A Complete
CONCORDANCE
to the Writings of
MARY BAKER EDDY
other than Science and Health with Key to the Scriptures

A Complete

CONCORDANCE

to the Writings of

MARY BAKER EDDY

other than Science and Health with Key to the Scriptures

Together with an Index to the Chapter Sub-titles, Headings,
and Titles of the Poems, and an Index to the Scriptural Quotations
contained in these Writings as finally revised
and arranged by their author

MARY BAKER EDDY

Discoverer and Founder of Christian Science

Marcas Registradas

Published by

THE FIRST CHURCH OF CHRIST, SCIENTIST

in Boston, Massachusetts, U.S.A.

Important Notice

If the user of this book does not readily find the
reference desired, the Compiler's Preface and List
of Abbreviations should be consulted.

The method employed in the Compilation of this
Concordance is carefully set forth in the Preface,
and instructions are given as to where certain
references may be found.

ISBN 0-87952-089-2

Compiler's Preface

The plan of this Concordance to the WRITINGS OF MARY BAKER EDDY, other than SCIENCE AND HEALTH, follows in every detail the plan of the Concordance to SCIENCE AND HEALTH, which was compiled in 1902 under the personal direction and supervision of MRS. EDDY. It therefore (with the exceptions noted below) contains every noun, verb, adjective, and adverb in the above-mentioned books, together with such pronouns, prepositions, and conjunctions as were deemed of sufficient importance to be introduced.

The books are indexed in the order in which they stand in the list of abbreviations on page viii.

The words are indexed in each book by page and line numbers. The titles of the poems in "Poems," and the titles of the chapters in the other books are not numbered; but all other lines including chapter sub-titles, headings and Scriptural quotations are numbered.

The numbers indicating page and line refer to the word under consideration and not necessarily to the beginning of the line quoted. The letters preceding some of the numbers are abbreviations of the titles of the books indexed, and indicate the books in which these references are to be found. Vacant spaces below the abbreviations indicate that the references are from the same book until a different abbreviation appears.

A special feature of the work is to be found in the fact that every noun of frequent occurrence is provided with sub-titles. These sub-titles are arranged in alphabetical order, under their respective nouns, and consist of adjectives or other qualifying words or phrases, preserving in every case the exact phraseology of the books from which they are taken. By this method all that is said on any given subject will be found grouped in one place.

For example: Man is often referred to as the "image and likeness" of God. More than fifty references to this subject will be found in the sub-title "and likeness" under the principal title "image." The sub-titles also enable those who are familiar with the text to look up passages by means of such words as God, Life, Truth, Love, Mind, matter, error, etc., without searching through several hundred references.

A few adjectives also, such as human, material, mortal, spiritual, etc., are furnished with sub-titles.

Certain words occurring in some places as nouns, are used in other places as verbs or adjectives. For example: the word "healing" is used as a noun, an adjective, and a participle. All such words appearing more than fifty times are classified and grouped under their respective parts of speech. If used less than fifty times in all, these words are not so separated.

The capitalization used in the sixteen books indexed presented many puzzling problems. Where a word referred to Deity when capitalized, and to humanity when not capitalized, it has been indexed under both headings, as for example: Life, life; Truth, truth; Love, love. The two headings have also been retained where the capitalization gave the word a different signification, as in such cases as Master, master; Physician, physician, where the capital referred to Christ Jesus. But where the word began a sentence, or was capitalized simply for emphasis, as in the headings in the Manual, or in the chapter sub-titles in the other books, and the capital did not change the meaning, the word has been indexed under the lower case heading only. For example: "Editor" and "editor" both appear under "editor." In some cases dual headings have been employed, as for example: "Masonic and masonic"; "Massachusetts and Mass."

All references to the Discoverer and Founder of Christian Science are arranged as sub-titles under the title "Eddy." Mrs. Eddy's signatures to various documents and communications will be found under "Eddy-signatures." A few references concerning Mrs. Eddy's childhood and the members of her family are indexed under "Baker" and "Glover."

For all Chapter Sub-titles, Headings, and Titles of the Poems in their entirety see Appendix "A." For individual words in same, consult the main body of the book.

Every Scriptural quotation is indexed under every important word in it, in the same manner as other words, and is followed by the book, chapter, and verse where it may be found in the Bible. A separate index of all the books, chapters, and verses of the Bible from which passages in quotation marks have been taken for use in the Writings of Mary Baker Eddy other than Science and Health will be found in Appendix "B."

All passages quoted by Mrs. Eddy from other authors, and also reports of church officials, letters, editorials, and other newspaper articles, etc., not written by Mrs. Eddy, are indexed in the usual way; but all such references may be identified by the * which precedes the lines taken from these sources. All signatures to documents not written by Mrs. Eddy will be found under the title "signatures."

The list of "Church Officers" on page 21, and also the "Application Forms," "Orders of Services," and "Deeds of Trusts" in the Appendix to the Church Manual, and the article entitled "Concord, N.H., to Mrs. Eddy and Mrs. Eddy's Reply" are indexed under their headings only. In indexing the Manual, the 1914 edition was used, and attention is called to the fact that the first three lines on page 85, are to be found at the bottom of page 84 in earlier editions. To find the name of any "Article" in the Manual consult the title "Church Manual." In these references the number of the line corresponds with the beginning of the line quoted. The names of the "Sections" will be found under the titles "Section I," "Sect. II," "Sect. III," etc.

Proper names are indexed under the surnames.

All dates containing years are indexed under "dates," and arranged chronologically; all dates containing months, but not years, are arranged chronologically under "months."

All values given in dollars and cents are indexed under "values."

All numbers consisting of one word, as "one, two, twenty, thirty, etc.," are indexed in their alphabetical places: all numbers consisting of more than one word, as "two thousand, one million, etc.," are indexed under "numbers."

Hours of the day are indicated by sub-titles under the title "time."

For the passages read from the BIBLE and SCIENCE AND HEALTH at the dedication of the extension to The Mother Church, consult "Lesson Sermon on Dedication Sunday."

Page numbers referring to SCIENCE AND HEALTH are indexed as sub-titles under "SCIENCE AND HEALTH."

All words used in the description of the organ in the original Mother Church are indexed as sub-titles under the word "organ."

Titles of more than one word, as "Falmouth and Norway Streets" are indexed in the place indicated by the first important word in the title. The above title is therefore to be found in the "F's."

The complete Concordance to all the writings of our beloved Leader and Teacher, published in book form, is embodied in the Concordance to SCIENCE AND HEALTH WITH KEY TO THE SCRIPTURES and the present volume.

ALBERT F. CONANT
Compiler

List of Abbreviations

The abbreviations made use of in this Concordance are as follows:—

These abbreviations appear at the left of the references and indicate the book in which the reference is found. Vacant space in this column following the abbreviation indicates that the references are from the same book until another abbreviation appears.

The words "Christian Science" and "Science and Health" have been abbreviated in the lines to C.S., and S. and H. respectively.

A Complete
CONCORDANCE
to the Writings of
MARY BAKER EDDY
other than Science and Health

A

Aaron's
  My. 127–15   even as *A·* rod swallowed up the
Abaddon
  Mis. 190–28   In the Hebrew, "devil" is . . . *A·* ;
abandon
  Mis. 27– 9   other systems . . . *a·* their own logic.
      250–12   which in their human *a·* become
      261–29   one will either *a·* his claim
  My. 40–13   * *a·* their strongholds of rivalry.
      249– 9   moral *a·* of hating even one's
abandoned
  Mis. 393–11   Soon *a·* when the Master
  Po. 51–16   Soon *a·* when the Master
  My. 140–22   *a·* so soon as God's Way-shower,
abandonment
  Mis. 205–25   *a·* of sin finally dissolves all
abased
  My. 140–24   This instructs us how to be *a·*
abashed
  Ret. 31–23   I gazed, and stood *a·*.
abate
  Mis. 324– 9   footfalls *a·*, the laughter ceases.
      366–27   *a·* dishonesty, self-will, envy, and
  Un. 54– 8   is to *a·* the fear of it ;
abated
  Mis. 366–26   never have *a·* . . . self-will, envy, and
abating
  Mis. 8– 2   we can aid in *a·* suffering
Abba
  Mis. 184–28   saith *A·*, Father, and *is* born of
abbess
  Pul. 32–13   * like any *a·* of old.
Abbott, D. D., Lyman
  Pan. 12– 4   Lyman *A·*, D.D., writes,
Abel
  No. 34–19   better things than that of *A·*.
Abercrombie, Dr.
  Peo. 6– 3   Dr. *A·*, . . . writes : "Medicine is the
ab extra
  My. 348– 6   not within but *a· e·*,
abhor
  Mis. 147–21   *a·* whatever is base or unworthy ;
  Po. 27– 4   I, dying, dare *a·* !"
abhors
  Mis. 317–29   My soul *a·* injustice,
abide
  Mis. 11– 4   to *a·* by our State statutes ;
      135– 6   and if we *a·* in these,
      149–30   shall *a·* steadfastly in the faith
      153–30   be and *a·* with this church.
      154–19   *A·* in His word,
      154–20   and it shall *a·* in you ;
      215–13   To *a·* by these we must first
      227–21   thoughts *a·* in tabernacles of
      265–24   Those who *a·* by them do well.
      270–19   the Word must *a·* in us,
      298–20   *A·* by the *morale* of absolute C. S.,
  Man. 60–16   love should *a·* in every heart

abide
  Ret. 56– 4   and that we must *a·* by them.
      64–24   It is scientific to *a·* in conscious
      82–16   and therein *a·*.
      88–26   *a·* in such a spiritual attitude
      92– 8   "If ye *a·* in me, — *John* 15 : 7.
      92– 9   my words *a·* in you, — *John* 15 : 7.
  Pul. 21–25   there *a·* in confidence and hope.
  '01. 34–22   be steadfast, *a·* and abound in
  '02. 9–20   should *a·* forever in man.
  Hea. 16–10   *a·* by your statements, and abound in
  Po. 43– 5   You in Him *a·*.
  My. 6– 6   To *a·* in our unselfed better self
      31– 5   * "*A·* with me ;"
      33–15   who shall *a·* in thy — *Psal.* 15 : 1.
      63–14   * to *a·* with us and enable us
      107–23   *a·* under the shadow of — *Psal.* 91 : 1.
      112– 7   those who *a·* in its teachings
      128–19   Christian Scientists *a·* by the laws of
      148– 7   be and *a·* with you henceforth.
      150–23   "If ye *a·* in me, — *John* 15 : 7.
      150–24   my words *a·* in you, — *John* 15 : 7.
      187–16   love of God be and *a·* with you
      192–14   be and *a·* with you.
      227–28   I *a·* by this rule and triumph by
      360–20   *A·* in fellowship with and obedience
abides
  Mis. 19–21   one who *a·* by his statements
  Un. 40–16   Hence Life *a·* in man,
      40–17   if man *a·* in good,
  '02. 9–17   and *a·* in Christlikeness.
  My. 124–16   *a·* in the hearts of these hearers
      160– 2   he *a·* in a right purpose,
      210–15   *a·* under the shadow of the Almighty.
      358– 1   C. S. *a·* by the definite rules
abideth
  Mis. 111–22   but the Word of God *a·*.
      367–32   and *a·* in Himself,
abiding
  Mis. 26– 2   hath life *a·* in it,
      100–29   *a·* faith, and affection,
      135– 7   *A·* in Love, not one of you can
      311–16   *a·* consciousness of health,
      331– 8   Thus *a·* in Truth,
  Ret. 23– 3   could be a real and *a·* rest.
  My. 140– 1   *a·* spiritual understanding
abilities
  Mis. 185– 7   *a·* or disabilities, pains or
ability
  and popularity
    Mis. 295–19   whose *a·* and popularity
  his
    No. 22–26   indicated his *a·* to cast it out.
  man's
    Mis. 16–12   man's *a·* to meet them is from God ;
      192–20   man's *a·* to prove the truth of
      199– 5   thence comes man's *a·* to
  might and
    Un. 42–17   might and *a·* to subdue material
  Mrs. Eddy's
    My. 273– 3   * proof of Mrs. Eddy's *a·*

ability

my
My. 42–19 * to the best of my *a*.
304–20 he knew my *a* as an editor.
natural
Mis. 183–18 but by the natural *a*, that
of Christians
Hea. 7–27 *a* of Christians to heal the sick ;
one's
Ret. 72– 5 it deteriorates one's *a* to do good,
No. 2–24 destroys one's *a* to heal mentally.
our
Mis. 236–18 to the best of our *a*,
student of
My. 320–10 * and as a student of *a*.
their
Mis. 351– 1 called on students to test their *a*
No. 40–19 forfeit their *a* to heal
My. 227–16 their *a* to cope with the claim,
this
My. 82–18 * would seem that this *a*
to comply
Mis. 286– 8 *a* to comply with absolute Science,
to demonstrate
Mis. 55– 5 *a* to demonstrate to the extent
'01. 4– 9 *a* to demonstrate Love according to
My. 242–13 forfeit your *a* to demonstrate it.
to gain
Mis. 38– 3 *a* to gain and maintain health,
to grasp
Man. 62–21 *a* to grasp the simpler meanings of
to rise
Mis. 97– 2 gives man *a* to rise above the
to teach
Hea. 14–23 to reach the *a* to teach ;
will give the
Mis. 115–26 God will give the *a* to overcome
your
My. 242–13 or you forfeit your *a* to
320–23 * spoke of your *a* without any

Mis. 335–16 the *a*, in belief, of evil

abject
My. 110–29 made his life an *a* failure.

abjure
Mis. 197–29 Let man *a* a theory that is
My. 97– 7 * of the sick who *a* medicine

abjured
My. 139–14 Justice, honesty, cannot be *a* ;

ablaze
My. 150–17 moon *a* with her mild glory.

able
Mis. 5– 8 *a* to produce perfect health
7–23 *a* to reach many homes
26–17 Matter is not intelligent, and thus *a*
42–16 *a* to communicate with and to
45– 6 is *a* to do more than to heal a
54–25 *Because none of your students have been a to*
93– 1 and by reason thereof is *a* to
114–32 and to be *a*, through Christ,
126–18 *a* editors of *The C. S. Journal*,
133–28 It affords me great joy to be *a* to attest
153–21 May you be *a* to say,
185– 2 *a* to discern fully and
200–20 Christians to-day should be *a* to say,
260– 4 and found *a* to heal them.
300–30 pays whatever he is *a* to pay
338– 4 to be *a* to lift others
342–32 *a* to make us wise unto salvation!
352– 6 it is *a* for the first time to discern
352– 8 *a* to behold the facts of Truth
359–16 insomuch as he was *a* to do this ;
Ret. 7–15 * As a lawyer he was *a* and learned,
44–14 *a* to maintain the church
84–20 and by reason thereof is *a* to
90–12 they were *a* to fulfil his behest
Un. 1–17 practically *a* to testify, by their lives,
7–13 I have been *a* to replace
24–24 *a* to see, taste, hear, feel, smell.
48–20 faintly *a* to demonstrate Truth
Pul. 29–24 * The discourse was *a*,
47– 2 *a* lectures upon Scriptural topics.
Rud. 14–15 only from those who were *a* to pay.
'01. 4–23 should be *a* to explain
Po. 79– 7 God *a* is To raise up seed
My. 15–15 all that you are *a* to bear now,
28– 1 *a* to make this announcement
29–12 * will ever be *a* to forget.
29–29 *a* to wait patiently for the
40– 3 * church *a* to give more adequate
51–14 * who is so *a* as she to lead us
99– 3 * faith which is *a* to raise its
99– 7 * cult *a* to promote its faith with
121–10 *a* to carry navies,

able
My. 137–30 *a* to select the Trustees I need
145–12 * I do not feel *a* to keep about.
147–20 *a* to heal both sin and disease.
156– 5 persuaded that He is *a* '' — *II Tim.* 1 : 12.
156– 5 ''*a* to do exceeding — *Eph.* 3 : 20.
156– 6 ''*a* to make all grace — *II Cor.* 9 : 8.
156– 9 ''*a* to keep that which — *II Tim.* 1 : 12.
162–17 was not *a* to finish.'' — *Luke* 14 : 30.
165–20 *a* to impart truth, health, and
177– 9 I am quite *a* to take the trip
196–13 *a* also to bridle the — *Jas.* 3 : 2.
228–29 *a* to keep that which — *II Tim.* 1 : 12.
273– 6 * fortunate in being *a* to point to
296– 2 The *a* discourse of our ''learned
316–22 under Mr. Flower's *a* guardianship
323–27 * not have been *a* to appreciate

ablution
Peo. 9– 3 not an *a* of the body,

ably
Man. 44–21 these periodicals are *a* edited
Ret. 42– 9 lectured so *a* on Scriptural topics
No. 45–18 these rights are *a* vindicated
My. 125–14 Principle they so *a* vindicate,

abnegation
My. 134– 1 *a*, constant battle against the

abnormal
Mis. 17–25 normal or *a* material conditions
32–10 The query is *a*, when
200– 4 and evil as the *a* ;
Man. 41– 4 is *a* in a Christian Scientist,

abode
Mis. 174–16 *a* of Spirit, the realm of the real.
Un. 32–22 truth *a* not in you. — *see John* 8 : 44.
Rud. 7–17 truth *a* not in him,'' — *see John* 8 : 44.
No. 24–23 truth *a* not in him.'' — *see John* 8 : 44.
36– 7 It *a* forever above,
Pan. 5–14 *a* not in the truth — *John* 8 : 44.

abolish
Mis. 286–15 To *a* marriage at this period,
My. 141–16 * *a* its famous communion seasons.

abolished
Mis. 258– 4 *a* this unrelenting false claim
Peo. 10–28 when African slavery was *a*
My. 141– 2 * chapter sub-title
141– 5 * has been *a* by order of
142– 4 * *a* the disappointment of
241– 2 * Class teaching will not be *a*

abolishing
My. 140–11 * chapter sub-title
142–11 *a* the communion season

abolition
Ret. 6–29 *a* of imprisonment for debt.

abolitionist
Peo. 11– 4 a new *a* struck the keynote

abomination
My. 229– 6 an *a* unto the Lord : — *Deut.* 18 : 12.

abominations
My. 229– 7 because of these *a* — *Deut.* 18 : 12.

abortive
Un. 11–10 this mind and its *a* laws.
44–13 This *a* ego, this fable of error,

abound
Mis. 135– 6 they will *a* in us,
'01. 33– 7 * ''Quackery and dupery do *a*
34–22 be steadfast, abide and *a* in faith,
Hea. 16–10 *a* in Love and Truth,
Po. 77– 5 Plenty and peace *a* at Thy behest,
My. 140–24 how to be abased and how to *a*.
156– 7 all grace *a* toward you ; — *II Cor.* 9 : 8.
156– 8 *a* to every good work,'' — *II Cor.* 9 : 8.
182–30 *a* in the righteousness of Love,

abounded
'01. 33– 9 * they have fearfully *a* ;

abounding
My. 139– 7 its *a*, increasing, advancing
140– 1 this *a* and abiding spiritual
155– 5 *a* in love and good works,

abounds
My. 88–15 * its dedication *a* in remarkable
124–15 What more *a* and abides in

about
Mis. 29–17 ranks of my *a* five thousand students.
32– 4 *what a that clergyman's remarks*
47– 2 *carry a this weight daily?*
69–28 for information *a* his case.
122–12 were hanged *a* his neck, — *Matt.* 18 : 6.
130–10 talking *a* it, thinking it over,
141–17 parties concerned *a* the legal quibble,
143–22 within *a* three months, donated

about

Mis.	154– 7	He will dig *a·* this little church,
	158– 6	the changes *a·* to be made.
	163– 8	Three years he went *a·* doing good.
	163–30	forever *a·* the Father's business ;
	177–13	What will you do *a·* it?
	178–15	* "I think it was *a·* a year ago
	225–28	In *a·* one hour he awoke, and was hungry.
	239– 5	*a·* to commence a large class
	248–11	simple falsehoods uttered *a·* me
	266–18	assertion that I have said hard things *a·*
	271–20	Much is said at this date, 1889, *a·*
	276–10	*a·* one thousand Christian Scientists,
	277–25	Though clouds are round *a·* Him,
	281– 2	*a·* to chant hymns of victory for triumphs.
	348–18	once in *a·* seven years
	349– 4	instructions included *a·* twelve lessons,
	349–31	no pay from my church for *a·*
	349–32	put into the church-fund *a·*
	350–14	second P. M. convened in *a·* one week
	353–26	at *a·* three years of scientific age,
	370–16	twines its loving arms *a·* the
	371– 4	wandering *a·* without a leader,
	375–10	* *a·* the wonderful new book
Man.	61–24	*a·* eight or nine minutes
	104– 9	and hedge it *a·* with divine Love.
Ret.	2–28	grandmother's stories *a·* General Knox,
	4– 4	farm of *a·* five hundred acres,
	8– 3	when I was *a·* eight years old,
	9– 4	Mother told Mehitable all *a·* this
	19–21	directions to his brother masons *a·*
	20– 8	my little son, *a·* four years of age,
	24–22	withdrew from society *a·* three years,
	40–10	stood by her side *a·* fifteen minutes
	48– 6	conscientious scruples *a·* diplomas,
	51– 3	*a·* twenty thousand dollars,
	52– 4	to build a hedge round *a·* it
	89– 0	scattered *a·* in cities and villages,
	93– 1	Jesus went *a·* doing good.
	93– 3	evangelists of those days wandered *a·*.
Un.	6–16	leading questions *a·* God and sin,
	6–21	*a·* the problems of Euclid,
	6–24	our declarations *a·* sin and Deity
	28–13	The common hypotheses *a·* souls
Pul.	47–26	* so picturesque all *a·* Concord
	54–28	NOTE :— *A·* 1868, the author
	58– 4	* Coming to Boston *a·* 1880,
	68–16	* organized in this city *a·* a year ago.
	69– 1	* came to Baltimore *a·* three years ago
	69– 3	* *a·* eighteen months ago.
	69–17	* to explain fully all *a·* it,
	71–12	* THE NEWS *A·* MRS. MARY BAKER EDDY,
	72–27	* going *a·* doing good and healing
	73– 2	* why should we worry ourselves *a·*
	86– 2	* *a·* six inches in each dimension,
Rud.	7–25	bring *a·* alteration of species
	8–20	also uttering falsehood *a·* good.
	11–28	He never talks *a·* the
No.	22– 1	"driven *a·* by every — *see Eph.* 4: 14.
	26– 5	infantile talk *a·* Mind-healing
'01.	16–28	one hundred falsehoods told *a·* it
	21– 9	* ideas *a·* the spiritual world
	32– 9	busy *a·* their Master's business,
	33–12	* that they were *a·* to die."
'02.	13– 7	*a·* one hundred and twenty thousand
	13–14	*a·* one half the price paid,
	14– 1	*A·* five thousand dollars
Hea.	9– 2	We should have no anxiety *a·*
	14– 3	in fine, much ado *a·* nothing.
	16–16	A word *a·* the five personal senses,
My.	vi– 7	* knows anything *a·* C. S. except
	24–18	* inquired *a·* the progress of the work
	27– 5	*a·* the time of our annual meeting
	29–28	* began to congregate *a·* the church
	38–12	* in *a·* twenty minutes,
	53–14	* *a·* two hundred and twenty-five.
	54–14	* were present *a·* eight hundred
	60– 7	* *a·* the early history of C. S.
	61–21	* One feature *a·* the work
	68– 6	* *a·* one mile and a half of pews.
	71– 8	* no need of fussing *a·* the underlying
	74– 7	* arrive in this city just *a·* in time
	83– 2	* of never going *a·* labelled.
	87–26	* There is one thing *a·* it :
	89– 9	* needs only an open space *a·* it,
	91–13	* and shed sunshine *a·* them
	95–13	* cost them *a·* two million dollars,
	95–20	* They go *a·* telling of miracles
	98–18	* This structure cost *a·* two million
	100– 5	* cost *a·* two million dollars
	114–16	read no other book . . . for *a·* three years.
	123–18	now *a·* twenty thousand dollars.
	135–18	*a·* forty thousand members,
	137–25	before . . . I knew aught *a·* them,
	137–26	consulted Lawyer Streeter *a·* the
	145–12	* I do not feel able to keep *a·*.

about

My.	162–13	*a·* eighty thousand dollars,
	169–18	call of *a·* three thousand believers
	173–19	number of visitors, *a·* four thousand,
	223–13	questions *a·* secular affairs,
	225–11	used in writing *a·* C. S.
	241–25	* beliefs I entertained *a·* it ;
	242– 2	in your statement *a·* yourself.
	308–22	as they were *a·* to start for church.
	312–21	and died in *a·* nine days.
	313– 8	stories told . . . *a·* my father
	313–10	and *a·* persons being hired to
	314–19	*a·* to have Dr. Patterson arrested
	315– 5	* conversation with him *a·* his wife,
	319–22	* *a·* the preparation of a theme,
	319–25	* which I did *a·* the twentieth of
	320– 6	* converse *a·* you and your work,
	322–10	* *a·* the Rev. James H. Wiggin's work
	323–10	* not going to lie *a·* anything
	324– 2	* *a·* you and your work,
	328–16	* how this came *a·* in Kinston
	331– 1	*a·* accompanying her on her sad
	344–19	If I harbored that idea *a·* a
	344–21	* heading
	345–24	*a·* advice on surgical cases."
	346–12	* several turns *a·* the court-house
		(*see also* **year**)

above

Mis.	ix–17	requires strength from *a·*,
	xii– 7	lift my readers *a·* the smoke of conflict
	12– 9	*a·* all, do not fancy that
	28–18	he arose *a·* the illusion of
	34– 3	metaphysics is *a·* physics.
	53–18	*a·* the standard of metaphysics ;
	67– 2	*A·* physical wants, lie the
	68–18	Does the gentleman *a·* mentioned
	87– 1	soar *a·*, as the bird
	97– 2	gives man ability to rise *a·* the
	102–18	in modes *a·* the human.
	106–13	On to the blest *a·*,
	106–25	*a·*, beyond, methinks I hear
	107– 8	As we rise *a·* the seeming mists
	120–17	heard *a·* the din of battle,
	139–16	with a portion of the *a·* Scripture
	143– 6	*a·* the plane of matter.
	156–27	Experience and, *a·* all, *obedience,*
	158– 4	the heavens *a·* the earth
	158– 4	is His wisdom *a·* ours.
	174–12	*A·* Arcturus and his sons,
	178–12	those things which are *a·*, — *Col.* 3: 1.
	187– 5	*a·* every sense of matter,
	192–23	as the *a·* Scripture plainly declares,
	206– 5	*A·* the waves of Jordan,
	216–13	might add to the *a·* definition
	234– 4	attempt to mount *a·* error by
	242– 2	article . . . having the *a·* caption,
	255–27	metaphysics is *a·* physics.
	267– 1	to make itself heard *a·* Truth's voice.
	277– 4	but Truth will soar *a·* it.
	277– 6	trying to be heard *a·* Truth,
	279– 7	but over and *a·* it all
	282–20	the *a·* rule of mental practice.
	286– 1	The *a·* prophecy, written years ago,
	291– 7	*a·* personal motives, unworthy aims
	306–18	* a member of the *a·* organization,
	307–17	and *a·* all, God's love
	309–22	infinitely *a·* a bodily form of
	312–21	this man must have risen *a·*
	317–19	my answers to the *a·* questions.
	323– 4	celestial city *a·* all clouds,
	331–22	*a·* the frozen crust of creed
	355–18	but to lift your head *a·* it,
	357– 9	*a·* the present status of religion
	368– 9	* keeping watch *a·* His own."
	374–11	*A·* the fogs of sense and
	376–19	*a·* the horizon, in the east,
	385– 2	* *A·* the sod Find peace in God,
	391– 4	For things *a·* the floor,
	392–17	As grandly rising to the heavens *a·*.
	394–12	God-given mandate that speaks from *a·*,
	395–19	May rest *a·* my head.
	395–23	Is registered *a·*.
Man.	40–17	*a·* Church Rule shall be read
	85–20	since receiving instruction as *a·*,
Ret.	18–17	May soar *a·* matter,
	67–13	rising *a·* corporeal personality,
	69–25	"*A·* error's awful din, blackness,
	73–14	lift thought *a·* physical personality,
	81–24	* *a·* all : To thine own self be true ;
	89–26	*A·* all, trespass not intentionally
Un.	18–16	from outside and *a·* ourselves?
	38–13	*a·* the living and true God.
	61– 1	*a·* the false, to the true evidence
Pul.	13–18	their heads *a·* the drowning wave.
	28– 4	* star of Bethlehem shines down from *a·*.

above

Pul.	28– 5	* *A·* this is a panel containing the
	41–24	* one hundred and twenty-six feet *a·* the
	42–20	* the choir gallery *a·* the platform,
	53–19	* *a·* the level of the brute,
	86–28	* Bible and the book alluded to *a·*,
Rud.	12– 3	*A·* all, he keeps unbroken the
No.	14–17	chapter sub-title
	14–26	Are frozen dogmas, . . . from *a·*?
	36– 7	It abode forever *a·*,
Pan.	2– 7	looms *a·* the mists of pantheism
	2– 8	higher than Mt. Ararat *a·* the deluge.
	6– 8	but lifteth his head *a·* it
	12–13	high *a·* the so-called laws of matter,
	13–23	who is *a·* all, — *Eph.* 4 : 6.
	14– 4	Set your affections on things *a·*;
'00.	5– 1	who is *a·* all, — *Eph.* 4 : 6.
	15– 4	are distinguished *a·* human title
'01.	18–20	teaches that . . . is *a·* a demonstration
	18–21	*a·* the grandeur of our great master
	33– 7	* *a·* all, in the more advanced
'02.	10–12	*a·* itself towards the Divine,
Hea.	11–28	excellence *a·* other systems.
Peo.	5–17	has risen *a·* the sod
	9–23	is seen to rise *a·* physics,
	11– 9	*A·* the platform of human rights
	12–16	*a·* the demands of matter.
Po.	9–10	wishing this earth more gifts from *a·*,
	10–13	Betokened from *a·*.
	16– 5	it blossoms *a·*;
	20–21	rising to the heavens *a·*.
	22– 4	and, beckoning from *a·*,
	23–10	*A·* the world's control?
	24–19	And from *a·*, Dear heart of Love,
	25–13	And breath of the living *a·*.
	28–11	*A·* the tempest's glee ;
	29–17	so far *a·* All mortal strife,
	30–17	a patient love *a·* earth's ire,
	34–20	in azure bright soar far *a·*;
	37– 2	* *A·* the sod Find peace in God,
	38– 3	For things *a·* the floor,
	45–16	mandate that speaks from *a·*,
	47– 7	Ever the gross world *a·*;
	58– 4	May rest *a·* my head.
	58– 8	Is registered *a·*.
	64– 8	May soar *a·* matter,
	67–21	flowers of feeling may blossom *a·*,
My.	6–24	*a·* the work of men's hands,
	14– 4	*a·* the song of angels,
	15–19	* Of unseen things *a·*,
	32–10	* *a·* the usual platform tone.
	38– 3	* every perfect gift cometh from *a·*,
	40–19	* wisdom that is from *a·* — *Jas.* 3 : 17.
	59– 7	* It was *a·* conception
	66– 3	* gives to the *a·* society the ownership
	66– 9	* by the *a·* society,
	67– 1	* raises its dome *a·* the city
	68–11	* two hundred and twenty-four feet *a·*
	68–22	* *a·* the Readers' special rooms.
	88– 7	* *a·* the average in intelligence.
	94–27	high *a·* the work of men's hands,
	99– 4	* *a·* the suffering of petty ills ;
	106– 8	I name those mentioned *a·* simply to
	106–10	over and *a·* matter in every mode
	114–24	Truth and Love, infinitely *a·* me,
	131–14	*a·* the symbol seize the spirit,
	143–14	*A·* all this fustian of either denying or
	156– 6	*a·* all that we ask or think,'' — *Eph.* 3 : 20.
	165–19	rise *a·* the oft-repeated inquiry,
	182–21	Love that reigns *a·* the shadow,
	186–10	point the path *a·* the valley,
	190–20	*a· matter* in healing disease,
	202– 2	soar *a·* it, pointing the path
	215– 2	I was *a·* begging
	217–15	complied with my request as *a·*
	227–21	The *a·* quotation by the editor-in-chief
	235–25	adopt as truth the *a·* statements?
	238–17	man rises *a·* the letter, law, or
	245– 1	*a·* the approved schools of
	245–17	*a·* the dire din of mortal
	248–16	rising *a·* theorems into the
	249– 5	When error strives to be heard *a·*
	250–26	impulsion of this action . . . from *a·*.
	252–29	the impetus comes from *a·*
	320–21	* at the time *a·* referred to,
	337–14	Betokened from *a·*.
	350–19	Thou infinite — dost doom *a·*.
	351–12	*morale* of Free Masonry is *a·* ethics
	354–26	* The *a·* lines were written
	360–30	God is *a·* your teacher, your healer,

above-ground

My.	110– 4	*a·* in material sense.

above-mentioned

My.	315–13	* was the *a·* woman.
	323– 2	* so well written in the *a·* letter.

above-named

Mis.	32–16	My sympathies extend to the *a·* class
	92–23	own a copy of the *a·* book
	301– 5	author of the *a·* book
	301–10	instances of the *a·* law-breaking
	349–11	student had taken the *a·* course
'00.	2– 3	springing up in the *a·* cities,
My.	238– 6	by reading the *a·* books
	319–26	* twentieth of the *a·* month.

Abraham

Mis.	189–14	"Before *A·* was, I am." — *John* 8 : 58.
	360–29	"Before *A·* was, I am," — *John* 8 : 58.
Chr.	55–15	Before *A·* was, I am. — *John* 8 : 58.
Ret.	26–19	He who antedated *A·*,
Pul.	82–16	* never called *A·* "Father,"
'01.	8–25	"Before *A·* was, I am." — *John* 8 : 58.
My.	161–11	when ye shall see *A·*, — *Luke* 13 : 28.

abreast

Man.	44–21	kept *a·* of the times.

abridge

Mis.	266– 5	to *a·* a single human right or

abroad

Mis.	39– 7	There are *a·* at this early date
	159–30	and some from *a·*,
	266–28	The spirit of lies is *a·*.
	370– 6	antagonistic spirit of evil is still *a·*;
	370– 7	greater spirit of Christ is also *a·*,
Ret.	85–24	and scatter the sheep *a·*;
Pul.	46– 1	* story has been *a·* that Judge Hanna
No.	2–28	not spread *a·* patchwork ideas
Po.	33–16	faith spreads her pinions *a·*,
	77– 9	blessings spreadst *a·*,
My.	3–11	scattered *a·* in Zion's waste places,
	74– 1	* from *a·* and from the far West

abrogate

No.	44–15	*a·* the rights of conscience

abrogated

Mis.	244–15	* "Has the law been *a·* that
'02.	4–20	a law never to be *a·*

absence

Mis.	27–21	for evil signifies the *a·* of good,
	65–28	for the *a·* of the other,
	289– 7	It is suppositional *a·* of good.
	353–15	in the overseer's *a·*,
	363– 6	supposition that the *a·* of good is
Ret.	58– 5	trying to compensate for the *a·* of
	60–12	It declares that evil is the *a·* of
Un.	4–12	destroys our sense . . . of His *a·*,
No.	17– 4	evil, is the *a·* of Spirit
My.	94–12	* *a·* of dissent among them
	193– 5	that you will not feel my *a·*.
	220–14	Injustice denotes the *a·* of law.
	312– 3	during her temporary *a·*.

absent

Mis.	78– 8	*taught to those who are a·?*
	116–26	Never *a·* from your post,
	278–19	students, who are *a·* from me,
	322–19	though I be present or *a·*,
	344–22	*a·* from the body, — *II Cor.* 5 : 8.
Man.	36–15	deceased, *a·*, or disloyal,
	111–17	deceased, *a·*, or disloyal,
Ret.	89–16	when he had been some time *a·*
Un.	59– 7	never *a·* from the earth and heaven ;
	60–21	He is neither *a·* from Himself
	62– 9	God, good, is never *a·*,
	63– 4	never *a·* for a moment.
No.	20–18	Love must seem *a·* to
'00.	1– 5	we may be *a·* from the body
	7–19	this Christ is never *a·*.
Po.	page 23	poem
My.	118–14	"*a·* from the body," — *II Cor.* 5 : 8.
	301–29	If mind be *a·* from the body,

absentness

Mis.	206–14	no illusive vision, no dreamy *a·*,

absolute

Mis.	99– 1	Science is *a·* and final.
	108– 7	attested the *a·* powerlessness
	136–17	the *a·* demonstration of C. S.
	148–20	*a·* doctrines destined for future
	156–17	Science is *a·*,
	177– 3	an *a·* consecration to the
	205–25	repentance and *a·* abandonment
	234–29	God is regarded more as *a·*,
	260–23	pure Mind as *a·* and entire,
	286– 8	ability to comply with *a·* Science,
	286–28	Until this *a·* Science of being
	288–15	and thence achieves the *a·*.
	298–20	the *morale* of *a·* C. S.,
	299–16	is the only *a·* good;
	299–17	is the only *a·* evil.
	307–20	this *a·* basis of C. S.;
	311–24	The works . . . contain *a·* Truth,

absolute

Mis.	318– 2	obsolete terms in *a·* C. S.,
	355– 9	This *a·* demonstration of Science
	359–23	The *way* is *a·* divine Science :
	364–28	If . . . there is no *a·* good.
Man.	3–17	*a·* doctrines destined for future
	63–10	must not deviate from the *a·*
Ret.	27– 7	the *a·* Science of Mind-healing,
	31– 5	The *a·* proof . . . of Truth
	83–30	deviating from *a·* C. S.
Un.	8–10	for this evidence is not *a·*,
	58–18	Thus the *a·* unreality of sin,
Pul.	vii–20	*a·* power of Truth
	75– 9	the *a·* antipode of C. S.,
Rud.	6–25	definite and *a·* form of healing,
	11–15	*a·* consciousness of harmony
No.	27–23	Who can say what the *a·* personality
Pan.	7–16	*a·* oneness and infinity of God,
'00.	4–22	found final, *a·*, and eternal.
'01.	1–24	gain the *a·* and supreme certainty
	2–13	*A·* certainty in the practice of divine
	22–30	its *a·* simple statement as to Spirit
'02.	5–18	This *a·* definition of Deity
My.	22–13	* shown the *a·* necessity of giving.
	79– 3	* kneeling . . . in *a·* stillness,
	146–19	the *a·* truth of his sayings
	241–15	* should be *a·* and correct teaching.
	242– 5	C. S. is *a·*;
	246–14	*a·* scientific unity which must exist
	260–10	the real, the *a·* and eternal,
	293–14	lack of the *a·* understanding
	293–16	the power of *a·* Truth
	349–23	God of nature in *a·* Science.
	357– 7	*a·* opposite of spiritual means,

absolutely

Mis.	22–12	*a·* refutes the amalgamation,
	50–13	*a·* no additional secret
	91– 5	not *a·* necessary to ordain
	92– 6	understood to be *a·* demonstrated.
	288–12	conclusion . . . is not *a·* right.
	317–12	not *a·* requisite for some people
Ret.	26–28	*a·* reduce the demonstration of
Un.	15– 6	*a·* cognizant of sin?
	29–13	*a·* immutable and eternal,
No.	6–24	is *a·* unreal.
'01.	3–10	loyal Christian Scientists *a·* adopt
My.	vi– 4	* to state truth *a·*
	77–27	* open its doors *a·* free of debt,
	85–27	* this structure, which is *a·* unique
	91–30	* is *a·* free from debt.
	98–20	* dedicated *a·* free of debt,
	104–23	of which a man knows *a·* nothing
	224–29	which is not *a·* genuine.
	284–24	*a·* and religiously opposed to war,
	338–28	Board of Lectureship is *a·*
	348– 1	*a·* healed of so-called disease

absolve

My.	274– 5	Death alone does not *a·* man from

absolved

My.	119– 8	but is *a·* by it.
	218–14	*a·* from death and the grave.

absorb

Ret.	80–18	will so *a·* it that this warning will be
Pul.	51–26	* C. S. cannot *a·* the world's

absorbed

Mis.	333– 5	could be *a·* in error!
Pul.	72–11	* very much *a·* in the work
No.	25–19	Man is not *a·* in Deity ;
My.	119– 7	man is not *a·* in the divine nature,

absorbing

My.	234– 3	*a·* one's time writing or reading
	336–19	* of *a·* interest to Christian Scientists

absorbs

Mis.	333– 8	it *a·* all the rays of light.

absorption

Mis.	22–13	*a·*, or annihilation of
	195– 2	*a·* of all action, motive, and

abstain

My.	114– 4	*a·* from alcohol and tobacco;
	339–26	Merely to *a·* from eating was not

abstinence

Mis.	288–31	*a·* from intoxicating beverages.
	289– 4	only temperance is total *a·*.

abstract

Mis.	38–15	such a *dry* and *a·* subject?
	38–17	is far from dry and *a·*.
	53–27	*a·* or difficult to perceive.
	82–21	comprehend only as *a·* glory.
	200–32	*a·* statement that all is Mind,
	222–25	Error is more *a·* than Truth.
	264–16	assimilate pure and *a·* Science
Ret.	67– 6	Sin is both concrete and *a·*.

abstract

Hea.	16–17	leave our *a·* subjects for this time.
My.	249– 1	You may condemn evil in the *a·*

abstraction

Mis.	53–28	Its seeming *a·* is the mystery of
	250–20	Love cannot be a mere *a·*,
My.	113–23	is C. S. a cold, dull *a·*,

abstractions

Mis.	174– 6	Let us have a clearing up of *a·*.
	195–27	were spiritual *a·*,
My.	218–16	introduction of pure *a·* into

abstruse

Ret.	7–10	* *a·* and metaphysical principles,
'02.	4–25	*a·* problems of Scripture,

absurd

Mis.	171– 7	is as *a·* as to think,
My.	111–20	be *a·* and unscientific?
	111–23	Were the apostles *a·* and
	111–29	they may pronounce it *a·*,
	344–12	*a·* to say that when a man dies,

absurdities

Un.	16– 3	unheard-of contradictions, — *a·*;

absurdly

Un.	17–23	Would it not *a·* follow

abundance

My.	36–19	* *a·* of salvation through His divine
	274–22	an *a·* of material presents ;
	340–29	are succeeded by our time of *a·*,

abundant

My.	198– 8	but their *a·* and ripened fruit.

abundantly

Pul.	1– 1	*They shall be a· satisfied* — *Psal.* 36 : 8.
	2–13	"they shall be *a·* satisfied," — *Psal.* 36 : 8.
	3–16	"They shall be *a·* satisfied — *Psal.* 36 : 8.
	4–26	"They shall be *a·* satisfied — *Psal.* 36 : 8.
	7–29	"They shall be *a·* satisfied — *Psal.* 36 : 8.
My.	156– 5	"able to do exceeding *a·* — *Eph.* 3 : 20.
	194–26	May divine Love *a·* bless you,
	209– 3	God will *a·* bless this willing

abuse

Mis.	31– 8	the *a·* of mental treatment,
	78–20	this *a·*, has become too common :
	282–29	The *a·* which I call attention to,
	289– 3	its slightest use is *a·*;
Pan.	4–13	will is capable of use and of *a·*,
'02.	9–28	bitter comment and personal *a·*
	11–10	*a·* of him who, having a new idea
My.	219–10	otherwise its use is *a·*.
	343–18	shower of *a·* upon my head,

abused

Mis.	238–12	unmentioned, save when he is *a·*
	250– 4	is the best become the most *a·*,
Hea.	6– 9	The spiritualists *a·* me for it

abuses

Mis.	284– 5	C. S., . . . is subject to *a·*.
	338–16	uses of good, to *a·* from evil ;
Ret.	45–15	uses and *a·* of organization.
	76–24	never *a·* the corporeal personality,

abusing

Ret.	85–20	of *a·* the practice of Mind-healing

abyss

Un.	60– 9	the dark *a·* of nothingness,
My.	200–24	bottomless *a·* of self-damnation,
	291–18	fathomed the *a·* of difficulties

academic

My.	310– 2	were given an *a·* education,
	310– 5	In addition to my *a·* training,

academics

Pan.	4–12	In *a·* and in religion it is patent
My.	217– 2	You will want it for *a·*,

academies

My.	175–14	up-to-date *a·*, humane institutions,

Academy of Greece

Pul.	5–27	in the *A· o· G·*,

accelerated

Pul.	13–22	comes back . . . with *a·* force,
My.	239–29	*a·* by the advent of C. S.,

accent

Mis.	116–15	As *crescendo* and . . . *a·* music,

accented

Pul.	24–11	* *a·* by stone porticos and turreted

accents

Mis.	107– 3	are earth's *a·*,
Ret.	17– 8	tremble with *a·* of bliss.
Po.	62– 8	tremble with *a·* of bliss.

accentuating

Mis.	206–20	*a·* harmony in word and deed,

accept

Mis.	27–13	Mortals *a·* natural science, wherein
	27–14	why not *a·* divine Science
	76–18	and *a·* it on other topics
	83–12	No person can *a·* another's belief,
	83–16	to reject or to *a·* this error ;
	132–21	inconvenient to *a·* your invitation
	137– 2	*A·* my thanks for your card of
	142–11	*A·* my thanks for the beautiful
	146– 9	I cannot *a·* hearsay,
	185–17	as *a·* the truth of being,
	189– 4	willing to *a·* the divine Principle
	191–32	*a·* the Scriptures in their broader,
	194–23	how to *a·* God's power and guidance,
	218–11	It is erroneous to *a·* the evidence
	242–10	Will the gentleman *a·* my thanks
	242–11	if I should *a·* his bid on Christianity,
	244–17	Will he *a·* my reply
	319–18	Will all the dear Christian Scientists *a·*
	349–24	before I would *a·* the slightest
Man.	51– 3	and if he neglect to *a·*
Ret.	50– 9	was finally led, . . . to *a·* this fee.
Un.	5– 9	not to *a·* any personal opinion
	43–20	I exhort them to *a·* Christ's promise,
Pul.	38–17	* Scientists do not *a·* the belief
	44–28	* refused to *a·* any further checks
	54–12	* We *a·* the statement of Hudson :
	76–27	* to *a·* the magnificent new edifice
	77–15	* invited to visit and formally *a·*
	78–14	* formally *a·* this testimonial
	87– 4	* to *a·* this offering,
	87–13	*a·* my profound thanks.
	87–19	*a·* your grand church edifice.
'00.	6–26	in the degree that you *a·* it,
'01.	3–13	we *a·* God, emphatically.
Hea.	18–13	the world would *a·* our sentiments ;
My.	24– 4	* all who *a·* its divine ministry.
	25–16	my dear correspondents *a·* this,
	51–20	* *a·* the pastorate for the ensuing
	85–11	* One does not need to *a·* the
	93–17	* who do not *a·* the doctrine of
	120– 7	*A·* my gratitude for the chance
	129–29	*A·* my counsel and teachings only as
	142–10	*A·* my thanks for your approval
	156– 2	*a·* my gratitude for your dear letter,
	160–11	*a·* dead truisms which can be
	167– 1	*A·* my deep thanks therefor,
	172–18	*a·* my thanks for your kind,
	172–21	* "I *a·* this gift in behalf of
	172–27	*a·* from me the accompanying gift
	175– 6	Please *a·* the enclosed check
	186–25	*A·* my thanks for your cordial card
	190–13	*a·* our Master as authority,
	191–30	*A·* my thanks.
	194–23	gratefully *a·* the spirit of it ;
	196– 6	*a·* my tender counsel in these words
	199–11	*a·* my grateful acknowledgment of
	201–27	Please *a·* a line from me in lieu of
	208– 3	*A·* my deep thanks for your
	215–14	begging me to *a·* it,
	224–24	not safe to *a·* the latter as standards.
	229–22	*a·* profound thanks for their swift
	231–28	*a·* my thanks for your interesting
	236– 2	*a·* my full heart's love for them
	237–10	wise to *a·* only my teachings
	253–15	*A·* my love and these words of
	253–21	*a·* my profound thanks
	273–13	I for one *a·* his wise deduction,
	274–20	*a·* my thanks for their magnificent
	285– 2	*a·* my thanks for your kind
	285– 5	*a·* my hearty congratulations.
	308–24	but declined to *a·* the stick,
	332– 8	* *a·* it as a tribute of grateful hearts
	341–10	*a·* your Leader's Spring greeting,
	347– 8	*a·* my heartfelt acknowledgment of
	352–27	*A·* my thanks for your

acceptable

Mis.	184–11	presenting our bodies holy and *a·*,
	262–11	*a·* to those who have hearts.
No.	28–10	*a·* time for beginning the lesson.
	41– 7	that is most *a·* to God
My.	17–12	*a·* to God by Jesus Christ. — I Pet. 2 : 5.
	36–12	* service that shall be *a·* unto God.
	167–17	be one *a·* in His sight,
	184–22	service *a·* in God's sight.
	250– 9	*a·* service as church Readers,

acceptably

Man.	89–14	practised C. S. healing *a·*
My.	37– 6	* can *a·* ascend heavenward
	310– 3	taught school *a·* at various times

acceptance

Mis.	110–23	obvious that the world's *a·*
	181–23	urges upon our *a·* this great fact :
	196–31	*a·* of the truths they present ;
Pul.	87–14	permit me, . . . to decline their *a·*,

acceptance

'01.	1– 9	nearer the whole world's *a·*.
My.	99–29	* no choice but the *a·* of them
	123– 8	urge the perfect model for your *a·*
	184–29	*a·* throughout the earth,

accepted

Mis.	5–28	is something not easily *a·*,
	19–13	*a·* the divine claims of Truth
	75–29	and the commonly *a·* view is
	81–10	in the commonly *a·* teachings
	132– 3	substance whereof you had already *a·*
	187–11	This rule of harmony must be *a·*
	237– 6	*a·* as the penalty for sin.
	247–23	is not so easily *a·*.
	297–19	and *a·* the claims of the marriage
	349–27	I *a·*, for a time, fifteen dollars
	349–30	I have *a·* no pay from my
Man.	18– 6	She *a·* the call, and was ordained
	81– 6	not *a·* by the Pastor Emeritus
Ret.	15–15	I *a·* the invitation and commenced
	16–19	She *a·* the call,
	44– 7	I *a·* the call, and was ordained
Un.	9–17	They have not *a·* the simple teaching
	55– 1	*a·* the one fact whereby
Rud.	6–16	* fact "almost universally *a·*,
No.	23–10	after the *a·* definition.
	31–24	forgiven in the generally *a·* sense,
My.	12–18	now is the *a·* time." — II Cor. 6 : 2.
	49–32	* Mrs. Eddy *a·* the call.
	53–18	* which invitation she *a·*.
	59–11	* tenets be *a·* wholly or in part by
	145– 6	showed it to me, and I *a·* it.
	236–16	uniformity with which they *a·* the
	324–26	* why he *a·* your invitation

accepting

Mis.	ix– 3	* prevent a man from *a·* charity ;
	101– 5	and *a·* spiritual truth,
	347–17	*a·* the premonition of one of them,
Rud.	5–24	*A·* the verdict of these material

accepts

Mis.	13–20	frail human reason *a·*.
	47–29	depends upon what one *a·* as
'00.	6–15	child not only *a·* C. S. more readily

access

Mis.	155– 9	find *a·* to the heart of humanity.

accessible

Mis.	x– 8	*a·* as reference,

accession

Mis.	204–28	Through the *a·* of spirituality,

accessions

Mis.	149–12	full of *a·* to your love,
My.	9– 1	* large *a·* to their membership.

accessories

My.	149–23	the Principle in its *a·*,

accessory

Mis.	119– 7	punish the dupe as *a·* to the fact.
Ret.	63–19	becomes *a·* to it.

accident

Mis.	24– 9	an injury caused by an *a·*,
	282–27	*a·*, when there is no time for
	380–13	an *a·*, called fatal to life,
Ret.	24–13	an injury caused by an *a·*,
Pul.	34– 6	* met with a severe *a·*,

accidental

Mis.	224–23	no . . . *a·* disturbance shall agitate or

accommodate

Mis.	66–31	I endeavor to *a·* my instructions to
'01.	22–17	nor say this to *a·* popular opinion
My.	22– 5	* *a·* the constantly increasing
	39– 1	* in order to *a·* those who
	80–25	* to *a·* the great throngs who
	82–12	* wagons enough to *a·* the demand.
	86–28	* *a·* the throng of participants.

accommodated

Mis.	136–26	will be *a·* by this arrangement.
My.	75– 6	* chapter sub-title

accommodation

My.	8–16	* to make reasonable *a·* for

accommodations

My.	75–15	* in the matter of securing *a·*.
	88–14	* its *a·* are so wide,
	123–20	my outdoor *a·* at Pleasant View

accompanied

Mis.	51– 5	*a·* by great mental depression,
	143–28	always *a·* with a touching letter
	177–24	* *a·* by Rev. D. A. Easton,
My.	31–23	* *a·* by the Second Reader,
	313–18	always *a·* by some responsible
	331– 7	* who *a·* her to the train

accompanies
  Mis. 47–15 *a·* thought with less impediment
accompaniment
  My. 23–26 * with its inseparable *a·*,
accompany
  Mis. 306– 3 * book which will *a·* the bell
  Un. 64–14 forever *a·* our being.
  My. 74–13 * *a·* them in their triumph of mind
  332–10 * to *a·* her only to New York,
accompanying
  Mis. 189–23 *a·* consciousness of spiritual power
  Ret. 19–22 *a·* her on her sad journey
  58– 8 an *a·* sense of power
  Un. 37–18 The evil *a·* physical personality
  Pul. 86–13 * *A·* the stone testimonial
  My. 172–28 accept from me the *a·* gift
  331– 1 *a·* her on her sad journey
accomplish
  Mis. 41– 4 to *a·* an evil purpose.
  69–23 in their effort to *a·* this result,
  137–23 To *a·* this, you must give much time
  148–21 absolute doctrines . . . might not *a·*.
  273–31 more than one person can well *a·*,
  Man. 3–18 absolute doctrines . . . might not *a·*.
  No. 2– 9 to *a·* this, you cannot begin by
  Hea. 13– 3 and *a·* less on either side.
  My. 150–12 can *a·* the full scale?
  308– 1 divine Love will *a·* what
accomplished
  Mis. 8– 3 we shall have *a·* much ;
  130–19 that they could have *a·*,
  130–21 such Herculean tasks as they have *a·*.
  171–16 the basis upon which are *a·*
  172–13 until the three measures be *a·*,
  238–10 All that ever was *a·*,
  273–18 have not yet *a·* all the good
  297– 6 more than has been *a·* by legally
  302–14 Much good has been *a·*
  Ret. 45– 9 and fellowship has *a·* its end,
  49– 7 having *a·* the worthy purpose for which
  86–21 If . . . the duty will *not be a·*.
  Pul. 21–11 faithfully struggle till it be *a·*
  44– 4 * The 'prayer in stone' is *a·*.
  54–17 * greatest good could be *a·*.''
  Pan. 10–23 *a·* by the grace of God,
  '02. 11–15 how much more is *a·* when
  14–12 *a·* on this solid basis.
  My. 45–14 * prophetically seen has been *a·*.
  59–30 * has *a·* such a work or
  61–16 * that the work would be *a·*
  78–12 * The seating is *a·* in a
  126–23 saw in spiritual vision will be *a·*.
  203–29 if you have not *a·* all you
  241– 3 * until it has *a·* that for which it
  247–28 The little that I have *a·*
  278– 6 this means and end will be *a·*.
  280–10 * *a·* through the righteous prayer
  283–22 *a·* when self is lost in Love
  292– 2 All that can be *a·*, and more
  298– 6 already reported of the good *a·*
  308– 2 can never prevent being *a·*
  321– 4 * had *a·* this great work.
accomplishing
  Mis. 122– 8 this holy (?) alliance for *a·* such a
  214–15 *a·* its purpose of Love,
  230–12 is no proof of *a·* much.
  273–19 good they are capable of *a·*;
  292–25 C. S., . . . is *a·* great good,
  358–25 *a·* the greatest work of the ages,
  Ret. 83– 2 is *a·* the divine purpose
  Pul. 15– 4 mental ways of *a·* iniquity.
accomplishment
  Man. 52–24 *a·* of what she understands is
accord
  Mis. 143–27 ''with one *a·* — Acts 2 : 1.
  238–29 I *a·* these evil-mongers due credit
  354–19 body and soul in *a·* with God.
  372–19 in *a·* with the ancient . . . artists.
  Man. 42–14 in *a·* with all of Mrs. Eddy's
  Ret. 24–21 in perfect scientific *a·* with divine law.
  45–15 in *a·* with my special request,
  76–22 when the disciples were of one *a·*.
  81– 6 keeping them in *a·* with Christ,
  Pul. 34–23 perfect scientific *a·* with the divine law.''
  Peo. 7–32 to *a·* with our thoughts.
  My. 3– 6 not alone in *a·* with human desire
  36–18 * with blessed *a·* we are come,
  157–16 * in *a·* with the expressed wish of
  212–19 ''with one *a·* — Acts 2 : 1.
  232–28 does that watch *a·* with Jesus' saying?
  362–15 * gathered in one place with one *a·*,
accordance
  Mis. 11–16 in *a·* with common law,

accordance
  Mis. 266–25 in *a·* with my students' desires,
  272–13 * In *a·* with Statutes of 1883,
  Man. 42–11 In *a·* with the C. S. textbooks,
  66– 5 then act in *a·* therewith.
  68–25 calls a student in *a·* with
  69– 7 to serve our Leader in *a·* with
  72–13 proper application, made in *a·* with
  80–10 in *a·* with the By-Laws
  100–15 in *a·* with said By-Laws.
  Un. 38– 5 not in *a·* with His law,
  Pul. 85–18 * in *a·* with the prayer and
  My. 78–17 * in *a·* with the custom of the
  112–23 not in *a·* with the Scriptures.
  212–16 they do not practise in strict *a·*
  323– 1 * in *a·* with what Mr. Bates has
  361–21 * in *a·* with your desire for a
accorded
  Ret. 6– 8 *a·* special household privileges.
  My. 284– 4 you may have *a·* me more than
according
  Mis. 17–24 *a·* to the timely or
  22–23 *a·* to the rules of its
  23–30 *a·* to natural science,
  27–20 *A·* to reason and revelation,
  30– 3 *a·* to Jesus' example
  44– 1 ''*a·* to the pattern — Heb. 8 : 5.
  61–21 *A·* to the Word, man is the
  66–10 *a·* to divine decree.
  68–21 *A·* to Webster, metaphysics is
  69–24 *A·* to their diagnosis,
  72– 7 *A·* to the beliefs of the flesh,
  76–11 *A·* to human belief the bodies
  91–26 answer them *a·* to it,
  104–12 *A·* to C. S., perfection is normal,
  114–16 enunciation of these *a·* to Christ.
  117–22 *A·* to my calendar, God's time
  147–15 *a·* as Truth and the voice of
  165–32 origin of man *a·* to divine Science,
  171– 7 *a·* to the report of some,
  191–10 *A·* to the Scripture,
  215–17 not *a·* to the infantile conception
  217–25 *A·* to Holy Writ, it is a kingdom
  219– 1 *A·* to lexicography, teleology is
  220–30 it would be *a·* to the woman's belief ;
  223– 4 *a·* to God's command.
  247–27 reflects harmony or discord *a·* to
  257–32 *a·* to this lawless law which
  261– 6 *A·* to divine law, sin and suffering
  265–13 demonstrates its Principle *a·* to rule,
  289–16 *a·* to the divine precept,
  309– 4 *A·* to C. S., material personality is
  334– 1 doeth *a·* to His will — Dan. 4 : 35.
  337–25 such as lived *a·* to his precepts,
  347– 1 *a·* to his folly, — Prov. 26 : 4.
  348–15 *a·* to his folly, — Prov. 26 : 5.
  360–21 ''the Israel *a·* to Spirit''
  366–28 *a·* to His mode of C. S. ;
  370–13 *a·* to humanity's needs.
  376–19 *A·* to terrestrial calculations,
  Man. 28–12 neither did *a·* to his will, — Luke 12 : 47.
  34– 8 *a·* to the platform and teaching
  39– 1 to live *a·* to its requirements
  39– 2 application for membership *a·* to
  42–22 practised *a·* to the Golden Rule :
  46– 5 *a·* to the laws of our land.
  48–19 *A·* to the Scripture they shall
  56– 3 *a·* to Article XI, Sect. 4.
  62–20 *a·* to their understanding or ability
  81–17 *a·* to the provisions in the
  98–13 published *a·* to copy ;
  100– 8 carried out *a·* to her directions.
  100–11 *a·* to these By-Laws,
  112–10 *a·* to the form on page 114.
  Ret. 1– 1 My ancestors, *a·* to the flesh,
  14– 9 *a·* to his views,
  28–20 *a·* to the law of God.
  36– 3 would not expound the gospel *a·* to
  71–20 *a·* to pure and undefiled religion.
  83–23 and be answered *a·* to it,
  89–20 even *a·* to his promise,
  Un. 2–20 *A·* to this same rule,
  6–13 Until the heavenly law of health, *a·* to
  11–21 *a·* to the ruder sort then prevalent,
  30– 9 suffers, *a·* to material belief,
  31–11 *A·* to C. S., the *first* idolatrous claim
  31–23 evil *does*, *a·* to belief,
  36–11 solved by C. S. *a·* to Scripture.
  36–16 demonstration, *a·* to C. S.,
  44–11 *a·* to Biblical history.
  Rud. 7–12 *A·* to the evidence of the so-called
  7–23 *A·* to divine Science,
  13–11 *a·* to their own belief
  No. v– 2 *a·* to the apostle's admonition,
  9–26 and *a·* to Webster, it is

according
No. 23–12 A· to Crabtre, these devils **were**
24– 3 A· to Spinoza's philosophy
24– 6 a· to Spinoza, man is an
24–10 A· to false philosophy and
25–13 a· to a law of "the survival
Pan. 2–10 A· to Webster the word
13– 6 demonstrated a· to Christ,
'01. 4– 9 demonstrate Love a· to Christ,
8–13 man, a· to C. S.,
8–18 a· to Holy Writ
10–28 faith a· to works.
11–27 a· to his folly, — *Prov.* 26 : 4.
16–17 a· to Holy Writ these qualities
23–15 a· to the Master's teaching and proof.
'02. 3–29 A· to Holy Writ, the first lie
Hea. 10–24 win or lose a· to your plea.
19–22 a· to the model on the mount,
Peo. 10–22 a· to the images that thought
My. 5– 2 a· to the Scriptural allegory,
13–12 A· to his description,
34–29 * are a· to the 1913 edition.
75–25 * A· to the custom of the
79–17 * A· to the despatches,
93–10 * a· to the pledges which it
126–17 a· to her works : — *Rev.* 18 : 6.
127– 5 to be judged a· to their works,
128–15 a· to the dictates of his own
128–29 God will reward your enemies a· to
141–20 A· to the following statement,
143–27 a· to His purpose. — *Rom.* 8 : 28.
167–16 a· to time-tables,
168– 2 worship God a· to the dictates of
186–15 all your needs a· to His riches
194–26 reward you a· to your works,
222– 1 Gospel a· to St. Matthew,
229–16 a· to this saying of Christ Jesus :
240–18 a· to the word of God.
241–24 * a· to the beliefs I entertained
243– 2 A· to reports, the belief is
247– 7 are a· to Christ Jesus ;
254–28 are a· to Christ Jesus ;
261– 6 a· to the custom of the age
268–11 a· to the Principle of law
277–13 shall be a· to His laws.
291–10 zeal a· to wisdom,
300– 4 overcome sin a· to the Scripture,
300–24 a· to Christ's command,
302– 3 a· to a man's belief,
(*see also* **Scriptures**)

accordingly
Mis. 165–25 a· as this account is settled
381–13 A·, her counsel asked the
Ret. 9– 1 A· she returned with me to
38–10 A·, I set to work,
'00. 14–30 you prepare a· for the festivity.
Peo. 1–17 a· as the understanding that we
My. 180–24 what we know is right, and act a·,
329– 2 * license was a· taken out.

accords
Ret. 65–20 It a· with the trend and tenor **of**
'01. 3–15 this a· with the literal sense of
'02. 7– 3 It a· all to God, Spirit,
My. 294–12 whatever a· not with a full faith

account
Mis. 65–25 balancing man's a· with his Maker.
115– 7 can a· for this state of mind
165–25 as this a· is settled with divine Love,
297– 1 Taking into a· the short time that
Ret. 2–24 full a· of the death and burial of
36– 8 This will a· for certain published
No. 41– 9 on a· of persecution,
My. 79– 8 * to read the a· of the dedication
81–26 * any a· of the marvellous cures
161– 7 balancing his a· with divine Love,
179– 4 an a· of the spiritual creation,
334–10 * a· of her husband's demise
351– 5 * on a· of its beautiful tribute to

accountant
Man. 77– 3 by an honest, competent a·.

accounted
Un. 17– 2 to be a· true.
My. 269– 6 which shall be a· worthy — *Luke* 20 : 35.

accounts
Mis. 131–24 opportunity to cancel a·.
131–30 to itemize or audit their a·,
221–16 This a· for many helpless
Pul. 54–18 * A careful reading of the a· of his
'02. 17–19 to square a· with each passing hour.
My. 9–27 what my heart gives to balance a·.

accredited
Pul. 73–25 * has been a· as having been deified.

accretion
Mis. 206–12 gained through growth, not a·.
accrue
Mis. 350–25 benefit that would otherwise a·.
accrues
Un. 2–11 pain which a· to him from it.
accumulates
Mis. 348–14 Error, left to itself, a·.
accumulating
Mis. 17–30 a· pains of sense,
Ret. 44–13 a· work in the College,
My. 276– 7 When a· work requires it,
accumulation
Ret. 82–19 an a· of power on his side
My. 12– 8 * a· of a sum sufficient to
accumulative
Mis. 316–18 Imperative, a·, sweet demands
My. 291– 2 Imperative, a·, holy demands
accurate
Pul. 67– 9 * a· census of the religious faiths
accurately
Un. 31– 1 or, more a· translated,
accuse
Ret. 73–22 or a· people of being unduly personal,
My. 285–24 whereof they now a· me. — *Acts* 24 : 13.
accused
Man. 52–12 guilty of that whereof he is a·
Pul. 12– 8 a· them before our God — *Rev.* 12 : 10.
My. 138–13 cruelly, unjustly, and wrongfully a·.
accuser
Mis. 191–26 define him as an "a·," — *Rev.* 12 : 10.
Pul. 12– 7 a· of our brethren — *Rev.* 12 : 10.
12–20 for the a· is not there,
'01. 16–16 defines *devil* as a·, *calumniator*;
33– 4 "a·" or "calumniator" — *Rev.* 12 : 10.
accusing
Un. 21– 3 a· or else excusing — *Rom.* 2 : 15.
accustomed
Mis. 135–29 in my a· place with you,
256–22 a· to think and to speak of
achieve
'02. 1– 4 no special effort to a· this result,
My. 89–10 * to a· its extreme of beauty.
292– 1 What cannot love . . . a· for the **race?**
achieved
Mis. xi– 7 by what they have hitherto a·
67–22 right practice of Mind-healing a·,
120–12 a· great guerdons in the vineyard
238–10 unselfed love a· for the race
297– 5 a· far more than has been
316–25 had my students a· the point
Ret. 78– 4 student has not yet a· the entire
88–16 a·, both by example and precept.
Pul. 32–29 * a· eminence as a lawyer.
'02. 14–12 the only success I have ever a·
Peo. 11– 7 this victory is a·, not with bayonet
achievement
Mis. 185– 9 a· of his spiritual identity
319–25 opportunity for the grandest a·
340–22 they work on to the a· of good ;
Un. 43– 9 a· of this ultimatum of Science,
Pul. 33–26 * to more than ordinary a·,
84–17 * Of the significance of this a·
84–26 * This a· is the result of long **years of**
'02. 14–20 a· after a· has been blazoned on
My. 37–16 * By reason of your spiritual a·,
43–29 * with wonder upon this grand a·,
86–18 * regarded as an extraordinary a·,
98–30 * has been a wonderful a·,
124– 8 growth, grandeur, and a·,
234–13 from faith to a·,
253– 5 What nobler a·, what greater **glory**
357–18 their success and glory of a·
achievements
Mis. v– 5 a· WHICH CONSTITUTE THE SUCCESS
10– 1 purposes and a· wherewith **to**
125–29 remarkable a· that have been
250–18 noble sacrifices and grand a·
My. 6–26 beauty, and a· of goodness.
10– 4 * a· of its followers.
64– 2 * a· of our beloved Leader
74–15 * one of the finest architectural **a·**
94–30 beauty, and a· of goodness."
134–11 Joy over good a·
256–14 pleasures, a·, and *aid*.
287–20 new possibilities, a·, and
achieves
Mis. 288–14 and thence a· the absolute.
My. 274–14 one a· the Science of Life,

achieving
Mis. 230–24 * Still *a*·, still pursuing,
266–22 who are toiling and *a*· success
My. 185– 6 * Still *a*·, still pursuing,
268– 9 affections are enduring and *a*·.

aching
Mis. 275– 9 bendeth his *a*· head ;
Po. 35–10 An *a*·, voiceless void,

acknowledge
Mis. 5–24 They *a*· an erring or mortal mind,
35– 8 *a*· and attest the blessings
77– 9 not only *a*· the incarnation,
98–25 to *a*· its divine Principle.
247–20 They *a*· the existence of mortal mind,
Man. 15– 6 We *a*· and adore one supreme
15– 7 We *a*· His Son, one Christ ;
15–10 We *a*· God's forgiveness of sin in
15–14 We *a*· Jesus' atonement as the
16– 1 we *a*· that man is saved through
16– 5 We *a*· that the crucifixion of Jesus
74–17 societies are required to *a*·
Un. 64– 3 God can no more behold it, or *a*· it,
Pul. 85– 8 will, in . . . time, see and *a*· it.
Rud. 10–26 learn to *a*· God in all His ways.
Pan. 1–19 shall know and *a*· one God
'01. 35– 1 all thy ways *a*· Him, — *Prov*. 3 : 6.
Peo. 12–12 *a*· only God in all thy ways,
My. 52– 8 * *a*· our indebtedness to her,
62–26 * We *a*· with many thanks
133– 5 at last come to *a*· God,
180–20 refuses to see . . . or to *a*· it,
280– 3 * We *a*· with rejoicing
352– 8 * *a*· our debt of gratitude to you

acknowledged
Mis. 49–12 *a*· and notable cases of
164– 8 until it be *a*·, understood,
166–27 even if not *a*·, has come to be
183– 4 must be *a*· and demonstrated.
349–21 students have openly *a*· this.
Man. 72–11 This church shall be *a*· publicly as
Pul. 71–16 * the *a*· C. S. Leader,
82–17 * *a*· woman as man's proper helpmeet.
No. 18– 3 *a*· God in all His ways.
My. 103– 2 reluctantly seen and *a*·.
146– 7 not been *a*· since the third century.
240– 3 *a*· throughout the earth.
307–12 He even *a*· this himself,

acknowledges
Mis. 62–21 *a*· this fact in her work

acknowledging
Mis. 53–15 which is virtually *a*· that
256– 7 *a*· the public confidence
260–23 *a*· pure Mind as absolute
Ret. 94– 7 though *a*· the true way,
My. 195– 4 *a*· your card of invitation
357–29 I thank you for *a*· me as

acknowledgment
Mis. 185– 9 *a*· and achievement of his
221–20 and *a*· of it in another
Ret. 41– 6 without even an *a*· of the benefit.
Un. 7–20 an *a*· of the perfection of
Pul. 69–21 * *a*· of certain Christian and
Po. vii–10 * grateful *a*·, . . . of this permission,
My. 19–26 with *a*· of exemplary giving,
75– 2 * respectful *a*· of its enthusiasm,
164– 6 chapter sub-title
184–13 I omitted to wire an *a*·
199–12 my grateful *a*· of the receipt of
283– 1 chapter sub-title
336–10 * She makes grateful *a*· of this
347– 8 *a*· of their beautiful gift

acknowledgments
Mis. 274–12 with grateful *a*· to the public
Man. 75– 9 she, with grateful *a*· thereof,

acme
Mis. 100–22 the *a*· of C. S.
122–14 The divine order is the *a*· of mercy :
176–28 act up to the *a*· of divine energy
252–17 C. S. is not only the *a*· of Science
355– 6 good healing is to-day the *a*· of
Un. 61–20 earthly *a*· of human sense.
My. 208–26 reaching the very *a*· of C. S.

aconite
Ret. 26– 6 preparation of poppy, or *a*·,
Hea. 13–11 We have attenuated a grain of *a*·
13–11 until it was no longer *a*·,

acoustic
My. 32– 7 * *a*· properties of the new structure
72– 1 * nicely adjusted *a*· properties
78–22 * The *a*· properties of the temple,

acoustics
No. 6–25 optics, *a*·, and hydraulics are

acquaint
Mis. 328–11 *a*· sensual mortals with the
342–30 *a*· themselves with the etiquette of
Ret. 28– 3 one must *a*· himself with God,
'02. 12–23 a privilege to *a*· communicants with
Peo. 6–24 "*a*· now thyself with Him — *Job* 22 : 21.
My. 7– 6 a privilege to *a*· communicants with
239– 6 *a*· the student with God.

acquaintance
Mis. 151–21 make Him thy first *a*·.
216–15 an *a*· with the author justifies
Un. 4–21 forbid man's *a*· with evil.
54–17 then *a*· with that claimant becomes
54–26 and disowned its *a*·,
'01. 31–12 long *a*· with the communicants of my
Po. v–18 * and who made her *a*·,
My. 223–12 with whom I have no *a*·
320–27 * proud of his *a*· with you.
322–29 * told me of his *a*· with you

acquaintances
Mis. 249–14 as well as my intimate *a*·.
Ret. 19–14 large circle of friends and *a*·,
My. 87–15 * congratulate these comfortable *a*·
330–26 large circle of friends and *a*·,

acquainted
Mis. 43– 4 *a*· with the mental condition of
151–19 art thou *a*· with God?
Un. 55– 5 and *a*· with grief," — *Isa*. 53 : 3.
56–25 become *a*· with that Love which is
My. 42– 9 * no doubt already *a*· with him
145– 2 You are by this time *a*· with
226–28 becomes better *a*· with C. S.,

acquaints
Mis. 175–25 healing which *a*· us with God

acquiescence
Mis. 213– 8 *a*· in the methods of divine Love.
291–10 A tacit *a*· with others' views
Un. 36–18 instead of *a*· therein
Rud. 3– 2 Hence their comparative *a*· in
My. 170– 3 simply my *a*· in the request of
292– 7 joy of *a*· consummated.
293– 7 in his loving *a*·, believed that

acquire
My. 229–11 *a*· in one year the Science that

acquired
Mis. ix– 9 *a*· by healing mankind morally,
Ret. 87– 8 more thoroughly and readily *a*· by
'00. 13–18 There Æsculapius, . . . *a*· fame ;
'01. 26–27 *a*· taste for what was problematic
My. 273–15 sense of rightness *a*· by experience

acquirements
Ret. 7–21 * from his talents and *a*·.

acquiring
Mis. 156–26 no aid to students in *a*· solid C. S.
'01. 2– 4 indispensable to the *a*· of greater

acquisition
My. 87–18 * *a*· of an edifice so handsome

acquitted
My. 125–21 have *a*· themselves nobly.

acre
Mis. 376–21 an *a*· of eldritch ebony.

acres
Mis. 140–26 Our title to God's *a*· will be safe
Ret. 4– 5 of about five hundred *a*·,
4– 7 One hundred *a*· of the old farm
4–21 covered areas of rich *a*·,

across
Mis. 71–29 shadows flitting *a*· the dial of time.
143– 7 *A*· lakes, into a kingdom,
Ret. 5– 1 just *a*· the bridge,
Pul. 44– 5 * *A*· two thousand miles of space,
48–10 * *a*· the farm, which stretches
My. 59–14 * gazing *a*· that sea of heads,
124–12 *a*· continents and oceans,
183–11 Beloved Brethren *a*· the Sea :
200–12 stretches *a*· the sea and rises
259–12 To this church *a*· the sea
342–17 * smaller parlor *a*· the hall,

Act
Mis. 272– 4 * under *A*· of 1874, Chapter 375,
272– 5 * "This *A*· was repealed from
272– 9 * till the repealing of said *A*·
272–11 * substance of this *A*· is at present

act
Mis. 32– 7 in what manner they should *a*·
43– 2 the capabilities of Mind to *a*·
85– 9 every thought and *a*· leading to good.
90–11 It is always right to *a*· rightly ;
108–25 Remember, and *a*· on, Jesus' definition
112–18 regarded his *a*· as one of simple

act

Mis.	117– 6	motive, and *a·* superinduced by the
	124–24	The last *a·* of the tragedy
	124–26	This grand *a·* crowned . . . Christianity :
	131–18	did not *a·* under that By-law ;
	134– 4	contrition for an *a·* which you
	139–27	it will be found that this *a·* was
	146–24	you will *a·*, relative to this matter,
	173–18	space to occupy, power to *a·*,
	176–28	*a·* up to the acme of divine energy
	197– 3	the motive-power of every *a·*.
	205–15	omnipotent *a·* drops the curtain on
	219–12	mortals think . . . and *a·* wickedly :
	272–29	I have endeavored to *a·* toward
	289–14	to *a·* as a whole and per agreement.
	300–17	When I consent to this *a·*,
	305–32	* we ask every one . . . *to a· at once.*
	352–17	enables the practitioner to *a·*
Man.	53– 1	or shall influence others thus to *a·*,
	66– 5	then *a·* in accordance therewith.
	98–22	*a·* under the direction of this
	99–22	*a·* as District Manager of the
	100–14	*a·* upon this important matter
Pul.	3– 8	power to think and *a·* rightly,
Hea.	7–11	begins with motive, instead of *a·*,
	7–12	it corrects the *a·* that results from
	7–16	begins in motive to correct the *a·*,
	7–20	regardless of any outward *a·*,
Peo.	10– 2	Thought is the essence of an *a·*,
My.	12–27	* "*a·* in the living present."
	13– 3	*a·* in God's time.
	108– 6	I challenge matter to *a·* apart from
	108– 8	as it is seen to *a·* apart from matter.
	180–24	and *a·* accordingly,
	250–23	wait for the favored moment to *a·*
	293– 4	*a·* as the different properties of
	293– 5	*a·* — one against the other
	327–20	* section of an *a·* in the Legislature
	328–23	.* machinery *a·* of the Legislature
	345–15	could be made to *a·* on me.
	359– 2	Directors do not *a·* contrary to
	362–18	* as their first *a·* send you their

acted

'01.	13– 6	ought not to be seen, felt, or *a·* :
	14–24	Wrong is thought before it is *a·* ;
Po.	33–15	If these resolutions are *a·* up to,
My.	345–17	they *a·* just the same

acting

Mis.	96–28	not one mind *a·* upon another mind ;
	117–15	basis of all right thinking and *a·* ;
	119– 3	this were no apology for *a·* evilly.
	130–13	*a·* thus regarding disease
	204–32	evil speaking and *a·* ;
	365–13	right thinking and right *a·*,
Ret.	31–14	Truth and Love, *a·* through C. S.
	81–11	false thinking, feeling, and *a·* ;
No.	12– 4	right thinking and right *a·*
	18– 9	Right thinking and right *a·*,
'00.	9– 9	right thinking and *a·* is open to
Hea.	3– 7	foundation of . . . right *a·*,
	15–19	*a·* oppositely to your prayer,
My.	7–18	* *a·* in behalf of ourselves
	12–22	lost in speaking or in *a·*,
	139– 3	living, loving, *a·*, enjoying.
	209– 6	in right thinking and right *a·*,
	254–12	reward of right thinking and *a·*,
	273–14	of thinking, feeling, and *a·*,
	274–11	right feeling, and right *a·*
	309– 5	even *a·* as counsel in a lawsuit

action

all
Mis.	195– 2	follow the absorption of all *a·*,
Hea.	12– 8	mind, the basis of all *a·*,

and effects
Mis.	12–21	*a·* and effects of this so-called

any
Ret.	89–28	to any *a·* not first made known

atomic
Mis.	23–21	is not a result of atomic *a·*,
	190– 1	Atomic *a·* is Mind, not matter.

before
Man.	66–10	before *a·* is taken

ceaseless
Mis.	224–16	the ceaseless *a·* and reaction

element of
Peo.	10– 2	the stronger element of *a·* ;

every
'01.	32–30	governing impulse of every *a·* ;
Peo.	8–18	governs every *a·* of the body

excess of
Mis.	353– 4	is either an excess of *a·* or

fading warmth of
Mis.	342– 6	their fading warmth of *a·* ;

form of
Man.	28– 7	form of *a·*, nations, individuals,

action

God's
Mis.	354–22	pride would regulate God's *a·*.

governed the
Ret.	33– 3	governed the *a·* of material medicine.

harmonious
No.	11– 6	their intelligent and harmonious *a·*,

human
Mis.	268– 3	queries give point to human *a·* :
	288–13	Wisdom in human *a·* begins with
Ret.	93–16	it becomes the model for human *a·*.
'00.	11–28	highest criticism on all human *a·*,

immediate
Man.	51–19	provides for immediate *a·*.

impulse, and
Rud.	3–20	all true volition, impulse, and *a·* ;

incentive for
My.	217– 5	generous incentive for *a·*,

independent
Mis.	289–14	surrenders independent *a·*

internal
Mis.	347– 4	foretell the internal *a·* of

is Science
Mis.	58–25	the *a·* is Science.

its
Mis.	222–16	mental argument and its *a·* on

legal
Man.	67–10	Unauthorized Legal *A·*.
	67–12	nor take legal *a·* on a case

legitimate
No.	9–10	to prevent their legitimate *a·*

liberal
My.	11–17	* because of prompt and liberal *a·*,

misguide
'00.	9–13	bias human judgment and misguide *a·*,

motives for
Mis.	51–17	the right motives for *a·*,

normal
Mis.	350–24	Hence it prevents the normal *a·*,
My.	218– 1	to its normal *a·*, functions, and

of fear
Mis.	41–22	through the *a·* of fear,

of God
Hea.	4– 7	we limit the *a·* of God to the

of man
Mis.	58–24	If God does not govern the *a·* of man,

of Mind
Mis.	70– 6	healing *a·* of Mind upon the body

of mind
Mis.	48–17	through the *a·* of mind alone.
	197–15	such an *a·* of mind would be of no
	220–28	in this *a·* of mind over mind,
	244–14	which are the *a·* of mind
	341– 1	right *a·* of mind or body.

of sickness
Mis.	353– 4	like the *a·* of sickness,

of the body
Peo.	8–18	governs every *a·* of the body

of the church
Mis.	310–23	will determine the *a·* of the church

of the churches
Man.	70–19	*a·* of the churches in said State.

of the divine Mind
Mis.	62–28	based on the *a·* of the divine Mind
My.	108– 7	*a·* of the divine Mind is salutary

of the divine Spirit
Mis.	40–16	namely, the *a·* of the divine Spirit,

organizing
Mis.	177– 9	in organizing *a·* against us.

origin and
Un.	32–10	cannot be separated in origin and *a·*.

points of
Hea.	13– 1	so weaken both points of *a·* ;

put into
Mis.	288– 8	before being put into *a·*.

right
Mis.	171–12	our right *a·* is not to condemn
	341– 1	right *a·* of mind or body.
	354–17	right *a·* of the mental mechanism,

rule of
My.	43– 6	* definite rule of *a·* whereby to

special
Man.	27– 6	shall order no special *a·* to be taken

sphere of
Ret.	89–25	to enlarge their sphere of *a·*.

stage of
'01.	17–22	next more difficult stage of *a·*

such
My.	362–22	* such *a·* as will unite the churches

systematizes
Mis.	235–16	systematizes *a·*, gives a keener sense
My.	287–23	systematizes *a·*, and insures

tending the
Mis.	353–20	tending the *a·* that He adjusts.

their
Man.	94– 5	the churches shall decide their *a·*.

action

their
My. 250–13 please send . . . notice of their *a*.
this
Mis. 166–26 This *a* of the divine energy,
214–11 This *a* of Jesus was stimulated by
220–28 in this *a* of mind over mind,
Pul. 45–27 * This *a*, it appears, was the result
My. 250–26 the impulsion of this *a* in
252–27 You are not aroused to this *a* by
thought and
(*see* **thought**)
thought or
Mis. 3–16 this line of thought or *a*.
260– 8 line of Jesus' thought or *a*.
My. 278–30 brings into human thought or *a*
308– 7 aroused to thought or *a* only by
unchristian
Mis. 81– 4 all unpleasant and unchristian *a*
unity of
My. 212–18 there would be unity of *a*.
unprecedented
Ret. 45–17 noble, unprecedented *a* of
without
Mis. 269–21 without Mind the body is without *a*;
wrong
Mis. 279– 4 prevent the wrong *a*
Pan. 4–14 of right and wrong *a*,
your
Mis. 146– 7 to direct your *a* on receiving or

Mis. 267–27 *a*, in obedience to God,
353– 5 excess of action or not *a* enough:
Man. 90– 7 *a* OF THE BOARD.
My. 278– 2 proper incentive to the *a* of all
361–20 * by *a* at its annual meeting

actions

Mis. 23–29 mirror repeats . . . the looks and *a*
220–10 sick man's thoughts, words, and *a*,
237– 7 wrought a change in the *a* of men.
280– 5 weigh the thoughts and *a* of men;
291–10 other people's thoughts and *a*.
My. 203–16 Our thoughts beget our *a*;
276–20 * seek to dictate the *a* of others.

active

Mis. 206–17 by the *a*, all-wise, law-creating,
250–16 call for *a* witnesses to prove it,
276–11 Scientists, *a*, earnest, and loyal,
278–30 withdrawing from *a* membership in
340–23 Be *a*, and, however slow, thy
Man. 73– 4 at least one *a* practitioner
73–17 unanimous vote of, the *a* members
85–19 *a* and loyal Christian Scientists
Ret. 33–22 is found to be even more *a*.
Pul. 14– 4 *a* yet unseen mental agencies
36– 6 * from *a* contact with the world.
68–10 * from *a* contact with the world.
'*00.* 3– 2 his thoughts are right, *a*, and
'*02.* 8–22 it makes man *a*,
My. 165–16 an *a* portion of one stupendous
230– 4 amid ministries aggressive and *a*,

actively

My. 272– 2 *a* strives for perfection,

activities

Mis. 24–19 increases the intellectual *a*,
362–32 or lessens the *a* of virtue.
My. 37–20 * supreme cause of all the *a* of
382–16 * enlarging the *a* of the Cause

activity

Mis. 250–21 or goodness without *a* and power.
329–21 challenging . . . shadows to *a*,
339–11 because of the supposed *a* of evil.
No. 39–15 purifies, and quickens *a*,
'*00.* 8–19 a percentage due to our *a*
My. 8–28 * religious denomination and its *a*.
37–24 * unbroken *a* of your labors,
66– 5 * considerable *a* has been going on
159–17 this is the only right *a*,
213– 3 spiritual growth and *a*.
213– 5 and give *a* to evil.
213– 6 *a* is by no means a right of evil
259–25 give the *a* of man infinite scope;
353–14 *a* and availability of Truth;

Act of 1874, Chapter 375, Section 4.

Mis. 272– 4 * under *A* of 1874, *C* 375, *S* 4.

actor

Mis. 199–24 but the *a* was human.

actors

Mis. 275– 1 chief *a* in scenes like these,
'*02.* 17–13 Earth's *a* change earth's scenes;

acts

Mis. 46–18 weight of his thoughts and *a*
51–16 Motives govern *a*,

acts

Mis. 119– 4 responsible for our thoughts and *a*;
130–23 and the majority of one's *a* are right,
147–26 for he *a* no studied part;
204–30 ambition, and *a* of the Scientist.
216– 2 inference from his *a*,
219–27 feels wickedly and *a* wickedly,
264–19 it *a* for a season.
278–12 when my motives and *a* are
Man. 40– 4 A Rule for Motives and *A*
40– 6 the motives or *a* of the members
Ret. 78– 1 *a* like a diseased physique,
79–10 in unselfish motives and *a*,
Hea. 5–22 of our own thoughts and *a*;
Peo. 11–19 as directly as men pass legislative *a*
My. 3–17 for it *a* and *a* wisely,
211–16 committal of *a* foreign to the
240–13 for it *a* and *a* wisely,
352–13 reflect in our thoughts and *a* the

actual

Mis. 71–14 All *a* causation must interpret
103–22 hides the *a* power,
129– 8 an imaginary or an *a* wrong,
164–23 in the *a* likeness of his Maker.
182– 6 perceive man's *a* existence
188–27 not . . . an *a* change in the realities
269–15 the *a* Science of Mind-healing
Un. 25–22 it is not individual, not *a*.
56–11 the *a* understanding of C. S.
Pul. vii–21 the *a* bliss of man's existence
55–29 * *a* members of different congregations
Rud. 13– 8 body is not the *a* individuality
No. 24–10 denies the *a* existence of both
31– 9 never *a* persons or real facts.
Hea. 16– 7 hath the most *a* substance,
My. 86–14 * before the *a* work was completed,
160–17 for *a* being, health, holiness, and
348–22 an *a*, unfailing causation,

actuality

Un. 19–16 without any *a* which Truth can know.

actually

Mis. 171– 6 To suppose that Jesus did *a* anoint
Ret. 61– 8 *a* conscious of the truth of C. S.,
My. 72–26 * before the work was *a* completed.

actuate

'*01.* 33–28 motives which *a* one sect to

actuated

'*02.* 8–11 unless he is *a* by love

actuating

Mis. 141–17 spirit of Christ *a* all the parties

acute

Mis. 6– 9 majority of the *a* cases
29–22 *a* diseases that had defied medical
41–23 a belief of chronic or *a* disease,
44– 6 Can C. S. cure *a* cases
204– 7 sometimes chronic, but oftener *a*.
Pan. 10–19 organic, chronic, and *a* diseases

Adam (*see also* Adam's)

Mis. 2–11 this *A* legacy must first be seen,
79–24 "As in *A* all die, — *I Cor.* 15 : 22.
109–19 allegory of *A* and Eve
179–10 "*A*, where art thou?" — *see Gen.* 3 : 9.
182– 9 man was never lost in *A*,
185–27 *The first man A* — *I Cor.* 15 : 45.
185–28 *last A was made* — *I Cor.* 15 : 45.
186– 3 In the creation of *A* from dust,
186–29 last *A* represented by the Messias,
188–29 she knew that the last *A*,
244– 1 from the side of *A*, — *see Gen.* 2 : 21.
258–19 Error, or *A*, might give names
Chr. 53–22 By *A* bid,
Ret. 55– 8 improves the race of *A*.
69–26 '*A*, where art thou?
Un. 30–14 "The first man *A* — *I Cor.* 15 : 45.
30–15 last *A was made* — *I Cor.* 15 : 45.
30–16 refers to the second *A* as
30–23 I discerned the last *A* as a
51–17 but not one . . . is an Eve or an *A*.
'*01.* 5–17 the material race of *A*,
'*02.* 8–28 of man not as the offspring of *A*,
Hea. 2–12 * "Old *A* is too strong for
17–14 The allegory of *A*,
17–16 sleep" that fell upon *A* — *Gen.* 2 : 21.
My. 33– 8 "*A*, Where Art Thou?" — *see Gen.* 3 : 9.

Adam-dream

Ret. 69– 5 was the *A*, the deep sleep,
My. 5– 1 *A* . . . in which man is supposed to
109– 4 *A* of mind in matter,
296–18 the waking out of his *A* of evil

Adam-race

'*00.* 3–16 *A* are not apt to worship the pioneer

Adam's

Ret.	67–22	in no way contingent on *A·* thought,
No.	20–23	*A·* mistiness and Satan's reasoning,

adaptability

Mis.	192–19	learned its *a·* to human needs,
	210–15	woman's special *a·* to lead on C. S.,
My.	250–21	discriminate as regards its *a·* to

adapted

Mis.	46– 7	*a·* to destroy the appearance of evil
	138–22	not so *a·* to the members of
	313–13	jewels of thought, so *a·* to the hour,
	314–31	such as is *a·* to that service.
	315– 3	especially *a·* to the occasion,
Man.	63– 6	*a·* to a juvenile class,
	104– 6	*a·* to The Mother Church only.
	104– 8	*a·* to form the budding thought
Ret.	49–10	S. and H. is *a·* to work this result ;
	82–30	better *a·* to spiritualize thought
Pul.	59–17	* was well *a·* for its purpose,
My.	127–31	a defence *a·* to all men,
	216–21	*a·* to your present unfolding
	233–12	better *a·* to deliver mortals from
	237–11	*a·* to the present demand.
	256– 4	*a·* to the key of my feeling

add

Mis.	135–19	*A·* one more noble offering to the
	216–13	might *a·* to the above definition
	306–17	* We would *a·*, as being of interest,
	314–25	and *a·* to this announcement,
Ret.	40–17	It is sufficient to *a·* her babe was
Pul.	39– 9	*a·* . . . a little poem that I consider
	45– 6	* but *a·* that they can get their
	50– 7	* thus *a·* her influence toward the
No.	8– 4	*a·* one more privilege
'00.	2–22	Here we *a·* : The doom of such
'01.	1–13	*a·* to your treasures of thought the
	26–26	allow me to *a·* I have read little of their
My.	20– 1	please *a·* to your givings
	122–10	and, you may *a·*, with tedious prosaics.
	134–15	And here let me *a·* :
	163–22	Here let me *a·* that,

added

Mis.	178–26	* pastor again came forward, and *a·*
	270–11	shall be *a·* unto you." — *Matt.* 6 : 33.
	339–19	*a·* one furrow to the brow of care?
Chr.	55–11	shall be *a·* unto you. — *Matt.* 6 : 33.
Pul.	69–14	* and *a·* : "This C. S. really is a
	72–25	* *a·* the speaker,
	81–11	* the woman of the past with an *a·* grace
No.	45– 4	*a·* : "Charity suffereth long, — *I Cor.* 13 : 4.
'00.	10–18	wisdom of our forefathers is not *a·*
'01.	2–30	been *a·* since last November
	22–16	I do not say that one *a·* to one is
'02.	1– 7	*a·* to our church during the year
Hea.	2–15	*a·* his testimony :
My.	8–30	* congregations have been *a·*,
	50–25	* members were *a·* to the church."
	69–14	* *a·* magnificent carvings to
	130–22	must have the author's name *a·*
	210– 5	plain that nothing can be *a·* to
	222–12	Also he *a·* : "This kind — *Matt.* 17 : 21.
	307– 2	*a·* to his copy when I corrected it.
	318– 3	where Mr. Wiggin *a·* words,

addenda

'01.	21– 3	They are not the *a·*,

addendum

Mis.	57–14	That this *a·* was untrue, is seen

addicted

Mis.	242–30	*a·* to the use of opium

adding

Ret.	44–29	*A·* to its ranks and influence,
My.	195–18	our only means of *a·* to that talent

addition

Mis.	30– 4	Should we adopt the "simple *a·*"
	60–15	to say that *a·* is not subtraction
	106–19	In *a·*, I can only bring
	234–23	in *a·* to this, she has
Man.	68–12	in *a·* to rent and board.
	99–21	he shall, in *a·* to his other duties,
Ret.	59– 8	It is like saying that *a·* means
	59– 9	and *a·* in another,
Un.	53–18	assertion that the rule of *a·* is
	54–22	distinct *a·* to human wisdom,
My.	16–13	* In *a·* to the members of
	67–19	* *a·* to The First Church of Christ,
	75–26	* big *a·* to The Mother Church
	299–13	In *a·* to this, C. S. presents
	310– 5	In *a·* to my academic training,

additional

Mis.	50–14	There is absolutely no *a·* secret
Un.	35–27	which can gather *a·* evidence of
Pul.	50–14	* no *a·* sums outside of the
My.	335–11	* *A·* facts regarding Major Glover,

Address

Mis.	98– 7	my *A·* at the National Convention
	106–15	chapter sub-title
	110–13	chapter sub-title
	116– 7	chapter sub-title
	120–26	chapter sub-title
	143–13	chapter sub-title
	251– 1	chapter sub-title
My.	131–17	chapter sub-title
	148– 9	chapter sub-title
	170–11	chapter sub-title

address

Mis.	63–13	*a·* himself to the healing of
	69–27	I will send his *a·* to any one
	144– 9	laid away a copy of this *a·*,
	155–25	when they *a·* me I shall be apt to
	253– 8	speakers that will now *a·* you
	280–23	brief *a·* by Mr. D. A. Easton,
	315–24	shall not . . . mentally *a·* the thought,
	322– 9	present to *a·* this congregation,
	368–19	silent *a·* of a mental malpractitioner
Man.	52– 9	shall *a·* a letter of inquiry
Pul.	5– 4	*a·* on C. S. from my pen,
	60– 4	* There was no *a·* of any sort,
	86–14	* *a·* from the Board of Directors :
My.	53–31	* so many different ones *a·* them
	64–22	* *a·* ourselves with renewed faith
	299– 4	kindly referring to my *a·*
	363–21	*a·* before the Christian Scientist

addressed

Mis.	60– 3	*the Bible is a· to sinners*
Man.	36–24	*A·* to Clerk.
	36–25	*a·* to the Clerk of the Church.
Ret.	90–10	St. John *a·* one of his epistles
Pul.	74–11	* *a·* to the editor of the *Herald :*
Rud.	15–23	who cannot be *a·* individually,
My.	140–12	* letter *a·* to Christian Scientists
	223–23	*a·* to the C. S. Board of Directors
	271–20	* *a·* this question, requesting the
	351– 3	* her letter of recent date, *a·* to

addresses

Ret.	15–22	made memorable by eloquent *a·*
My.	74–19	* not only evident from their *a·*

addressing

Mis.	320–21	*a·* to dull ears and undisciplined
My.	318–24	and, *a·* me, burst out with :

adds

Ret.	60– 9	Material sense *a·* that the
Un.	36– 1	only as it *a·* lie to lie.
Pul.	68–21	* *a·* interest to the Baltimore
Rud.	2– 4	He *a·*, that among Trinitarian
	6–15	he *a·* that this is not
Hea.	11–19	metaphysics *a·*, "until you arrive at
My.	121–22	C. S., however, *a·* to these graces,
	310–25	and *a·* that these "fits" were

adequacy

'02.	4– 6	their *a·* and correct analysis of

adequate

Mis.	4–18	*a·* to meet the requirement.
	43–11	trifling sense of it as being *a·* to
	341–31	neither . . . are *a·* to plead for
Man.	101– 6	who shall receive an *a·* salary
My.	22– 8	* sum of money *a·* to
	40– 4	* able to give more *a·* reception to
	56– 2	* be *a·* for years to come.
	243–14	who are *a·* to take charge of
	248–12	*a·* for the emancipation of the race.

adhere

Mis.	92–16	teacher should strictly *a·* to the
	233–28	they only who *a·* to that standard.
	284–10	Students who strictly *a·* to the right,
	307–27	*a·* to the divine Principle
	309–29	*a* to the Bible and S. and H.,
Ret.	8–12	*a·* to the orderly methods
'01.	2–17	these are they who will *a·* to it.
	22–19	I *a·* to my text, that one and one
Hea.	8–26	*a·* to the rule of this Principle
My.	111–18	Can Scientists *a·* to it,
	182–30	May this beloved church *a·* to
	251–29	*A·* to the teachings of the Bible,

adhered

Mis.	172–29	must be understood and *a·* to ;

adherence

Mis.	65–27	proves that strict *a·* to one is
	140– 9	their *a·* to the superiority of
	198–23	suffering is the fruit of . . . *a·* to
Man.	44– 2	show strict *a·* to the Golden Rule,
Ret.	50–21	*a·* to divine Truth and Love.
	87–13	implicit *a·* to fixed rules,
My.	84–19	* in numbers, . . . and faithful *a·*.
	94–11	* *a·* of its converts to the faith,

adherent
Mis. 62–20 An a· to this method honestly
Pul. 59–18 * not an a· of the order,

adherents
Mis. 213–18 a· of Truth have gone on rejoicing.
Man. 15– 3 As a· of Truth, we take the
Pul. 30–10 * is not limited to the Boston a·,
57–16 * a· of this church have proved
60–14 * thousands of a· who had come
79–11 * a· in every part of the civilized
My. 45– 4 * ultimate regeneration of its a·
59– 9 * should number its a· by
85– 7 * a· number probably a million,
93–31 * a· number hundreds of thousands,
96–17 * generosity of its a· towards

adheres
Ret. 84– 9 he strictly a· to the teachings in

adhering
Mis. 108–28 believing in, or a· to,
Man. 70– 6 a· strictly to her advice thereon.
My. 111–23 in a· to his premise
235– 7 a· to the imperative rules of

adieu
My. 347–13 * nor ever bid the Spring a·!

ad infinitum
Mis. 364–30 reality and power to evil a· i·.
Un. 41–27 phenomena appear to go on a· i·;
No. 21–19 perpetuate the supposed power. . . a· i·.
My. 245–19 majestic march of C. S. go on a· i·,

adipose
Mis. 47– 5 a· belief of yourself as substance ;

adjoining
Ret. 4– 5 a· towns of Concord and Bow,
9– 2 led my cousin into an a· apartment.
Pul. 34–15 * she walked into the a· room,
58–23 * A· the chancel is a pastor's
My. 12– 7 * land a· The Mother Church,
69–21 * A· this foyer are the

adjourn
Mis. 139– 1 recommend this honorable body to a·,

adjourned
Mis. 156–13 proposed to merge the a· meeting in

adjudged
Man. 44– 4 shall not be a· C. S.

adjust
Mis. 283– 5 upset, and a· his thoughts
317–20 Human desire is inadequate to a·

adjusted
Mis. 321– 9 balance a· more on the side of God,
My. 72– 1 * nicely a· acoustic properties

adjusting
Mis. 379–30 a· in the scale of Science

adjustment
My. 277–13 its a· shall be according to

adjusts
Mis. 353–20 the action that He a·.

ad libitum
Mis. 285–23 new-style conjugality, which, a· l·,
318– 9 affection for goodness must go on a· l·

administer
Mis. 90–22 a· the communion,
241–18 a· this alterative Truth :
Peo. 9–19 and then a· drugs
My. 129–21 Then will angels a· grace,

administered
Mis. 90–25 a· to his disciples the Passover,
'01. 18–11 who a· no remedy apart from Mind,
My. 247– 3 its government is a· by
254–24 its government is a· by

administering
Hea. 13–13 a· one teaspoonful of this water

administers
My. 107–15 homœopathist a· half a dozen or

administration
My. 69–22 * and the a· offices,

admirable
Pul. 29–19 * In his a· discourse Judge Hanna

admirably
My. 256– 4 a· adapted to the key of my feeling

Admiral
Mis. 281–12 A· Coligny, in the time of the

admiration
Mis. 167–22 in a· of his origin, he exclaims,
Pul. 61–21 * Much a· was expressed by all
My. 25–24 a· for and faith in the
31–16 * expressions of surprise and of a·
70–14 * stood in silent a· while

admire
My. 85–22 * to reverence and a·!
282– 4 I a· the faith and friendship of

admired
Po. 2–12 A· by all, still art thou drear

admirer
Mis. 294–26 an a· of Edgar L. Wakeman's

admirers
Pul. 47– 4 * her circle of pupils and a·

admires
My. 41–19 * affection which a· friends and hates

admiring
My. 86– 1 * the greeting of a· eyes,

admissible
Mis. 32–15 love alone is a· towards friend and
Ret. 21–28 may be a· and advisable ;

admission
Mis. 46– 1 The a· of the reality of evil
196–30 require more than a simple a·
346–16 mortal a· of the reality of evil
Man. 67– 3 candidates for a· to this Church,
88–18 applying for a· to this Board
91–14 President gives free a· to classes.
Pul. 60– 2 * waiting for a·.
No. 2–14 through such an a·,
My. 30– 2 * or awaiting a· to one.
30–29 * for a· at the ten o'clock service,
57–20 * more than the hitherto largest a·,
79–12 * to gain a· to the temple

admissions
Mis. 42–31 our own false a· prevent us

admit
Mis. 2– 9 a· the total depravity of mortals,
14–11 to a· this vague proposition,
57– 4 which you a· cannot discern
58–29 you a· that there is more than
59–15 to a· that it has been lost
74–30 If you will a·, with me,
76–25 You will a· that Soul is the
81– 3 scholarly physicians openly a·.
109– 9 how much of this claim you a·
193–22 to a· that all Christians are
Man. 36–23 may a· said applicant to membership.
Ret. 54– 6 to a· the claims of the
Un. 22– 9 Thou shalt not a· that error
22–11 To a· the existence of error
22–12 would be to a· the truth of a lie.
36–22 yet a· the reality of moral
54– 3 is to a· all there is of sickness ;
54–11 To a· that sin has any claim
54–12 is to a· a dangerous fact.
Pul. 56–10 * Space does not a· of an elaborate
No. 2–12 healers who a· that disease is real
31– 2 if you a· that God sends it
41–18 never a· such as come to steal
'01. 23– 4 a· that God is Spirit and infinite,
33–18 a· that they do not kill people with
'02. 10–17 Religions in general a· that man
Hea. 12–25 a· the higher attenuations are
18–25 You must a· that what is termed
My. 61–22 * as the workmen began to a· that
97– 1 * almost every one is inclined to a·.
97– 2 * a· the power of mind over matter.
315–27 which they a· has snatched me from

admits
Mis. 102–13 His character a· of no degrees
209–13 physics a· the so-called pains of
Ret. 54–14 when it a· Truth without
Un. 34– 4 Mortal mind a· that it sees only
Hea. 15–17 a· in statement what he denies in
My. 211–31 which a· of no intellectual culture

admittance
My. 39– 2 * those who could not gain a·
188–31 When divine Love gains a· to
265– 5 and that it finds a

admitted
Mis. 219–12 a· that mortals think wickedly
Man. 35– 6 may be a· to membership
Ret. 6–22 a· to the bar in two States,
13– 1 a· to the Congregational . . . Church,
54–17 if Truth is a·, but not understood,
Un. 23–16 evidence of . . . is not to be a·,
54–24 both knew and a· the dignity of
'01. 33– 5 must not be a· to the vineyard
My. 38–11 * no more were a· until the next
57–18 * number of candidates a·
57–21 * number a· during the last year
311– 5 knocked at the door and was a·.

admitting
Mis. 18–24 Only by a· evil as a
27–31 first a· that it is substantial.

admitting

Mis.	109–21	*a·* the existence of both, mortals
No.	2–10	you cannot begin by *a·* its reality.
	46–13	begin by *a·* individual rights.
Pan.	4–28	By *a·* self-evident affirmations
Hea.	5– 2	While *a·* that God is omnipotent,
My.	222–14	*a·* the claims of the senses
	329–23	* *a·* its interest in the movement,

admixtures

Pan.	8–25	are *a·* of matter and Spirit,

admonish

Mis.	107– 7	to *a·* them,
	141–25	I *a·* you : Delay not longer
Man.	56– 2	to *a·* that member according to
My.	106– 2	I *a·* Christian Scientists either to

admonished

Mis.	361–17	To this great end, Paul *a·*,
	366–20	even as Jesus *a·*.
Man.	51– 1	shall be *a·* in consonance with

admonishes

Mis.	339–15	The past *a·* us :
Peo.	10–25	and, as St. Paul *a·*,

admonition

Mis.	292–23	Charity thus serves as *a·* and
	328–27	observe the apostle's *a·*,
Man.	51– 4	if he neglect to accept such *a·*,
	78– 3	fails to heed this *a·*,
No.	v– 3	according to the apostle's *a·*,
My.	37–29	* its wise counsel and *a·*.
	287– 8	serving as *a·*, instruction, and

admonitions

My.	46–26	* *a·* of our Church Manual

ado

Hea.	14– 3	in fine, much *a·* about nothing.

adopt

Mis.	19–11	to *a·* them and bring them out in
	30– 4	Should we *a·* the "simple addition"
	215–28	nor *a·* the words, that Jesus used
Man.	59–11	to *a·* the aforenamed method for
	72– 2	Branch churches shall not *a·*,
Ret.	88–25	we should *a·* the spirit of
Un.	50–25	*A·* this rule of Science,
'01.	3–10	*a·* Webster's definition of God,
	30–28	and to *a·* Pope's axiom :
Hea.	18–14	would willingly *a·* the new idea,
My.	128–14	man's right to *a·* a religion,
	224–30	let us *a·* the classic saying,
	235–24	*a·* as truth the above statements?
	236– 9	please *a·* generally for your name,
	250– 7	*a·* this By-law in their churches,
	250–12	churches who *a·* this By-law

adopted

Mis.	x–26	*a·* that form of signature,
	111– 2	to demonstrate what you have *a·*
	111–32	or is a spiritually *a·* child,
	140–18	*a·* and urged only the
	359– 4	Christly method . . . must be *a·*.
Man.	18–23	The Church Tenets, . . . were *a·*.
	18–24	By-Law *a·* March 17, 1903,
	46– 3	who claims a spiritually *a·* child
	46– 3	or a spiritually *a·* husband or wife.
	105– 2	No new Tenet or By-Law shall be *a·*,
Ret.	43–10	my *a·* son, Ebenezer J. Foster-Eddy,
	44–25	proper measures were *a·* to
Hea.	2– 8	afterwards pardoned and *a·*,
My.	266–28	more spiritual modes . . . are *a·*.
	282– 9	Douma recently *a·* in Russia
	313–28	wounded her pride when I *a·* C. S.,

adopting

Mis.	77–20	In *a·* all this vast idea of
	193–21	a word which the people are now *a·*.
My.	250–20	churches *a·* this By-law will

adoption

Mis.	15– 6	"waiting for the *a·*, — *Rom.* 8 : 23.
	15–15	joyful *a·* of good ;
	95–22	"waiting for the *a·*, — *Rom.* 8 : 23.
	101– 6	that which blesses its *a·* by
	182–10	find their *a·* with the Father ;
	184–25	as the seal of man's *a·*.
Man.	46– 1	Illegal *A·*.
	46– 4	There must be legal *a·* and
Ret.	78–16	the *a·* of a worldly policy
Peo.	10–25	"waiting for the *a·*, — *Rom.* 8 : 23.

adopts

Man.	71–17	or *a·* The Mother Church's form of

adorable

Mis.	106–23	the most *a·*, but most unadored,
	331–30	this *a·*, all-inclusive God,

adoration

Pul.	5– 3	offered his audible *a·* in the words
No.	35– 6	through deep humility and *a·*

adore

Mis.	96–20	I reverence and *a·* Christ
	124–22	*a·* the white Christ,
Man.	15– 6	*a·* one supreme and infinite God.
Ret.	18–18	freely *a·* all His spirit hath made,
Un.	4– 1	He is near to them who *a·* Him.
Po.	64– 9	*a·* all His spirit hath made,

adoring

Pan.	14– 6	if daily *a·*, imploring, and

adoringly

Ret.	26– 3	*A·* I discerned the Principle of

adorn

Mis.	392– 3	Clouds to *a·* thy brow,
Po.	20– 3	Clouds to *a·* thy brow,
My.	121–16	gems that *a·* the Christmas ring
	195–30	continue to build, rebuild, *a·*, and

adorned

Pul.	48–20	* *a·* the mantel.
My.	125–26	the bride (Word) is *a·*,

adornment

Pul.	42–19	* was rich with the *a·* of flowers.
My.	71–11	* great *a·* to the city.

adorns

Pul.	76–14	* superb mantel . . . *a·* the south wall.
My.	285– 8	Whatever *a·* Christianity crowns the

adown

'02.	4–16	*a·* the corridors of time,

adulation

My.	302–24	and I refuse *a·*.

adult

Mis.	34–19	or the *a·* can return to his
	159–20	risen Christ, and the *a·* Jesus.
	241– 2	faith of both youth and *a·* should
Pul.	1– 8	An old year is time's *a·*,
No.	26– 7	identical with the *a·*,
'00.	6–16	more readily than the *a·*,
	6–19	sense which the *a·* entertains of it.

adulterate

Mis.	67– 6	thou shalt not *a·* Life, Truth, or
	268–25	let us not *a·* His preparations

adulterated

Man.	43–20	prevent C. S. from being *a·*.
Ret.	61–30	let not the milk be *a·*.

adulterating

Man.	43–13	No *A·* C. S.

adulterer

My.	106–25	a profane swearer, an *a·*,

adulterers

Mis.	324–13	Within this mortal mansion are *a·*,

adulteries

'01.	20–27	will handle its thefts, *a·*, and

adultery

Mis.	67– 5	shalt not commit *a·*;" — *Exod.* 20 : 14.
	335–18	murder, steal, commit *a·*,
Hea.	7–22	Jesus knew that *a·* is a crime,
My.	268–16	shalt not commit *a·*" — *Exod.* 20 : 14.
	314–16	cause nevertheless was *a·*.

advance

Mis.	xi– 6	are still in *a·* of their time ;
	6–15	will rank far in *a·* of allopathy
	21–12	As the ages *a·* in spirituality,
	22– 8	far in *a·* of human knowledge
	29–26	nor *a·* health and length of days.
	50–26	*a·* Christianity a hundredfold,
	108–16	and *a·* the second stage of
	118–14	*a·* individual growth,
	139–28	in *a·* of the erring mind's
	199–25	as we *a·* in the spiritual
	274– 9	more than my teaching would *a·* it :
	359–21	were in *a·* of the period
	366– 3	they would *a·* the world.
Ret.	54–21	is far in *a·* of their theory.
	70–12	or *a·* speculative theories
	94– 2	Having perceived, in *a·* of others,
'01.	33–28	persecute another in *a·* of it.
'02.	10– 7	call them false or in *a·* of the
Peo.	12–17	As our ideas of Deity *a·*
My.	20–11	name your gifts to her, in *a·*?
	21– 9	* *a·* the erection of many branch
	148–28	scourging the sect in *a·* of it.
	216–26	*a·* in the knowledge of self-support,
	252–25	was a step in *a·*.
	342–32	will *a·* nearer perfection."

advanced

Mis.	52–28	before solving the *a·* problem.
	234–16	never has *a·* man a single step
	295–24	The most *a·* ideas are
	308–12	*A·* scientific students are ready
	311–12	not quite ready to take this *a·* step
	345–21	against an *a·* form of religion,

advanced

Mis.	379–16	He certainly had *a·* views
Ret.	34–18	he is *a·* morally and spiritually.
Pul.	vii–12	telescope of that *a·* age,
'01.	33– 8	* in the more *a·* decaying stages
Hea.	1–11	to wait until the age *a·*
My.	22–24	* *a·* position taken by our
	44–15	* *a·* to the front of the platform,
	80– 5	* of consumption in its *a·* stages,
	95–21	* when "*a·*" clergymen of other
	139–23	you have *a·* from the audible to
	140–23	Christ, points the *a·* step.
	160–28	*a·* psychist knows that this hell is
	310– 2	sufficiently *a·* so that they

advancement

Mis.	6– 7	needed for the *a·* of the age.
Ret.	49– 2	for the *a·* of the world in Truth
	81–30	requisite at every stage of *a·*.
Pul.	50– 7	* toward the *a·* of better home life
Hea.	8–12	slow to perceive individual *a·* ;
My.	113–30	steady *a·* of this Science
	239–28	state and stage of mental *a·*,
	241– 8	* prevent their *a·* in this direction.
	281–25	* *a·* of the cause of arbitration."
	339–13	New Hampshire's *a·* is marked.

advances

Mis.	309–11	He *a·* most in divine Science who
My.	140–20	*a·* it spiritually.

advancing

Mis.	2– 1	the evolutions of *a·* thought,
	42–19	our joys and means of *a·*
	206–11	The *a·* stages of C. S.
	222– 5	to believe that he is *a·* while
	246–31	The *a·* faith and hope
	247– 3	*proofs of a· truth*
	360–32	No *a·* modes of human mind
	363–30	every *a·* epoch of Truth
Ret.	70–21	the *a·* idea of God,
Un.	61–12	Human perception, *a·* toward the
	61–15	neither *a·*, retreating, nor
No.	19– 8	second thought of *a·* humanity.
	33– 7	by *a·* the kingdom of Christ.
	39–24	*A·* in this light, we reflect it ;
	46– 6	The *a·* hope of the race,
'01.	1– 7	more extended, more rapidly *a·*,
	29– 5	mortals in the *a·* stages of their
'02.	10–12	*a·* above itself towards the Divine,
	11–20	Therefore it is thine, *a·* Christian,
Hea.	2– 7	condemned at every *a·* footstep,
My.	45–26	* each *a·* step has logically
	135–12	more peace in my *a·* years,
	135–27	cheer my *a·* years.
	139– 7	*a·* footsteps of progress,
	200– 2	rapidly *a·*, . . . the genius of C. S.
	242– 6	nor *a·* towards it ;
	322–25	* *a·* many good points in the Science,

advantage

Mis.	35–25	it is greatly to your *a·*
	156–14	no *a·*, but great disadvantage,
	255–17	chapter sub-title
	283– 2	one can to *a·* speak the
Pul.	62– 7	* *a·* of great economy of space,
No.	2–25	Taking *a·* of the present ignorance
	41–10	to the best *a·* for mankind
My.	37–11	* everlasting *a·* of this race.
	97–13	* Scientists have a little the *a·*

advantageous

Mis.	43–14	far more *a·* to the sick
Man.	52–25	of what she understands is *a·*
My.	244– 5	if a larger class were *a·* to

advantageously

Rud.	15–19	can *a·* enter a class,

advantages

Mis.	33–21	*What are the a· of your system*
	33–23	C. S. has the following *a·*:
	255–18	What are the *a·* of your system
	255–21	I claim . . . the following *a·*:
Ret.	34–10	following *a·*: . . . It does away with

advent

Mis.	10–26	this is the *a·* of spiritualization.
	162– 5	*a·* of a higher Christianity.
	320– 5	its earthly *a·* and nativity,
Ret.	70–21	spiritual *a·* of the advancing idea
	81–15	supreme *a·* of Truth in the heart,
Pul.	55– 8	* is the *a·* of C. S.
'01.	24–19	its earthly *a·* is called
My.	239–30	accelerated by the *a·* of C. S.,
	256–19	earthly *a·* and nativity of our Lord
	308– 3	*a·* of divine healing

adventure

My.	158– 9	in an age of Love's divine *a·*

adversary

'00.	2–24	than the *a·* can hope.

adverse

No.	6–22	more apparent than the *a·* but **true**
'01.	29–19	and *a·* winds are blowing,
'02.	11– 4	to and fro by *a·* circumstances,
My.	41– 9	* thoughts *a·* to the law of love.
	195– 5	*A·* circumstances, loss of help,
	213–25	*a·* influence of animal magnetism.

adversity

Mis.	8–22	* "Sweet are the uses of *a·*."
My.	139–10	Christian Scientist thrives in *a·* ;

advertise

Man.	46–10	which *a·* his business or profession,
	82–18	shall not *a·* as healers,
My.	191– 5	Your enemies will *a·* for you.

advertised

Man.	72–15	may be *a·* in *The C. S. Journal.*
	74–19	churches and . . . *a·* in said *Journal,*
My	57–23	* *a·* in *The C. S. Journal*
	57–25	* number of societies *a·*
	306–24	I *a·* that I would pay
	334– 8	* *a·* in every weekly issue of

Advertiser

Pul.	88–12	* *A·*, Calais, Me.
	88–13	* *A·*, Boston, Mass.
	88–25	* *A·*, New York City.

advertiser

Man.	82–12	without the request of the *a·*,

advertising

'02.	13–21	*a·* the property in the

advice

Mis.	137–18	dear ones, if you take my *a·*
	236– 8	giving *a·* on personal topics.
	236–16	to give, to one or the other, *a·*
	243–23	alludes to Paul's *a·* to Timothy.
	298–24	chapter sub-title
	350– 5	By and with *a·* of the very student
	350–10	There was no *a·* given,
Man.	70– 6	adhering strictly to her *a·*
'00.	9– 4	I sometimes withdraw that *a·*
My.	122– 1	*a·* that one gratuitously bestows
	313–24	nor did . . . seek my *a·*.
	345–24	about *a·* on surgical cases."

advisable

Mis.	53–11	*Do you sometimes find it a· to*
	89–10	*a·* in most cases that Scientists
Ret.	21–28	may be admissible and *a·* ;
	85– 3	Teachers of C. S. will find it *a·*

advise

Mis.	308–32	I earnestly *a·* all Christian Scientists
	347–15	Two individuals, . . . *a·* me.
Man.	87–12	No member . . . shall *a·* against **class**
No.	8–10	*A·* students to rebuke
'00.	8–30	I sometimes *a·* students not to
My.	360–17	I *a·* you with all my soul to

advised

'02.	15–26	*a·* me to drop both the book and **the**
My.	319–20	* may interest you to be *a·* that

advisers

Hea.	9–11	their moral *a·* talk for them

advises

My.	226–27	"Mrs. Eddy *a·*, until the public

advising

Rud.	15–12	*a·* diseased people not to enter a

advisory

My.	63– 4	* *a·* capacity in the later days ;

advocacy

Ret.	7–18	* *a·* of the side he deemed right.

advocate

Ret.	78–12	which *a·* materialistic systems ;

Æolian

Pul.	26–13	* with *Æ·* attachment,
	60–21	* having an *Æ·* attachment.

aerial

Ret.	11– 5	If fancy plumes *a·* flight,
Po.	60– 1	If fancy plumes *a·* flight,

Æsculapius (*see also* **Esculapius**)

'00.	13–18	*Æ·*, the god of medicine,
	13–19	serpent was the emblem of *Æ·*.
	13–23	school of Balaam and *Æ·* ;
My.	105– 4	This *Æ·*, defined Christianly
	205–17	spiritual *Æ·* and Hygeia, saith,

æsthetic

My.	88–28	* *æ·* debt to that great and growing

afar

Mis.	174–19	Is this kingdom *a·* off?
	342–20	fables flee, and heaven is *a·*
	393–16	From the shores *a·*, complete.
	397–13	From tired joy and grief *a·*,
Chr.	53– 2	Bright, blest, *a·*,

afar
Pul.	18–22	From tired joy and grief *a·*,
Po.	13– 1	From tired joy and grief *a·*,
	51–21	From the shores *a·*,
	68–23	whether near or *a·*.
	73–17	*a·* from life's turmoil its goal.
My.	183–25	Not *a·* off I am
	290– 4	near seems *a·*, the distant nigh,
	290–18	when all earthly joys seem most *a·*.

affair
Mis.	52–13	occasionally a love *a·*.

affairs
Mis.	204–25	all the minutiæ of human *a·*.
	267–23	human *a·* should be governed by
	297–12	reports of American *a·*
	312–14	* of divine Providence in human *a·*
Man.	69–24	or attend to other *a·* outside
	74– 9	interfere with its *a·*.
Pul.	55–28	* in the management of its own *a·*.
My.	43– 6	* order aright the *a·* of daily life.
	135– 9	attended to my secular *a·*,
	137–12	to my secular *a·*,
	137–19	*a·* carefully taken care of for
	216– 1	wisdom should temper human *a·*,
	223–13	questions about secular *a·*,
	340–25	rule righteously the *a·* of state.
	359–- 9	involved in the *a·* of the church

affect
Mis.	31– 5	disastrously *a·* the happiness of
Pul.	51–16	* *a·* the well-established methods.
My.	179–25	in no wise *a·* C. S.
	301–25	or *a·* cerebral conditions in any

affected
Ret.	33–17	patients not *a·* by a larger dose.

affecting
Ret.	71–13	know not what is *a·* them,
My.	328–11	* the law *a·* them passed by the

affection (*see also* affection's)
distinguishing
Ret.	94–26	distinguishing *a·* illustrated in

faith, and
Mis.	100–29	forgiveness, abiding faith, and *a·*,

faithful
Mis.	110– 6	innocence, unselfishness, faithful *a·*,

fervid
My.	248–12	honest, fervid *a·* for the race

gratitude and
Mis.	203– 5	mine through gratitude and *a·*.

growing
Mis.	337–18	unless it produces a growing *a·*

higher
Mis.	276–23	a purer, higher *a·* and ideal.

human
Mis.	287–20	foundations of human *a·*
My.	234–12	human *a·* to spiritual understanding,
	268– 8	If the motives of human *a·* are right,

its
Mis.	351–28	chastens its *a·*, purifies it,

just
Ret.	76–19	This just *a·* serves to

large
Mis.	318– 5	I have a large *a·*,

legitimate
Mis.	287– 9	discerning not the legitimate *a·*

may dwell
Ret.	18–20	the spot where *a·* may dwell
Po.	64–12	the spot where *a·* may dwell

miscall
Mis.	250– 5	Mortals misrepresent and miscall *a·*;

natural
Mis.	318– 9	natural *a·* for goodness

objects of
Ret.	31– 1	material objects of *a·*

of nations
My.	290– 7	live on in the *a·* of nations.

one
No.	39–18	include all mankind in one *a·*.

or love
Ret.	80– 1	an unselfish *a·* or love,

our
Ret.	80–28	in proportion to our *a·*.
My.	9–12	* declare the depth of our *a·*

permanence of
Mis.	160– 1	power and permanence of *a·*

preserve
Mis.	287–30	preserve *a·* on both sides.

pride and
Mis.	295–13	Scotchman's national pride and *a·*,

protection and
Mis.	263–12	divine protection and *a·*.

pure
Mis.	107–11	A pure *a·*, concentric,

pure in
Mis.	152–19	made ready for the pure in *a·*,

affection
real
Mis.	91–16	real *a·* for Jesus' character

reason and
Mis.	363–23	misguides reason and *a·*,

respect and
My.	37– 9	* gratitude, respect, and *a·*
	88–25	* turn with respect and *a·*.

same
No.	12–13	The same *a·*, desire, and

sentimental
My.	41–19	* rise from sentimental *a·* which

significance of
Mis.	250–22	the glorious significance of *a·*

so-called
Mis.	250– 6	so-called *a·* pursuing its

tender
My.	36–27	* tender *a·* for the cause of

this
Ret.	76–15	This *a·*, so far from being

true
Mis.	142–18	varying types of true *a·*,

undivided
Mis.	341– 3	undivided *a·* that leaves the

wealth of
My.	291–14	enfolded a wealth of *a·*,

zealous
Mis.	322–26	zealous *a·* for seeking good,

Mis.	154–29	Have no ambition, *a·*, nor

affectional
Ret.	81–12	spiritual sense, *a·* consciousness,

affectionate
Mis.	147–22	the trusty friend, the *a·* relative,
	240–21	*a·*, and generally brave.
Un.	48–13	the *a·* Father and Mother
Pul.	86– 6	* from her *a·* Students,
My.	322– 6	* Your *a·* student,

affectionately
Mis.	132– 6	A· yours,
	136–28	Yours *a·*,
	146–26	A· yours,
	151–29	A· yours in Christ,
	153–31	A· yours,

affection's
Mis.	388–17	A· wreath, a happy home;
Po.	21– 6	A· wreath, a happy home;
My.	258–10	bowed in strong *a·* anguish,

affections
aims and
Mis.	266– 3	unselfish and pure aims and *a·*.

alone in the
Mis.	145– 4	shall exist alone in the *a·*,

and desires
Ret.	79–12	purification of the *a·* and desires.

and lives
My.	156–22	receive into their *a·* and lives

and motives
Mis.	19–10	the *a·* and motives of men

and understanding
Un.	2–26	through their *a·* and understanding.

are enduring
My.	268– 8	*a·* are enduring and achieving.

changing the
Mis.	268–20	changing the *a·*, enlightening the

chastened
Mis.	356–10	chastened *a·*, and costly hopes,

chasten the
Ret.	21–18	to chasten the *a·*, to rebuke human

educate the
Mis.	235–23	educate the *a·* to higher resources,

enrich the
Man.	41–24	enrich the *a·* of all mankind,

false
My.	125– 2	false *a·*, motives, and aims,

foundation for the
Mis.	74– 7	spiritual foundation for the *a·*

human
(*see* human)

hypocrite's
Un.	56–22	The hypocrite's *a·* must first be

increased
Mis.	289–25	exalted and increased *a·*,

interests and
Mis.	289–29	Mutual interests and *a·* are the

my
Mis.	290–20	my *a·* involuntarily flow out
	310–13	While my *a·* plead for all
Ret.	23–18	my *a·* had diligently sought

new
Mis.	204–14	new purposes, new *a·*,

our
Mis.	174–10	Let us open our *a·* to the
Ret.	28–16	must be supreme in our *a·*,

affections
  our
    Pul. 35–20 must be supreme in our *a·*,
  permeate the
    Mis. 223–20 so permeate the *a·* of all
  purifies the
    My. 131– 1 that which purifies the *a·*
  union of the
    Mis. 52–16 it must be a union of the *a·*
  your
    Pan. 14– 4 Set your *a·* on things above ;
    Hea. 16–13 Life and Love will occupy your *a·*,

    Mis. 147–17 not guided merely by *a·*
    172–21 received through the *a·*,

affects
    Mis. 5–31 believe that the body *a·* the mind,
    5–32 than that the mind *a·* the body.
    247–26 believe that the body *a·* mind,

affidavit
    My. 137– 1 chapter sub-title
    137– 2 * *a·*, in the form of a letter
    314–31 *a·* by R. D. Rounsevel

affiliate
    Mis. 80–14 to *a·* with a wrong class

affinities
    Mis. 291– 4 personal channels, *a·*, self-interests,

affinity
    Mis. 296–24 *a·* for the worst forms of vice?
    Un. 57–16 neither held her error by *a·* nor

affirm
    Mis. 293–24 To *a·* mentally and audibly
    298– 5 as some *a·* that we say,
    374–24 frantically *a·* what is what :
    Man. 92– 5 demonstrates what we *a·* of C. S.,
    Un. 2–15 *a·* that the Mind which is good,
    49–25 than to *a·* it to be something which
    Peo. 3–11 would *a·* that these are natural,
    My. 217–23 all that the material senses *a·*.

affirmation
    Ret. 9– 7 and emphasized her *a·*.
    My. 22–18 * put its seal of *a·* upon

affirmations
    Mis. 65– 8 why not submit to the *a·*
    Pan. 4–28 By admitting self-evident *a*

affirmative
    Mis. 67–29 I modify my *a·* answer.
    193– 3 we reply in the *a·*
    337– 5 certain of so momentous an *a·*?
    Un. 45–17 *a·* to Truth's negative.
    My. 61– 1 * I gladly answered in the *a·*,

affirmed
    Mis. 169–14 She *a·* that the Scriptures
    345–22 pagan slanderers *a·* that
    My. 84–10 * has *a·* its wisdom.

affirming
    Un. 38–16 thus *a·* the existence and
    Pul. 31– 5 * in *a·* the present application of

affirms
    Un. 24–25 Whatever matter thus *a·*
    Pul. 30–18 * It *a·* the atonement;
    30–20 * *a·* the power of Truth

affixed
    Mis. x–13 To some articles are *a·* data,

afflatus
    Mis. 166– 7 in our midst a divine *a·*.
    Ret. 31–30 a present spiritual *a·*.

afflict
    Mis. 73– 6 doth not *a·* willingly."— *Lam. 3 : 33.*

afflicted
    Mis. 168– 8 hear not, and are *a·* with
    208–22 "Before I was *a·*—*Psal. 119 : 67.*
    My. 96– 6 * and none of them *a·* with

afflicteth
    Ret. 74– 8 *a·* me not wittingly :
    Rud. 10–20 know that He *a·* not willingly

affliction
    Mis. 9– 2 *a·* rightly understood,
    66–16 suffering is the lighter *a·*.
    151–- 8 the furnace of *a·*.
    276–20 Love is found in *a·*.
    My. 303–32 molten in the furnace of *a·*.

afflictions
    Mis. 327–25 consoling their *a·*, and helping

afford
    Mis. 13–26 to *a·* opportunity for proof
    35–11 *a·* the most concise, yet complete,
    64–19 philosophy and religion that *a·*
    120–24 as often as they can *a·* to

afford
    Mis. 136–19 You can well *a·* to give me up,
    224– 5 can hardly *a·* to be miserable for
    338– 6 not by "words,"— these *a·* no proof,
    338–13 *a·* the only rule I have found
    Man. 44–18 every member, who can *a·* it,
    Ret. 6–14 more space than this little book can *a·*.
    Un. 34–18 What evidence does mortal mind *a·*
    Rud. 5– 1 spiritual senses *a·* no such evidence,
    7–14 they *a·* the only true evidence
    '02. 14–28 and *a·* an open field and fair play.
    Hea. 16–20 senses *a·* no evidence of Truth
    My. 151– 8 these attacks *a·* opportunity for
    161–25 do not *a·* a sufficient defence
    179–30 They *a·* such expositions of
    219– 1 that which my books *a·*,
    224–28 cannot *a·* to recommend
    262–19 *a·* little divine effulgence,
    349–10 *a·* little aid in understanding

afforded
    Mis. 275–21 satisfaction that you *a·* me
    Ret. 83–11 *a·* by the Bible and my books,
    '02. 14–23 *a·* me neither favor nor

affords
    Mis. 72–31 passage quoted *a·* no evidence of
    106–29 *a·* the only strains that thrill
    133–28 It *a·* me great joy to be able
    164–31 Science *a·* the evidence that God **is**
    186–22 *a·* self-evident proof of immortality ;
    319–24 *a·* ample opportunity for
    Rud. 1–11 word *person a·* a large margin for
    No. 34–14 Physical torture *a·* but a slight
    '00. 7–27 Christ is found near, *a·* help,
    Hea. 19–18 *a·* him fresh opportunities
    My. 42–20 * It *a·* me great pleasure to
    91– 4 It *a·* refutation of the notion
    189– 6 it *a·* even me a perquisite of joy.

aflame
    Po. 22– 5 One hundred years, *a·* with **Love,**

afloat
    My. 144– 5 lies *a·* that I am sick,

aforenamed
    Man. 59–11 to adopt the *a·* method

aforesaid
    Mis. 302–24 copying of my writings as *a·*.
    371– 3 If, as the gentleman *a·* states,
    378–10 *en route* for the *a·* doctor
    Man. 43– 2 a second offense as *a·* shall
    75–18 own the *a·* premises
    My. 135–19 of this, the *a·* transaction.
    136–24 To my *a·* Trustees I have
    144– 7 either of the *a·* conditions
    284–18 the *a·* Memorial service

aforethought
    Mis. 227– 9 yet with malice *a·*
    248–15 malice *a·* of sinners."

aforetime
    Un. 11– 9 intended it, or ordered it *a·*,
    '01. 9–26 now, as *a·* — they cast out evils
    My. 185–20 Christ, as *a·*, heals the sick,
    204–29 based as *a·* on this divine Principle,
    219–17 healing, as *a·*, of all manner of
    239– 8 mankind will, as *a·*,

afraid
    Mis. 39–17 not *a·* to take their own medicine,
    109–29 "Be not *a·* !"— *Mark 6 : 50.*
    211–19 Or, are you *a·* to do this
    324–23 he is *a·* to go on
    335–20 *a·* of its supposed power,
    Ret. 9–12 I was *a·*, and did not answer.
    Un. 20– 9 *Third:* I am *a·* of it.
    Pul. 3–27 so small that I am *a·*.
    4– 2 "Be not *a·* "—*Mark 6 : 50.*
    33– 9 * was *a·* and did not reply.
    '02. 20– 3 be not *a·*.'"— *Mark 6 : 50.*
    My. 165–26 He who is *a·* of being too generous
    336– 4 * was *a·* to have her brother,

Africa
    My. 147–28 From the interior of *A·* to

African
    Mis. 88–25 * miraculous to the equatorial *A·*,
    Peo. 10–27 *A·* slavery was abolished on this

after
    Mis. x–20 *A·* my first marriage,
    24–13 ever *a·* was in better health
    32–20 seekers *a·* Truth whose teacher
    34– 1 none of the harmful "*a·* effects"
    42– 1 *A· the change called death*
    42– 5 *A·* the momentary belief of
    43– 4 *a·* having been made acquainted
    54–18 *a· one month's treatment*
    57–12 *a·* the truth of man had been demonstrated,

after

Mis.	60– 9	*a·* all other means have failed.
	67–30	*a·* all the footsteps requisite
	69–11	*a·* our likeness : — *Gen.* 1 : 26.
	82–13	*a· the destruction of mortal mind*
	87–17	*to look a· the students;*
	87–20	*A·* class teaching, he does best in
	88–18	like a benediction *a·* prayer,
	89–22	*I am a seeker a· Truth.*
	90–28	*a·* his resurrection,
	90–29	*a·* his disciples had left their
	105–10	*a·* showing us the way
	114– 2	to all seekers *a·* Truth.
	131–28	*A·* this financial year,
	149– 7	*a·* presenting the various offerings,
	149– 8	one *a·* another has opened his lips
	156– 4	readers, and seekers *a·* Truth.
	158– 9	*a·* His messenger has obeyed the
	162–23	*a·* the similitude of the Father,
	163–25	*A·* his brief brave struggle,
	186– 5	the embryo-man *a·* his birth,
	188–14	walk not *a·* the flesh, — *Rom.* 8 : 1.
	188–14	but *a·* the Spirit." — *Rom.* 8 : 1.
	197– 6	and to strive *a·* holiness.
	197–20	compel us to pattern *a·* both ;
	201– 9	reproduced his body *a·* its burial,
	201–25	more securely *a·* a robbery,
	201–26	*a·* losing those jewels of character,
	205–16	*A·* this, man's identity or
	216–22	* some time *a·* the rest of it had gone."
	219–14	think also *a·* a sickly fashion.
	225–13	Soon *a·* this conversation,
	226– 5	*a·* eating several ice-creams,
	235–18	and thirsting *a·* a better life,
	246–32	earnest seeking *a·* practical truth
	261–25	a kind of men *a·* man's own making.
	265–21	*A·* . . . explaining spiritual Truth
	272– 5	* *repealed* from and *a·* January 31,
	295–27	an institution which names itself *a·*
	302–22	at once *a·* said service.
	304– 7	* *A·* the close of the Exhibition
	315–16	look *a·* the welfare of his students,
	315–17	not only through . . . but *a·* it ;
	341– 7	*a·* much slipping and clambering,
	358–25	*a·* accomplishing the greatest work
	360–19	"Israel *a·* the flesh," — *I Cor.* 10 : 18.
	364–13	is not a search *a·* wisdom,
	378– 8	*A·* much consultation among
	379– 1	*A·* treating his patients, Mr. Quimby
	379–27	It was *a·* Mr. Quimby's death
Man.	17– 2	earnest seekers *a·* Truth
	26–22	*a·* the candidate is approved by
	36–21	*a·* which, the unanimous vote
	37– 4	*a·* the blank has been properly filled
	46– 9	*a·* his name on circulars,
	55–16	*a·* three years of exemplary character.
	62–14	*a·* reaching the age of twenty.
	64–22	nineteen hundred and three and *a·*,
	75–19	*A·* the first church was built,
	76– 1	*a·* the debts are paid,
	83–16	not only during the class . . . but *a·*
	84–10	*A·* 1907, the Board of Education
	86– 3	*A·* a student's pupil has been
	94– 7	no receptions nor festivities *a·* a
	109–12	*a·* being filled out by the
Ret.	7– 3	age of thirty-one, *a·* a short illness,
	10–11	*A·* my discovery of C. S.,
	14–30	*A·* the meeting was over
	19– 5	*A·* parting with the dear home circle
	20– 1	*A·* returning to the paternal roof
	20– 3	until *a·* my mother's decease.
	20–16	written *a·* this separation :
	20–25	*a·* our marriage his stepfather
	21– 1	*A·* his removal a letter was read
	24– 1	*a·* the death of the magnetic doctor,
	27– 7	*a·* my discovery of the
	31–10	hunger and thirst *a·* divine things,
	36– 5	Five years *a·* taking out my
	38– 7	*A·* months had passed,
	43– 6	No charter was granted . . . *a·* 1883.
	43–10	*A·* I gave up teaching,
	43–18	*a·* which I judged it best
	45– 8	*A·* this material form of cohesion
	47–18	*A·* having received instructions in
	49– 6	*a·* having accomplished the worthy
	49–27	*A·* due deliberation and earnest
	81–15	*A·* the supreme advent of Truth
	92– 6	*a·* that the full corn — *Mark* 4 : 28.
Un.	6– 3	fruit *a·* its kind." — *Gen.* 1 : 11.
	14– 5	long *a·* God made the universe,
	22– 2	made *a·* God's eternal likeness,
	60–14	who are made *a·* the — *see Jas.* 3 : 9.
Pul.	5– 6	one friendship *a·* another
	5–13	*A·* the publication of "S. and H.
	9–16	*A·* the loss of our late lamented
	14– 9	*a·* the woman, — *Rev.* 12 : 15.

after

Pul.	33–13	* and *a·* that it ceased.
	36– 1	* a year *a·* her founding of the
	41– 4	* *a·* the full amount needed
	43–13	* *A·* an organ voluntary,
	50–25	* *a·* a little skirmishing,
	51–10	* are searching *a·* religious truth.
	57–27	* who, *a·* many vicissitudes,
	64–19	* *A·* careful study she became
	69– 8	* *a·* several doctors had pronounced
	72–13	* she had practically been given up
	73– 6	* an ardent follower *a·* God.
	82–14	* because she was created *a·* man,
No.	12– 9	*A·* a lifetime of orthodoxy
	13–10	centuries passed *a·* those words were
	21– 7	It was not a search *a·* wisdom;
	23–10	*a·* the accepted definition.
	27–27	*a·* the change called death,
	28– 2	*a·* the transition called death,
	39– 6	*a·* the fashion of Baal's prophets,
Pan.	7– 8	belief, that *a·* God, Spirit, had
	10–13	*a·* graduation, the best students
	11– 5	*a·* the image of Him — *Col.* 3 : 10.
'00.	7–12	*a·* reading "S. and H.
	10– 4	that *a·* a fight vanisheth
	13–13	*a·* a series of wars
	15–10	*a·* this Passover cometh victory,
'01.	6–17	*a·* this model of personality?
	10–24	*a·* the pattern of the mount.
	10–30	*A·* Jesus had fulfilled his mission
	21–14	*a·* Mrs. Eddy has gone.
	28–29	*A·* a hard and successful career
	29– 2	Have we looked *a·* or even known
	31–12	*A·* a long acquaintance with the
'02.	13–19	*A·* the mortgage had expired
	14–20	achievement *a·* achievement has
	16– 1	*a·* the earthquake and the fire.
Hea.	4–15	*a·* infinite Spirit is
	4–18	*a·* a temporary lapse,
	13–18	*A·* these experiments you cannot
Peo.	9–14	*a·* the model of our Father,
My.	v–19	* *a·* nine years of arduous
	4– 8	followeth *a·* me, — *Matt.* 10 : 38.
	13–30	returns it unto them *a·* many days,
	16– 7	* *a·* paying out the sum of
	17–27	* *a·* which the following extracts
	30–20	* were returned *a·* having been
	32– 3	* *a·* five minutes of silent communion
	32–29	* *A·* the reading of the
	38–24	* Scientists said *a·* the service
	40– 5	* thirst *a·* practical righteousness ;
	47–10	* *A·* a work has been established,
	50–32	* committee met *a·* the services
	52–32	* "Day *a·* day flew by,
	53–18	* *A·* establishing itself as a church
	54–25	* Sunday *a·* Sunday."
	61–13	* but *a·* a while, in the night,
	91–30	* *A·* but a few years,
	105– 7	*A·* my discovery of C. S.,
	113–12	not *a·* the flesh, but *a·* — *Rom.* 8 : 1.
	114–19	I could not write . . . *a·* sunset.
	173– 3	* *a·* the visit of the Christian Scientists
	173– 9	*A·* the C. S. periodicals
	178– 2	do not mislead the seeker *a·* Truth.
	205– 3	not *a·* the flesh, but *a·* — *Rom.* 8 : 1.
	214–19	Four years *a·* my discovery of C. S.,
	229–18	and come *a·* me, — *Luke* 14 : 27.
	233–25	followeth *a·* me, — *Matt.* 10 : 38.
	241–25	* *a·* coming to the light of Truth,
	246– 1	*a·* receiving the first degree,
	247–26	*a·* many or a few days
	250– 9	*a·* three years of acceptable service
	251–12	if, *a·* examination in the Board of
	251–19	*a·* three years of good practice,
	285–25	*a·* the way which they call heresy,
	302–25	*a·* it was built and dedicated
	307–10	*A·* this I noticed he used that word,
	309–10	*A·* it was decided,
	309–24	*a·* the prevailing style of
	311– 7	Shortly *a·*, . . . my good housekeeper
	312– 7	* six months *a·* his marriage,
	313–30	*a·* my father's second marriage
	314– 3	says that *a·* my marriage
	314–18	*A·* the evidence had been
	320–28	* several times *a·* the class closed,
	327–19	* *A·* the amendment had been passed,
	328–26	* *a·* enumerating the different
	331–25	* bereaved widow *a·* his decease.
	331–31	* extended to her *a·* his death,
	332–24	* *A·* frequent searchings
	335–15	* for many years *a·* his death.
	336– 5	* *a·* her husband's death,
	336–12	"*A·* returning to the paternal roof
	336–14	*a·* my mother's decease."
	338–13	till *a·* the lecture was delivered
	342– 5	* and *a·* a kindly greeting

after
My.	342–25	* *a·* all now concerned in its
	343– 5	* *a·* a prolonged exordium.
	346–10	* *a·* I reached Concord
		(*see also* **death, manner**)

Afterglow
My.	250–14	chapter sub-title

afternoon
Mis.	168–27	* on the *a·* of October 26,
Ret.	16– 1	One memorable Sunday *a·*,
	38–15	The *a·* that he left Boston
Pul.	37– 9	* and drives in the *a·*.
My.	39– 3	* at two o'clock in the *a·*.
	56– 5	* were held, morning and *a·*,
	65– 7	* voted yesterday *a·* to raise.
	78– 4	* morning, *a·*, and evening
	80–29	* as early as three o'clock in the *a·*
	147– 5	morning and *a·* services
	171–13	at two o'clock in the *a·*,
	171–20	* on her regular *a·* drive

afterpiece
Mis.	xii– 5	this *a·* of battle.

aftersmile
Mis.	389–24	heaven's *a·* earth's tear-drops gain,
Po.	5– 4	heaven's *a·* earth's tear-drops gain,

afterward
Mis.	373– 7	A few days *a·*,
Man.	39– 9	*a·*, when sufficient time
	64–19	*a·* consented on the ground that
Ret.	9–12	*A·* I wept, and prayed that
Pul.	55–17	* *A·* she selected the name C. S.
	65–26	* exemplar *a·* became a saint.
Po.	v–23	* *for years a·*,

afterwards
Mis.	11– 8	*a·* assisting them pecuniarily,
	81–16	*a· to go up into the wilderness,*
	248–25	*A·*, the glorious revelations of
	285– 5	*A·*, by a blunder of the gentleman
	318–16	and *a·* studied thoroughly
	325–11	and *a·* try to kill him.
	332–19	*a·* to have formed an evil sense
	348–31	*a·* denied this and objected
Ret.	6–19	*a·* President of the United States ;
	24– 6	which I *a·* named C. S.
	38–12	As it *a·* appeared,
	40–12	*A·* they showed me the clothes
	40–18	The mother *a·* wrote to me,
	47–20	and *a·* studied thoroughly
'00.	3–23	Yahwah, *a·* transcribed Jehovah ;
'01.	13–24	as it is destroyed, and never *a·* ;
'02.	13–28	I *a·* gave to my church
Hea.	2– 8	*a·* pardoned and adopted,
My.	215–10	*A·*, with touching tenderness,
	307–18	*a·* I concluded that he only
	309– 7	Franklin Pierce, *a·* President
	311–20	*a·* Mrs. Judge Potter,
	319– 6	*a·* he wrote a kind

again
Mis.	10–12	if they fall they shall rise *a·*,
	50– 1	that God made all . . . is *a·* Scriptural ;
	54–22	But not to be subject *a·* to
	57– 1	created man over *a·*
	61– 6	*A·* : mortals are the embodiments
	73– 5	and *a·* "He doth not — *Lam.* 3 : 33.
	99–29	is *a·* casting out evils
	126– 4	I half wish for society *a·* ;
	127– 7	and *a·* earnestly request,
	135– 2	*A·* I repeat, person is not
	137–18	if you take my advice *a·*,
	139– 3	meet *a·* in three years.
	150–29	*A·*, this infinite Principle, with its
	154–21	*a·* be made manifest in the flesh
	178–24	* *a· to* preach, here or elsewhere.
	178–25	* the pastor *a·* came forward,
	180– 8	* Has Christ come *a·* on earth?"
	191–22	*A·*, our text refers to the devil as
	217–21	*A·*, that matter is both cause and
	221–18	*A·* : If error is the cause of disease,
	243–16	*A·*, the Professor quotes,
	246–27	*a·* deluge the earth in blood?
	261– 1	*A·* : evil, as *mind*, is doomed,
	261–13	is measured to him *a·*,
	298– 9	measured to you *a·* — *Matt.* 7 : 2.
	302– 5	seeks *a·* to "cast lots — *Matt.* 27 : 35.
	317–12	*A·*, it is not absolutely requisite
	324–26	rushes *a·* into the lonely streets,
	327–21	only to take them up *a·*,
	337–30	is *a·* reproduced in the character
	369–25	would find our Father's house *a·*
	370–14	Let the sentinels . . . shout once *a·*,
	380–15	I *a·*, in faith, turned to divine help,
	392–23	Scenes that I would see *a·*.
	394– 9	bless, and make joyful *a·*.

again
Man.	39–18	he shall not *a·* be received
Ret.	8–15	the call *a·* came,
	8–19	till *a·* the same call was
	9–10	when the voice called *a·*,
	9–15	When the call came *a·*
	9–16	never *a·* to the material senses
	20–24	dominant thought in marrying *a·*
	21– 6	We never met *a·* until he had
	62– 1	Unless . . . healing will *a·* be lost,
	89–17	once *a·* entered the synagogue
Un.	14– 3	do His work over *a·*,
	23– 6	God has no bastards to turn *a·* and
	34–18	*A·* I ask : What evidence
	61–14	retreats, and *a·* goes forward ;
Pul.	14–20	nor *a·* sink the world into the
	33– 8	* if she heard the voice *a·* to reply
	33–12	* reply if the call came *a·*.
	54– 1	* *A·*, in a poem entitled "The Master,"
	54– 5	* And we are whole *a·*.
	60–13	* The place was *a·* crowded,
No.	31–25	returned, to be *a·* forgiven ;
	44–21	or rule of error will *a·* unite
Pan.	6–18	*A·* : Did one Mind, or two
	7–26	*A·* : The hypothesis of mind in
	11–19	falls physically needs to rise *a·*
'00.	6–25	*A·*, that C. S. is the Science of
'01.	7– 8	*A·*, God being infinite Mind,
	8– 2	*A·* I reiterate this cardinal point :
	8–13	*A·* : Is man, according to C. S.,
	14– 2	*A·* : To assume there is no reality in
	22–28	*A·* : Even the numeration table of
	24– 9	*A·*, while descanting on the virtues of
	34–16	Give us, dear God, *a·* on earth
'02.	2–29	we shall meet *a·*, never to part.
	4– 3	I *a·* repeat, Follow your
	19– 4	*A·* : True to his divine nature,
Hea.	2–23	*A·*, they knew it was not
	3– 9	must *a·* become the head of
	4–17	to show itself infinite *a·*.
	7–19	*A·*, he charged home a crime
	16–23	*A·*, shall we say that God hath
Peo.	8–21	shall *a·* be swept by the divine
	8–23	Then shall C. S. *a·* appear,
	14–17	and behold once *a·* the power of
Po.	vi– 4	* *and a· in Boston*, in 1856.
	22– 6	*A·* shall bid old earth good-by
	41–20	just breaking, reecho *a·*
	45–12	bless, and make joyful *a·*.
	47– 1	Are the dear days ever coming *a·*,
	51– 5	Scenes that I would see *a·*.
	72– 3	ne'er *a·* Quench liberty that's just.
My.	12–22	it comes not back *a·*.
	18– 4	and *a·* earnestly request,
	36–10	* to consecrate all that we are
	37– 9	* declare *a·* our high appreciation
	54–22	* Hawthorne Rooms were *a·* secured.
	59–15	* listening *a·* to your words
	62–22	* we *a·* express our thankful
	104–13	*A·*, what shall be said of him who
	122–29	Christ, Truth, *a·* healing the sick
	128– 4	not laying *a·* the — *Heb.* 6 : 1.
	174– 7	in *a·* opening their spacious
	185–19	"was dead, and is alive *a·* ; — *Luke* 15 : 32.
	196–18	reviled not *a·* ; — *I Pet.* 2 : 23.
	214– 8	Christianity is *a·* demonstrating
	215–13	it was *a·* mailed to me in letters
	227–25	turn *a·* and rend you." — *Matt.* 7 : 6.
	256–17	*A·* loved Christmas is here,
	259– 1	look *a·* at your gift,
	280– 4	* which *a·* gives assurance of
	290–24	where the high and holy call you *a·*
	343–30	all back to union and love *a·*.

against (*see also* **'gainst**)
Mis.	2–29	beliefs that war *a·* Spirit,
	8–24	*a·* you *falsely*, for my sake ; — *Matt.* 5 : 11.
	25– 1	*a·* his holiness and health.
	31–18	argue *a·* his own convictions
	36–25	mortal mind] is enmity *a·* God ; — *Rom.* 8 : 7
	55–13	are using that power *a·*
	55–14	the sin *a·* the Holy Ghost
	56–17	a kingdom divided *a·* itself,
	61– 5	*a·* the material symbolic counterfeit
	68– 8	* *Christian would protest a·*
	89– 3	kingdom divided *a·* itself — *Matt.* 12 : 25.
	114–19	*a·* original sin,
	114–31	how to guard *a·* evil
	115– 2	an offense *a·* God and humanity.
	115–23	*a·* the subtler forms of evil,
	119–14	strives to tip the beam *a·* the
	119–15	the flesh strives *a·* Spirit,
	119–15	*a·* whatever or whoever opposes
	119–17	*a·* man's high destiny.
	121– 9	human struggles *a·* the divine,
	124– 8	warreth *a·* Spirit,

against

Mis.	130–25	sin that one can commit *a·*
	139–12	*exalteth itself a· the* — *II Cor.* 10 : 5.
	140–24	would not be found fighting *a·* God.
	141– 8	and *a·* this church temple
	144–20	shall not prevail *a·* it." — *Matt.* 16 : 18.
	148– 2	meditates evil *a·* us in his heart.
	150–21	who can be *a·* us?" — *Rom.* 8 : 31.
	152–23	beat *a·* this sure foundation.
	174– 3	to talk and disclaim *a·* Truth ;
	174–20	to declare *a·* this kingdom is
	177– 6	conspiracy *a·* the Lord
	177– 7	and *a·* His Christ,
	177–10	in organizing action *a·* us.
	177–11	sworn enmity *a·* the lives of
	197–26	that is divided *a·* itself,
	201–28	bar his door *a·* further robberies.
	206– 5	dashing *a·* the receding shore,
	212–18	currents of human nature rush in *a·*
	213–12	*a·* the evil which, if seen,
	214– 7	at variance *a·* his father, — *Matt.* 10 : 35.
	214– 7	the daughter *a·* her — *Matt.* 10 : 35.
	214– 8	the daughter-in-law *a·* — *Matt.* 10 : 35.
	216–17	a big protest *a·* injustice ;
	217–24	and man a rebel *a·* his Maker.
	217–26	kingdom divided *a·* itself,
	221–25	*a·* both evil and disease,
	222–19	This sin *a·* divine Science
	224–27	unless the offense be *a·* God.
	234–21	That one should . . . *a·* such odds,
	246–26	intolerance, arrayed *a·* the
	247–12	charges *a·* my views are false,
	254–11	whose children rise up *a·* her ;
	256– 8	in daily letters that protest *a·*
	281– 5	will-power that you must guard *a·*.
	284–19	*a·* human error and hate.
	293–13	*a·* the opposite claims of error.
	307–29	must guard *a·* the deification of
	309–18	*a·* falling into the error of
	312– 2	to guard *a·* that temptation.
	316– 1	to defend themselves *a·*
	319–12	protest *a·* the reality of sin,
	325–27	*a·* sensualism in its myriad forms.
	328–14	and closed it *a·* Truth,
	345– 4	*a·* the charge of atheism ;
	345–21	*a·* an advanced form of religion,
	355–17	To strike out . . . *a·* the mist,
	367–22	It was not *a·* evil,
	367–22	but *a· knowing* evil,
	383–11	beat in vain *a·* the immortal parapets
Man.	42– 6	*a·* aggressive mental suggestion,
	51–26	complaints *a·* church members ;
	52– 4	A complaint *a·* a member of
	52–20	Working *A·* the Cause.
	52–22	working *a·* the interests of
	77– 5	Prior to paying bills *a·* the
	84– 1	Defense *a·* Malpractice.
	84– 3	how to defend themselves *a·*
	87–13	No member . . . shall advise *a·*
Ret.	22–10	*a·* himself." — *Heb.* 12 : 3.
	63–16	is nothing but a conspiracy *a·*
	67–10	self-arrayed *a·* the infinite,
	67–11	the mortal *a·* immortality,
	78–23	is to conspire *a·* the blessings
	78–23	*a·* your own success
	78–24	*a·* the progress of the human race
	79– 1	*a· honest* metaphysical theory
	85–13	Guard yourselves *a·* the subtly
	85–24	who can be *a·* us?" — *Rom.* 8 : 31.
Un.	17– 6	fought *a·* Sisera. — *Judg.* 5 : 20.
	26–20	protest *a·* this stanza of Bowring's,
	36– 4	this lie was the false witness *a·*
	46–17	incensed the rabbins *a·* Jesus,
	60– 4	a kingdom divided *a·* itself.
Pul.	12–23	in our warfare *a·* error,
	50–23	* The opposition *a·* it from the
Rud.	8–20	falsity shuts *a·* him the Truth
	9–18	weighs *a·* his healing power ;
	9–28	that whatever militates *a·* health,
No.	2– 7	leaves you to work *a·* that which
	5–19	and yet is arrayed *a·* being,
	5–22	divided *a·* itself — *Luke* 11 : 17.
	9–15	*a·* too great leniency, on my part,
	18–25	This demand militates *a·* the
	23–22	can have no such warfare *a·* Himself.
	38–11	*a·* which the gates of hell cannot
'00.	9–23	no one can fight *a·* God, and win.
	11–16	measures himself *a·* deeper grief.
	12–18	somewhat *a·* thee, — *Rev.* 2 : 4.
'01.	3– 5	all manner of evil *a·* you — *Matt.* 5 : 11.
	14–23	*a·* the approach of thieves.
	15–17	measure of wickedness *a·* all light.
	18– 9	Those who laugh at or pray *a·*
	24–14	when the storms of disease beat *a·*
	25–29	kingdom divided *a·* itself,
	26–10	In one sentence he declaims *a·*

against

'02.	11–23	all manner of evil *a·* you — *Matt.* **5 : 11.**
	14– 7	shield *a·* the powers of darkness,
	16–22	in self-defense *a·* false witnesses,
	19–12	no person can commit an offense *a·*
Hea.	2– 4	prejudices arrayed *a·* it,
	11–16	before lifting its foot *a·* its neighbor,
Peo.	11–28	*a·* the liberty and lives of men.
My.	v–12	* *a·* the mesmerism of personal pride
	6– 2	knows will be turned *a·* himself.
	10–21	* to contribute money *a·* their will
	11– 6	* storms that have surged *a·* her
	33–20	reproach *a·* his neighbor. — *Psal.* 15 : 3.
	33–26	reward *a·* the innocent. — *Psal.* 15 : 5.
	40–29	* Human sense often rebels *a·* law,
	50–11	* *a·* the currents of dogma,
	64–20	* warn all her followers *a·* the
	104–31	all manner of evil *a·* you — *Matt.* **5 : 11.**
	130– 3	*a·* evil suggestions and *a·* malicious
	134– 2	battle *a·* the world,
	143–28	who can be *a·* us?" — *Rom.* 8 : 31.
	150–31	the disclaimer *a·* God
	151–16	who can be *a·* us?" — *Rom.* 8 : 31.
	156–10	unto Him *a·* that day." — *II Tim.* **1 : 12.**
	161–26	a sufficient defence *a·* it.
	162–30	rock of ages *a·* which the waves
	164–28	*a·* which envy, enmity, or malice
	193–18	Protesting *a·* error, you unite with
	196–21	contradiction . . . *a·* himself, — *Heb.* **12 : 3.**
	199– 7	I have naught *a·* thee.
	213–19	Be ever on guard *a·* this enemy.
	219–27	precautions *a·* the spread of
	224–26	"He that is not *a·* us — *Mark* 9 : 40.
	228–30	unto him *a·* that day" — *II Tim.* 1 : 12.
	229–31	measures the infinite *a·* the finite.
	232–31	watching *a·* a negative watch,
	233–23	should one watch *a·* such a result?
	234–29	and when the laws are *a·* it,
	292–18	*a·* the *modus operandi* of another,
	293– 5	one *a·* the other
	316– 8	all manner of evil *a·* you — *Matt.* **5 : 11.**
	339–28	and all that wars *a·* Spirit
	358– 8	whereby the conflict *a·* Truth is

Agassiz

Professor

'01.	27–27	Professor *A·* said : "Every great
My.	304–24	*A·*, the celebrated naturalist

Age

Mis.	231– 1	*A·*, on whose hoary head

age (*see also* **age's**)

advanced

Pul.	vii–12	telescope of that advanced *a·*,
Hea.	1–10	until the *a·* advanced to a more

advancement of the

Mis.	6– 8	needed for the advancement of the *a·*.

and Christianity

'01.	16–24	to handle . . . *a·* and Christianity!

and manhood

Mis.	257–24	childhood, *a·*, and manhood go

any

Pul.	75– 1	Whoever in any *a·* expresses most of

apostolic

'00.	12–27	in the apostolic *a·*

apprehension of the

Ret.	26–30	to the apprehension of the *a·*.

commercial

My.	91– 6	* in this so-called commercial *a·*.

custom of the

My.	261– 6	according to the custom of the *a·*

demand of the

Ret.	48–23	demand of the *a·* for something higher

early

Pul.	34– 1	* At an early *a·* Miss Baker was

eight years of

Pul.	33– 3	* When eight years of *a·* she began,

every

Mis.	213–17	In every *a·*, the pioneer reformer
	374–23	Extremists in every *a·* either
No.	44–26	In every *a·* and clime,
Peo.	2–21	people's belief of God, in every *a·*,
Po.	28– 1	Father of every *a·*,
My.	103–10	In every *a·* and at its every

four years of

Ret.	20– 8	my little son, about four years of *a·*,

his

'01.	28–26	among the worldlings in his *a·*,

legal

My.	217–13	shall have arrived at legal *a·*,

manhood, and

Mis.	324– 6	youth, manhood, and *a·* gayly tread

marvel of the

My.	85– 4	* this cult is the marvel of the *a·*.

material

My.	221– 2	earthly price . . . in a material *a·*

age

middle
Mis. 231– 2   middle *a·*, in . . . full fruition of

of miracles
My. 80– 2   * back to the *a·* of miracles.

of seventeen
My. 311–13   I joined the . . . at the *a·* of seventeen

of thirty-four
Ret. 21– 7   reached the *a·* of thirty-four,

of thirty-one
Ret. 7– 3   passed away at the *a·* of thirty-one,

of twelve
Man. 35– 2   arrived at the *a·* of twelve years,
Ret. 13– 1   At the *a·* of twelve I was admitted

of twenty
Man. 62–10   up to the *a·* of twenty years,
    62–15   after reaching the *a·* of twenty.

old
Mis. ix–19   There is an old *a·* of the heart,
My. 135– 6   may be applied to old *a·*,
    273– 3   * proof of Mrs. Eddy's ability in old *a·*

origin and
Mis. 185–23   by which to learn his origin and *a·*,

our
Chr. 53–50   So in our *a·*,

present
My. 63–24   * which has come to the present *a·*.

scientific
Mis. 353–27   about three years of scientific *a·*,

scoff of the
My. 204–22   which was then the scoff of the *a·*.

ten years of
Ret. 10– 4   At ten years of *a·* I was as

that
Mis. 21– 5   and in that *a·* culminates in
    161–21   or preach in public under that *a·*.
    187–17   writers and translators in that *a·*
Man. 62–12   may be received . . . up to that *a·*,
No. 14–22   to Jesus' students in that *a·*,
    38– 2   could be done in that *a·*,

this
Mis. 1–13   seer of this *a·* should be a sage.
    159– 2   God has given to this *a·* "S. and **H.**
    167– 1   The material questions at this *a·*
    222–29   cost of investigating, for this *a·*,
    232– 6   This *a·* is reaching out towards
    310– 6   Truth, amplified in this *a·* by
    370–13   In this *a·* it assumes,
    382–14   healed in this *a·* by C. S.
Pul. 14–21   In this *a·* the earth will help the
    77–14   * through you to this *a·*.
    78–13   * through you to this *a·*.
No. 14–23   but they extend to this *a·*,
'01. 28–27   not popular with them in this *a·* ;
My. vii– 8   * as the revelator to this *a·*
    40–16   * demand of this *a·* is for
    113–32   great men and women of this *a·*.
    146–22   not been demonstrated in this *a·*,
    213– 8   this *a·* is cursed with one rancorous
    323–21   * giving this *a·* such a Leader

twelve years of
My. 169– 6   Busy Bees, under twelve years of *a·*,
    311–15   culminate at twelve years of *a·*.

yellow with
Ret. 2–22   some newspapers, yellow with *a·*.

———

Mis. 4–17   is necessary for the *a·*,
    159–27   been unveiled to us, and to the *a·* !"
    161–20   when he was thirty years of *a·* ;
    171–10   When one comes to the *a·* with
    234–26   midst of an *a·* so sunken in sin
Un. 6–12   as the *a·* has strength to bear.
Pul. 32–20   * some sixty years of *a·*,
    73–12   * Biblical scholars of the *a·*.
Hea. 7–23   I wish the *a·* was up to his
    11–11   though it may seem to the *a·* like
My. 158– 9   *a·* of Love's divine adventure
    190– 7   The *a·* is fast answering this question :
    271–14   * at eighty-six years of *a·* the most
    272–25   * nearly eighty-seven years of *a·*,
    304–10   At sixteen years of *a·*,
    306–15   *A·*, with . . . patience and unselfed
    318–14   spiritual effect upon the *a·* of

aged
Mis. 226– 4   unbiased youth and the *a·* Christian
'01. 29– 7   The *a·* reformer should not be
My. 153–11   *a·* gentleman healed from the day
    271–19   * this *a·* woman of world-wide renown

agencies
Mis. 95–20   no human *a·* were employed,
    244–16   * visible *a·* for specific ends?"
Pul. 14– 5   active yet unseen mental *a·*

agency
Mis. 113– 7   free moral *a·* is lost ;
    119–19   a plea for free moral *a·*,

agency
Rud. 12–11   then restored through its *a·*.
No. 46–12   upon free moral *a·* ;
My. 14– 9   Godlike *a·* of man.
    91–12   * debased through its *a·*.

agent
Mis. 4– 3   remedial *a·* on the earth.
    83–15   you are a free moral *a·*
    272–14   * officer, *a·*, or servant of any
Rud. 2– 2   a self-conscious being ; a moral *a·* ;

agents
Un. 60–18   Mortals are free moral *a·*,
Rud. 2– 6   one of the three subjects, or *a·*,

age's
'02. 9–25   Did the *a·* thinkers laugh long over

ages
Mis. 21–11   As the *a·* advance in spirituality,
    112– 5   The *a·* are burdened with
    140–29   our church will stand the storms of *a·* :
    176– 7   has been exemplified in all *a·*,
    192–27   that extends to all *a·*
    194– 9   to heal in all *a·*,
    205–23   order of Science is the chain of *a·*,
    235–22   must push on the *a·* :
    319– 1   are in the darkness of all the *a·*,
    320–27   is the light of all *a·* ;
    346– 7   The origin of evil is the problem of *a·*.
    358–26   the greatest work of the *a·*,
    370–12   In different *a·* the divine idea
    374–19   brought a great light to all *a·*,
    383–13   it will go on with the *a·*,
Ret. 33–17   mixed with the faith of *a·*,
Un. 9–23   spiritual thinkers in all *a·*.
    26–14   * Man decays and *a·* move ;
Pul. 72–25   * dormant in mankind for *a·*,"
No. 12–14   true Christianity in all *a·*,
    31– 3   has for *a·* been a pretender,
    41–19   Through long *a·* people have
'00. 3– 5   does the thinking for the *a·*.
'01. 12–16   Christ's command to heal in all *a·*,
    21– 5   Science leading the *a·*.
Hea. 3–14   engrossed the attention of the *a·*.
My. 37–19   * philosophy of the *a·* transformed.
    103– 3   severest conflicts of the *a·*
    116–24   Had the *a·* helped their leaders
    129–19   ye who leap . . . from this rock of *a·*,
    152–20   even as the *a·* have shown.
    162–30   may it build upon the rock of *a·*
    180– 8   which applies to all *a·*,
    188–25   As you work, the *a·* win ;
    190–24   all peoples, in all *a·*,
    279– 9   reappearing in all *a·*,
    285–11   belong to the darker *a·*,
    288– 2   unselfs men and pushes on the *a·*.

aggregate
Mis. 62–12   making the *a·* positive,
My. 100– 3   * as remarkable in their *a·*

aggregates
No. 10– 9   it *a·*, amplifies, unfolds, and

aggregating
Pul. 40–17   * *a·* nearly six thousand persons,

aggregation
My. 99– 8   * *a·* of good and beneficial works,

aggressive
Mis. 284–26   Evil let alone grows more real, *a·*,
Man. 42– 6   against *a·* mental suggestion,
'01. 20– 2   yielding to its *a·* features.
My. 230– 3   amid ministries *a·* and active,

aggrieve
Man. 51– 8   *a·* or vilify the Pastor Emeritus

agitate
Mis. 224–23   no passing breath . . . shall *a·* or
Un. 5– 1   rudely or prematurely *a·* a theme

agitated
My. 266–26   are now *a·*, modified, and

agitation
Pul. 31–19   * central figure in all this *a·*
    51–11   * is more or less in a state of *a·*.
My. 318–22   manifested more and more *a·*,

aglow
Mis. 276–17   The wise will have their lamps *a·*,
    341–32   tended to keep *a·* the flame
'00. 1– 3   glad faces, *a·* with gratitude,

agnosticism
Mis. 56– 1   theories of *a·* and pantheism,
Ret. 23–21   *A·*, pantheism, and theosophy
My. 318–21   until I began my attack on *a·*.

ago
Mis. 165– 2   more than eighteen centuries *a·*,
    178–15   * it was about a year *a·* that I

ago

Mis.	182–32	more than eighteen centuries *a*.
	242–15	difficult tasks fifteen years *a*.
	248–24	Many years *a*· my regular
	281– 7	I learned long *a*· that the world could
	286– 1	prophecy, written years *a*·,
	321– 4	less of a miracle than eighteen centuries *a*· ;
	375–11	* Years *a*·, while in Italy,
Ret.	1– 7	English authoress of a century *a*·.
	16– 9	entered this church one hour *a*·
	41– 2	encountered a quarter-century *a*·,
Un.	6–22	Not much more than a half-century *a*·
Pul.	6–13	* "Six months *a*· your book,
	35– 9	* nineteen hundred years *a*·.
	36–20	* Several years *a*· Mrs. Eddy removed
	45–23	* A week *a*· Judge Hanna withdrew from
	53– 3	* nineteen hundred years *a*·,
	66– 5	* was founded fifteen years *a*·
	67–15	* Founded twenty-five years *a*·,
	68–16	* in this city about a year *a*·.
	69– 2	* came to Baltimore about three years *a*·
	69– 3	* about eighteen months *a*·.
	69– 8	* some twelve years *a*·,
	72–13	* healed a number of years *a*·
	79–10	* starting fifteen years *a*·, has already
	85– 1	* nearly thirty years *a*·
Rud.	8– 5	the lion of six thousand years *a*· ;
'01.	18– 6	the sneers forty years *a*·
	27–17	if . . . could start thirty years *a*·
Po.	3–15	Written many years *a*·.
	35–15	Written more than sixty years *a*·
My.	10– 6	* externalized itself, ten years *a*·,
	11–14	* A year *a*· she quietly alluded to
	14–11	* A few days *a*· we received a letter
	22–14	* almost forty years *a*·,
	43–21	* Forty years *a*· the Science of
	50–30	* more than twenty-six years *a*·,
	52–20	* Eighteen years *a*·, the Rev. . . . Wiggin,
	55–31	* Twelve years *a*· . . . the corner-stone
	59– 3	* nearly forty years *a*·.
	67–25	* temple, begun nearly two years *a*·,
	68–15	* old church . . . built twelve years *a*·,
	70– 5	* its first church . . . twelve years *a*·,
	72–29	* in Boston twelve years *a*·
	76–28	* twenty-seven years *a*· was founded
	85– 5	* Thirty years *a*· it was
	92–14	* it is but a few years *a*· that
	94–31	* few years *a*·, men there were who
	99–22	* Less than a generation *a*·
	104–28	to learn of her who, thirty years *a*·,
	109–10	If nineteen hundred years *a*·
	147– 4	Over a half century *a*·,
	176– 5	Long *a*· you of the dear South
	181–21	Thirty years *a*· (1866) C. S. was
	181–25	thirty years *a*· the death-rate was
	182– 1	Thirty years *a*· Chicago had few
	182– 4	Thirty years *a*· at my request
	237– 3	in the *Sentinel* a few weeks *a*·,
	237– 6	some twenty-five years *a*·
	297–21	as when he visited me a year *a*·.
	313– 2	a silly song of years *a*·.
	322–15	* Thanksgiving Day twenty years *a*·,
	325–12	* Years *a*· I offered my services
	342– 9	* to the portraits of twenty years *a*·,

agonies

Mis.	253–24	*a*· that gave that child birth
Rud.	17–11	of friendlessness, toil, *a*·, and
Pan.	12–19	*a*· whereby the way-seeker gains and

agony

Mis.	69–17	barely alive, and in terrible *a*·.
	70–12	Paradisaical rest from physical *a*·
	204– 1	*a*· struggles, pride rebels, and
	222–20	cancelled only through human *a*· :
Un.	58–11	what is humanly called *a*·.
No.	33–15	the brief *a*· of the cross ;
'01.	20–20	*a*· and death that it must sooner or
	35–12	From the human *a*· !
'02.	16–17	*a*· in the life of our Lord ;
My.	105–22	breathing at intervals in *a*·.
	132–15	no longer . . . to strive with *a*· ;
	335–29	* these nine days and nights of *a*·

agree

Mis.	58–29	if you *a*· that God is Mind,
	81– 7	let each society . . . *a*· to
	117–10	I *a*· with Rev. Dr. Talmage,
	243–13	I *a*· with the Professor, that every
	309– 6	All will *a*· with me that material
	365–23	Even doctors *a*· that infidelity,
No.	19– 5	doctors will *a*· that infidelity,
	45–21	we should *a*· to disagree ;
Pan.	4– 7	may *a*· with physics and anatomy
'02.	2–25	or at least *a*· to disagree, in love,
My.	7–19	* we *a*· to contribute any portion of
	71–10	* all *a*· that it is a stunning
	154–22	I *a*· with him ; and in our era

agree

My.	273–24	*a*· with me that the material body is

agreeable

Pul.	72–10	* a very pleasant and *a*· lady,
'00.	4–13	ought not this to be an *a*· surprise,
My.	74–10	* chapter sub-title
	74–12	* very interesting and *a*· visitors,
	342– 2	* warmth within . . . was *a*·.

agreeably

Ret.	15–28	*a*· informed the congregation that

agreed

My.	9– 4	* we have *a*· to contribute
	138– 3	*a*· . . . to take care of my property
	318–19	I *a*· not to question him
	320– 7	* *a*· with what you had told me.

agreement

Mis.	289–14	to act as a whole and per *a*·.
Man.	68–23	*A*· Required.
	69– 2	shall come under a signed . . . *a*· to
My.	vi–22	* under *a*· to pay all future profits
	138– 5	I consider this *a*· a great benefit
	168– 3	practical religion in *a*· with
	318–31	"you have broken our *a*·.

agreements

Mis.	289–12	partnerships are formed on *a*·

agrees

Un.	23– 9	*a*· with the word of Scripture,
Pan.	4– 1	*a*· with certain forms of pantheism

agriculture

Mis.	340–13	*a*· instead of litigation,
My.	216– 7	manufacture, *a*·, tariff, and
	265–28	*a*·, manufacture, commerce,

agriculturist

Mis.	26– 9	*a*· ponders the history of a seed,

aid

apply for

Man.	98–10	apply for *a*· to the Committee

best

Pul.	38–30	* their best *a*· and guidance,

different

Ret.	87–30	and different *a*· is sought.

divine

Peo.	9–18	invoke the divine *a*· of Spirit to heal
My.	166–20	divine *a*· is near.

his

Mis.	89–18	to some who sought his *a*· ;

juvenile

Pul.	8–30	By juvenile *a*·, . . . have come $4,460.

little

My.	349–10	afford little *a*· in understanding

material

Mis.	225–23	Looking away from all material *a*·,
My.	105–25	restored by me without material *a*·,

no

Mis.	31–13	no place in, and receives no *a*· from,
	156–25	is no *a*· to students in acquiring

no other

Mis.	270–17	Then you will need no other *a*·,
	282–28	and no other *a*· is near.

no personal

Mis.	283–26	he needs no personal *a*·.

no real

Mis.	267–25	is no real *a*· to being.

of mind

My.	301–28	without the *a*· of mind.

Mis.	3–17	never are needed to *a*·
	8– 2	If we can *a*· in abating suffering
	52– 2	such as seek . . . to *a*· the spiritual,
	57– 1	by the *a*· of mankind,
	58–19	*Does the theology of C. S. a*·
	62– 6	*a*· an artist in painting a landscape.
	80– 8	and possibly to *a*· individual rights
	98–11	mutually to *a*· one another
	143–25	in *a*· of our Church Building Fund,
	149–21	to send him to *a*· me.
	262– 5	you will *a*· our prospect
	263–23	lacks the *a*· and protection of
	264–27	to *a*· the mental development of
	266–26	thus we mutually *a*· each other,
	282–26	which may call for *a*· unsought,
	291–29	the solution of this problem,
	333–19	to *a*· in understanding and securing
	372–25	Not by *a*· of foreign device
Ret.	94– 7	*a*· the establishment of Christ's
Un.	17– 5	and all that is good will *a*·
'01.	29–26	To *a*· my students in starting
Po.	28–10	*A*· our poor soul to sing
My.	21–13	* *a*· the progress of our Cause
	155– 2	a mutual *a*· society,
	175– 7	to *a*· in repairing your church
	222–30	will *a*· the ejection of error,
	236–29	and it will greatly *a*· the students

aid
My.	256–15	pleasures, achievements, and *a*.
	283– 9	To *a* in this holy purpose is

aided
Ret.	33– 1	*a* by hints from homœopathy,
Rud.	12–13	*a* in this mistaken fashion,
Pan.	9–18	ought to be *a*, not hindered,
My.	181– 5	*a* only at long intervals with

aiding
Mis.	79–27	*a persons brought before the courts*
	119– 4	*a* other people's devices

aids
Mis.	64–23	*a* to a student of the Bible
	156–27	are the *a* and tests of growth
'01.	25–11	call *a* to divine metaphysics,
Hea.	14–15	are miserable medical *a*.
My.	217–25	*a* in taking the next step
	261–13	*a* in perpetuating purity and

ailing
Rud.	12– 3	of the body supposed to be *a*.

ailment
Mis.	66–25	like the more physical *a*.
	241– 9	the other having a physical *a*.
	241–28	easier to heal . . . than the moral *a*.
Pul.	6–17	* of an *a* of seven years' standing.
	69– 7	* cured . . . of a physical *a*
My.	145–13	* an old *a* my mother had."

ailments
Mis.	6–28	confined to the *a* of the body,
	45–17	effectual in treating moral *a*.
	168–10	buried in dogmas and physical *a*,
	268–24	antidotes for the *a* of mortal mind
Ret.	57–13	causes all bodily *a*,
Rud.	12–13	their *a* will return,

aim
Mis.	11– 5	*a* a ball at my heart,
	67–11	shalt not strike . . . with a malicious *a*,
	154–30	Have no . . . *a* apart from holiness.
	220– 9	*a* to refute the sick man's thoughts,
	267– 7	whose chief *a* is to injure me,
	277– 9	archers *a* at Truth's mouthpiece ;
	348– 1	But the Scientists *a* highest.
Ret.	22–17	He alone is our origin, *a*, and
Pul.	37–14	* it is her most earnest *a* to
My.	71–28	* *a* and object of the architect :
	213– 3	*a* of perverted mind-power,
	257–13	Christ's heavenly origin and *a*.

aimed
Mis.	372–24	I *a* to reproduce,
Ret.	48– 4	was *a* at its vital purpose,
'01.	32–14	they armed quickly, *a* deadly,
My.	128–28	shaft *a* at you or your practice

aiming
My.	126– 5	strong swimmer . . . *a* for Truth,

aims
Mis.	9–24	unworthy of human *a*.
	50–21	human affections, desires, and *a*,
	204–29	governs the *a*, ambition, and acts
	214–23	their motives, *a*, and tendency.
	227–17	wider *a* of a life made honest.
	266– 3	summit of unselfish and pure *a*
	291– 7	demonstrates above . . . unworthy *a*
	330–22	higher joys, holier *a*,
'02.	17–26	take its answer as to thy *a*,
My.	125– 2	false affections, motives, and *a*,

air
Mis.	7– 2	nor to breathe the cold *a*,
	7–19	so loaded with . . . seems the very *a*.
	69–13	over the fowl of the *a*." — *Gen.* 1 : 26.
	102–29	as one that beateth the *a*,
	240– 3	through the cold *a* the little one
	291–23	will at length dissolve into thin *a*.
	347– 7	hanging like a horoscope in the *a*,
	356– 8	from lack of *a* and freedom.
	356–18	and the birds of the *a*,
	357–15	The fowls of the *a* pick them up.
Ret.	2–15	comes that heart-stirring *a*,
	11–22	Free as the generous *a*,
Pul.	32–10	* wonderful tumult in the *a*
	49– 4	* *a* of hospitality that marks its
Po.	24– 2	Breathe through the summer *a*
	60–20	Free as the generous *a*,
	65– 8	And left but a parting in *a*.
My.	81– 2	* struck with the *a* of well-being
	110–14	navigation of the *a* ;
	341–27	* change from the misty *a* outside

air-castles
Mis.	230–18	in building *a* or floating off on

airy
Po.	34– 7	Bird of the *a* wing,
My.	110–16	early dreams of flying in *a* space,

aisles
Ret.	15–19	and benches were used in the *a*.
My.	56– 4	* many stood in the *a*,
	71–21	* neither nave, *a*, nor transept
	151–18	vaulted *a* by flaunting folly trod,

ajar
Mis.	394–19	* I fain would keep the gates *a*,
Ret.	9– 3	The door was *a*,
Po.	57– 5	* I fain would keep the gates *a*,

akin
Mis.	372–29	is *a* to its *Science :*
Un.	9–22	because ideas *a* to mine have been

alabaster
My.	258–31	beautiful statuette in *a*

alacrity
My.	236–15	with the sweet *a* and uniformity

alarm
Un.	40–20	Death can never *a* or even

alarmed
'02.	4–25	Alternately transported and *a* by

alarming
No.	43–15	*a* the hypocrite, and

alas
Mis.	223–15	But, *a*! for the mistake of
	231–29	But, *a*! for the desolate home ;
	344–13	*A* for such a material science
Pul.	13–14	*A* for those who break faith with
'01.	16–22	*A*! if now it is permitted
Po.	65–13	*A*! that from dreams so boundless
My.	257– 1	*a* for the broken household band!

Albany, N. Y.
Pul.	89– 3	* *Knickerbocker, A, N.Y.*
	89– 8	* *Press, A, N.Y.*

Albany (N. Y.) *Knickerbocker* (see also **Knickerbocker**)
My.	94–15	*[A (N. Y.) K]*

Albert (Baker)
(*see* **Baker**)

Albion's
Mis.	295–24	resound from *A* shores.

album
Mis.	280–20	elegant *a* costing fifty dollars,

alchemy
Mis.	78–13	occultism, magic, *a*, or

alcohol
Mis.	37–22	appetite for *a* yields to Science
	48–16	produce the effect of *a*,
Ret.	65– 9	odors of persecution, tobacco, and *a*
My.	106–24	not a brawler, an *a* drinker,
	114– 4	abstain from *a* and tobacco ;
	212–10	the evil effects of *a*.

alcoholic
Mis.	71– 4	an appetite for *a* drink
	243–27	tell you that *a* drinks cause
	297– 9	destroys the appetite for *a* drinks.
My.	212–10	The *a* habit is the use of

Alcott, A. Bronson
Pul.	5–12	the late A. Bronson *A*.

alcoves
Pul.	76– 9	* *a* are separated from the
	76–18	* One of the two *a* is a

alder
Ret.	18– 6	nestling *a* is whispering low,
	18–26	*a* growing from the bent branch
Po.	63–15	nestling *a* is whispering low,
	63–24	*a* growing from the bent branch

alders
Mis.	330–14	*a* bend over the streams to

alehouses
Mis.	296–10	barmaids of English *a*

alert
Mis.	374– 7	Keen and *a* was their indignation
My.	226–26	told by the *a* editor-in-chief of

alertness
Man.	42– 4	*A* to Duty.

Alexander the Great
'00.	12–16	night that *A the G* was born.
	13–12	*A the G* founded the city of

Alger, Rev. William R.
Pul.	6–24	the Rev. William R. *A* of Boston,

alias
Mis.	2–10	mortals, *a* mortal mind,
	41–25	for health, *a* harmony,
	75–28	mortal man (*a* material sense)
	257–11	*a* the minds of mortals.
Ret.	36– 6	Science of Mind-healing, *a* C. S.,
	43– 8	*a* the Science of Mind-healing.

alias

Ret. 63– 8 pleasure of sin, *a·* the reality of sin,
64– 6 to efface sin, *a·* the sinner,
67–13 Silencing self, *a·* rising above
67–24 the "devil" (*a·* evil), — *John* 8 : 44.
68– 5 *a·* an evil offspring.
Un. 22–21 *will-power,* — *a·* intelligent matter.
No. 26– 5 spirits, or souls, — *a·* gods.
32–17 A lie is negation, — *a·* nothing,
'01. 13–13 evil, *a·* devil, sin, is a lie
Peo. 11–17 Mortals, *a·* mortal minds,
My. 232–31 negative watch, *a·*, no watch,

alien

My. 260– 3 would make matter an *a·*

alight

Mis. 239–13 *a·* and take from his carriage
My. 160– 5 is seldom *a·* with love.

alighting

Po. v–16 * *a· from her carriage,*

alike

Mis. 200–29 were *a·* unreal to Jesus ;
268–21 curing *a·* the sin and the
Ret. 64–13 are *a·* simply nothingness ;
85–20 Christian Scientist is incapable *a·* of
Pul. 45–15 * of workman and onlooker *a·*
My. 220–31 should share *a·* liberty of conscience,
324– 7 * were too much *a·* for the book to

alive

Mis. 69–17 I found him barely *a·*,
79–25 shall all be made *a·*." — *I Cor.* 15 : 22.
Pul. 34–10 * no probability that she would be *a·*
'02. 18–30 made him keenly *a·* to the injustice,
My. 139– 4 *a·* to the reality of living,
185–19 "was dead, and is *a·* again ; — *Luke* 15 : 32.
275–15 *a·* to the truth of being

All

Mis. 16–21 God is a divine *Whole,* and *A·*,
24–24 when good is God, and God is *A·*
26–22 God is *A·*, in all.
26–22 What can be more than *A·*?
27–23 when God is really *A·*.
101–26 If God is *A·*, and God is good,
108– 5 that good is infinite, *A·*.
125–19 *A·* that is real is divine,
151–23 God is— what? Even *A.*
173–17 preexisted in the *A·* and Only
174–21 the *A·* of God, and His omnipresence
208– 5 God is *A·*, and by virtue of this
250– 1 the infinite *A·* of good,
258– 9 the great truth that God is *A·*,
258–14 God is One and *A·* ;
260–18 opposite to Him who is *A·*.
293–24 God is *A·* and there is no sickness
350–16 "God is *A·*;
Ret. 60– 6 Science reveals Spirit as *A·*,
60–11 God and His idea as the *A·*
63– 5 recognition that God *is A·*,
Un. 3–24 If He is *A·*, He can have no
4– 6 Truth is *A·*, and there is no error.
5– 2 involving the *A·* of infinity.
7–23 because God is *A·*,
18–25 I am *A·*.
24– 2 I am the infinite *A·*.
25–24 elements which belong to the eternal *A·*,
31– 5 If God is Spirit, and God is *A·*,
31– 6 for the divine *A·* must be Spirit.
34–11 God is *A·*, and God is Spirit ;
36– 5 the fact that Spirit is *A·*,
48–12 To me God is *A·*.
60– 6 God is *A·*, and there is none beside
Rud. 9–26 that He is *A·*,
11– 8 Therefore good is one and *A·*.
No. 16–18 Mortals do not understand the *A·* ;
16–20 He who is *A·*, understands all.
17– 6 God is good, ever-present, and *A·*.
24– 9 rests on God as One and *A·*,
25– 2 God becomes the *A·* and Only
30–11 God's law is . . . "I am *A·*,"
38– 7 God is *A·*, and He is good,
Pan. 13–21 life in Life, all in *A·*.
'00. 4–24 God is *One* and *A·*
'02. 7–16 *A·*, than which there is naught else.
Hea. 10–13 God is *A·*, and in all :
Po. 79–17 And God is *A·*.
My. 108–16 omnipotent, infinite, *A·*.
109– 7 God is one because God is *A·*.
178–13 Scripture declares that God is *A·*.
225–12 all belongs to God, for God is *A·* ;
299–19 and that God is *A·*

all (*see also* **all's**)

Mis. xi–18 to suit and savor *a·* literature.
1– 6 the scoffed of *a·* scoffers,

all

Mis. 3–10 applicable to *a·* the needs of
3–19 The Principle of *a·* cure is God,
5–16 I have done *a·* that can be done.
6–18 Mind governs *a·*.
6–30 *a·* that she can attend to in
7–15 if you cannot bring peace to *a·*,
8–16 that blesses infinitely one and *a·*?
9– 6 passes *a·* His flock under His rod
9–32 *a·* that an enemy or enmity can obtrude
11–18 in *a·* the manifestations wherein
11–22 not leaving *a·* retribution to
11–31 taking by the hand *a·* who
12– 9 above *a·*, do not fancy that you
12–30 doing good to *a·* ;
12–32 to *a·* within the radius of our
13– 3 so far as one and *a·* permit me
13–10 consideration of *a·* Christian Scientists.
19–14 *a·* the wicked endeavors of
20– 4 *a·* ye that labor— *Matt.* 11 : 28.
21–11 *a·* his words and works.
21–17 *A·* is infinite Mind and its
22–16 *a·* true thoughts revolve in
23–27 manifests *a·* His attributes
23–30 *A·* must be Mind and Mind's ideas ;
24–30 put down *a·* subtle falsities
25–13 rejects *a·* other theories of causation,
25–23 the Latin word meaning *a·*,
26–22 God is All, in *a·*.
27–11 (including *a·* inharmony,
27–25 and *a·* that really is,
30– 7 demonstrate *a·* the possibilities
32–17 If I had the time to talk with *a·*
32–22 to give to my own flock *a·* the
32–27 *a·* people can and should be just,
33– 5 *a·* ministers and ministries of Christ,
33– 7 *A·* clergymen may not understand
33–25 It does away with *a·* material
33–27 *a·* "the ills that flesh is heir to,"
34–23 *A·* that are called "communications
36–22 *a·* beliefs relative to the so-called
36–23 and *a·* material objects,
37– 5 in *a·* thoughts and desires
37–18 Its antidote for *a·* ills is God,
38– 2 *a· the good we can do*
39–12 *a·* her years in giving it birth.
40–14 *A·* true healing is governed by,
41–20 and produces *a·* harmony
41–28 sufficient for *a·* emergencies.
43– 6 *Do a· who at present claim to*
44–23 is but a dream at *a·* times.
45–21 *If God made a· that was made,*
48– 2 and avoid *a·* that works ill.
49–15 *If a· that is mortal is a dream*
49–19 spirit of Truth leads into *a·* truth,
50– 1 God made *a·* that was made,
51– 7 *A·* mesmerism is of one of three kinds ;
52– 9 beyond *a·* human means
53–22 *so that a· can readily understand it?*
54–12 power of C. S. over *a·* obstacles
54–17 *to keep well a· my life?*
55– 4 prove *a·* its possibilities.
55–22 *a·* that is unlike Spirit.
57– 1 *a·* was later made which *He*
57– 6 The creative "Us" made *a·*,
57–29 But *a·* that really is, always was
59–18 *Is not a· argument mind over mind?*
60– 9 after *a·* other means have failed.
61– 1 belief, in *a·* its manifestations,
61– 6 *A·* the knowledge and vain strivings
63– 8 Principle of *a·* pure theology ;
66–11 is verified in *a·* directions
67–30 after *a·* the footsteps requisite
71–14 *A·* actual causation must interpret
72–21 need of *a· these things,*" — *Matt.* 6 : 32.
73–20 *a·* subjective states of false sensation
74– 9 *a·* human systems of etiology
74–31 you may have *a·* that is left of it ;
77–20 In adopting *a·* this vast idea
78–22 *a·* the clearer for the purification
79– 1 *A·* these mortal beliefs will be
79– 8 reflects *a·* whereby we can know God.
79–24 "As in Adam *a·* die,— *I Cor.* 15 : 22.
79–24 shall *a·* be made alive." — *I Cor.* 15 : 22.
80–19 promotes and impels *a·* true reform ;
81– 4 *a·* unpleasant and unchristian action
81–17 *shall go forth into a· the cities*
81–19 *if a· this be a fair or correct view*
82–11 grasp and gather— in *a·* glory
83– 1 Principle, of *a·* real being ;
85– 6 *a·* that he knows of Life,
87– 3 To take *a·* earth's beauty into
89– 7 *be right to treat this patient at a· ;*
89–15 to do him *a·* the good you can ;
90– 4 you remove *a·* reality from its power.
90– 6 will save *a·* who understand it.

all

Mis. 91–13	It is imperative, at *a·* times
91–17	Be it remembered, that *a·* types
93–18	*a·* cause and effect are in God.
96– 4	an ever-present help in *a·* times of trouble,
96–21	*a·* who entertain this understanding
97–12	*A·* human control is animal magnetism,
97–14	more despicable than *a·* other methods
97–25	we have not seen *a·* of man ;
98–23	The lives of *a·* reformers attest
99– 2	it upsets *a·* that is not upright.
101–26	it follows that *a·* must be good ;
101–32	elements of *a·* forms and individualities,
102–21	which blots out *a·* our iniquities
102–21	and heals *a·* our diseases.
107– 9	*a·* the heart's homage belongs to God.
108–23	the conception of it at *a·* as
111– 4	as meekly, you have toiled *a·* night ;
113– 6	*a·* that is real and eternal.
113–19	so that *a·* are without excuse.
114– 2	value to *a·* seekers after Truth.
114–20	*a·* the *et cetera* of evil.
114–27	will test *a·* mankind on *a·* questions ;
116– 3	The God of *a·* grace be with you,
117–14	the basis of *a·* right thinking
118–24	they will uproot *a·* happiness.
119–20	full exemption from *a·* necessity to
119–25	demands of *a·* trespassers
122–28	He made *a·* that was made.
125– 6	since *a·* that is *real* is *right.*
125–14	that passeth *a·* understanding ;
131–19	not in existence *a·* of the year.
131–22	May God give unto us *a·* that
132–18	inquiries from *a·* quarters,
133–29	Love makes *a·* burdens light,
135– 1	Christians, and *a· true* Scientists,
135–10	conquers *a·* opposition,
135–11	surmounts *a·* obstacles,
136–17	*A·* our thoughts should be given to
137– 4	*a·* of which are complete.
137–27	give to the world the benefit of *a·* this,
138–26	to *a·* His soldiers of the cross
138–28	we *a·* shall take step and march on
139–25	like *a·* true wisdom,
139–29	As with *a·* former efforts in the
140– 7	*a·* spiritual good comes to
141–10	*A·* loyal Christian Scientists hail with
141–17	*a·* the parties concerned
141–19	to the satisfaction of *a·*.
143–26	quiet call . . . found you *a·*
147–22	at *a·* times the trusty friend,
147–28	In *a·* his pursuits, he knows
149– 4	Invite *a·* cordially and freely
149–22	*a·* the rich graces of the Spirit.
150–11	with *a·* who are with Truth,
150–27	Not more to one than to *a·*,
150–30	is *a·* that really is or can be ;
155–17	*a·* of her interesting correspondence,
155–23	give to us *a·* the pleasure of
156– 8	*A·* is well at headquarters,
156–23	the basis of *a·* true thought
156–27	and, above *a·*, *obedience*,
157–10	*a·* questions important for your case,
157–11	they furnish *a·* information
158–13	The meaning of it *a·*,
158–19	*A·* God's servants are minute men
159– 7	God of *a·* grace give you peace.
159–29	*a·* gifts of Christian Scientists
159–29	from *a·* parts of our nation,
163–27	idea which leadeth into *a·* Truth
164–32	*a·* that is real and eternal.
166– 4	but this is not *a·* of the
166–26	and *a·* materialism disappear.
167– 9	*a·* that resembles God.
169– 1	found *a·* the divine Science
169– 2	*a·* along the way of her researches
169–25	health and peace and hope for *a·*.
170–15	interpreted *a·* spiritually :
170–18	we also may *a·* partake of.
171–29	*a·* clad in the shining mail
172–10	charity, brooding over *a·*,
173– 6	who healeth *a·* our sickness
174– 7	removeth *a·* iniquities,
174– 8	and healeth *a·* our diseases.
174–11	moves *a·* in harmony,
174–32	that leadeth into *a·* Truth ;
175–32	remember God in *a·* thy ways,
176– 7	been exemplified in *a·* ages,
177– 2	God makes to us *a·*, right here,
177– 4	greatest and holiest of *a·* causes.
179–24	God does *a·* this through
182–24	possibility of *a·* finding their place
184–13	healeth *a·* thy diseases." — *Psal.* 103 : 3.
184–26	which casteth out *a·* fear,
185– 6	strips matter of *a·* claims,
185– 8	renunciation of *a·* that

all

Mis. 185–13	cleansing mortals of *a·* uncleanness,
186–14	that God made *a·* ;
189– 6	that leadeth into *a·* truth.
191– 5	*a·* the beasts of the field." — *see Gen.* 3 : 1.
191–21	*a·* consistent supposition
192– 8	disease and death, in *a·* their forms,
192–27	extends to *a·* ages
192–27	and throughout *a·* Christendom.
193– 4	Jesus did mean *a·*, and even more
193– 8	practicality of *a·* Christ's teachings
193–23	*a·* Christians are properly called
194– 9	command to heal in *a·* ages,
194–25	Love that casts out *a·* fear.
195– 2	the absorption of *a·* action,
198–25	*a·* of which is corrected
199–26	understanding that *a·* substance,
202– 1	basis of *a·* supposed miracles ;
204–14	*a·* pointing upward.
204–24	*a·* the minutiæ of human affairs.
204–31	it banishes forever *a·* envy,
205–24	and unites *a·* periods in the
205–26	dissolves *a·* supposed material life
206– 1	have turned *a·* revolutions,
206–25	and good is the reward of *a·* who
208–17	*A·* states and stages of human
211–29	"Drink ye *a·* of it," — *Matt.* 26 : 27.
211–29, 30	drink it *a·*, and let *a·* drink
213– 3	*A·* that I have written,
215– 5	I do it *a·* in love ;
217– 4	*a·* should conceive and understand
218– 9	*a·* its conceptions of life,
223– 3	I was saying *a·* the time,
223–20	*a·* those who have named
224–14	character, from *a·* the rest ;
225–23	away from *a·* material aid,
226– 3	* Father of *a·* will care for him.
228–14	momentary success of *a·* villanies,
229–14	*a·* other influences governing
230–14	*A·* successful individuals have
230–19	*a·* of which drop human life into
232– 1	God comfort them *a·*!
232–20	that most important of *a·* arts,
232–25	fixed Principle of *a·* healing
235–13	cut down *a·* that bringeth not
236–12	yield obedience to them in *a·*
236–13	rights of conscience, as we *a·* have,
236–13	follow God in *a·* your ways.
236–24	remedy for *a·* human discord.
236–27	blamed for *a·* that is not right :
237–13	*A·* the different phases of error
238– 5	for *a·* who dare to be true,
238–10	*A·* that ever was accomplished,
238–16	but what of *a·* that?
240–11	*A·* education should contribute
240–16	to the satisfaction of *a·*.
244–27	The teachings . . . were for *a·* peoples
245–19	in *a·* the good tendencies,
246– 3	*a·* unmitigated systems of crime ;
246– 5	blot out *a·* inhuman codes.
253– 1	and selleth *a·* that he hath
254– 5	*a·* that love which brooded
254– 6	for *a·* that love that hath fed them
258–12	*a·* law was vested in the
258–25	*a·* law, Life, Truth, and Love.
259–21	*a·* the sons of God shouted
259–29	applicable to *a·* the needs of man.
260–12	annulled *a·* other laws.
262– 2	happiness to *a·* households
262–24	*a·* the homage beneath the skies,
263–13	meet *a·* human needs
263–14	and reflect *a·* bliss.
265– 9	*A·* must have *one* Principle
265–10	*a· who follow the Principle*
267–16	Through *a·* human history,
267–26	exciting cause of *a·* defeat
270–15	*a·* these things shall be added — *Matt.* 6 : 33.
271–11	should eschew *a·* magazines . . . which
272– 2	* with *a·* the rights and privileges
272–19	* *A·* the mind-healing colleges
272–29	endeavored to act toward *a·* students
273–13	and gather *a·* my students, in the
273–18	not yet accomplished *a·* the good
274–10	therefore I leave *a·* for Christ.
275–16	and bless *a·* who mourn.
276– 4	like *a·* else, was purely Western
276– 5	I did not hold interviews with *a·*
276–24	I pray that *a·* my students shall
278–14	Job sinned not in *a·* he said,
279– 7	but over and above it *a·* are
279–21	evil is naught and good is *a·*.
279–24	they had *a·* to shout *together*
280–11	Because God does *a·*,
280–14	we imagine is well if we
284–32	thus it is with *a·* moral obligations.
284–32	I am opposed to *a·* personal attacks.

all

Mis.	289–12	A˙ partnerships are formed on
	290– 7	a˙ bonds that hinder progress.
	290–20	involuntarily flow out towards a˙.
	290–29	a˙ who are receptive share this
	291–13	growth and prosperity of a˙
	291–24	on the hearts and lives of a˙
	292–18	to shut out a˙ opposite sense.
	293– 3	a˙ the claims and modes of evil ;
	293–15	will not understand a˙ your instructions ;
	294–18	from . . . a˙ ravening beasts.
	296–18	to intemperance, as to a˙ immorality,
	297– 3	has distanced a˙ other religious
	297–21	a˙ the claims growing out of this
	297–28	a˙ that belongs to the rights of freedom.
	298– 1	with a˙ thine heart ; — *Prov.* 3 : 5.
	298–19	a˙ the claims of sensuality.
	302–21	a˙ destroyed the copies at once
	303–10	will rest upon us a˙.
	307– 5	you will have a˙ you need
	307– 9	assurance . . . to a˙ human fears,
	307–17	and above a˙, God's love
	307–22	easily-besetting sin of a˙ peoples.
	308–19	I thank you, each and a˙,
	308–32	I earnestly advise a˙
	309– 6	A˙ will agree with me that
	309–21	include a˙ obstacles to health,
	309–30	which contain a˙ and much more than
	310–14	plead for a˙ and every one,
	310–15	a˙ shall be redeemed,
	310–19	A˙ who desire its fellowship,
	310–27	cordially invite a˙ persons who
	311– 1	a˙ who love God and keep His
	311–16	would help a˙ to gain the abiding
	311–28	take the cup, drink a˙ of it,
	312– 1	sorry that I spoke at a˙,
	312– 6	lays a˙ upon the altar,
	312– 7	and alone, bears a˙ burdens,
	312– 7	suffers a˙ inflictions,
	312– 8	endures a˙ piercing for the sake
	314–18	shall read a˙ the selections
	315– 9	a˙ over the world,
	317– 4	we are a˙ of one kindred.
	318–23	demands on a˙ those who
	319– 1	the darkness of a˙ the ages,
	319–18	a˙ the dear Christian Scientists
	320–18	"healeth a˙ our — see *Psal.* 103 : 3.
	320–27	is the light of a˙ ages ;
	321–24	In reply to a˙ invitations
	321–30	infinitely beyond a˙ earthly
	323– 3	city above a˙ clouds,
	324–25	find the lights a˙ wasted
	325– 7	a˙ "drunken without wine." —see *Isa.* 29 : 9.
	326–16	Thus are a˙ mortals, . . driven out
	327–13	insisted upon taking a˙ of it
	327–23	A˙ this time the Stranger is
	329– 2	nature in a˙ her moods
	329–16	rippling a˙ nature in
	329–17	* "breath a˙ odor and cheek a˙ bloom."
	331– 7	over a˙ the earth" — *Gen.* 1 : 26.
	331–30	a˙ earth's hieroglyphics
	333– 8	it absorbs a˙ the rays
	334–11	a˙ its supposed power
	335– 1	Love that casteth out a˙ fear,
	336–22	cognomen of a˙ true religion,
	338– 7	A˙ must go and do likewise.
	339–21	venturing its a˙ of happiness
	339–24	Remember, that for a˙ this
	341–19	find Life eternal : you gain a˙.
	342–27	you shall receive a˙.
	343– 4	a˙ that we have to sacrifice,
	346–21	a˙ its divine requirements.
	347–14	with a˙ the goodness of
	349–19	My counsel to a˙ of them
	354–20	the Principle of a˙ that
	354–24	wherein a˙ is controlled,
	356–17	least of a˙ seeds," — *Matt.* 13 : 32.
	357– 2	and a˙ the *et cetera* of the
	357–20	the greatest of a˙ stages
	358–30	fulfilled a˙ the good ends
	361–12	overshadowed a˙ human philosophy,
	361–25	a˙ eternal individuality.
	362– 6	and reflects a˙ real mode,
	362–12	that God, having made a˙,
	362–12	a˙ that He made was good.
	362–25	We a˙ must find shelter
	364–16	governing a˙ identity,
	364–18	He made a˙ that was made,
	365–29	and more than a˙ else,
	366–23	a˙ mortal conclusions start from
	368–12	a˙ are not metaphysicians,
	369– 9	which governs a˙ effects,
	370–25	would gather a˙ sorts into a
	370–27	the good shepherd cares for a˙
	370–28	Shepherd does care for a˙,
	371–15	mixing a˙ grades of persons

all

Mis.	374– 9	justified of a˙ — *Luke* 7 : 35.
	374–19	brought a great light to a˙ ages,
	375–10	* I did not utter a˙ I felt
	375–32	* A˙ that I can say to you,
	379– 9	it was not at a˙ metaphysical
	379–15	Principle of a˙ healing.
	384– 5	And a˙ is morn and May.
	386–29	a˙ the crowned and blest,
	389–13	me, and mine, and a˙.
	393– 7	Science, a˙ unweary,
	398– 4	A˙ the rugged way.
	399– 2	Love wipes your tears a˙ away,
	399–10	A˙ thy sorrow and sickness
Man.	27–16	a˙ other C. S. literature
	28–18	If an officer fails to fulfil a˙ the
	31– 5	and of a˙ its branch churches
	32–22	read a˙ notices and remarks
	32–24	in a˙ the branch churches.
	36–24	A˙ applications for membership
	42–14	and in accord with a˙ of
	45– 3	occupation for a˙ its members.
	46–14	a˙ private communications
	47–17	a˙ thy diseases" — *Psal.* 103 : 3.
	47–24	Charity to A˙.
	49– 4	a˙ who understand the teachings
	59–17	a˙ sects and denominations
	60–17	each day of a˙ the years.
	66–19	if a˙ of the letter has been read,
	66–20	require a˙ of it to be read ;
	74–18	a˙ other C. S. churches
	77– 6	submit them a˙ to said committee
	77–20	a˙ the proceedings of the members
	90– 1	A˙ members of this class must
	91– 6	on a˙ certificates issued.
	92–10	be a˙ that we claim for it.
	99–15	By-Law applies to a˙ States except
	102–10	A˙ deeds of further purchases
	102–13	a˙ the trusts mentioned
	102–18	in a˙ such deeds
	110–10	A˙ names, whether of applicants,
	110–16	A˙ names must be written
	110–16	written the same in a˙ places
Chr.	53–12	That stills a˙ strife.
	55–10	a˙ these things shall — *Matt.* 6 : 33.
Ret.	5–19	in a˙ the walks of life.
	5–25	* was felt by a˙ around her.
	9– 4	told Mehitable a˙ about this
	18–18	a˙ His spirit hath made,
	19–20	remarked by a˙ observers.
	20– 1	lost a˙ my husband's property,
	20–19	life is dead, bereft of a˙,
	22–17	God is over a˙.
	22–20	a˙ the children of one parent,
	24– 8	to trace a˙ physical effects to
	24–10	a˙ causation was Mind,
	27– 8	like a˙ great truths,
	29– 3	I esteem a˙ honest people,
	30– 9	a˙ moral and religious reform.
	31–21	he is guilty of a˙." — *Jas.* 2 : 10.
	34–11	a˙ material medicines,
	34–12	antidote for a˙ sickness,
	34–14	a˙ the ills which befall mortals.
	38– 5	A˙ efforts to persuade him
	38–19	printed a˙ the copy on hand,
	42– 6	He forsook a˙ to follow
	46–10	A˙ the rugged way.
	47– 5	a˙ over our continent,
	47–12	In view of a˙ this,
	48– 4	a˙ that was aimed at its
	48– 9	a˙ these considerations moved me
	48–21	sent to a˙ parts of our country,
	49– 2	willing to sacrifice a˙
	49–17	a˙ that is unlike Christ
	49–28	a˙ debts of the corporation
	57–13	causes a˙ bodily ailments,
	57–20	sufficient to supply a˙
	57–22	A˙ must be of God,
	58– 4	a˙ this is like trying to
	59–19	and a˙ that is made by Him,
	60–14	good is a˙ that is real.
	61–13	the cause of a˙ sickness ;
	64–10	good is equally *one* and a˙,
	64–24	they are no claims at a˙.
	64–26	to a˙ the illusive forms,
	69– 5	The parent of a˙ human discord
	69–22	God created a˙ through Mind,
	69–22	and made a˙ perfect and eternal.
	70–28	virtually stands at the head of a˙
	80–11	* With exactness grinds He a˙.
	81–24	* This above a˙ :
	89–26	Above a˙, trespass not intentionally
	90–23	give a˙ her hours to those
	91–18	spiritual needs of a˙ who
	94–14	When a˙ fleshly belief is
Un.	3–22	He is a˙ the Life and Mind there is

all

Un.	4–12	diviner sense that God is *a·*
	8–11	*A·* that is beautiful and good
	8–17	*A·* forms of error are uprooted
	9– 9	that *a·* are without excuse who
	9–23	few spiritual thinkers in *a·* ages.
	10– 2	separates my system from *a·* others.
	11– 6	*a·* in direct opposition to
	14–21	*a·* cannot be good therein.
	15– 2	* death into the world, and *a·* our woe.
	17– 5	and *a·* that is good will aid
	17– 9	predestined from *a·* eternity ;
	19– 7	If God knows evil at *a·*,
	20–17	*a·* hate and the sense of evil.
	23–13	*a·* are partakers, — *Heb.* 12 : 8.
	24– 3	all consciousness, *a·* individuality
	24–17	Spirit is *a·* that endureth,
	24–20	constitute *a·* that exists.
	26– 7	*a·* responsibility for myself
	26–24	*A·* is real, *a·* is serious.
	27– 9	doubts *a·* existence except its own.
	29– 4	as does *a·* criminal law,
	29–13	*a·* that is absolutely immutable
	31–19	*a·* that denies and defies Spirit,
	35–16	immortal Mind, the Parent of *a·*.
	37–13	*a·* Life is eternal.
	38– 9	*a·* is real which proceeds from
	38–18	false sense of life is *a·* that dies,
	39–28	Science and . . . conflict at *a·* points,
	41–12	come to *a·* sooner or later ;
	41–22	*A·* Life is Spirit,
	42–14	*a·* the sons of God — *Job.* 38 : 7.
	43–16	till *a·* be fulfilled." — *Matt.* 5 : 18.
	45– 8	need most of *a·* to be rid of
	46– 3	*A·* Truth is from inspiration
	47– 5	*A·* that can exist is God and
	48– 9	He heals *a·* my ills,
	48–14	Father and Mother of *a·* He creates ;
	51–14	generic term for *a·* humanity.
	51–16	the generic term for *a·* women ;
	51–16	of *a·* these individualities
	53– 2	*a·* its forms are inverted good.
	54– 4	*a·* there is of sickness ;
	57–27	Science wipes away *a·* tears.
	58–14	over *a·* mortal mentality
	58–16	"in *a·* points tempted — *Heb.* 4 : 15.
	60– 2	mortal inventions, one and *a·*
	62–25	is *a·* that can be buried.
	64– 1	*A·* that *is*, God created.
Pul.	3–13	assurance ends *a·* warfare,
	3–23	*a·* human desires are quenched,
	4–20	lives in *a·* Life,
	4–29	used, in *a·* its public sessions,
	5–20	with a beauty *a·* its own
	8– 1	*A·* praise to the press of
	8–11	the donors *a·* touchingly told their
	10– 6	*a·* thine iniquities ;— *Psal.* 103 : 3.
	10– 7	*a·* thy diseases." — *Psal.* 103 : 3.
	11– 6	May *a·* whose means, energies, and
	12–22	by which we lay down *a·* for Truth,
	15–16	At *a·* times and under *a·* circumstances,
	15–20	will unite *a·* interests in the
	17– 9	*A·* the rugged way.
	21– 6	This we *a·* must do to be
	21–15	doing good in *a·* denominations
	22– 3	*A·* Christian churches have one bond
	25–12	The girders are *a·* of iron,
	29–20	* Judge Hanna said that while *a·* these
	30–10	* includes those *a·* over the country.
	31–19	* the central figure in *a·* this
	33–20	* *A·* inquiry in the neighborhood
	37– 3	* its attitude toward *a·* questions.
	38–26	* each and *a·* these movements,
	38–29	* good that each and *a·* shall prosper,
	39– 1	* that *a·* meet on common ground
	39– 5	* *a·* teach that one great truth,
	39–25	* 'mid them *a·* I only see *one* face,
	41–10	* *a·* the territory that lies between,
	41–13	* From *a·* New England the members
	41–20	* *a·* who wished had heard and seen ;
	41–27	* *A·* hail the power of Jesus' name,
	42– 2	* *a·* filled with a waiting multitude.
	43– 3	* numbering thirty-five singers in *a·*
	44–11	* While we *a·* rejoice, yet the mother
	44–12	* the mother in Israel, alone of us *a·*,
	44–18	* chapter sub-title
	44–25	* has flowed in from *a·* parts of the
	47–26	* picturesque *a·* about Concord
	49–11	* has come forth *a·* this beauty!
	51– 1	* C. S. does not strike *a·* as a system of
	51– 3	* the same impressions upon *a·*.
	52–23	* obliterated *a·* vital belief in his
	54–23	* "put them *a·* out," — *Luke* 8 : 54.
	55–19	* *a·* causation is of Mind,
	55–26	* others being branches,
	57–12	* and, indeed, in *a·* New England.

all

Pul.	58–18	* The floors are *a·* mosaic,
	58–20	* *a·* the windows are of colored **glass.**
	58–28	* furnished with *a·* conveniences
	60–15	* from *a·* parts of the country.
	61–21	* admiration was expressed by *a·*
	62–13	* and call forth *a·* the purity
	62–17	* They have *a·* the beauties of **a**
	62–22	* as they range in *a·* sizes,
	63–25	* Scientists *a·* over the country,
	64– 8	* Money came freely from *a·*
	68– 7	* from *a·* parts of the world,
	69–17	* to explain fully *a·* about it,
	70–16	* Scientists *a·* over the country.
	70–18	*a·* causation was Mind,
	71–13	* in fact *a·* over the country,
	73–21	* versed in *a·* their beliefs
	73–23	* but that *a·* comes from God.
	74–22	not at *a·* as I have heard her talk.
	75–21	* *a·* over North America
	76–19	* *a·* heavily plated with gold.
	79– 6	* the money was *a·* paid in
	80–29	* *a·* these ideas are Christian.
	81– 2	* *A·* hail the power of Jesus' name,
	81–10	* We *a·* know her — she is simply the
	81–15	* of *a·* those who scorn self
	81–16	* of *a·* those who seek the brightness
	81–21	* *a·* the harmonies of the universe
	81–25	* *a·* that the twelve have left undone.
	81–26	* of missions — the highest of *a·*
	84– 7	* *a·* that is worth living for,
	84–15	* *a·* predictions and prognostications
	84–19	* *A·* who are awake thereto have **some**
	84–23	* *a·* obstacles to its completion
	85–15	* gratitude and love of *a·*
	86–20	* students and *a·* contributors
Rud.	v– 4	RESPECTFULLY DEDICATED TO *a·*
	3– 4	obstinate resistance to *a·* efforts
	3–19	which gives *a·* true volition,
	4– 6	*Principle of a· science,*
	4–10	*A·* true Science represents a
	4–21	*a·* is God, and there is naught **beside**
	5– 5	then *a·* must be Mind,
	6– 6	*A·* beauty and goodness are
	7– 1	Not that *a·* healing is Science,
	8–15	In *a·* moral revolutions,
	9–20	lust, and *a·* fleshly vices.
	10–26	acknowledge God in *a·* His ways.
	12– 3	Above *a·*, he keeps unbroken the
	12–20	*a·* the conditions requisite for
	13–26	give *a·* their time to C. S. work,
	14– 3	must give Him *a·* their services,
	15–17	should be fortified on *a·* sides
No.	v– 7	transparent to the hearts of *a·*
	2– 9	rob disease of *a·* reality ;
	5– 1	*A·* true Christian Scientists are
	6–11	as *a·* understand who practise
	6–26	*a·* at war with the testimony of
	8– 4	faithful, and charitable with *a·*,
	8– 8	passeth *a·* understanding, — *Phil.* 4 : 7.
	9–24	and includes *a·* Truth.
	10–11	postulate of *a·* that I teach,
	10–12	Principle for *a·* scientific truth.
	10–25	turns . . . *a·* hope and faith to God,
	12–14	true Christianity in *a·* ages,
	12–27	removes *a·* limits from divine **power.**
	12–28	*a·* instead of a part of being,
	13– 5	the Principle of *a·* harmony,
	14– 6	*a·* sensible phenomena are merely
	15– 5	would convince *a·* that their purpose **is**
	16–20	He who is All, understands *a·*.
	16–22	can take in no more than *a·*.
	17–21	these two words *a·* and *nothing*,
	18– 3	acknowledged God in *a·* His ways.
	18– 5	*a·* presence, power, and glory,
	20–25	*a·* human philosophy.
	21–10	the Principle of *a·* phenomena,
	24– 2	loses *a·* place, person, and power.
	24– 8	*A·* these vagaries are at variance
	26–13	*A·* real being represents God,
	33–25	Jesus suffered for *a·* mortals
	34– 1	the delusion of *a·* human error,
	38–25	*A·* prayer that is desire is
	39–23	most of *a·*, it shows us what God **is.**
	41–12	sinners in *a·* societies,
	42– 8	supplies *a·* human needs.
	42–10	*a·* "the ills that flesh is heir to."
	42–11	*a·* the vain power of dogma
	43– 4	*a·* ye that labor — *Matt.* 11 : 28.
	45–19	with *a·* its sweet amenities
Pan.	1–18	even the day when *a·* people
	2–11	Greek words meaning "*a·*"
	3– 2	pantheism suits not at *a·* the
	4– 4	who possesses *a·* wisdom,
	4–25	*a·* thine iniquities ; — *Psal.* 103 : 3.
	4–25	healeth *a·* thy diseases. — *Psal.* 103 : 3.

all

Pan.	6– 2	more effectual than *a·* other
	6–17	made *a·* that was made,
	10–22	*A·* this is accomplished by
	12–14	it showeth to *a·* peoples
	12–25	*a·* that the term implies,
	12–25	*a·* that is real and eternal.
	13–13	Love *a·* Christian churches
	13–18	*a·* shall know Him,
	13–21	life in Life, *a·* in All.
	13–23	Father of *a·*,— *Eph.* 4 : 6.
	13–23	above *a·*, and through *a·*,— *Eph.* 4 : 6.
	13–24	and in you *a·*."— *Eph.* 4 : 6.
'00.	2–27	Well, *a·* that is good.
	4–28	reflects *a·* that really is,
	4–29	*a·* personality and individuality.
	5– 1	Father of *a·*, who is above *a·*,— *Eph.* 4 : 6.
	5– 1	through *a·*, and in you *a·*."— *Eph.* 4 : 6.
	5–25	*a·* systems of religion.
	7– 8	more Bibles sold than in *a·* the
	7–11	those in *a·* the walks of life,
	9–16	must be a hero at *a·* points,
	10– 2	*A·* that worketh good is
	11–28	criticism on *a·* human action,
	14–24	At *a·* times respect the character
	15–10	which of *a·* human experience is
	15–16	*a·* this time divine Love has been
'01.	1–18	*A·* that is true is a sort of
	2–24	*a·* their returning footsteps.
	5– 9	possesses the nature of *a·*,
	5–13	the divine Principle of *a·*.
	6–27	*a·* conceivable idea of Him
	7–23	The God whom *a·* Christians
	10– 3	For *a·* these things they will — *see Matt.* 10:17.
	12–16	command to heal in *a·* ages,
	14–26	To overcome *a·* wrong, it must
	15–17	wickedness against *a·* light.
	23– 6	If . . . the infinite is not *a·* ;
	24– 7	*a·* the ills of mortals
	24–11	* greatest of *a·* temporal blessings,
	25–15	matter minus, and God *a·*,
	25–17	*a·* such gilded sepulchres
	27– 2	independent of *a·* other authors
	27–24	taken out of its metaphysics *a·* matter
	28–22	*a·* that worketh or maketh a lie.
	29–10	*a·* the best of his earthly years.
	29–22	*A·* honor and success to those
	30– 1	*a·* other religious denominations
	30–13	birth to nothing and death to *a·*,
	30–19	destroying *a·* lower considerations.
	30–27	under *a·* circumstances to obey the
	32–12	to renounce *a·* for Him.
	33– 7	* above *a·*, in the more advanced
	33–18	judged (if at *a·*) by their works.
	34–29	with *a·* thine heart ;— *Prov.* 3 : 5.
	35– 1	In · thy ways— *Prov.* 3 : 6.
'02.	2–10	It is purifying *a·* peoples,
	4– 7	Let us *a·* pray . . . for more grace,
	4–23	applicable to *a·* periods
	5– 6	C. S. stills *a·* distress
	5–30	silences *a·* questions on this subject,
	6–13	Here *a·* human woe is seen to
	6–17	*a·* it includes is obliterated,
	6–20	*A·* Christian faith, hope, and
	6–20	*a·* devout desire, virtually petition,
	7– 3	It accords *a·* to God, Spirit,
	7–11	*omni*, which signifies *a·*,
	9– 4	*a·* law and gospel.
	12–15	conflicts not at *a·* with another
	14–27	silence *a·* private criticisms,
	14–28	*a·* unjust public aspersions,
	16–20	no darkness, but *a·* is light,
	17– 6	*a·* are ready to seek and obey
	17–27	will put to flight *a·* care
	18–28	death of *a·* his disciples
	19– 9	*a·* the malice of his foes.
	19–23	of *a·* these things."— *Matt.* 6 : 32.
	20–22	but in this, as *a·* else,
	20–24	meeting you *a· occasionally*
Hea.	2–18	*a·* ye that labor — *Matt.* 11 : 28.
	4–23	Principle of *a·* that is right,
	7–19	more than they *a·*."— *see Mark* 12 : 43.
	9–23	God made *a·* that was made,
	10–13	God is All, and in *a·* :
	11–23	Metaphysics places *a·* cause
	12– 8	mind, the basis of *a·* action,
	12–10	*a·* physical effects originate in
	14–27	in sympathy with *a·* that is right
	14–28	opposed to *a·* that is wrong,
	15– 5	understood, to heal *a·* ills
	15–14	why should man deny *a·* might to
	16– 3	for the benefit of *a·* who,
	17– 8	God made *a·* that was made ;
	17–10	with *a·* their evidences of sin,
	17–12	we shall *a·* learn this as we awake
	17–23	but *a·* appeared through the

all

Hea.	19–11	origin of *a·* mortal things.
Peo.	4– 1	*a·* systems of *materia medica*
	6– 1	* *a·* the better for mankind
	6– 1	* *a·* the worse for the fishes.
	6–26	for which we are to leave *a·*
	7– 2	We are *a·* sculptors;
	9–24	*a·* evidence of any other power
	11–23	*a·* the woes of mankind
	12–12	acknowledge only God in *a·* thy ways,
	12–13	*a·* thine iniquities ;— *Psal.* 103 : 3.
	12–13	healeth *a·* thy diseases."— *Psal.* 103 : 3.
Po.	vi–22	* *A· of the author's best-known hymns*
	2–10	With *a·* the strength of weakness
	2–12	Admired by *a·*, still art thou drear
	4–12	encircles me, and mine, and *a·*.
	9– 9	leaves *a·* faded, the fruitage shed,
	9–11	reason made right and hearts *a·* love.
	11– 3	Victorious, *a·* who live it,
	14– 8	*A·* the rugged way.
	16–19	when the winds are *a·* still.
	24–14	Is *a·* I need to comfort mine.
	29–18	so far above *A·* mortal strife,
	29–21	Fill us today With *a·* thou art
	32–20	comfort my soul *a·* the wearisome day,
	33– 8	vanity, folly, and *a·* that is wrong
	36– 4	And *a·* is morn and May.
	39– 1	Author of *a·* divine
	39–18	"Temples of Honor," *a·*,
	40– 1	"Good Templars" one and *a·*,
	41–18	didst call them to banish *a·* pain,
	46–16	Be *a·* thy life in music given,
	50–16	with *a·* the crowned and blest,
	51–12	Art and Science, *a·* unweary,
	53–19	dead are *a·* The vernal songs
	64– 9	*a·* His spirit hath made,
	75– 9	Love wipes your tears *a·* away,
	75–17	*A·* thy sorrow and sickness and sin."
My.	vi–22	* to pay *a·* future profits to
	vii–14	* *a·* Christian Scientists can render
	4–15	loves *a·* who love God, good ;
	5–10	God giving *a·* and man having *a·*
	6–10	overcome sin in *a·* its forms,
	8–21	* if they are *a·* to get in."
	11– 5	* constantly at her post during *a·*
	11–11	* we know that in *a·* this time
	13–20	*a·* thine iniquities ;— *Psal.* 103 : 3.
	13–20	*healeth a· thy diseases;*— *Psal.* 103 : 3.
	13–26	reverberating through *a·* cycles of
	15–15	*a·* that you are able to bear now,
	17– 4	*a·* malice, and *a·* guile,— *I Pet.* 2 : 1.
	17– 5	*a·* evil speakings,— *I Pet.* 2 : 1.
	18–21	Love *a·* Christian churches for the
	18–30	* *a·* other published writings of
	19–11	be with you *a·*.— *II Cor.* 13 : 14.
	20–13	Bring *a·* your tithes into
	21– 3	* We *a·* know of the loving
	21–10	* *a·* Christian Scientists will gladly
	21–26	* *a·* will rejoice in the glad reunion
	22– 6	* attendance at *a·* the services,
	22–27	* Is it not therefore the duty of *a·*
	24– 4	* is ready to heal *a·* who accept its
	25–16	Will one and *a·* of my dear
	25–25	*a·* vanity of victory disappears
	25–27	divinity appears in *a·* its promise.
	27–25	* pay *a·* bills in connection with
	30– 3	* *a·* the services were precisely
	30– 7	* Scientists from *a·* over the world,
	30– 7	* nearly *a·* the local Scientists,
	32– 5	* they began *a·* together,
	36–11	* *a·* that we are or hope to be
	36–26	* *a·* the beauty of color and design,
	37– 1	* natural healer of *a·* our diseases
	37–10	* appreciation of *a·* that you have
	37–20	* supreme cause of *a·* the activities
	38– 3	* in God is *a·* consolation
	38– 5	* our love for you and for *a·* that
	38– 6	* *a·* that you have done for us.
	38–10	* *a·* seating space had been filled
	38–18	* *a·* the seats in the body of the
	38–22	* their service was the same as *a·*
	39–12	* Lord's Prayer, in which *a·* joined.
	41–21	* love which is just and kind to *a·*
	47– 5	* from *a·* parts of the world,
	47–16	* victories . . . precious each and *a·*.
	48–25	* are *a·* forces that make for
	48–31	* to say, in *a·* fairness.
	50–24	* a very inspiring season to us *a·*,
	51– 5	* *a·* others now interested in
	51–30	* thanks and gratitude shared by *a·*
	52– 9	* *a·*, will make greater efforts
	59–32	* marvellous beyond *a·* imagining
	60–10	* expressed the thought of *a·*
	60–19	* "With *a·* thy getting get — *Prov.* 4 : 7.
	64– 7	* for *a·* that she has done.
	64–15	* In *a·* her writings, through *a·* the

all

My.
64–20   * Fearlessly does she warn *a*· her
64–24   * overcoming *a*· that is unlike God,
68–18   * color scheme for *a*· the auditorium
70– 7   * and they are *a*· paid for.
70–12   * The effect on *a*· within earshot
71– 9   * *a*· agree that it is a stunning
71–19   * In fact, nearly *a*· the traditions of
72– 9   * From *a*· the centres of Europe
72–14   * chapter sub-title
72–22   * members of the church *a*· over the
73– 4   * churches *a*· over this country
73–13   * flocking from *a*· over the world
73–21   * here the visitors will receive *a*·
73–23   * to which *a*· mail may be directed,
75–12   * *a*· the preliminary arrangements
75–17   * take it *a*· very good-naturedly.
76– 3   * the largest of them *a*·
76–14   * *a*· of which goes to show the
76–21   * *a*· contributions have been voluntary.
77– 1   * the cynosure of *a*· eyes
77– 9   * From *a*· over the world
77–23   * Scientists from *a*· quarters
78– 2   * in order that *a*· might participate
78–31   * apparently understanding *a*· they
80–27   * when these places had been filled,
82– 1   * they *a*· have the same stories
82– 6   * this morning it looked as though *a*·
84– 3   * practically *a*· the resources
84–12   * Scientists *a*· over the world.
88– 7   * It shows strength in *a*· parts,
88–22   * *a*· that increasing host
89– 4   * *a*· facts inhospitable to it
89– 5   * deemed . . . not to exist at *a*·.
89–18   * different from almost *a*· other
89–29   * greatest religious phenomenon of *a*·
90– 4   * *a*· these things are new,
90–10   * *A*· the passionate love for life
90–25   * from *a*· over the civilized world,
96– 2   * from *a*· parts of the world
96–29   * from *a*· parts of the United States.
98–19   * *a*· of the funds required
99–18   * from *a*· parts of the world,
100–8, 9   * coming from *a*·, or nearly *a*·,
104– 5   *a*· sorts of institutions flourish
106–27   the very antipode of *a*· these?
107–24   God made *a*· that was made,
110–14   *a*· the *et cetera* of mortal mind
113–24   *a*· around us is demonstrated
114–19   *A*· thoughts in the line of Scriptural
117–25   May *a*· Christian Scientists ponder
117–31   is *a*· that I ask of mankind.
119–17   "healeth *a*· thy diseases" — *Psal.* 103 : 3.
121–24   is not only polite to *a*· but is
125–11   *A*· honor to the members of our
127–11   than *a*· other religions since the
127–32   *a*· times, climes, and
129– 6   *a*· concomitants of C. S.
130–21   *A*· published quotations from
130–28   in *a*· your public ministrations,
131–24   "Bring ye *a*· the tithes — *Mal.* 3 : 10.
132–21   God *a*·, one, — one Mind
133– 5   So shall *a*· earth's children
133–27   my book is not *a*· you know of me.
134–17   Life lessens *a*· pride
137–14   selected *a*· my investments,
138–18   except I leave *a*· for Christ.
141–19   * from *a*· parts of the world.
143–10   one and *a*· of my beloved friends
143–14   *a*· this fustian of either denying or
146– 2   understood by *a*· Christians that
146–17   if they are true at *a*·,
148– 4   *A*· that we ask of any people
148– 7   God of *a*· grace, truth, and love
148–13   *a*· unthought of till the day had
151–26   discovery of *a*· cause and effect.
152–16   Principle of *a*· that really is,
152–18   there is none else and in whom is *a*·
152–25   God demands *a*· our faith and love ;
152–29   cause of *a*· that is rightly done.
153–28   to *a*· human thought and action,
154– 1   *a*· salvation from sin, disease,
154– 2   Science of *a*· healing is based on
156– 6   above *a*· that we ask — *Eph.* 3 : 20.
156– 7   *a*· grace abound — *II Cor.* 9 : 8.
156– 8   having *a*· sufficiency — *II Cor.* 9 : 8.
158–28   and *a*· who worship therein
159–29   *A*· rights reserved.
160–20   a hell for *a*· who persist in
161– 9   *a*· ye workers of — *Luke* 13 : 27.
161–12   and *a*· the prophets, — *Luke* 13 : 28.
162– 4   fulfil *a*· righteousness." — *Matt.* 3 : 15.
162–11   Scientists *a*· over the field,
163– 9   Not having the time to receive *a*·
163–25   *a*· and more than I anticipated.
164–12   *a*· within the human heart

all

My.
164–26   the sum of *a*· reality and good.
165– 1   promote and pervade *a*· his success.
166– 1   infinite source where is *a*·,
166–20   If *a*· our years were holidays,
167–19   Give to *a*· the dear ones
169– 2   I invite you, one and *a*·,
170–10   in the minds of *a*· present
171–11   invite *a*· my church communicants
173–21   my heart welcomed each and *a*·.
178–10   and prepared for *a*· peoples.
178–13   Then *a*· is Spirit and spiritual.
178–15   pronounces *a*· that God made
178–18   for He made *a*·
178–31   *a*· else reported as his sayings
179–11   *a*· of which divine Science shows
180– 8   which applies to *a*· ages,
181– 2   settle *a*· points beyond cavil,
183– 2   with *a*· thy heart, — *Luke* 10 : 27.
183– 2   with *a*· thy soul, — *Luke* 10 : 27.
183– 3   with *a*· thy strength, — *Luke* 10 : 27.
183– 3   with *a*· thy mind ; — *Luke* 10 : 27.
186–13   o'er *a*· victorious!
186–14   in whom dwelleth *a*· life, health,
186–15   will supply *a*· your needs
187– 8   exclude *a*· darkness or doubt,
187–17   be and abide with you *a*·.
188–27   convey *a*· impressions to man,
190–23, 24   *a*· peoples, in *a*· ages,
191–17   Love, which wipes away *a*· tears.
193– 6   mine to watch and work for *a*·,
193–18   unite with *a*· who believe in Truth.
195–16   To do good to *a*· because we love *a*·,
195–17   the one talent that we *a*· have,
199–16   *a*· loyal lovers of God and man.
201–24   *A*· the rugged way.
202– 8   "Render therefore to *a*· — *Rom.* 13 : 7.
203– 4   *a*· is in your textbooks.
203–10   *A*· that is worth reckoning
203–26   safe from *a*· chance of being
203–29   if you have not accomplished *a*· you
205–23   shorn of *a*· personality,
210–10   *a*· whom your thoughts rest upon
211– 9   *A*· that error asks is to
214–27   cast my *a*· into the treasury
216– 2   give *a*· their time to spiritual
216– 4   *A*· systems of religion stand on this
217–18   * "If *a*· matter is unreal, why do we
217–22   *a*· that the material senses affirm.
218– 4   fulfil *a*· righteousness." — *Matt.* 3 : 15.
219– 6   have *a*· the honor of their success
220–15   I pray for the pacification of *a*·
221–24   *A*· issues of morality,
223–17   *A*· such questions are superinduced
223–20   *A*· inquiries, coming directly or
223–29   Do *a*· Christian Scientists see or
225–12   In divine Science *a*· belongs to God,
225–15   distinguishes it from *a*· other names,
225–22   In this, as in *a*· that is right,
225–30   divine Principle includes them *a*·.
226–13   governs *a*· from the infinitesimal to
229– 5   *a*· that do these things
229–14   and thus lose *a*· selfishness,
230–10   but to one and *a*· equally.
230–27   *a*· taught of God." — *John* 6 : 45.
232– 7   whereby *a*· our debts are paid,
232–14   I say unto *a*·, Watch" — *Mark* 13 : 37,
234–21   *a*· our great Master's sayings
235–16   Did God make *a*· that was made?
237–23   I recommend its careful study to *a*·
239–14   *and a*· *are taught of God*
239–18   and so includes *a*· in one.
239–22   is the reflection of *a*· that is real
239–27   Spirit, who made *a*· that was made.
240–17   *a*· that is unlike God, good
241–29   * so that *a*· may know it."
242–17   *a*· inquiries . . . relating to C. S.
243–17   give *a*· possible time and attention
244– 9   any or *a*· of you who are ready
244–21   *a*· loyal students of my books
245–24   of *a*· who claim to teach C. S.
247–28   has *a*· been done through love,
249–14   *a*· this only to satiate its loathing
251–24   for *a*· is thine and mine.
252–29   *A*· hail to this higher hope
256– 9   I beg to send to you *a*· a
257–16   healing *a*· sorrow, sickness, and sin.
257–20   *a*· human hate, pride, greed,
258– 8   to *a*· of holiest worth.
258–24   sounded *a*· depths of love, grief,
259–13   *A*· our dear churches' Christmas
260–26   appeals to *a*· conditions,
263– 6   wishes you *a*· a *happy Christmas*,
265–30   reaching out to *a*· classes
266–17   *a*· codes, modes, hypotheses,
266–19   origin of *a*· that really is,
266–21   by the spiritualization of *a*·

all

My. 267– 6 the originator of a· that really is.
267–30 a· the divine modes, means, forms,
269–12 * A· are but parts of one stupendous
271– 5 little understood a· that I indited ;
271–23 * will be read with deep interest by a·
273– 7 * emerging . . . from a· attacks
275–20 is a· that prevents my daily drive.
275–27 charity brooding over a·,
276–12 to a· her dear friends and enemies.
277–20 can settle a· questions amicably
279– 9 reappearing in a· ages,
279–10 a· periods in the design of God.
279–13 is sufficient to still a· strife.
279–14 Had a· peoples one Mind,
280– 8 * reminder from you that a· the things
280–19 He will bless a· the inhabitants
280–22 bless a· with His own truth
281–10 brotherhood of a· peoples
282– 7 a· the ends of the earth.'' — Isa. 45 : 22.
283–15 remedies for a· earth's woe.
284–26 a· quarrels between nations
285– 7 in a· your wise endeavors for
286– 5 prayed that a· the peoples on earth
287– 9 governing a· that really is.
288–11 and He is the Father of a·.
288–31 because God made a·,
289– 1 A· education is work.
290–17 never so near as when a· earthly joys
291–11 the interests of a· peoples ;
292– 2 A· that can be accomplished,
294– 6 omnipresent, supreme over a·.
294–14 control a· the conditions of man
297– 4 a· that Miss Barton really is,
298– 7 distinguished a· my working years.
302– 1 a· modes of healing disease
302– 8 mind is the cause of a· effect
303–21 what feeds a few feeds a·.
303–25 pith and finale of them a·.
305–21 A· that I am in reality,
307– 5 word science was not used at a·,
308– 1 a· the powers of earth combined
309–31 * practically a· the intellectual life.
310– 1 A· my father's daughters were given
310– 3 they a· taught school acceptably
310–17 allegation . . . that a· the family,
315–30 a· this because the truth
316–25 and of a· that is right.
320–15 * the author of a· your works.
320–18 * did not endorse a· the statements
323–18 * a· that your wonderful life and
323–19 * Neither do I now feel at a· equal
325– 2 * when amidst a· your duties you
327–12 * it has made glad the hearts of a·
327–25 * "A· other professionals who
328–28 * "and a· other professionals who
330–11 * are appreciated by a·,
330–31 was remarked by a· observers.
332– 7 * yet it is a· we can award :
336–12 I lost a· my husband's property,
338– 3 Victorious, a· who live it,
338–23 But a· Christian Scientists deeply
338–29 charitable towards a·,
339–14 a· that it formerly signified,
339–28 and a· that wars against Spirit
340–26 Jesus' example in this, as in a· else,
341– 9 Beloved brethren a· over our land
341–14 A love for a·
341–26 * It had been raining a· day
342–25 * after a· now concerned in its
343–29 brought a· back to union and love
344– 3 then a· his rays collectively
345–26 They a· tend to newer, finer,
346–29 "S. and H. makes it plain to a·
347–19 in exchange for a· else.
347–20 with a· its sweet associations.
348– 4 a· effect must be the offspring of
348– 8 the greatest of a· questions
349–10 including a· law and supplying a· the
350–19 Thou a·, Thou infinite
351–27 divine Science is a· they need,
353– 9 I have given the name to a· the
353–26 the spiritual have a· place and
357–22 therefore Spirit is a·.
358–13 however much I desire to read a·
358–21 through whom a· my business is
359–11 a· of which can be read by the
360–17 I advise you with a· my soul to
361– 5 A· I say is stated in C. S.
362–13 Trustees and Readers of a· the
(see also **being, churches, consciousness, disease,
earth, error, evil, faith, good, mankind, manner,
men, Mind, minds, nations, power, Science,
sense, sin, space, suffering, things, time, way,
world**)

all-absorbing
Un. 6–17 such a grand and a· verity
allay
Mis. 45– 7 although its power to a· fear,
Ret. 26– 6 to a· the tortures of crucifixion.
allaying
My. 335–19 * in the hope of a· the excitement
all-conquering
My. 258–11 with Christ's a· love.
allegation
My. 310–17 the a· by McClure's Magazine
334– 5 * a· that copies of Mrs. Eddy's book,
allegations
My. 317– 4 * a· in the public press
allege
Mis. 199– 3 to a· that only mortal, erring mind
alleged
Mis. 48–13 It is a· that at one of his
248–20 is a· to have reported my demise,
My. 136–16 for which it is a· he was
315–24 her a· double or dummy
354– 2 because of a· misrepresentations
allegement
Mis. 238–25 public a· that I am "sick,
allegiance
Mis. 134–18 Firm in your a· to the reign of
276–32 firmer than ever in their a· to God.
Ret. 50–19 I mean this, — a· to God,
My. 42–27 * how faithful is her a· to God,
299– 9 * claim the a· of mankind.''
allegiant
My. 189–17 for love is a·,
alleging
Mis. 380–32 a· that the copyrighted works of
allegorical
My. 179– 7 In this a· document
allegories
'00. 11–27 His a· are the highest criticism
allegory
Mis. 24–28 or rather the a· describing it.
109–19 a· of Adam and Eve
323– 1 chapter sub-title
332–13 In the a· of Genesis,
Pan. 6–19 enter into the Scriptural a·,
Hea. 17–14 The a· of Adam,
17–24 Sin was first in the a·,
My. 5– 2 according to the Scriptural a·,
179– 6 second was an opposite story, or a·,
alleviate
Mis. 89–12 save him or a· his sufferings,
All-Father
Ret. 91–25 holy messages from the A·.
All-Father-Mother
Mis. 77–24 learn, . . . somewhat of the A· God.
ALL-God
No. 10–10 and expresses the A·.
all-harmonious
Mis. 18–16 the a· "male and female,'' — Gen. 1 : 27.
alliance
Mis. 122– 8 instrument in this holy (?) a·
allied
Mis. 97–12 It is in no way a· to divine power.
Un. 17– 5 Be a· to the deific power,
Pul. 83–18 * our own a· armies of evil
No. 14–12 is no more a· to C. S. than
Po. 10–17 A· by nations' grace,
My. 177–17 genesis of C. S. was a· to
337–18 A· by nations' grace,
allies
Mis. 288–28 temperance and truth are a·,
My. 129–22 and be thy dearest a·.
all-important
'01. 33– 1 a· consideration of their being,
Peo. 13– 8 This a· understanding is gained in
All-in-all
God is
(see **God**)

Mis. 25– 9 God is Truth, and A·.
45–25 imply Him to be, A·,
49–27 This belief . . . that God is not A·,
55–26 If God is Spirit, . . . and A·,
64– 1 Spirit might be found "A·."
115–20 since God, good, is A·.
183– 8 it will be found that Mind is A·,
200– 7 Spirit was to him A·,
366–12 because He is A·,

All-in-all
Ret.	34– 3	the *A·* of Spirit,
Un.	20–18	perception of God as *A·*.
	37–15	God is Life and *A·*.
	60–20	He will be unto them *A·*.
No.	18– 4	lie that denies Him as *A·*,
	36– 4	and therefore as the *A·* ;
My.	158–10	Love's divine adventure to be *A·*.

all-in-all
My.	5–15	are the *a·* of C. S.
	64–14	are the *a·* of C. S."

all-inclusive
Mis.	331–30	this adorable, *a·* God,
My.	46–26	* *a·* instructions and admonitions

all-in-one
My.	247– 1	*a·* and one-in-all.
	254–22	*a·* and one-in-all.

all-just
Mis.	124–13	unchangeable, all-wise, *a·*,

all-knowing
Mis.	71–15	omnipotence, the *a·* Mind.
	71–26	God, good, the *a·* Mind.
'01.	7– 8	*a·*, all-loving Father-Mother,

all-knowledge
Un.	27–15	His own all-presence, *a·*,

all-loving
'01.	7– 9	all-wise, all-knowing, *a·*

all-merciful
Mis.	124–14	all-wise, all-just, *a·* ;
Po.	28–14	*A·* and good, Hover the homeless

All-Mind
Un.	7–25	highest phenomena of the *A·*.

allness
Mis.	93– 8	declare the *a·* and oneness of God
	109– 2	the unity of Truth, and its *a·*
	188–24	up to its infinite meaning, its *a·*.
	206– 9	eternal existence, God's *a·*, and
	208– 6	by virtue of this nature and *a·*
	253–11	make amends . . . with the *a·* of Mind.
Man.	16– 7	even the *a·* of Soul, Spirit, and
Ret.	26–28	know yet more of . . . the *a·* of Spirit,
Un.	10– 1	you demonstrate the *a·* of God.
Rud.	10–27	understanding of the *a·* of God,
No.	30– 8	by virtue of the *a·* of God.
	35–12	*a·* of Love and the nothingness of
'01.	12–23	we then see the *a·* of Spirit,
'02.	16–15	the divine presence and *a·*.
My.	280–21	Out of His *a·* He must bless all
	349–15	he is conscious of the *a·* of God
	364–15	supremacy and *a·* of good.

allopath
My.	108– 3	the *a·* who depends upon drugs.

allopathic
Ret.	43–13	from Dr. W. W. Keen's (*a·*)
'01.	17–28	where the *a·* doses would not.

allopathy
Mis.	6–15	will rank far in advance of *a·*
	252– 4	medical systems of *a·* and
Ret.	33– 8	*a·*, homœopathy, hydropathy,
Pul.	47–12	* schools of *a·*, homœopathy, and
	64–17	* She investigated *a·*,
Hea.	11–16	recover from the heel of *a·*

allotted
Mis.	95–11	time so kindly *a·* me
My.	273– 6	* beyond the *a·* years of man,

allow
Mis.	108– 4	To *a·* sin of any sort is
	118– 9	then a one numeral to make
	303–14	*a·* to each and every one the same
	315–25	nor *a·* their students to do thus,
Man.	91– 2	shall not *a·* it or a copy of it
Ret.	82– 5	my students should not *a·* their
No.	7– 5	No personal considerations should *a·*
Pan.	11–12	When will the schools *a·* mortals
'01.	17–19	when the public sentiment would *a·*
	26–26	*a·* me to add I have read little of
'02.	12–21	*a·* me to interpolate some matters of
Po.	vii– 8	* *to a· a popular edition to be*
My.	7– 4	*a·* me to interpolate some matters of
	39–19	* You will *a·* me, however,
	41–12	* will *a·* no one to escape that
	53– 5	* would she *a·* printer and binder
	156– 3	*a·* me to reply in words of the
	163–11	must not *a·* myself the pleasure
	167–23	*A·* me to send forth a pæan of
	173– 5	*A·* me through your paper
	175–11	*A·* me to say to the good folk of
	213–18	*a·* himself to drift in the wrong
	256– 2	*a·* me to improvise some new notes,

allow
My.	274–21	*a·* me to say that I am not fond of
	315–25	*a·* me to thank the enterprising
	324–18	* too honorable to *a·* the thought

allowable
Mis.	297–10	Smart journalism is *a·*, . . . but

allowed
Mis.	7– 1	These children must not be *a·* to
	95– 5	* *a·* ten minutes in which to reply
	247– 4	be *a·* due consideration,
	289–31	*a·* to rise to the spiritual altitude
	296– 2	*a·* myself to be elected an associate
	302–18	I *a·*, till this permission was
	315– 6	No copies from my books are *a·*
	353– 1	the consciousness be *a·* to rejoice
Man.	60–23	No large gathering . . . shall be *a·*
	71–19	specially *a·* and named in this Manual.
	81–24	no evil speaking shall be *a·*.
	93–19	The Board of Lectureship is not *a·*
Ret.	88–28	Itinerancy should not be *a·* to
Un.	54–14	for if sin's claim be *a·*
'01.	29–27	I *a·* them for several years
	33–15	to be *a·* the rights of conscience
My.	311– 5	She begged to be *a·* to remain
	338–16	not *a·* to consult me relative to

alloweth
Ret.	94–19	that thing which he *a·*.— *Rom.* 14 : 22.

allowing
My.	173–26	*a·* the visitors to assemble on the
	211– 7	*a·* it first to smoulder,
	359–29	*a·* your students to deify you

allows
Mis.	245–24	but, if the pulpit *a·* the people
Man.	68–18	calls to her home or *a·* to visit

all-pervading
Mis.	16–21	an *a·* intelligence and Love,
Un.	45–15	its *a·* presence in certain forms of

All-power
Mis.	200– 7	understood omnipotence to be *A·* :
'02.	9– 3	the *A·* — giving life, health,
Peo.	9–26	omnipotence is the *A·*.

all-power
Mis.	14– 4	the ever-presence and *a·* of good ;
	25–24	this medicine is *a·* ;
	101–21	Science saith to man, "God hath *a·*."
	141– 5	revealed to you God's *a·*,
	173–21	Mind, God, is *a·* and all-presence,
	197–30	God as omnipotent, having *a·* ;
	332–29	The supposition is, that . . . are not *a·* ;
Ret.	60–19	God is *a·* and all-presence,
Un.	27–15	all-presence, all-knowledge, *a·*.
Rud.	11–23	*a·* and ever-presence of good,
'02.	7–12	signifies *a·*, all-presence,
Peo.	13– 9	the one God and His *a·*
My.	152–11	conception of Spirit and its *a·*.
	226–22	even as you value His *a·*,
	274– 9	its *a·*, all-presence, all-Science.

All-presence
'02.	9– 2	Then God becomes to him the *A·*

all-presence
Mis.	141– 5	God's all-power, *a·*, and all-science.
	173–22	Mind, God, is all-power and *a·*,
Ret.	60–19	God is all-power, and *a·*,
Un.	27–15	*a·*, all-knowledge, all-power.
'02.	7–13	signifies all-power *a·*,
My.	226–22	His all-power, *a·*, all-Science,
	274– 9	its all-power, *a·*, all-Science.

all's
My.	40–27	* "*A·* love, but *a·* law."

All-science
'02.	9– 4	*A·* — all law and gospel.

all-Science and all-science
Mis.	25–25	omniscience means as well, *a·*.
	141– 6	all-power, all-presence, and *a·*.
'02.	7–13	all-power, all-presence, *a·*.
My.	226–22	His all-power, all-presence, *a·*,
	274– 9	its all-power, all-presence, *a·*.

allude
Mis.	280–27	*a·* briefly to a topic of great import
	379–15	*a·* to God as the divine Principle

alluded
Mis.	57– 9	its spiritual Science is *a·* to
	301–31	to whom Isaiah *a·* thus :
Pul.	86–28	* Bible and the book *a·* to
'01.	25–14	*a·* to or required in such
My.	11–14	* she quietly *a·* to the need of

alludes
Mis.	243–23	*a·* to Paul's advice to Timothy.
Hea.	3–17	Josephus *a·* to several individuals

alluding
 My. 103–15 *A·* to this divine method,

all-unbeguiled
 Mis. 386– 9 Truth's new birth *A·*
 Po. 49–14 Truth's new birth *A·*

allurements
 My. 211–14 silent *a·* to health and holiness,
 252–27 *a·* of wealth, pride, or power ;

allusion
 Mis. 88–14 His *a·* to C. S. in the
 193–17 thankful even for his *a·* to

all-wise
 Mis. 124–13 unchangeable, *a·*, all-just,
 206–18 by the active, *a·*, law-creating,
 '01. 7– 8 He is the *a·*, all-knowing,
 Po. 28– 7 To Thy *a·* behest

Alma Mater
 Mis. 359– 1 follow the example of the *A· M·*.
 Ret. 49– 6 follow the example of the *A· M·*

Almighty
 Un. 57– 8 shadow of the *A·*." — *Psal.* 91 : 1.
 My. 107–23 shadow of the *A·*." — *Psal.* 91 : 1.
 210–16 abides under the shadow of the *A·*.

almighty
 Mis. 227–32 is the command of *a·* wisdom ;
 Hea. 15–16 he calls God *a·* and admits

Almighty God
 My. 147–19 will, in the name of *A· G·*,
 200– 6 our trust is in the *A· G·*,

almond-blossom
 Mis. 231– 1 *a·* formed a crown of glory ;

almost
 Mis. 159–30 *a·* marvel at the power and
 375–21 * an *a·* identical resemblance,
 Ret. 7– 9 * by intense and *a·* incessant study
 Pul. 29–27 * *a·* the entire congregation was
 49–16 *a·* as big as they are now,
 63–13 *a·* as big as they are now,
 Rud. 6–16 * fact "*a·* universally accepted,
 No. 41–22 Church seems *a·* chagrined that
 '01. 28–11 into *a·* every Christian tongue,
 '02. 5– 9 this *a·* unconceived light of
 Hea. 20– 7 * In notes *a·* divine."
 My. 22–14 * Since 1866, *a·* forty years ago,
 22–14 * *a·* forty years in the wilderness,
 38–21 * in *a·* perfect time.
 43–13 * was *a·* as marvellous as
 89–18 * different from *a·* all other
 89–19 * *a·* as constant as petitions for
 97– 1 * *a·* every one is inclined to admit.
 106– 7 organic diseases of *a·* every kind.
 225–20 Mankind *a·* universally gives
 248– 3 its grandeur *a·* surprises me.
 306–13 *a·* unutterable truths to translate,
 318– 2 In *a·* every case where Mr. Wiggin
 347–14 would *a·* suggest that nature had

alms
 Mis. ix– 4 * best *a·* are to show and to enable
 ix– 5 * enable a man to dispense with *a·*."

aloft
 Ret. 53– 5 designed to bear *a·* the standard of

alone
 Mis. 2–18 will be found *a·* the remedy for sin,
 4–18 *a·* adequate to meet the requirement.
 4–29 It is not *a·* the mission of C. S.
 28–16 he demonstrated that divine Science *a·*
 32–15 love *a·* is admissible.
 48–17 through the action of mind *a·*.
 66– 9 for the offender *a·* suffers,
 97–15 C. S. is not a remedy of faith *a·*,
 101– 3 He *a·* knows these wonders who
 104–31 This *a·* gives me the forces of God
 118–18 willing to work *a·* with God
 126– 8 *a·* he has his own thoughts to guard,
 137–21 to work out individually and *a·*,
 138–11 student should seek *a·* the guidance of
 142–16 Why the letter *a·*?
 145– 4 shall exist *a·* in the affections,
 166– 1 *a·* demonstrates the divine Principle
 198–26 all of which is corrected *a·* by
 236–22 but be guided by God *a·* ;"
 243–19 their works *a·* should declare them,
 244– 5 Mind *a·* constructing the human system,
 245–28 can walk *a·* the straight and
 250– 2 the *a·* God, is Love.
 266–13 dashing through space, headlong and *a·*.
 268–27 Right *a·* is irresistible,
 275–10 bereft wife or husband, silent and *a·*,
 284–26 Evil let *a·* grows more real,
 290– 2 Let other people's marriage relations *a·* :
 293– 5 leave . . . *a·*, and to the special care of

alone
 Mis. 301–32 trodden the winepress *a·* ; — *Isa.* 63 : 3.
 303– 8 governed by divine Love *a·*
 312– 7 speechless and *a·*, bears all burdens,
 318– 5 not *a·* for my students,
 319–26 feel themselves *a·* among the stars.
 324– 8 he *a·* who looks from that dwelling,
 328– 2 "Let them *a·* ; they must learn
 328–21 He *a·* ascends the hill of C. S.
 339–24 thou *a·* canst and must atone.
 352–23 Through the divine energies *a·*
 353–27 set up housekeeping *a·*.
 358–10 God *a·* is his help,
 359– 7 instantaneously, and through Spirit *a·*.
 365– 1 This philosophy *a·* will bear the strain
 365–11 for it rests *a·* on demonstration.
 365–19 for what immortal Mind *a·* can supply.
 373–31 it presents not words *a·*, but works,
 380– 2 if a divine Principle *a·* heals,
 388–10 For Love *a·* is Life ;
 Man. 40– 8 divine Love *a·* governs man ;
 51–26 and they *a·* shall vote on cases
 61–23 Music from the organ *a·* should
 71–12 The Mother Church stands *a·* ;
 95–22 The duties of a Reader are ample.
 104– 7 It stands *a·*, uniquely adapted
 111– 4 Initials *a·* will not be received.
 Ret. 22–17 He *a·* is our origin, aim, and being.
 25–15 because Soul *a·* is truly substantial.
 28– 1 became evident that the divine Mind *a·*
 30– 1 As the pioneer of C. S. I stood *a·*
 Un. 18–19 which *a·* enable Me to rebuke,
 31–23 God, or good, is Spirit *a·* ;
 35–24 Spirit is *spiritual* consciousness *a·*.
 38– 3 To God *a·* belong the indisputable realities
 38–15 by declaring that not He *a·* is Life,
 55– 1 Jesus accepted the one fact whereby *a·* the
 58– 6 "the winepress *a·*." — *Isa.* 63 : 3.
 Pul. 32–16 experiences which *a·* are significant.
 44–12 * mother in Israel, *a·* of us all,
 52–18 * The name C. S. *a·* is new.
 Rud. 6–25 can *a·* answer this question
 10– 5 know that God *a·* governs man ;
 No. 5– 7 As Truth *a·* is real, then it follows
 9– 9 let your opponents *a·*,
 18– 7 it rests *a·* on the demonstration of
 18–25 asks for what Mind *a·* can supply.
 25–23 immortal man *a·* is God's likeness,
 '01. 9–20 "Let us *a·* ;— *Mark* 1 : 24.
 19–19 through spiritual ascendency *a·*.
 20– 8 The Christian Scientist is *a·* with his
 30–24 working *a·* with God,
 '02. 10– 8 and reiterate, Let me *a·*.
 Hea. 18–26 death has been produced by a belief *a·*.
 Peo. 10–15 Mental Science *a·* grasps the standard
 10–19 they *a·* have fettered free limbs,
 Po. 7–10 For Love *a·* is Life ;
 page 8 poem
 8– 1 sitting *a·* where the shadows fall
 8– 7 I'm waiting *a·* for the bridal hour
 8–11 watching *a·* o'er the starlit glow,
 8–16 I'm dreaming *a·* of its changeful sky
 8–20 I'm thinking *a·* of a fair young bride,
 9– 3 picturing *a·* a glad young face,
 9– 8 weeping *a·* that the vision is fled,
 19– 3 God's eye is upon me — I am not *a·*
 66–12 'Tis breaking *a·*, but a young heart
 My. 3– 6 this not *a·* in accord with
 89–24 * not . . . of interest to that city *a·*,
 89–25 * not to the nation *a·*,
 89–25 * not to this time *a·*,
 92– 7 * brushed aside by ridicule *a·*.
 109–26 not *a·* by miracle and parable,
 116–24 let them *a·* in, God's glory,
 148–19 I, as usual at home and *a·*,
 148–24 Christianity is not *a·* a gift,
 180–13 It appeals *a·* to God,
 189–32 Am I not *a·* in soul?
 211– 9 All that error asks is to be let *a·* ;
 211–11 "Let us *a·* ; — *Mark* 1 : 24.
 247–22 it is Love *a·* that feeds them.
 249–20 I *a·* know what that means.
 263– 2 leaving one *a·* and without
 273–30 death *a·* does not awaken man
 273–31 *a·* gives the true sense of life
 274– 5 Death *a·* does not absolve man from
 277–20 words and deeds of men *a·*
 302–28 went *a·* . . . to the church,
 306–18 Divinity *a·* solves the problem
 309–26 * states : "*A·* of the Bakers, he
 332– 4 * silent gush of grateful tears *a·* can
 338–24 he stands *a·* in word and deed,
 342–22 in it *a·* is the simplicity of the

along
 Mis. 169– 2 all *a·* the way of her researches

along

Mis.	214–26	cannot . . . take error *a·* with Truth,
	250–26	little feet tripping *a·* the
	265–19	extends *a·* the whole line of
	274–29	rolls *a·* the streets besmeared with
	291–28	sentinels *a·* the lines of thought,
	295– 6	* "*a·* a gamut of isms and ists,
	339–26	sent *a·* the ocean of events
Ret.	15– 3	and my protest *a·* with me.
Pul.	66–18	* the mystical which, *a·* many lines,
No.	2–20	*a·* the shores of erudition ;
'01.	25–22	*a·* with this the
Hea.	19–24	*a·* the rugged way,
My.	308–17	* *a·* the highway,
	339–12	*A·* the lines of progressive

alongside

Pul.	51–28	* *a·* other great demonstrations

aloud

Mis.	266–29	Because Truth has spoken *a·*,
	388– 5	Love whose finger traced *a·*
Ret.	83–24	occasionally reading *a·* from the book
'02.	20–14	Love whose finger traced *a·*
Po.	7– 5	Love whose finger traced *a·*
	71–22	"Cry *a·*!" — *Isa.* 58 : 1.
My.	61–17	* I said *a·*, "Why, there is no fear ;

Alpha

Mis.	333–10	"*A·* and Omega" of C. S. — *Rev.* 1 : 8.
Un.	10–19	whereof God is the *A·* and Omega,
'02.	2–22	wherein Christ is *A·* and Omega.
My.	267– 9	not the *A·* and Omega of man
	267–12	no end, no *A·* and no Omega.

alphabet

Mis.	67– 2	beyond the mere *a·* of Mind-healing.
Ret.	11– 4	poem
Po.	vi–28	* poem
	page 60	poem

Alphabet and Bayonet

Po.	vi–28	* poem
	(see also **Appendix A**)	

Alpine

My.	257–29	monarch's palace, the *A·* hamlet,

Alps

Po.	65–20	O'er ocean or *A·*, the stranger

already

Mis.	7–25	A great work *a·* has been done,
	65–19	must be, and *a·* is, apprehended
	70–19	and had *a·* begun to die,
	98–13	interest *a·* felt in a higher mode
	101– 9	We *a·* have had two in this nation ;
	110–23	*a·* obvious that the world's acceptance
	113–21	*A·* I clearly recognize that mental
	131–30	these will be found *a·* itemized,
	132– 2	had *a·* accepted as a By-law.
	136– 8	*a·* brought to your earnest consideration,
	150– 3	*a·* you have the great Shepherd
	150–15	We have *a·* seen the salvation
	154–12	have *a·* proof of the prosperity of
	154–18	the reign of harmony *a·* within us.
	183–18	ability, that reflection *a·* has
	238–20	and it *a·* hath a benediction :
	261– 1	evil, as *mind*, is doomed, *a·*
	261–26	*a·* saved with an everlasting salvation.
	286– 1	above prophecy, . . . has *a·* been fulfilled.
	307–12	the rapid sale *a·* of two editions
	317–25	having *a·* seen in many instances
	335–27	I would have you *a·* out,
	362–16	evil mind *a·* doomed,
	379–20	I had *a·* experimented in medicine
Man.	65– 2	*a·* used in our periodicals.
Ret.	35–19	it *a·* was and is demonstrated
	38– 3	I had *a·* paid him
	38– 9	what I had *a·* observed
	40–12	*a·* prepared for her burial ;
	83– 2	*a·* been proven that this volume
	83– 9	are *a·* laid in their minds
	87–28	It is *a·* understood that
Un.	5– 4	*a·* gained of the wholeness of Deity,
	7– 2	as *a·* He is glorified
	12– 1	fields are *a·* white for the harvest ;
	48– 3	*a·* told a hundred times,
	52– 7	reign of harmony, *a·* with us.
Pul.	30– 5	* unite with churches *a·* established
	52– 3	* no sums except those *a·* subscribed
	79–10	* *a·* gained to itself adherents
	86–29	* *a·* ordained as our pastor.
	87–18	I *a·* speak to you each Sunday.
No.	39–23	what we *a·* have and are ;
Pan.	15– 1	*a·* murdering her peaceful seamen
'00.	1–16	C. S. *a·* has a hearing
	2– 1	are *a·* interested in C. S. ;
Peo.	3–14	*a·* spans the moral heavens
	8–25	*a·* charred, are fast fading into
My.	15–14	*A·* I have said to you

already

My.	22– 9	* Scientists have contributed *a·*
	42– 9	* You are no doubt a *a·* acquainted
	48–32	* *a·* manifest in their faces,
	57–30	* no sums except those *a·* subscribed
	74– 2	* are *a·* in Boston.
	75–12	* not *a·* been provided for.
	91– 3	* most of whom were *a·*
	106–17	It is *a·* proved that C. S.
	124–13	the "well done" *a·* yours, — *Matt.* 25 : 21.
	133–12	in sundries *a·* given out.
	135– 8	Perhaps you *a·* know that I have
	138– 5	a great benefit to me *a·*.
	139–23	*A·* you have advanced from
	147–23	*a·* dedicated to Christ's service,
	170–15	only that this gift is *a·* yours.
	177–11	(*a·* imputed to me),
	210– 5	added to the mind *a·* full.
	252–21	and are *a·* rich rays from
	253–25	you have His rich blessing *a·*
	282–14	we must practise what we *a·* know
	298– 5	*a·* reported of the good
	307–31	had *a·* dawned on me.
	339–13	*A·* Massachusetts has exchanged
	347– 1	*a·* been revealed in a degree

also

Mis.	11– 7	I thought, *a·*, that if I taught
	13–12	for sinners *a·* love — *Luke* 6 : 32.
	21–10	shall ye do *a·* ; " — *see John* 14 : 12.
	26–29	Saxon term for God is *a·* good.
	27– 9	Here *a·* is found the pith of
	28–15	*A·*, he demonstrated that
	29– 8	"for them *a·* which shall — *John* 17 : 20.
	36–22	*a·*, all beliefs relative to the
	50–22	*a·*, that there must be a change from
	63– 8	*a·*, that this divine trinity is
	66– 7	that shall he *a·* reap." — *Gal.* 6 : 7.
	68– 5	include *a·* man's changed appearance
	68– 9	* *He a· maintained that pain and*
	73–25	*ye a· shall sit upon* — *Matt.* 19 : 28.
	76–28	then shall ye *a·* appear — *Col.* 3 : 4.
	79–18	cause is perfect, its effect is perfect *a·* ;
	83–25	*a·* may glorify Thee." — *John* 17 : 1.
	87–17	*a·*, *that no one there was working*
	91–30	*a·* to require their pupils to study the
	105–30	that shall he *a·* reap." — *Gal.* 6 : 7.
	110– 7	You need *a·* to watch, and pray
	121–27	if I *a·* ask you, — *Luke* 22 : 68.
	124– 4	It is *a·* plain, that we should not
	125– 4	Then shall he *a·* reign with him :
	126–10	We *a·* have gained higher heights ;
	132–15	* and, by the way, from Mrs. Eddy, *a·*."
	136–23	*a·*, that hereafter you hold
	145–22	"The wolf *a·* shall dwell — *Isa.* 11 : 6.
	152– 5	includes *a·* His presence
	157– 4	shall *a·* reign with him." — *II Tim.* 2 : 12.
	157–22	trust *a·* in Him ; — *Psal.* 37 : 5.
	161–21	*A·*, it is natural to conclude
	170–12	So, *a·*, she spoke of the hades,
	170–18	we *a·* may all partake of.
	186–23	*a·*, that the Principle of man cannot
	191–26	*A·*, the original texts define him as
	192–10	*shall he do a·* ; — *John* 14 : 12.
	192–24	*A·*, the last chapter of Mark
	193–18	and *a·* of what had been said when
	195–19	shall he do *a·*." — *John* 14 : 12.
	196–15	*a·*, the character of the votaries
	197–21	*a·* in Christ Jesus." — *Phil.* 2 : 5.
	198–18	disease *a·* is treated and healed.
	201–12	he *a·* showed forth the error
	209–11	*a·* demonstrates this Principle
	219–14	think *a·* after a sickly fashion.
	221–24	*a·* contradicts the doctrine that we
	228–15	This will bring us *a·* to look on a
	234–14	*a·* his effort to steal from others
	242–26	*A·*, Mr. C. M. H——, of Boston,
	256–12	*a·*, that this must prevent
	260–16	*a·*, that pure Mind is the truth
	264–26	status of thought must be right *a·*.
	265– 7	*a·* predisposes his students to make
	269– 1	trust *a·* in Him ; — *Psal.* 37 : 5.
	281– 6	I find *a·* another mental condition
	284–21	It must *a·* be remembered that
	298– 7	causing others to go astray, we *a·*
	305–26	* She is *a·* asked to collect two dollars
	306– 7	* *a·* welcome suggestions of events
	311– 6	*A·*, I would extend a tender invitation
	314–10	*A·*, this First Reader shall
	314–18	*a·*, shall read all the selections from
	314–27	This form shall *a·* be observed at
	335–28	*a·*, to remember the Scripture
	347– 2	lest thou *a·* be like — *Prov.* 26 : 4.
	370– 7	spirit of Christ is *a·* abroad,
	382–26	*a·* the constitution and by-laws
Man.	16–10	which was *a·* in Christ Jesus ;

also

Man.	26– 1	a· for the editors and the manager
	27–18	It shall a· be the duty of the
	43–26	A· the spirit in which the writer
	46–15	a· such information as may come to
	46–24	A· he shall reasonably reduce his
	59–10	Members shall a· instruct their pupils
	64– 8	a· the literature published or sold by
	64–25	See a· Article XXV, Sect. 7.
	66–20	a· to have any authority supposed to
	73–13	A· members in good standing with
	78–11	A· important movements of the manager
	98–16	It shall a· be the duty of the
	102–17	A· there shall be incorporated in
Ret.	2–17	My childhood was a· gladdened by
	15– 2	the good clergyman's heart a· melted,
	27– 1	I wrote a·, at this period,
	38–28	must a· gain its spiritual significance,
	42– 9	a· taught a special Bible-class ;
	43–12	and who a· received a certificate from
	45–21	turn to him the other a·." — Matt. 5 : 39.
	45–23	I a· saw that Christianity has
	76–17	was a· in Christ Jesus," — Phil. 2 : 5.
	80– 3	This a· is proverbial,
	83–10	A·, they are prepared to receive
	83–25	It is a· highly important that
	85– 9	Of this a· rest assured,
Un.	2– 2	they a· declare that God pitieth
	4–19	was a· in Christ Jesus," — Phil. 2 : 5.
	7– 8	to make a· the following statement :
	14– 7	"the stars a·," — Gen. 1 : 16.
	26–18	how can it be a· true that
	37– 2	but a· "the life." — John 14 : 6.
	38–16	but that something else a· is life,
	43–25	in the third chapter of Philippians, we are a·
	53–15	it is a· self-destructive.
	56–14	He a· suffereth in the flesh,
Pul.	vii– 9	but a· a registry of the rise of
	3– 6	He a· said : "The kingdom of — Luke 17 : 21.
	4–20	Who lives in good, lives a· in God,
	5–23	a· the same in Great Britain,
	6–29	A· that renowned apostle of anti-slavery,
	7– 9	remember a· that God is just,
	9–10	warmed a· our perishless hope,
	14–28	should a· know the great delusion of
	47–16	* And she a· defines carefully the
	67–19	* In Canada, a·, there is a large number of
	73–17	* is a· a very prominent member
Rud.	8–19	is a· uttering falsehood about good.
	12–24	The practitioner should a· endeavor
No.	5–15	a· avers that Spirit, or Truth,
	6–21	a· that the error of the revolution of
	24– 5	A·, according to Spinoza, man is
	31–26	said a· : "If a man keep — John 8 : 51.
	32– 9	that shall he a· reap." — Gal. 6 : 7.
	35–10	conquered a· the drear subtlety of
	35–13	He lived that we a· might live.
	37–20	What God knows, He a· predestinates ;
	40– 5	they expect a· what is impossible,
Pan.	4– 9	a·, that the functions of
	4–16	but that man a· is a creator,
	6–22	if . . . evil a· is mind,
	12– 2	Then a· will it be learned that
'00.	3–23	a· that women's names contained this
	8– 5	the evil man a· exhales consciously
	9–27	A· that I strove earnestly to
	12–26	and a· in private houses.
	13– 5	which I a· hate." — Rev. 2 : 6.
'01.	3–13	A·, we accept God, emphatically,
	9–11	a· the mysticism complained of
	11–27	lest thou a· be like — Prov. 26 : 4.
	27– 3	My critic a· writes :
	27–18	a· sinners reformed and
Hea.	5–28	that shall he a· reap." — Gal. 6 : 7.
My.	6– 6	that shall he a· reap." — Gal. 6 : 7.
	11–20	* we have a· made good the pledge.
	16–28	"Judgment a· will I lay — Isa. 28 : 17.
	17– 3	* A·, 1 Peter 2 : 1–6,
	17–11	"Ye a·, as lively stones, — I Pet. 2 : 5.
	17–14	"Wherefore a· it is — I Pet. 2 : 6.
	20– 1	this a· that she hath done — Mark 14 : 9.
	21– 9	* a· advance the erection of many
	23–24	* not only to faith but a· to sight ;
	24– 7	* and a· to symbolize your
	37–21	* we a· recognize that He has
	40– 6	* will a· enlarge their hospitality,
	49–14	* a· the tenets and church covenant.
	52–16	* a· realize we must use more energy
	62–29	* a· the services of other members
	66– 2	* a· in the shape of a triangle,
	69–11	* a· placed on the two sides of
	71– 4	* There is a· a solo organ
	72–21	* a· through the C. S. Sentinel
	73–23	* There is here a· a post-office
	94–14	* a· much to convince the skeptic.
	131– 1	that which purifies . . . a· strengthens

also

My.	132–10	he a· knows they embark for
	132–24	Divine Love will a· rebuke and
	135–29	a· you spiritually and scientifically
	136–21	a· in Canada, Australia, etc.
	144– 1	* Mrs. Eddy a· sent the following
	152–24	It will a· be seen that this God
	153– 1	A· I hear that the loving hearts
	162–18	the love that rebukes praises a·,
	163–24	a· received from the leading people of
	164–17	that faith a· possesses them.
	170–22	Delight thyself a· in — Psal. 37 : 4.
	170–23	trust a· in Him ; — Psal. 37 : 5.
	173–28	a· to Mr. George D. Waldron,
	174– 2	a· for throwing open their doors for
	190–28	them a· which shall believe — John 17 : 20.
	196–13	able a· to bridle the — Jas. 3 : 2.
	196–16	"Christ a· suffered for us, — I Pet. 2 : 21.
	220–18	I a· have faith that my prayer
	221–23	shall he do a·." — John 14 : 12.
	222–12	A· he added : "This kind — Matt. 17 : 21.
	223– 4	A· that I neither listen to
	224–14	A· be sure that you are not
	224–27	a· speak in loving terms of their
	224–31	* "They a· serve who only stand and
	227–28	turn to him the other a·." — Matt. 5 : 39.
	231– 7	a· from the undeserving poor
	233–16	"They have healed a· — Jer. 6 : 14.
	256– 9	A· I beg to send to you all
	273–25	a· that the five personal senses
	276–18	* she has a· believed that in such
	280– 7	* We rejoice a· in this new reminder
	295–13	is a· the gift of gifts ;
	299–12	as a· whatever portions of truth
	308–29	McClure's Magazine a· declares
	312–11	* a· paid Mrs. Glover's fare
	314–25	I was a· the means of
	319–14	* and a· indicate what he
	319–28	* I a· recall very plainly the
	320– 5	* He a· seemed very much pleased
	320– 8	* He a· expressed himself freely
	321– 3	* a· your position as regards
	321–30	* I am a· pleased to have had
	322–12	* a· Mr. Edward P. Bates' letter
	328–12	* apt a· to be pleased with the fact
	336–11	* In this book (p. 20) she a· states,

altar

Mis.	87–31	imagine they can . . . steady God's a·
	149–24	whose a· is a loving heart,
	162–16	lay himself as a lamb upon the a·
	312– 6	which lays all upon the a·,
	343– 4	have laid upon the a·
	394– 6	at the a· or bower,
Ret.	86–16	when we offer our gift upon the a·.
Pul.	9– 7	May the a· you have built
'00.	15–19	and you kneel at its a·.
'01.	35– 6	and lay ourselves upon the a·
Hea.	2–27	and sprinkled the a· of Love
Po.	26–10	on her a· our loved Lincoln's own
	32–18	To kneel at the a· of mercy and pray
	39– 8	from its a· to Thy throne
	45– 8	at the a· or bower,
My.	36–21	* At this a·, dedicated to the only
	302–30	upon the steps of its a·.

altars

Mis.	120– 2	take off their shoes at our a· ;
	287–32	attempts to steady other people's a·,
	326–14	wrapping their a· in ruins.
	360–20	who partaketh of its own a·,
Hea.	11–13	burn upon the a· of to-day ;
My.	125– 1	kindle a· for human sacrifice.
	126–30	at our fire-sides, on our a·,
	184–21	lay upon its a· a sacrifice

alter

My.	41– 5	* nor in any wise a· its effects.

alteration

Rud.	7–25	bring about a· of species

alterative

Mis.	241– 9	the great a·, Truth :
	241–19	administer this a· Truth :
Pan.	12–19	without the a· agonies whereby

alternately

Mis.	314–16	a· in response to the congregation,
Man.	99– 1	a· appoint a Committee on
	99– 9	shall annually and a· appoint a
Pul.	28–20	* The reading is from the two a· ;
'02.	4–25	A· transported and alarmed by

alternative

Mis.	31–17	leaves the individual no a·

although

Mis.	xi– 5	a· a reproduction of what
	7–10	a· skepticism and incredulity
	45– 7	a· its power to allay fear,

although

Mis.	89–13	*a·* the medical attendant and friends
	243– 6	*a·* students treat sprains,
	260–24	evil is naught, *a·* it seems
	273– 3	*a·* it will cost him much,
	286–18	*a·* it is to-day problematic.
	371–16	*a·* he who has self-interest
	374– 3	*A·* clad in panoply of power,
	380–18	*A· I* could heal mentally,
Man.	18– 7	*A·* walking through deep waters,
	55–14	*A·* repentant and forgiven by the
Ret.	38–12	*a·* I had not thought of such a result,
	68– 1	*a·* as a serpent it claimed to
Pul.	37– 7	* and *a·* her hair is white,
'01.	6–15	must be One *a·* He is three.
	24–19	*a·* its earthly advent is called
Hea.	5–15	*a·* we have no evidence of the fact
	11–17	*a·* homœopathy has laid the
Po.	vi–13	*a· Boston has since been the pioneer*
My.	11– 3	* *a·* we may falter or stumble
	55– 7	* *a·* given up for a time,
	82–27	* *A·* the Scientists came to Boston
	89–13	* *a·* it cost two million dollars,
	94–24	* *A·* Mrs. Eddy, the Founder of C. S.,
	146–11	*a·* it has not been demonstrated
	281–29	*a·* its purpose is good will towards
	308–26	*A· McClure's Magazine* attributes
	314–13	*A·,* as *McClure's Magazine* claims,
	320–17	* *a·* he did not endorse all the
	336– 6	* *A·* he desired to go to her

altitude

Mis.	16–28	this new-born spiritual *a· ;*
	67– 1	until its *a·* reaches beyond the
	255–11	that *a·* of Mind which was in
	289–31	*a·* whence they can choose only good.
Ret.	76–12	to the *a·* which perceived a light
Pan.	6–26	the *a·* of mind gives it power,
	12–12	The *a·* of Christianity openeth,
My.	68–11	* reaches an *a·* twenty-nine feet
	110–24	mount higher in the *a·* of being.
	146–14	*a·* of its highest propositions
	272–10	is not the *a·* of the infinite.

altogether

Mis.	167– 6	the one *a·* lovely.
	342–12	"*a·* lovely," — *Song* 5 : 16.
Ret.	23–19	"*a·* lovely," — *Song* 5 : 16.
Pul.	66–17	* *A·* the belief and service are
'01.	6–30	"*a·* lovely," — *Song* 5 : 16.
Hea.	13–19	resigned the imaginary medicine *a·,*
Peo.	6–17	because He is found *a·* lovely.
My.	29–23	* assuming an *a·* different status
	154–25	*A·* it makes the church militant,

Alumni

Mis.	110–13	chapter sub-title

alway

Mis.	39–15	"Lo, I am with you *a·*" — *Matt.* 28 : 20.
	389–21	"Lo, I am with you *a·*," — *Matt.* 28 : 20.
Ret.	89–21	"Lo, I am with you *a·*!" — *Matt.* 28 : 20.
Pul.	10–30	God within you, — with you *a·,*
No.	46– 1	"Lo, I am with you *a·*," — *Matt.* 28 : 20.
'01.	35–10	Love is the way *a·.*
Po.	4–20	"Lo, I am with you *a·*," — *Matt.* 28 : 20.
	29–22	be thou our saint, Our stay, *a·.*
	65–16	moments most sweet are fleetest *a·,*
My.	44–12	* "Lo, I am with you *a·*," — *Matt.* 28 : 20.
	58–24	* "Lo, I am with you *a·*." — *Matt.* 28 : 20.
	159– 5	"Lo, I am with you *a·*, — *Matt.* 28 : 20.
	190–32	"Lo, I am with you *a·*" — *Matt.* 28 : 20.

always

Mis.	5–26	*a·* perfect in God,
	19– 3	lust, hatred, malice, are *a·* wrong,
	32–29	*a·* should try to bless their
	41–29	may not *a·* prove equal to
	57–30	*a·* was and forever is ;
	64–16	and are *a·* materialistic.
	66–10	*a·* according to divine decree.
	73–12	it is *a·* mental and moral,
	78–30	hypotheses are *a·* human vagaries,
	88–20	* have *a·* insisted that this Science
	90–11	It is *a·* right to act rightly ;
	95–17	have *a·* attended my life phenomena
	114–17	They must *a·* have on armor,
	117– 9	We *a·* know where to look
	117–10	and *a·* find him there.
	119–12	will *a·* be found arguing for itself,
	126–26	honesty *a·* defeats dishonesty.
	129–18	will *a·* find somebody in his way,
	138– 9	is not *a·* to cooperate,
	143–28	*a·* accompanied with a touching letter
	180–15	Truth is *a·* here,
	203– 8	it will *a·* mirror their love,
	236–18	*a·* with the purpose to restore
	237–24	is delayed, and *a·* has been ;
	260–26	Words are not *a·* the auxiliaries of

always

Mis.	261–23	spirit of sacrifice *a·* has saved,
	262–11	its language is *a·* acceptable
	263–12	*A·* bear in mind that His
	276–15	will *a·* be the bridal hour,
	278–16	is *a·* a blessing to the human race.
	281–22	*a·* as debtors to Christ, Truth.
	304–28	* It will *a·* ring at nine o'clock
	330–11	in the Lord *a·*." — *see Phil.* 4 : 4.
	343–20	are not *a·* destroyed by the
	345–19	* *a·* assured and reassured me
	347– 9	cannot *a·* discern the mental signs
	347–22	it is *a·* straight and narrow ;
	353– 8	human concept is *a·* imperfect ;
	371–22	error *a·* strives to unite,
	374– 6	*a·* the opposite of what it was.
Ret.	8– 8	Her answer was *a·*, "Nothing,
	8–23	She answered as *a·* before.
	44–22	danger to its members which must *a·*
	49–12	spiritual formation first, last, and *a·,*
	82– 9	have *a·* been attained by
	85–18	*a·* wait for God's finger to point the
	91–19	*a·* leading them into the divine
Un.	18–15	Is not our comforter *a·*
	59–18	the divine idea is *a·* present.
Pul.	26–28	* *a·* burning day and night.
	33–23	* and Mr. Parker *a·* believed,
	36–18	* and *a·* with this experience repeated.
No.	8–10	rebuke each other *a·* in love,
'00.	8–17	apathy is *a·* egotism and animality.
'01.	1–20	must *a·* characterize heroic hearts ;
	27–30	* they say they had *a·* believed it."
	31– 1	*a·* stung by a clear elucidation of
'02.	1–17	has *a·* met with opposition and
	2–29	I have *a·* taught the student
My.	vi–14	* *a·* has been and is now its guide,
	3–18	*a·* unfolding the highway of hope,
	21–21	* *a·* experienced much pleasure in
	28– 4	"Divine Love *a·* has met and *a·* will
	52–26	* has *a·* filled her coffers anew.
	73–9, 10	"Divine Love *a·* has met and *a·* will
	112– 2	Science has *a·* been first met with
	121–13	reliable, helpful, and *a·* at hand.
	121–18	*a·* a diamond of the first water ;
	125–17	which *a·* thrills the soul.
	148–24	Bear in mind *a·* that Christianity
	155– 5	*a·* abounding in love
	155–26	*a·* be gathering Easter lilies
	156– 7	*a·* having all sufficiency
	163– 8	I *a·* try to be just,
	214– 5	Divine Love *a·* has met and *a·* will
	228– 6	*a·* saying the unexpected to them.
	240–13	*a·* unfolding the highway of hope,
	248– 4	Let your watchword *a·* be :
	252– 4	*a·* distributing sweet things
	276–17	* has *a·* believed that those who
	283–18	It is *a·* safe to be just.
	290–25	Thou hearest me *a·*," — *John* 11 : 42.
	304–28	* say they have *a·* believed it."
	305– 6	"I have *a·* known it."
	313–18	*a·* accompanied by some responsible
	313–20	I have *a·* consistently declared
	320–14	* He *a·* spoke of you as the author
	320–22	* he *a·* referred to you as the author
	321– 3	*a·* referred to you as the one who
	321– 9	* and he *a·* gave you that position
	324–21	* we *a·* thought that Mr. Wiggin
	342–14	* and which are *a·* bright.
	345–32	* *a·* from the standpoint of C. S.,

amalgamation

Mis.	22–13	It absolutely refutes the *a·,*
'00.	13–25	* *a·* of different pagan religions
'01.	23–18	all error, *a·,* and compounds.

amaranth

Peo.	14– 4	*a·* blossoms, evergreen leaves,

amateur

My.	313–23	* never was "an *a·* clairvoyant,"

amazed

Mis.	325–20	*a·* beyond measure that anybody

amazement

Mis.	325–19	porter starts up in blank *a·*
	375–20	* to my *a·* and delight I find

Amazons

Pul.	83–16	* In olden times it was the *A·* who

ambassador

Mis.	141–25	As the *a·* of Christ's teachings,
Ret.	3– 3	held the position of *a·* to Persia.

ambiguous

My.	111–29	pronounce it absurd, *a·,*
	113– 6	Can such a book be *a·,*
	317–14	points that might seem *a·* to

ambition

Mis.	110– 9	What grander *a·* is there than to

ambition

Mis.	154–29	Have no *a·*, . . . apart from
	204–29	governs the aims, *a·*, and
	228–14	mad *a·* and low revenge.
	254–13	The victim of mad *a·*
	263–27	mad *a·* drives them to
	281– 1	and with laudable *a·* are about to
	281– 9	and I have now one *a·*
	281–10	But if one cherishes *a·* unwisely,
	296–21	or foster a feminine *a·*
	351–16	repeated attempts of mad *a·*
Ret.	79–13	Dishonesty, envy, and mad *a·*
Pul.	10–13	No dream of avarice or *a·*
'00.	15– 7	start forward with true *a·*.
'02.	3–28	the only true *a·* is to serve God
Po.	16– 7	*A·*, come hither!
	33– 9	*a·* that binds us to earth ;
My.	129– 9	counteract the trend of mad *a·*.
	202– 3	from human *a·*, fear, or distrust
	250– 5	promotes wisdom, quiets mad *a·*,
	262–23	mad *a·*, rivalry, and ritual of our

ambitions

Mis.	224–13	human wills, opinions, *a·*,
	291– 8	unworthy aims and *a·*.

ambitious

Po.	2– 7	who can fathom thee! *A·* man,

ambler

Mis.	183–11	silly *a·* to the so-called pleasures

Ambrose

Abigail Barnard

Ret.	4–23	Abigail Barnard *A·*, daughter of

Deacon

Pul.	32–25	* Deacon *A·*, her maternal grandfather,

Deacon Nathaniel

Ret.	4–24	Deacon Nathaniel *A·* of Pembroke,

Grandfather

Ret.	5– 3	Grandfather *A·* was a very religious

ambush

Mis.	126–25	strong race to run, and foes in *a·* ;
Pul.	15–11	telling mankind of the foe in *a·*?

amelioration

No.	8–22	pray for the *a·* of sin,

ameliorative

Mis.	235– 9	This Science is *a·* and regenerative,
My.	287–19	Philanthropy is loving, *a·*,

Amen

My.	19–11	be with you all. *A·*." — *II Cor.* 13 : 14.
	297– 6	I will say, *A·*, so be it.

amenable

Mis.	199– 7	*a·* only to moral and spiritual law,
Man.	67–23	break a rule . . . and are *a·* therefor.

amended

Man.	105– 3	nor any Tenet or By-Law *a·*
My.	15– 4	* has been *a·* to read as follows :

amende honorable

My.	236– 8	permit me to make the *a· h·*

amendment

Mis.	318–12	is an *a·* of the paragraph
Man.	105– 1	*A·* of By-Laws.
My.	15– 2	chapter sub-title
	327–17	* An *a·* was obtained by
	327–19	* After the *a·* had been passed,

amendments

My.	230–19	your approval of the *a·*

amends

Mis.	253–10	*a·* for the nothingness of matter

amenities

Man.	40– 9	reflects the sweet *a·* of Love,
No.	45–20	woman's hour, with all its sweet *a·*

America   (*see also* **America's**)

Mis.	170–21	history of Europe and *A·* ;
	295– 6	same power which in *A·* leads women
Ret.	2– 8	came to *A·* seeking "freedom to
Pul.	5–23	colleges, and universities of *A·* ;
	70–11	* most remarkable women in *A·*.
No.	23–14	eminent divines, in Europe and *A·*,
Po.	11– 1	Brave Britain, blest *A·*!
My.	79–11	* seat of learning of *A·* ;
	89– 2	* one of the largest . . . in *A·*,
	181–22	C. S. was discovered in *A·*.
	338– 1	Brave Britain, blest *A·*!

American

Mis.	295– 1	certain references to *A·* women
	295–14	has our *A·* correspondent lost
	296– 6	Was it ignorance of *A·* society
	296– 8	work and career of *A·* women,
	297–11	reports of *A·* affairs from
Ret.	2–24	for they were *A·* newspapers,
Pul.	67– 6	* said by a great *A·* writer.
Rud.	6–13	the young *A·* astronomer

American

My.	85–31	* sky-lines in an *A·* city,

American, The

Pul.	68–12	* *The A·*, Baltimore, Md.,

American Art Journal

Pul.	57–18	* *A· A· J·*, New York,

Americans

My.	271–24	* read with deep interest by all *A·*,

American Secretary

My.	282–18	Mr. Hayne Davis, *A· S·*,

America's

Pul.	8– 1	the press of *A·* Athens,

Amesbury

Pul.	54–29	at his home in *A·*,

amiable

My.	333–27	* He has left an *a·* wife,

amicable

My.	279–24	for the *a·* settlement of the war

amicably

Mis.	156–25	listening to each other *a·*,
My.	277–21	can settle all questions *a·*
	360–13	settle this church difficulty *a·*

amid   (*see also* **'mid**)

Mis.	ix–16	*a·* the uniform darkness of storm
	228– 7	is to be calm *a·* excitement,
	228– 7	just *a·* lawlessness,
	228– 7	pure *a·* corruption.
	277–28	one can be just *a·* lawlessness,
Hea.	2– 9	never seen *a·* the smoke of battle.
Po.	30–21	*a·* the hymning spheres of light,
My.	150–15	sleeping *a·* willowy banks
	182–27	*a·* the fair foliage of this vine
	230– 3	*a·* ministries aggressive and active,

amidst

No.	33–22	*a·* physical suffering and
Peo.	3– 6	eternal roasting *a·* noxious vapors ;
My.	262– 8	born in a manger *a·* the flocks and
	325– 2	* when *a·* all your duties you

Amiens

Pul.	65–18	* the story of the cathedral of *A·*,

amiss

Mis.	51–31	because ye ask *a·*, — *Jas.* 4 : 3.
No.	20–19	Hence this asking *a·*
	40– 2	because ye ask *a·*, — *Jas.* 4 : 3.
Hea.	15–24	because ye ask *a·* ;" — *Jas.* 4 : 3.
	15–24	is it not asking *a·* to pray for
Peo.	9–17	because we "ask *a·* ;" — *Jas.* 4 : 3.

among

Mis.	ix– 6	*a·* my thousands of students
	117–12	* enduring vivacity *a·* God's people."
	136–15	come out from *a·* them, — *II Cor.* 6 : 17.
	142– 9	*a·* other beautiful decorations,
	184– 6	made flesh and dwell *a·* mortals,
	203–11	waters that run *a·* the valleys,
	225– 6	*A·* the guests, were an
	270–29	*A·* the foremost virtues of
	281–23	*A·* the gifts of my students,
	296– 4	*a·* its constituents and managers
	319–27	feel themselves alone *a·* the stars.
	323–12	Venomous serpents hide *a·* the rocks,
	334– 2	and *a·* the inhabitants — *Dan.* 4 : 35.
	343–26	*A·* the manifold soft chimes
	371– 1	*a·* the first lessons on healing
	378– 8	After much consultation *a·* ourselves,
Man.	66– 8	If . . . shall arise *a·* the members
Ret.	2– 1	*a·* the Scotch Covenanters,
	2–21	*A·* grandmother's treasures were
	6– 9	*A·* the treasured reminiscences of
	6–27	*A·* other important bills which
	13– 8	*a·* those who were doomed
	15–23	*A·* other diseases cured
	23–20	"*a·* ten thousand." — *Song* 5 : 10.
	70–27	Preeminent *a·* men, he virtually
Un.	15– 9	Was evil *a·* these good things?
	39– 1	"made flesh" *a·* mortals, — *John* 1 : 14.
	62–23	*a·* the dead? — *Luke* 24 : 5.
Pul.	38–27	* they may differ *a·* themselves,
	43–27	* to discourage *a·* her followers
	46–17	* *A·* the many souvenirs that Mrs. Eddy
	51– 9	* numbered *a·* the many pioneers
	56– 5	* *a·* the members of all the churches
	60–14	* *a·* the thousands of adherents
	63–17	* people *a·* her devoted followers.
Rud.	2– 5	*a·* Trinitarian Christians the word
	16–24	springing up *a·* unchristian students,
No.	9– 3	which have sprung up *a·* Scientists
	9– 6	or established *a·* another class
	23–11	not one person was named *a·* them.
	42– 3	* will . . . God's power increase *a·* us."
	46–14	were *a·* the first settlers of
Pan.	13– 4	Chief *a·* the questions herein,

among
'00.   2– 5   *a·* the best people on earth
    5–15   way under heaven and *a·* men
    11– 7   jarring elements *a·* musicians
    14–18   Let no . . . bitterness spring up *a·* you,
'01.   27– 6   * arise *a·* the Christian Scientists
    28–25   *a·* the worldlings in his age,
    31–20   *A·* the list of blessings infinite
    31–28   *a·* whom were the Rev. . . . Burnham
'02.   3– 4   *a·* the educated classes
Po.   vi–26   * *A· her earliest poems*
My.   40– 9   * subsidence of criticism *a·* workers.
    40–14   * Through rivalries *a·* leaders
    53–23   * *a·* whom was the Rev. A. J. Peabody,
    53–27   * statements, *a·* which is this :
    53–29   * interest in C. S. *a·* the people,
    85–17   * *a·* the architectural beauties of
    87–10   * *a·* them visitors of title
    88– 7   * *a·* classes above the average
    90–30   * Prominent *a·* these is the
    94–13   * absence of dissent *a·* them
    95– 1   * soon be included *a·* the cults which
    97– 8   * than *a·* those who were
    100–13   * *a·* religious bodies,
    113–31   *a·* the scholarly and titled,
    164–19   wrought a resurrection *a·* you,
    177–23   prophecy . . . is fulfilled *a·* you :
    182–14   seemed the least *a·* seeds,
    197–19   else C. S. will disappear from *a·*
    212–15   dissension *a·* mental practitioners?
    243– 3   belief is springing up *a·* you
    244– 3   *a·* those who wish to share this
    274–24   unity *a·* brethren, and love to God
    274–28   health *a·* all nations." — *Psal.* 67 : 2.
    286–12   preserving peace *a·* nations.
    304– 6   *A·* my early studies were
    321–26   * I was *a·* your early students
    324–23   * *a·* his literary friends.
    331– 5   * *a·* whom she remembers the

amount
Mis.   43–22   rivalry does a vast *a·* of injury
    227–29   *a·* of happiness it has bestowed
    230– 4   great *a·* of time is consumed in
    305–27   * send with the *a·* the name of
    349–30   contributions, . . . doubled that *a·*.
Man.   76–11   *a·* of funds which the Church has
    76–12   the *a·* of its indebtedness
    76–23   *a·* of funds received by the
Ret.   50– 7   This *a·* greatly troubled me.
Pul.   41– 4   * full *a·* needed was received.
    64–10   * When the necessary *a·* was raised,
No.   23–24   *a·* of good or evil he possesses.
'02.   13–24   *a·* due on the mortgage.
My.   9–26   draw on God for the *a·* I owe you,
    10–15   * as to *a·* and date of payment.
    11–28   * the *a·* to be expended
    12–11   * *a·* to be expended
    14–14   * entire *a·* . . . had been paid in ;
    20–26   * expenditure of a large *a·*
    21– 1   * *a·* which they would have expended
    23– 4   * *a·* each shall send the Treasurer.
    23–10   * *A·* on hand June 1, 1905,
    23–14   * *A·* necessary to complete the sum
    123–18   *a·* is now about twenty thousand
    312–22   took with him the usual *a·* of money

amphitheatre
My.   59–19   * couple of pews in this grand *a·* ;

ample
Mis.   319–24   affords *a·* opportunity for
Man.   44–23   Church Organizations *A·*.
    82–20   *a·* time for faithful practice.
    95–23   duties alone of a Reader are *a·*.
Ret.   82–17   is *a·* to supply many practitioners,
'02.   15–14   income from literary sources was *a·*,
My.   10– 9   * in a beautiful *a·* building,
    13–19   with which to build an *a·* temple
    24– 5   * express in its *a·* auditorium
    56–15   * *a·* room for growth of attendance
    312–29   My salary . . . gave me *a·* support.
    318–28   *a·* fund of historical knowledge,
    342– 1   *a·*, richly furnished house

amplification
Mis.   261–11   every effect and *a·* of wrong will
No.   24– 3   According to . . . God is *a·*.
My.   288–24   *a·* of wrong will revert to the
    336–20   * as *a·* of the facts given by Mrs. Eddy

amplified
Mis.   310– 6   Truth, *a·* in this age by

amplifies
No.   10– 9   it aggregates, *a·*, unfolds, and

amplitude
Mis.   249–24   in the *a·* of His love ;
    322–24   shown you the *a·* of His mercy,
My.   236–18   opens wide on the *a·* of liberty

amply
My.   261– 5   seems to have *a·* provided for this,

amputation
My.   105–14   ready for their *a·*.

amuse
My.   325– 5   * that I think will *a·* you :

amusement
Mis.   230–11   or planning for some *a·*,
Man.   60– 9   *A·* or idleness is weariness.
'00.   2–13   He takes no time for *a·*,

amusements
Mis.   357– 2   no time for idle words, vain *a·*,

amusing
Mis.   62–25   which is *a·* to astute readers,
Peo.   6–12   * *a·* the patient while nature

analogy
Mis.   29–12   no *a·* between C. S. and

analysis
Pan.   2– 9   chapter sub-title
'02.   4– 7   correct *a·* of C. S.

analyzing
Ret.   30–11   *a·*, uncovering, and annihilating the
My.   319–24   * in *a·* and arranging the topics,

anarchy
My.   166– 2   will never end in *a·*

anathema
Mis.   105– 6   *a·* of priesthood and the senses ;
My.   104–29   *a·* spoken of in Scripture :

anatomical
Rud.   15–26   laid bare for *a·* examination.

anatomically
Un.   57– 3   *A·* considered, the design of

anatomy
Man.   47– 7   on the *a·* involved.
Un.   28– 4   *A·* has not descried nor described
    45–17   *A·* and physiology make mind-matter
Rud.   11–26   the subject of human *a·* ;
Pan.   4– 8   belief may agree with physics and *a·*

ancestors
Ret.   1– 1   My *a·*, according to the flesh,
Pul.   48–27   * She had a long list of worthy *a·*
No.   46–14   The author's *a·* were among the
My.   163–28   thank their *a·* for helping to

ancestral
Pul.   46–13   * in going back to the *a·* tree
My.   309–28   * at the *a·* home at Bow.

ancestry
Ret.   68–29   good, and pure constitute his *a·*.
Pul.   32–24   * from Scotch and English *a·*,
My.   270–10   records of my *a·* attest honesty and
    311–25   which is of my mother's *a·*.

anchor
No.   45–22   *a·* the Church in more spiritual
My.   132–11   and *a·* in omnipotence.

anchorage
Un.   43– 7   too finite for *a·* in infinite good,

anchored
My.   152– 3   *a·* its faith in troubled waters.

anchors
'00.   10–21   our hope *a·* in God who reigns,

ancient
Mis.   1– 2   *a·* Greek looked longingly for
    40–14   equal the *a·* prophets as healers.
    148–10   solemn conclave as in *a·* Sanhedrim.
    169– 4   bypaths of *a·* philosophies
    173– 1   *A·* and modern philosophy,
    333–30   The *a·* Chaldee hung his destiny
    333–31   but *a·* or modern Christians,
    344–16   *A·* and modern philosophies
    372–20   *a·* and most distinguished artists.
Man.   3– 6   solemn conclave as in *a·* Sanhedrim.
Ret.   2–23   were not very *a·*,
    10– 9   I received lessons in the *a·* tongues,
    34– 7   Neither *a·* nor modern philosophy
    57– 4   Neither *a·* nor modern philosophy
Pul.   8– 4   through the leaves of an *a·* oak,
    46–25   * looking into the *a·* languages,
    47–13   * No *a·* or modern philosophy
    52–14   * reviver of the *a·* faith
No.   11–23   *A·* and modern human philosophy
'01.   9– 6   *a·* worthies caught glorious glimpses
    28– 8   *a·* writers since the first century
Hea.   11–13   fires of *a·* proscription burn upon the
    19–12   *a·* question, Which is first,
Po.   10– 7   Thy palm, in *a·* day,
My.   70–21   * of both *a·* and modern masters,
    103–22   in *a·* or in modern systems
    178–32   *a· Logia*, or imputed sayings of
My.   337– 8   Thy palm, in *a·* day,

anciently
    Mis. 121–11 *A·*, the blood of martyrs was
    Pul. 20–21 *a·* one of the many dates selected
    '01. 12–10 was *a·* an opprobrium ;

ancients
    Mis. 191–6 *a·* changed the meaning of the term,

Andover Seminary
    Un. 7–4 by the changes at *A· S·*

Andover Theological School
    Mis. 178–3 a graduate . . . of *A· T· S·*.

Andrew, Governor
    Po. vi–19 *To-day, by order of Governor A·,*

anew
    Mis. 109–27 and consecrate one's life *a·*.
    125–9 Then shall he drink *a·* Christ's cup,
    246–16 to forge *a·* the old fetters ;
    343–17 burnishing *a·* the . . . gems of Love,
    346–8 It confronts each generation *a·*.
    384–6 Come Thou! and now, *a·*,
    Rud. 15–28 fill *a·* the individual mind.
    '00. 10–9 unconquerable right is begun *a·*,
    Hea. 4–19 to begin *a·* as infinite Life,
    Po. 36–5 Come Thou! and now, *a·*,
    My. 46–18 * pledge ourselves *a·* to this demand,
    52–26 * has always filled her coffers *a·*.
    97–21 * opened the eyes of the country *a·*
    307–19 referred to the *coming a·* of Truth,

angel (*see also* **angel's**)
    Mis. 141–31 O recording *a·*! write :
    275–6 Who— but God's avenging *a·*!
    374–31 my ideal of an *a·* is
    396–22 wake a white-winged *a·* throng
    Pul. 18–6 wake a white-winged *a·* throng
    '00. 13–29 *a·* of the church in Philadelphia
    14–20 *a·* that spake unto the churches
    15–22 may the *a·* of The Mother Church
    '02. 16–18 enigmatical seals of the *a·*,
    Peo. 5–15 in *a·* form, saying unto us,
    5–22 not entertain the *a·* unawares.
    7–11 * As an *a·* dream passed o'er him.
    Po. 12–6 wake a white-winged *a·* throng
    My. 126–3 purpose of the destroying *a·*,
    126–7 recording *a·*, standing with
    148–23 as with the pen of an *a·*
    153–8 *a·* of the church in— *Rev.* 3 : 7.

angelic
    Ret. 85–11 upon which *a·* thoughts ascend
    My. 163–3 *a·* song chiming chaste challenge

Angelico's
    Mis. 375–25 * hands and feet in *A·* 'Jesus,'

angel's
    Mis. 388–22 To fold an *a·* wings below ;
    '00. 11–23 * Like the close of an *a·* psalm,
    Po. 21–11 To fold an *a·* wings below ;

angels (*see also* **angels'**)
    Mis. 78–3 and the overture of the *a·*.
    106–26 the soft, sweet sigh of *a·* answering,
    111–3 work, well done, would dignify *a·*.
    145–29 and echo the song of *a·* :
    149–26 fellowship with saints and *a·*.
    152–27 no element of earth to cast out *a·*,
    166–14 for the overture of *a·*
    204–11 sings to the heart a song of *a·*.
    251–21 where *a·* are as men,
    251–21 and men as *a·*
    280–4 one of the *a·* presented himself
    280–6 not *a·* with wings, but messengers
    286–15 but are as the *a·*.
    306–22 chapter sub-title
    306–23 When *a·* visit us, we do not hear the
    306–29 shall give His *a·* — *Psal.* 91 : 11.
    374–14 *A·*, with overtures, hold charge
    375–3 are not my concepts of *a·*.
    386–20 *a·* beckoned me to this bright land,
    389–20 Seeking and finding, with the *a·* sing :
    391–21 When *a·* shall repeat it,
    Ret. 10–17 Prosody, the song of *a·*,
    Un. 28–10 peopled with demons or *a·*,
    Pul. 11–6 mingle with the joy of *a·*
    39–21 * sculptured *a·*, on the gray church
    No. 46–11 for joining the overture of *a·*.
    '00. 8–2 and with saints and *a·* shall be
    '01. 26–22 of men and of *a·*,— *I Cor.* 13 : 1.
    34–17 solace us with the song of *a·*
    '02. 3–25 and the lay of *a·*
    19–14 He entertains *a·* who listens to
    Peo. 1–11 are the *a·* of His presence,
    Po. 4–19 with the *a·* sing :
    10–14 List, brother! *a·* whisper
    38–20 When *a·* shall repeat it,
    50–5 *a·* beckoned me to this bright land,
    My. 14–4 blessing above the song of *a·*,

angels
    My. 46–29 * company of *a·*,— *Heb.* 12 : 22.
    122–23 Can we say with the *a·* to-day :
    129–21 Then will *a·* administer grace,
    148–20 What are the *a·* saying or singing
    155–24 sing as the *a·* heaven's symphonies
    189–1 warmest wish of men and *a·*.
    269–9 equal unto the *a·* ;— *Luke* 20 : 36.
    337–15 List, brother! *a·* whisper
    354–23 The tongue of *a·*

angels'
    Po. 30–22 and *a·* loving lays,
    My. 354–21 Give us not only *a·* songs,

Angelus
    My. 70–16 * "*A·* " had living reproductions

angel-vision
    Peo. 7–15 * He had caught the *a·*.
    7–23 * Our lives that *a·*."

anger
    Mis. 36–13 Appetites, passions, *a·*, revenge,
    123–13 to appease the *a·* of a so-called god
    223–26 "He that is slow to *a·* — *Prov.* 16 : 32.
    My. 196–10 "He that is slow to *a·* — *Prov.* 16 : 32.

angles
    Pul. 47–30 * *a·* and pitch of the roof,
    My. 69–6 * no sharp *a·* are visible,

Anglican
    Pul. 65–5 * Eastern churches and the *A·* fold

Anglo-Israel
    Po. 10–19 *A·*, lo ! Is marching under orders ;
    My. 337–20 *A·*, lo ! Is marching under orders ;

Anglo-Saxon
    Mis. 13–28 Seek the *A·* term for God,
    216–12 given to the *A·* tongue,
    Pul. 6–7 Good, the *A·* term for God,

angry
    Mis. 162–9 stem these rising *a·* elements,
    397–5 o'er earth's troubled, *a·* sea
    Pul. 18–14 o'er earth's troubled, *a·* sea
    Po. 12–14 o'er earth's troubled, *a·* sea
    46–4 blasts of winter's *a·* storm,
    My. 310–29 * "When do you ever see Mary *a·*?"

anguish
    Mis. 104–1 was on earth and in *a·*,
    237–5 mental *a·* is generally accepted as
    253–25 Can that child conceive of the *a·*,
    Un. 57–25 Mortal throes of *a·*
    Peo. 14–15 ye may go to the bed of *a·*,
    My. 258–10 bowed in strong affection's *a·*,
    350–16 This weight of *a·* which they

animal
    Mis. 23–6 * or dream in the *a·*,
    36–14 *a·* qualities of sinning mortals ;
    36–16 qualities of the so-called *a·* man ;
    37–13 leave the *a·* for the spiritual,
    156–22 through which the *a·* magnetizer preys,
    184–31 mortal mind purged of the *a·*
    217–14 vegetable, and *a·* kingdoms,
    257–4 dreams in the *a·*,
    281–3 this *a·* element flings open
    287–15 the spiritual over the *a·*,
    294–13 but he is a small *a·* :
    297–24 If the man is dominant over the *a·*,
    Ret. 70–2 confers *a·* names and natures
    Un. 38–24 mineral, vegetable, or *a·* kingdoms.
    No. 24–6 according to . . . man is an *a·* vegetable,
    Pan. 3–4 horned and hoofed *a·*,
    9–2 * dreams in the *a·*,
    '01. 19–14 That *a·* natures give force to
    Hea. 14–2 the bigger *a·* beats the lesser ;
    My. 245–14 *a·* elements manifested in ignorance,

animality
    Mis. 277–32 drunkenness produced by *a·*.
    375–2 personality blind with *a·*,
    Pul. 13–12 mortal beliefs, *a·*, and hate,
    '00. 8–17 apathy is always egotism and *a·*.

Animal Magnetism
    Mis. 350–9 "There is no *A· M·*."
    Ret. 37–22 the chapter on *A· M·*,
    Pul. 38–12 "Marriage," "*A· M·*,"

animal magnetism
    (*see* **magnetism**)

animals
    Mis. 36–6 *Do a· and beasts have a mind?*
    Un. 14–6 earth, man, *a·*, plants,
    Rud. 7–27 transforming . . . plants into *a·*,

animate
    My. 206–2 would unite dead matter with *a·*,

animated
    Mis. 325–21 that anybody is *a·* with a purpose,

animated

Peo.	5–23	not self-existent matter *a·* by mind,
My.	294–26	have *a·* the Church of Rome
	320–32	* he spoke in a very *a·* manner

animosities

Mis.	284–29	I deprecate personal *a·*

animosity

Man.	40– 5	Neither *a·* nor mere personal
My.	40–13	* forsake *a·*, and abandon their

animus

Mis.	38–18	Science that has the *a·* of Truth.
	48–18	as to the *a·* of animal magnetism
	113–32	spiritual *a·* is felt throughout the
	290– 4	so long as the *a·* of the contract is
Man.	31–13	spiritual *a·* so universally needed.
Pul.	3–30	unfitness for such a spiritual *a·*
	32– 9	* but a spiritual *a·*.
Pan.	11– 9	gauge the *a·* of man?
'00.	3–29	*a·* of heathen religion was not
My.	3–16	persuasive *a·*, an unerring impetus,
	26–24	to give the true *a·* of our church
	45–12	* *a·* and spirit of our movement.
	277–11	The mental *a·* goes on,
	339–27	The *a·* of his saying was :

annals

My.	45– 8	* in the *a·* of our history.
	98– 9	* such as religious *a·* hardly parallel
	148–10	In the *a·* of our denomination

annexed

My.	138–28	* contained in the *a·* letter

annihilate

Mis.	3–32	thus to *a·* hallucination.
	56– 6	would destroy Spirit and *a* man.
Ret.	64– 6	This, however, does not *a·* man,
My.	226–16	*a·* matter, and man . . . would remain

annihilated

Mis.	10–26	material tendencies . . . are thus *a·* ;
	42– 4	Man is not *a·*, nor does he lose
Ret.	94–14	When all fleshly belief is *a·*,
Un.	31–10	as emphatically as they *a·* sin.
	58– 4	before error is *a·*.
No.	26–18	If . . . he would be *a·*,

annihilates

Mis.	14–29	Science of Truth *a·* error,
Un.	39– 7	omnipotent Love which *a·* hate,
'01.	13– 3	*a·* its own embodiment :

annihilating

Mis.	141–14	even the *a·* law of Love.
Ret.	30–11	*a·* the false testimony of
My.	110–13	forces *a·* time and space,

annihilation

Mis.	22–14	or *a·* of individuality.
'01.	13– 4	this is the only *a·*.

anniversaries

Mis.	304–24	* *a·* of the days on which
	304–27	* on the *a·* of their death.

anniversary

Mis.	305–29	* the *a·* of the inauguration of
My.	174–19	one hundred and seventy-fifth *a·* of
	175– 2	this deeply interesting *a·*,
	270– 8	its one hundred and seventy-fifth *a·* ;

Anno Domini

Mis.	131–21	encountered in *A· D·* 1894,
Pul.	24–14	* erected *A· D·* 1894.
	84–14	* close of the year, *A· D·* 1894,

announce

Mis.	374–15	*a·* their Principle and idea.
Man.	32–13	*a·* the full title of the book
	59– 9	*a·* the name of the author.
Ret.	42– 5	to *a·* himself a Christian Scientist,
Pul.	86–17	* We are happy to *a·* to you
My.	242–16	I hereby *a·* to the C. S. field

announced

Mis.	114–11	*a·* in the Bible and their textbook,
	177–25	* who was *a·* to preach the sermon,
	256–13	as was *a·* in the October number of
Pul.	55–15	* the ninety-first edition is *a·*.
My.	31–28	* *a·* simply that they would sing
	81–11	* *a·* at the main meeting that
	91–20	* since C. S. was *a·*
	132– 3	We begin with the law as just *a·*,
	157–18	* first *a·* in the *Concord Monitor*
	237– 2	*a·* in the *Sentinel* a few weeks ago,

announcement

Mis.	168–25	* *a·* that the Rev. Mary B. G. Eddy
	314–25	this *a·*, "the C. S. textbook."
Man.	32–15	Such *a·* shall be made but once
My.	26– 2	* chapter sub-title
	27–22	* made by Mr. Chase
	28– 1	* make this *a·* coincident with
	61– 9	* *a·* that the services would be

announcement

My.	76– 8	* formal *a·* was made that no more
	83–23	* *a·*, which has just been made,
	98–15	* remarkable *a·* to the effect
	141–12	* *a·* in regard to the services
	163– 8	chapter sub-title
	281–18	* *a·* of peace between Russia and
	294–23	*a·* of the decease of Pope Leo XIII,

announcements

Mis.	84– 4	to receive startling *a·*.
Pul.	71–15	* *a·* in New York papers

announcing

Mis.	300– 5	*a·* the author's name,
	314–24	*a·* the full title of this book,
Man.	58–20	*A·* Author's Name.
No.	35–24	Jesus came *a·* Truth,
My.	26– 4	* takes pleasure in *a·* that
	134–24	* In *a·* this letter, he said :
	204–14	A LETTER *A·* THE PURPOSE OF

annoy

Po.	31– 6	Sad sense, *a·* No more the peace of

annual

Mis.	134–11	at the *a·* session of the
Man.	56–10	*A·* Meetings.
	76–11	report at the *a·* Church meeting
	95–16	*A·* Lectures.
	97–13	shall receive an *a·* salary,
'00.	7– 3	show the *a·* death-rate to have
'02.	20–17	our *a·* gathering at Pleasant View,
My.	8–25	* convened in *a·* business meeting
	23–19	* in *a·* business meeting assembled,
	25–19	at our *a·* communion
	26– 5	* on the date of the *a·* communion,
	32–26	* Reading of *a·* Message from
	37–27	* We have read your *a·* Message
	53–25	* *a·* report of the business committee
	57– 1	* *a·* meetings were overcrowded
	63–11	* Our *a·* communion and
	76–20	* assembled in their *a·* church meeting
	124– 6	Looking on this *a·* assemblage of
	133–11	my *a·* Message is swallowed up in
	140–13	* dropping the *a·* communion service
	141–17	* the *a·* communion season of
	170– 7	in my *a·* Message to the church
	207– 8	in *a·* conference assembled,
		(*see also* **meeting**)

annually

Mis.	136–24	hold three sessions *a·*,
	315–11	can teach *a·* three classes only.
Man.	29–17	salary . . . shall be at present . . . *a·*.
	44–13	pay *a·* a per capita tax
	56–12	shall be held *a·*, on Monday
	76–18	Its members shall be appointed *a·*
	77– 2	audited *a·* by an honest,
	79– 3	elect *a·* a Committee on Business,
	84–17	The associations . . . shall convene *a·*.
	88–11	vice-president shall be elected *a·*
	91–17	shall be paid over *a·* to
	93– 6	shall be elected *a·*
	95–18	branch churches shall call . . . *a·*
	97–10	He shall be elected *a·*
	98–26	shall *a·* and alternately appoint
	99– 8	shall *a·* and alternately appoint
'02.	12–27	who *a·* favor us with their presence
My.	7–10	who *a·* favor us with their presence
	141– 4	* held *a·* in The First Church
	284–19	has been held *a·* in some church
	328–14	* This license of five dollars *a·*,

Annual Meeting

Mis.	125–21	chapter sub-title
Man.	93– 7	on Monday preceding the *A· M·*,
My.	7–12	chapter sub-title
	22– 1	* chapter sub-title
	23–16	* *Greeting to Mrs. Eddy from the A· M·*
	38–27	* chapter sub-title
	131–17	chapter sub-title
	154–14	chapter sub-title
	156– 1	chapter sub-title

annuity

Ret.	40– 3	living on a small *a·*.

annul

Mis.	199– 6	to *a·* his own erring mental law,
My.	219–22	cannot *a·* nor make void the laws

annulled

Mis.	28–29	*a·* the claims of physique
	244–18	who *a·* the so-called laws of matter
	260–12	these laws *a·* all other laws.
	290– 4	nuptial vow is never *a·* so long as
Man.	105– 3	nor any Tenet or By-Law . . . *a·*,
Un.	11– 8	He *a·* the laws of matter,
	31– 8	*a·* the claims of matter,
Pan.	8–15	*a·* the so-called laws of matter,
My.	268– 3	should never be *a·* so long as

annulling
 Man. 28– 6 *a·* its Tenets and By-Laws.
 My. 340–17 immediately *a·* such bills

annuls
 Mis. 99– 3 It *a·* false evidence,
   103– 1 *a·* the testimony of the senses,
 My. 234– 6 personal worship which C. S. *a·*

anoint
 Mis. 171– 6 *a·* the blind man's eyes

anointed
 Mis. 161–13 Christ-Jesus, the Godlike, the *a·*.
   347–26 those whom He has *a·*.
   355–22 is unlike "the *a·*," — *see Acts* 10 : 38.
 Ret. 28–30 character and practice of the *a·* ;

anointing
 Mis. 258– 8 *a·* the wounded spirit with
 Pul. 27–21 * Mary *a·* the head of Jesus,

anointings
 Pul. 9–26 prayers, prophecies, and *a·*.

anoints
 Mis. 130–30 the meek and loving, God *a·*
 Chr. 53– 9 The Christ-idea, God *a·*
 Ret. 91– 1 He *a·* His Truth-bearers,
 My. 270–26 or by C. S., which *a·* with Truth,

anomalous
 Mis. 63– 2 and *a·* in the other.
   92– 1 To omit these important points is *a·*,
   108– 4 To allow sin of any sort is *a·*
   256–26 The assertion that . . . is *a·*.
 Ret. 83–27 is *a·*, when we consider the
 Pan. 2– 3 that C. S. is pantheism is *a·*

anonymous
 Mis. 295– 8 This *a·* talker further declares,
 '02 15– 1 *a·* letters mailed to me

another (*see also* another's)
 Mis. 1–20 reveals *a·* scene and *a·* self
   22–16 from one individual to *a·* ;
   29– 7 At *a·* time he prayed, not for
   37– 2 if there were in reality *a·* mind
   40–32 unintentionally harms himself or *a·*.
   43–21 If one student tries to undermine *a·*,
   58–28 even one human mind governing *a·* ;
   59–23 speaking often one to *a·*,
   59–24 one individual has with *a·*
   60–20 with *a·* who is awake.
   63– 4 claim that one erring mind cures *a·*
   67–27 by equivalent words in *a·* ;
   71– 7 and *a·* that he had sore eyes ;
   91–11 love for one *a·*.
   96–28 not one mind acting upon *a·*
   98–11 to aid one *a·* in finding ways
   104–30 I will love, if *a·* hates.
   111–31 or is *a·* Christ,
   129–16 an atom of *a·* man's indiscretion,
   147– 3 *A·* year has rolled on,
   147– 4 *a·* annual meeting has convened,
   147– 4 *a·* space of time has been given us,
   147– 5 has *a·* duty been done
   147– 6 *a·* victory won for time and
   147– 7 in unity, preferring one *a·*,
   148– 3 never . . . at variance with *a·*.
   148–12 one person might impose on *a·*.
   149– 8 one after *a·* has opened his lips
   155– 6 Sacrifice self to bless one *a·*,
   158– 8 *a·* change in your pulpit
   173–22 man is not met by *a·* power
   175–23 supposition . . . one mind controls *a·* ;
   175–24 one belief takes the place of *a·*.
   183–25 for it claims *a·* father.
   191– 3 embodies . . . in *a·* term, serpent,
   191–19 cast out of *a·* individual
   197–24 He believes there is *a·* power
   198–27 supposition of *a·* intelligence
   212–29 before letting *a·* know it.
   215– 3 to go from one extreme to *a·* :
   219–15 one person feels sick, *a·* feels
   219–27 *a·* knows that if he can change
   220– 4 whom *a·* would heal mentally.
   221–20 acknowledgment of it in *a·*
   221–30 Who would tell *a·* of a crime that
   224–29 wilfully attempt to injure *a·*,
   236–26 in one's efforts to help *a·*,
   238–27 *a·* evidence of the falsehoods
   242–15 I am in *a·* department of
   246–14 from *a·* direction there comes
   246–15 *a·* sharp cry of oppression.
   246–15 *A·* form of inhumanity
   248– 6 as, in *a·* Scripture,
   273–27 *a·* and a larger number would
   281– 6 But I find also *a·* mental condition
   283– 8 management of *a·* man's property.
   283–15 to treat *a·* student without his
   292– 5 That ye love one *a·*." — *John* 13 : 34.

another
 Mis. 311– 9 so, loving one *a·*, go forth
   311–20 as soon harm myself as *a·* ;
   325–13 patiently seeks *a·* dwelling,
   336–21 What is it but *a·* name for C. S.,
   395–18 Ere autumn blanch *a·* year,
 Man. 3– 8 one person might impose on *a·*.
   34–18 a member of *a·* Church of Christ,
   37–18 cannot recommend the pupil of *a·*
   45– 4 Joining *A·* Society.
   62–11 transfer from *a·* Church of Christ,
   84–24 shall not teach *a·* loyal
   99–14 with *a·* Church of Christ, Scientist.
   100–18 *a·* Committee to fill the vacancy ;
 Ret. 40–16 to be delivered of *a·* child.
   59– 9 and addition in *a·*,
   86–19 and *a·* one undertakes to carry his
   88– 3 professional intercourse . . . with one *a·*.
   88– 4 *A·* command of the Christ,
   88–17 *a·* part of C. S. work,
   89–23 employing *a·* student to take charge
   90– 6 while he is serving *a·* fold?
 Un. 3– 4 they awake only to *a·* sphere of
   3– 5 must pass through *a·* probationary
   6–28 and in less than *a·* fifty years
   8– 1 Let *a·* query now be considered,
   21– 3 excusing one *a·*." — *Rom.* 2 : 15.
   21– 7 good and evil talk to one *a·* ;
   26–22 *a·* line of this hymn,
   34–14 Take *a·* train of reasoning.
   38–13 must enthrone *a·* power,
   39–15 claims *a·* father, and denies
 Pul. 5– 6 light of one friendship after *a·*
   6–23 *A·* brilliant enunciator, seeker,
   14– 5 *a·* extreme mortal mood,
   14– 7 for one extreme follows *a·*.
   21– 2 inevitably love one *a·*
   27–20 * *A·* great window tells its
   33–24 * believed, . . . form from *a·* world.
   38–30 * one form of belief or *a·*
   42– 3 * At 10 : 30 o'clock *a·* service began,
   42– 4 * and at noon still *a·*.
   48–19 * *a·* distinguished relative,
   48–26 * many *a·* well-born woman's.
 No. 7–22 between one person and *a·*,
   9– 6 *a·* class who are clearer
   24–26 *a·* and more glorious truth,
   30–13 rebuke any claim of *a·* law.
   40–21 for one mind to meddle with *a·*
 Pan. 11– 3 "Lie not one to *a·*, — *Col.* 3 : 9.
   13–13 rebuke and exhort one *a·*.
   14– 5 Once more I write, . . . love one *a·* ;
 '00. 5–16 loving *a·* as himself.
   8–20 work that belongs to *a·*.
 '01. 5–14 This suggests *a·* query :
   13– 2 *a·* nonentity that belittles
   33–28 to persecute *a·* in advance of it.
 '02. 1– 1 *a·* year of God's loving providence
   7–22 chapter sub-title
   7–23 proceed to *a·* Scriptural passage
   7–26 love one *a·* ; — *John* 13 : 34.
   12–15 with *a·* of his sayings :
   12–25 *a·* united effort to purchase
   18–16 "Love one *a·*, — *John* 13 : 34.
 Hea. 2–14 And still *a·* Christian hero,
   4–26 and the opposite of it at *a·*,
   5–20 covered, in one way or *a·*,
   13–27 while it is supposed to cure *a·*,
   13–28 one lie getting the better of *a·*,
   15–15 *a·* mind perpetually at war
 Peo. 2– 8 gives *a·* letter to the word
   8– 5 prayer of one and not of *a·* ;
   11– 9 *a·* staging for diviner claims,
 Po. 43– 4 Loving God and one *a·*,
   58– 3 Ere autumn blanch *a·* year,
 My. 7– 8 before making *a·* united effort,
   14–12 * letter from a friend in *a·* city,
   18–21 rebuke and exhort one *a·*.
   69–20 * *A·* unusual feature is the foyer,
   81– 9 * laughingly give precedence to *a·*
   84–17 * *a·* great demonstration of
   85–20 * *A·* glory for Boston, *a·* "landmark"
   94– 1 * through *a·* decade
   113–19 Neither is it presumptuous . . . for *a·*,
   122–16 *a·* Christmas has come and gone.
   152– 1 turned to *a·* form of idolatry,
   167– 6 and unites us to one *a·*.
   187–15 we should love one *a·*." — *I John* 3 : 11.
   187–28 "that ye love one *a·*." — *John* 15 : 12.
   189–12 vibrating from one pulpit to *a·*
   189–12 from one heart to *a·*,
   202–11 but to love one *a·* : — *Rom.* 13 : 8.
   202–11 he that loveth *a·* hath — *Rom.* 13 : 8.
   216–19 indicates *a·* field of work
   218–28 to one no more than to *a·*.
   221–12 Earth has not known *a·* so great

another

My.	224–19	same time giving full credit to a·
	227– 6	minifying of his own goodness by a·.
	234–20	gives the subject quite a· aspect.
	240–15	I now repeat a· proof,
	267–21	a· with that of relief from fear
	267–22	still a· with a bitter sense of
	292–18	against the *modus operandi* of a·,
	292–21	belief unwittingly neutralizing a·,
	306–11	I have quite a· purpose in life
	311–24	I have a· coat-of-arms,
	346– 5	* a· opportunity for presenting a·

(*see also* **member, person**)

another's

Mis.	11–16	could save it . . . by taking a·,
	39–23	"one a· burdens, — *Gal.* 6 : 2.
	83–10	*your own thought or a·."*
	83–12	No person can accept a· belief,
	83–15	originated in a· mind,
	97– 6	transmitted to a· thought
	98–28	* a· heart would'st reach."
	127–19	finds one's own in a· good.
	184–27	not her own, but a· good ;
	213–16	chastened and illumined a· way
	223–30	arrow shot from a· bow
	224– 2	makes a· criticism rankle,
	224– 3	makes a· deed offensive,
	224– 4	feels hurt by a· self-assertion.
	338–23	* A· soul wouldst reach ;
Ret.	72– 2	that hazards a· happiness,
	88–23	to enter unasked a· pulpit,
No.	3–23	not so much thine own as a· good,
	29– 2	for his own sin, but not for a·.
	43–20	their own on a· foundation.
'00.	14–19	not only her own, but a· good.
'01.	34–19	seeketh not her own but a· good,
My.	18–16	finds one's own in a· good."
	19–23	not her own" but a· good, — *I Cor.* 13 : 5.
	188–24	one man's head lies at a· feet.
	227– 5	because of a· wickedness

answer (noun)

Mis.	4–16	has been devoted to their a·.
	23–11	The a· is self-evident,
	50– 2	therefore your a· is, that error
	55– 1	failed to get the right a·,
	67–29	I modify my affirmative a·.
	89–23	the proper a· to this question
	93–21	Your a· is, that neither fear nor
	96–25	This a· includes tóo much
	121–25	this a· to the questions of the
	127–16	fitness to receive the a· to its desire ;
	130– 4	She readily leaves the a· to
	310–11	My a· to manifold letters
	349–22	In a· to a question on the
	380–32	A· was filed by the defendant,
Man.	41– 9	"A soft a· turneth away — *Prov.* 15 : 1.
Ret.	8– 7	Her a· was always, "Nothing,
	30–17	The a· is plain.
	34– 5	If I sought an a· from the
Pul.	74–10	* preferred to prepare a written a·
Rud.	9–15	and an a· of the lips
Pan.	5–11	gave the proper a· for all time
'02.	17–26	take its a· as to thy aims,
Hea.	1–13	our a· was, "Then there were no
	9–21	only correct a· to the question,
My.	18–13	to receive the a· to its desire ;
	25–17	my a· to their fervid question :
	43–32	* The a· is, The way out of
	51–22	* "she gave no definite a·,
	59–26	* My a· has invariably been,
	107– 5	and you have the correct a·.
	113–29	emphasize the a· to this
	124–22	what shall the a· be?
	149–16	Epictetus made a·,
	271–27	heading
	277–12	a· to the sublime question as to
	292–13	My a· to the inquiry,
	323– 5	* written in a· to an unfair criticism
	343– 4	* in her own way, reaching an a·

answer (verb)

Mis.	41–19	We a·, Yes.
	51–11	cannot a· your question
	91–26	a· them according to it,
	92–14	students will a· them from the same
	121–27	ye will not a· me, — *Luke* 22 : 68.
	132–21	to accept your invitation to a·
	142–24	a· in a commonplace letter.
	145–10	a· to his name in this corner-stone
	155–18	and less wherein to a· it
	177–19	A· at once and practically,
	177–20	and a· aright!
	238–20	Let one's life a· well
	280–26	I met the class to a· some
	299– 9	simply a· the following question
	300– 7	We a·, It is a mistake ;

answer (verb)

Mis.	301–21	I a· : It is not right to copy my
	347– 1	"A· not a fool — *Prov.* 26 : 4.
	348–15	"A· a fool according — *Prov.* 26 : 5.
Ret.	9–12	I was afraid, and did not a·.
	9–15	a·, in the words of Samuel,
	14–24	I replied that I could only a·
	28– 2	the divine Mind alone must a·,
	68–20	We a· that it cannot.
Un.	6–15	not prepared to a· intelligently
	45– 7	We should a· : "Yes!
	48– 4	yet ask, and I will a·.
Pul.	74–14	to a· for myself,
Rud.	6–25	can alone a· this question
No.	46– 9	must a· the constant inquiry :
'00.	2–19	is supposed to a· smilingly :
'01.	11–26	"A· not a fool — *Prov.* 26 : 4.
	14– 7	We a·, Yes and No!
My.	83–15	* questions as to locality to a·,
	120– 8	a· your excellent letter.
	186–22	I will a· ;— *Isa.* 65 : 24.
	212–15	We a·, Because they do not
	223–14	about secular affairs, I do not a·.
	343– 8	I can a· that. It will be a man."
	343–10	"I cannot a· that now."
	351– 9	in which to a· it.
	360– 1	A· this letter immediately.

answered

Mis.	4–26	When it is a· that there is no
	218–28	echo a·, "Pretty well,
	249– 9	met and a· *legally.*
	281–17	She a· him, "It is wiser
	326–32	He a·, "The sight of thee
	327– 7	He a·, "I will."
	378–16	He a· kindly and squarely,
Ret.	8–18	I a· not, till again the same
	8–23	She a· as always before.
	9– 6	My cousin a· quickly,
	14–11	I a· without a tremor,
	25– 3	It a· my questions as to how I
	83–23	and be a· according to it,
Pul.	33–12	* a· as her mother had bidden her,
	34–27	It a· my questions as to
'00.	11–12	human sigh for peace and love is a·
'02.	5–15	can never be a· satisfactorily by
	5–17	a· this great question forever
	14–27	This pregnant question, a· frankly
Hea.	19–13	is a· by the Scripture,
My.	61– 1	* I gladly a· in the affirmative,
	105–26	When a· in the negative,
	133– 9	chapter sub-title
	190–16	He a·, "This kind — *Matt.* 17 : 21.
	218–21	chapter sub-title
	222– 8	the master Metaphysician, a·,
	339–20	he a· them in substance :

answereth

Mis.	152– 4	in water face a· to face," — *Prov.* 27 : 19.
	203– 9	in water face a· to face, — *Prov.* 27 : 19.

answering

Mis.	106–26	soft, sweet sigh of angels a·,
	132–17	or a· personally manifold letters
'00.	1– 7	I am with thee, heart a· to heart,
My.	190– 7	The age is fast a· this question :
	192–28	a· your prayers, crowning your

answers

Mis.	23– 6	Christianity a· this question.
	81–26	a· the human call for help ;
	92–16	questions and a· contained in
	95–13	confine myself to questions and a·.
	132–17	dictating a· through my secretary,
	167– 3	though their a· pertain to
	317–19	prompt my a· to the above
Man.	63– 5	questions and a· as are adapted to
Un.	8– 3	before Science a· it.
'00.	2–29	he a· : "I am not so successful
'01.	19– 1	God a· their prayers,
Peo.	8– 5	or that a· the prayer of one
My.	238– 1	chapter sub-title
	343– 1	* plain that the a· to questions

antagonism

Mis.	200–19	spiritual law and its a· to
	320–21	It doth meet the a· of error ;
My.	11– 8	* encountered the full force of a·.

antagonist

Ret.	7– 4	His noble political a·,
Un.	41–22	can never dwell in its a·, matter.

antagonistic

Mis.	78–30	views a· to the divine order
	217–22	but that the effect is a· to its
	296–17	C. S., a· to intemperance,
	370– 6	a· spirit of evil is still abroad ;
Ret.	78–12	works, a· to C. S.,
Un.	38– 5	not in accordance . . . but a· thereto.

antagonistic
No. 20–27 mortal hypotheses, *a·* to Revelation
My. 87–28 * nothing *a·* to it in this doctrine

antagonize
Mis. 85–21 Spirit and flesh *a·*.
Un. 21–13 This would *a·* individual

antagonized
Ret. 56– 1 *a·* by finite theories,
My. 306– 9 false should be *a·* only for

antagonizes
Mis. 309–23 human concept *a·* the divine.

antecedent
Mis. 26–24 Spirit, God, has no *a·* ;
No. 17– 1 consequent of an *a·* false assumption
17– 2 If God knows the *a·*,
My. 303–27 her duplicate, *a·*, or subsequent.

antedated
Mis. 182– 1 he *a·* his own existence,
Ret. 26–19 He who *a·* Abraham,

anteroom
Mis. 379– 2 Mr. Quimby would retire to an *a·*

anthem
Mis. 330– 3 What is the *a·* of human life?
My. 186–12 *a·* of one Father-Mother God,

anthems
Pul. 81–23 * the unwritten *a·* of love.

Anthony, Susan
Mis. 248–22 my property to Susan *A·*.

anthropomorphic
'01. 4–18 is not corporeal nor *a·*.
6–23 in the corporeal or *a·* sense.

anti-Christ
Mis. 111–30 The belief in *a·* :
309–18 falling into the error of *a·*.

anti-Christian
Un. 53–11 Matter and evil are *a·*,

anticipate
My. 219– 2 Nor should patients *a·* being

anticipated
My. 21–18 * forego their *a·* visit this year
21–22 * who have *a·* much joy in meeting
163–25 all and more than I *a·*.

anticipating
My. 346– 7 * Those who have been *a·* nature

anticipation
My. 219– 4 such an *a·* on the part of

anticipations
Ret. 81–28 the frailty of mortal *a·*,

antics
Mis. 369–15 indulge in mad *a·*.

antidote
Mis. 33–27 *a·* for sickness, as well as for sin,
37–18 Its *a·* for all ills is God,
44–29 applying this mental remedy or *a·*
255–23 fact that the *a·* for sickness,
255–26 because it is this divine *a·*,
334–24 Then it cannot *a·* error.
Ret. 34–12 recognizes the *a·* for all sickness,

antidotes
Mis. 3–23 *a·* and destroys these material
189–11 Love *a·* and destroys the errors of
195– 1 Truth that *a·* all error.
209– 1 penalties as its *a·* and remedies.
268–23 *a·* for the ailments of mortal mind

antiphonal
Pul. 59–15 * *A·* paragraphs were read from

antipode
Mis. 31– 3 and is the *a·* of C. S.
217–12 is the *a·* of Spirit,
267–24 *a·* of Spirit, which we name
308–30 human likeness is the *a·* of man
332–26 the *a·* of immortal man.
351–26 declares itself the *a·* of Love ;
351–30 Material life is the *a·* of
Ret. 29– 2 spiritualism is the *a·* of C. S.
60– 8 says that matter, His *a·*,
67–12 a sinner was the *a·* of God.
Un. 31–18 matter, the *a·* of Spirit,
Pul. 75– 9 the absolute *a·* of C. S.,
No. 5– 5 *a·*, — the reality of error ;
27–17 Mortal man is the *a·* of
35–19 matter, — which is the *a·* of God,
'02. 5–28 an *a·* of *infinite* Love
Hea. 13–25 is the *a·* of mesmerism,
My. 106–27 he is the very *a·* of all these
181–30 material earth or *a·* of heaven.
301– 1 a peaceable party quite their *a·*

antipodes
Mis. 34–25 are the *a·* of C. S. ;
55–20 these facts are the direct *a·* of
56– 1 the very *a·* of C. S.
Ret. 25–17 and its *a·*, or the temporal,
59–15 is the *a·* of Life, or God,
Un. 53–11 are anti-Christian, the *a·* of Science.
My. 85– 9 * meet in Europe and in the *a·*,

antique
Pul. 24–27 * with doors of *a·* oak richly carved.
59– 1 * behind an *a·* lamp,

anti-slavery
Pul. 6–29 that renowned apostle of *a·*,
Po. vi–14 *has since been the pioneer of a·*

antithesis
Pul. 6– 3 continue till the *a·* of Christianity,
Peo. 8–12 not more the *a·* of Christianity than

anxiety
Hea. 9– 2 We should have no *a·* about

anxious
Man. 39– 1 *a·* to live according to its
Ret. 8–12 my mother was perplexed and *a·*.

anxiously
Mis. 324–11 *a·* surveying him who waiteth

any
Mis. 5–17 There is no longer *a·* reason for
7–30 naturally without *a·* assistance.
8–14 or *a·* other creature separate you
17– 5 *a·* supposititious law of sin,
24–31 and thus destroy *a·* supposed effect
28–32 drink *a·* deadly thing, — *Mark* 16 : 18.
29–13 and *a·* speculative theory.
30–26 for *a·* seeming mysticism
46– 8 *a·* doctrine previously entertained.
48–16 effect of alcohol, or of *a·* drug,
53–15 by *a·* compromise with matter ;
54–23 to *a·* disease whatsoever,
57– 5 of *a·* other creation?
58– 2 *does that disease have a· more power*
59–21 *A·* copartnership with that Mind
60– 2 *God does not recognize a·*,
69–27 I will send his address to *a·* one
72–16 not have occasion *a·* more — *Ezek.* 18 : 3.
74–23 *a·* supposition that matter is
78–10 than can science in *a·* other direction.
78–28 *a·* more than goodness,
79–29 Beware of joining *a·* medical league
87–19 I never commission *a·* one to
96–25 to give you *a·* conclusive idea
98– 1 making this question . . . of *a·* importance,
103–21 *A·* inference of the divine
108– 4 To allow sin of *a·* sort is
113–15 refuses to be influenced by *a·*
128–10 if there be *a·* virtue, — *Phil.* 4 : 8.
128–10 if there be *a·* praise, — *Phil.* 4 : 8.
137–10 if you had *a·* questions to propose,
144–32 more than *a·* other institution,
170–28 as having *a·* power to see.
178–17 * If *a·* one had said to me
179– 9 *a·* other consciousness than
194–32 to exclude all faith in *a·* other
197–16 *a·* historical event or person.
229– 1 *a·* one is liable to have them
229– 3 prepares one to have *a·* disease
229–18 neither shall *a·* plague — *Psal.* 91 : 10.
229–26 *a·* other possible sanative method ;
230– 3 more than upon *a·* other one thing.
230–23 * With a heart for *a·* fate ;
241–21 *a·* man's bondage to sin and
249– 6 drink *a·* deadly thing, — *Mark* 16 : 18.
256–10 from *a·* other than Mrs. Eddy,
259– 2 was not *a·* thing made." — *John* 1 : 3.
260–17 destroys *a·* suppositional
263– 6 to be found in *a·* language
266–19 New York, or *a·* other place,
272–14 * *a·* officer, agent, or servant
272–14 * of *a·* corporation or
272–16 * *a·* diploma or degree,
272–21 * such as *a·* stock company
272–22 * for *a·* secular purposes ;
283–13 *A·* exception to the old wholesome **rule,**
284– 4 more than *a·* other system
288–12 *a·* conclusion drawn therefrom
291–16 If *a·* are not partakers thereof,
304–13 * *a·* great patriotic celebration
306– 5 * *a·* ideas on that subject
308– 6 love or hatred or *a·* other cause
309– 1 the personal sense of *a·* one,
314–11 give out *a·* notices from the pulpit,
318–14 *A·* student, having received instructions
322–15 By *a·* personal presence, or word
337–32 Sin of *a·* sort tends to hide from
349–17 I claim no jurisdiction over *a·*

any

Mis.	351– 9	and would not if I could, harm *a·* one
	351–10	method of Mind-healing, or in *a·* manner.
	353– 9	concept of me, or of *a·* one,
	371–21	To sympathize in *a·* degree with
	380–25	*a·* outward form of practice.
Man.	28–25	It is the duty of *a·* member
	29– 3	or of *a·* other officer in this
	45–16	shall not be a member of *a·* church whose
	49– 3	in *a·* church or locality,
	50–23	violating *a·* of the By-Laws
	51– 8	*A·* member whom shall unjustly aggrieve
	62– 4	*a·* special hymn selected
	62– 9	Sunday School classes of *a·*
	62–14	Sunday School of *a·* Church of
	65–16	comply with *a·* written order,
	66–20	*a·* authority supposed to come
	73–10	students in *a·* university
	74– 5	or control over *a·* other church.
	77–24	*a·* possible future deviation from
	78– 2	If *a·* Director fails to heed
	78–19	not exceeding $200 for *a·* one
	91–15	*A·* surplus funds left in the
	92–17	in *a·* class in the
	95– 6	*a·* member of this Board
	97–20	or circulated literature of *a·* sort.
	100– 6	to *a·* Committee on Publication,
	100–17	*a·* Church of Christ, Scientist,
	100–23	and *a·* Committee so named
	102–16	land purchased for *a·* purpose
	104–17	if a discrepancy appears in *a·*
	105– 2	nor *a·* Tenet or By-Law
Ret.	14–17	*a·* profession of religion,
	14–21	not designate *a·* precise time.
	14–27	*a·* wicked way in me, — *Psal.* 139 : 24.
	25–26	to form *a·* proper conception
	27– 6	never been read by *a·* one but myself,
	40– 2	refusing to take *a·* pay
	50–13	*a·* real equivalent for my instruction
	60–29	*A·* attempt to divide these
	61–12	fear or suffering of *a·* sort.
	64– 9	Need it be said that *a·* opposite
	78–18	or *a·* name given to it other than
	82–29	clearer than *a·* previous edition,
	85– 6	*a·* other organic operative method
	85–15	*a·* deviation from the order
	89–22	*a·* precedent for employing
	89–27	*a·* action not first made known
Un.	5– 9	not to accept *a·* personal opinion
	5–13	frightened sense of *a·* need
	10– 6	*a·* previous teachers, save Jesus
	10– 8	If there be *a· monopoly* in my
	13–10	in ethics *a·* more than in music.
	13–15	If God has *a·* real knowledge of
	14– 5	Can it be seriously held, by *a·*
	19–16	without *a·* actuality which
	29–16	*a·* standpoint of their own.
	43– 3	for *a·* strong demonstration over
	48– 7	no faith in *a·* other thing or being.
	54– 7	becomes as tangible as *a·* reality.
	54–12	To admit that sin has *a·* claim
	54–14	if sin's claim be allowed in *a·* degree,
	64– 1	If sin has *a·* pretense of existence,
Pul.	21–20	the welfare of *a·* one.
	21–28	cannot come from *a·* other source.
	21–29	aught that can darken in *a·* degree
	23– 5	* Most Unique Structure in *A·* City
	24– 6	* most unique structure in *a·* city.
	28–16	* not differ widely from that of *a·* other
	32– 8	* not by *a·* crude self-assertion,
	32–13	* like *a·* abbess of old.
	36–17	* walked *a·* conceivable distance.
	37– 1	* *a·* information for *The Inter-Ocean,*"
	37–22	* depending on *a·* one personality.
	42– 8	* at *a·* one of these services.
	44–26	* without *a·* special appeal,
	44–28	* refused to accept *a·* further checks
	47–13	* without receiving *a·* real satisfaction.
	47–14	* *a·* distinct statement of the Science
	50–19	* *A·* new movement will awaken some
	50–28	* live down *a·* attempted repression.
	53–16	* "That word, more than *a·* other,
	58–17	* Scarcely *a·* wood-work is to be found.
	60– 4	* There was no address of *a·* sort.
	72–17	* "I have not taken *a·* medicine
	72–17	* or drugs of *a·* kind,
	72–22	* *a·* power other than that which
	75– 1	Whoever in *a·* age expresses
	75– 8	to think or speak of me in *a·* manner as
	87– 2	* *a·* services that may be held therein.
Rud.	5–14	If there is *a·* such thing as matter,
	6–15	* "*a·* metaphysical subtlety,"
	7– 2	Not . . . is Science, by *a·* means ;
	12–25	from *a·* sense of subordination
	16– 7	in *a·* branch of education.
	16–16	*A·* departure from Science is

any

No.	5–26	*A·* contradictory fusion of Truth with
	7– 5	*a·* root of bitterness to spring up
	7– 6	nor cause *a·* misapprehension
	10– 4	*a·* proof that can be given
	14–20	more than *a·* other religious sect,
	15– 6	would enable *a·* one to prove
	17–15	or *a·* mode of mortal mind,
	30– 9	*a·* more than the legislator need
	30–12	to rebuke *a·* claim of another law.
	30–17	if He possessed *a·* knowledge of
	32–10	chapter sub-title
	38–23	*a·* other state or stage of being.
Pan.	6– 4	will never disappear in *a·* other way.
'00.	6– 9	*A·* mystery in C. S. departs when
'01.	7–26	nor can they gain *a·* evidence of ·
	19–23	to *a·* susceptible misuse of
	27–13	If *a·* one as yet has healed
'02.	3– 8	to *a·* lingering sense of the
	6– 1	the thought of *a·* other reality,
	14–11	success possible for *a·* Christian
	14–15	on *a·* other foundation,
	20–18	breaking *a·* seeming connection
Hea.	1– 3	*drink a· deadly thing, — Mark* 16 : 18.
	5–14	Does *a·* one think the departed
	7–20	regardless of *a·* outward act,
	7–25	drink *a·* deadly thing, — *Mark* 16 : 18.
	9–15	a duty for *a·* one to believe that
	15–11	drink *a·* deadly thing, — *Mark* 16 : 18.
	15–12	to *a·* one's perfect satisfaction
Peo.	9–24	all evidence of *a·* other power
	12– 3	drink *a·* deadly thing, — *Mark* 16 : 18.
My.	8– 1	* *a·* portion of two million dollars
	9– 5	* *a·* portion of two million dollars
	10–18	* in *a·* particular,
	11–30	* "*a·* portion of two million dollars
	33–11	*a·* wicked way in me, — *Psal.* 139 : 24.
	41– 5	* nor in *a·* wise alter its effects.
	41–21	* unable to cherish *a·* enmity.
	41–25	* Why should *a·* one postpone his
	42–10	* so that *a·* further words
	48– 1	* drink *a·* deadly thing, — *Mark* 16 : 18.
	61–20	* never more did I have *a·* doubt.
	67–26	* surpass *a·* church edifice erected
	69–19	* view of the platform from *a·* seat.
	70– 7	* than *a·* other denomination
	71–18	* different from *a·* other church
	72–15	* do not send us *a·* more money
	74–15	* in this or *a·* other city,
	79–14	* in the world on *a·* occasion;
	81–26	* to give *a·* account of the
	83– 9	* or insignia of *a·* kind.
	91–18	* this country or *a·* other country
	93– 8	* to attract *a·* class save the
	98–12	* if they would deal . . . with *a·* effect.
	98–24	* to *a·* of the latter-day methods of
	98–25	* record is one of which *a·* church
	104–26	in this or *a·* other country.
	106– 1	than *a·* material method.
	118– 5	*a·* imaginary benefit they receive
	119–11	Buddhism or *a·* other "ism."
	146– 4	drink *a·* deadly thing, — *Mark* 16 : 18.
	148– 5	All that we ask of *a·* people is to
	163–11	pleasure of receiving *a·* of them.
	182– 3	*a·* other city in the United States.
	185– 5	* With a heart for *a·* fate ;
	202–10	Owe no man *a·* thing,
	220– 2	to this century or to *a·* epoch,
	223– 7	or to *a·* class of individual discords.
	223–22	which relate in *a·* manner to
	224–28	cannot afford to recommend *a·*
	242–23	nor to reply to *a·* received,
	244– 9	*a·* or all of you who are ready for it,
	249– 2	without harming *a·* one
	267– 8	*a·* thing made that was — *John* 1 : 3.
	269– 9	can they die *a·* more : — *Luke* 20 : 36.
	272–28	* for *a·* publications outside of
	299– 6	* "If they . . . have *a·* truth to reveal
	301–26	in *a·* manner whatever.
	303– 8	Catholics, or *a·* other sect.
	305–21	claim no special merit of *a·* kind.
	306– 5	or to dissever *a·* unity that may
	313–11	Nor do I remember *a·* such stuff
	318–18	not ask him *a·* questions.
	320–24	* without *a·* hesitation or restriction.
	321–10	* without *a·* restriction.
	323–11	* nor willingly leave *a·* false
	324– 5	* *a·* idea for your book,
	324– 7	* book to have come from *a·* one but
	324–16	* had *a·* other thought but that you
	324–31	* could have done so *a·* better.
	325–12	* in *a·* capacity in which I could
	333–16	* nor by *a·* Christian Scientists
	344–27	Were vaccination of *a·* avail,
	344–29	more dangerous than *a·* material
	345–17	pellets without *a·* medication

any
My. 346– 4   * puzzled by a· question,
346–23   * had in mind a· particular person
351–25   a· assertions to the contrary are
353–24   of a· special interest.
359–10   in a· other way than through
360–30   your healer, or a· earthly friend.
363–26   a· other individual but the
363–28   A· deviation from this direct
364– 5   A· departure from this golden rule
364–12   a· other cause or effect
    (see also **man, part, time, way**)

anybody
Mis. 80–10   A· and everybody, who
87–30   imagine they can help a·
325–21   that a· is animated with a purpose,

anything
Mis. 45–29   without Him was not a· made — John 1: 3.
61–24   A culprit, a sinner, — a· but a man !
68–13   that pain and sickness are a·
236–23   by a· that is said to you,
281– 8   nor give me a·,
367–15   to claim that He is ignorant of a· ;
379– 3   if he indited a· pathological
Un.   3–24   of a· unlike Himself ;
8– 4   *Is a· real of which the physical*
23–21   a· so wholly unlike Himself
'01.   5–24   a· that is real, good, or true ;
'02.   5–27   on the existence of a· which is
Hea. 18–18   never did a· for sickness
My. vi– 7   * knows a· about C. S. except
98– 6   * a· that its foes try to prove
321–13   * that he has ever said a· whatever of
323–10   * not going to lie about a·

anywhere
My. 69–18   * a· in the vast space
79–14   * seldom witnessed a· in the world
98–21   * no member of the church a·,
129– 1   see if there be found a· a

anywise
Man. 93–19   not allowed in a· to meddle with

apace
My. 224–32   Our Cause is growing a·

apart
Mis. 34–12   They are wholly a· from it.
57– 3   a· from the evidence of that
71–26   nothing can be formed a· from God,
123–31   far a· from physical sensation
125–24   A· from the common walks of
154–30   Have no . . . aim a· from holiness.
183–24   Asserting a selfhood a· from God,
186–21   a· from its fundamental basis.
196– 3   claim no mind a· from God.
200–24   a· from the personal senses.
333– 2   sin — yea, selfhood — is a· from God,
364–20   nothing a· from this Mind,
Ret. 20–27   A plot . . . for keeping us a·.
31–11   better than matter, and a· from it,
60– 1   as something a· from God,
95– 7   * may'st consecrated be And set a·
Pul. 59–28   * seats were especially set a· for
Rud.   5–10   considered a· from Mind.
No. 35–16   a supposed existence a· from God.
'01. 18–12   no remedy a· from Mind,
24– 1   * Matter a· from conscious mind is an
'02.   6– 3   law, a· or other than God
7– 2   no origin or causation a· from God.
Hea. 11– 5   man is seen wholly a· from
My.   3–13   C. S. is not a dweller a·
5– 7   Wholly a· from this mortal dream,
108– 6   I challenge matter to act a· from
108– 8   as it is seen to act a· from matter.
115– 6   were I, a· from God, its author.
118–29   entirely a· from limitations,
133–25   and we live a·.
166–15   we will live on and never drift a·.
167– 6   which is a· from matter,
189–17   there is no loyalty a· from love.
205–24   a· from human hypotheses,
225–19   sacredly holding His name a· from
273–19   utterly a· from a material or
274– 3   a· from the so-called life of matter
357– 2   materiality is wholly a· from C. S.,

apartment
Ret.   9– 2   led my cousin into an adjoining a·.
Pul. 29– 9   * The spacious a· was thronged
42–13   * a superb a· intended for
76– 3   * a· known as the "Mother's Room,"
76– 9   * alcoves are separated from the a·
My. 231–23   not an empty a· in his house,

apartments
Mis. 275–29   floral offerings sent to my a·
329– 8   various a· are dismally dirty.
Pul. 27– 1   * a·, with full-length French mirrors

apathy
Mis. 115– 4   astounded at the a· of some students
Pul. 14– 4   present a· as to the tendency of
'00.   8–17   mental idleness or a· is always
My. 233–20   for a·, dishonesty, sin, follow

ape
Ret. 63–22   * "The devil is but the a· of God."
No. 42–18   said that the devil is the a· of God.

apes
Mis. 294–18   thy offerings from asps and a·,

aphorisms
Mis. 316–21   tired a· and disappointed ethics ;
My. 291– 5   than a mere rehearsal of a·,

aping
Mis. 61– 7   a· the wisdom and magnitude of
No. 42–21   false claimants, a· its virtues,

Apocalypse
Un.   3– 9   of which we read in the A·
Pul. 27–23   * woman spoken of in the A·,
38–16   Genesis, A·, and Glossary.
No. 21– 2   the vision of the A·.

Apocalyptic
No. 27– 8   similitude of the A· pictures.

Apocryphal New Testament
Ret. 22– 6   essayed in the A· N· T·

Apollo
'00. 13–24   in the city of Thyatira was A·.
Peo.   4–23   pagan priests appointed A·

Apollyon
Mis. 190–29   in the Greek, A·, serpent, liar,

apologist
Mis. 227– 5   without friend and without a·.

apology
Mis. 119– 2   this were no a· for acting evilly.
134– 6   To reiterate such words of a·
Pan.   7–21   or a vague a· for contradictions.
'01. 28–18   my only a· for trying to follow it
My. 288– 5   incentive and sacrifice need no a·.

apostate
My. 131–13   a· praise return to its first love,

apostle (see also **apostle's**)
Mis. 46–21   what the a· meant by the
51–30   The a· James said,
77– 8   in those few words of the a·.
96–14   to the a· who declared it,
180–25   Here, the a· assures us that
181–23   The a· urges upon our acceptance
182–22   The a· indicates no personal plan
185–30   the a· first spake from their
186–28   As the a· proceeds in this line
188–12   but the a· says,
190–30   The a· Paul refers to this
200–11   a· Paul insists on the rare rule
200–21   the sweet sincerity of the a·,
255–13   recognition of what the a· meant
307–23   The a· saith, "Little — I John 5: 21.
368–20   in these words of the a·,
Ret. 54–16   belief cannot say with the a·,
Un.   1– 5   as the a· Peter declared
30–15   a· refers to the second Adam as
Pul.   6–29   renowned a· of anti-slavery,
81–24   * She is the a· of the true,
No. 39–10   Prophet and a· have glorified God
40– 1   The a· James said :
Pan. 10– 2   But what saith the a·?
'00. 13–10   the a· justly regards as heathen,
Peo.   5– 1   the a· devoutly recommends

apostle's
Mis. 128– 6   with the a· injunction :
328–27   observe the a· admonition,
Un. 21– 1   a· description of mental processes
No. v– 2   according to the a· admonition,
'02.   8– 1   it emphasizes the a· declaration,
9–11   and fulfilling the a· saying :
Hea.   5–24   but on the a· rule,

apostles
Mis. 23– 7   the a·, demonstrated a divine
40–10   same method . . . Jesus and the a· used,
179–24   These flowers are floral a·.
Ret. 22– 6   Writers less wise than the a·
Un. 10– 6   Jesus and his a·, who have thus
56–18   a· suffered from the thoughts of
Pul. 65– 2   * is not confined to its original a·
85–14   * of Jesus and the a·,
Peo.   5– 4   prophets and a·, whose lives are
Po. 25–10   Fair floral a· of love,
My. 103–25   and the lives of prophets and a·.
106–32   prophets and a· and the Christians
111–23   Were the a· absurd and
153–31   flowers should be to us His a·,

apostleship
  My. 191–14   will seal your *a*.

apostolic
  Mis. 245–26   and rejects *a·* Christianity,
  Ret. 43– 2   since the *a·* days.
  Pul. 54–11   * as were necessary in *a·* times.
  '00. 12–27   Revelation of St. John in the *a·* age

apothecary
  Peo. 6– 8   * physician, surgeon, *a·*,

apothegm
  Mis. ix– 1   *a·* of a Talmudical philosopher

apparel
  Mis. 373–17   soft raiment or gorgeous *a·* ;

apparent
  Mis. 48– 6   One thing is quite *a·* ;
  60–11   make the unreality of both *a·*
  191–17   evils, *a·* wrong traits,
  239–21   Her *a·* pride at sharing in
  Man. 95– 4   When the need is *a·*,
  100–12   becomes *a·* to the C. S. Board
  Ret. 64– 7   makes *a·*, the real man,
  81–13   genuine goodness become so *a·*
  Un. 63– 5   kingdom, not *a·* to material sense,
  No. 6–22   is more *a·* than the adverse
  '02. 3– 4   in the Orient are *a·*.
  My. 87– 6   * *a·* to the most casual observer.
  94–16   * the *a·* permanency of C. S.
  222–26   as God's government becomes *a·*,
  239–14   *and see their a· identity as*
  265– 7   more *a·* to reason ;
  266–11   This flux . . . so generally *a·*,
  306–10   purpose of making the true *a·*.

apparently
  Mis. 3–27   in *a·* deluding reason,
  241–13   big enough *a·* to neutralize
  378– 5   returned *a·* well,
  Ret. 14– 6   He was *a·* as eager to
  Hea. 12–28   divide one's faith *a·* between
  My. 50–18   * over the *a·* discouraging outlook
  78–30   * *a·* understanding all they heard,
  92–28   * due *a·* to nothing save the

apparition
  Pul. 34–16   and that it was my *a·*,"

appeal
  Mis. 179– 6   This *a·* resolves itself into
  253–23   should it not *a·* to human sympathy?
  Man. 60–19   *a·* to daily Christian endeavors
  Ret. 54– 7   and *a·* to God for relief through
  Un. 49– 5   simple *a·* to human consciousness.
  Pul. 41– 2   * an *a·*, not for more money, but
  44–26   * without any special *a·*,
  83– 7   * courage to prosecute the *a·*.
  Peo. 7–25   *a·* to mind to improve its subjects
  My. 3–11   *a·* to reformers,
  10–15   * No *a·* has ever been made in
  32– 6   * in a heartfelt *a·* to the creator.
  90–14   * it is not the only source of *a·*.
  108–17   divine Mind is the sovereign *a·*,
  132–14   no longer to *a·* to human strength,
  219–31   *a·* to the gospel to save him from
  270–22   *a·* to Him as my witness to the truth
  316–17   dignified, eloquent *a·* to the press

appealed
  My. 29–15   * that *a·* more to the eye,
  29–21   * *a·* to and fired the imagination.
  86–16   * *a·* to his brethren to give no more
  288–19   He never *a·* to matter

appeals
  Mis. 63–25   *a·* to its hope and faith,
  105– 2   C. S., which *a·* intelligently to
  252–18   It *a·* to man as man ;
  Pul. 83– 5   * and *a·* from Philip drunk to
  '01. 35– 7   *a·* loudly to those asleep
  My. 153–20   *a·* to an unknown power
  180–13   It *a·* alone to God,
  260–26   *a·* to all conditions,

appear
  Mis. 56–19   will *a·* at the full revelation
  57–13   the postulate of error must *a·*.
  76–28   "When Christ, . . . shall *a·*,— *Col.* 3 : 4.
  76–29   shall ye also *a·*— *Col.* 3 : 4.
  78–22   C. S. will some time *a·*
  86– 5   but it doth not yet *a·*.
  97–31   hence, it doth not *a·*
  144– 9   subscription list on which *a·*
  175–11   and when this shall *a·*,
  196–21   Life that is God, good, shall *a·*,
  213–19   God's universal kingdom will *a·*,
  217–30   must *dis*appear, for Spirit to *a·*.
  229– 3   whenever there a *a·*
  232–13   next to *a·* as its divine origin.
  236–29   whatever else may *a·*,

appear
  Mis. 250–18   Unless these *a·*, I cast aside the
  252–12   and they should *a·* thus.
  285–28   may *a·* in the *rôle* of a superfine
  340–32   sickness, sin, and death still *a·*
  343–18   their pure perfection shall *a·*
  386– 2   Beyond the shadow, infinite *a·*
  Man. 47–21   testimonials which *a·* in the
  98– 9   desirable that this correction shall *a·*,
  Un. 40–21   Death can never alarm or even *a·*
  41–19   and when this Life shall *a·*
  41–27   these phenomena *a·* to go on
  49–18   One should *a·* real to us,
  49–20   * we make "the worse *a·* the better
  51– 1   everlasting facts of being *a·*,
  62–12   Then shall it *a·* that the true ideal
  No. 31– 6   *a·* to-day in subtler forms
  '00. 8–13   takes it off for his poverty to *a·*.
  Peo. 8–23   Then shall C. S. again *a·*,
  Po. 49– 4   Beyond the shadow, infinite *a·*
  My. 22–26   * *a·* in their proper perspective.
  92– 6   * makes it *a·* that Science
  110–10   and the daystar will *a·*,
  154–17   the new-old vesture in which to *a·*
  227– 7   but when charity does *a·*,
  265–15   *a·* full-orbed in millennial glory ;
  329–16   * as they *a·* in that paper

appearance
  Mis. 46– 7   adapted to destroy the *a·* of evil
  68– 5   include also man's changed *a·*
  147–25   He assumes no borrowed *a·*.
  379– 8   descriptive of the general *a·*,
  Pul. 58–12   * Its *a·* is shown in the pictures
  Rud. 1–17   in distinction from one's *a·*
  My. 69– 7   * presenting an oval and dome *a·*
  100–12   * since the C. S. sect made its *a·*
  195–12   under an *a·* of indifference.
  234– 5   they give the *a·* of personal worship

appeared
  Mis. 123–21   at-one-ment with Christ has *a·*
  164– 6   has *a·* in the ripeness of time,
  164–12   spiritual idea . . . *a·* as a star.
  214– 3   it *a·* hate to the carnal mind,
  216– 8   there *a·* a review of,
  239–17   sweet face *a·* in the vestibule,
  280– 2   Mind spake and form *a·*.
  359–22   period in which he personally *a·* ;
  Ret. 25– 6   Their spiritual signification *a·* ;
  38–12   As it afterwards *a·*,
  93– 3   Christ, or the spiritual idea, *a·*
  Un. 59–14   Jesus *a·* as a child,
  61– 5   Jesus first *a·* as a helpless
  Pul. 33–19   * suddenly *a·* at his side,
  83–27   * there *a·* a great wonder— *Rev.* 12 : 1.
  No. 36–26   in which he *a·* at his birth.
  '01. 27–10   nothing has since *a·* that is
  Hea. 17–23   *a·* through the false supposition of
  Po. vi– 8   * *a·* in a *Lynn, Mass., newspaper,*
  vi–25   * which *a·* in various publications
  My. 48–15   * *a·* in the *Methodist Review*
  138–26   * personally *a·* Mary Baker Eddy
  173– 2   * following letter *a·* in the
  232–10   *A·* IN THE C. S. SENTINEL,
  246–21   of the spirit and the Word *a·*,
  315–16   * personally *a·* R. D. Rounsevel
  319–19   * questions which have recently *a·*,
  329–11   * which *a·* in the *Wilmington*
  334–27   * obituary which *a·* in 1845
  346–19   * recent interview which *a·* in
  359–17   * *a·* under the heading "None good but

appearing
  Mis. 1– 3   Chaldee watched the *a·* of a star ;
  17–22   human birth is the *a·* of a mortal,
  33–10   *a·* in the womanhood as well as
  73–28   It is the *a·* of divine law
  76–30   Science of Soul, Spirit, involves this *a·*,
  114–19   sin, *a·* in its myriad forms :
  161–15   the *a·* of this dual nature,
  165– 7   The last *a·* of Truth will be a
  165–10   The daystar of this *a·* is the
  168–19   "We behold the *a·* of the star!"
  320– 7   Christ's *a·* in a fuller sense
  320–18   shall be the sign of his *a·*
  338– 1   *a·* of good in an individual
  373–15   delineates Christ's *a·* in the flesh,
  Ret. 70–20   The second *a·* of Jesus is,
  Un. 63– 2   interpreted this *a·* as a risen
  63– 7   so-called *a·*, disappearing, and
  Pan. 1–16   waiteth patiently the *a·*
  '00. 7–18   and hath Christ a second *a·*?
  7–29   wait for the full *a·* of Christ
  Po. vi– 1   * *a·*, . . . *in a book "Gems for You,"*
  My. 74–21   * intelligent and a happy *a·* body,
  103–11   In every age and at its every *a·*,
  185– 2   waited patiently for the *a·* of

appearing
My. 262–30 my conception of Truth's *a.*

appears
Mis. 14–21 What *a.* to mortals from their
15–25 the stature of man in Christ *a.*
41–20 produces all harmony that *a.*
77–30 where the miracle of grace *a.*,
105–24 Nothing *a.* to the physical senses but
147–27 is indeed what he *a.* to be,
165–16 perfect and eternal, *a.*
188–7 that which *a.* second, material, and
259–3 Whatever *a.* to be law,
276–22 and the bridegroom *a.*
291–12 at least it so *a.* in results.
371–14 he who deprecates their condition *a.* to,
Man. 104–17 if a discrepancy *a.* in any
Un. 25–10 and hence, whatever it *a.* to say
32–23 Here it *a.* that a *liar* was
38–18 is all that dies, or *a.* to die.
41–26 *a.* to both live and die,
Pul. 45–27 * This action, it *a.*, was
No. 6–24 has shown that what *a.* real,
24–20 Then *a.* the grand verity of C. S.:
Po. 16–3 hopeful though winter *a.*.
My. 25–27 divinity *a.* in all its promise.
94–5 * evidence *a.* in the concrete

appease
Mis. 123–12 to *a.* the anger of a so-called god
No. 35–11 It was not to *a.* the wrath of God,

appeased
Peo. 3–8 to be *a.* by the sacrifice and

appeases
Un. 15–26 as a criminal *a.*, with a money-bag,

appellative
Man. 64–20 this *a.* in the Church meant
'00. 3–24 contained this divine *a.*
My. 236–17 this *a.* seals the question of
302–15 the endearing *a.* ''Mother,''

append
Pul. 88–8 can *a.* only a few of the names

appendages
Mis. 17–9 lay aside your material *a.*,

appended
Mis. x–13 a few articles are herein *a.*.

appetite
Mis. 37–22 *a.* for alcohol yields to Science
71–4 an *a.* for alcoholic drink
71–5 saved many . . . from this fatal *a.*.
137–24 control *a.*, passion, pride, envy,
209–19 tend to rebuke *a.* and
297–8 destroys the *a.* for alcoholic drinks.
Ret. 65–11 gratification of *a.* and passion,
Po. 32–16 As reason with *a.*, pleasures deny,

appetites
Mis. 36–13 *A.*, passions, anger, revenge,
114–20 passion, *a.*, hatred, revenge,
231–7 rich viands made busy many *a.*;
240–22 Passions, *a.*, pride, selfishness,
296–28 and the bad *a.* of men
324–15 *A.* and passions have
Pan. 10–29 Sin, sickness, *a.*, and passions,
'00. 6–21 which destroys his false *a.*
'01. 27–19 habits and *a.* of mankind corrected,
30–22 or by the stress of the *a.*
Hea. 18–22 Pride, *a.*, passions, envy, and
My. 339–28 Silence *a.*, passion, and all that

appetizing
Mis. 275–29 and the fare is *a.*.

applause
Mis. 325–9 puffed up with the *a.* of the world:

apple
Mis. 22–28 A falling *a.* suggested to Newton
Ret. 24–14 was the falling *a.* that led me to
Rud. 8–1 No rock brings forth an *a.*;

apples
Mis. 346–23 like *a.* of gold — *Prov.* 25 : 11.
Ret. 4–15 orchards of *a.*, peaches, pears,

appliances
Mis. 243–10 removed these *a.* the same day
Pul. 9–9 whose *a.* warm this house,

applicable
Mis. 3–9 *a.* to all the needs of man.
29–4 Had it been *a.* only to his
138–20 My counsel is *a.* to the
200–13 *a.* to every stage and state of
259–29 *a.* to all the needs of man.
'02. 4–23 *a.* to all periods — past, present,
My. 19–30 These are *a.* words:
238–21 and *a.* to every human need.
302–18 name is not *a.* to me.

applicant
Mis. 256–18 send to each *a.* a notice
Man. 34–7 *a.* must be a believer in the
36–23 admit said *a.* to membership.
37–5 properly filled out by an *a.*.
37–10 shall send to the *a.* a notice of
109–17 the *a.* will be notified,
111–5 If the *a.* is a married woman
112–8 If the *a.* is not a member of a

applicants
Man. 35–16 evidence of the loyalty of the *a.*.
35–17 *A.* for membership who have not
38–9 *A.* for membership in this Church,
89–10 *a.* AND GRADUATES.
109–11 Those who approve *a.* should
109–13 after being filled out by the *a.*,
110–10 All names, whether of *a.*, . . . or
111–1 heading
111–14 *A.* will find the chief points of
Ret. 47–8 *a.* were rapidly increasing.

application
Mis. 25–10 in its direct *a.* to human needs.
38–19 *a.* to benefit the race,
44–9 and its *a.* direct.
170–21 the spiritual *a.* bears upon
216–1 in your *a.* of his words
289–10 at present the *a.* of scientific rules
298–13 special *a.* to Christian Scientists;
375–18 * conscientious *a.* to detail,
Man. 37–3 nor countersign an *a.* for membership
37–7 If an *a.* for membership with
38–7 the *a.* must be countersigned by
39–2 and make *a.* for membership
72–12 proper *a.* made in accordance with
73–16 may become members . . . by *a.* to,
111–2 In filling out the *a.* blank,
111–9 two regular forms of *a.*.
111–21 furnished special forms on *a.* to
112–9 fill out his *a.* . . . according to
113–1 heading
Ret. 36–1 its *a.* in all time to those who
Pul. 31–5 * present *a.* of the principles
'01. 27–12 The *a.* of C. S. is healing and
Peo. 12–22 proved the *a.* of its Principle
My. 41–22 * brings into present and hourly *a.*
103–18 C. S. and its *a.* to the treatment of
146–20 their present *a.* to mankind,
328–24 * *a.* for license was made

applications
Mis. 273–23 one hundred and sixty *a.*
Man. 35–3 whose *a.* are countersigned by
35–9 *a.* FOR MEMBERSHIP.
35–10 *A.* for membership with
36–4 *A.* for membership with
36–17 refuse to endorse their *a.*
36–24 All *a.* for membership must be
37–1 Endorsing *A.*.
38–10 whose *a.* are correctly prepared,
39–6 their *a.* shall be void.
71–7 nor written on *a.* for membership
109–2 *A.* for Church Membership.
109–6 eligible to countersign *a.*
109–12 should have *a.* returned to them
109–18 new *a.* will be required,
110–3 prevent *a.* being duplicated
111–19 whose teachers refuse, . . . to sign *a.*
Ret. 47–7 *a.* from persons desiring to

applied
Mis. 180–28 This term, as *a.* to man,
353–14 a man who *a.* for work,
Pul. 46–23 * *a.* herself, like other girls,
54–17 * *a.* it where the greatest good could
'00. 5–10 *A.* to Deity, Father and Mother are
My. 30–29 * *a.* for admission at the ten o'clock
135–6 declaration may be *a.* to old age,
162–13 *a.* to building, embellishing, and

applies
Mis. 203–14 medicine *a.* it physically,
Man. 32–24 This By-Law *a.* to Readers in all
47–21 This By-Law *a.* to testimonials which
65–17 *a.* to their official functions.
99–15 By-Law *a.* to all States except
Rud. 1–16 Blackstone *a.* the word *personal* to
My. 180–8 healing Christianity which *a.* to all
250–18 By-law *a.* only to C. S. churches in

apply
Mis. 39–1 Many who *a.* for help are
69–28 *a.* to him for information about
Man. 36–19 *a.* to the Clerk of this Church,
89–10 may *a.* to the Board of Education
95–10 may *a.* through their clerks
98–10 *a.* for aid to the Committee
102–16 this rule shall not *a.* to

apply

Ret.	59–11	even as mortals *a·* finite terms to God,
Un.	12– 4	*a·* to the waiting grain the
Pul.	51– 5	* *a·* themselves to a matter like
'01.	27– 7	* *a·* them more rationally to human
My.	220– 6	as to *a·*, on the basis of C. S.,
	230– 9	rules *a·* not to one member only,

applying

Mis.	44–28	*a·* this mental remedy or antidote
Man.	88–18	*a·* for admission to this Board
Ret.	59–10	then *a·* this rule to a
Un.	27–12	*A·* these distinctions to evil and
'01.	1–23	by feeling and *a·* the nature and

appoint

Mis.	335–10	*a·* him his portion — *Matt.* 24 : 51.
Man.	29–13	shall *a·* five suitable members
	69–16	*a·* a proper member of this Church
	94–16	shall *a·* a Circuit Lecturer.
	96– 2	not *a·* a lecture for Wednesday
	99– 1	*a·* a Committee on Publication
	99– 9	*a·* a Committee on Publication
	99–12	can *a·* a Committee on Publication
	100– 5	Readers shall *a·* said candidate.
	100–18	*a·* another Committee to fill the
	101– 5	*a·* an assistant manager,
My.	339–25	but he did not *a·* a fast.

appointed

Man.	17–14	Mrs. Eddy was *a·* on the committee
	76–18	Its members shall be *a·* annually
	97– 4	shall be *a·* by The Mother Church
	99–20	*a·* by the C. S. Board of Directors,
	99–26	*a·* by the First and Second Readers
Ret.	21– 3	a guardian was *a·* him,
	21–11	was *a·* United States Marshal
	32– 1	its divinely *a·* human mission,
Pul.	29–12	* Before the *a·* hour every seat in
No.	7–18	God has *a·* for Christian Scientists
'01.	19– 2	prayer is a divinely *a·* means of
Peo.	3–28	way that our Lord has *a·* ;
	4–23	pagan priests *a·* Apollo
My.	49–13	* Mrs. Eddy was *a·* on the committee
	340– 2	no record of his observing *a·* fasts.

appointee

Man.	69–17	*a·* shall go immediately

appointing

Mis.	208–19	in the way of God's *a·*.

appointment

Mis.	215–16	in the way of His *a·*,
Man.	80–19	the right to fill the same by *a·* ;
	99–24	*A·*.
My.	223– 3	without previous *a·* by letter.
	283– 1	chapter sub-title
	283– 6	Your *a·* of me as *Fondateur*
	310–13	*a·* on the staff of the Governor of

appointments

My.	143–13	by those with whom I have *a·*.

appoints

Mis.	130–30	God anoints and *a·* to
Chr.	53–11	The Way in Science He *a·*,
Ret.	90–30	He *a·* and He anoints His

appreciable

My.	107–14	without harm and without *a·* effect.

appreciate

Mis.	165–20	can neither *a·* nor appropriate his
	317– 6	to *a·* the signs of the times ;
Ret.	73–13	fail to *a·* individual character.
Pul.	87–15	I fully *a·* your kind intentions.
'00.	3–12	workers who *a·* a life,
My.	149–21	to *a·* or to demonstrate Christian
	174– 5	I greatly *a·* the courtesy
	194–22	I deeply *a·* it,
	323–27	* may not have been able to *a·*

appreciated

Mis.	88–11	whose thought is *a·* by many
	305–20	* will be particularly *a·*
	365–31	To be *a·*, it must be . . . understood
Pul.	10–21	If you are less *a·* to-day
No.	11–14	To be *a·*, Science must be understood
'00.	7–12	loved the Bible and *a·* its worth
'01.	1– 8	better *a·*, than ever before,
My.	26–14	unexpected . . . but not the less *a·*.
	61–31	* I *a·* as never before the faithful,
	330–11	* are *a·* by all,

appreciating

'02.	20–23	while gratefully *a·* the privilege

appreciation

Mis.	224–19	*a·* of everything beautiful,
	263–28	without credit, *a·*, or
Pul.	85–26	* the *a·* of her labors
My.	37– 9	* *a·* of all that you have done
	48–15	* splendid *a·* of her efforts
	51–26	* *a·* of Mrs. Eddy's tireless labors,

appreciation

My.	51–31	* *a·* of her earnest endeavors,
	62–23	* thankful *a·* of your wise counsel,
	176– 3	In *A·* of a Gift of Fifty Dollars
	197–11	*a·* of your labor and success
	316–24	sound *a·* of the rights of

apprehend

Ret.	28–10	in order to *a·* Spirit.
	88–12	*a·* the living beauty of Love,
Un.	43–23	enable us to *a·*, or lay hold upon,
Pul.	35–14	in order to *a·* Spirit.
Rud.	6–24	The proof of what you *a·*,
No.	v–13	*a·* the pure spirituality of Truth.
Peo.	3–21	begins wrongly to *a·* the infinite,
My.	282–13	to *a·* more, we must practise

apprehended

Mis.	65–20	*a·* by those who understand my
Ret.	25– 6	and I *a·* for the first time,
Un.	1–12	so little *a·* and demonstrated by
	43–25	"*a·* of . . . Christ Jesus," — *Phil.* 3 : 12.
Pul.	35– 1	I *a·* the spiritual meaning
No.	20– 9	may seem distant . . . until better *a·*.
'00.	6– 5	not myself to have *a·* : — *Phil.* 3 : 13.
'01.	7–25	He cannot be *a·* through
My.	90–29	* can be readily *a·*.

apprehending

Mis.	261–27	*a·* the moral law so clearly

apprehends

Un.	40–27	A sense material *a·* nothing
	58–13	*a·* Christ as "the way." — *John* 14 : 6.

apprehensible

Ret.	26–13	divinely natural and *a·* ;

apprehension

Mis.	74– 6	a new *a·* of the true basis
	139–28	in advance of the erring mind's *a·*.
	201– 2	beyond the common *a·* of sinners ;
	363–31	a more spiritual *a·* of the
Ret.	26–30	to the *a·* of the age.
	30–13	necessary to the right *a·* of
	32– 2	bearing . . . to my *a·*,
	47– 1	The *a·* of what has been,
	79– 4	nor cometh this *a·* from the
	81–17	blunders which arise from wrong *a·*.
Un.	5– 6	will increase their *a·* of God,
	7– 1	will be magnified in the *a·* of
	17–15	A right *a·* of the wonderful
	61–13	toward the *a·* of its nothingness,
'01.	11– 5	has risen to human *a·*,
	14–28	scientific *a·* of this grand verity.
My.	183–12	Spiritual *a·* unfolds, transfigures,

approach

Mis.	30–29	as we *a·* spirituality,
	180–13	shuddered at her material *a·* ;
	233–28	some fall short, others will *a·* it ;
	352–12	lengthen as they *a·* the light,
Un.	4– 3	*a·* Him and become like Him.
	13– 5	Men must *a·* God reverently,
	57– 4	warn mortals of the *a·* of danger
No.	16–24	in proportion as mortals *a·* Spirit,
'00.	4– 9	nearer *a·* to monotheism
'01.	14–23	against the *a·* of thieves.
Hea.	16–25	through which it is impossible to *a·*
Peo.	7–31	must spiritualize to *a·* Him,
My.	93–18	* prone to *a·* it in a spirit of
	178–29	nearest *a·* to the sayings of

approached

Pul.	26–20	* The "Mother's Room" is *a·* by
	76– 4	* *a·* through a superb archway of
'02.	15–13	*a·* the mythical.

approaches

Mis.	2–17	time *a·* when divine Life,
	363– 1	an erring so-called mind *a·*
Pul.	25–15	* and marble *a·*
	27– 3	* in marble *a·* and rich carving,
	49–28	* the visitor as he *a·* Pleasant View.
My.	344–15	gradual *a·* to Soul's perfection."

approaching

Mis.	321–28	offered upon this *a·* occasion.
'01.	28– 2	*a·* the last stage of the

approbation

Mis.	214–27	in the recognition or *a·* of it.
My.	166– 3	will continue with divine *a·*.

appropriate

Mis.	165–20	can neither appreciate nor *a·* his
	263–28	*a·* my ideas and discovery,
	280–23	who in *a·* language and metaphor
	304– 6	* the most *a·* place
	358– 6	the only *a·* seals for C. S.
Man.	61–20	of an *a·* religious character
Pul.	28–10	* in *a·* decorative effect.
My.	24–31	* could be no more *a·* time for
	80–17	* an *a·* reading from the Bible,

appropriate

My. 85–28 * in its symmetrical and a· design.
169–19 I was rejoiced at the a· beauty of
259–27 most a· and proper exercise.
281–19 * seems to offer an a· occasion for

appropriated

Mis. 150–26 God is universal ; . . . . a· by no sect.
249– 8 false report that I have a· other
Ret. 51– 4 to be a· for the erection,
My. 158– 1 to be a· in building a granite

appropriates

Mis. 203–15 metaphysics a· it topically as

appropriating

Mis. 299–32 does it justify you in a· them,
Ret. 75– 7 a· my language and ideas,

approval

Mis. 262–27 little need of words of a·
383– 4 met with the universal a·
Man. 25– 9 a· of the Pastor Emeritus.
28– 2 the a· of the Pastor Emeritus.
35–20 only by a· from students of
36–11 shall have the a· and signature of
63–22 the a· of Mary Baker Eddy.
65–24 the a· of Mary Baker Eddy.
78–14 the a· of Mary Baker Eddy.
78–26 shall be reported, . . . for their a·.
79–14 to Mrs. Eddy for her written a·.
80–21 subject to her a·.
85–21 a· of The C. S. Board of Directors.
88–15 a· of the Pastor Emeritus.
89– 8 on receiving her a· shall be elected
93– 7 subject to the a· of the
101– 4 with the a· of the Pastor Emeritus,
No. 40– 5 receive, a material sense of a· ;
'00. 13–30 being bidden to write the a· of
My. 36– 5 * rose as one to indicate their a·
142–11 Accept my thanks for your a· of
230–18 I read with pleasure your a·
359–25 * with the latter's unqualified a·.

approve

Man. 38– 1 qualified to a· for membership
109– 4 are eligible to a· candidates
109–11 Those who a· applicants should
My. 240–24 * Does Mrs. Eddy a· of class teaching :
358–30 a· the By-laws of The Mother Church,

approved

Man. 26–22 after the candidate is a· by
35– 3 who are a·, and whose applications
94–17 His term of office, if a·,
My. 49–22 * minutes . . . were read and a·.
245– 1 over and above the a· schools of

approver

Man. 38– 5 If the a· is not a loyal student

approvers

Man. 110–10 applicants, a·, or countersigners,

approves

Man. 82– 1 a·, and publishes the books and
My. 240–18 a· or disapproves according to

approximate

Un. 64–10 The nearer we a· to such a Mind,
Pul. 22–12 a· the understanding of C. S.
52– 6 * a faith a· to that of these
No. 38–17 as mortals a· the understanding of
My. 58– 1 * a faith a· to that of these

approximately

My. 96–19 * cost a· two million dollars.

approximates

Mis. 374–22 the one illustrating my poem a· it.
My. 31–11 * which a· two millions of dollars,

approximation

Mis. 161–12 Jesus' a· to this state of being

A Priest of the Church

My. 299– 3 signature "A P· of the C·,"

April

(see months)

April's

(see months)

apt

Mis. 155–25 I shall be a· to forward their letters
279– 6 too a· to weep with those who weep,
287–29 and he will be a· to please you ;
300–31 more a· to recover than he who
371–17 self-interest in this mixing is a· to
'00. 3–16 Adam-race are not a· to worship the
'01. 25– 6 is a· to be the cross,
My. 224– 9 not a· to be correctly drawn.
328–12 * a· also to be pleased with the fact

aptness

Mis. 264–16 a· to assimilate pure and abstract

Araby

Mis. 110– 2 The costly balm of A·,

Arbiter

Un. 30–27 reflect the Life of the divine A·.

arbiter

Mis. 83–16 you are the a· of your own fate,
152–12 as a dictator, a·, or ruler,

arbitrary

Mis. 148–11 not a· opinions nor dictatorial
Man. 3– 7 not a· opinions nor dictatorial
My. 49– 6 * and control, in no a· sense,

arbitrated

My. 286– 8 should be, a· wisely, fairly ;

arbitration

My. 281–25 * advancement of the cause of a·."
284–26 to conciliate by a· all quarrels

arbutus

Mis. 329–23 paint in pink the petals of a·,

archers

Mis. 277– 9 a· aim at Truth's mouthpiece ;

arches

My. 46– 1 * in symmetrical a·,
68– 5 * supported on four a·
68–26 * plaster work for the great a·
78– 9 * a· in the several facades.

archipelago

Mis. 368–16 upas-tree in the eastern a·.

architect

Mis. 41–19 Mind is the a· that builds its own
My. 16–19 * a· and the builder of the new
71–28 * aim and object of the a· :
89– 8 * a· has joined lightness and grace

architectural

Pul. 9–13 quibbled over an a· exigency,
65–19 * whose a· construction and
My. 67–21 * marvel of a· beauty.
68–22 * It has an a· stone screen
74–15 * one of the finest a· achievements
84–14 * crown for the other a· efforts
85–17 * among the a· beauties of
86– 2 * unaccustomed to fine a· effects,
88–13 * a· symbolisms of aspiration

architecturally

My. 87–18 * an edifice so handsome a·.

architecture

Pul. 24–24 * The a· is Romanesque throughout.
My. 31–17 * beauty and the grace of the a·.
71– 7 * chapter sub-title
71–10 * a stunning piece of a·
71–18 * For in its interior a· it is
71–20 * traditions of church interior a·
72– 3 * traditions of interior church a·.
77– 2 * its great size, beautiful a·,
309–23 * building of rudimentary a·."
309–25 style of a· at that date.

archway

Pul. 76– 4 * superb a· of Italian marble

Arctic

Pul. 76–16 * brought from the A· regions.

Arcturus

Mis. 174–12 Above A· and his sons,

ardent

Ret. 90–19 like the a· mother
Pul. 73– 5 * an a· follower after God.

ardently

My. 50– 5 * labored faithfully and a·,

arduous

Hea. 14–18 most a· task I ever performed.
My. v–19 * years of a· preliminary labor,
51–31 * earnest endeavors, her a· labors,

area

My. 67– 9 * A· of site . . . 40,000 sq. ft.

areas

Ret. 4–21 covered a· of rich acres,

argue

Mis. 31– 4 To mentally a· in a manner that
31–18 a· against his own convictions of
Hea. 10–20 a· with yourself on the side of
10–23 or to a· stronger for sorrow than

argued

My. 160–22 Physical science has sometimes a·

argues

'01. 24– 3 a· that matter is not *without* the

arguing

Mis. 119–12 always be found a· for itself,
Un. 21– 5 perpetually a· with ourselves ;
Hea. 1–12 before a· with the world
My. 6– 1 a· for the plaintiff in favor of

argument

Mis.	32– 1	with his wrong *a*,
	59–18	*Is not all a· mind over mind?*
	116–21	The ultimate . . . is not an *a*· :
	119–18	not an *a*· either for pessimism or
	220– 6	The healer begins by mental *a*·.
	221– 3	by a false mental *a*· ;
	222–15	The malicious mental *a*
	319– 5	closes the *a*· of aught besides Him,
	350–23	soundness of the *a*· used.
	352–25	or he must, through *a*· and
	359– 5	you continue the mental *a*· in
Ret.	21–30	*a*·, with its rightful conclusions,
Un.	20–10	By a reverse process of *a*·
Rud.	9–22	an audible or even a mental *a*·,
'01.	3–20	* but this is no *a*· that Love is
Hea.	7–28	it contains no *a*· for a creed
My.	318–27	continued with a long *a*·,

arguments

Mis.	12–22	human mind in its silent *a*·,
	220– 9	His mental and oral *a*· aim to
	350–26	I issue no *a*·,
	350–29	such *a*· only as promote health
	351– 6	*a*· which, perverted, are
Un.	9–14	their *a*· and conclusions as to
	33– 1	lesser *a*· which prove matter to be
My.	211–13	by unseen, silent *a*·.

aright

Mis.	51–18	they will lead him *a*· :
	84–28	and teaches Life's lessons *a*·.
	108–12	hence the utility of knowing evil *a*·,
	116–13	filling the measures of life's music *a*·,
	125–15	"to know *a*· is Life eternal,"
	177–20	and answer *a*· !
	235–20	learn God *a*·, and know
	235–23	must start the wheels of reason *a*·,
	299– 4	The error that is seen *a*· as error,
	352– 3	quickened to behold *a*· the error,
Un.	14– 4	it was not at first done *a*·.
Pul.	69–23	* must understand these laws *a*·.
No.	40–22	and control *a*· the thought
'02.	17– 7	When mortals learn to love *a*· ;
Peo.	6–16	when we learn God *a*·,
My.	43– 6	* to order *a*· the affairs of daily life.
	193– 2	Him whom to know *a*· is life
	203– 4	Pray *a*· and demonstrate your prayer ;
	248–22	to conceive God *a*· you must be good.
	261–12	mould *a*· the first impressions

arise

Mis.	196–26	*a*· to spiritual recognition of being,
	215– 7	*A*·, let us go hence ; — *John* 14 : 31.
	303–12	therefore no queries should *a*·
Man.	66– 8	*a*· among the members
Ret.	11–15	Hero and sage *a*· to show
	81–17	which *a*· from wrong apprehension.
Un.	52–18	From this falsehood *a*· the
Pul.	53–13	* "*A*·, go thy way : — *Luke* 17 : 19.
Rud.	10– 9	These beliefs *a*· from the subjective
No.	4–21	they do not *a*· from the
	45–11	*a*· from a spiritual lack,
'01.	27– 6	* I look to see some St. Paul *a*·
'02.	9– 9	Truth will *a*· in human thought
Peo.	8–22	I say unto thee, *a*·." — *Mark* 5 : 41.
·Po.	60–12	Hero and sage *a*· to show
	79–10	darkling sense, *a*·, go hence !
My.	183–26	"*A*·, shine ; for thy light — *Isa.* 60 : 1.
	359–27	Awake and *a*· from this temptation

arisen

My.	321–18	* circumstances which have *a*·
	346–23	* Various conjectures having *a*· as to

arises

Mis.	59–23	*a*· from the success that one
Ret.	60–30	*a*· .rom the fallibility of sense,
Un.	8–15	*a*· from their deleterious effects,
No.	5– 9	Disease *a*· from a false and material

arising

Mis.	24–32	supposed effect *a*· from false claims
Ret.	47– 9	had shown the dangers *a*· from
My.	335–20	* excitement which was fast *a*·,

aristocracy

My.	72– 8	* members of the titled *a*·

aristocratic

Pul.	46–12	* *A*· to the backbone,

Aristotle

Mis.	226–18	*A*· was asked what a person could

arithmetic

My.	8–18	* my faint knowledge of *a*·
	311–31	* reached long division in *a*·,"

ark

Mis.	92–28	attempting to steady the *a*· of Truth,
Ret.	84–16	attempting to steady the *a*· of Truth,
No.	20–25	emerged from the *a*·.

ark

My.	188– 9	your *a*· of the covenant will

Arlington, Massachusetts

Mis.	225– 2	Mr. Rawson, of *A*·, *M*·,

arm

Mis.	114–18	They cannot *a*· too thoroughly
	183–21	He to whom the *a*· of the Lord is
	389–13	His *a*· encircles me, and mine,
Un.	39–10	He to whom the *a*· of the Lord is
Pul.	7–15	with His outstretched *a*·.
No.	32–13	Mind-healing lifts with a steady *a*·,
	44–22	through the civil *a*· of government,
Pan.	14–17	right *a*· of His righteousness.
'01.	1– 5	never lack God's outstretched *a*·
'02.	14–26	outstretched *a*· of infinite Love
Peo.	8–20	controls the muscles of the *a*·.
Po.	4–12	His *a*· encircles me, and mine,
My.	42–30	* with an outstretched *a*·" — *Deut.* 26 : 8.
	355–11	strong supporting *a*· to religion

Armageddon

Mis.	177– 5	The great battle of *A*· is upon us.

armament

Un.	6–27	manual of their spiritual *a*·.
My.	127–25	Unlike Russia's *a*·, ours is
	286–11	*a*· of navies is necessary,
	355–14	the untiring spiritual *a*·.

armaments

Mis.	xii– 2	privileged *a*· of peace.

armed

Mis.	5–18	*a*· with the power of Spirit,
	10– 9	He has called His own, *a*· them,
'01.	32–14	they *a*· quickly, aimed deadly,
My.	277–23	*a*· with power girt for the hour.
	278–11	faith *a*· with the understanding

Armenians

Mis.	123– 2	butchers the helpless *A*·,

armies

Mis.	338–19	*a*· of earth press hard upon you.
Pul.	83–18	* overcome our own allied *a*· of evil

armor

Mis.	xii– 3	With *a*· on, I continue the march,
	114–17	They must always have on *a*·,
	120–15	with *a*· on, not laid down.
	171–30	keep bright their invincible *a*· ;
'02.	19–12	Meekness is the *a*· of a Christian,
Peo.	14–14	put on the whole of Truth ;
My.	189– 2	Clad in invincible *a*·,
	210– 8	Good thoughts are an impervious *a*· ;

armored

Mis.	176–29	divine energy wherewith we are *a*·

armors

My.	251–25	God gives, elucidates, *a*·, and tests

arms

Mis.	120–15	Christian success is under *a*·,
	124–23	stretch out our *a*· to God.
	140–23	put back into the *a*· of Love,
	370–16	babe that twines its loving *a*· about
	398–11	Take them in Thine *a*· ;
Ret.	46–22	Take them in Thine *a*· ;
	80–23	carries his lambs in his *a*·
Pul.	17–21	Take them in Thine *a*· ;
	48–21	* her family coat of *a*·
No.	15–10	have the civil and religious *a*·
Pan.	14–12	for her victory under *a*· ;
Po.	14–20	Take them in Thine *a*· ;
My.	113–19	in the *a*· of divine Love,
	124–11	world's *a*· outstretched to us,

Armstrong, Joseph

Pul.	43– 8	* Joseph *A*·, Stephen A. Chase, and
	59–21	* on the platform sat Joseph *A*·,
	86–10	* William B. Johnson, Joseph *A*·,
	87– 7	* signature
My.	21–29	* signature

Armstrong, C. S. D., Joseph

My.	296–11	Joseph *A*·, *C.S.D.*, is not dead,

army

Mis.	334– 2	in the *a*· of heaven, — *Dan.* 4 : 35.
Pul.	63–19	* great hold she has upon this *a*·
	80–21	* an *a*· of well-meaning people
	83–13	* as an *a*· with banners?" — *Song* 6 : 10.
My.	98– 3	* a twentieth of the C. S. *a*·
	175–15	provisions for the *a*·,

Arnold, Sir Edwin

Mis.	153–23	Sir Edwin *A*·, to whom I presented

aroma

Mis.	20– 3	*a*· of Jesus' own words,

arose

Mis.	28–18	he *a*· above the illusion of matter.
	164–30	*a*· from the testimony of the senses.
	249–20	The report that I was dead *a*·

arose
Mis. 345–28   thence a· the rumor that it was
     351–11   a· solely from mental malicious
Ret. 50–28   the blessings which a· therefrom.
Pul. 79–26   * But when C. S. a·,
Po. 68–19   When the star of our friendship a·

around
Mis. 54– 5   the planets to revolve a· it
     210– 8   post a· it placards warning people
     230–12   Rushing a· smartly is no proof of
     279–17   went seven times a· these walls,
Ret. 5–25   * was felt by all a· her.
Pul. 37–23   * not to centre too closely a·
     39– 6   * flows a· our incompleteness,
     42– 2   * sidewalks a· the church were
No. 6–18   revolves a· our planet,
     6–21   error of the revolution of the sun a·
Po. 25– 7   A· you in memory rise !
My. 13–11   * planets, revolving a· it.
     99–20   * baskets when passed a· were
     113–24   all a· us is demonstrated
     161– 1   hung a· the necks of the wicked.
     186– 5   cluster a· this rock-ribbed church
     192–15   My heart hovers a· your churches
     343– 3   * and works a· a question

arouse
Un. 6–25   declarations about sin . . . must a·,

aroused
Mis. 352–30   moral sense be a· to reject the
Ret. 13–10   a· by this erroneous doctrine,
No. 1–11   when public sentiment is a·,
'01. 26–16   land is reached and the world a·,
My. 252–27   You are not a· to this action by
     308– 7   man is a· to thought or action

arranged
No. 9–27   * it is "knowledge, duly a· and

arrangement
Mis. 136–27   will be accommodated by this a·.
     283– 8   and suit one's self in the a·
Ret. 82–28   a· of my last revision, in 1890,
Pul. 65–19   * a· of statuary and paintings
My. 83– 6   * members of the local a· committee

arrangements
Pul. 49–19   * something of her domestic a·,
My. 75–13   * all the preliminary a· for

arranging
Mis. 330–17   a· in the beauty of holiness
My. 173–26   for a· the details and allowing
     319–24   * in analyzing and a· the topics,

arrant
Mis. 163–10   a· hypocrite and to dull disciples

array
Mis. 299–19   a· myself in them, and
Po. 15–10   enchantment in beauty's a·,

arrayed
Mis. 246–26   a· against the rights of man,
No. 5–19   If disease . . . is a· against being,
Hea. 2– 4   prejudices a· against it,

arrest
Mis. 79–31   because they chance to be under a·
     117– 7   a· the former, and obey the latter.
     121–21   a·, trial, and crucifixion of
     231–18   to a· the peel !
     300–10   liable to a· for infringement of
My. 88–16   * which must a· public attention.
     314–22   prevented Dr. Patterson's a·

arrested
Mis. 40– 3   its power would be a· if one
'01. 17–13   would not have a· public attention
My. 13– 9   my attention was a· by
     222–15   Jesus was not a· . . . because of
     222–18   but he was a· because,
     227–10   a· for manslaughter because
     314–20   about to have Dr. Patterson a·

arrival
Mis. 69–16   Upon my a· I found him barely alive,
Ret. 40– 5   On my a· my hostess told me
My. 54– 9   * before the a· of the pastor,
     244– 1   I have awaited your a· before

arrive
Mis. 183–30   will a· at the true status of man
     198– 4   To a· at this point of unity
     341–11   to a· at the results of Science :
Hea. 4–21   a· at a proper conception of
     11–20   "until you a· at no medicine."
     14– 3   Medicine will not a· at the science of
My. 73–28   * due to a· in Boston to-night,
     74– 7   * who will a· in this city just about
     357– 3   a· at the spiritual fulness of God,

arrived
Mis. 142–13   Each day since they a· I have

arrived
Man. 35– 2   who have a· at the age of twelve
Ret. 23–13   when the moment a· of the heart's
My. 96–22   * day set for the dedication a·
     217–12   shall have a· at legal age,

arrives
Mis. 172–13   and he a· at fulness of stature ;

arrogance
My. 41– 9   * Pride, a·, and self-will are

arrogant
Mis. 92–27   in times past, a· ignorance and
Ret. 84–15   In times past, a· pride,
Un. 17–13   taught the a· Pharisees that,

arrogated
My. 340–14   has a· to itself the prerogative of

arrow
Mis. 223–30   mental a· shot from another's bow
     330– 6   wherein no a· wounds the dove
     387–12   a· that doth wound the dove
No. 3– 3   shoot its a· at the idea which
Po. 6– 7   a· that doth wound the dove
My. 290–22   where no a· wounds the eagle

art
Mis. 107– 4   A· must not prevail over Science.
     232– 7   is pushing towards perfection in a·,
     365– 7   what a child's love of pictures is to a·.
     372–17   * are truly a work of a·,
     372–26   Not by aid of . . . could I copy a·,
     372–27   but the a· of C. S.,
     373– 2   illustrate the simple nature of a·.
     374–12   and its a· will rise triumphant ;
     375– 5   The truest a· of C. S.
     375– 7   to delineate this a·.
     375–13   * and their great works of a·
     375–14   * an idea of what constitutes true a·.
     375–16   * the study of music and a·.
     375–19   * which is the foundation of true a·.
     375–22   * In other words, the a· is perfect.
     375–28   * to see produced to-day that a·
     375–29   * the only true a·
     376– 1   * the a· is perfect.
     376– 2   * It is the true a· of the oldest,
     393– 6   A· and Science, all unweary,
     393–17   A· hath bathed this isthmus-lordling
Ret. 95– 5   * skill In comfort's a· :
Pul. 65–24   * and so was memorialized in a·
     66– 1   * what they term the divine a· of healing,
     78– 3   * examples of the goldsmith's a·
No. 18–16   what a child's love of pictures is to a·.
'00. 11–16   his composition is the triumph of a·,
Peo. 6–11   * "The a· of medicine consists in
Po. 2– 4   chisel of the sculptor's a·
     51–12   A· and Science, all unweary,
     52– 1   A· hath bathed this isthmus-lordling
My. 70–20   * is replete with rare bits of a·,
     124–18   reflects man and a· pencils him,
     270–29   than I would because of his a·.
     270–31   control both religion and a·
     327–25   * who practise the a· of healing,"
     328–29   * practise the a· of healing for pay,

Article
Man. 36–13   provided for in Sect. 4 of this A·.
     72– 8   conformity with Sect. 7 of this A·,
     (see also **Church Manual**)

article
Mis. 88–10   the author of the a· in question
     132–26   I read in your a· these words :
     133– 2   at the close of your a·,
     242– 2   The a· of Professor T——,
Man. 48– 8   an a· that is uncharitable
     53–25   an a· that is false or unjust,
     71– 5   a· "The" must not be used
     82– 6   A book or an a· of which
     98– 3   corrected a false newspaper a·
     98–13   last proof sheet of such an a·
     98–15   papers containing such an a·,
     112– 4   The a· "the" . . . must not be
Pul. 29– 7   * speak, a little later, in this a·.
     55– 5   * In a previous a· we have referred
     74– 4   * a· published in the Herald
     84–18   * not undertake to speak in this a·.
'01. 21– 7   a· published in the New York Journal,
My. 237–21   The a· on the Church Manual by
     254–19   * following extract from your a·
     266–12   a· on the decrease of students in
     272–21   * an a· sent to us by Mrs. Eddy,
     303–13   his a·, of which I have seen only
     316–11   The a· in the January number of
     327–11   * I know the enclosed a· will
     328– 7   * The following a·, copied from

articles
Mis. x–10   most of these a· were
     x–12   a few a· are herein appended.

articles
Mis. x–13 To some *a·* are affixed data,
305–20 * *a·* of historic interest
313–15 I was impressed by the *a·*
Pul. 88–1 chapter sub-title
88–5 uniformly kind and interesting *a·*
88–9 whose *a·* are reluctantly omitted.
My. 18–29 It contained the following *a·* :
82–10 * trunks and smaller *a·* of baggage

articulate
Ret. 27–25 experience and confidence to *a·* it.
'01. 30–9 struggles to *a·* itself.
My. 133–26 this inmost something becomes *a·*,

articulated
Mis. 100–2 were *a·* in a decaying language,
163–14 His words were *a·* in the language of

articulates
Un. 60–5 With the same breath he *a·* truth and

artisans
Pul. 41–1 * forth from the hands of the *a·*
My. 66–19 * *A·* and artists are working

artist (*see also* **artist's**)
Mis. 62–6 an *a·* in painting a landscape.
230–28 needing but . . . the touch of an *a·*
270–5 What *a·* would question the skill of
372–17 * the *a·* seems quite familiar with
373–4 My *a·* at the easel objected,

artistic
Mis. 308–20 scholarly, *a·*, and scientific notices
374–32 is it less *a·* or less natural?
My. 67–24 * never was a more *a·* effect reached.

artist's
Mis. 393–4 Gives the *a·* fancy wings.
Po. 51–9 Gives the *a·* fancy wings.

artists
Mis. 372–10 from *a·* and poets.
372–20 and most distinguished *a·*.
Rud. 3–13 what the models . . . are to *a·*.
My. 66–19 * Artisans and *a·* are working

artless
Mis. 100–1 to *a·* listeners and dull disciples.
357–13 by the wayside, on *a·* listeners.
Ret. 35–22 beneath the stroke of *a·* workmen.

arts
Mis. 232–20 most important of all *a·*, — healing.
Pul. 47–20 * definitions of these two healing *a·*.
'00. 12–16 Magical *a·* prevailed at Ephesus ;

Asa
Mis. 245–5 *A·* . . . sought not to — *II Chron.* 16 : 12.
245–6 *A·* slept with his — *II Chron.* 16 : 13.

ascend
Mis. 232–16 meekly to *a·* the hill of Science,
323–18 Would ye *a·* the mountain,
327–17 *a·* faster than themselves,
356–13 songs should *a·* from the mount of
Ret. 85–11 upon which angelic thoughts *a·*
My. 34–1 Who shall *a·* into the hill — *Psal.* 24 : 3.
37–6 * *a·* heavenward from this house of God.

ascended
My. 119–16 to the *a·* Christ,

ascendency
'01. 19–19 through spiritual *a·* alone.

ascending
Mis. 57–28 *a·* the scale of being up to man.
151–27 on the *a·* scale of everlasting Life
292–10 a new tone on the scale of *a·*,
Ret. 8–5 three times, in an *a·* scale.
My. 211–12 in its *a·* steps of evil,

ascends
Mis. 96–12 as thought *a·* the scale of being
328–21 He alone *a·* the hill of C. S. who
My. 188–32 *a·* the scale of miracles
268–27 harmoniously *a·* the scale of life.

ascension
Mis. 28–18 great truth was shown by his *a·*
165–3 because of the *a·* of Jesus.
'02. 19–5 rebuked them on the eye of his *a·*,
My. 131–7 sacrament, sacrifice, and *a·*,
218–12 incorporeal idea, came with the *a·*.

ascent
Mis. 206–29 scaled the steep *a·* of C. S.,
265–31 must stop at the foot of the grand *a·*,
323–10 descent and *a·* are beset with peril,
327–14 which must greatly hinder their *a·*
347–23 *a·* is easy and the summit can be
'01. 19–22 From . . . to C. S. is a long *a·*,
Hea. 19–25 up the steep *a·*, on to heaven,
My. 117–9 to pursue the infinite *a·*,
189–3 you have started in this sublime *a·*,
229–21 steep *a·* of Christ's Sermon on the

ascertain
My. 53–16 * to *a·* if she would preach

ascribe
No. 18–5 nor does it *a·* to Him all presence,

ascribed
Mis. 191–28 opposite characters *a·* to him

ashes
Mis. 1–17 fire from the *a·* of dissolving self,
285–26 from the *a·* of free-love,
Peo. 8–26 are fast fading into *a·* ;
My. 178–27 If the world were in *a·*,
306–4 Far be it from me to tread on the *a·*
308–11 tread not ruthlessly on their *a·*.

Asheville, N. C.
My. 326–14 Elizabeth Earl Jones of *A·*, *N.C.*,
328–5 * 105 Bailey St., *A·*, *N.C.*,

Asia Minor
'00. 12–8 the capital of *A· M·*.

Asiatics
Pul. 66–26 * pre-Christian ideas of the *A·*

aside
Mis. 9–23 we voluntarily set it *a·*
15–8 Nothing *a·* from the spiritualization
17–8 lay *a·* your material appendages,
71–11 *Does C. S. set a· the law of*
72–4 Science sets *a·* man as a creator,
129–19 and try to push him *a·* ;
136–10 in turning *a·* for one hour
137–8 speaking a few words *a·* to your
179–28 must lay *a·* material consciousness,
250–19 I cast *a·* the word as a sham
335–31 seeking power or good *a·* from
361–17 "Let us lay *a·* — *Heb.* 12 : 1.
Ret. 81–18 loathes error, and casts it *a·* ;
90–2 most careful not to thrust *a·* Science,
Pul. 21–30 aught that can darken . . . must be set *a·*.
'00. 9–26 years I have desired to step *a·*.
15–1 Putting *a·* the old garment,
'01. 6–20 which is set *a·* to some degree,
My. vi–6 * no one on earth . . . *a·* from Mrs. Eddy,
67–18 laying *a·* all malice, — *I Pet.* 2 : 1.
67–18 * was set *a·* for the building of this
71–20 * have been set *a·* in this temple,
72–2 * set *a·* the traditions of
85–29 * *A·* from every other consideration,
92–7 * cannot be brushed *a·* by ridicule
191–17 With grave-clothes laid *a·*, Christ,
256–21 springs *a·* at the touch of Love.

ask
Mis. 51–30 "Ye *a·*, and receive not, — *Jas.* 4 : 3.
51–31 because ye *a·* amiss, — *Jas.* 4 : 3.
54–29 You would not *a·* the pupil in
89–21 I *a·* for information, not for
91–26 *a·* questions from it,
121–27 if I also *a·* you, — *Luke* 22 : 68.
145–9 let him *a·* himself,
149–5 *A·* them to bring what they possess of
157–10 *a·* them all questions important
195–15 We *a·* what is the authority
244–9 But, we *a·*, have those conditions
298–9 *A·* yourself : Under the same
299–24 The spectators may *a·*,
305–31 * we *a·* every one receiving this
307–2 Never *a·* for to-morrow :
307–7 More we cannot *a·* :
317–1 students whom I have not seen that *a·*,
359–29 To *a·* wisdom of God, is the
378–15 but she did *a·* him how
390–20 *A·* of its June, the long-hushed heart,
Ret. 20–22 compelled to *a·* for a bill of divorce,
50–12 *a·* my loyal students if they consider
71–15 *A·* the unbridled mind-manipulator
83–22 they should *a·* questions from it,
91–29 *A·*, rather, what has he *not* done.
92–9 shall *a·* what ye will, — *John* 15 : 7.
95–4 * *A·* God to give thee skill
Un. 34–18 Again I *a·* : What evidence does
35–14 I *a·*, Which was first,
48–1 to *a·* of every one a reason
48–3 yet *a·*, and I will answer.
Pul. 87–18 You *a·* too much when asking
Rud. 14–4 *a·* a suitable price for
No. 40–1 "Ye *a·*, and receive not, — *Jas.* 4 : 3.
40–2 because ye *a·* amiss, — *Jas.* 4 : 3.
41–6 as much as to *a·*,
42–28 Here a skeptic might well *a·*
Pan. 12–6 we naturally *a·*, how can Spirit
'00. 2–17 *A·* how he gets his money,
14–28 invited to a feast you naturally *a·*
'01. 19–8 "*A·*, and ye shall receive ;" — *John* 16 : 24.
19–9 continue to *a·*, and because of
33–13 Scientists . . . *a·* not to be judged on a
33–15 *a·* to be allowed the rights of

ask

'01. 33–17 they *a·* to be known by their works,
'02. 14–24 I *a·* : What has shielded and
Hea. 4– 9 even as we *a·* a person with
4–10 *a·* infinite wisdom to possess our
15–23 "Ye *a·*, and receive not,— *Jas.* 4 : 3.
15–24 because ye *a·* amiss ;"— *Jas.* 4 : 3.
Peo. 9–17 We *a·* and receive not,
9–17 because we "*a·* amiss ;"— *Jas.* 4 : 3.
Po. 34–15 Yet wherefore *a·* thy doom?
55–21 *A·* of its June, the long-hushed
My. 19–19 but I *a·* for more, even this :
20–30 *a·* the members to contribute
24– 1 * those who pass by are impelled to *a·*,
60–27 * may I *a·* a little of your time
73– 7 * If you *a·* a Christian Scientist
117–31 is all that I *a·* of mankind.
127– 4 who *a·* only to be judged according to
130–15 Therefore I *a·* the help of others
130–16 I *a·* that according to the Scriptures
133–23 and a question to *a·*.
138–14 *a·* me to receive persons whom I
148– 5 All that we *a·* of any people is to
149–31 while those . . . *a·* no praising.
150–18 *a·* God to enable you to reflect God,
150–24 ye shall *a·* what ye will,— *John* 15 : 7.
152–14 *A·* thyself, Do I enter by the door
156– 6 above all that we *a·* — *Eph.* 3 : 20.
175–18 May I *a·* in behalf of the public
221–31 earnestly *a·* : Shall we not believe
232–18 Here we *a·* : Are Christ's teachings
318–18 not *a·* him any questions.
329–25 * we *a·* you to give your readers the
343– 7 You would *a·*, perhaps,

asked

Mis. 33–14 question that is being *a·* every day.
40– 9 It is often *a·*, "If C. S.
137– 9 when, having *a·* in general assembly
180– 7 A dear old lady *a·* me,
226–18 When Aristotle was *a·* what a
255–18 sometimes *a·*, What are the advantages
287–22 When *a·* by a wife or a husband
299–26 have you *a·* yourself this question
305–16 * many persons are to be *a·*
305–24 * is *a·* to contribute one cent
305–26 * She is also *a·* to collect two dollars
316– 7 When will you . . . is often *a·*.
333–22 *a·* : "What communion— *II Cor.* 6 : 14.
346– 9 The question is often *a·*,
379– 4 *a·* if I could see his pennings
381–13 her counsel *a·* the defendant's
Ret. 8–22 *a·* her if she had summoned me
9– 5 *a·* if she really did hear Mary's
14–23 *a·* me to say how I felt when
30–10 often *a·* why C. S. was revealed to
40– 7 I *a·* permission to see her.
54– 1 *a·*, Why are faith-cures sometimes
82–27 often *a·* which revision of S. and H.
89–16 as Jesus was once *a·* to exhort,
Pul. 50–15 * no additional sums . . . are *a·* for.
Hea. 1–10 We have *a·*, in our selfishness,
Po. v–19 * *a· her what she was writing,*
My. 43–18 * it was *a·*, "What mean ye— *Josh.* 4 : 6.
59–24 * In years gone by I have been *a·*,
60–29 * I was *a·* by one of the Directors
96–23 * members were *a·* to quit giving.
98–22 * no member . . . was *a·* to contribute
105–25 he *a·* earnestly if I had a work
139–17 When I *a·* you to dispense with
160–19 I am *a·*, "Is there a hell?"
190–15 *a·* their great Teacher,
212–14 The question is often *a·*,
222– 7 When his disciples *a·* him why they
276–23 I am *a·*, "What are your politics?"
324–29 * When we *a·* him if he found you could

asking

Mis. 27–16 *a·*, "Do men gather— *Matt.* 7 : 16.
305–12 * *a·* for her personal cooperation
Ret. 50– 8 I shrank from *a·* it,
Pul. 87–19 *a·* me to accept your grand church
No. 20–19 Hence this *a·* amiss
39–17 True prayer is not *a·* God for love ;
Hea. 15–24 is it not *a·* amiss to pray for
My. 43–31 * many are *a·*, "What mean ye— *Josh.* 4 : 6.
148–20 and my heart is *a·* :
240– 6 * "Would it be *a·* too much of you
280–30 And why this *a·* ?

asks

Mis. 26–13 *a·*, Whence came the first seed,
127–14 faithfully *a·* divine Love to feed it
244–15 He *a·*, "Has the law been abrogated
315–26 *a·* for mental treatment.
353– 7 If one *a·* me, Is my concept of you
Ret. 60–16 Material sense *a·*, in its ignorance
Un. 15– 3 *a·* the poet-patriarch.

asks

No. 18–24 *a·* for what Mind alone can supply.
Pan. 6–15 and *a·*, If God is *infinite* good,
My. 18–11 *a·* divine Love to feed it with the
211– 9 All that error *a·* is to be let alone ;
235– 8 *a·* herself : Can I teach my child

asleep

Mis. 44–21 when awake, or when *a·* in a dream.
108– 2 or the so-called Christian *a·*,
325–14 only to find its inmates *a·*
392– 7 *a·* in night's embrace,
Ret. 61– 8 fall *a·*, actually conscious of
'01. 35– 7 appeals loudly to those *a·*
Po. 20– 9 *a·* in night's embrace,

aspect

My. 28–31 * changed the whole *a·* of medicine
89– 2 * in its size, if not in its *a·*,
234–20 gives the subject quite another *a·*.

aspects

Mis. 355– 3 presents two opposite *a·*,
Pul. 23–12 * under several different *a·*
My. 86–24 * in some of its *a·* the most notable

aspersion

Mis. 255– 4 no fairness or propriety in the *a·*.

aspersions

'02. 14–28 all unjust public *a·*,

aspirants

Mis. 351–14 of *a·* for place and power.
Rud. 16–25 class of *a·* which snatch at

aspiration

Pul. 23–21 * manifested in unrest or in *a·*,
My. 88–13 * symbolisms of *a·* and faith,
303–26 not the inspiration nor the *a·*

aspirations

My. 91–10 * no person's spiritual *a·*

aspire

Pul. 51–28 * *a·* to take its place alongside
My. 113–15 to *a·* to this knowledge of Christ

asps

Mis. 294–17 keep back thy offerings from *a·*
368–21 "the poison of *a·* — *Rom.* 3 : 13.

assail

'00. 10–15 *a·* even the new-old doctrines of

assailable

Mis. 122–15 it is neither questionable nor *a·* :

assailant

My. 331–15 * would have punished the *a·* of

assailed

'01. 32–12 When infidels *a·* them,
Po. vi–15 *and a· . . . William Lloyd Garrison*
My. 138–11 My personal reputation is *a·*

assails

Mis. 335–12 One mercilessly *a·* me for

assassin

Mis. 112–16 the *a·* of President Garfield,
226–29 red-tongued *a·* of radical worth ;

assemblage

Mis. 276–12 *a·* for the third convention of our
276–13 an *a·* found waiting and watching
My. 124– 6 annual *a·* of human consciousness,

assemble

Man. 84–21 or *a·* a selected number of them,
My. 27– 4 *A·* not at the residence of your
147– 9 a modest hall, in which to *a·*
173–27 allowing the visitors to *a·* on
284–21 desire to *a·* in my church building,

assembled

Mis. 279–11 *A·* FEB. 25, 1889,
Man. 98–20 in annual meeting *a·*.
Ret. 89– 7 Men *a·* in the one temple
My. 23–20 * in annual business meeting *a·*,
36– 9 * *a·* at this sacred time to commune
44–25 * in annual meeting *a·*,
46–22 * in the presence of this *a·* host,
65– 3 * *A·* in the largest church . . . meeting
76–20 * *a·* in their annual church meeting
88– 3 * *a·* at Boston to attend the
96– 2 * *a·* to participate in
171–22 * who were *a·* on the lawn of the
207– 9 * in annual conference *a·*,
352– 4 * Informally *a·*, we, the ushers

assemblies

Mis. 315– 8 either in private or in public *a·*,
Man. 50– 9 in public debating *a·*,
56–14 These *a·* shall be for listening to
Rud. 15–23 to promiscuous and large *a·*,

assembling

Mis. 144–22 *a·* of His people in this temple,
156–24 *A·* themselves together,

assembling
My.   79–12   * thirty thousand people *a·*
      85– 1   * character of the *a·* membership,
assembly
Mis. 137–10   having asked in general *a·* if you
Pul.   5– 5   in that unique *a·*.
      22– 6   with every praying *a·* on earth,
My.   46–30   * to the general *a·* — *Heb.* 12 : 23.
      79–17   * that *a·* was not a gathering of
      95–15   * During the great *a·* of
assent
Mis. 109– 3   *a·* where they should dissent ;
     240–13   without the *a·* of mind,
Ret. 14–13   if *a·* to this doctrine was essential
My. 291– 6   a quiet *a·* or dissent.
assented
Po. vii– 9   * *to which she a·.*
assert
Mis. 55–21   verities of Spirit *a·* themselves
Un.   40– 4   is to *a·* what we have not proved ;
Pul. 23–22   * *a·* that the end of a cycle,
Hea. 18–23   will cease to *a·* their Cæsar sway
My. 106–13   C. S. has healed cases that I *a·*
asserted
Mis. 77– 6   great truths *a·* of the Messiah :
Pul. 31– 6   * the principles *a·* by Jesus,
asserting
Mis. 183–24   *A·* a selfhood apart from God,
     335–21   by *a·* its nothingness,
'00. 10– 3   *a·* and developing good.
'01. 34– 4   Bible is our authority for *a·* this,
My. 143–14   this fustian of either denying or *a·*
assertion
Mis. 191–14   *a·* indicating the existence of
     256–25   The *a·* that matter is a law,
     266–18   *a·* that I have said hard things
Ret. 14–22   he persisted in the *a·* that I *had* been
Un.   6–22   the *a·* of universal salvation
      53–17   than would be the *a·* that the
My.   84– 1   * speak more plainly than mere *a·*
assertions
Un.   44– 5   The foundations of these *a·*,
My. 351–25   any *a·* to the contrary are false.
asserts
Mis. 59–26   who *a·* himself the least,
Pul. 70–17   * Mrs. Eddy *a·* that in 1866
assets
My.   vi–21   * *a·* valued at forty-five thousand
asseverated
Pul. 45–18   * repeatedly *a·* to the contrary.
assiduously
Mis. 262–14   at work conscientiously and *a·*,
     263–17   working *a·* for our common Cause,
     379–24   *a·* pondering the solution of
assigned
Man. 79–10   the business *a·* to them
      95–13   one shall be *a·* them by the Board.
Rud.   2–20   takes away the trammels *a·* to
My.   75–11   * where they were *a·* rooms
assigns
Peo.   3–24   and *a·* them mortal fetters
assimilate
Mis. 264–16   to *a·* pure and abstract Science
Ret. 28–29   *a·* the character and practice of
      84–12   *a·* this inexhaustible subject— C. S.
Un.   6–17   world is far from ready to *a·* such a
Rud. 15–21   *a·* what has been taught them.
assimilated
Mis. 213– 6   in the proportion that . . . are *a·*,
     317–16   Scarcely a moiety, . . . is yet *a·*
My. 292– 6   the right government is *a·*,
assimilation
Mis. 317–17   yet this *a·* is indispensable to
My. 230– 7   during the senses' *a·* thereof,
assist
Mis. 53–12   *a· in producing a cure,*
      79–30   which in any way obligates you to *a·*
My.   62–28   * ready to *a·* us in every way
     222–29   *a·* in the holding of crime in check,
     319–24   * to *a·* me in analyzing and
     320– 4   * he readily consented to *a·* me,
assistance
Mis.   7–30   naturally without any *a·*.
     349– 2   even the offer of pecuniary *a·*
My. 331–31   * the *a·* volunteered to
     336– 6   * he desired to go to her *a·*,
assistant
Man. 101– 3   If . . . the manager . . . needs an *a·*,
     101– 5   appoint an *a·* manager,

assistant
Ret. 43–20   the only *a·* teachers in the College.
assisted
My. 130–10   whom I have *a·* pecuniarily
     330–11   * *a·* by a Mason of good standing
assisting
Mis. 11– 9   afterwards *a·* them pecuniarily,
assists
Mis. 75–20   *a·* one to understand C. S.
associate
Mis. 296– 2   elected an *a·* life-member of
Ret. 24– 3   spiritualists would *a·* therewith,
associated
Mis. 296–19   is by no means *a·* therewith.
Pan. 14–15   those *a·* with his executive trust,
My.   45– 7   * significant events *a·* with this,
     153–14   imbued and *a·* with no intrinsic
Associated Press
My. 346–25   * gave the following to the *A· P·*,
Association
Mis. 111–28   call the attention of this *A·* to
     120–20   *A·* hereafter meet triennially :
     134– 9   chapter sub-title
     135–23   chapter sub-title
     137– 1   chapter sub-title
Pul. 37–25   * heading
My. 251–23   chapter sub-title
     252–18   chapter sub-title
     253–10   chapter sub-title
     283–12   fruits of said grand *A·*,
association
Mis. 272–15   * of any corporation or *a·*,
Man. 85– 6   may teach and receive into his *a·*
      86–12   who is not in charge of an *a·*
      86–14   conduct the meetings of their *a·*.
Pul. 58– 5   * gathered an *a·* of students,
'01. 23–29   * phenomena connected by *a·*
      31–24   my early *a·* with
'02. 19–28   and crowns the *a·* with
Association for International Conciliation
My. 282–22   in the success of the *A· for I· C·*
     283– 2   chapter sub-title
     283– 7   *Fondateur* of the *A· for I· C·*
     285–15   embodied in the *A· for I· C·*
associations
Mis. 137–29   organize their students into *a·*,
     315–22   shall form *a·* for this purpose ;
     358–22   organizing churches and *a·*.
Man. 84–16   *A·*.
      84–16   *a·* of the pupils of loyal teachers
      85– 3   attend each other's *a·*.
Ret. 50–25   organize churches, schools, and *a·*
      52–16   branch *a·* in other States,
      85– 4   band together their students into *a·*,
No.   41–13   for perfection in churches or *a·*.
My. 347–21   loving-cup with all its sweet *a·*.
assume
Mis.   x–19   to *a·* various *noms de plume*.
       2– 3   those *a·* most who have the least
     281–27   realized what a responsibility you *a·*
Man. 70–11   shall *a·* no general official control of
      71–14   branch church to *a·* such position
      83–12   shall not *a·* personal control of,
Pul. 65– 9   * whatever attitude Rome may *a·*
'01. 14– 2   To *a·* there is no reality in sin,
My. 334–20   "To *a·* there is no reality in sin,
assumed
Mis. 44–25   your belief *a·* a new form,
      63–30   Jesus *a·* for mortals the weakness of
Un.   45–11   evil ego, and his *a·* power,
      46–28   Jesus *a·* the burden of disproof
Pul. 68– 1   * Mrs. Eddy *a·* the pastorship of
My. 111– 9   now *a·* by many doctors
assumes
Mis. 39–28   Scientist, *a·* no more when claiming
     147–25   He *a·* no borrowed appearance.
     274–18   when the press *a·* the liberty to
     370–12   divine idea *a·* different forms,
     370–14   In this age it *a·*,
assuming
Un.   33–14   Brain, thus *a·* to testify,
Rud.   6– 3   *a· manifold forms and colors,*
My.   29–23   * *a·* an altogether different status
      42–12   * Mr. Gross, on *a·* office, said :
assumption
No.   17– 1   false *a·* of the realness of
'01. 13– 8   an *a·* that nothing is something.
assumptions
Un.   24– 6   Your *a·* insist that there is more than

assurance
Mis. 307– 8   *a·* is the "Peace, be still" — *Mark* 4 : 39.
     373–25   this *a·* is followed by
Un. 44–20   thus carrying out the serpent's *a·* :
     55–17   Job's faith . . . gained him the *a·*
Pul. 3–13   heavenly *a·* ends all warfare,
     9–21   O glorious hope and blessed *a·*,
     83–10   * With the *a·* of faith she prays,
My. 38– 4   * we rest in this satisfying *a·*,
     44–30   * and their confident *a·*
     65–11   * with both unanimity and *a·*.
     280– 4   * gives *a·* of your watchful care
     295– 3   blessed *a·* that life is not lost ;
     333–24   * *a·* of his willingness to die,
     356–15   I have given no *a·*,

assure
Ret. 24–19   could only *a·* him that the divine
My. 80– 4   * earnestly *a·* thousands of auditors
     362–21   * *a·* you that it is our intention to

assured
Mis. 10–16   more *a·* to press on safely.
     114–26   Rest *a·* that God in His wisdom
     160–i3   Of this we rest *a·*, that every trial
     276– 8   rest *a·* my heart's desire met
     303–25   I feel *a·* that many Christian Scientists
     345–19   * has always *a·* and reassured me
Ret. 85– 9   Of this also rest *a·*,
'01. 1– 4   rest *a·* you can never lack
Peo. 13–27   * "My heart has *a·* and reassured me
My. 139– 2   Rest *a·* that your Leader is living,
     151–12   Rest *a·* that the injustice done
     162– 1   God's mercy . . . is *a·* ;
     186–13   Rest *a·* that He in whom dwelleth all
     230–20   Be *a·* that fitness and fidelity
     252– 8   Rest *a·* that the good you do
     333–31   * "We are *a·* that reports of
     342–20   continuity of The . . . "is *a·*.

assuredly
My. 240–26   * She most *a·* does,

assures
Mis. 180–25   apostle *a·* us that man has power to
'01. 21–24   My faith *a·* me that God knows
Peo. 10–17   It *a·* us, of a verity, that

Assyrian Merodach
Mis. 123–14   The *A· M·*, or the god of sin,

astonished
Mis. 189–27   were *a·* at his doctrine :— *Matt.* 7 : 28.
Ret. 58–10   "were *a·* at his doctrine :— *Matt.* 7 : 28.
Un. 42–18   were *a·* at his doctrine ;— *Matt.* 7 : 28.

astonishing
My. 65– 2   * chapter sub-title
     65–10   * This *a·* motion was passed
     92–15   * *a·* revelation was made

astonishment
Ret. 15– 1   To the *a·* of many,

astounded
Mis. 115– 3   *a·* at the apathy of some students

astray
Mis. 208–22   I went *a·* :— *Psal.* 119 : 67.
     298– 7   causing others to go *a·*,

astrology
Mis. 334– 5   *A·* is well in its place,

astronomer
Mis. 363–26   confutes the *a·*,
Rud. 6–13   Langley, the young American *a·*

astronomy
Mis. 344– 5   have you studied music, *a·*, and
     344–27   Not through *a·* did he point out
Ret. 87– 6   in religion and scholarship as in *a·*
Un. 13– 2   same principle that it does in *a·*.
No. 6–25   *A·*, optics, acoustics, and

astute
Mis. 62–26   which is amusing to *a·* readers,

astutely
Mis. 71–23   St. Paul declares *a·*,

asunder
Mis. 335–10   "And shall cut him *a·*,— *Matt.* 24 : 51.

asylums
My. 301–21   are committed to insane *a·*

ate
Mis. 170–17   The bread he *a·*,

atheism
Mis. 345– 4   against the charge of *a·* ;
Pan. 3–22   It is opposed to *a·* and monotheism,
My. 90–15   * which teaches that hate is *a·*,

atheist
Mis. 45–12   *Can an a· or a profane man be cured*

Athenian
Pul. 26–27   * *A·* lamp over two hundred years old,

Athenians
Ret. 93–17   St. Paul said to the *A·*,

Athens
Mis. 344–30   when he stood on Mars' hill at *A·*,
Pul. 8– 1   the press of America's *A·*,
'02. 10–11   * not *A·*, but Calvary."

athirst
Mis. 324–28   Naked, hungry, *a·*, this time he
Pul. 14–15   weary wanderers, *a·* in the desert
No. v– 9   *a·* for the life-giving waters of

athletic
Pul. 5–14   his *a·* mind, scholarly and serene,

Athol (**Mass.**) *Transcript*
My. 97–24   * [*A·* (*M·*) *T·*]

athwart
Po. 43–16   Beacon beams — *a·* the weakly,

Atlanta
Ga.
Pul. 89–18   * *Journal, A·*, Ga.
Georgia
My. 187–21   chapter sub-title

Pul. 56– 4   * Scranton, Peoria, *A·*, Toronto, and
'00. 1–20   *A·*, New Orleans, Chicago,

Atlantic
Mis. 251– 5   from the Pacific to the *A·* shore,
     359–17   to step upon the *A·*
Ret. 2– 0   crossed the *A·* more than a score of
Pul. 88– 3   from the *A·* to the Pacific ocean,
My. 85– 9   * as from the *A·* to the Pacific

atmosphere
Mis. 12–32   the radius of our *a·* of thought.
     86–26   The *a·* of mortal mind
     129–17   send it into the *a·* of mortal mind
     174–13   higher than the *a·* of our planet,
     260–25   Pure Mind gives out an *a·* that heals
     355–28   from thine own mental *a·*.
     356– 3   illumine its own *a·* with spiritual
Man. 31–11   mental *a·* they exhale shall
Pul. 31–17   * Boston *a·* was largely thrilled
No. 9–26   Science is the *a·* of God ;
'00. 9–15   till the mental *a·* is clear.
'02. 3–29   Envy is the *a·* of hell.
My. 57– 6   * sacred *a·* of a church home.
     197–17   translucent *a·* of the former must
     265–24   the *a·* of the human mind,

atmospheres
Mis. 267–21   for rarefied *a·* and upward flight.

atom
Mis. 129–16   an *a·* of another man's indiscretion,
     173–28   Whence, then, is the *a·* or molecule
Un. 35–26   material *a·* is an outlined falsity of
My. 162– 7   unity and power are not in *a·* or in
     349–32   from *a·* and dust draws its conclusions

atomic
Mis. 23–20   is not a result of *a·* action,
     190– 1   *A·* action is Mind, not matter.

atoms
Mis. 26–14   Was it molecules, or material *a·*?
     224–17   of these different *a·*.

atone
Mis. 118–14   sympathy can neither *a·* for error,
     339–25   thou alone canst and must *a·*.
My. 104–22   but what can *a·* for the vulgar

atoned
No. 35–15   He *a·* for the terrible unreality of

atonement
Mis. 96–17   Do I believe in the *a·* of Christ?
     96–18   this *a·* becomes more to me
     123–20   majestic *a·* of divine Love.
     125– 3   then hath he part in Love's *a·*,
     261–16   the *a·* of Christ loses no efficacy.
Man. 15–14   We acknowledge Jesus' *a·* as the
Pul. 30–18   * It affirms the *a·* ;
No. 33–12   chapter sub-title
     34–19   The real *a·* — so infinitely beyond
     37–11   the vicarious *a·* of Jesus,
     37–18   would make the *a·* to be less than
     42–28   ask if the *a·* had lost its
'01. 10–22   *a·* of Christ, whereby good
Hea. 18–18   The doctrine of *a·* never

at-one-ment
Mis. 123–21   *a·* with Christ has appeared
Un. 54–15   *a·*, or oneness with God,
No. 33–19   sustains man's *a·* with God ;
     37–19   would make . . . less than the *a·*,

Atonement and Eucharist
Pul. 38–13   "Prayer," "*A· and E·*,"
My. 136– 6   depicted in the chapter *A· and E·*,

atones
My. 288–27 Love a· for sin through love
attach
Mis. 174– 8 Let us a· our sense of Science to
attached
Mis. 291– 9 Too much and too little is a· to me
Pul. 77– 6 * A· to the scroll is a golden key
78–21 * A· by a white ribbon to the scroll
My. 70–30 * A· to the organ is a set of
71– 5 * There is also a solo organ a·.
335– 7 * He was devotedly a· to Masonry,
attaches
Mis. 209– 1 a· to sin due penalties
attaching
My. 93–21 * a· meanwhile no importance to
attachment
Man. 40– 5 nor mere personal a· should impel
Pul. 26–13 * with Æolian a·,
60–21 * having an Æolian a·.
attack
Mis. 90–12 it is inexpedient to a·
316– 2 never to a· the malpractitioner,
Ret. 63– 7 We a· the sinner's belief in
63–10 we a· the belief of the sick in
My. 127–22 culminating in fierce a·,
143–22 I do not regard this a· upon me as
213–24 wiser and better through every a·
304–29 The first a· upon me was :
308–11 The a· on me and my late father
318–21 began my a· on agnosticism.
attacked
Mis. 11–15 If one's life were a·,
193–19 when critics a· me for
Ret. 19– 9 a· by this insidious disease,
My. 335–16 * Mr. Glover was a· with yellow fever
attacking
My. 300–32 or are they a· a peaceable party
attacks
Mis. 285– 1 I am opposed to all personal a·,
323–14 masters their secret and open a·
No. 5–23 a· a normal and real condition
My. 151– 2 present schoolboy epithets and a·
151– 8 these a· afford opportunity for
210– 9 shielded from the a· of error
273– 7 * emerging triumphantly from all a·
316–13 A· on C. S. and its Founder,
attain
Mis. 86– 4 the Christian will, must, a· it ;
147–30 rather fail of success than a· it by
Ret. 49–15 a· the bliss of loving unselfishly,
'01. 2–16 others will a· it,
24–30 I relinquished the form to a· the
'02. 16–13 To a· peace and holiness is
Hea. 14–26 to a· a mind in harmony with God,
My. 123–27 Seeing that we have to a· to the
149– 1 To a· to these works, men must
attained
Mis. 42–11 not a· by the death of the body,
46–28 thought has not yet wholly a· unto
86– 5 Until this be a·, the Christian
220–14 The end is a·, and the patient says
Ret. 82–10 a· by those loyal students who
No. 31–18 until a perfect consciousness is a·.
32–19 When this sense is a·, we shall no longer
Hea. 13–15 highest attenuation we ever a·
My. 237– 8 not a· the full understanding of
345–22 or rather a· by us,
attaining
My. 93–13 * or a· dominion over others,
attainment
Mis. 101–13 holiness, and the a· of heaven.
116–20 research and a· in divine Science
Un. 4– 9 but a· of the understanding of
Pan. 9–15 a· of scientific Christianity
My. 131– 5 courage, devotion, and a·.
attainments
Mis. 345–32 directed them to spiritual a·.
'00. 1–14 rich spiritual a·,
My. 64– 5 * to us through her spiritual a·
244–12 fresh impulse to our spiritual a·,
251– 1 duties and a· beckoning them.
attains
My. 103–13 a· the stature of man in Christ
228–27 He who strives, and a· ;
attempt
Mis. 18–27 a· to separate Life from God.
52–24 should a· to work out a rule
118–28 Every a· of evil to harm good
171– 5 with the second a·,
175–28 The a· to mix matter and Mind,

attempt
Mis. 216–27 * a· of phenomenism to conceive
216–29 * it is an a· to conceive a grin
224–29 He who can wilfully a· to injure
234– 4 a· to mount above error
234– 8 a· to seem what we have not
268– 5 but not vain enough to a·
Man. 83–13 a· to dominate his pupils,
Ret. 60–29 Any a· to divide these
71–28 one who is unaware of this a·,
78–19 an a· to demonstrate the facts of
Un. 10–21 To a· the calculation of His mighty
Rud. 16–10 None . . . should a· overmuch in their
No. 6– 3 to a· to destroy the realities of Mind
45–10 Such an a· indicates weakness,
'00. 7–25 ofttimes this a· measurably fails,
'01. 2– 8 To a· to twist . . . into harmony with
29–18 if they a· to help their parents,
My. 42–22 * I shall not a· to speak of the
74–24 * it would be idle to a· to deny them
81–26 * If an a· were made to give
110–28 Robert Ingersoll's a· to convict the
197– 4 A· nothing without God's help.
332– 3 * an a· at expressing the feelings of
340–16 this a· is shorn of some of its
attempted
Ret. 70– 6 is an a· infringement on infinity"
Pul. 50–28 * and live down any a· repression.
attempting
Mis. 92–27 a· to steady the ark of Truth,
277–15 the present mode of a· this
Ret. 84–15 a· to steady the ark of Truth,
Un. 5–13 a· to solve every Life-problem in
attempts
Mis. 62–23 a· to solve its divine Principle by
217– 4 neither philosophy nor reason a· to
233–11 and so strangled in its a·.
287–31 a· to steady other people's altars,
351–15 These repeated a· of mad ambition
'00. 9–22 Whosoever a· to ostracize C. S.
My. 59–22 * feeble a· to lead the singing.
305– 3 Failing in these a·,
306– 2 a· to narrow my life into
attend
Mis. 6–30 has all that she can a· to
209–25 happiness should still a· it.
Man. 30–18 the Board shall a· to the insurance
59–23 come to a· the morning services.
62–16 a· the Sunday School exercises.
69–23 or a· to other affairs outside
85– 3 a· each other's associations.
Pul. 40–12 * TO A· THE EXERCISES
81– 3 * We did not a·,
'00. 5–30 might and majesty a· every
'01. 7–22 a· their petitions to divine Love.
My. 25– 7 * children who a· the Sunday School
72–11 * who come to a· the dedication
72–20 * to a· the dedication exercises,
73–15 * a· the June meetings of The
88– 4 * a· the opening of their great new
105–19 I was wired to a· the patient of a
141– 9 * to a· the communion seasons
142–28 I will a· the meeting,
171–12 communicants who a· this communion,
173–16 Why not invite those who a· the
174–18 your kind invitation to a· the
285– 4 a· the Industrial Peace Conference,
289–23 It being inconvenient for me to a·
attendance
Mis. 279–12 WITH AN A· OF SIXTY-FIVE STUDENTS.
Man. 94– 3 unite in their a· on his lecture,
'01. 34– 5 d tains the patient from the a· of
My. 20–23 * a general a· of the members
22– 5 * increasing a· at all the services,
30–11 * the character of the a·.
55– 9 * not only was the a· rapidly
55–30 * a steady increase in a·.
56– 2 * A· at the Sunday service
56–16 * growth of a· in The Mother Church,
56–21 * a· at them and at The Mother Church
86–26 * The a· at the ceremonies
87– 1 * a· was greater than the
94–23 * many . . . were in a·.
94–25 * Mrs. Eddy, . . . was not in a·,
attendant
Mis. 89–13 the medical a· and friends
Un. 37–19 good a· upon spiritual individuality
attendants
Pul. 59– 7 * so long as there were a· ;
My. 53–19 * number of a· steadily increased.
56–18 * the number of a· increased
56–23 * a· at The Mother Church.

attended
Mis.	69–18	next day he a· to his business.
	95–17	There have always a· my life
	204– 7	a· throughout with doubt, hope,
Ret.	24–17	homœopathic physician who a· me,
My.	30– 4	* nobody a· more than one,
	51–30	* all who have a· the services,
	58–29	* a· the dedicatory services
	96–28	* a· by people from all parts of
	99–18	* a· the dedicatory exercises,
	135– 9	a· to my secular affairs,
	137–12	a· personally to my secular affairs,
	141– 6	* services a· last Sunday
	331–23	* a· him during his last sickness,
	333–23	* friends who a· him during his illness
	335–25	* a· cases of this terrible disease
	340– 1	Jesus a· feasts,

attending
Mis.	17–26	material conditions a· it.
Pul.	29– 8	* a· the service held in Copley Hall.
'01.	15–29	* of a· His solemn worship.
My.	140–15	* a· occasionally The Mother Church.
	140–27	occasionally a· this church.
	145–19	at home a· to the machinery

attends
Mis.	123–32	such as a· eating and drinking
Pul.	37–10	* a· to a vast correspondence ;

attent
My.	188– 6	a· unto the prayer — II Chron. 7 : 15.

attention
call
Mis.	282–29	The abuse which I call a· to,
My.	91–17	* serves to call a· to one of the most
	110–32	serve to call a· to that book,

call the
Mis.	111–27	Let me specially call the a· of

close
Mis.	127–31	need close a· and examination.
Pul.	12– 4	stillness . . . indicated close a·.

constant
My.	175– 5	requires my constant a· and time,

daily
My.	237–14	give daily a· thereto.

definite
Pul.	24– 2	* a keynote of definite a·.

direct
Mis.	319–26	Christian Scientists can direct a·,

directed
Ret.	5–27	* directed a· to themes at once pleasing

her
Pul.	72–12	* given so much of her a·.
Po.	v– 8	* that claimed her a·.

immediate
Mis.	146–16	but will give them immediate a·,

kind
My.	331–29	* recounting the kind a· paid to
	332–11	* or remit his kind a· until he

less
My.	259–15	they require less a· than packages

much
Mis.	353–11	People give me too much a·

my
Mis.	276– 7	circumstances demanded my a·
My.	13– 8	my a· was arrested by

no mean
Mis.	376– 1	* as one who gives no mean a· to

our
My.	27– 7	should engage our a· at this sacred

present
Mis.	299– 8	which demands our present a·.

profound
My.	250– 4	has received profound a·.

public
Mis.	171–28	obtruding upon the public a·
	221–31	or call public a· to that crime?
'01.	17–13	would not have arrested public a·
My.	88–17	* which must arrest public a·.
	316–18	appeal . . . demands public a·.

require
My.	177– 7	daily duties require a· elsewhere,

serious
Man.	43–18	not only calls more serious a· to

share of
Pul.	51–27	* the share of a· it deserves,

special
Rud.	13–20	then give special a· to
'02.	7–27	special a· to his new commandment.

their
Man.	67–18	who turn their a· from the

time and
(see time)

time or
Mis.	366–	time or a· that human hypotheses

attention
your
Mis.	121– 6	cup to which I call your a·,
	133– 8	I call your a· and
'00.	14–14	I call your a· to this to remind you
My.	224– 5	call your a· to this demand,
Pul.	2–11	Turning the a· from sublunary views,
	36–10	* such earnestness of a· as
	47– 1	* the a· of many clergymen
	65–13	* A· is directed to the progress
'02.	1–21	C. S., engaging the a· of
Hea.	3–14	engrossed the a· of the ages.
My.	v– 5	* a· of . . . world is fixed on C. S.,
	295–19	engages the a· and enriches the

attentive
My.	185–23	spoke to an a· audience

attenuate
My.	108–18	nothing in the divine Mind to a·.

attenuated
Un.	61–24	how a· are our demonstration and
Pul.	35–25	* the more a· the drug,
'01.	18– 2	a· one thousand degrees less
Hea.	13–10	We have a· a grain of aconite until

attenuation
Mis.	252– 5	gains no potency by a·,
	260–32	is the highest a· of evil.
	271– 2	a· of a drug up to the point of
	379–21	up to the highest a· in homœopathy,
Ret.	33–15	One drop of the thirtieth a· of
No.	16–26	its highest a· is mortal mind ;
'01.	17–27	and this a· in some cases
Hea.	13– 6	thirty times at every a·.
	13–15	highest a· we ever attained

attenuations
Ret.	33–18	drug disappears in the higher a·
'01.	17–25	In the highest a· of homœopathy
Hea.	11–28	higher a· of homœopathy
	12–23	higher a· prove that the power was
	12–26	higher a· are the most powerful.
	13– 8	reached soonest by the higher a·,
My.	107–10	the one thousandth a·
	107–12	the lower a· have so little

attest
Mis.	35– 8	acknowledge and a· the blessings
	98–24	lives of all reformers a· the
	106–27	"So live, that your lives a· your
	133–28	a· to the truth of Jesus' words.
Pul.	22– 9	If the lives of Christian Scientists a·
Pan.	10– 8	will a· its uplifting power,
Po.	31–16	but Truth and Love a·
My.	111–31	thousands upon thousands a·
	270–10	a· honesty and valor.

attestation
Mis.	220– 8	by audible explanation, a·, and

attested
Mis.	108– 7	a· the absolute powerlessness
	121–11	omnipotence of good, as divinely a·.
Man.	66–22	come from her satisfactorily a·.
My.	194–16	It stands . . . for Truth as a· by

attesting
Man.	66–14	Reading and A· Letters.
My.	96–12	* joy in a· their faith in the creed

attitude
Mis.	214–24	a· of mortal mind in being healed
	214–25	is the same as its a· physically.
	215–27	cannot in the beginning take the a·,
Man.	74–20	an a· of Christian fellowship.
Ret.	88–26	abide in such a spiritual a· as will
Pul.	37– 3	* in its a· toward all questions."
	65– 9	* whatever a· Rome may assume
My.	199–14	show explicitly the a· of this
	290–26	Hold this a· of mind,
	322–11	* work for and a· towards you ;
	329–24	* fair a· of the press everywhere,
	345– 7	* "What is your a· to science

Attleboro, Mass.
Pul.	88–23	* Sun, A·, M·.

attorney
Man.	67–11	shall not employ an a·,
Hea.	10–23	You are the a· for the case,

attract
My.	93– 8	* to a· any class save the

attracted
Pul.	47– 1	* a· the attention of many clergymen
	61–25	* a· quite a throng of people,

attracting
Pul.	46– 2	* that he was a· listeners

attraction
Mis.	173–29	Have a· and cohesion formed it?

attraction
  Un. 36– 2 This process it names material *a·*,
  My. 49– 5 * as by an irresistible *a·*.
      85–23 * become the great centre of *a·*,
    159–18 tend to check spiritual *a·*
    159–20 *a·* towards the temporary and

attribute
  Mis. 2–12 justice, the eternal *a·* of Truth,
  Pul. 53–11 * It is that *a·* of mind which

attributed
  Mis. 48– 3 If mesmerism has the power *a·* to it
  My. 312–32 rhyme *a·* to me by *McClure's*

attributes
  Mis. 1–18 Meekness heightens immortal *a·*
    23–27 manifests all His *a·* and power,
    69– 2 His essence, relations, and *a·*.
    69– 6 Mind, or God, and His *a·*.
  No. 10–15 or relates to its so-called *a·*,
  My. 308–26 *McClure's Magazine a·* to my father

attune
  My. 158– 8 in *a·* with faith's fond trust.

attuned
  Mis. 151– 2 their ears are *a·* to His call.

Auburn, N. Y.
  Pul. 88–26 * *Bulletin, A·, N. Y.*

audacious
  My. 97–16 * speaks of "the *a·*, stupendous,

audacity
  Un. 54–27 *a·* of diabolical and sinuous logic

audible
  Mis. 220– 8 by *a·* explanation, attestation, and
    222–13 listen complacently to *a·* falsehoods
    267– 2 *a·* and inaudible wail of evil
    319–11 mental and *a·* protest against the
    351–12 the *a·* falsehood designed to
  Ret. 9– 6 Mary's name pronounced in *a·* tones.
  Pul. 5– 3 offered his *a·* adoration in
  Rud. 9–22 an *a·* or even a mental argument,
  No. 39– 4 The *a·* prayer may be offered
    40–12 *a·* prayer of the right kind;
  My. 17–25 * *a·* repetition of the Lord's Prayer
    32–17 * *a·* repetition of the Lord's Prayer
    32–30 * *a·* repetition of the Lord's Prayer.
    39–11 * *a·* repetition of the Lord's Prayer,
    78–20 * *a·* repetition of the Lord's Prayer.
    139–23 from the *a·* to the inaudible prayer;

audibly
  Mis. 67–14 a lie, either mentally or *a·*,
    283– 3 speak the truth *a·*;
    293–24 affirm mentally and *a·* that God is
  Ret. 38–22 Not a word . . . *a·* or mentally,
  No. 2–14 by healing one case *a·*,
  My. 146–26 Scientist never mentally or *a·*

audience
  Mis. 48–15 informed his *a·* that he could
    95– 5 * was presented to Mr. Cook's *a·*,
    168–27 * drew a large *a·*.
  Ret. 15–18 not sufficient to seat the *a·*
  Pul. 12– 3 impressive stillness of the *a·*
  Hea. 17–18 claimed *a·* with a serpent.
  Po. vi– 7 * *and was sung by the a·*
  My. 81–17 * No more cosmopolitan *a·* ever
    185–23 spoke to an attentive *a·*

audience-room
  My. 9– 3 * *a·* in The Mother Church which will

audiences
  My. 68– 3 * impressing the *a·* with the beauty and

audit
  Mis. 131–30 to itemize or *a·* their accounts,

audited
  Man. 76–10 have the books . . . *a·* semi-annually,
    77– 2 books of the Church Treasurer *a·*
    77– 5 books are to be *a·* on May first.

Auditorium
  My. 77– 5 * In this respect it leads the *A·* of

auditorium
  Pul. 25– 8 * *a·*, seating eleven hundred people
    25–19 * entrances leading to the *a·*,
    25–21 * *a·* is seated with pews of
    27–12 * In the *a·* are two rose windows
    27–25 * One more window in the *a·*
    41–16 * The large *a·*, with its capacity for
    42–18 * pulpit end of the *a·* was rich with
    57– 5 * The *a·* is said to seat
    58–16 * main *a·* has wide galleries,
  My. 7–16 * *a·* for The Mother Church that will
    16–11 * The corner-stone of the new *a·*
    24– 5 * to express in its ample *a·*
    46– 2 * in exquisite and expansive *a·*,
    57– 4 * need was felt of an *a·* that would

auditorium
  My. 68– 4 * *a·*, with its high-domed ceiling,
    68–18 * color scheme for all the *a·* is
    69–16 * The *a·* contains seven galleries,
    71–21 * just one vast *a·* which will seat
    71–25 * every person seated in the *a·*,
    71–29 * *a·* that would seat five thousand
    80–11 * old *a·* of The Mother Church,
    80–21 * into the *a·* of the extension of
    80–31 * *a·* was comfortably filled.
    86–28 * Not even the great size of the *a·*

auditors
  Pul. 59–29 * the *a·* left by the rear doors,
  My. 80– 4 * earnestly assure thousands of *a·*

aught
  Mis. 10–31 that *a·* but good exists in Science.
    12–26 Whatever manifests *a·* else
    18–31 but to believe that *a·*
    27– 4 or *a·* that can result in evil
    72–29 cannot cognize *a·* material,
    124– 1 It is plain that *a·* unspiritual,
    171–26 Few people at present know *a·* of
    319– 5 This closes the argument of *a·*
    319– 5 *a·* else than good.
    344– 7 *a·* of that which leads to bliss,
    358–11 He that seeketh *a·* besides
    367–19 if He did know *a·* else,
    390– 9 Too pure for *a·* so mute.
  Un. 10–14 toward *a·* but infinite Deity.
    18–26 of *a·* beside Myself is impossible.
    38–21 in *a·* which is unlike God,
  Pul. 21–29 *a·* that can darken in any degree our
    74–21 If she said *a·* with intention to be
  No. 17–10 to be conscious of *a·* but good.
    27– 4 Matter is not Mind, to claim *a·*;
  Pan. 9– 4 no reality in *a·* else.
  '00. 5– 5 idolatry or *a·* besides God, good.
  '02. 6– 2 to have *a·* unlike the infinite.
  Po. 55–10 Too pure for *a·* so mute.
  My. 137–25 before . . . I knew *a·* about them,
    153–19 Faith in *a·* else misguides the
    261– 9 that Santa Claus has *a·* to do with
    300– 2 belief in sin or in *a·* besides God,

augment
  My. 10– 4 * and *a·* the achievements of its

augmented
  Mis. 289–30 they should be consulted, *a·*, and

August
  (*see* **months**)

august
  My. 294–27 The *a·* ruler . . . has now passed

Augusta, Me.
  Pul. 88–16 * *Kennebec Journal, A·, M·.*

Augustus, Emperor
  '00. 12–10 in the time of the Roman Emperor *A·.*

auspices
  Man. 88– 5 under the *a·* of Mary Baker Eddy,
    90–15 under the *a·* of this Board.
  Pul. 6–20 * He went out under the *a·* of
  My. 125–20 *a·* of the Massachusetts Metaphysical
    246– 6 examined under its *a·* by the Board

auspicious
  Pul. 44–10 * *a·* hour in your eventful career.
    60–15 * come to Boston for this *a·* occasion
  My. 201–28 on the *a·* occasion of the opening
    257–17 To this *a·* Christmastide,

Australia
  '00. 1–17 in *A·*, the Philippine Islands,
  My. 30–15 * from *A·*, from India, from England,
    136–21 also in Canada, *A·*, *etc.*
    208– 2 chapter sub-title

authentic
  Mis. 376– 2 * most *a·* Italian school, revived.
    376– 3 * I use the words *most a·*
    376– 7 * said to have been *a·*;

authentically
  My. 181–27 *a·* said that one expositor of

authenticate
  My. 179–20 *a·* Christ's Christianity as the

authenticated
  Mis. 347–30 only *a·* organ of C. S.

authenticity
  Mis. 98–24 attest the *a·* of their mission,
    193–10 the *a·* of the Gospels,
  Ret. 35–18 no authority for querying the *a·* of
    70– 8 We do not question the *a·* of

author (*see also* **author's**)
  Mis. 50– 3 God is not its *a·*,
    62–23 In that work the *a·* grapples with
    83– 6 "*Every sin is the a· of itself,*

author

Mis.	83–17	sin is the *a·* of sin.
	88– 7	*a· of that genuine critique in the*
	88– 9	*a·* of the article in question is
	196–13	God was not the *a·* of it ;
	216–15	an acquaintance with the *a·*
	296– 8	unknown *a·* cited by Mr. Wakeman
	361–20	Jesus the *a·* and finisher— *Heb.* 12 : 2.
	381–12	claim that Dr. Quimby was the *a·*
Ret.	70– 5	and claims God as their *a·* ;
Un.	26– 5	God is my *a·*, authority,
	26–10	Neither is He the *a·* of the material
Pul.	6–11	The *a·* of "Marriage of the Lamb,"
	39–11	*a·* of "The World Beautiful."
No.	42–24	would make a lie the *a·* of Truth,
'01.	4–12	God is the *a·* of Science
	17– 5	the *a·* and finisher of our faith,
Hea.	9–22	"Who is the *a·* of evil?"
Po.	39– 1	*A·* of all divine Gifts,
My.	258–13	Jesus the *a·* and finisher— *Heb.* 12 : 2.
	304– 6	*a·* of Sanborn's Grammar.
	304–24	the celebrated naturalist and *a·*,
	338–19	talented *a·* of this lecture has
	347–26	man is not the *a·* of Science,
	349–16	Jesus the *a·* and finisher— *Heb.* 12 : 2.
		(*see also* **Eddy**)

authoress

Ret.	1– 6	the pious and popular English *a·*
		(*see also* **Eddy**)

authoritative

My.	326– 6	* in an official and *a·* manner.

authoritatively

My.	346– 8	* may learn *a·* from the *Herald* that

authorities

Rud.	2– 9	word is used by the best *a·*,
'00.	13–27	* *a·* of the Judæo-Christian church."
Po.	vi–17	*a· could protect him nowhere but in*
My.	220– 7	reporting . . . to the proper *a·*
	332–25	* much interviewing with Masonic *a·*,
	335–20	* *a·* gave the cause of death as

authority

and law

Un.	26– 9	is not your *a·* and law.

and power

Mis.	333–25	God had *a·* and power,

any

Man.	66–21	any *a·* supposed to come from her

Biblical

Hea.	5–18	Such hypotheses ignore Biblical *a·*,

book as

Mis.	91–27	read from the book as *a·* for

brief

No.	22– 5	* clothed with a "brief *a·* ;"
My.	340–14	clad in a little brief *a·*,

cited as

Man.	104–18	these editions shall be cited as *a·*.

comes into

Un.	20– 6	Through these . . . evil comes into *a·* :

divine

Mis.	93–16	fear, . . . is without divine *a·*.
Un.	33– 7	we have it on divine *a·* :
'01.	14–27	wrong has no divine *a·* ;

for Christian Science

My.	305– 4	as the *a·* for C. S. !
	318–31	not find my *a·* for C. S. in history,

good

My.	14–13	* claimed to have good *a·* for

having

Mis.	189–28	as one having *a·*,— *Matt.* 7 : 29.
Ret.	58–11	as one having *a·*,— *Matt.* 7 : 29.
Un.	42–19	as one having *a·*,— *Matt.* 7 : 29.

his

Mis.	76–18	no man can rationally reject his *a·*

no

Ret.	35–18	There is no *a·* for querying the
'01.	20– 3	no *a·* in C. S. for

no Biblical

Mis.	274– 2	we have no Biblical *a·* for a

no legal

Mis.	141–28	had no legal *a·* for obtaining,

of God

Un.	31–17	usurps the *a·* of God, Spirit ;

of Jesus

'01.	8–11	we have the *a·* of Jesus for
Peo.	9–20	despite the *a·* of Jesus

of sin

Ret.	63–11	When we deny the *a·* of sin,

of their Church

Man.	87– 5	consent of the *a·* of their Church.

only

My.	104– 1	The Bible has been my only *a·*.

our

'01.	25–20	What, then, is our *a·* in
	34– 4	Bible is our *a·* for asserting **this,**

authority

position of

My.	343–22	"A position of *a·*," she went on,

recognized

Pul.	55–29	* Truth is the sole recognized *a·*.

Scriptural

'02.	7–17	Scriptural *a·* for divine metaphysics

true

My.	232–18	Are Christ's teachings the true *a·*

Mis.	109– 4	or who take me as *a·* for
	195–15	We ask what is the *a·* for
	265– 1	and gives me as *a·* for it ;
	291– 9	as *a·* for other people's thoughts
Man.	51–20	*A·*.
	66–17	or she is referred to as *a·* for
	66–24	shall not report on *a·* an order
	104–12	Seventy-third Edition the *A·*.
Un.	26– 5	God is my author, *a·*, governor,
My.	190–13	accept our Master as *a·*,

authorize

Mis.	195–13	does not *a·* us to expect the

authorized

Man.	49–22	a clergyman who is legally *a·*.
	80– 9	is *a·* to order its disposition
	86– 3	*A·* to Teach.
	86– 4	*a·* to be a teacher of C. S.,
	87– 9	by its By-Laws to teach C. S.,
	111–11	studied C. S. with an *a·* teacher ;
My.	vi–29	* and *a· Der Herold der C. S.*,

Authorized Version

'02.	16– 5	which is rendered in the *A·V·*

authorizes

Mis.	93–10	C. S. *a·* the logical conclusion
	272–15	* who confers, or *a·* to be conferred,

author's

Mis.	216–23	to illustrate the *a·* following point
Ret.	75–17	embraced in the *a·* own mental mood,
	76– 1	plagiarizing an *a·* ideas
My.	224–15	not caught in some *a·* net,
		(*see also* **Eddy**)

authors

Mis.	80– 1	*a·* of spurious works on
	264– 1	while they quote from other *a·*
	301– 7	Those *a·* and editors of pamphlets
Man.	59– 3	writings of *a·* who think at random
Ret.	75– 9	citing from the works of other *a·*
	91–10	or by the Scripture *a·*.
'01.	27– 2	of all other *a·* except the Bible.
My.	52–28	* sacrifices from which most *a·* would
	114–15	I consulted no other *a·*
	224–25	would not deny their *a·* a hearing,
	305–20	* of the foremost living *a·*."

authorship

Mis.	301–11	gospel-opposing system of *a·*,
No.	42–22	Denial of the *a·* of "S. and H.
'01.	21–13	improved in its teaching and *a·*
My.	306– 2	my character, education, and *a·*,
	317– 6	* in the *a·* of "S. and H.
	321–25	* knowledge of the *a·* of your works

autographs

Mis.	280–22	on each page, with their *a·*.

autopsy

Man.	50– 1	an *a·* shall be made by qualified

Autumn

Mis.	395–14	poem
Po.	vi–28	* poem
	page 58	poem

autumn

Mis.	142–18	shaded as *a·* leaves with bright hues
	332– 9	may its sober-suited *a·* follow
	395–18	Ere *a·* blanch another year,
Ret.	4–16	shone richly in the mellow hues of *a·*,
Po.	58– 3	Ere *a·* blanch another year,

autumnal

Mis.	355–30	at the close of a balmy *a·* day,

autumn's

Mis.	395–27	Enhancing *a·* gloom.
Po.	58–12	Enhancing *a·* gloom.

auxiliaries

Mis.	260–26	not always the *a·* of Truth.
Man.	43– 7	as *a·* to teaching C. S.

auxiliary

My.	246–22	is an *a·* to the College called
	288–18	matter was not the *a·* of Spirit.

avail

Mis.	7–13	of what can mortal opinion *a·* ?
	89–30	*a·* himself of the efficacy of Truth,
	165–26	is the sinner ready to *a·* himself of
	181–12	What *a·*, then, to quarrel over
	344–14	Of what *a·* would geometry be to

avail
My. 317–11 so as to *a·* myself of
344–27 Were vaccination of any *a·*,
availability
My. 353–15 universal activity and *a·* of Truth;
available
Mis. 62–13 by that much, less *a·*.
359–23 and is *a·* at the right time.
My. 54–18 * could be found that was *a·*,
availed
My. 318–10 I *a·* myself of the name of
availeth
My. 220–19 I also have faith that my prayer *a·*,
280–11 * righteous prayer which *a·* much.
avails
Mis. 33– 2 It is the righteous prayer that *a·*
avarice
Pul. 10–13 No dream of *a·* or ambition
ave
My. 204–10 sacred *a·* and essence of Soul
avenge
Mis. 129– 8 To *a·* an imaginary or an actual
227–31 Not to *a·* one's self upon one's
228– 5 and yet not to *a·* thyself,
avenging
Mis. 275– 6 Who — but God's *a·* angel!
My. 161–27 When evil was *a·* itself on its
Aventine
Pul. 10– 8 Rome's fallen fanes and silent *A·*
avenue
Mis. 185–12 good flows into every *a·* of being,
avenues
'01. 1– 3 through the mental *a·* of mankind
aver
Mis. 49–30 God is Truth, the Scriptures *a·*;
Rud. 13–19 To *a·* that harmony is the real
No. 2– 5 To *a·* that disease is normal,
My. 193–23 Here I *a·* that you have
300–14 or *a·* that there is no death,
average
Mis. 131– 7 of more than *a·* avoirdupois
Pan. 10–12 were the *a·* man and woman.
My. 88– 7 * above the *a·* in intelligence.
106–24 more than does the *a·* man,
averred
Pan. 10–13 best students in the class *a·*
averring
Ret. 60– 6 *a·* that there is nothing beside God;
avers
Mis. 253– 3 not merely a gift, as St. Paul *a·*,
295– 4 *a·* that the "cursed barmaid system"
No. 5–15 Material sense also *a·* that Spirit,
avert
Un. 19– 6 yet which He cannot *a·*.
No. 2–25 Conceit cannot *a·* the effects of deceit.
averts
Mis. 71–14 Science never *a·* law,
Po. 10–21 His hand *a·* the blow."
My. 337–22 His hand *a·* the blow."
avoid
Mis. 39– 4 To *a·* being *subject* to disease,
48– 2 and *a·* all that works ill.
127–25 cannot *a·* wielding it if we reflect
130–23 *a·* referring to past mistakes.
234–14 his effort to . . . *a·* hard work;
322– 7 To *a·* this, I may hereafter
347– 4 To *a·* danger from this source
363–22 *a·* the shoals of a sensual religion
Ret. 65–18 it will continue to *a·* whatever
84–29 *a·* leaving his own regular institute
No. 8– 6 *A·* voicing error;
35–15 and how to *a·* paying it.
My. 160–15 most men *a·* until compelled to
224–13 *A·* . . . public debating clubs.
226– 1 To *a·* using this word incorrectly,
244– 2 in order to *a·* the stir that might be
363–25 *a·* naming, in his mental treatment,
avoidance
Mis. 257–19 reliance where there should be *a·*,
Pul. 15– 6 to ensure the *a·* of the evil?
My. 211–23 reliance where there should be *a·*,
avoided
Mis. 80–10 A league which . . . should be *a·*.
240– 3 squills and bills would have been *a·*;
avoiding
Mis. 45– 8 *a·* the fatal results that frequently
300– 1 *a·* the cost of hiring or purchasing?

avoirdupois
Mis. 131– 7 man of more than average *a·*
avowal
Mis. 83–26 for the *a·* of this great truth,
avowals
No. 42– 4 Such sentiments are wholesome *a·* of
avowed
'01. 25–26 since been *a·* to be as real,
avowing
My. 95–22 * *a·* their disbelief in the miraculous.
200– 2 *a·* and consolidating the genius of
await
Mis. 241–14 else he will doubtingly *a·* the result;
Man. 66–12 to *a·* her explanation thereof.
My. 222–31 *a·* the end — justice and judgment.
awaited
My. 244– 1 I have *a·* your arrival before
244–13 I have *a·* the right hour,
318–13 confidently *a·* the years to declare
awaiting
Mis. 358–28 *a·*, with staff in hand, God's
360– 4 *a·* the hammering, chiselling, and
Ret. 85–22 *a·* only an opportunity
'00. 15– 3 for many years has been *a·* you.
My. 20– 9 *a·* on behalf of your Leader
30– 2 * or *a·* admission to one.
150– 2 and where its tender lesson is not *a·*
awaits
Mis. 246–21 *a·* the crouching wrong that
'02. 11– 7 *a·* with warrant and welcome,
19–24 a spiritual behest, in reversion, *a·*
My. 177–22 joy of many generations *a·* it,
230– 2 eternity *a·* our Church Manual,
290–21 He *a·* to welcome you where no arrow
awake
Mis. 15–21 and man *a·* in His likeness.
30–31 and *a·* in His likeness.
44–21 when *a·*, or when asleep in a dream.
47–17 with less impediment than when *a·*,
60–20 with another who is *a·*.
295–12 *a·*, and caught napping?
299– 1 *a·* to their cause and character.
331–29 As mortals *a·* from their dream
358–12 "*a·* in His likeness," — see *Psal.* 17 : 15.
400– 3 Slumbers not in God's embrace; Be *a·*;
Ret. 61–11 you cannot *a·* in fear or
Un. 2–21 *a·* from a sense of death
3– 4 they *a·* only to another sphere of
20–18 You will *a·* to the perception of
50–21 and *a·* from the troubled dream,
Pul. 84–19 * All who are *a·* thereto have
Rud. 11–16 *a·* from a night-dream;
11–17 just so you can *a·* from the dream of
No. 36– 5 when we *a·* in the divine likeness.
'00. 3–13 *a·* the slumbering capability of man.
8– 3 till we *a·* in his likeness.
'01. 15– 2 must *a·* from his belief in this awful
'02. 17–12 who should keep themselves *a·*
Hea. 17–12 we shall all learn this as we *a·* to
Peo. 14–12 *a·* to a higher and holier love for
Po. 76–14 Slumbers not in God's embrace; Be *a·*;
My. 356– 1 When will mankind *a·* to know their
359–27 *A·* and arise from this temptation
awaken
Mis. 42– 9 to *a·* with thoughts, and being,
100– 5 was to *a·* the dull senses,
106–30 and *a·* the heart's harpstrings.
Ret. 61– 6 as when you *a·* from sleep
Pul. 50–20 * will *a·* some sort of interest.
'01. 17– 2 *a·* the sufferer from the mortal
My. 204– 5 which storms *a·* to vigor and to
230–14 and to *a·* the sinner.
267–20 *a·* from his dream of life in matter
273–30 death alone does not *a·* man in God's
297–21 If we would *a·* to this recognition,
awakened
Mis. 4–19 Much interest is *a·* and expressed
16–24 This newly *a·* consciousness is wholly
123–19 there has risen to the *a·* thought
201–28 is *a·* to bar his door against
347–15 A true sense . . . has been *a·*.
No. 39–20 an *a·* desire to be and do good.
40– 9 pure pearls of *a·* consciousness,
'00. 15–13 *a·* to see through sin's disguise
15–18 a feast for this *a·* consciousness.
My. 155–20 an *a·* sense of the risen Christ.
257– 7 To the *a·* consciousness,
281– 2 and *a·* a wiser want,
awakening
Mis. 16–16 *a·* from the dream of life in matter,
Ret. 21–21 The *a·* from a false sense of life,
Pul. 23– 9 * The "great *a·*" of the time of

awakening
My. 316– 5 song of the Redeemer a· the nations,

awakes
Mis. 15– 3 until he a· from it.
222–18 the subject scarcely a· in time,
Un. 56–21 Until he a· from his delusion,
My. 273–28 "Man a· from the dream of death

award
My. 332– 7 * yet it is all we can a· :

aware
Mis. 148–23 not a· that the contribution box was
176–26 Are we duly a· of our own great
227–13 ere that one himself become a·,
335– 9 hour that he is not a· of,— Matt. 24 : 50.
Pul. 31–15 * in the early '80's that I became a·
34–11 * became a· of a divine illumination
My. 342– 2 * I became a· of a white-haired lady
358– 6 You are a· that animal magnetism is

away
Mis. 10–24 wherein old things pass a·
17– 7 before the flames have died a·
27–32 Take a· the mortal sense of
33–25 It does a· with all material
48–27 That persons have gone a· from
53–27 the thought educated a· from it
58–25 Take a· the theology of
58–26 and you take a· its science,
59–25 leading his thoughts a· from
74–19 rolled a· the stone from the door
77–26 belief that man has fallen a· from
84–27 takes them a·, and teaches
90– 3 Take a· this pleasure, and you
98– 4 should turn a· from inharmony,
99–21 earth shall pass a·,— Matt. 24 : 35.
99–22 shall not pass a· ;"— Matt. 24 : 35.
111–17 earth shall pass a·,— Matt. 24 : 35.
111–18 shall not pass a· ;"— Matt. 24 : 35.
120–25 a· from their own fields of labor.
121– 2 his words can never pass a· :
121–16 put a· the guilt— Deut. 19 : 13.
123–18 Divine Science has rolled a· the stone
144– 8 there are laid a· a copy of
144–14 laid a· as a sacred secret
156– 9 when the mist shall melt a·
163–19 earth shall pass a·,— Matt. 24 : 35.
163–19 shall not pass a· !"— Matt. 24 : 35.
168–29 * and many had to go a·
176–22 melted a· in the fire of love
179– 2 roll a· the stone?"— see Mark 16 : 3.
179– 3 The stone has been rolled a· by
189–18 quickening spirit takes it a· :
198– 5 turning a· from material gods ;
205– 5 and melting a· the shadows
210–14 and takes a· its sting.
212–14 One step a· from the direct line
222– 1 It takes a· a man's proper sense of
225–23 Looking a· from all material aid,
246–11 washed it divinely a· in C. S. !
254–19 take a· a third part of the stars
255–22 It does a· with material medicine,
275– 3 would you take a· even woman's
275– 4 Who can roll a· the stone
285– 4 I ordered to be laid a·
289–21 Rights that are bargained a·
292–15 a· from the open sepulchres of sin,
324–22 Stealing cautiously a· from his comrades,
325–11 seize his pearls, throw them a·,
325–17 dreaming a· the hours.
325–24 A· from this charnel-house
327–32 wipes a· the blood stains,
328–18 stumbled, and wandered a·?
333–15 a· from the only living and
333–17 a· from the divine source of being,
334–11 a· goes all its supposed power
335– 1 a· from this divine Principle
336–28 only to take a· its frailty.
343–12 a· from the sordid soil of self
343–15 picking a· the cold, hard pebbles
343–23 and tear them a· from their
345–31 turned men a· from the thought
357–16 what has been sown has withered a·,
359–10 I put a· childish things.— I Cor. 13 : 11.
360–16 When C. S. has melted a· the
370– 5 they went a· and took counsel
381–23 publishing, selling, giving a·,
385–24 and doomed To pass a·.
388– 4 What chased the clouds a·?
399– 2 Love wipes your tears all a·,
399–19 Rolled a· from loving heart
Man. 41– 9 turneth a· wrath."— Prov. 15 : 1.
48–20 a· from personality and numbering
94–10 should go a· contemplating truth ;
Chr. 53–53 To-day, as oft, a· from sin
Ret. 7– 3 passed a· at the age of thirty-one,
18–10 and perfume from buds burst a·,

away
Ret. 18–25 This life is a shadow, and hastens a·.
20– 8 was sent a· from me,
34–11 does a· with all material medicines,
42–13 In 1882 he passed a·.
80–25 sees the door and turns a· from it,
89–15 had been a· from the neighborhood ;
Un. 2– 9 takes a· man's fondness for sin
11–18 taking a· the material evidence.
14–23 infinite model would be taken a·.
25–25 evil can never take a·.
30–10 takes a· this belief and restores
34–19 Take a· mortal mind,
34–21 Take a· matter, and mortal mind
43–16 never "pass a·— see Matt. 5 : 18.
57–27 Science wipes a· all tears.
Pul. 7–16 and with power to wash a·,
14–10 carried a· of the— Rev. 12 : 15.
16– 4 Rolled a· from loving heart
36–16 * I came a· in a state of
49–20 * to get a· from her busy career
50–22 * thoroughly carried a· with
54–23 * He kept the unbelievers a·,
Rud. 2–20 takes a· the trammels assigned to
11–21 takes a· every human belief,
No. 1–16 flames die a· on the mount
7–12 a· from the enemy of sinning sense,
36–24 rolled a· the stone from the
40–17 never to take a· the rights,
43–23 which they go a· to disgrace.
Pan. 10– 1 it takes a· man's personality
'00. 11– 9 turns mortals a· from earth
'01. 7–20 have not taken a· their Lord,
9–17 taketh a· the sin of — John 1 : 29.
16–26 and go a· to pray?
26–12 a· from Christ's purely spiritual
31–27 yielded up . . . what He took a·.
'02. 19–20 troubled sea foams itself a·,
19–22 treasures, taken a· from you?
20–13 That swept the clouds a·?
Hea. 10– 1 he saw it pass a·,— an illusion.
Peo. 1– 5 crumbling a· of material elements
5– 5 have not taken a· our Lord,
5–18 points a· from matter and
9– 5 washing a· the motives for sin ;
11–13 gnawing a· life and hope ;
Po. 2–16 On wings of morning gladly flit a·,
7– 4 What chased the clouds a·?
15–11 whispering voices are calling a·
22–10 wipes the tears of time A·,
23–22 Bid error melt a· !
31–21 That wipes a· the sting of death
33–19 That waft me a· to my God.
41–14 sunny slopes of the woodland a· ;
48–20 and doomed To pass a·.
63–21 and perfume from buds burst a·,
64–22 This life is a shadow, and hastens a·.
65–18 and death like mist melt a·,
70– 1 a· In the dim distance,
70–14 A·, then, mortal sense !
75– 9 Love wipes your tears all a·,
76– 3 Rolled a· from loving heart
78–12 When to be wiped a·, Thou knowest
My. 4–21 the iron in human nature rusts a· ;
16–29 the hail shall sweep a·— Isa. 28 : 17.
24–26 * they have gone a· with the conviction
30–28 * hundreds had to be turned a·,
44– 4 * tears are being wiped a·,
45–25 * "He took not a· the— Exod. 13 : 22.
54– 2 * hundreds going a· who could not
69–31 * in Cambridge, some four miles a·.
82– 8 * trying to get a· at the same time.
82–19 * seem that this ability to get a·
83–10 * but this is usually hidden a·
92–22 * but one cannot sneer a· the
94– 6 * "One cannot sneer a· the
111–10 swept a· their illogical syllogisms
119–16 a· from the supposedly crucified
119–30 spirit of Truth that leadeth a· from
120–11 God's spiritual idea that takes a· all sin,
132–31 wipes a· the unavailing, tired tear,
135– 5 I put a· childish things."— I Cor. 13 : 11.
153–31 pointing a· from matter and man
166– 6 Religions may waste a·,
171– 7 sighing shall flee a·."— Isa. 35 : 10.
191–16 Love, which wipes a· all tears.
191–23 The stone is rolled a·.
193–16 Love gives nothing to take a·.
247–22 persuasion that takes a· their fear,
252–13 and run a· in the storm,
261–17 I put a· childish things."— I Cor. 13 : 11.
297–14 blows a· the baubles of belief,
313–25 to describe scenes far a·,
335–18 * at the end of nine days he passed a·.

awe
Mis. 249–28 I am in a· before it.

awe
Ret. 25–29 I beheld with ineffable *a*·
My. 63–21 * *a*· and of reverence beyond words,

awed
My. 78–28 * the little children, *a*· by the grandeur of

awe-filled
No. 10–2 I employ this *a*· word in both a

awestruck
Po. 71–10 Righteousness ne'er — *a*· or dumb

awful
Mis. 14–18 This *a*· deception is evil's umpire
17–1 *a*· detonations of Sinai.
99–8 cost Galileo, what? This *a*· price:
238–1 *a*· story that "he helped 'niggers'
Ret. 69–25 "Above error's *a*· din,
No. 35–14 the *a*· price paid by sin,
'01. 15–2 must awake from his belief in this *a*·
Po. 27–3 Bloated oppression in its *a*· hour,

awhile
Po. 33–11 (And mem'ry but part us *a*·),

awoke
Mis. 180–1 I *a*· from the dream of
225–28 In about one hour he *a*·,
Ret. 20–18 *A*· new beauty in the surge's roll !

axe
Mis. 37–17 C. S. lays the *a*· at the root of
235–12 It lays the *a*· at the root of
285–19 laying the *a*· at the root of error.

axe
'01. 13–15 C. S. lays the *a*· at the root of sin,
23–17 he laid the *a*· at the root of
My. 268–25 lays the *a*· at the root of all evil,
287–21 it lays the *a*· at the root of the
296–3 lays the *a*· "unto the root — *Matt. 3 : 10.*

axiom
'01. 30–28 and to adopt Pope's *a*· :
Hea. 11–18 it has established this *a*·,
My. 58–6 * proves the truth of the *a*·,
177–17 was allied to that olden *a*· :
236–10 An old *a*· says :
357–23 the *a*· of true C. S.,

axiomatic
Mis. 271–16 take in this *a*· truism :
Ret. 87–4 is so eternally true, so *a*·,

axioms
'01. 25–13 No Christly *a*·, practices, or

axis
Ret. 88–30 Mind revolves on a spiritual *a*·,

Ayer, D. D., Rev. Franklin D.
My. 174–13 To the Rev. Franklin D. *A*·, *D.D.*,

ayont
Po. 79–15 and lifteth me, *A*· hate's thrall :

azure
Mis. 323–3 city above all clouds, in serene *a*·
Po. 18–1 in the *a*· the eagle's proud wing,
34–20 in *a*· bright soar far above ;

B

Baal (*see also* Baal's)
Mis. 333–24 worshippers of *B*· worshipped the sun.

Baalites
My. 151–24 the *B*· or sun-worshippers failed to

Baal's
No. 39–6 after the fashion of *B*· prophets,

babbling
No. 1–8 *b*· brooks fill the rivers till they

babe
Mis. 72–2 For the innocent *b*· to be born
111–32 or is an incarnated *b*·,
159–19 not so much the Bethlehem *b*·,
164–13 *b*· Jesus seemed small to mortals ;
167–7 Is the *b*· a son, or daughter?
370–15 This is the *b*· we are to cherish.
370–16 *b*· that twines its loving arms
388–24 nurse the Bethlehem *b*· so sweet,
Chr. 53–24 O'er *b*· and crib.
Ret. 19–18 my *b*· was born.
20–20 *b*· of my soul.
31–28 as by the tearful lips of a *b*·.
40–15 at the birth of her last *b*·,
40–17 her *b*· was safely born,
70–9 Virgin-mother and Bethlehem *b*·,
90–19 comprehend the needs of her *b*·
Un. 6–21 talk to her *b*· about the problems of
61–6 appeared as a helpless human *b*· ;
Pul. 1–4 a *b*· of time, a prophecy
No. 26–7 than the *b*· is identical with
36–27 was a *b*· born in a manger
Po. 21–13 the Bethlehem *b*· so sweet,
29–12 The Bethlehem *b*· — Beloved,
70–20 As when this *b*· was born,
My. 257–7 the Bethlehem *b*· has left his
258–17 The memory of the Bethlehem *b*·
262–7 mortal *b*· — a *b*· born in a manger
262–10 This homely origin of the *b*· Jesus
330–30 my *b*· was born.

Babel
My. 245–15 and to their *B*· of confusion

babes
Mis. 167–26 revealed them unto *b*· !" — *Luke 10 : 21.*
Ret. 61–29 Let there be milk for *b*·,
Pul. 8–18 and *b*· gave kisses to
8–22 "Out of the mouths of *b*· — *Matt. 21 : 16.*
Rud. 8–3 or provides breast-milk for *b*·.
No. v–11 if you are *b*· in Christ,
45–2 revealed them unto *b*·." — *Luke 10 : 21.*
My. 6–21 evidencing the praise of *b*·
17–6 "As newborn *b*·, — *I Pet. 2 : 2.*

baby
Mis. 231–16 And the *b*· !
231–21 Now ! *b*· has tumbled,
231–26 That was a scientific *b*· ;

Babylon
'00. 3–22 Israelites in *B*· hesitated not

Babylonian
Pan. 8–3 *B*· sun god, moon god,
'00. 4–8 *B*· and Neoplatonic religion,

Babylonian Yawa
Mis. 123–15 *B*· *Y*·, or Jehovah,

Babylonish
My. 125–29 The doom of the *B*· woman,
126–24 The *B*· woman is fallen,

Bachelor
My. 245–29 degrees of *B*· and Doctor of C. S.,

back
Mis. xi–20 to fling it *b*· and forth.
23–3 the power *b*· of gravitation,
50–7 *is there a secret b· of what*
52–27 would be obliged to turn *b*·
93–6 *bring b· old beliefs of disease*
93–22 bring on disease or bring *b*· disease,
99–15 take not *b*· the words of Truth.
112–20 he sank *b*· in his chair,
140–23 and now it must be put *b*· into
169–6 *b*· to the inspired pages.
184–24 The Science of being gives *b*· the
184–32 giving *b*· the lost sense of
195–8 is held *b*· by reason of the lack of
211–18 to be pitied and brought *b*·
294–17 keep *b*· thy offerings from asps
324–23 he departs ; then turns *b*·,
327–1 When I went *b*· into the house
327–27 Obstinately holding themselves *b*·,
327–31 goes *b*· and kindly binds up their
328–4 will call thee *b*· to the path
328–17 turned *b*·, stumbled, and wandered
329–27 calling the feathered tribe *b*· to
365–28 held *b*· by the common ignorance
376–14 * You have given us *b*· our Jesus,
390–8 Gives *b*· some maiden melody,
Ret. 20–25 to get *b*· my child,
Un. 64–17 can never turn *b*· what Deity knoweth,
Pul. 13–21 comes *b*· to him at last
20–5 gave *b*· the land to the church.
46–13 * in going *b*· to the ancestral tree
No. 11–11 this system is held *b*· by
Hea. 6–3 and so come *b*· to the world?
6–24 lying *b*· in the unconscious thought,
Peo. 1–6 translation of law *b*· to its
Po. 23–7 Or give . . . *b*· An image of the soul,
55–9 Gives *b*· some maiden melody,
71–7 Corruption's band Is driven *b*· ;
My. 12–22 it comes not *b*· again.
47–13 * look *b*· to the picturesque,
47–16 * To-day we look *b*· over the years
59–16 * my mind was carried *b*· to
68–21 * great organ is placed *b*· of the
69–17 * and three at the *b*·,
80–1 * *b*· to the age of miracles.
84–6 * retards and holds *b*· work
132–32 brings *b*· the wanderer to
184–18 brought *b*· to me the odor of

back
My. 307– 5 *b·* of his magnetic treatment
    316–20 turn *b·* the foaming torrents of
    336– 5 * to take her *b·* to the North.
    342–18 * Mrs. Eddy sat *b·* to be questioned.
    343–29 brought all *b·* to union and love

Back Bay
Pul. 24– 3 * church is in the fashionable *B· B·*,
    57–23 * this new edifice on *B· B·*,
My. 77–29 * edifice in the *B· B·* district
    84–15 * in that section of the *B· B·*
    86–23 * edifice of the . . . on the *B· B·*
    325– 7 * very sure *B· B·* property would never
    325–11 * greater future than the new *B· B·*.

Back Bay Park
Mis. 139–19 near the beautiful *B· B· P·*,
Pul. 36–22 * at the entrance to the *B· B· P·*,

backbiteth
My. 33–19 He that *b·* not — *Psal.* 15 : 3.

backbone
Pul. 46–12 * Aristocratic to the *b·*,

background
Mis. 266–10 Stationary in the *b·*,
    376–25 on a *b·* of cerulean hue ;

backs
Mis. 325–17 or, flat on their *b·*,

back-to-back
Mis. 171– 8 *b·* seances with their patients,

backward
Mis. 340– 1 One *b·* step, one relinquishment of
Pul. vii–11 instructive to turn *b·* the

backwardness
Pul. 15– 5 Why this *b·*, since exposure is

bacteria
My. 344–16 * reject utterly the *b·* theory

bad
Mis. 25–29 then they are *b·* and unfit for man ;
    69–20 neutralized the *b·* effects of
    71–12 *good or b· influences on the unborn*
    72– 8 good and *b·* traits of the parents
    198–24 belief, fear, theory, or *b·* deed,
    243– 3 with no *b·* results,
    296–28 and the *b·* appetites of men
    345–10 * I cannot change from good to *b·*.''
    362–31 the influence of *b·* inclinations
Man. 63–24 shall have no *b·* habits,
Un. 15–23 *b·* deity, who seeks to do
Pul. 69–13 * leave no room there for the *b·*,
Hea. 10–14 question of a good and a *b·* side to
Peo. 13–20 * cannot change . . . from good to *b·*.''
My. 87–24 * not be a *b·* thing if all the world
    205–18 * as the thing made is good or *b·*,
    220– 1 save him from *b·* physical results.
    310–26 * mingled with *b·* temper.''

bade
Mis. 197–10 and *b·* his followers pursue.
Ret. 9– 9 *b·* me, when the voice called again,
    13–18 *b·* me lean on God's love,
Pul. 33– 7 * and *b·* her, if she heard the voice
My. 149– 3 by doing as he *b·* :
    156–13 he *b·* them say to the good man
    215– 5 He it was that *b·* me do what I did,
    215–24 he *b·* them take no scrip
    215–26 Next, . . . he *b·* them take scrip.

badge
Mis. 137– 3 your card of invitation, your *b·*,
Pul. 42–15 * each of them wore a white satin *b·*

badges
My. 83– 8 * has been no flaunting of *b·*

badly
Mis. 12– 5 If you have been *b·* wronged, forgive

badness
My. 123–29 small things in goodness or in *b·*,

baffle
Mis. 125–26 the controversies which *b·* it,

baffles
Mis. 221–22 *b·* the student of Mind-healing,

baggage
Mis. 327–12 These had heavy *b·* of their own,
    327–17 those who, having less *b·*,
    327–22 determined not to part with their *b·*.
    327–31 Then he who has no *b·* goes
'02. 10–21 discharges burdensome *b·*,
My. 82–10 * trunks and smaller articles of *b·*

Bailey St., 105
My. 328– 5 * 105 *B· S·*, Asheville, N. C.,

Baker
Abigail (Ambrose)
Pul. 32–18 * Mark and Abigail (Ambrose) *B·*,
Albert
Ret. 6–11 my second brother, Albert *B·*,
    6–15 My brother Albert was graduated at
    6–20 Albert spent a year in the office of
    7– 7 * Albert *B·* was a young man of
    10– 8 From my brother Albert I received
Pul. 32–28 * Albert *B·*, graduated at Dartmouth
My. 309–27 * [Albert] received a liberal education.
    310– 4 Albert was a distinguished lawyer.
    310–18 * all the family, ''excepting Albert,
Congressman
Pul. 48–17 * Congressman *B·* from New Hampshire,
George
My. 312–13 taken to . . . by her brother George.
George S.
My. 332–14 * signature
    336– 4 * her brother, George S. *B·*,
George Sullivan
My. 310– 9 youngest brother, George Sullivan *B·*,
Grandfather
Ret. 2–26 A relative of my Grandfather *B·*
Hon. Henry M.
My. 135–15 namely, the Hon. Henry M. *B·*,
    136–15 Hon. Henry M. *B·*, who won a suit
    137–22 namely, the Hon. Henry M. *B·*,
Hon. Henry Moore
Ret. 4– 9 brother of the Hon. Henry Moore *B·*
James
Ret. 4– 4 and with his brother, James *B·*,
Joseph
Ret. 1–18 an Englishman, named Joseph *B·*,
    2– 7 Joseph *B·* and his wife,
Mark (see also Baker's)
Ret. 4– 2 was my father, Mark *B·*,
    4–23 The wife of Mark *B·* was
Pul. 32–17 * daughter of Mark and Abigail . . . *B·*,
My. 172– 6 * grown on the farm of Mark *B·*,
    309– 9 and Mark *B·* for Bow.
    309–17 Mark *B·* was the youngest of
Mary (see also Eddy)
Ret. 8–10 I heard somebody call *Mary*,
Pul. 32–17 * Mary *B·* was the daughter of
    33– 2 * As a child Mary *B·* saw visions
My. 309–27 * Mary *B·* passed her first fifteen years at
    310–23 * Mary, a child ten years old,
    310–29 * ''When do you ever see Mary angry?''
    311–30 * ''Mary *B·* completed her education
Mary Morse
Mis. x–18 my Christian name, Mary Morse *B·*.
Mary's
Ret. 9– 5 if she really did hear Mary's name
Miss
Pul. 34– 1 * At an early age Miss *B·* was married
Mrs. Abigail Ambrose
Ret. 5–21 * character of Mrs. Abigail Ambrose *B·*
Mrs. Marion McNeil
Ret. 2– 1 Mrs. Marion McNeil *B·* was reared
Samuel D.
My. 310–15 My oldest brother, Samuel D. *B·*,
Uncle James
(see Baker's)

Ret. 5– 6 In the *B·* homestead at Bow
My. 309–21 describing the *B·* homestead at Bow :
    313–28 to a *B·* that was a sorry offence.

Baker's
Grandmother
Ret. 2–18 one of my Grandmother *B·* books,
    2–30 line of my Grandmother *B·* family
Mark
My. 309–20 Mark *B·* father paid the largest tax
Uncle James
Ret. 4– 8 owned by Uncle James *B·* grandson,

Bakers
My. 309–26 * ''Alone of the *B·*, he [Albert]

Balaam
'00. 12–29 It refers to the Hebrew *B·* as the
    13–23 school of *B·* and Æsculapius,

balance
Mis. 104–30 gain a *b·* on the side of good,
    263–21 poise the wavering *b·* on the right
    317–21 is inadequate to adjust the *b·*
    321– 9 *b·* adjusted more on the side of God,
    350– 2 the *b·* was never receipted for.
Man. 75–20 the *b·* of the building funds,
    75–23 *b·* of the church building funds,
No. 18–13 when weighed in the *b·*,
My. 9–27 what my heart gives to *b·* accounts.
    16– 6 * there was a *b·* of $226,285.73

balances
    Mis. 280– 5   with *b·* to weigh the thoughts and
         288– 7   should be dropped into the *b·* of God
         365– 5   weighed in the *b·* of God

balancing
    Mis. 65–25   *b·* man's account with his Maker.
         325–18   *B·* on one foot, with eyes half open,
    My. 161– 7   thus *b·* his account with divine Love,

bald
    Pan. 12–27   unpierced . . . by *b·* philosophy,

ball
    Mis. 11– 5   if a man should aim a *b·* at my heart,

Ballard, William P.
    My. 174–16   John C. Thorne, William P. *B·*,

balloon
    Mis. 129–16   will seek occasion to *b·* an atom of

balm
    Mis. 110– 1   The costly *b·* of Araby,
    No. 44–19   healing *b·* of Truth and Love
    Po. vii–14   * a *b·* to the weary heart.
         22–16   probe the wound, then pour the *b·*
         24– 3   A *b·* — the long-lost leaven
    My. 38– 1   * the *b·* of heavenly joy,
         129–12   brook, blossom, breeze, and *b·*
         175–22   Sweeter than the *b·* of Gilead,

balmy
    Mis. 355–30   at the close of a *b·* autumnal day,

Baltimore
  Md
    Pul. 68–12   * *The American*, *B·*, Md.,

         ————
    Pul. 68–21   * adds interest to the *B·* organization.
         68–24   * The *B·* congregation was organized
         69– 1   * the pastor, came to *B·*
    '00. 1–20   *B·*, Charleston, S. C., Atlanta,

Bancroft, S. P.
    My. 60–21   * signature

band
    Mis. 144– 6   a little *b·* called Busy Bees,
         279–16   Joshua and his *b·* before the walls
         279–24   in the case of Joshua and his *b·*
         386–19   o'er thy broken household *b·*,
    Man. 17– 1   little *b·* of earnest seekers
    Ret. 85– 4   to *b·* together their students
    Po. 50– 4   o'er thy broken household *b·*,
         71– 6   Corruption's *b·* Is driven back ;
    My. 50– 6   * little *b·* of prayerful workers.
         50– 9   * so this little *b·* of pioneers,
         50–21   * fresh courage to the earnest *b·*,
         158–24   will bless this dear *b·* of brethren.
         257– 2   alas for the broken household *b·* !

bandage
    Hea. 19– 9   removed the *b·* from his eyes,

bandages
    Mis. 243– 9   doctor had put on splints and *b·*

bands
    Un. 12– 5   bind it with *b·* of Soul.
    Rud. 4–13   "loose the *b·* of Orion." — *Job.* 38 : 31.

bane
    '00. 8– 9   comes forth a blessing or a *b·*
    '01. 20–15   This mental *b·* could not bewilder,
    My. 224– 7   *b·* which follows disobedience,

baneful
    Mis. 115–28   *b·* effects of sin on yourself,
    My. 301–22   *b·* effects of illusion on mortal

banish
    Po. 41–17   didst call them to *b·* all pain,
    My. 95–24   * *b·* faith in the supernatural,

banished
    Ret. 31–15   *b·* at once and forever the
    Po. 70–24   sin, and death are *b·* hence.

banishes
    Mis. 204–31   *b·* forever all envy, rivalry,

banishment
    Ret. 13– 9   doomed to perpetual *b·*

bank
    Ret. 5– 2   left *b·* of the Merrimac River.

bank-notes
    My. 78–15   * every basket piled high with *b·*,

bankrupt
    Mis. 374–20   homage is indeed due, — but is *b·*.
    My. 9–19   I am *b·* in thanks to you,

bankruptcy
    Mis. 122–24   Neither spiritual *b·* nor a

banks
    My. 150–15   willowy *b·* dyed with emerald.

banner
    Mis. 138–27   under the *b·* of His love,
         285–11   hold high the *b·* of Truth
    Po. 10– 1   fling thy *b·* To the billows
    My. 232– 2   unfurling your *b·* to the breeze
         291–21   bear its *b·* into the vast forever.
         337– 3   fling thy *b·* To the billows

banners
    Pul. 83–13   * as an army with *b·*'' — *Song* 6 : 10.

banquet
    Mis. 149– 4   to this *b·* of C. S.,
    Ret. 18–13   Oft plucked for the *b·*,
    Po. 64– 3   Oft plucked for the *b·*,

banquet-rooms
    Mis. 324– 8   parlors, dancing-halls, and *b·*.

bans
    Mis. 172– 8   regardless of the *b·* or clans

banter
    My. 322–23   * seemed inclined to *b·* me

baptism
    Mis. 30–31   bathe in the *b·* of Spirit,
         82– 8   out of the *b·* of Spirit,
         125– 2   be baptized with his *b·* !
         131–12   one faith, one God, one *b·*.
         203–17   *b·* serves to rebuke the senses
         203–19   *First :* The *b·* of repentance
         204–12   *Second :* The *b·* of the Holy Ghost
         205–13   *Third :* The *b·* of Spirit,
         213–18   must pass through a *b·* of fire.
         298–16   the material rite of water *b·*,
         328–20   wakened through the *b·* of fire
         345–12   through the *b·* of flame.
         345–24   a *b·* not of water but of
    Ret. 48–26   like the *b·* of Jesus,
         54–10   being baptized with his *b·*,
         94– 9   so Christ's *b·* of fire,
    Pul. 20–23   *b·* of our master Metaphysician,
    No. 34– 2   through the *b·* of suffering,
    '01. 1–15   The *b·* of the Spirit,
    '02. 5– 8   with the *b·* of Jesus.
    Hea. 10–27   for the true fount and Soul's *b·*.
    Peo. 1– 1   *one faith, one b·.* — *Eph.* 4 : 5.
         5– 3   one faith, one *b·.*" — *Eph.* 4 : 5.
         9– 1   one faith, one Lord, one *b·* ;
         9– 2   this *b·* is the purification of mind,
         9– 9   *b·* of Spirit that washes our robes
         13–22   went up through the *b·* of fire
         14–19   one *b·.*" — *Eph.* 4 : 5.
    My. 161–20   with the *b·* that I — *Matt.* 20 : 23.
         174–21   offered me to Christ in infant *b·*.

baptismal
    Mis. 206–31   *b·* font of eternal Love.
         292– 3   and its spirit is *b·* ;

baptismals
    Mis. 18– 1   *b·* that come from Spirit,

Baptist
    No. 41–24   a Boston *B·* clergyman,
    '01. 32– 3   Rev. Mr. Boswell, of Bow, N. H., *B·* ;
    My. 331– 6   * Mr. Reperton, a *B·* clergyman,
         339–18   disciples of St. John the *B·*
    (*see also* **John the Baptist**)

Baptist Tabernacle
    Ret. 15–14   *B· T·* of Rev. Daniel C. Eddy, D. D.,

baptized
    Mis. 81–13   *footsteps of Truth being b· of John,*
         125– 1   be *b·* with his baptism !
         194–25   Then are you *b·* in the Truth
         206– 7   saying forever to the *b·* of Spirit :
    Ret. 54–10   being *b·* with his baptism,
    No. 34–12   *b·* in the purification of persecution
    Pan. 14– 9   and be *b·* in Spirit.
    '01. 9– 7   truer sense of Christ *b·* them
         12– 5   he *b·* with the Holy Ghost
    My. 161–20   be *b·* with the baptism — *Matt.* 20 : 23.
         161–21   that I am *b·* with." — *Matt.* 20 : 23.

baptizing
    Mis. 184–29   John came *b·* with water.

bar
    Mis. 114–22   or *b·* their doors too closely,
         201–28   *b·* his door against further robberies.
    Ret. 6–22   admitted to the *b·* in two States,
    '00. 7–10   members of the *b·* and bench,
    Po. 46–17   While beauty fills each *b·*.

barbarisms
    Mis. 29–25   esoteric magic and Oriental *b·*
    Peo. 5–12   the *b·* of spiritless codes.

barbarous
    My. 278–26   War is in itself an evil, *b·*,
         286– 4   *b·* slaughtering of our fellow-beings ;

barbs
    Mis. 224– 1   unless our own thought *b·* it.

bard
Mis.	126–30	Hebrew *b·* spake after this manner :
	142–23	spiritual strains of the Hebrew *b·*.
	192–14	The Hebrew *b·* saith,
	297–29	The Hebrew *b·* wrote,
My.	273–10	King David, the Hebrew *b·*,

bare
Mis.	335–16	I lay *b·* the ability, in belief,
	348– 9	one should lay it *b·* ;
	391–16	With *b·* feet soiled or sore,
Un.	44–13	is laid *b·* in C. S.
Rud.	15–25	laid *b·* for anatomical examination.
'01.	35– 5	willing to *b·* our bosom to the blade
Po.	38–15	With *b·* feet soiled or sore,
My.	322–21	* in Boston on the *b·* hope of

barefaced
Mis.	43–28	the *b·* errors that are taught

barely
Mis.	69–17	I found him *b·* alive,
Ret.	50– 7	for tuition lasting *b·* three weeks.

bares
Ret.	17–16	*b·* a brave breast to the lightning
Po.	62–20	*b·* a brave breast to the lightning

bargained
Mis.	289–21	Rights that are *b·* away

bark
Mis.	385–10	thy *b·* is past The dangerous sea,
Pul.	6–25	as my lone *b·* rose and fell
No.	43–27	envy and hatred *b·* and bite at its
Po.	48– 1	thy *b·* is past The dangerous sea,
My.	184–15	birch *b·* on which it was written

barmaid
Mis.	295– 5	* "cursed *b·* system" in England
	296–29	*b·* and Christian Scientist

barmaids
Mis.	294–24	chapter sub-title
	296– 4	not *b·*, but bishops
	296–10	*b·* of English alehouses
	296–25	And the *b·* !

barren
Mis.	151–11	He saith of the *b·* fig-tree,
	228–12	seeking to raise those *b·* natures
	398– 9	Strangers on a *b·* shore,
Ret.	46–15	Strangers on a *b·* shore,
Pul.	17–14	Strangers on a *b·* shore,
	49–10	* yet from a *b·* waste
Po.	14–13	Strangers on a *b·* shore,
	24–17	The *b·* brood, O call With song of

barricaded
Pul.	2–17	in a poorly *b·* fort,

barriers
Mis.	269– 4	He cannot escape from *b·*
Pul.	22–16	doctrinal *b·* between the churches
No.	28– 5	will burst the *b·* of sense,

barrister
Mis.	340–12	*b·* who never brings out a brief.

barter
Mis.	270– 4	such as *b·* integrity and peace for

Bartimeus
Mis.	241–24	Then, like blind *B·*,

Barton
Miss
My.	297– 1	Now if Miss *B·* were not a
	297– 4	all that Miss *B·* really is,

Miss Clara
My.	296–24	chapter sub-title
	296–26	Miss Clara *B·* dipped her pen in

basal
Mis.	27–10	the pith of the *b·* statement,

base
Mis.	147–21	abhor whatever is *b·* or unworthy ;
	228– 2	a deception dark as it is *b·*
Pul.	25–24	* The *b·* and cap are of . . . marble.
Rud.	9–13	*b·* your practice on immortal Mind,
No.	40– 8	wise to hide from dull and *b·* ears

based
Mis.	34–13	C. S. is *b·* on divine Principle ;
	55–16	*Is C. S. b· on the facts of*
	55–18	C. S. is *b·* on the facts of Spirit
	62–28	The theology of C. S. is *b·* on
	71–18	*b·* on a mortal or material formation ;
	198–24	*b·* on physical material law,
Ret.	93– 5	human concept of Christ is *b·* on
Un.	9–13	have not *b·* upon revelation their
	46– 8	not *b·* on a human conception
Pul.	55–18	* It is *b·* upon what is held to be
Rud.	11–20	*b·* on a true understanding of God
No.	10–25	*b·* as it is on His omnipotence
'01.	25–20	metaphysics *b·* on materialism?
Peo.	2– 5	*b·* on material conceptions of

based
Peo.	2–14	*b·* on the evidences gained from
	3–20	A personal God is *b·* on finite
My.	96–13	* It is a faith *b·* upon reason,
	108–14	is *b·* on the law of divine Mind.
	116–17	*b·* upon personal sight or sense.
	119– 5	*b·* on one infinite God, and man,
	154– 2	Science of all healing is *b·* on Mind
	179–26	*b·* on the divine Principle of being,
	204–29	*b·* as aforetime on this divine
	205–27	it is forever *b·* on Love,
	283–27	*b·* on the enlightened sense of God's
	348–14	was *b·* upon her discovery

baseless
Mis.	48–29	is a *b·* fabrication
No.	43–19	build a *b·* fabric of their own

basement
Pul.	25– 4	* two large boilers in the *b·*
	58–14	* Inside is a *b·* room,
My.	69–23	* in the *b·* is a cloak-room

bases
Mis.	101–19	*b·* his conclusions on mortality,
	297– 7	*b·* its work on ethical conditions
Ret.	68–21	so long as it *b·* creation on

basic
Mis.	6–20	with that *b·* truth we conquer
Un.	49–19	Standing in no *b·* Truth,
My.	348–29	*b·* Principle of all Science,

basis
absolute
Mis.	307–20	on this absolute *b·* of C. S. ;

and support
No.	38–15	the *b·* and support of creation,

Biblical
My.	181– 2	Biblical *b·* that God is All-in-all ;

broad
Mis.	143– 2	broad *b·* and sure foundation of

Christian
Man.	80– 2	on a strictly Christian *b·*,

false
Mis.	209–24	on the false *b·* that evil should
	287–10	may place love on a false *b·*

firm
Mis.	232–24	its infinite value and firm *b·*.

former
Hea.	3– 8	reestablished on its former *b·*.

for others
Mis.	156–16	becoming the *b·* for others :

for teaching
Man.	86–16	*B·* for Teaching.

founded upon the
Mis.	13–18	founded upon the *b·* of material

fundamental
Mis.	186–21	torn apart from its fundamental *b·*.

heathen
My.	118–25	rests on a heathen *b·* for its Nirvana,

immortal
Hea.	1– 9	builds on less than an immortal *b·*,

its
My.	111–19	healing on its *b·*,

less
Un.	28–15	and have less *b·* ;

liberal
My.	245– 7	on a broad and liberal *b·*.

material
Mis.	254–22	mental healing on a material *b·*
	341– 4	unreal material *b·* of things,
Ret.	85–21	or of healing on a material *b·*.
No.	6–16	trying to heal on a material *b·*.

of a lie
'02.	6– 8	into the world on the *b·* of a lie,

of all action
Hea.	12– 8	mind, the *b·* of all action,

of Christian Science
Mis.	307–20	absolute *b·* of C. S. ;
Ret.	15– 5	built on the *b·* of C. S.,
Rud.	13– 5	Whatever saps, . . . this *b·* of C. S.,
My.	220– 6	as to apply, on the *b·* of C. S.,

of Christmas
My.	260–17	The *b·* of Christmas is the rock,
	260–22	*b·* of Christmas is love loving its

of divine liberty
Mis.	163–20	are the *b·* of divine liberty,

of fixed Principle
My.	106–17	rests on the *b·* of fixed Principle,

of harmony
Ret.	60–24	the only sure *b·* of harmony.

of his words
'02.	11–30	very *b·* of his words and works.

of hypnotism
Mis.	4– 5	healing on the *b·* of hypnotism,

of its demonstration
Mis.	357–32	the *b·* of its demonstration,

basis
  of its unreality
    Mis. 63–14 on the *b·* of its unreality
  of justice
    My. 283–21 unite . . . on the *b·* of justice,
  of malpractice
    Rud. 9–10 The *b·* of malpractice is in
  of *materia medica*
    Mis. 81– 2 not the *b·* of *materia medica*,
    379–21 beyond the *b·* of *materia medica*,
  of matter
    Mis. 243–21 who practise on the *b·* of matter,
  of Mind-healing
    Rud. 6–18 *Is not the b· of Mind-healing a*
  of nothingness
    '01. 13–16 destroys it on the very *b·* of nothingness.
  of Science
    My. 357– 1 He is the only *b·* of Science ;
  of the sentiments
    Chr. 55– 1 *b·* of the sentiments in the verses,
  only
    My. 357– 1 He is the only *b·* of Science ;
    357–24 only *b·* upon which this Science
  practical
    Ret. 48–19 healing on a purely practical *b·*,
  same
    Mis. 54–28 *they do not heal on the same b·*
    Un. 8–18 same *b·* whereby sickness is healed,
  scientific
    Mis. 148–18 hence their simple, scientific *b·*,
    267–27 rests on this scientific *b·* :
    269–17 Christian, mental, scientific *b·* ;
    Man. 3–15 hence their simple, scientific *b·*,
    Ret. 37–17 interpretation of the scientific *b·* for
    57– 5 furnishes a scientific *b·* for
  Scriptural
    My. 240–18 on a Scriptural *b·*,
  solid
    '02. 14–13 accomplished on this solid *b·*.
  sound
    My. v–15 * established the Cause on a sound *b·*
  spiritual
    Un. 25–19 material, not a spiritual *b·*.
    Hea. 1–21 more spiritual *b·* and tendency
  spirituality is the
    Mis. 156–23 Spirituality is the *b·* of all true
  such a
    My. 119– 3 or on such a *b·* to demonstrate
  that
    '01. 7–25 cannot be conceived of on that *b·* ;
  that Christ
    '02. 12– 5 on the *b·* that Christ is the Messiah,
    Hea. 18–21 on the *b·* that Christ, Truth, heals
  their
    Mis. 200–17 for the sole reason that it is their *b·*.
  this
    Mis. 289–11 human life seems to rest on this *b·*.
    Rud. 13– 5 Whatever saps, . . . this *b·* of C. S.,
    No. 5– 1 can only be — healed on this *b·*.
    37–22 on this *b·* Messiah and prophet
    My. 4– 9 On this *b·*, how many are following
    216– 5 systems of religion stand on this *b·*.
    281–10 On this *b·* the brotherhood of all
    300– 1 On this *b·* they endeavor to
  true
    Mis. 74– 6 apprehension of the true *b·* of being,

    Mis. 19–22 as high a *b·* as he understands,
    117–14 the *b·* of all right thinking
    171–16 seeking out of the *b·* upon which
    188–16 St. Paul first reasons upon the *b·*
    202– 1 *b·* of all supposed miracles ;
    289–27 on the *b·* of a bill of rights.
    333– 7 on the *b·* that black is not
    Ret. 35– 5 *b·* it laid down for physical and
    56–16 on the *b·* of the omnipotence
    No. 10–17 on the *b·* that all consciousness is
    38– 6 on the *b·* that God is All,
    Pan. 8–22 on the *b·* of the First Commandment
    '01. 27–11 the *b·* whereof cannot be traced
    My. 10–19 * on the *b·* of fretful or
    281–12 the *b·* on which and by which
    294– 4 on the *b·* that God has all power,

bask
  Po. 22–11 And *b·* in one eternal day.

basket
  Pul. 42–28 * large *b·* of white carnations
  My. 78–15 * *b·* piled high with bank-notes,

baskets
  Mis. 149–11 *b·* full of accessions to your love,
  My. 99–20 * *b·* when passed around

bastard
  Un. 23– 2 from his *b·* son Edmund

bastards
  Un. 23– 6 God has no *b·* to turn again and
    23–14 *b·*, and not sons.'' — *Heb.* 12 : 8.

bat
  Peo. 14– 8 * ''*b·* and owl on the bending stones,

bated
  Ret. 9– 3 I listened with *b·* breath.

Bates
  Caroline S.
    Pul. 77–20 * signature
    78–18 * signature
  Edward P. (*see also* **Bates'**)
    Pul. 59–25 * Edward P. *B·*, Stephen A. Chase,
    77–19 * signature
    78–17 * signature
    My. 322– 7 * signature
  Gen. Erastus N.
    Ret. 43–17 Gen. Erastus N. *B·* taught one Primary
  Mr.
    My. 172–20 * In reply Mr. *B·* said,
    323– 1 * what Mr. *B·* has so well written
  Mr. E. P.
    My. 171–25 * by the President, Mr. E. P. *B·*,
  President
    My. 172– 8 * this gavel to President *B·*,

Bates'
  Mr. Edward P.
    My. 322–12 * Mr. Edward P. *B·* letter to you

bath
  Hea. 5– 5 the neglect of a *b·*, and so on.
  Peo. 9– 6 The cool *b·* may refresh the body,

bathe
  Mis. 30–31 *b·* in the baptism of Spirit,
    323–20 and *b·* in its streams,

bathed
  Mis. 393–17 Art hath *b·* this isthmus-lordling
  Ret. 13–18 as she *b·* my burning temples,
  Po. 52– 1 Art hath *b·* this isthmus-lordling

bathes
  Mis. 203–14 Theology religiously *b·* in water,
    206–30 *b·* in the baptismal font of eternal
    227–27 *b·* it in the cool waters of peace
  Peo. 9–10 *b·* us in the life of Truth

bathing
  My. 228–19 *b·* the human understanding with

battle (*see also* **battle's**)
  Mis. xii– 5 this afterpiece of *b·*.
    99–18 and be in the *b·* every day
    105–19 follow this line of light and *b·*.
    120–17 be heard above the din of *b·*,
    136– 5 still with you on the field of *b·*,
    177– 5 *b·* of Armageddon is upon us.
    246–20 conflict more terrible than the *b·* of
    339–10 In the *b·* of life,
    348–13 and show the plan of *b·*.
  Ret. 3–11 neighboring *b·* of Chippewa,
    30– 4 they have won fields of *b·* from which
  Pan. 14–20 whether in camp or in *b·*.
  '02. 14–18 From the beginning of the great *b·*
  Hea. 2– 9 never seen amid the smoke of *b·*.
  My. 62– 2 * stood at the breastworks in the *b·*,
    134– 2 constant *b·* against the world,
    268–22 lively *b·* with ''the world, the flesh

battle-axe
  No. 32–14 cleaves sin with a broad *b·*.

Battle-Axe Plug
  Mis. 240–29 ''*B· P·*'' takes off men's heads ;

battledores
  Mis. xi–20 no *b·* to fling it back and forth.

battle-field
  Mis. 304–12 * the *b·* of New Orleans (1812),
    383–14 and on every *b·* rise higher

battle-ground
  Un. 46–27 It furnished the *b·* of the past,

battle-grounds
  Mis. xi–25 to old *b·*, there sadly to survey

battle-plan
  Po. 11– 2 Unite your *b·* ;
  My. 338– 2 Unite your *b·* ;

battle's
  My. 278– 3 to be subserved by the *b·* plan

battles
  Mis. xi–22 preliminary *b·* that purchased it.
  No. 7–21 students must now fight their own *b·*.
  Peo. 10–16 *b·* for man's whole rights,
    11– 5 scarcely done with their *b·* before

battle-worn
  Mis. 85– 1 To the *b·* and weary

battling
Mis. 321–22 And b· for a brighter crown.
baubles
My. 297–14 blows away the b· of belief,
bay
Ret. 17–17 While palm, b·, and laurel,
Pul. 26–26 * Before the great b· window
27–30 * A large b· window,
Po. 63– 1 While palm, b·, and laurel,
bayonet
Ret. 11– 4 poem
Peo. 11– 7 not with b· and blood,
Po. vi–29 * poem
page 60 poem
Bay State (see also **Massachusetts**)
Mis. 211–10 people in the old B· S·.
Po. 39–14 Sons of the old B· S·,
bay-tree
My. 95– 2 * like a green b·,
B. C.
Pul. 82–28 * The date is no longer B. C.
beach
Po. 73–11 Laving with surges thy silv'ry b·!
beacon
Po. 43–16 B· beams — athwart the weakly,
beacon-lights
No. 2–20 such teachers are becoming b·
Beacon St., No. 5
Mis. 242–27 Mr. C. M. H——, of Boston,...No. 5 B· S·,
beam
Mis. 119–14 nature strives to tip the b· against
212–27 cast the b· out of his own eye,
336–14 b· in your own eye that hinders
355–21 "Cast the b· out — see Matt. 7 : 5.
398–18 Till the morning's b· ;
Ret. 46–24 Till the morning's b· ;
Pul. 17–23 Till the morning's b· ;
Po. 14–22 Till the morning's b· ;
29–13 Thou gentle b· of living Love,
My. 277–19 mercy tips the b· on the right side,
beams
Ret. 87–26 Truth b· with such efficacy as to
Un. 58–19 revelation that b· on mortal sense
Po. 43–16 Beacon b· — athwart the weakly,
My. 62–12 * brightest b· on your pathway,
190– 5 morning b· and noonday glory of
269–21 b· of right have healing in their
bear
Mis. 39–23 b· "one another's — Gal. 6 : 2.
54–10 they b· witness to this fact.
67–13 not b· false witness ;" — Exod. 20 : 16.
93–24 B· in mind, however,
99–24 never b· into oblivion his words.
126–25 b· in mind that, in the long race,
144–27 so may our earthly sowing b· fruit
151– 8 Those who b· fruit He purgeth,
151– 9 that they may b· more fruit.
196–11 b· in mind that a serpent said that ;
211–32 refuses to b· the cross and
228–10 b· with patience the buffetings
263–12 b· in mind that His presence,
328–31 b· thy cross up to the throne
330–20 learn what report they b·,
365– 1 I will b· the strain of time
382–10 b· witness to this gift of God
Man. 48– 3 calls a member to b· testimony
53–20 shall b· witness to the offense
93–13 b· testimony to the facts
Ret. 22– 3 b· brief testimony even to the
25–27 "If I b· witness — John 5 : 31.
53– 5 to b· aloft the standard of
87–24 b· the weight of others' burdens,
Un. 6–13 as the age has strength to b·.
7–15 can b· witness to these cures.
33– 8 "If I b· witness — John 5 : 31.
Pul. 11– 1 b· you outward, upward,
'00. 9–29 "b· the burden — see Matt. 20 : 12.
'01. 15–25 * He is of purer eyes than to b· to
31–17 would b· loving testimony.
'02. 3– 2 b· testimony to this fact.
20–22 I can b· the cross,
Hea. 12–18 power of thought brought to b· on
Po. 15– 6 unless thou canst b· A message
26–17 "This record I will b·
35–13 Bird, b· me through the sky!
My. 15–15 all that you are able to b· now,
36–19 * b· witness to the abundance of
83–30 * to b· each his or her share of
120– 9 B· with me the burden of discovery
128–32 take no root . . . nor b· fruit.
148–24 B· in mind always that Christianity
202–29 that ye b· much fruit." — John 15 : 8.

bear
My. 229–17 doth not b· his cross, — Luke 14 : 27.
291–21 b· its banner into the vast forever.
297– 5 knowing that she can b· the blows
beard
Un. 11– 4 b· the lions in their dens.
Pul. 33–18 * an old man with a snowy b·
bearer
Man. 91– 9 b· of a card of free scholarship
bearest
Mis. 386– 7 "B· thou no tidings from
Po. 49–11 "B· thou no tidings from
beareth
Mis. 46–22 Spirit itself b· witness — Rom. 8 : 16.
218–19 b· witness of things spiritual,
255–14 Spirit itself b· witness — Rom. 8 : 16.
Man. 42–18 whereof the Scripture b· testimony.
bearing
Mis. 158–18 obedience in b· this cross.
357–17 and is b· fruit.
Ret. 32– 2 b· on its white wings,
54–12 without b· the fruits of goodness,
85–11 b· on their pinions of light
Un. 6– 3 "b· fruit after its kind." — see Gen. 1 : 11.
Pul. 26–11 * b· six . . . silver lamps,
26–24 * with sprays of fig leaves b· fruit.
27–17 * two small windows b· palms
31–26 * winning in b· and manner,
32–21 * elastic b· of a woman of thirty,
Hea. 19–23 b· the cross meekly
Po. 34–18 B· no bitter memory at heart ;
My. 49– 1 * their conversation, and their b·,
73–28 * b· the first instalments of
170–30 b· your sheaves with you.
bears
Mis. 21– 8 whereof C. S. now b· testimony.
170–21 b· upon our eternal life.
220–21 has power and b· fruit,
312– 7 b· all burdens, suffers all
320–14 calms man's fears, b· his burdens,
Ret. 11–10 No despot b· misrule.
Un. 40– 8 and b· the fruits of Love,
55–15 and the wounds it b·.
Pul. 78– 6 * It b· upon its face the following
No. 21–22 b· the strain of time,
Po. 60– 7 No despot b· misrule.
77–19 B· hence its sunlit glow
My. 258–17 b· to mortals gifts greater than
beast
Mis. 18– 3 efface the mark of the b·.
36–10 ferocious mind seen in the b·
36–12 for His b· is the lion that
113–10 name of the b·, — Rev. 13 : 17.
269–32 name of the b·, — Rev. 13 : 17.
'01. 20– 8 to harm either man or b·.
Hea. 10– 5 b· bowed before the Lamb :
beasts
Mis. 36– 6 Do animals and b· have a mind?
36– 7 B·, as well as men, express Mind
36–15 b· that have these propensities
191– 5 b· of the field." — see Gen. 3 : 1.
294–19 and all ravening b·.
323–12 b· of prey prowl in the path,
323–20 taming the b· of prey,
345– 8 * "I will set the b· upon you,
Ret. 64–17 like the b· that perish." — Psal. 49 : 20.
Un. 52–21 rabid b·, fatal reptiles, and
Hea. 14– 2 it is the fight of b·,
Peo. 13–18 let loose the wild b· upon him,
My. 245–13 poisonous reptiles and devouring b·,
beat
Mis. 152–23 b· against this sure foundation,
383–11 b· in vain against the immortal
'01. 24–13 storms of disease b· against
My. 162–31 waves and winds b· in vain.
164–29 enmity, or malice b· in vain.
beaten
Man. 28–13 b· with many stripes." — Luke 12 : 47.
'00. 4–18 b· path of human doctrines
Hea. 5– 4 saying He is b· by certain kinds of
beateth
Mis. 102–29 as one that b· the air,
Pan. 6– 7 not as one that b· the mist,
beating
'01. 1– 3 b· through the mental avenues of
My. 308–17 * regularly b· the ground with
341–13 And in her heart is b· A love for all
beatings
Peo. 1–14 b· of our heart can be heard ;
beatitude
My. 227–29 The sinner may sneer at this b·,

Beatitudes

Mis. 303–19	imbibe the spirit of Christ's B.
My. 129–31	Ten Commandments, the B,

beatitudes

Mis. 82–17	unfolding the endless b of Being ;
My. 200–13	glorious b of divine Love.

beats

Mis. 267–19	while the left b its way downward,
Hea. 14– 2	the bigger animal b the lesser;
My. 160– 4	The heart that b mostly for self

beauties

Mis. 87– 7	let us say of the b of
Pul. 62–17	* b of a great cathedral chime,
My. 85–17	* among the architectural b of
88–19	* striking as are its b,

beautifies

Mis. 390–18	When sunshine b the shower,
Po. 55–19	When sunshine b the shower,

Beautiful

My. 132–19	Divine Love hath opened the gate B

beautiful

Mis. 86–16	Earth is more spiritually b
139–19	near the b Back Bay Park,
141–32	how b are her feet!
142– 1	how b are her garments !
142– 7	a b boat presented by
142– 9	among other b decorations,
142–12	b boat and presentation poem.
169–29	* how b and inspiring are the
224–19	appreciation of everything b,
230–27	It was a b group!
280–21	b hand-painted flowers
281–24	one of the most b
321–25	hospitality of their b homes
355–29	more b than the rainbow
356– 1	radiant sunset, b as blessings
Ret. 4–20	singing brooklets, b wild flowers,
5–13	Park Cemetery of that b village.
6–13	To speak of his b character
17– 1	in the b suburbs of Boston.
23–22	Being was b,
27–26	natural manifestation is b
45– 2	more b became the garments
68–28	The b, good, and pure constitute
Un. 8–11	All that is b and good
52–24	b blossom is often poisonous,
52–25	b mansion is sometimes the home of
52–27	form the condition of b evil,
53– 1	which make a b lie.
Pul. 22–20	her most b garments,
23– 5	* A B TEMPLE AND ITS FURNISHINGS
24– 5	* It is one of the most b,
27– 3	* directors' room is very b
32– 5	* her b complexion and
36–23	* one of the most b residences
37– 6	* where she has a b residence,
37–17	* sat in the b drawing-room,
39–11	* author of "The World B."
40–14	* B ROOM WHICH THE CHILDREN BUILT
41– 7	* to help erect this b structure,
42–30	* filled with b pink roses.
48–11	* b meadows and pastures
57–12	* b buildings in Boston.
58– 7	* b estate called Pleasant View ;
58–22	* a b sunburst window.
61–15	* B suggestions greet you
65–16	* b structure of gray granite,
68–11	* lives in a b country residence
75–16	* B CHURCH AT BOSTON
76– 3	* b apartment known as
76– 6	* described as "particularly b,
81–20	* full of b possibilities as a
81–24	* apostle of the true, the b,
85–25	* a b and unique testimonial
86–11	* The b souvenir is encased in
Peo. 14– 2	we express them by objects more b.
Po. vii– 1	* in the b suburbs of Boston);
9– 6	birth of that b boy.
My. 10– 9	* in a b, ample building,
66–24	* from her b home, Pleasant View,
66–29	* many b houses of worship
68–17	* platform is of a b foreign marble,
70–24	* more b, more musical,
71– 3	* b effects by means of the bells.
77– 2	* its great size, b architecture,
84–27	* dedication of the b structure
87–24	* gives such serene, b expressions,
88–18	* and this b temple,
121–15	plain dealing is a jewel as b as
125–25	Zion must put on her b garments
155–29	sweet scents and b blossoms
157– 7	* to build a b church edifice
157–11	* commodious and b church home
157–14	* of the same b Concord granite

beautiful

My. 166–28	your gift to me of a b cabinet,
171–13	and view this b structure,
174– 1	b lawn surrounding their church
182–19	this b house of worship
184–15	The b birch bark on which
184–26	"How b upon the mountains — Isa. 52 : 7.
187–23	to consecrate your b temple
202–14	on the builders of this b temple,
258–23	b are the Christmas memories of him
258–30	b statuette in alabaster
347– 9	b gift to me, a loving-cup,
347–16	b pearls that crown this cup
351– 5	* b tribute to Free Masonry.

beautifully

Mis. 229–21	would thus become b less ;
231–12	mammoth turkey grew b less.
Ret. 73–10	human concept grew b less
'00. 4–29	St. Paul b enunciates this
My. 171–27	* b bound with burnished brass.
322–30	* spoke earnestly and b of you

beautify

Mis. 394– 9	b, bless, and make joyful again.
Peo. 7– 7	to b and exalt our lives.
Po. 45–12	b, bless, and make joyful again.
My. 134–19	b, bless, and inspire man's power.
173–15	b our new church building in

beautifying

Mis. 143– 5	participants in b this boat

beauty (see also beauty's)

and bounty

My. 260– 1	b and bounty of Life everlasting,

and goodness

Rud. 6– 6	b and goodness are in and of Mind,
6– 8	the nature of b and goodness

and perfume

Ret. 18–10	b and perfume from buds burst away,
Po. 46–12	yield its b and perfume
63–20	b and perfume from buds burst away,

and strength

My. 68– 3	* b and strength of the design.

and the grace

My. 31–16	* b and the grace of the architecture.

and use

My. 256–11	for those things of b and use

appropriate

My. 169–19	appropriate b of time and place

architectural

My. 67–21	* marvel of architectural b.

bowers of

Ret. 17– 4	zephyrs at play In bowers of b,
Po. 62– 3	zephyrs at play In bowers of b,

burdened with

My. 162–32	its goodly temple — burdened with b,

composite

Pul. 81–14	* She represents the composite b,

conception of

Mis. 86–22	Even the human conception of b,

divine

Mis. 86–24	It is next to divine b

earth's

Mis. 87– 3	To take all earth's b into
Ret. 18–14	Earth's b and glory delude
Po. 64– 5	Earth's b and glory delude

evidence of that

My. 88–20	* evidence of that b and serenity of

extreme of

My. 89–11	* to achieve its extreme of b.

fled

Mis. 396– 8	It voices b fled.
Po. 58–20	It voices b fled.

Helen's

Mis. 374–26	* "Helen's b in a brow of Egypt."

isle of

Mis. 392–20	Isle of b, thou art singing
393–21	Isle of b, thou art teaching
Po. 51– 2	Isle of b, thou art singing
52– 5	Isle of b, thou art teaching

is marred

Rud. 6– 9	the b is marred, through a false

label

Mis. 87– 4	and label b nothing,

new

Ret. 20–18	Awoke new b in the surge's roll !

new-born

Po. 30– 3	new-born b in the emerald sky,
My. 158–15	lends a new-born b to holiness,

of color

My. 36–26	* all the b of color and design,

of holiness

Mis. 197–18	understand the b of holiness,
330–18	arranging in the b of holiness
363–17	declare the b of holiness,
Ret. 32– 3	"the b of holiness," — Psal. 29 : 2.
No. 8– 7	the b of holiness, the joy of Love

beauty

'01.	33– 2	the original *b·* of holiness
'02.	17–21	to show man the *b·* of holiness
My.	41–32	* "*b·* of holiness," — *Psal.* 29 : 2.
	114–12	the *b·* of holiness is not yet won.
	196–29	The *b·* of holiness comes with
	197– 5	May the *b·* of holiness be upon this

of Love

Ret.	88–13	to apprehend the living *b·* of Love,

of the building

My.	24–23	* The *b·* of the building,

of the universe

Mis.	86–14	My sense of the *b·* of the universe is,

personal

Pul.	31–27	* with great claim to personal *b·*.

ravished with

Po.	8–10	Ravished with *b·* the eye of day.

rich

My.	69–15	* the rich *b·* of the interior.

spirit of

Pul.	2– 6	spirit of *b·* dominates The

spiritual

My.	141–29	has blossomed into spiritual *b·*,

strength and

My.	39–29	* strength and *b·* of her character.

strong

Mis.	393–18	In a *b·* strong and meek
Po.	52– 2	In a *b·* strong and meek

sweetness and

Mis.	107– 2	even the sweetness and *b·* in

this

Pul.	49–12	* has come forth all this *b·*!"

typifies holiness

Mis.	86–15	*b·* typifies holiness,

Mis.	87–13	*b·*, grandeur, and glory of the
Un.	52–22	elaborate in *b·*, color, and form,
Pul.	5–19	with a *b·* all its own
Peo.	7–22	* Its heavenly *b·* shall be our own,
Po.	46–17	While *b·* fills each bar.
My.	6–26	*b·*, and achievements of goodness.
	94–30	*b·*, and achievements of goodness."

beauty's

Po.	15– 9	enchantment in *b·* array,
	46– 8	A gem in *b·* diadem,

became

Mis.	153– 9	the rock *b·* a fountain ;
	162–11	Here the cross *b·* the emblem
	191– 7	serpent *b·* a symbol of wisdom.
	326–11	until they *b·* unmanageable ;
	359–10	when I *b·* a man, — *I Cor.* 13 : 11.
Ret.	1–18	*b·* my paternal grandmother,
	23– 6	As these pungent lessons *b·* clearer,
	28– 1	It *b·* evident that the divine Mind
	45– 2	more beautiful *b·* the garments
	73–12	corporeality *b·* less to me than
	91–24	a fishing-boat *b·* a sanctuary,
	91–25	The grove *b·* his class-room,
Pul.	31–14	* in the early '80's that I *b·* aware
	34–11	* she suddenly *b·* aware of a
	35–23	* Mrs. Eddy *b·* convinced of the
	46–28	* *b·* the wife of Asa Gilbert Eddy.
	64–20	* she *b·* convinced that
	65–26	* afterward *b·* a saint.
	70–17	* *b·* certain that "all causation was
No.	12 –11	it *b·* a sacred duty for her to
'01.	32– 5	I *b·* early a child of the Church,
'02.	13–20	the note therewith *b·* due,
	15–15	I *b·* poor for Christ's sake.
Hea.	18–17	until it *b·* popular.
Peo.	4– 7	belief that . . . infinity *b·* finity,
Po.	vii– 7	* *When this b· known to her friends,*
My.	40–15	* *b·* divided into warring sects ;
	43–11	* finally *b·* willingly obedient to
	76– 6	* *b·* evident to the Board
	135– 4	when I *b·* a man, — *I Cor.* 13 : 11.
	165– 4	in doing this the Master *b·*
	238–15	*b·* requisite in the divine order.
	245– 2	they *b·* deeply interested in it.
	261–17	when I *b·* a man, — *I Cor.* 13 : 11.
	304–18	Judge S. J. Hanna *b·* editor
	342– 2	* *b·* aware of a white-haired lady
	343–22	position of . . . "*b·* necessary.

because

Mis.	2– 5	*b·* they have so little of their own.
	3–25	*B·* God is supreme and
	7– 2	*b·* there is danger in it ;
	7–27	*b·* people do not understand
	9–29	*B·* it is the great and only danger
	10– 9	*B·* He has called His own,
	11–26	*B·* I can do much general good
	12– 1	*B·* I thus feel, I say to others :
	31–20	*b·* he has no faith in the
	35–21	Only *b·* both are important.
	51–31	*b·* ye ask amiss, — *Jas.* 4 : 3.

because

Mis.	52–26	*b·* the first rule was not easily
	53–24	*b·* of their great lack of spirituality.
	54–25	*B·* *none of your students have been*
	54–30	*b·* he failed to get the right **answer,**
	65– 7	this is *b·* Science is true,
	72– 3	*b·* of his parents' mistakes
	75– 9	*b·* it includes a rule that must
	75–15	*b·* Soul is a term for Deity,
	79–30	*b·* they chance to be under **arrest**
	93–27	*b·* it cannot go unpunished
	100–26	*b·* he loves God most.
	103–15	*b·* eternally conscious.
	105–31	*B·* God is Mind,
	122– 3	*b·* of offenses! — *Matt.* 18 : 7.
	132–16	*B·* of the great demand upon
	133–19	*b·* of my desire to set you **right**
	138–23	*B·* the growth of these
	142–16	*B·* your dear hearts expressed
	155–16	*B·* Mother has not the time
	156–14	*b·* I saw no advantage,
	165– 3	*b·* of the ascension of Jesus,
	165– 5	*b·* of the corruption of the **Church.**
	178– 5	*b·* he was not satisfied with a
	179–32	"*B·* he lives, — *see John* 14 : 19.
	183–31	arrive at the true status of man *b·*
	184–22	good *b·* it is of God,
	187–14	*b·* their transcribing thoughts
	188– 8	*B·* of human misstatement
	192– 2	*b·* the Hebrew term for Deity
	192– 4	*b·* the original text defines devil
	192–11	*b·* *I go unto my Father.* — *John* 14 : 12.
	194–20	"*b·* I go unto my Father." — *John* 14 : 12.
	194–20	"*B·*" in following him, you — *John* 14 : 12.
	196–25	*b·* the "I" does go unto the Father,
	199– 2	*b·* of this, we have the right to
	200– 7	*b·* Spirit was to him All-in-all,
	200–23	*b·* it compels me to seek the
	201– 2	*b·* it meets the immortal demands
	201–20	*b·* they were so many proofs
	201–32	*b·* it illustrates through the flesh
	210– 9	*b·* they have stings?
	211–16	*B·* you wish to save him from
	215–19	*b·* he is a somnambulist,
	222–14	*b·* the false seems true.
	229–16	"*B·* thou hast made — *Psal.* 91 : 9.
	233–24	*b·* unwilling to work hard
	242–14	*B·* I performed more difficult **tasks**
	244–31	*b·* of their medical discoveries?
	247–19	*b·* they do not understand that
	255–26	*b·* it is this divine antidote,
	262–29	*b·* I take so much pleasure
	266–28	*B·* Truth has spoken aloud,
	276– 6	solely *b·* so many people and
	280–10	*B·* God does all,
	281–24	*b·* you have signed your names.
	285– 4	*b·* I had been personal
	290–29	emits light *b·* it reflects ;
	297– 7	*b·* this Science bases its work on
	299–30	*b·* you have confessed that they **are**
	333– 8	*b·* it absorbs all the rays of light.
	334–15	*b·* it is a lie, without one word of
	334–28	*B·* I have uncovered evil,
	339–11	*b·* of the supposed activity of **evil.**
	340–12	*B·* he followed agriculture
	350–19	*b·* of the misconception of
	353–22	and *b·* it *is* thus governed,
	360– 6	good, *b·* fashioned divinely,
	366– 6	*b·* they contain and offer Science,
	366–12	And *b·* He is All-in-all,
	374–31	*B·* my ideal of an angel is a
	378–17	"*B·* it conveys *electricity* to them."
Chr.	55–16	dead *b·* of sin ; — *Rom.* 8 : 10.
	55–17	*b·* of righteousness. — *Rom.* 8 : 10.
Ret.	1–11	*b·* my great-grandmother wrote **a**
	25–10	*Christian, b·* it is compassionate,
	25–14	*b·* Soul alone is truly substantial.
	44–13	*b·* of accumulating work in the
	54– 3	*B·* faith is belief, and not
	63– 3	*B·* C. S. heals sin
	78–13	*b·* such works and words becloud **the**
	87–12	*b·* their religion demands implicit
	89–12	*b·* he was bidden to this privileged
Un.	2–23	*b·* their lives have grown so far
	3–25	*b·*, if He is omnipresent,
	4–21	*b·* evil is no part of the
	5– 7	*b·* their mental struggles and **pride**
	7–23	*b·* God is All,
	9–21	*b·* ideas akin to mine
	10– 3	*b·* they are not to be found in God,
	10–17	They live, *b·* He lives ;
	10–17	perfect, *b·* He is perfect,
	14– 3	*b·* it was not at first done aright.
	14–16	*b·* His created children proved **sinful ;**
	17–20	*b·* He knows all things ;
	21–16	*b·* there is nothing beside Him

because

Un.	22– 2	B· man is made after God's eternal
	24–18	no evil mind, b· Mind is God.
	28–15	b· material theories are built on the
	29– 6	Spirit never sins, b· Spirit is God.
	37–11	B· God is ever present,
	37–13	b· God is Life, all Life is eternal.
	41– 5	b· sin shuts out the real sense of
	41–23	b· God cannot be the opposite of
	42– 2	b· there is no place left for it.
	42– 7	b· it is not a living . . . reality.
	43– 7	b· mortals now believe in the
	43–18	B· of these profound reasons
	46–17	b· it was an indignity to
	48– 9	B· He lives, I live.
	54–22	b· the knowledge of evil would
	57–24	b· to suffer with him is to
	59–15	b· he could reach and teach mankind
	59–18	b· the divine idea is always present.
Pul.	3–29	B· of my own unfitness for
	12–14	b· he knoweth that he — *Rev.* 12 : 12.
	15– 6	B· people like you better
	21– 4	b· it *is* Love.
	43–26	* b·, as heretofore stated in
	56–17	* b· dogma and truth could not unite,
	81–12	* b· she thinks so much of herself
	82–14	* b· she was created after man,
Rud.	3– 1	b·, while mortals love to sin,
	3–11	more b· of his spiritual than his
	7–18	b· there is no material sense.
	10–21	punished b· of disobedience to His
	12–14	b· the relief is unchristian
	12–17	belief that they live in or b· of
	14–19	b· their first classes furnished students
	15– 5	B· the glad surprise
No.	4–19	b· they embody not the idea of
	11–21	b· they teach divine Science,
	16–16	b· it has no darkness to emit.
	21–18	b· by it we lose God's ways
	24–17	b· the evil that is hidden by
	24–18	b· evil, being thus uncovered,
	32– 5	b· *forgiveness*, in the popular sense
	33–10	b· they involve divine Science,
	35–17	b· of the shocking human idolatry
	40– 2	b· ye ask amiss, — *Jas.* 4 : 3.
	40– 3	B· of vanity and self-righteousness,
	40–24	mankind are better b· of this.
Pan.	5–14	b· there is no truth — *John* 8 : 44.
	6– 2	b· it was more effectual than
	6– 3	b· evil and disease will never
	8–27	suffering b· of it,
	11–30	And b· Christ's dear demand,
'00.	9– 5	not b· it is the best thing to do,
	9– 6	b· the student is not willing
	12–18	b· thou hast left thy — *Rev.* 2 : 4.
'01.	3– 9	b· their God is not a person.
	3–28	b· God is Love, Love is divine
	4–21	b· we understand that God is
	4–25	b· He is infinite ;
	4–25	b· He is Life, Truth, Love,
	6–16	b· He is not after this model
	7–18	B· Christian Scientists call their
	7–27	b· thou hast seen — *John* 20 : 29.
	11– 3	b· of Jesus' great work on earth,
	13– 6	b· it ought not, we must know
	13–17	b· he fears it or loves it.
	18–14	b· the substance of Truth transcends
	19– 9	b· of your often coming
	25–12	b· of their more spiritual import
	29–11	not b· reformers are not loved,
	29–11	well-meaning people
	34– 1	B· the effect of prayer.
'02.	7–28	B· it emphasizes the apostle's
Hea.	3–21	B· God is the Principle of
	6–23	b· it is lying back in the
	15–23	b· ye ask amiss ;" — *Jas.* 4 : 3.
	15–26	b· you do not understand God,
Peo.	4–11	b· a serpent said it.
	6–17	b· He is found altogether lovely.
	6–21	b· the grand realities of Life
	7–30	B· God is Spirit, our thoughts
	9–17	b· we "ask amiss ;" — *Jas.* 4 : 3.
	10– 3	simply b· it is more ethereal.
My.	10–24	* b· they recognize the importance
	11–17	* b· of prompt and liberal action,
	13–28	B· Christian Scientists virtually
	15–23	* B· I know 'tis true ;
	19–28	b· of that gift which you
	36–13	* Most of us are here b· we have
	39–28	* B· our own growth in love
	40–25	* b· she is an exact metaphysician.
	41– 8	* b· they have thoughts adverse to
	64– 9	* it is b· our Leader has
	77– 1	* b· of its great size,
	103– 2	B· Science is unimpeachable,
	104– 8	B· they could find no fault in him,

because

My.	105–10	declared incurable b· the lungs
	106–23	Is it b· he minds his own business
	106–27	b· he is the very antipode of
	106–28	Is it b· he heals the sick
	109–19	God is one b· God is All.
	112–21	b· of their uniformly pure morals
	113–16	b· he was not a disciple of
	114–10	Simply b· the treasures of
	116–10	B· it would dethrone the
	119–13	Mary of old wept b· she
	127–30	B· it is "on earth peace, — *Luke* 2 : 14.
	135–28	"Fret not thyself b· of — *Psal.* 37 : 1.
	137–27	b· I had implicit confidence in
	138– 2	b· I wanted it protected
	138–16	solely b· I find that I cannot
	146– 6	b· I understand it,
	151– 4	(1) B· I sympathize with their
	151– 6	(2) B· I know that no Christian can
	151– 8	(3) B· these attacks afford
	151–10	(4) B· it is written :
	161–25	b· one's thought and conduct
	178–10	b· Science is naturally divine,
	195–16	To do good to all b· we love all,
	212–16	B· they do not practise in strict
	213– 8	B· this age is cursed with
	217–21	b· we can meet this negation
	222– 4	b· of this Jesus rebuked them,
	222– 9	"B· of your unbelief" — *Matt.* 17 : 20.
	222–16	b· of his faith and his great
	222–18	he was arrested b·, as was said,
	223–14	b· I have not sufficient time to
	223–15	b· I do not consider myself
	227– 5	b· of another's wickedness
	227– 5	or b· of the minifying of his
	227–10	b· one out of three of their
	229– 6	b· of these abominations — *Deut.* 18 : 12.
	235–21	B· Spirit is God and *infinite;*
	236– 5	B· I suggested the name
	240–16	higher criticism b· it criticizes evil,
	241–20	* b· I referred to myself as an
	241–22	* b· I still lived in my flesh
	260–19	not b· of tradition, usage, or
	260–20	but b· of fundamental and
	260–21	b· of the heaven within us.
	270– 4	B· of the magnitude of their
	270–28	quarrel with a man b· of his religion
	270–29	than I would b· of his art.
	273–29	b· death alone does not awaken man
	276– 7	or b· of a preference to remain
	280–18	b· of oft speaking,
	280–30	B· a spiritual foresight of
	284– 1	B· of my rediscovery of C. S.,
	288–31	all is good b· God made all,
	290–15	he trusteth in Thee." — *Isa.* 26 : 3.
	294– 8	b· of their unbelief," — *Matt.* 13 : 58.
	294– 8	b· of the mental . . . elements,
	302–23	B· C. S. is not yet popular,
	313–30	b· after my father's second marriage
	316– 1	b· the truth I have promulgated
	316– 4	b· I still hear the harvest song
	316– 6	b· "blessed are ye, — *Matt.* 5 : 11.
	318– 8	b· at that date some critics
	326– 5	* not b· a favor has been extended,
	326– 5	* but b· their inherent rights are
	327–21	* b· the representative men of
	334– 7	* b· she has contradicted
	342–22	b· in it alone is the simplicity of
	349–15	b· he is conscious of the allness of
	349–22	b· they are spiritual,
	354– 2	b· of alleged misrepresentations
	355–27	Mrs. Eddy is happier b· of them;
	357– 6	b· matter is the absolute opposite

beck

My.	350– 2	at the b· of material phenomena,

beckoned

Mis.	386–20	angels b· me to this bright land,
Po.	50– 5	angels b· me to this bright land,

beckonest

Po.	30– 1	thou b· from the giant hills

beckoning

Po.	22– 3	and, b· from above,
My.	46– 4	* b· us on towards a higher
	251– 1	duties and attainments b· them.

beckons

Mis.	320–14	b· him on to Truth and Love

becloud

Ret.	78–13	b· the right sense of metaphysical
	78–21	To b· mortals, . . . is to conspire
Hea.	8–17	b· the light of revelation,
My.	161–23	Lest human reason b· spiritual

beclouds

Un.	40–20	A sense of death . . . b· it.

become

Mis.	xi–16	*b·* footsteps to joys eternal.
	4–13	a newspaper . . . has *b·* a necessity.
	7– 4	until their bodies *b·* dry,
	9–20	having tasted . . . we *b·* intoxicated ;
	9–20	*b·* lethargic, dreamy objects of
	9–27	*b·* educated to gratification
	10–24	and all things *b·* new.
	16– 8	requisite to *b·* wholly Christlike,
	35–17	*is one obliged to b· a student*
Mis.	78–20	this abuse, has *b·* too common :
	92– 5	*b·* sufficiently understood to be
	107–24	may *b·* morally blind,
	127–21	condition whereby to *b·* blessed,
	134– 2	have *b·* "wise— *II Tim.* 3 : 15.
	164–22	as it shall *b·* understood,
	164–26	*b·* so magnified to human sense,
	177–15	*b·* real and consecrated warriors
	178– 6	wanted to *b·* a God-like man.
	179–14	Truth has *b·* more to us,
	187–24	*b·* a clod, in order to
	188–31	This knowledge did *b·* to her
	189– 3	*b·* willing to accept the divine
	194–24	*b·* imbued with divine Love
	196–10	and thus *b·* material, sensual, evil.
	196–24	is *b·* the head stone— *Psal.* 118 : 22.
	197– 2	*b·* the motive-power of every act.
	217– 5	cannot *b·* less than Spirit ;
	217–28	must change in order to *b·*
	217–29	or to *b·* both finite and infinite ;
	227–13	ere that one himself *b·* aware,
	229–21	would thus *b·* beautifully less ;
	229–24	*b·* healthier, holier, happier,
	230–14	*b·* such by hard work ;
	235–19	and *b·* Christian Scientists ;
	236– 7	and *b·* weary with study to
	250– 3	the best *b·* the most abused,
	250–12	*b·* jealousy and hate.
	253–26	until she herself is *b·* a mother?
	289–30	the right to *b·* a mother ;
	294–26	*b·* an admirer of Edgar L. Wakeman's
	310–20	and to *b·* members of it,
	316–12	Until minds *b·* less worldly-minded,
	318–24	all those who *b·* teachers.
	344– 3	to *b·* one of his disciples.
	368–27	may *b·* the worst,
Man.	18– 2	is *b·* the head — *Matt.* 21 : 42.
	18– 1	to *b·* their pastor.
	34– 5	To *b·* a member of The Mother Church,
	45– 8	shall not hereafter *b·* members of
	73–15	may *b·* members of the
	110– 8	and *b·* a part thereof.
Ret.	16–19	to *b·* their pastor.
	28–10	It must *b·* honest,
	28–12	The first must *b·* last.
	38–24	grown disgusted . . . and *b·* silent.
	44– 7	call to me to *b·* their pastor.
	64–29	will *b·* the victims of error.
	76–29	I *b·* responsible, as a teacher,
	81–13	genuine goodness *b·* so apparent
	87– 4	that it has *b·* a truism ;
	87–22	*b·* a law unto themselves.
Un.	4– 3	approach Him and *b·* like Him.
	14–27	never said that man would *b·* better by
	15–19	*b·* only an echo of the divine?
	40–14	than they can *b·* perfect by
	52– 8	consciousness should *b·* divine,
	56–25	*b·* acquainted with that Love
	58– 3	and must *b·* *dis-eased,*
	64–12	mind-pictures would *b·* to us ;
Pul.	10–20	is *b·* the head — *Matt.* 21 : 42.
	35–14	It must *b·* honest,
	35–16	The first must *b·* last.
	73– 3	* If we *b·* sick, God will care for us,
	79–27	* *b·* materialistically "lopsided,"
	86–27	* to *b·* the permanent pastor of
Rud.	3– 6	and *b·* their Saviour.
	5–27	must either *b·* non-existent, or
No.	24–15	claims of evil *b·* both less and more
	38–14	is *b·* the head — *Matt.* 21 : 42.
'00.	5–24	it will *b·* the head of the corner,
'01.	5– 6	*b·* less coherent than the
	14–26	it must *b·* unreal to us :
	26–23	*b·* as sounding brass,— *I Cor.* 13 : 1.
Hea.	3– 9	again *b·* the head of the corner.
	4–15	and *b·* finite for a season ;
	4–18	*b·* finite, and have an end ;
	5–28	The more spiritual we *b·*
	8–25	If we work to *b·* Christians
	12–11	before they can *b·* manifest
Peo.	2–22	has their Deity *b·* good ;
	4–10	*b·* intelligent of good and evil,
	7–29	*b·* more or less perfect
	10– 6	matter will *b·* vague,
	14– 1	ideas of Deity *b·* more spiritual,
My.	4–26	*b·* as little children, — *Matt.* 18 : 3.

become

My.	41– 1	* to *b·* gladly obedient to law,
	49–11	* to Mrs. Eddy to *b·* its pastor.
	49–19	* to *b·* pastor of the church.
	60–13	* has *b·* the corner-stone of
	63–13	* has *b·* a part of our expanding
	85–22	* *b·* the great centre of attraction,
	107– 9	the old school has *b·* reconciled.
	111–19	*b·* successful healers and models of
	123– 2	they have *b·* a wonder !
	126–25	"is *b·* the habitation of — *Rev.* 18 : 2.
	150–19	to *b·* His own image and likeness,
	190–25	*b·* students of the Christ, Truth,
	190–25	thus *b·* God-endued with power
	236–12	may *b·* equivalent to no centre.
	251– 9	* to *b·* teachers of Primary classes
	253–28	*b·* one with his creator,
	267– 1	*b·* the one and the only religion
		(*see also* **power**)

becomes

Mis.	59–27	and thus *b·* a transparency
	96–13	God *b·* to me,
	96–18	this atonement *b·* more to me
	101– 2	how healing *b·* spontaneous,
	115–24	*b·* a means of grace.
	156–22	and in turn *b·* a prey.
	203– 5	*b·* mine through gratitude
	216–25	* "When philosophy *b·* fairy-land,
	218– 1	in which nature *b·* Spirit ;
	222–10	he *b·* morally paralyzed
	235– 6	*b·* the partaker of that Mind
	277– 8	*b·* the mark for error's shafts.
	284–25	not something . . . that *b·* more **real**
	293–23	*b·* the creator of the claim
	346–25	*b·* requisite to bring out Truth.
	351–25	joy that *b·* sorrow.
	363– 2	more conscious it *b·* of its
	391–13	And Love *b·* the substance,
Man.	100–12	*b·* apparent to the C. S. Board
Ret.	21–30	*b·* correspondingly obscure.
	63–19	*b·* accessory to it.
	80–14	heart *b·* obediently receptive
	93–16	*b·* the model for human action.
Un.	24–24	In my mortal mind, matter *b·*
	45–16	where it *b·* error's affirmative
	45–26	until it *b·* non-existent.
	54– 6	then disease *b·* as tangible as
	54–18	*b·* legitimate to mortals,
Pul.	79– 9	* it *b·* us as students of
No.	4–13	*b·* fable instead of fact.
	5–20	Disease *b·* indeed a stubborn
	25– 2	*b·* the All and Only of our being.
Pan.	6–21	what *b·* of theism in Christianity?
'01.	16–10	hatred gone mad *b·* imbecile
	25– 2	*b·* clear to the godly.
'02.	6–25	In the degree that man *b·*
	6–26	he *b·* Godlike.
	9– 2	God *b·* to him the All-presence
	10–17	man *b·* finally spiritual.
Po.	38–12	And Love *b·* the substance,
My.	133–26	this inmost something *b·* articulate,
	148–11	this church *b·* historic,
	165–23	Human reason *b·* tired and calls for
	179– 9	man *b·* both good and evil,
	183–19	when the forest *b·* a fruitful field,
	222–26	as God's government *b·* apparent,
	226–28	*b·* better acquainted with C. S.,
	308–10	It *b·* my duty to be just to the

becometh

My.	162– 4	thus it *b·* us to — *Matt.* 3 : 15.
	218– 3	thus it *b·* us to — *Matt.* 3 : 15.

becoming

Mis.	156–16	*b·* the basis for others :
	281–16	* wise to count the cost of *b·* a
	281–18	* cost of *not b·* a true Christian."
Pul.	83–12	* *b·* "as fair as the morn, — *see Song* 6 : 10.
No.	2–20	such teachers are *b·* beacon-lights
	3–25	*b·* odious to honest people ;
	30–14	not by *b·* human, and knowing sin,
My.	197– 2	but *b·* slaves to pleasure is.

bed

Mis.	127–32	human heart, like a feather *b·*,
	376–19	for me, on my *b·*
Ret.	17–12	heart of the pink — in its odorous *b·* ;
	40–11	the sick woman rose from her *b·*,
Peo.	14–15	ye may go to the *b·* of anguish,
Po.	62–15	heart of the pink — in its odorous *b·* ;

bedew

Pul.	5–15	was the first to *b·* my hope with a

bedewing

Po.	67– 7	*b·* these fresh-smiling flowers !

Bedford

My.	45–29	* granite and *B·* stone,

Bedford

My. 68–19　　* to harmonize with the *B·* stone
　　68–25　　* *B·* stone and marble form the
　　68–30　　* bronze, marble, and *B·* stone.

bedridden

Mis. 241–18　　to the *b·* sufferer administer

beds

Pul. 48– 3　　* dotted with *b·* of flowering shrubs,
　　54– 3　　* Is by our *b·* of pain ;
My. 36–14　　* delivered from *b·* of sickness
　　188–24　　like *b·* in hospitals,

bedside

Mis. 63–13　　go to the *b·* and address himself to
　　201–30　　Go to the *b·* of pain,
My. 105–23　　Her physician, who stood by her *b·*,
　　153–12　　my flowers visited his *b·* :

Bee

Pul. 89–24　　* *B·*, Omaha, Neb.

bee

Mis. 294–13　　a hived *b·*, with sting ready
My. 252– 4　　Then you will be toilers like the *b·*,

beefsteak

No. 42–27　　* eat *b·* and drink strong coffee

beehive

Pul. 42–16　　* golden *b·* stamped upon it,
　　42–16　　* and beneath the *b·* the words,

Beelzebub

Mis. 63– 3　　healed through *B·* ;
　　97–10　　casting out devils through *B·*.
'01. 10– 5　　"If they have called . . . *B·*,— *Matt.* 10 : 25.
Hea. 13–26　　antipode of mesmerism, *B·*.

beest

Hea. 8–16　　* "What thou seest, that thou *b·*."

Beethoven

'00. 11–14　　*B·* besieges you with tones

befall

Mis. 229–18　　there shall no evil *b·* thee,— *Psal.* 91 : 10.
Ret. 34–14　　all the ills which *b·* mortals.

befogs

Mis. 121–18　　whatever belittles, *b·*, or

befools

Mis. 173–24　　pains, fetters, and *b·* him.

before

Mis. 7–14　　Cast not your pearls *b·* swine ;
　　8–25　　which were *b·* you."— *Matt.* 5 : 12.
　　9–19　　to fall in fragments *b·* our eyes.
　　10–12　　stronger than *b·* the stumble.
　　14–15　　from evidences *b·* him
　　16–32　　You stand *b·* the awful detonations
　　17– 6　　And, *b·* the flames have died away
　　17–13　　meekly bow *b·* the Christ,
　　18–10　　no other gods *b·* me ;"— *Exod.* 20 : 3.
　　21– 3　　no other gods *b·* me."— *Exod.* 20 : 3.
　　23–13　　no other gods *b·* me."— *Exod.* 20 : 3.
　　24–14　　better health than I had *b·* enjoyed.
　　26–12　　*b·* it was in the earth."— *Gen.* 2 : 5.
　　28–21　　no other gods *b·* me,"— *Exod.* 20 : 3.
　　29–10　　even *b·* the Christian era ;
　　30– 2　　*b·* we prove it,
　　34– 7　　*b·* the body is renewed
　　34–16　　as they were *b·* death,
　　42– 2　　*do we meet those gone b·?*
　　42–10　　and being, as material as *b·*.
　　42–15　　with those gone *b·*,
　　42–17　　*b·* the change whereby we meet
　　45–27　　having "other gods *b·* me."— *Exod.* 20 : 3.
　　49– 3　　to withdraw *b·* its close.
　　49– 4　　*b·* entering the College,
　　52–28　　*b·* solving the advanced problem.
　　53– 3　　*b·* this false claim can be
　　79–27　　*persons brought b· the courts*
　　81–17　　*b· it shall go forth into all the cities*
　　89–17　　"pearls *b·* swine"— *Matt.* 7 : 6.
　　91–31　　study the lessons *b·* recitations.
　　92– 4　　Centuries will intervene *b·* the
　　92–20　　to study it *b·* the recitations ;
　　96–20　　I reverence and adore Christ as never *b·*.
　　96–30　　the evidence *b·* the personal senses,
　　99–10　　courage of his convictions fell *b·* it.
　　107–14　　*b·* poor humanity is regenerated
　　107–20　　pass through . . . *b·* yielding error.
　　109–14　　*b·* they can be reduced to
　　110–13　　chapter sub-title
　　112– 4　　*b·* they know it,
　　116– 7　　chapter sub-title
　　117–29　　make their moves *b·* God makes His,
　　123– 4　　no other gods *b·* me :"— *Exod.* 20 : 3.
　　132– 5　　are opening, even wider than *b·*,
　　134–14　　such as you never *b·* received.
　　151–24　　May mercy and truth go *b·* you :
　　153– 6　　God went forth *b·* His people,

before

Mis. 161– 3　　Sunday *b·* Christmas, 1888.
　　162– 7　　stepped suddenly *b·* the people
　　165–30　　*b·* man can truthfully conclude
　　166–31　　*b·* it could make him the glorified.
　　168–26　　* speak *b·* the Scientist denomination
　　169– 9　　*b·* Truth dawned upon her
　　169–16　　*b·* their message can be borne fully to
　　172– 7　　a higher sense than ever *b·*,
　　178–18　　* that to-day I should stand *b·* you
　　178–22　　* I should not be standing *b·* you :
　　179–26　　*b·* it sprang from the earth :
　　187–28　　*b·* he can be good ;
　　187–29　　dying, *b·* deathless ;
　　187–29　　material, *b·* spiritual ;
　　189–14　　"*B·* Abraham was,— *John* 8 : 58.
　　204– 3　　humble *b·* God, he cries,
　　206–28　　going *b·* you, has scaled the steep
　　208–21　　"*B·* I was afflicted — *Psal.* 119 : 67.
　　209–22　　having "other gods *b·* me,"— *Exod.* 20 : 3.
　　209–23　　but are punished *b·* extinguished.
　　210–31　　Charity never flees *b·* error,
　　212–28　　*b·* letting another know it.
　　214–17　　*b·* it could be returned
　　214–29　　*b·* they can be burned,
　　216–29　　* the attempt . . . may succeed, but not *b·* ;
　　218–10　　*b·* it can reach the immortality of
　　230–15　　improving moments *b·* they pass
　　238–28　　kept constantly *b·* the public.
　　239–12　　draw up *b·* a stately mansion ;
　　242–29　　*b·* leaving the class he took a patient
　　244– 6　　*b·* surgical instruments were invented,
　　249–28　　What a word ! I am in awe *b·* it.
　　251– 2　　chapter sub-title
　　251–27　　will fall *b·* Truth demonstrated,
　　251–29　　*b·* the evangel of Truth
　　251–30　　as the mountain mists *b·* the sun.
　　264–20　　*b·* they are quite free from the
　　271–15　　*B·* considering a subject that is
　　273–24　　lying on the desk *b·* me,
　　274–26　　are held up *b·* the rabble
　　277–19　　Benjamin Franklin's report *b·* the
　　277–23　　No evidence *b·* the material senses
　　278– 1　　vision of the Revelator is *b·* me.
　　279–16　　*b·* the walls of Jericho.
　　280–27　　some questions *b·* their dismissal,
　　284–24　　not something to fear and flee *b·*,
　　287– 3　　will go out *b·* the forever fact
　　288– 5　　*b·* you are sure of being a
　　288– 8　　*b·* being put into action.
　　288–19　　*b·* it is understood
　　307–21　　Cast not pearls *b·* the unprepared
　　312–12　　in his remarks *b·* that body,
　　316–24　　*B·* entering the . . . College,
　　318–19　　*B·* entering this sacred field of labor,
　　328–29　　which are *b·*."— *Phil.* 3 : 13.
　　330–15　　let mortals bow *b·* the creator,
　　330–31　　stoops meekly *b·* the blast ;
　　343– 3　　others *b·* us have laid upon the
　　345– 3　　had stood four hundred years *b·*,
　　347–20　　guardians of His presence go *b·* me.
　　349–24　　*b·* I would accept the slightest
　　352–29　　*uncovered b· it can be destroyed,*
　　360–29　　"*B·* Abraham was,— *John* 8 : 58.
　　361–19　　race that is set *b·* us,— *Heb.* 12 : 1.
　　370–14　　more intelligently than ever *b·*,
　　373– 9　　I had never *b·* seen it :
　　382– 4　　*B·* the publication of my first work
　　391–20　　Some good ne'er told *b·*,
Man. 26–16　　*b·* they are elected ;
　　30–19　　attend to the insurance *b·* it expires,
　　32–12　　*b·* commencing to read from this book,
　　52– 7　　shall be laid *b·* this Board,
　　57– 3　　may properly come *b·* these meetings,
　　57– 8　　*B·* calling a meeting of the members
　　57–16　　*b·* he can call said meeting.
　　66– 3　　*b·* presenting it to the Church
　　66–10　　*b·* action is taken it shall be the duty
　　66–16　　brought *b·* a meeting of this Church,
　　69– 8　　*b·* the expiration of the time
　　71– 6　　*b·* titles of branch churches,
　　79–12　　*B·* being eligible for office
　　93–17　　copies of his lectures *b·* delivering them.
　　109–16　　*b·* sending them to the Clerk
　　110–15　　sign "Miss" or "Mrs." *b·* their names
　　112– 6　　*b·* titles of branch churches.
Chr. 55–15　　*B·* Abraham was,— *John* 8 : 58.
Ret. 7– 4　　after a short illness, *b·* his election.
　　8–23　　answered as always *b·*.
　　9– 8　　That night, *b·* going to rest,
　　13– 5　　*B·* this step was taken,
　　16– 7　　she has not sung *b·* since she
　　20– 5　　*b·* my father's second marriage,
　　20–12　　The night *b·* my child was taken
　　22–11　　joy that was set *b·* him — *Heb.* 12 : 2.
　　26–12　　had *b·* seemed to me supernatural,

before

Ret. 26-18   *b·* the material world saw him.
     27-23   *b·* the mind can duly express it
     27-25   *b·* gathering experience and
     31-24   bent low *b·* the omnipotence of Spirit,
     35- 9   *b·* a work on this subject
     40- 4   called to speak *b·* the Lyceum Club,
     40-19   "I never *b·* suffered so little
     44- 9   five years *b·* being ordained.
     47-23   *b·* entering this field of labor
     55- 1   true sense of the great work *b·* them,
     67- 1   *b·* the human concept of sin
     71-25   *b·* the wheat can be garnered
     80-14   *b·* this heart becomes obediently
     83-26   study each lesson *b·* the recitation.
     84- 1   Centuries will intervene *b·* the
Un. 2-23   beyond what they possessed *b·* ;
     3- 6   *b·* it can be truly said of them :
     8- 2   *b·* Science answers it.
     10-22   evidence *b·* the material senses,
     42- 9   *b·* he can be virtuous,
     42-10   dying *b·* he can be deathless,
     42-10   material *b·* he can be spiritual,
     54-21   Satan held it up *b·* man
     58- 4   *b·* error is annihilated.
     58-13   *b·* he apprehends Christ as
     59-15   to suffer *b·* Pilate and on Calvary,
Pul. 6-15   * I had not read three pages *b·* I
     8-17   Little hands, never *b·* devoted to
     12- 8   accused them *b·* our— *Rev.* 12 : 10.
     12-19   than has ever *b·* reached high heaven,
     26-26   * *B·* the great bay window
     29-12   * *B·* the appointed hour every seat
     31-24   * *b·* Mrs. Eddy entered the room.
     34- 9   * *b·* proceeding to his morning service,
     38- 3   * *b·* being ordained in this church,
     39-24   * hurrying throng *b·* me pass,
     41-30   * *B·* this service had closed
     43-29   * *B·* presenting the sermon,
     45-11   * *b·* the close of the year
     45-16   * *b·* April or May of 1895.
     46-16   * not long *b·* the Revolution.
     54-15   * as no one *b·* him understood it ;
     59-29   * *B·* one service was over
     60- 6   * *b·* coming into this work,
     63-24   * paid for *b·* it was begun,
     65- 8   * and may have a future *b·* it.
     76-14   * *b·* the hearth is a large rug
     80-23   * did not believe in them *b·*.
Rud. 12- 9   until they hold stronger than *b·*
No. 8-24   *b·* this state of mortal mind,
     13-10   *b·* this reappearing of Truth,
     13-12   *b·* that saying is demonstrated
     39-22   more clearly than we saw *b·*,
     42- 6   to have other gods *b·* Him,
Pan. 9-10   no other gods *b·* me ;"— *Exod.* 20 : 3.
     10-14   stronger and better than *b·* it.
     10-16   broadened and brightened *b·* them,
'00. 5-20   no other gods *b·* me ;"— *Exod.* 20 : 3.
     6- 7   those things which are *b·*,— *Phil.* 3 : 13.
     8-22   *b·* we can successfully war with
     9-12   *b·* the time?"— *Matt.* 8 : 29.
     9-17   *b·* he can conquer others.
'01. 1- 8   better appreciated, than ever *b·*,
     8-25   "*B·* Abraham was,— *John* 8 : 58.
     14-24   thought *b·* it is acted ;
     22-22   rules, are *b·* the people,
     22-24   *b·* they have learned its numeration
     26-25   *B·* leaving this subject of the
     27-29   * say it has been discovered *b·*.
'02. 4-20   no other gods *b·* me,"— *Exod.* 20 : 3.
     5-30   no other gods *b·* me,"— *Exod.* 20 : 3.
     6-20   no other gods *b·* me."— *Exod.* 20 : 3.
     10- 6   *b·* the time?"— *Matt.* 8 : 29.
     11-26   which were *b·* you."— *Matt.* 5 : 12.
     12-25   *b·* making another united effort
     15-13   *B·* entering upon my great life-work,
Hea. 1-11   *b·* arguing with the world
     4- 4   *b·* calculating the results of an
     10- 5   But the beast bowed *b·* the Lamb :
     10- 7   fell *b·* the womanhood of God,
     11-16   *b·* lifting its foot against its neighbor,
     12-11   *b·* they can become manifest
     17-17   material sense that *b·* had claimed
     19-14   *b·* it was in the earth."— *Gen.* 2 : 5.
Peo. 2-26   constantly *b·* the people's mind,
     5-26   lecture *b·* the Harvard Medical
     7- 9   * With his marble block *b·* him ;
     7-17   * With our lives uncarved *b·* us,
     11- 3   scarcely done with their battles *b·*
Po. 38-19   Some good ne'er told *b·*,
My. 5-14   no other gods *b·* me,"— *Exod.* 20 : 3.
     7- 8   *b·* making another united effort
     9-24   I never *b·* felt poor in thanks,
     29-24   * different status *b·* the world !
     30-32   * *B·* half past seven the chimes

before

My. 37-15   * *b·* the gaze of universal humanity.
     43- 3   * wilderness was *b·* them,
     43-15   * Red Sea forty years *b·*.
     45-19   * Him who went *b·* you
     50- 1   * deliberation *b·* a Communion Sabbath
     50- 9   * knew not the trials *b·* them,
     50-14   * for deliberation *b·* Communion
     54- 8   * *b·* the service commenced,
     54- 9   * *b·* the arrival of the pastor,
     57-27   * Shortly *b·* the dedication of The
     59-27   * *b·* it was ever written.
     59-28   * *b·* it was ever printed."
     61- 8   * completed *b·* the end of summer,
     61-18   * I bowed my head *b·* the might of
     61-31   * I appreciated as never *b·* the
     64-10   * name an honored one *b·* the world.
     64-13   no other gods *b·* me,'— *Exod.* 20 : 3.
     64-19   * standing of C. S. *b·* the world.
     64-27   * members of The Mother Church *b·* men.
     66-30   * never *b·* has such a grand church
     72- 7   * Never *b·* has the city been
     72-26   * *b·* the work was actually completed.
     74-17   * paying for their church *b·*
     79- 2   * kneeling . . . *b·* the pews,
     79-22   * than it ever occupied *b·*.
     80-31   * *b·* seven the auditorium was
     81-14   * told to name, *b·* beginning,
     83-25   * even *b·* the building itself has
     86-14   * *b·* the actual work was completed,
     88- 5   * as now *b·* this continent,
     91- 9   * paid for *b·* they are dedicated.
     95-11   * *b·* the press gallery of
     96-21   * *b·* the day set for the dedication
     137-24   *b·* the present proceedings were
     138-30   * *B·* me : ALLEN HOLLIS,
     140- 5   darkness light *b·* them,— *Isa.* 42 : 16.
     149-18   emptied *b·* it can be refilled.
     150- 1   where Love has not been *b·* thee
     153-17   no other gods *b·* me"— *Exod.* 20 : 3.
     155-14   run in joy, . . . the race set *b·* it,
     186-21   "*B·* they call,— *Isa.* 65 : 24.
     197-20   hope set *b·* us in the Word
     221-18   no other gods *b·* me."— *Exod.* 20 : 3.
     227-24   your pearls *b·* swine,— *Matt.* 7 : 6.
     229- 8   from *b·* thee."— *Deut.* 18 : 12.
     234-28   *b·* the minds of the people are
     244- 1   *b·* informing you of my
     256- 2   *B·* the Christmas bells shall ring,
     257-14   Christ is, more than ever *b·*,
     258-14   joy that was set *b·* him— *Heb.* 12 : 2.
     260- 5   withdraw itself *b·* Mind.
     260- 6   would flee *b·* such reality,
     265- 4   knocks more loudly than ever *b·*
     270- 2   prophets which were *b·*— *Matt.* 5 : 12.
     270-11   nearer my consciousness than *b·*,
     273- 2   * to put *b·* its readers.
     278- 9   no other gods *b·* me,"— *Exod.* 20 : 3.
     279-12   no other gods *b·* me"— *Exod.* 20 : 3.
     298- 9   placing this book *b·* the public,
     299- 8   * *b·* they claim the allegiance of
     302-22   am less lauded, . . . than others *b·* me
     304-27   * say it has been discovered *b·*.
     306-25   *B·* his decease, in January, 1866,
     310- 8   died *b·* the election.
     315-19   * *B·* me, (Signed) H. M. MORSE,
     321-31   * knew you years *b·* I did,
     322-17   * I had seen you the day *b·* at
     323- 2   * *B·* we left that evening,
     323- 8   * How long must it be *b·* the
     329- 7   * *b·* a board of medical examiners.
     329-26   * It will put *b·* them some
     344-14   better than he was *b·* death.
     346-12   * drove into town . . . before returning.
     363-21   address *b·* the Christian Scientist
     364- 8   no other gods *b·* me."— *Exod.* 20 : 3.

beforehand

Mis. 338- 4   gained its height *b·*,

befriended

Pul. 7- 6   her laws have *b·* progress.

beg

Ret. 50-11   I *b·* disinterested people to
My. 118- 9   I *b·* to thank you for your
     165-12   I *b·* to thank the dear brethren
     256- 9   I *b·* to send to you all a

began

Mis. 33-16   when they *b·* treatment,
     101-10   *b·* and ended in a contest for
     168-30   * speaker *b·* by saying :
     182- 1   *b·* spiritually instead of
     237-13   as when this nation *b·*,
     345-17   * since the reign of Christianity *b·*
Ret. 43- 2   I *b·* by teaching one student
Pul. 33- 3   * she *b·*, like Jeanne d'Arc,

began

Pul.	42– 4	* At 10 : 30 o'clock another service *b·*,
	58– 4	* about 1880, she *b·* teaching,
	80– 6	* *b·* in the most intellectual city
	85– 1	* *b·* to lay the foundation of
'02.	2–27	I but *b·* where the Church left off.
	3–30	leap into perdition *b·* with
Po.	v–15	* *b· to take form in her thought,*
	v–17	* *seated herself . . . and b· to write.*
	1– 8	when first creation vast *b·*,
	70–16	discord ne'er in harmony *b·* !
My.	6–18	*b·* with the cross ;
	29–27	* *b·* to congregate about the church
	31– 1	* chimes . . . *b·* to play,
	32– 4	* *b·* to repeat the Lord's Prayer,
	32– 5	* they *b·* all together,
	61–22	* as soon as the workmen *b·* to admit
	72–28	* the way the Christian Scientists *b·*
	77–18	* *b·* to gather at daybreak
	114–14	*b·* with notes on the Scriptures.
	116–23	Every loss in . . . since time *b·*,
	162–16	"This man *b·* to build, — *Luke* 14 : 30.
	291– 7	His work *b·* with heavy strokes,
	291– 9	*b·* by warming the marble of
	304–10	I *b·* writing for the leading
	318–21	*b·* my attack on agnosticism.

begat
My.	132–15	"Of His own will *b·* He us — *Jas.* 1 : 18.

beget
Ret.	68– 4	it claimed to *b·* the offspring of
My.	203–16	Our thoughts *b·* our actions ;

begets
Mis.	210–19	Intemperance *b·* a belief of
Ret.	74– 1	and *b·* a fear of the senses
No.	39–20	Prayer *b·* an awakened desire to
Hea.	3–13	divine Principle that *b·* the quality,

beggar
Pul.	65–24	* half of the garment to a naked *b·* ;

beggared
My.	332– 3	* language would be but *b·* by

begged
My.	302–14	I *b·* the students who first
	311– 5	She *b·* to be allowed to remain

begging
Pul.	8–13	no urging, *b·*, or borrowing;
	31–20	* *b·* the favor of an interview
My.	215– 2	I was above *b·*
	215–13	in letters *b·* me to accept it,
	273–12	nor his seed *b·* bread." — *Psal.* 37 : 25.

begin
Mis.	14–13	we *b·* with the correct statement,
	32–24	and charity must *b·* at home.
	98–22	must *b·* with individual growth,
	106–24	and where shall *b·* that praise
	218–21	To *b·* with, the notion of
	335– 5	shall *b·* to smite — *Matt.* 24 : 49.
	380–11	call for help impelled me to *b·*
Man.	93– 9	The lecture year shall *b·* July 1
Ret.	63–12	we *b·* to sap it ;
Pul.	31– 7	* tempted to "*b·* at the beginning"
	44– 3	* At last you *b·* to see the fruition
	83–26	* *b·* to know what John on Patmos meant
No.	2–10	cannot *b·* by admitting its reality.
	37– 7	to *b·* and end, to know both
	46–13	*b·* by admitting individual rights.
'01.	22–15	I *b·* at the feet of Christ
'02.	4– 2	dishonesty in trusts, *b·* with
	20–17	*b·* omitting our *annual* gathering
Hea.	4–19	to *b·* anew as infinite Life,
My.	41–30	* and we *b·* to understand how
	41–32	* we *b·* to comprehend the
	42–25	* *b·* to comprehend, even in small degree,
	132– 2	*b·* with the law as just announced,
	203– 9	*b·* with work and never stop
	204– 8	can *b·* and never end.
	216–31	*b·* now to earn for a purpose
	274–13	To *b·* rightly enables one
	350– 3	*b·* with the divine noumenon, Mind,
	357–15	*b·* on a wholly spiritual foundation,

beginner
Mis.	66–25	*b·* in sin-healing must know this,

beginning
at the
Mis.	215–23	My students are at the *b·* of their
Pul.	31– 8	* tempted to "begin at the *b·*"
	52–18	* At the *b·* of Christianity it was
My.	78–14	* The offertory taken at the *b·* of
	107– 4	at the *b·* of the Christian era,

end for the
Mis.	215–11	if we take the end for the *b·*

from the
Mis.	56–27	*have existed from the b·*,
	108– 7	of Satan as a liar from the *b·*,

beginning
from the
Mis.	164–15	prophet beheld it from the *b·* as the
	208–23	He who knows the end from the *b·*,
	257–21	"a murderer from the *b·*." — *John* 8 : 44.
	363–14	Truth said, and said from the *b·*,
Un.	17–14	that, from the *b·*, their father,
	32–21	a murderer from the *b·*. — *John* 8 : 44.
	36– 4	From the *b·* this lie was the false
No.	24–23	"a murderer from the *b·*, — *John* 8 : 44.
Pan.	5–14	a murderer from the *b·*, — *John* 8 : 44.
'01.	13– 7	sin is a lie from the *b·*,
'02.	14–18	From the *b·* of the great battle
My.	187–15	ye heard from the *b·*, — *I John* 3 : 11.

in the
Mis.	60–26	Evil in the *b·* claimed the power,
	186–24	than it produced in the *b·*.
	196– 7	saying as in the *b·*,
	215–27	cannot in the *b·* take the attitude,
	258–32	as harmonious to-day as in the *b·*,
	359– 2	is requisite in the *b·* ;
Ret.	48–25	in the *b·* in this institution,
	50–30	in the *b·* of pioneer work.
'01.	18– 2	less than in the *b·*,
	25–25	which Satan demanded in the *b·*,
My.	117–18	"In the *b·* was the Word, — *John* 1 : 1.

its
My.	92– 4	* its *b·* has been impressive,

no
Mis.	167–13	Of his days there is no *b·*
Ret.	58–12	Life, as defined by Jesus, had no *b·* ;
Un.	42–21	Life had no *b·* ;
My.	267–11	eternal Mind that hath no *b·*

of Christian Science
My.	164–14	*b·* of C. S. in Chicago

of days
Chr.	55–20	neither *b·* of days, — *Heb.* 7 : 3.

of war
'02.	3–20	at the close than the *b·* of war.

of wisdom
Mis.	359–29	To ask wisdom . . . is the *b·* of wisdom.

or end
Mis.	189–31	Life without *b·* or end.
No.	37– 9	He cannot know *b·* or end.
My.	119–24	Life without *b·* or end of days.

the very
Un.	54–20	to know evil at the very *b·*,

without
Mis.	189–31	Life without *b·* or end.
Ret.	59– 6	eternal, without *b·* or ending.
Un.	13–17	"without *b·* of years — *see Heb.* 7 : 3.
	40–23	without *b·* and without end,
'02.	7–15	Love, without *b·* and without end,
Hea.	4–19	Life, without *b·* and without end.
Peo.	2–24	Life without *b·* or ending,
My.	119–24	Life without *b·* or end of days.

Mis.	47–25	a *b·* must have an ending.
	57–28	*b·* with the lowest form
	216–20	* *b·* with the end of the tail,
	219–13	it is *b·* to be seen by thinkers,
Man.	86–20	*b·* on page 330 of the revised
	88–12	*B·* with 1907, the teacher shall be
	91–24	once in three years *b·* A. D. 1907 ;
Ret.	60– 1	apart from God, and ending,
No.	28–11	acceptable time for *b·* the lesson.
My.	6–20	remains in the *b·* of this edifice,
	56–28	* Therefore, *b·* October 1, 1905,
	81–14	* been told to name, before *b·*,
	179– 1	the *b·* of the gospel writings.
	236–25	paragraph *b·* at line 30 of page 442

beginnings
My.	123–26	ofttimes small *b·* have large endings.
	303– 1	foresplendor of the *b·* of truth

begins
Mis.	15–13	*b·* with moments, and goes on with
	21– 1	C. S. *b·* with the First Commandment
	220– 5	The healer *b·* by mental argument.
	288–13	Wisdom in human action *b·* with
	347–11	Where my vision *b·* and is clear,
'00.	8–20	man *b·* to quarrel with himself
'01.	21–19	*b·* his calculation erroneously ;
Hea.	7–10	It *b·* with motive, instead of act,
	7–15	*b·* in mind to heal the body,
	7–15	*b·* in motive to correct the act.
Peo.	3–20	*b·* wrongly to apprehend the infinite,
My.	82– 5	* chapter sub-title
	216–28	that charity *b·* at home,
	225–17	*b·* in the minds of men
	253–26	that which *b·* in ourselves

begirt
Mis.	194– 7	*b·* with the Urim and Thummim of
	392– 5	With peaceful presence hath *b·* thee
'01.	12–13	Though a man were *b·* with
Po.	20– 6	With peaceful presence hath *b·* thee

begotten

Mis.	164–25	the only b· of the Father,
Ret.	26–24	It must be b· of spirituality,
Pul.	35– 9	"Divine Science is b· of

begs

Mis.	330–26	mere mendicant that boasts and b·,
My.	276– 4	she b· to say, in her own behalf,

beguile

Po.	33–14	Whose mercies my sorrows b·,
	35– 2	B· the lagging hours of weariness

begun

Mis.	16–25	is the new birth b· in C. S.
	70–19	and had already b· to die,
	141– 6	This building b·, will go up,
	302– 2	purpose to kill the reformation b·
	354–27	for a flight well b·,
	384–12	The reign of heaven b·,
Pul.	63–24	* was paid for before it was b·,
'00.	10– 9	unconquerable right is b· anew,
	15–29	The reign of heaven b·,
Po.	36–11	The reign of heaven b·,
My.	57–12	* was b· in October, 1903,
	67–25	* b· nearly two years ago,
	254– 2	have b· to be a Christian Scientist.

behalf

Mis.	23–17	Satan, the first talker in its b·,
	156– 1	in b· of a suffering race,
	292–20	what he is doing in their b·,
Man.	75– 5	in b· of The First Church of Christ,
Pul.	86–20	* In b· of your loving students
My.	7–18	* acting in b· of ourselves and
	10–16	* has ever been made in this b·,
	20– 9	awaiting on b· of your Leader
	99–12	* it must be said in their b·
	171–24	* greeted in b· of the church
	172–21	* "I accept this gift in b· of
	175–18	May I ask in b· of the public
	190–21	a divine decision in b· of Mind.
	216–16	on b· of the room of
	265–12	in b· of the sacred rights of
	276– 4	she begs to say, in her own b·,
	280– 5	* care and guidance in our b·
	285– 3	on b· of the Civic League of
	312–24	their provisions in my b·
	316–17	in b· of common justice and truth
	331–19	* in b· of the relatives and friends
	332– 6	* in b· of the unfortunate,

behave

No.	45– 5	not b· itself unseemly, — I Cor. 13 : 5.

beheld

Mis.	21– 7	b· "a new heaven — Rev. 21 : 1.
	82– 7	b· the forthcoming Truth,
	164–14	prophet b· it from the beginning
	188–32	for she b· the meaning of
	269–29	The Revelator b· the opening of
Ret.	25–29	I b· with ineffable awe our great
My.	148–14	Then we b· the omen,
	290–21	Through a . . . mist he b· the dawn.

behest

Mis.	385– 7	This is Thy high b· :
Ret.	90–12	until they were able to fulfil his b·
'02.	19–24	a spiritual b·, in reversion,
Po.	28– 7	To Thy all-wise b·
	31–18	The ever Christ, and glorified b·,
	37– 7	This is Thy high b· :
	77– 5	Plenty and peace abound at Thy b·,

behind

Mis.	141– 8	the power that is b· it ;
	160– 5	But a mother's love b· words
	170–11	This is the reality b· the symbol.
	232–10	never do to be b· the times
	302– 1	B· the scenes lurks an evil
	327–28	they fall b· and lose sight of
	328–28	things which are b·, — Phil. 3 : 13.
	368– 8	* and, b· the dim unknown,
	373– 3	placing the serpent b· the woman
	373–10	out of his mouth, b· the woman,
	374–28	Looking b· the veil,
Pul.	1–15	path b· thee is with glory crowned ;
	48– 1	* terrace that slopes b· the
	59– 1	* electric light, b· an antique lamp,
	60–19	* recess b· the spacious platform,
No.	23– 7	"Get thee b· me, Satan ;" — Matt. 16 : 23.
'00.	6– 6	things which are b·, — Phil. 3 : 13.
Po.	26– 2	track b· thee is with glory crowned ;
My.	38–19	* not a whit b· their elders,
	92–18	* would soon be left b·.
	94– 2	* every other sect will be left b·
	155–11	leave b· those things that are b·,
	242– 6	neither b· the point of perfection
	355–19	* "B· a frowning providence

behold

Mis.	vii– 6	* Then do I love thee, and b· thy ends

behold

Mis.	2–14	we b· but the first faint view
	16–31	and b· for the first time
	17–15	you b· for the first time
	107– 9	we b· more clearly that all the
	123–17	too pure to b· iniquity.
	133–32	b· the sick who are healed,
	134–23	Like Elisha, look up, and b· :
	159–25	Thy children grown to b· Thee!
	168–19	b· the appearing of the star !"
	210– 2	b· the result : evil, uncovered,
	213– 1	could not b· his immortal being
	322– 3	invite you . . . to preparation to b· it.
	323– 7	b· a Stranger wending his way
	326–27	B·, your house — Matt. 23 : 38.
	330–16	b· man in God's own image
	336–25	b· a better man, woman, or child.
	342–12	to b· the bridegroom,
	342–18	But how could they b· him?
	352– 3	to b· aright the error,
	352– 8	able to b· the facts of Truth
	367–30	too pure to b· iniquity ;
	371– 6	and b· the remedy,
	389–11	Can I b· the snare, the pit, the fall :
Chr.	55–26	B·, I stand at the — Rev. 3 : 20.
Ret.	42–15	and b· the upright :— Psal. 37 : 37.
	86–10	B· its vileness, and remember
	86–13	may b· the real man,
Un.	1–11	Does God know or b· sin,
	2– 1	too pure to b· iniquity — see Hab. 1 : 13.
	18– 8	too pure to b· iniquity,
	29–28	to b· Spirit as the sole origin
	55–20	and b· the truth of being,
	55–22	Now and here shall I b· God,
	64– 3	for God can no more b· it,
Pul.	2– 4	"B·, the half was not — I Kings 10 : 7.
Rud.	10– 7	too pure to b· iniquity,
No.	22–17	greater than the corporeality we b·.
	24–22	for b· evil (or devil) is,
Pan.	13– 7	b·, the kingdom of God — Luke 17 : 21.
'00.	7–21	we b· the Christ
	8– 1	b· more nearly the embodied Christ,
	14– 3	B·, I will make them — Rev. 3 : 9.
'02.	19– 2	Yet b· his love !
Hea.	17–12	as we awake to b· His likeness.
Peo.	14–17	b· once again the power of divine
Po.	4–10	Can I b· the snare, the pit,
My.	12–17	"B·, now is the accepted — II Cor. 6 : 2.
	16–24	saith the Lord God, B·, — Isa. 28 : 16.
	17–15	B·, I lay in Sion — I Pet. 2 : 6.
	122–24	b· the place where they — Mark 16 : 6.
	122–28	spiritualized to b· this Christ,
	191–20	B· the place where they laid me ;
	267–28	"B·, the kingdom of God — Luke 17 : 21.
	300– 1	than to b· evil." — Hab. 1 : 13.

beholding

Mis.	68– 5	visible to those b· him here.
	180– 6	b· me restored to health.
	182–18	b· the truth of being ;
	324–19	Startled beyond measure at b· him,
	342– 9	b· the bridal of Life and Love,
My.	274–23	blessed when b· Christian healing,

beholds

Un.	41– 1	and b· nothing but mortality,

behooves

Mis.	171–29	it b· all clad in the shining mail
Pul.	2–26	it b· us to defend our heritage.

Being

Mis.	82–18	endless beatitudes of B· ;
Ret.	56– 7	B· into beings, — is a misstatement
Un.	19– 3	must be one, in an infinite B·.
No.	26–20	reflect the supreme individual B·,
Pan.	4– 4	will of a self-existent divine B·,
'00.	12– 5	the radiance of glorified B·.
'01.	3–11	* definition of God, "A Supreme B·,"
	3–12	* Supreme B·, self-existent and
	3–19	fundamental, intelligent, divine B·,
Hea.	15– 4	omnipotence of the Supreme B·
	19–18	Tireless B·, patient of man's
Peo.	2– 5	people's . . . views of the Supreme B·.
	4–27	false ideals of the Supreme B·
	13– 5	Divine B· is more than a person,
		(see also Supreme Being)

being (noun)

actual

My.	160–17	for actual b·, health, holiness,

aid to

Mis.	267–25	is no real aid to b·.

aim, and

Ret.	22–17	He alone is our origin, aim, and b·.

all

Mis.	78– 6	His glory encompasseth all b·.
	104– 9	In Science all b· is individual ;
	399–12	Life of all b· divine :
Ret.	28– 2	Life, or Principle, of all b· ;

being (noun)

all
Un. 24- 4 all individuality, all b·.
29-10 Soul of all b·, the only Mind
Rud. 3-27 divine Principle of all b·,
Po. 75-19 Life of all b· divine :

altitude of
My. 110-24 higher in the altitude of b·.

arrayed against
No. 5-19 and yet is arrayed against b·,

avenue of
Mis. 185-12 good flows into every avenue of b·,

basis of
Mis. 74- 6 of the true basis of b·,

chain of
My. 202-18 onward and upward chain of b·.
339- 4 leads upward in the chain of b·.

cognizes
Rud. 5-19 consciousness which cognizes b·.

concrete
Mis. 82-20 Infinite progression is concrete b·,

conscious
Un. 56-19 Their conscious b· was not fully
No. 36- 6 Jesus' true and conscious b·

constituency of
No. 4-23 and true constituency of b·.

deathless
My. 195-24 lives, moves, and has deathless b·.

demonstration of
Ret. 26-29 demonstration of b·, in Science,

dome of
Mis. 1- 5 dawned on the dome of b·

dynamics of
Mis. 258-31 the eternal dynamics of b·,

enriches the
My. 295-20 enriches the b· of all men.

eternal
Un. 43- 1 eternal b· and its perfections,
No. 11- 4 Principle, and an eternal b·.

exhaustless
My. 149-12 mysteries of exhaustless b·.

fact of
Mis. 186-26 is not the scientific fact of b· ;
My. 109- 6 is not the spiritual fact of b·.

facts of
Mis. 37- 7 spiritual facts of b·.
187-26 primal facts of b· are eternal ;
234-24 into the spiritual facts of b·
Un. 51- 1 everlasting facts of b· appear,

fate to
No. 42-18 determine the fact and fate to b·.

finite
Mis. 102- 4 is only an infinite finite b·,

fragrance of
Mis. 330-23 freshen the fragrance of b·.

good in
My. 196-25 good in b·, . . . is your daily bread.

grounds of
Mis. 68-28 * the ultimate grounds of b·,

harmonious
Mis. 77-17 one eternal round of harmonious b·.
188- 5 grand chorus of harmonious b·.

harmony of
(see **harmony**)

her
Mis. 160- 7 paramount portion of her b·.

His
Mis. 102-11 His b· is individual,
Un. 13-17 in the very fibre of His b·,
32-14 the eternal qualities of His b·.

his
Mis. 85- 8 the divine Principle of his b·,
181- 4 reality of his b·, in divine Science
Ret. 69- 4 and Life is the law of his b·''
No. 36-17 reality and royalty of his b·,
Pan. 11-11 the divine Principle of his b·,
My. 164-29 lives, moves, and has his b· in God,

his own
'01. 20- 9 Scientist is alone with his own b·

human
(see **human**)

idea of
Mis. 166- 2 Principle and spiritual idea of b·.
188-10 divine Principle and idea of b·,

immortal
Mis. 213- 1 could not behold his immortal b·
Un. 57-26 forward the birth of immortal b· ;
No. 27-28 learn the definition of immortal b· ;
'02. 16-20 and man's immortal b·.

individual
Mis. 104- 2 his individual b·, the Christ,
No. 17- 9 is a spiritual and individual b·,
26-19 Man's individual b· must reflect the

infinite
My. 262-17 with the glory of infinite b·.

being (noun)

is God
Mis. 72-28 B· is God, infinite Spirit ;

is understood
Mis. 361-13 and b· is understood in startling

justice and
'02. 15-12 connection between justice and b·

knowledge, and
Ret. 32- 4 spiritual insight, knowledge, and b·.

law of
Mis. 181- 9 blind obedience to the law of b·,
259-18 the only law of b·.
No. 2- 8 is natural and a law of b·.
My. 217-31 not to destroy the law of b·,

laws of
Mis. 31- 7 subverts the scientific laws of b·.

Life and
Ret. 68-25 Life and b· are of God.

man's
Mis. 202- 4 lift man's b· into the sunlight of
Un. 53-15 harmony of man's b· is not built on
Rud. 9-14 divine Principle of man's b· ;
My. 4- 7 C. S., the truth of man's b·.
155- 1 Such communing uplifts man's b· ;
246-17 divine Mind or Principle of man's b·
257-22 make man's b· pure and blest.
274- 7 consummate man's b· with the

misapprehension of
Un. 53-13 is a misapprehension of b·,

my
My. 189-27 song and the dirge, surging my b·,
241-27 * and moved and had my b· in God,

of God
Un. 47- 4 with good, the b· of God,
Rud. 7-15 evidence of the b· of God and man,

one in
'02. 12-19 Father and son, are one in b·.

or consciousness
Un. 3-21 is perfect b·, or consciousness.

order of
Mis. 104-23 the divine law and order of b·.
Un. 40-11 imperative in the divine order of b·.

our
Mis. 8- 6 and have our b·,'' — Acts 17 : 28.
82-30 and have our b·.'' — Acts 17 : 28.
Ret. 93-18 and have our b·.'' — Acts 17 : 28.
Un. 64-14 forever accompany our b·.
Pul. 2-23 and have our b·'' — Acts 17 : 28.
No. 17- 7 and have our b· ;'' — Acts 17 : 28.
25- 3 becomes the All and Only of our b·.
Pan. 13-20 and have our b·'' — Acts 17 : 28.
'02. 12-20 and have our b·.'' — Acts 17 : 28.
My. 109-23 and have our b·.'' — Acts 17 : 28.

part of
No. 12-28 all instead of a part of b·,

personal
Ret. 25-21 personal b·, like unto man ;

phenomena of
No. 10-28 constitute the phenomena of b·,

power of
Pul. 4-25 with it cometh the full power of b·.

predicate of
Mis. 103- 6 ultimate and predicate of b·.

present
Un. 41-16 illumine our present b· with

Principle of
Mis. 93-17 by the unerring Principle of b·,
269-11 elucidate the Principle of b·,
Man. 67-19 from the divine Principle of b· to
My. 179-27 based on the divine Principle of b·,

problem of
(see **problem**)

problems of
Mis. 125-25 hitherto untouched problems of b·,

real
Mis. 83- 1 Principle, of all real b· ;
No. 26-13 All real b· represents God,

realities of
(see **realities**)

reality of
Mis. 367-11 reality of b· — goodness and harmony
Un. 38-27 reality of b·, whose Principle is
51- 5 reality of b· is neither seen, felt,
No. 16-25 Spirit, which is the reality of b·.

recognition of
Mis. 196-26 arise to spiritual recognition of b·,

regard
My. 178-14 those who regard b· as material.

resources of
Un. 9-15 as to the source and resources of b·,

right
'01. 2-11 a fair seeming for right b·,

rule of
Mis. 189- 4 divine Principle and rule of b·,

scale of
(see **scale**)

being (noun)

Science of
  (*see* **Science**)

scientific
  Mis. 288–19 consciousness of scientific *b·*
  My. 272– 8 ultimate of scientific *b·* presents,
      279– 8 is the chain of scientific *b·*

self-conscious
  Rud. 2– 2 *"a living soul; a self-conscious *b·*;

sense of
  (*see* **sense**)

source of
  Mis. 333–18 away from the divine source of *b·*,
  Ret. 69– 3 primitive and ultimate source of *b·*;
  Un. 46–12 spiritual sense and source of *b·*.

spiritual
  Mis. 105–15 his individual spiritual *b·*,
      113–13 scale of moral and spiritual *b·*,
      352– 1 it mocks the bliss of spiritual *b·*;
  Peo. 2– 6 material conceptions of spiritual *b·*,

stage of
  Mis. 288–22 in every state and stage of *b·*.
  No. 38–23 any other state or stage of *b·*.

statement of
  Ret. 94– 1 this scientific statement of *b·*.
  My. 19– 7 * scientific statement of *b·*,"
      33– 4 "the scientific statement of *b·*"
     111–26 "The scientific statement of *b·*"

state of
  Mis. 161–12 approximation to this state of *b·*
  No. 5–19 and is itself a state of *b·*,
     17–17 there is no fallen state of *b·*;

states of
  Mis. 357–20 of all stages and states of *b·*;

statuesque
  Pan. 10–28 promotes statuesque *b·*, health, and

substance of
  Un. 49–10 reality and substance of *b·* are *good*,

sum of
  Mis. 52–29 have the sum of *b·* to work out,

their
  '01. 33– 1 consideration of their *b·*,
  My. 200–28 save sinners and fit their *b·* to

to be eternal
  No. 4–25 *b·*, to be eternal, must be

true
  Mis. 104–31 on the side of good, my true *b·*.

true estimate of
  Ret. 21–20 joy and true estimate of *b·*.

truth of
  (*see* **truth**)

unrealities of
  Mis. 60– 7 as the woeful unrealities of *b·*,

upholds
  Mis. 105–15 It upholds *b·*, and destroys the

verities of
  (*see* **verities**)

verity of
  Mis. 261– 8 demonstrates this verity of *b·*;
     286–27 should recognize this verity of *b·*,

visible
  Mis. 205–18 whose visible *b·* is invisible to

was beautiful
  Ret. 23–22 *B·* was beautiful, its substance,

wonder of
  Un. 37–10 would reveal this wonder of *b·*.

your
  My. 139–28 redeem . . . your *b·* from sensuality;

  ———

  Mis. 42– 9 awaken with thoughts, and *b·*, as
     50–25 live thereby, and have *b·*.
     79– 9 we live, move, and have *b·*.
  Un. 48– 7 no faith in any other thing or *b·*.

being (ppr.)
  Mis. 14– 1 it fills all space, *b·* omnipresent;
     16–12 *b·* His likeness and image,
     24–17 this Life *b·* the sole reality of
     27–24 *b·* in and of Spirit,
     39– 4 To avoid *b·* *subject* to disease,
     42–29 *Can I be treated without b· present*
     43–11 as *b·* adequate to make safe
     46– 5 *b·* real, evil, good's opposite, is
     67–30 I believe in this removal *b·* possible
     79–10 origin and existence *b·* in Him,
     93–15 This *b·* true, sin has no power;
    108– 8 a lie, *b·* without foundation in fact,
    115– 9 and fear of *b·* found out.
    116–28 *b·* "faithful over a — *Matt.* 25 : 21.
    133– 8 As to *b·* "prayerless,"
    188– 6 presents as *b·* first that which
    193–17 *b·* a modification of silence
    206– 2 the former *b·* servant to the latter,
    209– 8 The Principle of divine Science *b·* Love,
    220–26 and speak of him as *b·* sick,
    221–18 Truth *b·* the cure,

being (ppr.)
  Mis. 259–12 to conceive of good as *b·* unlike
    271–21 *b·* the only chartered College of
    288– 5 *b·* a fit counsellor.
    300–30 pays . . . for *b·* healed,
    306–17 * We would add, as *b·* of interest,
    346–20 good *b·* real, its opposite is
    367– 7 fact of there *b·* no mortal mind,
    381– 6 the defendant *b·* present personally
  Man. 99– 5 dividing line *b·* the 36th parallel
  Ret. 1– 3 *b·* John McNeil of Edinburgh.
    15– 6 *b·* the chief corner-stone." — *Eph.* 2 : 20.
    19–11 *b·* a member in Saint Andrew's Lodge,
    34–19 body *b·* but the objective state of
    64–23 error *b·* a false claim,
    73– 1 The immortal man *b·* spiritual,
    73–22 or accuse people of *b·* unduly personal,
    76–15 so far from *b·* personal worship,
    78– 2 *b·* too fast or too slow.
    86– 6 There is but one way of *b·* good,
  Un. 29–28 Virgin-mother's sense *b·* uplifted
    30– 7 *b·* spiritual Life, never sins,
    31–14 *fourth*, that matter, *b·* so endowed,
    33– 6 Now these senses, *b·* material,
    42– 1 Life, God, *b·* everywhere,
    46–23 as *b·* equally identical and
    49– 4 as *b·* the eternally divine idea.
    49–22 *B·* destitute of Principle,
    53– 5 *B·* a lie, it would be truthful to
    53–14 *b·* self-contradictory, it is also
    58–16 *b·* "in all points tempted — *Heb.* 4 : 15.
  Pul. 1–18 To-day, *b·* with you in spirit,
    3– 1 Such *b·* its nature,
    4–13 in *b·* and doing right,
    26– 3 * the centre *b·* of pure white light,
    55–26 * all others *b·* branches,
    58–11 * every bill *b·* paid.
    59–10 * certain hymns and psalms *b·* omitted.
    62–15 * superb, *b·* rich and mellow.
    68– 2 * *b·* now known as the Rev. . . . Eddy.
    69– 7 * *b·* cured by Mrs. Eddy of a
    73–19 * *b·* of the same theory as Mrs. Copeland.
    76– 1 * *b·* that used in the doors and pews.
    86– 1 * *b·* of granite, about six inches in
  Rud. 5– 7 *b·* made in the image of Spirit,
    7–16 material evidence *b·* wholly false.
    14–25 People are *b·* healed by means of
  No. 13–17 not susceptible of *b·* held as
    24–18 evil, *b·* thus uncovered, is found out,
    25– 5 that *b·* dead wherein — *Rom.* 7 : 6.
    27– 3 and the claim, *b·* worthless,
  Pan. 4–26 This *b·* the case, what need have we
  '00. 4–20 *b·* demonstrable, they are undeniable ;
    5–17 This *b·* the divine Science of
  '01. 3–25 light, *b·* matter, loses the nature of
    6–18 The logic of divine Science *b·* faultless,
    7– 5 The trinity . . . *b·* Life, Truth, Love,
    7– 8 Again, God *b·* infinite Mind,
    9–24 and these things *b·* spiritual,
    10– 8 Christ *b·* the Son of God,
    23–30 * nature *b·* nothing more than
    27–15 rejoice in *b·* informed thereof.
    31– 6 *b·* neither personal nor human,
  '02. 8–18 evidence of *b·* Christian Scientists
    17–22 in *b·* and in doing good ;
  Po. v– 5 * *b· the spontaneous outpouring of*
    34– 2 soul of melody by *b·* blest
  My. 56–30 * second and third *b·* repetitions of
    66–15 * *b·* in a fine part of the city.
    165–27 power of *b·* magnanimous.
    179–14 *b·* translations, the Scriptures are
    179–26 *b·* contingent on nothing written
    212–18 *B·* like the disciples of old,
    238– 9 God *b·* Spirit, His language and
    273– 6 * in *b·* able to point to a Leader
    289–23 It *b·* inconvenient for me to
    315– 6 * *b·* a pure and Christian woman,
    315– 8 * separation *b·* wholly on his part ;
    320–12 * *b·* a very unique book,
    330–23 *b·* a member in St. Andrew's Lodge,
    356–28 God *b·* infinite, He is the only basis

beings
  Ret. 56– 7 Being into *b·*, — is a misstatement
  Un. 37–17 Human *b·* are physically mortal,
  Pul. 51– 7 * their inherent right as human *b·*,
  Rud. 4– 3 peopled with perfect *b·*,
  Peo. 1–18 that we are spiritual *b·* here
  Po. 17– 1 Blest *b·* departed!
  My. 294–28 The august ruler of . . . human *b·*
    303–14 divine rights in human *b·*.

belated
  My. 74– 6 * numbers of *b·* church members

belay
  Mis. 327–16 They stoutly *b·* those who,

belch
  Mis. 237– 9 *b·* forth their latent fires.
beleaguered
  Mis. 326–18 wanderers in a *b·* city,
belfry
  Pul. 58–13 * In the *b·* is a set of tubular
  Po. 71–14 Joy is in every *b·* bell
Belial
  Mis. 333–23 hath Christ with *B·*?" — II Cor. 6 : 15.
belial
  Hea. 6–28 in Hebrew it is *b·*,
belie
  No. 32–23 to *b·* and belittle C. S.,
  40–10 Words may *b·* desire,
belied
  Mis. 337–23 life of Jesus was belittled and *b·* by
  My. 139–13 when misrepresented, *b·*, and
belief
  according to
  Un. 32– 1 according to *b·*, obtain in matter ;
  adipose
  Mis. 47– 5 adipose *b·* of yourself as substance ;
  alone
  Hea. 18–26 produced by a *b·* alone.
  and service
  Pul. 66–17 * *b·* and service are well suited to
  and understanding
  Pul. 47–19 * the terms *b·* and understanding,
  another's
  Mis. 83–12 No person can accept another's *b·*,
  baubles of
  My. 297–14 blows away the baubles of *b·*,
  begets a
  Mis. 210–19 Intemperance begets a *b·* of
  blind
  Ret. 54–15 Blind *b·* cannot say with the apostle,
  bodily
  Mis. 352–16 supposed bodily *b·* of the patient
  called
  Ret. 54–17 in this mental state called *b·* ;
  called death
  Mis. 42– 5 passing through the *b·* called death.
  changed
  Mis. 237–6 This changed *b·* has wrought a change
  common
  Mis. 49–21 common *b·* in the opposite of
  concerning Deity
  Pan. 2–25 *b·* concerning Deity in theology.
  conditions of a
  Mis. 73–16 Belief fulfils the conditions of a *b·*,
  conscientious
  Peo. 6– 7 * "I declare my conscientious *b·*,
  darkness of
  Pul. 13–16 in the deep darkness of *b·*.
  desire or
  My. 292–21 effect of one human desire or *b·*
  destroy belief
  Mis. 334–25 Can *b·* destroy belief?
  destroy the
  Mis. 28– 6 Destroy the *b·* that you can walk,
  73–17 these conditions destroy the *b·*.
  Un. 35– 6 Destroy the *b·*, and . . . disappears.
  My. 132–25 destroy the *b·* of life in
  entertain a
  Man. 42–16 shall neither entertain a *b·* nor
  erring
  Mis. 186– 9 this erring *b·* even separates its
  erroneous
  Mis. 10–30 erroneous *b·* that you have enemies ;
  error of
  Mis. 45–27 This error of *b·* is idolatry,
  220–32 error of *b·* has not the power of
  No. 4–10 error of *b·*, named disease,
  even in
  Mis. 10–29 Even in *b·* you have but one
  evil
  Mis. 247–30 only an evil *b·* of mortal mind,
  Un. 53–10 evil *b·* that renders them obscure.
  except in
  Un. 51– 7 hair white or black, except in *b·* ;
  extension of
  Un. 7– 3 in the wide extension of *b·*
  fad of
  My. 218–22 fad of *b·* is the fool of mesmerism.
  faith is
  Ret. 54– 3 Because faith is *b·*, and not
  false
  Mis. 45–24 It is but a false *b·* ;
  48– 2 its demonstrations as a false *b·*,
  56–19 final destruction of this false *b·*
  63–16 to save them from *this false b·*;
  198–14 false *b·* of the personal senses ;
  233–30 must be understood as a false *b·*

belief
  false
  Mis. 332–23 second, a false *b·* ;
  Un. 50–21 which are but states of false *b·*,
  felon's
  Hea. 19– 8 Had they changed the felon's *b·*
  fervor of
  My. 81–30 * fervor of *b·* with which each
  finite
  No. 25–12 is beyond a finite *b·*.
  fleshly
  Ret. 94–14 When all fleshly *b·* is annihilated,
  fulfils
  Mis. 73–16 *B·* fulfils the conditions of a belief,
  her
  Pul. 73–28 * concise idea of her *b·*
  his
  '01. 15– 2 awake from his *b·* in this awful
  his own
  Mis. 83–13 with the consent of his own *b·*.
  human
    (*see* **human**)
  ignorant
  Ret. 54–19 same channel of ignorant *b·*.
  improved
  My. 217–25 "An improved *b·* is one step out
  in anti-Christ
  Mis. 111–30 The *b·* in anti-Christ :
  in Christian Science
  Pul. 57–22 * how extensive is the *b·* in C. S.
  in death
  Un. 40– 9 subordinates the *b·* in death,
  41–11 (that is, from the *b·* in death)
  in disease
  Mis. 256– 2 cured of their *b·* in disease,
  in evil
  Mis. 221–32 *b·* in evil and in the process of
  in God
  Pul. 79–25 * breath of his soul is a *b·* in God.
  Rud. 11– 4 *b·* in God as omnipotent ;
  in material origin
  Mis. 361– 3 *b·* in material origin, mortal mind,
  in material sense
  Mis. 37–10 we oppose the *b·* in material sense,
  in matter
  Mis. 56–19 this false *b·* in matter
  Un. 50– 8 pantheistic *b·* in matter
  in one God
  Pan. 3–21 In religion, it is a *b·* in one God,
  '02. 12–12 unites with the Jew's *b·* in one God,
  in safety
  Mis. 257–19 It fosters . . . a *b·* in safety
  My. 211–23 fosters . . . a *b·* in safety
  in sin
  Mis. 319– 8 not seeing their own *b·* in sin,
  Man. 15–12 *b·* in sin is punished so long as
  No. 32– 7 *b·* in sin — its pleasure, pain, or
  My. 233–13 from the effects of *b·* in sin
  300– 2 *b·* in sin or in aught besides God,
  in their reality
  Ret. 62– 6 than a *b·* in their reality has
  in the personality
  Pan. 3–18 Theism is the *b·* in the personality
  is strong
  Hea. 6–17 if the *b·* is strong enough to
  lasts
  Man. 15–13 punished so long as the *b·* lasts.
  law of
  Mis. 209–10 human belief fulfils the law of *b·*.
  Peo. 11–21 ignorant of the law of *b·*,
  man's
  My. 302– 3 according to a man's *b·*,
  material
  Mis. 60–28 material *b·* hints the existence of
  61– 1 it will be seen that material *b·*,
  186– 7 material *b·* has fallen far below
  Un. 30– 9 suffers, according to material *b·*,
  matter
  Mis. 60–28 its counterfeit in some matter *b·*.
  may attend
  '01. 7–22 in order that *b·* may attend their
  mere
  Pul. 9–27 spiritual understanding, not mere *b·*,
  mistaken
  Rud. 12–17 C. S. erases . . . their mistaken *b·*
  momentary
  Mis. 42– 6 After the momentary *b·* of dying
  mortal
    (*see* **mortal**)
  of chronic
  Mis. 41–23 *b·* of chronic or acute disease,
  of death
  Mis. 170– 1 salvation from the *b·* of death,
  of disease
  Mis. 198–20 a *b·* of disease is as much the
  of error
  Rud. 12– 8 encouraging them in the *b·* of error

belief

of eyesight
   Mis. 58–17 through a *b·* of eyesight ;
of life
   Un. 40– 6 *b·* of life in matter, must perish,
   My. 132–25 destroy the *b·* of life in matter.
of material existence
   Mis. 42–21 a *b·* of material existence
of material eyes
   Mis. 170–28 contempt for the *b·* of material eyes
of mind
   Mis. 26–19 *b·* of mind in matter is pantheism.
   179–21 It is the *b·* of mind in matter.
of nervousness
   Mis. 51– 5 *b· of nervousness, accompanied by*
of our brethren
   ’01. 8– 5 than the *b·* of our brethren,
of pain
   Mis. 44–18 could only have been a *b·* of pain
of pantheism
   Pan. 9– 1 reiterate the *b·* of pantheism,
of sensation
   Mis. 93–19 Fear is a *b·* of sensation in matter :
of the sick
   Ret. 63–10 *b·* of the sick in the reality of
old
   Hea. 18–15 if . . . reconciled with the old *b·* ;
one
   Mis. 175–23 one *b·* takes the place of another.
one form of
   Pul. 38–30 * in one form of *b·* or another
one’s
   Peo. 9– 7 religious rite may declare one’s *b·* ;
opposite
   Ret. 69–21 opposite *b·* is the prolific source of
our
   Mis. 234– 1 only by reason of our *b·* in it :
pantheistic
   Un. 50– 8 pantheistic *b·* in matter
people’s
   Peo. 2–20 people’s *b·* of God, in every age,
perpetuates the
   Mis. 46– 1 perpetuates the *b·* or faith in evil.
reason, or
   Un. 28–21 human reflection, reason, or *b·*
religious
   Pul. 50–16 * phase of religious *b·*
   51–21 * new project in religious *b·*
   51–29 * demonstrations of religious *b·*
   63–16 * new phase of religious *b·*,
revived
   Pul. 52–25 * revived *b·* in what he taught
self-constituted
   Mis. 186– 6 self-constituted *b·* of the Jews
sickness is a
   Ret. 61– 3 declares that sickness is a *b·*,
signify a
   Man. 42–16 nor signify a *b·* in more than one
sinner’s
   Ret. 63– 7 sinner’s *b·* in the pleasure of sin,
some
   Mis. 198–23 some *b·*, fear, theory, or bad deed,
stubborn
   My. 233–20 most stubborn *b·* to overcome,
that God
   Mis. 45–24 *b·* that God is not what the
   Un. 14– 2 *b·* that God must one day
   Peo. 4– 4 sprang from the *b·* that God is a form,
that intelligence
   Mis. 36–28 *b·* that intelligence, Truth, and
that it has
   Mis. 334– 7 *b·* that it has, deceives itself.
that Jesus
   Pan. 8– 6 *b·* that Jesus, . . . is God,
that Life
   Mis. 77–32 resurrecting . . . to the *b·* that Life,
that man
   Mis. 77–26 *b·* that man has fallen away from
that Mary
   Pan. 8– 8 *b·* that Mary was the mother of God
that matter
   Rud. 10–23 *b·* that matter can master Mind,
   No. 5–10 *b·* that matter has sensation.
that Mind
   Mis. 49–25 *b·*, that Mind is in matter,
that mind
   Ret. 69–27 *b·* that mind is in matter,
that produces
   Hea. 6–22 *b·* that produces this result may
that sees
   Mis. 58–16 as mortal mind, it is a *b·* that sees.
that Spirit
   Peo. 4– 6 *b·* that Spirit materialized into a
that the man
   My. 348–12 *b·* that the man Jesus, rather than

belief

their
   Mis. 256– 2 cured of their *b·* in disease,
   My. 273– 5 * enthusiastic in their *b·*,
their own
   Mis. 319– 8 not seeing their own *b·* in sin,
   Rud. 13–21 according to their own *b·*
theological
   Pan. 4– 7 theological *b·* may agree with physics
   My. 307–17 my theological *b·* was offended
this
   Mis. 49–26 This *b·* presupposes not only a
   72–10 this *b·* is as false as it is
   93–19 this *b·* is neither maintained by
   197–27 This *b·* breaks the First Commandment
   210–20 this *b·* serves to uncover and
   346–13 This *b·* is a species of idolatry,
   352–18 in destroying this *b·*.
   Ret. 63– 9 in order to destroy this *b·*
   Un. 30–10 understanding takes away this *b·*
   Rud. 5–21 this *b·* of seeing with the eye,
thought, or
   Mis. 70– 8 thought, or *b·*, was removed,
unreal
   No. 5–13 substitutes for Truth an unreal *b·*,
vital
   Pul. 52–23 * all vital *b·* in his teachings.
we call spiritualism
   Pul. 38–17 * the *b·* we call spiritualism.
woman’s
   Mis. 220–30 according to the woman’s *b·* ;
your
   Mis. 44–25 your *b·* assumed a new form,
   44–27 When your *b·* in pain ceases,
   44–29 antidote directly to your *b·*,
   59– 4 practise your *b·* of it in

   Mis. 18–26 can we in *b·* separate one man’s
   45– 4 matter is but a *b·*,
   50–22 *b·* that the heart is matter
   58– 8 *b·* in the power of disease
   60–14 *dead only in b·?*
   182– 3 putting him to death, only in *b·*,
   193–32 condition insisted upon is, first, ‘‘*b·*;’’
   197–16 a *b·* in any historical event or person.
   198–28 a *b·* in self-existent evil,
   210–24 *b·* in venereal diseases tears the
   293–23 Truth perverted, in *b·*, becomes the
   335–16 *b·*, of evil to break the Decalogue,
   346–12 It is but a *b·* that there is an
   Ret. 13–13 *b·* in a final judgment-day,
   54–14 *B·* is virtually blindness,
   64–20 in *b·* an illusion termed sin,
   Un. 26–11 *b·* in which leads to such teaching
   40–26 mortals die, in *b·*,
   41– 7 Knowledge of evil, or *b·* in it,
   Pul. 65– 1 * *b·* in that curious creed is
   80–26 * The *b·* that ‘‘thoughts are things,’’
   Rud. 12– 9 *b·* that they are first made sick by
   Pan. 6–27 the *b·* in more than one spirit,
   7– 8 *b·*, that after God, Spirit, had
   My. 74–25 * a *b·* in such emancipation,
   218–22 The *b·* that an individual can
   243– 3 *b·* is springing up among you that

beliefs

all
   Mis. 36–22 all *b·* relative to the so-called
and doctrines
   Pul. 73–21 * versed in all their *b·* and doctrines.
evil
   Mis. 191–29 could only be possible as evil *b·*,
false
   Mis. 111–28 false *b·* inclining mortal mind
   Peo. 3–10 false *b·* that have produced sin,
human
   Mis. 320–25 long night of human *b·*,
   Rud. 10– 8 material laws are only human *b·*,
   My. 44– 1 * the wilderness of human *b·*
   206– 8 human *b·* are not parts of C. S. ;
I entertained
   My. 241–24 * according to the *b·* I entertained
its own
   Mis. 47–15 when let loose from its own *b·*.
material
   Mis. 2–29 material *b·* that war against Spirit,
   5–29 mortal thought with material *b·*.
   334–27 remedies the ills of material *b·*.
mortal
   (*see* **mortal**)
of mortals
   My. 146–23 *b·* of mortals tip the scale of being,
of Scientists
   Pul. 73–20 * in the *b·* of Scientists,
of the flesh
   Mis. 28–14 destroy the *b·* of the flesh,

beliefs

of the flesh
Mis. 72– 7 According to the *b·* of the flesh,
old
Mis. 93– 6 *Can fear or sin bring back old b·*
producing the
Rud. 10–10 producing the *b·* of a mortal
religious
'02. 1–16 systems of religious *b·*
My. 163–27 I respect their religious *b·*,
271–24 * whatever their religious *b·*,
these
Rud. 10– 9 These *b·* arise from the subjective
undisciplined
Mis. 320–22 to dull ears and undisciplined *b·*

Mis. 28– 5 *b·* that mortals entertain.
Peo. 4–22 out of *b·* that are as material as
My. 241–28 * the *b·* of an earthly mortal.

belies
Mis. 121–18 whatever belittles, befogs, or *b·*

believe
Mis. 5–25 but *b·* it to be brain matter.
5–31 to *b·* that the body affects the
13–15 to *b·* in the reality of evil
18–30 to *b·* that aught that God sends is
22– 1 *b·* in one God, one Christ
24–27 God warned man not to *b·*
28–31 them that *b· ;— Mark* 16 : 17.
29– 3 Do you *b·* his words?
29– 8 which shall *b·* on me — *John* 17 : 20.
47– 1 How can I *b·* that there is no
50–18 *Do you b· in change of heart?*
50–19 We do *b·*, and understand
60– 1 *How can you b· there is no sin,*
60– 4 *How can you b· there is no sickness,*
63–15 to save such as *b·* in the
67–24 *Do you b· in translation?*
67–29 I *b·* in this removal being possible
68–11 * *to b· they are illusions.*
68–12 It is unchristian to *b·* that pain
70– 2 That the Bible is true I *b·*,
77– 4 verb *b·* took its original meaning,
77–20 To *b·* is to *be firm.*
77–22 To *b·* thus was to enter the
96– 7 Do I *b·* in a personal God?
96– 8 I *b·* in God as the Supreme Being.
96–17 Do I *b·* in the atonement of Christ?
121–26 ye will not *b· ;— Luke* 22 : 67.
132–23 as to what I *b·* and teach,
141–16 I *b·*, — yea, I understand,
170– 5 may still *b·* in death
180–22 *even to them that b· — John* 1 : 12.
192–29 follow them that *b· ;— Mark* 16 : 17.
194– 1 *b·* that the power of God equals
194–31 set forth in the text, namely, *b· ;*
196– 7 "*B·* in me, and I will make
196–28 *B· on the Lord Jesus — Acts* 16 : 31.
197–13 let us see what it is to *b·*
220–25 people *b·* that a man is sick
220–29 he will *b·* that he is sick,
222– 5 causes the victim to *b·* that
225–19 * I may be led to *b·*."
228–27 *b·* what others *b·*,
228–30 People *b·* in infectious and
229– 9 If only the people would *b·* that
238– 3 sometimes made to *b·* a lie,
244–28 as many as should *b·* in him.
247–21 but *b·* it to reside in matter
247–25 to *b·* that the body affects mind,
282–22 and they *b·* in the efficacy of
313–25 Humbly, and, as I *b·*, divinely
349–31 *b·* that I have put into the
Man. 34– 4 *B·* in C. S.
47–25 do not *b·* in the doctrines of
48– 1 those who do *b·* in such doctrines,
Ret. 10– 1 taught to *b·* that my brain was
16–15 follow them that *b·*." — *Mark* 16 : 17.
28–28 I *b·* in no ism.
49–23 which we *b·* will prove a healing
54– 4 easier to *b·*, than to understand
59– 2 to *b·* man has a finite and
90–26 * "I *b·* the proper thing for us to do
Un. 3– 2 and still *b·* in matter's reality,
19–11 But this we cannot *b·* of God ;
20–21 and *b·* that He can see
24– 5 To *b·* in minds many is to
37–14 Is it unchristian to *b·* there is no
37–15 unless it be a sin to *b·* that
38–11 It is unchristian to *b·* in the
38–30 no divine fiat commands us to *b·* in
40–12 Jesus declares that they who *b·*
41– 8 to know death, or to *b·* in it,
43– 8 now *b·* in the possibility that
45– 1 says . . . you shall *b·* a lie,

Un. 48– 5 *Do you b· in God?*
48– 6 I *b·* more in Him than do most
48–19 I *b·* that of which I am conscious
49– 1 *Do you b· in man?*
49 –2 I *b·* in the individual man,
49– 7 But I *b·* less in the sinner,
50– 3 *Do you b· in matter?*
50– 4 I *b·* in matter only as I *b·* in evil,
Pul. 38–18 * They *b·* those who have passed the
38–25 * what they *b·* to be the literal
51– 4 * Freedom to *b·* or to dissent
65–27 * expresses the faith of those who *b·*
71–10 * chapter sub-title
72–21 * nor did she *b·* that Mrs. Lathrop had,
73– 4 * *b·* in His unlimited and divine power.
79–16 * We *b·* there are two reasons for
80–22 * people to *b·* in God
80–23 * did not *b·* in them before.
85–16 * and who *b·* it to be possible to
Rud. 5–25 *b·* man and the universe to be the
10–28 to *b·* in the existence of matter,
No. 14–23 to as many as shall *b·* on him.
15–14 It is no easy matter to *b·* there are
26– 1 mind-quacks *b·* that mortal man is
29– 8 they *b· . . .* sinning sense to be
42– 2 * to *b·* all things written in the
Pan. 5–20 we should neither *b·* the lie,
5–20 nor *b·* that it hath embodiment
5–22 we should not *b·* that a lie,
9–23 (though they *b·* it not),
11–21 may *b·* that evil develops good,
'00. 2–27 however, I *b·* in working
4–24 Do religionists *b·* that God is *One*
7–23 we *b·* in the second coming,
'01. 5–14 Do Christian Scientists *b·* in
5–19 We *b·*, according to the Scriptures,
6–26 We *b·* in God as the infinite Person ;
7–21 They do not *b·* there must be
7–24 Christians now claim to *b·* in
12– 7 too transcendental for me to *b·*,
13–30 or *b·* in the power of sin,
14– 6 Do Christian Scientists *b·* that
18–30 they *b·* that God answers their prayers,
19– 2 They *b·* that divine power, besought,
22– 8 I do not *b·* in such a compound.
32–26 I *b·*, if those venerable Christians
'02. 3–30 began with "*B·* in me."
15–19 for I could never *b·* that a
Hea. 1– 1 *follow them that b· ;— Mark* 16 : 17.
6–26 follow them that *b· ;— Mark* 16 : 17.
7– 5 "Them that *b·*" — *Mark* 16 : 17.
9–15 Is it a duty for any one to *b·* that
15–20 and *b·* that sickness is something
18–28 *b·* he was bleeding to death.
19–27 follow them that *b· ;— Mark* 16 : 17.
Peo. 5–27 * "I firmly *b·* that if the whole
13– 3 *b·* that God is a personal Spirit.
My. 8–17 * I *b·* really, with my
47–30 * follow them that *b· ;— Mark* 16 : 17.
74–22 * if those outside are unable to *b·*
90– 9 * Thousands upon thousands *b·*
97– 3 * They *b·* that firm faith
107–16 he tells you, and you *b·* him,
119– 3 impossible in Science to *b·* this,
146– 5 I *b·* this saying because I
146–12 Few *b·* this saying.
146–12 Few *b·* that C. S. contains
190–29 them also which shall *b· — John* 17 : 20.
193–18 unite with all who *b·* in Truth.
212– 2 is led to *b·* and do what he
219–13 not be more preposterous than to *b·*
220–12 I *b·* in obeying the laws of the land.
221–31 Shall we not *b·* the Scripture,
234–20 I *b·* that all our great Master's
261– 8 not be taught to *b·* that Santa Claus
278–18 Japanese may *b·* in a heaven for
282– 3 *b·* strictly in the Monroe doctrine,
284–25 I do *b·* implicitly in the
293–31 *b·* that ye receive them, — *Mark* 11 : 24.
299–17 Do Christians, who *b·* in sin,
299–18 *b·* that God is good,
300–10 not *b·* in the reality of disease,
303– 2 I *b·* in one Christ,
303– 3 I *b·* in but one incarnation,
321–10 * I *b·* that Mr. Wiggin
321–13 * cannot *b·* that he has ever
345–18 *b·* in a science of drugs?"

believed
Mis. 44–23 *b·* that if the tooth were extracted,
77–21 to *know* in whom he *b·*.
108–29 who *b·* in the use of drugs,
121–12 was *b·* to be the seed of the Church.
183–20 "Who hath *b·* our — *Isa.* 53 : 1.
195–25 I once *b·* that the practice and

believed

Mis.	229– 4	If he *b·* as sincerely that health is
	333–24	They *b·* that something besides
Ret.	54–16	whom I have *b·*." — *II Tim.* 1 : 12.
	57– 6	Plato *b·* he had a soul,
Un.	3–14	Him in whom they have *b·*.
	33–15	and is *b·* to be mind
	35– 3	If every mortal mind *b·*
	39– 9	"Who hath *b·* our — *Isa.* 53 : 1.
	46–22	This evil ego they *b·* must
Pul.	33–23	* and Mr. Parker always *b·*,
	75–25	* *b·* to be the most nearly fire-proof
No.	36– 8	even while mortals *b·* it was here.
'01.	7–28	thou hast *b·* : — *John* 20 : 29.
	7–29	and yet have *b·*." — *John* 20 : 29.
	27–30	* say they had always *b·* it."
My.	79–27	* conviction that they would be *b·*,
	80– 9	* yet they were *b·*.
	118–17	and yet have *b·*." — *John* 20 : 29.
	156– 4	"I know whom I have *b·*, — *II Tim.* 1 : 12.
	228–28	I know whom I have *b·*, — *II Tim.* 1 : 12.
	276–17	* has always *b·* that those who
	276–19	* also *b·* that in such matters
	293– 8	*b·* that his martyrdom was
	293– 9	thousands of others *b·* the same,
	304–28	* say they have always *b·* it."

believer

Mis.	332–25	Is man the supposer, false *b·*,
Man.	34– 7	*b·* in the doctrines of C. S.,
Ret	28–28	Am I a *b·* in spiritualism?
My.	309–15	strong *b·* in States' rights,

believers

Mis.	325– 5	are *b·* of different sects,
Ret.	14– 8	elect *b·* converted and rescued
Pul.	40–11	* ENABLING SIX THOUSAND *B·* TO
	41–19	* nearly a thousand local *b·*.
	44–17	* chapter sub-title
	52–15	* *b·* receive light, health, and
	58– 8	* *b·* throughout this country
	66– 6	* the number of *b·* has grown
	67–17	* quarter of a million of *b·*,
	67–22	* single *b·* or little knots of them
	71– 8	* money comes from C. S. *b·*
My.	77–25	* nearly forty thousand *b·*
	95–11	* prosperous body of *b·*
	99– 4	* able to raise its *b·* above the
	169–18	three thousand *b·* of my faith,
	271–18	* beloved of thousands of *b·*

believes

Mis.	26–10	*b·* that his crops come from the
	197–23	Mortal man *b·* in, but does not
	197–24	He *b·* there is another power
	221–12	unless he *b·* that sin has produced
	223–12	to discern what it *b·*,
	229– 4	which he *b·* produce it.
Pul.	50– 3	* *b·* that "the laborer — *Luke* 10 : 7.
No.	29– 5	He *b·* that Spirit, or Soul,
Pan.	11–17	If . . . it matters not what he *b·* ;
'01.	5– 1	*b·* that three persons are defined
	5– 3	he *b·* three persons constitute the
'02.	12– 1	The Jew *b·* that the Messiah
	12– 2	Christian *b·* that Christ is come
	12– 7	The Jew who *b·* in the
	12–10	who *b·* in the First Commandment
My.	97–11	* *b·* that if the figures could be
	271– 9	what a man thinks or *b·* he knows ;
	297–16	Scientist who *b·* that he dies,
	300– 8	Does he who *b·* in sickness know
	300–13	Does he who *b·* in death understand

believeth

Mis.	192–10	*He that b· on me,* — *John* 14 : 12.
	193–27	"He that *b·* on me, — *John* 14 : 12.
	195–18	"He that *b·* on me, — *John* 14 : 12.
Chr.	55–28	liveth and *b·* in me — *John* 11 : 26.
No.	13– 8	liveth and *b·* in me — *John* 11 : 26.
Pan.	9–13	liveth and *b·* in me — *John* 11 : 26.
My.	16–26	he that *b·* shall — *Isa.* 28 : 16.
	17–16	he that *b·* on him shall — *I Pet.* 2 : 6.
	221–22	"He that *b·* on me, — *John* 14 : 12.

believing

Mis.	62– 9	*B·* a lie veils the truth from our
	68–14	penalty for *b·* in their reality
	77– 2	*depend merely on his b· that*
	77– 3	this *b·* was more than faith in
	93–25	by *b·* that sin is pardoned without
	108–12	is to be in danger of *b·* it ;
	108–27	*b·* in, or adhering to,
	108–32	an individual *b·* in that
	179– 5	*b·* we have lost sight of Truth,
	184–18	persisting in *b·* that he is sick
	223–15	But, alas! for the mistake of *b·*
	239–29	saying even more bravely, and *b·* it,
	288–20	*b·* otherwise would prevent
	832–27	false *b·*, suffering are not

believing

Mis.	362–11	make the mortal mistake of *b·* **that**
Ret.	54–12	Millions are *b·* in God, or good,
	69–17	*b·* that there is life in matter,
Un.	40–14	can no more receive . . . life by *b·*
	40–15	than they can become perfect by *b·*
Pul.	34–13	* *b·* her delirious.
	59–26	* The children of *b·* families
	69–10	* *b·* that disease comes from evil
'01.	14–20	from *b·* in what is unreal,
Peo.	6–14	*B·* that man is the victim of his
My.	51–22	* *b·* that it was for the interest of
	106– 8	to show the folly of *b·* that
	206–13	*b·* that you see an individual who
	285–27	*b·* all things which — *Acts* 24 : 14.

belittle

No.	32–23	great evil to belie and *b·* C. S.,

belittled

Mis.	337–22	Even the life of Jesus was *b·*

belittles

Mis.	121–18	whatever *b·*, befogs, or belies
Pan.	11–22	*b·* man's personality.
'01.	13– 3	another nonentity that *b·* itself

bell

Mis.	304– 8	* *b·* will pass from place to place
	304–22	* is the proposed use of the *b·* :
	305–14	* In creating the *b·* it is
	305–19	* can be made a part of the *b·* ;
	305–23	* with which to pay for the *b·*.
	305–25	* to be fused into the *b·*,
	305–28	* In order that the *b·* shall be
	306– 1	* material to be melted into the *b·*,
	306– 3	* book which will accompany the *b·*
Pul.	31–23	* rang the *b·* at a spacious house
Po.	71–14	Joy is in every belfry *b·*
My.	189–30	Wherefore, pray, the *b·* did toll?

bells

Mis.	120–18	sound of vintage *b·* to villagers
	356–15	sweeter than the sound of vintage *b·*.
Pul.	26–17	* chime of *b·* includes fifteen,
	62– 6	* cast *b·* of old-fashioned chimes.
	62– 8	* a chime of fifteen *b·*
	62–20	* to which these *b·* may be put.
	62–23	* down to little sets of silver *b·*
Po.	vi– 8	* poem
	vi–19	*b· are ringing to celebrate the*
	page 71	poem
My.	31– 7	* "Oh, the clanging *b·* of time ;"
	71– 4	* by means of the *b·*.
	89– 7	* a chime of *b·*,
	185– 3	harvest *b·* are ringing.
	256– 2	Christmas *b·* shall ring,
	302–28	with escort and the ringing of *b·*,

belly

'01.	11–28	him whose god is his *b·* :

belong

Mis.	22–18	untruths *b·* not to His creation,
	112–12	seem to *b·* to the latter days,
	228–23	*b·* to mind and not to matter.
Un.	10– 9	to whom *b·* all things.
	25–24	The elements which *b·* to
	38– 3	To God alone *b·* the
	61– 3	*b·* to mortal consciousness.
Pul.	8–29	They *b·* to the twentieth century.
Po.	29–10	No natal hour . . . To thee *b·*.
My.	242–24	leave these duties . . . to whom they *b·*.
	285–11	war, and . . . *b·* to the darker ages,

belonged

Man.	75–22	building funds, . . . *b·* to the Church,

belonging

Mis.	375–30	* *b·* to them exclusively,
Ret.	53– 2	and the funds *b·* thereto.
Un.	21–20	*b·* to true individuality,
	40–28	*b·* to the nature and office of Life.
Pul.	46–18	* *b·* to her grandparents
My.	100– 2	* facts and figures *b·* to it,
	340– 6	*b·* not to the Christian era,

belongs

Mis.	51–15	that sensation *b·* to matter.
	107–10	the heart's homage *b·* to God.
	190–25	*b·* to Mind instead of matter,
	192–23	*b·* to every period ;
	240–31	something which *b·* to nature,
	259–27	*b·* not to nature nor to God.
	297–29	*b·* to the rights of freedom.
Man.	52– 5	*if said member b· to no branch*
Pul.	57–26	* site . . . *b·* to the followers of
No.	42–11	All power *b·* to God ;
'00.	8–19	the work that *b·* to another.
My.	110– 1	*b·* not to a dispensation now ended,
	225–12	all *b·* to God, for God is All ;
	260–13	Nothing conditional . . . *b·* to it.
	340–24	which virtually *b·* to the past,

belongs
My. 354–22 But Science vast, to which b·

Beloved
Chr. 53–13 What the B· knew and taught,

beloved
Mis. 110– 4 B· children, the world has need of
121–22 crucifixion of His b· Son,
149–20 your b· pastor, Rev. Mr. Norcross,
151–18 Brother, sister, b· in the Lord,
152– 3 B· Pastor and Brethren:
156– 7 B· Christian Scientists:
157– 5 Reign then, my b· in the Lord.
170– 5 over the graves of their b·:
206– 7 "This is my b· — Matt. 3 : 17.
322–18 Therefore, b·, my often-coming
Man. 60–18 sacred words of our b· Master,
Pul. 10–29 this is His redeemed ; this, His b·.
24–15 * A testimonial to our b· teacher,
48– 5 * straight to her b· "lookout"
63–27 * "a testimonial to our b· teacher,
84–27 * our b· teacher and Leader,
86– 4 * "To our B· Teacher,
86–16 * our B· Teacher and Leader:
87–11 B· Directors and Brethren:
'00. 14– 9 B·, let him that hath an ear
'02. 18–20 B·, how much of what he did are we
Po. 29–13 B·, replete, by flesh embound
My. 5–23 B·, I am not with you
22–15 * our b· Leader and teacher,
23–17 * B· Teacher and Leader:
27– 2 To the B· Members of my Church,
36– 8 * B· Teacher and Leader:
42–13 * B· Friends: — Most unexpectedly
42–26 * inaugurated by our b· Leader,
43–22 * was revealed to our b· Leader,
44–23 * B· Teacher and Leader:
51–29 * to our b· pastor, Mrs. Eddy,
62–19 * B· Leader and Teacher:
64– 2 * achievements of our b· Leader
118– 1 b· members of my church who
129– 8 throughout our b· country
131– 1 B·, that which purifies the
134–26 * been secured from our b· Leader
135–26 My B· Church: — Your love
140–18 B· Christian Scientists: Take
142–10 B· Christian Scientist: — Accept my
143–10 my b· friends and followers
150–26 B· in Christ, what our Master said
157– 3 * B· Teacher and Leader:
162–10 such as my b· Christian Scientists
163– 9 b· ones who have so kindly come
170–27 b·, some of you have come long
193–15 B·: — The spiritual dominates the
207– 7 * B· Leader: — The representatives of
208–12 B· Christian Scientists: — Like the
210– 2 B· Christian Scientists, keep your
216–15 My B· Children: — Tenderly thanking
236– 5 B· Christian Scientists: — Because I
243–20 B· Christian Scientists: — Your prompt
254– 5 B·: — I am glad you enjoy the dawn
256– 7 This year, my b· Christian Scientists,
263– 5 B·: — A word to the wise
271–17 * b· of thousands of believers
279–22 Dearly B·: — I request that every
280– 3 * B· Leader: — We acknowledge
289–16 long honored, revered, b·.
290– 9 b· as this noble woman,
291– 3 b· President, William McKinley.
297–18 My b· Edward A. Kimball,
312–26 the remains of my b· one
315–29 and made me the b· Leader of
322– 9 * My B· Teacher: — I have just read
323–17 * B· Teacher: — My heart has
325–14 * in any way, b· Leader.
327–11 * B· Leader: — I know the enclosed
335– 9 * b· by his brothers and companions,
352– 4 * B· Leader: — Informally assembled,
352–19 B· Ushers of The Mother Church
352–27 B· Christian Scientists: — Accept my
358– 9 B·! you need to watch and pray
361–19 * B· Leader: — We rejoice that our
(see also brethren, church, student, students)

below
Mis. 53–18 seeks what is b· instead of above
95– 9 * and is transcribed b·.
186– 7 material belief has fallen far b·
388–22 To fold an angel's wings b· ;
Pul. 39–22 * Gaze on the world b·.
48–10 * whole landscape that lies b·,
No. 26–16 into something b· infinitude.
'00. 7–28 Thus it is we walk here b·,
Po. 21–11 To fold an angel's wings b· ;

Beman, Mr.
My. 63– 4 * of Mr. B· in an advisory capacity
Bemis
Mrs.
Pul. 43–24 * was then read by Mrs. B·.
43–29 * Mrs. B· read the following letter
57– 9 * sermon, . . . was read by Mrs. B·.
Mrs. Henrietta Clark
Pul. 43–10 * and Mrs. Henrietta Clark B·,
59–19 * read by . . . Mrs. Henrietta Clark B·,
bench
'00. 7–10 members of the bar and b·,
benches
Ret. 15–18 and b· were used in the aisles.
bend
Mis. 134–17 b· or outweigh your purpose
330–14 alders b· over the streams
387–11 And on the same branch b·.
Ret. 17– 4 In bowers of beauty, — I b· to thy lay,
No. 3– 2 sad it is that envy will b· its bow
Po. 6– 6 And on the same branch b·.
62– 3 In bowers of beauty, — I b· to thy lay,
My. 125– 6 to b· upward the tendrils
bended
Mis. 127–10 not verbally, nor on b· knee,
204– 3 falling on the b· knee of prayer,
My. 18 – 7 not verbally, nor on b· knee,
bendeth
Mis. 275– 9 b· his aching head ;
bending
Mis. 387–14 If thou the b· reed wouldst break
Ret. 4–14 broad fields of b· grain
Hea. 2–19 b· beneath the malice of the world.
Peo. 14– 9 * "bat and owl on the b· stones,
Po. 6– 9 If thou the b· reed wouldst break
bends
Mis. 240–17 The sapling b· to the breeze,
beneath (see also 'neath)
Mis. 55–29 in matter and b· a skull bone,
106–25 B·, above, beyond, methinks I hear
154–13 b· your own vine and fig-tree
195–21 cannot fall to the ground b· the
262–24 With all the homage b· the skies,
263– 9 "b· the shadow of — see Isa. 32 : 2.
389–18 B· the shadow of His mighty wing ;
396–16 B· the maple's shade.
Ret. 35–21 fall to the ground b· the stroke
79– 8 the material pigment b·
Pul. 27–14 * with six small windows b·,
27–17 * B· are two small windows
42–16 * and b· the beehive the words,
No. 14–16 chapter sub-title
14–24 were not from b·.
15– 2 Are the dews of . . . from b·?
'02. 17–29 like the sun b· the horizon,
Hea. 2–19 bending b· the malice of the world.
Po. 4–17 B· the shadow of His mighty wing ;
59– 8 B· the maple's shade.
My. 78– 9 * entrances b· a series of arches
350–23 foundations . . . Sunk from b· man,
benediction
Mis. 8–29 fulfilled through the gospel's b·.
81–15 b· of an honored Father,
81–29 This is the Father's b·.
88–17 like a b· after prayer,
143– 8 with this silent b· :
152– 8 silent b· over all the earth,
238–21 and it already hath a b· :
314–14 shall pronounce the b·.
320– 2 God will give the b·.
Pul. 87– 5 * with our humble b·.
No. 8–25 quietly, with b· and hope,
'01. 3– 3 b· of our Father-Mother God
'02. 11–21 this is thy Lord's b· upon it :
Po. 78–16 In that b· which knoweth best !
My. 19– 8 * and the b·, 2 Corinthians 13 : 14 :
33– 7 * The b·.
132–13 may there come this b· :
188–18 breathing a b· for God's largess.
202–13 b· of "Well done, — Matt. 25 : 23.
295–21 chapter sub-title
benedictions
Mis. 213–17 perfect their own lives by gentle b·
320– 8 with divine b· for mankind.
My. 167–13 their loving b· upon your lives.
256–17 Christmas . . . full of divine b·
benefactor
Mis. 161–18 of our Master as a public b·,
benefactors
My. 200–22 by pulling down its b·,

benefice
My. 245– 3 demand for this universal *b·* is

beneficence
Ret. 81– 2 threaten to paralyze its *b·*.
My. 340–30 *b·* of the laws of the universe

beneficent
My. 26–12 Your *b·* gift is the largest sum

beneficial
Mis. 348–27 drugs have no *b·* effect
Ret. 85– 7 useful to the Cause and *b·* to
My. 99– 8 * aggregation of good and *b·* works,

beneficially
Man 75–19 own the aforesaid premises . . . *b·*.

benefit
  brought a
  Pul. 51–20 * on the other hand, have brought a *b·*.
  great
  Pul. 14–27 great *b·* which Mind has wrought.
  My. 138– 5 a great *b·* to me already.
  imaginary
  My. 118– 5 any imaginary *b·* they receive is
  most
  Mis. 316–26 derived most *b·* from their pupilage,
  my
  My. 138– 8 not for my *b·* in any way,
  no personal
  '02. 13–11 I receive no personal *b·*
  of all
  Hea. 16– 3 *b·* of all who, having ears, hear
  of our Cause
  Man. 59–11 for the *b·* of our Cause.
  of our race
  Un. 13–20 for the *b·* of our race.
  of this Church
  Man. 76– 3 used for the *b·* of this Church,
  only
  Mis. 59–22 only *b·* in speaking often
  share the
  Mis. 290–26 share the *b·* of that radiation.

  Mis. 11–25 general effort to *b·* the race.
       35–19 *of what b· is your book?*
       38–19 application to *b·* the race,
       64–17 ethics . . . must *b·* every one ;
      137–27 give to the world the *b·* of
      227–20 odor they send forth to *b·* mankind ;
      241– 2 to *b·* the body,
      241– 3 as to *b·* the mind.
      271–26 * "To *b·* the community,
      290–24 one must *b·* those who
      302–25 *b·* which the student derived
      350–24 the *b·* that would otherwise accrue.
      351–17 nor *b·* mankind by such endeavors.
      378–16 how manipulation could *b·* the sick.
  Ret. 41– 6 an acknowledgment of the *b·*.
       72– 5 to *b·* himself and mankind.
  No. v– 2 to *b·* no favored class,
  '01. 20– 4 to serve God and *b·* mankind.
       21–23 whereby to *b·* the race
  My. 24–17 * state, for the *b·* of those who
      203–28 doing so much to *b·* mankind
      231– 7 whom she has labored much to *b·*

benefited
Mis. 35–24 You are *b·* by reading S. and H.,
     273– 3 neophyte will be *b·* by experience,
     291–15 has equal opportunity to be *b·*
Ret. 83– 7 seldom *b·* by the teachings of other
     85–14 *b·*, by any deviation from
My. 210–11 but all . . . are thereby *b·*.

benefiting
Mis. 130– 1 of thereby *b·* him
Pul. 15–10 doing right and *b·* our race.
My. 136–26 *b·* the human race ;

benefits
Pan. 9–23 this love *b·* its enemies
'00. 2–12 *b·* society by his example
'02. 1–19 honors God and *b·* mankind
My. 81– 7 * *b·* and the healing power of

benevolence
Mis. 50–28 *b·* and love for God and man ;
     199– 1 God does not reward *b·* . . . with penalties;
My. 165–24 Goodness and *b·* never tire.
     262–28 in quietude, humility, *b·*, charity,

benevolent
Man. 47– 1 he is *b·*, forgiving,

benighted
My. 234–17 success of C. S. in *b·* China,

benign
Mis. 63– 5 to hinder his *b·* influence
Peo. 2–27 a *b·* and elevating influence
My. 128– 8 less than God's *b·* government,

benison
My. 257–25 I group you in one *b·*

bent
Mis. 264–18 * "As the twig is *b·*,
Ret. 18–26 *b·* branch of a pear-tree.
     31–24 My heart *b·* low before the
Po. 63–24 *b·* branch of a pear-tree.

bequeathed
Mis. 248–21 and *b·* my property to

bequeathing
'01. 30– 5 is only the *b·* of itself to

bequests
Ret. 30– 3 The rare *b·* of C. S. are costly,

bereaved
My. 289–13 sympathy with the *b·* nation,
     331–20 * in behalf of . . . his *b·* lady,
     331–25 * *b·* widow after his decease.

bereavement
Ret. 19–16 in this terrible *b·*.
My. 290– 3 this sudden international *b·*,
     330–28 * in this terrible *b·*.

bereft (*see also* **'reft**)
Mis. 275–10 *b·* wife or husband,
     352– 1 *b·* of permanence and peace.
Ret. 20–19 life is dead, *b·* of all,
Un. 51–10 In pantheism the world is *b·* of
'01. 34–15 wantonly *b·* of the Word of God.

Berkeley (*see also* **Berkeley's**)
  Bishop
  Ret. 37–12 now declare Bishop *B·*, David Hume,
  No. 22– 5 Hegel, Spinoza, Bishop *B·*,
  '01. 21– 8 * Bishop *B·* of the Church of England
       23–23 Bishop *B·* published a book

  Mis. 361–15 Plato, Kant, Locke, *B·*,
  No. 22– 6 *B·* ended his metaphysical theory
  '01. 24–18 *B·*, Darwin, or Huxley.
  My. 349– 9 *B·*, Tyndall, and Spencer

Berkeley's
  Bishop
  '01. 24–14 Bishop *B·* metaphysics and

  '01. 24–21 I had not read one line of *B·*

Berlin
'00. 1–23 Dublin, Paris, *B·*, Rome,

berries
Ret. 4–19 green pastures bright with *b·*,

beseeching
Ret. 8– 6 *b·* her to tell me what she wanted.

beset
Mis. 318–26 Two points of danger *b·* mankind ;
     319– 9 *b·* with egotism and hypocrisy.
     323–10 descent and ascent are *b·* with
     361–18 doth so easily *b·* us, — *Heb.* 12 : 1.
Ret. 71– 7 temptations *b·* an ignorant or an
     79–17 If *b·* with misguided emotions,
No. 42–20 C. S. is *b·* with false claimants,
'01. 2–24 *b·* all their returning footsteps.

besetments
Mis. 10–18 with fear and the *b·* of evil ;

besets
'02. 19–24 A danger *b·* thy path?

beside
Mis. 63–20 none else *b·* Him," — *Deut.* 4 : 35.
     97–19 no God *b·* me." — *Isa.* 45 : 5.
    151–17 that I desire *b·* thee." — *Psal.* 73 : 25.
    206–32 *b·* the still waters," — *Psal.* 23 : 2.
    225–21 and sat down *b·* the sofa
    227–24 *b·* the still waters, on isles of
    322–15 *b·* the still waters." — *Psal.* 23 : 2.
    350–16 none *b·* Him." — *see Deut.* 4 : 35.
    357– 8 and rest *b·* still waters.
    366–12 *none b· Him."* — *see Deut.* 4 : 35.
Ret. 60– 7 that there is nothing *b·* God ;
     60–19 and there is nothing *b·* Him ;"
     63– 5 and there is none *b·* Him,
Un. 18–26 A knowledge of aught *b·* Myself
    21–16 there is nothing *b·* Him
    25–12 claiming to be something *b·* God,
    36– 5 *b·* which there is no other
    60– 6 and there is none *b·* Him,
    62– 9 there is none *b·* good.
Rud. 4–21 and there is naught *b·* Him.
     9–26 and that there can be none *b·* Him ;
    13–15 none else *b·* Him." — *Deut.* 4 : 35.
No. 16–13 for there is none *b·* God
    16–18 inference of some other existence *b·*
    17–20 "none *b·* Him." — *see Deut.* 4 : 35.
    24–28 As there is none *b·* Him,
    37–22 God, and none *b·* Him ;

beside
Peo.	5–15	it sitteth b· the sepulchre
Po.	67–13	B· you they walk while you weep,
My.	77– 5	* B· it the dome of the
	112–32	a book which lies b· the Bible
	129–26	green pastures b· still waters,
	162–26	b· the still waters.''— Psal. 23 : 2.
	247–15	when I stood silently b· it,

besides
Mis.	22–20	it dwelleth in Him b· whom
	27– 1	What can there be b· infinity?
	27–23	matter claims something b· God,
	37– 1	and no power b· God, good.
	93–12	there is in reality none b·
	173–25	whence, then, is something b· Him
	319– 5	the argument of aught b· Him,
	332–30	that there is something b· Him ;
	333–25	believed that something b· God had
	358–11	He that seeketh aught b· God,
Ret.	1– 9	b· other verses and enigmas
	60– 8	is something b· God.
	60–22	something b· Him, which
Un.	22–13	But there is something b·
Pul.	5– 3	b· listening to an address on C. S.
	47–21	* B· her Boston home, Mrs. Eddy has
	56– 5	* b· a large and growing number of
Rud.	14–21	doing charity work b·.
	15–13	Few were taken b· invalids
'00.	5– 5	or aught b· God, good.
'02.	6– 7	of something b· God, good,
Hea.	15–20	trying everything else b· God,
My.	300– 3	belief in sin or in aught b· God,

besieged
Mis.	274–17	press is gagged, liberty is b· ;
Pul.	2–17	fiercely b· by the enemy.
My.	54–24	* crowds had b· the doors

besieges
'00.	11–14	Beethoven b· you with tones

besmear
Mis.	337–31	sensualism, . . . would hide or b·.

besmeared
Mis.	274–29	the streets b· with blood.

besought
'01.	19– 3	They believe that divine power, b·,

bespeaks
My.	133–29	The spiritual b· our temporal

best
Mis.	ix– 4	* b· alms are to show and to enable
	2–32	decided views as to the b· method
	5– 2	devote our b· energies to the work.
	9–12	are virtually thy b· friends.
	10–17	b· lesson of their lives is gained by
	32–19	I would gladly do my b· towards
	43–10	who understands it b·,
	59–26	That individual is the b· healer who
	80–20	at the b· time, will redress wrongs
	87–20	he does b· in the investigation of
	156–17	b· understood through the study of
	216–17	but, the b· may be mistaken.
	233– 3	malpractice of the b· system
	236–17	and the b· way to overcome them,
	236–18	to the b· of our ability,
	236–21	though it be your b· friend ;
	250– 3	the b· become the most abused,
	257–14	repays our b· deeds with sacrifice
	267– 5	are the b· friends to our growth.
	268– 4	Who shall be b·?
	271–12	books which are less than the b·.
	273–25	I cannot do my b· work for a
	288– 2	convictions regarding what is b·
	293– 4	b· to leave the righteous unfolding
	295–28	unquestionably the b· queen on earth ;
	298–11	having my b· friend break troth
	307–14	thought b· to stop its publication.
	316–12	the hour b· for the student.
	349–17	should do as he deemed b·,
	368–26	But while the b·, perverted,
Ret.	43–19	judged it b· to close the institution.
	49–29	b· to dissolve this corporation,
	82–28	which revision . . . is the b·.
	83–12	and are their b· guides.
	93–13	b· spiritual type of Christly method
Un.	48–12	He is b· understood as Supreme
	50–11	At b·, matter is only a phenomenon
Pul.	38–30	* their b· aid and guidance,
	82–23	* sing b· by singing most for their
Rud.	2– 8	used by the b· authorities,
	6–23	Mind-healing is b· understood in
	15–15	to fill in the b· possible manner
No.	41–10	repeat his work to the b· advantage
	44– 6	having its b· interpretation in the
Pan.	9–27	the b· of people sometimes object to
	10–13	b· students in the class averred

best
Pan.	11–14	superior to the b· church-member
'00.	2– 5	among the b· people on earth
	3– 5	right thinker and worker does his b·,
	3–14	what the b· thinker and worker has said
	7– 9	b· and most scholarly men and
	9– 1	which I know it were b· not to do,
	9– 5	not because it is the b· thing
	9–22	challenge . . . workers to do their b·.
	10– 5	new birth of the greatest and b·.
'01.	17–15	the respect of our b· thinkers.
	27– 3	* ''The b· contributions that
	29–10	all the b· of his earthly years.
'02.	10–25	martyrdom of God's b· witnesses
	11–28	the b· Christian on earth,
Po.	28– 9	Knowing Thou knowest b·.
	77– 7	Thou knowest b· !
	77–13	of Thee, who knowest b· !
	77–20	Thou knowest b· !
	78– 7	Thou knowest b· !
	78–12	Thou knowest b· !
	78–16	that benediction which knoweth b· !
My.	8– 9	* the b· church in the world,
	8–10	* b· expression of the religion of
	8–11	* let us have the b· material symbol of
	8–12	* in the b· city in the world.
	10– 9	* b· of design, material, and
	12–12	* b· evidenced by the liberality and
	15–27	* For those who know it b·
	42–19	* to the b· of my ability.
	46– 8	* In the b· sense it stands in
	60–16	* as a reward for the b· paper on
	69–29	* b· point of view is on top of the
	97– 2	* b· physicians now admit the power of
	108–23	Master designated as his b· work,
	108–25	b· work of a Christian Scientist.
	112–31	chief cities and the b· families
	136– 5	it is b· explained by its fruits,
	145– 4	one of Concord's b· builders
	165– 3	namely, of choosing the b·,
	165– 8	The b· help the worst ;
	165–28	The b· man or woman is the most
	178–20	and this is the b· of it.
	180–26	misconstrues our b· motives,
	195–18	b· way to silence a deep discontent
	203–10	b· of everything is not too good,
	205–22	theology at its b· touches but the
	229–28	Thou knowest b· what we need most,
	237– 7	The b· mathematician has not
	249–25	individual b· fitted to perform this
	250– 7	The b· Christian Scientists will be
	253–26	We understand b· that which
	285–13	b·, bravest, most cultured men and
	288–30	can make the b· of what God has made.
	304–11	I wrote for the b· magazines
	305–13	b· and most distinguished men
	331– 5	* of Wilmington's b· citizens,
	331–13	* by Wilmington's b· men,
	332–30	* giving b· praises to his honorable
	358–11	your Leader and b· earthly friend.
	358–23	Give my b· wishes and love to

best-known
Po.	vi–22	* All of the author's b· hymns

bestow
Mis.	272–23	* b· no rights to confer degrees.
	291–20	to b· it upon others,
My.	38– 1	* b· upon you the balm of heavenly
	231– 2	b· her charities for such purposes

bestowal
My.	247–21	to receive your b·,

bestowed
Mis.	77–16	Love that He hath b· upon us,
	127– 5	hath His love been b· upon her ;
	183–18	reflection already has b· on him,
	227–29	happiness it has b· upon others.
	289–23	has b· on a wife the right to
Ret.	2–14	b· by Sir William Wallace,
Pul.	46–21	* sword had been b· by
Po.	74– 3	moments to memory b·
My.	18– 2	hath His love been b· upon her ;
	19–29	gift which you so sacredly b·
	157–12	* church home you have so freely b·.
	215– 3	b· without money or price.

bestows
Mis.	345– 1	The Spirit b· spiritual gifts,
Rud.	10– 3	you forfeit the power that Truth b·,
'01.	15–15	blessings that divine Love b·
Peo.	12–27	our Father b· heaven
My.	122– 1	advice that one gratuitously b·

Bethany
Ret.	31–26	Bethlehem and B·, Gethsemane and

Bethel
Un.	57–18	This is earth's B· in stone,

Bethlehem

Mis.	159–19	not so much the *B·* babe,
	320–23	star of *B·* is the star of Boston,
	320–27	star of *B·* is the light of all ages ;
	388–24	To nurse the *B·* babe so sweet,
Ret.	31–26	*B·* and Bethany, Gethsemane and
	70– 9	Virgin-mother and *B·* babe,
Pul.	28– 4	* star of *B·* shines down from above.
Po.	21–13	To nurse the *B·* babe so sweet,
	29–12	The *B·* babe — Beloved,
My.	110– 5	At the present time this *B·* star
	257– 7	the *B·* babe has left his
	258–17	The memory of the *B·* babe

betide

Po.	79– 5	pure peace is thine, Whate'er *b·*.

betimes

Mis.	206–32	As you journey, and *b·* sigh for rest
	327–18	and *b·* burden them with their own.

betokened

Po.	10–13	bless a bridal *B·* from above.
My.	337–14	bless a bridal *B·* from above.

betokens

My.	290– 1	It *b·* a love and a loss felt by

betray

Po.	2– 1	no soul those looks *b·* ;

betrayed

Ret.	90–14	*b·* him, and others forsook him.
My.	283–16	even though it be *b·*.

betrays

Mis.	212– 3	a caressing Judas that *b·* you,
Ret.	73–24	*b·* a violent and egotistical
My.	128–24	A lack of wisdom *b·* Truth

better

Mis.	24–14	ever after was in *b·* health
	42–27	a *b·* state of existence.
	45–20	*b·* both morally and physically.
	59– 8	without this Science there had *b·*
	80–12	It is *b·* to be friendly
	88– 4	the *b·* it is for that student.
	110– 1	Repentance is *b·* than sacrifice.
	122–11	"It were *b·* for him — *Matt.* 18 : 6.
	130– 6	understand how much *b·* it is to
	175– 9	giving *b·* views of Life ;
	194– 6	know Him *b·*, and love Him more.
	200– 5	the *b·* representatives of God
	218–27	*b·* than Pat's echo, when he said
	223–26	*b·* than the mighty." *Prov.* 16 : 32.
	229– 7	quite as surely and with *b·* effect
	229–25	a *b·* preventive of contagion
	235–18	and thirsting after a *b·* life,
	239– 4	I never was in *b·* health.
	252– 6	the more the *b·* in every case.
	268–12	in pursuit of *b·* means for healing
	269–10	who can *b·* define ethics,
	269–10	*b·* elucidate the Principle
	273–12	as well as the *b·* part of mankind,
	278–28	sooner this lesson is gained the *b·*.
	318– 7	*b·* than some of mine
	333–32	the prophet *b·* understood Him
	336–26	behold a *b·* man, woman, or child.
	343– 7	Thought must be made *b·*,
	365–14, 15	*b·* health and *b·* men.
	371– 8	guide Christian Scientists *b·* than
	371–16	not productive of the *b·* sort,
	376–14	* and in a much *b·* form.
	396–14	I hope it's *b·* made,
Man.	87–20	the *b·* it will be for both
	92– 3	Healing *B·* than Teaching.
Ret.	11– 2	suited my emotions *b·* than prose.
	31–11	higher and *b·* than matter,
	33–13	the *b·* the work is done ;
	47–17	a *b·* healer and teacher than
	62– 5	bring forth *b·* fruits of health,
	82–30	and it is therefore *b·* adapted to
	84–26	the *b·* it will be for both teacher and
Un.	1–15	had *b·* leave the subject untouched,
	14–27	never said that man would become *b·* by
	45–21	finally dies in order to *b·* itself.
	49–20	* "the worse appear the *b·* reason,"
Pul.	9–19	who, with his *b·* half, is a very
	15– 7	Because people like you *b·* when
	50– 8	* *b·* home life and citizenship.
	56–16	* It makes people *b·* and happier.
	69–24	* may gain a *b·* understanding than the
	82–11	* far *b·* than their teachers.
	83– 4	* our *b·* self is shamed and
	84–18	* It can be *b·* felt than expressed.
	85–10	* *b·* and higher conception of God
	85–16	* a *b·* and grander humanity,
Rud.	14–16	must of necessity do *b·* than
No.	3– 6	*b·* to fall into the hands of God,
	4– 4	had *b·* be undertaken in health
	18–11	need of *b·* health and morals.

better

No.	20– 9	distant or cold, until *b·* apprehended.
	29–16	*B·* far that we impute such doctrines
	34–18	The blood of Christ speaketh *b·* things
	40–24	mankind are *b·* because of this.
	40–27	made *b·* only by divine influence.
Pan.	10–14	stronger and *b·* than before it.
	10–20	*b·* still, they reform desperate cases
'00.	6–27	you are made *b·* physically,
	14–25	philanthropy of the *b·* class of M.D.'s
'01.	1– 8	*b·* appreciated, than ever before,
	1–21	the *b·* side of man's nature
	15–20	dis-ease in sin is *b·* than ease.
	17– 7	departed from his *b·* self
	21–23	Does this critic know of a *b·* way
'02.	9– 9	we shall have *b·* practitioners,
	11– 3	mortals who seek for a *b·* country
Hea.	3– 4	to make men *b·*, to cast out error,
	8–15	Plato did *b·* ; he said,
	9– 4	if we understood the Principle *b·*
	9– 7	the *b·* for mankind, morally
	11–19	"The less medicine the *b·*,"
	13–28	one lie getting the *b·* of another,
	15–28	as we understand God *b·*.
Peo.	6– 1	* all the *b·* for mankind
	7–26	and give to the body those *b·*
Po.	59– 6	I hope it's *b·* made,
My.	5–22	to love more and to serve *b·*.
	6– 7	To abide in our unselfed *b·* self
	26–16	I thought it *b·* to be brief
	39–29	* comprehend *b·* the strength and
	63–14	* enable us *b·* to work out the
	108–19	The more of this Mind the *b·*
	112–22	*b·* representatives of C. S.
	150– 8	* rendering the world happier and *b·*
	162– 8	is *b·* than a wilderness of dullards
	164–25	into the greater and *b·*,
	174–28	humbly pray to serve Him *b·*.
	196–10	*b·* than the mighty ; — *Prov.* 16 : 32.
	213–23	Thus you will grow wiser and *b·*
	215–26	Can we find a *b·* example
	221–13	can we find a *b·* moral philosophy,
	221–14	or a *b·* religion than his?
	226–28	becomes *b·* acquainted with C. S.,
	229–13	*B·* far that Christian Scientists
	233–10	are you not made *b·* by watching?
	233–12	*b·* adapted to deliver mortals from
	236–20	the more the *b·*.
	264–16	signifies . . . the Bible *b·* understood
	307–21	understood what I said *b·* than
	324–31	* no man could have done so any *b·*.
	329–21	* At no *b·* time than now,
	334–16	* no *b·* terms than to quote her own
	344–13	*b·* than he was before
	352–11	* is proved in *b·* lives.
	355–25	world is *b·* for this happy group

better-tended

Mis.	342– 8	*b·* lamps of the faithful.

between

Mis.	x–15	difference *b·* then and now,
	16–32	conflict *b·* the flesh and Spirit.
	19–25	*B·* the centripetal and centrifugal
	29–12	no analogy *b·* C. S. and
	29–13	*b·* it and any speculative theory.
	36–19	*distinction b· mortal mind and*
	42–21	The difference *b·* a belief of
	49–20	*b·* the real and the unreal.
	52– 4	divided *b·* catnip and Christ ;
	60–24	*b· them and real identity,*
	65–10	Every question *b·* Truth and error,
	95–16	*b·* the so-called dead and living.
	102–27	conflict *b·* sense and Soul.
	110–20	while leagues have lain *b·* us.
	111–23	*b·* his doctrines and those of Jesus,
	111–25	*b·* the Catholic and Protestant sects.
	117– 5	*b·* the thought, motive, and
	119–23	*b·* the real and the unreal
	124– 1	intervening *b·* God and man,
	168– 5	those halting *b·* two opinions
	178–29	wall *b·* the old and the new ;
	178–30	*b·* the old religion in which we
	179–19	*b·* us and the resurrection morning?
	188–11	a war *b·* the flesh and Spirit,
	188–12	a contest *b·* Truth and error
	203– 3	*b·* my students and your students ;
	256–17	intervals *b·* my class terms,
	257– 6	distinction *b·* that which is and
	269–18	his choice *b·* matter and Mind,
	271–27	* *b·* true and false teachers
	289– 9	mortals must first choose *b·*
	302–11	discriminate *b·* error and Truth,
	312–17	* *b·* religion and Science,
	319–28	*b·* the promise and event ;
	329– 7	*b·* taking up the white carpets and
	347–16	*B·* the two I stand still ;

between

Mis.	351–13	designed to stir up strife *b·* brethren,
	352–28	*b·* the healing of sin and the
	374–29	*b·* the thinker and his thought
Man.	41– 6	gulf *b·* C. S. and theosophy,
	75–12	*b·* the C. S. Board of Directors and
Ret.	38–22	Not a word had passed *b·* us,
	56–12	War is waged *b·* the evidences
	68– 9	great difference *b·* these opposites is,
Un.	5–22	spring up *b·* C. S. students and
	27– 4	have a shade of difference *b·* them.
	29–18	*b·* the true Science of Soul and
Pul.	2–16	the war *b·* China and Japan.
	20–15	warfare *b·* the flesh and Spirit,
	21–20	*b·* our denomination and other sects,
	22–16	doctrinal barriers *b·* the churches
	24– 3	* *b·* Commonwealth and Huntington
	38–20	* *b·* the embodied and disembodied
	41–10	* and all the territory that lies *b·*,
	47–17	* *b·* faith-cure and C. S.,
	55–30	* *b·* one hundred thousand and
	57– 6	* *b·* fourteen and fifteen hundred,
No.	7– 5	to spring up *b·* Christian Scientists,
	7–22	*b·* one person and another,
	14– 4	he would know that *b·* those who
	31–17	*b·* what is and is not,
Pan.	6–20	colloquy *b·* good and evil,
	13–15	the war *b·* flesh and Spirit,
	14–28	*b·* United States and Spain
’01.	5–12	metaphysics discriminates *b·*
	23–28	* “only the constant relation *b·*
’02.	4–10	peace *b·* Soul and sense
	8–12	*b·* the law and the gospel,
	8–13	*b·* the old and the new commandment,
	15–12	the connection *b·* justice and
	20–19	breaking any seeming connection *b·*
Hea.	1–20	The difference *b·* religions is,
	5–11	* “*b·* Christianity and spiritualism,
	6–12	*b·* the so-called dead and the
	12–28	*b·* matter and mind,
	18– 8	no connection *b·* Spirit and matter.
Peo.	1– 7	final unity *b·* man and God.
	9–13	*b·* matter and Spirit ;
My.	18–23	war *b·* flesh and Spirit,
	65– 9	* *b·* four and five thousand persons.
	108–10	difference *b·* metaphysics in
	124–19	*b·* these lines of thought
	147– 5	*b·* the morning and afternoon services
	180–30	*b·* divine theology and C. S.,
	181–18	line of justice *b·* the classes
	199–20	fourfold unity *b·* the churches
	200–25	gap *b·* this course and C. S.
	221– 3	moral distance *b·* Christianity and
	238– 5	degree of comparison *b·* the effects
	246–15	exist *b·* the teaching and letter of
	259– 3	on its pedestal *b·* my bow windows,
	265–10	peace *b·* nations,
	277– 3	*b·* the United States and Spain
	277– 7	difficulties *b·* individuals
	279–24	war *b·* Russia and Japan ;
	281–18	* peace *b·* Russia and Japan
	284–26	quarrels *b·* nations and peoples.
	306– 5	unity that may exist *b·* C. S. and
	309– 6	*b·* the towns of Loudon and Bow,
	310–22	* *b·* Mary, a child ten years old, and
	316– 3	Truth divides *b·* sect and Science

beverages

Mis.	288–32	abstinence from intoxicating *b·*.

beware

Mis.	39–10	false teachers . . . of such *b·*.
	79–29	*B·* of joining any medical league
	109– 2	*B·* of those who misrepresent facts ;
	307–27	should *b·* of unseen snares,
	366–18	“*b·* of the leaven of — *Matt.* 16 : 6.
No.	41– 1	chapter sub-title
	41– 4	warned the people to *b·* of Jesus,
My.	241– 7	* *b·* the net that is craftily laid

bewilder

’01.	20–15	This mental bane could not *b·*,

bewilderment

Pul.	34–14	* to their *b·* and fright,

beyond

Mis.	9–14	far *b·* the present sense
	12– 5	throughout time and *b·* the grave.
	46– 8	*b·* the power of any doctrine
	52– 9	*b·* all human means and methods.
	67– 1	until its altitude reaches *b·* the
	68–30	* soars *b·* the bounds of experience,”
	81–18	*many of the people from b· Jordan?*
	106–25	above, *b·*, methinks I hear
	111– 7	extended it *b·* safe expansion ;
	165– 4	grown *b·* the human sense of him,
	201–22	*b·* the common apprehension of sinners;
	202– 6	* *b·* the walks of common life,

beyond

Mis.	223– 9	Science proves, *b·* cavil, that
	228–17	and honest *b·* reproach,
	321–30	*b·* all earthly expositions
	324–19	Startled *b·* measure at beholding
	325–20	amazed *b·* measure that anybody
	339– 8	and is one day *b·* it,
	357– 9	*b·* the walks of common life,
	367–20	knows nothing *b·* Himself
	379–20	*b·* the basis of *materia medica*,
	385–12	moored at last — *B·* rough foam.
	386– 2	*B·* the shadow, infinite appear
Ret.	71– 1	exalts a mortal *b·* human praise,
	76–12	a light *b·* what others saw.
	89– 3	is proven *b·* a doubt
Un.	2–23	*b·* what they possessed before ;
Pul.	26– 6	* *b·* the power of words to depict.
	36–21	* just *b·* Massachusetts Avenue,
	40– 4	* *B·* the sapphire sea?
No.	4–17	* other systems of medicine,
	12–21	*b·* doctrine and ritual ;
	25–11	the infinite idea of Truth is *b·* a
	34–19	*b·* the heathen conception
’00.	12– 1	*b·* the power of the pen.
’01.	24–18	It dates *b·* Socrates,
	28–21	proven to me *b·* a doubt
’02.	4–27	*b·* the ken of mortals,
Hea.	8– 1	it implies no necessity *b·* the
Po.	1– 5	*B·* the ken of mortal e’er to tell
	48– 5	moored at last — *B·* rough foam.
	49– 4	*B·* the shadow, infinite appear
	70– 1	*B·* the clouds, away
My.	8– 6	* necessity here indicated is *b·*
	8– 7	* *b·* resistance in your thought.”
	14– 4	*b·* the ken of mortals
	45–22	* marvellous *b·* human ken.
	59– 7	* *b·* our mortal vision.
	59–32	* marvellous *b·* all imagining
	63–21	* awe and of reverence *b·* words,
	65–12	* *b·* two brief explanations
	77–11	* From *b·* the Rockies,
	91– 1	* established *b·* cavil.
	96–26	* *b·* the sneering point.
	97– 1	* C. S. just goes a little *b·*
	107–27	nothing *b·* illimitable divinity.
	108– 6	I have proved *b·* cavil that
	123– 2	gifts to me are *b·* comparison
	127–26	but it is rich *b·* price,
	180– 3	knows *b·* a doubt that its life-giving
	181– 2	settle all points *b·* cavil,
	190–20	remains *b·* questioning a divine
	250–29	have *b·* it duties and attainments
	273– 6	* *b·* the allotted years of man,
	349–20	*b·* the so-called natural sciences

bias

Mis.	264–21	*b·* of their first impressions,
’00.	9–13	Strong desires *b·* human judgment
Hea.	5– 7	*b·* a man’s character.

biased

Mis.	240–20	than the *b·* mind.

Bible (*see also* **Holy Bible**)

Mis.	24–11	I called for my *B·*,
	35–20	Why do we read the *B·*, and then go
	60– 3	*and the B· is addressed to sinners*
	64–14	the *B·*, and “S. and H.
	64–24	a student of the *B·* and of C. S.
	70– 2	That the *B·* is true I believe,
	114–12	in the *B·* and their textbook,
	130– 8	the *B·*, and in the C. S. textbook,
	169– 1	Within *B·* pages she had found all
	169–28	* Taking several *B·* passages, Mrs. Eddy
	170–19	The material record of the *B·*,
	170–32	“Hand,” in *B·* usage, — *Isa.* 59 : 1.
	180–20	chapter sub-title
	279–13	three picture-stories from the *B·*
	284–11	make the *B·* and S. and H. a study,
	300–27	the spiritual meaning of *B·* texts ;
	309–29	soberly adhere to the *B·* and
	313–26	I hereby ordain the *B·*, and
	314– 9	the chapter) in the *B·*,
	314–29	both the *B·* and the C. S. textbook
	318–21	a good *B·* scholar and a devout,
	322–11	the *B·*, and “S. and H.
	363–27	*B·* is the learned man’s masterpiece,
	366– 1	the *B·* and “S. and H.
	382–32	I ordained that the *B·*, and
	383– 7	its pastor is the *B·* and my book.
Man.	15– 4	the *B·* as our sufficient guide
	29–22	one to read the *B·*,
	32– 5	shall read the *B·* texts.
	34–12	The *B·*, together with S. and **H.**
	42–12	the *B·*, and S. and **H.**
	58– 5	ordain the *B·*, and S. and **H.**
	84–18	shall be guided by the *B·*, **and**
Ret.	25– 3	The *B·* was my textbook.

Bible

Ret.	26–12	The miracles recorded in the *B*·,
	27– 3	the Science of the *B*·,
	47–25	*B*· scholar and a consecrated Christian.
	76– 7	The *B*· is not stolen,
	83–11	afforded by the *B*· and my books,
	91– 9	compilers and translators of the *B*·,
Pul.	7–24	I have ordained the *B*· and
	25–27	* illuminated texts from the *B*· and
	28–19	* equal measure to its use of the *B*·.
	29–15	* selections from the *B*· and
	34–27	"the *B*· was my only textbook.
	45–26	* the *B*· and "S. and H.
	52–24	* The *B*· was a sealed book.
	58–25	* only pastor shall be the *B*·,
	60– 5	* no explanation of *B*· or
	65–20	* called the *B*· of that city.
	66–15	* the literal teachings of the *B*·
	69–20	* We find in this view of the *B*·
	70–19	* Taking her text from the *B*·,
	86–28	* the *B*· and the book alluded to
Rud.	5– 3	*B*· says: "Let God — *Rom.* 3 : 4.
	16– 9	the spiritual signification of the *B*·,
No.	11–15	If the *B*· and S. and H.
	15– 8	Fatiguing *B*· translations and
	33– 5	If the *B*· and my work
'00.	7–12	they never loved the *B*· and
'01.	3–14	definition derived from the *B*·,
	5– 8	named in the *B*· Life, Truth, Love
	8–23	follow the teachings of the *B*·.
	11–13	True, . . . the *B*·, and " S. and H.
	27– 2	all other authors except the *B*·.
	27–29	* people say it conflicts with the *B*·.
	31–22	daily *B*· reading and family prayer ;
	32–22	Such churchmen and the *B*·,
	34– 4	The *B*· is our authority
	34–12	or must we have a new *B*·
	34–23	study the *B*· and the textbook
'02.	4–28	thoughts of the *B*· utter our lives.
	5– 7	doubtful interpretations of the *B*· ;
Hea.	15–14	miracles recorded in the *B*·,
My.	34–15	* citations from the *B*· and "S. and H.
	39– 5	* read from the *B*· and S. and H.
	46–25	* sacred teachings of the *B*·
	48–12	* a prayerful study of the *B*·,
	48–19	* daily reading of the *B*·
	60–15	* little *B*· which you gave me
	80–18	* an appropriate reading from the *B*·,
	103– 6	our textbooks, the *B*· and "S. and H.
	103–25	The *B*· has been my only authority.
	112–27	S. and H. in connection with the *B*·.
	112–32	a book which lies beside the *B*·
	114–16	read no other book but the *B*·
	130–28	used as a companion to the *B*·
	147–15	*B*· and the C. S. textbook
	178– 1	Your *B*· and your textbook
	190–23	*B*· was written in order that all
	219–19	*B*· record of our great Master's life
	238– 2	*B*·, *if read and practised*,
	238–19	When the *B*· is thus read
	251–29	Adhere to the teachings of the *B*·,
	264–16	the *B*· better understood
	295– 8	chapter sub-title
	295–10	*B*·, PRINTED IN NUREMBERG IN 1733
	295–13	time-worn *B*· in German.
	295–17	The *B*· is our sea-beaten rock.
	299– 7	* by the church or the *B*·,
	299–15	Principle and rules of the *B*·,
	299–16	in the translations of the *B*·
	304–26	* say it conflicts with the *B*·
	308–29	*B*· was the only book in his

Bible-class

Ret.	42– 9	He also taught a special *B*· ;

Bible Lesson

Pul.	60– 8	* the *Quarterly B· L·*,

Bible Lessons

Mis.	180–20	chapter sub-title
Man.	104–13	the Committee on *B· L·*.

Bibles

'00.	7– 8	more *B*· sold than in all the
My.	354– 3	offering *B*· and other books

Biblical

Mis.	120–27	*B*· record of the great Nazarene,
	169–18	dual meaning to every *B*· passage,
	274– 2	we have no *B*· authority for
Man.	58–15	*B*· texts in the Lesson-Sermon
Un.	44–11	according to *B*· history.
Pul.	73–10	* delved deep into the *B*· passages,
	73–11	* one of the greatest *B*· scholars of
Hea.	5–18	Such hypotheses ignore *B*· authority,
My.	181– 2	*B*· basis that God is All-in-all ;

bid

Mis.	242–11	his *b*· on Christianity,
Chr.	53–22	earthly Eves, By Adam *b*·,

bid

Pul.	34– 8	* her pastor came to *b*· her good-by
Po.	22– 6	Again shall *b*· old earth good-by
	23–22	*B*· error melt away !
	53–13	*B*· faithful swallows come
My.	347–13	* nor ever *b*· the Spring adieu !

bidden

Mis.	158–14	when you were *b*· to be ordained,
Ret.	9–14	as my mother had *b*· me.
	89–12	*b*· to this privileged duty
Un.	16– 1	perfection which he is *b*· to imitate.
Pul.	33–13	* answered as her mother had *b*· her,
'00.	13–30	*b*· to write the approval of
My.	99– 9	* and *b*· Godspeed."

bidding

Mis.	269–26	Many are *b*· for it,
Hea.	19–20	*b*· man go up higher,

bids

Mis.	335–23	Watcher *b*· them watch,
	348– 8	God *b*· one uncover iniquity,
Un.	4–18	the Father *b*· man have the same Mind
Pul.	3–13	and *b*· tumult cease,
My.	27– 4	Divine Love *b*· me say:
	258– 7	*b*· her bind the tenderest tendril

bier

Ret.	18–13	but laid on the *b*·.
Pul.	1–17	Pass proudly to thy *b*· !
Peo.	14– 3	with flowers laid upon the *b*·,
Po.	26– 6	Pass proudly to thy *b*· !
	27–10	To brighten o'er thy *b*·?
	64– 4	but laid on the *b*·.
	65–21	gathers a wreath for his *b*· ;
My.	326–17	laid on his *b*· the emblems of a

big

Mis.	12–11	the future, *b*· with events.
	216–17	a *b*· protest against injustice ;
	231–16	Why, he made a *b*· hole,
	231–17	with two incisors, in a *b*· pippin,
	241–13	dose of error *b*· enough apparently
	253–14	This period is *b*· with events.
	276– 8	was not *b*· enough to fill the order ;
	400–19	To THE *B*· CHILDREN
Pul.	47–28	* *b*· house, so delightfully remodelled
	49– 1	* *b*·, sunny room which Mrs. Eddy calls
	49–15	"Look at those *b*· elms !
	49–16	almost as *b*· as they are now,
	57–24	* not far from the *b*· Mechanics Building
	63–13	almost as *b*· as they are now,
Po.	69– 7	To the *B*· Children
My.	65–13	* a *b*· church was required,
	75–24	* chapter sub-title
	75–26	* *b*· addition to The Mother Church
	125– 8	*b*· with promise ;

bigger

Mis.	134–15	is *b*· than the shadow,
	191–20	no *b*· than themselves.
Hea.	14– 1	the *b*· lie occupying the field
	14– 2	*b*· animal beats the lesser ;
My.	123–20	outdoor accommodations . . . are *b*· than

biggest

Mis.	123– 9	the serpent's *b*· lie !

bigoted

Un.	11–20	theologian of some *b*· sect,

bigotry

Mis.	365–24	infidelity, *b*·, or sham
Ret.	65– 7	lead to self-righteousness and *b*·,
Pul.	52–21	* wave of materialism and *b*·
My.	93– 4	* have little of the spirit of *b*·.

bilious

My.	335–21	* cause of death as *b*· fever,

bill

Mis.	131–25	itemize a *b*· of this church's gifts
	208–11	legislative *b*· that governs millions
	289–27	on the basis of a *b*· of rights.
	289–27	Can the *b*· of conjugal rights be
	300–14	spares you the printer's *b*·,
	380–27	a *b*· in equity was filed
Ret.	20–22	compelled to ask for a *b*· of divorce,
Pul.	58–11	* every *b*· being paid.
My.	327–15	* a medical *b*· was proposed

Bill of Rights

Peo.	10–12	our constitutional *B*· of *R*·.

billow

'02.	20– 2	mounting the *b*· or going down into

billows (*see also* **billows'**)

Mis.	153– 8	untouched by the *b*·.
	162–10	over their fretted, foaming *b*·.
Po.	10– 2	To the *b*· and the breeze ;
My.	337– 4	To the *b*· and the breeze ;

billows'

Po.	73–10	list the moan Of the *b*· foam,

billowy
Po. 24– 9   From out life's *b·* sea,

bills
Mis. 211–10   Inhuman medical *b·*,
   240– 2   doctor's squills and *b·*
Man. 77– 5   *b·* against the Church,
   77– 9   its endorsement of the *b·*
   78–18   *b·* of immediate necessity
   78–23   for the payment of such *b·*.
Ret. 6–27   Among other important *b·*
My. 27–25   * pay all *b·* in connection with
   30–21   * they were heaped high with *b·*,
   30–23   * Some . . . were one-hundred-dollar *b·*.
   340–17   immediately annulling such *b·*

bind
Mis. 396–20   whose measures *b·* The power of pain,
   398– 5   Thou wilt *b·* the stubborn will,
Ret. 46–11   Thou wilt *b·* the stubborn will,
Un. 12– 5   *b·* it with bands of Soul.
Pul. 17–10   Thou wilt *b·* the stubborn will,
   18– 4   whose measures *b·* The power of pain.
Rud. 4–12   "*b·* the sweet influences of — *Job* 38 : 31.
No. 31–28   "Whatsoever thou shalt *b·* — *Matt.* 16 : 19.
Peo. 11–25   "*b·* heavy burdens," — *Matt.* 23 : 4.
Po. 12– 4   whose measures *b·* The power of pain,
   14– 9   Thou wilt *b·* the stubborn will,
My. 258– 8   *b·* the tenderest tendril of
   350–16   anguish which they blindly *b·*

binder
My. 53– 5   * allow printer and *b·* to send forth

binding
Mis. 296–13   *b·* up the wounds of the
No. 43–14   * *b·* up the broken-hearted,

binds
Mis. 275–15   *b·* up the wounds of bleeding hearts,
   327–32   *b·* up their wounds,
Po. 33– 9   ambition that *b·* us to earth ;
   35– 6   Which *b·* to earth — infirmity of woe!
My. 132–29   It *b·* up the broken-hearted ;
   250–17   neither *b·* nor compels the

biographies
Pul. 33–14   * of which Catholic *b·* are full,

birch
Pul. 25–21   * with pews of curly *b·*,
My. 184–15   *b·* bark on which it was written

bird
Mis. 87– 1   as the *b·* in the clear ether of
   124–16   marking the unwinged *b·*,
   267–18   *b·* whose right wing flutters
No. 7–12   "flee as a *b·* — *Psal.* 11 : 1.
Pan. 3–12   lyre of *b·* and brooklet.
Hea. 19–13   Which is first, the egg or the *b·*?
Po. page 34   poem
   34– 1   O for thy wings, sweet *b·!*
   34– 7   *B·* of the airy wing,
   35–13   *B·*, bear me through the sky!
My. 126–27   every unclean . . . *b·*'" — *Rev.* 18 : 2.
   129–12   *b·*, brook, blossom, breeze,
   341–11   The *b·* of hope is singing
   347–15   bough, *b·*, and song, to salute me.

birds
Mis. 356–18   and the *b·* of the air,
   387–10   Like brother *b·*, that soar
Po. 6– 4   Like brother *b·*, that soar
My. 182–26   May the *b·* of passage rest

birth
commemorates the
My. 262– 7   commemorates the *b·* of a human,
conception and
Un. 46– 9   human conception and *b·*.
day of the
Pul. 20–23   day of the *b·* and baptism of our
forward the
Un. 57–26   forward the *b·* of immortal being ;
give
My. 133–16   give *b·* to the sowing of Solomon.
give it
Ret. 26–23   Woman must give it *b·*.
given
Mis. 166–20   given *b·* to the corporeal child
giving
'01. 30–13   giving *b·* to nothing and death to
giving it
Mis. 39–12   all her years in giving it *b·*.
his
Mis. 186– 5   embryo-man after his *b·*,
   278–15   cursed the hour of his *b·* ;
No. 36–26   in which he appeared at his *b·*.
human
Mis. 17–22   A material or human *b·* is the
material
Mis. 362– 3   material *b·*, growth, and decay :

birth
new
Mis. 15– 4   chapter sub-title
   15– 5   St. Paul speaks of the new *b·*
   15–13   The new *b·* is not the work of
   15–19   cannot complete, the new *b·* :
   16–25   new *b·* begun in C. S.
   18– 6   spiritual signs of the new *b·*
   386– 8   toiler tireless for Truth's new *b·*
'00. 10– 5   new *b·* of the greatest and best.
Po. 49–13   toiler tireless for Truth's new *b·*
My. 158–13   it points to the new *b·*,
of Christian Science
Pul. vii– 3   story of the *b·* of C. S.,
of Truth
My. 262–15   *b·* of Truth, the dawn of divine **Love**
second
Mis. 51–26   * as from a second *b·*,
spiritual
Mis. 17–18   spiritual *b·* opens to the enraptured
   17–27   With the spiritual *b·*,
their
Mis. 77–31   miracles of Jesus had their *b·*,
this
Mis. 17–23   This *b·* is more or less prolonged
welcome
Po. 24–10   A wave of welcome *b·*,
without
Chr. 53–39   Life, without *b·* and without end,
wondrous
Po. 31–12   veils the leaflet's wondrous *b·*

———

Mis. 18– 8   *b·* in the divine order of Science,
   253–25   agonies that gave that child *b·*
   286–21   Human procreation, *b·*, life, and
   321– 3   whose *b·* is less of a miracle than
Chr. 53–25   Yet wherefore signalize the *b·*
Ret. 40–15   at the *b·* of her last babe,
Po. 9– 6   at the *b·* of that beautiful boy.
My. 253–27   by education brightens into *b·*.

birthday
Mis. 225– 4   eighty-second *b·* of his mother
Po. 71–18   freedom's *b·* — blood-bought boon!
My. 148–12   February 22 — Washington's *b·*.

birthdays
Mis. 304–26   * *b·* of the "creators of liberty ;"
My. 235–26   meaningless commemoration of *b·*,

birthmark
'02. 2–23   kind of *b·*, to love the Church ;

birthplace
Pul. 48–14   * point out her own *b·*.
   58– 7   * in Concord, N. H., near her *b·*,
'02. 10–10   * *b·* of civilization is not Athens, **but**
My. 264–11   * *b·* of Thanksgiving Day,

birthright
Mis. 181–15   When we understand man's true *b·*,
Ret. 9–25   * redeemed her *b·* of the day,
My. 128–11   man's inalienable *b·* — **Liberty**.
   248–10   are they whose new-old *b·*
   283–13   find their *b·* in divine Science.

bishop
'01. 25– 9   the scholasticism of a *b·*,

bishops
Mis. 296– 5   not barmaids, but *b·*

bit
Mis. 159–23   a *b·* of what I said in 1890 :
   231–17   and *b·* the finger

bite
No. 43–27   envy and hatred bark and *b·* at its

bites
'00. 10– 1   Hatred *b·* the heel of love

biteth
Mis. 210–18   as it *b·* at the heel.

bits
My. 70–20   * replete with rare *b·* of art,

bitter
Mis. 27–19   sweet water and *b·*?" — *Jas.* 3 : 11.
   224–25   to neutralize what is *b·* in it,
Pul. 65–22   * one *b·* winter day,
'02. 9–27   Is it cause for *b·* comment
   11–19   gave our glorified Master a *b·* cup
Po. 1–16   Recalling oft the *b·* draft
   34–18   Bearing no *b·* memory at heart ;
My. 97–15   * *Zion's Herald*, a rather *b·* critic
   132–10   waters of Meribah here — *b·* waters ;
   230– 6   nutriment as both sweet and *b·*,
   230– 7   and *b·* in experience
   252– 5   which, if *b·* to sense,
   267–22   *b·* sense of lost opportunities
   350–17   this *b·* searing to the core of love ;

bitterly
    My. 218–24 false faith that will end *b*.
bitterness
    Mis. 287–26 it will spare you much *b*.
    Pul. 84– 4 * wrong be robbed of her *b*
    No. 7– 5 any root of *b* to spring up
    '00. 14–17 Let no root of *b* spring up
Black, Rev. Hugh
    '02. 10–10 Rev. Hugh *B* writes truly :
black
    Mis. 210–24 tears the *b* mask from the
    333– 8 basis that *b* is not a color
    Un. 51– 7 never make one hair white or *b*,
    Pul. 83–14 * under the *b* flag of oppression
blacken
    My. 130– 8 effort of disloyal students to *b*
blackness
    Ret. 69–25 "Above error's awful din, *b*,
    Pul. 52–22 * *b* of the Dark Ages,
Blackstone
    Mis. 340–14 forsook *B* for gray stone,
    Rud. 1–16 *B* applies the word *personal*
blade
    Mis. 195–23 He who never unsheathed his *b*
    215–31 while the corn is in the *b*,
    330–32 to put forth its slender *b*,
    Ret. 92– 5 "first the *b*,— *Mark* 4 : 28.
    '01. 35– 6 to bare our bosom to the *b*
Blair's Rhetoric
    My. 304– 8 book title
blame
    Pul. 80–20 * either to praise or *b*,
    No. 43–26 Science often suffers *b* through
blamed
    Mis. 111– 9 *b* others more than yourself.
    236–27 *b* for all that is not right :
blameless
    My. 40–31 * her own *b* and happy life,
blames
    Mis. 374–30 he that perceives . . . *b* him not.
blanch
    Mis. 395–18 Ere autumn *b* another year,
    Po. 58– 3 Ere autumn *b* another year,
blanched
    Ret. 31–23 *B* was the cheek of pride.
bland
    Mis. 31– 2 is a *b* denial of Truth,
blank
    Mis. 325–19 starts up in *b* amazement
    Man. 37– 4 *b* has been properly filled out
    111– 2 In filling out the application *b*,
blanketed
    My. 89–14 * not *b* with debts
blasphemous
    No. 18– 1 chapter sub-title
    My. 302–20 I regard self-deification as *b*.
blasphemy
    No. 18– 2 *B* has never diminished sin
    18– 3 *B* rebukes not the godless lie
blast
    Mis. 330–31 stoops meekly before the *b* ;
blasts
    Mis. 384–11 The cold *b* done,
    '00. 15–28 The cold *b* done,
    Po. 36–10 The cold *b* done,
    46– 4 Nor *b* of winter's angry storm,
blazoned
    '02. 14–21 *b* on the forefront of the world
    Po. 39–20 *b*, brilliant temperance hall
bleaching
    Mis. 393–23 To my heart that would be *b*
    Po. 52– 7 To my heart that would be *b*
bled
    Ret. 2–16 "Scots wha hae wi' Wallace *b*."
    Po. 15–19 pang in the bosom that *b*,
bleeding
    Mis. 243–30 *b*, vomiting, death.
    266– 1 struggle up, with *b* footprints,
    275–15 binds up the wounds of *b* hearts,
    Un. 58– 5 Jesus walked with *b* feet
    No. 34–23 Love bruised and *b*,
    Hea. 18–28 believe he was *b* to death.
    19– 8 belief that he was *b* to death,
    Po. 27–16 Hearts *b* ere they break
    78–10 Tears of the *b* slave
    My. 201–14 *b* brow of our blessed Lord,

blemish
    Ret. 94–15 and every spot and *b* . . . is removed,
    My. 197– 7 without spot or *b*.
blemished
    My. 192– 5 make spotless the *b*,
blemishes
    My. 121–17 Few *b* can be found in a true
blend
    Mis. 387– 9 'Neath which our spirits *b*
    No. 26– 3 that good and evil *b* ;
    Po. 6– 3 'Neath which our spirits *b*
    My. 291–27 Tears *b* with her triumphs.
blended
    Mis. 237–18 *b* with the murmuring winds
    Rud. 9– 6 more or less *b* with error ;
blending
    '01. 25–24 contradictory as the *b* of good and
    Hea. 5– 2 and of good and evil *b*.
    My. 183–25 *b* with thine my prayer
blends
    Chr. 53–37 faith's pale star now *b*
    Pul. 76– 6 * *b* harmoniously with the
    No. 14–10 *b* with its magic and enchantments.
    Po. 3– 1 starlight *b* with morning's hue,
bless
    Mis. 16– 3 so comfort, cheer, and *b* one,
    32–29 should try to *b* their fellow-mortals.
    127–22 inevitable condition . . . is to *b* others:
    155– 6 Sacrifice self to *b* one another,
    249–26 more tenderly to save and *b*.
    273–12 God *b* my enemies, as well as
    275–16 and *b* all who mourn.
    320–11 *b* man as he reaches forth for
    333–26 could heal and *b* ;
    348–10 divine Love will *b* this
    388–19 To *b* the orphan, feed the poor ;
    394– 9 beautify, *b*, and make joyful again.
    Ret. 11– 8 And live to *b* mankind.
    21–24 but for . . . I *b* God.
    Un. 60–13 "*b* we God,— *Jas.* 3 : 9.
    Pul. 87–22 our states of mind, to *b* mankind.
    No. 33– 3 lead us to *b* those who curse,
    Pan. 9–18 spiritual endeavor to *b* others,
    14–15 guide and *b* our chief magistrate,
    Hea. 4–12 to *b* what is unfit to be blessed.
    Po. 10–12 Returns to *b* a bridal
    21– 8 *b* the orphan, feed the poor ;
    33– 5 *b* me with Christ's promised rest ;
    45–12 beautify, *b*, and make joyful again.
    60– 5 And live to *b* mankind.
    68– 3 "I'm living to *b* thee ;
    My. 23– 7 * *b* us so long as we follow His
    132–22 and *b* our enemies.
    134–19 *b*, and inspire man's power.
    143–23 when these things cease to *b*
    158–24 will *b* this dear band of brethren.
    185–27 * we *b* Thee, Our God,
    194–26 May divine Love abundantly *b* you,
    197–28 God will *b* the work of your hearts
    202–29 God *b* this vine of His planting.
    203–20 God *b* this dear church,
    208–24 God *b* the courageous, far-seeing
    209– 3 God will abundantly *b* this
    220–21 I pray : "God *b* my enemies ;
    253–24 in three words : God *b* you.
    279–25 pray that God *b* that great nation
    280–19 He will *b* all the inhabitants
    280–22 Out of His allness He must *b* all
    337–13 Returns to *b* a bridal
    353–18 but to *b* all mankind.
    360–22 God will *b* and prosper you.
Blessed
    Mis. 337– 9 immaculate Son of the *B*
blessed
    Mis. 8–22 "*B* are ye, when— *Matt.* 5 : 11.
    8–29 "*B* are ye,"— *Matt.* 5 : 11.
    15– 7 "*B* are the pure— *Matt.* 5 : 8.
    93– 4 posterity shall call you *b*,
    127– 2 He has *b* her.
    127–21 condition whereby to become *b*,
    155– 7 even as God has *b* you.
    185–21 reveals man infinitely *b*,
    235–14 *b* is he, whosoever— *Matt.* 11 : 6.
    263– 8 How *b* it is to think of
    325– 2 "*B* are the poor in— *Matt.* 5 : 3.
    339–30 wisdom that might have *b* the past
    Ret. 42– 2 was a *b* and spiritual union,
    82– 7 practitioners of the same *b* faith.
    84–22 posterity will call him *b*,
    86–24 every man cared for and *b*.
    Un. 3– 6 "*B* are the dead — *Rev.* 14 : 13.
    30–16 the Messiah, our *b* Master,

blessed

Pul.	9–21	O glorious hope and b· assurance,
	15– 8	requires the spirit of our b· Master
	44– 9	* era in the b· onward work of C. S.
No.	33–14	The sacrifice of our b· Lord
'01.	3– 4	"B· are ye when — Matt. 5 : 11.
	7–28	b· are they that — John 20 : 29.
'02.	11–22	"B· are ye, when — Matt. 5 : 11.
Hea.	4–13	to bless what is unfit to be b·.
Peo.	12–20	Our b· Master demonstrated this
Po.	34–16	B· compared with me thou art
My.	3– 7	"B· are they that do — Rev. 22 : 14.
	13–31	their loving giving has been b·.
	17–30	He has b· her.
	21–26	* they too will be b·,
	25–21	I shall be with my b· church
	36–17	* with b· accord we are come,
	40–22	* "B· are the peacemakers : — Matt. 5 : 9.
	41– 7	* b· and comforted by divine Love.
	41–12	* "B· are the merciful," — Matt. 5 : 7.
	104–29	"B· are ye, when — Matt. 5 : 11.
	118–16	"B· are they that — John 20 : 29.
	143– 3	are b· in their results.
	158–24	God has b· and will bless this
	191–13	"B· are ye" — Matt. 5 : 11.
	199– 4	B· art thou.
	201–14	bleeding brow of our b· Lord,
	232– 8	mankind b·, and God glorified.
	274–23	I am cheered and b· when
	295– 3	b· assurance that life is not lost ;
	316– 6	"b· are ye, when — Matt. 5 : 11.
	328– 1	* God has dignified, b·, and
	345–16	came like b· relief to me,
	358– 4	you will be b· in your obedieuce.

blessedness

Mis.	209–26	goodness and b· are one :
	290–27	This individual b· and blessing
My.	40–11	* b· of peacemakers.
	41–13	* allow no one to escape that b·,
	41–24	* his real estate is one of b·.
	162–10	bond of b· such as my beloved
	208–15	in due expectation of just such b·,

blesses

Mis.	8–15	that b· infinitely one and all
	101– 5	that which b· its adoption by
	109–17	seeing the need of . . . b· mortals.
Pul.	21–13	which Christ organizes and b·.
Pan.	9–21	Christianity b· all mankind.
My.	151–14	when it no longer b· this

blessing

Mis.	11–23	and returning b· for cursing.
	18–30	Not to know what is b· you,
	133–22	I retire to seek the divine b·
	134–13	God will pour you out a b·
	139– 5	God will pour you out a b·
	212–12	they received the b·.
	278–16	always a b· to the human race.
	290–27	individual blessedness and b·
	291–19	I would part with a b·
	351– 5	of b· even my enemies,
Un.	60–16	b· and cursing. — Jas. 3 : 10.
Pul.	10–27	breathe Thou Thy b· on
	14–23	Those ready for the b· you impart
	74–18	and the b· it has been to mankind
'00.	8– 9	a b· or a bane upon individuals
'01.	2–19	b· the poor in spirit
	34–20	return b· for cursing ;
'02.	17– 9	is in b· others, and self-immolation
	19– 6	lifting up his hands and b· them,
My.	4–11	b· saint and sinner
	14– 4	b· above the song of angels,
	14– 5	a b· that two millions of
	21–19	* will receive a greater b·
	34– 6	He shall receive the b· — Psal. 24 : 5.
	52– 4	* b· them that curse her,
	66–25	* giving her b· to the structure.
	131–28	pour you out a b·, — Mal. 3 : 10.
	131–30	this great, great b· ;
	132– 5	pour you out a b·," — Mal. 3 : 10.
	154–11	that confers the b·,
	165– 7	I returned b· for cursing.
	165–16	goodness makes life a b·.
	182–15	through God's b· and the faithful
	192–14	May the b· of divine Love
	201– 1	God is b· you, my beloved students
	203–21	if it is ready for the b·.
	209– 6	faith in the b· of fidelity,
	224– 7	the b· which follows obedience
	253–24	you have His rich b· already
	258–26	hallowed by our Lord's b·.
	269–23	pouring out b· for cursing,
	269–28	pour you out a b·, — Mal. 3 : 10.
	297–16	rich b· of disbelief in death,
	323–23	* b· those who would destroy you

blessings

attest the

Mis.	35– 8	attest the b· of this mental system

beautiful as

Mis.	356– 1	radiant sunset, beautiful as b·.

brings

Mis.	85– 3	Life eternal brings b·.

filled with

No.	15– 7	filled with b· for the whole human

infinite

Mis.	56–24	and brings b· infinite.
	100–25	crown them with b· infinite.
	238–15	fraught with infinite b·,
Pul.	9–29	and call down b· infinite.
'01.	15–15	infinite b· that divine Love bestows
	31–20	Among the list of b· infinite
My.	281– 8	Faith . . . brings b· infinite,
	354–16	O b· infinite ! O glad New Year !

manifold

My.	262–32	and gives manifold b·.

my

Po.	33– 1	daily remember my b·

of the infinite

My.	118–21	supply the b· of the infinite,

our

My.	256–21	We count our b·

recognition of

My.	352– 1	* chapter sub-title

recognition of the

My.	352– 6	* express our recognition of the b·

rehearsal of

Man.	47–15	More than a mere rehearsal of b·,

rich

Mis.	165–27	to avail himself of the rich b·
My.	132–18	Oh, may these rich b· continue

richest

Mis.	166–28	diffusing richest b·.
My.	149–17	richest b· are obtained by labor.

spreadst

Po.	77– 8	b· spreadst abroad,

temporal

'01.	24–11	* greatest of all temporal b·,

which arose

Ret.	50–28	b· which arose therefrom.

Ret.	78–23	is to conspire against the b·
My.	42–17	* b· which have come into my life
	52– 9	* our indebtedness . . . for these b·,

blest

Mis.	106–13	On to the b· above,
	109–16	Ignorance is only b· by reason of
	205–30	lives on, God-crowned and b·.
	207– 3	heart meets heart reciprocally b·,
	212–12	When they were fit to be b·,
	385– 6	And I am b· !
	386–29	with all the crowned and b·,
Chr.	53– 2	Bright, b·, afar,
	53–49	As in b· Palestina's hour,
Po.	11– 1	Brave Britain, b· America !
	17– 1	B· beings departed !
	29– 1	B· Christmas morn, though murky
	30–15	shadows cast on Thy b· name,
	34– 3	soul of melody by being b·
	37– 6	And I am b· !
	44– 2	Crown the lives thus b·
	50–16	with all the crowned and b·,
My.	31– 5	"B· Christmas morn ;"
	170–28	to kneel with us . . . in b· communion
	202– 1	springs exultant on this b· morn.
	234– 2	Are the holidays b· by
	250–28	by the branch churches will be b·.
	257–22	make man's being pure and b·.
	338– 1	Brave Britain, b· America !

blight

Mis.	88– 1	tends to b· the fruits of
Chr.	53–57	No b·, no broken wing,

blighted

Mis.	360–18	b· flowers of fleeting joys,

blights

Ret.	7–22	* It b· too many hopes ;

blind

Mis.	22–25	and the b·, healed by it,
	66–28	yea, it is "the b· — Matt. 15 : 14.
	66–29	leading the b·." — see Matt. 15 : 14.
	107–24	may become morally b·,
	134–28	but, b· to its own fate,
	168– 4	b·, spiritually and physically,
	170–24	Jesus' proceedings with the b· man
	171– 5	and the b· saw clearly.
	171– 6	anoint the b· man's eyes
	181– 8	requirement of b· obedience
	210–30	Love opens the eyes of the b·,
	211–6, 7	else the b· will lead the b·
	234– 2	remain no longer to b· us

blind
Mis. 241–24　Then, like *b·* Bartimeus,
242– 9　give sight to one born *b·*.
244–20　make the *b·* to see,
258– 7　he restored sight to the *b·*,
275– 2　"Ye fools and *b·* !" — *Matt.* 23 : 17.
301–28　harden the heart, *b·* the eyes,
307–17　opening the eyes of the *b·*
326– 8　where the *b·* saw them not,
345–14　Methinks the infidel was *b·*
362– 8　Scholastic dogma has made men *b·*.
362– 9　gives sight to these *b·*,
368– 5　open the eyes of the *b·*,
370–19　chapter sub-title
375– 2　*b·* with animality,
Ret. 54–15　*B·* belief cannot say with the
Un. 10–25　He is not the *b·* force of a material
Pul. 55– 1　* "Not in *b·* caprice of will,
No. 8–23　who is too *b·* for instruction,
20–26　Human reason is a *b·* guide,
'01. 17–15　I healed the deaf, the *b·*,
Hea. 18–24　no *b·* Samson shorn of his locks.
Peo. 11–12　The lame, the *b·*, the sick,
13–23　The infidel was *b·* who said,
My. 22–11　* let us not be unconsciously *b·*
105–17　restored sight to the *b·*,
110–22　solve the *b·* problem of matter.
140– 2　"And I will bring the *b·* — *Isa.* 42 : 16.
152–18, 19　the *b·* is leading the *b·*,
153–22　This trembling and *b·* faith,
183–20　eyes of the *b·* see out of obscurity.
224–15　*b·* to his loss of the Golden Rule,
270–27　opening the eyes of the *b·*
311– 4　a girl, totally *b·*, knocked
311– 8　* "If this *b·* girl stays
311–10　to turn the *b·* girl out,

blinded
Mis. 332–20　*b·* the eyes of reason,

blinding
Rud. 17– 5　*b·* the people to the true character

blindly
Ret. 27–18　* Groping *b·* in the darkness,
My. 350–16　anguish which they *b·* bind

blindness
Ret. 54–14　Belief is virtually *b·*,
Un. 6–19　God's *b·* to error and
My. 80– 5　* they had been cured of *b·*,

Bliss
Mis. 153–29　* Far-off, infinite, *B·* !

bliss
Mis. 19–32　spiritual sense . . . of itself a *b·*,
83– 2　rhythmic round of unfolding *b·*,
160– 9　meet and mingle in *b·* supernal.
263–14　and reflect all *b·*.
287–12　Soul is the infinite source of *b·* :
328– 9　which from the summit of *b·*
330–12　possibilities are infinite, *b·* is eternal,
344– 7　aught of that which leads to *b·*,
352– 1　it mocks the *b·* of spiritual being ;
386–30　to reap, . . . Of *b·* the sum.
Ret. 17– 8　and tremble with accents of *b·*.
49–16　the *b·* of loving unselfishly,
Un. 57–17　gospel of suffering brought life and *b·*.
Pul. vii–21　the actual *b·* of man's existence
Rud. 14–10　except the *b·* of doing good.
'01. 35–15　And the *b·* of blotted-out sin
Po. 22– 9　*b·* that wipes the tears of time
31–15　Nor burdened *b·*, but Truth and Love
50–17　Of *b·* the sum.
62– 8　tremble with accents of *b·*.
67– 1　*b·* of life's little day
My. 120–10　*b·* of seeing the risen Christ,
192– 4　possession of unburdened *b·*.
267–17　infinite, boundless *b·*.

bloated
Mis. 123–10　pagan priests *b·* with crime ;
Po. 27– 3　*B·* oppression in its awful hour,

block
Peo. 7– 9　* With his marble *b·* before him ;
My. 65–19　* *b·* bounded by Falmouth, Norway, and
66– 4　* the ownership of the entire *b·*.
66–10　* the ownership of the entire *b·*.
66–14　* No *b·* is so well situated for

blood
bayonet and
Peo. 11– 8　not with bayonet and *b·*,
besmeared with
Mis. 274–29　the streets besmeared with *b·*.
brave
Pul. 48–25　* of blue and brave *b·*,
his
Mis. 65–31　shall his *b·* be shed." — *Gen.* 9 : 6.
My. 156–22　"drink of his *b·*" — *see John* 6 : 53.

blood
human
No. 33–18　human *b·* was inadequate to
33–20　shedding human *b·* brought to light
34–20　conception that God requires human *b·*
innocent
Mis. 121–17　the guilt of innocent *b·* — *Deut.* 19 : 13.
man's
Mis. 65–31　"whoso sheddeth man's *b·* — *Gen.* 9 : 6.
of Christ
No. 33–18　to represent the *b·* of Christ,
34–18　*b·* of Christ speaketh better things
34–26　significance of the *b·* of Christ.
of Jesus
No. 35– 1　This *b·* of Jesus is everything to
of martyrs
Mis. 121–12　*b·* of martyrs was believed to be
326–13　licking up the *b·* of martyrs
of the Lamb
Mis. 358–16　in the *b·* of the Lamb ;" — *Rev.* 7 : 14.
Pul. 12– 9　by the *b·* of the Lamb, — *Rev.* 12 : 11.
Peo. 9–10　in the *b·* of the Lamb ;
of the martyrs
My. 125–31　*b·* of the martyrs of Jesus," — *Rev.* 17 : 6.
177–17　* *b·* of the martyrs is the seed of
of the saints
My. 125–31　with the *b·* of the saints, — *Rev.* 17 : 6.
real
No. 34–22　The real *b·* or Life of Spirit
stained with
'02. 10– 9　footprints . . . are stained with *b·*.
14– 9　* not like Cæsar, stained with *b·*,
My. 248– 5　* not like Cæsar, stained with *b·*,
young
Pul. 7– 2　* "Had I young *b·* in my veins,
_____
Mis. 180–23　*were born, not of b·,* — *John* 1 : 13.
182–14　were born, not of *b·*, — *John* 1 : 13.
246–27　again deluge the earth in *b·* ?
327–32　wipes away the *b·* stains,
345–25　baptism not of water but of *b·*,
No. 34–27　*b·*, . . . purchasing the freedom of
Po. 22–21　and *b·* was not its price.

blood-bought
Po. 71–18　freedom's birthday — *b·* boon !

bloodgiving
No. 37–15　as a personal and material *b·*

bloodless
My. 124–12　*b·* sieges and tearless triumphs,

bloodshed
My. 285–10　*B·*, war, and oppression belong to

bloom
Mis. x– 1　coloring glory of perpetual *b·* ;
329–17　* "breath all odor and cheek all *b·*."
389– 1　To form the bud for bursting *b·*,
Chr. 53–31　Sharon's rose must bud and *b·*
Po. 21–15　To form the bud for bursting *b·*,
46–10　Thus may it ripen into *b·*,

Bloomington, Ill.
Pul. 89–35　* *Leader, B·, I·*.

blossom
Mis. 142– 3　to bud and *b·* as the rose !
227–18　fresh flowers of feeling *b·*,
Ret. 17–20　Its feathery *b·* and branches
18– 5　colored softly by *b·* and leaves ;
95– 2　will *b·* into greater freedom,
Un. 52–24　The most beautiful *b·* is often
Po. 15–16　Here smileth the *b·* and sunshine
63– 7　Its feathery *b·* and branches
63–13　colored softly by *b·* and leaves ;
67–21　flowers of feeling may *b·* above,
My. 129–12　brook, *b·*, breeze, and balm
201–11　repeat my legacies in *b·*.

blossomed
Pul. 22–21　budded and *b·* as the rose.
My. 141–28　*b·* into spiritual beauty,

blossoming
'02. 1–10　and *b·* as the rose.

blossoms
Mis. 332–15　stately palms, many-hued *b·*,
Pul. 4–19　crown the tree with *b·*.
Peo. 14– 4　amaranth *b·*, evergreen leaves,
Po. 16– 4　hath thy verdure, it *b·* above ;
32– 5　*b·* whose fragrance and charms
My. 155–29　beautiful *b·* in their Leader's love,
160–13　with *b·* on its branches
258–21　*b·* that mock their hope

blot
Mis. 246– 5　to *b·* out all inhuman codes.
Ret. 86–15　should be no *b·* on the escutcheon of
No. 7– 9　and *b·* it out of others.
'01. 5–16　We do not *b·* out the material race

blot
'01. 20–21 cannot b· out its effects on himself

blots
Mis. 102–20 which b· out all our iniquities

blotted
Pan. 14–25 b· out the Spanish squadron.

blotted-out
'01. 35–15 And the bliss of b· sin

blow
'02. 15– 2 contained threats to b· up the hall
Po. 10–21 His hand averts the b·.''
My. 51–11 * would be a serious b· to her Cause
337–22 His hand averts the b·.''

blowing
'01. 29–19 adverse winds are b·,

blows
My. 297– 5 knowing that she can bear the b·
297–13 b· away the baubles of belief,

blue
Mis. 87– 1 clear ether of the b· temporal sky.
330–28 violet lifts its b· eye to heaven,
376–25 faint, fairy b· and golden flecks
Pul. 32– 2 * and lighted by luminous b· eyes,
48–25 * of b· and brave blood,
Po. 67–19 like the b· hyacinth,
74– 5 O b· eyes and jet,
My. 110–19 higher in the boundless b·.

blue-gray
My. 342–13 * whether b· or grayish brown,

blunder
Mis. 285– 6 by a b· of the gentleman who
My. 228– 5 Evil minds signally b·

blunders
Ret. 81–17 b· which arise from wrong

blush
Mis. 296–32 his shame would not lose its b· !
Ret. 88–22 b· to enter unasked
Pan. 1– 9 roseate b· of joyous June
My. 115– 4 I should b· to write of

boa-constrictor
Mis. 62– 6 holding in thought the form of a b·

Board
Mis. 131–18 B· did not act under that By-law ;
Man. 26–21 a vacancy occurring on that B·
26–25 the discussions of this B·,
27–10 the written consent of said B·.
30–18 B· shall attend to the insurance
51–24 Only the members of this B·
52– 7 shall be laid before this B·,
52–15 shall be deemed sufficient by the B·.
57–15 must have the consent of this B·
69–14 If the author . . . call on this B·
69–15 the B· shall immediately appoint
78– 5 vacancy supplied by the B·.
80–15 such reasons as to the B· may
84–26 Outside of this B· each student
88–14 elected every third year by said B·,
88–19 applying for admission to this B·
90– 4 given certificates by this B·
90– 7 ACTION OF THE B·.
90–16 under the auspices of this B·.
95–13 shall be assigned them by the B·.
95–15 a member of the B· may lecture
100–22 privilege of this B· to name the
100–24 any Committee so named by the B·
101– 4 B· shall, . . . appoint an assistant
Ret. 48–12 B· of the Metaphysical College
My. 62–27 * services rendered to this B·

board
Mis. 231–32 vacant seat at fireside and b·
Man. 68–12 in addition to rent and b·.
My. 73–22 * concerning rooms and b·,
128– 6 coroner's inquest, a b· of health,
329– 6 * The b· only excused them from
329– 7 * b· of medical examiners.
340–13 a simple b· of health,

boarded
My. 315– 3 * b· with me in Littleton,
323–29 * Mr. Snider and myself b· in the

boarding
'02. 15– 7 rooming and b· indigent students

boarding-houses
My. 82– 9 * Hotels, b·, and private houses

Board of Directors
Christian Science
Mis. 126–17 obedience of the C. S. B· of D· ;
130–17 C. S. B· of D· has borne
131–25 have the C. S. B· of D· itemize
131–29 C. S. B· of D· to itemize
Man. 25–18 incorporation of the ''C. S. B· of D·.''

Board of Directors
Christian Science
Man. 26– 9 vote of the C. S. B· of D·
26–20 C. S. B· of D· shall consist of
27– 3 transacted by its C. S. B· of D·.
27–12 duty of the C. S. B· of D·
27–19 duty of the C. S. B· of D·
28–14 duty of the C. S. B· of D·
29– 7 If the C. S. B· of D· fails
35–14 signed by the C. S. B· of D·
38–12 vote of the C. S. B· of D·
39–15 vote of the C. S. B· of D·.
51–21 C. S. B· of D· has power
56–19 meeting of the C. S. B· of D·,
63–22 elected by the C. S. B· of D·,
65–22 vote of the C. S. B· of D·,
68–20 through the C. S. B· of D·
68–24 When the C. S. B· of D· calls a
75– 5 C. S. B· of D·, in behalf of
75–13 between the C. S. B· of D·
75–16 C. S. B· of D· owns the
76– 8 duty of the C. S. B· of D·
76–19 annually by the C. S. B· of D·
77– 1 books of the C. S. B· of D·
79– 2 C. S. B· of D· shall elect
80– 8 order of the C. S. B· of D·,
80–13 C. S. B· of D· shall have the power
81– 3 vote of the C. S. B· of D·,
81– 7 not accepted by . . . the C. S. B· of D·
82–13 vote of the C. S. B· of D·
85–22 approval of The C. S. B· of D·.
88–12 annually by the C. S. B· of D·.
89– 5 meeting of the C. S. B· of D·
95– 4 C. S. B· of D·, . . may call
97–11 vote of the C. S. B· of D·
99–17 elected only by the C. S. B· of D·.
99–20 appointed by the C. S. B· of D·,
100–13 apparent to the C. S. B· of D·,
100–16 The C. S. B· of D· may notify
101– 1 any time the C. S. B· of D· shall
Pul. 9– 4 Brothers of the C. S. B· of D·,
59–24 * members of the C. S. B· of D·
85–25 * from the C. S. B· of D·,
86– 6 * her . . . Students, the C. S. B· of D·.''
87– 9 * signature
'02. 13–30 to be known as ''The C. S. B· of D·.''
My. 16–14 * members of the C. S. B· of D·,
18–28 members of the C. S. B· of D·.
21–32 * signature
26– 3 * C. S. B· of D· takes pleasure in
63– 7 * signature
142–25 chapter sub-title
223–24 addressed to the C. S. B· of D·
242–20 should be sent to the C. S. B· of D·
358–31 and require the C. S. B· of D· to

Mis. 131–13 If our B· of D· is prepared to itemize
Man. 25– 5 a B· of D·, a President,
25–10 elected, . . . by the B· of D·
26–14 elected . . . by the B· of D·
27– 8 consulting with the full B· of D·
28–19 the B· of D· shall immediately call
29– 2 to inform the B· of D·
29–16 The salary . . . of the B· of D·
30– 8 majority vote of the B· of D·
30–16 The B· of D· shall pay from
36–22 unanimous vote of the B· of D·
50–10 the consent of the B· of D·.
50–18 a meeting of the B· of D·
53– 3 duty of the B· of D·
54– 2 and if, . . . the B· of D· finds
55–17 B· of D· may decide if his loyalty
56– 2 duty of the B· of D· to admonish
56–17 Meetings of B· of D·.
57–11 B· of D· and the Pastor Emeritus
62– 5 hymn selected by the B· of D·.
67–26 B· of D· shall immediately notify
77–13 shall be the duty of the B· of D·
77–25 shall visit the B· of D·,
78–13 sanctioned by the B· of D·
78–24 reported, . . . to the B· of D· and
104–13 B· of D·, the Committee on
Ret. 47–12 B· of D· of my College,
Pul. 43–10 * who compose the B· of D·,
86–14 * address from the B· of D· :
My. 26– 8 chapter sub-title
61–32 * earnest work of our noble B· of D·.
76– 6 * became evident to the B· of D·
199–10 B· of D· and Trustees of this church

Board of Education
Man. 35– 5 by a student of the B· of E·,
36– 8 loyal students . . . in the B· of E·,
36–10 examination by the B· of E·,
38– 6 or a student of the B· of E·
65–15 duty . . . of the B· of E·
84–10 After 1907, the B· of E· shall have

body

in the
    Rud. 13–19 to treat every organ in the *b·*.
is an expression
    Mis. 247–26 *b·* is an expression of mind,
is dead
    Chr. 55–16 the *b·* is dead because of — *Rom.* 8 : 10.
is governed
    Mis. 34– 6 *b·* is governed by mind ;
    256– 3 *b·* is governed by Mind,
is renewed
    Mis. 34– 7 before the *b·* is renewed
is the servant
    Mis. 47–18 *b·* is the servant of Mind,
its
    Peo. 11– 6 can free its *b·* from disease
its own
    Un. 45–19 telephones over its own *b·*,
limited
    Mis. 102– 7 could originate in a limited *b·*,
    No. 19–12 a limited mind nor a limited *b·*.
    Hea. 4– 2 cannot start from a limited *b·*.
manifest on the
    Mis. 219–26 made manifest on the *b·*,
    Ret. 61– 4 made manifest on the *b·*
man's
    Mis. 198–19 We know that man's *b·*, as matter,
material
    (*see* **material**)
matter, or the
    My. 349– 7 self-evident that matter, or the *b·*,
mind affects the
    Mis. 5–32 the mind affects the *b·*.
Mind and
    No. 40–20 obstruct the harmony of Mind and *b·*,
mind and
    (*see* **mind**)
mind or
    Mis. 59–25 away from the human mind or *b·*,
    97–28 a perfect man in mind or *b·*,
    103–22 either as mind or *b·*,
    341– 2 right action of mind or *b·*.
mind over
    Hea. 19– 2 to test the power of mind over *b·* ;
mortal
    Mis. 75–14 not in matter or the mortal *b·*.
    Ret. 34–19 mortal *b·* being but the objective
    Un. 28– 3 Is it a reality within the mortal *b·* ?
    Hea. 18– 2 both mortal mind and mortal *b·*
my
    Ret. 10– 2 too large for my *b·*
not in the
    Mis. 75– 7 *and that Soul is not in the b·*
of a female
    Man. 50– 3 the *b·* of a female shall be
of a subject
    Rud. 15–25 *b·* of a subject laid bare for
of believers
    My. 95–11 * prosperous *b·* of believers
of Christ
    My. 126– 1 the *b·* of Christ, Truth ;
    131– 7 For the *b·* of Christ,
of mind or of
    Hea. 9–25 either an error of mind or of *b·*.
of people
    Mis. 312–16 * *b·* of people known as . . . Scientists,
    My. 95–18 * well-dressed *b·* of people.
    99–11 * optimistic *b·* of people,
of Scientists
    My. 31–31 * great *b·* of Scientists joined in
of the church
    My. 38–18 * seats in the *b·* of the church,
    80–30 * in the main *b·* of the church,
of the holy Spirit
    Mis. 70–24 *b·* of the holy Spirit of Jesus was
of the infinite
    Hea. 3–27 the *b·* of the infinite,
one
    My. 316– 2 uniting in one *b·* those who
on the
    Un. 39– 2 is rendered practical on the *b·*.
    Rud. 10–15 thought manifested on the *b·* ;
    Hea. 7– 4 harmonious effect on the *b·*.
    Peo. 7– 3 impress of mind on the *b·*
our own
    Peo. 10–21 We possess our own *b·*,
over the
    Peo. 13–17 triumph of mind over the *b·*,
parts of the
    Rud. 12– 2 nor manipulates the parts of the *b·*
poor
    My. 132–30 heals the poor *b·*,
receptivity of the
    Mis. 229–15 governing the receptivity of the *b·*,
reconstructed the
    Ret. 28–22 Mind reconstructed the *b·*,

body

reconstructed the
    Pul. 35–21 Mind reconstructed the *b·*,
redemption of our
    Mis. 15– 6 redemption of our *b·*.'' — *Rom.* 8 : 23.
    95–23 the redemption of our *b·*,'' — *Rom.* 8 : 23.
    Peo. 10–26 redemption of our *b·*.'' — *Rom.* 8 : 23.
redemption of the
    Mis. 182–11 the redemption of the *b·*.
reflects God in
    Mis. 184– 7 when man reflects God in *b·*
refresh the
    Peo. 9– 6 The cool bath may refresh the *b·*,
religious
    Ret. 15– 4 My connection with this religious *b·*
    Pul. 50–26 * No one religious *b·* holds the
    My. 49– 5 * The religious *b·* which can direct,
resuscitating the
    My. 293–17 resuscitating the *b·* of the patient.
saviour of the
    My. 108–30 is the saviour of the *b·*.'' — *Eph.* 5 : 23.
scientific
    My. 59–12 * every religious and scientific *b·*
sense of the
    Mis. 47–15 In sleep, a sense of the *b·*
sick
    No. 29–12 * forgiven soul in a sick *b·*
Soul and
    No. 29– 5 false sense of Soul and *b·*.
Soul is not in
    Un. 51–27 whose Soul is not in *b·*,
soulless
    Ret. 74– 5 *corpus sine pectore* (soulless *b·*),
Spirit controls
    Mis. 247–20 understand that Spirit controls *b·*.
spiritual
    My. 218–11 *spiritual b·*, the incorporeal idea,
subjugating the
    '02. 10–13 subjugating the *b·*, subduing matter,
that
    Mis. 312–12 his remarks before that *b·*,
    Ret. 13– 3 having been members of that *b·*
thief's
    Mis. 70–22 The thief's *b·*, as matter,
this
    Mis. 44–20 You call this *b·* matter,
to heal the
    Hea. 7–15 begins in mind to heal the *b·*,
turns to the
    Mis. 101–19 He who turns to the *b·* for
upbuilding of the
    Mis. 169–13 was the upbuilding of the *b·*.
upon the
    Mis. 7–21 depicted in . . . time upon the *b·*.
    70– 6 healing action of Mind upon the *b·*
    Rud. 3–22 manifestation of Truth upon the *b·*
    Hea. 18– 1 destroy their effects upon the *b·*,
    My. 301–30 no curative effect upon the *b·*.
was interred
    My. 333–13 * where the *b·* was interred
whole
    My. 196–13 bridle the whole *b·*.'' — *Jas.* 3 : 2.
your
    Mis. 47–10 when moving your *b·*,
    Man. 47–12 ''Glorify God in your *b·*,— *I Cor.* 6 : 20.
    My. 139–27 redeem your *b·* from disease ;

    Mis. 3–22 and imparts these states to the *b·* ;
    42–12 not attained by the death of the *b·*,
    76– 9 mortal belief that soul is in *b·*,
    76–21 the so-called soul in the *b·*,
    269–21 without Mind the *b·* is without action ;
    Ret. 61–25 it cannot be found in the *b·*.
    Pul. 82– 1 * make the *b·* not the prison, but the
    Rud. 5–11 who has ever found Soul in the *b·*
    Peo. 4– 6 materialized into a *b·*,
    11–20 while the *b·*, obedient to
    My. 74–21 * intelligent and a happy appearing *b·*,
    91– 1 * immense membership of the *b·* is
    119–31 away from person — from *b·* to Soul,
    217–19 * and not the *b·* itself?''
    269–13 * Whose *b·* nature is, and God the Soul.

Boer
    '02. 3–19 British and *B·* may prosper

Bohemia
    My. 347–22 Special contribution to ''*B·*.''

boil
    '00. 8–23 will *b·* over the brim of life

boilers
    Pul. 25– 4 * two large *b·* in the basement

bold
    Ret. 17–15 hickory rears his *b·* form,
    Pul. 24–13 inscription carved in *b·* relief :
    Pan. 12–27 *b·* conjecture's sharp point,

bold
Po. 62–18 hickory rears his *b·* form,
71– 4 and guilt, grown *b·*,
boldly
No. 44–10 no hobby, however *b·* ridden
boldness
Ret. 7–17 * noted for his *b·* and firmness,
Bonaparte
Mis. 345–16 *B·* declared, "Ever since the
Peo. 13–24 *B·* said : "Since ever the
bond
Mis. 77–13 the indissoluble *b·* of union,
91–11 This *b·* is wholly spiritual
Ret. 76–19 and *b·* of perfectness.
Pul. 22– 3 Christian churches have one *b·*
My. 162–10 *b·* of blessedness such as
164–22 *unity, the b· of perfectness,*
bondage
Mis. 90–17 Break the yoke of *b·*
103–16 which must be ever in *b·*,
241–21 *b·* to sin and sickness.
Peo. 11–17 children of Israel still in *b·*.
My. 42–31 * from the *b·* of the Egyptians,
74–23 * *b·* of the material world,
bonds
Mis. 135–20 cement the *b·* of Love.
141–12 *b·* and methods of Truth,
150– 5 Yours in *b·* of Christ,
273–13 *b·* of love and perfectness,
290– 7 break all *b·* that hinder progress.
Pul. 22–17 *b·* of peace are cemented by
83–23 * "bound to her by *b·* dearer than
No. 8– 9 fellowship in the *b·* of Christ.
26–23 eternal *b·* of Science,
'02. 19– 3 burst the *b·* of the tomb
Po. 3–13 Till bursting *b·* our spirits part
My. 217– 8 invested in safe municipal *b·*
339– 2 *b·* of Christian brotherhood,
362–23 * in the *b·* of Christian love
bone
Mis. 44–17 What you thought was pain in the *b·*
55–29 and beneath a skull *b·*,
243–32 "He took a *b·* from— see Gen. 2 : 21.
bones
My. 80– 7 * when having broken *b·* set ;
105–11 diphtheria and carious *b·*
Bonney, Hon. Charles Carrol
Mis. 312–11 Hon. Charles Carrol *B·*, President of
Book
My. 183–20 deaf hear the words of the *B·*,
295–13 This *B·* of books is also the
book
above-named
Mis. 92–23 own a copy of the above-named *b·*
301– 5 author of the above-named *b·*
and author
Man. 32–10 Naming *B·* and Author.
and the title
'02. 15–27 both the *b·* and the title.
clerk's
My. 311–12 clerk's *b·* shows that I joined the
covers of the
My. 178–25 covers of the *b·* were burned up,
credit of the
Pul. 80–16 * rather to the credit of the *b·*
decry the
My. 114–10 and decry the *b·* which has
every
'01. 29–28 every *b·* of mine that they sold.
first
Rud. 16–20 the first *b·*, recorded in
Gerhardt C. Mars'
My. 351–23 have not read Gerhardt C. Mars' *b·*,
her
Mis. 54–14 The reading of her *b·*, "S. and H.
Pul. 58–25 * with her *b·*, called "S. and H.
80–12 * her *b·* has many a time
My. 52–29 * moral rightness of her *b·*."
53– 6 * send forth her *b·* to the world."
304–31 the contents of her *b·*,
336–10 * acknowledgment of this in her *b·*,
itself
My. 111–20 and yet the *b·* itself be absurd
large
Mis. 276– 1 large *b·* of rare flowers,
little
Ret. 6–14 than this little *b·* can afford.
35– 3 This little *b·* is converted into the
Rud. v– 1 THIS LITTLE *b·* IS . . . DEDICATED
My. 323– 7 * I have his little *b·* yet.
making a
Po. v– 5 * *not . . . with a view of making a b·*,

book
Mrs. Eddy's
Mis. 248–13 mistaken views of Mrs. Eddy's *b·*,
Pul. 28–17 * the use of Mrs. Eddy's *b·*,
38– 5 * first edition of Mrs. Eddy's *b·*,
60–12 * passages . . . from Mrs. Eddy's *b·*.
My. 334– 5 * Mrs. Eddy's *b·*, "Retrospection and
my
Mis. vii– 1 * that tak'st my *b·* in hand,
274– 4 revise my *b·* "S. and H.
301–21 It is not right to copy my *b·*
308–20 scientific notices of my *b·*.
314–15 shall read from my *b·*, "S. and H.
383– 7 its pastor is the Bible and my *b·*.
Ret. 38– 5 to persuade him to finish my *b·*
Pul. 6–12 thinking she . . . from my *b·*,
87–17 Through my *b·*, your textbook,
My. 133–26 my *b·* is not all you know of me.
228– 2 My *b·* S. and H. names disease,
266–23 My *b·*, "S. and H. with Key to the
318– 5 was not my proofreader for my *b·*
318– 9 critics declared that my *b·* was
343–17 In 1875 I wrote my *b·*.
name for the
'02. 15–21 to suggest a name for the *b·*
new
Mis. 375–11 * new *b·* you have given us.
no other
My. 114–16 and read no other *b·* but the Bible
of Revelation
Pul. 59–15 * read from the *b·* of Revelation
only
My. 308–29 Bible was the only *b·* in his
open
My. 126– 9 has in his hand a *b·* open
or an article
Man. 82– 6 A *b·* or an article of which
published a
'01. 23–23 Bishop Berkeley published a *b·*
read from the
Mis. 91–27 read from the *b·* as authority for
sealed
Pul. 52–24 * The Bible was a sealed *b·*.
small
Pul. 69–16 * It would take a small *b·* to explain
such a
My. 113– 6 Can such a *b·* be ambiguous,
Sibyl Wilbur's
My. 297–30 friends have read Sibyl Wilbur's *b·*,
that
Mis. 50– 7 *is contained in that b·*
92– 5 inexhaustible topics of that *b·*
No. 3–14 will put that *b·* in the hands of
'02. 15–28 God had led me to write that *b·*,
My. 111– 1 serve to call attention to that *b·*,
this
Mis. 50–17 the contents of this *b·*,
314–24 announcing the full title of this *b·*,
372–13 Knowing that this *b·* would
Man. 32–13 commencing to read from this *b·*,
Ret. 37– 7 "This *b·* is indeed wholly original,
38–25 learns the letter of this *b·*,
39– 1 demand for this *b·* increased,
83– 5 to the teachings of this *b·*,
Pul. 5–16 and pulpit cannonaded this *b·*,
5–21 This *b·*, in 1895,
5–28 This *b·* is the leaven
My. v–23 * copies of this *b·* have been sold
43–25 * teachings of this *b·*
53– 6 * This *b·* has now reached its
112–16 The earnest student of this *b·*,
112–25 student of this *b* will tell you
113– 4 practises the teachings of this *b·*
114–26 the higher meaning of this *b·*
114–28 Is it too much to say that this *b·*
178–24 snatched this *b·* from the flames.
298– 9 placing this *b·* before the public,
305–17 the demand for this *b·*
320–15 * the author of this *b·*
336–11 * In this *b·* (p. 20) she also states,
title of the
Man. 32–14 announce the full title of the *b·*
unique
Pul. v– 7 UNIQUE *b·* IS . . . DEDICATED BY
My. 320–12 * as being a very unique *b·*,
wonderful
Mis. 372–11 * pictures in your wonderful *b·*
write a
My. 105–27 urged me immediately to write a *b·*
your
Mis. 35–19 *of what benefit is your b·?*
83– 5 *In your b·, S. and H.,*
Pul. 6–13 * your *b·*, S. and H., was put
No. 43–10 * "Your *b·* leavens my sermons."
43–13 * "Your *b·* S. and H. is healing
My. 238– 3 *Will . . . heal as effectually as your b·,*

book

your
My. 323– 6   * criticism of you and your *b·*
324– 2   * especially your *b·* S. and H.
324– 6   * any idea for your *b·*,
324–17   * the author of your *b·*,

Mis. x– 8   republish them in *b·* form,
35–15   *Will the b· S. and H., ... heal the sick,*
285–17   *b·* that cast the first stone,
306– 3   * *b·* which will accompany the bell
314–22   shall name, . . . the *b·*, chapter, and
Ret. 38–12   finished my copy for the *b·*.
83–24   reading aloud from the *b·* to
Pul. 86–28   * Bible and the *b·* alluded to
Po. vi– 3   * *in a b· "Gems for You,"*
My. 13– 4   *b·* by Benjamin Wills Newton,
26–16   too short to be printed in *b·* form,
112–28   *b·* that through the good it does
112–32   a *b·* which lies beside the Bible in
115– 1   written or indicated in the *b·*.
178–26   not one word in the *b·* was effaced.
258–31   a child . . . reading a *b·*
324– 7   * *b·* to have come from any one but

book-borrowing
Ret. 75– 1   *b·* without credit

book-knowledge
Ret. 10– 3   I gained *b·* with far less labor

book-learning
Mis. 366–32   what Jesus had not, namely, mere *b·*,

Book of Life
My. 258– 1   Wherever . . . the *B· of L·* is loved,

books

my
Mis. 32–12   in my *b·*, on this very subject.
43–14   contemplative reading of my *b·*,
285– 6   who fills orders for my *b·*,
315– 6   No copies from my *b·* are allowed
378–20   readers of my *b·* cannot fail to
Ret. 83–11   afforded by the Bible and my *b·*,
Pul. 74–23   "My *b·* and teachings maintain
No. 15– 4   Reading my *b·*, without prejudice,
'00. 1–24   readers of my *b·* and those interested
'01. 25–12   regret their lack in my *b·*,
'02. 13–12   privilege of publishing my *b·*
My. 166–29   for my *b·*, placed in my room
219– 1   than that which my *b·* afford,
224–21   My *b·* state C. S. correctly.
244–22   all loyal students of my *b·*
296–11   the publisher of my *b·*,
318– 6   for only two of my *b·*.

Mis. vii –5   * well made choice of friends and *b·* ;
vii– 7   * making thy friends *b·*, and thy *b·* friends.
xi– 1   initial "G" on my subsequent *b·*.
64–14   through no *b·* except the Bible,
271–12   *b·* which are less than the best.
348– 1   infringe neither the *b·* nor the business
381–27   infringing *b·*, to the number of
382–16   the first *b·* on this subject ;
Man. 27–22   publication and sale of the *b·*
32– 9   not read from . . . but from the *b·*.
43–10   *b·* of the Discoverer and Founder of
44– 8   Obnoxious *B·*.
44–11   that has for sale obnoxious *b·*.
59– 8   *b·* or poems of our Pastor Emeritus,
71–22   shall not write . . . in their church *b·*,
76– 9   *b·* of the Church Treasurer audited
76–26   *b·* of the C. S. Board of Directors
77– 1   *b·* of the Church Treasurer
77– 3   *b·* are to be audited on May first.
81– 9   be connected with publishing her *b·*,
81–25   *B·* to be Published.
82– 1   publishes the *b·* . . . it sends forth.
82– 3   disapproves of certain *b·* or
Ret. 2–18   one of my Grandmother Baker's *b·*,
85– 9   *b·* and teaching are but a ladder
Pul. 45–29   * read from the two *b·* by Readers,
No. 15– 6   enable any one to prove these *b·* to
43– 9   * the good your *b·* are doing."
'00. 12–22   the magical *b·* in that city were
My. 28– 8   * treasurer's *b·* will show the dollars and
97–10   * kept no *b·* on the subject,
224–23   *b·* less correct and therefore less
238– 6   by reading the above-named *b·*
295–13   Book of *b·* is also the gift of gifts ;
354– 4   offering Bibles and other *b·* for sale
354– 8   *b·* for which my endorsement is

bookstore
Man. 44–10   *b·* that has for sale obnoxious books.

boon
Po. 71–19   freedom's birthday — blood-bought *b·* !

border
Pul. 26–23   * floor of white has a Romanesque *b·*

borders
Mis. 127– 6   and enlarging her *b·*.
142– 2   how hath He enlarged her *b·* !
154– 9   enlarge its *b·* with divine Love.
My. 18– 3   and enlarging her *b·*.

bore
Mis. 64– 4   Our Master *b·* the cross
162–18   Jesus *b·* our infirmities,
225–11   *b·* testimony to the power of Christ,
385–13   gales celestial, in sweet music *b·*
Ret. 94–29   Jesus' teachings *b·* much fruit,
Un. 55– 4   In his real self he *b·* no infirmities.
55– 6   he *b·* not *his* sins, but *ours,*
Po. 25–16   Whose heart *b·* its grief
48– 6   gales celestial, in sweet music *b·*
My. 326–18   *b·* his remains to their

born
Mis. 72– 2   For the innocent babe to be *b·*
161– 5   *unto us a child is b·,— Isa.* 9 : 6.
166–11   unto us a child *is b·,— Isa.* 9 : 6.
180–22   were *b·*, not *of blood,— John* 1 : 13.
181–16   "*b·*, not . . . of the will — *John* 1 : 13.
181–32   being *b·* not of the human will
182–14   were *b·*, not of blood, — *John* 1 : 13.
182–17   *B·* of no doctrine, no human faith,
183–10   Man is free *b·* :
184– 8   The child *b·* of a woman has the
184– 9   man *b·* of Spirit is spiritual,
184–28   and *is b·* of God !
205–29   man *b·* of the great Forever,
242– 9   would give sight to one *b·* blind.
253–18   devour the child as soon as it was *b·*,
317– 3   When *b·* of Truth and Love,
321– 3   "Unto us a child is *b·*," — *Isa.* 9 : 6.
370–10   "Unto us a child is *b·*, — *Isa.* 9 : 6.
Chr. 53–26   the birth Of him ne'er *b·* ?
55–14   *b·* of a woman — *Job* 14 : 1.
Ret. 5– 6   In the Baker homestead at Bow I was *b·*,
19–18   my babe was *b·*.
26–22   "*b·* of the flesh," — *John* 3 : 6.
40–17   her babe was safely *b·*,
Un. 23– 7   divine children are *b·* of law and order,
Pul. 32–18†   * Mary Baker . . . was *b·* in Concord, N. H.,
48–18   * *b·* and bred in that same
57–27   * *b·* of an old New Hampshire family,
No. 25–21   That which is *b·* of the flesh
36–27   a babe *b·* in a manger,
46–18   that we are *free b·*.
'00. 12–16   night that Alexander the Great was *b·*.
'01. 8–26   was *b·* of a virgin mother,
27–26   *b·* of the Spirit and not matter.
Hea. 3–16   *b·* in a remote province
10– 3   as soon as it was *b·*," — *Rev.* 12 : 4.
Peo. 1– 3   is not *b·* of human wisdom ;
10–13   "I was free *b·*." — *Acts* 22 : 28.
Po. 25– 2   Whence the dewdrop is *b·*,
29– 4   *b·* where storm enshrouds
70–20   As when this babe was *b·*,
My. 162–29   This church, *b·* in my nativity,
183–12   To-day a nation is *b·*.
228–13   none greater had been *b·*
239–25   so-called man *b·* of the flesh,
261–25   Christ was not *b·* of the flesh.
261–26   *b·* of God — *b·* of Spirit
261–27   the Galilean Prophet, was *b·* of
262– 8   *b·* in a manger amidst the flocks
262–11   never *b·* and never dying.
290– 9   *b·* in 1819, married in 1840,
330–30   my babe was *b·*.
357– 5   *b·* of God, the offspring of Spirit,

borne
Mis. 130–17   *b·* the burden in the heat of
147–10   worthy to be *b·* heavenward?
169–17   *b·* fully to our minds and hearts.
295–30   and *b·* the English sceptre.
356–17   has sprung up, *b·* fruit,
394– 2   *b·* on the zephyr at eventide's hour ;
Pul. 67– 7   * a fact *b·* out by circumstances.
71– 5   * is not *b·* out by the voluntary
No. 1–11   *b·* on by the current of feeling.
Po. 19– 5   upward and heavenward *b·*.
27–21   Thou hast *b·* burdens,
45– 1   *b·* on the zephyr at eventide's hour ;
My. 52– 4   * she has *b·* them bravely,

borrow
Mis. 117–27   *b·* oil of the more provident
121–30   *b·* their sense of justice from
342– 7   *b·* the better-tended lamps
My. 130–31   that you *b·* little else from it,

borrowed
Mis. 147–25   He assumes no *b·* appearance.

† *Incorrect newspaper account, quoted as published.*

borrowed
Mis. 371–25 error in *b·* plumes?
Ret. 57–15 Man shines by *b·* light.
Un. 17–12 consolation from *b·* scintillations.
17–17 despoil error of its *b·* plumes,
Hea. 11– 1 play in *b·* sunbeams,
My. 301– 2 it shines with *b·* rays

borrower
Ret. 30– 5 the dainty *b·* would have fled.
75–17 the *b·* from it is embraced in the

borrowing
Mis. 276–26 not one of them be found *b·* oil,
Pul. 8–13 no urging, begging, or *b·* ;
My. 130–23 *B·* from my copyrighted works,

borrows
My. 224–17 when he *b·* the thoughts,

bosom
Mis. 125–13 rest on the *b·* of God ;
145– 8 Does a single *b·* burn for fame
399– 1 it calls you, — "Come to my *b·*,
Pul. 13–21 has made his *b·* companion,
'01. 35– 5 bare our *b·* to the blade
'02. 9–20 in the *b·* of the Father,
Po. 8– 6 Her *b·* to fill with mortal woes.
15–18 in the *b·* that bled,
41– 1 * Come, rest in this *b·*,
44– 3 With the guerdon of Thy *b·*,
75– 8 it calls you, — "Come to my *b·*,
My. 203–26 buried . . . in the *b·* of earth
332– 4 * the feelings of a swelling *b·*.

Boston
Mass.
Mis. 150– 7 *B·*, MASS., 1889.
161– 2 CHICKERING HALL, *B·*, MASS.,
Man. 15– 2 *The First Church . . . B·, Mass.*
19– 1 THE FIRST CHURCH . . . *B·*, MASS.,
34– 6 The First Church . . . *B·*, Mass.,
37– 9 The First Church . . . *B·*, Mass.,
45–16 The First Church . . . *B·*, Mass.,
58– 8 The First Church . . . *B·*, Mass.,
65– 5 The First Church . . . *B·*, Mass.,
72–27 The First Church . . . *B·*, Mass.,
75– 6 The First Church . . . *B·*, Mass.,
92–21 The First Church . . . *B·*, Mass.
102–12 The First Church . . . *B·*, Mass.,
103– 2 The First Church . . . *B·*, Mass."
103– 5 The First Church . . . *B·*, Mass.,
104– 5 The First Church . . . *B·*, Mass.,
Pul. page 1 chapter heading
23– 8 * *B·*, Mass., December 28.
77–18 * "The First Church . . . *B·*, Mass.
78–16 * "The First Church . . . *B·*, Mass.
88–13 * *Advertiser*, *B·*, Mass.
88–19 * *Post*, *B·*, Mass.
My. vi–12 * The First Church . . . *B·*, Mass.,
15– 7 * The First Church . *B·*, Mass.,
23–19 * The First Church . . . *B·*, Mass.,
27–13 * The First Church . . . *B·*, Mass.,
27–19 * *B·*, MASS., June 2, 1906.
44–25 * The First Church . . . *B·*, Mass.,
46–32 * *B·*, MASS., June 12, 1906.
47– 3 * *The First Church . . . B·, Mass.:*
62–16 * *B·*, MASS., June 30, 1906.
63– 9 * *B·*, MASS., July 10, 1906.
135–25 THE FIRST CHURCH . . . *B·*, MASS.
142– 9 The Mother Church, *B·*, Mass.
172–10 * The First Church . . . *B·*, Mass.:
175– 2 my little church in *B·*, Mass.,
246–24 The Mother Church . . . *B·*, Mass.
280–13 * *B·*, MASS., June 13, 1905.
310–16 a large business in *B·*, Mass.
322– 8 * *B·*, MASS., November 21, 1906.
352–17 * *B·*, MASS., October 9, 1908.
Massachusetts
Mis. 147– 2 chapter sub-title
381–30 destroyed, in *B·*, Massachusetts.
My. 244–29 The . . . College of *B·*, Massachusetts,
289– 9 Mother Church . . . *B·*, Massachusetts,

Mis. 48–13 one of his recent lectures in *B·*
88–10 a *B·* gentleman whose thought is
125–22 chapter sub-title
132–11 *B·*, March 21, 1885.
133– 3 * prayerless Mrs. Eddy, of *B·*."
137– 5 a meagre reception in *B·*
139– 9 chapter sub-title
139–19 I gave a lot of land — in *B·*,
141–27 commence building our church in *B·* ;
141–31 Of our first church in *B·*,
143–17 "The First Church . . . in *B·*.
145–31 The Church of Christ, Scientist, in *B·*,
146– 5 chapter sub-title
148– 9 Manual of The First Church . . . *B·*,

Boston
Mis. 171–21 chapter sub-title
193–14 The Church of Christ, Scientist, in *B·*,
242– 6 the Metaphysical College in *B·*,
242–26 Also, Mr. C. M. H——, of *B·*,
249–17 since my residence in *B·* ;
300–23 The Church of Christ, Scientist, in *B·*,
310–13 gone out of The First Church . . . in *B·*,
311– 3 unite with The Mother Church in *B·*
316– 7 or speak to your church in *B·*
316– 8 I shall speak to my dear church at *B·*
320–23 star of Bethlehem is the star of *B·*,
380–28 the United States Circuit Court in *B·*,
382–21 edifice of this denomination in *B·* ;
Man. 3– 5 Manual of The First Church . . . *B·*,
26– 4 general Committee on Publication in *B·*
30–15 No. 385 Commonwealth Avenue, *B·*.
97– 6 loyal Christian Scientist who lives in *B·*,
98–18 in a leading *B·* newspaper
Ret. 6–21 the Hon. Richard Fletcher of *B·*.
15–13 I was called to preach in *B·*
16–16 charter for The Mother Church in *B·*
17– 2 in the beautiful suburbs of *B·*.
38–16 The afternoon that he left *B·*
38–16 I started for *B·*
38–20 he to find me *en route* for *B·*,
43– 5 Massachusetts Metaphysical College in *B·*,
45– 1 Church of Christ, Scientist, in *B·*,
46– 2 Church of Christ, Scientist, in *B·*.
51– 1 I gave a lot of land in *B·* to
Pul. v– 6 THE FIRST CHURCH . . . *B·*,
6–24 the Rev. William R. Alger of *B·*,
6–26 At a *conversazione* in *B·*,
7– 4 I love *B·*, and especially the
7– 8 praised and persecuted in *B·*,
7–27 The First Church . . . in *B·*,
8–28 The First Church . . . in *B·*,
20– 2 The First Church . . . in *B·*,
23– 3 * THE FIRST CHURCH . . . *B·*
24– 2 * first C. S. church erected in *B·*
30– 3 * when a *B·* clergyman remonstrated
30–10 * is not limited to the *B·* adherents,
30–25 * church in *B·* was organized by
31–17 * *B·* atmosphere was largely thrilled and
36– 2 * the Metaphysical College in *B·*,
36–23 * most beautiful residences in *B·*.
37–11 * superintends the church in *B·*,
40–19 * costly edifice erected in *B·*
41– 9 * these contributors came to *B·*,
47–21 * Besides her *B·* home, Mrs. Eddy has
49–21 * from her busy career in *B·*,
52–11 * The erection of a massive temple in *B·*
55–24 * *B·* congregation was organized
56–11 * the erection of the temple, in *B·*,
56–25 * C. S. church was dedicated in *B·*
57–12 * one of the most beautiful buildings in *B·*.
57–20 * excellent name given to a new *B·* church.
58– 4 * Coming to *B·* about 1880,
58– 9 * have joined The Mother Church in *B·*,
60–15 * had come to *B·* for this
63– 7 * BUILT IN HER HONOR AT *B·*
63–23 * was dedicated in *B·*.
64–24 * *B·* has just dedicated the first
65– 6 * should not overlook the *B·* sect
65–15 * by the dedication at *B·* of
65–26 * The *B·* church similarly expresses
67– 5 * a new faith, go to *B·*,"
67– 7 * *B·* can fairly claim to be the
68–19 * The dedication in *B·* last Sunday of
70–13 * very recently saw completed in *B·*,
70–26 * She has a palatial home in *B·*
75–17 * A BEAUTIFUL CHURCH AT *B·*
75–19 * took part in the ceremonies at *B·*
76–27 * The First Church . . . *B·*,
77–11 * erected . . . in the city of *B·*,
77–22 * "*B·*, January 6th, 1895."
77–26 * The First Church . . . at *B·*,
78–10 * erected . . . in the city of *B·*,
78–20 * "*B·*, January 6, 1895."
79– 4 * dedication in *B·*, of a C. S. temple
80– 8 * *B·* is emphatically the women's
81– 1 * chimes on the C. S. temple in *B·*
81– 8 * [*The New Century*, *B·*, February, 1895]
84–13 * The First Church . . . in *B·*,
85–23 * THE FIRST CHURCH . . . IN *B·*
85–25 * from the C. S. Board of Directors, *B·*,
86–15 * *B·*, March 20, 1895.
86–19 * The First Church . . . in *B·*.
87–13 "The First Church . . . in *B·*
No. 12– 8 Church of Christ, Scientist, in *B·*,
19– 7 C. S. is no "*B·* craze ;"
27–19 said, in a lecture in *B·*,
41–24 a *B·* Baptist clergyman
44–25 a Congregational clergyman of *B·*,
45–13 Let it not be heard in *B·*
'00. 1–19 *B·*, New York, Philadelphia,

Boston

'02.	13–14	The First Church . . . in *B·*,
	13–21	in the *B·* newspapers,
Po.	vi– 4	* *again in B·, in 1856.*
	vi–12	*In 1835 a mob in B·*
	vi–13	*B· has since been the pioneer of*
	vii– 2	* *in the beautiful suburbs of B·*
My.	8–26	* annual business meeting in *B·*,
	9–24	enlarge our church edifice in *B·*.
	13–15	The Mother Church . . . in *B·*.
	13–17	pledged to this church in *B·*
	16–12	* The Mother Church in *B·*
	20–25	* annual meeting in *B·*
	20–30	* usual large gathering in *B·*,
	21–11	* forego a visit to *B·* at this time,
	21–28	* the new edifice in *B·*.
	22–31	* The First Church . . . in *B·*
	27– 3	*Members of my Church, . . . in B· :*
	31–18	* by the Scientists in *B·*
	38–29	* The annual meeting . . . in *B·*,
	53–11	* 569 Columbus Avenue, *B·*.
	56–10	* in such suburbs of *B·* as would
	65– 4	* largest . . . meeting ever held in *B·*
	65– 6	* The First Church of Christ, . . . *B·*,
	67–20	* giving *B·* an edifice that is
	72– 5	* chapter sub-title
	72– 6	* gates of *B·* are open wide
	72–20	* Scientists who have come to *B·*
	72–29	* church in *B·* twelve years ago
	73–14	* from all over the world to *B·*
	73–28	* due to arrive in *B·* to-night,
	74– 3	* are already in *B·*.
	74–14	* *B·* is indebted to them for
	76–21	* annual church meeting in *B·*,
	76–25	* will be dedicated in *B·*
	76–29	* was founded in *B·* by
	77– 7	* leading landmark of *B·*,
	77–14	* pilgrims are pouring into *B·*,
	77–26	* believers had gathered in *B·*.
	79–10	* in the heart of the city of *B·*,
	79–15	* this occurred in staid old *B·*,
	80– 1	* close of their visit to *B·* ;
	81–17	* audience ever sat in *B·*.
	82– 7	* have been crowding *B·*
	82–21	* indications were that *B·*
	82–27	* came to *B·* in such numbers
	82–29	* to the residents of *B·*,
	83–19	* chapter sub-title
	84–12	* *B·* is the Mecca for
	84–17	* *B·* is near to another great
	85–14	* here in *B·* the zeal and
	85–20	* Another glory for *B·*,
	86– 4	* As *B·* has ever loved its
	86–10	* have been pouring into *B·*
	87– 5	* increase of the population of *B·*
	87–17	* *B·* is to be congratulated
	87–21	* in *B·* during the past few days.
	88– 4	* Scientists have assembled at *B·*
	88–10	* The dedication, Sunday, in *B·*,
	88–29	* a great church in *B·*.
	89–23	* The dedication . . . in *B·*
	90–23	* The Mother Church of C. S. at *B·*,
	91–16	* a C. S. temple at *B·*
	91–27	* just been dedicated at *B·*
	92–10	* convention of . . . Scientists in *B·*
	93– 5	* their great church in *B·*
	93–29	* now being held in *B·*
	94–18	* in the recent dedication in *B·*
	95–10	* magnificent C. S. church in *B·*
	95–16	* assembly of . . . Scientists in *B·*
	96– 1	* zeal . . . exhibited at *B·*,
	96–18	* The building they were in *B·* to
	96–28	* Mother Church extension in *B·*,
	97–21	* Mother Church . . . at *B·*
	97–25	* Scientists who descended upon *B·*
	97–28	* *B·* has not yet recovered from
	98–18	* recently dedicated at *B·*.
	98–28	* The erection in *B·* of the
	99–15	* a splendid cathedral in *B·*,
	100– 1	* a C. S. temple in *B·*
	100– 5	* temple recently dedicated at *B·*
	117–28	I left *B·* in the height of prosperity
	134–22	meeting of April 3, 1907, . . . in *B·*,
	135–17	First Reader of my church in *B·*,
	140–15	* The First Church . . . in *B·*,
	141– 9	* members . . . outside of *B·*
	141–15	* The First Church . . . in *B·*,
	141–18	* communion season of the *B·* church
	163–17	When I removed from *B·* in 1889
	172–24	* opened the following day in *B·*
	173– 8	members of my church, . . . in *B·*.
	173–17	attend the communion in *B·*
	216–18	The First Church of Christ, . . . *B·*,
	217– 7	The Mother Church . . . in *B·*,
	246–13	closed my College . . . left *B·*, and
	279–23	of The Mother Church . . . in *B·*,

Boston

My.	292–20	1901, Message to my church in *B·*,
	304–13	Chicago, *B·*, Portland,
	317– 4	* Rev. James Henry Wiggin of *B·*,
	319–21	* entered your Primary class at *B·*.
	322–21	* waiting months in *B·*
	325– 9	* old part of *B·* in which he lived
	338–14	lecture was delivered in *B·*,

Boston Daily Advertiser

My.	83–20	* [*B· D·A·*]

Boston Evening Record

My.	84–16	* [*B·E·R·*]

Boston Evening Transcript (see also **Boston Transcript**)

My.	57–28	* the *B· E· T·* said :
	70– 9	* [*B· E· T·*]
	73–25	* [*B· E· T·*]
	74– 9	* [*B· E· T·*]
	75–23	* [*B· E· T·*]

Boston Globe (see also **Boston Sunday Globe**, **Globe**)

My.	65–17	* [*B· G·*, April, 1903]
	69–25	* [*B· G·*]
	71–12	* [*B· G·*]
	72–13	* [*B· G·*]
	73–11	* [*B· G·*]
	75– 5	* [*B· G·*]
	78–25	* [*B· G·*]
	86– 8	* [*B· G·*]
	137– 5	* The *B· G·*, referring to this
	140–10	* [*B· G·*]
	141– 1	* [*B· G·*]
	264– 7	[*B· G·*, November 29, 1900]
	278–15	[*B· G·*, December, 1904]
	281–15	[*B· G·*, August, 1905]

Boston Herald

Pul.	40– 7	* [*B· H·*, January 7, 1895]
Po.	11– 5	*B· H·*, Sunday, May 15, 1898.
My.	29– 2	* Reprinted from *B· H·*
	79–23	* [*B· H·*]
	82– 4	* [*B· H·*]
	84–11	* [*B· H·*]
	85–19	* [*B· H·*]
	87–19	* [*B· H·*]
	264– 1	[*B· H·*, May 5, 1900]
	268– 1	[*B· H·*, March 5, 1905]
	274–16	* [*B· H·*, April, 1908]
	277– 1	[*B· H·*, March, 1898]
	337– 1	[*B· H·*, Sunday, May 15, **1898**]

Bostonians

Pul.	71– 2	* eight hundred of . . . are *B·*.

Boston Journal

Pul.	61–19	* [*B· J·*, January 7, 1895]
My.	65– 1	* [*B· J·*, June 19, 1902]
	71– 6	* [*B· J·*]
	304– 1	[*B· J·*, June 8, 1903]

Boston Post

My.	66–17	* [*B· P·*, June 6, 1906]
	67– 3	* [*B· P·*]
	70–18	* [*B· P·*]
	72– 4	* [*B· P·*]
	84–25	* [*B· P·*]
	86–21	* [*B· P·*]
	276–15	* [*B· P·*, November, 1908]

Boston Sunday Globe

Pul.	44–15	* [*B· S· G·*, January 6, 1895]

Boston Times

My.	99– 1	* *B· T·*, comments, it is but one of

Boston Transcript

Pul.	50– 9	* [*B· T·*, December 31, 1894]

Boston Traveler

Mis.	271–24	published in the *B· T·*
My.	54– 5	* *B· T·* contained the following

Boswell, **Rev. Mr.**

'01.	32– 3	Rev. Mr. *B·*, of Bow, N. H.,

both

Mis.	12–18	interest of *b·* good and evil
	16–18	higher sense of *b·* God and man.
	23–18	*b·* noumenon and phenomena,
	24–23	A knowledge of *b·* good and evil
	35–21	Only because *b·* are important.
	44–15	*the mind, or extracting, or b·*,
	45–20	better *b·* morally and physically.
	51–29	*Are b· prayer and drugs necessary to heal?*
	55–16	*Is C. S. based on the facts of b·*
	60–11	unreality of *b·* apparent
	65–22	C. S. demands *b·* law and gospel,
	65–23	*b·* in its demonstration,
	65–28	since *b·* constitute the divine law
	68– 3	it requires *b·* time and eternity.

both
Mis.	72– 7	*b·* good and bad traits
	85–31	way out of *b·* sickness and sin.
	109–22	but, admitting the existence of *b·*,
	118– 2	We cannot obey *b·*
	119– 6	rise and overthrow *b·*.
	121–32	Teacher of *b·* law and gospel
	128–12	have *b·* learned, and received,
	141–15	*b·* the law of God and the
	146–10	*b·* sides of the subject,
	158–11	we *b·* had first to obey,
	161–16	*b·* human and divinely endowed,
	165– 3	*b·* because of the ascension
	167– 8	*B·* son and daughter :
	173–14	says that man is *b·* matter and
	175–29	*b·* animal magnetism and
	180–28	*b·* a material and a spiritual sense.
	187– 1	regeneration of *b·* mind and body,
	187–17	Had *b·* writers and translators
	195– 8	*B·* the spirit and the letter
	197–20	compel us to pattern after *b·* ;
	197–25	that is *b·* good and evil ;
	198–22	knowledge of *b·* good and evil ;
	211– 7	will lead the blind and *b·* shall fall.
	213– 5	Suffering or Science, or *b·*,
	217–21	*b·* cause and effect,
	217–29	to become *b·* finite and infinite ;
	220–22	is patent *b·* to the
	220–23	*B·* should understand
	221–25	against *b·* evil and disease,
	222– 2	gives him a false sense of *b·*
	241– 1	the faith of *b·* youth and adult
	246– 7	*b·* human and divine rights,
	247– 2	*b·* human and divine rights ;
	249–10	*B·* in private and public life,
	267–20	*B·* wings must be plumed
	287–30	preserve affection on *b·* sides.
	292–26	great good, *b·* seen and unseen ;
	295–21	as *b·* untrue and uncivil.
	297–22	mutual consent of *b·* parties,
	314–28	selections from *b·* the Bible and
	333–12	Is it in *b·* evil and good,
	352– 5	*b·* material and spiritual,
	352–26	consciousness of *b·* evil and good,
	367–16	knowledge of *b·* good and evil,
	374–15	hold charge over *b·*,
	381–31	* *b·* founder and discoverer
Man.	37–18	so long as *b·* are loyal
	54–26	member of *b·* The Mother Church and
	74– 3	shall not be a member of *b·*
	87–21	for *b·* teacher and student.''
	92–12	If *b·* husband and wife are
	92–14	either one, not *b·*, should teach
Ret.	1– 1	from *b·* Scotland and England,
	5–11	names of *b·* father and mother
	14– 8	*b·* salvation and condemnation
	38–18	and were *b·* surprised,
	59–16	*b·* in idea and demonstration.
	64– 4	*b·* sinner and sin will be
	67– 6	Sin is *b·* concrete and abstract.
	67– 8	*b·* material and spiritual,
	81– 3	*b·* for the living and the dead.
	84–26	for *b·* teacher and student.
	88–16	*b·* by example and precept.
Un.	7– 7	due *b·* to C. S. and myself
	23–24	knowing *b·* evil and good ;
	24–11	which is *b·* evil and good.
	41–26	appears to *b·* live and die,
	46–19	regarded as *b·* good and evil,
	52– 6	of *b·* God and the universe.
	52–10	consciousness of *b·* good and evil,
	53–19	sums done under *b·* rules
	54–24	*b·* knew and admitted the
	61–23	C. S. is *b·* demonstration and
Pul.	1–10	Time past and time present, *b·*,
	2– 5	*B·* without and within,
	10– 2	healing *b·* mind and body,
	29– 4	* *b·* of whom had formerly been
	46–15	* *b·* in Scotland and England.
	53– 9	* the mind of *b·* healer and patient,
	69– 4	* *B·* were under the instruction of
Rud.	14–26	instructions, *b·* in and out of class.
No.	5–17	*b·* human health and life.
	5–27	in *b·* theory and practice,
	6–20	the evidence in *b·* cases
	10– 2	in *b·* a divine and human sense ;
	12–25	it makes *b·* sense and Soul,
	13– 6	declare *b·* the Principle and idea
	23–15	*b·* a literal and a moral meaning.
	24–10	and denies the actual existence of *b·*
	24–15	claims of evil become *b·* less and more
	31–19	but he treated them *b·*,
	37– 7	to know *b·* evil and good ;
	42–20	declaring itself *b·* true and good.
	45–19	by the noblest of *b·* sexes.
Pan.	5–19	It shows that evil is *b·* liar and lie,

both
'01.	4– 2	for *b·* have the nature of God.
	5–29	explains *b·* His person and nature,
	10–11	*b·* male and female.
	10–13	*b·* the divine and the human,
	10–18	as *b·* Father and Mother.
	28–13	*b·* in Catholic and Protestant
	34– 4	for asserting this, in *b·* cases.
'02.	4–15	*b·* ringing like soft vesper chimes
	8– 4	and *b·* will be fulfilled.
	15–27	*b·* the book and the title.
	17–10	*b·* the old and the new commandment,
Hea.	3– 2	wherewith to heal *b·* mind and body ;
	8– 2	heals *b·* mind and body ;
	8– 8	carrying out this government over *b·*
	10–22	be careful not to talk on *b·* sides,
	11–25	supposed to be *b·* mind and matter.
	13– 1	so weaken *b·* points of action ;
	13– 2	*b·* horns of the dilemma,
	18– 1	*b·* mortal mind and mortal body
My.	vi–29	* *b·* of which, . . . are the property of
	4–18	interests of *b·* medical faculty and
	8–11	* material symbol of *b·* of these,
	12–11	* *b·* as to the amount
	49– 1	* *b·* in public and private.
	62–31	* there was urgent need of *b·*.
	64–16	* *b·* by precept and example
	65–11	* with *b·* unanimity and assurance.
	70–21	* *b·* ancient and modern masters,
	108–19	for *b·* physician and patient.
	137– 9	* in *b·* substance and penmanship :
	147–20	able to heal *b·* sin and disease.
	152–19	and *b·* will stumble into doubt
	179–10	*b·* good and evil, *b·* mind and
	190–10	My experience in *b·* practices
	215–29	to test the effect of *b·* methods
	230– 6	as *b·* sweet and bitter,
	234–18	*b·* sides of the great question
	249–26	If *b·* the First and Second Readers
	251– 8	* *b·* Primary and Normal class
	270–30	control *b·* religion and art
	277– 6	satisfactory to *b·* nations
	292–22	*b·* are equally sincere.
	300– 6	*b·* to will and to do — *Phil.* 2 : 13.
	307–20	which we *b·* desired ;
	309– 9	*B·* entered their pleas,
	324–32	* *B·* Mr. and Mrs. Wiggin frequently
	335– 7	* retained his membership in *b·*
	349– 8	susceptible of *b·* ease and dis-ease,

Botticelli's
Mis.	375–26	* or *B·* 'Madonna' !

bottle
Hea.	18– 7	the *b·* will break and the wine
	18–16	put the new wine into the old *b·*

bottles
Mis.	178– 8	could not be put into old *b·*
No.	43–21	"new wine into old *b·* ;" — *Matt.* 9 : 17.
Hea.	18– 6	put new wine into old *b·* ;
	18–12	put the new wine into old *b·*.

bottom
Mis.	165–12	rends the veil . . . from top to *b·*.
Peo.	5–28	* sunk to the *b·* of the sea,
My.	52–25	* has reached her *b·* dollar,
	301– 8	solid Christianity at the *b·*

bottomless
Mis.	134–29	it will tumble into the *b·*.
No.	42–15	engulfing error in *b·* oblivion,
My.	53– 3	* a *b·* sea of corrections ;
	200–23	*b·* abyss of self-damnation,

bough
My.	347–15	primal presence, *b·*, bird, and song,

boughs
My.	347–10	exquisite design of *b·*
	347–12	* Ah happy, happy *b·*,

bought
Mis.	253– 3	but is *b·* with a price,
Pul.	36–23	* *b·* one of the most beautiful
	49–26	* Once *b·*, the will of the woman
My.	123–13	I had the property *b·* by
	265– 8	and is *b·* at par value ;
	314–10	*b·* a place in North Groton,
	325– 6	* that you had *b·* your house

bound
Mis.	101–18	opening the doors for them that are *b·*.
	143– 7	a closer link hath *b·* us.
	157–13	"as *b·* with you," — *see Heb.* 13 : 3.
	245–18	rights that man is *b·* to respect.
	262–21	to such as are *b·* ;
	275–18	open the prison to them that are *b·*,
	297–20	is held in C. S. as morally *b·*
	345–11	*b·* him to the stake.
Ret.	63–17	Do you not feel *b·* to expose

bound
Un.	7–11	has so *b·* me to Him
Pul.	83–23	* "*b·* to her by bonds dearer than
No.	31–28	shall be *b·* in heaven." — *Matt.* 16 : 19.
	45–15	rights which man is *b·* to respect.
Peo.	13–20	Them they *b·* him to the stake,
Po.	vii– 6	* *b·* volumes of her poems,
My.	48–30	* I am *b·* as an observer
	171–27	* *b·* with burnished brass.

boundaries
Hea.	11– 8	rebels at its own *b·* ;

boundary
Un.	37–11	no *b·* of time can separate

bounded
My.	65–19	* block *b·* by Falmouth,

bounding
Mis.	240– 4	*b·* with sparkling eyes,

boundless
Pul.	3– 4	Can Love be less than *b·* ?
Po.	65–13	from dreams so *b·*
My.	110–18	higher in the *b·* blue.
	267–17	infinite, *b·* bliss.

bounds
Mis.	68–30	* beyond the *b·* of experience,"
My.	138–19	the *b·* of propriety

bounteous
Chr.	53–33	Forever present, *b·*, free,

bounty
Pul.	9–23	a *b·* hidden from the world.
My.	260– 1	*b·* of Life everlasting,

bouquets
Mis.	112–22	* have brought to him *b·*,
	211– 8	supplies criminals with *b·*

Bouton, D. D., Rev. Nathaniel
'01.	32– 2	Rev. Nathaniel *B·*, D. D., of Concord,

Bow
N. H.
'01.	32– 3	Rev. Mr. Boswell, of *B·*, N. H.,
My.	172– 7	* grown on the farm . . . at *B·*, N. H.
	309– 7	towns of Loudon and *B·*, N. H.
Ret.	4– 6	towns of Concord and *B·*,
	5– 6	the Baker homestead at *B·*
Pul.	48–16	* on the brow of *B·* hill,
My.	172– 7	and Mark Baker for *B·*.
	309– 9	
	309–19	extensive farm situated in *B·*
	309–22	the Baker homestead at *B·* :
	309–28	* at the ancestral home at *B·*.

bow
Mis.	17–13	meekly *b·* before the Christ,
	223–30	arrow shot from another's *b·*
	330–15	let mortals *b·* before the creator,
	388– 6	A *b·* of promise on the cloud.
Pul.	42–28	* fastened with a broad ribbon *b·*.
No.	3– 2	envy will bend its *b·* and shoot
	8–17	*b·* down to the commandments
'02.	20–15	A *b·* of promise on the cloud.
Peo.	3–14	the *b·* of omnipotence
Po.	7– 6	A *b·* of promise on the cloud.
	28– 6	Help us to humbly *b·*
	67–11	Should *b·* thee, as winds *b·*
	77–14	to Thee we'll meekly *b·*,
My.	257–20	*b·* and declare Christ's power.
	259– 3	between my *b·* windows,

Bowdoin College
Mis.	178– 3	He is a graduate of *B· C·*

bowed
Mis.	339–22	*b·* the o'erburdened head
	386–18	*B·* to His will.
Hea.	10– 5	the beast *b·* before the Lamb :
Po.	46– 6	leaves have shed or *b·* the stem ;
	50– 2	*B·* to His will.
My.	61–18	* I *b·* my head before the
	258– 9	*b·* in strong . . . anguish,
	309–11	Mr. Pierce *b·* to my father

bowels
Mis.	69–22	even to move his *b·*,

bower
Mis.	354–31	the lark in her emerald *b·*
	394– 6	at the altar or *b·*,
Ret.	11–20	From erudition's *b·*.
Po.	8– 8	naiad from woodland *b·* ;
	18– 9	lark in her emerald *b·* ?
	35– 1	O take me to thy *b·* !
	45– 8	at the altar or *b·*,
	60–18	From erudition's *b·*.

bowers
Ret.	17– 4	In *b·* of beauty,
Po.	25– 9	From your green *b·* free,
	46– 3	Within life's summer *b·* !
	53– 1	Come to thy *b·*, sweet spring,

bowers
Po.	53–18	To empty summer *b·*,
	62– 3	In *b·* of beauty,

Bowring
Pul.	28–23	Robertson, Wesley, *B·*,

Bowring's
Un.	26–20	protest against this stanza of *B·*,

bows
Un.	16– 1	*b·* to the infinite perfection

box
Mis.	148–24	contribution *b·* was presented
Pul.	78–23	* in a white satin-lined *b·*
	86– 3	* contains a solid gold *b·*,
	86–12	* in an elegant plush *b·*.
My.	172–23	* The *b·* containing the gavel
	309–22	* a small, square *b·* building

Boxer's
My.	234–25	more fatal than the *B·* rebellion.

boy
Mis.	ix–20	a Love that is a *b·*,
	162–31	simple as the shepherd *b·*,
Po.	9– 7	the birth of that beautiful *b·*.
My.	60– 8	* "My *b·*, you will be ruined
	313–31	my little *b·* was not welcome in my

boyhood
Mis.	34–20	can return to his *b·*.

bracketed
Pul.	25–25	* On the walls are *b·*

Brahmanism
No.	14–10	from the Oriental philosophy of *B·*,

brain
Mis.	5–25	believe it to be *b·* matter.
	168– 9	"tympanum on the *b·*"
	247–22	believe it to reside in . . . *b·* ;
Ret.	10– 1	taught to believe that my *b·*
Un.	33–14	*B·*, thus assuming to testify,
Pul.	82– 2	* the *b·* for its great white throne.
Pan.	4– 9	located in the *b·* ;
	4–10	conditions of matter, or *b·*,
	4–14	it is patent . . . that *b·* is matter,
'02.	9–19	not the dream of a heated *b·* ;
Hea.	4–10	with softening of the *b·*
	5– 7	the developments of the *b·*
Po.	47–13	The weary of body and *b·* ?
My.	122– 3	from the *b·* of a dreamer.
	301–25	cannot of itself go to the *b·*
	302–11	the specific insanity is that *b·*,

brains
Mis.	210–19	a belief of disordered *b·*,
Un.	22–20	physical senses and material *b·*,
	33–16	that form of matter called *b·*,

branch
Mis.	114– 6	*Quarterly* as an educational *b·*.
	387–11	And on the same *b·* bend.
Man.	54–10	a member of a *b·* of
	54–15	*b·* church's list of membership
	54–26	and a *b·* Church of Christ,
	58–13	and of the *b·* Churches
	73–27	a member of one *b·* Church
	95–10	*b·* Churches of Christ, Scientist,
	95–17	*b·* churches shall call on
Ret.	18–26	from the bent *b·* of a pear-tree.
	52–16	*b·* associations in other States,
Pul.	67– 4	* THE MONTREAL *B·*
Rud.	16– 7	in any *b·* of education.
Po.	6– 6	And on the same *b·* bend.
	63–24	from the bent *b·* of a pear-tree.
My.	159– 9	rich fruit of this *b·* of his vine,
		(*see also* **church, churches**)

Branch Churches
(*see* **churches**)

branches
Mis.	154– 3	*b·* of The Church of Christ,
	154– 8	prune its encumbering *b·*,
	243– 5	mental *b·* taught in my college ;
	344–11	not studied those *b·*,
	356–19	have lodged in its *b·*.
Man.	45– 6	of The Mother Church and of its *b·*
Ret.	17–20	Its feathery blossom and *b·*
Pul.	46–14	* tracing those *b·* which
	55–27	* all others being *b·*,
Po.	63– 7	Its feathery blossom and *b·*
My.	125– 6	to rejuvenate the *b·*
	160–13	with blossoms on its *b·*,
	192–17	sits smilingly on these *b·*
	257– 1	green *b·* of the Christmas-tree.

Brande
Mis.	68–27	*B·* calls metaphysics "the science

brass
Mis.	316–23	pounding . . . love into sounding *b·* ;
Ret.	2–12	encased in a *b·* scabbard,
Pul.	46–19	* encased in a *b·* scabbard,
	62– 5	* tubes of drawn *b·*

brass
No. 45– 4 "as sounding *b*,— *I Cor.* 13 : 1.
'01. 26–23 as sounding *b*,— *I Cor.* 13 : 1.
My. 171–28 bound with burnished *b*.

brave
Mis. 163–25 After his brief *b* struggle,
183–29 He is bravely *b* who dares
240–22 affectionate, and generally *b*.
376–17 describe the *b* splendor of a
385–18 *B* wrestler, lone.
Chr. 53– 4 One lone, *b* star.
Ret. 17–16 bares a *b* breast to the lightning
Un. 39–20 be *b*, and let Science declare
Pul. 48–25 * a tincture of blue and *b* blood,
Pan. 14–19 remember our *b* soldiers,
14–23 as at Manila, where *b* men,
'00. 13– 6 that their words were *b*
Po. 11– 1 *B* Britain, blest America !
25–14 Flowers for the *b*
48–12 *B* wrestler, lone.
62–20 bares a *b* breast to the lightning
My. 291–19 was wise, *b*, unselfed.
338– 1 *B* Britain, blest America !

bravely
Mis. 137–17 to spread your own so *b*.
183–28 He is *b* brave who dares
239–26 so *b* confessing that she had
239–29 value of saying even more *b*,
'00. 11–29 His symbolic ethics *b* rebuke
My. 52– 4 * she has borne them *b*,

bravery
Ret. 2–15 whose patriotism and *b*

bravest
Pul. 5–10 *b* to endure, firmest to suffer,
My. 285–13 best, *b*, most cultured men and

brawler
My. 106–24 is not a *b*, an alcohol drinker,

braying
Mis. 370–21 *b* donkey whose ears stick out

breach
Mis. 283–16 *b* of good manners and morals ;

breaches
Mis. 316–21 *b* widened the next hour ;
My. 291– 6 uniting of *b* soon to widen,

bread
Mis. 127–12 hungry heart petitions . . . for *b*,
127–15 to feed it with the *b* of heaven,
170– 7 eating of *b* and drinking of wine
170–16 "I have *b* to eat — *see John* 4 : 32.
170–17 The *b* he ate, which was
175– 7 which says, I am sustained by *b*,
175–16 unleavened *b* of — *I Cor.* 5 : 8.
254– 7 *b* that cometh down from heaven,
399–15 the water, the *b*, and the wine.
Ret. 91–23 his . . . teaching was the *b* of Life.
Pul. 30–13 * outward symbols of *b* and wine,
Pan. 14– 8 *b* that cometh down from heaven,
Po. 75–22 the water, the *b*, and the wine.
My. 18– 9 hungry heart petitions . . . for *b*,
18–11 with the *b* of heaven, health,
131– 9 *b* of heaven whereof if a man eat
156–21 *b* that cometh down from heaven,
196–26 good in being, . . . is your daily *b*.
196–27 The poor toil for our *b*,
247–25 cast your *b* upon the waters
273–12 nor his seed begging *b*."— *Psal.* 37 : 25.

break
Mis. 19– 3 and will *b* the rule of C. S.
90–17 *B* the yoke of bondage
111– 5 and at *b* of day caught much.
123– 8 That man can *b* the forever-law
144–31 the universal dawn shall *b* upon
211–15 Why, then, do you *b* his peace
283–10 It would be right to *b* into a burning
283–12 and *b* through windows
290– 6 must ultimately *b* all bonds
298–12 my best friend *b* troth with me?
335–17 to *b* the Decalogue,
387–14 If thou the bending reed wouldst *b*
398– 8 *B* earth's stupid rest.
Man. 54–10 *b* the rules of its Tenets
67–22 *b* a rule . . . and are amenable
Ret. 46–14 *B* earth's stupid rest.
Un. 30–21 to *b* the cords of matter,
Pul. 9– 6 no Delphian lyre could *b* the full
13–14 Alas for those who *b* faith with
17–13 *B* earth's stupid rest.
Hea. 18– 7 if this be done, the bottle will *b*
Po. 6– 9 bending reed wouldst *b*
14–12 *B* earth's stupid rest.
15– 5 *B* not on the silence,
27–16 Hearts bleeding ere they *b*
79–18 The centuries *b*,

break
My. 117–10 will *b* one's own dream of
211– 8 *b* out in devouring flames.
221–17 *b* the First Commandment of

breaker
My. 282– 2 is its peace maker or *b*.

breaketh
Ret. 31–18 which *b* the divine commandments.
Pan. 7– 1 *b* the First Commandment

breakfast
Mis. 90–28 His spiritually prepared *b*,

breaking
Mis. 123– 3 *b* the First Commandment,
311–20 since by *b* Christ's command,
'02. 20–18 thus *b* any seeming connection
Po. 41–19 harpstring, just *b*, reecho again
66–12 'Tis *b* alone, but a young heart
My. 31– 3 * "The morning light is *b* ;"
160–20 persist in *b* the Golden Rule
223–22 *b* of one of the Church By-laws,
262–16 *b* upon the gloom of matter

breaks
Mis. 31– 6 *b* the Golden Rule and
101–17 *b* their chains,
176– 1 truth that *b* the dream of sense,
197–27 *b* the First Commandment of God.
274–19 outrages humanity, *b* common law,
301–26 *Second :* It *b* the Golden Rule,
'00. 6–20 and *b* God's commandments,
'01. 4–30 he *b* faith with his creed,

breast
Mis. 295–15 lost these sentiments from his own *b*?
306–24 feathery touch of the *b* of a dove ;
331–14 calls them to her *b*,
354–33 than the dream in his *b*.
389–23 drops down upon the troubled *b*,
398– 6 Wound the callous *b*,
Ret. 17–16 And bares a brave *b* to the
46–12 Wound the callous *b*,
Pul. 17–11 Wound the callous *b*,
Po. 5– 3 drops down upon the troubled *b*,
14–10 Wound the callous *b*,
18–12 as the dream in his *b* !
27–23 thy head on time's untired *b*.
34– 5 dear remembrance in a weary *b*.
62–20 bares a brave *b* to the lightning
78–11 Tears . . . poured on her *b*,
My. 191–24 Immortal courage fills the human *b*

breast-milk
Rud. 8– 2 or provides *b* for babes.

breasts
Mis. 240–18 sturdy oak, . . . *b* the tornado.
Po. 53–16 Their downy little *b*.

breastworks
My. 62– 1 * stood at the *b* in the battle,

breath
Mis. 51–22 * from the lips of Truth one mighty *b*
224–22 so settled that no passing *b*
233– 7 the *b* of mental malpractice,
296–30 who utters . . . in the same *b*?
328–10 with a *b* of heaven,
329–17 * "*b* all odor and cheek all bloom."
390–14 Thy breezes scent the rose's *b* ;
Ret. 9– 4 I listened with bated *b*
19–20 With his parting *b* he gave
48– 2 drew its *b* from me,
Un. 60– 5 With the same *b* he articulates
Pul. 79–24 * as his lungs call for *b* ;
79–24 the *b* of his soul is a belief in God.
No. 14–13 the sweet *b* of springtide,
Hea. 4– 4 We must give freer *b* to thought
Po. 16–23 *b* from the verdant springtime,
25–13 *b* of the living above.
30–19 and loudest *b* of praise
55– 5 Thy breezes scent the rose's *b* ;
My. 195–22 deep-drawn *b* fresh from God,
256–10 deep-drawn, heartfelt *b* of thanks
330–32 With his parting *b* he

breathe
Mis. 7– 2 nor to *b* the cold air,
152– 8 *b* a silent benediction over all
Pul. 10–27 *b* Thou Thy blessing on every
Po. 24– 2 *B* through the summer air
33–12 *b* forth a prayer that His love
My. 341– 1 and love to *b* it to the breeze

breathed
Mis. 189–15 supposition . . . Mind, is *b* into
396–24 and *b* in raptured song,
Pul. 18– 8 and *b* in raptured song,
'02. 5–21 and *b* in the Sermon on the Mount.
Po. 12– 8 and *b* in raptured song,

breathes
Mis.	175– 1	*b·* His presence and power,
'00.	11–21	Adelaide A. Proctor *b·* my thought :
Po.	68– 1	she *b·* in my ear,

breathing
Mis.	143–29	*b·* the donor's privileged joy.
	293– 2	*b·* new Life and Love
My.	105–22	*b·* at intervals in agony.
	188–18	*b·* a benediction for God's largess.
	270–18	*b·* love for his enemies,

breathings
Ret.	9–19	* my spirit's *b·* to control,

bred
Pul.	48–18	* was born and *b·* in that same

breeze
Mis.	51–23	* like a whirlwind, scatter in its *b·*
	240–17	The sapling bends to the *b·*,
	329–16	stirring the soft *b·* ;
	329–26	now chirps to the *b·* ;
Po.	10– 2	To the billows and the *b·* ;
	53– 4	Bring with thee brush and *b·*.
My.	29–26	* cooling *b·* to temper the heat,
	128–10	and whispers to the *b·*
	129–12	brook, blossom, *b·*, and balm
	208–13	refreshing *b·* of morn,
	232– 2	unfurling your banner to the *b·*
	337– 4	To the billows and the *b·* ;
	341– 2	and love to breathe it to the *b·*

breezes
Mis.	332–16	perfume-laden *b·*, and crystal
	390– 4	Thy *b·* scent the rose's breath ;
Po.	19– 2	*b·* that waft o'er its sky !
	55– 4	Thy *b·* scent the rose's breath ;

brethren
beloved
Mis.	109–28	Beloved *b·*, Christ, Truth,
	125–23	*Beloved B·, Children, and*
	129– 2	*Beloved B·* : — If a member
	148–23	*Beloved B·* : — Until recently,
	149–18	*My Beloved B·* : — Lips nor pen
	150–10	*Beloved B·* : — Space is no
	154– 3	*Beloved B·* : — The spreading
	251– 4	My beloved *b·*, who have come
	322– 5	*Beloved B·* : — People coming from
Man.	86–10	Those beloved *b·* whose teacher
Pan.	1– 5	Beloved *b·*, since last you
	13–10	Beloved *b·*, the love of our loving
'00.	1– 1	My beloved *b·*, methinks even I
	11– 3	Beloved *b·*, have no discord over
'01.	1– 1	Beloved *b·*, to-day I extend my
'02.	1– 1	Beloved *b·*, another year of
	20–16	Beloved *b·*, are you ready to
My.	3– 4	MY BELOVED *B·* : — The divine might
	9–20	thanks to you, my beloved *b·*,
	15–12	*My Beloved B·* : — My heart goes out
	18–18	"Beloved *b·*, the love of our loving
	19–18	*Beloved B·* : — It is conceded that
	47– 2	* *Beloved B· of The First Church*
	108–26	Finally, beloved *b·* in Christ,
	121– 2	MY BELOVED *B·* : — I have suggested
	122–16	Beloved *b·*, another Christmas has
	124– 6	*My Beloved B·* : — Looking on this
	131–18	*My Beloved B·* : — I hope I shall not
	133–22	*My Beloved B·* : — I have a secret
	139–17	*My Beloved B·* : — When I asked
	142–17	My beloved *b·* may some time
	144– 4	*My Beloved B·* : — Give yourselves
	148–10	*My Beloved B·* : — In the annals of
	151–23	*My Beloved B·* : — We learn from
	154–15	*My Beloved B·* : — At this, your
	155–17	*Beloved B·* : — May this glad Easter
	156– 2	*Beloved B·* : — You will accept my
	158– 7	*Beloved B·* : — This day
	159– 3	*Beloved B·* : — Never more sweet than
	164– 8	*My Beloved B·* : — I have yearned to
	165–12	*Beloved B·* : — I beg to thank
	166–10	*My Beloved B·* : — Your munificent gift
	166–27	*Beloved B·* : — I am for the first time
	167–23	*Beloved B·* : — Allow me to send
	170–12	*Beloved B·* : — Welcome home !
	172–11	"*My Beloved B·* — Permit me to
	172–27	"*My Beloved B·* : — You will please
	174–17	*Beloved B·* : — I have the pleasure of
	176– 5	*My Beloved B·* : — Long ago you
	177– 3	BELOVED *B·* : — Most happily would I
	183–11	*Beloved B· across the Sea :*
	183–18	*Beloved B·* : — I rejoice with you ;
	184– 3	*My Beloved B·* : — Have just received
	184– 8	*My Beloved B·* : — To-day I am
	186–25	*Beloved B·* : — Accept my thanks for
	187–22	*My Beloved B·* : — You have met to
	189–24	Beloved *b·*, I cannot forget that
	191–28	*My Beloved B·* : — Your card of
	193–22	*Beloved B·* : — Carlyle writes,

brethren
beloved
My.	195– 3	*Beloved B·* : — You will pardon my
	196– 3	*My Beloved B·* : — I congratulate you
	196–25	*My Beloved B·* : — The good in being,
	197–25	*My Beloved B·* : — At this dedicatory
	199–10	*Beloved B·* : — The Board of Directors
	200–11	*My Beloved B·* : — The chain of
	201–10	*My Beloved B·* : — Your Soul-full words
	201–27	*Beloved B·* : — Please accept a line
	202–21	*Beloved B·* : — I thank you for
	203– 3	*Beloved B·* : — I have nothing new to
	204–17	*Beloved B·* : — I congratulate you
	205–15	*Beloved B·* : — Love and unity
	207– 3	*Beloved B·* : — Your communication
	208– 3	*Beloved B·* : — Accept my deep thanks
	231–28	*Beloved B·* : — You will accept my
	253–11	*Beloved B·* : — I thank you.
	253–15	*Beloved B·* : — Accept my love
	283– 6	*My Beloved B·* : — Your appointment
	341– 9	Beloved *b·* all over our land
	360–10	*Beloved B·* : — In consideration of
	360–16	My beloved *b·* in First Church
	362– 4	*Beloved B·* : — I rejoice with you
Mis.	106–17	*Friends and B·* : — Your Sunday
	120–27	*Friends and B·* : — The Biblical
	128– 6	"Finally, *b·*, whatsoever — *Phil.* 4 : 8.
	152– 3	*Beloved Pastor and B· :*
	167–19	they who do the will of . . . are his *b·*.
	185–30	with the Corinthian *b·*,
	303–11	*b·* in the fullest sense of that word ;
	311– 4	welcomed, greeted as *b·*
	351–13	to stir up strife between *b·*,
Ret.	22–20	his *b·* are all the children of one parent,
Un.	60–16	My *b·*, these things — *Jas.* 3 : 10.
Pul.	12– 8	accuser of our *b·* — *Rev.* 12 : 10.
	87–11	*Beloved Directors and B· :*
Pan.	6– 5	Finally, *b·*, let us continue to
'01.	8– 5	than the belief of our *b·*,
	11–26	But, my *b·*, the Scripture saith,
	34–20	Finally, *b·*, wait patiently on God ;
'02.	18–15	least of these my *b·*, — *Matt.* 25 : 40.
	19–10	*B·*, even as Jesus forgave,
My.	21–22	* their *b·* from far and near,
	86–16	* *b·* to give no more money,
	125– 4	*B·*, our annual meeting is a
	147– 2	*Friends and B·* : — There are
	158–24	will bless this dear band of *b·*.
	165–12	I beg to thank the dear *b·*
	198– 3	*Beloved Students and B· :*
	199– 3	BELOVED STUDENTS AND *B·* :
	201– 1	beloved students and *b·*.
	274–24	unity among *b·*, and love to God
	301–10	unite as *b·* in one prayer :
	336– 8	* care of her husband's Masonic *b·*,
	357–13	When my dear *b·* in New York

brevity
My.	170– 6	The *b·* of my remarks was due to

bribe
Un.	15–25	whom therefore they wish to *b·* with

bric-a-brac
Pul.	76–17	* Pictures and *b·*

brick
My.	66– 2	* a four-story *b·* building

bridal
Mis.	276–16	will always be the *b·* hour,
	342– 9	the *b·* of Life and Love,
Ret.	23–14	heart's *b·* to more spiritual
Po.	8– 7	waiting alone for the *b·* hour
	10–12	to bless a *b·* Betokened from above.
My.	125–25	beautiful garments — her *b·* robes.
	190– 1	falling upon the *b·* wreath,
	337–13	to bless a *b·* Betokened from above.

bride
Ret.	19–19	devotion to his young *b·*
My.	125–26	the *b·* (Word) is adorned,
	153–27	"the Spirit and the *b·*," — *Rev.* 22 : 17.
		(*see also* **Eddy**)

bridegroom
Mis.	276–21	and the *b·* appears.
	342–12	expectancy was to behold the *b·*,
	342–17	"The *b·* cometh !" — *Matt.* 25 : 6.
Ret.	23–15	and, lo, the *b·* came !
My.	125–27	and lo, the *b·* cometh !

bridge
Ret.	5– 1	near Concord, just across the *b·*,

Bridgeport, Conn.
Pul.	88–14	* *Farmer, B·, C·.*

Bridgeport (**Conn.**) *Standard*
My.	99–26	* [*B· (C·.) S·*]

bridges
No. 1– 9 demolishing *b·* and overwhelming

bridle
My. 196–13 *b·* the whole body." — *Jas.* 3 : 2.

brief
Mis. 96–26 conclusive idea in a *b·* explanation.
111–22 The Christianity that . . . is *b·*;
163–25 After his *b·* brave struggle,
280–23 *b·* address by Mr. D. A. Easton,
295– 2 deserve and elicit *b·* comment.
340–12 barrister who never brings out a *b·*.
Ret. 5–17 The following is a *b·* extract from
19– 7 spared to me for only one *b·* year.
22– 3 Gospel narratives bear *b·* testimony
Pul. 30–11 * a *b·* "confession of faith,"
44– 8 * to receive this *b·* message of
46–11 * touched upon in this *b·* sketch.
No. 22– 5 * once clothed with a "*b·* authority ;"
33–15 the *b·* agony of the cross,
'02. 3–14 in its *b·* occupation of that pearl
Po. 67– 1 *b·* bliss of life's little day
My. 26–17 I thought it better to be *b·*
65–12 * beyond two *b·* explanations
113–10 declares . . . in these *b·* sentences :
312–17 * a *b·* season she taught school."
333–28 * the *b·* space of six months,
340–14 clad in a little *b·* authority,

briefly
Mis. 128– 4 to learn or to teach *b·* ;
280–27 allude *b·* to a topic of great import
285–20 to write *b·* on marriage,
'02. 4–22 *b·* consider these two commandments
My. 72–17 * B· that is the notice which
131–19 I wish to say *b·* that this
292–15 My answer . . . is *b·* this :
298– 3 I *b·* declare that nothing has
305– 8 *b·* express myself unmistakably

Brigham, Mr. Charles
My. 16–18 * Mr. Charles *B·* . . . the architect

bright
Mis. 142–19 with *b·* hues of the spiritual,
171–30 to keep *b·* their invincible armor ;
354–33 No vision more *b·* than the
386–20 beckoned me to this *b·* land,
397– 4 A world more *b·*.
Chr. 53– 2 *B·*, blest, afar,
55– 4 *b·* and morning star. — *Rev.* 22 : 16.
Ret. 4–19 green pastures *b·* with berries,
18–11 to the *b·*, laughing day ;
Un. 54– 1 The *b·* gold of Truth is
Pul. 18–13 A world more *b·*.
83–13 * as *b·* as the sun, — *see Song* 6 : 10.
Hea. 10–17 if you will look on the *b·* side ;
Po. 2–15 stars, so cold, so glitteringly *b·*,
12–13 A world more *b·*.
18–11 What vision so *b·* as the
27–17 right with *b·* eye met,
34–20 in azure *b·* soar far above ;
43–20 Safe in Science, *b·* with glory
46–15 *B·* as her evening star,
50– 5 beckoned me to this *b·* land,
63–22 to the *b·*, laughing day ;
65–14 dreams so boundless and *b·*
68–21 and *b·* as the star,
70– 3 A *b·* and golden shower
73–20 the *b·* truth of the soul.
My. 342–14 * those eyes . . . which are always *b·*.

brighten
Mis. 262– 4 to *b·* so pure a purpose,
Po. 27–10 To *b·* o'er thy bier ?
My. 155–22 *b·* their faith with a dawn
350–25 *B·* the horoscope of crumbling creeds,

brightened
Pan. 10–16 broadened and *b·* before them,

brightening
My. 253– 2 *b·* this lower sphere with the

brightens
My. 253–27 by education *b·* into birth.

brighter
Mis. 321–22 battling for a *b·* crown.
Ret. 6– 4 * to follow her to the *b·* world.
Po. 23–16 In *b·* morn will find

brightest
My. 62–12 * shed its *b·* beams on your pathway,

brightness
Mis. 78– 5 *b·* of His glory encompasseth
363–20 the *b·* of His coming.
376–29 the *b·* of His glory.
Un. 18– 4 I can see only the *b·* of

brightness
Pul. 81–16 * who seek the *b·* of truth

brilliant
Mis. 296– 5 profound philosophers, *b·* scholars.
Pul. 6–23 Another *b·* enunciator, seeker,
No. 14–13 *b·* coruscations of the northern sky
Po. 39–20 blazoned, *b·* temperance hall

brilliantly
No. 44–11 boldly ridden or *b·* caparisoned,

brim
'00. 8–23 will boil over the *b·* of life

brimming
Po. 66– 1 nectar our *b·* cup fill,

brimstone
Mis. 237– 2 opinion that hell is fire and *b·*,

bring
Mis. 6– 2 to *b·* man nearer to God,
7–14 but if you cannot *b·* peace to all,
8– 3 if we can *b·* to the general thought
18–32 *b·* to you at His demand
19–11 and *b·* them out in human lives.
75–24 does not *b·* out the meaning
93– 6 *Can fear or sin b· back old beliefs*
93–22 neither . . . can *b·* on disease
93–22 or *b·* back disease,
100–23 *b·* to earth a foretaste of heaven.
106–20 I can only *b·* crumbs
139– 4 *b·* your tithes into the storehouse,
149– 6 Ask them to *b·* what they possess
149–23 *b·* to your beloved church
153–18 *b·* forth the fruits of Spirit,
154–24 *B·* forth fruit
157–23 shall *b·* it to pass. — *Psal.* 37 : 5.
157–23 He shall *b·* forth — *Psal.* 37 : 6.
194–15 *b·* out the entire hues of Deity,
228–15 This will *b·* us also to look on
231–23 *b·* the soft little palms patting
262– 1 designed to *b·* health and happiness
265–20 can never *b·* forth the real fruits
269– 1 shall *b·* it to pass." — *Psal.* 37 : 5.
320–15 sweet immunity these *b·* from sin,
341– 1 they never *b·* out the right action
346–25 becomes requisite to *b·* out Truth.
365– 2 *b·* out the glories of eternity ;
369– 5 *b·* "on earth peace, — *Luke* 2 : 14.
Ret. 30–18 to *b·* him to Christ.
49–24 *b·* all men to a knowledge of the
62– 5 *b·* forth better fruits of health,
Un. 13–21 Such a view would *b·* us upon an outworn
43– 4 cannot *b·* out the infinite reality of
Pul. 14– 2 *b·* the hour when the people will chain,
51–14 * and with them *b·* different ideas.
Rud. 7–25 *b·* about alteration of species
No. 28–12 is found to *b·* with it health,
33–25 to *b·* in this glory ;
34–21 propitiate His justice and *b·* His mercy
39–12 nor *b·* His designs into mortal modes ;
'00. 8–14 "*B·* forth things — *see Matt.* 13 : 52.
'01. 12–21 *b·* out the entire hues of God.
21–22 Christ came not to *b·* death
35– 2 He shall *b·* forth thy — *Psal.* 37 : 6.
Hea. 5– 1 *b·* out our own erring finite sense
9–13 to *b·* out in their lives ?
Peo. 8– 9 we shall *b·* out these qualities
Po. 39– 5 An offering *b·* to Thee !
53– 4 *B·* with thee brush and breeze.
My. 14– 6 will *b·* to be discerned in the
20–12 *B·* all your tithes into
40–17 * to *b·* health and a cure
52–15 * *b·* out the perfection of all things,
74– 5 * night trains of Saturday will *b·*
131–24 "*B·* ye all the tithes — *Mal.* 3 : 10.
140– 2 "And I will *b·* the blind — *Isa.* 42 : 16.
170–24 He shall *b·* it to pass. — *Psal.* 37 : 5.
170–24 He shall *b·* forth thy — *Psal.* 37 : 6.
173–12 would *b·* thousands here
190– 2 *b·* the recompense of human woe,
193– 3 His presence with you will *b·* to
213–14 *b·* out glorious results.
222– 6 *b·* him hither to me." — *Matt.* 17 : 17.
361– 7 do not *b·* your Leader into a

bringeth
Mis. 235–13 *b·* not forth good fruit ;
Ret. 45– 3 "*b·* good tidings, — *Isa.* 52 : 7.
'02. 20– 4 *b·* us into the desired haven,
My. 184–27 *b·* good tidings, — *Isa.* 52 : 7.
287–22 tree that *b·* not forth good fruit ;

bringing
Mis. 41–30 *b·* out the result of the Principle
139–13 *b·* into captivity every — *II Cor.* 10 : 5.
201– 5 would oppose *b·* the qualities of
247–13 those *b·* them do not understand my
344–30 *b·* Christianity for the first time

bringing

Mis.	392–22	To my busy mem'ry *b·*
Un.	7–25	*b·* out the highest phenomena of
'02.	4– 9	*b·* music to the ear,
Hea.	8– 8	*b·* out the results of this higher
Po.	51– 4	To my busy mem'ry *b·*
My.	14– 3	*Then,* when this *b·* is consummated,
	150–21	*b·* the sinner to repentance,
	202–26	*b·* your sheaves into the storehouse.
	269–20	The vine is *b·* forth its fruit ;

brings

Mis.	9– 3	purification it *b·* to the flesh,
	12– 4	*b·* suffering upon suffering to
	56–24	and *b·* blessings infinite.
	71–16	Law *b·* out Truth, not error ;
	82– 4	*b·* the peace symbolized by a dove ;
	85– 2	Life eternal *b·* blessings.
	96–21	It *b·* to my sense, and to the
	102–22	Human pity often *b·* pain.
	109–11	knowledge . . . that *b·* on repentance
	184–12	*b·* to remembrance the Hebrew strain,
	189–12	*b·* to light the true reflection :
	204–25	*b·* with it wonderful foresight,
	205– 8	*b·* the light which dispels darkness.
	208–20	His rod *b·* to view His love,
	210–13	*b·* the serpent out of its hole,
	282– 3	*b·* to human view an enlarged sense
	292– 2	St. John's Gospel *b·* to view
	292–13	*b·* to human weakness might and
	293–18	*b·* greater torment than ignorance.
	337–16	Science *b·* out harmony ;
	338– 3	*b·* to humanity some great good,
	340–12	barrister who never *b·* out a brief.
	350– 6	*b·* up the question of this society,
	393– 2	Is the moral that it *b·* ;
Chr.	53–45	For C. S. *b·* to view
Ret.	35–14	*b·* out the hues of Deity.
	55– 6	*b·* out the nothingness of evil
	64– 7	*b·* to light, makes apparent,
Un.	7–24	and *b·* us nearer to God,
	38–19	*b·* to light Life and immortality.
	41– 6	*b·* in an unreal sense of suffering
Rud.	4–23	*b·* out the fruits of Spirit
	8– 1	No rock *b·* forth an apple ;
	11– 9	*b·* forward the next proposition
No.	21–23	*b·* in the glories of eternity ;
	24–26	*b·* with it another and more glorious
	26–11	*b·* forth its own sensuous conception.
'01.	19– 5	prayer *b·* the seeker into
Po.	51– 7	Is the moral that it *b·* ;
My.	41–22	* It *b·* into present and hourly
	116–16	*b·* on this contagion.
	132–32	*b·* back the wanderer to
	247–20	loving look which *b·* forth
	253– 4	*b·* to light the perfect original
	278–30	*b·* into human thought
	281– 8	Faith . . . *b·* blessings infinite,

Britain (*see also* Great Britain)

Po.	11– 1	Brave *B·*, blest America !
My.	338– 1	Brave *B·*, blest America !

British

Ret.	3– 2	prominent in *B·* politics,
'02.	3–19	*B·* and Boer may prosper in peace,

Britons

Mis.	296–19	Do manly *B·* patronize taprooms

broad

Mis.	32– 2	this *b·* road to destruction.
	81– 1	*b·* and sure foundation
	143– 1	*b·* basis and sure foundation
	154– 5	reaching out their *b·* shelter
	224–24	charity *b·* enough to cover
	253– 8	platform is not *b·* enough for me,
Ret.	4–11	a *b·* picturesque view of the
	4–13	*b·* fields of bending grain
Pul.	42–27	* fastened with a *b·* ribbon bow.
	48– 6	* *b·* piazza on the south side
No.	32–14	cleaves sin with a *b·* battle-axe.
Po.	71– 9	Spans our *b·* heaven of light.
My.	46– 2	* foyer and *b·* stairways,
	68–28	* seven *b·* marble stairways,
	194– 2	Christianity writes in *b·* facts
	245– 6	on a *b·* and liberal basis.
	338–21	unfamiliar with his *b·* views

broadcast

My.	129– 6	Christianity sown *b·*

broaden

Ret.	52– 3	seeking to *b·* its channels

broadened

Ret.	82– 1	lessons are changed, modified, *b·*,
Pan.	10–16	wonderfully *b·* and brightened

broader

Mis.	2–16	deeper and *b·* philosophy

broader

Mis.	136– 6	*b·* and higher views,
	174–13	*b·* than the solar system
	191–32	accept the Scriptures in their *b·*,
Ret.	52–10	the *b·* wants of humanity,

broke

Mis.	111– 6	net has been so full that it *b·* :
Ret.	27–24	Science first *b·* upon my sense,
	45– 2	A new light *b·* in upon it,
Pul.	10–13	*b·* their exalted purpose,
'02.	18–10	who *b·* not the bruised reed
My.	258–10	one word, "Mary," *b·* the gloom

broken

Mis.	111–14	it would not have *b·*.
	224– 7	*b·* the head of his statue
	282–11	would have our houses *b·* open
	285–25	notifies the public of *b·* vows.
	386–19	o'er thy *b·* household band,
Chr.	53–57	no *b·* wing, no moan,
Ret.	60– 4	defines life as a *b·* sphere,
Un.	61–26	the *b·* and contrite heart
Pul.	22–17	doctrinal barriers . . . are *b·*,
	56–21	* We tread upon life's *b·* laws,
	80–14	* fairly *b·* our mental teeth
	83– 9	* a million of *b·* pledges.
Po.	50– 3	o'er thy *b·* household band,
My.	44– 3	* shackles of sin are being *b·*,
	53–30	* must have been very much *b·*
	80– 7	* when having *b·* bones set ;
	232–17	to be *b·* through." — *Luke* 12 : 39.
	257– 2	alas for the *b·* household band !
	318–30	"you have *b·* our agreement.

broken-hearted

Mis.	296–13	binding up the wounds of the *b·*,
No.	43–14	* binding up the *b·*,
My.	132–29	It binds up the *b·* ;

Bronx

My.	363– 8	CHRISTIAN SCIENCE SOCIETY, *B·*,

bronze

Mis.	305–21	* silver, *b·*, copper, and nickel
My.	68–29	* *b·*, marble, and Bedford stone.
	68–31	* *B·* is used in the lighting fixtures,
	69– 2	* the eight *b·* chains,

brood

Mis.	152– 9	*b·* unconsciously o'er the work of
	254– 9	nest of the raven's callow *b·* !
	331–12	dove feeds her callow *b·*,
	356–21	nests of the raven's callow *b·*.
	387– 8	*B·* o'er us with Thy shelt'ring
Po.	6– 1	*B·* o'er us with Thy shelt'ring
	24–17	The barren *b·*, O call

brooded

Mis.	254– 5	love which *b·* tireless
	342–14	darkness profound *b·* over

brooding

Mis.	172–10	charity, *b·* over all,
My.	86– 6	* *b·* elevation, guarding as it were,
	275–27	charity *b·* over all,

brook

'02.	18–19	like the summer *b·*, soon gets dry.
My.	129–12	bird, *b·*, blossom, breeze,

brooklet

Mis.	329–30	*b·* sings melting murmurs
Ret.	27–22	like the *b·* in its meandering
Pan.	3–13	lyre of bird and *b·*.

brooklets

Mis.	395–24	languid *b·* yield their sighs,
Ret.	4–19	*b·*, beautiful wild flowers,
Po.	58– 9	languid *b·* yield their sighs,

BROOKLINE
Mass.

My.	142–23	Box G, *B·*, MASS., June 24, 1908.
	143– 6	*B·*, MASS., June 5, 1909.
	144–10	Box G, *B·*, MASS., June 7, 1909.
	168– 9	Box G, *B·*, MASS., April 12, 1909.
	208– 8	Box G, *B·*, MASS., July 15, 1909.
	208–21	Box G, *B·*, MASS., November 2, 1909.
	237–19	*B·*, MASS., December 24, 1909.
	263–10	Box G, *B·*, MASS., December 25, 1909.
	275– 9	*B·*, MASS., May 1, 1908.
	275–29	Box G, *B·*, MASS., May 15, 1908.
	351–29	Box G, *B·*, MASS., June 24, 1908.
	352–24	Box G, *B·*, MASS., October 12, 1908.
	353– 4	Box G, *B·*, MASS., November 16, 1908.
	354–11	Box G, *B·*, MASS., April 28, 1909.
	358–27	Box G, *B·*, MASS., July 12, 1909.
	359–14	*B·*, MASS., October 12, 1909.
	360– 5	*B·*, MASS., July 23, 1909.
	360–26	*B·*, MASS., November 13, 1909.
	361–13	*B·*, MASS., December 11, 1909.

Brooklyn
N. Y.
   My. 183–17   chapter sub-title

   My. 363– 5   First Church of Christ, . . . *B·*,
         363– 6   Fourth Church of Christ, . . . *B·*,

Brooklyn (N. Y.) Eagle
   My. 88–26   *[B· (N. Y.) E·]*

brooks
   No. 1– 8   babbling *b·* fill the rivers
   Hea. 10–26   hart panteth for the water *b·*,

brother (*see also* **brother's**)
   Mis. 50–30   and helping our *b·* man.
       129– 4   or to condemn his *b·* without cause,
       129– 7   forgive his *b·* and love his enemies.
      129–10   tell thy *b·* his fault
      151–18   *B·*, sister, beloved in the Lord,
      254–11   when *b·* slays *b·*,
      353–13   My *b·* was a manufacturer ;
      353–17   When my *b·* returned and saw it,
      387–16   Like *b·* birds, that soar and sing,
   Man. 64–21   a tender term such as sister or *b·*.
   Chr. 55–24   the same is my *b·*, — *Matt.* 12 : 50.
   Ret. 4– 3   and with his *b·*, James Baker,
       4– 8   *b·* of the Hon. Henry Moore Baker
       6–11   my second *b·*, Albert Baker,
       6–15   My *b·* Albert was graduated at
       7– 5   wrote of my *b·* as follows :
      10– 8   From my *b·* Albert I received
      10–10   My *b·* studied Hebrew
      19–21   directions to his *b·* masons
   Pul. 9– 9   *b·* whose appliances warm this house,
   Po. 6– 4   Like *b·* birds, that soar and sing,
      10– 1   Hail, *b·* ! fling thy banner
      10–14   List, *b·* ! angels whisper
   page 23   poem
   My. 46–24   * Christly love of God and our *b·*,
      296–10   lamented Christian Scientist *b·*
      310– 4   My *b·* Albert was a distinguished
      310– 9   my youngest *b·*, George . . . Baker,
      310–15   My oldest *b·*, Samuel D. Baker,
      312–13   * she was met . . . by her *b·* George.
      330–32   directions to his *b·* Masons
      336– 4   * her *b·*, George S. Baker,
      337– 3   Hail, *b·* ! fling thy banner
      337–15   List, *b·* ! angels whisper
      338–11   last lecture of our dear *b·*,

brotherhood
   Mis. 56–20   and the *b·* of man.
      318– 3   universal *b·* of man
      348– 7   help on the *b·* of men.
   Ret. 49–26   uniting them in one common *b·*.
   Peo. 13–10   *b·* of man in unity of Mind
   My. 85–27   * spirit of faith and *b·*
      220–16   I pray . . . for the *b·* of man,
      240– 2   one God and the *b·* of man
      265–10   *b·* of man should be established,
      279–18   will establish the *b·* of man,
      280– 9   * universal, loving *b·* on earth
      281–10   On this basis the *b·* of all peoples
      339– 3   cement the bonds of Christian *b·*,

brotherliness
   Man. 40–10   in true *b·*, charitableness, and

brotherly
   Mis. 149–22   Christianity, *b·* love, and
   Man. 77–19   wisdom, economy, and *b·* love
   '00. 14–14   signifies "*b·* love." — *Heb.* 13 : 1.
   My. 41–20   * *b·* love which is just and kind
      153– 9   the church of *b·* love,
      175–26   Let *b·* love continue.
      196– 6   "city of *b·* love."
      213– 2   *b·* love, spiritual growth and

brother's
   Mis. 131– 8   console this *b·* necessity by
   My. 329–14   * and of her *b·* letter,

brothers
   Mis. 142–28   I longed to say to the masonic *b·* :
      167–16   Who are his parents, *b·*, and
   Ret. 6–10   my much respected parents, *b·*, and
      13– 7   if my *b·* and sisters were to be
      14–16   with my *b·* and sisters,
   Pul. 9– 4   *B·* of the C. S. Board of Directors,
      32–28   * One of her *b·*, Albert Baker,
   My. 5– 6   the murderers of their *b·* !
      62– 8   * give it to my *b·* and sisters
      217– 3   help your parents, *b·*, or sisters.
      335– 9   * beloved by his *b·* and companions,

brought
   Mis. 3–13   *b·* to the understanding through
      56–18   that shall be *b·* to desolation.
      75–31   *b·* forth by human thought,
      79–27   *persons b· before the courts*
      89– 3   *b·* to desolation." — *Matt.* 12 : 25.

brought
   Mis. 98–10   *b·* us together to minister and to
      112–22   * visitors have *b·* to him bouquets,
      112–23   * you have *b·* what will do him good."
      136– 8   *b·* to your earnest consideration,
      170– 3   resurrection and life immortal are *b·*
      201– 6   Sin *b·* death ;
      211–18   pitied and *b·* back to life
      214–14   The very conflict his Truth *b·*,
      217–26   shall be *b·* to desolation.
      231–27   *b·* sunshine to every heart.
      237–12   *b·* to realize how impossible it is
      374–18   To him who *b·* a great light
   Man. 66–16   *b·* before a meeting of this Church,
   Ret. 2–11   With them they *b·* to New England
      20– 2   except what money I had *b·*
      72– 9   *b·* into desolation, — *Psal.* 73 : 19.
   Un. 57–17   gospel of suffering *b·* life
      59–11   the divine idea *b·* to the flesh
   Pul. 13–28   *b·* forth the man child. — *Rev.* 12 : 13.
      49–16   I had them *b·* here in warm weather,
      51–20   * it may, . . . have *b·* a benefit.
      56–15   * *b·* hope and comfort to many
      63–12   "I had them *b·* here in warm weather,
      76–16   * *b·* from the Arctic regions,
      80–24   * it has *b·* a hopeful spirit into
      83–29   * She *b·* to warring men the
   No. 5–22   *b·* to desolation ;" — *Luke* 11 : 17.
      33–17   the glory his sacrifice *b·*
   Pan. 5–25   *b·* sin, sickness, and death
   '01. 1–17   have *b·* you hither.
   '02. 6– 7   *b·* death into the world
      16– 2   *b·* to me Wyclif's translation of
   Hea. 12–18   power of thought *b·* to bear on
   My. 14– 2   *b·* their tithes into His storehouse.
      28–29   * who has *b·* to the world the
      43–12   * *b·* them into the promised land,
      43–25   * has *b·* us to this hour.
      50–20   * *b·* fresh courage to the
      95–10   * has *b·* that cheerful and
      100– 1   * *b·* out in connection with the
      104–27   What was it that *b·* together this
      137–25   before . . . proceedings were *b·*
      138– 6   This suit was *b·* without my
      149–32   canst be *b·* into no condition,
      184–18   *b·* back to me the odor of
      187–24   *b·* into the light and liberty of
      188– 9   *b·* out of the city of David,
      336–13   except what money I had *b·* with me ;
      343–18   It *b·* down a shower of abuse
      343–29   *b·* all back to union and love
   (*see also* **light**)

brow
   Mis. 210–25   the shameless *b·* of licentiousness,
      225–21   whereon lay the lad with burning *b·*,
      325–15   Robust forms, with manly *b·*
      339–20   added one furrow to the *b·* of care?
      340– 3   has torn the laurel from many a *b·*
      374–26   * "Helen's beauty in a *b·* of Egypt."
      386–22   kissed my cold *b·*,
      392– 3   Clouds to adorn thy *b·*,
   Chr. 53–44   Crowns the pale *b·*.
   Pul. 48–15   * on the *b·* of Bow hill,
      83–25   * royalty which shines from her *b·*.
   '02. 3–22   on the *b·* of good King Edward,
   Po. 20– 3   Clouds to adorn thy *b·*,
      23– 2   a shadow on thy *b·*
      50– 8   kissed my cold *b·*,
   My. 201–14   bleeding *b·* of our blessed Lord,

Brown, George T.
   Mis. 242–27   George T. *B·*, pharmacist,

brown
   My. 342–13   * blue-gray or grayish *b·*,

Browning
   Elizabeth Barrett
   Pul. 39– 8   * signature _____

bruise
   Mis. 336– 5   handle the serpent and *b·* its head ;
   Un. 45– 3   *B·* the head of this serpent,

bruised
   Mis. 275– 9   *b·* father bendeth his aching head ;
   Un. 55– 7   "He was *b·* for *our* — *Isa.* 53 : 5.
   No. 34–23   Love *b·* and bleeding,
   '02. 18–10   who broke not the *b·* reed

brush
   Mis. 373– 6   Soul's expression through the *b·*;
      377– 2   should move our *b·* or pen
   Po. 53– 4   Bring with thee *b·* and breeze.

brushed
   My. 92– 7   * Science cannot be *b·* aside by

brutality
   '02. 19– 1   treachery, and *b·* that he received.

brute
   Ret.   69– 1   His origin is not, . . . in *b·* instinct,
   Pul.   53–19   * above the level of the *b·*,

brute-force
   Mis.   41– 1   *b·* that only the cruel and evil can

bubbles
   Mis.   328–10   to burst the *b·* of earth

bucket
   Mis.   353–15   to pour a *b·* of water

buckler
   '02.   19–13   his shield and his *b·*.

bud
   Mis.   142– 3   to *b·* and blossom as the rose !
         389– 1   form the *b·* for bursting bloom,
   Chr.   53–31   Sharon's rose must *b·* and bloom
   Po.   21–15   form the *b·* for bursting bloom,
        53– 3   The *b·*, the leaf and wing

budded
   Pul.   22–21   *b·* and blossomed as the rose.

Buddha
   My.   118–25   The doctrine of *B·*,

Buddhism
   '02.   3–5   *B·* and Shintoism are said to be
   My.   119–11   towards *B·* or any other "ism."

budding
   Mis.   330–18   arranging . . . each *b·* thought.
   Man.   104– 8   adapted to form the *b·* thought

buds
   Ret.   18–10   beauty and perfume from *b·*
   Po.   63–20   beauty and perfume from *b·*
   My.   125– 6   and to vivify the *b·*,

Buffalo
   N. Y.
   Pul.   89– 4   * *News, B·,* N. Y.

   Pul.   56– 2   * New York, Chicago, *B·,* Cleveland,

buffetings
   Mis.   228–11   the *b·* of envy or malice

bugle-call
   Rud.   2–24   *b·* to thought and action,

build
   Mis.   5–16   There is nothing to *b·* upon.
       43–24   to *b·* on the downfall of others.
       98–19   *b·* up, through God's right hand,
      133– 4   to *b·* a sentence of so few words
      135–13   though you should *b·* to the heavens,
      135–13   you would *b·* on sand.
      144–19   I will *b·* my church ; — *Matt.* 16 : 18.
      176–18   to *b·* upon the rock of Christ,
      263– 7   I will *b·* my church;" — *Matt.* 16 : 18.
      264– 5   They *b·* for time and eternity.
      298–15   To *b·* on selfishness is to *b·* on sand.
      309– 8   unfitness for fable or fact to *b·* upon.
   Ret.   48– 8   should *b·* on his own foundation,
      52– 4   to *b·* a hedge round about it
   Un.   64– 5   To *b·* the individual spiritual
   Pul.   8–12   helping to *b·* The Mother Church.
      49–22   * *b·* a substantial home that should
   No.   12–16   *b·* on the new-born conception of
      43–19   *b·* a baseless fabric of their own
   '02.   2–14   The wise builders will *b·* on the
      13–13   on which to *b·* The First Church
   Peo.   11– 9   let us *b·* another staging for
   Po.   53–14   And *b·* their cozy nests,
   My.   13–18   with which to *b·* an ample temple
      13–24   to *b·* a temple
      48–21   * will certainly *b·* such truth as
      65– 8   * to *b·* in this city a church
      77–28   * to *b·* the imposing edifice
      98–19   * all of the funds required to *b·* it
     112– 7   and *b·* on its chief corner-stone.
     157– 6   * to *b·* a beautiful church edifice
     162–16   "This man began to *b·*, — *Luke* 14 : **30.**
     162–29   may it *b·* upon the rock of ages
     165–30   the means that *b·* to the heavens,
     187–26   *b·* a house unto Him whose name
     192– 1   Ye *b·* not to an unknown God.
     195–25   its united efforts to *b·* an edifice
     195–30   continue to *b·*, rebuild, adorn, and
     357–13   desire to *b·* higher,
     357–18   as they *b·* upon the rock of Christ,

builded
   Mis.   244– 1   *b·* up the woman." — *Gen.* 2 : 21.
   My.   24–10   * *b·* by the prayers and offerings of

builder (God)
   Ret.   48– 9   the one *b·* and maker, God,

builder
   My.   16–20   * the *b·* of the new edifice.
      63– 2   * services of Mr. Whitcomb as *b·*
     162–20   would say to the *b·* of the

builders
   Mis.   5–20   stone that the *b·* have rejected,
     196–24   stone which the *b·* — *Psal.* 118 : 22.
   Man.   18– 1   stone which the *b·* — *Matt.* 21 : 42.
   Pul.   10–19   stone which the *b·* — *Matt.* 21 : 42.
     65–17   * its *b·* call it their "prayer in
   No.   38–13   rock which the *b·* rejected ;
   '00.   5–23   which the *b·* reject for a season ;
   '01.   25– 6   stone which the *b·* reject
   '02.   2–14   The wise *b·* will build on the stone
   Hea.   3– 9   stone which the *b·* rejected
   My.   25–23   *b·* of this church edifice,
     60–12   * stone which the *b·* — *Matt.* 21 : **42.**
     71– 3   * discoveries of organ *b·*
     129–20   stone which the *b·* — *Matt.* 21 : 42.
     145– 4   one of Concord's best *b·*
     188– 1   stone which the *b·* rejected
     202–14   on the *b·* of this beautiful temple,
     301– 9   a foundation for the *b·*.

Building
   (*see* **Mother Church**)

building (noun)
   ample
   My.   10– 9   * in a beautiful, ample *b·*,
   beauty of the
   My.   24–23   * The beauty of the *b·*,
   box
   My.   309–23   * a small, square box *b·*
   brick
   My.   66– 2   * a four-story brick *b·* also in the
   burning
   Mis.   283–10   to break into a burning *b·*
   My.   178–22   on a table in a burning *b·*.
   church
   Pul.   30–29   * its own magnificent church *b·*,
   My.   27–15   * the completion of the church *b·*,
     60–26   * dedication of our new church *b·*,
     173–15   beautify our new church *b·*
     174– 1   lawn surrounding their church *b·*,
     175– 7   in repairing your church *b·*.
     208–19   prospect of erecting a church *b·*,
     284–14   service . . . held in my church *b·*,
     284–22   to assemble in my church *b·*,
   College
   Mis.   249–15   to remain in my College *b·*
   cost of the
   My.   76– 8   * the entire cost of the *b·*,
   land and
   Mis.   140– 1   provisions for the land and *b·*
   Mother Church
   My.   357–11   crowned The Mother Church *b·*
   new
   My.   11–24   * the new *b·* will be erected,
     16– 9   * the site of the new *b·*.
     72–25   * subscribed for the new *b·*,
   same
   Man.   27–21   located in the same *b·*,
   My.   123–12   rooms in the same *b·*.
   size of the
   My.   11–26   * The size of the *b·* was decided
   size of this
   My.   69–27   * an idea of the size of this *b·*
   some
   My.   55– 5   * to obtain by purchase some *b·*,
   such a
   My.   22– 8   * adequate to erect such a *b·*
   suitable
   Man.   27–13   suitable *b·* for the publication of
   this
   Mis.   141– 6   This *b·* begun, will go up,
     144– 4   northeast corner of this *b·*,
   My.   28–17   * The significance of this *b·*
     89–13   * remarkable thing in this *b·*
   within the
   My.   69–12   * Everywhere within the *b·*

   ———

   Pul.   57– 2   * The *b·* is fire-proof,
     57– 9   * the significance of the *b·*,
   My.   24– 5   * congratulate you that the *b·* is to
     24–20   * erection of the *b·* is proceeding
     24–29   * *b·* with a seating capacity of
     28– 2   * the completion of the *b·*
     61– 2   * been in the *b·* part of every
     61– 7   * seemed impossible for the *b·* to be
     65–13   * why the *b·* was needed.
     68– 7   * dome surmounting the *b·*
     69–31   * From this point the *b·* and dome
     83–25   * even before the *b·* itself has
     87– 2   * greater than the *b·* could contain.
     89– 5   * The *b·* is of light stone,
     96–18   * The *b·* they were . . . to dedicate
     100– 8   * were present in the *b·*,
     359–21   * then occupied offices in the *b·*

building (adj.)
Man. 75–20 the balance of the *b·* funds,
76– 1 *b·* funds, which can be spared
My. 11–29 date for commencing *b·* operations.
14–25 * *b·* operations have been commenced,
19–14 * their local church *b·* funds
(*see also* **fund**)

building (ppr.)
Mis. 141–26 to commence *b·* our church
143–24 toward *b·* The Mother Church.
144– 3 money for *b·* "Mother's Room,"
230–18 in *b·* air-castles or floating off
263–10 *b·* on His foundation,
Ret. 51– 4 *b·* on the premises
Pul. 44–21 * *b·* a church by voluntary
64– 6 * funds for the *b·* of a new church,
'01. 25– 3 *B·* on the rock of Christ's
My. v– 4 * stirring times of church *b·*,
21– 6 * *b·* church homes of their own,
28–12 * to the *b·* of this church.
57–11 * *b·* a suitable edifice
67–18 * for the *b·* of this addition
85–16 * the *b·* of a church structure
88–29 * the *b·* of a great church
98–17 * for the *b·* of the church
158– 1 in *b·* a granite church
162–13 applied to *b·*, embellishing,
192–29 *b·* for you a house
321– 1 * *b·* this church for your followers.

Building Committee
Man. 102– 3 *B· C·*.
102– 4 There shall be a *B· C·*

Building Fund (*see also* **fund**)
Mis. 140–15 contributions to the *B· F·*
143–26 in aid of our Church *B· F·*,
My. 23–10 * *B· F·* : Amount on hand
27–10 * chapter sub-title
27–18 * *Treasurer of the B· F·*.

Buildings and **buildings**
Man. 27–11 Publishing *B·*.
75–19 aforesaid premises and *b·*,
Pul. 45– 7 * get their *b·* finished on time,
48– 1 * slopes behind the *b·*,
57–12 * one of the most beautiful *b·*
62–21 * concert halls, and public *b·*,
My. 90– 2 * *b·* should be filled at every
236– 1 history of our church *b·*.

builds
Mis. 5–19 *b·* on the stone that the
41–19 Mind is the architect that *b·*
Hea. 1– 9 *b·* on less than an immortal basis,
Peo. 9– 2 *b·* on Spirit, not matter ;
My. 164–27 It *b·* upon the rock,
194–10 *b·* that which reaches heaven.
195–27 unselfed love that *b·* without

built
Mis. 131–11 being *b·* upon the rock
140–22 on which our church was to be *b·*
140–28 *B·* on the rock, our church
149–29 *b·* the first temple for C. S. worship
319–22 Our church edifice must be *b·* in 1894.
349–23 and *b·* up the church,
383–10 and *b·* upon the rock of Christ.
Man. 19– 2 is designed to be *b·* on the Rock,
75–20 After the first church was *b·*,
103– 7 the site where it was *b·*,
Ret. 15– 5 *b·* on the basis of C. S.,
Un. 9–16 but have *b·* instead upon the sand
10– 4 *b·* on Him as the sole cause.
28–15 material theories are *b·* on the
53–16 not *b·* on such false foundations,
Pul. 9– 7 May the altar you have *b·*
24–22 * church is *b·* of Concord granite
40–15 * ROOM WHICH THE CHILDREN *B·*
63– 6 * RECENTLY *B·* IN HER HONOR
63–26 * *b·* as "a testimonial to our
77–13 * *b·* as a testimonial to Truth,
78–11 * *b·* as a testimonial to Truth,
85– 9 * *b·* up in human consciousness
No. 38–10 on which he *b·* his Church
'00. 5–22 On this rock C. S. is *b·*.
Hea. 1– 9 whoso builds on . . . hath *b·* on sand.
2–26 magnifies his name who *b·*, on Truth,
11– 9 immortal superstructure is *b·* on
My. 15– 8 from the site where it was *b·*,
17–11 *b·* up a spiritual house,— *I Pet. 2 : 5.*
23–26 * is being *b·* in our day ;
66–30 * has such a grand church been *b·*
67–28 * it is so proportionately *b·*
68– 1 * *B·* in the Italian Renaissance style,
68–14 * old church . . . *b·* twelve years ago,
71– 9 * *b·* the C. S. cathedral.
95– 4 * church which has been *b·* upon the
95–12 * They have *b·* a huge church,

built
My. 97–27 * *b·* at a cost of two million dollars,
99–14 * *b·* a splendid cathedral in Boston,
157–14 * The church will be *b·* of the
172– 3 * It was *b·* in 1761,
184–10 having *b·* First Church of Christ,
187–30 you have *b·* this house
188– 4 house, which thou hast *b·*,—*I Kings 9 : 3.*
302–25 The Mother Church after it was *b·* and

bullet
My. 277–10 A *b·* in a man's heart never
293–11 feared that the *b·* would

Bulletin
Pul. 88–26 * *B·*, Auburn, N. Y.
89–25 * *B·*, San Francisco, Cal.

bulwark
Mis. 145– 2 *b·* of civil and religious liberty.

bulwarks
Pul. 9– 2 you are the *b·* of freedom,

bumper
Mis. 232– 2 in a *b·* of pudding-sauce

Bunker Hill
Mis. 304–11 * Then it will go to *B· H·*
My. 45–31 * loftier than the *B· H·* monument,

buoyancy
Mis. 371–24 with Truth, to give it *b·*.

buoyant
My. 110–16 *b·* with liberty and the luxury of

burden
Mis. 130–18 borne the *b·* in the heat of
327–18 *b·* them with their own.
Ret. 86–20 undertakes to carry his *b·*
Un. 47– 1 Jesus assumed the *b·* of disproof
Pan. 12–15 lifteth the *b·* of sharp experience
'00. 9–29 "bear the *b·* — *see Matt. 20 : 12.*
My. 120– 9 Bear with me the *b·* of discovery
138– 3 relieved of the *b·* of doing this.
158–18 *b·* of proof that C. S. is
161–29 "My *b·* is light." — *Matt. 11 : 30.*

burdened
Mis. 112– 5 ages are *b·* with material modes.
251–22 who, *b·* for an hour,
328–16 *b·* by pride, sin, and self,
'02. 19–16 To the *b·* and weary, Jesus saith :
Po. 31–15 Nor *b·* bliss, but Truth and Love
My. 162–32 *b·* with beauty, pointing to the

burdens
Mis. 39–23 bear "one another's *b·*, — *Gal. 6 : 2.*
133–29 Love makes all *b·* light,
262–25 yet were our *b·* heavy but for
312– 7 speechless and alone, bears all *b·*,
320–14 calms man's fears, bears his *b·*,
351– 2 to lift the *b·* imposed by
374–19 and named his *b·* light,
397– 2 sweet mercies show Life's *b·* light.
Ret. 87–23 They feel their own *b·* less,
87–24 bear the weight of others' *b·*,
Pul. 18–11 sweet mercies show Life's *b·* light.
Peo. 11–25 "bind heavy *b·*," — *Matt. 23 : 4.*
Po. 12–11 sweet mercies show Life's *b·* light.
27–21 Thou hast borne *b·*,
My. 44– 3 * heavy *b·* are being laid down,
223–27 *b·* that time will remove.

burdensome
'02. 10–21 discharges *b·* baggage,

Burgess
Un. 14–10 as *B·*, the boatbuilder, remedies

burial
Mis. 201– 9 reproduced his body after its *b·*,
Man. 50– 3 shall be prepared for *b·* by
Ret. 2–25 death and *b·* of George Washington.
40–13 clothes already prepared for her *b·* ;
'02. 17– 2 knells tolling the *b·* of Christ.
My. 312–11 * received a decent *b·*.

buried
Mis. 78– 1 Life, God, is not *b·* in matter.
168– 9 *b·* in dogmas and physical ailments,
212–31 and *b·* it out of their sight.
393–15 When the *b·* Master hails us
Ret. 21– 2 that his mother was dead and *b·*.
66– 4 no longer *b·* in materiality.
Un. 62–26 matter, is all that can be *b·*
63– 2 The I AM was neither *b·* nor
No. 37–24 *b·* in a false sense of being.
'02. 18–25 and it should be *b·*.
Peo. 5–13 The right ideal is not *b·*,
Po. 51–20 When the *b·* Master hails us
My. 110– 4 *b·* above-ground in material sense.
159–15 The infinite will not be *b·* in
160–11 dead truisms which can be *b·*
164–18 *b·* in the depths of the unseen,

buried
My. 203–25 and *b·* . . . in the bosom of earth
275–14 is dead, and should be *b·.*

burlesque
My. 278–25 *b·* of uncivil economics.

Burlington, Iowa
Pul. 89–30 * *Gazette, B·, I·.*

burn
Mis. 145– 8 Does a single bosom *b·* for fame
Hea. 11–13 *b·* upon the altars of to-day ;
My. 160–31 Only the makers of hell *b·* in their fire.
256–23 the Yule-fires *b·,*

burned
Mis. 214–30 before they can be *b·,*
'00. 12–15 temple was *b·* on the night that
12–22 books in that city were publicly *b·.*
My. 48–26 * *b·* indelibly upon the mind of
178–25 covers of the book were *b·* up,
332–28 * where they were *b·* ;

Burnham, Rev. Abraham
'01. 32– 1 Rev. Abraham *B·* of Pembroke, N. H.,

burning
Mis. 92–11 his own lamp trimmed and *b·.*
225–21 with *b·* brow, moaning in pain.
276–25 their lamps trimmed and *b·*
283–10 right to break into a *b·* building
335–25 get out of a *b·* house,
Ret. 13–18 as she bathed my *b·* temples,
84– 8 his own lamp trimmed and *b·.*
Un. 34–16 yet put your finger on a *b·* coal,
Pul. 26–28 * which will be kept always *b·*
39–15 * The sunset, *b·* low,
59– 1 * perpetually *b·* in her honor ;
My. 125–28 Are our lamps trimmed and *b·*?
160–26 *b·* in torture until the sinner is
178–22 on a table in a *b·* building.

burnished
My. 171–27 * bound with *b·* brass.

burnishing
Mis. 343–16 *b·* anew the hidden gems of Love,

burns
My. 249–12 heat of hate *b·* the wheat,

burnt
Mis. 51– 3 *B·* offerings and drugs,

burst
Mis. 283–11 but wrong to *b·* open doors
326– 6 The door is *b·* open,
328–10 to *b·* the bubbles of earth with
376–18 *b·* through the lattice
Ret. 18–10 perfume from buds *b·* away,
No. 27– 7 will *b·* upon us in the similitude of
28– 5 will *b·* the barriers of sense,
'02. 19– 2 as he *b·* the bonds of the tomb
Po. 63–20 perfume from buds *b·* away,
My. 202–15 *b·* upon the spiritual sense of
318–24 and, addressing me, *b·* out with :

bursting
Mis. 178– 8 into old bottles without *b·* them,
389– 1 To form the bud for *b·* bloom,
'00. 12– 2 *b·* paraphrases projected from
Po. 3–13 Till *b·* bonds our spirits part
21–15 To form the bud for *b·* bloom,
My. 81– 7 * *b·* with a desire to testify to
162–32 *b·* into the rapture of song

bury
Mis. 129–13 dead *b·* their dead,'' — *Matt.* 8 : 22.
169–30 dead *b·* their dead ; — *Matt.* 8 : 22.
292–16 It calls loudly on them to *b·* the
311– 9 so, *b·* the dead past ;
Man. 60–18 dead *b·* their dead,'' — *Matt.* 8 : 22.
Ret. 87– 1 dead *b·* their dead ; — *Matt.* 8 : 22.
'01. 16–12 Then let the dead *b·* its dead,
'02. 9– 5 dead *b·* their dead ;'' — *Matt.* 8 : 22.
My. 353–25 dead *b·* their dead,'' — *Matt.* 8 : 22.

burying-ground
My. 333–13 * from thence to the Episcopal *b·,*

busier
Mis. 7– 5 mother of one child is often *b·*

busiest
'00. 2–21 are my *b·* workers ;

Business
(see **Committee on Business**)

business
assigned
Man. 79–10 the *b·* assigned to them
authority for
Man. 66–18 referred to as authority for *b·,*
conduct the
Man. 79–23 and conduct the *b·* of
Father's
Mis. 163–31 forever about the Father's *b·* ;

business
God's
Mis. 140–13 but this was God's *b·,*
her own
My. 276–11 she is minding her own *b·,*
his
Mis. 69–19 he attended to his *b·.*
Man. 46–10 leaflets, which advertise his *b·*
his own
My. 106–23 because he minds his own *b·*
large
Ret. 7–16 * practice of a very large *b·.*
My. 310–15 carried on a large *b·* in Boston,
lucrative
'00. 2–22 will leave a lucrative *b·*
man of
Mis. 147–23 the conscientious man of *b·,*
Master's
'01. 32– 9 busy about their Master's *b·,*
matters of
'02. 12–21 interpolate some matters of *b·*
My. 7– 4 interpolate some matters of *b·*
much
My. 309– 4 called upon to do much *b·*
my
My. 358–22 through whom all my *b·* is
of others
Mis. 348– 5 the books nor the *b·* of others ;
other
Man. 56–20 electing officers and other *b·,*
57– 2 transaction of such other *b·*
other people's
Mis. 357– 1 trafficking in other people's *b·,*
profits of the
Man. 80– 5 profits of the *b·* shall be paid
regular
My. 8–16 * accommodation for the regular *b·*
such
Man. 79– 6 such *b·* as Mrs. Eddy,
your own
Mis. 283–14 * "Mind your own *b·,*"

Mis. 13– 4 special care to mind my own *b·.*
141–22 rule this *b·* transaction,
252–28 encourages and empowers the *b·* man
Man. 27– 1 The *b·* of The Mother Church
70– 3 nor enter into a *b·* transaction with
Ret. 19– 8 He was in Wilmington, . . . on *b·,*
Pul. 59–22 * *b·* manager of the Publishing Society,
'02. 13– 8 *b·* of The C. S. Publishing Society
My. 8–25 * convened in annual *b·* meeting
23–19 * in annual *b·* meeting assembled,
30–12 * *b·* men come from far distant points
49–15 * first *b·* meeting of the church was
50–31 * *b·* committee met after the services
53–25 * annual report of the *b·* committee
62–27 * by the members of the *b·* committee,
65– 3 * largest church *b·* meeting
81–32 * hard-headed shrewd *b·* men.
96– 6 * in the social and *b·* world,
106–26 dishonest politician or *b·* man?
137–28 as to honesty and *b·* capacity.
312–19 While on a *b·* trip to Wilmington,
330–18 * who died there while on *b·*

Buskirk's, Hon. Clarence A.
My. 296– 1 chapter sub-title

bustle
Mis. 316–20 my retirement from life's *b·.*
Po. 16–11 *b·* and toil for its pomp and its pride.

busy
Mis. 231– 7 made *b·* many appetites ;
392–22 To my *b·* mem'ry bringing
Ret. 4–13 But change has been *b·.*
Un. 26–13 * Chance and change are *b·* ever,
Pul. 49–20 * get away from her *b·* career
'01. 32– 9 *b·* about their Master's business,
Po. 51– 4 To my *b·* mem'ry bringing
My. 75– 7 * Yesterday was a *b·* day at
187– 4 too *b·* to think of doing so
252– 3 Keep yourselves *b·* with divine Love.
338–17 owing to my *b·* life,

Busy Bees
Mis. 144– 6 a little band called *B· B·,*
Pul. 8–23 workers were called "*B· B·.*"
42–14 * are known . . . as the "*B· B·,*"
My. 169– 6 *B· B·,* under twelve years of age,
216–23 drop the insignia of "*B· B·,*"

busybody
Mis. 356–32 Humility is no *b·* :

butcher
Mis. 250– 7 a *b·* fattening the lamb

butchers
Mis. 123– 2 *b·* the helpless Armenians,

buttons
My. 83– 7 * wore tiny white, unmarked *b·*,

buy
Mis. 113– 9 "no man might *b·* — *Rev.* 13 : 17.
140–11 No one could *b·*, sell, or mortgage
149– 2 come ye, *b·*, and eat ; — *Isa.* 55 : 1.
149– 2 *b·* wine and milk — *Isa.* 55 : 1.
269–28 mortals to *b·* error at par value.
269–31 "no man might *b·* — *Rev.* 13 : 17.
342–24 *b·* for yourselves." — *Matt.* 25 : 9.
Man. 43–22 shall neither *b·*, sell, nor circulate
My. 334– 7 * that efforts are being made to *b·*
354– 8 under no obligation to *b·*

buyeth
Mis. 253– 1 all that he hath and *b·* it.
253– 1 *B·* it ! Note the scope

buying
Pul. 50– 5 * one of her motives in *b·*
My. 298– 2 request the privilege of *b·*,

By-Law and By-law
Mis. 131–16 that you waive the church *B·*
131–18 did not act under that *B·* ;
132– 3 had already accepted as a *B·*.
Man. 18–24 *B·* adopted March 17, 1903,
28– 9 hence the necessity of this *B·*
29– 8 to fulfil the requirements of this *B·*,
32–24 This *B·* applies to Readers in
37– 6 A member who violates this *B·*
43–17 This *B·* not only calls
44– 5 the spirit or letter of this *B·*
47–21 This *B·* applies to testimonials
51–18 unless a *B·* governing the case
65–18 Disobedience to this *B·* shall be
68–21 This *B·* takes effect on Dec. 15, 1908.
70– 2 shall not make a church *B·*,
99– 3 For the purposes of this *B·*,
99–15 This *B·* applies to all States except
105– 2 No new Tenet or *B·* shall be
105– 3 nor any Tenet or *B·* amended
My. 15– 2 chapter sub-title
230–11 each Rule and *B·* in this Manual
231–29 interesting report regarding the *B·*,

By-Law and By-law
My. 250– 2 The *B·* of The Mother Church
250– 8 adopt this *B·* in their churches,
250–12 churches who adopt this *B·*
250–15 The *B·* of The Mother Church
250–18 *B·* applies only to C. S. churches in
250–21 churches adopting this *B·*

By-Laws and by-laws
Mis. 132– 5 to the light of Love — and *B·*.
148– 8 Rules and *B·* in the Manual
382–25 wrote its constitution and *b·*,
382–26 the constitution and *b·* of
Man. 3– 3 Rules and *B·* in the Manual
18–22 Church Tenets, Rules, and *B·*,
18–26 *B·* pertaining to "Executive Members"
28– 6 annulling its Tenets and *B·*.
32–26 Enforcement of *B·*.
33– 4 enforce the discipline and *b·*
36– 3 Article VI, Sect. 2, of these *B·*.
39– 3 according to its *B·*.
50–22 Violation of *B·*.
50–23 found violating any of the *B·*
67–13 case not provided for in its *B·*
71–11 in its *B·* and self-government,
72– 5 A member . . . who obeys its *B·*
78– 2 comply with the *B·* of the Church.
78– 9 debts as are specified in its *B·*.
80–10 *B·* contained in this Manual.
87– 9 authorized by its *B·* to teach
92–24 Article XXVI of these *B·*
100–11 obligations . . . according to these *B·*,
100–15 in accordance with said *B·*.
105– 1 Amendment of *B·*.
My. 15– 4 * Article XLI . . . of the Church *B·*
49–14 * formulate the rules and *b·*,
223–23 breaking of one of the Church *B·*,
254–18 * preamble to our *B·*,
255– 6 publish the foregoing in their *B·*.
343–24 I made a code of *b·*,
358–30 approve the *B·* of The Mother Church,

bypaths
Mis. 169– 4 *b·* of ancient philosophies
No. 20–28 straying into forbidden *b·*

C

cabalistic
No. 9–22 *c·* insignia of philosophy ;

cabinet
My. 166–28 gift to me of a beautiful *c·*,

cable
'02. 11–13 a steam engine, a submarine *c·*,

cabled
My. 259– 6 received the following *c·* message :

Cablegram
My. 295–22 [Copy of *C·*]

cactus
Ret. 18– 4 While *c·* a mellower glory
Po. 63–12 While *c·* a mellower glory

Cæsar (see also Cæsar's)
Mis. 374–24 one renders not unto *C·*
Ret. 71– 5 "Render to *C·* the things — *Mark* 12 : 17.
'02. 14– 9 * not like *C·*, stained with blood,
Hea. 18–23 will cease to assert their *C·* sway
My. 220–10 'Render to *C·* the things — *Mark* 12 : 17.
248– 5 * not like *C·*, stained with blood,
344–25 'Render to *C·* the things — *Mark* 12 : 17.

Cæsar's
Mis. 374–25 things that are *C·* ;" — *Mark* 12 : 17.
376– 9 * taken by Fra Angelico from *C·* Cameo,
Ret. 71– 6 things that are *C·*, — *Mark* 12 : 17.
My. 220–10 things that are *C·*,' — *Mark* 12 : 17.
344–25 things that are *C·*.' — *Mark* 12 : 17.

cage
My. 126–27 *c·* of every unclean . . . bird" — *Rev.* 18 : 2.

Calais, Me.
Pul. 88–12 * *Advertiser, C·, M·*.

calamity
Mis. 347– 8 To escape from this *c·*
Ret. 7–23 * It is a public *c·*
71– 2 with the tax it raises on *c·*

calcareous
My. 108– 1 *c·* salts formed by carbonate and

calculated
'02. 1–15 Whatever seems *c·* to displace
My. 97–30 * *c·* to impress the most determined
327–15 * *c·* to limit or stop the

calculating
Hea. 4– 4 before *c·* the results of

calculation
Un. 10–21 attempt the *c·* of His mighty ways,
'01. 21–19 begins his *c·* erroneously ;

calculations
Mis. 376–19 According to terrestrial *c·*,

calculus
Mis. 22–11 infinite *c·* defining the line,
104–10 *c·* of forms and numbers.
'01. 22–20 infinite *c·* of the infinite God.

Calderon
Ret. 32–11 *C·*, the famous Spanish poet,

Caledonia
'02. 13–17 Falmouth and *C·* (now Norway) Streets ;

calendar
Mis. 117–23 According to my *c·*,

calf
Mis. 145–24 *c·* and the young lion and the
307–25 not intended for a golden *c·*,

California and Cal.
Man. 99– 3 State of *C·* shall be considered as
(*see also* **Los Angeles, Oakland, San Francisco, San Jose**)

call (noun)
accepted the
Man. 18– 6 accepted the *c·*, and was ordained
Ret. 16–19 She accepted the *c·*,
44– 7 I accepted the *c·*,
My. 49–32 * Mrs. Eddy accepted the *c·*.
came
Ret. 9–14 When the *c·* came again
Pul. 33– 9 * The *c·* came, but the little maid
33–11 * if the *c·* came again.
clarion
Mis. 120–16 the clarion *c·* of peace
Ret. 12– 1 nobler far than clarion *c·*
'01. 35– 8 a clarion *c·* to the reign of
Po. 60–21 nobler far than clarion *c·*
cooing
My. 341–12 A lightsome lay, a cooing *c·*,
expert
My. 172–19 your kind, expert *c·* on me."

call (noun)

extended a
Man.	18– 5	extended a c· to Mary Baker Eddy
Ret.	16–18	extended a c· to Mary B. G. Eddy
	44– 7	extended a c· to me

heart's
Po.	53–17	Come at the sad heart's c·,

His
Mis.	151– 2	their ears are attuned to His c·.

human
Mis.	81–26	answers the human c· for help ;
Un.	13– 4	coming at human c· ;

imperative
Mis.	273–32	the imperative c· is for my

imperious
Mis.	177– 1	solemn and imperious c·

kind
Pul.	87–12	kind c· to the pastorate of

Love's
My.	129–13	They come at Love's c·.

mysterious
Ret.	9–16	never again . . . was that mysterious c·

quiet
Mis.	143–25	A quiet c· from me for this extra

same
Ret.	8–19	the same c· was thrice repeated.

spiritual
My.	172–14	material symbol of my spiritual c·

that
My.	172–15	and this is that c· :

this
Mis.	99–14	Then obey this c·.
Man.	68– 7	or who declines to obey this c·

to lecture
Man.	96–10	a c· to lecture in a place where he

to serve
My.	42–14	* the c· to serve you in this

unexplained
My.	243–21	at my unexplained c·

Man.	57– 7	upon the c· of the Clerk.
	69–18	in obedience to the c·.
Ret.	8–15	the c· again came,
Pul.	8– 9	responded to the c· for this church
My.	118–12	In a c· upon my person,
	169–18	c· of about three thousand

call (verb)

Mis.	9–16	Whom we c· friends seem to
	26–23	this is just what I c· matter,
	44–20	You c· this body matter,
	83–20	Why did Jesus c· himself
	93– 3	posterity shall c· you blessed,
	98–24	and the world to acknowledge
	110–28	how fleeting is that which men c· great ;
	111–27	Let me specially c· the attention of
	121– 6	cup to which I c· your attention,
	131–28	when you c· on the members of the
	133– 8	I c· your attention and
	181– 1	Jesus said to c· no man father ;
	203–12	coaxed in their course to c· on me,
	221–31	or c· public attention to that crime?
	233– 5	c· themselves metaphysicians
	239– 1	C· at the . . . Metaphysical College,
	250–16	c· for active witnesses to prove it,
	258–20	and c· Mind by the name of matter,
	282–26	which may c· for aid unsought,
	282–29	The abuse which I c· attention to,
	287– 6	"C· no man your father — Matt. 23 : 9.
	317– 2	"May I c· you mother?"
	328– 4	will c· thee back to the path
	330– 9	should c· his race as gently
	368–13	who c· themselves so.
	380–11	c· for help impelled me to begin
	387– 3	To c· her home,
Man.	28–20	shall immediately c· a meeting
	53– 4	immediately to c· a meeting,
	57–16	before he can c· said meeting.
	69–14	c· on this Board for household help
	76– 4	as the right occasion may c· for it.
	84–20	shall not c· their pupils together,
	95– 5	Mother Church may c· on any member
	95–17	shall c· on the Board of Lectureship
Ret.	8– 9	"Mother, who did c· me?
	8–10	I heard somebody c· Mary,
	68–13	"c· no man your father — Matt. 23 : 9.
	69–11	into what I c· matter,
	84–22	posterity will c· him blessed,
Un.	10–28	and c· in vain for the mountains of
	32–16	which I prefer to c· mortal mind.
	32–26	which I c· mortal mind ;
	44–15	Human theories c·, or miscall,
	49–24	right to c· evil a negation,
	53– 5	would be truthful to c· itself a lie ;
	53–26	"C· no man your father — Matt. 23 : 9.
	60– 7	We c· God omnipotent and
Pul.	9–28	and c· down blessings infinite.

call (verb)

Pul.	38–17	* the belief we c· spiritualism.
	52–17	* We c· it new.
	62–13	* and c· forth all the purity
	65–17	* c· it their "prayer in stone,"
	79–24	* as much as his lungs c· for breath ;
	81–12	* dearest ones c· her "selfish"
Rud.	9–11	outcome of what I c· mortal mind,
	16–26	c· it their first-fruits,
Pan.	8–18	"C· no man your father — Matt. 23 : 9.
	11–26	are content to c· man,
'00.	3–22	to c· the divine name Yahwah,
	14–14	I c· your attention to this
'01.	7–18	c· their God "divine Principle,"
	10– 5	much more shall they c· — Matt. 10 : 25.
	18–26	Truth, Love — whom men c· God
	25–10	certain individuals c· aids to
'02.	10– 7	c· them false or in advance of the
Hea.	16–21	shall we c· that reliable evidence
Po.	16–22	And c· to my spirit
	24–17	O c· With song of morning lark ;
	41–17	Was it then thou didst c· them
	50–21	To c· her home,
My.	49–30	* to c· Mrs. Eddy to the pastorate
	50–32	* to c· a general meeting of the
	91–17	* serves to c· attention to one of
	104–11	of a man that should c· St. Paul a
	104–13	who shall c· a Christian Scientist a
	110–32	may serve to c· attention to
	150–31	c· this "a subtle fraud,"
	152–23	Principle of good, that we c· God,
	163– 1	c· the worshipper to seek the
	186–21	"Before they c·, I will — Isa. 65 : 24.
	224– 5	c· your attention to this demand,
	228– 1	I c· disease by its name
	229– 1	I c· none but genuine . . . Scientists,
	240– 7	* c· C. S. the higher criticism
	251–24	c· you mine, for all is thine and
	256–23	Parents c· home their loved ones,
	285–26	way which they c· heresy, — Acts 24 : 14.
	290–24	where the high and holy c· you again
	319–23	* you suggested that I c· on the
	347–16	c· to mind the number of our

called

Mis.	10– 9	Because He has c· His own,
	24–10	I c· for my Bible,
	34–23	All that are c· "communications
	68– 8	* metaphysical healing being c· C. S.
	69–14	once c· to visit a sick man
	84–17	was c· the Son of man,
	89– 4	If Scientists are c· upon to care for
	99–13	c· to voice a higher order of
	112–17	mental state c· moral idiocy.
	131– 3	will be c· a moral nuisance,
	139–21	c· The Church of Christ, Scientist.
	144– 6	a little band c· Busy Bees,
	161– 6	his name shall be c· — Isa. 9 : 6.
	162– 2	Jacob was c· Israel ;
	164–17	"His name shall be c· — Isa. 9 : 6.
	173–28	atom or molecule c· matter
	174–21	Shall that be c· heresy which
	176–10	been c· for and manifested.
	180–27	month is c· the son of a year.
	193–23	Christians are properly c· Scientists
	205– 5	c· sin, disease, and death.
	205–28	mortal molecules, c· man,
	234–20	metaphysical healing, c· C. S.,
	248–10	the person they c· slanderer,
	257–20	c· it "a murderer — John 8 : 44.
	265–27	constantly c· to settle questions
	272–21	* which may be c· a charter,
	294–12	sometimes c· a man,
	310–22	and upon a meeting being c·,
	312–17	* c· to declare the real harmony
	321– 5	shall be c· Wonderful, — Isa. 9 : 6.
	337–12	"Jesus c· a little child — Matt. 18 : 2.
	351– 1	c· on students to test their ability
	380–13	an accident, c· fatal to life,
	380–20	people generally, c· for a sign
Man.	17– 3	a church without creeds, to be c·
	50–19	a meeting . . . shall be c·,
	57– 8	C· only by the Clerk.
	64–18	objected to being c· thus,
	65– 5	shall not be c· Leader
	69– 6	has been c· to serve our Leader
	73–19	When c· for, a member of the
	89– 6	shall immediately be c·,
	94– 2	within the city whither he is c·
	95–14	If c· for, a member of the Board
Ret.	9–10	when the voice c· again,
	14– 2	John Calvin rightly c· his own tenet
	15–13	I was c· to preach in Boston
	25–11	God I c· immortal Mind.
	25–13	sensuous nature, I c· error
	25–18	Spirit I c· the reality ;
	27– 3	my work c· S. and H.,

called

Ret.	33– 7	as it has been well c·.
	40– 4	c· to speak before the Lyceum
	44– 3	to be c· the Church of Christ, Scientist,
	47–12	a meeting was c· of the Board
	52–20	was c· Journal of C. S.
	53– 2	The C. S. Journal, as it was now c·,
	54–17	in this mental state c· belief ;
	67–16	until the false claim c· sin is
	88– 7	c· the physical man from the tomb
	91– 3	c· "the pearl of parables,"
	91– 5	c· "the diamond sermon."
Un.	15–16	God is commonly c· the sinless,
	22–21	c· human intellect and will-power,
	33– 5	existence of a substance c· matter.
	33–16	that form of matter c· brains,
	38–11	transition c· material death,
	46– 1	mortal error, c· mind,
	54– 3	a false claim, c· sickness,
	58–11	through what is humanly c· agony.
Pul.	8–23	youthful workers were c· "Busy Bees."
	24– 7	* as it is officially c·,
	28–21	* c· the "C. S. Hymnal,"
	33– 4	* she heard her name c·
	37– 6	* residence, c· Pleasant View.
	44–21	* students, as they are c·,
	47– 6	* It was c· the Journal of C. S.,
	51–18	* c· forth the implements of
	55–16	* Her discovery was first c·,
	58– 7	* beautiful estate c· Pleasant View ;
	58–25	* her book, c· "S. and H."
	58–27	* and c· "Mother's Room,"
	62–20	* They can be c· into requisition in
	65– 3	* what is c· the New England mind
	65–14	* progress . . . made by what is c· C. S.
	65–20	* c· the Bible of that city.
	65–25	* c· the divine spirit of giving,
	68–19	* C. S. church, c· The Mother Church,
	72– 5	* reporter c· upon a few of the
	82–16	* Jews who never c· Abraham "Father,"
Rud.	3–15	c· the Sermon on the Mount,
	5–16	either mind which is c· matter,
No.	16–12	c· mortal mind or matter,
	31–23	evils c· sin, sickness, and death
	41– 4	and contemptuously c· him
'00.	5–29	casting out God's opposites, c· evils,
'01.	3–19	c· in Scripture, Spirit, Love.
	7– 7	divine intelligence c· God.
	9– 1	Christ Jesus, c· in Scripture the
	9–12	crucified Jesus and c· him a
	10– 4	"If they have c· the — Matt. 10 : 25.
	13– 2	The outcome of evil, c· sin,
	24– 4	is generally c· matter
	24–20	is c· the Christian era.
'02.	7–27	c· his disciples' special attention to
	19– 6	c· one a "fool" — see Luke 24 : 25.
Peo.	4–14	a third person, c· material man,
	7–24	objects of sense c· sickness and
Po.	v– 7	* c· forth by some experience
My.	13– 4	c· "Thoughts on the Apocalypse,"
	21–24	* c· upon to make no less sacrifice
	40–22	* c· the children of God." — Matt. 5 : 9.
	122–13	It c· forth flattering comment
	143–26	according to His purpose. — Rom. 8 : 28.
	148– 3	c· to do your part wisely
	193–27	c· thee by thy name ; — Isa. 43 : 1.
	196– 5	c· the "city of brotherly love."
	201– 3	whereunto divine Love has c· us
	206–25	Him who hath c· you — I Pet. 2 : 9.
	228–26	Who shall be c· to Pleasant View?
	228–31	such a one was never c· to
	229– 9	Scientists, c· to the home of
	240– 9	I c· C. S. the higher criticism
	244–13	c· of God to contribute my part
	244–20	"Many are c·, — Matt. 22 : 14.
	245–11	c· out of their hiding-places those
	246–22	c· the Board of Education
	247–19	c· you to be a fisher of men.
	269– 2	image or likeness, c· man,
	269– 4	divine Principle, Love, c· God,
	291–26	c· to mourn the loss of her
	309– 3	c· upon to do much business for
	311–32	I was c· by the Rev. R. S. Rust,
	317–23	has been c· original.
	320–20	* I c· on Mr. Wiggin several times
	325– 3	* c· to inquire of his welfare
	334–18	* while being c· unreal.
	343–14	"I have been c· a pope,
		(see also **death**)

calleth

Hea.	11– 4	A dream c· itself a dreamer,

calling

Mis.	4– 6	c· this method "mental science."
	245–11	c· forth the vox populi
	329–27	c· the feathered tribe back

calling

Mis.	333–18	c· on matter to work out the
	348– 2	towards the mark of a high c·.
	365–18	that mortal mind is c· for what
Man.	57– 9	Before c· a meeting of the
	86–13	who is ready for this high c·,
Ret.	8– 4	c· me distinctly by name,
	8–18	"Your mother is c· you !"
	8–21	your mother is c· you !"
Un.	53– 6	c· the knowledge of evil good,
Pul.	21–27	spirit of Christ c· us together.
	23–15	* and ingenuously c· out a
	74–13	c· for an interview
'00.	6– 8	of the high c· of God — Phil. 3 : 14.
'01.	4–28	c· God "divine Principle,"
	5–13	c· one the divine Principle
Hea.	6–11	but they take pleasure in c· me a
Po.	15–11	whispering voices are c· away
My.	3–23	Christian Scientist verifies his c·.
	147–30	hearts are c· on me for help,
	201– 2	Press on towards the high c·
	229– 2	unless I mistake their c·.
	320– 3	* Upon c· on Mr. Wiggin,

callous

Mis.	398– 6	Wound the c· breast,
Ret.	46–12	Wound the c· breast,
Pul.	17–11	Wound the c· breast,
Po.	14–10	Wound the c· breast,

callow

Mis.	254– 9	nest of the raven's c· brood !
	331–12	dove feeds her c· brood,
	356–21	nests of the raven's c· brood.

calls

Mis.	27– 2	Science of good c· evil nothing.
	68–27	c· metaphysics "the science which
	110–29	that which God c· good.
	132–20	teaching C. S., receiving c·,
	230– 9	making lingering c·,
	274– 7	and which God c· me to
	283–31	seldom c· on his teacher or
	292–16	It c· loudly on them to
	325–20	c· out, rubs his eyes,
	331–14	c· them to her breast,
	370– 1	when their feebleness c· for help,
	370–17	and c· forth infinite care from
	399– 1	Mourner, it c· you,
	399– 6	Sinner, it c· you,
Man.	43–18	c· more serious attention to the
	48– 3	whenever God c· a member to
	68–18	c· to her home or allows to visit
	68–24	C. S. Board of Directors c· a student
	95– 2	c· FOR LECTURES.
Ret.	69–26	voice of Truth still c·:
Un.	34–20	could not feel what it c· substance.
	59–21	illusion which c· sin real,
	59–22	illusion which c· sickness real,
Pul.	49– 1	* room which Mrs. Eddy c· her den
Rud.	8–18	man who c· himself a Christian Scientist,
Hea.	1– 8	c· to higher duties,
	15–16	at the same time he c· God almighty
Peo.	11–21	c· its own enactments "laws
Po.	75– 7	Mourner, it c· you,
	75–13	Sinner, it c· you,
My.	84– 3	* the interest on which c· for
	165–23	becomes tired and c· for rest.
	180–26	misconstrues . . . and c· them unkind.
	228– 7	The evil mind c· it "skulking,"
	310– 8	c· my youngest brother,
	314– 1	c· Dr. Daniel Patterson,

calm

Mis.	200–25	holy c· of Paul's well-tried hope
	227–21	wherein c·, self-respected thoughts
	228– 6	is to be c· amid excitement,
	229–25	A c·, Christian state of mind
	338–17	and c· strength will enrage evil.
Ret.	60–16	and there is a great c·.
'00.	11–25	* With a touch of infinite c·.
'01.	30–25	far-seeing vision, the c· courage,
'02.	19–20	underneath is a deep-settled c·.
Hea.	2– 2	a c· and steadfast communion with
Po.	22–17	life perfected, strong and c·.
My.	127– 8	c· coherence in the ranks of C. S.
	139–14	Life, — c·, irresistible, eternal.
	150–20	c·, clear, radiant reflection of
	204– 5	power which lies concealed in the c·
	333–22	* "His end was c· and peaceful,

calmly

Mis.	247– 9	I c· challenge the world,
My.	350– 8	c· and rationally, though faintly,

calms

Mis.	320–13	c· man's fears, bears his burdens,
My.	106–20	divine Mind c· . . . with a word.
	166–19	c· of human existence.

calumniator

Mis.	191–27	define him as . . . "c",
'01.	16–17	defines *devil* as *accuser*, c;
	33– 4	"c" must not be admitted to
My.	305– 3	Failing in . . . the c has resorted to
	330– 6	* The c who informed you

calumny

My.	308– 6	It is c on C. S. to say

Calvary

Mis.	124–24	last act of the tragedy on C
Ret.	31–26	Bethany, Gethsemane and C,
Un.	59–15	to suffer before Pilate and on C,
'02.	10–11	* not Athens, but C."

Calvin, John

Ret.	14– 1	as John C rightly called his

Calvinistic

Ret.	2– 3	C devotion to Protestant liberty

Cambridge

Mass.

My.	53–24	* A. J. Peabody, D.D., of C, Mass.
	60–22	* C, Mass., June 12, 1906.
My.	56–13	* C, Chelsea, and Roxbury.
	69–30	* in Mt. Auburn cemetery in C,
	318–11	the University Press, C,

came

Mis.	24– 5	c to me in an hour of great need ;
	26–13	Whence c the first seed,
	26–15	Whence c the infinitesimals,
	82– 8	c up out of the baptism of
	105– 9	c from the testimony of the
	143–27	Each donation c promptly ;
	144– 5	c from the dear children
	176–22	which c down from heaven.
	176–23	c to establish a nation in
	177–26	* c on the platform.
	178– 8	and he c to us.
	178–25	* the pastor again c forward,
	184–29	John c baptizing with water.
	188–24	c to her through a spiritual sense
	190–11	*And it c to pass,* — *Luke* 11 : 14.
	196–12	that saying c not from Mind,
	214– 5	c not to send peace, — *Matt.* 10 : 34.
	242– 3	c not to my notice until January
	261–18	"I c not to destroy — see *Matt.* 5 : 17.
	281–26	it c to me more clearly
	327– 3	I c hither, hoping that I might
	360–28	c from the Father," — see *John* 16 : 28.
	372–15	From them c such replies
	376–25	c out on a background of
Ret.	2– 7	c to America seeking
	8–15	the call again c,
	9–11	The voice c ; but I was afraid,
	9–14	When the call c again
	13–21	glow of ineffable joy c over me.
	14–30	After the meeting was over they c
	21– 9	and c to see me in Massachusetts.
	23–16	and, lo, the bridegroom c !
	24– 6	discovery c to pass in this way.
	45–14	c my clue to the uses and
Un.	15– 1	c "death into the world,
	59– 9	one who c down from heaven,
	60– 2	Christ Jesus c to save men,
	62– 4	and c to save me ;"
Pul.	8–14	and forth c the money,
	9–11	c to the rescue as
	29–16	* Then c his sermon, which dealt
	32–23	* On her father's side Mrs. Eddy c from
	33– 9	* The call c, but the little maid
	33–12	* reply if the call c again.
	33–12	* It c, and she answered
	33–22	* as to whence the stranger c
	34– 7	* There c a Sunday morning when
	34– 8	* her pastor c to bid her good-by
	35– 1	c to me with a new meaning,
	35– 6	* Mrs. Eddy c to perceive that
	36– 7	* To this College c hundreds
	36–15	* I c away in a state of exhilaration
	41– 1	* c forth from the hands of the
	41– 7	c to help erect this
	41– 8	* these contributors c to Boston,
	41–15	* c parties of forty and fifty.
	43–19	* few minutes of silent prayer c next,
	46– 3	* c to hear him preach.
	46–16	* Her family c to this country
	55– 6	* cyclic changes that c during the
	57– 4	* contributions for its erection c from
	64– 8	* Money c freely from all parts of
	68– 6	* Students or to it in hundreds
	69– 1	* the pastor, c to Baltimore
	69– 3	* Miss Cross c from Syracuse, N. Y.,
	72–22	* other than that which c from God
	73–11	* c from her seclusion
No.	42–25	clergyman c to be healed.

came

'01.	18–19	he c to do "the will of — *Matt.* 12 : 50.
	21–22	Christ c not to bring death
	31– 9	"I c not to send peace — *Matt.* 10 : 34.
'02.	9–22	and knew not whence it c
	13–16	I c to the rescue,
	15–22	Its title, S. and H., c to me
	15–30	voice" that c to Elijah — *I Kings* 19 : 12.
Hea.	11–22	Mind c in as the remedy,
	17–27	If sickness . . . c through mind,
Po.	47– 2	As sweetly they c of yore,
My.	5–11	Whence, then, c the creation of
	38–18	* when it c to the singing,
	42–13	* unexpectedly to me c the call to
	43–19	* Israel c over this Jordan
	53– 1	* from every quarter c important
	61– 9	* Then c the announcement
	61–16	* conviction . . . c to me so clearly,
	63–20	* there c a deeper feeling,
	82–27	* c to Boston in such numbers
	117–15	and c unto thee?" — *Matt.* 25 : 39.
	163–18	and c to Concord, N. H.,
	164– 1	far from my purpose, when I c here,
	171–23	* carriage c to a standstill on
	173–15	it c to me: Why not invite
	184–12	c when I was so occupied
	217–30	He c to the world not to
	218–11	c with the *ascension*.
	247–15	c out in orderly line to the
	256–22	and see whence they c
	258–11	Then c her resurrection and
	275–18	since I c to Massachusetts.
	310–13	His . . . title of Colonel c from
	328–16	* how this c about in Kinston
	343–17	light of the Science c first to me.
	345–15	c like blessed relief to me,
	350– 8	c to the writer's rescue,
		(*see also* **Jesus**)

camels

My.	211– 3	and swallowing c.
	218–20	and swallowing c.
	235– 5	one may swallow c.
	276– 9	strain at gnats or swallow c

Cameo, Cæsar's

Mis.	376– 9	* the face . . . from Cæsar's C,

camera

Mis.	264– 8	like c shadows thrown upon the

camera obscura

My.	164–11	c o, a thing focusing light

camomile

Mis.	227–19	like the c, the more trampled

camp

Pan.	14–20	whether in c or in battle.

Campbell, Miss Maurine R.

Mis.	144– 7	organized by Miss Maurine R. C.

Canada and Can.

Man.	94–18	lecture in the United States, in C,
	97– 8	throughout the United States, C,
	98–26	United States and in C
Pul.	44–26	* United States and C
	67–19	* In C, also, there is a large
	88– 3	From C to New Orleans,
My.	77–12	* from C, from Great Britain,
	136–21	also in C, Australia, *etc.*
	250–20	in the United States and C.
		(*see also* **London, Montreal, Toronto**)

Canadian

My.	253–14	chapter sub-title

cancel

Mis.	131–24	opportunity to c accounts.
No.	7– 9	c error in our own hearts,

cancelled

Mis.	222–20	c only through human agony :
	261– 7	c by repentance or pardon.

cancels

Mis.	338–12	c not sin until it be destroyed,
'02.	12– 4	c the disagreement,

cancer

Un.	7–12	a c which had eaten its way to
Hea.	6–17	whether . . . a flower or a c,
My.	80– 6	* they had been cured . . . of c ;
	105–14	I have healed at one visit a c
	310–18	* "excepting Albert, died of c,"
	310–21	as caused by c.
	315–23	declared dying of c,

cancers

Ret.	15–24	they specified c.

candidate

Man.	26–22	after the c is approved by
	65–23	c shall be subject to the approval
	88–14	c shall be subject to the approval

candidate
Man.	100– 4	*c·* for its Committee on Publication,
	100– 5	Readers shall appoint said *c·*.
Pul.	83– 2	* promise as lover and *c·*

candidates
Mis.	146– 8	receiving or dismissing *c·*.
Man.	26–15	names of its *c·* before they are
	26–17	if she objects, said *c·* shall not
	56–22	Regular meetings for electing *c·*
	67– 3	*c·* for admission to this Church,
	109– 4	are eligible to approve *c·*
Ret.	14– 3	examination of *c·* for membership
My.	57–17	* The number of *c·* admitted June 5

candle
Pul.	28– 4	* by the light of a single *c·*,

candle-power
My.	69– 4	* each lamp of thirty-two *c·*.

candlestick
'00.	12–19	will remove thy *c·* — *Rev.* 2 : 5.

candlesticks
'00.	12– 5	seven golden *c·''* — *Rev.* 2 : 1.

candor
Mis.	147–27	full of truth, *c·*, and humanity.

cane
My.	308–25	saying, "I never use a *c·*."

canker
'02.	3–23	triumph *c·* not his coronation,

cannonaded
Pul.	5–16	press and pulpit *c·* this book,

cannon's
Po.	26–20	Purged by the *c·* prayer ;

canny
Mis.	xi–15	will find herein a "*c·*" crumb ;

canon
My.	199–12	receipt of their Christian *c·*

canonical
'01.	34–11	*c·* writings of the Fathers,

canonized
My.	104– 4	Mars' Hill orator, the *c·* saint,
	268–24	Truth, *c·* by life and love,

cant
Mis.	374– 5	To them it was *c·* and caricature,

canvas
Mis.	230–27	*c·* and the touch of an artist
	374–30	thinker and his thought on *c·*,
Ret.	79– 7	effaced from the *c·* of mortal mind ;

cap
Mis.	329–22	put the fur *c·* on pussy-willow,
Pul.	25–24	* The base and *c·* are of . . . marble.

capabilities
Mis.	43– 1	recognizing the *c·* of Mind
	193–30	man's *c·* and spiritual power.
Peo.	2– 1	we learn our *c·* for good,

capability
Mis.	66–32	to the present *c·* of the learner,
'00.	3–13	awake the slumbering *c·* of man.

capable
Mis.	13– 1	of which I feel at present *c·*,
	273–10	so *c·* of relieving my tasks
	273–19	good they are *c·* of accomplishing ;
Pul.	25– 9	* *c·* of holding fifteen hundred ;
	58–14	* *c·* of division into seven
Pan.	4–13	will is *c·* of use and of abuse,
My.	65– 9	* a church edifice *c·* of seating
	70–24	* or more *c·* instrument.
	223–16	do not consider myself *c·* of

capacities
Ret.	82–21	Their liberated *c·* of mind
'02.	10– 2	Utilizing the *c·* of the human mind
My.	259–26	in which human *c·* find the most

capacity
Mis.	49–16	our *c·* for formulating a dream,
	49–29	*c·* to err proceeds from
	49–31	never created error, or such a *c·*,
	76– 2	destitute of . . . derived *c·* to sin.
	204–18	It develops individual *c·*,
	228–12	to a *c·* for a higher life.
	316–14	profited up to their present *c·*
Un.	26– 2	and the *c·* to evolve mind.
	36– 3	double *c·* of creator and creation.
	43–23	divine power to human *c·*,
Pul.	41–16	* large auditorium, with its *c·* for
No.	21–12	reflecting God and the divine *c·*.
My.	8–20	* should have a seating *c·*
	24–29	* seating *c·* of five thousand.
	42–14	* the call to serve you in this *c·*,
	53–13	* seating *c·* of which place was
	55–25	* seating *c·* of six hundred and

capacity
My.	56– 1	* thought the seating *c·* would be
	57– 5	* would be of great seating *c·*,
	63– 4	* of Mr. Beman in an advisory *c·*
	67–10	* Seating *c·* . . . 5,000
	67–22	* exceeds it in seating *c·*,
	68–14	* seating *c·* of twelve hundred,
	69–23	* a cloak-room of the *c·* of
	77– 4	* seating *c·* of over five thousand.
	78– 1	* seating *c·* of the temple is
	137–29	as to honesty and business *c·*
	216–21	to your present unfolding *c·*.
	230–13	invigorate his *c·* to heal the sick,
	296–29	standing and seating *c·*,
	325–12	* any *c·* in which I could serve you,

caparisoned
No.	44–11	boldly ridden or brilliantly *c·*,

capital
Mis.	48–31	enemy is trying to make *c·* out of
	304– 9	* coming first to the *c·*
Pul.	7– 5	whereof this city is the *c·*.
	47–23	* New Hampshire's quiet *c·*,
	75–23	* in the great New England *c·*
'00.	2–20	his dupes are his *c·* ;
	3– 7	hoards this *c·* to distribute gain."
	12– 8	the *c·* of Asia Minor.
My.	157– 7	*c·* city of your native State.
	199–15	attitude of this church in our *c·*
	225– 7	A correct use of *c·* letters
	225–10	where *c·* letters should be used in
	265– 8	loses *c·*, and is bought at par
	270– 6	my first religious home in this *c·*
	289–27	meeting to be held in the *c·*

capitalization
My.	225– 6	chapter sub-title
	225–14	the *c·* which distinguishes it from
	318– 1	liberty that I have taken with *c·*,

capitalized
Man.	112– 5	*c·* (The), or small (the),

caprice
Pul.	55– 1	* "Not in blind *c·* of will,

caps
My.	225– 7	*c·* the climax of the old

capsicum
Mis.	348–19	thea (tea), *c·* (red pepper) ;

capsize
Pul.	80– 2	* it is ready to *c·*.

caption
Mis.	242– 2	having the above *c·*,

captive
Mis.	30–19	opened the door to the *c·*,
	101–17	and sets the *c·* free,
	124–16	opening the prison doors to the *c·*,
	168– 1	he giveth liberty to the *c·*,
No.	43–15	* preaching deliverance to the *c·*,
Po.	71–15	Joy for the *c·* ! Sound it long !
My.	110–26	"led captivity *c·*," — *Psal.* 68 : 18.
	133–15	set the *c·* sense free from self's

captives
Mis.	153–17	as *c·* are they enchained.
My.	110–20	if bodily sensation makes us *c·* ?

captivity
Mis.	139–13	*bringing into c· every* — *II Cor.* 10 : 5.
'00.	3–21	during the period of *c·*
My.	110–26	"led *c·* captive," — *Psal.* 68 : 18.

captured
Ret.	79–28	its spiritual gates not *c·*,

car
Mis.	274–28	*c·* of the modern Inquisition
My.	219–13	to ride to church on an electric *c·*,

carbonate
My.	108– 1	*c·* and sulphate of lime ;

Card
Mis.	256– 6	chapter sub-title
	310–10	chapter sub-title
	321–23	chapter sub-title
My.	25–15	chapter sub-title
	136–12	chapter sub-title
	173– 1	chapter sub-title
	316–10	chapter sub-title
	331–17	* heading

card
Mis.	137– 3	my thanks for your *c·* of invitation,
	157– 9	their *c·* in *The C. S. Journal*),
Man.	73– 4	whose *c·* is published in
	74–16	a *c·* in *The C. S. Journal*,
	91–10	*c·* of free scholarship from the
	91–13	on presentation of the *c·* to the
My.	184–11	Your kind *c·*, inviting me to
	186–26	your cordial *c·* inviting me to

card
My 191–28 Your *c·* of invitation to this
195– 4 acknowledging your *c·* of invitation
332–17 * paper containing this *c·* is

cardinal
Mis. 27–10 the *c·* point in C. S.,
107–14 Three *c·* points must be gained
Un. 9–27 What is the *c·* point of the
No. 25– 3 this *c·* point of divine Science,
'01. 8– 2 I reiterate this *c·* point :
My. 339– 4 The *c·* points of C. S.

cards
Man. 46– 9 on circulars, *c·*, or leaflets,
49–14 *c·* of such persons may be
82–10 Removal of *C·*.
82–10 No *c·* shall be removed . . . without
My. 223–10 practitioners whose *c·* are in

care
all
'02. 17–27 will put to flight all *c·* for
and providence
Pan. 3–29 *c·* and providence by which he
and responsibility
My. 123–14 *c·* and responsibility of purchasing it,
and worry
My. 48–25 * the discouragement of *c·* and worry,
brow of
Mis. 339–20 added one furrow to the brow of *c·*?
depressing
Mis. 133–26 In the midst of depressing *c·*
first
Mis. 370–29 His first *c·* is to separate the
His
Mis. 154– 7 God's love . . . is manifest in His *c·*.
his
Ret. 91–19 placed themselves under his *c·*,
infinite
Mis. 370–17 calls forth infinite *c·* from
of nurse
Ret. 90–17 to the *c·* of nurse or stranger.
of pupils
Man. 83– 8 *C·* of Pupils.
of the sick
Man. 49–13 can take proper *c·* of the sick.
special
Mis. 11–27 I do it with earnest, special *c·*
13– 4 special *c·* to mind my own business.
293– 5 special *c·* of the unerring modes
take
Mis. vii– 1 * take *c·*, that tak'st my book in hand,
39–13 *Can you take c· of yourself?*
Man. 69–23 shall not take *c·* of their churches
My. 138– 2 my property to take *c·* of
138– 4 to take *c·* of my property
takes
My. 166– 8 God takes *c·* of our life.
203–19 for God takes *c·* of it.
tender
'01. 29– 7 need the watchful and tender *c·*
under my
Mis. 33–17 place themselves under my *c·*,
under the
Mis. 304–10 * under the *c·* of our society.
304–18 * under the *c·* of the Daughters of the
Ret. 20– 9 under the *c·* of our family nurse,
87–29 under the *c·* of a regular physician,
watchful
My. 280– 5 * your watchful *c·* and guidance

Mis. 89– 4 *Scientists are called upon to c· for*
139–30 I took *c·* that the provisions for the
226– 3 * Father of all will *c·* for him.''
238–16 Who should *c·* for everybody?
238–17 enough, say they, to *c·* for a few.
370–28 *good* Shepherd does *c·* for all,
371– 6 the *c·* of the great Shepherd,
Ret. 20–28 family to whose *c·* he was
Pul. 73– 3 * God will *c·* for us,
79– 7 * no debt had to be taken *c·* of
Hea. 1– 8 not discharge from *c·* ;
My. 60–30 * *c·* to do a little watching
87– 3 * to *c·* for the multitudes
137–19 carefully taken *c·* of
331–24 * extended their *c·* and sympathy
336– 8 * entrusted herself to the *c·* of

cared
Ret. 86–24 every man *c·* for and blessed.

careening
Po. 18– 5 *C·* in liberty higher and higher

career
Mis. 212– 6 left his glorious *c·* for our
266–12 An erratic *c·* is like the comet's
296– 7 work and *c·* of American women,
Ret. 94–26 affection illustrated in Jesus' *c·*,

career
Pul. 44–11 * in your eventful *c·*.
49–20 * her busy *c·* in Boston,
70– 4 * *C·* OF REV. MARY BAKER EDDY,
No. 34–17 the endeavor to crush out of a *c·*
'01. 28–29 After a hard and successful *c·*

careers
Mis. 356–11 give promise of grand *c·*.
Un. 4– 1 guides every event of our *c·*.
'01. 29– 6 in the advancing stages of their *c·*

careful
Mis. 43–13 *c·*, . . . reading of my books,
Ret. 45–14 From *c·* observation and experience
90– 1 student should be most *c·* not to
Pul. 54–18 * A *c·* reading of the accounts of
64–20 * After *c·* study she became convinced
73–20 * made a *c·* and searching study
'00. 8– 6 hence, be *c·* of your company.
Hea. 10–22 be *c·* not to talk on both sides,
My. 237–23 I recommend its *c·* study to all

carefully
Mis. 306– 3 * entered *c·* in a book
315–13 thirty-three students, *c·* selected,
Man. 83– 9 shall *c·* select for pupils
Ret. 44–17 Examining the situation . . . *c·*,
Pul. 47–16 * defines *c·* the difference
62–15 * The tubes are *c·* tuned,
My. 31–31 * As though trained *c·* under
38– 8 * *c·* trained corps of ushers,
137–19 affairs *c·* taken care of
330–13 * *c·* investigated the points

careless
Man. 41– 3 *C·* comparison . . . to Christ Jesus

carelessly
Mis. 339–25 *C·* or remorselessly thou mayest
My. 12–21 the reliable *now* is *c·* lost

cares
Mis. 341–29 neither the *c·* of this world nor
370–27 good shepherd *c·* for all
Hea. 4–10 not to forget his daily *c·*.
My. 52–23 * Little *c·* she, if only

caressing
Mis. 212– 2 a *c·* Judas that betrays you,

carfare
My. 65–16 * passing out a nickel for *c·*.

caricature
Mis. 87– 4 ignorantly to *c·* God's creation,
374– 5 To them it was cant and *c·*,

caring
Man. 85– 4 *C·* for Pupils of Strayed Members.
Rud. 12–20 *c·* for all the conditions requisite
My. 243–18 *c·* for their own flocks.

carious
My. 105–11 *c·* bones that could be dented

Carlyle
'01. 33– 6 *C·* writes : "Quackery and dupery
My. 154–18 *C·* wrote : "Wouldst thou plant for
193–22 *C·* writes, "Give a thing time ;

carnage
Po. 27– 1 "Convulsion, *c·*, war ;

carnal
Mis. 36–24 "The *c·* mind . . . is enmity — *Rom.* 8 : 7.
38–12 reap your *c·* things?'' — *I Cor.* 9 : 11.
54– 1 The *c·* mind cannot discern
139–10 *not c·, but mighty* — *II Cor.* 10 : 4.
169–26 the reading of the *c·* mind.
182–16 neither from dust nor *c·* desire.
214– 3 appeared hate to the *c·* mind,
Ret. 78– 8 *c·* and sinister motives, entering
'01. 9–24 disturb the *c·* and destroy it ;

carnality
'02. 10–27 human error, *c·*, opposition to
Hea. 2–22 his spirituality rebuked their *c·*,

carnally
Mis. 24– 3 to be *c·* minded is death ;— *Rom.* 8 : 6.
'02. 6–27 to be *c·* minded is death ;— *Rom.* 8 : 6.

carnations
Pul. 42–29 * large basket of white *c·*

carnival
Mis. 274–23 quill-drivers . . . hold high *c·*.

carobs
Mis. 369–23 *c·* which he shared with the swine,

Carpenter (*see also* **Carpenter's**)
Mr.
Mis. 48– 7 Mr. *C·* deserves praise for his
48–14 Mr. *C·* made a man drunk on water,

carpenter
Mis. 166–31 a good *c·*, and a good man,

Carpenter's, Professor
   Mis. 47–27   *Professor C· exhibitions of*

carpenters
   My. 145–10   One day the c· foreman said to me :

carpets
   Mis. 329– 7   between taking up the white c· and

carriage
   Mis. 239–12   I observed a c· draw up
         239–13   and take from his c· the ominous
   Po.   v–16   * *and alighting from her c·,*
   My. 171–23   * Her c· came to a standstill
         275–17   I go out in my c· daily,
         302–29   went alone in my c· to the church,
         346–11   * Mrs. Eddy's c· drove into town

carried
   Mis. 113–13   c· to the depths of perdition
         191–25   and c· the question with Eve.
         226– 5   c· the case on the side of God ;
         284–31   those rules must be c· out ;
         292–30   and c· out my ideal.
         364–28   This error, c· to its ultimate,
   Man. 100– 8   c· out according to her directions.
   Ret.   6–28   c· through the Legislature by
   Pul. 14–10   c· away of the flood. — *Rev.* 12 : 15.
         50–21   * thoroughly c· away with
   Peo.   8–14   we say that Life is c· on through
   My.   8–22   * motion was c· unanimously.
         12– 2   * c· the implication that work should
         14–26   * will be c· on without interruption
         44–18   * motion was c· unanimously
         59–16   * my mind was c· back to
         68– 2   * c· out with the end in view of
         80– 1   * cures that c· one back
         138– 7   c· on contrary to my wishes.
         145–10   and saw them c· out.
         310–15   c· on a large business in Boston,
         333–18   * Major Glover's remains were c·

carries
   Mis. 346– 2   c· this thought even higher,
         353–24   divine Principle c· on His harmony.
   Ret.   7–22   * c· with it too much of sorrow
         80–22   c· his lambs in his arms

carry
   Mis.   7–19   These descriptions c· fears
         47– 2   *and c· about this weight*
         117–18   to c· out a divine commission
         162–28   To c· out his holy purpose,
         356–20   c· the fruit of this tree into
   Ret. 44–25   measures were adopted to c·
         86–20   undertakes to c· his burden
   '01. 16–22   to c· a most vital point.
   Hea. 10–22   take the side you wish to c·,
   My. 38–25   * c· with them the memory of it.
         121–10   the ocean, able to c· navies,
         211–19   to c· out the designs of
         214–28   with which to c· on a Cause
         328–27   * to c· them on in this State,

carrying
   Mis. 19– 6   c· out what He teaches
   Ret. 16–14   c· them on their shoulders.
   Un. 44–19   c· out the serpent's assurance :
   Hea.   8– 7   and c· out this government

carve
   Peo.   7–20   * c· it then on the yielding stone

carved
   Mis. 325– 1   a massive c· stone mansion,
   Pul. 24–13   * inscription c· in bold relief :
         24–28   * doors of antique oak richly c·.
         26– 9   * with richly c· seats
         76–12   * in special designs, elaborately c·,
   Peo.   7–12   * c· the dream on that shapeless stone

carving
   Mis. 231–11   Under the skilful c· of the
   Pul. 27– 4   * marble approaches and rich c·,

carvings
   My. 69–14   * sculptor added magnificent c·
         78–11   * decorative c· peculiarly rich

Case, Mr. Henry Lincoln
   Pul. 43– 5   * direction, . . . of Mr. Henry Lincoln C·

case
  attorney for the
   Hea. 10–24   You are the attorney for the c·,
  carried the
   Mis. 226– 5   carried the c· on the side of God ;
  contagious
   My. 220– 7   reporting of a contagious c· to the
  difficult
   Rud.   7– 4   as the most difficult c· so treated.
  done with the
   Ret. 87–30   until he has done with the c·
  either
   Mis. 219–17   remove this feeling in either c·,

case
  either
   My. 302– 5   produces the result in either c·.
  every
   Mis. 40–19   same results follow not in every c·,
         40–20   student does not in every c·
         44–10   in every c· of disease,
         252– 7   the more the better in every c·.
   My. 318– 3   In almost every c· where Mr. Wiggin
  following
   Mis. 49– 1   out of the following c·.
  given up the
   Ret. 40– 9   The physicians had given up the c·
  governing the
   Man. 51–18   By-Law governing the c·
  her
   Mis. 378–13   signally failed in healing her c·.
   Pul. 34– 6   * her c· was pronounced hopeless
  his
   Mis. 69–29   for information about his c·.
   Ret. 19–10   which in his c· proved fatal.
   Pul. 69– 9   * pronounced his c· incurable.
  Mrs. Stebbin's
   Mis. 157–21   relative to Mrs. Stebbin's c·.
  my
   Mis. 379– 5   his pennings on my c·.
   My. 307–25   At first my c· improved
  nature of the
   Mis. 379– 9   and the nature of the c· :
   Pul. 80– 6   * inevitable in the nature of the c·.
  never loses a
   My. 132–29   Divine Love . . . never loses a c·.
  of dropsy
   Hea. 13–18   we cured an inveterate c· of dropsy.
  offender's
   Man. 50–20   offender's c· shall be tried
  of Jairus' daughter
   Pul. 54–22   * In the c· of Jairus' daughter
  of lunacy
   My. 190–15   a severe c· of lunacy,
         222– 3   a violent c· of lunacy.
  of malignant disease
   My. 227–15   taking a c· of malignant disease.
  of necessity
   Man. 100–25   C· of Necessity.
  of sprain
   Mis. 243– 7   c· of sprain of the wrist-joint,
  one
   Mis. 40– 1   in the one c· as in the other.
         63– 2   which is infidel in the one c·,
   No.   2–13   by healing one c· audibly,
  particulars of the
   Mis. 51–10   We have not the particulars of the c·
  rested
   Mis. 140–12   Thus the c· rested,
  said
   Man. 67–13   if said c· relates to the person
  second
   My. 335–18   * the second c· of the dread disease
  seldom the
   Mis. 283–22   but this is seldom the c·
  simplest
   Rud.   7– 2   the simplest c·, healed in Science,
  single
   Mis. 242–20   if he will heal one single c·
  such a
   Mis. 242–25   cured precisely such a c· in 1869.
  takes up the
   Mis.   5–19   takes up the c· hopefully
  that
   Mis. 52–27   In that c· he would be obliged
   My. 222– 8   why they could not heal that c·,
  the only
   Mis. 49–10   This is the only c· that could be
  this
   Mis. 190–23   In this c· it was the evil of
  this being the
   Pan.   4–26   This being the c·, what need have we
  your
   Mis. 157–10   questions important for your c·,

   Mis. 41–21   There is no other healer in the c·.
         195–24   unfit to judge in the c· ;
         279–24   in the c· of Joshua and his band
         282–26   is a c· from accident,
         283– 3   then the c· is not exceptional.
   Man. 47– 6   c· he cannot fully diagnose,
         67–12   c· not provided for in its By-Laws
         77–23   In c· of any . . . deviation from
         110–15   as the c· may be.
   My. 105– 8   a c· which the M.D.'s,
         335–27   * the c· was one of yellow fever

cases
  acute
   Mis.   6– 9   the majority of the acute c·
         44– 6   *Can C. S. cure acute c·*

cases

both
No. 6–20 evidence in both c· to be unreal.
'01. 34– 4 Bible is our authority . . . in both c·.
chronic
Man. 46–25 in chronic c· of recovery,
desperate
Ret. 41– 4 Many were the desperate c·
Pan. 10–20 desperate c· of intemperance,
exceptional
Mis. 39–21 There may be exceptional c·,
Man. 36–14 Exceptional C·.
96– 9 Exceptional C·.
extreme
Mis. 112–15 in extreme c·, moral idiocy.
healed
My. 106– 6 The list of c· healed by me
106–13 C. S. has healed c· that
his
My. 108– 3 in healing his c· without drugs
hopeless
'01. 27–14 has healed hopeless c·,
many
Mis. 222– 7 in many c· causes the victim
most
Mis. 45–15 more in this than in most c· ;
89–10 advisable in most c· that Scientists
notable
Mis. 49–13 notable c· of insanity have been
of candidates
Man. 67– 2 c· of candidates for admission
of discipline
Man. 67– 2 not . . . on c· of discipline,
My. 359– 8 not . . . in c· of discipline,
of disease
Mis. 60– 9 healing c· of disease and sin
one hundred
My. 127–17 out of one hundred c· I healed
some
'01. 17–28 this attenuation in some c·
such
Mis. 6–11 such c· should certainly prove
236–20 In such c· we have said,
Man. 36–12 such c· as are provided for
71–18 except in such c· as are specially
100–21 In such c· it shall be the privilege
surgical
My. 345–24 about advice on surgical c·."
these
Ret. 15–26 I had not heard of these c·
those
Mis. 6–10 those c· that are pronounced

Mis. 43– 3 enables one to heal c· without even
Man. 46–25 in c· where he has not effected a
52– 1 shall vote on c· involving
67– 4 c· of those on trial for dismissal
Ret. 15–24 The c· described had been
My. 335–25 * attended c· of this terrible disease

cash

Man. 78–21 a petty c· fund, to be used by him

casket

Pul. 77– 6 * plush c· with white silk linings.
My. 171–27 * a handsome rosewood c·
171–29 * The c· contained a gavel

cast

Mis. 7–13 C· not your pearls before swine ;
105–23 the shadow c· by this error.
111–11 c· their nets on the right side,
212–11 c· their nets on the right side.
212–27 c· the beam out of his own eye,
250–18 c· aside the word as a sham
254–20 and c· them to the earth.
280–14 if we c· something into the scale
285–17 the book that c· the first stone,
302– 5 "c· lots for his vesture,"— see Matt. 27 : 35.
305–29 * In order that the bell shall be c·
307–21 C· not pearls before the unprepared
326– ⁴ And they c· him out.
336–15 how to c· the mote of evil out of
355–21 "C· the beam out — see Matt. 7 : 5.
355–22 Learn what . . . and c· it out ;
360– 8 c· in the moulds of C. S. :
Un. 29–24 "Why art thou c· down,— Psal. 42 : 11.
Pul. 6–17 * I c· from me the false remedy
12– 8 accuser . . . is c· down,— Rev. 12 : 10.
13–28 c· unto the earth,— Rev. 12 : 13.
62– 6 * c· bells of old-fashioned chimes.
No. 8–23 no longer c· your pearls before this
22–21 That Jesus c· several persons out of
22–26 indicated his ability to c· it out.
23–11 Jesus c· seven devils ;
Pan. 4–21 "Why art thou c· down,— Psal. 42 : 11.
5–27 He . . . c· it out of mortal mind,
'01. 26–17 and they c· lots for it?

cast

Hea. 7–19 "She hath c· in more— see Mark 12 : 43.
Po. 30–15 shadows c· on Thy blest name,
My. 190–16 "Why could not we c·— Matt. 17 : 19.
191– 8 and love will c· it out.
206–10 they divide . . . and c· lots for it.
214–27 c· my all into the treasury
227–23 "Neither c· ye your pearls— Matt. 7 : 6.
247–25 c· your bread upon the waters

cast out

Mis. 40–21 power to c· out the disease.
70– 4 c· out the sick man's illusion,
131– 5 darkness in one's self must first be c· out,
152–27 no element of earth to c· out angels,
175–30 in thy name c· out devils.
190–21 c· out of another person ;
190–24 c· out by the spiritual truth
191–19 c· out of another individual
326– 1 c· out devils,— Matt. 10 : 8.
336–13 c· out your own dislike and hatred
373–10 serpent c· out of his mouth,
Pul. 14– 8 c· out of his mouth— Rev. 12 : 15.
14–12 c· out of his mouth.— Rev. 12 : 16.
29–18 * c· out demons."— see Matt. 10 : 8.
29–23 * c· out the demons of evil thought.
66–13 * c· out demons."— see Matt. 10 : 8.
No. 14–19 c· out devils" !— Matt. 10 : 8.
15–15 c· out of another person.
22–18 c· out devils."— Matt. 10 : 8.
22–23 the evils which were c· out.
23–18 in order to c· out this devil
40–23 Truth and Love that c· out fear
41–21 c· out devils ;"— Matt. 10 : 8.
Pan. 11– 2 c· out the unreal or counterfeit.
'01. 9–26 c· out evils and heal the sick.
Hea. 1– 2 shall they c· out devils ;— Mark 16 : 17.
6–27 shall they c· out devils."— Mark 16 : 17.
Peo. 4–27 cannot heal the sick and c· out
My. 47–30 * shall they c· out devils ;— Mark 16 : 17.
192– 5 c· out fashionable lunacy.
288–22 c· out devils and healed the sick.
300– 2 c· out the belief in sin
300–26 c· out devils."— Matt. 10 : 8.
(see also **error, evil, Jesus**)

caste

Mis. 246– 8 interests of wealth, religious c·,

casteth

Mis. 184–26 c· out all fear, all sin,
229–27 "c· out fear"— I John 4 : 18.
334–32 Love that c· out all fear,
Ret. 61–17 c· out fear.' "— I John 4 : 18.
Un. 20–16 "c· out fear,"— I John 4 : 18.
Peo. 6–16 c· out fear ;"— I John 4 : 18.

casting

Mis. 25–18 healing the sick, c· out evil,
77–31 healing the sick, c· out evils,
89–16 c· "pearls before swine"— Matt. 7 : 6.
97– 9 c· out devils through Beelzebub.
99–29 c· out evils and healing the sick ;
139–11 c· down imaginations,— II Cor. 10 : 5.
165– 1 c· out evils and healing,
175– 1 c· out error and healing
187– 2 c· out evils, healing the sick,
190–11 c· out a devil,— Luke 11 : 14.
191–13 c· out devils— Mark 9 : 38.
192– 7 in c· out error,
268–13 healing the sick and c· out error.
Ret. 65–23 c· out evils and healing the sick ;
66– 2 utilized . . . in c· out error,
No. 12–18 c· out evil, healing the sick,
'00. 5–28 c· out God's opposites,
Peo. 13– 7 c· out error and healing the sick.
My. 110– 2 c· out evils, healing the sick,
113–26 men are found c· out the evils of
126–13 c· out evil and healing the sick.
153–26 c· out evil and healing the sick.

castle

Un. 28– 9 declare some old c· to be

Cast out Demons

Pul. 28– 8 * and "C· out D·."— see Matt. 10 : 8.

casts

Mis. 68–17 error which Truth c· out.
73– 3 when Mind c· out the suffering.
191–18 traits, that Christ, Truth, c· out.
193–13 heals the sick, c· out error,
194–25 divine Love that c· out all fear.
210–30 rebukes error, and c· it out.
241– 6 c· out sickness as well as sin
Man. 15–12 that c· out evil as unreal.
17–17 c· out error, heals the sick,
Ret. 61–20 Love that c· out fear.
81–18 loathes error, and c· it aside ;
Hea. 13–23 truth of being that c· out error

casts
　My. 260–25　c· out evils, heals the sick,

casual
　My. 87– 6　* apparent to the most c· observer.

casualties
　'01. 24– 8　ills of mortals and the c· of earth.

casualty
　Mis. 35– 5　her recovery, . . . from a severe c·

cat
　Mis. 216–30　* to conceive a grin without a c·.''
　　　218–23　"grin without a c· ;''
　　　218–23　a grin expresses the nature of a c·,

cataracts
　Ret. 9–22　* From the far c·

catch
　Mis. 229– 6　would c· their state of feeling
　Pul. 47–24　* when she wishes to c· a glimpse of
　No. 39– 5　ostensibly to c· God's ear,
　Hea. 11– 8　would c· the meaning of Spirit.
　My. 81–10　* first to c· the Reader's eye.
　　　155– 9　May it c· the early trumpet-call,
　　　227–18　to c· them in their sayings ;
　　　342–13　* shade of which is so hard to c·,

catching
　Mis. 228–29　Common consent . . . makes disease c·.
　　　229– 5　If he believed . . . that health is c·
　My. 6–28　love c· a glimpse of glory.
　　　344 -20　think myself in danger of c· it.''
　　　344–28　the fear of c· smallpox is more

catechized
　My. 241–19　* c· by a C. S. practitioner

categories
　No. 22– 8　circumlocution and cold c· of Kant

category
　Mis. 252–12　Continuing this c·, we learn
　　　296–11　same c· with noble women
　'02. 7– 6　enter not into the c· of creation

cathedral
　Pul. 62–17　* beauties of a great c· chime,
　　　65–18　* story of the c· of Amiens,
　My. 67–16　* Corner-stone of c· laid . . . 1904
　　　67–17　* C· to be dedicated . . . 1906
　　　71– 1　* is a set of c· chimes,
　　　71– 9　* that built the C. S. c·.
　　　71–14　* enter this new c· or temple
　　　76–27　* c· erected by the devotees of
　　　99–14　* recently built a splendid c·
　　　182–18　large membership and majestic c·.
　　　188–20　walls of your grand c·

cathedrals
　My. 89–10　* finds in the English c·,

Catholic
　Mis. 111–25　C· and Protestant sects.
　Pul. 33–14　* C· biographies are full,
　'01. 28–13　C· and Protestant oratories.
　My. 4–15　Scientist loves Protestant and C·,
　　　270–25　promoted by C·, by Protestant,

Catholics
　My. 303– 8　Protestants, C·, or any other sect.

catnip
　Mis. 52– 5　divided between c· and Christ ;

caught
　Mis. 111– 5　at break of day c· much.
　　　228–22　must be c· through mind ;
　　　231–19　Then he was c· walking !
　　　295–12　*awake*, and c· napping?
　　　326– 7　flames c· in the dwelling
　Ret. 16– 2　a soprano, . . . c· my ear.
　Un. 15–14　very knowledge c· from God,
　Pul. 6–12　mistake of thinking she c·
　　　48–21　* c· her family coat of arms
　'01. 9– 6　c· glorious glimpses of the
　Peo. 7–15　* c· the angel-vision.
　My. 31–21　* sight which the visitors c·
　　　224–15　c· in some author's net,

causation
　Mis. 25–13　all other theories of c·,
　　　71–15　c· must interpret omnipotence,
　Ret. 24–10　that all c· was Mind,
　Pul. 55–19　* that all c· is of Mind,
　　　70–18　certain that "all c· was Mind,
　'02. 7– 2　no origin or c· apart from God.
　Hea. 19–12　Spirit is c·,
　My. 348–22　an actual, unfailing c·,

Cause
　great
　'01. 17–14　started the great C· that to-day
　'02. 14–25　prospered preeminently our great C·,
　My. 47–18　* inception of this great C·,
　　　204–21　when starting this great C·,

Cause
　of Christian Science
　Mis. 153– 2　establishing the C· of C. S·
　　　278–10　connected with the C· of C. S·
　Man. 52–26　advantageous . . . to the C· of C. S.,
　'02. 12–30　movements of the C· of C. S.,
　My. 10–17　* It is doubtful if the C· of C. S.
　　　37–17　* C· of C. S. has been organized
　　　143–20　The C· of C. S. is prospering
　　　163–20　labor for the C· of C. S.,
　　　199–15　towards the C· of C. S.,
　　　362–17　* C· of C. S. in this community,

　our
　Mis. x–16　the progress of our C·.
　　　32–27　for the individual, and for our C·.
　　　110–22　unprecedented prosperity of our C·.
　　　148–17　dignity and defense of our C· ;
　　　274– 9　might hinder the progress of our C·
　　　351–16　may retard our C·, but they never
　Man. 3–14　dignity and defense of our C· ;
　　　59–12　for the benefit of our C·.
　Ret. 85–25　our C·, is highly prosperous,
　'01. 17–23　more difficult stage . . . for our C·.
　'02. 13– 3　Christ and our C· my only incentives,
　My. 21–13　* our C· throughout the world.
　　　24–27　* structure is worthy of our C·
　　　45– 3　* for the furtherance of our C·,
　　　224–32　Our C· is growing apace
　　　316–16　a grand defence of our C·
　　　352–15　* testimony of the efficacy of our C·

　—————

　Mis. 38– 7　to support one's self and a C·
　　　43–22　a vast amount of injury to the C·.
　　　43–30　on the C·, and on the health of
　　　98–16　and the progress of our common C·
　　　263–18　working . . . for our common C·,
　Man. 48– 4　and to defend the C· of Christ,
　　　52–20　Working Against the C·.
　Ret. 85– 7　commend itself as useful to the C·
　　　85–25　The C·, . . . is highly prosperous,
　Un. 5–17　neither will it promote the C· of Truth
　Pul. 85–27　* in the C· of their common faith.
　No. 9– 4　to the hindrance of the C· of Truth.
　　　32–24　a C· which is healing its thousands
　'01. 35– 5　sacrifice self for the C· of Christ,
　My. v– 6　* growth and prosperity of the C·
　　　v–15　* established the C· on a sound basis
　　　10–25　* importance of . . . to the C·.
　　　10–31　* general welfare of the C·.
　　　47–20　* a C· that has rooted itself in so many
　　　50–28　* willing to labor for the C·.
　　　51–11　* would be a serious blow to her C·
　　　51–23　* it was for the interest of the C·,
　　　55–10　* C· itself was spreading over
　　　58– 8　* magnificent growth of this C·,
　　　58–12　* shows the growth of this C·,
　　　157– 9　* prosperity of the C·
　　　214–28　means with which to carry on a C·
　　　214–29　To desert the C· never occurred

cause (noun)
　and cure
　Hea. 11–23　places all c· and cure as mind ;
　　　11–24　where c· and cure are supposed to
　and effect
　Mis. 79–18　c· and effect in Science are
　　　93–18　all c· and effect are in God.
　　　155– 2　but one c· and effect.
　　　173–12　Mind is its own . . . c· and effect.
　　　217–22　that matter is both c· and effect,
　　　361–30　are inseparable as c· and effect.
　　　364–15　thought, extension, c·, and effect ;
　My. 151–26　discovery of all c· and effect.
　　　181– 4　or material c· and effect,
　and effects
　My. 212– 8　to expose the c· and effects of
　and end
　Mis. 218–21　Spirit as c· and end,
　central
　Mis. 295– 9　declares, that the central c· of this
　Christ's
　Mis. 302–19　working faithfully for Christ's c·
　establishment of a
　Mis. 238–14　labor for the establishment of a c·
　evil
　Pul. 56–19　* "And still we love the evil c·,
　exciting
　Mis. 69–25　the exciting c· of the inflammation
　　　267–26　exciting c· of all defeat and
　Ret. 44–18　predisposing and exciting c· of its
　final
　Mis. 219– 2　science of the final c· of things ;
　for bitter comment
　'02. 9–27　Is it c· for bitter comment and
　for joy
　'02. 3– 4　It is c· for joy that among the

cause (noun)

for rejection
Man. 37–13   to report the *c·* for rejection.
for rejoicing
Mis. 72–10   It is *c·* for rejoicing that this belief
glorious
Po. 39–15   Work for our glorious *c·* !
great
Mis. 79–17   If the great *c·* is perfect,
    173–12   its own great *c·* and effect.
greatness of a
'00. 10– 7   signs . . . of the greatness of a *c·*
holy
Mis. 273–17   labor for a good and holy *c·*.
in effect
Mis. 219– 3   neither reveals . . . *c·* in effect,
My. 149–23   Losing . . . *c·* in effect, and faith in
    349–32   inductive . . . seeks *c·* in effect,
insufficient
Man. 36–17   whose teachers, for insufficient *c·*,
intelligent
My. 108– 5   the intelligent *c·* in pathology?
into effect
Mis. 362–16   Philosophy . . . puts *c·* into effect,
its
Mis. 217–23   antagonistic to its *c·* ;
judging a
Pan. 11– 7   judging a *c·* by its effects?
latent
Hea. 6–25   latent *c·* producing the effect
mental
Ret. 24– 9   physical effects to a mental *c·* ;
mind is the
My. 302– 8   mind is the *c·* of all effect
no
'01. 28–18   no *c·* for not following it ;
My. 339–21   and have no *c·* to mourn ;
of all disease
Un. 9– 1   mortal mind is the *c·* of all disease.
of all sickness
Ret. 61–13   fear, . . . the *c·* of all sickness ;
of arbitration
My. 281–25   * advancement of the *c·* of arbitration."
of Christ
My. 165– 6   endured for the *c·* of Christ,
of Christian Science
Mis. 288–27   strong impulse from the *c·* of C. S.:
Man. 95– 8   as the *c·* of C. S. demands.
of death
My. 335–20   * *c·* of death as bilious fever,
of disease
Mis. 66–29   Ignorance of the *c·* of disease
    221–18   If error is the *c·* of disease,
of human weal
My. 36–27   * for the *c·* of human weal,
of its tear
Po. 65–23   *man* is the *c·* of its tear.
of temperance
Mis. 288–26   *c·* of temperance receives
of the mischief
My. 211–27   unless the *c·* of the mischief is
of the separation
My. 315– 7   * *c·* of the separation being wholly
of Truth
My. 49–28   * labors in the *c·* of Truth,"
one
Mis. 25– 3   one *c·* and one effect,
    155– 2   there is but one *c·* and effect.
    271– 9   one *c·* and one effect.
only
Mis. 23–19   the first and only *c·*.
    36– 9   only *c·* is the eternal Mind,
    97–32   The only *c·* for making this
or effect
My. 364–12   of any other *c·* or effect save
other
Mis. 308– 6   love or hatred or any other *c·*
My. 364–12   of any other *c·* or effect save
present
My. 152–29   remote, predisposing, and present *c·*
primal
Mis. 22–31   primal *c·*, or Mind-force,
remove that
Mis. 66–30   can neither remove that *c·* nor its
removing the
Mis. 41–14   removing the *c·* in that so-called
righteous
Mis. 99–16   ready to suffer for a righteous *c·*,
sole
Un. 10– 5   is built on Him as the sole *c·*.
sufficient
Man. 65–19   sufficient *c·* for the removal of the
    111–19   refuse, without sufficient *c·*, to
supreme
My. 37–20   * God is the supreme *c·* of all

cause (noun)

their
Mis. 288–28   and their *c·* prospers in proportion
    299– 2   until one is awake to their *c·*
this
My. 348– 6   I sought this *c·*, not within but
true
Mis. 266– 9   The true leader of a true *c·*
underlying
Mis. 169– 8   underlying *c·* of the long years of
universal
My. 226– 9   an effect of one universal *c·*,
    348– 5   the offspring of a universal *c·*.
which governs
Mis. 369– 9   *c·* which governs all effects,
without
Mis. 129– 4   condemn his brother without *c·*,
without a
Mis. 9–11   who have hated thee without a *c·*
    217– 3   effect without a *c·* is inconceivable;

Mis. 33–26   mortal mind is the *c·* of all "the ills
    46–15   that which is formed is not *c·*, but
    83– 7   *c·* of his own sufferings."
    217– 7   whose *c·* is the self-created Principle,
    255– 6   is not *c·*, but effect ;
Man. 49–25   the *c·* thereof be unknown,
Ret. 23–22   its substance, *c·*, and currents
'01. 24– 7   *c·* of all the ills of mortals
Po. 39–13   The *c·* she elevates.
My. 295–26   have *c·* to lament the demise of
    314–15   the *c·* nevertheless was adultery.

cause (verb)
Mis. 51–18   *c·* him to love them,
    66– 3   may *c·* the innocent to suffer
    67–15   nor *c·* it to be thought.
    211–16   *c·* him to suffer in coming to life?
    243–27   *c·* the coats of the stomach to
    331– 6   *c·* them to wait patiently
    350–26   *c·* none to be used in mental practice,
    368– 5   and *c·* the deaf to hear.
    373–11   *c·* her to be river-borne."
Man. 43– 3   *c·* the name of said member to be
    48– 8   nor *c·* to be published,
    87–11   or *c·* or permit others to solicit,
Ret. 29– 1   can *c·* a surrender of this effort.
Pul. 3–10   who or what can *c·* you to sin
    14–10   *c·* her to be carried away — *Rev.* 12 : 15.
No. 7– 6   nor *c·* any misapprehension as to
'01. 17– 4   *c·* him to return to the Father's
    20–21   sooner or later *c·* the perpetrator,
My. 349– 7   matter, . . . cannot *c·* disease,

caused
Mis. x–19   *c·* me, as an author, to
    xi– 3   *c·* me to retain the initial "G"
    24– 9   an injury *c·* by an accident,
    33– 3   high priests of old *c·* the crucifixion
    44–15   *c·* the pain to cease
    89–17   *c·* our Master to refuse help to
    157– 7   *c·* my secretary to write,
    212– 9   *c·* them to remember the
    231–14   *c·* unconditional surrender.
    267– 8   *c·* me to exercise most patience.
    374– 2   *c·* even the publicans to justify
Ret. 3– 7   *c·* that prolonged contest
    24–13   an injury *c·* by an accident,
    40–14   condition was *c·* by an injury
    47– 3   *c·* me to dread the . . . popularity of
Pul. 33–10   * This *c·* her tears of remorse
    80–21   * an army of well-meaning people to
Pan. 11– 2   It *c·* St. Paul to write,
'01. 32–17   *c·* me to love their doctrines.
'02. 18–11   who *c·* not the feeble to fall,
My. 135–13   *c·* me to select a Board of Trustees
    307–29   This . . . might have *c·* my illness.
    310–21   as *c·* by cancer.

causeless
Hea. 9–15   * "the curse *c·* cannot come"

causes
Mis. 12–20   *c·* that at former periods in
    18–29   *c·* much that must be repented of
    41– 6   *c·* "the wrath of man" — *Psal.* 76 : 10.
    62–31   its own disease, or that which it *c·*,
    68–26   * and *c·* of all things existing,"
    138– 1   if it *c·* thought to wander
    177– 4   greatest and holiest of all *c·*.
    222– 5   *c·* the victim to believe that he is
    222– 7   *c·* the victim great physical suffering ;
    229– 2   certain predisposing or exciting *c·*.
    289– 1   *c·* him to degenerate physically
    290–21   cease to judge of *c·* from a
    292–14   Divine Love eventually *c·* mortals to
Man. 53–24   publishes, or *c·* to be published,
Ret. 57–13   *c·* all bodily ailments,

causes
Un.	8–21	heredity and other physical *c·*.
Rud.	10–16	*c·* sickness and suffering.
Pan.	2–20	the deification of natural *c·*,
	8– 2	*c·* a man to be mentally deranged ;
My.	150–30	if the wisdom you manifest *c·*

causing
Mis.	2– 8	*c·* great obscuration of Spirit.
	244–19	*c·* him to walk the wave,
	298– 7	*c·* others to go astray,
	328–23	*c·* to stumble, fall, or faint,
My.	316– 6	*c·* man to love his enemies ;

caution
Mis.	6–26	*c·* is observed in regard to diet,
	240– 7	by that flippant *c·*,
Hea.	14– 9	*c·* should be exercised in

cautiously
Mis.	324–22	Stealing *c·* away from
Ret.	4–17	the crow caws *c·*,
My.	245– 5	it should be met . . . *c·*,

cave
Mis.	370– 8	and the *c·* of ignorance.

caves
Mis.	347– 8	people prepare shelter in *c·*

cavil
Mis.	193– 3	If this be the *c·*, we reply
	223– 9	Science proves, beyond *c·*,
My.	8– 7	* The necessity . . . is beyond *c·* ;
	91– 1	* established beyond *c·*.
	108– 7	I have proved beyond *c·* that
	181– 2	settle all points beyond *c·*,

caws
Ret.	4–17	the crow *c·* cautiously,

cease
Mis.	11– 9	did not *c·* teaching the wayward
	44–16	*caused the pain to c·*
	44–24	You believed . . . the pain would *c·* :
	180– 2	and strive to *c·* my warfare.
	290–21	When will the world *c·* to judge of
Ret.	60–17	raging of the material elements *c·*?"
	60–21	when will my sufferings *c·*?
Pul.	3–14	and bids tumult *c·*,
	52– 1	* Wonders will never *c·*.
No.	1–15	stir of contending sentiments *c·*,
	32–20	and shall *c·* to love it.
	35– 7	When human struggles *c·*,
	41– 8	Not that he would *c·* to do the will of
Hea.	18–23	will *c·* to assert their Cæsar sway
Po.	35– 8	never dry or *c·* to flow ;
My.	57–29	* "Wonders will never *c·*.
	110–25	mortals will *c·* to be mortal.
	143–23	when these things *c·* to bless
	143–24	they will *c·* to occur.
	151–13	injustice done by press . . . will *c·*,
	280–16	*c·* special prayer for the peace of
	280–17	and *c·* in full faith that God
	280–28	to *c·* praying for the peace of

ceased
Mis.	330– 4	Has love *c·* to moan over the
Ret.	8–16	though I had *c·* to notice it.
Pul.	33–13	* and after that it *c·*.
	82–30	* *c·* to kiss the iron heel of wrong.
My.	231–12	*c·* practice herself in order to

ceaseless
Mis.	224–15	the *c·* action and reaction
	250–24	the silent, *c·* prayer ;
	329–17	rippling all nature in *c·* flow,
Ret.	30– 5	*C·* toil, self-renunciation, and
Peo.	1–15	*c·* throbbings and throes of thought

ceases
Mis.	28– 7	and volition *c·* ;
	34–22	not a moment when he *c·* to exist.
	44–14	*and then the pain c·*,
	44–27	When your belief in pain *c·*,
	324–10	footfalls abate, the laughter *c·*.
Ret.	67–15	testimony of . . . personal sense *c·*,

ceasing
Mis.	154–25	Pray without *c·*.
	356–30	"pray without *c·*," — *I Thess.* 5 : 17.
No.	40– 1	"Pray without *c·*" — *I Thess.* 5 : 17.
My.	340– 4	"Pray without *c·*." — *I Thess.* 5 : 17.

ceiling
Pul.	25–17	* In the *c·* is a sunburst
	25–29	* sunburst in the centre of the *c·*
	58–22	* In the *c·* is a beautiful sunburst
My.	68– 4	* with its high-domed *c·*,
	69– 5	* *c·* or roof and side walls

ceilings
My.	68–26	* the great arches and *c·*.

celebrate
Mis.	91– 1	*c·* in commemoration of the Christ.

celebrate
Mis.	176–14	The day we *c·* reminds us of
	225– 4	*c·* the eighty-second birthday of
Chr.	53–18	To *c·* As Truth demands,
Po.	vi–19	*bells are ringing to c· the*
My.	262–12	I *c·* Christmas with my soul,

celebrated
Mis.	306– 7	* suggestions of events to be *c·*
Pul.	30–13	* not *c·* by outward symbols of
	31– 1	* on January 6 shall be *c·*.
	75–21	* *c·* the dedication of the church
My.	50–23	* *c·* her Communion Sabbath as
	304–24	Agassiz, the *c·* naturalist

celebration
Mis.	304–13	* any great patriotic *c·*

celestial
Mis.	100–24	unite terrestrial and *c·* joys,
	311– 5	as we journey to the *c·* city.
	323– 3	*c·* city above all clouds,
	376–29	spangled the gloom in *c·* space
	385–13	Soft gales *c·*, in sweet music bore
Ret.	87–19	to obey the *c·* injunction,
No.	26–24	Man is a *c·* ;
Pan.	3–17	* fair wisdom, that *c·* maid."
	3–28	denotes the *c·* harmony of
	3–32	his man-face, the *c·* world.
Po.	19– 2	*C·* the breezes that waft o'er its
	31– 3	*c·* seed dropped from Love's throne.
	48– 6	Soft gales *c·*, in sweet music bore
My.	186–11	on to the *c·* hills,

celibacy
Mis.	288–16	Is marriage nearer right than *c·*?
	341–24	takes the most solemn vow of *c·*

cell
Mis.	112–16	I visited in his *c·* the assassin of
	294–15	hides it in his *c·* of ingratitude.
Po.	1– 7	sustains thee in thy rock-bound *c·*.

cells
Ret.	18–11	And ope their closed *c·* to the
Po.	63–22	And ope their closed *c·* to the

cement
Mis.	135–20	so *c·* the bonds of Love.
	145– 1	at present is the *c·* of society,
Pul.	9– 2	*c·* of society, the hope of
	15–20	*c·* of a higher humanity
My.	189–14	encircle and *c·* the human race.
	339– 2	*c·* the bonds of Christian

cemented
Pul.	22–17	bonds of peace are *c·* by

cemeteries
Peo.	14– 4	our *c·* with amaranth blossoms,

cemetery
Po.	vi– 2	* poem
	page 15	poem
My.	69–30	* Mt. Auburn *c·* in Cambridge,
	312–27	followed the remains . . . to the *c·*.

censor
Mis.	297–12	surly *c·* ventilating his lofty scorn

censure
Mis.	278–11	never given occasion for a single *c·*,
Pul.	51– 8	* though they cannot escape *c·*,
No.	8– 6	whenever it can substitute *c·*.

census
Mis.	29–18	The *c·* since 1875
Pul.	67– 9	* *c·* of the religious faiths

cent
Mis.	305–25	* asked to contribute one *c·*
My.	72–26	* every *c·* of it was paid in
	73– 6	* very few of them owe a *c·*.
	86–13	* every *c·* of the estimated cost
	99–17	* not a *c·* of indebtedness left.
	216–11	without a *c·* to sustain it
	216–13	or his truth not worth a *c·*.

Centennial Day
Ret.	43–22	*C· D·* of our nation's freedom.

central
Mis.	162–12	*c·* point of his Messianic mission
	295– 9	*c·* cause of this "same original
	357–12	no *c·* emblem, no history.
Un.	57– 9	The cross is the *c·* emblem of
Pul.	28– 2	* The *c·* panel represents her
	31–19	* *c·* figure in all this agitation
	42–10	* children in the *c·* pews.
My.	73–29	* *c·* and western sections of
	236– 6	name for one *c·* Reading Room,

centre
Mis.	241– 2	should *c·* as steadfastly in God
	308– 1	divine Mind as its sole *c·*
	346– 1	Life, . . . the very *c·* of its faith.
Ret.	83– 6	than try to *c·* their interest on

centre
 Un. 10–19 Alpha and Omega, the *c·* and
 Pul. 25–29 * sunburst in the *c·* of the ceiling
   26– 3 * the *c·* being of pure white light,
   37–23 * not to *c·* too closely around
   42–22 * with a *c·* of white immortelles,
   56– 5 * and nearly every other *c·* of
   62–23 * placed on a small *c·* table.
 My. 13–10 * like a sun in the *c·* of its system,
   75– 4 * holding the *c·* of the stage
   85–23 * great *c·* of attraction,
   98– 8 * *c·* of an enthusiasm and reverence
   236–12 may become equivalent to no *c·*.

centre-piece
 Pul. 8–26 even its *c·*,— Mother's Room

centres
 Mis. 113–28 systematized *c·* of C. S.
 Pul. 8– 8 unemployed in our money *c·*,
 My. 72– 9 * From all the *c·* of Europe
   236–12 Too many *c·* may become
   341–21 * interest *c·* in the personality of

centrifugal
 Mis. 19–25 centripetal and *c·* mental forces

centripetal
 Mis. 19–25 *c·* and centrifugal mental forces

cents
 Mis. 305–25 * and twenty-five *c·* to pay for it.
 '01. 29–27 fifty *c·* on every book
 My. 28– 8 * dollars and *c·* received by him,

centuries
 break
 Po. 79–18 *c·* break, the earth-bound wake,
 Christian
 My. 112– 5 in the early Christian *c·*
 combined
 My. 127–22 siege of the combined *c·*,
 coming
 '01. 30– 5 bequeathing . . . to the coming *c·*.
 dumb
 My. 268–18 as silent as the dumb *c·*
 early
 '01. 18–23 followers in the early *c·*,
 eighteen
 Mis. 81–12 *Are not the last eighteen c·*
   165– 2 more than eighteen *c·* ago,
   182–32 more than eighteen *c·* ago.
   321– 4 less . . . than eighteen *c·* ago ;
 eighteenth
 Ret. 2–20 the seventeenth and eighteenth *c·*.
 entire
 Mis. 196– 6 through the entire *c·*,
   312–26 throughout the entire *c·*,
 fifteen
 Pul. 52–22 * over the world for fifteen *c·*,
 first
 '01. 33–26 what it was in the first *c·*
 forthcoming
 Ret. 94–30 and the forthcoming *c·*,
 genius of the
 Un. 9–12 talent and genius of the *c·*
 lead on the
 My. 347– 3 lead on the *c·* and reveal my
 nineteen
 My. 48– 4 * Not until nineteen *c·* had passed
   220–28 nineteen *c·* have greatly improved
 of spiritual growth
 Mis. 380– 8 as if *c·* of spiritual growth
 pass
 No. 27–11 Until *c·* pass, and this vision
 passed
 No. 13– 9 *c·* passed after those words were
 preceding
 Pul. 55– 6 * last quarter of preceding *c·*.
 race of the
 My. 126–31 win we the race of the *c·*.
 will intervene
 Mis. 92– 4 *C·* will intervene before the
 Ret. 84– 1 *C·* will intervene before the

 Mis. 80–25 in successive generations for *c·*,
   99–23 winds of time sweep clean the *c·*,
   203–13 served the imagination for *c·*.
 Ret. 17–19 sturdy horse-chestnut for *c·* hath
 Po. 63– 5 sturdy horse-chestnut for *c·* hath
 My. 117–23 lost to the *c·* except by
   272– 5 pushes onward the *c·* ;

century
 ago
 Ret. 1– 7 English authoress of a *c·* ago.
 My. 147– 4 Over a half *c·* ago,
 closing
 Pan. 12–10 This closing *c·*, and its successors,

century
 coming
 My. 266– 4 confronting the coming *c·*
 every
 Pul. 23–19 * closing years of every *c·*
 first
 Mis. 40–12 first *c·* of the Christian era?"
   189–30 not confined to the first *c·* ;
 Ret. 93– 1 first *c·* of the Christian era
   94–28 first *c·* of the Christian era
 Pan. 8–15 demonstrated in the first *c·* by
 '01. 28– 8 first *c·* of the Christian era
 My. 107– 1 the Christians in the first *c·*
   127–11 other religions since the first *c·*.
   180– 5 practised in the first *c·* by him
   300–29 from the first *c·* churches,
 half
 Mis. 295–29 who for a half *c·* has
 My. 147– 4 a half *c·* ago, . . . the grand old elm
   229–12 might cost them a half *c·*.
 hence
 Pul. vii– 5 Three quarters of a *c·* hence,
 new
 '01. 1– 6 first communion in the new *c·*
 Po. page 22 poem
 My. 260–10 the first month of the new *c·*.
 nineteenth
 Mis. 99–12 Men and women of the nineteenth *c·*,
   382–12 latter half of the nineteenth *c·*
 Pul. vii– 8 latter half of the nineteenth *c·*
   23–18 * last quarter of the nineteenth *c·*.
   55– 7 * Of our remarkable nineteenth *c·*
 '00. 1–10 last year of the nineteenth *c·*
 My. 127–21 latter days of the nineteenth *c·*.
   131–23 latter days of the nineteenth *c·*,
   257–18 the close of the nineteenth *c·*,
   264–13 * Thanksgiving Day of the nineteenth *c·*
 patient
 Po. 22– 1 God-crowned, patient *c·*,
 present
 Pul. 23–23 * latter part of the present *c·*,
 quarter
 My. 89–28 * marvels of the last quarter *c·*.
 quarter of a
 My. 294–27 animated . . . for one quarter of a *c·*.
 quarter of the
 Pul. 56–14 * the last quarter of the *c·*.
 third
 My. 146– 7 acknowledged since the third *c·*.
 this
 Mis. 43–20 great ordeal of this *c·*.
   166–24 named in this *c·* C. S.,
 '01. 16–24 Shall it be said of this *c·*
   33–25 proof that a religion in this *c·* is
 My. 192–10 mystery and . . . rule not this *c·*.
   220– 2 Whatever changes come to this *c·*
   264–15 last Thanksgiving Day of this *c·*
   302–19 I stand in relation to this *c·* as
 twentieth
 Pul. vii– 6 elders of the twentieth *c·*,
   8–30 They belong to the twentieth *c·*.
   22–10 I predict that in the twentieth *c·*
 '00. 9–20 twentieth *c·* in the ebb and flow of
 '02. 5– 5 spiritual dawn of the twentieth *c·*
 My. 95–20 * miracles . . . in this twentieth *c·*
   155–16 take step with the twentieth *c·*,
   199–18 on the verge of the twentieth *c·*,
   229–23 twentieth *c·* Church Manual
   248–15 sponsors for the twentieth *c·*,
   264– 9 * threshold of the twentieth *c·*,

cerebellum
 Un. 45–18 a habitant of the *c·*,

cerebral
 My. 301–25 drug cannot . . . affect *c·* conditions

ceremonial
 Mis. 81–14 *c· (or ritualistic) waters*
   91– 8 not as a perpetual . . . *c·* of the
 Pul. 30–11 * The *c·* of uniting is to sign a
 No. 34– 4 We shall leave the *c·* law when we
 My. 88–11 * a *c·* of far more than usual
   170– 2 no formal church *c·*,

ceremonials
 Mis. 91–14 to perpetuate no *c·* except as

ceremonies
 Mis. 17–11 material religion with its . . . *c·*,
 Ret. 89– 8 for sacrificial *c·*, not for sermons.
 Pul. 40–16 * simple *c·*, four times repeated,
   64–27 * to participate in the *c·*,
   75–19 * *c·* at Boston last Sunday
 No. 12–10 doctrines, rites, and *c·*,
 My. 29–15 * *c·* that appealed more to the eye,
   86–12 * take part in the subsequent *c·*
   86–26 * The attendance at the *c·*
   333–14 * with the usual *c·*.

ceremoniously
   My. 147–25 never stop *c·* to dedicate halls.
ceremony
   Mis. 143–15 with quiet, imposing *c·*,
      282–27 when there is no time for *c·*
   Man. 49–19 A Legal *C·*.
      49–20 the *c·* shall be performed by
      60–25 Let the *c·* be devout.
   Ret. 19– 3 the *c·* taking place under the
   Pul. 38– 3 * *c·* took place in 1881.
   My. 19– 6 * The *c·* concluded with
certain
   Mis. ix– 1 A *c·* apothegm of a Talmudical
      7– 2 not be allowed to eat *c·* food,
     64–28 as to be *c·* that he *is* in a state of
     71– 8 *c·*, that he healed others who
     71–22 mythical origin and *c·* end.
     80–24 In a *c·* sense, we should
    107–27 in *c·* morbid instances
    159–16 where I deposit *c·* recollections
    166–22 leaven that a *c·* woman hid
    193–15 *c·* clergyman charitably expressed it,
    220–10 in *c·* directions, and turn them
    229– 1 *c·* predisposing or exciting causes.
    229–11 how much more *c·* would be
    242– 7 if either would reset *c·* dislocations
    272–31 If *c·* natures have not profited
    289–12 agreements to *c·* compacts:
    295– 1 *c·* references to American women
    337– 4 how can you be *c·* of so momentous
    349– 3 a *c·* regular-school physician,
    353–27 *C·* students, being too much
   Man. 82– 3 disapproves of *c·* books or
   Ret. 1– 8 *c·* manuscripts containing Scriptural
     36– 8 This will account for *c·* published
     37–13 or *c·* German philosophers,
   Un. 4– 8 in a *c·* finite human sense,
     7–18 *C·* self-proved propositions
    29– 4 all criminal law, to a *c·* extent.
    45–15 *c·* forms of theology and philosophy,
   Pul. 13–13 sweet and *c·* sense that God is Love.
    14– 4 *c·* active yet unseen mental agencies
    29–20 * injunctions could, under *c·* conditions,
    59–10 * *c·* hymns and psalms being omitted.
    69–22 * *c·* Christian and scientific laws,
    70–17 * in 1866 she became *c·* that
    76–10 * in *c·* lights has a shimmer of silver.
   Rud. 16–24 originated with *c·* opposing factions,
    17– 1 Like *c·* Jews whom St. Paul
   Pan. 3– 8 *C·* moods of mind find an
    4– 1 *c·* forms of pantheism and polytheism.
   '00. 8–30 advise students not to do *c·* things
    10–11 *C·* elements in human nature
   '01. 25–10 *c·* individuals call aids to
   Hea. 5– 4 by *c·* kinds of food,
   Peo. 3–25 implanted in our religions *c·*
   My. 44– 8 * but one thing is *c·*,
    70– 3 * One thing is *c·* :
    93–27 * *c·* statistics brought to light
    105–32 proved to be more *c·*
    111–27 *c·* class of professionals
    116– 6 *c·* individuals are inclined
    210–19 *C·* individuals entertain the
    221– 4 *c·* purely human views.
    259–23 *C·* occasions, considered
    294– 7 In a *c·* city the Master
    303–13 not wasted in *c·* directions.
    334–12 * *c·* circumstances in 1843,
    342–10 * no mistaking *c·* lines
certainly
   Mis. 6–11 should *c·* prove to all minds
    28–22 It *c·* does not signify a
    38– 5 as this teaching *c·* does,
    61–17 * *c·* I saw him, or his effigy,
    87–18 *which is c· a mistake.*
    379–16 He *c·* had advanced views
   Un. 4–20 which was *c·* the divine Mind ;
    33–12 it is *c·* not the Mind of Christ,
   Pul. 10–23 as progress *c·* demands,
    24– 5 * *c·* the most unique structure in
    31– 2 * *c·* a very remarkable retrospect.
    33–15 * *c·* offer food for meditation.
    33–25 * *c·* true that many and many persons,
   No. 6– 2 *c·* would contradict the Science of
    22– 2 has *c·* not touched the hem
   Pan. 7–22 *c·* gives to matter and evil
    11–18 as *c·* as the man who
   My. 48–21 * will *c·* build such truth
    70– 1 * it *c·* looks imposing.
    75– 4 * *c·* holding the centre of the
    79–19 * *c·* must be something more
    87–26 * *c·* imbued with the spirit of
    95–19 * faith of these people is *c·* great.
    244–26 will *c·* not exceed three
    273– 5 * *C·*, Christian Scientists,

certainly
   My. 307– 1 *c·* read like words that
    324–19 * He *c·* never gave us the
certainty
   Mis. 210– 5 with mathematical *c·*
    220–31 with the *c·* of Science
    279– 3 *c·* of individual punishment
   Ret. 24–10 I gained the scientific *c·*
    31– 4 showing this solemn *c·*
   Pul. 55–19 * held to be scientific *c·*,
    83–10 * the *c·* of inspiration
   '01. 2– 1 *c·* that Christianity is now
    2–13 Absolute *c·* in the practice of
   My. 190–19 *c·* of the divine laws of
    295– 5 the *c·* of immortality.
    348–20 *c·* of its value to the race
certificate
   Mis. x–25 *c·* of membership made out to
   Man. 85–13 unless he has a *c·* to show
    91–21 not having the *c·* of C.S.D.
   Ret. 43–13 received a *c·* from Dr. W. W. Keen's
   My. 251–22 receive a *c·* of the degree C.S.D.
    329–18 * by the *c·* of a notary public
certificates
   Man. 85–11 Teachers must have *C·*.
    90– 3 *C·*.
    90– 4 given *c·* by this Board
    91– 6 shall be on all *c·* issued.
   My. 240–28 * who have received *c·* from
    245–23 students . . . have received *c·*,
cerulean
   Mis. 376–26 on a background of *c·* hue ;
cessation
   Pul. 41– 3 * *c·* of the tide of contributions
chaff
   Mis. 79– 6 sift the *c·* from the wheat,
   My. 111–11 as *c·* is separated from the wheat.
chagrined
   No. 41–22 Church seems almost *c·* that
chain
   Mis. 205–23 order of Science is the *c·* of ages,
   Pul. 14– 2 hour when the people will *c·*,
   Po. 15–15 or die in their *c·*.
    26–19 *c·* and charter I have lived to see
    34–19 Wearing no earthly *c·*,
    72– 1 O not too soon is rent the *c·*
   My. 200–11 The *c·* of Christian unity,
    202–18 onward and upward *c·* of being.
    279– 8 *c·* of scientific being
    339– 4 leads upward in the *c·* of being.
chained
   Mis. 102– 7 If . . . Mind would be *c·* to finity,
chains
   Mis. 101–17 undermines the . . . breaks their *c·*,
    262–20 looseth the *c·* of sickness and sin,
   Un. 56–23 be made to fret in their *c·* ;
   Peo. 11–14 their *c·* are clasped by the false
   My. 69– 2 * the eight bronze *c·*,
chair
   Mis. 112–20 he sank back in his *c·*,
   Ret. 8–14 I sat in a little *c·* by her side,
   Pul. 48– 7 * sit in her swinging *c·*,
   Po. 3– 8 I watch thy *c·*, and wish thee here ;
   My. 49–20 * with Mrs. Eddy in the *c·*.
Chairman and **chairman**
   My. 173–28 *c·* of the prudential committee
    333– 2 * in the possession of the *c·*
    361–26 * CHARLES DEAN, *C·*,
    362– 2 CHARLES A. DEAN, *C·* BOARD OF TRUSTEES,
chairs
   Mis. 325–16 nodding on cushioned *c·*,
   Pul. 29–13 * *c·* pressed into service
Chaldee
   Mis. 1– 3 The *C·* watched the appearing
    333–30 *C·* hung his destiny out upon
challenge
   Mis. 247– 9 I calmly *c·* the world,
   '00. 9–21 *c·* the thinkers, speakers,
   My. 108– 5 I *c·* matter to act apart from
    163– 3 angelic song chiming chaste *c·*
    248–28 *c·* universal indifference,
challenged
   My. 203–27 all chance of being *c·*.
    233– 7 when *c·* by Truth,
challenges
   Mis. 131– 1 *c·* the errors of others
challenging
   Mis. 329–20 *c·* the sedentary shadows

chamber
Mis.	159–13	Into this upper c·,
	159–15	In this c· is memory's wardrobe,
	202– 5	* c· where the good man meets
	257–29	Even the c· where the good man
	279–23	met together in an upper c· ;
Pul.	54–26	* in the c· with him,

Chamberlin
Hon. Judge
My.	137–10	HON. JUDGE C·, CONCORD, N. H.

Honorable Judge
My.	138–29	* directed to Honorable Judge C·

Judge Robert N.
My.	137– 3	* Judge Robert N. C· of the

chambers
Mis.	292–28	searched the secret c· of sense?
	343–27	haunted the c· of memory,
Ret.	8– 2	throng the c· of memory.
Pul.	5– 9	holds in her secret c· those
Po.	26–18	the dim c· of eternity
My.	156–19	the upper c· of thought

chamois
Ret.	11–21	Farther than feet of c· fall,
Po.	60–19	Farther than feet of c· fall,

chance
Mis.	79–30	because they c· to be under arrest
Ret.	14–15	take my c· . . . with my brothers and
Un.	17– 1	A lie has only one c· of
	26–13	* C· and change are busy ever,
	26–18	how can it be also true that c·
	26–23	what place has c· in the divine
Rud.	5–25	football of c· and sinking into
My.	49– 7	* c· of sweeping the world
	120– 7	Accept my gratitude for the c·
	203–26	safe from all c· of being challenged.
	248–28	indifference, c·, and creeds.

chancel
Pul.	26– 8	* corresponding to the c· of
	58–23	* Adjoining the c· is a pastor's

chancery
Mis.	122–24	Neither . . . nor a religious c·

chandeliers
Pul.	25–30	* takes the place of c·.

change (noun)
actual
Mis.	188–27	not . . . an actual c· in the realities

and the grave
Mis.	339–29	C· and the grave may part us ;

another
Mis.	158– 8	another c· in your pulpit

before the
Mis.	42–17	If, before the c· whereby we meet

called death
Mis.	42– 1	*After the c· called death,*
No.	27–27	go on after the c· called death,

chance and
Un.	26–13	* Chance and c· are busy ever,
	26–18	can it be . . . that *chance* and c· are

in the actions
Mis.	237– 7	wrought a c· in the actions of men.

in the time
My.	121– 3	suggested a c· in the time for

no present
My.	343– 6	* "No present c· is contemplated

of consciousness
Un.	11–11	c· of consciousness and evidence,

of death
Pul.	38–19	* passed the c· of death

of heart
Mis.	50–18	*Do you believe in c· of heart?*
	50–25	c· of heart would deliver man
	51– 1	c· of heart is essential to
Ret.	14–20	experienced a c· of heart ;

small
My.	78–16	* none proffering small c·.

this
Mis.	50–25	This c· of heart would
	51– 1	This c· of heart is essential
Un.	11–12	effected this c· through the
'02.	20–20	I shall be the loser by this c·,

to health
No.	40–25	comes with the c· to health,

Mis.	50–20	must be a c· from human affections,
	50–22	must be a c· from the belief that
	82–31	not subject to growth, c·, or
Ret.	4–12	But c· has been busy.
Un.	30–22	c· in the mortal sense of things,
	37– 9	a c· in human consciousness,
No.	40–24	If a c· in the religious views of
'01.	23–13	as would a c· of the denominations
My.	60–11	* What a c· in the Christian world !
	341–27	* c· from the misty air outside

change (verb)
Mis.	19–15	can never c· the current of that
	23–31	could not c· its species
	26–31	How, then, can this conclusion c·,
	118–15	nor c· this immutable decree of Love :
	217–28	nature of God must c· in order to
	217–32	and our convictions c· :
	218– 8	mortal mind must c· all its
	219–17	must c· his patient's consciousness
	219–20	must c· the patient's sense of
	219–28	he can c· this evil sense and
	298–30	false consciousness does not c· the
	345–10	* I cannot c· from good to bad."
Un.	35– 2	Let mortal mind c·, and say
	35– 5	C· the mind, and the quality changes.
	56–24	c· from flesh to Spirit,
Rud.	6– 8	when we c· the nature of beauty
No.	39–12	Prayer can neither c· God, nor
	39–13	can and does c· our modes
'02.	17–13	Earth's actors c· earth's scenes ;
Peo.	13–19	* cannot c· at once from
Po.	67–19	c· not with years ;
My.	41– 4	* No one can c· the law of
	321–19	* to c· my opinion one iota

changeableness
Peo.	8– 3	If c· that repenteth itself ;

changed
Mis.	x–17	My signature has been slightly c·
	26–32	or be c·, to mean that good
	50–28	c· from self to benevolence
	50–29	c· to having but *one* God
	52–18	*not dispelled, but only c·,*
	65–17	*Have you c· your instructions*
	68– 5	include also man's c· appearance
	191– 6	c· the meaning of the term,
	220–16	c· his patient's consciousness
	235– 1	man has a c· recognition of
	237– 6	c· belief has wrought a change in
Man.	18–24	c· the title of "First Members"
	64–13	The Title of Mother C·.
Ret.	30– 7	motive of my . . . labors has never c·.
	64–18	God's ways . . . have never c·,
	82– 1	c·, modified, broadened,
Rud.	17–15	ways of Christianity have not c·.
No.	1– 5	only as our natures are c·
Hea.	19– 7	Had they c· the felon's belief
My.	28–31	* c· the whole aspect of medicine
	325–14	* my desire has never c·.
	327–21	* an old law, . . . was c·
	327–24	* was c· to read as follows :

changeful
Pul.	32– 6	* c· expression cannot thus be
Po.	8–16	dreaming alone of its c· sky
	31–14	vassal of the c· hour,
	46– 5	Nor April's c· showers,

changeless
Un.	26–21	If God be c· *goodness,*

changes
Mis.	158– 6	c· about to be made.
	170– 6	which never c· to death.
	175– 9	Science c· this false sense,
	363–13	the c· of matter, or evil.
Un.	7– 4	c· at Andover Seminary
	26–10	the material c·, the *phantasma,*
	35– 6	Change the mind, and the quality c·.
Pul.	55– 5	* cyclic c· that came during
Rud.	7–23	Spirit no more c· its species,
Hea.	5– 5	by c· of temperature,
Peo.	1–16	c· from material to spiritual
My.	66–12	* number of c· will be made
	220– 1	Whatever c· come to this century

changeth
My.	33–24	and c· not. — *Psal.* 15 : 4.

changing
Mis.	268–20	c· the affections,
Un.	11–10	the need of c· this mind
Pan.	6–13	c· the order and harmony of
Hea.	4–27	demonstrate a c· Principle?
My.	215–31	we have no hint of his c·

channel
Mis.	309–15	not the c· through which
	373–18	out of its proper c·,
Ret.	54–19	same c· of ignorant belief.

channels
Mis.	212–20	flow not into one of their c·.
	220–11	turn them into c· of Truth.
	291– 4	forced into personal c·,
	351–29	turns it into the opposite c·.
	359–13	proper c· for development,
Man.	45– 1	supplies within the wide c· of
Ret.	52– 4	seeking to broaden its c·
	79–16	Through the c· of material sense,
No.	44–15	and choke the c· of God.

channels
'01. 19–27 flow through no such *c·.*

chant
Mis. 281– 2 *c·* hymns of victory for triumphs.
Po. 34– 9 Wouldst *c·* thy vespers

chants
Mis. 321– 2 watchful shepherd *c·* his welcome

chaos
Chr. 53– 3 O'er the grim night of *c·*
Ret. 69–25 awful din, blackness, and *c·,*
Un. 13–14 reduce the universe to *c·.*
56– 1 The *c·* of mortal mind
Pul. 14–21 deep waters of *c·* and old night.
Po. 1–10 from *c·* dark set free,

chapel
My. 172– 3 * first *c·* of the college.
184–23 Your rural *c·* is a social success

chapels
Mis. 150–17 *C·* and churches are dotting the

chaplain
My. 309–12 For several years father was *c·* of

chaplet
Mis. 163– 6 its *c·,* a grave

Chapter
115
Mis. 272–12 * Public Statutes, *C·* 115, Section 2,
268
Mis. 272–14 * Statutes of 1883, *C·* 268,
375
Mis. 272– 4 * under Act of 1874, *C·* 375,

My. 335– 9 * officer of the Lodge and *C·,*

Chapter
Mis. 32–13 In Mark, ninth *c·,*
57– 9 in the first *c·* of Genesis.
92–13 in the *c·* on Recapitulation.
92–17 contained in that *c·* of "S· and H·
191– 8 John, sixth *c·* and seventieth verse,
191–12 In Mark, ninth *c·* and
192–25 last *c·* of Mark is emphatic on this
314– 8 *c·* (or portion of the *c·*)
314–22 the book, *c·,* and verses.
332–13 Genesis, third *c·* and ninth verse,
Man. 86–17 teach from the *c·* "Recapitulation"
86–24 said *c·* on "Recapitulation"
Ret. 35– 3 *c·* on Recapitulation in S. and H.
37–22 the *c·* on Animal Magnetism,
38– 2 I had finished . . . as far as that *c·,*
38– 8 in my last *c·* a partial history of
38–21 closing *c·* of my first edition of
83–19 the *c·* for the class-room,
84–10 in the *c·* on Recapitulation.
Un. 43–24 in the third *c·* of Philippians,
Pul. 27–24 * in the Apocalypse, *c·* 12,
Pan. 7–19 the third *c·* of Genesis,
'00. 12– 6 In Revelation, second *c·,*
'02. 7– 5 In the first *c·* of Genesis,
My. 60–17 * the first *c·* of Genesis.
136– 6 as depicted in the *c·*
222– 1 the seventeenth *c·* of the Gospel

chapters
Pul. 38– 9 * It consists of fourteen *c·,*
My. 179– 3 first and second *c·* of Genesis,

character
and divinity
Mis. 197–18 the *c·* and divinity which Jesus
and philanthropy
'00. 14–24 respect the *c·* and philanthropy
and practice
Ret. 28–30 assimilate the *c·* and practice of
and sovereignty
Pan. 7–11 lose the *c·* and sovereignty of
beautiful
Ret. 6–13 To speak of his beautiful *c·*
cause and
Mis. 299– 2 awake to their cause and *c·.*
Christian
My. 332–31 * record and Christian *c·* was found ;
concrete
Mis. 337–25 understood the concrete *c·* of
consecrated
Pul. 32–28 * saintly and consecrated *c·.*
distinguished
Pul. 1– 9 was a distinguished *c·,*
divine
Un. 1–17 nearer to the divine *c·,*
Hea. 4–22 conception of the divine *c·,*
elevated
Ret. 5–25 * She gave an elevated *c·* to
enduring
My. 24–24 * substantial and enduring *c·* of

character
exemplary
Man. 55–17 three years of exemplary *c·.*
give force to
'01. 19–14 That animal natures give force to *c·*
granite
My. 163–26 friendship, and granite *c·.*
health and
Peo. 7–28 health and *c·* of man
her
Ret. 2– 2 had in her *c·* that sturdy
My. 39–30 * strength and beauty of her *c·.*
high-principled
My. 319– 9 for his high-principled *c·*
His
Mis. 102–13 His *c·* admits of no degrees
his
Mis. 148– 3 one part of his *c·* at variance
293–16 if evil dominates his *c·,*
309–11 contemplation of his *c·.*
hue and
Mis. 372–28 with true hue and *c·* of the
human
Mis. 151– 7 purifies the human *c·,*
Un. 29– 2 hypothesis as to its human *c·.*
'00. 8– 9 so the human *c·* comes forth
My. 246–18 revealed through the human *c·.*
identical in
My. 78– 3 * six services, identical in *c·,*
individual
Mis. 81–22 Every individual *c·,*
Ret. 73–14 fail to appreciate individual *c·.*
No. 7–25 distinctions of individual *c·*
Jesus'
Mis. 91–16 real affection for Jesus' *c·*
jewels of
Mis. 201–27 losing those jewels of *c·,*
man's
Hea. 5– 7 saying . . . bias a man's *c·.*
my
My. 306– 2 misrepresents my *c·,*
nature and
Un. 1–12 nature and *c·* of God
3–21 in His own nature and *c·,*
6–18 concerning the divine nature and *c·*
31–18 the nature and *c·* of matter,
of a liar
Mis. 226–21 *c·* of a liar and hypocrite
of Christ
Mis. 367–27 in logic, or in the *c·* of Christ.
of Jesus
Mis. 360–10 and the *c·* of Jesus,
Ret. 22– 8 St. Paul summarized the *c·* of Jesus
of nations
Peo. 2–28 influence upon the *c·* of nations
of the Christ
Ret. 23–16 *c·* of the Christ was illuminated by
of the votaries
Mis. 196–15 the *c·* of the votaries to
of true greatness
My. 150–5 of the *c·* of true greatness :
phases of
Mis. 127–30 Mortal mind presents phases of *c·*
previous
Man. 52–12 and his previous *c·* has been good,
qualities of
Peo. 8– 9 bring out these qualities of *c·*
refines
My. 131– 3 that which refines *c·*
religious
Man. 61–20 of an appropriate religious *c·*
scholarship, and
My. 104–26 talents, scholarship, and *c·*
straightforward
Mis. 233–19 fair-seeming for straightforward *c·,*
subdued
Mis. 354–16 a *c·* subdued, a life consecrated,
true
Rud. 17– 5 true *c·* of C. S.,
My. 121–18 can be found in a true *c·,*
unstable
Mis. 147–18 a loose and unstable *c·.*
whatever
No. 24– 5 He is extension, of whatever *c·.*

———

Mis. 26–27 in the Greek Testament, *c·.*
67– 9 with his rights of mind and *c·.*
120–28 whose *c·* we to-day commemorate,
224–14 constitution, culture, *c·,*
337–30 again reproduced in the *c·*
Ret. 5–21 * *c·* of Mrs. Abigail Ambrose Baker
My. 4–21 unfolding the true metal in *c·,*
30–11 * the *c·* of the attendance.
85– 1 * remarkable in the *c·* of the
179–22 *c·* of the Nazarene Prophet

characteristic
'02.   2–22   inherent c· of my nature,
Hea.   12–15   c· peculiarities and
My.   82–20   * c· of Christian Scientists,
     137– 8   * c· in both substance and
     184–16   c· of our Granite State,

characteristics
Pul.   48–25   * one of her c·,
'00.   8– 7   c· of tree and flower,
My.   87– 7   * c· of this crowd of visitors.

characterize
Mis.   126–21   should c· Christian Scientists.
     134– 6   c· justice and Christianity.
     301–12   c· the writings of a few professed
Man.   77–19   c· all the proceedings of
Pan.   14–13   to c· her government,
'01.   1–20   must always c· heroic hearts ;
My.   4–22   c· the seeker and finder of C. S.
     245– 7   Law and order c· its work

characterized
Mis.   84– 4   This wisdom, which c· his sayings,
     112–30   is c· in this Scripture :
     199–31   c· and dated the Christian era.
     363–31   c· by a more spiritual apprehension
Ret.   25– 5   God I c· as individual entity,
Un.   1– 9   may justly be c· as *wonderful*.
Peo.   6–28   Periods and peoples are c· by
Po.   vii– 2   * c· by the same lofty trend of
My.   331–27   * c· the people of the South,

characterizes
My.   308–31   whom *McClure's Magazine* c· as

characterizing
Man.   59– 2   or without c· their origin

characters
Mis.   191–28   opposite c· ascribed to him
     357–23   whose Christian c· and lives
     360– 7   colossal c·, Paul and Jesus.
Pul.   5– 9   those c· of holiest sort,
Peo.   3– 2   our ideals form our c·,
My.   48–22   * into the marrow of their c·.
     186– 3   writes in living c· their lessons
     277–14   c· and lives of men determine the

charge
Mis.   38– 1   *Why do you c· for teaching C. S.*,
     132–19   having c· of a church,
     155–30   to contemplate the universal c·
     306–29   give His angels c· — *Psal.* 91 : 11.
     335–13   others c· upon me with
     345– 4   against the c· of atheism ;
     374–15   Angels, . . . hold c· over both,
Man.   52–11   as to the validity of the c·.
     63–20   take c· of the Reading Rooms
     69–11   whatsoever she may c·
     86–12   who is not in c· of an association
Ret.   84–27   A teacher should take c· only of
     89–23   to take c· of their students,
Pul.   87– 1   * take c· of any services that may
'00.   14–27   this sin to their c·." — *Acts* 7 : 60.
'02.   15– 6   Healing . . . without c·,
Po.   33– 1   remember my blessings and c·,
My.   12– 6   * those having the work in c·
     16–15   * who have the work directly in c·,
     73–20   * It is in c· of G. D. Robertson,
     135–14   to take the c· of my property ;
     137–21   to take c· of my property ;
     219–18   I would not c· Christians with
     243–14   who are adequate to take c· of
     244–27   No c· will be made for my services.

chargeable
Mis.   363–16   God is not c· with imperfection.

charged
Hea.   7–19   he c· home a crime to mind,

charges
Mis.   247–12   The c· against my views are false,
     311–32   who were reporting false c·,
My.   237–15   chapter sub-title
     237–17   their c· for treatment equal to

charging
My.   204–23   the c· of the sick whom you

chariot
My.   115– 2   mighty c· of divine Love,

chariot-paths
Pul.   7– 1   from the c· of justice,

chariots
Un.   17–10   ties its . . . to the divine c·,

chariot-wheels
My.   127– 7   speed of the c· of Truth

charitable
Rud.   14– 8   never sought c· support,
No.   8– 4   faithful, and c· with all.
My.   245–16   let Christian Scientists be c·.

charitable
My.   338–29   instructed to be, c· towards all,
     358–20   to a worthy and c· purpose.

charitableness
Man.   40–10   in true brotherliness, c·,

charitably
Mis.   78–16   We will c· hope, however,
     172– 3   Dispensing the Word c·,
     193–15   clergyman c· expressed it,
My.   106– 3   speak c· of all mankind

charities
Mis.   245–20   c·, and reforms of to-day.
My.   231– 2   endeavors to bestow her c·

charity
Mis.   ix– 3   * "The noblest c· is to
     ix– 4   * prevent a man from accepting c· ;
     7– 7   Great c· and humility is necessary
     13– 2   mercy and c· toward every one,
     32–23   and c· must begin at home.
     130– 2   long-suffering, meekness, c·,
     130–27   he who exercises the largest c·,
     172–10   white-winged c·, brooding over all,
     209–30   egotism and false c·
     210–27   C· has the courage of conviction ;
     210–29   C· is Love ;
     210–31   C· never flees before error,
     211– 7   sickly c· that supplies criminals
     224–24   c· broad enough to cover the
     267– 6   C· students, for whom I have
     292–23   C· thus serves as admonition
     311–12   in the full spirit of that c·
     330–27   boasts and begs, and God denies c·.
     335–14   having too much c· ;
     338–12   c· that suffereth long and is
     369–21   white-winged c· that heals and
Man.   47–24   C· to All.
Ret.   50–15   my list of indigent c· scholars
Rud.   14– 1   fed, clothed, and sheltered by c·.
     14–21   doing c· work besides.
No.   45– 3   St. Paul said that without c· we
     45– 4   "C· suffereth long, — *I Cor.* 13 : 4.
'00.   14–19   c· that seeketh not only her own,
     15–24   and c·, and service, — *Rev.* 2 : 19.
'01.   12–14   yet should not have c·,
     26–20   a sound faith and c·,
     26–20   the greatest of which is c·
     26–23   and have not c·, — *I Cor.* 13 : 1.
     32– 8   Full of c· and good works,
     34–18   sweet c· which seeketh not
My.   19–22   that her c·, . . . shall reap richly
     149–22   to demonstrate Christian c·.
     158–15   holiness, patience, c·, love.
     175–24   fraternity, and Christian c·.
     187–12   c· out of a pure heart, — *I Tim.* 1 : 5.
     215– 9   without having c· scholars
     216–28   that c· begins at home,
     227– 6   C· is quite as rare as wisdom,
     227– 7   but when c· does appear,
     231– 1   chapter sub-title
     231–17   "C· suffereth long — *I Cor.* 13 : 4.
     231–18   wisdom must govern c·,
     262–28   humility, benevolence, c·,
     275–27   c· brooding over all,

charlatan
My.   106–28   * is the Christian Scientist a c· ?

charlatanism
Mis.   368–14   C·, fraud, and malice
'00.   12–23   to purge our cities of c·.
Hea.   14–14   ignorance and c· are miserable

charlatans
Mis.   80– 7   defense of medical c· in general,
     243–20   There are c· in "mind-cure,"

Charles
Pul.   39–16   * Throws o'er the C· its flood of

Charleston
S. C.
Pul.   34– 2   * Colonel Glover, of C·, S. C.,
'00.   1–20   cities, such as . . . C·, S. C.,
My.   312–19   resided in C·, S. C.
     330–13   * Christian Scientist of C·, S. C.,
     330–16   * who she states was of C·, S. C.,
     335– 3   * resided in C·, S. C.,
     335–13   * a resident of C·, S. C.

South Carolina
Mis.   x–21   Glover of C·, South Carolina,
Ret.   19– 2   Glover of C·, South Carolina,
'02.   15–17   Glover, of C·, South Carolina,

'02.   3– 8   put an end, at C·, to any
My.   332–21   * A Christian Scientist in C· was
     335–22   * to take the remains to C·.

Charlestown, Mass.
My.   49–16   * August 16, 1879, in C·, M·,

charm

Mis.	390– 3	Thou hast a Naiad's *c* ;
	393– 1	Chief, the *c* of thy reflecting,
Pul.	81–11	* an added grace—a newer *c*.
Pan.	3– 7	loneness lacks but one *c*
Po.	51– 6	Chief, the *c* of thy reflecting,
	55– 3	Thou hast a naiad's *c* ;
My.	258–27	A transmitted *c* rests on them

charms

'00.	13–20	included *c* and incantations.
Po.	32– 5	blossoms whose fragrance and *c*

charnel-house

Mis.	293–28	the *c* of sensuality,
	325–25	Away from this *c* of the

charred

Peo.	8–25	material systems, already *c*,
My.	178–24	Instantly the table sank a *c* mass.

chart

Mis.	356–28	the *c* of its divine Principle

charter

Mis.	272– 1	* obtained a college *c*
	272–21	* grant, which may be called a *c*,
	382–17	obtained the first *c* for the
	382–21	obtained the first and only *c* for a
Man.	18– 3	*c* for the Church was obtained
Ret.	16–16	*c* for The Mother Church
	43– 5	No *c* was granted for
	44– 4	*c* for this church was obtained
	49–19	thank the State for its *c*,
Pul.	20– 7	and reobtain its *c*
	38– 1	* *c* obtained the following June.
	67–28	* and a *c* was obtained
Po.	26–19	chain and *c* I have lived to see
	72– 2	*c*, trampling right in dust !
My.	49– 9	* The *c* of this little church

chartered

Mis.	271–22	only *c* College of Metaphysics.
	272–25	* but one legally *c* college of
Ret.	43– 5	College in Boston, *c* in 1881.
	48–17	College, *c* in January, 1881,
'00.	1–11	this first church . . . *c* in 1879,
My.	244–30	College . . . was *c* A.D. 1881.

charters

Mis.	272– 8	* no *c* were granted for
	272–22	* these so-called *c* bestow no rights to
	272–24	* institutions, under such *c*,

Chase

Mr.

My.	27–22	* announcement made by Mr. *C*

Stephen A.

Pul.	43– 9	* On the platform . . . Stephen A. *C*,
	59–25	* on the platform . . . Stephen A. *C*,
	86–10	* signatures of . . . and Stephen A. *C*,
	87– 8	* signature
My.	16– 2	* The report of Mr. Stephen A. *C*,
	21–30	* signature
	27–17	* signature
	72–17	* the notice which Stephen A. *C*,

Chase, C.S.D.

Stephen A.

My.	39–16	* Treasurer, Stephen A. *C*, C.S.D. ;

chase

Ret.	17–18	*C* tulip, magnolia, and fragrant
Po.	63– 3	*C* tulip, magnolia, and fragrant

chased

Mis.	388– 4	What *c* the clouds away?
Po.	7– 4	What *c* the clouds away?

chaste

My.	163– 3	chiming *c* challenge to praise

chastely

Pul.	77– 3	* one of the most *c* elegant

chasten

Ret.	21–18	is to *c* the affections,

chastened

Mis.	209–20	False pleasure will be, is, *c* ;
	213–15	has *c* and illumined
	281–10	one will be *c* for it.
	356–10	cultured intellects, *c* affections,
Ret.	31–27	spoke to my *c* sense

chasteneth

Mis.	18– 4	Lord loveth He *c*,— *Heb.* 12 : 6.
	73– 5	Lord loveth He *c* ;"— *Heb.* 12 : 6.
	125– 4	Lord loveth He *c*."— *Heb.* 12 : 6.
	208–20	Lord loveth He *c*."— *Heb.* 12 : 6.
Ret.	80– 5	Lord loveth He *c*,— *Heb.* 12 : 6.
Un.	23–12	whom the father *c* not— *Heb.* 12 : 7.

chastening

Un.	23–10	"If ye endure *c*,— *Heb.* 12 : 7.

chastens

Mis.	126–14	ordeal refines while it *c*.

chastens

Mis.	351–28	*c* its affection, purifies it,
	387–25	*c* pride and earth-born fear,
Po.	6–20	*c* pride and earth-born fear,

chastisement

Un.	23–13	if ye be without *c*,— *Heb.* 12 : 8.

chastisements

Mis.	102–18	His *c* are the manifestations of
My.	282–10	Through the wholesome *c* of **Love,**

Chattanooga, Tenn.

My.	323–15	* *C*, *T*, December 4, 1906.

chattel

Pul.	82–13	* they treated woman as a *c*,

cheating

'00.	2–19	"By *c*, lying, and crime ;

check

My.	26– 9	*c* of five thousand dollars,
	159–18	Material theories tend to *c*
	175– 6	Please accept the enclosed *c*
	222–30	holding of crime in *c*,
	289– 4	*c* for five hundred dollars
	318–20	He held himself well in *c*

checking

My.	67–11	* *C* facilities . . . 3,000 garments

checks

Pul.	44–28	* refused to accept any further *c*

cheek

Mis.	11–29	When smitten on one *c*,
	329–17	"breath all odor and *c* all bloom."
Ret.	31–23	Blanched was the *c* of pride
	45–21	on thy right *c*,— *Matt.* 5 : 39.
Po.	8–19	parting the ringlets to kiss my *c*.
My.	227–27	on thy right *c*,— *Matt.* 5 : 39.

cheeks

Mis.	240– 4	sparkling eyes, and ruby *c*

cheer

Mis.	16– 3	so comfort, *c*, and bless one,
	118–24	Be of good *c* ;
	157–18	I am glad that you are in good *c*.
	213–27	Christian Scientists, be of good *c* :
	231–23	look of *c* and a toy from
	320–11	to *c*, guide, and bless man
'02.	17–30	*c* the heart susceptible of light
Po.	10–18	*c* the hosts of heaven ;
	32–21	*c* me with hope when 'tis done ;
	66–14	Might *c* it, perchance,
My.	132– 7	be of good *c* ;— *John* 16 : 33.
	135–26	*c* my advancing years.
	175–12	growth and . . . of our city *c* me.
	202–21	I thank you for the words of *c*
	261– 3	*c* the children's Christmas
	337–19	"Wouldst *c* the hosts of heaven ;

cheered

Mis.	xii– 5	Supported, *c*, I take my pen and
My.	11–19	* she will be *c* and encouraged
	274–23	I am *c* and blessed when
	302–22	I am less lauded, . . . and *c*

cheerful

Ret.	5–24	* like the gentle dew and *c* light,
My.	84–21	* *c* optimism and energy of its
	87–20	* *c* looking groups of people
	87–29	* *c* doing of good.
	91–12	* Its communicants are *c*
	95–10	* *c* and prosperous body of

cheerfully

My.	87– 9	* *c* contented multitude
	118– 2	who *c* obey God
	222–31	*c* await the end— justice and
	360–14	*c* subscribe these words of love :

cheerfulness

My.	31–14	* of light and *c*,

cheering

Mis.	150–15	The outlook is *c*.
My.	234–18	regarded on one side only, is *c*,

cheers

My.	202–23	The taper . . . *c* the darkness.

Chelsea

My.	56–13	* Cambridge, *C*, and Roxbury.

chemicalization

Mis.	10–23	This destruction is a moral *c*,
Pul.	5–30	This spiritual *c* is the upheaval

chemist

Peo.	6– 9	* *c*, druggist, or drug

Chemistry and chemistry

Rud.	12–22	with the *c* of food?
My.	304– 8	*C*, Blair's Rhetoric,

cherish

Mis.	253–29	*C* these new-born children

cherish

Mis.	356–30	C· humility, "watch," — Matt. 26 : 41.
	370–15	This is the babe we are to c·.
Man.	48– 1	c· no enmity toward those who
Ret.	6–13	his beautiful character as I c· it,
My.	41–21	* unable to c· any enmity
	251–28	C· steadfastly this fact.
	331–22	* gratitude we owe and c· towards
	362–21	* We revere and c· your friendship,

cherished

Ret.	2–29	for whom she c· a high regard.
My.	40–12	* relinquish their c· resentments,
	195–11	deep love which I c· for you

cherishes

Mis.	131– 1	and c· his own,
	281–10	if one c· ambition unwisely,
'02.	19– 8	Scientist c· no resentment ;

cherries

Ret.	4–15	apples, peaches, pears, and c·

cherubim

My.	188–15	under the wings of the c·,

Cheshire Cat

Mis.	216–19	story of the C· C·,

Chestnut Hill

Mass.

Po.	vii–17	* C· H·, Mass., September 24, 1910.
My.	140– 9	C· H·, Mass.
	140–29	C· H·, Mass., June 21, 1908.
	143–31	C· H·, Mass., June 7, 1909.
	198– 9	C· H·, Mass., June 26, 1909.
	207–26	C· H·, Mass., January 6, 1909.
	255–11	C· H·, Mass., March 6, 1909.
	352– 3	* C· H·, Mass.
	355–16	C· H·, Mass., February 7, 1910.
	356–10	C· H·, Mass., April 20, 1910.
	356–19	C· H·, Mass., July 18, 1910.
	361–18	* Mrs. Mary Baker Eddy, C· H·, Mass.
	362– 7	C· H·, Mass., January 20, 1910.
	362–11	* Mrs. Mary Baker Eddy, C· H·, Mass.

chews

Mis.	240–28	nothing but . . . naturally c· tobacco.

Chicago

Ill.

Pul.	89–27	* Elite, C·, Ill.
	90– 9	* Times, C·, Ill.
My.	177– 2	chapter sub-title
	191–27	chapter sub-title
	208–23	chapter sub-title

Mis.	98– 7	at the National Convention in C·,
	98–16	progress of our common Cause in C·,
	134–18	to be in C· on June 13.
	156–14	in the one held at C·,
	157–19	Mr. E. A. Kimball, C. S. D., of C·,
	266–19	loyal students in C·, New York,
	275–22	at the grand meeting in C·
	275–26	C· is the wonder of the western
	304– 7	* coming World's Exposition at C·
	321–24	In reply to all invitations from C·
Pul.	4–29	Parliament of Religions, held in C·,
	23– 1	Daily Inter-Ocean, C·,
	28–27	* Judge Hanna, formerly of C·,
	56– 2	* New York, C·, Buffalo, Cleveland,
	79– 1	* [The Union Signal, C·]
'00.	1–21	C·, St. Louis, Denver,
My.	36– 4	* Mr. Edward A. Kimball of C·,
	77– 5	* leads the Auditorium of C·,
	146– 1	my dedicatory letter to the C·
	146– 8	in my letter to the church in C·,
	164– 7	heading
	164–15	beginning of C. S. in C·,
	177– 6	First Church of Christ, . . . in C·.
	181–23	it is estimated that C· has
	182– 1	Thirty years ago C· had few
	182–12	Scientist Association in C·,
	183– 5	in this great city of C·,
	192–16	hovers around your churches in C·,
	304–13	in New York City, C·, Boston,
	304–21	In a lecture in C·, he said :

Chickering Hall

Mis.	161– 2	in C· H·, Boston, Mass.,
Pul.	28–28	* held its meetings in C· H·,
My.	54–27	* concluded to engage C· H·
	54–31	* Sunday service held in C· H·
	55–10	* attendance . . . in C· H·,
	55–19	* services were held in C· H·,
	55–23	* as C· H· was to be remodelled.
	57–15	* in C· H·, October 3, 1893,
	80–15	* Howe and Woolson Halls, C· H·.
	80–24	* Woolson Hall, and C· H·,

chides

Hea.	1–18	* At fifty, c· his infamous delay,

chief

Mis.	163–23	Truth, the c· cornerstone.
	267– 7	whose c· aim is to injure me,
	275– 1	c· actors in scenes like these,
	393– 1	C·, the charm of thy reflecting,
Man.	17–15	the c· corner-stone whereof is,
	111–14	c· points of these instructions
Ret.	15– 6	the c· corner-stone." — Eph. 2 : 20.
Pul.	10–18	c· corner-stone in the house of
	43–23	* c· feature of the dedication,
No.	38–15	This is the c· corner-stone,
Pan.	13– 4	C· among the questions herein,
	14–15	guide and bless our c· magistrate,
Po.	51– 6	C·, the charm of thy reflecting,
	78–14	mourners, while yet the c·,
My.	17–15	a c· corner stone, — I Pet. 2 : 6.
	112– 8	and build on its c· corner-stone.
	112–30	c· cities and the best families
	158–25	He has laid the c· corner-stone
	166–15	Life's ills are its c· recompense ;
	182– 9	Truth, as the c· corner-stone.
	282– 5	friendship of our c· executive
	290–19	our nation's c· magistrate,
	292–10	comfort the c· mourner

chiefest

Ret.	23–19	"the c·," the only, — Song 5 : 10.

chiefly

Mis.	6–27	conversation c· confined to the
	176– 8	c· in the great crises of nations
Hea.	5–12	* the question c· is concerning
My.	159–28	thought c· regards material things,

child (see also child's)

adopted

Mis.	111–32	or is a spiritually adopted c·,
Man.	46– 3	claims a spiritually adopted c·

another

Ret.	40–17	be delivered of another c·.

appeared as a

Un.	59–14	Jesus appeared as a c·,

complaining

Mis.	236–10	c· complaining of his parents

corporeal

Mis.	166–20	to the corporeal c· Jesus,

give the

Mis.	226– 2	* "Give the c· what he relishes,

God's

Mis.	181–28	preexistence as God's c· ;
Un.	15– 9	Man is God's c· and image.
'02.	8–29	not as . . . but as God's c·.

govern a

Mis.	51–12	govern a c· metaphysically?

her

Mis.	253–24	Can a mother tell her c· one tithe

His

No.	30–14	love of a Father for His c·,

his

Un.	48–16	than the . . . enters into his c·.

in sleep

Mis.	215–18	as when a c· in sleep walks

is born

Mis.	161– 5	unto us a c· is born, — Isa. 9 : 6.
	166–10	unto us a c· is born, — Isa. 9 : 6.
	321– 3	"Unto us a c· is born," — Isa. 9 : 6.
	370–10	"Unto us a c· is born, — Isa. 9 : 6.

little

Mis.	145–25	little c· shall lead them." — Isa. 11 : 6.
	337–12	"Jesus called a little c· — Matt. 18 : 2.
	337–14	as this little c·, — Matt. 18 : 4.
	344–26	as a little c·, — Luke 18 : 17.

looks up

My.	257–30	Wherever the c· looks up

man

Pul.	13–29	brought forth the man c·. — Rev. 12 : 13.

Mother, and

Mis.	18–19	whereby Father, Mother, and c·

my

Mis.	331–21	Keep Thou my c· on upward wing
	372–12	* book has healed my c·."
	389– 9	Keep Thou my c· on upward wing
Ret.	20–12	night before my c· was taken
	20–25	was to get back my c·,
Po.	4– 7	Keep Thou my c· on upward wing
My.	235– 8	Can I teach my c· the correct

of God

(see God)

one

Mis.	7– 5	mother of one c· is often

poor

Mis.	239–19	looking up quaintly, the poor c·

spake as a

Mis.	359– 9	I spake as a c·, — I Cor. 13 : 11.
My.	135– 3	I spake as a c·, — I Cor. 13 : 11.
	261–16	I spake as a c· — I Cor. 13 : 11.

child

spiritual
Mis. 18–15 as God's spiritual *c·* only,
sweet
Mis. 239–26 What if that sweet *c·*,
that
Mis. 253–24 agonies that gave that *c·* birth
253–25 Can that *c·* conceive of the anguish,
this
Mis. 166–10 And what of *this c·*?
166–13 This *c·*, or spiritual idea,
thought as a
Mis. 359– 9 I thought as a *c·* :— *I Cor.* 13 : 11.
My. 135– 4 I thought as a *c·* :— *I Cor.* 13 : 11.
tired
Po. 47–14 Weary of sobbing, like some tired *c·*
to devour the
Mis. 253–17 stood ready to devour the *c·*
Hea. 10– 3 "to devour the *c·* — see *Rev.* 12 : 4.
unborn
Mis. 71–13 *influences on the unborn c·?*
understood as a
Mis. 359– 9 I understood as a *c·*, — *I Cor.* 13 : 11.
My. 135– 3 I understood as a *c·*, — *I Cor.* 13 : 11.
261–17 I understood as a *c·*, — *I Cor.* 13 : 11.
wife and
Mis. 225– 7 clergyman, his wife and *c·*.
will demonstrate
My. 113–21 A *c·* will demonstrate C. S.
woman, or
Mis. 336–26 a better man, woman, or *c·*.
Rud. 2– 4 * a corporeal man, woman, or *c·* ;
young
My. 122–19 to find where the young *c·* lies,

Mis. 184– 8 The *c·* born of a woman
339–19 Art thou a *c·*,
359– 8 "When I was a *c·*, — *I Cor.* 13 : 11.
No. 18–16 A *c·*, in his ignorance, may
'00. 6–12 A *c·* can measurably understand
6–15 *c·* not only accepts C. S.
My. 135– 3 "When I was a *c·*, — *I Cor.* 13 : 11.
258–31 *c·* with finger on her lip reading a
261–16 "When I was a *c·*, — *I Cor.* 13 : 11.
312–15 * with a *c·*, but entirely without
(*see also* **Eddy**)

child-birth
Ret. 40–19 suffered so little in *c·*."

childhood (*see also* **childhood's**)
Mis. 257–24 *c·*, age, and manhood
395–15 Written in *c·*, in a maple grove
Ret. 1– 8 I remember reading, in my *c·*,
2–17 My *c·* was also gladdened by
5– 9 During my *c·* my parents
8– 2 events connected with my *c·*
11– 1 From *c·* I was a verse-maker.
31– 9 From my very *c·* I was
89–18 which he had frequented in *c·*.
My. 184–18 the odor of my *c·*,
261–12 inclining thought of *c·*.

childhood's
Mis. 238– 4 contrast with that *c·* wrong
Ret. 6– 6 My *c·* home I remember
'01. 31–19 chapter sub-title
My. 147– 7 over my *c·* Sunday noons.

childish
Mis. 237–30 *c·* fear clustered round his
310– 1 *c·* pleasure of studying Truth
359–10 put away *c·* things. — *I Cor.* 13 : 11.
My. 135– 5 put away *c·* things." — *I Cor.* 13 : 11.
261–18 put away *c·* things." — *I Cor.* 13 : 11.

childlike
Mis. 15–15 *c·* trust and joyful adoption
133–25 with *c·* confidence that

children (*see also* **children's**)
are destined
Pul. 8–28 The *c·* are destined to witness
beloved
Mis. 110– 4 Beloved *c·*, the world has need
My. 216–15 *My Beloved C· :*
big
Mis. 400–19 To the Big C·
Po. 69– 7 *To the Big C·*
Christmas for the
My. 261– 1 chapter sub-title
created
Un. 14–16 His created *c·* proved
dear
Mis. 144– 5 came from the dear *c·*
145–32 and to the dear *c·*
My. 217– 8 for my dear *c·* contributors
230–24 education of the dear *c·*,
258–25 To the dear *c·* let me say :

children

divine
Un. 23– 7 divine *c·* are born of
dusky
'02. 3–16 her dusky *c·* are learning
education of
Mis. 286–11 education of *c·* will serve
family of
Mis. 6–29 Take a large family of *c·*
four thousand
Mis. 353–26 the Mother's four thousand *c·*,
gifts from the
My. 25– 6 * chapter sub-title
God's
Mis. 170– 9 spiritual refreshment of God's *c·*
her
Mis. 152–14 for the welfare of her *c·*,
354– 9 "justified of her *c·*." — *Matt.* 11 : 19.
374–10 justified of all her *c·*." — *Luke* 7 : 35.
Ret. 1–20 thus mingling in her *c·*.
6– 1 * to the education of her *c·*.
90–16 never willingly neglects her *c·*
90–22 and happiness of her *c·*?
90–24 till her *c·* can walk steadfastly
My. 66–25 * welcoming her *c·* and
228–22 justified of her *c·*." — *Matt.* 11 : 19.
His
Mis. 373–14 should, does, guide His *c·*.
My. 187–25 light and liberty of His *c·*,
lessons of the
Man. 62–25 The first lessons of the *c·*
like
'01. 29–13 They are like *c·* that go out
little
Mis. 189– 3 When, as little *c·*, we are
307–23 "Little *c·*, keep — *I John* 5 : 21.
400–13 Gift to the Little C·
Po. 69–1 *Gift to the Little C·*
My. 4–26 become as little *c·*, — *Matt.* 18 : 3.
78–28 * little *c·*, awed by the grandeur
loving
Mis. 238– 2 Even the loving *c·* are
My
Un. 18–12 tears from the eyes of My *c·*.
new-born
Mis. 254– 1 Cherish these new-born *c·*
of darkness
My. 191–10 you are not *c·* of darkness.
of God
Mis. 46–23 we are the *c·* of God :— *Rom.* 8 : 16.
199– 9 liberty of the *c·* of God." — *Rom.* 8 : 21.
255–15 we are the *c·* of God :— *Rom.* 8 : 16.
My. 40–23 * called the *c·* of God." — *Matt.* 5 : 9.
242–11 that mortals are the *c·* of God,
269–10 and are the *c·* of God." — *Luke* 20 : 36.
of Israel
Ret. 79–25 *c·* of Israel were saved by
Peo. 11–16 *c·* of Israel still in bondage.
My. 42–31 * *c·* of Israel delivered from the
of light
Mis. 342–29 wiser than the *c·* of light ;" — *Luke* 16 : 8.
Ret. 90–29 one of the *c·* of light.
My. 191– 9 C· of light, you are
206–31 walk as *c·* of light." — *Eph.* 5 : 8.
of men
Rud. 10–20 *c·* of men, who are punished
My. 90–11 * nature endows the *c·* of men,
193– 9 to the *c·* of men." — *Psal.* 107 : 8.
of one parent
Ret. 22–20 all the *c·* of one parent,
of our Lord
Mis. 244–31 especially the *c·* of our Lord
of this period
Mis. 253–27 Do the *c·* of this period dream
of this world
Mis. 342–28 "The *c·* of this world — *Luke* 16 : 8.
of to-day
Pul. vii– 5 *c·* of to-day are the elders of
precious
Pul. 8–24 precious *c·*, your loving hearts
rise up
Mis. 254–10 whose *c·* rise up against her ;
Sabbath School
Man. 62–19 The Sabbath School *c·* shall
six
Ret. 5– 7 youngest of my parents' six *c·*
Sunday School
Po. page 43 poem
My. 155–26 May the dear Sunday School *c·*
162–12 the dear Sunday School *c·*,
teaching the
Man. 62–18 Teaching the C·.
teach the
Mis. 240–24 Teach the *c·* early self-government,
their
Mis. 5– 9 perfect morals in their *c·*

children

their
Pul. 21– 1 their *c·* and grandchildren
82–26 * their husbands, their *c·*, and
these
Mis. 7– 1 These *c·* must not be allowed to
Pul. 42–14 * These *c·* are known in the
thirteen
Ret. 4– 1 grandmother had thirteen *c·*,
Thy
Mis. 159–25 sense of Thy *c·* grown to
two
Mis. 6–32 families of one or two *c·*,
Ret. 21– 7 had a wife and two *c·*,
understood by the
Mis. 53–26 readily understood by the *c·* ;
who forget
'01. 29–15 *c·* who forget their parents'
women and
Pul. 45– 1 * Men, women, and *c·*
64– 9 * Men, women, and *c·* contributed,
your
My. 344–30 let your *c·* be vaccinated,

Mis. 18–17 as *c·* of one common Parent,
46–24 if *c·*, then heirs ;— *Rom.* 8: 17.
110– 5 more as *c·* than as men
125–23 *Beloved Brethren, C·, and*
240–20 *C·* not mistaught, naturally love
255–15 if *c·*, then heirs ;— *Rom.* 8: 17.
315– 1 shall be preached to the *c·*,
354–12 the *c·* are tending the regulator ;
397–15 where Thine own *c·* are,
Man. 35– 1 *C·* when Twelve Years Old.
35– 2 *C·* who have arrived at the age
Pul. v– 3 TWO THOUSAND AND SIX HUNDRED *C·*
8–16 Even the *c·* vied with their
9– 1 *c·*, you are the bulwarks of freedom,
18–24 where Thine own *c·* are,
40–14 * ROOM WHICH THE *C·* BUILT
42–10 * presence of several hundred *c·*
59–26 * *c·* of believing families
'02. 2–11 making the *c·* our teachers.
Po. 13– 3 where Thine own *c·* are,
My. 25– 7 * great interest exhibited by the *c·*
133– 5 all earth's *c·* at last come to
216–14 chapter sub-title
258–30 *c·* who sent me that beautiful
261– 8 *c·* should not be taught to believe
310–28 for her other *c·* to imitate,
345– 2 vaccination will do the *c·* no harm.

children's

Mis. 72–14 *c·* teeth are set on edge— *Ezek.* 18: 2.
240– 4 freshness out of the *c·* lives by
252–29 It is the dear *c·* toy
315– 4 The *c·* service shall be
Man. 63– 9 instruction given by the *c·* teachers
My. 12–29 The dear *c·* good deeds are
38–16 * It was "*c·* day" at noon,
78–26 * chapter sub-title
261– 3 How shall we cheer the *c·* Christmas

child's

Mis. 51–15 a declaration to the *c·* mind
51–17 If you make clear to the *c·* thought
365– 7 what a *c·* love of pictures is to art.
No. 18–16 what a *c·* love of pictures is to art.

chill

Pul. 10–24 rejoice that *c·* vicissitudes have not
Po. 26– 7 *C·* was thy midnight day,

chime

Pul. 26–17 * *c·* of bells includes fifteen,
62– 8 * a *c·* of fifteen bells
62–17 * beauties of a great cathedral *c·*,
My. 89– 7 * a *c·* of bells, and

chimed

Pul. 41–28 * were *c·* until the hour for

chimerical

Ret. 70–11 give *c·* wings to his imagination,
My. 347–26 that a phenomenon is *c·*,

chimes

Mis. 126– 5 soft music of our Sabbath *c·*
343–26 Among the manifold soft *c·*
Pul. 8– 4 church *c·* repeat my thanks
16– 1 Set to the Church *C·*
41–23 * *c·* in the great stone tower,
58–13 * In the belfry is a set of . . . *c·*.
61–20 * chapter sub-title
61–22 * listen to the first peal of the *c·*
61–27 * The *c·* were made by
62– 6 * cast bells of old-fashioned *c·*.
62–10 * old-fashioned *c·* required a strong
81– 1 * *c·* on the C. S. temple
'02. 4–15 ringing like soft vesper *c·*

chimes

My. 30–32 * Before half past seven the *c·*
70–10 * chapter sub-title
70–11 * *c·* for the new C. S. temple
70–15 * while the *c·* were being tested
71– 1 * a set of cathedral *c·*,
77–21 * pealed from the *c·* a first hymn
256– 1 chapter sub-title

chiming

My. 163– 3 *c·* chaste challenge to praise him

China

Pul. 2–16 war between *C·* and Japan.
5–25 Greece, Japan, India, and *C·* ;
6–20 * missionary to *C·*, in 1884.
My. 234–15 chapter sub-title
234–17 C. S. in benighted *C·*,
234–25 war on religion in *C·*

Chinese

Un. 57– 1 More obnoxious than *C·* stenchpots

chinked

'00. 1– 3 *c·* within the storied walls of

Chippewa

Ret. 3–12 neighboring battle of *C·*,

chirps

Mis. 329–26 now *c·* to the breeze ;

chisel

Peo. 7– 8 * "*C·* in hand stood a sculptor-boy,
Po. 2– 4 *c·* of the sculptor's art
My. 69–14 * hammer and *c·* of the sculptor

chiseled

Po. 76– 8 (Heaven *c·* squarely good)

chiselled

Mis. 399–24 (Heaven *c·* squarely good)
Pul. 16– 9 (Heaven *c·* squarely good)

chiselling

Mis. 360– 4 awaiting the hammering, *c·*,
Peo. 7– 4 *c·* to higher excellence,

chivalry

My. 331–13 * Southern *c·* would have scorned to

choice

Mis. vii– 5 * well made *c·* of friends and books ;
19–28 Which, then, shall be our *c·*,
227–16 their *c·* of self-degradation
269–17 his *c·* between matter and Mind,
Man. 87– 5 *C·* of patients is left to
Ret. 71–14 freedom of *c·* and self-government.
Pul. 66–20 * largely Oriental in its *c·*.
Pan. 3–15 * *C·* of the prudent !
Hea. 14– 9 in the *c·* of physicians.
My. 96–13 * creed of the church of their *c·*.
99–29 * no *c·* but the acceptance of
283–30 *c·* of folly never fastens on the

choicest

'01. 28–12 *c·* memorials of devotion

choir

Ret. 16– 7 not sung before since she left the *c·*
Pul. 26– 6 * organ and *c·* gallery is spacious
37–19 * *c·* of the new church,
42–19 * On the wall of the *c·* gallery
42–25 * In the *c·* and the
43– 2 * the *c·* of the homo church,
59–11 * There was singing by a *c·*
Po. 66– 9 To join with the neighboring *c·* ;

choir organ

(*see* **organ**)

choirs

Pul. 43– 1 * Two combined *c·*

choke

Mis. 343–22 *c·* the coming clover.
No. 44–15 and *c·* the channels of God.

choose

Mis. 19–27 *c·* our course and its results.
271–13 " *C·* you this day — *Josh.* 24: 15.
289– 9 mortals must first *c·* between evils,
289– 9 of two evils *c·* the less ;
289–32 whence they can *c·* only good.
338–10 cannot *c·* but to labor and love ;
Un. 60–18 to *c·* whom they would serve.
'01. 31–12 then I cannot *c·* but obey.
My. 3–23 *C· ye!*
5–27 Continue to *c·* whom ye will serve.
165– 3 helping others thus to *c·*.

choosing

My. 165– 2 namely, of *c·* the best,

chord

Mis. 187–10 a *c·* is manifestly the reality of
Ret. 82– 2 law of the *c·* remains unchanged,
'00. 3– 4 unless he loses the *c·*.
'01. 34–16 the lost *c·* of Christ ;

chord

My. 150–11 hallowed by one *c·* of C. S.,

chords

Mis. 106–29 strains that thrill the *c·* of feeling
116–16 varied strains of human *c·*
142–21 *c·* of feeling too deep for words.
Ret. 17– 7 Wake *c·* of my lyre,
Pul. 9– 6 break the full *c·* of such a rest.
'02. 9–13 Loving *c·* set discords in harmony.
Peo, 8–20 trembling *c·* of human hope
Po. 62– 7 Wake *c·* of my lyre,
66– 7 Wake gently the *c·* of her lyre,

chorus

Mis. 188– 5 grand *c·* of harmonious being.
My. 59–20 * mighty *c·* of five thousand voices,

chose

Pul. 49–24 * She *c·* the stubbly old farm

chosen

Mis. 151–23 Ye are a *c·* people,
161–14 prophet whose words we have *c·*
191–10 " Have not I *c·* you — John 6 : 70.
197– 4 Our *c·* text is one
200–12 that we have *c·* for a text ;
327– 8 " thou hast *c·* the good part ;
Man. 26–17 said candidates shall not be *c·*.
Ret. 42–12 untiring in his *c·* work.
91–22 students whom he had *c·*,
Pul. 85–14 * as the one *c·* of God to this end,
No. 22–25 " Have I not *c·* you — John 6 : 70.
My. 17–10 *c·* of God, and precious, — I Pet. 2 : 4.
70–20 * *c·* from the works of
125–10 with the sling of Israel's *c·* one
127–24 garrisoned by God's *c·* ones,
206–23 " Ye are a *c·* generation, — I Pet. 2 : 9.
244–21 but few are *c·*." — Matt. 22 : 14.

Christ (see also Christ's)

according to
Mis. 114–16 enunciation of these according to *C·*.
Pan. 13– 6 demonstrated according to *C·*,
'01. 4–10 demonstrate Love according to *C·*,
adore
Mis. 96–20 I reverence and adore *C·*
and our Cause
'02. 13– 2 *C·* and our Cause my only incentives,
appearing of
'00. 7–29 wait for the full appearing of *C·*
as an example
Pul. 72–26 * we take *C·* as an example,
ascended
My. 119–17 to the ascended *C·*, to the Truth
as "the way"
Un. 58–13 *C·* as "the way." — John 14 : 6.
atonement of
Mis. 96–17 Do I believe in the atonement of *C·*?
261–16 atonement of *C·* loses no efficacy.
'01. 10–22 atonement of *C·*, whereby good
at-one-ment with
Mis. 123–21 at-one-ment with *C·* has appeared
basis that
Hea. 18–21 on the basis that *C·*, Truth,
behold the
'00. 7–22 behold the *C·* walking the wave
be in you
Chr. 55–16 If *C·* be in you, — Rom. 8 : 10.
beloved in
My. 150–26 Beloved in *C·*, what our Master said
blood of
No. 33–19 to represent the blood of *C·*,
34–18 blood of *C·* speaketh better things
34–26 significance of the blood of *C·*.
body of
My. 126– 1 the church, — the body of *C·*, Truth ;
131– 8 For the body of *C·*,
bonds of
Mis. 150– 5 Yours in bonds of *C·*,
No. 8– 9 fellowship in the bonds of *C·*.
brethren in
My. 108–26 Finally, beloved brethren in *C·*,
bring him to
Ret. 30–18 schoolmaster, to bring him to *C·*.
burial of
'02. 17– 2 knells tolling the burial of *C·*.
came
'01. 21–21 *C·* came not to bring death but life
cannot leave
Mis. 270–21 we cannot leave *C·* for
catnip and
Mis. 52– 5 divided between catnip and *C·* ;
Cause of
Man. 48– 4 to defend the Cause of *C·*,
'01. 35– 5 sacrifice self for the Cause of *C·*,
cause of
My. 165– 7 endured for the cause of *C·*,

Christ

character of
Mis. 367–27 or in the character of *C·*.
character of the
Ret. 23–16 character of the *C·* was illuminated
Christianity of
My. 37–12 * rule of the Christianity of *C·*
179–32 ethics, and Christianity of *C·*
Church of
(see **Church of Christ; Church of Christ, Scientist**)
church of
'00. 13– 3 * Gentiles entered the church of *C·*'"
closely with
'00. 7–24 would walk more closely with *C·* ;
comes
Chr. 53–34 *C·* comes in gloom ;
commandments of
No. 8–18 bow down to the commandments of *C·*,
command of
Mis. 318–19 so fulfil the command of *C·*.
Ret. 47–23 so fulfil the command of *C·*.
Pul. 29–17 * dealt directly with the command of *C·*
'00. 5–21 to obey . . . the command of *C·* :
command of the
Ret. 88– 4 Another command of the *C·*,
conception of the
No. 12–16 new-born conception of the *C·*,
cross of
Ret. 30–21 and the cross of *C·*.
cup of
Mis. 144–28 wine poured into the cup of *C·*.
No. 34–11 They drink the cup of *C·*
days of
Un. 9–26 not . . . since the days of *C·*.
dear
Po. 29– 7 Dear *C·*, forever here and near,
debtors to
Mis. 281–22 always as debtors to *C·*, Truth.
declaration of
'02. 12–14 This declaration of *C·*, understood,
demands
My. 232–29 watching as *C·* demands
demonstration of
Man. 47–16 illustrates the demonstration of *C·*,
direct line in
'01. 2–23 departure from the direct line in *C·*
disciple of
'00. 6–23 meek and loving disciple of *C·*,
divine
My. 36–20 * salvation through His divine *C·*.
doctrines of
Mis. 188– 1 opposed the doctrines of *C·*
embodied
'00. 8– 2 behold more nearly the embodied *C·*,
enjoins
Mis. 292–19 *C·* enjoins it upon man to help
eternal
My. 262–11 my sense of the eternal *C·*,
even
My. 182– 9 the same, even *C·*, Truth,
ever-present
Mis. 328– 8 ever-present *C·*, the spiritual idea
existed
'01. 8–25 *C·* existed prior to Jesus,
faith in
Rud. 11– 4 leading . . . first to faith in *C·* ;
feet of
'01. 22–15 I begin at the feet of *C·*
follow
Ret. 65–13 if they would follow *C·*,
follower of
Un. 56–13 every follower of *C·* shares his cup
following
Mis. 170– 2 for by following *C·* truly,
245–24 thinking that it was following *C·* ;
No. 34– 5 sense of following *C·* in spirit,
follows
'01. 34–26 only so far as she follows *C·*.
'02. 4– 4 only so far as she follows *C·*.
found
My. 119–32 St. John found *C·*, Truth,
given by
No. 28–15 way of salvation given by *C·*,
gospel of
Mis. 18– 7 law and gospel of *C·*, Truth.
'02. 5–21 reiterated in the gospel of *C·*,
has said
Mis. 258– 2 *C·* has said that love is the
has told
Pul. 72–27 * *C·* has told us to do his work,
healed by
My. 63–30 * had been healed by *C·*, Truth,
healed the sick
Pul. 66– 2 * as it did when *C·* healed the sick.
healing
Mis. 154–20 the healing *C·* will again be

Christf

healing
Pan. 7– 5 demonstration that the healing C·,
'00. 6–12 interprets the healing C·.
'02. 9–19 spirit of the healing C·,
My. 122–17 healing C· that saves from sickness

heart of
Pul. 12–20 nearer to the great heart of C· ;

His
Mis. 177– 7 against the Lord and against His C·,
193–24 commands of our Lord and His C·,
Pul. 12– 7 power of His C·:— Rev. 12: 10.
My. 260–28 It leaves . . . to God and His C·,

human concept of
Ret. 93– 5 human concept of C· is based on

ideal
Mis. 166– 7 ideal C· — or impersonal infancy,
No. 36–28 while the divine and ideal C· was

ideal, or
Mis. 124–12 rest in the spiritual ideal, or C·.

idea of the
No. 21–26 demonstrably the true idea of the C·,

identify
My. 119–19 could not identify C· spiritually,

I love
'01. 28–19 I love C· more than all the world,

in accord with
Ret. 81– 6 keeping them in accord with C·,

incorporeal
Mis. 164– 7 reveals the incorporeal C· ;

is come
'02. 12– 2 Christian believes that C· is come

is divine
'01. 8– 3 C· is divine— the Holy Ghost, or

is here
My. 44–10 * The C· is here,

is incorporeal
My. 260–30 C· is incorporeal.

is individual
Pul. 74–25 " C· is individual, and one with God,

is meekness
My. 247–11 C· is meekness and Truth enthroned.

is not God
'01. 8–11 C· is not God, but an impartation of

is One
'01. 8– 1 chapter sub-title

is rejected
'01. 9–18 yet C· is rejected of men !

is risen
My. 122–25 Scientist can say his C· is risen

is speaking
My. 257–12 The C· is speaking for himself

is the head
My. 108–29 "C· is the head of the— Eph. 5: 23.

is the idea
Hea. 3–15 C· is the idea of Truth ;

is the Messiah
'02. 12– 5 on the basis that C· is the Messiah,

is the Truth
My. 261–25 C· is the Truth and Life born of God

is Truth
Mis. 180– 9 "C· is Truth, and Truth is always

joint-heirs with
Mis. 46–25 joint-heirs with C·."— Rom. 8: 17.
255–16 joint-heirs with C·."— Rom. 8: 17.

kingdom of
No. 33– 7 by advancing the kingdom of C·.

knowledge of
Mis. 360–15 with the true knowledge of C·
360–32 with the true knowledge of C·.
My. 113–15 to aspire to this knowledge of C·
239–14 comes into the knowledge of C·

law of
Mis. 39–24 so fulfil the law of C·."— Gal. 6: 2.
Ret. 45–23 fulfil the law of C· in
No. 30– 2 law of Life . . . is the law of C·,

leading you to
Rud. 11– 3 schoolmaster, leading you to C· ;

leave all for
Mis. 274–10 therefore I leave all for C·.
My. 138–18 except I leave all for C·.

led to
Mis. 85–30 sick often are thereby led to C·,

Life in
Un. 2–22 to a sense of Life in C·,

life in
Mis. 197–24 does not understand life in, C·.

Life is
My. 185–20 for Life is C·,

life of
No. 10–10 life of C· is the predicate and
41–14 life of C· is the perfect example ;

live in
Mis. 84–25 To lose error thus, is to live in C·,

looks up for
My. 119–15 The Mary of to-day looks up for C·,

Christf

lost chord of
'01. 34–17 again on earth the lost chord of C· ;

love of
Mis. 246–11 when the love of C· would have
Rud. 17– 3 to convert . . . to the love of C·,

loveth
Pul. 21– 3 love wherewith C· loveth us ;

loving
'00. 7–27 tender, loving C· is found near,

lowly in
Mis. 168–11 to the poor — the lowly in C·,

loyal to
Mis. 264– 3 students, who are loyal to C·,

man in
Mis. 15–25 fulness of the stature of man in C·
No. 19–25 fulness of the stature of man in C·.

material
My. 122–26 not the material C· of creeds,

Messiah or
'01. 9– 7 glimpses of the Messiah or C·,

Messiah or the
'02. 12– 1 believes that the Messiah or the C·

metaphysics of
'01. 24–27 metaphysics of C· — healing all

Mind of
Un. 33–12 it is certainly not the Mind of C·,

mind of
My. 142–2 we have the mind of C·.' — I Cor. 2: 16.

ministries of
Mis. 33– 6 ministers and ministries of C·,

ministry of
My. 327–30 * dignify the ministry of C·

must be spiritual
'01. 10– 9 C· must be spiritual, not material.

name of
Mis. 19–12 has named the name of C·,
223–21 named the name of C·
Pul. 81– 4 * we learn that the name of C·
Hea. 16– 9 named the name of C·

nativity of
My. 262–31 splendor of this nativity of C·

never died
Un. 62–18 In Science, C· never died.

never left
Mis. 180– 9 "C· never left," I replied;

nothing in
Mis. 155– 4 that has nothing in C·.
My. 4–25 that hath nothing in C·.

obedience of
Mis. 139–14 to the obedience of C·.— II Cor. 10: 5.

obey
My. 241–27 * to obey C· was not to

office of
Mis. 366–28 is the office of C·, Truth,

one
Mis. 22– 1 believe in one God, one C·
Man. 15– 7 We acknowledge His Son, one C· ;
42–11 One C·.
42–17 a belief in more than one C·,
Pul. 75– 1 never can be but one God, one C·,
'00. 7–17 Is there more than one C·,
7–18 There is but one C·.
'01. 8– 3 There is but one C·,
My. 109–20 can be but one God, one C·,
155– 8 have one God, one C·,
191–12 one God and one C·.
303– 2 I believe in one C·, teach one C·,
303– 3 know of but one C·.
303–18 one God, one C·, no idolatry,
344– 8 There can be but one C·."

one in
My. 204–11 which makes them one in C·.

oneness of
My. 342–23 the oneness of C· and

organizes
Pul. 21–12 which C· organizes and blesses.

our Lord and
Mis. 276–14 full coming of our Lord and C·.

our Model
Mis. 159–27 our Model, C·, been unveiled to us,

perfect
My. 11– 2 * followers of the perfect C·,

perfectibility through
'00. 7–16 Science of perfectibility through C·,

points the way
Mis. 211– 3 C· points the way of salvation.

power of
(see power)

prefers
Ret. 65–19 and prefers C· to creed.

Principle of
My. 149– 6 The Principle of C· is divine Love,

proving the
Ret. 31– 8 paramount . . . in proving the C·.

Christ

reach the
Mis. 309–16 through which we reach the *C·*,
real
No. 36–12 The real *C·* was unconscious of
reappearing
No. 46– 7 and the reappearing *C·*,
redemptive
'01. 11– 8 Through this redemptive *C·*,
reign of the
My. 64–22 * ideal manhood — the reign of the *C·*
reigns
My. 183– 7 "When *C·* reigns, and not till then,
rejoiceth
My. 159– 6 *C·* rejoiceth and comforteth us.
respects the
My. 259–28 Christmas respects the *C·*
rest in
'02. 19–18 rest in *C·*, a peace in Love.
return of
My. 181–29 the year . . . for the return of *C·*
reveals
My. 119–15 the Principle that reveals *C·*.
risen
Mis. 159–20 the man of God, the risen *C·*,
179–31 revealed to me this risen *C·*,
Un. 63– 2 this appearing as a risen *C·*.
Peo. 5– 9 spiritual ideal, the risen *C·*,
Po. 31– 5 Prolong the strain "*C·* risen !"
My. 120–11 bliss of seeing the risen *C·*,
155–20 awakened sense of the risen *C·*.
192– 8 The risen *C·* is thine.
risen with
Mis. 178–11 be risen with *C·*, — *Col.* 3 : 1.
robe of
My. 192– 7 ideal robe of *C·* is seamless.
robes of
My. 247–12 Put on the robes of *C·*,
rock of
    (*see* **rock**)
said
Mis. 210– 9 *C·* said, "They shall take — *Mark* 16 : 18.
sake of
No. 42–14 in the name and for the sake of *C·*,
Science of
My. 103– 9 indeed Science, — the Science of *C·*,
second coming of
'00. 6–30 the second coming of *C·*.
serving
Mis. 7–13 if serving *C·*, Truth,
sitteth
Mis. 178–12 where *C·* sitteth on the — *Col.* 3 : 1.
spirit of
    (*see* **spirit**)
spiritual
Mis. 84–12 The spiritual *C·* was infallible ;
spiritual sense of
My. 257–10 to the spiritual sense of *C·*
spoke of the
Un. 59– 8 spoke of the *C·* as one who
stand for
My. 344– 4 rays collectively stand for *C·*,
statement of the
Pul. 74–24 and statement of the *C·*
stature in
Pan. 11–10 shall his stature in *C·*,
'01. 11– 1 fulness of his stature in *C·*,
stature of
Mis. 102– 2 nature and stature of *C·*,
steadfast in
My. 155– 5 steadfast in *C·*, always abounding
students of the
My. 190–25 become students of the *C·*,
suffer for
Mis. 157– 3 worthy to suffer for *C·*, Truth.
Un. 57–24 worthy to suffer for *C·* ;
summons thee
Chr. 53–54 *C·* summons thee !
taught
My. 109–10 *C·* taught his followers to heal
teachings of
Pul. 38–25 * the literal teachings of *C·*.
the ever
Po. 31–18 The ever *C·*, and glorified
this
Mis. 328–13 Hast not thou heard this *C·*
'00. 7–19 this *C·* is never absent.
My. 122–28 spiritualized to behold this *C·*,
through
Mis. 3–14 to the understanding through *C·*,
41–11 purged through *C·*, Truth,
114–32 and to be able, through *C·*,
Man. 16– 1 man is saved through *C·*,
Un. 51– 9 through *C·* as perfect manhood.
Rud. 3– 5 to save them from sin through *C·*,
'01. 15– 8 overcomes them through *C·*,

Christ

through
'02. 6–23 Through *C·*, . . . points the way,
My. 9–17 * way of salvation through *C·*."
161–16 is saved through *C·*, Truth.
349– 5 gained through *C·*, Truth ;
to prove
My. 119–21 the prints of the nails, to prove *C·*,
truer sense of
'01. 9– 7 truer sense of *C·* baptized them
trust
Mis. 369–17 devout enough to trust *C·*
Truth, or
Pul. 12–23 lay down all for Truth, or *C·*,
My. 118–27 Truth, or *C·*, finds its paradise
understand
Ret. 36– 2 understand *C·* as the Truth
Un. 59–11 By this we understand *C·* to be
understanding of
Mis. 164–20 grew in the understanding of *C·*,
My. 344– 2 to my understanding of *C·*
understanding of the
My. 262–14 human understanding of the *C·*
unlike
Ret. 49–17 conquering all that is unlike *C·*
veritable
My. 119–23 the veritable *C·*, Truth,
walketh
'02. 19–30 *C·* walketh over the wave ;
was not born
My. 261–25 *C·* was not born of the flesh.
was not crucified
Chr. 53–29 *C·* was not crucified
was not human
'01. 10–12 The *C·* was not human.
was "the way"
Mis. 75– 2 *C·* was "the way ;" — *John* 14 : 6.
what concord hath
Mis. 333–23 what concord hath *C·* with — *II Cor.* 6 : 15.
white
Mis. 124–22 adore the white *C·*,
212–23 Love, the white *C·*, is the
will command
Pul. 14–24 *C·* will command the wave.
will give
Pul. 22–13 *C·* will give to Christianity
will rechristen
Pul. 8–20 *C·* will rechristen them with
words of
My. 105– 1 even more than the words of *C·*,
works of
Mis. 196–23 we shall do the works of *C·*,

Mis. 2–20 *C·*, the spiritual idea of God,
17–13 meekly bow before the *C·*,
63–22 If *C·* was God, why did Jesus
63–26 *C·* as the Son of God was divine.
76–28 "When *C·*, who is our life, — *Col.* 3 : 4.
79–24 even so in *C·* — *I Cor.* 15 : 22.
84–13 Jesus, as material manhood, was not *C·*.
84–15 *C·*, was the Son of God ;
84–20 *to live is C·*, — *Phil.* 1 : 21.
91– 1 in commemoration of the *C·*.
96–32 It is *C·* come to destroy the
104– 2 individual being, the *C·*, was at rest
107– 8 plant the feet steadfastly in *C·*.
109–28 *C·*, Truth, saith unto you,
111–31 or is another *C·*,
151–26 wedded to the spiritual idea, *C·* ;
151–29 Affectionately yours in *C·*,
161–11 senses could not cognize the *C·*,
162–23 The spiritual man, or *C·*, was
162–27 dethroned his power as the *C·*.
163–26 *C·* or spiritual idea which leadeth
166–15 *C·*, the incorporeal idea of God,
166–29 spiritual idea, or *C·*, entered into
180– 8 * Has *C·* come again on earth?"
189–13 *C·* plainly declared, through Jesus,
191–17 that *C·*, Truth, casts out.
195– 1 *C·*, the Truth that antidotes all
234–29 *C·* is clad with a richer illumination
292–22 leading them, if *possible*, to *C·*,
310– 5 substituting personality for the *C·*,
365– 3 which is *C·*, Truth.
365– 8 whose schoolmaster is not *C·*,
396–17 poem
397– 6 I see *C·* walk,
399–13 Thou the *C·*, and not the creed ;
Man. 19– 3 to be built on the Rock, *C·* ;
42–17 even that *C·* whereof the
Chr. 53–17 Thus *C·*, eternal and divine,
Ret. 65–17 ruled *C·* out of the synagogues,
93– 3 *C·*, or the spiritual idea, appeared
Un. 42–19 With *C·*, Life was not merely a
59– 5 the *C·* (that is, the divine idea
60–24 if *C·* be not raised, — *I Cor.* 15 : 17.

Christ

Un.	60–26	*C·* cannot come to mortal and
	62– 3	saith, "*C·* (God) died for me,
Pul.	18– 1	poem
	18–15	I see *C·* walk,
	74–14	'Am I the second *C·* ?'
	75– 8	in any manner as a *C·*,
No.	v–11	and if you are babes in *C·*,
	18–19	If the schoolmaster is not *C·*,
	22– 2	not touched the hem of the *C·* garment.
'00.	7–17	hath *C·* a second appearing?
'01.	8–24	*C·* was Jesus' spiritual selfhood ;
	9–17	it is the *C·*, Comforter,
	10– 8	*C·* being the Son of God.
	26– 5	only on *C·*, Truth,
	28–21	*C·*, Truth, is indeed the way
'02.	2–21	wherein *C·* is Alpha and Omega.
	6– 9	*C·*, Truth, demonstrated
	10–24	proof that *C·*, Truth, is the way.
Po.	page 12	poem
	12–15	I see *C·* walk,
	75–20	Thou the *C·*, and not the creed ;
	78–13	Thou who in the *C·* hallowed its
My.	20– 3	Gratefully yours in *C·*,
	104–15	healer of men, the *C·*, the Truth,
	109–12	*C·* is "the same— *Heb.* 13 : 8.
	110–25	*C·* will have "led— *Psal.* 68 : 18.
	129–19	plant thy steps in *C·*, Truth,
	135–20	Lovingly yours in *C·*,
	140–22	*C·*, points the advanced step.
	168– 4	*C·*, the Holy One of Israel,
	174–11	offered me to *C·* in infant baptism.
	185–20	*C·*, as aforetime, heals the sick,
	191–17	*C·*, Truth, has come forth from the
	196–16	"*C·* also suffered for us,— I *Pet.* 2 : 21.
	205– 4	*C·* hath made us free."— *Gal.* 5 : 1.
	219–15	*C·*, Truth, the ever-present
	219–22	*C·*, the great demonstrator of
	238–14	C. S.— the *C·* Science,
	248–22	*C·* mode of understanding Life
	257–13	To-day the *C·* is, more than ever
	260–32	Neither . . . can be or is *C·*.
	339–22	those who have not the *C·*,
	343–13	* heading
	344– 2	been spoken of as a *C·*,
	344– 6	God the Father is greater than *C·*,
	344– 6	*C·* is 'one with the Father,'
	351–18	Lovingly yours in *C·*,
	357– 5	*C·*, born of God,

(*see also* **Messiah, Model, Saviour, Son, Vine**)

Christ and Christmas

Mis.	32– 5	*clergyman's remarks on* "*C·ʼ and C·ʼ*"
	33– 8	illustrations in "*C·ʼ and C·ʼ* ;"
	307–13	rapid sale . . . of "*C·ʼ and C·ʼ*,"
	308–12	are ready for "*C·ʼ and C·ʼ* ;"
	371–26	chapter sub-title
	372– 7	"*C·ʼ and C·ʼ*" voices C. S.
	372–19	find "*C·ʼ and C·ʼ*" in accord with
	372–22	spirit and mission of "*C·ʼ and C·ʼ*."
	375– 9	illustrations of "*C·ʼ and C·ʼ*" :
Chr.	page 53	poem

Christ-basis

My.	46–16	* heal the sick on the *C·*

Christendom

Mis.	192–27	to all ages and throughout all *C·*.
Pul.	22–14	*C·* will be classified as
'01.	34– 2	prayer, whereby *C·* saves sinners,
My.	4–13	woman has put into *C·* and medicine.
	40–14	* *C·* became divided into
	150 30	wisdom you manifest causes *C·*
	151– 3	attacks of a portion of *C·* :
	339–12	Along the lines of progressive *C·*,

christened

Mis.	121–22	*c·* by John the Baptist,
Un.	17–11	that its vileness may be *c·* purity,
Pul.	8–20	these lambs my prayers had *c·*,

christening

Mis.	320–28	Love, to-day *c·* religion undefiled,

Christ-healing

Mis.	29–10	*C·* was practised even before
Pul.	69–27	* demonstrating the *C·*."
Peo.	3–12	that Christianity and *C·* are
My.	23–26	* with its . . . accompaniment, the *C·*,

Christian (*see also* **Christian's**)

advancing
'02.	11–21	it is thine, advancing *C·*,

aged
Mis.	226– 4	unbiased youth and the aged *C·*

any
'02.	14–11	only . . . success possible for any *C·*

armor of a
'02.	19–13	Meekness is the armor of a *C·*,

Christian

believes
'02.	12– 2	*C·* believes that Christ is come

best
'02.	11–28	the best *C·* on earth,

consecrated
Mis.	318–22	a devout, consecrated *C·*.
Ret.	47–25	Bible scholar and a consecrated *C·*.

hero, and
Mis.	166– 5	philanthropist, hero, and *C·*.

impels the
My.	9– 8	* impels the *C·* to turn

Jew and
'02.	11–29	while to-day Jew and *C·* can unite

mission of a
Pul.	73–13	* mission of a *C·*, to do good

quickening the
No.	43–16	* and quickening the *C·*."

the word
'01.	12–10	the word *C·* was anciently

true
Mis.	68– 7	* *A true C· would protest*
	281–16	* cost of becoming a true *C·*."
	281–18	* of *not* becoming a true *C·*."
'01.	31– 7	Every true *C·* in the near future
My.	28–14	* qualities which mark the true *C·*,

venerable
Mis.	225–17	he said to this venerable *C·* :

who believes
'02.	12–10	The *C·* who believes in the

Mis.	39–28	A *C·*, or a Christian Scientist,
	86– 4	the *C·* will, must, attain it ;
	108– 2	*C·* asleep, thinks too little of sin.
	234– 9	not lifted ourselves to *be*, . . . a *C·*.
Ret.	28–29	my endeavor, to be a *C·*,
Un.	62– 3	*C·* saith, "Christ . . . died for me,
Rud.	9– 3	not a *C·*, in the highest sense,
Peo.	2–16	make a *C·* only in theory,
My.	151– 6	I know that no *C·* can or
	160– 1	The *C·*, . . . strives for the spiritual ;
	160–30	the *C·* has no part in it.
	228– 9	how one can be a *C·* and yet

Christian (adj.)

basis
Man.	80– 2	on a strictly *C·* basis,

brotherhood
My.	339– 3	bonds of *C·* brotherhood,

canon
My.	199–12	*C·* canon pertaining to the hour.

centuries
My.	112– 5	Master in the early *C·* centuries

character
My.	332–31	* honorable record and *C·* character

characters
Mis.	357–23	whose *C·* characters and lives

charity
My.	149–22	to demonstrate *C·* charity.
	175–24	fraternity, and *C·* charity.

church
Pul.	22–11	every *C·* church in our land,

churches
Pul.	22– 3	*C·* churches have one bond
Pan.	13–13	Love all *C·* churches
My.	18–21	Love all *C·* churches
	89–18	* all other of the *C·* churches,

clergymen
'01.	31–24	distinguished *C·* clergymen,

compact
Mis.	91–10	The real *C·* compact is love

demonstration
Mis.	156–18	the daily *C·* demonstration

denominations
Mis.	21–13	trend of other *C·* denominations
My.	v– 9	* by other *C·* denominations,

Discoverer
My.	302–19	*C·* Discoverer, Founder, and Leader.

education
My.	230–24	*C·* education of the dear children,

endeavors
Man.	60–19	daily *C·* endeavors for the living

endeavor society
Pul.	21–12	Let this be our *C·* endeavor society,

era

(*see* **era**)

example
Ret.	26– 4	*C·* example on the cross,
My.	52– 6	* her *C·* example, as well as

faith
Ret.	6– 5	* living illustration of *C·* faith.
Pul.	51– 2	* Neither does the *C·* faith
'02.	6–20	All *C·* faith, hope, and prayer,

fellowship
Man.	51– 7	Violation of *C·* Fellowship.
	51–10	does not live in *C·* fellowship with

Christian (adj.)

fellowship
- *Man.* 74–20 an attitude of *C·* fellowship.
- *Ret.* 15–20 we parted in *C·* fellowship,

folk
- *Pul.* 52– 5 * pity some of our practical *C·* folk
- *My.* 58– 1 * pity some of our practical *C·* folk

healers
- *Mis.* 370–26 true fold for *C·* healers,
- *'01.* 9– 9 made seers of men, and *C·* healers.

healing
(*see* **healing**)

hero
- *Mis.* 85– 2 battle-worn and weary *C·* hero,
- *'01.* 30–26 heart of the unselfed *C·* hero.
- *Hea.* 2–14 And still another *C·* hero,

history
- *Ret.* 45– 8 earliest periods in *C·* history.

idea
- *'02.* 12– 9 Jew unites with the *C·* idea that

lady
- *My.* 320– 9 * high regard for you as a *C·* lady,

life
- *'01.* 28– 9 none lived a more devout *C·* life
- *My.* 200–17 What holds us to the *C·* life is the

lives
- *My.* 213–11 to live pure and *C·* lives,

love
- *My.* 362–23 * bonds of *C·* love and fellowship,

manner
- *Man.* 97–16 to correct in a *C·* manner

metaphysics
- *Mis.* 205–21 termed in *C·* metaphysics the ideal
- 365–26 *C·* metaphysics is hampered by
- *No.* 11– 8 my system of *C·* metaphysics
- *My.* 41– 4 * the law of *C·* metaphysics,

motives
- *Man.* 50–17 shall from *C·* motives make

name
- *Mis.* x–18 *C·* name, Mary Morse Baker.
- *Man.* 111– 6 sign her own *C·* name,

names
- *Man.* 111– 3 one of the *C·* names

people
- *Pul.* 50–17 * number of *C·* people,
- *My.* 60–10 * *C·* (?) people at that time.

practice
- *Ret.* 54–20 whose *C·* practice is far in advance
- *'01.* 11–19 enough for *C·* practice.

religion
- *Pan.* 6–22 the *C·* religion has at least
- *My.* 220–18 establishment of *C·* religion

sacraments
- *Mis.* 345–26 purpose of *C·* sacraments.

Science
(*see* **Science**)

Scientist
(*see* **Scientist**)

Scientist's
(*see* **Scientist's**)

Scientists
(*see* **Scientists**)

Scientists'
(*see* **Scientists'**)

sense
- *Pan.* 3– 2 the *C·* sense of religion.

sentiments
- *My.* 316–19 freedom of *C·* sentiments,

service
- *My.* 36–11 * to a holy *C·* service

spirit
- *Man.* 77–26 in a *C·* spirit and manner,

standard
- *Un.* 38–27 the *C·* standard of Life,

standpoint
- *No.* 12– 2 a purely *C·* standpoint.

state
- *Mis.* 229–25 calm, *C·* state of mind is a

students
(*see* **students**)

success
- *Mis.* 120–14 *C·* success is under arms,

system
- *My.* 244–31 success of this *C·* system

Theism
- *Mis.* 13–13 chapter sub-title

tongue
- *'01.* 28–12 into almost every *C·* tongue,

unity
- *My.* 200–11 The chain of *C·* unity,

warfare
- *Mis.* 40–26 In this *C·* warfare the student
- 281–19 whatever . . . is hard in the *C·* warfare
- *Ret.* 44–23 danger to its . . . in *C·* warfare.

woman
- *My.* 315– 7 * a pure and *C·* woman,

Christian (adj.)

work
- *Mis.* 5– 7 themselves to this *C·* work.
- 242–15 another department of *C·* work,

world
- *My.* 60–11 * What a change in the *C·* world!
- 103 chapter sub-title

worship
- *Mis.* 345–29 rumor that . . . a part of *C·* worship
- *Un.* 15–28 Surely this is no *C·* worship!
- *My.* 47–26 * an era of *C·* worship founded on

zeal
- *My.* 187– 1 fidelity, faith, and *C·* zeal

- *Mis.* 22–22 That C. S. is *C·*,
- 30–23 * "is neither *C·* nor science!"
- 68–11 * *not C·* to believe they are
- 269–16 on a *C·*, mental, scientific basis;
- 350–13 deliberations were, as usual, *C·*,
- *Ret.* 25–10 *C·*, because it is compassionate,
- *Pul.* 69–22 * certain *C·* and scientific laws,
- 80–30 * all these ideas are *C·*.
- *No.* 10– 7 are "*C·*" and "Science."
- *Pan.* 7–15 Mosaic, the *C·*, and the
- *'02.* 11–12 neither *C·* nor Science.
- *My.* 216– 6 *C·*, civil, and educational means,
- 245– 5 This *C·* educational system
- 257–29 the *C·* traveller's resting-place.

Christianity (*see also* **Christianity's**)

adorns
- *My.* 285– 9 Whatever adorns *C·* crowns the

advance
- *Mis.* 50–27 advance *C·* a hundredfold.

age and
- *'01.* 16–24 to handle with garrulity age and *C·*!

altitude of
- *Pan.* 12–12 altitude of *C·* openeth, . . . a door

and materialism
- *My.* 221– 3 distance between *C·* and materialism

and Science
- *Pul.* 56–16 * Welding *C·* and Science,
- *My.* 179–25 *C·* and Science, being contingent on

and spiritualism
- *Hea.* 5–11 * "between *C·* and spiritualism,

antithesis of
- *Pul.* 6– 3 continue till the antithesis of *C·*,
- *Peo.* 8–12 not more the antithesis of *C·* than

apostolic
- *Mis.* 245–26 and rejects apostolic *C·*,

as taught
- *Pan.* 8–14 *C·*, as taught and demonstrated
- *'00.* 4–17 *C·* as taught by our great Master;

authority in
- *'01.* 25–20 What, . . . is our authority in *C·* for

beginning of
- *Pul.* 52–19 * At the beginning of *C·* it was taught

bringing
- *Mis.* 344–30 bringing *C·* for the first time

Christ's
- *Mis.* 241– 5 Christ's *C·* casts out sickness
- *My.* 179–21 Christ's *C·* as the perfect ideal.
- 220–18 Christian religion — Christ's *C·*.

contemporary of
- *Mis.* 22– 8 what, but the contemporary of *C·*,

crown of
- *Mis.* 252–18 C. S. is . . . the crown of *C·*.

crowns
- *Mis.* 124–27 crowned and still crowns *C·*:

demanded
- *Mis.* 374– 8 demanded *C·* in life and religion.

demonstrated
- *My.* 348–25 demonstrated *C·* and proved

demonstration of
- *Mis.* 149–21 refreshing demonstration of *C·*,
- *Pan.* 9–21 demonstration of *C·* blesses all

demonstrator of
- *'01.* 26– 4 demonstrator of *C·* is the Master,

divine Principle of
- *Mis.* 30– 1 understand the divine Principle of *C·*

elucidates
- *'02.* 8– 2 elucidates *C·*, illustrates God,

ends of
- *No.* 12–20 these are the ends of *C·*.

entered
- *Mis.* 373–21 *C·* entered into synagogues,

equity of
- *My.* 181–20 universal equity of *C·*.

essential to
- *Mis.* 51– 1 change of heart is essential to *C·*,

ethics and
- *My.* 129– 5 spirit of humanity, ethics, and *C·*

Founder of
- *Pul.* 53– 2 * by the Founder of *C·*
- *My.* 279– 3 The Founder of *C·* said:

genius of
- *Hea.* 2– 2 genius of *C·* is works more than

Christianity

genuine
'02. 18–27 ended in the downfall of genuine *C·*,
given to
Pul. vii–16 impetus thereby given to *C·* ;
godliness or
'01. 34–26 Godliness or *C·* is a human necessity :
grandeur of
Pan. 12– 9 chapter sub-title
has withstood
Ret. 45–24 *C·* has withstood less the
healing
My. 180– 7 healing *C·* which applies to all
heart of
Mis. 25– 5 it is the heart of *C·*,
heaven-crowned
Mis. 328– 7 the mountain is heaven-crowned *C·*,
higher
Mis. 162– 5 advent of a higher *C·*.
Hea. 8– 8 results of this higher *C·*,
higher sense of
Mis. 195–30 have given me a higher sense of *C·*.
history of
Peo. 13–25 * "Since ever the history of *C·*
hope of
Mis. 246–31 advancing faith and hope of *C·*,
ideal of
My. 40–25 * has presented . . . the ideal of *C·*,
infant
Mis. 15–29 developed into an infant *C·* ;
is Christlike
Mis. 25–19 *C·* is Christlike only as it
is consistent
'01. 6–19 its consequent *C·* is consistent with
is divine Science
'01. 4–15 and *C·* is divine Science,
is fit only
Mis. 345–14 * "*C·* is fit only for women and
Peo. 13–23 * "*C·* is fit only for women and
is the summons
My. 148–28 *C·* is the summons of divine Love
justice and
Mis. 134– 6 as characterize justice and *C·*.
letter of
My. 246–15 teaching and letter of *C·*
life of
Mis. 199–30 outflowing life of *C·*,
lost
Hea. 3–11 it lost *C·* and the power to heal ;
lower order of
Peo. 13– 4 have a lower order of *C·* than he who
manifestations of
Ret. 65–25 practical manifestations of *C·*
means of
Mis. 269–23 is the proper means of *C·*,
model of
Ret. 22– 9 Jesus as the model of *C·*,
morals and
Mis. 283–20 as well as its morals and *C·*.
nature of
My. 179–19 nature of *C·*, as depicted in
new-old
My. 301– 3 C. S. is the new-old *C·*,
no
'01. 4–16 else there is no Science and no *C·*.
of Christ
My. 37–12 * rule of the *C·* of Christ
179–31 ethics, and *C·* of Christ
one
Pan. 1–19 acknowledge one God and one *C·*.
paragons of
Mis. 316–28 would be on earth paragons of *C·*,
perfect
Mis. 1– 9 ordeal of a perfect *C·*,
pioneers of
My. 104–19 on the pioneers of *C·*
possibilities of
Mis. 30– 7 all the possibilities of *C·*
power of
Mis. 193–26 spirit and power of *C·*.
193–29 power of *C·* to heal ;
No. 44– 7 power of *C·* to heal.
My. 239–10 redemptive power of *C·*
practical
Mis. 232–10 a more perfect and practical *C·*
My. 362–25 * thus demonstrating practical *C·*.
practice of
My. 239– 6 rules, and practice of *C·*
practising
Mis. 5–10 scientific method of practising *C·*.
precedents of
No. 35– 2 how poor the precedents of *C·*!
present
My. 339–21 rejoice in their present *C·*
primitive
Mis. 192–24 as primitive *C·* confirms.

Christianity

primitive
Man. 17–12 should reinstate primitive *C·*
Pul. 69–16 * return to the ideas of primitive *C·*.
Peo. 5–10 ideals of primitive *C·* are nigh,
My. 46–12 should reinstate primitive *C·*
111–16 C. S. maintains primitive *C·*,
245–20 doing the works of primitive *C·*,
Principle of
Mis. 16– 9 The Principle of *C·* is infinite :
144–30 life-giving Principle of *C·*,
privilege of
Hea. 3– 3 The primitive privilege of *C·* was
professed
Mis. 247– 8 I have professed *C·* a half-century ;
progress and
Hea. 7–24 so important to progress and *C·*.
progress of
No. 32– 2 retarded the progress of *C·*
proof of
Hea. 2–23 and gave this proof of *C·*
pure
Mis. 270–16 Gain a pure *C·* ;
Peo. 5–25 a Truth-filled mind makes a pure *C·*
My. 152–12 restoration of pure *C·*
purity of
My. 178– 5 invincible process and purity of *C·*
quintessence of
Mis. 336–23 C. S., . . . the quintessence of *C·*,
realism of
Mis. 374– 2 Immanuel and the realism of *C·*,
reality of
Mis. 251–15 rights and radiant reality of *C·*,
records of
My. 184–21 on the glowing records of *C·*,
reign of
Mis. 345–17 * "Ever since the reign of *C·* began
reinstated
My. 46–17 * requirement of a reinstated *C·*.
requires
Hea. 3– 1 Such *C·* requires neither hygiene nor
reveals God
Ret. 65–30 *C·* reveals God as ever-present Truth
Science and
Peo. 2– 9 unites Science and *C·*,
Science in
My. 127– 2 upward to Science in *C·*,
Science of
(*see* **Science**)
scientific
Pan. 8–13 chapter sub-title
9–15 attainment of scientific *C·*
'02. 8–21 Scientific *C·* works out the rule of
solid
My. 301– 8 leaving a solid *C·* at the bottom
specific
'01. 6–15 Is this pure, specific *C·*?
spirit of
My. 246–16 spirit of *C·*, dwelling forever in
spiritual
(*see* **spiritual**)
standard of
'01. 34–10 look for the standard of *C·*
support the
No. 15–12 to support the *C·* that heals the sick
system of
'01. 34–13 and a new system of *C·*,
Teacher of
My. 338–26 great Teacher of *C·*,
tendency of
Un. 31– 7 tendency of *C·* is to spiritualize
their
My. 107– 1 as a token of their *C·*.
theism in
Pan. 6–21 if . . . what becomes of theism in *C·*?
this
'00. 4–20 Principle and rules of this *C·*
to elucidate
'02. 16–25 fail to elucidate *C·* :
true
Mis. 113–24 evil can be resisted by true *C·*.
No. 12–14 stimulated true *C·* in all ages,
My. 91–14 * no insignificant element in true *C·*.
turned men
Mis. 345–31 *C·* turned men away from the
unbiased
Mis. 235–24 *C·* unbiased by the superstitions
understanding of
My. 51–15 * to the higher understanding of *C·*,
vital
'01. 30– 4 the object of vital *C·* is
32– 6 lover and student of vital *C·*.
vital spark of
Mis. 132–29 is a vital spark of *C·*.
watchword of
No. 44–27 must be the watchword of *C·*.

Christianity

ways of
Rud. 17–15   ways of *C·* have not changed.
which heals
My. 300–23   teach the *C·* which heals,
will give to
Pul. 22–14   Christ will give to *C·* his
womanhood and
My. 330–11   * whose womanhood and *C·*
womanhood of
Mis. 16– 7   manhood or womanhood of *C·*,
work of
My. 30–26   * by evangelists for the work of *C·*,
would commingle
'00. 4– 6   precedent that would commingle *C·*,
writes
My. 194– 1   only that which *C·* writes

Mis. 16–23   *C·* is a divine Science.
23– 6   *C·* answers this question.
29–25   will neither flavor *C·* nor
29–29   they are the signs following *C·*,
107– 4   *C·* is not superfluous.
111–21   The *C·* that is merely of sects,
193–20   supplying the word Science to *C·*,
242–11   if I should accept his bid on *C·*,
253– 2   *C·* is not merely a gift,
307–16   inquiry of mankind as to *C·*
345–19   * *C·* must be a divine reality."
357–11   Without . . . *C·* has no central emblem,
Un. 15–28   In *C·*, man bows to the infinite
Pul. 6– 8   unites Science to *C·*.
Pan. 8–17   *C·* then had one God and one law,
8–21   *C·*, as he taught and demonstrated
9– 6   in *C·* they signify
13– 5   *C·* be demonstrated according to
'01. 2– 1   *C·* is now what Christ Jesus taught
2–18   *C·* is ever storming sin
Hea. 11–27   *C·* of metaphysical healing,
14– 6   What has . . . physics done for *C·*
Peo. 3–11   *C·* and Christ-healing are
13–28   * *C·* must be a divine reality."
My. 4–18   of both medical faculty and *C·*,
40–16   * *C·* may more widely reassert its
107– 2   Has *C·* improved upon its
148–24   *C·* is not alone a gift, but
214– 8   *C·* is again demonstrating the Life
219–20   since *C·* must be predicated of
221–24   All issues of morality, of *C·*,
239– 4   relegates *C·* to its primitive proof,
267– 2   *C·* is fully demonstrated to be
279– 8   *C·* is the chain of scientific

Christianity's
Mis. 373–19   a sketch of *C·* state,

Christianization
Mis. 15– 9   *C·* — of thought and desire,
'02. 6–15   *C·* of mortals, whereby

Christianized
Mis. 269–20   can only be *C·* through Mind ;

Christianly
Mis. 259–24   physically, morally, and *C·*,
Pul. 2–27   do this *C·* scientific work?
'02. 7–20   proposition can be *C·* entertained.
My. 105– 4   defined *C·* and demonstrated

Christian's
Mis. 23–15   matter is not the *C·* God,
123–16   The *C·* God is neither,
155–11   valiant in the *C·* warfare,

Christians
Mis. 29–30   *C·*, like students in mathematics,
82– 9   Such *C·* as John cognize the
135– 1   *C·*, and all *true* Scientists,
193–23   *C·* are properly called Scientists
200–20   *C·* to-day should be able to say,
333–31   ancient or modern *C·*, instructed in
345–23   slanderers affirmed that *C·* took
345–26   *C·* met in midnight feasts
383–15   and in the hearts of *C·*.
Man. 30– 3   exemplary *C·* and good English
38– 2   known to them to be *C·*,
Un. 5–22   between C. S. students and *C·*
14–12   *C·* are commanded to *grow in grace.*
26–19   Many ordinary *C·* protest against
43–18   I urge *C·* to have more faith in
48– 6   I believe more in Him than do most *C·*,
Pul. 9–23   *C·* rejoice in secret,
Rud. 2– 5   among Trinitarian *C·* the word
No. 41– 1   chapter sub-title
42– 1   * *C·* more and more learn their duty
'01. 7–23   all *C·* now claim to believe
18–30   *C·* and clergymen pray for sinners ;
30– 3   since ever the primitive *C·*,
32– 7   Why I loved *C·* of the old sort was
32–27   if those venerable *C·* were here

Christians
'02. 8– 8   are neither *C·* nor Scientists.
Hea. 7–27   duty and ability of *C·* to heal
8–25   If we work to become *C·*
Po. 25–18   Aye, the *C·* who wind
My. 91– 3   * were already nominal *C·*,
95–28   * days of the primitive *C·*,
106–32   the *C·* in the first century
146– 3   understood by all *C·*
151–13   this denomination of *C·*
162–22   in them *C·* may worship God,
162–23   not that *C·* may worship church
179–17   *C·* and Christian Scientists know
190–13   *C·* who accept our Master
219–18   I would not charge *C·* with
292–13   "Why did *C·* of every sect
299–17   Do *C·*, who believe in sin,

Christian Science
(*see* **Science**)

Christian Science and Spiritualism
Pul. 38–11   "*C· S·* and *S·*,"

Christian Science and the Bible
My. 323– 4   * entitled "*C· S· and the B·*,"

Christian Science Board of Directors
(*see* **Board of Directors**)

Christian Science Board of Education
(*see* **Board of Education**)

Christian Science Board of Lectureship
(*see* **Board of Lectureship**)

Christian Science Church
(*see* **Church**)

Christian Science Hall
My. 145– 5   the plan for *C· S· H·*

Christian Science Hymnal
(*see* **Hymnal**)

Christian Science Journal, The
(*see* **Journal**)

Christian Science Monitor, The
(*see* **Monitor**)

Christian Science Platform
Man. 86–19   and from the *C· S· P·*,

Christian Science Practice
Pul. 38–14   "*C· S· P·*,"

Christian Science Publishing Society, The
(*see* **Publishing Society**)

Christian Science Quarterly
(*see* **Quarterly**)

Christian Science Quarterly Lessons
Man. 63– 7   may be found in the *C· S· Q· L·*,

Christian Science Reading Room
My. 236–10   for your name, *C· S· R· R·*.

Christian Science Sentinel
(*see* **Sentinel**)

Christian Science Society
Bronx
My. 363– 8   * signature
Flushing, L. I.
My. 363– 9   * signature

Christian Science *versus* Pantheism
p. 13
My. 18–25   (*C· S· v· P·*, p. 13.)

Christian Scientist
(*see* **Scientist**)

Christian Scientist Association
Mis. 116– 7   chapter sub-title
271–23   Publishing Committee of the *C· S· A·*
278–30   membership in the *C· S· A·*.
382–24   organized the first *C· S· A·*,
Man. 17– 8   At a meeting of the *C· S· A·*,
Ret. 43–21   The first *C· S· A·*
43–24   At a meeting of the *C· S· A·*,
45–17   action of the *C· S· A·*
52–14   delegations from the *C· S· A·*
52–19   official organ of the *C· S· A·*
Pul. 37–26   * The first *C· S· A·* was organized
67–25   * first *C· S· A·* was organized by
My. 182–12   formed a *C· S· A·* in Chicago.
363–19   chapter sub-title
363–21   My address before the *C· S· A·*
(*see also* **National Christian Scientist Association**)

Christian Scientist's
(*see* **Scientist's**)

Christian Scientists
(*see* **Scientists**)

Christian Scientists'
(*see* **Scientists'**)

Christian Scientists' Association
Mis. 135–26 To the Members of the *C· S· A·*

Christ-idea
Mis. 81–11 *C· mingled with the teachings*
260– 1 intelligent *C·* illustrated by
Chr. 53– 9 The *C·*, God anoints
Pul. 14–19 flood to drown the *C·*?

Christ-image
Mis. 8–18 dethrones the *C·* that you

Christ Jesus (see also Christ Jesus')
Mis. 70–16 *C· J·* lived and reappeared.
77–21 adopting all this vast idea of *C· J·*,
188–14 them which are in *C· J·*,— *Rom.* 8: 1.
197–21 was also in *C· J·*."— *Phil.* 2: 5.
201–18 Spirit of life in *C· J·* — *Rom.* 8: 2.
255–11 Mind which was in *C· J·*.
321–15 Spirit of life in *C· J·* — *Rom.* 8: 2.
326– 2 Spirit of life in *C· J·* — *Rom.* 8: 2.
Man. 15–16 unity with God through *C· J·*
16–10 which was also in *C· J·* ;
41– 1 *C· J·* the Ensample.
41– 4 irreverent reference to *C· J·* is
Ret. 70–10 the Messianic mission of *C· J·* ;
76–18 was also in *C· J·*,"— *Phil.* 2: 5.
Un. 2–25 stature of manhood in *C· J·*,
4–19 was also in *C· J·*,"— *Phil.* 2: 5.
43–26 grasped by] *C· J·*,"— *Phil.* 3: 12.
60– 2 *C· J·* came to save men,
Pul. 75– 4 that Mind which was in *C· J·*.
Pan. 8–12 infringe the sacredness of one *C· J·*
'00. 4– 7 the righteous Galilean, *C· J·*,
6– 8 calling of God in *C· J·*'"— *Phil.* 3: 14.
'01. 2– 1 what *C· J·* taught and demonstrated
9– 1 the spiritual and material *C· J·*,
9–10 "Spirit of life in *C· J·*,"— *Rom.* 8: 2.
9–14 *C· J·* possessed it, practised it,
10–13 but the *C· J·* represented both
10–20 salvation comes through . . . *C· J·*.
11– 5 the divine nature of *C· J·*
25–17 *C· J·*, denounced all such
28–25 *C· J·*, who was not popular
28–28 is not a student of *C· J·*.
'02. 7–24 *C· J·* saith, "A new — *John* 13: 34.
8– 9 The new commandment of *C· J·*
8–16 life of *C· J·*, his words
8–26 *C· J·* reckoned man in Science,
9–12 Spirit of life in *C· J·* — *Rom.* 8: 2.
Hea. 3–18 *C· J·* was an honorary title ;
My. 24– 2 * truth which *C· J·* revealed
41–23 * Spirit of life in *C· J·*,"— *Rom.* 8: 2.
103–13 stature of man in *C· J·*
113–12 them which are in *C· J·*,— *Rom.* 8: 1.
113–13 Spirit of life in *C· J·* — *Rom.* 8: 2.
129–32 teachings and example of *C· J·*.
139– 6 founded upon the rock, *C· J·*,
161– 1 *C· J·* paid our debt
161– 9 Hence these words of *C· J·* :
205– 2 them which are in *C· J·*,— *Rom.* 8: 1.
219–20 what *C· J·* taught and did ;
221–12 great and good as *C· J·*.
229–17 according to this saying of *C· J·* :
247– 7 are according to *C· J·* ;
254–28 are according to *C· J·* ;
260–17 The basis . . . is the rock, *C· J·*,
272– 6 Spirit of life in *C· J·* — *Rom.* 8: 2.
293–29 Spirit of life in *C· J·* — *Rom.* 8: 2.
318–26 * was such a man as *C· J·*?'"
339– 6 supreme, infinite, and one *C· J·*.
347– 1 revealed in a degree through *C· J·*

Christ-Jesus
Mis. 161–13 that made him the *C·*,

Christ Jesus'
Mis. 74–13 *C· J·* sense of matter was
No. 34–27 vital currents of *C· J·* life,
'01. 18–11 of questioning *C· J·* healing,

Christlike
Mis. 16– 8 to become wholly *C·*,
25–19 Christianity is *C·* only as it
193–29 this is *C·*, and includes
373–28 promise that the *C·* shall
Ret. 78–15 wholly *C·* and spiritual,
95–12 * comforters . . . Of *C·* touch.
Pul. 21–19 only that which is *C·*,
'01. 27–25 purely spiritual, *C·*
My. 148–29 summons . . . for man to be *C·*
149– 7 must be *C·*, or C. S.
220–26 religion, which . . . cannot be *C·*

Christlikeness
Mis. 162–26 demoralizing his motives and *C·*,
245–25 in the direction of *C·*,
313– 8 May the *C·* it reflects
357– 8 These long for the *C·* that
'02. 9–17 leaves the minor . . . and abides in *C·*.

Christliness
Ret. 86–15 the escutcheon of our *C·*
92– 7 unloose the latchets of his *C·*,

Christ-love
Mis. 262–25 burdens heavy but for the *C·*

Christly
Mis. 318– 8 who are less lovable or *C·*.
359– 3 *C·* method of teaching
Ret. 48–28 whose *C·* spirit has led to higher
93–13 best spiritual type of *C·*
'01. 25–13 No *C·* axioms, practices, or
My. 46–23 * more sincere and *C·* love
364– 5 treat this mind to be *C·*.

Christ-majesty
Po. 30– 9 With thy still fathomless *C·*.

Christmas
Mis. 159–10 chapter sub-title
159–18 This is my *C·* storehouse.
161– 1 chapter sub-title
161– 3 Sunday before *C·*, 1888.
309–27 My *C·* poem and its illustrations
320– 3 chapter sub-title
Man. 67–21 Thanksgiving, *C·*, New Year,
Chr. 53–23 Make merriment on *C·* eves,
Pul. 37–17 * said a gentleman to me on *C·* eve,
Po. page 29 poem
29– 1 Blest *C·* morn, though murky clouds
My. 31– 5 "Blest *C·* morn ;"
121–16 gems that adorn the *C·* ring
122–16 another *C·* has come and gone.
256– 2 Before the *C·* bells shall ring,
256– 9 total exemption from *C·* gifts.
256–16 chapter sub-title
256–17 Again loved *C·* is here,
257–23 chapter sub-title
257–24 your manifold *C·* memorials,
257–26 my *C·* gift, two words enwrapped,
258–23 beautiful are the *C·* memories of him
258–25 Your *C·* gifts are hallowed by
259– 9 * Loving, grateful *C·* greetings
259–13 dear churches' *C·* telegrams
259–14 most pleasing *C·* presents,
259–22 chapter sub-title
259–28 *C·* respects the Christ too much to
260– 3 *C·* would make matter an alien
260– 9 In C. S., *C·* stands for the real,
260–17 basis of *C·* is the rock, Christ Jesus ;
260–22 basis of *C·* is love loving its
260–24 true spirit of *C·* elevates
261– 1 chapter sub-title
261– 3 cheer the children's *C·*
261–22 chapter sub-title
261–23 *C·* involves an open secret,
262– 6 *C·* commemorates the birth of a
262–12 I celebrate *C·* with my soul,
262–20 *C·* to me is the reminder of God's
262–24 ritual of our common *C·*
262–27 I love to observe *C·* in quietude,
263– 3 chapter sub-title
263– 6 Mother wishes you all a *happy C·*,

Christmas, 1900
My. 256–16 chapter sub-title

Christmas-tide and Christmastide
Mis. 369– 6 chapter sub-title
My. 257–17 To this auspicious *C·*,

Christmas-tree
My. 257– 1 green branches of the *C·*.

Christ-principle
My. 149– 9 the meekness of the *C·* ;

Christ's
command
(*see* **command**)
healing
(*see* **healing**)
Sermon
Mis. 21– 4 with *C·* Sermon on the Mount,
25– 9 *C·* Sermon on the Mount,
93–30 *C·* Sermon on the Mount,
Rud. 12– 4 practises *C·* Sermon on the Mount.
My. 180– 6 uttered *C·* Sermon on the Mount,
229–22 ascent of *C·* Sermon on the Mount,
teachings
(*see* **teachings**)

Mis. 30–30 cleanse our lives in *C·* righteousness ;
91– 4 to organize materially *C·* church.
125– 9 Then shall he drink anew *C·* cup,
199–12 *distresses for C· sake.* — *II Cor.* 12: 10.
241– 5 *C·* Christianity casts out sickness
273–14 one grand family of *C·* followers
302–19 working faithfully for *C·* cause
303–18 and imbibe the spirit of *C·* Beatitudes.
320– 7 *C·* appearing in a fuller sense

Christ's

Mis.	330–10	to the springtide of *C·* dear love.
	358–15	*C·* vestures are put on only when
	362– 8	*C· logos* gives sight to these blind,
	373–15	clearly delineates *C·* appearing
Chr.	53–43	*C·* silent healing, heaven heard,
	53–59	Eternal swells *C·* music-tone,
Ret.	65–21	tenor of *C·* teaching and example,
	94– 9	so *C·* baptism of fire,
	94–27	aid the establishment of *C·* kingdom
Un.	43–20	I exhort them to accept *C·* promise,
	52–13	*C·* immortal sense of Truth,
Pul.	4–14	Each of *C·* little ones reflects
	13–11	He that touches the hem of *C·* robe
	14–17	a cup of cold water in *C·* name,
No.	41–20	have slumbered over *C·* commands,
	43– 1	and if *C·* power to heal was not
Pan.	11– 30	And because *C·* dear demand,
'01.	6–19	is consistent with *C·* hillside sermon,
	10–22	Love spans the dark passage . . . with *C·*
	21–23	better way than *C·* . . . to benefit the race?
	26–12	turns away from *C·* purely spiritual
	26–14	to preserve *C·* vesture unrent ;
	28–16	followed exclusively *C·* teaching,
	34– 7	spiritual obedience to *C·* mode
'02.	15–16	I became poor for *C·* sake.
Po.	33– 5	And bless me with *C·* promised rest ;
My.	147–24	already dedicated to *C·* service,
	150–20	clear, radiant reflection of *C·* glory,
	153– 5	if these kind hearts . . . do this in *C·*
	179–21	*C·* Christianity as the perfect ideal.
	183– 1	infinite uses of *C·* creed,
	191–13	*C·* "Blessed are ye" — *Matt.* 5 : 11.
	220–18	Christian religion — *C·* Christianity.
	225–17	The coming of *C·* kingdom on earth
	257–13	*C·* heavenly origin and aim.
	257–21	should bow and declare *C·* power,
	258–11	with *C·* all-conquering love.
	262–26	in commemoration of *C·* coming.
	269–11	*C·* plan of salvation from divorce.
	279– 6	C. S. reinforces *C·* sayings
	300–17	to health in *C·* name,

Christs

Mis.	175–19	There are false *C·* that would

Christ Science

(*see* **Science** *under sub-title* **Christ**)

Christ-spirit

Mis.	40–20	possess sufficiently the *C·*
Ret.	85–12	bearing on their pinions . . . the *C·*.
My.	265– 9	the *C·* will cleanse the earth of

Christ-thought

Mis.	178–31	new, living, impersonal *C·*

Christus

Chr.	53–21	For heaven's *C·*, earthly Eves,

Christward

Mis.	85–18	feeble flutterings of mortals *C·*
My.	148–25	Christianity . . . is a growth *C·* ;

chronic

Mis.	29–22	*c·* and acute diseases that had
	41–23	belief of *c·* or acute disease,
	54–18	*was healed of a c·* trouble
	204– 6	sometimes *c·*, but oftener acute.
	355– 7	*c·* recovery ebbing and flowing,
Man.	46–25	in *c·* cases of recovery,
Pan.	10–18	*c·*, and acute diseases that

Chronicle

Pul.	89–26	* *C·*, San Francisco, Cal.
My.	333–22	* The *C·* states:
	333–30	* the *C·*, dated September 25,

chronicles

Mis.	292– 4	he *c·* this teaching,

chronologically

My.	349– 1	divine Mind was first *c·*,

Church (*see also* **Church's**)

Christian Science

Man.	18–16	reorganized, . . . the C. S. *C·*
Pul.	28–15	* order of service in the C. S. *C·*
	30– 6	* C. S. *C·* did not recruit itself from
	37–13	* recognized head of the C. S. *C·*.
	56–24	* chapter sub-title
	70–27	* C. S. *C·* has a membership of
	76–24	* MEMORIALIZED BY A C. S. *C·*

Clerk of the

Man.	36–26	addressed to the Clerk of the *C·*.
	37–10	Clerk of the *C·* shall send
	52– 9	Clerk of the *C·* shall address a
	52–17	Clerk of the *C·* shall immediately
	78–17	through the Clerk of the *C·*,
	98–16	a copy to the Clerk of the *C·*.
	109–17	to the Clerk of the *C·*.

this

Man.	18–20	were elected members of this *C·*,

Church

this

Man.	26– 1	Treasurer of this *C·*
	27– 7	in the Manual of this *C·*
	28–16	that the officers of this *C·*
	28–23	shall be dismissed from this *C·*,
	28–25	duty of any member of this *C·*,
	29– 4	or of any other officer in this *C·*
	29– 9	a member of this *C·*
	29–14	five suitable members of this *C·*
	34–18	This *C·* will receive a member of
	35–20	can unite with this *C·* only by
	36–19	can apply to the Clerk of this *C·*,
	38– 6	a Director of this *C·*,
	38–10	for membership in this *C·*,
	38–19	been members of this *C·*,
	38–22	may be received into this *C·*
	39–19	not again be received into this *C·*.
	40–11	members of this *C·* should daily
	41–20	duty of every member of this *C·*
	42– 5	duty of every member of this *C·*
	42–15	members of this *C·* shall neither
	43–14	member of this *C·* shall not
	43–22	member of this *C·* shall neither
	44– 9	member of this *C·* shall not
	44–19	which are the organs of this *C·* ;
	44–24	Members of this *C·* shall not unite
	46– 2	be a member of this *C·*
	46–13	Members of this *C·* shall hold
	47– 5	If a member of this *C·* has
	47–25	members of this *C·* do not
	48– 7	member of this *C·* shall not
	50– 8	member of this *C·* shall not debate
	50–14	If a member of this *C·* shall
	51–12	regular standing with this *C·*,
	52–21	If a member of this *C·* shall,
	52–25	advantageous to this *C·*
	53– 8	If a member of this *C·*
	53–16	Members of this *C·* shall not
	53–18	excommunicated from this *C·*.
	54– 5	from his or her office in this *C·*
	54–10	member of a branch of this *C·*
	54–20	If a member of this *C·*,
	55–22	If a member of this *C·* is found
	56– 6	dropped from the roll of this *C·*.
	57– 9	meeting of the members of this *C·*
	58– 9	continue to preach for this *C·*
	59– 7	duty of every member of this *C·*,
	65– 6	by members of this *C·*,
	65–10	duty of the officers of this *C·*,
	65–26	If the Clerk of this *C·* shall
	66– 7	If at a meeting of this *C·*
	66–17	before a meeting of this *C·*,
	66–24	Members of this *C·* shall not
	67– 1	executive bodies of this *C·*.
	67– 3	for admission to this *C·*,
	67–11	member of this *C·* shall not
	67–18	Members of this *C·* who
	67–22	break a rule of this *C·*
	68– 2	member of this *C·* at least three
	69–17	appoint a proper member of this *C·*
	72– 5	member of this *C·* who obeys its
	76– 4	used for the benefit of this *C·*,
	76–17	three members of this *C·*
	76–23	real estate owned by this *C·*
	77– 6	Treasurer of this *C·* shall submit
	78– 9	Donations from this *C·*
	79–21	Pastor Emeritus of this *C·*,
	82–16	Members of this *C·* who practise
	85– 7	of another member of this *C·*
	85–12	member of this *C·* shall not
	87– 2	nor a member of this *C·*.
	87–12	No member of this *C·* shall
	92– 7	that each member of this *C·*
	92–23	who are members of this *C·*
	93– 4	This *C·* shall maintain a
	93–16	mail to the Clerk of this *C·*
	97–19	Mrs. Eddy or members of this *C·*
	109– 5	to unite with this *C·*.
Mis.	121–12	believed to be the seed of the *C·*.
	144–32	The *C·*, more than any other institution,
	165– 6	because of the corruption of the *C·*.
	245–23	I have loved the *C·* and followed it,
	313–24	chapter sub-title
Man.	18– 3	charter for the *C·* was obtained
	18– 8	the little *C·* went steadily on,
	18–19	students and members of her former *C·*
	19– 6	*C·* Universal and Triumphant.
	25–12	the annual meeting of the *C·*.
	33– 8	Rules, and discipline of the *C·*.
	37–12	neither the Clerk nor the *C·* shall
	40–16	To be Read in *C·*.
	41–15	disqualifies . . . for office in the *C·*
	44– 6	involves schisms in our *C·*
	51–13	withdraw from the *C·* or be
	52–19	shall dismiss a member from the *C·*.

Church

Man. 55–14 and forgiven by the *C*·
    56–21 annual meeting of the *C*·.
    61–17 MUSIC IN THE *C*·.
    64–20 this appellative in the *C*·
    66– 3 before presenting it to the *C*·
    66–18 it shall be the duty of the *C*·
    67– 5 on trial for dismissal from the *C*·.
    67– 8 to a member of her *C*·
    75–13 between the . . . Directors and said *C*·
    75–22 belonged to the *C*·,
    76–12 funds which the *C*· has on hand,
    77– 5 paying bills against the *C*·,
    78– 2 comply with the By-Laws of the *C*·.
    78–18 pay from the funds of the *C*·
    87– 5 of the authority of their *C*·.
    102–19 phrase, "Mary Baker Eddy's *C*·,
    110– 8 recorded in the history of the *C*·
Ret. 13– 2 Congregational (Trinitarian) *C*·,
Pul. 69–24 * than the *C*· has had in the past.
No. 12–15 to goodness, in or out of the *C*·,
    38–11 built his *C*· of the new-born,
    41–22 *C*· seems almost chagrined that
    41–26 * as the faith of the *C*· increases,
    44–21 will again unite *C*· and State,
    45–22 anchor the *C*· in more spiritual
'01. 32– 6 I became early a child of the *C*·,
'02. 2–23 to love the *C*· ;
    2–24 and the *C*· once loved me.
    2–26 I never left the *C*·,
    2–27 I but began where the *C*· left off.
My. 8–23 * chapter sub-title
    27– 2 *To the Beloved Members of my C*·,
    135–26 *My Beloved C*· :— Your love
    177–18 * is the seed of the *C*· ;"
    183–24 *Beloved Students and C*· :— Thanks
    299– 2 chapter sub-title
    (*see also* **Mother Church, The First Church of Christ, Scientist, First Church of Christ, Scientist, Second Church of Christ, Scientist, etc.**)

Church (adj.)

Man. 18–14 *C*· members met and reorganized,
    21– 1 heading
    25– 1 heading
    25– 4 The *C*· officers shall consist of
    28– 3 Duties of *C*· Officers.
    28–24 written on the *C*· records.
    30–17 shall pay from the *C*· funds
    33– 5 *C*· Reader shall not be a Leader,
    44–16 *C*· Periodicals.
    44–23 *C*· Organizations Ample.
    46–18 the offender to *C*· discipline.
    51– 6 from the roll of *C*· membership.
    51–15 No *C*· discipline shall ensue until
    51–26 complaints against *C*· members ;
    52–14 compliance with our *C*· Rules
    53– 6 from the roll of *C*· membership.
    54– 5 suspended . . . from *C*· membership.
    63– 8 read in *C*· services.
    75–18 *C*· members own the aforesaid
    76– 6 proper management of the *C*· funds :
    76–11 to report at the annual *C*· meeting
    77–11 If it be found that the *C*· funds
    79–11 shall be paid from the *C*· funds.
    98–20 letter sent to . . . by the *C*· members
My. 15– 4 Section 3 . . . of the *C*· By-laws
    223–23 breaking of one of the *C*· By-laws,

Church, Walter

Mis. 313–17 "The Lamp," by Walter *C*·,

church (see also church's)

action of the
Mis. 310–23 will determine the action of the *c*·
affairs of the
My. 359– 9 involved in the affairs of the *c*·
and society
Pul. 20– 2 purchased by the *c*· and society.
and State
My. 196– 8 to be engrafted in *c*· and State :
any
Man. 45–17 of any *c*· whose Readers are not
    49– 3 healing work in any *c*· or locality,
My. 98–25 * record is one of which any *c*·
any other
Man. 74– 5 or control over any other *c*·.
My. 71–18 * different from any other *c*·
around the
Pul. 42– 2 * sidewalks around the *c*· were all
at Ephesus
'00. 13– 4 commends the *c*· at Ephesus
at Jerusalem
My. 13– 9 * "The *c*· at Jerusalem, like a sun
beautiful
Pul. 75–17 * BEAUTIFUL *C*· AT BOSTON
beloved
Mis. 149–23 bring to your beloved *c*· a vision of

church

beloved
My. 133–10 My beloved *c*· will not receive a
    169– 2 MY BELOVED *C*· :— I invite you,
    172–14 spiritual call to this my beloved *c*·
    182–30 May this beloved *c*· adhere to
    197– 6 may this beloved *c*· be glorious,
best
My. 8– 9 * the best *c*· in the world,
big
My. 65–13 * a big *c*· was required,
    75–24 * chapter sub-title
blessed
My. 25–21 I shall be with my blessed *c*·
body of the
My. 38–18 * seats in the body of the *c*·,
    80–30 * in the main body of the *c*·,
Boston
Pul. 57–20 * name given to a new Boston *c*·.
    65–27 * The Boston *c*· similarly expresses
My. 141–18 * communion season of the Boston *c*·
branch
Man. 52– 6 *belongs to no branch c*·
    54–17 The Mother Church or a branch *c*·
    71–14 for a branch *c*· to assume such
    72–22 each branch *c*· shall continue its
    72–26 A branch *c*· of The First Church
    74– 3 of both a branch *c*· and a society ;
    74– 6 In C. S. each branch *c*· shall
    100–24 shall be elected by the branch *c*·.
    112– 9 not a member of a branch *c*·,
My. 142–15 communion of branch *c*· communicants
building a
Pul. 44–21 * building a *c*· by voluntary
building of the
My. 98–17 * for the building of the *c*·
building, or
My. 55– 5 * purchase some building, or *c*·,
built up the
Mis. 349–24 and built up the *c*·,
celebrated
My. 50–23 * The *c*· celebrated her Communion
ceremonial of the
Mis. 91– 8 indispensable ceremonial of the *c*·.
Chicago
My. 146– 2 dedicatory letter to the Chicago *c*·
Christian
Pul. 22–11 every Christian *c*· in our land,
Christian Science
Mis. 382–18 charter for the first C. S. *c*·,
Pul. 24– 1 * completion of the first C. S. *c*·
    56–25 * A great C. S. *c*· was dedicated
    68–19 * C. S. *c*·, called The Mother Church,
My. 8–17 * business of the C. S. *c*·,
    30–31 * entire body of the C. S. *c*·.
    58–30 * services at the C. S. *c*·
    65–22 * to the ownership of the C. S. *c*·,
    66– 8 * conveyed by deed to the C. S. *c*·,
    77–20 * temple of the C. S. *c*·,
    78–18 * custom of the C. S. *c*·,
    95–10 * magnificent C. S. *c*·
    99–23 * not a C. S. *c*· in the land.
    329– 2 * healers of the C. S. *c*·,
Christ's
Mis. 91– 5 organize materially Christ's *c*·.
Clerk of the
Mis. 310–22 to the Clerk of the *c*· ;
    322– 9 Clerk of the *c*· can inform
Concord
My. 157– 4 * The members of the Concord *c*·
    171– 9 Concord *c*· is so nearly completed
conducting the
My. 49–25 * mode of conducting the *c*·."
connection with the
My. 321–23 * my connection with the *c*·,
construction of the
My. 63– 3 * the construction of the *c*·,
cooling of the
Pul. 25– 1 * lighting and cooling of the *c*·
costly
My. 87–16 * their costly *c*· fully paid for,
dear
Mis. 125–28 turns to her dear *c*·,
    150– 4 my forever-love to your dear *c*·.
    316– 8 I shall speak to my dear *c*·
My. 19–20 That this dear *c*· shall be
    155–18 the members of this dear *c*·
    196– 6 May this dear *c*· militant
    203–20 God bless this dear *c*·,
dedication of the
Pul. 75–22 * celebrated the dedication of the *c*·
doors of the
My. 31–10 * doors of the *c*· were thrown open
drag on a
My. 84– 2 * Nothing is more of a drag on a *c*·
each
Mis. 314– 5 Each *c*·, or society formed for

church

each
Man. 55– 5 Each c· shall separately and
63–14 Each c· of the C. S. denomination
99–10 Each c· is not necessarily
My. 343–28 I wrote to each c· in tenderness,
enter even the
My. 126– 1 would enter even the c·,
entire
Pul. 27– 9 * the entire c· is a testimonial,
Episcopal
Pul. 26– 8 * chancel of an Episcopal c·
experience of the
Ret. 48– 7 recent experience of the c·
feature of the
Pul. 76– 2 * A striking feature of the c·
filled the
Pul. 41–21 * vast congregations filled the c·
fire-proof
Pul. 70–14 * a handsome fire-proof c·
75–26 * the most nearly fire-proof c·
first
Mis. 141–31 Of our first c· in Boston,
Man. 75–20 After the first c· was built,
Pul. 64–24 * dedicated the first c· of
'00. 1–10 first c· of our denomination,
My. 47–24 * Mrs. Eddy founded her first c·
67–14 * First c· organized . . . 1879
67–15 * First c· erected . . . 1894
70– 5 * its first c· only twelve years ago,
72–29 * when they erected the first c·
289–10 first c· of C. S. known on earth,
first such
Ret. 44– 4 first such c· ever organized.
form a
Man. 72– 7 to form a c· in conformity with
forming the
My. 49–13 * interested in forming the c·,
founded a
Ret. 15– 5 till I founded a c· of my own,
Frankish
Pul. 65–21 * Frankish c· was reared upon the
grand
My. 66–30 * never before has such a grand c·
great
My. 88–29 * in the building of a great c·
93– 5 * dedication of their great c·
head of the
My. 108–29 the head of the c· :— Eph. 5 : 23.
her
My. vi–23 * all future profits to her c· ;
vi–24 * she presented to her c·
40– 3 * desired for years to have her c·
48–14 * future growth of her c·,
144– 2 * members of her c· in Concord,
172– 9 * to the members of her c·,
His
Mis. 399–25 on this rock . . . Stands His c·,
Pul. 16–10 on this rock . . . Stands His c·,
Po. 76– 9 on this rock . . . Stands His c·,
My. 20–12 what God gives to His c·.
his
My. 300–21 are common to his c·,
history of the
My. 57–19 * largest in the history of the c·
284–16 * first time in the history of the c·
home
Pul. 43– 2 * the choir of the home c·,
huge
My. 95–12 * They have built a huge c·,
in Boston
Mis. 141–31 our first c· in Boston,
316– 7 speak to your c· in Boston?
Pul. 30–25 * c· in Boston was organized by
37–11 * superintends the c· in Boston,
My. 13–17 pledged to this c· in Boston
135–17 First Reader of my c· in Boston,
175– 2 my little c· in Boston, Mass.,
292–20 Message to my c· in Boston,
in Chicago
My. 146– 8 in my letter to the c· in Chicago,
infant
My. 343–28 are dangerous in an infant c·.
in Philadelphia
'00. 13–29 angel of the c· in Philadelphia
14–13 except the c· in Philadelphia
My. 153– 8 c· in Philadelphia,"— Rev. 3 : 7.
199– 6 of the c· in Philadelphia :
is the mouthpiece
My. 247– 6 c· is the mouthpiece of C. S.,
254–27 c· is the mouthpiece of C. S.,
Judæo-Christian
'00. 13–28 * of the Judæo-Christian c·."
known in the
Pul. 42–14 * children are known in the c· as

land, and the
Mis. 140– 4 The land, and the c· standing on it,
large
'01. 31–13 communicants of my large c·,
My. 132–18 every member of this large c·.
little
Mis. 149–28 little c· that built the first
154– 7 He will dig about this little c·,
My. 47–25 * And this little c·, God's word
49– 9 * The charter of this little c·
50– 1 * first meeting of this little c·
50–26 * little c· in the wilderness,
154–16 congratulate this little c·
155– 4 May this dear little c·,
175– 2 my little c· in Boston,
184–20 God grant that this little c·
185–25 spoke of the little c·
186– 9 tells the tale of your little c·,
local
Man. 55– 4 members of their local c· ;
96–11 local c· is unable to meet the
magnificent
My. 98– 7 * but that magnificent c·,
maintain the
Ret. 44–15 found able to maintain the c·
meeting of the
Man. 100– 2 If prior to the meeting of the c·
My. 49–15 * first business meeting of the c·
50–32 * to call a general meeting of the c·
51–19 * meeting of the c·, December 15, 1880,
57–14 * first annual meeting of the c·
93–28 * meeting of the c· now being held
member of the
Mis. 129– 2 If a member of the c· is inclined
Pul. 73–18 * prominent member of the c·.
My. 98–21 * no member of the c· anywhere,
members of a
Mis. 90–23 members of a c· not organized
members of the
My. 33– 2 * despatch from the members of the c·
55–14 * twelve of the members of the c·
62–29 * services of other members of the c·,
72–22 * members of the c· all over the
141– 8 * Of late years members of the c·
memorial
Pul. 71– 6 * a memorial c· for Mrs. Eddy,
Message to the
My. 57– 7 * Mrs. Eddy's Message to the c·
170– 8 annual Message to the c·
militant
Pul. 3–18 No longer are we of the c· militant,
My. 125–23 grateful that the c· militant
133– 7 c· militant rise to the
154–25 it makes the c· militant,
196– 6 May this dear c· militant
Mind-healing
Ret. 44– 2 Mind-healing c·, without a creed,
misfortune of a
Pul. 37–22 * misfortune of a c· depending on
my
Mis. 126–27 God hath indeed smiled on my c·,
144–19 I will build my c· ;— Matt. 16 : 18.
263– 7 I will build my c· ;" — Matt. 16 : 18.
349–31 accepted no pay from my c·
Ret. 44–11 my c· increased in members,
45– 5 the prosperity of my c·,
'01. 2–28 my c· of over twenty-one thousand
31–17 every member of my c· would
'02. 13–28 gave to my c· through trustees,
14– 3 is to save it for my c·.
My. 13–29 not only to my c· but to Him who
26–11 ever received from my c·,
118– 2 members of my c· who cheerfully
122–11 my c· tempted me tenderly
135–17 the First Reader of my c·
171– 1 dear members of my c· :
173– 7 to the members of my c·,
215–20 to give my c· The C. S. Journal,
230–21 in the officials of my c·
280–16 that the members of my c· cease
280–28 In no way . . . did I request my c·
281– 3 the daily prayer of my c·,
292–20 Message to my c· in Boston,
my own
Ret. 16–11 occurrence in my own c·
needed a place
My. 55– 3 * c· needed a place of its own,
new
Mis. 149–24 a vision of the new c·,
Pul. 37–19 * for the choir of the new c·,
64– 6 * for the building of a new c·,
79– 3 * chapter sub-title
85–28 * corner-stone of the new c·
My. 30–32 * the chimes of the new c·
70–20 * The new c· is replete with

church

new
My. 72–11 * dedication of the new c·
97–22 * growth of the new c·
new-old
My. 182– 8 establishing a new-old c·,
Nicolaitan
'00. 12–30 Nicolaitan c· presents the
13–11 denounces the Nicolaitan c·.
no other
Man. 71–13 that no other c· can fill.
74– 8 no other c· shall interfere
obedient
My. 209– 4 this willing and obedient c·
of brotherly love
My. 153– 9 the c· of brotherly love,
of Christ
'00. 13– 3 * entered the c· of Christ"
of Christian Science
Mis. 383– 6 wherever a c· of C. S. is
My. 289–10 first c· of C. S. known
of Ephesus
'00. 12– 7 commence with the c· of Ephesus.
of Jerusalem
My. 13–13 c· of Jerusalem seems to
of our faith
My. 163–29 in this city a c· of our faith
of the firstborn
My. 46–30 * c· of the firstborn." — Heb. 12: 23.
of their choice
My. 96–13 * of the c· of their choice.
old
Mis. 178– 4 He has left his old c·,
My. 68–13 * The old c· at the corner of
80–23 * crowded . . . into the old c·,
one
Man. 71– 4 where more than one c· is
My. 67–21 * But one c· in the country
85– 5 * one c· and a mere handful
243– 5 come together and form one c·.
243– 9 should be more than one c· in it.
organize a
Man. 17–10 organize a c· designed to
Ret. 44– 1 voted to organize a c· to
My. 46–10 organize a c· designed to
organized a
Pul. 58– 5 * and organized a c·.
or individuals
Pul. 21–21 close the door on c· or individuals
or society
Mis. 314– 5 Each c·, or society formed for
orthodox
Mis. 111–26 I love the orthodox c· ;
our
Mis. 91– 9 If our c· is organized,
126–15 Perhaps our c· is not yet
129–10 the rule of our c· is to
140–14 Our c· was prospered by
140–21 foundation on which our c· was
140–28 our c· will stand the storms of ages :
141–26 to commence building our c·
'02. 1– 7 added to our c· during the year
20–19 between the sacrament in our c· and
My. 26–24 the true animus of our c·
352–21 for ushering into our c· the
361–19 * We rejoice that our c· has
parent
My. 10–26 * a prosperous parent c·,
pastorate of the
Pul. 45–24 * from the pastorate of the c·,
My. 49–31 * to the pastorate of the c·,
pastor of the
Pul. 29– 5 * first pastor of the c· here
43–30 * from a former pastor of the c· :
My. 49–19 * to become pastor of the c·.
pastorship of the
Pul. 68– 1 * assumed the pastorship of the c·
pastor to the
Pul. 28–28 * pastor to the c· in this city,
Pergamene
'00. 13–22 The Pergamene c· consisted of
prayer in
Man. 42– 1 Prayer in C·.
purity of the
'00. 13– 1 unity and the purity of the c·.
Reader in
Man. 55–13 a Reader in c· or a teacher
Readers in
My. 249–21 chapter sub-title
refers to the
'00. 13–21 refers to the c· in this city as
removed
My. 55–24 * the c· removed to Copley Hall
reorganized the
My. 55–15 * reorganized the c·, and named it

church

reorganize the
Pul. 20– 7 I had to . . . reorganize the c·,
rock-ribbed
My. 186– 5 cluster around this rock-ribbed c·
ruling
My. 13–12 * a *mother* and a ruling c·."
said
My. 51– 6 * now interested in said c·,
Science
My. 85–22 * The Science c· has become the
seats in the
Man. 59–16 welcomes to her seats in the c·,
some
My. 284–19 has been held annually in some c·
South Congregational
My. 289–24 in the South Congregational c·
students and
My. 358–24 to your dear students and c·.
such a
Man. 72–15 the services of such a c·
Pul. 57–16 * organization of such a c·,
supplied
My. 309–29 * The c· supplied the only
that
Mis. 111–26 that c· will love C. S.
Man. 100–20 shall be the duty of that c·
their
My. 74–17 * paying for their c· before
86–20 * maintain towards their c·.
96–18 * generosity . . . towards their c·.
214– 2 on the walls of their c·.
their own
My. 359– 4 individuals in their own c·
this
Mis. 127– 2 in proportion as this c·
144– 1 granite for this c· was taken from
146–20 cannot be the conscience for this c· ;
153–30 peace be and abide with this c·.
310–18 one's connection with this c·,
382–19 I donated to this c· the land
Man. 72–11 This c· shall be acknowledged
Ret. 15–15 by the pastor of this c·.
16– 8 When she entered this c·
44– 5 charter for this c· was obtained in
44–20 to defend this c· from the envy and
Pul. 7–27 so long as this c· is satisfied with
8–10 responded to the call for this c·
20–13 prosperity of this c· is unsurpassed.
20–21 This c· was dedicated on January 6,
24– 3 * This c· is in the fashionable Back Bay,
28–10 * The cost of this c· is
38– 3 * being ordained in this c·,
57–17 * the adherents of this c· have
66–22 * the dedication of this c·,
86–21 * present this c· to you
86–27 * permanent pastor of this c·,
'00. 13– 6 It is written of this c·
13–14 The Revelator writes of this c·
14– 1 approval of this c· by our Master
15–23 write of this c· :
'02. 12–24 financial transactions of this c·,
13–10 yield this c· a liberal income.
My. vii– 5 * its Leader has done for this c· ;
6–27 this c· is the one edifice on
7– 7 financial transactions of this c·,
13–17 pledged to this c· in Boston
17–30 in proportion as this c· has
28–12 * to the building of this c·.
37–23 * that this c· owes itself and
37–27 * your annual Message to this c·.
46– 9 * primary declaration of this c·
47– 6 * steps by which this c· has
55– 9 * rapidly growing in this c·
57–17 * membership of this c·
68– 2 * the interior of this c· is
85–29 * this c·, with its noble dome
89– 1 * This c· is one of the largest
140–27 occasionally attending this c·.
148–11 this c· becomes historic,
155– 8 May this c· have one God,
162–29 This c·, born in my nativity,
163–10 come to the dedication of this c·,
165–13 thank the dear brethren of this c·
165–18 may each member of this c·
165–29 God grant that this c·
177–20 nurtured and nourished this c·
182– 7 my early love for this c·
186–19 May our God make this c·
195–24 praiseworthy success of this c·,
199–11 Trustees of this c· will please
199–14 attitude of this c· in our
230– 9 This c· is impartial.
259–12 To this c· across the sea
321– 1 * building this c· for your

church

to examine the
My. 38–15   * tarry to examine the *c.*
to leave the
My. 56–27   * obliged to leave the *c·*
to ride to
My. 219–12   To say that it is sin to ride to *c·*
triumphant
Pul. 3–19   but of the *c·* triumphant ;
My. 133– 7   rise to the *c·* triumphant,
    154–26   foreshadowing of the *c·* triumphant.
    174–30   rejoice in the *c·* triumphant ?
two-million-dollar
My. 86–12   * new two-million-dollar *c·*,
    98–28   * two-million-dollar *c·* of the
unique
Pul. 61–16   * every part of this unique *c·*,
Unitarian
My. 171–22   * the lawn of the Unitarian *c·*
    173–29   committee of the Unitarian *c·*,
unite with the
Ret. 14–13   could I unite with the *c·*,
vestibule of the
My. 320–31   * in the vestibule of the *c·*
voted
My. 53–15   * the *c·* voted to wait upon
    57– 9   * *c·* voted to raise any part of
was filled
My. 30–27   * Though the *c·* was filled
    38–11   * The *c·* was filled for each service
was founded
Pul. 37–28   * 1879, the *c·* was founded
    67–27   * The *c·* was founded in April,
went into the
Ret. 16–13   pale cripples went into the *c·*
will be built
My. 157–14   * The *c·* will be built of the
without creeds
Man. 17– 3   forming a *c·* without creeds,
work of the
My. 51–26   * this very early work of the *c·*,
yields to the
Pul. 6– 5   yields to the *c·* established by
your
Mis. 155– 9   win the . . . stranger to your *c·*,
    159– 5   read this letter to your *c·*,
    316– 7   or speak to your *c·* in Boston ?
My. 23–18   * The members of your *c·*,
    36– 9   * The members of your *c·*
    62–20   * We, the Directors of your *c·*,
    191–29   the dedication of your *c·*
    192–21   at the dedication of your *c·*,
    194–18   fair escutcheon of your *c·*.
    194–27   guide and guard you and your *c·*
    195– 5   dedicatory services of your *c·*.
    352– 5   * we, the ushers of your *c·*,
    360–19   unite with those in your *c·*

Mis. 35–20   and then go to *c·* to hear it
    129–12   drop this member's name from the *c·*,
    131– 8   kneels on a stool in *c·*,
    132–19   having charge of a *c·*,
    349–25   When the *c·* had sufficient
Man. 29– 1   the First Reader of a *c·*,
    33– 4   the *c·* in which he is Reader.
    33– 9   shall not be a President of a *c·*.
    96– 8   paid by the *c·* that employs him.
    99–27   Readers of the *c·* employing said
    100– 3   send to the First Reader of the *c·*
Ret. 44–24   recommended that the *c·* be dissolved.
Un. 26–12   the hymn-verse so often sung in *c·* :
Pul. 20– 5   gave back the land to the *c·*.
    20–10   regive the land to the *c·*.
    24–22   * *c·* is built of Concord granite
    30– 8   * *c·* numbers now four thousand
    44–22   * *c·* which will be dedicated to-day
    52– 1   * Here is a *c·* whose treasurer
    63– 6   * C· COSTING $250,000
    77– 1   * which the *c·* has just erected.
Pan. 14–10   chapter sub-title
Peo. 14–12   thou of the *c·* of the new-born ;
My. 8–19   * *c·* of twenty-four thousand members
    14–27   * until the *c·* is finished.
    29–28   * began to congregate about the *c·*
    30– 8   * drawn to the *c·* from curiosity,
    36– 3   * telegram from the *c·* to Mrs. Eddy
    49–20   * August 27 the *c·* held a meeting,
    50–23   * her Communion Sabbath as a *c·*,
    50–25   * members were added to the *c·*."
    50–31   * her farewell sermon to the *c·*.
    53– 9   * voted that the *c·* hold its
    53–19   * establishing itself as a *c·*
    53–26   * business committee of the *c·*,
    55–22   * *c·* was obliged to seek other
    57–29   * *c·* whose Treasurer has

church

My. 61– 1   * watching at the *c·*.
    66–13   * will enable the *c·* to expand,
    69– 1   * *c·* is unusually well lighted,
    75–27   * No *c·* has ever yet been
    91–24   * the *c·* has continued to grow.
    94– 4   * figures given out by the *c·*
    94–26   * "crowning ultimate" of the *c·*
    95– 4   * *c·* which has been built upon the
    123–22   less sufficient to receive a *c·* of
    171–25   * greeted in behalf of the *c·* by
    171–26   * as a love-token for the *c·*
    172–21   * in behalf of the *c·*,
    173–30   and to the *c·* itself,
    174–22   until I had a *c·* of my own,
    187– 3   *c·* in Salt Lake City hath not
    259–10   * members London, England, *c·*.
    299– 7   * by the *c·* or the Bible,
    302–29   went alone . . . to the *c·*,
    308–23   as they were about to start for *c·*.
    328–22   * a prominent healer of the *c·*,

church (adj.)

Mis. 131–16   that you waive the *c·* By-law
    141– 8   and against this *c·* temple
    177–23   hour for the *c·* service
    284–30   rules of *c·* government,
    310–19   comply with the *c·* rules.
Man. 70– 2   shall not make a *c·* By-Law,
    71–22   in their *c·* books,
    72– 9   *c·* services conducted by
    72–18   under one *c·* government.
    75– 1   heading
    75–23   balance of the *c·* building funds,
Ret. 89– 6   There was no *c·* preaching,
Pul. 8– 4   *c·* chimes repeat my thanks
    9–17   *c·* services were maintained by
    16– 1   Set to the C· Chimes
    20–11   ministry and *c·* government.
    29–26   * heading
    39–21   * on the gray *c·* tower,
    44–19   * chapter sub-title
    66– 4   * first *c·* organization of this faith
    75–26   * most nearly fire-proof *c·* structure
    77– 7   * golden key of the *c·* structure.
    78–22   * gold key to the *c·* door.
'02. 1– 4   our *c·* communicants constantly
My. v– 4   * stirring times of *c·* building,
    vi–12   * devised its *c·* government,
    19–14   * their local *c·* building funds
    19–29   * towards its *c·* building fund.
    21– 6   * building *c·* homes of their own,
    29–13   * more gorgeous *c·* pageantries
    29–15   * have been *c·* ceremonies that
    49–14   * tenets and *c·* covenant.
    50– 4   * left their former *c·* homes,
    65– 3   * largest *c·* business meeting
    66–15   * so well situated for *c·* purposes
    71–19   * all the traditions of *c·* interior
    72– 3   * interior *c·* architecture.
    74– 6   * numbers of belated *c·* members
    76–11   * by the thousands of *c·* members
    76–17   * support of their *c·* work,
    76–20   * in their annual *c·* meeting
    83–31   * necessary expense of *c·* work,
    84– 5   * how a "*c·* debt" cramps and
    85–16   * in the building of a *c·* structure
    121– 4   our semi-annual *c·* meetings,
    170– 2   no formal *c·* ceremonial,
    170– 4   request of my *c·* members that
    171–11   invite all my *c·* communicants
    186–26   on the day of your *c·* dedication.
    203– 7   C· laws which are obeyed without
    223– 5   which pertain to *c·* difficulties
    236– 1   history of our *c·* buildings.
    250– 3   three years' term for *c·* Readers,
    250–10   acceptable service as *c·* Readers,
    311–16   my first *c·* membership.
    352– 7   * enjoy in this *c·* work.
    360–13   settle this *c·* difficulty amicably
    (see also **building, edifice, edifices, home**)

Church-building
Man. 102– 1   heading

Church Building Fund
Mis. 143–26   in aid of our C· B· F·,

Church Business
Man. 27– 1   C· B·.

Church Directors
    (see **Directors**)

Churches and churches (see also **churches'**)
action of the
Man. 70–20   unity and action of the *c·*
all
Pul. 69–25   * All *c·* have prayed for the cure of

Churches and **churches**
all the
Mis. 383– 2	pastor, on this planet, of all the *c.*
Pul. 56– 7	* members of all the *c·*
'00. 14–12	inspired rebuke to all the *c·*
'01. 11–14	the pastor for all the *c·*
My. 301– 9	I would that all the *c·* on earth
342–21	It will embrace all the *c·*,

and associations
Mis. 358–22	organizing *c·* and associations.

and societies
Man. 74–17	*c·* and societies are required to
74–18	other C. S. *c·* and societies
My. 207– 7	* representatives of *c·* and societies
362–23	* will unite the *c·* and societies

are united
Pan. 13–14	*c·* are united in purpose,
My. 18–22	*c·* are united in purpose.

branch
Man. 31– 3	AND OF ITS BRANCH *C·*.
31– 6	Readers . . . of all its branch *c·*
32–17	Readers in Branch *C·*.
32–25	Readers in all the branch *c·*.
40–18	the branch *c·* by the First Reader
45–21	branch *c·* of this denomination
48–19	nor that of the branch *c·*.
54–25	Members of Branch *C·*.
61–11	Communion of Branch *C·*.
61–13	be observed in the branch *c·* on
70– 8	heading
71– 1	Branch *c·* of The Mother Church
71– 7	before titles of branch *c·*,
71–17	no Church . . . that has branch *c·*
71–21	Branch *c·* shall not write the
72– 1	Branch *c·* shall not adopt,
72–16	branch *c·* shall be individual,
72–26	Organizing Branch *C·*.
73–23	branch *c·* shall not confine their
74–13	or rooms in the branch *c·*,
93–18	No Disruption of Branch *C·*.
94– 1	organization of branch *c·*.
95– 9	From Branch *C·*.
95–10	branch *C·* of Christ, Scientist,
95–17	branch *c·* shall call on
98–24	In Branch *C·*.
98–25	three largest branch *c·* in each
99– 8	its three largest branch *c·*,
112– 1	When branch *c·* are designated by
112– 6	before titles of branch *c·*.
120– 2	heading
125– 2	heading
127– 3	heading
'02. 1– 9	our branch *c·* are multiplying
My. 10–27	* prosperity of the branch *c·* ;
19–13	* branch *c·* which contributed
21– 4	* made by many of the branch *c·*
21– 9	* erection of many branch *c·*.
40– 6	* we are sure that now the branch *c·*
56–10	* necessary to organize branch *c·*
56–12	* three branch *c·* were organized,
56–18	* organization of branch *c·*
56–22	* more branch *c·* were established
57–22	* total number of branch *c·*
141–26	"The branch *c·* continue their
243– 7	of the rules for branch *c·*.
250–18	nor compels the branch *c·* to
250–23	the branch *c·* can wait for the
250–28	is done . . . by the branch *c·*
359– 5	with the members of branch *c·*.

chapels and
Mis. 150–17	Chapels and *c·* are dotting the

Christian
Pul. 22– 3	Christian *c·* have one bond
Pan. 13–13	Love all Christian *c·*
My. 18–21	Love all Christian *c·*
89–18	* almost all other of the Christian *c·*,

Christian Science
Man. 32– 2	First Readers in the C. S. *c·*
42– 2	prayers in C. S. *c·* shall be
64– 5	Reading Rooms of C. S. *C·*;
71–10	its relation to other C. S. *c·*,
74–18	all other C. S. *c·* and societies
My. 250–19	applies only to C. S. *c·* in
255– 5	C. S. *c·* have my consent to
362–13	* Readers of all the C. S. *c·*
363–15	C. S. *c·* in Greater New York

conference of
Man. 70–16	No conference of *c·* shall be held,

Congregational
My. 182– 2	Chicago had few Congregational *c·*.

dear
My. 164–16	Now [1904] six dear *c·* are there,
175–13	Its dear *c·*, reliable editors,

dedicate
Mis. 91– 6	ordain pastors and to dedicate *c·* ;

dozens of
My. 73– 4	* They have erected dozens of *c·*

Churches and **churches**
each other's
Man. 85– 2	Pupils may visit each other's *c·*,

Eastern
Pul. 65– 4	* Eastern *c·* and the Anglican fold

erect
Pul. 45– 6	* effect cures . . . and erect *c·*,

evangelical
Mis. 249–13	devout members of evangelical *c·*
Man. 17– 5	were members of evangelical *c·*,
Ret. 64–30	If evangelical *c·* refuse
My. 182– 6	recommendation to evangelical *c·*

first century
My. 300–30	from the first century *c·*,

five
My. 343–26	they had five *c·* under discipline.

form
Mis. 137–30	My students can *now* . . . form *c·*,

from halls to
Mis. 125–30	the rapid transit from halls to *c·*,

halls and
Ret. 40–23	a hearing in their halls and *c·*.

have risen
My. 85– 8	* its *c·* have risen by hundreds,

messages to the
'00. 12– 7	his messages to the *c·*

more
Man. 63–16	two or more *c·* may unite in
My. 243–15	to take charge of three or more *c·*.

new
My. 8–30	* one hundred and five new *c·*

old
Mis. 179– 1	The old *c·* are saying,

or associations
No. 41–13	perfection in *c·* or associations.

organize
Ret. 50–24	continue to organize *c·*, schools,

organizing
Mis. 358–22	organizing *c·* and associations.
Man. 72– 4	Organizing *C·*.

other
Man. 70–12	no . . . official control of other *c·*,
Ret. 44–21	molestation of other *c·*,
Pul. 30– 7	* not recruit itself from other *c·*
66–10	* conversions from other *c·*,
My. 13–10	* other *c·*, like so many planets,
284–23	only as other *c·* had done.

our
Mis. 91– 3	observed at present in our *c·*.
113–29	Our *c·*, The C. S. Journal, and
158–29	as our *c·* ordain ministers.
Man. 70– 1	our *c·*, located in the same
My. 189– 9	The silent prayers of our *c·*,
214– 2	Otherwise, as our *c·* multiply,
249–29	What our *c·* need is

pastors of
Mis. 143–20	editors, and pastors of *c·*,

seven
'00. 14– 6	He goes on to portray seven *c·*,

several
My. 243– 4	the several *c·* in New York City

shall decide
Man. 94– 5	the *c·* shall decide their action.

small
Man. 72–18	not more than two small *c·* shall

some
Pul. 56– 7	* In some *c·* a majority of

some of the
My. 10–12	* and some of the *c·*

strong
Pul. 67–20	* Toronto and . . . have strong *c·*,

such
Man. 71– 8	nor written . . . in naming such *c·*.
My. 99–24	* hundreds of such *c·*.

their
Man. 69–23	take care of their *c·* or attend to
94– 4	for their *c·* a less lecture fee ;
My. 76–18	* dedicate their *c·* free of debt
250– 8	adopt this By-law in their *c·*,

these
My. 182– 3	said to have a majority of these *c·*

Unitarian
Pul. 28–26	* hymn-books of the Unitarian *c·*.

unity with
Pul. 21–26	Our unity with *c·* of other

unto the
'00. 11–27	saith unto the *c·*."— Rev. 2: 7.
14–10	what the Spirit saith unto the *c·* ;
14–20	angel that spake unto the *c·*

within the city
Man. 94– 2	can invite *c·* within the city

your
My. 192–16	My heart hovers around your *c·*
214– 4	on the walls of your *c·*.

Mis. 158–26	directions sent out to the *c·*.

Churches and churches

churches'

Churches and Societies of C. S. in Missouri

Churches of Christ, Scientist

church-fund

churchman

Church Manual (*see also* **Manual**)

Church Manual

church-member

church-members

Church Membership

churchmen

Church of Christ

Church of Christ, Scientist

Church of England
  '01. 21– 9   * Berkeley of the *C· of E·*
Church Officers
  Man. 21– 1   names of
         25– 1   heading
         28– 3   Duties of *C· O·.*
Church of Rome
  My. 294–26   animated the *C· of R·*
Church Purposes
  Man. 136– 2   heading
Church Rule
  Man. 40–17   *C· R·* shall be read in
Church's
  Man. 75– 8   this *C·* love and gratitude,
church's
  Mis. 131–26   bill of this *c·* gifts to Mother ;
  Man. 54–15   branch *c·* list of membership
  Ret. 44–18   noting the *c·* need, and the
  Pul. 45–13   * declared that the *c·* completion
         87–24   our *c·* tall tower detains the sun,
  My. 123– 1   this *c·* gifts to me are
Church Services
  Man. 58– 1   heading
Church Tenets
  Man. 18–22   The *C· T·*, Rules, and
         40–20   the *C· T·* are to be read.
Church Treasurer
  Man. 44–15   forwarded each year to the *C· T·.*
         76– 9   the books of the *C· T·*
         77– 1   books of the *C· T·* audited annually
         (*see also* **Treasurer**)
Church Universal and Triumphant
  Man. 19– 6   reflect . . . the *C· U· and T·.*
church-yards
  Peo. 14– 6   dismal gray stones of *c·*
cigarette
  Mis. 240–26   If they see their father with a *c·*
Cincinnati
  Pul. 56– 2   * Buffalo, Cleveland, *C·,*
cipher
  My. 235– 9   and never name a *c·* ?
circle
  Ret. 19– 5   parting with the dear home *c·*
         19–14   lamented by a large *c·* of friends
  Un. 12– 5   sickle of Mind's eternal *c·,*
  Pul. 47– 4   * her *c·* of pupils and admirers
  '02. 2–28   in the *c·* of love, we shall meet
  My. 330–26   lamented by a large *c·* of friends
circles
  Ret. 5–26   * in the *c·* in which she moved,
  Pul. 51–17   * a sensation in religious *c·,*
         57–21   * Few people outside its own *c·*
circling
  Chr. 53– 1   Fast *c·* on, from zone to zone,
  '02. 1–21   C. S., . . . is *c·* the globe,
  My. 115– 2   is *c·* the whole world.
Circuit Lecturer
  Man. 94–14   *C· L·.*
         94–16   Mother Church shall appoint a *C· L·.*
circuitous
  Mis. 139–23   transferred in a *c·,* novel way,
circular
  Mis. 305–11   * this *c·* is sent to every member
         305–31   * every one receiving this *c·*
  Pul. 24–10   * Romanesque tower with a *c·* front
circulars
  Man. 46– 9   on *c·,* cards, or leaflets,
circulate
  Man. 43–22   shall neither buy, sell, nor *c·*
         98–14   *c·* in large quantities the papers
  My. 298–11   to publish and *c·* this work.
circulated
  Mis. 285– 4   and not one of them *c·,*
  Man. 97–20   or *c·* literature of any sort.
  My. 305–10   "vulgar" defamers have *c·,*
circulates
  Mis. 126–23   yet nothing *c·* so rapidly :
circulating
  My. 136–20   *c·* in the five grand divisions of
         297–29   said to be *c·* regarding my history,
         298– 2   buying, *c·,* and recommending it
circulation
  Mis. 382– 6   manuscripts of mine were in *c·.*
  Pul. 47– 7   * *c·* with the members of this
  My. 76– 4   * notices . . . had been in *c·,*
         175–27   counterfeit letters in *c·,*
         333–32   * reports of . . . are in *c·.*"

circumference
  Un. 10–20   God is . . . the centre and *c·.*
circumlocution
  No. 22– 8   The *c·* and cold categories
circumscribed
  Un. 21–11   said, . . . your intellect will be *c·*
circumstance
  Mis. 91–13   at all times and under every *c·,*
         117–32   hasten to follow under every *c·.*
         118– 7   Honesty . . . under every *c·,*
         119–12   more stubborn than the *c·,*
         155– 3   pride of *c·* or power
         160– 6   through time and *c·,*
  Ret. 40–24   This *c·* is cited simply to show
  Pul. 55– 8   * not the least eventful *c·*
  My. 248–18   No fatal *c·* of idolatry can
         330–22   * Mrs. Eddy says of this *c·* :
circumstances
  Mis. 17–25   the timely or untimely *c·,*
         90–12   under *c·* exceptional,
         146–10   would need to know the *c·*
         178–28   but will yield to *c·.*
         200–26   met no obstacle or *c·* paramount
         229– 4   *c·* which he believes produce it.
         276– 7   *c·* demanded my attention
         288–14   nearest right under the *c·,*
         298–10   Under the same *c·,*
         326–16   under every hue of *c·,*
  Man. 46–20   shall not, under pardonable *c·,*
  Ret. 8– 1   Many peculiar *c·* and events
         13– 4   some *c·* are noteworthy.
         38– 1   will be seen in the following *c·.*
         38–25   motives and *c·* unknown to me.
         53– 4   prosperous under difficult *c·,*
  Pul. 15–16   At all times and under all *c·,*
         67– 7   * fact borne out by *c·.*
  '01. 30–27   under all *c·* to obey
  '02. 11– 4   to and fro by adverse *c·,*
  My. 37– 3   * no pride of *c·* has place
         52–31   * peculiar knowledge of the *c·.*
         118–14   such *c·* embarrass the
         195– 5   Adverse *c·,* loss of help,
         204–20   recommend it under the *c·.*
         321–17   * nothing in the *c·* which have
         334–12   * this critic places certain *c·*
citadel
  Pul. 2–20   strengthen your *c·* by every means
  My. 213–22   strengthen your own *c·*
citadels
  Mis. 211–27   Jesus stormed sin in its *c·*
  '01. 2–19   ever storming sin in its *c·,*
citations
  My. 34–14   * *c·* from the Bible and "S. and H.
cite
  Mis. 300–25   I gave permission to *c·,*
  My. 107– 7   I will *c·* a modern phase of
cited
  Mis. 296– 9   unknown author *c·* by Mr. Wakeman
  Man. 104–18   shall be *c·* as authority.
  Ret. 40–24   circumstance is *c·* simply to show the
         76– 7   it is *c·,* and quoted deferentially.
  My. 281– 6   I *c·,* as our present need, faith
cites
  '00. 6–29   *c·* 1875 as the year of the
         14–20   angel that spake . . . *c·* Jesus as
cities
  Mis. 81–17   *c·* and towns of Judea,
         257–26   Earthquakes engulf *c·,* churches,
  Ret. 82–14   locate in large *c·,* in order to
         82–16   population of our principal *c·*
         89– 9   scattered about in *c·* and villages,
  Pul. 5–23   public libraries of the principal *c·,*
         79–13   * or village — to say nothing of *c·*
  No. 1– 9   demolishing bridges and . . . *c·.*
  '00. 1–19   in most of the principal *c·,*
         2– 3   springing up in the above-named *c·,*
         12–23   to purge our *c·* of charlatanism.
  My. 112–31   into the chief *c·*
citing
  Ret. 75– 8   *c·* from the works of other authors
citizen
  Mis. 147–24   the public-spirited *c·.*
  My. 277–22   every *c·* would be a soldier
citizens
  '01. 33–29   Christian Scientists are harmless *c·*
  My. 173– 6   to thank the *c·* of Concord for
         227–21   *c·* are arrested for manslaughter
         331– 5   * of Wilmington's best *c·,*
         333– 5   * found by one of your own *c·,*

citizenship
   Pul. 50– 8 * better home life and *c*.

city
  above the
    My. 67– 1 * raises its dome above the *c*
  American
    My. 85–31 * sky-lines in an American *c*,
  another
    My. 14–12 * from a friend in another *c*,
  any
    Pul. 23– 5 * Most Unique Structure in Any *C*
       24– 6 * most unique structure in any *c*.
  beleaguered
    Mis. 326–18 wanderers in a beleaguered *c*,
  best
    My. 8–12 * and in the best *c* in the world.
  capital
    My. 157– 8 * capital *c* of your native State.
  celestial
    Mis. 311– 5 as we journey to the celestial *c*.
       323– 3 celestial *c* above all clouds,
  certain
    My. 294– 7 In a certain *c* the Master
  convention
    My. 83– 4 * residing in the convention *c*.
  entire
    '00. 12–26 The entire *c* is now in ruins.
    My. 69–29 * seems to dominate the entire *c*,
  great
    My. 183– 5 in this great *c* of Chicago,
  guests of the
    My. 74–26 * are as the guests of the *c*,
  heavenly
    Pul. 27–13 * one representing the heavenly *c*
  historic
    My. 85–25 * this historic *c* is the Mecca
  home
    My. 157– 9 * the Cause in your home *c*,
      174–11 editors in my home *c*
  illustrious
    '00. 12– 8 Ephesus as an illustrious *c*,
  intellectual
    Pul. 80– 7 * in the most intellectual *c*
  light of the
    No. 27–10 Spirit will be the light of the *c*,
  other
    My. 74–15 * in this or any other *c*,
      182– 3 any other *c* in the United States.
  our
    My. 154–17 this little church in our *c*,
      175–12 growth and prosperity of our *c*
  picturesque
    My. 175–17 Our picturesque *c*, however,
  pleasant
    My. 163–24 people of this pleasant *c*
  renowned
    My. 177–16 In your renowned *c*,
  streets of a
    Mis. 324– 3 streets of a *c* made with hands.
  that
    Ret. 19– 8 when the yellow-fever raged in that *c*,
    Pul. 65–20 * called the Bible of that *c*
    '00. 12–22 the magical books in that *c*
      12–24 During St. Paul's stay in that *c*
      13– 3 church of Christ" in that *c*.
    My. 89–24 * not . . . to that *c* alone,
      92–11 * than it has evoked in that *c*,
      335–19 * the dread disease in that *c*,
  this
    Mis. 251–10 voicing the friendship of this *c*
    Pul. 7– 5 whereof this *c* is the capital.
      28–28 * pastor to the church in this *c*,
      50–12 * house of worship in this *c*,
      68–16 * was organized in this *c*
      71–13 * Christian Scientists in this *c*,
      72– 4 * feeling of Scientists in this *c*
      78– 1 * Mary Baker Eddy of this *c*,
    '00. 12–11 items concerning this *c*.
      13–21 refers to the church in this *c* as
      13–25 * "In this *c* the amalgamation of
    My. 65– 9 * to build in this *c* a church edifice
      67–27 * surpass any church . . . in this *c*.
      74– 7 * who will arrive in this *c*
      77–10 * rapidly gathering in this *c*
      83–21 * Christian Scientists in this *c*
      141– 5 * held annually . . . in this *c*,
      148– 1 your pioneer work in this *c*.
      158– 3 church edifice for . . . in this *c*.
      163–29 in this *c* a church of our faith
      164– 4 give to many in this *c* a church
      328–19 * C. S. healers in this *c*.
  town and
    My. 92– 1 * in every important town and *c*
  within the
    Man. 94– 2 can invite churches within the *c*

city
  your
    My. 177–10 able to take the trip to your *c*,
      187– 1 Church of Christ, . . . in your *c*.
      187– 4 at some near future visit your *c*,
      330–10 * Christian Scientist of your *c*,
      331– 9 * irreproachable standing in your *c*

    Mis. 323– 2 "a *c* set upon a hill," — *see Matt.* 5 : 14.
    Ret. 20–23 in the *c* of Salem, Massachusetts.
    Pul. 77–11 * in the *c* of Boston,
      78–10 * in the *c* of Boston,
    '00. 13–12 founded the *c* of Smyrna,
      13–17 *c* of Pergamos was devoted to a
      13–24 deity in the *c* of Thyatira was Apollo.
    '01. 28–17 persecuted from *c* to *c*.
    My. 3–10 gates into the *c*." — *Rev.* 22 : 14.
      46–28 * *c* of the living God, — *Heb.* 12 : 22.
      66–16 * in a fine part of the *c*.
      70– 1 * in their relation to the *c* itself,
      71–11 * great adornment to the *c*.
      72– 7 * Never before has the *c* been more
      75– 9 * into the *c* from every direction
      78– 8 * from every quarter of the *c*.
      79–10 * in the heart of the *c* of Boston,
      82–26 * trains pulled out of the *c*
      122–15 in our good *c* of Concord.
      123–11 finest localities in the *c*,
      188–10 brought out of the *c* of David,
      196– 5 "*c* of brotherly love."
      196–12 that taketh a *c*." — *Prov.* 16 : 32.
      206–20 "The *c* had no need of — *Rev.* 21 : 23.
      270– 7 this capital *c* of Concord, N. H.,
      271–13 * in the *c* of Concord,
      285–23 nor in the *c* :— *Acts* 24 : 12.

city (adj.)
    Po. vi–17 *that the c authorities could*
    My. 174– 8 the efficient *c* marshal and his
      175–19 favor of our *c* government ;

City of Mexico, Mex.
    My. 95– 8 *[Mexican Herald, C of M, M.]*

civic
    '00. 10–12 *c*, social, and religious rights
    My. 285– 8 industrial, *c*, and national peace.

Civic League of San Francisco
    My. 285– 3 on behalf of the *C L of S F*,

civil
    Mis. 145– 2 *c* and religious liberty.
      206– 2 natural, *c*, or religious.
      246– 5 *c* and religious reform,
      246– 9 *c* and political power.
      251–12 *c* and religious freedom,
    Ret. 70–28 *c*, moral, and religious reform.
    Pul. 20–17 *c*, and religious reform
    No. 15–10 *c* and religious arms
      44–22 the *c* arm of government,
    My. 216– 6 *c*, and educational means,
      268–13 the justice of *c* codes,

civilization
    Pul. 66–27 * with which our *c* has developed.
    '02. 10–10 * "The birthplace of *c* is not
    My. 29–14 * and in an older *c* ;
      265–10 that *c*, peace between nations,
      278–20 elevating power of *c*
      278–24 have no right to engraft into *c*

civilized
    Pul. 79–11 * in every part of the *c* world,
    My. 59–12 * scientific body in the *c* world.
      77–13 * practically every *c* country,
      90–25 * from all over the *c* world,
      273– 9 * covers practically the *c* world.

Civil War
    My. 332–27 * during the *C W* many Masonic

clad
    Mis. 104–16 *c* in a false mentality,
      162–14 *C* with divine might,
      171–29 all *c* in the shining mail
      234–29 *c* with a richer illumination
      262– 7 *c* in Truth-healing's new
      373–16 as *c* not in soft raiment
      374– 3 *c* in panoply of power,
    Ret. 28–16 we must be *c* with divine power.
    Pul. 1– 5 promise *c* in white raiment,
      15–18 *C* in the panoply of Love,
      35–20 we must be *c* with divine power.
    No. 29–22 though *c* in soft raiment,
    My. 189– 1 *C* in invincible armor,
      191–18 *c* in immortality.
      210– 8 *c* therewith you are completely
      340–13 *c* in a little brief authority,

claim (noun)

any
Un. 54–12 To admit that sin has any *c·*
No. 30–12 to rebuke any *c·* of another law.

being worthless
No. 27– 3 and the *c·*, being worthless,

claimant or a
Mis. 259– 8 that evil is a claimant or a *c·*.

cope with the
My. 227–17 their ability to cope with the *c·*,

diviner
Mis. 140–25 The diviner *c·* and means for

evil
Mis. 284–22 neither an evil *c·* nor an

false
Mis. 53– 1 out of this dream or false *c·*
53– 3 before this false *c·* can be
108–11 Not to know that a false *c·* is false,
258– 5 unrelenting false *c·* of matter
Ret. 64–23 and error being a false *c·*,
67– 1 Sin existed as a false *c·*
67–16 until the false *c·* called sin is
Un. 32– 2 and that evil is a false *c·*,
32–15 misnamed mind is a false *c·*,
32–26 but the false *c·* to personality,
47– 5 false *c·* to existence or consciousness.
54– 3 To say there *is* a false *c·*, called
54– 4 it is nothing but a false *c·*.
54– 5 one must lose sight of a false *c·*.
54– 8 regard sickness as a false *c·*
No. 16– 7 If God knows evil even as a false *c·*,
17–24 If God could know a false *c·*,
27– 3 It issues a false *c·* ;
'01. 14– 8 evil, as a false *c·*, false entity,
'02. 6–14 is seen to obtain in a false *c·*,

falsity of the
Un. 32–28 demonstrate the falsity of the *c·*.

fraudulent
Mis. 272–25 * is a fraudulent *c·*.

great
Pul. 31–27 * with great *c·* to personal beauty.

his
Mis. 261–29 one will either abandon his *c·*
381–12 evidence to support his *c·*

idolatrous
Un. 31–11 *first* idolatrous *c·* of sin is,

illusive
Pan. 6– 6 illusive *c·* that God is not supreme,

its
Mis. 31–11 Its *c·* to power is in proportion to
108–13 reducing its *c·* to its proper
Ret. 35–20 its *c·* is substantiated,

mortal
Mis. 198–10 the mortal *c·* to life, substance, or

no
No. 27– 4 is in reality no *c·* whatever.
'00. 15–14 thence to see that sin has no *c·*,
My. 272– 9 no *c·* that man is equal to God,

no other
Mis. 193–10 established on no other *c·*

of error
Mis. 100–10 *c·* of error for Truth to deny
293–23 creator of the *c·* of error.
Un. 8–20 nothingness of every *c·* of error,
54–10 insensible to every *c·* of error.
'01. 15– 5 We must condemn the *c·* of error

of evil
Mis. 55– 9 is the universal *c·* of evil
115–18 delivered from every *c·* of evil,
Ret. 64–11 as the opposite *c·* of evil is one.

of insanity
Mis. 49–11 distorted into the *c·* of insanity

of matter
Mis. 258– 5 unrelenting false *c·* of matter
Un. 32– 3 Hence the *c·* of matter usurps the

of sin
Un. 31–11 *c·* of sin is, that matter exists ;
'00. 15–14 awakened to see . . . the *c·* of sin,
'01. 13–28 first detect the *c·* of sin ;

pushed that
Un. 54–27 serpent, who pushed that *c·*

sin, as a
Ret. 63–19 Sin, as a *c·*, is more dangerous

sin's
Un. 54–14 for if sin's *c·* be allowed

their
No. 38– 5 by knowing their *c·*.
My. 134–14 will never lose their *c·* on us.

this
Mis. 39–10 risen up in a day to make this *c·* ;
109– 9 how much of this *c·* you admit

to error
No. 30–20 forbids . . . even a *c·* to error.

valid
Mis. 261–30 or else make the *c·* valid.

---

claim (noun)
Mis. 63– 4 the *c·* that one erring mind cures
Ret. 35–21 a *c·* too immanent to fall to the
Un. 32–26 a *c·* which C. S. uncovers.
54– 6 If the *c·* be present to the thought,
54– 9 the so-called fact of the *c·*

claim (verb)
Mis. 3– 3 shall *c·* no especial gift from our
43– 6 *Do all who at present c· to be*
196– 3 *c·* no mind apart from God.
199– 4 erring mind can *c·* to do thus,
255–20 I *c·* for healing by C. S.
303–16 privileges that we *c·* for ourselves.
349–17 I *c·* no jurisdiction over any
367–14 to *c·* that He is ignorant of anything ;
Man. 92–11 Science to be all that we *c·* for it.
Ret. 34–10 I *c·* for healing scientifically the
Pul. 66–11 * *c·* to have been rescued from death
67– 8 * Boston can fairly *c·* to be the hub
74–16 *c·* nothing more than what I am,
No. 27– 4 Matter is not Mind, to *c·* aught ;
'01. 7–24 God whom all Christians now *c·*
Hea. 15–15 why should man . . . *c·* another mind
My. 26–21 or that I *c·* their homage.
245–24 all who *c·* to teach C. S.
299– 8 * *c·* the allegiance of mankind.''
299–18 those who *c·* to pardon sin.
305–21 I *c·* no special merit of any kind.
320–16 * *c·* to be a Christian Scientist,
354– 4 which they *c·* have been endorsed by

claimant
Mis. 259– 8 supposition that evil is a *c·*
Un. 54–17 even as a false *c·*,
54–18 then acquaintance with that *c·*
No. 24–22 evil has no . . . and was never a *c·* ;

claimants
Mis. 263–27 especially by unprincipled *c·*,
No. 42–21 C. S. is beset with false *c·*,

claimed
Mis. 60–26 Evil in the beginning *c·* the power,
349–15 which he *c·* to be practising ;
352–16 what has *c·* to produce it,
Ret. 25–17 The real I *c·* as eternal ;
68– 2 as a serpent it *c·* to originate
68– 4 it *c·* to beget the offspring of evil,
Un. 46–19 as is still *c·* by the worldly-wise.
Pul. 72–21 * had never *c·*, nor did she believe
82–12 * In olden times the Jews *c·* to be
Hea. 17–18 had *c·* audience with a serpent.
18–19 or *c·* to reach that woe ;
Po. v– 7 * *experience that c· her attention.*
My. 14–13 * *c·* to have good authority for
73– 6 * it is *c·* that very few of them
303– 5 and I have never *c·* to be.
330–18 * as *c·* in your issue
333–16 It has never been *c·* by Mrs. Eddy
354– 9 for which my endorsement is *c·*.

claiming
Mis. 39–29 *c·* to work with God
108– 5 *c·*, as they do, that good is
174– 3 it is a lie, *c·* to talk
184– 1 by *c·* that God is Spirit,
223–16 *c·* full faith in the divine
255–10 not *c·* equality with,
Un. 25–12 *c·* to be something beside God,

claims (noun)

accepted the
Mis. 297–19 accepted the *c·* of the marriage

all
Mis. 185– 7 it strips matter of all *c·*,

all the
Mis. 293– 3 all the *c·* and modes of evil ;
297–21 morally bound to fulfil all the *c·*
298–19 all the *c·* of sensuality.

divine
Mis. 19–13 accepted the divine *c·* of Truth

diviner
Peo. 11–10 another staging for diviner *c·*,

erroneous
My. 161–18 to destroy its erroneous *c·*.

false
Mis. 24–32 effect arising from false *c·*
109–26 to escape from the false *c·* of sin.

higher
Mis. 67– 3 higher *c·* of the law and gospel
Peo. 11– 4 struck the keynote of higher *c·*,

his
No. 2–18 student . . . is modest in his *c·*

infinite
Mis. 16–11 Principle hath infinite *c·* on man,

its
Mis. 284–26 aggressive, and enlarges its *c·* ;

lawful
Pul. 82–18 * women had few lawful *c·*

claims (noun)

Mrs. Eddy's
My. 332–24   * corroborate Mrs. Eddy's *c*.

no
Ret. 64–23   they are no *c*· at all.
No. 24–21   evil has no *c*·

of envy
My. 167–28   illegitimate *c*· of envy, jealousy,

of error
Mis. 293–13   against the opposite *c*· of error.
Ret. 64–22   supposititious *c*· of error ;

of evil
Mis. 114–23   deliverance from the *c*· of evil.
No. 23–10   we need to discern the *c*· of evil,
    24–15   *c*· of evil become both less and more

of matter
Un. 31– 9   annulled the *c*· of matter,
    36–18   rejection of the *c*· of matter

of physique
Mis. 28–29   annulled the *c*· of physique

of politics
My. 266– 5   *c*· of politics and of human power,

of sense
Mis. 172– 8   defeat the *c*· of sense and sin,

of Spirit
Mis. 140–10   superiority of the *c*· of Spirit

of the corporeal senses
Ret. 54– 6   the *c*· of the corporeal senses

of the law
Mis. 67– 3   higher *c*· of the law and gospel
    348– 3   *c*· of the law and the gospel.

of the senses
My. 222–14   from admitting the *c*· of the senses

of these senses
Mis. 198–15   if we deny the *c*· of these senses

other
Mis. 286–28   shut out all sense of other *c*·.

Scientist
My. 81–24   * demonstration of the Scientist *c*·,

sensible
No. 38– 4   that . . . and death are sensible *c*·,

statements and
Mis. 78–19   false statements and *c*·.

strong
Pan. 12–11   will make strong *c*· on religion,

such
Mis. 297–22   unless such *c*· are relinquished by

their
Mis. 172– 1   their *c*· and lives steadfast in

these
Mis. 16–11   these *c*· are divine, not human ;
Ret. 54– 9   deny these *c*· and learn the divine
No. 23–21   fight these *c*·, . . . as illusions ;

Mis. 181–10   *c*· of the divine Principle.

claims (verb)
Mis. 27–22   matter *c*· something besides God,
    62–15   *mind-cure c· to heal without it?*
    109– 9   how much, sin *c*· of you ;
    138–12   divine Principle which he *c*·
    183–25   for it *c*· another father.
    243–14   *c*· more than it practises.
    363– 4   "ego" that *c*· selfhood in error,
Man. 46– 2   who *c*· a spiritually adopted child
Ret. 56–21   Whatever else *c*· to be mind,
    70– 5   and *c*· God as their author ;
Un. 39–15   *c*· another father, and denies
Pul. 47–15   * She *c*· that no human reason has
    72–12   * *c*· to have been healed
No. 3– 3   which *c*· only its inheritance,
My. 300–20   If, as this kind priest *c*·,
    314–13   as *McClure's Magazine c*·,

clairvoyant
My. 313–23   * never was "an amateur *c*·,"

clambering
Mis. 341– 8   after much slipping and *c*·,

clamor
No. 45–25   The people *c*· to leave cradle
'02. 2– 4   without *c*· for distinction or

clamorous
My. 203– 7   not *c*· for worldly distinction.

clanging
My. 31– 7   * "Oh, the *c*· bells of time ;"

clans
Mis. 172– 9   regardless of the bans or *c*·
    274–21   inordinate, unprincipled *c*·.

clap
Mis. 168–20   pure in heart *c*· their hands.
    330– 1   the leaves *c*· their hands,

Clarendon Street
My. 55–24   * Copley Hall on *C*· *S*·,

---

clarion
Mis. 120–16   the *c*· call of peace
Ret. 12– 1   nobler far than *c*· call
'01. 35– 8   It is a *c*· call to the reign of
Po. 60–21   nobler far than *c*· call

clasp
Mis. 143– 8   I reach out my hand to *c*· yours,
    152– 4   in love continents *c*· hands,
    392– 3   skies *c*· thy hand,
Pul. 84– 5   * revenge shall *c*· hands with pity,
Po. 20– 4   skies *c*· thy hand,

clasped
Peo. 11–14   their chains are *c*· by the false

claspeth
Po. 65–17   love *c*· earth's raptures not long,

clasping
Mis. 306–27   it is not the *c*· of hands,

Class

(*see* **Primary Class**)

class (noun)

another
No. 9– 6   or established among another *c*·

any
Man. 92–17   instructions in C. S. in any *c*·
My. 93– 8   * to attract any *c*· save the
    223– 7   any *c*· of individual discords.

better
'00. 14–25   the better *c*· of M.D.'s

certain
My. 111–27   may irritate a certain *c*· of

College
Mis. 49– 1   A young lady entered the College *c*·
Man. 90–13   members of the College *c*·

each
Mis. 315–12   Each *c*· shall consist of

enter a
Rud. 15–13   diseased people not to enter a *c*·.
    15–20   can advantageously enter a *c*·,

first
My. 59– 3   * member of your *first c*· in Lynn,

healed in a
Rud. 15– 3   student, if healed in a *c*·,

healed in the
Rud. 14–28   and were healed in the *c*· ;

her
Mis. 49–14   have been cured in her *c*·.

higher
'01. 30–17   higher *c*· of critics in theology

his
Mis. 92–13   textbook of C. S. into his *c*·,
    92–21   When closing his *c*·, the teacher

in Christian Science
Mis. 239– 6   commence a large *c*· in C. S.
    316– 6   When will you take a *c*· in C. S.
    316–10   The date of a *c*· in C. S.
My. 182–11   In 1884, I taught a *c*· in C. S.

juvenile
Man. 63– 6   are adapted to a juvenile *c*·,

larger
My. 244– 5   if a larger *c*· were advantageous

my
My. 104–24   in my *c*· on C. S. were many

my last
My. 125–22   The students in my last *c*·

no favored
No. v– 2   to benefit no favored *c*·,

Normal
Mis. 143–19   Normal *c*· graduates of my College,
    264–13   enter the Normal *c*· of my College
Man. 84–11   Normal *c*· not exceeding thirty
    86–17   teachers of the Normal *c*· shall
    90– 1   eligible to enter the Normal *c*·.
    90–19   be given to each Normal *c*·
    91–22   may enter the Normal *c*· in
Ret. 47–18   Normal *c*· student who partakes
My. 251– 8   * Primary and Normal *c*· instruction
    251–13   eligible to enter the Normal *c*·,
    323–31   * Normal *c*· in the fall of 1887?

Obstetric
Ret. 43–17   taught the . . . Obstetric *c*·

of aspirants
Rud. 16–25   fusing with a *c*· of aspirants

of people
Mis. 80–15   with a wrong *c*· of people.

of students
Mis. 32–16   the above-named *c*· of students

one
Man. 84– 8   shall teach but one *c*· yearly,
    84–11   shall have one *c*· triennially,
    92–14   should teach yearly one *c*·.
Ret. 50–16   as many as seventeen in one *c*·.
No. 9– 5   errors of one *c*· of thinkers
My. 215–10   a dozen or upward in one *c*·.

class (noun)
  or creed
    My. 157–10   * without regard to *c·* or creed,
  Primary
    Mis. 273–24   applications . . . for the Primary *c·*
    273–29   if I should teach that Primary *c·*,
    280–18   students of this Primary *c·*,
    318–15   instructions in a Primary *c·*
    Man. 86–23   teachers of the Primary *c·*
    89–12   taught in a Primary *c·* by Mrs. Eddy
    Ret. 43–18   taught one Primary *c·*, in 1889,
    47–16   A Primary *c·* student,
    47–19   instructions in a Primary *c·*
    Rud. 14–13   never taught a Primary *c·* without
    My. 245–32   given to students of the Primary *c·* ;
    319–21   * I entered your Primary *c·*
    320–21   * while I was in your Primary *c·*
    322–19   * to enter the next Primary *c·*
  privileged
    Mis. 244–27   not for a privileged *c·* or
  read to the
    Man. 90–22   shall be read to the *c·*,
  same
    My. 111– 7   same *c·* of minds to deal with
  second
    My. 323–31   * studying in the second *c·*
  this
    Man. 90– 1   All members of this *c·* must
    My. 104–27   that brought together this *c·*
    254–14   faithful teacher of this *c·*
  your
    My. 321–22   * and entered your *c·*.
    324–27   * to sit through your *c·*.

    Mis. 49–12   in a *c·* of Mrs. Eddy's ;
    92–19   point out the lesson to the *c·*,
    242–29   before leaving the *c·* he took
    273–26   *c·* which contains that number.
    280–26   met the *c·* to answer some questions
    316– 5   chapter sub-title
    317–13   to be taught in a *c·*,
    Man. 84– 9   *c·* shall consist of not more than
    90–21   One student in the *c·* shall
    Ret. 84–11   When closing the *c·*,
    Rud. 14–26   both in and out of *c·*.
    Pan. 10–13   best students in the *c·* averred
    My. 93– 1   * Christian Scientists, as a *c·*,
    100–15   * of a *c·* who are reputable,
    243–19   chapter sub-title
    254–24   chapter sub-title
    254– 9   chapter sub-title
    319– 6   nothing further from him in the *c·*,
    320–28   * several times after the *c·* closed,

class (adj.)
    Mis. 11–10   at close of the *c·* term,
    211–10   medical bills, *c·* legislation,
    256–17   intervals between my *c·* terms,
    273–28   waiting for the same *c·* instruction ;
    274–24   shout for *c·* legislation,
    315–17   not only through *c·* term, but
    Man. 83–16   not only during the *c·* term but
    87–13   against *c·* instruction.
    91– 8   Tuition of *c·* instruction
    Pul. 36– 9   * I was present at the *c·* lectures
    Rud. 16– 7   to thorough *c·* instruction
    My. 128– 6   or *c·* legislation is less than the
    340–12   and her frown on *c·* legislation.
    (see also **teaching***)*

classed
    '01. 28–12   *c·* with the choicest memorials of
    My. 340– 4   He *c·* the usage of special days

classes
    Mis. 41–18   *Can all c· of disease be healed*
    256–13   that this must prevent my *c·*
    273–29   the other three *c·*
    296–15   This writer *c·* C. S. with
    315–11   can teach annually three *c·* only.
    Man. 62– 9   received in the Sunday School *c·*
    87–12   shall not solicit, . . . for their *c·*,
    90–15   no Primary *c·* shall be taught under
    91–14   President gives free admission to *c·*.
    Rud. 14–11   The only pay . . . was from *c·*,
    14–19   No discount . . . made on higher *c·*,
    14–19   their first *c·* furnished students with
    14–24   unprepared to enter higher *c·*.
    '02. 3– 5   among the educated *c·*
    My. 88– 7   * among *c·* above the average in
    181–18   *c·* and masses of mankind,
    251–10   * become teachers of Primary *c·*?"
    265–30   reaching out to all *c·* and peoples.
    318–16   to visit one of my *c·*

classic
    Ret. 86– 8   as said the *c·* Grecian motto.
    Hea. 1–15   A *c·* writes, — "At thirty, man
    My. 224–30   let us adopt the *c·* saying,

classical
    Ret. 17–17   palm, bay, and laurel, in *c·* glee,
    Po. 63– 1   palm, bay, and laurel, in *c·* glee,

classification
    My. 107–25   entitled to a *c·* as truth or
    109– 7   When this scientific *c·* is
    224–18   borrows the thoughts, words, and *c·*

classifications
    Mis. 86–13   scientific *c·* of the unreal

classified
    Mis. 112–13   strictly *c·* in metaphysics as
    Pul. 22–15   Christendom will be *c·* as
    Pan. 4– 8   reason and will are properly *c·* as

classifies
    Mis. 252– 8   C. S. *c·* thought thus :

classify
    Mis. 36– 3   *c·* evil and error as mortal mind,
    Ret. 64–21   *c·* sin, sickness, and death as

class-room
    Mis. 91–25   textbook with him into the *c·*,
    279–27   We, to-day, in this *c·*,
    Ret. 83–19   the chapter for the *c·*,
    91–26   The grove became his *c·*,

class-rooms
    Pul. 27– 7   * opening from it are three large *c·*
    58–15   * division into seven excellent *c·*,

claws
    Mis. 294–21   their stings, and jaws, and *c·* ;

clay
    Mis. 326–17   driven out of their houses of *c·*
    Pan. 11–12   allow mortals to turn from *c·* to
    Po. 2– 3   to sport at mortal *c·*
    67– 4   cold in this spot as the spiritless *c·*,
    My. 344–10   inhabiting *c·* and then withdrawn

clean
    Mis. 79– 4   swept *c·* by the winds of history.
    99–23   The winds of time sweep *c·*
    398–20   Shepherd, wash them *c·*.
    Ret. 46–26   Shepherd, wash them *c·*.
    Pul. 17–25   Shepherd, wash them *c·*.
    Po. 14–24   Shepherd, wash them *c·*.
    My. 34– 3   He that hath *c·* hands, — *Psal.* 24 : 4.
    228–20   washing it *c·* from the taints of

cleanliness
    Mis. 184–30   a type of physical *c·*

cleanse
    Mis. 30–30   *c·* our lives in Christ's
    271–13   *C·* your mind of the cobwebs
    399– 7   *C·* the foul senses within ;
    Ret. 86–11   *C·* every stain from this
    Pul. 29–18   * *c·* the lepers, — *Matt.* 10 : 8.
    29–22   * to *c·* the leprosy of sin,
    66–12   * *c·* the lepers, — *Matt.* 10 : 8.
    Po. 39–12   will watch to *c·* from dross
    75–14   *C·* the foul senses within ;
    My. 265– 9   *c·* the earth of human gore;
    300–26   *c·* the lepers, — *Matt.* 10 : 8.

cleansed
    Mis. 153–14   Israel, . . . *c·* of the flesh,
    153–21   *c·* my heart in vain." — *Psal.* 73 : 13.
    168– 7   moral lepers are *c·* ;
    Pul. 53–11   * When the ten lepers were *c·*
    No. 1–20   healed the sick and *c·* the sinful.
    My. 265–25   *c·* of self and permeated with

cleanseth
    Mis. 322–21   healeth the sick and *c·* the sinner.

Cleanse the Lepers
    Pul. 28– 8   * "*C· the L·*," — *Matt.* 10 : 8.

cleansing
    Mis. 124–17   healing the sick, *c·* the leper,
    185–12   *c·* mortals of all uncleanness,
    204–13   spirit of Truth *c·* from all sin ;

clear
    Mis. 51–16   If you make *c·* to the child's thought
    79– 6   until it is *c·* to human comprehension
    87– 1   as the bird in the *c·* ether of the
    140–27   * "read our title *c·*"
    181–31   *c·* discernment of divine Science :
    211– 1   Our own vision must be *c·*
    215–14   and be *c·* that it is Love,
    347–11   Where my vision begins and is *c·*,
    357–22   it has been *c·* to my thought
    Man. 66– 4   and obtain a *c·* understanding of
    Ret. 16– 1   a soprano, — *c·*, strong, sympathetic,
    34– 7   Neither ancient nor . . . could *c·* the clouds
    93–20   It is quite *c·* that as yet this
    Pul. 21–24   a *c·* expression of God's likeness,
    59–19   * in a *c·* emphatic style.
    60– 7   * *c·*, manly, and intelligent tones,
    Rud. 9–25   imbued with a *c·* conviction of

clear

No.	13–14	c· and profound deduction from
'00.	9–16	till the mental atmosphere is c·.
'01.	25– 2	becomes c· to the godly.
	30–25	like the c·, far-seeing vision,
	31– 1	by a c· elucidation of truth,
My.	113–22	have a c· perception of it.
	137– 7	* c·, plain-speaking English."
	149–19	c· perception of divine justice,
	150–20	calm, c·, radiant reflection of
	155–19	a c· vision of heaven here,
	234– 5	they only cloud the c· sky,
	297–18	c·, correct teaching of C. S.
	342–20	* she said, in her c· voice,

cleared

Ret.	30– 6	have c· its pathway.

clearer

Mis.	13–23	and reveals in c· divinity the
	13–27	c· discernment of good.
	78–23	will some time appear all the c· for
	84–30	a c· and nearer sense of Life
	277– 4	Truth is speaking louder, c·,
	324–17	c· pane of his own heart
Ret.	23– 6	As these pungent lessons became c·,
	82–29	makes the subject-matter c·
Un.	25– 4	nothing can be c· than the
	49–24	gives me a c· right to call evil a
Pul.	12–19	rises c· and nearer to the
No.	9– 7	c· and more conscientious
My.	207–11	* for the c· understanding and
	265–27	in c· skies, less thunderbolts,
	324–11	* c· nomenclature for S. and H.

clear-headed

Mis.	266–13	c· and honest Christian Scientist

clearing

Mis.	174– 6	a c· up of abstractions.
	343–13	c· the gardens of thought
My.	57–11	* The labor of c· the land

clearly

Mis.	37– 8	recognized this relation so c·
	42–10	S. and H. c· states that
	92–1C	He who sees most c·
	95–19	but I c· understand that no
	107– 9	we behold more c· that
	113–21	Already I c· recognize that
	156–10	will see c· the signs of Truth
	164– 8	continue to be seen more c·
	171– 5	and the blind saw c·.
	186–18	let us not lose this . . . but gain it c· ;
	261–28	apprehending the moral law so c·
	281–26	came to me more c· this morning
	336–15	that hinders your seeing c·
	373–15	One great master c· delineates
Ret.	50–23	I see c· that students in C. S.
	84– 7	He who sees c· and enlightens
Un.	7– 9	When I have most c· seen
Pul.	12–24	This rule c· interprets God as
No.	1–17	read more c· the tablets of Truth.
	39–22	It shows us more c· than we
'01.	9– 4	C. S. shows c· that God is
	27– 7	* who will interpret . . . more c·,
My.	45–22	* As c· as in retrospect we see the
	61–16	* conviction . . . came to me so c·,
	225–27	In their textbook it is c· stated
	317–14	enable me to explain more c·
	322–26	* which were so c· stated that I

clearness

Mis.	220–23	understand with equal c·,

clears

Mis.	75–20	*sense* for *soul* c· the meaning,
	355–17	To strike . . . never c· the vision ;

cleave

Mis.	2– 7	determination of mankind to c· to

cleaves

No.	32–13	c· sin with a broad battle-axe.

cleaving

No.	42–21	c· to their own vices.

clemency

Mis.	274–19	it discounts c·, mocks morality,
	295–29	dignity, virtue, c·, and

clergy

Mis.	225– 1	chapter sub-title
Ret.	6– 7	to the c· were accorded
	40–22	so stirred the doctors and c·

clergyman (*see also* clergyman's)

Mis.	193–15	c· charitably expressed it,
	225– 6	c·, his wife and child.
Man.	49–21	a c· who is legally authorized.
Pul.	30– 3	* when a Boston c· remonstrated
No.	41–24	a Boston Baptist c·,
	42–25	distinguished c· came to be healed.

clergyman

No.	44–24	Congregational c· of Boston,
'01.	21–12	This c· gives it as his opinion
My.	84– 4	* Many a c· can testify
	118– 8	chapter sub-title
	331– 6	* Rev. Mr. Reperton, a Baptist c·,

clergyman's

Mis.	32– 4	*what about that c· remarks on*
	32–31	c· comments on my illustrated poem,
	225–13	c· son was taken violently ill.
	225–14	Then was the c· opportunity to
	226– 6	c· son returned home — *well.*
	229–12	c· conversion of sinners.
	300–13	gives you the c· salary
Ret.	15– 2	the good c· heart also melted,

clergymen

Mis.	33– 7	All c· may not understand the
Ret.	42–10	c· of other denominations
Pul.	5– 1	one of the very c· who had
	29– 4	* formerly been Congregational c·.
	47– 1	* c· of other denominations
'01.	18–30	Christians and c· pray for sinners ;
	31–25	distinguished Christian c·,
Hea.	5–11	One of our leading c·
My.	53–22	* by c· of different denominations,
	95–21	* c· of other denominations

clerical

Mis.	246– 1	pulpit and press, c· robes and

Clerk (*see also* Clerk's)

Mis.	310–21	send in their petitions . . . to the C·
	322– 9	the C· of the church can inform
Man.	25– 6	a President, a C·, a Treasurer.
	25–15	C· and Treasurer.
	25–16	The term of office for the C·
	29–10	shall complain thereof to the C·
	36–19	can apply to the C· of this Church,
	36–24	Addressed to the C·
	36–26	addressed to the C· of the Church.
	37–10	C· of the Church shall send to the
	37–11	neither the C· nor the Church shall
	52– 8	C· of the Church shall address a
	52–16	C· of the Church shall immediately
	56–15	reports of Treasurer, C·, and
	57– 7	upon the call of the C·.
	57– 8	Called only by the C·.
	57–11	shall be the duty of the C·
	57–14	C· must have the consent of
	65–26	If the C· of this Church shall
	66–11	duty of the C· to report to her
	78–17	through the C· of the Church,
	78–21	sum of $500 with the C·,
	93–16	mail to the C· of this Church
	98–16	sending a copy to the C·
	109–17	before sending them to the C·
	111–21	on application to the C·.
Ret.	49–31	C. A. FRYE, C·.
My.	38– 7	* WILLIAM B. JOHNSON, C·.
	39–14	* list of officers . . . was read by the C·
	39–16	* C·, William B. Johnson, C.S.D.
	46–31	* WILLIAM B. JOHNSON, C·.
	47– 1	* heading
	49–17	* August 22 the C·, by instructions
	49–30	* voted to instruct the C· to call
	51–16	* It was moved to instruct the C· to
	242–23	leave these duties to the C· of The
	280–12	* WILLIAM B. JOHNSON, C·.
	283– 5	MR. JOHN D. HIGGINS, C·.
	289– 7	MR. WILLIAM B. JOHNSON, C.S.B., C·.
	361–27	* ARTHUR O. PROBST, C·.

clerk (*see also* clerk's)

My.	314–21	instructed the c· to record the

Clerk of the Court

My.	137– 4	* in the office of the C· of the C·,

Clerk's

My.	22– 2	* *Extract from the C· Report*

clerk's

My.	311–12	c· book shows that I joined the

clerks

Man.	95–11	may apply through their c·

Cleveland

Ohio

Ret.	52–23	its meeting in C·, Ohio,
Pul.	89–36	* *Leader,* C·, Ohio.
My.	195– 2	chapter sub-title
Pul.	56– 2	New York, Chicago, Buffalo, C·.

clew

Pul.	64–18	* without finding a c· ;

Cliff

Mis.	393–12	Crowns life's C· for such as we.
	393–24	To thy whiteness, C· of Wight.
Po.	51–17	Crowns life's C· for such as we.
	52– 8	To thy whiteness, C· of Wight.

cliffs
Mis. 323–19 climbing its rough *c*,

climax
No. 17–13 Man is the *c* of creation ;
My. 225– 8 caps the *c* of the old

climb
Mis. 215–10 not seek to *c* up some other way,
327– 5 "Wilt thou *c* the mountain,
Un. 64–15 Mortals may *c* the smooth glaciers,
No. 44– 9 To *c* up by some other way
My. 152–15 or do I *c* up some other way?

climbed
Pul. 9–13 a woman *c* with feet and hands

climbing
Mis. 323–19 *c* its rough cliffs,
My. 61–14 * I was *c* over stones and

clime
No. 44–26 In every age and *c*,

climes
My. 127–32 all times, *c*, and races.

cling
Mis. 310– 8 rather than *c* to personality
Pul. 40– 2 * thoughts of you forever *c* to me :
My. 116– 7 inclined to *c* to the personality

clinging
Mis. 275– 4 *c* faith in divine power

clings
Mis. 308– 6 *c* to my material personality,
Ret. 73–19 He who *c* to personality,
'01. 14– 3 that *c* fast to iniquity.
My. 334–21 that *c* fast to iniquity.

clip
Ret. 88–28 not be allowed to *c* the wings of

cloak
'01. 30–24 * man "clouting his own *c*"

cloak-room
My. 69–23 * in the basement is a *c*

clod
Mis. 187–25 Did the substance . . . become a *c*,
395– 7 His home the *c* !
Po. 57–14 His home the *c* !

clog
Mis. 234– 2 and *c* the wheels of progress.

clogging
Rud. 17– 4 *c* the wheels of progress by
My. 215–22 *c* the wheels of C. S.

clogs
Mis. 156–20 *c* the progress of students,

close
Mis. 11–10 at *c* of the class term,
49– 3 to withdraw before its *c*.
127–31 need *c* attention and examination.
128– 5 Therefore I *c* here, with the
133– 2 at the *c* of your article,
136–23 *c* your meetings for the summer ;
137– 6 at the *c* of the first convention
185–21 so-called material senses would *c*,
271–18 chapter sub-title
273– 5 I *c* my College in order to work in
274–13 I *c* my College.
277–23 No evidence . . . can *c* my eyes to
280–19 at *c* of the lecture on the fourth
304– 7 * After the *c* of the Exhibition
355–30 at the *c* of a balmy autumnal day,
Man. 73–22 No *C* Communion.
Ret. 3–12 towards the *c* of the War of 1812.
6–17 talented, *c*, and thorough
15–19 At the *c* of my engagement
43–19 judged it best to *c* the institution.
48–10 to *c* my flourishing school,
Un. 55–10 must keep *c* to his path,
Pul. 12– 4 stillness . . . indicated *c* attention.
21–21 and *c* the door on church or
31–15 * *c* contact with public feeling
34–10 * that she would be alive at its *c*.
45–12 * one month before the *c* of the year
84–13 * *c* of the year, Anno Domini 1894,
No. 45–27 material history is drawing to a *c*.
Pan. 7–18 *c* study of the . . . Testaments
13–15 *c* the war between flesh and
'00. 2– 8 *c* observer reports three types
11–23 * Like the *c* of an angel's psalm,
'02. 3–18 *c* of the conflict in South Africa ;
3–20 wiser at the *c* than the beginning
Hea. 20– 1 following hymn was sung at the *c* :
My. 15–16 I *c* with Kate Hankey's . . . hymn,
18–23 *c* the war between flesh and
29–31 * until the *c* of the evening service,
78–17 * At the *c* of the Lesson-Sermon,
80– 1 * *c* of their visit to Boston :

close
My. 81–25 * a fitting *c* to a memorable week.
108–28 and will *c* with his own words :
256–12 *c* the door of mind
257–17 *c* of the nineteenth century,

closed
Mis. 214–12 *c* — to the senses — that wondrous
244– 1 *c* up the wound — *see Gen.* 2 : 21.
317–11 when my College *c*.
328–14 and *c* it against Truth,
332– 6 doors that *c* on C. S.
358–26 Metaphysical College, . . . is *c*.
Man. 69–27 shall hereafter be *c* to visitors.
Ret. 18–11 ope their *c* cells to the bright,
Pul. 36– 4 * *c* (in 1889) in the very zenith of
42– 1 * had *c* the large vestry room
68– 8 * The college was *c* in 1889,
'02. 9–24 opened my *c* eyes.
Hea. 2– 5 synagogues as of old *c* upon it,
Po. 63–22 ope their *c* cells to the bright,
My. 79– 3 * in absolute stillness, their eyes *c*
246–12 *c* my College in the midst of
320–28 * several times after the class *c*,
333–15 * which was *c* in due form."
353–23 shall hereafter be *c* to visitors.

closely
Mis. 114–22 or bar their doors too *c*,
376– 5 * very *c* resemble in detail
Pul. 37–23 * not to centre too *c* around
'00. 7–24 would walk more *c* with Christ ;
My. 10–30 * is *c* interwoven with the

closer
Mis. 143– 7 a *c* link hath bound us.
Un. 1–18 *c* to the true understanding of God
Pul. 23–15 * calling out a *c* inquiry into
'01. 19– 6 *c* proximity with divine Love,

closes
Mis. 88–18 *c* the task of talking to deaf ears
276–30 it *c* the door on itself.
304–16 * until that Exhibition *c*.
319– 5 *c* the argument of aught besides
324– 2 His converse . . . in the valley *c*,

closest
Pul. 54–24 * with his *c* friends and followers,

closet
Mis. 133–14 enter into thy *c*, — *Matt.* 6 : 6.

closing
Mis. 92–21 When *c* his class,
244– 7 *c* the incisions of the flesh.
Ret. 38–21 *c* chapter of my first edition of
84–11 When *c* the class, each member
Pul. 23–19 * *c* years of every century
Pan. 3–12 evening's *c* vespers.
12–10 This *c* century, and its successors,
My. 29– 7 * Such was the *c* incident
185–26 *c* my remarks with the words of

cloth
Mis. 233–14 new *c* of metaphysics ;
'01. 2– 8 new-old *c* of Christian healing.

clothe
No. 26–26 *c* the grass of the field, — *Matt.* 6 : 30.
26–27 much more *c* you, — *Matt.* 6 : 30.
Peo. 14– 2 we *c* our thoughts of death with
My. 154–18 to *c* the human race.

clothed
Mis. 6–30 keeping them *c* and fed,
104–14 *C*, and in its right Mind,
185–16 and man be *c* with might,
251–21 *c* more lightly,
Pul. 83–27 * a woman *c* with the sun, — *Rev.* 12 : 1.
Rud. 13–27 to be fed, *c*, and sheltered
No. 22– 5 *c* with a "brief authority ;"
'00. 6–23 *c* and in his right mind,
'01. 29– 1 housed, fed, *c*, or visited
My. 117–14 or naked, and *c* thee? — *Matt.* 25 : 38.
349–14 at the feet of Jesus *c* in truth,

clothes
Ret. 40–12 *c* already prepared for her burial ;

clothing
Mis. 294–18 from wolves in sheep's *c*
323–13 wolves in sheep's *c* are ready to
325– 6 Christian Scientists in sheep's *c* ;
370–21 a wolf in sheep's *c*
Hea. 4– 7 *C* Deity with personality,
My. 215–21 wolves in sheep's *c*," — *see Matt.* 7 : 15.

cloud
Mis. ix–16 darkness of storm and *c*
149–28 Guided by the pillar and the *c*,
204– 2 a dark, impenetrable *c* of error ;
257–23 Electricity, . . . sparkles on the *c*,
277–30 the *c* of the intoxicated senses.

cloud
Mis.	347– 6	A conical c·, hanging like a
	360–16	When C. S. has melted away the c· of
	386–28	farewells c· not o'er our ransomed rest
	388– 6	A bow of promise on the c·.
Ret.	23– 7	c· of mortal mind seemed to
No.	21–28	like a c· without rain,
'02.	20–15	A bow of promise on the c·.
Peo.	3–17	like a promise upon the c·,
Po.	7– 6	A bow of promise on the c·.
	50–14	farewells c· not o'er our ransomed rest
My.	45–20	* by day in a pillar of c·
	45–25	* pillar of c· by day, — see Exod. 13 : 22.
	178– 3	c· not the spiritual meaning
	234– 5	they only c· the clear sky,

cloud-crowned
Po.	1–13	Proud from yon c· height

cloudless
Mis.	395–26	sunny days and c· skies,
Po.	58–11	sunny days and c· skies,

clouds
Mis.	277–25	Though c· are round about Him,
	323– 3	celestial city above all c·,
	355–26	Let no c· of sin gather
	377– 5	in c· and darkness !
	388– 4	What chased the c· away?
	392– 3	C· to adorn thy brow,
Ret.	9–26	* And won, through c·, to Him,
	18–24	But c· are a presage,
	34– 7	Neither . . . could clear the c·,
Pul.	9–12	as sunshine from the c· ;
'02.	20–13	That swept the c· away ;
Po.	7– 4	What chased the c· away?
	20– 3	C· to adorn thy brow,
	29– 2	though murky c· Pursue thy way,
	30–18	Piercing the c· with its triumphal
	54– 3	O come to c· and tears
	64–20	But c· are a presage,
	70– 1	Beyond the c·, away
My.	149–27	C· parsimonious of rain,
	252–14	work midst c· of wrong,

clouting
'01.	30–23	* "c· his own cloak"

clover
Mis.	343–22	to choke the coming c·.

club-house
My.	174– 7	opening their spacious c·

clubs
Mis.	336– 6	resort to stones and c·,
My.	224–14	Avoid . . . public debating c·.

clue
Ret.	45–14	my c· to the uses and abuses of

cluster
My.	186– 5	c· around this rock-ribbed church

clustered
Mis.	237–30	fear c· round his coming.

coal
Un.	34–16	put your finger on a burning c·,

coast
Pul.	41– 9	* from the far-off Pacific c·
My.	30–17	* from Hawaii, from the c· States.

coat
Pul.	48–21	* her family c· of arms

coated
Pul.	25–14	* are of iron, c· with plaster ;

coat-of-arms
My.	311–18	facts regarding the McNeil c·
	311–21	presented me my c·,
	311–23	with her own family c·.
	311–24	I have another c·, which is

coats
Mis.	243–27	the c· of the stomach to thicken

coax
Mis.	119– 6	If a criminal c· the unwary

coaxed
Mis.	203–12	you have c· in their course
My.	152–32	florist has c into loveliness

cobelievers
Pul.	71–22	* By her followers and c· she is

cobwebs
Mis.	271–14	Cleanse your mind of the c·

cocaine
Mis.	244–30	discoverers of quinine, c·, etc.,

code
Mis.	257–15	It is a c· whose modes
My.	343–23	I made a c· of by-laws,

codes
Mis.	246– 5	to blot out all inhuman c·.
Peo.	5–12	barbarisms of spiritless c·.
	11–19	as men . . enact penal c· ;
My.	266–17	all c·, modes, hypotheses,
	268–13	the justice of civil c·, and the

coelbow
Mis.	138–10	but sometimes to c· !

coequal
Mis.	319– 4	can neither be coeval nor c·

coercive
Mis.	80–16	unjust c· legislation
	297– 6	by legally c· measures,

coeternal
Mis.	79–23	coexistent and c· with God.
	360–30	coexistent and c· with God,
Ret.	59–23	as coexistent and c· with God,
No.	25–18	coexistent and c· with Him.

coeval
Mis.	93–15	its c·, is without divine authority.
	319– 4	can neither be c· nor coequal,

coexist
Un.	64– 4	than the sun can c· with darkness.
'00.	4–26	Man and the universe c· with God
'02.	8–24	Love, purity, meekness, c· in
My.	349–22	and c· with the God of nature

coexistence
Mis.	47–24	spiritual c· with his Maker.

coexistent
Mis.	57–26	if he was c· with God?
	79–23	c· and coeternal with God.
	190– 8	man is c· with Mind,
	360–29	c· and coeternal with God,
Ret.	59–23	c· and coeternal with God,
Un.	49– 4	man is c· with God,
No.	25–17	c· and coeternal with Him.
'01.	5–25	are c· and eternal,
'02.	7–18	man and the universe c· with God.
My.	5– 9	His idea, c· with Him

coexists
My.	239– 2	The Science of . . . c· with God ;

coffea
Mis.	348–19	not even c· (coffee),

coffee
Mis.	348–19	not even coffea (c·),
No.	42–27	* and drink strong c· to support

coffers
My.	52–26	* has always filled her c· anew.

cognate
My.	106–11	the folly of the c· declaration

cognizance
Mis.	28– 8	Matter takes no c· of matter.
	218–13	can take no c· of Spirit
	228–21	in any way takes c· of,
Ret.	60–26	no c· of the spiritual facts
Un.	28–18	five senses take no c· of Soul,
	28–19	so they take no c· of God.
	38– 1	no c· of spiritual individuality,
No.	6– 8	take c· of their own phenomena,
	19–22	A sinner can take no c· of

cognizant
Mis.	208– 6	He is c· only of good.
Un.	8– 4	of which the physical senses are c·?
	15– 6	declare Him absolutely c· of sin?

cognize
Mis.	72–29	it cannot c· aught material,
	74–12	how did Jesus, . . . c· it?
	82– 9	c· the symbols of God,
	97–26	more than personal sense can c·,
	161–11	could not c· the Christ,
Un.	23–25	has no sense whereby to c·
	28– 7	The five physical senses do not c· it.
	34–22	could not c its own so-called
No.	25– 9	c· through the material senses.

cognized
Mis.	22–29	simple fact c· by the senses,

cognizes
Rud.	5–19	consciousness which c· being.

cognomen
Mis.	108–26	This c· makes it less dangerous ;
	336–22	c· of all true religion,

coherence
My.	127– 8	calm c· in the ranks of C. S.

coherent
'01.	5– 6	and become less c· than the

cohesion
Mis.	173–29	Have attraction and c· formed it?
Ret.	45– 8	this material form of c·

coin
 My. 170–16 It is His *c·*, His currency ;

coincide
 Mis. 223– 8 logic, and revelation *c·*.
 '02. 8–25 Lust, hatred, revenge, *c·* in
 My. 278– 1 To *c·* with God's government

coincidence
 Mis. 100–21 *c·* of the divine with the human,
 Un. 52– 9 in the *c·* of God and man,
 Pul. 55–12 * regard it as a mere *c·*
 '02. 8–12 The *c·* between the law and
 My. 114–17 a strange *c·* or relationship
  181–31 It is a marked *c·* that those dates
  265–22 *c·* of the human and divine,
  327– 3 Is it not a memorable *c·*

coincident
 My. 28– 1 * *c·* with the completion of the
  326– 8 * this recognition should be *c·*

coincides
 '00. 5– 3 *c·* with the First Commandment

colaborers
 My. 173–30 his *c* on said committee

cold
 Mis. 7– 2 nor to breathe the *c·* air,
  239–10 * chapter sub-title
  239–20 * "I've got *c·*, doctor."
  240– 1 "I have *not* got *c·*."
  240– 3 through the *c·* air the little one
  240– 8 flippant caution, "You will get *c·*."
  240–13 If a *c·* could get into the body
  339–16 with finger grim and *c·* it points
  343–15 picking away the *c·*, hard pebbles
  384–11 The *c·* blasts done,
  386–22 kissed my *c·* brow,
  398–13 So, when day grows dark and *c·*,
 Ret. 46–19 So, when day grows dark and *c·*,
 Un. 34–19 is hot or *c·*?
 Pul. 14–17 Give them a cup of *c·* water
  16–18 *C·*, silent, stately stone,
  17–18 So, when day grows dark and *c·*,
  21–20 To perpetuate a *c·* distance
  82– 3 * the *c·* haunts of sin and sorrow,
 No. 20– 9 it may seem distant or *c·*,
  22– 8 *c·* categories of Kant
 '00. 15–28 The *c·* blasts done,
 Hea. 5– 8 if a man has taken *c·* by doing good
  5– 9 will punish him now for the *c·*,
 Peo. 5– 7 into the *c·* materialisms of dogma
  10– 5 as we struggle through the *c·* night of
 Po. 2–15 so *c·*, so glitteringly bright,
  14–17 So, when day grows dark and *c·*,
  26–14 phantom finger, grim and *c·*,
  36–10 The *c·* blasts done,
  50– 7 kissed my *c·* brow,
  67– 5 Grow *c·* in this spot as the
 My. 113–23 Then, is C. S. a *c·*, dull
  252–31 by the *c·* impulse of a lesser gain !
  265–28 extremes of heat and *c·* ;

Cole
 Mrs.
 Pul. 73–20 Mrs. *C·* has made a careful
 Mrs. Henrietta N.
 Pul. 73–17 * Mrs. Henrietta N. *C·* is also a very

Coligny, Admiral
 Mis. 281–12 Admiral *C·*, in the time of the

collapse
 Un. 10–15 they cannot *c·*, or lapse into
 No. 26–14 man can no more relapse or *c·*
 My. 106–15 Without . . . the universe would *c·* ;

collect
 Mis. x– 5 to *c·* my miscellaneous writings
  148–25 *c·* no moneyed contributions from
  305–26 * to *c·* two dollars from others,

collected
 Pul. 59–27 * *c·* the money for the Mother's Room,
 My. 21– 5 * money which had been *c·* for
  185–23 an attentive audience *c·* in

collection
 Man. 62– 3 time required to take the *c·*.
 Po. vi–23 * *are included in this c·*,
 My. 32–23 * *C·*.

collections
 Mis. 159–17 and rare grand *c·*
 My. 30–19 * The six *c·* were large,
  30–25 * record *c·* secured by evangelists

collective
 Ret. 67–21 *c·* as well as individual.

collectively
 Mis. 164–28 reveal man *c·*, as individually,
 Man. 42– 3 offered for the congregations *c·*

collectively
 My. 134– 9 keep the faith individually and *c·*,
  259–23 considered either *c·* or
  344– 4 then all his rays *c·* stand for

College and **college**
 Mis. 4–14 come to the *C·* and to the
  5– 5 Our *C·* should be crowded with
  35–23 and then study it at *c·*?
  38–13 *How happened you to establish a c·*
  49– 1 A young lady entered the *C·* class
  49– 4 before entering the *C·*,
  64– 9 *prospective students of the C·*
  135–23 chapter sub-title
  143–19 Normal class graduates of my *C·*,
  243– 6 mental branches taught in my *c·*
  249–15 None are permitted . . . in my *C·*
  249–22 students, expelled from my *C·*
  264–13 enter the Normal class of my *C·*
  272– 1 * obtained a *c·* charter in January, 1881,
  272– 6 * Mrs. Eddy's grant for a *c·*,
  272–25 * but one legally chartered *c·* of
  273– 5 I close my *C·* in order to work in
  274– 4 when I opened my *C·*.
  274– 8 outside of *C·* work,
  274–13 I close my *C·*.
  317–11 was shut when my *C* closed.
  349– 2 to take lessons outside of my *C·*,
  349–10 mode of obstetrics taught in my *C·*.
  358–24 only *C·* for teaching C· S·
  382–22 for a metaphysical medical *c·*,
 Man. 35–10 Students of the *C·*.
  73–10 students in any university or *c·*,
  73–12 at such university or *c·*,
  73–15 graduates of said university or *c·*,
  73–18 the rules of the university or *c·*
  73–20 said university or *c·* organization.
  89– 1 Presidency of *C·*.
  90–13 teacher and members of the *C·* class
  91– 5 and of the President of the *C·*
 Ret. 10–11 studied Hebrew during his *c·* vacations.
  43– 7 It is the only *C·*, hitherto, for
  43–10 taught two terms in my *C·*.
  43–20 the only assistant teachers in the *C·*.
  44–13 accumulating work in the *C·*,
  45–18 connected with my *C·*
  47– 4 unprecedented popularity of my *C·*.
  47– 7 persons desiring to enter the *C·*,
  47–13 Board of Directors of my *C·*,
  49–20 only one ever granted to a *legal c·*
  50– 6 one course of lessons at my *C·*,
 Pul. 36– 7 * To this *C·* came hundreds
  68– 8 * The *c·* was closed in 1889,
 No. 43–22 Such students come to my *C·* to
 '01. 29–30 * our tuition for the *c·* course."
 My. 172– 3 * the first chapel of the *c·*.
  246–12 closed my *C·* in the midst of
  246–22 the result is an auxiliary to the *C·*

College Association
 Mis. 135–23 chapter sub-title

College of Metaphysics
 Mis. 271–22 the only chartered *C· of M·*.

colleges
 Mis. 38–21 metaphysics at other *c·* means,
  272– 8 * no . . . granted for similar *c·*,
  272–19 * "All the mind-healing *c·*
  272–24 * Hence to name these . . . *c·*,
 Pul. 5–23 *c·*, and universities of America ;

collisions
 Mis. 339–13 In the mental *c·* of mortals
 Un. 6–12 forcible *c·* of thought
 Peo. 1–12 intellectual wrestling and *c·*

colloquialism
 Pul. 31– 7 * At the risk of *c·*,

colloquy
 Mis. 168–15 Here ends the *c·* ;
 Un. 27– 2 word employed in the foregoing *c·*.
 Pan. 6–20 *c·* between good and evil,

Colonel
 Mis. x–20 my first marriage, to *C·* Glover
 Ret. 19– 1 *C·* George Washington Glover
  19–19 *C·* Glover's tender devotion
 Pul. 34– 1 was married to *C·* Glover,
 '02. 15–16 My husband, *C·* Glover,
 My. 310–13 His military title of *C·* came from
  330–30 *C·* Glover's tender devotion

Colonial
 Pul. 48–27 * *C·* and Revolutionary days,

colony
 My. 309–20 paid the largest tax in the *c·*.

color
 Mis. 86–19 sensations . . . of form and *c·*,
  87–10 substance of form, light, and *c·*,
  147–18 give the *c·* of virtue to

color

Mis.	333– 8	basis that black is not a *c·*
Un.	52–22	elaborate in beauty, *c·*, and form,
Rud.	6–14	* He says that "*c·* is in *us*,"
My.	36–26	* all the beauty of *c·* and design,
	68–18	* *c·* scheme for all the auditorium

Colorado and Col.

Pul.	60– 6	* who was a *C·* lawyer

(*see also* **Colorado Springs, Denver**)

Colorado Springs, Col.

My.	19–17	First Church of . . . *C· S·, C·.*

colored

Mis.	246–13	The cry of the *c·* slave
Ret.	18– 5	light *c·* softly by blossom and
Pul.	58–21	* windows are of *c·* glass,
Peo.	11– 3	rights of the *c·* man
Po.	63–13	light *c·* softly by blossom and

coloring

Mis.	ix–22	*c·* glory of perpetual bloom ;
Pul.	32–21	* *c·* and the elastic bearing of
	48–10	* gorgeous October *c·* of the

colors

Rud.	6– 4	*assuming manifold forms and c·,*

colossal

Mis.	360– 7	unpretentious yet *c·* characters,

Columbia

My.	332–28	* records were transferred to *C·,*

Columbian Liberty Bell

Mis.	304– 4	* to create a *C· L· B·,*

Columbian Liberty Bell Committee

Mis.	304– 1	* *C· L· B· C·,* . . . Washington, D. C.

Columbus (Avenue)

Pul.	36–20	* from *C·* to Commonwealth Avenue,

Columbus Avenue

569

My.	53–11	* 569 *C· A·,* Boston.

571

Mis.	132–10	571 *C· A·,* Boston,
	279–11	Metaphysical College, 571 *C· A·,*

Pul.	31–24	* at a spacious house on *C· A·,*

Columbus, Ohio

Pul.	89–33	* *Journal, C·, O·.*
My.	204–13	chapter sub-title

columns

My.	vi–19	* principal contributor to its *c·* ;
	331–18	* Through the *c·* of your paper,
	346–19	* in the *c·* of the *New York Herald,*

combat

Mis.	216– 2	your own state of *c·* with error.
	241–15	by constant *c·* and direful struggles,
Pul.	2–19	single-handed to *c·* the foe
Po.	71–12	Injustice to the *c·* sprang ;

combated

My.	94– 6	* concrete and cannot be *c·.*

combating

Mis.	285– 1	*c·* evil only, rather than person.

combination

'02.	16– 6	Wyclif's use of that *c·* of words,
My.	70–25	* it is a *c·* of six organs,

combination pedals

(*see* **organ**)

combinations

Un.	9–15	its *c·*, phenomena, and outcome,

combine

My.	225–29	Mind, Soul, which *c·* as *one.*

combined

Mis.	245– 8	*c·* efforts of the materialistic
	249–21	from the *c·* efforts of
Pul.	43– 1	* Two *c·* choirs — that of
Pan.	2–17	* *c·* forces and laws which
'02.	1–11	*c·* in formidable conspiracy,
My.	127–22	siege of the *c·* centuries,
	308– 2	all the powers of earth *c·*

combines

Mis.	97–16	*c·* faith with understanding,
	217– 1	*c·* in logical sequence,
'01.	26– 9	that *c·* matter with Spirit.

combustible

Pul.	75–26	* the only *c·* material used

come

Mis.	4–14	*c·* to the College and to the
	16– 4	heaven to *c·* down to earth.
	18– 1	baptismals that *c·* from Spirit,
	20– 4	"*C·* unto me, — *Matt.* 11 : 28.
	22–17	they *c·* from God and return to
	26–10	believes that his crops *c·* from the
	34–18	can no more *c·* to those they have

come

Mis.	42–14	shall have *c·* upon the same plane
	55– 6	will *c·* when the student possesses
	59–19	"*C·* now, and let us reason — *Isa.* 1 : 18.
	63–11	*why did Jesus c· to save sinners?*
	70–12	rest from physical agony would *c·*
	70–15	paradise of Spirit would *c·* to Jesus,
	80–30	*c·* to understand the medical system
	83–24	the hour is *c·* ; — *John* 17 : 1.
	83–26	The hour had *c·* for the avowal of
	96–32	It is Christ *c·* to destroy the
	98–17	*c·* to strengthen and perpetuate our
	99–28	and *c·* up hither."
	107– 6	these *c·* to the rescue of mortals,
	112– 3	not knowing whence they *c·*,
	116–15	tones whence *c·* glad echoes
	120–17	and *c·* more sweetly to our ear
	122– 4	needs be that offenses *c·* ; — *Matt.* 18 : 7.
	122–18	that good may *c·* ! — *Rom.* 3 : 8.
	135– 2	*c·* into the ranks !
	136–15	"Wherefore *c·* out — *II Cor.* 6 : 17.
	143– 9	May the kingdom of heaven *c·*
	146–22	that desired to *c·*, into its fold,
	149– 1	*c·* ye to the waters, — *Isa.* 55 : 1.
	149– 1	*c·* ye, buy, and eat ; — *Isa.* 55 : 1.
	149– 2	*c·*, buy wine and milk — *Isa.* 55 : 1.
	163–28	must needs *c·* in C. S.,
	166–28	to be seen as diffusing
	168–16	seems to say, "*C·* and see." — *Rev.* 6 : 1.
	169–11	had *c·* physical rejuvenation.
	174– 7	Let us *c·* into the presence of Him
	174–25	"Thy kingdom *c·* ;" — *Matt.* 6 : 10.
	176– 2	*c·* in with healing, and peace,
	177– 4	The hour is *c·.*
	179–21	*c·* into the spiritual resurrection
	180– 8	* Has Christ *c·* again on earth?"
	195–11	Son of man is *c·* — *Matt.* 18 : 11.
	199– 8	*c·* into their rightful heritage,
	208–11	*c·* into sympathy with it,
	211–31	"Thy kingdom *c·*." — *Matt.* 6 : 10.
	214– 5	"Think not that I am *c·* to — *Matt.* 10 : 34
	214– 6	For I am *c·* to — *Matt.* 10 : 35.
	223– 3	"*C·* not thou into — *Gen.* 49 : 6.
	229–19	*c·* nigh thy dwelling." — *Psal.* 91 : 10.
	251– 4	who have *c·* all the way from
	253– 9	*c·*, let us kill him, — *Luke* 20 : 14.
	254–14	*c·*, let us kill him, — *Luke* 20 : 14.
	254–26	will *c·* and destroy — *Mark* 12 : 9
	279– 1	"Offenses will *c·* : — *Luke* 17 : 1.
	279– 2	through whom they *c·*." — *Luke* 17 : 1.
	280– 9	You have *c·* to be weighed ;
	281–15	to *c·* out and confess his faith,
	281–28	But, whatever may *c·* to you,
	293– 7	punishing of sin must, will *c·*,
	298– 5	that good may *c·* ? — *Rom.* 3 : 8.
	299–10	that this query has finally *c·*
	311– 2	*c·* and unite with The Mother Church
	312–14	* has *c·* in recent years,
	332– 5	seedtime has *c·* to enrich earth
	335– 7	shall *c·* in a day — *Matt.* 24 : 50.
	335–29	that good may *c·*,
	339–30	may *c·* too late.
	345–10	* "Let them *c·* ; I cannot change
	350–18	If harm could *c·* from the
	356–13	the harvest hour has *c·* ;
	362–22	revelation must *c·* tc the rescue
	365–30	impostors that *c·* in its name.
	384– 1	poem
	384– 2	*C·*, in the minstrel's lay ;
	384– 6	*C·* Thou ! and now, anew,
	384–18	* "The seasons *c·* and go :
	386– 4	Where mortal yearnings *c·* not,
	386–27	Thy child, shall *c·*
	387–24	*C·* from that Love, divinely near,
	397– 7	And *c·* to me, and tenderly,
	399– 1	"*C·* to my bosom,
	399– 6	"*C·* to this fountain,
Man.	41–21	"Thy kingdom *c·* ;" — *Matt.* 6 : 10.
	46–16	*c·* to them by reason of their relation
	57– 2	as may properly *c·* before these
	59–18	*c·* to listen to the Sunday sermon
	59–23	*c·* to attend the morning services.
	66–21	authority supposed to *c·* from her
	69– 1	said student shall *c·* under a
Chr.	55–27	I will *c·* in to him, — *Rev.* 3 : 20.
Ret.	22–16	but this triumph will *c·* !
	38–19	and had *c·* to tell me
	38–24	He had *c·* to a standstill
	44–19	I saw that the crisis had *c·*
	49– 8	the hour has *c·* wherein the
	79–19	*c·* short of the wisdom requisite
Un.	1–18	*c·* closer to the true understanding
	9– 7	That time has partially *c·*,
	10–10	how could it have *c·* into the world?
	22–17	Whatever exists must *c·* from God,
	26– 4	From Him *c·* my forms,

come

Un.	41–12	must *c·* to all sooner or later ;
	45–10	egotist must *c·* down and learn,
	58– 7	*c·* down from the cross."— *Mark* 15 : 30.
	59– 1	why did the Messiah *c·*
	59–17	never saw the Saviour *c·* and go,
	60–26	Christ cannot *c·* to mortal and
Pul.	5–17	* "I have *c·* to comfort you."
	9– 1	into the building fund have *c·*
	12– 6	Now is *c·* salvation, — *Rev.* 12 : 10.
	12–13	the devil is *c·* down— *Rev.* 12 : 12.
	18–16	And *c·* to me, and tenderly,
	21–28	It cannot *c·* from any other source.
	22– 7	"Thy kingdom *c·*.— *Matt.* 6 : 10.
	35–28	* a physician who had *c·* into
	40– 3	* wonder how the seasons *c·* and go
	41–29	* hour for the dedication service had *c·*.
	49–11	* has *c·* forth all this beauty !"
	53–18	* salvation in the world to *c·*;
	60–14	* thousands of adherents who had *c·*
Rud.	9–19	and similar effects *c·* from pride,
No.	v–10	"*C·* and drink ;"
	11–13	those who *c·* falsely in its name.
	18–10	physical and . . . *c·* with Science,
	31–25	"*C·* out of him, — *Mark* 9 : 25.
	34–15	pangs which *c·* to one upon whom
	41–18	will never admit such as *c·* to steal
	43– 4	"*C·* unto me, — *Matt.* 11 : 28.
	43–22	Such students *c·* to my College to
	46–10	he that should *c* ?"— *Matt.* 11 : 3.
Pan.	1– 6	winter winds have *c·* and gone ;
'00.	2–23	doom of such workers will *c·*,
	9–11	art thou *c·* hither — *Matt.* 8 : 29.
	15– 2	you have *c·* to a sumptuous feast,
	15–18	To-day you have *c·* to Love's feast,
'01.	9–21	art thou *c·* to destroy us? — *Mark* 1 : 24.
	28–30	Has the thought *c·* to Christian Scientists,
'02.	5–23	"Think not that I am *c·* — *Matt.* 5 : 17.
	5–24	am not *c·* to destroy, — *Matt.* 5 : 17.
	10– 6	"Art thou *c·* hither to — *Matt.* 8 : 29.
	12– 1	believes . . . Christ has not yet *c·* ;
	12– 2	believes that Christ is *c·*
	12– 9	the Christian idea that God is *c·*,
	19–16	"*C·* unto me."— *Matt.* 11 : 28.
Hea.	2–17	"*C·* unto me, — *Matt.* 11 : 28.
	6– 3	and so *c·* back to the world?
	9–16	* "the curse causeless cannot *c·*"?
	10–16	when sorrow seems to *c·*,
	16–13	*c·* nearer your hearts
Peo.	13–19	* "Let them *c·* ; I cannot change
Po.	6–19	*C·* from that Love, divinely near,
	12–16	And *c·* to me, and tenderly,
	16– 7	Ambition, *c·* hither !
	16–23	They *c·* with a breath
	22– 2	Thine hour hath *c·* !
	23– 6	*C·* ever o'er thy heart?
	24– 1	*C·* to me, joys of heaven !
	24– 8	*C·* to me, peace on earth !
	24–15	*C·* when the shadows fall,
page 36		poem
	36– 1	*C·*, in the minstrel's lay ;
	36– 5	*C·* Thou ! and now, anew,
	36–17	* "The seasons *c·* and go :
	41– 1	* *C·*, rest in this bosom,
	49– 6	Where mortal yearnings *c·* not,
	50–13	Thy child, shall *c·*
	53– 1	*C·* to thy bowers, sweet spring,
	53–13	Bid faithful swallows *c·*
	53–17	*C·* at the sad heart's call,
	54– 3	O *c·* to clouds and tears
	73– 2	I *c·* to thee O'er the moonlit sea,
	75– 7	"*C·* to my bosom,
	75–13	"*C·* to this fountain,
My.	3–21	good which has *c·* into his life,
	22–23	* In years to *c·* the moral and
	30–12	* *c·* from far distant points
	34–13	King of glory shall *c·*— *Psal.* 24 : 9.
	36–18	* we are *c·*, in humility, to
	42–17	* blessings which have *c·* into my life
	44–10	* *c·* to individual consciousness ;
	49– 2	* '*C·* thou with us, and we will
	56– 2	* adequate for years to *c·*.
	62– 6	* Whence did it *c·*?
	63–23	* has *c·* to the present age.
	63–27	* of the thousands who had *c·*,
	66–23	* will *c·* from her beautiful home,
	69– 5	* roof and side walls *c·* together
	72–11	* who *c·* to attend the dedication
	72–20	* Scientists who have *c·* to Boston to
	73–15	* for several days to *c·*,
	93–24	* part it has *c·* to play in the
	93–29	* *c·* in the nature of a revelation.
	116–23	has *c·* from injustice and
	118–24	should *c·* from conscience.
	122–16	another Christmas has *c·* and gone.
	125– 8	You *c·* from feeding your flocks,

come

My.	125– 9	you *c·* with the sling of Israel's
	125–26	hour is *c·* ; the bride (Word) is
	126–14	"*C·* out of her, my people"— *Rev.* 18 : 4.
	126–20	plagues *c·* in one day, — *Rev.* 18 : 8.
	129–13	They *c·* at Love's call.
	132–13	may there *c·* this benediction :
	133– 5	at last *c·* to acknowledge God,
	142– 8	* communicants who *c·* long distances
	153– 7	have *c·* to fulfil the whole law.
	153–29	*C·*, and I will give thee rest,
	155–24	heaven's symphonies that *c·* to
	156–19	may these communicants *c·* with
	163–10	so kindly *c·* to the dedication
	166–14	of shade and shine may *c·* and go,
	170–27	*c·* long distances to kneel with us
	171– 4	*c·* to Zion with songs — *Isa.* 35 : 10.
	171–12	to *c·* to Concord,
	173–13	gifts had *c·* from Christian Scientists
	183–19	day has *c·* when the forest
	183–27	for thy light is *c·*, — *Isa.* 60 : 1.
	191–18	*c·* forth from the tomb of the past,
	219–24	"Think not that I am *c·* to — *Matt.* 5 : 17.
	219–25	I am not *c·* to destroy, — *Matt.* 5 : 17.
	220– 2	Whatever changes *c·* to this century
	221–25	must *c·* through a correct or
	225– 2	*c·* to the surface to pass off,
	229– 3	No mesmerist . . . is fit to *c·* hither.
	229–18	and *c·* after me, — *Luke* 14 : 27.
	232–15	the thief would *c·*, — *Luke* 12 : 39.
	243– 4	*c·* together and form one church.
	244–23	teachers have *c·* so to regard them.
	247–24	Do you *c·* to your little flock
	273–26	lapse and relapse, *c·* and go,
	277–12	that the answer . . . shall *c·* from God
	281– 4	"Thy kingdom *c·*.— *Matt.* 6 : 10.
	288–26	lest a worse thing *c·* — *John* 5 : 14.
	319–17	* not *c·* under the observation of
	324– 7	* *c·* from any one but yourself.
	336– 5	* *c·* to her after her husband's death,
	352– 6	* blessings that have *c·* to us

comeliness

Mis.	302– 8	the form without the *c·*,
My.	42– 2	* depicted its form and *c·*.
	257– 9	*c·* of the divine ideal,

comers

My.	223– 2	no *c·* are received . . . without

comes

Mis.	1–12	new idea that *c·* welling up from
	5–18	Then metaphysics *c·* in, armed with
	9– 2	*c·* through affliction rightly understood,
	10–27	Heaven *c·* down to earth,
	26–29	From this premise *c·* the
	69–30	Now *c·* the question :
	73–29	the spiritualization that *c·* from
	140– 7	good *c·* to Christian Scientists,
	158–10	*c·* the interpretation thereof.
	171–10	When one *c·* to the age with
	178– 1	I have met one who *c·* from
	199– 5	thence *c·* man's ability to annul
	215– 3	*c·* into the intermediate space,
	218–17	Truth *c·* to the rescue of reason
	227– 8	crime *c·* within its jurisdiction.
	231–31	through which the loved one *c·* not,
	246–14	there *c·* another sharp cry of
	276–19	Out of the gloom *c·* the glory
	276–21	the true sense *c·* out,
	287–31	mischief *c·* from attempts to
	290–27	blessedness and blessing *c·*
	335–24	when the hour of trial *c·*
	339– 7	out of defeat *c·* the secret of
	340–28	*c·* out in the darkness to shine
	341–13	*c·* of honesty and humility.
	346–10	whence *c·* the evil?
	394– 8	It *c·* through our tears,
Chr.	53–34	Christ *c·* in gloom ;
Ret.	2–15	*c·* that heart-stirring air,
	81–16	there *c·* an overwhelming sense
Un.	4– 9	that God *c·* to us and pities us ;
	15–13	his destruction *c·* through the
	20– 6	Through . . . evil *c·* into authority :
	27– 1	From various friends *c·* inquiry
	34–10	Here *c·* in the summary of the
	40–22	*c·* through our ignorance of Life,
	56– 5	all suffering *c·* from mind,
	62– 5	that neither *c·* nor goes,
Pul.	13–21	*c·* back to him at last
	26–12	* The great organ *c·* from Detroit.
	48–24	* lawful pride that *c·* with
	69–10	* believing that disease *c·* from
	71– 7	* money *c·* from C. S. believers
	73–23	* but that all *c·* from God.
	82– 3	* she *c·* like the south wind
No.	1– 4	which *c·* to our recognition
	40–25	*c·* with the change to health.

comes
Pan.	12– 3	*c* from the rejection of evil
'00.	8– 9	so the human character *c* forth
'01.	1–19	Truth *c* from a deep sincerity
	10–19	man's salvation *c* through
Hea.	6–28	The word *devil c* from
Po.	2– 5	* but *c* not to the heart."
	45–10	It *c* through our tears,
My.	5– 8	C. S. to reveal man as God's
	12–22	it *c* not back again.
	54– 3	* inconvenience that *c* from crowding,
	66– 8	* now *c* the purchase of the last
	118–17	saving faith *c* not of a person,
	134–18	Love *c* to our tears like a
	147– 3	past *c* forth like a pageant
	196–29	The beauty of holiness *c*
	208–13	*c* your dear letter to my waiting
	239–13	*c into the knowledge of Christ*
	252–28	the impetus *c* from above
	292– 4	*c* from God and human faith in

comest
Mis.	326–31	"Wherefore *c* thou hither?"

cometh
Mis.	37–19	whence *c* all evil.
	101–11	Now *c* a third struggle ;
	109–31	and thus, *c* repentance,
	118–32	*c* out of the mouth, — *Matt.* 15 : 11.
	122– 5	the offense *c* !" — *Matt.* 18 : 7.
	145– 3	But the time *c* when the
	149–24	that *c* down from heaven,
	251–16	kingdom of God *c* — *Luke* 17 : 20.
	254– 7	that *c* down from heaven,
	286–19	The time *c*, and now is,
	321–13	"The hour *c*, — *John* 4 : 23.
	340– 9	that which *c* from God,
	342–17	"The bridegroom *c* !" — *Matt.* 25 : 6.
Ret.	79– 4	nor *c* this apprehension from
	79–17	Through . . . pride, *c* no success in
Un.	11–28	*then c* the harvest,
	22–19	*c* not from the eternal Spirit,
Pul.	4–25	with it *c* the full power of being.
	27–13	* "*c* down from God — *see Rev.* 3 : 12.
No.	34– 9	"The hour *c*, — *John* 4 : 23.
Pan.	14– 8	bread that *c* down from heaven,
'00.	15–11	after this Passover *c* victory,
'01.	12–11	"When the Son of man *c*, — *Luke* 18 : 8.
'02.	18– 3	wilt know when the thief *c*.
Hea.	10–18	and joy *c* with the light.
	16–28	man *c* unto the Father,
My.	38– 2	* every perfect gift *c* from above,
	125–27	and lo, the bridegroom *c* !
	156–21	bread that *c* down from heaven,
	257–15	*c* into the world," — *John* 1 : 9.
	364–12	save that which *c* from God.

comet's
Mis.	266–12	is like the *c* course,

comfort (see also comfort's)
Mis.	16– 3	so *c*, cheer, and bless one,
	118–20	His rod and His staff *c* you.
	232– 1	God *c* them all !
	275–15	*c*, encourage, and bless all
Pul.	5–18	* "I have come to *c* you."
	56–15	* brought hope and *c* to many
	87–16	If it will *c* you in the least,
'00.	3– 6	no heart his *c*.
Po.	24–14	Is all I need to *c* mine.
	32–20	*c* my soul all the wearisome day,
	78–15	Give to the pleading hearts *c*
My.	38– 3	* in God is all consolation and *c*,
	92–29	* for some such *c* as it promises.
	174– 2	open their doors for the *c* and
	206–18	words of the Scriptures *c* you:
	230–13	to *c* such as mourn,
	292– 9	His rod and His staff *c* the living
	292–10	may His love shield, . . . and *c*

comfortable
Mis.	ix– 8	their *c* fortunes are acquired by
Pul.	58–17	* in its exceedingly *c* pews.
	58–20	* rather dark, . . . for *c* reading,
My.	87–15	* these *c* acquaintances

comfortably
My.	71–23	* and seat them *c*.
	80–31	* the auditorium was *c* filled.

comforted
Pul.	50–19	* *c* and strengthened by them.
My.	41– 7	* blessed and *c* by divine Love.

Comforter
Mis.	174–31	Divine Science ; the *C* ;
	189– 6	*C* that leadeth into all truth.
	195–32	by divine Science, the *C*,
Man.	15– 8	Holy Ghost or divine *C* ;
'01.	9–17	it is the Christ, *C*,

comforter
Un.	18–15	our *c* always from outside and above

comforters
Ret.	95–11	* And *c* are needed much

comforteth
My.	159– 7	Christ rejoiceth and *c* us.

comforting
Mis.	124–15	*c* such as mourn,
My.	154–10	*c* to the dear sick,

comfortless
Mis.	249–24	will never leave me *c*,

comfort's
Ret.	95– 5	* give thee skill In *c* art :

comforts
My.	132–31	*c* such as mourn,
	295– 2	knowing our dear God *c* such

comical
Mis.	239–22	Her apparent pride . . . was *c*.

coming
Mis.	81–13	*c up straightway out of the*
	136–26	members *c* from a distance
	211–16	cause him to suffer in *c* to life?
	213–26	when he seeth the wolf *c*.
	237–30	fear clustered round his *c*.
	249–25	*c* nearer in my need,
	276–14	*c* of our Lord and Christ.
	304– 6	* in the *c* World's Exposition
	304– 9	* *c* first to the capital
	322– 5	People *c* from a distance
	323– 9	working and watching for his *c*.
	335– 4	delayeth his *c* ; — *Matt.* 24 : 48.
	343–22	to choke the *c* clover.
	363–21	brightness of His *c*.
Man.	36– 5	*c* from pupils of loyal students
Chr.	55– 6	The hour is *c*, — *John* 5 : 25.
Un.	13– 3	*c* at human call ;
	28–12	going in or *c* out.
	58– 8	*c* down from the cross,
	61– 2	*C* and going belong to
Pul.	44–27	* and it kept *c* until the custodian
	58– 3	* *C* to Boston about 1880,
	60– 6	* before *c* into this work,
	82– 9	* could stop the *c* of spring.
'00.	6–29	the second *c* of Christ.
	7–23	we believe in the second *c*,
'01.	19–10	because of your often *c*
	30– 5	bequeathing . . . to the *c* centuries.
Po.	47– 1	Are the dear days ever *c* again,
My.	17– 9	"To whom *c*, as unto — *I Pet.* 2 : 4.
	20– 8	The holidays are *c*,
	25– 3	* special effort during the *c* week
	30– 2	* either *c* from a service or
	42– 6	* President for the *c* year,
	73–26	* chapter sub-title
	87– 4	* multitudes going and *c*.
	99–18	* *c* from all parts of the world,
	100– 8	* *c* from all, or nearly all, parts
	223–20	All inquiries, *c* directly or
	225–17	The *c* of Christ's kingdom on earth
	241–25	* after *c* to the light of Truth,
	262–26	in commemoration of Christ's *c*.
	266– 4	dangers confronting the *c* century
	307–19	referred to the *c* anew of Truth,

command
another
Ret.	88– 4	Another *c* of the Christ,

Christ's
Mis.	194– 9	permanence of Christ's *c*
	311–21	since by breaking Christ's *c*,
Ret.	71–17	transgressing Christ's *c*.
'01.	12–15	Christ's *c* to heal in all ages,
My.	227–26	side by side with Christ's *c*,
	300–24	according to Christ's *c*,

divine
Mis.	10–14	If they mistake the divine *c*,
Ret.	71– 5	obedient to the divine *c*,
My.	224– 6	the human need, the divine *c*,
	351–11	is indeed a divine *c*,

first
Mis.	347– 1	this first *c* of Solomon,

full
Mis.	193–25	no one is following his full *c*

God's
Mis.	223– 5	according to God's *c*.
	298–17	he did not say that it was God's *c* ;
Peo.	7–18	* Waiting the hour when at God's *c*

His
Mis.	153– 9	At His *c*, the rock became

his
Mis.	282–15	metaphysical tone of his *c*,

Jesus'
Ret.	35–24	perpetuity of Jesus' *c*,
	45–20	following Jesus' *c*,

command
Lord's
Ret. 88–25 The Lord's *c·* means this,
Master's
My. 233– 2 spirit of our Master's *c·*?
obedience to the
My. 43–15 * In obedience to the *c·*
of Christ
Mis. 318–18 and so fulfil the *c·* of Christ.
Ret. 47–22 and so fulfil the *c·* of Christ.
Pul. 29–17 * dealt directly with the *c·* of Christ
'00. 5–21 to obey . . . the *c·* of Christ :
of the Master
My. 128–20 following the *c·* of the Master,
prime
Ret. 88– 5 his prime *c·*, was that his
proper
Mis. 138–26 God will give . . . the proper *c·*,
remains
Mis. 23–12 and the *c·* remains,
sacred
'02. 5–29 sacred *c·*, "Thou shalt have— *Exod.* 20 : 3.
second
Mis. 158–15 second *c·*, to drop the use of notes,
this
Ret. 88–10 significance of this *c·*,
My. 156–18 In obedience to this *c·*
transverse
Mis. 348–14 Solomon's transverse *c·* :

Mis. xii– 3 *c·* and countermand ;
56–25 Why did God *c·*,
214–13 the *c·*, "Put up thy sword." — *John* 18 : 11.
227–32 *c·* of almighty wisdom ;
Pul. 14–24 Christ will *c·* the wave.
My. 122–13 such as to *c·* respect everywhere.
325–14 * *C·* me at any time, in any way,

commanded
Ret. 4–10 *c·* a broad picturesque view of
87–16 as the Master *c·*.
Un. 11– 6 he *c·* the winds,
14–12 are *c·* to *grow in grace*.
'01. 19–17 *c·* even the winds and waves,
'02. 9– 5 Jesus *c·*, "Follow me ; — *Matt.* 8 : 22.
My. 106–31 *c·* his followers to do likewise.

commanding
'00. 11–15 tones intricate, profound, *c·*.

Commandment
Mis. 292– 1 chapter sub-title
'02. page 1 heading
(see also **First Commandment***)*

commandment
Mis. 28–24 Then the *c·* means,
73–13 and a *c·* to the wise.
292– 4 "A new *c·* I give— *John* 13 : 34.
292– 7 Love had a new *c·* even for him.
Man. 43–18 more serious attention to the *c·*
Ret. 69–30 and keeping His *c·*? ' "
'02. 4–14 new *c·* in the gospel of peace,
5–12 subordinated to this *c·*,
7–25 "A new *c·* I give— *John* 13 : 34.
7–27 special attention to his *new c·*.
8– 9 *c·* of Christ Jesus shows what
8–14 between the old and the new *c·*,
17–10 obey both the old and the new *c·*,
My. 64–17 * how to obey this *c·* and rule,
109– 8 *c·*, "Love thy neighbor— *Lev.* 19 : 18.
153–16 the great and first *c·*,
187–12 end of the *c·* is charity — *I Tim.* 1 : 5.
187–27 would glorify in a new *c·*
364– 7 includes and inculcates the *c·*,

Commandments
(see **Ten Commandments***)*

commandments
Mis. 67–15 Obedience to these *c·* is
118–16 "Keep My *c·*."— *John* 15 : 10.
123–25 love God, and keep His *c·*,
268– 8 hearkened to My *c·* !— *Isa.* 48 : 18.
311– 1 love God and keep His *c·*,
318–11 love God and keep His *c·*.
Ret. 31–18 which breaketh the divine *c·*.
No. 8–17 it will bow down to the *c·*
'00. 6–20 licentious, and breaks God's *c·*,
'01. 32–20 love God and keep His *c·*
'02. 4–22 briefly consider these two *c·*
17– 3 keep my *c·*."— *John* 14 : 15.
My. 3– 8 they that do His *c·*,— *Rev.* 22 : 14.
130–26 to him who keeps the *c·*.
160–21 or in disobeying the *c·*
268–14 Two *c·* of the Hebrew Decalogue,

commands
Mis. 18–11 These *c·* of infinite wisdom,
193–24 who follow the *c·* of our Lord
301–30 the *c·* of our hillside Priest,

commands
Mis. 358–29 awaiting, with staff in hand, God's *c·*.
Un. 3–10 those who have obeyed God's *c·*,
38–21 no divine fiat *c·* us to believe
49–26 *c·* mortals to shun or relinquish,
No. 14–21 are obeying these *c·* ;
41–20 have slumbered over Christ's *c·*,
Pan. 12–12 inspired Scriptural *c·* be fulfilled.
'01. 17–14 *c·* the respect of our best thinkers.
'02. 8– 3 *c·* man to love as Jesus loved.
My. 23– 8 * so long as we follow His *c·*.
47–27 * founded on the *c·* of Jesus :
52–17 * to establish these our Master's *c·*
118–13 spiritual sense demands and *c·* us ;
131– 4 humbles, exalts, and *c·* a man,
226–12 *c·* the waves and the winds,

commemorate
Mis. 120–28 whose character we to-day *c·*,
159–18 *c·*, . . . the man of God,
251–12 To-day we *c·* not only
Man. 17–10 *c·* the word and works of our Master,
Ret. 44– 1 *c·* the words and works of our Master,
'01. 1–10 *c·* in unity the life of our Lord,
My. 46–10 *c·* the word and works of our Master,
131– 8 life that we *c·* and would emulate,
158–26 temple which to-day you *c·*,
262–13 and so *c·* the entrance into

commemorated
Mis. 306– 8 * names to be *c·*.
My. 235–29 *c·* in deed or in word

commemorates
Mis. 166– 3 *c·* the earthly life of a martyr ;
My. 262– 6 *c·* the birth of a human, . . . babe

commemorating
No. 34– 8 *c·* his death with a material rite.

commemoration
Mis. 91– 1 in *c·* of the Christ.
Pul. 64–25 * in *c·* of the Founder of that sect,
My. 188– 8 Your feast days will not be in *c·*,
235–26 meaningless *c·* of birthdays,
262–25 in *c·* of Christ's coming.

commence
Mis. 15–18 Time may *c·*, but it cannot complete,
51–25 * reign of Mind *c·* on earth,
141–26 Delay not longer to *c·* building
198– 5 one must *c·* by turning away from
239– 5 about to *c·* a large class in C. S.
314–24 *c·* by announcing the full title of
'00. 12– 7 *c·* with the church of Ephesus.
'01. 16–27 Shall the hope for our race *c·* with

commenced
Mis. 380–15 and *c·* teaching.
Ret. 15–16 accepted the invitation and *c·* work.
My. 12– 2 * work should be *c·* as soon as
14–26 * building operations have been *c·*,
54– 8 * one hour before the service *c·*,

commences
Mis. 327–15 The journey *c·*.

commencing
Mis. 32–13 *c·* at the thirty-third verse,
Man. 32–12 before *c·* to read from this book,
Un. 10–23 It is like *c·* with the minus sign,
My. 11–28 * date for *c·* building operations.
12–12 * the date of *c·* work,

commend
Mis. 97–22 I *c·* the Icelandic translation :
Ret. 83– 4 *c·* students and patients to
85– 7 *c·* itself as useful to the Cause

commendable
Mis. 297–10 Smart journalism . . . is *c·* ;

commendation
Mis. 313– 1 chapter sub-title

commending
My. 124– 3 *c·* ourselves to every — *II Cor.* 4 : 2.

commends
'00. 13– 3 *c·* the church at Ephesus

commensurate
Mis. 261– 2 suffering is *c·* with evil,
My. 288–22 suffering is *c·* with sin ;

comment
Mis. 295– 2 which deserve and elicit brief *c·*.
No. 44– 2 incapacitates him for correct *c·*.
'01. 11–18 read each Sunday without *c·*
'02. 9–27 Is it cause for bitter *c·*
My. v– 7 * wonderment and frequent *c·*,
122–14 It called forth flattering *c·*
209– 1 chapter sub-title
232–10 *C·* ON AN EDITORIAL WHICH APPEARED

commentaries
No. 15– 8 *c·* are employed to explain

commentators
My. 95–11 * the press gallery of c·.

comments
Mis. 32–31 in regard to some clergyman's c·
Ret. 27– 1 I wrote . . . c· on the Scriptures,
27– 5 If these notes and c·,
27–10 These early c· are valuable
My. 99– 1 * contemporary, the *Boston Times*, c·,

commerce
'02. 4– 1 Competition in c·, deceit in councils,
My. 265–28 agriculture, manufacture, c·,

Commercial
Pul. 89–17 * C·, Louisville, Ky.

commercial
My. 91– 6 * in this so-called c· age.

commingle
Mis. 333– 3 The supposition is, that . . . c·,
'00. 4– 5 This precedent that would c·

commingled
Mis. ix–13 sigh, and smile c·,
379–16 they c· error with truth,

commingling
My. 189–13 c· in one righteous prayer,

commiserate
Mis. 80–24 c· the lot of regular doctors,

commission
Mis. 87–19 I never c· any one to
117–18 to carry out a divine c·

commissioned
Pul. 81–24 * c· to complete all that the

commissions
Mis. 18–32 or that those whom He c·

commit
Mis. 19–19 most fearful sin that mortals can c·.
52–19 *if . . . why not c· suicide?*
61–13 image of God, does not c· sin.'
67– 5 shalt not c· adultery ;"— *Exod.* 20 : 14.
119– 7 unwary man to c· a crime,
130– 7 to be wronged, than to c· wrong?
130–25 greatest sin that one can c·
157–22 "C· thy way unto— *Psal.* 37 : 5.
261–10 suffer from the wrong they c·,
268–32 "C· thy way unto— *Psal.* 37 : 5.
335–17 to murder, steal, c· adultery,
Man. 79– 8 such business as . . . shall c· to it.
'01. 14– 2 To assume . . . and yet c· sin,
'02. 19–11 c· an offense against me that I
My. 170–23 C· thy way unto— *Psal.* 37 : 5.
252– 9 the wrong you may c· must,
268–15 shalt not c· adultery"— *Exod.* 20 : 14.
334–20 "To assume . . . and yet c· sin,

commits
Mis. 61–14 * *What c· theft? Or who does murder?*
113–16 c· his way to God,
212– 3 betrays you, and c· suicide.
269– 4 c· his moral sense to a dungeon.
'01. 16–11 outdoes itself and c· suicide.

committal
My. 211–16 c· of acts foreign to the

committed
Mis. 163–15 c· to the providence of God.
222–22 The crimes c· under this
Man. 54– 3 finds that the offense has been c·,
Ret. 20–28 family to whose care he was c·
Pul. 7–18 c· in the name of religion.
20–12 c· to the providence of God,
'01. 20–23 crimes c· under this new-old
My. 136–24 c· the hard earnings of my pen,
156– 9 have c· unto Him— *II Tim.* 1 : 12.
196–19 c· himself to Him that— *I Pet.* 2 : 23.
228–29 have c· unto him— *II Tim.* 1 : 12.
231–16 They are c· to the waste-basket
248–25 I have largely c· to you,
301–20 c· to insane asylums

Committee and committee
Mis. 114– 2 C· on Sunday School Lessons
271–23 the Publishing C· of
305– 1 * c· of women representing
Man. 17–14 Mrs. Eddy was appointed on the c·
27– 6 action to be taken by said C·
77– 7 submit them all to said c·
77– 7 This c· shall decide thereupon
79– 9 While the members of this C· are
98– 5 which has been forwarded to this C·
98– 9 C· shall immediately apply for aid
99–12 in selecting this C·,
99–18 C· for the counties in which London,
100– 1 church employing said C·.
100–19 another C· to fill the vacancy ;
100–22 name the C· if it so desires,
100–23 any C· so named by the Board

Committee and committee
Man. 102– 5 this c· shall not be dissolved until
102– 7 This c· shall elect, dismiss, or
My. 49–13 * Mrs. Eddy was appointed on the c·
50–31 * business c· met after the services
53–25 * annual report of the business c·
62–28 * by the members of the business c·,
83– 6 * members of the local arrangement c·
141–14 * Alfred Farlow of the publication c·
173–29 chairman of the prudential c·
173–30 to his colaborers on said c·
242–18 publication c· work, reading-room work,
282–19 International Conciliation C·,
333– 3 * the C. S. publication c·.
363–10 * *By the C·.*
(*see also* **Building Committee, Publication Committee, State Committee**)

Committee on Bible Lessons
Man. 104–13 the C· on B· L·, and the Board

Committee on Business
Man. 79– 1 C· on B·.
79– 3 elect annually a C· on B·,
98–10 apply for aid to the C· on B·.

Committee on Finance
Man. 76–16 There shall be a C· on F·,
77–25 C· on F· shall visit the
78–25 Board of Directors and the C· on F·,

Committee on Publication
Man. 26– 3 manager of the general C· on P·
27– 4 manager of the general C· on P·
29– 2 the failure of the C· on P·
78–12 the manager of the C· on P·
79– 7 C· on P· shall commit to it
97– 1 heading
97– 4 C· on P·, which shall consist of
97–16 duty of the C· on P· to correct
98– 1 C· on P· shall be responsible for
98– 6 the correction by the C· on P·
98–11 the C· on P· shall read
98–17 duty of the C· on P· to have published
98–22 under the direction of this C· on P·.
99– 1 appoint a C· on P· to serve
99– 9 appoint a C· on P·
99–13 can appoint a C· on P·
99–16 C· on P· is elected only by the
100– 4 candidate for its C· on P·,
100– 7 special request to any C· on P·,
100– 9 If the C· on P· neglects to
100–18 to remove its C· on P·
100–26 not obtainable for C· on P·,
101– 3 manager of the general C· on P·

Committees and committees
Man. 56–16 reports of Treasure, Clerk, and C·,
My. 208–23 chapter sub-title
208–24 The C· :
208–25 God bless the courageous, . . . c·

Committees on Publication
Man. 65–13 members of the C· on P·,
82– 4 The C· on P· are in no manner
97– 7 manager of the C· on P·
98–21 The State C· on P·
99–22 District Manager of the C· on P·
99–24 C· on P· shall consist of men

committing
Mis. 53– 3 C· suicide to dodge the question
115– 1 is c· an offense against God
221–31 a crime that he himself is c·,
331– 3 c· their way unto Him who
Rud. 16–13 some impostors are c· this error.
My. 130– 5 This hidden method of c· crime

commodious
My. 46– 1 * in c· foyer and broad stairways,
157–11 * c· and beautiful church home

common
Mis. 11–16 in accordance with c· law,
18–18 children of one c· Parent,
26–26 in the c· version of Hebrews
40–27 those elements of evil too c·
49–21 the c· belief in the opposite of
78–15 this abuse, has become too c· :
98–15 the progress of our c· Cause
125–24 Apart from the c· walks of mankind,
138–11 the guidance of our c· Father
145–19 may melt into one, and c· dust,
155–26 to Him as our c· Parent,
201–22 beyond the c· apprehension of
202– 6 * beyond the walks of c· life,
219–14 In c· parlance, one person feels
228–28 C· consent is contagious,
247–24 seems, to the c· estimate, solid
263–18 working assiduously for our c· Cause,
274–20 outrages humanity, breaks c· law,
285–27, 28 c· law, c· sense, and c· honesty,
300– 7 in c· parlance, it is an *ignorant*

common

Mis.	348–22	*Natrum muriaticum* (*c·* salt).
	357–10	beyond the walks of *c·* life,
	365–17	form the *c·* want,
	365–28	is held back by the *c·* ignorance
	371– 9	guidance of our *c·* Father,
Ret.	49–25	uniting them in one *c·* brotherhood.
	75–25	no warrant in *c·* law and
Un.	28–13	The *c·* hypotheses about souls
Pul.	23–13	* each having the *c·* identity of
	39– 1	* all meet on *c·* ground in the
	85–27	* in the Cause of their *c·* faith.
No.	1– 1	*c·* sentiment of regard for the
	3–25	so *c·* it is becoming odious
	11–12	*c·* ignorance of what it is
	18–22	health and . . . are the *c·* wants ;
	20–20	*c·* idolatry of man-worship.
'02.	14–16	so counter to the *c·* convictions of
My.	165–24	a relapse into the *c·* hope.
	168– 4	with the demand of our *c·* Christ,
	189– 6	in the *c·* walks of life,
	220– 3	safely submit . . . to *c·* justice,
	226– 1	not be written or used as a *c·* noun
	226– 6	termed in *c·* speech the principle of
	247– 4	by the *c·* consent of the governed,
	254–25	by the *c·* consent of the governed,
	262–24	ritual of our *c·* Christmas
	300–21	are *c·* to his church,
	316–17	in behalf of *c·* justice and truth
		(*see also* **sense**)

commonly

Mis.	75–29	*c·* accepted view is that *soul*
	81–10	*c·* accepted teachings of the day,
	280–13	As we *c·* think,
Ret.	91– 7	*c·* known as the Sermon on the Mount,
Un.	15–16	God is *c·* called the *sinless,*
	32– 7	By matter is *c·* meant mind,

commonplace

Mis.	142–24	send my answer in a *c·* letter.
	379– 7	The composition was *c·*,

Commonwealth and Huntington Avenues

Pul.	24– 4	* between *C· and H· A·*.

Commonwealth Avenue

No. 385

Man.	30–15	No. 385 *C· A·*, Boston.

Pul.	36–21	* removed from Columbus to *C· A·*,
My.	325– 7	* your house on *C· A·*,

commotion

Ret.	79–19	quicksands of worldly *c·*,
My.	121– 5	*c·* of the season's holidays.

commune

Pan.	14– 5	*c·* at the table of our Lord
My.	36– 9	* assembled at this sacred time to *c·*

communicants

'00.	1–12	sixteen thousand *c·* in unity,
'01.	2–19	over twenty-one thousand . . . *c·*
	31–13	*c·* of my large church,
'02.	1– 4	our church *c·* constantly increase
	12–13	a privilege to acquaint *c·* with
My.	7– 6	a privilege to acquaint *c·* with
	90–24	* tremendous outpouring of eager *c·*
	91–12	* Its *c·* are cheerful
	141–25	forty-eight thousand *c·*,
	142– 5	* *c·* who come long distances
	142–15	communion of branch church *c·*
	148–17	membership of seventy-four *c·*,
	156–18	In obedience to . . . may these *c·*
	171–11	invite all my church *c·*
	175– 3	thirty-six thousand *c·*,

communicate

Mis.	34–15	If the departed were to *c·* with us,
	42–16	then we shall be able to *c·* with
	60–20	or for one who sleeps to *c·* with
My.	203– 3	I have nothing new to *c·* ;

communicates

Ret.	83–15	*c·*, . . . his misconception of Truth,

communicating

Mis.	60–18	reveals the impossibility of . . . . *c·*,
'02.	10–28	like sentencing a man for *c·* with

communication

Mis.	132–12	In your *c·* to *Zion's Herald,*
Man.	65–26	*c·* from the Pastor Emeritus
	67– 7	*c·* from the Pastor Emeritus
Pul.	38–21	* no possibility of *c·*.
My.	207– 3	Your *c·* is gratefully received.
	272–24	* will be interested in this *c·*
	329–25	* give your readers the following *c·*.

communications

Mis.	34–23	called "*c·* from spirits,"
Man.	46–14	all private *c·* made to them
	65–25	Understanding *C·*.

communications

Man.	66– 6	Interpreting *C·*.
	66– 9	*c·* of the Pastor Emeritus
	67– 6	Private *C·*.
Hea.	5–13	* trustworthiness of the *c·*,

communing

Mis.	171–14	This does not mean *c·* with spirits
My.	154–27	*C·* heart with heart,
	154–30	Such *c·* uplifts man's being ;

Communion and communion (noun)

1898

Pan.	1– 3	heading

January 2, 1898

My.	121– 1	chapter sub-title

June 4, 1899

My.	124– 5	chapter sub-title

1904

My.	15–11	chapter sub-title

Mis.	60–13	*deny the possibility of c· with*
	90–22	*administer the c·,*
	90–24	*shall . . . receive the c·?*
	90–30	*c·* which . . . Scientists celebrate
	149–25	whose *c·* is fellowship with saints
	282–18	person with whom you hold *c·*
	333–22	"What *c·* hath light with — *II Cor. 6 : 14.*
	344– 1	chapter sub-title
Man.	61– 7	*C·.*
	61– 8	No more *C·.*
	61–11	*C·* of Branch Churches.
	61–12	*C·* shall be observed in the
	73–22	No Close *C·.*
Ret.	15– 3	he received me into their *c·*,
	18–21	sacred *c·* with home's magic spell !
Pul.	30–21	* *c·*, which is not celebrated by
'01.	1– 6	Our first *c·* in the new century
	1–16	human in *c·* with the Divine,
Hea.	2– 3	calm and steadfast *c·* with God ;
Po.	64–14	sacred *c·* with home's magic spell !
My.	19–10	*c·* of the Holy Ghost, — *I Cor. 13 : 14.*
	20–24	* at the *c·* and annual meeting
	25–19	at our annual *c·*
	26– 5	* on the date of the annual *c·*,
	26–17	This *c·* and dedication include
	29– 4	* kneeling in silent *c·* ;
	32– 3	* after five minutes of silent *c·*
	32–29	* After the reading . . . silent *c·*,
	38–24	* than the silent *c·*.
	54–13	* *c·* was held at Odd Fellows Hall,
	61– 8	* *c·* would likely be postponed
	63–11	* Our annual *c·* and the dedication
	78–19	* congregation knelt in silent *c·*,
	79– 2	* kneeling for silent *c·*
	139–25	material to the spiritual *c·* ;
	140–11	* chapter sub-title
	140–20	Relinquishing a material form of *c·*
	140–25	Dropping the *c·* of The Mother Church
	141–29	*c·* universal and divine.
	142–15	*c·* of branch church communicants
	154–26	embodied in a visible *c·*,
	170–28	to kneel with us . . . in blest *c·*
	171–12	communicants who attend this *c·*,
	173–16	invite those who attend the *c·*

Communion and communion (adj.)

Mis.	120–26	chapter sub-title
	314–28	observed at the *C·* service ;
	398–21	poem
Man.	40–20	On *C·* day the Church Tenets
	61–10	shall observe no more *C·* seasons.
'02.	4– 8	pray at this *C·* season for
Po.	page 75	poem
My.	5–24	memorable dedication and *c·* season,
	27– 6	our annual meeting and *c·* service,
	29– 3	* chapter sub-title
	56–32	* Our *c·* services and annual meetings
	140–13	* dropping the annual *c·* service
	141– 2	* chapter sub-title
	141– 3	* general *c·* service of the
	141–10	* not . . . to attend the *c·* seasons
	141–16	* to abolish its famous *c·* seasons.
	141–17	* *c·* season of the Boston church
	141–26	branch churches continue their *c·*
	141–27	no more *c·* season in The
	142–11	abolishing the *c·* season of The
	142–14	The Mother Church *c·* season

Communion Day

Mis.	315– 5	on the Sunday following *C· D·*.

Communion Doxology

My.	33– 1	* Singing the *C· D·*.

Communion Hymn

My.	31– 1	* first the "*C· H·*,"
	32–24	* Solo, "*C· H·*,"
		(*see also* **Appendix A**)

communions
    My. 91– 4 * did not find in other *c*.
Communion Sabbath
    My. 50– 1 * *C· S·* was held at the home of
          50–14 * for deliberation before *C· S·*
          50–23 * church celebrated her *C· S·*
Communion Services
  in Branch Churches
    Man. 125– 1 heading
Communion Sunday
    Mis. 314–32 first Sunday of . . . except *C· S·*,
     02. 12–27 their presence on *C· S·*.
    My. 7–11 their presence on *C· S·*.
         50–19 * *C. S.*, . . . brought fresh courage
communities
    My. 95– 7 * intelligence of many *c·*
community
    Mis. 43–31 the health of the *c·*.
       115–11 ignorance of the *c·* on this subject
       271–26 * "To benefit the *c·*,
    No. 3–21 to be safe members of the *c·*.
     01. 31–16 individual and the *c·*.
    My. 94–10 * growth of the sect in every *c·*
       362–17 * Cause of C. S. in this *c·*,
compact
    Mis. 91–10 The real Christian *c·* is love for
       290– 1 *c·* of two hearts.
    Ret. 47– 3 wars with Love's spiritual *c·*,
compacts
    Mis. 289–13 agreements to certain *c·* :
companion
    Pul. 13–21 has made his bosom *c·*,
    My. 124–24 time-table, log, traveller's *c·*,
       130–28 used as a *c·* to the Bible
companionless
    Po. 35–13 in the cringing crowd *C·* !
companions
    My. 335–10 * beloved by his brothers and *c·*,
company
    Mis. 153–12 great was the *c·* of — *Psal.* 68 : 11.
       272–21 * such as any stock *c·* may obtain
       324–21 he seeks to leave the odious *c·*
       378– 9 in *c·* with several other patients,
    Pul. 66–26 * to supplant those in *c·* with
     00. 8– 7 be careful of your *c·*.
     01. 12– 9 only . . . would be seen in such *c·*."
    My. 46–29 * innumerable *c·* of angels, — *Heb.* 12 : 22.
comparative
    Rud. 3– 2 Hence their *c·* acquiescence
     01. 17–21 *c·* ease of healing
comparatively
    Pul. 67–21 * have strong churches, *c·*,
     00. 9– 9 but few, *c·*, see it ;
    My. 29–22 * A *c·* new religion
       85– 5 * it was *c·* unknown ;
      271– 8 of *c·* little importance
compare
    Man. 109–14 *c·* them with the forms here given,
    No. 41–14 to *c·* mortal lives with this model
     01. 21–18 or to *c·* its literature.
    My. 107– 3 *C·* the lives of its professors with
      164–14 *c·* the beginning of C. S.
compared
    Mis. 67– 9 *c·* with his rights of mind and
      239–22 her dividend, when *c·* with
      317–15 *c·* with the whole of the Scriptures
    No. 22–11 *C·* with the inspired wisdom
    Po. 34–16 Blessed *c·* with me thou art
    My. 96– 8 * in no sense, save one, be *c·* with
comparing
    Mis. 382– 8 *c·* those with the joy of
    My. 127–11 *C·* our scientific system of
      197–15 *C·* such students with those
comparison
    Mis. 102–14 admits of no degrees of *c·*.
      294–24 chapter sub-title
    Man. 41– 3 Careless *c·* or irreverent reference
    My. 92–19 * give a feeble impression in *c·* with
      96–15 * *c·* with other creeds.
      123– 2 gifts to me are beyond *c·*
      127– 9 On *c·*, it will be found that C. S.
      238– 5 *c·* between the effects produced by
comparisons
    Mis. 267–15 * *C·* are odorous. — SHAKESPEARE.
    My. 338–22 his *c·* and ready humor.
compass
    Ret. 70–15 No person can *c·* or fulfil the
    Un. 58–16 test the full *c·* of human woe,
    Pul. 26–13 * It is one of vast *c·*,
      60–22 * It is of three-manual *c·*,

compass
    Pul. 60–23 * pedal *c·*, C. C. C. to F. 30.
    Hea. 4-- 6 the *c·* of infinite Life,
    Po. 18–10 higher he soareth to *c·* his rest,
       (*see also* **organ**)
compassed
    '02. 14–15 *c·* on any other foundation,
compassion
    My. 39–26 * Our hearts were thrilled by her *c·*,
compassionate
    Ret. 25–10 *c·*, helpful, and spiritual.
    Pan. 15– 3 as she has been *c·* in peace.
    '02. 18–13 Jesus was *c·*, true,
    My. 37– 5 * incense of gratitude and *c·* love
compatible
    Mis. 289–18 *c·* with home and heaven.
compel
    Mis. 197–20 *c·* us to pattern after both ;
compelled
    Ret. 20–22 *c·* to ask for a bill of divorce,
    Un. 50–13 though we are *c·* to use the phrase
    Pul. 64–11 * *c·* to refuse further contributions,
    No. 42– 6 mortals are not *c·* to have other gods
    My. 160–16 until *c·* to glance at it.
compelling
    Ret. 80–24 under his *c·* rod.
compels
    Mis. 85–27 pain *c·* human consciousness to
      200–23 *c·* me to seek the remedy for it,
      209–15 *c·* mortals to learn that
      265–32 until suffering *c·* the downfall of
    My. 3–21 *c·* him to think genuine,
      250–17 nor *c·* the branch churches to
      308–13 *c·* me . . . to speak.
compensate
    Mis. 65–27 is inadequate to *c·* for the
      111–12 *c·* loss, and gain a higher sense
      322–25 to *c·* your zealous affection for
    Ret. 58– 4 trying to *c·* for the absence of
    My. 212–26 tries to *c·* himself for his own loss
compensated
    '00. 11–12 answered and *c·* by divine love.
compensates
    My. 21–15 * divine Love more than *c·* for
compensateth
    Mis. 363– 8 *c·* vanity with nothingness.
compensation
    Mis. 38–10 should expect no *c·*.
compete
    Ret. 31– 3 Nothing can *c·* with C. S.,
      82–25 *c·* with ecclesiastical fellowship
competent
    Man. 77– 2 by an honest, *c·* accountant.
competition
    '02. 4– 1 *C·* in commerce, deceit in councils,
    My. 266– 7 insufficient freedom of honest *c·* ;
competitor
    Mis. 22–19 It hath no peer, no *c·*,
compilation
    Mis. 300– 6 reading it publicly as your own *c·*,
    Pul. 28–20 * *c·* called the "C. S. Hymnal,"
compilations
    No. 3–26 such *c·*, instead of possessing
compilers
    Ret. 91– 8 *c·* and translators of the Bible,
compiling
    Mis. xi–27 In *c·* this work, I have tried
      300– 3 *c·* them in connection with
      301– 1 *c·* and delivering that sermon
complacently
    Mis. 222–13 listen *c·* to audible falsehoods
     01. 20–13 People may listen *c·* to the
complain
    Man. 29–10 shall *c·* thereof to the Clerk
    Pul. 56–20 * And of the just effect *c·* ;
complainant
    Mis. 381–18 ordered that the *c·* (Mrs. Eddy)
    Man. 29– 6 the name of the *c·*.
complained
    Man. 52–10 to the member *c·* of
     01. 9–11 the mysticism *c·* of
complaining
    Mis. 236–10 the child *c·* of his parents
complains
     01. 11–28 St. Paul *c·* of him whose god is

complaint

Man.	29–10	and the *c·* be found valid,
	52– 4	A *c·* against a member of
	52– 6	and if this *c·* is not for
	53–1, 2	upon her *c·* or the *c·* of a member
	53–10	upon her *c·* that member should
	53–18	No member shall enter a *c·* of
	54– 1	upon *c·* by another member,
	54–12	on *c·* of Mrs. Eddy
	54–13	this *c·* being found valid,
	68– 8	upon Mrs. Eddy's *c·* thereof
'02.	19–19	The thought of it stills *c·* ;

complaints

Mis.	6– 4	but little time free from *c·*
Man.	50–12	C·.
	51–25	*c·* against Church members ;
	82–15	for the examination of *c·*.
No.	9–14	repeated *c·* and murmurings
My.	223– 4	that I neither listen to *c·*,
	354– 2	In view of *c·* from the field,

complete

Mis.	15–18	it cannot *c·*, the new birth :
	35–11	most concise, yet *c·*, summary
	50–10	a *c·* textbook of C. S. ;
	75–17	used and make *c·* sense.
	137– 4	all of which are *c·*.
	393–16	From the shores afar, *c·*.
Ret.	37– 2	the *c·* statement of C. S.,
	60– 3	Science reveals Life as a *c·* sphere,
	78– 6	is *c·* in S. and H. ;
Un.	43– 9	*c·* triumph over death,
Pul.	73–27	* *c·* and yet concise idea
	81–25	* commissioned to *c·* all that the
No.	37– 3	nature and manhood were forever *c·*,
'00.	14– 7	signifies a *c·* time or number
Po.	51–21	From the shores afar, *c·*.
My.	14–14	* entire amount required to *c·*
	14–24	* the building fund is not *c·*,
	22–12	* in order to *c·* this great work,
	23–14	* Amount necessary to *c·* the sum
	29–17	* *c·* unanimity of thought
	58– 5	* no more funds are needed to *c·*
	66–21	* spacious and elegant edifice *c·*
	81– 5	* so *c·* this self-abnegation,
	113– 9	truth of the *c·* system of C. S.
	158–26	to-morrow *c·*, and thereafter dedicate
	194–11	a *c·* subordination of self.
	212–13	to *c·* the sum total of sin.
	221–13	a more *c·*, natural, and divine

completed

Man.	102– 7	new church edifice is *c·*.
Pul.	45–15	* that it could not be *c·* before
	70–13	* very recently saw *c·* in Boston,
	84–24	* and that our temple is *c·*
	86– 1	* the new church . . . just *c·*,
My.	20–28	* should be *c·* as early as possible,
	40– 1	* this *c·* extension of
	61– 7	* for the building to be *c·*
	72–27	* work was actually *c·*
	76–31	* structure, which is now *c·*,
	83–26	* building itself has been *c·*.
	86–14	* before the actual work was *c·*,
	148–11	having *c·* its organization
	171–10	church is so nearly *c·*
	311–30	* *c·* her education when she

completely

Pul.	71–20	* Mrs. Eddy has resigned herself *c·* to
My.	v–17	* reforming the sinner . . . *c·*,
	59–31	* or so *c·* vindicated.
	127–13	divine metaphysics *c·* overshadows
	210– 8	*c·* shielded from the attacks of

completeness

No.	10– 5	of the *c·* of Science.

completing

My.	24–31	* appropriate time for *c·* the
	197–11	*c·* and dedicating your church

completion

Mis.	158–25	you will find the forthcoming *c·*
Pul.	23– 3	* C· OF THE FIRST CHURCH OF CHRIST,
	24– 1	* *c·* of the first C. S. church
	45–13	* *c·* within the year 1894
	84–14	* 1894, witnessed the *c·* of
	84–23	* all obstacles to its *c·*
	86–18	* the *c·* of The First Church of Christ,
My.	21– 8	* *c·* of The Mother Church,
	21–27	* *c·* of the new edifice
	27–14	* *c·* of the church building,
	28– 2	* coincident with the *c·* of
	43–30	* *c·* and dedication of our
	62–11	* which crowns the *c·* of this
	62–21	* *c·* of the magnificent extension

complex

My.	239–20	compound, *c·* idea or likeness of

complexion

Mis.	379– 8	general appearance, height, and *c·*
Pul.	32– 5	* her beautiful *c·* and

compliance

Mis.	244– 9	without *c·* to ordained conditions.
Man.	52–14	his *c·* with our Church Rules
Peo.	9– 6	as *c·* with a religious rite may
My.	180–23	drop *c·* with their desires,
	204–15	IN C· WITH THE STATE LAWS
	231– 3	Giving merely in *c·* with

complied

Man.	110– 6	conditions be exactly *c·* with,
My.	217–15	provided he has *c·* with my request

compliment

Ret.	89–14	hortatory *c·* to a stranger,

compliments

My.	184–17	I treasure it next to your *c·*.

comply

Mis.	x– 5	*c·* with an oft-repeated request ;
	109–10	claim you admit . . . or *c·* with.
	194–30	we must *c·* with the first condition
	286– 8	ability to *c·* with absolute Science,
	310–19	one must *c·* with the church rules.
Man.	65–15	*c·* with any written order,
	78– 1	*c·* with the By-Laws of the Church.
	100–20	duty of that church to *c·* with
'00.	9– 1	they *c·* with my counsel ;
My.	177– 3	Most happily would I *c·* with your

compose

Ret.	76– 6	he cannot dishonestly *c·* C. S.
Pul.	43– 9	* who *c·* the Board of Directors,

composed

Mis.	106–17	Sunday Lesson, *c·* of Scripture and
	381– 3	manuscripts originally *c·* by
Pul.	27–30	* *c·* of three separate panels,
	29–28	* entire congregation was *c·* of
	76–15	* rug *c·* entirely of skins of
My.	276–10	try to be *c·* and resigned

composite

Pul.	81–14	* represents the *c·* beauty,
My.	359–19	* quotations from a *c·* letter,

composition

Mis.	379– 6	The *c·* was commonplace,
'00.	11–15	his *c·* is the triumph of art,
My.	225– 7	correct use of capital letters in *c·*

compound

Mis.	167– 8	*c·* idea of all that resembles God.
Pul.	74–26	Love and its *c·* divine ideal.
'01.	22– 8	I do not believe in such a *c·*.
	22– 9	Truth and Truth is not a *c·* ;
My.	239–20	*c·*, complex idea or likeness of
	269– 2	*c·* idea, image or likeness,
	292–16	a *c·* of prayers in which
	292–29	mind is a *c·* of faith and doubt,
	293– 6	this *c·* of mind and matter

compounded

Mis.	248–12	falsehoods uttered about me were *c·*,
	271– 7	notion that *c·* metaphysics
Rud.	1–14	Latin verb *personare* is *c·* of

compounds

Mis.	270–27	chapter sub-title
	271– 1	exclusion of *c* from its pharmacy,
	271–14	which spurious " *c·* " engender.
'01.	22–10	Spirit and matter, are *c·*
	23–18	all error, amalgamation, and *c·*.

comprehend

Mis.	23–24	who *c·* what C. S. means by
	82–21	see and *c·* only as abstract glory.
	197–12	to *c·* the meaning of the text,
	255–12	He should *c·*, in divine Science,
Ret.	90–18	*c·* the needs of her babe
My.	39–29	* enables us to *c·* better the
	41–32	* *c·* the "beauty of — *Psal.* 29 : 2.
	42–25	* begin to *c·*, even in small degree,
	225– 9	reader who does not *c·* where

comprehended

Mis.	164– 9	Saviour, which is Truth, be *c·*.
	187–17	fully *c·* the later teachings
Ret.	75–16	If one's spiritual ideal is *c·*
No.	20–13	As the divine Principle is *c·*,
My.	110– 9	darkness *c·* it not." — *John* 1 : 5.

comprehendeth

Mis.	368– 4	the darkness *c·* it not,
Un.	63–11	the darkness *c* it not.

comprehending

Mis.	46–20	but *c·* at every point,
My.	117– 9	the *c·* of the divine order

comprehends
Mis. 362– 6 c· and reflects all real mode,
Pul. 44–12 * c· its full significance.
No. 9–25 More . . . than this period c·.

comprehension
Mis. 79– 7 until it is clear to human c·
200–15 remote from the general c· of
Pul. 84–22 * unfold it to the c· of mankind.
No. 15– 5 The c· of my teachings would
28–22 neither the c· of its Principle nor

comprehensive
My. 45– 2 * c· means by you provided
149–22 Losing the c· in the technical,

comprise
Mis. 101–32 c· the elements of all forms
No. 4– 7 c· the whole of mortal existence,

comprised
My. 107–26 c· in a knowledge or understanding
306–24 these c· the manuscripts which

compromise
Mis. 53–15 by any c· with matter ;
101–15 enters into no c· with
My. 41–16 * makes no c· with evil,

compromises
Pul. 51–22 * c· have been welcomed.

compulsory
My. 344–30 Where vaccination is c·,

compute
My. 23– 3 * c· by the total membership of

comrades
Mis. 324–23 Stealing cautiously away from his c·,

Comstock's Natural Philosophy
My. 304– 7 book title

con
Pul. vii–16 to c· the facts surrounding the

Conant
Mrs.
My. 32– 8 * Mrs. C· could be heard perfectly
34–17 * read by Mr. McCrackan and Mrs. C· :
Mrs. Laura Carey
My. 31–24 * Second Reader, Mrs. Laura Carey C·,

conceal
My. 335–27 * could not c· the fact that the case

concealed
Mis. 22–32 c· in the treasure-troves of
209–25 false basis that evil should be c·
My. 160–32 C· crimes, the wrongs done
166–18 virtues that lie c· in the
204– 5 the power which lies c·
241-- 8 * cunningly c· to prevent

concede
No. 23–14 c· that the Scriptures have
My. 347–24 Most thinkers c· that Science is

conceded
Mis. 13–25 only needs to be c·,
218–12 when it is c· that the five
My. 19–18 It is c· that our shadows

concedes
'02. 7– 2 c· no origin or causation apart from

conceit
Mis. 234–13 his vain c·, the Phariseeism of
267–18 c·, cowardice, or dishonesty.
348–16 wise in his own c·." — Prov. 26 : 5.
No. 2–24 C· cannot avert the effects of

conceivable
Pul. 25– 7 * as literally fire-proof as is c·.
36–17 * walked any c· distance.
'01. 6–27 lose all c· idea of Him as
7– 1 consistently c· as the
My. 212–27 hindering in every way c·
259– 2 sweetest sculptured face and form c·,

conceive
Mis. 96–11 worship that of which I can c·,
216–27 * to c· the universe as a
216–29 * to c· a grin without a cat."
217– 4 all should c· and understand
253–25 Can that child c· of the anguish,
259–11 too evil to c· of good
Un. 23–23 c· of God only as like itself,
Pul. 66–14 * what they c· to be the literal
Rud. 2–12 We do not c· rightly of God, if we
No. 18–18 Thus falsely may the human c· of
20– 1 so far as he can c· of personality.
23– 2 To c· of God as resembling
'01. 4–24 c· of God as One
6–11 Who can c· either of three
14–19 to c· of error as either right or
15–17 I can c· of little short of

conceive
'02. 5–26 why should mortals c· of a law,
My. 248–22 to c· God aright you must

conceived
Mis. 71–21 Whatever is humanly c·
108–14 c· of only as a delusion.
108–21 that which is truly c· of,
No. 13–20 No greater opposites can be c· of,
Pan. 2–16 * the universe, c· of as
2–20 c· as one personified nature,
'01. 7–24 cannot be c· of on that basis ;
My. 262–14 c· of Spirit, of God

conceives
Un. 40–28 It c· and beholds nothing but

concentrated
Mis. 242–22 in its most c· form,
Ret. 93–12 c· and immovably fixed
Hea. 12–17 the c· power of thought

concentric
Mis. 107–12 A pure affection, c·,

concept
human
(see **human**)

Mis. 89–25 Mortal man is a false c·
353– 7 If one asks me, Is my c· of you
Ret. 67– 2 hence one's c· of error is
67– 5 human or physical c·.
68– 1 material c· was never a creator,
68–10 human material c· is unreal,
68–10 divine c· or idea is spiritually
Un. 32– 7 universe, is His spiritual c·.
41– 2 has but a feeble c· of immortality.
No. 23– 1 incorrect c· of the nature of evil
36–25 from human sense to a higher c·
36–27 Mankind's c· of Jesus was
'01. 24– 2 * impossible and unreal c·."
'02. 6–16 mortal c· and all it includes
My. 224–11 its right or its wrong c·,

conception
above
My. 59– 7 * It was above c·
convey a
My. 81–29 * impossible to convey a c· of
divine
Mis. 287– 1 the most exalted divine c·.
false
Rud. 6–10 beauty is marred, through a false c·,
frail
Mis. 87–11 Matter is a frail c· of mortal mind ;
heathen
No. 34–20 infinitely beyond the heathen c·
'00. 3–26 In the heathen c· Yahwah,
higher
Pul. 85–10 * a better and higher c· of God
holier
Mis. 17–19 much higher and holier c· of
human
(see **human**)
humanized
Ret. 54– 8 a humanized c· of His power,
infantile
Mis. 215–17 not according to the infantile c·
maturing
My. 181– 8 Progress is the maturing c· of
my
Mis. 354– 2 It exceeds my c· of human nature.
My. 262–29 express my c· of Truth's appearing.
no possible
'01. 5– 1 has no possible c· of ours,
of God
Ret. 25–20 I knew the human c· of God to be
Pul. 85–10 * better and higher c· of God
of man
Mis. 186–10 even separates its c· of man from
of sin
'01. 13–18 destroy the c· of sin as something,
of Spirit
My. 152–10 c· of Spirit and its all-power.
of the Christ
No. 12–16 new-born c· of the Christ,
of Truth
Ret. 83–13 may mistake in his c· of Truth,
original
Mis. 263–29 or a single original c·,
proper
Ret. 25–26 inadequate to form any proper c· of
Hea. 4–21 can we ever arrive at a proper c·
sensual
Mis. 361– 4 When the belief in . . . sensual c·,
sensuous
No. 26–11 brings forth its own sensuous c·.
spiritual
Mis. 286–11 more spiritual c· and education

conception
true
Mis. 108–15 This true *c·* would remove
My. 267–25 to darken the true *c·* of
your own
Mis. 8–12 the object of your own *c·*?

Mis. 108–22 *c·* of it at all as something

conceptions
Mis. 6–19 *c·* of Life, Truth, and Love
68–22 * science of the *c·* and relations
170–14 wrong and foolish, *c·* of God
218– 9 mortal mind must change all its *c·*
325– 7 small *c·* of spiritual riches,
375– 2 material *c·* and personality
Rud. 7– 5 infinite and subtler *c·*
No. 15–16 These *c·* of Deity and devil
Peo. 2– 6 material *c·* of spiritual being,
2–14 It is the false *c·* of Spirit,
8– 8 our *c·* of Deity,
8–13 finite and material *c·* of Deity.
12–17 advance to truer *c·*,

concepts
Mis. 71–28 even human *c·*, mortal shadows
294– 3 the *c·* of his own creating,
351–19 chapter sub-title
353– 3 Human *c·* run in extremes ;
361–10 spiritual *c·* testifying to
375– 3 are not my *c·* of angels.
My. 293– 2 but differing human *c·*

concern
Rud. 12–22 *c·* themselves with the chemistry of
'02. 9– 7 pride, and ease *c·* you less,
My. 104–17 of the utmost *c·* to the world
143– 9 *To Whom It May C·* :
276– 2 chapter sub-title
354– 1 chapter sub-title

concerned
Mis. 141–17 actuating all the parties *c·*
My. 99–13 * whenever their . . . religion is *c·*.
342–25 * all now *c·* in its government
351–26 Scientists are not *c·* with

concerning
Mis. 65– 9 *c·* the greater subject of human weal
72–13 proverb *c·* the land of — *Ezek.* 18 : 2.
78–23 of the public thought *c·* it.
79–13 error *c·* himself and his origin :
197–14 an opinion entertained *c·* Jesus
236–16 to give, . . . advice *c·* difficulties
287–23 important questions *c·* their
311–31 when rehearsing facts *c·* others
335–28 remember the Scripture *c·* those
372–22 declaration *c·* the spirit and
Un. 6–17 *c·* the divine nature and character
23–16 when they testify *c·* Spirit,
33– 7 from their own evidence, and *c·*
44– 1 misrepresentations are made *c·* my
Pul. 47–10 * knowledge *c·* the physical side
57–15 * *c·* the organization of
No. 24–26 great fact *c·* all error
Pan. 2–25 belief *c·* Deity in theology.
'00. 12–11 St. Paul's life furnished items *c·*
'01. 18– 4 woeful warnings *c·* C. S. healing
Hea. 5–12 * the question chiefly is *c·*
Peo. 8–15 speculate *c·* material forces.
My. 73–22 * information *c·* rooms and board,
220– 9 *c·* obedience to human law,
329–27 * facts *c·* Mrs. Mary Baker Eddy,
330–13 * *c·* Major Glover's history

concerns
Mis. 63–18 the great reality that *c·* man,
65–12 your query *c·* a negative
321–30 wisdom . . . that *c·* me, and you,
Ret. 88–11 The spiritual . . . most *c·* mankind.
88–18 a part which *c·* us intimately,

concert
Mis. 314– 9 repeat in *c·* with the congregation
Pul. 62–21 * *c·* halls, and public buildings,

concession
Mis. 91– 7 let it be in *c·* to the period,

conciliate
My. 284–26 efficacy of divine Love to *c·*

Conciliation
My. 282–19 International *C·* Committee,

concise
Mis. 35–11 most *c·*, yet complete, summary
Pul. 73–27 * *c·* idea of her belief

conclave
Mis. 148–10 originated not in solemn *c·*
Man. 3– 5 originated not in solemn *c·*

conclude
Mis. 47–27 *What should one c· as to*
56–13 to *c·* that Spirit constitutes
161–22 it is natural to *c·* that
165–31 before man can truthfully *c·*
327–19 they *c·* to stop and
'01. 4–30 we naturally *c·* that he breaks faith

concluded
Mis. 169–19 divines of the world have *c·* ;
Pul. 70–21 * *c·* that the way of salvation
My. 19– 6 * ceremony *c·* with the
32–30 * *c·* with the audible repetition of
54–27 * *c·* to engage Chickering Hall
307–18 afterwards I *c·* that he only

concluding
My. 135– 6 *c·* declaration may be applied to

conclusion
any
Mis. 288–12 any *c·* drawn therefrom is not
correct
Mis. 344–19 would seek a correct *c·*.
final
Ret. 33– 2 my final *c·* that mortal belief,
follows
Mis. 269–22 *c·* follows that the correct
his
My. 111–24 proving that his *c·* was logical
illogical
My. 225–24 and by no illogical *c·*,
inevitable
Un. 38–25 Hence the inevitable *c·* that
latter
Rud. 5–28 latter *c·* is the simple solution
logical
Mis. 26– 6 The only logical *c·* is that
26–30 logical *c·* that God is
93–11 logical *c·* drawn from the
'02. 7–19 No other logical *c·* can be
must be met
Ret. 94– 4 the *c·* must be met that
of the sermon
Mis. 178–25 * At the *c·* of the sermon,
one
Pul. 74–23 teachings maintain but one *c·*
opposite
Mis. 367–25 opposite *c·*, that darkness dwelleth
premise and
Mis. 101–28 On this proof rest premise and *c·*
195–21 one correct premise and *c·*,
200– 9 an error of premise and *c·*,
My. 112–14 with its logical premise and *c·*,
premise and in
My. 111–17 logical in premise and in *c·*.
rash
Mis. 288– 9 A rash *c·* that regards only
such a
Mis. 195–15 the authority for such a *c·*,
this
Mis. 9–10 Wherein is this *c·* relative to
25–11 Christ's Sermon . . . confirms this *c·*.
26–31 How, then, can this *c·* change,
119–17 This *c·* is not an argument
My. 340– 1 The fact that . . . confirms this *c·*.

Mis. 216–16 justifies one in the *c·* that he
245–11 The *c·* cannot now be pushed,
'01. 3–23 is not lost by the *c·*,
3–27 the *c·* is not properly drawn.

conclusions
Mis. 27– 6 *c·* that destroy their premise
46–13 premises or *c·* of C. S.,
101–19 bases his *c·* on mortality,
228–26 reliability of its *c·*,
291–32 over his emotions and *c·*.
309– 5 must result in erroneous *c·*.
312–23 *c·* which . . . cannot fasten upon.
366–23 mortal *c·* start from this false
Ret. 21–28 if spiritual *c·* are separated from
21–30 argument, with its rightful *c·*,
Un. 5–16 No stubborn purpose to force *c·*
9–14 their arguments and *c·* as to the
My. 175–29 to *c·* the very opposite of
224– 8 Hurried *c·* on to the public thought
350– 1 draws its *c·* of Deity and man,

conclusive
Mis. 96–25 any *c·* idea in a brief explanation.
192–28 Nothing can be more *c·* than this :
My. 85–13 * This is *c·* ;
321–25 * *c·* to me in every detail,

conclusively
Un. 9– 1 it proves my view *c·*,
My. 103– 8 show *c·* that C. S. is indeed
348– 4 proved *c·* that all effect must be

concomitants
   Mis. 14–16   facts of existence and its *c·* :
   Un. 46–21   sickness, and death were evil's *c·*.
   My. 129– 6   all *c·* of C. S.

Concord (*see also* **Concord's**)
New Hampshire
   Mis. 203– 3   Pleasant View, in *C·*, New Hampshire,
   Pul. 43–11   * a native of *C·*, New Hampshire.
N. H.
   Mis. xii–10   *C·*, N. H. January, 1897
   116– 5   Pleasant View, *C·*, N. H.,
   138–32   *C·*, N. H., May 13, 1890.
   251– 2   chapter sub-title
   294–25   Since my residence in *C·*, N. H.
   Pul. 32–18†   * and was born in *C·*, N. H.,
   37– 5   * in her removal to *C·*, N. H.,
   43–25   * remained at her home in *C·*, N. H.,
   58– 6   * she has lived in *C·*, N. H.,
   63–12   * country home in *C·*, N. H.,
   70–27   * a country-seat in *C·*, N. H.
   74– 4   * *C·*, N. H., February 4, 1895.
   76–21   * *C·*, N. H., February 27, 1895
   77–23   * *People and Patriot*, *C·*, N. H.,
   '01. 32– 2   Nathaniel Bouton, D. D., of *C·*, N. H.,
   Po. 22–22   *C·*, N. H., *January*, 1901.
   24–22   Pleasant View, *C·*, N. H., 1899.
   25–20   *C·*, N. H., *May* 21, 1904.
   31–23   *C·*, N. H., *April* 18, 1900.
   44– 5   *C·*, N. H., *April* 3, 1899.
   79–22   *C·*, N. H., *January*, 1900.
   My. 9–29   *C·*, N. H., July 21, 1902.
   20– 5   *C·*, N. H., September 1, 1904.
   20–20   *C·*, N. H., October 31, 1904.
   25–29   *C·*, N. H., April 8, 1906.
   26–27   *C·*, N. H., April 23, 1906.
   44–22   * Pleasant View, *C·*, N. H.
   58–27   * Pleasant View, *C·*, N. H.
   60–24   * Pleasant View, *C·*, N. H.
   62–18   * Pleasant View, *C·*, N. H.
   66–24   * Pleasant View, in *C·*, N. H.,
   91–21   * Mary Baker Eddy of *C·*, N. H.
   123–10   To-day in *C·*, N. H., we have a
   133–19   *C·*, N. H., May 11, 1903.
   135–22   *C·*, N. H., March 22, 1907.
   136–10   *C·*, N. H., April 2, 1907.
   136–23   National State Capital Bank, *C·*, N. H.
   136–30   *C·*, N. H., April 3, 1907.
   137–10   Hon. Judge Chamberlin, *C·*, N. H.
   138–23   *C·*, N. H., May 16, 1907.
   144– 2   * her church in *C·*, N. H. :
   144– 3   First Church . . . *C·*, N. H.
   145– 5   C. S. Hall in *C·*, N. H.
   162–15   our church edifice in *C·*, N. H.
   163–18   and came to *C·*, N. H.,
   165–14   First Church . . . in *C·*, N. H.
   166–12   First Church . . . *C·*, N. H.,
   166–30   First Church . . . *C·*, N. H.
   169– 3   *C·*, N. H., on July 5,
   169–11   *C·*, N. H., June 30, 1897.
   169–17   I was happy to receive at *C·*, N. H.,
   171–17   *C·*, N. H., June 11, 1904.
   173– 2   * in the *C·* (N. H.) newspapers
   174–15   Congregational Church, *C·*, N. H.,
   174–20   Congregational Church in *C·*, N. H.,
   175– 8   *C·*, N. H., November 14, 1905.
   187–18   *C·*, N. H., November 16, 1898.
   193–11   *C·*, N. H., November 20, 1902.
   197–29   *C·*, N. H., July 27, 1907.
   230–28   *C·*, N. H., November 14, 1904.
   236–21   *C·*, N. H., July 8, 1907.
   259– 8   * Pleasant View, *C·*, N. H.
   261–19   *C·*, N. H., December 28, 1905.
   270– 7   in this capital city of *C·*, N. H.,
   271–14   * in the city of *C·*, N. H.,
   272–17   Pleasant View, *C·*, N. H.
   279–29   *C·*, N. H., June 13, 1905.
   280–- 2   * Pleasant View, *C·*, N. H.
   280–24   *C·*, N. H., June 27, 1905.
   282–29   *C·*, N. H., April 3, 1907.
   284– 8   *C·*, N. H., April 22, 1907.
   284–20   in some church in *C·*, N. H.
   284–29   *C·*, N. H., May 28, 1907.
   285–31   Pleasant View, *C·*, N. H.
   289–21   *C·*, N. H., January 27, 1901.
   290–30   *C·*, N. H., September 14, 1901.
   295–30   *C·*, N. H., August 31, 1907.
   296– 7   *C·*, N. H., October 14, 1907.
   296–22   *C·*, N. H., December 10, 1907.
   297– 9   *C·*, N. H., January 10, 1908.
   299– 5   First Church . . . *C·*, N. H.,
   301–12   *C·*, N. H., March 22, 1899.
   309–19   situated in Bow and *C·*, N. H.
   327– 6   *C·*, N. H., October 16, 1903.
   335– 2   * formerly of *C·*, N. H.

---
† *Incorrect newspaper account, quoted as published.*

Concord
N. H.
   My. 346–16   * *C·*, N. H., Tuesday, April 30, 1901.
   351–20   *C·*, N. H., February 9, 1906.

   Mis. 251– 9   welcomed you to *C·* most graciously,
   Ret. 4– 5   adjoining towns of *C·* and Bow,
   5– 1   near *C·*, just across the bridge,
   5–10   eighteen miles from *C·*,
   7– 5   Hon. Isaac Hill, of *C·*,
   Pul. 24–22   * church is built of *C·* granite
   47–26   * so picturesque all about *C·*
   49–23   * do honor to that precinct of *C·*.
   49–24   * old farm on the road from *C·*,
   '02. 20–20   a pilgrimage to *C·* ?
   My. 122–15   in our good city of *C·*.
   145–15   Mr. George H. Moore of *C·*,
   148– 6   May the good folk of *C·*
   153– 2   Christian Scientists in *C·*
   153– 7   gospel ministry of my students in *C·*
   157– 4   * members of the *C·* church
   157–14   * of the same beautiful *C·* granite
   158– 6   chapter sub-title
   162–21   Scientists' church edifice in *C·* :
   164–10   gift to First Church . . . in *C·*,
   169– 1   chapter sub-title
   169–14   chapter sub-title
   170–10   minds of all present here in *C·*.
   171– 8   chapter sub-title
   171– 9   *C·* church is so nearly completed
   171–12   invite all . . . to come to *C·*,
   171–19   * heading
   173– 6   thank the citizens of *C·*
   173–15   our new church building in *C·*,
   175–11   say to the good folk of *C·*
   243–21   Your prompt presence in *C·*
   284–18   Since my residence in *C·*,
   346–10   * Soon after I reached *C·*

concord
   Mis. 116–18   gain of its sweet *c·*,
   333–23   what *c·* hath Christ with — *II Cor.* 6 : 15.

Concord Church
   My. 148– 9   chapter sub-title
   157– 2   * chapter sub-title

Concord Evening Monitor
   Pul. 85–20   * [*C· E· M·*, March 23, 1895]

Concord Monitor
   My. 157–18   * first announced in the *C· M·*

Concord* (N. H.) *Daily Patriot
   My. 284–10   [*C· (N.H.) D· P·*]

Concord* (N. H.) *Monitor
   My. 88– 9   * [*C· (N.H.) M·*]
   157– 1   * [*C· (N.H.) M·*]
   266–10   [*C· (N.H.) M·*, July, 1902]

Concord (N. H.) Street Fund
   My. 176– 4   towards the *C·* (*N.H.*) *S· F·*

Concord Publishing Company
   My. 298– 8   Miss Wilbur and the *C· P· C·*

Concord's
   My. 145– 4   one of *C·* best builders
   163–20   opportunity in *C·* quiet

Concord School of Philosophy
   Pul. 5–11   founder of the *C· S· of P·*

concourse
   Mis. 225– 3   *c·* of friends had gathered

concrete
   Mis. 82–20   Infinite progression is *c·* being,
   337–25   understood the *c·* character of
   Ret. 67– 6   Sin is both *c·* and abstract.
   My. 92–20   * so huge and *c·* a demonstration
   94– 5   * evidence appears in the *c·*

concur
   '02. 8– 4   The law and the gospel *c·*,

concurrence
   My. 148–16   and the father of our nation in *c·*.
   246–20   light and might of the divine *c·*

condemn
   Mis. 22–26   is incompetent to *c·* it;
   55– 1   and then, . . . *c·* the pupil
   126–22   Most people *c·* evil-doing,
   129– 3   or to *c·* his brother without **cause,**
   171–12   right action is not to *c·*
   '01. 15– 5   must *c·* the claim of error
   My. 249– 1   You may *c·* evil in the abstract
   249– 2   *c·* persons seldom, if ever.

condemnation
   Mis. 188–13   now no *c·* to them — *Rom.* 8 : 1.
   285– 5   because I had been personal in *c·*.
   300–14   does it spare you our Master's *c·* ?
   Ret. 14– 9   salvation and *c·* depended,
   Pan. 13–11   stern *c·* of all error,

condemnation

My. 18–19 stern *c·* of all error,
113–11 now no *c·* to them — *Rom.* 8 : 1.
205– 2 now no *c·* to them — *Rom.* 8 : 1.

condemned

Mis. 48– 5 should be conscientiously *c·*.
Man. 42–10 and justified or *c·*.
Un. 29– 3 Jewish law *c·* the sinner to death,
54–25 *c·* the knowledge of sin
No. 23– 3 personality that Jesus *c·* as
Hea. 2– 7 *c·* at every advancing footstep,
My. 196–14 shalt be *c·*.'' — *Matt.* 12 : 37.

condemneth

Ret. 94–18 he that *c·* not himself — *Rom.* 14 : 22.

condemning

Mis. 95– 6 * public letter *c·* her doctrines ;
Man. 40–13 prophesying, judging, *c·*,
93–13 reply to public topics *c·* C. S.,

condition

diseased
Ret. 40–14 said the diseased *c·* was caused by
every
Mis. 118– 6 Honesty in every *c·*,
'02. 9–14 Every *c·* implied by the
first
Mis. 109–18 Ignorance was the first *c·* of sin
194–30 first *c·* set forth in the text,
form the
Un. 52–26 The senses, . . . form the *c·* of
higher
Rud. 8–15 higher *c·* of thought and action.
inevitable
Mis. 127–21 inevitable *c·* whereby to become
its
Ret. 44–19 exciting cause of its *c·*,
mental
(*see* **mental**)
no
My. 149–32 canst be brought into no *c·*,
normal
Ret. 13–23 in a normal *c·* of health.
of mortality
Mis. 64–25 *put into this c· of mortality?*
of salvation
Mis. 192–26 making healing a *c·* of salvation,
of sin
Mis. 109–18 Ignorance was the first *c·* of sin
overcrowded
My. 56–11 * relieve the overcrowded *c·* of
56–25 * the overcrowded *c·* of
perplexed
Pul. 8– 6 Notwithstanding the perplexed *c·* of
present
Mis. 98– 3 whereby to improve his present *c·* ;
real
No. 5–23 normal and real *c·* of man,
spiritual
Un. 7–13 In the same spiritual *c·* I have
their
Mis. 371–13 he who deprecates their *c·*
this
Mis. 64–25 *into this c· of mortality?*
Pul. 79–28 * this *c·* can never long continue.
wretched
Mis. 52–15 wretched *c·* of human existence.

Mis. 193–31 The *c·* insisted upon is,
Pul. 53– 7 * *c·* which Jesus of Nazareth,
My. 318–18 on *c·* that I should not ask

conditional

My. 260–12 Nothing *c·* or material belongs to

conditioned

Mis. 64–28 wherefore man is thus *c·*,

conditions

aforesaid
My. 144– 7 either of the aforesaid *c·*
all
My. 260–26 appeals to all *c·*,
all the
Rud. 12–20 as caring for all the *c·*
My. 294–14 to control all the *c·*
certain
Pul. 29–21 * could, under certain *c·*, be
cerebral
My. 301–26 or affect cerebral *c·* in any manner
ethical
Mis. 297– 8 bases its work on ethical *c·*
fulfils the
Mis. 73–16 Belief fulfils the *c·* of a
fulfil the
Mis. 212– 1 to fulfil the *c·* of our
intermediate
No. 28– 7 intermediate *c·* — the purifying

conditions

its own
Rud. 11– 1 or . . . frame its own *c·*,
material
(*see* **material**)
mental
Mis. 91–15 types of these mental *c·*,
Un. 56–27 Such mental *c·* as ingratitude,
mortal
Un. 59–17 this conformity to mortal *c·* ;
of environment
Pul. 54–20 * *c·* of environment and harmonious
of matter
Pan. 4–10 depend on *c·* of matter,
of mortals
No. 22– 9 fail to improve the *c·* of mortals,
of salvation
Mis. 244–11 are the *c·* of salvation mental,
ordained
Mis. 244– 9 compliance to ordained *c·*.
other
My. 212–21 impossible under other *c·*,
requisite
Pul. 54–10 * *c·* requisite in psychic healing
Rud. 12–20 *c·* requisite for the well-being of man.
strict
Man. 110– 5 these seemingly strict *c·*
their
My. 250–22 its adaptability to their *c·*.
these
Mis. 73–17 these *c·* destroy the belief.
those
Mis. 244–10 those *c·* named in Genesis

My. 69–12 * where *c·* permitted it

condolence

My. 289–25 send a few words of *c·*,

conduct

Mis. 297–25 consequences of his own *c·* ;
301–27 a divine rule for human *c·*.
Man. 31–16 duty of the First Readers to *c·* the
53– 7 No Unchristian *C·*.
54–11 unjust and unmerciful *c·*
73–11 form and *c·* a C. S. organization
79–23 and *c·* the business of
81–20 Rule of *C·*.
86–14 *c·* the meetings of their association.
88–19 nor on their course or *c·*.
'00. 1–15 fast forming themselves into *c·*.
'02. 18–25 ignoble *c·* of his disciples
My. 71–26 * two Readers who *c·* the services
161–25 because one's thought and *c·*
223– 1 chapter sub-title

conducted

Mis. 44–10 *c·* by one who understands
314– 4 *c·* by Readers in lieu of pastors.
Man. 72– 9 church services *c·* by reading the
81–17 copyrighted and *c·* according to
My. 16–21 * *c·* by the First Reader,

conducting

My. 49–25 * mode of *c·* the church.''

confer

Mis. 262– 3 *c·* increased power to be good
272–23 * bestow no rights to *c· degrees.*
272–26 * with powers to *c·* diplomas
Man. 47– 9 to *c·* with an M.D. on Ontology,
70–18 *c·* on a statute of said State,
70–18 *c·* harmoniously on individual unity
88–20 students can *c·* with their teachers
My. 362–15 * to *c·* harmoniously and unitedly

conference

Man. 70–15 No *c·* of churches shall be held,
My. 207– 9 * in annual *c·* assembled,
208–23 chapter sub-title
208–25 God bless the . . . committees in *c·*

conferred

Mis. 90–27 this prerogative being *c·* by
272–16 * or authorizes to be *c·*,
Man. 67–15 personally *c·* with her
Ret. 78–23 the blessings otherwise *c·*,
My. 42–15 * the honor *c·* upon me.
245–30 *c·* by the President

conferring

My. 244– 8 prior to *c·* on any or all

confers

Mis. 272–15 * *c·*, or authorizes to be conferred,
Ret. 70– 1 *c·* animal names and natures
Un. 7–21 *c·* a power nothing else can.
'02. 17–24 what God gives, . . . *c·* happiness :
My. 154–11 not he . . . that *c·* the blessing,

confess
Mis. 281–15 come out and c· his faith,
My. 88–27 * stoutest enemies of C. S. will c·
285–25 this I c· unto thee, — Acts 24 ; 14.

confessed
Mis. 299–30 c· that they are the property of

confessedly
Un. 23–17 c· incompetent to speak.

confessing
Mis. 239–26 c· that she had something that she
344–10 On Justin's c· that he had not

confession
Man. 52–13 his c· of his error and
Pul. 30–11 * a brief "c· of faith,"
30–15 * The "c· of faith" includes
My. 42– 8 * " witnessed a good c·" — I Tim. 6 : 13.

confessions
Peo. 13–15 forcing . . . shameful c·,

confidence
Mis. 33–18 Patients naturally gain c· in
133–25 c· that He will reward
137–28 teach with increased c·.
229–20 The c· of mankind in
256– 7 acknowledging the public c·
257–17 suspicion where c· is due,
323–15 meets . . . attacks with serene c·.
Man. 46–13 shall hold in sacred c· all
Ret. 15– 7 In c· of faith, I could say
27–25 before gathering experience and c·
Pul. 3–11 Our surety is in our c·
21–25 abide in c· and hope.
Peo. 9–19 full c· in their efficacy,
My. 44–29 * unshaken c· in the unerring
137–27 because I had implicit c· in
208–25 their c· in His ways
332–23 * we had full c· that it would
340–25 tend to enhance their c·

confident
My. 21–25 * we are c· that they too
37–26 * c· and favorable expectation.
44–30 * and their c· assurance

confidently
My. 318–12 c· awaited the years to declare the

confine
Mis. 95–12 c· myself to questions and answers.
339– 2 If people would c· their talk to
Man. 73–24 shall not c· their membership to the

confined
Mis. 6–27 conversation chiefly c· to the
42–30 Mind is not c· to limits ;
60–21 c· and conformed to the Science of
150–25 God is universal ; c· to no spot,
189–29 not c· to the first century ;
Man. 99–11 church is not necessarily c· to
Pul. 65– 1 * not c· to its original apostles
No. 14–22 not c· to Jesus' students

confines
My. 37– 4 * sacred c· of this sanctuary.

confining
Un. 62–25 Mortal sense, c· itself to matter,

confirm
Mis. 13–20 what the shifting mortal senses c·
153– 3 God will c· His inheritance.
'02. 7–24 serves to c· C. S.
My. 319–13 * c· her statement regarding the

confirmation
Un. 57–20 Suffering was the c· of Paul's

confirms
Mis. 25–10 c· this conclusion.
192–24 as primitive Christianity c·.
Un. 36– 6 it unwittingly c· Truth,
'02. 8–14 c· the fact that God and Love are
My. 339–30 c· this conclusion.

conflict
Mis. xii– 7 above the smoke of c·
16–31 c· between the flesh and Spirit.
45–19 in a single instance decides the c·,
73– 7 materially, these passages c· ;
102–27 c· between sense and Soul.
105–12 Science would have no c· with Life
184– 4 Science and sense c·,
195–24 unequal to the c·,
214–14 The very c· his Truth brought,
246–20 c· more terrible than the battle of
Ret. 30– 2 I stood alone in this c·,
Un. 39–28 Science and material sense c·
'00. 10– 5 C· and persecution are the truest
10– 8 Such c· never ends till
'02. 3–19 close of the c· in South Africa ;
Po. 77–12 joy and tears, c· and rest,

conflict
My. 306– 3 into a c· for fame.
358– 8 whereby the c· against Truth
361– 8 into a personal c·.

conflicting
No. 2–27 c· theories and practice.
My. 134– 9 c· elements must be mastered.
293–13 c· states of the human mind,

conflicts
Mis. 260– 2 By c·, defeats, and triumphs,
'01. 27–28 * people say it c· with the Bible.
'02. 12–14 c· not at all with another
My. 103– 3 severest c· of the ages
304–26 * people say it c· with the Bible.

conform
Mis. 114–10 Teachers must c· strictly to the
Un. 59–20 to which he seemed to c· :

conformed
Mis. 21–23 c· to the text of the
60–21 c· to the Science of being.
127–15 it will be c· to a fitness
My. 18–12 c· to a fitness to receive
221–21 Our Master c· to this law,

conforming
Mis. 138– 6 detail of c· to society,
Man. 62– 2 the offertory c· to the time

conformity
Mis. 315–28 educate their students in c· to
Man. 72– 7 to form a church in c· with
83–19 in c· with the unerring laws of God,
Un. 59–16 this c· to mortal conditions ;

confounded
Mis. 4–21 in many minds it is c· with
No. 27–18 the two should not be c·.
My. 17–16 shall not be c·." — I Pet. 2 : 6.
245–16 Babel of confusion worse c·,

confounding
Rud. 7–27 thus confusing and c· the

confront
Pul. 2–25 The enemy we c· would
My. 229–24 Heaps upon heaps of praise c· me,

confronted
My. 214–21 I was c· with the fact that I

confronting
My. 266– 3 imminent dangers c· the

confronts
Mis. 346– 7 c· each generation anew.
346– 8 It c· C. S.

Confucius
No. 21– 6 C· and Plato but dimly discerned,

confuse
My. 211–25 into his mind, fret and c· it,
218–18 tends to c· the mind of

confused
My. 170– 8 should not be c· with other

confusing
Rud. 7–27 thus c· and confounding the

confusion
Man. 110– 4 c· that might result therefrom.
My. 38– 9 * was no c· in finding seats,
245–15 Babel of c· worse confounded,

confutes
Mis. 363–26 c· the astronomer, exposes the

congenial
My. 87– 8 * pleasant, c·, quietly happy,

congratulate
'02. 4– 5 I cordially c· our Board
My. 24– 4 * We c· you that the building
87–15 * c· these comfortable acquaintances
154–16 permit me to c· this little church
184– 9 to c· the Christian Scientists
196– 3 I c· you upon erecting
204–17 I c· you tenderly on the
208–18 I c· you on the prospect of
270– 9 the leading editors . . . c· me ;

congratulated
My. 87–17 * Boston is to be c· upon the
309–11 bowed to my father and c· him.

congratulation
Pul. 44– 8 * receive this brief message of c·.

congratulations
Pul. 44– 6 * I send my hearty c·.
My. 62–20 * send you loving greetings and c·
63–18 * even the greetings and c· of
197–27 I send loving c·,
234– 3 writing or reading c· ?
281–20 * expression of c· and views
285– 5 and accept my hearty c·.

congratulatory
Man. 67–20 sending gifts, *c·* despatches

congregate
My.   29–27 * thousands who began to *c·*
       289–11 should upon this solemn occasion *c·* ;

congregation
Mis. 150–13 dwelleth in the *c·* of the faithful,
       314–10 repeat in concert with the *c·*
       314–17 alternately in response to the *c·*,
       322– 9 present to address this *c·*,
Ret. 15–17 The *c·* so increased in number
        15–28 agreeably informed the *c·*
Pul. 29–10 * a *c·* whose remarkable earnestness
        29–27 * I was told that almost the entire *c·*
        30– 4 * enticing a separate *c·*
        41–30 * At 9 a. m. the first *c·* gathered.
        43–16 * hymn, . . . was sung by the *c·*.
        45–30 * elected each year by the *c·*.
        55–24 * Boston *c·* was organized
        59–11 * singing by a choir and *c·*.
        59–13 * *c·* repeating one sentence
        68–15 * C. S. *c·* was organized
        68–24 * The Baltimore *c·* was organized
        74– 7 * pastor of the C. S. *c·*
My.   29– 6 * rising in unison from the vast *c·*,
        31–27 * *c·* had taken their seats,
        32– 4 * *c·* began to repeat the
        35–28 * read to the *c·* the . . . Message
        54–26 * large *c·* was present.
        55–28 * *c·* worshipped in Copley Hall
        78–19 * *c·* knelt in silent communion,
        78–21 * *c·* singing in perfect unison.
        81– 3 * prosperity of the great *c·*.
        97–18 * evidently wealthy *c·*
       188–12 your tabernacle of the *c·*
       249–30 thought which spiritualizes the *c·*.

Congregational
Ret. 13– 1 admitted to the *C·* . . . Church,
Pul. 29– 4 * formerly been *C·* clergymen.
No.   44–24 Rev. S. E. Herrick, a *C·* clergyman
My. 182– 1 Chicago had few *C·* churches.

Congregational Church
Mis. 178– 2 the *C· C·*.
Ret.   5– 4 first *C· C·* in Pembroke.
'01. 31–21 my early culture in the *C· C·* ;
My. 174–23 I was a member of the *C· C·*
       182– 4 I received from the *C· C·*
       311–13 I joined the Tilton *C· C·*

Congregationalist
'01. 32– 4 Rev. Corban Curtis, *C·* ;

Congregationalists
'01. 32– 2 of Concord, N. H., *C·* ;

congregations
Man. 42– 3 offered for the *c·* collectively
Pul. 40–17 * presence of four different *c·*,
        41–21 * four vast *c·* filled the church
        55–29 * members of different *c·*
My.   8–30 * one hundred and five new . . . *c·*
        30–12 * In those huge *c·* were
        30–21 * having been through the *c·*,
        85– 8 * its *c·* meet in Europe and in
        91–31 * *c·* in every important town

Congress and **congress**
Ret.   7– 1 nomination to *C·* on a majority vote
Pan. 14–16 give to our *c·* wisdom,
Po.   vi–20 *resolution in C· prohibiting*
My. 278–13 President and *C·* of our favored land
       310– 7 was nominated for *C·*,

congressman
Mis. 253– 9 the speakers . . . one a *c·*

conical
Mis. 347– 6 A *c·* cloud, hanging like a

conjectural
Mis. 290–22 *c·* and misapprehensive !

conjecture's
Pan. 12–27 unpierced by bold *c·* sharp point,

conjectures
Un.   28–14 than ordinary material *c·*,
My. 346–22 * Various *c·* having arisen

conjoined
'01. 23–29 * *c·* by the operations of the

conjugal
Mis. 289–26 Science touches the *c·* question
       289–27 Can the bill of *c·* rights be fairly

conjugality
Mis. 285–23 may conjure up a new-style *c·*,
       285–29 the *rôle* of a superfine *c·* ;

conjure
Mis. 285–22 may *c·* up a new-style conjugality,
Un.   60– 8 and then *c·* up, from the dark

Conn. (State)
     (*see* **Bridgeport, Hartford, New Haven, New London**)

connected
Mis. 278– 9 in my history as *c·* with the
       309–20 and whatever is *c·* therewith,
Man. 27–24 and of other literature *c·* therewith.
        74–14 nor in rooms *c·* therewith.
        81– 8 shall in no manner be *c·* with
        82– 5 are in no manner *c·* with these
Ret.   3– 4 *c·* with Capt. John Lovewell
         6–17 ever *c·* with that institution.
         8– 1 events *c·* with my childhood
        24– 4 in no wise *c·* with this event,
        45–18 Association *c·* with my College
Un.   47– 3 Nowhere in Scripture is evil *c·* with
Pul. 59–25 * gentlemen officially *c·* with the
'01. 23–28 * phenomena *c·* by association
My. 125–12 Board of Lectureship *c·* with The
       175– 4 organizations *c·* therewith,
       321– 3 * in a way *c·* with your work,

connecting
Mis. 393– 3 Nature, with the mind *c·*,
Po.   51– 8 Nature, with the mind *c·*,

connection
Mis.   x–27 in *c·* with my published works.
        60–23 *what is the c· between*
       127– 3 Throughout my entire *c·* with
       300– 4 compiling them in *c·* with
       310–18 one's *c·* with this church,
Man. 65– 7 used in *c·* with C. S.
Ret. 13– 3 In *c·* with this event,
        15– 3 My *c·* with this religious body
Un.   7–19 in *c·* with these experiences ;
Pul. 86–27 * in *c·* with the Bible.
Pan.   7–18 in *c·* with the original text
'02. 15–12 *c·* between justice and being
        20–19 breaking any seeming *c·* between
Hea. 18– 8 no *c·* between Spirit and matter.
My.   17–31 Throughout my entire *c·* with
        27–25 * in *c·* with the extension of
       100– 1 * brought out in *c·* with the
       112–26 S. and H. in *c·* with the Bible.
       200–28 *c·* with its divine Principle,
       311–22 in *c·* with her own family
       315– 2 is of interest in this *c·* :
       321–22 * my *c·* with the church,

connects
My. 205–19 This idealism *c·* itself with

conquer
Mis.   6–20 we *c·* sickness, sin, and death.
        40–30 requires more . . . to *c·* this sin
       163– 1 to *c·* the three-in-one of error :
       235– 4 to *c·* sin, sickness, and death ;
Un.   18–24 and thus I *c·* death ;
'00.   9–18 before he can *c·* others.
My. 125– 2 Have you learned to *c·* sin,

conquered
Mis. 74–28 He met and *c·* the resistance of
Pul. 83–16 * Amazons who *c·* the invincibles,
No.   35–10 *c·* also the drear subtlety of death.
        36–23 nor could he have *c·* the malice
'00.   9–17 and he must have *c·* himself
My.   43– 3 * that wilderness must be *c·*.

conquering
Ret. 49–16 *c·* all that is unlike Christ

conqueror
'02. 19–15 happier than the *c·* of a world.

conquerors
Mis. 176–17 not as the flying nor as *c·*,

conquers
Mis. 126–13 sustains us, and finally *c·*
       135–10 *c·* all opposition, surmounts all
'01. 13–20 fear, unconquered, *c·* him.

conquest
Pul. 12–18 mighty *c·* over all sin?
My. 127–28 it is not . . . surrendered in *c·*,
       192–11 *c·* over sin and mortality,

conscience (*see also* **conscience'**)
Mis. 43–23 at the expense of his *c·*,
       146–20 I cannot be the *c·* for this church ;
       147–16 Truth and the voice of his *c·*
       176–24 true freedom, in the rights of *c·*.
       228–16 just person, faithful to *c·*
       236–12 but you have the rights of *c·*,
       237–11 such a cup of gall that *c·* strikes
       237–16 is not essentially one of *c·* :
       246–17 to shackle *c·*, stop free speech,
       299–30 but does this silence your *c·* ?
       339–27 surge dolefully at the door of *c·*,
Un.   5–19 Let us respect the rights of *c·*
        25– 3 stultify my intellect, insult my *c·*,

conscience

Pul.	10– 3	that raised the deadened *c·*,
	10–12	they planted . . . the rights of *c·*,
No.	44–15	and so abrogate the rights of *c·*
'01.	33–15	allowed the rights of *c·*
'02.	18– 1	at the temple gate of *c·*,
Peo.	13–14	putting man to the rack for his *c·*,
My.	118–24	should come from *c·*.
	124– 4	to every man's *c·*." — *II Cor.* 4*:* 2.
	128–16	dictates of his own rational *c·*
	160–25	even the fire of a guilty *c·*,
	168– 3	the dictates of enlightened *c·*,
	187–13	and of a good *c·*, — *I Tim.* 1*:* 5.
	197– 3	which is least distinct to *c·*.
	220–31	should share alike liberty of *c·*,
	222–27	liberty of *c·* held sacred.

conscience'

Mis. 261–28	for *c·* sake, one will either

consciences

Mis. 274–22	those quill-drivers whose *c·*

conscientious

Mis.	80–12	cultured and *c·* medical men,
	147–23	the *c·* man of business,
	220–22	to the *c·* Christian Scientist
	340–20	The *c·* are successful.
	375–18	* *c·* application to detail,
Ret.	48– 5	*c·* scruples about diplomas,
Un.	25–21	Evil is not conscious or *c·* Mind ;
	31–16	Hence my *c·* position,
Pul.	51– 5	* a number of *c·* followers
No.	v– 7	hearts of all *c·* laborers
	2–18	is modest . . . *c·* in duty,
	9– 7	more *c·* in their convictions ;
Peo.	6– 6	* "I declare my *c·* belief,
My.	112–26	result of his *c·* study
	213–10	*c·* in their desire to do right

conscientiously

Mis.	48– 5	should be *c·* condemned.
	146– 6	I cannot *c·* lend my
	262–14	who are at work *c·*
	365–31	it must be *c·* understood
Ret.	55– 2	enter . . . and work *c·*.
Rud.	14– 5	and then *c· earn their wages*,
No.	11–14	understood and *c·* introduced.

conscious

Mis.	42– 7	still in a *c·* state of existence ;
	42–12	but by a *c·* union with God.
	42–15	same plane of *c·* existence
	73– 1	or that God is *c·* of it.
	103–15	true substance, because eternally *c·*,
	219–29	a good sense, or *c·* goodness,
	283–18	*c·* trespass on the rights of mortals.
	283–25	*c·*, meanwhile, that God worketh
	363– 1	the more *c·* it becomes of
Ret.	61– 8	actually *c·* of the truth of C. S.,
	64–24	scientific to abide in *c·* harmony,
Un.	4–17	if God be *c·* of it?
	13–13	If God could be *c·* of sin,
	18–24	to be ever *c·* of Life
	18–25	is to be never *c·* of death.
	24–24	becomes *c·*, and is able to see,
	25–16	honors *c·* human individuality
	25–21	Evil is not *c·* or conscientious
	36–23	to say that the divine Mind is *c·* of
	36–23	yet is not *c·* of matter,
	44–22	[you shall be *c·* matter],
	45–13	teaching that matter can be *c·* ;
	45–14	*c·* matter implies pantheism.
	45–28	Matter is not truly *c·*,
	48–13	as infinite and *c·* Life,
	48–19	I believe that of which I am *c·*
	50–24	Matter and evil cannot be *c·*,
	56–19	Their *c·* being was not fully exempt
	57–28	The only *c·* existence in the flesh
	64– 5	*c·* of only health, holiness, and
	64– 7	which is *c·* of sickness, sin, and
Pul.	13– 8	*c·* of the supremacy of Truth,
No.	17–10	*c·* of aught but good.
	19–14	gratefully and lovingly *c·* of
	36– 6	Jesus' true and *c·* being
	36–13	was *c·* only of God,
	36–17	*c·* reality and royalty of his
	36–21	Had he been as *c·* of these
'01.	23–30	* nothing more than *c·* experience.
	24– 1	* Matter apart from *c·* mind
'02.	8–30	*c·* that God is his Father,
	17–24	*c·* worth satisfies the hungry heart,
My.	221–26	since matter is not *c·* ;
	294–18	*c·* understanding of omnipotence,
	349–15	*c·* of the allness of God

consciously

Mis.	212–24	If, *c·* or unconsciously, one is
Ret.	81–19	is *c·* untrue to the light,
'00.	8– 5	exhales *c·* and unconsciously his

consciousness

accompanying

Mis. 189–23	accompanying *c·* of spiritual **power**

affectional

Ret. 81–12	spiritual sense, affectional *c·*,

all

Ret.	56–18	All *c·* is Mind,
Un.	4–16	we lose all *c·* of error,
	24– 3	proceedeth all Mind, all *c·*,
	24–12	All *c·* is Mind ;
No.	10–18	all *c·* is Mind and eternal,

and life

Un.	36– 1	evidence of *c·* and life
My.	203– 6	distinct in our *c·* and life,

any other

Mis. 179– 9	any other *c·* than that of good?

awakened

Mis.	16–24	awakened *c·* is wholly spiritual ;
No.	40– 9	pure pearls of awakened *c·*,
'00.	15–18	feast for this awakened *c·*.
My.	257– 7	To the awakened *c·*, the Bethlehem

being, or

Un. 3–21	and is perfect being, or *c·*.

change of

Un. 11–11	demanded a change of *c·*

disk of

Ret. 94–15	blemish on the disk of *c·*

divine

(*see* **divine**)

diviner

Mis. 96–13	ascends the scale . . . to diviner *c·*,

evil in

Un. 49–14	So long as I hold evil in *c·*,

existence or

Un. 47– 5	false claim to existence or *c·*.

false

Mis.	222– 6	This state of false *c·*
	298–30	false *c·* does not change the **fact**,
Un.	52–10	false *c·* of both good and

falsity of

Un. 35–27	outlined falsity of *c·*,

finite

Un.	24–10	*Evil.* I am a finite *c·*,
	24–13	and not a finite *c·*.
	24–16	There is . . . no finite *c·*.

force the

Mis. 288–18	to force the *c·* of scientific

glorified

Un. 49–12	a glorified *c·* of the only

His

No. 17–25	would be a part of His *c·*.

his

Mis. 352–24	his *c·* is the reflection of the **divine**,

His own

No. 16–21	no . . . inference but His own *c·*,

his own

Mis.	302– 6	preserves in his own *c·*
My.	161–15	within his own *c·*,
	364–10	excludes from his own *c·*,

human

(*see* **human**)

idea in

My. 263– 1	spiritual idea in *c·*,

identity or

Mis. 205–17	man's identity or *c·* reflects **only**

individual

Un.	8–12	individual *c·* is permanent.
	21–13	individual *c·* and existence.
	21–17	Individual *c·* in man is
	24–14	reflected in individual *c·*,
'01.	1–12	rise . . . higher in the individual *c·*
My.	42–24	* unfolds in each individual *c·*
	44–10	* has come to individual *c·* ;

individual in

My. 119– 9	individual in *c·* — in Mind,

infinite

Mis. 258–24	infinite *c·*, ever-presence,
No. 37– 6	eternal God and infinite *c·*

in Science

My. 117– 9	divine order and *c·* in Science,

interchange of

No. 14– 6	can be no interchange of *c·*,

is Mind

Ret.	56–18	All *c·* is Mind,
Un.	24–12	All *c·* is Mind ;
No.	10–18	all *c·* is Mind and eternal,

left to

'02. 7–14	nothing is left to *c·* but Love,

material

Mis.	179–28	We must lay aside material *c·*,
Un.	42– 6	results of material *c·* ;
	42– 6	material *c·* can have no real

mental

Ret. 94–13	no matter, to the mental *c·*.

misguide

'01. 20–16	bewilder, darken, or misguide *c·*,

consciousness

misled
  Mis. 222–12   In this state of misled *c·*,

mode of
  Un. 8– 6   What you see, . . . is a mode of *c·*,

modes and
  Mis. 268– 1   materializes human modes and *c·*,

mortal
  Un. 61– 3   belong to mortal *c·*.
  Po. 35– 5   mortal *c·* Which binds to earth

my
  Mis. 222–31   Truth had flowed into my *c·*
  My. 270–11   nearer my *c·* than before,

no
  Mis. 259– 9   no *c·* or knowledge of evil ;
  Un. 3–24   no *c·* of anything unlike Himself ;
  21–15   With Him is no *c·* of evil,
  No. 36–22   no *c·* of human error,

of corporeality
  Mis. 309–19   The *c·* of corporeality,

of disease
  Mis. 308–26   holding in mind the *c·* of disease

of ease
  Mis. 219–18   *c·* of ease and loss of suffering ;

of error
  Un. 4–14   lose our own *c·* of error.
  4–16   we lose all *c·* of error,

of evil
  Un. 21–15   With Him is no *c·* of evil,
  50–19   The less *c·* of evil . . . mortals have,

of God
  Mis. 352–11   quickens the true *c·* of God,
  '02. 8–30   *c·* of God as Love gives man power

of good
  Mis. 9– 1   *c·* of good, grace, and peace,
  259– 9   *c·* of good has no . . . knowledge of

of harmony
  Rud. 11–15   absolute *c·* of harmony

of health
  Mis. 311–17   to gain the abiding *c·* of health,
  My. 349– 4   health is a *c·* of health,

of heaven
  My. 118–28   *c·* of heaven within us

of Life
  Un. 41– 3   true knowledge and *c·* of Life,

of light
  No. 30–22   *c·* of light is like the

of Mind
  My. 131–31   I say with the *c·* of Mind

of sickness
  Mis. 179–16   Have we left the *c·* of sickness

of the unreality
  Rud. 11–13   *c·* of the unreality of pain

of Truth
  My. 63–13   * our expanding *c·* of Truth,

old
  Mis. 179–12   This is the old *c·*.
  179–22   old *c·* of Soul in sense.

one
  No. 38–20   Having one God, one Mind, one *c·*,

our
  Mis. 179– 8   Is our *c·* in matter or in God?
  179–11   We are wrong if our *c·* is in sin,
  290–24   it should not, to our *c·*,
  My. 203– 6   distinct in our *c·* and life,

patient's
  Mis. 219–18   change his patient's *c·* of dis-ease
  220–17   changed his patient's *c·* from

perfect
  No. 31–18   until a perfect *c·* is attained.

plane of
  Pul. 38–19   * entirely different a plane of *c·*

pure
  Un. 57–14   His pure *c·* was discriminating,

real
  Rud. 5–18   Soul is the only real *c·*

realm and
  No. 21–17   mingle in the same realm and *c·*.

rise in
  My. 116– 3   endeavor to rise in *c·*

roused
  Ret. 31–15   acting . . . on my roused *c·*,

same
  Mis. 364–27   it has the same *c·*,

sensation and
  Mis. 228–23   perception, sensation, and *c·*
  360–23   spiritual sensation and *c·*.

sense and
  Mis. 219–28   change this evil sense and *c·*

sense or
  Mis. 93–29   a sinning sense or *c·*
  Un. 7–24   the sense or *c·* of sin,

sensual
  Un. 9– 5   Material and sensual *c·* are

silences
  Mis. 198– 9   *c·* silences the mortal claim

consciousness

spiritual
  Un. 23–25   good and spiritual *c·*
  35–24   Spirit is *spiritual c·* alone.
  35–25   spiritual *c·* can form nothing unlike

spiritualize
  No. 11–27   spiritualize *c·* with the dictum and

stages of
  Un. 50–16   states or stages of *c·*,

state of
  Mis. 219–25   state of *c·* made manifest
  367–22   evil is a different state of *c·*.
  '02. 9–16   urging a state of *c·* that

supercilious
  '00. 15–12   supercilious *c·* that saith

supreme in
  My. 205–20   makes God more supreme in *c·*,

temporary
  Un. 4– 7   To gain a temporary *c·* of

their
  Mis. 267– 3   steadfast in their *c·* of the

the only
  Un. 21–20   and this is the only *c·*

this
  Mis. 180– 4   through this *c·*, I was delivered
  278– 8   There is great joy in this *c·*,
  Un. 24–13   This *c·* is reflected in
  My. 258–27   this *c·* of God's dear love

true
  Mis. 298–25   true *c·* is the true health.
  352–11   quickens the true *c·* of God,
  Un. 4–13   God is all true *c·* ;

untrue
  '02. 6–14   a false claim, an untrue *c·*,

without
  Mis. 47–11   without *c·* of its weight

your own
  '01. 1–23   define God to your own *c·*

  Mis. 205–20   individual Spirit-substance and *c·*
  330–12   *c·* thereof is here and now
  352–32   the *c·* be allowed to rejoice
  Ret. 56–21   claims to be mind, or *c·*,
  69–26   *C·*, where art thou?
  Un. 50–22   a *c·* which is without Mind
  50–24   *c·* should not be evil.
  '01. 30– 8   *c·* which is most imbued
  '02. 7– 6   category of creation or *c·*.
  My. 349– 4   a *c·* gained through Christ,

consecrate
  Mis. 5– 6   willing to *c·* themselves to this
  109–27   *c·* one's life anew.
  Hea. 5–26   elevate, and *c·* man;
  My. 36–10   * *c.* all that we are or hope to be
  187–22   to *c·* your beautiful temple

consecrated
  Mis. x– 2   *c·* life wherein dwelleth peace,
  177–15   become real and *c·* warriors
  318–22   a devout, *c·* Christian.
  350–30   My life, *c·* to humanity
  354–17   character subdued, a life *c·*,
  Man. 55–20   consistent, *c·* Christian Scientist.
  Ret. 47–25   good Bible scholar and a *c·* Christian.
  95– 6   * That thou may'st *c·* be
  Pul. 32–27   * a saintly and *c·* character.
  My. 28–19   * *c·* leadership of Mrs. Eddy,

consecrates
  Mis. 8–19   sanctifies, and *c·* human life,
  252–26   *c·* and inspires the teacher

consecrating
  Mis. 291–26   refreshing, and *c·* mankind.

consecration
  Mis. 177– 3   an absolute *c·* to the greatest
  Pul. 30–30   * its *c·* service on January 6
  59– 5   * sentence or prayer of *c·*,
  85– 2   * devotion and *c·* to God
  My. 41–28   * through long years of *c·*
  46–23   * pledge ourselves to a deeper *c·*,

consecutive
  Man. 68–14   remain with her three *c·* years,
  91–25   diplomas are for three *c·* years
  Ret. 6–27   faithfully for two *c·* years.

consecutively
  Man. 68– 5   to remain . . . three years *c·*.

consent
  Mis. 77– 7   and *c·* to that infinite demand
  83–13   with the *c·* of his own belief.
  113–14   depths of perdition by his own *c·*.
  119–27   Would you *c·* that others should tear
  228–28   Common *c·* is contagious,
  282– 8   without their knowledge or *c·*?
  283– 6   without his knowledge or *c·*,
  289–22   except by mutual *c·*.

consent

Mis.	289–25	by mutual *c·*, . . . she may win
	297–22	by mutual *c·* of both parties,
	300–17	When I *c·* to this act,
	301– 3	without the author's *c·*,
	301–22	and read it publicly *without my c·*.
	349– 1	received my *c·* and even the offer of
Man.	26–10	the *c·* of the Pastor Emeritus
	27–10	the written *c·* of said Board.
	30– 9	the *c·* of the Pastor Emeritus,
	43– 1	without her or their *c·*
	50–10	the *c·* of the Board of Directors.
	53–13	unnecessarily and without her *c·*,
	57–15	the *c·* of this Board and the
	67– 9	without her written *c·*.
	68– 7	without the Directors' *c·*
	76–20	the *c·* of the Pastor Emeritus.
	78–10	written *c·* of the Pastor Emeritus.
	81– 3	the *c·* of the Pastor Emeritus
	82– 9	without her knowledge or written *c·*.
	87– 4	*c·* of the authority of their Church.
	97–11	the *c·* of the Pastor Emeritus
	103– 7	written *c·* of the Pastor Emeritus,
	104–11	written *c·* of its author.
	105– 4	written *c·* of Mary Baker Eddy,
Ret.	71–10	without the *c·* or knowledge of
	71–16	if he would *c·* to this ;
	88–24	without the *c·* of the stated occupant
Pan.	8– 1	or by the *c·* of Mind !
My.	15– 9	written *c·* of the Pastor Emeritus,
	61–24	* the human mind was giving its *c·*.
	247– 4	the common *c·* of the governed,
	254–25	the common *c·* of the governed,
	255– 5	churches have my *c·* to publish
	302–16	But without my *c·*, the use of
	356–16	nor *c·* to have my picture issued,

consented

Man.	64–19	afterward *c·* on the ground that
My.	164– 3	demand increased, and I *c·*,
	284–22	I *c·* thereto only as other
	318–17	he *c·* on condition that I
	320– 4	* he readily *c·* to assist me,

consents

'00.	4– 4	unwittingly *c·* to many minds

consequence

Pan.	8–28	and dying in *c·* of it.
My.	56– 4	* in *c·* two services were held,

consequences

Mis.	108–16	mortals' ignorance and its *c·*,
	109–21	knowledge of sin and its *c·*,
	297–24	count the *c·* of his own conduct ;
Pul.	14–17	and never fear the *c·*.
No.	17– 3	He must produce its *c·*.
'02.	6–13	God made neither evil nor its *c·*.

consequent

Mis.	26–24	God's *c·* is the spiritual cosmos.
	337–18	*c·* disaffection for all evil,
No.	6–11	the *c·* cure of the sick,
	16–28	Death is the *c·* of an
'01.	6–18	its *c·* Christianity is consistent
My.	266–13	*c·* vacancies occurring in the

consequently

Mis.	31–12	*c·* to the lack of faith in good.
Ret.	6–22	He was *c·* admitted to the bar
	59– 3	*c·* a mortal mind and soul
	68–23	*c·* no transference of mortal thought
Un.	34–12	*c·* there is no matter.
Pul.	46– 4	* *C·* the new rules were formulated.
No.	17– 7	*c·* it is impossible for the true man
My.	14–16	* *c·* further payments or

conservation

My.	226– 7	*c·* of number in geometry,

conservative

Mis.	226–30	*c·* swindler, who sells himself
My.	345–24	*c·* about advice on surgical cases."

conservators

Pul.	82–12	* *c·* of the world's morals

consider

Mis.	31– 1	*c· to be mental malpractice?*
	65–14	not *c·* the false side of existence
	131–19	just to *c·* the great struggles with
	297–25	will *c·* the effects, on himself
Chr.	55–13	neither *c·* the operation — *Isa.* 5 : 12.
Ret.	22– 9	" *C·* him that endured — *Heb.* 12 : 3.
	50–12	if they *c·* three hundred dollars
	83–28	when we *c·* the necessity of
Pul.	39– 9	poem that I *c·* superbly sweet
	49– 3	* *c·* her their spiritual Leader
No.	28–15	The proof . . . I *c·* well established.
'02.	4–22	*c·* these two commandments
My.	138– 4	I *c·* this agreement a great benefit
	196–20	" *C·* him that endured — *Heb.* 12 : 3.

consider

My.	223–15	do not *c·* myself capable of
	227–16	*c·* well their ability to cope with
	236–27	I *c·* the information there given
	237– 6	I do not *c·* a precedent for

considerable

Pul.	64– 5	* There is usually *c·* difficulty in
My.	66– 5	* *c·* activity has been going on
	74– 5	* will bring *c·* numbers of

consideration

Mis.	13–10	urge upon the solemn *c·*
	133– 9	*c·* to the following Scripture,
	134–17	Let no *c·* bend or outweigh
	136– 9	brought to your earnest *c·*,
	247– 4	*proofs* . . . be allowed due *c·*,
	350– 8	subject given out for *c·*
	350–19	the *c·* of these two topics,
Ret.	88–17	leads inevitably to a *c·* of
'01.	33– 1	piety was the all-important *c·*
My.	54–28	* *c·* of places for meeting
	85–29	* Aside from every other *c·*,
	297– 4	in *c·* of all that Miss Barton
	360–10	In *c·* of the present momentous

considerations

Mis.	317–19	These *c·* prompt my answers
Ret.	48– 9	all these *c·* moved me to
No.	7– 4	No personal *c·* should allow
'01.	30–20	destroying all lower *c·*.

considered

Mis.	289–15	This fact should be duly *c·*
	378– 3	A patient *c·* incurable left that
Man.	44– 1	spirit . . . shall be definitely *c·*.
	53–14	it shall be *c·* an offense.
	53–22	shall be *c·* a sufficient evidence
	71–16	no Church . . . shall be *c·* loyal that
	99– 4	*c·* as though it were two States,
Un.	8– 1	Let another query now be *c·*,
	57– 3	Anatomically *c·*, the design of
Rud.	5–10	*c·* apart from Mind.
'02.	5–13	God must be intelligently *c·*
	15–17	My husband, . . . was *c·* wealthy,
My.	54–17	* different places were *c·*,
	55– 6	* Several places were *c·*,
	259–23	occasions, *c·* either collectively
	314– 7	*c·* a rarely skilful dentist.
	319–27	* I *c·* the time an important

considering

Mis.	92– 1	*c·* the necessity for
	271–15	*c·* a subject that is unworthy
My.	319–18	* *c·* the questions which have

consign

Mis.	350–27	which *c·* people to suffering.

consigned

My.	273–27	at length they are *c·* to dust.

consigning

Ret.	90–17	*c·* them to the care of nurse

consigns

Mis.	293–28	*c·* sensibility to the charnel-house

consist

Mis.	315–13	class shall *c·* of not over
Man.	25– 5	The Church officers shall *c·* of
	26–20	Board of Directors shall *c·* of
	63– 5	The next lessons *c·* of
	64– 5	literature sold . . . shall *c·* only of
	76–16	shall *c·* of three members of
	79– 4	shall *c·* of not less than three
	84– 9	class shall *c·* of not more than
	97– 5	*c·* of one loyal Christian Scientist
	99–25	Committees on . . . shall *c·* of men
Pul.	45–28	* sermons hereafter will *c·* of

consisted

'00.	13–22	The Pergamene church *c·* of
My.	34–14	* The Lesson-Sermon *c·* of

consistencies

Rud.	7– 5	conceptions and *c·* of C. S.

consistency

'01.	26– 1	unity and *c·* of Jesus' theory
My.	214–16	letters questioning the *c·* of

consistent

Mis.	191–21	destroys all *c·* supposition of
	223–15	disbelieves in . . . and is *c·*.
	312– 4	Love is *c·*, uniform,
Man.	55–20	*c·*, consecrated Christian Scientist.
'01.	6–19	*c·* with Christ's hillside sermon,
Hea.	4–28	*c·* with our inconsistent statement
My.	vii–11	* *c·* and constant right thinking
	94–10	* steady, *c·* growth of the sect
	291–17	uniform, *c·*, sympathetic,

consistently

Mis.	105–13	if this sense were *c·* sensible.
'01.	4–24	Scientists *c·* conceive of God as One

consistently
'01. 7– 1 c· conceivable as the personality of
7–14 c· say, "Our Father-Mother God"
My. 313–20 I have always c· declared

consisting
Mis. 132–16 c· in part of dictating answers
Man. 88– 7 c· of three members,
102– 4 c· of not less than three members,
My. 80–17 * services were identical, c· of

consists
Un. 4–23 "life eternal" c· in— John 17 : 3.
22– 3 this likeness c· in a sense of
Pul. 38– 8 * It c· of fourteen chapters,
'02. 17–22 Happiness c· in being . . . good ;
Peo. 6–12 * "The art of medicine c· in
My. 108–11 c· in this forcible fact :

consolation
Un. 17–12 c· from borrowed scintillations.
My. 38– 3 * in God is all c· and comfort,
283–27 C· and peace are based on
290–13 for your support, c·, and victory.

console
Mis. 131– 8 let the leaner sort c· this brother's
275–18 c· the innocent, and throw wide the
Un. 18–13 in order to c· it.
18–14 you oftenest c· others in
'02. 19– 3 hastened to c· his unfaithful

consolidate
Man. 72–18 shall c· under one church

consolidating
My. 200– 3 c· the genius of C. S.

consoling
Mis. 327–24 c· their afflictions, and helping

consonance
Mis. 364– 1 c· with the textbook of C. S.
Man. 51– 2 in c· with the Scriptural demand
72–23 in c· with The Mother Church Manual.
Ret. 93– 7 in c· with their Principle.

consonant
My. 277–16 Killing men is not c· with

conspicuous
Mis. 83–21 meekness was as c· as
My. 272–26 * and leads with such c· success

conspicuously
My. 85–13 * it is c· manifest.
356– 3 where God dwells most c·

conspiracy
Mis. 177– 6 leagued together in secret c·
Ret. 63– 6 nothing but a c· against man's
63–18 feel bound to expose this c·,
'02. 1–11 combined in formidable c·,

conspirator
My. 128–25 as effectually as does a subtle c· ;

conspire
Ret. 78–22 to c· against the blessings

conspires
Peo. 11–27 Scientific guessing c· unwittingly

constancy
Po. page 3 poem
My. 37–14 * c· of your obedience during

constant
Mis. 115–16 c· watchfulness and prayer
147–14 one who makes it his c· rule
236–15 yielding to c· solicitations
241–15 c· combat and direful struggles,
263–18 their c· petitions for the same,
Ret. 32–17 * Whose most c· substance seems
38– 7 I yielded to a c· conviction
Pul. 9–25 c· prayers, prophecies, and
No. 46– 9 must answer the c· inquiry:
'01. 23–28 * "only the c· relation between
'02. 18– 4 c· spectacle of sin thrust upon
Po. 15–20 c· as love that outliveth the
16– 2 c· and hopeful though winter
My. vii–11 * consistent and c· right thinking
48–18 * c· daily reading of the Bible
86– 3 * will be c· and sincere.
89–19 * almost as c· as petitions
134– 1 c· battle against the world,
160– 6 in c· relation with the divine,
175– 4 requires my c· attention and time,
192–24 c· recurring demands upon my time
294–19 in spite of the c· stress of

Constantine
Mis. 224– 7 courtier told C· that a mob

constantly
Mis. 62– 4 opposite image . . . kept c· in mind,
133–27 I turn c· to divine Love
160–11 gaining c· in the knowledge
177–29 I am c· homesick for heaven.

constantly
Mis. 206–19 Scientist is c· accentuating harmony
238–28 falsehoods kept c· before the public.
265–27 c· called to settle questions
353–30 they c· go to her for help,
Ret. 73–21 C· to scrutinize physical
82– 2 yet their core is c· renewed ;
Un. 30– 3 c· uses the word soul
Rud. 9– 4 c· sowing the seeds of discord
Pan. 8–28 They c· reiterate the belief of
12– 6 how can Spirit be c· passing
'02. 1– 5 church communicants c· increase
Hea. 5–19 grand truth which is c· covered,
9– 5 We are c· thinking and talking
Peo. 2–26 held c· before the people's
My. 11– 5 * has been c· at her post
22– 5 * the c· increasing attendance
76– 5 * new contributions were c· being
95– 5 * c· strengthened by members
211–24 lies, poured c· into his mind,
231–19 Mrs. Eddy is c· receiving
305–17 demand for this book c· increases.
308–27 household law, c· enforced,

constellation
Mis. 340–27 Every luminary in the c· of

constituency
No. 4–22 true c· of being.

constituent
No. 4– 7 human error, a c· part of

constituents
Mis. 296– 4 among its c· and managers
My. 340–23 has suggested to his c·

constitute
Mis. v– 6 c· THE SUCCESS OF A STUDENT
65–28 c· the divine law of healing.
234–25 c· physical and mental perfection,
Ret. 65–25 c· the only evangelism.
67– 4 human thought does not c· sin,
68–29 good, and pure c· his ancestry.
76–20 c· the Mind-healer a wonder-worker,
Un. 24–20 God and the universe— c· all
56–27 c· the miasma of earth.
No. 10–27 c· the phenomena of being,
11– 6 c· his individuality in the
38–21 and loving . . . c· C. S.,
Pan. 10–30 c· no part of man, but obscure man.
'01. 1–14 c· mental and physical perfection.
5– 4 he believes three persons c· the
My. 5–16 c· a Christian Scientist,
88–17 * externals c· the smallest feature of
136–13 c· the Board of Trustees
259–19 c· man, and nothing less is man

constituted
Mis. 56–14 c· laws to that effect,
217–15 nature is c· of and by Spirit.
Man. 79–19 c· by a Deed of Trust
Ret. 65–16 If the religion of to-day is c· of
My. 80– 8 * c· a severe tax upon
167–26 The c· religious rights in
318– 2 c· a new style of language.

constitutes
Mis. 9–30 false sense of what c· happiness
56–13 to conclude that Spirit c·
86–27 c· our mortal environment.
86–29 c· their present earth and heaven :
185– 8 c· a so-called material man,
206–16 nor lack of what c· true manhood.
233–26 rule of C. S. is what c· its utility :
375–14 * idea of what c· true art.
Man. 28– 4 Law c· government,
Ret. 28–20 increases, diminishes, c·, and
67– 4 c· the human or physical concept.
Un. 53– 7 it c· the lie an evil.
Pul. 53–21 * c· the power of the human soul
'01. 2–14 Absolute certainty . . . c· its utility.
7– 5 c· the individuality of the infinite
My. 64–18 * c· the high standing of C. S.

constituting
Mis. 56–11 Every indication of matter's c· life
364–15 c· and governing all identity,
Rud. 2– 6 subjects, or agents, c· the

Constitution
My. 128– 7 C· of the United States,
200– 2 individual rights under the C·
222–22 C· of the United States
282– 3 in our C·, and in the laws of God.

constitution
Mis. 224–14 different history, c·, culture,
382–25 wrote its c· and by-laws,
382–26 also the c· and by-laws of
Pul. 79–22 * something in the c· of man

constitutional
'01. 33–16 c· laws of their land ;
Peo. 10–12 our c· Bill of Rights.
My. 227–22 justice, c· individual rights,
340–18 through c· interpretations.

constrained
My. 360–12 I am c· to say, if I can settle this

construct
Mis. 330–32 c· the stalk, instruct the ear,
My. 71–28 * c· an auditorium that would

constructed
Pul. 75–22 * the church c· in the great
My. 157–16 * Building in Washington is c·.

constructing
Mis. 244– 5 Mind alone c· the human system,

construction
Pul. 65–19 * whose architectural c·
76– 1 * material used in its c·
My. 24–24 * enduring character of its c·,
63– 3 * the c· of the church,
71–15 * been in process of c·,
75–29 * any part of the expense of its c·
83–24 * the c· of the new temple
318–12 to defend my grammatical c·,
338–21 may have overlooked the c· that

construed
Mis. 121–32 c· the substitution of a good man
291–11 is often c· as direct orders,
No. 9–26 humanly c·, and according to Webster,
My. 329– 1 * This was c· to include

construes
Mis. 301– 9 what the law c· as crime.

consult
Man. 47– 7 may c· with an M. D. on the anatomy
'02. 17–25 C· thy every-day life ;
My. 338–16 not allowed to c· me relative to

consultation
Mis. 378– 8 After much c· among ourselves,

consulted
Mis. 146–13 have hitherto declined to be c·
289–30 Mutual interests . . . should be c·,
348–32 student who c· me on this
349–12 he c· me on the feasibility of
Man. 67– 2 is not to be c· on cases of
70– 1 Pastor Emeritus to be C·.
87– 7 is not to be c· on this subject.
88–16 President is not to be C·.
88–17 President is not to be c·
My. 114–15 I c· no other authors and
137–26 c· Lawyer Streeter about the method.

consulting
Man. 27– 8 without c· with the full Board
70– 5 without first c· her on said subject

consume
Mis. 51–31 that ye may c· it — Jas. 4 : 3.
366– 3 attention that human hypotheses c·,
No. 40– 2 c· it on your lusts." — see Jas. 4 : 3.
My. 124–31 that they c· in their own fires
160–23 will eventually c· this planet.

consumed
Mis. 82–26 is c· as a moth,
230– 4 great amount of time is c· in
326–12 they c· the next dwelling ;
Ret. 72–10 c· with terrors." — Psal. 73 : 19.
My. 25–18 the time c· in travel,
105–10 the lungs were mostly c·.
160–26 until the sinner is c·,

consumes
Mis. 117–21 each step be taken, c· time,
Ret. 94–10 c· whatsoever is of sin.

consuming
Mis. 151– 6 God is a c· fire.
326–15 "God is a c· fire." — Heb. 12 : 29.
Ret. 79– 6 In this c· heat false images
'02. 18–12 nor spared . . . the c· tares.

consummate
Mis. 194–29 c· naturalness of the Life
200– 1 c· naturalness of Truth
213– 7 c· the joys of acquiescence
355–10 To c· this desideratum,
Ret. 82–22 to c· much good or else evil ;
My. 23– 6 * to c· the erection of the
274– 7 so c· man's being with the

consummated
Ret. 20–27 A plot was c· for
My. 14– 3 when this bringing is c·,
292– 7 and the joy of acquiescence c·.

consummates
'02. 6–18 and c· the First Commandment,

consummation
Mis. 98–22 * "c· devoutly to be wished."
322–22 For this c· He hath given you
Un. 17–19 * c· devoutly to be wished."
Pul. 8–19 earn a few pence toward this c·.
45–11 * features of this glorious c·
My. 60–28 * to perform in this wonderful c·.
181–16 * c· devoutly to be wished"
283–11 prayed and labored for the c· of

consumption
Mis. 58– 1 If one has died of c·,
58– 7 learns that c· did not kill him.
Ret. 16– 8 since she . . . was in c· !
Pul. 54–30 of incipient pulmonary c·.
'01. 17–16 the last stages of c·, pneumonia,
My. 80– 5 * cured of blindness, of c·
105– 7 I healed c· in its last stages,

contact
Mis. 110– 9 lose them not through c· with the
229– 5 catching when exposed to c· with
236– 7 from c· with family difficulties,
Pul. 31–15 * close c· with public feeling
36– 6 * to retire from active c· with
68–10 * to retire from active c· with

contagion
Mis. 228–20 chapter sub-title
229–26 a better preventive of c·
My. 116– 1 chapter sub-title
116– 5 fact . . . realized will stop a c·.
116– 8 it is a c· — a mental malady,
116–15 danger and darkness of personal c·.
116–16 Forgetting . . . brings on this c·.
116–23 from injustice and personal c·.
118– 4 the disobedient spread personal c·,

contagious
Mis. 228–28 Common consent is c·,
228–30 infectious and c· diseases,
229–10 good is more c· than evil,
229–20 confidence of mankind in c· disease
My. 116– 2 At a time of c· disease,
116–20 not a symptom of this c· malady,
190– 9 of c· and organic diseases?
219–28 infectious and c· diseases
220– 7 reporting of a c· case to
226–30 infectious or c· diseases."
344–23 infectious and c· diseases.

contain
Mis. 16–20 more than a person, . . . can c· ;
76–12 but they c· immortal souls !
309–30 which c· all and much more
311–23 The works . . . c· absolute Truth,
366– 6 they c· and offer Science,
Hea. 4– 1 finite cannot c· the infinite,
12– 1 c· no medicinal properties,
My. 50–21 * records . . . these simple . . . words,
87– 2 * greater than the building could c·.
179–13 Testaments c· self-evident truths
334–10 * still c· the original account of

contained
Mis. 50– 7 c· in that book,
92–16 c· in that chapter of "S. and H.
199–27 so-called miracles c· in Holy Writ
302–29 divine teachings c· in "S. and H.
Man. 34– 9 teaching c· in the C. S. textbook,
43– 9 is c· in the books of the
63–10 C. S. c· in their textbook.
80–10 By-Laws c· in this Manual.
Ret. 2–24 c· a full account of the
91– 6 c· in what is commonly known as
Pul. 53–10 * c· in the one word — faith.
55–22 * c· in the volume entitled "S. and H.
'00. 3–24 c· this divine appellative
'02. 15– 1 letters mailed to me c· threats
My. 17–14 c· in the scripture, — I Pet. 2 : 6.
18–28 It c· the following articles :
54– 5 * Boston Traveler c· the following
138–28 * statements c· in the annexed letter
171–29 * The casket c· a gavel
199–13 joint resolutions c· therein

containing
Mis. 217–18 presuppose . . . person c· infinite
280–21 c· beautiful hand-painted flowers
Man. 98–15 papers c· such an article,
Ret. 1– 9 manuscripts c· Scriptural sonnets,
37– 2 c· the complete statement of C. S.,
Pul. 28– 5 * c· the C. S. seal,
60–20 * c· pneumatic wind-chests
My. 172–23 * box c· the gavel was opened
223–13 c· questions about secular affairs,
332–17 * paper c· this card is now in

contains
Mis. 273–26 class which c· that number.
Un. 2–18 c· neither discord nor disease.

contains

Un.	14– 1	platform, which *c·* such planks as
Pul.	vii– 1	*c·* scintillations from press and
	86– 2	* *c·* a solid gold box,
'01.	6–14	We hear . . . this Person *c·* three
Hea.	7–28	it *c·* no argument for a creed
My.	53–26	* *c·* some very interesting
	68– 6	* *c·* about one mile and a half of pews.
	69–16	* auditorium *c·* seven galleries,
	98–14	* *c·* a . . . remarkable announcement
	112–18	*c·* a Science which is demonstrable
	146–13	C. S. *c·* infinitely more than
	180–12	C. S. *c·* no element whatever of
	299–11	*c·* the entire truth of

contaminating

Ret.	52– 5	*c·* influences of those who

contemned

My.	33–22	vile person is *c·* ; — *Psal.* 15 : 4.

contemplate

Mis.	16–28	earnestly to *c·* this new-born
	155–29	were they to *c·* the universal
	321–29	wisdom and Love to *c·*,
'01.	15–14	to *c·* the infinite blessings

contemplated

My.	137–24	I had *c·* doing this
	237– 1	*c·* reference in S. and H.
	343– 6	* "No present change is *c·*

contemplating

Mis.	64–12	Persons *c·* a course at the
	308–25	*c·* personality impedes spiritual
	380– 7	When *c·* the majesty and
Man.	94–10	should go away *c·* truth ;
Po.	v–10	* *c· this lofty New Hampshire crag,*
My.	216–30	C· these important wants,
	290– 2	*c·* this sudden international

contemplation

Mis.	98– 3	that his *c·* regarding himself
	136–11	turning aside for one hour from *c·*
	309–10	true *c·* of his character.
	322– 2	earnestly invite you to its *c·*

contemplative

Mis.	43–13	*c·* reading of my books,

contemporary

Mis.	22– 7	what, but the *c·* of Christianity,
My.	98–30	* our *c·*, the *Boston Times,*

contempt

Mis.	170–27	expressing the utmost *c·*.
	170–28	recorded as having expressed *c·*
My.	324– 4	* thought of *c·* for the unlearned,

contemptible

Mis.	226–21	liar and hypocrite is so *c·*,
	230– 8	one of which is *c·*,

contemptuously

No.	41– 4	Pharisees . . . *c·* called him

contending

No.	1–15	noise and stir of *c·* sentiments
Hea.	9–13	C· for the reality of
My.	148–27	to gain power over *c·* sects

content

Pan.	11–20	Mortals, *c·* with something less
	11–26	lost image that mortals are *c·* to
My.	151–26	They were *c·* to look no higher

contented

My.	80– 2	* prosperous, *c·* men and women,
	87– 9	* and cheerfully *c·* multitude
	95–17	* *c·* and well-dressed body of people.

contentiously

Mis.	156–25	listening . . . amicably, or *c·*,

contents

Mis.	9–21	the *c·* of this cup of selfish
	50–16	understanding of the *c·* of this book,
My.	178–27	*c·* of "S. and H. with Key to the
	304–30	she has stolen the *c·* of
	338–11	The *c·* of the last lecture

contest

Mis.	101–10	they began and ended in a *c·* for
	188–11	a *c·* between Truth and error ;
Ret.	3– 7	caused that prolonged *c·*
	56–13	this *c·* must go on until

contests

Peo.	2–19	demoniacal *c·* over religion.

context

Mis.	194–19	The *c·* of the foregoing
Hea.	8– 9	perceive the meaning of the *c·*,

contexts

My.	110–32	torn from their necessary *c·*,

continent

Ret.	47– 5	Students from all over our *c·*,
Pul.	75–26	* most nearly fire-proof . . . on the *c·*,

continent

Peo.	10–28	slavery was abolished on this *c·*,
My.	85–10	* Atlantic to the Pacific on this *c·*.
	88– 5	* C. S., as now before this *c·*,

continents

Mis.	152– 4	in love *c·* clasp hands,
My.	124–12	heart meeting heart across *c·*
	194– 2	in broad facts over great *c·*

contingent

Ret.	67–22	in no way *c·* on Adam's thought,
No.	43– 3	Truth is not *c·* on matter.
My.	179–26	being *c·* on nothing written
	293–23	*c·* on the power of God,

continual

Mis.	316–20	*c·* recapitulation of tired aphorisms
Un.	41–17	*c·* presence and power of good,
No.	37–17	demands His *c·* presence,

continually

Mis.	92– 7	needs *c·* to study this textbook.
	130–10	looking *c·* for a fault in
	151–25	*c·* be full of oil,
	362–20	*c·*, until self-extinguished by
Man.	48–13	*c·* stroll by her house,
Un.	9–24	Healing has gone on *c·* ;
No.	20–28	*c·* straying into forbidden by-paths
My.	9–11	* *c·* move us to utter our gratitude
	130–14	to be *c·* pursuing a lie
	346– 1	* her views, . . . were *c·* surprising.

continuance

Peo.	2– 2	which insures man's *c·*
My.	198– 7	God grant not only the *c·* of

continue

Mis.	xii– 3	With armor on, I *c·* the march,
	42– 2	*does life c· in thought only*
	86– 6	must *c·* to strive with sickness,
	92–23	to *c·* the study of this textbook.
	154–23	C· in His love.
	164– 7	this will *c·* to be seen
	164–22	Thus it will *c·*, . . . until man
	256–18	*c·* to send to each applicant
	273–19	*c·*, as at present, to send
	286– 7	will *c·* unprohibited in C. S.
	304–16	* will *c·* until that Exhibition closes.
	310–18	To *c·* one's connection with this
	312–25	Truth that will *c·* to reverberate
	359– 5	you *c·* the mental argument
Man.	58– 9	will *c·* to preach for this Church
	61–23	should *c·* about eight or nine minutes
	72–22	*c·* its present form of government
	90–12	will *c·* not over one week.
Ret.	22–15	*c·* till its involved errors are
	50–24	*c·* to organize churches,
	65–18	it will *c·* to avoid whatever
	81– 7	and our friendship will surely *c·*.
	84– 4	should *c·* to study this textbook,
	84–12	*c·* to study and assimilate this
	85– 4	to *c·* the organization of churches,
Pul.	6– 3	it will *c·* till the antithesis of
	79–28	* this condition can never long *c·*.
	83– 1	* *c·* to demand woman's love
No.	7– 7	and *c·* to do so unto the end.
	46–22	I shall *c·* to labor and wait.
Pan.	6– 5	let us *c·* to denounce evil
	6– 6	*c·* to fight it until it disappears,
	14–12	*c·* to characterize her government,
'01.	19– 9	*c·* to ask, and because of your
My.	5–27	C· to choose whom ye will serve.
	13–32	it will *c·* to "prosper"— *Isa.* 55 : 11.
	37–10	* all that you have done and *c·* to do
	122– 9	plant will *c·* to grow.
	123– 4	I must *c·* to prize love even more
	123– 8	*c·* to urge the perfect model
	132–18	Oh, may these rich blessings *c·*
	141–26	branch churches *c·* their communion
	166– 3	will *c·* with divine approbation
	175–26	Let brotherly love *c·*.
	191– 8	C· steadfast in love
	195–29	*c·* to build, rebuild, adorn, and
	200–29	For this I shall *c·* to pray.
	246– 2	*c·* for three years as practitioners
	261– 7	Let it *c·* thus with one exception :
	267– 4	Nothing can . . . *c·* forever which is

continued

Mis.	110–21	thanksgiving for the *c·* progress
	192–16	name shall be *c·* — *Psal.* 72 : 17.
Man.	60– 3	C· Throughout the Year.
	60– 5	*c·* twelve months each year.
Ret.	8–10	*c·* until I grew discouraged,
	45– 9	*c·* organization retards spiritual
Pul.	37–21	* "Mother feels very strongly," he *c·*,
	41– 4	* contributions which *c·* to flow in
	49–15	* she *c·* : "Look at those big elms !
	64–12	* to stop the *c·* inflow of money

continued

No. 20–26   c' series of mortal hypotheses,
Po. v–22   * c' to reach the author
My. 44–28   * desire to express their c' loyalty
    55–20   * c' there until March, 1894,
    56–31   * c' growth, this c' overcrowding,
    91–24   * the church has c' to grow.
  222–10   c' : "If ye have faith— Matt. 17 : 20.
  318–27   would have c' with a long argument,

continues

Mis. 188–22   c' the explanation of the power
  365–21   but it c', and increases,
No. 19– 4   That it c' to rise,
'00. 9–14   reformer c' his lightning,
'02. 6–10   c' to demonstrate this grand
My. 5–21   c' to love more and to serve
  94– 1   * growth c' in like proportion
  236– 7   this name c' to be multiplied,

continuing

Mis. 252–12   C' this category, we learn

continuity

Pan. 4– 3   owes its origin and c' to
My. 53–29   * even though the c' of thought
  342–19   c' of The Church of Christ,

continuous

Pul. 59– 6   * c' services were held from nine to

continuously

Man. 85–18   members who have not been c'

contract

Mis. 243–28   and the organ to c' ;
  289–16   when by the marriage c'
  290– 5   animus of the c is preserved
  297–21   claims growing out of this c',
  297–23   or this c' is legally dissolved.

contractors

Mis. 289–22   must not be retaken by the c',

contracts

My. 12– 4   * justified the letting of c'.

contradict

Mis. 190–17   will c' the interpretations that
  382– 2   my experience would c' it
Rud. 7–14   Science and spiritual sense c' this,
No. 6– 2   would c' the Science of Mind-healing

contradicted

Mis. 295–21   not only be queried, but flatly c',
My. 334– 7   * allegation . . . she has c' herself,

contradicting

Pan. 4–28   By admitting . . . and then c' them,
  6–12   talking serpent, c' the word of God
My. 294–10   unrighteous c' minds of mortals,
  330– 8   * thus c' his own statement,

contradiction

Mis. 83–11   please explain this seeming c'?
  361–14   c' of human hypotheses ;
Ret. 22–10   endured such c' of sinners— Heb. 12 : 3.
Un. 38– 4   Death is a c' of Life,
My. 196–20   endured such c' of sinners— Heb. 12 : 3.

contradictions

Un. 16– 3   unheard-of c',— absurdities ;
Pan. 7–21   or a vague apology for c'.
Hea. 4–23   with such self-evident c'?

contradictory

Mis. 190–15   too limited and c'.
  372– 2   incorrect, c', unscientific,
Ret. 34– 6   the reply was dark and c'.
  59– 4   have no c' significations.
No. 5–26   Any c' fusion of Truth with error,
'01. 25–23   as c' as the blending of good and

contradicts

Mis. 14– 3   material view which c' the
  96–31   Science c' this evidence ;
  195–17   divine logic, . . . c' this inference,
  221–24   Such denial also c' the doctrine
Ret. 60–25   Material sense c' Science,
  94– 5   and yet c' divine Science

contradistinction

Mis. 36– 4   in c' to good and Truth,
  73–30   in c' to the testimony of
Un. 52– 1   in c' to the supposition that
  52– 9   c' to the false consciousness of
'01. 24–24   In c' to his views I
'02. 2– 8   in c' to all error,

contrary

Mis. 29–28   on the c', they fulfil His laws ;
  350–12   On the c', our deliberations were,
  350–28   On the c', I cannot serve two
Man. 55–23   c' to the statement thereof
  86–22   shall teach nothing c' thereto.
Ret. 38–10   I set to work, c' to my inclination,
  72– 4   is c' to the law of God ;

contrary

Un. 4–18   on the c', the Father bids man
  14–28   but the c', that by this knowledge,
  19– 5   are c' to His creative will,
  19–15   On the c', evil is only a delusive
Pul. 45–18   * repeatedly asseverated to the c'.
  54–13   * On the c', the whole transaction
  84–16   * to the c' notwithstanding.
Rud. 11– 1   c' to the law of Spirit.
No. 21– 1   c' to the life and teachings
'00. 9– 3   c' to their inclination.
My. 106–12   On the c', C. S. has healed cases
  138– 7   carried on c' to my wishes.
  215–25   on the c', he bade them take script.
  308–30   On the c', my father was
  351–25   any assertions to the c' are false.
  359– 2   These Directors do not act c' to

contrast

Mis. 238– 4   to c' with that childhood's wrong

contrasted

Ret. 30–14   as c' with the foibles
  41– 2   as c' with its present welcome

contribute

Mis. 156– 1   they would c' oftener to the pages
  240–12   All education should c' to
  305–24   * asked to c' one cent
My. 7–19   * we agree to c' any portion of
  9– 5   * agree to c' any portion of
  9–22   to c' any part of two millions
  10–20   * not expected to c' money against
  20–30   * to ask the members to c' to
  21–12   * in order to c' more liberally
  96–20   * invited to c' what they could
  98–22   * no member . . . was asked to c'
  216–24   and no longer c' to The
  244–14   to c' my part towards this result.

contributed

Mis. 203– 2   pretty pond c' to Pleasant View,
Pul. 64– 9   * Men, women, and children c',
My. 19–13   * of the many branch churches which c'
  22– 9   * Christian Scientists have c' already
  28– 6   * experience of many who have c'
  31–12   * c' from over the entire world.
  58–13   * c' to the erection of these mighty
  86–14   * c' before the actual work was

contributes

My. 68–23   * c' not a little to the imposing

contributing

My. 78–16   * high with bank-notes, everybody c',

contribution

Mis. 143–25   call from me for this extra c',
  148–24   I was not aware that the c' box
Pul. 71– 5   * c' of a quarter of a million dollars
My. 12–14   * promptness of his own c'.
  99–19   * c' baskets when passed around
  347–22   Special c' to "Bohemia."

contributions

Mis. 140–15   c' to the Building Fund
  143–21   c' of one thousand dollars each,
  148–26   c' from the people present
  156– 8   send in your c' as usual
  303–26   will respond to this letter by c'.
  305–16   * small c' from many persons
  305–17   * rather than large c' from a few.
  306–12   * C' should be sent to the
  349–29   the c', when I preached,
  350– 1   two thousand dollars of my own c'.
Man. 96–13   and trust to c' for his fee.
Pul. v– 4   c' OF $4,460 WERE DEVOTED
  41– 3   * a cessation of the tide of c'
  44–21   * building a church by voluntary c',
  57– 4   * c' for its erection came from
  63–24   * by the voluntary c' of
  64–12   * compelled to refuse further c',
'01. 27– 3   * "The best c' that have been made
My. 14–29   * c' to the building fund
  23– 1   * to delay our c'
  25– 9   * their c' to the building fund.
  30–22   * Some of these c' were
  76– 5   * c' were constantly being received ;
  76– 9   * no more c' to the building fund
  76–21   * all c' have been voluntary.
  98–23   * C' were entirely voluntary.

contributor

Mis. 305–28   * name of each c'.
My. 217–11   in equal shares to each c'.
  217–13   each c' will receive his dividend
    (see also Eddy)

contributors

Mis. 141–29   to the several c',
  313–12   c' to The C. S. Journal
Pul. 41– 8   * four thousand of these c'

contributors
Pul.	42–11	* little *c·* to the building fund,
	86–20	* all *c·* wherever they may be,
My.	27–10	* chapter sub-title
	27–11	* The *c·* to the building fund
	42–10	* helpful *c·* to our periodicals,
	216–14	chapter sub-title
	217– 9	bonds for my dear children *c·*
	217–12	*c·* shall have arrived at legal age,

contrite
Un.	61–27	*c·* heart soonest discerns this truth,

contrition
Mis.	134– 3	as you have expressed *c·*

control
Mis.	37–11	under the *c·* of God,
	45– 4	enables you to *c·* pain.
	69–32	want of *c·* over "the fish — *Gen.* 1 : 26.
	97–13	All human *c·* is animal magnetism,
	137–24	*c·* appetite, passion, pride,
	140– 1	such as error could not *c·*.
	199–20	manifest in the *c·* it gave him
	220–13	harmonious thought has the full *c·*
Man.	70–12	no . . . *c·* of other churches,
	74– 5	or *c·* over any other church.
	83–12	shall not assume personal *c·* of,
Ret.	9–19	* my spirit's breathings to *c·*,
Pul.	32– 8	* to dominate, to lead, to *c·*,
Rud.	16– 1	If publicity and material *c·* are
No.	40–21	*c·* aright the thought
'01.	14–24	*c·* it in the first instance,
	14–25	or it will *c·* you in the second.
Po.	23–10	Above the world's *c·*
My.	49– 5	* *c·*, in no arbitrary sense,
	159–26	could not *c·* human will,
	270–30	*c·* both religion and art in unity
	293–25	law of Spirit to *c·* matter,
	294–14	*c·* all the conditions of man
	318–23	could *c·* himself no longer

controlled
Mis.	66–18	material sense must be *c·* by
	354–24	all is *c·*, . . . by wisdom, Truth, and
Man.	70–13	shall be *c·* by none other.
Ret.	82– 6	not . . . be *c·* by other students,
My.	275– 7	until they are *c·* by divine Love ;

controller
Rud.	10– 2	throne of the *c·* of all mankind.

controllers
No.	11– 2	not the creators, *c·*, nor

controls
Mis.	5–24	reality that Mind *c·* the body.
	175–23	supposition . . . that one mind *c·*
	247–20	understand that Spirit *c·* body.
Man.	87–18	"The less the teacher personally *c·*
Ret.	84–24	The less the teacher personally *c·*
Rud.	12–18	*c·* the health or existence of
'01.	17–27	must be mind that *c·* the effect ;
Hea.	6–19	Man thinks . . . disease *c·* his body
Peo.	8–19	*c·* the muscles of the arm.

controversies
Mis.	125–26	the *c·* which baffle it,

controversy
Mis.	89–22	*for information, not for c·,*
Un.	5–21	Let no enmity, no untempered *c·*,
No.	8–19	hold no *c·* or enmity over
'00.	12–30	presents the phase of a great *c·*,
	13– 2	* "a *c·* was inevitable when
My.	129–32	Refrain from public *c·* ;
	306– 8	newspaper *c·* over a question

controvert
Mis.	109– 6	try to reverse, . . . or *c·*, Truth ;

controverted
My.	322– 4	* facts which cannot be *c·*

contusions
Mis.	243– 7	students treat sprains, *c·*, etc.,

convene
Mis.	315–23	*c·* as often as once in three months.
Man.	57–14	for which the members are to *c·*.
	70–17	*c·* to confer on a statute
	84–17	pupils of loyal teachers shall *c·*
My.	289–12	*c·* for the sacred purpose of

convened
Mis.	147– 4	another annual meeting has *c·*,
	350–14	second P. M. *c·* in about one week
My.	8–25	* *c·* in annual business meeting
	251–26	You have *c·* only to convince
	333– 7	* was *c·* for the purpose of

convenience
Pul.	27– 2	* French mirrors and every *c·*.
My.	174– 3	*c·* of the Christian Scientists

conveniences
Pul.	58–28	* furnished with all *c·* for living,

convenient
Mis.	52–12	That it is often *c·*,
	150–17	*C·* houses and halls can now
'00.	2–27	working when it is *c·*."
	9–10	and wait for a more *c·* season ;
My.	119– 1	It is *c·* for history to record
	211– 2	sticklers for a false, *c·* peace,

conveniently
Man.	27–20	provide suitable rooms, *c·* and

convening
Mis.	136–24	*c·* once in four months ;

convention
Mis.	137– 6	close of the first *c·* of the
	138– 4	to prepare for this national *c·*
	276–12	the third *c·* of our National
	370–25	gather . . . into a "national *c·*"
Ret.	52–17	general *c·* at New York City,
My.	83– 3	* the holding of a great *c·*
	83– 4	* residing in the *c·* city.
	92– 9	* prodigious *c·* of Christian Scientists

converge
Un.	10–13	Spiritual phenomena never *c·* toward

convergence
Pul.	22– 4	one nucleus or point of *c·*,

conversant
My.	319–16	* I am *c·* with some facts

conversation
Mis.	6–27	*c·* chiefly confined to the
	225– 8	*c·* drifted to . . . C. S. ;
	225–13	Soon after this *c·*,
Man.	91–26	under Mrs. Eddy's daily *c·*
Ret.	5–26	* elevated character to the tone of *c·*
Pul.	5–19	*c·* with a beauty all its own
My.	48–32	* manifest in their faces, their *c·*,
	315– 5	* *c·* with him about his wife,
	319–22	* in *c·* with you about the
	319–29	* recall very plainly the *c·*
	320–29	* last *c·* I had with him
	322–13	* reminds me of a *c·* I had with

conversations
Pul.	72– 6	* number of very interesting *c·*
My.	306–30	holding long *c·* with him
	307– 3	In his *c·* with me
	320–24	* *c·* were at times somewhat long
	321–24	* my many *c·* with you,
	321–30	* *c·* with people who knew you

conversazione
Pul.	6–26	At a *c·* in Boston, he said,

converse
Mis.	148–28	Let the invitation to this sweet *c·*
	324– 1	His *c·* with the watchers
Pul.	72–10	* agreeable lady, ready to *c·*,
My.	320– 6	* to *c·* about you and your work,

conversed
My.	149–15	* *c·* with many wise men,"

conversion
Mis.	229–12	clergyman's *c·* of sinners.
My.	82– 2	* same stories of their *c·*,

conversions
Pul.	66– 9	* than from *c·* from other churches,

convert
Mis.	279–27	enough to *c·* the world if we are
Rud.	17– 2	Jews whom St. Paul had hoped to *c·*

converted
Mis.	281–13	was *c·* to Protestantism through
Ret.	14– 8	*c·* and rescued from perdition ;
	35– 3	*c·* into the chapter on Recapitulation
Pul.	69– 6	* *c·* to C. S. by being cured
My.	92– 6	* large numbers . . . *c·* to it

convertible
'01.	4– 3	major premise must be *c·* to the

converting
Mis.	39–30	than in *c·* the sinner.

converts
Pul.	70–13	* over one hundred thousand *c·*,
My.	94–12	* adherence of its *c·* to the faith,
	343–19	it won *c·* from the first.

convey
My.	44–26	* *c·* to you their sincere greetings
	78–27	* No mere words can *c·* the
	81–29	* impossible to *c·* a conception of
	188–27	*c·* all impressions to man,
	226– 5	and *c·* its meaning in C. S.

conveyed
Mis.	140– 4	must be *c·* through a type
	140–12	my gift as I had it *c·*.
Man.	79–23	manage the property therein *c·*,

conveyed
Ret. 51– 5 on the premises thereby c·,
'02. 13–27 land legally c· to me,
My. 66– 7 * estates having been c· by deed
77–26 * Word was c· to them that
157–23 which c· to them the sum of
324–24 * Everything he said c· this

conveying
Mis. 133– 5 c· ideas more opposite to the fact.
Man. 136– 1 heading

conveys
Mis. 378–17 "Because it c· electricity
No. 20–12 fully c· the ideas of God,

convict
My. 110–28 Robert Ingersoll's attempt to c·

convicting
No. 43–15 * c· the infidel, alarming the

conviction
Mis. 210–27 Charity has the courage of c· ;
222– 8 c· of his wrong state of
222– 9 failing of c· and reform,
299–11 with the courage of c·
Ret. 30–13 Why was this c· necessary to
38– 7 I yielded to a constant c·
48– 7 growing c· that every one should
Un. 7–20 and here is one such c· :
55–21 as expressed in his c·,
Pul. 34–18 * From that hour dated her c· of
Rud. 9–25 clear c· of the omnipotence
No. 40–12 thoughts are our honest c·.
'00. 15–15 it yields to sharp c·
My. 24–26 * have gone away with the c· that
61–15 * and the c· that the work
79–27 * c· that they would be believed,
121– 8 a true, tried mental c·

convictions
Mis. 31–19 against his own c· of good
99– 9 courage of his c· fell
116–19 the courage of honest c·,
217–32 and our c· change :
238– 6 honest to their c·,
247– 3 his honest c· and proofs
288– 2 sincere and courageous c·
Ret. 71–22 they proceed from false c·
Un. 5–12 following upward individual c·,
No. 9– 7 conscientious in their c· ;
'00. 1–14 right c· fast forming
'01. 32–13 courage of their c· was seen.
32–15 Their c· were honest,
'02. 14–17 counter to the common c· of mankind

convince
No. 15– 4 c· all that their purpose is right.
My. 94–14 * much to c· the skeptic.
251–27 c· yourselves of this grand verity :

convinced
Mis. 6–23 once c· of the uselessness of
358–31 c· that by leaving the material
Pul. 35–23 * Mrs. Eddy became c· of the
64–20 * that the curative Principle was
'01. 24–11 * that under Providence I
My. 146–18 I am c· of the absolute truth of

convinces
Un. 4–13 c· us that, as we get still nearer

convincing
Ret. 93–24 give to the world c· proof of

convulsion
Po. 27– 1 "C·, carnage, war ;

convulsions
My. 201–17 scan the c· of mortal mind,

cooing
My. 341–12 A lightsome lay, a c· call,

Cooke, Mr.
My. 332– 9 * Many thanks are due Mr. C·,

Cook's, Mr.
Mis. 95– 5 * was presented to Mr. C· audience,

cool
Mis. 225–26 a c· perspiration spread over it,
227–27 bathes it in the c· waters of peace
323–21 rest in its c· grottos,
332–14 walking in the c· of the day
Ret. 18– 3 C· waters at play with the
Peo. 9– 6 The c· bath may refresh the body,
14– 5 c· grottos, smiling fountains,
Po. 63–10 C· waters at play with the

cooling
Pul. 25– 1 * lighting and c· of the church
25– 2 * for c· is a recognized feature
My. 29–26 * c· breeze to temper the heat,

coolly
Mis. 285–25 c· notifies the public of

cooperate
Mis. 138– 9 is not always to c·,
152– 8 c· with the divine power,
364–23 must either c· or quarrel

cooperates
Peo. 11–11 wherein man c· with and

cooperation
Mis. 40– 2 healing demands such c· ;
305–12 * asking for her personal c·
My. 162– 9 Unity is spiritual c·,

copartnership
Mis. 59–21 Any c· with that Mind

cope
Mis. 183– 9 there is no matter to c· with.
My. 227–16 their ability to c· with the claim,

Copeland
Mrs.
Pul. 72– 9 * Mrs. C· is a very pleasant and
72–12 * Mrs. C· claims to have been healed
72–16 * past eleven years," said Mrs. C·,
72–19 * In regard to Mrs. Eddy, Mrs. C· said
73–19 * of the same theory as Mrs. C·.

Mrs. D. W.
Pul. 72– 8 * Mrs. D. W. C· of University Avenue

Copernicus
No. 6–23 C· has shown that what appears

copied
Mis. 381– 2 but had been c· by her,
Pul. 88– 8 To those which are c·
My. 317–16 Mr. Calvin A. Frye c· my writings,
328– 7 * following article, c· from the
331–10 * c· from the Wilmington Chronicle

copies
Mis. 300–12 from c· of my publications
301–13 have read c· of my works
302–21 destroyed the c· at once
315– 6 No c· from my books
376–12 * c· of an engraving cut in a stone.
Man. 32– 8 shall not read from c·
93–16 c· of his lectures
Ret. 37– 9 edition numbered one thousand c·.
Pul. 5–22 edition of one thousand c·.
My. v–22 * over four hundred thousand c·
53– 8 * each of one thousand c·.
329–13 * photographed c· of the notice
334– 5 * allegation that c· of Mrs. Eddy's

Copley Hall
Pul. 29– 1 * held its meetings . . . later in C· H·,
29– 9 * service held in C· H·.
My. 55–24 * the church removed to C· H·
55–29 * congregation worshipped in C· H·

Copley Square
Pul. 29– 2 * Studio Building on C· S·.

copper
Mis. 305–21 * gold, silver, bronze, c·, and

copy
Mis. 92–22 to own a c· of the above-named book
144– 8 laid away a c· of this address,
153–23 to whom I presented a c· of
281–13 through a stray c· of the Scriptures
299–13 * "Is it right to c· your works
300– 4 taking this c· into the pulpit,
300– 9 If you should print and publish your c·
300–19 Your manuscript c· is liable,
301–20 "Is it right to c· your works
301–21 It is not right to c· my book
302–26 derived from making his c·,
372–26 Not by aid of . . . could I c· art,
379– 6 I read the c· in his presence,
Man. 91– 2 shall not allow it or a c· of it
98–14 published according to c· ;
98–16 sending a c· to the Clerk of the
104–15 a c· of the Seventy-third Edition
Ret. 38–11 finished my c· for the book.
38–14 finished printing the c· he had
38–17 with my finished c·.
38–19 printed all the c· on hand,
84–11 should own a c· of S. and H.,
'02. 13–30 A c· of this deed is published in our
16– 8 happy possessor of a c· of Wyclif,
Po. v–21 * each requested a c·,
My. 189–28 from which I c· this verse :
295– 9 GIFT OF A C· OF MARTIN LUTHER'S
295–22 [C· of Cablegram]
307– 3 which I, . . . added to his c·
333–30 * we c· the following :

copying
Mis. 300– 3 C· my published works
302–20 c· and reading my works
302–23 desist from further c· of my

copyright

Mis.	300–10	arrest for infringement of *c*,
	302– 5	encourages infringement of my *c*,
Ret.	36– 5	after taking out my first *c*,
	39– 2	the *c* was infringed,
	39– 3	entered a suit at law, and my *c* was
	76– 3	nor would protection by *c* be
My.	116–25	*C*, 1909, by Mary Baker Eddy.
	159–29	*C*, 1904, by Mary Baker G. Eddy.
	210–22	*C*, 1909, by Mary Baker Eddy.
	273–32	*C*, 1907, by Mary Baker G. Eddy.

copyrighted

Mis.	xi– 2	*c* at the date of its issue, 1875,
	381– 1	*c* works of Mrs. Eddy
Man.	43–16	from Mary Baker Eddy's *c* works
	71–20	Tenets *C*.
	71–25	*c* in S. AND H. WITH KEY TO THE
	81–16	*c* and conducted according to
	104– 6	written by Mary Baker Eddy and *c*,
Ret.	35– 1	I *c* the first publication on
	76– 2	C. S. is not *c* ;
My.	130–23	Borrowing from my *c* works,

cord

My.	105–16	so that it stood out like a *c*.

cordial

My.	177– 4	comply with your *c* invitation
	184–14	and to return my *c* thanks
	186–25	Accept my thanks for your *c* card

cordiality

Mis.	276– 4	purely Western in its *c*

cordially

Mis.	149– 4	Invite all *c* and freely to this
	306– 9	* Very *c* yours,
	310–27	would *c* invite all persons who
Pul.	87– 1	* most *c* invite you to be present
'02.	4– 5	I *c* congratulate our Board

cords

Un.	30–22	to break the *c* of matter,
'02.	3– 3	loosening *c* of non-Christian

core

Mis.	251–10	loyal to the heart's *c* to religion,
Ret.	82– 1	yet their *c* is constantly renewed ;
My.	350–17	bitter searing to the *c* of love ;

Corinthian

Mis.	185–29	reasoning . . . with the *C* brethren.

Corinthians

first epistle to (xv. 45)

Un.	30–13	In his first epistle to the *C* (xv. 45)

II. (13 : 14)

My.	19– 8	* benediction, 2 *C* 13 : 14 :

corn

Mis.	215–31	while the *c* is in the blade,
	330–31	patient *c* waits on the elements
	331– 1	crown the full *c* in the ear,
Ret.	92– 6	full *c* in the ear." — *Mark* 4 : 28.

corner

Mis.	144– 4	tower on the northeast *c*
	196–24	head stone of the *c*," — *Psal.* 118 : 22.
	306–13	* *c* Liberty and West Streets,
Man.	18– 2	the head of the *c*." — *Matt.* 21 : 42
Ret.	7–12	* explored their every nook and *c*,
Pul.	10–20	the head of the *c*." — *Matt.* 21 : 42.
	61–23	* *c* of Falmouth and Norway Streets,
No.	38–14	the head of the *c*." — *Matt.* 21 : 42.
'00.	5–25	will become the head of the *c*,
'01.	25– 7	the crown and the head of the *c*.
'02.	2–15	on the stone at the head of the *c* ;
	13–17	*c* of Falmouth and Caledonia
Hea.	3–10	become the head of the *c*.
My.	16–26	a precious *c* stone, — *Isa.* 28 : 16.
	17–15	a chief *c* stone, — *I Pet.* 2 : 6.
	29– 9	* *c* of Falmouth and Norway Streets,
	48– 7	* "the head of the *c*'" — *Matt.* 21 : 42.
	67– 1	* *c* of Falmouth and Norway Streets.
	68–13	* *c* of Falmouth and Norway Streets,
	70–16	* on every *c* in the neighborhood.
	73–19	* *c* of Huntington and Massachusetts
	188– 2	have made the head of the *c*.

corners

Mis.	133–13	*c* of the streets, — *Matt.* 6 : 5.
Pul.	24–12	* stone porticos and turreted *c*.

Corner Stone and corner-stone

Mis.	143–13	chapter sub-title
	143–15	*c* of "The First Church of Christ,
	145–10	in this *c* of our temple :
	163–23	eternal as Truth, the chief *c*.
	399–17	*c* of The Mother Church
Man.	17–16	the chief *c* whereof is,
	60–22	Laying a *C* *S*.
	60–24	when laying the *C* *S* of a Church
Ret.	15– 6	being the chief *c*." — *Eph.* 2 : 20.

Corner Stone and corner-stone

Un.	14–20	but the *c* of living rock,
Pul.	10–18	*c* in the house of our God.
	16– 2	poem
	43–15	* for the *c* laying last spring,
	85–28	* It was a facsimile of the *c*
No.	38–15	This is the chief *c*,
Po.	76– 1	the *c* of The Mother Church.
My.	16–10	* chapter sub-title
	16–11	* *c* of the new auditorium
	18–27	* The *c* was then laid by the
	55–32	* the *c* of The Mother Church
	57–12	* the *c* was laid July 16, 1904.
	60–13	* *c* of this wonderful temple
	67–16	* *C* of cathedral laid . . . 1904.
	112– 8	and build on its chief *c*.
	158– 6	chapter sub-title
	158–25	He has laid the chief *c* of the
	182–10	Christ, Truth, as the chief *c*.
	203–24	You have laid the *c* of

coronals

My.	258–20	*c* of meekness, diadems of love.

coronation

'02.	3–23	triumph canker not his *c*,

coroner's

My.	128– 6	*c* inquest, a board of health,

corporation

Mis.	272–15	* agent, or servant of any *c*
Ret.	49–28	all debts of the *c* have been
	49–29	deemed best to dissolve this *c*,

corporeal

Mis.	51–21	to resort to *c* punishment.
	97–30	*c* man is this lost image ;
	102– 3	A *c* God, as often defined
	152–11	I, as a *c* person, am not in
	161– 4	*C* and Incorporeal Saviour.
	162–18	*c* Jesus bore our infirmities,
	163–26	crucifixion of the *c* man,
	164– 2	incorporeal and *c* are distinguished
	166–20	given birth to the *c* child Jesus,
	205–15	the last scene in *c* sense.
	205–27	*c* or mortal man disappears
	308–29	invisible to *c* sense.
	309–20	*C* falsities include all obstacles
Ret.	45–11	even as the *c* organization
	54– 7	the claims of the *c* senses
	73– 2	material, *c*, and temporal.
	76–24	never abuses the *c* personality,
	89–29	*C* and selfish influence is human,
	91–21	His power . . . was spiritual, not *c*.
Rud.	2– 3	* a *c* man, woman, or child ;
'01.	4–18	is not *c* nor anthropomorphic.
	6–23	the *c* or anthropomorphic sense.
	12–26	embodies itself in the so-called *c*,
My.	109–15	whose person is not *c*,
	257–10	has passed from a *c* to the
	260–19	tradition, usage, or *c* pleasures,
		(see also **personality***)*

corporeality

Mis.	162–24	without *c* or finite mind.
	165– 9	fetters of the flesh, or *c*.
	165–14	The material *c* disappears ;
	309– 2	their own or others' *c*,
	309–19	The consciousness of *c*,
Ret.	25–16	but His *c* I denied.
	73–12	personal *c* became less to me
	73–21	sure victim of his own *c*.
	74– 1	increases one's sense of *c*,
	74– 6	the false sense of *c*,
No.	22–17	greater than the *c* we behold.

corporeally

Mis.	60–19	even if touching each other *c* ;
	123–32	as attends eating and drinking *c*.

corps

My.	38– 8	* carefully trained *c* of ushers,

corpse

My.	302– 7	Neither . . . can be produced on a *c*,

corpuscle

No.	26–21	never originated in molecule, *c*,

corpus sine pectore

Ret.	74– 4	defines it by his own *c* *s* *p*

correct

Mis.	14–13	we begin with the *c* statement,
	65– 6	If man's *ipse dixit* . . . is *c*,
	81–19	*if all this be a fair or c view*
	86– 9	*Is it c to say of material objects,*
	86–11	words which need *c* definition.
	195–20	but one *c* premise and conclusion,
	202– 3	are found to *c* the discords of
	264–21	whether those be *c* or incorrect.
	266–24	If I *c* mistakes which may be made
	269–23	*c* Mind-healing is the proper means
	344–19	would seek a *c* conclusion.

correct

Man.	43–24	C. S. literature which is not c·
	97–16	to c· in a Christian manner
	109–17	If not c·, the applicant will be
Un.	7–17	views here promulgated . . . are c·.
	25– 1	thus affirms is mainly c·.
Rud.	5– 3	Which testimony is c·?
No.	v– 4	c· involuntary as well as voluntary
	44– 2	incapacitates him for c· comment.
'01.	3–22	The first proposition is c·,
	27–10	nothing . . . that is c· on this subject
'02.	4– 6	c· analysis of C. S.
	10–19	his predicate tending thereto is c·,
Hea.	7–16	begins in motive to c· the act,
	9–21	only c· answer to the question,
	16–27	gain our . . . from the c· source.
Peo.	4–17	mysterious ideas . . . are far from c·,
My.	107– 5	and you have the c· answer.
	130– 1	c· the false with the true
	221–25	c· or incorrect state of thought,
	224–20	more fashionable but less c·.
	224–23	books less c· and therefore less
	225– 7	A c· use of capital letters in
	235– 8	c· numeration of numbers
	237–11	my teachings that I know to be c·
	241–15	* absolute and c· teaching
	242– 2	scientifically c· in your statement
	249– 3	c· sin through your own perfectness.
	249–24	The report . . . I desire to c·.
	267– 3	Nothing can be c· . . . which
	284–17	next issue please c· this mistake.
	297–18	clear, c· teaching of C. S.
	301–23	supposition that we can c· insanity by
	317–10	to c· my diction.
	349–27	is c· only as it is spiritual,
	356–28	only possible c· version of C. S.

corrected

Mis.	109–13	must be seen . . . in order to be c·;
	141–18	it can easily be c·
	198–25	is c· alone by Science,
	256– 4	mortal mind must be c· in order to
	285– 7	mistaken for the c· edition,
	356– 3	a life c· illumine its own
Man.	98– 2	c· a false newspaper article
Ret.	81– 9	c· by a diviner sense of liberty
	83–14	is sure to be c·.
'01.	27–20	and appetites of mankind c·,
My.	304– 2	chapter sub-title
	307– 3	his copy when I c· it.

correcting

Man.	98– 2	shall be responsible for c·
Ret.	57– 7	would be like c· the principle of
No.	1–21	c· the individual thought,
Hea.	7– 3	c· error in thought,
	7–12	and there c· the motive,
My.	322–10	* your statement c· mistakes

correction

Mis.	137–24	self-examination and c·;
Man.	98– 6	If the c· by the Committee
	98– 8	desirable that this c· shall appear,
My.	217–16	chapter sub-title
	284–11	chapter sub-title

corrections

Mis.	133– 1	you will not delay c· of the
My.	53– 3	* a bottomless sea of c·;
	272–22	* with the c· on the manuscript

correctly

Mis.	43– 7	Do all . . . teach it c·?
	58–11	read and studied c·,
Man.	38–11	whose applications are c· prepared,
	110– 2	that are not c· made out.
Rud.	16–18	Whatever is said and written c·
'01.	22–29	is not taught c· by those who
My.	224– 9	are not apt to be c· drawn.
	224–21	My books state C. S. c·.
	242–13	you must state its Principle c·,
	298– 4	experience which, if c· narrated
	313– 2	C· quoted, it is as follows,

correctness

Mis.	13–26	opportunity for proof of its c·
	56–23	proves the c· of my statements,

corrects

Mis.	37–19	Mind, which c· mortal thought,
	287–11	Science c· this error with the
	363–25	This Word c· the philosopher,
'01.	12– 3	and it c· the material sense
Hea.	7–12	it c· the act that results from

correlated

Mis.	241– 4	Body and mind are c·

correlative

Mis.	106–18	its c· in "S. and H.
Man.	32– 3	c· texts in S. AND H.
Man.	58–15	c· Biblical texts in the

correlative

My.	33– 5	* c· Scripture, 1 John 3 : 1–3.

correlatives

My.	218–16	introduction of . . . without their c·,

correspond

Mis.	32–18	If I had the time to . . . c· with
	217– 8	c· in quality and quantity.

correspondence

Mis.	74– 1	divine c· of noumenon and
	155–17	all of her interesting c·,
	205–23	maintain their obvious c·,
Pul.	23– 8	* December 28. — Special Correspondence.
	37–10	* attends to a vast c·;
My.	279– 9	its obvious c· with the Scriptures

correspondent

Mis.	295–14	has our American c· lost
My.	341–25	* received the Herald c·.

correspondents

Mis.	155–15	chapter sub-title
	322–10	Clerk of the church can inform c·.
My.	25–16	Will one and all of my dear c·

corresponding

Mis.	279–18	c· to the seven days of creation :
Pul.	26– 7	* c· to the chancel of
'00.	12–11	C· to its roads, its gates,

correspondingly

Ret.	22– 1	becomes c· obscure.

corresponds

Mis.	158–28	c· to the example of our Master.
Chr.	55– 2	whereto their number c·.

corridors

Mis.	xi–25	through the dim c· of years,
'02.	4–16	adown the c· of time,
My.	189–10	through the dim c· of time,

corroborate

Ret.	83–24	to c· what they teach.
My.	332–23	* c· Mrs. Eddy's claims.
	338– 9	* will fully c· this statement.

corroborating

'00.	5– 6	words of our Master c· this

corroborative

My.	317–20	quoting c· texts of Scripture.

corrupt

Mis.	223– 7	impure streams flow from c· sources.

corruption (see also corruption's)

Mis.	165– 5	because of the c· of the Church.
	228– 8	and pure amid c·.
No.	14– 8	Theosophy is a c· of Judaism.
	14– 8	This c· had a renewal in the
'00.	12– 1	His types of purity pierce c·

corruption's

Po.	71– 6	C· band Is driven back ;

Corser, Rev. Enoch

'01.	32– 4	Rev. Enoch C·, . . . Congregationalists ;

coruscations

No.	14–13	brilliant c· of the northern sky

Cosmopolitan

My.	272–18	* [C·, November, 1907]
	272–20	* The C· presents this month
	272–32	* C· gives no editorial indorsement

cosmopolitan

My.	81–16	* No more c· audience ever

cosmos

Mis.	26–25	God's consequent is the spiritual c·.
	362–25	spiritual c· and Science of Soul.
Un.	56– 2	to the c· of immortal Mind.
My.	180–32	the whence and why of the c·
	226–19	immortality of man and the c·
	350–10	the c· and Science of man.

cost

Mis.	84– 8	This c· them their lives,
	99– 7	It c· Galileo, what?
	165–24	This c·, none but the sinner can pay ;
	199–15	c· him the hatred of the rabbis.
	211–22	protects himself at his neighbor's c·,
	212–15	One step away . . . c· them — what?
	222–29	I shall not forget the c· of
	236–29	doing our duty, . . . at whatever c·.
	273– 4	although it will c· him much,
	281–16	* to count the c· of becoming a true
	281–17	* to count the c· of *not* becoming a
	288–21	To reckon the universal c· and gain,
	300– 1	and so avoiding the c· of hiring
	342–25	It should c· you something :
	381–19	recover of the defendant her c· of
	382– 7	c· more than thirty years of
Man.	96– 7	the c· of hall shall be paid by
Pul.	26–14	* c· eleven thousand dollars.
	28–10	* The c· of this church is
	50–13	* c· two hundred thousand dollars,

cost

Pul.	52–12	* *c·* of over two hundred thousand
	57– 3	* *c·* over two hundred thousand
	58–10	* *c·* over two hundred thousand
	60–17	* at a *c·* of eleven thousand dollars,
	62– 7	* economy of space, as well as of *c·*,
	63–22	* *c·* of two hundred and fifty thousand
	68–20	* *c·* over two hundred thousand
	70–15	* *c·* two hundred and fifty thousand
'00.	11– 1	*c·* me a tear !
Hea.	11– 2	Did we survey the *c·* of sublunary
My.	31–11	* the *c·* of which approximates
	67– 6	* C · . . . $2,000,000
	76– 8	* entire *c·* of the building,
	76–19	* estimated *c·* of the extension
	86–13	* every cent of the estimated *c·*
	89–14	* although it *c·* two million dollars,
	90–23	* paid-up *c·* of two million dollars
	91–27	* The temple . . . *c·* two million dollars,
	95–13	* *c·* them about two million dollars,
	96–19	* *c·* approximately two million dollars.
	97–27	* at a *c·* of two million dollars,
	98–18	* *c·* about two million dollars,
	99–15	* at a *c·* of two million dollars,
	100– 5	* *c·* about two million dollars
	123–16	original *c·* of the estate was
	127–26	not costly as men count *c·*,
	167– 2	self-sacrifice it may have *c·*
	229–12	might *c·* them a half century.

costing

Mis.	280–20	album *c·* fifty dollars,
Pul.	30–29	* *c·* over two hundred thousand
	63– 6	* CHURCH C· $250,000
	79– 5	* *c·* over two hundred thousand
My.	166–28	*c·* one hundred and seventy-five

costly

Mis.	110– 1	The *c·* balm of Araby,
	117–22	experiments ofttimes are *c·*.
	262– 8	new and *c·* spring dress.
	281–24	most beautiful and the most *c·*,
	356–11	chastened affections, and *c·* hopes,
Ret.	30– 4	bequests of C. S. are *c·*,
Pul.	40–18	* *c·* edifice erected in Boston
	87–11	your *c·* offering, and kind call
My.	87–16	* their *c·* church fully paid for,
	127–25	not *c·* as men count cost,

costs

Mis.	108–23	conception of it . . . *c·* much.
	138– 6	*c·* you what it would
'01.	2–23	*c·* a return under difficulties ;

cot

My.	287–12	Love lived in a court or *c·*

cottage

My.	113– 2	sinners in court and in *c·*,

couch

Mis.	388–23	And hover o'er the *c·* of woe ;
Po.	21–12	And hover o'er the *c·* of woe ;
My.	313–13	with a *c·* or cradle

cough

Mis.	239–18	suffused eyes, *c·*, and tired look,

councils

'01.	10– 4	deliver you up to the *c·*'' — *Matt.* 10 : 17.
'02.	4– 1	deceit in *c·*, dishonor in nations,

counsel

Mis.	138–20	My *c·* is applicable to the state of
	146– 7	I cannot conscientiously lend my *c·*
	146–22	and *c·* and help him to
	236– 8	weary with study to *c·* wisely
	236–20	"Take no *c·* of a mortal,
	243–24	Did he refer to that questionable *c·*,
	263–16	The need of their teacher's *c·*,
	301–18	my private *c·* they disregard,
	347–18	I follow his *c·*, take a few steps,
	349–19	My *c·* to all of them was
	359–28	Men give *c·* ; but they give not
	370– 5	they went away and took *c·*
	381– 6	present personally and by *c·*.
	381– 8	gave notice through his *c·*
	381–11	to inquire of defendant's *c·*
	381–13	her *c·* asked the defendant's *c·*
	381–17	drawn up and signed by *c·*.
Man.	83–19	and patiently *c·* his pupils
Ret.	81–23	puts this pious *c·* into a father's
Un.	1–13	I *c·* my students to defer this
Pul.	33–20	* high *c·* and serious thought.
No.	8–11	*c·* each other to work out his
	8–28	This *c·* is not new,
Pan.	13–12	I *c·* thee, rebuke and exhort
'00.	9– 2	and they comply with my *c·* ;
'01.	30–27	I *c·* Christian Scientists under all
'02.	13–19	paying for it . . . through my legal *c·*.
	13–21	were instituted by my *c·*
	13–27	conveyed to me, by my *c·*.

counsel

My.	18–20	I *c·* thee, rebuke and exhort
	37–29	* its wise *c·* and admonition.
	44– 9	* *c·* of our ever faithful Leader.
	49– 6	* but through sane *c·*,
	55–15	* upon Mrs. Eddy's *c·*, reorganized
	62–23	* appreciation of your wise *c·*,
	129–29	Accept my *c·* and teachings only as
	196– 7	accept my tender *c·* in these words
	309– 5	even acting as *c·* in a lawsuit
	309– 8	was the *c·* for Loudon

counseling

Man.	40–14	condemning, *c·*, influencing

counselling

My.	362–20	* we rejoice . . . in your wise *c·*.

Counsellor

Mis.	161– 7	C ·, *The mighty God*, — *Isa.* 9 : 6.
	164–18	C ·, *The mighty God*, — *Isa.* 9 : 6.
	321– 5	C ·, *The mighty God*, — *Isa.* 9 : 6.

(see also **Eddy***)*

counsellor

Mis.	288– 5	sure of being a fit *c·*.

(see also **Eddy***)*

count

Mis.	8–17	*c·* your enemy to be that which
	149–11	*c·* the baskets full of accessions
	281–16	* "It is wise to *c·* the cost of
	281–17	* wiser to *c·* the cost of *not*
	281–19	we must *c·* as nothing,
	281–21	*c·* ourselves always as debtors to
	297–24	he will *c·* the consequences of his
	391– 8	Will *c·* their mercies o'er,
'00.	6– 4	"I *c·* not myself to have — *Phil.* 3 : 13.
'01.	31–20	blessings infinite I *c·* these dear :
Po.	38– 7	Will *c·* their mercies o'er,
My.	127–26	not costly as men *c·* cost,
	256–21	We *c·* our blessings and see

counted

Mis.	176–15	*c·* not their own lives dear
Man.	55–16	shall not be *c·* loyal till after

countenance

Mis.	148– 1	never shows us a smiling *c·*
Ret.	42–14	smile . . . resting on his serene *c·*.
Un.	29–26	health of my *c·*, — *Psal.* 42 : 11.
Pan.	4–24	health of my *c·*, — *Psal.* 42 : 11.
My.	249–17	*c·* such evil tendencies.

counter

Mis.	301–30	*c·* to the commands of our
'02.	14–16	so *c·* to the common convictions of

counteract

Mis.	7–21	A periodical of our own will *c·*
	291–30	*c·* the influence of envious minds
My.	129– 9	*c·* the trend of mad ambition.
	249– 7	*c·* its most gigantic falsities.

counteracting

Mis.	223–22	no *c·* influence can hinder
My.	294– 9	because of the mental *c·* elements,

counteracts

'02.	9–29	*c·* ignorance and superstition

counterfeit

Mis.	60–28	has its *c·* in some matter belief.
	61– 5	against the material . . . *c·* sciences.
	71–27	is the *c·* of the divine,
	173–26	the *c·* of man's creator
	250–19	cast aside the word as a . . . *c·*,
	375– 4	*c·* of the spiritual
No.	25–25	sinful mortal is but the *c·* of
Pan.	11– 2	to cast out the unreal or *c·*.
My.	175–27	am sure that the *c·* letters

counterfeits

Mis.	351–20	Evil *c·* good :
Rud.	4– 5	of which . . . are the *c·*.

countermand

Mis.	xii– 4	command and *c·* ;
	10–15	*c·* their order, retrace their
	119–29	reverse your rules, *c·* your orders,
	124– 3	would tend to . . . *c·* the Scripture
	346–26	*c·* this first command of Solomon,

counterpart

Mis.	173–26	not the *c·* but the counterfeit

counterpoised

My.	129–16	*c·* his origin from dust,

countersign

Man.	37– 3	*c·* an application for membership
	109– 6	No persons are eligible to *c·*

countersigned

Man.	35– 4	*c·* by one of Mrs. Eddy's loyal
	38– 8	application must be *c·* by

countersigners
  Man. 110–11 applicants, approvers, or c·,
Countess of Dunmore and Family
  My. 295–23 C· of D· and F·, 55 Lancaster Gate
counties
  Man. 99–18 Committee for the c· in which
counting
  My. 178–12 * "c· the legs of insects"?
countless
  My. vi– 1 * to well-nigh c· numbers
        42–17 * gratitude for the c· blessings
countries
  Pul. 53– 3 * though practised in other c·
  My. 73– 5 * in other c· since that time,
        94–23 * foreign c· were in attendance.
       315–30 in our own and in other c·,
country (*see also* **country's**)
  Mis. 251–11 religion, home, friends, and c·.
        303–24 profitable to the heart of our c·.
  Ret.   7–15 * distinguished men in the c·.
        48–22 and sent to all parts of our c·,
  Pul. 23–11 * has swept over the c·,
        30–10 * includes those all over the c·.
        36– 8 * from Europe as well as this c·.
        46–16 * Her family came to this c·
        47–22 * Mrs. Eddy has a delightful c· home
        47–26 * driving rather into the c·,
        58– 8 * believers throughout this c·
        60–16 * from all parts of the c·.
        62– 2 * a novelty in this c·,
        63–12 * her delightful c· home in Concord,
        63–25 * Christian Scientists all over the c·,
        66– 8 * societies in every part of the c·.
        66–19 * uncommon development in this c·
        68–11 * c· residence in her native State.
        70–16 * Christian Scientists all over the c·.
        71–14 * and in fact all over the c·,
        78– 3 * ever wrought in this c·.
        80– 7 * the freest c· in the world
  Pan.   3–27 patron of c· life,
        14–10 chapter sub-title
        14–11 Pray for the prosperity of our c·,
        14–20 Oh, may their love of c·,
  '00. 10–29 serving his c· in that torrid zone
  '02. 11– 3 mortals who seek for a better c·
        15– 5 protection of the laws of my c·.
  My. 29–14 * pageantries have been seen in this c·
        67–22 * But one church in the c· exceeds
        71–17 * church edifices in the c·
        73– 5 * churches all over this c·
        74– 1 * western sections of this c·.
        77–13 * practically every civilized c·,
        79–19 * intelligence and wisdom of the c·
        85–18 * architectural beauties of the c·.
        91–18 * this c· or any other c·
        92–18 * every other sect in the c·
        97–21 * has opened the eyes of the c·
        98– 4 * C. S. army in this c·
        98–22 * in this c· or elsewhere,
       100– 9 * nearly all, parts of the c·,
       104–27 in this or any other c·.
       129– 8 throughout our beloved c·
       167–30 In our c· the day of heathenism,
       234–24 teaching C. S. in her c·.
       278–19 him who dies in defence of his c·,
       284–16 * history of the church in this c·
       291–30 work for their own c·,
       311– 3 his c· home in North Groton, N. H.,
       313–23 * nor did "the superstitious c· folk
       329–22 * when the whole c· is recognizing
country's
  Po. 10– 8 Didst rock the c· cradle
  My. 337– 9 Didst rock the c· cradle
Country-Seat and **country-seat**
  Ret. page 17 poem
  Pul. 70–26 * c· in Concord, N. H.
  Po. vi–29 * poem
        page 62 poem
county
  Man. 99– 6 Each c· of Great Britain
couple
  My. 59–18 * scarce fill a c· of pews
       118–30 which would . . . c· evil with good.
       314–26 the means of reconciling the c·.
coupled
  '02. 17– 1 c· with selfishness, worldliness,
couplers
  (*see* **organ**)
couples
  '00.   4– 1 misnomer c· love and hate,
  My. 108–13 c· faith with spiritual understanding

couplet
  Un. 44– 7 if the . . . c· may be so paraphrased
  My. 347–11 illustrated by Keats' touching c·,
courage
  Mis. 30–26 Take c·, dear reader,
        99– 9 c· of his convictions fell
       116–18 the c· of honest convictions,
       210–27 Charity has the c· of conviction ;
       257–18 fear where c· is requisite,
       294–22 but thank God and take c·,
       299–11 come with the c· of conviction
  Pul. 83– 6 * moral strength and c·
  '01. 30–25 far-seeing vision, the calm c·,
        32–13 c· of their convictions was seen.
  My. 50–20 * brought fresh c· to the
       131– 5 gives him c·, devotion, and
       140–18 *Christian Scientists :* — Take c·.
       191–24 Immortal c· fills the human breast
       209– 7 fidelity, c·, patience, and grace.
       211–22 fear where c· should be
courageous
  Mis. 288– 2 and c· convictions regarding
  My. 208–24 God bless the c·, far-seeing
course
  above-named
  Mis. 349–11 had taken the above-named c·
  college
  '01. 29–30 * our tuition for the college c·."
  comet's
  Mis. 266–12 career is like the comet's c·,
  erroneous
  Mis. 352– 8 error of its present erroneous c·,
  free
  Man. 91–12 a free c· in this department
  No. 45–24 Let the Word have free c·
  native
  Pul.   6–30 the native c· of whose mind
  of lessons
  Ret. 50– 5 one c· of lessons at my College,
  Primary
  Mis. 264–14 not fitted for it by the Primary c·.
  regular
  Rud. 14–27 regular c· of instruction from me,
  right
  Mis. 212–19 rush in against the right c· ;
  straight to the
  Mis. 268–14 Scientist keeps straight to the c·.
  such a
  Mis. 349– 7 Such a c· with such a teacher
  their
  Mis. 41–13 keep the faith and finish their c·.
       203–12 you have coaxed in their c·
       280–29 the rocks and sirens in their c·,
  Man. 88–19 nor on their c· or conduct.
  Ret. 11–14 That widen in their c·.
  Po. 60–11 That widen in their c·.
  this
  Mis. 220–12 He persists in this c· until the
  My. 200–25 gap between this c· and C. S.
  unswerving
  Mis. 291–22 true and unswerving c· of a

  Mis. ix–15 To preserve a long c· of years
        19–27 choose our c· and its results.
        39– 2 c· of instruction in C. S.
        64–12 Persons contemplating a c· at the
        79–26 *What c· should Christian Scientists*
       225– 8 In the c· of the evening,
  Man. 68–13 members whom she teaches the c·
  Ret. 14– 4 I was of c· present.
  Pul. 32– 9 * Of c· such a personality,
        82– 9 * no more turn her from her c· than
  No. 45– 9 is of c· out of the question.
  Po. 19– 1 My c·, like the eagle's,
        68–22 Be its c· through our heavens,
  My. 12– 1 * of c· carried the implication
        21– 7 * c· suggested will not only
        92– 1 * Of c· the new idea will never
       232– 1 you are recognizing the proper c·,
       304– 5 finished my c· of studies under
       343–21 but of c· the term pope is
courses
  Un. 17– 6 the stars in their c· — *Judg.* 5 : 20.
Court
  Mis. 380–29 by decree and order of the C·,
       381–22 under the seal of the said C·,
  My. 137– 4 * office of the Clerk of the C·,
       327– 3 in the C· of New Hampshire,
       (*see also* **Superior Court**)
court
  Rud.   1–17 appearance (in c·, for example)
  Pan.   3–17 * We c· fair wisdom,

court

My. 113– 2 in c· and in cottage,
188–23 C. S. has a place in its c·,
287–12 Love lived in a c· or cot is
294–30 c· of the Vatican mourns him ;
314–13 the c· record may state
314–17 who were present in c·
314–20 the c· instructed the clerk to

courtesy

Ret. 88– 1 The same c· should be observed
Pul. 36–15 * by her hospitable c·,
36–27 * to whose c· I am much indebted
My. 123–13 by the c· of another person
174– 6 c· extended to my friends
174– 8 c· of the efficient city marshal
271–21 * requesting the c· of a reply :
271–28 To your c· and to your question
341– 2 breathe it to the breeze as God's c·.

court-house

My. 346–12 * made several turns about the c·

courtier

Mis. 224– 7 c· told Constantine that a mob

court-room

My. 185–12 in the pulpit, in the c·,

courts

Mis. 79–27 *persons brought before the c·*
373–18 as living feebly, in kings' c·.
Man. 48–10 impertinent towards . . . the c·,
My. 326– 3 * legislatures and c· are thus
340–17 c· immediately annulling such

cousin

Ret. 3– 9 A c· of my grandmother
8–13 One day, when my c·, Mehitable
8–17 surprised, my c· turned to me
8–24 my c· had heard the voice,
9– 2 led my c· into an adjoining
9– 6 My c· answered quickly,
Pul. 48–17 * her c·, was born and bred in that

covenant

Mis. 285–24 severs the marriage c·,
297–19 claims of the marriage c·,
My. 49–15 * also the tenets and church c·.
131–13 seals the c· of everlasting love.
177–24 everlasting c· with them."— *Isa.* 61 : 8.
188– 9 your ark of the c· will not be

cover

Mis. 19–18 wherewith to c· iniquity,
147–26 He seeks no mask to c· him,
172–10 shall c· with her feathers
209–31 to c· iniquity and punish it not,
210–29 foolhardiness to c· iniquity.
224–24 to c· the whole world's evil,
263– 8 "He shall c· thee— *Psal.* 91 : 4.
Pul. 86– 3 * upon the c· of which
86– 8 * On the under side of the c·
My. 127–31 a c· and a defence adapted to
212–31 he says this to c· his crime of

covered

Mis. 263–11 and c· from the devourer
352–31 while sickness must be c· with the
Ret. 4–21 herds, c· areas of rich acres,
'01. 10– 7 there is nothing c·,— *Matt.* 10 : 26.
Hea. 5–19 grand truth which is constantly c·,

covereth

Mis. 153–16 wherein violence c· men
213– 9 "He that c· his sins— *Prov.* 28 : 13.

covering

Mis. 335–21 notion that one is c· iniquity
Pul. 26– 1 * c· one hundred and forty-four
52–22 * c· it with the blackness of the
My. 328–23 * act of the Legislature c· it

coverings

Mis. 7– 4 loaded down with c·

covers

Mis. 208– 4 it c· all sin and its effects.
246– 2 that cradles and c· the sins of
Ret. 63–19 Whosoever c· iniquity becomes
My. 178–25 c· of the book were burned up,
273– 9 * c· practically the civilized world.

covert

Mis. 144–16 c· from the tempest ;— *Isa.* 32 : 2.
My. 182–29 and a c· from the tempest.

coveted

My. 163–23 retirement I so much c·,

covetousness

Mis. 19– 2 c·, lust, hatred, malice,
118–21 c·, envy, revenge, are foes to
123– 6 idolatry, envy, jealousy, c·,

coward

My. 225– 1 in which the c· and the hypocrite

cowardice

Mis. 210–28 neither the c· nor the foolhardiness
211–21 C · is selfishness.
267–18 from individual conceit, c·, or
'02. 18– 8 c· and self-seeking of his disciples

cowardly

Mis. 211– 4 His mode is not c·, uncharitable,
My. 211– 4 too c·, too ignorant, or too wicked

coworker

Pan. 6–18 creator or c· with God?

coworkers

'01. 29–15 grand c· for mankind,

cozy

Po. 53–14 And build their c· nests,

Crabtre

No. 23–12 According to C ·, these devils were

cradle

Mis. 321– 2 over the c· of a great truth,
329–20 rocking the oriole's c· ;
331–15 remember *their* c· hymns,
Ret. 11–18 The c· of her power,
Pul. vii–17 c· of this grand verity
No. 45–25 to leave c· and swaddling-clothes.
'01. 31–23 my c· hymn and the Lord's Prayer,
Po. 10– 8 Didst rock the country's c·
29– 8 No c· song, No natal hour
60–15 The c· of her power,
My. 257– 5 the new c· of an old truth.
257– 6 from c· to crown.
313–13 with a couch or c·
315–28 from the c· and the grave,
337– 9 Didst rock the country's c·

cradled

My. 122–21 not . . . finitized, cribbed, or c·,

cradles

Mis. 246– 2 c· and covers the sins of the world,

craft

'01. 30–15 they have no c· that is in danger.

craftily

My. 241– 7 * beware the net that is c· laid

craftiness

Mis. 191– 1 "dishonesty, c·,— see II Cor. 4 : 2.
'01. 16–15 world's god as dishonesty, c·,
My. 124– 1 not walking in c·,— II Cor. 4 : 2.

craftsmen

My. 66–20 * c· are hurrying on with their

crag

Po. v–11 * this lofty New Hampshire c·,

cramps

My. 84– 6 * a "church debt" c· and retards

crannies

My. 186– 6 in the c· of the rocks,

crass

Pul. 79–18 * from the c· materialism of

crave

Mis. 369–28 c· the privilege of saying to

craving

Mis. 227–26 the mind c· a higher good,
No. 46– 6 c· health and holiness,

cravings

Mis. 16– 2 the c· for immortality,
287–13 can satisfy immortal c·.
325– 8 few c· for the immortal,
My. 189–20 satisfies the immortal c·

craze

No. 19– 8 C. S. is no "Boston c· ;"
My. 302–10 c· is that matter masters mind ;

create

Mis. 25–28 if He could c· them otherwise,
26–18 to evolve or c· itself :
174– 1 to evolve or to c· matter
187–25 c· a sick, sinning, dying man?
304– 4 * c· a Columbian Liberty Bell,
306–25 love they c· in our hearts.
362–10 and out of nothing would c·
Un. 23–21 can He c· anything so wholly unlike
Pan. 5– 6 What, then, can matter c·,
5– 8 Did God c· evil?
My. 122– 2 this would c· for one's self
149–11 tides of truth . . . c· and govern it ;

created

Mis. 25–27 If God c· drugs good,
25–29 and if He c· drugs for healing
49–31 Truth never c· error,
56–30 first spiritually c· the universe,
56–30 implies that Spirit, . . . c· man over
57–23 universe with man c· spiritually.
57–24 and the universe c· materially.
61–12 was c· in the image of God,

created

Mis.	97– 23	"He *c·* man in the image and
	97– 24	likeness of Mind *c·* He him."
	182– 16	*c·* neither from dust nor
	186– 2	*c·* man in His own image
	247– 29	Everything that God *c·*,
	346– 9	If God *c·* only the good,
Ret.	22– 18	nor is he ever *c·* through the flesh ;
	60– 9	sense adds that the divine Spirit *c·*
	67– 18	The sinner *c·* neither himself nor
	67– 19	sin *c·* the sinner ;
	69– 22	God *c·* all through Mind,
Un.	14– 16	*c·* children proved sinful ;
	15– 8	God *c·* all things,
	20– 7	*First:* The Lord *c·* it.
	23– 20	unless God has *c·* them?
	64– 1	All that *is,* God *c·*.
Pul.	82– 14	* because she was *c·* after man,
	82– 15	* was *c·* solely for man.
No.	17– 9	*c·* in the eternal Science of being
Pan.	7– 9	*c·* all things spiritually,
	11– 6	Him that *c·* him." — *Col.* 3 : 10.
'01.	5– 12	the creator and the *c·*,
	18– 17	If God *c·* drugs for medical use,
Hea.	16– 24	shall we say that God hath *c·*
	17– 7	personal senses were *c·* by God?
My.	87– 12	* The impression *c·* is that of
	122– 14	*c·* surprise in our good city of
	182– 22	that *c·* and governs the universe
	232– 25	man *c·* by and of Spirit,
	239– 26	spiritual man, *c·* by God,

creates

Mis.	27– 4	That God, good, *c·* evil,
	27– 5	or that Spirit *c·* its opposite,
Un.	48– 14	Father and Mother of all He *c·* ;
My.	189– 16	love it *c·* in the heart of man ;
	225– 19	the names of that which He *c·*.
	262– 1	God *c·* man perfect and eternal

creating

Mis.	37– 2	*c·* or governing man or the universe.
	294– 4	the concepts of his own *c·*,
	305– 13	* In *c·* the bell it is particularly

Creation

Pul.	38– 10	"*C·*," "Science of Being,"

creation (*see also* creation's)

bases
Ret.	68– 21	it bases *c·* on materiality"

category of
'02.	7– 6	not into the category of *c·*

climax of
No.	17– 13	Man is the climax of *c·* ;

creator and
Un.	36– 3	double capacity of creator and *c·*.
My.	103– 10	of the creator and *c·*.

error of
Mis.	57– 23	The false sense and error of *c·*

every
Mis.	60– 27	every *c·* or idea of Spirit

Genesis of
Mis.	258– 12	In the spiritual Genesis of *c·*,

God's
Mis.	87– 5	to caricature God's *c·*,
	286– 13	in the dawn of God's *c·*,
Pan.	6– 14	order and harmony of God's *c·*.

His
Mis.	22– 18	untruths belong not to His *c·*,
	362– 14	part and parcel of His *c·*?
Un.	30– 17	interpretation of God and His *c·*
	48– 15	no more enters into His *c·* than
	48– 16	His *c·* is not the Ego,
Pan.	3– 20	reveals Himself . . . to His *c·*,
	9– 3	means one God and His *c·*,
'02.	7– 8	understanding . . . of God and His *c·*,

His own
Mis.	354– 21	to govern His own *c·*,

impossible
'02.	6– 15	human woe . . . an impossible *c·*,

its own
Un.	45– 20	imaginary sphere of its own *c·*

law of
Mis.	258– 15	This is the law of *c·* :
	259– 14	Lawgiver was the only law of *c·*,

material
Pan.	7– 9	belief, . . . a material *c·* took place,

named in the
'00.	14– 7	number of days named in the *c·*,

no other
My.	235– 22	no other creator and no other *c·*.

of Adam
Mis.	186– 3	In the *c·* of Adam from dust,

of the schools
'01.	34– 14	but a *c·* of the schools

other
Mis.	57– 5	what evidence . . . of any other *c·*?

creation

Principle of
Mis.	361– 27	God, . . . divine Principle of *c·*,

reckons
My.	349– 31	reckons *c·* as its own creator,

reflection is
Mis.	23– 23	God, whose reflection is *c·*,

regards
Mis.	362– 15	regards *c·* as its own creator,

Science of
Mis.	57– 22	Science of *c·* is the universe with
	57– 27	Science of *c·* is stated in

seven days of
Mis.	279– 18	to the seven days of *c·* :

spiritual
My.	179– 5	account of the spiritual *c·*,

support of
No.	38– 15	the basis and support of *c·*,

true
Mis.	57– 8	the true *c·* was finished,

understood
Mis.	286– 32	*c·* understood as the most exalted

vast
Po.	1– 8	when first *c·* vast began,

work of
'00.	3– 28	improved on his work of *c·*,

Mis.	8– 10	thing outside thine own *c·*?
	23– 11	Was it Mind or . . . that spake in *c·*,
	27– 23	*C·*, evolution, or manifestation,
	57– 25	*a c· of the sixth and last day,*
	185– 31	namely, that *c·* is material :
	188– 4	*c·* joined in the grand chorus
My.	5– 11	Whence, then, came the *c·* of matter,

creation's

Mis.	388– 2	Which swelled *c·* lay :
'02.	20– 11	Which swelled *c·* lay,
Po.	7– 2	Which swelled *c·* lay :
	70– 19	To hail *c·* glorious morn

creations

Ret.	69– 18	believing that . . . are *c·* of God,

creative

Mis.	57– 5	The *c·* "Us" made all,
	361– 27	is by no means a *c·* partner
Un.	19– 5	contrary to His *c·* will,

creator

and creation
Un.	36– 3	double capacity of *c·* and creation.
My.	103– 10	Science . . . of the *c·* and creation.

and preserver
Pan.	4– 5	*c·* and preserver of man.

and the created
'01.	5– 12	God and man, the *c·* and the created,

before the
Mis.	330– 16	let mortals bow before the *c·*,

evil is not a
Un.	25– 20	Evil is not a *c·*.

his
Mis.	46– 19	in the scale *with* his *c·* ;
	294– 11	and honors his *c·*.
Un.	14– 26	which is everlasting in his *c·*
	15– 15	for his likeness to his *c·*.
My.	247– 5	whereby man governed by his *c·* is
	254– 1	one with his *c·*,
	254– 26	whereby man governed by his *c·* is

intelligent
Pan.	6– 18	intelligent *c·* or coworker with God?

its own
Mis.	362– 16	regards creation as its own *c·*,
My.	349– 32	reckons creation as its own *c·*,

man's
Mis.	173– 26	counterfeit of man's *c·*

Mind was the
Mis.	57– 6	and Mind was the *c·*.

no other
My.	235– 22	no other *c·* and no other creation.

of man
Pan.	4– 16	He is the *c·* of man,

of the claim
Mis.	293– 23	*c·* of the claim of error.

one
Mis.	361– 11	testifying to one *c·*,

the only
Mis.	56– 9	Life is God, the only *c·*,
	286– 27	Spirit, God, is the only *c·* :
Un.	25– 21	God, good, is the only *c·*.
	32– 6	Spirit is the only *c·*,
	35– 26	Spirit is the only *c·*.
No.	6– 6	God is the only *c·*,

underived from its
Mis.	46– 16	no power underived from its *c·*.

was never a
Ret.	68– 1	material concept was never a *c·*,

creator
Mis.	26–32	or the *c·* of evil?
	72– 4	Science sets aside man as a *c·*,
Un.	25–18	*Evil.* I am a *c·*,
	32– 4	saying, "I am a *c·*.
Pan.	4–16	but that man also is a *c·*,
My.	32– 6	* in a heartfelt appeal to the *c·*.
	235–20	Is mortal man a *c·*,

creators
Mis.	57–19	ye shall be as gods," *c·*.— *Gen.* **3** : 5.
	304–26	* birthdays of the "*c·* of liberty ;"
No.	11– 2	desire, and fear, are not the *c·*,
Pan.	4–17	making two *c·* ;

creature
Mis.	8–10	Is it a *c·* or a thing
	8–14	or any other *c·* separate you
	175– 4	showeth them unto the *c·*,
Ret.	25– 1	and show them to the *c·*,
Un.	15–14	and the *c·* is punished for
'01.	9–23	showeth them unto the *c·* ;
My.	47–29	* gospel to every *c·*.— *Mark* 16 : 15.
	253–28	Let the *c·* become one with
	300–25	gospel to every *c·*," — *Mark* 16 : 15.

credentials
Man.	89–15	such *c·* as are required to
My.	245–24	these *c·* are still required

credible
My.	85–26	* Last Sunday it was entirely *c·*

credibly
Mis.	49– 3	We are *c·* informed that,

credit
Mis.	238–29	I accord these evil-mongers due *c·*,
	263–28	without *c·*, appreciation, or a
	264– 1	and give them *c·* for every
Ret.	75– 1	book-borrowing without *c·*
	75– 8	give *c·* when citing from the works
Pul.	73–23	* She placed no *c·* whatever in the
	80–16	* rather to the *c·* of the book
My.	vi–12	* *c·* for this extraordinary work.
	70– 6	* fine church edifices to its *c·*
	130–24	without *c·*, is inadmissible.
	224–19	at the same time giving full *c·*

credited
Mis.	226–19	* "Not to be *c·* when he
My.	118–22	*c·* only by human belief,

credulity
My.	80– 9	* severe tax upon frail human *c·*,

creed
Mis.	176–21	frozen ritual and *c·* should forever
	195–28	but deed, not *c·*, and
	331–13	frozen crust of *c·* and dogma,
	338–31	* A great and noble *c·*."
	399–13	Thou the Christ, and not the *c·* ;
Ret.	44– 3	Mind-healing church, without a *c·*,
	65–19	and prefers Christ to *c·*.
	65–26	and they need no *c·*.
Pul.	65– 1	* belief in that curious *c·*
'01.	5– 1	he breaks faith with his *c·*,
	5–28	necessitates a *c·* to explain both
	33–14	platform, a *c·*, or a diploma
Hea.	7–28	contains no argument for a *c·*
Po.	71– 2	Or cruel *c·*, or earth-born taint :
	75–20	Thou the Christ, and not the *c·* ;
My.	47–26	* in the wilderness of dogma and *c·*,
	50–12	* against the currents of dogma, *c·*,
	85–15	* followers of this *c·*
	87–28	* whatever one's special *c·* may be,
	96–12	* attesting their faith in the *c·*
	148–25	it is not a *c·* or dogma,
	157–10	* without regard to class or *c·*,
	183– 1	infinite uses of Christ's *c·*,
	205–24	human hypotheses, matter, *c·* and
	266– 7	ritual, *c·*, and trusts in place of
	288–15	*c·*, dogma, or *materia medica*.
	301– 7	dogma and *c·* will pass off in scum,

creedal
Ret.	14–18	even if my *c·* doubts left me outside

creeds
Man.	17– 3	forming a church without *c·*,
Pul.	67–12	* enumeration of John Bull's *c·*.
No.	15– 9	explain and prop old *c·*,
	15–13	notions . . . to be found in *c·*
	24–16	human philosophies or *c·* :
'00.	7– 5	*c·* and dogmas have been sifted,
My.	96–15	* comparison with other *c·*.
	122–26	not the material Christ of *c·*,
	248–28	indifference, chance, and *c·*.
	299–13	portions of truth may be found in *c·*.
	299–16	and lacking in the *c·*.
	307–27	*materia medica*, dogma, and *c·*,
	350–25	horoscope of crumbling *c·*,

creeping
Mis.	111– 6	human pride, *c·* into its meshes,

crept
Mis.	326–13	*c·* unseen into the synagogue,

crescendo
Mis.	116–15	As *c·* and *diminuendo* accent music,

crescent
Mis.	276– 2	and the *c·* with a star.

crest
Un.	45– 5	rears its *c·* proudly,
Po.	1– 2	unfallen still thy *c·* !

crib
Chr.	53–24	O'er babe and *c·*.

cribbed
My.	122–21	finitized, *c·*, or cradled.

cricket's
Mis.	396– 5	*c·* sharp, discordant scream
Po.	58–17	*c·* sharp, discordant scream

cried
Pul.	44–27	* custodian of funds *c·* "enough"
My.	81–16	* "Dresden !" "Peoria !" they *c·*.
	211–10	unclean spirits *c·* out,
	290–16	have I *c·* unto Thee." — *Psal.* 130 : 1.

cries
Mis.	204– 4	humble before God, he *c·*,
Ret.	4–17	now the lone night-bird *c·*,

crieth
'01.	9–20	*c·* out, "Let us alone ; — *Mark* 1 : 24.

crime
Mis.	61–15	* is held responsible for the *c·* ;
	112–12	The mental stages of *c·*,
	112–18	He had no sense of his *c·* ;
	119– 7	coax the unwary man to commit a *c·*,
	122– 1	to suffer for evil-doers — a *c·*
	122–22	lessens not . . . the criminal's *c·* ;
	123–10	pagan priests bloated with *c·* ;
	221–30	Who would tell another of a *c·* that
	221–31	or call public attention to that *c·*?
	227– 3	no fraternity where its *c·* may stand
	227– 8	*c·* comes within its jurisdiction.
	246– 3	all unmitigated systems of *c·* ;
	301– 9	for what the law construes as *c·*.
	362–30	And pleasure is no *c·* except when
Pul.	7–17	power to wash away, . . . every *c·*,
No.	32– 6	can neither extinguish a *c·* nor
'00.	2–19	"By cheating, lying, and *c·* ;
Hea.	7–20	he charged home a *c·* to mind,
	7–22	knew that adultery is a *c·*,
Po.	71– 2	When earth, inebriate with *c·*,
My.	130– 5	hidden method of committing *c·*
	212–31	he says this to cover his *c·*
	222–29	holding of *c·* in check,

crimes
Mis.	222–22	*c·* committed under this new
'01.	20–23	*c·* committed under this new-old
	20–29	darkest and deepest of human *c·*.
My.	160–32	Concealed *c·*, the wrongs done

criminal (*see also* **criminal's**)
Mis.	70–13	rest . . . would come to the *c·*, if
	119– 6	If a *c·* coax the unwary man to
	211–17	Then, if a *c·* is at peace,
Un.	15–26	*c·* appeases, with a money-bag,
	29– 4	as does all *c·* law,
No.	30–10	*c·* who is punished by the law
	32– 4	pardon may encourage a *c·*
Hea.	7–22	and *mind* is the *c·*.
My.	276– 3	watched, as one watches a *c·*

criminal's
Mis.	122–21	hater's hatred nor the *c·* crime ;

criminals
Mis.	211– 8	supplies *c·* with bouquets

crimson
Mis.	376–27	gold, orange, pink, *c·*, violet ;
Ret.	17– 9	peers out, from her *c·* repose,
'00.	11–22	* It flooded the *c·* twilight
Po.	16–12	flitting through far *c·* glow,
	62– 9	peers out, from her *c·* repose,

cringing
Po.	35–12	And in the *c·* crowd

cripples
Ret.	16–12	Many pale *c·* went into the church
Peo.	3– 5	helpless invalids and *c·*.

crises
Mis.	176– 8	in the great *c·* of nations

crisis
Ret.	44–19	I saw that the *c·* had come

crisp
My.	137– 7	* *c·*, clear, plain-speaking English."

critic
Mis. 88–14 *c·* who knows whereof he speaks.
'01. 21–14 I am sorry for my *c·*,
21–23 Does this *c·* know of a better
27– 3 My *c·* also writes :
My. 97–15 * a rather bitter *c·* of Mrs. Eddy
330–15 * are questioned by this *c·*,
334–12 * since this *c·* places certain

critical
Mis. 245–12 directing more *c·* observation to

critically
Rud. 15–25 may be dissected more *c·*

criticise
Mis. 353–31 *c·* and disobey her ;
'01. 21–18 manifest unfitness to *c·* it

criticism
Mis. 88–16 glows in the shadow of darkling *c·*
216–16 conclusion that he is a power in *c·*,
224– 2 makes another's *c·* rankle,
Pan. 6–15 But the higher *c·* is not satisfied
'00. 11–27 His allegories are the highest *c·*
My. 3–19 higher *c·*, the higher hope ;
40– 8 * subsidence of *c·* among workers.
118–15 embarrass the higher *c·*.
136–28 spiritual thought and the higher *c·*.
237– 2 reference . . . to the "higher *c·*"
240– 5 chapter sub-title
240– 8 * call C. S. the higher *c·*
240– 9 I called C. S. the higher *c·*
240–16 higher *c·* because it criticizes evil,
323– 6 * unfair *c·* of you and your book
329–29 * *c·* of this good woman

criticisms
'01. 18– 4 weak *c·* and woeful warnings
'02. 14–28 forever silence all private *c·*,
My. 317–12 so as to avail myself of his *c·*
317–13 which *c·* would enable me to

criticized
My. 142–13 important events are *c·*.
146– 9 has been quoted and *c·* :
179–15 the Scriptures are *c·*.
276– 5 therefore to be *c·* or judged

criticizes
My. 240–16 higher criticism because it *c·* evil,

critics
Mis. 66–22 Cynical *c·* misjudge my meaning
193–19 when *c·* attacked me for
372– 1 *c·* declared that it was incorrect,
372–14 I sought the judgment of sound *c·*
Ret. 37– 6 the *c·* took pleasure in saying,
'01. 30–17 higher class of *c·* in theology
My. 95–23 * higher *c·* and the men of science
98–10 * *c·* who seek the light
318– 8 *c·* declared that my book was

critique
Mis. 88– 7 *author of that genuine c· in*

crook
Pan. 3–29 his shepherd's *c·*,

crooked
My. 140– 5 *c·* things straight. — *Isa.* 42 : 16.

crops
Mis. 26–10 believes that his *c·* come from the

Cross, Miss
Pul. 69– 2 * Miss *C·* came from Syracuse,

cross
agony of the
No. 33–15 the brief agony of the *c·* ;
and the crown
Mis. 135–15 take this *c·*, and the crown
Pul. 28– 9 * The *c·* and the crown and the star
bearing the
Hea. 19–23 bearing the *c·* meekly along the
bear the
Mis. 211–32 refuses to bear the *c·* and to
'02. 20–23 but in this, . . . I can bear the *c·*,
bore the
Mis. 64– 4 Our Master bore the *c·*
down from the
Un. 58– 7 come down from the *c·*." — *Mark* 15 : 30.
58– 9 coming down from the *c·*,
endured the
Ret. 22–12 endured the *c·*, — *Heb.* 12 : 2.
My. 258–15 endured the *c·*, — *Heb.* 12 : 2.
example on the
Ret. 26– 5 Christian example on the *c·*,
glorifies the
'02. 19–28 divine Science glorifies the *c·*
his
Ret. 86–18 taking up his *c·* and following
My. 4– 8 taketh not his *c·*, — *Matt.* 10 : 38.
229–17 doth not bear his *c·*, — *Luke* 14 : 27.

cross
his
My. 233–24 taketh not his *c·*, — *Matt.* 10 : 38.
is the central emblem
Un. 57– 9 *c·* is the central emblem of
kiss the
Mis. 397– 3 I kiss the *c·*, and wake to know
Pul. 18–12 I kiss the *c·*, and wake to know
Po. 12–12 I kiss the *c·*, and wake to know
last at the
Mis. 100– 5 woman, "last at the *c·*,"
388–20 Last at the *c·* to mourn her Lord,
No. 45–14 woman, "last at the *c·*,"
Po. 21– 9 Last at the *c·* to mourn her Lord,
39–10 And she — last at the *c·*,
no
Hea. 1–13 "Then there were no *c·* to take up,
of Christ
Ret. 30–21 and the *c·* of Christ.
soldiers of the
Mis. 138–26 to all His soldiers of the *c·*
Un. 39–20 As soldiers of the *c·* we must
take up the
Mis. 115–13 take up the *c·* as I have done,
Ret. 65–12 Mortals must take up the *c·*
No. 2–11 deny self, sense, and take up the *c·*.
this
Mis. 135–15 Then take this *c·*,
158–18 obedience in bearing this *c·*.
thy
Mis. 328–31 bear thy *c·* up to the throne
to crown
My. 163– 5 from *c·* to crown, from sense to Soul,
wait at the
My. 305–22 I still wait at the *c·* to learn
without the
Mis. 357–11 Without the *c·* and healing,

Mis. 135–14 Is it a *c·* to give one week's time
138–16 love made perfect through the *c·*.
162–11 *c·* became the emblem of Jesus'
212–30 friends took down from the *c·*
'01. 25– 6 the *c·*, which they reject
My. 6–19 modest edifice . . . began with the *c·* ;
155–30 in the flowers and the *c·* from
180–27 But this is the *c·*.

cross-bearing
Mis. 213– 4 through *c·*, self-forgetfulness,
Ret. 54– 5 It demands less *c·*,

crossed
Mis. 285–15 first *c·* swords with free-love,
Ret. 2– 9 *c·* the Atlantic more than a
2–23 nor had they *c·* the ocean ;

crossing
Mis. 10–17 *c·* swords with temptation,
My. 43–12 * The *c·* of the Jordan

Croton oil
Mis. 69–15 given three doses of *C· o·*,
My. 292–23 *c· o·* is not mixed with morphine

crouching
Mis. 246–21 awaits the *c·* wrong that refused

croup
Mis. 44– 7 *acute cases . . . as in membranous c·?*

crow
Ret. 4–17 the *c·* caws cautiously,
Pul. 48–15 * Straight as the *c·* flies,

crowd
Mis. 339–12 The elbowing of the *c·*
Ret. 16– 4 pushing their way through the *c·*,
Po. 35–12 in the cringing *c·* Companionless
My. 30–29 * the largest *c·* of the day
87– 7 * the characteristics of this *c·*

crowded
Mis. 5– 6 *c·* with students who are
Pul. 60– 1 * vestibule and street . . . were *c·*
60–13 * The place was again *c·*,
My. 54– 8 * *c·* one hour before the service
55– 1 * at this service . . . the hall was *c·*.
55–21 * was *c·* to overflowing.
75–19 * *C·* as the hall was yesterday,
80–21 * *c·* into the auditorium
304–12 lectured in large and *c·* halls

crowding
My. 54– 4 * inconvenience that comes from *c·*,
82– 7 * *c·* Boston the last week
323–20 * *c·* thoughts of gratitude

crowds
My. 30– 1 * held large *c·* of people,
54–24 * *c·* had besieged the doors
73–29 * *c·* of Christian Scientists
82–17 * edifice was emptied of its *c·*

crown

Mis.	100–25	*c·* them with blessings infinite.
	135–15	take this cross, and the *c·* with it.
	155–12	and peace will *c·* your joy.
	231– 2	formed a *c·* of glory ;
	252–18	the *c·* of Christianity.
	295–30	worn the English *c·*
	321–22	And battling for a brighter *c·*.
	330–29	and *c·* imperial unveils its regal
	331– 1	*c·* the full corn in the ear,
	340– 9	win and wear the *c·* of the faithful.
	388–16	Her dazzling *c·*, her sceptred throne,
	389– 2	The hoary head with joy to *c·* ;
	392– 9	her noonday glories *c·*?
Ret.	85–26	will *c·* the effort of to-day
	86– 2	to *c·* patient toil, and rejoice in
Pul.	4–19	*c·* the tree with blossoms.
	4–22	his diadem a *c·* of crowns.
	28– 9	* The cross and the *c·* and the star
	83–29	* a *c·* of twelve stars.'' — *Rev.* 12 : 1.
'00.	13–15	give thee a *c·* of life.'' — *Rev.* 2 : 10.
	14– 5	that no man take thy *c·*.'' — *Rev.* 3 : 11.
'01.	25– 7	whereby is won the *c·*
'02.	18– 9	helped *c·* with thorns the life of
Hea.	2–15	passed from his execution to a *c·*,
Po.	20–13	her noonday glories *c·*?
	21– 4	Her dazzling *c·*, her sceptered
	21–16	The hoary head with joy to *c·* ;
	44– 2	*C·* the lives thus blest
My.	6–19	its excelsior extension is the *c·*.
	84–14	* Its stately cupola is a fitting *c·*
	125–22	stars in my *c·* of rejoicing.
	128–13	No *c·* nor sceptre nor rulers
	150– 9	joy and *c·* of such a pilgrimage
	163– 5	from cross to *c·*, from sense to
	180–27	Take it up, — it wins the *c·* ;
	201–13	Even the *c·* of thorns,
	253– 9	* manhood's glorious *c·* to gain.''
	257– 6	from cradle to *c·*.
	274–25	this is my *c·* of rejoicing,
	347–16	beautiful pearls that *c·* this cup

crowned

Mis.	124–26	*c·* and still crowns Christianity :
	320– 4	*c·* with the history of Truth's idea,
	360–14	When shall earth be *c·* with
	376–21	*c·* with an acre of eldritch ebony.
	386–29	with all the *c·* and blest,
Pul.	1–15	path behind thee is with glory *c·* ;
'00.	1–11	*c·* with unprecedented prosperity ;
Po.	26– 3	track behind thee is with glory *c·* ;
	50–16	with all the *c·* and blest,
My.	256–18	*c·* with the dearest memories
	350–26	Truth delightful, *c·* with endless
	357–11	*c·* The Mother Church building

crowneth

My.	13–21	who *c·* thee with — *Psal.* 103 : 4.

crowning

My.	6–22	Its *c·* ultimate rises to
	94–26	''*c·* ultimate'' of the church
	192–28	*c·* your endeavors, and
	208–15	*c·* the hope and hour of
	323–22	* Your *c·* triumph over error

crowns

Mis.	118–27	obedience *c·* persistent effort
	124–27	crowned and still *c·* Christianity :
	267–29	and *c·* them with success ;
	393–12	*C·* life's Cliff for such as we.
Chr.	53–44	*C·* the pale brow.
Ret.	71– 1	not the forager . . . that God thus *c·*,
Pul.	4–22	his diadem a crown of *c·*.
'02.	19–28	*c·* the association with our Saviour
Po.	51–17	*C·* life's Cliff for such as we.
My.	62–11	* glory which *c·* the completion of
	250– 6	and *c·* honest endeavors.
	285– 9	*c·* the great purposes of life

crucial

My.	225– 1	This is a *c·* hour,

crucible

Mis.	79– 2	dissolved in the *c·* of Truth,

crucified

Mis.	187–32	such as *c·* our Master,
	345–28	and talked of the *c·* Saviour ;
Chr.	53–29	Christ was not *c·*
Un.	56– 7	''*c·* the Lord of glory,'' — *I Cor.* 2 : 8.
'01.	9–12	rabbis, who *c·* Jesus
	14– 5	self-righteousness *c·* Jesus.
My.	119–16	away from the supposedly *c·*
	333–25	* on the merits of a *c·* Redeemer.
	334–23	self-righteousness *c·* Jesus.''

crucifixion

Mis.	33– 4	*c·* of even the great Master ;
	63–28	through the *c·* of the human,

crucifixion

Mis.	121–21	arrest, trial, and *c·* of
	122– 2	foretelling his own *c·*,
	163–25	*c·* of the corporeal man,
Man.	16– 5	We acknowledge that the *c·* of
Ret.	26– 7	to allay the tortures of *c·*.

crucifixions

Mis.	107– 6	self-denials, and *c·* of the flesh.

crucify

Mis.	270–22	schools which *c·* him,

crude

Mis.	360– 3	encumbered with *c·*, rude fragments,
Un.	4–28	at the present *c·* hour,
Pul.	32– 8	* not by any *c·* self-assertion,
My.	111– 5	false psychics, *c·* theories or modes

cruder

Pul.	79–19	* materialism of the *c·* science

crudest

Peo.	3– 3	*c·* ideals of speculative theology

cruel

Mis.	19– 1	is unjust, — is wrong and *c·*.
	41– 1	brute-force that only the *c·* and evil
	257–13	is *c·* and merciless.
	324–21	odious company and the *c·* walls.
Un.	23– 1	*c·* treatment received by old Gloster
Po.	29–19	*c·* creed, or earth-born taint :

cruelly

Man.	53– 9	disrespectfully and *c·*,
My.	138–13	*c·*, unjustly, and wrongfully accused.

crumb

Mis.	xi–15	will find herein a ''canny'' *c·* ;
	369–19	*c·* that falleth from his table.

crumble

Mis.	140–30	though . . . should *c·* into dust,
Pul.	7–22	tabernacles *c·* with dry rot.

crumbled

Peo.	14– 7	churchyards have *c·* into decay,

crumbling

Peo.	1– 5	*c·* away of material elements
My.	200–21	on *c·* thrones of justice
	350–25	horoscope of *c·* creeds,

crumbs

Mis.	106–20	*c·* fallen from this table of Truth,
My.	133–12	These *c·* and monads will feed the

crush

No.	34–16	the endeavor to *c·* out of a career its

crushed

Ret.	32– 8	is *c·* as the moth.
My.	128– 9	Truth *c·* to earth springs . . . upward,

crushing

My.	350–18	This *c·* out of health and peace,

crust

Mis.	331–23	frozen *c·* of creed and dogma,

crutches

Mis.	168– 6	or hobbling on *c·*,
Ret.	16–13	went into the church leaning on *c·*

cry

Mis.	63–22	*why did Jesus c· out,*
	64– 2	human *c·* which voiced that struggle ;
	81–23	*c·* in the desert of earthly joy ;
	209–16	and *c·*, ''Peace, peace ; — *Jer.* 6 : 14.
	246–13	The *c·* of the colored slave
	246–15	another sharp *c·* of oppression.
	342–19	Hear that human *c·* :
	369– 6	chapter sub-title
Pul.	82–28	* remain deaf to their *c·*?
'00.	7–26	fails, and we *c·*, ''Save, — *Matt.* 8 : 25.
	9–11	or as of old *c·* out :
'02.	10– 5	and mortals *c·* out,
Po.	71–22	''*C·* aloud !'' — *Isa.* 58 : 1.
	73–13	The sea-mew's lone *c·*,

crying

Mis.	99–26	voice of one *c·* in the wilderness,
	231–22	instead of a real set-to at *c·*,
	246–23	was heard *c·* in the wilderness,

crystal

Mis.	332–16	*c·* streams of the Orient,
Pul.	7–15	Those *c·* globes made morals for

crystallized

No.	2– 2	that *c·* expression, C. S.
My.	13–31	*c·* into a foundation for our

C. S.

Man.	46– 7	Use of Initials ''C. S.''
	46– 9	the initials ''C. S.'' after his name

C. S. B.
Man. 92–19 nor receive the degree of *C. S. B.*
My. 245–32 The first degree (*C. S. B.*) is given

C. S. D.
Man. 89–17 to receive the degree of *C. S. D.*
    91–22 not having the certificate of *C. S. D.*,
    92–19 the degree of C. S. B. or *C. S. D.*,
My. 244– 9 the degree of *C. S. D.*,
    246– 1 second degree (*C. S. D.*) is given to
    251–22 certificate of the degree *C. S. D.*

Cuba
Pan. 14–29 for the liberty of *C.*
'02. 3–12 inauguration of home rule in *C.*,
My. 81–15 * "Des Moines !" "Glasgow !" "*C.* !"

Cubans
My. 278– 4 so that the *C.* may learn to

cuckoo
Mis. 329–26 *c.* sounds her invisible lute,

Cullis, Dr.
Mis. 132–15 * "like to hear from Dr. *C.* ;
    132–28 * misrepresented either Dr. *C.* or

culminate
Mis. 366–25 *c.* in sickness, sin, disease, and
My. 311–15 seemed to *c.* at twelve years

culminates
Mis. 21– 5 *c.* in the Revelation of
    85–13 it *c.* in the fulfilment of

culminating
My. 127–22 *c.* in fierce attack,

culpable
Mis. 115– 5 *c.* ignorance of the workings of
    234– 7 nor gained by a *c.* attempt
    283–17 mistaken kindness, a *c.* ignorance,

culprit
Mis. 61–23 A *c.*, a sinner, — anything but a

cult
My. 77– 2 * the *c.* which it represents.
    77–11 * feature in the life of their *c.*
    85– 4 * growth of this *c.* is the marvel of
    88–28 * debt to that great and growing *c.*,
    94–18 * magnificent new temple of the *c.*
    96–26 * evident that the *c.* will soon
    97–16 * critic of Mrs. Eddy and her *c.*,
    99– 7 * a *c.* able to promote its faith
    100–10 * number of the followers of the *c.*
    341–22 * the Founder of the *c.*

cultivated
Ret. 4– 7 are still *c.* and owned by
My. 309– 3 *c.* in mind and manners.

cultivation
No. 1–13 silent *c.* of the true idea

cults
My. 95– 1 * included among the *c.*

culture
Mis. v– 5 INDISPENSABLE TO THE *c.* AND
    88–12 intellectual *c.*, reading, writing,
    224–14 constitution, *c.*, character,
    265–26 is not in the *c.* but the soil.
    317–26 *c.*, and singleness of purpose
'01. 31–21 my early *c.* in the Congregational
My. 211–31 admits of no intellectual *c.*
    304–23 * sound education and liberal *c.*"

cultured
Mis. 80–12 better to be friendly with *c.*
    356–10 My students, with *c.* intellects,
My. 285–14 most *c.* men and women

cumbereth
Mis. 151–12 why *c.* it the ground?" — *Luke* 13 : 7.

cunning
Pul. 55– 2 * Not in *c.* sleight of skill,

cunningly
My. 241– 7 * craftily laid and *c.* concealed

cup
bitter
  '02. 11–19 gave our glorified Master a bitter *c.*
Christ's
  Mis. 125– 9 Then shall he drink anew Christ's *c.*,
drain the
  Ret. 30–21 No one else can drain the *c.*
drop in the
  '02. 19–30 no redundant drop in the *c.*
his
  Mis. 212–32 had not yet drunk of his *c.*,
  Un. 56–14 shares his *c.* of sorrows.
Jesus'
  Ret. 54– 9 drinking Jesus' *c.*,
life's
  Mis. 9–16 friends seem to sweeten life's *c.*

cup
Master's
  Mis. 125– 1 indeed drink of our Master's *c.*,
  My. 258–21 they who drink their Master's *c.*
my
  Mis. 211–26 drink indeed of my *c.*" — *Matt.* 20 : 23.
  My. 161–20 drink indeed of my *c.*, — *Matt.* 20 : 23.
of Christ
  Mis. 144–28 wine poured into the *c.* of Christ.
  No. 34–11 They drink the *c.* of Christ
of cold water
  Pul. 14–16 Give them a *c.* of cold water
of gall
  Mis. 237–11 earth gives them such a *c.* of gall
of martyrdom
  Mis. 121– 7 even the *c.* of martyrdom :
of salvation
  Pan. 14– 9 drink of the *c.* of salvation,
of their Lord
  My. 161–17 *c.* of their Lord and Master
take the
  Mis. 311–28 ought not that one to take the *c.*,
this
  Mis. 9–17 We lift this *c.* to our lips ;
    9–22 this *c.* of selfish human enjoyment
    211–28 He drank this *c.* giving thanks,
  Ret. 30–24 without tasting this *c.*
  My. 347–11 design . . . encircling this *c.*,
    347–16 pearls that crown this *c.*

  Mis. 121– 6 is not the *c.* to which I call your
  Po. 66– 1 pure nectar our brimming *c.* fill,
  My. 126–18 *c.* which she hath filled — *Rev.* 18 : 6.
    131–10 *c.* red with loving restitution,

cupola
My. 84–14 * Its stately *c.* is a fitting crown

curative
Ret. 25– 1 reveal the great *c.* Principle,
    33–21 Mind, the *c.* Principle, remains,
    34– 1 utility of using a material *c.*
Pul. 64–16 * search for the great *c.* Principle.
    64–20 * the *c.* Principle was the Deity.
    70–20 * to find the great *c.* Principle
Hea. 13–20 Mind as the only *c.* Principle.
My. 105–28 my *c.* system of metaphysics.
    106– 1 proved to be more certain and *c.*
    301–30 drugs can produce no *c.* effect

cure (noun)
all
  Mis. 3–19 The Principle of all *c.* is God,
cause and
  Hea. 11–23 places all cause and *c.* as mind ;
    11–25 where cause and *c.* are supposed
effected the
  Mis. 243–11 effected the *c.* in less than one week.
instantaneous
  Mis. 355– 8 not guesswork, . . . but instantaneous *c.*
inventor of this
  Pul. 71– 7 * Mrs. Eddy, the inventor of this *c.*
its
  Mis. 343– 6 to find disease . . . and its *c.*,
not effected a
  Man. 46–26 where he has not effected a *c.*
of disease
  Pul. 69–25 * prayed for the *c.* of disease,
  Rud. 3– 1 harder than the *c.* of disease ;
    3–18 He wrought the *c.* of disease
of the sick
  No. 6–11 the consequent *c.* of the sick,
    30–26 *c.* of the sick demonstrates
Principle of
  Mis. 209–12 demonstrates this Principle of *c.*
Principle of his
  Mis. 260–11 Principle of his *c.* was God,
producing a
  Mis. 53–12 *to assist in producing a c.*,
Truth being the
  Mis. 221–19 Truth being the *c.*,
work a
  Pul. 69–13 * if they . . . they can work a *c.*
    69–22 * to work a *c.* the practitioner must

  Pul. 69–10 * but rely on Mind for *c.*,
  My. 40–18 * power to bring health and a *c.* to
    82– 2 * through a *c.* to themselves or
    268– 2 chapter sub-title

cure (verb)
Mis. 37–16 *Can your Science c. intemperance?*
    38–28 to *c.* his present disease,
    44– 6 *Can C. S. c. acute cases*
    48–26 Mind-healing would *c.* the insane.
    62–31 can *c.* its own disease,
    242–24 to *c.* that habit in three days,

cure (verb)

Mis.	359– 6	until you can c· without it
	399– 9	That exalts thee, and will c·
Ret.	33–17	would c· patients not affected by
Pul.	53–11	* Can drugs suddenly c· leprosy?
Rud.	8–24	whom he is supposed to c·.
	12– 7	strengthen . . . instead of c· it ;
Hea.	12– 9	when matter cannot c· it,
	13–27	while it is supposed to c· another,
Po.	75–16	That exalts thee, and will c·
My.	106–14	impossible for the surgeon . . . to c·.
	190–14	Jesus' students, failing to c· a
	222– 3	once failed mentally to c·

cured

Mis.	45–12	*profane man be c· by metaphysics,*
	49–14	have been c· in her class.
	242–25	I c· precisely such a case in 1869.
	243– 2	c· her perfectly of this habit,
	256– 2	c· of their belief in disease,
Ret.	15–24	Among other diseases c·
Pul.	69– 7	* being c· by Mrs. Eddy of a
	73– 6	* c· herself of a deathly disease
Hea.	13–14	c· the incipient stage of fever.
	13–17	c· an inveterate case of dropsy.
My.	80– 5	* c· of blindness, of consumption
	81–19	* gratitude for ills c·,
	90– 9	* it has c· them of diseases many
	228– 1	and have c· it thus ;

cures

Mis.	40–11	perform as instantaneous c· as
	63– 4	claim that one erring mind c·
	255–25	and c· where they fail,
Ret.	34–15	c· when they fail, or only relieve ;
	54– 2	some of the c· wrought through
Un.	7–16	bear witness to these c·.
Pul.	45– 6	* can effect c· of disease
Hea.	12– 9	c· it thus when matter cannot
Peo.	6–12	* while nature c· the disease."
My.	79–28	* told of c· from diseases,
	80– 1	* c· that carried one back
	81–27	* account of the marvellous c·
	227–31	Statistics show that C. S. c·

curing

Mis.	33–30	c· where these fail,
	54–15	c· hundreds at this very time ;
	268–21	c· alike the sin and the

curiosity

Mis.	348–24	I wanted to satisfy my c·
	379– 2	I had a c· to know
My.	30– 9	* from c·, and from sympathy, too.

curious

Pul.	23–19	* History shows the c· fact that
	65– 1	* belief in that c· creed

curly

Pul.	25–21	* with pews of c· birch,

currency

My.	14– 5	two millions of love c·
	170–16	It is His coin, His c· ;
	216– 9	regulated by a government c·,

current

Mis.	19–16	can never change the c· of that life
	126–24	even gold is less c·.
	228–25	Floating with the popular c·
	234–22	even the entire c· of mortality,
Ret.	2–19	with the phraseology c· in the
No.	1–12	borne on by the c· of feeling.
My.	19– 2	c· numbers of *The Christian Science Journal,*
	214–25	to meet my own c· expenses.

currents

Mis.	135–16	Sending forth c· of Truth,
	157–28	the eternal c· of Truth.
	212–18	c· of human nature rush in
Ret.	23–22	its substance, cause, and c·
Un.	11– 3	c· of matter, or mortal mind.
No.	34–27	the vital c· of Christ Jesus' life,
'01.	19–26	c· of God flow through no such
My.	50–11	* against the c· of dogma,

curse

Mis.	17–17	from under the c· of materialism,
	278–15	a c· on sin is always a blessing
	292–21	and therefore c· him ;
Un.	60–14	therewith c· we men, — *Jas.* 3 : 9.
No.	33– 4	lead us to bless those who c·,
'02.	6– 4	c· . . . was pronounced upon a lie,
Hea.	9–15	* "the c· causeless cannot come"
My.	52– 4	* blessing them that c· her,

cursed

Mis.	278–14	he c· the hour of his birth ;
	295– 5	* "c· barmaid system" in England
Hea.	9–17	God never c· man,
My.	213– 8	Because this age is c· with

cursing

Mis.	11–23	returning blessing for c·
Un.	60–16	blessing and c·.— *Jas.* 3 : 10.
'01.	34–21	return blessing for c· ;
My.	165– 7	I returned blessing for c·.
	269–23	pouring out blessing for c·,

curtail

Mis.	302–25	injunction did not c· the benefit

curtailed

My.	127–27	it is not c· in peace,

curtain

Mis.	205–16	drops the c· on material man
	346–26	lift the c·, let in the light,
	395–11	The c· drops on June ;
'02.	17–14	the c· of human life should be
Po.	57–18	The c· drops on June ;
My.	268–25	lifts the c· on the Science of being,
	305–31	to lift the c· on wrong,

curtains

My.	296–27	lifting the c· of mortal mind,

Curtice, Rev. Corban

'01.	32– 4	Rev. Corban C·, Congregationalist ;

curve

Pul.	26–10	* following the sweep of its c·,

curved

My.	69– 7	* gently c· and panelled surface,

curving

Un.	12– 4	c· sickle of Mind's eternal circle,

cushioned

Mis.	325–15	nodding on c· chairs,

custodian

Pul.	44–27	* kept coming until the c· of funds
	64–11	* the c· of the funds was

custodians

Man.	77–17	of which they are the c·.

custom

Ret.	89–13	It was the c· to pay this
Pul.	43–27	* her c· to discourage among her
My.	75–25	* c· of the Christian Scientists,
	78–18	* c· of the C. S. church,
	83– 2	* c· Christian Scientists have
	96–25	* It is the c· to sneer at C. S.,
	202– 9	c· to whom c· ; — *Rom.* 13 : 7.
	261– 6	according to the c· of the age

cut

Mis.	151–11	"C· it down ; — *Luke* 13 : 7.
	233–16	into a more fashionable c·
	235–13	to c· down all that bringeth not
	335–10	shall c· him asunder, — *Matt.* 24 : 51.
	335–24	would c· off somebody's ears.
	376–12	* an engraving c· in a stone.
Un.	11–17	c· off this vain boasting
	28– 6	nor c· with the dissecting-knife.
Pul.	25–30	* There is a disc of c· glass in
	78– 6	* inscription, c· in script letters :
My.	122– 7	To c· off the top of a plant

cuts

My.	160–14	trenchant truth that c· its way

cycle

Pul.	23–22	* assert that the end of a c·,
My.	270– 3	c· of good obliterates the

cycles

Un.	11–24	Jesus required neither c· of time
My.	13–26	all c· of systems and spheres.
	160–28	This may take millions of c·,

cyclic

Pul.	55– 5	* c· changes that came during

cyclone

Mis.	347– 7	foreshadows a c·.

cyclones

Mis.	257–27	C· kill and destroy,

cymbal

No.	45– 4	or a tinkling c· ;"— *I Cor.* 13 : 1.
'01.	26–24	or a tinkling c·."— *I Cor.* 13 : 1.

cynical

Mis.	66–22	C· critics misjudge my meaning

cynically

Mis.	255– 2	It is sometimes said, c·,
My.	93–10	* It has been said c·

cynosure

My.	77– 1	* been the c· of all eyes

cypress

Po.	16– 1	gentle c·, in evergreen tears,
	67–17	The c· may mourn with

D

dabbled
My. 313–22   * never "d· in mesmerism,"

Daily
Pul. 88–27   * D·, York, Pa.

daily
Mis.   7–10   has d· to be exemplified ;
   19–14   is d· departing from evil ;
   29–20   D· letters inform me that a perusal
   47– 3   *and carry about this weight d·*
   102–30   proves d· that "one on God's side
   127– 9   pray d· for themselves ;
   156–18   d· Christian demonstration thereof.
   256– 8   confidence manifested in d· letters
   294–26   I have read the d· paper,
   307– 2   they give you d· supplies.
   311–15   My deepest desires and d· labors
   366–30   and this is being done d·.
   373–31   d· demonstration of Truth and Love.
   397–17   My prayer, some d· good to do
Man.   40–12   should d· watch and pray
   41–19   D· Prayer.
   42– 6   to defend himself d· against
   60–19   appeal to d· Christian endeavors
   91–26   under Mrs. Eddy's d· conversation
   97–19   by the d· press, by periodicals or
Ret.   83–20   to God's d· interpretation.
Pul.   4–11   and d· demonstrate this.
   19– 1   My prayer, some d· good to do
   31–16   * editorial work in d· journalism
   37– 2   * "for it is the great d· that is
   37– 9   * she takes a d· walk and
   79–13   * a d· paper in town or village
No.   43– 2   d· meat and drink.
   43–13   specimen of those received d· :
Pan.   14– 6   if d· adoring, imploring, and
'01.   31–22   d· Bible reading and family prayer ;
Hea.   4–10   not to forget his d· cares.
Po.   13– 5   My prayer, some d· good to do
   28–16   Give us this day our d· food
   33– 1   To d· remember my blessings
My.   15–13   d· desire that the Giver of all good
   18– 6   pray d· for themselves ;
   36–23   * devotion to the d· life and purpose
   42–29   * performance of her d· tasks.
   43– 6   * order aright the affairs of d· life.
   48–19   * constant d· reading of the Bible
   77–13   * d· trainloads of pilgrims are
   128–30   Watch, and pray d· that evil
   134– 7   inasmuch as our d· lives serve to
   143–11   am seen d· by the members of my
   175– 5   with the exception of a d· drive.
   177– 6   d· duties require attention
   196–26   The good . . . is your d· bread.
   233– 4   in yourself, in your d· life,
   237–14   give d· attention thereto.
   244–12   need of which I d· discern.
   275–17   I go out in my carriage d·,
   275–20   that prevents my d· drive.
   276– 6   d· drive or a dignified stay at home,
   281– 3   d· prayer of my church,
   286– 3   I have prayed d· that there be
   352–14   * that our d· living may be
   353– 2   and read our d· newspaper.

Daily Inter-Ocean (*see also Inter-Ocean*)
Pul. 23– 1   D· I·, Chicago, December 31, 1894

dainty
Mis. 329–22   Her d· fingers put the fur cap on
Ret.   30– 5   the d· borrower would have fled.
Po.   47– 3   the olden and d· refrain,

daisies
Mis. 329–19   turning up the d·,

dale
Po.   32– 7   scattered o'er hillside and d· ;

Dallas, Tex.
Pul. 89–22   * Times-Herald, D·, T·.

damaging
Mis. 43–29   d· effects these leave

damnation
Mis. 122–18   whose d· is just." — Rom. 3 : 8.
   298– 6   whose d· is just." — Rom. 3 : 8.
   335–29   "whose d· is just ;" — Rom. 3 : 8.
No.   14–26   the doctrine of eternal d·,
My.   6– 9   smile and deceit of d·.

damned
Mis. 368–26   the destinies of the d·.

damning
My. 211– 1   error that is d· men.

damp
My. 341–26   * raining all day and was d·

damsel
Peo.   8–22   "D·, I say unto thee, — Mark 5 : 41.

dancing-halls
Mis. 324– 7   d·, and banquet-rooms.

danger
Mis.   7– 3   because there is d· in it ;
   9–29   great and only d· in the path
   12–19   d· of yielding to temptation
   67–20   if you see the d· menacing
   108–11   is to be in d· of believing it ;
   126– 1   from d· to escape,
   240– 9   Predicting d· does not dignify life,
   257–20   where there is most d·.
   284–11   in no d· of mistaking their way.
   318–26   Two points of d· beset mankind ;
   319– 7   mortals are in d· of not
   347– 4   To avoid d· from this source
Ret.   13–14   in the d· of endless punishment,
   44–22   from the d· to its members
   54–16   There is d· in this mental state
Pul.   15–14   stewards who have seen the d·
   37–21   * feels very strongly," . . . "the d·
Un.   57– 4   warn mortals of the approach of d·
No.   23– 4   is fraught with spiritual d·.
'01.   18–11   d· of questioning Christ Jesus'
   30–15   they have no craft that is in d·.
'02.   19–23   A d· besets thy path?
My.   116–14   Hence the sin, the d· and
   129– 3   I reluctantly foresee great d·
   211–24   where there is most d· ;
   234–23   there would be no d· in
   234–30   is fraught with d·.
   344–20   I should think myself in d· of

dangerous
Mis.   7–18   reflects that it is d· to live,
   108–27   This cognomen makes it less d· ;
   209–14   that destroy its more d· pleasures.
   252– 6   its largest dose is never d·,
   385–11   thy bark is past The d· sea,
Ret.   63–20   is more d· than sickness,
Peo.   71–24   selfish motives . . . are d· incentives ;
Un.   8– 9   d· to rest upon the evidence of
   54–12   is to admit a d· fact.
Po.   48– 3   thy bark is past The d· sea,
My.   179–15   Some d· skepticism exists as to
   224–10   is helpful or d· only in
   283–29   Lured by fame, . . . success is d·,
   343–27   Dissensions are d·
   344–29   more d· than any material infection,
   364– 1   is more or less d·.

dangers
Ret.   47– 9   Example had shown the d·
My.   266– 3   To my sense, the most imminent d·

dangle
Mis.   61–22   or d· at the end of a rope?

dangling
Mis.   61–17   * d· at the end of a rope.

Daniel's
My.   181–28   one expositor of D· dates

Dante
No.   18–17   may imagine the face of D· to be

dare
Mis.   22– 5   Who d· say that matter or mortals
   238– 5   for all who d· to be true,
Peo.   9–18   d· to invoke the divine aid of Spirit
Po.   27– 4   I, dying, d· abhor !"
My.   253–27   D· to be faithful to God

dared
Mis.   110–26   d· the perilous defense of Truth,

dares
Mis.   183–29   d· at this date refute the evidence
Un.   28– 8   Who, then, d· define Soul as

daring
Ret.   2– 4   poetic d· and pious picturesqueness

dark
Mis.   51–24   * d· pile of human mockeries ;
   53–30   but to . . . the ungodly, it is d·
   117–25   he works somewhat in the d· ;
   180– 5   the d· shadow and portal of death,
   204– 2   a d·, impenetrable cloud of error ;
   228– 2   a deception d· as it is base
   250–28   lighting the d· places of earth.
   265– 5   He grows d·, and cannot regain,
   276–31   In the d· hours, . . . stand firmer

dark

Mis.	330– 2	make melody through *d·* pine groves.
	360–28	to sensitive ears and *d·* disciples,
	385–21	The *d·* unknown.
	398–13	So, when day grows *d·* and cold,
Ret.	4–18	low requiems through *d·* pine groves.
	18– 8	*D·* sentinel hedgerow is guarding
	20–13	knelt by his side throughout the *d·* hours,
	23–10	The world was *d·*.
	34– 6	the reply was *d·* and contradictory.
	46–19	So, when day grows *d·* and cold,
Un.	40– 4	*d·* shadow of material sense,
	60– 8	the *d·* abyss of nothingness,
	64–15	leap the *d·* fissures,
Pul.	17–18	So, when day grows *d·* and cold,
	32– 1	* her face, framed in *d·* hair
	58–19	* It is rather *d·*, often too much so
'01.	10–21	Divine Love spans the *d·* passage of sin,
Po.	1–10	from chaos *d·* set free,
	14–17	So, when day grows *d·* and cold,
	22–18	The *d·* domain of pain
	24–16	And night grows deeply *d·* ;
	26–15	*d·* record of our guilt unrolled,
	30–15	And stern, *d·* shadows cast
	34– 8	In what *d·* leafy grove
	42– 3	sunshine without a *d·* spot ;
	48–15	The *d·* unknown.
	63–17	*D·* sentinel hedgerow is guarding
	67–15	o'er the *d·* wavy grass.
My.	61–26	* *d·* stillness of the night,
	222–15	in those *d·* days Jesus was not
	256–24	the gifts glow in the *d·* green
	297–13	*d·* hour that precedes the dawn.
	340–27	*d·* days of our forefathers
	350–12	did'st not Thou the *d·* wave treading

Dark Ages

Pul.	52–23	* the blackness of the *D· A·*,

darken

Ret.	18–24	they *d·* my lay :
Pul.	21–29	aught that can *d·* in any degree
'01.	20–15	could not bewilder, *d·*, or
Po.	64–20	they *d·* my lay :
My.	206– 9	*d·* the discernment of Science ;
	267–25	*d·* the true conception of man's

darkened

Mis.	169– 5	insight had been *d·* thereby,
Ret.	35–15	*d·* the glow and grandeur
My.	350–20	mortal sense is *d·* unto death

darkens

Mis.	291– 6	*d·* the understanding that

darker

My.	285–11	war, and . . . belong to the *d·* ages,

darkest

'01.	20–28	*d·* and deepest of human crimes.

darkling

Mis.	88–16	the shadow of *d·* criticism
Po.	79–10	*d·* sense, arise, go hence !

darkly

Mis.	359–11	see through a glass, *d·* ; — *I Cor.* 13 : 12.

darkness

and death
Po.	65–18	*d·* and death like mist melt away,

and doubt
Ret.	68–20	*D·* and doubt encompass thought,

and gloom
Mis.	320–20	wading through *d·* and gloom,

cannot see
Mis.	367–24	sees light, and cannot see *d·*.

cheers the
My.	202–23	taper unseen in . . . cheers the *d·*.

children of
My.	191–10	you are not children of *d·*.

clouds and
Mis.	377– 5	radiant relief in clouds and *d·* !

coexist with
Un.	64– 4	than the sun can coexist with *d·*.

danger and
My.	116–14	danger and *d·* of personal contagion.

deeper
Ret.	81–20	so sinks into deeper *d·*.

discern
Mis.	131– 6	in order rightly to discern *d·*

dispels
Mis.	205– 9	light which dispels *d·*.

doubt and
Mis.	342– 4	thus they were in doubt and *d·*.
'00.	7–20	In doubt and *d·* we say as did Mary
My.	152–20	stumble into doubt and *d·*,

flies in
Mis.	145–15	hooded hawk which flies in *d·*.

for light
Mis.	174–27	We do not look into *d·* for light.

darkness

illumine the
Mis.	276–18	light will illumine the *d·*.

in one's self
Mis.	131– 4	*d·* in one's self must first be

its
Un.	17–11	and its *d·* get consolation from

light and
Mis.	34–27	as direct opposites as light and *d·*.

light with
Mis.	333–22	hath light with *d·* ? — *II Cor.* 6 : 14.

melt into
Mis.	264– 9	they melt into *d·*.

mental
Mis.	355–18	Mental *d·* is senseless error,

no
Mis.	113– 3	spiritual light, wherein is no *d·*.
No.	16–17	because it has no *d·* to emit.
	30–21	light wherein there is no *d·*,
'02.	16–20	in whom there is no *d·*,

of belief
Pul.	13–16	in the deep *d·* of belief.

or doubt
My.	187– 8	exclude all *d·* or doubt,

our
My.	232–13	as living lights in our *d·* :

out of
Mis.	130–31	out of *d·* into light.
My.	206–25	called you out of *d·* — *I Pet.* 2 : 9.

pierce the
Mis.	320–25	pierce the *d·* and melt into dawn.

place of
My.	199– 4	In place of *d·*, light hath

power of
My.	206–29	from the power of *d·*, — *Col.* 1 : 13.

powers of
'02.	14– 8	against the powers of *d·*,

profound
Mis.	342–14	*d·* profound brooded over

shineth in
Mis.	368– 3	let the light that shineth in *d·*,
Un.	63–10	that light which shineth in *d·*,
My.	110– 8	"shineth in *d·* ; — *John* 1 : 5.

sometimes
My.	206–30	" Ye were sometimes *d·*, — *Eph.* 5 : 8.

that
Ret.	27–19	* Touch God's right hand in that *d·*,
	81–22	how great is that *d·* !" — *Matt.* 6 : 23.
Un.	19–15	how great is that *d·* !" — *Matt.* 6 : 23.

to daylight
Mis.	126– 3	yea, from *d·* to daylight,

walked in
Chr.	55– 8	that walked in *d·* — *Isa.* 9 : 2.

within
No.	30–21	holding *d·* within itself.

works of
Rud.	4–24	extinguishes forever the works of *d·*

Mis.	ix–16	*d·* of storm and cloud and tempest,
	165–14	neither *d·*, doubt, disease, nor
	212–16	reign of difficulties, *d·*, and
	319–15	in the *d·* of all the ages,
	340–29	comes out in the *d·* to shine
	367–25	conclusion, that *d·* dwelleth in light,
	368– 4	the *d·* comprehendeth it not,
Ret.	27–18	* Groping blindly in the *d·*,
	61–15	you are *d·*, nothingness,
	81–21	light that is in thee be *d·*, — *Matt.* 6 : 23.
Un.	19–14	light that is in thee be *d·*, — *Matt.* 6 : 23.
	63–11	the *d·* comprehendeth it not.
'00.	6–24	is not *d·* but light.
'01.	2–23	*d·*, doubt, and unrequited toil
My.	110– 8	*d·* comprehended it not." — *John* 1 : 5.
	140– 4	I will make *d·* light — *Isa.* 42 : 16.

Dartmouth

Pul.	32–29	* Albert Baker, graduated at *D·*

Dartmouth College

Ret.	6–15	graduated at *D· C·* in 1834,

darts

Mis.	387–13	*D·* not from those who watch
Po.	6– 8	*D·* not from those who watch

Darwin

Mis.	361–15	Berkeley, Tyndall, *D·*,
'01.	24–18	Leibnitz, Berkeley, *D·*,

dashing

Mis.	206– 5	*d·* against the receding shore,
	266–12	comet's course, *d·* through space,

dastardly

My.	340–20	paltering, timid, or *d·* policy,

data

Mis.	x–13	To some articles are affixed *d·*,
Pul.	36–28	* some of the *d·* of this paper.

date

Mis. xi– 2   the *d·* of its issue, 1875,
    xii– 2   and to retain at this *d·* the
    4–12   At this *d·*, 1883,
    29–16   Since that *d·* I have known of
    29–18   the *d·* of the first publication
    39– 8   abroad at this early *d·*
    81–23   at some *d·* must cry in the
    139– 2   to three years from this *d·* ;
    183–29   who dares at this *d·* refute the
    271–20   Much is said at this *d·*, 1889,
    293– 7   will come, at some *d·*,
    314– 3   From this *d·* the Sunday services
    316–10   The *d·* of a class in C. S. should
    316–16   the word spoken at this *d·*.
    366–16   At this *d·*, poor jaded humanity
    372– 9   *d·* of its publication in December,
Ret. 26–19   gave the world a new *d·* in the
Pul. 53– 4   * in other countries at an earlier *d·*.
    67–23   * *d·* of the Declaration of Independence,
    82–28   * The *d·* is no longer B. C.
    86–11   * with the *d·*, "1895."
'00. 15– 2   a new one that is up to *d·*.
Po. vi– 9   * *under the d· of February* 3, 1865.
My. 10–15   * as to amount and *d·* of payment.
    11–28   * *d·* for commencing building
    12–12   * and the *d·* of commencing work,
    16– 6   * $226,285.73 on hand on that *d·*,
    26– 5   * on the *d·* of the annual communion,
    26–22   should *d·* some special reform,
    55– 1   * This *d·* is memorable as the one
    56– 6   * The *d·* of the inauguration of
    57–16   * membership at that *d·* was 1,545.
    148–13   Memorable *d·*, all unthought of
    169– 7   requested to visit me at a later *d·*,
    184–14   my cordial thanks at an earlier *d·*.
    216–22   I request that from this *d·*
    217–14   dividend with interest thereon up to *d·*,
    266–26   points . . . at that *d·* undisturbed.
    307–16   At that *d·* I was a staunch orthodox,
    309–25   style of architecture at that *d·*.
    311–16   *d·* of my first church membership.
    318– 8   because at that *d·* some critics
    334– 3   * newspaper reports of that *d·*
    351– 3   * publish her letter of recent *d·*,

dated

Mis. 163– 8   He who *d·* time, the Christian era,
    199–31   *d·* the Christian era.
Man. 41– 2   He who *d·* the Christian era
Pul. 34–18   * From that hour *d·* her conviction of
My. 138–29   * and *d·* May 16, 1907,
    180– 8   by him . . . who *d·* time.
    333–30   * *Chronicle*, *d·* September 25, 1844,
    359–19   * composite letter, *d·* July 19,

dates

145 (A. D.)
My. 178–31   written in A.D. 145,
325
'02. 18–28   about the year 325,
1620
My. 183– 6   what John Robinson wrote in 1620
1710
'01. 23–23   published a book in 1710
1722–1725
Ret. 3– 7   Indian troubles of 1722–1725,
1733
My. 295–11   PRINTED IN NUREMBERG IN 1733
1761
My. 172 –4   * It was built in 1761,
1812
Mis. 304–12   * battle-field of New Orleans (1812),
Ret. 3–12   towards the close of the War of 1812.
1814
Ret. 3–11   and won distinction in 1814
1819
My. 290– 9   this noble woman, born in 1819,
1820–'30
Pul. 32–19   * in the early decade of 1820–'30.
1834
Ret. 6–16   at Dartmouth College in 1834,
1835
Po. vi–12   *In 1835 a mob in Boston*
1837
Ret. 6–23   In 1837 he succeeded to the
1840
My. 290–10   married in 1840,
1841
Ret. 6–30   In 1841 he received further
1843
Ret. 19– 1   In 1843 I was united to my first husband,
My. 330– 8   * in Wilmington in 1843,
    330–18   * in 1844, not in 1843, as claimed
    334–13   * certain circumstances in 1843,
1844
Pul. 34– 3   * to her father's home — in 1844

dates

1844
'02. 15–19   sell them at his decease in 1844,
My. 189–28   a poem written in 1844,
    330–18   * in 1844, not in 1843, as claimed
    332–30   * George Washington Glover in 1844
    334–13   * records show really existed in 1844,
1844, June
My. 312– 7   * in *J·*, 1844, . . . he died
    333– 6   * twenty-eighth day of *J·*, 1844,
    335–16   * Wilmington, N. C., in *J·*, 1844,
1844, July 3
My. 333–19   * *Wilmington Chronicle* of *J·* 3, 1844,
1844, August 21
My. 329–17   * issues of July 3 and *A·* 21, 1844,
    331–11   * *Wilmington Chronicle* of *A·* 21, 1844,
1844, September 25
My. 333–30   * *Chronicle*, dated *S·* 25, 1844,
1845
My. 334–27   * obituary which appeared in 1845
1850
Po. vi– 4   * *in Manchester, N. H., in* 1850,
1853
Peo. 10– 8   succored a fugitive slave in 1853,
My. 13– 6   in London, England, in 1853,
1856
Po. vi– 4   * *and again in Boston, in* 1856.
1862
Mis. 378– 1   About the year 1862, while the author
My. 306–22   In 1862, when I first visited
1865
Po. page 26   poem
1866
Mis. 179–31   In 1866, when God revealed to me
    246–23   the spiritual famine of 1866,
    379–28   I discovered, in 1866, the momentous
Ret. 24– 9   and in the latter part of 1866
Pul. vii– 3   birth of C. S., in 1866,
    5– 1   my form of prayer since 1866 ;
    34– 4   * until 1866 no special record is
    34– 5   * In 1866, while living in Lynn,
    64–15   * she discovered C. S. in 1866.
    70–17   * Mrs. Eddy asserts that in 1866
Po. vi– 6   * *in Lynn, Mass., in* 1866,
My. v–15   * discovered C. S. in 1866,
    22–14   * Since 1866, almost forty years ago,
    67–13   * C. S. discovered . . . 1866
    181–21   (1866) C. S. was discovered
    181–28   fixed the year 1866 or 1867
    343–16   It was in 1866 that the light of
1866–'69
Pul. 34–24   * From 1866–'69 Mrs. Eddy withdrew
1866, January
My. 306–26   *J·*, 1866, Dr. Quimby had
1866, February
Ret. 24– 1   in *F·*, 1866, and after the death
1867
Mis. 29–15   In 1867, I taught the first
Ret. 43– 1   In 1867 I introduced the first
My. 181–28   fixed the year 1866 or 1867
1868
Pul. 54–28   About 1868, the author of S. and H.
Po. page 28   poem
1869
Mis. 242–25   cured precisely such a case in 1869.
My. 105–19   About the year 1869, I was wired
1870
Ret. 35– 1   In 1870 I copyrighted the first
1874
Mis. 272– 4   * Act of 1874, Chapter 375, Section 4.
My. 315– 3   * About the year 1874, Dr. Patterson,
1875
Mis. xi– 2   at the date of its issue, 1875,
    29–18   The census since 1875
    285–14   about the year 1875 that S. and H.
Ret. 27– 4   S. and H., published in 1875.
    37– 5   was published in 1875.
Pul. 38– 6   * S. and H., was issued in 1875.
    55–14   * have been published in 1875.
Rud. 16–20   which I published in 1875.
'00. 6–29   cites 1875 as the year of
My. v–19   * in 1875, after nine years of
    266–24   "S. and H. . . . published in 1875.
    343–17   In 1875 I wrote my book.
1876
Ret. 43–22   and six of my students in 1876,
1876, July 4
Pul. 37–27   * was organized on *J·* 4, 1876,
    67–24   * when on *J·* 4, 1876, the first
1877
Ret. 42– 4   last marriage . . . in the year 1877.
Pul. 35–27   * In 1877 Mrs. Glover married
    46–27   * marriage was in the spring of 1877.
My. 266–22   Since 1877, these special "signs

dates

1878
Ret. 15–13 In the year 1878 I was called
No. 3– 9 in 1878, some irresponsible people
1879
Man. 17– 1 In the spring of 1879, a little band
38–20 organized in 1879 by Mary Baker Eddy,
'00. 1–11 first church . . . chartered in 1879,
My. 67–14 * First church organized . . . 1879
1879, April
Pul. 37–28 * *A·*, 1879, the church was founded
67–27 * church was founded in *A·*, 1879,
1879, April 12
Man. 17– 9 *A·* 12, 1879, on motion of
Ret. 43–24 *A·* 12, 1879, it was voted
Pul. 30–26 * meeting held on *A·* 12, 1879.
55–25 * was organized *A·* 12, 1879,
1879, June
Man. 18– 4 was obtained *J·*, 1879,
Ret. 16–17 was obtained *J·*, 1879,
44– 5 was obtained in *J·*, 1879,
1879, August 16
My. 49–16 * was held *A·* 16, 1879,
1879, August 23
My. 49–10 * was obtained *A·* 23, 1879,
1879, October 19
My. 49–26 * meeting held *O·* 19, 1879,
1880
Pul. 58– 4 * Coming to Boston about 1880,
Peo. 10–10 practice of medicine in 1880.
'80's
Pul. 31–14 * some year in the early '80's
1880, January 2
My. 50– 3 * Communion . . . *J·* 2, 1880.
1880, January 4
My. 50–22 * "Sunday, *J·* 4, 1880.
1880, May 23
My. 50–29 * record of *M·* 23, 1880,
1880, December 15
My. 51–19 * meeting . . . *D·* 15, 1880,
1881
Man. 18– 7 was ordained A.D. 1881.
Ret. 16–20 was ordained A. D. 1881.
43– 5 chartered in 1881.
44– 8 was ordained in 1881,
Pul. 38– 4 * ceremony took place in 1881.
68– 2 * and in 1881 was ordained,
68– 5 * by Mrs. Eddy in 1881,
My. 244–30 was chartered A.D. 1881.
1881, January
Mis. 272– 2 * charter in *J·*, 1881,
272– 9 * from *J·*, 1881, till
Ret. 48–17 chartered in *J·*, 1881,
1881, July 20
My. 51–27 * record . . . of *J·* 20, 1881,
1882
Ret. 42–13 In 1882 he passed away,
Pul. 36– 1 * Dr. Eddy died in 1882,
47– 3 * He died in 1882.
1882, January
Mis. 272–10 * said Act in *J·*, 1882.
1882, January 31
Mis. 272– 6 * from and after *J·* 31, 1882.
1882, September 8
My. 53– 9 * *S·* 8, 1882, it was voted
1883
Mis. 4–12 At this date, 1883,
35– 7 In 1883, a million of people
272–14 * In accordance with Statutes of 1883,
Ret. 43– 6 No charter was . . . after 1883.
My. vi–18 * founded *The C. S. Journal* in 1883,
304–16 1883, I started *The C. S. Journal,*
1883, April
Mis. x– 7 published . . . since *A·*, 1883,
139–15 *A·*, 1883, I started the *Journal*
380–27 *A·*, 1883, a bill in equity was
Ret. 52–21 I started it, *A·*, 1883,
1883, October 22
My. 53–15 * At a meeting *O·* 22, 1883,
1883, November
My. 53–12 * until *N·*, 1883,
1884
Pul. 6–20 * a missionary to China, in 1884.
My. 182–11 In 1884, I taught a class in
1884, December
Mis. 242–28 he was my student in *D·*, 1884;
1885
Mis. 39– 5 In 1885, this knowledge
245– 9 the pulpit and press in 1885,
1885, February 8
My. 54–13 * *F·* 8, 1885, communion was held
1885, March 16
Mis. 95– 3 * on Monday, *M·* 16, 1885,
1885, October 18
My. 54–26 * On *O·* 18, 1885, the rooms

dates

1885, October 25
My. 54–32 * first Sunday service . . . *O·* 25, 1885.
1885, December 7
My. 53–26 * year ending *D·* 7, 1885,
1886
Ret. 52–12 to my students, in 1886,
1886, February 11
Ret. 52–18 at New York City, *F·* 11, 1886.
1887
My. 306–24 manuscripts which in 1887
323–31 * Normal class in the fall of 1887
1887, January
My. 319–21 * *J·*, 1887, I entered your
1887, Jan. 10
My. 322–19 * Primary class (*J·* 10, 1887).
1888
Mis. 134–11 and meet *en masse*, in 1888,
161– 3 SUNDAY BEFORE CHRISTMAS, 1888.
274–22 At this period, 1888, those quill-drivers
275–23 Scientist Association in 1888.
My. 185–22 In 1888 I visited these
1888, June 13
Mis. 98– 8 Convention in Chicago, *J·* 13, 1888.
1889
Mis. 239– 2 Metaphysical College, in 1889,
271–20 Much is said at this date, 1889,
Ret. 43–18 taught one Primary class, in 1889,
Pul. 36– 4 * and it was closed (in 1889)
68– 8 * The college was closed in 1889,
My. 163–17 I removed from Boston in 1889
246–11 In the year 1889, to gain a
284–18 my residence in Concord, 1889,
1889, Feb. 25
Mis. 279–12 THAT ASSEMBLED *F·* 25, 1889,
1889, June
Ret. 52–23 in Cleveland, Ohio, *J·*, 1889,
1889, Oct. 29
Ret. 48–13 College Corporation, *O·* 29, 1889,
1889, December
Ret. 51– 1 In *D·*, 1889, I gave a lot of
1889, December 10
Mis. 139–18 *D·* 10, 1889, I gave
1890
Mis. 159–23 a bit of what I said in 1890:
309–32 See the revised edition of 1890,
379–32 revised edition of 1890,
Ret. 82–28 my last revision, in 1890,
My. 92–15 * since 1890 its following had
93–29 * In 1890 the faith had but
1891, April 15
My. 178–21 *A·* 15, 1891, the C. S. textbook
1891, June 3
Mis. 135–25 Association, *J·* 3, 1891.
1891, September
Ret. 37–10 *S·*, 1891, it had reached
1892
Ret. 51– 3 valued in 1892 at about
Pul. 20– 6 In 1892 I had to recover the land
1892, September
Man. 18–12 twenty-third day of *S·*, 1892,
My. 55–13 * twenty-third day of *S·*, 1892,
1892, September 1
My. 55–11 * *S·* 1, 1892, Mrs. Eddy gave
1893
Pul. 1– 8 1893 was a distinguished character,
4–28 In 1893 the World's Parliament of
My. 172– 4 * razed in 1893 to make room for
304–18 In 1893, Judge S. J. Hanna became
1893, October 3
My. 57–15 * Chickering Hall, *O·* 3, 1893,
1893, December
Mis. 372– 9 its publication in *D·*, 1893,
1894
Mis. x–24 In 1894, I received from the
131–21 encountered in Anno Domini 1894,
310–26 year of religious jubilee, 1894,
319–22 edifice must be built in 1894.
382–20 1894 was erected the first church
Man. 103– 4 The edifice erected in 1894 for
Pul. 1–12 garner the memory of 1894;
6–13 wrote to me in 1894,
24–15 * erected Anno Domini 1894.
42–24 * "Love-Children's Offering — 1894."
45–13 * completion within the year 1894
78– 8 * During the year 1894 a church
84–14 * year, Anno Domini 1894,
My. 15– 6 * edifice erected in 1894 for The
23– 6 * of the present edifice in 1894,
67–15 * First church erected . . . 1894
eighteen hundred and ninety-four
Pul. 77– 9 * year *e· h· and n·*

dates

1894, February 27
  Pul. 68–26   * meeting . . . on *F.* 27, 1894.
1894, March
  My. 55–20   * continued there until *M.*, 1894,
1894, 21st day of May, A. D.
  Mis. 143–15 On the 21st *d.* of *M.*, A. D. 1894,
1894, December 30
  My. 55–28   * for occupancy, *D.* 30, 1894.
1895
  Mis. 382–32 In 1895 I ordained that the Bible,
  Pul.   5–21 In 1895, book, is in its ninety-first
      20–10 In 1895 I reconstructed my
      45–16   * before April or May of 1895.
      86–11   * with the date, "1895."
  '00.   7– 6 In 1895 it was estimated that
  My. 57–28   * before the dedication . . . in 1895,
      76–14   * time of the dedication . . . in 1895,
    320–31   * time of the dedication . . . in 1895.
1895, February
  Pul. 78–15   * *F.*, 1895, at high noon.
eighteen hundred and ninety-five
  Man. 64–14 year *e. h.* and *n.*,
eighteen hundred and ninety-five, February
  Pul. 77–16   * *F.*, *e. h.* and *n.*,
eighteen hundred and ninety-five, March
  Pul. 87– 4   * *M.*, *e. h.* and *n.*,
1895, March 20
  Man. 75– 4 Whereas, on *M.* 20, 1895,
1896
  Mis. 383– 8 In 1896 it goes without saying,
1896, April 26
  My. 56– 7   * The date of . . . was *A.* 26, 1896.
1897
  My. 121–17 by my students in 1897.
1897, October
  My. 145– 3 in *O.*, 1897, I proposed to
1897, October 29
  My. 145– 7 From that time, *O.* 29, 1897,
1898
  Mis. 347–31 *The C. S. Journal* . . . up to 1898.
  My. vi–20   * Publishing Society, which in 1898,
    125–22 students in my last class in 1898
1898, January twenty-fifth
  Man. 79–22 on *J. t.*, 1898,
1898, January 31
  My. 157–22 On *J.* 31, 1898, I gave a
1898, March 19
  My. 157–19   * *Concord Monitor* of *M.* 19, 1898.
1898, November 21
  My. 104–24 On *N.* 21, 1898, in my class
1899, Oct. 12
  My. 217–17 the last *Sentinel* [*O.* 12, 1899]
1900
  Mis. 304–14   * until 1900, when it will be sent to
  My.   8–29   * "Since the last report, in 1900,
    256–16 chapter sub-title
1901
  My. 334–19   * Message to The Mother Church [1901] :
1901, May 16
  My. 346–26   * Associated Press, *M.* 16, 1901 :
1901, June
  My. 292–19 In the *J.*, 1901, Message
1901, August
  My. 330– 2   * in your paper in *A.*, 1901.
1902
  Man. 86–21 revised editions since 1902,
  '02. 20–17 in 1902 to begin omitting our *annual*
  My. 22– 3   * In the year 1902 our Leader
      23–15   * pledged at the annual meeting, 1902,
      57– 7   * Message to the church in 1902
      76–21   * church meeting in Boston, in 1902,
    259–17 I hope that in 1902 the churches
1902, June
  '02.   1– 8 during the year ending *J.*, 1902,
  My. 22– 7   * annual meeting in *J.*, 1902,
1902, June 19
  My. 23–12   * total receipts *J.* 19, 1902
1903
  My. 13– 6 was presented to me in 1903
    305–18 in the *National Magazine* (1903)
    327– 5 in 1903, made it legal to
nineteen hundred and three
  Man. 64–22 year *n. h.* and *t.*
1903, March
  Man. 102–15 deeds given by . . . in *M.*, 1903 ;
1903, March 1
  My. 25–12   * *M.* 1, 1903 to February 29, 1904,
1903, March 17
  Man. 18–24 By-Law adopted *M.* 17, 1903,
1903, June
  My. 57–21   * 2,194 more than . . . of *J.*, 1903.
1903, July 16
  My. 347–10 presented *J.* 16, 1903.
1903, October
  My. 57–12   * was begun in *O.*, 1903,

dates

1903, October 24
  My. 329–12   * appeared . . . *O.* 24, 1903.
1904
  My. 67–16   * Corner-stone . . . 1904
    159–29 Copyright, 1904, by
    164–16 Now [1904] six dear churches are
    173– 4   * visit of . . . Scientists in 1904 :
    254–20   * in the June *Journal* of 1904,
1904, February 29
  My. 25–12   * March 1, 1903 to *F.* 29, 1904,
1904, March 1
  My. 25–13   * *M.* 1, 1904 to February 28, 1905,
1904, May 31
  My. 16– 5   * up to and including *M.* 31, 1904,
1904, June 1
  My. 23–11   * expenditures *J.* 1, 1904
1904, June 13
  My. 171–14 Monday, *J.* 13, 1904.
1904, July 16
  My. 16–12   * Saturday, *J.* 16, 1904,
     57–13   * corner-stone . . . laid *J.* 16, 1904.
1905
  My. 56–24   * In the spring of 1905
    270– 5 In 1905, the First Congregational
1905, February 28
  My. 25–13   * March 1, 1904 to *F.* 28, 1905,
1905, March 1
  My. 25–13   * *M.* 1, 1905 to February 28, 1906,
1905, May 31
  My. 23–11   * June 1, 1904 to *M.* 31, 1905,
1905, June 1
  My. 23–10   * Amount on hand *J.* 1, 1905,
     23–13   * June 19, 1902 to *J.* 1, 1905,
1905, September 23
  My. 232–11 SENTINEL, *S.* 23, 1905
1905, October 1
  My. 56–28   * beginning *O.* 1, 1905,
1906
  My. 67–17   * Cathedral to be dedicated . . . 1906
1906, February 28
  My. 25–14   * March 1, 1905 to *F.* 28, 1906,
1906, April 23
  My. 26–10 generous check . . . *A.* 23, 1906,
1906, June 10
  My. 26– 6   * annual communion, . . . *J.* 10, 1906.
    240–11 Message . . . *J.* 10, 1906,
1906, December 1
  My. 317– 2   * *Sentinel* of *D.* 1, 1906,
1907
  Man. 84–10 After 1907, the Board of Education
     88–12 Beginning with 1907, the teacher
     91–24 beginning A.D. 1907 ;
  My. 273–32 Copyright, 1907, by
1907, January
  My. 308–13 *McClure's Magazine*, *J.*, 1907,
1907, April 3
  My. 134–21   * meeting of *A.* 3, 1907,
1907, May
  My. 138–26   * sixteenth day of *M.*, 1907,
1907, May 16
  My. 138–29   * and dated *M.* 16, 1907,
1908
  Mis. 21–24 1908 edition of S. and H.
1908, January 6
  My. 296–25 *New York American*, *J.* 6, 1908,
1908, February 29
  My. 236–27 will be issued *F.* 29 [1908].
1908, July 8
  Man. 18–26 On *J.* 8, 1908, the By-Laws
1908, Dec. 15
  Man. 68–22 takes effect on *D.* 15, 1908.
1909
  Mis. 318–28 See edition of 1909.
  My. 116–25 Copyright, 1909, by
    210–22 Copyright, 1909, by
1909, June 7
  My. 142–28 annual meeting . . . *J.* 7, 1909.
1909, July 31
  My. 359–17   * In the *Sentinel* of *J.* 31, 1909,
1909, August 30
  My. 361–10 not written to her since *A.* 30, 1909.
1910, May
  Po. vii– 5   * In *M.*, 1910, Mrs. Eddy requested
1910, September 10
  My. 237–22 in the *Sentinel* of *S.* 10 [1910]
1913
  My. 34–30   * according to the 1913 edition.

———

  Mis. 148–14 were written at different *d.*,
  Man. 3–10 were written at different *d.*,
  Pul. 20–22 one of the many *d.* selected
  '01. 24–18 It *d.* beyond Socrates,
  My. 67–12   * *Notable D.* in C. S.
    181–28 one expositor of Daniel's *d.*
    181–31 those *d.* were the first two years of

dates
    My. 319–26   * These *d·* are very well fixed in
      (*see also* **months**)

dates — addresses
1888, June 13
  Mis. 98– 8
1895, June 3
  Mis. 116– 6

dates — affidavits
1902, Jan'y
  My. 315–16 *
1907, May 16
  My. 138–24

dates — chapter sub-titles
1885, January 18
  Mis. 171–22
1893
  Mis. 116– 9
1895
  Mis. 110–14
1895, May 26
  Mis. 106–16
1896
  Mis. 125–22
1896, January
  Mis. 120–26
1897
  Mis. 251– 3
1897, July 4
  My. 169– 1
1897, December 12
  My. 147– 1
1898
  My. 243–19
1898, January 2
  My. 121– 1
1898, December
  My. 256– 1
1899
  My. 339–11
1899, February
  My. 148– 9
1899, April 19
  My. 151–21
1899, June 4
  My. 124– 5
1899, June 6
  My. 131–17
1900
  My. 256–16
1900, January 11
  My. 154–14
1901
  My. 169–14
1902
  My. 155–16
1902, June 15
  My. 7– 2
1903
  My. 251–23
      252–18
1903, June
  My. 133–21
      170–11
1903, July 20
  My. 294–22
1904
  My. 15–11
      167–14
      171– 8
      253–10
      253–14
1904, July 17
  My. 159– 2
1904, December
  My. 253–20
1905
  My. 254– 4
      254– 9
1905, January 6
  My. 156– 1
1906, June 10
  My. 3– 3

dates — headings
1895, January 6
  Pul. page 1
1898
  Pan. 1– 3
1902, June 18
  My. 7–13
1904, June 14
  My. 16– 1 *
1905, May
  My. 20–22 *

dates — headings
1905, June 13
  My. 22– 1 *
1906, June 12
  My. 38–27 *

dates — interview
1901, April 30
  My. 346–17 *

dates — letters from Mrs. Eddy
1885, March 21
  Mis. 132–11
1889
  Mis. 150– 7
1890, May 23
  Mis. 138–32
1895, Feb. 12
  Mis. 146–28
1895, March 25
  Pul. 87–28
1895, Sept. 30
  Mis. 148– 6
1897, June 30
  My. 169–12
1898, November 16
  My. 187–19
1899, March 22
  My. 301–13
1902, July 21
  My. 9–30
1902, November 20
  My. 193–12
1903, May 11
  My. 133–20
1903, October 16
  My. 327– 9
1904, June 11
  My. 171–18
1904, September 1
  My. 20– 6
1904, October 31
  My. 20–21
1904, November 14
  My. 230–29
1905, June 13
  My. 279–30
1905, June 27
  My. 280–25
1905, November 14
  My. 175– 9
1905, December 28
  My. 261–20
1906, February 9
  My. 351–21
1906, April 8
  My. 25–30
1906, April 23
  My. 26–28
1907, March 22
  My. 135–23
1907, April 2
  My. 136–11
1907, April 3
  My. 136–31
      282–30
1907, April 22
  My. 284– 9
1907, May 28
  My. 284–30
1907, July 8
  My. 236–22
1907, July 27
  My. 197–30
1908, June 21
  My. 140–30
1908, June 24
  My. 142–24
1908, October 12
  My. 352–25
1908, November 16
  My. 353– 5
1909, March 6
  My. 255–12
1909, April 12
  My. 168–10
1909, June 5
  My. 143– 7
1909, June 7
  My. 144–11
1909, June 26
  My. 198–10
1909, July 12
  My. 358–28
1909, July 15
  My. 208– 9

dates — letters from Mrs. Eddy

1909, July 23
My. 360– 6
1909, November 2
My. 208–22
1909, December 11
My. 361–14
1909, December 25
My. 263–11
1910, January 20
My. 362– 8
1910, February 7
My. 355–17
1910, April 20
My. 356–11 *

dates — letters to a newspaper

1844, August 12
My. 332–16 *

dates — letters to Mrs. Eddy

1895, January 6
Pul. 77–22 *
      78–20 *
1895, March 20
Pul. 86–15 *
1903, October 11
My. 328– 6 *
1905, June 13
My. 280–13 *
1906, June 12
My. 60–22 *
1906, June 30
My. 62–16 *
1906, July 10
My. 63– 9 *
1906, November 21
My. 322– 8 *
1906, December 4
My. 323–16 *
1906, December 7
My. 325–20 *
1908, October 9
My. 352–17 *
1910, January 19
My. 361–29 *
1910, February 5
My. 363–12 *

dates — newspaper articles

1894, December 31
Pul. 23– 1 *
      50– 9 *
1895, January
Pul. 84– 9 *
1895, January 6
Pul. 44–15 *
1895, January 7
Pul. 40– 7 *
      61–19 *
1895, January 9
Pul. 71– 3 *
1895, January 10
Pul. 65–10 *
1895, January 12
Pul. 75–13 *
1895, January 14
Pul. 68–12 *
1895, January 18
Pul. 70– 1 *
1895, January 19
Pul. 56–23 *
1895, January 20
Pul. 52– 8 *
1895, January 26
Pul. 57–18 *
1895, February
Pul. 81– 8 *
1895, February 1
Pul. 71– 9 *
1895, February 2
Pul. 63– 1 *
      67– 1 *
1895, February 6
Pul. 74– 1 *
1895, February 7
Pul. 64–22 *
1895, February 27
Pul. 76–21 *
      77–23 *
1895, March 23
Pul. 85–20 *
1895, July
My. 363–17
1898, March
My. 277– 1
1900, May 5
My. 264– 1

dates — newspaper articles

1900, November 29
My. 264– 7
1900, December
My. 266– 1
1901, May 1
My. 341–17 *
1902, June 19
My. 65– 1 *
1902, July
My. 266–10
1903, April
My. 65–17 *
1903, May 16
My. 10– 1 *
      11–22 *
1903, May 30
My. 12–15 *
1903, June 8
My. 304– 1
1904, January 2
My. 14–10 *
1904, March 5
My. 15– 1 *
1904, December
My. 278–15
1905, February
My. 267–13
1905, March 5
My. 268– 1
1905, June 17
My. 279–20
1905, July 1
My. 280–14
1905, July 22
My. 280–26
1905, August
My. 281–15 *
1905, November 25
My. 24–16 *
1906, March 17
My. 25– 5 *
1906, April 14
My. 26– 1
1906, April 28
My. vii–15 *
      26– 7 *
1906, June 6
My. 66–17 *
1906, June 9
My. 27–20 *
1906, June 16
My. 29– 1 *
1906, June 23
My. 63–10 *
1906, November
My. 269–15
1907, January 19
My. 316– 9
1907, August
My. 271–11 *
1907, November
My. 272–18 *
1908, April
My. 274–16 *
1908, May
My. 286– 1
1908, May 1
My. 275–10
1908, May 15
My. 275–30
1908, May 16
My. 276– 1
1908, November
My. 276–15 *
1908, November 25
My. 353– 7
1909, November 13
My. 360–27
      363–18
1910, July 18
My. 356–20

dates — notices

1906, June 2
My. 27–19 *
1908, June 24
My. 351–30
1909, April 28
My. 354–12
1909, June 7
My. 143–32
1909, October 12
My. 359–15
1909, December 24
My. 237–19
1910, September 28
My. 242–26

dates—poem by Lilian Whiting
1888, April 15
  Pul. 40– 6 *

dates—poems by Mrs. Eddy
1865, February 3
  Po. vi–10
    72– 5
1865, August 24
  Po. 68–24
1865, December 7
  Po. 78–17
1866, January 1
  Po. 27–25
1866, August 4
  Po. 40– 5
1866, August 25
  Po. 66–15
1866, September 3
  Po. 9–12
1866, November 8
  Po. 23–23
1866, December 8
  Po. 46–18
1867, March 3
  Po. 74– 7
1868, January 1
  Po. 28–18
1868, February 19
  Po. 42– 8
1871, April
  Po. 70–26
1871, September 3
  Po. 47–23
1876, May 6
  Po. 21–19
1898, May 15
  Po. 11– 5
  My. 337– 1
1898, December
  Po. 29–23
1899
  Po. 24–22
1899, April 3
  Po. 44– 5
1900, January
  Po. 79–22
1900, April 18
  Po. 31–23
1901, January
  Po. 22–22
1904, May 21
  Po. 25–20
1910, January 1
  My. 354–14

dates—prefaces
1895, February
  Pul. vii–24
1897, January
  Mis. xii–11
1910, September 24
  Po. vii–17 *

dates—telegrams, cablegrams
1895, February 4
  Pul. 74– 4 *
1901, December 24
  My. 259–11 *
1906, June 12
  My. 46–32 *
1909, January 5
  My. 207–19 *
1909, January 6
  My. 207–17

dates—tributes
1901, January 27
  My. 289–22
1901, September 14
  My. 290–31
1907, August 31
  My. 295–31
1907, October 14
  My. 296– 8
1907, December 10
  My. 296–23
1908, January 10
  My. 297–10

dating
  Mis. xi–12 *d·* the unseen, and enabling
  Man. 26– 4 *d·* from the time of election
    80–25 *d·* from the time of election
  Po. v– 3 * *d· from her early girlhood*

daughter
  Mis. 126–28 my church,— this *d·* of Zion :
    167– 7 Is the babe a son, or *d·*?
    167– 8 Both son and *d·* :

daughter
  Mis. 214– 7 *d·* against her mother,— *Matt.* 10 : 35.
  Ret. 1–15 Marion Moor McNeil had a *d·*,
    4–24 *d·* of Deacon Nathaniel Ambrose
    16– 6 "Did you hear my *d·* sing?
  Pul. 27–16 * the raising of the *d·* of Jairus.
    32–17 * Mary Baker was the *d·* of
    54–22 * In the case of Jairus' *d·*
    54–27 * he raised the *d·* to life.
  My. 233–17 the *d·* of my people— *Jer.* 6 : 14.
    282–24 importance to every son and *d·*

daughter-in-law
  Mis. 214– 8 the *d·* against her — *Matt.* 10 : 35.

Daughter of the Revolution
  (*see* **Eddy**)

daughters
  Mis. 182–26 the Elohim, His sons and *d·*.
    295–16 the dignity of her *d·*
  Pul. 83–17 * we must look now to their *d·*
  Po. 40– 2 Good "Sons," and *d·*, too,
  My. 185–29 *d·* of the Granite State
    310– 1 All my father's *d·* were

Daughters and Sons of the American Revolution
  Mis. 305– 4 * *D· and S· of the A· R·*,

Daughters of the American Revolution
  Mis. x–24 from the *D· of the A· R·*
    304– 3 * To ᴛʜᴇ *D· of the A· R·* :
    304–18 * care of the *D· of the A· R·*.
    304–30 * of the *D· of the A· R·*.
    305–10 * of the *D· of the A· R·*

Daughters of the Revolution
  Pul. 48–22 * Society of the *D· of the R·*.

dauntless
  Pan. 14–23 led by the *d·* Dewey,
  My. 50–10 * *d·* Leader and teacher,

David (*see also* **David's**)
  Mis. 151–15 *D·* sang, "Whom have I— *Psal.* 73 : 25.
    162–30 Of the lineage of *D·*,
    196–23 and, in the words of *D·*,
    208–21 *D·* said, "Before I was— *Psal.* 119 : 67.
    229–16 would teach man as *D·* taught :
  Chr. 55– 4 the offspring of *D·*,— *Rev.* 22 : 16.
  Un. 30–12 restoreth my soul," says *D·*.— *Psal.* 23 : 3.
  Pul. 83–19 * *D·* sang — "God shall help— *Psal.* 46 : 5.
  '00. 14–21 hath the key of *D·* ;— *Rev.* 3 : 7.
  My. 188–10 out of the city of *D·*,
    244–15 place," whereof *D·* sang,— *Psal.* 91 : 1.
    273–10 King *D·*, the Hebrew bard, sang,

David's
  Ret. 15– 7 I could say in *D·* words,

Davis
Dr.
  My. 105–20 Dr. *D·* of Manchester, N. H.
Mr.
  My. 282–21 *Dear Mr. D· :*— Deeply do I thank you
Mr. Hayne
  My. 282–18 Mʀ. Hᴀʏɴᴇ *D·*, American Secretary,

dawn
  Mis. 78– 2 the spiritual *d·* of the Messiah,
    144–31 the universal *d·* shall break
    174–28 Death can never usher in the *d·*
    286–13 the *d·* of God's creation,
    313–10 *d·*, kindling its glories in the east,
    320–26 pierce the darkness and melt into *d·*.
    390– 6 lark's shrill song doth wake the *d·* :
  Un. 61–10 twilight and *d·* of earthly vision,
  No. 20–15 omnipresence will *d·* on mortals,
    22–14 as Stygian night to the kindling *d·*.
  '01. 35–14 Doth it *d·* on you and me?
  '02. 5– 1 As silent night foretells the *d·*
    5– 4 *d·* of the twentieth century
    20– 5 hues of heaven, tipping the *d·*
  Po. 17– 1 Ye echoes at *d·* !
    27– 8 *d·* with wisdom's light
    29– 6 Nor *d·* nor day !
    55– 7 lark's shrill song doth wake the *d·* :
  My. 110– 9 But the day will *d·*
    155–22 *d·* that knows no twilight
    254– 5 am glad you enjoy the *d·* of C. S. ;
    262–16 *d·* of divine Love breaking upon
    282–10 no uncertain ray of *d·*.
    290–21 Through a . . . mist he beheld the *d·*.
    297–13 dark hour that precedes the *d·*.
    350–26 *D·* Truth delightful, crowned with

dawned
  Mis. 1– 4 *d·* on the dome of being
    24– 6 daystar that *d·* on the night of
    24–12 healing Truth *d·* upon my sense ;
    169– 9 Truth *d·* upon her understanding.

dawned

Ret.	14–24	the new light d· within me.
No.	46–20	has d· on the sick-bound and
My.	265–14	Science of Christianity has d·
	307–31	had already d· on me.

dawning

Mis.	320–13	d· upon human imperfection,
	385–27	radiant glory sped The d· day.
Po.	28– 5	Of truth, this d· year !
	49– 2	radiant glory sped The d· day.

dawns

Mis.	17–28	d· on human thought,
	84–11	which d· by degrees on mortals.
	213–28	night is far spent, the day d· ;
	222–32	as easily as d· the morning light
'00.	6–10	d· the spiritual meaning thereof ;
	7–30	morning d· on eternal day.
My.	185– 3	day d· and the harvest bells are

Day

My.	252–25	in England on New Year's D·,

day (see also day's)

after day

My.	52–32	* "D· after day flew by,

all

My.	341–26	* It had been raining all d·

ancient

Po.	10– 7	Thy palm, in ancient d·,
My.	337– 8	Thy palm, in ancient d·,

and night

Mis.	177– 9	are engaged d· and night in
	341–26	replenished with oil d· and night,
Pul.	12– 9	d· and night. — Rev. 12: 10.
	26–28	* kept always burning d· and night.

autumnal

Mis.	355–30	close of a balmy autumnal d·,

before

My.	322–17	* I had seen you the d· before

before the

My.	96–21	* before the d· set for the

break of

Mis.	111– 5	and at break of d· caught much.

busy

My.	75– 7	* Yesterday was a busy d· at the

by day

My.	31– 6	* "D· by day the manna fell ;"
	207–10	* strive more earnestly, d· by day,

children's

My.	38–16	* It was "children's d·" at noon,

Communion

Man.	40–20	On Communion d· the Church Tenets

cool of the

Mis.	332–14	walking in the cool of the d·

dawning

Mis.	385–27	radiant glory sped The dawning d·.
Po.	49– 2	radiant glory sped The dawning d·.

dawns

Mis.	213–28	night is far spent, the d· dawns ;
My.	185– 3	d· dawns and the harvest bells

dedication

Pul.	79– 7	* taken care of on dedication d··
My.	77–17	* chapter sub-title
	77–22	* It was dedication d·,

distant

My.	59– 6	* might be true in some far distant d·
	147– 8	And now, at this distant d·,

during the

Pul.	43–25	* in Concord, N. H., during the d·,
My.	29–11	* repeated six times during the d·.
	174– 4	Christian Scientists during the d·.

each

Mis.	142–12	Each d· since they arrived
Man.	41–21	duty of . . . to pray each d· :
	60–16	should abide in every heart each d·
My.	161–23	sufficient unto each d· is the
	174–27	Each d· I know Him nearer,
	220–14	Each d· I pray for the
	220–21	Each d· I pray : " God bless my
	279–24	pray each d· for the . . . settlement of

endless

Mis.	399– 5	glories of one endless d·."
Po.	75–12	glories of one endless d·."

eternal

'00.	7–30	morning dawns on eternal d·.
Po.	22–11	And bask in one eternal d·.

everlasting

Mis.	vii–18	sprung from Spirit, In everlasting d· ;
'02.	20– 6	tipping the dawn of everlasting d·,

every

Mis.	33–14	that is being asked every d·.
	99–18	and be in the battle every d·
	348–20	every d·, and especially at dinner,
My.	48–11	* make, every d·, a prayerful study
	48–27	* every d· through its reading.
	145– 8	I inspected the work every d·,

day

every

My.	167–21	this and every d·.
	340– 3	every d· and every hour.

eye of

Po.	8–10	Ravished with beauty the eye of d·.

facts of

My.	110–21	unfold in part the facts of d·,

following

'02.	15–25	The following d· I showed it to my
My.	172–24	* was opened the following d·

glad

My.	158– 8	it is a glad d·, in attune with
	173–21	It was a glad d· for me

grayest

My.	87–23	* make sunshine on the grayest d·.

grows dark

Mis.	398–13	So, when d· grows dark and cold,
Ret.	46–19	So, when d· grows dark and cold,
Pul.	17–18	So, when d· grows dark and cold,
Po.	14–17	So, when d· grows dark and cold,

has come

My.	183–18	d· has come when the forest becomes

heat of the

Mis.	130–18	the burden in the heat of the d·,
'00.	9–30	heat of the d·." — Matt. 20: 12.

hours of the

My.	94–21	* at different hours of the d·,

in Concord

My.	171–19	* heading

interesting

Mis.	320– 4	This interesting d·, crowned with

is at hand

My.	202– 7	and the d· is at hand.

is not distant

Pan.	1–17	d· is not distant in the horizon

last

Mis.	57–26	the sixth and last d·,

laughing

Ret.	18–11	to the bright, laughing d· ;
Po.	63–23	to the bright, laughing d· ;

little

Po.	67– 2	brief bliss of life's little d·

memorable

Mis.	144– 8	On this memorable d· there are

midnight

Po.	26– 7	Chill was thy midnight d·,

next

Mis.	69–18	next d· he attended to his

night and

My.	66–19	* artists are working night and d·

no

My.	129–10	there is no d· but in His smile.

no distant

Mis.	6–14	At no distant d·, Christian healing

of dedication

Pul.	57– 7	* services on the d· of dedication.

of heathenism

My.	167–30	In our country the d· of heathenism,

of rest

Mis.	279–20	the seventh is the d· of rest,

of the birth

Pul.	20–23	d· of the birth and baptism of our

one

Mis.	339– 8	and is one d· beyond it,
	353–13	one d· a workman in his mills,
Ret.	8–13	One d·, when my cousin,
Un.	14– 2	the belief that God must one d·
Pul.	33–17	* at work in a field one d·
My.	126–21	plagues come in one d·, — Rev. 18: 8.
	145–10	One d· the carpenters' foreman
	307– 5	till one d· I declared to him

one especial

My.	325– 2	* spoke of one especial d· when

oppressive

My.	29–30	* inconveniences of an oppressive d·.

or night

Pul.	58–29	* make it a home by d· or night.

or two

Pul.	75–20	* and for the d· or two following,

other

My.	70–15	* were being tested the other d·.
	96–28	* The dedication of . . . the other d·,

our

My.	23–27	* is being built in our d· ;

pillar by

My.	164–21	pillar by d·, kindling, guiding,

same

Mis.	243–10	removed these appliances the same d·

seventh

My.	336– 2	* would have died on the seventh d·.

sixteenth

My.	138–26	* On the sixteenth d· of May, 1907,

teachings of the

Mis.	81–11	accepted teachings of the d·,

tenth

My.	319–20	* On the tenth d· of January, 1887,

day

that
Mis. 70–25 That *d·* the thief would be with
304–30 * organization on that *d·* of the
Pul. 60– 9 * happened that *d·* to be on Jesus'
Po. vi–26 * *various publications of that d·.*
My. 156–10 against that *d·.*" — *II Tim.* 1 : 12.
228–30 against that *d·*" — *II Tim.* 1 : 12.
that thou eatest
Mis. 367–17 "In the *d·* that thou eatest — *Gen.* 2 : 17.
the other
Hea. 6– 4 When I was told the other *d·,*
third
Mis. 24–10 On the third *d·* thereafter,
My. 335–23 * third *d·* of her husband's illness,
this
Mis. 271–13 "Choose you this *d·* — *Josh.* 24 : 15.
Po. 28–16 Give us this *d·* our daily food
My. 158– 7 This *d·* drops down upon the
158–10 This *d·* is the natal hour of my
three times a
Mis. 133–22 Three times a *d·,* I retire to seek
throughout the
My. 31– 2 * following hymns throughout the *d·* :
20th
Pul. 78–14 * on the 20th *d·* of February, 1895,
twentieth
Pul. 77–16 * on the twentieth *d·* of February,
twenty-eighth
My. 333– 6 twenty-eighth *d·* of June, 1844,
twenty-fourth
Pul. 87– 3 * on the twenty-fourth *d·* of March,
twenty-third
Man. 18–12 On the twenty-third *d·* of September,
My. 55–13 * On the twenty-third *d·* of September,
wearisome
Po. 32–20 all the wearisome *d·,*
we celebrate
Mis. 176–14 The *d·* we celebrate reminds us
when all people
Pan. 1–18 even the *d·* when all people
will dawn
My. 110– 9 *d·* will dawn and the daystar
winter
Pul. 65–22 * bitter winter *d·,* a Roman soldier

Mis. 7–17 the newspapers of the *d·,*
39–10 risen up in a *d·* to make this claim ;
57–16 "In the *d·* that thou eatest — *Gen.* 2 : 17.
226–16 * must follow, as the night the *d·,*
335– 7 *d·* when he looketh not — *Matt.* 24 : 50.
Ret. 9–25 * redeemed her birthright of the *d·,*
81–25 * must follow, as the night the *d·,*
Un. 5–13 every Life-problem in a *d·.*
17–22 in the *d·* when they should partake of
44–20 "In the *d·* ye eat thereof — *Gen.* 3 : 5.
Po. vi–27 * poem
29– 6 Nor dawn nor *d·* !
page 32 poem
My. 30–29 * by far the largest crowd of the *d·*
45–19 * by *d·* in a pillar of cloud
45–25 * pillar of cloud by *d·,* — *see Exod.* 13 : 22.
75–20 * and warm as the *d·* was,
148–13 unthought of till the *d·* had passed !
153–12 healed from the *d·* my flowers
173–17 on the *d·* when there are no formal
186–26 on the *d·* of your church dedication.
187–24 Since the *d·* in which you were
327–29 * and look forward to the *d·,*

daybreak
Un. 27–14 fleeing like a shadow at *d·* ;
My. 77–19 * began to gather at *d·*

day-dream
Mis. 47–13 tend to elucidate your *d·,*

day-dreams
Ret. 12– 5 echoes still my *d·* thrill,
Po. 61– 3 echoes still my *d·* thrill,
My. 109– 3 Matter has no . . . in our *d·*

day-god
Po. 16–14 when the *d·* is low ;

daylight
Mis. 126– 3 yea, from darkness to *d·,*

day's
My. 92–12 * hardly more than a *d·* wonder.

days (see also days')

apostolic
Ret. 43– 2 since the apostolic *d·.*
beginning of
Chr. 55–20 neither beginning of *d·,* — *Heb.* 7 : 3.
dark
My. 222–15 Even in those dark *d·* Jesus was not
340–27 The dark *d·* of our forefathers
dear
Po. 47– 1 Are the dear *d·* ever coming again,

days

early
Mis. 345–27 midnight feasts in the early *d·,*
My. 63– 3 * early *d·* of the construction of
eight
My. 323–32 * eight *d·* in Mr. and Mrs. Wiggin's
endless
My. 350–26 crowned with endless *d·,*
end of
Un. 13–18 or end of *d·.*" — *see Heb.* 7 : 3.
My. 119–25 without beginning or end of *d·.*
feast
My. 188– 7 Your feast *d·* will not be in
few
Mis. 80–17 must be "of few *d·,* — *Job* 14 : 1.
373– 7 A few *d·* afterward, the following
Chr. 55–14 is of few *d·,* — *Job.* 14 : 1.
My. 14–11 * A few *d·* ago we received a
86–10 * into Boston in the past few *d·*
87–22 * in Boston during the past few *d·.*
145–12 * "I want to be let off for a few *d·.*
247–26 after many or a few *d·*
319–22 * A few *d·* later, in conversation
for prayer
My. 340– 3 St. Paul's *d·* for prayer were
full number of
'00. 14– 7 full number of *d·* named in the
later
My. 63– 4 * advisory capacity in the later *d·* ;
319–22 * A few *d·* later, in conversation
latter
Mis. 112–13 seem to belong to the latter *d·,*
My. 127–21 latter *d·* of the nineteenth century.
131–22 in this hour of the latter *d·*
length of
Mis. 29–26 nor advance health and length of *d·.*
67–17 happiness, and length of *d·.*
many
My. 13–30 returns it unto them after many *d·,*
may be few
Po. 33–17 I ponder the *d·* may be few
nine
My. 312–21 and died in about nine *d·.*
335–17 * and at the end of nine *d·*
335–29 * In these nine *d·* and nights
of Christ
Un. 9–25 since the *d·* of Christ.
of Eden
Un. 44–10 In the *d·* of Eden, humanity was
of shade
My. 166–13 *D·* of shade and shine may come
pioneer
Mis. x–10 in the early pioneer *d·,*
Revolutionary
Pul. 48–28 * in Colonial and Revolutionary *d·,*
seven
Mis. 279–18 corresponding to the seven *d·* of
several
My. 73–15 * as they have been for several *d·*
73–15 * will be for several *d·* to come,
six
Mis. 279–18 the six *d·* are to find out the
special
My. 340– 5 usage of special *d·* and seasons
sunny
Mis. 395–26 Of sunny *d·* and cloudless skies,
Po. 58–11 Of sunny *d·* and cloudless skies,
ten
Man. 52– 8 within ten *d·* thereafter,
68– 3 to go in ten *d·* to her,
My. 76– 3 * Up to within ten *d·*
these
Pul. 51– 4 * a great privilege in these *d .*
those
Ret. 89– 5 In those *d·* preaching and
93– 2 The evangelists of those *d·*
Pul. 82–18 * In those *d·* women had few lawful
three
Mis. 242–24 cure that habit in three *d·,*
Pul. 3– 5 in three *d·* I will — *John* 2 : 19.
thy
My. 252–16 "As thy *d·,* so shall thy — *Deut.* 33 : 25.
270–17 "as thy *d·,* so shall thy — *Deut.* 33 : 25.

Mis. 167–13 Of his *d·* there is no beginning
304–24 * anniversaries of the *d·* on which
Pul. 34–20 * *d·* when Jesus of Nazareth
'02. 15–12 *d·* wherein the connection between
My. 95–28 * since the *d·* of the primitive

days'
Mis. 239– 5 had but four *d·* vacation
My. 74– 4 * within two or three *d·* ride,
214–11 Jesus' three *d·* work in the sepulchre
322–22 * few *d·* instruction by Mrs. Eddy

dayspring

Pul.	10–25	descended like *d·* from on high.
Po.	30– 7	O gladsome *d·* ! 'reft of mortal sigh

daystar

Mis.	24– 6	*d·* that dawned on the night of
	165–10	*d·* of this appearing is the light of
'02.	2– 2	sees through the mist . . . this *d·*,
My.	110–10	*d·* will appear, lighting the gloom,

dazzling

Mis.	162– 6	From this *d·*, God-crowned summit,
	376–22	over a deeply *d·* sunlight,
	388–16	Her *d·* crown, her sceptred throne,
'02.	3–21	The *d·* diadem of royalty
Po.	21– 4	Her *d·* crown, her sceptered throne,
My.	193– 7	*d·* glory in the Occident,

D. C. (District of Columbia)
(*see* **Washington**)

D. D.

My.	4–15	Protestant and Catholic, *D.D.* and

D. D. S.

My.	314– 9	He had the degree *D.D.S.*,

deacon

My.	60– 7	* my uncle, the good old *d·* of

Deacons

My.	174–16	Ballard, . . . Morrison, *D·*.

dead

Mis.	25–19	and raising the spiritually *d·*.
	28–28	healed the sick and raised the *d·*.
	60–13	*d· only in belief?*
	74–19	he raised the *d·*, and
	95–16	the so-called *d·* and living.
	124–18	raising the *d·*, saving sinners.
	129–13	*d·* bury their *d·*," — *Matt.* 8 : 22.
	168– 9	the *d·*, those buried in dogmas
	169–30	*d·* bury their *d·* ; — *Matt.* 8 : 22.
	170– 4	to us there can be no *d·*.
	187– 2	*healing the sick*, and raising the *d·*.
	237–27	in honor of the *d·* hero
	238–27	allegement that I . . . am *d·*,
	244–21	and the *d·* to be raised
	248–19	not more true than that I am *d·*,
	249–20	The report that I was *d·* arose
	292–17	bury the *d·* out of sight ;
	311– 9	so, bury the *d·* past ;
	326– 1	raise the *d·* ; — *Matt.* 10 : 8.
	385–20	Man is not mortal, never of the *d·*:
Man.	60–18	*d·* bury their *d·*," — *Matt.* 8 : 22.
Chr.	53– 7	rouse the living, wake the *d·*,
	55– 6	*d·* shall hear the voice — *John* 5 : 25.
	55–16	body is *d·* because of — *Rom.* 8 : 10.
Ret.	20–19	life is *d·*, bereft of all, with thee,
	21– 2	was *d·* and buried.
	66– 2	in casting out error, in raising the *d·*.
	81– 3	both for the living and the *d·*.
	87–1, 2	*d·* bury their *d·*." — *Matt.* 8 : 22.
	88– 5	"raise the *d·*." — *Matt.* 10 : 8.
	88– 8	so-called *d·* forthwith emerged into a
	88–11	"Raise the *d·*," — *Matt.* 10 : 8.
Un.	3– 7	"Blessed are the *d·* — *Rev.* 14 : 13.
	41–11	Resurrection from the *d·*
	61– 8	neither *d·* nor risen.
	62–24	the living among the *d·* ? — *Luke* 24 : 5.
Pul.	9–29	without works is *d·*." — *James* 2 : 26.
	29–18	* raise the *d·*, — *Matt.* 10 : 8.
	66–13	* raise the *d·*, — *Matt.* 10 : 8.
No.	25– 5	that being *d·* wherein — *Rom.* 7 : 6.
	37–23	saved the sinner and raised the *d·*,
'01.	16–12	Then let the dead bury its *d·*,
	19–17	healed the sick, raised the *d·*
'02.	9–5, 6	*d·* bury their *d·* ;" — *Matt.* 8 : 22.
Hea.	2–24	not in the power of . . . a *d·* rite
	6–12	the so-called *d·* and the living.
Peo.	12–21	healing the sick and raising the *d·*
Po.	15–17	blossom and sunshine not *d·*
	25–12	Fragrance fresh round the *d·*,
	48–14	Man is not mortal, never of the *d·* :
	53–19	and *d·* are all The vernal songs
	67–10	memory of dear ones deemed *d·*
	78– 1	our honored *d·* fought on
My.	110– 3	healing the sick, and raising the *d·*
	128– 4	repentance from *d·* works." — *Heb.* 6 : 1.
	133–14	"*d·* in trespasses — *Eph.* 2 : 1.
	139– 3	She is neither *d·* nor
	150–22	*d·* in trespasses and sins
	158–20	letter without the spirit is *d·* :
	160–11	willingly accept *d·* truisms
	185–18	"was *d·*, and is alive — *Luke* 15 : 32.
	189–31	*D·* is he who loved me dearly ;
	191–19	The sepulchres give up their *d·*.
	192– 5	raise the living *d·*,
	206– 1	would unite *d·* matter with
	218–10	The power . . . to raise the *d·*
	219–16	spiritual idea, who raises the *d·*,

dead

My.	269– 7	resurrection from the *d·*, — *Luke* 20 : 35.
	270–15	Mary Baker Eddy is not *d·*,
	275–14	is *d·*, and should be buried.
	296–12	Joseph Armstrong, C.S.D., is not *d·*,
	300–26	raise the *d·*, — *Matt.* 10 : 8.
	306– 4	to tread on the ashes of the *d·*
	353–25	*d·* bury their *d·*," — *Luke* 9 : 60.

deadened

Pul.	10– 3	raised the *d·* conscience,
My.	91–11	* no person's . . . were ever *d·*

deadly

Mis.	28–32	drink any *d·* thing, — *Mark* 16 : 18.
	177–10	Their feeling and purpose are *d·*,
	249– 6	drink any *d·* thing, — *Mark* 16 : 18.
	368–16	more *d·* than the upas-tree
Un.	54–16	its most potent and *d·* enemy.
'01.	32–15	they armed quickly, aimed *d·*,
Hea.	1– 3	*drink any d· thing,* — *Mark* 16 : 18.
	7–26	drink any *d·* thing, — *Mark* 16 : 18.
	15–11	drink any *d·* thing, — *Mark* 16 : 18.
Peo.	12– 4	drink any *d·* thing, — *Mark* 16 : 18.
My.	48– 1	* drink any *d·* thing, — *Mark* 16 : 18.
	146– 4	drink any *d·* thing, — *Mark* 16 : 18.

deaf

Mis.	22–24	with the sick, the lame, the *d·*,
	88–18	task of talking to *d·* ears
	168– 7	the *d·* — those who, having ears,
	244–21	the *d·* to hear, the lame to walk,
	362– 9	ears to these *d·*, feet to these lame,
	368– 6	and cause the *d·* to hear.
Pul.	82–28	* remain *d·* to their cry?
'00.	11–13	The *d·* Beethoven besieges you with
'01.	17–15	It was that I healed the *d·*,
My.	105–17	sight to the blind, hearing to the *d·*,
	183–19	the *d·* hear the words of the Book,

deal

Mis.	4–25	must require a great *d·* of faith
	64–19	are those which *d·* with facts
Peo.	12–10	*D·*, then, with this fabulous law
My.	98–12	* would *d·* with the phenomenon
	111– 7	same class of minds to *d·* with

dealeth

Un.	23–11	*d·* with you as with sons ; — *Heb.* 12 : 7.

dealing

Ret.	71–19	is not *d·* justly and loving
	82– 3	*d·* with a simple Latour exercise
My.	121–14	Peace, like plain *d·*,
	121–15	plain *d·* is a jewel as beautiful as
	181– 4	*d·* with human hypotheses,

dealt

Mis.	12–23	*d·* with by divine justice.
	211– 8	*d·* with summarily by
	284–16	so *d·* with at the outset.
	284–20	sin must now be *d·* with as evil,
Pul.	29–17	* *d·* directly with the command of

Dean, Charles

My.	361–26	* signature

Charles A.

My.	362– 2	Charles A. *D·*, Chairman

dear

Mis.	16–27	*d·* reader, pause for a moment
	30–26	Take courage, *d·* reader,
	42–17	we meet the *d·* departed,
	61–11	* "*D· Mrs. Eddy:* — In the October
	81– 5	by right of God's *d·* love,
	132–12	*D· Sir:* — In your communication
	134– 3	*d·* sir, as you have expressed
	137–17	*d·* ones, if you take my advice
	142–17	your *d·* hearts expressed in their
	145–18	friendship, delicate as *d·*,
	176–15	counted not their own lives *d·*
	180– 7	A *d·* old lady asked me,
	239– 1	let me say to you, *d·* reader :
	252–29	It is the *d·* children's toy
	262– 1	*D·* readers, our *Journal* is designed to
	266–22	They are essentially *d·* to me,
	313– 8	rest on the *d·* readers,
	317– 9	The *d·* ones whom I would have
	319–18	Will all the *d·* Christian Scientists
	320– 6	*d·* to the heart of Christian Scientists ;
	328– 6	*D·* reader, dost thou suspect that
	330–10	the springtide of Christ's *d·* love.
Ret.	19– 5	parting with the *d·* home circle
	21–13	It is well to know, *d·* reader,
Un.	20–15	Try this process, *d·* inquirer,
Pul.	v– 2	To THE *D·* . . . CHILDREN
	7–10	were our *d·* Master in our
	44– 2	* "*D· Teacher, Leader, Guide:*
	77– 9	* "*D· Mother:* — During the year
	78– 8	* "*D· Mother:* — During the year 1894
	82–11	* many things *d·* to the soul

dear

Pan.	11–30	because Christ's *d·* demand,
'01.	31–20	of blessings infinite I count these *d·* :
'02.	20–21	faces of my *d·* church-members ;
Po.	24–20	*D·* heart of Love,
	29– 7	*D·* Christ, forever here and near,
	34– 5	*d·* remembrance in a weary breast.
	47– 1	Are the *d·* days ever coming again,
	67– 9	memory of *d·* ones deemed dead
	77–17	some *d·* lost guest
My.	12–29	*d·* children's good deeds are gems
	25–16	all of my *d·* correspondents
	58–28	* *My D· Teacher :* — Of the many
	60–25	* *D· Leader and Guide:*
	82– 3	* one near and *d·* to them.
	90–12	* for self or *d·* ones.
	118– 9	*My D· Sir :* — I beg to thank you
	122–12	deportment of its *d·* members
	145– 2	*D·* EDITORS:— You are by this time
	148–21	of this *d·* little flock,
	154–10	comforting to the *d·* sick,
	155– 4	May this *d·* little church,
	155–26	*d·* Sunday School children
	156– 3	my gratitude for your *d·* letter,
	158–24	will bless this *d·* band of brethren.
	162–11	*d·* Sunday School children,
	163–17	*D· Editor :* — When I removed from
	164–16	Now . . . six *d·* churches are there,
	165–12	I beg to thank the *d·* brethren
	166–22	*d·* ones, let us together sing
	167– 2	may have cost the *d·* donors.
	167–19	Give to all the *d·* ones my love,
	168– 6	people of my *d·* old New Hampshire.
	171– 1	*d·* members of my church :
	173– 5	*D· Mr. Editor :* — Allow me
	175–12	Its *d·* churches, reliable editors,
	175–23	*d·* as the friendship of
	175–29	minds of this *d·* people
	176– 5	Long ago you of the *d·* South
	189– 4	So *d·*, so due, to God is *obedience,*
	197– 5	be upon this *d·* people,
	199–16	C. S., so *d·* to our hearts
	202–25	From the *d·* tone of your letter,
	206–30	kingdom of His *d·* Son." — *Col.* 1 : 13.
	208–14	your *d·* letter to my waiting heart,
	213–30	*d·* Churches of Christ, Scientist.
	254–14	this class and its *d·* members.
	254–17	* *D· Leader :* — May we have permission
	257– 3	His *d·* love that heals the
	258–28	consciousness of God's *d·* love for you
	259–13	*d·* churches' Christmas telegrams
	270–18	words of our *d·*, departing Saviour,
	274–10	*D·* reader, right thinking,
	274–20	Will the *d·* Christian Scientists
	275–21	my *d·* friends' and my *d·* enemies'
	276–12	all her *d·* friends and enemies.
	282–21	*D· Mr. Davis :* — Deeply do I thank
	284–12	*D· Editor :* — In the issue of
	290–12	*D· Mrs. Mckinley :* — My soul reaches
	302–27	*d·* members wanted to greet me
	319–16	* *D· Teacher :* — I am conversant
	326–12	*D· Editor :* — I send for publication
	327–22	* representative men of our *d·* State
327–31*,	328– 1	* as lived by our *d·*, *d·* Leader,
	338–11	lecture of our *d·* brother,
	357–13	When my *d·* brethren in New York

(*see also* **children, church, God, student, students**)

dearer
Pul.	83–23	* by bonds *d·* than freedom,"

dearest
Ret.	6–12	the very *d·* of my kindred.
Pul.	81–12	* Some of her *d·* ones
My.	129–22	and be thy *d·* allies.
	256–18	*d·* memories in human history
	271–22	* "What is nearest and *d·*
	271–30	what is "nearest and *d·*''

dearly
Chr.	53–15	understanding, *d·* sought,
My.	189–31	Dead is he who loved me *d·* :
	279–22	*D· Beloved :* — I request that
	313–27	My oldest sister *d·* loved me,

dearth
Po.	33– 7	selfishness, sinfulness, *d·*,

death (*see also* **death's**)
after
Mis.	2–21	Man's probation after *d·*
	2–24	If man should not progress after *d·*,
	28–18	shown by his ascension after *d·*,
	34–17	after *d·*, they can no more come
	222–19	suffer its full penalty after *d·*.

agony and
'01.	20–20	Even the agony and *d·* that it

alone
My.	273–30	*d·* alone does not awaken man
	274– 5	*D·* alone does not absolve man

death

and burial
Ret.	2–25	*d·* and burial of George Washington.

and humanity
My.	258–24	love, grief, *d·*, and humanity.

and the grave
Un.	30–19	victorious over *d·* and the grave.
Peo.	5–14	overcome *d·* and the grave,
My.	218–15	absolved from *d·* and the grave.

before
Mis.	34–16	see them as they were before *d·*,
My.	344–14	better than he was before *d·*.

belief in
Un.	40–10	subordinates the belief in *d·*,
	41–12	(that is, from the belief in *d·*)

belief of
Mis.	170– 1	salvation from the belief of *d·*,

believes in
My.	300–14	Does he who believes in *d·*

believing in
Un.	40–14	by believing in *d·*,

bleeding to
Hea.	18–28	believe he was bleeding to *d·*.
	19– 8	belief that he was bleeding to *d·*,

brought
'02.	6– 7	brought *d·* into the world

called
Mis.	42– 1	*After the change called d·*
	42– 5	through the belief called *d·*.
	42–13	passed the ordeal called *d·*,
Un.	2–28	this transition, called *d·*,
	40– 4	shadow of material sense, called *d·*,
No.	14– 5	the transition called *d·*,
	27▾27	after the change called *d·*,
	28– 3	after the transition called *d·*,
My.	206–14	through the shadow called *d·*,

came
Un.	15– 2	came "*d·* into the world,

can be nowhere
Un.	42– 1	must follow that *d·* can be nowhere ;

can never
Mis.	174–27	*D·* can never usher in the dawn of
Un.	40–20	*D·* can never alarm or

cause of
My.	335–21	* cause of *d·* as bilious fever,

changed, by
Mis.	52–19	*but only changed, by d·*,

change of
Pul.	38–19	* passed the change of *d·*

conquer
Un.	18–24	saith, . . . thus I conquer *d·* ;

darkness and
Po.	65–18	darkness and *d·* like mist melt away,

demonstration over
Un.	43– 4	strong demonstration over *d·*,

deprives
Un.	48–10	deprives *d·* of its sting,

destroy
Mis.	193–13	C. S., . . . will destroy *d·*.

destroys
Mis.	235– 5	reflect Him who destroys *d·*
	336–24	heals disease . . . and destroys *d·!*

disbelief in
My.	297–17	blessing of disbelief in *d·*,

disease and
(*see* **disease**)

disease, nor
Mis.	165–14	darkness, doubt, disease, nor *d·*.

disease, sin, and
Un.	10– 1	*unreality of disease, sin, and d·*,
My.	106–20	expressed in disease, sin, and *d·*,

dissolving
Po.	24– 4	Dissolving *d·*, despair !

does not destroy
Mis.	28–14	*d·* does not destroy the beliefs of

door named
Mis.	84–30	through the door named *d·*,

dream of
Mis.	58– 6	Waking from the dream of *d·*,
My.	273–28	"Man awakes from the dream of *d·*

early
My.	335–10	* who mourn his early *d·*.

ends in
Mis.	361– 6	its miscalled life ends in *d·*,
Ret.	69–15	false sense . . . which ends in *d·*''

error and
Hea.	8– 5	that destroy error and *d·*.

fear of
'02.	3–22	the muffled fear of *d·*

has lost
My.	191–23	*D·* has lost its sting,

has no
Un.	38–20	*D·* has no quality of Life ;
	41–14	second *d·* has no power.

death

her husband's
My. 329–14 * notice of her husband's *d·*
    336– 5 * come to her after her husband's *d·*,
his
Mis. 71– 4 John B. Gough . . . until his *d·* ;
    84– 5 did not prophesy his *d·*,
Ret. 7–18 * His *d·* will be deplored,
No. 34– 5 by commemorating his *d·* with a
My. 331–31 * extended to her after his *d·*,
    335–15 * for many years after his *d·*.
illness and
My. 335–12 * regarding . . . his illness and *d·*,
illusion that
Un. 59–23 illusion that *d·* is as real as
into Life
Un. 41–18 portal from *d·* into Life ;
is a contradiction
Un. 38– 4 *D·* is a contradiction of Life,
is at war
Mis. 217–23 *d·* is at war with Life,
is not the goal
Un. 45–22 *d·* is not the goal which Truth seeks.
issues of
Mis. 222– 1 holds the issues of *d·* to the
is the consequent
No. 16–28 *D·* is the consequent of an
itself
Mis. 361– 6 *d·* itself is swallowed up in
jaws of
Pan. 14–25 victoriously through the jaws of *d·*
know
Un. 41– 8 to know *d·*, or to believe in it,
last enemy
My. 185–21 destroys the last enemy, *d·*.
law of
My. 154– 6 transcending the law of *d·*.
leadership and
Ret. 3– 6 whose gallant leadership and *d·*,
lead to
Mis. 61– 7 vain strivings . . . that lead to *d·*,
life and
    (*see* **life**)
life from
My. 139–29 redeem . . . your life from *d·*.
life nor
My. 302– 6 Neither life nor *d·*, health nor
Life, not
Un. 39–24 and embodies Life, not *d·*.
My. 239– 1 it demonstrates Life, not *d·* ;
life, not
Mis. 346– 1 Life, not *d·*, was and is the
Life, not of
Un. 3–19 of Life, not of *d·*.
Life over
Mis. 61–10 and of Life over *d·*.
    321–12 of Life over *d·*,
material
Un. 38–12 transition called *material d·*,
Mr. Quimby's
Mis. 379–27 It was after Mr. Quimby's *d·*
must know
Un. 18–22 Error says God must know *d·*
never changes to
Mis. 170– 7 which never changes to *d·*.
never conscious of
Un. 18–25 is to be never conscious of *d·*.
never see
Mis. 76– 5 shall never see *d·*.''— *John* 8 : 51.
No. 31–27 shall never see *d·*;''— *John* 8 : 51.
My. 300–19 shall never see *d·*.''— *John* 8 : 51.
no
Mis. 179–32 this Life that knows no *d·*,
    183– 3 Love, and . . . that know no *d·*.
    194–27 sense of Life that knows no *d·*,
Un. 37–14 to believe there is no *d·*?
    39– 8 that Life which knows no *d·*.
    43– 5 namely, that there is no *d·*,
    43–27 Life which knows no *d·*,
    55– 3 namely, that there is no *d·*.
No. 13–13 in Life that knows no *d·*,
My. 297–11 chapter sub-title
    297–15 no evil, no disease, no *d·* ;
    300–14 aver that there is no *d·*,
no spiritual
Un. 29– 8 there can be, no spiritual *d·*.
not through
Un. 41–20 not through *d·*, but through Life ;
My. 181–11 not through *d·*, but through the
not to bring
'01. 21–22 came not to bring *d·* but life
of an individual
'01. 21–15 *d·* of an individual who loves God
of a sparrow
Mis. 184– 4 from . . . to the *d·* of a sparrow.

death

of her husband
My. 329– 9 * reference to the *d·* of her husband,
of Pope Leo XIII
My. 294–22 chapter sub-title
of sinners
Un. 50–27 maturity, and *d·* of sinners,
or the grave
Mis. 104– 5 not subject . . . to *d·*, or the grave.
pain or
My. 90–12 * pain or *d·* for self or dear ones.
pangs of
Peo. 1–17 Even the pangs of *d·* disappear,
physical
Mis. 37–21 leads to moral or physical *d·*.
portal of
Mis. 180– 5 dark shadow and portal of *d·*,
power over
Mis. 64– 4 to show his power over *d·* ;
No. 33–22 Love and its power over *d·*.
putting him to
Mis. 182– 3 impossibility of putting him to *d·*,
put to
No. 29– 2 put to *d·* for his own sin,
'02. 11–3 put to *d·* the Galilean Prophet,
recording the
My. 332–29 * papers recording the *d·* of
rescued from
Pul. 66–11 * claim to have been rescued from *d·*
second
Mis. 2–26 second *d·* hath no power''— *Rev.* 20 : 6.
Un. 3– 8 the second *d·*, of which we read
    41–14 the second *d·* has no power.
sense of
Un. 2–22 awake from a sense of *d·*
    40–19 A sense of *d·* is not requisite
shadow of
Chr. 55– 9 land of the shadow of *d·*,— *Isa.* 9 : 2.
My. 294–29 passed through the shadow of *d·*
sickness and
    (*see* **sickness**)
sickness, disease, or
Mis. 65– 4 sin, sickness, disease, or *d·*,
sickness or
Peo. 12– 6 The only law of sickness or *d·*
sickness, sin, and
    (*see* **sickness**)
sin and
    (*see* **sin**)
sin brought
Mis. 201– 7 Sin brought *d·* ; and death is an
sin, disease, and
    (*see* **sin**)
sin, disease, or
My. 146–27 the side of sin, disease, or *d·*.
sin, or
Mis. 30–11 they were without pain, sin, or *d·*.
Un. 62–16 sin, or *d·* is a false sense of
sin, sickness, and
    (*see* **sin**)
sin, sickness, or
Mis. 17– 6 law of sin, sickness, or *d·*.
Un. 4– 3 finite sense of sin, sickness, or *d·*,
Hea. 9– 7 less . . . of sin, sickness, or *d·*,
    16–18 evidence . . . of sin, sickness, or *d·*
sin unto
Mis. 120– 9 whether of sin unto *d·*, or — *Rom.* 6 : 16.
source of
Ret. 59– 7 *Life* never means . . . source of *d·*,
sting of
Po. 31–21 wipes away the sting of *d·*
stung to
Pul. 13–24 The dragon is at last stung to *d·*
subjection to
Mis. 67–28 without his subjection to *d·*,
subtlety of
No. 35–10 also the drear subtlety of *d·*.
suffering and
Un. 41– 6 unreal sense of suffering and *d·*.
My. 161–32 triumph over . . . suffering, and *d·*.
surrenders to
Mis. 257–30 where the good man surrenders to *d·*
their
Mis. 304–28 * anniversaries of their *d·*.
thoughts of
Peo. 14– 3 clothe our thoughts of *d·* with
to all
'01. 30–13 birth to nothing and *d·* to all,
tragic
My. 312– 4 the tragic *d·* of my husband,
triumph over
Un. 43–10 complete triumph over *d·*,
twin sister of
Po. 65–11 Ah, sleep, twin sister of *d·*
ultimate
Mis. 257–16 lead to immediate or ultimate *d·*.

death

until
Mis. 286– 4   * "until *d·* do us part ;"
unto
Mis. 351–25   life that leads unto *d·*,
'00. 13–15   faithful unto *d·*, — Rev. 2 : 10.
My. 80– 8   * that when wasted unto *d·*
350–20   sense is darkened unto *d·*
unto the
Pul. 12–11   their lives unto the *d·*. — Rev. 12 : 11.
violent
'02. 18–28   violent *d·* of all his disciples
what is termed
Hea. 18–26   You must admit that what is termed *d·*
word
My. 235– 3   without using the word *d·*,

———

Mis. 17– 3   the material law of *d·* ;
23– 9   disease, *d·*, winds, and waves,
24– 3   carnally minded is *d·* ; — Rom. 8 : 6.
27–12   inharmony, sin, disease, *d·*
30–11   *D·* was not the door to
42–11   not attained by the *d·* of the body,
76–14   theory that *d·* must occur,
76–27   wages of sin is *d·*." — Rom. 6 : 23.
76–32   overcame the last enemy, *d·*.
96– 3   robbed . . . *d·* of its sting.
105–16   its opposites — *d·*, disease, and
105–28   the thought of sin, sickness, *d·*,
123–17   not through the *d·* of a man,
170– 5   may still believe in *d·* and
174–26   did not teach us to pray for *d·*
180–17   of Life, and not of *d·*.
196–27   not through *d·*, but Life,
201– 7   *d·* is an element of matter,
211–17   wish to save him from *d·*.
243–30   bleeding, vomiting, *d·*.
259– 6   law of Life, not of *d·* ;
332–24   third, suffering ; fourth, *d·*.
Ret. 24– 2   after the *d·* of the
Un. 29– 4   condemned the sinner to *d·*,
37– 7   *d·* is not the real stepping-stone
38– 6   *D·*, then, is error, opposed to
58– 1   sin, pain, *d·*, — a false sense of
No. 13– 7   *d·* must be swallowed up in Life,
17–27   Then . . . *d·* as real as Life ;
Pan. 12– 7   passing out of mankind by *d·*
'01. 21–20   *D·* is neither the predicate nor
'02. 6–27   carnally minded is *d·* ; — Rom. 8 : 6.
My. 126–21   *d·*, and mourning, and — Rev. 18 : 8.
180–17   C. S. meets . . . *d·* with Life,
192–12   living way to Life, not to *d·*.
248–24   and their penalty, *d·*
288–21   Jesus cast out evil, disease, *d·*,
310–19   there was never a *d·* in my

death-bed
Mis. 24– 6   give it to you as *d·* testimony

death-blow
Mis. 299– 4   The error . . . has received its *d·* ;

death-couch
Mis. 385–25   faith triumphant round thy *d·*
Po. 48–21   faith triumphant round thy *d·*

death-dealing
Mis. 257–25   go down in the *d·* wave.

deathless
Mis. 75–30   accepted view is that *soul* is *d·*,
104–15   individuality is sinless, *d·*,
184– 3   that Deity is *d·*,
187–29   dying, before *d·* ;
Ret. 64–25   *d·* Truth and Love.
Un. 39–26   that Deity is *d·*,
40– 7   in order to prove man *d·*,
41–23   Life, therefore, is *d·*,
42– 3   Soul, Spirit, is *d·*.
42–10   dying before he can be *d·*,
Pul. 4–22   His existence is *d·*,
5– 8   the glow of some *d·* reality.
No. 29– 4   and a *d·* sense of being.
Peo. 5– 6   they have resurrected a *d·* life
Po. 28– 3   Help us to write a *d·* page
29–16   living Love, And *d·* Life !
My. 195–24   lives, moves, and has *d·* being.
214–12   He proved Life to be *d·*

deathly
Pul. 73– 7   * cured herself of a *d·* disease

death-penalty
Un. 40–22   *d·* comes through our ignorance of

death-rate
'00. 7– 3   statistics show the annual *d·*
My. 181–26   the *d·* was at its maximum.

death's
Mis. 386–13   "When, severed by *d·* dream,
Po. 49–19   "When, severed by *d·* dream,

deaths
Mis. 29–16   but fourteen *d·* in the ranks of
48–21   tragic events and sudden *d·*

death's-head
Mis. 233– 8   *d·* at the feast of Truth ;
'01. 2–18   *d·* at the feast of Love,

debar
My. 140–15   * need not *d·* distant members from

debased
My. 91–11   * or his moral standards *d·*

debate
Man. 50– 8   shall not *d·* on C. S. in public

debaters
Mis. 88–19   deaf ears and dull *d·*.

debating
Man. 50– 6   *d·* IN PUBLIC.
50– 7   No Unauthorized *D·*.
50– 9   in public *d·* assemblies,
My. 224–14   Avoid . . . public *d·* clubs.

débris
Mis. 393– 5   Soul, sublime 'mid human *d·*,
Po. 51–10   Soul, sublime 'mid human *d·*,

debt
Mis. xi– 8   one's *d·* of gratitude to God,
261–12   pays his full *d·* to divine law,
Man. 78– 6   *D·* and Duty.
Ret. 6–29   abolition of imprisonment for *d·*.
Pul. 44–24   * dedicated to-day . . . and free of *d·*.
79– 6   * no *d·* had to be taken care of
My. 75–27   * dedicated to-morrow free from *d·*.
76–18   * free of *d·* without exception.
77–27   * open its doors absolutely free of *d·*,
84– 3   * heavy *d·*, the interest on which
84– 5   * "church *d·*" cramps and retards
84– 9   * until it be wholly free from *d·*.
88–28   * æsthetic *d·* to that great and
91–30   * Church is absolutely free from *d·*.
94–20   * the structure was free from *d·*.
98– 8   * dedicated free from *d·*,
98–21   * dedicated absolutely free of *d·*,
98–30   * and its dedication free from *d·*
161– 2   paid our *d·* and set us free
352– 8   * acknowledge our *d·* of gratitude

debtor
Mis. 382–11   comparing those . . . I am the *d·*.

debtors
Mis. 281–22   always as *d·* to Christ, Truth.
My. 161– 3   for which we are still his *d·*,

debts
Man. 76– 2   after the *d·* are paid,
78– 7   not . . . responsible for the *d·* of
78– 8   except such *d·* as are specified
Ret. 49–28   all *d·* of the corporation
My. 81–18   * *d·* of gratitude for ills cured,
89–14   * not blanketed with *d·*
232– 7   whereby all our *d·* are paid,

decade
Pul. 23–10   * paralleled during the last *d·* by
32–19   * in the early *d·* of 1820–'30.
66–20   * during the last *d·*,
67–16   * practically unknown a *d·* since,
'02. 2–12   Within the last *d·* religion
My. 94– 2   * through another *d·*

Decalogue
Mis. 254– 2   to which the *D·* points
335–17   to break the *D·*, — to murder,
Man. 43–19   commandment of the *D·*,
Ret. 65–12   in the gospel or the *D·*.
Pan. 7– 2   First Commandment in the *D·*.
'00. 5– 4   First Commandment of the *D·*,
5–19   First Commandment of the *D·* :
'01. 32–22   First Commandment of the *D·*,
My. 221–18   First Commandment of the *D·*,
264–18   First Commandment of the *D·*

decapitated
Mis. 274–24   *d·* reputations, headless trunks,

decay
Mis. 362– 3   material birth, growth, and *d·* :
395–20   Touched by the finger of *d·*
Ret. 81–12   and falsity must thus *d·*,
Peo. 14– 7   churchyards have crumbled into *d·*,
Po. 58– 5   Touched by the finger of *d·*
My. 189–20   that which defies *d·*

decaying
Mis. 100– 3   articulated in a *d·* language,
121– 1   written in a *d·* language,
'01. 33– 8   * *d·* stages of religion,

decays
Un. 26–14   * Man *d·* and ages move ;
26–19   that *man d·* ?

decease

Man.	49–18	MARRIAGE AND *d·*.
	49–23	Sudden *D·*.
	49–24	If a member . . . shall *d·* suddenly,
Ret.	20– 4	until after my mother's *d·*.
'02.	15–19	I declined to sell them at his *d·*
My.	294–23	*d·* of Pope Leo XIII,
	306–26	Before his *d·*, in January, 1866,
	312–23	At his *d·* I was surrounded by
	331–25	* bereaved widow after his *d·*.
	335– 7	* membership in both till his *d·*.
	336–15	after my mother's *d·*."

deceased

Man.	36–15	*d·*, absent, or disloyal,
	111–17	*d·*, absent, or disloyal,
My.	290–10	*d·* the first month of the new
	331–23	* towards those friends of the *d·*
	331–30	* the *d·* during his late illness,
	333–12	* the residence of the *d·*,

deceit

No.	2–25	cannot avert the effects of *d·*.
'02.	4– 1	*d·* in councils, dishonor in nations,
	18–17	no emulation, no *d·*, enters into
My.	5–32	Indulging *d·* is like the defendant
	6– 9	smile and *d·* of damnation.
	261–10	*d·* or falsehood is never wise.

deceitfully

Mis.	191– 2	word of God *d·*." — *II Cor.* 4 : 2.
'01.	16–15	handling the word of God *d·*.
My.	34– 5	nor sworn *d·*." — *Psal.* 24 : 4.
	124– 2	word of God *d·* ; — *II Cor.* 4 : 2.

deceive

Mis.	78–15	which would *d·*, if possible,
	175–20	"*d·*, if it were — *see Matt.* 24 : 24.
	341–14	Do human hopes *d·*?
My.	258–19	hopes that cannot *d·*,

deceived

My.	212–22	are being *d·* and misled.

deceiver

'01.	9–12	called him a "*d·*." — *Matt.* 27 : 63.

deceives

Mis.	334– 7	the belief that it has, *d·* itself.

deceiveth

Pan.	10– 4	he *d·* himself." — *Gal.* 6 : 3.

December

(*see* **months**)

decent

My.	312–11	* and thus received a *d·* burial.

decently

Mis.	310–16	*d·* and in order." — *I Cor.* 14 : 40.

deception

Mis.	14–18	This awful *d·* is evil's umpire
	228– 2	a *d·* dark as it is base
	338–16	will subject one to *d·* ;
Un.	17– 1	one chance of successful *d·*,
	19–16	evil is only a delusive *d·*,

decide

Mis.	65–11	Science must and will *d·*.
	81– 8	patiently wait on God to *d·*,
Man.	55–18	may *d·* if his loyalty has been
	77– 8	This committee shall *d·*
	94– 5	the churches shall *d·* their action.

decided

Mis.	2–32	While we entertain *d·* views
	243– 3	with *d·* improvement in health.
	306– 5	* motto has not yet been *d·* upon,
Man.	55–11	it may be *d·* that a teacher has
My.	11–26	* The size of the building was *d·*
	20–29	* *d·* to omit this year the
	54–29	* *d·* that this hall was too large,
	237– 3	I have since *d·* not to publish.
	309–10	After it was *d·*, Mr. Pierce bowed to
	324– 9	* so original and so very *d·*

decides

Mis.	45–19	when Science in a single instance *d·*

decision

Mis.	65–11	Left to the *d·* of Science,
Ret.	50–11	the wisdom of this *d·* ;
My.	6– 1	*d·* which the defendant knows will
	11–27	* there still remained for definite *d·*
	12– 9	* *d·* of these remaining problems.
	76–13	* A similar *d·* was reached
	190–21	divine *d·* in behalf of Mind.
	204–18	*d·* you have made as to the
	314–17	the *d·* was given by the judge

declaims

'01.	26–10	In one sentence he *d·* against

declaration

Mis.	28–30	his *d·*, "These signs — *Mark* 16 : 17.
	46–22	apostle meant by the *d·*,

declaration

Mis.	48–17	*d·* as to the animus of
	51–14	virtually a *d·* to the child's mind
	76–16	rendered void by Jesus' divine *d·*,
	172–30	*d·* in Scripture that God is good ;
	187–30	is but the *d·* of the material senses
	192–30	*d·* of our Master settles the
	193–28	unmistakable *d·* of the right
	201– 3	*d·* resolves the element misnamed
	278–13	*d·* that Job sinned not
	372–21	gives no uncertain *d·* concerning
	373–26	is followed by Jesus' *d·*,
	381–32	*d·* were either a truism or a rule,
Ret.	35–19	the authenticity of this *d·*,
Un.	30–24	understood the meaning of the *d·*
	32–20	To this *d·* C. S. responds,
Pul.	4–16	therefore is the seer's *d·* true,
	30–15	* "confession of faith" includes the *d·*
No.	13–13	the *d·* is nevertheless true,
Pan.	2– 2	a *d·* from the pulpit that
'01.	15– 1	*d·* that evil is unreal,
'02.	8– 1	*d·*, "God is Love," — *I John* 4 : 8.
	12–14	This *d·* of Christ, understood,
My.	46– 9	* primary *d·* of this church
	106–11	folly of the cognate *d·* that
	135– 6	*d·* may be applied to old age,
	190–17	This *d·* of our Master,
	326– 8	* the *d·* of this recognition

Declaration of Independence

Pul.	67–24	* from the date of the *D· of I·*,

declarations

Un.	6–24	our *d·* about sin and Deity
Pul.	45–20	* oft-repeated *d·* of our textbooks,

declare

Mis.	23–18	Reason and revelation *d·* that
	46– 2	Scriptures *d·*, "To whom — *Rom.* 6 : 16.
	55–26	Spirit, as the Scriptures *d·*,
	63–21	as the Scriptures *d·*.
	93– 8	Scriptures plainly *d·* the allness
	141–28	you yourselves *d·* you have had no
	166–17	how to *d·* its spiritual origin,
	172– 4	*d·* the positive and the negative
	174–20	first to *d·* against this kingdom
	183–32	Scriptures *d·* reflects his Maker,
	189–20	Scriptures *d·* Life to be the
	243–19	works alone should *d·* them,
	258–23	did *d·* a mighty individuality,
	312–17	* to *d·* the real harmony between
	346–17	and the Scriptures *d·* that
	362–12	Scriptures *d·* that all that He made
	363–17	His modes *d·* the beauty of
Man.	80–14	to *d·* vacancies in said trusteeship,
Ret.	37–12	*d·* Bishop Berkeley, David Hume,
Un.	2– 1	*d·* that God is too pure to
	2– 2	they also *d·* that God pitieth
	15– 6	may *d·* Him absolutely cognizant of
	25–13	this lie I *d·* an illusion.
	28– 9	As well might you *d·* some old castle
	39–21	*d·* the immortal status of man,
	56– 3	suffered, as the Scriptures *d·*,
Pul.	13–23	Scriptures *d·* that evil is temporal,
	74–16	to *d·* in His infinite mercy.
	75– 7	they can justly *d·* it.
No.	5– 8	to *d·* error real would be to
	13– 5	*d·* both the Principle and idea
Pan.	5– 4	The Scriptures plainly *d·*,
	11–10	shall his stature . . . *d·* him?
'01.	7–11	as the Scriptures *d·*,
	7–17	as the Scriptures *d·* He will
	15– 1	*d·* that he must awake from his
Hea.	3–24	The Scriptures *d·* that
Peo.	5–17	to *d·* His omnipotence."
	6– 6	* "I *d·* my conscientious belief,
	9– 7	religious rite may *d·* one's belief ;
My.	9–12	* *d·* the depth of our affection
	37– 9	* *d·* again our high appreciation
	127–16	I deliberately *d·* that when I
	155– 9	Saviour whom the Scriptures *d·*.
	242– 4	*d·* yourself to be immortal
	257–21	bow and *d·* Christ's power,
	271– 1	If, as the Scriptures *d·*,
	298– 3	*d·* that nothing has occurred in my
	300– 8	*d·* that there is no sickness or
	305– 5	defamer will *d·* as honestly (?),
	318–13	*d·* the moral and spiritual effect
	359– 8	I hereby publicly *d·*

declared

Mis.	24–29	*d·* that his followers should handle
	30–12	gates thereof he *d·* were inlaid
	57–18	*d·*, "God doth know — *Gen.* 3 : 5.
	83–22	he *d·* his sonship with God :
	96–14	as to the apostle who *d·* it,
	121–16	prophet *d·*, "Thou shalt — *Deut.* 19 : 13.
	172–26	*d·* on the side of immutable right,

declared

Mis.	189–13	Christ plainly d·, through Jesus,
	201–17	d· that "the law of the — Rom. 8 : 2.
	225–16	what the Christian Scientist had d· ;
	345–16	Bonaparte d·, "Ever since the
	372– 1	critics d· that it was incorrect,
Ret.	8–23	earnestly d· my cousin had heard the
	15–11	hitherto have I d· — Psal. 71 : 17.
	30–17	St. Paul d· that the law was
	56–14	until peace be d· by
Un.	1– 5	such as the apostle Peter d·
	37– 1	Jesus not only d· himself
Pul.	45–12	* d· that the church's completion
	45–17	* hopeful, trustful ones, who d·
	53– 9	* d· to be essential,
Pan.	7–10	d· that man should die,
'01.	23–27	In later publications he d·
'02.	12–13	is not God, as he himself d·,
Hea.	8–20	what the Scriptures have d·,
My.	45–17	* d· you to be in extremis.
	94–26	* greetings in which she d·
	98– 2	* but these, it is d·, are but
	105– 9	d· incurable because the lungs
	105–23	d· that she could not live.
	152– 6	and our Master d·,
	228–14	Referring to . . . our Master d· :
	307– 5	till one day I d· to him
	313–20	I have always consistently a·
	315–23	d· dying of cancer,
	318– 9	some critics d· that my book
		(see also Jesus)

declares

Mis.	26–11	even while the Scripture d·
	30–20	law of Life, which St. Paul d·
	71–23	St. Paul d· astutely,
	122–17	denounces him that d·,
	123–29	Holy Writ d· that God is Love,
	176– 2	harmony of Science that d· Him,
	192–24	as the above Scripture plainly d·,
	217–13	Nature d·, throughout the mineral,
	218– 5	visible universe d· the invisible
	218– 6	by reversion, as error d· Truth.
	259–12	d· that God knows iniquity !
	295– 9	anonymous talker further d·,
	309– 7	this d· its unfitness for fable
	351–26	d· itself the antipode of Love ;
Ret.	60–12	d· that evil is the absence of
	60–28	d· that there is but one Truth,
	61– 3	d· that sickness is a belief,
Un.	4– 5	d· that Truth is All,
	4–23	John's Gospel d· (xvii. 3) that
	17–21	d· God told our first parents
	29–10	Science d· God to be the Soul
	29–20	d· can never be seen or measured
	31– 2	"God is Spirit"), d· the Scripture
	32–17	d· itself material, in sin, sickness,
	33–26	d· that matter sees through the
	34– 2	d· that matter is the master
	40–12	d· that they who believe
Pul.	63–26	* d· that it was built as
	64–16	* she d·, in a search for the
Pan.	5–25	as the Scripture d·,
'02.	1–12	The Scripture d·,
My.	107–24	Scripture d·, God made all
	113– 9	Paul d· the truth of the
	178–12	The Scripture d· that God is All.
	224–25	since the Scripture d·,
	308–29	McClure's Magazine also d·
	334–19	* She d· in her Message

declaring

Mis.	108–30	while d· that they have no
	109– 1	d· the unity of Truth,
	334– 9	does this as a lie d· itself,
	354– 1	d· they "never disobey Mother" !
Ret.	14–12	d· that never could I unite with
Un.	38–15	by d· that not He alone
No.	42–19	by d· itself both true and good.
My.	116–18	D· the truth regarding an
	326– 3	* courts as thus d· the liberties of
	346– 7	* d· Mrs. Eddy non-existent

decline

Mis.	342– 6	hence the steady d· of
Pul.	87–14	permit me, respectfully, to d·
My.	138–15	d· to receive solely because I
	194–24	but I must d· to receive
	226–29	d· to doctor infectious or

declined

Mis.	146–12	hence I have hitherto d· to
Man.	75–10	d· to receive this munificent gift,
Pul.	71– 4	* The idea that C. S. has d·
'02.	15–18	I d· to sell them at his decease
My.	302–28	but I d· and went alone
	308–24	d· to accept the stick,
	336– 7	* she d· on this ground,

declines

Man.	68– 7	or who d· to obey this call

declineth

Ret.	21–17	shadow when it d·." — see Psal. 102 : 11.

declining

Mis.	163–14	language of a d· race,
'02.	15–15	d· dictation as to what I should

decoction

No.	21– 4	an unsafe d· for the race.

decomposition

My.	107–31	stops d·, removes enteritis,

decorated

Pul.	26–24	* d· with sprays of fig leaves
	28– 6	* d· with emblematic designs,

decoration

Pul.	76– 7	* pale green and gold d·
	76–14	* Mexican onyx with gold d·

decorations

Mis.	142– 9	among other beautiful d·,

decorative

Pul.	26– 1	* disc of cut glass in d· designs,
	28–10	* in appropriate d· effect.
My.	78–11	* in soft gray with d· carvings

decrease

My.	266–12	article on the d· of students in

decreased

My.	181–27	Since that time it has steadily d·.

decree

Mis.	66–10	always according to divine d·.
	118–15	this immutable d· of Love :
	121–14	a divine d·, a law of Love !
	122–11	predestined to fulfil a divine d·,
	341–20	implicit treason to divine d·.
	380–28	by d· and order of the Court,
	381–16	a d· in favor of Mrs. Eddy
Ret.	14– 1	"horrible d·" of predestination

decry

My.	114– 9	d· the book which has moulded their

dedicate

Mis.	v– 4	d· THESE PRACTICAL TEACHINGS
	91– 6	to ordain pastors and to d· churches ;
Po.	39–21	temperance hall To Thee we d·.
	40– 3	We d· this temperance hall
My.	13–19	an ample temple d· to God,
	76–17	* enables them to d· their churches
	96–18	* building they were in Boston to d·
	97–26	* to d· the new temple,
	147–25	never stop ceremoniously to d·
	158–27	d· to Truth and Love.
	182–19	d· this beautiful house of worship
	193– 1	d· your temple in faith unfeigned,

dedicated

Pul.	v– 7	THIS UNIQUE BOOK IS TENDERLY d· BY
	11– 5	d· to the ever-present God
	20–21	church was d· on January 6,
	40–22	* to the worship of God.
	44–23	* church which will be d· to-day
	50–13	* which will be d· to-morrow.
	56–25	* church was d· in Boston
	59– 3	* d· on New Year's Sunday
	61–24	* Church . . . d· yesterday.
	63–23	* Church . . . was d· in Boston.
	64–24	* has just d· the first church of
Rud.	v– 3	TENDERLY AND RESPECTFULLY d·
My.	26– 5	* will be d· on the date of the
	36–21	* d· to the only true God,
	67–17	* Cathedral to be d· . . . 1906
	75–26	* d· to-morrow free from debt,
	75–28	* d· by this denomination
	76–25	* d· in Boston to-morrow
	84– 8	* may not be formally d· until
	91– 9	* paid for before they are d·.
	91–27	* which has just been d· at Boston
	98– 7	* church, . . . d· free from debt,
	98–17	* was recently d· at Boston.
	98–20	* d· absolutely free of debt,
	99–16	* when it was d· there was not
	100– 4	* temple recently d· at Boston
	147–24	already d· to Christ's service,
	193–25	d· to God and humanity,
	302–26	after it was built and d·

dedicating

My.	74–17	* paying for their church before d· it.
	193–17	You are d· yours to Him.
	197–12	completing and d· your church

dedication (noun)

at Boston

Pul.	65–14	* by the d· at Boston of

attend the

My.	72–11	* attend the d· of the new church

dedication (noun)
church
   My. 186–27 on the day of your church *d·*.
communion and
   My. 26–18 communion and *d·* include enough
completion and
   My. 43–30 * completion and *d·* of our
day of
   Pul. 57– 7 * four services on the day of *d·*.
historical
   My. 26–22 This historical *d·* should date
in Boston
   Pul. 68–18 * The *d·* in Boston last Sunday
       79– 4 * *d·*, in Boston, of a C. S. temple
   My. 94–17 * in the recent *d·* in Boston
in June
   My. 25–19 the *d·* in June next of
its
   My. 88–15 * its *d·* abounds in remarkable
      184–12 to be present at its *d·*,
of the church
   Pul. 75–21 * celebrated the *d·* of the church
of the edifice
   My. 86–22 * The *d·* of the edifice of the
of the extension
   My. 3– 2 chapter sub-title
      29–25 * the *d·* of the extension of
      63–11 * the *d·* of the extension of
      96– 3 * the *d·* of the extension of
of The Mother Church
   Pul. 40– 9 * chapter sub-title
      88– 6 the *d·* of The Mother Church.
   My. 57–27 * the *d·* of The Mother Church
      76–14 * the *d·* of The Mother Church
      90–22 * The *d·* of The Mother Church
of this church
   Pul. 66–22 * marked by the *d·* of this church,
   My. 163–10 come to the *d·* of this church,
of your church
   My. 191–29 the *d·* of your church
      192–21 present at the *d·* of your church,
recent
   My. 99–30 * recent *d·* of a C. S. temple
your
   My. 183–25 Thanks for invitation to your *d·*.

   Pul. 43–24 * chief feature of the *d·*,
      56–12 * *d·* taking place on the 6th of
      75–16 * D· TO THE FOUNDER OF THE ORDER
      81– 3 * morning of the *d·*.
   Po. vi– 5 * poem
    page 39 poem
   My. 26– 2 * chapter sub-title
      29– 3 * chapter sub-title
      38–23 * impressive feature of the *d·*
      45–10 * physically present at the *d·*
      60–26 * *d·* of our new church building,
      73–16 * *d·* of the new temple.
      77–15 * will participate in the *d·*.
      78– 2 * all might participate in the *d·*,
      79– 9 * to read the account of the *d·*
      84–26 * *d·* of the beautiful structure on
      86–11 * to be present at the *d·*
      88–10 * The *d·*, Sunday, in Boston,
      89–22 * *d·* of the new Mother Church
      91–16 * *d·* of a C. S. temple
      92–20 * the *d·* of this vast temple.
      93– 5 * *d·* of their great church in Boston
      95– 9 * *d·* of the magnificent C. S. church
      96–22 * before the day set for the *d·*
      96–27 * The *d·* of what is known as
      98–29 * its *d·* free from debt
     100– 7 * On the Sunday of the *d·*,
     159– 1 chapter sub-title
     177– 5 *d·* of First Church of Christ,
     198– 4 *d·* of your magnificent church
     320–30 * *d·* of the first Mother Church

dedication (adj.)
   Pul. 41–29 * hour for the *d·* service
      79– 7 * no debt . . . on *d·* day,
   My. 5–24 *d·* and communion season,
      72–21 * to attend the *d·* exercises,
      77–17 * chapter sub-title
      77–22 It was *d·* day,

Dedication of a Temperance Hall
   Po. vi– 5 * poem
    (*see also* **Appendix A**)

dedicatory
   Pul. 59–28 * at the second *d·* service.
   Po. vi– 8 * *sung . . . as a d· hymn.*
   My. 29– 7 * closing incident of the *d·* services
      31–29 * opening of the *d·* service.
      36– 1 * *d·* Message from her teacher
      58–29 * attended the *d·* services
      64–11 * *d·* Message to The Mother Church,

dedicatory
   My. 82–14 * *d·* services of The Mother Church
      94–20 * *d·* services were being held
      99–18 * attended the *d·* exercises,
     146– 1 In explanation of my *d·* letter
     195– 4 *d·* services of your church.
     197–25 *d·* season of your church edifice
     240–10 *d·* Message to The Mother Church,
deduced
   My. 349–28 induced by love and *d·* from God,
deduction
   No. 13– 5 scientific *d·* from the Principle of
     13–14 profound *d·* from C. S.
   My. 273–13 I for one accept his wise *d·*,
deductive
   My. 349–27 *d·* reasoning is correct only as it
deed
   Mis. 195–28 *d·*, not creed, and practice more than
     198–24 belief, fear, theory, or bad *d·*,
     206–20 harmony in word and *d·*,
     224– 3 that makes another's *d·* offensive,
     250–23 unselfish *d·* done in secret ;
     384– 7 To thought and *d·* Give sober speed,
     399–14 Thou the Truth in thought and *d·* ;
   Ret. 79–22 temperate in thought, word, and *d·*.
   '02. 13–30 A copy of this *d·* is published in
   Hea. 5–10 reward of his good *d·* hereafter.
   Po. 36– 6 To thought and *d·* Give sober speed,
     75–21 Thou the Truth in thought and *d·* ;
     79– 8 in thought and *d·*
   My. 9– 9 * glory in every good *d·* and thought
     65–22 * *d·* being taken by Ira O. Knapp
     66– 7 * conveyed by *d·* to the C. S. church,
     157–18 * in her original *d·* of trust,
     157–22 I gave a *d·* of trust to three individuals
     205–18 * "As the thought is, so is the *d·* ;
     235–29 commemorated in *d·* or in word
     260–29 the Way, in word and in *d·*,
     338–25 he stands alone in word and *d·*,

Deed Conveying Land
for Church Purposes
   Man. 136– 1 heading
deeded
   My. 217– 6 I have *d·* in trust to
Deed of Trust
   Man. 25–17 See under "*D· of T·*" for
     79–19 constituted by a *D· of T·*
     81–18 the provisions in the *D· of T·*
     128– 1 heading
deeds
   Mis. 210–14 Good *d·* are harmless.
     257–14 and repays our best *d·* with
     292–23 by loving words and *d·*.
     341– 7 then put . . . words into *d·* ;
     370– 4 saw Jesus do such *d·* of mercy,
   Man. 102–10 Designation of *D·*.
     102–10 All *d·* of further purchases of
     102–14 in the *d·* given by Albert Metcalf
     102–18 shall be incorporated in all such *d·*
   No. 27–21 old man and his *d·*," — *see Col. 3 : 9.*
   Pan. 11– 4 old man with his *d·* ; — *Col. 3 : 9.*
   '00. 13– 5 *d·* of the Nicolaitanes, — *Rev. 2 : 6.*
     13– 7 words were brave and their *d·* evil.
   '01. 2–11 substitute good words for good *d·*,
     26– 6 supported it by his words and *d·*.
   '02. 8–17 his *d·*, demonstrate Love.
   Hea. 19–26 rays in the sunlight of our *d·* ;
   My. vii–10 * *D·*, not words, are the sound test
     12–29 dear children's good *d·* are gems
     218– 3 and in explanation of his *d·* he said,
     277–20 immortal words and *d·* of men
     283–14 Right thoughts and *d·* are the
     309– 4 making out *d·*, settling quarrels,
     350–27 in prayer, in word, and *d·*.
deem
   Mis. 80–27 of what they *d·* pathology,
     112– 4 may *d·* these delusions verities,
   Po. 47–18 reaping the harvest we *d·*,
   My. 289– 8 *Beloved Student :* — I *d·* it proper that
     306– 7 I *d·* it unwise to enter into a
deemed
   Mis. 193– 5 or *d·* it safe to say at that time.
     228– 3 by those *d·* at least indebted friends
     349–17 he should do as he *d·* best,
     386–14 She *d·* I died, and could not know
   Man. 52–15 *d·* sufficient by the Board
     85– 8 so strayed as justly to be *d·*,
     92–25 *d·* loyal teachers of C. S.
   Ret. 7–18 advocacy of the side he *d·* right.
     45–11 *d·* requisite in the first stages of
     49–29 *d·* best to dissolve this corporation,
   Peo. 6–23 should no longer be *d·* treason to

deemed
Po. 49–21 She d· I died, and could not know
67–10 memory of dear ones d· dead
My. 89– 4 * are d· by its professors not to exist

deems
Po. 31–19 which d· no suffering vain

deep
Mis. ix–17 d· draughts from the fount of
3–31 d· demand for the Science of
107–26 and of *repentance* therefor, d·,
133– 9 d· consideration to the following
142–21 chords of feeling too d· for words.
225–26 The d· flush faded from the face,
285–18 d· down in human consciousness,
387– 2 joy divinely fair, the high and d·,
388–18 The right to worship d· and pure,
Ret. 17– 5 while I worship in d· sylvan spot,
42–11 listened to him with d· interest.
69– 6 the Adam-dream, the d· sleep,
Un. 29–22 d· meaning of the Scriptures
Pul. 13–16 in the d· darkness of belief.
73–10 * d· into the Biblical passages,
76–10 * hangings of d· green plush,
Rud. 15–10 and d· systematic thinking
No. 34–25 this is the d· significance of the
35– 5 through d· humility and adoration
'01. 1–19 Truth comes from a d· sincerity that
'02. 20– 2 or going down into the d·,
Hea. 17–16 "d· sleep" — Gen. 2 : 21.
Po. 2–19 thy d· silence is unbroken still.
21– 7 The right to worship d· and pure,
23–12 With utterance d· and strong,
31– 8 D· loneliness, tear-filled tones of
50–20 divinely fair, the high and d·,
53– 6 On vale and woodland d· ;
62– 5 while I worship in d· sylvan spot,
68–11 Enchant d· the senses,
My. 42–22 * d· significance of this momentous
44–26 * greetings and their d· love.
113–31 the d· thinkers, the truly great
154–19 * d· infinite faculties of man."
157– 5 * d· gratitude that your generous
167– 1 Accept my d· thanks therefor,
195–11 d· love which I cherished for you
195–18 best way to silence a d· discontent
197–11 express my d· appreciation
203–18 A d· sincerity is sure of success,
208– 3 Accept my d· thanks for your
248–15 reaching d· down into the universal
271–23 * read with d· interest by all
289–13 expressing our d· sympathy with
348– 4 induced a d· research,
(see also **waters**)

deep-drawn
My. 195–22 d· breath fresh from God,
256–10 d·, heartfelt breath of thanks

deeper
Mis. 2–16 a d· and broader philosophy
Ret. 81–20 so sinks into d· darkness.
Pul. 2– 9 a thought higher and d·
36– 5 * d· foundation of her religious work
'00. 11–17 measures himself against d· grief.
Po. 34–12 thy love-lorn note — In d· solitude,
My. 46–22 * to a d· consecration,
63–21 * there came a d· feeling,

deepest
Mis. 311–15 My d· desires and daily labors
'01. 20–28 darkest and d· of human crimes.

deeply
Mis. 176– 6 d· and solemnly expounded
256–10 I feel, d·, that of necessity this
274–11 D· regretting the disappointment
317–24 My sympathies are d· enlisted
376–22 over a d· dazzling sunlight,
392–16 d· rooted in a soil of love ;
Pul. 1–13 and records d· engraven.
Po. v– 6 * outpouring of a d· poetic nature
20–20 d· rooted in a soil of love ;
24–16 And night grows d· dark ;
My. 6–16 d· do I thank you for this proof
28– 2 * will be d· significant.
37–28 * We are d· touched by its
58–30 * one so d· impressed
125–23 d· grateful that the church militant
149–20 too d· read in scholastic theology
175– 1 d· interesting anniversary,
194–22 I d· appreciate it,
245– 2 became d· interested in it.
282–21 D· do I thank you
326–13 d· interesting letter from
326–19 D· grateful, I recognize the divine
338–23 Christian Scientists d· recognize

deep-settled
'02. 19–20 underneath is a d· calm.

deep-toned
Mis. 204–16 freedom, d· faith in God ;

deer
Po. 41– 1 * my own stricken d·.

defaces
Mis. 8–18 defiles, d·, and dethrones the

defacing
Mis. 337–23 possessing these d· deformities.

defame
'01. 32–10 to d· their fellow-men.

defamer
My. 305– 5 Lastly, the d· will declare

defamers
'01. 16–12 surviving d· share our pity.
My. 305–10 "vulgar" d· have circulated,

defeat
Mis. 172– 7 d· the claims of sense and sin,
204– 8 hope, sorrow, joy, d·, and triumph.
267–26 cause of all d· and victory
339– 7 out of d· comes the secret of
'00. 10– 1 Success in sin is downright d·.
My. 134–10 D· need not follow victory.
278–26 Victory in error is d· in Truth.

defeats
Mis. 126–26 honesty always d· dishonesty.
260– 3 By conflicts, d·, and triumphs,
268– 2 divine Principle . . . d· them.
268– 7 victories of rivalry . . . are d·
My. 43– 9 * in the wilderness they suffered d·

defence (see also **defense**)
My. 127–31 a d· adapted to all men,
161–26 a sufficient d· against it.
264– 2 chapter sub-title
278–19 dies in d· of his country,
316–15 grand d· of our Cause

defend
Mis. 112– 9 can neither d· the innocent nor
115–22 relying on God to d· us
295–16 d· the dignity of her daughters
315–32 how to d· themselves against
371–20 has no truth to d·.
Man. 42– 5 d· himself daily against aggressive
48– 4 to d· the Cause of Christ,
84– 2 how to d· themselves against
Ret. 44–20 to d· this church from the envy
Pul. 2–26 behooves us to d· our heritage.
My. 318–12 to d· my grammatical construction,
364–13 to d· themselves from all evil,

defendant (see also **defendant's**)
Mis. 380–32 Answer was filed by the d·,
381– 6 d· being present personally
381– 7 testimony on the part of the d·
381–19 recover of the d· her cost of suit,
381–22 restraining the d· from directly or
My. 5–32 like the d· arguing for
6– 2 decision which the d· knows will be

defendant's
Mis. 381–10 inquire of d· counsel why he
381–13 asked the d· counsel this question,

defenders
Peo. 11– 2 d· of the rights of the

defending
Mis. 345–13 d· himself against the charge of
My. 207–23 mastering evil and d· good,

defends
My. 316–18 It d· human rights

defense (see also **defence**)
Mis. 80– 7 d· of medical charlatans in general,
110–26 dared the perilous d· of Truth,
115–16 protection and d· from sin
148–17 dignity and d· of our Cause ;
229–28 Love" . . . is a sure d·.— I John 4 : 18.
238– 7 no time to give in d· of his own
258–16 "My d· is of God, — Psal. 7 : 10.
338–18 move majestically to your d·
Man. 3–14 dignity and d· of our Cause ;
84– 1 D· against Malpractice.
Ret. 91– 1 God is their sure d· and refuge.
Pul. 2–21 remain within the walls for its d·
No. 15–10 religious arms in their d· ;

defenses
Mis. 10–10 furnished them d· impregnable.

defer
Un. 1–14 to d· this infinite inquiry,

deference
Mis. 60– 6 To regard . . . death with less d·,
My. 225–14 giving unto His holy name due d·,

deferentially
   Ret. 76– 8 cited, and quoted *d·*.

deferred
   Mis. 17–29 travail of mortal mind, hope *d·*,
        262–19 heart grown faint with hope *d·*.
        389–15 For hope *d·*, ingratitude, disdain !
   Po. 4–14 For hope *d·*, ingratitude, disdain !

defiance
   Pul. 54– 7 * not in *d·*, suppression, or

defiant
   Mis. 190– 4 Life, *d·* of error or matter.
   Un. 42–24 Truth, *d·* of error or matter,
   No. 2–23 the most *d·* forms of disease.

deficiency
   Mis. 115– 6 even the teacher's own *d·*

defied
   Mis. 29–22 diseases that had *d·* medical skill.
        199–17 denied and *d·* their superstition.
        223– 2 mystery of error . . . at first *d·* me.

defies
   Mis. 86–23 is something that *d·* a sneer.
   Un. 31–19 all that denies and *d·* Spirit,
   My. 189–20 that which *d·* decay

defiled
   Un. 50– 2 how can infinite Mind be *d·*?

defilement
   Mis. 109– 7 a sure pretext of moral *d·*.
   Un. 50– 2 implies the possibility of its *d·* ;

defiles
   Mis. 8–17 *d·*, defaces, and dethrones

defileth
   Mis. 118–32 *d·* a man ;— *Matt.* 15 : 11.
        119– 1 this *d·* a man."— *Matt.* 15 : 11.

define
   Mis. 13–29 then *d·* good as God,
        191–26 the original texts *d·* him as
        269–10 a man who can better *d·* ethics,
   Ret. 59–20 five material senses *d·* Mind and
   Un. 28– 8 Who, then, dares *d·* Soul as
        29–16 that which the senses cannot *d·*
   Rud. 1– 1 *How would you d· C. S.?*
   '01. 1–22 As Christian Scientists you seek to *d·*
        3–16 to *d·* Love in divine Science
   '02. 7–13 Use these words to *d·* God,
   Po. 42– 6 Without heart to *d·* man;
   My. 235– 4 to *d·* truth and not name its

defined
   Mis. 68–21 metaphysics is *d·* thus :
        102– 3 A corporeal God, as often *d·*
        150–25 God is . . . . *d·* by no dogma,
        180–27 word "son" is *d·* variously ;
        193–12 as *d·* and practised by Jesus,
   Ret. 32–11 is graphically *d·* by Calderon,
        58–12 Life, as *d·* by Jesus,
   Un. 42–21 As *d·* by Jesus, Life had no
   No. 9–25 Divinely *d·*, Science is the
        22–24 Jesus *d·* devil as a mortal who
   '01. 5– 2 *d·* strictly by the word Person,
        5–15 their personality is *d·* spiritually,
        6– 1 human person, as *d·* by C. S.,
        6– 6 Person is *d·* differently by
   My. 105– 4 Æsculapius, *d·* Christianly and

defines
   Mis. 68–24 Worcester *d·* it as "the philosophy
        102–32 Science *d· omnipresence* as
        190–31 and then *d·* this god as
        191– 4 then *d·* this serpent as
        192– 5 *d·* devil as a "liar."— *John* 8 : 44.
        300–11 law *d·* and punishes as theft.
   Ret. 59–23 Science *d·* man as immortal,
        60– 1 *d·* life as something apart from
        60– 4 sense *d·* life as a broken sphere,
        74– 4 *d·* it by his own *corpus sine pectore*
   Un. 29–17 C. S. *d·* as material sense ;
   Pul. 47–16 * carefully the difference
   Rud. 2–18 Science *d·* the individuality of
   '01. 16–14 St. Paul *d·* this world's god as
        16–16 original text *d· devil* as *accuser*,
   My. 180–32 *d·* noumenon and . . . spiritually,

defining
   Mis. 22–11 infinite calculus *d·* the line,
   Rud. 2– 9 in *d· person* as especially a
   My. 248– 8 grasping and *d·* the demonstrable,
        317– 2 * *d·* her relations with the

definite
   Un. 49– 3 man is as *d·* and eternal as God,
   Pul. 24– 2 * keynote of *d·* attention.
   Rud. 6–25 *d·* and absolute form of healing,
   No. 23–26 He is *d·* and individual,
   Peo. 8–11 *d·* form of a national religion,
   My. 11–27 * remained for *d·* decision

definite
   My. 43– 5 * *d·* rule of action whereby to
        51–22 * "she gave no *d·* answer,
        343–11 * Here, then, was the *d·* statement
        358– 1 C. S. abides by the *d·* rules

definitely
   Man. 44– 1 spirit . . . shall be *d·* considered.
        57–13 state *d·* the purpose for which
   Rud. 2– 7 God is *d·* individual,
   My. 235–12 should *d·* name the error,
        305–23 to learn *d·* more from my

definition
   Mis. 68–31 is a further *d·*.
        86–12 which need correct *d·*.
        108– 6 in his *d·* of Satan
        108–26 Jesus' *d·* of sin as a *lie*.
        190–14 Its *d·* as an individual is
        216–13 might add to the above *d·*
        258–29 the divine *d·* of Deity
        371–23 in a *d·* of purpose,
   Rud. 1–12 misapprehension, as well as *d·*.
   No. 22–26 His *d·* of evil indicated
        23–10 not a *devil*, after the accepted *d·*.
        27–28 learn the *d·* of immortal being ;
   Pan. 5– 7 chapter sub-title
        5–18 Jesus' *d·* of devil (evil) explains
   '01. 3–11 adopt Webster's *d·* of God,
        3–12 Standard dictionary's *d·* of God,
        3–14 higher *d·* derived from the Bible,
   '02. 5–19 This absolute *d·* of Deity
   My. 221–10 establish the *d·* of omnipotence,

definitions
   Mis. 52–14 Marriage is susceptible of many *d·*.
   Pul. 47–20 * of these two healing arts.
   Rud. 2– 1 Other *d·* of *person*,
        2–21 introduces us to higher *d·*.
   No. 25–12 Man outlives finite mortal *d·* of

deformed
   Mis. 107–26 lack of seeing one's *d·* mentality,
        167– 5 Is he *d·*?

deformities
   Mis. 337–23 possessing these defacing *d·*.

deformity
   Mis. 203–22 rends the veil that hides mental *d·*.
        332–20 masked with *d·* the glories of
   My. 121–21 No *d·* exists in honesty.

defrauds
   Rud. 15– 1 has shown that this *d·* the scholar,

deft
   Pul. 8–25 loving hearts and *d·* fingers

degenerate
   Mis. 289– 1 causes him to *d·* physically

degrade
   Pan. 10–28 does not *d·* man's personality.

degree
  any
   Mis. 371–22 To sympathize in any *d·* with error,
   Un. 54–14 if sin's claim be allowed in any *d·*,
   Pul. 21–29 aught that can darken in any *d·* our
  C.S.D.
   My. 251–22 a certificate of the *d·* C.S.D.
  diploma or
   Mis. 272–16 * who confers, . . . any diploma or *d·*,
  final
   Mis. 86– 3 final *d·* of regeneration is saving,
  first
   My. 245–31 first *d·* (C.S.B.) is given to
      246– 2 after receiving the first *d·*,
  great
   Pul. 37– 8 * retains in a great *d·* her energy
  greater
   Pul. 75– 6 a greater *d·* of this spirit than in
  highest
   Mis. 334–20 of the highest *d·* of nothingness :
   Un. 50–12 of which evil is the highest *d·* ;
  holds a
   Man. 38– 7 student . . . who holds a *d·*.
  large
   My. 74– 2 * to a large *d·* are already in Boston.
  last
   Mis. 85–16 The last *d·* of regeneration rises
  of comparison
   My. 238– 5 exact *d·* of comparison between
  of C.S.B.
   Man. 92–18 nor receive the *d·* of C.S.B.
  of C.S.D.
   Man. 89–16 to receive the *d·* of C.S.D.
   My. 244– 9 conferring . . . the *d·* of C.S.D.,
  of M. D.
   Mis. 349– 6 students with the *d·* of M. D.,
  receive the
   Man. 68–15 receive the *d·* of the . . . College.
       89–16 to receive the *d·* of C.S.D.

degree

remarkable
Ret. 83– 3 purpose to a remarkable *d*·.
My. 287– 6 used in a remarkable *d*·

second
My. 246– 1 the second *d*· (C.S.D.)

small
Rud. 7– 3 as . . . scientific, in a small *d*·,
No. 38– 3 to-day proving in a small *d*·,
'00. 7–15 lived, and learned, in a small *d*·,
My. 42–25 * comprehend, even in small *d*·,

smallest
Rud. 13– 7 even in the smallest *d*·.

some
Mis. 195–10 every one can prove, in some *d*·,
Man. 19– 6 thus to reflect in some *d*· the
Un. 39–17 must reflect, in some *d*·, the power
Pul. 31–10 * some *d*· of familiarity with the
'01. 6–20 which is set aside to some *d*·,
My. 63–19 * in some *d*· sharing in our joy.
112–17 demonstrates in some *d*· the truth

Man. 109– 9 who have been given a *d*·,
Pul. 85–12 * in the *d*· in which she has
'00. 6–26 in the *d*· that you accept it,
'02. 6–25 In the *d*· that man becomes
My. 314– 9 He had the *d*· D.D.S.,
335– 5 * *d*· of a Royal Arch Mason
347– 1 been revealed in a *d*· through

degrees
Mis. 84–12 dawns by *d*· on mortals.
86– 7 strive . . . though in lessening *d*·
102–13 admits of no *d*· of comparison.
165– 3 spiritual idea . . . disappeared by *d*·;
272– 3 * (*including the right to grant d*·)
272–23 * bestow no rights to *confer d*·.
272–26 * to confer diplomas and *d*·,
359–25 Science is demonstrated by *d*·,
'01. 18– 2 attenuated one thousand *d*· less
My. 245–27 *d*· that follow the names of
245–29 indicate, . . . *d*· of Bachelor and

de Hirsch
Baron and Baroness
My. 287– 2 chapter sub-title
287– 4 the late Baron and Baroness *de H*·

My. 289– 5 *De H*· monument fund.

deific
Mis. 45–16 *d*· law that supply invariably meets
Ret. 70– 6 usurps the *d*· prerogatives
Un. 17– 5 Be allied to the *d*· power,
Pul. 4–13 thus demonstrating *d*· Principle.
Rud. 1– 9 these are the *d*· Principle.
My. 262–19 *d*· presence or power.

deification
Mis. 307–11 chapter sub-title
307–29 the *d*· of finite personality.
Pul. 72– 4 * the reported *d*· of Mrs. Eddy,
74–24 statement of the Christ and the *d*· of
Rud. 17– 9 pride, rivalry, or the *d*· of self.
Pan. 2–20 the *d*· of natural causes.

deified
Mis. 308–11 revelators . . . will not be *d*·.
Pul. 6– 9 not the *d*· drug, but the goodness of
71–10 * chapter sub-title
73–25 * accredited as having been *d*·.

deify
My. 359–29 allowing your students to *d*·

deities
Mis. 255– 3 on pedestals, as so many petty *d*·;
No. 36– 2 did not teach that there are two *d*·,
Peo. 4–23 as material as the heathen *d*·.
4–25 inquired of these heathen *d*·

Deity
and man
My. 350– 1 draws its conclusions of *D*· and man,
applied to
'00. 5–10 Applied to *D*·, Father and Mother are
belief concerning
Pan. 2–25 belief concerning *D*· in theology.
conceptions of
No. 15–16 These conceptions of *D*· and devil
Peo. 8– 9 if . . . are our conceptions of *D*·,
8–14 material conceptions of *D*·.
definition of
Mis. 258–29 divine definition of *D*·
'02. 5–19 This absolute definition of *D*·
dethrone
Mis. 260–22 seeking to dethrone *D*·.
dethroning
Mis. 3–28 denying . . . and dethroning *D*·.

Deity
drugs to
My. 139–25 advanced . . . from drugs to *D*·;
entertained of
Hea. 8–17 mistaken views entertained of *D*·
essence of
Mis. 121–19 nature and essence of *D*·,
fact of
'00. 4–30 this fundamental fact of *D*· as the
foreknows
Un. 19– 3 What *D*· *foreknows*, Deity must
good
Un. 15–23 who worship not the good *D*·,
hues of
Mis. 194–15 bring out the entire hues of *D*·,
Ret. 35–14 brings out the hues of *D*·.
ideal of
Peo. 6–18 spiritual and true ideal of *D*·
ideas of
Ret. 56– 1 The following ideas of *D*·,
Peo. 12–17 As our ideas of *D*· advance
14– 1 As our ideas of *D*· become more
infinite
Un. 10–14 toward aught but infinite *D*·.
is deathless
Mis. 184– 3 claiming . . . *D*· is deathless, but
Un. 39–26 presuppose . . . *D*· is deathless, but
its
Peo. 2–17 and form its *D*· out of the worst
knoweth
Un. 64–18 can never turn back what *D*· knoweth,
misconception of
Mis. 124–11 Moslem's misconception of *D*·,
monument of
Po. 1–12 Ye rose, a monument of *D*·,
must foreordain
Un. 19– 3 *foreknows*, *D*· must *foreordain*;
name of
Mis. 75–24 name of *D*· used in that place
nature of
Mis. 79– 1 antagonistic to . . . the nature of *D*·.
192– 9 terms and nature of *D*· and devil
not absorbed in
No. 25–19 Man is not absorbed in *D*·;
personal
No. 19–10 chapter sub-title
possible in
Un. 15–17 if . . . could be possible in *D*·,
recognition of
Mis. 1–16 to a higher recognition of *D*·.
relation to
Mis. 181–21 his spiritual relation to *D*·:
scoff at
Mis. 69– 3 sneer at metaphysics is a scoff at *D*·;
sense of
(*see* **sense**)
signify
No. 20– 8 Principle is used to signify *D*·
sin and
Un. 6–24 our declarations about sin and *D*·
statement of
Hea. 5– 1 our inconsistent statement of *D*·,
term for
Mis. 75–15 Soul is a term for *D*·,
192– 3 Hebrew term for *D*· was "good,"
their
Peo. 2–22 has their *D*· become good;
to indicate
Ret. 59–13 *Life* is a term used to indicate *D*·;
truth of
Peo. 9–27 This truth of *D*·, understood,
understanding of
Un. 13–13 gain the true understanding of *D*·.
was forever
Mis. 218– 3 fact that *D*· was forever Mind,
wholeness of
Un. 5– 4 of the wholeness of *D*·,
would fashion
No. 20– 6 Error would fashion *D*· in a manlike

Mis. 217–18 and that *D*· is a finite person
218–15 they make *D*· unreal and
Ret. 25– 2 great curative Principle, — *D*·.
Un. 15–18 would *D*· then be sinless
19–13 if . . . there would be sin in *D*·,
Pul. 64–21 * curative Principle was the *D*·.
70–20 * great curative Principle — the *D*·
No. 23–22 *D*· can have no such warfare
Hea. 4– 7 Clothing *D*· with personality,
15–22 as if drugs were superior to *D*·.
Peo. 12–25 As if *D*· would not if He could,

deity
Mis. 123–16 Jehovah, was the Jewish tribal *d*·.
Un. 15–24 the bad *d*·, who seeks to do
Pan. 2–24 mythological *d*· of that name;

deity
Pan.	3– 1	mythical *d·* may please the fancy,
	3– 3	Pan, as a *d·*, is supposed to
'00.	13–24	principal *d·* in the city of
Peo.	13– 2	have a more material *d·*,
My.	189– 8	You worship no distant *d·*,

delay
Mis.	133– 1	you will not *d·* corrections
	141–26	*D·* not longer to commence building
	151–20	*d·* not to make Him thy
	341–22	the evil of inaction and *d·*.
Hea.	1–18	* chides his infamous *d·*,
My.	23– 1	* not necessary for us to *d·* our
	195– 3	You will pardon my *d·*

delayed
Mis.	237–24	Honor to faithful merit is *d·*,
	273–30	classes . . . would be *d·*.
Pul.	83– 8	* sunlight cannot long be *d·*.

delayeth
Mis.	335– 4	*d·* his coming ; — *Matt.* 24 : 48.

delegates
Mis.	276–10	My students, our *d·*,

delegations
Ret.	52–14	*d·* from the . . . Association

deleterious
Un.	8–15	arises from their *d·* effects,

deliberately
My.	127–16	I *d·* declare that when I was

deliberation
Ret.	49–27	due *d·* and earnest discussion
	85–18	without due *d·* and light,
My.	50– 1	* meeting of this little church for *d·*
	50–14	* "The tone of this meeting for *d·*

deliberations
Mis.	350–12	On the contrary, our *d·*
Man.	17– 2	went into *d·* over forming

delicacy
Mis.	133–20	I should feel a *d·* in making

delicate
Mis.	145–18	friendship, *d·* as dear,

delicious
Mis.	9–26	*d·* forms of friendship,
	231–14	*d·* pie, pudding, and fruit

delight
Mis.	375–21	* to my amazement and *d·*
Ret.	50–17	Loyal students speak with *d·* of
Pul.	46–12	* Mrs. Eddy takes *d·* in
	61–26	* people, who listened with *d·*.
My.	170–21	*D·* thyself also in — *Psal.* 37 : 4.

delighted
Mis.	372–18	*d·* to find "Christ and Christmas"

delightful
Pul.	47–21	* a *d·* country home one mile from
	63–11	* *d·* country home in Concord,
My.	350–26	Truth *d·*, crowned with endless days,

delightfully
Pul.	47–28	* big house, so *d·* remodelled

delighting
Pul.	46–24	* *d·* in philosophy, logic, and

delights
Mis.	131–23	sense of gratitude which *d·* in

delineate
Mis.	375– 7	it demands more . . . to *d· this* art.

delineated
Mis.	309–10	been so unnaturally *d·*
Ret.	82–13	orderly methods herein *d·*.

delineates
Mis.	373–15	*d·* Christ's appearing in the flesh,

delineations
Mis.	372–18	* *d·* from the old masters."
Peo.	7–26	give to the body those better *d·*.

delirious
Pul.	34–13	* believing her *d·*.

delirium
Mis.	243– 1	without it . . . she would have *d·*

deliver
Mis.	50–26	would *d·* man from heart-disease,
	81–28	*d·* mortals out of the depths of
	114–28	He will *d·* us from temptation
	298–18	Trials purify mortals and *d·* them
	301– 2	you *d·* without the author's consent,
Ret.	91–13	Where did Jesus *d·* this great lesson
'01.	10– 3	*d·* you up to the councils" — *Matt.* 10 : 17.
My.	150– 4	to save, to heal, and to *d·*,
	233– 6	"*D·* us from evil" — *Matt.* 6 : 13.
	233–12	better adapted to *d·* mortals from

deliverance
Mis.	114–23	*d·* from the claims of evil.
No.	43–15	* preaching *d·* to the captive,
Po.	33– 6	To hourly seek for *d·* strong
My.	43– 1	* but this *d·* did not put them in

delivered
Mis.	115–18	*d·* from every claim of evil,
	161– 2	*D·* IN CHICKERING HALL,
	171–21	chapter sub-title
	178–10	* *d·* an interesting discourse
	180– 4	I was *d·* from the dark shadow
	211–13	I *d·* thee." — *Psal.* 81 : 7.
	281–31	righteous shall be *d·*." — *Prov.* 11 : 21.
Man.	40–12	pray to be *d·* from all evil,
Ret.	40–16	*d·* of another child.
Pul.	1—	chapter heading
No.	25– 5	we are *d·* from the law, — *Rom.* 7 : 6.
'01.	14–20	*d·* from believing in what is unreal,
Hea.	19– 1	felon was *d·* to them for experiment
My.	36–13	* *d·* from beds of sickness
	36–22	* we who have been *d·* from the
	42–31	* children of Israel *d·* from the
	206–28	*d·* us from the power of — *Col.* 1 : 13.
	338–13	after the lecture was *d·*

deliverer
Mis.	399–11	Strongest *d·*, friend of the
Po.	75–18	Strongest *d·*, friend of the
My.	132–15	this benediction : . . . I am thy *d·*.
	252–15	wait on God, the strong *d·*,

delivering
Mis.	235–10	*d·* mankind from all error
	301– 1	compiling and *d·* that sermon
Man.	93–17	his lectures before *d·* them.

delivers
Mis.	298–21	then Truth *d·* you from the

dell
Mis.	390–13	Through woodland, grove, and *d·* ;
Po.	55–14	Through woodland, grove, and *d·* ;

Delphian
Pul.	9– 5	no *D·* lyre could break the

Delsarte
Pul.	31–28	* flexible . . . as that of a *D·* disciple ;

delude
Ret.	18–14	Earth's beauty and glory *d·*
Po.	64– 5	Earth's beauty and glory *d·*

deluded
Mis.	107–21	*d·* sense must first be shown its
	254–24	filling with hate its *d·* victims,
'01.	15–19	waken such a one from his *d·* sense ;
	15–19	for all sin is a *d·* sense,

deluding
Mis.	3–27	*d·* reason, denying revelation,
	260–20	*d·* reason and denying revelation,

deluge
Mis.	246–27	again *d·* the earth in blood?
	355–25	like the dove from the *d·*.
Pan.	2– 8	higher than Mt. Ararat above the *d·*.

delusion
Mis.	11– 1	wake from his *d·* to suffer
	15– 3	endure the effects of his *d·*
	108–15	conceived of only as a *d·*.
	109–32	your superiority to a *d·* is won.
Ret.	32–15	* Fleeting pleasure, fond *d·*,
	69– 6	in which originated the *d·*
Un.	30– 4	under the *d·* that the senses
	33–16	only through error and *d·*.
	53–14	which will die of its own *d·* ;
	56–21	Until he awakes from his *d·*,
Pul.	14–28	the great *d·* of mortal mind,
No.	4– 8	material sensation and mental *d·*.
	34– 1	*d·* of all human error,
Pan.	5–19	liar and lie, a *d·* and illusion.
Hea.	17–26	did not mind originate the *d·* ?
My.	5– 8	this illusion and *d·* of sense,

delusions
Mis.	112– 4	may deem these *d·* verities,

delusive
Mis.	65– 1	*d·* evidence, Science has dethroned
Un.	19–16	evil is only a *d·* deception,

delved
Pul.	73– 9	* *d·* deep into the Biblical passages,

delving
Mis.	340–14	dug into soils instead of *d·* into

demand
accommodate the
My.	82–13	* enough to accommodate the *d·*.

and example
No.	14–24	The *d·* and example of Jesus

and supply
My.	216– 8	subsist on *d·* and supply,

demand

dear
Pan. 11–30 because Christ's dear *d·*,
deep
Mis. 3–31 Hence the deep *d·* for the Science of
every
My. 41–29 * has obeyed its every *d·*,
feasibility of the
Hea. 19–21 or doubts the feasibility of the *d·*.
for this book
Ret. 39– 1 *d·* for this book increased,
My. 305–17 *d·* for this book . . . increases.
great
Mis. 132–16 great *d·* upon my time,
His
Mis. 18–32 bring to you at His *d·* that which
his
My. 339–27 not sufficient to meet his *d·*.
immediate
Mis. 148–16 immediate *d·* for them as a help
Man. 3–12 immediate *d·* for them as a help
imperative
My. 134–13 some imperative *d·* not yet met.
increased
My. 164– 3 But the *d·* increased, and I
infinite
Mis. 77– 7 infinite *d·* made upon the eunuch
its
Mis. 8–27 its *d·* and sentence,
Master's
Mis. 287– 5 and the Master's *d·*,
meets
Mis. 45–16 law that supply invariably meets *d·*,
meet the
Mis. 91– 9 it is to meet the *d·*
Ret. 48–23 to meet the *d·* of the age
Pul. 8–17 vied with . . . to meet the *d·*.
No. 39–28 silent prayer can meet the *d·*,
met the
Mis. 276– 9 my heart's desire met the *d·*.
of mortal thought
Mis. 44–24 *d·* of mortal thought once met,
of the times
Mis. 232–21 healing, . . . is a *d·* of the times.
of this age
My. 40–15 * *d·* of this age is for peacemaking,
of this hour
My. 132– 1 Love . . . is the *d·* of this hour
present
My. 237–11 adapted to the present *d·*.
Scriptural
Man. 51– 2 consonance with the Scriptural *d·*
special
My. 132– 2 fulfilment of . . . the special *d·*.
spiritual
Pul. 23–14 * common identity of spiritual *d·*.
Hea. 19–20 makes a more spiritual *d·*,
that
My. 224– 2 understand the importance of that *d·*
this
No. 18–25 This *d·* militates against the
My. 46–18 * pledge ourselves anew to this *d·*,
224– 5 call your attention to this *d·*,
wide
My. 245– 3 wide *d·* for this universal benefice
would diminish
Mis. 365–21 If . . . the *d·* would diminish ;

Mis. 136– 4 as society and our societies *d·*.
225–15 opportunity to *d·* a proof of
232–23 would desire and *d·* it,
247– 1 *d·* for man his God-given heritage,
Man. 78– 1 *d·* that each member thereof
Ret. 61–26 Posterity will have the right to *d·*
Pul. 83– 1 * *d·* woman's love and woman's help
No. 19– 4 and the *d·* to increase,
Pan. 12–11 and *d·* that the inspired Scriptural
'01. 10–28 This is what the Scriptures *d·*
My. 168– 4 with the *d·* of our common Christ,
219–30 I recommend, if the law *d·*,

demanded

Mis. 19– 5 obedience *d·* of His servants
158– 8 change in your pulpit would be *d·*.
276– 7 circumstances *d·* my attention
283–12 if no emergency *d·* this.
298–18 implied that the period *d·* it.
374– 8 *d·* Christianity in life and
Un. 11–11 *d·* a change of consciousness
'01. 25–25 which Satan *d·* in the beginning,
My. 103– 5 The faith and works *d·* of man
348–18 since Science *d·* a rational proof

demanding

Mis. 23– 2 Science, *d·* more, pushes the
Ret. 26– 1 *d·* neither obedience to

demanding

Pul. 82–24 * They are *d·* the right to help
My. 231–15 letters from invalids *d·* her help

demands (noun)

dictatorial
Mis. 148–11 not . . . opinions nor dictatorial *d·*,
Man. 3– 7 not . . . opinions nor dictatorial *d·*,
eternal
My. 159–22 only legitimate and eternal *d·*
Father's
Peo. 3–27 obedience to our Father's *d·*,
great
Mis. 204–20 great *d·* of spiritual sense are
My. 222–17 his great *d·* on the faith of
highest
No. 45–26 urging its highest *d·* on mortals,
holy
My. 291– 2 Imperative, accumulative, holy *d·*
immortal
Mis. 201– 2 meets the immortal *d·* of Truth.
important
My. 231–20 important *d·* on her time
increasing
Pul. 37– 4 * increasing *d·* of the public
My. 135–11 increasing *d·* upon my time
137–17 increasing *d·* upon my time,
indispensable
Mis. 318–23 These are the indispensable *d·*
manifold
Mis. x– 9 manifold *d·* on my time
of Love
Peo. 9– 8 or meet the *d·* of Love.
of matter
No. 18–26 so-called *d·* of matter,
Peo. 12–16 lifts man above the *d·* of matter.
of the hour
Mis. 70–18 not equal to the *d·* of the hour ;
of the law
My. 43– 7 * Obedience to the *d·* of the law
recurring
My. 192–24 recurring *d·* upon my time and
sacred
My. 163–14 sacred *d·* on my time and
strong
Mis. 250–16 I make strong *d·* on love,
sweet
Mis. 316–19 sweet *d·* rest on my retirement

My. 46–14 * *d·* of this early pronouncement
118–20 furnishing the *d·* upon the finite
275–19 *d·* upon my time at home,

demands (verb)

Mis. 2–13 the outlook *d·* labor,
3– 2 shall express these views as duty *d·*,
16–29 this statement *d·* demonstration.
37–29 least difficult of the labor that C. S. *d·*.
40– 2 healing *d·* such cooperation ;
45–14 moral status of the man *d·* the
65–21 C. S. *d·* both law and gospel,
65–30 The Jewish religion *d·* that
67–19 mercy *d·* that if you see the danger
112–11 this knowledge *d·* our time and attention.
119–25 *d·* of all trespassers upon the
123–11 a religion that *d·* human victims
215–12 C. S. *d·* order and truth.
244–15 * *d·* the employment of visible
264–12 *d·* oneness of thought and action.
299– 7 which *d·* our present attention.
317– 8 demonstrate, as this period *d·*,
318– 4 and *d·* to be demonstrated.
375– 6 it *d·* more than a Raphael
Man. 95– 8 as the cause of C. S. *d·*.
Chr. 53–19 To celebrate As Truth *d·*,
Ret. 54– 5 It *d·* less cross-bearing,
57– 1 *d·* mighty wrestlings with mortal
87–12 *d·* implicit adherence to fixed rules,
Pul. 10–23 as progress certainly *d·*,
No. 37–16 *d·* His continual presence,
Pan. 11–26 *d·* man's unfallen spiritual
My. 3– 5 *d·* well-doing in order to
118–13 spiritual sense *d·* and commands
152–25 God *d·* all our faith and love ;
232–29 Can watching as Christ *d·*
316–18 truth *d·* public attention.
355– 9 However, if the occasion *d·* it,

dematerialized

Peo. 2–21 has been *d·* and unfinited
8– 1 Religion and medicine must be *d·*

dematerializing

No. 10–24 *d·* and spiritualizing mortals

demean

Mis. 32– 3 *How shall we d· ourselves towards*

dementia

Mis. 113–22 insanity. *d·*, or moral idiocy.

demerit

Mis. 80–14 on its own merit or *d·*,
My. 306–17 Human merit or *d·* will find its

demise

Mis. 248–21 alleged to have reported my *d·*,
My. 295–26 lament the *d·* of Lord Dunmore ;
334–10 * account of her husband's *d·*

democratic

Man. 74– 7 distinctly *d·* in its government,
My. 247– 3 Essentially *d·*, its government is
254–24 Essentially *d·*, its government is
361–21 * *d·* and liberal government.

demolish

My. 127–23 cannot *d·* our strongholds.

demolished

Man. 103– 6 *d·*, nor removed from the site
Pul. 3– 2 *d·*, or even disturbed?
My. 15– 7 *d·* nor removed from the site

demolishing

No. 1– 8 *d·* bridges and overwhelming cities.

demon

'01. 16– 8 whereby the *d·* of this world,

demoniacal

Peo. 2–19 *d·* contests over religion.

demons

Mis. 19–15 endeavors of suppositional *d·*
Un. 28–10 peopled with *d·* or angels,
Pul. 29–19 * cast out *d·*.'' — *see Matt.* 10 : 8.
29–23 * cast out the *d·* of evil thought.
66–13 * cast out *d·*.'' — *see Matt.* 10 : 8.

demonstrable

Mis. 26– 3 truth, as *d·* as mathematics.
150–27 God *d·* as divine Life, Truth, and
193– 7 self-evident *d·* truth.
Man. 49–10 *d·* knowledge of C. S. practice,
Ret. 56– 3 *d·* rules in C. S.,
Un. 49– 5 This is *d·* by the simple appeal to
Pan. 2– 6 neither hypothetical nor . . . but *d·*,
'00. 4–20 being *d·*, they are undeniable.
'01. 2–15 divine and *d·* Principle and rule
21– 5 students of a *d·* Science
My. 58–20 * revealed a *d·* way of salvation.
112–19 it contains a Science which is *d·*
143–21 an eternal and *d·* Science,
179–32 as make even God *d·*,
248– 8 grasping and defining the *d·*,
260–20 fundamental and *d·* truth,
299–14 presents the *d·* divine Principle
348–26 a *d·* Principle and given rule.

demonstrably

Mis. 12–27 aught else . . . *d·* is not Love.
80–32 C. S. Mind-healing rests *d·* on
Rud. 7– 3 as *d·* scientific, in a small degree,
No. 10– 3 C. S. is *d·* as true,
21–25 Divine philosophy is *d·* the true
28–20 What is *d·* true cannot be gainsaid ;
Pan. 12–23 is *d·* the self-existent Life,
My. 4–31 divinely natural and *d·* true,

demonstrate

Mis. v– 7 AND *d·* THE ETHICS OF C. S.
3– 7 *d·* in our lives the power of
22–27 a willing sinner, cannot *d·* it.
30– 7 *d·* all the possibilities of
30–19 enabled man to *d·* the law of
44–11 to *d·* its highest possibilities.
52–23 failing to *d·* one rule
55– 5 ability to *d·* to the extent
59– 3 can neither understand nor *d·* its
65–22 in order to *d·* healing,
75–10 or it is impossible to *d·* the
111– 2 to *d·* what you have adopted
115–19 till you intelligently know and *d·*,
138–12 Principle which he claims to *d·*,
148–19 requisite to *d·* genuine C. S.,
181– 5 power to *d·* his divine Principle,
185– 3 to discern fully and *d·* fairly
195– 6 is unable to *d·* this Science ;
201–30 you can *d·* the triumph of good
220– 1 *d·* this rule, which obtains in
243–16 can *d·* only in proportion as he
247–16 *d·* this Science by healing the sick ;
258–21 could neither name nor *d·* Spirit.
264–11 and to *d·* the divine One,
282– 1 going out to *d·* a living faith,
283–27 genius of C. S. to *d·* good,
317– 6 to *d·* self-knowledge and
317– 8 and to *d·*, as this period demands,
322–13 the Love they *d·*,
334–32 *d·* the might of perfect Love
344–20 the Science of Life,
366– 5 *d·* what they teach
380– 9 to *d·* what I had discovered :

demonstrate

Man. 3–15 so requisite to *d·* genuine C. S.,
92– 8 *d·* by his or her practice,
Chr. 53–20 this living Vine Ye *d·*.
Ret. 28– 6 to *d·*, even in part,
38–29 in order to *d·* C. S.
78–19 an attempt to *d·* the facts
88–15 its power to *d·* immortality.
Un. 8–21 You *d·* the process of Science
10– 1 you *d·* the allness of God.
32–27 to *d·* the falsity of the claim.
48–20 faintly able to *d·* Truth and Love.
55–10 *d·* "the way" — *John* 14 : 6.
Pul. 4–11 and daily *d·* this.
Rud. 8– 7 *How should I undertake to d· C. S.*
No. 11–19 and *d·* what these works teach,
11–24 are inadequate . . . to *d·* it.
12– 6 to understand and to *d·* God.
26– 9 to *d·* my metaphysics.
33– 9 and *d·* what these volumes teach,
38–22 must *d·* the nothingness of
Pan. 11–14 will *d·* man to be superior
'00. 4–23 Does it *d·* its doctrines?
6– 2 Principle and rules which *d·* it.
'01. 4– 9 destroys the ability to *d·* Love
15– 3 to understand and *d·* its unreality.
23–14 cannot *d·* C. S. except
24–26 to *d·* the divine Science of
'02. 6–10 to *d·* this grand verity,
8–17 his deeds, *d·* Love.
Hea. 3–23 or we cannot *d·* it in part.
4–27 how can we *d·* a changing Principle?
Peo. 13– 6 can *d·* in part this great
My. 3– 5 in order to *d·* truth,
5–29 they cannot *d·* the omnipotence
111–16 shows how to *d·* it,
113–21 A child will *d·* C. S.
119– 3 or on such a basis to *d·* the
149–21 or to *d·* Christian charity.
187–10 to *d·* the perfect man
203– 4 Pray aright and *d·* your prayer ;
233–13 can you *d·* over the effects of
234–27 to teach and to *d·* C. S.
242– 3 You can never *d·* spirituality until
242– 9 you have no Principle to *d·*
242–12 or you forfeit your ability to *d·* it.
254– 7 Watch, pray, *d·*.
279–18 *d·* "on earth peace, — *Luke* 2 : 14.
303–17 to *d·* Science and its pure
357–14 *d·* C. S. to a higher
358– 1 which *d·* the true following of
(*see also* **Principle**)

demonstrated

Mis. 22–23 *d·* it, according to the rules
23– 7 *d·* a divine intelligence
25– 6 that Jesus taught and *d·*.
28–16 he *d·* that divine Science alone can
40–15 and *d·* on, the same Principle
41–28 if *d·*, is sufficient for all
52–26 first rule was not easily *d·*?
54– 5 discovered, *d·*, and teaches C. S.?
57–13 after the truth of man had been *d·*,
70– 3 I *d·* its truth when I
74–26 the lifelessness of matter,
76– 6 is true, and remains to be *d·* ;
92– 6 sufficiently . . . to be absolutely *d·*.
101– 3 divine Mind is understood and *d·*
104–26 divine Principle and idea are *d·*,
107–15 is regenerated and C. S. is *d·* :
172–21 understood, and *d·* in our lives.
183– 5 must be acknowledged and *d·*.
188– 2 that *d·* the opposite, Truth.
251–27 will fall before Truth *d·*,
258– 9 he *d·* the healing power and
270– 9 He who *d·* his power over sin,
286–29 *d·* in the offspring of divine Mind,
318– 4 is stated and demands to be *d·*.
334–26 By the substitution of Truth *d·*,
342– 2 the joy of divine Science *d·*.
359–25 Science is *d·* by degrees,
367–12 goodness and harmony — is *d·*.
Man. 16– 2 Love as *d·* by the Galilean Prophet
17–17 taught and *d·* by our Master,
Ret. 26– 9 *d·* for all time and peoples
35–19 was and is *d·* as practical,
61–27 stated and *d·* in its godliness
71–26 wheat can be garnered and C. S. *d·*.
84– 3 sufficiently understood to be fully *d·*.
93–21 has not been fully *d·*,
Un. 1–13 little apprehended and *d·* by mortals,
53– 9 they are here to be seen and *d·* ;
55– 2 rule of Life can be *d·*,
Pul. 21– 8 live, to see this love *d·*.
63–19 * *d·* in a very tangible and
70–22 * way of salvation *d·* by Jesus

demonstrated

Pul.	85– 9	* unfolded and *d·* divine Love,
	85–13	* she has *d·* the system of healing
No.	13–12	before that saying is *d·* in Life
	14– 2	nor misconceived, when properly *d·*.
	21–10	Science *d·* the Principle of all
	28–18	Truth, as *d·* by Jesus,
	36– 1	*d·* the infinite as one,
Pan.	8–14	Christianity, as taught and *d·* in
	8–21	Christianity, as he taught and *d·* it,
	9– 8	that hath *d·* one God
	11–29	grand realism . . . is *d·* by C. S.
	13– 5	When shall Christianity be *d·*
'01.	2– 2	what Christ Jesus taught and *d·*
	4–14	and *d·* as divine Love ;
	23–20	he *d·* his power over matter, sin,
	23–22	as no other person has ever *d·* it.
	25–21	He *d·* what he taught.
'02.	6– 9	Christ, Truth, *d·* and continues to
Peo.	12–20	Our blessed Master *d·* this great
My.	37–15	* you have *d·* this Science
	103–20	I have *d·* through Mind
	105– 4	defined Christianly and *d·*
	105– 5	rules *d·* prove one's faith
	112–20	is fully understood when *d·*.
	113–24	is *d·* on a fixed Principle
	146–13	infinitely more than has been *d·*,
	146–21	has not been *d·* in this age.
	152–28	understood and *d·*, is found to be
	162–12	have *d·* in gifts to me
	181–14	which, *d·* on the Golden Rule,
	205–27	it is *d·* by perfect rules ;
	238– 9	discerned, understood, and *d·*.
	267– 3	fully *d·* to be divine Science?
	275–27	spiritually understood and *d·*,
	300–12	Principle of C. S., *d·*, heals
	348–24	*d·* Christianity and proved
	357–25	upon which this Science can be *d·*.
		(*see also* **Jesus**)

demonstrates

Mis.	67–18	gospel of healing *d·* the law of Love.
	85– 7	and *d·* what he understands.
	98–20	*d·* God and the perfectibility of man.
	101–22	omnipotence *d·* but one power,
	116–26	Obeying the divine . . . *d·* Truth.
	166– 1	which alone *d·* the divine Principle
	189–31	*d·* Life without beginning or end.
	190– 5	*d·* Mind as dispelling a false sense
	209– 9	rule of this Principle *d·* Love,
	209–11	Metaphysics also *d·* this Principle
	252–22	*d·* the divine Principle, rules and
	259–24	Truth *d·* good, and is natural ;
	261– 8	*d·* this verity of being ;
	265–13	*d·* its Principle according to rule,
	291– 6	*d·* above personal motives,
	300–29	C. S. *d·* that the patient
	338–14	only rule . . . which *d·* C. S.
Man.	92– 4	*d·* what we affirm of
Ret.	65–21	it *d·* the power of Christ
	88–28	Mind *d·* omnipresence and
Un.	40–10	*d·* Life as imperative in the
No.	4–14	Science *d·* the reality of Truth
	6–28	and C. S. *d·* this.
	30–26	cure of the sick *d·* this grand
Pan.	9–16	Whoever *d·* the highest humanity,
'01.	15–11	*d·* the Science of Christianity.
	22– 2	whosoever *d·* the truth of these
'02.	6–24	points the way, *d·* heaven here,
My.	5–19	understanding which *d·* C. S.,
	112–17	*d·* in some degree the truth of
	181– 9	it *d·* the scientific, sinless
	238–19	Science is reached that *d·* God.
	238–23	is Science, for it *d·* Life,
	274– 1	*d·* the Principle of life eternal ;
	274–14	*d·* health, holiness, and
	274–25	for it *d·* C. S.
	275– 5	it lives love, it *d·* love.
	279– 7	Principle of C. S. *d·* peace.
	285– 9	and *d·* the Science of being.
	288– 9	*d·* Truth and reflects divine Love.

demonstrating

Mis.	42–31	false admissions prevent us from *d·*
	54–11	she is *d·* the power of C. S.
	64– 5	*d·* the nothingness of sickness,
	116–22	doing, the Word — *d·* Truth
	147– 7	*d·* the divine Principle of C. S.
	163–28	*d·* the spiritual healing of body
	185–13	*d·* the true image and likeness,
	270–12	used in *d·* Life scientifically,
	380– 3	human modus for *d·* this,
	380–24	*d·* the Science of metaphysical
Man.	45–12	*d·* the rules of divine Love.
Ret.	37–17	*d·* the spiritual Principle of
	79–20	*d·* the victory over self and sin.
Pul.	4–13	thus *d·* deific Principle.

demonstrating

Pul.	69–27	* *d·* the Christ-healing.''
Rud.	1– 3	*d·* the divine Principle
No.	4– 3	*d·* it understandingly
Hea.	9– 4	employed our thoughts more in *d·* it.
	16– 6	How much are you *d·* of this
	16–11	unless you do this you are not *d·* the
My.	214– 8	*d·* the Life that is Truth,
	297–23	*d·* the fundamental truth of C. S.
	362–24	* thus *d·* practical Christianity.

demonstration

absolute
Mis.	136–18	absolute *d·* of C. S.
	355– 9	absolute *d·* of Science must be

and fruition
Un.	61–23	C. S. is both *d·* and fruition,

Christian
Mis.	156–19	daily Christian *d·* thereof.

daily
Mis.	373–32	daily *d·* of Truth and Love.

demands
Mis.	16–29	this statement demands *d·*.

dethrones
Mis.	221–22	Such denial dethrones *d·*,

feeble
Mis.	30– 2	in at least some feeble *d·* thereof,

gospel, or
Mis.	367– 1	letter without law, gospel, or *d·*,

grand
My.	321– 1	* grand *d·* in building this church

great
My.	84–17	* near to another great *d·* of

higher
Mis.	355–16	gives scope to higher *d·*.
No.	44– 5	higher *d·* of medicine and religion.

his
Mis.	3–11	his *d·* hath taught us
	74–20	His *d·* of Spirit
	192– 7	his *d·* of Truth in casting out
	215–29	used at the *end* of his *d·*.
'01.	11– 3	his *d·* over sin, disease, and death,

idea and
Ret.	59–17	both in idea and *d·*.

inquiry and
Mis.	268–15	His whole inquiry and *d·*

its
Mis.	19– 4	and prevent its *d·* ;
	56–22	its *d·* proves the correctness
	65–23	I have taught them both in its *d·*,
	214–13	summed up its *d·* in the command,
	357–32	Divine Love . . . the basis of its *d·*,
Ret.	31– 3	C. S., and its *d·*,
	94– 3	a struggle for its *d·*.
Un.	25–13	Truth and its *d·* in C. S.,
My.	113–16	knowledge of Christ and its *d·*,
	242–10	and no rule for its *d·*.
	361–20	* has promptly made its *d·*

manifestation, and
My.	357– 8	manifestation, and *d·*.

marvellous
No.	37–14	this most marvellous *d·*,

of being
Ret.	26–29	*d·* of being, in Science,

of Christ
Man.	47–16	illustrates the *d·* of Christ,

of Christianity
Mis.	149–21	refreshing *d·* of Christianity,
Pan.	9–20	*d·* of Christianity blesses all

of Christian Science
Mis.	136–18	absolute *d·* of C. S.
	338– 6	but by *d·* of C. S.,
Man.	43–25	rules and the *d·* of C. S.
Ret.	78–10	will prevent the *d·* of C. S.
'01.	23–12	Principle, rule, or *d·* of C. S.,
	28–20	my *d·* of C. S. in healing
My.	136– 3	At this period my *d·* of C. S.

of divine Life
No.	18–14	*d·* of divine Life and Love ;

of divine power
Mis.	268–10	the *d·* of divine power,

of God
(*see* **God**)

of healing
'01.	18–21	is above a *d·* of healing,

of infinity
Ret.	59–12	in *d·* of infinity.

of Jesus
Mis.	244–26	teachings and *d·* of Jesus

of Love
Mis.	214– 2	was full of Love, and a *d·* of Love,

of the Science
Rud.	11–18	*d·* of the Science of Mind-healing

of the science
Ret.	59–10	*d·* of the science of numbers ;

demonstration

of the truth
Mis. 87–27 indispensable to the *d·* of the truth

of the unreality
Ret. 62– 7 A *d·* of the *unreality* of evil

of Truth
Mis. 192– 7 and to his *d·* of Truth
373–32 *d·* of Truth and Love.
Ret. 75–11 writings on ethics, and *d·* of Truth,
No. 11–28 dictum and the *d·* of Truth

origin and
Mis. 58–23 not human, in origin and *d·*.

our
Mis. 359–25 our *d·* rises only as we rise
Un. 61–24 our *d·* and realization of this

perfection and
Ret. 57–30 perfection and *d·* of metaphysical,

practical
Un. 36–26 interfere with its practical *d·*.
Rud. 6–23 best understood in practical *d·*.
My. 81–24 * It was a practical *d·* of the

prevents the
Pan. 7– 5 and thus prevents the *d·*

Principle and
Mis. 69– 7 Science rests on Principle and *d·*.

progress is
Mis. 235– 8 progress is *d·*, not doctrine.

rule and
Mis. 336–12 insist on the rule and *d·* of
Ret. 94–24 in Principle, rule, and *d·*.

rule, and the
My. 272–14 rule, and the *d·* of this idealism.

rules for
Mis. 307–28 Principle and rules for *d·*.

scientific
Mis. 288–20 would prevent scientific *d·*.
Ret. 40–21 This scientific *d·* so stirred the
Pul. 45–19 * indeed, then, a scientific *d·*.

strong
Un. 43– 3 for any strong *d·* over death,

supreme in
Ret. 28–15 For Spirit to be supreme in *d·*,
Pul. 35–19 For Spirit to be supreme in *d·*,

teaching and
Ret. 25– 7 Jesus' teaching and *d·*,

that
My. 79–22 * higher pedestal by that *d·*

their
Mis. 215–23 at the beginning of their *d·*;

thereof
Mis. 30– 2 some feeble *d·* thereof,
55– 4 understanding and *d·* thereof
156–19 daily Christian *d·* thereof.
Ret. 87–13 in the orderly *d·* thereof.
Peo. 5–20 *d·* thereof in healing the sick.
My. 348–20 the *d·* thereof was made,

this
Mis. 105– 7 this *d·* is the foundation of C. S.
Man. 92– 6 nothing can substitute this *d·*.
Rud. 11–19 This *d·* is based on a true

understanding and
Mis. 55– 4 least understanding and *d·* thereof
Man. 19– 3 understanding and *d·* of divine Truth,

wonderful
My. 95–29 * wonderful *d·* of religious faith

Mis. 252–15 My proof of these . . . is *d·*,
346– 3 *d·* of moral and spiritual healing
365–12 for it rests alone on *d·*.
Un. 36–16 is the *d·*, according to C. S.,
No. 13– 4 *d·* of moral and physical growth,
18– 8 *d·* of God's supremacy
'01. 25–14 *d·* of matter minus, and God all,
Hea. 3– 6 a *d·*, more than a doctrine.
My. 25– 4 * of this feature of the *d·*.
47–22 * *d·* of the knowledge of God,
92–20 * so huge and concrete a *d·*
221– 9 the *d·* which was to destroy sin,

demonstrations

Mis. 4–26 faith to make your *d·*."
48– 1 I measure its *d·* as a false belief,
70–28 wonderful *d·* of divine power,
105– 5 Master's individual *d·* over sin,
172– 1 to keep their *d·* modest,
187–18 the later teachings and *d·* of
263–25 Science is hampered by immature *d·*,
Un. 31– 8 *d·* of Jesus annulled the
Pul. 51–29 * other great *d·* of religious belief
'01. 17–11 my first *d·* of C. S.
My. 103–24 *d·* of our great Master
111–31 attest with their individual *d·*.

demonstratively

Mis. 288– 3 must be *d·* right yourself,

demonstrator

'00. 6– 3 Only the *d·* can mistake or
'01. 26– 3 great teacher, preacher, and *d·*
My. 219–23 great *d·* of C. S., said,
338–25 visible discoverer, founder, *d·*,
348–27 The human *d·* of this Science

demoralize

Ret. 81– 9 tends to *d·* mortals,

demoralized

My. 122–20 our sense of Truth is not *d·*,

demoralizes

Ret. 71–28 *d·* the person who does this,

demoralizing

Mis. 162–26 *d·* his motives and Christlikeness,

Demosthenes

Mis. 345– 4 place where *D·* had pleaded

demurrer

My. 307–17 I entered a *d·* which rebuked him.

den

Pul. 49– 1 * which Mrs. Eddy calls her *d·*

denial

Mis. 31– 2 malpractice is a bland *d·* of Truth,
183–24 is a *d·* of man's spiritual sonship ;
194–10 this *d·* would dishonor that office
221–19 *d·* of this fact in one instance
221–21 Such *d·* dethrones demonstration,
221–23 Such *d·* also contradicts the doctrine
247–32 must be met, . . . with a *d·* by Truth.
Un. 25–14 This *d·* enlarges the human intellect
31–16 in the *d·* of matter,
45–12 These falsities need a *d·*.
No. 29–16 a *d·* of God's power?
42–22 *D·* of the authorship of "S. and H.
My. 275–12 chapter sub-title

denials

Pul. 83– 9 * not be disheartened by a thousand *d·*

denied

Mis. 7–26 Oftentimes we are *d·* the
184–20 he has *d·* the power of Truth,
199–17 *d·* and defined their superstition.
348–31 afterwards *d·* this and objected to
Ret. 25–16 His corporeality I *d·*.
35–24 and *d·* the perpetuity of Jesus'
Un. 21–12 your personal senses be *d·*.
50– 5 something to be *d·* and destroyed
54–13 Hence the fact must be *d·*;
Pul. 46– 5 * at C. S. headquarters this is *d·* ;
Pan. 5–27 He *d·* it, cast it out of mortal mind,
'00. 14– 2 hast not *d·* my name.— *Rev.* 3 : 8.
My. 195–13 We must resign . . . what we are *d·*,

denies

Mis. 31–14 *d·* the grand verity of this Science,
102–23 supports harmony, *d·* suffering,
211–32 when the heart *d·* it,
221–14 if he *d·* it, the good effect is lost.
330–27 boasts and begs, and God *d·*
Un. 31–19 all that *d·* and defies Spirit,
39–16 and *d·* spiritual sonship ;
Rud. 12–12 *d·* the Principle of Mind-healing.
No. 18– 4 lie that *d·* Him as All-in-all,
24– 9 *d·* . . . both matter and evil.
'01. 24– 2 He *d·* the existence of matter,
Hea. 15–17 admits in . . . what he *d·* in proof?

denominated

Mis. 112–15 *d·*, in extreme cases, moral idiocy.
190–28 "devil" is *d·* Abaddon ;— *Luke* 11 : 14.
Ret. 25–14 Soul I *d·* *substance*.

denomination (see also denomination's)

Mis. 168–26 * would speak before the Scientist *d·*
314– 3 Sunday services of our *d·*
334–21 reduce this falsity to its proper *d·*,
382–20 first church edifice of this *d·*
383– 3 all the churches of the C. S. *d·*.
Man. 34–20 member from a different *d·*
45–21 read in branch churches of this *d·*
48–23 The periodicals of our *d·*
63–15 Each church of the C. S. *d·*
Ret. 28–18 to their own mental *d·*,
Un. 35–10 Reduced to its proper *d·*,
Pul. 21–20 between our *d·* and other sects,
24–20 * and the first pastor of this *d·*."
31– 3 * the Founder of this *d·*
40–14 * Mary Baker Eddy, Founder of the *D·*
41–13 * members of the *d·* gathered ;
45– 9 * a publication of the new *d·* :
64– 4 * the first pastor of this *d·*."
70–10 * first pastor of the C. S. *d·*,
'00. 1–10 this first church of our *d·*,
2– 3 Churches of this *d·* are
'01. 11–15 churches of the C. S. *d·*,
34–24 Bible and the textbook of our *d·* ;

denomination
   My.   8– 4   * "Our *d·* is palpably outgrowing
          8–28   * Leader of our religious *d·*
        26–24   animus of our church and *d·*.
        65– 6   * Mother Church of the *d·*,
        70– 7   * any other *d·* in the world,
        75–28   * been dedicated by this *d·*
        90–27   * the Founder of a great *d·*
        96– 4   * The Mother Church of that *d·*.
        99–24   * *d·* has grown with a rapidity
      141–11   * communion service of the C. S. *d·*,
      148–10   In the annals of our *d·*
      151–13   injustice done . . . to this *d·*
      151–14   when it no longer blesses this *d·*.
      189–25   first church edifice of our *d·*
      194–17   attested by the Founder of your *d·*
      196– 4   the first edifice of our *d·*
      199–21   between the churches of our *d·*

denominational
   Mis. 32–25   *d·* and social organizations
      155–28   reading-matter for our *d·* organ.
      382–28   our *d·* form of Sunday services,
   My. 139–21   the *d·* to the doctrinal,
      173–18   exercises at the *d·* headquarters

denomination's
   My. 90–30   * *d·* peculiar department of healing,

denominations
   Mis. 21–13   trend of other Christian *d·*
   Man. 34–17   Free from Other *D·*.
       59–17   persons of all sects and *d·*
   Ret. 42–10   clergymen of other *d·* listened
   Pul. 21–15   in all *d·* of religion,
      21–26   unity with churches of other *d·*
      47– 1   * many clergymen of other *d·*
   '01. 23–13   change of the *d·* of mathematics ;
      30– 2   as all other religious *d·* have
   My. v– 9   * extended . . . by other Christian *d·*,
      53–23   * by clergymen of different *d·*,
      74–16   * other *d·* might profit by
      84– 7   * It is a rule in some *d·*
      91– 7   * a good example to other *d·*
      95–21   * clergymen of other *d·* are avowing
     112– 8   Our religious *d·* interpret the

denominator
   Mis. 108–13   reducing its claim to its proper *d·*,

denotes
   Pan. 3–28   *d·* the celestial harmony of
   My. 220–14   Injustice *d·* the absence of law.

denounce
   Pan. 6– 5   let us continue to *d·* evil
   My. 210–21   and only *d·* error in general,

denounced
   Mis. 57–15   is seen when Truth, God, *d·* it,
   Ret. 65–16   hence Jesus *d·* it.
   '01. 25–17   *d·* all such gilded sepulchres
   My. 218–19   ultimates in what Jesus *d·*,

denounces
   Mis. 122–17   Holy Writ *d·* him that declares,
   '00. 13–11   he *d·* the Nicolaitan church.

dens
   Un. 11– 5   beard the lions in their *d·*.

densely
   Mis. 168–28   * Hawthorne Hall was *d·* packed,

dented
   My. 105–12   could be *d·* by the finger,

dentist
   My. 314– 2   * second husband, "an itinerant *d·*."
      314–10   considered a rarely skilful *d·*.
      315– 3   * Dr. Patterson, a *d·*, boarded with

dentistry
   Mis. 45–11   in the practice of *d·*.

denunciation
   Ret. 63–12   this *d·* must precede its
   '01. 32–15   aimed deadly, and spared no *d·*.
   My. 104–22   what can atone for the vulgar *d·*

denunciations
   My. 112– 2   always been first met with *d·*.

Denver
   Mis. 152– 2   chapter sub-title
   '00. 1–21   St. Louis, *D·*, Salt Lake City,

Denver (Col.) *News*
   My. 89–21   * [*D· (C·) N·*]

Denver (Col.) *Republican*
   My. 99–10   * [*D· (C·) R·*]

deny
   Mis. 58–11   *d· the evidences of the senses*
      60–12   *to d· the possibility of communion*
     100–11   for Truth to *d·* or to destroy.
     171–13   not to condemn and *d·*, but to

deny
   Mis. 193– 7   Doctrines that *d·* the substance
     194– 8   yet should *d·* the validity or
     198–15   if we *d·* the claims of these senses
     199– 2   *d·* the supposed power of matter to
     335–18   Those who *d·* my wisdom or right
     374–23   doggedly *d·* or frantically affirm
   Ret. 54– 8   *d·* these claims and learn the
     63–11   When we *d·* the authority of sin,
   Un. 10– 3   these so-called existences I *d·*,
     25– 1   If you, O good, *d·* this,
     25– 1   then I *d·* your truthfulness.
     36–21   To *d·* the existence or reality of
     38–22   or to *d·* that He is Life eternal.
     39–21   *d·* the evidence of the material senses,
     46– 7   I do not *d·*, I maintain, the
   Rud. 3–17   they will . . . prescribe drugs, or *d·* God.
     5– 2   but *d·* the testimony of the
   No. 2–11   *d·* self, sense, and take up the cross.
   Pan. 5–22   *d·* it and prove its falsity.
     8– 9   *d·* the self-existence of God?
   '01. 12–15   *d·* the validity and permanence of
     23–25   to *d·*, on received principles of
   Hea. 15–14   why should man *d·* all might to
   Po. 32–16   reason with appetite, pleasures *d·*,
   My. 74–24   * to *d·* them the satisfaction
     217–18   * why do we *d·* the existence of
     217–21   We *d· first* the existence of disease,
     224–25   We would not *d·* their authors a

denying
   Mis. 3–28   deluding reason, *d·* revelation,
     198– 5   *d·* material so-called laws and
     260–21   deluding reason and *d·* revelation,
     333–13   *d·* that God, good, is supreme,
   Un. 25–12   *d·* Truth and its demonstration
   No. 6–14   healed by *d·* its validity ;
   My. 143–14   *d·* or asserting the personality
     211– 5   by *d·* that this evil exists.

Deo volente
   Mis. 67–21   you shall, *D· v·*, inform them
   My. 123–19   I will see you in this hall, *D· v·*;

depart
   Mis. 21–13   to *d·* from the trend of
     215– 7   let us *d·* from the material sense
     270– 6   Shall we *d·* from the example of
     270–20   We cannot *d·* from his holy example,
     316–13   and *d·* farther from the primitives
     398–19   White as wool, ere they *d·*,
     399–21   Lifted higher, we *d·*,
   Man. 50–14   If a member of this Church shall *d·*
     94–12   opportunity to *d·* in quiet *thought*
   Ret. 46–25   White as wool, ere they *d·*,
     90–12   and *d·* on their united pilgrimages.
   Un. 24– 5   to *d·* from the supreme sense of
   Pul. 16– 6   Joyous, risen, we *d·*
     17–24   White as wool, ere they *d·*
   '01. 4– 6   To *d·* from the rule of mathematics
   Po. 14–23   White as wool, ere they *d·*,
     24– 7   A sign that never can *d·*.
     31– 9   *D·* ! Glad Easter glows with gratitude
     76– 5   Lifted higher, we *d·*,
   My. 161– 9   "*D·* from me, — *Luke* 13 : 27.
     228– 9   yet *d·* from Christ's teachings.

departed
   Mis. 34–15   If the *d·* were to communicate with
     34–19   than we, . . . can go to the *d·*
     42–17   change whereby we meet the dear *d·*,
     60–13   *d· friends — dead only in belief*
     171–15   supposed to have *d·* from the earth,
     385– 9   poem
   No. 12–22   in nothing else has she *d·* from the
   '01. 17– 7   prodigal — *d·* from his better self
     22–29   those who have *d·* from its
   Hea. 5–14, 15   think the *d·* are not *d·*,
   Po. 17– 1   Blest beings *d·* ! Ye echoes at dawn !
     34–22   O'er joys *d·*, unforgotten love.
     page 48   poem
   My. 97–28   * have mostly *d·*, but Boston
     267–17   the *d·* enter heaven in proportion to
     290– 5   The *d·* Queen's royal and imperial
     302– 7   a corpse, whence mind has *d·*.
     308–10   my duty to be just to the *d·*

departeth
   Mis. 335–30   whoso *d·* from divine Science,

departing
   Mis. 19–14   is daily *d·* from evil ;
     101– 4   *d·* from the thraldom of the senses
   Ret. 58– 2   then *d·* from this statement
   Pul. 83–30   * and he, *d·*, left his scepter
   My. 82–28   * *d·* with such remarkable expedition,
     270–18   words of our dear, *d·* Saviour,
     292– 9   comfort the living as it did the *d·*.

department

Mis. 115– 7 deficiency in this d·.
242–15 At present, I am in another d·
Man. 91–12 a free course in this d·
Rud. 15–15 to fill . . . the d· of healing.
My. 90–30 * denomination's peculiar d· of

departments

Rud. 15–16 should have separate d·,

departs

Mis. 268–11 who d· from Mind to matter,
324–23 Stealing cautiously away . . . he d· ;
325–28 As he d·, he sees robbers
'00. 6– 9 Any mystery in C. S. d· when
My. 220–25 which d· from the instructions
254– 1 mysticism d·, heaven opens,

departure

Mis. 71–21 is a d· from divine law ;
136– 2 it was a d·, socially, publicly,
234–28 In this new d· of metaphysics,
247–10 to furnish a single instance of d·
Man. 41–13 A d· from this rule
44– 4 A d· from the spirit or letter of this
50–13 D· from Tenets.
Ret. 78–21 d· from the Science of Mind-healing.
Pul. 31– 9 * and take, as the point of d·,
66–21 * d· from long respected views
Rud. 16–16 d· from Science is an irreparable
'01. 2–22 a d· from the direct line in Christ
4– 7 a d· from the Principle and rule
6– 5 Here is the d·.
6–25 Our d· from theological personality
14–10 Our only d· from ecclesiasticism
19–15 flat d· from Jesus' practice
23–11 This d·, however, from the
'02. 8–28 a d· from God, or His lost likeness,
My. 151–27 This d· from Spirit, . . . was
181–10 d· from matter to Spirit,
197– 1 comes with the d· of sin.
289–14 in the sudden d· of the late
300–29 C. S. is not a d· from
331– 8 * to the train on her d·,
348–11 d· from divine Science sprang from
348–14 writer's d· from such a religion
364– 6 d· from this golden rule is

departures

Mis. 265–29 growing out of the d· from Science
278–32 and led to some startling d·
Ret. 57–24 Human systems . . . are d· from C. S.

depend

Mis. 77– 1 *Did the salvation of the eunuch d·*
316–10 d· on the fitness of things,
Pul. 13–26 must d· upon sin's obduracy.
Pan. 4–10 d· on conditions of matter,
My. 226–23 d· on Him for your existence.
244–25 This, however, must d· on results.
342–11 * d· upon the osseous structure ;

depended

Ret. 14– 9 salvation and condemnation d·,

dependence

Ret. 28–14 and d· on spiritual things.
Pul. 35–18 and d· on spiritual things.
Peo. 3–26 such as d· on personal pardon

dependent

Mis. 28– 5 d· on the beliefs that
Ret. 59–21 mutually d·, each on the other,
No. 3–12 People d· on the rules of this
5–14 d· on material conditions.
'02. 15– 9 while d· on the income from the

depending

Pul. 37–22 * d· on any one personality.

depends

Mis. 47–29 d· upon what one accepts as
88–28 d· upon what kind of a doctor it is.
230– 2 Success in life d· upon persistent
Man. 31– 9 prosperity of C. S. largely d·.
Pul. 82–26 * d· the welfare of their husbands,
My. 108– 4 allopath who d· upon drugs.

depict

Ret. 76–26 sees each mortal in an impersonal d·.
Pul. 26– 7 * beyond the power of words to d·.

depicted

Mis. 7–20 d· in some future time upon the
142–26 symbols of freemasonry d· on the
My. 42– 1 * d· its form and comeliness.
136– 6 as d· in the chapter Atonement
179–19 as d· in the life of our Lord,
296–28 she d· its rooms, guests,

depictive

Po. 43– 1 picture d· of Isaiah xi.

depicts

Rud. 11–27 never d· the muscular, vascular,

deplorable

Mis. 107–24 this d· mental state is moral idiocy.
'01. 15–14 d· sight is to contemplate the

deplorably

Mis. 25–25 sick are more d· situated than

deplored

Ret. 7–19 * His death will be d·,

deportment

My. 122–12 The d· of its dear members

deposit

Mis. 159–16 where I d· certain recollections
159–20 Here I d· the gifts that
Man. 76– 2 should remain on safe d·,
78–20 keep on d· the sum of $500

deposits

My. 135–10 investments, d·, expenditures,
137–13 investments, d·, expenditures,

depot

Ret. 38–17 We met at the Eastern d· in Lynn,

depraved

Mis. 354–10 When d· reason is preferred to
Rud. 7–13 material, fallen, sick, d·,

depravity

Mis. 2–10 admit the total d· of mortals,
112–32 exemplification of total d·,

deprecate

Mis. 97–12 Such suppositional healing I d·.
284–29 I d· personal animosities

deprecates

Mis. 371–13 he who d· their condition

depressing

Mis. 133–26 In the midst of d· care and labor

depression

Mis. 51– 6 *accompanied by great mental d·,*

deprivation

My. 21–16 * every seeming trial and d·

deprive

Mis. 281– 8 could neither d· me of something nor
291–20 could not d· them of it.
My. vii– 6 * not unwittingly made to d·

deprives

Mis. 14–29 d· evil of all power,
41– 7 It d· those who practise it
Un. 48–10 d· death of its sting,

depth

Mis. 8–14 Can height, or d·, or any other
122–13 in the d· of the sea'' — *Matt. 18 : 6.*
My. 9–12 * declare the d· of our affection
81–21 * the d· of sincerity,
128– 2 d· of desire can find no other

depths

Mis. 81–28 out of the d· of ignorance
111–11 like Peter, they launch into the d·,
113–14 d· of perdition by his own consent.
211–13 "Out of the d· — *Psal. 130 : 1.*
Ret. 73– 9 great fact leads into profound d·.
My. 36–22 * have been delivered from the d·
37– 8 * d· of tenderest gratitude,
164–19 buried in the d· of the unseen,
194–28 guard you . . . through the d· ;
200–27 spare this plunge, lessen its d·,
258–24 all d· of love, grief, death, and
290–16 "Out of the d· — *Psal. 130 : 1.*

deputy

Rud. 1–18 (in court, for example) by d·

deranged

Pan. 8– 3 causes a man to be mentally d· ;

Derby's, J. C.

Pul. 78–26 * window of J. C. D· jewelry store.

deride

Mis. 126–28 to d· her is to incur the penalty
Man. 94–10 who goes to hear and d· truth,

derided

No. 41– 7 work most d· and envied

derision

Mis. 126–32 shall have them in d·.'' — *Psal. 2 : 4.*

derisively

My. 162–17 This was spoken d·.

derivation

Pan. 2–12 Webster's d· of the English word

derivative

Mis. 14–25 cannot be, the d· of good.
14–26 neither a primitive nor a d·,

derive

Mis. 33–20 recognize the help they d·

derived

Mis.	76– 2	self-created or d· capacity
	103–21	Any inference of the divine d· from
	162–15	his power, d· from Spirit,
	244–17	d· from the life and teachings of
	302–26	d· from making his copy,
	316–26	could have d· most benefit from
Un.	6– 7	higher selfhood, d· from God,
No.	10– 1	* and from which it is d·.''
Pan.	2–10	d· from two Greek words
'01.	3–14	definition d· from the Bible,
Hea.	3–15	was d· from the word good.

derives

My.	189–15	government of divine Love d· its

dernier ressort

Mis.	357– 5	the schoolroom is the d· r·.

descant

Un.	60–11	yet we d· upon sickness, sin,
No.	46–12	Theologians d· pleasantly upon

descanting

'01.	24– 9	d· on the virtues of tar-water,

Descartes

No.	22– 4	Leibnitz, D·, Fichte,

descend

Ret.	85–11	angelic thoughts ascend and d·,

descendants

No.	46–16	As dutiful d· of Puritans,

descended

Pul.	10–25	which d· like day-spring
My.	97–25	* Christian Scientists who d· upon

descending

My.	342– 3	* lady slowly d· the stairs.

descent

Mis.	323–10	d· and ascent are beset with
Chr.	55–20	without mother, without d·,— Heb. 7 : 3.

describe

Mis.	376–17	d· the brave splendor of a
My.	313–25	I never went into a trance to d·

described

Ret.	15–24	cases d· had been treated
	25–18	the temporal, I d· as unreal.
Un.	28– 5	has not descried nor d· Soul.
Pul.	60–20	* and is d· as containing
	62–22	* from those d· down to little sets
	76– 6	* d· as ''particularly beautiful,
My.	95–16	* were d· in the newspapers
	315–24	dummy heretofore d·?

describes

Mis.	259–20	rhythm that the Scripture d·,
My.	271–12	* chapter sub-title

describing

Mis.	24–28	or rather the allegory d· it.
My.	105–25	a work d· my system of healing.
	309–21	d· the Baker homestead

descried

Un.	28– 4	has not d· nor described Soul.

description

Mis.	306– 2	* send fullest historical d·.
	376– 9	* from a d·, in The Galaxy,
Man.	47–18	shall not include a d· of
Un.	21– 1	we read the apostle's d· of
Pul.	23– 4	* D· OF THE MOST UNIQUE
	57–11	* From the d· we judge that
My.	v–24	* record for a work of this d· ;
	13–13	According to his d·, the church
	67– 4	* chapter sub-title
	150– 5	Pliny gives the following d·
	297– 6	said d· of her soul-visit,

descriptions

Mis.	7–19	These d· carry fears to many
Man.	48–23	d· of our church edifices,
My.	306–23	his scribblings were d· of

descriptive

Mis.	379– 7	d· of the general appearance,

desert

Mis.	81–23	in the d· of earthly joy ;
	150–22	and the d· a resting-place
	154–26	never d· the post of spiritual
	246–22	to yield its prey the peace of a d·,
	325–24	grieve Him in the d·.'' — Psal. 78 : 40.
Pul.	14–15	weary wanderers, athirst in the d·
'00.	15–16	it waits in the d·
My.	214–29	To d· the Cause never
	332–10	* but did not d· her

desertion

My.	314–15	granted on the ground of d·,

deserts

'01.	3–25	d· its premise, and expresses
My.	167–10	Love . . . which never d· us.
	361– 2	and though it be through d·

deserve

Mis.	295– 2	which d· and elicit brief comment.
My.	160–10	than that we d· it.

deserved

My.	83–22	* takes on a tone of d· satisfaction,
	258– 4	lifts a system . . . to d· fame?
	284– 4	accorded me more than is d·,

deserves

Mis.	48– 7	Mr. Carpenter d· praise for his
Pul.	50– 4	* he d· to have a home and
	51–27	* get the share of attention it d·,
Hea.	4–12	d· to be punished,
Peo.	9–15	sin that d· to be punished
My.	130– 7	and punished as it d·.
	150– 6	* ''Doing what d· to be written,
	150– 7	* writing what d· to be read ;

deserving

My.	46–20	* obedient, d· disciples.

Desha

Mary

Mis.	306–10	* signature

Miss Mary

Mis.	306–15	* notification . . . to Miss Mary D·,

desideratum

Mis.	355–10	To consummate this d·,

design

Mis.	205–24	all periods in the divine d·.
	249–23	of their mental d· to do this
Un.	57– 3	the d· of the material senses
Pul.	24–10	* the d· a Romanesque tower
	25–26	* silver lamps of Roman d·,
Rud.	3–18	in its nature, method, and d·.
My.	10– 9	* embodying the best of d·,
	36–26	* all the beauty of color and d·,
	68– 3	* the beauty and strength of the d·.
	85–28	* symmetrical and appropriate d·.
	190– 3	merciful d· of divine Love,
	279–10	all periods in the d· of God.
	347–10	exquisite d· of boughs

designate

Ret.	14–21	could not d· any precise time.
Pul.	15–13	d· those as unfaithful stewards

designated

Man.	112– 1	branch churches are d· by number,
My.	108–23	our Master d· as his best work,
	137–20	I have d· by my last will,

designation

Man.	102–10	D· of Deeds.
My.	268–30	the d· man meaning woman as well,

designed

Mis.	84–24	discipline of the flesh is d· to
	262– 1	is d· to bring health and happiness
	351–13	falsehood d· to stir up strife
Man.	17–10	church d· to commemorate the word
	19– 2	d· to be built on the Rock, Christ ;
Ret.	53– 5	d· to bear aloft the standard of
Pul.	25–10	* d· for the exclusive use of
	28– 1	* d· to be wholly typical of the
My.	46–10	church d· to commemorate the word
	244–11	This opportunity is d· to impart
	353–11	d· to put on record the

designs

Pul.	26– 1	* cut glass in decorative d·,
	28– 6	* decorated with emblematic d·,
	76– 8	* floor is of mosaic in elegant d·,
	76–12	* white mahogany in special d·,
No.	39–12	nor bring His d· into mortal modes ;
My.	211–19	tools to carry out the d· of
	212–32	in furtherance of unscrupulous d·.

desirable

Mis.	4– 3	potent and d· remedial agent
	97–10	by no means a d· . . . healer.
	109–20	Their mental state is not d·,
	139–23	I had this d· site transferred
Man.	98– 8	periodical in which it is d· that
Un.	54–21	Satan held it up . . . as something d·
My.	14–29	* it is d· that the contributions
	121–15	peace is d·, and plain dealing is a

desire (noun)

and fear

No.	11– 2	human will, intellect, d·, and fear,

and motives

No.	12–13	The same affection, d·, and motives

and thought

Pul.	55–20	* has its origin in d· and thought.

awakened

No.	39–20	an awakened d· to be and do good.

desire (noun)

carnal
  Mis. 182–16 neither from dust nor carnal *d*.
daily
  My. 15–13 daily *d*. that the Giver of all
depth of
  My. 128– 2 depth of *d*. can find no other
devout
  '02. 6–21 all devout *d*., virtually petition,
due to a
  My. 170– 6 was due to a *d*. on my part
for notoriety
  Mis. 296–26 from a *d*. for notoriety and a
for services
  My. 54–21 * *d*. for services was so great
for something
  Ret. 31–10 *d*. for something higher
heart's
  Mis. 276– 9 my heart's *d*. met the demand.
hope and
  My. 9–16 * modestly renew the hope and *d*.
human
  Mis. 317–20 Human *d*. is inadequate to adjust
        360– 1 Meekness, moderating human *d*.,
  My. 3– 7 not alone in accord with human *d*.
        292–21 the effect of one human *d*.
humble
  '01. 14– 4 Publican's wail won his humble *d*.,
  My. 334–22 Publican's wail won his humble *d*.,
its
  Mis. 127–16 to receive the answer to its *d*. ;
  My. 18–13 to receive the answer to its *d*. ;
kindling
  No. 38–26 kindling *d*. loses a part of its
may belie
  No. 40–10 Words may belie *d*.,
my
  Mis. 133–19 my *d*. to set you right on this
        291–17 and is far from my *d*. ;
        310–14 my *d*. is that all shall be
  My. 128– 1 cannot quench my *d*. to say this ;
        159– 8 every pulse of my *d*. for the
        325–13 * my *d*. has never changed.
        352–29 My *d*. is that every
no
  Mis. 198– 2 will have no *d*. to sin.
        321–27 no *d*. to see or to hear what
no time or
  '01. 32–10 no time or *d*. to defame their
prayer is a
  Peo. 9–22 Silent prayer is a *d*., fervent,
quenchless
  Po. 18– 6 unfolding a quenchless *d*.
retain a
  '00. 8–28 retain a *d*. to follow your own
rightful
  Mis. 179– 4 rightful *d*. in the hour of loss,
stronger
  Mis. 235–17 and a stronger *d*. for it.
tender
  My. 292–17 one earnest, tender *d*. works
their
  Mis. 239– 1 due credit for their *d*.,
  My. 213–11 in their *d*. to do right
        284–21 the Veterans indicated their *d*.
thought and
  Mis. 15–10 Christianization — of thought and *d*.,
to be just
  Mis. 132–29 Even the *d*. to be just is a
to testify
  My. 81– 7 * bursting with a *d*. to testify
untamed
  Ret. 31–18 untamed *d*. which breaketh the
worldly
  Mis. 354–29 inflated with worldly *d*.
your
  My. 361–21 * in accordance with your *d*. for

  No. 38–25 All prayer that is *d*. is
  My. 23– 5 * divine Love that prompted the *d*.,
        92–28 * nothing save the *d*. in the human heart
        275–14 (and I trust the *d*. thereof)

desire (verb)

  Mis. 90–15 Do you *d*. to be freed from sin?
        148–25 I specially *d*. that you collect no
        151–17 *d*. beside thee.'' — *Psal.* 73 : 25.
        232–23 would *d*. and demand it,
        274– 4 I *d*. to revise my book
        282–21 If the friends of a patient *d*. you to
        291–12 I *d*. the equal growth and prosperity
        294–22 *d*. to help even such as these.
        310–20 All who *d*. its fellowship,
        363–15 a perfect man would not *d*. to
  Man. 89–19 pupils who so *d*. may apply to
  Ret. 74– 9 for I *d*. never to think of it,

desire (verb)

  Pul. 85–16 * *d*. a better and grander humanity,
        87– 3 * We especially *d*. you to be present
        87–20 more of earth now, than I *d*.,
  '00. 9– 4 "You may do it if you *d*.''
  '02. 13–12 no personal benefit . . . and *d*. none
  My. 12–30 The good they *d*. to do,
        17– 6 *d*. the sincere milk — *I Pet.* 2 : 2.
        42–14 * *d*. to improve this opportunity
        44–28 * *d*. to express their continued
        138–15 persons whom I *d*. to see
        204– 1 not accomplished all you *d*.,
        249–24 The report . . . I *d*. to correct.
        293–31 "What things soever ye *d*., — *Mark* 11 : 24.
        352– 5 * *d*. to express our recognition
        357–13 brethren in New York *d*. to
        358–13 however much I *d*. to read all

desired

  Mis. 86–16 beauty . . . is something to be *d*.
        127– 7 One thing I have greatly *d*.,
        146–21 every reformed mortal that *d*.
        276– 6 all with whom I *d*. to,
        305–14 * *d*. that the largest number of
  Un. 53– 6 and greatly to be *d*.,
  '00. 9–26 I have *d*. to step aside
  '02. 20– 4 bringeth us into the *d*. haven,
  My. 14–17 * further payments . . . were not *d*.
        18– 4 "One thing I have greatly *d*.,
        40– 3 * She has *d*. for years to
        164– 3 retirement I so much *d*.
        292–19 would prevent the result *d*.
        307–20 Truth, which we both *d*. ;
        336– 6 * he *d*. to go to her assistance,

desires

  Mis. 32– 1 if indeed he *d*. success in this
        37– 5 manifest in all thoughts and *d*.
        50–20 human affections, *d*., and aims,
        71–12 *law of transmission, prenatal d*.,
        155–18 (however much she *d*. thus to do),
        235–11 It gives to the race loftier *d*.
        266–26 in accordance with my students' *d*.,
        282–18 should know that the person . . . *d*. it.
        311–15 My deepest *d*. and daily labors
        356–18 uplifted *d*. of the human heart,
        371–19 Whoever *d*. to say, "good right,
  Man. 69– 3 remain with Mrs. Eddy if she so *d*.,
        100–23 name the Committee if it so *d*.,
  Ret. 79–12 purification of the affections and *d*.
  Pul. 3–23 when all human *d*. are quenched,
  '00. 9–13 Strong *d*. bias human judgment
  My. 12–11 * that his individual *d*.,
        170–22 *d*. of thine heart. — *Psal.* 37 : 4.
        180–23 drop compliance with their *d*.,
        287–20 wakens lofty *d*., new possibilities,
        359–12 individual who *d*. to inform himself

desiring

  Ret. 47– 7 persons *d*. to enter the College,
        86–17 *d*. growth in the knowledge of Truth,

desirous

  My. 170– 1 *d*. that it should be understood

desist

  Mis. 302–23 *d*. from further copying of my
        358–22 or to *d*. from organizing churches

desk

  Mis. 273–24 applications lying on the *d*.
        283– 7 to enter a house, unlock the *d*.,
        379– 2 and write at his *d*.
  Pul. 42–26 * *d*. was wreathed with ferns

Des Moines

  My. 81–15 * "*D. M*.!" "Glasgow!" "Cuba!"

desolate

  Mis. 231–30 But, alas ! for the *d*. home ;
        326–28 left unto you *d*.'' — *Matt.* 23 : 38.
  Po. 34–14 Divinely *d*. the shrine to paint?
  My. 292–11 mourner at the *d*. home !

desolating

  Mis. 257–27 *d*. the green earth.

desolation

  Mis. 56–18 that shall be brought to *d*.
        81–25 *d*. of human understanding,
        89– 3 is brought to *d*.'' — *Matt.* 12 : 25.
        217–27 shall be brought to *d*.
  Ret. 72– 9 brought into *d*., — *Psal.* 73 : 19.
  No. 5–22 brought to *d*. ;'' — *Luke* 11 : 17.

despair

  Mis. 30– 5 *d*. of ultimately reaching them,
        275–11 looks in dull *d*. at the vacant
  Un. 64–13 the hope . . . must yield to *d*.,
  Po. 24– 4 Dissolving death, *d*. !
  My. 150– 2 Therefore *d*. not nor murmur,
        350–13 Lift from *d*. the struggler

despairing
Mis. 327–18 *D·* of gaining the summit,

despatch
Pul. 74–13 *d·* is given me, calling for
My. 33– 2 * *d·* from the members of the church
44–16 * read the following *d·*,
44–20 * The *d·* was as follows :
65–15 * pledged with the readiness and *d·*
184– 3 Have just received your *d·*.

despatches
Man. 67–20 congratulatory *d·* or letters
My. 79–17 * According to the *d·*,
223–11 Letters and *d·* from individuals

desperate
Mis. 177– 8 Large numbers, in *d·* malice,
Ret. 41– 4 Many were the *d·* cases
Pan. 10–20 *d·* cases of intemperance,

despicable
Mis. 97–13 more *d·* than all other

despise
Mis. 269– 8 and *d·* the other. — *Matt.* 6 : 24.
My. 356–23 and *d·* the other. — *Matt.* 6 : 24.

despising
Ret. 22–12 *d·* the shame, — *Heb.* 12 : 2.
My. 258–15 *d·* the shame, — *Heb.* 12 : 2.

despite
Ret. 45– 5 *D·* the prosperity of my church,
Un. 11–13 *d·* the boastful sense of
Pul. 59–30 * (*d·* the snowstorm)
Pan. 8– 1 *d·* of Mind, or by the consent of
Peo. 9–20 *d·* the authority of Jesus
My. 91–23 * *d·* the obstacles put in the way
153– 1 *d·* our winter snows.

despitefully
Mis. 11–22 persecute and *d·* use one,
147–12 hate you and *d·* use you
Man. 41–10 However *d·* used and misrepresented
Ret. 29– 4 "*d·* use you — *Matt.* 5 : 44.
My. 6–11 men may revile us and *d·* use us,
52– 5 * loving them that *d·* use her,

despoil
Un. 17–17 *d·* error of its borrowed plumes,

despot
Ret. 11–10 No *d·* bears misrule,
Po. 60– 7 No *d·* bears misrule,

despotic
Mis. 48– 7 its so-called power is *d·*,

despotism
My. 260– 5 The *d·* of material sense

destined
Mis. 148–20 doctrines *d·* for future generations
Man. 3–17 doctrines *d·* for future generations
Pul. 8–28 The children are *d·* to witness
Pul. 33–26 * whose life has been *d·* to more than
'02. 11– 2 Our heavenly Father never *d·*
My. 266–29 C. S. is *d·* to become the one and

destines
Mis. 147–20 *d·* him to do nothing but what is

destinies
Mis. 368–25 working out the *d·* of the damned.
My. 291– 4 Presiding over the *d·* of a nation

destiny
Mis. 1– 4 to him, no higher *d·* dawned
119–17 in the scale against man's high *d·*.
232–12 standard . . . that regulates human *d·*.
333–30 Chaldee hung his *d·* out upon
Ret. 48–21 fulfilled its high and noble *d·*,
No. 34–17 endeavor to crush . . . its divine *d·*.
45–23 and so fulfil her *d·*.
46–19 Man has a noble *d·* ;
46–20 full-orbed significance of this *d·*
Po. 78– 9 star whose *d·* none may outrun ;
My. 122– 3 *d·* more grand than can issue from
229–30 Truth is strong with *d·* ;

destitute
Mis. 76– 2 *d·* of . . . derived capacity to sin.
Un. 49–22 Being *d·* of Principle,
50–18 Like evil, it is *d·* of Mind,
No. 16–13 *d·* of time and space ;

destroy
Mis. 4–30 but to *d·* sin in mortal thought.
24–31 thus *d·* any supposed effect
27– 6 conclusions that *d·* their premise
28– 6 *D·* the belief that you can walk,
28–14 death does not *d·* the beliefs
31–19 so *d·* his power to be or to do good,
37–20 God can and does *d·* the
40–17 power of Truth to *d·* error,
45– 8 *d·* the necessity for ether
46– 7 to *d·* the appearance of evil

destroy
Mis. 47–22 Truth does not *d·* but substantiates
56– 5 disorganization would *d·* Spirit
60– 8 is the only way to *d·* them ;
73–17 these conditions *d·* the belief.
85–29 tends to *d·* error :
97– 1 to *d·* the power of the flesh ;
97– 4 and *d·* mortal discord with
100–11 for Truth to deny or to *d·*.
105– 3 disdain the fears and *d·* the discords
105–28 *D·* the thought of sin, sickness,
105–29 and you *d·* their existence.
116– 1 *d·* your own sensitiveness to the
157–27 Error has no power but to *d·* itself.
193–13 casts out error, and will *d·* death.
201–11 its powerlessness to *d·* good,
209–13 that *d·* its more dangerous pleasures.
209–19 *d·* the peace of a false sense.
254–26 will come and *d·* — *Mark.* 12 : 9.
257–27 Cyclones kill and *d·*,
261–19 to *d·* the law," — *Matt.* 5 : 17.
334–25 Can belief *d·* belief?
352–20 enable one to *d·* it and its effects.
365–11 If C. S. lacked . . . it would *d·* itself ;
366–27 To *d·* sin and its sequence,
Man. 91– 3 but shall *d·* this paper.
Ret. 55– 4 sufficient knowledge of error to *d·* it
63– 9 to *d·* this belief and save him
Un. 9– 2 *D·* the mental sense of the disease,
9– 3 *D·* the sense of sin,
18– 8 and *d·* everything that is unlike
18–20 eventually . . . every supposition of
20–17 then see if this Love does not *d·*
25–19 *Evil.* . . . I give life, and I can *d·* life.
35– 6 *D·* the belief, and the
49–27 relinquish, lest it *d·* them.
54– 8 does not *d·* the so-called fact of the
62–15 *D·* this sense of sin,
62–16 *D·* this trinity of error,
Pul. 3– 5 "*D·* this temple, — *John* 2 : 19.
Rud. 5–21 *d·* this belief of seeing with the
5–26 *D·* the five senses as
10–25 an error which Truth will *d·*.
No. 5–17 material conditions can and do *d·*
6– 3 attempt to *d·* the realities of
30–16 could not *d·* our woes totally if
31–15 *d·* the works of — *I John* 3 : 8.
'00. 3–19 would *d·* this man's goodness.
13– 1 ready to *d·* the unity and
'01. 9–21 art thou come to *d·* us? — *Mark* 1 : 24.
9–25 they disturb the carnal and *d·* it ;
13–10 take possession of us and *d·* us,
13–18 *d·* the conception of sin as
13–19 and you *d·* the fear
'02. 5–23 to *d·* the law, — *Matt.* 5 : 17.
5–24 not come to *d·*, — *Matt.* 5 : 17.
6– 8 Love and Truth *d·* this
16–26 they never *d·* one iota of hypocrisy,
Hea. 8– 5 that *d·* error and death.
18– 1 *d·* their effects upon the body,
My. 132–24 will also rebuke and *d·* disease,
132–25 *d·* the belief of life in matter.
161– 5 would *d·* himself eternally,
161–18 to *d·* its erroneous claims.
217–31 not to *d·* the law of being,
218– 9 to *d·* all disease and
219–24 to *d·* the law, — *Matt.* 5 : 17.
219–25 not come to *d·*, — *Matt.* 5 : 17.
221– 9 demonstration which was to *d·* sin,
269–25 not *d·* the fruits of — *Mal.* 3 : 11.
296–14 to harm, to hinder, or to *d·*
301–28 Drugs cannot . . . *d·* disease
323–24 * blessing those who would *d·* you

destroyed
Mis. 37–22 sin of every sort, is *d·* by Truth.
42–13 or *d·* this last enemy,
58– 9 When the belief . . . is *d·*,
67–23 discerned, disarmed, and *d·*.
118–19 until all error is *d·*
194– 4 sickness, disease, and death are *d·* ;
210– 6 when found out, is two-thirds *d·*,
213–13 evil which, if seen, can be *d·*.
302–21 each and all *d·* the copies
338–13 but cancels not sin until it be *d·*,
343–20 not always *d·* by the first uprooting ;
352–30 uncovered before it can be *d·*,
355–14 Error found out is two-thirds *d·*,
356– 7 that they be *d·* through suffering ;
381–29 and their unlawful existence *d·*,
Ret. 64– 5 *d·* by the supremacy of good.
64–28 illusion, error, may be *d·* ;
Un. 11–18 and *d·* human pride by
15–12 If man must be *d·* by the
50– 5 something to be denied and *d·*
Pul. 81–17 * not as the moth to be *d·*
No. 29–21 sin, disease, and death are *d·*.

destroyed
No. 30– 5   will not let sin go until it is d·,
'01. 13–24   never punishes it only as it is d·,
16– 6   till the sin is d·.
Peo. 9–15   can be d· only through suffering.
My. 108–22   if they did . . . they would be d·.
111– 5   cannot be d· by false psychics,
130–18   lie left to itself is not so soon d·
160–27   sinner is consumed, — his sins d·.
207–13   * by which sin and sickness are d·
211–28   cause . . . is found out and d·.

destroyer
Mis. 210–26   save him from his d·.
My. 161– 5   The intentional d· of others
161–28   avenging itself on its d·,

destroyers
No. 11– 3   nor d· of life or its harmonies.

destroying
Mis. 40– 7   Truth is as effectual in d· sickness
70–18   sin was d· itself,
185–13   d· all suffering,
214–28   prevent the possibility of d· the
261–21   by Truth's d· error.
352–18   in d· this belief.
Ret. 57– 8   for the purpose of d· discord.
71–30   will end in d· health and morals.
94–12   divine mercy, d· all error.
Un. 47– 1   d· sin, sickness, and death,
No. 30– 2   d· all sense of sin and death.
Pan. 15– 2   d· millions of her money,
'01. 30–19   d· all lower considerations.
Peo. 6–22   d· sin, sickness, and death ;
My. 126– 3   purpose of the d· angel,
194– 9   healing sickness and d· sin,
265–18   mitigating and d· sin, disease, and

destroys
Mis. 3–23   d· these material elements
14–20   that good, . . . forcibly d·.
14–30   d· all error, sin, sickness,
41– 8   d· their own possibility of
78– 4   d· all sense of sin, sickness, and
101–24   This virtually d· matter and evil,
102–23   denies suffering, and d· it
105–15   d· the too common sense of
107–30   so severe that it d· them,
184–21   d· his self-deceived sense
189–11   antidotes and d· the errors of
189–25   d· sin, disease, and death.
191–21   d· all consistent supposition of
194–26   in the Truth that d· all error,
235– 5   to reflect Him who d· death
260–17   d· any suppositional or
283–29   mandate of Truth which d· all error.
297– 8   d· the appetite for alcoholic drinks.
336–23   heals disease and sin and d· death !
Ret. 62– 8   A demonstration of . . . d· evil.
67–14   reforms the sinner and d· sin.
Un. 4– 7   Truth d· every phase of error.
4–11   d· our sense of imperfection,
32–12   d· all sense of matter as substance,
48–10   heals all my ills, d· my iniquities,
54–14   if . . . then sin d· the at-one-ment,
56–12   C. S. first eliminates and then d·.
Rud. 3–20   d· the mental error made manifest
No. 2–24   Dishonesty d· one's ability to heal
4–12   d· the feasibility of disease ;
13– 2   d· sin quickly and utterly.
30– 8   God's law reaches and d· evil
30– 9   He need not know the evil He d·,
32–22   domination of good d· the
Pan. 11–24   good supreme d· all sense of evil,
'00. 6–21   which d· his false appetites
'01. 4– 7   To depart from . . . d· the proof of
4– 9   d· the ability to demonstrate
10–23   whereby good d· evil,
13–12   such a sense of its nullity as d· it.
13–16   d· it on the very basis of
18–27   if God d· the popular triad
Peo. 9–27   d· discord with the higher and
My. 119–12   C. S. d· such tendency.
119–23   d· the false sense with the
185–21   d· the last enemy, death.
212–25   d· the true sense of Science,
233–22   d· his peace in error,
278–20   civilization d· such illusions
288–27   through love that d· sin.
(see also error, Truth)

destructibility
Un. 50– 1   notion of the d· of Mind

destruction
Mis. 10–23   This d· is a moral chemicalization,
32– 2   in this broad road to d·.
40– 7   as in the d· of sin.

destruction
Mis. 55–22   in the final d· of all that
56–18   final d· of this false belief
82–13   after the d· of mortal mind
215– 1   and the final d· of error
237–22   can only work out its own d· ;
Man. 15–11   forgiveness of sin in the d· of sin
Ret. 63–13   denunciation must precede its d·.
Un. 1– 7   unto their own d·." — II Pet. 3 : 16
15–13   then his d· comes through the
Rud. 6–18   d· of the evidence of the
No. 6–10   indispensable to the d· of false
23– 1   hinders the d· of evil.
24–20   exposure is nine points of d·.
31–12   which is the sure d· of sin ;
31–13   I insist on the d· of sin
42–10   God's pardon is the d· of
'01. 15–24   * swallowed up in everlasting d·.
My. 13–21   thy life from d· ; — Psal. 103 : 4.
218– 6   the d· of the human body,
219–14   the d· of disease germs.
249–11   let loose for one's own d·.
360– 1   It will be your d· if you

destructive
Mis. 103– 7   materiality, and d· forces,

detail
Mis. 35–26   who explains it in d·.
138– 5   The d· of conforming to society,
148–18   simple, scientific basis, and d·
375–18   * conscientious application to d·,
376– 5   * very closely resemble in d·
Man. 3–15   simple, scientific basis, and d·
Un. 31–22   It can be shown, in d·,
Pul. 46–10   * much is told of herself in d·
My. 320–25   * d· regarding your work,
321–26   * conclusive to me in every d·,

detailed
Mis. 299– 8   I have no time for d· report

details
My. 145– 9   suggested the d· outside and inside
173–26   for arranging the d· and

detains
Pul. 87–24   church's tall tower d· the sun,
'01. 34– 5   interval that d· the patient from

detect
Mis. 112– 9   neither defend the innocent nor d·
'01. 13–27   first d· the claim of sin ;

detected
Un. 57–16   for it was d· and dismissed.

deter
Mis. 236–28   must not d· us from doing our duty,

deteriorates
Ret. 72– 5   d· one's ability to do good,

determination
Mis. 2– 7   d· of mankind to cleave to
My. 273– 8   * remarkable skill, d·, and energy

determine
Mis. 310–23   will d· the action of the church
Man. 101– 2   C. S. Board of Directors shall d·
Ret. 65–27   As well expect to d·, without a
No. 42–17   with power to d· the fact
My. 277–14   characters and lives of men d· the
306–12   Time and goodness d· greatness.

determined
Mis. 224–25   d· not to be offended when no
304– 4   * It has been d· to create a
327–21   d· not to part with their baggage.
My. 11–26   * The location is, therefore, d·.
92– 2   * d· its real position in the
98– 1   * impress the most d· skeptic.
238– 7   can only be d· by personal proof.

determines
Pul. 80–29   * d· where we shall be hereafter
No. 6–19   Science d· the evidence in both
My. 117– 4   d· the right or the wrong of
270–24   What we love d· what we are.

deterrent
My. 129– 1   a d· of Truth and Love,

dethrone
Mis. 260–21   and seeking to d· Deity.
No. 21–13   philosophy would d· perfection,
30–24   would d· God as Truth,
My. 116–10   would d· the First Commandment,

dethroned
Mis. 65– 2   delusive evidence, Science has d·
162–27   would have d· his power
Un. 20–10   evil must be d· :

dethrones
Mis.	8–18	defiles, defaces, and *d·* the
	221–22	Such denial *d·* demonstration,
My.	193–16	Nothing *d·* His house.

dethroning
Mis.	3–28	denying revelation, and *d·* Deity.

detonation
Mis.	356– 6	need no terrible *d·* to free them.

detonations
Mis.	17– 1	before the awful *d·* of Sinai.

detract
Mis.	302–26	nor *d·* from the good that
	349– 9	nor *d·* from the metaphysical mode

detraction
'02.	1–18	met with opposition and *d·* ;

Detroit
Mich.
Pul.	89–29	* *Free Press, D·*, Mich.
My.	183–23	chapter sub-title

Pul.	26–13	* great organ comes from *D·*.
	56– 3	* Philadelphia, *D·*, Toledo,
	60–17	* Farrand & Votey in *D·*,

Deuteronomy
26 : 1, 2, 5–10 (first sentence)
My.	32–15	* *D·* 26 : 1, 2, 5–10 (first sentence).

Rud.	13–14	In *D·* (iv. 35) we read :

devastating
Mis.	343–21	they reappear, like *d·* witch-grass,

develop
Mis.	14–10	through which to *d·* good.
	18– 2	*d·*, step by step, the original
Un.	42–26	mortal does not *d·* the immortal,
No.	37– 2	offspring had to grow, *d·* ;
Hea.	14–19	educate and *d·* the spiritual sense
My.	166–16	they *d·* hidden strength.
	342–28	Its government will *d·* as

developed
Mis.	15–28	*d·* into an infant Christianity ;
	201–23	they tested and *d·* latent power.
	247–18	healing force *d·* by C. S.
	278–31	This has *d·* higher energies
Ret.	27– 9	Science *d·* itself to me until
Pul.	66–27	* which our civilization has *d·*.
	69–20	* power fully *d·* to heal the sick.
No.	24– 6	*d·* through the lower orders of
My.	358– 9	conflict . . . is engendered and *d·*.

developing
'00.	10– 3	asserting and *d·* good.
'01.	1–21	man's nature *d·* itself.

development
Mis.	75– 5	man's possible earthly *d·*.
	264–27	aid the mental *d·* of the student ;
	356–22	second stage of mental *d·* is
Mis.	359–13	proper channels for *d·*,
Pul.	31–10	* *d·* of some degree of familiarity
	53– 1	* fresh *d·* of a Principle that
	66–19	* has shown an uncommon *d·*
	79–17	* reasons for this remarkable *d·*,
My.	48–20	* a means of spiritual *d·*
	84–24	* Its hold and *d·* are most notable.
	88– 6	* is the *d·* of a short lifetime.
	88–20	* material *d·* in evidence of

developments
Hea.	5– 6	Phrenology will be saying the *d·* of

develops
Mis.	204–18	It *d·* individual capacity,
Pan.	11–21	may believe that evil *d·* good,

deviate
Man.	63– 9	children's teachers must not *d·* from
Rud.	3–14	will no more *d·* morally from

deviating
Mis.	92– 3	present liability of *d·* from C. S.
Ret.	83–29	liability of *d·* from absolute C. S.

deviation
Man.	77–24	In case of any . . . *d·* from duty,
Ret.	85–15	any *d·* from the order prescribed by
My.	363–28	Any *d·* from this direct rule

device
Mis.	372–25	Not by aid of foreign *d·*

devices
Mis.	119– 4	instead of aiding other people's *d·*
	159–28	rich *d·* in embroidery, silver,
Pan.	4–18	chapter sub-title

devil
Mis.	68–15	Jesus cast out a *d·*,
	97– 8	"He is a *d·*," — *see John* 6 : 70.
	163– 2	the world, the flesh, and the *d·*.
	190–11	*casting out a d·*, — *Luke* 11 : 14.
	190–12	*d· was gone out*, — *Luke* 11 : 14.
	190–13	meaning of the term "*d·*" — *Luke* 11 : 14.
	190–21	the *d·* herein referred to was
	190–28	In the Hebrew, "*d·*" — *Luke* 11 : 14.
	191– 2	the term "*d·*" — *Luke* 11 : 14.
	191– 9	refers to a wicked man as the *d·* :
	191–10	one of you is a *d·* ?" — *John* 6 : 70.
	191–11	if *d·* is an individuality,
	191–12	if . . . there is more than one *d·*.
	191–15	indicating . . . more than one *d·* ;
	191–22	existence of one personal *d·*.
	191–23	our text refers to the *d·* as dumb ;
	191–24	the original *d·* was a great talker,
	192– 4	we mean not that he is a personal *d·*,
	192– 5	defines *d·* as a "liar." — *John* 8 : 44.
	192– 9	nature of Deity and *d·* be understood.
	248–11	word synonymous with *d·*.
Ret.	63–22	* "The *d·* is but the ape of God."
	67–24	the "*d·*" (*alias* evil), — *John* 8 : 44.
Un.	17–14	the *d·*, was the would-be murderer
	52–11	good and evil, God and *d·*,
	52–18	world, the flesh, and the *d·*.
Pul.	12–13	*d·* is come down — *Rev.* 12 : 12.
	13–22	the *d·* knoweth his time is short.
No.	15–17	conceptions of Deity and *d·*
	22–15	chapter sub-title
	22–19	shows that the term *d·* is generic,
	22–20	that there is more than one *d·*.
	22–24	*d·* as a mortal who is full of evil.
	22–25	one of you *is a d·* ?" — *John* 6 : 70.
	23– 9	and therefore was not a *d·*,
	23–17	moral sense of the word *d·*,
	23–18	in order to cast out this *d·* ?
	24–22	for behold evil (or *d·*) is,
	31–15	the works of the *d·*" — *I John* 3 : 8.
	32–16	the *d·* was "a liar, — *John* 8 : 44.
	42–18	said that the *d·* is the ape of God.
Pan.	5–12	your father, the *d·*, — *John* 8 : 44.
	5–18	Jesus' definition of *d·* (evil)
'00.	5– 8	opposite of God . . . named *d·*
'01.	13–14	evil, *alias d·*, sin, is a lie
	16–13	In the Greek *d·* is named *serpent*
	16–16	defines *d·* as *accuser*,
Hea.	6–27	word *d·* comes from the Greek
Peo.	3–13	mysterious God and a natural *d·*.
	4–13	personal God and a personal *d·*
	7– 1	by their God and their *d·*.
My.	14–20	* If the *d·* were really an entity,
	60– 9	* it is the work of the *d·*."
	252– 3	and you will have no *d·*.
	268–22	"the world, the flesh and the *d·*,"

devilish
No.	23– 4	that Jesus condemned as *d·*,
My.	278–26	War is . . . barbarous, *d·*.

devils
Mis.	97– 9	casting out *d·* through Beelzebub.
	175–30	in thy name cast out *d·*,
	191–14	casting out *d·* — *Mark* 9 : 38.
	326– 1	cast out *d·*, — *Matt.* 10 : 8.
No.	14–19	cast out *d·*"! — *Matt.* 10 : 8.
	22–18	cast out *d·*." — *Matt.* 10 : 8.
	23–11	Jesus cast seven *d·* ;
	23–12	these *d·* were the diseases
	41–21	cast out *d·* ;" — *Matt.* 10 : 8.
Hea.	1– 2	*shall they cast out d·* ; — *Mark* 16 : 17.
	6–27	shall they cast out *d·*." — *Mark* 16 : 17.
Peo.	4–28	and cast out *d·*, error.
My.	47–30	* shall they cast out *d·* ; — *Mark* 16 : 17.
	126–26	the habitation of *d·*, — *Rev.* 18 : 2.
	288–23	cast out *d·* and healed the sick.
	300–27	cast out *d·*." — *Matt.* 10 : 8.

devious
My.	260–14	philosophy may pursue paths *d·*,

deviously
Mis.	111–29	inclining mortal mind more *d·* :

devise
My.	51– 1	* to *d·* means to pay our pastor,

devised
My.	vi–12	* *d·* its church government,

devoid
Un.	49–23	it is *d·* of Science.

devote
Mis.	5– 2	*d·* our best energies to the work.
Man.	31– 6	*d·* a suitable portion of their time
	82–20	*d·* ample time for faithful practice
My.	358–19	I shall *d·* it to a worthy

devoted

Mis.	4–16	has been *d·* to their answer.
	4–17	periodical *d·* to this work
	37–26	Her time is wholly *d·* to instruction,
	48–19	purpose to which it can be *d·*,
	318– 7	love some of those *d·* students
Pul.	v– 4	WERE *d·* TO THE MOTHERS'S ROOM
	8–17	never before *d·* to menial
	42–18	* was *d·* to the "Mother's Room,"
	58– 2	* *d·* herself to imparting this
	58–27	* a room *d·* to her,
	63–17	* among her *d·* followers.
	71–22	* thousands . . . are now so entirely *d·*.
'00.	13–17	*d·* to a sensual worship.
My.	30–14	* professional men, *d·* women
	49–28	* *d·* labors in the cause of Truth,"
	88–19	* by a noble and *d·* woman,
	272–23·	* Mrs. Eddy's own *d·* followers,
	321– 7	* your *d·* and faithful friends,
	328– 3	* With *d·* love,

devotedly

My.	335– 7	* He was *d·* attached to Masonry,

devotees

Un.	15–22	There are, or have been, *d·* who
Pul.	79– 8	* never have been, *d·* of
My.	76–27	* erected by the *d·* of a religion

devotes

Pul.	44–18	* chapter sub-title

devoting

Mis.	375–15	* *d·* every moment to the study of

devotion

Mis.	176– 9	supreme *d·* to Principle
	177– 2	fervent *d·* and an absolute
	342– 1	keep aglow the flame of *d·*
Ret.	2– 3	that sturdy Calvinistic *d·* to
	19–19	tender *d·* to his young bride
Pul.	85– 2	* *d·* and consecration to God
'01.	28–13	choicest memorials of *d·*
My.	30–10	* *d·* of the members to their
	36–23	* the measure of our *d·* to
	41–31	* supports such selfless *d·*,
	86–19	* the generosity of the *d·*
	131– 5	courage, *d·*, and attainment.
	330–30	Colonel Glover's tender *d·* to his

devotional

Pul.	28–22	* those *d·* hymns from Herbert,
	28–24	* other recognized *d·* poets,

devour

Mis.	82–28	the errors which *d·* it.
	253–17	stood ready to *d·* the child
	323–13	wolves . . . are ready to *d·* ;
Hea.	10– 3	*d·* the child as soon — *see Rev.* 12: 4.
	10– 4	ready to *d·* the idea of Truth.

devourer

Mis.	263–11	covered from the *d·* by
'00.	12–29	Balaam as the *d·* of the people.
My.	269–24	"I will rebuke the *d·* — *Mal.* 3: 11.

devouring

My.	211– 8	break out in *d·* flames.
	245–12	poisonous reptiles and *d·* beasts,

devout

Mis.	249–12	The most *d·* members of
	318–22	a *d·*, consecrated Christian.
	337–24	Only the *d·* Marys, and such as
	369–17	*d·* enough to trust Christ
Man.	60–25	Let the ceremony be *d·*.
	64– 1	and a *d·* Christian Scientist.
Ret.	54–20	The faith-cure has *d·* followers,
Pul.	10–22	if you are as *d·* as they,
	80–24	* women more thoughtful and *d·* ;
'00.	3–30	not the incentive of the *d·* Jew
	14–26	as the *d·* St. Stephen said :
'01.	28– 9	none lived a more *d·* Christian life
	31–21	*D·* orthodox parents;
'02.	6–21	hope, and prayer, all *d·* desire,
My.	5–19	enables the *d·* Scientist to
	38–24	* *D·* Scientists said after the service
	90– 3	* *d·* worshippers, wooed by no
	249–29	*d·*, unselfed quality of thought

devoutly

Mis.	98–23	* "consummation *d·* to be wished."
Un.	17–19	* consummation *d·* to be wished."
Peo.	5– 2	*d·* recommends the more spiritual
My.	181–16	* consummation *d·* to be wished"

dew

Mis.	291–23	The *d·* of heaven will fall gently
	394– 3	It falls on the heart like the *d·*
Ret.	5–24	* like the gentle *d·* and cheerful light,
Po.	3– 3	I miss thee as the flower the *d·* !
	45– 3	It falls on the heart like the *d·*

dewdrop

Ret.	17–11	*d·* is shed On the heart of the pink
Pul.	4–14	A *d·* reflects the sun.
Po.	25– 2	Whence the *d·* is born,
	62–13	*d·* is shed On the heart of the pink

Dewey

Pan.	14–24	led by the dauntless *D·*,

dews

Mis.	154– 8	water it with the *d·* of heaven,
	343–11	watered by the heavenly *d·* of Love,
	360–17	*d·* of divine grace, falling upon
Ret.	95– 1	watered by *d·* of divine Science,
No.	14–26	*d·* of divine Truth,
My.	208–12	Like the gentle *d·* of heaven

dewy

Po.	73–12	Night's *d·* eye,

dexterous

Mis.	231–13	*d·* use of knife and fork,

dexterously

My.	6–13	*d·* and wisely provided for

diabolical

Mis.	41– 2	is given vent in the *d·* practice of
Un.	54–27	audacity of *d·* and sinuous logic

diabolism

Mis.	334–18	*d·* of suppositional evil
'01.	20–24	new-old *régime* of necromancy or *d·*

diabolos

Hea.	6–28	word *devil* comes from the Greek *d·*;

diadem

Ret.	85–27	with a *d·* of gems from the
Pul.	4–21	his *d·* a crown of crowns.
'02.	3–21	The dazzling *d·* of royalty
Po.	46– 8	A gem in beauty's *d·*,
My.	201–15	with a *d·* of duties done.

diadems

My.	258–20	coronals of meekness, *d·* of love.

diagnose

Man.	47– 6	case he cannot fully *d·*,

diagnosed

My.	310–25	these "fits" were *d·* by Dr. Ladd

diagnoses

Hea.	12– 8	he *d·* disease as mind,

diagnosis

Mis.	69–25	According to their *d·*,

dial

Mis.	71–29	flitting across the *d·* of time.
Ret.	23–11	were indicated by no floral *d·*.

diameter

My.	68– 8	* having a *d·* of eighty-two feet

diametrical

Mis.	220–18	*d·* opposite of what it was

diametrically

Pul.	38–22	* They are *d·* opposed

diamond

Mis.	376–27	*d·*, topaz, opal, garnet,
Ret.	91– 5	be called "the *d·* sermon."
No.	13–25	and sparkle like a *d·*,
My.	121–18	a *d·* of the first water ;

diamonds

Pul.	8–14	forth came the money, or *d·*,
My.	175–23	richer than the *d·* of Golconda,

Diana

'00.	12–14	*D·*, the tutelary divinity

diapason

Mis.	206–21	repeating this *d·* of heaven :
My.	189–11	a *d·* of heart-beats,
		(*see also* **organ**)

Dickey

Adam H.

Po.	vii–16	* signature

Mr. Adam

My.	240–24	* through her student, Mr. Adam *D·*,
	358–21	Mr. Adam *D·* is my secretary,

dictate

My.	223– 5	nor *d·* replies to letters which
	276–19	* no one should seek to *d·* the

dictated

My.	114–24	which *d·* "S. and H. with Key to

dictates

My.	128–16	*d·* of his own rational conscience
	168– 2	*d·* of enlightened conscience,

dictating

Mis.	132–17	*d·* answers through my secretary,

dictation

'02.	15–15	declining *d·* as to what I should write,

dictator
  Mis. 152–12 as a *d·*, arbiter, or ruler,

dictatorial
  Mis. 148–11 arbitrary opinions nor *d·* demands,
  Man. 3– 7 arbitrary opinions nor *d·* demands,

diction
  Mis. 341–28 and the *d·* purely Oriental.
  Ret. 27–15 express in feeble *d·* Truth's ultimate.
  My. 317–10 to correct my *d·*.
  317–17 left my *d·* quite out of the
  317–22 My *d·*, as used in explaining C. S.,

dictionary (*see also* **dictionary's**)
  Mis. 252–30 the wise man's spiritual *d·* ;
  363–29 the ignorant man's *d·*,

dictionary's
  '01. 3–12 Standard *d·* definition of God,

dictum
  Mis. 133–18 following the *d·* of Jesus ;
  No. 11–28 *d·* and the demonstration of Truth

did
  Mis. 40–12 as *d·* those in the first century of
  47–10 *d·* this without consciousness of
  54–26 as Jesus and his disciples *d·*,
  55– 6 to the extent that Jesus *d·*,
  77– 3 It *d·* ; but this believing was more
  165–19 rich legacy of what he said and *d·*,
  178– 4 left his old church, as I *d·*,
  182–31 will yield to it, even as they *d·*
  237–27 dead hero who *d·* the hard work,
  244–22 he *d·* this for man's example ;
  253– 4 knoweth as *d·* our Master
  283–23 the person who *d·* it.
  311–25 I *d·* this even as a surgeon
  373– 5 objected, as he often *d·*,
  Man. 28–12 neither *d·* according to — *Luke* 12 : 47.
  Ret. 9–10 bade me, . . . to reply as he *d·*,
  89–11 he *d·* so informally, and because
  90–13 This he *d·*, even though one of the
  Un. 32–21 even as *d·* our Master.
  50– 9 We should subjugate it as Jesus *d·*,
  62–20 Jesus seemed to die, though he *d·* not.
  Pul. 33– 8 * bade her, . . . reply as he *d·* :
  34–13 * and reluctantly they *d·* so,
  51– 2 * If it *d·*, it would be a prodigy.
  66– 2 * exists as much to-day as it *d·* when
  74–11 * which she *d·* in this letter,
  No. 31– 7 in subtler forms than they *d·*
  46–17 rejoicing, as Paul *d·*,
  '00. 7–12 as they *d·* after reading
  7–20 we say as *d·* Mary of old :
  '02. 11–28 for the truths he said and *d·* :
  18–21 how much of what he *d·*
  Hea. 8–15 Plato *d·* better ; he said,
  18–18 never *d·* anything for sickness
  My. 3–22 to think genuine, whoever *d·* it.
  59–25 * Some say she *d·* not."
  59–27 * "Send those who say she *d·* not
  112– 5 *d·* just what he enjoined
  190–28 would remain, even as it *d·*,
  212–18 If they *d·*, there would be unity
  215– 5 bade me do what I *d·*,
  219–21 what Christ Jesus taught and *d·* ;
  220–32 seems more divine to-day than it *d·*
  235–16 Did God make all . . . He *d·*.
  292– 9 as it *d·* the departing.
  294– 7 "*d·* not many mighty — *Matt.* 13 : 58.
  307–21 better than some others *d·*.
  313–14 *d·* everything they could think of
  319–14 * work which the Rev. Mr. Wiggin *d·*
  319–25 * which I *d·* about the twentieth of
  320– 5 * consented to assist me, which he *d·*.
  321–31 * knew you years before I *d·*,

die
  Mis. 57–17 thou shalt surely *d·*." — *Gen.* 2 : 17.
  58– 7 and that he did not *d·* ;
  69–16 and then had left him to *d·*.
  70–17 He was too good to *d·* ;
  70–19 and had already begun to *d·*,
  75–28 it shall *d·*," — *Ezek.* 18 : 4.
  75–29 mortal man . . . that sinneth, shall *d·* ;
  76–13 hence these bodies must *d·*
  76–23 sense, which sinneth and shall *d·* ;
  76–26 Now if Soul sinned, it would *d·* ;
  79–24 "As in Adam all *d·*, — *I Cor.* 15 : 22.
  84–20 and to *d·* is gain." — *Phil.* 1 : 21.
  208– 3 "Thou shalt surely *d·*." — *Gen.* 2 : 17.
  209–22 Evil passions *d·* in their own flames,
  235– 3 to sin, be sick, and *d·*
  258– 1 lawless law which dooms man to *d·*
  367–17 thou shalt surely *d·*." — *Gen.* 2 : 17.
  Chr. 55–28 shall never *d·*." — *John* 11 : 26.
  Un. 2–21 if they *d·* in the Lord
  3– 7 which *d·* in the Lord." — *Rev.* 14 : 13.

die
  Un. 17–23 declares . . . they must surely *d·*.
  22– 7 ye shall not touch it, lest ye *d·*.
  28– 2 it shall *d·*." — *Ezek.* 18 : 4.
  37– 4 Must man *d·*, then, in order to
  38–18 all that dies, or appears to *d·*.
  40–13 who believe his sayings will never *d·* ;
  40–26 mortals *d·*, in belief,
  41–26 matter appears to both live and *d·*,
  53–14 will *d·* of its own delusion ;
  62–19 The fleshly Jesus seemed to *d·*,
  Pul. 3– 3 Can Life *d·* ?
  No. 1–16 flames *d·* away on the mount of
  13– 9 shall never *d·*." — *John* 11 : 26.
  28–26 it shall *d·*." — *Ezek.* 18 : 20.
  Pan. 7–11 declared that man should *d·*
  9–13 shall never *d·*." — *John* 11 : 26.
  '01. 33–12 * that they were about to *d·*."
  Po. 15–14 or *d·* in their chain.
  My. 128–15 to live or to *d·* according to
  164–30 man must live, he cannot *d·* ;
  195–22 mortals expect to live and *d·*,
  269– 9 neither can they *d·* — *Luke* 20 : 36.
  333–24 * assurance of his willingness to *d·*,

died
  Mis. 17– 7 before the flames have *d·*
  58– 1 *If one has d· of consumption,*
  58– 6 proves to him who thought he *d·*
  238–26 or that I *d·* of palsy,
  248–21 said that I *d·* of poison,
  386–14 She deemed I *d·*,
  Un. 62– 3 saith, "Christ (God) *d·* for me,
  62–18 In Science, Christ never *d·*.
  62–19 In material sense Jesus *d·*,
  Pul. 34–15 "and they thought I had *d·*,
  36– 1 * Dr. Eddy *d·* in 1882,
  47– 3 * He *d·* in 1882.
  49–17 big elms ! . . . and not one *d·*."
  63–14 and not one *d·*."
  '01. 11– 3 never suffered and never *d·*.
  Po. 49–21 She deemed I *d·*,
  My. 97– 8 * a larger proportion have *d·*
  189–26 There my husband *d·*,
  241–24 * lived or *d·* according to the
  297–23 and realize that he never *d·* ;
  310– 8 * but *d·* before the election.
  310–18 * "excepting Albert, *d·* of cancer,"
  312– 8 * he *d·* of yellow fever.
  312–21 *d·* in about nine days.
  330–17 * *d·* there while on business
  333– 9 * *d·* on the night of the
  333–21 * *d·* on Thursday night,
  335– 1 * *D·* at Wilmington, N. C., on the
  336– 1 * would have *d·* on the seventh day.

dies
  Mis. 2–22 for good *d·* not
  184– 3 by claiming that . . . man *d·*.
  209–10 and *d·* of its own physics.
  268–30 error *d·* of its own elements.
  277– 7 its voice *d·* out in the distance.
  Ret. 25–12 That which sins, suffers, and *d·*,
  Un. 38–18 false sense of life is all that *d·*,
  39–22 which testify that man *d·*.
  39–26 presuppose . . . that man *d·*.
  40– 2 It is mortality only that *d·*.
  40– 5 but man in Science never *d·*.
  41–25 hence matter neither lives nor *d·*.
  43–14 that man *d·* not,
  45–21 until it finally *d·* in order to
  45–22 But Truth never *d·*,
  62– 4 God *d·* not, and is the ever-presence
  No. 29– 3 mortal sense, sins and *d·*.
  My. 194– 5 The letter of your work *d·*,
  227–12 *d·* while the others recover,
  278–18 *d·* in defence of his country,
  297–16 Scientist who believes that he *d·*,
  344–13 absurd to say that when a man *d·*,

diet
  Mis. 6–27 observed in regard to *d·*,

differ
  Mis. 117–23 God's time and mortals' *d·*.
  252– 4 allopathy and homœopathy *d·*.
  288–30 People will *d·* in their opinions
  Un. 5–23 wholly or partially *d·* from them
  Pul. 28–16 * does not *d·* widely from that of
  38–27 * may *d·* among themselves,

difference
  Mis. x–15 *d·* between then and now,
  42–21 The *d·* between a belief of
  111–23 no greater *d·* existed between
  271–27 * *d·* between true and false teachers
  352–28 *d·* between the healing of sin and
  Ret. 68– 8 *d·* between these opposites
  Un. 9–27 the cardinal point of the *d·* in

difference

Un.	10– 2	This *d·* wholly separates my
	27– 4	really have a shade of *d·*
Pul.	47–17	* defines carefully the *d·*
	57–14	* whatever *d·* of opinion there may be
Rud.	16–23	shades of *d·* in Mind-healing
Hea.	1–20	The *d·* between religions is,
My.	75–16	* it would not make much *d·*,
	108–15	* *d·* between metaphysics in
	319– 2	would make no *d·* to me.

different

Mis.	60–18	sleepers, in *d·* phases of thought,
	100–30	*d·* stages of man's recovery
	148–13	were written at *d·* dates,
	191–29	*d·* phases of sin or disease
	224–12	thousand million *d·* human wills,
	224–13	each person has a *d·* history,
	224–16	action . . . of these *d·* atoms.
	237–13	All the *d·* phases of error
	325– 5	These are believers of *d·* sects,
	367–21	evil is a *d·* state of consciousness.
	370–12	In *d·* ages the divine idea assumes *d·*
Man.	3–10	were written at *d·* dates,
	34–20	church member from a *d·* denomination
Ret.	33– 7	I sought knowledge from the *d·* schools,
	61– 4	*d·* forms of fear or disease.
	80– 7	As the poets in *d·* languages have
	87–30	and *d·* aid is sought.
Un.	9–23	So they have, but in a far *d·* form.
Pul.	23–12	* under several *d·* aspects
	38–19	* entirely a plane of consciousness
	40–17	* four *d·* congregations
	47–11	* *d·* schools of allopathy,
	51–13	* others who have *d·* methods,
	51–14	* with them bring *d·* ideas.
	55–29	* members of *d·* congregations
'00.	13–25	* amalgamation of *d·* pagan religions
'01.	7–13	thoughts that express the *d·* mentalities
	22–23	and the *d·* religious sects
Po.	v– 2	* *were written at d· periods*
My.	24–22	* fifteen *d·* trades represented.
	29–23	* *d·* status before the world !
	47–22	* many of *d·* races and tongues
	53–22	* clergymen of *d·* denominations,
	53–31	* *d·* ones address them on the
	54–17	* *d·* places were considered,
	71–18	* *d·* from any other church
	89–17	* *d·* from almost all other
	94–21	* held at *d·* hours of the day,
	95– 7	* in *d·* parts of the world.
	179–24	*d·* renderings or translations of
	293– 4	act as the *d·* properties of drugs
	315– 5	* During his stay, at *d·* times,
	328–26	* enumerating the *d·* professions

differently

'01.	6– 6	defined *d·* by theology,

differing

Mis.	380–17	practised in slightly *d·* forms.
'01.	7–16	*d·* needs of the individual mind
	22–23	and the *d·* schools of medicine
Hea.	11–24	*d·* in this from homœopathy,
My.	293– 2	*d·* human concepts as to the
	321–15	* said anything . . . *d·* from what he

differs

Mis.	258–29	*d·* essentially from the human.

difficult

Mis.	37–28	is in reality the least *d·* of
	52– 3	It is *d·* to say how much
	52– 5	but not so *d·* to know that
	52–25	a rule farther on and more *d·*
	53–12	*when it is d· to start the*
	53–24	*d·* to make the rulers understand,
	53–28	abstract or *d·* to perceive.
	54– 1	to . . . the ungodly, it is dark and *d·*.
	117–18	It is *d·* for me to carry out a
	133– 4	*d·* to build a sentence of
	242–14	I performed more *d·* tasks
	245–20	It is *d·* to say which may be
Ret.	53– 4	prosperous under *d·* circumstances,
	63–20	more subtle, more *d·* to heal.
	83–17	find it more *d·* to rekindle
Un.	10– 5	It would be *d·* to name any
Pul.	37–23	* *d·* not to centre too closely
Rud.	7– 4	as the most *d·* case so treated.
'01.	17–20	overcome a *d·* stage of the work,
	17–22	more *d·* stage of action
Po.	27–13	let today grow *d·* and vast

difficulties

Mis.	53–16	acknowledging that under *d·*
	131–20	perplexities and *d·* which
	212–16	return under the reign of *d·*,
	236– 7	shrunk from contact with family *d·*,
	236–16	advice concerning *d·* and the
'01.	2–23	costs a return under *d·* ;

difficulties

'01.	29–27	a tithe of my own *d·*,
My.	220–15	pacification of all national *d·*,
	223– 5	which pertain to church *d·*
	277– 3	*d·* between the United States and
	277– 7	*d·* between individuals and
	291–18	fathomed the abyss of *d·*
	359– 3	trouble me with their *d·*

difficulty

Mis.	379–30	there remained the *d·* of
Pul.	64– 5	* considerable *d·* in securing
My.	134– 1	*D·*, abnegation, constant battle
	360–13	settle this church *d·* amicably

diffusing

Mis.	166–28	*d·* richest blessings.

dig

Mis.	154– 7	*d·* about this little church,

digest

Mis.	313– 5	It is a *d·* of good manners,
Rud.	3–15	that divine *d·* of Science

digested

My.	230– 8	*d·* only when Soul silences the

digestion

My.	229–19	chapter sub-title
	230– 5	*d·* of spiritual nutriment

dignified

Mis.	226–26	*d·* natures cannot stoop to
Man.	61–22	*d·* and suitable manner.
My.	276– 6	daily drive or a *d·* stay at home,
	309– 2	The man . . . was uniformly *d·*
	316–16	a *d·*, eloquent appeal to the press
	327–27	* this *d·* legal protection
	328– 1	* *d·*, blessed, and prospered it,

dignify

Mis.	111– 3	work, well done, would *d·* angels.
	199– 4	and *d·* the result with the name of
	240– 9	Predicting danger does not *d·* life,
My.	327–30	* will *d·* the ministry of Christ

dignitaries

Pul.	71–17	* various *d·* of the faith.

dignity

Mis.	126–12	lift us to that *d·* of Soul
	148–17	*d·* and defense of our Cause ;
	295–16	defend the *d·* of her daughters
	295–29	such *d·*, clemency, and virtue
Man.	3–13	*d·* and defense of our Cause ;
Un.	54–24	admitted the *d·* of evil.
My.	39–24	* her graciousness and *d·*.
	58–11	* *d·* of this church edifice

dilates

Mis.	356– 2	*d·* and kindles into rest.

dilemma

Mis.	134– 5	you are placed in this *d·* :
Hea.	13– 2	both horns of the *d·*,
My.	350– 7	It was in this *d·* that

diligence

My.	340–31	which man's *d·* has utilized.

diligently

Mis.	154–26	Watch *d·* ; never desert the
	206–26	all who *d·* seek God.
Ret.	23–18	He whom my affections had *d·*
	31–12	seek *d·* for the knowledge of God
My.	122–18	Are we still searching *d·*

dim

Mis.	xi–25	the *d·* corridors of years,
	368– 8	* behind the *d·* unknown,
	383–13	go down the *d·* posterns of time
Chr.	53–58	Truth's fane can *d·* ;
Ret.	9–20	* His presence in the vast and *d·*
	33– 5	*d·* mazes of *materia medica*,
Po.	18– 7	Would a tear *d·* his eye,
	26–18	the *d·* chambers of eternity
	70– 2	In the *d·* distance, lay
My.	189–10	the *d·* corridors of time,

dimension

Mis.	22–12	fourth *d·* of Spirit.
Pul.	86– 2	* about six inches in each *d·*,

dimensions

My.	77– 8	* its *d·* are only half as great.

diminish

Mis.	365–21	the demand would *d·* ;
Un.	5– 8	their . . . will proportionately *d·*.

diminished

No.	18– 2	never *d·* sin and sickness,
'00.	7– 4	death-rate to have gradually *d·*.

diminishes

Ret.	28–19	*d·*, constitutes, and sustains,
	67–16	sin *d·*, until the false claim

diminishing
   Mis.   8– 2 abating suffering and *d·* sin,
   No. 32–25 *d·* the percentage of sin.
   My. 107–17 *d·* of the drug does not disprove

diminuendo
   Mis. 116–15 *crescendo* and *d·* accent music,

diminution
   Mis. 82–31 not subject to growth, change, or *d·*,

dimly
   Mis. 87–10 what I now through you discern *d·* ;
   Pul. 39–17 * *D·*, as in a dream, I watch the flow
        39–23 * *D·*, as in a dream, I see the
   No. 21– 6 Plato but *d·* discerned,

dimmed
   Mis. 92–28 have *d·* the power and glory of
      324–16 have so *d·* their sight
   Un. 54– 1 bright gold of Truth is *d·* by

dims
   Mis.   1–19 removing the dust that *d·* them.
      291– 5 it *d·* the true sense of God's
      354–30 No tear *d·* his eye

din
   Mis. 120–17 heard above the *d·* of battle,
   Ret. 69–25 "Above error's awful *d·*,
   '02.   5– 1 foretells the dawn and *d·* of morn ;
   My. 245–18 dire *d·* of mortal nothingness,

dine
   My. 322–16 * to *d·* with the Wiggin family.

dinner
   Mis. 230–26 chapter sub-title
      348–21 every day, and especially at *d·*,

dinner-table
   Mis. 231– 6 Four generations sat at that *d·*.

dip
   My. 125–11 *d·* my pen in my heart to say,

diphtheria
   My. 105–11 I healed malignant *d·*
      107–32 pneumonia, *d·*, and ossification

diploma
   Mis. 272–16 * any *d·* or degree,
   Pul. 48–22 * *d·* given her by the Society of
   '01. 33–14 platform, a creed, or a *d·*

diplomacy
   My. 277– 5 by statesmanship and *d·*,

diplomas
   Mis. 272–26 * with powers to confer *d·*
   Man. 91–25 provided their *d·* are for three
   Ret. 48– 6 conscientious scruples about *d·*,

dipped
   My. 296–26 Clara Barton *d·* her pen in my heart,

dire
   My. 245–17 the *d·* din of mortal nothingness,

direct
   Mis. 25–10 *d·* application to human needs,
      34–26 as *d·* opposites as light and darkness.
      44– 9 and its application *d·*.
      55–20 *d·* antipodes of the so-called facts
      56–12 *d·* opposite of immortal Life,
    146– 7 to *d·* your action on receiving or
    147–29 the fair, open, and *d·* one,
    157– 6 He that marketh . . . will *d·* thy way.
    212–14 One step away from the *d·* line
    282– 9 *d·* rule for practice of C. S.
    291–11 is often construed as *d·* orders,
    319–26 Christian Scientists can *d·* attention,
   Ret. 37–16 Scriptures gave no *d·* interpretation
   Un. 11– 7 in *d·* opposition to human philosophy
   Pul. 50–22 * simple and *d·* as they are,
   Rud.   9–22 without a *d·* effort,
   '01.   2–23 departure from the *d·* line in Christ
      35– 1 He shall *d·* thy paths ;" — *Prov.* 3 : 6
   My. 49– 5 * The religious body which can *d·*,
    129–29 Trust God to *d·* your steps.
    161–27 "He shall *d·* thy paths." — *Prov.* 3 : 6.
    177–23 "I will *d·* their work — *Isa.* 61 : 8.
    361– 3 He will *d·* you into the paths of
    363–28 Any deviation from this *d·* rule

directed
   Mis. 264–19 As mortal mind is *d·*,
      313–25 as I believe, divinely *d·*,
      345–32 *d·* them to spiritual attainments.
   Ret.   5–26 * *d·* attention to themes
   Pul. 65–13 * Attention is *d·* to the progress
   Pan.   2–22 the religious sentiment is *d·*.
   Hea. 15– 8 spiritual power divinely *d·*.
   My. 73–23 * to which all mail may be *d·*,
    138–28 * *d·* to Honorable Judge Chamberlin
    156–11 Jesus *d·* his disciples to
    342–29 * *d·* by a single earthly ruler?"

directing
   Mis. 245–12 *d·* more critical observation to

direction
   Mis. 78–10 than can science in any other *d·*.
      80– 9 aid individual rights in a wrong *d·*
    115–32 Using mental power in the right *d·*
    127–23 know yourself, under God's *d·*,
    156–28 growth and understanding in this *d·*.
    172–17 nor of human *d·*.
    212–25 If, . . . one is at work in a wrong *d·*,
    229–13 encourage faith in God in this *d·*,
    245–25 to go no further in the *d·* of
    246–14 from another *d·* there comes
    297– 5 In the *d·* of temperance it has
    304–31 * and the *d·* of its use,
    347–16 Take the opposite *d·* !
    381– 2 copied by her, or by her *d·*,
   Man. 98–22 under the *d·* of this Committee
   Ret. 84–29 place themselves under his *d·* ;
   Pul. 43– 4 * led the singing, under the *d·*,
   No. 39–15 in the *d·* that is unerring.
   '01. 13–21 conquers him, in whatever *d·*.
   Hea. 14– 8 encourage faith in an opposite *d·?*
   My. 10–13 * have taken steps in this *d·*,
      75– 9 * into the city from every *d·*
    117– 7 helping a leader in God's *d·*,
    117–27 only in the right *d·* !
    146–25 in the right or in the wrong *d·*.
    213–18 to drift in the wrong *d·*
    215–31 no hint of his changing this *d·* ;
    241– 9 advancement in this *d·*.
    250–27 whatever is done in this *d·*
    266–15 flux and flow in one *d·*,

directions
   Mis. 33–18 and follow the *d·* given.
      66–11 precept is verified in all *d·*
      89– 8 *to follow the doctor's d·?*
    158–26 divine *d·* sent out to the churches.
    220–10 words, and actions, in certain *d·*,
    273– 5 in order to work in other *d·*,
   Man. 100– 8 carried out according to her *d·*.
   Ret. 19–21 pathetic *d·* to his brother masons
   My. 231– 5 working in wrong *d·*.
    303–13 wit was not wasted in certain *d·*.
    330–32 pathetic *d·* to his brother Masons
    361– 1 Follow the *d·* of God

directly
   Mis. 37–23 yields to Science as *d·* and
      44–29 applying this . . . *d·* to your belief,
    381–22 *d·* or indirectly printing,
   Pul. 29–17 * dealt *d·* with the command of
   Hea.   8–25 as *d·* upon a divine Principle,
      8–27 as *d·* as we do to the rule of
    12–13 God, *d·* or indirectly, through His
    19– 5 is governed *d·* and entirely by
   Peo.   8–19 as *d·* as it moves a planet
    11–18 as *d·* as men pass legislative acts
   My. 16–15 * have the work *d·* in charge,
     82–30 * leading *d·* to Horticultural Hall.
    223–20 All inquiries, coming *d·* or

Director
   Man. 29– 5 *D·* shall not make known the
     35– 5 by a *D·*, or by a student of
     38– 6 a *D·* of this Church, or a student of
     78– 2 If any *D·* fails to heed this

Directors (*see also* **Board of Directors, Directors'**)
   Mis. 131–21 difficulties which the *D·* encountered
     322– 8 notify the *D·* when I shall be present
   Man. 26–17 The *D·* shall fix the salaries of
     26–19 *D·*.
     29–11 the *D·* shall resign their office or
     30– 1 *D·* shall select intelligible Readers
     44–20 the duty of the *D·* to see that these
     75–22 remained in the hands of the *D·*,
     75–23 not solely to the *D·*.
     76– 7 Report of *D·*.
     79– 7 such business as Mrs. Eddy, the *D·*, or
     95– 3 From the *D·*.
    100–14 it shall be the duty of the *D·*
    109– 8 *D·*, and students of the Board of
   Pul. 20–10 and through *D·* regive the land
     86– 9 * facsimile signatures of the *D·*,
     87–11 *Beloved D· and Brethren :*
   My. 20–22 * chapter sub-title
     60–30 * was asked by one of the *D·*
     62–19 * We, the *D·* of your church,
     82–16 * pride of the Church *D·* that the
    359– 1 *D·* do not act contrary to the
    360–18 support the *D·* of The Mother Church.
    360–20 supporting The Mother Church *D·*.

Directors'
   Man. 68– 6 without the *D·* consent

directors'
Pul. 25–11 * "d· room," and the vestry.
25–20 * "Mother's Room," and the d· room.
27– 3 * d· room is very beautiful
directory
Mis. 363–29 the wise man's d·.
directs
Mis. 117–31 Be sure that God d· your way ;
My. 143– 2 Watch and pray that God d· your
231–14 as God, not man, d·.
direful
Mis. 241–16 by constant combat and d· struggles,
Pul. 2–15 d· scenes of the war
dirge
Mis. 400– 7 D· and song and shoutings low
Pul. 16–19 D· and song and shoutings low,
Po. 76–18 D· and song and shoutings low
My. 189–27 the song and the d·,
326–18 in long procession with tender d·
dirty
Mis. 329– 9 various apartments are dismally d·.
disabilities
Mis. 185– 7 abilities or d·, pains or pleasures.
disable
My. 4– 5 dishonesty, sin, d· the student ;
disadvantage
Mis. 156–15 I saw no advantage, but great d·,
disaffection
Mis. 337–18 consequent d· for all evil,
disaffections
Mis. 265–27 questions and d· toward C. S.
disagree
Mis. 81– 7 agree to d·, and then patiently
243–25 Even doctors d· on that
327–16 encumbered travellers halt and d·,
345–16 even infidels may d·.
No. 45–22 we should agree to d· ;
'02. 2–25 at least agree to d·, in love,
Peo. 13–24 infidels d· ; for Bonaparte said :
disagreement
Man. 66– 7 a doubt or d· shall arise
Un. 41–28 implies perpetual d· with Spirit.
'02. 12– 4 cancels the d·, and settles the
disagreements
My. 286– 8 National d· can be, and
disallowed
My. 17– 9 d· indeed of men, — I Pet. 2 : 4.
disappear
Mis. 28– 1 and the stone itself would d·,
41–24 the effect or disease will d·
72–19 *do they d· only to the natural sense?*
165–16 eternal, appears — never to d·.
166–26 and all materialism d·.
198–17 the temptation will d·.
217–30 matter must d·, for Spirit to appear.
290–10 whatever is false should d·.
361– 9 When every form and mode of evil d·
367– 9 will d· in the proportion that
395–16 Quickly earth's jewels d· ;
Un. 60–23 Without Him, the universe would d·,
No. 16–23 sin, sickness, and death — d·
17–23 would d·, and the eternal, infinite
20–17 and the notion . . . will d·.
Pan. 6– 3 will never d· in any other way.
Hea. 9–14 Contending for . . . what should d·
18– 5 mortality shall d· and immortality be
Peo. 1–17 Even the pangs of death d·,
Po. 58– 1 Quickly earth's jewels d· ;
My. 197–18 else C. S. will d· from
260– 8 the inaccuracy of . . . would d·.
disappearance
Mis. 68– 4 means more than mere d·
271– 3 the point of its d· as matter
disappeared
Mis. 165– 3 spiritual idea . . . d· by degrees ;
Un. 63– 6 never d· to spiritual sense,
disappearing
Mis. 338– 2 involves the d· of evil.
Un. 63– 8 appearing, d·, and reappearing
My. 266–27 agitated, modified, and d·,
disappears
Mis. 165–15 The material corporeality d· ;
205–27 mortal man d· forever.
Ret. 33–18 d· in the higher attenuations of
73– 7 as the fleshly nature d·
Un. 9– 3 and the disease itself d·.
9– 4 and sin itself d·.

disappears
Un. 35– 7 Destroy the belief, and the quality d·.
50–27 as the history of man, d·,
57– 5 as this sense d· it foresees the
62–15 Destroy this sense of sin, and sin d·.
No. 38–19 and material incumbrance d·.
Pan. 6– 7 continue to fight it until it d·,
'01. 13–20 destroy the fear . . . and sin d·.
13–29 sin d·, and its unreality is **proven.**
Hea. 12–24 drug d· by your process
My. 25–26 all vanity of victory d·
232–24 material error finally d·,
disappointed
Mis. 316–21 aphorisms and d· ethics ;
322– 7 People . . . are frequently d·.
'02. 11– 3 d· travellers, tossed to and fro
My. 229–28 my d· hope and grateful joy.
disappointment
Mis. ix–12 joy, sorrow, hope, d·,
274–11 Deeply regretting the d·
My. 142– 4 * has only abolished the d·
disappointments
My. 43–10 * suffered defeats and met with d·,
disapprove
Mis. 109– 4 as authority for what I d·,
disapproves
Man. 82– 2 d· of certain books
My. 240–18 approves or d· according to
disarm
Mis. 134–27 can neither silence nor d· God's
162–31 to d· the Goliath.
'02. 19– 4 and to d· their fears.
disarmed
Mis. 67–23 discerned, d·, and destroyed.
My. 364– 9 are d· by the practitioner who
disarrangement
Pan. 8– 2 it follows that the d· of matter
disastrous
Mis. 9–31 more d· to human progress
Man. 71–14 such position would be d· to C. S.
disastrously
Mis. 31– 4 a manner that can d· affect
disband
My. 216–22 that from this date you d·
disbelief
My. 95–22 * their d· in the miraculous.
297–16 blessing of d· in death,
disbelieves
Mis. 223–14 individual d· in Mind-healing,
disbursal
My. 217–11 This d· will take place when the
disbursed
My. 217–10 on interest till it is d·
disbursements
My. 14–30 * keep pace with the d·.
disc
Pul. 25–30 * There is a d· of cut glass in
discern
Mis. 1– 7 d· the face of the — Matt. 16 : 3.
1– 8 d· the signs of — Matt. 16 : 3.
2– 1 d· the power of Truth and Love
49–20 to d· between the real and the
54– 1 carnal mind cannot d· spiritual
57– 4 that which you admit cannot d·
66–17 to d· God's perfect ways
73– 8 once d· their spiritual meaning,
77– 7 d· and consent to that infinite
87–10 what I now through you d·
103–25 so far as material sense could d·
109–26 must d· the nothingness of evil,
117– 5 d· between the thought, motive, and
131– 5 in order rightly to d· darkness
185– 3 shall be able to d· fully
188–28 that we can d· more of them.
223–12 sufficiently strong to d· what
287–16 until progress lifts mortals to d·
347– 9 d· the face of the skies
347–10 cannot always d· the mental signs
352– 6 able for the first time to d·
355–23 then thou wilt d· the error
Un. 62–27 Mary had risen to d· faintly
No. 23–20 need to d· the claims of evil,
34–12 who d· his true merit,
'00. 9– 2 I d· that this obedience is
My. 45–23 * we now d· the fulfilment of
114– 1 d· the signs of — Matt. 16 : 3.
244–12 need of which I daily d·.

discerned

Mis.	30– 8	St. John spiritually *d·* and
	67–23	*d·*, disarmed, and destroyed.
	169–16	truths . . . must be spiritually *d·*,
	172–24	*d·*, understood, and obeyed.
	199–24	divine Principle is *d·* in C. S.
Ret.	26– 4	Adoringly I *d·* the Principle
Un.	28–11	never a light or form was *d·*
	30–23	then I *d·* the last Adam
No.	20– 3	neither self-created, nor *d·* through
	21– 6	Confucius and Plato but dimly *d·*,
	34–23	The real blood . . . is not yet *d·*.
'00.	15– 8	Passover, spiritually *d·*, is a
'01.	18–15	*d·* only through divine Science.
My.	14– 6	to be *d·* in the near future
	151–30	*d·* its idolatrous tendencies.
	238– 9	*d·*, understood, and demonstrated.
	350– 9	she spiritually *d·* the divine idea

discerneth

'00.	14– 9	(that *d·* spiritually)

discerning

Mis.	287– 9	*d·* not the legitimate affection of
	326–29	*D·* in his path the penitent one
Peo.	10–12	*D·* the God-given rights of

discernment

Mis.	13–27	and the clearer *d·* of good.
	112–29	intellectual, and spiritual *d·*,
	181–31	a clear *d·* of divine Science :
	215–32	spiritual *d·* must be used
	312–21	and his own spiritual *d·*,
My.	22–21	* spiritual *d·* of the needs of
	206– 9	they darken the *d·* of Science ;

discerns

Un.	61–27	contrite heart soonest *d·* this

discharge

Hea.	1– 8	not *d·* from care ;

discharged

No.	8–11	Having *d·* this duty,
My.	119–21	*d·* evidence of material sense

discharges

'02.	10–21	*d·* burdensome baggage,

disciple

Mis.	28–15	proved to his doubting *d·*,
	151– 2	In the words of the loving *d·*,
Pul.	32– 1	* as that of a Delsarte *d·*;
'00.	6–23	meek and loving *d·* of Christ,
'01.	28–24	enough for the *d·* — *Matt.* 10 : 25.
My.	44–11	* faithful *d·* rejoices in prophecy
	113– 8	not an immediate *d·* of our Lord,
	113–17	not a *d·* of the personal Jesus
	119–18	doubting *d·* could not identify
	229–18	cannot be my *d·*." — *Luke* 14 : 27.
	244–21	In the highest sense of a *d·*,

disciples (*see also* **disciples'**)

and prophets

Mis.	84– 7	*d·* and prophets thrust disputed

dark

Mis.	360–28	to sensitive ears and dark *d·*,

deserving

My.	46–20	* faithful, obedient, deserving *d·*.

dull

Mis.	100– 2	artless listeners and dull *d·*.
	163–11	to arrant hypocrite and to dull *d·*
	337–27	to itching ears and to dull *d·*

first

My.	347–17	our great Master's first *d·*,

her

My.	48–20	* has given to her *d·* a means of

his

Mis.	54–26	*healing as Jesus and his d· did,*
	90–25	administered to his *d·* the Passover,
	90–29	after his *d·* had left their nets
	212–31	His *d·*, who had not yet drunk
	274– 1	history of Jesus and of his *d·*,
	344– 4	the wish to become one of his *d·*.
Ret.	90– 7	towns whither he sent his *d·* ;
Pul.	52–20	* practised by Jesus and his *d·*.
'00.	10–16	of Jesus and his *d·*.
'01.	18–12	and taught his *d·* none other.
	18–18	Jesus and his *d·* would have
	23–19	and taught his *d·* and followers
'02.	18– 9	self-seeking of his *d·*
	18–25	ignoble conduct of his *d·*
	18–28	all his *d·* save one.
My.	150–27	our Master said unto his *d·*,
	156–11	directed his *d·* to prepare
	180– 7	taught his *d·* the healing
	190–22	Jesus gave his *d·* (students)
	222– 7	When his *d·* asked him
	339–24	Jesus said to his *d·*,

disciples

immediate

Mis.	29– 5	only to his immediate *d·*,
Ret.	91–16	primarily to his immediate *d·*.

Jesus'

'01.	2–21	Jesus' *d·* of old experienced,

met together

Mis.	279–22	picture is of the *d·* met together

Mrs. Eddy's

Pul.	68–14	* chapter sub-title

my

My.	156–16	passover with my *d·*? — *Luke* 22 : 11.
	339–20	My *d·* rejoice in their

of Christian Science

Pul.	41– 6	* love-offerings of the *d·* of C. S.

of Jesus

My.	222– 2	even the *d·* of Jesus once failed

of Mary Baker Eddy

Pul.	52–13	* of the *d·* of Mary Baker Eddy,

of old

'01.	2–21	Jesus' *d·* of old experienced,
My.	212–19	Being like the *d·* of old,

of St. John

My.	339–17	*d·* of St. John the Baptist said

thy

My.	339–19	thy *d·* fast not?" — *Matt.* 9 : 14.

true

Mis.	171–18	By these signs are the true *d·*
Mis.	279–26	the *d·*, too, were of one mind.
Ret.	76–21	the *d·* were of one accord.

disciples'

'02.	7–27	called his *d·* special attention

discipleship

My.	188–30	be God-endowed for *d·*.

discipline

Mis.	6– 2	*d·* to bring man nearer to God,
	84–23	*d·* of the flesh is designed to
Man.	33– 3	to enforce the *d·* and by-laws of
	33– 7	Rules, and *d·* of the Church.
	40– 1	heading
	41–16	renders this member liable to *d·*
	46–18	subject the offender to Church *d·*.
	46–22	on penalty of *d·*
	51–15	No Church *d·* shall ensue until
	51–21	Board of Directors has power to *d·*,
	52– 2	involving The Mother Church *d·*.
	55– 6	and independently *d·* its own
	67– 2	not to be consulted on cases of *d·*,
Ret.	77– 1	for laxity in *d·* and
	80–15	receptive of the heavenly *d·*.
'00.	8–13	till God's *d·* takes it off
My.	343–27	had five churches under *d·*
	359– 8	not to interfere in cases of *d·*,

disciplined

Man.	37– 6	member who . . . shall be *d·*.
	43– 1	A member . . . shall be *d·*,
	54–22	shall immediately be *d·*,

disclaim

Mis.	174– 3	claiming to talk and *d·* against

disclaimer

My.	150–30	or the *d·* against God

disclaims

Ret.	56–15	Divine Science *d·* sin,

disclose

My.	224–13	the future must *d·* and dispel.

discomfited

Pul.	71–14	* startled and greatly *d·*

discomfort

Mis.	219–21	a sense of *d·* in sin
My.	233–11	Is not *d·* from sin

discomforted

Mis.	241–30	sick who are dis-eased, *d·*,

discomforts

My.	75–22	* *d·* they might have endured

disconnected

Ret.	93–11	is not fragmentary, *d·*,

disconsolate

Mis.	262–17	and hope to the *d·* ;

discontent

Mis.	332– 7	* long winter of our *d·*,"
My.	195–19	deep *d·* with our shortcomings.

discontinue

Hea.	9–12	subjects they would gladly *d·* to

discontinued

Ret.	47–15	voted that the school be *d·*.
My.	51–12	* to have the public services *d·*
	141–22	* these gatherings will be *d·* :

discord

Mis.	40–17	*d·* of whatever sort.
	65– 3	no more proof of human *d·*,
	97– 4	destroy mortal *d·* with immortal
	187– 8	*d·*, as seen in disease and death,
	187–11	and *d·* the unreality.
	187–27	extinguished in a night of *d·*.
	236–24	the remedy for all human *d·*.
	247–27	and reflects harmony or *d·*
	265–18	whose minds . . . disturbed by this *d·*,
	283–28	good, not evil, — harmony, not *d·* ;
	287– 8	To an ill-attuned ear, *d·* is harmony ;
Ret.	57– 8	for the purpose of destroying *d·*.
	69– 5	parent of all human *d·*
Un.	2–19	contains neither *d·* nor disease.
	13– 8	principle . . . knows nothing of *d·*.
	18–21	every supposition of *d·*.
Rud.	9– 5	the seeds of *d·* and disease.
	13–20	and *d·* is the unreal,
No.	16– 4	and *d·* must be eternal.
'00.	11– 3	have no *d·* over music.
Peo.	9–27	destroys *d·* with the higher and
Po.	70–16	*d·* ne'er in harmony began !
My.	90–15	* that *d·* is poisonous,

discordant

Mis.	396– 5	cricket's sharp, *d·* scream
Peo.	10–22	harmonious or *d·* according to
Po.	58–17	cricket's sharp, *d·* scream

discords

Mis.	105– 3	*d·* of this material personality.
	202– 3	correct the *d·* of sense,
No.	10–22	earth's *d·* have not the reality
'02.	9–13	Loving chords set *d·* in harmony.
My.	223– 7	any class of individual *d·*.

discount

Rud.	14–18	No *d·* on tuition was made

discountenanced

'00.	13–26	* *d·* by the authorities of

discounts

Mis.	274–18	it *d·* clemency, mocks morality,

discourage

Pul.	43–27	* *d·* . . . that sort of personal worship

discouraged

Ret.	8–11	continued until I grew *d·*,

discouragement

My.	48–24	* with the *d·* of care and worry,

discouraging

My.	50–18	* apparently *d·* outlook of the

discourse

Mis.	149– 9	has opened his lips to *d·*
	178–10	* delivered an interesting *d·*
Pul.	29–19	* In his admirable *d·* Judge Hanna
	29–24	* *d·* was able, and helpful
My.	155–23	May those who *d·* music to-day,
	296– 2	able *d·* of our "learned judge,"

discourses

Mis.	126– 2	from fragmentary *d·* to one

discoursing

My.	339– 8	wise in *d·* on the great subject

discourteous

My.	327–22	* did not wish to be "*d·*

discover

Mis.	380–14	had driven me to *d·* the Science of
Un.	50–26	you will *d·* the material origin,

discovered

Mis.	34–30	*d·* the Science of healing
	54– 5	Who is it that *d·*, demonstrated,
	75–26	she *d·* the spiritual origin of man.
	165–29	secret stores of wisdom must be *d·*,
	188–21	found it, when she *d·* C. S.
	337– 1	Have I *d·* and founded at this period
	370–29	What manner of man . . . has *d·* an
	379–27	I *d·*, in 1866, the momentous facts
	380–10	to demonstrate what I had *d·* :
	382–12	I *d·* the Science of Christianity
Ret.	24– 4	I *d·* the Science of divine
Un.	30–21	When I *d·* the power of Spirit
Pul.	64–14	* she *d·* C. S. in 1866.
	70– 3	* chapter sub-title
Pan.	5– 3	Can . . . be *d·* in matter?
'01.	27–29	* say it has been *d·* before.
Hea.	12–10	*d·* that all physical effects
My.	v–14	* Mary Baker Eddy *d·* C. S.
	41–27	* not only *d·* C. S., but
	61–29	* As I *d·* the many intricate
	67–13	* C. S. in . . . 1866
	103–19	just as I have *d·* them.
	133–29	even as your heart has *d·* it.
	181–21	C. S. was *d·* in America.
	304–27	* say it has been *d·* before.

dis-covered

Mis.	334–28	and *d·* for you divine Science,

Discoverer
(*see* **Eddy**)

discoverer

Mis.	381–32	both founder and *d·* of
My.	143–18	the *d·* of an eternal truth
	338–25	visible *d·*, founder, demonstrator,
		(*see also* **Eddy**)

discoverers

Mis.	244–30	Are the *d·* of quinine,

discoveries

Mis.	244–32	because of their medical *d·* ?
No.	39–21	new and scientific *d·* of God,
	41–22	by new *d·* of Truth sin is losing
My.	71– 2	* intricate *d·* of organ builders
	237– 9	in his earliest studies or *d·*.

discovering

Pul.	35–24	* *d·* that the more attenuated the

discovers

Mis.	352– 9	when it *d·* the truth,

discovery

Mis.	22– 9	the *d·* of even a portion of it
	121–10	up to a point of *d·* ;
	188–29	At the moment of her *d·*,
	263–25	by the infancy of its *d·*,
	263–28	to appropriate my ideas and *d·*,
	297– 2	elapsed since the *d·* of C. S.,
	310– 6	amplified in this age by the *d·* of C. S.
	379–29	and named my *d·* C. S.
	382– 4	prior to my *d·* of this Science.
	382– 6	The *d·* and founding of C. S.
Ret.	10–11	After my *d·* of C. S.,
	24– 6	The *d·* came to pass in this way.
	24– 8	During twenty years prior to my *d·*
	24–15	the *d·* how to be well myself,
	26–21	*d·* of the Science of being
	26–23	divine Science must be a *d·*.
	27– 7	*d·* of the absolute Science of
	27–13	I had not fully voiced my *d·*.
Pul.	55–16	* Her *d·* was first called,
'01.	27– 1	experience, and final *d·*,
'02.	9–25	Morse's *d·* of telegraphy?
Peo.	7–27	Scientific *d·* and the inspiration of
My.	66–28	* Since the *d·* by Mrs. Eddy,
	91–20	* a *d·* of Mary Baker Eddy
	105– 7	After my *d·* of C. S.,
	120–10	Bear with me the burden of *d·*
	151–26	thus missing the *d·* of all cause
	181–32	first two years of my *d·* of C. S.
	214–19	Four years after my *d·* of C. S.,
	238–13	*d·*, and presentation of C. S.
	296–29	gave her *d·* to the press.
	348– 1	My *d·* that mankind is absolutely
	348–15	was based upon her *d·* that

discredit

Mis.	223–13	and to say, if it must, "I *d·*
'02.	1–15	calculated to displace or *d·*

discrepancy

Man.	104–17	if a *d·* appears in any
Un.	29–18	herein lies the *d·* between

discretion

Mis.	287–32	venturing on valor without *d·*,
Man.	96– 5	left to the *d·* of the lecturer.

discriminate

Mis.	302–11	*d·* between error and Truth,
My.	250–21	*d·* as regards its adaptability

discriminates

Mis.	119–23	*d·* between the real and the unreal
'01.	5–11	*d·* between God and man,

discriminating

Un.	57–14	His pure consciousness was *d·*,

discriminations

No.	7–26	*d·* and guidance thereof

discussed

Man.	90–23	thoroughly *d·*, and understood ;
My.	271–15	* most *d·* woman in all the world.

discussing

'01.	22–23	schools of medicine are *d·* them

discussion

Ret.	49–27	deliberation and earnest *d·*
Un.	6–23	provoked *d·* and horror,
My.	107– 7	general subject under *d·*,

discussions

Man.	26–25	shall neither report the *d·* of
Un.	1–14	in their *d·* of C. S.

disdain

Mis.	105– 3	*d·* the fears and destroy the discords
	389–15	hope deferred, ingratitude, *d·* !
Po.	4–14	hope deferred, ingratitude, *d·* !

disdainfully

My.	129–18	O ye who leap *d·* from this rock

disease

acute

Mis.	41–23	belief of chronic or acute *d·*,

all

Un.	9– 1	mortal mind is the cause of all *d·*.
No.	4–26	All *d·* must be . . . healed on this
My.	204–30	its therapeutics, . . . heals all *d·*.
	218–10	to destroy all *d·* and to raise the

all classes of

Mis.	41–18	*Can all classes of d· be healed*

all manner of

Ret.	60–18	saith to all manner of *d·*,
My.	239–10	by healing all manner of *d·*,
	245– 1	system of healing all manner of *d·*,

and death

Mis.	14–31	sin, sickness, *d·*, and death.
	36–21	includes all evil, *d·*, and death ;
	187– 3	sin, sickness, *d·*, and death.
	187– 8	discord, as seen in *d·* and death,
	194– 4	*d·*, and death are destroyed ;
No.	6– 9	sickness, *d·*, and death.
Pan.	10–27	no necessity for *d·* and death.
My.	172–17	cast out evil, *d·*, and death ;
	180–16	sin, sickness, *d·*, and death.
	240–17	it criticizes evil, *d·*, and death

and sin

Mis.	60– 9	healing cases of *d·* and sin
	105–16	opposites — death, *d·*, and sin.
	336–23	heals *d·* and sin and destroys death !
No.	31– 6	*D·* and sin appear to-day in subtler
	31– 8	*d·* and sin are unreal,

any

Mis.	54–23	not to be subject again to any *d·*
	229– 3	prepares one to have any *d·*

arises

No.	5– 9	*D·* arises from a false and material

becomes

Un.	54– 6	then *d·* becomes as tangible as
No.	5–20	*D·* becomes indeed a stubborn

belief in

Mis.	256– 2	not only cured of their belief in *d·*,

belief of

Mis.	198–20	belief of *d·* is as much the product of

beliefs of

Mis.	93– 6	*beliefs of d· that have been healed*

bring back

Mis.	93–22	neither . . . can . . . bring back *d·*,

bring on

Mis.	93–22	neither fear nor sin can bring on *d·*

cannot cause

My.	349– 7	the body, cannot cause *d·*,

cast out

Mis.	6– 4	Jesus cast out *d·* as evil.

cast out the

Mis.	40–21	power to cast out the *d·*.

cause of

Mis.	66–29	Ignorance of the cause of *d·*
	221–18	If error is the cause of *d·*,

consciousness of

Mis.	308–26	holding . . . the consciousness of *d·*

contagious

Mis.	229–20	confidence . . . in contagious *d·*
My.	116– 2	At a time of contagious *d·*,

controls

Hea.	6–19	when he is sick, *d·* controls

cure of

Pul.	69–26	* prayed for the cure of *d·*,
Rud.	3– 1	harder than the cure of *d·* ;
	3–19	He wrought the cure of *d·* through

cures of

Pul.	45– 6	* they can effect cures of *d·*

cures the

Peo.	6–13	* says : . . . nature cures the *d·*.''

deathly

Pul.	73– 7	* cured herself of a deathly *d·*

destroy

My.	132–24	will also rebuke and destroy *d·*,
	301–28	or destroy *d·* without the aid of

diagnoses

Hea.	12– 8	he diagnoses *d·* as mind,

discord and

Rud.	9– 5	seeds of discord and *d·*.

discord nor

Un.	2–19	contains neither discord nor *d·*.

dread

My.	335–19	* the second case of the dread *d·*

effect or

Mis.	41–24	the effect or *d·* will disappear

disease

eradicate

No.	31– 1	you cannot eradicate *d·* if you

every case of

Mis.	44–10	heal in every case of *d·*,

evidence for

No.	6–19	as . . . real as the evidence for *d·* ;

evidence of

No.	6–13	error indicates, the evidence of *d·*

evil and

Mis.	221–25	struggle against both evil and *d·*,
Un.	37–16	Evil and *d·* do not testify of
Pan.	6– 1	His treatment of evil and *d·*,
	6– 3	because evil and *d·* will never

fear or

Ret.	61– 5	different forms of fear or *d·*.

feasibility of

No.	4–13	destroys the feasibility of *d·* ;

feel

Mis.	234– 1	feel *d·* only by reason of our belief

forms of

No.	2–23	the most defiant forms of *d·*.

heal

My.	117–11	heal *d·*, and make one a
	180–18	overcome evil and heal *d·*.
	300– 9	Does he . . . thus heal *d·* ?
	300–11	heal *d·*, for the reason that

healed

No.	31–19	He healed *d·* as he healed sin ;

healed of

My.	113– 5	and thereby is healed of *d·*.

healed of the

Mis.	34– 5	not only healed of the *d·*,

healing

Mis.	33–22	*ordinary methods of healing d·?*
	51– 3	effect physically . . . healing *d·*.
My.	190–20	divine laws . . . in healing *d·*,
	302– 1	all modes of healing *d·*

healing of

Mis.	63–14	to the healing of *d·*,

health nor

My.	302– 6	life nor death, health nor *d·*,

health, not

My.	239– 1	Life, not death ; health, not *d·* ;

heart

My.	80– 6	* been cured . . . of heart *d·*,

his

Ret.	34–18	not only healed of his *d·*, but

idea about a

My.	344–19	harbored that idea about a *d·*,

in error

Mis.	85–29	*D·* in error, more than ease

insidious

Ret.	19– 9	attacked by this insidious *d·*,
My.	334– 3	* some insidious *d·* was raging

in the body

Mis.	343– 5	turn from *d·* in the body

in the mortal mind

Mis.	343– 6	to find *d·* in the mortal mind,

intruding

My.	221–29	open to the intruding *d·*,

is more

No.	4– 6	*D·* is more than *imagination* ;

is treated

Hea.	14– 4	until *d·* is treated mentally

is unreal

Rud.	12–28	in Science, *d·* is unreal ;
No.	4–16	proposition, . . . that *d·* is unreal ;

itself

Mis.	40–31	nullify either the *d·* itself or
Un.	9– 2	the *d·* itself disappears.

its own

Mis.	62–31	notion that . . . can cure its own *d·*,

loaded with

Mis.	7–18	so loaded with *d·* seems the

malignant

My.	227–15	taking a case of malignant *d·*.

material

Rud.	10–12	of material *d·* and mortality.

medium of

Hea.	6–19	thinks he is a medium of *d·* ;

mental

Mis.	112–24	This mental *d·* at first shows

more

No.	2–15	I have healed more *d·* by the

named

No.	4–10	error of belief, named *d·*,

name of the

Man.	47–20	the generic name of the *d·*

names

My.	228– 3	S. and H. names *d·*,

no

Mis.	93–23	since there is in reality no *d·*.
	334–14	since there is no *d·* ?

disease

no
Un. 7–10 the infinite recognizes no *d*,
My. 297–15 in reality no evil, no *d*,

nor death
Mis. 165–14 darkness, doubt, *d*, nor death.

one
Hea. 13–26 Mesmerism makes one *d* while it

on the body
Hea. 6–13 mind produces *d* on the body,

origin of
Hea. 19–11 The illusive origin of *d*

pain and
Mis. 68–10 * *maintained that pain and d are not*
68–15 is the very pain and *d*.
Rud. 11–14 the unreality of pain and *d* ;

pain or
Rud. 10–14 see, or report pain or *d*.

power of
Mis. 58– 9 belief in the power of *d*

present
Mis. 38–28 in order to cure his present *d*,

producing
My. 302– 2 vehicle . . . of producing *d*.

propagation of
My. 344–17 * theory of the propagation of *d*?"

regarding
Mis. 130–13 acting thus regarding *d*

return of the
Mis. 54–21 return of the *d* that you were

said to
No. 31–25 but Jesus said to *d* :

same
My. 227–11 patients, having the same *d*

seizure of
My. 336–16 * seizure of *d* was so sudden

sense of
Ret. 61–24 If you rule out every sense of *d*
Rud. 12– 7 strengthen the sense of *d*, instead of

sense of the
Un. 9– 2 Destroy the mental sense of the *d*,

sickness and
Pul. 73– 2 * worry . . . about sickness and *d*?
Peo. 7–24 To remove . . . sickness and *d*,
My. 364–16 heals all manner of sickness and *d*,

sickness or
My. 300– 9 there is no sickness or *d*,

sickness, . . . or death
Mis. 65– 4 sin, sickness, *d*, or death,

sin and
Mis. 101–25 evil, including sin and *d*.
No. 4–19 Sin and *d* are not scientific,
My. 147–21 able to heal both sin and *d*,
221–20 with which to heal sin and *d*.

sin, and death
Un. 10– 1 *unreality of d, sin, and death,*
My. 106–19 expressed in *d*, sin, and death,

sin, . . . and death
(*see* **sin**)

sin or
Mis. 191–30 phases of sin or *d* made manifest.

sin, . . . or death
My. 146–27 the side of sin, *d*, or death.

sin, sickness, and
Mis. 251–29 Sin, sickness, and *d* flee before

smites with
Mis. 257–28 pitiless power smites with *d*

so-called
My. 228– 4 so-called *d* is a sensation of mind,
348– 2 absolutely healed of so-called *d*

spread
My. 336– 3 * The *d* spread so rapidly

storms of
'01. 24–13 when the storms of *d* beat against

subject to
Mis. 39– 4 To avoid being *subject* to *d*,

terrible
My. 335–25 * attended cases of this terrible *d*

that
Mis. 58– 2 *and he has no remembrance of that d*
58– 2 *does that d have any more power*

their
Ret. 25–30 as to their *d* or its symptoms,
'01. 33–11 * was not the health . . . but their *d*,

to rob
No. 2– 9 scientific to rob *d* of all reality ;

treat
Mis. 334–13 Why do Christian Scientists treat *d*

treating
Mis. 35– 9 mental system of treating *d*.
65–18 *the right way of treating d*?
97–14 all other methods of treating *d*.
368–18 Science of treating *d* through Mind.
Hea. 14– 4 at the science of treating *d*

disease

treatment of
Hea. 14–21 the metaphysical treatment of *d* ;
My. 103–19 application to the treatment of *d*

treatment of a
My. 204–23 The too long treatment of a *d*,

unreal
No. 4– 5 chapter sub-title
13– 3 makes *d* unreal, and this heals it.

worse than the
My. 118– 7 remedy is worse than the *d*.

———

Mis. 23– 9 *d*, death, winds, and waves,
27–12 inharmony, sin, *d*, death
58– 9 belief . . . destroyed, *d* cannot return.
66–23 *D* that is superinduced by sin
181–26 *d*, sickness, sin, and death
198–18 *d* also is treated and healed.
228–28 and it makes *d* catching.
334–13 Why . . . treat disease *as d*,
Pul. 69–10 * believing that *d* comes from evil
Rud. 10–15 *D* is a thing of thought
11–11 What seem to be *d*, vice, and
No. 2– 6 To aver that *d* is normal,
2–12 healers who admit that *d* is real
5– 5 and *d* is one of the severe
5–18 If *d* is as real as health,
6– 1 If *d* is real it is not illusive,
6–14 If, . . . then *d* cannot be healed by
Peo. 11– 6 can free its body from *d*
My. v–25 * has healed multitudes of *d*
139–27 redeem your body from *d* ;
217–19 * deny the existence of *d*
217–21 deny *first* the existence of *d*,
219–14 the destruction of *d* germs.
228– 1 I call *d* by its name and have
288–21 cast out evil, *d*, death,
300–11 do not believe in the reality of *d*,
349– 5 while *d* is a mental state
349– 8 *d* is in a sense susceptible of

dis-ease

Mis. 219–18 his patient's consciousness of *d*
'01. 15–20 *d* in sin is better than ease.
My. 233–11 should we prefer, ease or *d* in sin?
349– 9 susceptible of both ease and *d*,

diseased

Ret. 40–14 *d* condition was caused by
78– 1 acts like a *d* physique,
Rud. 13–21 according to their own belief is *d*,
15–12 advising *d* people not to enter a
My. 106–18 overcomes the evidence of *d*
218– 1 He restored the *d* body to its

dis-eased

Mis. 241–30 the sick who are *d*,
Un. 58– 3 must become *d*, disquieted,

diseases

acute
Mis. 29–22 chronic and acute *d* that had defied
Pan. 10–19 acute *d* that M.D.'s have failed to

all manner of
'01. 2– 5 Science of healing all manner of *d*.
24–27 healing all manner of *d*.
34– 3 in the healing of all manner of *d*.
'02. 15– 6 Healing all manner of *d* without
My. 190–23 power over all manner of *d* ;
214–21 and for healing all manner of *d*,
219–18 healing, . . . all manner of *d*.

contagious
Mis. 228–30 in infectious and contagious *d*,
My. 219–28 so-called infectious and contagious *d*
226–30 to doctor infectious or contagious *d*."
344–23 of infectious and contagious *d*.

cures from
My. 79–28 * Scientists told of cures from *d*,

healeth all our
Mis. 174– 8 and healeth all our *d*.

imaginary
My. 106–12 limited to imaginary *d* !

infectious
My. 344–21 * heading

inflammatory
My. 107–30 organic and inflammatory *d*,

inveterate
Rud. 9–23 oftentimes healed inveterate *d*.
My. 300–13 heals the most inveterate *d*.

malignant
My. 227–32 a larger per cent of malignant *d*

many
My. 90– 9 * has cured them of *d* many

mysterious
Mis. 221–17 practitioners and mysterious *d*.

of mortal mind
Rud. 10–13 *d* of mortal mind, and not of

diseases

organic
My. 106– 1 in functional and organic *d·*
106– 7 organic *d·* of almost every kind.
190– 9 of contagious and organic *d·*?

other
Ret. 15–24 Among other *d·* cured

our
Mis. 102–21 and heals all our *d·*.
320–19 all our *d·* ;"— see *Psal.* 103 : 3.
My. 37– 1 * natural healer of all our *d·*

their
My. 28–27 * and healed them of their *d·*

thy
Mis. 184–13 healeth all thy *d·*."— *Psal.* 103 : 3.
Man. 47–17 healeth all thy *d·*."— *Psal.* 103 : 3.
Pul. 10– 7 healeth all thy *d·*."— *Psal.* 103 : 3.
Pan. 4–25 healeth all thy *d·*."— *Psal.* 103 : 3.
Peo. 12–14 healeth all thy *d·*."— *Psal.* 103 : 3.
My. 13–20 *healeth all thy d· ;— Psal.* 103 : 3.
119–17 "healeth all thy *d·*'" — *Psal.* 103 : 3.

venereal
Mis. 210–24 belief in venereal *d·* tears the

———

No. 23–12 these devils were the *d·*

disembodied
Mis. 205–19 *d·* individual Spirit-substance
Pul. 38–20 * between the embodied and *d·*

disengage
Mis. 344– 8 *d·* the soul from objects of sense,

disgorging
My. 82–10 * *d·* trunks and smaller articles

disgrace
Mis. 41– 5 malpractice would *d·* Mind-healing,
No. 43–23 which they go away to *d·*.

disgraces
Mis. 226–27 *d·* human nature more than

disguise
Pan. 11–22 whatever strips off evil's *d·*
'00. 15–13 awakened to see through sin's *d·*
My. 121–20 to *d·* internal vulgarity and

disguised
My. 180–24 the *d·* or the self-satisfied mind,

disguises
Mis. 210– 2 strips off its *d·*,

disgusted
Ret. 38–23 had grown *d·* with my printer,

disgusting
Mis. 233– 5 feverish, *d·* pride of those who

disheartened
Mis. 264– 4 will not be *d·* in the midst
325–13 Somewhat *d·*, he patiently
Pul. 83– 8 * will not be *d·* by a thousand

dishonest
Mis. 288–23 the shift of a *d·* mind,
Hea. 12–28 it would be *d·* and divide one's
My. 106–26 *d·* politician or business man?

dishonestly
Ret. 76– 6 he cannot *d·* compose C. S.

dishonesty
Mis. 126–26 honesty always defeats *d·*.
191– 1 "*d·*, craftiness, — see *II Cor.* 4 : 2.
267–18 conceit, cowardice, or *d·*.
366–27 *d·*, self-will, envy, and lust.
Ret. 75–20 *d·* retards spiritual growth
79–13 *D·*, envy, and mad ambition
No. 2–24 *D·* destroys one's ability to heal
3–19 *D·* necessarily stultifies
39– 8 no *d·* or vanity influences the
'01. 16–15 defines this world's god as *d·*,
'02. 4– 2 dishonor . . . *d·* in trusts,
My. 4– 5 *d·*, sin, disable the student ;
124– 1 hidden things of *d·*,— *II Cor.* 4 : 2.
203–16 *D·* is a mental malady
233–20 *d·*, sin, follow in its train.

dishonor
Mis. 194–10 denial would *d·* that office
236–19 restore harmony and prevent *d·*.
'01. 12–16 he would *d·* that office
'02. 4– 1 *d·* in nations, dishonesty

dishonored
Mis. 163– 6 a grave to mortal sense *d·*
Pul. 83– 4 * better self is shamed and *d·*,
No. 43–17 C. S. Mind-healing is *d·* by

dishonors
Mis. 367–14 it *d·* God to claim that He

disinterested
Ret. 50–11 I beg *d·* people to ask my

disk
Ret. 94–15 on the *d·* of consciousness

dislike
Mis. 336–13 *d·* and hatred of God's idea,

dislocated
Un. 7–14 able to replace *d·* joints

dislocations
Mis. 242– 7 reset certain *d·* without the

disloyal
Mis. 32– 4 *the students of d· students?*
Man. 36–16 are deceased, absent, or *d·*,
111–18 are deceased, absent, or *d·*,
'01. 20–11 he is *d·* to God and man ;
'02. 3– 2 ten thousand loyal . . . to one *d·*,
My. 130– 4 *d·* to the teachings of C. S.
130– 8 The effort of *d·* students
229– 3 nor *d·* Christian Scientist

dismal
Peo. 14– 6 *d·* gray stones of church-yards

dismally
Mis. 329– 9 various apartments are *d·* dirty.

dismayed
Mis. 278– 3 but I am not *d·*,
My. 294–16 faithful M.D. is not *d·* by a

dismiss
Man. 26–24 shall *d·* a member.
52–18 shall *d·* a member from the Church.
102– 8 This committee shall elect, *d·*, or

dismissal
Mis. 101– 6 and the *d·* of sorrow.
280–27 some questions before their *d·*,
Man. 28–23 his *d·* shall be written on the
41–17 *d·* from The Mother Church.
67– 4 on trial for *d·* from the Church.
My. 182– 5 letter of *d·* and recommendation

dismissed
Mis. 280–18 *d·* the fifth of March,
344–11 he was *d·* by the professor.
Man. 28–23 shall be *d·* from this Church,
39– 7 Members once *D·*.
78– 3 he may be *d·* from office
Un. 57–16 for it was detected and *d·*.

dismissing
Mis. 146– 7 on receiving or *d·* candidates.

disobedience
Mis. 267–29 *d·* to this divine Principle
Man. 28– 4 *d·* to the laws of The Mother Church
65–18 *D·* to this By-Law shall be
Un. 15– 1 by man's first *d·*, came
Rud. 10–21 *d·* to His spiritual law.
My. 159–23 enforcing obedience and punishing *d·*.
224– 8 and the bane which follows *d·*.

disobedient
Mis. 117–29 The *d·* make their moves before
My. 118– 4 *d·* spread personal contagion,

disobey
Mis. 73–13 The foolish *d·* moral law,
208–16 and so *d·* the divine order.
353–31 criticise and *d·* her ;
354– 1 declaring they "never *d·* Mother"!

disobeying
My. 160–20 *d·* the commandments of God.

disordered
Mis. 210–19 begets a belief of *d·* brains,
375– 1 Pictures which present *d·* phases
My. 301–27 cannot . . . restore *d·* functions,

disorderly
My. 131–19 I hope I shall not be found *d·*,

disorganization
Mis. 56– 5 if . . . *d·* would destroy Spirit

disorganize
Mis. 137–19 *D·* the National . . . Association !
139– 2 adjourn, if it does not *d·*,
139– 3 if it does *d·*, to meet again
Un. 34– 1 *D·* the so-called material structure,

disowned
Un. 54–26 and *d·* its acquaintance,

disparagement
No. 29–15 Is not this a *d·* of the person

dispassionately
My. 249– 6 Meet *d·* the raging element of

dispel
Mis. 368– 4 *d·* this illusion of the senses,
My. 224–13 future must disclose and *d·*.

dispelled
Mis. 52–18 *If this life is a dream not d·*,
53– 3 false claim can be wholly *d·*.

dispelling
Mis. 190– 5   as d· a false sense
Un.   42–24   Science, d· a false sense

dispels
Mis. 205– 9   the light which d· darkness.
Un.   7–23   realization of this fact d· even

dispensation
Ret. 87–22   In this orderly, scientific d·
My. 110– 2   belongs not to a d· now ended,
     221– 7   foresaw the new d· of Truth

dispense
Mis. ix– 5   * enable a man to d· with alms.''
My. 139–17   When I asked you to d· with

dispensing
Mis. 172– 3   D· the Word charitably,

dispersed
Po.   vi–14   In 1835 a mob . . . d· a meeting

displace
Mis. 283– 7   unlock the desk, d· the furniture,
'02.   1–15   Whatever seems calculated to d·

displacing
Mis. 294– 5   and d· his fellows.

display
Man. 60–23   No large gathering of people nor d·

displayed
Mis. 66– 5   the genius whereof is d· in
Ret. 88–30   and its power is d·

displays
Mis. 142– 9   boat d·, among other beautiful

displeasure
Pul. 15– 9   and so risk human d·

disporting
Mis. 112– 1   d· itself with the subtleties of

disposal
Man. 80– 4   D· of Funds.
My. 167–24   noble d· of the legislative question
     281– 6   faith in God's d· of events.

dispose
My.   25– 3   * d· fully and finally of this feature

disposed
Mis.   4–14   questions important to be d· of
My.   93–19   * too often d· to touch upon it

disposer
Un.   26– 5   author, authority, governor, d·.

disposing
Mis. 381–24   d· of, the enjoined pamphlet,

disposition
Man. 80– 9   is authorized to order its d·
My. 211–26   spoiling that individual's d·,
     310–27   often presented my d· as
     311– 2   as illustrative of my d· :

dispositions
Un.   57– 1   d· which offend the spiritual sense.

dispossess
Pul.   3– 8   nothing can d· you of this
No.   42–12   to d· the divine Mind of

dispraise
Mis. 245–22   the praise or the d· of men.

disproof
Un.   47– 1   Jesus assumed the burden of d·

disprove
Mis. 101–29   d· the evidence of the senses.
My. 107–18   does not d· the efficiency of

disproved
My. 303–16   If . . . C. S. would be d· ;

dispute
Un.   25– 3   and d· self-evident facts ;
'02. 10– 7   and mortals . . . d· the facts,

disputed
Mis. 84– 7   prophets thrust d· points
Peo. 12– 9   d· and trampled under the feet
My. 111– 8   d· his teachings on practically

disputing
My. 285–21   in the temple d· with — Acts 24 : 12.

disqualifies
Man. 41–14   d· a member for office

disquieted
Un.   58– 3   must become dis-eased, d·,
Pan.   4–22   why art thou d· within — Psal. 42 : 11.

disregard
Mis. 301–18   my private counsel they d·.
Ret. 72– 3   To d· the welfare of others
My.   41–25   * d· his lawful inheritance,

disrespectfully
Man. 53– 9   to treat the author of our textbook d·

disrupt
Man. 93–20   to meddle with nor to d· the

disruption
Man. 93–18   No D· of Branch Churches.

dissected
Rud. 15–24   mind of the pupil may be d·

dissecting-knife
Un.   28– 6   nor cut with the d·.

dissension
My. 212–15   Why is there so much d·

dissensions
My. 343–27   D· are dangerous in an infant church.

dissent
Mis. 109– 3   assent where they should d· ;
Pul. 51– 4   * Freedom to believe or to d·
My.   94–12   * absence of d· among them
     291– 6   a quiet assent or d·.

dissented
My. 317–19   d· from what I had written,

dissenting
Ret. 44–26   passing without a d· voice.

dissever
My. 306– 5   to d· any unity that may exist

dissimulation
Un.   56–26   Love which is without d·

dissolve
Mis. 70–23   d· into its native nothingness ;
     291–23   will at length d· into thin air.
     358–21   to d· their organizations,
Ret. 49–29   deemed best to d· this corporation,
      87–26   such efficacy as to d· error.
Un.   60–28   must yield . . . and so d·.

dissolved
Mis. 53– 6   d· only as we master error
      79– 2   beliefs will be purged and d·
     297–23   or this contract is legally d·.
     350–17   I d· the society,
     364–25   impossible partnership is d·.
Man. 34–21   until that membership is d·.
     102– 6   shall not be d· until the
Ret. 44–24   recommended that the church be d·.
      49–30   and the same is hereby d·.

dissolves
Mis. 205–26   d· all supposed material life
     361– 4   d· through self-imposed suffering,

dissolving
Mis.   1–17   from the ashes of d· self,
     290– 9   Mistaken views ought to be d· views,
Ret. 45–18   when d· that organization,
Po.   24– 4   D· death, despair !

distance
Mis.   x–15   as mile-stones measuring the d·,
      79–14   he cannot get out of the focal d· of
     120–21   members reside a long d· from
     136–26   members coming from a d·
     263–17   especially by those at a d·,
     277– 7   its voice dies out in the d·
     322– 5   People coming from a d·
Ret. 65–28   magnitude and d· of the stars,
Un.   20–22   outside of His own focal d·.
Pul. 21–20   To perpetuate a cold d· between
      36–17   * could have walked any conceivable d·.
      47–23   * an easy driving d· for her
'02. 10–21   shortens the d·,
Po.   70– 2   In the dim d·, lay
My. 221– 2   moral d· between Christianity and
     332– 1   * restore her to her friends at a d·

distanced
Mis. 297– 3   has d· all other religious

distances
My. 142– 5   * communicants who come long d·
     170–27   some of you have come long d·

distant
Mis.   6–14   At no d· day, Christian healing
     347– 3   d· rumbling and quivering of the
Pul. 41–15   * and even from the d· States
No.   20– 9   it may seem d· or cold,
Pan.   1–17   day is not d· in the horizon of
Po.   31– 8   tear-filled tones of d· joy,
My.   30–12   * come from far d· points
      47–21   * rooted itself in so many d· lands,
      59– 6   * true in some far d· day
     140–15   * need not debar d· members from
     140–26   does not prevent its d· members
     147– 8   And now, at this d· day,
     189– 8   You worship no d· deity,
     290– 4   the near seems afar, the d· nigh,
     327–29   * not far d·, when the laws

distilled

Mis.	278– 2	are the *d·* spirits of evil,
Pul.	8–25	*d·* the nectar and painted the
My.	178– 9	*d·* in the laboratory of

distinct

Mis.	32–25	*D·* denominational and social
Ret.	34– 8	or give me one *d·* statement
	59–21	define Mind and matter as *d·*,
Un.	54–22	*d·* addition to human wisdom,
Pul.	47–14	* gave her any *d·* statement of
	64–19	* gave her no *d·* statement of
My.	179– 3	were in two *d·* manuscripts.
	197– 3	is least *d·* to conscience.
	203– 6	should be *d·* in our consciousness

distinction

Mis.	36–19	*What is the d· between*
	203– 3	I make no *d·* between my
	227–10	is the nice *d·* by which
	257– 6	*d·* between that which
Ret.	3–11	won *d·* in 1814 at the
Rud.	1–17	in *d·* from one's appearance
'02.	2– 4	without clamor for *d·* or
My.	87–11	* visitors of title and *d·*,
	203– 7	not clamorous for worldly *d·*.
	343–15	I have sought no such *d·*.

distinctions

Un.	27–12	Applying these *d·* to evil and
No.	7–25	*d·* of individual character

distinctive

'00.	13–10	*d·* feature the apostle justly regards
My.	100–12	* as a *d·* organization

distinctly

Man.	32–13	*d·* announce the full title
	74– 7	*d·* democratic in its government,
Ret.	8– 4	calling me *d·* by name,
	14–14	*D·* do I recall what followed.
Un.	17–13	Jesus *d·* taught the arrogant
Pul.	33– 5	* heard her name called *d·*,
My.	39–27	* even more *d·* may we realize

distinguish

Ret.	74– 5	fails to *d·* the individual,
Un.	14–28	learning to *d·* evil from good,

distinguished

Mis.	68–25	* *d·* from that of matter,
	68–29	* *d·* from its phenomenal modifications."
	164– 3	incorporeal and . . . are *d·* thus :
	168–29	* The *d·* speaker began by saying :
	372–20	the ancient and most *d·* artists.
Ret.	5–21	* *d·* for numerous excellences.
	7–14	* made himself one of the most *d·* men
Pul.	1– 8	1893 was a *d·* character,
	43–11	* Mrs. Henrietta Clark Bemis, a *d·*
	48–19	* Hon. Hoke Smith, another *d·* relative,
No.	42–25	A *d·* clergyman came to be healed.
	43–10	A *d·* Doctor of Divinity said :
'00.	7– 9	*d·* members of the bar and bench,
	14–29	being told they are *d·* individuals,
	15– 4	*d·* above human title
'01.	31–24	with *d·* Christian clergymen,
My.	105–20	the patient of a *d·* M.D.,
	174–10	*d·* editors in my home city
	298– 7	has *d·* all my working years.
	305–13	best and most *d·* men
	310– 4	Albert was a *d·* lawyer.
	335–24	* sent for the *d·* physician

distinguishes

Pul.	69–13	* He *d·* C. S. from the
My.	225–14	capitalization which *d·* it

distinguishing

Man.	59– 3	*d·* them from the writings of
Ret.	94–25	the modesty and *d·* affection
My.	82–19	* is a *d·* characteristic of

distorted

Mis.	49–11	*d·* into the claim of insanity
	250–11	is *d·* into human qualities,

distorting

Mis.	345–25	thus *d·* or misapprehending the

distress

'02.	5– 6	C. S. stills all *d·*

distresses

Mis.	199–12	in *d·* for Christ's sake. — II Cor. 12 : 10.

distribute

Mis.	149– 9	*d·* what God has given him
'00.	3– 8	hoards this capital to *d·* gain."

distributed

Pul.	25– 4	* by the four systems

distributing

Mis.	381–24	selling, giving away, *d·*, or
Ret.	36– 7	and *d·* them unsparingly.
My.	252– 4	like the bee, always *d·* sweet

distribution

Man.	77–16	proper *d·* of the funds
Po.	vii– 7	* *her poems, for private d·.*

district

My.	77–29	* edifice in the Back Bay *d·*
	309–30	* the *d·* school practically all the

District Manager

Man.	99–22	act as *D· M·* of the Committees

distrust

My.	202– 3	from human ambition, fear, or *d·*
	211–21	suspicious *d·* where honor is due,

disturb

Mis.	124– 2	would tend to *d·* the divine order,
'01.	9–24	they *d·* the carnal and destroy it ;

disturbance

Mis.	224–23	no passing breath nor accidental *d·*

disturbed

Mis.	265–18	must be, *d·* by this discord,
Pul.	3– 2	be demolished, or even *d·* ?
My.	126– 4	the *d·* human mind

ditch

Mis.	230–20	drop human life into the *d·*

diverged

Mis.	322–17	must not be diverted or *d·*,

divergence

Mis.	265– 5	if he . . . this *d·* widens.
Rud.	17– 1	slight *d·* is fatal in Science.

diverges

Mis.	265– 2	if he *d·* from Science
Ret.	56– 5	*d·* from the one divine Mind,

diverse

Mis.	265– 8	*D·* opinions in Science are
My.	90–10	* of diseases many and *d·*.

diversions

My.	309–30	* supplied the only social *d·*,

diversities

Mis.	347–13	*d·* of operation by the same spirit.

diverted

Mis.	322–16	must not be *d·* or diverged,

divest

Mis.	14– 2	*D·* your thought, then, of the mortal

divests

Mis.	92–32	*d·* himself of pride and self,
Ret.	84–19	*d·* himself most of pride and self,

divide

Mis.	194–14	to *d·* the rays of Truth,
Ret.	60–30	Any attempt to *d·* these
	85–23	to *d·* the ranks of C. S.
'01.	12–20	to *d·* the rays of Truth,
Hea.	12–28	dishonest and *d·* one's faith
My.	206–10	they *d·* Truth's garment

divided

Mis.	52– 4	*d·* between catnip and Christ;
	56–17	a kingdom *d·* against itself,
	89– 2	*d·* against itself — *Matt.* 12 : 25.
	197–26	that is *d·* against itself,
	217–26	a kingdom *d·* against itself,
	237–20	a period of . . . *d·* interests,
Un.	33–23	find them *d·* in evidence,
	60– 4	a kingdom *d·* against itself.
No.	5–21	*d·* against itself — *Luke* 11 : 17.
'01.	25–29	a kingdom *d·* against itself,
My.	40–15	* *d·* into warring sects ;

dividend

Mis.	239–22	her *d·*, when compared with
My.	217–13	will receive his *d·* with interest

divides

Ret.	28–19	*d·*, subdivides, increases,
	35–13	*d·* its rays and brings out the
	56– 6	Whatever . . . *d·* Mind into minds,
Rud.	10– 7	*d·* His power with nothing evil
My.	316– 3	*d·* between sect and Science

dividing

Man.	99– 5	*d·* line being the 36th parallel
Peo.	9–12	*d·* our homage and obedience

Divina

My.	268–19	centuries without a living *D·*.

Divine

Un.	50– 6	and is unknown to the *D·*.
Rud.	4– 6	*or only of D· or C. S.?*
No.	18–19	the human conceive of the *D·*.
'01.	1–17	human in communion with the *D·*,
'02.	10–13	above itself towards the *D·*,

divine

adventure

My.	158– 9	an age of Love's *d·* adventure

afflatus

Mis.	166– 7	moves in our midst a *d·* afflatus.

divine

aid
Peo. 9–18 invoke the d· aid of Spirit
My. 166–20 When we . . . d· aid is near.
All
Un. 31– 6 the d· All must be Spirit.
antidote
Mis. 255–26 because it is this d· antidote,
appellative
'00. 3–24 contained this d· appellative
approbation
My. 166– 3 will continue with d· approbation.
Arbiter
Un. 30–27 reflect the Life of the d· Arbiter.
art
Pul. 66– 1 * what they term the d· art of healing,
authority
Mis. 93–16 fear, . . . is without d· authority.
Un. 33– 7 yet we have it on d· authority :
'01. 14–27 wrong has no d· authority ;
beauty
Mis. 86–24 It is next to d· beauty
Being
Pan. 4– 4 a self-existent d· Being,
'01. 3–19 intelligent, d· Being,
benedictions
Mis. 320– 8 with d· benedictions for mankind.
My. 256–17 full of d· benedictions
blessing
Mis. 133–22 to seek the d· blessing
capacity
No. 21–12 reflecting God and the d· capacity.
character
Un. 1–16 draw nearer to the d· character,
Hea. 4–22 conception of the d· character,
chariots
Un. 17–10 evil ties its . . . to the d· chariots,
children
Un. 23– 7 d· children are born of law and
Christ
My. 36–20 * salvation through His d· Christ.
claims
Mis. 19–13 accepted the d· claims of Truth
Comforter
Man. 15– 8 Holy Ghost or d· Comforter ;
command
Mis. 10–14 If they mistake the d· command,
Ret. 71– 5 obedient to the d· command,
My. 224– 6 the human need, the d· command,
351–11 is indeed a d· command,
commandments
Ret. 31–18 breaketh the d· commandments.
commission
Mis. 117–18 to carry out a d· commission
concept
Ret. 68–10 d· concept . . . is spiritually real.
conception
Mis. 287– 1 most exalted d· conception.
concurrence
My. 246–20 d· concurrence of the spirit and
consciousness
Mis. 366–14 or can be d· consciousness.
Un. 51–20 The Ego is d· consciousness.
No. 4–22 do not arise from the d· consciousness
16– 1 found in the d· consciousness.
17–16 d· consciousness and God's verity.
correspondence
Mis. 74– 1 d· correspondence of noumenon and
decision
My. 190–21 d· decision in behalf of Mind.
declaration
Mis. 76–16 void by Jesus' d· declaration,
decree
Mis. 66–10 always according to d· decree.
121–14 even a d· decree, a law of Love !
122–10 predestined to fulfil a d· decree,
341–20 implicit treason to d· decree.
definition
Mis. 258–28 d· definition of Deity
design
Mis. 205–24 unites all periods in the d· design.
destiny
No. 34–17 to crush out . . . its d· destiny.
digest
Rud. 3–15 that d· digest of Science
directions
Mis. 158–26 d· directions sent out to the
economy
Un. 26–23 chance in the d· economy?
efficacy
Rud. 17– 6 its d· efficacy to heal.
effulgence
My. 262–19 d· effulgence, deific presence
element
Mis. 337–21 they obscure its d· element,

divine

emanation
'01. 10– 8 a spiritual, d· emanation,
energies
Mis. 176–12 more of the d· energies of good,
352–23 Through the d· energies alone
360–22 fill earth with the d· energies,
Ret. 88–13 its practicality, its d· energies,
'02. 10– 4 spiritual forces, the d· energies,
energy
Mis. 166–27 This action of the d· energy,
176–28 up to the acme of d· energy
208– 3 This law is a d· energy.
292–13 partly illustrate the d· energy
343– 8 for the d· energy to move it
My. 355–13 in our ranks of d· energy,
Esse
My. 202–25 the underived glory, the d· Esse.
essence
Mis. 163–30 This idea or d· essence was,
Un. 39– 6 quenched in the d· essence,
ever-presence
My. 192–28 d· ever-presence, answering your
Father
Mis. 33–11 our d· Father and Mother.
Father-Mother
Mis. 102–15 loving, d· Father-Mother God.
127–11 petitions the d· Father-Mother God
My. 18– 8 petitions the d· Father-Mother God
fiat
Un. 38–21 no d· fiat commands us to
food
My. 247–24 so filled with d· food
God is
Pan. 4–12 reason and will are human ; God is d·.
good
Mis. 164– 4 idea that represents d· good,
Ret. 56–11 omnipresence of God, or d· good.
80– 2 this is the pledge of d· good
Un. 24– 4 My Mind is d· good,
government
Mis. 56–15 opposed to the d· government.
grace
Mis. 360–17 and the dews of d· grace,
hand
Ret. 27–29 d· hand led me into a new world
My. 326–20 I recognize the d· hand in
healing
Mis. 2–17 a more rational and d· healing
Ret. 28– 7 the perfect Mind and d· healing.
Pul. 34–17 * heading
34–19 * the Principle of d· healing,
67–13 * the Principle of d· healing,
My. 308– 3 the advent of d· healing
help
Mis. 39–30 D· help is as necessary in the one
158–17 a lack of faith in d· help,
380–15 I again, in faith, turned to d· help,
history
Ret. 10–15 d· history, voicing the idea of
honors
Mis. 358– 5 will graduate under d· honors,
idea
Mis. 18–20 divine Principle and d· idea,
186–16 the d· idea named man ;
370–12 d· idea assumes different forms,
Un. 49– 4 as being the eternally d· idea.
59– 5 d· idea of the divine Principle
59–11 d· idea brought to the flesh
59–18 the d· idea is always present.
No. 26– 8 than . . . belief resembles the d· idea.
My. 350– 9 spiritually discerned the d· idea
357– 4 even the d· idea of C. S.,
ideal
Mis. 103–26 exchanges this . . . for the d· ideal,
Un. 51–26 d· ideal, whose Soul is not in body,
Pul. 74–26 Love and its compound d· ideal.
My. 257– 9 form and comeliness of the d· ideal,
272–11 and ever shall be the d· ideal,
illumination
Pul. 34–11 * became aware of a d· illumination
impetus
My. 248–21 fall for lack of the d· impetus.
import
'00. 14–11 seek thou the d· import of the
infinitude
Un. 20–20 as you realize the d· infinitude
influence
No. 40–27 are made better only by d· influence.
influx
My. 206– 4 hinder the d· influx and lose
intelligence
Mis. 23– 8 demonstrated a d· intelligence
82–11 d· intelligence, or Principle, of all
336–27 the fiat of d· intelligence,
'01. 7– 6 infinite Person or d· intelligence

divine

interpretation
  My. 114–21 the influx of *d·* interpretation

justice
  Mis. 12–24 dealt with by *d·* justice.
    277–25 *d·* justice and judgment are
    289–19 Neither *d·* justice nor human
  My. 149–20 clear perception of *d·* justice,
    227–13 turn to *d·* justice for support

knowledge
  Un. 4–22 no part of the *d·* knowledge.

largess
  My. 349–12 a *d·* largess, a gift of God

law
  Mis. 65–28 constitute the *d·* law of healing.
    71–22 is a departure from *d·* law ;
    73–28 It is the appearing of *d·* law
    104–23 *d·* law and order of being.
    107–23 oft-repeated violations of *d·* law,
    119–25 prominent statute in the *d·* law,
    261– 6 According to *d·* law, sin and
    261–12 pays his full debt to *d·* law,
  Ret. 24–21 perfect scientific accord with *d·* law.
    26–16 the operation of the *d·* law.
  Un. 13– 6 in obedience to *d·* law,
    18–17 I show My pity through *d·* law,
    56–16 but the *d·* law is supreme,
  Pul. 34–24 scientific accord with the *d·* law.''
    35– 7 * natural fulfilment of *d·* law
  No. 26–23 immutable harmony of *d·* law.
  My. 106– 4 for love fulfils *d·* law
    129–22 *d·* law gives to man health
    131–23 much of the *d·* law and the gospel.
    131–24 The *d·* law has said to us :
    153–23 unmindful of the *d·* law of Love,
    154– 8 to infringe the *d·* law of Love
    190–26 with power (knowledge of *d·* law)

laws
  My. 190–19 certainty of the *d·* laws of Mind

liberty
  Mis. 163–20 and are the basis of *d·* liberty,

Life
  Mis. 2–17 The time approaches when *d·* Life,
    123–27 but through a *d· Life,*
    150–27 God demonstrable as *d·* Life,
    167–17 His Father and Mother are *d·* Life,
    331–19 O Life *d·*, that owns each waiting
    389– 7 O Life *d·*, that owns each waiting
  Un. 61–12 nightless radiance of *d·* Life.
  Pul. 30–22 * the possibilities of the *d·* Life.
  No. 15–24 estranges mortals from *d·* Life
    18–14 demonstration of *d·* Life and Love ;
    33–21 efficacy of *d·* Life and Love
  Pan. 14– 7 living the *d·* Life, Truth, Love,
  '01. 18–26 The *d·* Life, Truth, Love
  Peo. 2–23 but the *d·* Life, Truth, and Love,
    14–17 power of *d·* Life and Love
  Po. 4– 3 O Life *d·*, that owns each waiting
    22– 8 New themes seraphic, Life *d·*,
  My. 109–21 reflex images of this *d·* Life,
    150–14 to reflect the *d·* Life, Truth, and
    153–32 up to the one source, *d·* Life
    257–22 the reign of Truth and Life *d·*
    348–29 *D·* Life, Truth, Love is the basic

life
  Po. 70– 6 Making this life *d·*,

light
  Mis. 113– 7 and *d·* light to be obscured,
    223– 8 *d·* light, logic, and revelation
  Un. 6–11 presented to the people in *d·* light,
  My. 187– 6 May the *d·* light of C. S.
    194–14 human self lost in *d·* light,
    258– 7 seems illuminated . . . with *d·* light.

likeness
  Ret. 60– 2 as very far from the *d·* likeness.
  Un. 39–27 losing the *d·* likeness.
  No. 36– 5 when we awake in the *d·* likeness.
  My. 121–23 and reflects the *d·* likeness.

logic
  Mis. 195–17 Master's *d·* logic, as seen in
  My. 350– 5 minus *d·* logic and plus human

Love
  Mis. ix–18 draughts from the fount of *d·* Love.
    20– 2 with the radiance of *d·* Love ;
    28–27 together with his *d·* Love,
    81–26 *d·* Love hears and answers the human
    111– 8 losing hold of *d·* Love, you lost
    113–24 *D·* Love is our hope, strength, and
    121–28 greater than human pity, is *d·* Love,
    122–20 Love *d·* spurned, lessens not the
    122–27 *D·* Love knows no hate ;
    123–20 majestic atonement of *d·* Love.
    125–13 rest, in the understanding of *d·* Love
    127–14 faithfully asks *d·* Love to feed it
    127–17 the tributary of *d·* Love,
    133–27 I turn constantly to *d·* Love

divine

Love
  Mis. 144–29 To-day I pray that *d·* Love,
    154–10 and enlarge its borders with *d·* Love.
    154–16 the purpose of *d·* Love to resurrect
    155–30 wherewith *d·* Love has entrusted us,
    158–10 has obeyed the message of *d·* Love,
    160–11 knowledge of Truth and *d·* Love.
    165–26 this account is settled with *d·* Love,
    186–15 that God is *d·* Love :
    186–15 *d·* Love is the divine Principle
    194–25 *d·* Love that casts out all fear.
    208–13 motion of the law of *d·* Love
    209–32 *D·* Love, . . . pursues the evil
    213– 8 acquiescence in the methods of *d·* Love.
    223–20 *d·* Love so permeate the affections
    236–23 seek in *d·* Love the remedy
    261–21 No greater type of *d·* Love can be
    262–19 *d·* Love which looseth the chains of
    276–20 *d·* Love is found in affliction.
    292–14 *D·* Love eventually causes mortals to
    303– 7 be governed by *d·* Love alone
    307– 3 *d·* Love is an ever-present help ;
    317–28 *d·* Love will open the way
    328–25 Whatever . . . *d·* Love will remove ;
    335–15 path made luminous by *d·* Love.
    348– 9 *d·* Love will bless this
    351–27 Love *d·* punishes the joys of
    357–31 *D·* Love is the substance of C. S.,
    384–15 Light, Love *d·* Is here,
    386– 3 infinite appear Life, Love *d·*,
  Man. 40– 7 *d·* Love alone governs man ;
    45–12 demonstrating the rules of *d·* Love.
    104– 9 hedge it about with *d·* Love.
  Un. 55–22 here shall I behold God, *d·* Love.
  Pul. 3–15 *d·* Love gives us the true sense of
    3–21 is a tributary of *d·* Love,
    74–26 with God, in the sense of *d·* Love
    77–14 * as revealed by *d·* Love through you
    78–12 * as revealed by *d·* Love through you
    85– 9 * unfolded and demonstrated *d·* Love,
  Rud. 12–19 induces rest in God, *d·* Love,
  No. 19–18 feel no sensation of *d·* Love.
    35– 8 to the purpose of *d·* Love,
  Pan. 14–22 May the *d·* Love succor and
  '00. 4–28 *d·* Love includes and reflects all
    5–17 divine Science of *d·* Love,
    5–28 utilize the power of *d·* Love in
    15– 6 partake of what *d·* Love hath
    15–17 all this time *d·* Love has
  '01. 1–24 practical possibilities of *d·* Love;
    4–14 demonstrated as *d·* Love;
    4–28 Principle,'' meaning *d·* Love,
    7–23 may attend their petitions to *d·* Love.
    9–14 the spirit of *d·* Love,
    10–20 *D·* Love spans the dark passage of sin,
    15–15 blessings that *d·* Love bestows
    17– 5 quickly to return to *d·* Love,
    19– 6 closer proximity with *d·* Love,
    21–27 or felt the incipient touch of *d·* Love
    35–11 Love *d·* that plucks us From the human
  '02. 2– 5 to wait on *d·* Love ;
    5–10 almost unconceived light of *d· Love,*
    6–22 image and likeness of *d·* Love.
    7– 9 the true idea of God — *d·* Love
    11– 6 *D·* Love waits and pleads to save
    19–22 It is *d·* Love that doeth it,
    20– 9 with the fulness of *d·* Love.''
  Po. 3–14 Love *d·* doth fill my heart.
    24–12 O Love *d·*, This heart of Thine
    36–14 Love *d·* Is here, and thine ;
    49– 5 infinite appear Life, Love *d·*,
  My. 4–12 with the leaven of *d·* Love
    12–26 Faith in *d·* Love supplies the
    18–11 faithfully asks *d·* Love to
    18–14 the tributary of *d·* Love,
    21–15 * *d·* Love more than compensates for
    23– 4 * The *d·* Love that prompted the desire,
    27– 3 *D·* Love bids me say :
    28– 4 ''*D·* Love always has met
    41– 7 * blessed and comforted by *d·* Love.
    61–19 * the might of *d·* Love,
    63–15 * to work out the purposes of *d·* Love.
    73– 9 ''*D·* Love always has met
    113–19 in the arms of *d·* Love,
    115– 2 mighty chariot of *d·* Love,
    123– 5 great guerdon of *d·* Love,
    132– 1 fulfilment of *d·* Love in our lives
    132–16 *D·* Love has strengthened the hand
    132–19 *D·* Love hath opened the gate
    132–24 *D·* Love will also rebuke and
    132–28 *D·* Love is our only physician,
    135–30 understand that God is *d·* Love,
    138–11 test my trust in *d·* Love.
    139–27 so doth the *d·* Love redeem your body
    148–29 Christianity is the summons of *d·* Love
    149– 6 Principle of Christ is *d·* Love,

divine

Love

My.	153–18	spiritual help of *d·* Love.
	161– 7	balancing his account with *d·* Love,
	162–28	their understanding of *d·* Love.
	179–32	the *d·* Love practical,
	181– 9	maturing conception of *d·* Love ;
	182–20	*d·* Love that reigns above the
	184–25	precious in the sight of *d·* Love,
	188–31	When *d·* Love gains admittance to
	189–15	government of *d·* Love derives its
	190– 3	merciful design of *d·* Love,
	192– 3	thou ransomed of *d·* Love,
	192–15	May the blessing of *d·* Love
	194–25	May *d·* Love abundantly bless
	197–20	I thank *d·* Love for the hope
	200–14	the glorious beatitudes of *d·* Love.
	201– 3	whereunto *d·* Love has called us
	204–10	in one Principle, *d·* Love,
	214– 5	*D·* Love always has met
	223–28	Just now *d·* Love and wisdom saith,
	240– 1	all men shall know Him (*d·* Love)
	252– 3	Keep yourselves busy with *d·* Love.
	262– 4	inherent unity with *d·* Love,
	262–16	dawn of *d·* Love breaking upon
	265–20	*d·* Love, impartial and universal,
	265–26	and permeated with *d·* Love,
	270–10	*D·* Love, nearer my consciousness
	275– 4	As the sequence of *d·* Love
	275– 7	they are controlled by *d·* Love ;
	278– 7	government of *d·* Love is supreme.
	284–25	in the full efficacy of *d·* Love
	287– 6	as instruments of *d·* Love,
	287– 7	*D·* Love reforms, regenerates,
	287– 9	*D·* Love is the noumenon
	288– 9	and reflects *d·* Love.
	288–20	the functions of Spirit, *d·* Love.
	290–17	*D·* Love is never so near as when
	292– 5	Through *d·* Love the right government
	293–24	power of *d·* Love to overrule the
	295– 4	*d·* Love holds its substance safe
	295–25	*D·* Love is your ever-present help.
	301– 4	and is the revelation of *d·* Love.
	308– 1	*d·* Love will accomplish what
	350–24	Love *d·*, whose kindling mighty **rays**

love

Mis.	388– 9	Fed by Thy love *d·* we live,
'00.	11–12	and compensated by *d·* love.
Po.	7– 9	Fed by Thy love *d·* we live,

Master

Mis.	187–19	our human and *d·* Master,

means

No.	21–14	for *d·* means and ends.

mercy

Mis.	11–14	Love metes . . . but *d·* mercy.
Ret.	94–11	this purgation of *d·* mercy,
My.	89–20	* constant as petitions for *d·* mercy.

metaphysics

Mis.	38–20	makes *d·* metaphysics needful,
	68–19	know the meaning of *d·* metaphysics,
	69– 1	*D·* metaphysics is that which
	70– 7	only explanation in *d·* metaphysics.
	252– 3	mental medicine of *d·* metaphysics
	293– 8	teacher of *d·* metaphysics should impart
Ret.	30–19	the mazes of *d·* metaphysics
'01.	2–13	in the practice of *d·* metaphysics
	5–11	*d·* metaphysics discriminates between
	8–21	logic of *d·* metaphysics makes
	10–14	Science of *d·* metaphysics removes the
	24–15	from *d·* metaphysics to tar-water !
	25–11	call aids to *d·* metaphysics,
'02.	5–16	*D·* metaphysics and St. John
	6–23	*d·* metaphysics points the way,
	7– 1	*D·* metaphysics concedes no
	7–17	authority for *d·* metaphysics
My.	109–23	*D·* metaphysics is not to be scoffed
	115– 7	harmonies of heaven in *d·* metaphysics,
	127–13	*d·* metaphysics completely overshadows
	206– 5	lose the Principle of *d·* metaphysics
	228– 5	signally blunder in *d·* metaphysics ;
	279–17	understood in its *d·* metaphysics,
	287–10	practice of *d·* metaphysics.
	294– 3	on the subject of *d·* metaphysics ;
	301–16	Is faith in *d·* metaphysics insanity?
	349–11	*d·* metaphysics or its therapeutics.

method

My.	103–15	Alluding to this *d·* method,

might

Mis.	138–19	unity is *d·* might,
	162–14	Clad with *d·* might,
My.	3– 4	*d·* might of Truth demands well-doing

Mind

Mis.	33–29	mortal mind's opposite, — the *d·* Mind.
	39–18	for this medicine is *d·* Mind ;
	56– 8	substance of Spirit is *d·* Mind.
	59–28	*d·* Mind, who is the only physician ;
	59–28	*d·* Mind is the scientific healer.

divine

Mind

Mis.	62–29	the action of the *d·* Mind,
	75–30	Soul is the *d·* Mind,
	95–20	*d·* Mind reveals itself to humanity
	101– 2	how the *d·* Mind is understood
	103–14	which dwell forever in the *d·* Mind
	113–15	influenced by any but the *d·* Mind,
	199–19	the qualities of the *d·* Mind
	205– 3	practical C. S. is the *d·* Mind,
	255–24	may be found in God, the *d·* Mind.
	257–10	force of immortal and *d·* Mind.
	260– 9	The *d·* Mind was his only
	264–29	must take its hue from the *d·* Mind,
	269–18	*d·* Mind to be the only physician.
	269–22	Science is a law of *d·* Mind.
	286–30	demonstrated in the offspring of *d·* **Mind,**
	308– 1	*d·* Mind as its sole centre and
	363– 3	*d·* Mind and true happiness.
	364–19	it is good, reflects the *d·* Mind,
Ret.	28– 1	*d·* Mind alone must answer,
	56– 5	diverges from the one *d·* Mind.
Un.	4–20	which was certainly the *d·* Mind ;
	36–23	to say that the *d·* Mind is
Pul.	3–24	pleasing to the *d·* Mind.
	15– 2	good resident in *d·* Mind,
	58– 2	* healed by the power of *d·* Mind,
Rud.	3–19	cure of disease through the *d·* **Mind,**
	11–11	no . . . death in the *d·* Mind.
	12–26	*d·* Mind, not material law,
No.	24– 1	immeasurable idea of *d·* Mind.
	25–16	immortal mode of the *d·* Mind.
	27–16	*d·* Mind and that Mind's idea.
	37–16	is known to the *d·* Mind,
	42–12	to dispossess the *d·* Mind of
Pan.	3–24	* proceeding from the *d·* Mind
'01.	7–12	our heavenly Parent — the *d·* Mind
	20– 6	guided by . . . Truth, the *d·* Mind.
Hea.	15–14	why . . . deny all might to the *d·* **Mind,**
Peo.	4– 5	an infinite and *d·* Mind ;
My.	3–15	This Science is a law of *d·* Mind,
	5–30	*d·* Mind that heals the sick
	61– 5	* of the power of *d·* Mind
	106–20	*d·* Mind calms . . . with a word.
	108– 7	action of the *d·* Mind is salutary
	108–14	based on the law of *d·* Mind.
	108–16	*d·* Mind is the sovereign appeal,
	108–18	nothing in the *d·* Mind to attenuate.
	153–25	as the *d·* Mind, not as matter,
	221–28	shall we have no faith . . . in the *d·* **Mind,**
	221–29	forgetting that the *d·* Mind,
	240–11	"This Science is a law of *d·* Mind,
	241–21	* immortal idea of the one *d·* Mind.
	246–17	dwelling forever in the *d·* Mind
	279–13	God is the *d·* Mind.
	288–15	*d·* Mind was his only instrumentality
	292–27	*d·* Mind is the same yesterday,
	348–18	proof that the *d·* Mind heals
	349– 1	*d·* Mind was first chronologically,
	349–23	The laws of God, or *d·* Mind,

Mind-force

Mis.	331–23	*d·* Mind-force, filling all space

ministry

My.	24– 4	* all who accept its *d·* ministry.

mission

Pul.	71–23	* having a *d·* mission to fulfil,

modes

Mis.	361–32	*d·* modes and manifestations
My.	267–30	all the *d·* modes, means, forms,
	349–20	*D·* modes or manifestations

music is

'00.	11–18	Music is *d·*.

mystery

No.	38– 9	This *d·* mystery of godliness

name

'00.	3–22	to call the *d·* name Yahwah,

nature

Mis.	104–22	In obedience to the *d·* nature,
	392– 4	Nature *d·*, in harmony profound,
Un.	6–18	verity concerning the *d·* nature
No.	37– 2	his *d·* nature and manhood
'01.	11– 4	the *d·* nature of Christ Jesus
'02.	11– 4	Again : True to his *d·* nature,
Hea.	17– 4	get nearer his *d·* nature
Po.	20– 5	Nature *d·*, in harmony profound,
My.	110– 1	it is the *d·* nature of God,
	119– 8	is not absorbed in the *d·* nature,

noumenon

My.	350– 4	To begin with the *d·* noumenon,

One

Mis.	264–11	to demonstrate the *d·* One,

oneness

Mis.	131–12	upon the rock of *d·* oneness,
No.	1–19	*d·* oneness of the trinity,

order

Mis.	18– 8	in the *d·* order of Science,
	79– 1	views antagonistic to the *d·* **order**

divine

order

Mis.	122–14	d· order is the acme of mercy :
	124– 2	tend to disturb the d· order,
	136–14	its fulfilment of d· order.
	208–16	and so disobey the d· order.
Ret.	87–17	they must follow the d· order
	91–19	always leading them into the d· order,
Un.	40–10	imperative in the d· order of being.
	56–13	In the d· order of Science
My.	117– 9	comprehending of the d· order
	238–15	became requisite in the d· order.

origin

Mis.	3– 3	no especial gift from our d· origin,
	232–13	next to appear as its d· origin.
Ret.	56–10	is of human instead of d· origin.
Pul.	39– 3	* the d· origin of humanity
'02.	9–23	was the proof of its d· origin,

overtures

My.	13–25	reach the stars with d· overtures,

pardon

No.	31–11	d· pardon is that divine presence

Parent

Un.	48–14	d· Parent no more enters into His

peace

Peo.	11– 8	not by . . . warfare, but in d· peace.

perfection

Mis.	320–12	infant idea of d· perfection

Person

My.	117–29	and to seek the one d· Person,

persons

'01.	6– 2	theology's three d· persons,

philosophy

Mis.	364–12	It is the soul of d· philosophy,
	364–32	reproduces the d· philosophy of Jesus
No.	21–25	D· philosophy is demonstrably the

potency

Ret.	89– 2	d· potency of this spiritual mode

power

Mis.	17–21	man reflects the d· power to heal
	59– 7	d· power understood, as in C. S. ;
	63– 6	and to hide his d· power.
	69– 9	man shall utilize the d· power.
	70–29	wonderful demonstrations of d· power,
	97–12	in no way allied to d· power.
	152– 9	cooperate with the d· power,
	171– 9	for the d· power to filter from
	175–29	both animal magnetism and d· power,
	183–23	equips man with d· power
	194–16	lens of Science magnifies the d· power
	201–32	illustrates through the flesh the d· power
	225–24	through the d· power, she healed him.
	244– 5	was performed by d· power.
	268–10	the demonstration of d· power,
	275– 4	clinging faith in d· power?
	360– 2	and procures d· power.
Ret.	26– 3	the d· power which heals.
	28–16	we must be clad with d· power.
	50– 4	knowledge of that d· power
Un.	43–22	This will interpret the d· power
Pul.	35–20	we must be clad with d· power.
	73– 5	* His unlimited and d· power.
Rud.	12–21	As power d· is the healer,
No.	12–27	It removes all limits from d· power.
	29–19	shocking reflection on the d· power.
'01.	2–10	into harmony with d· power,
	12–22	magnifies the d· power to human
	19– 3	They believe that d· power, besought,
	24– 5	impression produced by d· power
	33–22	might and majesty of d· power
'02.	18– 7	d· power manifested through man ;
Hea.	15–25	to pray for a proof of d· power,
My.	114–23	d· power of Truth and Love,
	131– 3	endues with d· power ;
	293– 3	d· power and purpose of
	293–19	The d· power and poor human sense
	315–27	of the d· power of C. S.,

precept

Mis.	235–27	tried to follow the d· precept,
	289–16	according to the d· precept,

presence

Mis.	71–19	not the factors of d· presence
	110–17	when encompassed by d· presence,
Pul.	10–27	D· presence, breathe Thou Thy
No.	31–12	divine pardon is that d· presence
Pan.	14–14	Pray that the d· presence may still
'02.	16–14	is to recognize the d· presence

presumption

My.	228–27	has the d· presumption to say :

Principle

Mis.	17–16	d· Principle that redeems man
	18–19	d· Principle and divine idea,
	19– 9	d· Principle and rules of C. S.
	22– 5	law of God, its d· Principle.
	22–23	the rules of its d· Principle,
	30– 1	the d· Principle of Christianity

divine

Principle

Mis.	32– 9	rules and d· Principle of C. S.
	34–13	C. S. is based on d· Principle ;
	41–27	d· Principle which governs the universe,
	46–25	represents his d· Principle,
	46–29	the Father, his d· Principle, is perfect.
	62–24	attempts to solve its d· Principle
	71–16	Law . . . unfolds d· Principle,
	77–12	d· Principle and spiritual idea ;
	79–22	immortal man's d· Principle.
	85– 8	the d· Principle of his being,
	87–22	d· Principle and rules of
	89–29	saved on this d· Principle,
	96–14	d· Principle, — which I worship ;
	98–25	acknowledge its d· Principle.
	104–26	d· Principle and idea are demonstrated,
	116–25	Obeying the d· Principle which
	118–26	d· Principle worketh with you,
	120– 5	d· Principle of life's long problem,
	121–30	justice from the d· Principle
	138–12	d· Principle which he claims to
	140–32	a perpetual type of the d· Principle
	147– 8	demonstrating the d· Principle of
	164– 1	Its d· Principle interprets the
	165–10	as eternal as its d· Principle.
	166– 1	d· Principle and spiritual idea of
	181– 6	power to demonstrate his d· Principle,
	181–11	the claims of the d· Principle.
	182– 6	in and of his d· Principle,
	185– 3	demonstrate fairly the d· Principle
	186–16	d· Principle of the divine idea
	188–10	d· Principle and idea of being,
	189– 4	d· Principle and rule of being,
	195– 3	d· Principle of metaphysical healing.
	198–26	d· Principle, and its spiritual laws.
	199–24	d· Principle is discerned in C. S.,
	200–28	involved in its d· Principle, God :
	204–28	God, the d· Principle of C. S.,
	221– 6	learns more of its d· Principle.
	223–16	full faith in the d· Principle,
	252–22	demonstrates the d· Principle,
	268– 1	while disobedience to this d· Principle
	290–11	d· Principle, which is Love,
	290–13	misapprehension of the d· Principle
	307–28	adhere to the d· Principle
	308–15	healing the sick on its d· Principle.
	308–28	is taught through its d· Principle,
	309–16	true idea of man's d· Principle.
	335– 1	you turn away from this d· Principle
	353–23	d· Principle carries on His harmony.
	354–13	the knowledge of the d· Principle
	356–28	its d· Principle and rule of practice.
	361–26	the only substance and d· Principle
	364–11	a postulate of the d· Principle,
	379–15	the d· Principle of all healing.
	380– 2	if a d· Principle alone heals,
	380– 4	d· Principle heals the sick,
Man.	43–24	its statement of the d· Principle
	62–22	simpler meanings of the d· Principle
	67–18	from the d· Principle of being
	83–15	the understanding of d· Principle,
Ret.	55– 7	vindicates the d· Principle,
	56– 8	unerring d· Principle of Science,
	57–25	Mistaking d· Principle for
	58– 1	Stating the d· Principle,
	82–10	rest on d· Principle for guidance,
	93– 6	incorporeal d· Principle of man,
Un.	10–16	for God is their d· Principle.
	46– 8	but I do so on a d· Principle,
	51–27	God, — the d· Principle of man.
	59– 6	d· Principle which made heaven
	61–14	but the d· Principle and Spirit
Pul.	4– 9	protected by his d· Principle, God
	13– 1	interprets God as d· Principle,
	85–11	* the d· Principle of all things
Rud.	1– 3	demonstrating the d· Principle
	3–26	d· Principle of all being,
	9–14	the d· Principle of man's being ;
No.	4–20	embody not the idea of d· Principle,
	11– 4	d· Principle, and an eternal being.
	20– 8	term d· Principle is used to signify
	20–13	As the d· Principle is comprehended,
	25–14	the eternal idea of his d· Principle,
	26–15	his d· Principle, or Father,
Pan.	11–10	Governed by the d· Principle of his
'00.	4–20	The d· Principle and rules of this
'01.	3–17	phrase for God — d· Principle.
	3–28	Love is d· Principle ;
	4– 1	d· Principle or Person stands for God
	4–28	calling God "d· Principle,"
	5–13	the d· Principle of all.
	7–18	call their God "d· Principle,"
	8– 4	spiritual idea of the d· Principle,
	22–21	its d· Principle and rules,
	23–12	d· Principle, rule, or demonstration
Hea.	3–13	d· Principle that begets the quality,

divine

Principle

Hea.	3–22	understand in part this *d·* Principle,
	8–26	as directly upon a *d·* Principle,
	14– 7	the *d·* Principle of healing
Peo.	2–11	*d·* Principle, — Life, Truth, Love ;
	4–19	three terms for one *d·* Principle
	6–20	*d·* Principle, understood in part,
My.	40–27	* She has obeyed the *d·* Principle,
	45–16	* fidelity to the *d·* Principle
	105– 5	the *d·* Principle whose rules
	109–14	the ever-operative *d·* Principle
	116–13	God is *d·* Principle, Love.
	116–16	Forgetting *d·* Principle brings on
	117–24	sinking its *d·* Principle in
	119– 4	demonstrate the *d·* Principle
	125–13	Loyal to the *d·* Principle
	149– 2	know somewhat of the *d·* Principle
	152–16	*d·* Principle of all that really is,
	152–22	Then the *d·* Principle of good,
	152–27	the *d·* Principle of nature
	179–27	based on the *d·* Principle of being,
	180–14	*d·* Principle, or Life, Truth, and
	200–29	with its *d·* Principle, Love.
	204–29	based . . . on this *d·* Principle,
	205–26	full idea of its *d·* Principle,
	218–13	demonstrated the *d·* Principle
	218–17	leaves the *d·* Principle of C. S.
	225–21	C. S. names God as *d·* Principle,
	225–27	God is *d·* Principle
	225–29	*d·* Principle includes them all.
	226–15	Withdraw God, *d·* Principle, from
	226–20	intelligent *d·* Principle, Love.
	239– 5	reason, revelation, the *d·* Principle,
	248–29	found nearest the *d·* Principle,
	267–26	man's *d·* Principle, Love,
	269– 3	infinite *d·* Principle, Love,
	270–29	The *d·* Principle of C. S. will
	272–13	C. S. reveals the *d·* Principle,
	299–16	the demonstrable *d·* Principle
	299–22	the *d·* Principle of C. S.
	300–11	the *d·* Principle of C. S.,
	303– 9	following the *d·* Principle
	348–12	rather than his *d·* Principle,
	348–23	enshrined in the *d·* Principle

process

| *Un.* | 11–23 | neither . . . hindered the *d·* process. |

protection

| *Mis.* | 263–11 | by *d·* protection and affection. |

Providence

| *Mis.* | 312–14 | * interposition of *d·* Providence |
| | 320– 1 | seize them, trust the *d·* Providence, |

purpose

| *Ret.* | 37–23 | *d·* purpose that this should be done, |
| | 83– 3 | accomplishing the *d·* purpose |

realism

| *Mis.* | 87– 6 | unjust . . . to the *d·* realism. |

reality

| *Mis.* | 345–20 | * Christianity must be a *d·* reality.'' |
| *Peo.* | 13–28 | * Christianity must be a *d·* reality.'' |

rebuke

| *Ret.* | 80–12 | *d·* rebuke is effectual to the |

reflection

| *'00.* | 1– 8 | in the glow of *d·* reflection. |
| *My.* | 129–13 | richly fraught with *d·* reflection. |

repentance

| *Un.* | 14– 1 | such planks as the *d·* repentance, |

requirements

| *Mis.* | 261–19 | *d·* requirements typified in |
| | 346–21 | grasped in all its *d·* requirements. |

retreat

| *Pan.* | 3–14 | * ''O sacred solitude ! *d·* retreat ! |

rights

Mis.	246– 7	both human and *d·* rights,
	247– 2	both human and *d·* rights ;
My.	303–14	eschews *d·* rights in human beings.

royalty

| *Mis.* | 121–24 | shameless insult to *d·* royalty, |

rule

Mis.	85–13	this *d·* rule in Science :
	209– 8	the *d·* rule of this Principle
	301–26	a *d·* rule for human conduct.

ruling

| *Mis.* | 204–30 | *d·* ruling gives prudence and energy ; |

scale

| *My.* | 146–31 | in the *d·* scale of being |

Science

(*see* **Science**)

Science is

Mis.	58–22	All Science is *d·*,
	172–16	Science is *d·* :
	219– 3	(and all Science is *d·*)
	261–31	All Science is *d·*.
My.	260–11	Science is *d·* ;

Scientist

| *Ret.* | 26–17 | a natural and *d·* Scientist. |

divine

sense

| *Un.* | 21–21 | true individuality, or a *d·* sense of being. |
| *'02.* | 6–17 | lets in the *d·* sense of being, |

significance

| *Mis.* | 250–10 | The *d·* significance of Love |

sin

| *Un.* | 16– 2 | such terms as *d·* *sin* and |

source

Mis.	19–17	flowing on to God, its *d·* source.
	22– 7	if not from the *d·* source,
	333–18	the *d·* source of being,
Pul.	4–11	sense of unity with your *d·* source,

Spirit

Mis.	40–16	action of the *d·* Spirit,
	49–23	opposes the leadings of the *d·* Spirit
	55– 7	as much of the *d·* Spirit as
Ret.	24–19	*d·* Spirit had wrought the miracle
	60– 9	adds that the *d·* Spirit created
Pul.	20–16	whose substance is the *d·* Spirit,
	34–21	*d·* Spirit had wrought a miracle,''
No.	42– 7	*d·* Spirit supplies all human needs.
My.	225–20	gives to the *d·* Spirit the name God.
	294–14	ever-present power of *d·* Spirit

spirit

| *Pul.* | 65–25 | * the *d·* spirit of giving, |

standard

| *Mis.* | 50–21 | change from . . . to the *d·* standard, |

statute

| *'02.* | 4–20 | a *d·* statute for yesterday, and |

statutes

| *Peo.* | 12– 2 | these *d·* statutes of God : |

strength

Mis.	170–17	was refreshment of *d·* strength,
	358–15	humility, and love are *d·* strength.
Un.	39–12	removes human weakness by *d·* strength,

substance

| *Mis.* | 68– 1 | *d·* substance, intelligence, Life, |

Talitha cumi

| *Peo.* | 8–21 | swept by the *d·* *Talitha cumi*, |

teachings

| *Mis.* | 302–29 | *d·* teachings contained in ''S. and **H**. |

theology

| *My.* | 180–30 | between *d·* theology and C. S., |

things

| *Ret.* | 31–10 | hunger and thirst after *d·* things, |

thought

| *Un.* | 5– 6 | toward the perfect thought *d·*. |

tone

| *'00.* | 11–19 | if the *d·* tone be lacking, |

trinity

| *Mis.* | 63– 8 | this *d·* trinity is one infinite remedy |

Truth

Mis.	241–28	When *d·* Truth and Love heal,
	284–18	vindicated *d·* Truth and Love
Man.	19– 4	demonstration of *d·* Truth,
	41–22	reign of *d·* Truth, Life, and Love
	87–20	trusts them to the *d·* Truth and **Love**,
Ret.	50–21	strict adherence to *d·* Truth
	84–25	trusts them to the *d·* Truth and **Love**,
	93–14	and imparting *d·* Truth,
No.	15– 1	dews of *d·* Truth,

understanding

| *Mis.* | 40–29 | it requires more *d·* understanding to |
| *Un.* | 30–10 | till *d·* understanding takes away |

Us

| *Mis.* | 18–20 | *d·* ''Us''— one in good, and good in **One**. |

verities

| *Mis.* | 81–27 | utters the *d·* verities of being |

visions

| *Ret.* | 18–15 | of real joy and of visions *d·* ; |
| *Po.* | 64– 6 | of real joy and of visions *d·* ; |

way

| *Ret.* | 54– 9 | and learn the *d·* way, |
| *No.* | 12–20 | *d·* way impels a spiritualization |

Whole

| *Mis.* | 16–21 | God is a *d·* *Whole*, and *All*, |

will

| *Mis.* | 141–21 | but let the *d·* will . . . rule |

wisdom

Mis.	209– 4	prerogative of *d·* wisdom,
	293– 6	unerring modes of *d·* wisdom.
My.	5–31	may . . . mislead man ; *d·* wisdom, never.
	215–32	his *d·* wisdom should temper

Word

Mis.	192–19	practicability of the *d·* Word,
Pul.	73– 9	* meditated over His *d·* Word.
No.	29–17	Better . . . than to the *d·* Word.

Mis.	16–11	and these claims are *d·*,
	16–22	Love, a *d·*, infinite Principle ;
	63–27	the Son of God was *d·*.
	69– 8	The Principle of C. S. is *d·*.
	71–28	is the counterfeit of the *d·*,
	99–20	seemed Jesus of Nazareth more *d·*
	100–21	coincidence of the *d·* with the human,

divine

Mis.	103–21	Any inference of the d·
	121– 9	the human struggles against the d·,
	121–19	whatever belittles, . . . is not d·
	125–20	All that is real is d·,
	163–16	less human and more d·
	172–12	D· and unerring Mind measures man,
	184–32	submerged in the humane and d·,
	199–23	Principle of these marvellous works is d· ;
	208–18	d· Truth's negativing error
	212–22	human will is lost in the d· ;
	234–12	things most essential and d·.
	309–24	human concept antagonizes the d·.
	337– 6	its effect on yourself to be — d·.
	338– 7	that its Principle is d·.
	352–25	consciousness is the reflection of the d·,
	353– 9	relinquish your human . . . and find the d·,
	394–11	rainbow of rapture, o'erarching, d· ;
	399–12	Life of all being d· :
Man.	15–15	evidence of d·, efficacious Love,
Chr.	53–17	Thus Christ, eternal and d·,
Ret.	24– 5	Science of d· metaphysical healing
	28–26	Its Principle is d·, not human,
	37– 4	d·, or spiritual, Science of
	50–20	subordination of the human to the d·,
	89–30	but incorporeal impulsion is d·,
Un.	10–15	Their gradations are spiritual and d· ;
	15–20	become only an echo of the d·?
	42– 8	a d· and intelligent — reality.
	52– 8	consciousness should become d·,
Pul.	70–24	* the d· or spiritual Science of
Rud.	13– 9	the d· and spiritual image of God.
No.	10– 2	in both a d· and human sense ;
	13– 6	both the Principle and idea to be d·.
	21–17	modes, wherein the human and d·
	30–18	His sympathy is d·, not human.
	36–18	mortal as unreal, and the d· as real.
	36–28	while the d· and ideal Christ was
Pan.	3– 7	but one charm to make it half d·
	7– 6	the omnipotence of one d·, infinite
	8– 7	one the d·, infinite Person,
	12–22	this d· infinite Principle,
'00.	15–10	of all human experience is the most d· ;
'01.	2–14	it has a d· and demonstrable Principle
	4–13	The Science of God must be, is, d·,
	5– 7	one d· infinite triune Principle,
	8– 1	chapter sub-title
	8– 3	one Christ, and Christ is d·
	10–13	both the d· and the human,
	31– 7	neither personal nor human, but d·.
'02.	8–20	The energy that saves . . . is d·.
Hea.	20– 7	* In notes almost d·."
Peo.	10–16	d· as well as human.
Po.	39– 1	of all d· Gifts, lofty, pure,
	45–14	rainbow of rapture, o'erarching, d· ;
	75–19	Life of all being d· :
My.	27– 6	the d· and not the human
	111–25	conclusion was logical and d·
	132–21	one Mind and that d· ;
	139–22	from the human to the d·.
	141–29	communion universal and d·.
	160– 6	constant relation with the d·,
	178–10	Science is naturally d·,
	186– 3	prophetic of the finger d·
	220–30	That the innocent . . . seems less d·,
	220–31	seems more d· to-day than
	221–17	other than the spiritual and d·,
	226–10	the one d· intelligent Principle
	244–19	put off the human for the d·.
	252–29	it is moral, spiritual, d·.
	265–22	coincidence of the human and d·,
	283–26	only as it patterns the d·.

Divine Being

Peo.	13– 5	D· B· is more than a person,

divinely

Mis.	26–30	naturally and d· infinite good.
	81–24	be heard d· and humanly.
	121–11	good, as d· attested.
	161–16	both human and d· endowed,
	163– 4	preparing to heal and teach d· ;
	192–13	words of him who spake d·,
	209–22	To suffer for . . . is d· wise.
	246–11	would have washed it d· away
	313–25	and, as I believe, d· directed,
	360– 6	good, because fashioned d·,
	387– 2	With joy d· fair,
	387–24	Come from that Love, d· near,
	397– 8	and tenderly, D· talk.
Ret.	26–13	d· natural and apprehensible ;
	32– 1	d· appointed human mission,
Pul.	18–17	and tenderly, D· talk.
No.	9–25	D· defined, Science is the
Pan.	12–28	It is d· true, and every hour
'01.	19– 1	d· appointed means of grace
Hea.	15– 7	spiritual power d· directed.

divinely

Po.	6–19	that Love, d· near,
	12–17	and tenderly, D· talk.
	34–14	D· desolate the shrine to paint?
	50–20	With joy d· fair,
	77–10	Love, and Truth, — d· God !
My.	4–31	Whatever is not d· natural
	28–28	* labors of one d· guided woman,
	258–22	D· beautiful are the Christmas
	267– 4	which is not d· scientific,
	288–10	Good is d· natural.
	349–13	d· natural to him who sits
	351–13	hem of his garment who spake d·.

diviner

Mis.	68– 5	changed appearance and d· form
	96–13	ascends . . . to d· consciousness,
	140–25	The d· claim and means for
	330–22	purer peace and d· energy,
	385–17	To Soul's d· sense,
Ret.	81– 1	d· sense of liberty and light.
Un.	4–12	a d· sense that God is all
No.	3–11	but I obeyed a d· rule.
Peo.	5–19	d· sense of Life and Love,
	11–10	another staging for d· claims,
Po.	48–11	To Soul's d· sense,

diviners

Mis.	363–27	and drives d· mad.

divines

Mis.	169–19	most eminent d· of the world
No.	23–14	eminent d·, in Europe
'01.	31–28	taught by some grand old d·,
My.	149–20	and d· be too deeply read

Divine Science

Mis.	174–31	The leaven . . . is D· S· ;
	336–20	chapter sub-title
Rud.	14– 6	strictly practising D· S·,

divine Science

(see Science)

Divinity (see also Doctor of Divinity)

Man.	68–13	teaches the course in D·,

divinity

Mis.	13–23	reveals in clearer d· the
	63–27	This d· was reaching humanity
	96– 1	reveals the infinitude of d·
	102–24	destroys it with the d· of Truth.
	197–18	character and d· which Jesus
	292– 2	d· of St. John's Gospel
	372–30	shades to the shadows of d·,
Ret.	57–29	status and rule of d·,
	91–14	lessons . . . on humanity and d·
Pul.	15–21	unite all interests in the one d·.
No.	v–10	life-giving waters of a true d·,
	7– 2	The rule of d· is golden :
Pan.	11– 1	required the d· of our Master
'00.	6– 4	proving its power and d·.
	12– 2	projected from d· upon humanity,
	12–14	tutelary d· of Ephesus.
Hea.	4–13	to drop d· long enough to
Peo.	14–11	our ideas of d· form our
My.	25–26	and the glory of d· appears
	63–23	* revelation of d· which has come
	107–28	nothing beyond illimitable d·.
	118–26	represents not the d· of
	179–23	Principle and practice of a true d·
	291–16	weighed in the scales of d·,
	306–18	D· alone solves the problem
	307–30	want of d· in scholastic theology,

division

Pul.	58–14	* d· into seven excellent class-rooms,
My.	311–31	* reached long d· in arithmetic,"

divisions

'00.	1–17	five grand d· of the globe ;
My.	136–20	five grand d· of our globe ;

divorce

Ret.	20–22	to ask for a bill of d·,
My.	268– 2	chapter sub-title
	268– 5	frequency of d· shows that
	268–11	D· and war should be exterminated
	268–17	will eliminate d· and war.
	269–11	Christ's plan of salvation from d·.
	314–14	my d· from Dr. Patterson
	314–21	to record the d· in my favor.
	314–30	up to the time of the d·.

divorced

Mis.	289–19	nor human equity has d·
Pul.	56–17	* Christianity and Science, hitherto d·
My.	349–26	human will d· from Science.

divorces

Mis.	221–23	and d· his work from Science.

divulged

Ret.	15–27	persons who d· their secret joy

do

Mis.	4— 9	its power to *d·* good, not evil.
	5— 2	It cannot fail to *d·* this if we
	5—15	says, "I can *d·* no more.
	6— 7	C. S. practitioners have plenty to *d·*,
	10— 6	whatever these try to *d·*, shall
	11—20	*d·* them good whenever opportunity
	11—26	I can *d·* much general good to such
	11—27	I *d·* it with earnest, special care
	21— 9	that I *d·* shall ye *d·* — *see John* 14 : 12.
	29— 3	I *d·*, and that his promise is
	31—20	power to be or to *d·* good,
	32—19	gladly *d·* my best towards helping those
	37—23	as directly and surely as *d·*
	38— 2	*all the good we can d·*
	41— 3	power of liberated thought to *d·* good,
	45— 6	*d·* more than to heal a toothache ;
	52— 4	how much one can *d·* for himself,
	52— 6	he could *d·* vastly more.
	57—11	*d·* quickly." — *John* 13 : 27.
	67—27	If your question refers to . . . I *d·*.
	71— 9	unquestionably right to *d·* right ;
	71—10	is a very right thing to *d·*.
	89—15	to *d·* him all the good you can ;
	90—14	should *d·* to you, — *Matt.* 7 : 12.
	90—14	*d·* ye even so — *Matt.* 7 : 12.
	91—30	sufficiently to *d·* this,
	93—18	Sin can *d·* nothing :
	96—18	I *d·* ; and this atonement becomes
	108— 5	Scientists, claiming, as they *d·*,
	112—23	* have brought what will *d·* him good."
	116— 1	as you would have them *d·* to you,
	119—32	should *d·* to you, — *Matt.* 7 : 12.
	119—32	*d·* ye even so — *Matt.* 7 : 12.
	122—18	"Let us *d·* evil, — *Rom.* 3 : 8.
	127—20	one must *d·* good to others.
	127—23	*d·* His will even though
	128—13	and seen in me, *d·* : — *Phil.* 4 : 9.
	130—22	Where the motive to *d·* right exists,
	131—15	prepared to itemize . . . let it *d·* so ;
	135—10	as ye would they should *d·* unto you,
	137—18	you will *d·* — what?
	146— 8	To *d·* this, I should need to be
	146—19	should *d·* unto you, — *see Matt.* 7 : 12.
	146—19	*d·* ye even so — *Matt.* 7 : 12.
	147—20	*d·* nothing but what is honorable,
	148—10	which will *d·* for the race what
	155—19	she desires thus to *d·*
	158—11	to *d·* this through faith,
	158—23	and God will *d·* the rest.
	167—18	they who *d·* the will of his Father
	175—25	nothing to *d·* with the Science of
	177—13	What will you *d·* about it?
	180—18	Let us *d·* our work ;
	192—10	*that I d· shall he d·* — *John* 14 : 12.
	192—11	*than these shall he d· ;* — *John* 14 : 12.
	193—27	that I *d·* shall he *d·*," — *John* 14 : 12.
	195—19	that I *d·* shall he *d·* — *John* 14 : 12.
	196—22	we shall *d·* the works of Christ,
	199— 3	supposed power of matter to *d·* it,
	199— 4	erring mind can claim to *d·* thus,
	208—14	But who is willing to *d·* His will
	211—19	Or, are you afraid to *d·* this
	214—22	need to *d·* this even to understand
	215— 5	I *d·* it all in love ;
	215—11	as we shall *d·* if we take
	218—28	"How *d·* you *d·* ?"
	221—11	The evil-doer can *d·* little at
	226—28	more than to *d·* most vices.
	228— 5	is to *d·* good to thyself ;
	228—26	we *d·* what others *d·*,
	230— 6	as to what one should *d·*.
	232—10	never *d·* to be behind the times
	235—28	should *d·* unto you, — *see Matt.* 7 : 12.
	235—29	*d·* ye even so — *Matt.* 7 : 12.
	238—18	the love that foresees more to *d·*,
	241—12	and try to make others *d·* likewise,
	248—25	could *d·* no more for me.
	249—23	of their mental design to *d·* this
	251—16	that I *d·* shall he *d·*" ; — *John* 14 : 12.
	251—23	good they would *d·*, that they *d·*,
	251—24	and the evil they would not *d·*,
	251—24	that they *d·* not.
	254—26	Lord of the vineyard *d·* ? — *Mark* 12 : 9.
	262— 4	to be good and to *d·* good.
	265—24	Those who abide by them *d·* well.
	265—25	If others, . . . *d·* ill,
	266—12	that nobody else can or will *d·*.
	273— 7	where none other can *d·* the work.
	273—25	I cannot *d·* my best work for a
	274— 5	in order to *d·* this I must
	282—10	should *d·* to you, *d·* ye." — *Luke* 6 : 31.
	282—23	it is sometimes wise to *d·* so,
	284— 1	for each one to *d·* his own work well,
	287—27	pleasanter to *d·* right than wrong ;
	298— 5	Let us *d·* evil, — *Rom.* 3 : 8.

do

Mis.	299—25	permission to *d·* this,
	299—27	What right have I to *d·* this?
	301— 6	would have others *d·* unto you?
	315—25	nor allow their students to *d·* thus,
	317— 5	to *d·* their own work ;
	317—22	"What I *d·* — *John* 13 : 7.
	323—18	"What *d·* ye here?
	334—26	understanding is required to *d·* this.
	335—29	who *d·* evil that good may come,
	338— 7	All must go and *d·* likewise.
	349—16	he should *d·* as he deemed best,
	358—27	*d·* their present work,
	359—16	as he was able to *d·* this ;
	370— 4	saw Jesus *d·* such deeds of mercy,
	384— 9	Thy will to know, and *d·*.
	397—12	My prayer, some daily good to *d·*
Man.	3—16	will *d·* for the race what
	16—11	to *d·* unto others
	16—11	as we would have them *d·* unto us ;
	28—22	then failing to *d·* either,
	29—13	Failing to *d·* thus,
	41— 8	*d·* it, but without hard words.
	41—12	*d·* good unto your enemies
	42—23	should *d·* to you, — *Matt.* 7 : 12.
	42—24	*d·* ye even so — *Matt.* 7 : 12.
	46—17	failure to *d·* this shall subject the
	48— 5	he shall *d·* it with love
Chr.	55—23	For whosoever shall *d·* — *Matt.* 12 : 50.
Ret.	5—16	the pen can never *d·* justice.
	9—13	resolving to *d·*, next time,
	13—20	as I was wont to *d·*,
	64—25	To *d·* this, mortals must first
	68—25	In C. S., man can *d·* no harm,
	72— 5	deteriorates one's ability to *d·* good,
	75—14	which shall *d·* a miracle — *Mark* 9 : 39.
	78— 3	to *d·* either too much or too little.
	82—15	in order to *d·* the greatest good
	86— 5	and that is to *d·* it !
	86—20	carry his burden and *d·* his work,
	87—20	should *d·* to you, — *Matt.* 7 : 12.
	87—21	*d·* ye even so — *Matt.* 7 : 12.
	90—27	* " I believe the proper thing for us to *d·*
Un.	14— 2	must one day *d·* His work over again,
	15—24	who seeks to *d·* them mischief,
	17—10	or seeks so to *d·*,
	21—11	If you *d·* not, your intellect will be
	44— 4	know not what they *d·*." — *Luke* 23 : 34.
	46— 8	I *d·* so on a divine Principle,
	48— 6	I believe more in Him than *d·* most
Pul.	2—21	Likewise should we *d·* as
	2—27	How can we *d·* this Christianly
	19— 1	My prayer, some daily good to *d·*
	21— 6	This we all must *d·*
	32— 4	* No photographs can *d·* the least
	49—22	* *d·* honor to that precinct of Concord.
	50— 6	* *d·* something for the toilers,
	72—28	* Christ has told us to *d·* his work,
	73—13	* to *d·* good and heal the sick.
Rud.	14— 4	To *d·* this, they must at present
	14—12	in order to *d·* gratuitous work.
	14—16	must of necessity *d·* better
No.	7— 8	and continue to *d·* so
	39—20	desire to be and *d·* good.
	41— 8	to *d·* the will of his Father
Pan.	5—13	ye will *d·*. — *John* 8 : 44.
	9—14	wise enough to *d·* himself no harm,
	13—20	we *d·* "live, and move, — *Acts* 17 : 28.
'00.	6— 5	this one thing I *d·*, — *Phil.* 3 : 13.
	8—30	not to *d·* certain things
	9— 1	know it were best not to *d·*,
	9— 4	"You may *d·* it if you desire."
	9— 6	not because it is the best thing to *d·*,
	9—21	workers to *d·* their best.
	14—17	should *d·* to you, *d·* ye." — *Luke* 6 : 31.
'01.	5—15	They *d·*, but their personality is
	9—15	taught his followers to *d·* likewise.
	9—20	what have we to *d·* with — *Mark* 1 : 24.
	11—23	forgets what Christian Scientists *d·* not,
	18—19	he came to *d·* "the will of — *Matt.* 12 : 50.
	23—20	and followers to *d·* likewise ;
	27—23	than others *d·* in proportion,
'02.	18—20	what more could he *d·* ?
	18—22	that I *d·* shall he *d·*." — *John* 14 : 12.
Hea.	5—23	to *d·* our work for us,
	8—27	as directly as we *d·* to the rule of
	8—28	*d·* more than we are now doing,
	12— 6	it can *d·* nothing,
	16—11	unless you *d·* this you are
Po.	13— 5	some daily good to *d·*
	36— 8	Thy will to know, and *d·*.
My.	vii— 4	* can never *d·* for its Leader what
	3— 8	*d·* His commandments, — *Rev.* 22 : 14.
	9—25	but I *d·* now,
	13— 1	The good they desire to *d·*,
	15—25	* As nothing else can *d·*.

do

My.	37–10	* you have done and continue to *d·*
	49– 3	* and we will *d·* thee good,'
	60– 5	* she would doubtless *d·* so.
	60–30	* care to *d·* a little watching
	61–27	* "What cannot God *d·*?"
	66–14	* to *d·* so it was necessary to have
	72– 2	* To *d·* this it was necessary to
	73– 7	* If you ask . . . how they *d·* it,
	106–31	his followers to *d·* likewise.
	114– 5	*D·* unto others as ye
	114– 6	would have others *d·* to you.
	129–21	*d·* thy errands, and
	140– 6	These things will I *d·* — *Isa.* 42 : 16.
	147–26	I have a work to *d·*
	148– 1	to *d·* your pioneer work in
	148– 3	called to *d·* your part wisely
	149– 3	"Go, and *d·* thou likewise." — *Luke* 10 : 37.
	153– 4	*d·* this in Christ's name,
	156– 5	"able to *d·* exceeding — *Eph.* 3 : 20.
	163–15	which I think *d·* them more good.
	170–20	in the Lord, and *d·* good ; — *Psal.* 37 : 3.
	180–29	know not what they *d·*." — *Luke* 23 : 34.
	191– 2	"No man can *d·* these — *John* 3 : 2.
	194– 5	as *d·* all things material,
	195–14	for we cannot *d·* more than we
	195–15	To *d·* good to all
	200–14	Striving to be good, to *d·* good,
	203–10	All that is worth . . . is what we *d·*,
	211–11	what have we to *d·* with — *Mark* 1 : 24.
	212– 2	victim is led to believe and *d·*
	212– 3	never, otherwise, think or *d·*
	212–11	matter, wherewith to *d·* evil ;
	213–11	in their desire to *d·* right
	213–12	be more zealous to *d·* good,
	214–24	which I yearned to *d·*,
	215– 5	bade me *d·* what I did,
	216–10	What, then, can a man *d·*
	216–20	by which you can *d·* much good
	221–21	that I *d·* shall he *d·* — *John* 14 : 12.
	229– 5	all that *d·* these things — *Deut.* 18 : 12.
	235–10	cannot *d·* this in mathematics,
	235–25	Do you adopt as truth . . . I *d·*.
	246–25	"What I *d·* thou knowest not — *John* 13 : 7.
	251– 2	"What I *d·* thou knowest not — *John* 13 : 7.
	252– 8	good you *d·* unto others you *d·* to
	258–12	to know and to *d·* God's will,
	261– 9	aught to *d·* with this pastime.
	264– 4	may *d·* so honestly and not
	266– 9	should *d·* to you, — *Matt.* 7 : 12.
	266– 9	*d·* ye even so — *Matt.* 7 : 12.
	270–20	know not what they *d·*." — *Luke* 23 : 34.
	274– 6	holiness, and love *d·* this,
	275–24	as we would that they *d·* by us,
	276–18	* entitled to vote should *d·* so,
	281–21	* Will you *d·* us the kindness
	283–23	"To *d·* justly, — *Mic.* 6 : 8.
	288– 6	The good done and the good to *d·*
	289– 2	what we *d·*, not what we say.
	300– 6	both to will and to *d·* — *Phil.* 2 : 13.
	303–29	proved by the good I *d·*.
	305–25	simply how to *d·* his works.
	307– 8	nothing to *d·* with matter,
	309– 4	called upon to *d·* much business
	310–31	* "Read it, for it will *d·* you good.
	314–23	imploring him not to *d·* it.
	319–28	* and *d·* so still.
	320–13	* having had something to *d·*
	324–29	* if he found you could *d·* so,
	345– 2	will *d·* the children no harm.
	345– 4	I *d·* not suppose their
	358–14	I have not the time to *d·* so.
	360– 1	if you do not *d·* this.

dock root

My.	122– 7	Sin is like a *d· r·*.

Doctor

Man.	45–25	titles of Reverend and *D·*,
My.	245–29	degrees of Bachelor and *D·*

doctor (*see also* **doctor's**)

Mis.	88–27	*to treat with a d·?*
	88–28	depends upon what kind of a *d·*
	239–20	* "I've got cold, *d·*."
	243– 8	regular *d·* had put on splints
	252–27	equips the *d·* with safe and
	378–11	the aforesaid *d·* in Portland.
Ret.	13–11	family *d·* was summoned,
	24– 2	magnetic *d·*, Mr. P. P. Quimby,
No.	29– 9	and then they *d·* this soul
'01.	18–20	*d·* who teaches that a human
My.	226–30	decline to *d·* infectious or
	314– 5	* The *d·* practised in several towns,

doctored

Ret.	57– 6	which must be *d·* in order to

Doctor of Divinity

No.	43–10	A distinguished *D· of D·* said :

doctor's

Mis.	89– 7	*to follow the d· directions?*
	229–11	more certain would be the *d·* success,
	240– 2	*d·* squills and bills would have

doctors

Mis.	80–25	regular *d·*, who, in successive
	88–30	drop one of these *d·* when you
	240– 6	Parents and *d·* must not take the
	243–25	Even *d·* disagree on that
	365–23	Even *d·* agree that infidelity,
Ret.	40–21	demonstration so stirred the *d·*
Pul.	69– 8	* *d·* had pronounced his case incurable.
No.	19– 5	Even *d·* will agree that infidelity,
My.	111–10	now assumed by many *d·* and
	345–14	*d·* said I would live if the

doctrinal

Pul.	22–16	*d·* barriers between the churches
'01.	33–14	not to be judged on a *d·* platform,
'02.	12– 3	explains these *d·* points,
My.	139–21	the denominational to the *d·*,

doctrine

Mis.	46– 8	*d·* previously entertained.
	76–10	That *d·* is not theism,
	121–13	would make this fatal *d·* just
	182–17	Born of no *d·*,
	189–16	a pantheistic *d·* that presents
	189–27	astonished at his *d·* : — *Matt.* 7 : 28.
	221–24	contradicts the *d·* that we must
	235– 9	demonstration, not *d·*.
	366– 5	to learn the *d·* of theology,
	382– 5	my first work on this *d·*,
Ret.	13– 5	the *d·* of unconditional election,
	13–10	aroused by this erroneous *d·*,
	14–13	if assent to this *d·* was essential
	15–20	if not in full unity of *d·*.
	58–10	astonished at his *d·* : — *Matt.* 7 : 28.
Un.	1– 1	no *d·* of C. S. rouses so much
	8–20	even the *d·* of heredity
	42–18	astonished at his *d·* ; — *Matt.* 7 : 28.
	54– 1	*d·* of mind in matter.
Pul.	52–26	* No new *d·* is proclaimed,
No.	12–21	method, beyond *d·* and ritual ;
	14–25	the *d·* of eternal damnation,
	22– 1	wind of *d·*." — *Eph.* 4 : 14.
Pan.	2–15	* "The *d·* that the universe,
	2–20	pantheism is the *d·* of the
	4– 2	the *d·* that the universe
	8–10	*d·* that Mohammed is the only prophet
'00.	13– 8	system supported by their *d·*
'01.	19– 5	I love this *d·*, for I know
	24–29	to prove the *d·* of Jesus,
'02.	2–26	either in heart or in *d·* ;
	5–26	formulate a *d·*, or speculate
	11–29	Jew and Christian can unite in *d·*
Hea.	3– 6	a demonstration, more than a *d·*.
	7–28	no argument for a creed or *d·*,
	18–18	The *d·* of atonement never
Peo.	5– 7	cold materialisms of dogma and *d·*
	5–18	points away from matter and *d·*,
My.	87–29	* this *d·* of health, happiness,
	93–17	* who do not accept the *d·* of
	112– 9	interpret the Scriptures to fit a *d·*,
	118–25	The *d·* of Buddha,
	148– 5	judge our *d·* by its fruits.
	221– 4	precludes Jesus' *d·*, now as then,
	282– 3	believe strictly in the Monroe *d·*,
	300–22	make known his *d·* to the world,

doctrines

absolute

Mis.	148–20	absolute *d·* destined for future
Man.	3–17	absolute *d·* destined for future

and hypotheses

Ret.	56– 2	theories, *d·*, and hypotheses,

and traditions

No.	8–20	enmity over *d·* and traditions,

beliefs and

Pul.	73–22	* versed in all their beliefs and *d·*.

effete

Ret.	79–11	ridding the thought of effete *d·*,

erroneous

Mis.	366–26	Erroneous *d·* never have abated

goodness, not

Pul.	9–27	goodness, not *d·*,

her

Mis.	95– 7	* public letter condemning her *d·* ;

his

Mis.	111–24	his *d·* and those of Jesus,

human

'00.	4–18	beaten path of human *d·*
My.	262–18	Human *d·* or hypotheses

its

'00.	4–23	Does it demonstrate its *d·*?

doctrines

my
Un. 44– 2 made concerning my d·,
Pul. 75–11 more of heathenism than of my d·.
new-old
'00. 10–16 new-old d· of the prophets
of Christ
Mis. 188– 1 teachings opposed the d· of Christ
of Christian Science
Man. 34– 8 believer in the d· of C. S.,
of men
Mis. 366–19 "beware of . . . d· of men,— Matt. 16: 6.
of theosophy
Man. 47–25 not believe in the d· of theosophy,
of the world
My. 92– 3 * real position in the d· of the world
opinions and
Mis. 17– 9 human opinions and d·,
personal
Mis. 232–15 theories, personal d· and
Presbyterian
Ret. 14– 6 of the strictest Presbyterian d·.
such
Man. 48– 2 those who do believe in such d·,
No. 29–17 Better far that we impute such d· to
taught
My. 112– 9 d· taught by divine Science
that deny
Mis. 193– 7 D· that deny the substance and
their
'01. 32–17 caused me to love their d·.

No. 12–10 d·, rites, and ceremonies,
Pan. 8–24 d· that embrace pantheism,
11– 8 d·, and dogmas of men
My. 85–11 * the d· of Mrs. Eddy

document
My. 137– 6 *Boston Globe*, referring to this d·,
179– 7 In this allegorical d· the power

dodge
Mis. 53– 4 to d· the question is not

doer
My. 210–15 the proud talker and d·.

doers
My. 125– 3 not only sayers but d· of the law?
197–21 in the Word and in the d· thereof,
352–22 the hearers and the d· of God's Word.

does
Mis. 6–13 surely d·, to many thinkers,
15–19 eternity d· this ;
33–25 d· away with all material medicines,
37–26 She now d· not.
38– 5 as this teaching certainly d·,
43–22 d· a vast amount of injury to
61–23 If not, what d·?
87–20 he d· best in the investigation of
92–31 That teacher d· most for his students
145– 8 D· a single bosom burn for fame
179–24 God d· all this through His
190– 7 nor d· the material ultimate in
229– 7 and with better effect than he d·
240–10 forecasting liberty and joy d· ;
255–22 It d· away with material medicine,
266– 7 Whoever d· this may represent
280–11 Because God d· all,
334– 8 d· this as a lie declaring itself,
365–29 what it is and of what it d·,
369–18 to trust Christ more than it d· drugs.
Ret. 34–11 It d· away with all material medicines,
71–28 demoralizes the person who d· this,
74– 3 He who d· this is ignorant of the
75– 5 d· violence to the ethics of C. S.
84–19 That teacher d· most for his students who
86–19 If he d· this not, and another one
Un. 13– 2 on the same principle that it d·
29– 4 as d· all criminal law,
30– 4 This it d· under the delusion
46–27 as it d· of the present.
Rud. 5–20 Human belief says that it d· ;
No. 11–12 what it is and what it d·,
18– 6 C. S. d· this.
30– 3 It d· more than forgive the
'00. 3– 4 thinker and worker d· his best,
3– 5 d· the thinking for the ages.
'01. 18–29 d· it and so proves their nullity.
22– 7 since Science d· not
29–24 d· most, and sacrifices most
Peo. 2– 7 what God is, and what God d·.
Po. 43– 2 Jesus loves you ! so d· mother :
My. 106–23 more than d· the average man,
108– 3 as d· the allopath who depends upon
112–28 through the good it d·
122– 8 To cut off the top . . . d· no good ;

does
My. 128–18 Men cannot punish . . . God d· that.
128–25 as d· a subtle conspirator ;
227–32 than d· *materia medica*.
232–26 Does the textbook . . . It d·.
232–29 does that watch accord . . . It d· not.
240–26 * She most assuredly d·,
271– 9 the good that a man d·
273–29 "Man awakes . . . d· he not?"

doest
Mis. 57–11 "That thou d·,— *John* 13: 27.
334– 3 What d· Thou?"— *Dan.* 4: 35.
347–28 None can say unto Him, What d· Thou?
Po. 77–16 learned of Truth what Thou d· now
My. 191– 3 miracles that thou d·,— *John* 3: 2.
200– 8 "What d· thou?"— *Dan.* 4: 35.
280–21 nor say unto Him, What d· Thou?

doeth
Mis. 334– 1 "He d· according to His— *Dan.* 4: 35.
'02. 19–22 It is divine Love that d· it,
My. 33–19 nor d· evil to his— *Psal.* 15: 3.
33–26 He that d· these things— *Psal.* 15: 5.
99– 5 * merry heart that d· good

doff
Mis. 177–14 d· your lavender-kid zeal,

doggedly
Mis. 374–23 d· deny or frantically affirm
My. 308–16 * tramping d· along the highway,

dogma
Mis. 150–26 defined by no d·, appropriated by no
331–23 frozen crust of creed and d·,
362– 8 Scholastic d· has made men blind.
Ret. 31– 7 paramount to rubric and d·
65– 6 Ritualism and d· lead to
Pul. 56–17 * d· and truth could not unite,
No. 24–17 evil that is hidden by d· and
42–12 vain power of d· and philosophy
Peo. 5– 7 cold materialisms of d· and
5–19 from matter and doctrine, or d·,
My. 47–26 * in the wilderness of d· and creed,
50–11 * against the currents of d·,
148–26 it is not a creed or d·,
205–24 wholly apart from . . . creed and d·,
288–15 creed, d·, or *materia medica*.
301– 7 d· and creed will pass off in scum,
307–27 *materia medica*, d·, and creeds,

dogmas
Mis. 168– 9 buried in d· and physical ailments,
232–15 personal doctrines and d·,
Ret. 14– 7 unbelievers in these d· lost,
No. 14–25 frozen d·, persistent persecution,
Pan. 11– 8 doctrines, and d· of men
'00. 7– 5 creeds and d· have been sifted,

dogmatical
Pan. 2– 6 neither hypothetical nor d·,

dogmatism
'02. 2–20 d·, relegated to the past,

doing
Mis. 9–13 they are d· thee good
67–12 but shalt know that by d· thus
114–24 Thus d·, Scientists will silence
115–32 d· to others as you would have
116–22 not merely saying, but d·,
131– 9 console . . . by d· likewise.
135– 9 d· unto others as ye would they
153– 4 not weary in well d·."— see *Gal.* 6: 9.
199– 8 so d·, male and female come into
215–22 and what he was d·.
223–17 while d· unto others what
230– 5 in talking nothing, d· nothing,
230–22 * "Let us, then, be up and d·,
236–28 not deter us from d· our duty,
262–15 for the good you are d·.
263– 1 much pleasure in thus d· ;
266– 7 may represent me as d· it ;
266–11 d· the work that nobody else can
284– 2 hinder others from d· theirs
290–19 this person was d· well,
292–20 who know not what he is d·
301– 4 d· to the author of the
317– 3 Yes, if you are d· God's work.
Ret. 84–22 Thus d·, posterity will call him
85– 2 for d· their own work well.
87–17 In so d· they must follow the
Un. 13– 5 d· their own work in obedience
45– 4 as Truth and . . . are d· in C. S.,
58– 8 This was the very thing he *was d·*,
Pul. 4–13 in being and d· right,
15–10 for the sake of d· right
Rud. 14–21 d· charity work besides.
No. 41–26 * and it is d· it to-day ;
43– 9 * the good your books are d·."

doing

'00.
3–15 not far from saying and *d·*.
8–18 *d·* rightly by yourself and others.
8–19 *d·* the work that belongs to another.
'02. 18–21 how much of what he did are we *d·*?
Hea. 9– 1 more than we are now *d·*,
12– 5 to learn what matter is doing
My. v–17 * *d·* this work "without money — *Isa.* 55 : 1.
12–24 God prepares the way for *d·* ;
13– 1 they insist upon *d·* now.
14–20 * was entirely right in *d·* so.
28–20 * *d·* the works which Jesus
64–18 * her success in so *d·*
87–29 * the cheerful *d·* of good.
99– 3 * good things that this sect is *d·*.
137–24 I had contemplated *d·* this
138– 3 relieved of the burden of *d·* this.
142–12 sought God's guidance in *d·* it,
149– 3 by *d·* as he bade :
150– 6 * "*D·* what deserves to be written,
165– 4 But in *d·* this the Master
185– 4 * Let us, then, be up and *d·*,
187– 5 too busy to think of *d·* so
203–28 *d·* so much to benefit mankind
204– 1 nor will you be long in *d·* more.
245–20 *d·* the works of primitive
252–12 to make one enjoy *d·* right,
275–24 *D·* unto others as we would
358– 3 *d·* as you say you are,
363–25 sure that one is not *d·* this,
(see also **good**)

doinge
Mis. 253–12 * chapter sub-title

doings
My. 279– 6 Christ's sayings and *d·*.

doleful
Ret. 14–11 ready for his *d·* questions,

dolefully
Mis. 339–27 surge *d·* at the door of

dollar
Man. 44–14 tax of not less than one *d·*
Mis. 141–27 or else return every *d·*
My. 52–25 * reached her bottom *d·*,
98–23 * asked to contribute a *d·*.
(see also **values**)

dollars
My. 28– 8 * will show the *d·* and cents
53– 3 * hundreds of *d·* were sunk
(see also **values**)

domain
Mis. 320–24 the zenith of Truth's *d·*,
Po. 22–18 *d·* of pain and sin
My. 278–27 War is not in the *d·* of good ;

dome
Mis. 1– 4 dawned on the *d·* of being
Pul. 2– 8 soft shimmer of its starlit *d·*.
Po. 39– 6 A temple, whose high *d·*
My. 29–20 * the *d·* of the great edifice
36–25 * by this sheltering *d·* ;
46– 3 * towering, overshadowing *d·*,
61–26 * stood under the great *d·*,
67– 1 * raises its *d·* above the city
68– 7 * *d·* surmounting the building
68– 8 * twice the size of the *d·* on
68–10 * *d·* is two hundred and twenty-four feet
69– 7 * presenting an oval and *d·* appearance
69–28 * in which the *d·* seems to dominate
69–31 * building and *d·* can be seen
70–12 * are worthy of the *d·*.
77– 6 * *d·* of the Massachusetts State House,
78– 6 * massive *d·* rising to a height of
81–23 * rose tingling to the great *d·*,
85–30 * noble *d·* of pure gray tint;
86– 5 * loved its golden State House *d·*,
89– 6 * *d·* over two hundred and twenty feet
95–13 * *d·* which rivals that of the
186– 8 Though neither *d·* nor turret

domestic
Pul. 49–19 * something of her *d·* arrangements,

dominance
Pul. 31–18 * in the *d·* of mind over matter,
No. 33– 3 gives the *d·* to God,

dominant
Mis. 293–14 If spiritual sense is not *d·* in
297–24 If the man is *d·* over the animal,
Ret. 20–24 My *d·* thought in marrying again
31– 2 sunders the *d·* ties of earth
Un. 50– 9 by a *d·* understanding of Spirit.

dominate
Man. 83–13 or attempt to *d·* his pupils,
Pul. 32– 7 * to *d·*, to lead, to control,
My. 69–28 * seems to *d·* the entire city,

dominates
Mis. 293–15 if evil *d·* his character,
Pul. 2– 6 spirit of beauty *d·* The
My. 96– 9 * where fanaticism *d·* everything
193–15 The spiritual *d·* the temporal.

dominating
Pul. 32–13 * *d·* her followers like any abbess
Pan. 7–27 lapses into evil *d·* good,
My. 309– 1 * *d·*, passionate, fearless."

domination
No. 32–22 *d·* of good destroys the sense of evil.

dominion
Mis. 16–14 reflect the full *d·* of Spirit
69–12 let them have *d·* — *Gen.* 1 : 26.
69–30 Had that sick man *d·* over the fish
125– 8 *d·* over his own sinful sense
145–12 to whom God gave "*d·* — *Gen.* 1 : 26.
167–22 He has *d·* over the whole earth ;
183–28 in proof of man's "*d·* — *Gen.* 1 : 26.
331– 7 rich heritage, — "*d·* over — *Gen.* 1 : 26.
373–24 God gave man *d·* over all things,
Un. 39–18 giveth man *d·* over all the earth.
Pul. 53–19 * *d·* over the physical world.
Peo. 12– 3 Let them have "*d·* — *Gen.* 1 : 26.
My. 93–13 * or attaining *d·* over others,
119–18 gives *d·* over all the earth.

donated
Mis. 140–20 The lot of land which I *d·*
143–23 *d·* the munificent sum of
382–19 I *d·* to this church the land

donating
Pul. 64–10 * others *d·* large sums.

donation
Mis. 143–27 Each *d·* came promptly ;
My. 10–14 * *d·* to be specifically subscribed

donations
Man. 78– 9 *D·* from this Church
My. 12– 5 * spontaneous and liberal *d·*

done
Mis. 5– 1 This work well *d·* will elevate
5–16 I have *d·* all that can be *d·*.
7–25 great work already has been *d·*,
7–26 work yet remains to be *d·*.
8– 7 we shall have *d·* more.
11–13 I had *d·* my whole duty to students.
23–11 "and it was *d·*" — *Psal.* 33 : 9.
38– 2 *must be* d· *freely?*
41–17 struggle with sin is forever *d·*.
42–18 proves to have been well *d·*,
45– 2 This is not *d·* by will-power,
57– 8 This work had been *d·* ;
91– 6 but if this be *d·*, let it be in
96–24 How is the healing *d·* in C. S.?
96–27 some means by which it is not *d·*.
111– 3 work, well *d·*, would dignify angels.
115–13 take up the cross as I have *d·*,
122–25 or the "Well *d·*, — *Matt.* 25 : 23.
129– 6 having *d·* this, one will naturally,
141–19 Let this be speedily *d·*.
141–30 what shall be *d·* with their money.
147– 5 and has another duty been *d·*
175–31 and *d·* many wonderful works?
198– 8 must be *d·* with the understanding
208– 1 chapter sub-title — *Matt.* 6 : 10.
208–12 and to let His will be *d·*.
208–15 to do His will or to let it be *d·*
212–21 but Thine, be *d·*," — *Luke* 22 : 42.
213–30 be *d·* on earth as in heaven.
216– 4 must first have *d·* our work,
223–18 we would resist to the hilt if *d·*
236–17 *d·* this to the best of our ability,
238–18 the good *d·*, and the love that
250–23 unselfish deed *d·* in secret ;
274– 7 The work that needs to be *d·*,
283–22 *d·* without incriminating the
292–30 as to just how this should be *d·*,
308– 2 Until this be *d·*, man will
308–21 messenger has *d·* its work,
310–16 be *d·* decently — *I Cor.* 14 : 40.
334–15 This is *d·* only as one gives
334–21 and you have *d·* with it.
335–31 has *d·* himself harm.
355–1 "well *d·* ;" — *Matt.* 25 : 21.
359– 3 when it has *d·* its work,
366–30 and this is being *d·* daily.
380–22 that something was being *d·*
384–11 The cold blasts *d·*,
391–11 That when a wrong is *d·* us,
391–19 Then if we've *d·* to others
399–18 *Laus Deo*, it is *d·* !
Man. 97–18 injustices *d·* Mrs. Eddy or members of
Ret. 28–23 How it was *d·*,

done

Ret.	33–13	the better the work is *d·* ;
	37–23	divine purpose that this should be *d·*,
	50–18	what it has *d·* for them,
	52–14	This was immediately *d·*,
	62– 7	than *a belief . . . has ever d·.*
	64–28	if this is not *d·*, mortals will
	87–30	until he has *d·* with the case
	91–28	teacher, *d·* for the human race?
	91–29	Ask, rather, what has he *not d·*.
	92–10	it shall be *d·* unto you." — *John* 15 : 7.
Un.	14– 3	was not at first *d·* aright.
	53–19	sums *d·* under both rules would
	58–11	*d·* through what is humanly called
Pul.	9– 5	your tireless tasks are *d·* — well *d·*
	16– 3	*Laus Deo,* it is *d·* !
	21–22	however much this is *d·* to us
	22– 7	Thy will be *d·* — *Matt.* 6 : 10.
	25– 3	* are *d·* by electricity,
	43–14	* "*Laus Deo,* it is *d·* !"
	44– 2	* '*Laus Deo,* it is *d·* !'
	51–19	* While it has *d·* this,
	51–29	* which have *d·* something good
	53– 5	* that which is *d·* — *Eccl.* 1 : 9.
	53– 6	* that which shall be *d·* : — *Eccl.* 1 : 9.
	69–26	* have not *d·* so in an intelligent
No.	1– 3	but this must be *d·* gradually,
	9– 8	but this one thing can be *d·*,
	37–26	but he could not have *d·* this if
	38– 1	so far as this could be *d·*
	40–26	our Father has *d·* this ;
Pan.	13–17	and *d·* on earth as in heaven.
'00.	3–15	worker has said and *d·*,
	15–28	The cold blasts *d·*,
'01.	27–20	why was it not *d·* ?
'02.	17–15	duty *d·* and life perfected,
	18–14	ye have *d·* it unto — *Matt.* 25 : 40.
	18–15	*d·* it unto me." — *Matt.* 25 : 40.
Hea.	7–21	would not have *d·* to-day.
	14– 6	What has physiology, ... *d·*
	18– 7	if this be *d·*, the bottle will break
	18–13	If that could be *d·*
Peo.	11– 3	scarcely *d·* with their battles
Po.	26–16	And smiling, say'st, " 'Tis *d·* !
	27–20	Thy work is *d·*, and well :
	32–21	with hope when 'tis *d·* ;
	36–10	The cold blasts *d·*,
	38–10	That when a wrong is *d·* us,
	38–18	Then if we've *d·* to others
	76– 2	LAUS DEO, it is *d·* !
My.	vii– 4	* what its Leader has *d·* for
	6– 7	is to be *d·* forever with the sins
	8–15	* something *d·*, and *d·* immediately,
	12–23	Whatever needs to be *d·*
	12–23	which cannot be *d·* now,
	12–25	that which can be *d·* now,
	18–25	and *d·* on earth as in heaven."
	20– 1	this also that she hath *d·* — *Mark* 14 : 9.
	24–28	* as well as this can be *d·* by a
	37–10	* of all that you have *d·*
	38– 6	* all that you have *d·* for us.
	53– 5	* that her duty was wholly *d·*,
	58–23	* as she has *d·*, verifying
	61–23	* to admit that the work could be *d·*,
	62– 2	* "Well *d·*," — *Matt.* 25 : 23.
	64– 7	* gratitude and love for all that she has *d·*.
	78–10	* an interior *d·* in soft gray
	84– 7	* that would otherwise be *d·*.
	98–11	* must have *d·* with scoffs and jeers
	122– 9	Now I am *d·* with homilies
	124–13	"well *d·*" — *Matt.* 25 : 23.
	134–11	and work well *d·* should not
	136–27	and I have so *d·* that I may have
	142–19	as they so often have *d·*,
	150–25	it shall be *d·* unto you." — *John* 15 : 7.
	151–12	injustice *d·* by press and pulpit
	152–30	of all that is rightly *d·*.
	160–32	the wrongs *d·* to others,
	162–21	"Well *d·*," — *Matt.* 25 : 23.
	201–15	crowned with a diadem of duties *d·*.
	202–13	"Well *d·*," — *Matt.* 25 : 23.
	207–21	"Well *d·*," — *Matt.* 25 : 21.
	225– 4	"Well *d·*," — *Matt.* 25 : 23.
	229–16	as she has *d·*,
	235–11	it cannot be *d·* in metaphysics,
	235–28	Had I known what was being *d·*
	240–27	* when the teaching is *d·* by those who
	247–29	has all been *d·* through love,
	250–27	whatever is *d·* in this direction
	261–11	Too much cannot be *d·* towards
	281– 4	Thy will be *d·* — *Matt.* 6 : 10.
	284–23	only as other churches had *d·*.
	288– 6	The good *d·* and the good to do
	315– 8	* if he had *d·* as he ought,
	319–30	* told me that he had *d·* some literary
	320– 7	* statement of what he had *d·* for you

done

My.	324–31	* no man could have *d·* so any better.
	327–14	* This is the result of the work *d·* at
	345–21	"The work *d·* by the surgeon

donkey

Mis.	370–21	braying *d·* whose ears stick out

donor (*see also* **donor's**)

Pul.	26–16	* healing of the wife of the *d·*.

donor's

Mis.	143–29	breathing the *d·* privileged joy.

donors

Mis.	142– 6	chapter sub-title
	142–13	Let me write to the *d·*,
Pul.	8–11	*d·* all touchingly told their
My.	167– 2	it may have cost the dear *d·*.

doom

Mis.	354– 5	lead the innocent to *d·* ?
Chr.	53–29	that *d·* Was Jesus' part ;
Un.	57– 6	it foresees the impending *d·*
Pul.	7–21	stumble onward to their *d·* ;
'00.	2–23	*d·* of such workers will come,
Po.	34–15	Yet wherefore ask thy *d·* ?
My.	125–29	The *d·* of the Babylonish woman,
	211–27	and sealing his *d·*,
	350–19	Thou infinite — dost *d·* above.

doomed

Mis.	261– 1	evil, as *mind*, is *d·*,
	362–19	an evil mind already *d·*,
	385–23	flesh was weak, and *d·* To pass away.
Ret.	13– 8	among those who were *d·* to
Po.	48–19	flesh was weak, and *d·* To pass away.

dooms

Mis.	258– 1	this lawless law which *d·* man to

door

Mis.	30–12	Death was not the *d·* to this
	30–18	opened the *d·* to the captive,
	74–19	rolled away the stone from the *d·*
	83–14	error which knocks at the *d·*
	84–30	through the *d·* named death,
	106–12	Out through the *d·* of Love,
	133–15	when thou hast shut thy *d·*, — *Matt.* 6 : 6.
	155– 8	woo the weary wanderer to your *d·*,
	180–14	I found the open *d·* from this
	201–28	is awakened to bar his *d·*
	250–26	out of a side *d·* ;
	250–27	the *d·* that turns toward want
	275– 5	from the *d·* of this sepulchre
	276–29	quickly learned when the *d·* is shut.
	276–30	and it closes the *d·* on itself.
	303–14	knock instead of push at the *d·*
	317–10	*d·* to my teaching was shut when
	324– 5	The *d·* is shut.
	324–12	him who waiteth at the *d·*.
	326– 6	The *d·* is burst open,
	328–13	heard this Christ knock at the *d·* of
	339–27	at the *d·* of conscience,
	342–22	The *d·* is shut.
	391–18	Find items at our *d·*.
	398–11	We would enter by the *d·*,
Chr.	55–26	I stand at the *d·*, — *Rev.* 3 : 20.
	55–27	and open the *d·*, — *Rev.* 3 : 20.
Ret.	9– 3	The *d·* was ajar,
	23–14	When the *d·* opened,
	46–17	We would enter by the *d·*,
	80–24	sees the *d·* and turns away from it,
Pul.	17–16	We would enter by the *d·*,
	21–21	and close the *d·* on church or
	26–21	over the *d·*, . . . is the word "Love."
	35–30	* on the sign at his *d·*.
	78–22	* gold key to the church *d·*.
Pan.	12–13	a *d·* that no man can shut ;
'01.	14–23	even as one guards his *d·* against
Peo.	5–11	are nigh, even at our *d·*.
Po.	14–15	We would enter by the *d·*,
	38–17	Find items at our *d·*.
My.	54–11	* was turned from the *d·*
	90–13	* the *d·* to this gospel for many,
	152–14	Do I enter by the *d·*
	210– 5	no *d·* through which evil can enter,
	221–28	thus throwing the *d·* wide open to
	256–12	close the *d·* of mind on this subject,
	311– 5	knocked at the *d·* and was admitted.

doors

Mis.	101–18	opening the *d·* for them that
	114–22	or bar their *d·* too closely,
	124– 6	opening the prison *d·* to the
	262–21	opening the prison *d·* to such as
	280–30	*d·* of animal magnetism open wide
	281– 3	*d·* that this animal element
	283–12	wrong to burst open *d·*
	325–30	without watchers and the *d·* unbarred !
	332– 6	*d·* that closed on C. S.
Ret.	14–18	even if . . . left me outside the *d·*.

doors

Pul.	24–27	* with *d·* of antique oak
	59–30	* auditors left by the rear *d·*,
	76– 2	* that used in the *d·* and pews.
No.	41–17	trying to force the *d·* of Science
My.	29–29	* for the opening of the *d·*
	31– 9	* *d·* of the church were thrown open
	34–11	ye everlasting *d·* ; — *Psal.* 24 : 9.
	54–24	* crowds had besieged the *d·*
	77–27	* open its *d·* absolutely free of
	·94–19	* *d·* were opened to the public,
	110–22	open the prison *d·*
	174– 2	throwing open their *d·* for the
	276– 8	preference to remain within *d·*

dormant

Pul.	72–24	* power of Christ has been *d·* in
My.	211–19	Other minds are made *d·* by it,
	260–25	raises the *d·* faculties,

dose

Mis.	241–10	give to the immoralist a mental *d·*
	241–13	so taking a *d·* of error
	252– 6	its largest *d·* is never dangerous,
Ret.	33–18	not affected by a larger *d·*.
'01.	18– 3	that was my favorite *d·*.
Hea.	12–19	made the infinitesimal *d·* effectual.
	13–17	with this original *d·* we cured an

dosed

My.	345–13	I was *d·* with drugs until

doses

Mis.	69–15	given three *d·* of Croton oil,
	249– 2	some large *d·* of morphine,
	348–21	*d·* of *Natrum muriaticum*
	348–26	Hence I tried several *d·* of
'01.	17–28	where the allopathic *d·* would not.

dotted

Pul.	48– 3	* *d·* with beds of flowering shrubs,

dotting

Mis.	150–17	churches are *d·* the entire land.

dottings

My.	252–19	Your letter and *d·* are an

double

Un.	36– 3	endows with the *d·* capacity of
My.	82–26	* trains pulled out . . . in *d·* sections.
	126–17	*d·* unto her *d·* — *Rev.* 18 : 6.
	126–19	fill to her *d·* — *Rev.* 18 : 6.
	315–24	or is it her alleged *d·* or

doubled

Mis.	349–30	contributions, . . . *d·* that amount.

doubleminded

Mis.	198–23	the "*d·*" senses, — *Jas.* 4 : 8.

doubly

My.	85–31	* this church, . . . is *d·* welcomed.

doubt

and darkness

Mis.	342– 4	they were in *d·* and darkness.
'00.	7–19	In *d·* and darkness we say as did
My.	152–19	will stumble into *d·* and darkness,

any

My.	61–20	* never more did I have any *d·*.

beyond a

Ret.	89– 4	is proven beyond a *d·*
'01.	28–21	has proven to me beyond a *d·*
My.	180– 4	knows beyond a *d·* that its

darkness and

Ret.	68–20	Darkness and *d·* encompass thought,

darkness or

My.	187– 8	exclude all darkness or *d·*,

every

Mis.	120–29	puts to flight every *d·* as to the

excludes

My.	293– 2	The knowledge that . . . excludes *d·*,

faith and

My.	292–29	is a compound of faith and *d·*,

fear or

No.	8–13	his own salvation, without fear or *d·*,

natural

Un.	1– 2	rouses so much natural *d·*

no

Mis.	6–19	we exist in God, . . . there is no *d·*,
	49– 6	no *d·* she could have been
	52– 8	has no *d·* of God's power,
	249–20	no *d·* from the combined efforts of
	319–28	No *d·* must intervene
My.	19–27	no *d·* fill the memory
	42– 9	* no *d·* already acquainted with him
	74– 5	* no *d·* the night trains

of their reality

Hea.	5–14	* not the *d·* of their reality."

or disagreement

Man.	66– 7	If . . . a *d·* or disagreement shall

doubt

period of

Mis.	237–19	This is a period of *d·*, inquiry,

prayer of

Mis.	59–16	prayer of *d·* and mortal belief

single

My.	294–13	would mightily rebuke a single *d·*

without

Pul.	70–10	* is without *d·* one of the

Mis.	30– 5	and *d·* its higher rules,
	165–14	darkness, *d·*, disease, nor death.
	204– 7	attended throughout with *d·*,
	226– 2	* *d·* not that the Father of all
	250– 6	and *d·* what it is.
	341–20	To *d·* this is implicit treason
Pul.	54– 8	* That Jesus . . . we cannot *d·*.
'01.	2–24	*d·*, and unrequited toil will beset
	22– 2	Science is Science, who can *d·* ;

doubted

My.	311–23	I never *d·* the veracity of

doubtful

Un.	23–15	*d·* or spurious evidence of
'02.	2–13	Protestantism to *d·* liberalism.
	5– 6	*d·* interpretations of the Bible ;
My.	10–17	* It is *d·* if the Cause of C. S.
	58–30	* it is *d·* if there was one so
	95–28	* It is *d·* if, since the days of
	260–15	*d·* sense that falls short of

doubting

Mis.	28–15	our Master proved to his *d·* disciple,
	241–24	*d·* heart looks up through faith,
	307– 4	if you wait, never *d·*,
My.	119–18	The *d·* disciple could not identify
	219–18	not charge Christians with *d·*

doubtingly

Mis.	241–14	else he will *d·* await the result ;

doubtless

Mis.	137–11	Since then you have *d·* realized
	239–24	*d·* their familiarity with
Ret.	49– 6	will *d·* follow the example of
Pul.	50–18	* and *d·* have been comforted
	51–23	* erection of this temple will *d·* help
My.	60– 5	* she would *d·* do so.
	83–14	* policemen, who will *d·* have fewer
	215–29	*D·* to test the effect of both
	250–20	*D·* the churches adopting this

doubts

Ret.	14–18	even if my creedal *d·*
	33–24	insufficient to satisfy my *d·*
Un.	27– 9	which *d·* all existence except
Hea.	19–21	*d·* the feasibility of the demand.

Douma

My.	282– 9	The *D·* recently adopted in

dove (see also dove's)

Mis.	81–21	*hear this voice, or see the d·,*
	82– 5	peace symbolized by a *d·* ;
	306–24	touch of the breast of a *d·* ;
	330– 6	no arrow wounds the *d·*?
	331–12	*d·* feeds her callow brood,
	355–25	like the *d·* from the deluge.
	387–12	arrow that doth wound the *d·*
Po.	6– 7	arrow that doth wound the *d·*
	10–11	Our eagle, like the *d·*,
	24–21	Send us thy white-winged *d·*.
	43– 7	Gentle as the *d·*,
My.	192–16	the *d·* of peace sits smilingly
	337–12	Our eagle, like the *d·*,

dove-like

Mis.	ix–14	now hope sits *d·*.

dove's

Po.	28–13	The *d·* to soar to Thee !

doves

Mis.	210–11	harmless as *d·*." — *Matt.* 10 : 16.
	270– 3	them that sold *d·*," — *Matt.* 21 : 12.
My.	150–29	harmless as *d·*." — *Matt.* 10 : 16.
	205– 6	harmless as *d·*." — *Matt.* 10 : 16.

Dowager Empress

My.	234–22	If the *D· E·* could hold her nation

down

Mis.	5–28	weighed *d·* as is mortal thought
	7– 4	loaded *d·* with coverings
	10–27	Heaven comes *d·* to earth.
	16– 4	heaven to come *d·* to earth.
	24–30	put *d·* all subtle falsities
	36–12	lion that lieth *d·* with the lamb.
	120–15	with armor on, not laid *d·*.
	125–11	shall sit *d·* at the Father's right hand :
	125–12	*sit d·*; not stand waiting
	139–11	*pulling d· of strong holds* ; — *II Cor.* 10 : 4.

down

Mis.	139–11	*casting d· imaginations,*— *II Cor.* **10**: 5.
	145–23	lie *d·* with the kid ;— *Isa.* **11**: 6.
	151–11	"Cut it *d·* ; — *Luke* **13**: 7.
	212–30	friends took *d·* from the cross
	225–20	sat *d·* beside the sofa whereon
	235–13	cut *d·* all that bringeth not forth
	250–15	taken *d·* on rare occasions
	257–13	and strikes *d·* the hoary saint.
	257–25	*d·* in the death-dealing wave.
	261–14	pressed *d·*, and running over.
	285–18	deep *d·* in human consciousness,
	320– 9	The star that looked lovingly *d·*
	320–24	looketh *d·* on the long night of
	321–21	Still treading each temptation *d·*,
	327–20	lay *d·* a few of the heavy weights,
	329– 8	putting *d·* the green ones,
	356–25	gone *d·* in his own esteem.
	373–28	sit *d·* at the right hand of the **Father.**
	376–10	* handed *d·* from the *living reality.*
	383–13	*d·* the dim posterns of time
	389–23	No night drops *d·* upon
	392– 8	pouring *d·* Thy sheltering shade,
Ret.	22–12	set *d·* at the right hand of — *Heb.* **12**: 2.
	35– 5	basis it laid *d·* for physical and
	40–23	notices for a second lecture pulled *d·*,
	80–13	pulling *d·* of sin's strongholds,
	85–10	a ladder let *d·* from the heaven **of**
Un.	1– 4	this may be set *d·* as
	12– 1	I say, Look up, not *d·*,
	29–24	"Why art thou cast *d·*,— *Psal.* **42**: 11.
	45–10	The egotist must come *d·* and learn,
	58– 7	come *d·* from the cross." — *Mark* **15**: 30.
	58– 8	coming *d·* from the cross,
Pul.	9–28	and call *d·* blessings infinite.
	12– 8	accuser of . . . is cast *d·*,— *Rev.* **12**: 10.
	12–13	for the devil is come *d·* — *Rev.* **12**: 12.
	12–22	Self-abnegation, by which we lay *d·* all
	27–13	* "cometh *d·* from God — *see Rev.* **3**: 12.
	28– 4	* star of Bethlehem shines *d·* from above.
	45–24	* gladly laid *d·* his responsibilities
	49– 8	* Looking *d·* from the windows
	50–28	* live *d·* any attempted repression.
	60–11	* as set *d·* for him,
	62–22	* from those described *d·* to
Rud.	16–19	practice laid *d·* in S. and H.,
No.	8–17	bow *d·* to the commandments **of**
	19– 3	the premium would go *d·*.
Pan.	4–21	"Why art thou cast *d·*,— *Psal.* **42**: 11.
'01.	16– 1	* at this moment drop *d·* into
'02.	18–19	Jesus laid *d·* his life for mankind ;
	20– 2	or going *d·* into the deep,
Po.	2–13	The moon looks *d·* upon
	5– 2	No night drops *d·* upon the
	20–11	from thy lofty summit, pouring *d·*
	41– 6	earth-stricken lay *d·* their woes,
My.	21–19	* "good measure, pressed *d·*,— *Luke* **6**: 38
	44– 4	* heavy burdens are being laid *d·*,
	110– 5	looks *d·* upon the long night of
	119–13	she *stooped d·* and looked into the
	127–28	nor laid *d·* at the feet of progress
	155–11	lay *d·* the low laurels of vain glory,
	158– 7	This day drops *d·* upon
	200–22	by pulling *d·* its benefactors,
	212– 9	put *d·* the evil effects of alcohol.
	248–15	reaching deep *d·* into the universal
	258–16	set *d·* at the right hand of — *Heb.* **12**: 2.
	343–18	It brought *d·* a shower of abuse
		(*see also* **heaven**)

downfall

Mis.	43–24	or to build on the *d·* of others,
	265–32	compels the *d·* of his self-conceit.
'02.	18–27	*d·* of genuine Christianity,

downright

'00.	10– 1	Success in sin is *d·* defeat.

downtrodden

Mis.	127–24	even though your pearls be *d·*.
	331– 4	When *d·* like the grass,

downward

Mis.	267–20	while the left beats its way *d·*,
	323– 7	Stranger wending his way *d·*,
	362–24	millstone that is dragging them *d·*,

downy

Po.	53–16	Their *d·* little breasts.

Doxology

My.	31– 8	* following hymns . . . *D·*.

dozen

My.	81–13	* up leaped half a *d·* Scientists.
	107–15	administers half a *d·* or less
	215–10	sometimes a *d·* or upward in **one**
	243–12	duties of half a *d·* or more

dozens

My.	73– 4	* have erected *d·* of churches

Dr.——

Mis.	218–30	*D·* says : "The recognition **of**

Dr.——'s

Mis.	218–27	illustrate *D·* views

draft

Man.	17–15	committee to *d·* the Tenets **of**
Po.	1–16	Recalling oft the bitter *d·*

drag

My.	84– 2	* Nothing is more of a *d·* on **a**

dragged

Mis.	237–26	through which Garrison was *d·*

dragging

Mis.	362–23	millstone that is *d·* them downward,

dragon

Mis.	253 -17	*d·* that stood ready to devour
	254–18	great red *d·* of this hour,
Pul.	13–24	*d·* is at last stung to death
	13–27	when the *d·* saw that — *Rev.* **12**: 13.
	14–12	flood which the *d·* — *Rev.* **12**: 16.
	14–18	What if the old *d·* should
Hea.	10– 2	The *d·* that was wroth

drain

Ret.	30–21	No one else can *d·* the cup

drama

My.	281– 1	foresight of the nations' *d·*

drank

Mis.	121– 5	*d·* from their festal wine-cup.
	211–28	*d·* this cup giving thanks,
	232– 3	*d·* to peace, and plenty,
'02.	11–19	which he *d·*, giving thanks,

draped

Mis.	237–26	*d·* in honor of the dead hero

drapery

Mis.	376– 5	* face, figure, and *d·* of Jesus,
	376– 6	* face, figure, and *d·* of that

drap'ry

Po.	65–12	My thoughts 'neath thy *d·*

draughts

Mis.	ix–17	deep *d·* from the fount

draw

Mis.	37– 5	*d·* mankind toward purity,
	239–12	I observed a carriage *d·* up
Ret.	88–27	as will *d·* men unto us.
	93– 9	will *d·* all men unto — *John* **12**: 32.
Un.	1–16	until they *d·* nearer to the
No.	7–21	*d·* no lines whatever between
My.	9–25	*d·* on God for the amount
	202– 6	may his salvation *d·* near,
	247–13	will *d·* all men unto you.

drawing

Pul.	64–26	* *d·* together six thousand **people**
No.	45–27	material history is *d·* to a close.

drawing-room

Pul.	37–17	* sat in the beautiful *d·*,

drawings

My.	335–14	* *d·* and specifications of which

drawn

Mis.	93–11	conclusion *d·* from the Scriptures,
	214–17	the sword must have been *d·*
	288–12	conclusion *d·* therefrom is not
	341–22	parable is *d·* from the sad history **of**
	381–17	decree in favor of Mrs. Eddy was *d·*
Pul.	46– 7	* no such inference is to be *d·*
	62– 5	* substitution of tubes of *d·* brass
'01.	3–27	conclusion is not properly *d·*.
	26–27	I was not *d·* to them by a
'02.	7–19	No other logical conclusion can be *d·*
My.	30– 8	* other faiths, *d·* to the church
	49– 4	* one is wholly *d·* over,
	185– 9	sword of the Spirit is *d·* ;
	189–23	we are *d·* towards God.
	224– 9	are not apt to be correctly *d·*.

draws

Peo.	1– 4	it *d·* not its life from human
Po.	22– 3	Eternity *D·* nigh
My.	350– 1	*d·* its conclusions of Deity and

dread

Mis.	396– 6	Fills mortal sense with *d·* ;
Ret.	47– 3	to *d·* the unprecedented popularity
Un.	64–12	hope of ever eluding their *d·* presence
Po.	58–18	Fills mortal sense with *d·* ;
My.	335–18	* second case of the *d·* disease

dreaded

Ret.	13–16	to win me from *d·* heresy.

dream

angel
  Peo.   7–11   * angel *d·* passed o'er him.
apart from the
  Hea. 11– 5   wholly apart from the *d·*.
asleep in a
  Mis. 44–21   or when asleep in a *d·*.
calleth itself
  Hea. 11– 4   *d·* calleth itself a dreamer,
carved the
  Peo.   7–12   * He carved the *d·* on that
death's
  Mis. 386–13   "When, severed by death's *d·*,
  Po.   49–19   "When, severed by death's *d·*,
disease or
  Mis. 58– 2   *no remembrance of that disease or d·,*
formulating a
  Mis. 49–16   *capacity for formulating a d·,*
has no place
  Ret. 21–15   *d·* has no place in the Science
has passed
  Hea. 11– 4   but when the *d·* has passed,
life
  Peo.   7–19   * Our life *d·* passes o'er us.
life is a
  Mis. 28–11   so-called life is a *d·* soon told.
  52–18   *If this life is a d·*
like a
  Ret. 10–13   vanished like a *d·*.
material
  Mis. 28–12   this mortal and material *d·*,
memory's
  Po.   66– 5   songs float in memory's *d·*.
mortal
  Mis. 393– 8   Lighting up this mortal *d·*.
  Po.   51–13   Lighting up this mortal *d·*.
  My.   5– 7   apart from this mortal *d·*,
  296–16   mortal *d·* of life, substance, or
nothingness of the
  Mis. 49–24   the nothingness of the *d·*,
of avarice
  Pul. 10–12   No *d·* of avarice or ambition
of death
  Mis. 58– 5   Waking from the *d·* of death,
  My. 273–28   "Man awakes from the *d·* of death
of dying
  Mis. 70–13   if the *d·* of dying should
of life
  Mis. 16–16   the *d·* of life in matter,
  Hea.   9–27   the *d·* of life in matter,
  Peo. 14–16   this *d·* of life in matter,
  My. 267–20   his *d·* of life in matter
  296–16   mortal *d·* of life, substance, or
of material sensation
  Mis. 331–29   their *d·* of material sensation,
of other dreams
  Ret. 32–18   * But the *d·* of other dreams.
of sense
  Mis. 176– 1   that breaks the *d·* of sense,
of sickness
  Rud. 11–17   awake from the *d·* of sickness ;
of Spirit
  Mis. 180– 1   the *d·* of Spirit in the flesh
of suffering
  Mis. 70–14   from the *d·* of suffering.
one's own
  My. 117–10   one's own *d·* of personal sense,
or error
  Mis. 49–15   *is a d· or error,*
passing
  My.   46– 7   * it were but a passing *d·*.
this
  Mis. 53– 1   out of this *d·* or false claim
  Hea.   9–26   sickness, and death are this *d·*.
  17–15   explains this *d·* of material life,
  Peo. 14–16   this *d·* of life in matter,
troubled
  Un.   50–22   awake from the troubled *d·*,
vanish as a
  Mis. 205–29   molecules, . . . vanish as a *d·* ;
waking from a
  Mis. 58– 4   Waking from a *d·*, one learns
waking from the
  Mis. 58– 5   Waking from the *d·* of

  Mis. 23– 5   * or *d·* in the animal,
  42– 3   *only as in a d·?*
  42–22   is a *d·* and unreal,
  44–23   is but a *d·* at all times.
  58– 7   proves to him . . . that it was a *d·*,
  253–27   Do the children of this period *d·* of
  354–33   more bright than the *d·* in his breast.
  Pul. 39–17   * Dimly, as in a *d·*, I watch the flow
  39–23   * Dimly, as in a *d·*,
  '02.   9–18   man is not the *d·* of a heated brain ;

dream

  Hea.   9–25   Life in matter is a *d·* :
  10–19   Then will your sorrow be a *d·*,
  17–11   sickness, and death, are but a *d·*,
  17–15   *d·* of the "deep sleep" — *Gen.* 2 : 21.
  Po.   3–10   To *d·* of thee, to *d·* of thee !
  18–11   as the *d·* in his breast !
  47–21   and the gladness a *d·*,
  My. 109– 5   *d·* which is mortal and God-condemned
  132–28   satisfied to sleep and *d·*.

dreamed

  Mis. 78–12   never *d·* that either of these
  91–24   never *d·*, until informed thereof,
  Pul. 33– 2   * saw visions and *d·* dreams.

dreamer

  Hea. 11– 4   dream calleth itself a *d·*,
  My. 122– 4   from the brain of a *d·*.
  132–26   It will waken the *d·*

dreaming

  Mis. 325–17   *d·* away the hours.
  Po.   8–16   I'm *d·* alone of its changeful sky
  My. 132–26   sinner, *d·* of pleasure in sin ;
  132–27   the sick, *d·* of suffering matter ;

dreams

  Mis. 28– 8   In *d·*, things are only what
  28–10   phenomena of mortal life are as *d·* ;
  36–28   as in the *d·* of sleep.
  209–16   neither oblivion nor *d·* can
  252–10   possessing the nature of *d·*.
  257– 4   *d·* in the animal,
  Ret. 21–14   history is but the record of *d·*,
  32–18   * But the dream of other *d·*.
  Un.   26–25   a product of human *d·*.
  Pul.   8–29   which will eclipse Oriental *d·*.
  33– 2   * saw visions and dreamed *d·*.
  Pan.   9– 2   * *d·* in the animal,
  Hea. 10–28   Earth's fading *d·* are empty streams,
  Po.   65– 5   meeting with loved ones in *d·*
  65–13   *d·* so boundless and bright
  My. 110–16   my early *d·* of flying
  236– 2   Let us have no more of echoing *d·*.

dreamt

  Pul.   6–28   * more than is *d·* of

dreamy

  Mis.   9–21   *d·* objects of self-satisfaction ;
  206–14   manifests . . . no *d·* absentness,

drear

  No.   35–10   also the *d·* subtlety of death.
  Po.   2–12   still art thou *d·* and lone !

dreary

  Po.   65– 9   enchained to life's *d·* night,
  65–15   We waken to life's *d·* sigh.

dregs

  Ret. 30–22   cup which I have drunk to the *d·*

Dresden

  My.   81–16   * "*D·* !" "Peoria !" they cried.

dress

  Mis. 262– 8   new and costly spring *d·*.
  Pul. 54– 2   * The healing of his seamless *d·*

dressed

  Mis. 24–13   I rose, *d·* myself, and
  Ret. 13–22   I rose and *d·* myself,
  40–11   rose from her bed, *d·* herself,

drew

  Mis. 121–24   *d·* from the great Master this answer
  168–27   * *d·* a large audience.
  340–16   *d·* up·logs instead of leases.
  Ret. 48– 1   *d·* its breath from me,
  My. 145– 5   He *d·* the plan,

drift

  Mis. 81– 5   *d·*, by right of God's dear love,
  Un.   24– 5   and cannot *d·* into evil.
  Peo.   1–13   *d·* into more spiritual latitudes.
  My. 166–15   will live on and never *d·* apart.
  213–18   to *d·* in the wrong direction

drifted

  Mis. 225– 8   conversation *d·* to . . . C. S. ;

drifting

  No.   45–21   *D·* into intellectual wrestlings,
  My. 307–27   and *d·* whither I knew not.

driftwood

  No.   29–23   *d·* on the ocean of thought ;

drilled

  Un.   6–26   not yet thoroughly *d·* in the

drills

  Peo. 12–23   Having faith in drugs and hygienic *d·*,

drink

  Mis. 28–32   *d·* any deadly thing, — *Mark* 16 : 18.
  71– 4   an appetite for alcoholic *d·*

drink
Mis.	125– 1	he will indeed *d·* of our Master's cup,
	125– 9	Then shall he *d·* anew Christ's cup,
	207– 3	*d·* with me the living waters of the
	211–26	"Ye shall *d·* indeed — *Matt.* 20 : 23.
	211–29	"*D·* ye all of it," — *Matt.* 26 : 27.
	211–29, 30	*d·* it all, and let all *d·* of it.
	245– 4	What shall we *d·*?" — *Matt.* 6 : 31.
	249– 6	*d·* any deadly thing, — *Mark* 16 : 18.
	289– 2	Strong *d·* is unquestionably an evil,
	311–28	to take the cup, *d·* all of it,
	323–21	and *d·* from its living fountains?
	328–14	*d·* with the drunken" — *Matt.* 24 : 49.
	335– 6	*d·* with the drunken ; — *Matt.* 24 : 49.
Ret.	26– 5	on the cross, when he refused to *d·*
Pul.	1– 2	*d·* of the river of — *Psal.* 36 : 8.
	3–17	*d·* of the river of — *Psal.* 36 : 8.
	3–23	We *d·* of this river when all
	7–30	*d·* of the river of — *Psal.* 36 : 8.
	9–20	"*d·* from the river — *see Psal.* 36 : 8.
	14–16	watching for rest and *d·*.
No.	v–10	it saith tenderly, "Come and *d·* ; "
	34–11	They *d·* the cup of Christ
	42–27	* eat beefsteak and *d·* strong coffee
	43– 2	to the power of daily meat and *d·*.
Pan.	14– 9	*d·* of the cup of salvation,
'02.	11–20	gave it to his followers to *d·*.
Hea.	1– 3	*d·* any deadly thing, — *Mark* 16 : 18.
	7–25	*d·* any deadly thing, — *Mark* 16 : 18.
	15–11	*d·* any deadly thing, — *Mark* 16 : 18.
Peo.	12– 3	*d·* any deadly thing, — *Mark* 16 : 18.
Po.	32– 1	and *d·* in the view
My.	48– 1	* *d·* any deadly thing, — *Mark* 16 : 18.
	126– 6	such as *d·* of the living water.
	146– 4	*d·* any deadly thing, — *Mark* 16 : 18.
	156–22	"*d·* of his blood" — *see John* 6 : 53.
	161–17	*d·* sufficiently of the cup
	161–19	"Ye shall *d·* indeed — *Matt.* 20 : 23.
	258–21	who *d·* their Master's cup

drinker
My.	106–24	a brawler, an alcohol *d·*,

drinking
Mis.	90– 9	*for d· and smoking?*
	123–32	eating and *d·* corporeally.
	170– 7	eating of bread and *d·* of wine
Ret.	54– 9	*d·* Jesus' cup, being baptized
No.	19–19	*d·* in the nature and essence of
'01.	12– 5	came neither eating nor *d·*,
My.	78–30	* *d·* in every word of the

drinks
Mis.	15–30	it *d·* in the sweet revealings
	243–27	will tell you that alcoholic *d·*
	297– 9	appetite for alcoholic *d·*.
'01.	12– 2	spiritual sense *d·* it in,

drive
Man.	48–13	shall not haunt Mrs. Eddy's *d·*
My.	171–20	* While on her regular afternoon *d·*
	175– 5	with the exception of a daily *d·*.
	229– 7	doth *d·* them out from — *Deut.* 18 : 12.
	275–18	have omitted my *d·* but twice
	275–20	is all that prevents my daily *d·*.
	276– 6	judged by either a daily *d·* or
	276– 9	because . . . she omits her *d·*,

driven
Mis.	326–17	*d·* out of their houses of clay
	328–15	Hast thou been *d·* by suffering
	380–14	had *d·* me to discover the
No.	22– 1	"*d·* about by every wind — *see Eph.* 4 : 14.
Po.	71– 7	Corruption's band Is *d·* back ;

drives
Mis.	263–27	mad ambition *d·* them to
	363–27	and *d·* diviners mad.
Pul.	37– 9	* and *d·* in the afternoon.

driving
Pul.	47–23	* an easy *d·* distance for her
	47–25	* *d·* rather into the country,
My.	313–12	*d·* into Franklin, N. H.,

drooped
Mis.	385–23	Thy pinions *d·* ; the flesh was weak,
Po.	48–18	Thy pinions *d·* ; the flesh was weak,

drooping
Mis.	376–22	*d·* over a deeply dazzling sunlight,
Pul.	4– 5	Can ne'er refresh a *d·* earth,
Po.	3– 9	Till sleep sets *d·* fancy free

droops
Mis.	329–18	Whatever else *d·*, spring is gay :

drop
Mis.	42–26	*d·* our false sense of Life in sin
	88–30	*d·* one of these doctors when you
	129–12	*d·* this member's name from the church,
	158–16	command, to *d·* the use of notes,
	230–20	*d·* human life into the ditch of

drop
Man.	45–24	*d·* the titles of Reverend and Doctor,
	53– 4	*d·* forever the name of the member
	65– 1	*d·* the word *mother*
Ret.	33–14	One *d·* of the thirtieth attenuation
Pul.	4– 4	'So small a *d·* as I
	4–18	*d·* of water may help to hide the stars,
	5–15	bedew my hope with a *d·* of humanity.
'01.	16– 1	* at this moment *d·* down into hell,
'02.	12–16	*d·* of water is one with the ocean,
	15–26	advised me to *d·* both the book and
	19–30	no redundant *d·* in the cup
Hea.	4–13	to *d·* divinity long enough to
	13–12	*d·* of this harmless solution,
My.	180–22	*d·* compliance with their desires,
	202–24	a *d·* from His ocean of love,
	216–23	*d·* the insignia of "Busy Bees,"

dropped
Mis.	x–21	I *d·* the name of Morse
	288– 6	*d·* into the balances of God
Man.	43– 3	name of said member to be *d·*
	51– 6	his name shall be *d·* from the roll
	56– 5	his or her name shall be *d·*
Hea.	7–18	*d·* her mite into the treasury,
	13–11	*d·* into a tumblerful of water
Po.	31– 3	celestial seed *d·* from

dropping
My.	140–13	* *d·* the annual communion
	140–25	*D·* the communion of

drops
Mis.	1–17	mounting sense . . . *d·* the world.
	205–15	*d·* the curtain on material man
	389–23	No night *d·* down upon the
	395–11	The curtain *d·* on June ;
Pul.	7–13	sacred *d·* were but enshrined
Po.	5– 2	No night *d·* down upon the
	57–18	The curtain *d·* on June ;
	66– 1	But *d·* of pure nectar
My.	158– 7	This day *d·* down upon the

dropsy
Hea.	13–18	an inveterate case of *d·*.

dross
Mis.	151– 6	separates the *d·* from the gold,
	205– 8	separates the *d·* from the gold,
Ret.	94– 9	As *d·* is separated from gold,
Po.	39–12	will watch to cleanse from *d·*

drove
My.	346–11	* Mrs. Eddy's carriage *d·* into town

drown
Pul.	14–19	flood to *d·* the Christ-idea?
	14–19	can neither *d·* your voice
My.	126– 4	to *d·* the strong swimmer

drowned
Mis.	122–12	and that he were *d·* — *Matt.* 18 : 6.
My.	48–28	* *d·* in frivolity, or paralyzed by
	91– 6	* has been *d·* out in this so-called

drowning
Mis.	211–14	*d·* man just rescued from
Pul.	13–18	their heads above the *d·* wave.

drowsy
Po.	30– 5	murmurs from the *d·* rills

drug
any
Mis.	48–16	effect of alcohol, or of any *d·*,

attenuated the
Pul.	35–25	* the more attenuated the *d·*,

attenuation of a
Mis.	271– 2	attenuation of a *d·* up to

diminishing of the
My.	107–18	diminishing of the *d·* does not

disappears
Ret.	33–18	The *d·* disappears in the higher
Hea.	12–24	for when the *d·* disappears

gives the
My.	154– 4	not the person who gives the *d·*

had no effect
Mis.	249– 4	"The *d·* had no effect upon me

instead of the
Ret.	33– 3	mortal belief, instead of the *d·*,

killed by a
My.	302– 4	can he be . . . killed by a *d·* ;

knife or the
My.	294–17	use of the knife or the *d·*,

power of a
Mis.	194– 2	power of a *d·* to heal the sick !

so-called
Hea.	13–10	then the so-called *d·* loses its power

Mis.	45–10	follow the use of that *d·*
	229–26	is a better preventive . . . than a *d·*,
	249–17	neither purchased nor ordered a *d·*
Pul.	6– 9	not the deified *d·*, but

drug

'01.	17–26	the *d·* is utterly expelled,
	18– 1	one grain of the *d·* was
Hea.	12–21	cannot shake the poor *d·* without
	13–16	leave the *d·* out of the question
Peo.	6– 9	* chemist, druggist, or *d·*
My.	107–12	have not an iota of the *d·* left
	154– 4	nor the *d·* itself that heals,
	301–25	*d·* cannot of itself go to the brain

drugged

My.	48–28	* are not *d·* by scandal,

drugging

Mis.	233–13	to put into the old garment of *d·*
Ret.	48–24	higher than physic or *d·* ;

drugging-doctor

Mis.	19–20	more faith in an honest *d·*,

druggist

Peo.	6– 9	* chemist, *d·*, or drug

drugs

administer

Peo.	9–19	and then administer *d·* with

and prayers

Mis.	40– 5	hygienic rules, *d·*, and prayers

depends upon

My.	108– 4	allopath who depends upon *d·*.

dosed with

My.	345–13	I was dosed with *d·* until

effect of

Mis.	348–25	curiosity as to the effect of *d·* on

faith in

Mis.	6–22	overcome the patient's faith in *d·*
Peo.	12–23	faith in *d·* and hygienic drills,

healing by

My.	345–12	false science — healing by *d·*.

healing with

Mis.	88–29	Mind-healing, and healing with *d·*,

hygiene and

Peo.	4– 3	more faith in hygiene and *d·* than

hygiene nor

Hea.	3– 1	requires neither hygiene nor *d·*

hygiene or

Hea.	15– 6	no faith in hygiene or *d·* ;

if God created

Mis.	25–27	If God created *d·* good,
'01.	18–17	If God created *d·* for medical use,

inanimate

'01.	19–22	the use of inanimate *d·* to

medicine or

Pul.	72–17	* medicine or *d·* of any kind,

more effectual than

Mis.	33–30	It is more effectual than *d·* ;
	255–25	It is more effectual than *d·*,
Ret.	34–15	It is more effectual than *d·*,

never recommended

'01.	25–19	He never recommended *d·*,

no

Mis.	348–19	I use no *d·* whatever,

no remedies in

Mis.	96– 6	no remedies in *d·*,

partook not of

Mis.	260– 8	His faith partook not of *d·*,

poisonous

'01.	33–19	not kill people with poisonous *d·*,

prayer and

Mis.	51–29	*Are both prayer and d· necessary*

prescribe

Rud.	3–17	manipulate invalids, prescribe *d·*,

prescribing

Ret.	26– 2	nor prescribing *d·* to support

properties of

My.	293– 5	different properties of *d·*

those

My.	292–24	those *d·* are supposed to

to Deity

My.	139–25	advanced . . . from *d·* to Deity ;

use of

Mis.	108–30	believed in the use of *d·*,
My.	301–24	use of *d·* is in itself a species

without

My.	106–29	because he heals the sick without *d·*?
	108– 3	healing his cases without *d·*

Mis.	3–16	*D·*, inert matter, never are needed
	8– 4	*d·* do not, cannot, produce health
	29–29	if He created *d·* for healing
	51– 3	and *d·*, God does not require.
	52– 2	to such as . . . take *d·* to
	245– 2	or recommended others to use, *d·* ;
	248–28	since which time I have not taken *d·*,
	348–27	*d·* have no beneficial effect
	366–22	*d·*, electricity, and animal magnetism
	369–18	trust Christ more than it does *d·*.
Pul.	53–10	* Can *d·* suddenly cure leprosy?
Pan.	4–26	what need have we of *d·*,

drugs

Hea.	15–21	as if *d·* were superior to Deity.
Peo.	4–25	inquired . . . what *d·* to prescribe.
My.	301–26	*D·* cannot remove inflammation,
	301–29	*d·* can produce no curative effect
	345–14	if the *d·* could be made to act on me.
	345–19	How could I believe in . . . *d·* ?"
	348– 2	*d·*, surgery, hygiene, electricity,

drunk

Mis.	48–14	made a man *d·* on water,
	212–32	had not yet *d·* of his cup,
	225–10	who had *d·* at its fount,
Ret.	30–22	which I have *d·* to the dregs
Pul.	83– 5	* from Philip *d·* to Philip sober,
My.	125–32	"*d·* with the wine of — *Rev.* 17 : 2.

drunkard

Mis.	71– 5	yet he saved many a *d·*

drunkards

'02.	20– 6	"No *d·* within, no sorrow, no pain ;

drunken

Mis.	325– 7	"*d·* without wine." — see *Isa.* 29 : 9.
	328–15	drink with the *d·*" — *Matt.* 24 : 49.
	335– 6	drink with the *d·* ; — *Matt.* 24 : 49.
My.	125–30	"*d·* with the blood of — *Rev.* 17 : 6.
	212– 5	which makes mankind *d·*.

drunkenness

Mis.	277–31	*d·* produced by animality.
	289– 4	*D·* is sensuality let loose,
	324–14	*d·*, witchcraft, variance, envy,

Dr. Vail's Hydropathic Institute

Mis.	378– 2	*D· V· H· I·* in New Hampshire,

dry

Mis.	7– 5	until their bodies become *d·*,
	38–15	*such a d· and abstract subject*
	38–17	far from *d·* and abstract.
	251–28	as *d·* leaves fall to enrich the soil
Pul.	7–22	tabernacles crumble with *d·* rot.
'02.	18–19	like the summer brook, soon gets *d·*.
Po.	35– 8	streams will never *d·* or cease to
My.	43–20	* over this Jordan on *d·* ground.

dual

Mis.	161–15	the appearing of this *d·* nature,
	169–18	*d·* meaning to every Biblical passage,
	322–10	Your *d·* and impersonal pastor,
'01.	8–28	as to his *d·* personality,

Dublin

'00.	1–22	Edinburgh, *D·*, Paris,

duck

Pul.	76–16	* skins of the eider-down *d·*,

due

Mis.	x–11	without *d·* preparation.
	122–23	for the suffering *d·* to sin.
	209– 1	attaches to sin *d·* penalties
	238–29	I accord these evil-mongers *d·* credit
	242–10	thanks *d·* to his generosity ;
	247– 4	be allowed *d·* consideration,
	257–17	suspicion where confidence is *d·*,
	308–23	only to reappear in *d·* season.
	373–21	in *d·* time Christianity entered into
	374–20	homage is indeed *d·*,
Man.	39–11	gives *d·* evidence of having
Ret.	1–17	in *d·* time was married to an
	49–22	everlasting gratitude is *d·* to
	49–27	After *d·* deliberation and earnest
	85–18	*d·* deliberation and light,
Un.	7– 7	*d·* both to C. S. and myself
Pul.	1–11	For *d·* refreshment garner the
	21–14	While we entertain *d·* respect
	32–22	* *d·* to the principles of C. S.
'00.	8–19	We lose a percentage *d·* to
'02.	13–20	note therewith became *d·*,
	13–24	amount *d·* on the mortgage.
Peo.	2– 4	*d·* to the people's improved views of
My.	20–16	rich portion in *d·* season.
	73–27	* trains are *d·* to arrive
	83– 1	* This fact will be *d·* to the
	92–27	* *d·* apparently to nothing save
	116–19	praise to whom praise is *d·*,
	170– 6	*d·* to a desire on my part
	173–25	Special thanks are *d·*
	189– 5	so *d·*, to God is *obedience*,
	202– 9	to whom tribute is *d·* ; — *Rom.* 13 : 7.
	208–14	waiting in *d·* expectation of just
	211–21	distrust where honor is *d·*,
	225–14	unto His holy name *d·* deference,
	332– 9	* Many thanks are *d·* Mr. Cooke,
	333–15	* which was closed in *d·* form."
	354– 5	it is *d·* the field to state that

dues

My.	202– 8	to all their *d·* : — *Rom.* 13 : 7.

dug
   Mis. 340–14   *d·* into soils instead of

dull
   Mis. 88–19   deaf ears and *d·* debaters.
        100– 1   artless listeners and *d·* disciples.
        100– 5   was to awaken the *d·* senses.
        163–11   arrant hypocrite and to *d·* disciples
        275–11   looks in *d·* despair at the vacant
        320–21   addressing to *d·* ears and
        324– 9   the music is *d·*, the wine is unsipped,
        337–27   to itching ears and to *d·* disciples
   No. 40– 8   to hide from *d·* and base ears
   My. 113–23   is C. S. a cold, *d·* abstraction,

dullards
   My. 162– 8   better than a wilderness of *d·*

dulness
   '02.   5– 2   *d·* of to-day prophesies renewed

Duluth, Minn.
   Pul. 90– 1   * *News-Tribune, D·, M·.*
   My. 186–17   chapter sub-title
        186–18   *First Church of Christ, . . . D·, M·:*

duly
   Mis. 176–26   Are we *d·* aware of our own great
        289–15   This fact should be *d·* considered
   Man. 86– 4   *d·* authorized to be a teacher of
        91–20   Students of C. S., *d·* instructed
        92–12   *d·* qualified to teach C. S.,
   Ret. 27–23   can *d·* express it to the ear,
   No.   9–27   * "knowledge, *d·* arranged and
   '00.   3– 9   worker's servitude is *d·* valued,
   My. 26–10   generous check . . . is *d·* received.
        191–29   invitation . . . was *d·* received.
        192–21   Your kind letter, . . . *d·* received.
        240–27   * by those who are *d·* qualified,
        351– 8   letter was handed to me *d·*.
        358–12   have been *d·* informed by me

dumb
   Mis. 68–15   cast out a devil, and the *d·* spake ;
        190–11   *a devil, and it was d·.— Luke* 11 : 14.
        190–12   *the d· spake.— Luke* 11 : 14.
        191–23   refers to the devil as *d·* ;
   '01. 16–20   refer to an evil spirit as *d·*,
        17–16   the blind, the *d·*, the lame,
   Po. 71–10   Righteousness ne'er — awestruck or *d·*
   My. 105–17   hearing to the deaf, speech to the *d·*,
        149–28   with *d·* thunderbolts,
        268–18   as silent as the *d·* centuries

dumbness
   Mis. 190–23   it was the evil of *d·*,

dummy
   My. 315–24   * her alleged double or *d·*

Duncan, Mrs. Elizabeth Patterson
   Ret. 20– 6   to Mrs. Elizabeth Patterson *D·*,

dungeon
   Mis. 99–14   Go, if you must, to the *d·* or
        269– 5   commits his moral sense to a *d·*.
   No. 44–14   sentence men to the *d·* or stake

Dunmore
  Countess of
   My. 295–23   Countess of *D·* and Family,
  Lord
   My. 295–26   lament the demise of Lord *D·* ;

Dunstable
   Ret.   3– 5   Capt. John Lovewell of *D·*,

duodecillions
   Pul.   4–12   as important a factor as *d·*

dupe
   Mis. 119– 7   our laws punish the *d·* as

dupery
   '01. 33– 7   * "Quackery and *d·* do abound

dupes
   '00.   2–20   his *d·* are his capital ;

duplicate
   Mis. 306–14   * a *d·* letter written,
   My. 303–27   her *d·*, antecedent, or

duplicated
   Man. 110– 3   to prevent applications being *d·*

Dura lex, sed lex
   My. 40–30   * hence the proverb : *D· l·, s· l·*

during
   Mis. 42–29   *without being present d· treatment?*
        241–15   *d·* which interim, by constant combat
        321–25   *d·* the great wonder of the world,
   Man. 30–13   *d·* his term of Readership,
        32–16   made but once *d·* the lesson.
        60– 6   *d·* the months of July and August
        69– 3   *d·* the time specified in the
        69–11   *d·* the time of such service.
        83–16   not only *d·* the class term but after

during
   Man. 95–21   *d·* his term of Readership.
   Ret.   5– 9   *D·* my childhood my parents removed
        10–10   *d·* his college vacations.
        24– 7   *D·* twenty years prior to my discovery
        44– 5   *d·* the same month the members,
        50–13   *d·* twelve half-days,
   Pul. vii– 4   *d·* the ensuing thirty years.
        23–10   * paralleled *d·* the last decade by
        31–14   * *d·* some year in the early '80's
        34–10   * *D·* this time she suddenly
        34–26   "*D·* this time," she said,
        38– 6   * *D·* these succeeding twenty years it
        43–25   * in Concord, N. H., *d·* the day,
        53– 8   * *d·* the three years of his ministry
        55– 6   * cyclic changes that came *d·* the
        66–19   * *d·* the last decade,
        68– 1   * of the church *d·* its early years,
        77– 9   * *D·* the year eighteen hundred and
        78– 8   * *D·* the year 1894
        81– 5   * than it was *d·* those services,
        85– 3   * *d·* the intervening years
   '00.   3–21   *d·* the period of captivity
        7– 7   *d·* the past three years
        12–24   *D·* St. Paul's stay in that city
   '02.   1– 7   *d·* the year ending June, 1902,
        13– 5   *D·* the last seven years
   Po. vi–24   * *d· the years she resided in Lynn,*
   My. 11– 5   * *d·* all the storms that have
        11– 8   * *d·* these years she has not
        25– 3   * special effort *d·* the coming week
        29–11   * six times *d·* the day.
        35–27   * *D·* the progress of each service,
        37–14   * obedience *d·* forty years
        43– 8   * their sojourn in the
        52– 1   * *d·* the past year.
        54–16   * *D·* the summer vacation,
        55–21   * *d·* the last year the hall was
        55–28   * *D·* the months that the
        57–21   * admitted *d·* the last year
        66– 5   * *D·* the past two weeks
        78– 3   * *d·* the morning, afternoon, and
        87–21   * *d·* the past few days.
        90– 1   * *d·* her lifetime ;
        91–22   * *d·* the first years of her
        95–15   * *D·* the great assembly of
        97–30   * incidents witnessed *d·* the week
        174– 3   convenience of . . . *d·* the day.
        230– 7   *d·* the senses' assimilation
        312– 2   *d·* her temporary absence.
        314– 4   * *D·* the following nine years
        315– 4   * *D·* his stay,
        321–22   * *D·* that time, from my
        321–28   * *d·* the past twenty years.
        322–19   * *D·* the evening my friend spoke of
        323–30   * *d·* the time of our studying in
        331–23   * *d·* his last sickness,
        331–30   * *d·* his late illness,
        332–26   * *d·* the Civil War
        333–23   * attended him *d·* his illness

dusky
   '02.   3–16   her *d·* children are learning

dust
   Mis. vii–10   And mankind from the *d·* ;
        1–19   removing the *d·* that dims them.
        23–21   it is not organized *d·*.
        57– 7   Man originated not from *d·*,
        140–30   though the . . . should crumble into *d·*,
        145–19   melt into one, and common *d·*,
        145–21   to quicken even *d·* into
        170–25   he is said to have spat upon the *d·*.
        182–16   created neither from *d·* nor
        186– 4   In the creation of Adam from *d·*,
        325–26   wipes off the *d·* from his feet
        363– 9   compensateth . . . *d·* with *d·* !
   Ret. 22–18   The real man is not of the *d·*,
        71– 1   monuments which weigh *d·*,
        86–22   wipe the *d·* from his feet
   Pul. 10– 9   pomp and power lie low in *d·*.
   No. 26–28   *d·* returning to *d·*,
   Po. 31–13   rare footprints on the *d·* of earth.
        72– 2   trampling right in *d·* !
   My.   5– 3   man is supposed to start from *d·*
        129–16   counterpoised his origin from *d·*,
        162– 7   not in atom or in *d·*.
        179– 7   allegory, of . . . and man made of *d·*.
        179– 9   enters non-intelligent *d·*
        273–27   they are consigned to *d·*.
        350– 1   from atom and *d·* draws its

duties
   Man. 25– 3   Names, election, and *d·*.
        28– 3   *D·* of Church Officers.
        29– 4   to perform his official *d·*.
        31– 2   *d·* of readers of the
        31–15   First Readers' *D·*.

duties

Man.	64–10	heading
	93– 3	ORGANIZATION AND d·.
	95–22	d· alone of a Reader are ample.
	97–15	D·.
	99–22	in addition to his other d·,
Hea.	1– 8	they are calls to higher d·,
My.	49–24	* d· in the Church of Christ,
	177– 6	daily d· require attention
	201–15	crowned with a diadem of d· done.
	242–23	leave these d· to the Clerk of The
	243–12	the d· of half a dozen or more
	250–29	d· and attainments beckoning them.
	325– 2	* when amidst all your d·
	358–16	It is part of their d· to relieve

dutiful

Mis.	255– 7	it is possible, and d·,
Man.	45– 2	d· and sufficient occupation
No.	46–16	As d· descendants of Puritans,
My.	308–13	compels me as a d· child

duty

Mis.	3– 2	shall express these views as d· demands,
	11–13	I had done my whole d· to students.
	46–17	man's d·, so to throw the weight of
	147– 5	and has another d· been done
	147–15	rule to follow the road of d·,
	236–28	must not deter us from doing our d·,
	293–22	includes the whole d· of man :
Man.	27–12	d· of the C. S. Board of Directors
	27–18	d· of the C. S. Board of Directors
	28–14	d· of the C. S. Board of Directors
	28–25	d· of any member of this Church,
	31–16	d· of the First Readers to conduct the
	33– 1	d· of every member of The
	41–19	d· of every member of this Church
	42– 4	Alertness to D·.
	42– 5	d· of every member of this Church
	42– 8	nor to neglect his d· to God,
	44–17	privilege and d· of every member,
	44–20	shall be the d· of the Directors
	45– 5	d· of the members of The
	47– 4	D· to Patients.
	53– 3	d· of the Board of Directors
	56– 2	d· of the Board of Directors
	57–11	d· of the Clerk to inform the
	59– 6	d· of every member of this Church,
	59–21	d· and privilege of the local members
	64–24	d· of Christian Scientists to drop the
	65–10	d· of the officers of this Church,
	66–11	d· of the Clerk to report to her
	66–18	d· of the Church to inquire
	67–17	D· to God.
	68– 3	d· of the member thus notified
	68– 8	or who declines to obey this call to d·,
	76– 8	d· of the C. S. Board of Directors
	77–12	d· of the Board of Directors
	77–24	possible future deviation from d·,
	78– 6	Debt and D·.
	93–10	D· of Lecturers.
	93–10	d· of the Board of Lectureship
	97–15	d· of the Committee on Publication
	98–17	d· of the Committee on Publication
	100–13	d· of the Directors immediately to act
	100–20	d· of that church to comply with this
Ret.	70–29	post of d·, unpierced by vanity,
	86–20	the d· will not be accomplished.
	88–20	d· should not be so warped
	89–13	d· at that particular moment.
Pul.	73–13	* this d· she faithfully performed.
	81–16	* love and her handmaiden d·
No.	2–18	conscientious in d·, waiting and
	8–11	Having discharged this d·,
	12–11	sacred d· for her to impart to others
	42– 1	* Christians more and more learn their d·
'00.	2–26	says : "It is my d· to take some time
'01.	32–21	the whole d· of man.
'02.	17–15	d· done and life perfected,
Hea.	7–27	d· and ability of Christians to heal
	9–15	Is it a d· for any one to believe that
	9–16	Then it is a higher d· to know that
My.	22–27	* Is it not therefore the d· of
	39–22	* it was my pleasant d· to preside at
	51– 7	* Mrs. Eddy, feels it her d· to
	51–23	* her d·, to go into new fields
	53– 4	* satisfied that her d· was
	85–25	* Mecca of their love and d·.
	161–23	each day is the d· thereof.
	248–27	labor, d·, liberty, and love,
	308–10	d· to be just to the departed

dwarf

Mis.	278–26	and so d· their experience.
My.	118–30	would d· individuality in personality

dwell

Mis.	103–14	d· forever in the divine Mind
	145–23	d· with the lamb, — Isa. 11 : 6.

dwell

Mis.	152–16	mercy, and love d· forever in the
	184– 6	and d· among mortals, only when
	290–24	it should not, ... d· elsewhere,
	309– 1	not to d· in thought upon their own
	400– 9	D· serene, — and sorrow? No,
Chr.	55– 8	they that d· in the land — Isa. 9 : 2.
Ret.	18–20	the spot where affection may d·
Un.	22– 4	in which no evil can possibly d·.
	41–22	never d· in its antagonist, matter.
Pul.	12–12	ye that d· in them. — Rev. 12 : 12.
	16–21	D· serene, — and sorrow? No,
	84– 5	* love shall d· in the tents of hate ;
Po.	16–22	my spirit with seraphs to d· ;
	32– 3	home where I d· in the vale,
	64–13	the spot where affection may d·
	76–20	D· serene, — and sorrow? No,
My.	33–16	d· in thy holy hill? — Psal. 15 : 1.
	33–29	they that d· therein. — Psal. 24 : 1.
	170–20	d· in the land, — Psal. 37 : 3.
	228–23	d· in Thy holy hill? — Psal. 15 : 1.

dweller

Mis.	189–21	not a d· in matter.
Po.	1– 3	Primeval d· where the wild
My.	3–13	C. S. is not a d· apart

dwellers

Mis.	325– 2	saith unto the d· therein,
Ret.	18–12	d· in Eden, earth yields
Pul.	3–12	indeed d· in Truth and Love,
	13–16	d· still in the deep darkness of
Po.	64– 1	d· in Eden, earth yields

dwelleth

Mis.	x– 2	consecrated life wherein d· peace,
	22–20	for it d· in Him
	93–10	in Him d· no evil
	134–14	He who d· in eternal light
	150–12	God d· in the congregation of
	367–23	He d· in light ;
	367–25	conclusion, that darkness d· in
Un.	64–19	d· in the eternal Mind.
My.	186–14	in whom d· all life, health,

dwelling

Mis.	227–22	d· upon a holy hill,
	229–19	come nigh thy d·." — Psal. 91 : 10.
	324– 4	at the threshold of a palatial d·,
	324–10	from the window of this d·
	324–17	he alone who looks from that d·,
	325–14	he patiently seeks another d·,
	325–29	finding ready ingress to that d·
	326– 8	flames caught in the d· of luxury,
	326–12	they consumed the next d· ;
	326–30	groped his way from the d· of
Ret.	69–27	Art thou d· in the belief that
	82–24	found d· together in harmony,
Un.	18– 4	D· in light, I can see only the
Pul.	47–18	* d· particularly upon the terms
'00.	13–21	church in this city as d·
My.	246–16	d· forever in the divine Mind

dwelling-house

My.	335–13	* where he erected a fine d·,

dwelling-place

Mis.	206–30	the d· of our God,
	326– 5	Once more he seeks the d·

dwellings

Mis.	201–25	We protect our d· more securely

dwells

Mis.	290–23	When thought d· in God,
Po.	23– 1	D· there a shadow on thy brow
My.	356– 3	where God d· most conspicuously

dwelt

No.	37– 3	d· forever in the Father.
'02.	9–19	d· forever in the bosom of the Father,
Hea.	18–10	good and evil never d· together.

dye

Ret.	17–14	flowers with exquisite d·.
Po.	62–17	flowers with exquisite d·.

dyed

My.	150–16	willowy banks d· with emerald.

dying

Mis.	36– 1	erring, sinful, sick, and d·,
	42– 6	belief of d· passes from mortal mind,
	70–10	when he said to the d· thief,
	70–13	if the dream of d· should startle
	70–20	The d· malefactor and our Lord
	79–19	A mortal who is sinning, sick, and d·,
	187–25	a sick, sinning, d· man?
	187–28	d·, before deathless ;
Ret.	9–21	* where d· thunders roll
	40– 6	her next-door neighbor was d·.
Un.	2–21	the d· — if they die in the Lord

dying

Un.	7–14	raise the *d·* to instantaneous health.
	42–10	*d·* before he can be deathless,
	43–19	more faith in living than in *d·*.
Pan.	8–28	and *d·* in consequence of it.
Peo.	4–21	sinning, sick, and *d·* mortals.
Po.	27– 4	I, *d·*, dare abhor !''
My.	58–10	* statements . . . that "C. S. is *d·* out."
	105–21	The patient was pronounced *d·*
	262–12	Truth, never born and never *d·*.
	267–17	The *d·* or the departed
	300–16	and raise the *d·* to health?

dying

My.	300–16	Scientists raise the *d·* to health
	315–23	declared *d·* of cancer,

dynamics

Mis.	258–31	eternal *d·* of being,
'01.	17–24	*d·* of medicine is Mind.

dysentery

My.	292–24	not mixed with . . . to remedy *d·*,

dyspepsia

My.	230– 8	silences the *d·* of sense.

E

each

Mis.	xi–14	At *e·* recurring holiday
	26– 4	*E·* successive period of progress
	38–27	not necessary to make *e·* patient **a**
	81– 6	let *e·* society of practitioners,
	117–21	then watch that *e·* step be taken,
	119– 8	*E·* individual is responsible for
	120– 4	*e·* and every injunction of the
	137–20	and *e·* one return to his place
	137–25	*e·* one of the innumerable errors
	138–10	*E·* student should seek alone
	143– 9	May the kingdom of heaven come in *e·*
	143–21	contributions of one thousand dollars *e·*,
	143–27	*E·* donation came promptly ;
	144–21	be this hope in *e·* of our hearts,
	224–13	*e·* person has a different history,
	256–18	continue to send to *e·* applicant
	280–21	hand-painted flowers on *e·* page,
	283–24	*E·* student should, must, work out his
	284– 1	*e·* one to do his own work well,
	289–13	*e·* party voluntarily surrenders
	290–26	and *e·* share the benefit of
	291–14	*e·* and every one has equal
	294–14	with sting ready for *e·* kind touch,
	302–21	*provided*, they *e·* and all
	303–14	and allow to *e·* and every one
	305– 1	* women representing *e·* State and
	305– 2	* representative from *e·* Republic
	305–28	* the name of *e·* contributor.
	308–19	I thank you, *e·* and all,
	314– 5	*E·* church, or society formed **for**
	314–21	shall name, at *e·* reading,
	314–32	On the first Sunday of *e·* month,
	315–12	*E·* class shall consist of not over
	321– 7	*e·* receding year sees the steady
	321– 9	*e·* recurring year witnesses the
	321–21	Still treading *e·* temptation down,
	330–18	arranging . . . *e·* budding thought.
	330–21	With *e·* returning year,
	331–19	that owns *e·* waiting hour ;
	338–28	* Speak truly, and *e·* word of thine
	342–11	*E·* moment's fair expectancy
	346– 8	It confronts *e·* generation anew.
	349–28	fifteen dollars *e·* Sunday
	375–20	* I went on to study *e·* illustration
	389– 7	that owns *e·* waiting hour,
Man.	26– 4	one year *e·*, dating from the
	29–17	two thousand five hundred dollars *e·*
	40–19	on the first Sunday of *e·* month.
	55– 5	*E·* church shall separately and
	63–14	*E·* church of the C. S. denomination
	70–14	*E·* Church of Christ, Scientist,
	72–21	*e·* branch church shall continue its
	74– 6	In C. S. *e·* branch church
	80–25	one year *e·*, dating from the
	84–26	*e·* student occupies only his own
	85– 2	Pupils may visit *e·* other's churches,
	85– 3	attend *e·* other's associations,
	90–19	shall be given to *e·* Normal class
	93–11	include in *e·* lecture a true and
	98–25	largest branch churches in *e·* State
	99– 6	*E·* county of Great Britain and Ireland,
	99–10	*E·* church is not necessarily
	99–25	*E·* State Committee shall be appointed
	104–14	shall *e·* keep a copy of
	110–13	given names of *e·*, written in full.
Ret.	50– 5	price for *e·* pupil in one course
	59–22	dependent, *e·* on the other,
	70–18	*E·* individual must fill his own niche
	76–26	sees *e·* mortal in an impersonal depict.
	82–19	the prosperity of *e·* worker ;
	83–26	study *e·* lesson before the recitation.
	86–22	God will help *e·* man who
Un.	21– 5	*e·* mortal is not two personalities,
Pul.	4–14	*E·* of Christ's little ones
	23–13	* *e·* having the common identity
	26– 4	* *e·* ray under prisms which reflect
	38–26	* Yet *e·* and all these movements,

each

Pul.	38–29	* good that *e·* and all shall prosper,
	41–21	* *e·* of the four vast congregations
	42–15	* *e·* of them wore a white satin badge
	55–27	* *e·* is entirely independent in the
	60–10	* *E·* paragraph he supplemented
	60–26	* 61 pipes *e·*.
	60–30	* 61 pipes *e·*.
	61– 3	* 61 pipes *e·*.
	61– 5	* 30 pipes *e·*.
	86– 2	* about six inches in *e·* dimension,
	87–18	I already speak to you *e·* Sunday.
Rud.	5–22	with *e·* of the physical senses.
No.	v– 1	*e·* edition of this pamphlet
	7–20	performance of *e·* one of them.
	22–16	*E·* is greater than the corporeality
Pan.	7–15	Does not *e·* of these religions
'01.	5– 8	*e·* of these possesses the nature of
	11–17	read *e·* Sunday without comment
'02.	11–14	*e·* in turn has helped mankind,
	13– 3	*e·* success incurred a sharper fire
	17–19	square accounts with *e·* passing hour.
Po.	v– 5	* *e·* *poem being the spontaneous*
	v–21	* *e·* *requested a copy*,
	4– 3	that owns *e·* waiting hour,
	46–17	While beauty fills *e·* bar.
My.	11–11	* to grow into readiness for *e·* step,
	12–10	* *E·* person interested must remember,
	23– 4	* what amount *e·* shall send
	35–27	* During the progress of *e·* service,
	38–12	* church was filled for *e·* service
	42–24	* in *e·* individual consciousness
	45–26	* advancing step has logically
	47–16	* are precious *e·* and all.
	47–18	* by *e·* landmark of progress
	52– 9	* *e·* and all, will make greater efforts
	53– 7	* *e·* of one thousand copies.
	56–12	* *e·* of the following named places :
	56–29	* three services were held *e·* Sunday,
	69– 2	* *e·* suspending seventy-two lamps,
	69– 3	* *e·* lamp of thirty-two candle-power.
	71–30	* *e·* of whom could see the Readers,
	72– 1	* *e·* person could hear what was said.
	74–30	* and *e·* is interesting,
	80–16	* At *e·* of the meetings the
	81–30	* *e·* tells his or her experience.
	83–31	* bear *e·* his or her share
	86–29	* At *e·* of the identical services,
	114–30	trace its teachings in *e·* step
	137–28	implicit confidence in *e·* one
	148–21	and what is *e·* heart in this
	173–21	my heart welcomed *e·* and all.
	215– 8	tuition of three hundred dollars *e·*,
	216– 9	by which *e·* is provided for
	217–11	in equal shares to *e·* contributor.
	217–13	and *e·* contributor will receive his
	230–11	*e·* Rule and By-law in this Manual
	330–19	* by Masonic records in *e·* place
	343–24	*e·* one was the fruit of experience
	343–28	I wrote to *e·* church in tenderness,
	344– 4	*e·* separate ray for men and women.
		(*see also* **day, member, year**)

each other

Mis.	4– 8	and their relation to *e·* other.
	60–19	even if touching *e·* other corporeally **;**
	156–25	listening to *e·* other amicably,
	224–16	action and reaction upon *e·* other
	236–22	Be not estranged from *e·* other
	266–26	thus we mutually aid *e·* other,
	327–29	grumbling, and fighting *e·* other,
No.	8–10	Advise students to rebuke *e·* other
	8–12	counsel *e·* other to work out
My.	120– 5	and know *e·* other there,
	173–22	fellow-citizens vied with *e·* other

eager

Mis.	98–14	to watch with *e·* joy the
Ret.	14– 6	He was apparently as *e·* to have

eager
'01. 32– 6 an *e·* lover and student of
My. 90–24 * outpouring of *e·* communicants

eagle (*see also* **eagle's**)
Mis. 354–26 Go gaze on the *e·*,
Po. 10–11 Our *e·*, like the dove,
My. 290–22 where no arrow wounds the *e·*
337–12 Our *e·*, like the dove,

eagle-plumed
Mis. 385–22 hope soared high, and joy was *e·*,
Po. 48–16 hope soared high, and joy was *e·*,

eagle's
Po. 18– 1 in the azure the *e·* proud wing,
19– 1 My course, like the *e·*,
28–12 Give us the *e·* fearless wing,
My. 13–24 renewed like the *e·*,"— *Psal.* 103 : 5.

eaglet
Ret. 18–16 as the *e·* that spurneth the sod,
Po. 64– 7 as the *e·* that spurneth the sod,

ear
Mis. 120–18 come more sweetly to our *e·*
126– 6 Sabbath chimes saluting the *e·*
127–28 on the *e·* or heart of the hearer ;
166–14 has evolved a more ready *e·*
215–32 nor yet when it is in the *e·* ;
287– 8 To an ill-attuned *e·*, discord is
331– 1 construct the stalk, instruct the *e·*,
331– 2 crown the full corn in the *e·*,
Ret. 16– 3 a soprano, . . . caught my *e·*.
27–23 can duly express it to the *e·*,
79– 3 Not by the hearing of the *e·*
92– 6 "first the blade, then the *e·*,— *Mark* 4 : 28.
92– 6 the full corn in the *e·*."— *Mark* 4 : 28.
Un. 28–22 nor *e·* heard."— *I Cor.* 2 : 9.
Pul. 9– 6 gain the *e·* and right hand of
Rud. 5–14 in the material *e·*,
No. 39– 6 ostensibly to catch God's *e·*,
'00. 14– 9 Beloved, let him that hath an *e·*
'02. 4– 9 bringing music to the *e·*,
Peo. 13–12 On the startled *e·* of humanity
Po. 68– 2 she breathes in my *e·*,
My. 109–16 by the hearing of the *e·*,
184– 5 have not heard with the *e·*,

earlier
Pul. 53– 4 * in other countries at an *e·* date.
'00. 12–15 The *e·* temple was burned
My. 45–23 * in retrospect we see the *e·* leading,
107– 2 improved upon its *e·* records,
184–14 cordial thanks at an *e·* date.

earliest
Ret. 30– 7 motive of my *e·* labors
45– 7 *e·* periods in Christian history.
Hea. 6– 7 From my *e·* investigations
Po. vi–26 * *Among her e· poems*
16–25 waken my joy, as in *e·* prime.
My. 237– 9 in his *e·* studies or discoveries.
351– 8 my *e·* moment in which to

early
Mis. ix– 6 In the *e·* history of C. S.,
x–10 my time in the *e·* pioneer days,
x–18 Timidity in *e·* years caused me,
39– 8 There are abroad at this *e·* date
43–17 The sad fact at this *e·* writing is,
141–20 Do not, . . . stain the early history of
169– 6 *E·* training, through the
240–16 incline the *e·* thought rightly,
240–24 Teach the children *e·*
345–27 midnight feasts in the *e·* days,
373–20 *e·* part of the Christian era,
Ret. 22– 7 history of the *e·* life of Jesus.
27–10 These *e·* comments are valuable to me
32– 5 *E·* had I learned that whatever
90–17 in their *e·* and sacred hours,
Pul. vii–14 on the *e·* footsteps of C. S.
31–14 * during some year in the *e·* '80's
32–19 * in the *e·* decade of 1820–'30.
33–28 * voices or visions in their *e·* youth.
34– 1 * At an *e·* age Miss Baker was married
51–15 * It is too *e·* to predict where this
68– 2 * the church during its *e·* years,
83–20 * and that right *e·*."— *Psal.* 46 : 5.
Pan. 3–12 the gentle murmur of *e·* morn,
'01. 18–23 his followers in the *e·* centuries,
31–21 my *e·* culture in the Congregational
31–24 my *e·* association with distinguished
32– 5 I became *e·* a child of the Church,
34– 1 *e·* employment of an M.D.
'02. 12–29 institutions and *e·* movements of
Po. v– 3 * *dating from her e· girlhood*
19– 6 Written in *e·* years.
My. 20–28 * completed as *e·* as possible,
29–28 * as *e·* as half past five in the
46–14 * this *e·* pronouncement

early
My. 51–25 * *e·* work of the church,
60– 1 * knew of your *e·* struggles.
60– 2 * *e·* history of C. S.
63– 3 * *e·* days of the construction of
80–29 * as *e·* as three o'clock
82–25 * to the utmost from *e·* morning,
86–30 * at intervals from *e·* morning
110–16 * dreams of flying in airy space,
112– 5 in the *e·* Christian centuries
155–10 catch the *e·* trumpet-call,
182– 7 my *e·* love for this church
217– 4 *e·*, generous incentive for action,
256– 1 chapter sub-title
273–16 should be *e·* presented to youth
304– 3 I was *e·* a pupil of
304– 7 Among my *e·* studies were
321–26 * I was among your *e·* students
335–10 * who mourn his *e·* death.
350–22 old foundations of an *e·* faith

earn
Pul. 8–18 to *e·* a few pence toward
Rud. 14– 6 *conscientiously e· their wages,*
My. 125–14 they *e·* their laurels.
216– 4 must *e·* it in order to help
216–31 you should begin now to *e·*

earned
Pul. 53–24 * *e·* the title of Saviour
Hea. 8–23 receive only what we have *e·*.
My. 215–16 I *e·* the means with which

earnest
Mis. 11–27 I do it with *e·*, special care
87–26 to be honest, *e·*, loving, and
106–22 long been a question of *e·* import,
136– 9 brought to your *e·* consideration,
156– 3 a vast number of *e·* readers,
177–14 equally in *e·* for the truth?
246–32 *e·* seeking after practical truth
276–11 Scientists, active, *e·*, and loyal,
317–21 subjects of such *e·* import.
Man. 17– 1 band of *e·* seekers after Truth
Ret. 49–27 due deliberation and *e·* discussion
Un. 8– 2 much trouble to many *e·* thinkers
Pul. 32– 4 * she was magnetic, *e·*, impassioned.
37–14 * it is her most *e·* aim to
'02. 2– 1 *e·*, honest investigator sees
Po. 23– 7 Or give those *e·* eyes
My. v–11 * *e·* and loyal Christian Scientists
50–21 * fresh courage to the *e·* band,
51–31 * appreciation of her *e·* endeavors,
61–31 * *e·* work of our noble Board
96–11 * Scientists are thoroughly in *e·*
112–16 The *e·* student of this book,
150–13 be honest and in *e·*
240– 6 An *e·* student writes to me :
292–17 one *e·*, tender desire works
352–12 * It is our *e·* prayer that

earnestly
Mis. 16–27 *e·* to contemplate this
127– 7 and again *e·* request,
308–32 *e·* advise all Christian Scientists
322– 2 *e·* invite you to its contemplation
Ret. 8–23 Then I *e·* declared
14–29 This was so *e·* said,
Pul. 49–18 * talked *e·* of her friendships.
'00. 9–28 I strove *e·* to fit others
Hea. 19–22 let us work more *e·*
My. vi– 3 * those who are *e·* seeking Truth ;
18– 4 and again *e·* request,
80– 4 * *e·* assure thousands of auditors
105–25 he asked *e·* if I had a work
207–10 * strive more *e·*, day by day,
221–31 *e·* ask : Shall we not believe
264– 5 honestly and not too *e·*,
322–29 * spoke *e·* and beautifully of you

earnestness
Pul. 29–10 * *e·* impressed the observer.
36–10 * such *e·* of attention
My. 52–24 * More than once, in her *e·*,
76–15 * show the *e·* and loyalty

earnings
'02. 13– 1 my own private *e·*
My. 136–25 hard *e·* of my pen,

earns
'00. 2–14 *e·* his money and gives it wisely
2–16 idler *e·* little and is stingy ;

ears
Mis. 88–18 deaf *e·* and dull debaters.
99– 4 and *e·* ye hear not ;— *see Mark* 8 : 18.
151– 1 their *e·* are attuned to His call.
168– 8 those who, having *e·*, hear not,
170–29 and *e·*, ye hear not,
301–29 the *e·* of understanding,

ears

Mis.	320–21	dull e· and undisciplined beliefs
	335–24	would cut off somebody's e·.
	337–27	to itching e· and to dull disciples
	360–28	saying to sensitive e·
	362– 9	e· to these deaf, feet to these lame,
	370–21	braying donkey whose e· stick out
Man.	58–21	To pour into the e· of listeners
Ret.	91– 6	ever fell upon human e·
No.	40– 8	to hide from dull and base e·
Hea.	16– 3	having e·, hear and understand.
My.	188– 6	mine e· attent unto the— *II Chron.* **7 : 15.**

earshot
My.	70–12	* The effect on all within e· is

earth (*see also* **earth's**)
above the
Mis.	158– 4	than the heavens above the e·
Pul.	41–24	* which rises . . . above the e·,

again on
Mis.	180– 8	* Has Christ come again on e·?''
'01.	34–16	Give us, dear God, again on e·

all the
Mis.	145–13	over all the e·,''— *Gen.* **1 : 26.**
	152– 8	silent benediction over all the e·,
	183–28	over all the e·.''— *Gen.* **1 : 26.**
	331– 8	over all the e·''— *Gen.* **1 : 26.**
Un.	39–19	dominion over all the e·.
Peo.	12– 3	over all the e·.''— *Gen.* **1 : 26.**
My.	119–18	gives dominion over all the e·.
	185–10	reign triumphant over all the e·.
	208– 7	its heavenly rays over all the e·.

and heaven
Mis.	30– 9	He saw the real e· and heaven.
	86–29	their present e· and heaven :
	228–18	existence fit for e· and heaven.
Un.	59– 7	never absent from the e· and heaven ;

and in heaven
Mis.	113–26	to enjoy on e· and in heaven.
	151–15	on e· and in heaven.
'00.	2– 6	best people on e· and in heaven.

and mortals
Un.	52–22	Why are e· and mortals so

and sky
Rud.	6– 3	*sounds and glories of e· and sky,*

armies of
Mis.	338–19	armies of e· press hard upon you.

best Christian on
'02.	11–28	the best Christian on e·,

best queen on
Mis.	295–28	unquestionably the best queen on e· ;

bind on
No.	31–28	thou shalt bind on e·— *Matt.* **16 : 19.**
My.	350–17	which they blindly bind On e·,

binds to
Po.	35– 6	consciousness Which binds to e·

binds us to
Po.	33– 9	ambition that binds us to e· ;

bosom of
My.	203–26	in the bosom of e· safe from

bring to
Mis.	100–23	bring to e· a foretaste of heaven.

brotherhood on
My.	280–10	* loving brotherhood on e·

bubbles of
Mis.	328–10	to burst the bubbles of e·

came to
Un.	59– 5	Jesus came to e· ;

cast unto the
Pul.	13–28	cast unto the e·,— *Rev.* **12 : 13.**

casualties of
'01.	24– 8	and the casualties of e·.

caves of the
Mis.	347– 8	shelter in caves of the e·.

Christian Scientist on
'01.	27–17	without a Christian Scientist on e·,

cleanse the
My.	265– 9	will cleanse the e· of human gore ;

comes down to
Mis.	10–27	Heaven comes down to e·,

come to
My.	155–25	heaven's symphonies that come to e·.

commence on
Mis.	51–25	* reign of Mind commence on e·,

crushed to
My.	128– 9	Truth crushed to e· springs

dark places of
Mis.	250–29	lighting the dark places of e·.

deluge the
Mis.	246–27	again deluge the e· in blood?

down to
Mis.	16– 5	enough of heaven to come down to e·.

drooping
Pul.	4– 5	Can ne'er refresh a drooping e·,

dust of
Po.	31–13	footprints on the dust of e·.

earth
elements of
Mis.	9– 8	from the elements of e·.
	383–11	elements of e· beat in vain

ends of the
My.	282– 8	all the ends of the e·.'' — *Isa.* **45 : 22.**

enrich
Mis.	332– 8	seedtime has come to enrich e·

face of the
Peo.	6–10	* or drug on the face of the e·,

fair
Mis.	329–29	fair e· and sunny skies.

falls to the
Mis.	267–20	The bird . . . falls to the e·.

fall to the
My.	166– 5	fail . . . and fall to the e·.

fill
Mis.	360–22	fill e· with the divine energies,

from the
Mis.	30–28	a mist from the e·— *Gen.* **2 : 6.**
	171–15	to have departed from the e·,
	179–26	before it sprang from the e· :
	378–23	than the . . . is from the e·.
Ret.	93– 9	lifted up from the e·, — *John* **12 : 32.**

gives
Mis.	237–10	e· gives them such a cup of gall

green
Mis.	257–27	desolating the green e·.

has not known
My.	221–11	E· has not known another

heaven and
(*see* **heaven**)

held
Po.	68– 7	E· held but this joy,

helped the woman
Pul.	14–10	e· helped the woman,— *Rev.* **12 : 16.**

holds the
Rud.	4–11	holds the e· in its orbit
My.	226–11	holds the e· in its orbit

inhabitants of the
Mis.	334– 2	inhabitants of the e· ;— *Dan.* **4 : 35.**
My.	280–20	all the inhabitants of the e·,

inhabiters of the
Pul.	12–13	inhabiters of the e·— *Rev.* **12 : 12.**

inherit the
Mis.	145–14	"inherit the e·." — *Psal.* **37 : 11.**
'01.	26–19	the meek that inherit the e· ;
My.	228–18	Who shall inherit the e·?
	228–22	they shall inherit the e·,

in the
Mis.	26–12	before it was in the e·." — *Gen.* **2 : 5.**
	266–29	running to and fro in the e·,
	277– 6	walking to and fro in the e·,
Hea.	19–15	before it was in the e·." — *Gen.* **2 : 5.**

is full
Mis.	361–11	e· is full of His glory,

is the Lord's
My.	33–28	The e· is the Lord's, — *Psal.* **24 : 1.**

kingdom on
My.	225–17	coming of Christ's kingdom on e·

known on
Pul.	20–18	greatest . . . reform ever known on e·.
My.	289–10	first church of C. S. known on e·,

known to
Ret.	80–26	no greater miracles known to e·

launched the
My.	182–22	launched the e· in its orbit,

mantled the
Ret.	31–26	humility, . . . mantled the e·.

material
My.	181–30	material e· or antipode of heaven.

matter and the
Mis.	179–27	yet we look into matter and the e·

meekest man on
Mis.	163– 9	was the meekest man on e·.

miasma of
Un.	56–28	constitute the miasma of e·.

ministry on
Pul.	53– 8	* three years of his ministry on e·,

more of
Pul.	87–20	more of e· now, than I desire,

new
Mis.	21– 7	new heaven and a new e·,"— *Rev.* **21 : 1.**

no element of
Mis.	152–27	there enters no element of e·

old
Po.	22– 6	Again shall bid old e· good-by

omnipotent on
'01.	25– 4	omnipotent on e·, encompassing time

on the
Ret.	94–28	Christ's kingdom on the e·.
'01.	12–12	find faith on the e·?"— *Luke* **18 : 8.**
My.	126– 8	his left foot on the e·," — *Rev.* **10 : 2.**

opened her mouth
Pul.	14–11	the e· opened her mouth, — *Rev.* **12 : 16.**

earth

our
　My. 160–22　internal fires of our *e·*

parts of the
　My. 147–28　to the utmost parts of the *e·*,

passes from
　Pul. 5– 7　passes from *e·* to heaven,

peace on
　　(*see* **peace**)

peoples .
　Po. 1–15　insignificance that peoples *e·*,

powers of
　Mis. 134–20　the powers of *e·* and hell
　My. 308– 2　powers of *e·* . . . can never prevent

quivering of the
　Mis. 347– 3　rumbling and quivering of the *e·*

reach
　Mis. 275–18　Thy light and Thy love reach *e·*,

rejoice
　Mis. 277–22　let the *e·* rejoice."— *Psal.* 97 : 1.

replenish the
　Mis. 56–26　*and replenish the e·,"*— *Gen.* 1 : 28.

revolution of the
　Un. 40– 1　from the revolution of the *e·*

solidity of the
　Pan. 3–31　goat's feet, the solidity of the *e·* ;

things of
　Mis. 390–24　like things of *e·*,
　Po. 56– 3　like things of *e·*,

this
　Mis. 368–28　this *e·* shall some time rejoice
　Po. 9–10　wishing this *e·* more gifts from

throughout the
　My. 185– 1　acceptance throughout the *e·*,
　　240– 4　and acknowledged throughout the *e·*.

ties of
　Ret. 31– 2　sunders the dominant ties of *e·*

to heaven
　Pul. 5– 7　passes from *e·* to heaven,
　'00. 11– 9　away from *e·* to heaven ;
　'02. 10–16　and rise . . . from *e·* to heaven.
　　19– 7　he rose from *e·* to heaven.
　My. 202– 3　the path from *e·* to heaven

tumult on
　Hea. 2– 3　tumult on *e·*,— religious factions

upheaves the
　Mis. 331–24　having all power, upheaves the *e·*.

upon
　Mis. 151–16　there is none upon *e·*— *Psal.* 73 : 25.
　Pul. 85–18　* kingdom of heaven upon *e·*
　'01. 28– 5　heaven within us and upon *e·*,
　My. 200– 7　ruleth in heaven and upon *e·*,
　　274–28　may be known upon *e·*,— *Psal.* 67 : 2.

upon the
　Mis. 287– 6　father upon the *e·* :— *Matt.* 23 : 9.
　Ret. 68–14　father upon the *e·* :— *Matt.* 23 : 9.
　Un. 53–27　father upon the *e·* :— *Matt.* 23 : 9.
　Pan. 8–19　father upon the *e·*,— *Matt.* 23 : 9.

verdant
　My. 129–11　The oracular skies, the verdant *e·*

walked the
　Pul. 34–20　* Jesus of Nazareth walked the *e·*.

was without form
　Mis. 280– 1　when the *e·* was without form,

whole
　Mis. 167–22　has dominion over the whole *e·* ;
　　330–30　grass, inhabiting the whole *e·*,
　Pul. 84– 3　* shall subdue the whole *e·*

will help the woman
　Pul. 14–21　the *e·* will help the woman ;

writ on
　Po. 22–12　'Tis writ on *e·*, on leaf and flower :

yields
　Ret. 18–12　*e·* yields you her tear,
　Po. 64– 1　*e·* yields you her tear,

　　————

　Mis. 4– 3　desirable remedial agent on the *e·*.
　　21– 6　while on *e·* and in the flesh,
　　86–16　*E·* is more spiritually beautiful
　　104– 1　while his personality was on *e·*
　　145–27　*e·* will float majestically
　　145–29　on *e·* peace,— *Luke* 2 : 14.
　　213–10　and *His* will be done on *e·* as in heaven.
　　254–20　and cast them to the *e·*.
　　302–19　for Christ's cause on *e·*,
　　316–27　there would be on *e·* paragons of
　　329– 6　sets the *e·* in order ;
　　337– 8　Wonder in heaven and on *e·*,
　　339– 4　would happen very frequently on *e·*,
　　360–14　When shall *e·* be crowned with the
　　360–31　then will the *e·* be filled with
　　369– 5　"on *e·* peace,— *Luke* 2 : 14.
　　373–27　in heaven and in *e·*,"— *Matt.* 28 : 18.
　　386– 7　tidings from our loved on *e·*,
　　392– 7　Guard'st thou the *e·*,
　Ret. 87–12　most systematic . . . people on *e·*,

earth

　Un. 14– 6　*e·*, man, animals, plants,
　Pul. 22– 7　every praying assembly on *e·*,
　　22– 8　Thy will be done in *e·*,— *Matt.* 6 : 10.
　　41–25　* "On *e·* peace,— *Luke* 2 : 14.
　No. 6–17　evidence that the *e·* is motionless
　　6–22　revolution of the sun around the *e·*
　　36– 7　never left heaven for *e·*.
　　44–26　"On *e·* peace,— *Luke* 2 : 14.
　Pan. 3–25　* heaven, *e·*, sea, the eternal fire,
　　11–15　to the best church member . . . on *e·*,
　　13–17　and done on *e·* as in heaven
　'01. 11– 3　because of Jesus' great work on *e·*,
　　35– 9　to the kingdom of heaven . . . on *e·*,
　Po. 20– 9　Guard'st thou the *e·*,
　　49–12　tidings from our loved on *e·*,
　　67–22　yield *e·* the fragrance of goodness
　　71– 2　When *e·*, inebriate with crime,
　My. vi– 6　* That no one on *e·* to-day,
　　6–27　the one edifice on *e·* which most
　　18–25　and done on *e·* as in heaven."
　　90–19　* "on *e·* peace,— *Luke* 2 : 14.
　　127–30　"on *e·* peace,— *Luke* 2 : 14.
　　158–11　natal hour of my lone *e·* life ;
　　159–12　greatest man or woman on *e·*
　　167–11　"on *e·* peace,— *Luke* 2 : 14.
　　279–19　"on *e·* peace,— *Luke* 2 : 14.
　　281– 4　Thy will be done in *e·*,— *Matt.* 6 : 10.
　　281– 9　"on *e* peace,— *Luke* 2 : 14.
　　283–11　"on *e·* peace,— *Luke* 2 : 14.
　　286– 5　prayed that all the peoples on *e·*
　　301– 9　I would that all the churches on *e·*
　　346–28　I did not mean any man to-day on *e·*.
　　355–22　are the happiest group on *e·*.

earth-born
　Mis. 387–25　chastens pride and *e·* fear,
　Po. 6–20　chastens pride and *e·* fear,
　　29–19　cruel creed, or *e·* taint :

earth-bound
　Mis. 328–16　*e·*, burdened by pride,
　Po. 79–18　centuries break, the *e·* wake,

earth-life
　Mis. 86–25　It lives with our *e·*,

earthliness
　Ret. 32– 8　hope, if tinged with *e·*,

earthly
　Mis. 74–15　His *e·* mission was to
　　75– 5　man's possible *e·* development.
　　81–24　must cry in the desert of *e·* joy ;
　　86–17　more *e·* to the eyes of Eve.
　　144–26　may our *e·* sowing bear fruit
　　166– 4　the *e·* life of a martyr ;
　　268– 4　*E·* glory is vain ;
　　320– 5　its *e·* advent and nativity,
　　321–30　infinitely beyond all *e·* expositions
　　395–21　Is every *e·* love ;
　Chr. 53–21　For heaven's *Christus, e·* Eves,
　Ret. 10–17　and no *e·* or inglorious theme.
　　20–20　Star of my *e·* hope,
　　23– 3　things *e·* must ultimately yield
　　47– 9　placed on *e·* pinnacles,
　Un. 61–11　twilight and dawn of *e·* vision,
　　61–19　*e·* acme of human sense.
　'01. 24–19　its *e·* advent is called
　　29–10　all the best of his *e·* years.
　Po. 34–19　Wearing no *e·* chain,
　　58– 6　Is every *e·* love ;
　My. 221– 1　*e·* price of spirituality
　　241–28　* the beliefs of an *e·* mortal.
　　256–19　*e·* advent and nativity of
　　290–17　when all *e·* joys seem most afar.
　　342–30　* directed by a single *e·* ruler ?"
　　358–11　Leader and best *e·* friend.
　　361– 1　above . . . any *e·* friend.

earthquake
　Un. 46–24　This ego was in the *e·*,
　'02. 16– 1　after the *e·* and the fire.

earthquakes
　Mis. 257–25　*E·* engulf cities,
　Un. 52–20　lightnings, *e·*, poisons,
　Po. 18–17　and *e·* may shock,

earth-road
　Un. 58– 5　Jesus walked . . . the thorny *e·*,

earth's
　Mis. 65– 5　that the *e·* surface is flat,
　　87– 3　To take all *e·* beauty into
　　107– 2　sweetness and beauty . . . are *e·* accents,
　　144–25　from *e·* pillows of stone,
　　313–10　the east, lightens *e·* landscape.
　　331– 3　tosses *e·* mass of wonders into
　　331–30　*e·* hieroglyphics of Love,
　　342–15　over *e·* lazy sleepers.
　　342–20　*e·* fables flee, and heaven is

earth's

Mis.	374–13	envy, and hatred — *e·* harmless thunder
	389–24	*e·* tear-drops gain,
	394–13	No place for *e·* idols,
	395–16	Quickly *e·* jewels disappear ;
	397– 5	And o'er *e·* troubled, angry sea
	398– 8	Break *e·* stupid rest.
Ret.	18–14	*E·* beauty and glory delude
	21–17	heavenly intent of *e·* shadows
	46–14	Break *e·* stupid rest.
Un.	57–18	This is *e·* Bethel in stone,
Pul.	17–13	Break *e·* stupid rest.
	18–14	And o'er *e·* troubled, angry sea
No.	10–22	*e·* discords have not the reality of
'00.	7–22	walking the wave of *e·* troubled sea,
'02.	17–13	*E·* actors change *e·* scenes ;
	19–21	*e·* pleasures, its ties and
	20– 7	the glory of *e·* woes is risen
Hea.	10–28	*E·* fading dreams are empty streams,
Po.	5– 4	*e·* tear-drops gain,
	12–14	o'er *e·* troubled, angry sea
	14–12	Break *e·* stupid rest.
	30–17	a patient love above *e·* ire,
	45–17	No place for *e·* idols,
	58– 1	*e·* jewels disappear ;
	64– 5	*E·* beauty and glory delude
	65–17	love claspeth *e·* raptures not long,
My.	133– 5	So shall all *e·* children
	189–19	how soon *e·* fables flee
	283–15	sovereign remedies for all *e·* woe.
	290–20	has passed *e·* shadow

earth-stricken

Po.	41– 5	Where the weary and *e·*

earth-task

Mis.	64– 5	relinquished his *e·* of teaching

earthward

My.	154–29	not looking nor gravitating *e·*,

earth-weary

'02.	11– 8	the *e·* and heavy-laden

earth-weights

Mis.	328–27	give up thy *e·* ;

ease

Mis.	85–29	Disease in error, more than *e·*
	219–19	to a consciousness of *e·*
	219–20	patient's sense of sinning at *e·*
	241–29	the sinner who is at *e·* in sin,
	293–29	*e·*, self-love, self-justification,
	343– 2	the temptation of *e·* in sin ;
Ret.	82–20	the *e·* and welfare of the workers.
Un.	58– 2	if at *e·* in so-called existence,
'00.	2–13	takes no time for amusement, *e·*,
'01.	15–13	A sinner ought not to be at *e·*,
	15–20	dis-ease in sin is better than *e·*.
	17–22	the comparative *e·* of healing
	30–21	by the hope of *e·*, pleasure, or
'02.	9– 7	pride, and *e·* concern you less,
My.	233–11	should we prefer, *e·* or dis-ease in
	233–13	better adapted . . . than *e·* in sin?
	253– 8	* "Thou art not here for *e·* or pain,
	308– 7	only by *e·*, pleasure, or recompense.
	349– 8	susceptible of both *e·* and dis-ease,

easel

Mis.	ix–10	*e·* of time presents pictures
	373– 5	My artist at the *e·*

easier

Mis.	5–30	*e·* for people to believe that
	240–19	*e·* to incline the early thought
	241–27	*e·* to heal the physical than
	247–25	*e·* for people to believe that
Ret.	54– 4	it is *e·* to believe, than to
Un.	50–20	the *e·* it is for them to evade
'02.	3–21	diadem of royalty will sit *e·* on the

easily

Mis.	5–27	is something not *e·* accepted,
	52–26	first rule was not *e·* demonstrated?
	141–18	it can *e·* be corrected
	222–32	as *e·* as dawns the morning light
	247–23	is not so *e·* accepted.
	361–18	which doth so *e·* beset us, — *Heb.* 12 : 1.
'01.	20–24	are not *e·* reckoned.

easily-besetting

Mis.	307–22	Idolatry is an *e·* sin

East

Ret.	80–22	The kindly shepherd of the *E·*
Pul.	20–22	dates selected and observed in the *E·*
My.	193– 6	from *E·* to West,

east

Mis.	313–10	kindling its glories in the *e·*,
	376–20	above the horizon, in the *e·*,
Pul.	83– 7	* But the *e·* is rosy,
My.	63–28	* "from the *e·*, and from — *Psal.* 107 : 3.

East Boston

Mis.	243–12	107 Eutaw Street, *E· B·*.

Easter

Mis.	177–21	chapter sub-title
	180–16	I *love* the *E·* service :
Man.	60–12	*E·* Observances.
	60–14	nor gifts at the *E·* season
	67–22	Christmas, New Year, or *E·*,
Pul.	42–26	* palms and ferns and *E·* lilies.
Po.	page 30	poem
	31– 9	Glad *E·* glows with gratitude
My.	155–16	chapter sub-title
	155–17	May this glad *E·* morn
	155–27	gathering *E·* lilies of love
	191–15	This glad *E·* morning witnesseth
	202– 5	him who hallowed this *E·* morn.

Eastern

Ret.	38–17	We met at the *E·* depot in Lynn,
Pul.	65– 4	* In inviting the *E·* churches and

eastern

Mis.	368–16	in the *e·* archipelago.

Eastern States

Pul.	88–11	* heading

Easter Sunday

My.	54– 7	* had their meeting *E· S·*

Eastertide

Po.	43– 3	Glad thy *E·* :

Easton

Mr.

Mis.	177–27	* introduced Mr. *E·* as follows :
	178–10	* Mr *E·* then delivered an

Mr. D. A.

Mis.	280–23	brief address by Mr. D. A. *E·*,

Rev. D. A.

Mis.	177–25	* accompanied by Rev. D. A. *E·*,
Pul.	9–17	lamented pastor, Rev. D. A. *E·*,
	29– 3	* Rev. D. A. *E·* and

Eastport, Me.

Pul.	88–22	* *Sentinel, E·, M·*.

eastward

Pul.	48–13	* truant river, as it wanders *e·*.

easy

Mis.	200– 2	that made his healing *e·* and
	262–26	and renders the yoke *e·*.
	347–23	ascent is *e·* and the summit can be
Pul.	47–23	* an *e·* driving distance for her
No.	15–14	It is no *e·* matter to believe
Hea.	2–11	* the parting will be *e·*."

eat

Mis.	7– 2	not be allowed to *e·* certain food,
	149– 2	come ye, buy, and *e·* ; — *Isa.* 55 : 1.
	170–16	" I have bread to *e·* — see *John* 4 : 32.
	245– 4	What shall we *e·* ? — *Matt.* 6 : 31.
	328–14	"*e·* and drink with the — *Matt.* 24 : 49.
	335– 6	*e·* and drink with the — *Matt.* 24 : 49.
	345–29	to kill and *e·* a human being.
Un.	21–10	"Ye shall *e·* of every tree — see *Gen.* 3 : 1.
	22– 5	*e·* of Godlikeness,
	22–10	to *e·* or be eaten, to see or be seen,
	44–20	" In the day *e·* thereof — *Gen.* 3 : 5.
Rud.	12–23	what ye shall *e·*." — *Matt.* 6 : 25.
No.	42–26	* and have to *e·* beefsteak
My.	131– 9	whereof if a man *e·*
	156–15	where I shall *e·* the passover — *Luke* 22 : 11.
	186–20	those that plant the vineyard *e·*

eaten

Mis.	72–14	have *e·* sour grapes, — *Ezek.* 18 : 2.
Un.	7–12	*e·* its way to the jugular vein.
	22–10	to eat or be *e·*, to see or be seen,
My.	105–15	*e·* the flesh of the neck

eatest

Mis.	57–16	day that thou *e·* thereof — *Gen.* 2 : 17.
	367–17	day that thou *e·* thereof, — *Gen.* 2 : 17.

eating

Mis.	69–26	*e·* smoked herring.
	123–32	*e·* and drinking corporeally.
	170– 7	*e·* of bread and drinking of wine
	226– 5	after *e·* several ice-creams,
'01.	12– 5	came neither *e·* nor drinking,
My.	216– 3	live without *e·*, and obtain their
	339–26	Merely to abstain from *e·* was not

ebb

Mis.	384–21	* But knows no *e·* and flow.
'00.	9–20	the *e·* and flow of thought
Po.	36–20	* But knows no *e·* and flow.

ebbing

Mis.	355– 8	chronic recovery *e·* and flowing,
My.	183–13	no *e·* faith, no night.

ebony

Mis.	376–21	with an acre of eldritch *e·*.

eccentric
  Ret. 37–11 sneered at it, as foolish and *e·*,

ecclesiastic
  '01. 32–19 They fill the *e·* measure,
  My. 88–12 * more than usual *e·* significance.

ecclesiastical
  Ret. 82–25 *e·* fellowship and friendship.
  No. 44–16 *E·* tyranny muzzled the

ecclesiasticism
  Mis. 193–22 The next step for *e·* to take,
  '01. 14–10 Our only departure from *e·*
  '02. 2–19 present modifications in *e·*

echo
  Mis. 145–28 *e·* the song of angels :
  218–27 Pat's *e·*, when he said
  218–28 *e·* answered, "Pretty well,
  231–28 *e·* such tones of heartfelt joy
  Un. 15–20 an *e·* of the divine?
  Po. 30–21 *E·* amid the hymning spheres of

echoes
  Mis. 116–15 whence come glad *e·*
  Ret. 12– 5 *e·* still my day-dreams thrill,
  17– 6 Muses' soft *e·* to kindle the grot.
  Po. 17– 1 Ye *e·* at dawn !
  61– 3 *e·* still my day-dreams thrill,
  62– 6 Muses' soft *e·* to kindle the grot.

echoing
  '02. 4–16 *e·* and reechoing through the
  Po. 15– 3 *e·* moans from the footsteps of time !
  My. 115– 7 scribe *e·* the harmonies of heaven
  186–11 *e·* the Word welling up from
  236– 2 Let us have no more of *e·* dreams.

eclipse
  Pul. 8–29 which will *e·* Oriental dreams.

eclipsed
  Ret. 10–14 so illumined, that grammar was *e·*.
  My. 134–12 not be *e·* by some lost opportunity,

eclipses
  Mis. 105–22 *e·* the other with the shadow cast by

economics
  My. 278–25 burlesque of uncivil *e·*.

economy
  Mis. 286– 5 this verity in human *e·*
  Man. 77–19 God requires wisdom, *e·*, and
  Un. 26–23 chance in the divine *e·*?
  51–18 in the *e·* of God's wisdom and
  Pul. 62– 7 * advantage of great *e·* of space,
  My. 93–25 * *e·* of our social and religious life.
  203–11 is *e·* and riches.

Eddy
Asa G.
  Ret. 43– 9 Asa G. *E·*, taught two terms in my
Asa Gilbert
  Ret. 42– 1 marriage was with Asa Gilbert *E·*,
  Pul. 46–28 * became the wife of Asa Gilbert *E·*.
Dr.
  Ret. 42– 4 Dr. *E·* was the first student publicly
  Pul. 36– 1 * Dr. *E·* died in 1882,
  43–18 * read by Judge Hanna and Dr. *E·*.
Dr. and Mrs.
  My. 49–27 * voted that "Dr. and Mrs. *E·* merited
Dr. Asa G.
  Mis. 35–10 words of . . . the late Dr. Asa G. *E·*,
Dr. Asa Gilbert
  Pul. 35–27 * Mrs. Glover married Dr. Asa Gilbert *E·*,
Rev. Daniel C.
  Ret. 15–14 Tabernacle of Rev. Daniel C. *E·*, D. D.,

Eddy (*see also* **Baker, Eddy's, Glover**)
Mary Baker
  Mis. x–26 made out to Mary Baker *E·*,
  Man. 3– 2 *By Mary Baker E·*
  18– 5 extended a call to Mary Baker *E·*
  27–23 books of which Mary Baker *E·* is,
  38–21 organized in 1879 by Mary Baker *E·*,
  58– 5 I, Mary Baker *E·*, ordain.
  63– 3 Interpretation by Mary Baker *E·*,
  63–23 the approval of Mary Baker *E·*.
  64– 7 *S. and H.* . . . by Mary Baker *E·*,
  65–17 signed by Mary Baker *E·*,
  65–24 the approval of Mary Baker *E·*.
  67–15 the property of Mary Baker *E·*
  78–15 the approval of Mary Baker *E·*.
  82– 2 If Mary Baker *E·* disapproves of
  88– 6 under the auspices of Mary Baker *E·*,
  103– 8 the Pastor Emeritus, Mary Baker *E·*.
  104– 6 written by Mary Baker *E·*
  105– 4 written consent of Mary Baker *E·*,
  Pul. 23– 2 * chapter sub-title
  52–15 * the disciples of Mary Baker *E·*,
  63– 4 * MARY BAKER *E·* THE "MOTHER"
  My. v–14 * Mary Baker *E·* discovered C. S.

Eddy
Mary Baker
  My. 3– 1 chapter sub-title
  15–10 Pastor Emeritus, Mary Baker *E·*.
  17–18 * "S. and H. . . . by Mary Baker *E·*,
  58–19 * Leader and teacher, Mary Baker *E·*,
  66–23 * the words of Mary Baker *E·* will come
  91–21 * Mary Baker *E·* of Concord, N. H.
  116–25 Copyright, 1909, by Mary Baker *E·*
  138–27 * personally appeared Mary Baker *E·*
  143–15 presence of Mary Baker *E·*,
  210–22 Copyright, 1909, by Mary Baker *E·*,
  270–15 Mary Baker *E·* is not dead,
Mary Baker G.
  My. 159–29 Copyright, 1904, by Mary Baker G. *E·*.
  273–32 Copyright, 1907, by Mary Baker G. *E·*.
  315–12 * Mary Baker G. *E·*, the Discoverer
Mary B. G.
  Ret. 16–18 extended a call to Mary B. G. *E·*
Mrs.
  Mis. 37–25 *Does Mrs. E· take patients?*
  54– 3 *Has Mrs. E· lost her power to heal?*
  58–10 *How does Mrs. E· know that*
  61–11 * *"Dear Mrs. E· :— In the October*
  95–10 * Mrs. *E·* responding, said :
  132–15 * by the way, from Mrs. *E·*, also."
  132–28 * either Dr. Cullis or Mrs. *E·*.
  133– 3 * prayerless Mrs. *E·*, of Boston."
  169–28 * Mrs. *E·* showed how beautiful and
  238–24 chapter sub-title
  256–10 from any other than Mrs. *E·*,
  306–17 * Mrs. *E·* is a member of
  381– 1 copyrighted works of Mrs. *E·*
  381– 5 taken on the part of Mrs. *E·*,
  381–10 Later, Mrs. *E·* requested her lawyer
  381–17 a decree in favor of Mrs. *E·*
  381–18 the complainant (Mrs. *E·*)
  Man. 17– 9 on motion of Mrs. *E·*, it was voted,
  17–14 Mrs. *E·* was appointed on the committee
  18–23 By-Laws, as prepared by Mrs. *E·*,
  26–24 or the request of Mrs. *E·*
  26–26 nor those with Mrs. *E·*.
  30–12 Unless Mrs. *E·* requests otherwise,
  30–21 so long as Mrs. *E·* does not occupy
  34–13 and other works by Mrs. *E·*,
  35–21 approval from students of Mrs. *E·*,
  38– 5 not a loyal student of Mrs. *E·*,
  54–12 on complaint of Mrs. *E·*
  59–16 Mrs. *E·* welcomes to her seats
  64–18 Mrs. *E·* objected to being called thus,
  66–25 an order from Mrs. *E·*
  67–26 the Pastor Emeritus, Mrs. *E·*,
  68– 5 remain with Mrs. *E·* three years
  69– 1 home of their Leader, Mrs. *E·*,
  69– 2 agreement to remain with Mrs. *E·*
  69–10 shall pay to Mrs. *E·* whatsoever
  69–21 Students with Mrs. *E·*.
  69–22 Students employed by Mrs. *E·*
  72–19 the Pastor Emeritus, Mrs. *E·*,
  79– 7 Mrs. *E·*, the Directors, or the
  79–14 presented to Mrs. *E·* for her
  82– 7 of which Mrs. *E·* is the author
  85–14 that he has been taught by Mrs. *E·*
  86– 6 the personal instruction of Mrs. *E·*,
  87– 7 Mrs. *E·* is not to be consulted on this
  89–13 taught in a Primary class by Mrs. *E·*
  94–15 written request of Mrs. *E·*,
  97–18 injustices done Mrs. *E·*
  100– 2 If . . . Mrs. *E·* shall send to the
  109– 7 except loyal students of Mrs. *E·*,
  Pul. 5– 2 * "the prayerless Mrs. *E·*,"
  25–11 * for the exclusive use of Mrs. *E·* ;
  28– 2 * wholly typical of the work of Mrs. *E·*.
  28–12 * the land — a gift from Mrs. *E·*
  29– 6 * pastor of the church here was Mrs. *E·*
  30–12 * written by Mrs. *E·*,
  30–25 * was organized by Mrs. *E·*,
  31– 8 * my own knowledge of Mrs. *E·*,
  31–13 * heading
  31–20 * central figure in all this . . . was Mrs. *E·*.
  31–25 * Mrs. *E·* entered the room.
  32– 5 * the least justice to Mrs. *E·*.
  32–23 * Mrs. *E·* came from Scotch and
  33– 1 * heading
  34– 5 * Mrs. *E·* met with a
  34–24 * From 1866–'69 Mrs. *E·* withdrew
  35– 6 * Mrs. *E·* came to perceive that
  35–12 * of this experience, Mrs. *E·* has said :
  35–23 * became convinced of the
  36– 5 * Mrs. *E·* felt it essential to the
  36–14 * the evening that I first met Mrs. *E·*
  36–18 * met Mrs. *E·* many times since then,
  36–20 * years ago Mrs. *E·* removed from
  37– 4 * demands of the public on Mrs. *E·*
  37–16 * "On this point, Mrs. *E·* feels very
  37–27 * by seven persons, including Mrs. *E·*.

Eddy
Rev. Mary Baker
Man.	79–20	given by Rev. Mary Baker *E·*,
	91–11	the President, Rev. Mary Baker *E·*,
Pul.	page 1	heading
	page 16	heading
	page 20	heading
	24–16	* beloved teacher, the Rev. Mary Baker *E·*,
	31– 3	* Rev. Mary Baker *E·*, the Founder
	40–13	* SERMON BY REV. MARY BAKER *E·*,
	40–22	* Founder of C. S., Rev. Mary Baker *E·*,
	44– 1	* "To Rev. Mary Baker *E·*.
	57– 2	* Founder of C. S., the Rev. Mary Baker *E·*,
	63– 9	* Rev. Mary Baker *E·*, the "Mother" of C. S.,
	63–27	* beloved teacher, Rev. Mary Baker *E·*,
	64– 7	* experience of Rev. Mary Baker *E·*,
	64–26	* Founder . . . the Rev. Mary Baker *E·*,
	68– 3	* known as the Rev. Mary Baker *E·*.
	70– 4	* CAREER OF REV. MARY BAKER *E·*
	70– 6	* Rev. Mary Baker *E·*, Discoverer and
	75–24	* Founder of C. S., Rev. Mary Baker *E·*,
	76–23	* REV. MARY BAKER *E·* MEMORIALIZED BY
	76–25	* Rev. Mary Baker *E·*, Discoverer of C. S.,
	78–19	* "To the Rev. Mary Baker *E·*,
	85–22	* To REV. MARY BAKER *E·*, FROM THE
	85–24	* Rev. Mary Baker *E·* received
My.	18–31	* writings of the Rev. Mary Baker *E·*,
	32–14	* Words by the Rev. Mary Baker *E·*.
	32–25	* words by the Rev. Mary Baker *E·*,
	32–27	* Message from . . . Rev. Mary Baker *E·*.
	34–16	* by the Rev. Mary Baker *E·*,
	36– 7	* REV. MARY BAKER *E·*, *Pastor Emeritus*.
	43–23	* Leader, the Rev. Mary Baker *E·*.
	44–21	* To THE REV. MARY BAKER *E·*,
	54–10	* pastor, the Rev. Mary Baker *E·*,
	62–17	* REV. MARY BAKER *E·*, Pleasant View,
	140–13	* Rev. Mary Baker *E·* explains
	172– 6	* father of the Rev. Mary Baker *E·*,
	280– 1	* REV. MARY BAKER *E·*, Pleasant View,
	338– 6	* views of the Rev. Mary Baker *E·*
	346–20	* Rev. Mary Baker *E·*, Discoverer and

Rev. Mary Baker G.
Mis.	177–24	* pastor, Rev. Mary Baker G. *E·*,
	272– 1	* "Rev. Mary Baker G. *E·* obtained a

Rev. Mary Baker Glover
Pul.	57–26	* of Rev. Mary Baker Glover *E·*,

Rev. Mary B. G.
Mis.	168–25	* Rev. Mary B. G. *E·* would speak
Ret.	48–30	President, the Rev. Mary B. G. *E·*,

Rev. Mrs.
Mis.	272–28	* of which Rev. Mrs. *E·* is founder
My.	259– 7	* REV. MRS. *E·*, PLEASANT VIEW,

author
Mis.	x–19	caused me, as an *a·*, to assume
	34–29	*a·* of "S. and H. with Key to the
	35–26	taught its Science by the *a·*
	144–12	other works written by the same *a·*,
	301– 5	the *a·* of the above-named book
	314–25	with the name of its *a·*,
	315– 8	except by their *a·*.
	378– 1	the *a·* of this work was at Dr. Vail's
	378– 9	*a·*, in company with several other
	378–15	never occurred to the *a·* to learn his
	382–16	*a·* and publisher of the first books
Man.	27–23	is, or may be, the *a·*,
	32–10	Naming Book and *A·*
	53– 8	the *a·* of our textbook
	53–20	*a·* of S. AND H. shall bear witness
	59–10	announce the name of the *a·*.
	64– 8	and other writings by this *a·* ;
	64–15	given to the *a·* of their textbook,
	69–13	If the *a·* of the C. S. textbook call on
	71–23	they give the name of their *a·*
	82– 7	of which Mrs. Eddy is the *a·*
	104–11	the written consent of its *a·*.
	105– 5	the *a·* of our textbook, S. AND H.
Ret.	70–17	No person can take the place of the *a·*
	75–13	misunderstand or misrepresent the *a·*.
Pul.	5–17	introduced himself to its *a·*
	24–17	* *a·* of "S. and H. with Key to the
	52–14	* *a·* of the textbook from which,
	54–28	About 1868, the *a·* of S. and H.
	64– 1	* *a·* of its textbook, 'S. and H.
	70– 7	* *a·* of its textbook, "S. and H.
	86–24	* *a·* of its textbook, "S. and H.
	88– 4	From Canada to . . . the *a·* has
Rud.	14– 8	*a·* never sought charitable support,
Po.	v– 3	* *in the life of the a·*,
	v–10	* *written while the a· was*
	v–23	* *requests continued to reach the a·*
	vi–10	* *A note from the a·*,
	vii–13	* *from this spiritually-minded a·*
My.	23–2	* Founder of C. S. and *a·* of its
	115– 6	were I, apart from God, its *a·*.
	224–18	borrows . . . of one *a·* without
	305–15	I am the *a·* of the C. S. textbook,

Eddy
author
My.	310–32	* it so resembles the *a·*."
	320–10	* *a·*, and as a student of ability.
	320–14	* always spoke of you as the *a·*
	320–15	* *a·* of all your works.
	320–23	* referred to you as the *a·* of
	324–17	* that you were the *a·* of

authoress
My.	53– 4	* yet not until the *a·* was satisfied

author's
Mis.	300– 5	announcing the *a·* name,
	300–28	a special privilege, and the *a·* gift.
	301– 3	without the *a·* consent,
Man.	32–14	and give the *a·* name.
	58–20	Announcing *A·* Name.
No.	12– 9	of the *a·* religious experience.
	46–14	The *a·* ancestors were
Po.	vi–22	* *All of the a· best-known hymns*
My.	130–22	must have the *a·* name added

bride
Po.	8–20	thinking alone of a fair young *b·*,
My.	312– 6	* took his *b·* to Wilmington,
	330–31	devotion to his young *b·*

child
Mis.	386–12	What of my *c·*?"
	386–27	Thy *c·*, shall come
Ret.	2–28	listening, when a *c·*, to grandmother's
	8– 8	"Nothing, *c·*! What do you mean?"
Pul.	33– 1	* heading
	33– 2	* As a *c·* Mary Baker saw visions
'01.	32– 5	I became early a *c·* of the Church,
Po.	49–18	What of my *c·*?"
	50–13	Thy *c·*, shall come
My.	308–13	compels me as a dutiful *c·*
	310–23	* Mary, a *c·* ten years old,
	341– 3	a *c·* of the Republic,
	345–13	I was a sickly *c·*.

contributor
My.	vi–19	* principal *c·* to its columns ;

Counsellor
My.	362–12	* *Revered Leader, C·, and Friend:*

counsellor
My.	vi–16	* wise and unerring *c·*.

Daughter of the Revolution
My.	341– 3	a *D·* of the *R·*,

Discoverer
Mis.	144–13	*D·* and Founder of C. S. ;
Man.	43–10	*D·* and Founder of C. S.
Ret.	30–22	*D·* and teacher of C. S. ;
	70–17	*D·* and Founder of C. S.
Pul.	24–16	* *D·* and Founder of C. S. ;
	31– 4	* *D·* of C. S., as they term her
	40–21	* *D·* and Founder of C. S.,
	57– 1	* *D·* and Founder of C. S.,
	64– 1	* *D·* and Founder of C. S.,
	70– 6	* *D·* and Founder of C. S.,
	74– 9	* the C. S. "*D·*," to-day.
	74–17	*D·* and Founder of C. S.,
	75–23	* *D·* and Founder of C. S.,
	76–25	* *D·* of C. S., has received from the
	84–29	* *D·* and Founder of C. S.,
	86– 5	* *D·* and Founder of C. S.,
	86–23	* *D·* and Founder of C. S.,
Rud.	17–10	*D·* of this Science could tell you
My.	18–31	* *D·* and Founder of C. S. ;
	23–21	* *D·* and Founder of C. S.
	143–17	history of its *D·* and Founder.
	229–10	*D·* and Founder of C. S.,
	302–19	*D·*, Founder, and Leader.
	315–12	* *D·* and Founder of C. S.,
	346–21	* *D·* and Founder of C. S.,
	359– 6	*D·* and Founder of C. S.

discoverer
Mis.	383–10	*is founded by its d·*,
'01.	16–25	its greatest *d·* is a woman

editor
Mis.	382–23	*e·* and proprietor of the first
Ret.	52–21	as *e·* and publisher.
Pul.	47– 5	* *e·* and publisher of the first official
My.	vi–18	* was its first *e·* and for years
	304–17	sole *e·* of that periodical.
	304–20	he knew my ability as an *e·*.

Founder
Mis.	34–28	*Who is the F· of mental healing?*
	39–11	the *F·* of genuine C. S. has been
	40–21	The *F·* of C. S. teaches her
	144–13	Discoverer and *F·* of C. S.
	295–32	*F·* of this system of religion,
Man.	43–10	Discoverer and *F·* of C. S.
	64–16	author of their textbook, the *F·* of C. S.,
Ret.	70–18	Discoverer and *F·* of C. S.
Pul.	24– 7	* termed by its *F·*, "Our prayer
	24–16	* Discoverer and *F·* of C. S. ;
	31– 3	* the *F·* of this denomination
	40–13	* *F·* OF THE DENOMINATION

Eddy

Founder

Pul.	40–21	* Discoverer and *F·* of C. S.,
	57– 1	* Discoverer and *F·* of C. S.,
	64– 1	* Discoverer and *F·* of C. S.,
	64–25	* in commemoration of the *F·* of that
	69– 5	* the *F·* of the movement.
	70– 6	* Discoverer and *F·* of C. S.,
	71–17	* Mary Baker Eddy, *F·* of the Faith
	72–20	* was the *F·* of the faith,
	74–17	Discoverer and *F·* of C. S.,
	75–16	* Dedication to the *F·* of the
	75–23	* Discoverer and *F·* of C. S.,
	78– 1	* the *F·* of C. S.,
	84–29	* Discoverer and *F·* of C. S.,
	86– 5	* Discoverer and *F·* of C. S.,
	86–23	* Discoverer and *F·* of C. S.,
My.	19– 1	* Discoverer and *F·* of C. S. ;
	22–16	* Mrs. Eddy, the *F·* of C. S.,
	23–21	* Discoverer and *F·* of C. S.
	90–27	* *F·* of a great denomination
	94–24	* Mrs. Eddy, the *F·* of C. S.,
	143–17	history of its Discoverer and *F·*.
	194–16	*F·* of your denomination
	229–10	Discoverer and *F·* of C. S.,
	249–19	I am the *F·* of C. S.
	271–16	* *F·* and Leader of C. S.,
	302–19	Discoverer, *F·*, and Leader.
	315–13	* Discoverer and *F·* of C. S.,
	316–13	Attacks on C. S. and its *F·*,
	341–22	* the *F·* of the cult.
	346–21	* Discoverer and *F·* of C. S.,
	359– 7	Discoverer and *F·* of C. S.

founder

Mis.	272–28	* of which Rev. Mrs. Eddy is *f·*
My.	305–30	the *f·* of C. S.

Friend

My.	362–12	* *Leader, Counsellor, and F· :*

guardian

My.	vi–15	* its guide, *g·*, Leader, and

Guide

Pul.	44– 2	* *"Dear teacher, Leader, G· :*
My.	60–25	* *Dear Leader and G· :*

guide

My.	vi–15	* its *g·*, guardian, Leader, and

head

Man.	72–20	her place as the *h·* or Leader of
Pul.	37–13	* *h·* of the C. S. Church.

helper

My.	229–14	go to help their *h·*, and thus

her

Mis.	35– 1	healing embodied in *h·* works.
	35– 2	revealed to *h·* the fact that Mind,
	35– 4	and subsequently *h·* recovery,
	35–10	the following words of *h·* husband,
	35–13	* are the outgrowths of *h·* life.
	37–26	*H·* time is wholly devoted to instruction,
	37–27	leaving to *h·* students the work of
	39–12	been all *h·* years in giving it birth.
	40–22	teaches *h·* students that they must
	48–30	solely to injure *h·* or *h·* school.
	49–14	have been cured in *h·* class.
	54– 3	*Has Mrs. Eddy lost h· power to heal?*
	54– 9	are *h·* students, and they bear witness
	54–11	Instead of losing *h·* power to heal,
	54–13	malice would fling in *h·* path.
	54–13	reading of *h·* book, "S. and H.
	58–12	*She had to use h· eyes to read.*
	95– 7	* public letter condemning *h·* doctrines ;
	125–28	turns to *h·* dear church,
	130– 2	Has *h·* life exemplified long-suffering,
	130– 5	to those who know *h·*.
	131–26	let *h·* state the value thereof,
	141– 4	and of your hearts' offering to *h·*
	155–17	all of *h·* interesting correspondence,
	155–19	you, *h·* students' students,
	155–21	write such excellent letters to *h·*,
	169– 2	the way of *h·* researches therein,
	169– 3	whenever *h·* thoughts had wandered
	169– 5	*h·* spiritual insight had been
	169– 9	dawned upon *h·* understanding,
	188–24	this power came to *h·* through
	188–29	At the moment of *h·* discovery,
	188–31	This knowledge did become to *h·*
	254–11	whose children rise up against *h·* ;
	353–30	they constantly go to *h·* for help,
	353–31	criticise and disobey *h·* ;
	378–12	seemed at first to relieve *h·*,
	378–13	failed in healing *h·* case.
	378–18	the sum of what he taught *h·*
	381– 2	were not original with *h·*,
	381– 2	copied by *h·*, or by *h·* direction,
	381–10	Mrs. Eddy requested *h·* lawyer to inquire
	381–12	was the author of *h·* writings !
	381–13	*h·* counsel asked the defendant's
	381–19	*h·* cost of suit, taxed at

Eddy

her

Mis.	386–11	This hour looks on *h·* heart
	386–25	the remembrance of *h·* loyal life,
	387– 3	To call *h·* home,
	389–25	And mother finds *h·* home
Man.	18–14	twelve of *h·* students
	18–15	reorganized, under *h·* jurisdiction,
	18–19	and members of *h·* former Church
	26–11	given in *h·* own handwriting.
	30–23	are satisfactory to *h·*.
	43– 1	treats our Leader or *h·* staff
	43– 1	without *h·* or their consent
	43–16	without *h·* permission,
	43–17	shall not plagiarize *h·* writings.
	48–14	continually stroll by *h·* house,
	48–14	or make a summer resort near *h·*
	53– 1	upon *h·* complaint or the
	53– 2	complaint of a member for *h·*
	53–10	upon *h·* complaint that member should
	53–11	without *h·* having requested
	53–12	shall trouble *h·* on subjects
	53–13	and without *h·* consent,
	59–16	to *h·* seats in the church,
	66– 2	he shall inform *h·* of this fact
	66–11	report to *h·* the vexed question
	66–12	await *h·* explanation thereof.
	66–21	authority supposed to come from *h·*
	67– 8	to a member of *h·* Church
	67– 9	without *h·* written consent.
	67–16	personally conferred with *h·*
	68– 3	to go in ten days to *h·*,
	68– 6	leaves *h·* in less time without
	68–14	remain with *h·* three consecutive
	68–18	calls to *h·* home or allows to visit
	69– 8	leaves *h·* before the expiration
	69–22	employed by Mrs. Eddy at *h·* home
	69–24	affairs outside of *h·* house.
	70– 5	without first consulting *h·*
	70– 6	adhering strictly to *h·* advice
	71–23	*h·* permission to publish them
	72–20	*h·* place as the head or Leader
	79–14	for *h·* written approval.
	80–21	subject to *h·* approval.
	81– 4	given in *h·* own handwriting.
	81– 9	connected with publishing *h·* books,
	82– 8	without *h·* knowledge or written
	89– 2	resign over *h·* own signature
	89– 3	or vacate *h·* office of President
	89– 7	on receiving *h·* approval
	97–12	given in *h·* own handwriting,
	100– 8	according to *h·* directions.
Ret.	19–22	accompanying *h·* on *h·* sad journey
	49–23	for *h·* great and noble work,
	90–23	Mother in Israel give all *h·* hours
	90–24	till *h·* children can walk steadfastly
Pul.	23– 6	* Mrs. Eddy's Work and *H·* Influence
	28– 2	* The central panel represents *h·*
	31– 4	* as they term *h·* work in affirming
	31– 9	* my first meeting with *h·*
	31–11	* familiarity with the work of *h·* life
	31–20	* To a note which I wrote *h·*,
	31–27	* *H·* figure was tall,
	32– 1	* *h·* face, framed in dark hair
	32– 5	* *h·* beautiful complexion and
	32–10	* *h·* large and enthusiastic following
	32–13	* was dominating *h·* followers
	32–14	* She told me the story of *h·* life,
	32–20	* At the time I met *h·*
	32–23	* On *h·* father's side
	32–25	* was a relative of *h·* grandmother.
	32–25	* Deacon Ambrose, *h·* . . . grandfather,
	32–26	* *h·* mother was a religious enthusiast,
	32–28	* One of *h·* brothers,
	33– 4	* for a year she heard *h·* name
	33– 5	* would often run to *h·* mother
	33– 6	* the mother related to *h·* the story of
	33– 7	* bade *h·*, if she heard the voice
	33–10	* caused *h·* tears of remorse
	33–12, 13	* as *h·* mother had bidden *h·*,
	34– 3	* returned to *h·* father's home
	34– 6	* *h·* case was pronounced hopeless
	34– 8	* *h·* pastor came to bid *h·* good-by
	34–12	* She requested those with *h·* to
	34–13	* they did so, believing *h·* delirious.
	34–18	* From that hour dated *h·* conviction
	35–29	* sympathy with *h·* own views,
	36– 1	* a year after *h·* founding of the
	36– 6	* foundation of *h·* religious work
	36–11	* given to *h·* morning talks by
	36–14	* by *h·* hospitable courtesy,
	36–15	* I went to *h·* peculiarly fatigued.
	37– 5	* in *h·* removal to Concord,
	37– 7	* *H·* health is excellent,
	37– 7	* although *h·* hair is
	37– 8	* *h·* energy and power ;

Eddy
her

Pul.	37–14	* it is *h·* most earnest aim to
	43–25	* remained at *h·* home in Concord,
	43–26	* it is *h·* custom
	43–27	* to discourage among *h·* followers
	44–18	* chapter sub-title
	46–16	* *H·* family came to this country
	46–18	* belonging to *h·* grandparents
	46–23	* applied herself, . . . to *h·* studies,
	46–27	* *H·* last marriage was in the
	47– 4	* Mrs. Eddy is known to *h·* circle of
	47– 9	* In recounting *h·* experiences
	47–14	* No ancient . . . philosophy gave *h·* any
	47–21	* Besides *h·* Boston home,
	47–24	* easy driving distance for *h·*
	48– 5	* straight to *h·* beloved "lookout"
	48– 7	* can sit in *h·* swinging chair,
	48–14	* pleased *h·* to point out *h·* own
	48–15	* Straight as the crow flies, from *h·* piazza,
	48–17	* Congressman Baker . . . *h·* cousin,
	48–21	* *h·* family coat of arms
	48–22	* diploma given *h·* by the
	48–25	* one of *h·* characteristics,
	48–29	* figure largely in *h·* genealogy,
	49– 1	* which Mrs. Eddy calls *h·* den
	49– 2	* speaking of *h·* many followers
	49– 3	* consider *h·* their spiritual Leader
	49– 7	* gifts of *h·* loving pupils.
	49–18	* talked earnestly of *h·* friendships.
	49–19	* *h·* domestic arrangements,
	49–20	* *h·* busy career in Boston,
	49–21	* return to *h·* native granite hills.
	50– 1	* using *h·* money to promote
	50– 5	* one of *h·* motives in buying
	50– 7	* thus add *h·* influence toward
	55–16	* *H·* discovery was first called,
	58– 3	* imparting this faith to *h·*
	58– 7	* near *h·* birthplace,
	58–25	* the Bible, with *h·* book,
	58–27	* a room devoted to *h·*,
	58–30	* portrait of *h·* in stained glass ;
	59– 1	* burning in *h·* honor ;
	59– 2	* has not yet visited *h·* temple,
	59–16	* book of Revelation and *h·* work
	63– 6	* RECENTLY BUILT IN *H·* HONOR
	63–11	* shade *h·* delightful country home
	63–17	* among *h·* devoted followers.
	64–18	* modern philosophy gave *h·* no
	68– 9	* interests of *h·* religious work
	68–11	* country residence in *h·* native State.
	70–14	* a testimonial to *h·* labors,
	70–19	* Taking *h·* text from the Bible,
	71–22	* *h·* followers and cobelievers
	72– 1	* inspired in *h·* great task
	73– 7	* through the mediation of *h·* God.
	73–11	* came from *h·* seclusion
	73–12	* *H·* mission was then the mission of
	73–15	* fulfilled His promises to *h·*
	73–28	* concise idea of *h·* belief
	80–12	* *h·* book has many a time been sent
	85– 5	* in part, understand *h·* mission,
	85– 6	* gratitude to *h·* for *h·* great work,
	85–26	* the appreciation of *h·* labors
	86– 6	* from *h·* affectionate Students,
Rud.	14– 9	fully seven-eighths of *h·* time
	14–10	The only pay taken for *h·* labors
	17–13	miraculous vision to sustain *h·*,
No.	12–11	sacred duty for *h·* to impart to
	12–15	nerved *h·* purpose to
Po.	v– 3	* *dating from h· early girlhood*
	v– 7	* *that claimed h· attention,*
	v–15	* *take form in h· thought,*
	v–16	* *alighting from h· carriage,*
	v–18	* *who made h· acquaintance,*
	v–19	* *asked h· what she was writing,*
	vi–26	* *Among h· earliest poems*
	vii– 4	* *in h· later productions.*
	vii– 5	* *requested h· publisher to prepare*
	vii– 6	* *a few bound volumes of h· poems,*
	vii– 8	* *this became known to h· friends,*
	vii– 8	* *they urged h· to allow a popular*
	5– 6	mother finds *h·* home and
	9– 1	glance of *h·* husband's watchful eye
	49–15	gathered from *h·* parting sigh :
	49–16	looks on *h·* heart with pitying eye,
	50–11	remembrance of *h·* loyal life,
	50–21	To call *h·* home,
My.	vi– 8	* from *h·* and from *h·* writings ;
	vi– 9	* only as they give *h·* full credit
	vi–23	* all future profits to *h·* church ;
	vi–24	* she presented to *h·* church
	vi–27	* for the publishing of *h·* works ;
	11– 5	* has been constantly at *h·* post
	11– 6	* storms that have surged against *h·*
	20–11	and name your gifts to *h·*.

Eddy
her

My.	20–12	Send *h·* only what God gives
	20–14	would expend for presents to *h·*,
	20–16	let this suffice for *h·* rich portion
	20–17	Send no gifts to *h·*
	22–19	* justification of *h·* labors is the fruit.
	28–20	* and following *h·* example,
	39–24	* *h·* graciousness and dignity.
	39–25	* harmonious tones of *h·* gentle voice.
	39–25	* were thrilled by *h·* compassion,
	39–27	* realize *h·* presence with us to-day.
	39–29	* beauty of *h·* character.
	40– 2	* evidence to us of *h·* hospitable love.
	40– 3	* desired for years to have *h·* church
	40–31	* *h·* own blameless and happy life,
	40–32	* as well as by *h·* teachings,
	41–30	* as well as for *h·* own ;
	42– 1	* to be truly grateful to *h·*
	42–27	* faithful is *h·* allegiance to God,
	42–28	* how untiring are *h·* efforts,
	42–29	* performance of *h·* daily tasks.
	47–24	* Mrs. Eddy founded *h·* first church
	48– 9	* *h·* textbook, "S. and H.
	48–11	* insisted that *h·* students
	48–14	* future growth of *h·* church,
	48–15	* appreciation of *h·* efforts
	48–18	* in *h·* insistence upon the constant
	48–19	* and *h·* own writings,
	48–20	* has given to *h·* disciples a means of
	50–23	* celebrated *h·* Communion Sabbath
	51– 1	* so as to keep *h·* with us,
	51– 2	* who could take *h·* place
	51– 7	* feels it *h·* duty to tender *h·*
	51–11	* serious blow to *h·* Cause
	51–23	* *h·* duty, to go into new fields
	51–31	* *h·* earnest endeavors, *h·* arduous labors,
	52– 4	* blessing them that curse *h·*,
	52– 5	* them that despitefully use *h·*,
	52– 6	* giving in *h·* Christian example,
	52– 6	* as well as *h·* instructions,
	52– 8	* acknowledge our indebtedness to *h·*,
	52–10	* to sustain *h·* in *h·* work.
	52–23	* if only through *h·* work
	52–24	* More than once, in *h·* earnestness,
	52–25	* reached *h·* bottom dollar,
	52–26	* to hear *h·* word
	52–26	* has always filled *h·* coffers anew.
	52–29	* the moral rightness of *h·* book."
	53– 4	* satisfied that *h·* duty was
	53– 6	* send forth *h·* book to the world."
	53–22	* by *h·* students and by clergymen
	58–21	* May *h·* example inspire us
	58–21	* to follow *h·* in preaching,
	59–27	* I heard *h·* talk it before
	64– 2	* *h·* relation to the experiences
	64– 5	* through *h·* spiritual attainments
	64– 5	* and *h·* years of toil,
	64–11	* In *h·* dedicatory Message
	64–15	* In all *h·* writings,
	64–15	* all the years of *h·* leadership,
	64–16	* has been teaching *h·* followers
	64–18	* *h·* success in so doing
	64–20	* warn all *h·* followers against
	66–24	* *h·* beautiful home, Pleasant View,
	66–25	* welcoming *h·* children and giving *h·*
	90– 1	* thousands during *h·* lifetime ;
	90–28	* and the sources of *h·* power
	91–22	* the first years of *h·* preaching
	97–16	* Mrs. Eddy and *h·* cult.
	97–19	* their teacher and *h·* utterances."
	104–28	to learn of *h·* who, thirty years ago,
	134–27	* a letter from *h·* to me.
	134–29	* it shows *h·* usual mental
	144– 2	* to the members of *h·* church
	157–17	* in *h·* original deed of trust,
	171–20	* *h·* regular afternoon drive
	171–23	* *H·* carriage came to a standstill
	172– 9	* to the members of *h·* church,
	231– 2	endeavors to bestow *h·* charities
	231–15	invalids demanding *h·* help
	231–15	letters from . . . do not reach *h·*.
	231–16	committed to the waste-basket by *h·*
	231–20	important demands on *h·* time
	231–22	unwise for *h·* to undertake
	240–23	* replies, through *h·* student,
	270–16	*H·* life is proven under trial,
	271–12	* chapter sub-title
	271–19	* has made *h·* famous.
	272–22	* reproduced in *h·* own handwriting.
	272–26	* *h·* very great following.
	273– 4	* vindicate in *h·* own person
	273– 4	* the value of *h·* teachings.
	273– 7	* from all attacks upon *h·*,
	276– 4	begs to say, in *h·* own behalf,
	276– 8	or because . . . she omits *h·* drive,

Eddy

her

My.	276–11	she is minding *h·* own business,
	276–12	all *h·* dear friends and enemies.
	276–22	* expression of *h·* political views,
	304–30	the contents of *h·* book,
	309–28	* passed *h·* first fifteen years at
	310–23	*h·* father, a gray-haired man
	311–30	* completed *h·* education when
	312–13	* *h·* father's home by *h·* brother
	312–14	* *H·* position was an embarrassing one.
	315– 6	* He spoke of *h·* being a pure and
	315–24	or is it *h·* alleged double
	317– 3	* defining *h·* relations with the
	319–13	* confirm *h·* statement regarding
	319–14	* which the Rev. Mr. Wiggin did for *h·*,
	326–10	* which Mrs. Eddy has made *h·* home.
	328– 2	* blessed, and prospered it, and *h·*.
	329– 9	* the death of *h·* husband,
	329–13	* has in *h·* possession
	329–14	* notice of *h·* husband's death
	329–14	* and of *h·* brother's letter,
	329–28	* some incidents of *h·* life
	330–16	* relating to *h·* husband
	331– 1	accompanying *h·* on *h·* sad journey
	331– 7	* accompanied *h·* to the train
	331– 8	* on *h·* departure,
	331– 8	* *h·* irreproachable standing
	331–31	* sympathy extended to *h·*
	332– 1	* to restore *h·* to *h·* friends.
	332–10	* who engaged to accompany *h·*
	332–11	* but did not desert *h·*
	332–11	* until he saw *h·* in the
	332–12	* in the fond embrace of *h·* friends.
	334–10	* account of *h·* husband's demise
	334–16	* to quote *h·* own words.
	334–17	* Nothing could be further from *h·*
	334–19	* She declares in *h·* Message
	335–23	* third day of *h·* husband's illness,
	335–29	* save the life of *h·* husband.
	335–30	* for *h·* husband's recovery,
	336– 1	* but for *h·* prayers
	336– 4	* *h·* brother, George S. Baker,
	336– 5	* come to *h·* after *h·* husband's
	336– 5	* to take *h·* back to the North.
	336– 6	* he desired to go to *h·* assistance,
	336– 8	* *h·* husband's Masonic brethren,
	336– 9	* performed their obligation to *h·*.
	336–10	* acknowledgment of this in *h·* book,
	338– 8	* held and expressed by *h·*.
	338– 9	* reference to *h·* writings will
	342–20	* she said, in *h·* clear voice,
	343– 4	* a question in *h·* own way,
	345–32	* *h·* views, strictly and always
	346– 2	* has lived with *h·* subject
	346– 5	* another view of *h·* religion.
	346–15	* expression of . . . was on *h·* face.
	346–22	* *h·* successor would be a man.
	348–15	was based upon *h·* discovery
	351– 3	* publish *h·* letter of recent date,
	354–27	* The members of *h·* household
	355– 1	* were with *h·* at the time,
	355– 2	* in *h·* spiritualized thought

hers

Mis.	272– 8	* similar colleges, except *h·*,

herself

Man.	30–22	does not occupy the house *h·*
Pul.	29– 6	* Mrs. Eddy *h·*, of whose work I
	46–10	* much is told of *h·* in detail
	46–23	* applied *h·*, like other girls,
	49– 4	* that marks its hostess *h·*.
	58– 1	* found *h·* . . . healed by the power of
	58– 2	* devoted *h·* to imparting this
	71–19	* resigned *h·* completely to the study
	73– 6	* cured *h·* of a deathly disease
	73– 8	* secluded *h·* from the world
	73–14	* She of *h·* had no power.
	73–26	* Mrs. Eddy had *h·* written,
Po.	v–16	* seated *h·* by the roadside
My.	vi–27	* reserving for *h·* only a
	231–12	has ceased practice *h·*
	334– 8	* allegation . . . has contradicted *h·*,
	336– 7	* entrusted *h·* to the care of
	342– 8	* but Mrs. Eddy *h·*.
	343–12	* like *h·*, be the ruler.

hostess

Pul.	49– 4	* that marks its *h·* herself.

I

Mis.	11–28	with tears have *I* striven for it.
	238–26	or that *I* died of palsy,
	239–15	"Ah !" thought *I*, "somebody has to
	248–21	have said that *I* died of poison,
	277–29	*I* thunder His law to the sinner,
	299–27	What right have *I* to do this?
	303–16	If ever *I* wear out from serving
	350–17	*I* dissolved the society,

Eddy

I

Mis.	371–12	*I* as their teacher can say,
	372–26	Not by aid of . . . could *I* copy art,
	376–30	Then thought *I*, What are we,
Man.	58– 4	*I*, Mary Baker Eddy, ordain
Ret.	13– 9	So perturbed was *I* by the
	24– 5	which *I* afterwards named C. S.
	28–28	Am *I* a believer in spiritualism?
	38–18	*I* to learn that he had printed
	73–10	as *I* floated into more spiritual
Un.	9–21	it is said, . . . that *I* monopolize;
	40– 3	To say that you and *I*, as mortals
Pul.	1–19	Were *I* present, methinks
	74–14	'Am *I* the second Christ?'
Pan.	13–25	Have *I* wearied you with the
'02.	2–27	*I* but began where the Church
	2–28	When the churches and *I*
Hea.	14–18	most arduous task *I* ever performed.
My.	20–10	May *I* relieve you of selecting,
	62– 8	* may *I* not take this precious truth
	115– 6	were *I*, apart from God, its author.
	127–16	*I* deliberately declare that when
	129– 3	*I* reluctantly foresee great danger
	148–18	*I*, as usual at home and alone,
	163–23	retirement *I* so much coveted,
	164– 2	retirement *I* so much desired.
	166–16	Had *I* never suffered for
	173–11	*I* scarcely supposed that a note,
	174– 5	*I* greatly appreciate the courtesy
	189–32	Am *I* not alone in soul?
	194–22	*I* deeply appreciate it,
	201–19	Rich hope have *I* in him
	214–25	*I* therefore halted from necessity.
	219– 7	*I* by no means would pluck their plumes.
	220–18	*I* also have faith that
	223– 4	*I* neither listen to complaints, . . . nor
	228– 8	*I* fail to know how one can
	233– 9	*I* surely should.
	235–28	Had *I* known what was being done
	249–20	*I* alone know what that means.
	256– 8	that *I* be permitted total exemption
	260–31	Neither the you nor the *I* in the
	264– 3	*I* even hope that those who are
	271– 5	*I* little understood all that *I*
	295–25	You, *I*, and mankind have cause
	302–14	*I* begged the students who first
	306–22	when *I* first visited Dr. Quimby
	307– 2	and which *I*, at his request,
	313–13	*I* only know that my father and
	313–27	but *I* wounded her pride
	315–25	If indeed it be *I*, allow me to
	318– 7	*I* especially employed him on
	344–18	If *I* harbored that idea
	351–15	May you and *I* and all mankind

I abide

My.	227–28	*I* abide by this rule

I accepted

Mis.	349–27	*I* accepted, for a time,
Ret.	15–15	*I* accepted the invitation
	44– 7	*I* accepted the call,
My.	145– 6	showed it to me, and *I* accepted it.

I accord

Mis.	238–29	*I* accord these evil-mongers

I add

Pul.	39– 9	*I* add on the following page

I adhere

'01.	22–19	*I* adhere to my text,

I admire

My.	282– 4	While *I* admire the faith and

I admonish

Mis.	141–25	*I* admonish you :
My.	106– 2	*I* admonish Christian Scientists

I adopted

My.	313–28	when *I* adopted C. S.,

I advertised

My.	306–24	*I* advertised that I would pay

I advise

My.	360–17	*I* advise you with all my soul

I afterwards

'02.	13–28	*I* afterwards gave to my church

I again

Mis.	380–15	*I* again, in faith, turned to
'02.	4– 3	*I* again repeat, Follow your

I agree

Mis.	117–10	*I* agree with Rev. Dr. Talmage,
	243–13	*I* agree with the Professor
My.	154–22	*I* agree with him :

I agreed

My.	318–19	*I* agreed not to question him

I aimed

Mis.	372–24	*I* aimed to reproduce, . . . the modest

I allowed

Mis.	302–18	*I* allowed, . . . the privilege of
'01.	29–27	*I* allowed them for several years

Eddy

I already
Pul. 87–18   I already speak to you each Sunday.
I also saw
Ret. 45–23   I also saw that Christianity has
I always try
My. 163–12   I always try to be just,
I am
Mis. 22– 1   I am strictly a theist
48– 8   I am opposed to it,
88– 9   I am pleased to inform this inquirer,
115– 3   I am astounded at the apathy of
133– 6   your statement that I am a pantheist,
136– 5   I am still with you on the field
150–11   I am with all who are with Truth,
157–18   I am glad that you are in good cheer.
177–29   I am constantly homesick for heaven.
193–15   of which I am pastor,
193–17   I am thankful even for his allusion
238–25   allegement that I am "sick,
242–15   I am in another department
248–16   that I am an infidel.
248–19   not more true than that I am dead,
249–28   I am in awe before it.
262–15   I am grateful to you for giving to
265–27   I am constantly called to
273– 2   I am thankful that the neophyte
284–32   I am opposed to all personal
295–32   I am a Christian Scientist,
372–18   I am delighted to find
382–11   I am the debtor.
385– 6   And I am blest !
Ret. 94–25   I am persuaded that only by
Un. 48–19   that of which I am conscious
Pul. 21– 8   I am seeking and praying for it
74–15   What I am is for God to declare
74–17   claim nothing more than what I am,
No. 28– 8   Of his intermediate . . . I am ignorant.
'00. 1– 1   I am touched with the tone of your
1– 6   I am with thee, heart answering to
1– 9   I am grateful to say that in the
'01. 21–14   I am sorry for my critic,
22– 7   I am a spiritual homœopathist
'02. 16– 7   To-day I am the happy possessor of
Po. 37– 6   And I am blest !
73– 8   I am with thee in spirit
My. 5–24   I am with you "in spirit — John 4 : 23.
9–19   I am bankrupt in thanks
9–26   till I am satisfied with
122– 9   Now I am done with homilies
136–13   I am pleased to say that the
144– 5   lies afloat that I am sick,
144– 6   public report that I am in
146–18   I am convinced of the absolute
146–20   I am equally sure that
147–30   and I am helping them.
151– 1   I am patient with the newspaper
160–19   I am asked, "Is there a hell?"
166–27   I am for the first time informed of
170– 1   I am especially desirous that
175–27   I am sure that the counterfeit
177– 7   and I am glad to say
177– 9   I am quite able to take the trip
183–25   I am blending with thine my prayer
184– 8   To-day I am privileged to
203–20   and I am sure that He will
219– 1   unless I am personally present.
228– 6   hence I am always saying
230–11   I am sure, that each Rule
233–10   made better by watching?   I am.
235–24   Are you a Christian Scientist?   I am.
248– 2   I am more than satisfied
249–19   I am the Founder of C. S.
254– 5   I am glad you enjoy the dawn of
268–18   I am as silent as the
274–22   I am cheered and blessed
275–13   the report that I am sick
275–15   I am well and keenly alive
276–23   I am asked, "What are your politics?"
284–23   But here let me say that I am
289–27   I am interested in a meeting
295–12   I am in grateful receipt of your
302–21   I am less lauded, pampered,
303–28   What I am remains to be proved
305–15   I am the author of the
305–17   I am rated in the
305–21   All that I am in reality,
313–11   stories . . . I am ignorant of.
316–21   I am pleased to find this
345–23   At present I am conservative
360–12   I am constrained to say,
I am not
Mis. 95–15   I am not, and never was.
133–18   I hope I am not wrong
249–11   I am not a spiritualist,
253– 6   I am not enough the new woman

Eddy

I am not
Mis. 265–22   I am not morally responsible for
278– 3   but I am not dismayed,
310–15   I am not unmindful that
Po. 19– 3   I am not alone
My. 5–23   Beloved, I am not with you
119–28   for I am not there.
274–21   I am not fond of an abundance of
303– 4   I know that I am not that one,
359– 8   I am not personally involved
I answer
Mis. 301–21   I answer : It is not right
I answered
Ret. 14–11   I answered without a tremor,
I answered not
Ret. 8–18   I answered not, till again
I anticipated
My. 163–25   more than I anticipated.
I apprehended
Ret. 25– 6   I apprehended for the first time,
Pul. 35– 1   I apprehended the spiritual meaning
I approve
My. 358–30   I approve the By-laws
I, as a
Mis. 152–11   I, as a corporeal person,
152–11   I, as a dictator, arbiter, or
152–12   but I, as a mother
I as an individual
Mis. 310–26   I as an individual would
I ask
Un. 34–18   I ask : What evidence does
35–14   I ask, Which was first, matter or
'02. 14–24   I ask : What has shielded and
My. 19–19   I ask for more, even this :
117–31   is all that I ask of mankind.
130–15   Therefore I ask the help of others
130–16   I ask that according to
175–18   May I ask in behalf of the public
I asked
Ret. 40– 7   I asked permission to see her.
My. 139–17   When I asked you to dispense with
I a spiritualist?
Mis. 95–14   Am I a spiritualist?
I assert
My. 106–13   I assert it would have been
I availed
My. 318–10   I availed myself of the name of
I aver
My. 193–23   Here I aver that you have
I awoke
Mis. 180– 1   I awoke from the dream of Spirit
I became
'01. 32– 5   I became early a child of the
'02. 15–15   I became poor for Christ's sake.
I become
Ret. 76–29   I become responsible, as a teacher,
I beg
Ret. 50–11   I beg disinterested people to
My. 118– 9   I beg to thank you for your
165–12   I beg to thank the dear brethren
256– 9   I beg to send to you all a
I began
Ret. 43– 2   I began by teaching one
My. 304–10   I began writing for the leading
318–21   I began my attack on agnosticism.
I begin
'01. 22–15   I begin at the feet of Christ
I beheld
Ret. 25–29   I beheld with ineffable awe
I behold
Mis. 389–11   Can I behold the snare, the pit,
Po. 4–10   Can I behold the snare, the pit,
I believe
Mis. 67–29   I believe in this removal being
70– 2   That the Bible is true I believe,
96– 7   Do I believe in a personal God?
96– 8   I believe in God as the Supreme
96–17   Do I believe in the atonement of
132–23   what I believe and teach,
141–16   I believe, — yea, I understand,
313–25   as I believe, divinely directed,
Ret. 28–28   I believe in no ism.
Un. 48– 6   I believe more in Him than
48–19   I believe that of which I am
49– 2   I believe in the individual man,
49– 7   I believe less in the sinner,
50– 4   I believe in matter only as
50– 4   only as I believe in evil,
'01. 32–26   I believe, if those venerable
My. 146– 5   I believe this saying
220–12   I believe in obeying the laws
234–20   I believe that all our great
282– 3   I believe strictly in the Monroe
303– 2   I believe in one Christ,

Eddy

I believe
My.	303– 3	I believe in but one incarnation,
	345–18	could I believe in a science of

I bend
Ret.	17– 4	I bend to thy lay,
Po.	62– 3	I bend to thy lay,

I be present
Mis.	322–19	though I be present or absent,

I bless God
Ret.	21–24	for those lucid . . . I bless God.

I briefly
My.	298– 3	I briefly declare that nothing has
	305– 7	I briefly express myself

I by firing first
Mis.	11– 6	and I by firing first could kill him

I call
Mis.	26–23	I call matter, *nothing.*
	121– 6	to which I call your attention,
	133– 8	I call your attention and
	282–29	abuse which I call attention to,
Un.	32–26	which I call *mortal mind;*
Rud.	9–11	of what I call *mortal mind,*
'00.	14–14	I call your attention to this
My.	228– 1	I call disease by its name
	229– 1	I call none but genuine Christian
	251–24	I call you mine, for all is

I called
Mis.	24–10	I called for my Bible,
Ret.	25–11	God I called *immortal Mind.*
	25–13	sensuous nature, I called *error*
	25–18	Spirit I called the *reality;*
My.	240– 9	I called C. S. the higher criticism

I calmly
Mis.	247– 9	I calmly challenge the world,

I came
'02.	13–15	I came to the rescue,
My.	164– 1	far from my purpose, when I came
	275–18	since I came to Massachusetts.

I can
Mis.	11–26	I can do much general good
	62– 2	I can improve my own,
	96–11	that of which I can conceive,
	96–26	I can name some means by which
	106–20	I can only bring crumbs fallen from
	115– 7	I can account for this state of mind
	239– 3	I can talk — and laugh too !
Un.	44– 3	I can only repeat the Master's
Rud.	8–10	I can give you here nothing but
'01.	15–17	I can conceive of little short of
	31–14	I can use the power that God gives
'02.	14– 4	I can neither rent, mortgage, nor
	20–22	I can bear the cross,
My.	145–22	I can serve equally my friends and
	192–26	Of this, however, I can sing :
	268–21	I can only solace the sore ills of
	270–22	I can appeal to Him as my witness
	277– 6	I can see no other way of
	343– 8	I can answer that.
	360–12	if I can settle this
	360–14	as many students think I can,

I cannot
Mis.	136– 9	I cannot feel justified in turning
	146– 6	I cannot conscientiously lend my
	146– 9	I cannot accept hearsay,
	146–20	I cannot be the conscience for this
	266–21	I cannot find it in my heart not to
	273–25	I cannot do my best work for
	277–30	I cannot help loathing the
	318– 6	I cannot but love some of those
	350–28	I cannot serve two masters ;
Ret.	5–15	I cannot speak as I would,
Un.	43–12	I *cannot* speak of myself as
	49–14	So long as . . . I cannot be wholly good.
'01.	31–12	then I cannot choose but obey.
'02.	19–12	no person . . . that I cannot forgive.
My.	25–18	I cannot be present *in*
	115– 8	I cannot be super-modest in
	127–32	I cannot quench my desire to say
	138–16	I cannot "serve two — *Matt.* 6 : 24.
	138–17	I cannot be a . . . Scientist except
	145–18	but I cannot go upon the
	163–12	and I cannot show
	189–24	I cannot forget that yours is the first
	233–15	by indifference thereto ? I cannot.
	234– 4	I cannot watch and pray while
	251– 1	What these are I cannot yet say.
	285– 6	I cannot spare the time requisite to
	307–13	saying what I cannot forget
	343–10	"I cannot answer that now."

I cast
Mis.	250–18	I cast aside the word as a sham

I celebrate
My.	262–12	I celebrate Christmas with my soul,

I challenge
My.	108– 5	I challenge matter to act

Eddy

I characterized
Ret.	25–15	God I characterized as

I cherish
Ret.	6–13	beautiful character as I cherish it,

I cherished
My.	195–11	deep love which I cherished

I cited
My.	281– 6	I cited, as our present need,

I claim
Mis.	255–20	I claim for healing by C. S.
	349–17	I claim no jurisdiction over any
Ret.	34–10	I claim for healing scientifically
Pul.	74–16	I claim nothing more than
My.	26–21	or that I claim their homage.
	305–21	I claim no special merit

I claimed
Ret.	25–16	The real I claimed as eternal ;

I clearly
Mis.	95–19	I clearly understand that no
	113–21	I clearly recognize that

I close
Mis.	128– 5	Therefore I close here,
	273– 5	I close my College in order to
	274–13	I close my College.
My.	15–16	I close with Kate Hankey's
	256–12	Thus may I close the door

I closed
My.	246–11	I closed my College

I come
Po.	73– 2	I come to thee

I commend
Mis.	97–22	I commend the Icelandic

I comply
My.	177– 3	Most happily would I comply

I concluded
My.	307–18	But afterwards I concluded that

I congratulate
My.	196– 3	I congratulate you upon erecting
	204–17	I congratulate you tenderly
	208–18	I congratulate you on the

I consent
Mis.	300–17	When I consent to this act,

I consented
My.	164– 3	demand increased, and I consented,
	284–22	I consented thereto only as other

I consider
Pul.	39– 9	that I consider superbly sweet
No.	28–15	I consider well established.
My.	138– 4	I consider this agreement
	236–27	I consider the information there

I consulted
My.	114–15	I consulted no other authors

I continue
Mis.	xii– 3	I continue the march,

I copy
My.	189–28	from which I copy this verse :

I copyrighted
Ret.	35– 1	I copyrighted the first publication

I cordially
'02.	4– 5	I cordially congratulate our Board

I correct
Mis.	266–24	If I correct mistakes which may be

I corrected
My.	307– 3	his copy when I corrected it.

I could
Mis.	19–22	than I could or would have
	106– 4	if I could write the history in
	351– 9	would not if I could,
	379– 4	asked if I could see his pennings
	380–18	Although I could heal mentally,
Ret.	14–24	I could only answer him in the
	15– 7	I could say in David's words,
	24–19	I could only assure him that
	50– 2	I could think of no financial
'02.	15–19	I could never believe that a

I could not
Mis.	351– 8	I could not if I would,
Ret.	14–21	I could not designate any precise
	24–18	I could not then explain the *modus*
Pul.	34–22	"How, I could not tell,
'01.	32– 7	I could not help loving them.
My.	114–18	I could not write these notes after
	311– 7	I could not refuse her.

I counsel
Un.	1–13	I counsel my students to defer
Pan.	13–12	I counsel thee, rebuke and
'01.	30–27	I counsel Christian Scientists
My.	18–20	I counsel thee, rebuke and

I count
'01.	31–20	I count these dear :

I cured
Mis.	242–24	I cured precisely such a case

I daily
My.	244–12	need of which I daily discern.

Eddy

I declare
'01. 15– 1   *I* declare that he must awake

I declared
My. 307– 5   one day *I* declared to him

I declined
'02. 15–18   *I* declined to sell them
My. 302–28   *I* declined and went alone in my

I dedicate
My. 182–19   *I* dedicate this beautiful house

I deem
My. 289– 8   *I* deem it proper that The
306– 7   *I* deem it unwise to enter into

I demonstrated
Mis. 70– 3   *I demonstrated* its truth when I

I denied
Ret. 25–16   His corporeality *I* denied.

I denominated
Ret. 25–14   Soul *I* denominated *substance*,

I deny
Un. 10– 3   reality of these . . . *I* deny,

I deposit
Mis. 159–16   *I* deposit certain recollections
159–20   Here *I* deposit the gifts that my

I deprecate
Mis. 97–12   Such . . . healing *I* deprecate.
284–29   *I* deprecate personal animosities

I described
Ret. 25–18   temporal, *I* described as unreal.

I desire
Mis. 274– 4   *I* desire to revise my book
291–12   *I* desire the equal growth and
Ret. 74– 9   *I* desire never to think of it,
Pul. 87–20   more of earth now, than *I* desire,
My. 138–15   persons whom *I* desire to see
249–24   The report . . . *I* desire to correct.
358–13   however much *I* desire to read all

I desired
Mis. 276– 6   all with whom *I* desired to,

I did
Mis. 178– 4   left his old church, as *I* did,
311–25   *I* did this even as a surgeon
Ret. 9–15   *I* did answer, in the words of
My. 215– 5   bade me do what *I* did,
312–30   *I* did open an infant school,
346–27   "*I* did say that a man would be

I did not
Mis. 276– 5   *I* did not hold interviews with all
Ret. 35– 7   *I* did not venture . . . until later,
My. 346–28   *I* did not mean any man

I disapprove
Mis. 109– 4   authority for what *I* disapprove,

I discern
'00. 9– 2   *I* discern that this obedience

I discerned
Ret. 26– 3   Adoringly *I* discerned the Principle
Un. 30–23   *I* discerned the last Adam as a

I discovered
Mis. 337– 1   Have *I* discovered and founded
379–27   *I* discovered, . . . the momentous facts
382–12   *I* discovered the Science of
Ret. 24– 4   *I* discovered the Science of
Un. 30–21   When *I* discovered the power of Spirit

I do
Mis. 11–27   *I* do it with earnest, special care
29– 3   Do you believe his words? *I* do,
67–27   If your question refers to . . . *I* do.
96–18   Do I believe in the . . . *I* do ;
Un. 46– 8   *I* do so on a divine Principle,
My. 9–25   but *I* do now,
219–21   *I* do say that C. S. cannot annul
235–25   Do you adopt as truth . . . *I* do.
284–24   *I* do believe implicitly in the
303–29   to be proved by the good *I* do.

I donated
Mis. 140–20   The lot of land which *I* donated
382–19   *I* donated to this church the land

I do not
Mis. 267– 9   * those whom *I* do not love,"
358–20   Be it understood that *I* do not
Ret. 76–28   but if *I* do not insist upon
Un. 46– 7   *I* do not deny, . . . the individuality
'01. 22– 6   *I* do not try to mix matter and
22– 8   *I* do not believe in such a compound.
22–16   *I* do not say that one added to one
My. 143–22   *I* do not regard this . . . as a trial,
223–13   secular affairs, *I* do not answer.
223–15   *I* do not consider myself capable of
223–19   either of which *I* do not entertain.
237– 6   *I* do not consider a precedent for
242–10   *I* do not mean that mortals are
255– 7   *I* do not mean that minor officers
318–31   *I* do not find my authority for
345– 3   *I* do not suppose their
361– 4   *I* do not presume to give you

Eddy

I dropped
Mis. x–21   *I* dropped the name of Morse

I dwell
Po. 32– 3   home where *I* dwell in the vale,

I earned
My. 215–16   *I* earned the means with which to

I earnestly
Mis. 308–32   *I* earnestly advise . . . Scientists
322– 2   *I* earnestly invite you to its
Ret. 8–23   Then *I* earnestly declared

I employ
No. 10– 1   *I* employ this awe-filled word

I employed
My. 307–11   terms which *I* employed
317– 9   mistake to say that *I* employed

I enclose
Mis. 157–18   *I* enclose you the name of
My. 289– 4   *I* enclose a check for

I endeavor
Mis. 66–31   *I* endeavor to accommodate my

I endeavored
Ret. 73–14   *I* endeavored to lift thought above

I engaged
My. 317–11   *I* engaged Mr. Wiggin so as to

I enjoin
No. 8–19   *I* enjoin it upon my students to

I enter
Mis. 299–18   If *I* enter Mr. Smith's store
347–20   *I* enter the path.
My. 188–17   In spirit *I* enter your inner

I entered
Ret. 39– 3   *I* entered a suit at law,
My. 307–17   *I* entered a demurrer which

I entertain
Mis. 292–12   higher sense *I* entertain of Love,

I entitled
My. 353–12   the second *I* entitled *Sentinel*,

I esteem
Ret. 29– 2   *I* esteem all honest people,

I exercised
Mis. 70– 3   when *I* exercised my power

I exhort
Un. 43–19   *I* exhort them to accept Christ's

I exist
My. 143–11   *I* exist in the flesh,

I experimented
Mis. 249– 2   *I* experimented by taking

I extend
'01. 1– 1   to-day *I* extend my

I fain
Mis. 394–19   * *I* fain would keep the gates ajar,
Po. 57– 5   * *I* fain would keep the gates ajar,

I fed
My. 247–16   *I* fed these sweet little thoughts

I feel
Mis. 13– 1   only justice of which *I* feel
146–23   *I* feel sure that as Christian Scientists
256–10   *I* feel, . . . this imposes on me the
266–20   *I* speak of them as I feel,
303–24   *I* feel assured that many
My. 138– 7   *I* feel that it is not for my benefit

I felt
Mis. 281–25   *I* felt the weight of this yesterday,
Ret. 14–23   asked me to say how *I* felt
Pul. 34–20   "*I* felt that the divine Spirit

I find
Mis. 132–20   *I* find it inconvenient to
281– 6   *I* find also another mental
My. 137–30   *I* find myself able to select
138–16   solely because *I* find that I

I first proved
Mis. 338– 5   *I* first proved to myself,

I follow
Mis. 347–18   *I* follow his counsel,

I followed
My. 343–19   *I* followed it up, teaching

I foresaw
My. 185–24   Then and there *I* foresaw this hour,

I foresee
Mis. 363–30   *I* foresee and foresay that
My. 26–20   as *I* foresee, the need of it.

I for one
Mis. 131–24   *I*, for one, would be pleased
My. 273–13   *I* for one accept his wise

I found
Mis. 69–16   *I* found him barely alive,
180–14   *I* found the open door from this
247– 7   *I* found health in just
348–23   When *I* found myself under this
Ret. 24–21   *I* found to be in perfect scientific
33–10   *I* found, in the two hundred and
56– 2   *I* found to be demonstrable
Pul. 34–23   *I* found it to be in perfect scientific
'01. 24–24   *I* found it necessary to follow
My. 343–26   *I* found at one time that they had

Eddy

I found
My .	345–16	but *I* found that when I
	348– 6	*I* found it was God made manifest

I founded
Ret.	15– 4	till *I* founded a church of my own,

I fully
Pul.	87–15	*I* fully appreciate your kind

I furnished
'02.	12–30	*I* furnished the money

I gained
Ret.	10– 3	*I* gained book-knowledge
	24– 9	*I* gained the scientific certainty

I gave
Mis.	137– 5	*I* gave you a meagre reception
	139–18	*I* gave a lot of land
	300–25	*I* gave permission to cite,
Ret.	43–10	After *I* gave up teaching,
	51– 1	*I* gave a lot of land in Boston
'02.	15–27	To this, . . . *I* gave no heed,
My.	138– 1	*I* gave them my property to
	157–22	*I* gave a deed of trust

I gazed
Ret.	31–22	*I* gazed, and stood abashed.

I give
Mis.	24– 5	*I* give it to you as
My.	119–26	Should *I* give myself the pleasant

I go
My.	275–17	*I* go out in my carriage daily,

I greatly rejoice
Mis.	137–14	*I* greatly rejoice over the growth of

I greet
Mis.	251– 6	beloved brethren, . . . *I* greet you ;

I grew discouraged
Ret.	8–10	until *I* grew discouraged,

I group
My.	257–25	*I* group you in one benison

I had
Mis.	11–13	*I* had done my whole duty
	24–14	better health than *I* had before
	32–17	If *I* had the time to talk with all
	139–23	*I* had this desirable site transferred
	140–11	as *I* had it conveyed.
	237–30	*I* had heard the awful story
	285– 4	because *I* had been personal
	300–23	which *I* had organized
	300–24	*I* had for many years been pastor,
	373– 9	*I* had never before seen it :
	379– 2	*I* had a curiosity to know if he
	379–20	*I* had already experimented
	380–10	demonstrate what *I* had discovered :
Ret.	8–16	though *I* had ceased to notice it.
	10– 6	latter *I* had to repeat every Sunday.
	10–12	knowledge *I* had gleaned from
	14–19	when *I* had experienced a change
	14–20	tearfully *I* had to respond
	14–22	*I had* been truly regenerated,
	20– 2	except what money *I* had brought
	20–10	*I* had no training for self-support,
	23–23	*I* had touched the hem of C. S.
	24– 8	*I* had been trying to trace
	28– 9	*I* had learned that thought must
	28–22	*I* had learned that Mind reconstructed
	38– 1	*I* had finished that edition as far as
	38– 3	*I* had already paid him
	38– 9	*I* had already observed
	38–23	*I* had grown disgusted with
	40– 9	*I* had stood by her side
	44– 8	though *I* had preached five years
Pul.	20– 6	In 1892 *I* had to recover the land
	34–15	they thought *I* had died,
	35–13	"*I* had learned that thought must
	35–21	*I* had learned that Mind reconstructed
	49–15	*I* had them brought here
	63–12	"*I* had them brought here
'01.	17–19	*I* had overcome a difficult stage
	17–24	*I* had learned that the dynamics
'02.	13–25	price *I* had paid for it,
	15–22	book *I* had been writing.
My.	13– 7	first that *I* had even heard of it.
	105–25	he asked earnestly if *I* had a
	123–13	*I* had the property bought
	137–23	*I* had contemplated doing this
	137–25	*I* had consulted Lawyer Streeter
	137–27	*I* had implicit confidence in each one
	174–22	until *I* had a church of my own,
	214–21	*I* had no monetary means
	214–27	*I* had cast my all into the treasury of
	271– 7	truth of what *I* had written.
	317–19	dissented from what *I* had written,
	336–13	except what money *I* had brought
	348–21	*I* had found unmistakably an

I had not
Mis.	290–18	*I* had not thought of the writer
Ret.	15–26	*I* had not heard of these cases
	27–13	*I* had not fully voiced my

Eddy

I had not
Ret.	38–12	although *I* had not thought of
'01.	24–21	*I* had not read one line of Berkeley's

I half wish
Mis.	126– 4	*I* half wish for society again ;

I hate no one
Mis.	311–18	*I* hate no one ;

I have
Mis.	xi–27	In compiling this work, *I* have
	11–29	When smitten on one cheek, *I* have
	11–30	*I* have but two to present.
	13– 7	*I* have long endured at the hands of
	24–16	*I* have since tried to make plain to
	29–16	*I* have known of but fourteen
	39–14	*I* have faith in His promise,
	47–30	*I* have no knowledge of mesmerism,
	65–23	*I* have taught them both in its
	115–13	take up the cross as *I* have done,
	127– 1	*I* have observed that in proportion as
	127– 4	*I* have seen, that in the ratio of
	127– 7	One thing *I* have greatly desired,
	142–13	since they arrived *I* have said,
	146–12	*I* have hitherto declined to be
	157– 7	*I* have written, or caused my
	177–30	*I* have met one who
	213– 3	All that *I* have written,
	231– 9	would *I* have had the table
	239– 4	*I* have had but four days' vacation
	245–23	*I* have loved the Church
	247– 8	*I* have professed Christianity
	249– 8	false report that *I* have appropriated
	249–16	*I* have neither purchased nor
	249–23	*I* have proof, but no fear.
	266–18	assertion that *I* have said
	267– 6	for whom *I* have sacrificed the most
	272–29	*I* have endeavored to act toward all
	278–10	can be proven that *I* have never
	278–15	*I* have learned that a curse on sin
	278–24	*I* have felt for some time that
	278–29	*I* have been gradually withdrawing
	281– 9	*I* have now one ambition
	294–25	*I* have read the daily paper,
	299– 8	*I* have no time for detailed report
	307–13	*I* have thought best to stop its
	308–24	The knowledge that *I* have gleaned
	311–23	works *I* have written on C. S.
	311–32	*I* have been sorry that I spoke
	318– 4	*I* have a large affection,
	321–27	*I* have no desire to see or to hear what
	321–29	*I* have a world of . . . to contemplate,
	334–28	Because *I* have uncovered evil,
	338–13	only rule *I* have found which
	348–18	*I* have to repeat this,
	348–29	*I* have by no means encouraged
	349– 5	*I* have students with the degree of
	349–30	*I* have accepted no pay from my
	349–31	*I* have put into the church-fund
	351– 1	*I* have sometimes called on
	351– 7	*I* have no skill in occultism ;
Ret.	28–25	*I* have since understood it.
	30–21	the cup which *I* have drunk
	50–16	*I* have had as many as seventeen in
	52– 1	*I* have endeavored to find new ways
	52– 7	*I* have worked to provide a home for
	76–27	*I* have long remained silent
	83– 7	Students whom *I* have taught
Un.	7– 8	When *I* have most clearly seen
	7–13	*I* have been able to replace
	43–12	*I* have by no means spoken of myself,
	48– 6	*I* have no faith in any other thing
Pul.	7–24	*I* have ordained the Bible and
	74–22	not what *I* have taught her,
	74–22	not at all as *I* have heard her talk.
	87–19	*I* have more of earth now, than
Rud.	8– 9	*I* have given you only an epitome of
No.	2–15	*I* have healed more disease by
	8–11	in love, as *I* have rebuked them.
	9–16	*I* have opposed occasionally
	40–12	*I* have no objection to audible prayer
Pan.	13–26	*I* have only traversed my subject that
'00.	9–25	*I* have desired to step aside
	10–25	*I* have learned it was a private
'01.	11–13	True, *I* have made the
	26–14	*I* have passed through deep waters
	26–26	*I* have read little of their writings.
	26–28	What *I* have given to the world
	27–14	*I* have in one to three interviews
	27–22	*I* have put less of my own
	27–23	*I* have taken out of its
'02.	2–29	*I* have always taught the student to
	13– 5	*I* have transferred to The Mother Church,
	14–12	only success *I* have ever achieved
Po.	65– 5	in dreams *I* have had,
My.	15–14	Already *I* have said to you
	17–29	"Hitherto, *I* have observed that in

Eddy

I have

My.	18– 1	*I* have seen, that in the ratio of
	18– 4	"One thing *I* have greatly desired,
	25–23	*I* have faith in the givers
	26–13	that *I* have ever received
	103–18	*I* have set forth C. S.
	103–19	just as *I* have discovered them.
	103–20	*I* have demonstrated through Mind
	103–22	*I* have found nothing in ancient or
	104– 1	*I* have had no other guide
	105–14	*I* have healed at one visit a cancer
	105–16	*I* have physically restored sight
	105–32	*I* have proved to be more certain
	108– 6	*I* have proved beyond cavil
	114–25	*I* have been learning the higher
	115– 5	blush to write of . . . as *I* have, were it
	119–28	*I* have risen to look and wait
	121– 2	*I* have suggested a change
	125–11	*I* have only to dip my pen in my
	125–16	*I* have felt the touch of the
	130–10	whom *I* have assisted pecuniarily
	130–13	*I* have neither the time nor the
	133–22	*I* have a secret to tell you
	135– 8	*I* have heretofore personally
	136–24	To my . . . Trustees *I* have committed
	136–27	*I* have so done that I may have
	137–11	*I* have attended personally to my
	137–14	*I* have personally selected all my
	137–20	*I* have designated by my last will,
	143– 9	*I* have the pleasure to report
	145–17	*I* have worked even harder
	147– 8	*I* have provided for you a
	147–22	*I* have purchased a pleasant place
	147–26	*I* have a work to do
	152–31	*I* have the sweet satisfaction of
	163–23	*I* have also received from
	164– 8	*I* have yearned to express my
	174–17	*I* have the pleasure of thanking you
	203– 3	*I* have nothing new to communicate ;
	217– 5	*I* have deeded in trust to The
	219–26	*I* have expressed my opinion
	223–11	with whom *I* have no acquaintance
	223–12	of whom *I* have no knowledge,
	229– 3	*I* have no use for such,
	236–13	*I* have the joy of knowing that
	237– 3	*I* have since decided not to publish.
	242–21	*I* have requested my secretary not to
	244– 1	*I* have awaited your arrival
	244–13	*I* have awaited the right hour,
	244–24	What *I* have to say may not require
	247–28	The little that *I* have accomplished
	248–24	*I* have largely committed to you,
	250–26	*I* have faith that whatever is done
	259– 4	*I* have named it my *white student.*
	270–21	*I* have returned good for evil,
	276–23	*I* have none, in reality,
	286– 3	*I* have prayed daily that there be no
	303– 4	and *I* have never claimed to be.
	303–12	of which *I* have seen only extracts,
	304–12	*I* have lectured in large and crowded
	306–10	*I* have quite another purpose
	311–24	*I* have another coat-of-arms,
	313– 3	so *I* have been told ;
	313–19	*I* have always consistently declared
	314–28	just as *I* have stated them.
	316– 1	the truth *I* have promulgated
	317–23	liberty that *I* have taken with
	318– 3	*I* have erased them in my revisions.
	341– 1	*I* have one innate joy,
	343–14	"*I* have been called a pope,
	343–14	*I* have sought no such distinction.
	343–15	*I* have simply taught as I learned
	344– 1	*I* have even been spoken of as a
	353– 9	*I* have given the name to all the
	356–15	*I* have given no assurance,
	357–11	*I* have crowned The Mother Church
	357–28	*I* have just finished reading your

I have not

Mis.	32–21	But *I* have not moments enough
	65–19	*I* have not ; and this important fact
	97–27	*I* have not seen a perfect man
	243– 5	*I* have not yet made surgery one of
	248–28	*I* have not taken drugs,
	264–14	whom *I* have not fitted for it
	317– 1	students whom *I* have not seen
My.	138–19	Trusting that *I* have not exceeded
	165– 6	which *I* have not endured for the
	195– 9	privileges *I* have not had time to
	223–14	*I* have not sufficient time to waste
	243–13	*I* have not yet had the privilege of
	297–27	*I* have not had sufficient interest in the
	303–26	*I* have not the inspiration nor
	351–23	*I* have not read Gerhardt C. Mars' book,
	351–24	therefore *I* have not endorsed it,
	355– 8	*I* have not infrequently hinted at

I have not

My.	358–13	*I* have not the time to do so.
	361– 9	*I* have not seen Mrs. Stetson for

I healed

Ret.	40– 1	four successive years I healed,
'01.	17–15	It was that *I* healed the deaf,
My.	105– 7	*I* healed consumption in its last stages,
	105–10	*I* healed malignant diphtheria
	127–17	*I* healed ninety-nine to the ten of
	145–13	*I* healed him on the spot.

I hear

Mis.	106–25	methinks *I* hear the soft, sweet
Po.	16–20	'Mid graves do *I* hear the glad
My.	153– 1	*I* hear that the loving hearts

I heard

Ret.	8– 9	*I* heard somebody call *Mary,*
'02.	9–21	When first *I* heard the life-giving **sound**
My.	319– 5	*I* heard nothing further from him

I hereby

Mis.	297–16	*I* hereby state, in unmistakable
	313–25	*I* hereby ordain the Bible, and
My.	171–11	*I* hereby invite all my church
	223– 2	*I* hereby notify the public that
	242–16	*I* hereby announce to the C. S. field
	359– 8	and *I* hereby publicly declare that

I herewith

My.	289–25	*I* herewith send a few words of
	360–14	*I* herewith cheerfully subscribe these

I hold

Mis.	350– 1	*I* hold receipts for $1,489.50
Un.	49–13	So long as *I* hold evil in
My.	319– 8	*I* hold the late Mr. Wiggin in
	344–12	*I* hold it absurd to say that when

I hope

Mis.	133–18	*I* hope I am not wrong in
	391– 3	*I* hope the heart that's hungry
	396–14	*I* hope it's better made,
Po.	38– 2	*I* hope the heart that's hungry
	59– 6	*I* hope it's better made,
My.	120– 4	*I* hope and trust that you and I
	131–18	*I* hope I shall not be found disorderly,
	169– 7	date, which *I* hope soon to name
	259–16	*I* hope that in 1902 the churches

I impart

Mis.	292–11	Could *I* impart to the student

I implore

Mis.	141–19	Do not, *I* implore you,

I indited

My.	271– 5	little understood all that *I* indited ;

I indulge

Mis.	348–21	*I* indulge in homœopathic doses of

I infer

Mis.	32– 6	*I* infer that some of my students

I inferred

Mis.	379–10	from his remarks *I* inferred that

I inform

My.	135–18	*I* inform you of this,

I insist

Mis.	283–19	*I* insist on the etiquette of C. S.,
Un.	43–13	*I* insist only upon the fact,
No.	10– 3	*I* insist that C. S. is
	31–13	*I* insist on the destruction of sin

I insisted

Mis.	158– 6	When *I* insisted on your speaking
	373– 3	*I* insisted upon placing the serpent

I inspected

My.	145– 8	*I* inspected the work every day,

I instantly

Ret.	41– 4	desperate cases *I* instantly healed,

I instruct

No.	40–14	*I* instruct my students to pursue

I intervened

My.	343–27	*I* intervened.

I introduce

Mis.	247–14	of the Science *I* introduce,

I introduced

Ret.	43– 1	in 1867 *I* introduced the first

I invite

My.	169– 2	*I* invite you, one and all,

I invited

My.	318–16	*I* invited Mr. Wiggin

I issue

Mis.	350–26	*I* issue no arguments,

I joined

My.	311–13	*I* joined the Tilton Congregational

I judged

Ret.	43–18	*I* judged it best to close the

I just

Mis.	262–13	*I* just want to say, I thank you,

I kiss

Mis.	397– 3	*I* kiss the cross, and wake to know
Pul.	18–12	*I* kiss the cross, and wake to know
Po.	12–12	*I* kiss the cross, and wake to know

I knelt

Ret.	20–13	*I* knelt by his side throughout

Eddy

I knew

Mis.	140– 1	*I* knew that to God's gift,
	267–12	when *I* knew they were secretly
	290–19	*I* knew that this person was
Ret.	25–20	*I* knew the human conception of
Hea.	6– 8	*I* knew it was misinterpreted,
My.	137–25	or *I* knew aught about them,

I knew not

My.	307–28	drifting whither *I* knew not.

I know

Mis.	78–10	*I* know not how to teach either
	157–25	This *I* know, for God is for us.
'00.	8–30	*I* know it were best not to do,
'01.	19– 5	*I* know that prayer brings the
'02.	12–24	so far as *I* know them,
My.	7– 7	so far as *I* know them,
	138– 9	*I* know it was not needed
	151– 6	*I* know that no Christian can
	174–27	Each day *I* know Him nearer,
	223–17	that of which *I* know nothing.
	237–10	that *I* know to be correct
	271–29	insomuch as *I* know myself,
	303– 4	*I* know that I am not that one,
	357–30	*I* know that every true follower
	360–22	This *I* know, for He has proved it

I know not

Mis.	96– 8	*I* know not what the person of

I lay

Mis.	335–16	*I* lay bare the ability, in belief,

I leaned

'02.	15– 5	*I* leaned on God, and was safe.

I learned

Mis.	24–18	*I* learned that mortal thought
	281– 7	*I* learned long ago that the world
Ret.	25–24	*I* learned that these material senses
	32– 5	Early had *I* learned that
Hea.	6–13	*I* learned how mind produces
	6–14	*I* learned how it produces the
My.	271– 7	then *I* learned the truth
	343–15	I have simply taught as *I* learned

I leave all

Mis.	274–10	therefore *I* leave all for Christ.
My.	138–17	except *I* leave all for Christ.

I led

Ret.	30–19	Even so was *I* led into the

I left

My.	117–28	*I* left Boston in the height of

I listened

Ret.	9– 3	*I* listened with bated breath.

I little knew

Mis.	158– 7	*I* little knew that so soon another

I little thought

Mis.	158– 5	*I* little thought of the changes

I live

Un.	48– 9	Because He lives, *I* live.

I lived

My.	314–28	*I* lived with Dr. Patterson

I'll think

Po.	17– 3	*I'll* think of its glory, and rest

I long

Pul.	21– 7	*I* long, and live, to see

I longed

Mis.	142–28	*I* longed to say to the masonic

I look

Mis.	159–28	*I* look at the rich devices in
	203– 6	as *I* look on this smile of C. S.,

I lost

Ret.	20– 1	*I* lost all my husband's property,
My.	311–11	so *I* lost my housekeeper.
	336–12	*I* lost all my husband's property,

I love

Mis.	33– 5	*I* love all ministers and
	111–25	*I* love the orthodox church ;
	180–16	*I love* the Easter service :
	311–16	*I* love my enemies
	397–16	*I* love to be.
Pul.	7– 4	*I* love Boston, and especially the
	18–25	*I* love to be.
'01.	19– 5	*I* love this doctrine,
	28–19	*I* love Christ more than all
Po.	13– 4	*I* love to be.
	35– 4	as *I* love life less !
My.	105–30	and *I* love them ;
	133–23	Do you know how much *I* love
	163–25	*I* love its people
	234– 7	know how much *I* love them,
	262–27	*I* love to observe Christmas
	270–24	*I* love the prosperity of Zion,

I loved

'01.	32– 7	*I* loved Christians of the old sort

I love *you*

Mis.	11–32	"*I* love *you*, and would

I lovingly

Mis.	v– 4	I LOVINGLY DEDICATE THESE

Eddy

I'm

Po.	page 8	poem
	8– 1	*I'm* sitting alone where the shadows
	8– 7	*I'm* waiting alone for the bridal
	8–11	*I'm* watching alone o'er the starlit
	8–16	*I'm* dreaming alone of its changeful
	8–20	*I'm* thinking alone of a fair young
	9– 3	*I'm* picturing alone a glad young
	9– 8	*I'm* weeping alone that the vision is

I made

My.	343–23	*I* made a code of by-laws,

I maintain

Un.	46– 7	I do not deny, *I* maintain,

I make

Mis.	203– 3	*I* make no distinction between
	250–16	*I* make strong demands on love,
	299–20	can *I* make this right by saying,

I may

Mis.	58–16	*I* may read the Scriptures through a
	142–29	If as a woman *I* may not unite with
	143– 6	*I* may hope that a closer link
	322– 7	*I* may hereafter notify the Directors
Po.	33–12	that His love *I* may know,
My.	120– 4	that you and *I* may meet in truth
	136–27	that *I* may have more peace,
	146–10	*I* may then be even younger
	187– 3	*I* may at some near future
	302–20	*I* may be more loved,

I mean

Mis.	261–24	by mankind *I* mean mortals,
Ret.	50–19	By loyalty in students *I* mean this,
Rud.	3–26	*I* mean the infinite and divine
	8–25	By this *I* mean that mortal mind

I measure

Mis.	48– 1	as *I* measure its demonstrations

I met

Mis.	280–26	*I* met the class to answer some

I might

My.	163–18	that *I* might find retirement

I miss

Po.	3– 3	*I* miss thee as the flower

I mistake

My.	229– 2	unless *I* mistake their calling.

I modify

Mis.	67–29	*I* modify my affirmative answer.

I must

Mis.	58–17	*I* must spiritually understand them
	105–18	*I* must ever follow this line
	274– 6	*I* must stop teaching at present.
	307–20	*I* must stand on this absolute
Ret.	34– 1	*I* must know more of the
	38– 8	*I* must insert in my last chapter
My.	123– 4	*I* must continue to prize love
	194–24	*I* must decline to receive that

I must not

Mis.	301–16	*I* must not leave persistent
My.	163–10	*I* must not allow myself the

I name

My.	106– 7	*I* name those mentioned above

I named

Ret.	25–10	*I* named it *Christian*, because
	25–12	*I* named *mortal mind*.
My.	353–15	the next *I* named *Monitor*,

individual

Mis.	266–11	this *i·* is doing the work that
'01.	21–15	an *i·* who loves God and man ;
My.	116–18	the truth regarding an *i·*

I need

Po.	24–14	Is all *I* need to comfort mine.
My.	137–30	to select the Trustees *I* need
	234– 8	*I* need every hour wherein to

I need not

My.	130–24	But *I* need not say this
	200–19	*I* need not say this to you,

I neglect

Mis.	351– 5	The fact is, . . . *I* neglect myself.

I never

Mis.	87–19	*I* never commission any one to
	91–24	*I* never dreamed, until informed
	94– 3	*I* never knew a person who
	239– 3	*I* never was in better health.
	292–28	*I* never knew a student who
	349–28	*I* never received more than
	351– 5	*I* never have practised by
	374–20	*I* never looked on my ideal of
	379–13	*I* never heard him say that
'00.	10–24	from a person *I* never saw.
'02.	2–26	*I* never left the Church,
	15– 2	yet *I* never lost my faith
My.	9–24	*I* never before felt poor in
	311–23	*I* never doubted the veracity
	313–21	*I* never was especially interested,
	313–24	*I* never went into a trance

I noticed

My.	307–10	*I* noticed he used that word,

Eddy

I now
Mis.	13– 9	This law *I* now urge upon the
	158–25	completion (as *I* now think)
	273– 6	*I* now seem to be most needed,
	311–19	As *I* now understand C. S.,
No.	9–19	*I* now point steadfastly to the
My.	240–15	*I* now repeat another proof,
	280–16	*I* now request that the members

instructor
Pul.	58–24	* their prime *i·* has ordained

I obeyed
No.	3–11	*I* obeyed a diviner rule.

I objected
Mis.	349–13	*I* objected on the ground that

I observed
Mis.	239–11	*I* observed a carriage

I offer
Mis.	242–19	*I* offer him three thousand dollars

I often
Mis.	159–14	*I* often retreat, sit silently,

I omitted
My.	184–13	so occupied that *I* omitted

I once
Mis.	138–17	*I* once thought that in unity
	195–25	*I* once believed that
	278–13	*I* once wondered at the Scriptural

I opened
Mis.	274– 3	when *I* opened my College.

I ordained
Mis.	382–32	*I* ordained that the Bible,

I ordered
Mis.	285– 3	pamphlets *I* ordered to be laid away

I ought
My.	224– 6	knowing a little, as *I* ought,

I owe
My.	9–26	for the amount *I* owe you,

I paid
Pul.	20– 4	therefore *I* paid it,

I performed
Mis.	242–14	*I* performed more difficult tasks

I ponder
Po.	33–17	'Twill be sweet when *I* ponder

I practise
My.	220–12	*I* practise and teach this

I practised
My.	204–20	*I* practised gratuitously
	271– 6	*I* practised its precepts,

I pray
Mis.	144–29	*I* pray that divine Love,
	151–19	*I* pray thee as a Christian Scientist,
	276–24	*I* pray that all my students
My.	167–11	*I* pray that heaven's messages of
	220–15	*I* pray for the pacification of
	220–21	Each day *I* pray : "God bless my

I prayed
Ret.	13–21	*I* prayed ; and a soft glow of
My.	283–10	Many years have *I* prayed and labored

I preached
Mis.	349–23	*I* preached four years,
	349–28	each Sunday when *I* preached.
	349–29	contributions, when *I* preached,
'02.	15– 2	the hall where *I* preached ;

I predict
Pul.	22–10	*I* predict that in the twentieth century

I prefer
Un.	32–16	which *I* prefer to call *mortal mind.*
Rud.	2–14	*I* prefer to retain the proper sense of
My.	249–22	The report that *I* prefer to have a

I prescribed
My.	345–16	*I* prescribed pellets without any

I present
My.	216–19	which *I* present to your thought,

I presented
Mis.	153–23	to whom *I* presented a copy of

I proceeded
My.	318–21	As *I* proceeded, Mr. Wiggin

I proposed
Mis.	156–13	*I* proposed to merge the
My.	145– 4	*I* proposed to one of

I published
Rud.	16–20	a work which *I* published in 1875.
'01.	24–21	when *I* published my work S. and H.,

I query
My.	299–17	*I* query : Do Christians, who believe

I quickly saw
Mis.	49– 2	*I* quickly saw, had a tendency to

I quieted
My.	317–20	*I* quieted him by quoting

I reach
Mis.	143– 8	*I* reach out my hand to clasp yours,
Un.	49–11	*I* reach, in thought,

I read
Mis.	24–11	As *I* read, the healing Truth
	58–13	*I* read the inspired page
	132–26	*I* read in your article these words:

Eddy

I read
Mis.	379– 5	*I* read the copy in his presence,
My.	230–18	*I* read with pleasure your approval

I realized
Mis.	281–27	*I* realized what a responsibility

I rebuke
Mis.	277–32	*I* rebuke it wherever I see it.

I recall
Ret.	14–14	*I* recall what followed.
Pul.	7– 7	Yet when *I* recall the past,

I receive
'02.	13–10	*I* receive no personal benefit

I received
Mis.	x–24	*I* received from the Daughters of
	137–10	*I* received no reply.
Ret.	10– 9	*I* received lessons in the ancient
'00.	10–23	*I* received a touching token
My.	182– 4	*I* received from the Congregational Church
	259– 6	*I* received the following cabled

I recognize
Mis.	102–15	*I* recognize the loving, divine
My.	326–19	*I* recognize the divine hand

I recollect
My.	309–13	as *I* recollect it, he was justice of

I recommend
Mis.	120–20	*I* recommend that this Association
	131–16	*I* recommend that you waive the
	136–22	*I* recommend that the June session
	139– 1	*I* recommend this honorable body
	302–32	*I* recommend that students stay
Man.	92– 7	*I* recommend that each member
Ret.	78–11	*I* recommend students not to
No.	7–21	*I* recommend that Scientists draw no
My.	219–29	*I* recommend, if the law demand,
	237–23	*I* recommend its careful study to all
	354– 5	*I* recommend nothing but what is

I recommended
Ret.	44–23	*I* recommended that the church

I reconstructed
Pul.	20–10	In 1895 *I* reconstructed my

I redeemed
Mis.	140–20	*I* redeemed from under mortgage.
'02.	14– 2	the land when *I* redeemed it.

I refer
My.	292–20	*I* refer to the effect of one

I refuse
My.	302–24	and *I* refuse adulation.

I regard
My.	302–20	*I* regard self-deification as

I regarded
Ret.	20–11	my home *I* regarded as very

I regret
My.	245–11	*I* regret to say,

I reiterate
'01.	8– 2	*I* reiterate this cardinal point :

I rejoice
Mis.	279– 6	*I* rejoice with those who rejoice,
'01.	14–28	*I* rejoice in the scientific
'02.	3– 7	*I* rejoice that the President
My.	183–18	*Brethren :*— *I* rejoice with you ;
	199– 3	BRETHREN :— *I* rejoice with thee.
	285– 7	*I* rejoice with you in all your wise
	362– 4	*I* rejoice with you in the victory of

I relinquished
'01.	24–29	*I* relinquished the form to attain

I remain
My.	108–28	*I* remain steadfast in St. Paul's faith.
	138–21	*I* remain most respectfully yours,
	175–25	must remain so long as *I* remain.

I remember
Mis.	137– 9	*I* remember my regret,
	237–23	*I* remember, when a girl,
Ret.	1– 8	*I* remember reading, in my childhood,
	6– 6	My childhood's home *I* remember as
My.	313–11	Nor do *I* remember any such stuff

I removed
Mis.	69–19	*I* removed the stoppage,
My.	163–17	*I* removed from Boston in 1889

I repeat
Mis.	135– 2	*I* repeat, person is not in the
My.	170–30	*I* repeat to these dear members
	285–20	In the words of St. Paul, *I* repeat :

I repeatedly
Ret.	8– 4	*I* repeatedly heard a voice,

I replied
Mis.	180– 9	"Christ never left," *I* replied ;
Ret.	14–24	*I* replied that I could only answer

I reply
Mis.	353– 7	*I* reply, The human concept is
My.	251– 5	*I* reply to the following question

I request
Mis.	133– 7	*I* request you to read my sermons
My.	216–21	*I* request that from this date
	236–24	*I* request the Christian Scientists

Eddy

I request
  My. 279–22 I request that every member of The
  280–28 In no way nor manner did *I* request
I requested
  Mis. 158– 5 When *I* requested you to be
I respect
  Mis. 223–11 I respect that moral sense which
  My. 163–27 I respect their religious beliefs,
I respectfully
  My. 224– 5 I respectfully call your attention to
I rest
  My. 250–25 I rest peacefully in knowing that
I retain
  '02. 14– 3 only interest *I* retain in this property
I retire
  Mis. 133–22 I retire to seek the divine blessing
I retired
  Mis. 136– 1 I retired from the field of labor,
I return
  My. 259–12 I return my heart's wireless love.
I returned
  Ret. 19–16 A month later *I* returned
  My. 165– 7 I returned blessing for cursing.
  215–12 I returned this money
  330–28 I returned to New Hampshire,
I reverence
  Mis. 96–20 I reverence and adore Christ
I revised
  No. 3– 8 When *I* revised "S. and H.
I rose
  Mis. 24–13 I rose, dressed myself,
  Ret. 13–22 I rose and dressed myself.
  '02. 15–24 I rose and recorded the
I said
  Mis. 159–23 what *I* said in 1890 :
  180–11 I said, in the words of
  380–22 I said, "Suffer it to be so— *Matt.* 3 : 15.
  Hea. 6– 9 misinterpreted, and *I* said it.
  My. 229–25 That which *I* said in my heart
  240–11 June 10, 1906, when *I* said,
  307– 1 words that *I* said to him,
  307–21 and understood what *I* said
  318–30 "Now, Mr. Wiggin," *I* said,
I sat
  Ret. 8–14 I sat in a little chair by her
I saw
  Mis. 156–14 because *I* saw no advantage,
  267–10 when *I* saw an opportunity
  Ret. 44–19 I saw that the crisis had come
  45–21 I saw these fruits of Spirit,
  Hea. 6–11 I saw the impossibility,
  6–15 I saw how the mind's ideals
I say
  Mis. 12– 1 *Because* I thus feel, *I say*
  249– 4 I say with tearful thanks,
  282–15 I say, When you enter
  298–26 I say, You mistake ;
  321–26 I say, Do not expect me.
  Un. 11–28 I say, Look up,
  17– 4 I say, Be allied to the
  '01. 29–11 I say this not because reformers
  '02. 19–11 I say it with joy,
  My. 131–31 I say with the consciousness of
  216–12 I say : The purpose of God
  344–25 "I say, 'Render to Caesar— *Mark* 12 : 17.
  344–29 I say : Where vaccination is
  361– 5 All *I* say is stated in C. S.
I see
  Mis. 277–32 I rebuke it wherever *I* see it.
  347–19 I see the way now.
  397– 6 I see Christ walk,
  Ret. 50–23 I see clearly that students
  Un. 49– 8 the more *I* see it to be sinless,
  Pul. 18–15 I see Christ walk,
  Rud. 16–11 but *I* see that some novices,
  '00. 5–14 I see no other way
  Po. 12–15 I see Christ walk,
  17– 3 and rest till *I* see
  My. 216–30 I see that you should begin now
I seek
  My. 118–13 hence *I* seek to be
I seldom
  My. 215– 8 I seldom taught without having
  313–19 but *I* seldom took one.
I selected
  My. 137–27 I selected said Trustees because
I send
  Mis. 142–23 So *I* send my answer in a
  My. 159– 7 Sitting at his feet, *I* send
  197–26 I send loving congratulations,
  253–23 I send with this a store of wisdom
  326–12 I send for publication in our
I sent
  Ret. 52–23 June, 1889, *I* sent a letter,

Eddy

I set to work
  Ret. 38–10 I set to work, contrary to my
I shall
  Mis. 95–12 I shall confine myself to questions
  132– 3 I shall take this as a favorable
  155–25 I shall be apt to forward their
  256–18 I shall continue to send to each
  263– 2 I shall have the unselfish joy
  278– 6 I shall fulfil my mission,
  316– 8 I shall speak . . . very seldom.
  322– 8 when *I* shall be present
  No. 46–22 I shall continue to labor and wait.
  '01. 27–15 I shall rejoice in being informed
  '02. 4–21 I shall briefly consider these two
  20–20 I shall be the loser by this change,
  My. 25–21 I shall be with my blessed church
  147–25 I shall be with you personally
  154– 7 I shall scarcely venture to send
  177–11 I shall then be even younger
  200–29 For this *I* shall continue to pray.
  240–20 I shall refer to this.
  347–20 I shall treasure my loving-cup
  358–19 I shall devote it to a worthy
I shall not
  Mis. 222–29 I shall not forget the cost of
  My. 131–18 I hope I shall not be found disorderly
I should
  Mis. 19–20 I should have more faith in an
  133–20 I should feel a delicacy in
  146– 8 I should need to be with you.
  242–11 if *I* should accept his bid on
  273–28 if *I* should teach that Primary class,
  302–22 When *I* should so elect
  311–22 I should lose my hope of heaven.
  Pul. 1–18 what need that *I* should be present
  2– 1 I should be much like the Queen of
  '02. 15–15 as to what *I* should write,
  My. 115– 4 I should blush to write of
  249–27 I should prefer that student who is
  297– 3 I should shrink from such salient
  307–23 I should still think that it was
  319– 2 I should still know that
  344–19 I should think myself in danger of
  344–27 I should tremble for mankind ;
I should not
  '01. 21–26 I should not have known
  My. 318–18 on condition that *I* should not ask
I showed
  '02. 15–26 I showed it to my literary friends,
I shrank
  Ret. 50– 8 I shrank from asking it,
I shuddered
  Mis. 180–12 I shuddered at her material
I smiled
  Hea. 6– 4 pardon me if *I* smiled.
I sometimes
  '00. 8–29 I sometimes advise students not to
  9– 3 I sometimes withdraw that advice
I sought
  Mis. 372–13 I sought the judgment of
  Ret. 33– 7 I sought knowledge from the
  34– 5 If *I* sought an answer from the
  My. 142–12 I sought God's guidance
  348– 5 I sought this cause, not within but
I speak
  Mis. 266–20 I speak of them as I feel,
  My. 107– 9 Here *I* speak from experience.
I specially desire
  Mis. 148–25 I specially desire that you
I spoke
  Mis. 312– 1 sorry that *I* spoke at all,
I stand
  Mis. 158–20 I stand with sandals on and staff
  347–16 Between the two *I* stand still;
  392– 2 at whose feet *I* stand,
  Po. 20– 2 at whose feet *I* stand,
  My. 302–18 I stand in relation to this century
I started
  Mis. 139–15 April, 1883, *I* started the *Journal*
  Ret. 38–16 I started for Boston
  52–20 I started it, April, 1883,
  My. 304–16 I started *The C. S. Journal*,
I still
  My. 302–17 I still must think the name is not
  305–22 I still wait at the cross
  316– 4 I still hear the harvest song
I stood
  Ret. 30– 1 I stood alone in this conflict,
  My. 247–14 when *I* stood silently beside it,
  247–16 to the rim where *I* stood.
I stopped him
  My. 318–29 but *I* stopped him.
I stoutly
  Ret. 14–14 I stoutly maintained that

Eddy

I strove
'00.   9–27   *I* strove earnestly to fit others
I struggled
'02.   15– 8   *I* struggled on through many
I submit
My.   26–19   enclosed notice *I* submit to you,
      299–10   *I* submit that C. S. has
I suggest
'02.   14– 6   *I* suggest as a motto for every
My. 236–14   the one which *I* suggest,
I suggested
Ret.   52–11   *I* suggested to my students,
My. 236– 5   *I* suggested the name
I supposed
Mis.   91–28   *I* supposed that students had
      140–12   *I* supposed the trustee-deed
I sympathize
My. 151– 4   Because *I* sympathize with
      295– 1   *I* sympathize with those who
I take
Mis.   xii– 5   *I* take my pen and
      231– 8   *I* take no stock in spirit-rappings
      248–16   That *I* take opium ; . . . is not
      262–29   *I* take so much pleasure in
I talk
Mis. 159–22   Here *I* talk once a year,
I taught
Mis.   11– 8   if *I* taught indigent students
      29–15   *I* taught the first student
      382–14   *I* taught the first student
Ret.   36– 5   *I* taught the Science of
'02.   15– 8   indigent students that *I* taught
My. 182–11   In 1884, *I* taught a class
I teach
Mis. 247– 7   in just what *I* teach.
      350–28   *I* teach the use of such
Un.   9–25   healing, as *I* teach it,
No.   10–11   postulate of all that *I* teach,
I temporarily
Mis. 350– 3   *I* temporarily organized a
I thank
Mis. 262–13   *I* thank you, my dear students,
      308–18   *I* thank you, each and all,
      313–12   *I* thank the contributors to *The*
My.   6–16   *I* thank you for this proof of your
      142–26   *I* thank you for your kind
      159–10   *I* thank God who hath sent forth His
      174–10   *I* thank the distinguished editors
      197–20   *I* thank divine Love for the hope
      201–12   *I* thank you out of a full heart.
      202–21   *I* thank you for the words of cheer
      253–11   *Brethren :* — *I* thank you.
      254–13   *I* thank the faithful teacher
      270–21   *I* thank God that for the
      282–21   Deeply do *I* thank you for the
      295–16   *I* thank you for it.
      298– 8   *I* thank Miss Wilbur and the Concord
      341– 3   *I* thank God that He has
      352–20   *I* thank you not only for your
      357–29   *I* thank you for acknowledging me as
      358–18   *I* thank you for the money
I then left
Ret.   8–21   *I* then left the room,
I then withdrew
Ret.   24–22   *I* then withdrew from society
I think
Pul.   74–20   "*I* think Mrs. Lathrop was not
Po.   3– 6   *I* think of thee, *I* think of thee !
My. 133– 3   *I* think of this in the great light of
      163–15   which *I* think do them more good.
      171–10   *I* think you would enjoy seeing it.
I thought
Mis.   11– 7   *I* thought, also, that if *I*
Ret.   8– 5   *I* thought this was my mother's
My.   26–16   *I* thought it better to be brief
I thus feel
Mis.   12– 1   *Because I* thus feel, I say to
I thus speak
Un.   7– 6   though *I* thus speak, and from my
I took
Mis. 139–30   *I* took care that the provisions for
      248–24   prescribed morphine, which *I* took,
My. 313–19   when *I* took an evening walk,
I touch
No.   32–11   when *I* touch this subject
I tread
Mis. 395–17   The turf, whereon *I* tread,
Po.   58– 2   The turf, whereon *I* tread,
I treasure
My. 184–16   *I* treasure it next to your
I tried
Mis. 348–26   *I* tried several doses of medicine,
I trow
Mis. 395– 8   And yet *I* trow,
Po.   57–15   And yet *I* trow,

Eddy

I trow
My.   20– 8   *I* trow you are awaiting
I trust
My. 167–27   will, *I* trust, never be marred
      275–13   (and *I* trust the desire thereof)
I try
Un.   45–15   *I* try to show its all-pervading
I turn
Mis. 133–27   *I* turn constantly to divine Love
I understand
Mis.   34–14   so far as *I* understand it,
      95–15   *I* understand the impossibility of
      96– 3   *I* understand that God is an
      141–16   I believe, — yea, *I* understand,
Ret.   29– 1   As *I* understand it, spiritualism is the
Un.   49– 2   *I* understand that man is as
      49– 8   *I* understand true humanhood,
My.   13–16   *I* understand that the members
      146– 6   because *I* understand it,
      313– 1   is, *I* understand, a paraphrase
I unite
Ret.   14–12   never could *I* unite with the
I unveil
Un.   45–14   This pantheism *I* unveil.
I urge
Mis.   75– 8   *I* urge this fundamental fact
Un.   43–18   *I* urge Christians to have more faith
I use
Mis. 348–18   *I* use no drugs whatever,
Pul.   5– 3   adoration in the words *I* use,
I used to think
Mis.   11– 4   *I* used to think it sufficiently just
I've
Mis. vii–19   Wherefore, *I've* more to glory,
Po.   18– 1   *I've* watched in the azure
I vindicate
Mis. 141–15   *I* vindicate both the law of God
No.   2– 1   only Mind-healing *I* vindicate ;
I visited
Mis. 112–15   *I* visited in his cell the
My. 185–22   *I* visited these mountains
I waited
'02.   15–21   Six weeks *I* waited on God
Hea.   14–22   *I* waited many years for a
I wandered
Ret.   33– 5   *I* wandered through the dim mazes
I want
'00.   11–17   *I* want not only quality,
I wanted
Mis. 348–24   *I* wanted to satisfy my curiosity
My. 138–2   *I* wanted it protected
I warn
Mis. 309–18   *I* warn students against
I was
Mis.   69–14   *I* was once called to visit a
      180– 4   *I* was delivered from the dark shadow
      223– 2   *I* was saying all the time,
      249–20   The report that *I* was dead
      311–26   *I* was a scribe under orders ;
      313–14   *I* was impressed by the articles
      349–15   *I* was willing, and said so,
Ret.   2–27   *I* was fond of listening,
      5– 6   at Bow *I* was born,
      8– 3   when *I* was about eight years old,
      9–12   *I* was afraid, and did not answer.
      10– 4   *I* was as familiar with
      11– 1   *I* was a verse-maker.
      13– 1   *I* was admitted to the Congregational
      13– 6   *I* was unwilling to be saved, if
      13–20   as *I* was wont to do,
      14– 4   *I* was of course present.
      14–10   *I* was ready for his doleful questions,
      14–15   *I* was willing to trust God,
      15–13   *I* was called to preach in Boston
      19– 1   *I* was united to my first husband,
      20–22   *I* was compelled to ask for a bill of
      21– 4   *I* was then informed that my son
      23–15   *I* was waiting and watching ;
      25– 4   questions as to how *I* was healed ;
      31– 9   *I* was impelled, by a hunger
      33– 6   *I* was weary of "scientific
      40– 4   *I* was called to speak before the
      44–10   When *I* was its pastor,
      46– 1   Lines penned when *I* was pastor of
      48– 2   *I* was yearning for retirement.
      50– 4   *I* was led to name three hundred
Pul.   34–28   by which *I* was restored to health ;
'00.   11– 5   Once *I* was passionately fond of
'01.   26–26   *I* was not drawn to them by
Hea.   6– 3   *I* was told the other day,
My. 105–19   *I* was wired to attend the patient of
      115– 6   *I* was only a scribe echoing the
      127–16   when *I* was in practice,
      169–17   *I* was happy to receive at Concord,
      169–19   *I* was rejoiced at the appropriate

Eddy

I was
My.	174–23	*I* was a member of the Congregational
	184–12	came when *I* was so occupied that
	214–21	*I* was confronted with the fact that
	215– 2	*I* was above begging
	304– 3	*I* was early a pupil of
	306–29	while *I* was his patient in Portland
	307–16	*I* was a staunch orthodox,
	307–26	*I* was gradually emerging from
	310– 5	*I* was privately tutored by him.
	311– 3	*I* was living with Dr. Patterson
	311–25	When *I* was last in Washington,
	311–31	*I* was called by the
	312–21	*I* was with him on this trip.
	312–23	*I* was surrounded by friends,
	313–15	to help me when *I* was ill.
	313–16	*I* was never "given to long and
	313–17	*I* was always accompanied by
	313–29	*I* was obliged to be parted from
	314– 7	When *I* was married to him,
	314–25	*I* was also the means of
	343–20	*I* was the mother,
	345–12	*I* was a sickly child.
	345–13	*I* was dosed with drugs until
	348– 8	Then *I* was healed.

I was not
Mis.	148–23	*I* was not aware that the
My.	313–20	*I* was not a medium for spirits.

I watch
Po.	3– 8	*I* watch thy chair, and wish

I ween
Mis.	393– 6	Paints the limner's work, *I* ween,
Po.	51–11	Paints the limner's work, *I* ween,

I welcome
My.	154–23	*I* welcome the means and methods,

I went
Ret.	13–19	if *I* went to Him in prayer,
	19– 5	*I* went with him to the South ;
	40– 8	*I* went to the invalid's house.

I wept
Ret.	9–12	*I* wept, and prayed that God would

I were
Mis.	146–20	if *I* were, I would gather every
	312– 1	wished *I* were wise enough to

I will
Mis.	33– 1	*I* will say : It is the righteous
	69–27	*I* will send his address to any one
	104–29	*I* will love, if another hates.
	104–30	*I* will gain a balance on the side of
	158– 2	In reply to your letter *I* will say :
	349–22	*I* will state that I preached
	398– 1	*I* will listen for Thy voice,
	398– 3	*I* will follow and rejoice
Ret.	46– 7	*I* will listen for Thy voice,
	46– 9	*I* will follow and rejoice
Un.	48– 3	yet ask, and *I* will answer.
Pul.	17– 6	*I* will listen for Thy voice,
	17– 8	*I* will follow and rejoice
Po.	14– 5	*I* will listen for Thy voice,
	14– 7	*I* will follow and rejoice
My.	107– 7	*I* will cite a modern phase of
	123–19	Ere long *I* will see you in this hall,
	142–28	*I* will attend the meeting,
	146– 2	*I* will say : It is understood by all
	214–18	In reply . . . *I* will say :
	277– 6	*I* will say I can see no other way
	297– 6	*I* will say, Amen, so be it.
	310–18	*I* will say that there was never a
	311– 1	*I* will relate the following incident,
	355– 9	*I* will repeat that men are very

I wish
Hea.	7–23	*I* wish the age was up to his
My.	131–19	*I* wish to say briefly that this meeting

I wished
Mis.	178–27	*I* wished to be excused from

I withdraw
Mis.	273– 7	*I* withdraw from an overwhelming

I wonder
Pul.	7– 9	*I* wonder whether, were our dear

I worship
Mis.	96–10	*I* worship that of which
	96–15	divine Principle, — which *I* worship ;
Ret.	17– 5	while *I* worship in deep sylvan spot,
Po.	62– 5	while *I* worship in deep sylvan spot,

I would
Mis.	11–31	*I* would enjoy taking by the hand
	32–19	*I* would gladly do my best towards
	146–21	*I* would gather every reformed mortal
	291–19	*I* would part with a blessing
	311– 6	*I* would extend a tender invitation
	311–19	*I* would as soon harm myself as
	317– 9	dear ones whom *I* would have
	335–27	*I* would have you already out,
	349–24	before *I* would accept the slightest
	350–11	which *I* would hesitate to

Eddy

I would
Mis.	351– 8	and I could not if *I* would,
	392–23	Scenes that *I* would see again.
Ret.	5–15	I cannot speak as *I* would,
	8– 9	Then *I* would say,
Pan.	9–19	*I* would kiss the feet of such a
'01.	17–20	*I* would put patients into the
Po.	15–14	*I* would live in their empire,
	51– 5	Scenes that *I* would see again.
My.	166–17	she nor *I* would be practising
	170–14	*I* would present a gift
	175– 1	*I* would love to be with you
	244– 4	to whom *I* would gladly give it
	270–28	*I* would no more quarrel with
	270–29	than *I* would because of his art.
	301– 9	*I* would that all the churches
	306–25	I advertised that *I* would pay
	345–14	doctors said *I* would live if

I would not
Mis.	280– 9	*I* would not weigh you,
Ret.	27–11	which *I* would not have effaced.
My.	219–18	*I* would not charge Christians

I write
Pan.	14– 4	Once more *I* write,
Po.	32–12	inspires my pen as *I* write ;
My.	258–32	To the children . . . *I* write :

I wrote
Ret.	27– 1	*I* wrote also, at this period,
My.	114–17	What *I* wrote had a strange
	146–21	what *I* wrote is true,
	215– 6	*I* wrote "S. and H. with Key to
	237– 5	What *I* wrote on C. S.
	271– 4	When *I* wrote "S. and H.
	304–11	for many years *I* wrote
	343–17	In 1875 *I* wrote my book.
	343–28	*I* wrote to each church

I yearned
My.	214–24	which *I* yearned to do,

I yielded
Ret.	38– 7	*I* yielded to a constant conviction

lady
My.	271–15	* This *l·* with sweet smile and
	320– 9	* regard for you as a Christian *l·*,
	331–21	* and his bereaved *l·*,
	342– 3	* *l·* slowly descending the stairs.

Leader
Mis.	159–22	and to their lone *L·*.
Man.	37–19	loyal to their *L·* and to the
	42– 8	his duty to God, to his *L·*, and
	42–26	malpractises upon or treats our *L·*
	54– 1	injurious, to C. S. or to its *L·*,
	54–21	to or of the *L·* and Pastor Emeritus,
	65– 1	and to substitute *L·*,
	67–24	Opportunity for Serving the *L·*.
	68–10	Members thus serving the *L·*
	69– 1	to the home of their *L·*,
	69– 6	has been called to serve our *L·*
	72–20	her place as the head or *L·*
Pul.	44– 2	* "*Dear Teacher, L·, Guide :* — 'Laus Deo,
	49– 3	* consider her their spiritual *L·*
	71–17	* the acknowledged C. S. *L·*,
	84–28	* our beloved teacher and *L·*,
	86–17	* *our Beloved Teacher and L·:*
'01.	34–25	follow your *L·* only so far as she
'02.	4– 3	Follow your *L·*, only so far as she
My.	vi–15	* its guide, guardian, *L·*,
	vii– 4	* can never do for its *L·*
	vii– 4	* what its *L·* has done for
	vii– 7	* not . . . to deprive their *L·* of
	vii–14	* service which . . . can render their *L·*.
	6–20	The room of your *L·* remains
	8–27	* *L·* of our religious denomination
	11– 4	* *L·* of this movement,
	20– 9	awaiting on behalf of your *L·*
	22– 3	* our *L·* saw the need of a larger
	22–15	* our beloved *L·* and teacher,
	22–25	* our Pastor Emeritus and *L·*,
	23–17	* *Beloved Teacher and L·:*
	28– 3	* Our *L·* has said in S. and H.
	36– 1	* Message from their teacher and *L·*,
	36– 8	* *Beloved Teacher and L·:*
	40–24	* Our *L·*, Mrs. Eddy, has presented
	40–32	* our *L·* has induced a multitude
	41–27	* Our *L·* and teacher not only
	42– 6	* faithful follower of this *L·*
	42–27	* inaugurated by our beloved *L·*,
	43–22	* revealed to our beloved *L·*
	44– 9	* counsel of our ever faithful *L·*.
	44–17	* forwarded at once to our *L·*,
	44–23	* *Beloved Teacher and L·:*
	50–10	* guided by their dauntless *L·*
	58–19	* our revered *L·* and teacher,
	60–25	* *Dear L· and Guide :*
	62–19	* *Beloved L· and Teacher:*
	64– 2	* achievements of our beloved *L·*

Eddy

Leader

My.	64– 9	* it is because our *L·* has made the
	129–28	Lean not too much on your *L·*.
	134–26	* been secured from our beloved *L·*
	139– 2	Rest assured that your *L·*
	143– 3	your *L·* will then be sure
	157– 3	* "Beloved Teacher and *L·* :
	170– 4	might see the *L·* of C. S.
	207– 7	* *Beloved L· :* — The representatives
	210– 1	chapter sub-title
	241–17	* instruction from their *L·*
	244– 1	unity with your *L·*.
	254–17	* *Dear L· :* — May we have permission
	256–12	to send to your *L·*.
	271–17	* Founder and *L·* of C. S.,
	273– 6	* being able to point to a *L·*
	280– 3	* *Beloved L· :* — We acknowledge
	302–20	Discoverer, Founder, and *L·*.
	308–14	and the *L·* of C. S.
	315–29	beloved *L·* of millions of
	316–16	defence of our Cause and its *L·*.
	323–21	* giving this age such a *L·*
	325–15	* Command me . . . beloved *L·*.
	326– 2	* enclosures received from our *L·*
	327–11	* *Beloved L· :* — I know the enclosed
	328– 1	* as lived by our dear, dear *L·*,
	351– 1	* chapter sub-title
	352– 4	* *Beloved L· :* — Informally assembled,
	357–30	acknowledging me as your *L·*,
	358– 2	true following of their *L·* ;
	358–11	cannot separate you from your *L·*
	358–25	Lovingly your teacher and *L·*,
	359– 6	My province as a *L·*
	361– 7	do not bring your *L·* into
	361–19	* *Beloved L· :* — We rejoice that
	362–12	* *L·, Counsellor, and Friend :*

leader

Mis.	266– 9	true *l·* of a true cause
My.	116– 8	personality of its *l·*.
	116–18	regarding an individual or *l·*,
	117– 7	whereas helping a *l·*
	117– 8	and giving this *l·* time

Leader's

Mis.	129–22	*L·* precepts and example !
Man.	59–15	The *L·* Welcome.
My.	9–18	chapter sub-title
	155–29	blossoms in their *L·* love,
	341–10	your *L·* Spring greeting,
	351– 2	* With our *L·* kind permission,

Mary

My.	119–15	*M·* of to-day looks up for Christ,

me

Mis.	x– 4	for *m·* to comply with an
	x–19	caused *m·*, as an author,
	xi– 3	caused *m·* to retain the initial "G"
	11–27	general good to such as hate *m·*,
	11–28	since they permit *m·* no other way,
	11–31	all who love *m·* not,
	13– 3	so far as one and all permit *m·* to
	13– 8	wrought out for *m·* the law of
	16–27	pause for a moment with *m·*,
	19–22	more faith in an honest . . . healing *m·*,
	24– 5	came to *m·* in an hour of great need ;
	29–21	Daily letters inform *m·* that a
	38–16	Metaphysics, as taught by *m·* at the
	48–11	enough for *m·* to know that
	74–30	If you will admit, with *m·*,
	94– 4	to understand *m·*, or himself.
	95–11	the time so kindly allotted *m·*
	96–13	God becomes to *m·*,
	96–18	this atonement becomes more to *m·*
	102– 5	a theory to *m·* inconceivable.
	104–31	gives *m·* the forces of God
	109– 4	who take *m·* as authority for
	111–27	Let *m·* specially call the attention
	112–21	The jailer thanked *m·*, and said,
	117–18	difficult for *m·* to carry out a
	132–30	inspire *m·* with the hope
	133– 3	when referring to *m·*,
	133–28	It affords *m·* great joy to be able to
	135– 8	not one . . . can be separated from *m·* ;
	135–28	You may be looking to see *m·*
	136–12	seem to you as to *m·*,
	136–19	can well afford to give *m·* up,
	142–13	Let *m·* write to the donors,
	142–30	nor you with *m·* in C. S.,
	143–18	It gives *m·* great pleasure to **say**
	143–25	A quiet call from *m·* for this
	145–32	let *m·* say, 'T is sweet to
	149–19	the joy you give *m·*
	149–21	to send him to aid *m·*.
	155–25	when they address *m·* I shall be apt
	157–26	Write *m·* when you need *m·*,
	180– 6	beholding *m·* restored to health.
	180– 7	A dear old lady asked *m·*,
	180–11	person, more material, met *m·*,
	180–16	it speaks to *m·* of Life,
	193–19	when critics attacked *m·*
	195–29	given *m·* a higher sense
	203–12	in their course to call on *m·*,
	207– 3	drink with *m·* the living waters
	223– 2	mystery of error . . . at first defied *m·*.
	239– 1	let *m·* say to you, dear reader :
	242– 5	offered *m·*, as President of
	247– 7	those who know *m·*, know that
	248–11	falsehoods uttered about *m·*
	248–25	he could do no more for *m·*.
	248–26	revelations of C. S. saved *m·*
	248–27	and made *m·* well,
	249– 5	drug had no effect upon *m·*
	249–22	combined efforts . . . to kill *m·* :
	249–24	will never leave *m·* comfortless,
	253– 8	platform is not broad enough for *m·*,
	256–11	imposes on *m·* the severe task of
	262–28	little need of . . . encouragement from *m·*.
	262–28	Perhaps it is even selfish in *m·*
	265– 1	and gives *m·* as authority for it ;
	266– 7	may represent *m·* as doing it ;
	266– 8	but he mistakes *m·*,
	266–22	They are essentially dear to *m·*,
	267– 7	whose chief aim is to injure *m·*,
	267– 8	caused *m·* to exercise most patience.
	267– 9	When they report *m·* as
	267–13	secretly striving to injure *m·*.
	273–24	lying on the desk before *m·*,
	274– 3	This point, . . . had not impressed *m·*
	274– 7	which God calls *m·* to
	275–22	satisfaction that you afforded *m·*
	275–25	moved *m·* to speechless thanks.
	278– 1	vision of the . . . is before *m·*.
	278– 4	my peace returns unto *m·*.
	278–19	who are absent from *m·*,
	281– 7	fills *m·* with joy.
	281– 8	neither deprive *m·* of something
	281– 8	nor give *m·* anything,
	281–26	but it came to *m·* more clearly
	290–15	A person wrote to *m·*,
	291– 9	is attached to *m·* as authority
	299–10	the following question sent to *m·* ;
	299–22	but you must pay *m·*,
	303–22	oblige *m·* by giving place in your *Journal*
	308– 4	Whosoever looks to *m·* personally
	308–22	mayhap taught *m·* more than
	309– 6	All will agree with *m·* that
	311–19	more than they can love *m·*.
	313– 2	Permit *m·* to say that your editorial
	318–15	from *m·*, or from a loyal student
	319–19	grant *m·* this request,
	319–21	without one gift to *m·*.
	321–27	Do not expect *m·*.
	321–30	that concerns *m·*, and you,
	322– 2	its contemplation with *m·*,
	322– 6	expecting to hear *m·* **speak**
	335–12	One mercilessly assails *m·*
	335–13	others charge upon *m·*
	335–15	neither moves *m·* from
	347–15	Two individuals, . . . advise *m·*.
	347–20	The guardians . . . go before *m·*.
	348–32	A student who consulted *m·*
	349–12	consulted *m·* on the feasibility
	349–26	and refused to give *m·* up
	353– 7	If one asks *m·*, Is my concept of
	353– 9	your human concept of *m·*,
	353–11	People give *m·* too much attention
	373– 9	New Testament was handed to *m·*,
	376–18	burst through the lattice for *m·*,
	380– 9	to enable *m·* to elucidate
	380–11	call for help impelled *m·* to
	380–14	driven *m·* to discover the Science
	380–24	taught *m·* the impossibility of
	389–13	His arm encircles *m·*,
	389–14	O make *m·* glad for every
	392–12	of life, that teacheth *m·*
	397– 7	And come to *m·*, and tenderly,
	397– 9	Thus Truth engrounds *m·*
	397–20	God leadeth *m·*
	397–22	Shepherd, show *m·* how to go
	398–25	And was found by you and *m·*
Chr.	53–35	grace towards you and *m·*,
Ret.	8– 4	a voice, calling *m·* distinctly
	8– 7	to tell *m·* what she wanted.
	8– 9	"Mother, who *did* call *m·*?
	8–17	my cousin turned to *m·*
	8–22	asked her if she had summoned *m·* ?
	9– 1	said that mother wanted *m·*.
	9– 1	she returned with *m·* to
	9– 8	my mother read to *m·*
	9– 9	bade *m·*, when the voice called **again,**
	9–13	prayed that God would forgive *m·*,

Eddy

me

Ret.	9–14	as my mother had bidden *m·*.
	10– 2	kept *m·* much out of school,
	13– 6	predestination, greatly troubled *m·* ;
	13–11	pronounced *m·* stricken with fever.
	13–16	to win *m·* from dreaded heresy.
	13–19	bade *m·* lean on God's love,
	13–19	which would give *m·* rest,
	13–22	ineffable joy came over *m·*.
	14– 2	forever lost its power over *m·*.
	14–18	doubts left *m·* outside the doors.
	14–19	wished *m·* to tell him
	14–23	asked *m·* to say how I felt
	14–24	when the new light dawned within *m·*.
	15– 1	they came and kissed *m·*.
	15– 2	received *m·* into their communion,
	15– 3	and my protest along with *m·*.
	18–20	Oh, give *m·* the spot where
	19– 6	he was spared to *m·* for only
	19–16	helped to support *m·* in this
	20– 3	money I had brought with *m·* ;
	20– 8	was sent away from *m·*,
	20–13	before my child was taken from *m·*,
	20–23	granted *m·* in the city of Salem,
	20–26	he should have a home with *m·*.
	21– 9	came to see *m·* in Massachusetts.
	23– 1	too eventful to leave *m·* undisturbed
	24–14	the falling apple that led *m·* to
	24–17	physician who attended *m·*,
	25– 4	had to *m·* a new meaning,
	26–13	had before seemed to *m·* supernatural,
	27– 9	Science developed itself to *m·*
	27–11	valuable to *m·* as waymarks
	27–29	divine hand led *m·* into a new world
	28–24	It was a mystery to *m·* then,
	30–11	why C. S. was revealed to *m·*
	34– 8	give *m·* one distinct statement of
	36–10	did not originate with *m·*.
	37– 3	the term employed by *m·* to
	38– 2	the printer informed *m·*
	38–15	started for Lynn to see *m·*.
	38–19	come to tell *m·* he wanted more,
	38–20	to find *m· en route* for Boston,
	38–26	circumstances unknown to *m·*.
	40– 6	my hostess told *m·* that
	40–12	they showed *m·* the clothes
	40–13	told *m·* that her physicians
	40–19	The mother afterwards wrote to *m·*,
	40–23	refused *m·* a hearing in their halls
	44– 7	call to *m·* to become their pastor.
	46– 3	Shepherd, show *m·* how to go
	47– 3	caused *m·* to dread the
	47–19	instructions in a Primary class from *m·*,
	48– 2	drew its breath from *m·*,
	48–10	moved *m·* to close my flourishing
	50– 1	impelled *m·* to set a price on
	50– 8	This amount greatly troubled *m·*.
	50–10	God has since shown *m·*,
	73–13	corporeality became less to *m·*
	74– 8	afflicteth *m·* not wittingly :
	74–10	and it cannot think of *m·*.
	81– 5	Nothing . . . can separate them from *m·*.
	81–29	led *m·* to the feet of C. S.,
	87– 7	Experience has taught *m·* that
	90–26	One of my students wrote to *m·* :
Un.	7–10	has not separated *m·* from God,
	7–11	has so bound *m·* to Him as to
	7–11	enable *m·* instantaneously to heal
	9–21	by those who fail to understand *m·*,
	48–12	To *m·* God is All.
	49–10	To *m·* the reality and substance of
	49–24	gives *m·* a clearer right to call evil a
Pul.	2–12	think for a moment with *m·* of
	5– 2	who had publicly proclaimed *m·*
	5–20	his conversation . . . reassured *m·*.
	6–13	wrote to *m·* in 1894,
	6–25	signalled *m·* kindly as my lone bark rose
	17– 2	Shepherd, show *m·* how to go
	18–16	And come to *m·*, and tenderly,
	18–18	Truth engrounds *m·* on the rock,
	19– 4	God leadeth *m·*.
	21–10	Who will unite with *m·*
	35– 1	it came to *m·* with a new meaning,
	74–13	"A despatch is given *m·*,
	74–15	"Even the question shocks *m·*.
	75– 7	But to think or speak of *m·*
	87–14	But permit *m·*, respectfully,
	87–16	make *m·* your *Pastor Emeritus,*
	87–19	when asking *m·* to accept your
Rud.	14–27	course of instruction from *m·*,
No.	31–11	To *m· divine pardon* is
'00.	10–26	soldier who sent to *m·*,
	10–30	send *m·* some of his hard-earned
	11– 1	cost *m·* a tear !
	11– 1	it gave *m·* more pleasure than

Eddy

me

'00.	11– 7	weaned *m·* from this love
	11– 8	wedded *m·* to spiritual music,
	11–15	To *m·* his composition is the triumph
	11–20	human tone has no melody for *m·*.
'01.	21–24	My faith assures *m·* that God
	26–26	allow *m·* to add I have read little of
	28–21	proven to *m·* beyond a doubt
	29–29	students wrote *m·*,
	31–11	Has God entrusted *m·* with a
	31–14	they regard *m·* with no vague,
	31–15	the power that God gives *m·*
	32–17	caused *m·* to love their doctrines.
	35–14	Doth it dawn on you and *m·*?
'02.	2–24	and the Church once loved *m·*.
	12–21	allow *m·* to interpolate some matters
	13–27	land legally conveyed to *m·*,
	14–23	afforded *m·* neither favor nor
	15– 1	anonymous letters mailed to *m·*
	15–11	paid *m·* not one dollar of royalty
	15–23	came to *m·* in the silence of night,
	15–26	advised *m·* to drop both
	15–28	God had led *m·* to write that book,
	15–30	It was to *m·* the "still, — *I Kings* 19 : 12.
	16– 2	brought to *m·* Wyclif's translation
	19–12	no . . . offense against *m·* that I
	20–16	are you ready to join *m·*
	20–21	for it gives *m·* great joy
Hea.	6– 4	pardon *m·* if I smiled.
	6– 9	spiritualists abused *m·* for it then,
	6–11	calling *m·* a medium.
Peo.	7–28	have taught *m·* that the health
Po.	4–12	His arm encircles *m·*,
	4–13	O make *m·* glad for every
	12–16	And come to *m·*, and tenderly,
	12–18	Thus Truth engrounds *m·*
	13– 8	God leadeth *m·*.
	14– 1	Shepherd, show *m·* how to go
	17– 4	in glory still waiting for *m·*.
	19– 3	God's eye is upon *m·*
	20–16	of life, that teacheth *m·*
	24– 1	Come to *m·*, joys of heaven !
	24– 6	To *m·* thou art
	24– 8	Come to *m·*, peace on earth !
	32–21	And cheer *m·* with hope
	33– 5	And bless *m·* with Christ's
	33–19	That waft *m·* away to my God.
	34–16	Blessed compared with *m·*
	35– 1	O take *m·* to thy bower !
	35– 4	To make *m·* love thee
	35–13	bear *m·* through the sky !
	43– 1	*sent m· the picture depictive of*
	64–12	Oh, give *m·* the spot where
	page 65	poem
	65– 1	O sing *m·* that song !
	65–10	sing *m·* "Sweet hour of
	68– 1	So one heart is left *m·*
	74– 2	Think kindly of *m·*,
	74– 4	Smile on *m·* yet,
	75– 5	was found by you and *m·*
	79–14	Love looseth thee, and lifteth *m·*,
My.	7– 4	allow *m·* to interpolate some matters
	13– 6	was presented to *m·* in 1903
	26–21	*the lie that students worship m·*
	27– 4	Divine Love bids *m·* say :
	31– 3	"Shepherd, show *m·* how to go ;"
	105–24	restored by *m·* without material aid,
	105–27	urged *m·* immediately to write a book
	106– 6	The list of cases healed by *m·*
	110–15	remind *m·* of my early dreams of
	114–20	leave *m·* until the rising of the sun.
	114–24	divine power . . . infinitely above *m·*,
	117–31	To give *m·* this opportunity
	118–11	with which you honor *m·*.
	118–12	you would not see *m·*, for
	119–28	you would not see *m·* thus,
	120– 2	Those who look for *m·* in person,
	120– 3, 4	lose *m·* instead of find *m·*.
	120– 7	gratitude for the chance you give *m·*
	120– 9	Bear with *m·* the burden of discovery
	120–10	share with *m·* the bliss of seeing the
	121–17	Christmas ring presented to *m·*
	122–11	tempted *m·* tenderly to be proud !
	123– 2	this church's gifts to *m·* are
	123– 3	To *m·*, however, love is the greater
	123– 8	this encourages *m·* to continue
	130– 8	effort of . . . to blacken *m·* and
	130–12	failed too often for *m·* to fear it.
	131–12	given to *m·* in a little symbol,
	131–20	this meeting is very joyous to *m·*.
	131–22	something suggestive to *m·*
	133–11	will not receive a Message from *m·*
	133–27	my book is not all you know of *m·*.
	134–15	And here let *m·* add :
	135–13	caused *m·* to select a Board of Trustees

Eddy

me

My.	136– 1	enough for you and *m·* to know
	137–21	influenced *m·* to select a Board of Trustees
	137–29	No person influenced *m·* to make
	138– 4	agreed with *m·* to take care of my
	138– 5	a great benefit to *m·* already.
	138–14	ask *m·* to receive persons whom I
	138–20	statements herein made by *m·*,
	142–18	learn this and rejoice with *m·*,
	143–23	do not regard this attack upon *m·* as a
	145– 6	He drew the plan, showed it to *m·*,
	145–11	carpenters' foreman said to *m·* :
	145–21	makes *m·* the servant of the race
	147–30	calling on *m·* for help,
	147–31	You have less need of *m·* than
	148– 1	must not expect *m·* further to do
	154–16	permit *m·* to congratulate this little
	156– 3	allow *m·* to reply in words of
	159– 4	seem to *m·*, and must seem to thee,
	162–12	have demonstrated in gifts to *m·*
	163–22	Here let *m·* add that,
	165–14	presented to *m·* for First Church of
	166–28	gift to *m·* of a beautiful cabinet,
	167–23	Allow *m·* to send forth a pæan
	169– 7	to visit *m·* at a later date,
	172–11	Permit *m·* to present to you
	172–19	your kind, expert call on *m·*."
	172–28	accept from *m·* the accompanying gift
	173– 5	Allow *m·* through your paper to
	173–16	it came to *m·* : Why not invite
	173–21	It was a glad day for *m·*
	174– 9	extended to *m·* throughout.
	174–21	my parents first offered *m·* to Christ
	174–27	and omnipotence enfolds *m·*.
	175–11	Allow *m·* to say to the good folk of
	175–12	and prosperity of our city cheer *m·*.
	177–11	fourscore (already imputed to *m·*),
	184–11	inviting *m·* to be present
	184–15	beautiful birch bark . . . pleased *m·* ;
	184–18	brought back to *m·* the odor of
	186–26	inviting *m·* to be with you
	186–27	It gives *m·* great pleasure to know
	188–19	He surely will not shut *m·* out
	188–21	cannot prevent *m·* from entering
	188–22	heart of a Southron has welcomed *m·*.
	189– 6	affords even *m·* a perquisite of joy.
	189–29	why throng in pity round *m·*?
	189–31	Dead is he who loved *m·* dearly :
	192–20	inviting *m·* to be present
	192–22	It would indeed give *m·* pleasure
	192–25	demands upon . . . pin *m·* to my post.
	194–20	you present to *m·* the princely gift
	198– 4	informing *m·* of the dedication of
	199–15	towards *m·* and towards the Cause
	201–27	Please accept a line from *m·* in lieu of
	214–29	To desert . . . never occurred to *m·*,
	215– 5	bade *m·* do what I did,
	215–11	sent *m·* the full tuition money.
	215–13	it was again mailed to *m·*
	215–14	in letters begging *m·* to accept it,
	218–30	receiving instruction from *m·*,
	219– 2	anticipate being helped by *m·*
	223– 8	not read by *m·* or by my
	228– 7	when to *m·* it is wisdom to
	229–25	heaps of praise confront *m·*,
	232– 1	It rejoices *m·* that you are
	234– 9	give *m·* the holidays for this work
	236– 7	you will permit *m·* to make
	240– 6	An earnest student writes to *m·* :
	244– 7	invited hither to receive from *m·*
	247–14	must have felt *m·* when I . . . silently
	247–17	thoughts that, not fearing *m·*,
	247–18	sought their food of *m·*.
	248– 3	its grandeur almost surprises *m·*.
	253– 1	It rejoices *m·* to know that you
	254–11	to your kind letter, let *m·* say :
	256– 2	allow *m·* to improvise some new
	256– 8	you must grant *m·* my request
	258–25	To the dear children let *m·* say :
	258–30	children who sent *m·* that beautiful
	258–32	Fancy yourselves with *m·* ;
	259–14	Christmas telegrams to *m·* are
	259–15	and give *m·* more time to think and work
	259–17	churches will remember *m·* only thus.
	261–22	chapter sub-title
	261–23	To *m·* Christmas involves an open
	262–20	Christmas to *m·* is the reminder of
	264– 4	kind enough to speak well of *m·*
	270– 7	kindly invited *m·* to its
	270– 9	leading editors . . . congratulate *m·* ;
	271–29	to your question permit *m·* to say
	273–24	You will agree with *m·* that the
	274–21	allow *m·* to say that I am not fond of
	275–13	Permit *m·* to say, the report that I
	283– 6	Your appointment of *m·* as *Fondateur*

Eddy

me

My.	284– 4	you may have accorded *m·* more
	284–23	But here let *m·* say that I
	289–23	inconvenient for *m·* to attend the
	295–15	kind of you to give it to *m·*.
	297–21	he visited *m·* a year ago.
	298– 5	nothing . . . could injure *m·* ;
	302–15	gave *m·* the endearing appellative
	302–16	not to name *m·* thus.
	302–18	name is not applicable to *m·*.
	302–22	than others before *m·*
	302–26	My first visit to . . . pleased *m·*,
	302–27	wanted to greet *m·* with escort
	303– 5	It suffices *m·* to learn the Science of
	304–29	The first attack upon *m·* was :
	305–22	All that I am . . . God has made *m·*.
	306– 4	Far be it from *m·* to tread on
	307– 4	In his conversations with *m·*
	307–12	startled *m·* by saying
	307–31	had already dawned on *m·*.
	308–11	attack on *m·* and my late father
	308–13	compels *m·* as a dutiful child
	311– 6	to be allowed to remain with *m·*,
	311– 8	my good housekeeper said to *m·* :
	311–21	presented *m·* my coat-of-arms,
	312–28	took *m·* to my father's home
	312–29	My salary . . . gave *m·* ample support.
	312–32	rhyme attributed to *m·* by
	313–11	being hired to rock *m·*,
	313–13	cradle for *m·* in his wagon.
	313–15	to help *m·* when I was ill.
	313–27	My oldest sister dearly loved *m·*,
	314–23	was a letter from *m·* to
	314–26	A Christian Scientist has told *m·*
	314–29	he was kind to *m·* up to the time of
	315–25	allow *m·* to thank the enterprising
	315–28	snatched *m·* from the *cradle* and the
	315–29	made *m·* the beloved Leader of
	317–13	enable *m·* to explain more clearly
	318–20	refrained from questioning *m·*.
	318–24	addressing *m·*, burst out with:
	319– 2	would make no difference to *m·*.
	330–27	helped to support *m·* in this
	336–14	money I had brought with *m·* ;
	338–13	unknown to *m·* till after the
	338–16	not allowed to consult *m·*
	343–17	light of . . . came first to *m·*.
	343–20	and trust in *m·* grew.
	345–14	until they had no effect on *m·*.
	345–15	if . . . could be made to act on *m·*.
	345–16	came like blessed relief to *m·*,
	347– 9	their beautiful gift to *m·*,
	347–15	bird, and song, to salute *m·*.
	348–10	the hope that was within *m·*.
	351– 8	letter was handed to *m·* duly.
	351–15	to remember *m·* as the widow of a
	352–21	your tender letter to *m·*,
	354– 5	claim have been endorsed by *m·*,
	357–29	acknowledging *m·* as your Leader,
	358–12	have been duly informed by *m·*
	358–13	to read all that you send to *m·*,
	358–17	to relieve *m·* of so much labor.
	358–18	for the money you send *m·*
	359– 3	neither do they trouble *m·* with
	359–29	temptation . . . to deify you and *m·*.
	360–23	for He has proved it to *m·*

messenger

Mis.	158– 9	now, after His *m·* has obeyed

mine

Mis.	13– 9	the law of loving *m·* enemies.
	87–19	to teach students of *m·*.
	140–14	God's business, not *m·*.
	203– 5	*m·* through gratitude and affection.
	225– 5	a friend of *m·*,
	243– 9	a student of *m·* removed these
	264– 2	random thought in line with *m·*.
	266– 8	state of his own mind for *m·*.
	283–15	For a student of *m·* to
	318– 2	*M·* and thine are obsolete terms
	318– 8	some of *m·* who are less lovable
	322–16	personal presence, or word of *m·*,
	329– 2	*M·* is an obstinate *penchant* for
	382– 6	a few manuscripts of *m·*
	389–10	Love is our refuge ; only with *m·* eye
	389–13	encircles me, and *m·*, and all.
Ret.	43–19	These students of *m·* were the only
Un.	9–22	ideas akin to *m·* have been held
No.	26–11	*M·* is the spiritual idea which
'00.	1– 7	and *m·* to thine in the glow of
'01.	29–28	every book of *m·* that they sold.
Po.	4– 9	Love is our refuge ; only with *m·* eye
	4–12	encircles me, and *m·*, and all.
	24–14	Is all I need to comfort *m·*.
My.	119–27	the opportunity of seeing *m·*,
	163–28	for helping to form *m·*.

Eddy

mine

My.	193– 5	privilege remains *m·* to watch
	251–18	A Primary student of *m·*
	251–24	I call you *m·*,
	251–25	for all is thine and *m·*.
	313– 1	The rhyme . . . is not *m·*,

Mother

Mis.	125–27	*M·*, thought-tired, turns to-day to
	128–14	With love, *M·*,
	131–26	a bill of this church's gifts to *M·* ;
	141– 4	It will speak to you of the *M·*,
	155–16	Because *M·* has not the time
	353–29	They do not love *M·*,
	354– 2	declaring they "never disobey *M·*" !
Man.	64–13	The Title of *M·* Changed.
	64–17	endearing term of *M·*.
Pul.	37–21	* "*M·* feels very strongly,"
	63– 4	* THE "*M·*" OF THE IDEA
	63–10	* the "*M·*" of C. S.,
	77– 9	* *Dear M·* : — During the year
	78– 8	* "*Dear M·* : — During the year
My.	169– 5	as simply seeing *M·*.
	169– 9	With love, *M·*,
	263– 5	*M·* wishes you all a *happy*
	302–15	endearing appellative " *M·*,"

mother

Mis.	389–25	And *m·* finds her home
Man.	65– 1	to drop the word *m·*
Chr.	53–48	gleaming through Mind, *m·*, man.
Ret.	21– 2	informing him that his *m·*
	21– 8	learned that his *m·* still lived,
Po.	5– 6	And *m·* finds her home
	43– 2	Jesus loves you ! so does *m·* :
My.	343–20	I was the *m·*, but of course

Mother in Israel

Ret.	90–23	Thus must the *M· in I·*

mother in Israel

Pul.	44–11	* yet the *m· in I·*, alone

Mother's

Mis.	253–28	the spiritual *M·* sore travail,
	353–25	*M·* four thousand children,
	354– 8	When the *M·* love can no longer
	389– 5	poem
	400–13	*M·* NEW YEAR GIFT TO THE
Po.	page 4	poem
	69– 1	*M· New Year Gift to the*

(*see also* **Mother's Room** and **room**)

mother's

Po.	9– 4	young face, Upturned to his *m·*

my

Mis.	vii–17	*M·* world has sprung from Spirit,
	ix– 2	suits *m·* sense of doing good.
	ix– 6	among *m·* thousands of students
	x– 6	to collect *m·* miscellaneous
	x– 9	manifold demands on *m·* time
	x–17	*M·* signature has been
	x–17	changed from *m·* Christian name,
	x–20	After *m·* first marriage, to
	x–22	to retain *m·* maiden name,
	x–27	connection with *m·* published works.
	xi– 2	in *m·* name of Glover,
	xi– 3	initial "G" on *m·* subsequent books.
	xii– 5	I take *m·* pen and pruning-hook,
	xii– 7	lift *m·* readers above the smoke of
	11– 6	aim a ball at *m·* heart,
	11– 7	and save *m·* own life,
	11–11	if *m·* instructions had healed them
	11–13	I had done *m·* whole duty
	13– 4	special care to mind *m·* own business.
	21–15	*M·* first plank in the platform of
	24– 8	wrought *m·* immediate recovery
	24–11	I called for *m·* Bible,
	24–12	Truth dawned upon *m·* sense ;
	25– 5	to *m·* understanding it is the heart of
	29–17	in the ranks of *m·*
	29–19	first publication of *m·* work.
	29–21	perusal of *m·* volume is healing the
	32– 6	I infer that some of *m·* students
	32–12	*m·* books, on this very subject.
	32–14	you will find *m·* views
	32–15	*M·* sympathies extend
	32–19	I would gladly do *m·* best towards
	32–22	in which to give to *m·* own flock
	33– 1	comments on *m·* illustrated poem,
	33–11	to place themselves under *m·* care,
	43–14	contemplative reading of *m·* books,
	46–11	A reader of *m·* writings would not
	56–23	the correctness of *m·* statements,
	62– 1	*right* idea of man in *m·* mind,
	62– 2	I can improve *m·* own,
	65–20	*m·* instructions on this question.
	66–22	critics misjudge *m·* meaning
	66–31	to accommodate *m·* instructions
	67–29	I modify *m·* affirmative answer.
	68–13	*M·* proof of this is,

Eddy

my

Mis.	69–16	Upon *m·* arrival I found him
	70– 4	exercised *m·* power over the fish,
	86–14	*M·* sense of the beauty of
	86–17	spiritually beautiful to *m·* gaze
	87–22	*M·* students are taught the
	88– 1	to blight the fruits of *m·* students.
	89–24	in *m·* published works.
	91–29	had followed *m·* example,
	95–17	always attended *m·* life phenomena
	96–21	to *m·* sense, and to the sense of all
	97–25	To *m·* sense, we have not seen all of
	98– 7	*m·* Address at the National Convention
	104–31	on the side of good, *m·* true being.
	105–20	C. S. is *m·* only ideal ;
	106–15	chapter sub-title
	110–15	*M· Beloved Students :* — Weeks have
	112–19	*M·* few words touched him ;
	115–13	May God enable *m·* students to
	116–11	*M· Beloved Students :* — This question,
	116–12	ever nearest to *m·* heart,
	117–22	According to *m·* calendar,
	126–27	hath indeed smiled on *m·* church,
	127– 3	*m·* entire connection with The
	129– 2	*M· Beloved Brethren :*
	132–16	the great demand upon *m·* time,
	132–17	answers through *m·* secretary,
	132–24	to *m·* various publications,
	132–24	and to *m·* Christian students.
	133– 7	read *m·* sermons and publications.
	133–10	voices *m·* impressions of prayer :
	133–19	were it not because of *m·* desire
	133–23	with *m·* face toward the Jerusalem
	135–28	*M· Beloved Students :* — You may be
	135–29	to see me in *m·* accustomed place
	136– 9	so grow upon *m·* vision that I
	136–14	necessity for *m·* seclusion,
	136–19	*m·* last revised edition of S. and H.
	137– 2	*M· Dear Students and Friends :*
	137– 2	Accept *m·* thanks
	137– 9	I remember *m·* regret,
	137–14	rejoice over the growth of *m·* students
	137–17	dear ones, if you take *m·* advice
	137–28	*M·* students can *now* organize
	138–20	*M·* counsel is applicable to the
	139–25	to *m·* spiritual perception,
	140–11	No one could . . . mortgage *m·* gift
	142–11	Accept *m·* thanks for the
	142–15	*M·* first impression was to indite
	142–15	*m·* second, a psalm ;
	142–16	*m·* third, a letter.
	142–19	*m·* Muse lost her lightsome lyre,
	142–23	So I send *m·* answer
	143– 4	*M·* dear students may have explained
	143– 8	I reach out *m·* hand to clasp yours,
	143–19	class graduates of *m·* College,
	144– 2	New Hampshire, *m·* native State.
	145–32	children that *m·* heart folds within it,
	146– 6	*M· Beloved Students :* — I cannot
	146– 7	conscientiously lend *m·* counsel
	146–11	not *m·* present province ;
	147– 3	*M· Beloved Students :* — Another year
	149–18	*M· Beloved Brethren :* — Lips nor
	150– 4	*m·* forever-love to your dear church.
	153–24	*m·* first edition of "S. and H.
	155–24	If *m·* own students cannot spare time
	156–18	through the study of *m·* works
	157– 2	*M· Dear Student :* — It is a great
	157– 7	or caused *m·* secretary to write,
	157–15	Yes, *m·* student, *m·* Father is your
	158– 2	*M· Beloved Student :* — In reply to
	159–11	*M·* heart has many rooms :
	159–12	sacred to the memory of *m·* students.
	159–21	the gifts that *m·* dear students
	160–13	It satisfies *m·* present hope.
	177–30	In *m·* long journeyings I have met
	178– 1	the place of *m·* own sojourning
	178–27	*M·* friends, I wished to be excused
	180– 3	and strive to cease *m·* warfare.
	180– 5	*m·* friends were frightened
	180–12	in the words of *m·* Master,
	180–13	then *m·* heart went out to God,
	203– 4	*m·* students and your students ;
	203– 6	From *m·* tower window,
	203– 7	this gift from *m·* students
	207– 4	the spirit of *m·* life-purpose,
	213– 4	*m·* faith in the right.
	213–14	May *m·* friends and *m·* enemies
	214–19	*M·* students need to search the
	214–22	even to understand *m·* works,
	215–23	*M·* students are at the beginning of
	222–31	flowed into *m·* consciousness
	224–31	a question in *m·* mind,
	227–15	Would that *m·* pen or pity
	237–29	he visited *m·* father,

Eddy

my

Mis. 238– 5 reverence of *m·* riper years
239– 8 *m·* shadow is not growing less ;
242– 4 came not to *m·* notice until January
242– 6 one of *m·* students,
242–10 Will the gentleman accept *m·* thanks
242–28 he was *m·* student in December,
243– 6 mental branches taught in *m·* college ;
243–18 *M·* Christian students are proverbially
243–19 *m·* system of medicine
244–17 Will he accept *m·* reply
247– 6 Those familiar with *m·* history
247–10 in one of *m·* works
247–12 charges against *m·* views are false,
247–13 do not understand *m·* statement
248–17 or that *m·* hourly life is prayerless,
248–20 to have reported *m·* demise.
248–22 and bequeathed *m·* property to
248–24 *m·* regular physician prescribed
249– 9 that I have . . . in *m·* works,
249–11 especially through *m·* teachings,
249–14 *m·* intimate acquaintances.
249–15 remain in *m·* College building
249–17 since *m·* residence in Boston ;
249–17 and to *m·* knowledge,
249–18 not one has been sent to *m·* house,
249–22 expelled from *m·* College
249–23 *M·* heavenly Father will
249–25 coming nearer in *m·* need,
251– 4 *M·* beloved brethren, who have come
251– 6 *m·* hand may not touch yours to-day
251– 7 *m·* heart will with tenderness
251–10 and of *m·* native State
252–14 *M·* proof of these novel propositions
256–13 prevent *m·* classes from forming
256–17 intervals between *m·* class terms,
262–13 I thank you, *m·* dear students,
262–29 to relieve *m·* heart of its secrets,
263– 1 but if *m·* motives are sinister.
263–28 *m·* ideas and discovery,
264– 3 *M·* noble students, who are loyal to
264–13 Normal class of *m·* College
264–15 taught their first lessons by *m·* students ;
264–20 Some students leave *m·* instructions
265–23 *M·* teachings are uniform.
266–18 about *m·* loyal students
266–21 I cannot find it in *m·* heart
266–23 *m·* own endeavors and prayers.
266–26 accordance with *m·* students' desires,
272–31 not profited by *m·* rebukes,
273– 5 I close *m·* College in order to
273– 8 *M·* students have never expressed so
273– 9 grateful a sense of *m·* labors
273–10 capable of relieving *m·* tasks
273–12 God bless *m·* enemies,
273–13 and gather all *m·* students,
273–25 cannot do *m·* best work for
273–32 call is for *m·* exclusive teaching.
274– 4 when I opened *m·* College.
274– 4 I desire to revise *m·* book
274– 9 more than *m·* teaching would
274–13 I close *m·* College.
275–29 floral offerings sent to *m·* apartments
276– 7 circumstances demanded *m·* attention
276– 7 *m·* personality was not big enough
276– 9 *m·* heart's desire met the demand.
276–10 *M·* students, our delegates,
276–24 I pray that all *m·* students
277–10 No evidence . . . can close *m·* eyes
278– 4 *m·* peace returns unto me.
278– 6 I shall fulfil *m·* mission,
278– 9 throughout *m·* labors,
278– 9 in *m·* history as connected with
278–11 when *m·* motives and acts are
278–12 seen as *m·* Father seeth them.
278–18 *m·* beloved students, who are absent
278–19 shared less of *m·* labors
278–25 perpetual instruction of *m·* students
278–25 might substitute *m·* own for
279–13 *M·* students, three picture-stories
279–14 present themselves to *m·* thought ;
281–23 Among the gifts of *m·* students,
285– 6 who fills orders for *m·* books,
287–23 the substance of *m·* reply is :
290–20 *m·* affections involuntarily flow out
291–15 to be benefited by *m·* thoughts
291–17 this is not *m·* fault,
291–17 and is far from *m·* desire ;
292–29 who fully understood *m·* instructions
293– 1 and carried out *m·* ideal.
294–25 Since *m·* residence in Concord,
300– 3 Copying *m·* published works
300– 9 your copy of *m·* works,
300–12 from copies of *m·* publications
300–15 You literally publish *m·* works

Mis. 300–26 from *m·* work S. and H.,
301– 8 made up of *m·* publications,
301–13 *M·* Christian students who have read
301–14 copies of *m·* works
301–18 *m·* private counsel they disregard.
301–19 question of *m·* true-hearted students,
301–21 It is not right to copy *m·* book
301–22 publicly *without m· consent.*
301–22 *M·* reasons are as follows :
302– 4 infringement of *m·* copyright,
302– 9 *M·* students are expected
302–20 copying and reading *m·* works
302–24 from further copying of *m·* writings
308– 6 clings to *m·* material personality,
308–20 scientific notices of *m·* book.
309–27 *M·* Christmas poem and its
310– 2 neither the intent of *m·* works
310–11 *M·* answer to manifold letters
310–13 *m·* affections plead for all
310–14 *m·* desire is that all shall be
311–15 *M·* deepest desires and daily labors
311–16 I love *m·* enemies and would help all
311–22 I should lose *m·* hope of heaven.
311–24 *m·* necessity was to tell it ;
311–31 never escaped from *m·* lips,
314–15 First Reader shall read from *m·* book,
315– 6 No copies from *m·* books are allowed
316– 8 I shall speak to *m·* dear church
316–17 *M·* juniors can tell others
316–19 rest on *m·* retirement
316–25 had *m·* students achieved the point
317– 2 *m·* heart replies, *Yes,* if you
317–10 the door to *m·* teaching was shut
317–11 when *m·* College closed.
317–19 *m·* answers to the above questions.
317–24 *M·* sympathies are deeply enlisted
317–29 *M·* soul abhors injustice,
318– 1 chapter sub-title
318– 5 not alone for *m·* students,
318–21 latest editions of *m·* works,
319–18 accept *m·* tender greetings
321– 7 *M·* heart is filled with joy,
322–14 Shepherd that feedeth *m·* flock,
322–18 *m·* often-coming is unnecessary ;
322–23 *m·* past poor labors and love.
329–10 Spring is *m·* sweetheart,
331–21 Keep Thou *m·* child on upward wing
335–16 In *m·* public works I
335–18 Those who deny *m·* wisdom
347–11 Where *m·* vision begins and is clear,
348–24 I wanted to satisfy *m·* curiosity
349– 1 received *m·* consent and even
349– 2 take lessons outside of *m·* College,
349–10 obstetrics taught in *m·* College.
349–16 notwithstanding *m·* objection,
349–19 *M·* counsel to all of them was
349–26 or to receive *m·* gratuitous services,
349–30 accepted no pay from *m·* church
350– 1 two thousand dollars of *m·* own
350–13 and like *m·* public instruction.
350–30 *M·* life, consecrated to humanity
350–32 its own proof of *m·* practice.
351– 5 blessing even *m·* enemies,
353–13 *M·* brother was a manufacturer ;
353–16 When *m·* brother returned
354– 2 It exceeds *m·* conception of
355–29 rainbow seen from *m·* window
356–10 *M·* students, with cultured
356–19 Now let *m·* faithful students
357–22 it has been clear to *m·* thought
371–14 *m·* heart pleads for them
373– 4 *M·* artist at the easel objected,
373– 5 *m·* sense of Soul's expression
374–20 never looked on *m·* ideal of the
374–22 the one illustrating *m·* poem
374–31 *m·* ideal of an angel is
375– 3 not *m·* concepts of angels.
376–19 for me, on *m·* bed?
378–20 The readers of *m·* books cannot
379– 5 see his pennings on *m·* case.
379–29 named *m·* discovery C. S.
380–17 *M·* students at first practised
380–19 *m·* students' patients, and people
382– 1 *m·* experience would contradict it
382– 4 *m·* discovery of this Science,
382– 5 *m·* first work on this doctrine,
383– 7 pastor is the Bible and *m·* book.
385– 5 Oh, Thou hast heard *m·* prayer ;
385– 9 poem
389– 9 Keep Thou *m·* child on upward
392–11 To *m·* lone heart thou art a
392–14 and patient be *m·* life as thine ;
392–21 To *m·* sense a sweet refrain ;
392–22 To *m·* busy mem'ry bringing

Eddy

my

Eddy

my

My.

26–11	imagine *m·* gratitude and emotion
26–13	ever received from *m·* church,
26–15	*M·* Message for June 10 is ready
27– 2	*To the Beloved Members of m· Church,*
62– 8	* and give it to *m·* brothers
103–23	on which to found *m·* own,
103–25	Bible has been *m·* only authority.
104–24	in *m·* class on C. S.
105– 7	After *m·* discovery of C. S.,
105–26	work describing *m·* system
105–28	*m·* curative system of metaphysics.
110–16	remind me of *m·* early dreams
114–14	*M·* first writings on C. S. began
114–22	pour in upon *m·* spiritual sense
115– 8	*m·* estimate of the C. S. textbook.
118– 1	*M·* soul thanks the loyal,
118– 2	beloved members of *m·* church
118– 9	*M· Dear Sir :* — I beg to thank you
118–12	In a call upon *m·* person,
120– 3	or elsewhere than in *m·* writings,
120– 7	Accept *m·* gratitude for the chance
120– 9	*m·* honest position.
121– 2	*M· Beloved Brethren :* — I have
121–17	presented to me by *m·* students
122–11	*m·* church tempted me tenderly
123–19	*m·* outdoor accommodations at
123–21	*M·* little hall, which holds
124– 6	*M· Beloved Brethren :* — Looking on
125–11	dip *m·* pen in *m·* heart to say,
125–21	students in *m·* last class in 1898
125–22	stars in *m·* crown of rejoicing.
127–32	I cannot quench *m·* desire to say
129–29	Accept *m·* counsel and teachings
130– 8	effort . . . to keep *m·* works from
130–17	*m·* students reprove, rebuke, and
130–21	published quotations from *m·* works
130–23	Borrowing from *m·* copyrighted works,
130–31	hence *m·* request, that you
131–18	*M· Beloved Brethren :* — I hope
133–10	*M·* beloved church will not receive
133–11	for *m·* annual Message is
133– 2	*M· Beloved Brethren :* — I have a secret
133–24	*m·* sacred secret is incommunicable,
133–26	*m·* book is not all you know of me.
133–28	uncovers *m·* life,
134– 2	tell *m·* long-kept secret
135– 9	to *m·* secular affairs, — to *m·* income,
135–10	to *m·* employees.
135–11	increasing demands upon *m·* time
135–12	*m·* yearning for more peace
135–12	in *m·* advancing years,
135–14	take the charge of *m·* property;
135–17	First Reader of *m·* church
135–26	*M· Beloved Church :* — Your love
135–26	cheer *m·* advancing years.
136– 3	*m·* demonstration of C. S.
136–14	Trustees who own *m·* property :
136–24	To *m·* aforesaid Trustees I have
136–25	hard earnings of *m·* pen,
137–12	*m·* secular affairs, to *m·* income,
137–13	to *m·* employees.
137–14	selected all *m·* investments
137–17	increasing demands upon *m·* time,
137–18	*m·* property and affairs
137–20	designated by *m·* last will,
137–22	take charge of *m·* property ;
138– 1	I gave them *m·* property to
138– 4	to take care of *m·* property
138– 6	suit was brought without *m·*
138– 7	carried on contrary to *m·* wishes.
138– 8	not for *m·* benefit in any way,
138– 8	but for *m·* injury,
138– 9	not needed to protect *m·* person or
138–10	test *m·* trust in divine Love.
138–11	*M·* personal reputation is assailed
138–12	some of *m·* students and trusted
139–17	*M· Beloved Brethren :* — When I asked
139–18	purpose of *m·* request was sacred.
142–10	Accept *m·* thanks for your approval
142–17	*M·* beloved brethren may some time
143–10	one and all of *m·* beloved friends
143–12	by the members of *m·* household
144– 4	*M· Beloved Brethren :* — Give yourselves
145– 2	*M· Dear Editors :* — You are
145–22, 23	*m·* friends and *m·* enemies.
146– 1	*m·* dedicatory letter to the Chicago
146– 8	statement in *m·* letter to the church
146–10	"If wisdom lengthens *m·* sum of years
146–17	and *m·* poor prophecy,
147– 7	*m·* childhood's Sunday noons.
148–10	*M· Beloved Brethren :* — In the annals of
148–20	and *m·* heart is asking :
151–23	*M· Beloved Brethren :* — We learn
152–32	flowers that *m·* skilful florist has
153– 3	floral offerings in *m·* name to
153– 7	gospel ministry of *m·* students
153–12	healed from the day *m·* flowers
153–14	from *m·* poor personality.
154–15	*M· Beloved Brethren :* — At this, **your**
155– 4	nestled so near *m·* heart
156– 2	*m·* gratitude for your dear letter,
158–10	natal hour of *m·* lone earth life ;
159– 8	every pulse of *m·* desire for
162–10	such as *m·* beloved Christian Scientists
162–29	This church, born in *m·* nativity,
163–13	cannot show *m·* love for them in
163–14	sacred demands on *m·* time
164– 1	was far from *m·* purpose,
164– 8	*M· Beloved Brethren :* — I have **yearned**
164– 8	yearned to express *m·* thanks
166–10	*M· Beloved Brethren :* — Your **munificent**
166–22	*m·* dear ones, let us together sing
166–29	for *m·* books, placed in *m·* room
167– 1	Accept *m·* deep thanks therefor,
167–19	*m·* love, and *m·* prayer
167–26	by the laws of *m·* native State.
168– 5	of *m·* dear old New Hampshire.
169– 2	*M· Beloved Church :* — I invite **you,**
169– 6	*M·* precious Busy Bees,
169–18	believers of *m·* faith,
170– 3	simply *m·* acquiescence in
170– 3	request of *m·* church members
170– 6	brevity of *m·* remarks was due **to**
170– 6	desire on *m·* part that the
170– 7	in *m·* annual Message to the **church**
170–13	your home in *m·* heart !
170–18	it is *m·* sacred motto,
171– 1	dear members of *m·* church:
171–11	invite all *m·* church communicants
172–11	"*M· Beloved Brethren :* — Permit me
172–13	symbol of *m·* spiritual call
172–14	to this *m·* beloved church
172–18	please accept *m·* thanks for your
172–27	"*M· Beloved Brethren :* — You will **please**
173– 7	to the members of *m·* church,
173–20	exceeded *m·* expectation,
173–20	*m·* heart welcomed each and all.
173–22	*m·* fellow-citizens vied with
174– 6	courtesy extended to *m·* friends **by**
174–10	editors in *m·* home city
174–21	where *m·* parents first offered
174–22	until I had a church of *m·* own,
174–25	*m·* soul can only sing and soar,
175– 2	*m·* little church in Boston, Mass.,
175– 4	requires *m·* constant attention
175–25	song of *m·* soul must remain
175–28	purporting to have *m·* signature,
175–30	opposite of *m·* real sentiments.
176– 5	*M· Beloved Brethren :* — Long ago
176– 6	way to *m·* forever gratitude,
177– 8	of *m·* personal presence at your
177–10	lengthens *m·* sum of years to
181–32	of *m·* discovery of C. S.
182– 4	Thirty years ago at *m·* request
182– 6	*m·* early love for this church
183–26	blending with thine *m·* prayer
184– 3	*M· Beloved Brethren :* — Have just
184– 8	*M· Beloved Brethren :* — To-day I am
184– 9	Christian Scientists of *m·* native State
184–14	to return *m·* cordial thanks
184–18	brought back to me the odor of *m·*
185–26	closing *m·* remarks with the words **of**
186–25	Accept *m·* thanks for your cordial
187–22	*M· Beloved Brethren :* — You have
189–26	sunny South — once *m·* home.
189–26	There *m·* husband died,
189–27	and the dirge, surging *m·* being,
190– 9	*M·* experience in both practices
191–28	*M· Beloved Brethren :* — Your card
191–30	Accept *m·* thanks.
192–15	*M·* heart hovers around your
192–25	demands upon *m·* time
192–25	demands upon . . . pin me to *m·* **post**
192–26	*M·* love can fly on wings of joy
193– 4	that you will not feel *m·* absence.
195– 3	You will pardon *m·* delay in
195– 7	hitherto prevented *m·* reply.
196– 3	*M· Beloved Brethren :* — I congratulate
196– 7	accept *m·* tender counsel
196–25	*M· Beloved Brethren :* — The good in
197–11	*m·* deep appreciation of your labor
197–25	*M· Beloved Brethren :* — At this
197–26	in the home of *m·* heart,
199– 3	*M· Beloved Students and Brethren :*
199–11	accept *m·* grateful acknowledgment
200– 1	*M· Beloved Brethren :* — The chain of
201– 1	God is blessing you, *m·* beloved
201–10	*M· Beloved Brethren :* — Your Soul-full

Eddy
my

Eddy

my

My.	317–16	Calvin A. Frye copied *m·* writings,
	317–17	left *m·* diction quite out of the
	317–22	*M·* diction, as used in explaining
	318– 4	I have erased them in *m·* revisions.
	318– 5	not *m·* proofreader for *m·* book
	318– 6	for only two of *m·* books.
	318– 9	critics declared that *m·* book was
	318–12	defend *m·* grammatical construction,
	318–16	to visit one of *m·* classes
	318–21	began *m·* attack on agnosticism.
	318–31	find *m·* authority for C. S.
	319– 5	*M·* saying touched him,
	326–14	the State where *m·* husband,
	327– 4	*m·* native State,
	330–23	"*M·* husband was a Free Mason,
	330–29	where, . . . *m·* babe was born.
	336–12	I lost all *m·* husband's property,
	336–14	remained with *m·* parents until
	336–15	after *m·* mother's decease."
	338–17	owing to *m·* busy life,
	343– 7	whether *m·* successor will be
	343–17	In 1875 I wrote *m·* book.
	343–18	shower of abuse upon *m·* head,
	344– 2	to *m·* understanding of Christ
	346–27	would be *m·* future successor.
	347– 3	and reveal *m·* successor,
	347– 8	accept *m·* heartfelt acknowledgment
	347–20	I shall treasure *m·* loving-cup
	348– 1	*M·* discovery that mankind is
	351– 8	*m·* earliest moment in which to
	352–27	*m·* thanks for your successful plans
	352–29	*M·* desire is that every
	354– 8	books for which *m·* endorsement is
	356–16	nor consent to have *m·* picture
	357–13	When *m·* dear brethren in New York
	358–21	Mr. Adam Dickey is *m·* secretary,
	358–22	through whom all *m·* business is
	358–23	Give *m·* best wishes and love to
	359– 6	*M·* province as a Leader
	359–10	*m·* written and published rules,
	359–27	*M· Dear Student:* — Awake and
	360–16	*M·* beloved brethren in First Church
	360–17	I advise you with all *m·* soul
	360–29	*M· Dear Student:* — Your favor
	363–21	*M·* address . . . has been misrepresented

myself

Mis.	24–13	I rose, dressed *m·*,
	95–12	shall confine *m·* to questions
	263– 2	they will harm *m·* only,
	291–20	would part with a blessing *m·*
	296– 2	have allowed *m·* to be elected
	299–19	array *m·* in them,
	299–20	put *m·* and them on exhibition,
	311–20	as soon harm *m·* as another ;
	338– 5	I first proved to *m·*,
	348–23	found *m·* under this new *régime*
	348–27	so proved to *m·* that drugs
	351– 5	for want of time, . . . I neglect *m·*.
Ret.	13–23	I rose and dressed *m·*,
	24–15	how to be well *m·*,
	27– 6	never been read by any one but *m·*,
	43–22	organized by *m·* and six of my
Un.	7– 7	both to C. S. and *m·*
	43–12	by no means spoken of *m·*,
	43–13	I *cannot* speak of *m·* as
Pul.	74–14	an interview to answer for *m·*,
'02.	3– 1	used no other means *m·* ;
My.	114–23	not *m·*, but the divine power
	119–26	give *m·* the pleasant pastime of
	137–30	I find *m·* able to select the
	138– 2	and *m·* relieved of the burden of
	163–11	must not allow *m·* the pleasure of
	223–15	I do not consider *m·* capable of
	271–30	as I know *m·*, what is "nearest and
	276–25	and my neighbor as *m·*.
	305– 8	I briefly express *m·*
	311–26	Mrs. Judge Potter and *m·* knelt
	315–22	Is it *m·*, the veritable Mrs. Eddy,
	317–12	to avail *m·* of his criticisms
	318–10	I availed *m·* of the name of
	344–19	I should think *m·* in danger of

one

Mis.	54– 6	That *o·*, whoever it be,
	234–18	That *o·* should have ventured
My.	48– 4	* *o·* ready to receive the inspiration,
	58–19	* the *o·* through whom God has revealed
	62–10	* thank God enough for such an *o·*,
	321– 4	* referred to you as the *o·* who had
	346– 2	* as *o·* who has lived with her subject

organizer

Pul.	29– 5	* The *o·* and first pastor of

our

Mis.	3– 3	shall claim no especial gift from *o·*
	195–17	divine logic, as seen in *o·* text,

Eddy

our

Mis.	197– 4	*O·* chosen text is one
	236– 3	Throughout *o·* experience
	236–18	to the best of *o·* ability,

Pastor

Pul.	1——	chapter heading

pastor

Mis.	177–24	* the *p·*, Rev. Mary Baker G. Eddy,
	177–26	* The *p·* introduced Mr. Easton
	178–25	* the *p·* again came forward,
	193–15	of which I am *p·*,
	300–25	had for many years been *p·*,
	382–19	and was its first *p·*.
Man.	18– 6	to become their *p·*.
Ret.	16–19	to become their *p·*.
	44– 7	to become their *p·*.
	44–10	When I was its *p·*,
	46– 1	Lines penned when I was *p·*
Pul.	24–19	* first *p·* of this denomination."
	29– 5	* and first *p·* of the church
	64– 4	* first *p·* of this denomination."
	70– 9	* *p·* of the C. S. denomination,
	86–27	* the permanent *p·* of this church,
My.	49–11	* Mrs. Eddy to become its *p·*.
	49–19	* to become *p·* of the church.
	50– 2	* held at the home of the *p·*,
	50–30	* "Our *p·*, Mrs. Eddy, preached **her**
	51– 1	* devise means to pay our *p·*,
	51– 7	* sincerely regret that our *p·*,
	51–17	* have our *p·* remain with us
	51–29	* tender to our beloved *p·*,
	52–14	* taught and expressed by our *p·*,
	53–32	* When our *p·* preached for us
	54– 9	* before the arrival of the *p·*,

Pastor Emeritus

Man.	25– 5	*P· E·*, a Board of Directors,
	25– 9	approval of the *P· E·*,
	26–10	consent of the *P· E·*
	26–15	shall inform the *P· E·*
	26–22	approved by the *P· E·*.
	28– 2	approval of the *P· E·*.
	29– 9	If . . . the *P· E·* shall complain
	29–13	the *P· E·* shall appoint five
	30– 9	the consent of the *P· E·*,
	30–14	the house of the *P· E·*,
	51– 9	aggrieve or vilify the *P· E·*
	52–23	or the interests of our *P· E·*
	54–12	on complaint of Mrs. Eddy our *P· E·*
	54–21	represents falsely to . . . *P· E·*,
	55– 3	to The Mother Church, or to the *P· E·*,
	57–12	Board of Directors and the *P· E·*
	57–15	consent of this Board and the *P· E·*,
	59– 8	books or poems of our *P· E·*,
	64–11	heading
	66– 1	communication from the *P· E·*
	66–10	communications of the *P· E·*
	66–15	or a message from the *P· E·*
	67– 1	*P· E·* is not to be consulted
	67– 7	communication from the *P· E·*
	67–20	or letters to the *P· E·*
	67–25	written request of the *P· E·*,
	70– 1	*P· E·* to be Consulted.
	72–19	If the *P· E·*, . . . should relinquish
	76–20	with the consent of the *P· E·*.
	78–11	written consent of the *P· E·*.
	79–20	the *P· E·* of this Church,
	80–17	*P· E·* reserves the right to fill the
	81– 3	and the consent of the *P· E·*
	81– 6	who is not accepted by the *P· E·*
	87– 2	Neither the *P· E·* nor a member
	88–15	to the approval of the *P· E·*
	93– 8	to the approval of the *P· E·*.
	93–15	pertaining to the life of the *P· E·*.
	97–12	and the consent of the *P· E·*
	98–19	letter sent to the *P· E·*
	101– 5	with the approval of the *P· E·*,
	103– 8	written consent of the *P· E·*,
Pul.	87–16	make me your *P· E·*, nominally.
My.	15– 9	written consent of the *P· E·*
	22–25	* position taken by our *P· E·*
	27– 5	residence of your *P· E·*
	32–26	* Message from the *P· E·*,
	36– 7	* REV. MARY BAKER EDDY, *P· E·*.
	39–23	* *P· E·*, Mrs. Eddy, was present.
	133–21	chapter sub-title
	216–17	the room of the *P· E·*
	217– 9	the room of the *P· E·*.
	223–25	and not to the *P· E·*.

pastor's

Pan.	1– 1	heading
My.	52–17	* and our *p·* teachings,

President

Mis.	242– 5	*P·* of the Metaphysical College
Man.	88– 6	*P·* of the . . . Metaphysical **College**
	88–16	*P·* not to be Consulted.

Eddy

President

Man.	88–17	*P·* is not to be consulted
	89– 2	Should the *P·* resign
	89– 3	or vacate her office of *P·*
	91– 5	of the *P·* of the College
	91–10	free scholarship from the *P·*,
	91–14	Only the *P·* gives free
Ret.	48–30	*P·*, the Rev. Mary B. G. Eddy,
	49–23	gratitude is due to the *P·*,
My.	245–30	conferred by the *P·* or

president

Mis.	272–28	* Rev. Mrs. Eddy is founder and *p·*."
	382–23	its first and only *p·* ;
Man.	88– 7	a *p·*, vice-president, and teacher
Pul.	24–18	* *p·* of the . . . Metaphysical College,
	64– 3	* *p·* of the . . . Metaphysical College,
	70– 8	* *p·* of the . . . Metaphysical College,

proprietor

Mis.	382–23	*p·* of the first C. S. periodical ;
My.	304–17	*p·* and sole editor of

publisher

Mis.	382–16	author and *p·* of the first
Ret.	52–21	I started it, ... as editor and *p·*.
Pul.	47– 5	* editor and *p·* of the first official

pupil

My.	304– 3	*p·* of Miss Sarah J. Bodwell,

revelator

My.	vii– 7	* her rightful place as the *r·*

scribe

Mis.	311–26	I was a *s·* under orders ;
My.	115– 7	I was only a *s·* echoing the

she

Mis.	37–26	*S·* now does not.
	54–11	*s·* is demonstrating the power of
	58–10	*How does Mrs. Eddy know that s·*
	58–12	*S·* had to use her eyes to read.
	130– 4	*S·* readily leaves the answer to
	155–18	however much *s·* desires thus to do
	155–19	*s·* hereby requests : First,
	169– 1	Within Bible pages *s·* had found
	169– 2	all the divine Science *s·* preaches ;
	169– 6	till *s·* was God-driven back
	169– 9	years of invalidism *s·* endured
	169–14	*S·* affirmed that the Scriptures
	170–19	So, also, *s·* spoke of the hades,
	170–19	material record of the Bible, *s·* said,
	170–31	*s·* explained as the putting forth
	188–21	when *s·* discovered C. S.
	188–22	And *s·* has *not* left it,
	188–29	*s·* knew that the last Adam,
	188–32	*s·* beheld the meaning of
	210–17	*s·* puts her foot on the head of
	234–23	*s·* has made some progress,
	378–15	*s·* did ask him how manipulation
	386–14	*S·* deemed I died,
	386–22	*S·* that has wept o'er thee.
	387– 4	*S·* shall mount upward unto
Man.	18– 6	*S·* accepted the call,
	26–16	and if *s·* objects,
	43–11	Sometimes *s·* may strengthen the faith
	48–13	not haunt Mrs. Eddy's drive when *s·*
	52–24	what *s·* understands is advantageous
	66–17	or *s·* is referred to as authority
	66–25	an order . . . that *s·* has not sent,
	68–13	members whom *s·* teaches the course
	68–19	those individuals whom *s·* engages
	69– 3	remain with Mrs. Eddy if *s·* so desires,
	69–10	whatsoever *s·* may charge
	69–11	what *s·* has taught him or her
	75– 9	*s·*, with grateful acknowledgments
	75–11	*s·* now understands the financial
	80–19	but if *s·* does not elect to
	100– 6	if *s·* shall send a special request
Ret.	16–19	*S·* accepted the call,
Pul.	31–21	* *s·* most kindly replied,
	31–22	* *s·* would receive me.
	31–25	* *S·* impressed me as . . . graceful
	32– 3	* *s·* was magnetic, earnest,
	32– 7	* *s·* had the temperament to dominate,
	32–12	* What had *s·* originated?
	32–14	* *S·* told me the story of her life,
	32–20	* *s·* must have been some sixty years
	32–20	* yet *s·* had the coloring and the
	32–22	* this, *s·* told me, was due to
	33– 3	* *s·* began, like Jeanne d'Arc,
	33– 4	* *s·* heard her name called
	33– 6	* questioning if *s·* were wanted.
	33– 7	* if *s·* heard the voice again
	33–11	* *s·* prayed for forgiveness,
	33–12	* It came, and *s·* answered as
	34– 2	* *S·* returned to her father's home
	34–10	* no probability that *s·* would be alive
	34–11	* *s·* suddenly became aware of a
	34–12	* *S·* requested those with her to
	34–14	* *s·* walked into the adjoining room,

Eddy

she

Pul.	34–16	* they thought I had died, ... *s·* said.
	34–21	* *s·* said, in reference to this
	34–26	* *s·* said, in reply to my questions,
	35–10	* begotten of spirituality," *s·* says,
	36–23	* *s·* bought one of the most beautiful
	37– 6	* where *s·* has a beautiful residence,
	37– 8	* *s·* retains in a great degree her
	37– 9	* *s·* takes a daily walk
	37– 9	* *S·* personally attends to a vast
	37–12	* *s·* is the recognized head of the
	46–28	* *s·* became the wife of
	47–10	* *s·* states that *s·* sought knowledge
	47–15	* *S·* claims that no human reason has
	47–16	* *s·* also defines carefully
	47–24	* when *s·* wishes to catch a glimpse of
	47–25	* *s·* lives very much retired,
	48– 7	* *s·* can sit in her swinging chair,
	48–16	* *s·* paused and reminded the reporter
	48–26	* *S·* had a long list of worthy
	49–13	* "Four years !" *s·* ejaculated ;
	49–15	* *s·* continued : "Look at those
	49–19	* *S·* told something of her domestic
	49–20	* *s·* had long wished to get away
	49–24	* *S·* chose the stubbly old farm
	49–29	* *S·* employs a number of men
	50– 2	* in whom *s·* takes a vital interest.
	50– 6	* that *s·* might do something for
	55–14	* Since then *s·* has revised it
	55–17	* Afterward *s·* selected the name
	58– 4	* about 1880, *s·* began teaching,
	58– 6	* *s·* has lived in Concord, N. H.,
	58–29	* should *s·* wish to make it a home
	59– 2	* *s·* has not yet visited her temple,
	63– 4	* *S·* HAS AN IMMENSE FOLLOWING
	63–10	* *s·* pointed to a number of large elms
	63–19	* hold *s·* has upon this army
	64–14	* Mrs. Eddy says *s·* discovered C. S.
	64–15	* *S·* studied the . . . *s·* declares,
	64–16	* *S·* investigated allopathy,
	64–20	* *s·* became convinced that
	68– 5	* *s·* taught the principles of the
	68–10	* *S·* now lives in a beautiful
	70–11	* *S·* has within a few years
	70–17	* in 1866 *s·* became certain that
	70–19	* *s·* endeavored in vain to find
	70–21	* *s·* concluded that the way of
	70–25	* Mind-healing, which *s·* termed C. S.
	70–25	* *S·* has a palatial home in Boston
	71–10	* chapter sub-title
	71–22	* *s·* is unquestionably looked upon as
	72–19	* *s·* was the Founder of the faith,
	73– 6	* *S·* had faith in Him,
	73– 6	* *s·* cured herself of a deathly disease
	73– 8	* *s·* secluded herself from the world
	73– 9	* *S·* delved deep into the
	73–13	* this duty *s·* faithfully performed.
	73–14	* of herself had no power.
	74–11	* which *s·* did in this letter,
	85– 8	* *s·* has unfolded and demonstrated
	85–13	* *s·* has demonstrated the system
	85–14	* surely *s·*, as the one chosen of God
	88– 8	* can append only a few of
Rud.	14–12	*S·* has never taught . . . without
	17–12	*s·* needed miraculous vision to
No.	12–22	in nothing else has *s·* departed from
'01.	34–25	only so far as *s·* follows Christ.
'02.	4– 4	only so far as *s·* follows Christ.
Po.	v–16	* *s·* seated herself by the roadside
	v–19	* asked her what *s·* was writing,
	v–19	*s·* replied by reading the poem
	vi–24	* years *s·* resided in Lynn,
	vii– 9	* to which *s·* assented.
	49–21	*S·* deemed I died,
	50– 7	*S·* that has wept o'er thee,
	50–22	*S·* shall mount upward unto
My.	v–20	* *s·* wrote and published the
	vi–19	* *s·* organized The C. S. Publishing
	vi–22	* *s·* made over to trustees
	vi–23	* *s·* presented to her church
	vi–28	* *s·* established the *C. S. Sentinel*
	11– 7	* *S·* has been the one of all the world
	11– 9	* *s·* has not tried to guide us by
	11–11	* in all this time *s·* has never
	11–14	* *s·* quietly alluded to the need of
	11–15	* *S·* knew that we were ready ;
	11–16	* *s·* expressed much gratification
	11–18	* *s·* will be cheered and encouraged
	22–18	* purpose *s·* has set in motion,
	22–20	* *s·* has shown wisdom, faith, and
	40– 2	* *S·* has desired for years to
	40–25	* *s·* is an exact metaphysician.
	40–26	* *S·* has illustrated what the poet
	40–27	* *s·* has obeyed the divine Principle,
	42–28	* and how successful *s·* is in the

Eddy

she

My.	43–23	* s· gave us our textbook,
	48–13	* s· founded the future growth of
	51– 8	* s· has not met with the support
	51– 9	* s· should have reason to expect,
	51–10	* hope s· will remain with us.
	51–14	* who is so able as s· to lead us
	52– 2	* s· had many obstacles to
	52– 4	* s· has borne them bravely,
	52–23	* Little cares s·, if only
	52–24	* s· has reached her bottom dollar,
	52–27	* s· has made sacrifices
	53– 5	* would s· allow printer and binder
	53–16	* ascertain if s· would preach for
	53–18	* which invitation s· accepted.
	53–21	* when s· could give the time to
	54– 4	* eternal truth s· taught them."
	57– 7	* s· suggested the need of a larger
	58–23	* as s· has done, verifying Jesus'
	59–25	* Some say s· did not."
	59–27	* "Send those who say s· did not to me.
	60– 4	* s· would doubtless do so.
	64– 7	* for all that s· has done.
	64–16	* s· has been teaching her followers
	64–20	* Fearlessly does s· warn all her
	94–25	* s· sent greetings in which s·
	139– 3	S· is neither dead nor
	139– 4	s· is keenly alive to the reality of
	155–29	their Leader's love, which s· sends
	171–24	* s· was greeted in behalf of
	171–26	* s· presented as a love-token for
	229–15	lose all selfishness, as s· has
	229–16	as s· has done, according to
	231– 6	s· has suffered most from those
	231– 6	whom s· has labored much to
	231– 8	to whom s· has given large sums
	231– 9	S· has, therefore, finally resolved
	231–11	S· has qualified students for
	240–26	* S· most assuredly does,
	270–15	of those who say that s· is
	275–12	chapter sub-title
	276– 4	s· begs to say, in her own behalf,
	276– 5	that s· is neither ;
	276– 8	When . . . s· omits her drive,
	276–11	s· is minding her own business,
	276–18	* s· has also believed that in such
	276–22	* s· has given out this statement :
	304–30	second, s· has stolen the contents
	311–30	* when s· finished Smith's grammar
	312– 9	* S· was far from home
	312–12	* s· was met and taken to her father's
	312–14	* S· was a grown woman,
	312–17	* a brief season s· taught school."
	330–16	* who s· states was of Charleston,
	331– 5	* among whom s· remembers
	334– 7	* because s· has contradicted
	334–18	* S· declares in her Message
	336– 7	* s· declined on this ground,
	336– 9	* S· makes grateful acknowledgment
	336–11	* In this book . . . s· also states,
	342– 4	* S· entered with a gracious smile,
	342–15	* for weak s· was not.
	242–20	* s· said, in her clear voice,
	343– 2	* S· has a rapt way of talking,
	343– 5	* S· explained : "No present change
	343–22	* position of authority," s· went on,
	346– 2	* S· talks as one who has
	346– 9	* s· is in the flesh and in health.
	346–13	* S· was inside, and as s· passed
	346–23	* as to whether s· had in mind any
	350– 9	s· spiritually discerned the divine

sister

My.	331–29	* to Mrs. Glover (my s·)

St. Catherine

Pul.	32–12	* this modern St. C·,

student

My.	320–10	* as a s· of ability.

Teacher

Pul.	44– 2	* "Dear T·, Leader, Guide :
	86– 4	* "To our Beloved T·,
	86–17	* Beloved T· and Leader :
My.	23–17	* Beloved T· and Leader :
	36– 8	* Beloved T· and Leader :
	44–23	* Beloved T· and Leader :
	58–28	* Dear T· : — Of the many thousands
	62–19	* Beloved Leader and T· :
	157– 3	* "BELOVED T· AND LEADER :
	319–16	* Dear T· : — I am conversant
	322– 9	* Beloved T· : — I have just
	323–17	* Beloved T· : — My heart has

teacher

Mis.	137– 9	a few words aside to your t·.
	138–30	Your loving t·,
	144–12	the same author, your t·,
	280–20	presented their t· with an

Eddy

teacher

Mis.	280–25	thanks to their t·.
	302–12	sparing their t· a task
	371–12	I as their t· can say,
Ret.	77– 1	I become responsible, as a t·,
Pul.	24–15	* testimonial to our beloved t·,
	41–12	* sent them by the t·
	63–27	* testimonial to our beloved t·,
	84–28	* our beloved t· and Leader,
My.	22–15	* our beloved Leader and t·,
	36– 1	* from their t· and Leader,
	41–27	* Our Leader and t· not only
	50–10	* dauntless Leader and t·,
	58–19	* revered Leader and t·,
	97–19	* their t· and her utterances."
	323–21	* such a Leader and t·
	358–25	Lovingly your t· and Leader,
	360– 3	As ever, lovingly your t·,

thee

Po.	68– 3	"I'm living to bless t· ;

toiler

Mis.	386– 8	t· tireless for Truth's new birth
Po.	49–13	t· tireless for Truth's new birth

we

Mis.	2–32	w· entertain decided views
	3– 2	w· shall claim no especial gift
	35–28	w· refer you to "S. and H."
	36– 3	w· shall classify evil and error
	41–19	W· answer, Yes.
	48–19	has, w· trust, been made in season
	49– 3	W· are credibly informed that,
	161–14	whose words w· have chosen
	193– 3	w· reply in the affirmative
	195–15	W· ask what is the authority
	197– 6	w· fear . . . this text is not yet recognized.
	200–12	that w· have chosen for a text ;
	236– 4	w· have been made the repository
	236–10	w· have said, "Love and honor thy
	236–17	w· have done this to the best of our
	236–20	In such cases w· have said,
	244– 9	But, w· ask, have those conditions
	285–20	W· have taken the precaution to write
	286– 7	W· look to future generations for
	300– 7	W· answer, It is a mistake ;
	368–12	W· regret to be obliged to say that
Pan.	7–14	W· know of but three theistic
	10–21	which, w· regret to say,
'00.	2–22	Here w· add : The doom of such
Hea.	12–10	w· discovered that all physical effects
	12–12	w· learned from the Scripture
	12–17	w· saw at once the concentrated
	13–10	W· have attenuated a grain of
	13–15	highest attenuation w· ever
	13–17	w· cured an inveterate case of
	13–19	w· resigned the imaginary medicine
My.	212–15	W· answer, Because they do not
	300–21	w· propose that he make known his

who

Mis.	35–26	author of that work, w· explains it
My.	272–25	w·, nearly eighty-seven years of

widow

My.	331–25	* lone, feeble, and bereaved w·
	335–15	* were kept by his w·
	351–15	as the w· of a Mason.

wife

Mis.	386–26	my w·, Thy child, shall come
Pul.	46–28	* became the w· of Asa Gilbert Eddy.
Po.	50–12	my w·, Thy child, shall come
My.	312– 8	He left his young w· in
	315– 6	* conversation with him about his w·,
	315–11	* no knowledge of who his w· was.
	333–27	* He has left an amiable w·,
	335–30	* young w· prayed incessantly for

woman

Pul.	7– 3	* I would help that w·."
	44–18	* chapter sub-title
	49–26	* the will of the w· set at work,
'01.	16–25	its greatest discoverer is a w·
My.	4–12	w· has put into Christendom
	28–29	* one divinely guided w·,
	85–12	* this wonderful w· is a world power.
	88–24	* a noble and devoted w·,
	89–30	* That a w· should found a
	231–21	one w· is sufficient to
	271–15	* most discussed w· in all the
	271–19	* aged w· of world-wide renown
	271–26	* personality of this remarkable w·.
	272–25	* w· who, nearly eighty-seven years
	304–22	* a w· of sound education and
	305–12	* w· in New Hampshire."
	312–15	* She was a grown w·,
	315– 7	* a pure and Christian w·,
	315–14	* the above-mentioned w·.
	330– 1	* criticism of this good w·

Eddy

writer
Mis. 188–21   where the present w· found it,

writer's
My. 348–14   w· departure from such a religion
350– 8   came to the w· rescue,

you
Mis. 4–24   is often said, "Y· must have
31– 1   *What do y· consider to be mental*
35–15   *S. and H. that y· offer for sale*
35–18   *if one is obliged to study under y·,*
38– 1   *Why do y· charge for teaching C. S.,*
38–13   *How happened y· to establish a*
39–13   *Can y· take care of yourself?*
46–10   *Do y· teach that y· are equal with*
50–18   *Do y· believe in change of heart?*
52–11   *What do y· think of marriage?*
53– 1   *Do y· sometimes find it advisable*
60– 1   *How can y· believe there is no sin,*
60– 3   *How can y· believe there is no*
64–10   *Do y· regard the study of*
65–17   *Have y· changed your instructions*
67–24   *Do y· believe in translation?*
75– 6   *Why do y· insist that there is but*
83– 5   *y· say: "Every sin is the*
83– 8   *y· say: "Sickness is a*
83–10   *Will y· please explain this*
87–15   *if y· sent Mrs. —— to ——.*
87–16   *She said that y· sent her there*
112–22   * y· have brought what will do him good."
180– 7   * "How is it that y· are restored
299–24   Did he give y· permission
299–25   or loan them to y·?
299–26   have y· asked yourself this question
299–30   because y· have confessed that
299–32   and y· wished to handle them,
299–32   does it justify y· in appropriating
317– 2   "May I call y· mother?"
353– 7   Is my concept of y· right?
375–11   * new book y· have given us.
375–32   * "All that I can say to y·,
376–14   * Y· have given us back our Jesus,

Ret. 8– 8   "Nothing, child! What do y· mean?"
8–18   "Your mother is calling y·!"
8–20   "Why don't y· go?
8–21   your mother is calling y·!"
90–28   * in the path y· have pursued!"

Un. 48– 5   *Do y· believe in God?*
49– 1   *Do y· believe in man?*
50– 3   *Do y· believe in matter?*
51–13   *What say y· of woman?*
52–15   *What say y· of evil?*

Pul. 5–18   * "I have come to comfort y·."
44– 3   * y· begin to see the fruition of that *y·*
44– 6   * Y· are fully occupied, but
44– 7   * I thought y· would willingly pause
77–14   * revealed by divine Love through y·
77–14   * Y· are hereby most lovingly invited
78–12   * revealed by divine Love through y·
78–13   * Y· are hereby most lovingly invited
86–17   * We are happy to announce to y·
86–22   * we hereby present this church to y·
86–26   * extend to y· the invitation
86–29   * which y· have already ordained as
87– 1   * invite y· to be present

Rud. 1– 1   *How would y· define C. S.?*
1–10   *Do y· mean by this that God*
3–24   *do y· mean that God has*

Hea. 6– 4   * "People say y· are a medium,"

My. 8–26   * send our greeting to y·,
23–20   * loving greetings to y·,
24– 5   * We congratulate y·
24– 8   * which inspires y· to welcome all
24–12   * we know that y· rejoice in
37–11   * Through y· has been revealed
37–14   * y· have demonstrated this Science
38– 1   * and bestow upon y· the balm of
38– 5   * story of our love for y·
38– 6   * and for all that y· are
38– 6   * and all that y· have done for us.
44–26   * convey to y· their sincere
45–16   * divine Principle revealed to y·
45–17   * mortal sense declared y· to be
45–18   * Y· followed unswervingly
45–19   * of Him who went before y·
59– 2   * whom y· will recall as a member
59– 4   * y· told us that the truth
59–14   * which has been reared by y·,
60– 6   * Possibly y· may remember the
60– 8   * told that I had studied with y·.
60–15   * little Bible which y· gave me
60–27   * to tell y· of the interesting
62–10   * ever thank y· enough for your
62–20   * send y· loving greetings and
63– 1   * through y· we were enabled to
117–16   But when may we see y·,

Eddy

you
My. 157–10   * y· are so highly esteemed,
157–12   * y· have so freely bestowed.
157–12   * We thank y· for this
207– 9   * unite in loving greetings to y·,
207–12   * truth which y· have unfolded
240– 7   * "Would it be asking too much of y·
240– 7   * explain more fully why y· call
280– 8   * in this new reminder from y·
307–14   * "I see now what y· mean,
307–14   * I see that I am John, and that y·
311– 9   * "If this blind girl stays with y·,
319–19   * may interest y· to be advised that
319–22   * later, in conversation with y·
319–23   * y· suggested that I call on
319–29   * conversation with y· in general
319–30   * Y· told me that he had done some
320– 1   * literary work for y·
320– 6   * pleased to converse about y·
320– 7   * of what he had done for y·
320– 8   * agreed with what y· had told me.
320– 9   * as to his high regard for y·
320–14   * spoke of y· as the author of
320–22   * he always referred to y· as
320–27   * proud of his acquaintance with y·.
321– 4   * referred to y· as the one who
321– 8   * one who knew who and what y· are,
321– 9   * he always gave y· that position
321–14   * of y· and your relations to your
321–21   * twenty years since I first saw y·
321–24   * many conversations with y·,
321–31   * who knew y· years before I did,
322– 2   * told me she knew y· when y· were
322–12   * attitude towards y·;
322–12   * Edward P. Bates' letter to y·
322–17   I had seen y· the day before
322–30   * of y· and your work.
323– 6   * criticism of y· and your book
323– 8   * y· have so identified yourself with
323– 9   * y· are not going to lie
323–18   * to tell y· in words all that your
323–24   * blessing those who would destroy y·
323–24   * if God did not hold y· up
323–28   * I wonder if y· will remember
323–31   * in the second class with y·
324– 2   * about y· and your work,
324– 5   * had given y· any idea for
324– 6   * he said y· and your ideas were
324– 8   * said y· were so original and so
324–10   * of much service to y·,
324–12   * telling y· of this, and y· explained
324–13   * y· had waited on the Lord
324–14   * those very terms revealed to y·.
324–16   * that y· were the author of
324–19   * had helped y· write it.
324–22   * Mr. Wiggin regarded y· as quite
324–23   * pleased in numbering y· among his
324–25   * regarded y· as entirely unique
324–29   * we asked him if he found y· could
325– 1   * kindnesses y· had shown them,
325– 2   * y· personally called to inquire
325– 5   * that I think will amuse y·:
325– 6   * troubled that y· had bought
325– 8   * never be worth what y· then paid
325–12   * I offered my services to y·
325–13   * in which I could serve y·,
343– 9   * "Can y· name the man?"
344–16   * "Do y· reject utterly the
345– 7   * Do y· oppose it?"
352– 8   * our debt of gratitude to y·
362–18   * send y· their loving greetings.
362–21   * assure y· that it is our intention

your
Mis. 4–26   to make y· demonstrations."
33–21   *advantages of y· system of healing,*
35–17   *under y· personal instruction*
35–19   *of what benefit is y· book?*
37–16   *Can y· Science cure intemperance?*
38–25   *Is it necessary to study y· Science*
41–18   *healed by y· method*
54–17   *Must I study y· Science in order to*
54–19   *treatment by one of y· students.*
54–25   *Because none of y· students have*
65–17   *Have you changed y· instructions*
83– 5   *In y· book, S. and H.,*
87–15   *inform us, through y· Journal,*
88– 6   *give us, through y· Journal,*
255–18   of y· system of healing?
290–16   * "I felt the influence of y· thought
299–13   * "Is it right to copy y· works
299–28   it saves y· purchasing these
299–30   does this silence y· conscience?
301–20   "Is it right to copy y· works
316– 7   speak to y· church in Boston?
372–11   * pictures in y· wonderful book

Eddy

your

Mis.	372–16	* "The illustrations of *y·* poem
	375–17	* impressed me in *y·* illustrations
Ret.	8–18	" *Y·* mother is calling you !"
	8–19	*y·* mother is calling you !"
Pul.	6–13	* "Six months ago *y·* book,
	44–10	* in *y·* eventful career.
	86–20	* In behalf of *y·* loving students
	86–22	* gratitude for *y·* labors
No.	43– 9	* the good *y·* books are doing."
	43–10	" *Y·* book leavens my sermons."
	43–13	* " *Y·* book S. and H. is healing the
My.	23–17	* The members of *y·* church,
	24– 7	*y·* unmeasured love for humanity,
	36– 8	* The members of *y·* church
	36–30	* a sign of *y·* understanding
	37–14	* constancy of *y·* obedience
	37–16	* By reason of *y·* spiritual
	37–22	* through *y·* spiritual perception
	37–24	* unbroken activity of *y·* labors,
	37–27	* We have read *y·* annual Message
	44–28	* loyalty to *y·* teachings,
	44–30	* wisdom of *y·* leadership,
	59– 1	* magnitude of *y·* work
	59– 3	* member of *y· first* class in Lynn,
	59–15	* listening again to *y·* words
	60– 1	* knew of *y·* early struggles.
	60– 2	* by many of *y·* followers
	60–18	* on the fly-leaf in *y·* handwriting,
	60–27	* may I ask a little of *y·* time
	62–10	* for *y·* unselfed love.
	62–12	* brightest beams on *y·* pathway,
	62–13	* fill *y·* heart with the joy of
	62–14	* *Y·* sincere follower,
	62–20	* We, the Directors of *y·* church,
	62–23	* appreciation of *y·* wise counsel,
	63– 6	* gratefully *y·* students,
	117–17	out of *y·* personality?
	157– 5	* gratitude that *y·* generous gift
	157– 7	* church edifice for *y·* followers
	157– 8	* capital city of *y·* native State.
	157– 9	* Cause in *y·* home city,
	157–13	* evidence of *y·* unselfish love."
	215–14	* " *Y·* teachings are worth much more
	238– 3	as *y·* book, "S. and H.
	254–19	* following extract from *y·* article
	271–22	* dearest to *y·* heart to-day?"
	276–23	I am asked, "What are *y·* politics?"
	280– 4	* the receipt of *y·* message,
	280– 5	* *y·* watchful care and guidance
	280– 5	* of *y·* loving solicitude for
	319–18	* of many of *y·* students,
	319–21	* I entered *y·* Primary class
	320– 6	* converse about you and *y·* work,
	320–15	* author of all *y·* works.
	320–18	* statements in *y·* textbook;
	320–20	* while I was in *y·* Primary class
	320–23	* as the author of *y·* works
	320–23	* and spoke of *y·* ability
	320–26	* regarding *y·* work,
	320–32	* *y·* grand demonstration in
	321– 1	* building this church for *y·*
	321– 3	* connected with *y·* work,
	321– 7	* one of *y·* devoted and
	321– 8	* also *y·* position as regards
	321– 9	* *y·* published works ;
	321–14	* *y·* relations to *y·* published
	321–22	* and entered *y·* class.
	321–25	* authorship of *y·* works
	321–26	* I was among *y·* early students
	321–32	* their knowledge of *y·* work.
	322– 6	* *Y·* affectionate student,
	322– 9	* I have just read *y·* statement
	322–18	* and received *y·* permission to
	322–30	* of you and *y·* work.
	323– 6	* criticism of you and *y·* book
	323–12	* *y·* living witness to Truth
	323–18	* *y·* wonderful life and sacrifice
	323–22	* *Y·* crowning triumph over error
	323–26	* should mean to *y·* older students
	324– 2	* *y·* work, especially *y·* book
	324– 6	* any idea for *y·* book,
	324– 6	* said you and *y·* ideas were
	324–17	* the author of *y·* book,
	324–26	* why he accepted *y·* invitation
	324–27	* to sit through *y·* class.
	325– 2	* when amidst all *y·* duties
	325– 6	* that you had bought *y·* house
	325–16	* ever faithfully *y·* student,
	327–12	* will make *y·* heart glad,
	345– 7	* "What is *y·* attitude to science
	352– 5	* we, the ushers of *y·* church,
	352– 8	* for *y·* life of spirituality,
	361–21	* in accordance with *y·* desire for a
	362–20	* **in** *y·* **inspired leadership,**

Eddy

your

My.	362–20	* in *y·* wise counselling.
	362–21	* revere and cherish *y·* friendship,

yours

Mis.	376–12	* *Y·* is a palpitating, living
Pul.	44–13	* "*Y·* lovingly,
	87– 6	* Lovingly *y·*,
My.	60–20	* Respectfully and faithfully *y·*,
	362–26	* Gratefully *y·*,

yourself

Mis.	39–13	*Can you take care of y·?*
	299–26	Then have you asked *y·*
My.	323– 9	* identified *y·* with the truth
	324– 8	* to have come from any one but *y·*.

Eddy's

Mary Baker

Man.	43–15	Mary Baker *E·* copyrighted works
	102–19	phrase, "Mary Baker *É·* Church,

Mrs.

Mis.	35–13	* "Mrs. *E·* works are the outgrowths
	48–28	* by Mrs. *E·* teachings,"
	49– 9	that "Mrs. *E·* teachings had not
	49–12	in a class of Mrs. *E·* ;
	248–13	mistaken views of Mrs. *E·* book,
	271–20	Much is said . . . about Mrs. *E·*
	272– 6	* Mrs. *E·* grant for a college,
Man.	18–18	twenty others of Mrs. *E·* students
	35– 4	one of Mrs. *E·* loyal students,
	42–15	with all of Mrs. *É·* teachings,
	48–12	shall not haunt Mrs. *E·* drive
	68– 8	upon Mrs. *E·* complaint thereof
	69–25	Mrs. *E·* Room.
	91–26	under Mrs. *E·* daily conversation
Pul.	6–27	* Mrs. *E·* metaphysical teachings
	23– 6	* Mrs. *E·* WORK AND HER INFLUENCE
	24–24	* Mrs. *E·* native State.
	25–27	* and from Mrs. *E·* "S. and H.
	28–17	* includes the use of Mrs. *E·* book,
	36– 9	* by Mrs. *E·* kind invitation,
	36–13	* heading
	38– 5	* first edition of Mrs. *E·* book,
	46– 8	* Mrs. *E·* personal reminiscences,
	55–13	* first edition of Mrs. *E·* S. and H.
	60–12	* selected for him from Mrs. *E·* book.
	68–14	* chapter sub-title
	72–25	* it was Mrs. *E·* mission to revive it.
'01.	27– 5	* have been by Mrs. *E·* followers.
My.	7– 1	chapter sub-title
	17–28	* extracts from Mrs. *E·* writings
	51–26	* Mrs. *E·* tireless labors,
	52–22	* Mrs. *E·* future reputation,
	53–10	* in the parlors of Mrs. *E·* home,
	55–14	* upon Mrs. *E·* counsel, reorganized
	57– 7	* Mrs. *E·* Message to the church
	68–15	* Mrs. *E·* famous room will be
	134–28	* in Mrs. *E·* own handwriting,
	135– 1	heading
	137– 1	chapter sub-title
	137– 8	* in Mrs. *E·* own handwriting
	140–17	* following is Mrs. *E·* letter :
	142– 7	chapter sub-title
	143– 8	chapter sub-title
	157– 2	* chapter sub-title
	159– 2	chapter sub-title
	207– 6	* chapter sub-title
	207–20	heading
	241–13	* and Mrs. *E·* reply thereto.
	241–17	* question and Mrs. *E·* reply
	242– 1	heading
	255– 4	heading
	263– 3	chapter sub-title
	264–14	heading
	271–23	* Mrs. *E·* reply will be read
	271–27	heading
	272–23	* Mrs. *E·* own devoted followers,
	273– 3	* proof of Mrs. *E·* ability
	275–12	chapter sub-title
	281–26	heading
	283– 1	chapter sub-title
	297–26	chapter sub-title
	317– 8	chapter sub-title
	326–11	chapter sub-title
	329– 9	* Mrs. *E·* reference to the
	330–15	* Mrs. *E·* statements, relating to her
	332–24	* corroborate Mrs. *E·* claims.
	334– 5	* copies of Mrs. *E·* book,
	334–15	* state Mrs. *E·* teaching on the
	343– 2	* would be in Mrs. *E·* own spirit.
	343–11	* that Mrs. *E·* immediate successor
	346–11	* Mrs. *E·* carriage drove into
	346–18	* chapter sub-title
	352–18	heading
	352–26	chapter sub-title
	353–21	MRS. *E·* ROOM.

Eddy's
Mrs.
My. 355–21 Christian Scientists at Mrs. *E·*
361–15 chapter sub-title
362– 1 heading
362– 9 * chapter sub-title
363–13 heading
Rev. Mrs.
Mis. 272–20 * (except Rev. Mrs. *E·*)
Pul. 87–10 * heading

Eddy-signatures
Letters to branch churches
Mis. 151–30 MARY BAKER EDDY.
153–32 " " "
155–14 " " "
My. 20– 4 " " "
144– 9 " " "
158–30 " " "
168– 8 " " "
169–10 " " "
284– 7 " " "
360–25 " " "
_____
Mis. 150– 6 MARY BAKER G. EDDY.
Letters to students
Mis. 159– 9 MARY BAKER EDDY.
My. 20–19 " " "
135–21 " " "
142–22 " " "
171–16 " " "
263– 9 " " "
285–30 " " "
351–19 " " "
358–26 " " "
360– 4 " " "
361–12 " " "
362– 6 " " "
363–16 " " "
_____
Mis. 160–17 MARY BAKER G. EDDY.
_____
Mis. 156–30 MARY B. G. EDDY.
157–30 " " "
Letters to the . . . Christian Scientist Association
Mis. 135–22 MARY BAKER EDDY.
My. 364–18 " " "
_____
Mis. 138–31 MARY BAKER G. EDDY.
_____
Mis. 139– 7 M. B. G. E.
Letters to the Directors
Pul. 87–27 MARY BAKER EDDY.
My. 26–26 " " "
143– 6 " " "
Letters to The Mother Church
Mis. 132– 7 MARY BAKER EDDY.
142– 5 " " "
146–27 " " "
149–15 " " "
Pan. 15–11 " " "
My. 9–28 " " "
27– 9 " " "
133–18 " " "
136– 9 " " "
140–28 " " "
279–28 " " "
280–23 " " "
_____
Mis. 128–15 MARY BAKER G. EDDY.
Letters to the Press
Pul. 75–12 MARY BAKER EDDY.
My. 158– 5 " " "
272–16 " " "
276–14 " " "
282–16 " " "
284–28 " " "
316–26 " " "
327– 7 " " "
339–10 " " "
353–19 " " "
356–18 " " "
_____
Mis. 274–14 MARY BAKER G. EDDY.
Letter to the College Association
Mis. 136–29 MARY B. G. EDDY.
to an Affidavit
My. 138–22 MARY BAKER EDDY.
to a Notice
Mis. 303–27 MARY BAKER EDDY.
to Dedications
Mis. v– 9 MARY BAKER EDDY.
Pul. v– 8 " " "
Rud. v– 8 " " "
to Inscriptions
My. 214– 7 MARY BAKER EDDY.
214–10 " " "
214–14 " " "

Eddy-signatures
to Poems
Mis. vii–21 MARY BAKER EDDY.
My. 354–25 " " "
to Prefaces
Mis. xii– 9 MARY BAKER EDDY.
Pul. vii–23 " " "
No. v–14 " " "
to Tenets
Man. 16–13 MARY BAKER EDDY.
to the First (or Executive) Members
Mis. 148– 5 MARY BAKER EDDY.
My. 140– 8 " " "
to Tributes
My. 289–20 MARY BAKER EDDY.
290–29 " " "
295–29 " " "
296– 6 " " "
296–21 " " "
297– 8 " " "
297–25 " " "
298–12 " " "
Miscellaneous signatures
Mis. 143–12 MARY BAKER EDDY.
156– 5 " " "
My. 25–28 " " "
136–29 " " "
143–30 " " "
240–21 " " "
242–25 " " "
282–28 " " "
351–28 " " "
352–23 " " "
353– 3 " " "
353–27 " " "
354–10 " " "
355–15 " " "
356– 9 " " "
359–13 " " "
_____
Mis. 134– 8 MARY BAKER G. EDDY.
256–20 " " "
_____
Pul. 39–12 M. B. EDDY.
54–30 " " "

Eden
Mis. 109–19 Adam and Eve in the garden of *E·*.
287–12 and restores lost *E·*.
Ret. 18–12 dwellers in *E·*, earth yields you
Un. 44–10 In the days of *E·*, humanity was
Po. 64– 1 dwellers in *E·*, earth yields you

Edgar
Un. 23– 5 His lawful son, *E·*,

edge
Mis. 72–15 teeth are set on *e·*? — *Ezek.* 18 : 2.
195–23 to try the *e·* of truth in C. S.,
381–28 put under the *e·* of the knife,

edict
My. 278– 8 and its *e·* hath gone forth:

edifice
church
Mis. 139–21 erected thereon a church *e·*
319–22 church *e·* must be built in 1894.
382–20 church *e·* of this denomination
Man. 75– 3 Church *E·* a Testimonial.
75– 8 church *e·* as a Testimonial
102– 7 new church *e·* is completed.
102–17 erection of a church *e·*.
Ret. 51– 5 church *e·* to be used as a
Pul. 24–21 * heading
77–10 * a church *e·* was erected at
78– 8 * a church *e·* was erected at
87–19 to accept your grand church *e·*.
'02. 12–26 and enlarge our church *e·*
14– 4 nor sell this church *e·*
My. 7– 9 and enlarge our church *e·*
9–24 to enlarge our church *e·*
25–24 builders of this church *e·*,
55– 7 * thought of obtaining a church *e·*,
57– 8 * need of a larger church *e·*,
58–11 * the dignity of this church *e·*
65– 9 * to build in this city a church *e·*
67–26 * any church *e·* erected in this city.
84– 8 * church *e·* may not be formally
157– 7 * to build a beautiful church *e·*
158– 2 in building a granite church *e·*
162–14 furnishing our church *e·* in Concord,
162–20 church *e·* in Concord :
167–17 in our new church *e·*,
173–17 to take a peep at this church *e·*
189–25 first church *e·* of our denomination

edifice
church
My. 194–21 church e· in New York City,
197–12 and dedicating your church e·,
197–26 dedicatory season of your church e·
198– 5 your magnificent church e·,
201–29 opening of your new church e·.
203–25 corner-stone of your church e·
215–19 the site for a church e·,
costly
Pul. 40–18 * the unique and costly e·
dedication of the
My. 86–22 * dedication of the e· of the
elegant
My. 66–21 * spacious and elegant e·
first
My. 196– 4 first e· of our denomination in
grand
My. 194–13 engraven on your grand e·
great
My. 29–20 * dome of the great e·
handsome
Pul. 63–23 * This handsome e· was paid for
imposing
My. 77–29 * to build the imposing e·
larger
My. 22– 4 * saw the need of a larger e·
56–32 * proved the need of a larger e·.
magnificent
My. 45–15 * The magnificent e· stands a
modest
My. 6–17 modest e· of The Mother Church
Mother Church
Pul. 84–12 * The Mother Church e·
My. 55–27 * until The Mother Church e· was
55–32 * corner-stone of The Mother Church e·
320–30 * of the first Mother Church e·
new
Pul. 57–23 * this new e· on Back Bay,
77– 1 * magnificent new e· of worship
My. 16–20 * builder of the new e·.
21–27 * completion of the new e·
22–30 * erection of the new e· of The
23–23 * the walls of our new e·
one
My. 6–27 the one e· on earth which
present
My. 23– 6 * erection of the present e·
sacred
My. 63–20 * within our sacred e· there came
stone
My. 92–23 * two-million-dollar stone e·
94– 7 * two-million-dollar stone e·
suitable
My. 57–11 * building a suitable e·.
this
Pul. 58–10 * erected this e· at a cost of
77–13 * This e· is built as a testimonial
78–11 * This e· is built as a testimonial
My. 6–20 in the beginning of this e·,
24– 1 * What means this e·?
to build an
My. 195–25 to build an e· in which to worship
was emptied
My. 82–17 * e· was emptied of its crowds in

Mis. 131–14 since the erection of the e·
Man. 103– 4 The e· erected in 1894
Pul. 2–10 a thought higher . . . than the e·.
25– 7 * e· is therefore . . . fire-proof
My. 10– 7 * an e· for The Mother Church.
15– 6 The e· erected in 1894 for
67–20 * an e· that is a marvel of
76– 2 * new two-million-dollar e·,
87–18 * an e· so handsome architecturally.
88–12 * The e· itself is so rich in
89– 9 * and the e· needs only an

edifices
church
Man. 48–22 Our Church E·.
48–24 descriptions of our church e·,
75–16 owns the church e·,
Pul. 68–22 * many other church e·
My. 70– 6 * more fine church e·
71–16 * one of the most imposing church e·
91– 8 * church e· to be fully paid for
162–22 reason for church e· is,
162–24 not . . . worship church e·!

Edinburgh
Scotland
My. 208–11 chapter sub-title
304–15 London, England, and E·, Scotland.

Edinburgh
Ret. 1– 3 John McNeil of E·.
'00. 1–22 London, E·, Dublin, Paris,
Peo. 6– 4 Royal College of Physicians in E·,

edited
Mis. 4–12 newspaper e· and published by
Man. 44–21 ably e· and kept abreast of the

editing
Mis. 132–19 e· a magazine, teaching C. S.,
Man. 81– 9 nor with e· or publishing The

Edition and edition
Mis. xi– 1 first e· of S. and H. having been
21–24 1908 e· of S. and H.
35–30 * See the sixth e·.
83–28 * Quoted from the sixteenth e·.
136–20 in my last revised e· of S. and H.
153–24 I presented a copy of my first e· of
285– 3 An e· of one thousand pamphlets
285– 8 mistaken for the corrected e·,
309–32 See the revised e· of 1890,
318–28 See e· of 1909.
379–32 revised e· of 1890,
Man. 104–12 Seventy-third E· the Authority.
104–15 keep a copy of the Seventy-third E·
104–17 appears in any revised e·,
Ret. 37– 1 first e· of my most important work,
37– 9 first e· numbered one thousand
37–21 in my first e· of S. and H.,
38– 1 I had finished that e· as far as
38–21 closing chapter of my first e·
82–29 clearer than any previous e·,
Pul. 5–21 ninety-first e· of one thousand copies.
38– 5 * first e· of Mrs. Eddy's book,
38– 8 * now in its ninety-first e·.
55–13 * first e· of Mrs. Eddy's
55–15 * ninety-first e· is announced.
No. v– 1 each e· of this pamphlet
v– 7 import of this e· is,
9–17 first e· of this little work
'02. 15–11 royalty on its first e·.
Po. vii– 9 * to allow a popular e· to be issued,
My. 15– 3 * Article XLI (XXXIV in revised e·)
34–30 * according to the 1913 e·.
53– 7 * reached its four hundredth e·,
230–30 Sections 2 and 3 in 89th e·.
236–26 e· of S. and H. which will be
240–19 In the next e· of S. and H.
310–29 When the first e· of S. and H.

editions
Mis. 307–12 two e· of "Christ and Christmas,"
318–20 latest e· of my works,
379–33 pp. 152, 153 in late e·.
Man. 86–21 revised e· since 1902,
104–16 subsequent e· of the Church Manual;
104–18 these e· shall be cited as authority.
Ret. 37–10 it had reached sixty-two e·.
47–24 latest e· of my works,
'01. 21– 3 or new e· of old errors;
My. 320–14 something to do with some e·.

editor (see also editor's)
Mis. 177–22 * e· of The C. S. Journal
303–21 E· of C. S. Journal:
313– 2 E· of The C. S. Journal:
391– 2 Written to the E· of the Item,
Pul. 9–18 e· of The C. S. Journal
43– 6 * Judge S. J. Hanna, e· of The
74–12 * to the e· of the Herald:
Po. vi–12 "Mr. E·:— In 1835 a mob
38– 1 To the e· of the Item,
My. 142– 6 * E· Sentinel.
157–20 * an inquiry from the e· of
163–17 Dear E·:— When I removed from
173– 5 Dear Mr. E·— Allow me
250–13 send to the E· of our periodicals
271–20 * e· of The Evening Press
271–21 E· of The Evening Press:
281–27 To the E· of the Globe:
284–12 Dear E·:— In the issue of
304–19 e· of The C. S. Journal,
316–15 scholarly e·, Mr. B. O. Flower,
326–12 Dear E·:— I send for publication
329–21 * To the E·:— At no better time than
338–10 * E· Sentinel.
355– 4 * E· Sentinel.
356–13 E· C. S. Sentinel:
(see also Eddy)

editorial
Mis. 313– 3 your e· in the August number
Pul. 31–16 * e· work in daily journalism
My. 11–22 * E· in C. S. Sentinel,
14–10 * E· in C. S. Sentinel,
24–16 * E· in C. S. Sentinel,
27–20 * E· in C. S. Sentinel,
58–25 * chapter sub-title

editorial

My.	63–10	* *E·* in *C. S. Sentinel,*
	88– 1	* chapter sub-title
	232–10	COMMENT ON AN *E·* WHICH APPEARED
	272–32	* gives no *e·* indorsement to
	334–27	* extract from an *e·* obituary
	353– 6	Extract from the leading *E·*

editor-in-chief

My.	136–19	*e·* of the C. S. periodicals,
	226–26	*e·* of the *C. S. Sentinel,*
	227–21	above quotation by the *e·*

editor's

Mis.	168–21	chapter sub-title
My.	272–20	* *E·* NOTE. — The *Cosmopolitan* presents

editors

Mis.	126–18	able *e·* of *The C. S. Journal,*
	143–20	teachers, *e·*, and pastors
	155–22	*e·* of *The C. S. Journal*
	301– 7	authors and *e·* of pamphlets
Man.	26– 1	also for the *e·* and the manager
	65–11	*e·* of the *C. S. Journal,*
	80–22	*E·* and Manager.
	80–23	term of office for the *e·*
Pul.	36–26	* *e·* of *The C. S. Journal,*
My.	83–19	* chapter sub-title
	145– 2	MY DEAR *E·* :— You are by this time
	174–10	I thank the distinguished *e·*
	175–13	Its dear churches, reliable *e·*,
	270– 8	leading *e·* and newspapers of

Edmund

Un.	23– 2	his bastard son *E·*

educate

Mis.	51–19	*e·* him to love God, good,
	235–23	*e·* the affections to higher
	315–27	strive to *e·* their students
Hea.	14–19	*e·* and develop the spiritual sense

educated

Mis.	9–27	wherewith mortals become *e·* to
	53–27	only the thought *e·* away from it
	178–30	in which we have been *e·*,
Man.	32–20	read understandingly and be well *e·*.
	64– 1	shall be well *e·*, and a devout
'01.	32–24	*e·* my thought many years,
'02.	3– 5	among·the *e·* classes
My.	246– 7	Students . . . must be well *e·*

Education

(see **Board of Education**)

education

Mis.	38– 8	our whole system of *e·*,
	61– 4	*e·* of the future will be
	240–11	All *e·* should contribute to
	273–21	from these sources of *e·*,
	286–11	more spiritual . . . *e·* of children
Ret.	5–30	* to the *e·* of her children.
Rud.	16– 7	in any branch of *e·*.
My.	217– 2	for your own school *e·*,
	230–24	Christian *e·* of the dear children,
	252–11	entire purpose of true *e·*
	253–27	by *e·* brightens into birth.
	289– 1	All *e·* is work.
	304–22	* a woman of sound *e·*
	306– 2	my character, *e·*, and authorship,
	309–27	* received a liberal *e·*.
	310– 2	were given an academic *e·*,
	311–30	* completed her *e·* when she

educational

Mis.	114– 5	*Quarterly* as an *e·* branch.
	263–23	*e·* system of C. S.
My.	216– 6	Christian, civil, and *e·* means,
	245– 6	This Christian *e·* system
	312–31	starting that *e·* system

educed

Mis.	122–20	Good is not *e·* from its opposite :
Pan.	12– 2	good is not *e·* from evil,

Edward, King

'02.	3–22	on the brow of good King *E·*,

Edwards, Jonathan

Pul.	23–10	* of the time of Jonathan *E·*
'01.	15–22	thunderbolt of Jonathan *E·* :

e'en

Po.	30–10	*E·* as Thou gildest gladdened joy,
	43– 8	Fondling *e·* the lion furious,

e'er

Po.	1– 5	Beyond the ken of mortal *e·* to tell
	73–20	*E·* to mock the bright truth

E. E. Sturtevant Post

My.	284–14	Memorial service of the *E· E· S· P·*

efface

Mis.	18– 3	*e·* the mark of the beast.
Ret.	64– 6	to *e·* sin, *alias* the sinner,

effaced

Ret.	6– 3	* impressions . . . can never be *e·*,
	27–12	I would not have *e·*.
	79– 7	false images are *e·*
My.	178–26	not one word in the book was *e·*.

effect

all

My.	302– 9	mind is the cause of all *e·*
	348– 4	all *e·* must be the offspring of

any

My.	98–12	* if they would deal . . . with any *e·*.

appreciable

My.	107–14	and without appreciable *e·*.

artistic

My.	67–24	* never was a more artistic *e·*

better

Mis.	229– 7	and with better *e·* than he

cause and

(see **cause**)

cause in

Mis.	219– 4	neither reveals . . . cause in *e·*,
My.	149–23	cause in *e·*, and faith in sight,
	349–32	seeks cause in *e·*,

cause into

Mis.	362–16	puts cause into *e·*,

cause or

My.	364–12	of any other cause or *e·*

controls the

'01.	17–27	mind that controls the *e·* ;

curative

My.	301–30	no curative *e·* upon the body.

decorative

Pul.	28–10	* in appropriate decorative *e·*.

every

Mis.	261–11	every *e·* and amplification of wrong
Ret.	24–11	every *e·* a mental phenomenon.
Pul.	55–20	* every *e·* has its origin in desire
	70–18	every *e·* a mental phenomenon."
My.	288–24	every *e·* or amplification of wrong

fails in

Mis.	129–11	If this rule fails in *e·*,

good

Mis.	221–14	if he denies it, the good *e·* is lost.

harmonious

Hea.	7– 4	harmonious *e·* on the body.

imposing

My.	68–24	* imposing *e·* of the interior.

is antagonistic

Mis.	217–22	the *e·* is antagonistic to its cause ;

its

Mis.	51– 2	will have its *e·* physically
	66–30	that cause nor its *e·*.
	79–17	its *e·* is perfect also ;
	218–22	and end, with matter as its *e·*,
	249– 4	see if . . . could not obviate its *e·* ;
	337– 5	By proving its *e·* on yourself
Ret.	62– 3	Test C. S. by its *e·* on society,
My.	3–20	its *e·* on man is mainly this

just

Pul.	56–20	* And of the just *e·* complain ;

laws to that

Mis.	56–14	constituted laws to that *e·*,

manifestation in

Mis.	271– 4	its manifestation in *e·* as a thought,

no

Mis.	249– 5	drug had no *e·* upon me
My.	345–14	until they had no *e·* on me.

no beneficial

Mis.	348–28	drugs have no beneficial *e·*

of a fear

Ret.	61– 7	experiencing the *e·* of a fear

of alcohol

Mis.	48–16	could produce the *e·* of alcohol,

of both methods

My.	215–29	to test the *e·* of both methods

of drugs

Mis.	348–25	as to the *e·* of drugs on one who

of mesmerism

Mis.	59– 5	produces the *e·* of mesmerism.

of power

Mis.	334–10	may have the *e·* of power ;

of prayer

'01.	34– 1	*e·* of prayer, . . . as salutary in the

of self-mesmerism

My.	118– 5	is the *e·* of self-mesmerism,

of sin

Mis.	221–11	removing the *e·* of sin on himself,

one

Mis.	25– 4	one cause and one *e·*,
	271– 9	one cause and one *e·*.

on society

Ret.	62– 3	Test C. S. by its *e·* on society.

opposite

My.	348–24	never producing an opposite *e·*,

effect

or disease
Mis. 41–24 the *e·* or disease will disappear
pictorial
Pul. 25– 1 * are very rich in pictorial *e·.*
produced the
Mis. 221–13 sin has produced the *e·*
producing the
Hea. 6–25 cause producing the *e·* we see.
slightest
Mis. 221– 1 does not, produce the slightest *e·,*
spiritual
My. 318–14 the moral and spiritual *e·* upon the
supposed
Mis. 24–31 thus destroy any supposed *e·*
takes
Man. 68–22 By-Law takes *e·* on Dec. 15, 1908.
this
Mis. 310–21 send in their petitions to this *e·*
Un. 38–26 the popular views to this *e·*
took
Mis. 383– 4 ordinance took *e·* the same year,

Mis. 46–15 is not cause, but *e·,*
217– 3 *e·* without a cause is inconceivable ;
255– 6 is not cause, but *e·* ;
277–16 through which to *e·* the purposes of
Pul. 45– 5 * can *e·* cures of disease
No. 28– 8 necessary to *e·* this end
Pan. 10–22 other . . . teachers are unable to *e·.*
10–23 the *e·* of God *understood.*
My. 70–12 * The *e·* on all within earshot is
98–15 * announcement to the *e·* that
226– 9 an *e·* of one universal cause,
281–23 * *e·* on the two parties
292–20 *e·* of one human desire or belief
317– 5 * to the *e·* that Mr. Wiggin

effected

Mis. 243–10 *e·* the cure in less than one week.
Man. 46–26 where he has not *e·* a cure.
Un. 11–12 *e·* this change through the
No. 13–22 S. and H. has *e·* a revolution

effecting

Mis. 261–22 *e·* so glorious a purpose.

effective

'02. 18–23 we shall have more *e·* healers
My. 28–25 * it is as *e·* to-day as it was
155– 2 which is *e·* here and now.
233– 5 which prevents an *e·* watch?

effects

action and
Mis. 12–22 The action and *e·* of this
after
Mis. 34– 1 none of the harmful "after *e··"*
all
Mis. 369– 9 cause which governs all *e·,*
architectural
My. 86– 2 * to fine architectural *e·,*
bad
Mis. 69–20 neutralized the bad *e·*
baneful
Mis. 115–28 baneful *e·* of sin
My. 301–22 baneful *e·* of illusion
beautiful
My. 71– 4 * produce the most beautiful *e·*
cause and
My. 212– 8 expose the cause and *e·* of
consider the
Mis. 297–25 consider the *e·,* on himself
damaging
Mis. 43–29 damaging *e·* these leave
deleterious
Un. 8–15 from their deleterious *e·,*
demonstrate over the
My. 233–14 can you demonstrate over the *e·*
harmonious
'02. 8–10 its harmonious *e·* on the sick
its
Mis. 12–27 in its *e·* upon mankind,
208– 5 covers all sin and its *e·.*
352–21 to destroy it and its *e·.*
Pul. 35–26 * the more potent was its *e·.*
Pan. 11– 8 judging a cause by its *e·* ?
'01. 20–21 cannot blot out its *e·* on himself
My. 41– 6 * nor in any wise alter its *e·.*
350– 6 human hypothesis, with its *e·,*
natural
My. 205–29 Hence . . . are its natural *e·.*
occasions
Mis. 350–22 occasions *e·* on patients which
of alcohol
My. 212–10 the evil *e·* of alcohol.
of an injury
Ret. 24–12 the *e·* of an injury caused by

effects

of belief
My. 233–12 the *e·* of belief in sin
of Christian Science
Pan. 10– 6 *e·* of C. S. on the lives
of deceit
No. 2–25 cannot avert the *e·* of deceit.
of his delusion
Mis. 15– 3 endure the *e·* of his delusion
of infinite Love
Hea. 4– 5 the *e·* of infinite Love,
of Truth
Mis. 188–17 *e·* of Truth on the material senses ;
My. 103–20 *e·* of Truth on the health,
opposite
Ret. 57–27 such opposite *e·* as good and evil,
My. 292–26 and so to produce opposite *e·.*
physical
(*see* **physical**)
produced
My. 97–29 * *e·* produced by that stupendous
238– 5 *e·* produced by reading the
similar
Rud. 9–19 similar *e·* come from pride,
their
Hea. 18– 1 to destroy their *e·* upon the body,
witness the
Mis. 241–11 and witness the *e·.*

Mis. 222–17 From the *e·* of mental malpractice
My. 107–32 *e·* of calcareous salts

effectual

Mis. 33–30 It is more *e·* than drugs ;
40– 7 as *e·* in destroying sickness
45–17 *e·* in treating moral ailments.
255–25 It is more *e·* than drugs,
263–19 should be met in the most *e·* way.
Ret. 34–14 It is more *e·* than drugs,
80–12 Though the divine rebuke is *e·*
Pul. 87–22 More *e·* than the forum
No. 40–13 but the inaudible is more *e·.*
Pan. 6– 2 more *e·* than all other means ;
Hea. 12–19 made the infinitesimal dose *e·.*

effectually

My. 128–24 as *e·* as does a subtle
238– 2 *Will the Bible, . . . heal as e·*

effervescing

Hea. 18–16 if it could prevent its *e·*

effete

Ret. 12– 4 Are loosed, and not *e·* ;
79–11 ridding the thought of *e·* doctrines,
Po. 61– 2 Are loosed, and not *e·* ;

efficacious

Mis. 97–11 by no means a desirable or *e·* healer.
Man. 15–15 evidence of divine, *e·* Love,

efficacy

Mis. 3–27 their only supposed *e·* is in
89–30 avail himself of the *e·* of Truth,
261–17 atonement of Christ loses no *e·.*
282–22 they believe in the *e·* of
Ret. 83– 5 and the healing *e·* thereof,
87–26 Truth beams with such *e·* as to
Rud. 17– 6 and its divine *e·* to heal.
No. 4–17 and the *e·* of my system,
33–21 the *e·* of divine Life and Love
34– 7 meaning and *e·* of Truth and Love,
37–20 work of Jesus would lose its *e·*
43– 1 if the atonement had lost its *e·*
Peo. 9–19 with full confidence in their *e·,*
My. 90–31 * the *e·* of which to some extent is
284–25 full *e·* of divine Love
352–14 * testimony of the *e·* of our Cause

efficiency

My. 107–18 does not disprove the *e·* of the
107–19 It enhances its *e·,*

efficient

Mis. 126–19 to our *e·* Publishing Society.
'01. 19–13 notion that . . . is wise or *e·,*
My. 4– 6 practice or *e·* teaching of C. S.,
174– 8 courtesy of the *e·* city marshal

efficiently

Man. 79– 6 transact . . . *e·* such business as

effigy

Mis. 61–17 * certainly I saw him, or his *e·,*

effort

Mis. 11–25 general *e·* to benefit the race.
69–23 their *e·* to accomplish this result,
115–25 every *e·* to hurt one will only help
118–27 obedience crowns persistent *e·* with
171– 1 Jesus' first *e·* to realize Truth
230– 2 depends upon persistent *e·,*
234–14 his *e·* to steal from others

effort

Mis.	303–17	e· to help them to obey
Ret.	29– 1	cause a surrender of this e·.
	85–27	crown the e· of to-day
Un.	46–28	The fight was an e· to
Pul.	84–27	* zealous e· on the part of our
Rud.	9–22	without a direct e·,
No.	8– 4	To this small e· let us add
	9–13	whereas you may err in e·,
'02.	1– 4	With no special e· to achieve this
	12–25	united e· to purchase more land
My.	7– 8	united e· to purchase more land
	9–14	* the e· for righteous reform,
	25– 3	* making a special e·
	47–19	* showed a forward e· into the
	55–16	* This e· of Mrs. Eddy was
	130– 7	e· of disloyal students to
	164– 2	knowing that such an e· would
	312–16	* one e· at self-support.
	332– 6	* for so noble an e· in behalf of

efforts

Mis.	139–29	e· in the interest of C. S.,
	236–26	in one's e· to help another,
	245– 8	The combined e· of the
	249–21	e· of some malignant students,
Ret.	5–28	* untiring in her e· to
	27–14	e· to express in feeble diction
	38– 5	e· to persuade him to finish
	71–27	Secret mental e· to obtain help
	87–10	unsettled and spasmodic e·
Rud.	3– 4	obstinate resistance to all e·
No.	45–11	such e· arise from a spiritual lack,
Hea.	14–13	and his e· are salutary ;
Po.	32–17	health may my e· repay ;
My.	28–10	* a hint of the unselfish e·,
	42–28	* how untiring are her e·,
	48–15	* appreciation of her e·
	52–10	* will make greater e·
	55– 4	* e· were made to obtain
	62–30	* freely of their time and e·
	84–15	* for the other architectural e·
	93– 3	* without e· at proselytizing ;
	166– 2	e· to be great will never
	195–25	e· to build an edifice
	224–27	speak in loving terms of their e·,
	284– 2	honest e· (however meagre)
	334– 6	* e· are being made to buy

effulgence

Mis.	336–25	wherever one ray of its e·
My.	262–19	afford little divine e·,

egg

Hea.	19–13	Which is first, the e· or the bird?

Ego

Un.	48–16	His creation is not the E·,
	48–17	but the reflection of the E·.
	48–17	The E· is God Himself,
	51–20	The E· is divine consciousness,
	51–22	The E· is revealed as Father,

ego

Mis.	196– 1	e· is found not in matter
	196–25	the e· does arise to
	363– 4	"e·" that claims selfhood in error,
	363– 5	is no e·, but is simply
	375– 3	What is the material e·,
Un.	44–13	This abortive e·, this fable of
	45–11	evil e·, and his assumed power,
	45–24	evil e· has but the visionary
	46–20	evil was even more the e· than
	46–22	evil e· they believed must extend
	46–24	This e· was in the earthquake,
	52–16	God is not the so-called e· of evil ;
No.	26–17	Man's real e·, or selfhood, is
'02.	8–23	the e·, or I, goes to the Father,
Peo.	5–23	The e· is not self-existent

egoism

Un.	27– 8	E· is a more philosophical word,

egoist

Un.	27–10	An e·, therefore, is one

egoistic

Un.	26– 1	Evil. . . . and matter is e·,
	27–14	while God is e·, knowing only His

egotism

Mis.	209–29	e· and false charity say,
	224– 3	our e· that feels hurt by
	319–10	are beset with e· and hypocrisy.
Un.	27– 6	E· implies vanity and self-conceit.
'00.	8–17	is always e· and animality.

egotist

Un.	27– 6	e· is one who talks much of himself.
	45–10	e· must come down and learn,

egotistic

Ret.	74– 6	sense of corporeality, or e· self.
Un.	27–13	we shall find that evil is e·,

egotistical

Mis.	265–14	e· theorist or shallow moralist
Ret.	73–24	violent and e· personality,
	74– 2	a perpetually e· sensibility.

egregious

'01.	19–15	e· nonsense — a flat departure

Egypt

Mis.	374–26	* "Helen's beauty in a brow of E·."
Hea.	11–12	like the great pyramid of E·,
My.	127–16	rods of the magicians of E·.

Egyptians

My.	43– 1	* from the bondage of the E·,

eider-down

Pul.	76–16	* entirely of skins of the e· duck,

eight

Mis.	7– 6	busier than the mother of e·.
	341–23	a little girl of e· years,
Man.	61–24	about e· or nine minutes
Ret.	8– 3	when I was about e· years old,
Pul.	26–12	* silver lamps, e· feet in height.
	33– 3	* When e· years of age she began,
	62– 9	* not more than five by e· feet.
My.	16–13	* at e· o'clock in the forenoon.
	69– 2	* the e· bronze chains,
	323–32	* We were at that time some e· days
		(see also **numbers**)

eighteen

Mis.	81–12	Are not the last e· centuries
	165– 2	more than e· centuries ago,
	182–32	more than e· centuries ago.
	321– 4	than e· centuries ago ;
Ret.	5–10	e· miles from Concord,
Pul.	69– 3	* about e· months ago.
My.	52–20	* E· years ago, the Rev. . . . . Wiggin,
		(see also **dates**)

eighteenth

Ret.	2–19	seventeenth and e· centuries.

eighth

Pul.	78– 5	* an e· of an inch thick.
My.	305–19	* e· in a list of twenty-two

eighties

'02.	15– 1	In the e·, anonymous letters

eighty

(see **values**)

eighty-four

(see **numbers**)

eighty-second

Mis.	225– 4	e· birthday of his mother

eighty-seven

My.	272–25	* nearly e· years of age,

eighty-six

My.	271–14	* at e· years of age

eighty-two

My.	68– 9	* a diameter of e· feet

either

Mis.	14– 6	e· to the origin or ultimate
	40–30	nullify e· the disease itself or
	47–29	what one accepts as e· useful or
	55–30	e· a godless and material Mind, or
	67–14	shalt not utter a lie, e· mentally or
	78–11	e· Euclid or the Science of Mind
	78–12	never dreamed that e· of these
	83– 9	e· your own thought or another's."
	86–12	They e· mean formations of
	93–28	cannot go unpunished e· here or
	103–22	the human, e· as mind or body,
	105–21	If e· is misunderstood or maligned,
	105–27	has no right e· to be pitied or
	107–32	e· too much or too little of sin.
	119–18	not an argument e· for pessimism or
	123– 5	it is e· idolizing something
	132–28	e· Dr. Cullis or Mrs. Eddy,
	214–27	e· in the recognition or
	218–16	e· as mind or matter ;
	219–17	remove this feeling in e· case,
	221–14	E· of these states of mind
	241–12	E· he will hate you,
	242– 7	one thousand dollars if e·
	242– 9	two thousand dollars if e·
	250– 4	e· as a quality or as an entity?
	257– 1	e· excludes God from the universe, or
	257– 8	e· a moral or an immoral force.
	261–29	one will e· abandon his claim
	268–29	e· vacillating good or
	260– 7	e· he will hate the one, — Matt. 6 : 24.
	293–25	makes mortals e· saints or sinners.
	309– 2	e· as good or evil.

either

Mis.	315– 7	*e·* in private or in public assemblies,
	318–27	seem *e·* too large or too little :
	319–13	*e·* be overcoming sin in themselves,
	335–19	*e·* willing participants in wrong,
	352–23	*e·* get out of himself and into God
	353– 4	*e·* an excess of action or
	364–23	*e·* cooperate or quarrel
	364–29	This error, . . . would *e·* extinguish God
	374–23	*e·* doggedly deny or
	382– 1	*e·* a truism or a rule,
Man.	28–20	*e·* to resign his place or
	28–22	failing to do *e·*, said officer shall
	43– 9	Whatever is requisite for *e·* is
	51–12	*e·* withdraw from the Church or
	54–20	*e·* by word or work,
	66–26	*e·* to the Boards or to the
	92–13	*e·* one, not both, should teach
	112– 4	*e·* capitalized (The), or small
Ret.	64–18	*e·* in Principle or practice.
	78– 3	*e·* too much or too little.
	82–23	their examples *e·* excel or fall short
Pul.	26–11	* with a lamp stand . . . on *e·* end,
	29–28	* persons who had *e·* been
	80–20	* *e·* to praise or blame,
Rud.	5–15	*e·* mind which is called matter, or
	5–27	*e·* become non-existent, or
No.	3– 5	error murders *e·* friend or foe
	23–26	through the person of *e·*.
'01.	4– 1	Love as *e·* divine Principle or
	6–11	*e·* of three persons as one
	6–29	That God is *e·* inconceivable, or
	13–17	*e·* because he fears it or loves it.
	14–19	To conceive of error as *e·* right or
	19–13	*e·* in medicine or in religion,
	20– 7	to harm *e·* man or beast.
	23– 8	evil must *e·* exist in good, or
	33–30	*e·* by their practice or by ;
'02.	2–26	*e* in heart or in doctrine ;
Hea.	9–10	has not saved them from *e·*,
	9–24	*e·* an error of mind or of body.
	13– 3	accomplish less on *e·* side.
My.	30– 2	* *e·* coming from a service or
	69–16	* two on *e·* side
	71–25	* *e·* on floor or galleries,
	82– 2	* *e·* through a cure to themselves or
	106– 2	I admonish . . . Scientists *e·* to
	114–32	these progressive steps *e·* written or
	143–14	fustian of *e·* denying or asserting
	144– 7	*e·* of the aforesaid conditions
	146–25	*e·* in the right or in the wrong
	216–11	*E·* his life must be a miracle
	218–23	belief that an individual can *e·*
	223–18	*e·* of which I do not entertain.
	225–24	*e·* in speaking or in writing,
	259– 3	on *e·* side lace and flowers.
	259–23	considered *e·* collectively or
	275–19	*E·* my work, . . . or the weather,
	276– 6	judged by *e·* a daily drive or
	302– 5	produces the result in *e·* case.
	356–22	*e·* he will hate the one, — *Matt.* **6 : 24.**

ejaculated

Pul.	49–13	* "Four years !" she *e·* ;

ejection

My.	222–30	will aid the *e·* of error,

elaborate

Un.	52–22	*e·* in beauty, color, and form,
Pul.	56–10	* Space does not admit of an *e·*
My.	66–21	* *e·* observances of Sunday,
	68–26	* with *e·* plaster work

elaborately

Pul.	76–12	* special designs, *e·* carved,

elaborates

Mis.	13–14	theology *e·* the proposition

elaborating

Mis.	38–22	*e·* a man-made theory,

elapsed

Mis.	297– 1	short time that has *e·* since
Man.	39–10	when sufficient time has *e·*

elastic

Pul.	32–21	* *e·* bearing of a woman of thirty,

elate

Po.	39–16	be your waiting hearts *e·*,

elbow

Mis.	32–28	should never envy, *e·*, slander,

elbowed

Mis.	80–28	*e·* by a new school of practitioners,

elbowing

Mis.	294– 3	*e·* the concepts of his own creating,
	339–12	The *e* of the crowd

elders

Pul.	vii– 5	*e·* of the twentieth century,
'00.	12–12	the Ephesian *e·* travelled to
My.	38–20	* not a whit behind their *e* ,
	261– 4	The wisdom of their *e·*,
	340–19	Not the tradition of the *e·*,

eldritch

Mis.	376–21	with an acre of *e·* ebony.

elect

Mis.	78–16	if possible, the very *e·*.
	175–20	the very *e·*," — *Matt.* **24 : 24.**
	302–22	When I should so *e·*
	314– 6	shall *e·* two Readers :
Man.	79– 2	Directors shall *e·* annually
	80–19	but if she does not *e·* to
	86–11	can *e·* an experienced
	102– 7	This committee shall *e·*,
Ret.	14– 7	to have *e·* believers converted
	90–10	"the *e·* lady" — *II John* 1 : 1.
My.	17–15	corner stone, *e·* — *I Pet.* 2 : 6.
	229–30	should be happier than the *e·*.

elected

Mis.	296– 2	have allowed myself to be *e·*
Man.	18–20	were *e·* members of this Church,
	18–21	others that have since been *e·*
	25– 9	The President shall be *e·*,
	26– 7	or new officers *e·*,
	26–13	Readers shall be *e·*
	26–16	its candidates before they are *e·* ;
	38–11	*e·* by majority vote
	63–21	*e·* by the C. S. Board of Directors,
	81– 1	or new officers *e·*,
	88–11	vice-president shall be *e·* annually
	88–13	teacher shall be *e·* every third year
	89– 8	*e·* to fill the vacancy.
	93– 6	members of which shall be *e·* annually
	97– 9	He shall be *e·* annually
	99–17	Committee . . . is *e·* only by
	100–24	*e·* by the branch church.
	100–27	suitable woman shall be *e·*.
Ret.	6–25	soon *e·* to the Legislature
Pul.	45–30	* *e·* each year by the congregation.

electing

Man.	56–19	*e·* officers and other business,
	56–22	meetings for *e·* candidates
My.	49–17	* for the purpose of *e·* officers.

election

Man.	25– 3	NAMES, *e·*, AND DUTIES.
	25–13	eligible for *e·* but once in
	26– 5	dating from the time of *e·*
	29–20	*E·*
	37–15	RECOMMENDATION AND *e·*.
	38– 9	*E·*.
	80–25	dating from the time of *e·*
	88–10	*E·*.
	93– 4	*E·*.
	100– 2	for the *e·* of officers,
Ret.	7– 4	before his *e·*.
	13– 6	doctrine of unconditional *e·*,
Peo.	3– 6	the *e·* of the minority to be saved
My.	310– 8	died before the *e·*.

electric

Pul.	25– 5	* systems with motor *e·* power.
	26– 2	* *e·* lights in the form of a star,
	58–30	* *e·* light, behind an antique
	62–11	* rung from an *e·* keyboard,
My.	219–12	to ride to church on an *e·* car,

electrical

My.	110–13	*e·* forces annihilating time and

electricity

Mis.	257–22	*E·*, governed by this so-called law,
	366–22	drugs, *e·*, and animal magnetism
	378–17	"Because it conveys *e·* to them."
	379–14	*e·* was not as potential or
Ret.	33– 8	homœopathy, hydropathy, *e·*, and
Pul.	25– 3	* are done by *e·*,
	64–17	* allopathy, homœopathy, and *e·*,
My.	307– 8	nothing to do with matter, *e·*, or
	345–10	* *e·*, engineering, the telephone,
	348– 3	*e·*, magnetism, or will-power,

elects

Peo.	8– 4	*e·* some to be saved and others to be

elegant

Mis.	280–20	*e·* album costing fifty dollars,
Pul.	76– 8	* floor is of mosaic in *e·* designs,
	76–22	chapter sub-title
	77– 3	* one of the most chastely *e·*
	86–12	* encased in an *e·* plush box.
My.	66–21	* spacious and *e·* edifice

element

animal

Mis.	281– 3	doors that this animal *e·* flings open

element

divine
Mis. 337–21 they obscure its divine *e*,

essential
Pul. 53–20 * the essential *e* of success

great
Peo. 1– 3 The great *e* of reform

lost
Mis. 252–25 restores its lost *e*,
Man. 17–13 its lost *e* of healing.
My. 46–12 its lost *e* of healing."

magnetic
'01. 2– 9 the fatal magnetic *e*

male
My. 355–11 The male *e* is a strong

material
Hea. 3–10 the personal and material *e*

misnamed matter
Mis. 201– 4 resolves the *e* misnamed matter

mortal
Mis. 2–28 out of evil, their mortal *e*,

no
Mis. 152–27 there enters no *e* of earth
My. 180–12 no *e* whatever of hypnotism

no insignificant
My. 91–13 * no insignificant *e* in true

of action
Peo. 10– 2 the stronger *e* of action ;

of brute-force
Mis. 40–32 An *e* of brute-force that

of error
Un. 58– 3 their native *e* of error,

of matter
Mis. 201– 7 death is an *e* of matter,

of personality
Pul. 37–14 * eliminate the *e* of personality

opposing
'01. 31 - 3 The only opposing *e* that
My. 293–22 possessed no opposing *e*,

raging
My. 249– 6 raging *e* of individual hate

religious
Mis. 145– 3 when the religious *e*,

spiritual
Ret. 65– 7 which freeze out the spiritual *e*.

My. 278–30 an *e* opposed to Love,

elementary
Mis. 260–18 *e* opposite to Him who
My. 181– 5 are aided . . . with *e* truths,

elements

animal
My. 245–14 Towards the animal *e*

angry
Mis. 162– 9 stem these rising angry *e*,

certain
'00. 10–11 Certain *e* in human nature

conflicting
My. 134– 9 conflicting *e* must be mastered.

counteracting
My. 294– 9 mental counteracting *e*,

English
Ret. 1–19 Scotch and English *e*

grosser
Peo. 2– 7 yields its grosser *e*,

its own
Mis. 268–30 error dies of its own *e*.

jarring
'00. 11– 6 jarring *e* among musicians

material
Mis. 3–24 material *e* of sin and death.
Ret. 60–17 raging of the material *e*
Peo. 1– 5 crumbling away of material *e*

of all forms
Mis. 101–32 comprise the *e* of all forms

of earth
Mis. 9– 8 refuge at last from the *e* of earth.
383–10 *e* of earth beat in vain against

of evil
Mis. 40–27 has to master those *e* of evil

pent-up
Mis. 356– 5 pent-up *e* of mortal mind

self-destroying
Un. 52–19 self-destroying *e* of this world,

spiritual
Mis. 2–30 putting on the spiritual *e*

such
Ret. 65–17 constituted of such *e* as
My. 201–11 Such *e* of friendship, faith, and

these
'00. 10–15 These *e* assail even the new-old

waits on the
Mis. 330–32 patient corn waits on the *e*

Un. 25–24 *e* which belong to the eternal All,

elevate
Mis. 5– 1 will *e* and purify the race.
38– 4 *e* man in every line of life,
Hea. 5–26 purify, *e*, and consecrate man ;

elevated
Ret. 5–25 * She gave an *e* character to
93– 6 Science has *e* this idea
My. 255– 9 *e* to offices for which they are not

elevates
Pul. 53–18 * attribute of mind which *e* man
Po. 39–13 The cause she *e*.
My. 130–13 the lever which *e* mankind.
260–24 *e* medicine to Mind ;

elevating
Mis. 3– 1 *e* the race physically, morally,
Pan. 6–26 It is plain that *e* evil to the
Peo. 2–27 a benign and *e* influence
My. 278–19 *e* power of civilization

elevation
Ret. 88–11 an *e* of the understanding
My. 86– 6 brooding *e*, guarding as it were,

elevator
Mis. 259–23 spiritual *e* of the human race,
My. 288– 8 *e* of the human race ;

eleven
Pul. 72–16 * "And for the past *e* years,"
(*see also* **numbers, values**)

elicit
Mis. 295– 2 deserve and *e* brief comment.

eligibility
Man. 30– 1 E.
89–23 furnish evidence of their *e*

eligible
Man. 25–13 *e* for election but once in
39–13 *e* to probationary membership
72– 7 is *e* to form a church
74–15 In order to be *e* to a card in *The*
79–12 Before being *e* for office
89–16 *e* to receive the degree of C.S.D.
89–23 *e* to enter the Normal class.
109– 4 *e* to approve candidates
109– 6 No persons are *e* to countersign
My. 251–13 *e* to enter the Normal class,
251–21 if found *e*, receive a certificate

Elijah
'02. 16– 1 came to E. after the earthquake

eliminate
Pul. 37–14 * to *e* the element of personality
My. 268–16 will *e* divorce and war.

eliminated
Mis. 218–26 neither *e* nor retained by Spirit.
259–11 not a quality to be known or *e* by
My. 268–30 sex or gender *e* ;

eliminates
Un. 56–12 first *e* and then destroys.

Elisha
Mis. 134–23 Like E., look up, and behold :

Elite
Pul. 89–27 * E., Chicago, Ill.

Elizabeth's, Queen
No. 44–13 In Queen E. time Protestantism could

Ellen
Po. page 65 poem

elm
My. 147– 6 old *e* on North State Street

elms
Pul. 49–15 "Look at those big *e* !
63–11 * pointed to a number of large *e*
My. 174– 4 The wide-spreading *e*

elocutionist
Pul. 43–11 * Mrs. . . . Bemis, a distinguished *e*,
59–18 * read by a professional *e*,

Elohim
Mis. 182–25 eternal heritage of the E.,

eloping
My. 314–20 for *e* with his wife,

eloquence
Mis. 345– 6 immortal strains of *e*.
Hea. 2–24 it was not in the power of *e*
My. 90– 4 * wooed by no *e* of orator
247–21 not so much *e* as

eloquent
Mis. 101– 1 feeble lips are made *e*,
Ret. 15–21 memorable by *e* addresses
Pul. 1–10 time *improved* is *e* in God's
46– 1 * that Judge Hanna was so *e*
My. 262–28 *e* silence, prayer, and praise
316–16 *e* appeal to the press

eloquently
Pul.	5–18	Then *e·* paraphrasing it,
My.	46– 4	* *e·* beckoning us on

else
Mis.	9–21	*e·*, the contents of this cup of
	12–27	Whatever manifests aught *e·*
	63–20	none *e·* beside Him," — *Deut.* 4 : 35.
	64–16	are narrow, *e·* extravagant,
	70– 1	*e·* the Scriptures misstate man's power.
	97–19	and there is none *e·*, — *Isa.* 45 : 5.
	128– 1	*e·* it grows hard and
	130–10	for a fault in somebody *e·*,
	141–27	or *e·* return every dollar that
	178–20	* 'Much learning' — or something *e·*
	192–31	*e·* we are entertaining the startling
	211– 6	*e·* the blind will lead the blind
	236– 5	little *e·* than the troubles,
	236–29	doing our duty, whatever *e·* may
	241–14	*e·* he will doubtingly await the result ;
	260–20	Then, whatever *e·* seemeth to be
	261–30	or *e·* make the claim valid.
	265– 4	or wiser than somebody *e·*,
	266–11	work that nobody *e·* can or will do.
	269– 7	he will hold to — *Matt.* 6 : 24.
	276– 4	like all *e·*, was purely Western
	319– 6	aught *e·* than good.
	319–15	*e·* they are self-deceived sinners
	329–18	Whatever *e·* droops, spring is gay :
	365–30	more than all *e·*,
	367–19	if He did know aught *e·*,
Man.	43–12	as no one *e·* can.
Ret.	23– 4	or *e·* be merged into the
	28– 5	*e·* we cannot understand the
	30–21	No one *e·* can drain the cup
	48– 3	Who *e·* could sustain this institute,
	56–21	Whatever *e·* claims to be mind,
	81–18	or *e·* that heart is consciously untrue
	82–23	consummate much good or *e·* evil ;
Un.	19– 4	*e·* He is not omnipotent,
	19–10	*e·* how could it have come
	21– 3	*e·* excusing one another." — *Rom.* 2 : 15.
	38–16	but that something *e·* also is
	53–22	or *e·* he has lost his true
	53–24	*e·* the immortal and unerring
Pul.	33–22	* no one *e·* had seen him,
Rud.	12– 7	*e·* quiet the fear of the sick
	13–15	none *e·* beside Him." — *Deut.* 4 : 35.
	16–27	or *e· post mortem* evidence.
No.	27–28	*e·* their present mistakes would
Pan.	9– 4	no reality in aught *e·*.
'00.	9–14	misguide action, *e·* they uplift
	9–29	no one *e·* has seemed equal to
'01.	4–15	*divine*, . . . *e·* there is no Science
'02.	7–16	than which there is naught *e·*.
	20–22	but in this, as all *e·*,
Hea.	15–19	everything *e·* besides God,
	19– 5	*e·* those functions could not
Peo.	2–17	*e·* of wood or stone.
	6–27	for which we are to leave all *e·*.
My.	10–22	* on the part of some one *e·*.
	37– 4	* Naught *e·* than the grandeur
	90– 7	* Whatever *e·* it is, this faith
	96–10	* dominates everything *e·*.
	130–31	that you borrow little *e·*
	152–18	than which there is none *e·*
	153–19	Faith in aught *e·* misguides
	178–31	all *e·* reported as his sayings
	197–18	*e·* C. S. will disappear
	231–18	*e·* love's labor is lost
	340–26	example in this, as in all *e·*,
	347–19	in exchange for all *e·*.
	356–23	*e·* he will hold to the one, — *Matt.* 6 : 24.
		(*see also* **nothing**)

elsewhere
Mis.	127– 9	Scientists, here and *e·*,
	178–24	* *to* preach, here or *e·*."
	290–24	and it should not, . . . dwell *e·*,
My.	18– 5	Scientists, here and *e·*,
	74– 7	* from New York and *e·*
	98–22	* in this country or *e·*,
	120– 3	or *e·* than in my writings,
	177– 7	daily duties require attention *e·*,
	243–16	students in New York and *e·*

elucidate
Mis.	47–13	tend to *e·* your day-dream,
	159– 3	to *e·* His Word.
	269–11	*e·* the Principle of being,
	380– 9	to enable me to *e·* or
Man.	87–16	*e·* the Principle and rule of C. S.,
Ret.	83– 1	*e·* scientific healing and teaching.
Un.	29–22	Often we can *e·* the
Rud.	13–17	*e·* my meaning.
'02.	16–25	fail to *e·* Christianity :

elucidates
Mis.	261– 8	C. S. not only *e·* but
	309–26	"S. and H. . . . *e·* this topic.
	361–28	He *e·* His own idea,
Rud.	16–21	*e·* a pathological Science
'02.	8– 1	*e·* Christianity, illustrates God,
My.	251–25	What God gives, *e·*, armors, and

elucidation
'01.	31– 1	by a clear *e·* of truth,
My.	241– 4	* *e·* of the Principle and rule of

eluding
Un.	64–12	*e·* their dread presence

emanate
Rud.	11–24	whence *e·* health, harmony, and

emanates
Mis.	16–24	*e·* from Soul instead of body,

emanating
Rud.	6– 7	beauty and goodness . . . *e·* from God ;
No.	1– 2	spiritual idea *e·* from the infinite,
My.	29–19	* *e·* from the thousands who
	154–24	*e·* from the pulpit and press.

emanation
'01.	10– 8	a spiritual, divine *e·*,
My.	226–10	an *e·* of the one . . . Principle

emancipate
Mis.	385–14	Spirit *e·* for this far shore
Po.	48– 7	Spirit *e·* for this far shore
My.	267–27	whereby soul is *e·*

emancipating
My.	190– 4	*e·* it with the morning beams

emancipation
Pul.	55–10	* *e·* from many of the thraldoms,
Peo.	10–23	*e·* of our bodies from sickness
My.	74–25	* springs from a belief in such *e·*.
	248–13	adequate for the *e·* of the race.

emasculation
Mis.	206–14	no *e·*, no illusive vision,

embark
My.	132–10	knows they *e·* for infinity

embarrass
My.	118–15	*e·* the higher criticism.

embarrassing
My.	312–14	* position was an *e·* one.

embellishing
My.	162–14	building, *e·*, and furnishing

emblazoned
No.	2– 1	on its standard have *e·*
My.	194–17	*e·* on the fair escutcheon
	341–17	*e·* on the escutcheon

emblem
Mis.	162–11	the cross became the *e·*
	357–12	no central *e·*, no history.
Un.	57– 9	The cross is the central *e·*
'00.	13–19	the *e·* of Æsculapius.

emblematic
Pul.	27–14	* *e·* of the six water-pots
	28– 6	* decorated with *e·* designs,

emblems
My.	326–17	the *e·* of a master Mason,

embodied
Mis.	34–30	Science of healing *e·* in her works.
Pul.	38–20	* between the *e·* and disembodied
'00.	8– 2	behold more nearly the *e·* Christ,
My.	154–25	*e·* in a visible communion,
	285–15	*e·* in the Association for

embodies
Mis.	191– 2	The Hebrew *e·* the term
Un.	39–24	and *e·* Life, not death.
'01.	12–26	Incorporeal evil *e·* itself

embodiment
Mis.	61–28	Naming these His *e·*,
Un.	3–23	every *e·* of Life and Mind.
Pan.	5–21	nor believe that it hath *e·*
'00.	7–24	so far from the *e·* of Truth
'01.	13– 4	annihilates its own *e·* :
Peo.	5– 4	the *e·* of a living faith,
My.	130–29	*e·* and substance of the truth

embodiments
Mis.	61–26	mortals are the *e·* . . . of error,

embody
No.	4–19	because they *e·* not the idea

embodying
My.	10– 9	* *e·* the best of design,

embound
Po.	29–13	Beloved, replete, by flesh *e·*

embrace
Mis. 392– 7 earth, asleep in night's *e*,
400– 2 Slumbers not in God's *e* ;
Pul. 16–14 Slumbers not in God's *e* ;
66–10 * most of those who *e* the faith
Pan. 8–24 doctrines that *e* pantheism,
Po. 20–10 earth, asleep in night's *e*,
76–13 Slumbers not in God's *e* ;
My. 332–12 * fond *e* of her friends.
342–21 It will *e* all the churches,

embraced
Mis. 103–30 individuality is *e* in Mind,
Ret. 43–15 *e* the teachings of C. S.,
75–17 *e* in the author's own mental mood,
Un. 6–18 as is *e* in the theory of

embraces
Mis. 2–15 *e* a deeper and broader philosophy
'02. 4–13 My subject to-day *e* the

embracing
My. 86– 6 * *e* as it may be, the hosts of

embroidery
Mis. 159–28 rich devices in *e*, silver, gold,

embryo
Mis. 15–26 In mortal . . . goodness seems in *e*.

embryo-man
Mis. 186– 5 Soul is supposed to enter the *e*

emerald
Mis. 354–31 To gaze on the lark in her *e* bower
Po. 18– 9 To gaze on the lark in her *e* bower
30– 3 new-born beauty in the *e* sky,
My. 150–16 willowy banks dyed with *e*.

emerge
'01. 10–27 we *e* gently into Life everlasting.

emerged
Ret. 88– 8 *e* into a higher manifestation of
No. 20–24 *e* from the ark,

emergencies
Mis. 5–14 do not fail in the greatest *e*.
41–28 is sufficient for all *e*.
Man. 78–16 *E*.

emergency
Mis. 283–12 if no *e* demanded this.

emerges
My. 200–16 man *e* from mortality

emerging
My. 273– 7 * *e* triumphantly from all attacks
307–26 *e* from *materia medica*,

Emeritus
(see **Eddy, Pastor Emeritus**)

Emerson (see also **Emerson's**)
Ralph Waldo
Ret. 37–13 David Hume, Ralph Waldo *E*,
My. 306– 7 for such was Ralph Waldo *E* ;

Un. 17– 4 *E* says, "Hitch your wagon to a

Emerson's
Ralph Waldo
My. 305– 4 Ralph Waldo *E* philosophy

eminence
Pul. 32–29 * achieved *e* as a lawyer.

eminent
Mis. 169–18 most *e* divines of the world
346– 4 spiritual healing as *e* proof
No. 23–14 The most *e* divines, in Europe

eminently
My. 97–17 * good-looking, *e* respectable,

emissaries
My. 213– 7 by no means a right of . . . its *e*,

emit
No. 16–17 because it has no darkness to *e*.
'00. 8– 7 odors *e* characteristics of

emits
Mis. 290–29 it *e* light because it reflects ;

emitting
Chr. 53–40 Life, . . . *E* light !
My. 282–15 to all mankind a light *e* light.
301– 2 from Light *e* light.

emoluments
Mis. 44– 3 are not working for *e*,

emotion
My. 26–11 imagine my gratitude and *e*

emotionalism
My. vii–12 * untainted by the *e* which

emotions
Mis. 291–31 his *e* and conclusions.
Ret. 11– 2 Poetry suited my *e* better
79–18 If beset with misguided *e*,

emotions
My. 296–27 its *e*, motives, and object.
332– 5 * *e* of the thankful heart,

emperor
Mis. 224– 8 The *e* lifted his hands to his head,
'01. 30–23 no *e* is obeyed like the

Emperor Augustus
'00. 12–10 in the time of the Roman *E* *A*.

emperors
My. 112–29 palaces of *e* and kings,

emphasis
Mis. 312–26 reverberate and renew its *e*
Pul. 57–10 * truths which will find *e*

emphasize
My. 113–29 *e* the answer to this
291–20 *e* humane power, and

emphasized
Ret. 9–7 and *e* her affirmation.
13–13 theology *e* belief in a
Pul. 73–18 * When seen yesterday she *e*
My. 170– 9 *e* in the minds of all present

emphasizes
Pul. 33–15 * which history not infrequently *e*,
'02. 7–28 *e* the apostle's declaration,

emphasizing
Mis. 116–13 *e* its grand strains,

emphatic
Mis. 192–25 last chapter of Mark is *e* on this
Pul. 59–19 * in a clear *e* style.
Rud. 2–26 * purpose of C. S. is the
3–10 His history is *e* in our hearts,
My. 12–17 This was an *e* rule of St. Paul :

emphatically
Un. 31– 9 as *e* as they annihilated sin.
Pul. 80– 8 * Boston is *e* the women's paradise,
'01. 3–13 Also, we accept God, *e*, in the
My. 14–18 * *e* pronounced the story a
256– 5 *e* phrasing strict observance

empire
Mis. 14–19 evil's umpire and *e*,
Po. 15–14 I would live in their *e*,

Empire City
My. 243– 8 The *E* *C* is large,
(see also **New York**)

empires
Mis. 268–27 From lack of moral strength *e* fall.
Peo. 2–19 Such a theory has overturned *e*
My. 162– 9 stronger than the might of *e*.

empirical
Mis. 234–15 *E* knowledge is worse than useless :

employ
Mis. 25–30 why did not Jesus *e* them
78–17 that some people *e* the
89– 1 when you *e* the other.
270–11 To seek or *e* other means
Man. 41–11 *e* no violent invective,
67–11 shall not *e* an attorney,
70– 4 a Christian Scientist in the *e* of
Ret. 85– 6 at present they can *e*
No. 10– 1 I *e* this awe-filled word
42– 6 and *e* material forms to
Hea. 14–10 If you *e* a medical practitioner,
My. 128–15 man's right . . . to *e* a physician,

employed
Mis. 49– 7 friends *e* a homœopathist,
75–16 this term should seldom be *e*
91–17 *e* in the service of C. S.
95–20 no human agencies were *e*,
184–29 He *e* a type of physical
191–20 The term, being here *e* in its
Man. 69–22 Students *e* by Mrs. Eddy
Ret. 21– 5 Every means . . . was *e* to find him,
37– 3 term *e* by me to express
59–14 name . . . if properly *e*,
Un. 27– 2 *e* in the foregoing colloquy.
No. 15– 9 commentaries are *e*
Hea. 9– 4 and *e* our thoughts more in
13–20 *e* Mind as the only curative
My. 307–11 other terms which I *e*
317– 9 great mistake to say that I *e*
318– 7 I especially *e* him on

employees
Man. 81– 5 Suitable *E*.
My. 135–10 personally attended . . . to my *e*.
137–14 attended personally . . . to my *e*.

employing
Mis. 89– 5 *who is e a regular physician,*
Man. 99–27 church *e* said Committee.
Ret. 89–23 for *e* another student to take
Hea. 15– 4 *e* no other remedy than Truth,

employment
Mis. 118–26 it gives one plenty of e,
244–16 * the e of visible agencies
'01. 34– 1 or by preventing the early e of
employs
Man. 96– 8 paid by the church that e him.
Pul. 49–29 * She e a number of men
emporium
'00. 12– 9 especially flourished as an e
empowered
Mis. 235– 3 e to conquer sin, sickness,
empowers
Mis. 252–28 and e the business man
Empress of India
My. 289–16 Queen of Great Britain and E of I,
289–29 Queen of Great Britain and E of I.
emptied
Mis. 168–13 e of vainglory and vain knowledge,
My. 38–13 * and was e in twelve,
82–17 * edifice was e of its crowds
82–22 * would be e of its twenty thousand
149–18 must be e before it can be refilled.
emptiness
Ret. 86– 2 to offset boastful e,
empty
Mis. 93– 1 to e his students' minds,
Ret. 84–21 to e his students' minds of error,
Rud. 15–27 as are required to e and to
Hea. 10–28 Earth's fading dreams are e streams,
Po. 53–18 To e summer bowers,
My. 231–23 has not an e apartment in his
emulate
Mis. 7– 9 we must strive to e.
My. 131– 9 that we commemorate and would e,
148–30 to e the words and the works of
emulation
Mis. 324–14 envy, e, hatred, wrath,
'02. 18–17 no e, no deceit, enters into
enable
Mis. ix– 4 * e a man to dispense with alms."
115–12 May God e my students
352–20 in order to e one to destroy it
380– 9 requisite to e me to elucidate
Ret. 82–22 e Christian Scientists to
88–12 will e thought to apprehend
Un. 7–11 to e me instantaneously to
18–19 which alone e Me to rebuke,
43–23 e us to apprehend, or lay hold
No. 15– 6 would e any one to prove
'00. 5–18 it would e man to escape
My. 63–14 * e us better to work out the
66–13 * will e the church to expand,
71– 3 * e the organist to produce
150–18 ask God to e you to reflect God,
317–13 e me to explain more clearly
enabled
Mis. 30–19 e man to demonstrate the law of
201–17 e him to triumph over them,
'01. 29–15 e them to be grand coworkers
My. 12– 5 * liberal donations with e
63– 1 * e to secure the services of
122–17 Has it e us to know more of the
enables
Mis. 43– 3 e one to heal cases without
45– 4 e you to control pain.
49–19 e man to discern between
125– 7 This knowledge e him to
352–17 e the practitioner to act
369– 7 e us to stand erect
Pan. 11–23 God e us to know that
'00. 5–27 e one to utilize the power of
Hea. 15– 9 it e mind to govern matter,
My. 5–19 e the devout Scientist to worship,
39–28 * e us to comprehend better the
76–17 * e them to dedicate their churches
274–13 To begin rightly e one to end rightly,
enabling
Mis. xi–12 e him to walk the untrodden
Pul. 40–11 * E Six Thousand Believers to Attend
My. 161– 2 and set us free by e us to pay it ;
300– 3 e the sinner to overcome sin
enact
Peo. 11–19 pass legislative acts and e penal
enacted
No. 30–11 is punished by the law e.
enactments
Peo. 11–21 calls its own e "laws of
encased
Ret. 2–12 sword, e in a brass scabbard,
Pul. 46–19 * sword, e in a brass scabbard,

encased
Pul. 77– 5 * e in a handsome plush casket
78–23 * e in a white satin-lined box
86–11 * is e in an elegant plush box.
enchained
Mis. 153–17 and as captives are they e.
Po. 65– 9 is e to life's dreary night,
enchant
Po. 68–11 E deep the senses,
enchanting
Pul. 2–12 sublunary views, however e,
enchantment
Mis. 394–20 * So full of sweet e are
Po. 15– 9 Here gloom hath e
41–21 a strain of e that flowed
57– 6 * So full of sweet e are
enchantments
No. 14–11 blends with its magic and e.
encircle
My. 189–14 e and cement the human race.
encircles
Mis. 389–13 His arm e me, and mine,
Po. 4–12 His arm e me, and mine,
encircling
My. 347–11 design of boughs e this cup,
enclose
Mis. 157–18 I e you the name of
My. 289– 4 I e a check for five hundred
enclosed
Pul. 60–30 * e in separate swell-box,
My. 26–19 The e notice I submit to you,
172–25 e note from Mrs. Eddy was read :
175– 6 Please accept the e check
327–11 * I know the e article will
enclosures
My. 326– 2 * e received from our Leader.
encompass
Ret. 68–20 Darkness and doubt e thought,
encompassed
Mis. 110–17 when e by divine presence,
153–15 e not with pride, hatred,
My. 64– 6 * The glories of . . . e us,
encompasseth
Mis. 78– 5 brightness of His glory e
encompassing
'01. 25– 5 e time and eternity.
encounter
Mis. 210–32 lest it should suffer from an e.
237–14 must e and help to eradicate
'01. 31– 4 opposing element that . . . can e
encountered
Mis. 131–21 e in Anno Domini 1894,
Ret. 41– 1 which C. S. e a quarter-century
50–30 e in the beginning of pioneer work.
My. 11– 7 * e the full force of antagonism.
encourage
Mis. 229–13 e faith in God in this direction,
275–16 e, and bless all who mourn.
No. 32– 4 pardon may e a criminal to
Hea. 14– 7 and e faith in an opposite
My. 217– 4 Further to e your early,
encouraged
Mis. 348–29 I have by no means e
Un. 5– 9 Every one should be e not to
My. 6–16 Greatly impressed and e thereby,
11–19 * cheered and e to know that,
132–17 the heart of every member
141– 9 * have not been e to attend the
213– 7 ought not to be e in it.
encouragement
Mis. 262–27 words of approval and e
'01. 14–30 evil-doer receives no e from
My. 62–24 * words of e when they were so
356–15 I have given no assurance, no e
encourages
Mis. 252–27 it e and empowers the business man
302– 4 e infringement of my copyright,
Ret. 63–24 recollect that it e sin to say,
My. 123– 7 this e me to continue to
encouraging
Mis. 262–18 e the heart grown faint
Rud. 12– 8 e them in the belief of error
encroachment
Pul. 66–24 * this e upon prevailing faiths,
encumbered
Mis. 327–15 e travellers halt and disagree.
360– 3 e with crude, rude fragments,
Pul. 1– 6 e with greetings

encumbering
Mis. 154– 8 prune its e· branches,
205–28 e· mortal molecules,

end (noun)
accomplished its
Ret. 45– 9 has accomplished its e·,
await the
My. 222–31 will cheerfully await the e·
beginning or
Mis. 189–32 Life without beginning or e·.
No. 37–10 He cannot know beginning or e·.
My. 119–25 without beginning or e· of days.
cause and
Mis. 218–21 notion of Spirit as cause and e·,
certain
Mis. 71–22 mythical origin and certain e·.
either
Pul. 26–11 * a lamp stand . . . on either e·,
for the beginning
Mis. 215–11 if we take the e· for the beginning
gaining the
Ret. 54–10 gaining the e· through persecution
great
Mis. 361–17 To this great e·, Paul admonished,
have an
Hea. 4–18 to become finite, and have an e· ;
his
My. 333–22 * "His e· was calm and peaceful,
institutional
My. 8– 5 * outgrowing the institutional e·
in view
My. 68– 2 * with the e· in view of
is attained
Mis. 220–14 e· is attained, and the patient says
knows the
Mis. 208–23 knows the e· from the beginning,
means and
My. 278– 5 this means and e· will be
no
My. 267–12 hath no beginning and no e·,
of a cycle
Pul. 23–22 * assert that the e· of a cycle,
of a rope
Mis. 61–18 * dangling at the e· of a rope.
61–23 or dangle at the e· of a rope?
of days
Un. 13–17 or e· of days." — see Heb. 7 : 3.
My. 119–25 Life without beginning or e· of days.
of four months
Ret. 19–17 at the e· of four months, my babe
My. 330–29 at the e· of four months, my babe
of his demonstration
Mis. 215–28 at the e· of his demonstration.
of idolatry
My. 220–16 e· of idolatry and infidelity,
of life
Chr. 55–21 nor e· of life ; — Heb. 7 : 3.
of nine days
My. 335–17 * at the e· of nine days he passed away.
of summer
My. 61– 8 * completed before the e· of summer,
of that man
Ret. 42–15 the e· of that man is — Psal. 37 : 37.
of the period
Pul. 73–10 * and at the e· of the period
of the service
My. 32– 3 * communion at the e· of the service,
of the world
My. 44–12 * unto the e· of the world." — Matt. 28 : 20.
pulpit
Pul. 42–18 * The pulpit e· of the auditorium
put an
'02. 3– 8 has put an e·, at Charleston, to any
My. 248–10 is to put an e· to falsities
steadfast to the
Ret. 26– 8 Way-shower, steadfast to the e·
successful
'02. 14–15 successful e· could never have been
this
Ret. 21–27 To this e·, but only to this e·,
88–15 This e· Jesus achieved,
Pul. 85–15 * chosen of God to this e·,
No. 28– 8 revolutions necessary to effect this e·
My. 10–23 * the money necessary to this e·,
178– 8 it hastens hourly to this e·.
unto the
Chr. 57– 2 my works unto the e·, — Rev. 2 : 26.
Ret. 89–20 and guarded them unto the e·,
No. 7– 8 and continue to do so unto the e·.
My. 44–12 * even unto the e· — Matt. 28 : 20.
159– 6 even unto the e·." — Matt. 28 : 20.
285–18 my works unto the e·, — Rev. 2 : 26.
without
Chr. 53–39 without birth and without e·,
Un. 40–23 without beginning and without e·,

end (noun)
without
'02. 7–15 without beginning and without e·,
Hea. 4–20 without beginning and without e·.

Mis. 140– 8 to the e· of taxing their faith
216–20 * beginning with the e· of the tail,
282–23 sometimes . . . e· justifies the means ;
Un. 19–13 this would be the e· of infinite
Pul. 13–19 What must the e· be?
My. 99–25 * and the e· is not yet.
187–11 e· of the commandment is — I Tim. 1 : 5.
344–12 preserving individuality . . . to the e·.
345– 6 will overthrow false . . . in the e·."

end (verb)
Mis. vii–11 Till time shall e· more timely,
106–25 praise that shall never e·
113–22 will e· in insanity, dementia, or
Ret. 71–29 will e· in destroying health and
Pul. 3– 3 Can eternity e·?
No. 37– 7 to begin and e·,
My. 166– 2 will never e· in anarchy
204– 8 can begin and never e·.
218–24 false faith that will e· bitterly.
274–13 enables one to e· rightly,
279–18 e· wars, and demonstrate
281–28 War will e· when nations are
296–19 evil will e· in harmony,
350– 4 to e· with the phenomenon, matter,

endearing
Man. 64–17 individual, e· term of Mother.
My. 302–15 e· appellative "Mother,"

endeavor
Mis. 41–15 scales the mountain of human e·,
66–31 I e· to accommodate my
204–27 gives . . . success to e·.
227–11 e· to get their weighty stuff
348–10 divine Love will bless this e·
Man. 49– 2 shall not e· to monopolize the
Ret. 28–29 my e·, to be a Christian,
Un. 10–27 would e· to hide from His presence
50–14 the e· to express the underlying
Pul. 21–12 our Christian e· society,
53–21 * in every field of human e·.
Rud. 12–24 practitioner should also e· to
No. 8– 3 should e· to be long-suffering,
34–16 in the e· to crush out
Pan. 9–17 spiritual e· to bless others,
'02. 13– 2 In this e· self was forgotten,
Hea. 19–17 spiritualize thought, motive, and e·.
My. 42–18 * I shall e· to perform this service
116– 2 e· to rise in consciousness
253– 6 can nerve your e·
282–26 May God guide . . . this good e·.
300– 2 On this basis they e· to cast out

endeavored
Mis. 272–29 I have e· to act toward all
Ret. 52– 1 I have e· to find new ways
73–14 I e· to lift thought above
Pul. 70–19 * she e· in vain to find
Rud. 14–14 has e· to take the full price of

endeavoring
Mis. 311– 4 e· to walk with us hand in hand,
Ret. 30– 2 e· to smite error with the
89–27 by e· to influence other minds

endeavors
Mis. 19–15 wicked e· of suppositional demons
227–14 responsible for kind(?) e·.
266–23 in unison with my own e·
351–18 nor benefit mankind by such e·.
365– 6 their highest e· are to Science
Man. 60–20 Christian e· for the living
Rud. 3– 3 in your e· to heal them of
No. 18–15 highest e· are, to divine Science,
My. 51–31 * appreciation of her earnest e·,
192–29 crowning your e·, and
231– 2 e· to bestow her charities
250– 6 and crowns honest e·.
285– 7 wise e· for industrial, civic,

ended
Mis. 85–25 the warfare is not e·
101–10 e· in a contest for the true idea,
285–17 warfare of sensuality was not then e·
No. 22– 6 Berkeley e· his metaphysical theory
'02. 18–27 e· in the downfall of genuine
My. 39–19 * my modest task will be e·.
110– 2 not to a dispensation now e·,
291–12 and it e· with a universal good

ending
Mis. 47–25 That . . . must have an e·.
167–13 there is no beginning and no e·.
216–21 * and e· with the grin,
Ret. 59– 6 without beginning or e·.

ending

Ret.	60– 2	apart from God, beginning and *e*,
'02.	1– 7	during the year *e* June, 1902,
Peo.	2–24	Life without beginning or *e*,
My.	53–26	* the year *e* December 7, 1885,
	281–22	* on the *e* of the war,

endings

My.	123–26	small beginnings have large *e*.

endless

Mis.	77–16	it holds man in *e* Life
	82–17	the *e* beatitudes of Being ;
	104–10	for individuality is *e* in the
	399– 5	Midst the glories of one *e* day."
Ret.	13–14	in the danger of *e* punishment,
Po.	75–12	Midst the glories of one *e* day."
My.	202–17	*e* hopes, and glad victories
	340– 7	fables, and *e* genealogies.
	350–26	crowned with *e* days,

endorse

Man.	36–17	refuse to *e* their applications
	37– 2	shall not *e* nor countersign an
My.	320–18	* did not *e* all the statements

endorsed

My.	59–31	* so thoroughly *e* or so
	351–24	therefore I have not *e* it,
	354– 4	they claim have been *e* by me,

endorsement

Man.	77– 9	and its *e* of the bills shall
My.	354– 8	books for which my *e* is claimed.

endorsing

Man.	37– 1	*E* Applications.

endowed

Mis.	161–16	both human and divinely *e*,
	161–23	specially *e* with the Holy Spirit ;
Un.	31–14	matter, being so *e*,
My.	14–21	* *e* with genius and inspiration,

endows

Un.	36– 2	*e* with the double capacity of
'01.	26–10	in the next he *e* it with
My.	90–11	* nature *e* the children of men,

ends

Mis.	vii– 6	* I love thee, and behold thy *e*
	62–25	fails, and *e* in a parody
	102–30	outmasters it, and *e* the warfare.
	112–28	it *e* in a total loss of
	118–29	*e* in the fiery punishment of the
	122–30	and he *e* — with suicide.
	137–22	the sublime *e* of human life.
	168–15	Here *e* the colloquy ;
	244–16	* visible agencies for specific *e* ?"
	288–31	to promote the *e* of temperance ;
	347–12	grows indistinct and *e*.
	358–30	fulfilled all the good *e* of
	361– 6	miscalled life *e* in death,
Ret.	32–16	* Short-lived joy, that *e* in sadness,
	47–11	promotion of spiritual *e*.
	69–15	false sense . . . which *e* in death"
Pul.	3–13	assurance *e* all warfare,
No.	12–20	these are the *e* of Christianity.
	21–14	for divine means and *e*.
'00.	10– 9	Such conflict never *e* till
'01.	25–15	*e* in some specious folly.
My.	259–29	temporary means and *e*.
	260–12	with human means and *e*,
	282– 8	all the *e* of the earth." — *Isa.* 45 : 22.

endues

My.	131– 2	and *e* with divine power ;

endurance

Mis.	238– 9	silent *e* of his love.
My.	227– 8	known by its patience and *e*.

endure

Mis.	15– 2	*e* the effects of his delusion
	192–15	"His name shall *e* — *Psal.* 72 : 17.
Un.	23–10	"If ye *e* chastening, — *Heb.* 12 : 7.
Pul.	5–10	bravest to *e*, firmest to suffer,
My.	52– 3	* many mental hardships to *e*,

endured

Mis.	13– 7	*e* at the hands of others
	169– 9	long years of invalidism she *e*
Ret.	22–10	"Consider him that *e* — *Heb.* 12 : 3.
	22–11	*e* the cross, — *Heb.* 12 : 2.
My.	75–22	* discomforts they might have *e*
	165– 6	*e* for the cause of Christ, Truth,
	196–20	"Consider him that *e* — *Heb.* 12 : 3.
	258–15	*e* the cross, — *Heb.* 12 : 2.

endures

Mis.	312– 7	*e* all piercing for the sake of
Ret.	90–20	*e* with her patience,

endureth

Un.	24–17	Spirit is all that *e*,
	56–26	and *e* all things.

endureth

Pul.	7–23	word of the Lord *e* — *I Pet.* 1 : 25.
Hea.	10–17	sorrow *e* but for the night,
Po.	16– 6	it *e* and liveth in love.
My.	158–12	it *e* all things ;

enduring

Mis.	117–12	* wit, humor, and *e* vivacity
Ret.	21–23	lucid and *e* lessons of Love
My.	24–23	* *e* character of its construction,
	36–29	* stand as an *e* monument,
	54– 3	* *e* the inconvenience
	268– 9	affections are *e* and achieving.

enemies (*see also* enemies')

forgiving

Ret.	45–19	forgiving *e*, returning good for

friends and

My.	276–13	all her dear friends and *e*.

harmless

My.	205–21	and *e* harmless.

hates

My.	41–20	* admires friends and hates *e*,

his

Mis.	129– 8	forgive his brother and love his *e*.
'00.	3–28	revenged himself upon his *e*.
My.	4–16	and he loves his *e*.
	270–19	breathing love for his *e*,
	316– 6	causing man to love his *e* ;

its

Mis.	124–26	*Love forgiving its e*.
Pan.	9–22	it loves its *e*
	9–23	and this love benefits its *e*
My.	260–22	love loving its *e*,

love your

Mis.	8– 8	chapter sub-title
	210–32	Love your *e*, or you will

mine

Mis.	13– 9	the law of loving mine *e*.

my

Mis.	213–14	May my friends and my *e*
	273–12	God bless my *e*,
	311–16	go to prove that I love my *e*
	351– 5	purpose of blessing even my *e*,
My.	145–23	my friends and my *e*.
	220–21	"God bless my *e* ;

no

Mis.	9–10	"Thou hast no *e*."
	10– 4	We have no *e*.
	10–28	"I have no *e*."

of Christian Science

My.	88–27	* stoutest *e* of C. S. will confess
	297–28	the *e* of C. S. are said to be

one's

Mis.	11–24	doing good to one's *e*
	227–31	one's self upon one's *e*,
'02.	17–19	to hate no man, to love one's *e*,
My.	204–27	loving one's *e*, and overcoming
	249– 9	hating even one's *e* excludes

our

Mis.	11–18	We must love our *e*
Ret.	29– 4	and hold to loving our *e*
No.	7– 7	We must love our *e*,
Pan.	15– 7	midst of our *e*," — see *Psal.* 23 : 5.
My.	132–23	and bless our *e*.

their

Mis.	371–21	* "men are known by their *e*."
Pul.	21– 5	Moreover, they love their *e*,

thine

Mis.	9– 9	"Love thine *e*" — see *Matt.* 5 : 44.

worst

Mis.	267– 5	Our worst *e* are the best friends
My.	211–19	the designs of their worst *e*,

your

Man.	41–13	do good unto your *e*
My.	128–29	God will reward your *e* according to
	191– 5	Your *e* will advertise for you.

Mis.	10–31	erroneous belief that you have *e* ;

enemies'

My.	275–22	my dear *e* health, happiness, and

enemy (*see also* enemy's)

Mis.	8– 9	Who is thine *e*
	8–11	Can you see an *e*,
	8–12	except you first formulate this *e*
	8–17	count your *e* to be that which
	8–20	Whatever purifies, . . . is not an *e*,
	9–32	all that an *e* or enmity can
	10–30	and this one *e* is yourself
	10–32	Soon or late, your *e* will wake
	42–14	or destroyed this last *e*.
	48–31	The *e* is trying to make capital
	76–32	overcame the last *e*, death.
	170– 1	the last *e* to be overthrown ;
	223–27	* "If I wished to punish my *e*,
Un.	54–16	its most potent and deadly *e*.

enemy

Pul.	2–18	fiercely besieged by the *e*.
	2–25	*e*· we confront would overthrow
No.	7–13	away from the *e*· of sinning sense,
My.	185–21	destroys the last *e*·, death.
	213–19	Be ever on guard against this *e*·.
	283–15	Sin is its own *e*·.
	300–15	overcome "the last *e*·"—*I Cor.* 15 : 26.
	358–10	pray that the *e*· of good cannot

enemy's

Mis.	xi–27	sadly to survey . . . the *e*· losses.

energies

Mis.	5– 3	devote our best *e*· to the work.
	97– 3	eternal *e*· of Truth,
	176–12	of the divine *e*· of good,
	278–31	This has developed higher *e*·
	352–23	Through the divine *e*· alone
	360–22	fill earth with the divine *e*·,
Ret.	30–14	infinite *e*· of Truth and Love,
	88–14	its practicality, its divine *e*·,
Pul.	11– 7	means, *e*·, and prayers helped
'02.	10– 4	divine *e*·, and their power over
My.	287–21	new possibilities, . . . and *e*· ;

energize

Ret.	86– 1	To *e*· wholesome spiritual warfare,

energizing

Mis.	291–26	truth which is *e*·, refreshing, and

energy

divine
(*see* **divine**)

Mis.	23–21	material force or *e*· ;
	190– 2	It is neither the *e*· of matter,
	204–31	gives prudence and *e*· ;
	245–11	giving it new impetus and *e*· ;
	330–22	a purer peace and diviner *e*·,
Ret.	6–28	carried . . . by his persistent *e*·
Pul.	36–16	* state of exhilaration and *e*·
	37– 8	* retains in a great degree her *e*·
'00.	10–10	gained fresh *e*· and final victory.
'02.	5– 2	prophesies renewed *e*· for to-morrow,
	8–19	The *e*· that saves sinners and heals
My.	24–21	* being pushed with the utmost *e*·,
	52–16	* more *e*· and unselfish labor
	75– 3	* its enthusiasm, its *e*·, and
	84–21	* optimism and *e*· of its followers
	273– 8	* skill, determination, and *e*·
	294–25	moral, and religious *e*·

enfolded

My.	291–14	*e*· a wealth of affection,

enfolds

Pul.	74–19	which eternity *e*·.
My.	174–27	and omnipotence *e*· me.
	290–14	Him whose love *e*· thee.

enforce

Man.	33– 3	to *e*· the discipline and by-laws
Pul.	82–25	* at least to help *e*· the laws
Peo.	11–15	that *e*· new forms of oppression

enforced

Mis.	6–26	laws of health are strictly *e*·,
My.	308–27	his household law, constantly *e*·,

enforcement

Man.	32–26	*E*· of By-Laws.
My.	343–25	Entrusting their *e*· to others,

enforcing

My.	159–23	spiritual laws *e*· obedience

engage

My.	27– 7	should *e*· our attention at this
	54–27	* concluded to *e*· Chickering Hall

engaged

Mis.	177– 9	*e*· day and night in organizing
Man.	79– 9	are *e*· in the transaction of the
	82–19	*e*· in the work of C. S.
Pul.	37–11	* *e*· on further writings on C. S.
My.	317–11	I *e*· Mr. Wiggin so as to
	332– 9	* Mr. Cooke, who *e*· to accompany her

engagement

Ret.	15–19	At the close of my *e*·

engages

Man.	68–19	only those individuals whom she *e*·
My.	295–19	It *e*· the attention and

engaging

'02.	1–21	*e*· the attention of philosopher

engender

Mis.	271–15	which spurious "compounds" *e*·.

engendered

Mis.	105– 1	faith *e*· by C. S.,
	291–21	False views, however *e*·,
My.	191– 8	*e*· by their fear,
	358– 9	conflict against Truth is *e*·

engendering

Pul.	6– 3	*e*· the limited forms of a

engenders

My.	213– 5	starts factions and *e*· envy

engine

'02.	9–27	inventor of a steam *e*·
	11–13	a steam *e*·, a submarine cable,
My.	345–11	* the telephone, the steam *e*·

engineering

My.	345–10	* electricity, *e*·, the telephone,

engirdle

My.	164–24	bond . . . that will *e*· the world,

England

Mis.	295– 5	"cursed barmaid system" in *E*·
Ret.	1– 2	from both Scotland and *E*·,
Pul.	5–26	Victoria Institute, *E*· ;
	46–15	* both in Scotland and *E*·.
	62– 4	* especially in *E*·.
My.	30–15	* from India, from *E*·, from Germany
	252–24	instituted in *E*· on New Year's
	289–17	is heard no more in *E*·,
		(*see also* **London**)

English

Mis.	294–24	chapter sub-title
	295– 3	noted *E*· leader, whom he quotes
	295–21	*E*· sentiment is not wholly
	295–30	worn the *E*· crown
	295–30	and borne the *E*· sceptre.
	296–10	barmaids of *E*· alehouses
Man.	30– 3	Christians and good *E*· scholars.
	90– 2	must be thorough *E*· scholars.
Ret.	1– 6	pious and popular *E*· authoress
	1–19	Scotch and *E*· elements
Un.	27– 3	two *E*· words, often used as if they
Pul.	32–24	* Scotch and *E*· ancestry,
Pan.	2–12	*derivation* of the *E*· word "pantheism"
'02.	7–11	*omni,* . . . used as an *E*· prefix
My.	89–10	* finds in the *E*· cathedrals,
	137– 7	* crisp, clear, plain-speaking *E*·."

English Barmaids

Mis.	294–24	chapter sub-title

Englishman

Ret.	1–17	was married to an *E*·,

engraft

Mis.	10– 1	or *e*· upon its purposes and
No.	43–21	can never *e*· Truth into error.
My.	278–24	no right to *e*· into civilization

engrafted

My.	196– 8	*e*· in church and State:
	268– 7	some fundamental error is *e*·

engraved

Mis.	121– 3	*e*· upon eternity's tablets.
Pul.	77– 5	* scroll of solid gold, suitably *e*·,

engraven

Mis.	376–13	* living Saviour *e*· on the heart.
Pul.	1–13	and records deeply *e*·,
My.	194–13	The tender memorial *e*· on
	341– 5	*e*· on her granite rocks,

engraving

Mis.	376–12	* an *e*· cut in a stone.

engrossed

Hea.	3–13	*e*· the attention of the ages.

engrounds

Mis.	397– 9	Truth *e*· me on the rock,
Pul.	18–18	Truth *e*· me on the rock,
Po.	12–18	Truth *e*· me on the rock,

engulf

Mis.	257–26	Earthquakes *e*· cities,

engulfing

No.	42–15	While Science is *e*· error

enhance

Mis.	10– 2	wherewith to . . . . *e*· its sorrows.
	154–11	to *e*· the means and measure
My.	134– 7	our daily lives serve to *e*·
	340–24	tend to *e*· their confidence

enhances

My.	107–19	It *e*· its efficiency,

enhancing

Mis.	395–27	*E*· autumn's gloom.
Po.	58–12	*E*· autumn's gloom.

enigmas

Ret.	1–10	other verses and *e*·

enigmatical

02.	16–18	*e*· seals of the angel,

enjoin

Mis.	24– 1	*e*· the First Commandment ;
	310–16	that the Scriptures *e*·,
	315–29	shall *e*· upon them habitually

enjoin
Man. 83–21   e· them habitually to study
No.   8–19   I e· it upon my students
Peo.   6–24   the Scriptures e· us to

enjoined
Mis. 381–25   disposing of, the e· pamphlet,
Ret. 76–16   e· upon the Galatians.
'01.   33–23   e· his students to teach
My. 112– 6   did just what he e·

enjoining
Peo.   8–11   Judaism, e· the limited and

enjoins
Mis. 292–19   Christ e· it upon man to help
    292–21   e· taking them by the hand

enjoy
Mis. 11–31   I would e· taking by the hand
    113–26   but everything to e· on earth
    200–22   e· the touch of weakness,
My. 169– 4   if you would e· so long a trip
    171–10   I think you would e· seeing it.
    252–12   to make one e· doing right,
    254– 5   glad you e· the dawn of
    352– 7   * the peculiar privileges we e·

enjoyed
Mis. 24–14   than I had before e·.

enjoying
Pul. 51– 6   * they are e· that liberty
My. 139– 3   living, loving, acting, e·.
    197– 1   E· good things is not evil,

enjoyment
Mis.   9–22   this cup of selfish human e·
    209–18   loss of gustatory e·
    210–23   pretense of . . . innocent e·,
'02.   3–13   the e· of self-government

enjoys
'01. 14– 9   something that e·, suffers,

enkindling
Po. 32– 8   sunbeams e· the sky

enlarge
Mis. 154– 9   and e· its borders with
Ret. 89–25   to e· their sphere of action.
'02. 12–26   and e· our church edifice
Po. 33– 4   my faith and my vision e·,
My.   7– 9   and e· our church edifice
    9–23   to e· our church edifice
    10– 3   * e· the favorable expectation,
    40– 6   * also e· their hospitality,
    357–14   to e· their phylacteries

enlarged
Mis. 142– 1   how hath He e· her borders !
    193–26   this e· sense of the spirit
    282– 3   an e· sense of Deity.
Un. 31–21   This subject can be e·.
Pul. 38– 7   * greatly revised and e·,
My. 129–16   And how is man, . . . e·,

enlarges
Mis. 284–26   aggressive, and e· its claims ;
Un. 25–14   e· the human intellect
Rud.   2–19   e· our sense of Deity,
No. 12–24   so e· our sense of God
'02.   9–30   Whatever e· man's facilities

enlarging
Mis. 127– 6   and e· her borders.
My. 18– 3   and e· her borders.
    362–16   * e· the activities of the Cause

enlighten
Mis. 38–19   e· and reform the sinner,
    82– 8   to e· and redeem mortals.
Ret. 83–18   to rekindle his own light or to e·
Un.   5–18   or e· the individual thought.
No.   3–16   students, whom it would e·.

enlightened
Mis.   7–32   not . . . e· on this great subject.
    173– 3   most e· sense herein sees
    340–31   have not sufficiently e· mankind.
    343–19   freshness and sunshine of e· faith
Ret. 81–17   The e· heart loathes error,
Pul.   9–30   foundation of e· faith is
No. 45–16   measure of e· understanding
Hea. 14–12   as a physician is e· and liberal
Peo. 11– 5   mind, e· and spiritualized,
My. 95–30   * religious faith and e· zeal
    128–16   conscience and e· understanding.
    168– 2   dictates of e· conscience,
    187– 7   lighteth every e· thought
    249–16   marvel is, that at this e· period
    283–27   e· sense of God's government.

enlightening
Mis. 268–20   e· the misguided senses,
'02.   2–17   e· the world with the
My. 245–20   and e· the world.

enlightenment
Mis.   4–16   Further e· is necessary
    162– 1   even as, at times of special e·,
    246– 4   requires the e· of these worthies,
Pan.   2– 2   At this period of e·,
My. 340– 9   The e·, the erudition,

enlightens
Mis. 92–10   e· other minds most readily,
Ret. 84– 7   sees clearly and e· other minds
My. 147–16   e· the people's sense of C. S.

enlisted
Mis. 317–24   My sympathies are deeply e·
'01. 15– 7   Scientist has e· to lessen sin,

enlists
My. 108–12   e· faith in the pharmacy of
    287– 4   e· my hearty sympathy.

en masse
Mis. 134–10   Meet together and meet e· m·,

enmity
Mis.   9–32   all that an enemy or e· can
    36–25   is e· against God ; — Rom. 8: 7.
    74– 5   e· of mortal man toward God.
    169–26   carnal mind, which is e· toward God,
    177–11   sworn e· against the lives of our
Man. 48– 1   cherish no e· toward those who
Ret. 61– 1   e· to God and divine Science.
    81– 1   envy, ingratitude, and e·,
Un.   5–21   no e·, no untempered controversy,
No.   8–20   e· over doctrines and traditions,
'02. 13– 4   incurred a sharper fire from e·.
My. 41–21   * unable to cherish any e·.
    164–28   rock, against which envy, e·, or

ennobling
Mis. 41–12   ready for victory in the e· strife.

enormous
My. 67–27   * Notwithstanding its e· size,
    130–27   has an e· strain put upon it,

enormously
My. 90–18   * The world is e· richer for this

enough
Mis. 16– 4   this is e· of heaven
    32–22   But I have not moments e·
    39–20   e· of the leaven of Truth to
    48–11   e· for me to know that
    224–24   charity broad e· to cover the
    224–25   sweet e· to neutralize what is bitter
    224–31   e· of a flatterer, a fool, or
    233–25   unwilling to work hard e·
    238–17   It is e·, say they,
    241–13   e· apparently to neutralize
    253– 6   I am not e· the new woman
    253– 8   platform is not broad e· for me,
    268– 5   not vain e· to attempt
    271– 6   understand e· of this to keep out
    276– 8   not big e· to fill the order ;
    279–27   e· to convert the world
    294–19   just e· to reform and transform them,
    307– 3   it is e· that divine Love is an
    312– 1   and wished I were wise e· to
    353– 5   excess of action or not action e· ;
    369–17   This method is devout e· to
Un.   6–11   is radical e· to promote as
Pul. 44–27   * the custodian of funds cried "e·"
    61–22   * fortunate e· to listen to the
    84–22   * It is e· for us now to know that
Rud. 15–14   until there were e· practitioners
No. 16–25   It is not e· to say that matter
    25– 1   uttering this great thought is not e· !
    27– 6   When we get near e· to God
    39– 7   speaking loud e· to be heard ;
Pan.   9–14   What mortal to-day is wise e·
'00.   2–30   but I work hard e· to be so."
    10–28   Surely it is e· for a soldier
'01. 11–19   would be e· for Christian practice.
    28–23   e· for the disciple — Matt. 10: 25.
Hea.   4–14   to drop divinity long e· to hate.
    6–18   if . . . is strong e· to manifest it.
My. 26–18   include e· of their own.
    62– 9   * How can we ever thank God e·
    62–10   * ever thank you e· for your
    72–16   * do not send . . . money — we have e· !"
    76– 7   * e· money was on hand to provide for
    82–12   * e· to accommodate the demand.
    86–17   * no more money, since he had e·.
    86–18   * which indicates plainly e· the
    124–15   e· to make this hour glad.
    131–28   room e· to receive it." — Mal. 3: 10.
    136– 1   e· for you and me to know
    221–23   This is e·.
    264– 3   kind e· to speak well of me
    268–28   Look high e·, and you see the
    268–29   Look long e·, and you see
    269–28   room e· to receive it." — Mal. 3: 10.

Enquirer		
Pul.	89–28	* E·, Oakland, Cal.

enrage

Mis.	338–17	calm strength will e· evil.

enraptured

Mis.	17–18	opens to the e· understanding
	390–11	E· by thy spell,
Po.	55–12	E· by thy spell,

enrich

Mis.	154– 9	e· its roots, and enlarge its
	251–28	to e· the soil for fruitage.
	332– 8	seedtime has come to e· earth
Man.	41–24	e· the affections of all mankind,

enriched

Ret.	84–23	tired tongue of history be e·.

enriches

My.	295–19	e· the being of all men.

enrobe

Mis.	332– 8	e· man in righteousness;

en route

Mis.	378–10	left the water-cure, e· r· for
Ret.	38–20	to find me e· r· for Boston,
My.	124–27	and the number e· r·.

Ensample

Mis.	258– 4	Our great E·, Jesus of Nazareth,
Man.	41– 1	Christ Jesus the E·.
	41– 2	is the E· in C. S.

enshrined

Pul.	7–13	but e· for future use,
My.	348–22	e· in the divine Principle

enshrouds

Po.	29– 5	born where storm e·

ensign

Mis.	135– 2	marching under whatsoever e·,
	313–19	The field waves its white e·,
My.	291–23	our nation's e· of peace
	341– 6	the e· of religious liberty

ensigns

Mis.	xii– 1	signs and e· of war,

enslave

Peo.	10–14	injustice and error e· him.

ensnare

My.	14–22	* lie with which to e·
	252– 7	which weaves webs that e·.

ensue

Man.	51–15	No Church discipline shall e· until
My.	127–20	e· a purer Protestantism

ensuing

Pul.	vii– 4	during the e· thirty years.
My.	20–17	no gifts to her the e· season,
	39–13	* officers for the e· year
	51–21	* pastorate for the e· year;

ensure

Pul.	15– 6	to e· the avoidance of the evil?

entails

My.	20–25	* e· the expenditure of a

enter

Mis.	3–15	e· this line of thought or action.
	77–22	e· the spiritual sanctuary
	77–29	e· unshod the Holy of Holies,
	88–23	* who do not e· into its sublimity
	115–17	that you e· not into temptation
	122–26	e· thou into the joy — *Matt.* 25 : 23.
	133–14	e· into thy closet, — *Matt.* 6 : 6.
	186– 4	Soul is supposed to e· the
	241– 5	man will no more e· heaven sick than
	262– 3	wherein it is permitted to e·,
	264–13	e· the Normal class of my College
	274–16	and equity cannot e·. — *Isa.* 59 : 14.
	280–32	when you are ready to e·
	282–14	"When ye e· a house, — see *Matt.* 10 : 12.
	282–16	When you e· mentally the personal
	283– 4	no more right to e· the mind of a
	283– 6	than one has to e· a house,
	296–25	Do they e· this line of
	299–18	If I e· Mr. Smith's store
	318–17	can e· upon the gospel work of
	328–25	are striving to e· the path,
	342– 1	to e· into the joy of divine Science
	343– 2	that we e· not into the temptation
	344–26	shall in no wise e· — *Luke* 18 : 17.
	347–21	I e· the path.
	348–30	to e· medical schools,
	398–11	We would e· by the door,
Man.	49– 5	to e· this holy work,
	53–18	No member shall e· a complaint
	70– 3	nor e· into a business transaction
	89–23	eligible to e· the Normal class.

enter

Man.	91–22	may e· the Normal class
Ret.	46–17	We would e· by the door,
	47– 7	persons desiring to e· the College,
	47–21	can e· upon the gospel work of
	54–18	error may e· through this same channel
	55– 1	e· this strait and narrow path,
	88–23	blush to e· unasked another's
Un.	37– 4	to inherit eternal life and e· heaven
	40– 3	will not e· this dark shadow
	50– 7	pray that we e· not into the
Pul.	17–16	We would e· by the door,
Rud.	14–24	unprepared to e· higher classes.
	15– 5	to immediately e· upon its
	15–13	diseased people not to e· a class.
	15–20	can advantageously e· a class,
No.	31–26	e· no more into him." — *Mark* 9 : 25.
	41–17	trying to force the doors . . . and e· in ;
Pan.	6–19	e· into the Scriptural allegory,
'01.	14–22	that he e· not into temptation
	28– 6	e· the strait and narrow way,
'02.	7– 6	e· not into the category
Peo.	4– 9	could e· finite man through his
Po.	14–15	We would e· by the door,
	22–10	will e·, when they may,
	22–19	Love doth e· in,
My.	3– 9	e· in through the gates — *Rev.* 22 : 14.
	4–27	ye shall not e· into — *Matt.* 18 : 3.
	6–15	wherein to e· and pray.
	40–10	* shall willingly e· into the
	62– 3	* e· thou into the joy — *Matt.* 25 : 23.
	71–14	* When these people e· this
	126– 1	would e· even the church,
	152–14	Ask thyself, Do I e· by the door
	159–14	struggling to e· into the
	188–17	In spirit I e· your
	207–21	e· thou into the joy — *Matt.* 25 : 21.
	210– 4	death cannot e· them.
	210– 6	no door through which evil can e·,
	218–28	an individual should not e·
	244–18	mortals do not e· without a
	246– 5	Students who e· the . . . College,
	251–13	eligible to e· the Normal class,
	267–17	e· heaven in proportion to
	306– 8	I deem it unwise to e· into
	322–18	* received your permission to e·
	348–31	nothing that worketh ill can e·
	358– 5	e· not into temptation." — *Matt.* 26 : 41.

entered

Mis.	49– 1	A young lady e· the College class
	166–29	e· into the minutiæ of
	206–24	you have e· the path.
	216– 5	e· into our rest,
	260– 7	never e· into the line of
	297–18	voluntarily e· into wedlock,
	306– 2	* e· carefully in a book
	327–10	Many there were who had e· the
	349–18	He e· the medical school,
	373–22	in due time Christianity e· into
Ret.	16– 8	e· this church one hour ago
	39– 3	I e· a suit at law,
	89–17	once again e· the synagogue which
	90– 7	ever e· the towns whither he sent
Pul.	31–25	* Mrs. Eddy e· the room.
'00.	13– 2	* Gentiles e· the church of Christ"
Hea.	18– 9	Spirit never e· and it never
Peo.	4– 7	belief . . . eternal e· the temporal.
	4–13	error that . . . personal devil e·
My.	92–24	* worshippers who e· its portals
	94– 8	* worshippers who e· its portals
	178–23	e· the house through a window
	235–30	would never have e· into the history
	302–29	e· it, and knelt in thanks
	307–17	and I e· a demurrer
	309– 9	Both e· their pleas,
	319–21	* I e· your Primary class
	321–22	* I first saw you and e· your class.
	342– 4	* She e· with a gracious smile,
	355– 4	* on which we have just e·.

entereth

Pan.	12–17	that he who e· it may run

entering

Mis.	18–25	e· into a state of evil
	49– 4	before e· the College,
	262– 6	e· upon its fifth volume,
	316–24	Before e· the Massachusetts
	318–19	Before e· this sacred field
	342– 8	e· the guest-chamber of Truth,
	348–31	and objected to their e·
	349–12	feasibility of e· a medical school ;
Ret.	47–23	before e· this field of labor
	71–21	selfish motives e· into mental
	78– 9	sinister motives, e· into this
No.	28–13	to-day is none too soon for e·
'02.	15–13	Before e· upon my great life-work,

entering
My. 81– 1   * Upon *e·* The Mother Church
188–21   cannot prevent me from *e·*

enteritis
Mis. 69–19   healed him of *e·*,
My. 107–31   removes *e·*, gastritis,

enterprising
My. 315–25   to thank the *e·* historians

enters
Mis. 101–15   *e·* into no compromise with
152–27   there *e·* no element of earth
208– 9   *e·* unconsciously the human heart
325– 1   *e·* a massive carved stone mansion.
325–31   Next he *e·* a place of worship,
Un. 48–15   no more *e·* into His creation
48–16   than the human father *e·*
'02. 18–17   no deceit, *e·* into the heart that
My. 68–19   * *e·* so largely into the
179– 9   *e·* non-intelligent dust

entertain
Mis. 2–32   While we *e·* decided views as to
9–14   present sense which thou canst *e·* of
16–18   we must *e·* a higher sense of
18–23   necessarily *e·* habitual love for
28– 6   beliefs that mortals *e·*.
47– 5   *e·* an adipose belief of yourself as
74–14   opposite of that which mortals *e·* :
96–21   all who *e·* this understanding
292–12   higher sense I *e·* of Love,
Man. 42–16   shall neither *e·* a belief nor
Un. 8– 7   than the sense you *e·* of it.
Pul. 21–14   *e·* due respect and fellowship for
Peo. 5–22   and not *e·* the angel unawares.
My. 74–31   * Whatever opinions we many *e·*
210–19   Certain individuals *e·* the notion
223–19   either of which I do not *e·*.

entertained
Mis. 46– 9   any doctrine previously *e·*.
197–14   It means more than an opinion *e·*
Ret. 5–29   * She ever *e·* a lively sense of
'02. 7–21   no other . . . can be Christianly *e·*.
Hea. 8–17   mistaken views *e·* of Deity
My. 241–24   * according to the beliefs I *e·*
331–12   * love and respect *e·* for Mrs. Eddy

entertaining
Mis. 49–20   *E·* the common belief in
192–31   else we are *e·* the startling

entertainment
My. 82–19   * when the *e·* is over

entertains
'00. 6–19   sense which the adult *e·* of it.
'02. 19–13   He *e·* angels who

enthrall
'01. 10–15   used to *e·* my sense of the Godhead,
My. 4– 4   world's *nolens volens* cannot *e·* it.

enthrone
Mis. 74– 7   affections which *e·* the Son of man
Un. 38–13   such misbelief must *e·* another
46–28   The fight was an effort to *e·* evil.
No. 42–16   material senses would *e·* error as

enthroned
Mis. 66–19   and Truth be *e·*,
277–26   justice and judgment are *e·*.
My. 201– 7   are *e·* now and forever.
247–12   meekness and Truth *e·*.

enthrones
Un. 32–13   *e·* God in the eternal qualities of

enthusiasm
My. 75– 2   * respectful acknowledgment of its *e·*,
79–13   * shows an *e·* for C. S.
85–15   * zeal and *e·* of the followers
98– 8   * centre of an *e·* and reverence
322–24   * to banter me on such *e·*,

enthusiast
Pul. 32–27   * her mother was a religious *e·*,

enthusiastic
Pul. 32–10   * her large and *e·* following
64–13   * money from *e·* Christian Scientists.
My. 273– 5   * Scientists, *e·* in their belief,

enthusiasts
My. 99–13   * *e·* whenever their form of religion

entices
My. 211–13   *e·* its victim by unseen, silent

enticing
Pul. 30– 4   * *e·* a separate congregation

entire
Mis. 50– 6   *e· method of metaphysical healing,*
92–15   Throughout his *e·* explanations,
118–10   to make incorrect your *e·* problem,

entire
Mis. 127– 3   Throughout my *e·* connection with
150–17   churches are dotting the *e·* land.
154– 5   broad shelter to the *e·* world.
194–15   bring out the *e·* hues of Deity,
196– 6   subtleties through the *e·* centuries,
201– 1   supports the *e·* wisdom of the text ;
234–21   the *e·* current of mortality,
260–23   Mind as absolute and *e·*,
312–26   throughout the *e·* centuries,
382–30   *e·* system of teaching and
Ret. 78– 4   *e·* wisdom of Mind-practice.
84– 9   Throughout his *e·* explanations
Pul. 27– 9   * the *e·* church is a testimonial,
29–27   * almost the *e·* congregation was
30–23   * *e·* membership of Christian Scientists
'00. 12–26   The *e·* city is now in ruins.
'01. 12–21   bring out the *e·* hues of God.
My. 10–14   * for this *e·* donation to be
14–14   * *e·* amount required to complete
17–31   Throughout my *e·* connection with
30–30   * representative of the *e·* body of the
31–13   * from over the *e·* world.
45–11   * small part of the *e·* body
66– 4   * ownership of the *e·* block.
66–10   * ownership of the *e·* block.
69–29   * dominate the *e·* city,
76– 8   * the *e·* cost of the building,
78–19   * the *e·* congregation knelt
137– 7   * *e·* letter is in Mrs. Eddy's own
232–23   *e·* mortal, material error
252–10   *e·* purpose of true education
299–11   contains the *e·* truth of the
301–19   *e·* testimony of the material

entirely
Mis. 71– 1   *when I am not e· well myself?*
Pul. 30–30   * and *e·* paid for when its
38–19   * in so *e·* different a plane
55–27   * though each is *e·* independent
57– 3   * It is *e·* paid for,
71–22   * are now so *e·* devoted.
76–15   * rug composed *e·* of skins
Hea. 19– 5   governed directly and *e·* by mind,
My. 14–20   * was *e·* right in doing so.
83–12   * men go *e·* unadorned.
85–26   * it was *e·* credible that the
93–24   * many of us have missed *e·*
98–23   * Contributions were *e·* voluntary.
118–29   *e·* apart from limitations,
312– 9   * and *e·* without money
312–15   * but *e·* without means
323– 1   * *e·* in accordance with what
324–25   * *e·* unique and original.
344–18   "Oh," . . . "*e·*.

entitled
Mis. 62–22   her work *e·* "Mind-cure on a
313–15   *e·* "The New Pastor," by
Man. 45–20   is not *e·* to hold office
91–11   shall be *e·* to a free course
Ret. 35– 2   *e·* "The Science of Man."
75–23   is he *e·*, when he leaves the
Pul. 28–17   * Mrs. Eddy's book, *e·* "S. and H.
54– 1   * in a poem *e·* "The Master,"
55–22   * volume *e·* "S. and H.
85–15   * *e·* to the gratitude and love of all
'01. 23–23   book . . . *e·* "Treatise Concerning the
My. 107–25   *e·* to a classification as truth
250– 4   was *e·* to and has received
276–18   * those who are *e·* to vote
316–12   *e·* "The Recent Reckless and
323– 3   * pamphlet *e·* C. S. and the Bible,"
353–12   the second I *e· Sentinel,*

entity
Mis. 45–23   It never . . . existed as an *e·*.
250– 4   either as a quality or as an *e·*.
346–12   Evil never did exist as an *e·*.
Ret. 25–16   God I characterized as individual *e·*,
'01. 13–12   Sin can have neither *e·*, verity, nor
14– 8   evil, as a false claim, false *e·*, and
My. 14–21   If the devil were really an *e·*,

entrance
Mis. 100–31   and his *e·* into Science
170–10   *e·* into their understanding is
280–31   open wide for the *e·* of error,
Pul. 25–16   * *e·* to this magnificent temple.
26–20   * an *e·* of Italian marble,
36–22   * at the *e·* to the Back Bay Park,
My. 54– 2   * could not obtain *e·* ;
221–30   Truth and Life, can guard the *e·*
262–13   *e·* into human understanding of the

entrances
Pul. 24–26   * The *e·* are of marble,
25–18   * *e·* leading to the auditorium,
My. 78– 9   * *e·* beneath a series of arches

entreaty
Mis. 254– 3 gentle *e·*, the stern rebuke
My. 10–22 * *e·* on the part of some one else.
37–28 * deeply touched by its sweet *e·*,

entrusted
Mis. 155–30 wherewith divine Love has *e·* us,
Ret. 6– 2 * especially *e·* to her watch-care,
'01. 31–11 *e·* me with a message to mankind
My. 336– 7 * *e·* herself to the care of

entrusting
My. 343–25 *E·* their enforcement to others,

enumerated
Ret. 33–11 remedies *e·* by Jahr,

enumerating
My. 328–26 * *e·* the different professions

enumeration
Pul. 67–11 * Max O'Rell's famous *e·* of

enunciated
Pul. 54– 9 * Jesus *e·* and exemplified the

enunciates
'00. 4–30 St. Paul beautifully *e·* this

enunciating
My. 188–15 *e·*, "God is Love." — *I John* 4 : 8.

enunciation
Mis. 114–15 *e·* of these according to Christ.

enunciator
Pul. 6–23 Another brilliant *e·*, seeker, and

envied
No. 41– 7 work most derided and *e·*

envies
My. 17– 5 hypocrisies, and *e·*, and — *I Pet.* 2 : 1.

envious
Mis. 129–15 If a man is jealous, *e·*, or
291–30 counteract the influence of *e·* minds

environed
Ret. 50–29 Students are not *e·* with such
My. 267–27 *e·* with everlasting Life.

environment
Mis. 85–22 *e·* of mortals, suggests
86–27 constitutes our mortal *e·*.
372–26 Not by aid of foreign device or *e·*
Un. 56– 9 quickened sense of false *e·*,
Pul. 54–20 * the conditions of *e·* and
54–27 * most perfect obtainable *e·*,

environments
Mis. 76–15 set a human soul free from its *e·*,
263–22 without a full knowledge of the *e·*.
My. 257– 8 swaddling-clothes (material *e·*)

envy
Mis. 10– 4 Whatever *e·*, hatred, revenge
19– 1 *E·*, evil thinking, evil speaking,
32–28 they should never *e·*, elbow,
54–12 over all obstacles that *e·* and malice
118–22 *e·*, revenge, are foes to grace,
123– 6 spirit of idolatry, *e·*,
137–25 passion, pride, *e·*, evil-speaking,
204–31 banishes forever all *e·*, rivalry,
222– 3 It inflames *e·*, passion,
228–11 the buffetings of *e·* or malice
254–18 *E·*, the great red dragon of
274–20 gives impulse to violence, *e·*,
277–17 the purposes of *e·* and malice
278– 2 The wines of fornication, *e·*, and
281– 4 rivalry, jealousy, *e·*, revenge.
324–14 witchcraft, variance, *e·*,
337–19 evil-speaking, lust, *e·*, hate.
343–14 weeds of passion, malice, *e·*,
347–31 Loyal Scientists are targets for *e·*,
356– 6 *E·*, rivalry, hate need no
357– 1 no place for *e·*,
366–27 self-will, *e·*, and lust.
368–25 Others, from malice and *e·*,
374–13 ignorance, *e·*, and hatred
383–9 preeminent over ignorance or *e·*,
Ret. 44–21 *e·* and molestation of other
79–13 *e·*, and mad ambition are
81– 1 *e·*, ingratitude, and enmity,
Rud. 9–20 *e·*, lust, and all fleshly vices.
No. 3– 2 How sad it is that *e·* will bend its
43–27 while *e·* and hatred bark and bite
Pan. 3–15 * *e·* of the great !
'01. 16– 9 lusts, falsities, *e·*, and hate,
'02. 3–28 *E·* is the atmosphere of hell.
11–10 *E·* or abuse of him who,
14–20 with mockery, *e·*, rivalry, and falsehood
16–27 pride, self-will, *e·*, or hate.
Hea. 10– 4 the vision of *e·*, sensuality, and
17– 2 the pride of life, *e·*, hypocrisy,
18–22 Pride, appetites, passions, *e·*,
My. 164–28 rock, against which *e·*, enmity, or

envy
My. 167–28 the illegitimate claims of *e·*,
213– 5 starts factions and engenders *e·*
228–21 self-righteousness, hypocrisy, *e·*,
252–14 wrong, injustice, *e·*, hate ;
316–20 foaming torrents of ignorance, *e·*,

enwrapped
My. 257–26 Christmas gift, two words *e·*,

Ephesian
'00. 12–12 whence the *E·* elders travelled

Ephesus
'00. 12– 7 commence with the church of *E·*.
12– 8 records *E·* as an illustrious city,
12–15 the tutelary divinity of *E·*.
12–17 Magical arts prevailed at *E·* ;
13– 4 commends the church at *E·*

Epictetus
My. 149–15 *E·* made answer, "And I with many
159–25 *E·*, a heathen philosopher

Epicurean
Mis. 162– 8 Gnostic, *E·*, and Stoic.

epicycle
My. 270– 3 obliterates the *e·* of evil.

Epigram
Mis. vii– 3 * BEN JONSON : *E· I.*
vii– 8 * BEN JONSON : *E· 86.*

Episcopal
Pul. 26– 8 * chancel of an *E·* church
My. 333–12 * thence to the *E·* burying-ground,

epistle
Un. 30–13 his first *e·* to the Corinthians

epistles
Ret. 90–11 addressed one of his *e·*

epithet
'01. 4–29 If . . . we merit the *e·* "godless,"
Hea. 3–19 which *e·* the great goodness and
My. 104– 6 That *e·* points a moral.

epithets
My. 151– 2 present schoolboy *e·* and attacks

epitome
Rud. 8– 9 only an *e·* of the Principle,

epitomize
Pul. vii– 2 *e·* the story of the birth of

epitomizes
My. 364–16 *e·* what heals all manner of

epoch
Mis. 363–30 every advancing *e·* of Truth
Man. 18– 9 at every *e·* saying,
Ret. 93– 4 At the present *e·* the human concept
My. 66–27 * an *e·* in the history of C. S.
220– 2 to this century or to any *e·*,

epoch-making
My. 30–19 * in gratitude for the *e·* event.

epoch-marking
My. 47–14 * *e·* stages of its growth,

equal
Mis. 40–14 *e·* the ancient prophets as healers.
41–29 may not always prove *e·* to
46–10 *Do you teach that you are e· with*
46–14 Man is not *e·* with his Maker ;
53–16 former is not *e·* to the latter.
62–11 offsets an *e·* positive quantity,
70–18 thief was not *e·* to the demands
70–29 none could *e·* his glory.
90–19 are *e·* to your motives ;
138–25 *e·* to the march triumphant,
220–23 understand with *e·* clearness,
255– 5 Man is not *e·* to his Maker.
291–13 *e·* growth and prosperity of all
291–15 *e·* opportunity to be benefited
Ret. 34– 9 Human reason was not *e·* to it.
Un. 38–27 or *e·* to the reality of being,
Pul. 28–19 * *e·* measure to its use of the Bible.
47–16 * no human reason has been *e·* to
84– 6 * side by side, *e·* partners in
Rud. 6– 2 * inference that there is no matter.
No. 43– 2 *e·* to the power of daily meat and
'00. 9–29 But no one else has seemed *e·* to
'01. 16– 7 scarcely *e·* the modern nondescripts,
27–18 an *e·* number of sick healed.
My. 190– 8 Does C. S. *e· materia medica* in
217–11 *e·* shares to each contributor.
219–14 to believe that . . . is not *e·* to
219–16 is *e·* to the giving of life and health
237–17 charges for treatment *e·* to those of
247– 8 *e·* rights and privileges,
255– 1 *e·* rights and privileges,
269– 9 *e·* unto the angels ; — *Luke* 20 : 36.
272– 9 no claim that man is *e·* to God,

equal
My. 323–19 * Neither do I now feel at all *e·* to
324–22 * as quite his literary *e·*,

equality
Mis. 255–10 not claiming *e·* with,
294–29 true ideas of humanity and *e·*.
My. 247– 9 *e·* of the sexes, rotation in office.''
255– 2 *e·* of the sexes, rotation in office.''

equalled
Pul. 36–12 * I never saw *e·*.

equalling
My. 190–12 not only *e·* but vastly excelling

equally
Mis. 46–20 not weighing *e·* with Him,
177–13 Will you be *e·* in earnest for the
290–30 all who are receptive share this *e·*.
Ret. 64–10 good is *e·* one and *all*,
Un. 46–23 being *e·* identical and
No. 15–11 should not these be *e·* extended to
My. 145–22 I can serve *e·* my friends and
146–20 *e·* sure that what I wrote is true,
230–10 but to one and all *e·*.
292–22 though both are *e·* sincere.

equals
Mis. 194– 1 believe that the power of God *e·*

equanimity
Mis. 224–22 with an *e·* so settled that
No. 8–26 while you walk on in *e·*,

equations
Mis. 54–29 not ask the pupil in simple *e·* to

equatorial
Mis. 88–25 * miraculous to the *e·* African,

equipoise
Mis. 65–25 restoring the *e·* of mind and body,

equipped
Mis. 10– 9 armed them, *e·* them, and
88–13 have *e·* him as a critic
Hea. 14–13 In proportion . . . is he *e·* with Truth,

equips
Mis. 183–23 *e·* man with divine power
252–27 *e·* the doctor with safe and sure

equitable
My. 277– 9 wholesome tribunals, *e·* laws,

equity
Mis. 274–16 *and e· cannot enter.— Isa.* 59 : 14.
289–19 Neither divine justice nor human *e·*
380–27 April, 1883, a bill in *e·* was filed
My. 181–20 universal *e·* of Christianity.
277–18 eternal scale of *e·* and mercy

equivalent
Mis. 67–26 by *e·* words in another,
300–31 withholds a slight *e·* for health.
Ret. 50– 3 I could think of no financial *e·*
50–13 *e·* for my instruction
Rud. 1–12 In French the *e·* word is *personne.*
My. 236–12 may become *e·* to no centre.

era

Christian
Mis. 29–11 even before the Christian *e·* ;
40–12 first century of the Christian *e·* ?''
163– 8 dated time, the Christian *e·*,
199–31 and dated the Christian *e·*.
373–20 early part of the Christian *e·*,
Man. 41– 2 He who dated the Christian *e·*
Ret. 26–20 a new date in the Christian *e·*,
93– 1 In the first century of the Christian *e·*
94–28 In the first century of the Christian *e·*
'01. 24–20 advent is called the Christian *e·*.
28– 9 first century of the Christian *e·*
My. 107– 5 at the beginning of the Christian *e·*,
340– 7 belonging not to the Christian *e·*,
340–27 suffices for the Christian *e·*.

Pul. 44– 9 * an *e·* in the blessed onward work
My. 29–23 * launching upon a new *e·*,
47–26 * an *e·* of Christian worship
154–23 in our *e·* of the world
212– 6 In this *e·* it is taking the place of

eradicate
Mis. 237–15 encounter and help to *e·*.
No. 31– 1 cannot *e·* disease if you admit

eradicated
My. 122– 8 the roots must be *e·* or the

erased
Man. 54–14 her name shall be *e·* from The
My. 318– 3 I have *e·* them in my revisions.

erases
Rud. 12–16 C. S. *e·* from the minds of invalids

ere
Mis. 227–13 *e·* that one himself become aware,
395–18 *E·* autumn blanch another year,
398–19 White as wool, *e·* they depart,
Ret. 46–25 White as wool, *e·* they depart,
81–12 falsity must thus decay, *e·* spiritual
Un. 56–24 *e·* he can change from flesh to
Pul. 17–24 White as wool, *e·* they depart
51–20 * *E·* this many a new project
Hea. 2–14 *e·* he passed from his execution to a
Peo. 8–26 will *e·* long stop trusting where
Po. 14–23 White as wool, *e·* they depart,
27– 6 *E·* thou grow tremulous with
27–16 Hearts bleeding *e·* they break
58– 3 *E·* autumn blanch another year,
My. 123–18 *E·* long I will see you
130– 6 will *e·* long be unearthed
181–15 would have solved *e·* this

erect
Mis. 79–16 is *e·* in goodness and perpetual in
369– 7 enables us to stand *e·*
383–12 *E·* and eternal, it will go on
Pul. 8–15 to *e·* this ''miracle in stone.''
11– 7 helped *e·* The Mother Church,
41– 7 * to help *e·* this beautiful
45– 6 * can effect cures . . . and *e·* churches,
My. 22– 8 * to *e·* such a building
287– 3 movement to *e·* a monument to
308–18 My father's person was *e·*

erected
Mis. 139–21 having *e·* thereon a church edifice
382–20 was *e·* the first church edifice
Man. 103– 4 The edifice *e·* in 1894
Pul. 2– 2 house Solomon had *e·*.
24– 2 * first C. S. church *e·* in Boston
24–14 * *e·* Anno Domini 1894.
40–19 * costly edifice *e·* in Boston
58–10 * *e·* this edifice at a cost of
63–21 * *e·* at a cost of
77– 2 * which the church has just *e·*.
77–10 * a church edifice was *e·* at the
78– 9 * 1894 a church edifice was *e·*
84–13 * The First Church . . . is *e·*.
My. 11–24 * the new building will be *e·*,
15– 6 edifice *e·* in 1894 for The
66–29 * houses of worship have been *e·*,
67–15 * First church *e·* . . . 1894
67–26 * surpass any church edifice *e·* in
70– 4 * *e·* its first church only
72–29 * when they *e·* the first church
73– 4 * have *e·* dozens of churches
76–27 * cathedral *e·* by the devotees of
186–28 *e·* a Church of Christ, Scientist,
189–25 *e·* in the sunny South
195–26 temples *e·* first in the hearts of
335–13 * where he *e·* a fine dwelling-house.

erecting
Ret. 5– 4 gave the money for *e·* the
My. 196– 3 I congratulate you upon *e·* the
208–18 *e·* a church building,

erection
Mis. 131–14 since the *e·* of the edifice of
Man. 102–17 *e·* of a church edifice.
Ret. 51– 4 to be appropriated for the *e·*,
Pul. 50–12 * *e·* of a visible house of worship
51–23 * The *e·* of this temple will
52–11 * *e·* of a massive temple in
56–11 * *e·* of the temple, in Boston,
57– 4 * contributions for its *e·* came from
85– 4 * have made its *e·* possible.
My. 21– 9 * *e·* of many branch churches.
22–29 * *e·* of the new edifice of The
23– 6 * *e·* of the present edifice in 1894,
23–28 * in the work of its *e·*.
24–19 * *e·* of the building is proceeding
58–14 * *e·* of these mighty walls.
98–28 * The *e·* in Boston of the

err
Mis. 49–29 that the capacity to *e·* proceeds from
168–22 *Ye do e·, not knowing the— Matt.* 22 : 29.
219– 6 ''Ye do *e·, not knowing the— Matt.* 22 : 29.
No. 9–13 whereas you may *e·* in effort,
37– 4 ''Ye do *e·, not knowing the— Matt.* 22 : 29.
'01. 30– 4 We *e·* in thinking the object of

errancy
Ret. 73–24 Such *e·* betrays a violent and

errand
Mis. 250–25 on an *e·* of mercy,

errands
My. 129–21 do thy *e·*, and be thy dearest

erratic
Mis. 266–12 An *e·* career is like the

erring

Mis.	3–20	the e· or mortal thought holds in itself
	5–25	an e· or mortal mind,
	13–22	testimony of the five e· senses,
	27–28	To e· material sense, No !
	36– 1	e·, sinful, sick, and dying,
	63– 4	claim that one e· mind cures
	97–10	E· human mind is by no means a
	139–28	the e· mind's apprehension.
	186– 9	this e· belief even separates its
	199– 4	only mortal, e· mind can claim
	199– 6	annul his own e· mental law,
	257–11	immoral force of e· mortal mind,
	260–14	Jesus knew that e· mortal thought
	286–22	states of the human e· mind ;
	362–24	refute e· reason with the spiritual
	362–32	an e· so-called mind
Ret.	59– 2	a finite and e· mind,
Rud.	9–10	in e· human will,
No.	4– 9	an e· sense of existence,
	5– 4	In e· mortal thought
Hea.	5– 1	our own e· finite sense of God,

erroneous

Mis.	10–30	e· belief that you have enemies ;
	73– 3	this supposition is proven e·
	218–11	It is e· to accept the evidence of
	309– 5	must result in e· conclusions.
	352– 8	error of its present e· course,
	366–26	E· doctrines never have
Ret.	13–10	aroused by this e· doctrine,
Un.	36–14	matter is e·, transitory, unreal.
	36–24	or to say that . . . is e·.
Rud.	10–23	e· physical and mental state.
No.	10–20	former position, . . . is proven e·.
My.	161–18	to destroy its e· claims.
	219– 3	Such practice would be e·,

erroneously

Mis.	276–27	or at work e·,
Man.	40–15	influencing or being influenced e·.
'01.	21–19	begins his calculation e· ;

error (see also error's)

above

Mis.	234– 4	we attempt to mount above e· by

absorbed in

Mis.	333– 6	could be absorbed in e· !

against

My.	193–18	Protesting against e·, you unite with

all

Mis.	14–30	and thereby destroys all e·,
	104–32	wherewith to overcome all e·.
	118–19	until all e· is destroyed
	194–26	the Truth that destroys all e·,
	195– 2	the Truth that antidotes all e·.
	235–10	delivering mankind from all e·
	251–26	all e·, physical, moral, or
	283–29	Truth which destroys all e·.
	301–28	All e· tends to harden the heart,
Ret.	94–12	divine mercy, destroying all e·,
Un.	17– 2	Evil seeks to fasten all e· upon
Pul.	70–23	* power of Truth over all e·,
No.	9–23	it excludes all e· and
	24–26	This great fact concerning all e·
Pan.	13–11	stern condemnation of all e·,
'01.	23–17	laid the axe at the root of all e·,
	31– 5	Truth opposed to all e·,
'02.	2– 8	in contradistinction to all e·,
My.	18–20	stern condemnation of all e·,

all forms of

Un.	8–17	All forms of e· are uprooted

always strives

Mis.	371–22	e· always strives to unite,

and death

Hea.	8– 5	that destroy e· and death.

and delusion

Un.	33–15	only through e· and delusion.

and nothingness

Mis.	201–12	e· and nothingness of supposed life

and shadow

Ret.	25–13	senses, . . . I called e· and shadow.

and sickness

Mis.	221– 9	e· and sickness are one,

and sin

No.	37–26	if e· and sin existed in the
My.	323–22	* triumph over e· and sin,

and Truth

Mis.	302–11	discriminate between e· and Truth,

annihilates

Mis.	14–29	Science of Truth annihilates e·,

antagonism of

Mis.	320–21	doth meet the antagonism of e· ;

asks

My.	211– 9	All that e· asks is to be let alone ;

atone for

Mis.	118–14	sympathy can neither atone for e·,

error

attacks of

My.	210– 9	shielded from the attacks of e·

before

Mis.	210–31	Charity never flees before e·,

belief of

Rud.	12– 9	encouraging them in the belief of e·

belief or

Mis.	79–13	cannot lapse into a . . . belief or e·

bid

Po.	23–22	Bid e· melt away !

blended with

Rud.	9– 6	more or less blended with e· ;

blindness to

Un.	6–19	theory of God's blindness to e·

cancel

No.	7– 9	we can cancel e· in our own hearts,

cannot antidote

Mis.	334–24	Then it cannot antidote e·.

casting out

Mis.	175– 2	casting out e· and healing the sick.
	192– 7	casting out e·,— sickness, sin,
	268–13	healing the sick and casting out e·.
Ret.	66– 2	healing the sick, in casting out e·,
Peo.	13– 7	casting out e· and healing the sick.

cast out

Mis.	247– 1	truth that shall cast out e·
No.	42–13	or to cast out e· with error,
Hea.	2–25	cast out e· and heal the sick.
	3– 4	to make men better, to cast out e·,
	7– 3	power of Truth to cast out e· ;
Peo.	8– 2	cast out e· and heal the sick.

casts out

Mis.	193–13	heals the sick, casts out e·,
Man.	17–18	casts out e·, heals the sick,
Hea.	13–24	casts out e· and thus heals

claim of

(see claim)

claims of

Mis.	293–13	opposite claims of e·.
Ret.	64–23	supposititious claims of e· ;

claim to

No.	30–20	existence of even a claim to e·.

cloud of

Mis.	204– 2	impenetrable cloud of e· ;

combat with

Mis.	216– 3	your own state of combat with e·.

commingled

Mis.	379–17	they commingled e· with truth,

conceive of

'01.	14–19	to conceive of e· as either right or

concept of

Ret.	67– 2	hence one's concept of e· is

consciousness of

Un.	4–15	lose our own consciousness of e·.
	4–16	we lose all consciousness of e·,

could not control

Mis.	140– 1	such as e· could not control.

declares

Mis.	218– 6	as e· declares Truth.

denounce

My.	210–21	only denounce e· in general,

despoil

Un.	17–17	despoil e· of its borrowed plumes,

destroy

Mis.	40–17	power of Truth to destroy e·,
	85–30	tends to destroy e· :
Hea.	8– 5	that destroy e· and death.

destroying

Mis.	261–21	by Truth's destroying e·.

destroys

Mis.	105–24	Truth destroys e·.
	204– 5	neutralizes and destroys e·.
	299– 3	To know the . . . destroys e·.
	370–30	by which e· destroys e·,
Ret.	61–20	Truth that destroys e·
My.	232–23	Truth which destroys e·,

destroys the

Mis.	241–21	Truth destroys the e· that insists on

destruction of

Mis.	215– 1	final destruction of e· through this

discern the

Mis.	355–23	then thou wilt discern the e·

disease in

Mis.	85–29	Disease in e·, more than ease

dissolve

Ret.	87–27	such efficacy as to dissolve e·.

dose of

Mis.	241–13	taking a dose of e· big enough

dream or

Mis.	49–15	all that is mortal is a dream or e·,

ejection of

My.	222–30	will aid the ejection of e·,

element of

Un.	58– 3	in their native element of e·,

error

engulfing
    No. 42–15 engulfing *e·* in bottomless oblivion,
entrance of
    Mis. 280–31 open wide for the entrance of *e·*,
every
    No. 7–11 to see every *e·* they possess,
every phase of
    Un. 4– 7 destroys every phase of *e·*.
evil and
    Mis. 36– 3 classify evil and *e·* as mortal mind,
evil, or
    Ret. 57–19 Evil, or *e·*, is not Mind ;
existence of
    Un. 22–11 To admit the existence of *e·*
expose
    Mis. 335–19 right to expose *e·*,
fable of
    Un. 44–13 This abortive ego, this fable of *e·*,
fails
    Mis. 6–17 ultimately succeed where *e·* fails.
faith in
    My. 292–30 faith in truth and faith in *e·*.
fall into
    No. 9–16 students who fall into *e·*,
find
    Mis. 334–17 You must find *e·* to be *nothing* :
firm of
    Mis. 361–28 by no means . . . in the firm of *e·*,
form of
    Mis. 48– 9 as to every form of *e·*,
found out
    Mis. 355–13 *E·* found out is two-thirds destroyed,
froth of
    Mis. 78–21 we will hope it is the froth of *e·*
fundamental
    Ret. 31–16 fundamental *e·* of faith in things
    My. 268– 7 fundamental *e·* is engrafted on it.
giveth no light
    Mis. 276–29 *E·* giveth no light,
handle the
    Mis. 221– 4 opportunity to handle the *e·*,
has no hobby
    No. 44–10 *E·* has no hobby, however boldly
has no life
    Un. 38– 8 *E·* has no life, and is virtually
has no power
    Mis. 157–26 *E·* has no power but to destroy
her
    Un. 57–15 he neither held her *e·* by affinity nor
his
    Man. 52–13 his confession of his *e·*
human
    (*see* **human**)
illusion and
    Mis. 68–17 illusion and *e·* which Truth casts out.
in borrowed plumes
    Mis. 371–24 *e·* in borrowed plumes
incapable of
    Mis. 210– 1 as unconscious as incapable of *e·*,
indicates
    No. 6–13 If, as the *e·* indicates,
injustice and
    Peo. 10–14 injustice and *e·* enslave him.
in practice
    Mis. 66–28 is met with *e·* in practice ;
in premise
    Mis. 66–27 *E·* in premise is met with
        265–19 An *e·* in premise can never
        309– 5 personality is an *e·* in premise,
in thought
    Hea. 7– 3 correcting *e·* in thought,
is annihilated
    Un. 58– 4 before *e·* is annihilated.
is not Mind
    Mis. 367– 8 showing that *e·* is not Mind,
    Ret. 57–19 Evil, or *e·*, is not Mind ;
is not Truth
    '01. 14–17 self-evident that *e·* is not Truth ;
is the unreal
    Hea. 10–15 Truth is the real ; *e·* is the unreal.
is walking
    Mis. 277– 5 *E·* is walking to and fro
its own
    Mis. 145–16 wounded sense of its own *e·*,
Jesus said of
    Mis. 57–11 Jesus said of *e·*,
knowledge of
    Ret. 55– 4 sufficient knowledge of *e·* to
    My. 232–21 "A knowledge of *e·* and of its
lapse or
    Peo. 2–25 Truth without a lapse or *e·*,
last
    Mis. 293–17 last *e·* will be worse than the first
likeness of
    Rud. 13–11 but the likeness of *e·*

error

loathes
    Ret. 81–18 The enlightened heart loathes *e·*,
material
    My. 232–24 material *e·* finally disappears,
may enter
    Ret. 54–18 *e·* may enter through this same
may say
    Un. 18– 6 *E·* may say that God can never
meets
    My. 180–16 C. S. meets *e·* with Truth,
mental
    Rud. 3–21 mental *e·* made manifest physically,
mists of
    No. 28– 4 mists of *e·*, . . . will melt
mortal
    Mis. 21–19 matter is mortal *e·*.
        56–15 to conclude that . . . is a mortal *e·*,
        77–28 could fall into mortal *e·* ;
    Un. 46– 1 mortal *e·*, called *mind*, is not
mystery of
    Mis. 223– 1 the metaphysical mystery of *e·*
name the
    My. 235–12 definitely name the *e·*, uncover it,
negation, or
    Mis. 334–22 How shall we treat a negation, or *e·*
negativing
    Mis. 208–18 by divine Truth's negativing *e·*
neutralizing
    Pul. 6– 2 when Truth is neutralizing *e·*
never created
    Mis. 49–31 that Truth never created *e·*,
never to repeat
    Mis. 346–25 rule in C. S. never to repeat *e·*
ninety-nine parts of
    No. 21– 3 philosophy has ninety-nine parts of *e·*
no
    Mis. 77–18 Truth that knows no *e·*,
    Un. 4– 6 Truth is All, and there is no *e·*.
    No. 5– 7 To Truth there is no *e·*.
no sympathy for
    No. 30–25 Truth has no sympathy for *e·*.
nothingness of
    Pul. 13– 9 nothingness of *e·* is seen ;
        13–10 nothingness of *e·* is in proportion to
not through
    Un. 41–21 not through *e·*, but through Truth.
of anti-Christ
    Mis. 309–18 falling into the *e·* of anti-Christ.
of belief
    Mis. 45–27 This *e·* of belief is idolatry,
        220–31 he knows that an *e·* of belief
    No. 4– 9 *e·* of belief, named disease,
of believing
    Ret. 69–17 *e·* of believing that there is life in
of creation
    Mis. 57–23 The false sense and *e·* of creation
of material sense
    Mis. 190–23 dumbness, an *e·* of material sense,
of mind
    Hea. 9–24 an *e·* of mind or of body.
of premise
    Mis. 200– 8 an *e·* of premise and conclusion,
        344–18 from *e·* of premise would seek a
of sickness
    Mis. 62–18 *e·* of sickness, sin, and death,
of statement
    Mis. 56–21 Organic life is an *e·* of statement
of supposed life
    Mis. 53– 5 *e·* of supposed life . . . in matter,
of the revolution
    No. 6–21 *e·* of the revolution of the sun
of the senses
    Un. 42–11 is an *e·* of the senses ;
of thought
    No. 4–13 hence *e·* of thought becomes fable
    My. 211–15 mortal mind into *e·* of thought,
opaque
    Mis. 347–11 peer through the opaque *e·*.
opposite
    Mis. 57–17 The opposite *e·* said, "I am true,"
or Adam
    Mis. 258–19 *E·*, or Adam, might give names to
or evil
    Mis. 259–25 *e·*, or evil, is really non-existent,
or false sense
    Mis. 76–24 it is an *e·* or false sense of
or matter
    Mis. 190– 4 Life, defiant of *e·* or matter.
    Un. 42–24 Truth, defiant of *e·* or matter,
outside of the
    Mis. 352– 9 facts of Truth outside of the *e·* ;
overcome
    Mis. 89–27 saved from error, or *e·* overcome.
pantheistic
    Ret. 69– 8 pantheistic *e·*, or so-called

error

peace in
My. 233–23 destroys his peace in *e·*,
penalty of
Un. 11– 2 from the penalty of *e·*.
phase of
Mis. 25– 8 matter is a phase of *e·*,
phases of
Mis. 237–13 All the different phases of *e·*
postulate of
Mis. 57–13 postulate of *e·* must appear.
qualities of
Mis. 332–28 but are qualities of *e·*.
rage
My. 270–14 Let *e·* rage and imagine a vain
rebukes
Mis. 210–30 rebukes *e·*, and casts it out.
No. 43– 6 Truth rebukes *e·* ;
remain in
Mis. 2–25 If man . . . should remain in *e·*,
renders
Mis. 333– 6 this renders *e·* a palpable falsity,
repeats itself
'00. 10–17 History shows that *e·* repeats itself
results of
Mis. 288–11 works out the results of *e·*.
root of
Mis. 285–19 laying the axe at the root of *e·*.
rule of
No. 44–21 no Reign of Terror or rule of *e·*
saved from
Mis. 89–27 saved from *e·*, or error overcome.
says
Mis. 367–13 *E·* says that knowing all things
Un. 17–20 *E·* says God must know evil
18–13 *E·* says you must know grief
18–22 *E·* says God must know death
seen aright as
Mis. 299– 4 error that is seen aright as *e·*,
see the
Mis. 352– 7 must first see the *e·* of its
self-assertive
Mis. 268–30 self-assertive *e·* dies of its own
self-destroying
No. 10–16 matter, . . . is a self-destroying *e·*.
selfhood in
Mis. 363– 4 "ego" that claims selfhood in *e·*,
senseless
Mis. 355–19 Mental darkness is senseless *e·*,
sense of
Mis. 352–31 aroused to reject the sense of *e·* ;
Un. 1–19 they lose all sense of *e·*.
side of
My. 146–28 Others who take the side of *e·*
smite
Ret. 30– 2 endeavoring to smite *e·* with
statements of
Un. 20– 4 We undo the statements of *e·* by
states of
Mis. 367– 5 states of *e·* or mortal mind.
strives
My. 249– 4 When *e·* strives to be heard
subtlety of
Ret. 64–27 forms, methods, and subtlety of *e·*,
such an
Mis. 276–28 Such an *e·* and loss will be
suggestion of
My. 243– 5 This is a suggestion of *e·*,
supersedes
Un. 40– 8 As Truth supersedes *e·*,
surging sea of
Pul. 13–17 They are in the surging sea of *e·*,
take
Mis. 214–26 cannot . . . take *e·* along with Truth,
tempest of
Hea. 2– 7 and stills the tempest of *e·* ;
that
My. 197– 2 That *e·* is most forcible which
that is seen
Mis. 299– 3 *e·* that is seen aright as error,
their
Mis. 212– 9 had suffered, and seen their *e·*.
the unreal
Hea. 18–11 Truth is the real ; *e·*, the unreal.
this
Mis. 45–27 This *e·* of belief is idolatry,
83–16 to reject or to accept this *e·* ;
105–23 shadow cast by this *e·*.
184–21 suffer for this *e·* until he learns
212–26 and open his eyes to see this *e·*?
265– 6 This *e·* in the teacher
287–11 Science corrects this *e·*
288–10 this *e·* works out the results of
364–28 This *e·*, carried to its ultimate,
Ret. 69–13 This *e·* has proved itself to be

error

this
Ret. 75– 3 This *e·* violates the law
83–14 this *e·* . . . is sure to be corrected.
Un. 36–24 This *e·* stultifies the logic of
42–12 very opposite of this *e·* is the
Rud. 9– 6 this *e·* will spring up in the
16–13 impostors are committing this *e·*.
No. 5– 6 severe realities of this *e·*.
Pan. 7–24 the logical sequence of this *e·*
My. 268– 7 What is this *e·*?
thrall of
No. 11–26 rescue reason from the thrall of *e·*.
three-in-one of
Mis. 163– 1 to conquer the three-in-one of *e·*:
throe of
Mis. 285–22 some extra throe of *e·* may
to buy
Mis. 269–28 mortals to buy *e·* at par value.
to declare
No. 5– 8 it follows that to declare *e·* real
to lose
Mis. 84–25 To lose *e·* thus, is to live in Christ,
to mix with
Hea. 4–15 expect infinite Truth to mix with *e·*,
to pay for
Mis. 342–25 to pay for *e·* and receive nothing
trespassing
No. 3– 5 while the trespassing *e·* murders
trinity of
Un. 62–17 Destroy this trinity of *e·*,
Truth and
Mis. 65–10 question between Truth and *e·*,
188–12 contest between Truth and *e·* ;
'01. 22–10 Truth and *e·*, Spirit and matter,
truth and
Un. 60– 5 he articulates truth and *e·*.
Pan. 8–26 matter and Spirit, truth and *e·*,
Truth, not
Mis. 71–16 Law brings out Truth, not *e·* ;
297–28 Trust Truth, not *e·* ;
My. 239– 1 Truth, not *e·* ; Love, not hate.
Truth over
(see **Truth***)*
Truth to
Mis. 208– 2 the law of Truth to *e·*,
268–12 from Truth to *e·*, in pursuit of
Truth versus
Mis. 346–22 chapter sub-title
unconcemned
'01. 15– 4 *E·* uncondemned is not nullified.
uncovers the
Mis. 352–10 uncovers the *e·* and quickens the
unfolding of
Mis. 293– 4 the righteous unfolding of *e·*
unreality of
No. 17–19 Hence the unreality of *e·*,
unreality of the
No. 4–15 the unreality of the *e·*.
versus
Mis. 332–22 *E·* versus Truth :
victory in
My. 278–26 Victory in *e·* is defeat in Truth.
voicing
No. 8– 6 Avoid voicing *e·* ;
voluntary
No. v– 5 involuntary as well as voluntary *e·*.
warfare against
Pul. 12–23 in our warfare against *e·*,
warfare with
Mis. 215–24 they have a long warfare with *e·*
ways of
Un. 55–16 self-destroying ways of *e·*
we master
Mis. 53– 6 only as we master *e·* with Truth.
when found out
Mis. 210– 5 certainty that *e·*, when found out,
whole of
Ret. 67– 3 is not the whole of *e·*.
will hate
Mis. 278– 5 *E·* will hate more as it realizes
witnesses for
Un. 33–21 Examine these witnesses for *e·*,
workings of
Mis. 51– 9 malicious workings of *e·*
would enthrone
No. 42–16 material senses would enthrone *e·*
would fashion
No. 20–5 *E·* would fashion Deity in a manlike
wrestle with
Mis. 336– 4 your province to wrestle with *e·*,
yielding
Mis. 107–20 pass through . . . before yielding *e·*.
yields
Mis. 204– 9 *e·* yields up its weapons

error
Mis. 24—22 e·, the opposite of Truth ;
36—30 The belief that . . . is an e· ;
49—18 *wrong, sinful, or an e·?*
50— 2 e· is an illusion of mortals ;
61—27 of e·, not of Truth ;
80— 2 By rendering e· such a service,
83—13 e· which knocks at the door of
105—26 senses join issue with e·,
112— 8 e·, given new opportunities,
118—19 willing to suffer patiently for e·
134—25 E· is only fermenting,
141—12 e·, which hates the bonds
177—19 salvation of the world from e·,
221— 6 E· produces physical sufferings,
221—18 If e· is the cause of disease,
222—24 E· is more abstract than Truth.
222—30 methods and power of e·.
258—20 e· could neither name nor
266— 6 to abridge a . . . privilege is an e·.
266—29 e·, running to and fro
269—27 E· is vending itself on trust,
298—22 the seeming power of e·,
299— 3 the what, when, and how of e·,
348—13 E·, left to itself, accumulates.
352— 4 to behold aright the e·,
352— 4 the e· of regarding Life,
354—10 e· to Truth, and evil to good,
371—22 To sympathize in any degree with e·,
Ret. 57—17 Matter is substance in e·,
59— 3 mortal mind . . . is e·.
64—23 e· being a false claim,
64—28 e·, may be destroyed ;
64—29 will become the victims of e·.
67—19 e· made its man mortal,
69—10 saying, . . . I will make e· as real
69—14 proved itself to be e·.
71—11 an e· of much magnitude.
84—21 empty his students' minds of e·,
Un. 22— 8 would taste and know e· for
22— 9 not admit that e· is something
22—18 *Evil. . . . E·,* even, is His offspring.
38— 6 Death, then, is e·,
57—17 existence in the flesh is e·
Rud. 8—17 e· has the majority.
10— 3 if you have power in e·,
10—25 e· which Truth will destroy.
No. 5— 5 an antipode, — the reality of e· ;
5—26 contradictory fusion of Truth with e·,
42—13 or to cast out error with e·,
43—21 can never engraft Truth into e·.
'01. 22—12 Truth is true, . . . e·, is not ;
Hea. 17—20 Sin, sickness, and death are e· ;
Peo. 4—13 the e· that a personal God
4—28 and cast out devils, e·.
Po. 70—15 Then, e·, get thee hence,
My. 211— 1 of e· that is damning men.
217—25 improved belief is one step out of e·,
235— 4 not name its opposite, e·.
349 —6 e· that Truth destroys.

error's
Mis. 277— 3 becomes the mark for e· shafts.
Ret. 69—25 "Above e· awful din,
81—16 overwhelming sense of e· vacuity,
Un. 45—16 it becomes e· affirmative

errors
are based
Mis. 71—18 E· are based on a mortal or
barefaced
Mis. 43—29 barefaced e· that are taught
his
Mis. 212—28 tries to show his e· to him
My. 233—22 to know what his e· are ;
history of the
Mis. 277—21 * history of the e· of the human mind."
innumerable
Mis. 137—26 each one of the innumerable e·
involved
Ret. 22—15 till its involved e· are vanquished
of flesh
Mis. 189—11 destroys the e· of flesh,
of others
Mis. 131— 1 challenges the e· of others
236— 6 indiscretions, and e· of others ;
of the members
Man. 55— 3 e· of the members of their
of thought
Rud. 10—12 Mortal ills are but e· of thought,
old
'01. 21— 4 or new editions of old e· ;
our own
Mis. 224—28 Nothing short of our own e· should
prejudices, and
No. 9— 5 prejudices, and e· of one class of
these
Man. 55— 5 strive to overcome these e·.

errors
which devour
Mis. 82—28 the e· which devour it.

Mis. 234—15 e· which can never find a place in
errs
Mis. 308— 7 greatly e·, stops his own progress,
Ret. 59—15 Whatever e· is mortal,
94— 7 seems to be good, and yet e·,
erudite
Ret. 31—28 E· systems of philosophy and
erudition (see also **erudition's**)
No. 2—21 beacon-lights along the shores of e· ;
My. 340— 9 The enlightenment, the e·,
erudition's
Ret. 11—20 From e· bower.
Po. 60—18 From e· bower.
escape
Mis. 53— 8 e· the weariness and wickedness of
64— 3 way he made for mortals' e·.
76—14 to e· and be immortal.
85—27 to e· from sense into the
105—11 to e· from the material body.
109—25 to e· from the false claims of sin.
113—18 of e· from the latter-day ultimatum
119—30 and e· the penalty therefor?
126— 1 from danger to e·,
162—20 to e· from the sins of the flesh.
261— 3 evil finds no e· from itself ;
269— 4 He cannot e· from barriers
347— 5 e· from their houses to the open
347— 7 To e· from this calamity
Un. 14—24 How then could man e·,
14—25 or hope to e·,
64—18 nor e· from identification with
Pul. 15—13 E· from evil, and designate those
51— 8 * though they cannot e· censure,
No. 17— 4 From this logic there is no e·.
17—18 no e· from the focal radiation of
Pan. 12—14 way of e· from sin, disease, and
'00. 5—18 enable man to e· from idolatry
My. 41—13 * no one to e· that blessedness,
escaped
Mis. 311—30 never e· from my lips,
Hea. 18— 9 never e· from matter;
My. 74—22 * e· from the bondage of the
escapes
My. 159—15 the true thought e· from
eschew
Mis. 271—11 e· all magazines and books which
eschewed
My. 288—17 so-called laws of matter he e· ;
eschewing
Peo. 4—28 E· a materialistic and idolatrous
eschews
Mis. 80— 9 A league . . . which C. S. e·
My. 303—14 e· divine rights in human beings.
escort
My. 302—27 wanted to greet me with e·
312—28 The Free Masons selected my e·,
Esculapius (see also **Æsculapius**)
Peo. 4—24 Apollo and E· the gods of medicine,
escutcheon
Ret. 86—15 no blot on the e· of our Christliness
My. 194—17 fair e· of your church.
341— 4 on the e· of this State,
esoteric
Mis. 29—24 e· magic and Oriental barbarisms
especial
Mis. 3— 3 shall claim no e· gift from
My. 325— 2 * and spoke of one e· day
329—10 * gives e· interest to the
especially
Mis. 62—26 e· when she tells them that she
128— 4 e· within the limits of a letter.
138—13 e· should he prove his faith
176— 9 devotion to Principle has e·
244—30 e· the children of our Lord
249—10 and e· through my teachings,
263—17 e· by those at a distance,
263—26 e· by unprincipled claimants,
276— 1 e· the large book of rare flowers,
277—26 Love is e· near in times of hate,
315— 2 e· adapted to the occasion,
320— 6 e· dear to the heart of
348—20 every day, and e· at dinner,
Man. 28—26 e· of one who has been or
Ret. 5—30 * e· in regard to the education of
6— 2 * e· entrusted to her watch-care,
Un. 23—16 e· when they testify concerning

especially

Pul.	7– 4	and e· the laws of the State
	59–28	* seats were e· set apart for them
	62– 3	* in the Old Country, e· in England.
	87– 2	* We e· desire you to be present
Rud.	2– 3	* e·, a living human being,
	2–10	as e· a finite *human being;*
No.	9–17	e· in the first edition
'00.	12– 9	It e· flourished as an emporium
'01.	32–22	e· the First Commandment of the
'02.	12–24	e· before making another united
My.	7– 8	e· before making another united
	167– 1	e· for the self-sacrifice
	170– 1	I am e· desirous that it should
	299–18	e· those who claim to pardon sin,
	313–17	* e· at night," as stated by
	313–21	I never was e· interested in
	318– 7	I e· employed him on "S. and H.
	324– 2	* e· your book S. and H.
	326– 7	* It is e· gratifying to them
	351– 5	* This letter is e· interesting

essayed

Ret.	22– 6	e· in the Apocryphal New Testament

Esse

My.	202–25	underived glory, the divine E·.

essence

Mis.	69– 2	His e·, relations, and attributes.
	121–18	belies the nature and e· of Deity,
	163–30	This idea or divine e· was, and is,
	394– 4	infinite e· from tropic to pole,
Ret.	33–20	rarefied to its fatal e·,
Un.	39– 6	quenched in the divine e·,
No.	12– 3	e· of this Science is right thinking
	19–19	e· of the individual infinite.
'00.	5–13	the e· and source of the
'01.	4–26	and these three are one in e·
Peo.	10– 1	Thought is the e· of an act,
Po.	45– 5	infinite e· from tropic to pole,
My.	159–27	* "What is the e· of God?
	178– 8	This Science is the e· of religion,
	204–10	that sacred *ave* and e· of Soul
	212– 5	the e·, or spirit, of evil,
	342–27	Its e· is evangelical.

essences

Peo.	10– 4	E· are refinements that lose
My.	345–28	They seek the finer e·.

essential

Mis.	13–16	e· to a rounded sense of the
	50–15	it is e· that the student
	51– 1	This change of heart is e·
	61–22	Does God's e· likeness sin,
	62–15	*hold that their theology is e· to*
	76–30	e· to the fulfilment of this
	232–11	behind the times in things most e·,
	234–12	to things most e· and divine.
	264–10	Unity is the e· nature of C. S.
	349– 8	not necessitate e· materialization
Man.	88–21	subjects e· to their progress.
Ret.	14–13	if assent to this doctrine was e·
	83–27	That these e· points are
Un.	22–14	e· to happiness and life.
Pul.	36– 5	* as Mrs. Eddy felt it e· to
	53– 9	* which Jesus . . . declared to be e·,
	53–20	* the e· element of success
	54–21	* that are e· to success.
	72–28	* naming as one great e·
'01.	1–12	most e· to your growth
	30– 6	are e· to its propagation.
My.	46–17	* e· requirement of a reinstated
	99– 6	* a pleasure and an e· ;
	303–19	it is e· to understand the spiritual

essentially

Mis.	237–16	This period is not e· one of
	258–29	differs e· from the human.
	266–22	They are e· dear to me,
Ret.	94–17	preaching, and practice be e· one.
My.	247– 2	E· democratic, its government
	254–24	E· democratic, its government

essentials

Pul.	39– 2	* great e· of love to God
No.	3–27	possessing the e· of C. S.,
My.	93–26	* have overlooked these e· of

establish

Mis.	38–13	*How happened you to e· a college*
	176–23	The Pilgrims came to e· a nation
	234–19	to e· this mighty system of
Pul.	85–17	* believe it to be possible to e·
Pan.	6– 1	Science will restore and e·,
	15– 7	e· us in the most holy faith,
My.	52–17	* to e· these our Master's commands
	111–18	e· their practice of healing
	214–23	or to e· a C. S. home
	215–18	to e· a Metaphysical College,

establish

My.	221–10	e· the definition of omnipotence,
	279–17	e· the brotherhood of man,

established

Mis.	187– 6	He e· health and harmony,
	193–10	can be e· on no other claim
	383– 6	wherever a church of C. S. is e·,
Man.	41–22	e· in me, and rule out of me all sin ;
	49–15	under rules e· by the publishers.
	71– 4	more than one church is e· in the
Ret.	93– 7	e· its rules in consonance with
Un.	6– 8	e· on everlasting foundations.
	33–25	every word may be e·." — *Matt.* 18 : 16.
Pul.	6– 5	church e· by the Nazarene Prophet
	30– 5	* unite with churches already e·
No.	9– 6	must not be introduced or e· among
	28–15	The proof . . . I consider well e·.
	38– 6	He e· the only true idealism
Hea.	11–18	it has e· this axiom,
	15– 3	e· upon this Principle,
	18–20	he e· his Messiahship on the basis
My.	v–15	* e· the Cause on a sound basis
	vi–28	* she e· the C. S. *Sentinel*
	9– 1	* those previously e· have had
	33–30	e· it upon the floods. — *Psal.* 24 : 2.
	47–10	* After a work has been e·,
	56–20	* foregoing named churches were e·,
	56–22	* more branch churches were e·
	90–31	* e· beyond cavil.
	241– 4	* that for which it was e· ;
	245– 6	e· on a broad and liberal basis.
	265–11	brotherhood of man should be e·,
	281–11	brotherhood of all peoples is e· ;
	348–21	its value to the race firmly e·.

establishes

Mis.	73–10	e· the reality of what is spiritual,
	101–14	scientific sense of being which e·
Rud.	3–21	e· the opposite manifestation

establishing

Mis.	153– 2	e· the Cause of C. S.
	177–17	work of e· the truth,
Ret.	63– 4	e· the recognition that God *is All,*
My.	53–18	* After e· itself as a church
	163–29	e· in this city a church
	182– 8	by e· a new-old church,

establishment

Mis.	238–14	labor for the e· of a cause
Man.	63–14	E·.
Ret.	48– 4	e· of *genuine* C. S. healing
	94–27	the e· of Christ's kingdom
Un.	8–18	by the e·, through reason,
Rud.	v– 6	e· OF THE SCIENCE OF MIND-HEALING
'01.	30–20	the e· of a new-old religion
My.	220–17	e· of Christian religion
	280– 9	* things which make for the e· of
	310–12	manufacturing e· in Tilton,

estate

Mis.	64– 7	and rose to his native e·,
	77–26	fallen away from his first e· ;
	167–20	Is he heir to an e· ?
	182–13	his perfect and eternal e·.
Pul.	49–27	* a strikingly well-kept e·
	50– 6	* in buying so large an e·
	58– 7	* e· called Pleasant View ;
My.	41–24	* his real e· is one of blessedness.
	123–16	The original cost of the e·
		(see also **real estate**)

estates

My.	66– 7	* ten e· having been conveyed

esteem

Mis.	84– 9	the world's temporary e· ;
	356–25	gone down in his own e·.
Ret.	29– 2	I e· all honest people,
'01.	24–10	* "I e· my having taken this
My.	9–13	* depth of our affection and e·.

esteemed

Ret.	19–13	highly e· and sincerely lamented
My.	157–10	* where, . . . you are so highly e·,
	330–25	highly e· and sincerely lamented

esteems

Mis.	289–24	if the wife e· not this privilege,

Esther

Pul.	82–20	* there were Miriam and E·,

Esthers

Pul.	82–22	* there are ten thousand E·,

estimable

My.	324–15	* neither Mr. Wiggin nor his e· wife

estimate

Mis.	247–24	seems, to the common e·,
	248– 9	Greeks showed a just e· of
Ret.	21–20	to spiritual joy and true e· of being.

estimate
Ret. 49–14   must learn to lose their *e·* of
Pul. 30– 9   * but this *e·*, as I understand,
No. 43– 8   * He who knows all things can *e·*
Hea. 7–11   where Jesus formed his *e·* ;
My. 115– 8   my *e·* of the C. S. textbook.
357–17   proportionally *e·* their success

estimated
Mis. 131–27   if, indeed, it could be *e·*.
'00. 7– 7   *e·* that during the past three years
My. 76–18   * *e·* cost of the extension
77–14   * it is *e·* that not less than
77–25   * *e·* that nearly forty thousand
86–13   * every cent of the *e·* cost
181–22   *e·* that Chicago has gained from

estimation
Mis. 383–14   in the *e·* of thinkers

estranged
Mis. 236–22   Be not *e·* from each other

estrangement
'02. 18–16   No *e·*, no emulation,

estranges
No. 15–24   *e·* mortals from divine Life

et cetera
Mis. 78–17   some people employ the *e· c·* of
114–20   and all the *e· c·* of evil.
357– 2   all the *e· c·* of the ways and means
My. 25–18   consumed in travel, *e· c·*,
110–15   all the *e· c·* of mortal mind
124–24   log, traveller's companion, *e· c·*,

et ceteras
'01. 21– 3   They are not the *addenda*, the *e· c·*,

eternal
absolute and
'00. 4–22   found final, absolute, and *e·*.
My. 260–10   the real, the absolute and *e·*,
All
Un. 25–24   elements which belong to the *e·* **All**,
and divine
Chr. 53–17   Thus Christ, *e·* and divine,
as God
Un. 49– 3   as definite and *e·* as God,
59–13   Salvation is as *e·* as God.
No. 17–28   would be as *e·* as God.
as Truth
Mis. 163–23   are as *e·* as Truth,
attribute
Mis. 2–12   the *e·* attribute of Truth,
being
Un. 43– 1   *e·* being and its perfections,
No. 11– 4   divine Principle, and an *e·* being.
bliss is
Mis. 330–12   why not, since . . . bliss is *e·*,
bonds
No. 26–22   God holds man in the *e·* bonds of
Christ
My. 262–11   my sense of the *e·* Christ, Truth,
Christian Science
My. 357–21   to salvation and *e·* C. S.
Christmas
My. 260– 3   An *e·* Christmas would make matter an
circle
Un. 12– 5   curving sickle of Mind's *e·* circle,
coexistent and
'01. 5–26   are coexistent and *e·*,
currents
Mis. 157–28   cannot stop the *e·* currents of Truth.
damnation
No. 14–26   doctrine of *e·* damnation,
day
'00. 7–30   morning dawns on *e·* day.
Po. 22–11   And bask in one *e·* day.
definite and
Un. 49– 3   man is as definite and *e·* as God,
demands
My. 159–22   legitimate and *e·* demands upon man ;
dynamics
Mis. 258–31   explains the *e·* dynamics of being,
energies
Mis. 97– 3   *e·* energies of Truth,
erect and
Mis. 383–12   Erect and *e·*, it will go on
existence
Mis. 206– 9   interpret man's *e·* existence,
286–19   spiritual and *e·* existence
fact
My. 143–16   the *e·* fact of C. S.
fire
Pan. 3–25   * heaven, earth, sea, the *e·* fire,
God
No. 37– 6   *e·* God and infinite consciousness
God is
No. 37– 8   evil is temporal and God is *e·*,

eternal
good
(*see* **good**)
harmonies
Mis. 72– 5   unfolds the *e·* harmonies of the
harmonious and
Mis. 5– 4   spiritual, harmonious, and *e·*.
235–21   the real man, harmonious and *e·*,
Rud. 4– 4   perfect beings, harmonious and *e·*,
No. 6– 6   spiritual, harmonious, and *e·*,
My. 119– 5   is real, harmonious, and *e·*
146–29   voices the harmonious and *e·*,
harmony
(*see* **harmony**)
haven
Ret. 57– 2   as we sail into the *e·* haven
heritage
Mis. 182–25   *e·* heritage of the Elohim,
idea
Mis. 79–12   the *e·* idea of Truth,
Un. 61– 7   even the *e·* idea of God,
No. 25–14   Man is the *e·* idea of
identity
No. 25–22   flesh is not man's *e·* identity.
image
'01. 5–27   His *e·* image and likeness.
immutable and
Un. 29–13   absolutely immutable and *e·*,
No. 11– 1   immutable and *e·* laws of God ;
individuality
Mis. 361–25   and all *e·* individuality.
infinite and
Peo. 4– 9   Life, which is infinite and *e·*,
My. 159–20   towards God, the infinite and *e·*
inseparable and
Mis. 182–28   man and . . . are inseparable and *e·*.
intact and
'02. 7– 1   nature of Love intact and *e·*.
joys
Mis. xi–16   become footsteps to joys *e·*.
justice
Ret. 80– 3   though *e·* justice be graciously
law
Mis. 123–23   through the *e·* law of justice ;
No. 30–22   like the *e·* law of God,
laws
No. 11– 1   immutable and *e·* laws of God ;
Life
(*see* **Life**)
life
(*see* **life**)
Life is
Un. 37–13   God is Life, all Life is *e·*.
light
Mis. 134–14   He who dwelleth in *e·* light
Po. 70–10   Truth is *e·* light,
likeness
Un. 22– 2   made after God's *e·* likeness,
lore
Mis. 125–17   the *e·* lore of Love ;
Love
Mis. 206–31   baptismal font of *e·* Love.
286–10   the unity of *e·* Love.
man is
Mis. 287– 3   forever fact that man is *e·*
mansion
Pul. 3–12   Truth and Love, man's *e·* mansion.
meridian
My. 177–12   and nearer the *e·* meridian
Mind
(*see* **Mind**)
noon
Mis. 385– 4   * And one *e·* noon."
Po. 37– 4   And one *e·* noon."
perfect and
Mis. 165–16   perfect and *e·*, appears
182–13   recognize his perfect and *e·* estate,
187–23   self-existent, perfect, and *e·*
369–26   perfect and *e·* Principle of man.
Ret. 69–23   made all perfect and *e·*.
No. 28– 6   man be found perfect and *e·*.
My. 262– 1   God creates man perfect and *e·*
presence
Un. 60–28   must yield to His *e·* presence,
Principle
Mis. 369–26   *e·* Principle of man.
Pul. 4–23   unfolding its *e·* Principle.
punishment
'01. 16– 4   a future and *e·* punishment
qualities
Un. 32–14   the *e·* qualities of His being.
real and
(*see* **real**)
reality
Un. 36–12   Spirit is Truth and *e·* reality ;
49–11   Through the *e·* reality of existence

eternal
real nor
  Mis. 286–25   and neither real nor *e*.
right and
  Mis. 71–30   Whatever is real is right and *e*;
       341– 5   that is real, right, and *e*
roasting
  Peo. 3– 6   *e* roasting amidst noxious vapors;
round
  Mis. 77–17   *e* round of harmonious being.
scale
  My. 277–18   weighs in the *e* scale of equity
Science
  No. 17– 9   in the *e* Science of being
self-existent and
  '01. 3–13   * Being, self-existent and *e*."
self-sustaining and
  My. 275–26   is self-sustaining and *e*.
sense
  Mis. 67–11   not strike at the *e* sense of Life
sermon
  Mis. 126– 2   from . . . to one *e* sermon;
somethingness
  Ret. 55– 7   brings out . . . the *e* somethingness,
Son of God
  '01. 11– 2   *e* Son of God, that never suffered
Spirit
  Un. 22–19   cometh not from the *e* Spirit,
spiritual and
  Mis. 188– 8   is primal, spiritual, and *e*.
       286–19   for spiritual and *e* existence
  Rud. 5– 7   man is spiritual and *e*,
  No. 25–16   for he is spiritual and *e*,
       37– 1   Son of God, spiritual and *e*.
stillness
  Ret. 89– 1   *e* stillness and immovable Love.
sunshine
  Mis. 279– 7   *e* sunshine and joy unspeakable.
  My. 252–21   the *e* sunshine of Love,
supersensible
  Un. 10–11   Spirit, the supersensible *e*.
Truth
  Mis. 182–30   *e* Truth will be understood;
  Un. 17– 3   make the lie seem part of *e* Truth.
       61– 2   takes hold of *e* Truth.
  No. 10–14   rests on Mind, the *e* Truth.
truth
  My. 54– 4   * for the sake of the *e* truth
       143–18   discoverer of an *e* truth
unity
  Mis. 77–11   *e* unity of man and God,
upright and
  Mis. 79–15   God is upright and *e*,
verities
  Mis. 55–21   the *e* verities of Spirit assert
       363–19   in glimpses of the *e* verities.
  No. 27–15   *e* verities of God and man
verity
  My. 232–24   *e* verity, man created by

  Mis. 19–30   spiritual, joy-giving, and *e*
       61– 3   priceless, *e*, and just at hand.
       70–24   holy Spirit of Jesus was *e*.
       93–12   is in reality none besides the *e*,
      100–18   and teach the *e*.
      103– 5   while the other is *e*,
      103–19   Neither does the temporal know the *e*.
      104–15   sinless, deathless, harmonious, *e*.
      136– 8   The *e* and infinite, already
      165–10   *e* as its divine Principle.
      187–26   primal facts of being are *e*,
      217–11   that matter and Spirit are one and *e*;
      268–28   is irresistible, permanent, *e*.
  Chr. 53–59   *E* swells Christ's music-tone,
  Ret. 25–17   The real I claimed as *e*;
      59– 5   Life is not temporal, but *e*,
      60– 3   as *e*, self-existent Mind.
      68–12   One is temporal, but the other is *e*.
      73– 2   spiritual, individual, and *e*,
      90– 1   divine, infallible, and *e*.
  Un. 13–16   they must be *e*;
      24–21   must be spiritual, perfect, *e*.
      51– 4   and hence that sin is *e*,
      62– 7   which are not seen are *e*." — *II Cor.* 4 : 18.
  Pul. 2–11   are temporal, not *e*.
      2–14   *e* in the heavens." — *II Cor.* 5 : 1.
      13–24   evil is temporal, not *e*.
  No. 4–25   being, to be *e*, must be harmonious.
      10–18   all consciousness is Mind and *e*,
      16– 4   then . . . discord must be *e*.
      17–23   the *e*, infinite harmony
  '00. 5–14   *e*, infinite individuality.
  '01. 9– 3   his *e* spiritual selfhood
      25– 4   superstructure *e* in the heavens,
  Peo. 2–25   Love universal, infinite, *e*.

eternal
  Peo. 4– 7   and the *e* entered the
  My. 44– 5   * promised land of *e*, harmonious
      139–15   Life, — calm, irresistible, *e*.
      143–21   an *e* and demonstrable Science,
      160– 7   the spiritual, and the *e*,
      179–28   are, irrefutable and *e*.
      188–14   *e* in the heavens;" — *II Cor.* 5 : 1.
      192–29   "*e* in the heavens." — *II Cor.* 5 : 1.
      194– 8   *e* in the heavens," — *II Cor.* 5 : 1.
      195–28   *e* in the heaven of Spirit.
      248– 9   defining the demonstrable, the *e*.
      259–30   It represents the *e* informing Soul
      348–29   the law of God — infallible, *e*.
eternally
  Mis. 103–15   because *e* conscious.
  Ret. 87– 3   poet's line, . . . is so *e* true,
      94–23   since Science is *e* one,
  Un. 10–17   and they are *e* perfect,
      49– 4   being the *e* divine idea.
      51–20   *e* radiating throughout all space
  No. 16– 2   must truly and *e* exist.
  Peo. 3– 7   majority to be *e* punished;
      8– 8   punishes man *e*,
  My. 126–28   One thing is *e* here;
      161– 6   would destroy himself *e*,
eternity (*see also* **eternity's**)
all
  Un. 17– 9   predestined from all *e*;
awaits
  My. 230– 2   *e* awaits our Church Manual,
chambers of
  Po. 26–18   To the dim chambers of *e*
enfolds
  Pul. 74–19   mankind which *e* enfolds.
glories of
  Mis. 365– 2   bring out the glories of *e*;
  No. 21–23   brings in the glories of *e*;
hoary with
  Mis. 336–28   hoary with *e*, touches time only to
inhabits
  Mis. 189–31   extends to all time, inhabits *e*,
keep pace with
  Mis. 107–19   it cannot keep pace with *e*.
of joy
  Mis. 135–18   is in itself an *e* of joy
plant for
  '01. 33– 4   To plant for *e*,
  My. 154–19   * "Wouldst thou plant for *e*,
rounds of
  '02. 4–17   the measureless rounds of *e*.
seal of
  My. 214–12   set the seal of *e* on time.
shoreless
  Mis. 82– 6   as a river into a shoreless *e*.
shore of
  Mis. 82–11   stand upon the shore of *e*,
spanned
  Mis. 163– 9   He who . . . spanned *e*,
takes hold of
  No. 13–18   It takes hold of *e*,
time and
       (*see* **time**)
time and for
  '02. 5–19   the theme for time and for *e*;

  Mis. 15–19   *e* does this; for progress is the law
      292–10   such as *e* is ever sounding.
  Pul. 3– 2   Can *e* end? Can Life die?
  Pan. 13– 1   in time and in *e* will witness more
  Po. 22– 2   *E* Draws nigh
      30– 8   To glorify all time — *e*
eternity's
  Mis. 121– 3   engraved upon *e* tablets.
  Hea. 2–26   on Truth, *e* foundation stone,
ether
  Mis. 26– 7   worlds, in the most subtle *e*,
      45– 8   and destroy the necessity for *e*
      87– 1   as the bird in the clear *e*
ethereal
  '02. 5– 9   It is this *e* flame,
  Peo. 10– 4   simply because it is more *e*.
etherialized
  My. 345–27   more *e* ways of living.
ethical
  Mis. 295–23   high and pure *e* tones
      297– 8   bases its work on *e* conditions
  My. 178– 1   *e* tenets, do not mislead
ethically
  Mis. 138–13   *e*, physically, and spiritually.
ethics
  Mis. v– 7   AND DEMONSTRATE THE *e* OF C. S.
      64–17   *e* which guide thought spiritually

ethics
Mis. 247–11 from the highest possible *e·*.
264–30 mistake . . . in *e·*, is more fatal than
265–21 explaining spiritual Truth and its *e·*
269–10 who can better define *e·*,
316–21 tired aphorisms and disappointed *e·* ;
340–30 Material philosophy, human *e·*,
344– 3 Pythagorean professor of *e·*,
Ret. 21–26 illustrate the *e·* of Truth.
75– 5 does violence to the *e·* of C. S.
75–11 and one's writings on *e·*,
Un. 13–10 not infringed in *e·* any more than in
No. 44– 8 swerves not from the highest *e·*
'00. 11–29 His symbolic *e·* bravely rebuke
'02. 2–10 religions, *e·*, and learning,
2–16 *e·*, medicine, and religion,
My. 4–32 in *e·*, philosophy, or religion,
114–31 each step . . . in religion and *e·*,
129– 5 humanity, *e·*, and Christianity
179–31 therapeutics, *e·*, and Christianity
260–27 hygiene, medicine, *e·*,
351–12 *morale* of Free Masonry is above *e·*

etiology
Mis. 74–10 systems of *e·* and teleology.

etiquette
Mis. 283–19 I insist on the *e·* of C. S.,
342–30 the *e·* of the exchange,

Eton of America
Pul. 49–25 * "*E·* of *A·*," St. Paul's School.

Etta
Po. page 46 poem

etymology
Ret. 10–15 *E·* was divine history,

Eucharist
Pul. 38–13 "Atonement and *E·*,"
My. 136– 7 chapter Atonement and *E·*,

Euclid
Mis. 78–11 either *E·* or the Science of Mind
Un. 6–21 about the problems of *E·*.

eulogy
Ret. 5–17 *e·* of the Rev. Richard S. Rust,

eunuch
Mis. 77– 1 *Did the salvation of the e·*
77– 8 demand made upon the *e·*
77–21 the *e·* was to *know* in whom

euphonious
Ret. 27–26 manifestation is beautiful and *e·*,

euphony
My. 291–20 renew *e·*, emphasize humane power,

Europe (see also **Europe's**)
Mis. 170–20 history of *E·* and America ;
345– 1 bringing Christianity . . . into *E·*.
Ret. 47– 5 all over our continent, and from *E·*,
Pul. 36– 8 * students, from *E·* as well as this
No. 23–14 eminent divines, in *E·* and America,
My. 72– 9 * From all the centres of *E·*
85– 9 * meet in *E·* and in the antipodes,

Europe's
Pul. 49– 6 * some of *E·* masterpieces,

Eutaw Street
Mis. 243–12 107 *E· S·*, East Boston.

evade
Mis. 226–25 manages to *e·* the law,
227– 8 Thus, to *e·* the penalty of law,
300–16 and thus *e·* the law,
Un. 50–20 *e·* sin, sickness, and death,

evangel
Mis. 251–29 flee before the *e·* of Truth
My. 113– 3 not less the *e·* of C. S.
188–15 your oracle, . . . is Truth's *e·*,

evangelic
Ret. 65–20 C. S. is the pure *e·* truth.

evangelical
Mis. 193– 9 Doctrines that deny . . . cannot be *e·* ;
193– 9 *e·* religion can be established
194–11 and misinterpret *e·* religion.
249–13 devout members of *e·* churches
Man. 17– 5 They were members of *e·* churches,
Ret. 35–15 glow and grandeur of *e·* religion.
64–30 If *e·* churches refuse fellowship
'01. 12–17 and misinterpret *e·* religion.
34–11 Have we misread the *e·* precepts
My. 182– 6 recommendation to *e·* churches
342–27 Its essence is *e·*.

evangelism
Ret. 65–26 constitute the only *e·*,

evangelistic
Ret. 88–20 *e·* duty should not be so warped

evangelists
Ret. 93– 2 *e·* of those days wandered about.
My. 30–25 * record collections secured by *e·*

Eve
Mis. 86–18 more earthly to the eyes of *E·*.
109–18 allegory of Adam and *E·*.
191–25 carried the question with *E·*.
Un. 51–17 not one . . . is an *E·* or an **Adam.**

eve
Pul. 37–17 * Christmas *e·*, as I sat in the
'02. 19– 5 he rebuked them on the *e·* of
Po. 53–11 Till heard at silvery *e·*

eve-bird's
Mis. 390– 7 The *e·* forest flute
Po. 55– 8 The *e·* forest flute

even (see also **e'en**)
Mis. 4–21 with isms, and *e·* infidelity,
6– 2 *e·* though sickness often leaves
10–29 *E·* in belief you have but one
11–19 must *e·* try not to expose their
16–14 *e·* its supremacy over sin,
18–14 *e·* in substance ;
18–20 *e·* the divine "Us"
22– 9 discovery of *e·* a portion of it?
23–16 Matter cannot *e·* talk ;
23–27 *e·* as the human likeness
26–11 *e·* while the Scripture declares
29–10 *e·* before the Christian era ;
30– 6 *e·* though failing at first to
33– 4 crucifixion of *e·* the great Master ;
43– 3 heal cases without *e·* having seen the
45–24 *e·* the belief that God is not
46–26 *e·* as the idea of sound,
46–29 man is perfect *e·* as the Father,
52– 8 *e·* the might of Truth,
58–28 *e·* one human mind governing another,
60–18 *e·* if touching each other
61– 7 *e·* when aping the wisdom
62– 9 *e·* as in mathematics,
63–24 *E·* as the struggling heart,
69–11 His physicians had failed *e·*
70–28 *e·* in the silent tomb,
71–28 *e·* human concepts,
77–11 *e·* the eternal unity of man and God,
79–24 *e·* so in Christ shall — *I Cor.* 15: 22.
84–29 *e·* though it be through the
85–14 *e·* as your Father — *Matt.* 5: 48.
86–22 *E·* the human conception of beauty,
86–30 *e·* this pleasing thraldom,
88– 2 *e·* sometimes feel the need of
90–14 do ye *e·* so to them." — *Matt.* 7: 12.
93–29 to indulge . . . *e·* one moment.
93–31 *e·* if you suffer for it
95–12 *e·* a synopsis of C. S.,
103–32 *E·* while his personality was
107– 1 *e·* the sweetness and beauty in
109–12 *E·* a mild mistake must be seen
109–25 *e·* the power to escape from the
112– 3 *E·* honest thinkers, not knowing
114–29 *e·* its utter nothingness.
115– 6 *e·* the teacher's own deficiency
116–22 *e·* as the fruits of watchfulness,
119–22 *e·* in the least,
119–32 do ye *e·* so to them." — *Matt.* 7: 12.
121– 7 *e·* the cup of martyrdom:
121–14 *e·* a divine decree, a law of Love !
126–23 *e·* gold is less current.
127–19 *e·* that joy which finds one's
127–23 *e·* though your pearls be downtrodden.
132– 5 *e·* wider than before,
132–28 *E·* the desire to be just
137–19 *E·* this : Disorganize the
138–11 *e·* the divine Principle which
139– 5 as you *e·* yet have not received.
140– 7 *e·* after the manner that all
141–14 *e·* the annihilating law of Love.
145–14 *E·* vanity forbids man to be vain ;
145–21 remains, to quicken *e·* dust
146–19 do ye *e·* so to them." — *Matt.* 7: 12.
151–23 God is — what? *E·* All.
154–14 that vine whereof our Father is
155– 6 *e·* as God has blessed you.
155–17 Mother has not the time *e·* to
162– 1 *e·* as, at times of special
166–18 Judæan religion *e·* required the
166–27 *e·* if not acknowledged,
167– 8 *e·* the compound idea of
175–13 *e·* as the leaven expands the loaf.
180–22 *e· to them that believe* — *John* 1: 12.
181– 2 your Father," *e·* God. — *Matt.* 23: 9.
182–18 *e·* the understanding that
182–31 *e·* as they did . . . centuries ago.
184–17 *e·* as when saying,
184–31 *e·* mortal mind purged of the

even

Mis. 186– 9 e· separates its conception of man
186–31 e· the sense of the real man
187– 9 e· as in Science a chord is
191–25 supposed to have out-talked e· Truth,
193– 4 Jesus did mean all, and e· more
193–17 thankful e· for his allusion to truth ;
194– 2 e· the power of a drug to heal
214–22 e· to understand my works,
217– 6 e· the ideal world
222–25 E· the healing Principle,
224–27 when no wrong is meant, nor e· when
226–22 e· of those who have lost their honor
228–11 e· while seeking to raise those
229–17 e· the most High — Psal. 91 : 9.
234–21 e· the entire current of mortality,
235–29 do ye e· so to them,'' — Matt. 7 : 12.
236–20 e· though it be your best friend ;
238– 2 E· the loving children are
239–29 value of saying e· more bravely,
243–25 E· doctors disagree on that
244– 4 e· a ''surgical operation''
247–15 to be taught it, e· gratuitously.
251–13 e·, the liberty of the sons of God,
251–27 e· as dry leaves fall to enrich the
253– 2 e· that Christianity is not merely
254– 7 e· the bread that cometh down
257–29 E· the chamber where the good man
258–24 e· the everlasting Father,
261–29 e· a knowledge of this Science,
262–22 e· through this white-winged messenger,
262–28 Perhaps it is e· selfish in me
275– 3 e· woman's trembling, clinging faith
278–14 e· when he cursed the hour of his birth ;
284– 6 E· the humanitarian at work
286–30 e· as the Father is perfect,
288– 1 E· your sincere . . . convictions
292– 8 a new commandment e· for him.
294–23 desire to help e· such as these.
296–17 by no means identical — nor e· similar.
308–14 e· they know its practicality only
308–25 e· as holding in mind the
309– 7 often fails to express e· mortal man,
310– 4 E· the teachings of Jesus
311–25 I did this e· as a surgeon
312– 5 e· that which lays all upon the
313– 9 e· as the dawn,
319– 3 e· as God is good,
329–11 e· as the heart may be ;
330–24 and e· pride should sanction
333– 4 e· that every ray of Truth,
336–13 e· that you first cast out your
337–22 E· the life of Jesus was belittled
345–15 but e· infidels may disagree.
346– 2 C. S. carries this thought e· higher,
348–19 not e· coffea (coffee), thea (tea),
349– 1 e· the offer of pecuniary assistance
351– 5 blessing e· my enemies,
363–19 E· through the mists of mortality
365–23 E· doctors agree that infidelity,
366–19 e· as Jesus admonished.
368– 3 E· so, Father, let the light
369–19 e· a crumb that falleth from
374– 2 caused e· the publicans to justify
380–13 E· as when an accident,
Man. 16– 7 e· the allness of Soul, Spirit,
19– 3 e· the understanding and
31–13 e· that spiritual animus
42–17 one Christ, e· that Christ whereof
42–24 do ye e· so to them.'' — Matt. 7 : 12.
Ret. 14–18 e· if my creedal doubts
14–29 e· the oldest church-members wept.
15– 9 e· of Thine only. — Psal. 71 : 16.
22– 3 bear brief testimony e· to the
23– 8 not e· fringed with light.
24–17 E· to the homœopathic physician
28– 7 demonstrate, in part,
30–18 E· so was I led into the mazes of
32– 3 e· the possibilities of spiritual
33–21 is found to be e· more active.
37–16 E· the Scriptures gave no direct
41– 6 without e· an acknowledgment of the
45–11 e· as the corporeal organization
50–14 or e· in half as many lessons.
59–11 e· as mortals apply finite terms to
64– 8 e· God's ''image and — see Gen. 1 : 26.
64–10 e· as the opposite claim of evil is one.
68– 7 e· the spiritual idea, or ideal man,
70–24 e· the reflection,
82– 6 e· if they are teachers and
82–25 if e· they compete with
83–16 communicates, e· unintentionally,
84–16 e· the power and glory of the
87–21 do ye e· so to them.'' — Matt. 7 : 12.
89–20 e· according to his promise,
90–13 e· though one of the twelve

even

Un. 6–14 e· the thinkers are not
7–23 dispels e· the sense or
8–20 e· the doctrine of heredity
22–18 Evil. . . .Error, e·, is His offspring.
28–13 are e· more vague than
32–20 responds, e· as did our Master :
38– 6 e· the unreality of mortal mind,
40–21 can never alarm or e· appear
46–20 To them evil was e· more the ego
54–17 e· as a false claimant,
58–12 E· the ice-bound hypocrite
60–13 e· the Father ; — Jas. 3 : 9.
61– 7 e· the eternal idea of God,
61–27 e· as the helpless sick are
64–10 e· if it were (or could be) God,
Pul. 2–14 e· the ''house not — II Cor. 5 : 1.
3– 2 demolished, or e· disturbed?
7–17 e· when mistakenly committed in
8–16 E· the children vied with their
8–26 e· its centre-piece, — Mother's Room
20–15 e· that shadow whose substance
21– 5 e· those that hate them.
41–14 * and e· from the distant States
42– 7 * scarcely e· a minor variation
45– 7 * e· when the feat seems impossible
50–27 * show e· some one side of it
62–12 * e· when rung by hand
67–11 * e· Max O'Rell's famous enumeration
74–15 ''E· the question shocks me.
Rud. 9– 5 E· the truth he speaks is
9–22 or e· a mental argument,
13– 6 e· in the smallest degree.
No. 16– 7 If God knows evil e· as a
19– 5 E· doctors will agree that
24– 1 e· the immeasurable idea of
25–11 e· as the infinite idea of Truth is
29–10 as if it were not e· a material sense.
30–19 of e· a claim to error.
33– 1 e· the wrath of man shall praise Him.
36– 7 e· while mortals believed it was here.
36–28 e· while the divine and ideal Christ
39–26 e· as photography grasps the solar
42–14 e· in the name and for the sake of
Pan. 1–18 e· the day when all people
9–11 e· as your Father — Matt. 5 : 48.
10– 2 what saith the apostle? — e· this :
'00. 1– 1 methinks e· I am touched with the
10–15 assail e· the new-old doctrines
'01. 6–21 its theory e· seldom named.
7–17 e· as the Scriptures declare He will
8–15 e· as your Father — Matt. 5 : 48.
12– 9 e· the word Christian was anciently
14–22 e· as one guards his door
15–21 may e· need to hear the following
17– 6 loves e· the repentant prodigal
19–18 commanded e· the winds and waves,
20–20 E· the agony and death that
22–28 E· the numeration table of C. S.
28–25 well to know that e· Christ Jesus,
29– 3 or e· known of his sore necessities?
29– 9 e· as he has sacrificed for others
30– 1 persecuted e· as all other
30–16 E· religion and therapeutics
'02. 7–15 e· the forever I AM,
11–16 e· the knowledge of salvation
12–18 e· so God and man,
19–10 Brethren, e· as Jesus forgave,
Hea. 4– 9 e· as we ask a person with
10–19 e· the triumph of Soul over sense.
17–15 dream of material life, e· the dream
Peo. 1–16 E· the pangs of death disappear,
3–21 e· the quality or the quantity of
5–10 are nigh, e· at our door.
9–17 e· dare to invoke the divine aid
10– 2 e· as steam is more powerful than
11–10 e· the supremacy of Soul
Po. vii– 2 * yet, e· these are characterized by
My. 5–21 understanding e· in part,
6–24 e· the outcome of their hearts,
13– 7 first that I had e· heard of it.
18–15 e· that joy which finds one's
19–20 but I ask for more, e· this :
29–25 * E· the sun smiled kindly upon the
34–10 e· lift them up, — Psal. 24 : 9.
39–26 * But e· more distinctly may we
40– 9 * It may e· imply that some who
42–25 * comprehend, e· in small degree,
44–12 * e· unto the end — Matt. 28 : 20.
53–29 * e· though the continuity of thought
56– 8 * e· this provision was inadequate
56–27 * there was not e· standing-room.
63–17 * e· the greetings and congratulations
63–26 * e· more impressive than this
65–12 * It was not e· talked over,
73– 2 * e· to return more than

even

My. 74–12 * *e·* to those who are unable to
74–21 * *e·* if those outside are unable
83–25 * *e·* before the building itself has
84–22 * impress *e·* the man who
86–28 * Not *e·* the great size of the
89–15 * *e·* to the flagstones in front
91–25 * but *e·* stranger is its increase
92–10 * worthy of perhaps *e·* more interest
94–28 *e·* the outcome of their hearts,
105– 1 *e·* more than the words of Christ,
110–23 *e·* mortals can mount higher
119–31 *e·* to the true image
122–26 Truth, *e·* as Jesus declared ;
123– 4 prize love *e·* more than the gifts
126– 1 would enter *e·* the church,
127–14 *e·* as Aaron's rod swallowed up the
133–28 *e·* as your heart has discovered it.
139– 6 *e·* the spiritual idea of Life,
145–18 worked *e·* harder than usual,
146–11 be *e·* younger than now.
150–20 *e·* the calm, clear, radiant reflection
152–20 *e·* as the ages have shown.
154– 9 to infringe . . . *e·* in thought.
159– 5 *e·* unto the end." — *Matt.* 28 : 20.
159–25 *E·* Epictetus, a heathen philosopher
160–12 *e·* though it be a sapling
160–25 *e·* the fire of a guilty conscience,
177–12 I shall then be *e·* younger
179–32 make *e·* God demonstrable,
182– 9 *e·* Christ, Truth, as the chief
185–18 *e·* that which "was dead, — *Luke* 15 : 32.
188–11 *e·* the omniscience of
189– 6 affords *e·* me a perquisite of joy.
190–28 would remain, *e·* as it did,
196–25 *e·* the spiritually indispensable,
200–13 *e·* to the glorious beatitudes
201–13 *E·* the crown of thorns,
211– 9 *e·* as in Jesus' time
211–19 their worst enemies, *e·* those who
214–24 *e·* to meet my own current expenses.
216–31 to earn for a purpose *e·* higher,
218–10 *e·* the self-same Lazarus.
220–10 *e·* while you render
222– 2 *e·* the disciples of Jesus
222–15 *E·* in those dark days
226–22 *e·* as you value His all-power,
232– 6 *e·* the way of Truth and Love
233– 1 *e·* the spirit of our Master's
244–17 *e·* the inner sanctuary
249– 9 hating *e·* one's enemies excludes
264– 3 I *e·* hope that those who are
266– 9 do ye *e·* so to them." — *Matt.* 7 : 12.
269–22 rays of reality — *e·* C. S.,
274– 2 *e·* the Life that is Soul
274– 9 *e·* its all-power, all-presence,
281– 2 *e·* to know how to pray
283–16 *e·* though it be betrayed.
293–11 *E·* the physicians may have feared this.
307–12 He *e·* acknowledged this himself,
309– 5 *e·* acting as counsel in a lawsuit
328– 1 * *e·* as God has dignified, blessed,
340–29 *e·* the full beneficence of the laws
344– 1 I have *e·* been spoken of as a
357– 4 *e·* the divine idea of C. S.,

evening (*see also* evening's)

Mis. 148–25 presented at your Friday *e·* meetings.
225–8 In the course of the *e·*,
389– 5 poem
Man. 31–18 and the Wednesday *e·* meetings.
31–21 part of the Wednesday *e·* services,
47–23 at the Wednesday *e·* meeting.
96– 1 No Wednesday *E·* Lectures.
96– 3 not appoint a lecture for Wednesday *e·*.
Un. 61– 9 *e·* and the morning of human thought,
Pul. 31–22 * *e·* on which she would receive me.
36–14 * the *e·* that I first met Mrs. Eddy
Pan. 3–16 * or in thy *e·* shade,
Po. 3– 7 With *e·*, memories reappear
page 4 poem
46–15 Bright as her *e·* star,
My. 29–31 * until the close of the *e·* service,
78– 4 * morning, afternoon, and *e·*.
79–24 * chapter sub-title
87– 1 * from early morning until the *e·*,
134–21 * At the Wednesday *e·* meeting
241–19 * "Last *e·* I was catechized by a
289–25 on Sunday *e·*, February 3,
313–19 when I took an *e·* walk.
322–19 * During the *e·* my friend spoke of
323– 3 * Before we left that *e·*,

Evening Monitor
Pul. 76–21 * [*E· M·*, Concord, N. H.,

Evening Reporter
Pul. 88–29 * *E· R·*, Lebanon, Pa.

evening's

Pan. 3–12 the *e·* closing vespers,

event

Mis. 162– 3 third *e·* of this eventful period,
197–17 belief in any historical *e·*
319–29 between the promise and *e·* ;
Ret. 7–21 * This sad *e·* will not be soon forgotten.
13– 4 In connection with this *e·*,
24– 4 in no wise connected with this *e·*,
Un. 3–28 and guides every *e·* of our
Pul. 79– 7 * The dedication, . . . is a notable *e·*.
No. 37–13 full-orbed glory of that *e·* ;
My. 21– 2 * expended in such an *e·*.
30–19 * gratitude for the epoch-making *e·*.
60–25 * the great *e·*, the dedication
90–25 * is an *e·* of impressiveness
100– 2 * in connection with the *e·*
284–16 * first time . . . that such an *e·*

eventful

Mis. 162– 3 third event of this *e·* period,
Ret. 23– 1 too *e·* to leave me undisturbed
Pul. 44–11 * auspicious hour in your *e·* career.
55– 7 * not the least *e·* circumstance

eventide (*see also* eventide's)

Po. 66– 6 Sweet spirit of love, at soft *e·*

eventide's

Mis. 394– 2 borne on the zephyr at *e·* hour ;
Po. 45– 1 borne on the zephyr at *e·* hour ;

events

Mis. 12–11 the future, big with *e·*.
48–21 hidden nature of some tragic *e·*
148–15 the logic of *e·*,
209–29 scientific logic and the logic of *e·*,
253–14 This period is big with *e·*.
269–13 in relation to human *e·*?
304–24 * days on which great *e·* have
306– 7 * welcome suggestions of *e·* to be
339–26 mayest have sent along the ocean of *e·*
Man. 3–12 the logic of *e·*,
Ret. 8– 1 *e·* connected with my childhood
21–25 personal *e·* are frivolous
70–13 recurrence of such *e·*.
Un. 19– 5 *e·* which are contrary to His
Pul. 32–15 * so far as outward *e·* may
'02. 20– 1 on the ocean of *e·*,
My. 31–22 * one of the *e·* of their lives.
45– 7 * associated with this,
142–13 most important *e·* are criticized
224– 4 should wait on the logic of *e·*
272– 4 logic of *e·* pushes onward the
281– 7 faith in God's disposal of *e·*.

eventually

Mis. 292–14 Divine Love *e·* causes mortals to
323–16 Stranger *e·* stands in the valley
Ret. 32– 6 corporeal personality, is *e·* lost.
Un. 18–20 *e·* destroy, every supposition of
Pul. 13–19 must *e·* expiate their sin
66–26 * *e·* to supplant those in
My. 160–23 will *e·* consume this planet.

ever (*see also* e'er)

Mis. ix–21 a Psyche who is *e·* a girl.
24–13 *e·* after was in better health than
27–13 no species *e·* produces its opposite.
27–22 though God is *e·* present ;
46–18 be *e·* found in the scale *with*
48–23 *Was e· a person made insane by*
49–11 *e·* having occurred in a class
56–14 or *e·* has constituted laws to that
85– 4 *Is a Christian Scientist e· sick,*
103–16 must be *e·* in bondage,
105–18 I must *e·* follow this line of light
116–11 question, *e·* nearest to my heart,
147–22 we find him *e·* the same,
149–18 Lips nor pen can *e·* express
157–29 *E·* with love,
172– 7 a higher sense than *e·* before,
173– 7 Who has *e·* learned of the schools that
173– 8 Who has *e·* learned from the schools,
182–20 since he is and *e·* was the image and
185–24 how much of a man he *e·* has been :
238–10 All that *e·* was accomplished,
245– 1 no record showing that our Master *e·*
276–32 stand firmer than *e·* in their
277– 5 more imperatively than *e·*.
292–10 such as eternity is *e·* sounding.
303–16 If *e·* I wear out from serving students,
327–21 more than *e·* determined
345–16 * "*E·* since the reign of Christianity
370–14 more intelligently than *e·* before,
386– 6 Thine, *e·* thine.
386–17 a hope that *e·* upward yearns,
Ret. 5–29 * She *e·* entertained a lively sense
6– 7 The needy were *e·* welcome,

ever

Ret.	6–17	e· connected with that institution.
	22–18	nor is he e· created through the
	44– 4	first such church e· organized.
	49–20	only one e· granted to a *legal college*
	62– 7	than *a belief in their reality has* e· *done.*
	83–27	That these essential points are e·
	90– 7	to show that Jesus e· entered
	91– 6	e· fell upon human ears
Un.	18–24	to be e· conscious of Life
	23– 5	Edgar, was to his father e· loyal.
	26–13	* Chance and change are busy e·,
	28–11	not a spectre had e· been seen
	37–11	Because God is e· present,
	60–21	God is e· present,
	64–12	e· eluding their dread presence
Pul.	12–19	than has e· before reached high heaven,
	20–18	greatest . . . religious reform e· known
	72–30	* e· hear of Jesus' taking medicine
	77– 4	* elegant memorials e· prepared,
	78– 3	* of the goldsmith's art e· wrought in
Rud.	5–11	who has e· found Soul in the body
	5–12	who has e· seen spiritual substance
No.	20–18	Ever-present Love must seem e· absent to
	20–23	Satan's reasoning, e· since the
	30–12	this perfect law is e· present to
Pan.	8–22	must e· rest on the basis of the
	12– 5	* Spirit, is e· in universal nature.''
'01.	1– 8	better appreciated, than e· before,
	2–19	e· storming sin in its citadels,
	23–22	as no other person has e· demonstrated
	27– 9	the first e· published on C. S.,
	30– 2	since e· the primitive Christians,
'02.	12–10	that God is come, and is e· present.
	14–12	the only success I have e· achieved
	17–17	Who of the world's lovers e· found
Hea.	4–21	e· arrive at a proper conception of
	6–10	abused me for it then, and have e· since;
	13–15	highest attenuation we e· attained
	14–18	most arduous task I e· performed.
Peo.	13–25	* ''Since e· the history of Christianity
Po.	23– 6	Come e· o'er thy heart?
	23–11	So may their gaze be e· fraught
	31–18	The e· Christ, and glorified
	32– 6	fragrance and charms e· new
	43–11	*E·* thus as Thine !
	47– 1	Are the dear days of e· coming again,
	47– 5	Oh, e· and nevermore?
	47– 6	*E·* to gladness and never to tears,
	47– 7	*E·* the gross world above ;
	47– 9	*E·* to Truth and to Love?
	47–11	Outside this e· of pain?
	49–10	Thine, e· thine.
	50– 1	hope that e· upward yearns,
My.	vii– 3	* Strive it e· so hard,
	10–15	* No appeal has e· been made in this
	10–17	* none will be made or e· be needed.
	15–13	goes out to you as e·
	26–13	that I have e· received
	29–12	* will e· be able to forget.
	37–13	* which has e· healed the sick.
	38–25	* they would e· carry with them
	44– 9	* of our e· faithful Leader.
	56–19	* increased faster than e·.
	59–28	* before it was e· written.
	59–28	* before it was e· printed.''
	62– 9	* How can we e· thank God enough
	62–10	* thank you enough for your
	62–28	* who were e· ready to assist us
	65– 3	* e· held in Boston
	65– 4	* e· held in the United States
	75–27	* e· yet been dedicated by
	79–22	* than it e· occupied before.
	81–17	* No more cosmopolitan audience e·
	86– 4	* As Boston has e· loved its
	87–20	* I do not think I have e· seen
	91–11	* spiritual aspirations were e·
	91–19	* country has e· known.
	110– 2	e· present, casting out evils,
	136–17	highest fee e· received by
	144– 8	With love, e· yours,
	145–16	* ''I am as well as I e· was.''
	148– 2	and more than e· persistently,
	149–32	no condition, be it e· so severe,
	159– 6	Thus may it e· be that Christ
	213–19	Be e· on guard against this enemy.
	239–29	going on since e· time was.
	249– 3	condemn persons seldom, if e·.
	257–14	Christ is, more than e· before,
	265– 4	knocks more loudly than e· **before**
	272–11	e· shall be the divine ideal,
	282–26	prosper e· this good endeavor.
	292– 3	All good that e· was written,
	310–28	* ''When do you e· see Mary angry?''
	318–25	* ''How do you know that there e·
	321–13	* cannot believe that he has e· said
	325–16	* e· faithfully your student,

ever

My.	347–13	* nor e· bid the Spring adieu !
	360– 3	As e·, lovingly your teacher,

ever-conscious

Un.	18–23	God saith, I am e· Life,

ever-flowing

Mis.	360–23	e· tides of spiritual sensation
My.	149–10	its might is the e· tides of truth

evergreen

Mis.	ix–22	is not the e· of Soul ;
Peo.	14– 4	amaranth blossoms, e· leaves,
Po.	16– 1	gentle cypress, in e· tears,
	67–17	cypress may mourn with her e· tears,
My.	139– 9	verdure and e· that flourish when

everlasting

Mis.	vii–18	sprung from Spirit, In e· day ;
	74–26	was an e· victory for Life ;
	105–17	C. S. is an e· victor,
	118–28	persistent effort with e· victory.
	161– 7	*The* e· *Father,* — *Isa.* 9 : 6.
	163– 7	a sublime and e· victory !
	164–18	The e· Father, — *Isa.* 9 : 6.
	258–24	even the e· Father,
	261–26	already saved with an e· salvation.
	277–11	right wins the e· victory.
	321– 6	The e· Father, — *Isa.* 9 : 6.
	328–31	up to the throne of e· glory.
	336–29	That it rests on e· foundations,
Ret.	14–28	lead me in the way e·.''–*Psal.* 139 : 24.
	49–22	And e· gratitude is due to the
Un.	6– 9	established on e· foundations.
	14–20	firmer than e· hills.
	14–25	a knowledge which is e·
	40–13	can no more receive e· life by
	51– 1	and the e· facts of being appear,
Pul.	12–21	her primal and e· strain.
No.	25–20	but what this e· individuality is,
	34–26	Nameless woe. e· victories,
'00.	7–18, 19	from e· to e· this Christ is never
'01.	15–24	* swallowed up in e· destruction.
'02.	20– 6	tipping the dawn of e· day,
My.	33–12	lead me in the way e·.'' — *Psal.* 139 : 24.
	34–11	ye e· doors : — *Psal.* 24 : 9.
	37–10	* e· advantage of this race.
	129–23	gives to man health and life e·
	131–13	seals the covenant of e· love.
	171– 5	songs and e· joy — *Isa.* 35 : 10.
	177–24	e· covenant with them.'' — *Isa.* 61 : 8.
	193– 3	whom to know aright is life e·.
	206–19	unto thee an e· light, — *Isa.* 60 : 19.
	253– 3	higher and e· harmony,
		(*see also* **Life**)

ever-living

Mis.	124–14	the ever-loving, e· Life,

ever-loving

Mis.	124–14	the e·, ever-living Life,

evermore

Mis.	100–20	the e· of Truth is triumphant.
	384–13	And Love, the e·.
Pul.	53–30	* Is e· the same.
'00.	15–30	And love, the e·.
Po.	36–12	And Love, the e·.
	47–19	*E·* gathering in woe

ever-operative

My.	109–13	the e· divine Principle

ever-presence

Mis.	14– 3	the e· and all-power of good;
	196–19	e· and power of God,
	258–25	as infinite consciousness, e·,
Un.	62– 4	e· that neither comes nor goes,
	62–27	to discern faintly God's e·,
	63– 8	so-called . . . reappearing of e·,
Rud.	11–23	all-power and e· of good,
Peo.	13–10	His all-power and e·,
My.	192–28	whisper to you of the divine e·.

ever-present

Mis.	174–19	No : it is e· here.
	183– 2	e· good, omnipotent Love,
	238–19	and are an e· reward.
	268–18	the omnipotent and e· good.
	307– 3	divine Love is an e· help ;
	328– 8	the Stranger the e· Christ,
Ret.	31–13	e· relief from human woe.
	60–13	good is God e·,
	65–30	reveals God as e· Truth and **Love**,
Un.	43–26	e· Life which knows no death,
	52– 7	the e· reign of harmony,
	60– 2	through e· and eternal good.
	62–13	omnipotent and e· good
Pul.	11– 5	dedicated to the e· God
Rud.	3–27	e· I AM, filling all space,
No.	17– 6	God is good, e· and All.

ever-present

No.	17–14	God is not without an *e·* witness,
	20–18	*E·* Love must seem
	20–18	ever absent to *e·* selfishness
'00.	1– 5	*e·* Love filling all space, time,
'02.	16–19	spiritual idea of the *e·* God
My.	219–15	Truth, the *e·* spiritual idea,
	254–13	will find the *e·* God
	273–23	*e·* good, and therefore life eternal.
	288– 6	good done and . . . are his *e·* reward.
	294–14	*e·* power of divine Spirit
		(*see also* **help**)

ever-recurring

'02.	5–14	*e·* human question and wonder,

ever-self

Mis	385–19	Now see thy *e·* ; Life never fled ;
Po.	48–13	Now see thy *e·* ; Life never fled ;

every

Mis	v– 3	SCIENTISTS IN THIS AND *e·* LAND
	13– 2	mercy and charity toward *e·* one,
	18– 4	scourgeth *e·* son whom — *Heb.* 12 : 6.
	18–13	its opposite, in *e·* God-quality,
	26–11	"*e·* plant of the field — *Gen.* 2 : 5.
	37–21	sin of *e·* sort, is destroyed by
	38– 4	elevate man in *e·* line of life,
	39–14	God giveth to *e·* one this *puissance;*
	46–20	comprehending at *e·* point,
	48– 9	opposed to it, as to *e·* form of error,
	56–11	*E·* indication of matter's constituting
	60–27	*e·* creation or idea of Spirit
	60–28	*E·* material belief hints the existence of
	64–18	must benefit *e·* one ;
	65–10	*E·* question between Truth and error,
	67–19	Justice uncovers sin of *e·* sort ;
	81–22	*E·* individual character, like the
	83– 6	"*E· sin is the author of itself,*
	83– 6	*and e· invalid the cause of his own*
	85– 9	*e·* thought and act leading to good.
	86– 8	manifest growth at *e·* experience.
	89– 2	"*E·* kingdom divided — *Matt.* 12 : 25.
	90–17	Break the yoke of bondage in *e·* wise
	91–13	and under *e·* circumstance,
	115–18	delivered from *e·* claim of evil,
	115–25	*e·* effort to hurt one will only help
	117–32	follow under *e·* circumstance.
	118– 6	Honesty in *e·* condition,
	118– 7	under *e·* circumstance,
	118–28	*E·* attempt of evil to harm good
	120– 5	obey implicitly each and *e·* injunction
	120–29	puts to flight *e·* doubt
	139–12	*e· high thing that* — *II Cor.* 10 : 5.
	139–13	*into captivity e· thought* — *II Cor.* 10 : 5.
	141–27	or else return *e·* dollar that you
	146–21	*e·* reformed mortal that desired to come,
	148–29	"Ho, *e·* one that thirsteth, — *Isa.* 55 : 1.
	152–13	pulsates with *e·* throb of theirs
	157–12	*E·* true Christian Scientist will feel
	160–13	*e·* trial of our faith in God
	169–18	dual meaning to *e·* Biblical passage,
	175–12	increase by *e·* spiritual touch,
	179–25	and He made *e·* flower
	183–16	can fulfil the Scriptures in *e·* instance ;
	185–12	flows into *e·* avenue of being,
	187– 5	over and above *e·* sense of matter,
	192–23	belongs to *e·* period ;
	195–10	*e·* one can prove, in some degree,
	197– 3	the motive-power of *e·* act.
	200–13	applicable to *e·* stage and state
	200–19	*e·* supposed material law.
	220– 1	in *e·* line of mental healing,
	232–22	*e·* woman would desire and demand it,
	241– 6	as well as sin of *e·* sort.
	243–13	*e·* system of medicine claims
	247–31	must be met, in *e·* instance,
	256–23	while *e·* quality of matter
	257– 2	in *e·* mode and form of evil.
	264– 1	*e·* random thought in line with mine.
	288–22	in *e·* state and stage of being.
	291–14	each and *e·* one has equal opportunity
	303–15	*e·* one the same rights and
	305–31	* *e·* one receiving this circular
	307– 5	will have all you need *e·* moment.
	307– 9	to suffering of *e·* sort.
	307–30	*E·* human thought must turn
	310–14	plead for all and *e·* one,
	317–18	progress of *e·* Christian Scientist.
	326–16	under *e·* hue of circumstances,
	333– 4	even that *e·* ray of Truth,
	339–16	it points to *e·* mortal mistake ;
	340–27	*E·* luminary in the constellation
	353–16	*e·* ten minutes on the regulator.
	360–19	lift *e·* thought-leaflet
	361– 9	*e·* form and mode of evil
	361–18	lay aside *e·* weight, — *Heb.* 12 : 1.
	363–30	*e·* advancing epoch of Truth

every

Mis.	375–15	* *e·* moment to the study of music
	383–14	and on *e·* battle-field rise higher
	389–14	glad for *e·* scalding tear,
	389–16	Wait, and love more for *e·* hate,
	391–15	That *e·* ragged urchin,
	295–21	Is *e·* earthly love ;
Man.	18– 9	and at *e·* epoch saying,
	26–12	*E·* third year Readers shall be
	88–13	shall be elected *e·* third year
Ret.	7–12	* explored their *e·* nook and corner,
	10– 7	the latter I had to repeat *e·* Sunday.
	21– 4	*E·* means within my power was
	28– 5	guiding our *e·* thought and action ;
	35–16	true followers in *e·* period,
	44–10	and in the pulpit *e·* Sunday,
	48– 8	*e·* one should build on his own
	52– 8	*e·* true seeker and honest worker
	59–13	*e·* other name for the Supreme
	61–24	If you rule out *e·* sense of
	76–25	thinks of *e·* one in his real quality,
	80– 6	scourgeth *e·* son whom — *Heb.* 12 : 6.
	81–30	at *e·* stage of advancement.
	86–11	Cleanse *e·* stain from this wanderer's
	94–14	*e·* spot and blemish on the disk of
Un.	3–23	*e·* embodiment of Life and Mind.
	3–28	guides *e·* event of our careers.
	4– 7	Truth destroys *e·* phase of error.
	5– 9	*E·* one should be encouraged
	5–13	*e·* Life-problem in a day.
	8–20	nothingness of *e·* claim of error,
	18–20	*e·* supposition of discord.
	21–10	*e·* tree of the garden." — *Gen.* 3 : 1.
	29– 1	in this relation to *e·* hypothesis
	33–25	*e·* word may be — *Matt.* 18 : 16.
	35– 3	If *e·* mortal mind believed
	47– 4	with *e·* passing hour it is
	48– 1	fair to ask of *e·* one a reason for
	54–10	insensible to *e·* claim of error.
	56–13	*e·* follower of Christ shares his cup
Pul.	2–20	by *e·* means in your power,
	7–17	power to wash away, . . . *e·* crime,
	13– 3	*E·* mortal at some period,
	22– 6	*e·* praying assembly on earth,
	22–10	*e·* Christian church in our land,
	23–19	* the closing years of *e·* century
	27– 2	* French mirrors and *e·* convenience.
	29–12	* *e·* seat in the hall was filled
	37–12	* In *e·* sense she is the recognized
	41– 2	* with *e·* stone paid for
	41– 5	* From *e·* State in the Union,
	45–12	* *e·* evidence of material sense
	51–11	* *E·* truth is more or less in a
	53–21	* *e·* field of human endeavor.
	56– 4	* nearly *e·* other centre of population,
	57– 4	* from *e·* State in the Union,
	58–11	* *e·* bill being paid.
	74– 7	* meets *e·* Sunday in Hodgson Hall,
	80–10	* socially, indeed *e·* way.
Rud.	10–23	removes *e·* erroneous physical and
	11–21	takes away *e·* human belief,
	13–18	to treat *e·* organ in the body.
No.	3–16	*E·* teacher must pore over it in secret,
	7–11	to see *e·* error they possess,
	7–13	stubborn will, and *e·* imperfection
	7–16	*E·* loving sacrifice for the good of
	8–15	*e·* germ of goodness will at last
	8–16	*e·* sin will so punish itself
	20–24	specimens of *e·* kind emerged
	22– 1	*e·* wind of doctrine." — *Eph.* 4 : 14.
	44–20	pours the healing . . . into *e·* wound.
'00.	5–19	escape from idolatry of *e·* kind,
	5–30	attend *e·* footstep of C. S.
'01.	15– 5	the claim of error in *e·* phase
	20–11	he has *e·* opportunity to
	27–27	* "*E·* great scientific truth
	28–12	into almost *e·* Christian tongue,
	29–28	*e·* book of mine that they sold.
	31– 7	*E·* true Christian in the
	32–30	governing impulse of *e·* action ;
'02.	9–14	*E·* condition implied by the
	9–15	*e·* promise fulfilled, was loving and
	14– 6	motto for *e·* Christian Scientist,
	14–18	*e·* forward step has been met
Hea.	2– 7	condemned at *e·* advancing footstep,
	5– 4	limiting His power at *e·* point,
	13– 6	thirty times at *e·* attenuation.
	19– 4	*e·* organ of the system, *e·* function of
	19–14	"*e·* plant of the field — *Gen.* 2 : 5.
Peo.	8–18	governs *e·* action of the body
Po.	4–13	glad for *e·* scalding tear,
	4–15	Wait, and love more for *e·* hate,
	28– 2	Of *e·* rolling sphere,
	38–14	That *e·* ragged urchin,
	43–18	Temper *e·* trembling footfall,
	58– 6	Is *e·* earthly love ;
	71–14	Joy is in *e·* belfry bell

every

My.	9– 9	* glory in *e·* good deed
	21–15	* compensates for *e·* seeming trial
	22–18	* *e·* purpose she has set in motion,
	28– 5	will meet *e·* human need,"
	30– 3	* precisely the same in *e·* respect,
	31–16	* were heard on *e·* hand
	38– 2	* *e·* perfect gift cometh from above,
	38–21	* In *e·* respect their service was
	41–29	* has obeyed its *e·* demand,
	47–28	* to *e·* creature. — *Mark* 16 : 15.
	53– 1	* from *e·* quarter came important
	56– 3	* until *e·* seat was filled
	59–11	* *e·* religious and scientific body
	61– 2	* in the building part of *e·* night
	62–28	* to assist us in *e·* way possible ;
	63–17	* as friend met friend at *e·* turn
	70–16	* living reproductions on *e·* corner
	71–24	* *e·* person seated in the auditorium,
	72–25	* *e·* cent of it was paid
	73–10	will meet *e·* human need."
	75– 9	* poured into the city from *e·*
	77–12	* practically *e·* civilized country,
	77–28	* *e·* penny of the two million
	78– 7	* from *e·* quarter of the city.
	78–15	* *e·* basket piled high with
	78–30	* *e·* word of the exercises
	83– 4	* patent to *e·* one residing in
	85–29	* Aside from *e·* other consideration,
	86–13	* *e·* cent of the estimated cost
	90– 2	* should be filled at *e·* meeting
	91–31	* in *e·* important town and city
	92–17	* *e·* other sect in the country
	94– 2	* *e·* other sect will be left behind
	94–10	* in *e·* community in which
	94–22	* from *e·* State in the Union
	97– 1	* almost *e·* one is inclined to
	103–11	and at its *e·* appearing,
	106– 7	diseases of almost *e·* kind.
	106–10	matter in *e·* mode and form,
	112–14	ninety-nine out of *e·* hundred
	116–22	*E·* loss in grace and growth
	124– 3	to *e·* man's conscience." — *II Cor.* 4 : 2.
	126–26	*e·* foul spirit, — *Rev.* 18 : 2.
	126–27	a cage of *e·* unclean — *Rev.* 18 : 2.
	149–30	solicit *e·* root and *e·* leaf
	156– 8	to *e·* good work," — *II Cor.* 9 : 8.
	159– 8	the throbbing of *e·* pulse
	187– 7	lighteth *e·* enlightened thought
	210– 9	attacks of error of *e·* sort.
	212–27	hindering in *e·* way conceivable
	213–23	through *e·* attack of your foe,
	214– 5	will meet *e·* human need.
	238–22	applicable to *e·* human need.
	249– 3	Improve *e·* opportunity
	255– 8	removed *e·* three years,
	260–26	supplies *e·* need of man.
	277–22	*e·* citizen would be a soldier
	282–24	to *e·* son and daughter
	292–13	"Why did Christians of *e·* sect
	300–25	to *e·* creature," — *Mark* 16 : 15.
	304–22	* from *e·* point of view a woman of
	304–25	* "*E·* great scientific truth
	321–12	* told the same story to *e·* one
	321–25	* is conclusive to me in *e·* detail,
	327–29	* when the laws of *e·* State will
	334– 9	* advertised in *e·* weekly issue of
	339– 3	whose *e·* link leads upward
	340–32	light their fires in *e·* home.
	341– 9	all over our land and in *e·* land,
	345– 5	But *e·* thought tells,
	352–29	My desire is that *e·* . . . Scientist,
	357–30	I know that *e·* true follower

(*see also* **age, case, day, effect, heart, hour, man, member, part, step**)

everybody

Mis.	80–10	Anybody and *e·*, who will
	238–16	Who should care for *e·* ?
	313– 7	pinnacle, that *e·* needs.
My.	78–15	* *e·* contributing,

every-day

'02.	17–25	Consult thy *e·* life ;

everything

Mis.	113–26	*e·* to enjoy on earth and in heaven.
	217–31	To the material sense, *e·* is matter ;
	224–19	appreciation of *e·* beautiful,
	247–30	*E·* that God created,
	364–10	C. S. refutes *e·* that is not
Un.	8– 5	*E·* is as real as you make it,
	18– 8	*e·* that is unlike Myself.
	27–10	uncertain of *e·* except his own
	44–17	into *e·* that exists,
No.	35– 1	is *e·* to human hope and faith.
Hea.	15–19	trying *e·* else besides God,
My.	61–23	* *e·* seemed to move as by magic ;

everything

My.	89–15	* *E·*, even to the flagstones
	96–10	* where fanaticism dominates *e·*
	203–11	best of *e·* is not too good,
	313–14	did *e·* they could think of
	324–24	* *E·* he said conveyed this impression

everywhere

Mis.	173–20	If God . . . is *e·*, matter is nowhere
	385– 8	Thou, here and *e·*.
Ret.	61–18	God is *e·*.
Un.	42– 1	Life, God, being *e·*, it must follow
Pul.	51–24	* Pilgrims from *e·* will go
	76–17	* Pictures and bric-a-brac *e·*
No.	35–27	God's kingdom is *e·* and supreme,
'02.	1–10	branch churches are multiplying *e·*
	12– 7	*now* and *forever*, here and *e·*.
Po.	37– 8	Thou, here and *e·*.
My.	40– 7	* seekers may be satisfied.
	69–12	* *E·* within the building
	122–13	such as to command respect *e·*.
	128–12	God is *e·*.
	173–14	from Christian Scientists *e·*
	329–24	* fair attitude of the press *e·*,

everywhere-present

No.	20–15	notion of an *e·* body

Eves

Chr.	53–21	For heaven's *Christus*, earthly *E·*,

eves

Chr.	53–23	Make merriment on Christmas *e·*,

evidence

accept the

Mis.	218–11	It is erroneous to accept the *e·* of

according to the

Rud.	7–12	According to the *e·* of the so-called

all

Peo.	9–24	remove all *e·* of any other power

another

Mis.	238–27	another *e·* of the falsehoods

appears

My.	94– 5	* *e·* appears in the concrete

built on the

Un.	28–15	built on the *e·* of the material

consciousness and

Un.	11–11	change of consciousness and *e·*

contradicts this

Mis.	96–31	Science contradicts this *e·* ;

delusive

Mis.	65– 1	delusive *e·*, Science has dethroned

deny the

Un.	39–21	deny the *e·* of the material senses,

destruction of the

Rud.	6–18	*destruction of the e· of the material*

discharged

My.	119–21	discharged *e·* of material sense

divided in

Un.	33–23	find them divided in *e·*,

due

Man.	39–11	due *e·* of having genuinely repented

false

Mis.	99– 3	It annuls false *e·*,
No.	6–10	destruction of false *e·*,

falsity of the

No.	38– 3	falsity of the *e·* of the . . . senses

for disease

No.	6–19	as the *e·* for disease ;

furnish

Man.	89–22	furnish *e·* of their eligibility

in both cases

No.	6–19	*e·* in both cases to be unreal.

its

Un.	25–15	by removing its *e·*

material

Mis.	380–21	material *e·* wherewith to
Un.	11–19	taking away the material *e·*.
Rud.	7–16	material *e·* being wholly false.
My.	93– 6	* material *e·* of their prosperity ;

mistaken

Mis.	66– 3	false testimony or mistaken *e·*

mortal

Mis.	13–19	basis of material and mortal *e·*

my

Un.	7–16	Herein is my *e·*,

no

Mis.	72–31	passage quoted affords no *e·* of
	277–23	No *e·* before the material senses
	381–15	"There is no *e·* to present."
Ret.	90– 6	There is no *e·* to show
	90– 8	no *e·* that he there taught
'02.	8–17	We have no *e·* . . . except
Hea.	5–16	we have no *e·* of the fact
	16–20	the senses afford no *e·* of

no such

Rud.	5– 1	spiritual senses afford no such *e·*

evidence

of consciousness
    Un. 36– 1 additional *e·* of consciousness
of disease
    No. 6–13 If, . . . *e·* of disease is not false,
of his compliance
    Man. 52–14 *e·* of his compliance with
of His presence
    '01. 7–26 gain any *e·* of His presence
of Life
    Un. 61– 1 to the true *e·* of Life,
of material sense
    Mis. 47–19 reverses the *e·* of material sense
           183–29 refute the *e·* of material sense
    Pul. 45–12 * every *e·* of material sense
    My. 119–21 *e·* of material sense gave the
of mortal sense
    My. 61–12 * with the *e·* of mortal sense
of Soul
    My. 119–24 *e·* of Soul, immortality,
of spiritual verity
    Pul. 3–26 *e·* of spiritual verity in me
of that beauty
    My. 88–20 * *e·* of that beauty and serenity
of the loyalty
    Man. 35–15 *e·* of the loyalty of the applicants.
of the senses
    Mis. 65– 7 *e·* of the senses is false.
          97– 2 rise above the *e·* of the senses,
        101–29 disprove the *e·* of the senses.
    Un. 8– 9 to rest upon the *e·* of the senses,
        11–15 nor to the *e·* of the senses.
        13– 1 Science reverses the *e·* of the senses
        23–15 spurious *e·* of the senses
only
    Mis. 64–29 only *e·* of the existence of a
    Hea. 16–17 only *e·* we have of sin,
overcomes the
    My. 106–18 overcomes the *e·* of diseased
post mortem
    Rud. 16–27 or else *post mortem e·.*
present
    Mis. 381–11 why he did not present *e·* to
rebuke the
    Ret. 26–22 in order to rebuke the *e·.*
reliable
    Hea. 16–22 shall we call that reliable *e·*
renewed
    My. 157–13 * renewed *e·* of your unselfish love.''
Science affords the
    Mis. 164–31 Science affords the *e·* that God is
slightest
    My. 75–20 * not the slightest *e·* of temper,
stand in
    My. 305–11 and the manuscripts . . . stand in *e·.*
sufficient
    Man. 53–22 considered a sufficient *e·* thereof.
their
    No. 38– 5 God substantiates their *e·*
their own
    Un. 33– 6 can only testify from their own *e·,*
this
    Un. 8–10 this *e·* is not absolute,
transcending the
    Un. 29– 9 Transcending the *e·* of the
transcends the
    '01. 18–14 transcends the *e·* of the
true
    Un. 61– 1 the true *e·* of Life,
    Rud. 6–20 true *e·* of spiritual sense
        7–15 afford the only true *e·* of
unseen
    My. 260–16 things hoped for and the *e·* unseen.
what
    Un. 34–18 What *e·* does mortal mind afford

    Mis. 57– 3 what *e·* have you — apart from the *e·* of
        96–30 the *e·* before the personal senses,
       101–19 He who turns to the body for *e·,*
       131–11 *e·* of its being built upon the rock
    Man. 15–14 *e·* of divine, efficacious Love,
    Un. 10–22 *e·* before the material senses,
        21–12 *e·* of your personal senses
    Pul. 45–21 * *e·* of the mortal senses is
        52–16 * *e·* of the rapid growth of the new
    No. 6–17 The *e·* that the earth is
    My. 40– 2 * *e·* to us of her hospitable love.
        134– 3 *e·* a heart wholly in protest
       226–19 *e·* of the immortality of man
       314–18 After the *e·* had been submitted

evidenced
    My. 12–13 * *e·* by the liberality

evidences
based on the
    Peo. 2–15 based on the *e·* gained from the

evidences
in Christian Science
    Peo. 9–28 more potent *e·* in C. S. of
of Life
    Hea. 16–26 gain our *e·* of Life from
of sin
    Hea. 17–10 with all their *e·* of sin,
of Spirit
    Ret. 56–12 waged between the *e·* of Spirit and
of the senses
    Mis. 58–11 *deny the e· of the senses?*
    Hea. 15– 1 repudiates the *e·* of the senses
other
    My. 83–27 * other *e·* of the strength and
trial, and
    My. 270–17 proven under trial, and *e·*

    Mis. 14–15 from *e·* before him he is
        172–18 *e·* whereof are taken in by
    Ret. 56–13 *e·* of the five physical senses ;
        56– 3 *e·* of the physical senses,
    My. 20–17 *e·* of glorious growth in C. S.
        58– 7 * *e·* of the magnificent growth of

evidencing
    My. 6–21 *e·* the praise of babes

evident
    Man. 50–18 from Christian motives make this *e·,*
    Ret. 28– 1 It became *e·* that the divine Mind
    My. 56– 8 * It was soon *e·* that even this
        74–19 * not only *e·* from their addresses
        76– 6 * *e·* to the Board of Directors
        96–26 * *e·* that the cult will soon be
       215–31 That he preferred the latter is *e·,*

evidently
    Mis. 75–25 It was *e·* an illuminated sense
       216–11 Phare Pleigh *e·* means more than
    Pul. 72–10 * *e·* very much absorbed in the work
    My. 97–18 * *e·* wealthy congregation
       251–16 *e·* some misapprehension
       363–22 *e·* misunderstood by some students.

evil (see also evil's)
absolute
    Mis. 299–17 is the only absolute *e·.*
abuses from
    Mis. 338–16 uses of good, to abuses from *e·* ;
accompanying
    Un. 37–18 *e·* accompanying physical personality
acquaintance with
    Un. 4–21 man's acquaintance with *e·.*
activity of
    Mis. 339–11 the supposed activity of *e·.*
Adam-dream of
    My. 296–19 waking out of his Adam-dream of *e·*
admitting
    Mis. 18–25 Only by admitting *e·* as a reality,
against
    Mis. 367–22 It was not against *e·,* but against
alias
    Ret. 67–24 the "devil" (*alias e·*), — *John 8 : 44.*
all
    Mis. 36–21 Mortal mind includes all *e·,*
        37–19 whence cometh all *e·.*
        97– 7 that holds within itself all *e·.*
       125– 8 the world, the flesh, and all *e·,*
       337–19 disaffection for all *e·,*
    Man. 40–13 to be delivered from all *e·,*
    My. 37– 2 * salvation of all men from all *e·.*
       268–25 axe at the root of all *e·,*
       357– 9 magnetism, — the name of all *e·,*
       364–24 defend themselves from all *e·,*
all manner of
    Mis. 8–24 all manner of *e·* — *Matt. 5 : 11.*
    '01. 3– 5 all manner of *e·* — *Matt. 5 : 11.*
    '02. 11–23 all manner of *e·* — *Matt. 5 : 11.*
    My. 104–31 all manner of *e·* — *Matt. 5 : 11.*
       316– 8 all manner of *e·* — *Matt. 5 : 11.*
and disease
    Mis. 221–25 against both *e·* and disease,
    Un. 37–16 *E·* and disease do not testify of
    Pan. 5–28 His treatment of *e·* and disease,
       6– 3 because *e·* and disease will never
and error
    Mis. 36– 3 we shall classify *e·* and error
and God
    Un. 27–12 these distinctions to *e·* and God,
and good
    Mis. 222– 2 false sense of both *e·* and good.
       333–12 Is it in both *e·* and good,
       352–26 consciousness of both *e·* and good,
    Un. 23–24 knowing both *e·* and good ;
       24–11 consciousness, . . . both *e·* and good.
    No. 37– 8 to know both *e·* and good ;

evil

and matter
Mis. 27–20 e· and matter are negation :
'01. 25–28 excludes e· and matter.
appearance of
Mis. 46– 7 destroy the appearance of e·
armies of
Pul. 83–18 * our own allied armies of e·
as a false claim
'01. 14– 8 e·, as a false claim, false entity, and
as a lie
'01. 14–14 We regard e· as a lie,
as a supposition
Un. 52–16 e·, as a supposition, is the father of
as mind
Mis. 261– 1 e·, as mind, is doomed,
as personified
Pan. 6–10 chapter sub-title
attempt of
Mis. 118–28 Every attempt of e· to harm good
attenuation of
Mis. 260–32 is the highest attenuation of e·.
author of
Hea. 9–22 "Who is the author of e·?"
avoidance of the
Pul. 15– 6 ensure the avoidance of the e·
beautiful
Un. 52–27 form the condition of beautiful e·,
belief in
Mis. 221–32 belief in e· and in the process of
belief . . . that
Ret. 69–28 the belief . . . that e· is mind,
believe that
Pan. 11–21 believe that e· develops good,
'01. 14– 6 Do . . . Scientists believe that e·
besetments of
Mis. 10–19 with fear and the besetments of e· ;
call
Un. 49–24 clearer right to call e· a negation,
calls
Mis. 27– 2 Science of good calls e· nothing.
can neither
No. 23– 4 E· can neither grasp
can never
Un. 25–25 e· can never take away.
casting out
Mis. 25–18 healing the sick, casting out e·,
No. 12–18 Living a true life, casting out e·,
My. 126–13 casting out e· and healing the sick.
153–26 casting out e· and healing the sick.
cast out
Mis. 211– 5 to handle serpents and cast out e·.
Pan. 5–24 our Master cast out e·,
My. 114– 5 cast out e· and heal the sick ;
172–17 cast out e·, disease, and death ;
288–21 Jesus cast out e·, disease, death,
casts out
Man. 15–12 understanding that casts out e· as
claim of
Mis. 55– 9 is the universal claim of e·
115–18 delivered from every claim of e·,
Ret. 64–11 as the opposite claim of e·
claims of
Mis. 114–23 deliverance from the claims of e·.
No. 23–20 we need to discern the claims of e·,
24–15 claims of e· become both less and
combating
Mis. 285– 1 combating e· only, rather than
comes
Un. 20– 5 e· comes into authority :
commensurate with
Mis. 261– 2 suffering is commensurate with e·,
condemn
My. 249– 1 You may condemn e· in the abstract
consciousness of
Un. 50–19 The less consciousness of e·
conscious of
Un. 36–23 to say that . . . is conscious of e·,
counterfeits good
Mis. 351–20 E· counterfeits good : it says,
criticizes
My. 240–16 because it criticizes e·, disease,
cruel and
Mis. 41– 1 only the cruel and e· can
dealt with as
Mis. 284–20 must now be dealt with as e·,
definition of
No. 22–26 His definition of e· indicated
Pan. 5– 7 chapter sub-title
deliver us from
My. 233– 6 "Deliver us from e·"— Matt. 6 : 13.
denounce
Pan. 6– 5 let us continue to denounce e·
departing from
Mis. 19–14 is daily departing from e· ;

evil

deprives
Mis. 14–29 deprives e· of all power,
destroys
Ret. 62– 8 demonstration of . . . destroys e·.
No. 30– 8 reaches and destroys e· by
'01. 10–23 whereby good destroys e·,
destruction of
No. 23– 2 hinders the destruction of e·.
dignity of
Un. 54–24 and admitted the dignity of e·.
disappearing of
Mis. 338– 2 involves the disappearing of e·.
does not obtain
Un. 31–22 e· does not obtain in Spirit,
doeth
My. 33–20 nor doeth e· to his— Psal. 15 : 3.
dominates
Mis. 293–15 if e· dominates his character,
drift into
Un. 24– 5 and cannot drift into e·.
ego of
Un. 52–16 not the so-called ego of e· ;
elements of
Mis. 40–27 has to master those elements of e·
elevating
Pan. 6–26 It is plain that elevating e·
enrage
Mis. 338–17 calm strength will enrage e·.
enthrone
Un. 46–28 an effort to enthrone e·.
epicycle of
My. 270– 3 obliterates the epicycle of e·.
error, or
Mis. 259–25 error, or e·, is really non-existent,
escape from
Pul. 15–13 Escape from e·, and designate
et cetera of
Mis. 114–21 and all the et cetera of e·.
explains
Pan. 5–18 Jesus' definition . . . explains e·.
fact that
'01. 14–12 takes hold of the fact that e·
faith in
Mis. 31–11 is in proportion to the faith in e·,
31–18 to relinquish his faith in e·,
31–22 in order to retain his faith in e·
46– 2 perpetuates the belief or faith in e·.
346–17 perpetuates faith in e· ;
falsity of
Mis. 201–10 myth or material falsity of e· ;
familiar with
Un. 14–21 if this Mind is familiar with e·,
fear of
Mis. 279– 5 and not the fear of e·,
finds
Mis. 261– 3 e· finds no escape from itself;
No. 27– 5 e· finds no place in good.
flesh, and
Mis. 2– 8 the world, the flesh, and e·,
My. 134– 2 the world, the flesh, and e·,
foreknow
Un. 19–12 predestine or foreknow e·,
for evil
Mis. 12– 8 Never return e· for evil ;
316– 2 never to return e· for evil ;
Man. 84– 4 never to return e· for evil,
My. 128–26 Return not e· for evil,
form of
Mis. 257– 3 every mode and form of e·.
forms of
Mis. 115–23 against the subtler forms of e·,
from good
Un. 14–28 to distinguish e· from good,
fruit of
Un. 17–23 partake of the fruit of e·,
full of
No. 22–24 a mortal who is full of e·.
gives
'00. 5– 5 It gives e· no origin,
good and
    (see **good**)
good for
    (see **good**)
good, not
Mis. 4–10 its power to do good, not e·.
42–24 learn that good, not e·, lives
101–23 this power is good, not e· ;
283–27 to demonstrate good, not e·,
good or
Mis. 309– 3 corporeality, either as good or e·.
No. 23–24 amount of good or e· he possesses.
good or of
No. 22–16 the person of good or of e·.
good over
Ret. 26–10 supremacy of good over e·,

evil

great
  No. 32–23   It seems a great *e·* to belie

growing
  Ret. 76–27   a growing *e·* in plagiarism ;

guard against
  Mis. 114–31   guard against *e·* and its silent modes,

gust of
  My. 297–12   A suppositional gust of *e·*

handling
  Mis. 292–30   on this point of handling *e·*,

hands of
  My. 128–24   betrays Truth into the hands of *e·*

has no claims
  No. 24–21   namely, that *e·* has no claims

has no power
  My. 296–13   *E·* has no power to harm,

He destroys
  No. 30– 9   He need not know the *e·* He destroys,

hidden
  My. 288– 3   and uncovers hidden *e·*.

immunity from
  Mis. 298–28   than immunity from *e·*.

impersonal
  Mis. 190–22   referred to was an impersonal *e·*,

impotence of
  Mis. 121–10   namely, the impotence of *e·*,

incapable of
  Pan. 4–14   while God is incapable of *e·* ;

in consciousness
  Un. 49–13   So long as I hold *e·* in consciousness,

incorporeal
  '01. 12–26   Incorporeal *e·* embodies itself in

indulged
  Mis. 94– 3   a person who knowingly indulged *e·*,

infirmity of
  Mis. 294– 2   last infirmity of *e·* is so-called
  '02. 10–26   is the infirmity of *e·*,

in human nature
  '01. 9–19   The *e·* in human nature foams

insists
  Mis. 366–20   *e·* insists on the unity of good and

introduces
  Pan. 6–11   Mosaic theism introduces *e·*,

is a false claim
  Un. 32– 1   and that *e·* is a false claim,

is a lie
  Pan. 5–25   Knowing that *e·* is a lie,

is a negation
  Mis. 107–17   *E·* is a negation :

is a quality
  No. 23–18   *E·* is a quality, not an individual.

is egotistic
  Un. 27–13   we shall find that *e·* is *egotistic*,

is illusion
  '00. 10– 4   *E·* is illusion, that after a fight

is impotent
  Mis. 119–10   *E·* is impotent to turn the righteous
  Hea. 10– 9   therefore *e·* is impotent.

is naught
  Mis. 260–24   *e·* is naught, although it seems to
     279–20   *e·* is naught and good is all.
  Un. 21– 8   *e·* is naught, and good only is

is never present
  Mis. 367–21   To good, *e·* is never present;

is no part
  Un. 4–21   *e·* is no part of the divine

is not a creator
  Un. 25–20   *E·* is not a creator.

is not a quality
  Mis. 259–10   *e·* is not a quality to be known

is not Mind
  Rud. 4–16   Good is Mind, but *e·* is not Mind.

is not self-made
  Pan. 5– 9   Since *e·* is not self-made,

is not something
  Mis. 284–24   *E·* is not something to fear

is not spiritual
  Un. 25–22   *E·* is not spiritual, and therefore

is not the medium
  Pan. 11–24   *e·* is not the medium of good,

is powerless
  Mis. 336– 3   this lesson . . . *e·* is powerless,

is self-destroying
  No. 26–18   for *e·* is self-destroying.

is self-destructive
  Mis. 2–22   and *e·* is self-destructive,

is temporal
  Mis. 93–13   *E·* is temporal : it is the illusion
  Pul. 13–23   *e·* is temporal, not eternal.
  No. 37– 8   *e·* is temporal and God is eternal,

is the absence
  Ret. 60–12   *e·* is the absence of good ;
  No. 17– 4   *e·*, is the absence of Spirit

is unnatural
  My. 288–10   *E·* is unnatural ; it has no origin

evil

is unreal
  Ret. 60–13   *e·* is unreal and good is all
  '01. 15– 1   declaration that *e·* is unreal,
  Hea. 9–23   statement that *e·* is unreal ;
  My. 178–19   revelation . . . that *e·* is unreal ;

knowing
  Mis. 108–12   utility of knowing *e·* aright,
     367–14   implies the necessity of knowing *e·*,
     367–23   but against *knowing e·*,

knowledge of
     (*see* **knowledge**)

know not
  Un. 18– 3   therefore I know not *e·*.

knows
  Un. 15–10   If God knows *e·*, so must man,
     18– 1   God must perish, if He knows *e·*
     19– 7   If God knows *e·* at all,
  No. 16– 7   If God knows *e·* even as a false

lapses into
  Pan. 7–27   lapses into *e·* dominating

league with
  My. 200–25   to relinquish its league with *e·*.

let alone
  Mis. 284–25   *E·* let alone grows more real,

licensed
  My. 211– 7   mistaken way, . . . has licensed *e·*,

lie of
  No. 42–19   lie of *e·* holds its own by declaring

like
  Un. 50–18   Like *e·*, it is destitute of Mind,

likeness of
  Ret. 67–20   the image and likeness of *e·*,

loses all place
  No. 24– 2   *e·* loses all place, person, and

loss of faith in
  Mis. 204–17   marked loss of faith in *e·*,

lurks an
  Mis. 302– 1   Behind the scenes lurks an *e·*

made
  Mis. 362–12   believing that God, . . . made *e·* ;
  Pan. 5–10   who or what hath made *e·* ?

made neither
  '02. 6–12   God made neither *e·* nor its

make
  No. 23– 5   nor make *e·* omnipotent and

manifest
  No. 16– 8   this knowledge would manifest *e·*

manifestations of
  Mis. 362–20   material manifestations of *e·*,

mastering
  My. 207–23   mastering *e·* and defending good,

master of
  Mis. 209–28   good is the master of *e·*.

material world and
  Rud. 3– 7   the material world and *e·*.

matter and
     (*see* **matter**)

matter, or
  Mis. 363–13   changes of matter, or *e·*.
  No. 17– 4   Matter, or *e·*, is the absence of

meditates
  Mis. 148– 2   while he meditates *e·* against us

mental
  My. 212–13   highest form of mental *e·*,

mode of
  Mis. 361– 9   every form and mode of *e·*

modes as
  Mis. 364–27   same power or modes as *e·*,

modes of
  Mis. 293– 3   all the claims and modes of *e·* ;

moral
  Un. 36–22   and yet admit . . . moral *e·*, sin, or

more contagious than
  Mis. 229–10   good is more contagious than *e·*,

more natural than
  Mis. 199–29   goodness is more natural than *e·*.
     222–28   should seem more natural than *e·*.

mote of
  Mis. 336–15   mote of *e·* out of other eyes.

must be dethroned
  Un. 20–10   *e·* must be dethroned :

mysterious
  Mis. 237–21   marvellous good, and mysterious *e·*.

mythology of
  Mis. 363–10   mythology of *e·* and mortality

named
  Mis. 196– 9   separate mind . . . named *e·* ;
  Ret. 63–16   Its opposite, nothing, named *e·*,
  Un. 60– 9   presence named *e·*.
  No. 32–18   its opposite, named *e·*, must

nature of
  No. 23– 1   incorrect concept of the nature of *e·*

never did exist
  Mis. 346–11   *E·* never did exist as an entity.

evil

never made
Un. 20–12 *First:* God never made *e*.
    45–11 God never made *e*.

no
Mis. 93–10 in Him dwelleth no *e*.
    229–18 shall no *e* befall thee,— *Psal.* 91 : 10.
    311–13 charity which thinketh no *e* ;
Ret. 63– 6 there is in reality no *e*,
Un. 22– 4 in which no *e* can possibly dwell.
    46–15 In his identity there is no *e*.
    62–14 there is no *e*.
No. 24–28 there can be no *e*.
    45– 6 thinketh no *e*,— *I Cor.* 13 : 5.
'01. 34–19 yea, which *knoweth* no *e*.
My. 297–14 for there is in reality no *e*,

no compromise with
My. 41–17 * C. S. makes no compromise with *e*,

no consciousness of
Un. 21–16 With Him is no consciousness of *e*,

no faith in
Mis. 118– 4 We shall have no faith in *e*

no intelligent
Mis. 36–30 for there is no intelligent *e*,

no Life in
Un. 62–11 learn that there is no Life in *e*.

non-intelligent
Mis. 267–25 *matter*, or *non-intelligent e*,

no reality in
Un. 59– 1 there is no reality in *e*,

not educed from
Pan. 12– 2 good is not educed from *e*,

nothingness of
Mis. 108– 8 attested the . . . nothingness— of *e* :
    109–27 must discern the nothingness of *e*,
    176–11 learn . . . the nothingness of *e*,
Ret. 55– 7 brings out the nothingness of *e*

not overcome of
Mis. 334–30 "Be not overcome of *e*,— *Rom.* 12 : 21.
'01. 34–21 be not overcome of *e*,

of dumbness
Mis. 190–23 it was the *e* of dumbness,

offspring of
Ret. 68– 4 claimed to beget the offspring of *e*,

of inaction
Mis. 341–22 *e* of inaction and delay.

one
Mis. 112– 1 in other words, the one *e*
My. 130–15 the one *e* or the evil one.

opposes
Mis. 119–16 whatever or whoever opposes *e*,

or error
Ret. 57–19 *E*, or error, is not Mind ;

original
Mis. 295–10 * cause of this "same original *e*"
Ret. 68– 3 claimed to originate . . . original *e* ;

origin of
Mis. 24–25 Speaking of the origin of *e*,
    346– 6 chapter sub-title
    346– 7 origin of *e* is the problem of ages.

or sin
'01. 12–25 chapter sub-title

outcome of
'01. 13– 2 The outcome of *e*, called sin,

out of
Mis. 2–27 those who progress . . . out of *e*,

overcome
Mis. 66–27 "overcome *e* with good."— *Rom.* 12 : 21.
    116– 1 will overcome *e* with good,
    334–30 overcome *e* with good,"— *Rom.* 12 : 21.
    352–27 through argument . . . overcome *e*.
Man. 47– 2 seeks to overcome *e* with good.
Pul. 15–16 overcome *e* with good.
No. 9–20 overcome *e* with good.
    33– 4 thus we may overcome *e* with good.
'01. 34–22 overcome *e* with good ;
'02. 2–30 overcome *e* with good,
My. 128–27 "overcome *e* with good."— *Rom.* 12 : 21.
    180–18 overcome *e* and heal disease.
    228– 8 "overcome *e* with good."— *Rom.* 12 : 21.
    278–21 overcome *e* with good.

overcoming
My. 204–28 overcoming *e* with good,
    291–13 universal good overcoming *e*.

persists in
Mis. 184–20 If he . . . persists in *e*,

personal
Rud. 7–17 Jesus said of personal *e*,

personality of
Mis. 190–30 Paul refers to this personality of *e*

phenomenal
My. 349–25 phenomenal *e*, which is lawless and

point out the
Pul. 15– 3 point out the *e* in human thought,

possible
Mis. 302–28 intended to forestall the possible *e*

evil

powerless
My. 296–19 *e* powerless, and God, . . . omnipotent

powerlessness of
Mis. 114–29 show us the powerlessness of *e*,

powers of
Mis. 177– 5 powers of *e* are leagued together

presence of
Mis. 103– 1 precludes the presence of *e*.

proceedeth not
Mis. 198–13 *e* proceedeth not from God,

process of
Mis. 221–32 belief . . . in the process of *e*,

punishment of
My. 296–18 and punishment of *e*

pursues the
Mis. 210– 1 pursues the *e* that hideth

really
Ret. 94– 8 and yet errs, . . . is really *e*.

reduction of
No. 33– 2 The reduction of *e*, in Science,

regard
My. 119– 2 to regard *e* as real,

rejection of
Pan. 12– 3 comes from the rejection of *e*

resists
My. 210–14 Goodness involuntarily resists *e*.

result in
Mis. 27– 5 or aught that can result in *e*,

return of
Mis. 13– 6 sharp return of *e* for good

reward of
Mis. 340– 4 Good is never the reward of *e*,

said of
Pan. 5–12 He said of *e* : "Ye are of— *John* 8 : 44.

seeks
Un. 17– 2 *E* seeks to fasten all error upon

seems as real
Mis. 108–19 wherein *e* seems as real as good,

seems to predominate
Mis. 113– 6 when *e* seems to predominate

seething
Mis. 338–11 in the midst of seething *e* ;

self-existent
Mis. 198–28 a belief in self-existent *e*,
Pan. 5– 8 or is *e* self-existent,

sense of
    (*see* **sense**)

sensible
Ret. 73–17 where sensible *e* is lost

should not be
Un. 50–25 consciousness should not be *e*.

signifies
Mis. 27–21 *e* signifies the absence of good,

spirit of
Mis. 370– 6 spirit of *e* is still abroad ;
My. 212– 5 the essence, or spirit, of *e*,

spirits of
Mis. 278– 2 the distilled spirits of *e*,

states of
No. 16–12 The subjective states of *e*,

subordinates good
No. 24–13 *e* subordinates good in personality.

substratum of
No. 16–26 matter is the substratum of *e*,

suppositional
Mis. 334–19 diabolism of suppositional *e*
    367– 8 the lie of suppositional *e*,

supposition of
Mis. 260–15 holds . . . the supposition of *e*,

supposition that
Mis. 259– 8 silences the supposition that *e*

that is hidden
No. 24–17 *e* that is hidden by dogma

this
Mis. 113–23 this *e* can be resisted
    254–16 kill this *e* in "self"
    284–15 The hour has passed for this *e* to
    368–17 This *e* obtains in the present
Un. 44–15 miscall, this *e* a child of God.
No. 32–26 reduce this *e* to its lowest terms,
My. 211– 6 denying that this *e* exists.

to attack
Mis. 90–13 inexpedient to attack *e*.

to behold
My. 300– 1 than to behold *e*."— *Hab.* 1 : 13.

to cognize
Un. 24– 1 whereby to cognize *e*.

to know
Un. 54–20 God forbade man to know *e*

to produce
Mis. 174– 2 than has good to produce *e*.

treatment of
Pan. 5–28 His treatment of *e* and disease,

ultimating in
Mis. 122–16 nor good ultimating in *e*.

evil
  ultimatum of
    Mis. 113–19   latter-day ultimatum of *e·*,
  uncontaminated with
    Man. 31–11   uncontaminated with *e·*,
  uncovered
    Mis. 210– 2   *e·*, uncovered, is self-destroyed.
         334–28   Because I have uncovered *e·*,
  unreality of
    Mis. 319– 2   the unreality of *e·* is lost.
    Ret. 62– 7   demonstration of the *unreality* of *e·*
    My. 334–16   * teaching on the unreality of *e·*
  unseen
    '01. 20–19   This unseen *e·* is the sin of sins ;
  victory over
    Pul. 15–18   occasion for a victory over *e·*.
  wail of
    Mis. 267– 2   wail of *e·* never harms Scientists,
  was avenging
    My. 161–27   When *e·* was avenging itself on its
  was even more
    Un. 46–20   To them *e·* was even more the ego
  was loquacious
    '01. 16–20   in its origin *e·* was loquacious,
  where is
    Pan. 6–16   what and where is *e·*?
  whisper
    Mis. 119– 2   If malicious suggestions whisper *e·*
  wholly
    No. 23– 9   could not have been wholly *e·*,
  with good
    Mis. 217–23   at war with Life, *e·* with good,
    My. 118–30   and couple *e·* with good.
        204–28   overcoming *e·* with good,
         (*see also sub-title* **overcome**)
  world's
    Mis. 224–24   to cover the whole world's *e·*,

    Mis.   2–23   therefore *e·* must be mortal
         3– 5   good as more natural than *e·*,
         6– 5   Jesus cast out disease as *e·*.
       10–31   erroneous belief . . . that *e·* is real ;
       13–15   proposition that *e·* is a factor of
       13–16   to believe in the reality of *e·*
       14– 2   neither place nor power left for *e·*.
       14– 6   where will you see or feel *e·*,
       14–10   that requires *e·* through which to
       14–17   to him *e·* is as real and eternal as
       14–22   to be the necessity for *e·*,
       14–24   *e·*, good's opposite, has no Principle,
       14–26   *e·* is neither a primitive nor a
       14–32   he makes a great reality of *e·*,
       22–15   transmitting human ills, or *e·*,
       26–32   to mean that good is *e·*,
       27– 1   or the creator of *e·*?
       27– 4   That God, good, creates *e·*,
       45–22   *where did e· originate?*
       45–26   opposite intelligence . . . termed *e·*.
       46– 1   admission of the reality of *e·*
       46– 5   *e·*, good's opposite, is unreal.
       49–22   that *e·* is as real as good,
       60–26   *E·* in the beginning claimed the
     107–22   knowledge of evil as *e·*, so-called.
     108–22   of what we need to know of *e·*,
     115–19   *e·* has neither prestige, power, nor
     116– 2   sensitiveness to the power of *e·*.
     122–15   it is not *e·* producing good,
     122–18   "Let us do *e·*, — *Rom.* 3 : 8.
     123– 3   *E·* was, and is, the illusion of
     174– 4   Matter is . . . *e·*, having presence
     181–29   not of God's opposite, — *e·*,
     184– 3   by claiming that . . . man is *e·* ;
     184–23   self-deceived sense of power in *e·*.
     196–10   and make you know *e·*,
     196–11   thus become material, sensual, *e·*.
     200– 4   and *e·* as the abnormal ;
     209–24   false basis that *e·* should be concealed
     213–12   against the *e·* which, if seen,
     251–23   and the *e·* they would not do,
     259– 7   of good, not of *e·*.
     259–16   moral power of good, not of *e·* :
     261– 3   and lasts as long as the *e·*.
     287–14   should preponderate over the *e·*,
     289– 2   Strong drink is unquestionably an *e·*,
     289– 2   and *e·* cannot be used temperately:
     289– 7   What is *e·*?   It is suppositional
     298– 5   Let us do *e·*, — *Rom.* 3 : 8.
     299–16   the *e·* which these senses see not
     335–17   ability, in belief, of *e·* to break the
     335–29   concerning those who do *e·*
     346–10   whence comes the *e·*?
     346–16   mortal admission of the reality of *e·*
     354–11   error to Truth, and *e·* to good,
     362–13   Then, was *e·* part and parcel of
     364–23   matter of Spirit and *e·* of good ;
     364–30   or give reality and power to *e·*

evil
    Mis. 367–21   *e·* is a different state of consciousness.
    Ret. 55– 5   *E·* is not mastered by *e·* ;
         57–10   it is the flesh that is *e·*.
         64– 4   such is the unity of *e·* ;
         82–23   consummate much good or else *e·* ;
    Un.   3–18   likeness of good, not of *e·* ;
         15– 9   Was *e·* among these good things?
         17– 9   *e·* ties its wagon-load of offal
         17–20   Error says God must know *e·*
         18– 1   *e·* necessarily leads to extinction
         19–15   *e·* is only a delusive deception,
         21–10   *E·*.   God hath said,
         22– 1   *E·*.   Why is this so?
         22– 8   *E·*.   But I would taste and know
         22–13   *E·*.   But there is something besides
         23–19   *E·*.   But mortal mind and sin really
         24–10   *E·*.   I am a finite consciousness,
         24–22   *E·*.   I am something separate from
         25–18   *E·*.   I am a creator,
         25–21   *E·* is not conscious or conscientious
         26– 1   *E·*.   I am intelligent matter ;
         26– 7   shirk all responsibility . . . as *e·*,
         26– 9   *Good.* You mistake, O *e·* !
         31–23   *e· does*, according to belief,
         39–26   They presuppose that . . . man is *e·*,
         41– 4   Of *e·* we can never learn it,
         44–18   Human wisdom says of *e·*,
         47– 3   Nowhere . . . is *e·* connected with **good,**
         49–22   *E·* is without Principle.
         50– 4   only as I believe in *e·*,
         50–12   mortal mind, of which *e·* is the
         51–22   and not of His opposite, *e·*.
         52–15   *What say you of e·?*
         53– 2   So *e·* and all its forms are
         53– 4   or it would not be *e·*.
         53– 7   constitutes the lie an *e·*.
         53–12   that *e·* is Mind, is a
    Rud.   4–17   Good is not in *e·*, but in God only.
         6–10   to the material senses, *e·* takes the place
    No. 16– 9   matter, *e·*, sin, sickness and death
        17–26   Then *e·* would be as real as good,
        21–19   supposed power and reality of *e·*
        24– 4   *e·* in human thought.
        24–12   By the same token, *e·* is not only
        24–18   *e·*, being thus uncovered, is
        24–22   for behold *e·* (or devil) is,
        24–25   never a moment in which *e·* **was real.**
        26–18   If man's individuality were *e·*,
    Pan.   5– 8   Did God create *e·* ?
        5–15   no truth [reality] in him [*e·*].
        5–18   Jesus' definition of devil (*e·*)
        5–19   shows that *e·* is both liar and lie,
        6–22   For if . . . *e·* also is mind,
        6–25   what power hath *e·* ?
    '00.   5– 8   *e·* — "is a liar, — *John* 8 : 44.
    '01. 12–27   *E·* is neither quality nor quantity :
        13–13   *e·*, *alias* devil, sin, is a lie
        23– 7   yet that *e·* exists and is real,
        23– 8   thence it would follow that *e·*
    '02.   1–10   *E·*, though combined in
    Peo.   4–12   was named a person, and *e·* another
    My. 178–16   therefore if *e·* exists,
       197– 2   Enjoying good things is not *e·*,
       210– 6   no door through which *e·* can **enter,**
       210– 6   no space for *e·* to fill
       211–12   in its ascending steps of *e·*,
       212–11   wherewith to do *e·* ;
       213– 5   and give activity to *e·*.
       213– 7   is by no means a right of *e·*
       265– 7   *e·* flourishes less, invests less
       278–25   War is in itself an *e·*,
       288–31   *e·* is not a fatherly grace.
       334–17   * than that *e·* could be indulged

evil (adj., adv.)
    Mis. 11– 1   to suffer for his *e·* intent ;
       18–25   entering into a state of *e·* thoughts,
     19–1, 2   *e·* thinking, *e·* speaking,
       41– 4   to accomplish an *e·* purpose.
       72– 1   nothing *e·*, or unlike Himself.
       89–16   "be *e·* spoken of." — *Rom.* 14 : 16.
     103– 2   which say that sin is an *e·* power,
     113–17   suggestions from an *e·* source.
     114–24   Scientists will silence *e·* suggestions,
     187–28   That man must be *e·* before he
     191–29   could only be possible as *e·* beliefs,
     204–32   *e·* thinking, *e·* speaking
     209–22   *E·* passions die in their own **flames,**
     219–28   if he can change this *e·* sense
     227–10   to extend their *e·* intent,
     247–30   Hence *that* is only an *e·* belief
     252–11   *e·* thoughts are impotent,
     259–11   iniquity, too *e·* to conceive of **good**
     284–21, 22   neither an *e·* claim nor an *e·* **person**
     332–19   to have formed an *e·* sense

evil (adj., adv.)

Mis.	335– 3	"But and if that *e·* servant— *Matt.* 24 : 48.
	340– 1	relinquishment of right in an *e·* hour,
	340–21	through *e·* or through good report,
Man.	81–24	no *e·* speaking shall be allowed.
Ret.	68– 5	*alias* an *e·* offspring.
	75–15	lightly speak *e·* of me."— *Mark* 9 : 39.
Un.	23–22	An *e·* material mind, so-called,
	43– 8	the possibility that Life can be *e·*.
	45–11	*e·* ego, and his assumed power,
	45–24	*e·* ego has but the visionary
	46–16	only as . . . not as material or *e·*.
	46–22	This *e·* ego they believed must
	53–10	*e·* belief that renders them obscure.
Pul.	29–23	* cast out the demons of *e·* thought.
	56–19	* "And still we love the *e·* cause,
	69–11	* *e·* and sick-producing thoughts,
Rud.	10– 8	with nothing *e·* or material ;
No.	7– 3	*e·* influences waver the scales
Pan.	9– 7	a good Spirit and an *e·* spirit.
'00.	8– 5	but the *e·* man also
	8– 6	exhales . . . his *e·* nature
	13– 7	words were brave and their deeds *e·*.
'01.	16–20	once refer to an *e·* spirit as *dumb,*
Hea.	10–11	it has no *e·* side ;
My.	17– 5	all *e·* speakings,— *I Pet.* 2 : 1.
	128–30	*e·* suggestions, in whatever guise,
	130– 3	guard . . . against *e·* suggestions
	210–12	self-seeking pride of the *e·* thinker
	210–14	The *e·* thinker is the proud talker
	211–32	induced by this secret *e·* influence
	212– 9	effects of this *e·* influence,
	212–10	the *e·* effects of alcohol.
	223–18	or by "*e·* suggestions,"
	228– 5	*E·* minds signally blunder
	249–17	countenance such *e·* tendencies.
	297–12	gust of evil in this *e·* world
		(*see also* **mind**)

evil-doer

Mis.	118–30	punishment of the *e·*.
	221–11	*e·* can do little at removing
	222– 1	issues of death to the *e·*.
	284–20	not as an *e·* or personality.
'01.	14–30	*e·* receives no encouragement from

evil-doers

Mis.	122– 1	good man to suffer for *e·*
My.	135–28	because of *e·* ;"— *Psal.* 37 : 1.

evil-doing

Mis.	126–22	condemn *e·*, evil-speaking ;

evilly

Mis.	119– 3	no apology for acting *e·*.
'00.	2–17	means, but he uses them *e·*.

evil-minded

Ret.	36–10	the *e·* would insinuate

evil-mongers

Mis.	238–29	I accord these *e·* due credit

evil one

Mis.	111–32	The belief in . . . is the *e· o·*
My.	14–19	* a fabrication of the *e· o·*,
	130–15	the one evil or the *e· o·*.

evil's

Mis.	14–18	*e·* umpire and empire,
Un.	46–21	Sin, sickness, and death were *e·*
Pul.	15– 3	*e·* hidden mental ways
Pan.	11–22	whatever strips off *e·* disguise

evils

called

'00.	5–29	God's opposites, called *e·*,

called sin

No.	31–23	If the *e·* called sin, sickness,

casting out

Mis.	77–32	healing the sick, casting out *e·*,
	99–30	casting out *e·* and healing the sick ;
	165– 2	casting out *e·* and healing,
	187– 2	casting out *e·*, *healing the sick,*
Ret.	65–23	casting out *e·* and healing the sick ;
My.	110– 3	casting out *e·*, healing the sick,

cast out

No.	31–17	Jesus cast out *e·*,
'01.	9–26	cast out *e·* and heal the sick.

casts out

My.	260–25	casts out *e·*, heals the sick,

choose between

Mis.	289– 9	must first choose between *e·*,

of mortal thought

My.	113–27	casting out the *e·* of mortal thought,

refer to the

No.	22–23	passage must refer to the *e·*

these

No.	36–21	Had he been as conscious of these *e·*

two

Mis.	289– 9	of two *e·* choose the less ;
	302–16	of two *e·* the less would be

evils

what

Un.	59– 2	from what *e·* was it his purpose to
		—————
Mis.	191–17	*e·*, apparent wrong traits,
Un.	59– 4	*e·* from which he saves

evil-speaking

Mis.	126–23	Most people condemn evil-doing, *e·* ;
	137–25	envy, *e·*, resentment, and
	222– 3	inflames envy, passion, *e·*, and
	337–19	*e·*, lust, envy, hate.

evinced

My.	293–14	*e·* a lack of . . . understanding

evoked

My.	92–11	* more interest than it has *e·* in

evokes

Mis.	364– 4	naturally *e·* new paraphrase

evolution (*see also* **evolution's**)

Mis.	27–24	Creation, *e·*, or manifestation,
Pul.	23–17	* potent factors in the social *e·*

evolution's

Mis.	vii–13	Thenceforth to *e·* Geology,

evolutions

Mis.	1–21	by the *e·* of advancing thought,

evolve

Mis.	22– 6	say that . . . mortals can *e·* Science?
	23–32	Spirit, could not . . . *e·* matter.
	26–18	not . . . able to *e·* or create itself :
	174– 1	no more power to *e·* or to create
Un.	26– 2	the capacity to *e·* mind.
My.	190– 3	so help to *e·* that larger sympathy
	342–27	"It will *e·* scientifically.

evolved

Mis.	166–13	has *e·* a more ready ear
	295– 5	is *e·* by the same power
	331–25	divine Science *e·* nature as thought,
Hea.	6–16	were *e·* and made tangible ;
My.	226–11	by *e·* spiritual power,

evolves

Mis.	24–18	*e·* a subjective state
	190– 7	mortal *e·* not the immortal,
	364–20	or *e·* the universe.

evolving

Rud.	7–24	by *e·* matter from Spirit,

Ewing, Judge William G.

My.	8– 8	* Judge William G. *E·*, in seconding the

exact

Mis.	78–27	the *e·* nature of its Principle,
My.	40–25	* she is an *e·* metaphysician.
	238– 5	*e·* degree of comparison between
	311–16	as to the *e·* date of my first
	322–30	* The *e·* words I do not recall,

exactly

Man.	110– 6	conditions be *e·* complied with,
Pul.	67–23	* It was *e·* one hundred years
My.	71–22	* *e·* five thousand and twelve people
	317– 2	* *e·* defining her relations with the
	320– 7	* *e·* agreed with what you had told me.

exactness

Mis.	233–24	with the *e·* of the rule
Ret.	80–11	* With *e·* grinds He all.

exaggerating

Mis.	112–27	an *e·* sense of other people's.

exalt

Peo.	7– 7	to beautify and *e·* our lives.

exalted

Mis.	130–28	renews his strength, and is *e·*
	162–32	in the strength of an *e·* hope,
	196–26	is *e·*,— not through death,
	287– 1	as the most *e·* divine conception.
	289–25	*e·* and increased affections,
	341–10	and its strength in *e·* purpose.
Ret.	91– 6	No purer and more *e·* teachings
	92– 2	nor was his power so *e·*
Pul.	10–13	No dream . . . broke their *e·* purpose,
	71–17	* *e·* by various dignitaries
My.	335– 5	* soon *e·* to the degree of

exalteth

Mis.	139–12	*high thing that e· itself*— *II Cor.* 10 : 5.
	167–29	he *e·* the lowly ;

exalts

Mis.	399– 9	That *e·* thee, and will cure
Ret.	70–29	*e·* a mortal beyond human praise,
No.	12– 3	heals the sick and *e·* the race.
Po.	75–16	That *e·* thee, and will cure
My.	131– 4	*e·*, and commands a man,

examination

Mis.	127–31	need close attention and *e·*.
Man.	36–10	*e·* by the Board of Education,

examination
Man.	51–25	meetings for the *e·* of complaints
	77– 7	shall submit them . . . for *e·*.
	82–14	or for the *e·* of complaints.
Ret.	14– 3	*e·* of candidates for membership,
Un.	35– 8	senses are found, upon *e·*, to be
Rud.	15–26	laid bare for anatomical *e·*.
My.	3–21	*e·* compels him to think genuine,
	251–12	after *e·* in the Board of Education,
	310–20	by physician or post-mortem *e·*
	329– 7	* excused them from a medical *e·*

examine
Mis.	109– 8	*E·* yourselves, and see what,
Un.	33–16	*E·* that form of matter called *brains*,
	33–21	*E·* these witnesses for error,
Pul.	50–18	* tempted to *e·* its principles,
'01.	3– 9	Let us *e·* this.
My.	38–14	* to *e·* the church.
	128–32	Ofttimes *e·* yourselves, and see if
	233–30	Let us *e·* it for ourselves.

examined
Man.	90– 3	Students are *e·* . . . by this Board
My.	246– 6	are *e·* under its auspices
	251–20	*e·* in the Board of Education,

examiners
My.	329– 8	* before a board of medical *e·*.

examines
Hea.	12– 4	feels the pulse, *e·* the tongue, etc.,

examining
Ret.	44–17	*E·* the situation prayerfully

example
and precept
Ret.	88–16	both by *e·* and precept.

and suffering
Mis.	165–27	*e·*, and suffering of our Master.

better
My.	215–26	Can we find a better *e·*

character and
Mis.	91–16	Jesus' character and *e·*.

Christ as an
Pul.	72–26	* we take Christ as an *e·*,

Christian
Ret.	26– 5	his holy heroism and Christian *e·*
My.	52– 6	* in her Christian *e·*, as well as

demand and
No.	14–24	The demand and *e·* of Jesus were

follows the
Ret.	65–18	follows the *e·* of our Lord

follow the
Mis.	359– 1	follow the *e·* of the *Alma Mater*.
Ret.	49– 6	follow the *e·* of the *Alma Mater*
	55– 3	Let us follow the *e·* of Jesus,

give
Mis.	216– 6	as the Scriptures give *e·*.

good
Mis.	126–21	silent lesson of a good *e·*.
My.	91– 7	* Christian Scientists set a good *e·*

had shown
Ret.	47– 8	*E·* had shown the dangers

her
Peo.	10–11	States had followed her *e·*
My.	28–20	* and following her *e·*,
	58–21	* May her *e·* inspire us to follow

his
Mis.	165–19	the heirs to his *e·* ;
	359–22	but his *e·* was right,
Rud.	3–12	His *e·* is, to Christian Scientists,
'00.	2–12	benefits society by his *e·*

holy
Mis.	270–21	cannot depart from his holy *e·*,

instructions and
My.	220–25	the instructions and *e·* of the

Jesus'
Mis.	30– 3	according to Jesus' *e·*
My.	340–26	Jesus' *e·* in this, as in all else,

man's
Mis.	244–23	he did this for man's *e·* ;

my
Mis.	91–29	had followed my *e·*,

of our Master
Mis.	158–28	corresponds to the *e·* of our Master.

of the Master
Mis.	270– 7	*e·* of the Master in C. S.,

our
Mis.	212– 7	glorious career for our *e·*.

particular
My.	83–30	* But of this particular *e·*

perfect
No.	41–14	life of Christ is the perfect *e·* ;

precept and
'01.	18–22	Metaphysician's precept and *e·*,
My.	64–17	* by precept and *e·* how to obey

example
precepts and
Mis.	129–22	your Leader's precepts and *e·* !
	269–12	whose precepts and *e·* have

previous
Mis.	52–28	and work out the previous *e·*,

teaching and
Ret.	65–21	Christ's teaching and *e·*,

teachings, and
Pul.	75– 6	my writings, teachings, and *e·*
My.	127–10	Christ's teachings and *e·*
	129–32	teachings and *e·* of Christ Jesus.

their
My.	74–16	* might profit by their *e·* of

this
Mis.	149–26	This *e·* of yours is a light

your
Mis.	110–11	to know that your *e·*,

Ret.	49–17	Christ and the *e·* he gave ;
Rud.	1–18	(in court, for *e·*)
My.	137– 6	* an *e·* of crisp, clear,
	196–16	leaving us an *e·*,— *I Pet.* 2 : 21.
	272–13	reveals . . . the *e·*, the rule,

examples
Mis.	223–23	or taint their *e·*.
Ret.	82–23	their *e·* either excel or
Pul.	78– 2	* one of the most magnificent *e·*
My.	218– 6	Neither . . . furnishes reasons or *e·*

exceed
Mis.	111–18	Jesus' faith . . . must not *e·* that of
Man.	84–14	shall not *e·* $100.00 per pupil.
My.	208–16	nothing can *e·* its ministrations of
	244–26	certainly not *e·* three in number.

exceeded
'01.	17–12	*e·* that of other methods,
My.	138–19	Trusting that I have not *e·* the
	173–20	*e·* my expectation,

exceedeth
Pul.	2– 5	*e·* the fame which— *I Kings* 10 : 7.

exceeding
Man.	78–19	not *e·* $200 for any one transaction,
	84–12	Normal class not *e·* thirty
Ret.	80– 9	* Yet they grind *e·* small ;
'02.	11–24	and be *e·* glad :— *Matt.* 5 : 12.
My.	156– 5	to do *e·* abundantly — *Eph.* 3 : 20.
	270– 1	and be *e·* glad :— *Matt.* 5 : 12.

exceedingly
Pul.	58–17	* in its *e·* comfortable pews.
Pan.	13–14	*e·* glad that the churches
My.	18–22	*e·* glad that the churches
	139–26	Rejoice and be *e·* glad,

exceeds
Mis.	354– 2	It *e·* my conception of
Pul.	30–24	* *e·* two hundred thousand people.
My.	67–22	* But one church in the country *e·*

excel
Ret.	82–23	examples either *e·* or fall short

excellence
Mis.	340– 5	There is no *e·* without labor ;
Man.	61–21	standard of musical *e·* ;
Hea.	11–28	this *e·* above other systems.
Peo.	7– 4	chiselling to higher *e·*,

excellences
Ret.	5–22	* distinguished for numerous *e·*.

excellent
Mis.	155–20	who write such *e·* letters
	313–22	more laborers of the *e·* sort,
Pul.	9–17	*e·* sermons from the editor
	37– 7	* Her health is *e·*,
	57–20	* Such is the *e·* name
	58–14	* into seven *e·* class-rooms,
My.	15–17	Kate Hankey's *e·* hymn,
	110–10	for your most *e·* letter.
	120– 8	to answer your *e·* letter.

excelling
My.	190–12	vastly *e·* the former.

excelsior
My.	6–19	its *e·* extension is the crown.

except
Mis.	x–27	*e·* in connection with my
	8–11	*e·* you first formulate this enemy
	21–14	*e·* by increase of spirituality.
	64–14	*e·* the Bible, and "S. and H."
	75–16	*e·* where the word *God* can be
	83–12	*e·* it be with the consent of
	91–14	*e·* as types of these mental
	226–27	cannot stoop to notice, *e·* legally,
	272– 8	* no charters were granted . . . *e·* hers,
	272–19	* colleges (*e·* Rev. Mrs. Eddy's)
	289–22	*e·* by mutual consent.

except
Mis.	314–32	e· Communion Sunday,
	315– 8	e· by their author.
	315–25	e· the individual needing it
	362–29	e· when it is necessary to
	362–30	pleasure is no crime e· when
Man.	36–12	e· in such cases as are
	37–20	e· as provided for in Article V,
	45– 9	e· those specified in the
	45–22	e· by invitation.
	45–25	e· those who have received
	46–11	e· as a C. S. practitioner.
	62–15	None e· the officers, teachers, and
	71–18	e· in such cases as are specially
	71–22	e· they give the name
	78– 8	e· such debts as are specified
	82–12	e· by a majority vote of the
	84–25	e· it be in the Board of Education.
	87– 4	e· it be with the written consent of
	99– 6	e· as hereinafter specified,
	99–15	all States e· Massachusetts,
	109– 7	e· loyal students of Mrs. Eddy,
Ret.	20– 2	e· what money I had brought
	81– 4	Nothing e· sin, in the students
Un.	2– 6	no refuge from sin, e· in God,
	27– 9	doubts all existence e· its own.
	27–11	everything e· his own existence.
	42– 5	nothing e· the results of material
	51– 7	hair white or black, e· in belief;
Pul.	52– 2	* no sums e· those already subscribed
Rud.	14– 9	e· the bliss of doing good.
'00.	12–20	e· thou repent." — Rev. 2 : 5.
	14–13	e· the church in Philadelphia
'01.	6–13	e· He be a Person,
	20– 4	e· it be to serve God
	23–15	e· on its fixed Principle
	27– 2	all other authors e· the Bible.
	31–15	in no way e· in the interest of
'02.	8–18	e· we possess this inspiration,
	13–11	e· the privilege of publishing
Hea.	5–16	no evidence of the fact e·
My.	vi– 7	* e· as he has learned it
	4–26	"E· ye . . . become as — Matt. 18 : 3.
	57–30	* e· those already subscribed
	82–30	* e· perhaps those living in the
	103–23	e· the teachings and demonstrations
	117–24	lost to the centuries e· by
	137–15	e· in one or two instances,
	138–17	e· I leave all for Christ.
	141–10	* e· on the triennial gatherings,
	191– 3	e· God be with him." — John 3 : 2.
	261–24	unutterable e· in C. S.
	336–13	e· what money I had brought

excepting
Man.	57–10	(e· its regular sessions)
	82–18	e· those members who
Pul.	47–29	* nothing is left e· the angles
My.	310–18	* that all the family, "e· Albert,

exception
Mis.	7– 1	sickness is by no means the e·.
	248–28	with the following e· :
	282–19	the following is an e·
	283–13	e· to the old wholesome rule,
	382– 2	contradict it and prove an e·.
Ret.	82– 8	e· to this rule should be very rare.
Hea.	19–11	is not an e· to the origin
My.	76–18	* free of debt without e·.
	83–13	* Therefore, with the e· of the
	175– 5	with the e· of a daily drive.
	261– 8	continue thus with one e· :

exceptional
Mis.	39–21	There may be e· cases,
	90–12	under circumstances e·,
	283– 4	then the case is not e·.
Man.	36–14	E· Cases.
	96– 9	E· Cases.

exceptions
Mis.	282–18	There are solitary e· to most
Man.	94– 8	there may occur e·.

excess
Mis.	353– 4	either an e· of action or
My.	340–10	in e· of other States,

exchange
Mis.	76–20	e· the term soul for sense
	78–20	taking its money in e· for this
	274–26	in e· for money, place, and
	342–30	with the etiquette of the e·,
My.	236–14	will e· the present name for
	347–19	in e· for all else.

exchanged
My.	36–15	* e· the tears of sorrow for
	339–14	Massachusetts has e· Fast Day,

exchanges
Mis.	103–26	e· this human concept of Jesus

excite
Pul.	66–23	* may reasonably e· wonder

excited
Pul.	32–11	* that her . . . following e·,
My.	75–18	* They do not get e· over trifles.

excitement
Mis.	228– 7	is to be calm amid e·
My.	121– 5	e· and commotion of the season's
	335–19	* in the hope of allaying the e·

exciting
Mis.	69–25	e· cause of the inflammation
	229– 2	predisposing or e· causes.
	267–26	predisposing and e· cause of all
Ret.	44–18	predisposing and e· cause of its

exclaim
Mis.	326–25	Well might this heavenly messenger e·,
Pul.	3–19	with Job of old we e·,

exclaimed
Un.	30– 1	e·, "My soul...doth magnify — Luke 1 : 46.
Pul.	49– 9	* e· : "You have lived here only four

exclaims
Mis.	167–23	e·, "I thank Thee, O Father, — Luke 10 : 21.

exclamation
Mis.	75–21	e·, "My soul doth magnify — Luke 1 : 46.

exclude
Mis.	194–32	e· all faith in any other remedy
My.	187– 8	e· all darkness or doubt,

excluded
Un.	4–27	the vision of sin is wholly e·.

excludes
Mis.	257– 2	either e· God from the universe, or
Ret.	75–18	Science of Mind e· opposites,
No.	9–23	e· all error and includes all Truth.
'01.	25–28	e· evil and matter.
My.	249– 9	hating even one's enemies e· goodness.
	293– 1	The knowledge that . . . e· doubt,
	364–10	e· from his own consciousness,

exclusion
Mis.	271– 1	e· of compounds from its pharmacy,
Man.	49– 3	not . . . to the e· of others,

exclusive
Mis.	273–32	call is for my e· teaching.
Pul.	25–10	* designed for the e· use of
	28–11	* e· of the land
No.	4–25	rests on the e· truth that being,

exclusively
Mis.	375–30	* as belonging to them e·,
Man.	42– 3	collectively and e·.
Pul.	71– 8	* from C. S. believers e·.
'01.	28–15	those who have followed e·

ex-common sense
Mis.	112– 7	microbes, X-rays, and e· s·,

excommunicate
Man.	51–23	e· members of The Mother Church.

excommunicated
Man.	39– 9	who has been e· once,
	50–21	put on probation, or e·.
	51–13	withdraw from the Church or be e·.
	53–10	that member should be e·.
	53–17	on penalty of being e· from
	68– 9	e· from The Mother Church.

excommunication
Man.	39–17	twice notified of his e·,

excursion
My.	312–23	would need on such an e·.

excuse
Mis.	113–20	so that all are without e·.
Un.	9– 9	so plain that all are without e·
'01.	29–20	this is no e· for waiting
My.	211– 5	and e· themselves by denying

excused
Mis.	178–27	I wished to be e· from speaking
My.	329– 6	* The board only e· them from

excusing
Un.	21– 3	or else e· one another." — Rom. 2 : 15.

executed
My.	222–16	was not arrested and e·

execution
Hea.	2–15	passed from his e· to a crown.

executive
Man.	66–26	to the Boards or to the e· bodies
Pan.	14–15	associated with his e· trust,
My.	281–29	is not an e· power,
	282– 5	friendship of our chief e·

Executive Members (*see also* **Executive Members'**)
Man. 18–25 "First Members" to "*E. M.*."
    18–26 pertaining to "*E. M.*"
My. 347– 7 *E. M.* of The Mother Church

Executive Members'
My. 139–18 the *E. M.* meeting,

exegesis
'00 6–28 e· on the prophetic Scriptures.

Exemplar
My. 106–30 Our great *E·*, the Nazarene Prophet,
    180–28 in the spirit of our great *E·* pray:
    217–28 Thus it is that our great *E·*,

exemplar
Pul. 65–26 * unbelieving e· afterward became

exemplary
Man. 30– 2 Readers who are e· Christians
    55–17 after three years of e· character.
    72– 6 loyal e· Christian Scientist
My. 19–26 with acknowledgment of e· giving,
    310–27 presented my disposition as e·

exemplification
Mis. 112–32 e· of total depravity,
Ret. 86– chapter sub-title

exemplified
Mis. 7–10 has daily to be e·;
    130– 2 Has her life e· long-suffering,
    176– 7 has been e· in all ages,
    293–21 sum total of Love reflected is e·,
Pul. 54– 9 * enunciated and e· the Principle;
My. 287–13 Love lived . . . is God e·,

exemplify
Mis. 333–29 e· the power of Truth and Love.
Man. 60–20 whereby to e· our risen Lord.
My. 181–19 e· in all things the universal equity
    182– 6 e· my early love for this church

exemplifying
Mis. 311–10 e· what we profess.

exempt
Mis. 257–30 is not e· from this law.
Un. 56–19 not fully e· from physicality

exemption
Mis. 119–19 full e· from all necessity to
My. 256– 8 total e· from Christmas gifts.

exercise
Mis. 13– 3 permit me to e· these sentiments
    137– 3 badge, and order of e·,
    152–30 *E·* more faith in God
    267– 8 caused me to e· most patience.
Man. 74– 4 neither shall he e· supervision
    80–19 not elect to e· this right,
Ret. 82– 4 dealing with a simple Latour e· or
Pan. 4–11 depend on . . . for their proper e·.
My. 259–27 appropriate and proper e·.

exercised
Mis. 70– 3 e· my power over the fish,
Hea. 14– 9 caution should be e· in the choice of

exercises
Mis. 130–27 he who e· the largest charity,
Man. 62–17 attend the Sunday School e·.
Pul. 40–12 * TO ATTEND THE *E·*
    42– 7 * variation in the e·
    43– 7 * presided over the e·.
    43–13 * simplicity marked the e·.
    59– 8 * e· four times repeated.
My. 72–21 * to attend the dedication e·,
    78–30 * every word of the e·
    86–13 * ceremonies and e·.
    99–19 * attended the dedicatory e·,
    173–18 when there are no formal e·

exercising
Mis. 24–32 e· their supposed power

exerted
My. 281–24 * which President Roosevelt has e·

exhale
Man. 31–12 the mental atmosphere they e·

exhales
'00. 8– 5 e· consciously and unconsciously

exhaling
Mis. 20– 3 e· the aroma of Jesus' own

exhaustion
My. 165–26 and never stop from e·.
    232–27 produces fear or e·

exhaustless
Mis. 39–18 this saving, e· source
My. 149–12 mysteries of e· being.

exhibit
Mis. 299–23 pay me, not him, for this e·?

exhibited
Man. 64– 4 e· in the Reading Rooms
    81–21 e· in the rooms where
My. 25– 7 * great interest e· by the
    95–30 * as that e· at Boston,

Exhibition
Mis. 304– 7 * After the close of the *E·*
    304–16 * until that *E·* closes.

exhibition
Mis. 299–20 and put myself and them on e·,
Pul. 78–25 * The scroll is on e·

exhibitions
Mis. 47–28 *Professor Carpenter's* e·
    322– 1 earthly expositions or e·.

exhibits
'01. 21–17 e· a startling ignorance of

exhilaration
Pul. 36–16 * a state of e· and energy

exhort
Mis. 197– 5 e· people to turn from sin
Ret. 89–16 as Jesus was once asked to e·,
Un. 43–19 I e· them to accept Christ's promise,
No. v– 3 "reprove, rebuke, e·," — *II Tim.* 4 : 2.
Pan. 13–12 rebuke and e· one another.
My. 18–20 rebuke and e· one another.
    130–17 my students reprove, rebuke, and e·.

exhortation
Pan. 13– 9 chapter sub-title
My. 343–29 in tenderness, in e·, and in rebuke,

exigencies
My. 224– 3 to meet the e· of the hour

exigency
Pul. 9–13 quibbled over an architectural e·,

exiled
Po. 2–13 upon thine e· height ;

exist
Mis. 6–18 we e· in God, perfect,
    34–23 not a moment when he ceases to e·.
    50–24 we e· in Mind, live thereby,
    86–10 *e· only in imagination?*
    101–28 no other . . . intelligence can e·.
    105–27 no right either to be pitied or to e·,
    105–27 and what does not e· in Science.
    145– 4 shall e· alone in the affections,
    173–17 Does an evil mind e·
    183– 4 the verities of being e·,
    190–27 and e· in Mind.
    337–20 Where these e·, C. S. has no sure
    346–12 Evil never did e· as an entity.
Ret. 61–16 saith to fear, . . . You do not e·,
    61–17 and have no right to e·,
Un. 23–19 *Evil.* But mortal mind and sin . . . *e·* !
    23–20 *Good.* How can they e·,
    47– 6 All that can e· is God and His idea.
Pul. 85–12 * all things which really e·,
Rud. 5–28 in Mind only ;
No. 16– 3 must truly and eternally e·.
    16– 3 If . . . matter can e· in Mind,
Pan. 5– 6 how can it e·?
'01. 14– 9 evil, as a false claim, . . . does e·
    23– 8 either e· in good, or e· outside of
My. 89– 5 * deemed by its professors not to e·
    143–11 I e· in the flesh, and am seen daily
    226–16 and the universe would no longer e·.
    246–15 scientific unity which must e·
    306– 5 any unity that may e· between

existed
Mis. 5–29 That which never e·,
    45–23 never originated or e·
    56–26 *e· from the beginning,*
    57–30 e· in and of the Mind that
    111–23 no greater difference e·
    382– 3 No works on the subject of C. S. e·,
Ret. 67– 1 Sin e· as a false claim,
No. 37–27 if error and sin e· in
'01. 8–25 Christ e· prior to Jesus,
My. 319– 1 If there had never e· such a
    334–13 * which records show really e·

existence
acknowledge the
Mis. 247–20 They acknowledge the e· of
actual
Mis. 182– 6 perceive man's actual e·
No. 24–10 denies the actual e· of both
admitting the
Mis. 109–22 but, admitting the e· of both,
all
Un. 27– 9 doubts all e· except its own.
and rulership
Un. 38–16 affirming the e· and rulership

existence

conscious
Mis. 42–15 same plane of conscious e·
Un. 57–28 The only conscious e· in the flesh
consciousness and
Un. 21–14 individual consciousness and e·.
denies the
'01. 24– 2 He denies the e· of matter,
eternal
Mis. 206– 9 interpret man's eternal e·,
286–20 spiritual and eternal e·
evidence of the
Mis. 64–29 The only evidence of the e· of
facts of
Mis. 14–16 facts of e· and its concomitants :
false side of
Mis. 65–14 not consider the false side of e·
form of
Mis. 309–23 above a bodily form of e·,
genuine
No. 30–19 forbids the genuine e· of
goal of
Mis. 85–11 Perfection, the goal of e·,
harmonious
My. 44– 6 * eternal, harmonious e·.
health or
Rud. 12–19 health or e· of mankind,
hints the
Mis. 60–29 hints the e· of spiritual reality;
his
Mis. 122–30 his e· is a parody,
Pul. 4–22 His e· is deathless,
his own
Mis. 182– 1 antedated his own e·,
Un. 27–11 everything except his own e·.
human
(see **human**)
indicating the
Mis. 191–15 assertion indicating the e· of
individual
Mis. 85–17 spiritual, individual e·.
in relation to
Mis. 218– 7 testimony of . . . in relation to e·
intelligence and
Ret. 59–22 for intelligence and e·.
its
Mis. 14– 6 or find its e· necessary
legitimate
My. 37–21 * activities of legitimate e·,
life or
Mis. 105–14 Man's real life or e·
man's
Mis. 52–21 Man's e· is a problem to be
Pul. vii–21 bliss of man's e· in Science.
material
Mis. 42–21 a belief of material e·
Ret. 30–16 finite mind and material e·.
32–10 termed mortal and material e·
mortal
(see **mortal**)
no longer in
My. 332–26 * lodge was no longer in e·,
no other
Un. 36– 6 beside which there is no other e·.
of anything
'02. 5–27 or speculate on the e· of anything
of a substance
Un. 33– 5 as to the e· of a substance called
of error
Un. 22–11 To admit the e· of error
of God
Mis. 69– 1 treats of the e· of God,
of good
Mis. 13–16 rounded sense of the e· of good.
13–23 e· of good only ;
or consciousness
Un. 47– 5 false claim to e· or consciousness.
origin and
Mis. 79–10 Man's origin and e· being in Him,
origin nor
No. 15–22 have neither origin nor e·
origin or
Un. 45–27 It has no origin or e· in Spirit,
or reality
Un. 36–21 deny the e· or reality of matter,
other
No. 16–18 inference of some other e·
plane of
Mis. 34–25 on this present plane of e·,
power, nor
Mis. 115–20 neither prestige, power, nor e·,
present
Mis. 196–19 illumines our present e·
pretence of
Un. 64– 2 If sin has any pretence of e·,

existence

real
Mis. 30–14 understanding of man's real e·,
Ret. 21–14 not of man's real e·,
25–23 witnesses to . . . the real e· of
Un. 42– 7 can have no real e·,
realities of
Mis. 53– 2 spiritual realities of e·,
reality of
Mis. 24–18 the sole reality of e·.
Un. 49–11 eternal reality of e·
roving
My. 314– 5 * led a roving e·.
sense of
(see **sense**)
sensual side of
Peo. 1– 9 pass from the sensual side of e· to
so-called
Un. 58– 2 Mortals, if at ease in so-called e·,
spiritual
Mis. 17–28 primitive, sinless, spiritual e·
182–16 man's primal, spiritual e·,
Ret. 23–14 heart's bridal to more spiritual e·.
stages of
Mis. 56–28 successive stages of e·
statement of
Mis. 182–26 metaphysical statement of e·
state of
Mis. 34–19 in our present state of e·,
34–21 We may pass on to their state of e·,
42– 7 in a conscious state of e· ;
42–28 and recognize a better state of e·.
states of
Un. 49–17 two opposite states of e·.
supposed
No. 35–16 supposed e· apart from God.
supposition of the
Mis. 191–22 supposition of the e· of
196– 4 supposition of the e· of many minds
their
Mis. 105–29 and you destroy their e·.
My. 99–28 * their e· points out their meaning
Truth of
Mis. 182– 7 receive the Truth of e· ;
unlawful
Mis. 381–29 their unlawful e· destroyed,
unstimulating
My. 309–29 * a lonely and unstimulating e·.
310– 1 * "lonely and unstimulating e·."
weave an
Mis. 228–18 weave an e· fit for earth and
without
Un. 38– 9 is virtually without e·.
your
My. 226–23 depend on Him for your e·.

Mis. 131–18 it was not in e· all of the year.
Ret. 61– 7 a fear whose e· you do not realize ;
69–15 false sense of an e· which ends in
Rud. 4–26 testify to the e· of matter.
10–28 to believe in the e· of matter,
Hea. 10–14 of a good and a bad side to e·.
My. 217–19 * deny the e· of disease
217–21 We deny first the e· of disease,

existences
Un. 10– 3 these so-called e· I deny,

existent
Mis. 12–21 at former periods . . . were not e·.
Un. 46–14 taught no selfhood as e· in matter.

existing
Mis. 68–27 * causes of all things e·,"
Un. 37–20 E· here and now,
No. 9–18 e· wrongs of the nature referred to.
Pan. 2–18 * manifested in the e· universe."
My. 165–22 and my reason for e·.

exists
Mis. 10–32 that aught but good e· in Science.
25– 8 neither one really e·,
42–25 e· only in spiritual perfection,
72–26 it e· only to material sense.
93–20 and e· only as fable.
111–24 e· between the Catholic and Protestant
130–22 Where the motive to do right e·,
354–21 Principle of all that really e·,
Ret. 61–21 reveals the fact that, if suffering e·,
Un. 22–16 Whatever e· must come from God,
24–20 constitute all that e·.
31–12 claim of sin is, that matter e· ;
43–14 fact, as it e· in divine Science,
44–17 into everything that e·,
62–14 Sin e· only as a sense,
Pul. 66– 2 * e· as much to-day as it did when
No. 29– 6 believes that . . . Soul, e· in matter.
'01. 14– 6 Do . . . Scientists believe that evil e· ?

exists
'01. 23– 7 yet that evil e' and is
My. 95–25 * no religion . . . e' without faith
121–21 No deformity e' in honesty,
178–16 if evil e', it e' without God.
179–15 Some dangerous skepticism e'
180–30 No warfare e' between divine
211– 6 by denying that this evil e'.

exits
My. 68–28 * There are twelve e'

exodus
My. 82– 5 * chapter sub-title

Exodus 20: 3 — 17
Man. 63– 1 Ten Commandments (E' 20 : 3–17),

ex officio
My. 250– 9 their Readers will retire e' o',

exonerated
Man. 50–20 said member e', put on probation, or

exordium
My. 343– 5 * after a prolonged e'.

expand
My. 66–13 * will enable the church to e',

expanding
My. 63–13 * our e' consciousness of Truth,

expands
Mis. 175–13 as the leaven e' the loaf.
My. 202–28 but it e' as we walk in it.

expansion
Mis. 111– 7 extended it beyond safe e' ;
Ret. 52– 2 e' of scientific Mind-healing,
My. 164–23 e' that will engirdle the world,

expansive
My. 46– 2 * exquisite and e' auditorium,

expatiates
My. 129–27 e', strengthens, and exults.

expect
Mis. 7–12 where one would least e' it,
38– 6 is it unreasonable to e'
38– 9 should e' no compensation.
136– 1 this you must no longer e'.
195–14 does not authorize us to e' the
321–27 Do not e' me.
Ret. 65–27 As well e' to determine, without
65–28 e' to obtain health, harmony,
Rud. 14–17 yet will e' and require others to
No. 40– 4 mortals seek, and e' to receive,
40– 5 they e' also what is impossible,
Hea. 4–13 We e' infinite Love to
4–14 We e' infinite Truth to
4–17 We e' infinite Life to
15–18 but should you e' this when you
My. 21–17 * it is but right to e' that
51– 9 * should have reason to e',
147–31 must not e' me further to do
195–21 by which we poor mortals e'

expectancy
Mis. 342–11 Each moment's fair e' was
My. 230– 6 sweet in e' and bitter in experience

expectation
My. 10– 4 * enlarge the favorable e',
37–26 * confident and favorable e'.
54–20 * e' that some place would
173–20 number . . . exceeded my e',
208–14 waiting in due e' of
218–29 e' of receiving instruction

expectations
Mis. 224–18 with the smallest e',

expected
Mis. 130–19 it ought not to be e'
226–23 e' that from the violation of
302–10 e' to know the teaching of C. S.
Ret. 7–20 * e' no more than they realized
Rud. 13–25 not be e', more than others,
My. 10–20 * not e' to contribute money
216–27 it is to be e' you will feel more
225–23 e' to stick to their text,

expecting
Mis. 322– 6 e' to hear me speak

expedient
Man. 80–15 to the Board may seem e'.

expedition
My. 82–28 * with such remarkable e',

expelled
Mis. 249–21 e' from my College
'01. 17–26 the drug is utterly e',

expend
My. 20–14 what you would e' for presents
217– 1 money that you e' for flowers.

expended
Pul. 44–23 * quarter of a million dollars e'
My. 11–28 * the amount to be e'
12–12 * the amount to be e'
21– 2 * which they would have e'

expending
Ret. 84–30 e' his labor where there are other

expenditure
My. 20–25 * e' of a large amount of money,

expenditures
Man. 76–13 of its e' for the last year.
My. 23–11 * e' June 1, 1904 to May 31, 1905,
135–10 investments, deposits, e',
137–13 investments, deposits, e',

expense
Mis. 43–23 at the e' of his conscience,
135–14 to give one week's time and e'
Man. 96–12 unable to meet the e',
Pul. 62–18 * with infinitely less e'.
My. 75–29 * e' of its construction
83–31 * his or her share of the necessary e'

expenses
Man. 96– 6 E'.
96– 7 The lecturer's traveling e'
'02. 13– 1 to meet the e' involved.
My. 123–17 repairs and other necessary e'
214–25 to meet my own current e'.
215–29 with, provision for their e'

experience
and wisdom
My. 273–15 acquired by e' and wisdom,
another sphere of
Un. 3– 5 awake only to another sphere of e',
benefited by
Mis. 273– 3 neophyte will be benefited by e',
bitter in
My. 230– 7 sweet in expectancy and bitter in e'
bounds of
Mis. 68–31 * soars beyond the bounds of e',"
conscious
'01. 24– 1 * nothing more than conscious e'.
dwarf their
Mis. 278–26 and so dwarf their e'.
every
Mis. 86– 8 manifest growth at every e'.
fruit of
My. 343–24 each one was the fruit of e'
gathering
Ret. 27–25 gathering e' and confidence
has shown
Rud. 14–28 e' has shown that this defrauds
has taught
Ret. 87– 7 E' has taught me that the rules of
her
My. 81–30 * tells his or her e'.
his own
My. 84– 5 * can testify from his own e'
holy
My. 63–13 * this happy and holy e'
human
'00. 15–10 of all human e' is the most divine ;
is victor
Mis. 339– 6 E' is victor, never the vanquished ;
learned from
My. 21–14 * Scientists have learned from e'
43–10 * but they learned from e'
43–26 * We have learned from e',
learn from
Mis. 359–20 He had to learn from e' ;
mortal
Mis. 205– 7 In mortal e', the fire of
my
Mis. 382– 1 my e' would contradict it
My. 190– 9 My e' in both practices
319–28 * important one in my e',
my life's
My. 298– 4 occurred in my life's e'
need of
Mis. 73–16 we have need of e'.
observation and
Ret. 45–14 careful observation and e'
of many
My. 28– 6 * true in the e' of many
84– 9 * e' of many generations
our
Mis. 236– 3 Throughout our e'
past
Un. 14– 8 gain wisdom and power from past e'
personal
My. 105–32 from personal e' I have proved
proves
Mis. 309–13 E' proves this true.
recent
Ret. 48– 6 recent e' of the church

experience

religious
No.	12– 9	of the author's religious *e·*.
My.	311–14	my religious *e·* seemed to

rich in
Mis.	231– 4	grandmother, rich in *e·*,

sharp
Pan.	12–16	it lifteth the burden of sharp *e·*
My.	244–18	without a struggle or sharp *e·*,

short
Mis.	24–15	That short *e·* included a glimpse of

shows
Mis.	354–22	*E·* shows that humility is the first

some
Po.	v– 7	* *called forth by some e·*

standpoint of
No.	9–10	from their own standpoint of *e·*,

this
Mis.	212– 9	This *e·* caused them to remember
Pul.	34–22	* in reference to this *e·*.
	35–12	* In writing of this *e·*, Mrs. Eddy
	36–19	* always with this *e·* repeated.
My.	43–13	* this *e·* was almost as marvellous
	321–27	* have had this *e·*

verdict of
Mis.	73–18	Hence the verdict of *e·* :

wisdom or
Mis.	2– 4	have the least wisdom or *e·* ;

Mis.	124–29	to patience, *e·* ;
	124–29	to *e·*, hope ;
	149–10	what God has given him of *e·*,
	156–26	*E·* and, above all, *obedience,*
	293–12	*E·* weighs in the scales of God
	380–23	*E·*, however, taught me
Man.	63–24	shall have had *e·* in the Field,
Pul.	64– 7	* not the *e·* of Rev. Mary Baker Eddy.
'01.	27– 1	*e·*, and final discovery,
My.	107– 9	Here I speak from *e·*.
	205– 7	won through faith, prayer, *e·* ;

experience-acquired
My.	306–16	Age, with *e·* patience

experienced
Man.	86–11	can elect an *e·* Christian Scientist,
Ret.	14–19	*e·* a change of heart ;
'01.	2–21	What Jesus' disciples of old *e·*,
My.	21–21	* always *e·* much pleasure in

experiences
Mis.	165–22	by their own growth and *e·*.
Ret.	79– 4	from the *e·* of others.
Un.	7–19	in connection with these *e·* ;
Pul.	32–15	* translate those inner *e·*
	33–14	* *e·*, of which Catholic biographies
	33–27	* have had *e·* of voices or visions
	47– 9	* her *e·* as the pioneer of C. S.,
My.	64– 3	* her relation to the *e·* of the hour
	236–30	in their individual *e·*.

experiencing
Ret.	61– 7	*e·* the effect of a fear
My.	109– 4	mortals are *e·* the Adam-dream

experiment
Hea.	19– 1	felon was delivered to them for *e·*

experimental
Ret.	80–21	golden scholarship of *e·* tuition.

experimented
Mis.	249– 2	*e·* by taking some large doses of
	379–20	I had already *e·* in medicine

experiments
Mis.	117–22	and *e·* ofttimes are costly.
Hea.	13–18	After these *e·* you cannot

expert
My.	172–19	your kind, *e·* call on me."
	335–25	* an *e·* (Dr. McRee we think it was),
	335–31	* was told by the *e·* physician

experts
Man.	50– 2	shall be made by qualified *e·*.

expiate
Pul.	13–19	*e·* their sin through suffering.

expiration
Man.	39– 3	at the *e·* of said one year,
	69– 8	before the *e·* of the time
Ret.	21–11	and at its *e·* was appointed

expired
Mis.	381– 8	The time . . . having nearly *e·*,
'02.	13–19	After the mortgage had *e·*

expires
Mis.	341–27	so that the flame never *e·*.
Man.	30–19	attend to the insurance before it *e·*,

expiring
Po.	27–19	Thou fast *e·* year.

explain
Mis.	50– 6	Does "S. and H. . . . . *e·* the entire
	68–26	* object is to *e·* the principles
	83–10	*Will you please e· this seeming*
	84–19	*Please e· Paul's meaning in the*
	317–22	words of our Master *e·* this hour :
Ret.	24–18	I could not then *e·* the *modus*
	83–19	should *e·* only Recapitulation,
Pul.	69–16	* would take a small book to *e·* fully
No.	15– 9	to *e·* and prop old creeds,
'01.	4–23	should be able to *e·* God's
	5–29	to *e·* both His person and nature,
	32–18	*e·* in a few words a good man.
My.	105–28	*e·* to the world my curative system
	240– 7	* to *e·* more fully why you call
	317–13	would enable me to *e·* more clearly

explained
Mis.	30–27	is *e·* in the Scripture,
	143– 4	*e·* to the kind participants
	163–11	he *e·* the Word of God,
	169–31	passages *e·* metaphysically.
	170–31	*e·* as the putting forth of power,
My.	136– 5	it is best *e·* by its fruits,
	324–12	* you *e·* how long you had waited
	343– 5	* She *e·* : "No present change is
	344– 7	mystery is scientifically *e·*.

explaining
Mis.	265–21	thoroughly *e·* spiritual Truth
My.	59–15	* your words *e·* the Scriptures,
	151– 8	opportunity for *e·* C. S. :
	317–22	diction, as used in *e·* C. S.,

explains
Mis.	25–14	*e·* the teachings . . . of our Lord.
	35–26	author of that work, who *e·* it in detail.
	194–19	Scriptural text *e·* Jesus' words,
	258–30	*e·* the eternal dynamics of being,
Pan.	5–18	Jesus' definition . . . *e·* evil.
'01.	2–27	*e·* its rapid growth.
	5–29	God *e·* Himself in C. S.
	8–27	*e·* that mystic saying of the Master
	9– 2	*e·* it as referring to his eternal
	10–17	C. S. *e·* the nature of God
'02.	12– 3	*e·* these doctrinal points,
Hea.	15–12	*e·* to any one's perfect satisfaction
	17–15	*e·* this dream of material life,
My.	140–13	* Rev. Mary Baker Eddy *e·*
	275– 4	it *e·* love, it lives love,

explanation
Mis.	70– 6	its only *e·* in divine metaphysics.
	96–26	any conclusive idea in a brief *e·*.
	188–22	continues the *e·* of the power of Spirit
	220– 8	by audible *e·*, attestation, and
Man.	66–12	to await her *e·* thereof.
Ret.	78– 5	The textual *e·* of this practice
Pul.	60– 5	* *e·* of Bible or their textbook.
My.	146– 1	In *e·* of my dedicatory letter
	218– 2	in *e·* of his deeds he said,
	280–27	chapter sub-title

explanations
Mis.	92–15	Throughout his entire *e·*,
Ret.	84– 9	Throughout his entire *e·* he
My.	65–12	* beyond two brief *e·*

explanatory
Man.	32–21	no remarks *e·* of the Lesson-Sermon

explicitly
My.	199–14	show *e·* the attitude of this church

explored
Ret.	7–12	* *e·* their every nook and corner,

expose
Mis.	11–19	even try not to *e·* their faults,
	335–19	my wisdom or right to *e·* error,
Ret.	63–17	feel bound to *e·* this conspiracy,
Pul.	15– 3	*e·* evil's hidden mental ways
My.	212– 8	*e·* the cause and effects of this evil

exposed
Mis.	229– 5	*e·* to contact with healthy people,
My.	105–15	and *e·* the jugular vein

exposes
Mis.	363–26	*e·* the subtle sophist,
	367– 7	*e·* the lie of suppositional evil,

expositions
Mis.	322– 1	infinitely beyond all earthly *e·*
My.	179–30	*e·* of the therapeutics, ethics, and

expositor
Pan.	12– 4	scholarly *e·* of the Scriptures,
My.	181–28	one *e·* of Daniel's dates

exposure
Mis.	48– 8	praise for his public *e·* of it.
	129–26	spare his *e·* so long as a hope
Pul.	15– 5	since *e·* is necessary to ensure
No.	24–19	*e·* is nine points of destruction.

expound
  Ret. 36– 3 *e·* the gospel according to Jesus.
expounded
  Mis. 35–21 go to church to hear it *e·*
      176– 6 so deeply and solemnly *e·*
  My. 59– 4 * the truth you *e·*
expounder
  Ret. 14– 5 pastor was an old-school *e·* of
expounding
  Mis. 159– 2 reading the Scriptures and *e·* them ;
ex-President
  Mis. 306–20 * Mrs. Harrison, wife of the *e·*,
express
  Mis. 3– 2 *e·* these views as duty demands,
      26–25 phrase, ''*e·* image,''— *Heb.* 1 : 3.
      36– 7 Beasts, as well as men, *e·* Mind
      36–15 *e·* the lower qualities of the
      50–12 necessity to *e·* the metaphysical in
      74–25 recognize or *e·* pain and pleasure.
      78–27 *e·* the exact nature of its Principle,
      116–16 *e·* life's loss or gain,
      145– 5 need no organization to *e·* it.
      145– 7 to *e·* Soul and substance.
      149–18 *e·* the joy you give me
      181–10 *e·* the claims of the divine Principle.
      218–25 matter does not *e·* the nature of
      250– 8 What the lower propensities *e·*,
      262–22 more grateful than words can *e·*,
      309– 7 often fails to *e·* even mortal man,
      365–27 terms in which to *e·* what it means.
      375–27 * joy as no words can *e·*,
  Ret. 27–15 *e·* in feeble diction Truth's ultimate.
      27–23 can duly *e·* it to the ear,
      37– 3 to *e·* the divine, or spiritual,
  Un. 50–14 to *e·* the underlying thought.
  Pul. 81– 7 * *e·* image of God for love.
  No. 39– 1 if the lips try to *e·* it.
  '01. 7–13 *e·* the different mentalities of man
  '02. 16–23 *e·* the life of Godlikeness.
  Peo. 14– 1 *e·* them by objects more beautiful.
  My. 24– 5 * to *e·* in its ample auditorium
      42–15 * *e·* my thanks for the honor
      44–28 * *e·* their continued loyalty
      62–22 * *e·* our thankful appreciation
      82–12 * secured *e·* wagons enough
      123– 5 gifts which would *e·* it.
      164– 8 to *e·* my thanks for your
      195–10 I have not had time to *e·*,
      197–10 * my deep appreciation
      234– 8 wherein to *e·* this love
      262–29 *e·* my conception of Truth's
      305– 8 *e·* myself unmistakably
      317–18 * wouldn't *e·* it that way.''
      318– 1 capitalization, in order to *e·*
      331–21 * *e·* the feeling of gratitude
      352– 5 * desire to *e·* our recognition of
expressed
  Mis. 4–19 interest is awakened and *e·*
      102–17 His pity is *e·* in modes above the
      102–20 fully *e·* in divine Science,
      134– 3 as you have *e·* contrition
      142–17 Because your dear hearts *e·*
      170–27 *e·* contempt for the belief of
      171–11 *e·* in literal or physical terms,
      177– 7 *e·* and operative in C. S.
      193–16 clergyman charitably *e·* it,
      273– 8 *e·* so grateful a sense of my
      280–24 *e·* his fellow-students' thanks
      344– 3 *e·* the wish to become one of
  Ret. 80– 7 different languages have *e·* it :
  Un. 55–20 as *e·* in his conviction,
  Pul. vii–20 *e·* in the absolute power of Truth
      61–21 * Much admiration was *e·*
      66–15 * Bible as *e·* in its poetical
      84–19 * It can be better felt than *e·*.
  My. 8–13 * *e·* the universal voice of
      11–16 * she *e·* much gratification
      24–13 * purpose which is thus *e·*,
      52–14 * taught and *e·* by our pastor,
      60–10 * *e·* the thought of all the
      106–19 *e·* in disease, sin, and death,
      157–16 * *e·* wish of Mrs. Eddy,
      219–26 *e·* my opinion publicly
      252–25 It *e·* your thanks,
      320– 8 * He also *e·* himself freely
      338– 8 * uniformly held and *e·* by her.
expresses
  Mis. 67–25 *e·* the sense of words
      218–23 a grin *e·* the nature of a cat,
  Pul. 53–16 * *e·* the whole law of
      65–27 * *e·* the faith of those who
      75– 1 Whoever in any age *e·* most
  No. 10– 9 unfolds, and *e·* the ALL-God.
  '01. 3–23 Love *e·* the nature of God ;

expresses
  '01. 3–26 *e·* God only in metaphor,
  My. 76–12 * feebly *e·* the gratification.
expressing
  Mis. 170–26 method of *e·* the utmost contempt.
  My. 289–13 *e·* our deep sympathy with the
      323–19 * *e·* the crowding thoughts of
      332– 3 * *e·* the feelings of a swelling bosom.
expression
  Mis. 4–28 we meet with an *e·* of incredulity.
      247–26 body is an *e·* of mind,
      373– 6 my sense of Soul's *e·*
  Ret. 27–27 written *e·* increases in power
  Pul. 21–24 a clear *e·* of God's likeness,
      32– 6 * beautiful complexion and changeful *e·*
      38–28 * higher spirituality seeking *e·*.
      67–14 * to give *e·* to a higher spirituality.
  No. 2– 2 that crystallized *e·*, C. S.
      11– 8 In its literary *e·*, my system
  Pan. 8– 4 find *e·* in sun worship, lunacy,
  Peo. 4–15 the error . . . obtained *e·*.
  My. 8–10 * the best *e·* of the religion of
      90– 6 * in the history of religious *e·*.
      189–27 gave *e·* to a poem written in 1844,
      248–30 nearest the scientific *e·* of Truth.
      267–30 divine modes, means, forms, *e·*,
      276–21 * an *e·* of her political views,
      281–19 * for the *e·* of congratulations
      346–13 * same *e·* of looking forward,
expressionless
  Mis. 376–11 * *e·* copies of an engraving
expressions
  Mis. 275–24 *e·* of love and loyalty
  My. 31–15 * *e·* of surprise and of admiration
      87–24 * gives such serene, beautiful *e·*,
expressive
  Mis. 124–21 *e·* silence wherein to muse His
  Un. 44–17 whether or not *e·* of the Mind
  Pul. 2– 2 In the *e·* language of Holy Writ,
  My. 124–22 *E·* silence, or with finger pointing
expunged
  Ret. 22– 2 and the material record *e·*.
exquisite
  Ret. 17–14 To sprinkle the flowers with *e·* dye.
  Po. 62–17 To sprinkle the flowers with *e·* dye.
  My. 46– 2 * in *e·* and expansive auditorium,
      347–10 The *e·* design of boughs
extant
  Ret. 36– 9 unpublished manuscripts *e·*,
extemporaneously
  My. 354–26 * above lines were written *e·*
Extempore
  Mis. 176– 5 *E·* REMARKS
  My. 354–13 poem
extend
  Mis. 32–16 My sympathies *e·* to the
      98–13 to quicken and *e·* the interest
      227–10 to *e·* their evil intent,
      311– 6 I would *e·* a tender invitation to
  Man. 58–16 shall *e·* from Genesis to Revelation.
  Un. 46–22 must *e·* throughout the universe,
  Pul. 86–26 * *e·* to you the invitation
  No. 14–22 but they *e·* to this age,
  '01. 1– 1 I *e·* my heart-and-hand-fellowship to
  Peo. 8–10 *e·* their influence to others.
  My. 331–14 * *e·* such unrestrained hospitality
extended
  Mis. 111– 7 *e·* it beyond safe expansion ;
  Man. 18– 5 *e·* a call to Mary Baker Eddy
  Ret. 16–18 *e·* a call to Mary B. G. Eddy
      44– 6 *e·* a call to me
  No. 15–11 should not these be equally *e·* to
  '01. 1– 7 new century finds C. S. more *e·*,
  Hea. 18–20 Jesus' mission *e·* to the sick
  My. v– 8 * *e·* to this people by other Christian
      49–10 * members *e·* a unanimous invitation to
      51–20 * an invitation was *e·* to Mrs. Eddy
      173– 7 generous hospitality *e·*
      174– 6 courtesy *e·* to my friends
      174– 9 courtesy . . . *e·* to me throughout.
      326– 5 * not because a favor has been *e·*,
      331–24 * *e·* their care and sympathy
      331–30 * sympathy *e·* to her after his death,
extends
  Mis. 189–30 it *e·* to all time,
      192–26 salvation, that *e·* to all ages
      265–18 which *e·* along the whole line of
extension
  Mis. 364–15 thought, *e·*, cause, and effect ;
  Un. 7– 3 glorified in the wide *e·* of belief
  No. 21– 9 space, immortality, thought, *e·*.

extension

No.	24– 5	He is *e·*, of whatever character.
My.	3– 2	chapter sub-title
	6–19	its excelsior *e·* is the crown.
	24–19	* progress of the work on the *e·*
	26– 4	* *e·* of The Mother Church
	27–11	* fund for the *e·* of The
	27–25	* all bills in connection with the *e·*
	29– 8	* dedicatory services of the *e·*
	29–26	* dedication of the *e·* of The
	38–29	* in the *e·* of The Mother Church.
	40– 1	* completed *e·* of The Mother Church
	42–21	* in the *e·* of The Mother Church.
	58– 5	* *e·* of The Mother Church,
	61–10	* held in the new *e·* on June 10.
	62–21	* completion of the magnificent *e·*
	63–11	* dedication of the *e·*
	67– 4	* chapter sub-title
	67– 5	* *E·* of The Mother Church
	76–19	* estimated cost of the *e·*
	80–10	* Meetings were held in the *e·*
	80–11	* in the *e·* vestry,
	80–22	* the *e·* of The Mother Church,
	82–15	* services of The Mother Church *e·*
	96– 3	* dedication of the *e·* of The
	96–28	* known as The Mother Church *e·*

extensive

Mis.	88–12	reading, writing, *e·* travel,
Pul.	57–21	* Few people . . . realize how *e·* is
My.	309–18	an *e·* farm situated in Bow

extent

Mis.	7–22	will counteract to some *e·* this
	46– 8	to an *e·* beyond the power of
	55– 5	to the *e·* that Jesus did,
	64–23	and languages, to a limited *e·*,
	366–23	To a greater or less *e·*,
Un.	29– 5	all criminal law, to a certain *e·*.
Pul.	65– 4	* penetrated . . . to an unlooked-for *e·*.
No.	9– 3	would have prevented, to a great *e·*,
'01.	5–23	to the *e·* of extinguishing
	22– 3	to some *e·* a Christian Scientist.
My.	90–31	* the efficacy of which to some *e·* is
	357–15	demonstrate C. S. to a higher *e·*,

exterminate

Mis.	348– 9	uncover iniquity, in order to *e·* it,
'00.	8–21	We must *e·* self

exterminated

No.	31–21	as mortal beliefs to be *e·*.
'00.	10–17	error repeats itself until it is *e·*.
My.	268–11	Divorce and war should be *e·*
	277–17	wrong and injustice are . . . *e·*.

exterminating

My.	248–23	*e·* sin and suffering

external

'01.	23–26	of an *e·* material world.
My.	88–16	* remarkable *e·* manifestations
	121–19	*e·* gentility and good humor

externalized

My.	10– 6	* impulse for good . . . *e·* itself,

externals

My.	88–17	* *e·* constitute the smallest feature

extinction

Un.	18– 2	and evil necessarily leads to *e·*
'01.	20–22	till he suffers up to its *e·*

extinguish

Mis.	199–17	*e·* whatever denied and defied
	337–22	and thus seem to *e·* it.
	364–29	would either *e·* God and
No.	28– 1	would *e·* human existence.
	32– 6	can neither *e·* a crime nor the

extinguished

Mis.	84–22	so far *e·* the latter as
	187–26	never *e·* in a night of discord.
	209–23	but are punished before *e·*.
'00.	8–24	and the fire . . . will be *e·*.

extinguishes

Ret.	81–10	*e·* false thinking,
Rud.	4–23	*e·* forever the works of darkness

extinguishing

'01.	5–23	to the extent of *e·* anything that

extolling

Mis.	372– 9	letters *e·* it were pouring in

extra

Mis.	143–25	for this *e·* contribution,
	285–22	some *e·* throe of error may
My.	73–27	* *e·* sections of trains are due

extract

Mis.	106–15	chapter sub-title
	148– 7	chapter sub-title
	159–10	chapter sub-title
	171–21	chapter sub-title

extract

Mis.	375– 8	*e·* from a letter reverting to
Man.	3– 1	heading
Ret.	5–17	following is a brief *e·* from
Pul.	40– 8	* from *Boston Herald*
	44–16	* from *Boston Sunday Globe*
	50–10	* from *Boston Transcript*
	52– 9	* from *Jackson Patriot*
	63– 2	* from *The Republic*
	64–23	* from *New York Tribune*
	65–11	* from *Journal*, Kansas City, Mo.
	67– 2	* from *Montreal Daily Herald*
	68–13	* from *The American*, Baltimore, Md.
	70– 2	* from *The Reporter*, Lebanon, Ind.
	75–14	* from *The Globe*, Toronto, Canada
	79– 2	* from *The Union Signal*, Chicago
	84–10	* from *Christian Science Journal*
No.	43–12	following *e·* from a letter
My.	7– 3	from Mrs. Eddy's Message, June 1902.
	16– 1	* chapter sub-title
	22– 2	* *E·* from the Clerk's Report
	23– 9	* *E·* from the Treasurer's Report
	241–11	* *e·* from a letter to Mrs. Eddy,
	254–19	* following *e·* from your article
	334–26	* *e·* from an editorial
	341–18	* from *New York Herald*
	353– 6	*E·* from the leading Editorial

extracted

Mis.	44–14	*until I have the tooth e·,*
	44–24	if the tooth were *e·*,

extracting

Mis.	44–15	*has the mind, or e·, or both,*

extracts

Mis.	168–21	chapter sub-title
	216– 9	some *e·* from, "Scientific Theism,"
	216–19	One of these *e·* is the story of
My.	17–27	* *e·* from Mrs. Eddy's writings
	303–12	of which I have seen only *e·*,
	336–19	* These letters and *e·* are of

extra-natural

Mis.	88–23	* supernatural, or *e·*,

extraordinary

My.	vi–10	* full credit for this *e·* work.
	69– 2	* one of the *e·* features is
	86–17	* regarded as an *e·* achievement,
	272–24	* communication from the *e·* woman

extravagant

Mis.	64–16	theories are narrow, else *e·*,

extreme

Mis.	42– 8	a moment of *e·* mortal fear,
	112–15	in *e·* cases, moral idiocy.
	112–24	shows itself in *e·* sensitiveness ;
	215– 3	go from one *e·* to another :
Pul.	14– 6	another *e·* mortal mood,
	14– 7	one *e·* follows another.
	80– 3	* pendulum that has swung to one *e·*
My.	89–11	* to achieve its *e·* of beauty.

extremes

Mis.	206– 4	from *e·* to intermediate.
	353– 3	Human concepts run in *e·* ;
My.	265–27	*e·* of heat and cold ;

extremists

Mis.	374–23	*E·* . . . either doggedly deny or

exuberant

Mis.	231– 3	infancy, *e·* with joy,
Rud.	15– 8	satisfies the thought with *e·* joy.

exudes

Mis.	144–27	*e·* the inspiration of the wine

exultant

Ret.	32– 8	*E·* hope, if tinged with earthliness
My.	201–29	Hope springs *e·* on this blest morn.

exultation

My.	63–16	* to repress a feeling of *e·*

exults

My.	129–27	expatiates, strengthens, and *e·*.

ex-Vice-President General, D. A. R.

Mis.	306–11	* MARY DESHA, *e· G·*, D. A. R.

eye (*see also* eye's)

blue

Mis.	330–28	violet lifts its blue *e·* to heaven,

bright

Po.	27–17	and right with bright *e·* wet,

dewy

Po.	73–12	Night's dewy *e·*,

God's

Po.	18–13	God's *e·* is upon him.
	19– 3	God's *e·* is upon me

hath not seen

Mis.	82–12	what *e·* hath not seen.
	205–18	*e·* hath not seen it,
Un.	28–22	"*e·* hath not seen, — *I Cor. 2 : 9.*

eye

his
Mis. 354–26 the eagle, his e· on the sun,
    354–30 No tear dims his e·,
Po. 18– 7 Would a tear dim his e·,

his own
Mis. 212–27 cast the beam out of his own e·,

mind's
Pul. 2–15 With the mind's e· glance at the

mine
Mis. 389–10 only with mine e· Can I behold
Po. 4– 9 only with mine e· Can I behold
My. 109–17 "But now mine e· — *Job* 42 : 5.

my
Pul. 48–21 * my e· caught her family coat of arms

of day
Po. 8–10 Ravished with beauty the e· of day.

pitying
Mis. 228–13 We should look with pitying e· on
    386–11 looks on her heart with pitying e·,
Po. 49–17 looks on her heart with pitying e·,

Reader's
My. 81–10 * first to catch the Reader's e·.

seeing with the
Rud. 5–21 this belief of seeing with the e·,

spiritual
Po. 32–11 illumines my spiritual e·,

thine own
Mis. 355–21 out of thine own e·." — *Matt.* 7 : 5.

to eye
Mis. 117–15 We see e· to eye and know as we

watchful
Po. 9– 1 her husband's watchful e·

your own
Mis. 336–14 the beam in your own e·

Mis. 58–15 As matter, the e· cannot see ;
Rud. 5–13 who has ever seen . . . with the e·,
Po. 70– 8 glory that e· cannot see.
My. 29–16 * appealed more to the e·,
    184– 5 neither hath the e· seen, what God

eye's
Un. 34– 5 pictured on the e· retina.

eyes

admiring
My. 86– 1 * greeting of admiring e·,

all
My. 77– 1 * the cynosure of all e·

blind man's
Mis. 171– 6 anoint the blind man's e· with

blind the
Mis. 301–29 blind the e·, stop the ears

blue
Pul. 32– 2 * lighted by luminous blue e·,
Po. 74– 5 O blue e· and jet,

closed
'02. 9–24 opened my closed e·.

earnest
Po. 23– 7 give those earnest e· yet back

face and
Mis. 285–27 in the face and e· of common law,

green
Mis. 129–18 for other green e· to gaze on :

half open
Mis. 325–18 with e· half open, the porter

having
Mis. 58–13 "Having e·, see ye not?" — *Mark* 8 : 18.
    99– 4 "Having e· ye see not, — *see Mark* 8 : 18.
    170–29 Having e·, ye see not ;

her
Mis. 58–12 *She had to use her e· to read.*
    366–17 needs to get her e· open
Ret. 16– 5 tears of joy flooding her e·

his
Mis. 83–24 lifted up his e· to heaven,
    212–26 open his e· to see this error
    325–20 calls out, rubs his e·,
    371– 5 opened his e· to see the need of

his
Ret. 86–13 and the tears from his e·,
Hea. 19– 9 removed the bandage from his e·,

material
Mis. 170–28 belief of material e· as having any

mine
My. 188– 4 mine e· and mine heart — *I Kings* 9 : 3.
    188– 6 mine e· shall be open, — *II Chron.* 7 : 15.

my
Mis. 277–24 No evidence . . . can close my e· to
My. 61–15 * I raised my e·,

of Eve
Mis. 86–18 more earthly to the e· of Eve.

of My children
Un. 18–12 tears from the e· of My children.

of reason
Mis. 332–20 blinded the e· of reason,

of sinful mortals
No. 7–10 e· of sinful mortals must be opened

of the blind
Mis. 307–17 God's love opening the e· of the blind
    368– 5 open the e· of the blind,
My. 183–20 e· of the blind see out of obscurity.
    270–27 opening the e· of the blind

of Truth
Mis. 233–17 worse in the e· of Truth

one's
My. 213–15 Unless one's e· are opened to the

opened the
My. 97–21 * has opened the e· of the country

opens the
Mis. 210–30 Love opens the e· of the blind,

open the
Mis. 48–20 to open the e· of the people
    211– 6 to open the e· of others,
    277–18 open the e· to the truth of
    368– 5 open the e· of the blind,
Pul. 15– 1 to open the e· of the people

other
Mis. 336–16 mote of evil out of other e·.

our
Mis. 9–19 to fall in fragments before our e·.

pure
'01. 15–28 * provoking His pure e· by

purer
'01. 15–25 * He is of purer e· than to bear to
My. 300– 1 "of purer e· than to — *Hab.* 1 : 13.

sore
Mis. 71– 8 that he had sore e· ;

sparkling
Mis. 240– 4 bounding with sparkling e·,

suffused
Mis. 239–18 red nose, suffused e·, cough,

tear-filled
Mis. 231–30 tear-filled e· looking longingly

tears flood the
Mis. 203–22 Tears flood the e·, agony struggles,

their
Mis. 253–29 opened their e· to the light
Ret. 64–26 must first open their e·
'00. 9–10 shut their e· and wait for a
My. 79– 3 * kneeling . . . their e· closed

those
My. 342–12 * those e· the shade of which

wet
My. 326–16 with wet e· the Free Masons

your
Mis. 57–18 your e· shall be opened, — *Gen.* 3 : 5.
    196–10 shall open your e·
Un. 44–21 your e· shall be opened — *Gen.* 3 : 5.

My. 33–22 In whose e· a vile person — *Psal.* 15 : 4.
    342–12 * there is no mistaking the e·

eyesight
Mis. 58–17 through a belief of e· ;

Ezekiel
Mis. 72–12 saith, through the prophet E·,

F

F——, Mrs. M. A.
Mis. 243–11 Reference, Mrs. M. A. F·,

Faber
Pul. 28–23 * F·, Robertson, Wesley, Bowring,

fable
Mis. 93–21 and exists only as f·.
    309– 8 its unfitness for f· or fact
Un. 44–13 This abortive ego, this f· of error,
No. 4–13 error of thought becomes f·
My. 301–18 insanity which mistakes f· for fact

fables
Mis. 64–20 resist speculative opinions and f·.
    191–31 St. Paul's injunction to reject f·,
    342–20 no light ! earth's f· flee,
Ret. 30–15 the foibles and f· of finite mind
My. 189–19 to see how soon earth's f· flee
    340– 7 to traditions, old-wives' f·,

fabric
Mis. 228–17 as the only suitable f·
Pul. 8–26 in the f· of this history,
No. 43–19 or think to build a baseless f·

fabrication
Mis. 48–30 baseless *f·* offered solely to injure
    334–10 whole *f·* is found to be a lie,
Pul. 2–29 true temple is no human *f·*,
My. 14–19 * pronounced the story a *f·*

fabulous
Peo. 12–11 Deal, then, with this *f·* law

Fabyan House
My. 185–23 in the hall at the *F· H·*.

Fabyans, N. H.
My. 314–32 White Mountain House, *F·, N. H.,*

facades
My. 78–10 * arches in the several *f·*.

face
and eyes
Mis. 285–27 in the *f·* and eyes of common law,
and form
My. 259–2 sweetest sculptured *f·* and form
answereth to
Mis. 152–3 *f·* answereth to *f·,"* — *Prov.* 27 : 19.
    203–9 *f·* answereth to *f·,* — *Prov.* 27 : 19.
familiar
Mis. 177–29 greets with joy a familiar *f·*.
her
Pul. 32–1 * her *f·*, framed in dark hair
My. 346–15 * expression of . . . was on her *f·*.
human
Po. v–12 * *resemble the profile of a human f·*.
its
Pul. 78–6 * bears upon its *f·* the following
lit up
Peo. 7–10 * his *f·* lit up with a smile of joy
looks out
Mis. 324–11 from the window . . . a *f·* looks out,
my
Mis. 133–23 my *f·* toward the Jerusalem of Love
of Dante
No. 18–17 may imagine the *f·* of Dante to be
of Jesus
Mis. 309–9 The *f·* of Jesus has uniformly
No. 18–18 the rapt *f·* of Jesus.
of mortals
Mis. 332–21 shamed the *f·* of mortals.
of the earth
Peo. 6–9 * on the *f·* of the earth,
of the Nazarite
Mis. 374–21 the *f·* of the Nazarite Prophet ;
of the skies
Mis. 347–9 They who discern the *f·* of the skies
of the sky
Mis. 1–7 discern the *f·* of the sky ;— *Matt.* 16 : 3.
one
Pul. 39–25 * 'mid them all I only see *one f·*,
portray the
No. 39–27 portray the *f·* of pleasant thought.
shining
My. 355–20 * He hides a shining *f·*."
sweet
Mis. 239–17 Just then a tiny, sweet *f·* appeared
thy
My. 34–9 seek thy *f·*, O Jacob.— *Psal.* 24 : 6.
to face
Mis. 16–30 you stand *f·* to face with the laws of
    359–11 but then *f·* to face." — *I Cor.* 13 : 12.
young
Po. 9–3 I'm picturing alone a glad young *f·*,

Mis. 99–17 take the front rank, *f·* the foe,
    112–5 look the illusions in the *f·*.
    225–26 The deep flush faded from the *f·*,
    376–4 **f·*, figure, and drapery of Jesus,
    376–6 **f·*, figure, and drapery of that
    376–8 * the *f·* having been taken by
My. 99–30 * at their *f·* value.
    248–26 *f·* the foe with loving look

faces
'00. 1–3 and can see your glad *f·*,
'02. 20–21 to look into the *f·* of my
My. 48–32 * already manifest in their *f·*,
    74–20 * but reflected in their *f·*,
    79–4 * little *f·* turned upward.
    81–5 * No pessimistic *f·* there !
    87–22 * Their happy *f·* would make
    124–8 garlanded with glad *f·*,
    355–22 *f·* shine with the reflection of

facetiousness
My. 93–20 * with the tongue of *f·*.

facilities
'02. 10–1 *f·* for knowing and doing good,
My. 67–11 * Checking *f· . . .* 3,000 garments
    82–24 * Transportation *f·* at the two
    87–2 * transportation *f·* of the town

facing
'01. 29–22 won for them by *f·* the winds.

facsimile
Pul. 85–28 **f·* of the corner-stone of
    86–8 **f·* signatures of the Directors,
My. 272–21 **f·* of an article sent to us

fact
accessory to the
Mis. 119–8 punish . . . as accessory to the *f·*.
against the
Un. 36–5 false witness against the *f·*
change the
Mis. 298–30 false . . . does not change the *f·*,
confirms the
'02. 8–14 confirms the *f·* that God and Love
curious
Pul. 23–19 * History shows the curious *f·*
dangerous
Un. 54–13 is to admit a dangerous *f·*.
determine the
No. 42–18 power to determine the *f·*
eternal
My. 143–16 stands the eternal *f·* of C. S.
fable for
My. 301–19 which mistakes fable for *f·*
fable or
Mis. 309–8 for fable or *f·* to build upon.
faith in the
Mis. 77–4 faith in the *f·* that Jesus was the
far from the
My. 206–16 far from the *f·* that portrays Life,
final
Mis. 63–18 and understand the final *f·*,
forcible
My. 108–12 consists in this forcible *f·* :
forever
Mis. 287–3 forever *f·* that man is eternal
My. 41–6 * forever *f·* that the meek and lowly
    226–17 would remain the forever *f·*,
foundation in
Mis. 108–9 being without foundation in *f·*,
fundamental
Mis. 75–8 I urge this fundamental *f·*
'00. 4–30 enunciates this fundamental *f·*
further
My. 20–26 * further *f·* that it is important
great
Mis. 8–4 to the general thought this great *f·*
    16–17 great *f·* that *God is the only Life;*
    24–15 included a glimpse of the great *f·*
    43–1 demonstrating this great *f·*.
    181–23 The apostle urges . . . this great *f·* :
Ret. 73–9 great *f·* leads into profound depths.
No. 24–26 great *f·* concerning all error
Peo. 9–25 whereby we learn the great *f·*
    12–8 When this great *f·* is understood,
My. 116–5 this great *f·* in C. S. realized
    266–20 since this great *f·* is to be verified
ignorant of the
Mis. 295–23 Nor is the world ignorant of the *f·*
important
Mis. 65–19 and this important *f·* must be,
instead of
No. 4–14 becomes fable instead of *f·*.
is found out
Hea. 13–8 until the *f·* is found out
is made obvious
Ret. 64–12 In C. S. the *f·* is made obvious
matter of
My. 14–24 * As a matter of *f·*, the building fund
    310–10 As a matter of *f·*, he was
metaphysical
Mis. 237–3 yielded . . . to the metaphysical *f·*
must be denied
Un. 54–13 Hence the *f·* must be denied ;
no evidence of the
Hea. 5–16 we have no evidence of the *f·*
notable
'00. 6–17 This notable *f·* proves that the
noticeable
Mis. 6–25 It is a noticeable *f·*,
notwithstanding the
My. 11–1 * Notwithstanding the *f·* that as
of being
Mis. 186–25 is not the scientific *f·* of being ;
My. 109–6 not the spiritual *f·* of being.
of divine substance
Mis. 68–1 up to the . . . *f·* of divine substance,
of its nothingness
Mis. 93–25 sin and the *f·* of its nothingness,
one
Un. 55–1 accepted the one *f·* whereby
one more
Mis. 277–20 * one more *f·* to be recorded

fact

opposite to the
Mis. 133– 5 ideas more opposite to the *f·*.
overlook the
My. 227–17 should not overlook the *f·* that
prove the
Mis. 45– 1 prove the *f·* that Mind is supreme.
really remains
Un. 62– 1 when the *f·* really remains,
recognizes the
Mis. 33–26 recognizes the *f·* that, as mortal
255–23 recognizes the *f·* that the antidote
recognize the
My. 85–12 * to recognize the *f·* that
remains
Mis. 372– 4 *f·* remains, that the textbook
Hea. 6–20 the *f·* remains, in metaphysics,
rests in the
My. 204– 2 rests in the *f·* that He is infinite
rests on the
Un. 31–17 rests on the *f·* that matter usurps
reveals the
Ret. 61–21 C. S. reveals the *f·* that,
No. 28–16 reveals the *f·* that Truth is
sad
Mis. 43–17 sad *f·* at this early writing is,
scientific
Mis. 186–25 not the scientific *f·* of being ;
Ret. 94– 2 perceived, . . . this scientific *f·*,
self-evident
My. 302– 8 self-evident *f·* is proof that
shocking
My. 276–11 resigned to the shocking *f·*
significant
Pul. 79–12 * significant *f·* that one cannot
simple
Mis. 22–29 simple *f·* cognized by the senses,
so-called
Un. 54– 9 does not destroy the so-called *f·*
spiritual
Mis. 42–22 and the spiritual *f·* of Life is,
My. 109– 6 not the spiritual *f·* of being.
state the
Pul. 80–18 * but simply state the *f·*.
that evil
'01. 14–12 takes hold of the *f·* that evil
that Mind
Mis. 35– 2 *f·* that Mind, instead of matter,
this
Mis. 27–16 Scriptures maintain this *f·*.
54–10 they bear witness to this *f·*.
62–21 acknowledges this *f·* in her work
82– 4 Understanding this *f·* in C. S.,
221–19 denial of this *f·* in one instance
289–15 This *f·* should be duly considered
Man. 66– 3 shall inform her of this *f·*
89–16 as are required to verify this *f·*,
Ret. 82–18 This *f·* interferes in no way with
Un. 7–23 realization of this *f·* dispels even
No. 6–27 This *f·* intimates that the laws of
'02. 3– 2 bear testimony to this *f·*.
My. 83– 1 * This *f·* will be due to
117–25 Christian Scientists ponder this *f·*,
251–29 Cherish steadfastly this *f·*.
275– 6 senses do not perceive this *f·* until
unfolds the
Mis. 218– 2 Science unfolds the *f·* that Deity
was heralded
My. 79–15 * *f·* was heralded in flaming
welcome the
My. 52–12 * welcome the *f·* of the spreading
well-known
My. 145–21 This well-known *f·* makes me
witnesses of the
Mis. 150–23 with living witnesses of the *f·*

Mis. 334– 6 in *f·*, no intelligence ;
351– 4 *f·* is, that for want of time,
367– 6 *f·* of there being no mortal mind,
Ret. 33–13 a *f·* which seems to prove
Un. 1–15 In *f·*, they had better leave the
43–14 I insist only upon the *f·*,
Pul. 67– 7 * *f·* borne out by circumstances.
71–13 * in *f·* all over the country,
Rud. 6–16 *f·* "almost universally accepted,
My. 20–23 * In view of the *f·* that a general
24–20 * in *f·*, it is being pushed
27–26 * *f·* that he has been able to
38–13 * in spite of the *f·* that many
58– 3 * The *f·* that a notice was published
71–19 * In *f·*, nearly all the traditions of
87–16 * the *f·* that they have their costly
96–31 * The *f·* is that C. S. just
110–14 in *f·*, all the *et cetera* of mortal
214–21 I was confronted with the *f·* that I
275–15 *f·* that I am well and keenly alive

fact

My. 302–14 It is a *f·* well understood that I
328–12 * *f·* that the law recognizes them
335–27 * he could not conceal the *f·* that
339–29 *f·* that he healed the sick man

factions

Rud. 16–24 opposing *f·*, springing up
No. 9– 3 the *f·* which have sprung up
Hea. 2– 4 religious *f·* and prejudices
My. 213– 5 starts *f·* and engenders envy

factor

Mis. 13–15 proposition that evil is a *f·*
Pul. 4–12 is as important a *f·* as
37– 5 * *f·* in her removal to Concord,

factors

Mis. 71–19 not the *f·* of divine presence
Un. 26–19 can it be . . . are universal *f·*,
Pul. 23–17 * one of the most potent *f·*
My. 355–10 important *f·* in our field of labor

facts

additional
My. 335–11 * Additional *f·* regarding Major Glover,
all
My. 89– 4 * all *f·* inhospitable to it
and figures
My. 99–27 * *F·* and figures are stubborn things,
100– 2 * some of the *f·* and figures belonging
based on the
Mis. 55–16 *Is C. S. based on the f· of both*
55–18 C. S. is based on the *f·* of Spirit
broad
My. 194– 2 which Christianity writes in broad *f·*
circumstances and
Mis. 146–10 circumstances and *f·* regarding both
con the
Pul. vii–17 to con the *f·* surrounding the
deal with
Mis. 64–19 are those which deal with *f·*
demonstrate the
Ret. 78–19 an attempt to demonstrate the *f·*
dispute the
'02. 10– 7 dispute the *f·*, call them false
following
My. 314–18 and who know the following *f·* :
foundational
Mis. 200–18 foundational *f·* of C. S.
given
My. 336–20 * the *f·* given by Mrs. Eddy
historical
My. v–13 * recalling the following historical *f·* :
immortal
Mis. 14– 5 take in only the immortal *f·*
interesting
My. 329–27 * put before them some interesting *f·*
misrepresent
Mis. 109– 3 Beware of those who misrepresent *f·* ;
momentous
Mis. 379–28 momentous *f·* relating to Mind
No. 28– 9 these momentous *f·* in the Science
nor supported by
Mis. 93–20 nor supported by *f·*,
of being
Mis. 37– 7 spiritual *f·* of being.
187–26 primal *f·* of being are eternal ;
234–24 into the spiritual *f·* of being
Un. 51– 1 everlasting *f·* of being appear,
of day
My. 110–21 unfold in part the *f·* of day,
of existence
Mis. 14–16 knowing the *f·* of existence
of Science
Mis. 183–30 with the *f·* of Science,
Un. 30– 5 spiritual *f·* of Science,
of Spirit
Mis. 55–18 C. S. is based on the *f·* of Spirit
of Truth
Mis. 352– 8 able to behold the *f·* of Truth
opposite
Un. 36– 9 opposite *f·*, or phenomena.
real
No. 31–10 never actual persons or real *f·*.
rehearsing
Mis. 311–31 rehearsing *f·* concerning others
self-evident
Un. 25– 4 and dispute self-evident *f·* ;
so-called
Mis. 55–20 so-called *f·* of matter ;
some
My. 319–16 * I am conversant with some *f·*
speak
My. 84– 1 * *f·* speak more plainly than
spiritual
     (see **spiritual**)

facts

testimony to the
Man. 93–14   to bear testimony to the *f·*
these
Mis. 24– 1   These *f·* enjoin the
    55–20   these *f·* are the direct antipodes of
My. 314–28   related these *f·* to her
two
Hea. 7–24   two *f·*, so important to progress

Mis. 101–29   *f·* that disprove the evidence of
  105– 2   *f·* of man's spirituality,
My. vi– 1   * *f·* which prove, (1) that S. and H.
  124–25   *f·* relating to the thitherward,
  311–18   *f·* regarding the McNeil coat-of-arms
  322– 4   * *f·* which cannot be controverted
  332–19   * *f·* regarding Major Glover's
  359–12   desires to inform himself of the *f·*.

faculties

Mis. 332–27   not *f·* of Mind,
Pan. 4–10   functions of these *f·* depend on
'01. 23– 3   little left that the sects and *f·*
My. 154–20   * infinite *f·* of man."
  260–25   raises the dormant *f·*,

faculty

Mis. 80–11   who will fight the medical *f·*,
  243–26   some of the medical *f·* will tell you
Man. 73– 9   members of the *f·*, instructors, or
No. 2– 4   ostracized by the medical *f·*,
Hea. 9–19   not a *f·* or power underived from
  14–20   spiritual sense or perceptive *f·*
My. 4–18   both medical *f·* and Christianity,
  175–13   intelligent medical *f·*,

fad

My. 79–20   * more than a *f·* in C. S.,
  218–22   *f·* of belief is the fool of mesmerism.

fade

Ret. 18–19   radiance and glory ne'er *f·*.
  79– 8   material pigment beneath *f·* into
Po. 64–11   radiance and glory ne'er *f·*.

faded

Mis. 225–26   flush *f·* from the face,
  396– 9   Yet here, upon this *f·* sod,
Po. 9– 9   leaves all *f·*, the fruitage shed,
  59– 1   Yet here, upon this *f·* sod,

fadeless

'02. 17–16   wherein joy is real and *f·*.

fading

Mis. 15–27   gradual *f·* out of the mortal
  342– 5   their *f·* warmth of action ;
Un. 8–13   is illusive and *f·*.
'01. 33– 3   seems to be *f·* so sensibly
Hea. 10–28   Earth's *f·* dreams are empty streams,
Peo. 8–26   fast *f·* into ashes ;

fagots

Mis. 345–11   set fire to the *f·*,
Peo. 13–21   set fire to the *f·*,

fail

Mis. 5– 2   It cannot *f·* to do this if we
  5–13   Truth and Love, and these do not *f·*
  34– 1   curing where these *f·*,
  44– 9   It cannot *f·* to heal in every case
  78–27   cannot *f·* to express the exact nature of
  135–12   or *f·* to fulfil this Golden Rule,
  147–30   rather *f·* of success than attain it by
  255–26   and cures where they *f·*,
  378–20   readers of my books cannot *f·* to
Ret. 6– 3   * can hardly *f·* to induce them to follow
  31–15   and cures when they *f·*,
  73–13   who *f·* to appreciate individual
Un. 9–20   by those who *f·* to understand me,
Pul. 13–15   and *f·* to strangle the serpent of sin
No. 22– 9   cold categories of Kant *f·*
'00. 6– 3   demonstrator can mistake or *f·*
  9–23   Whosoever attempts . . . will signally *f·* ;
'02. 16–24   *f·* to elucidate Christianity :
Hea. 6– 2   should this rule *f·* hereafter,
My. 111–28   professionals who *f·* to understand it,
  166– 4   *f·* to succeed and fall to the earth.
  175–28   must *f·* to influence the minds
  205–29   The practitioner may *f·*,
  271–25   * cannot *f·* to be impressed by the
  292–14   *f·* in their prayers to save

failed

Mis. 55– 1   *f·* to get the right answer,
  60–10   after all other means have *f·*.
  69–21   His physicians had *f·*
  267–11   never was a time when I . . . *f·* to
  282–25   when other means have *f·*.
  378–13   signally *f·* in healing her case.
Pan. 10–19   that M.D.'s have *f·* to heal ;
My. 130–12   has *f·* too often for me to fear it.

failed

My. 151–24   Baalites or sun-worshippers *f·* to
  222– 2   even the disciples of Jesus once *f·*
  306–27   to get them published and had *f·*.

failest

Mis. 63–25   Why *f·* thou me?

failing

Mis. 30– 6   even though *f·* at first
  52–23   *f·* to demonstrate one rule
  220–28   publish . . . that he is *f·*,
  222– 9   *f·* of conviction and reform,
Man. 28–22   *f·* to do either, said officer
  29–13   *F·* to do thus, the Pastor
My. 190–14   Jesus' students, *f·* to cure a
  305– 2   *F·* in these attempts,

fails

Mis. 6–17   ultimately succeed where error *f·*.
  62–25   *f·*, and ends in a parody on
  129–11   If this rule *f·* in effect,
  309– 7   often *f·* to express even mortal man,
Man. 28–18   If an officer *f·* to fulfil
  29– 7   If the C. S. Board of Directors *f·*
  78– 3   If any Director *f·* to heed
Ret. 74– 5   *f·* to distinguish the individual,
Pul. 4– 1   is naught and my faith *f·*."
'00. 7–26   this attempt measurably *f·*,
My. 130–19   Truth never falters nor *f·* ;
  130–20   it is our faith that *f·*.
  165–15   Goodness never *f·* to receive its

failure

Mis. 9–25   And wherefore our *f·*
Man. 29– 2   *f·* of the Committee on Publication
  46–17   A *f·* to do this shall subject the
No. 44– 3   This *f·* should make him modest.
My. 110–29   made his life an abject *f·*.

failures

Mis. 285–10   too short for foibles or *f·*.

fain

Mis. 394–19   I *f·* would keep the gates ajar,
Po. 57– 5   * I *f·* would keep the gates ajar,

faint

Mis. ix–11   once fragmentary and *f·*
  2–15   first *f·* view of a more spiritual
  262–18   heart grown *f·* with hope deferred.
  328–24   causing to stumble, fall, or *f·*,
  376–24   Fleecy, *f·*, fairy blue and golden
My. 8–17   * with my *f·* knowledge of
  123–32   "We *f·* not ;— II Cor. 4 : 1.
  132–31   whose whole heart is *f·* ;
  196–21   lest ye be wearied and *f·* — Heb. 12 : 3.
  254– 8   not be weary, walk and not *f·*.

fainting

Mis. 212–30   the *f·* form of Jesus,

faintly

Un. 48–20   *f·* able to demonstrate Truth
  62–27   discern *f·* God's ever-presence,
My. 350– 9   calmly and rationally, though *f·*,

fair

Mis. 81–19   *if all this be a f· or correct view*
  132– 4   a *f·* token that heavy lids
  147–29   no path but the *f·*, open, and direct one,
  239– 7   *f·* proof that my shadow is not
  247– 9   the world, upon *f·* investigation,
  329–29   prophesies of *f·* earth and sunny skies.
  342–11   Each moment's *f·* expectancy
  387– 2   With joy divinely *f·*,
Ret. 18–22   are fragrant and *f·*,
Un. 48– 1   It is *f·* to ask of every one a reason
Pul. 37– 2   * it is the great daily that is so *f·*
  82–29   * and in this *f·* land at least
  83–12   * "as *f·* as the morn, — see Song 6 : 10.
Pan. 3–17   * *f·* wisdom, that celestial maid."
'01. 2–11   a *f·* seeming for right being,
  31–27   my *f·* fortune to be often taught by
'02. 2–25   remain friends, or . . . part *f·* foes.
  14–29   an open field and *f·* play.
Po. 8–20   thinking alone of a *f·* young bride,
  25–10   *F·* floral apostles of love,
  46– 1   *F·* girl, thy rosebud heart
  50–20   With joy divinely *f·*,
  64–17   are fragrant and *f·*,
My. 154– 9   Send flowers and all things *f·*
  182–27   amid *f·* foliage of this vine
  194–17   *f·* escutcheon of your church.
  329–24   * *f·* attitude of the press

fairly

Mis. 185– 3   demonstrate *f·* the divine Principle
  269–16   has *f·* proven his knowledge
  289–28   *f·* stated by a magistrate,
Pul. 67– 8   * Boston can *f·* claim to be
  80–14   * *f·* broken our mental teeth
My. 81– 3   * Scientists *f·* radiate good nature

fairly
    My. 124—25   prove *f·* the facts relating to
         187— 2   faith, and Christian zeal *f·* indicate
         286— 9   arbitrated wisely, *f·* ;

fairness
    Mis. 255— 4   no *f·* or propriety in the aspersion.
         377— 2   brush or pen to paint frail *f·*
    My. 48—31   * to say, in all *f·*,

fair-seeming
    Mis. 233—19   *f·* for straightforward character,

fairy
    Mis. 376—24   *f·* blue and golden flecks

fairy-land
    Mis. 216—25   * "When philosophy becomes *f·*,

fairy-peopled
    Mis. 390—10   The *f·* world of flowers,
    Po. 55—11   The *f·* world of flowers,

faith (*see also* faith's)
abiding
    Mis. 100—29   abiding *f·*, and affection,
abound in
    '01. 34—22   abound in *f·*, understanding, and
all
    Mis. 194—32   exclude all *f·* in any other remedy
         348—26   one who had lost all *f·* in them.
    Hea. 15— 7   reposes all *f·* in mind,
    Peo. 9—23   rest all *f·* in Spirit,
    My. 158—16   Having all *f·* in C. S.,
ancient
    Pul. 52—14   * reviver of the ancient *f·*
and doubt
    My. 292—29   is a compound of *f·* and doubt,
and friendship
    My. 282— 5   *f·* and friendship of our chief
and good works
    '00. 15—11   victory, *f·*, and good works.
    '02. 20— 9   thy unfaltering *f·* and good works
and hope
    Mis. 246—31   *f·* and hope of Christianity,
    Un. 55—17   Job's *f·* and hope gained him
    My. 201—12   friendship, *f·*, and hope
and Love
    Mis. 152—24   strong tower of hope, *f·*, and Love,
and love
    Mis. 176—17   steadfast in *f·* and love,
    My. 64—23   * with renewed *f·* and love
         152—25   God demands all our *f·* and love ;
         156—20   with hope, *f·*, and love ready
and purity
    '00. 6—13   through his simple *f·* and purity,
and resolve
    Mis. 319—29   *f·* and resolve are friends to Truth ;
and understanding
    Mis. 149—10   hope, *f·*, and understanding,
         162—32   hope, *f·*, and understanding,
    Ret. 28—17   *f·*, and understanding must
    My. 132— 8   spiritual *f·* and understanding
         187— 7   illumine your *f·* and understanding,
         222— 3   cure by their *f·* and understanding
and works
    My. 103— 5   The *f·* and works demanded of man
armed
    My. 278—11   *f·* armed with the understanding
aspiration and
    My. 88—14   * symbolisms of aspiration and *f·*,
assurance of
    Pul. 83—10   * With the assurance of *f·* she prays,
banish
    My. 95—24   * may think they can banish *f·*
blessed
    Ret. 82— 7   practitioners of the same blessed *f·*.
blind
    My. 153—22   This trembling and blind *f·*,
break
    Pul. 13—14   Alas for those who break *f·* with
breaks
    '01. 4—30   conclude that he breaks *f·* with
Christian
    Ret. 6— 5   * living illustration of Christian *f·*.
    Pul. 51— 3   * Neither does the Christian *f·* produce
    '02. 6—20   Christian *f·*, hope, and prayer,
Christian Science
    My. 88—11   * Mother Church of the C. S. *f·*
         88—18   * smallest feature of the C. S. *f·*,
         97—20   * Mother Church of the C. S. *f·*
clinging
    Mis. 275— 4   woman's trembling, clinging *f·*
common
    Pul. 85—27   * in the Cause of their common *f·*.
confession of
    Pul. 30—12   * sign a brief "confession of *f·*,"
         30—15   * The "confession of *f·*" includes the
confidence of
    Ret. 15— 7   In confidence of *f·*, I could say

faith
converts to the
    My. 94—12   * adherence of its converts to the *f·*,
couples
    My. 108—13   couples *f·* with spiritual understanding
dignitaries of the
    Pul. 71—18   * various dignitaries of the *f·*.
early
    My. 350—22   old foundations of an early *f·*
ebbing
    My. 183—13   no more sea, no ebbing *f·*, no night.
embrace the
    Pul. 66—10   * most of those who embrace the *f·*
encourage
    Hea. 14— 8   and encourage *f·* in an opposite
enlightened
    Mis. 343—19   sunshine of enlightened *f·*?
    Pul. 9—30   enlightened *f·* is Christ's teachings
expresses the
    Pul. 65—27   * expresses the *f·* of those who believe
false
    Mis. 31—13   false *f·* finds no place in,
    My. 218—24   false *f·* that will end bitterly.
fast-increasing
    Pul. 47— 8   * members of this fast-increasing *f·*.
firm
    My. 97— 3   * They believe that firm *f·*
foundation of the
    Pul. 71—20   * foundation of the *f·* to which
Founder of the
    Pul. 71—12   * FOUNDER OF THE F·
         72—20   * she was the Founder of the *f·*,
full
    Mis. 223—16   full *f·* in the divine Principle,
         270—18   full *f·* in his prophecy,
    My. 280—18   in full *f·* that God does not
         294—12   accords not with a full *f·*
full-fledged
    My. 281— 7   F· full-fledged, soaring to the
great deal of
    Mis. 4—25   must require a great deal of *f·*
growth of a
    Pul. 65—12   * chapter sub-title
half-persuaded
    My. 166— 4   It is insincerity and a half-persuaded *f·*
have
    Mis. 33—12   *Must I have f· in C. S.*
         39—15   I have *f·* in His promise,
    Pul. 72—29   * we have *f·* in him.
         73— 4   * send to us those who have *f·*,
         73—16   * If you have *f·*, you can
    '01. 21— 1   they have *f·*, but they have Science,
    My. 25—23   I have *f·* in the givers
         158—17   we must have *f·* in whatever
         220—19   I also have *f·* that my prayer
         222—10   "If ye have *f·* as a— *Matt.* 17 : 20.
         250—27   So I have *f·* that whatever
having
    Hea. 4—26   having *f·* in it, how can we
    Peo. 12—23   Having *f·* in drugs and hygienic
healing
    My. 153—15   healing *f·* is a saving faith ;
Hebrew
    Un. 14—15   Jehovah of limited Hebrew *f·*
his
    Mis. 31—18   to relinquish his *f·* in evil,
         31—22   in order to retain his *f·* in evil
         99—20   his *f·* in the immortality of
         138—13   prove his *f·* by works,
         260— 8   His *f·* partook not of drugs,
         281—15   come out and confess his *f·*,
    Peo. 8—27   gorging his *f·* with skill
    My. 4— 1   by losing his *f·* in matter
         222—16   because of his *f·* and his great
         294—20   reason for his *f·* in what
holy
    Pan. 15— 7   establish us in the most holy *f·*,
hope and
    (*see* hope)
human
    Mis. 182—18   Born of . . . no human *f·*,
    My. 292— 4   human *f·* in the right.
illumed by
    Mis. 396—24   thoughts, illumed By *f·*,
    Pul. 18— 8   thoughts, illumed By *f·*,
    Po. 12— 8   thoughts, illumed By *f·*,
illumined
    Mis. 338— 9   F· illumined by works ;
implicit
    Mis. 105— 1   implicit *f·* engendered by C. S.,
inactive
    Pul. 10— 3   paralyzed by inactive *f·*,
in Christ
    Rud. 11— 4   first to *f·* in Christ ;

faith

in Christian Science
Mis. 33–12 *Must I have f· in C. S.*
My. 158–16 Having all f· in C. S.,

in divine Love
My. 12–26 F· in divine Love supplies the

in drugs
Mis. 6–22 overcome the patient's f· in drugs
Peo. 12–23 f· in drugs and hygienic drills,

in error
My. 292–30 faith in truth and f· in error.

in evil
(see **evil**)

inexplicable
My. 97–17 * stupendous, inexplicable f·

in God
(see **God**)

in Him
Pul. 72–23 * f· in Him and His teachings.
73– 6 * She had f· in Him,

in him
Pul. 72–29 * we have f· in him.

in His promise
Mis. 39–15 I have f· in His promise,

in humanity
Mis. 338–15 a pure f· in humanity

in hygiene
Hea. 15– 6 It places no f· in hygiene
Peo. 4– 3 more f· in hygiene and drugs

in man
My. 152– 9 By reposing f· in man

in matter
Mis. 334– 9 mortals' f· in matter may
Peo. 9–20 showing our greater f· in matter,
My. 4– 1 losing his f· in matter and sin,

in metaphysics
My. 301–15 chapter sub-title

in Mind
Mis. 229–14 f· in Mind over all other influences

in omnipotence
Peo. 12–24 we lose f· in omnipotence,

in sight
My. 149–24 Losing . . . f· in sight, we lose the

insufficient
My. 292–16 Insufficient f· or spiritual

interesting
Pul. 65– 8 * undoubtedly an interesting f·

in the blessing
My. 209– 6 f· in the blessing of fidelity,

in the givers
My. 25–23 I have f· in the givers

in the pharmacy
My. 108–12 enlists f· in the pharmacy of

in things material
Ret. 31–16 error of f· in things material ;

in truth
My. 292–30 f· in truth and faith in error.

iris of
Mis. 355–29 iris of f·, more beautiful than

is belief
Ret. 54– 3 Because f· is belief,

is divided
Mis. 52– 4 whose f· is divided between

is fruition
My. 253–24 If f· is fruition, you have

its
Mis. 346– 2 the very centre of its f·.
My. 75– 3 * its f· in its fundamentals.
99– 7 * a cult able to promote its f·
152– 3 anchored its f· in troubled waters.
155–15 finds the full fruition of its f·,

Jesus'
Mis. 111–18 Jesus' f· in Truth

keep the
Mis. 41–13 keep the f· and finish their course.
278– 7 and keep the f·.
My. 134– 8 To triumph in truth, to keep the f·

kept the
Hea. 2–16 I have kept the f·.” — II Tim. 4 : 7.

lack of
Mis. 31–12 lack of f· in good.
158–16 rebuke a lack of f· in divine help,
My. 222– 9 unbelief” (lack of f·) ; — Matt. 17 : 20.

little
No. 26–27 O ye of little f· ?” — Matt. 6 : 30.

live by the
Un. 61–21 I live by the f· of — Gal. 2 : 20.

living
Mis. 197– 1 they require a living f·,
282– 1 to demonstrate a living f·,
Ret. 69–29 art thou in the living f·
Pul. 30–21 * and the need of living f·
Peo. 5– 4 embodiment of a living f·,

lofty
Peo. 13–16 But the lofty f· of the

faith

loss of
Mis. 204–16 marked loss of f· in evil,

members of that
Pul. 75–21 * by which the members of that f·

members of the
Pul. 72– 6 * leading members of the f·

meritorious
Mis. 118–17 guerdon of meritorious f·

molecule of
My. 278–10 Let us have the molecule of f·

more
Mis. 19–20 I should have more f· in an
152–30 Exercise more f· in God
Un. 43–19 more f· in living than in dying.
Peo. 4– 3 more f· in hygiene and drugs
My. 162– 2 our want of more f· in His

more than
Mis. 4–28 more than f· is necessary,
77– 3 more than f· in the fact

mounts upward
My. 129–26 where f· mounts upward,

my
Mis. 213– 5 and my f· in the right.
Pul. 4– 1 you may say, . . . my f· fails.”
63– 8 “My f· has the strength to
'01. 21–24 My f· assures me that God
'02. 15– 3 never lost my f· in God,
Hea. 5–24 my f· by my works.” — Jas. 2 : 18.
Po. 33– 3 Increase Thou my f·
My. 169–18 three thousand believers of my f·,
204– 1 My f· in God and in His

new
Pul. 67– 5 * found a new f·, go to Boston,”
My. 92–13 * swift growth of the new f·

no
Mis. 31–20 because he has no f· in the
33–16 had no f· whatever in the Science,
89–14 have no f· in your method,
118– 4 We shall have no f· in evil
Un. 48– 7 have no f· in any other thing
Hea. 15– 6 no f· in hygiene or drugs ;
15–25 that you have little or no f·
My. 221–27 shall we have no f· in God,

not of
Ret. 94–19 whatsoever is not of f· — Rom. 14 : 23.

not sufficient
Mis. 5–12 but have not sufficient f·

of ages
Ret. 33–17 mixed with the f· of ages,

of Christian Science
My. 69– 9 * illustrative of the f· of C. S.

of his followers
My. 222–17 demands on the f· of his followers,

of the Church
No. 41–26 * as the f· of the Church increases,

of these people
My. 95–19 * The f· of these people is

one
Mis. 131–12 one f·, one God, one baptism.
Peo. 1– 1 one f·, one baptism. — Eph. 4 : 5.
5– 3 one f·, one baptism.” — Eph. 4 : 5.
9– 1 C. S. has one f·, one Lord,
14–19 one f·, one baptism.” — Eph. 4 : 5.

one's
Hea. 12–28 divide one's f· apparently between
My. 105– 6 prove one's f· by his works.

only
Un. 61–19 Only f· and a feeble understanding

on the earth
'01. 12–12 find f· on the earth?” — Luke 18 : 8.

our
Mis. 160–14 every trial of our f· in God
361–21 finisher of our f·.” — Heb. 12 : 2.
'01. 14–11 our f· takes hold of the fact that
17– 6 author and finisher of our f·,
My. 63–18 * of those not of our f·
130–20 it is our f· that fails.
152–25 God demands all our f· and love ;
163–29 a church of our f·
258–14 finisher of our f· ; — Heb. 12 : 2.
349–16 finisher of our f·.” — Heb. 12 : 2.

patient
'01. 35–18 do we walk in Patient f·

Paul's
Un. 57–20 confirmation of Paul's f·.

power of
Pul. 80–22 * in God and the power of f·,

power of the
My. 81– 8 * healing power of the f·,

prayer of
No. 41–25 * prayer of f· shall save — Jas. 5 : 15.
My. 221–32 prayer of f· shall save — Jas. 5 : 15.

primeval
My. 139– 8 primeval f·, hope, love.

faith

principles of the
Pul. 68– 6 * taught the principles of the f·
pure
Mis. 338–15 a pure f· in humanity
Peo. 13–21 and his pure f· went up
reasonable
Mis. 200–27 triumph of a reasonable f·
reason for the
Un. 48– 1 a reason for the f· within.
receivers of the
Pul. 56– 6 * receivers of the f· among the
religious
My. 89–27 * this form of religious f·
95–30 * demonstration of religious f·
301– 5 present flux in religious f·
saving
My. 118–17 saving f· comes not of
153–16 healing faith is a saving f· ;
serenity of
My. 88–21 * beauty and serenity of f·,
service, and
'00. 15–24 service, and f·, — Rev. 2 : 19.
sound
'01. 26–20 sound f· and charity,
My. 164–17 not only possess a sound f·,
spirit of
My. 85–26 * spirit of f· and brotherhood
spreads
Po. 33–16 f· spreads her pinions abroad,
St. Paul's
My. 108–28 remain steadfast in St. Paul's f·,
strengthen the
Man. 43–12 she may strengthen the f· by
strong
Mis. 345–12 his pure and strong f· rose
sublime
Mis. 131–11 substance of our sublime f·,
system of
My. 59– 8 * new system of f· and worship,
that
My. 89– 3 * held to symbolize that f· which
164–17 that f· also possesses them.
their
Mis. 140– 8 taxing their f· in God,
Pul. 57–17 * proved their f· by their works.
My. 30–11 * the devotion . . . to their f·,
74–18 * to the sincerity of their f· ;
79– 8 * stagger their f· not a little
90–12 * grips hold of their f·
96–12 * take joy in attesting their f·
155–22 brighten their f· with a dawn
162–27 may their f· never falter
162–28 their f· in and their understanding
222– 3 by their f· and understanding
this
Pul. 58– 3 * imparting this f· to her
66– 4 * church organization of this f·
Peo. 9– 2 this f· builds on Spirit,
My. 90– 8 * this f· is real and is given
103– 7 the practicality of this f·
through
Mis. 158–11 do this through f·, not sight.
241–25 doubting heart looks up through f·,
Pul. 72–23 * through f· in Him and His teachings.
My. 205– 7 Wisdom is won through f·,
thy
Pul. 53–13 * thy f· hath made — Luke 17 : 19.
My. 3–12 "Show me thy f· — Jas. 2 : 18.
152– 6 "Thy f· hath made — Matt. 9 : 22.
153–13 Thy f· hath healed thee.
trembling
My. 293–14 trembling f·, hope, and of fear,
triumphant
Mis. 385–25 f· triumphant round thy
Po. 48–21 f· triumphant round thy
unfaltering
Mis. 163–17 in his unfaltering f· in the
'02. 20– 9 glorifying thy unfaltering f·
My. 155– 6 unfaltering f· in the prophecies,
unfeigned
Mis. 136–11 and of the f· unfeigned.
My. 187–13 and of f· unfeigned ;" — I Tim. 1 : 5.
193– 1 your temple in f· unfeigned,
unflinching
My. 62– 1 * unflinching f· and unfailing
unity of
My. 170–29 unity of f·, understanding,
uplift
Man. 16– 6 served to uplift f·
vested in
Mis. 298–22 f· vested in righteousness
waning
Mis. 312–18 * restore the waning f· of many
without
My. 95–25 * without f· in the things unseen.

faith

without proof
'02. 18–24 f· without proof loses its life,
without works
Pul. 9–29 "F· without works is dead." — Jas. 2 : 26.
My. 3–10 sear leaves of f· without works,
with understanding
Mis. 97–16 combines f· with understanding,
your
Mis. 154– 5 Your f· has not been without works,
Un. 60–25 your f· is vain ; — I Cor. 15 : 17.
My. 148– 4 let your f· be known by your works.
187– 7 illumine your f· and understanding,

Mis. 97–15 C. S. is not a remedy of f· alone,
118– 5 when f· finds a resting-place
124–29 to experience, hope ; to hope, f· ;
124–30 to f·, understanding ;
149–30 shall abide steadfastly in the f·
210–15 He who has f· in woman's special
229–22 f· in the power of God to heal
241– 1 the f· of both youth and adult
380–15 in f·, turned to divine help,
385– 1 * "F·, hope, and tears, triune,
387– 7 For f· to kiss, and know ;
Pul. 37–15 * to eliminate . . . from the f·.
52– 4 * f· of the mustard-seed variety.
52– 6 * have not a f· approximate to
53–10 contained in the one word — f·.
'01. 10–28 f· according to works.
Po. 6–16 For f· to kiss, and know ;
37– 1 * "F·, hope, and tears, triune,
My. 3–18 hope, f·, understanding.
6–28 self-abnegation, hope, f· ;
22–20 * she has shown wisdom, f·, and
23–24 * not only to f· but also to sight ;
25–24 f· in the grandeur and sublimity of
57–31 * f· of the mustard-seed variety.
58– 1 * a f· approximate to that of
89– 3 * that faith which is so much a f·
90–14 * A f· which teaches that hate is
93–30 * In 1890 the f· had but
96–13 * It is a f· based upon reason,
99– 3 * "A f· which is able to raise
99–17 * Thirty thousand of the f·,
153–18 F· in aught else misguides the
187– 1 fidelity, f·, and Christian zeal
189–19 and f· grows wearisome,
202– 4 f·, meekness, and might of him who
203– 5 sing in f·.
234–13 from f· to achievement,
240–14 hope, f·, understanding."
281– 6 f· in God's disposal of events.
301–16 f· in divine metaphysics

faith-cure
Ret. 54–19 The f· has devout followers,
Pul. 47–17 * between f· and C. S.,
69–14 * distinguishes C. S. from the f·,
69–21 * It is not f·, but it is an

faith-cures
Ret. 54– 1 Why are f· sometimes more speedy

faith-curists
'01. 21– 1 mind-curists, nor f· ;

faithful
Mis. 7–15 if f· laborers in His vineyard.
88– 1 A f· student may even
110– 6 unselfishness, f· affection,
114–28 if found f·, He will deliver us
116–28 "f· over a few things." — Matt. 25 : 23.
122–25 good and f· servant, — Matt. 25 : 23.
150–13 in the congregation of the f·,
155–11 pressing meekly on, be f·,
158–15 in reward for your f· service,
158–22 Let us be f· and obedient,
213–18 But the f· adherents of Truth
228–16 just person, f· to conscience
237–24 Honor to f· merit is delayed,
238–22 Are you f· ? Do you love?
275– 8 the f·, stricken mother,
287–26 Be f· over home relations ;
317–17 by the most f· seekers ;
339–17 f· over a few things." — Matt. 25 : 23.
340–10 wear the crown of the f·.
340–16 He has not been f· over a few things.
340–24 hast been f· over a few things.
342– 8 better-tended lamps of the f·.
342–32 f· over the few things of Spirit,
343–28 "Thou hast been f· !" — Matt. 25 : 23.
354– 6 f· Christian Scientists
356–19 Now let my f· students
392–14 F· and patient be my life as thine ;
Man. 38– 2 f·, loyal students of the textbook,
82–21 devote ample time for f· practice.
Ret. 90– 4 Does the f· shepherd forsake
Pul. 5– 8 Memory, f· to goodness,

faithful

Pul.	13– 6	*f·* over a few things, — *Matt.* 25 : 23.
No.	8– 3	*f·*, and charitable with all.
Pan.	14–21	and their *f·* service thereof,
'00.	13–14	"Be thou *f·* unto death, — *Rev.* 2 : 10.
'01.	1– 2	heart-and-hand-fellowship to the *f·*,
'02.	18– 1	*f·* at the temple gate of conscience,
	18–13	*f·* to rebuke, ready to forgive.
Po.	20–18	F· and patient be my life
	53–13	Bid *f·* swallows come
	79– 9	in thought and deed — To *f·* His.
My.	6– 4	Are we honest, just, *f·* ?
	42– 5	* a *f·* follower of this Leader
	42–27	* how *f·* is her allegiance to God,
	44– 9	* counsel of our ever *f·* Leader.
	44–11	* *f·* disciple rejoices in prophecy
	46–19	* are we *f·*, obedient, deserving
	61–31	* the *f·*, earnest work of our noble
	62– 3	* good and *f·* servant ; — *Matt.* 25 : 23.
	84–19	* wealth, vigor, and *f·* adherence.
	158–21	makes the heart tender, *f·*, true.
	162–21	"Well done, good and *f·*." — *Matt.* 25 : 23.
	167– 9	in that Love which is *f·*,
	182–15	*f·* labor of loyal students,
	202–13	"Well done, good and *f·*," — *Matt.* 25 · 23.
	205–21	friends more *f·*,
	207–21	"Well done, thou good and *f·* — *Matt.* 25 : 21.
	225– 5	"Well done, good and *f·*," — *Matt.* 25 : 23.
	226–25	Our *f·* laborers in the field
	230–23	*f·* over foundational trusts,
	235– 6	guided by love, *f·* to her instincts,
	244–23	your wise, *f·* teachers
	248–25	committed to you, my *f·* witnesses.
	253–28	Dare to be *f·* to God and man.
	254–14	thank the *f·* teacher of this class
	294–16	skilful surgeon or the *f·* M.D.
	321– 7	* your devoted and *f·* friends,
	335– 8	* *f·* as a member and officer
	355–13	the strong, the *f·*, the untiring

faithfully

Mis.	111– 4	F·, as meekly, you have toiled
	127–14	*f·* asks divine Love to feed it
	302–19	working *f·* for Christ's cause
	318–20	student must have studied *f·*
	340–20	They follow *f·*;
Man.	28–21	to perform his office *f·* ;
	29–12	or perform their functions *f·*.
Ret.	6–26	he served the public interests *f·*
	19–24	performed their obligations most *f·*.
Pul.	21–11	*f·* struggle till it be accomplished
	73–14	* and this duty she *f·* performed.
'01.	31–26	used *f·* God's Word,
My.	18–11	*f·* asks divine Love to feed it
	50– 5	* had labored *f·* and ardently,
	52–10	* more *f·* to sustain her
	60–20	* Respectfully and *f·* yours,
	148– 1	F· and more than ever persistently,
	325–16	* ever *f·* your student,
	331– 3	performed their obligations most *f·*."
	336– 8	* *f·* performed their obligation to her.

faithless

Mis.	340– 2	*f·* tarrying, has torn the laurel
Ret.	81–19	*f·* to itself and to others,
My.	222– 5	"O *f·* and perverse — *Matt.* 17 : 17.

faith-lighted

Mis.	15–22	What a *f·* thought is this !

faith's

Chr.	53–37	*f·* pale star now blends
My.	158– 8	in attune with *f·* fond trust.

faiths

Mis.	251–25	falling leaves of old-time *f·*
	331–22	falling leaves of old-time *f·*,
Pul.	66–25	* encroachment upon prevailing *f·*,
	67– 9	* census of the religious *f·*
Peo.	1–13	collisions with old-time *f·*,
My.	30– 8	* but many hundreds of other *f·*,

falchion

Ret.	30– 3	smite error with the *f·* of Truth.

falcon

Po.	2– 8	trained *f·* in the Gallic van,

fall

Mis.	xl–19	intolerance will *f·* to the ground,
	9–18	to *f·* in fragments before our eyes.
	10–11	if they *f·* they shall rise again,
	22–30	to which it seemed to *f·*
	77–28	could *f·* into mortal error ;
	80–13	who leave C. S. to rise or *f·*
	115–30	you will *f·* the victim of your own
	127–27	garrulous talk may *f·* to the ground,
	157– 5	He that marketh the sparrow's *f·*
	195–21	and it cannot *f·* to the ground
	211– 7	will lead the blind and both shall *f·*.
	215–21	would *f·* immediately if he knew

fall

Mis.	231– 5	had seen sunshine and shadow *f·* upon
	233–27	if some *f·* short, others will approach
	251–27	will *f·* before Truth demonstrated,
	251–28	as dry leaves *f·* to enrich the soil
	268–27	From lack of moral strength empires *f·*.
	279–25	in order that the walls might *f·* ;
	291–24	dew of heaven will *f·* gently on the
	296–23	Why *f·* into such patronage,
	325–10	*f·* upon the Stranger.
	327–28	they *f·* behind and lose sight of
	328–24	causing to stumble, *f·*, or faint,
	355–27	Let no clouds of sin gather and *f·*
	357–13	seeds of Truth *f·* by the wayside,
	357–14	*f·* on stony ground and shallow soil.
	389–11	behold the snare, the pit, the *f·* :
Ret.	11–21	Farther than feet of chamois *f·*,
	35–21	too immanent to *f·* to the ground
	61– 8	but if you *f·* asleep,
	82–23	their examples either excel or *f·* short
Un.	40– 1	to the *f·* of a sparrow.
No.	3– 6	better to *f·* into the hands of God,
	9–16	students who *f·* into error,
	26–16	than his divine Principle, . . . can *f·*
	44–10	To climb up by . . . is to *f·*.
'01.	2–15	if some *f·* short of Truth,
	24–15	and great was the *f·*
'02.	18–11	who caused not the feeble to *f·*,
Po.	4–10	the snare, the pit, the *f·* :
	8– 2	alone where the shadows *f·*
	24–15	Come when the shadows *f·*,
	60–19	Farther than feet of chamois *f·*,
My.	128–29	it will *f·* powerless,
	166– 4	and *f·* to the earth.
	194–30	* Ne'er in a sunny hour *f·* off."
	226–13	that marks the sparrow's *f·*,
	248–21	*f·* for lack of the divine impetus.
	262– 3	an ideal which cannot *f·*
	278–28	*f·*, pierced by its own sword.
	323–31	* Normal class in the *f·* of 1887

fallacy

Mis.	74–22	he proved the *f·* of the theory
	217–10	*f·* of an unscientific statement
My.	307–29	*f·* of *materia medica,*

fallen

Mis.	14– 9	has *f·* into the imperfection
	77–26	has *f·* away from his first estate ;
	78–25	*Has man f· from a state of*
	106–20	crumbs *f·* from this table of Truth,
	181–29	God's opposite, — evil, or a *f·* man,
	186– 7	material belief has *f·* far below
	259–19	man is not *f·* : he is governed in
	262–17	lifting the *f·* and strengthening the
	274–16	*Truth is f· in the street,* — *Isa.* 59 : 14.
	328–26	uplift the *f·* and strengthen the
	357–17	*f·* into the good and honest hearts
Pul.	10– 8	Rome's *f·* fanes and silent
Rud.	7–13	material, *f·*, sick, depraved,
No.	17–17	In Science there is no *f·* state
Pan.	11–16	If man is spiritually *f·*,
	11–29	image of God, not *f·* or inverted
My.	126–24	The Babylonish woman is *f·*,

falleth

Mis.	369–20	crumb that *f·* from his table.

fallibility

Mis.	351–19	chapter sub-title
Ret.	60–30	arises from the *f·* of sense,

fallible

Mis.	332– 5	Mind is Love, — but not *f·* love.
	353– 5	Human concepts . . . are *f·* ;
	353–11	of the misguided, *f·* sort,
Ret.	89–29	and selfish influence is human, *f·*,

falling

Mis.	22–28	A *f·* apple suggested to Newton
	174–11	from the *f·* of a sparrow.
	204– 2	*f·* on the bended knee of prayer,
	251–25	*f·* leaves of old-time faiths
	309–18	*f·* into the error of anti-Christ.
	331–22	*f·* leaves of old-time faiths,
	360–17	*f·* upon the blighted flowers of
Ret.	24–14	the *f·* apple that led me to
No.	15– 1	*f·* on the sick and sinner,
My.	190– 1	*f·* upon the bridal wreath,

falls

Mis.	267–20	*f·* to the earth.
	390–14	soft thy footstep *f·* upon
	394– 3	*f·* on the heart like the dew
No.	34–16	*f·* with its leaden weight
Pan.	11–19	the man who *f·* physically
Po.	45– 3	*f·* on the heart like the dew
	55–15	soft thy footstep *f·* upon
My.	260–15	sense that *f·* short of substance,
	262–10	*f·* far short of my sense of the

Falmouth
    '02. 13–17 corner of *F·* and Caledonia

Falmouth and Norway Streets
    Pul. 61–23 * corner of *F· and N· S·*,
          77–11 * intersection of *F· and N· S·*,
          78– 9 * intersection of *F· and N· S·*,
    My. 29– 9 * corner of *F· and N· S·*,
          30– 1 * *F· and N· S·* held large crowds
          67– 2 * corner of *F· and N· S·*.
          68–13 * corner of *F· and N· S·*,

Falmouth, Norway, and St. Paul Streets
    My. 65–19 * bounded by *F·, N·, and St. P· S·*,

Falmouth Street
    95 and 97
    My. vi–25 * property at 95 and 97 *F· S·*,

    My. 84–27 * beautiful structure on *F· S·*,

false
    Mis. 24–32 effect arising from *f·* claims
          31–12 *f·* faith finds no place in,
          32– 8 the students of *f·* teachers,
          39– 8 incorrect and *f·* teachers
          42–31 *f·* admissions prevent us from
          57–19 This was *f·* ; and the Lord God never
          65– 8 evidence of the senses is *f·*.
          65–14 We must not consider the *f·* side of
          66– 2 *f·* testimony or mistaken evidence
          67–17 not bear *f·* witness ;" — *Exod.* 20 : 16.
          72–11 as *f·* as it is remorseless.
          73–20 subjective states of *f·* sensation
          76– 8 or proven true upon a *f·* premise,
          78–18 *f·* statements and claims,
          89–25 Mortal man is a *f·* concept
          89–26 saved from . . . whatever is *f·*.
          99– 3 It annuls *f·* evidence,
        104–16 clad in a *f·* mentality,
        104–20 stand the friction of *f·* selfhood
        107–19 *f·* senses pass through three
        108–11 Not to know that a false claim is *f·*,
        109–26 to escape from the *f·* claims of sin.
        111–28 *f·* beliefs inclining mortal mind
        118– 3 *f·* suggestions, self-will,
        171–28 ignorance or *f·* knowledge
        175–19 There are *f·* Christs that would
        209–20 *F·* pleasure will be, is, chastened ;
        209–24 has no foothold on the *f·* basis
        209–30 egotism and *f·* charity say,
        210–22 under the *f·* pretense of human need,
        218– 7 in relation to existence is *f·* ;
        218–14 *F·* realistic views sap the Science
        220– 3 and a *f·* rule the opposite way.
        221– 3 to harm by a *f·* mental argument ;
        222– 6 This state of *f·* consciousness
        222–15 because the *f·* seems true.
        226–12 *f·* to themselves as to others?
        226–17 * canst not then be *f·* to any man.
        247–12 charges against my views are *f·*,
        249– 8 *f·* report that I have appropriated
        260–20 whatever else seemeth to be . . . is *f·*,
        266–20 is utterly *f·* and groundless.
        271–27 * *f·* teachers of mental healing,
        287–10 may place love on a *f·* basis
        290–10 whatever is *f·* should disappear.
        291–21 *F·* views, however engendered,
        298–30 *f·* consciousness does not change the
        311–32 others who were reporting *f·* charges,
        332–25 Is man the supposer, *f·* believer,
        332–27 Supposing, *f·* believing, suffering
        351–24 pleasure that is *f·*,
        358–17 hounded footsteps, *f·* laurels.
        360–17 the cloud of *f·* witnesses ;
        366–24 start from this *f·* premise,
        366–31 *f·* theories whose names are legion,
    368–17, 18 present *f·* teaching and *f·* practice
    Man. 53–25 an article that is *f·* or unjust,
          98– 2 corrected a *f·* newspaper article
    Ret. 30–12 *f·* testimony of the physical senses.
          58– 5 physical, *f·*, and finite substitute.
          68–11 One is *f·*, while the other is true.
          71–22 they proceed from *f·* convictions
          73–18 whereby the *f·* personality is laid off.
          79– 6 In this consuming heat *f·* images
          81–11 Truth extinguishes *f·* thinking,
          81–26 * canst not then be *f·* to any man.
          94– 6 seems true, and yet . . . is *f·* ;
    Un. 32– 2 *f·* to God, *f·* to Truth and Life.
          32– 8 but a *f·* form of mind.
          33–20 self-testimony of . . . senses is *f·*.
          36– 4 this lie was the *f·* witness
          36– 8 C. S., which reverses *f·* testimony
          39–14 That selfhood is *f·* which opposes
          44–10 misled by a *f·* personality,
          46– 2 These are the shadowy and *f·*,
          51– 3 Reasoning from *f·* premises,

false
    Un. 52–10 *f·* consciousness of both good and
          53–16 not built on such *f·* foundations,
          54–17 even as a *f·* claimant,
          55–19 how *f·* are the pleasures and pains
          56– 9 a quickened sense of *f·* environment,
          61– 1 Rising above the *f·*, to the true
          63– 9 *f·* human sense of that light
    Pul. 6–18 * I cast from me the *f·* remedy
          7–20 *f·* prophets in the present
          75– 9 statement would not only be *f·*,
    Rud. 6–10 marred, through a *f·* conception,
          7–16 material evidence being wholly *f·*.
          8–19 yet is *f·* to God and man,
          9–12 *f·* and temporal sense of Truth,
        12– 8 else quiet the fear . . . on *f·* grounds,
    No. 5– 9 a *f·* and material sense,
          6–10 destruction of *f·* evidence,
          6–13 If, . . . evidence of disease is not *f·*,
        17– 1 *f·* assumption of the realness of
        17–25 *f·* knowledge would be a part of
        24–11 *f·* philosophy and scholastic theology,
        42–21 C. S. is beset with *f·* claimants,
    '00. 6–21 which destroys his *f·* appetites
    '01. 14– 8 *f·* entity, and utter falsity,
          15– 6 to prove it *f·*, therefore unreal.
         19–14 The notion . . . is proven *f·*.
         22–11 if one is true, the other is *f·*.
         26– 2 my tired sense of *f·* philosophy
    '02. 6– 5 *f·* knowledge, the fruits of the flesh
         10– 7 dispute the facts, call them *f·*
        16–22 self-defense against *f·* witnesses,
        18–12 nor spared from *f·* pity
    Hea. 17–23 appeared through the *f·* supposition
    Peo. 2–14 *f·* conceptions of Spirit,
          3– 9 *f·* beliefs that have produced sin,
         4–26 *f·* ideals of the Supreme Being
        11–14 are clasped by the *f·* teachings,
        11–15 *f·* theories, *f·* fears,
    Po. 79–12 *F·* fears are foes
    My. 111– 5 cannot be destroyed by *f·* psychics,
        112– 3 A fiction or a *f·* philosophy
        125– 2 *f·* affections, motives, and aims,
        130– 1 correct the *f·* with the true
        144– 7 The public report . . . is utterly *f·*.
        211– 2 a *f·*, convenient peace,
        218–24 *f·* faith that will end bitterly.
        274– 5 a *f·* material sense of life,
        306– 9 The *f·* should be antagonized
        323–11 * leave any *f·* impression.
        345– 6 C. S. will overthrow *f·* knowledge
        345–12 *f·* science — healing by drugs.
        351–25 assertions to the contrary are *f·*.
        (*see also* **belief, claim, sense**)

falsehood
    Mis. 13– 5 *f·*, ingratitude, misjudgment,
        226–19 by uttering a *f·*
        248– 8 chapter sub-title
        248–23 The opium *f·* has only this to it :
        269– 3 By using *f·* to regain his liberty,
        277– 3 *F·* is on the wings of the winds,
        348–17 To quench the growing flames of *f·*,
        351–12 *f·* designed to stir up strife
    Un. 52–18 From this *f·* arise the
    Rud. 8–20 uttering *f·* about good.
    '01. 20–14 suggestion of the inaudible *f·*,
    '02. 14–20 mockery, envy, rivalry, and *f·*
    My. 261–10 deceit or *f·* is never wise.
        306– 1 *f·* which persistently misrepresents

falsehoods
    Mis. 222–13 *f·* that once he would have resisted
        238–27 another evidence of the *f·*
        248–11 *f·* uttered about me
        277–15 by slanderous *f·*, and
    '01. 16–27 one hundred *f·* told about it

falsely
    Mis. 8–24 against you *f·*, — *Matt.* 5 : 11.
    Man. 54–21 represents *f·* to or of the Leader
    Ret. 25–24 material senses testify *f·*,
    Un. 39–25 material senses testify *f·*.
    Rud. 8–25 mortal mind should not be *f·*
    No. 11–13 those who come *f·* in its name.
        18–18 Thus *f·* may the human conceive of
    '01. 3– 6 against you *f·*, — *Matt.* 5 : 11.
    '02. 11–24 against you *f·*, — *Matt.* 5 : 11.
    My. 104–31 against you *f·*, — *Matt.* 5 : 11.
        316– 8 against you *f·*, — *Matt.* 5 : 11.

falsities
    Mis. 24–30 put down all subtle *f·*
        309–21 Corporeal *f·* include all obstacles to
    Un. 10–28 under their own *f·*,
        45–12 An evil ego, and . . . are *f·*.
        45–12 These *f·* need a denial.
    '01. 16– 8 its lusts, *f·*, envy, and hate,

falsities
My.	248–10	put an end to *f·* in a wise way
	249– 8	counteract its most gigantic *f·*.

falsity
Mis.	57–20	history of a *f·* must be told
	65– 2	by repeated proofs of its *f·*.
	84–26	A true sense of the *f·* of material
	107–21	must first be shown its *f·*
	108– 9	since a lie, . . . is merely a *f·* ;
	201– 8	element of matter, or material *f·*,
	201–10	myth or material *f·* of evil ;
	333– 7	renders error a palpable *f·*,
	334–20	reduce this *f·* to its proper
Ret.	61–14	you are a self-constituted *f·*,
	81–11	and *f·* must thus decay,
	86– 9	Note well the *f·* of this mortal self !
Un.	32–28	to demonstrate the *f·* of the claim.
	33–21	witnesses for error, or *f·*,
	35–27	an outlined *f·* of consciousness,
	45–13	The *f·* is the teaching that
Rud.	8–20	*f·* shuts against him the Truth
No.	38– 3	*f·* of the evidence of the material
Pan.	5–23	deny it and prove its *f·*.
'01.	14– 8	false entity, and utter *f·*,
My.	161–30	*f·* of supposititious life

falter
Mis.	135–12	If you *f·*, or fail to fulfil this
My.	11– 3	* although we may *f·* or stumble
	162–28	may their faith never *f·*
	248–19	No . . . can fold or *f·* your wings.

faltering
Mis.	331–20	guards the nestling's *f·* flight !
	389– 8	guards the nestling's *f·* flight !
Po.	4– 5	guards the nestling's *f·* flight !

falters
My.	130–19	Truth never *f·* nor fails ;

fame
Mis.	145– 8	Does a single bosom burn for *f·*
	270– 4	such as barter . . . for money and *f·*.
	327–12	and to search for wealth and *f·*.
Ret.	2–27	Henry Knox of Revolutionary *f·*.
Pul.	2– 5	the *f·* which I heard.'' — *I Kings* 10 : 7.
	46–22	* Wallace of mighty Scottish *f·*.
No.	43–19	motives, for wealth and *f·*,
'00.	13–18	the god of medicine, acquired *f·* ;
Hea.	16– 7	wealth and *f·*, or Truth and Love?
Po.	42– 5	for glory and *f·*, Without heart
My.	258– 4	lifts a system . . . to deserved *f·*
	283–29	Lured by *f·*, pride, or gold,
	306– 3	into a conflict for *f·*.

fame-honored
Ret.	17–15	*f·* hickory rears his bold form,
Po.	62–18	*f·* hickory rears his bold form,

familiar
Mis.	177–29	greets with joy a *f·* face.
	247– 6	Those *f·* with my history
	364– 9	and posterity your *f·* !
	372–14	critics *f·* with the works of masters
	372–17	* seems quite *f·* with delineations
Ret.	10– 5	*f·* with Lindley Murray's Grammar
Un.	14–21	if this Mind is *f·* with evil,
Pul.	41–27	* Old *f·* hymns — ''All hail
My.	92–14	* has in general way been *f·* ;
	134–29	* with which I have been *f·* for several

familiarity
Mis.	239–24	their *f·* with what the stock paid,
Pul.	31–10	* *f·* with the work of her life

families
Mis.	6–25	*f·* where laws of health are strictly
	6–32	small *f·* of one or two children,
Pul.	30– 1	* members of their own *f·*,
	59–26	* children of believing *f·*
My.	112–31	chief cities and the best *f·*

family
all the
My.	310–18	all the *f·*, ''excepting Albert,

grand
Mis.	273–14	one grand *f·* of Christ's followers.

her
Ret.	1– 5	her *f·* is said to have been
	5–29	* to secure the happiness of her *f·*.
Pul.	46–16	* Her *f·* came to this country

his
My.	308–12	my late father and his *f·*

his father's
My.	309–17	the youngest of his father's *f·*,

home and
Pul.	50– 5	* a home and *f·* of his own.

human
Mis.	18–27	of the whole human *f·*,
	98–12	helping the whole human *f·* ;
No.	15– 7	blessings for the whole human *f·*.
My.	208–20	prayer for the whole human *f·*.

family
large
Mis.	6–29	large *f·* of children where the

member of the
Mis.	89– 5	*to care for a member of the f·,*

my father's
My.	310–19	a death in my father's *f·*

New Hampshire
Pul.	57–27	* born of an old New Hampshire *f·*,

peace in the
Mis.	354– 9	promote peace in the *f·*,

remained
Ret.	5–10	and there the *f·* remained

same
My.	227–12	same disease and in the same *f·*,

Wiggin
My.	322–16	* to dine with the Wiggin *f·*.

Mis.	236– 7	shrunk from . . . *f·* difficulties,
Ret.	2–30	my Grandmother Baker's *f·*
	13–11	the *f·* doctor was summoned,
	17– 1	while visiting a *f·* friend
	20– 9	under the care of our *f·* nurse,
	20–27	*f·* to whose care he was
Pul.	48–21	* her *f·* coat of arms
'01.	31–22	daily Bible reading and *f·* prayer ;
'02.	3–10	reinstating the old national *f·* pride
Po.	vii– 1	* *while visiting a f· friend*
My.	295–23	Countess of Dunmore and *F·*,
	311–22	her own *f·* coat-of-arms.

famine
Mis.	246–23	the spiritual *f·* of 1866,
	338–27	* Shall the world's *f·* feed ;
Ret.	23–20	Soulless *f·* had fled.
My.	126–21	and mourning, and *f·* ; — *Rev.* 18 : 8.
	263– 7	feast of Soul and a *f·* of sense.

famishing
No.	43– 6	whether stall-fed or *f·*,

famous
Ret.	32–11	Calderon, the *f·* Spanish poet,
Pul.	67–11	* Max O'Rell's *f·* enumeration of
'01.	21– 8	* ''To the *f·* Bishop Berkeley
My.	68–16	* Mrs. Eddy's *f·* room will be
	95–14	*f·* old Massachusetts State House.
	141–16	* its *f·* communion seasons.
	271–19	* thought that has made her *f·*.

fan
Po.	30–12	*f·* Thou the flame Of right

fanatic
Po.	71– 8	Rescued by the ''*f·*'' hand,

fanaticism
Mis.	48–10	whether of ignorance or *f·*,
My.	79–25	* without a trace of *f·*,
	96– 7	* slightest trace of *f·*.
	96– 9	* where *f·* dominates everything else.

fancied
Ret.	12– 6	Woke by her *f·* feet.
Po.	61– 4	Woke by her *f·* feet.
My.	314–11	which he *f·*, for a summer home.

fancies
Mis.	15– 1	*f·* he finds pleasure in it,

fancy
Mis.	12– 9	do not *f·* that you have been wronged
	393– 4	Gives the artist's *f·* wings.
	396– 3	And frightened *f·* flees,
Ret.	11– 5	If *f·* plumes aerial flight,
Un.	18–10	Many *f·* that our heavenly Father
Pan.	3– 1	mythical deity may please the *f·*,
Po.	3– 9	Till sleep sets drooping *f·* free
	51– 9	Gives the artist's *f·* wings.
	58–15	And frightened *f·* flees,
	60– 1	If *f·* plumes aerial flight,
My.	258–32	*F·* yourselves with me ;

fane
Chr.	53–58	Truth's *f·* can dim ;
My.	151–17	* ''Pass ye proud *f·* by,

fanes
Pul.	10– 8	Rome's fallen *f·* and silent

fanned
Mis.	233– 7	*f·* by the breath of mental

Fantasie in E minor, Merkel
My.	32–11	* organ voluntary — *F· in E m·*, *M·*

fantastic
Un.	26–24	there is in God naught *f·*.

far
Mis.	6–15	will rank *f·* in advance of allopathy
	9–14	good *f·* beyond the present sense
	12–32	imparting, so *f·* as we reflect them,
	13– 2	just so *f·* as one and all permit me

far

Mis.	19– 8	task of healing the sick is *f·* lighter
	22– 8	*f·* in advance of human knowledge
	34–13	so *f·* as I understand it,
	38–17	*f·* from dry and abstract.
	43–14	*f·* more advantageous to the sick
	84–22	so *f·* extinguished the latter as
	103– 4	*f·* more impregnable and solid than
	103–24	so *f·* as material sense could
	123–31	*f·* apart from physical sensation
	158– 3	not as our ways ; but higher *f·*
	180– 2	so *f·* as to take the side of Spirit,
	186– 7	material belief has fallen *f·* below
	213–28	the night is *f·* spent,
	234–24	has seen *f·* into the spiritual facts of
	291–17	and is *f·* from my desire ;
	297– 5	has achieved *f·* more than
	344–23	Such philosophy is *f·* from
	352–24	out of himself and into God so *f·* that
	371–12	They know *f·* more of C. S. than
	385–14	emancipate for this *f·* shore
	385–16	and *f·* from mortal joys,
Ret.	9–22	* From the *f·* cataracts?
	10– 3	with *f·* less labor than is usually
	12– 1	nobler *f·* than clarion call
	38– 1	I had finished that edition as *f·*
	54–20	*f·* in advance of their theory.
	60– 2	very *f·* from the divine likeness.
	76–15	This affection, so *f·* from being
	87– 8	can be *f·* more thoroughly and
Un.	2–24	their lives have grown so *f·* toward the
	6–16	and the world is *f·* from ready to
	9–23	but in a *f·* different form.
	45– 9	very *f·* from God's likeness.''
Pul.	3–28	so *f·* from victory over the flesh
	32–14	* so *f·* as outward events may translate
	57–24	* not *f·* from the big Mechanics Building
	82–11	* *f·* better than her teachers.
Rud.	6–21	so *f·* as you perceive and understand
No.	15–13	are *f·* more mystic than
	20– 1	so *f·* as he can conceive of
	29–16	Better *f·* that we impute such
	38– 1	so *f·* as this could be done
Pan.	1–17	The night is *f·* spent,
'00.	3–15	not *f·* from saying and doing.
	7–24	find ourselves so *f·* from the
'01.	34–25	only so *f·* as she follows Christ.
'02.	4– 4	only so *f·* as she follows Christ.
	12–24	so *f·* as I know them,
Peo.	4–16	are *f·* from correct.
Po.	1– 9	And *f·* the universal fiat ran,
	16–12	through *f·* crimson glow,
	22– 7	*f·* heaven is nigh !
	25– 8	*F·* do ye flee,
	29–17	so *f·* above All mortal strife,
	34–20	in azure bright soar *f·* above ;
	48– 7	emancipate for this *f·* shore
	48– 9	and *f·* from mortal joys,
	60–21	Strains nobler *f·* than clarion call
My.	7– 7	so *f·* as I know them,
	21–22	* their brethren from *f·* and near,
	30–12	* business men come from *f·* distant
	30–28	* by *f·* the largest crowd of the day
	41–13	* howsoever *f·* he may stray,
	59– 6	* might be true in some *f·* distant day
	74– 2	* from abroad and from the *f·* West
	75–21	* no matter how *f·* they had travelled
	79– 6	* chapter sub-title
	79–21	* placed upon a *f·* higher pedestal
	88–12	* of *f·* more than usual ecclesiastic
	93– 1	* so *f·* as the writer knows them,
	97– 4	* *f·* towards making the patient well.
	97–13	* the advantage so *f·* as this goes.
	152– 7	*f·* lower in the scale of thought,
	163–29	was *f·* from my purpose, when I came
	197–13	ready hands of our *f·* Western
	202– 6	for the night is *f·* spent
	206–16	belief, which is *f·* from the fact
	229–13	Better *f·* that Christian Scientists
	242–12	I do not mean that . . . *f·* from it.
	262–10	*f·* short of my sense of the
	273– 6	* a Leader *f·* beyond the allotted years of
	291–18	and so *f·* as it fathomed
	306– 4	*F·* be it from me to tread on the
	312– 9	* She was *f·* from home
	313–25	to describe scenes *f·* away,
	322–20	* journeying from the *f·* South,
	323– 7	* some minister in the *f·* West
	327–29	* to the day, not *f·* distant,
	346– 4	* and so *f·* from being puzzled

farce

Mis.	288–25	real suffering would stop the *f·*.

fare

Mis.	275–28	and the *f·* is appetizing.
My.	312–12	* Masons also paid Mrs. Glover's *f·*

farewell

Po.	27–24	Illustrious year, *f·* !
My.	50–30	* her *f·* sermon to the church.

farewells

Mis.	386–28	Where *f·* cloud not o'er
Po.	50–14	Where *f·* cloud not o'er

Farlow

Alfred

My.	141–13	* Alfred *F·* of the publication committee

Mr. Alfred

My.	16–16	* Mr. Alfred *F·*, President of The

farm

Ret.	4– 4	inherited my grandfather's *f·*
	4– 7	One hundred acres of the old *f·*
Pul.	33–18	* on his father's *f·* at Lexington,
	48–11	* that lies below, across the *f·*,
	49–24	* She chose the stubbly old *f·*
	49–30	* to keep the grounds and *f·*
My.	172– 5	* grown on the *f·* of Mark Baker,
	309–18	an extensive *f·* situated in Bow

Farmer

Pul.	88–14	* *F·*, Bridgeport, Conn.
	88–30	* *F·*, Bridgeport, N. Y.

farm-house

Ret.	4–10	*f·*, situated on the summit of

far-off

Mis.	153–29	* music of this *F·*, infinite, Bliss !
Pul.	22–11	and a few in *f·* lands,
	41– 9	* from the *f·* Pacific coast

Farrand & Votey

Pul.	60–16	* organ, made by *F·* & *V·*

far-reaching

My.	236–18	a *f·* motive and success,

far-seeing

Mis.	254– 3	loving warning, the *f·* wisdom,
'01.	30–25	clear, *f·* vision, the calm courage,
My.	208–24	courageous, *f·* committees

farther

Mis.	52–25	a rule *f·* on and more difficult
	73–15	can get no *f·* than to say,
	316–13	depart *f·* from the primitives of
	378–21	*f·* removed from such thoughts
Ret.	11–21	*F·* than feet of chamois fall,
Po.	60–19	*F·* than feet of chamois fall,

Far West

Ret.	20–29	then regarded as the *F· W·*.

fascinated

Pul.	32–11	* *f·* the imagination.

fashion

Mis.	219–14	think also after a sickly *f·*.
	354–32	Whenever he soareth to *f·* his nest,
Rud.	12–13	aided in this mistaken *f·*,
No.	20– 5	Error would *f·* Deity in a manlike
	39– 6	after the *f·* of Baal's prophets,
My.	121–14	is somewhat out of *f·*.

fashionable

Mis.	111–22	sects, the pulpit, and *f·* society,
	233–16	into a more *f·* cut
Pul.	24– 3	* church is in the *f·* Back Bay,
My.	192– 6	cast out *f·* lunacy.
	224–20	more *f·* but less correct.

fashioned

Mis.	360– 6	good, because *f·* divinely,

fashions

Mis.	376–30	He who *f·* forever such forms

fast

Mis.	117–24	inclined to be too *f·* or too slow :
	154– 4	*f·* reaching out their broad shelter
	307–18	*f·* fitting all minds for the
	354–27	*F·* gathering strength for a flight
	363–24	hold *f·* to the Principle of C. S.
	400–24	Be it slow or *f·*,
Chr.	53– 1	*F·* circling on, from zone to zone,
Ret.	78– 2	being too *f·* or too slow.
'00.	1–14	right convictions *f·* forming
	14– 5	Hold that *f·* which thou — *Rev.* 3 : 11.
'01.	14– 3	sin itself, that clings *f·* to
	31–25	held *f·* to whatever is good,
Peo.	8–26	*f·* fading into ashes ;
Po.	27–19	Thou *f·* expiring year,
	69–12	Be it slow or *f·*,
My.	44– 7	* our progress may be *f·* or
	82–11	* disgorging trunks . . . so *f·* that
	129– 2	"hold *f·* that which — *I Thess.* 5 : 21.
	190– 7	*f·* answering this question :
	201– 3	*f·* fulfilling the promises.
	205– 3	"Stand *f·* therefore — *Gal.* 5 : 1.
	334–21	that clings *f·* to iniquity.
	335–20	* excitement which was *f·* arising,
	339–19	Pharisees *f·* oft, — *Matt.* 9 : 14.

fast
My. 339–19   thy disciples *f·* not?" — *Matt.* 9 : 14.
339–25   but he did not appoint a *f·*.
339–30   observance of a material *f·*

Fast Day
in New Hampshire, 1899
My. 339–11   chapter sub-title
————
My. 339–14   has exchanged *F· D·*,

fasten
Mis. 312–24   which reason . . . cannot *f·* upon.
Ret. 18–17   soar above matter, to *f·* on God,
Un. 17– 2   seeks to *f·* all error upon God,
Po. 64– 8   soar above matter, to *f·* on God,

fastened
Pul. 42–27   * pure white roses *f·* with

fastens
My. 283–30   never *f·* on the good

faster
Mis. 327–17   ascend *f·* than themselves,
Hea. 9– 1   and progress *f·* than we are
My. 56–19   * increased *f·* than ever.

fast-increasing
Pul. 47– 7   * members of this *f·* faith.

fasting
Mis. 156–21   by prayer and *f·*." — *Matt.* 17 : 21.
'02. 16–23   *F·*, feasting, or penance,
My. 190–17   by prayer and *f·*." — *Matt.* 17 : 21.
222–13   by prayer and *f·*" — *Matt.* 17 : 21.
339–25   by prayer and *f·*," — *Matt.* 17 : 21.

fasts
'00. 15–16   and *f·* in the wilderness.
My. 340– 2   of his observing appointed *f·*.

fat
Mis. 326–11   fed by the *f·* of hypocrisy

fatal
Mis. 24– 9   pronounced *f·* by the physicians.
45– 9   *f·* results that frequently follow
71– 5   from this *f·* appetite.
72–10   to impart to man this *f·* power.
93–28   Nothing is more *f·* than to
121–13   would make this *f·* doctrine just
222–16   malicious mental argument . . . is *f·*,
233–14   *f·* magnetic force of mortal mind,
264–30   more *f·* than a mistake in physics.
380–14   an accident, called *f·* to life,
Ret. 19–10   which in his case proved *f·*.
33–20   its *f·* essence, mortal mind ;
71–23   false convictions and a *f·* ignorance.
Un. 52–21   rabid beasts, *f·* reptiles, and mortals
Rud. 17– 1   A slight divergence is *f·* in Science.
'01. 2– 9   *f·* magnetic element of human will
34– 7   cannot be *f·* to the patient,
My. 234–25   more *f·* than the Boxers' rebellion.
248–18   No *f·* circumstance of idolatry
249–13   mental miasma *f·* to health,
293–11   that the bullet would prove *f·*.

fate
Mis. 83–17   arbiter of your own *f·*,
134–28   blind to its own *f·*, it will
202– 5   * where the good man meets his *f·*
230–23   * With a heart for any *f·* ;
291–18   is the irony of *f·*,
Ret. 23– 4   yield to the irony of *f·*,
No. 42–18   fact and *f·* to being.
My. 165– 2   Of two things *f·* cannot rob us;
185– 5   * With a heart for any *f·* ;

Father (*see also* **Father's**)
adoption with the
Mis. 182–10   their adoption with the *F·* ;
and Mother
Mis. 33–11   God, our divine *F·* and Mother.
96–11   as a loving *F·* and Mother ;
113– 5   Spirit is our *F·* and Mother,
154–23   thy *F·* and Mother, God.
167–17   *F·* and Mother are divine Life,
186–14   the universal *F·* and Mother of man ;
Un. 48–14   *F·* and Mother of all He creates ;
'00. 5–10   *F·* and Mother are synonymous
'01. 10–18   God as both *F·* and Mother.
and son
'02. 12–18   *F·* and son, are one in being.
begotten of the
Mis. 164–26   the only begotten of the *F·*,
bids man
Un. 4–18   *F·* bids man have the same Mind
bosom of the
'02. 9–20   forever in the bosom of the *F·*,
came from the
Mis. 360–29   "I came from the *F·*," — *see John* 16 : 28.
even the
Un. 60–13   "bless we God, even the *F·* ; — *Jas.* 3 : 9.

Father
everlasting
Mis. 161– 7   *The everlasting F·*, — *Isa.* 9 : 6.
164–19   The everlasting *F·*, — *Isa.* 9 : 6.
258–24   even the everlasting *F·*,
321– 6   The everlasting *F·*, — *Isa.* 9 : 6.
God is
My. 279–16   God is *F·*, infinite, and
God the
My. 344– 5   God the *F·* is greater than Christ,
goes to the
'02. 8–23   the ego, or I, goes to the *F·*,
go to the
Mis. 195–31   The "I" will go to the *F·* — *John* 14 : 12.
Un. 41–20   and we shall go to the *F·*,
great
My. 50–18   * feeling of trust in the great *F·*,
heavenly
Mis. 72–20   *heavenly F· knoweth* — *Matt.* 6 : 32.
249–24   My heavenly *F·* will never leave me
Ret. 37–18   until our heavenly *F·* saw fit,
Un. 18–10   Many fancy that our heavenly *F·*
'02. 11– 2   Our heavenly *F·* never destined
My. 9– 9   * thankfulness to his heavenly *F·*
36–10   * with our infinite heavenly *F·*
327–27   * We thank our heavenly *F·*
his
Mis. 74– 8   Son of man in the glory of his *F·* ;
167–17   His *F·* and Mother are divine Life,
167–18   they who do the will of his *F·*
Ret. 69– 4   God is his *F·*,
Un. 53–25   or else . . . God, is not his *F·* ;
No. 41– 8   to do the will of his *F·*
41–11   and the glory of his *F·*.
'01. 9–29   the spirit of his *F·* speaketh
'02. 8–30   conscious that God is his *F·*,
honored
Mis. 81–15   *benediction of an honored F·*,
is perfect
Mis. 286–31   even as the *F·* is perfect,
live in the
'01. 6– 2   live in the *F·* and have no
loved of the
Hea. 2–21   Jesus, the loved of the *F·*,
love of a
No. 30–14   love of a *F·* for His child,
loving
Mis. 96–11   as a loving *F·* and Mother ;
Un. 53–25   man's origin and loving *F·*,
man's
Un. 53–23   Man's *F·* is not a mortal mind
my
Mis. 37– 9   "I and my *F·* are one." — *John* 10 : 30.
157–15   my *F·* is your Father ;
192–11   *I go unto my F·*. — *John* 14 : 12.
194–20   I go unto my *F·*." — *John* 14 : 12.
278–12   as my *F·* seeth them.
Chr. 55–23   the will of my *F·* — *Matt.* 12 : 50.
Un. 46–13   "I and my *F·* are one." — *John* 10 : 30.
Pan. 8–20   "My *F·* is greater than I." — *John* 14 : 28.
'01. 8– 8   "I and my *F·* are one," — *John* 10 : 30.
8– 8   "my *F·* is greater than I," — *John* 14 : 28.
'02. 12–15   "I and my *F·* are one," — *John* 10 : 30.
My. 202–28   "Herein is my *F·* — *John* 15 : 8.
of all
Mis. 226– 3   * *F·* of all will care for him."
Pan. 13–23   *F·* of all, who is above — *Eph.* 4 : 6.
'00. 4–30   "*F·* of all, who is above — *Eph.* 4 : 6.
My. 288–11   and He is the *F·* of all.
of lights
Un. 14–17   "the *F·* of lights, — *Jas.* 1 : 17.
of man
Mis. 164–32   God is the *F·* of man,
of the universe
My. 148–15   the *F·* of the universe
one
My. 198– 6   gratitude to our one *F·*.
one with the
Un. 61– 7   he was one with the *F·*,
My. 344– 6   Christ is 'one with the *F·*,'
our
Mis. 100–30   symptoms by which our *F·*
113– 5   Spirit is our *F·* and Mother,
151–13   God is our *F·* and our Mother,
154–14   our *F·* is husbandman.
369–27   the vine which our *F·* tends.
Rud. 1– 7   our *F·* which is in heaven.
No. 40–26   our *F·* has done this ;
'02. 19–30   cup that our *F·* permits us.
Peo. 8–24   We thank our *F·* that to-day
9–14   after the model of our *F·*,
12–27   our *F·* bestows heaven
our common
Mis. 138–11   guidance of our common *F·*
371– 9   guidance of our common *F·*,

Father
  prayer to the
    Mis. 133–24   in silent prayer to the *F·*
  Principle, or
    No. 25–14   his divine Principle, or *F·*.
       26–15   his divine Principle, or *F·*,
  relation to the
    No. 36–16   higher self and relation to the *F·*,
  represented by the
    Pul. 13– 1   Life, represented by the *F·* ;
  similitude of the
    Mis. 162–24   after the similitude of the *F·*,
  their
    Mis. 278–18   reflect the image of their *F·*.
  thy
    Mis. 133–15   pray to thy *F·* — *Matt.* 6 : 6.
      133–16   thy *F·* which seeth in — *Matt.* 6 : 6.
      154–23   thy *F·* and Mother, God.
  unto the
    My. 206–26   "Giving thanks unto the *F·*, — *Col.* 1 : 12.
  was glorified
    Ret. 94–29   the *F·* was glorified therein.
  will of the
    '01. 18–19   "the will of the *F·*." — see *Matt.* 12 : 50.
  worship the
    Mis. 124– 4   those who worship the *F·*
      150–19   worship the *F·* "in spirit — *John* 4 : 23.
      321–14   worship the *F·* in spirit — *John* 4 : 23.
    Ret. 65–13   worship the *F·* "in spirit — *John* 4 : 23.
    No. 34–10   worship the *F·* in spirit — *John* 4 : 23.
  your
    Mis. 85–14   your *F·* which is in heaven — *Matt.* 5 : 48.
      157–15   my Father is your *F·* ;
      181– 1   "for one is your *F·*," — *Matt.* 23 : 9.
      287– 7   for one is your *F·*, — *Matt.* 23 : 9.
    Ret. 68–14   for one is your *F·*, — *Matt.* 23 : 9.
    Un. 53–27   for one is your *F·*, — *Matt.* 23 : 9.
    Pan. 8–19   for one is your *F·*, — *Matt.* 23 : 9.
      9–12   your *F·* which is in heaven — *Matt.* 5 : 48.
    '01. 8–16   your *F·* which is in heaven — *Matt.* 5 : 48.

    Mis. 18–19   *F·*, Mother, and child are the
      46–29   man is perfect even as the *F·*,
      83–24   *F·*, the hour is come ; — *John* 17 : 1.
      103–31   therefore is forever with the *F·*.
      167–23   "I thank Thee, O *F·*, — *Luke* 10 : 21.
      182–22   than he hath seen the *F·*.
      184–28   that saith Abba, *F·*,
      196–25   the "I" does go unto the *F·*, — *John* 14 : 12.
      206– 6   the *F·* and Mother's welcome,
      275–17   *F·*, we thank Thee that
      368– 3   Even so, *F·*, let the light
      373–29   at the right hand of the *F·*.
      397–15   *F·*, where Thine own children are,
    Un. 51–22   The Ego is revealed as *F·*, Son, and
    Pul. 18–24   *F·*, where Thine own children are,
      82–16   * who never called Abraham "*F·*,"
    No. 8– 1   *F·*, whose wisdom is unerring
      37– 4   and dwelt forever in the *F·*.
      44–28   "I thank Thee, O *F·*, — *Luke* 10 : 21.
    '00. 5–11   *F·*, Son, and Holy Ghost
    Hea. 16–28   cometh unto the *F·*, — *John* 14 : 6.
    Po. 13– 3   *F·*, where Thine own children are,
      43–10   *F·*, in Thy great heart hold them
    My. 180–28   "*F·*, forgive them ; — *Luke* 23 : 34.
      270–19   "*F·*, forgive them ; — *Luke* 23 : 34.
      301–10   *F·*, teach us the life of Love.
      350–12   *F·*, did'st not Thou the dark wave

father (*see also* **father's**)
  and mother
    Ret. 5–11   names of both *f·* and mother
      22–19   his *f·* and mother are the one Spirit,
    Pul. 54–24   * permitting only the *f·* and mother,
    '01. 29–23   who honor their *f·* and mother.
    My. 313–14   I only know that my *f·* and mother
  another
    Mis. 183–25   for it claims another *f·*.
    Un. 39–15   claims another *f·*,
  bruised
    Mis. 275– 9   bruised *f·* bendeth his aching
  chasteneth not
    Un. 23–12   the *f·* chasteneth not? — *Heb.* 12 : 7.
  Franklin Pierce's
    My. 308–21   President Franklin Pierce's *f·*,
  her
    My. 310–23   * her *f·*, a gray-haired man of fifty,
  her late
    My. 311–27   on the mound of her late *f·*,
  his
    Mis. 214– 7   variance against his *f·*, — *Matt.* 10 : 35.
    Ret. 22–19   his *f·* and mother are the one Spirit,
    Un. 23– 5   was to his *f·* ever loyal.
  human
    Un. 48–16   than the human *f·* enters into his

father
  Mark Baker's
    My. 309–20   Mark Baker's *f·* paid the largest tax
  my
    Mis. 237–29   and he visited my *f·*,
    Ret. 4– 2   youngest of whom was my *f·*,
      5–14   My *f·* possessed a strong intellect
      10– 1   My *f·* was taught to believe
    My. 308–20   my *f·* was visiting Governor Pierce,
      308–23   My *f·* thanked the Governor,
      308–26   attributes to my *f·* language
      308–30   my *f·* was a great reader.
      309–10   and my *f·* won the suit.
      309–11   Mr. Pierce bowed to my *f·*
      309–14   My *f·* was a strong believer in
      313– 9   stories . . . about my *f·*
      313–14   know that my *f·* and mother
  my late
    My. 308–12   my late *f·* and his family
  of every age
    Po. 28– 1   *F·* of every age,
  of itself
    Un. 52–17   evil, . . . is the *f·* of itself,
  of lies
    Rud. 7–21   "the *f·* of lies ;" — see *John* 8 : 44.
  of man
    Mis. 77–28   or, that man is the *f·* of man.
    Ret. 68– 6   neither indeed can be, the *f·* of man.
  of nothingness
    '01. 13–14   and the *f·* of nothingness.
  of our nation
    My. 148–15   and the *f·* of our nation
  or mother
    Man. 69–19   loveth *f·* or mother more — *Matt.* 10 : 37.
  their
    Mis. 240–25   see their *f·* with a cigarette
    Un. 17–14   their *f·*, the devil,
    '01. 29–23   honor their *f·* and mother.
  was chaplain
    My. 309–12   several years *f·* was chaplain
  without
    Chr. 55–20   Without *f·*, without mother, — *Heb.* 7 : 3.
  your
    Mis. 287– 6   "Call no man your *f·* — *Matt.* 23 : 9.
    Ret. 68–14   "call no man your *f·* — *Matt.* 23 : 9.
    Un. 53–26   "Call no man your *f·* — *Matt.* 23 : 9.
    Pan. 5–12   "Ye are of your *f·*, — *John* 8 : 44.
      5–13   lusts of your *f·* ye will — *John* 8 : 44.
      8–18   "Call no man your *f·* — *Matt.* 23 : 9.

    Mis. 24–27   and the *f·* of it." — *John* 8 : 44.
      83–18   and the *f·* of it — *John* 8 : 44.
      121–19   Who, then, shall *f·* or favor
      181– 1   Jesus said to call no man *f·* ;
      196–14   and the *f·* of it." — *John* 8 : 44.
      259– 5   and the *f·* of it." — *John* 8 : 44.
    Ret. 67–25   and the *f·* of it." — *John* 8 : 44.
    Un. 32–23   and the *f·* of it." — *John* 8 : 44.
    No. 32–16   and the *f·* of it." — *John* 8 : 44.
    Pan. 5–16   and the *f·* of it — *John* 8 : 44.
    '00. 5– 8   and the *f·* of it" — *John* 8 : 44.
    My. 172– 6   * *f·* of the Rev. Mary Baker Eddy,
      270–16   are the *f·* of their *wish*.

fatherliness
    Mis. 234–31   God's *f·* as Life, Truth, and Love,
    No. 19–14   *f·* of this Supreme Being.

fatherly
    My. 288–32   evil is not a *f·* grace.

Father-Mother
    Mis. 102–15   loving, divine *F·* God.
      127–11   petitions the divine *F·* God
      400–14   *F·* God, Loving me,
      400–20   *F·* good, lovingly Thee I seek,
    Rud. 4– 1   Mind, the one *F·* God.
    Pan. 15– 5   May our *F·* God, who in times past
    '01. 3– 3   benediction of our *F·* God
      7– 9   all-knowing, all-loving *F·*,
      7–15   consistently say, "Our *F·* God"
    Po. 69– 2   *F·* God, Loving me,
      69– 8   *F·* good, lovingly Thee I seek,
    My. 18– 8   petitions the divine *F·* God
      186–12   anthem of one *F·* God,
      265–31   we thank our *F·* God.
      281–13   God, good, the *F·* Love,
      347– 4   likeness of the *F·* God,

Father's
    Mis. 77–15   This is the *F·* great Love
      81–29   This *is* the *F·* benediction.
      125–11   sit down at the *F·* right hand :
      150– 1   your *F·* good pleasure — *Luke* 12 : 32.
      163–31   forever about the *F·* business ;
      321–11   your *F·* good pleasure — *Luke* 12 : 32.
      326–18   forced to seek the *F·* house,
      369–25   we would find our *F·* house

Father's

Ret.	50–27	it was the *F·* opportunity
Pul.	9–22	your *F·* good pleasure— *Luke* 12 : 32.
'01.	17– 4	to return to the *F·* house
Peo.	3–27	obedience to our *F·* demands,
My.	133– 1	*F·* house in which are many

father's

Mis.	124–17	with more than a *f·* pity ;
Ret.	1– 3	great-grandfather, on my *f·* side,
	13–13	My *f·* relentless theology
	20– 5	my *f·* second marriage,
	81–23	puts this pious counsel into a *f·*
Pul.	32–23	* On her *f·* side Mrs. Eddy came
	33–18	* one day on his *f·* farm
	34– 3	* returned to her *f·* home
My.	308–15	my *f·* "tall, gaunt frame"
	308–18	My *f·* person was erect
	309–17	youngest of his *f·* family,
	309–18	inherited his *f·* real estate,
	309–23	*f·* house had a sloping roof,
	310– 1	All my *f·* daughters were
	310–19	death in my *f·* family
	312–13	* taken to her *f·* home by her
	312–28	took me to my *f·* home
	313–30	after my *f·* second marriage
	313–31	not welcome in my *f·* house.

Fathers

'01.	34–12	canonical writings of the *F·*,

(*see also* **Pilgrim Fathers**)

fathers (*see also* fathers')

Mis.	72–14	*f·* have eaten sour grapes,— *Ezek.* 18 : 2.
	96–16	manner of my *f·*,— see *Acts* 24 : 14.
	245– 6	slept with his *f·*."— II *Chron.* 16 : 13.
Ret.	64–15	generation of his *f·* ;— *Psal.* 49 : 19.
'02.	6–11	Jesus said a lie *f·* itself,
My.	43– 8	* revealed the God of their *f·*,
	192–13	God of our *f·*, the infinite Person
	285–26	God of my *f·*,— *Acts* 24 : 14.

fathers'

My.	185–28	Our God, our *f·* God !

fathom

Po.	2– 7	Ah, who can *f·* thee !

fathomed

No.	17–24	infinite harmony would be *f·*.
My.	291–18	so far as it *f·* the abyss of

fathomless

'02.	4–10	*f·* peace between Soul and sense
Po.	30– 9	With thy still *f·* Christ-majesty.

fatigued

Man.	60– 8	Scientist is not *f·* by prayer,
Pul.	36–15	* I went to her peculiarly *f·*.

fatiguing

No.	15– 7	*F·* Bible translations

fatling

Mis.	145–24	young lion and the *f·*— *Isa.* 11 : 6.
My.	177–20	as a *f·* of the flock.

fatness

Pul.	1– 1	*with the f· of Thy house;— Psal.* 36 : 8.
	3–16	with the *f·* of Thy house ;— *Psal.* 36 : 8.
	4–26	with the *f·* of Thy house."— *Psal.* 36 : 8.
	7–29	with the *f·* of Thy house ; — *Psal.* 36 : 8.

fattened

Mis.	240– 5	*f·* by metaphysical hygiene.

fattening

Mis.	250– 7	*f·* the lamb to slay it.

fatuous

Un.	10–22	To attempt the calculation . . . is *f·*.

fault

Mis.	38– 8	whole system . . . is at *f·*,
	129–10	to tell thy brother his *f·*
	130–10	for a *f·* in somebody else,
	233–24	finds *f·* with the exactness of
	265–25	the *f·* is not in the culture
	284–18	and told him his *f·*,
	291–17	this is not my *f·*,
	335–22	is a *f·* of zealots,
	340–11	law-school is not at *f·* which
Rud.	14–23	it is their own *f·*,
My.	104– 9	they could find no *f·* in him,

faultless

'01.	6–18	logic of divine Science being *f·*,

faults

Mis.	11–20	try not to expose their *f·*,
	112–27	inability to see one's own *f·*,
	129–20	will see somebody's *f·* to magnify
	223–29	To punish ourselves for others' *f·*,
	224– 5	wounded by our own *f·* ;
	224– 6	to be miserable for the *f·* of others.
	317–28	penalty for other people's *f·* ;

faults

Ret.	72– 7	portrays the result of secret *f·*,
Pul.	15– 9	to tell a man his *f·*,

faulty

Mis.	66– 2	obedience thereto may be found *f·*,

favor

Mis.	121–19	father or *f·* this sentence
	164–21	it grew in *f·* with them.
	285– 1	in *f·* of combating evil only,
	381–16	a decree in *f·* of Mrs. Eddy
Pul.	31–21	* begging the *f·* of an interview
'02.	12–27	annually *f·* us with their presence
	14–23	neither *f·* nor protection
My.	6– 1	in *f·* of a decision which we
	7–10	annually *f·* us with their presence
	92–26	* things to be said in *f·* of C. S.
	175–19	this *f·* of our city government ;
	221– 4	now as then, from finding *f·* with
	314–21	to record the divorce in my *f·*.
	326– 5	* because a *f·* has been extended,
	341–24	* a special *f·* that Mrs. Eddy
	360–29	Your *f·* of the 10th instant

favorable

Mis.	132– 4	I shall take this as a *f·* omen,
	370–20	What figure is less *f·* than
My.	10– 4	* enlarge the *f·* expectation,
	37–26	* confident and *f·* expectation.

favorably

Pul.	62– 3	*f·* known in the Old Country,

favored

Pul.	10–10	Our land, more *f·*,
No.	v– 2	benefit no *f·* class,
My.	219– 3	through some *f·* student.
	250–23	wait for the *f·* moment to act
	278–13	Congress of our *f·* land

favorite

Ret.	10– 7	My *f·* studies were
'01.	18– 3	that was my *f·* dose.
Peo.	3– 9	torture of His *f·* Son,

favors

Hea.	1– 7	Heaven's *f·* are formidable :
My.	198– 7	the continuance of His *f·*,

fear (noun)

abate the

Un.	54– 8	is to abate the *f·* of it ;

action of

Mis.	41–22	through the action of *f·*,

all

Mis.	184–26	which casteth out all *f·*,
	194–25	Love that casts out all *f·*.
	335– 1	Love that casteth out all *f·*,

allay

Mis.	45– 7	although its power to allay *f·*,

and hope

My.	292–30	compound of . . . *f·* and hope,

and trembling

My.	300– 5	with *f·* and trembling.— *Phil.* 2 : 12.

and weakness

Mis.	245–15	indicate *f·* and weakness,

casteth out

Mis.	229–28	"casteth out *f·*."— I *John* 4 : 18.
Ret.	61–17	casteth out *f·*.' "— I *John* 4 : 18.
Un.	20–16	"casteth out *f·*,"— I *John* 4 : 18.
Peo.	6–16	casteth out *f·* ;"— I *John* 4 : 18.

cast out

No.	40–23	cast out *f·* and heal the sick,

casts out

Ret.	61–20	Love that casts out *f·*.

childish

Mis.	237–30	childish *f·* clustered round his

desire, and

No.	11– 2	intellect, desire, and *f·*,

destroy the

'01.	13–19	you destroy the *f·* and the

earth-born

Mis.	387–25	chastens pride and earth-born *f·*,
Po.	6–20	chastens pride and earth-born *f·*,

effect of a

Ret.	61– 7	experiencing the effect of a *f·*

has ceased

Pul.	82–30	*f·* has ceased to kiss the iron heel

is a belief

Mis.	93–18	*F·* is a belief of sensation in

is the procurator

Rud.	10–16	*f·* is the procurator of the

is the weapon

Mis.	99–10	*F·* is the weapon in the

latent

Ret.	61– 4	a latent *f·*, made manifest

man's

'01.	13–20	A man's *f·*, unconquered,

mortal

Mis.	42– 9	moment of extreme mortal *f·*,

fear

no
Mis. 249–23 I have proof, but no f·.
My. 61–17 * said aloud, "Why, there is no f·;
144– 4 Give yourselves no f·

nor sin
Mis. 93–21 neither f· nor sin can bring on

of death
'02. 3–22 the muffled f· of death

of evil
Mis. 279– 5 love of God, and not the f· of evil,

of the senses
Ret. 74– 1 begets a f· of the senses

of the sick
Rud. 12– 7 quiet the f· of the sick

or disease
Ret. 61– 5 different forms of f· or disease.

or distrust
My. 202– 3 human ambition, f·, or distrust

or doubt
No. 8–12 without f· or doubt,

or exhaustion
My. 232–27 produces f· or exhaustion

or malice
No. 45–10 weakness, f·, or malice;

or sin
Mis. 93– 6 *Can f· or sin bring back old beliefs*

or suffering
Ret. 61–11 cannot awake in f· or suffering
My. 267–22 relief from f· or suffering,

removes
My. 131– 2 removes f·, subdues sin,

sin and
No. 40–20 Only when sickness, sin, and f·

that
Mis. 237– 9 but remove that f·, and the

their
Mis. 10–21 their f· is self-immolated.
My. 191– 8 engendered by their f·,
247–22 *persuasion* that takes away their f·,

this
Ret. 61– 5 This f· is formed unconsciously
Rud. 10–17 Remove this f· by the true

without
Man. 48– 5 do it with love and without f·.
No. 8–12 without f· or doubt,

Mis. 10–18 with f· and the besetments of evil;
93–15 f·, its coeval, is without divine
99– 9 His f· overcame his loyalty;
115– 9 and f· of being found out.
198–24 to some belief, f·, theory, or
237– 8 serve God (or try to) from f·;
257–17 f· where courage is requisite,
Ret. 61–13 saith to f·, "You are the cause of
My. 211–21 f· where courage should be
293–14 trembling faith, hope, and of f·,
344–28 f· of catching smallpox is more

fear (verb)

Mis. 109–29 f· not sin, lest thereby it
109–30 only f· to sin.
113–25 We have nothing to f· when Love is
149–30 "F· not, little flock;— *Luke* 12 : 32.
197– 6 we f· the full import of this
284–24 Evil is not something to f·
321–16 "F· not, little flock;— *Luke* 12 : 32.
325–10 f· not to fall upon the Stranger,
389–16 f· No ill,— since God is good,
Un. 2– 3 God pitieth them who f· Him;
20–14 *Third:* We therefore need not f· it.
Pul. 14–17 never f· the consequences.
'01. 10– 6 F· them not therefore :— *Matt.* 10 : 26.
Peo. 6–15 Believing that . . . we naturally f·
Po. 4–15 f· No ill,— since God is good,
My. 33–23 them that f· the Lord.— *Psal.* 15 : 4.
130–12 failed too often for me to f· it.
193–27 "F· not :— *Isa.* 43 : 1.

feared

Mis. 284–23 is neither to be f· nor
Po. 71–11 F· for an hour the tyrant's heel !
My. 293–10 f· that the bullet would
293–12 physicians may have f· this.

fearful

Mis. 19–19 most f· sin that mortals can
368–24 and at a f· stake.

fearfully

'01. 33– 9 * they have f· abounded;

fearing

'01. 14–20 delivered . . . from f· it,
My. 247–17 not f· me, sought their food of me

fearless

Mis. 213–20 f· wing and firm foundation.
'01. 2–26 f· wing and a sure reward.

fearless

Po. 28–12 Give us the eagle's f· wing,
My. 309– 1 * dominating, passionate, f·,"

fearlessly

No. 5– 2 Scientists are vindicating, f· and
My. 64–19 * F· does she warn all her followers
160– 4 and follows Truth f·.

fears

Mis. 7–19 descriptions carry f· to many minds,
105– 3 disdain the f· and destroy the
307– 9 to all human f·, to suffering
320–14 calms man's f·, bears his burdens,
Un. 10–27 pursued by their f·,
'00. 7–28 and we are saved from our f·.
'01. 13–17 because he f· it or loves it.
'02. 19– 4 to disarm their f·.
Peo. 11–15 false theories, false f·,
Po. 47– 8 Never to toiling and never to f·,
79–12 False f· are foes
My. 182–26 f· turn hither with satisfied hope.

feasibility

Mis. 349–12 f· of entering a medical school;
No. 2–13 test the f· of what they say
4–12 destroys the f· of disease;
10–21 f· and immobility of C. S.
Hea. 19–21 doubts the f· of the demand.

feast

Mis. 121– 4 partook of the Jews' f·
149– 5 this f· and flow of Soul.
175–14 keep the f· of Life,
233– 8 the death's-head at the f·
Pan. 1– 6 at the f· of our Passover,
'00. 14–28 When invited to a f·
15– 3 come to a sumptuous f·,
15– 5 and this f· is a Passover.
15–17 Love has been preparing a f·
15–19 you have come to Love's f·,
'01. 2–18 the death's-head at the f·
My. 188– 7 Your f· days will not be in
191–29 invitation to this f· of soul
263– 6 a f· of Soul and a famine of sense.

feasting

Ret. 65–10 F· the senses, gratification of
'02. 16–23 Fasting, f·, or penance,

feasts

Mis. 345–27 Christians met in midnight f·
Chr. 55–12 are in their f· :— *Isa.* 5 : 12.
'00. 13– 7 orgies of their idolatrous f·
My. 340– 1 Jesus attended f·.

feat

Pul. 45– 7 * even when the f· seems impossible

feather (see also feather's)

Mis. 127–32 human heart, like a f· bed,

feathered

Mis. 329–27 calling the f· tribe back

feather's

Mis. 372– 3 had not one f· weight

feathers

Mis. 152–26 He will hide you in His f·
172–10 shall cover with her f·
263– 6 two words . . . *rock* and f·:
263– 8 cover thee with His f·."— *Psal.* 91 : 4.
374–32 without f· on her wings,

feather-some

Po. 18– 3 majestic, and f· fling

feathery

Mis. 306–24 nor feel the f· touch
Ret. 17–20 f· blossom and branches
Po. 63– 7 f· blossom and branches

feature

Pul. 25– 2 * cooling is a recognized f·
27– 8 * remarkable f· of this temple.
43–23 * chief f· of the dedication,
76– 2 * striking f· of the church
'00. 13–10 f· the apostle justly regards as
My. 25– 4 * this f· of the demonstration.
38–23 * no more impressive f· of the
61–21 * One f· about the work
69–20 * Another unusual f· is the foyer,
77–11 * notable f· in the life of their cult.
88–18 * smallest f· of the C. S. faith,
96–16 * A remarkable f·,

features

Mis. 112–14 many f· and forms of
Pul. vii–19 f· of the vast problem of
25– 8 * The principal f· are
45–10 * grandest and most helpful f·
'01. 20– 2 yielding to its aggressive f·.
My. 32– 2 * striking f· of the services.
69– 2 * one of the extraordinary f·
78–21 * remarkable f· of the services

February
(see **months***)*

fed
Mis.	6–31	keeping them clothed and *f*·,
	106–19	Your Sunday Lesson, . . . has *f*· you.
	153– 7	they were *f*· with manna :
	254– 6	love that hath *f*· them with Truth,
	326–11	*f*· by the fat of hypocrisy
	369–24	whom he *f*· that wholesome . . . food.
	388– 9	*F*· by Thy love divine we live,
Rud.	13–27	to be *f*·, clothed, and sheltered
Pan.	15– 1	*f*· her starving foe,
'01.	29– 1	Have we housed, *f*·, clothed, or
Po.	7– 9	*F*· by Thy love divine we live,
My.	170–21	verily thou shalt be *f*·.— *Psal.* 37 : 3.
	247–16	*f*· these sweet little thoughts

fee
Man.	94– 4	a less lecture *f*· ;
	96– 4	Lecture *F*·.
	96– 4	lecture *f*· shall be left to the
	96–13	trust to contributions for his *f*·.
Ret.	50– 9	finally led, . . . to accept this *f*·.
My.	136–17	highest *f*· ever received by
	204–24	a full *f*· for treatment,
	328–29	* shall pay a license *f*·
	329– 6	* from paying this *f*·,

feeble
Mis.	30– 2	in at least some *f*· demonstration
	85–18	*f*· flutterings of mortals Christward
	100–32	*f*· lips are made eloquent,
	104–16	wages *f*· fight with his
	172–19	*f*· sense of the infinite law
	196–31	*f*· acceptance of the truths
Ret.	27–15	to express in *f*· diction
	27–17	* But the *f*· hands and helpless,
Un.	41– 1	*f*· concept of immortality,
	61–19	faith and a *f*· understanding
'02.	18–11	caused not the *f*· to fall,
My.	59–22	* *f*· attempts to lead the singing.
	92–19	* statistics give a *f*· impression
	162–25	Shepherd of this *f*· flock
	331–25	* lone, *f*·, and bereaved widow

feebleness
Mis.	101–16	with finiteness and *f*·.
	370– 1	their *f*· calls for help,

feeblest
Peo.	11– 5	it was found that the *f*· mind,

feebly
Mis.	80–21	Tyranny can thrive but *f*· under
	373–18	living *f*·, in kings' courts.
My.	76–11	* *f*· expresses the gratification.
	174–29	seeking and finding (though *f*·),

feed
Mis.	127–14	faithfully asks divine Love to *f*· it
	338–27	* Shall the world's famine *f*· ;
	388–19	To bless the orphan, *f*· the poor ;
	397–21	poem — *John* 21 : 16.
	397–25	How to *f*· Thy sheep ;
	398–17	*F*· the hungry, heal the heart,
Ret.	page 46	poem — *John* 21 : 16.
	46– 6	How to *f*· Thy sheep ;
	46–23	*F*· the hungry, heal the heart,
Pul.	17– 1	poem — *John* 21 : 16.
	17– 5	How to *f*· Thy sheep ;
	17–22	*F*· the hungry, heal the heart,
Po.	page 14	poem — *John* 21 : 16.
	14– 4	How to *f*· Thy sheep ;
	14–21	*F*· the hungry, heal the heart,
	21– 8	bless the orphan, *f*· the poor ;
My.	18–11	asks divine Love to *f*· it
	48–30	* They *f*· the higher nature
	123–24	to *f*· the multitude ;
	133–13	monads will *f*· the hungry,

feedeth
Mis.	322–14	Shepherd that *f*· my flock,
	322–19	God that *f*· the hungry heart,

feeding
Mis.	15–29	*f*· at first on the milk of
My.	125– 8	You come from *f*· your flocks,

Feed My Sheep
(see **Appendix A***)*

feeds
Mis.	150–31	He guards, guides, *f*·,
	331–12	dove *f*· her callow brood,
Pul.	21–30	*f*· and fills the sentiment
My.	247–23	Love alone that *f*· them.
	303–20	what *f*· a few *f*· all.

feel
Mis.	12– 1	*Because* I thus *f*·, I say to others :
	13– 1	The only justice of which I *f*·
	14– 6	where will you see or *f*· evil,
	28– 3	neither see, hear, *f*·, taste, nor

feel
Mis.	86–28	What mortals hear, see, *f*·,
	88– 2	*f*· the need of physical help,
	133–20	*f*· a delicacy in making the following
	136–10	I cannot *f*· justified in
	142–30	yet as friends we can *f*· the
	146–23	I *f*· sure that as Christian Scientists
	157–13	true Christian Scientist will *f*·
	218– 8	can neither see, hear, nor *f*·,
	224– 5	Well may we *f*· wounded by
	224–10	* I don't *f*· hurt in the least."
	234– 1	that we see and *f*· disease only by
	237–17	few *f*· and live now as when
	256–10	I *f*·, deeply, . . . the severe task
	266–20	I speak of them as I *f*·,
	279–29	will *f*· the influence of this Mind ;
	303–24	I *f*· assured that many
	306–24	nor *f*· the feathery touch of the
	306–26	Oh, may you *f*· *this* touch,
	319–26	and *f*· themselves alone among
	326– 9	but the flesh at length did *f*· them ;
Ret.	9–20	* And *f*· His presence in the vast
	61– 7	awaken from sleep and *f*· ill,
	63–17	Do you not *f*· bound to expose this
	85–16	*f*· that God ordains you.
	87–23	They *f*· their own burdens less,
	90–18	Who can *f*· and comprehend
Un.	4– 8	to *f*·, in a certain finite human
	8– 6	What you see, hear, *f*·, is a
	22–11	to see or be seen, to *f*· or be felt.
	24–25	taste, hear, *f*·, smell.
	34–15	says that matter cannot *f*· matter ;
	34–17	material nerves, *do f*· matter.
	34–20	matter could not *f*· what it calls
	57– 5	the pain they *f*· and occasion ;
Pul.	3–27	I *f*· so far from victory over the
	6–21	* I *f*· the truth is leading us to
	36–17	* made me *f*· I could have
Rud.	10– 5	must *f*· and know that
	10–14	cannot *f*·, see, or report pain
No.	19–17	*f*· no sensation of divine Love,
Hea.	16–21	They can neither see, hear, *f*·,
My.	21–10	* We therefore *f*· sure that all
	21–24	* will *f*· that they have been called
	51– 8	* while we *f*· that she has not
	64– 8	* we *f*· a pardonable pride
	87–17	* we *f*· that Boston is to be
	138– 7	I *f*· that it is not for my benefit
	145–12	* I do not *f*· able to keep about.
	193– 4	you will not *f*· my absence.
	216–28	you will *f*· more than at present
	323–19	* Neither do I now *f*· at all equal

feeling
Mis.	106–29	that thrill the chords of *f*·
	142–21	chords of *f*· too deep for words.
	177–10	Their *f*· and purpose are deadly,
	219–16	if he would remove this *f*·
	222– 8	conviction of his wrong state of *f*·
	227–18	flowers of *f*· blossom,
	229– 7	would catch their state of *f*·
	343–18	Are we *f*· the vernal freshness
Ret.	18–22	flowers of *f*· are fragrant
	81–11	false thinking, *f*·, and acting ;
Pul.	31–15	* close contact with public *f*·
	51–21	* religious belief has stirred up *f*·,
	72– 3	* learning the *f*· of Scientists
No.	1–12	borne on by the current of *f*·.
	6–24	to material sense and *f*·,
'01.	1–23	by *f*· and applying the nature
'02.	15–28	*f*· sure that God had led me
Po.	64–16	flowers of *f*· are fragrant
	67–21	flowers of *f*· may blossom
My.	50–17	* there was a *f*· of trust
	63–16	* to repress a *f*· of exultation
	63–21	* there came a deeper *f*·,
	63–21	* a *f*· of awe and of reverence
	145–13	* I am *f*· an old ailment
	256– 5	adapted to the key of my *f*·
	273–14	spiritual sense of thinking, *f*·,
	274–10	right thinking, right *f*·,
	331–21	* express the *f*· of gratitude
	331–26	* the high *f*· of honor

feelingly
Ret.	15–22	from persons who *f*· testified

feelings
My.	332– 3	* attempt at expressing the *f*·

feels
Mis.	219–15	one person *f*· sick,
	219–15	another *f*· wicked.
	219–27	*f*· wickedly and acts wickedly,
	220–15	patient says and *f*·, "I am well,
	224– 4	our egotism that *f*· hurt by
	228–21	Whatever man sees, *f*·, or
Ret.	25–25	neither sees, hears, nor *f*· Spirit,

feels
Un.	11–17	looks very real and *f·* very real ;"
	25– 9	It sees, hears, *f·*, tastes, smells
Pul.	37–15	* Mrs. Eddy *f·* very strongly,"
	37–21	* "Mother *f·* very strongly,"
'00.	3– 6	No hand that *f·* not his help,
Hea.	12– 4	matter-physician *f·* the pulse,
My.	51– 7	* Mrs. Eddy, *f·* it her duty to

fees
My.	204–15	TO PRACTISE WITHOUT *F·*

feet
and hands
Pul.	9–14	climbed with *f·* and hands

another's
My.	188–24	lies at another's *f·*.

bare
Mis.	391–16	With bare *f·* soiled or sore,
Po.	38–15	With bare *f·* soiled or sore,

bleeding
Un.	58– 5	Jesus walked with bleeding *f·*

eight
Pul.	26–12	* eight *f·* in height.
	62– 9	* not more than five by eight *f·*.

eighty-two
My.	68– 9	* a diameter of eighty-two *f·*

fancied
Ret.	12– 6	Woke by her fancied *f·*.
Po.	61– 4	Woke by her fancied *f·*.

fifty-one
My.	68– 9	* and a height of fifty-one *f·*.

goat's
Pan.	3–31	goat's *f·*, the solidity of the earth ;

hands and
Mis.	375–24	* hands and *f·* of the figures
	375–25	* hands and *f·* in Angelico's 'Jesus,'

her
Mis.	142– 1	how beautiful are her *f·* !
Pul.	83–25	* the moon under her *f·*, — *Rev.* 12 : 1.

his
Mis.	325–26	wipes off the dust from his *f·*
Ret.	86–13	wipe the dust from his *f·*
My.	159– 7	Sitting at his *f·*,

hundred and twenty-six
Pul.	41–24	* rises one hundred and twenty-six *f·*

Jesus'
Mis.	388–25	The right to sit at Jesus' *f·* ;
Po.	21–14	The right to sit at Jesus' *f·* ;

kiss the
Mis.	124–22	to kiss the *f·* of Jesus,
Pan.	9–19	kiss the *f·* of such a messenger,

kneeling at the
Peo.	13–15	Galileo kneeling at the *f·* of

little
Mis.	250–26	little *f·* tripping along the sidewalk ;
	329–18	her little *f·* trip lightly on,
	400–17	Guide my little *f·*
Po.	69– 5	Guide my little *f·*

Master's
Mis.	110– 2	poured on our Master's *f·*,
	369–19	we kneel at our Master's *f·*,
My.	222–21	the sandals of thy Master's *f·*.

of Christ
'01.	22–15	I begin at the *f·* of Christ

of Christian Science
Ret.	81–29	led me to the *f·* of C. S.,

of Jesus
Mis.	17–12	to sit at the *f·* of Jesus.
	124–22	to kiss the *f·* of Jesus,
	361–16	sit at the *f·* of Jesus.
Pul.	27–22	*Mary washing the *f·* of Jesus,
My.	349–13	to him who sits at the *f·* of Jesus

of Love
Mis.	204– 9	and kisses the *f·* of Love,

of progress
My.	127–28	nor laid down at the *f·* of progress

of Truth
Peo.	12–10	trampled under the *f·* of Truth.
My.	228–19	meek, who sit at the *f·* of Truth,

one hundred and twenty
Pul.	24–25	* tower is one hundred and twenty *f·* in

our
Mis.	339–12	plants our *f·* more firmly.
Pan.	15– 8	plant our *f·* firmly on Truth,

their
Mis.	176–20	planted their *f·* on Plymouth Rock,
	325–16	their *f·* resting on footstools,
	326–24	to wash their *f·*,
My.	227–25	under their *f·*, — *Matt.* 7 : 6.

thirty-two
My.	70–30	* which is thirty-two *f·* long.

to these lame
Mis.	362– 9	ears to these deaf, *f·* to these lame,

twenty-nine
My.	68–11	* altitude twenty-nine *f·* higher

feet
twenty-one and one half
Pul.	24–26	* twenty-one and one half *f·* square.

two hundred and twenty
My.	89– 6	* over two hundred and twenty *f·* high,

two hundred and twenty-four
My.	45–30	* two hundred and twenty-four *f·*,
	68–10	* two hundred and twenty-four *f·*
	78– 7	* two hundred and twenty-four *f·*

Way-shower's
My.	161– 4	washing the Way-shower's *f·*

Mis.	107– 8	plant the *f·* steadfastly in Christ.
	392– 2	at whose *f·* I stand,
Ret.	11–21	Farther than *f·* of chamois fall,
Po.	20– 2	at whose *f·* I stand,
	60–19	Farther than *f·* of chamois fall,
My.	129–25	whose *f·* can never be moved.
	184–27	*f·* of him that bringeth — *Isa.* 52 : 7.

felicity
Pul.	53–16	* expresses the whole law of human *f·*

fell
Mis.	99–10	courage of his convictions *f·*
	281–14	copy of . . . that *f·* into his hands.
	285–15	and the latter *f· hors de combat;*
Ret.	91– 6	ever *f·* upon human ears
Pul.	6–25	as my lone bark rose and *f·*
'01.	24–15	he *f·*, and great was the fall
Hea.	10– 7	*f·* before the womanhood of God,
	17–16	sleep" that *f·* upon Adam — *Gen.* 2 : 21.
My.	31– 6	* "Day by day the manna *f·* ;"
	194– 3	*f·* forests and remove mountains,
	220–27	*f·* a victim to those laws.
	303– 1	*f·* mysteriously upon my spirit.

fellow
No.	41– 5	called him "this *f·*." — *Luke* 23 : 2.
My.	104– 5	a "pestilent *f·*," — *Acts* 24 : 5.
	104– 6	of this "pestilent *f·*." — *Acts* 24 : 5.

fellow-apostle
Un.	1– 5	taught by his *f·* Paul,

fellow-being
Mis.	31– 5	affect the happiness of a *f·*

fellow-beings
Pul.	58– 3	* imparting this faith to her *f·*.
My.	286– 5	no more . . . slaughtering of our *f·* ;

fellow-citizens
My.	173–22	my *f·* vied with each other to

fellow-man
Mis.	18–24	habitual love for his *f·*.

fellow-men
Mis.	170–15	conceptions of God and our *f·*.
'01.	32–10	or desire to defame their *f·*.

fellow-mortals
Mis.	32–30	should try to bless their *f·*.
	213–12	forewarn and forearm our *f·*
'02.	11–12	hastens to help on his *f·*,

Fellow of the Royal College of Physicians
Peo.	6– 3	Dr. Abercrombie, *F·* of the *R· C·* of *P·*

fellows
Mis.	294– 5	and displacing his *f·*.

fellow-saint
Ret.	86–14	*f·* of a holy household.

fellow-servants
Mis.	335– 5	begin to smite his *f·*, — *Matt.* 24 : 49.

fellowship
Mis.	149–25	*f·* with saints and angels.
	310–20	All who desire its *f·*,
	357–24	should receive full *f·* from us,
Man.	51– 7	Violation of Christian *F·*.
	51–10	does not live in Christian *f·*
	74–21	attitude of Christian *f·*.
	99–13	who is in good *f·* with another
Ret.	15–20	we parted in Christian *f·*,
	45– 9	material form of cohesion and *f·*
	64–30	refuse *f·* with the Church
	82–26	with ecclesiastical *f·*
Pul.	21–14	entertain due respect and *f·*
No.	8– 9	*f·* in the bonds of Christ.
My.	v– 8	* hand of *f·* is being extended
	275– 2	chapter sub-title
	275– 4	does produce universal *f·*.
	360–20	Abide in *f·* with and
	362–24	* Christian love and *f·*,

fellow-students
Mis.	280–24	expressed his *f·* thanks

felon (see also **felon's**)
Hea.	19– 1	A *f·* was delivered to them

felon's
Hea.	19– 8	*f·* belief that he was bleeding

felt

Mis.	98–13	already *f·* in a higher mode of
	113–32	animus is *f·* throughout the land.
	127–29	but a tender sentiment *f·*,
	183– 7	seen and *f·* in health, happiness, and
	263–16	*f·* by students, especially by those
	278–24	I have *f·* for some time that
	281–25	I *f·* the weight of this yesterday,
	290–16	* "I *f·* the influence of your thought
	312– 3	may the love that is talked, be *f·* !
	375–10	* I did not utter all I *f·*
	398–23	*F·* ye the power of the Word?
Ret.	5–24	* was *f·* by all around her.
	14–23	and asked me to say how I *f·*
	89– 1	its presence *f·* in eternal stillness
Un.	7– 9	most sensibly *f·* that the infinite
	22–11	to see or be seen, to feel or be *f·*.
	34–24	Nothing would remain to be seen or *f·*.
	51– 5	is neither seen, f·, heard, nor
	57–12	must have *f·* the influence
	57–13	for it is written that he *f·* that
Pul.	34–20	"I *f·* that the divine Spirit
	36– 5	* as Mrs. Eddy *f·* it essential to the
	68– 9	* as Mrs. Eddy *f·* it necessary
	84–18	* can be better *f·* than expressed.
No.	45–11	*f·*, though unacknowledged.
'01.	12– 2	it is not *f·* with the fingers ;
	13– 5	it ought not to be seen, *f·*, or
	21–27	or *f·* the incipient touch of
Po.	75– 3	*F·* ye the power of the Word?
My.	3–17	Its presence is *f·*,
	9–24	never before *f·* poor in thanks,
	50– 7	* Pilgrims *f·* the strangeness of
	50–12	* *f·* a peculiar sense of isolation,
	55– 3	* it was *f·* that the church needed a
	57– 4	* need was *f·* of an auditorium
	80– 6	* that they had *f·* no pain
	125–16	*f·* the touch of the spirit of
	165–31	*f·* the infinite source where is *all*,
	185–11	thought, *f·*, spoken, or written,
	240–12	Its presence is *f·*,
	247–14	must have *f·* me when
	290– 1	a love and a loss *f·* by
	291–15	not talked but *f·* and lived.

female

Mis.	18–16	all-harmonious "male and *f·*," — *Gen.* 1 : 27.
	199– 8	male and *f·* come into their rightful
	295– 7	* from *f·* suffrage, past a score of
	295–10	* "a *f·* passion for some manner of
	296–27	a wish to promote *f·* suffrage
	314– 6	two Readers : a male, and a *f·*.
Man.	50– 3	body of a *f·* shall be
'01.	7–11	made them male and *f·*
	10–12	generic term for both male and *f·*.
My.	268–30	and you see male and *f·* one

Female Anti-Slavery Society

Po.	vi–14	*a meeting of the F· A· S·,*

feminine

Mis.	296–20	note or foster a *f·* ambition
Un.	32–24	neither masculine nor *f·*.

fermentation

My.	301– 6	found to be a healthy *f·*,

fermenting

Mis.	134–25	Error is only *f·*,
Pul.	5–28	is the leaven *f·* religion ;
'02.	2–17	rapidly *f·*, and enlightening the world

fern

Ret.	4–22	scrub-oak, poplar, and *f·* flourish.

Fernald, Mr. Josiah E.

My.	135–16	namely, . . . Mr. Josiah E. *F·*.
	136–22	Josiah E. *F·*, justice of the peace
	137–23	namely, . . . Mr. Josiah E. *F·*.

ferns

Pul.	42–26	* palms and *f·* and Easter lilies.
	42–27	* with *f·* and pure white roses

ferocious

Mis.	36–10	*f·* mind seen in the beast

fervent

Mis.	xi– 9	the *f·* heart and willing hand
	177– 2	*f·* devotion and an absolute
Un.	58–12	hypocrite melts in *f·* heat,
No.	28– 4	in the *f·* heat of suffering,
Peo.	9–22	a desire, *f·*, importunate :

fervently

Mis.	114–22	cannot . . . pray to God too *f·*,
'00.	14–18	hold in your full hearts *f·*
My.	293–21	Had prayer so *f·* offered

fervid

My.	25–17	my answer to their *f·* question :
	248–12	*f·* affection for the race

fervor

'01.	3– 2	virtue, *f·*, and fidelity.
My.	81– 6	* that at the very height of *f·*,
	81–30	* conception of the *f·* of belief

festal

Mis.	121– 5	drank from their *f·* wine-cup.
My.	170– 2	this was no *f·* occasion,

festive

Po.	77–17	Why from this *f·* hour
My.	256–24	the *f·* boards are spread,

festivities

Man.	60–14	no special observances, *f·*, nor gifts
	94– 7	no receptions nor *f·* after

festivity

Mis.	324– 6	sounds of *f·* and mirth ;
'00.	14–30	prepare accordingly for the *f·*.

fetishism

My.	248–19	No *f·* with a symbol can fetter

fetter

My.	248–20	No fetishism . . . can *f·* your flight.

fettered

Peo.	10–19	they alone have *f·* free limbs,

fetters

Mis.	165– 8	without the *f·* of the flesh,
	173–24	pains, *f·*, and befools him.
	237–28	loosing the *f·* of one form of
	246–16	to forge anew the old *f·* ;
	359–14	or by holding it in *f·*.
	394– 7	And loosens the *f·* of pride
Pul.	14– 2	will chain, with *f·* of some sort,
Peo.	3–24	and assigns them mortal *f·*
	11–13	their *f·* are gnawing away life
Po.	45– 9	loosens the *f·* of pride

fever

Ret.	13–12	pronounced me stricken with *f·*.
	13–22	The *f·* was gone, and I rose
Hea.	13–15	cured the incipient stage of *f·*.
My.	312– 8	* he died of yellow *f·*.
	312–20	was suddenly seized with yellow *f·*
	335–17	* was attacked with yellow *f·*
	335–21	* cause of death as bilious *f·*,
	335–27	* case was one of yellow *f·*

fevered

'00.	11–24	* And it lay on my *f·* spirit

feverish

Mis.	233– 5	*f·*, disgusting pride of those
'01.	2–17	*f·* pride of sects and systems

few

Mis.	ix– 7	among my thousands of students *f·*
	x–12	a *f·* articles are herein
	2–14	the laborers seem *f·*.
	23–24	*F·* there are who comprehend what
	139–24	a *f·* persons have since scrupled ;
	171–26	*F·* people at present know
	237– 7	Not a *f·* individuals serve God
	237–16	*f·* feel and live now as when
	238–17	It is enough, say they, to care for a *f·*.
	301–12	a *f·* professed Christian Scientists.
	305–17	* large contributions from a *f·*.
	323– 8	a *f·* laborers in a valley
	323–23	and *f·* there be that find it."
	325– 8	*f·* cravings for the immortal,
	327–20	lay down a *f·* of the heavy weights,
	347–18	take a *f·* steps,
	354–16	a *f·* truths tenderly told,
	378– 4	in a *f·* weeks returned
	382– 5	a *f·* manuscripts of mine
Ret.	20– 5	*f·* months before my father's
	90– 8	taught a *f·* hungry ones,
Un.	9–22	a *f·* spiritual thinkers
	12– 3	laborers are *f·* in this vineyard of
Pul.	8–19	to earn a *f·* pence toward this
	22–11	and a *f·* in far-off lands,
	43–19	* A *f·* minutes of silent prayer
	49– 6	* a *f·* of which had been the gifts
	57–21	* *F·* people outside its own circles
	72– 5	* a *f·* of the leading members
	82–18	* women had *f·* lawful claims
	88– 8	can append only a *f·* of the names
Rud.	15–13	*F·* were taken besides invalids for
'00.	9– 9	but *f·*, comparatively, see it ;
'01.	28– 7	*f·* there be that find it." — *Matt.* 7 : 14.
'02.	4–22	a *f·* of their infinite meanings,
Peo.	8– 7	the sins of a *f·* tired years
	12–14	*F·* there be who know what a power
Po.	vii– 6	* *to prepare a f· bound volumes*
	33–18	I ponder the days may be *f·*
My.	17–24	* *f·* moments of silent prayer
	47– 7	* a *f·* of the stages of its progress,
	50–26	* and *f·* knew of its teachings,
	50–27	* those *f·* saw the grandeur
	51–17	* remain with us for a *f·* Sundays

few

My.	52–27	* Within a *f·* months she has made
	73– 6	* very *f·* of them owe a cent.
	80–28	* A *f·* were upon the scene
	85–31	* one of the *f·* perfect sky-lines
	91–21	* The *f·* thousand persons who followed
	121–17	*F·* blemishes can be found in a
	146–12	*F·* believe this saying.
	146–12	*F·* believe that C. S. contains
	182– 1	Chicago had *f·* Congregational
	237– 2	in the *Sentinel* a *f·* weeks ago,
	244–20	but *f·* are chosen.'' — *Matt.* 22 : 14.
	261–24	an open secret, understood by *f·*
	290– 5	and the tried and true seem *f·*.
	290– 8	*F·* sovereigns have been as venerable,
	303–20	what feeds a *f·* feeds all.
	322–21	* a *f·* days' instruction by Mrs. Eddy
	327–18	* a *f·* other Scientists who stayed
	334– 6	* allegation that copies . . . are *f·*,

(*see also* **days, things, words, years**)

fewer
My.	83–14	* will doubtless have *f·* questions

fiat
Mis.	336–27	Science is the *f·* of divine
Un.	38–21	no divine *f·* commands us to
'01.	5–18	leave all sin to God's *f·*
Po.	1– 9	far the universal *f·* ran,

fibre
Un.	13–17	in the very *f·* of His being,

fibres
Mis.	142–27	touched tender *f·* of thought,

Fichte
No.	22– 4	Leibnitz, Descartes, *F·*,

fiction
My.	48–29	* or paralyzed by sentimental *f·*.
	112– 3	A *f·* or a false philosophy

fidelity
Mis.	270–23	*F·* to his precepts and practice
	286– 4	the solemn vow of *f·*,
	339– 1	chapter sub-title
	341– 9	*F·* finds its reward
Ret.	91–17	and with such *f·*,
Pul.	22– 9	attest their *f·* to Truth,
	38–24	* They hold with strict *f·* to
	66–13	* They hold with strict *f·* to
'01.	3– 2	virtue, fervor, and *f·*,
My.	5–26	your generosity and *f·*,
	37–13	* By your *f·* and the constancy of
	45–16	*·f·* to the divine Principle
	62– 1	* unflinching faith and unfailing *f·*
	90–12	* insures *f·* in pain or death
	135–26	Your love and *f·* cheer my
	187– 1	your *f·*, faith, and Christian zeal
	209– 6	*f·*, courage, patience, and grace.
	230–21	fitness and *f·* such as thine
	243–21	witnesses your *f·* to C. S.

Field
Man.	56–16	general reports from the *F·*.
	64– 1	experience in the *F·*,
	72– 7	Scientist working in the *F·*,

field
at work in a
Pul.	33–17	* at work in a *f·* one day

beasts of the
Mis.	191– 5	beasts of the *f·*.'' — *see Gen.* 3 : 1.

complaints from the
My.	354– 2	In view of complaints from the *f·*,

every
Pul.	53–21	* every *f·* of human endeavor.

fruitful
My.	183–19	forest becomes a fruitful *f·*,

grass of the
No.	26–26	clothe the grass of the *f·*, — *Matt.* 6 : 30.

occupying the
Hea.	14– 1	occupying the *f·* for a period ;

of battle
Mis.	136– 5	with you on the *f·* of battle,

of labor
Mis.	136– 1	I retired from the *f·* of labor,
	318–19	entering this sacred *f·* of labor,
Man.	84–23	A Single *F·* of Labor.
	85– 1	occupies only his own *f·* of labor.
Ret.	47–23	before entering this *f·* of labor
No.	7–25	in this *f·* of labor.
My.	347–19	purchases our *f·* of labor
	355–10	factors in our *f·* of labor

of medicine
Mis.	366–17	imposition in the *f·* of medicine

of Mind-healing
Rud.	8–17	in the *f·* of Mind-healing.

of Science
My.	226–25	laborers in the *f·* of Science

of work
My.	216–19	indicates another *f·* of work

field
open
'02.	14–29	an open *f·* and fair play.

plant of the
Mis.	26–12	"every plant of the *f·* — *Gen.* 2 : 5.
Hea.	19–14	"every plant of the *f·* — *Gen.* 2 : 5.

student in the
My.	355– 6	letter from a student in the *f·*

this
Mis.	284– 7	in this *f·* of limitless power
Ret.	47–23	before entering this *f·* of labor
No.	7–25	in this *f·* of labor.
My.	362–23	* churches and societies in this *f·*

whole
My.	297–20	inspiration to the whole *f·*,

Mis.	54– 8	*f·* of metaphysical healing,
	313–19	The *f·* waves its white ensign,
My.	162–11	Scientists all over the *f·*,
	195– 6	problems to be worked out for the *f·*,
	242–16	I hereby announce to the C. S. *f·*
	327–18	* Scientists who stayed on the *f·*
	354– 5	it is due the *f·* to state that I
	355– 2	as it will be to the *f·*,

fields
Mis.	xi–14	unexplored *f·* of Science.
	xi–26	to survey the *f·* of the slain
	80–26	sown and reaped in the *f·*
	120–25	from their own *f·* of labor.
	302–32	stay within their own *f·*
Ret.	4–13	Where once stretched broad *f·*
	30– 4	have won *f·* of battle
Un.	12– 1	your *f·* are already white
My.	51–23	* her duty, to go into new *f·*
	243–17	remain in their own *f·* of labor

fierce
Chr.	53–16	With *f·* heart-beats ;
My.	127–22	culminating in *f·* attack,

fiercely
Pul.	2–17	*f·* besieged by the enemy.

fiery
Mis.	118–29	*f·* punishment of the evil-doer.

fifteen
Mis.	242–14	more difficult tasks *f·* years ago.
Ret.	40–10	stood by her side about *f·* minutes
Pul.	26–17	* chime of bells includes *f·*,
	30–27	* and within *f·* years it has grown
	52–22	* over the world for *f·* centuries,
	62– 8	* a chime of *f·* bells
	66– 5	* was founded *f·* years ago
	79–10	* starting *f·* years ago,
My.	24–22	*·f·* different trades represented.
	309–28	* passed her first *f·* years at

(*see also* **numbers, values**)

fifth
Mis.	262– 7	entering upon its *f·* volume,
	280–18	dismissed the *f·* of March,
	280–26	On the morning of the *f·*,
My.	122–11	On the *f·* of July last,

Fifth Avenue
542
My.	282–20	542 *F· A·*, New York City.

Fifth Church of Christ, Scientist
My.	363– 3	* signature

fifty
Mis.	221–26	that five times ten are *f·*
	221–27	saying . . . ten times five are not *f·* ;
Un.	6–28	in less than another *f·* years
Pul.	41–15	* parties of forty and *f·*.
Hea.	1–18	* At *f·*, chides his infamous delay,
My.	234– 1	*f·* telegrams per holiday
	310–24	* a gray-haired man of *f·*

(*see also* **numbers, values**)

fifty-one
My.	68– 9	* a height of *f·* feet.

fig
Pul.	26–24	* with sprays of *f·* leaves

fight
Mis.	41–12	The good *f·* must be fought
	80–11	will *f·* the medical faculty,
	104–17	wages feeble *f·* with his
	204– 8	When the good *f·* is fought,
	278–6, 7	*f·* the good *f·*,
	321–20	Untiring in your holy *f·*,
Un.	46–28	The *f·* was an effort to enthrone evil.
Pul.	3–14	good *f·* we have waged is over,
No.	7–20	must now *f·* their own battles.
	23–21	*f·* these claims, not as realities.
Pan.	6– 7	continue to *f·* it until it disappears,
	13–16	*f·* the good *f·*
'00.	9–23	no one can *f·* against God,
	10– 4	illusion, that after a *f·* vanisheth

fight
'02. 10– 2 has a *f·* with the flesh.
Hea. 2–16 "I have fought a good *f·,* — *II Tim.* 4:7.
14– 2 it is the *f·* of beasts.
Po. 10–10 The hoar *f·* is forgotten ;
My. 18–24 to *f·* the good *f·* till God's will
212– 7 A harder *f·* will be necessary
337–11 The hoar *f·* is forgotten ;

fighting
Mis. 140–24 not be found *f·* against God.
327–29 grumbling, and *f·* each other,
My. 278–22 Nothing is gained by *f·,*

figs
Mis. 27–17 or *f·* of thistles?" — *Matt.* 7:16.
336–18 nor *f·* of thistles.

fig-tree
Mis. 151–11 He saith of the barren *f·,*
154–13 beneath your own vine and *f·*

figurative
Pul. 66–15 * highly *f·* language.

figuratively
Mis. 258– 7 *f·* and literally spat upon matter ;
My. 343–21 the term pope is used *f·.*

figure
Mis. 370–20 What *f·* is less favorable than
376– 4 * face, *f·,* and drapery of Jesus,
376– 6 * the face, *f·,* and drapery of
376– 9 * the *f·* and garments from a
392–13 love the Hebrew *f·* of a tree.
Pul. 31–19 * central *f·* in all this agitation
31–27 * Her *f·* was tall, slender, and
48–28 * *f·* largely in her genealogy,
Po. 20–17 love the Hebrew *f·* of a tree.

figures
Mis. 375–24 * "The hands and feet of the *f·*
My. 8–18 * and the relationship of *f·,*
25–10 * *f·* are taken from the report
94– 3 * *f·* given out by the church
96– 5 * many of them prominent *f·* in
97–11 * if the *f·* could be given
99–27 * Facts and *f·* are stubborn things,
100– 2 * some of the facts and *f·*
345–29 make them our *f·* of speech.

filed
Mis. 380–27 a bill in equity was *f·*
380–32 Answer was *f·* by the defendant,
My. 137– 4 following affidavit, . . . was *f·*

filial
Mis. 254– 1 *f·* obedience to which the Decalogue

fill
Mis. 9–17 *f·* it with the nectar of the gods.
39–19 they intend to *f·* the human mind
43–23 *f·* one's pocket at the expense of
276– 8 not big enough to *f·* the order ;
343–26 *f·* the haunted chambers of memory,
360–22 *f·* earth with the divine energies,
386–15 to *f·* That waking with a love
Man. 26–21 They shall *f·* a vacancy occurring
29–14 five suitable members . . . to *f·*
71–13 position that no other church can *f·.*
80–18 reserves the right to *f·* the same
80–20 trustees shall *f·* the vacancy,
89– 8 shall be elected to *f·* the vacancy.
100–19 Committee to *f·* the vacancy ;
112– 9 *f·* out his application
Ret. 70–19 *f·* his own niche in time and eternity.
Pul. 60–19 * to *f·* the recess behind the
69–12 * *f·* the mind with good thoughts
Rud. 15–15 to *f·* in the best possible manner
15–28 to *f·* anew the individual mind.
No. 1– 8 *f·* the rivers till they rise in floods,
45–16 right of woman to *f·* the highest
Pan. 15– 9 and *f·* us with the life and
'01. 32–19 They *f·* the ecclesiastic measure,
Po. 3–14 Love divine doth *f·* my heart.
8– 6 Her bosom to *f·* with mortal woes.
29–20 *F·* us today With all thou art
49–23 to *f·* That waking with a love
66– 2 our brimming cup *f·,*
My. 19–27 no doubt *f·* the memory
59–18 * would scarce *f·* a couple of pews
62–13 * *f·* your heart with the joy of Love's
126–18 *f·* to her double — *Rev.* 18:6.
167–12 may *f·* your hearts
195–30 *f·* these spiritual temples with grace,
210– 6 and no space for evil to *f·*
270–19 Those words . . . *f·* my heart :

filled
Mis. 93– 2 that they may be *f·* with Truth.
111–14 had He *f·* the net,
124–19 man's true sense is *f·* with peace,
183–17 if he open his mouth it shall be *f·*

filled
Mis. 321– 7 My heart is *f·* with joy,
360–31 *f·* with the true knowledge of
386– 5 and hearts are found and *f·,*
Man. 37– 4 after the blank has been properly *f·*
109–12 *f·* out by the applicants,
Ret. 84–21 that they may be *f·* with Truth.
Pul. 28–27 * has *f·* the office of pastor
29–13 * the hall was *f·*
41–21 * vast congregations *f·* the church
42– 3 * *f·* with a waiting multitude.
42–30 * *f·* with beautiful pink roses.
53–29 * power that *f·* his garment's hem
No. 15– 7 *f·* with blessings for the whole
Po. 49– 9 hearts are found and *f·,*
My. 30–27 * church was *f·* for the service
38–10 * seating space had been *f·*
38–12 * church was *f·* for each service
38–17 * They *f·* all the seats
42–16 * a heart *f·* with gratitude
52–26 * always *f·* her coffers anew.
56– 3 * until every seat was *f·*
77–19 * *f·* the streets leading to the
80–27 * these places had all been *f·,*
80–32 * auditorium was comfortably *f·.*
90– 2 * great buildings should be *f·*
126–18 cup which she hath *f·* — *Rev.* 18:6.
157– 4 * are *f·* with profound joy
210– 3 *f·* with Truth and Love,
210– 7 in a mind *f·* with goodness.
247–24 so *f·* with divine food
250–28 have *f·* this sacred office
291–25 sheaves garnered, her treasury *f·,*
362–19 * *f·* with gratitude to God,

filling
Mis. 116–12 *f·* the measures of life's music
254–23 *f·* with hate its deluded victims,
331–24 *f·* all space and having all power,
Man. 111– 2 *f·* out the application blank,
Rud. 3–27 ever-present I AM, *f·* all space,
'00. 1– 6 ever-present Love *f·* all space,
'01. 15–16 *f·* up the measure of wickedness
My. 255– 7 *f·* their positions satisfactorily

fills
Mis. 13–30 it *f·* all space, being omnipresent ;
173–20 God is Mind and *f·* all space,
228–10 *f·* the world with its fragrance,
281– 7 *f·* me with joy,
285– 6 *f·* orders for my books,
396– 6 *F·* mortal sense with dread ;
Pul. 21–30 *f·* the sentiment with unworldliness,
Po. 46–17 While beauty *f·* each bar.
58–18 *F·* mortal sense with dread ;
My. 191–24 Immortal courage *f·* the human breast

filter
Mis. 171– 9 *f·* from vertebræ to vertebræ.

final
Mis. 55–22 the *f·* destruction of all that
56–18 *f·* destruction of this false belief
63–18 and understand the *f·* fact,
86– 3 This *f·* degree of regeneration
99– 1 Science is absolute and *f·.*
116–19 *f·* obedience to spiritual law.
205–13 *f·* immersion of human consciousness
215– 1 the *f·* destruction of error
219– 2 science of the *f·* cause of things ;
318–10 third and fourth and *f·* generation
361–21 So shall mortals soar to *f·* freedom,
Ret. 13–14 belief in a *f·* judgment-day,
33– 2 my *f·* conclusion that mortal belief,
47– 2 *f·* outcome of material organization,
56–14 by the *f·* triumph of Spirit
78–24 your own success and *f·* happiness,
'00. 4–22 *f·,* absolute, and eternal.
10–10 gained fresh energy and *f·* victory.
'01. 5–18 *f·* manifestation of the real
27– 1 experience, and *f·* discovery,
Peo. 1– 7 *f·* unity between man and God.
My. 266–17 *f·* spiritualization of all things,

__finale__
Un. 2–11 as the *f·* in Science :
My. 303–24 rather is it the pith and *f·* of

finally
Mis. 100–15 *f·* show the fruits of Love.
126–12 and *f·* conquers them ;
128– 6 "*F·,* brethren, — *Phil.* 4:8.
136– 2 socially, publicly, and *f·,*
205–26 abandonment of sin *f·* dissolves all
299–10 that this query has *f·* come
369– 4 God's law, . . . shall be *f·* understood ;
373– 6 but, as usual, he *f·* yielded.
373–28 *f·* sit down at the right hand
Ret. 45–12 mortal existence is *f·* laid off,

finally
Ret.	50– 8	was *f·* led, . . to accept this fee.
	67–16	*f·* lost for lack of witness.
Un.	45–21	until it *f·* dies in order to
Pul.	14– 5	*f·* be shocked into another
	50–25	* skirmishing, *f·* subsides.
Rud.	11– 5	*f·* to the *understanding* of God
No.	9–12	separate wisely and *f·* ;
Pan.	6– 5	*F·*, brethren, . . . denounce evil
'01.	20–26	flagrance will *f·* be known,
	34–20	*F·*, brethren, wait patiently
'02.	10–15	will *f·* gain the scope of
	10–17	becomes *f·* spiritual.
Po.	vi– 1	* *f· found its way into print,*
My.	25– 4	* to dispose fully and *f·*
	43–11	* *f·* became willingly obedient
	108–26	*F·*, beloved brethren
	174–29	*f·* may we not together
	231– 9	*f·* resolved to spend no
	232–24	material error *f·* disappears,
	278–28	*f·* fall, pierced by its own

Finance
(see **Committee on Finance***)*

finance
Mis.	327–11	policy, religion, politics, *f·*,

Finance Committee
Man.	76–15	*F· C·.*

finances
Mis.	131–17	By-law relating to *f·*
Pul.	8– 7	condition of our nation's *f·*,

financial
Mis.	131–14	a report of the first *f·* year
	131–28	After this *f·* year, when you
Man.	75–11	understands the *f·* situation
	75–15	*F·* Situation.
Ret.	50– 3	no *f·* equivalent for
'02.	12–23	*f·* transactions of this church,
My.	7– 7	*f·* transactions of this church,

find
Mis.	xi–15	will *f·* herein a "canny" crumb ;
	11– 2	to *f·* that, though thwarted,
	13–29	you will *f·* it to be good ;
	13–30	will *f·* that good is omnipotence,
	14– 6	or *f·* its existence necessary
	28–25	*f·* neither pleasure nor pain therein.
	32–14	will *f·* my views on this subject ;
	38–14	*other institutions f· little interest in*
	53–11	*Do you sometimes f· it advisable*
	76–22	will *f·* the right meaning indicated.
	86–30	and *f·* wings to reach the glory of
	89–23	will *f·* the proper answer to this
	98–18	and to *f·* strength in union,
	117–10	and always *f·* him there.
	124– 5	cannot *f·* God in matter,
	124–11	*f·* rest in the spiritual ideal,
	129–19	*f·* somebody in his way,
	130– 7	What do we *f·* in the Bible,
	132–21	I *f·* it inconvenient to accept
	133–28	I turn constantly to . . . and *f·* rest.
	147–21	we *f·* him ever the same,
	148– 2	We shall never *f·* one part of
	155– 9	*f·* access to the heart of humanity.
	157– 8	*f·* their card in *The C. S. Journal*
	158–25	*f·* the forthcoming completion
	176– 1	*f·* the truth that breaks the dream
	182– 9	*f·* their adoption with the Father ;
	200–24	to seek . . . and to *f·* happiness,
	211–24	*f·* the Life that cannot be lost.
	217– 4	nor reason attempts to *f·* one ;
	220– 2	*f·* that a good rule works one way,
	227–13	*f·* himself responsible for kind(?)
	234–15	which can never *f·* a place in Science.
	266–21	cannot *f·* it in my heart not to love
	279–19	*f·* out the nothingness of matter ;
	281– 6	But I *f·* also another mental condition
	287–17	*f·* the highway of holiness.
	298–26	One says, "I *f·* relief from pain in
	323–24	and few there be that *f·* it."
	324–22	and to *f·* the Stranger.
	324–25	only to *f·* the lights all wasted
	325–14	only to *f·* its inmates asleep
	327–26	for my sake, shall *f·* it." — *Matt. 10 : 39.*
	334–17	You must *f·* error to be *nothing:*
	341–19	and you *f·* Life eternal :
	343– 6	to *f·* disease in the mortal mind,
	353– 9	and *f·* the divine,
	357– 7	and yearn to *f·* living pastures
	362–25	We all must *f·* shelter from the
	369–20	would *f·* our Father's house again
	372–19	to *f·* "Christ and Christmas"
	375–21	* *f·* an almost identical resemblance,
	385– 3	* *F·* peace in God,
	390–22	And thou wilt *f·* that harmonies,
	391– 5	Will *f·* within its portals

find
Mis.	391–18	*F·* items at our door.
Man.	111–14	Applicants will *f·* the chief points
Ret.	2– 5	*f·* so graphically set forth in the
	18–23	*f·* a happiness rare ;
	21– 5	employed to *f·* him,
	24–23	*f·* the Science of Mind
	38–20	to *f·* me *en route* for Boston,
	52– 1	endeavored to *f* new ways and **means**
	62– 4	*f·* that the views here set forth
	83–17	he will *f·* it more difficult to
	85– 3	Teachers of C. S. will *f·* it advisable
	89–22	*f·* any precedent for employing
	90–28	It is gladdening to *f·*, in such a **student**,
Un.	20–19	*f·* yourself losing the knowledge
	21– 4	we shall *f·* that we are perpetually
	26–12	as we *f·* in the hymn-verse
	33–17	and you *f·* no mind therein.
	33–23	*f·* them divided in evidence,
	62–17	and you *f·* Truth.
Pul.	4–12	will *f·* that one is as important a
	6–27	* *f·* in Mrs. Eddy's metaphysical
	11– 8	*f·* within it home, and *heaven.*
	38–30	* *f·* in one form of belief or another
	57–10	* truths which will *f·* emphasis
	69–19	* We *f·* in this view of the Bible
	70–20	* to *f·* the great curative Principle
	75– 5	"If Christian Scientists *f·* in my
	80– 3	* will surely *f·* the other.
No.	7–14	*f·* rescue and refuge in Truth
	36–16	*f·* rest from unreal trials in
Pan.	3– 9	*f·* an indefinable pleasure in
	8– 4	*f·* expression in sun worship,
	13–19	*f·* life in Him in whom we
'00.	7–24	*f·* ourselves so far from the
'01.	2–12	*f·* the standard of Christ's healing
	12–12	*f·* faith on the earth?" — *Luke 18 : 8.*
	28– 7	few there be that *f·* it." — *Matt. 7 : 14.*
'02.	11– 8	*f·* and point the path
	12–22	*f·* no place in my Message.
	19–27	*f·* divine Science glorifies the
Peo.	4–20	*f·* no reflection in
Po.	23–16	In brighter morn will *f·*
	37– 3	* *F·* peace in God,
	38– 4	Will *f·* within its portals
	38–17	*F·* items at our door.
	56– 1	thou wilt *f·* that harmonies,
	64–18	*f·* a happiness rare ;
My.	7– 5	that ordinarily *f·* no place in
	23– 2	* in order to *f·* out how much **our**
	71–15	* they will *f·* themselves in one of
	86– 5	* *f·* pleasure in this new symbol,
	91– 4	* something they did not *f·* in other
	104– 9	they could *f·* no fault in him,
	105– 3	*f·* in them man's only medicine
	114–31	and *f·* these progressive steps
	120– 2	and there we *f·* him.
	120– 4	lose me instead of *f·* me.
	122–19	to *f·* where the young child lies,
	127–13	we *f·* that divine metaphysics
	128– 2	*f·* no other outlet to liberty.
	137–30	I *f·* myself able to select the
	138–16	I *f·* that I cannot
	142– 5	* and then *f·* no seats in The
	155–17	May this glad Easter morn *f·*
	155–28	To-day may they *f·* some **sweet**
	163–18	that I might *f·* retirement from
	182–28	*f·* shelter from the storm
	184–29	*f·* utterance and acceptance
	212–28	will *f·* this practitioner saying
	215–26	Can we *f·* a better example
	221–13	can we *f·* a better moral philosophy,
	233–27	for my sake shall *f·* it." — *Matt. 10 : 39.*
	254–13	*f·* the ever-present God
	259–27	in which human capacities *f·* the
	283–13	*f·* their birthright in divine Science.
	306–17	Human merit or demerit will *f·*
	316–21	I am pleased to *f·* this
	318–31	I do not *f·* my authority for
	323– 8	* before the people *f·* out that
	361– 6	Please *f·* it there, and do not

finder
My.	4–22	seeker and *f·* of C. S.

findeth
Mis.	252–32	if a man *f·*, he goeth and selleth

finding
Mis.	98–11	*f·* ways and means for helping
	182–24	*f·* their place in God's great love,
	324–26	*F·* no happiness within,
	324–27	seeking peace but *f·* none.
	325–28	sees robbers *f·* ready ingress to
	389–20	Seeking and *f·*, with the angels sing :
Pul.	64–18	* without *f·* a clew ;
'02.	4–28	and past *f·* out.
Po.	4–19	Seeking and *f·*, with the angels sing :

finding

My.	38– 9	* no confusion in *f·* seats,
	174–29	seeking and *f·* (though feebly),
	188–29	and *f·* it, be God-endowed
	221– 4	precludes . . . from *f·* favor with

finds

Mis.	15– 1	fancies he *f·* pleasure in it,
	16– 7	one *f·* so much lacking,
	31–13	false faith *f·* no place in,
	53–27	*f·* it abstract or difficult to
	118– 5	when faith *f·* a resting-place
	127–19	*f·* one's own in another's good.
	233–23	*f·* fault with the exactness of
	261– 3	evil *f·* no escape from itself ;
	341–10	Fidelity *f·* its reward
	389–25	And mother *f·* her home
Man.	54– 2	*f·* that the offense has been committed,
Pul.	39–3, 4	* *f·* no rest until it *f·* the peace of
No.	15–20	*f·* Spirit neither in matter nor
	27– 5	evil *f·* no place in good.
Pan.	10–25	individual who *f·* the highest joy,
'01.	1– 7	*f·* C. S. more extended,
	19– 7	thus he *f·* what he seeks,
'02.	10–20	reformer who *f·* the more spiritual
Po.	5– 6	And mother *f·* her home
My.	4– 1	*f·* the spirit of Truth,
	18–16	*f·* one's own in another's good."
	88–21	* *f·* its temple in the heart of
	89–10	* *f·* in the English cathedrals,
	118–27	*f·* its paradise in Spirit,
	155–14	*f·* the full fruition of its faith,
	265– 4	and that it *f·* admittance ;

fine

Mis.	272–17	* shall be punished by a *f·*
Pul.	26–17	* of *f·* range and perfect tone.
Hea.	14– 3	in *f·*, much ado about nothing.
My.	66–16	* in a *f·* part of the city.
	70– 6	* C. S. has more *f·* church edifices
	86– 2	* *f·* architectural effects,
	320– 1	* he was a *f·* literary student
	335–13	* erected a *f·* dwelling-house,

finely

Pul.	29–16	* were *f·* read by Judge Hanna.

finer

My.	345–27	*f·*, more etherealized ways of
	345–27	They seek the *f·* essences.

finesse

Mis.	373–12	Neither material *f·*, standpoint, nor

finest

Pul.	8–25	painted the *f·* flowers in the
My.	74–15	* *f·* architectural achievements
	91–28	* one of the *f·* places of worship
	123–11	in one of the *f·* localities

finger

Mis.	129– 4	let him put his *f·* to his lips,
	166– 3	monument whose *f·* points upward,
	231–17	and bit the *f·*
	339–16	with *f·* grim and cold it points
	388– 5	'T was Love whose *f·* traced aloud
	395–20	Touched by the *f·* of decay
Ret.	85–18	wait for God's *f·* to point the way.
Un.	34–15	yet put your *f·* on a burning coal,
'02.	20–14	'T was Love whose *f·* traced aloud
Po.	7– 5	'Twas Love whose *f·* traced aloud
	26–13	Thou point'st thy phantom *f·*,
	58– 5	Touched by the *f·* of decay
My.	105–12	could be dented by the *f·*,
	121–11	yielding to the touch of a *f·*.
	124–23	with *f·* pointing upward,
	186– 3	prophetic of the *f·* divine
	258–31	a child with *f·* on her lip

fingers

Mis.	329–22	Her dainty *f·* put the fur cap on
Pul.	8–25	your loving hearts and deft *f·*
'01.	12– 2	is not felt with the *f·* ;
Peo.	11–27	"with one of their *f·*."— *Matt.* 23 : 4.
	14–10	* white *f·* pointing upward."

finish

Mis.	41–13	keep the faith and *f·* their course.
	215–25	long warfare with error . . . to *f·*,
Ret.	38– 5	to persuade him to *f·*
My.	68–20	* largely into the interior *f·*.
	68–25	* form the interior *f·*,
	162–17	was not able to *f·*."— *Luke* 14 : 30.

finished

Mis.	57– 8	the true creation was *f·*,
Ret.	38– 1	I had *f·* that edition
	38–11	*f·* my copy for the book.
	38–14	*f·* printing the copy
	38–17	started for Boston with my *f·* copy.
Pul.	45– 7	* get their buildings *f·* on time,
My.	14–27	* until the church is *f·*.

finished

My.	45–13	* The great temple is *f·* !
	45–28	* The great temple is *f·* !
	68–29	* and *f·* with bronze,
	126–11	how the first is *f·*
	145– 8	remodelling of the house was *f·*,
	304– 5	*f·* my course of studies
	311–30	* when she *f·* Smith's grammar
	357–28	I have just *f·* reading your

finisher

Mis.	361–20	*f·* of our faith."— *Heb.* 12 : 2.
'01.	17– 6	the author and *f·* of our faith,
My.	258–14	*f·* of our faith ;— *Heb.* 12 : 2.
	349–16	*f·* of our faith."— *Heb.* 12 : 2.

finishes

Hea.	10–13	that *f·* the question

finishing

My.	66–18	* chapter sub-title

finite (noun)

Mis.	75–13	infinite is not within the *f·* ;
	173–16	Can the infinite be within the *f·* ?
Ret.	67–10	*f·* was self-arrayed against the
Hea.	3–28	the *f·* cannot contain the infinite,
My.	118–21	the demands upon the *f·*
	230– 1	measures the infinite against the *f·*.
	272– 9	the *f·* is not the altitude of the infinite.

finite (adj.)

Mis.	16–20	more than a person, or *f·* form,
	70–25	*f·* and material sense of relief ;
	82–20	which *f·* mortals see and comprehend
	102– 4	is only an infinite *f·* being,
	102– 8	and the infinite forever *f·*.
	162–24	without corporeality or *f·* mind.
	172–19	presents but a *f·*, feeble sense of
	182–23	no personal plan . . . partial and *f·* ;
	217–18	and that Deity is a *f·* person
	217–29	or to become both *f·* and infinite ;
	219– 6	or that the personality of . . . is *f·*
	307–29	deification of *f·* personality.
	308–31	a *f·* person is not the model
	309–14	Pondering on the *f·* personality of
Ret.	30–15	foibles and fables of *f·* mind
	56– 1	antagonized by *f·* theories,
	58– 3	taking the rule of *f·* matter,
	58– 6	physical, false, and *f·* substitute.
	59– 2	to believe man has a *f·* and
	59–11	even as mortals apply *f·* terms
	73– 3	Physical personality is *f·* ;
Un.	4– 8	in a certain *f·* human sense,
	24–10	*Evil.* I am a *f·* consciousness,
	24–13	infinite, and not a *f·* consciousness.
	24–15	There is no really *f·* mind,
	24–16	no *f·* consciousness.
	43– 7	too *f·* for anchorage in infinite
Rud.	2–10	especially a *f·* *human being;*
	2–13	The human person is *f·* ;
	2–21	assigned to God by *f·* thought,
	3–25	*do you mean that God has a f· form?*
No.	20–16	starting from a *f·* body,
	25–11	is beyond a *f·* belief.
	25–12	Man outlives *f·* mortal definitions
	36– 3	one infinite and the other *f·* ;
Pan.	8– 8	a human *f·* personality?
'01.	4–19	God is not *f·* ;
	6– 7	reckons . . . the infinite in a *f·* form,
	6– 9	infinite Mind inhabit a *f·* form?
	6–10	a *f·* or an infinite Person?
	6–28	idea of Him as a *f·* Person
Hea.	4– 8	we limit . . . to the *f·* senses.
	4–15	and become *f·* for a season ;
	4–18	expect infinite Life to become *f·*,
Peo.	3–20	is based on *f·* premises,
	4– 9	said that . . . could enter *f·* man
	8–13	our *f·* and material conceptions of Deity.
My.	109–15	is not corporeal, not *f·*.
	159–15	will not be buried in the *f·* ;
	159–21	the temporary and *f·*.
		(*see also* **sense**)

finiteness

Mis.	101–15	no compromise with *f·*
Ret.	73– 4	without *f·* of form or **Mind.**
Un.	25–15	from *f·* into infinity.

finitized

My.	122–21	*f·*, cribbed, or cradled,

finity

Mis.	102– 7	Mind would be chained to *f·*,
Ret.	67–10	manifestation of sin was a *f·*,
Peo.	4– 7	belief that . . . infinity became *f·*,

fire

Mis.	1–17	*f·* from the ashes of dissolving self,
	125– 2	be purified as by *f·*,
	151– 6	God is a consuming *f·*.

fire

Mis.	172– 9	clans pouring in their *f·* upon us ;
	176–22	melted away in the *f·* of love
	205– 7	the *f·* of repentance first
	213–18	pass through a baptism of *f·*.
	215– 2	the sifting and the *f·*.
	237– 2	that hell is *f·* and brimstone,
	326– 7	that house is on *f·* !
	326–11	"God is a consuming *f·*."— *Heb.* 12 : 29.
	328–20	wakened through the baptism of *f·* ?
	345–11	set *f·* to the fagots,
Ret.	94–10	so Christ's baptism of *f·*,
Pan.	3–25	* heaven, earth, sea, the eternal *f·*,
'00.	8–23	*f·* that purifies sense with Soul
'01.	12– 6	with the Holy Ghost and with *f·*,
'02.	13– 4	a sharper *f·* from enmity.
	16– 1	after the earthquake and the *f·*.
Peo.	13–21	set *f·* to the fagots,
	13–22	through the baptism of *f·*
My.	45–21	* by night in a pillar of *f·*
	45–25	* pillar of *f·* by night,"— *Exod.* 13 : 22.
	160–24	unpunished sin is this internal *f·*,
	160–25	even the *f·* of a guilty conscience,
	160–31	makers of hell burn in their *f·*.
	164–13	What is this . . . phœnix *f·*,
	300–31	Are the churches opening *f·* on

fired

My.	29–22	* *f·* the imagination.

fire-proof

Pul.	25– 7	* as literally *f·* as is conceivable.
	57– 2	* The building is *f·*,
	70–14	* a handsome *f·* church
	75–25	* believed to be the most nearly *f·*

fires

Mis.	125– 2	the *f·* of suffering ;
	237–10	belch forth their latent *f·*.
Pul.	9– 8	kindle perpetually its *f·*.
'02.	5– 7	lights the *f·* of the Holy Ghost,
	19–26	Master triumphed in furnace *f·*.
Hea.	11–13	*f·* of ancient proscription
My.	124–31	they consume in their own *f·*
	160–22	internal *f·* of our earth
	340–32	light their *f·* in every home.

fireside

Mis.	231–32	vacant seat at *f·* and board

firesides

My.	126–29	need it in our homes, at our *f·*,

firing

Mis.	11– 6	by *f·* first could kill him

firm

Mis.	77– 5	to be *f·*,— yea, to *understand*
	77–20	To *believe* is to *be f·*.
	134–18	*F·* in your allegiance to
	213–20	fearless wing and *f·* foundation.
	232–24	its infinite value and *f·* basis.
	299–31	property of a noted *f·*,
	361–27	partner in the *f·* of error,
'01.	2–25	Only a *f·* foundation in Truth can
My.	97– 3	* *f·* faith on the part of a

firmer

Mis.	160–14	*f·* in understanding and obedience.
	276–32	*f·* than ever in their allegiance to
Un.	14–20	*f·* than everlasting hills.

firmest

Pul.	5–10	bravest to endure, *f·* to suffer,

firmly

Mis.	225–11	*f·* bore testimony to the power
	339–12	plants our feet more *f·*.
Un.	6–14	Until . . . is *f·* grounded,
Pan.	15– 8	plant our feet *f·* on Truth,
Peo.	5–27	* "I *f·* believe that if the whole
My.	299–20	*f·* subscribe to this statement ;
	348–21	value to the race *f·* established.

firmness

Ret.	7–17	* noted for his boldness and *f·*,

First

Man.	99–26	by the *F·* and Second Readers
	112– 3	must be written *F·*, Second,
Pul.	37–25	* heading
My.	249–26	the *F·* and Second Readers

first

Mis.	x–20	After my *f·* marriage, to
	xi– 1	*f·* edition of S. and H. having been
	2–11	Adam legacy must *f·* be seen,
	2–14	but the *f·* faint view of a
	8–11	except you *f·* formulate this enemy
	11– 6	by firing *f·* could kill him
	15–29	feeding at *f·* on the milk of the
	21–15	My *f·* plank in the platform of C. S.
	23–17	Satan, the *f·* talker in its behalf,
	23–19	the *f·* and only cause.

first

Mis.	26–13	Whence came the *f·* seed,
	27–31	*f·* admitting that it is substantial.
	29–15	In 1867, I taught the *f·* student
	29–18	the *f·* publication of my work,
	30– 6	even though failing at *f·* to
	33–25	*F·* : It does away with all material
	36– 8	The *f·* and only cause is
	52–26	because the *f·* rule was not easily
	56–29	*f·* spiritually created the universe,
	57– 2	If the *f·* record is true,
	57– 9	in the *f·* chapter of Genesis.
	59–10	is worse than the *f·*.
	63– 5	was at *f·* gotten up to hinder his
	67– 4	*F·* is law, which saith :
	75– 8	*F·* : I urge this fundamental fact
	77–26	has fallen away from his *f·* estate ;
	85–17	*f·* feeble flutterings of mortals
	90–18	*F·*, be sure that your means for
	93–31	suffer for it in the *f·* instance,
	94– 5	He must *f·* see himself and the
	96–11	*f·*, as a loving Father and Mother ;
	106–15	chapter sub-title
	107–21	must *f·* be shown its falsity
	108–17	*f·* state, . . . knowledge of one's self,
	109–18	Ignorance was the *f·* condition
	112–24	This mental disease at *f·*
	117– 4	*f·* separate the tares from the wheat ;
	129– 5	One's *f·* lesson is to
	131– 5	darkness in one's self must *f·* be
	131–14	*f·* financial year since the erection
	137– 6	close of the *f·* convention of the
	138– 5	*f·* and last lesson of C. S. is love,
	138–24	growth of these at *f·* is more gradual ;
	142–15	My *f·* impression was to indite a poem ;
	149–29	*f·* temple for C. S. worship
	151–21	make Him thy *f·* acquaintance.
	153–24	my *f·* edition of "S. and H.
	153–28	* Hear the *f·* music of this
	155–19	she hereby requests : *F·*, that you,
	158–11	we both had *f·* to obey,
	164–13	At *f·*, the babe Jesus seemed small
	171– 3	Jesus' *f·* effort to realize Truth
	172–28	*f·* and fundamental rule of Science
	174–20	*f·* to declare against this kingdom
	176–20	When *f·* the Pilgrims
	179– 4	The *f·* rightful desire
	185–27	*The f· man Adam— I Cor.* 15 : 45.
	185–30	*f·* spake from their standpoint of
	187–14	presuppose a material man to be the *f·*
	188– 4	when the stars *f·* sang together,
	188– 6	presents as being *f·* that which
	188–16	St. Paul *f·* reasons upon the basis
	188–30	was the *f·*, the only man.
	189– 1	"The last shall be *f·*,— *Matt.* 20 : 16.
	189– 1	and the *f·* last."— *Matt.* 20–16.
	189–13	"the *f·* man,"— *I Cor.* 15 : 45.
	191–16	and by omitting the *f·* letter,
	193–31	condition insisted upon is, *f·*,
	194–30	must comply with the *f·* condition
	203–19	*F·* : The baptism of repentance
	205– 7	repentance *f·* separates the dross
	215–13	must *f·* understand the Principle
	216– 4	must *f·* have done our work,
	223– 2	mystery of error . . . at *f·* defied me.
	231–26	his *f·* sitting-at-table on Thanksgiving
	249– 1	*f·* undertaken by a mesmerist,
	255–22	*F·* : It does away with material
	264–15	are taught their *f·* lessons by my
	264–21	the bias of their *f·* impressions,
	270–14	"Seek ye *f·* the kingdom— *Matt.* 6 : 33.
	272– 7	* the *f·* on record in history,
	279–15	The *f·* is that of Joshua
	285–15	*f·* crossed swords with free-love,
	285–18	book that cast the *f·* stone,
	289– 8	mortals must *f·* choose between
	293–17	last error will be worse than the *f·*
	301–24	*F·* : This method is an unseen
	304– 9	* coming *f·* to the capital
	305–19	* *F·* : Material that can be made a
	305–30	* the *f·* President of the United States,
	314–31	On the *f·* Sunday of each month,
	315–23	*f·* few years, convene as often as
	326–23	*f·*, to meet with joy his own,
	330–23	Nature's *f·* and last lessons
	332–22	*f·*, a supposition ;
	336–13	even that you *f·* cast out your
	338– 2	*f·* brings to humanity some great
	338– 5	I *f·* proved to myself,
	341– 6	*F·* purify thought,
	343–21	not . . . by the *f·* uprooting ;
	347– 1	*f·* command of Solomon,
	350– 8	The *f·* subject given out for
	350–15	in about one week from the *f·*
	352– 7	But it must *f·* see the error of its
	354–23	humility is the *f·* step in C. S.,

first

Mis.	355–12	*F·*, self-knowledge.
	358–23	the *f·* and only College for
	360–13	stars of the *f·* magnitude
	366–20	From *f·* to last, evil insists on
	370–29	*f·* care is to separate the sheep
	371– 1	among the *f·* lessons on healing
	372– 1	When the latter was *f·* issued,
	375–17	* "The *f·* thing that impressed me
	378–12	treatment seemed at *f·* to relieve her,
	380–12	teach the *f·* student in C. S.
	380–17	My students at *f·* practised in
	382– 5	my *f·* work on this doctrine.
	382–13	*f·* patient healed in this age by
	382–15	I taught the *f·* student in C. S.
	382–16	the *f·* books on this subject ;
	382–17	obtained the *f·* charter for
	382–17	the *f·* C. S. church,
	382–19	and was its *f·* pastor.
	382–20	erected the *f·* church edifice
	382–21	obtained the *f·* and only charter
	382–22	its *f·* and only president ;
	382–23	the *f·* C. S. periodical
	382–24	*f·* Christian Scientist Association,
	386–15	At *f·* to fill That waking with
	388–21	*F·* at the tomb to hear his word :
Man.	40–19	*f·* Sunday of each month.
	56–12	following the *f·* Sunday in June.
	57– 4	preceding the *f·* Sunday in June,
	57– 5	*f·* Friday in November of each year.
	59– 9	*f·* to announce the name of the
	62–24	The *f·* lessons of the children
	64–18	At *f·* Mrs. Eddy objected to being
	70– 5	without *f·* consulting her on said
	77– 4	books are to be audited on May *f·*.
	78–24	on the *f·* of the following month,
	90–10	on the *f·* Wednesday of December.
	110–13	Initials only of *f·* names will not
Chr.	55–10	seek ye *f·* the kingdom — *Matt.* 6 : 33.
Ret.	5– 4	*f·* Congregational Church in Pembroke.
	19– 1	I was united to my *f·* husband,
	26–26	could *f·* state this Principle,
	27–14	*f·* jottings were but efforts to
	27–21	ripples in one's *f·* thoughts of it
	27–24	Science *f·* broke upon my sense,
	28–12	The *f·* must become last.
	31–13	*f·* spontaneous motion of Truth
	34–11	*F·* : It does away with all material
	35– 1	copyrighted the *f·* publication on
	36– 5	after taking out my *f·* copyright,
	37– 1	*f·* edition of my most important work,
	37– 6	When it was *f·* printed,
	37– 9	*f·* edition numbered one thousand copies.
	37–21	in my *f·* edition of S. and H.,
	38–21	closing chapter of my *f·* edition
	42– 4	Dr. Eddy was the *f·* student publicly
	42– 7	He was the *f·* organizer of
	43– 1	*f·* purely metaphysical system
	43–21	The *f·* Christian Scientist Association
	44– 4	The *f·* such church ever organized.
	45–12	deemed requisite in the *f·* stages of
	49–12	spiritual formation *f·*, last, and
	49–13	in human growth material . . . is *f·* ;
	52–19	The *f·* official organ of the
	64–26	mortals must *f·* open their eyes to
	67– 9	*f·* . . . manifestation of sin was
	81–28	*f·* led me to the feet of C. S.,
	81–30	Though our *f·* lessons are changed,
	87– 3	* "Order is heaven's *f·* law,"
	87–15	*F·* : Christian Scientists are to
	89–28	action not *f·* made known to them
	90–23	to those *f·* sacred tasks,
	92– 5	"*f·* the blade, then the ear, — *Mark* 4 : 28.
Un.	14– 3	because it was not at *f·* done
	15– 1	man's *f·* disobedience,
	17–21	God told our *f·* parents that
	20– 7	*F·* : The Lord created it.
	20–12	*F·* : God never made evil.
	30–13	*f·* epistle to the Corinthians
	30–14	"The *f·* man Adam — *I Cor.* 15 : 45.
	30–25	*f·* shall be last," — *Matt.* 19 : 30.
	31–11	*f·* idolatrous claim of sin is,
	35–15	Which was *f·*, matter or power?
	35–15	That which was *f·* was God,
	56–12	*f·* eliminates and then destroys.
	56–23	*f·* be made to fret in their chains ;
	61– 5	Jesus *f·* appeared as a helpless
Pul.	1——	chapter heading
	5–15	the *f·* to bedew my hope with a
	7–28	This is my *f·* ordination.
	20– 2	was *f·* purchased by the church
	20–14	From *f·* to last The Mother Church
	24– 1	* completion of the *f·* C. S. church
	24–19	* *f·* pastor of this denomination."
	29– 5	* *f·* pastor of the church here
	30–26	* *f·* meeting held on April 12, 1879.

first

Pul.	31– 9	* my *f·* meeting with her
	35–16	The *f·* must become last.
	35–29	* the *f·* to place "Christian Scientist" on
	36–14	* evening that I *f·* met Mrs. Eddy
	37–26	* *f·* Christian Scientist Association
	38– 5	* *f·* edition of Mrs. Eddy's book,
	41–30	* At 9 a. m. the *f·* congregation
	44–22	* the *f·* of its kind ;
	46–29	* He was the *f·* organizer of a
	47– 5	* publisher of the *f·* official organ
	49–27	* *f·* impression given to the visitor
	55–13	* the *f·* edition of Mrs. Eddy's
	55–16	* Her discovery was *f·* called,
	60–10	* Each paragraph he supplemented *f·*
	61–22	* *f·* peal of the chimes in the tower
	64– 4	* the *f·* pastor of this denomination."
	67–25	* *f·* Christian Scientist Association
	70– 9	* *f·* pastor of the C. S. denomination,
	72– 9	* one of the *f·* to be seen.
	79–18	* The *f·* is that a revolt was inevitable
Rud.	9– 2	worse than the *f·*." — *Matt.* 12 : 45.
	11– 4	*f·* to faith in Christ ;
	12–10	belief that they are *f·* made sick
	14–19	*f·* classes furnished students with
	16–20	This was the *f·* book,
	17–13	when taking the *f·* footsteps
No.	6– 1	last state . . . worse than the *f·*.
	9–17	the *f·* edition of this little work
	45–14	and *f·* at the sepulchre,"
	46–14	the *f·* settlers of New Hampshire.
Pan.	6– 1	*f·*, because it was more effectual
	6–11	*f·*, in the form of a talking serpent,
	9– 9	four *f·* rules pertaining thereto,
'00.	7– 2	"S. and H. . . . was *f·* published.
	8–26	learn *f·* what obedience is.
	10–26	in the name of a *f·* lieutenant of the
	12–19	hast left thy *f·* love — *Rev.* 2 : 4.
	15–23	not left thy *f·* love, — *see Rev.* 2 : 4.
	15–26	more than the *f·*." — *Rev.* 2 : 19.
'01.	1– 6	*f·* communion in the new century
	3–22	The *f·* proposition is correct,
	3–24	last . . . does not illustrate the *f·*,
	13–27	*f·* detect the claim of sin ;
	14–24	control it in the *f·* instance, or
	17–11	my *f·* demonstrations of C. S.
	27– 9	the *f·* ever published on C. S.,
	27–28	* *F·*, people say it conflicts with
	28– 1	Having passed through the *f·* two stages,
	33–13	Christian Scientists *f·* and last
	33–26	just what it was in the *f·* centuries
'02.	2– 5	to write truth *f·* on the
	3–30	the *f·* lie and leap into perdition
	7– 5	In the *f·* chapter of Genesis,
	9–21	When *f·* I heard the life-giving sound
	15–11	not one dollar of royalty on its *f·*
	16– 6	This was my *f·* inkling of Wyclif's
Hea.	11–14	the *f·* to be intolerant.
	13–28	that one is worse than the *f·* ;
	14–19	You must *f·* mentally educate and
	17–24	Sin was *f·* in the allegory,
	19–13	Which is *f·*, the egg or the bird?
Peo.	4–11	When *f·* good, God, was named a
Po.	1– 8	when *f·* creation vast began,
	3–11	Since *f·* we met, in weal or woe
	21–10	*F·* at the tomb to hear his word :
	39–11	*F·* at the tomb, who waits
	49–23	At *f·* to fill That waking with a
My.	vi–18	* was its *f·* editor and
	13– 7	the *f·* that I had even heard of it.
	31– 1	* *f·* the "Communion Hymn,"
	31–10	* public had its *f·* glimpse of the
	31–13	* *f·* impression was of vastness,
	31–20	* *f·* sight which the visitors caught
	40–19	* *f·* pure, then peaceable, — *Jas.* 3 : 17.
	42–20	* welcome you to our *f·* annual meeting
	49–15	* *f·* business meeting of the church
	49–32	* *f·* meeting of this little church
	54–23	* stated that from the *f·* of September
	54–31	* *f·* Sunday service held in Chickering
	56–30	* being repetitions of the *f·* service.
	57–14	* The *f·* annual meeting of the church
	59– 3	* your *f·* class in Lynn, Mass.,
	59–16	* back to that *f·* public meeting
	60–17	* of the *f·* chapter of Genesis.
	61– 6	* At *f·* I thought that,
	68–27	* floors of the *f·* story are of marble.
	73–28	* the *f·* instalments of the crowds
	74– 8	* in time for the *f·* Sunday service.
	76–26	* *f·* great monument to C. S.,
	77–21	* *f·* hymn of thanksgiving at six o'clock
	81–10	* *f·* to catch the Reader's eye.
	91–22	* the *f·* years of her preaching
	95– 4	* tenets *f·* presented by Mrs. Eddy
	112– 2	Science has always been *f·* met with
	114–14	My *f·* writings on C. S. began

first

My.	121–19	a diamond of the *f·* water ;
	126–11	how the *f·* is finished
	131–14	praise return to its *f·* love,
	153–16	the great and *f·* commandment,
	154–14	chapter sub-title
	154–15	your *f·* annual meeting,
	157–18	* *f·* announced in the *Concord Monitor*
	167–15	your *f·* Thanksgiving Day,
	172– 3	* *f·* chapel of the college.
	174–21	my parents *f·* offered me to Christ
	179– 3	*f·* and second chapters of Genesis,
	179– 4	The *f·* gave an account of
	181–31	*f·* two years of my discovery of
	189–24	cannot forget that yours is the *f·*
	193–24	taking the *f·* by the forelock
	195–26	temples erected *f·* in the hearts of
	196– 4	*f·* edifice of our denomination in
	202–27	The way is narrow at *f·*,
	211– 8	allowing it *f·* to smoulder,
	215–18	to plant our *f·* magazine,
	215–23	*f·* sent forth his students,
	215–28	*f·* without, and then with, provision
	217–21	We deny *f·* the existence of disease,
	217–29	*f·* takes up the subject.
	217–30	step to be taken *f·*.
	223–14	*F·*, because I have not . . . time
	236–16	they accepted the *f·* name.
	245–31	The *f·* degree (C.S.B.) is given to
	246– 2	after receiving the *f·* degree,
	250– 7	*f·* to adopt this By-law
	261–13	*f·* impressions of innocence,
	267–20	One individual may *f·* awaken from
	270– 6	my *f·* religious home in this capital
	290–10	*f·* month of the new century.
	302–15	*f·* gave me the endearing appellative
	302–25	My *f·* visit to The Mother Church
	303–27	*f·* or second Virgin-mother
	304–26	* *F·*, people say it conflicts with
	304–29	The *f·* attack upon me was :
	306–22	when I *f·* visited Dr. Quimby
	307–11	seemed at *f·* new to him.
	307–25	At *f·* my case improved
	309–28	* passed her *f·* fifteen years at
	310–29	*f·* edition of S. and H.
	311–16	date of my *f·* church membership.
	312– 4	Regarding my *f·* marriage
	312–18	My *f·* husband, Major George W. Glover,
	320–30	* dedication of the *f·* Mother Church
	321–21	* twenty years since I *f·* saw you
	328–20	* *f·* to be issued to the healers of
	343–17	Science came *f·* to me.
	343–19	it won converts from the *f·*.
	347–17	our great Master's *f·* disciples,
	349–1, 2	*f·* chronologically, is *f·* potentially,
	352–28	*f·* issue of *The C. S. Monitor.*
	353–10	The *f·* was *The C. S. Journal*,
	362–18	* as their *f·* act send you their

(*see also* **century, church, time**)

firstborn

My. 46–30 * church of the *f·*." — *Heb.* 12 : 23.

First Cause

Ret. 57–26 ingrafting upon one *F· C·*

First Church

Man. 112– 2 *F· C·*, Second Church, etc.,

First Church of Christ, Scientist

Atlanta, Georgia
My. 187–20 chapter sub-title
Brooklyn
My. 363– 5 * signature
Brooklyn, N. Y.
My. 183–16 chapter sub-title
Chicago, Ill.
My. 177– 1 chapter sub-title
Cleveland, Ohio
My. 195– 1 chapter sub-title
Colorado Springs, Col.
My. 19–16 heading
Columbus, Ohio
My. 204–12 chapter sub-title
Concord, N. H.
My. 144– 3 heading
166–30 *F· C· of C·, S·,* Concord, N. H.
Detroit, Mich.
My. 183–22 chapter sub-title
Duluth, Minn.
My. 186–16 chapter sub-title
186–18 *F· C· of C·, S·, Duluth, Minn.:*
Edinburgh, Scotland
My. 208–10 chapter sub-title
in Chicago
My. 177– 5 *F· C· of C·, S·,* in Chicago.
in Concord
My. 164– 9 to *F· C· of C·, S·,* in Concord,

First Church of Christ, Scientist

in Concord, N. H.
My. 165–14 *F· C· of C·, S·,* in Concord, N. H.
299– 4 *F· C· of C·, S·,* in Concord, N. H.,
in Denver
Mis. 152– 1 chapter sub-title
in Lawrence
Mis. 154– 1 chapter sub-title
in London
My. 259– 5 *F· C· of C·, S·,* in London,
in Oconto
Mis. 149–16 chapter sub-title
in Scranton
Mis. 150– 8 chapter sub-title
London, England
My. 183– 9 chapter sub-title
198– 1 chapter sub-title
200– 9 chapter sub-title
203–22 chapter sub-title
Los Angeles, Cal.
My. 192–18 chapter sub-title
Milwaukee, Wis.
My. 207– 1 chapter sub-title
New London, Conn.
My. 166–25 heading
New York City
My. 283– 4 *F· C· of C·, S·,* NEW YORK CITY,
360– 8 *F· C· of C·, S·,* NEW YORK CITY.
360–11 *F· C· of C·, S·,* New York City,
360–16 *F· C· of C·, S·,* New York City,
362– 3 *F· C· of C·, S·,* NEW YORK CITY.
New York, N. Y.
My. 165–11 heading
193–20 chapter sub-title
201– 8 chapter sub-title
361–24 * signature
Oakland, Cal.
My. 202–19 chapter sub-title
of Concord, N. H.
My. 166–11 *F· C· of C·, S·,* of Concord, N. H.,
of New York
Pul. 43– 1 * *F· C· of C·, S·,* of New York,
My. 359–22 * *F· C· of C·, S·,* of New York,
Ottawa, Ontario
My. 209– 1 chapter sub-title
Philadelphia, Pa.
My. 199– 1 chapter sub-title
Pittsburgh, Pa.
My. 196– 1 chapter sub-title
Salt Lake City, Utah
My. 186–23 chapter sub-title
San Jose, Cal.
My. 197– 8 chapter sub-title
Staten Island
My. 363– 7 * signature
St. Louis, Mo.
My. 196–23 chapter sub-title
Sydney, Australia
My. 208– 1 chapter sub-title
Toronto, Canada
My. 184– 1 chapter sub-title
Washington, D. C.
My. 199– 8 chapter sub-title
203– 1 chapter sub-title
Wilmington, N. C.
My. 176– 1 chapter sub-title
197–23 chapter sub-title

Man. 71– 2 title of *F· C· of C·, S·* ;
My. 158– 2 edifice for *F· C· of C·, S·*,
182–17 *F· C· of C·, S·,* with its large
183– 4 Thus may *F· C· of C·, S·,*
184–10 having built *F· C· of C·, S·,*
362–27 * signature

(*see also* **The First Church of Christ, Scientist**)

First Commandment

Mis. 21– 1 C. S. begins with the *F· C·*
23–14 the Me spoken of in the *F· C·*,
24– 1 These facts enjoin the *F· C·* ;
28–20 The *F· C·*, "Thou shalt have— *Exod.* 20 : 3.
123– 3 the illusion of breaking the *F· C·*,
197–27 This belief breaks the *F· C·* of God.
Pan. 7– 1 breaketh the *F· C·* in the Decalogue.
8–22 rest on the basis of the *F· C·*
'00. 5– 3 coincides with the *F· C·*
5–19 obey the *F· C·* of the Decalogue :
'01. 32–22 especially the *F· C·* of the
'02. 4–13 My subject to-day embraces the *F· C·*
4–19 The *F· C·*, "Thou shalt have— *Exod.* 20 : 3.
5–10 that heaven husbands in the *F· C·*.
6–19 consummates the *F· C·*,
7–10 sufficiently to fulfil the *F· C·*.
12– 7 Jew who believes in the *F· C·*
12–11 Christian who believes in the *F· C·*
My. 5–12 *F· C·* of the Hebrew Decalogue,

First Commandment
My. 64–12 *F· C·* of the Hebrew Decalogue,
116–10 would dethrone the *F· C·*,
221–17 *F· C·* of the Decalogue,
264–17 *F· C·* of the Decalogue
279–11 *F· C·* in the Hebrew Decalogue

First Congregational Church
My. 60– 7 * deacon of the *F· C· C·*
147– 5 afternoon services of the *F· C· C·*,
174–12 chapter sub-title
174–14 Pastor of the *F· C· C·*,
174–20 our time-honored *F· C· C·*
270– 5 In 1905, the *F· C· C·*,

firstfruits
Mis. 131–17 this year of your *f·*.
Rud. 16–26 call it their *f·*, or else

First Members
Mis. 147– 1 chapter sub-title
310–23 *F· M·* will determine the action
Man. 18–21 were known as "*F· M·*"
18–25 changed the title of "*F· M·*"
My. 289–12 special meeting of its *F· M·*

First Reader (*see also* **First Reader's**)
Mis. 314–10 *F· R·* shall give out any notices
314–15 *F ·R·* shall read from my book,
Man. 29– 1 the *F· R·* of a church,
30–12 *F· R·* of The Mother Church shall
33– 2 *F· R·* in a Church of Christ,
40–18 by the *F· R·* on the first Sunday
100– 3 send to the *F. R·* of the church
My. 16–17 * Prof. Hermann S. Hering, *F· R·* ;
16–22 * conducted by the *F· R·*,
31–23 *F· R·* William D. McCrackan,
31–27 * the *F· R·* announced simply
35–27 *F· R·* William D. McCrackan read
134–23 *F· R·*, Mr. William D. McCrackan,
135–17 *F· R·* of my church in Boston,
142– 9 *F· R·*, The Mother Church,
247–10 chapter sub-title
249–23 for *F· R·* in The Church of Christ,

First Reader's
Man. 30–11 *F· R·* Residence.

First Readers (*see also* **First Readers'**)
Man. 31–16 shall be the duty of the *F· R·*
31–19 The *F· R·* shall read, as a part of
32– 1 *F· R·* in the C. S. churches shall

First Readers'
Man. 31–15 *F· R·* Duties.

fish (*see also* **fish's**)
Mis. 69–12 over the *f·* of the sea, — *Gen.* 1 : 26.
69–31 dominion over the *f·*
69–32 "the *f·* of the sea" — *Gen.* 1 : 26.
70– 4 exercised my power over the *f·*,
393–14 Those who *f·* in waters deep,
Ret. 18– 3 at play with the gold-gleaming *f·* ;
Po. 51–19 Those who *f·* in waters deep,
63–11 at play with the gold-gleaming *f·* ;

fisher
My. 247–19 God has called you to be a *f·* of men.

fishermen
My. 295–18 It guides the *f·*.

fishers
Mis. 111–10 "*f·* of men" — *Mark* 1 : 17.
My. 295–17 Christian Scientists are *f·* of men.

fishes
Mis. 111– 8 you lost your *f·*,
Pul. 60– 9 * Jesus' miracle of loaves and *f·*.
Peo. 6– 1 * and all the worse for the *f·*."
My. 123–24 "five loaves and two *f·*" — *Matt.* 14 : 17.
247–14 The little *f·* in my fountain

fishing-boat
Ret. 91–23 a *f·* became a sanctuary,

fish's
My. 216– 3 obtain their money from a *f·* mouth,

fissures
Un. 64–16 leap the dark *f·*,

fit
Mis. 212–12 When they were *f·* to be blest,
228–18 an existence *f·* for earth and heaven.
288– 5 sure of being a *f·* counsellor.
315–10 who are letterly *f·*
344– 9 *f·* habitation for the intelligences
345–15 * *f·* only for women and weak men" ;
Man. 55–12 so strayed as not to be *f·* for the
Ret. 37–18 until our heavenly Father saw *f·*,
Rud. 16– 5 to *f·* students for practice
'*00.* 9–28 strove earnestly to *f·* others for
Peo. 13–23 * *f·* only for women and weak-minded
My. 112– 9 the Scriptures to *f·* a doctrine,
200–28 and *f·* their being to recover its
229– 3 No mesmerist . . . is *f·* to come hither.

fitful
Po. 65– 3 Life's pulses move *f·* and slow ;

fitly
Mis. 346–23 "A word *f·* spoken — *Prov.* 25 : 11.
My. 24–14 * "*f·* framed together — *Eph.* 2 : 21.

fitness
Mis. 127–16 *f·* to receive the answer to its
316–11 should depend on the *f·* of things,
Un. 11–25 to mature *f·* for perfection
My. 18–12 *f·* to receive the answer to its
230–20 Be assured that *f·* and fidelity
267–18 in proportion to their *f·*

fits
My. 310–25 * these "*f·*" were diagnosed by

fitted
Mis. 197– 9 no man can be wholly *f·* for
264–14 whom I have not *f·* for it
315–10 spiritually *f·* for teachers,
My. 249–25 individual best *f·* to perform this

fittest
Mis. 140–30 the *f·* would survive,
No. 25–13 * "the survival of the *f·*."
My. 166– 6 but the *f·* survives ;

fitting
Mis. 307–18 is fast *f·* all minds for the
374–11 most *f·* that Christian Scientists
Pul. 25–16 * vestibule is a *f·* entrance
My. 45–15 * edifice stands a *f·* monument of
58–15 * *f·* testimonial in stone,
81–25 * a *f·* close to a memorable week.
84–14 * stately cupola is a *f·* crown
352–14 * *f·* testimony of the efficacy of

five
Mis. 13–22 testimony of the *f·* erring senses,
28– 4 Perception by the *f·* personal senses
65– 1 gathered from the *f·* personal senses.
99– 3 saith to the *f·* material senses,
100–12 *f·* personal senses, that grasp neither
172–18 taken in by the *f·* personal senses,
172–25 Science, and the *f·* personal senses,
218–13 *f·* personal senses can take no
221–26 *f·* times ten are fifty
221–26 while ten times *f·* are not
351–23 *f·* senses give to mortals pain,
Man. 26–20 Board of Directors shall consist of *f·*
29–14 *f·* suitable members of this Church
Ret. 25–22 *f·* physical senses are so many
36– 5 *F·* years after taking out my
44– 8 though I had preached *f·* years
56–13 evidences of the *f·* physical senses ;
59–20 the *f·* material senses define
Un. 25– 5 testimony of the *f·* senses.
28– 6 *f·* physical senses do not cognize it.
28–18 *f·* senses take no cognizance of Soul,
Pul. 38– 2 * in other parishes for *f·* years
62– 9 * not more than *f·* by eight feet.
Rud. 4–26 *f·* material senses testify to the
5–26 Destroy the *f·* senses as
'*00.* 1–17 *f·* grand divisions of the globe ;
'*01.* 18–15 of the *f·* personal senses,
26– 7 *f·* personal senses can have
Hea. 16–16 about the *f·* personal senses,
My. 29–28 * half past *f·* in the morning
32– 3 * *f·* minutes of silent communion
123–23 the "*f·* loaves — *Matt.* 14 : 17.
136–20 in the *f·* grand divisions
273–25 the *f·* personal senses are
273–29 of the *f·* personal senses,
343–26 *f·* churches under discipline.
356–14 within the last *f·* years
(*see also* **numbers, values**)

five-dollar
'*00.* 10–27 ten *f·* gold pieces

fix
Man. 26–18 *f·* the salaries of the Readers.
Ret. 11– 6 Go *f·* thy restless mind
Po. 60– 2 Go *f·* thy restless mind

fixed
Mis. 147–19 is guided by a *f·* Principle,
232–24 *f·* Principle of all healing is God ;
240–18 with form and inclination *f·*,
320–17 *f·* in the heavens of divine Science,
360–13 *f·* stars in the heavens of Soul.
366– 7 with *f·* Principle, given rule, and
Ret. 87–13 implicit adherence to *f·* rules,
93–12 immovably *f·* in Principle.
No. 11–21 with *f·* Principle, given rule, and
33–10 divine Science, with *f·* Principle,
'*01.* 23–15 its *f·* Principle and given rule,
My. v– 5 * attention . . . is *f·* on C. S.,
106–18 rests on the basis of *f·* Principle,
113–24 demonstrated on a *f·* Principle

fixed
My. 122— 5   *f·* in one's own moral make-up.
181—28   *f·* the year 1866 or 1867 for the
319—26   * well *f·* in my memory,
347—27   manifestation of a *f·* Principle

fixtures
My. 68—31   * Bronze is used in the lighting *f·*,

flag
Pul. 83—14   * black *f·* of oppression
Po. 71—20   O war-rent *f·* ! O soldier-shroud !

flagrance
'01. 20—26   its hidden modus and *f·*

flagstones
My. 89—15   * even to the *f·* in front

flame
Mis. 82—27   treacherous glare of its own *f·*
341—27   so that the *f·* never expires.
341—32   to keep aglow the *f·* of devotion
345—13   though the baptism of *f·*.
'02. 5— 9   It is this ethereal *f·*,
Po. 30—13   fan Thou the *f·* Of right with might ;

flames
Mis. 17— 7   before the *f·* have died away
209—23   Evil passions die in their own *f·*,
237— 5   in place of material *f·* and odor,
326— 7   *f·* caught in the dwelling
348—17   quench the growing *f·* of falsehood,
No. 1—16   *f·* die away on the mount of
Hea. 9—14   furnishing fuel for the *f·*.
My. 178—24   snatched this book from the *f·*.
211— 9   break out in devouring *f·*.

flaming
My. 79—16   * fact was heralded in *f·* headlines

flash
My. 296— 2   his *f·* of flight and insight,

flat
Mis. 65— 5   that the earth's surface is *f·*,
325—16   or, *f·* on their backs,
'01. 19—15   a *f·* departure from Jesus' practice

flatly
Mis. 295—20   *f·* contradicted, as both untrue and

flatterer
Mis. 224—31   a *f·*, a fool, or a liar,
363— 7   greatest *f·*, identification,

flattering
My. 122—14   called forth *f·* comment

flattery
'02. 17—28   world's soft *f·* or its frown.

flaunting
Mis. 295—18   *f·* and floundering statements
My. 83— 8   * has been no *f·* of badges
151—18   * aisles by *f·* folly trod,

flavor
Mis. 9—23   enjoyment having lost its *f·*,
29—25   neither *f·* Christianity nor

flavored
Mis. 294—28   *f·* with the true ideas

flax
'02. 18—11   quenched not the smoking *f·*,

flecked
Ret. 4—20   and *f·* with large flocks

flecks
Mis. 376—25   golden *f·* came out on a

fled
Mis. 112—21   his flippancy had *f·*.
324—26   all wasted and the music *f·*.
385—19   see thy ever-self ; Life never *f·* ;
396— 8   It voices beauty *f·*.
Ret. 23—21   Soulless famine had *f·*.
30— 5   borrower would have *f·*.
Pan. 1— 9   frown and smile . . . have *f·* ;
'02. 15—24   when slumber had *f·*,
Po. 9— 8   weeping alone that the vision is *f·*,
41—15   waters had *f·* to the sea,
47—17   Watching the husbandman *f·* ;
48—13   see thy ever-self ; Life never *f·* ;
58—20   It voices beauty *f·*.
65— 7   it *f·* with the light,

fledgling
Po. 18—15   notice the frail *f·* hath.

flee
Mis. 222—32   light and shadows *f·*,
251—29   Sin, sickness, and disease *f·*
284—24   to fear and *f·* before,
342—20   earth's fables *f·*,
No. 7—12   "*f·* as a bird to your — *Psal.* 11 : 1.
Po. 3— 5   length'ning shadows *f·*,
25— 8   Far do ye *f·*,

flee
My. 171— 7   shall *f·* away." — *Isa.* 35 : 10.
189—19   how soon earth's fables *f·*
260— 6   would *f·* before such reality,
350—23   whither shall he *f·* ?

fleecy
Mis. 376—24   *F·*, faint, fairy blue

fleeing
Un. 27—13   *f·* like a shadow at daybreak ;

flees
Mis. 210—31   Charity never *f·* before error,
396— 3   And frightened fancy *f·*,
Po. 58—15   And frightened fancy *f·*,

fleet
Mis. 396—10   O happy hours and *f·*,
Po. 59— 2   O happy hours and *f·*,

fleetest
Po. 65—16   moments most sweet are *f·*

fleeth
Mis. 213—25   *f·* when he seeth the wolf

fleeting
Mis. ix—21   The *f·* freshness of youth,
9—25   to relish this *f·* sense,
110—28   You have learned how *f·* is that which
360—18   blighted flowers of *f·* joys,
Ret. 32—15   * *F·* pleasure, fond delusion,

flesh
according to the
Ret. 1— 1   My ancestors, according to the *f·*,
after the
Mis. 188—14   walk not after the *f·*, — *Rom.* 8 : 1.
360—20   "Israel after the *f·*." — *I Cor.* 10 : 18.
My. 113—12   walk not after the *f·*, — *Rom.* 8 : 1.
205— 3   walk not after the *f·*, — *Rom.* 8 : 1.
and evil
Mis. 2— 8   the world, the *f·*, and evil,
My. 134— 2   the world, the *f·*, and evil,
and Spirit
Mis. 16—32   conflict between the *f·* and Spirit.
188—11   a war between the *f·* and Spirit,
Pul. 20—15   warfare between the *f·* and Spirit,
Pan. 13—16   war between *f·* and Spirit,
My. 18—24   war between *f·* and Spirit,
and the devil
Mis. 163— 2   the world, the *f·*, and the devil.
Un. 52—18   world, the *f·*, and the devil.
My. 268—22   "the world, the *f·* and the devil,"
beliefs of the
Mis. 28—14   not destroy the beliefs of the *f·*,
72— 7   According to the beliefs of the *f·*,
born of the
Ret. 26—22   to one "born of the *f·*," — *John* 3 : 6.
No. 25—22   That which is born of the *f·*
My. 239—26   so-called man born of the *f·*,
261—25   Christ was not born of the *f·*.
brings to the
Mis. 9— 3   purification it brings to the *f·*,
brought to the
Un. 59—11   divine idea brought to the *f·*
cleansed of the
Mis. 153—14   cleansed of the *f·*,
crucifixions of the
Mis. 107— 6   self-denials, and crucifixions of the *f·*.
discipline of the
Mis. 84—23   discipline of the *f·* is designed to
errors of
Mis. 189—11   destroys the errors of *f·*,
fetters of the
Mis. 165— 8   man, without the fetters of the *f·*,
fight with the
'02. 10— 2   has a fight with the *f·*.
fruits of the
'02. 6— 6   fruits of the *f·* not Spirit.
human will or
Mis. 181—32   born not of the human will or *f·*,
incisions of the
Mis. 244— 7   closing the incisions of the *f·*.
in the
Mis. 21— 6   while on earth and in the *f·*,
103—24   Jesus' personality in the *f·*,
162—20   and suffered in the *f·*,
167— 3   manner of a mother in the *f·*,
178—28   In the *f·*, we are as a partition
180— 2   the dream of Spirit in the *f·*
214—21   personal Jesus' labor in the *f·*
292— 7   he gave his life (in the *f·*)
373—16   Christ's appearing in the *f·*,
Un. 55—12   "The way," in the *f·*." — *John* 14 : 6.
56—14   He also suffereth in the *f·*
57—28   conscious existence in the *f·*
61—21   now live in the *f·* — *Gal.* 2 : 20.
'01. 10—30   fulfilled his mission in the *f·*
My. 143—11   I exist in the *f·*, and am seen daily

flesh

in the
My. 260–31 Neither the you nor the I in the *f·*
346– 9 * she is in the *f·* and in health.
(*see also sub-title* **manifest in the**)

is heir
Mis. 33–27 * "the ills that *f·* is heir to,"
No. 42–10 * ills that *f·* is heir to."
Hea. 15– 6 all ills that *f·* is heir to.

leaves no
Ret. 94–12 destroying all error, leaves no *f·*,

lust of the
Un. 39– 5 lust of the *f·* and the pride of
My. 205–25 lust of the *f·* and the pride of

lusts of the
Mis. 182–32 lusts of the *f·* and the pride of
Ret. 79–14 "lusts of the *f·*," — *see I John* 2 : 16.
Hea. 17– 2 lusts of the *f·*, the pride of life,

made
Mis. 182–29 When the Word is made *f·*,
184– 6 The Word will be made *f·*
Un. 39– 1 "the Word" is "made *f·*" — *John* 1 : 14.

manifest in the
Mis. 44–20 thought made manifest in the *f·*
78– 4 God is made manifest in the *f·*,
154–21 be made manifest in the *f·*
Chr. 53–61 manifest in the *f·*." — *I Tim.* 3 : 16.
'01. 9–16 God is made manifest in the *f·*,
12–27 and thus is manifest in the *f·*.
My. 109–25 "manifest in the *f·*," — *I Tim.* 3 : 16.
124–28 "manifest in the *f·*," — *I Tim.* 3 : 16.
348– 7 God made manifest in the *f·*,

matter, or the
Mis. 124– 7 by means of matter, or the *f·*,

my
Un. 55–21 in my *f·* shall I see God ;" — *Job* 19 : 26.
Pul. 3–20 in my *f·* shall I see God." — *Job* 19 : 26.
My. 218– 5 "In my *f·* shall I see God." — *Job* 19 : 26.
241–23 * I still lived in my *f·*,
241–23 * I did not live in my *f·*,
241–24 * my *f·* lived or died according to

not of the
Mis. 181–18 of Spirit, and not of the *f·* ;

of the neck
My. 105–15 that had eaten the *f·* of the neck

one
Mis. 94– 7 the twain that are one *f·*,
289–17 twain shall be one *f·*." — *Matt.* 19 : 5.

out of the
Un. 55–12 suffering which leads out of the *f·*.
No. 33–26 show them that the way out of the *f·*,

over the
Mis. 30–18 superiority of Mind over the *f·*,
356–23 This virtue triumphs over the *f·* ;
Pul. 3–28 so far from victory over the *f·*

prevailed
My. 293–20 to mortal sense the *f·* prevailed.

sense of the
Un. 55–14 from the false sense of the *f·*

sin and
'00. 8– 1 if sin and *f·* are put off,

sins of the
Mis. 162–21 to escape from the sins of the *f·*.
My. 6– 8 with the sins of the *f·*,

somebody in the
Mis. 111–30 belief . . . that somebody in the *f·*

Spirit and
Mis. 85–21 Spirit and *f·* antagonize.

spirit and the
My. 293–20 the spirit and the *f·* — struggled,

strives
Mis. 119–15 for the *f·* strives against Spirit,

suffering of the
Mis. 200–23 pain, and all suffering of the *f·*,

sufferings of the
Un. 3–12 through the sufferings of the *f·*
55–18 sufferings of the *f·* are unreal.
'01. 11–10 the sins and sufferings of the *f·*,

temptations of the
Mis. 104– 4 to the temptations of the *f·*,

thorn in the
Mis. 71– 6 Paul had a thorn in the *f·* :
Un. 57–21 "a thorn in the *f·*" — *II Cor.* 12 : 7.

through the
Mis. 201–32 it illustrates through the *f·*
Ret. 22–19 nor is he ever created through the *f·* ;
Rud. 3– 7 through the *f·*, from the flesh,

to Spirit
Un. 56–24 change from *f·* to Spirit,

unknown to the
My. 167– 3 is unknown to the *f·*,

vale of the
Mis. 328–10 surveys the vale of the *f·*,

veil of the
Mis. 165–12 rends the veil of the *f·*

flesh

was weak
Mis. 385–23 the *f·* was weak, and doomed
Po. 48–18 the *f·* was weak, and doomed

weakness of
Mis. 64– 1 Jesus assumed . . . weakness of *f·*,

will of the
Mis. 180–23 *nor of the will of the f·,* — *John* 1 : 13.
181–16 of the will of the *f·,* — *John* 1 : 13.
182–15 nor of the will of the *f·.*" — *John* 1 : 13.

Mis. 96–32 not of the *f·*, but of the Spirit.
97– 1 to destroy the power of the *f·* ;
125– 8 overcome the world, the *f·*, and
153–19 the fruits of Spirit, not *f·* ;
326– 9 but the *f·* at length did feel them ;
Ret. 57–10 it is the *f·* that is evil.
Un. 36–13 the *f·* at war with Spirit ;
46– 4 from Spirit, not from *f·*.
Rud. 3– 7 the *f·*, — the material world and evil.
Po. 29–13 Beloved, replete, by *f·* embound
My. 108– 9 *f·* profiteth nothing." — *John* 6 : 63.
119– 9 Man is free from the *f·*
260– 6 the *f·* would flee before such

fleshly
Mis. 86– 2 these have no *f·* nature.
345–32 from the thought of *f·* sacrifice,
Ret. 73– 6 as the *f·* nature disappears
94–14 When all *f·* belief is annihilated,
Un. 46–11 subordinate the *f·* perceptions
62–19 The *f·* Jesus seemed to die,
Rud. 9–20 envy, lust, and all *f·* vices.

Fletcher, Hon. Richard
Ret. 6–21 Hon. Richard *F·* of Boston.

flew
My. 52–32 * "Day after day *f·* by,

flexible
Pul. 31–28 * tall, slender, and as *f·* in movement

flies
Mis. 145–15 hawk which *f·* in darkness.
Pul. 48–15 * Straight as the crow *f·*,

flight
Mis. 120–29 puts to *f·* every doubt as to the
267–21 rarefied atmospheres and upward *f·*.
331–20 guards the nestling's faltering *f·* !
354–27 strength for a *f·* well begun,
356– 2 blessings when they take their *f·*,
389– 8 guards the nestling's faltering *f·* !
Ret. 11– 5 If fancy plumes aerial *f·*,
'02. 17–27 will put to *f·* all care for the
Po. 4– 6 guards the nestling's faltering *f·* !
60– 1 If fancy plumes aerial *f·*,
My. 186– 7 preen their thoughts for upward *f·*.
248–20 No fetishism . . . can fetter your *f·*.
296– 3 his flash of *f·* and insight,

fling
Mis. xi–20 no battledores to *f·* it back and forth.
54–13 malice would *f·* in her path.
Po. 10– 1 *f·* thy banner To the billows and
18– 4 majestic, and feathersome *f·*
My. 337– 3 *f·* thy banner To the billows

flings
Mis. 281– 3 this animal element *f·* open

flippancy
Mis. 112–20 his *f·* had fled.

flippant
Mis. 240– 7 by that *f·* caution,

flit
Po. 2–16 On wings of morning gladly *f·*

flitting
Mis. 71–29 *f·* across the dial of time.
Po. 16–12 The tired wings *f·* through

float
Mis. 145–28 earth will *f·* majestically
Po. 66– 5 *f·* in memory's dream.

floated
Ret. 73–10 *f·* into more spiritual latitudes
Po. 8–17 rainbows of rapture *f·* by !

floating
Mis. 228–24 *F·* with the popular current
230–19 *f·* off on the wings of sense :
Ret. 16– 2 *f·* up from the pews,

flock
Mis. 9– 6 passes all His *f·* under His rod
32–22 in which to give to my own *f·*
146–23 to walk in the footsteps of His *f·*.
150– 1 "Fear not, little *f·* ; — *Luke* 12 : 32.
154– 6 God's love for His *f·* is manifest
303– 6 and tends his own *f·*.
321–17 "Fear not, little *f·* ; — *Luke* 12 : 32.

flock

Mis.	322–14	Shepherd that feedeth my *f·*,
	399–27	and understood By His *f·*.
Ret.	90– 5	salary for tending the home *f·*
Pul.	9–20	giving this *f·* "drink — *Psal.* 36 : 8.
	16–12	and understood By His *f·*.
Rud.	17–17	and the footsteps of His *f·*.
Po.	76–11	and understood By His *f·*.
My.	148–21	of this dear little *f·*,
	162–25	loving Shepherd of this feeble *f·*
	167–18	good will for yourselves, your *f·*,
	177–20	this church as a fatling of the *f·*.
	247–24	Do you come to your little *f·*

flocking

My.	73–13	* *f·* from all over the world

flocks

Mis.	371– 3	large *f·* of metaphysicians are
Ret.	4–20	flecked with large *f·* and herds,
Pan.	3–28	guardian of *f·* and herds.
My.	125– 8	You come from feeding your *f·*,
	186–19	make this church the fold of *f·*,
	243–18	caring for their own *f·*.
	262– 8	*f·* and herds of a Jewish village.

flood

Mis.	203–22	Tears *f·* the eyes,
	339–27	will some time *f·* thy memory,
Pul.	14– 9	water as a *f·*, — *Rev.* 12 : 15.
	14–10	carried away of the *f·*. — *Rev.* 12 : 15.
	14–12	swallowed up the *f·* — *Rev.* 12 : 16.
	14–19	a new *f·* to drown the Christ-idea?
	39–16	* its *f·* of golden light.
No.	20–24	ever since the *f·*,
My.	106–20	in tempest and in *f·*,

flooded

'00.	11–22	* It *f·* the crimson twilight

flood-gates

Mis.	185–11	opens the very *f·* of heaven ;
'01.	32–29	through the *f·* of Love ;

flooding

Ret.	16– 5	tears of joy *f·* her eyes
	47– 5	Students . . . were *f·* the school.
No.	2–27	*f·* our land with conflicting theories

floods

Mis.	257–23	F· swallow up homes and
Pul.	7–17	in *f·* of forgiveness,
No.	1– 8	fill the rivers till they rise in *f·*,
'02.	5– 8	*f·* the world with the baptism of
My.	33–31	established it upon the *f·*. — *Psal.* 24 : 2.

floor

Mis.	231–22	soft as thistle-down, on the *f·* ;
	325–17	lie stretched on the *f·*,
	391– 4	For things above the *f·*,
Un.	44–21	[when you, lie, get the *f·*].
Pul.	25–22	* *f·* is in white Italian mosaic,
	26–23	* mosaic marble *f·* of white has a
	76– 8	* The *f·* is of mosaic
Po.	38– 3	For things above the *f·*,
My.	71–23	* people on *f·* and galleries,
	71–25	* either on *f·* or galleries,

flooring

Pul.	2– 7	from its mosaic *f·* to the

floors

Pul.	25– 6	* *f·* of marble in mosaic
	58–18	* The *f·* are all mosaic,
My.	68–27	* The *f·* of the first story

Flora

Ret.	17–13	F· has stolen the rainbow
Po.	62–16	F· has stolen the rainbow

floral

Mis.	179–24	These flowers are *f·* apostles.
	275–29	The *f·* offerings sent to my
Ret.	23–11	indicated by no *f·* dial.
'00.	8– 7	in the *f·* kingdom odors emit
Po.	25–10	Fair *f·* apostles of love,
My.	153– 3	send these *f·* offerings in my name

florist

My.	152–32	flowers that my skilful *f·*

floundering

Mis.	295–18	flaunting and *f·* statements

flourish

Ret.	4–22	scrub-oak, poplar, and fern *f·*.
My.	95– 2	* cults which *f·* for a time
	104– 5	institutions *f·* under the name of
	139– 9	that *f·* when trampled upon,

flourished

'00.	12– 9	*f·* as an emporium

flourishes

My.	112– 3	false philosophy *f·* for a time
	265– 7	signifies . . . that evil *f·* less,

flourishing

Ret.	48–10	moved me to close my *f·* school,

flow

Mis.	127–16	then will *f·* into it the
	149– 5	this feast and *f·* of Soul.
	160– 8	Thus may our lives *f·* on
	212–19	happiness, and like *f·* not into
	223– 7	impure streams *f·* from corrupt
	290–20	my affections involuntarily *f·* out
	329–17	rippling all nature in ceaseless *f·*,
	384–21	* But knows no ebb and *f·*.
	387–23	Whence joys supernal *f·*,
Ret.	11–13	from this fount the streamlets *f·*,
	18– 7	lap of the pear-tree, with musical *f·*.
Pul.	3–22	and *f·* into everlasting Life.
	7–12	O ye tears ! Not in vain did ye *f·*.
	39–17	* as in a dream, I watch the *f·*
	39–20	* Repeats its glory in the river's *f·* ;
	41– 4	* which continued to *f·* in
'00.	9–20	in the ebb and *f·* of thought
'01.	19–26	*f·* through no such channels.
Po.	6–18	Whence joys supernal *f·*,
	8–12	O'er the silv'ry moon and ocean *f·* ;
	35– 9	will never dry or cease to *f·* ;
	36–20	* But knows no ebb and *f·*.
	60–10	from this fount the streamlets *f·*,
	63–16	with musical *f·*.
My.	18–13	then will *f·* into it the
	266–15	This flux and *f·* in one direction,

flowed

Mis.	213– 4	*f·* through cross-bearing,
	222–31	Truth had *f·* into my consciousness
Pul.	44–25	* money has *f·* in from all parts
Po.	41–21	strain of enchantment that *f·*

Flower (*see also* Flower's)

Mr. B. O.

My.	316–15	scholarly editor, Mr. B. O. *F·*,

flower

Mis.	179–25	He made every *f·* in Mind
	394– 3	like the dew on the *f·*,
'00.	8– 8	characteristics of tree and *f·*,
Hea.	6–17	whether that ideal is a *f·* or a
Po.	3– 3	I miss thee as the *f·* the dew !
	22–12	'Tis writ on earth, on leaf and *f·* :
	45– 4	like the dew on the *f·*,
My.	216–25	The Mother Church *f·* fund.

flowering

Pul.	48– 3	* dotted with beds of *f·* shrubs,

Flower's, Mr.

My.	316–22	under Mr. *F·* able guardianship

flowers

Mis.	179–24	These *f·* are floral apostles.
	227–18	fresh *f·* of feeling blossom,
	276– 1	large book of rare *f·*,
	280–21	hand-painted *f·* on each page,
	294–15	the *f·* of human hearts
	360–18	blighted *f·* of fleeting joys,
	390–10	The fairy-peopled world of *f·*,
	394–15	* "The *f·* of June
	394–17	* The *f·* of June
	394–21	* The *f·* of June."
Ret.	4–20	beautiful wild *f·*,
	17–14	sprinkle the *f·* with exquisite dye.
	18–22	*f·* of feeling are fragrant
Pul.	8–26	and painted the finest *f·*
	42–19	* rich with the adornment of *f·*.
Peo.	14– 3	with *f·* laid upon the bier,
Po.	15–18	F· fresh as the pang in the bosom
page 25		poem
	25–14	F· for the brave
	25–17	F· for the kind
	53–20	The vernal songs and *f·*.
	55–11	fairy-peopled world of *f·*,
	57– 1	* The *f·* of June
	57– 3	* The *f·* of June
	57– 7	* The *f·* of June.
	62–17	sprinkle the *f·* with exquisite dye.
	64–16	*f·* of feeling are fragrant
	67– 8	bedewing these fresh-smiling *f·* !
	67–21	*f·* of feeling may blossom above,
My.	152–32	*f·* that my skilful florist has
	153–12	my *f·* visited his bedside .
	153–13	*f·* were imbued and associated with
	153–30	*f·* should be to us His apostles,
	154– 7	I shall scarcely venture to send *f·*
	154– 9	Send *f·* and all things fair
	154–11	it is not he who gives the *f·*
	155–30	which she sends . . . in the *f·*
	217– 1	money that you expend for *f·*.
	259– 4	and on either side lace and *f·*.

floweth

Mis.	82– 5	this peace *f·* as a river

flowing
  Mis. 19–16 steadfastly *f·* on to God,
    165–27 blessings *f·* from the teaching,
    355– 8 chronic recovery ebbing and *f·*,
flows
  Mis. 185–12 *f·* into every avenue of being,
    316–11 tide which *f·* heavenward,
  Ret. 18– 9 songlet and streamlet that *f·*
  Pul. 39– 6 * God's greatness *f* around our
  Po. 63–19 songlet and streamlet that *f·*
flung
  Mis. 332– 8 doors that closed . . . are open *f·*.
  My. 147– 7 *f·* its foliage in kindly shelter
flush
  Mis. 225–26 deep *f·* faded from the face,
Flushing, L. I.
  My. 363– 9 C. S. Society, *F·*, *L. I.*,
flute
  Mis. 390– 7 The eve-bird's forest *f·*
  Po. 55– 8 The eve-bird's forest *f·*
flutterings
  Mis. 85–18 *f·* of mortals Christward
flutters
  Mis. 267–19 right wing *f·* to soar,
  My. 268–20 This time-world *f·* in my thought
flux
  Mis. 206– 3 from *f·* to permanence,
  My. 266–15 *f·* and flow in one direction,
    301– 5 present *f·* in religious faith
fly
  Hea. 6– 6 *f·* too high or too low.
  My. 192–26 My love can *f·* on wings of joy
flying
  Mis. 176–17 not as the *f·* nor as
  My. 110–16 dreams of *f·* in airy space,
fly-leaf
  My. 60–18 * this inscription on the *f·*
foam
  Mis. 385–12 moored at last Beyond rough *f·*.
  Po. 48– 5 moored at last Beyond rough *f·*.
    73–10 list the moan Of the billows' *f·*,
foaming
  Mis. 162–10 over their fretted, *f·* billows.
  My. 316–20 *f·* torrents of ignorance, envy, and
foams
  '01. 9–19 *f·* at the touch of good ;
  '02. 19–19 life's troubled sea *f·* itself away,
focal
  Mis. 79–14 *f·* distance of infinity.
  Un. 20–22 outside of His own *f·* distance.
  No. 17–18 *f·* radiation of the infinite.
focusing
  My. 164–11 a thing *f·* light
foe
  Mis. 32–15 towards friend and *f·*.
    99–17 take the front rank, face the *f·*,
    114–17 resist the *f·* within and without.
    206–12 idleness is the *f·* of progress.
    290–26 whether it be friend or *f·*,
  Ret. 31–17 unseen sin, the unknown *f·*,
  Pul. 2–19 single-handed to combat the *f·* ?
    15–11 telling mankind of the *f·* in ambush
    15–12 informer one who sees the *f·* ?
  No. 3– 5 error murders either friend or *f·*
  Pan. 15– 1 which fed her starving *f·*,
  Po. 33–10 kindly pass over a wound, or a *f·*
  My. 213– 9 lurking *f·* to human weal,
    213–24 through every attack of your *f·*,
    248–26 face the *f·* with loving look
foes
  Mis. 118–22 envy, revenge, are *f·* to grace,
    126–25 race to run, and *f·* in ambush ;
    214– 9 a man's *f·* shall be — *Matt.* 10 : 36.
  No. 36–24 conquered the malice of his *f·*,
  '02. 2–26 why not . . . part fair *f·*.
    19–10 the malice of his *f·*.
  Po. 79–12 False fears are *f·*
  My. 98– 6 * anything that its *f·* try to prove
fog
  '00. 6–17 proves that the so-called *f·*
fogs
  Mis. 374–11 Above the *f·* of sense
foibles
  Mis. 285–10 too short for *f·* or failures.
  Ret. 30–15 *f·* and fables of finite mind
fold
  Mis. 9– 7 under His rod into His *f·* ;
    146–22 that desired to come, into its *f·*

fold
  Mis. 244–25 which are not of this *f·*." — *John* 10 : 16.
    270–19 one *f·*, and one shepherd ;" — *John* 10 : 16.
    303– 5 kindly shepherd has his own *f·*
    310–28 all persons who have left our *f·*,
    357– 6 having strayed from the true *f·*,
    357–28 that have sought the true *f·*
    370–26 the true *f·* for Christian healers,
    388–22 To *f·* an angel's wings below ;
    398–15 Lead Thy lambkins to the *f·*,
  Chr. 55–25 one *f·*, and one shepherd. — *John* 10 : 16.
  Ret. 46–21 Lead Thy lambkins to the *f·*,
    80–23 older sheep pass into the *f·*
    90– 6 while he is serving another *f·* ?
  Pul. 17–20 Lead Thy lambkins to the *f·*,
    65– 5 * Anglican *f·* to unity with Rome,
  Po. 14–19 Lead Thy lambkins to the *f·*,
    21–11 *f·* an angel's wings below ;
    34– 7 and *f·* thy plumes?
    41– 3 Was that *f·* for the lambkin
  My. 186–19 God make this church the *f·*
    248–18 can *f·* or falter your wings.
folds
  Mis. 145–32 that my heart *f·* within it,
    151– 1 *f·* the sheep of His pasture ;
  Ret. 52–11 provide *f·* for the sheep
  Un. 7– 5 of other religious *f·*.
foliage
  Po. 15– 1 zephyrs through *f·* and vine !
  My. 147– 7 flung its *f·* in kindly shelter
    182–27 amid the fair *f·* of this vine
folk
  Pul. 52– 5 * our practical Christian *f·*
  My. 58– 1 * our practical Christian *f·*
    148– 6 May the good *f·* of Concord
    175–11 say to the good *f·* of Concord
    313–24 * "the superstitious country *f·*
folks
  Mis. 117–20 *modus operandi*, of other *f·*.
    238– 2 * 'niggers' kill the white *f·* !"
    353–18 Some people try to tend *f·*,
follow
  Mis. 28–31 "These signs shall *f·* — *Mark* 16 : 17.
    33–18 *f·* the directions given.
    40–18 reason that the same results *f·* not
    45– 9 fatal results that frequently *f·* the
    89– 7 *f· the doctor's directions?*
    90–30 left their nets to *f·* him,
    105–19 I must ever *f·* this line
    117–30 or make them too late to *f·* Him.
    117–31 *f·* under every circumstance.
    127–18 great growth in C. S. will *f·*,
    136– 7 with the hope that you will *f·*.
    147–15 to *f·* the road of duty,
    151– 3 and they *f·* me ; — *John* 10 : 27.
    169–30 *f·* thou me," — *see Matt.* 8 : 22.
    170– 3 If we *f·* him, to us there can be no
    192–29 these signs shall *f·* — *Mark* 16 : 17.
    193–24 *f·* the commands of our Lord
    195– 2 Thence will *f·* the absorption
    213–22 and they *f·* me :— *John* 10 : 27.
    215–30 If you would *f·* in his footsteps,
    219–30 the fruits of goodness will *f·*,
    226–16 * And it must *f·*, as the night the day,
    235–27 tried to *f·* the divine precept,
    236–13 must *f·* God in all your ways."
    237–25 but it is sure to *f·*.
    265–10 all *who f· the Principle and rule*
    270–22 and yet *f·* him in healing.
    311– 8 so, should we *f·* Christ's teachings ;
    321– 1 The wise men *f·* this guiding star ;
    327– 3 hoping that I might *f·* thee
    327– 9 hast chosen the good part ; *f·* me."
    332–10 autumn *f·* with hues of heaven,
    340–20 They *f·* faithfully ;
    347–18 I *f·* his counsel,
    359– 1 *f·* the example of the *Alma Mater*.
    398– 3 I will *f·* and rejoice
  Man. 60–19 "*F·* thou me," — *John* 21 : 22.
  Ret. 6– 4 * can hardly fail to induce them to *f·*
    16–15 *f·* them that believe." — *Mark* 16 : 17.
    42– 6 He forsook all to *f·* in this line
    46– 9 I will *f·* and rejoice
    49– 6 *f·* the example of the *Alma Mater*
    55– 3 Let us *f·* the example of Jesus,
    65–13 if they would *f·* Christ,
    81–25 * And it must *f·*, as the night the day,
    87– 1 Master said, "*F·* me ; — *Matt.* 8 : 22.
    87–17 they must *f·* the divine order
    90–27 * to *f·*, as nearly as we can,
  Un. 17–23 Would it not absurdly *f·* that
    42– 1 must *f·* that death can be nowhere ;
  Pul. 17– 8 I will *f·* and rejoice
  '00. 8–28 a desire to *f·* your own

follow

'01.	8–22	if we f· the teachings of the
	23– 8	thence it would f· that evil
	24–25	necessary to f· Jesus' teachings,
	28–19	only apology for trying to f· it is
	34–25	f· your Leader only so far as she
'02.	3–26	It does not f· that power must
	4– 3	F· your Leader, only so far as she
	9– 5	Jesus commanded, "F· me ;— Matt. 8 : 22.
	16–12	"F· peace with all men,— Heb. 12 : 14.
	18–26	showing their unfitness to f· him,
Hea.	1– 1	And these signs shall f· — Mark 16 : 17.
	6–26	"And these signs shall f· — Mark 16 : 17.
	19–26	and "these signs shall f· — Mark 16 : 17.
Peo.	10–24	f· the mind's freedom from sin ;
Po.	14– 7	I will f· and rejoice
My.	4–10	We f· Truth only as we
	4–10	f· truly, meekly, patiently,
	9–16	* that we may worthily f· with you
	18–15	great growth in C. S. will f·,
	19–19	our shadows f· us in the sunlight
	23– 7	* so long as we f· His commands.
	47–29	* And these signs shall f· — Mark 16 : 17.
	58–21	* inspire us to f· her in preaching,
	122– 1	If one would f· the advice
	125–15	their works will f· them.
	134–10	Defeat need not f· victory.
	196–17	should f· his steps :— I Pet. 2 : 21.
	201–23	I will f· and rejoice
	233–21	dishonesty, sin, f· in its train.
	241–18	* question and Mrs. Eddy's reply f·.
	245–27	degrees that f· the names of
	250–18	nor compels the branch churches to f·
	278–17	F· that which is good.
	296–13	and his works do f· him.
	297– 6	which may f· said description
	361– 1	F· the directions of God

followed

Mis.	11–11	f· them with precept upon precept ;
	73–23	ye which have f· me,— Matt. 19 : 28.
	91–29	supposed that students had f· my
	245–23	loved the Church and f· it,
	340–13	f· agriculture instead of
	373–25	is f· by Jesus' declaration,
Ret.	14–14	Distinctly do I recall what f·.
	44–27	This measure was immediately f· by
	45–16	f· that noble, unprecedented action
Pul.	43–19	* f· by the recitation of the
	59– 9	* program was for some reason not f·,
'01.	28–15	f· exclusively Christ's teaching,
Peo.	10–11	if the sister States had f·
My.	17–24	* f· by a few moments of
	32–17	* Silent prayer, f· by the
	39–11	* Then f· a short silent prayer
	45–18	* f· unswervingly the guidance
	45–26	* logically f· the preceding one.
	76– 2	* would be f· with this new
	78–19	* f· by the audible repetition
	91–22	* few thousand persons who f·
	312–26	f· the remains of my beloved one
	343–19	I f· it up, teaching and

follower

Mis.	152–20	worshipper in truth, the f· of
Un.	56–13	every f· of Christ shares
Pul.	73– 5	* ardent f· after God.
My.	42– 5	* a faithful f· of this Leader
	62–14	* Your sincere f·,
	113– 8	St. Paul was a f· but not
	330– 4	* noteworthy f· of our Lord
	357–30	I know that every true f·

followers

Christ's
Mis.	273–15	grand family of Christ's f·.

conscientious
Pul.	51– 5	* a number of conscientious f·

devoted
Pul.	63–18	* among her devoted f·.
My.	272–23	* Mrs. Eddy's own devoted f·,

devout
Ret.	54–20	The faith-cure has devout f·,

friends and
Pul.	54–25	* closest friends and f·,
My.	143–10	my beloved friends and f·

her
Pul.	32–13	* was dominating her f·
	43–27	* discourage among her f·
	71–22	* her f· and cobelievers
My.	64–16	* has been teaching her f·
	64–20	* Fearlessly does she warn all her f·

His
Mis.	179–25	God does all this through His f· ;
My.	204– 2	My faith in God and in His f·
	204– 3	He gives His f· opportunity to

followers

his
Mis.	24–29	declared that his f· should
	165–19	makes his f· the heirs to his example ;
	197–10	way which Jesus . . . bade his f·
	211–29	and he said to his f·,
Ret.	88– 5	command, was that his f· should
'00.	8–14	Our Master saith to his f· :
'01.	2–21	his f· of to-day will prove,
	9–15	taught his f· to do likewise.
	18–23	his f· in the early centuries,
'02.	11–20	then gave it to his f· to drink.
My.	28–21	* mark the lives of his f·.
	106–31	commanded his f· to do likewise.
	109–10	Christ taught his f· to heal
	111–22	unwittingly misguide his f·?
	221–21	and instructed his f·, saying,
	222–17	demands on the faith of his f·,
	330– 6	* he prophesied that his f· would be

hundred thousand
Pul.	70– 5	* OVER ONE HUNDRED THOUSAND F·

its
My.	10– 5	* achievements of its f·.
	37–18	* its f· have been prospered,
	84–21	* optimism and power and energy of its f·
	89–31	* that its f· should number
	107– 4	its f· at the beginning of

many
Pul.	49– 3	* speaking of her many f·

Mrs. Eddy's
'01.	27– 5	* have been by Mrs. Eddy's f·.

of the Master
My.	112– 4	f· of the Master in the early

of this creed
My.	85–15	* enthusiasm of the f· of this creed

true
Mis.	278–32	on the part of true f·,
Ret.	35–16	his true f· in every period,
My.	204– 9	unites its true f· in one Principle,
	213–21	into harmony with His true f·.

unfaithful
'02.	19– 4	to console his unfaithful f·

will gain
Pul.	50–27	* will gain f· and live down any

your
My.	60– 2	* solicited by many of your f·
	157– 7	* church edifice for your f·
	321– 2	* building this church for your f·.

Pul.	57–26	* f· of Rev. Mary Baker Glover Eddy,
'01.	23–20	taught his disciples and f·
My.	11– 2	* as yet but imperfect f· of the
	100–10	* of the f· of the cult.
	271–18	* f· of the thought that has

followeth

My.	4– 8	f· after me,— Matt. 10 : 38.
	233–25	f· after me,— Matt. 10 : 38.

following (noun)

Mis.	357–21	irrespective of self, rank, or f·.
Pul.	32–11	* her large and enthusiastic f·
	63– 5	* SHE HAS AN IMMENSE F·
Pan.	6–13	obtaining . . . a large f·,
'00.	1–16	C. S. already has a hearing and f· in
My.	90–29	* sources of her power and f·
	92–16	* since 1890 its f· had increased
	93–30	* had but an insignificant f·.
	117– 5	right or the wrong of this f·.
	272–27	* her very great f·.
	358– 2	true f· of their Leader ;

following (adj.)

Mis.	33–23	Healing by C. S. has the f· advantages:
	35– 9	f· words of her husband,
	48–31	to make capital out of the f·
	61–12	* In the . . . Journal I read the f· :
	88–15	His allusion to C. S. in the f·
	111–28	to the f· false beliefs
	133– 9	consideration to the f· Scripture,
	178–26	* came forward, and added the f· :
	216–23	illustrate the author's f· point?
	248–28	with the f· exception :
	255–20	I claim for . . . C. S. the f·
	271–25	in the Boston Traveler the f· :
	271–28	* the f· history and statistics
	272–12	* with the f· important restrictions :
	282–19	the f· is an exception to
	297–16	the f· statute in the morale of
	299– 7	f· mistake, which demands
	299– 9	simply answer the f· question
	303–22	giving place . . . to the f· notice.
	304–22	* The f· is the proposed use of
	318–12	f· is an amendment of the
	349–22	to a question on the f· subject,
	372–16	came such replies as the f· :
	373– 7	f· from Rotherham's translation

following (adj.)

Mis.	375– 8	The *f.* is an extract from a letter
	376– 4	* *most authentic* in the *f.* sense :
Man.	76– 5	The *f.* indicates the proper management
	78–24	reported, on the first of the *f.* month,
Ret.	5–17	The *f.* is a brief extract from
	11– 2	*f.* is one of my girlhood
	20–14	The *f.* lines are taken from
	34–10	I claim for . . . the *f.* advantages :
	37–24	seen in the *f.* circumstances.
	48–11	the *f.* resolutions were passed :
	48–13	the *f.* are some of the resolutions
	56– 1	The *f.* ideas of Deity,
Pul.	12– 1	*f.* selections from ''S. and H.
	24–12	* the *f.* inscription carved in
	38– 1	* charter obtained the *f.* June.
	39– 9	on the *f.* page a little poem
	45– 8	* Read the *f.*, from a
	75–20	* and for the day or two *f.*,
	78– 6	* upon its face the *f.* inscription,
	86–13	* *f.* address from the Board of Directors :
No.	43–12	The *f.* extract from a letter
'01.	15–21	to hear the *f.* thunderbolt of
'02.	15–25	The *f.* day I showed it to my
Hea.	20– 1	*f.* hymn was sung at the close :
My.	v–13	* the *f.* historical facts :
	7–14	* offered the *f.* motion :
	13– 9	attention was arrested by the *f.* :
	17–27	* *f.* extracts from Mrs. Eddy's
	18–29	It contained the *f.* articles :
	25– 9	* The *f.* figures are taken from
	31– 2	* succeeded by the *f.* hymns
	34–14	* *f.* citations from the Bible
	39–13	* *f.* list of officers for
	44–16	* read the *f.* despatch,
	48–14	* *f.* splendid appreciation of her
	51– 4	∗ *f.* resolutions were passed :
	54– 5	* *Boston Traveler* contained the *f.*
	56–13	* in each of the *f.* named places :
	136–13	*f.* members constitute the Board
	137– 2	* *f.* affidavit, in the form of
	140–16	* The *f.* is Mrs. Eddy's letter :
	141–25	hence the *f.* :
	150– 5	Pliny gives the *f.* description of
	172–23	* opened the *f.* day in Boston
	213–18	The *f.* three quotations from
	217–17	was the *f.* question :
	219–28	my opinion . . . in the *f.* words :
	232–12	Master left to us the *f.* sayings
	251– 5	I reply to the *f.* question from
	254–18	* *f.* extract from your article
	259– 6	received the *f.* cabled message :
	274–18	* has sent the *f.* to the *Herald :*
	311– 1	I will relate the *f.* incident,
	314– 4	* During the *f.* nine years
	314–18	who know the *f.* facts :
	314–31	*f.* affidavit by R. D. Rounsevel
	319–12	* *f.* letters from students
	326– 1	* publish the *f.* interesting letter
	326–13	*f.* deeply interesting letter from
	328– 7	* The *f.* article, copied from
	329–25	* to give your readers the *f.*
	333–31	* we copy the *f.* :
	334–26	* *f.* extract from an editorial
	338– 6	* *f.* views of the Rev. Mary Baker Eddy
	346–25	* the *f.* to the Associated Press,
		(*see also* **letter, signs, statement**)

following (ppr.)

Mis.	133–18	*f.* the dictum of Jesus ;
	170– 2	for by *f.* Christ truly,
	193–25	is *f.* his full command
	194–21	in *f.* him, you understand God
	245–24	thinking that it was *f.* Christ ;
	315– 5	on the Sunday *f.* Communion Day.
Man.	56–12	Monday *f.* the first Sunday in June.
Ret.	45–20	in *f.* Jesus' command,
	86–18	taking up his cross and *f.* Truth.
Un.	5–11	by *f.* upward individual convictions,
Pul.	26– 9	* seats *f.* the sweep of its curve,
No.	34– 5	truer sense of *f.* Christ in spirit,
'00.	14–15	*f.* the more perfect way,
'01.	14–21	from fearing it, *f.* it, or
	28–18	no cause for not *f.* it ;
My.	4– 9	how many are *f.* the Way-shower?
	28–19	* and *f.* her example,
	32–11	* *F.* the organ voluntary
	45–21	* results of such *f.* have been
	128–20	*f.* the command of the Master,
	303– 9	*f.* the divine Principle

follows

Mis.	21–16	My first plank . . . is as *f.* :
	88–17	*f.* like a benediction
	95– 4	* as will be seen by what *f.*,
	101–26	it *f.* that all must be good ;
	123–30	it *f.* that those who worship Him,

follows

Mis.	168–24	* *The C. S. Journal* reported as *f.* :
	177–27	* introduced Mr. Easton as *f.* :
	220–29	it *f.* that he will believe that he
	245– 3	his words, and the prophet's, as *f.* :
	269–22	The conclusion *f.* that the
	301–23	My reasons are as *f.* :
	328–22	who *f.* the Way-shower,
Man.	75–14	said Church to be as *f.* :
Ret.	7– 6	wrote of my brother as *f.* :
	65–18	*f.* the example of our Lord
	68–18	transference of thought, as *f.* :
Un.	2–11	Then *f.* this, as the *finale* in
	13–19	*f.* that He knows something which
Pul.	14– 7	for one extreme *f.* another.
	38– 9	* chapters, whose titles are as *f.* :
Rud.	8–12	it *f.* thou wilt be strong in God,
No.	5– 8	*f.* that to declare error real would
	22–20	it *f.* that there is more than one
	35–27	it *f.* that the human kingdom is
Pan.	8– 2	*f.* that the disarrangement of matter
'01.	14–17	then it *f.* that it is untrue ;
	34–25	only so far as she *f.* Christ.
'02.	4– 4	only so far as she *f.* Christ.
Po.	vi–11	* *A note from the author,* . . . *read as f.* :
My.	15– 4	* been amended to read as *f.* :
	16–22	* order of the services, . . . was as *f.* :
	19–15	* Mrs. Eddy wrote as *f.* :
	32–12	* order of service was as *f.* :
	39– 5	* Bible and S. and H. as *f.* :
	44–20	* The despatch was as *f.* :
	52–21	* wrote as *f.* : ''Whatever is to be
	141–14	* The announcement . . . as *f.* :
	146– 9	statement in my letter . . . as *f.*,
	160– 3	and *f.* Truth fearlessly.
	172– 9	* Mrs. Eddy spoke as *f.*
	224– 7	blessing which *f.* obedience
	224– 8	bane which *f.* disobedience.
	311–19	The facts are as . . . *f.* :
	313– 2	Correctly quoted, it is as *f.*,
	327–21	* was changed as *f.*,
	327–25	* was changed to read as *f.* :
	328–17	* in the *Kinston Free Press* as *f.* :
	359–26	* wrote to Mrs. Stetson as *f.* :

folly

Mis.	223–30	is superlative *f.*.
	327–24	showing them their *f.*,
	347– 2	according to his *f.*, — *Prov.* 26 : 4.
	348–15	according to his *f.*, — *Prov.* 26 : 5.
	353–23	*f.* of tending it is no mere jest.
'01.	11–27	according to his *f.*, — *Prov.* 26 : 4.
	25–16	ends in some specious *f.*.
Po.	33– 8	vanity, *f.*, and all that is wrong
My.	106– 8	simply to show the *f.* of
	106–11	*f.* of the cognate declaration that
	151–18	* aisles by flaunting *f.* trod,
	283–30	choice of *f.* never fastens on

fond

Ret.	2–27	I was *f.* of listening,
	7–10	* He was *f.* of investigating
	32–15	* Fleeting pleasure, *f.* delusion,
'00.	11– 6	*f.* of material music,
My.	124–10	''What a *f.* fool is hope''?
	158– 9	in attune with faith's *f.* trust.
	274–22	I am not *f.* of an abundance of
	332–12	* in the *f.* embrace of her friends.

Fondateur

My.	283– 2	chapter sub-title
	283– 7	Your appointment of me as *F.*

fondest

'02.	17–26	thy aims, motives, *f.* purposes,

fondling

Po.	43– 8	*F.* e'en the lion furious,

fondness

Un.	2– 9	takes away man's *f.* for sin

font

Mis.	206–31	baptismal *f.* of eternal Love.

food

Mis.	7– 2	not be allowed to eat certain *f.*,
	369–24	wholesome but unattractive *f.*.
Pul.	33–16	* offer *f.* for meditation.
Rud.	12–22	with the chemistry of *f.*?
Hea.	5– 5	certain kinds of *f.*,
Po.	28–16	Give us this day our daily *f.*
My.	154–20	*''If the poor . . . toil that we have *f.*,
	247–18	sought their *f.* of me.
	247–25	so filled with divine *f.*

fool

Mis.	30–24	*f.* hath said in his heart, — *Psal.* 14 : 1.
	112–30	*f.* hath said in his heart, — *Psal.* 14 : 1.
	212– 2	is a *f.* that saith in his heart,
	224–31	a flatterer, a *f.*, or a liar,
	347– 1	''Answer not a *f.* — *Prov.* 26 : 4.

fool
Mis. 348–15   "Answer a *f·* — *Prov.* 26 : 5.
'01. 11–27   "Answer not a *f·* — *Prov.* 26 : 4.
     18–24   *f·* hath said in his heart, — *Psal.* 14 : 1.
'02. 19–6   called one a "*f·*" — *see Luke* 24 : 25.
Hea. 1–16   man suspects himself a *f·* ;
My. 124–10   "What a fond *f·* is hope"?
     218–22   fad of belief is the *f·* of mesmerism.
     227–29   *f·* hath said in his heart, — *Psal.* 14 : 1.

foolhardiness
Mis. 210–28   neither the cowardice nor the *f·*

fooling
Mis. 271–17   * "Trust her not, she's *f·* thee ;"

foolish
Mis. 73–13   The *f·* disobey moral law,
     170–14   wrong and *f·*, conceptions of God
     342–3   The *f·* virgins had no oil
     342–23   and they said to the *f·*,
Ret. 37–11   formerly sneered at it, as *f·*

fools
Mis. 226–11   he loses the homage of *f·*,
     275–2   "Ye *f·* and blind !" — *Matt.* 23 : 17.

foot
Mis. 210–17   her *f·* on the head of the serpent,
     265–31   stop at the *f·* of the grand ascent,
     274–28   rights are trodden under *f·*,
     323–8   valley at the *f·* of the mountain
     323–17   valley at the *f·* of the mountain.
     324–30   valley at the *f·* of the mountain,
     325–18   Balancing on one *f·*,
     328–16   to the *f·* of the mount,
     369–1   *f·* of the mount of revelation,
Ret. 11–11   knowledge plants the *f·* of power
Pan. 6–8   putteth his *f·* upon a lie.
Hea. 11–16   lifting its *f·* against its neighbor,
Peo. 10–9   put her humane *f·* on a
Po. 60–8   knowledge plants the *f·* of power
My. 45–30   * one *f·* loftier than
     126–8   "right *f·* upon the sea, — *Rev.* 10 : 2.
     126–8   his left *f·* on the earth," — *Rev.* 10 : 2.

football
Rud. 5–25   believe . . . to be the *f·* of chance

footfall
Po. 43–18   Temper every trembling *f·*,

footfalls
Mis. 324–9   wine is unsipped, the *f·* abate,

foothold
Mis. 209–24   no *f·* on the false basis that
     337–20   has no sure *f·* :
My. 94–11   * in which it has found a *f·*.

footprints
Mis. 266–2   struggle up, with bleeding *f·*,
'02. 10–8   Hence the *f·* of a reformer are
Po. 31–13   rare *f·* on the dust of earth.

footstep
Mis. 390–14   And soft thy *f·* falls upon
'00. 5–30   might and majesty attend every *f·*
Hea. 2–7   condemned at every advancing *f·*,
Po. 55–15   And soft thy *f·* falls upon

footsteps
Mis. xi–16   become *f·* to joys eternal.
     67–30   *f·* requisite have been taken
     81–13   *f·* of *Truth being baptized of John,*
     146–23   to walk in the *f·* of His flock.
     215–30   If you would follow in his *f·*,
     358–9   hounded *f·*, false laurels.
     398–2   Lest my *f·* stray ;
Ret. 46–8   Lest my *f·* stray ;
Pul. vii–14   on the early *f·* of C. S.
     17–7   Lest my *f·* stray ;
Rud. 17–13   the first *f·* in this Science.
     17–17   and the *f·* of His flock.
'01. 2–25   beset all their returning *f·*.
     29–25   who soonest will walk in his *f·*.
Hea. 17–1   through the *f·* of Truth.
Peo. 1–8   *f·* of thought, as they pass from
Po. 14–6   Lest my *f·* stray ;
     15–3   echoing moans from the *f·* of time !
My. 117–30   *f·* from sense to Soul.
     139–7   advancing *f·* of progress,
     201–22   Lest my *f·* stray ;
     205–11   * He plants His *f·* in the sea
     224–11   and the forward *f·* it impels
     355–23   their *f·* are not weary ;
     356–7   * "He plants His *f·* in the sea

Footsteps of Truth
Pul. 38–10   "*F· of T·*," "Creation,"

footstools
Mis. 325–16   their feet resting on *f·*,

forager
Ret. 71–3   *f·* on others' wisdom

forbade
Un. 54–20   God *f·* man to know evil

forbearance
No. 8–28   gained from your *f·*.

forbearing
Mis. 84–1   was shown by his *f·* to speak,

forbid
Un. 4–20   *f·* man's acquaintance with evil.
'01. 26–17   cast lots for it?   God *f·* !

forbidden
Man. 43–5   Formulas *F·*.
     45–14   *F·* Membership.
Un. 3–14   This knowledge is not the *f·* fruit
     4–17   God has not *f·* man to know **Him** ;
     54–19   this knowledge would not be *f·* ;
No. 20–28   straying into *f·* by-paths
'02. 6–4   The knowledge of . . . is *f·*.

forbids
Mis. 145–14   Even vanity *f·* man to be vain ;
No. 30–19   *f·* the genuine existence of even
'01. 30–7   The magnitude of its meaning *f·*
'02. 6–1   *f·* the thought of any other reality,

force
Mis. 23–21   atomic action, material *f·* or
     220–7   he supports this silent mental *f·*
     233–15   magnetic *f·* of mortal mind,
     247–18   healing *f·* developed by C. S.
     257–8   a moral or an immoral *f·*.
     257–9   a moral and spiritual *f·*.
     257–11   *f·* of erring mortal mind,
     257–12   This so-called *f·*, or law,
     288–18   But to *f·* the consciousness
Ret. 79–27   violent take it by *f·* !" — *Matt.* 11 : 12.
Un. 5–16   to *f·* conclusions on this subject
     10–26   He is not the blind *f·* of a
     35–13   *F·*.   What is gravitation?
     35–14   a material power, or *f·*,
Pul. 13–22   at last with accelerated *f·*,
Rud. 4–10   a moral and spiritual *f·*,
     4–11   This *f·* is Spirit.
No. 41–17   trying to *f·* the doors of
Pan. 6–24   how can matter be *f·*
'01. 19–14   That animal natures give *f·* to
My. 11–8   * the full *f·* of antagonism.
     74–11   * Scientists are here in *f·*,
     344–26   cannot *f·* perfection on the

forced
Mis. 291–3   *f·* into personal channels,
     326–18   *f·* to seek the Father's house,
     373–17   *f·* out of its proper channel,
Hea. 4–16   *f·* in and out of matter
My. 11–10   * by means of *f·* marches,

forces
Mis. 19–25   mental *f·* of material and **spiritual**
     100–15   leads on irresistible *f·*,
     103–7   destructive *f·*, such as sin,
     104–31   gives me the *f·* of God
     173–30   are these *f·* laws of matter,
Un. 35–17   *f·* of Truth are moral and
     35–18   not the merciless *f·* of matter.
     35–19   the so-called *f·* of matter?
     52–19   its unkind *f·*, its tempests,
Pan. 2–17   * combined *f·* and laws which **are**
'02. 3–12   our military *f·* withdrawing,
     10–4   unfolds spiritual *f·*,
Peo. 8–16   speculate concerning material *f·*.
My. 48–25   * *f·* that make for righteousness.
     110–13   electrical *f·* annihilating time and

forcible
Un. 6–12   as *f·* collisions of thought
My. 108–11   consists in this *f·* fact :
     197–3   That error is most *f·* which

forcibly
Mis. 14–19   that good, . . . *f·* destroys.

forcing
Mis. 359–12   Growth is restricted by *f·* humanity
Peo. 13–14   *f·* from the lips of manhood

fore
My. 341–20   * C. S. has been so much to the *f·*

forearm
Mis. 213–11   forewarn and *f·* our fellow-mortals
My. 273–17   forewarn and *f·* humanity.

forecasting
Mis. 240–9   *f·* liberty and joy

foreclosed
'02. 13–26   the mortgage was *f·*,

forefathers (*see also* **forefathers'**)
Pul. 10–21   less appreciated . . . than your *f·*,
'00. 10–18   wisdom of our *f·* is not added
My. 340–27   dark days of our *f·*

forefathers'
   Mis. 237–18   our *f·* prayers blended with the
forefelt
   Mis.   1– 8   for he *f·* and foresaw the ordeal
forefront
   '02.   14–21   blazoned on the *f·* of the world
   My.   9–14   * you, who are standing in the *f·* of
forego
   My.   21–11   * *f·* a visit to Boston at this time,
          21–17   * to *f·* their anticipated visit
foregoing
   Mis. 194–19   context of the *f·* Scriptural text
        349–20   in substance the same as the *f·*,
   Un.   27– 2   word employed in the *f·* colloquy.
   My.   56–19   * three *f·* named churches
       255– 6   publish the *f·* in their By-laws.
foreign
   Mis. 177–28   homesick traveller in *f·* lands
        372–25   *f·* device or environment
   Ret. 48–22   our country, and into *f·* lands,
   Un.   23–22   unlike Himself and *f·* to
       26–21   its sentiment is *f·* to C. S.
   '02.   10–29   communicating with *f·* nations
       11– 1   to leave on a *f·* shore.
   My.   68–17   * a beautiful *f·* marble,
       94–23   * and from many *f·* countries
      112–31   in our own and in *f·* lands,
      129– 8   country and in *f·* lands,
      211–16   committal of acts *f·* to
foreknew
   Un.   19– 8   if He *f·* it, He must virtually
foreknow
   Un.   19–12   could predestine or *f·* evil,
foreknowing
   '01.   21–16   such foreseeing is not *f·*,
foreknowledge
   Un.   19– 1   With God, *knowledge* is necessarily *f·*;
      19– 2   *f·* and *foreordination* must
      19– 7   have had *f·* thereof ;
foreknows
   Un.   19– 3   What Deity *f·*, Deity must
forelock
   My. 193–24   taking the first by the *f·*
foreman
   My. 145–11   carpenters' *f·* said to me :
foremost
   Mis.   57–31   wherein man is *f·*.
      270–29   Among the *f·* virtues of
   Pul. 67–26   * of whom the *f·* was Mrs. Eddy.
   My. 305–19   * the *f·* living authors."
forenoon
   My.   16–13   * eight o'clock in the *f·*.
      39– 1   * at ten o'clock in the *f·*,
      73–19   * open to visitors this *f·*
foreordain
   Un.   19– 3   What . . . Deity must *f·* ;
foreordained
   Mis. 122–10   God *f·* and predestined
   Un.   19– 9   ordered it aforetime, — *f·* it ;
foreordination
   Un.   19– 2   *foreknowledge* and *f·* must
foresaw
   Mis.   1– 9   he forefelt and *f·* the
   My. 185–24   Then and there I *f·* this hour,
      201– 6   as the Revelator *f·*,
      221– 7   *f·* the new dispensation
foresay
   Mis. 363–30   I foresee and *f·* that every
foresee
   Mis. 363–30   I *f·* and foresay that every
   My.   26–20   trust that you will see, as I *f·*,
      129– 3   I reluctantly *f·* great danger
foreseeing
   '01.   21–16   such *f·* is not foreknowing,
foresees
   Mis. 238–18   love that *f·* more to do,
   Un.   19– 5   *f·* events which are contrary to
      57– 6   it *f·* the impending doom
foreshadow
   Mis. 184–30   to *f·* metaphysical purity,
foreshadowed
   Mis.   1– 5   *f·* by signs in the heavens.
      278–23   since necessities and . . . are *f·*.
   '02.   5– 4   but *f·* the spiritual dawn
foreshadowing
   My. 154–26   the *f·* of the church triumphant.
      303–30   *f·* and foretasting heaven

foreshadows
   Mis. 232–13   *f·* what is next to appear
      347– 7   A conical cloud, . . . *f·* a cyclone.
   My. 194– 7   *f·* the idea of God,
foresight
   Mis. 204–25   It brings with it wonderful *f·*,
   My. 173–31   kindly *f·* in granting permission,
      281– 1   *f·* of the nations' drama
foresplendor
   My. 302–30   *f·* of the beginnings of truth
forest
   Mis. 237–19   murmuring winds of their *f·* home.
      390– 7   The eve-bird's *f·* flute
   Po.   55– 8   The eve-bird's *f·* flute
   My. 183–19   *f·* becomes a fruitful field,
forestall
   Mis. 302–28   to *f·* the possible evil of
forestalling
   Mis. 107–13   forgiving wrongs and *f·* them,
forests
   Pan.   3– 5   poetical phase of the genii of *f·*.
   My.   50– 8   * vast gloom of the mysterious *f·*,
      186– 2   *f·* of our native State
      194– 3   fell *f·* and remove mountains,
foretaste
   Mis. 100–24   bring to earth a *f·* of heaven.
foretasting
   My. 303–31   foreshadowing and *f·* heaven
foretell
   Mis. 347– 3   *f·* the internal action of
foretelling
   Mis.   82– 7   He who knew the *f·* Truth,
      122– 2   *f·* his own crucifixion,
foretells
   Un.   57– 6   and *f·* the pain.
   '02.   5– 1   silent night *f·* the dawn
foretold
   Mis. 164–17   In our text Isaiah *f·*,
      214–30   Jesus *f·* the harvest hour
   Po.   71– 1   the hour they then *f·*
Forever
   Mis. 205–29   man born of the great *F·*,
forever
   abide
   '02.   9–20   should abide *f·* in man.
   abode
   No.   36– 7   It abode *f·* above,
   accompany
   Un.   64–14   *f·* accompany our being.
   at once and
   Ret. 31–16   banished at once and *f·*
   at strife
   Mis. 333– 3   commingle, and are *f·* at strife ;
   banishes
   Mis. 204–31   it banishes *f·* all envy,
   based
   My. 205–27   it is *f·* based on Love,
   cling
   Pul. 40– 2   * thoughts of you *f·* cling to me :
   complete
   No.   37– 3   were *f·* complete,
   continue
   My. 267– 4   Nothing can . . . continue *f·* which is
   disappears
   Mis. 205–28   mortal man disappears *f·*.
   done
   Mis.   41–17   struggle with sin is *f·* done.
   My.   6– 7   done *f·* with the sins of the flesh,
   drop
   Man. 53– 4   drop *f·* the name of the member
   dropped
   Man. 43– 4   dropped *f·* from The Mother Church.
   dwell
   Mis. 103–14   dwell *f·* in the divine Mind
      152–16   mercy, and love dwell *f·*
   dwelling
   My. 246–16   dwelling *f·* in the divine Mind
   dwelt
   No.   37– 4   dwelt *f·* in the Father.
   '02.   9–19   dwelt *f·* in the bosom of the Father,
   endureth
   Pul.   7–23   endureth *f·*."—*I Pet.* 1 : 25.
   extinguishes
   Rud.   4–24   extinguishes *f·* the works of
   fact
   Mis. 287– 3   *f·* fact that man is eternal
   My.   41– 6   * a *f·* fact that the meek
      226–17   would remain the *f·* fact,
   fashions
   Mis. 376–30   fashions *f·* such forms

forever

finite
Mis. 102– 8 and the infinite *f·* finite.
forbids
'02.   5–30 and *f·* forbids the thought of
good
Mis. 104–12 and good is *f·* good.
great
Mis. 183– 4 In the great *f·*, the verities
My. 267–10 supreme, infinite, the great *f·*,
294–29 passed . . . into the great *f·*.
harmonious
No. 26–25 individual and *f·* harmonious.
here
Po. 29– 7 *f·* here and near,
higher
My. 110–18 higher and *f·* higher
I AM
'02.   7–15 without end, even the *f· I AM*,
individual
Ret. 70–24 *f·* individual, incorporeal
No. 25–19 he is *f·* individual ;
26–25 he is *f·* individual
learn
Mis. 125–18 learn *f·* the infinite meanings
live
My. 131–10 shall live *f·*,'' — *John* 6 : 51.
lose
Un.   4–14 *f·* lose our own consciousness of
lost
Ret. 14– 2 *f·* lost its power over me.
Mind
Mis. 218– 3 Deity was *f·* Mind, Spirit ;
near
Po. 70–11 A help *f·* near ;
now and
No. 35–23 one with Him now and *f·*.
'02. 12– 6 this ideal of God is *now* and *f·*, *here*
My. 201– 7 enthroned now and *f·*.
of happiness
Po. 47–10 Can the *f·* of happiness be
permeated
Mis. 205–21 *f·* permeated with eternal life,
present
Chr. 53–33 *F·* present, bounteous, free,
reflection
Rud. 11– 7 the *f·* reflection of goodness.
reflects
Un. 39–23 man *f·* reflects and embodies Life,
reigns
Un. 63– 5 lives and reigns *f·*.
remained
Un. 63– 7 remained *f·* in the Science of being.
saith
Un. 62–21 saith *f·*, ''I am the living God,
silence
'02. 14–27 *f·* silence all private criticisms,
stands
My. 143–21 stands *f·* as an eternal and
to-day and
Ret. 94–23 to-day, and *f·*,'' — *Heb.* 13 : 8.
Un. 61– 4 to-day, and *f·*.'' — *Heb.* 13 : 8.
'02.   4–21 yesterday, and to-day, and *f·*.
My. 109–13 to-day, and *f·*.'' — *Heb.* 13 : 8.
292–28 yesterday, to-day, and *f·* ;
unfoldeth
No. 45–28 it unfoldeth *f·*.
unfolding
Mis. 82–17 man is *f·* unfolding
Pul.   4–22 *f·* unfolding its eternal Principle.
vast
Mis. 312–27 into the vast *f·*.
My. 291–22 bear its banner into the vast *f·*.
yesterday and
My. 246–29 to-day as yesterday and *f·*.

Mis. 57–30 always was and *f·* is ;
79– 4 will know them no more *f·*,
83– 2 holding man *f·* in the rhythmic
84–22 *f·* to quench his love for it.
90–13 This rule is *f·* golden :
103–31 is *f·* with the Father.
156–12 harmony be supreme and *f·* yours.
163–30 *f·* about the Father's business ;
176–21 should *f·* have melted away in the
188– 3 perfect now, and henceforth, and *f·*,
192–15 name shall endure *f·* : — *Psal.* 72 : 17.
197–32 neither be sick nor *f·* a sinner.
206– 7 saying *f·* to the baptized of
368– 7 * ''Truth *f·* on the scaffold,
368– 7 * Wrong *f·* on the throne.
Un. 62– 5 man is *f·* His image and likeness.
No. 16–16 *f·* giving forth more light,
'00. 10–22 habitation of His throne *f·*,
'02.   5–18 answered this great question *f·*
My. 126–29 supreme to-day, to-morrow, *f·*.

forever

My. 168– 5 *f·* the privileges of the people
176– 6 paved the way to my *f·* gratitude,
188– 4 put my name there *f·* ; — *I Kings* 9 : 3.
193– 8 and to thank God *f·*

forever-existing

Mis. 362– 3 *f·* realities of divine Science ;

forever-law

Mis. 123– 8 the *f·* of infinite Love,

forever-love

Mis. 150– 4 Give my *f·* to your dear church.

forewarn

Mis. 213–11 *f·* and forearm our fellow-mortals
My. 273–17 *f·* and forearm humanity.

forewarned

Mis. 367–23 against *knowing* evil, that God *f·*.

forfeit

Rud. 10– 3 *f·* the power that Truth bestows,
No. 40–18 *f·* their ability to heal in Science.
My. 242–13 *f·* your ability to demonstrate it.

forfeited

Mis. 67–13 by doing thus . . . shall be *f·*.

forfeits

Mis. 268–29 human pride *f·* spiritual power,

forgave

'02. 19–10 as Jesus *f·*, forgive thou.

forge

Mis. 246–16 to *f·* anew the old fetters ;

forget

Mis. 12– 6 If . . . wronged, forgive and *f·* :
154–30 *F·* not for a moment, that
155– 7 *F·* self in laboring for mankind ;
222–29 I shall not *f·* the cost of
292–17 to forgive and *f·* whatever is
343– 3 not *f·* that others before us have
353– 2 but something to *f·*.
368–27 let us not *f·* that the Lord reigns,
Man. 42– 7 not be made to *f·* nor to neglect
'01. 29–16 *f·* their parents' increasing years
Hea.   4–10 not to *f·* his daily cares.
Po. 27–11 Or we the past *f·*,
My. v– 2 * Lest we *f·* — lest we *f·* !
29–13 * will ever be able to *f·*.
63– 1 * not *f·* that it was through you
189–24 I cannot *f·* that yours is the first
225–25 to *f·* their prayer,
227–19 neither should they *f·* that
259–18 Do not *f·* that an honest, wise zeal,
307–13 by saying what I cannot *f·*

forgets

'01. 11–23 *f·* what Christian Scientists do not,

forgettest

Mis. 339–23 and *f·* to be grateful?

forgetting

Mis. 107–12 *f·* self, forgiving wrongs and
328–28 ''*F·* those things which — *Phil.* 3 : 13.
'00.   6– 5 *f·* those things which — *Phil.* 3 : 13.
My.   5–28 *F·* the Golden Rule and indulging sin,
116–16 *F·* divine Principle brings on
221–29 *f·* that the divine Mind,

forgive

Mis. 12– 6 If . . . *f·* and forget :
118–12 human affections yearn to *f·*
129– 5 *f·* others as he would *be*
129– 7 *f·* his brother and love his enemies.
292–17 to *f·* and forget whatever is
Ret.   9–13 prayed that God would *f·* me,
No. 30– 3 It does more than *f·*
'02. 18–13 faithful to rebuke, ready to *f·*.
19–10 even as Jesus forgave, *f·* thou.
19–12 no person . . . that I cannot *f·*.
Hea.   4–11 We ask infinite wisdom to . . . *f·*
My. 120– 8 *F·*, if it needs forgiveness,
180–28 ''Father, *f·* them ; — *Luke* 23 : 34.
201–16 mercifully *f·*, wisely ponder,
270–19 ''Father, *f·* them ; — *Luke* 23 : 34.

forgiven

Mis. 129– 5 forgive others as he would *be f·*.
Man. 55–14 repentant and *f·* by the Church
No. 29–12 * ''The *f·* soul in a sick body
30– 1 chapter sub-title
30– 6 until nothing is left to be *f·*,
30– 6 *F·* thus, sickness and sin
31–23 *f·* in the generally accepted sense,
31–25 returned, to be again *f·* ;
42– 9 ''Thy sins are *f·* thee ; — *see Luke* 5 : 23.
'01. 20–19 sin of sins ; it is never *f·*.

forgiveness

Mis. 100–29 patience, *f·*, abiding faith,
227– 2 can retire for *f·* to no fraternity

forgiveness
Man.	15–10	We acknowledge God's f· of sin
	40–11	charitableness, and f·.
	52–16	deemed sufficient by the Board for f·
Pul.	7–17	wash away, in floods of f·,
	30–20	* the f· of sin by God,
	33–11	* she prayed for f·,
No.	32– 5	f·, in the popular sense of the word,
My.	120– 8	Forgive, if it needs f·,

forgiveth
Pul.	10– 6	f· all thine iniquities ; — Psal. 103 : 3.
Pan.	4–24	f· all thine iniquities ; — Psal. 103 : 3.
Peo.	12–13	f· all thine iniquities ; — Psal. 103 : 3.
My.	13–19	f· all thine iniquities ; — Psal. 103 : 3.

forgiving
Mis.	107–12	forgetting self, f· wrongs
	124–26	Love f· its enemies.
Man.	47– 1	he is benevolent, f·,
Ret.	45–19	f· enemies, returning good for

forgotten
Mis.	54– 4	Has the sun f· to shine,
	92–26	It must not be f· that
	283–21	may momentarily be f· ;
	295–15	Has he f· how to honor
Ret.	7–22	* sad event will not be soon f·.
'02.	13– 2	In this endeavor self was f·,
Po.	10–10	The hoar fight is f· ;
My.	55– 8	* given up for a time, was not f·.
	95– 3	* and are then f·.
	149–28	seen and f· in the same hour ;
	337–11	The hoar fight is f· ;

fork
Mis.	231–14	dexterous use of knife and f·.

form (noun)
according to the
Man.	112–10	according to the f· on page 114.

and color
Mis.	86–19	sensations . . . of f· and color,

and comeliness
My.	42– 1	* depicted its f· and comeliness.
	257– 9	f· and comeliness of the divine ideal,

and inclination
Mis.	240–18	with f· and inclination fixed,

and individuality
Mis.	103–12	f· and individuality are never lost,

and tangibility
Mis.	56– 7	substance, f·, and tangibility,

angel
Peo.	5–16	beside the sepulchre in angel f·,

another
Mis.	246–15	Another f· of inhumanity
My.	152– 1	turned to another f· of idolatry,

appeared
Mis.	280– 1	Mind spake and f· appeared.

better
Mis.	376–15	* and in a much better f·."

bodily
Mis.	309–23	above a bodily f· of existence,

bold
Ret.	17–15	hickory rears his bold f·,
Po.	62–19	hickory rears his bold f·,

book
Mis.	x– 8	republish them in book f·,
My.	26–16	too short to be printed in book f·,

color, and
Un.	52–23	elaborate in beauty, color, and f·,

concentrated
Mis.	242–22	in its most concentrated f·,

definite
Peo.	8–11	definite f· of a national religion,

denominational
Mis.	382–29	our denominational f· of

different
Un.	9–24	but in a far different f·.

diviner
Mis.	68– 5	changed appearance and diviner f·

due
My.	333–15	* which was closed in due f·."

every
Mis.	48– 9	as to every f· of error,
	361– 9	every f· and mode of evil

face and
My.	259– 2	sweetest sculptured face and f·

fainting
Mis.	212–31	the fainting f· of Jesus,

finite
Mis.	16–20	more than a person, or finite f·,
Rud.	3–25	that God has a finite f· ?
'01.	6– 7	reckons . . . the infinite in a finite f·,
	6– 9	infinite Mind inhabit a finite f· ?

finiteness of
Ret.	73– 5	without finiteness of f· or

hero
Po.	78– 6	Till molds the hero f· ?

form (noun)
highest
My.	212–12	highest f· of mental evil,

its
Mis.	382–18	originated its f· of government,
My.	vi–13	* originated its f· of public worship,
	42– 1	* depicted its f· and comeliness.

lowest
Mis.	57–28	beginning with the lowest f·

material
Ret.	45– 8	this material f· of cohesion
My.	140–20	a material f· of communion
	140–21	The material f· is a

mode and
Mis.	257– 3	every mode and f· of evil.
My.	106–10	above matter in every mode and f·,

new
Mis.	44–26	your belief assumed a new f·,

octagonal
Pul.	24–11	* circular front and an octagonal f·,

of a boa-constrictor
Mis.	62– 6	the f· of a boa-constrictor

of action
Man.	28– 7	Without a proper . . . f· of action,

of a gold scroll
Pul.	78– 4	* in the f· of a gold scroll,

of a letter
My.	137– 2	* affidavit, in the f· of a letter

of a quotation
My.	73– 8	* in the f· of a quotation from

of a star
Pul.	26– 2	* electric lights in the f· of a star,

of a talking serpent
Pan.	6–11	first, in the f· of a talking serpent,

of Christian healing
Mis.	370–14	the f· of Christian healing.

of error
Mis.	48– 9	as to every f· of error,

of evil
Mis.	257– 3	every mode and f· of evil.

of Godlikeness
Mis.	213– 2	in the f· of Godlikeness.

of godliness
Mis.	145– 5	this f· of godliness seems as
'02.	16–27	The mere f· of godliness,

of government
Mis.	382–18	originated its f· of government,
Man.	70–15	its own f· of government.
	71–18	The Mother Church's f· of government
	72–23	its present f· of government

of healing
Rud.	6–25	definite and absolute f· of healing,

of matter
Un.	33–16	that f· of matter called brains,

of mind
Un.	32– 8	a false f· of mind.

of practice
Mis.	380–25	any outward f· of practice.

of prayer
Pul.	4–29	my f· of prayer since 1866 ;

of religion
Mis.	345–22	an advanced f· of religion,
My.	99–13	* whenever their f· of religion is

of Truth
Mis.	310– 6	impersonal f· of Truth,

one
Mis.	237–28	one f· of human slavery.
Pul.	38–30	* in one f· of belief or another

personality, or
No.	23– 3	in personality, or f·

pleasing
My.	vi– 5	* simpler or more pleasing f·.

relinquished the
'01.	24–30	I relinquished the f· to attain

spiritual
Pul.	33–24	* that his visitor was a spiritual f·

substance of
Mis.	87– 9	spiritual reality and substance of f·,

take
Po.	v–15	* began to take f· in her thought,

that
Mis.	x–26	adopted that f· of signature,
Un.	33–16	that f· of matter called brains,

this
Mis.	145– 5	this f· of godliness seems as
	314–27	This f· shall also be observed
My.	89–27	* this f· of religious faith

unseen
Mis.	301–24	an unseen f· of injustice

veiled
Mis.	250–25	veiled f· stealing on an errand of

whatever
Mis.	289– 5	in whatever f· it is made manifest.

without
Mis.	280– 1	earth was without f·,

form (noun)

without the comeliness
Mis. 302– 8   the *f·* without the comeliness,
worst
Mis. 233– 4   in the worst *f·* of medicine.
My. 335–28   * yellow fever in its worst *f·*,

Mis. 181–14   who can tell what is the *f·* of
362– 6   reflects all real mode, *f·*,
Un. 28–10   never a light or *f·* was discerned
Peo. 4– 4   the belief that God is a *f·*,

form (verb)

Mis. 137–30   My students can *now* . . . *f·* churches,
146–11   to *f·* a proper judgment.
193– 6   *f·* propositions of self-evident
315–22   Teachers shall *f·* associations
365–16   *f·* the common want,
389– 1   To *f·* the bud for bursting bloom,
Man. 72– 7   is eligible to *f·* a church
73–10   *f·* and conduct a C. S. organization
104– 8   to *f·* the budding thought
Ret. 25–26   to *f·* any proper conception of
Un. 35–25   can *f·* nothing unlike itself, Spirit,
52–26   *f·* the condition of beautiful
Peo. 2–17   and *f·* its Deity out of the worst
3– 2   our ideals *f·* our characters,
4–14   would *f·* a third person,
14–11   *f·* our models of humanity.
Po. 21–15   *f·* the bud for bursting bloom,
32–13   *f·* resolutions, with strength from
My. 68–25   * stone and marble *f·* the interior
163–28   for helping to *f·* mine.
243– 5   and *f·* one church.

Form 1

Man. 111–15   instructions illustrated in *F·* 1

Form 2

Man. 111–15   illustrated in Form 1 and *F·* 2,

formal

My. 29–20   * edifice whose *f·* opening
76– 8   * *f·* announcement was made that
170– 2   no *f·* church ceremonial
173–18   there are no *f·* exercises

formally

Pul. 76–27   * an invitation *f·* to accept
77–15   * *f·* accept this testimonial
78–14   * *f·* accept this testimonial
My. 84– 8   * may not be *f·* dedicated

formation

Mis. 71–18   based on a mortal or material *f·* ;
184– 8   has the *f·* of his parents ;
287–16   discern the Science of mental *f·*
Ret. 49–12   spiritual *f·* first, last, and always,

formations

Mis. 86–12   *f·* of . . . vague human opinions,
No. 6– 5   God's *f·* are spiritual,

formed

Mis, vii– 9   If worlds were *f·* by matter,
46–15   that which is *f·* is not cause,
71–26   nothing can be *f·* apart from
75–31   Soul cannot be *f·* or
104– 5   *F·* and governed by God,
173–29   Have attraction and cohesion *f·* it?
231– 1   almond-blossom *f·* a crown of glory ;
255– 5   That which is *f·* is not cause,
276–11   *f·* a goodly assemblage
289–12   partnerships are *f·* on agreements
314– 5   society *f·* for Sunday worship,
332–19   afterwards to have *f·* an evil sense
350– 7   with advice of . . . it was *f·*.
Man. 28– 1   *f·* by The Mother Church,
Ret. 61– 5   This fear is *f·* unconsciously
67– 2   a false claim before . . . sin was *f·* ;
Un. 35–23   matter, is not *f·* by Spirit ;
No. 19–26   Person is *f·* after the manner of
Hea. 7–11   where Jesus *f·* his estimate ;
My. 55– 2   * Sunday School was *f·*.
108– 1   calcareous salts *f·* by
182–12   *f·* a Christian Scientist Association
185–15   Love *f·* this trinity,
333–11   * "A procession was *f·*,

former

Mis. 12–20   at *f·* periods in human history
42–22   the *f·* is a dream and unreal,
53–16   the *f·* is not equal to the latter.
104–19   the *f·* revolve in their own orbits,
117– 8   arrest the *f·*, and obey the latter.
139–29   all *f·* efforts in the interest of
164– 3   the *f·* is the spiritual idea
206– 2   the *f·* being servant to the latter,
264–23   influence of their *f·* teacher.
Man. 18–19   members of her *f·* Church
86– 7   jurisdiction of his *f·* teacher.
Pul. 43–30   * from a *f·* pastor of the church :

former

Rud. 16– 3   the *f·* can never give a thorough
No. 10– 7   The *f·* is the highest style of man ;
10–18   *f·* position, that sense is organic
Hea. 3– 8   reestablished on its *f·* basis.
My. 39–21   * thoughts revert to a *f·* occasion,
50– 4   * left their *f·* church homes,
108–12   *f·* enlists faith in the pharmacy of
128–23   without the *f·* the latter were
141–17   * In *f·* years, the annual communion
190–12   vastly excelling the *f·*.
197–17   translucent atmosphere of the *f·*
318–10   name of the *f·* proofreader for

formerly

Mis. 242–26   *f·* partner of George T. Brown,
Man. 69–26   *f·* known as "Mother's Room"
Ret. 37–11   Those who *f·* sneered at it,
Pul. 28–26   * Judge Hanna, *f·* of Chicago,
29– 4   *f·* been Congregational clergymen.
59–22   * Joseph Armstrong, *f·* of Kansas,
My. 56–23   * *f·* been attendants at The
327–23   * *f·* read, "pretended healers,"
335– 2   * *f·* of Concord, N. H.
339–14   and all that it *f·* signified,
353–22   *f·* known as "Mother's Room"

formidable

Pan. 15– 3   will be as *f·* in war as
'02. 1–11   combined in *f·* conspiracy,
Hea. 1– 7   But Heaven's favors are *f·* :
My. 185–11   Truth, Life, and Love are *f·*,

forming

Mis. 256–13   from *f·* as frequently as
Man. 17– 3   *f·* a church without creeds,
Ret. 52–12   *f·* a National . . . Association.
'00. 1–14   right convictions fast *f·*
My. 49–12   * interested in *f·* the church,
69– 7   * and *f·* a gently curved
85–30   * *f·* one of the few perfect sky-lines
256–11   *f·* themselves in your thoughts

forms (noun)

all
Mis. 101–32   the elements of all *f·*
Un. 8–17   All *f·* of error are uprooted in
all its
Un. 53– 3   evil and all its *f·* are
My. 6–10   overcome sin in all its *f·*,
and colors
Rud. 6– 4   *assuming manifold f· and colors,*
and hues
Mis. 377– 1   such *f·* and hues of heaven,
and numbers
Mis. 104–10   calculus of *f·* and numbers.
and representations
Mis. 55–19   its *f·* and representations,
application
Man. 113– 1   heading
certain
Un. 45–16   in certain *f·* of theology
Pan. 4– 1   certain *f·* of pantheism
delicious
Mis. 9–26   delicious *f·* of friendship,
different
Mis. 370–13   assumes different *f·*,
Ret. 61– 4   in different *f·* of fear
differing
Mis. 380–18   in slightly differing *f·*.
features and
Mis. 112–14   some of the many features and *f·*
fresh
Mis. 1–16   mounting sense gathers fresh *f·*
here given
Man. 109–15   compare them with the *f·* here given,
illusive
Ret. 64–26   all the illusive *f·*, methods, and
limited
Pul. 6– 4   the limited *f·* of a national
majestic
Mis. 385–26   But faith . . . shed Majestic *f·* ;
Po. 49– 1   But faith . . . shed Majestic *f·* ;
material
Mis. 358–32   by leaving the material *f·*
No. 42– 7   material *f·* to meet a mental want.
milder
'01. 19–28   the milder *f·* of animal magnetism
moods and
Mis. 329– 3   nature in all her moods and *f·*,
my
Un. 26– 4   my *f·*, near or remote.
myriad
Mis. 114–19   appearing in its myriad *f·* :
325–27   sensualism in its myriad *f·*.
361– 7   whose myriad *f·* are neither
new
Peo. 11–15   that enforce new *f·* of oppression,

forms (noun)
of disease
  No.   2–23   the most defiant *f·* of disease.
of matter
  My. 212–11   use of higher *f·* of matter,
of religion
  '02. 16–24   merely outside *f·* of religion,
of sin
  No. 41–16   subtlest *f·* of sin are trying
other
  Ret. 71–29   the same as other *f·* of stealing,
  My. 212– 7   and other *f·* of intoxication.
regular
  Man. 111– 9   regular *f·* of application.
robust
  Mis. 325–15   Robust *f·*, with manly brow
special
  Man. 111–20   will be furnished special *f·*
spiritual
  Mis. 91–19   the most spiritual *f·* of thought
subtler
  Mis. 115–23   against the subtler *f·* of evil,
  No. 31– 6   appear to-day in subtler *f·*
their
  Mis. 192– 8   disease, and death, in all their *f·*,
varied
  Mis. 198– 7   its varied *f·* of pleasure and pain.
various
  Ret. 75– 1   various *f·* of book-borrowing
worse
  No. 31– 8   will multiply into worse *f·*,
worst
  Mis. 296–24   the worst *f·* of vice
  My. 190– 8   in healing the worst *f·* of

  My. 267–30   of all the divine modes, means, *f·*,
forms (verb)
  My. 265–22   *f·* the coincidence of the human and
formulas
  Man. 43– 5   *F·* Forbidden.
        43– 6   No member shall use written *f·*,
formulate
  Mis.   8–11   except you first *f·* this enemy
  '02.   5–26   *f·* a doctrine, or speculate on
  My. 49–14   * *f·* the rules and by-laws,
formulated
  Mis. 78–30   *f·* views antagonistic to
  Pul. 46– 4   * the new rules were *f·*.
formulating
  Mis. 49–16   *our capacity for f· a dream,*
fornication
  Mis. 278– 1   wines of *f·*, envy, and
  My. 125–32   with the wine of her *f·*,'' — *Rev.* 17 : 2.
fornicator
  My. 106–25   swearer, an adulterer, a *f·*,
fornicators
  Mis. 324–13   adulterers, *f·*, idolaters ;
forsake
  Mis. 123–24   repent, *f·* sin, love God,
  Ret. 85–17   Never *f·* your post without due
        90– 4   Does the faithful shepherd *f·* the
  '01. 15– 3   repent and *f·* it, in order to
  My. 40–13   * *f·* animosity, and abandon their
      140– 6   and not *f·* them.'' — *Isa.* 42 : 16.
      258–22   and friends that *f·*.
forsaken
  Mis. 63–23   *why hast Thou f· me?''* — *Mark* 15 : 34.
  Po. 41–11   When the herd had *f·*,
  My. 273–12   not seen the righteous *f·*, — *Psal.* 37 : 25.
forsaking
  My. 221–27   like a watchman *f·* his post,
forsook
  Mis. 340–13   *f·* Blackstone for gray stone,
  Ret.   7–11   * he never *f·* them until he
       42– 6   He *f·* all to follow in this line
       90–15   and others *f·* him.
fort
  Pul.   2–17   in a poorly barricaded *f·*,
forth
  Mis. xi–20   to fling it back and *f·*.
       27–18   ''Doth a fountain send *f·* — *Jas.* 3 : 11.
       41– 1   only the cruel and evil can send *f·*,
       75–31   Soul cannot be formed or brought *f·*
       81–17   *before it shall go f·*
     131–10   so shadow *f·* the substance of
     135–16   Sending *f·* currents of Truth,
     153– 6   When God went *f·* before His people,
     153–18   Christian Scientists bring *f·* the
     154–24   Bring *f·* fruit

forth
  Mis. 156–21   ''this kind goeth not *f·* — *see Matt.* 17 : 21.
     157–23   And He shall bring *f·* — *Psal.* 37 : 6.
     162–30   like him he went *f·*,
     170–31   explained as the putting *f·* of power.
     187–16   as set *f·* in original Holy Writ.
     194–31   first condition set *f·* in the text,
     201–12   he also showed *f·* the error
     224–17   Then, we should go *f·* into life
     227–20   the sweeter the odor they send *f·*
     235–13   that bringeth not *f·* good fruit ;
     237– 9   belch *f·* their latent fires.
     245–11   calling *f·* the *vox populi*
     265–20   can never bring *f·* the real fruits of
     311– 9   go *f·* to the full vintage-time,
     313–21   to send *f·* more laborers
     320–12   reaches *f·* for the infant idea
     328–29   reaching *f·* unto those — *Phil.* 3 : 13.
     330–32   to put *f·* its slender blade,
     339–28   and pour *f·* the unavailing tear.
     340–11   sends *f·* a barrister who never
     368–15   sending *f·* a poison more deadly
     370– 2   ''Stretch *f·* thy hand, — *Matt.* 12 : 13.
     370–17   calls *f·* infinite care from
  Man. 51– 1   Rules herein set *f·*.
      82– 2   literature it sends *f·*.
  Ret.   2– 5   find so graphically set *f·* in the
     11–13   *F·* from this fount the streamlets
     27– 2   setting *f·* their spiritual
     56–22   The sun sends *f·* light,
     62– 4   find that the views here set *f·*
     62– 5   bring *f·* better fruits of health,
     70– 4   puts *f·* its own qualities,
  Un.   5–25   shadowed *f·* in scientific thought.
     42–28   *f·* in the radiance of eternal being
     45–20   goes *f·* into an imaginary sphere
  Pul.   2–18   Would you rush *f·* single-handed to
     8–14   and *f·* came the money,
     12–21   Love sends *f·* her primal and
     13–29   brought *f·* the man child. — *Rev.* 12 : 13.
     14–18   send *f·* a new flood to drown the
     41– 1   * *f·* from the hands of the artisans
     47–12   * homœopathy, and so *f·*,
     49–11   * has come *f·* all this beauty !''
     51–18   * called *f·* the implements of
     54–22   * they are fully set *f·*.
     62–13   and call *f·* all the purity
     80–19   * speak of the system it sets *f·*,
     81– 6   * set *f·* as the power of God
  Rud.   7– 6   set *f·* in my work S. and H.
     8– 1   No rock brings *f·* an apple ;
     8– 5   in Science, Spirit sends *f·* its own
  No. 16–16   forever giving *f·* more light,
     26–11   brings *f·* its own sensuous conception.
     40–11   and pour *f·* a hypocrite's prayer ;
  '00.   6– 6   reaching *f·* to those — *see Phil.* 3 : 13.
     8– 9   comes *f·* a blessing or a bane
     8–14   ''Bring *f·* things — *see Matt.* 13 : 52.
  '01. 35– 2   He shall bring *f·* thy — *Psal.* 37 : 6.
  Hea. 4– 2   infinite can neither go *f·* from,
     20– 3   * could we sound the glories *f·*,
  Po.   v– 7   * *called f· by some experience*
     33–12   To breathe *f·* a prayer that
     60–10   *F·* from this fount the streamlets
  My. 53– 6   * send *f·* her book to the world.''
     72–19   * sent *f·* to the thirty thousand
    103–18   I have set *f·* C. S.
    122–14   called *f·* flattering comment
    147– 3   past comes *f·* like a pageant
    150–27   he sent them *f·* to heal
    151–20   * Go *f·*, and worship God.''
    159–10   sent *f·* His word to heal
    167–23   send *f·* a pæan of praise
    170–25   He shall bring *f·* thy — *Psal.* 37 : 6.
    179– 2   Scriptures, as set *f·* in the
    189–10   go *f·* in waves of sound,
    191–18   come *f·* from the tomb of the past,
    206–24   show *f·* the praises — *I Pet.* 2 : 9.
    208– 5   mirrored *f·* by your loving hearts,
    215– 4   God stretched *f·* His hand.
    215–23   first sent *f·* his students,
    215–28   Why did he send *f·* his students
    216– 1   set *f·* in the Scriptures.
    247–20   a loving look which brings *f·*
    248–26   You go *f·* to face the foe
    249–12   sends *f·* a mental miasma
    269– 3   showing *f·* the infinite
    269–20   vine is bringing *f·* its fruit ;
    269–22   sending *f·* their rays of reality
    278– 8   its edict hath gone *f·* :
    287–22   bringeth not *f·* good fruit ;
forthcoming
  Mis. 82– 7   beheld the *f·* Truth,
    158–25   will find the *f·* completion
    319–19   greetings for the *f·* holidays,
  Ret. 94–30   this period and the *f·* centuries,

forthwith
Ret. 88– 8 so-called dead *f·* emerged into
My. 334– 1 **f·* strives to give the impression

fortified
Rud. 15–17 should be *f·* on all sides

fortify
My. v–11 **f·* themselves against the mesmerism

fortress
Pul. 2–25 would overthrow this sublime *f·*,

forts
My. 127–23 *f·* of C. S., garrisoned by God's

fortunate
Pul. 61–21 * those *f·* enough to listen to the
My. 241–16 * Christian Scientists are *f·*
273– 6 **f·* in being able to point to a

fortune
'01. 31–27 my fair *f·* to be often taught by

fortunes
Mis. ix– 8 their comfortable *f·* are acquired by

forty
Pul. 41–15 * parties of *f·* and fifty.
'01. 18– 6 the sneers *f·* years ago
Hea. 1–17 * Knows it at *f·*, and reforms his
My. 22–14 * 1866, almost *f·* years ago,
22–14 * almost *f·* years in the wilderness,
37–14 * your obedience during *f·* years
43–15 **f·* years before.
43–21 **F·* years ago the Science of
59– 3 * nearly *f·* years ago.
59– 8 * in less than *f·* years
137–11 It is over *f·* years that I have
174–22 For nearly *f·* years
270–21 *f·* years I have returned good for
360–23 for *f·* years in succession.
(*see also* **values**)

forty-eight
Mis. 243– 2 in *f·* hours cured her perfectly
(*see also* **numbers**)

forty-five
(*see* **numbers, values**)

forty-four
(*see* **numbers**)

Forty-second Psalm
Un. 29–23 *soul, as in the F· P· :*

forty-two
(*see* **values**)

forum
Pul. 87–22 More effectual than the *f·*

forward
Mis. 18– 8 prominent laws which *f·* birth
136– 5 taking *f·* marches, broader and
155–25 I shall be apt to *f·* their letters
178–26 * pastor again came *f·*, and added the
212–25 who will step *f·* and open his
227–12 one may give it a *f·* move,
348– 1 They press *f·* towards the mark
Un. 57–26 *f·* the birth of immortal being ;
61–14 retreats, and again goes *f·* ;
Pul. 43–23 * which was looked *f·* to as
Rud. 11– 9 brings *f·* the next proposition
'00. 4–11 the new and *f·* steps in religion,
15– 7 Christian Scientists start *f·* with
'02. 3–11 Our nation's *f·* step was the
14–18 every *f·* step has been met
My. 14–28 **work will be pushed *f·*
47–19 * that showed a *f·* effort
155–12 *f·* in the onward march of Truth,
224–11 the *f·* footsteps it impels
327–28 * look *f·* to the day,
346–14 * expression of looking *f·*,

forwarded
Man. 44–15 which shall be *f·* each year
98– 4 *f·* to this Committee
Pul. 77–26 *f·* to Mrs. Mary Baker Eddy
My. 44–17 **f·* at once to our Leader,
359–23 * This letter was *f·* to Mrs. Eddy

forwarding
Mis. 306– 1 * In *f·* material to be melted

fossil
Mis. 30–23 the *f·* of wisdomless wit,

fossils
Peo. 8–25 *f·* of material systems,

Foster, Bishop
No. 27–18 Bishop *F·* said, in a lecture

foster
Mis. 296–20 *f·* a feminine ambition

Foster-Eddy, Ebenezer J.
Ret. 43–11 adopted son, Ebenezer J. *F·*,

fosters
Mis. 257–17 *f·* suspicion where confidence is due,
Rud. 12–11 This *f·* infidelity,
My. 211–21 *f·* suspicious distrust

fought
Mis. 41–12 The good fight must be *f·*
204– 8 When the good fight is *f·*,
Ret. 3–10 general who *f·* at Lundy's Lane,
Un. 17– 6 *f·* against Sisera. — *Judg.* 5 : 20.
46–26 Pharisees *f·* Jesus on this issue.
Hea. 2–16 "I have *f·* a good fight, — *II Tim.* 4 : 7.
10– 6 it was supposed to have *f·* the
Po. 78– 1 our honored dead *f·* on in gloom !
My. 61–12 * I *f·* hard with the evidence of

foul
Mis. 206– 3 from *f·* to pure, from torpid to
354– 7 to overbalance this *f·* stuff.
399– 7 Cleanse the *f·* senses within ;
Po. 75–14 Cleanse the *f·* senses within ;
My. 126–26 hold of every *f·* spirit, — *Rev.* 18 : 2.

found
Mis. xi–17 be *f·* to surpass imagination,
2–18 will be *f·* alone the remedy for sin,
10–20 *f·* their strength made perfect in
15–23 until man is *f·* to be the image of
25– 7 it is *f·* that matter is a phase of
27– 9 Here also is *f·* the pith of
28–13 will be *f·* to be the only Life.
32–11 are to be *f·* in the Scriptures,
33–28 *f·* in mortal mind's opposite,
46– 6 *f·* true, and adapted to destroy the
46–19 *f·* in the scale *with* his creator ;
53–23 *f·* it difficult to make the rulers
61– 2 *f·* the type and representative of
64– 1 Spirit might be *f·* "All-in-all."
66– 2 obedience thereto may be *f·* faulty,
69–17 I *f·* him barely alive,
80–23 until right is *f·* supreme.
96– 5 have *f·* Him so ;
112–16 *f·* him in the mental state called
114–27 then, if *f·* faithful,
115– 9 and fear of being *f·* out.
119–12 always be *f·* arguing for itself,
119–21 is *f·* powerless in C. S.
131–30 these will be *f·* already itemized,
139–27 it will be *f·* that this act was
140–24 we would not be *f·* fighting against
143–26 *f·* you all "with one accord — *Acts* 2 : 1.
157– 2 to be *f·* worthy to suffer for
164–23 *f·* in the actual likeness of
165–31 *f·* in the order, mode, and
169– 1 she had *f·* all the divine Science
178– 7 He *f·* that the new wine
178–21 * If I had not *f·* C. S. a new gospel,
178–23 * if I had not *f·* it truth,
180–14 *f·* the open door from this sepulchre
183– 8 will be *f·* that Mind is All-in-all,
188–21 where the present writer *f·* it,
189– 6 will be *f·* to be the Comforter
190–18 these terms will be *f·* to include the
191–16 name of his satanic majesty is *f·*
195–16 not to be *f·* in the Scriptures.
196– 1 ego is *f·* not in matter
202– 3 are *f·* to correct the discords of
210– 5 error, when *f·* out, is two-thirds
227– 6 Law has *f·* it necessary to offer to
236– 1 has not *f·* that human passions
247– 7 know that I *f·* health in just what I
248– 5 *f·* in the "new tongue," — *see Mark* 16 : 17.
255–10 Man should be *f·* not claiming
255–24 *f·* in God, the divine Mind.
260– 4 and *f·* able to heal them.
263– 6 the sweetest similes to be *f·*
276–13 an assemblage *f·* waiting and
276–20 divine Love is *f·* in affliction.
276–26 not one of them be *f·* borrowing oil,
279–20 when it is *f·* that evil is naught
286– 9 *f·* to be man's oneness with God,
288– 8 and not be *f·* wanting,
290– 3 *f·* within their precincts.
291–24 who are *f·* worthy to suffer for
303– 3 sought and *f·* as healers
308– 2 *f·* harmonious and immortal.
312– 4 we be not *f·* wanting.
334–11 fabrication is *f·* to be a lie,
338–14 afford the only rule I have *f·*
348–23 *f·* myself under this new *régime*
355–14 Error *f·* out is two-thirds destroyed,
361– 5 its substances are *f·* substanceless,
365– 6 Human theories . . . are *f·* wanting ;
386– 5 and hearts are *f·* and filled,
398–25 And was *f·* by you and me
Man. 29–11 and the complaint be *f·* valid,
30– 6 be *f·* at any time inadequate
39– 4 If, . . . they are *f·* worthy,

found

Man.	39– 5	but if not *f·* worthy
	50–15	be *f·* having the name without
	50–23	*f·* violating any of the By-Laws
	52–11	If a member is *f·* guilty of
	54–13	and this complaint being *f·* valid,
	55–22	is *f·* trying to practise or to
	63– 7	*f·* in the C. S. Quarterly Lessons,
	77–11	If it be *f·* that the Church funds
	89– 7	vice-president of . . . being *f·* worthy,
	90– 4	if *f·* qualified to receive them.
	92–12	*f·* duly qualified to teach C. S.,
Ret.	24–21	*f·* to be in perfect scientific accord
	28– 2	*f·* as the Life, or Principle,
	33–10	I *f·*, in the . . . remedies
	33–21	is *f·* to be even more active.
	44–14	*f·* able to maintain the church
	56– 2	*f·* to be demonstrable rules in C. S.,
	61–25	it cannot be *f·* in the body.
	69–14	Its life is *f·* to be not Life,
	73– 7	man is *f·* in the reflection of
	82–24	*f·* dwelling together in harmony,
	94–16	immortal Truth be *f·* true,
Un.	3–17	man is *f·* in the image and
	10– 4	they are not to be *f·* in God,
	15–21	*f·* in heathen religious history.
	30–26	shall be *f·* a quickening Spirit ;
	35– 8	so-called material senses are *f·*,
	51–23	Truth is *f·* only in divine Science,
	57–23	rejoiced that he was *f·* worthy
Pul.	6–15	* realized I had *f·* that for which
	28–25	* are *f·* in the hymn-books of the
	34–23	*f·* it to be in perfect scientific accord
	58– 1	* *f·* herself in Lynn, Mass.,
	58–18	* Scarcely any woodwork is to be *f·*.
	67– 5	* "If you would *f·* a new faith,
	67–10	* faiths which are to be *f·* there
	67–22	* little knots of them are to be *f·*.
Rud.	5–11	who has ever *f·* Soul in the body
	5–13	who has *f·* sight in matter,
No.	8–23	If one be *f·* who is too blind for
	12–27	be *f·* all instead of a part of being,
	15–13	notions of personality to be *f·* in
	16– 1	*f·* in the divine consciousness.
	18–14	Human theories, . . . are *f·* unequal to
	20–11	Principle is *f·* to be the only
	24–19	being thus uncovered, is *f·* out,
	28– 6	man be *f·* perfect and eternal.
	28–12	is *f·* to bring with it health,
Pan.	5– 1	is *f·* in scholastic theology.
	12– 1	it will be *f·* possible to fulfill it.
	13–12	condemnation of all error, wherever *f·*.
'00.	1–11	is *f·* crowned with unprecedented
	4–21	and they must be *f·* final, absolute,
	7–27	loving Christ is *f·* near,
'01.	24–24	I *f·* it necessary to follow Jesus'
	26–11	quality not to be *f·* in God !
'02.	17–17	Who . . . ever *f·* her true?
Hea.	12– 2	*f·* out that Mind instead of
	13– 9	*f·* out they have taken no medicine,
Peo.	6–17	because He is *f·* altogether lovely.
	6–22	are *f·* destroying sin, sickness, and
	11– 1	liberty of the sons of God as *f·* in C. S.
	11– 5	was *f·* that the feeblest mind,
Po.	vi– 1	* *finally f· its way into print*,
	49– 8	and hearts are *f·* and filled,
	75– 5	was *f·* by you and me
My.	4–16	*f·* that, instead of opposing,
	18–20	all error, wherever *f·*.
	28–17	* not to be *f·* in the material
	42– 2	* We have *f·* it true that
	43–27	* *f·* in C. S. that which heals
	53–32	* it was *f·* that the Hawthorne Rooms
	54–18	* no place suitable could be *f·*
	56– 9	* *f·* necessary to organize
	63–30	* *f·* the kingdom of God.
	73– 1	* *f·* necessary to issue a
	78–15	* *f·* every basket piled high
	78–23	* were *f·* to be perfect.
	88–22	* *f·* the truths of C. S. to be
	89–30	* *f·* a religious movement
	94–11	* in which it has *f·* a foothold.
	103–22	I have *f·* nothing in ancient or
	103–23	on which to *f·* my own,
	111–12	will tell you that he has *f·*
	113–26	men are *f·* casting out the evils
	119–32	St. John *f·* Christ, Truth,
	121–18	Few blemishes can be *f·*
	127– 9	it will be *f·* that C. S.
	129– 1	see if there be *f·* anywhere a
	131–18	I hope I shall not be *f·* disorderly,
	147–20	*f·* able to heal both sin and
	152–23	*f·* an ever-present help
	152–28	is *f·* to be the remote,
	165–31	*f·* and felt the infinite
	185–19	lost, and is *f·* ;" — *Luke* 15 : 32.

found

My.	189–21	is sought and *f·*.
	211–27	is *f·* out and destroyed.
	229– 4	cannot be *f·* at Pleasant View
	241–26	* I had *f·* that I lived and moved
	248–12	*f·* adequate for the emancipation
	248–29	*f·* nearest the divine Principle
	251–13	your pupils are *f·* eligible to
	251–21	if *f·* eligible, receive a
	285–21	they neither *f·* me in — *Acts* 24 : 12.
	291–16	His humanity, . . . was not *f·* wanting.
	299–13	may be *f·* in creeds.
	301– 5	*f·* to be a healthy fermentation,
	320– 6	* I *f·* that his statement
	324–29	* if he *f·* you could do so,
	330–15	* *f·* Mrs. Eddy's statements,
	332–31	* a roll of papers . . . was *f·* ;
	333– 5	* *f·* by one of your own citizens,
	343–26	I *f·* at one time that they had
	345–16	I *f·* that when I prescribed
	348– 6	I *f·* it was God made manifest
	348–21	I had *f·* unmistakably

foundation

and superstructure

Mis.	140– 2	*f·* and superstructure,
	357–32	yea, its *f·* and superstructure.

another's

No.	43–20	on another's *f·*.

deeper

Pul.	36– 5	* deeper *f·* of her religious work

firm

Mis.	213–20	fearless wing and firm *f·*.
'01.	2–25	Only a firm *f·* in Truth can give

for our temple

My.	13–31	a *f·* for our temple,

for the builders

My.	301– 8	a *f·* for the builders.

His

Mis.	263–11	building on His *f·*,

his own

Ret.	48– 8	build on his own *f·*,

in nature

Mis.	367–26	neither precedent nor *f·* in nature,

laid the

Ret.	27– 3	so laid the *f·* of my work
Hea.	11–17	homœopathy has laid the *f·* stone of

no

Mis.	334– 6	Necromancy has no *f·*,

of all systems

'00.	5–25	the *f·* of all systems of religion.

of Christian Science

Mis.	105– 7	demonstration is the *f·* of C. S.
My.	117–22	is the *f·* of C. S.

of Love

Pul.	2–30	reared on the *f·* of Love,

of repentance

My.	128– 4	*f·* of repentance from — *Heb.* 6 : 1.

of right thinking

Hea.	3– 6	It was the *f·* of right thinking

of Science

Mis.	81– 1	broad and sure *f·* of Science ;

of the world

My.	185–17	from the *f·* of the world," — *Rev.* 13 : 8.

of this temple

Pul.	85– 1	* to lay the *f·* of this temple,

of true art

Mis.	375–19	* the *f·* of true art.

of unbelief

Mis.	169–23	often is the *f·* of unbelief

other

Mis.	365– 2	"other *f·* can no man — *I Cor.* 3 : 11.
Un.	64– 8	"other *f·* can no man — *I Cor.* 3 : 11.
No.	21–23	other *f·* can no man — *I Cor.* 3 : 11.
'02.	14–16	on any other *f·*,

solid

My.	45–32	* In solid *f·* in symmetrical

spiritual

(*see* **spiritual**)

study and

Pul.	71–20	* study and *f·* of the faith

sure

Mis.	81– 1	broad and sure *f·* of Science ;
	143– 2	broad basis and sure *f·*
	152–23	beat against this sure *f·*,
My.	16–26	corner stone, a sure *f·* : — *Isa.* 28 : 16.

without

Mis.	108– 8	being without *f·* in fact,
My.	334– 8	* allegation . . . is without *f·*.

Mis.	140–21	The *f·* on which our church
Pul.	9–30	*f·* of enlightened faith is
	52–15	* with the New Testament at the *f·*,
Hea.	2–27	Truth, eternity's *f·* stone,
My.	16–25	for a *f·* a stone, — *Isa.* 28 : 16.

foundational
Mis. 200–17 The f· facts of C. S.
My. 230–23 faithful over f· trusts,

foundations
everlasting
Mis. 336–29 it rests on everlasting f·,
Un. 6– 9 established on everlasting f·.
false
Un. 53–16 not built on such false f·,
its
My. 187–30 laid its f· on the rock
of Christian Science
My. 191–11 f· of C. S. — one God and one Christ.
of human affection
Mis. 287–19 lays the f· of human affection
of mortality
Mis. 101–16 undermines the f· of mortality,
of their testimony
Un. 33–22 observe the f· of their testimony,
of these assertions
Un. 44– 5 The f· of these assertions,
old
My. 350–22 old f· of an early faith
scientific
Ret. 83– 8 scientific f· are already laid
sure
Mis. 82–10 reach the sure f· of time,

Mis. 163–22 yet the f· he laid are
Un. 64– 6 on the f· of an eternal Mind
Hea. 13–22 the f· of metaphysical healing
My. 145– 9 from the f· to the tower,
182– 8 the f· of which are the same,

founded
Mis. 13–18 f· upon the basis of material and
152–22 f· upon the rock of Christ,
337– 1 f· at this period C. S.,
383– 9 C. S. is f· by its discoverer,
Ret. 15– 4 till I f· a church of my own,
Pul. 37–28 * f· with twenty-six members,
66– 4 * was f· fifteen years ago
67–15 * F· twenty-five years ago,
67–27 * The church was f· in April, 1879,
68– 4 * College was f· by Mrs. Eddy
68–24 * C. S. was f· by Mrs. Mary Baker Eddy.
70–12 * has within a few years f· a sect that
No. 10– 1 * principles on which it is f·,
'00. 13–12 f· the city of Smyrna,
'01. 26– 4 f· his system of metaphysics
Peo. 3–19 religion f· upon C. S.
6– 7 * f· on long observation
My. vi–17 * f· The C. S. Journal in 1883,
33–30 hath f· it upon the seas, — Psal. 24 : 2.
47–24 * Mrs. Eddy f· her first church
47–27 * f· on the commands of Jesus :
48–13 * f· the future growth of her church,
76–28 * f· . . . by Mrs. Mary Baker Eddy
112–10 f· squarely . . . on the Scriptures.
139– 5 f· upon the rock, Christ Jesus,

Founder
Pul. 53– 2 * by the F· of Christianity
My. 279– 3 The F· of Christianity said :
(see also **Eddy**)

founder
Mis. 381–31 * both f· and discoverer
Pul. 5–11 f· of the Concord School of
My. 305– 2 and that he is the f· of
338–25 discoverer, f·, demonstrator,
(see also **Eddy**)

founding
Mis. 382– 7 discovery and f· of C. S.
Pul. 36– 1 * a year after her f· of the
'02. 12–29 f· the institutions and early

fount
Mis. ix–18 from the f· of divine Love.
92– 9 open f· of Truth and Love.
225–11 had drunk at its f·,
Ret. 11–13 from this f· the streamlets flow,
18–15 shrine Or f· of real joy
84– 6 this open f· of Truth and Love.
Hea. 10–27 for the true f· and Soul's baptism.
12– 7 metaphysician goes to the f·
Po. 60–10 from this f· the streamlets flow,
64– 6 shrine Or f· of real joy

fountain
Mis. 27–18 "Doth a f· send forth — Jas. 3 : 11.
117–28 God is the f· of light,
153– 9 the rock became a f· ;
399– 6 it calls you, — "Come to this f·,
Pul. 48– 4 * with here and there a f· or
Hea. 7–14 makes pure the f·,
Po. 41– 7 f· and leaflet are frozen

fountain
Po. 75–13 it calls you, — "Come to this f·,
My. 79–10 * supposed f· of knowledge
247–14 little fishes in my f·

fountains
Mis. 113–29 life-giving f· of truth.
223– 6 necessarily have pure f· ;
323–22 drink from its living f· ?
Ret. 31–28 Frozen f· were unsealed.
Hea. 10–28 f· play in borrowed sunbeams,
Peo. 14– 5 cool grottos, smiling f·,
Po. 9– 5 unsealed f· of grief and joy
My. 186– 2 meadows, f·, and forests

four
Mis. 136–25 convening once in f· months ;
231– 6 F· generations sat at that
239– 4 but f· days' vacation for the past year,
304–27 * at f· o'clock it will toll on the
349–23 will state that I preached f· years,
Man. 73– 2 f· of whom are members of The
Ret. 19–17 at the end of f· months,
20– 8 my little son, about f· years of age,
40– 1 f· successive years I healed,
65–22 as taught in the f· Gospels.
89–22 Nowhere in the f· Gospels
Un. 11–27 ye say, There are yet f· months,
Pul. 25– 4 * distributed by the f· systems
27–20 * pictorial story of the f· Marys
40–12 * THE SERVICE REPEATED F· TIMES
40–16 * simple ceremonies, f· times repeated,
40–17 * presence of f· different congregations,
41–21 * f· vast congregations filled the
49–10 * "You have lived here only f· years,
49–13 "F· years !" she ejaculated ;
57– 7 * was thronged at the f· services
59– 6 * were held from nine to f· o'clock,
59– 8 * exercises f· times repeated.
Pan. 9– 9 f· first rules pertaining thereto,
'01. 4– 5 f· times three is twelve,
4– 6 three times f· is twelve.
My. 68– 5 * f· arches springing from the
69–30 * some f· miles away.
70–25 * six organs, with f· manuals,
214–19 F· years after my discovery
330–29 where, at the end of f· months,
(see also **numbers, values**)

fourfold
My. 199–20 f· unity between the churches

fourscore
Po. 71–16 Ye who have wept f·
My. 146–10 sum of years to f·,
177–11 sum of years to f·

four-story
My. 66– 2 * f· brick building also

fourteen
Mis. 29–16 but f· deaths in the ranks
Pul. 8– 9 within f· months, responded
38– 8 * consists of f· chapters,
(see also **numbers, values**)

fourth
Mis. 22–12 f· dimension of Spirit.
176– 4 chapter sub-title
280–19 close of the lecture on the f·
309–25 third and f· paragraphs,
318–10 f· and final generation
332–24 third, suffering ; f·, death.
Un. 31–14 f·, that matter, being so endowed,

Fourth Church of Christ, Scientist
Brooklyn
My. 363– 6 * signature

My. 363– 2 * signature

Fourth of July
Mis. 251– 1 chapter sub-title

fowl
Mis. 69–12 over the f· of the air." — Gen. 1 : 26.

fowler
Mis. 389–22 no f·, pestilence or pain ;
Po. 5– 1 no f·, pestilence or pain ;

fowls
Mis. 357–15 f· of the air pick them up.

foxes
My. 123–30 "the little f· — Song 2 : 15.

foyer
My. 46– 1 * f· and broad stairways,
69–20 * unusual feature is the f·,
69–21 * Adjoining this f· are

Fra Angelico
Mis. 376– 8 * having been taken by F· A·

fraction
Mis. 269–14   f· of the actual Science
No.   30–20   more than a f· of himself.
fragmentary
Mis. ix–11   pictures — once f· and faint
     126– 2   from f· discourses
Ret.   93–11   Truth is not f·,
fragments
Mis.   9–18   fall in f· before our eyes.
     106–21   and gather up the f·.
     149–11   gather up the f·, and count
     360– 4   with crude, rude f·,
My. 133–13   f· gathered therefrom
fragrance
Mis. 228–10   fills the world with its f·,
     330–23   freshen the f· of being.
Po.   25–12   F· fresh round the dead,
     32– 5   blossoms whose f· and charms
     67–22   f· of goodness and love ;
fragrant
Ret.   17–18   magnolia, and f· fringe-tree ;
     18–22   flowers of feeling are f· and fair,
Peo. 14– 5   f· recesses, cool grottos,
Po.   46–11   Fresh as the f· sod,
     63– 3   magnolia, and f· fringe-tree ;
     64–16   flowers of feeling are f· and fair,
frail
Mis. 13–18   This f· hypothesis is founded upon
     13–20   f· human reason accepts.
     87–11   f· conception of mortal mind ;
     377– 2   brush or pen to paint f· fairness
Po.   18–15   notice the f· fledgling hath.
My.   80– 9   * tax upon f· human credulity,
     342–14   * when I say f·, let it not
frailer
My. 342– 7   *f·, but Mrs. Eddy herself.
frailty
Mis. 336–28   only to take away its f·.
Ret. 81–28   f· of mortal anticipations,
frame
Rud. 11– 1   f· its own conditions,
     11–28   nervous operations of the human f·.
My. 308–16   * "tall, gaunt f·"
framed
Pul.   32– 1   * her face, f· in dark hair
My.   24–14   * "fitly f· together — Eph. 2 : 21.
     68–29   * f· of iron and finished with
     318–28   long argument, f· from his
frames
Pul. 25–13   * window f· are of iron,
     76–11   * furniture f· are of white
France
Mis. 304–15   * takes place at Paris, F·.
     372–15   masters in F· and Italy.
Pul.   5–24   F·, Germany, Russia,
Frankish
Pul. 65–21   * F· church was reared upon the spot
Franklin
N. H.
My. 313–12   driving into F·, N. H.,
     314– 8   was located in F·, N. H.
     314–12   owned a house in F·, N. H.

My. 314– 4   * then moved to F·.
Franklin's, Benjamin
Mis. 277–18   truth of Benjamin F· report
frankly
'02. 14–27   answered f· and honestly,
frantically
Mis. 374–23   f· affirm what is what :
fraternity
Mis. 227– 2   no f· where its crime may
My. 175–24   f·, and Christian charity.
fraud
Mis. 368–14   Charlatanism, f·, and malice
My. 143–19   cannot be a temporal f·.
     150–31   to call this "a subtle f·,"
fraudulent
Mis. 51– 8   the ignorant, the f·,
     272–24   * Hence . . . is a f· claim.
fraught
Mis. 238–14   f· with infinite blessings,
     253–14   F· with history, it repeats the
     320– 8   f· with divine benedictions
No.   23– 4   f· with spiritual danger.
Po.   23–11   may their gaze be ever f·
My. 129–13   f· with divine reflection.
     234–29   is f· with danger.
     258– 6   so f· with opposites,

free
Mis.   6– 3   leaves mortals but little time f·
     30–20   "hath made me f· from — Rom. 8 : 2.
     76–15   to set a human soul f· from its
     83–15   you are a f· moral agent
     90–15   Then help others to be f· ;
     101–18   and sets the captive f·,
     103–17   eternal Mind is f·, unlimited,
     113– 7   f· moral agency is lost ;
     119–19   a plea for f· moral agency,
     154–19   Through the word . . . are you made f·.
     157–13   f· in Truth and Love,
     183–10   Man is f· born :
     185–22   upright, pure, and f· ;
     201–19   hath made me f· from — Rom. 8 : 2.
     241–23   truth shall make you f·.' " — John 8 : 32.
     246– 2   and the prohibiting of f· speech,
     246–17   stop f· speech, slander, vilify ;
     264–20   before they are quite f· from
     316– 3   to know the truth that makes f·,
     321–16   hath made me f· from — Rom. 8 : 2.
     326– 3   hath made you f· from — see Rom. 8 : 2.
     356– 6   need no terrible detonation to f· them.
     388– 8   'T· us from human strife.
     398–24   'T was the Truth that made us f·,
Man.   34–17   F· from Other Denominations.
     84– 5   to know the truth that makes f·,
     91– 7   Remuneration and F· Scholarship.
     91–10   card of f· scholarship from
     91–12   a f· course in this department
     91–14   gives f· admission to classes.
Chr.   53–33   Forever present, bounteous, f·,
Ret.   11–12   In our God-blessed f· school.
     11–22   F· as the generous air,
Un.   60–18   Mortals are f· moral agents,
Pul.   44–24   * a church . . . f· of debt.
Rud.   12–24   f· the minds of the healthy
     13–22   it will f· his patient.
     14–14   sometimes seventeen, f· students in it ;
No.   45–24   Let the Word have f· course
     46–12   upon f· moral agency ;
     46–18   rejoicing, . . . that we are f· born.
'01.   10– 2   truth shall make you f·." — John 8 : 32.
'02.   9–12   hath made me f· from — Rom. 8 : 2.
     15– 7   keeping a f· institute,
Peo.   10–13   Paul said, " I was f· born." — Acts 22 : 28.
     10–14   Justice and truth make man f·,
     10–19   they alone have fettered f· limbs,
     11– 6   can f· its body from disease
Po.   1–11   from chaos dark set f·,
     3– 9   sleep sets drooping fancy f·
     7– 8   F· us from human strife.
     25– 9   From your green bowers f·,
     39– 2   Gifts, lofty, pure, and f·,
     47–12   Will the hereafter from suffering f·
     60– 9   In our God-blessed f· school.
     60–20   F· as the generous air,
     75– 4   'Twas the Truth that made us f·,
My.   24– 3   * the truth which makes f·
     75–27   * dedicated to-morrow f· from debt.
     76–18   * dedicate their churches f· of debt
     77–27   * absolutely f· of debt,
     84– 9   * until it be wholly f· from debt.
     91–30   * is absolutely f· from debt.
     94–19   * structure was f· from debt.
     98– 8   * dedicated f· from debt,
     98–21   * absolutely f· of debt,
     98–29   * its dedication f· from debt
     113–14   hath made me f· from — Rom. 8 : 2.
     117–26   give their talents . . . f· scope
     119– 8   Man is f· from the flesh
     133–15   set the captive sense f·
     161– 2   set us f· by enabling us to
     205– 5   Christ hath made us f·." — Gal. 5 : 1.
     272– 6   hath made me . . . f· from — Rom. 8 : 2.
     293–29   hath made me f· from — Rom. 8 : 2
     350–15   the pathway glad and f·

freed
Mis. 90–15   Do you desire to be f· from sin?
freedom (see also **freedom's**)
air and
Mis. 356– 9   stifled from lack of air and f·.
and greatness
Mis. 331–11   its springtide of f· and greatness.
No.   8–16   struggle into f· and greatness,
and supremacy
Ret. 45–13   gain spiritual f· and supremacy.
bulwarks of
Pul.   9– 2   you are the bulwarks of f·,
dearer than
Pul. 83–23   * by bonds dearer than f·,"
final
Mis. 361–21   So shall mortals soar to final f·,
from pain
Mis. 298–28   gains f· from pain

freedom

from sin
Peo. 10–24 mind's *f·* from sin ;
great
Mis. 120–14 great *f·* for the race ;
greater
Ret. 95– 2 blossom into greater *f·*,
growing
Ret. 31– 4 solemn certainty in growing *f·*
heritage of
My. 128–14 vital heritage of *f·*
insufficient
My. 266– 2 chapter sub-title
266– 7 and insufficient *f·* of honest
missionary of
Mis. 304– 9 * as a missionary of *f·*,
nation's
Ret. 43–23 Centennial Day of our nation's *f·*.
native
My. 120–12 gives to soul its native *f·*.
of choice
Ret. 71–14 *f·* of choice and self-government.
of health
Mis. 101–12 for the *f·* of health, holiness, and
of mortals
No. 34–28 *f·* of mortals from sin and death.
pleaded for
Mis. 345– 5 pleaded for *f·* in immortal strains
Principle of
Mis. 258–18 this infinite Principle of *f·*,
reigned
Mis. 259–14 *f·* reigned, and was the heritage of
religious
Mis. 251–13 civil and religious *f·*,
My. 167–22 chapter sub-title
rights of
Mis. 297–29 belongs to the rights of *f·*.
strength and
Mis. 240–12 physical strength and *f·*.
struggling for
No. 40–22 the thought struggling for *f·*.
this
Mis. 259–16 this *f·* was the moral power of
to believe
Pul. 51– 3 * *F·* to believe or to dissent
to worship
Ret. 2– 8 seeking "*f·* to worship God ;"
My. 168– 1 *F·* to worship God according to
341– 6 * "*F·* to worship God."
true
Mis. 176–23 to establish a nation in true *f·*,

Mis. 141–13 *f·*, might, and majesty of Spirit,
204–15 *f·*, deep-toned faith in God ;
My. 154–22 * he have light, . . . *f·*, immortality ?"
316–19 the *f·* of Christian sentiments,

freedom's
Ret. 11– 9 sword is sheathed, 't is *f·* hour,
12– 2 Wake *f·* welcome,
Po. 60– 6 sword is sheathed, 'tis *f·* hour,
60–22 Wake *f·* welcome,
71–18 *f·* birthday — blood-bought boon !

free-love
Mis. 285–15 first crossed swords with *f·*,
285–26 up from the ashes of *f·*,

freely
Mis. 38– 2 *good we can do must be done f·*
149– 4 Invite all cordially and *f·*
Ret. 18–18 *f·* adore all His spirit hath made,
Pul. 64– 8 * Money came *f·* from all parts
Po. 64– 9 *f·* adore all His spirit hath made,
My. 62–30 * gave *f·* of their time and efforts
69–21 * where five thousand people can *f·*
157–12 * church home you have so *f·* bestowed.
172–17 '*F·* ye have received, — *Matt.* 10 : 8.
172–18 *f·* give.' — *Matt.* 10 : 8.
320– 9 * He also expressed himself *f·*
321–15 * talked so *f·* in my presence.
324– 1 * He often spoke his thoughts *f·*

Free Mason
My. 312–10 Glover, however, was a *F· M·*,
330–23 "My husband was a *F· M·*,

freemason
Ret. 19–11 My husband was a *f·*,

Free Masonry
My. 351– 6 * its beautiful tribute to *F· M·*.
351–11 *morale of F· M·* is above ethics

freemasonry
Mis. 142–26 symbols of *f·* depicted on
142–29 I may not unite with you in *f·*,

Free Masons
My. 312–27 *F· M·* selected my escort,
326–17 *F· M·* laid on his bier the emblems

Freemason's Monthly Magazine
My. 334–28 * appeared in 1845 in the *F· M· M·*,

Free Press
Pul. 89–29 * *F· P·*, Detroit, Mich.
90–13 * *F· P·*, London, Can.

freer
Hea. 4– 4 must give *f·* breath to thought

freest
Pul. 80– 7 * *f·* country in the world

freeth
Un. 56–16 *f·* him from the law of sin

freeze
Mis. 88–26 * had never seen water *f·*."
Ret. 65– 7 *f·* out the spiritual element.

French
Pul. 27– 2 * *F·* mirrors and every convenience.
Rud. 1–12 In *F·* the equivalent word is

French Commisioners
Mis. 277–19 report before the *F· C·*

French Huguenots
Mis. 281–12 in the time of the *F· H·*,

frequency
My. 268– 4 The *f·* of divorce shows

frequent
Mis. 238–25 The *f·* public allegement that I am
Man. 84–22 for more *f·* meetings.
Pul. 25–26 * *f·* illuminated texts from the
My. v– 7 * wonderment and *f·* comment,
332–24 * After *f·* searchings and much

frequented
Ret. 89–18 he had *f·* in childhood.
My. 72– 7 * *f·* by members of the

frequently
Mis. 6–21 *F·* it requires time to
45– 9 fatal results that *f·* follow
197– 4 text is one more *f·* used
256–13 classes from forming as *f·* as
322– 7 are *f·* disappointed.
339– 4 would happen very *f·* on earth,
No. 32–11 *F·* when I touch this subject
'01. 4–29 meaning divine Love, more *f·* than
My. 83– 9 * Scientists *f·* wear a small pin,
310–24 * *f·* set the house in an uproar,"
313–24 * *f·*'' seek my advice.
324–32 * Mr. and Mrs. Wiggin *f·* mentioned

fresh
Mis. 1–16 mounting sense gathers *f·* forms
51–26 * *f·*, as from a second birth,
144–24 *f·* as a summer morn,
227–18 *f·* flowers of feeling blossom,
240–23 over the *f·*, unbiased thought.
Ret. 27–30 a *f·* universe — old to God,
48– 7 experience . . . *f·* in my thoughts,
Pul. 53– 1 * *f·* development of a Principle
'00. 10–10 *f·* energy and final victory.
Hea. 19–19 *f·* opportunities every hour ;
Po. 15–18 Flowers *f·* as the pang in the bosom
25–12 Fragrance *f·* round the dead,
46–11 *F·* as the fragrant sod,
My. 50–20 * brought *f·* courage to the
155–19 a pure peace, a *f·* joy,
195–22 breath *f·* from God,
244–11 designed to impart a *f·* impulse

freshen
Mis. 330–23 *f·* the fragrance of being.

freshness
Mis. ix–21 fleeting *f·* of youth,
240– 6 must not take the sweet *f·* out
269–13 perpetual *f·* in relation to
343–18 vernal *f·* and sunshine

fresh-smiling
Po. 67– 7 bedewing these *f·* flowers !

fret
Un. 56–23 made to *f·* in their chains;
My. 135–28 "*F·* not thyself — *Psal.* 37 : 1.
211–25 *f·* and confuse it, spoiling that

fretful
My. 10–19 * *f·* or reluctant sacrifice

fretfulness
Mis. 6– 4 free from complaints and *f·*,

fretted
Mis. 162–10 over their *f·*, foaming billows.

friction
Mis. 104–20 the *f·* of false selfhood
224–20 the *f·* of the world

Friday
Mis. 148–24 at your *F·* evening meetings.
Man. 57– 3 held on the *F·* preceding

Friday
  Man. 57– 5   the first *F·* in November
  Pul. 85–24   * received *F·*, from the C. S. Board

Friend
  (*see* **Eddy**)

friend
  and foe
    Mis. 32–15   admissible towards *f·* and foe.
  best
    Mis. 236–21   though it be your best *f·* ;
         298–12   best *f·* break troth with me?
  earthly
    My. 358–11   your Leader and best earthly *f·*.
         361– 1   your healer, or any earthly *f·*.
  family
    Ret. 17– 1   while visiting a family *f·*
    Po. vii– 1   * *while visiting a family f·*
  happy
    Mis. 385–10   "Joy for thee, happy *f·* !
    Po. 48– 1   Joy for thee, happy *f·* !
  met friend
    My. 63–16   as *f·* met friend at every turn
  my
    Pul. 39–10   from my *f·*, Miss Whiting,
    My. 322–20   * During the evening my *f·* spoke of
  of mine
    Mis. 225– 5   his mother— a *f·* of mine,
  or foe
    Mis. 290–26   whether it be *f·* or foe,
    No. 3– 5   error murders either *f·* or foe
  our
    My. 14–18   * Our *f·* very promptly and
  trusty
    Mis. 147–22   at all times the trusty *f·*,
  without
    Mis. 227– 5   without *f·* and without apologist.
  your
    Mis. 364– 8   made the public your *f·*,
    My. 332–13   * Your *f·* and obedient servant,

    Mis. 89– 5   or a *f· in sickness, who is*
         118–13   and pass a *f·* over it smoothly,
         339–13   Hast thou a *f·*, and forgettest to be
         399–11   Strongest deliverer, *f·* of the
    Pul. 33–23   * so a *f·* has told me,
    Pan. 3– 7   a *f·*, with whom to whisper,
    Po. 75–18   Strongest deliverer, *f·* of the
    My. 14–11   * we received a letter from a *f·*
         322–15   a *f·* and I were the guests

friendless
  Mis. 399–11   friend of the *f·*,
  Po. 41– 9   And the mountains more *f·*,
      75–18   friend of the *f·*,

friendlessness
  Rud. 17–11   *f·*, toil, agonies, and

friendly
  Mis. 80–12   It is better to be *f·*
      294–17   O *f·* hand ! keep back thy
      330– 9   man, more *f·*, should call his
  My. 320–19   * but his tendency was *f·*.

friends (*see also* **friends'**)
  admires
    My. 41–20   * admires *f·* and hates enemies,
  and books
    Mis. vii– 5   * well made choice of *f·* and books ;
  and brethren
    Mis. 106–17   *F·* and Brethren : — Your Sunday Lesson,
        120–27   *F· and Brethren :—* The Biblical record
    My. 147– 2   *F· and Brethren :—* There are
  and country
    Mis. 251–11   religion, home, *f·*, and country.
  and enemies
    My. 276–12   all her dear *f·* and enemies.
  and followers
    Pul. 54–25   * with his closest *f·* and followers,
    My. 143–10   my beloved *f·* and followers
  beloved
    My. 42–13   * *Beloved F· :—* Most unexpectedly
       143–10   my beloved *f·* and followers
  best
    Mis. 9–13   are virtually thy best *f·*.
       267– 5   are the best *f·* to our growth.
  circle of
    Ret. 19–14   lamented by a large circle of *f·*
    My. 330–26   lamented by a large circle of *f·*
  concourse of
    Mis. 225– 3   happy concourse of *f·* had gathered
  departed
    Mis. 60–13   *departed f· — dead only in belief*
  faithful
    My. 321– 7   * your devoted and faithful *f·*,
  her
    Mis. 49– 7   Her *f·* employed a homœopathist,
       49– 9   opinion given to her *f·*,

friends
  her
    Po. vii– 8   * *When this became known to her f·*,
    My. 332– 1   * to restore her to her *f·*
       332–12   * in the fond embrace of her *f·*.
  indebted
    Mis. 228– 4   deemed at least indebted *f·*
  interested
    Pul. 80–13   * sent us by interested *f·*,
  literary
    '02. 15–26   I showed it to my literary *f·*,
    My. 324–23   * among his literary *f·*.
  loving
    Pul. 76–18   * the tribute of loving *f·*.
  my
    Mis. 178–27   My *f·*, I wished to be excused from
       180– 5   my *f·* were frightened
       213–14   May my *f·* and my enemies
    Po. 73– 1   inscribed to my *f·* in Lynn.
    My. 145–22   serve equally my *f·* and my enemies.
       174– 6   courtesy extended to my *f·*
       297–30   my *f·* have read Sibyl Wilbur's book,
  number of
    Ret. 7–20   * by a large number of *f·*,
  of a patient
    Mis. 282–21   If the *f·* of a patient desire
  other
    Pul. 37–20   * one or two other *f·* were gathered.
  our
    Mis. 11–19   whereby we love our *f·* ;
    Ret. 80–27   We love our *f·*, but ofttimes we
    My. 332– 8   * will our *f·* at Wilmington
  personal
    My. 138–12   students and trusted personal *f·*
  pitying
    Mis. 212–30   Pitying *f·* took down from the
  relatives and
    My. 331–19   * relatives and *f·* of the late
  remain
    '02. 2–25   Then why not remain *f·*,
  students and
    Mis. 137– 2   *My Dear Students and F· :*
       142–11   *Beloved Students and F· :*
  surrounded by
    My. 312–24   I was surrounded by *f·*,
  that forsake
    My. 258–22   and *f·* that forsake.
  their
    My. 76–11   * church members and their *f·*
  those
    My. 331–22   * those *f·* of the deceased
       333–23   * those *f·* who attended him during
  Thy
    My. 220–22   make them Thy *f·* ;
  thy
    Mis. vii– 7   * In making thy *f·* books,
  to Truth
    Mis. 319–29   faith and resolve are *f·* to Truth ;
  truest
    My. 213–10   are the truest *f·* of mankind,
  various
    Un. 27– 1   From various *f·* comes inquiry
  were requested
    My. 98–16   * *f·* were requested to send no
  without money or
    My. 312–10   * and entirely without money or *f·*.

    Mis. vii– 7   * and thy books *f·*.
        9–16   *f·* seem to sweeten life's cup
       89–13   *f·* have no faith in your method,
       142–30   as *f·* we can feel the touch of heart
       177–28   *F· :—* The homesick traveller in
       253– 6   *F·*, I am not enough the new woman
       308–18   *F·*, strangers, and
    Hea. 4–21   *F·*, can we ever arrive at a
       16–25   *F·*, it is of the utmost importance
    Po. 74– 1   *F·*, will not ye Think kindly of me,
    My. 27–15   * *f·* are requested to send no more
       44– 7   * *F·*, our progress may be fast or
       189–29   *F·*, why throng in pity round me?
       205–21   *f·* more faithful, and

friends'
  My. 275–21   praying for my dear *f·*

friendship (*see also* **friendship's**)
  Mis. 9–26   delicious forms of *f·*,
      100–23   Pure humanity, *f·*, home,
      145–18   In our rock-bound *f·*,
      251– 9   voicing the *f·* of this city
  Ret. 80–27   perfection and an unbroken *f·*.
      81– 7   our *f·* will surely continue.
      82–26   ecclesiastical fellowship and *f·*.
  Pul. 5– 6   light of one *f·* after another
  Po. 68–19   star of our *f·* arose
  My. 124–10   The fruition of *f·*,
      163–26   *f·*, and granite character.

friendship
My. 175–23 the f· of those we love,
201–11 Such elements of f·, faith,
282– 5 f· of our chief executive
362–21 * revere and cherish your f·,

friendship's
Mis. 143– 2 f· "level" and the "square"

friendships
Pul. 49–18 * talked earnestly of her f·.
My. 204– 7 mutual f· such as ours

frieze
Pul. 25–23 * with f· of the old rose,

fright
Pul. 34–14 * to their bewilderment and f·,

frighten
'01. 14–12 cannot be made so real as to f·

frightened
Mis. 180– 6 f· at beholding me restored
396– 3 And f· fancy flees,
Un. 5–12 undisturbed by the f· sense
Po. 58–15 And f· fancy flees,
My. 123–25 is not f· at miracles,

frightens
My. 160–14 a live truth, ... f· people.
216–12 a miracle that f· people,
233– 7 challenged by Truth, f· you,

fringed
Ret. 23– 8 was not even f· with light.

fringe-tree
Ret. 17–18 magnolia, and fragrant f· ;
Po. 63– 3 magnolia, and fragrant f· ;

frivolity
'00. 2–14 no time for amusement, ease, f· ;
My. 48–29 * drugged by scandal, drowned in f·,
260– 7 shadow of f· and the

frivolous
Ret. 21–25 personal events are f·

frocks
My. 83–11 * laces of the women's f·,

front
Mis. 23–29 actions of the object in f· of it.
99–17 take the f· rank, face the foe,
106– 9 Priestcraft in f· of them,
Un. 6–25 if hastily pushed to the f·
Pul. 24–10 * tower with a circular f·
24–12 * On the f· is a marble tablet,
59–30 * the f· vestibule and street
My. 31–19 * a place in the f· rank of the
31–26 * Stepping to the f· of the platform,
44–16 * advanced to the f· of the platform,
71–27 * in f· of the great organ,
89–16 * even to the flagstones in f·
110–15 mortal mind pressing to the f·,
313– 9 road in f· of his house

frost
Mis. 240–15 takes the f· out of the ground

froth
Mis. 78–21 f· of error passing off ;

frown
Pan. 1– 8 f· and smile of April,
'02. 17–28 world's soft flattery or its f·.
My. 129–10 no night but in God's f· ;
134–17 pride— its pomp and its f·
340–12 her f· on class legislation.

frowning
My. 355–19 * "Behind a f· providence

frozen
Mis. 176–21 f· ritual and creed should forever
331–23 f· crust of creed and dogma,
Ret. 31–28 F· fountains were unsealed.
No. 14–25 f· dogmas, persistent persecution,
Po. 41– 7 fountain and leaflet are f· and

fruit
bear
Mis. 144–27 may our earthly sowing bear f·
151– 8 Those who bear f· He purgeth,
My. 128–32 in your thought nor bear f·.
bearing
Mis. 357–18 and is bearing f·.
Un. 6– 3 "bearing f· after its kind."— see Gen. 1 : 11.
Pul. 26–24 * sprays of fig leaves bearing f·.
bears
Mis. 220–21 has power and bears f·,
borne
Mis. 356–17 has sprung up, borne f·,
bring forth
Mis. 154–24 Bring forth f·
eat the
My. 186–20 plant the vineyard eat the f·

fruit
forbidden
Un. 3–14 knowledge is not the forbidden f·
good
Mis. 235–14 bringeth not forth good f· ;
My. 287–22 bringeth not forth good f· ;
hothouse
My. 325– 4 * and to leave luscious hothouse f·.
its
Mis. 223–10 tree is known by its f· ;
My. 111–21 Is not the tree known by its f· ?
112–24 The tree is known by its f·.
269–20 vine is bringing forth its f· ;
300–28 The tree is known by its f·.
legitimate
'02. 14–14 growth and . . . are its legitimate f·
more
Mis. 151– 9 that they may bear more f·.
much
Ret. 94–29 Jesus' teachings bore much f·,
My. 202–29 that ye bear much f·."— John 15 : 8.
of evil
Un. 17–22 partake of the f· of evil,
of experience
My. 343–24 each one was the f· of experience
of Godlikeness
Un. 22– 5 may eat of the f· of Godlikeness,
of righteousness
My. 40–20 * the f· of righteousness— Jas. 3 : 18.
of rightness
My. 281– 9 is the f· of rightness,
of the Spirit
My. 167– 4 "the f· of the Spirit."— Gal. 5 : 22.
of the tree
Mis. 198–21 f· of the tree of the knowledge
367–15 this f· of the tree of knowledge
of this tree
Mis. 356–20 carry the f· of this tree into the
of ungodliness
Un. 22– 5 but as to the f· of ungodliness,
pudding, and
Mis. 231–14 delicious pie, pudding, and f·
rich
My. 159– 9 rich f· of this branch of his vine,
ripened
My. 198– 8 their abundant and ripened f·.

Un. 3–15 it is the f· which grows on the
My. 22–19 * justification of . . . is the f·.
218–26 f· of which all mankind may share.

fruitage
Mis. 251–28 to enrich the soil for f·.
308–24 I have gleaned from its f·
Po. 9– 9 leaves all faded, the f· shed,

fruite
Mis. 253–12 * chapter sub-title

fruitful
Mis. 56–25 f·, and multiply,— Gen. 1 : 28.
338–29 * Shall be a f· seed ;
343– 8 human life more f·,
'00. 3– 2 right, active, and they are f· ;
My. 183–19 the forest becomes a f· field,

fruition
Mis. 231– 2 the full f· of happiness ;
281– 1 the f· of your labors,
Ret. 92– 8 reach the f· of his promise :
Un. 61–23 both demonstration and f·,
Pul. 44– 3 * At last you begin to see the f·
No. 9–13 may err . . . and lose your f·.
My. 19–21 f· of her unselfed love,
124–10 The f· of friendship,
155–14 the full f· of its faith,
253–24 If faith is f·, you have His

fruitless
Pul. 33–22 * All inquiry . . . was f· ;
'01. 31–14 no vague, f·, inquiring wonder.
My. 294–17 by a f· use of the knife

fruits
blight the
Mis. 88– 1 to blight the f· of my students.
immortal
My. 182–15 sprang immortal f· through
its
My. 136– 5 is best explained by its f·,
136–26 labor that is known by its f·,
148– 5 judge our doctrine by its f·.
204–28 these are its f· ;
260–18 its f· are inspiration and
of Christian Science
Mis. 343–11 f· of C. S. spring upward,
My. 204–26 are not the f· of C. S.,
213– 1 f· of C. S. Mind-healing

fruits

of goodness
Mis. 219–29 *f·* of goodness will follow,
Ret. 54–13 without bearing the *f·* of goodness,

of health
Ret. 62– 5 bring forth better *f·* of health,

of Love
Mis. 100–15 finally show the *f·* of Love.
Un. 40– 8 and bears the *f·* of Love,

of Spirit
Mis. 153–18 bring forth the *f·* of Spirit,
303–10 peace and joy, the *f·* of Spirit,
331–10 will ripen the *f·* of Spirit,
Ret. 45–22 I saw these *f·* of Spirit,
Rud. 4–23 brings out the *f·* of Spirit

of the flesh
'02. 6– 6 *f·* of the flesh not Spirit.

of Truth
Mis. 265–20 bring forth the real *f·* of Truth.

of watchfulness
Mis. 116–23 *f·* of watchfulness, prayer,

of your ground
My. 269–25 *f·* of your ground.'' — *Mal. 3 : 11.*

of your labors
'00. 2–28 what of the *f·* of your labors?

prove
Mis. 354–14 whose *f·* prove the nature of their

purpose, and
Mis. 223– 2 its hidden paths, purpose, and *f·*

their
Mis. 90–20 then judge them by their *f·*.
Man. 49– 6 ''by their *f·* ye shall — *Matt. 7 : 20.*
No. 15– 2 ''By their *f·* ye shall — *Matt. 7 : 20.*
Pan. 10– 5 ''By their *f·* ye shall — *Matt. 7 : 20.*
My. 233– 4 ''by their *f·* ye shall — *Matt. 7 : 20.*
306–19 ''By their *f·* ye shall — *Matt. 7 : 20.*

My. 136–25 the *f·* of honest toil,
283–12 *f·* of said grand Association,
309–32 what were the *f·* of this

Frye
C. A.
Ret. 49–31 signature
Mr. Calvin A.
My. 138–14 Mr. Calvin A. *F·* and other students
317–16 Mr. Calvin A. *F·* copied my writings,

fuel
Hea. 9–14 furnishing *f·* for the flames.

fugitive
Peo. 10– 8 succored a *f·* slave in 1853,

fulfil
Mis. 29–28 on the contrary, they *f·* His laws ;
39–24 *f·* the law of Christ.'' — *Gal. 6 : 2.*
122–10 to *f·* a divine decree,
135–12 If you falter, or fail to *f·* this
183–15 man can *f·* the Scriptures
212– 1 *f·* the conditions of our petition
261–10 ''but to *f·* — *Matt. 5 : 17.*
278– 6 I shall *f·* my mission,
284–31 to *f·* that trust those rules must be
297–21 *f·* all the claims growing out of this
318–18 so *f·* the command of Christ.
Man. 28–18 If an officer fails to *f·* all the
29– 8 *f·* the requirements of this By-Law,
100–10 *f·* the obligations of his office
Ret. 38–11 to *f·* this painful task,
45–22 *f·* the law of Christ
47–22 so *f·* the command of Christ.
70–15 No person can compass or *f·*
90–12 until they were able to *f·* his
Un. 13– 6 *f·* the intended harmony of being.
Pul. 72– 1 * having a divine mission to *f·*,
83– 3 * what we never *f·* as husband and
No. 45–23 and so *f·* her destiny.
Pan. 12– 1 it will be found possible to *f·* it.
'02. 5–24 but to *f·*. — *Matt. 5 : 17.*
7–10 to *f·* the First Commandment.
My. 46–19 * *f·* the pledge in righteous living,
153– 5 will *f·* the law in righteousness.
153– 7 have come to *f·* the whole law.
162– 4 *f·* all righteousness.'' — *Matt. 3 : 15.*
217–31 but to *f·* it in righteousness.
218– 4 *f·* all righteousness.'' — *Matt. 3 : 15.*
219–25 but to *f·*.'' — *Matt. 5 : 17.*

fulfilled
Mis. 8–28 can only be *f·* through the
84–10 but the prophecies were *f·*,
141– 1 will be the prophecy *f·*,
286– 2 has already been *f·*.
308–21 *f·* its mission, retired with honor
358–30 When students have *f·* all the
Ret. 48–21 *f·* its high and noble destiny,
Un. 43–17 till all be *f·*.'' — *Matt. 5 : 18.*
Pul. 5–20 *That prophecy is f·.*

fulfilled
Pul. 13– 7 *f·*, when we are conscious of
29–21 * interpreted and *f·* literally,
73–15 * God has *f·* His promises to her
No. 13– 8 and the prophecy of Jesus *f·*,
37–28 and it must be *f·*.
Pan. 12–12 Scriptural commands be *f·*.
'00. 12–20 This prophecy has been *f·*.
'01. 10–30 After Jesus had *f·* his mission
'02. 4– 8 a more *f·* life and spiritual
8– 4 and both will be *f·*.
9–15 every promise *f·*, was loving and
18–23 prophecy of the great Teacher is *f·*
My. 36–28 * have *f·* a high resolve
44–11 * rejoices in prophecy *f·*,
125–30 The doom . . . is being *f·*.
171– 3 To-day is *f·* the prophecy of Isaiah :
177–23 this prophecy of Isaiah is *f·*
193–27 may the prophecy of Isaiah be *f·*:
202–11 hath *f·* the law.'' — *Rom. 13 : 8.*

fulfilling
Mis. 11– 3 Love is the *f·* of the law :
12–30 *f·* the law of Love,
155–27 thus *f·* their moral obligation to
258– 2 love is the *f·* of the law.
262– 5 aid our prospect of *f·* it by
285– 9 Love is the *f·* of the law.
304–20 * *f·* its mission throughout the
Ret. 65–23 Love, *f·* the law
'02. 9–11 *f·* the apostle's saying :
My. 131–23 *f·* much of the divine law
190–31 who are *f·* Jesus' prophecy
201– 3 and is fast *f·* the promises.

fulfilment
Mis. 76–30 the *f·* of this glorious prophecy
85–13 in the *f·* of this divine rule
136–14 and its *f·* of divine order.
192–22 The *f·* of the grand verities of
208– 4 Mortals cannot prevent the *f·* of
Pul. 9–11 and nerved its grand *f·*.
35– 7 * natural *f·* of divine law
My. 45–24 * the *f·* of the later prophecy,
132– 1 *f·* of divine Love in our lives
133– 4 might and light of the present *f·*.

fulfils
Mis. 66– 4 *f·* the law in righteousness,
73–16 Belief *f·* the conditions of a belief,
117–15 it *f·* the law.
209–10 belief *f·* the law of belief,
Ret. 76–16 *f·* the law of Love which Paul
'02. 6–18 *f·* the law in righteousness,
6–29 *f·* the law and the gospel,
My. 106– 4 love *f·* divine law
265–23 *f·* the saying of our great Master,
275–25 self-oblivious love *f·* the law

full
Mis. 16–13 reflect the *f·* dominion of Spirit
45– 3 The *f·* understanding that God is
46–21 *f·* significance of what the apostle
56–19 the *f·* revelation of Spirit,
80–18 and *f·* of trouble.'' — *Job 14 : 1.*
95– 7 * which reply was taken in *f·*
111– 6 net has been so *f·* that it broke :
119–19 *f·* exemption from all necessity to
147–27 *f·* of truth, candor, and
149–12 *f·* of accessions to your love,
151–25 lamp of your life continually be *f·*
164–26 *f·* of grace and Truth,
192–18 Principle of a *f·* salvation.
193–25 following his *f·* command
197– 6 the *f·* import of this text is not yet
197– 7 It means a *f·* salvation,
214– 2 While Jesus' life was *f·* of Love,
220–13 Thought has the *f·* control
222–19 suffer its *f·* penalty after death.
223–16 *f·* faith in the divine Principle,
227–28 grows into the *f·* stature of wisdom,
231– 2 and the *f·* fruition of happiness ;
261–12 pays his *f·* debt to divine law,
261–13 *f·*, pressed down, and
263–22 without a *f·* knowledge of the
270–18 have *f·* faith in his prophecy,
276–14 the *f·* coming of our Lord and Christ.
292–25 C. S., *f·* of grace and truth,
311–10 go forth to the *f·* vintage-time,
311–12 in the *f·* spirit of that charity
314–24 announcing the *f·* title of this book,
331– 1 crown the *f·* corn in the ear,
331– 6 *f·* of good odor,
338–25 * To give the lips *f·* speech.
357–24 should receive *f·* fellowship from us,
361–11 earth is *f·* of His glory,
377– 4 yet so near and *f·* of radiant relief
394–20 * So *f·* of sweet enchantment

full

Man.	27– 8	without consulting with the f· Board
	32–13	announce the f· title of the book
	39– 5	received into f· membership,
	39– 7	A f· member or a probationary member,
	110–13	given names of each, written in f·.
	111– 3	names must be written in f·.
Chr.	55–14	few days, and f· of trouble. — Job 14 : 1.
Ret.	2–24	contained a f· account of the
	15–20	if not in f· unity of doctrine.
	92– 6	the f· corn in the ear.'' — Mark 4 : 28.
Un.	51–23	the f· Truth is found only in
	58–16	f· compass of human woe,
Pul.	4–25	with it cometh the f· power of being.
	9– 6	the f· chords of such a rest.
	33–15	* Catholic biographies are f·,
	41– 4	* after the f· amount needed was
	44–12	* comprehends its f· significance.
	81–20	* she is as f· of beautiful possibilities
Rud.	14–15	to take the f· price of tuition
No.	22–24	as a mortal who is f· of evil.
	31–13	the only f· proof of its pardon.
'00.	7–29	wait for the f· appearing
	14– 6	f· numbers of days named
	14–18	hold in your f· hearts fervently
'01.	32– 8	F· of charity and good works,
'02.	9– 8	f· significance of this saying
Peo.	9–19	f· confidence in their efficacy,
	11– 1	f· liberty of the sons of God
Po.	57– 6	* So f· of sweet enchantment
My.	vi– 9	* only as they give her f· credit
	11– 8	* the f· force of antagonism.
	96–22	* fund was f· to overflowing
	107–13	a vial f· of the pellets
	149–18	vessel f· must be emptied
	150–12	can accomplish the f· scale ;
	155–14	finds the f· fruition of its faith,
	167–17	f· of love, peace, and good will
	201–13	I thank you out of a f· heart.
	204–24	charging . . . a f· fee for treatment,
	205–26	f· idea of its divine Principle,
	210– 5	added to the mind already f·.
	215–11	sent me the f· tuition money.
	224–19	giving f· credit to another
	236– 3	accept my f· heart's love
	237– 8	not attained the f· understanding
	256–17	f· of divine benedictions and
	261– 6	f· supply of juvenile joy.
	280–17	and cease in f· faith that God
	284–25	f· efficacy of divine Love to
	294–12	f· faith and spiritual knowledge
	323–17	* My heart has been too f· to
	332–23	* as we had f· confidence that it
	333–25	* f· reliance for salvation on the
	338–19	a heart f· of love towards God
	340–30	f· beneficence of the laws of the

fuller

Mis.	320– 7	Christ's appearing in a f· sense

fullest

Mis.	169–32	In their f· meaning,
	223–21	name of Christ in its f· sense,
	303–11	brethren in the f· sense
	306– 2	* f· historical description.

full-fledged

Mis.	335–13	charge upon me with f· invective
My.	281– 7	Faith f·, soaring to the

full-length

Pul.	27– 2	* with f· French mirrors

full-orbed

Mis.	355– 3	f· promise, and a gaunt want.
No.	37–12	unfolds the f· glory of that event;
	46–19	f· significance of this destiny
'01.	8–10	but it is not the f· sun.
My.	265–15	to appear f· in millennial glory ;

fully

Mis.	102–20	f· expressed in divine Science,
	169–17	borne f· to our minds and hearts.
	185– 3	discern f· and demonstrate fairly
	187–17	f· comprehended the later teachings
	292–28	who f· understood my instructions
Man.	47– 6	case he cannot f· diagnose,
	66– 2	which he does not f· understand,
Ret.	27–13	had not f· voiced my discovery.
	84– 3	sufficiently . . . to be f· demonstrated.
	93–21	has not been f· demonstrated.
Un.	40–21	to him who f· understands Life.
	56–19	not f· exempt from physicaiity
Pul.	44– 6	* You are f· occupied,
	54–22	* they are f· set forth.
	69–16	* take a small book to explain f·
	69–20	* power f· developed to heal
	87–15	f· appreciate your kind intentions.
Rud.	14– 9	f· seven-eighths of her time

fully

No.	20–12	f· conveys the ideas of God,
	27–12	f· interpreted by divine Science,
My.	25– 3	* to dispose f· and finally of
	87–16	* their costly church f· paid for,
	91– 8	* church edifices to be f· paid for
	112–19	f· understood when demonstrated.
	136– 4	cannot be f· understood,
	146–16	are not f· scaled.
	240– 7	* to explain more f· why you
	242– 8	Unless you f· perceive that
My.	267– 2	since Christianity is f· demonstrated
	286– 9	wisely, fairly ; and f· settled.
	338– 9	* her writings will f· corroborate

fulness

Mis.	15–25	f· of the stature of man
	172–14	arrives at f· of stature ;
Pul.	85– 7	* will, in the f· of time, see
No.	19–24	f· of the stature of man
'01.	11– 1	f· of his stature in Christ,
'02.	20– 9	with the f· of divine Love.''
Po.	vii– 4	* f· in her later productions.
My.	33–28	and the f· thereof ; — Psal. 24 : 1.
	357– 3	the spiritual f· of God,

function

Un.	34– 8	whole f· of material sight
Hea.	19– 4	every f· of the body,
My.	249–26	perform this important f·.

functional

Rud.	13– 2	hence Life is not f·,
Pan.	10–18	heal f·, organic, chronic,
My.	106– 1	in f· and organic diseases

functions

Mis.	260–27	performs the vital f·
Man.	28–16	f· of their several offices
	29–12	perform their f· faithfully.
	65–17	applies to their official f·.
	82– 6	connected with these f·.
Pan.	4– 9	the f· of these faculties
Hea.	19– 6	else those f· could not
My.	218– 2	its normal action, f·, and
	288–19	to perform the f· of Spirit,
	301–27	restore disordered f·,
	303–30	love to perform the f· of

fund (see also Building Fund)

building

Pul.	9– 1	into the building f· have come
	42–12	* contributors to the building f·,
My.	14–15	* building f· had been paid in ;
	14–24	* the building f· is not complete,
	14–30	* contributions to the building f·
	16– 3	* treasurer of the building f·
	19–15	* The Mother Church building f·,
	19–30	towards its church building f·.
	20–15	The Mother Church building f·,
	20–27	* building f· of The Mother Church
	21– 1	* contribute to the building f·
	21–12	* contribute . . . to the building f·
	22–11	* further needs of the building f·,
	24–31	* completing the building f·
	25– 9	* contributions to the building f·.
	27–11	* contributors to the building f·
	27–24	* treasurer of the building f·,
	28– 7	* contributed to the building f·.
	72–18	* treasurer of the building f·
	76– 9	* contributions to the building f·
	86–15	* building f· of the great temple

Man.	78–22	as a petty cash f·,
My.	10–11	* paid in towards the f·,
	21– 5	* transferring to this f· the money
	27–16	* no more money to this f·.
	28–13	* the giving to this f· has
	96–22	* f· was full to overflowing
	176– 4	Concord (N. H.) Street F·
	216–25	The Mother Church flower f·.
	289– 5	De Hirsch monument f·.
	318–28	f· of historical knowledge,

fundamental

Mis.	75– 8	I urge this f· fact
	172–28	first and f· rule of Science
	186–21	torn apart from its f· basis.
	221– 8	f· Principle of C. S. ;
	233– 1	without knowing its f· Principle.
Ret.	31–16	f· error of faith in things material
	49–11	f· principle for growth in C. S.
Pul.	69–17	* f· idea is that God is Mind,
'00.	4–30	enunciates this f· fact
'01.	3–18	f·, intelligent, divine Being,
My.	260–20	f· and demonstrable truth,
	268– 6	some f· error is engrafted
	297–23	f· truth of C. S.
	347–23	chapter sub-title

fundamentals
My. 75– 3 * its faith in its *f.*

funds
Man. 30–17 shall pay from the Church *f.*
  75– 1 heading
  75–21 the balance of the building *f.*,
  76– 1 balance of the church building *f.*,
  76– 6 management of the Church *f.* :
  76–11 *f.* which the Church has on hand,
  76–23 and the amount of *f.* received
  76–25 individually responsible for said *f.*.
  77–11 If it be found that the Church *f.*
  77–16 proper distribution of the *f.*
  78–18 pay from the *f.* of the Church
  79–11 shall be paid from the Church *f.*.
  80– 4 Disposal of *F.*.
  91–15 Surplus *F.*.
  91–15 Any surplus *f.* left in the
Ret. 53– 2 and the *f.* belonging thereto.
Pul. 44–27 * until the custodian of *f.*
  64– 6 * securing sufficient *f.* for
  64–11 * the custodian of the *f.* was
'*02.* 13– 6 my personal property and *f.*,
  13–15 when a loss of *f.* occurred,
My. 19–14 * their local church building *f.*
  27–14 * sufficient *f.* have been received
  27–23 * sufficient *f.* have been received
  58– 4 * no more *f.* are needed
  98–19 * the *f.* required to build it

fungus
Mis. 131– 3 a *f.*, a microbe, a mouse

fur
Mis. 329–22 the *f.* cap on pussy-willow,

furious
Po. 43– 8 Fondling e'en the lion *f.*,

furnace
Mis. 151– 8 through the *f.* of affliction.
  278–17 are tried in the *f.*
'*02.* 19–26 triumphed in *f.* fires.
My. 269–18 molten in the *f.* of Soul.
  303–32 molten in the *f.* of affliction.

furnish
Mis. 155–28 to *f.* some reading-matter
  157–11 *f.* all information possible.
  247–10 to *f.* a single instance of
Man. 30–19 suitably *f.* the house,
  89–22 *f.* evidence of their eligibility
No. 9–20 "*f.* a table in — *Psal.* 78 : 19.
My. 166–11 with which to *f.* First Church
  173–14 to help *f.* and beautify our
  180– 1 *f.* rules whereby man can

furnished
Mis. 10–10 *f.* them defenses impregnable.
Man. 111–20 will be *f.* special forms
Un. 46–26 *f.* the battle-ground of
Pul. 58–28 * *f.* with all conveniences
Rud. 14–19 *f.* students with the means
No. 2–19 Institutes *f.* with such teachers
'*00.* 12–11 *f.* items concerning this city.
'*02.* 12–30 I *f.* the money from my own
Hea. 16–18 is *f.* by these senses ;
My. 123–15 *f.* him the money to pay for it.
  156–10 upper room *f.* : — *Luke* 22 : 12.
  342– 1 * the ample, richly *f.* house

furnishes
Mis. 242–18 C. S. that *f.* its own proof.
  258–27 *f.* man with the only suitable
  350–31 *f.* its own proof of my practice.
Ret. 57– 4 *f.* a scientific basis for the
My. 218– 6 *f.* reasons or examples for the

furnishing
Ret. 50–27 *f.* a new rule of order
Pul. 76– 5 * The *f.* of the "Mother's Room"
Hea. 9–14 like *f.* fuel for the flames.
My. 118–20 *f.* the demands upon the finite
  162–14 embellishing, and *f.* our church

furnishings
Pul. 23– 6 * Beautiful Temple and Its *F.*

furniture
Mis. 283– 7 unlock the desk, displace the *f.*,
Pul. 76–11 * *f.* frames are of white mahogany

furrow
Mis. 339–19 added one *f.* to the brow of care?

further
Mis. 4–16 *F.* enlightenment is necessary
  68–31 is a *f.* definition.
  201–28 bar his door against *f.* robberies.
  244– 8 He *f.* states that God cannot

further
Mis. 245–25 to go no *f.* in the direction of
  295– 9 anonymous talker *f.* declares,
  302–23 desist from *f.* copying of my
Man. 102–11 *f.* purchases of land
Ret. 6–30 *f.* political preferment,
Un. 36–16 A *f.* proof of this is the
Pul. vii–19 scan *f.* the features of the
  30– 2 * I was *f.* told that once
  37–11 * *f.* writings on C. S.
  44–28 * refused to accept any *f.* checks
  64–12 * refuse *f.* contributions,
My. 14–16 * *f.* payments or subscriptions
  20–26 * *f.* fact that it is important
  22–11 * *f.* needs of the building fund,
  42–11 * *f.* words of mine are unnecessary.
  50–17 * as the records *f.* relate,
  56–26 * still *f.* provision must be made,
  148– 1 must not expect me *f.* to
  217– 4 *F.* to encourage your
  319– 5 heard nothing *f.* from him
  328–28 * The section, ... *f.* says,
  333–10 * record this *f.* proceeding :
  334–17 * Nothing could be *f.* from
  334–26 * Of *f.* interest in this matter

furtherance
Ret. 50–25 *f.* and unfolding of Truth,
'*02.* 9– 2 gives man power with untold *f.*.
My. 45– 2 * for the *f.* of our Cause,
  212–32 in *f.* of unscrupulous designs.

furthermore
Man. 98–11 *F.*, the Committee on Publication

fury
Po. vi–16 *such f. that the city authorities*

fused
Mis. 305–22 * copper, and nickel can be *f.*.
  305–25 * to be *f.* into the bell,

fusing
Rud. 16–25 *f.* with a class of aspirants

fusion
No. 5–26 Any contradictory *f.* of

fussing
My. 71– 8 * no need of *f.* about the

fustian
My. 143–14 Above all this *f.* of either

futile
Mis. 118–29 attempt of evil to harm good is *f.*,

future
Mis. 7–20 to be depicted in some *f.* time
  12–11 the *f.*, big with events.
  61– 4 The education of the *f.* will be
  100– 8 Past, present, *f.*, will show the
  139–26 transaction will in *f.* be regarded
  148–20 destined for *f.* generations
  230– 6 If one would be successful in the *f.*,
  253–15 and portends much for the *f.*.
  264–23 the *f.* mental influence of their
  281–32 You will need, in *f.*, *practice*
  285–22 In the present or *f.*,
  285–30 will have no past, present, or *f.*.
  286– 8 We look to *f.* generations for
  339– 9 robes the *f.* with hope's rainbow
  368– 8 * Yet that scaffold sways the *f.*,
Man. 3–18 destined for *f.* generations
  77–23 Provision for the *F.*.
  77–24 any possible *f.* deviation
Pul. 7–13 were but enshrined for *f.* use,
  65– 8 * may have a *f.* before it,
  84–21 * the *f.* will tell the story
No. 28–16 The present, as well as the *f.*,
Pan. 10–15 present and *f.* of those students
'*01.* 16– 3 chapter sub-title
  16– 4 a *f.* and eternal punishment
  31– 8 in the near *f.* will learn
'*02.* 4–24 past, present, and *f.*.
Hea. 2–26 Past, present, *f.* magnifies his
My. vi–23 * *f.* profits to her church ;
  12–20 We own no past, no *f.*,
  13– 2 on the past, present, nor *f.*,
  14– 6 to be discerned in the near *f.*
  22–22 * needs of the present and of the *f.*
  43–17 * In *f.* generations when it was asked,
  48–13 * the *f.* growth of her church,
  52–22 * to be Mrs. Eddy's *f.* reputation
  85–21 * for *f.* generations to reverence
  187– 4 at some near *f.* visit your city,
  220–24 Past, present, or *f.* philosophy
  224–13 *f.* must disclose and dispel.
  325–10 * as having a greater *f.*
  346–27 would be my *f.* successor.

G

Gabriel
Hea. 20– 6   * vie with *G·*, while he sings,

gagged
Mis. 274–17   When the press is *g·*,

gain (noun)
Mis.   6–24   once convinced . . . the *g·* is rapid.
    84–20   *and to die is g·." — Phil.* 1 : 21
  116–17   express life's loss or *g·*,
  288–21   reckon the universal cost and *g·*,
  321– 8   *g·* of Truth's idea in C. S. ;
  358– 7   their *g·* is loss to the . . . Scientist.
  389–17   since God is good, and loss is *g·*.
Pul. vii–13   *g·* of intellectual momentum,
'00.   3– 8   to distribute *g·*."
'02. 17–20   Then thy *g·* outlives the sun,
Po.   4–16   since God is good, and loss is *g·*.
My. 252–31   cold impulse of a lesser *g·* !

gain (verb)
Mis. 33–18   Patients naturally *g·* confidence in C. S.
  38– 3   ability to *g·* and maintain health,
  40–23   must *g·* the power over sin
  50–16   *g·* the spiritual understanding of
  53– 9   *g·* heaven, the harmony of being.
  65–15   to *g·* the true solution of Life
  86–19   until we *g·* the glorified sense of
  104–28   or would not *g·* the true ideal of Life
  104–30   I will *g·* a balance on the side of
  111–12   *g·* a higher sense of the true idea.
  116–18   *g·* of its sweet concord,
  172–28   To *g·* this scientific result,
  174–26   whereby to *g·* heaven.
  181–27   in the proportion that they *g·* the
  186–18   but *g·* it clearly ;
  203–20   *g·* severe views of themselves ;
  215– 8   *g·* a spiritual understanding
  226–18   asked what a person could *g·* by
  227– 1   traffic by which he can *g·* nothing.
  234– 9   we *g·* a true sense of Love as God ;
  254–16   *g·* the kingdom of God.
  270–16   *G·* a pure Christianity ;
  311–16   *g·* the abiding consciousness of
  341–19   and you find Life eternal : you *g·* all.
  389–24   aftersmile earth's tear-drops *g·*,
Ret. 34– 3   to *g·* the Science of Mind,
  38–28   must also *g·* its spiritual significance,
  45–13   *g·* spiritual freedom and supremacy.
  55– 4   *g·* sufficient knowledge of error
Un.   2–18   *g·* that spiritual sense of harmony
  4– 7   To *g·* a temporary consciousness of
  13–12   as we *g·* the true understanding
  14– 8   *g·* wisdom and power from past
Pul.   9–28   *g·* the ear and right hand of
  50–27   * will *g·* followers and live down any
  69–24   * may *g·* a better understanding than
No. 23–16   Which . . . is the more important to *g·*,
  34– 4   when we *g·* the truer sense
'01.   1–24   to *g·* the absolute and supreme
  7–26   nor can they *g·* any evidence of
'02. 10–15   *g·* the scope of Jacob's vision,
Hea.   4–22   *g·* a right idea of the Principle
  16–22   evidence through which we can *g·* no
  16–26   *g·* our evidences of Life from
Po.   5– 5   aftersmile earth's tear-drops *g·*,
  43–19   Till they *g·* at last
My. 39– 2   * *g·* admittance at that hour
  48–21   * build such truth as they do *g·*
  79–12   * to *g·* admission to the temple
  148–27   struggling to *g·* power over
  194–11   *g·* greatness who *g·* themselves
  246–11   to *g·* a higher hope for the race,
  253– 9   manhood's glorious crown to *g·*."
  287–15   In love for man we *g·* the only

gained
Mis. vii–15   Nothing have we *g·* therefrom,
  10–17   *g·* by crossing swords with
  24–21   knowledge *g·* from mortal sense
  43–17   letter is *g·* sooner than the spirit
  80– 3   you lose much more than can be *g·*
  107–14   Three cardinal points must be *g·*
  126–11   We also have *g·* higher heights ;
  206–11   are *g·* through growth, not
  226– 9   What has an individual *g·* by
  234– 7   nor *g·* by a culpable attempt to
  278–27   the sooner this lesson is *g·*
  293–10   *g·* from instruction, observation,
  298– 2   Nothing is *g·* by wrong-doing.
  338– 3   must have *g·* its height beforehand,
  347–24   and the summit can be *g·*.
  353–10   you have *g·* the right one
Ret. 10– 3   *g·* book-knowledge with far less
  24– 9   I *g·* the scientific certainty

gained
Ret. 30–23   neither can . . . be *g·* without
Un.   5– 4   understanding they have already *g·*
  51– 9   *g·* through Christ as perfect
  55–17   *g·* him the assurance that
Pul. 79–11   * *g·* to itself adherents
No.   8–28   *g·* from your forbearance.
  12– 1   C. S. Mind-healing can only be *g·* by
'00. 10–10   *g·* fresh energy and final victory.
Peo.   2–15   evidences *g·* from the material
  13– 8   understanding is *g·* in C. S.,
My. 181–23   *g·* from a population of 238,000 to
  278–22   Nothing is *g·* by fighting,
  349– 5   consciousness *g·* through Christ,

gaining
Mis. 113–12   not *g·* a higher sense of Truth
  160–10   knowing that one is *g·* constantly
  327–19   Despairing of *g·* the summit,
Ret. 54–10   *g·* the end through persecution and
My. 233– 1   *g·* the spirit of true watching,

gains
Mis. 17–31   *g·* a truer sense of Spirit
  41–15   *g·* the summit in Science
  43–12   sense one *g·* of this Science
  182–11   man *g·* the power to become the
  221– 5   *g·* in the rules of metaphysics,
  252– 5   *g·* no potency by attenuation,
  298–28   *g·* freedom from pain
Ret. 76–23   *g·* the God-crowned summit of C. S.
Un.   2–12   *g·* a higher sense of God,
  36– 8   and *g·* a knowledge of God
Pan. 12–20   *g·* and points the path.
My. 83–29   * made steady *g·* in recent years.
  112– 4   where Science *g·* no hearing.
  161–14   He who *g·* self-knowledge,
  188–31   When divine Love *g·* admittance to
  297–16   *g·* a rich blessing of disbelief in

gainsaid
No. 16–11   positives that cannot be *g·*.
  28–21   What is . . . true cannot be *g·* ;

gainsay
Mis. 265–14   Nobody can *g·* this.

'gainst
Mis. 397–11   *'G·* which the winds and waves
Pul. 18–20   *'G·* which the winds and waves
Po. 12–20   *'G·* which the winds and waves

Galatians
Ret. 76–17   Paul enjoined upon the *G·*.

gales
Mis. 385–13   *g·* celestial, in sweet music bore
Po. 48– 6   *g·* celestial, in sweet music bore

Galilean
'00.   4– 7   teaching of the righteous *G·*,

Galilean Prophet
Man. 16– 3   as demonstrated by the *G· P·*
'02. 11–27   Jews put to death the *G· P·*,
My. 111– 6   master Metaphysician, the *G· P·*,
  220–26   example of the great *G· P·*,
  261–27   Jesus, the *G· P·*, was born of
  288–12   The great *G· P·* was,
  319– 1   such a person as the *G· P·*,

Galilee
Pan.   8– 6   Jesus, the man of *G·*,

Galileo
Mis. 99– 7   It cost *G·*, what?
  269– 3   *G·* virtually lost it.
Peo. 13–15   *G·* kneeling at the feet of

gall
Mis. 237–11   earth gives them such a cup of *g·*
Ret. 26– 6   "vinegar and *g·*," — *see Matt.* 27 : 34.

gallant
Ret.   3– 6   *g·* leadership and death,

galleries
Pul. 25–13   * *g·* are in plaster relief,
  26– 5   * *g·* are richly panelled
  58–16   * auditorium has wide *g·*,
My. 69–16   * auditorium contains seven *g·*,
  71–23   * five thousand . . . on floor and *g·*.
  71–25   * either on floor or *g·*,
  78–13   * mahogany pews and in triple *g·*.

gallery
Pul. 26– 6   * organ and choir *g·* is spacious
  27–27   * In the *g·* are windows
  42–19   * On the wall of the choir *g·*
My. 59–13   * *g·* of that magnificent temple,
  95–11   * the press *g·* of commentators.

Gallic
    Po.   2– 8 falcon in the *G·* van,

gamesters
    My. 203–14 hero is a mark for *g·*,

gamut
    Mis. 295– 7 * a *g·* of isms and ists,

gap
    My. 200–25 Wide yawns the *g·* between

garbling
    No. 43–23 Stealing or *g·* my statements

garden
    Mis. 109–19 Adam and Eve in the *g·* of Eden.
    Un. 21–11 every tree of the *g·*." — *Gen.* 3 : 1.

gardener
    Mis. 343–22 O stupid *g·* ! watch their

gardens
    Mis. 343–13 clearing the *g·* of thought

Garfield, President
    Mis. 112–16 assassin of President *G·*,

garlanded
    My. 124– 8 *g·* with glad faces,

garment (*see also* **garment's**)
    Mis. 75– 2 touched the hem of the *g·*
        97–17 touch the hem of His *g·* ;
     153–16 covereth men as a *g·*,
     233–13 put into the old *g·* of drugging
    Pul. 65–23 * gave half of the *g·* to a
    No. 22– 3 touched the hem of the Christ *g·*.
    '00. 8–12 and wear the purloined *g·*
      15– 1 Putting aside the old *g·*,
      15–20 a wedding *g·* new and old,
      15–21 touch of the hem of this *g·*
    '01. 2– 7 trying to put into the *old g·*
    Hea. 16–15 touch but the hem of Truth's *g·*.
    My. 108–21 the *g·* of Christian Scientists,
     206–10 they divide Truth's *g·*
     351–12 touches the hem of his *g·*

garment's
    Pul. 53–29 * power that filled his *g·* hem

garments
    Mis. 142– 1 how beautiful are her *g·* !
     299–18 *g·* that are on sale,
     299–21 These *g·* are Mr. Smith's ;
     299–28 saves your purchasing these *g·*,
     376– 9 * the figure and *g·* from a
    Ret. 45– 3 more beautiful became the *g·*
      86–11 wanderer's soiled *g·*,
    Pul. 22–20 put on her most beautiful *g·*,
    Pan. 1–12 outgrown, wornout, or soiled *g·*
    My. 67–11 * Checking facilities . . . 3,000 *g·*
     125–25 put on her beautiful *g·*

garner
    Mis. 313–22 *g·* the supplies for a world.
    Pul. 1–11 *g·* the memory of 1894 ;

garnered
    Ret. 71–25 before the wheat can be *g·*
    Po. v– 1 * *g· up in this little volume*
    My. 291–25 sheaves *g·*, her treasury filled,

garnet
    Mis. 376–28 opal, *g·*, turquoise, and sapphire

Garrison
    William Lloyd
    Po. vi–16 *the person of William Lloyd G·*

    Mis. 237–26 streets through which *G·* was dragged

garrisoned
    My. 127–24 *g·* by God's chosen ones,

garrisons
    Mis. 303– 9 *g·* these strongholds of C. S.,

garrulity
    '01. 16–23 to handle with *g·* age and

garrulous
    Mis. 127–27 Wise sayings and *g·* talk

gas
    Mis. 347– 4 action of pent-up *g.*

gastric
    Mis. 243–29 secretions of the *g·* juice,

gastritis
    My. 107–31 removes enteritis, *g·*, hyperæmia,

gate
    '02. 18– 1 at the temple *g·* of conscience,
    My. 132–19 Divine Love hath opened the *g·*

gates
    Mis. 30–12 *g·* thereof he declared were inlaid
     141– 8 "the *g·* of hell" — *Matt.* 16 : 18.
     144–20 the *g·* of hell — *Matt.* 16 : 18.
     146– 3 and her *g·* with praise !

gates
    Mis. 150–13 and loveth the *g·* of Zion.
     185–20 opens the *g·* of paradise
     275–19 throw wide the *g·* of heaven.
     394–16 * The *g·* of memory unbar :
     394–19 * I fain would keep the *g·* ajar,
    Ret. 71– 3 to open the *g·* of heaven.
      79–28 its spiritual *g·* not captured,
      86–11 within thy *g·*." — *Exod.* 20 : 10.
    No. 38–11 against which the *g·* of hell
    '00. 12–12 its *g·*, whence the Ephesian elders
    Po. 57– 2 * The *g·* of memory unbar :
      57– 5 * I fain would keep the *g·* ajar,
    My. 3– 9 enter in through the *g·* — *Rev.* 22 : 14.
      34–10 your heads, O ye *g·* ; — *Psal.* 24 : 9.
      72– 5 * chapter sub-title
      72– 6 * The *g·* of Boston are open wide

Gath
    My. 123–13 "Tell it not in *G·*" ! — *II Sam.* 1 : 20.

gather
    Mis. 27–17 "Do men *g·* grapes of — *Matt.* 7 : 16.
      82–11 grasp and *g·* — in all glory
     106–21 and *g·* up the fragments.
     146–21 I would *g·* every reformed mortal
     149–11 *g·* up the fragments,
     215–31 must not try to *g·* the harvest while
     273–13 and *g·* all my students, in the
     336–17 we *g·* not grapes of thorns,
     355–26 Let no clouds of sin *g·*
     370–25 would *g·* all sorts into a
     397–24 How to *g·*, how to sow,
    Ret. 46– 5 How to *g·*, how to sow,
    Un. 12– 2 and *g·* the harvest by mental,
      35–27 which can *g·* additional evidence
    Pul. 17– 4 How to *g·*, how to sow,
    Hea. 10–15 *g·* the importance of this saying,
    Po. 14– 3 How to *g·*, how to sow,
    My. 77–18 * multitude which began to *g·*
     208–19 to *g·* in praise and prayer

gathered
    Mis. 64–30 *g·* from the five personal senses.
     200–18 are *g·* from the supremacy of
     225– 3 concourse of friends had *g·*
     386–10 *g·* from her parting sigh :
    Pul. 37–20 * one or two other friends were *g·*.
      41–14 * members of the denomination *g·* ;
      41–30 * At 9 a. m. the first congregation *g·*.
      58– 4 * *g·* an association of students,
    Pan. 1– 5 since last you *g·* at the feast
    Po. 49–15 *g·* from her parting sigh :
    My. 29–21 * they had *g·* to observe,
      47– 4 * *g·* here from all parts
      77–26 * believers had *g·* in Boston.
     133–13 the fragments *g·* therefrom
     362–14 * *g·* in one place with one accord,

gathering
    Mis. 354–27 *g·* strength for a flight
    Man. 60–23 No large *g·* of people nor display
    Ret. 27–25 *g·* experience and confidence
    '02. 20–18 *annual g·* at Pleasant View,
    Po. 47–19 Evermore *g·* in woe
    My. 20–29 usual large *g·* in Boston,
      73–12 * chapter sub-title
      77–10 * rapidly *g·* in this city
      79–18 * that assembly was not a *g·* of
      84–20 * story which the *g·* here tells.
      84–26 * The *g·* of Christian Scientists
      87–13 * a great *g·* of people
      96– 7 * The *g·* can in no sense,
      96–17 * the most remarkable, of the *g·*
      97–29 * produced by that stupendous *g·*.
     141–18 * *g·* of vast multitudes
     155–26 *g·* Easter lilies of love
     173–10 *g·* at this annual meeting

gatherings
    My. 22– 6 * *g·* at the annual meeting ;
      45– 8 * *g·* of Christian Scientists
     141–10 * except on the triennial *g·*,
     141–21 * these *g·* will be discontinued :

gathers
    Mis. 1–16 mounting sense *g·* fresh forms
    Po. 65–21 *g·* a wreath for his bier ;

gauge
    Pan. 11– 9 *g·* the animus of man?

gaunt
    Mis. 355– 4 full-orbed promise, and a *g·* want.
    My. 308–15 * my father's "tall, *g·* frame"

gave
    Mis. 17–14 *g·* of the power of God to heal
      75– 3 *g·* us, through a human person,
     137– 2 *g·* you a meagre reception in Boston
     139–18 I *g·* a lot of land
     142–20 *g·* place to chords of feeling

gave
Mis. 145–12 to whom God g· "dominion— Gen. 1 : 26.
153–11 "the Lord g· the word :— Psal. 68 : 11.
180–21 g· he power to become— John 1 : 12.
181–24 g· he power to become— John 1 : 12.
185–18 g· he power to become— John 1 : 12.
185–25 g· he power to become— John 1 : 12.
199–21 is manifest in the control it g· him
253–24 agonies that g· that child birth?
292– 6 who so loved the world that he g·
300–25 I g· permission to cite,
373–24 God g· man dominion over all things ;
375–27 * "It g· me such a thrill of joy
381– 8 g· notice through his counsel
382–27 and g· it The C. S. Journal ;
388– 1 who g· that word of might
Ret. 2– 3 g· those religionists the
5– 4 g· the money for erecting the
5–25 * She g· an elevated character to the
19–21 he g· pathetic directions to
26–19 g· the world a new date in the
37–16 Even the Scriptures g· no direct
43–10 After I g· up teaching,
49–17 Christ and the example he g· ;
51– 1 I g· a lot of land in Boston to
90–11 he g· personal instruction,
90–11 and g· in plain words,
Un. 39–18 who g· and giveth man dominion
Pul. 8–18 and babes g· kisses to
20– 5 g· back the land to the church.
29– 8 * Last Sunday I g· myself the pleasure of
47–14 * g· her any distinct statement of
53–23 * g· to mankind the key to health
64–18 * modern philosophy g· her no
65–23 * g· half of the garment to
Rud. 14– 8 g· fully seven-eighths of her time
No. 23– 8 he to whom our Lord g· the keys of the
Pan. 5–11 g· the proper answer for all time
7– 5 demonstration that . . . Truth, g·
'00. 11– 1 it g· me more pleasure than
'02. 11–18 g· our glorified Master a bitter cup
11–19 g· it to his followers to drink.
13–28 I afterwards g· to my church
15–27 To this, however, I g· no heed,
20–10 'T was God who g· that word
Hea. 2–22 g· this proof of Christianity
Po. 7– 1 Through God, who g· that word
41–24 to welcome the murmur it g·
43– 6 through Him who g· you to us,
My. 30–18 * They g· generously of their means
30–24 * g· a sum surpassing some of
43–23 * she g· us our textbook,
51–21 * "she g· no definite answer,
55–11 * Mrs. Eddy g· the plot of ground
60–15 * little Bible which you g· me
62–30 * g· freely of their time and efforts
119–22 g· the real proof of his Saviour,
138– 1 I g· them my property to
157–22 I g· a deed of trust to
179– 4 The first g· an account of
189–27 g· expression to a poem
190–22 Jesus g· his disciples (students)
215– 1 or g· it a halfpenny.
252–26 and g· to the "happy New Year"
296–29 g· her discovery to the press.
302–15 g· me the endearing appellative
312–29 salary for writing g· me ample
321– 9 * he always g· you that position
323– 3 * Mr. Wiggin g· me a pamphlet
324–20 * never g· us the impression that
330–32 he g· pathetic directions to his
333–23 * he g· the repeated assurance of his
335–20 * authorities g· the cause of death as
346–25 * Mrs. Eddy g· the following to

gavel
My. 171–29 * The casket contained a g·
172– 2 * wood of the head of the g·
172– 8 * presenting this g· to President Bates,
172–23 * The box containing the g·

gay
Mis. 329–18 Whatever else droops, spring is g· :
376–23 softened, grew gray, then g·,

gayly
Mis. 324– 7 manhood, and age g· tread the

gaze
Mis. 86–17 spiritually beautiful to my g·
129–18 for other green eyes to g· on :
354–26 Go g· on the eagle,
354–31 To g· on the lark in her
355–28 Hold thy g· to the light,
Pul. 39–22 * G· on the world below.
Po. 18– 9 To g· on the lark in her
23–11 So may their g· be ever
32– 8 To g· on the sunbeams

gaze
My. 37–15 * the g· of universal humanity.
114–12 to the g· of many men,

gazed
Ret. 31–22 I g·, and stood abashed.

Gazette
Pul. 89–30 * G·, Burlington, Iowa.

gazing
Mis. 231–32 g· silently on the vacant seat
My. 59–14 * g· across that sea of heads,

gem
Po. 46– 8 A g· in beauty's diadem,
My. 184–20 church shall prove a historic g·
351–10 the title of your g· quoted,

gems
Mis. 343–17 the hidden g· of Love,
Ret. 85–27 with a diadem of g· from the
Po. vi– 3 * book "G· for You,"
vii–12 * these g· of purest thought
My. 12–29 children's good deeds are g·
121–16 g· that adorn the Christmas ring

Gems for You
Po. vi– 3 * in a book "G· for Y·,"

gender
Un. 32–24 liar was in the neuter g·,
My. 239–23 G· means a kind.
268–30 sex or g· eliminated ;

genealogies
My. 340– 8 old-wives' fables, and endless g·.

genealogy
Pul. 48–29 * figure largely in her g·,

General
Ret. 2–26 G· Henry Knox of Revolutionary fame.
2–28 stories about G· Knox,
Pul. 48–28 the McNeils and G· Knox
My. 311–27 G· John McNeil, the hero of

general
Mis. 8– 4 if we can bring to the g· thought
11–25 g· effort to benefit the race.
11–26 Because I can do much g· good to
80– 8 medical charlatans in g·,
137–10 having asked in g· assembly if you
138–20 applicable to the state of g· growth
155–21 as a g· rule, send them to
200–15 g· comprehension of mankind
236–27 as a g· rule, one will be blamed
291–14 and the world in g· ;
293– 5 (as a g· rule)
293– 9 g· knowledge that he has gained from
379– 7 descriptive of the g· appearance,
Man. 26– 3 g· Committee on Publication
27– 4 g· Committee on Publication
56–16 g· reports from the Field.
70–12 shall assume no g· official control
101– 3 g· Committee on Publication
Ret. 3–10 John Macneil, the New Hampshire g·
40– 2 and taught in a g· way,
52–17 g· convention at New York City,
82– 5 A g· rule is, that my students
No. 9–28 * referred to g· truths
'02. 10–17 Religions in g· admit that
Hea. 12–16 g· and moral symptoms
My. v– 7 * matters of g· wonderment
10–31 * g· welfare of the Cause.
20–23 * g· attendance of the members
46–29 * to the g· assembly — Heb. 12 : 23.
50–32 * a g· meeting of the church
88– 1 * chapter sub-title
92–14 * the public has in a g· way
107– 6 g· subject under discussion,
141– 3 * g· communion service of the
159–28 The g· thought chiefly regards
210–21 denounce error in g·,
302–10 g· craze is that matter masters
319–29 * conversation with you in g·
345– 7 * your attitude to science in g·?

General Assembly
My. 329– 4 * last G· A· of North Carolina

General Association
My. 251–23 chapter sub-title
253–10 chapter sub-title

General Committee
Mis. 305–11 * representing . . . upon the G· C·,

generally
Mis. 6–31 and health is g· the rule ;
89–15 but your good will g·
237– 5 g· accepted as the penalty
240–21 affectionate, and g· brave.
243–20 my system . . . is not g· understood.
380–20 people g·, called for a sign
Man. 99–25 shall consist of men g·.

generally
Pul.	68–15	* It is not *g·* known that a
No.	31–24	in the *g·* accepted sense,
Pan.	10–12	The students . . ., *g·*, were the average
'01.	24– 4	that which is *g·* called matter
My.	100–15	* *g·* of a class who are reputable,
	178– 7	is not *g·* understood,
	236– 9	please adopt *g·* for your name,
	266–16	so *g·* apparent,
	272–23	* public *g·*, will be interested

generate
My.	194– 1	song and sermon *g·* only that

generated
Pul.	25– 3	* *g·* by two large boilers

generating
'01.	9– 5	*g·* or regenerating power.

generation
Mis.	74– 4	false sense of *g·*,
	286–16	maintain morality and *g·*,
	287– 2	offspring of an improved *g·*,
	318– 6	students of the second *g·*.
	318–10	final *g·* of those who
	342–28	in their *g·* wiser — *Luke* 16 : 8.
	346– 8	confronts each *g·* anew.
Ret.	64–15	*g·* of his fathers ; — *Psal.* 49 : 19.
Un.	43– 3	This *g·* seems too material
Pul.	vii–15	the pathway of this *g·* ;
My.	11– 6	* surged against her for a *g·*.
	34– 8	*g·* of them that seek — *Psal.* 24 : 6
	49– 8	* sweeping the world within a *g·*.''
	59–30	* No human being in this *g·*
	88–24	* revelation given to this *g·*
	99–22	* Less than a *g·* ago
	206–23	a chosen *g·*, — *I Pet.* 2 : 9.
	222– 5	perverse *g·*, — *Matt.* 17 : 17.
	272–31	* so much influence on this *g·*.

generations
Mis.	80–25	in successive *g·* for centuries,
	148–21	doctrines destined for future *g·*
	231– 6	Four *g·* sat at that dinner-table.
	286– 9	We look to future *g·* for
Man.	3–18	doctrines destined for future *g·*
Pul.	21– 2	grandchildren to the latest *g·*,
My.	43–18	* In future *g·* when it was asked,
	84–10	* And the experience of many *g·*
	85–21	* in the illustrious list for future *g·*
	177–22	the joy of many *g·* awaits it,

generic
Man.	47–20	*g·* name of the disease
Un.	51–14	the *g·* term for all humanity,
	51–15	the *g·* term for all women ;
No.	22–19	the term devil is *g·*,
'01.	10–11	*g·* term for both male and female.
My.	185–14	Love is the *g·* term for God.
	239–19	*g·* term for men and women.
	347– 5	man the *g·* term for mankind.''

generosity
Mis.	242–10	my thanks due to his *g·* ;
Pul.	85–27	* her labors and loving *g·*
My.	5–26	thanking your *g·* and fidelity,
	86–19	* *g·* of the devotion that the
	96–17	* *g·* of its adherents towards
	331–27	* the noble *g·* of heart which

generous
Mis.	231–11	skilful carving of the *g·* host,
	347–14	all the goodness of *g·* natures,
Ret.	11–22	Free as the *g·* air,
No.	3– 4	modest, *g·*, and sincere !
Po.	60–20	Free as the *g·* air,
My.	14–23	* to ensnare a *g·* and loyal people.
	26– 9	*g·* check of five thousand dollars.
	46– 1	* in *g·* hallways, in commodious foyer
	121–12	*g·*, reliable, helpful,
	157– 5	* *g·* gift of one hundred thousand
	163–12	I always try to be just, if not *g·* ;
	165–27	He who is afraid of being too *g·*
	173– 6	*g·* hospitality extended yesterday
	217– 4	your early, *g·* incentive

generously
Mis.	140–16	*g·* poured into the treasury.
My.	28–11	* those who have given so *g·*
	30–18	* They gave *g·* of their means

Genesis
Mis.	57–10	in the first chapter of *G·*.
	69–10	In *G·* i. 26, we read :
	244–10	those conditions named in *G·*
	258–12	In the spiritual *G·* of creation,
	332–13	In the allegory of *G·*,
	366–10	from *G·* to Revelation,
	373–24	In *G·* we read that God
Man.	58–17	shall extend from *G·* to Revelation.

Genesis
Pul.	38–16	*G·*, Apocalypse, and Glossary.
No.	37–21	From *G·* to Revelation the Scriptures
Pan.	7–20	in the third chapter of *G·*,
'02.	7– 5	In the first chapter of *G·*,
My.	60–17	* of the first chapter of *G·*.
	179– 3	first and second chapters of *G·*,

genesis
Mis.	57–27	In its *g·*, the Science of creation
My.	177–16	*g·* of C. S. was allied to

genial
Mis.	224–20	with a temper so *g·* that
'01.	30–19	kindles the inner *g·* life of a man,
Po.	2–17	sun's more *g·*, mighty ray ;

genii
Pan.	3– 5	poetical phase of the *g·* of forests.

genius
Mis.	66– 5	*g·* whereof is displayed in the
	283–26	It is the *g·* of C. S.
	354–29	*g·* inflated with worldly desire.
	356–23	it is the *g·* of C. S.
	365–12	Its *g·* is right thinking
Un.	9–12	talent and *g·* of the centuries
Pul.	83–11	* with the patience of *g·* she waits.
'00.	9–18	Sincerity is more successful than *g·*
Hea.	2– 1	*g·* of Christianity is works
Po.	18– 6	*g·* unfolding a quenchless desire.
My.	14–21	* endowed with *g·* and inspiration,
	200– 3	consolidating the *g·* of C. S.

Gennesaret
Mis.	212– 7	On the shore of *G·*

Gentiles
'00.	13– 2	* *G·* entered the church of Christ''

gentility
My.	121–19	external *g·* and good humor

gentle
Mis.	153–27	* Souls that are *g·* and still
	213–16	by *g·* benedictions.
	250–27	the *g·* hand opening the door
	254– 3	the *g·* entreaty, the stern rebuke
	330–28	When *g·* violet lifts its blue eye
	331–18	O *g·* presence, peace and joy
	389– 6	O *g·* presence, peace and joy
	390– 2	Whence are thy wooings, *g·* June?
Ret.	5–24	* *g·* dew and cheerful light,
	80– 4	though . . . justice be graciously *g·*,
Pul.	82– 8	* she is soft and *g·*,
Pan.	3–11	the *g·* murmur of early morn,
Hea.	2–12	Said the more *g·* Melanchthon :
Po.	4– 1	O *g·* presence, peace and joy
	16– 1	*g·* cypress, in evergreen tears,
	29–15	Thou *g·* beam of living Love,
	43– 7	*G·* as the dove,
	55– 1	thy wooings, *g·* June
My.	28–13	* *g·* qualities which mark the true
	39–25	* harmonious tones of her *g·* voice.
	93– 2	* happy, *g·*, and virtuous.
	208–12	Like the *g·* dews of heaven

gentleman (*see also* **gentleman's**)
Mis.	48– 3	by the *g·* referred to,
	68–18	Does the *g·* above mentioned
	88–10	Boston *g·* whose thought is
	239–13	a portly *g·* alight, and take
	242–10	Will the *g·* accept my thanks
	285– 6	*g·* who fills orders for my books,
	371– 3	the *g·* aforesaid states,
Pul.	37–16	* said a *g·* to me on Christmas eve,
	60–18	* a wealthy Universalist *g·*,
My.	153–11	would say to the aged *g·*

gentleman's
Mis.	296–21	in this unknown *g·* language,

gentlemen
Pul.	59–25	* *g·* officially connected with the

gentleness
Ret.	80–16	mingled sternness and *g·*

gently
Mis.	137–15	kind of you to part so *g·* with the
	240–14	nature would take it out as *g·*,
	291–24	will fall *g·* on the hearts
	330– 9	should call his race as *g·*
	387– 1	the heart-strings *g·* sweep,
Un.	5– 5	work gradually and *g·* up
Pan.	12–18	pass *g·* on without the
'01.	10–27	emerge *g·* into Life everlasting.
Po.	30– 1	*G·* thou beckonest from the
	50–19	the heartstrings *g·* sweep
	66– 7	Wake *g·* the chords of her lyre.
My.	69– 7	* *g·* curved and panelled surface,
	162–26	*g·* into ''green pastures — *Psal.* 23 : 2.

genuine

Mis.	39–11	the Founder of *g*· C. S. has
	88– 7	*author of that g· critique in the*
	148–19	requisite to demonstrate *g*· C. S.,
	207– 5	the *g*· recognition of practical,
Man.	3–16	requisite to demonstrate *g*· C. S.,
Ret.	48– 5	establishment of *g*· C. S. healing
	53– 5	bear aloft the standard of *g*· C. S.
	81–13	*g*· goodness become so apparent
	87–10	*G*· Christian Scientists are,
Un.	22–15	*g*· as Truth, though not so legitimate
	42–12	is the *g*· Science of being.
	49–13	only living God and the *g*· man.
Rud.	3–14	*G*· Christian Scientists will no more
No.	3–14	which sustains the *g*· practice,
	30–19	forbids the *g*· existence of even
'02.	14–11	only *g*· success possible for
	18–27	downfall of *g*· Christianity,
My.	3–22	compels him to think *g*·,
	4–14	A *g*· Christian Scientist loves
	111–12	*g*· Christian Scientist will tell you
	224–29	which is not absolutely *g*·.
	229– 1	I call none but *g*· Christian Scientists,

genuinely

Man.	39–12	evidence of having *g*· repented

genuineness

Mis.	39– 6	can be obtained in its *g*·

genus

Mis.	26–21	neither a *g*· nor a species

geology

Mis.	vii–14	to evolution's *G*·, we say,

geometry

Mis.	344– 6	music, astronomy, and *g*·,
	344–14	Of what avail would *g*· be
My.	226– 8	conservation of number in *g*·,

George

(see **Baker**)

Georgia and Ga.

(see **Atlanta**)

germ

No.	8–15	rejoice that every *g*· of goodness

German

Ret.	37–13	or certain *G*· philosophers,
My.	295–10	TRANSLATION INTO *G*· OF THE
	295–13	time-worn Bible in *G*·.

Germany

Pul.	5–24	France, *G*·, Russia,
My.	30–15	* from England, from *G*·,

germinating

My.	261–11	guarding and guiding well the *g*·

germs

Ret.	79–14	which uproot the *g*· of growth
My.	219–15	destruction of disease *g*·.

get

Mis.	55– 1	he failed to *g*· the right answer,
	73–15	can *g*· no farther than to say,
	79–14	cannot *g*· out of the focal distance of
	169–19	to *g*· at the highest, or
	225–30	* "Wait until we *g*· home,
	227–11	to *g*· their weighty stuff into the
	240– 8	flippant caution, "You will *g*· cold."
	240–13	If a cold could *g*· into the body
	241–16	you *g*· the victory and Truth heals
	280–13	We must *g*· rid of that notion.
	335–25	*g*· out of a burning house,
	352–23	one must either *g*· out of himself
	366–16	humanity needs to *g*· her eyes open
Ret.	20–24	was to *g*· back my child,
Un.	4–14	as we *g*· still nearer Him,
	17–12	its darkness *g*· consolation from
	44–20	[when you, lie, *g*· the floor],
Pul.	45– 7	* *g*· their buildings finished
	49–20	* long wished to *g*· away from
	51–27	* *g*· the share of attention it deserves,
No.	23– 7	"*G*· thee behind me, Satan ;" — *Matt.* 16 : 23.
	27– 6	*g*· near enough to God to see this,
'01.	13–29	and then we *g*· the victory,
Hea.	17– 4	*g*· nearer his divine nature
Po.	70–15	Then, error, *g*· thee hence,
My.	8–21	* if they are all to *g*· in."
	22–28	* to *g*· immediately into the
	60–19	* *g*· understanding." — *Prov.* 4 : 7.
	69–27	* If one would *g*· an idea of the size
	75–18	* They do not *g*· excited over trifles.
	82– 8	* were trying to *g*· away at the
	82–19	* this ability to *g*· away
	117–16	to *g*· some good out of
	306–26	tried to *g*· them published
	359–30	*g*· your students to help you

Gethsemane

Ret.	31–26	Bethany, *G*· and Calvary,

gets

Mis.	52–19	if one *g*· tired of it,
	365– 8	*g*· things wrong,
No.	18–20	If . . . the school *g*· things wrong,
'00.	2–18	Ask how he *g*· his money,
'02.	18–19	the summer brook, soon *g*· dry.

getting

Mis.	368–14	*g*· into the ranks of the good
No.	28–21	*g*· the letter and omitting the spirit
Hea.	13–28	one lie *g*· the better of another,
My.	60–19	* "With all thy *g*· — *Prov.* 4 : 7.
	97– 5	* *g*· well without the use of medicine.

Gettysburg

Mis.	246–20	more terrible than the battle of *G*·

ghosts

Mis.	396– 4	Where *g*· and goblins stalk.
Po.	58–16	Where *g*· and goblins stalk.

giant

Mis.	55–13	This *g*· sin is the sin against the
Po.	30– 2	thou beckonest from the *g*· hills
My.	76–24	* chapter sub-title
	341– 6	lifted to her *g*· hills the ensign

gift

accompanying

My.	172–28	accept from me the accompanying *g*·

author's

Mis.	300–28	privilege, and the author's *g*·.

beautiful

My.	347– 9	their beautiful *g*· to me,

beneficent

My.	26–12	Your beneficent *g*· is the largest

Christmas

My.	257–26	and send you my Christmas *g*·,

from Mrs. Eddy

Pul.	28–12	* a *g*· from Mrs. Eddy

generous

My.	157– 5	* gratitude that your generous *g*·

God's

Mis.	140– 2	I knew that to God's *g*·,

great

My.	262–21	reminder of God's great *g*·,

healing

Pul.	53–27	* That healing *g*· he lends to them

her

My.	311–23	never doubted the veracity of her *g*·.

invaluable

'02.	16– 8	Wyclif, the invaluable *g*· of

little

My.	172–12	present to you a little *g*·

lovely

Mis.	142–17	expressed in their lovely *g*·

Mrs. Eddy's

My.	157– 2	* chapter sub-title
	159– 2	chapter sub-title

munificent

Man.	75–11	to receive this munificent *g*·,
My.	164– 9	thanks for your munificent *g*·
	166–10	munificent *g*· of ten thousand

my

Mis.	140–11	my *g*· as I had it conveyed.

New Year

Mis.	400–13	MOTHER'S NEW YEAR *G*· TO THE
Po.	69– 1	*Mother's New Year G· to the*

no especial

Mis.	3– 3	we shall claim no especial *g*·

of gifts

My.	295–14	This Book . . . the *g*· of gifts ;

of God

Mis.	382–11	this *g*· of God to the race,
'01.	11– 9	it is the *g*· of God ;
My.	349–12	a divine largess, a *g*· of God

of joy

Po.	28– 8	Whate'er the *g*· of joy or woe,

one

Mis.	319–21	pass without one *g*· to me.

our

Ret.	86–16	we offer our *g*· upon the altar.

perfect

My.	38– 2	* every perfect *g*· cometh from

personal

Mis.	181– 3	sonship a personal *g*· to man,
	181–22	it is not, then, a personal *g*·,

princely

My.	194–20	princely *g*· of your magnificent

that

My.	19–28	because of that *g*· which you

this

Mis.	203– 7	this *g*· from my students
	382–11	this *g*· of God to the race,
My.	170–15	this *g*· is already yours.

gift

this

My.	170–17	This *g·* is a passage of
	172–21	* "I accept this *g·* in behalf of

your

Mis.	203– 2	your *g·* of the pretty pond
My.	166–28	your *g·* to me of a beautiful
	259– 1	look again at your *g·*,

Mis.	140– 5	the true nature of the *g·* ;
	253– 3	Christianity is not merely a *g·*,
Pul.	26–14	* *g·* of a single individual
	60–17	* *g·* of a wealthy Universalist
	85–21	* chapter sub-title
My.	148–25	Christianity is not alone a *g·*,
	170–14	I would present a *g·* to you
	176– 3	A *G·* OF FIFTY DOLLARS IN GOLD
	262–22	a *g·* which so transcends mortal,
	295– 9	*G·* OF A COPY OF MARTIN LUTHER'S
	347– 6	chapter sub-title

gifted

Ret.	7– 8	*G·* with the highest order of
Pul.	37–24	* a highly *g·* personality."

gift-giving

My.	259–26	mere merry-making or needless *g·*

gifts

Mis.	131–26	this church's *g·* to Mother;
	159–21	*g·* that my dear students offer
	159–29	*g·* of Christian Scientists
	281–23	Among the *g·* of my students,
	345– 1	Spirit bestows spiritual *g·*,
Man.	60–14	nor *g·* at the Easter season
	67–19	*g·*, congratulatory despatches or
Pul.	49– 7	* *g·* of her loving pupils.
'01.	29– 3	*G·* he needs not.
Po.	9–10	more *g·* from above,
	39– 2	*G·*, lofty, pure, and free,
My.	20– 7	chapter sub-title
	20–11	name your *g·* to her,
	20–16	Send no *g·* to her
	25~ 6	* chapter sub-title
	123– 2	this church's *g·* to me
	123– 4	even more than the *g·*
	162–12	have demonstrated my *g·* to me
	164– 6	chapter sub-title
	173–15	as many *g·* had come from
	256– 9	exemption from Christmas *g·*.
	256–24	*g·* glow in the dark green branches
	257–23	chapter sub-title
	258–18	*g·* greater than those of
	258–25	Your Christmas *g·* are hallowed by
	262–32	Material *g·* and pastimes tend to
	274–21	my thanks for their magnificent *g·*,
	295–14	is also the gift of *g·* ;

gigantic

Po.	1– 1	*G·* sire, unfallen still thy crest !
My.	249– 7	counteract its most *g·* falsities.

gilded

Mis.	366–31	*g·* with sophistry and what
'01.	25–18	denounced all such *g·* sepulchres

gildest

Po.	30–10	as Thou *g·* gladdened joy,

Gilead

My.	175–22	Sweeter than the balm of *G·*,

gilt

Pul.	42–17	* "Mother's Room," in *g·* letters.

girders

Pul.	25–12	* The *g·* are all of iron,

girl

Mis.	ix–21	Psyche who is ever a *g·*.
	237–29	I remember, when a *g·*,
	341–23	a little *g·* of eight years,
Po.	46– 1	Fair *g·*, thy rosebud heart
My.	311– 4	a *g·*, totally blind,
	311– 8	* "If this blind *g·* stays with you,
	311–10	to turn the blind *g·* out,

girlhood

Ret.	11– 3	one of my *g·* productions.
Pul.	6–16	* for which I had hungered since *g·*,
Pan.	3–23	(one of my *g·* studies),
Po.	v– 3	* *dating from her early g·*
	vi–24	* *many poems written in g·*
	33–20	Written in *g·*.
	59– 9	Written in *g·*, in a maple grove.

girls

Pul.	46–23	* applied herself, like other *g·*,

girt

Ret.	35–23	Though a man were *g·* with the
Peo.	14–16	*g·* with a higher sense of
My.	277–23	armed with power *g·* for the hour.

gist

My.	363–23	*g·* of the whole subject

give

Mis.	11–17	would one sooner *g·* up his own?
	15–10	can *g·* the true perception of God
	17–10	*g·* up your more material religion
	20– 5	and I will *g·* you rest." — *Matt.* 11 : 28.
	24– 5	*g·* it to you as death-bed testimony
	32–22	to *g·* to my own flock all the
	80– 6	obligates its members to *g·* money
	88– 6	*Please g· us, through your Journal,*
	96–25	to *g·* you any conclusive idea
	114– 3	cannot *g·* too much time and
	115–26	for God will *g·* the ability to
	131–22	May God *g·* unto us all that loving
	135–14	Is it a cross to *g·* one week's time
	136–19	You can well afford to *g·* me up,
	137– 7	simply to *g·* you the privilege,
	137–23	*g·* much time to self-examination
	137–27	*g·* to the world the benefit of
	138– 7	to *g·* time and attention to hygiene
	138–25	God will *g·* to all His soldiers
	146–16	but will *g·* them immediate attention,
	147–17	may some time *g·* the color of virtue to
	149–19	the joy you *g·* me in parting . . . with
	150– 2	to *g·* you the kingdom." — *Luke* 12 : 32.
	150– 2	May He soon *g·* you a pastor ;
	150– 4	*G·* my forever-love to your dear
	155–23	*g·* to us all the pleasure of
	159– 7	God of all grace *g·* you peace.
	160– 5	it may *g·* no material token,
	177–16	*g·* yourselves wholly and irrevocably
	179–27	to *g·* us these smiles of God !
	183–19	to *g·* utterance to Truth.
	190–18	interpretations that the senses *g·*
	196– 8	will *g·* you a separate mind from
	213–23	*g·* unto them eternal life ; — *John* 10 : 28.
	215– 6	*g·* I unto thee. — *see John* 14 : 27.
	216– 5	as the Scriptures *g·* example.
	226– 2	* "*G·* the child what he relishes,
	227–12	may *g·* it a forward move,
	231– 9	*g·* a spiritual groan for the
	236–16	to *g·*, to one or the other, advice
	238– 7	no time to *g·* in defense of his own
	239– 7	*g·* fair proof that my shadow is not
	241–10	*g·* to the immoralist a mental dose
	242– 9	would *g·* sight to one born blind.
	254–27	will *g·* the vineyard unto — *Mark* 12 : 9.
	258–19	might *g·* names to itself,
	264– 1	and *g·* them credit for every
	268– 3	*g·* point to human action :
	281– 8	nor *g·* me anything,
	292– 5	I *g·* unto you, — *John* 13 : 34.
	296–12	*g·* their time and strength to
	297–28	and Truth will *g·* you all that
	299–24	Did he *g·* you permission to do this,
	302–23	so elect and *g·* suitable notice,
	306–29	"He shall *g·* His angels — *Psal.* 91 : 11.
	307– 2	and in turn, they *g·* you daily supplies.
	314–11	*g·* out any notices from the pulpit,
	320– 2	God will *g·* the benediction.
	321–17	to *g·* you the kingdom." — *Luke* 12 : 32.
	322–12	and the Life these *g·*,
	328–26	Therefore, *g·* up thy earth-weights ;
	338–25	* To *g·* the lips full speech.
	349–26	refused to *g·* me up or to
	351–23	the five senses *g·* to mortals pain,
	353–11	People *g·* me too much attention
	356–11	*g·* promise of grand careers.
	359–28	Men *g·* counsel ;
	359–28	they *g·* not the wisdom to
	364–29	or *g·* reality and power to evil
	366– 9	Scriptures *g·* the keynote of C. S.
	371–24	with Truth, to *g·* it buoyancy.
	384– 8	*G·* sober speed,
	388– 7	to whose power our hope we *g·*,
Man.	32–14	and *g·* the author's name.
	48–25	or *g·* incidental narratives.
	59–22	to *g·* their seats, if necessary,
	71–23	*g·* the name of their author
Chr.	55–18	such as I have *g·* I — *Acts* 3 : 6.
	57– 2	I *g·* power over the — *Rev.* 2 : 26
	57– 4	*g·* him the MORNING STAR. — *Rev.* 2 : 28.
Ret.	13–19	which would *g·* me rest,
	18–20	*g·* me the spot where affection
	26–23	Woman must *g·* it birth.
	34– 8	or *g·* me one distinct statement
	37–21	My reluctance to *g·* the public,
	38–20	to *g·* him the closing chapter of
	48–17	*g·* instruction in scientific methods
	70–11	*g·* chimerical wings to his
	75– 8	*g·* credit when citing from the
	90–23	Mother in Israel *g·* all her hours to
	93–24	*g·* to the world convincing proof of
	95– 4	* Ask God to *g·* thee skill

give

Un.	25–19	*Evil. . . .* I *g·* life,
	33– 4	*g·* the only pretended testimony
Pul.	9–22	to *g·* you the kingdom." — *Luke* 12 : 32.
	14–16	G· them a cup of cold water
	22– 1	can *g·* peace and good will towards
	22–13	Christ will *g·* to Christianity
	37– 1	* pleasure to *g·* any information
	67–14	* *g·* expression to a higher spirituality.
	81–19	* those who have so much to *g·*
	87–23	God *g·* you grace.
Rud.	8–10	*g·* you here nothing but an outline
	13–20	and then *g·* special attention to
	13–26	to *g·* all their time to C. S.
	14– 3	They must *g·* Him all their services,
	16– 3	can never *g·* a thorough knowledge of
No.	20– 5	imagination, and revelation *g·* us no
	43– 5	and I will *g·* you rest." — *Matt.* 11 : 28.
Pan.	14–16	*g·* to our congress wisdom,
'00.	13–15	*g·* thee a crown of life." — *Rev.* 2 : 10.
'01.	2–25	Truth can *g·* a fearless wing
	13–28	hold it invalid, *g·* it the lie,
	19–14	That animal natures *g·* force to
	26– 2	*g·* my tired sense of false philosophy
	34–16	G· us, dear God, again on earth
'02.	7– 9	can *g·* man the true idea of God
	7–25	I *g·* unto you, — *John* 13 : 34.
	17–23	what we *g·* ourselves and others
Hea.	2–19	and I will *g·* you rest." — *Matt.* 11 : 28.
	4– 4	must *g·* freer breath to thought
Peo.	7–26	and *g·* to the body those better
	12–24	and *g·* the healing power to
	12–26	*g·* health to man ;
Po.	7– 7	to whose power our hope we *g·*,
	23– 7	*g·* those earnest eyes yet back
	23–21	G· peaceful triumph to the truth,
	28–12	G· us the eagle's fearless wing,
	28–16	G· us this day our daily food
	30–12	G· risen power to prayer ;
	36– 7	To thought and deed G· sober speed,
	64–12	*g·* me the spot where affection may
	70–23	G· God's idea sway,
	78–15	G· to the pleading hearts comfort
My.	vi– 9	* only as they *g·* her full credit
	26–23	*g·* the true animus of our church
	28– 9	* they can *g·* no more than a hint of
	37–30	* *g·* heed and ponder and obey.
	40– 3	* *g·* more adequate reception to
	45–21	* pillar of fire to *g·* you light,
	53–21	* *g·* the time to preach,
	62– 8	* *g·* it to my brothers and sisters?"
	80–26	* wanted to *g·* testimony
	81– 9	* *g·* precedence to another
	81–26	* to *g·* any account of the
	86–16	* to *g·* no more money,
	92–19	* *g·* a feeble impression
	117–25	and *g·* their talents
	117–31	To *g·* me this opportunity
	119–26	*g·* myself the pleasant pastime
	119–27	or *g·* you the opportunity of
	120– 7	chance you *g·* me to
	133–16	*g·* birth to the sowing of
	144– 4	G· yourselves no fear
	153–29	Come, and I will *g·* thee rest,
	164– 4	to *g·* to many in this city
	167–19	G· to all the dear ones
	170–22	and He shall *g·* thee — *Psal.* 37 : 4.
	172–18	freely *g·*." — *Matt.* 10 : 8.
	191–19	sepulchres *g·* up their dead.
	192–22	*g·* me pleasure to visit you,
	193–22	* Carlyle writes, "G· a thing time ;
	213– 4	*g·* activity to evil.
	215–19	to *g·* my church *The C. S. Journal,*
	216– 2	Till Christian Scientists *g·* all
	220–22	*g·* them to know the joy and
	230–21	*g··*my solitude sweet surcease.
	234– 5	and they *g·* the appearance of
	234– 9	would gladly *g·* me the holidays
	237–14	and *g·* daily attention thereto.
	241–28	* Please *g·* the truth in the *Sentinel,*
	243–17	*g·* all possible time and attention
	244– 5	to whom I would gladly *g·* it
	257– 2	God *g·* to them more of His dear love
	258–28	*g·* you the might of love,
	259–15	*g·* me more time to think
	259–24	*g·* the activity of man infinite
	279– 4	peace I *g·* unto you :— *John* 14 : 27.
	279– 4	*g·* I unto you." — *John* 14 : 27.
	285–19	to him will I *g·* power — *Rev.* 2 : 26.
	295–15	kind of you to *g·* it to me.
	324–10	* thought he could *g·* a clearer
	329–25	* we ask you to *g·* your readers
	334– 1	* strives to *g·* the impression that
	348– 9	to *g·* a reason for the hope
	354–21	G· us not only angels' songs,
	358–23	G· my best wishes and love

give

My.	361– 4	I do not presume to *g·* you personal
		(*see also* **thanks**)

given

Mis.	6– 9	acute cases are *g·* to the M. D.'s,
	8– 1	thought is *g·* to material illusions
	33–18	and follow the directions *g·*.
	41– 2	*g·* vent in the diabolical practice of
	49– 9	his opinion *g·* to her friends,
	59–13	God *has g·* all things to
	69–15	had *g·* three doses of Croton oil,
	112– 8	error, *g·* new opportunities, will
	120–29	what is *g·*, puts to flight every
	127–12	it is not *g·* a stone,
	128– 1	and *g·* a variety of *turns,*
	136–17	All our thoughts should be *g·*
	147– 5	another space of time has been *g·*
	149–10	what God has *g·* him of experience,
	158–27	order therein *g·* corresponds to
	159– 2	God has *g·* to this age "S. and H.
	161– 5	*unto us a son is g·* :— *Isa.* 9 : 6.
	161–23	he was *g·* the new name,
	165–30	reproduced and *g·* to the world,
	166–11	unto us a son *is g·* :— *Isa.* 9 : 6.
	166–20	*g·* birth to the corporeal child
	168–18	"Unto us a son is *g·*." — *Isa.* 9 : 6.
	178–32	has been *g·* to the world to-day.
	195–29	have *g·* me a higher sense of
	216–12	*g·* to the Anglo-Saxon tongue,
	227– 4	*g·* to the hisses of the multitude,
	242–16	no signs be *g·* them," — *see Matt.* 12 : 39.
	278–11	never *g·* occasion for a single censure,
	282–19	exceptions to most *g·* rules :
	286–14	nor are *g·* in marriage,
	307– 6	*g·* to us through the understanding
	322–22	He hath *g·* you C. S.,
	350– 8	The first subject *g·* out for
	350–10	There was no advice *g·*,
	350–15	subject *g·* out at that meeting
	370–11	unto us a son is *g·*." — *Isa.* 9 : 6.
	373–26	power is *g·* unto me — *Matt.* 28 : 18.
	375–11	* new book you have *g·* us.
	376–14	* You have *g·* us back our Jesus,
	387–20	that wisdom's rod is *g·*
Man.	26–11	*g·* in her own handwriting.
	47–22	*g·* at the Wednesday evening meeting.
	63– 8	instruction *g·* by the children's
	64–15	Christian Scientists had *g·* to the author
	79–20	a Deed of Trust *g·* by Rev. . . . Eddy,
	81– 4	*g·* in her own handwriting.
	90– 4	*g·* certificates by this Board
	90–19	*g·* to each Normal class
	91– 1	this paper shall be *g·* to the teacher,
	95–21	No lecture shall be *g·* by a Reader
	97–12	*g·* in her own handwriting.
	102–14	deeds *g·* by Albert Metcalf and
	109– 9	who have been *g·* a degree,
	109–15	compare them with the forms here *g·*,
	110–12	one, at least, of the *g·* names
Ret.	15–25	treated and *g·* over by physicians
	17–19	*g·* Its feathery blossom
	40– 9	physicians had *g·* up the case
	44–20	time and attention must be *g·*
	75– 4	violates the law *g·* by Moses,
	78–18	or any name *g·* to it other than C. S.,
	91– 8	this name has been *g·* it by
Pul.	vii– 7	inclination *g·* their own thoughts
	vii–16	impetus thereby *g·* to Christianity ;
	8–10	Not a mortgage was *g·*
	15–14	yet have *g·* no warning.
	36–11	* *g·* to her morning talks by the
	40– 9	* chapter sub-title
	43–21	* as *g·* in the C. S. textbook.
	48–22	* diploma *g·* her by the Society of
	49–28	* first impression *g·* to the visitor
	57–20	* name *g·* to a new Boston church.
	61– 1	* the name *g·* by Mrs. Eddy,
	72–11	* work to which she has *g·* so much
	72–14	* *g·* up by a number of well-known
	74–13	"A despatch is *g·* me,
Rud.	2– 1	definitions of *person,* as *g·* by
	8– 9	I have *g·* you only an epitome
No.	10– 5	as any proof that can be *g·*
	12–14	and *g·* impulse to goodness,
	13–23	and *g·* impulse to reason
	28–15	way of salvation *g·* by Christ,
'00.	10– 6	are the truest signs that can be *g·* of
	11– 2	than millions of money could have *g·*.
'01.	15–26	* There is no other reason to be *g·*
	15–30	* nothing else . . . *g·* as a reason
	19– 3	*g·* to them in times of trouble,
	19–10	it shall be *g·* unto you ;
	26–29	What I have *g·* to the world
Hea.	2–23	that religions had not *g·*.
	16– 1	and *g·* its spiritual version,

given

Peo.	4– 1	It has g· to all systems of
Po.	6–15	wisdom's rod is g·
	41–16	but one g· to suffer and be?
	46–16	Be all thy life in music g·,
	63– 6	for centuries hath g·
	68– 6	to my lone heart was g·,
My.	17–26	* as g· in the C. S. textbook,
	18– 9	it is not g· a stone,
	23– 2	* how much our neighbor has g·,
	28–11	* those who have g· so generously
	32–18	* as g· in the C. S. textbook.
	43– 4	* The law was g· that they might
	48–20	* has g· to her disciples a means of
	55– 7	* although g· up for a time,
	56–18	* branch churches had g·,
	88–24	* revelation g· to this generation
	90– 8	* and is g· very real tests.
	94– 3	* figures g· out by the church
	97–11	* if the figures could be g·
	131–12	g· to me in a little symbol,
	133–12	in sundries already g· out.
	141–21	* just g· out to the press,
	170–16	God hath g· it to all mankind.
	173– 9	C. S. periodicals had g· notice
	199– 6	reward of thy hands is g· thee
	218–25	My private life is g· to a
	231– 8	g· large sums of money,
	236–27	information there g· to
	245–32	g· to students of the Primary class ;
	246– 1	second degree (C.S.D.) is g· to
	253–17	whom Thou hast g· me,— John 17 : 11.
	269– 8	nor are g· in marriage :— Luke 20 : 35.
	276–22	* she has g· out this statement :
	310– 2	g· an academic education,
	313–16	* I was never "g· to
	314–17	decision was g· by the judge
	315–26	testimony they have thereby g·
	324– 5	* Mr. Quimby had g· you
	336–20	* amplification of the facts g· by
	353– 9	I have g· the name to
	356–15	I have g· no assurance,
	358–19	g· you by your students.
		(see also rule)

Giver

My.	15–13	desire that the G· of all good
	127– 6	We thank the G· of all good

giver

Pul.	4–24	the lord and g· of Life.
My.	205– 8	and God is the g·.

givers

My.	25–23	I have faith in the g·
	123– 7	will reward these g·,

gives

Mis.	25–17	It g· God's infinite meaning to
	50–14	that g· one the power to heal ;
	81–29	It g· lessons to human life,
	97– 2	g· man ability to rise above the
	104–31	This alone g· me the forces of God
	113– 2	God's presence g· spiritual light,
	118–25	g· one plenty of employment,
	124–28	it g· to suffering, inspiration ;
	143–18	It g· me great pleasure to say that
	181– 5	g· him power to demonstrate
	184–23	g· back the lost likeness and
	189–22	g· him not merely a sense of
	204–26	g· steadiness to resolve,
	204–30	divine ruling g· prudence
	208–13	the law of divine Love g·,
	213–20	C. S. g· a fearless wing
	221– 4	it g· one opportunity to
	222– 2	g· him a false sense of both
	235–11	It g· to the race loftier desires
	235–16	g· a keener sense of Truth
	237–11	g· them such a cup of gall that
	260–25	g· out an atmosphere that heals
	265– 1	and g· me as authority for it ;
	274–20	g· impulse to violence, envy,
	299–28	g· to the public new patterns
	300–12	g· you the clergyman's salary
	307– 1	God g· you His spiritual ideas,
	334–15	only as one g· the lie to a lie ;
	355–15	g· scope to higher demonstration.
	362– 9	g· sight to these blind,
	372–21	C. S. Journal g· no uncertain
	372–29	S. and H. g· scopes and shades to
	375–32	* one who g· no mean attention to
	390– 5	Old Time g· thee her palm.
	390– 8	G· back some maiden melody,
	393– 4	G· the artist's fancy wings.
Man.	39–11	g· due evidence of having
	91–14	Only the President g· free admission
Ret.	66– 3	C. S. g· vitality to religion,
Un.	8– 1	g· much trouble to many
	49–24	This g· me a clearer right to call evil a

gives

Pul.	3–15	divine Love g· us the true sense
	53–19	* g· dominion over the physical
Rud.	3–19	which g· all true volition,
No.	32–14	It g· the lie to sin,
	33– 2	g· the dominance to God,
	37– 6	Mortal thought g· the
Pan.	2–13	g· the meaning of pantheism
	6–26	altitude of mind g· it power,
	7– 6	gave and g· in proof of
	7–22	It certainly g· to matter and evil
'00.	2–11	he g· little time to society
	2–14	earns his money and g· it wisely
	5– 5	g· evil no origin, no reality.
'01.	20– 7	g· neither moral right nor might to
	21–12	clergyman g· it as his opinion
'02.	2–20	g· place to a more spiritual
	9– 1	g· man power with untold
	17– 5	when obedience g· him happiness.
	20–21	for it g· me great joy to
Hea.	7– 9	g· the spiritual instead of the
Peo.	2– 8	g· another letter to the word God
Po.	51– 9	G· the artist's fancy wings.
	55– 6	Old Time g· thee her palm.
	55– 9	G· back some maiden melody,
My.	9–27	with what my heart g·
	12– 7	* g· promise of the speedy
	12–27	g· the power to "act in the
	66– 3	* g· to the above society the
	66–10	* g· them the ownership of the
	87–23	* If C. S. g· such serene,
	118–19	Soul, not sense, receives and g· it.
	119–18	g· dominion over all the earth.
	120–12	g· to soul its native freedom.
	129–22	divine law g· to man health
	129–23	g· a soul to Soul,
	131– 5	g· him courage, devotion, and
	150– 5	Pliny g· the following description
	154– 3	not the person who g· the drug
	154–11	not he who g· the flowers
	186–27	It g· me great pleasure to
	193–16	Love g· nothing to take away.
	204– 3	He g· His followers opportunity
	225–20	g· to the divine Spirit the name God.
	234–20	g· the subject quite another aspect.
	262–32	and g· manifold blessings.
	268–23	g· man the victory over himself.
	272–32	* g· no editorial indorsement to the
	273–31	g· the true sense of life
	280– 4	* g· assurance of your watchful care
	288– 4	g· little thought to self-defence ;
	328–13	* it g· them a license to heal.
	329–10	* g· especial interest to the
		(see also God)

giveth

Mis.	39–14	g· to every one this puissance ;
	133–30	it g· a peace that passeth
	153–19	g· this "new name"— Rev. 3 : 12.
	167–28	He g· power, peace, and holiness ;
	167–29	he g· liberty to the captive,
	213–11	opportunities which God g·,
	215– 6	not as the world g·,— John 14 : 27.
	276–29	Error g· no light, and it closes the
	317–31	g· not the Spirit by— John 3 : 34.
	322–20	that g· grace for grace,
Ret.	65– 8	Spirit g· Life.
Un.	39–18	gave and g· man dominion
'01.	9–30	the spirit g· him liberty :
Po.	77–12	g· joy and tears, conflict and rest,
My.	156–23	which g· victory over sin,
	279– 4	not as the world g·,— John 14 : 27.

giving

Mis.	9– 7	g· them refuge at last from the
	39–12	all her years in g· it birth.
	121–20	g· the signet of God to the
	138–19	g· to human power, peace.
	175– 9	g· better views of Life ;
	184–32	g· back the lost sense of man in
	186– 1	not at this point g· the history of
	190– 5	g· the true sense of itself, God,
	204–13	g· mortals new motives,
	211–28	He drank this cup g· thanks,
	236– 8	g· advice on personal topics.
	245–10	g· it new impetus and energy ;
	262–15	g· to the sick relief from pain ;
	262–16	for g· joy to the suffering
	287–20	g· them strength and permanence.
	300–27	passages g· the spiritual meaning
	303–22	by g· place in your Journal to
	320–29	g· to it a new name,
	381–23	publishing, selling, g· away,
Pul.	9–20	with the Sunday School g· this
	33–20	* g· him high counsel and serious
	45– 2	* some g· a mite and some
	64– 9	* some g· a pittance,

giving

Pul.	65–25	* called the divine spirit of *g*,
	73– 1	* or *g* it to others?''
Rud.	14– 1	*g* only a portion of their time to
No.	16–16	yet forever *g* forth more light,
'01.	30–13	*g* birth to nothing and death to
'02.	9– 3	*g* life, health, holiness ;
	11–19	which he drank, *g* thanks,
	13–22	*g* opportunity for those who
Hea.	12–27	*g* the unmedicated sugar
Peo.	13–16	and *g* the lie to science.
Po.	70– 8	*G* the glory that eye cannot see.
My.	5–10	God *g* all and man having all
	6–25	*g* to the material a spiritual
	13–30	their loving *g* has been blessed.
	19–27	acknowledgment of exemplary *g*,
	22–19	* the absolute necessity of *g*.
	28–13	* that the *g* to this fund
	49–24	* *g* some useful hints as to
	52– 5	* *g* in her Christian example,
	61–24	* human mind was *g* its consent.
	66–25	* and *g* her blessing to the
	67–20	* in *g* Boston an edifice
	94–29	*g* to the material a spiritual
	96–23	* members were asked to quit *g*.
	117– 7	*g* this leader time and retirement
	131– 7	we unite in *g* thanks.
	182–23	guarding, guiding, *g* grace,
	206–26	''*G* thanks unto the — *Col.* 1 : 12.
	219–16	*g* of life and health to man
	224–19	*g* full credit to another
	225–13	*g* unto His holy name
	231– 3	*G* merely in compliance with
	231–18	else love's labor is lost and *g* is
	262–22	mortal, material, sensual *g*
	287– 7	*g* to human weakness strength,
	323–21	* *g* this age such a Leader
	332–30	* *g* best praises to his

givings

My.	20–14	please add to your *g*

glaciers

Un.	64–15	may climb the smooth *g*,
My.	196–28	Over the *g* of winter

glad

Mis.	93– 5	heart of history shall be made *g* !
	116–15	tones whence come *g* echoes
	157–12	They will be *g* to help you.
	157–18	I am *g* that you are in good cheer.
	262–19	We are made *g* by the
	299–10	*g*, indeed, that this query has
	329–10	whose voices are sad or *g*,
	357–29	ready and *g* to help them
	369– 4	and the gospel of *g* tidings
	387– 5	waiting, in what *g* surprise,
	389–14	*g* for every scalding tear,
	398–22	Heard ye the *g* sound?
Ret.	13–24	Mother saw this, and was *g*.
Pul.	51–12	* are *g* to welcome others
Rud.	15– 6	*g* surprise of suddenly regained
Pan.	13–14	*g* that the churches are united
'00.	1– 3	*g* faces, aglow with gratitude,
	13–15	A *g* promise to such as wait
'01.	29– 9	who are not *g* to sacrifice for him
'02.	11–24	and be exceeding *g* : — *Matt.* 5 : 12.
Po.	4– 3	*g* for every scalding tear,
	9– 3	picturing alone a *g* young face,
	16–20	hear the *g* voices that swell,
	31– 9	*G* Easter glows with gratitude
	43– 3	*G* thy Eastertide :
	50–23	waiting, in what *g* surprise,
	66–13	but a young heart and *g*
	70– 5	the soul's *g* immortality,
	70–18	while the *g* stars sang
	75– 2	Heard ye the *g* sound?
My.	18–22	*g* that the churches are united
	21–27	* rejoice in the *g* reunion
	37–31	* We would be *g* if our prayers,
	124– 8	garlanded with *g* faces,
	124–15	enough to make this hour *g*.
	139–26	Rejoice and be exceedingly *g*,
	155–17	May this *g* Easter morn
	155–30	which she sends to them this *g* morn
	158– 8	it is a *g* day, in attune with
	173–21	It was a *g* day for me
	177– 7	and I am *g* to say
	191–15	This *g* Easter morning
	202–17	endless hopes, and *g* victories
	241–11	* We are *g* to have the privilege of
	254– 5	*g* you enjoy the dawn of C. S. ;
	270– 1	and be exceeding *g* : — *Matt.* 5 : 12.
	321–26	* *g* that I was among your early
	326– 1	* *g* to publish the following
	327–12	* will make your heart *g*,
	327–12	* as it has made *g* the hearts of

glad

My.	350–15	pathway *g* and free
	354–17	O *g* New Year !
	355– 3	* a symbol of the *g* New Year

gladdened

Ret.	2–17	My childhood was also *g* by
Po.	30–10	E'en as Thou gildest *g* joy,

gladdening

Mis.	377– 3	glow with *g* gleams of God,
Ret.	90–28	*g* to find, in such a student,

gladly

Mis.	32–19	I would *g* do my best towards
Ret.	21–19	turn it *g* from a material, false
Pul.	45–24	* *g* laid down his responsibilities
'02.	17– 4	*g* obeys when obedience gives him
Hea.	9–12	subjects they would *g* discontinue
	11– 3	*g* waken to see it was unreal.
Po.	2–16	On wings of morning *g* flit away,
My.	21–11	*g* forego a visit to Boston
	41– 2	* become *g* obedient to law,
	61– 1	* I *g* answered in the affirmative,
	145–21	*g* thus, if in this way
	234– 9	*g* give me the holidays
	244– 4	to whom I would *g* give it

gladness

Po.	47– 6	Ever to *g* and never to tears,
	47–20	are the sheaves and the *g*
My.	171– 6	obtain joy and *g*, — *Isa.* 35 : 10.
	194– 4	songs of joy and *g*

gladsome

Po.	30– 7	O *g* dayspring !

glance

Pul.	2–15	With the mind's eye *g* at the
Po.	9– 1	*g* of her husband's watchful eye
My.	160–16	until compelled to *g* at it.

glare

Mis.	82–27	treacherous *g* of its own flame

glared

No.	2– 4	naturally *g* at by the pulpit,

Glasgow

My.	81–15	* ''Des Moines !'' ''*G* !'' ''Cuba !''

glass

Mis.	359–11	through a *g*, darkly ; — *I Cor.* 13 : 12.
Pul.	vii– 9	rise of the mercury in the *g*
	24–28	* The windows of stained *g*
	25–30	* There is a disc of cut *g* in
	58–21	* windows are of colored *g*,
	58–30	* portrait of her in stained *g* ;

gleam

Mis.	1–11	kindle all minds with a *g* of
My.	14– 6	as a *g* of reality ;
	163– 6	from *g* to glory, from matter to

gleaming

Chr.	53–47	*g* through Mind, mother, man.

gleams

Mis.	377– 3	with gladdening *g* of God,
My.	258–19	*g* of glory, coronals of meekness,

glean

Ret.	79– 5	We *g* spiritual harvests

gleaned

Mis.	308–24	have *g* from its fruitage
Ret.	10–12	*g* from schoolbooks
My.	47– 8	* as *g* from the pages of its history.

glee

Ret.	17–17	bay, and laurel, in classical *g*,
Po.	28–11	Above the tempest's *g* ;
	63– 2	bay, and laurel, in classical *g*,
My.	350–21	shadow of a world of *g*) ;

glide

Mis.	110–25	increase rapidly as years *g* on.

glided

Mis.	376–23	*g* into a glory of

glimpse

Mis.	24–15	a *g* of the great fact
Pul.	47–24	* to catch a *g* of the world.
My.	6–29	love catching a *g* of glory.
	31–11	* *g* of the great structure,

glimpses

Mis.	363–19	in *g* of the eternal verities.
'01.	9– 6	glorious *g* of the Messiah

glittering

Un.	54–27	*g* audacity of diabolical . . . logic

glitteringly

Po.	2–15	stars, so cold, so *g* bright,

Globe (*see also* **Boston Globe**)
The
Pul. 75–13 * *The G·*, Toronto, Canada,

My. 264–10 * send through the G· to the people
281–27 To the Editor of the G· :

globe
Ret. 85–26 rapidly spreading over the g· ;
'00. 1–17 five grand divisions of the g· ;
'02. 2– 1 is circling the g·,
My. 77–23 * from all quarters of the g·
136–21 five grand divisions of our g· ;

globes
Pul. 7–15 Those crystal g· made morals for

globules
My. 107–16 dozen or less of these same g·,

gloom
Mis. 276–19 Out of the g·comes the glory of
320–20 through darkness and g·,
342– 7 the midnight g· upon them,
376–28 spangled the g· in celestial space
395–27 Enhancing autumn's g·.
399– 3 will lift the shade of g·,
Chr. 53–34 Christ comes in g· ;
Peo. 1–11 guardians of the g· are the
Po. 15– 9 Here g· hath enchantment in
58–12 Enhancing autumn's g·.
75–10 will lift the shade of g·,
78– 2 fought on in g· !
My. 50– 8 * g· of the mysterious forests,
90–16 * teaches . . . that g· is sin,
110–10 will appear, lighting the g ,
158–11 to-day hath its g· and glory :
191–22 Mortality's thick g· is pierced.
192– 9 mystery and g· of his glory
257– 6 has traversed night, through g·
258–10 one word, ''Mary,'' broke the g·
262–16 breaking upon the g· of matter

glooms
Pan. 3– 6 My sense of nature's rich g·
Po. 34–10 chant thy vespers 'mid rich g·?

glories
Mis. 313–10 kindling its g· in the east,
332–21 the g· of revelation,
365– 2 bring out the g· of eternity ;
392– 9 shade, her noonday g· crown?
399– 5 the g· of one endless day.''
Rud. 6– 3 g· of earth and sky,
No. 21–23 brings in the g· of eternity ;
Hea. 20– 3 * could we sound the g· forth,
Po. 20–12 shade, her noonday g· crown?
75–12 the g· of one endless day.''
My. 64– 4 * The g· of the realm of
158– 8 upon the g· of summer ;

glorieth
Mis. 270–26 ''He that g·, — I Cor. 1 : 31.

glorified
Mis. 86–20 gain the g· sense of substance
154–22 Christ will again be . . . . g·.
166–32 before it could make him the g·.
Ret. 85–14 the Son of man will be g·,
94–29 the Father was g· therein.
Un. 7– 2 as already He is g· in the
49–12 a g· consciousness of the only
Pul. 82– 7 * one whom her love had g·
No. 39–10 Prophet and apostle have g· God
45–24 have free course and be g·.
'00. 12– 5 the radiance of g· Being.
'02. 11–18 gave our g· Master a bitter cup
16–18 a g· spiritual idea of the
Po. 31–18 The ever Christ, and g· behest,
79–19 God's glorified ! Who doth His will
My. 52–24 * through her work Truth may be glorified.
133– 8 church triumphant, and Zion be glorified.
202–28 ''Herein is my Father glorified, — John 15 : 8.
232– 8 mankind blessed, and God glorified.
355–27 glorified in His reflection

glorifies
'02. 19–28 g· the cross and crowns

glorify
Mis. 83–25 g· Thy Son, — John 17 : 1.
83–25 Son also may g· Thee.'' — John 17 : 1.
Man. 47–11 ''G· God in your body, — I Cor. 6 : 20.
'02. 1–12 Evil, . . . is made to g· God.
Po. 30– 8 To g· all time — eternity
My. 187–27 g· in a new commandment

glorifying
'02. 20– 8 g· thy unfaltering faith

glorious
Mis. 76–31 fulfilment of this g· prophecy
105–14 Life and its g· phenomena.
151–22 G· things are spoken of you

glorious
Mis. 159–24 ''O g· Truth ! O Mother Love !
199– 9 ''into the g· liberty — Rom. 8 : 21.
212– 6 left his g· career for our example.
234–32 makes His sovereignty g·.
245–17 remove with g· results.
248–26 the g· revelations of C. S.
250–22 g· significance of affection
261–22 effecting so g· a purpose.
307– 5 a g· inheritance is given to us
386– 1 ''Intensely grand and g·
387–22 greetings g· from high heaven,
Chr. 53–27 rehearse the g· worth
Pul. 9–21 O g· hope and blessed assurance,
45–11 * features of this g· consummation
No. 24–27 another and more g· truth,
35–20 The g· truth of being
'01. 9– 6 g· glimpses of the Messiah
'02. 19–17 O g· hope ! there remaineth a rest
Peo. 4–18 g· Godhead is Life, Truth, and Love,
Po. 6–17 greetings g· from high heaven,
39–15 Work for our g· cause !
49– 3 grand and g· life's sphere,
70–19 To hail creation's g· morn
My. 20–17 g· growth in C. S.
154–21 * high and g· toil for him
197– 6 may this beloved church be g·,
200–13 g· beatitudes of divine Love.
213–14 bring out g· results.
253– 9 * manhood's g· crown to gain.''

gloriously
My. 114–22 as g· as the sunlight on the

glory (*see also* **glory's**)
abstract
Mis. 82–21 only as abstract g·.
all
Mis. 82–12 and gather — in all g·
and fame
Po. 42– 4 will be victor, for g· and fame,
and permanence
Mis. 47– 7 g· and permanence of Spirit :
another
My. 85–20 * Another g· for Boston,
beauty and
Ret. 18–14 Earth's beauty and g· delude
Po. 64– 5 Earth's beauty and g· delude
bright with
Po. 43–20 Safe in Science, bright with g·
Christ's
My. 150–20 radiant reflection of Christ's g·,
coloring
Mis. ix–22 coloring g· of perpetual bloom ;
crowned
Pul. 1–15 path behind thee is with g· crowned ;
Po. 26– 3 track behind thee is with g· crowned ;
crown of
Mis. 231– 2 formed a crown of g· ;
dazzling
My. 193– 7 dazzling g· in the Occident,
earthly
Mis. 268– 5 Earthly g· is vain ;
everlasting
Mis. 328–32 the throne of everlasting g·.
full-orbed
No. 37–12 full-orbed g· of that event ;
giving the
Po. 70– 8 Giving the g· that eye cannot see.
gleams of
My. 258–19 gleams of g·, coronals of meekness,
gleam to
My. 163– 6 gleam to g·, from matter to Spirit.
glimpse of
My. 6–29 love catching a glimpse of g·.
gloom and
My. 158–12 to-day hath its gloom and g· :
gloom to
My. 257– 6 through gloom to g·,
God's
My. 117– 1 let them alone in, God's g·,
gone
My. 189–22 last-drawn sigh of a g· gone,
grace and
'02. 11– 7 warrant and welcome, grace and g·,
My. 339–16 joy, grace, and g· of liberty.
grandeur, and
Mis. 87–13 grandeur, and g· of the immortal
greater
My. 253– 5 what greater g· can nerve your
His
Mis. 78– 5 His g· encompasseth all being.
361–12 earth is full of His g·,
376–29 with the brightness of His g·.
My. 263– 2 leaving one alone and without His g·.

glory

his
Mis. 70–30   in which none could equal his *g*.
    73–24   *in the throne of his g*., — *Matt.* 19 : 28.
My. 15–20   * Of Jesus and his *g*,
    192– 9   mystery and gloom of his *g*·

His riches in
My. 186–15   according to His riches in *g*.

imperishable
Pul. 10–12   rights of conscience, imperishable *g*.

insure the
No. 33–16   insufficient to insure the *g*·

invested with
My. 349–17   great Way-shower, invested with *g*,

its
Po. 17– 3   Then I'll think of its *g*,
My. 134– 8   to enhance or to stay its *g*.

King of
My. 34–11   King of *g*· shall come in. — *Psal.* 24 : 9.
    34–12   Who is this King of *g*·? — *Psal.* 24 : 10.
    34–13   he is the King of *g*·. — *Psal.* 24 : 10.

lean
My. 245–15   persecution, and lean *g*,

Lord of
Un. 56– 8   "crucified the Lord of *g*.," — *I Cor.* 2 : 8.

loved ones in
Po. 17– 4   My loved ones in *g*·

marvel of
Mis. 163– 5   mission was a marvel of *g* :

Master's
'01. 35–13   O the Master's *g*· won thus,

mellower
Ret. 18– 4   While cactus a mellower *g*· receives
Po. 63–12   While cactus a mellower *g*· receives

mild
My. 150–17   moon ablaze with her mild *g*.

millennial
My. 265–16   appear full-orbed in millennial *g*· ;

modest
Mis. 372–25   the modest *g*· of divine Science.

My own
Un. 18– 5   brightness of My own *g*·.

noonday
My. 190– 5   noonday *g*· of C. S.

of achievement
My. 357–18   success and *g*· of achievement

of divinity
My. 25–26   *g*· of divinity appears in all its

of earth's woes
'02. 20– 7   *g*· of earth's woes is risen

of God
My. 206–21   *g*· of God did lighten it, — *Rev.* 21 : 23.

of good
My. 4–28   *g*· of good, healing the sick

of his Father
Mis. 74– 8   in the *g*· of his Father ;
No. 41–10   and the *g*· of his Father.

of His presence
My. 177–10   *g*· of His presence rests upon it,
    356– 5   liberty and *g*· of His presence,

of human life
No. 33–23   The *g*· of human life is in

of immortality
Peo. 2– 2   is the true *g*· of immortality.

of infinite
My. 262–17   with the *g*· of infinite being.

of mottled marvels
Mis. 376–24   glided into a *g*· of mottled marvels.

of our Lord
Mis. 276–19   comes the *g*· of our Lord,

of the Lord
My. 183–27   *g*· of the Lord is risen — *Isa.* 60 : 1.

of the resurrection
My. 202–15   *g*· of the resurrection morn

of the strife
Mis. 341–12   *g*· of the strife comes of honesty

power and
Mis. 92–28   power and *g*· of the Scriptures,
Ret. 84–17   power and *g*· of the Scriptures,
No. 18– 5   all presence, power, and *g*·.

presence and
No. 20–22   only power, presence, and *g*·.

radiance and
Ret. 18–19   radiance and *g*· ne'er fade.
Po. 64–10   radiance and *g*· ne'er fade.

radiant
Mis. 385–26   radiant *g*· sped The dawning day.
Po. 49– 1   radiant *g*· sped The dawning day.

reflected
My. 301– 1   C. S. is a reflected *g*· ;

reflection and
Mis. 187–24   man is their reflection and *g*·.

repeats its
Pul. 39–20   * Repeats its *g*· in the river's flow ;

scenes of
My. 15–30   * And when, in scenes of *g*·,

glory

songs of
My. 176–10   palms of victory and songs of *g*·.

task of
My. 258–12   resurrection and task of *g*·,

temptation nor
Un. 57–10   neither temptation nor *g*·.

that
My. 122– 5   That *g*· only is imperishable which

this
No. 33–25   all mortals to bring in this *g*· ;
My. 303–31   This *g*· is molten in the furnace

throne of
No. 34–24   yet mounting to the throne of *g*·

thy
My. 206–20   thy God thy *g*·." — *Isa.* 60 : 19.

to God
Mis. 145–29   "*G*· to God in the — *Luke* 2 : 14.

underived
My. 202–24   underived *g*·, the divine *Esse*.

unfathomable
Mis. 323– 4   serene azure and unfathomable *g*· :

unseen
No. 34–13   unseen *g*· of suffering for others.

wonder of
No. 37–13   to regard this wonder of *g*·,

      ———

Mis. vii–19   Whereof, I've more to *g*·,
    76–29   appear with him in *g*·." — *Col.* 3 : 4.
    86–31   the *g*· of supersensible Life ;
    231–13   His was the *g*· to vie with guests in
    270–26   let him *g*· in the Lord." — *I Cor.* 1 : 31.
    320–20   through . . . gloom, on to *g*·.
'02.   2–18   *g*· of untrammelled truth.
Po. 16– 9   The sequel of power, of *g*·,
    71–21   Thine be the *g*·
My.   4–29   *G*· be to Thee, Thou God most high
    9– 9   * *g*· in every good deed and thought
    62–11   * *g*· which crowns the completion of

glory's
Pul. 10– 8   silent Aventine is *g*· tomb ;

Glossary
Chr. page 55   heading
Pul. 38–16   Apocalypse, and *G*·.

Gloster
Un. 23– 1   treatment received by old *G*·

Glover (*see also* **Glover's**)

Brother
My. 335– 3   * Brother *G*· resided in Charleston,

Brother George W.
My. 333– 8   * respect to Brother George W. *G*·,

Colonel
Mis. x–20   my first marriage, to Colonel *G*·
Pul. 34– 2   * was married to Colonel *G*·,
'02. 15–16   My husband, Colonel *G*·,

Colonel George Washington
Ret. 19– 2   husband, Colonel George Washington *G*·

George Washington
My. 312– 5   * "He [George Washington *G*·] took his
    332–30   * death of George Washington *G*·

Jane
My. 313– 4   * Go to Jane *G*·, Tell her I love her ;

Major
My. 335–11   * facts regarding Major *G*·,

Major George W.
My. 312–18   Major George W. *G*·, resided in
    326–15   Major George W. *G*·, passed on
    329–10   * her husband, Major George W. *G*·,
    331–20   * the late Major George W. *G*·
    333–20   * Major George W. *G*·, died
    335– 2   * Major George W. *G*·, formerly

Mr.
My. 335–16   * Mr. *G*· was attacked with yellow fever
    336–15   * Mr. *G*· had made no will

Mrs. (*see also* **Eddy**)
Pul. 35–27   * Mrs. *G*· married Dr. Asa Gilbert Eddy,
My. 312–16   * Mrs. *G*· made only one effort at
    331–28   * yet when we listen to Mrs. *G*·
    335–23   * Mrs. *G*· (now Mrs. Eddy)
    336– 3   * disease spread so rapidly that Mrs. *G*·

      ———

Mis. xi– 3   in my name of *G*·,
My. 312–10   * *G*·, however, was a Free Mason,

Glover's

Colonel
Ret. 19–19   Colonel *G*· tender devotion to
My. 330–30   Colonel *G*· tender devotion to

Major
My. 330–14   * concerning Major *G*· history
    332–19   * facts regarding Major *G*·
    333–17   * never been claimed . . . that Major *G*·
    334–25   * heading

Glover's
Mrs. (*see also* **Baker, Eddy**)
My. 312–12   * Mrs. *G·* fare to New York City,

glow
Mis.   x– 1   spiritual *g·* and grandeur of
356– 4   spiritual *g·* and understanding.
377– 3   words that *g·* with gladdening
Ret. 13–21   a soft *g·* of ineffable joy
35–15   *g·* and grandeur of evangelical
Pul.   5– 7   *g·* of some deathless reality.
'00.   1– 8   in the *g·* of divine reflection.
Po.   8–11   watching alone o'er the starlit *g·*,
16–13   flitting through far crimson *g·*,
77–19   Bears hence its sunlit *g·*
My. 256–24   gifts *g·* in the dark green branches

glowed
Po. 74– 6   when parting thy sympathy *g·* !

glowing
My. 184–20   *g·* records of Christianity,

glows
Mis. 88–16   *g·* in the shadow of darkling
Po. 31– 9   Glad Easter *g·* with gratitude
My. 196–29   Over the glaciers . . . the summer *g·*.

gnashing
My. 161–11   weeping and *g·* of teeth, — *Luke* 13 : 28.

gnats
My. 211– 2   straining at *g·* and swallowing
218–20   straining at *g·* and swallowing
235– 5   Straining at *g·*, one may
276– 9   do not strain at *g·* or

gnawing
Mis. 131– 4   *g·* at the vitals of humanity.
Peo. 11–13   their fetters are *g·* away life

Gnostic
Mis. 162– 8   *G·*, Epicurean, and Stoic.

go
Mis. 19–26, 27   we *g·* into or we *g·* out of materialism
34–19   than we, . . . can *g·* to the departed
35–20   *g·* to church to hear it expounded
37–12   we *g·* on to leave the animal for the
37–14   "*G·* ye into all the world — *Mark* 16 : 15.
41–14   Mental purgation must *g·* on :
63–13   *g·* to the bedside and address
81–16   *to g· up into the wilderness,*
81–17   *g· forth into all the cities*
93–27   because it cannot *g·* unpunished
99–14   *G·*, if you must, to the dungeon
121–27   nor let me *g·*." — *Luke* 22 : 68.
134–19   *g·* to its rescue.
141– 6   This building begun, will *g·* up,
151–24   May mercy and truth *g·* before you :
166–19   Virgin-mother to *g·* to the temple
168– 3   *G·*, and tell what things ye shall see
168–28   * *g·* away unable to obtain seats.
192–11   *I g· unto my Father. — John* 14 : 12.
194–20   I *g·* unto my Father." — *John* 14 : 12.
195–31   The "I" will *g·* to the — *John* 14 : 12.
196–25   the "I" does *g·* unto — *John* 14 : 12.
201–30   *G·* to the bedside of pain,
215– 3   *g·* from one extreme to another :
215– 7   Arise, let us *g·* hence ; — *John* 14 : 31.
224–17   we should *g·* forth into life with
245–25   allows the people to *g·* no further
257–25   *g·* down in the death-dealing wave.
273–16   *g·* on in their present line of labor
281–30   shall not *g·* unpunished : — *see Prov.* 11 : 21.
286–31   human speculation will *g·* on,
287– 2   will *g·* out before the forever fact
298– 7   causing others to *g·* astray,
304–11   * Then it will *g·* to Bunker Hill
311– 9   *g·* forth to the full vintage-time,
311–15   *g·* to prove that I love my
318– 9   goodness must *g·* on *ad libitum*
324–24   he is afraid to *g·* on
325–32   "*G·* ye into all the world ; — *Mark* 16 : 15.
338– 7   All must *g·* and do likewise.
341– 8   you will *g·* up the scale of Science
342–23   "*G·* to them that sell, — *see Matt.* 25 : 9.
347–15   One says, *G·* this way ;
347–20   The guardians of . . . *g·* before me.
353–29   interested in themselves . . . *g·* their way.
353–30   they constantly *g·* to her for help,
354–26   *G·* gaze on the eagle,
356–24   One can never *g·* up, until
383–12   Erect and eternal, it will *g·* on
383–13   *g·* down the dim posterns of time
384–18   * "The seasons come and *g·* :
397–22   Shepherd, show me how to *g·*
Man. 68– 3   to *g·* in ten days to her,
69–17   shall *g·* immediately in obedience to
94–10   should *g·* away contemplating truth ;
Ret.   8–20   said sharply, "Why don't you *g·* ?
11– 6   *G·* fix thy restless mind

go
Ret. 15– 8   *g·* in the strength — *Psal.* 71 : 16.
38– 3   could not *g·* on with my work.
46– 3   Shepherd, show me how to *g·*
56–14   must *g·* on until peace be declared
64–15   "He shall *g·* to the — *Psal.* 49 : 19.
88–21   signify that we must or may *g·*,
Un. 41–19   and we shall *g·* to the Father,
41–27   appear to *g·* on *ad infinitum* ;
42–28   *g·* forth in the radiance of
59–17   never saw the Saviour come and *g·*,
Pul. 17– 2   Shepherd, show me how to *g·*
21–23   *G·* not into the way of the
40– 3   * I wonder how the seasons come and *g·*
51–15   * predict where this movement will *g·*,
51–24   * will *g·* there in search of truth,
53–13   * "Arise, *g·* thy way : — *Luke* 17 : 19.
67– 5   * found a new faith, *g·* to Boston,"
No. 14–18   "*G·* ye into all the world" — *Mark* 16 : 15.
19– 3   the premium would *g·* down.
27–27   probation of mortals must *g·* on
30– 5   will not let sin *g·* until it is
41–20   "*G·* ye into all the world, — *Mark* 16 : 15.
43–23   a system which they *g·* away to disgrace.
'00.   8– 3   *g·* on till we awake in his likeness.
'01. 16–26   *g·* to mock, and *g·* away to pray
19–22   to *g·* from the use of inanimate
29–13   *g·* out from the parents
29–17   *g·* not to help mother but to
Hea.   4– 2   can neither *g·* forth from,
9–11   why do they *g·* on thus,
17–28   so must they *g·* ;
19–20   bidding man *g·* up higher,
Peo. 14–15   *g·* to the bed of anguish,
Po. 14– 1   Shepherd, show me how to *g·*
36–17   * "The seasons come and *g·* :
60– 2   *G·* fix thy restless mind
79–10   darkling sense, arise, *g·* hence !
My. 19–19   sunlight wherever we *g·* ;
31– 4   "Shepherd, show me how to *g·* ;"
47–27   * "*G·* ye into all the world, — *Mark* 16 : 15.
51–23   * to *g·* into new fields to teach
83–11   * *g·* entirely unadorned.
95–19   * They *g·* about telling of
97– 4   * will *g·* far towards making the
118– 3   *g·* on promoting the true Principle
128– 3   *g·* on unto perfection ; — *Heb.* 6 : 1.
128–21   they *g·* into all the world,
132– 5   and we *g·* to the Gospels,
145–18   cannot *g·* upon the platform
149– 3   "*G·*, and do thou — *Luke* 10 : 37.
151–20   * *G·* forth, and worship God."
166–14   shade and shine may come and *g·*,
172–16   '*G·* ye into all the world,' — *Mark* 16 : 15.
229–14   *g·* to help their helper,
245–19   *g·* on *ad infinitum*,
248–26   *g·* forth to face the foe with
273–26   lapse and relapse, come and *g·*,
275–17   I *g·* out in my carriage daily,
300–24   "*G·* ye into all the world, — *Mark* 16 : 15.
301–25   cannot of itself *g·* to the brain
313– 4   * *G·* to Jane Glover,
313– 7   * I will *g·* to her.
324–18   * to allow the thought to *g·* out
336– 6   * to *g·* to her assistance,

goal
Mis. 63–25   reaching toward a higher *g·*,
85–11   Perfection, the *g·* of existence,
Un.   3–13   reached the *g·* in divine Science,
45–22   death is not the *g·* which Truth
58–15   was immortality's *g·*.
No. 44– 9   swerves not . . . from the spiritual *g·*.
Hea. 11–21   When you have reached this high *g·*
Po. 73–17   afar from life's turmoil its *g·*.

goat (*see also* goat's)
Pan.   3– 4   half *g·* and half man,

goat's
Pan.   3–31   *g·* feet, the solidity of the

goats
Mis. 370–29   separate the sheep from the *g·* ;

goblins
Mis. 396– 4   Where ghosts and *g·* stalk.
Po. 58–16   Where ghosts and *g·* stalk.

God (*see also* God's)
accept
'01.   3–13   we accept *G·*, emphatically,
acceptable to
No. 41– 8   most acceptable to *G·* ?
My. 17–13   acceptable to *G·* by — *I Pet.* 2 : 5.
acceptable unto
My. 36–12   * shall be acceptable unto *G·*.
accords all to
'02.   7– 3   It accords all to *G·*, Spirit,

God

acknowledge
Rud. 10–26 learn to acknowledge G·
My. 133– 5 come to acknowledge G·,

acquainted with
Mis. 151–19 art thou acquainted with G·?

acquaints us with
Mis. 175–26 which acquaints us with G·

action of
Hea. 4– 8 we limit the action of G·

against
Mis. 115– 2 offense against G· and humanity.
140–24 not be found fighting against G·.
224–27 unless the offense be against G·.
'00. 9–23 no one can fight against G·,
My. 150–31 or the disclaimer against G·

all
My. 132–21 G· all, one, — one Mind

allegiance to
Mis. 276–32 in their allegiance to G·.
Ret. 50–20 allegiance to G·, subordination
My. 42–27 * faithful is her allegiance to G·,

all-inclusive
Mis. 331–30 adorable, all-inclusive G·,

all is
Rud. 4–21 all is G·, and there is naught beside

allness of
Un. 10– 1 demonstrate the allness of G·.
Rud. 10–27 understanding of the allness of G·,
No. 30– 8 by virtue of the allness of G·.
My. 349–15 conscious of the allness of G·

All of
Mis. 174–22 the All of G·, and His omnipresence?

allude to
Mis. 379–15 allude to G· as the divine

alone
Mis. 236–21 be guided by G· alone ;''
250– 2 the *alone* G·, is Love.
358– 9 G· alone is his help,
Un. 38– 3 To G· alone belong the indisputable
Rud. 10– 5 G· alone governs man ;

alone to
My. 180–13 It appeals alone to G·,

alone with
Mis. 118–18 willing to work alone with G·
'01. 30–24 working alone with G·,

and a serpent
Pan. 6–20 between . . . G· and a serpent?

and devil
Un. 52–10 good and evil, G· and devil,

and good
Mis. 27– 3 terms G· and good, as Spirit,

and heaven
Un. 37– 7 G· and heaven, or Life, are present,

and His creation
Un. 30–17 interpretation of G· and His creation
Pan. 9– 3 one G· and His creation,
'02. 7– 8 of G· and His creation,

and His idea
Mis. 13–24 that is, of G· and His idea.
332–29 supposition is, that G· and His idea
Ret. 23–23 were G· and His idea.
60–11 C. S. reveals G· and His idea as
63– 1 G· and His idea are the only realities,
Un. 47– 6 All . . . is G· and His idea.

and His ideas
Un. 24–19 G· and His ideas

and His universe
Mis. 186–26 sense of G· and His universe

and humanity
Mis. 115– 2 offense against G· and humanity.
Pul. 85– 2 * consecration to G· and humanity
'01. 1– 4 for G· and humanity ;
My. 158–29 stand . . . for G· and humanity !
193–26 dedicated to G· and humanity,

and Love
'02. 8–14 G· and Love are *one.*

and man
Mis. 16–19 higher sense of both G· and man.
50–29 and love for G· and man ;
77–25 to understand G· and man :
82– 2 G· and man as the Principle and idea
124– 1 intervening between G· and man,
126– 6 with love for G· and man.
188– 9 misconception of G· and man,
189– 9 inseparability of G· and man,
361–29 Principle and idea, G· and man,
362– 4 wherein G· and man are perfect,
369–10 strong in the unity of G· and man.
Un. 52– 4 Science of G· and man is the
52– 9 in the coincidence of G· and man,
Rud. 7–15 evidence of the being of G· and man,
8–19 yet is false to G· and man,
11– 5 *understanding* of G· and man
No. 10– 8 reveals and interprets G· and man ;
27–15 eternal verities of G· and man

and man
'01. 5–12 discriminates between G· and man,
5–24 G· and man in divine Science,
10–14 divine and the human, G· and man.
20–11 he is disloyal to G· and man ;
21–16 individual who loves G· and man ;
'02. 8– 2 ''G· and man as His likeness,
9–18 The unity of G· and man is
12–18 even so G· and man, Father and son,
Peo. 4–16 mysterious ideas of G· and man
14–13 holier love for G· and man ;
Po. 11– 4 The love for G· and man.
My. 103–10 the Science of G· and man,
119– 6 one infinite G·, and man,
158–17 manifests love for G· and man.
159–14 perfect love of G· and man.
199–17 loyal lovers of G· and man.
200–17 the love of G· and man.
253–28 be faithful to G· and man.
274–24 and love to G· and man ;
295–27 the servant of G· and man,
338– 4 The love for G· and man.
338–20 love towards G· and man.

and Saviour
My. 155– 8 that one the G· and Saviour

and sin
Un. 6–16 leading questions about G· and sin,

and the universe
Mis. 190– 6 G·, and the universe ;
218–18 real nature of G· and the universe
Un. 24–19 G· and the universe — constitute all
34–25 reality of G· and the universe
52– 6 harmony of both G· and the universe.

anoints
Mis. 130–29 meek and loving, G· anoints
Chr. 53– 9 The Christ-idea, G· anoints

answers
'01. 19– 1 G· answers their prayers,

antipode of
Ret. 67–12 a sinner was the antipode of G·.
No. 35–19 which is the antipode of G·,

apart from
Mis. 71–26 nothing can be formed apart from G·,
183–24 Asserting a selfhood apart from G·,
196– 3 claim no mind apart from G·.
333– 2 sin — yea, selfhood — is apart from G·,
Ret. 60– 1 as something apart from G·,
No. 35–16 supposed existence apart from G·.
'02. 7– 3 no . . . causation apart from G·.
My. 115– 6 were I, apart from G·, its author.

ape of
Ret. 63–23 * ''The devil is but the ape of G·.''
No. 42–19 the devil is the ape of G·.

appeal to
Ret. 54– 7 and appeal to G· for relief

apprehension of
Un. 5– 7 increase their apprehension of G·,

approach
Un. 13– 5 Men must approach G· reverently,

as a person
No. 20– 4 and of G· as a person,
Hea. 3–12 and the qualities of G· as a person,

aside from
Mis. 335–31 seeking power or good aside from G·,

as infinite
No. 36– 4 He knew G· as infinite,

as its source
Un. 25–17 by showing G· as its source.

ask
Ret. 95– 4 * Ask G· to give thee skill
My. 150–18 ask G· to enable you to

as Love
'02. 4–18 chapter sub-title
9– 1 consciousness of G· as Love
My. 152–16 Do I understand G· as Love,

as old as
'01. 24–19 It is as old as G·,

as omnipotent
Mis. 197–30 recognize G· as omnipotent,

assigned to
Rud. 2–20 assigned to G· by finite thought,

assured that
Mis. 114–26 Rest assured that G· in His wisdom

as Truth
No. 30–25 sickness would dethrone G· as Truth,

atmosphere of
No. 9–26 Science is the atmosphere of G· ;

at-one-ment with
No. 33–20 man's at-one-ment with G· ;

aught besides
Mis. 358–11 He that seeketh aught besides G·,
'00. 5– 5 idolatry or aught besides G·,

authority of
Un. 31–17 matter usurps the authority of G·,

God

avails with
 Mis. 33– 2 prayer that avails with *G·*.
balances of
 Mis. 288– 7 dropped into the balances of *G·*
  365– 5 weighed in the balances of *G·*
banishment from
 Ret. 13– 9 perpetual banishment from *G·*.
becomes
 Mis. 96–13 *G·* becomes to me,
 No. 25– 2 *G·* becomes the All and Only of our
 '02. 9– 2 *G·* becomes to him the All-presence
before
 Mis. 117–30 their moves before *G·* makes His,
  204– 3 humble before *G·*, he cries,
behold
 Un. 55–22 Now and here shall I behold *G·*,
being infinite
 My. 356–28 *G·* being infinite, He is the only basis of
being is
 Mis. 72–28 Being is *G·*, infinite Spirit ;
being of
 Un. 47– 4 good, the being of *G·*,
 Rud. 7–15 of the being of *G·* and man,
belief in
 Pul. 79–25 * breath of his soul is a belief in *G·*.
 Rud. 11– 4 belief in *G·* as omnipotent ;
belief of
 Peo. 2–21 belief of *G·*, in every age,
belief that
 Mis. 45–24 even the belief that *G·* is not
 Un. 14– 2 the belief that *G·* must one day
 Peo. 4– 4 the belief that *G·* is a form,
believe in
 Un. 48– 5 *Do you believe in G·?*
 Pul. 80–22 * believe in *G·* and the power of
 '01. 6–27 We believe in *G·* as the infinite
believe that
 Peo. 13– 3 those who believe that *G·* is a
belongs to
 Mis. 107–10 the heart's homage belongs to *G·*.
 No. 42–11 All power belongs to *G·*;
 My. 225–12 all belongs to *G·*, for God is All ;
bereft of its
 Un. 51–10 bereft of its *G·*, whose place is
beside
 Ret. 60– 7 there is nothing beside *G·* ;
 Un. 25–12 claiming to be something beside *G·*,
 No. 16–13 there is none beside *G·*
  16–19 beside *G·* and His true likeness,
besides
 Mis. 27–23 claims something besides *G·*,
  37– 1 no power besides *G·*, good.
  333–25 believed that something besides *G·*
 Ret. 60– 8 says . . . is something besides *G·*.
 '02. 6– 7 of something besides *G·*, good,
 Hea. 15–20 trying everything else besides *G·*,
 My. 300– 3 or in aught besides *G·*,
bids one
 Mis. 348– 8 When *G·* bids one uncover iniquity,
bless
 Mis. 273–12 *G·* bless my enemies,
 Ret. 21–24 but for those . . . I bless *G·*.
 My. 202–29 *G·* bless this vine of His planting.
  203–19 *G·* bless this dear church,
  208–24 *G·* bless the courageous,
  220–21 "*G·* bless my enemies ;
  253–23 three words : *G·* bless you.
  279–25 *G·* bless that great nation
bless we
 Un. 60–13 "bless we *G·*,— *Jas.* 3 : 9.
born of
 Mis. 184–28 and *is* born of *G·* !
 My. 261–26 Truth and Life born of *G·*
  357– 5 born of *G·*, the offspring of Spirit,
bosom of
 Mis. 125–13 but rest on the bosom of *G·* ;
breeze of
 My. 232– 2 banner to the breeze of *G·*,
called
 '01. 7– 7 divine intelligence called *G·*.
 My. 269– 4 Principle, Love, called *G·*,
called of
 My. 244–13 called of *G·* to contribute
calling
 '01. 4–28 calling *G·* "divine Principle,"
calls
 Mis. 274– 7 work . . . which *G·* calls me to
 Man. 48– 3 whenever *G·* calls a member to
 Hea. 15–16 calls *G·* almighty and admits
calls good
 Mis. 110–29 that which *G·* calls good.
came from
 Pul. 72–23 * that which came from *G·*
cannot believe of
 Un. 19–11 But this we cannot believe of *G·* ;

God

cannot be obscured
 Mis. 333– 6 *G·* cannot be obscured,
caught from
 Un. 15–14 knowledge caught from *G·*,
channels of
 No. 44–16 choke the channels of *G·*.
character of
 Un. 1–12 nature and character of *G·*
child of
 Mis. 185–10 identity as the child of *G·*,
 Un. 22–16 not so legitimate a child of *G·*.
  44–15 miscall, this evil a child of *G·*.
  53–23 as a perfect child of *G·*.
 My. 242– 9 the child of *G·*, hence perfect,
children of
 (*see* **children**)
chosen of
 Pul. 85–14 * chosen of *G·* to this end,
 My. 17–10 but chosen of *G·*,— *I Pet.* 2 : 4.
Christian's
 Mis. 23–16 matter is not the Christian's *G·*,
  123–16 The *Christian's G·* is neither,
Christ is not
 '01. 8–12 Christ is not *G·*, but an impartation
claims
 Ret. 70– 5 claims *G·* as their author ;
coeternal with
 Mis. 79–24 coexistent and coeternal with *G·*.
  360–30 coexistent and coeternal with *G·*,
 Ret. 59–24 coexistent and coeternal with *G·*,
coexistent with
 Mis. 57–26 *he was coexistent with G·*
 Un. 49– 4 man is coexistent with *G·*,
 '02. 7–18 universe coexistent with *G·*.
coexists with
 My. 239– 2 Science of the . . . coexists with *G·* ;
coexist with
 '00. 4–26 Man and the universe coexist with *G·*
come from
 Mis. 22–17 come from *G·* and return to Him,
 Un. 22–17 Whatever exists must come from *G·*,
 My. 277–13 shall come from *G·*
comes from
 Pul. 73–23 * that all comes from *G·*.
 My. 292– 4 All good . . . comes from *G·*
comes to us
 Un. 4– 9 that *G·* comes to us and pities us ;
cometh down from
 Pul. 27–13 * "cometh down from *G·*— *see Rev.* 3 : 12.
cometh from
 Mis. 340– 9 than that which cometh from *G·*,
 My. 364–13 save that which cometh from *G·*.
comfort them
 Mis. 232– 1 *G·* comfort them all !
commandments of
 My. 160–21 disobeying the commandments of *G·*.
communion with
 Hea. 2– 3 steadfast communion with *G·* ;
conceive of
 Un. 23–23 can conceive of *G·* only as
 No. 23– 2 To conceive of *G·* as resembling
 '01. 4–24 consistently conceive of *G·* as One
conception of
 Ret. 25–20 the human conception of *G·*
 Pul. 85–11 * conception of *G·* as Life,
conceptions of
 Mis. 170–15 conceptions of *G·* and our
consciousness of
 Mis. 352–11 the true consciousness of *G·*,
 '02. 9– 1 consciousness of *G·* as Love
conscious only of
 No. 36–13 and was conscious only of *G·*,
control of
 Mis. 37–11 ourselves under the control of *G·*,
corporeal
 Mis. 102– 3 corporeal *G·*, as often defined
coworker with
 Pan. 6–18 creator or coworker with *G·* ?
created
 Mis. 25–27 If *G·* created drugs good,
  247–29 Everything that *G·* created,
  346– 9 If *G·* created only the good,
 Ret. 69–22 *G·* created all through Mind,
 Un. 15– 8 *G·* created all things,
  64– 1 All that *is*, *G·* created.
 '01. 18–17 If *G·* created drugs for
created by
 Hea. 17– 7 personal senses were created by *G·* ?
 My. 239–26 spiritual man, created by *G·*,
creates
 My. 262– 1 *G·* creates man perfect and eternal
currents of
 '01. 19–26 currents of *G·* flow through no such
dealeth
 Un. 23–11 *G·* dealeth with you as— *Heb.* 12 : 7.

God

dear
'01. 34–16 Give us, dear G·, again on earth
Po. 22–14. Dear G·! how great, how good
30–11 Thou gildest gladdened joy, dear G·,
My. 62– 7 * "Dear G·, may I not
295– 2 knowing our dear G· comforts such
declares
Un. 17–21 declares G· told our first parents
29–10 declares G· to be the Soul of all being,
declare that
Un. 2– 1 declare that G· is too pure to
dedicated to
My. 193–26 lofty temple, dedicated to G·
dedicate to
My. 13–19 an ample temple dedicate to G·,
deduced from
My. 349–28 deduced from G·, Spirit ;
defense is of
Mis. 258–16 "My defense is of G·,— Psal. 7 : 10.
definition of
'01. 3–11 Webster's definition of G·,
3–12 dictionary's definition of G·,
demands
My. 152–25 G· demands all our faith and love ;
demonstrable
Mis. 150–27 G· demonstrable as divine Life,
My. 179–32 make even G· demonstrable,
demonstrate
No. 12– 6 to understand and to demonstrate G·.
demonstrates
Mis. 98–20 Science demonstrates G·
My. 238–19 Science . . . that demonstrates G·.
demonstration of
Mis. 63–29 momentous demonstration of G·,
186–30 Messias whose demonstration of G·
Ret. 66– 6 scientific demonstration of G·.
Un. 51– 8 demonstration of G·, as in C. S.,
My. 221– 8 demonstration of G· in His
denies
Mis. 330–26 A mere mendicant that . . . G· denies
denounced it
Mis. 57–14 G·, denounced it, and said :
deny
Rud. 3–17 prescribe drugs, or deny G·.
departure from
'02. 8–28 Adam, a departure from G·,
derived from
Un. 6– 7 higher selfhood, derived from G·,
design of
My. 279–10 all periods in the design of G·.
destroys
'01. 18–27 if G· destroys the popular triad
dies not
Un. 62– 4 yet G· dies not,
directions of
My. 361– 1 Follow the directions of G·
directs
Mis. 117–31 Be sure that G· directs your way ;
My. 143– 2 pray that G· directs your meetings
discoveries of
No. 39–21 new and scientific discoveries of G·,
dishonors
Mis. 367–14 says . . . that it dishonors G· to
divinely
Po. 77–11 Love, and Truth,— divinely G·!
does
Peo. 2– 7 what God is, and what G· does.
My. 128–18 Men cannot punish . . . G· does that.
does all this
Mis. 280–11 Because G· does all,
does all this
Mis. 179–24 G· does all this through His
does forbid
Un. 4–20 but G· does forbid man's
does not limit
Mis. 282– 2 a sense that does not limit G·,
does not recognize
Mis. 60– 1 G· does not recognize any,
74–11 If G· does not recognize matter,
dominance to
No. 33– 3 gives the dominance to G·,
doth lighten it
Mis. 323– 6 for G· doth lighten it.
due, to
My. 189– 5 so due, to G· is obedience,
duty to
Man. 42– 8 nor to neglect his duty to G·,
67–17 Duty to G·.
dwelleth in
Mis. 150–12 G· dwelleth in the congregation of
dwells
My. 356– 2 where G· dwells most conspicuously
dwells in
Mis. 290–23 When thought dwells in G·,

God

emanating from
Rud. 6– 7 in and of Mind, emanating from G· ;
enables us
Pan. 11–23 G· enables us to know that
enmity against
Mis. 36–25 is enmity against G· ;— Rom. 8 : 7.
enmity to
Ret. 61– 1 enmity to G· and divine Science.
enmity toward
Mis. 169–27 mind, which is enmity toward G·,
enthrones
Un. 32–13 enthrones G· in the eternal
entrusted
'01. 31–11 Has G· entrusted me with a message
essence of
My. 159–27 * "What is the essence of G·? Mind."
eternal
No. 37– 6 eternal G· and infinite consciousness
eternal as
Un. 49– 3 as definite and eternal as G·,
59–13 Salvation is as eternal as G·.
No. 17–28 would be as eternal as G·.
even
Mis. 181– 2 is your Father," even G·.— Matt. 23 : 9.
My. 179–32 make even G· demonstrable,
ever-present
Ret. 60–13 good is G· ever-present,
Pul. 11– 5 dedicated to the ever-present G·
'02. 16–19 spiritual idea of the ever-present G·
My. 254–13 find the ever-present G·
evil and
Un. 27–12 these distinctions to evil and G·,
excludes
Mis. 257– 2 excludes G· from the universe, or
exemplified
My. 287–13 Love lived . . . is G· exemplified,
existence of
Mis. 69– 2 treats of the existence of G·,
exist in
Mis. 6–18 we exist in G·, perfect,
explains
'01. 5–29 G· explains Himself in C. S.
extinguish
Mis. 364–29 would either extinguish G· and His
faith in
Mis. 140– 9 taxing their faith in G·,
152–30 Exercise more faith in G·
160–14 every trial of our faith in G·
204–16 deep-toned faith in G· ;
229–13 would encourage faith in G·
345–18 * a practical faith in G·."
'02. 15– 3 never lost my faith in G·,
Peo. 13–26 * had a practical faith in G· ;"
My. 204– 2 My faith in G· and in His
221–28 shall we have no faith in G·,
false to
Un. 32– 2 false to G·, false to Truth
Rud. 8–19 yet is false to G· and man,
fasten on
Ret. 18–17 soar above matter, to fasten on G·,
Po. 64– 8 soar above matter, to fasten on G·,
Father-Mother
Mis. 102–16 divine Father-Mother G·.
127–12 petitions the divine Father-Mother G·
400–14 Father-Mother G·, Loving me,
Rud. 4– 1 Mind, the one Father-Mother G·.
Pan. 15– 5 May our Father-Mother G·,
'01. 3– 3 benediction of our Father-Mother G·
7–15 "Our Father-Mother G·"
Po. 69– 2 Father-Mother G·, Loving me,
My. 18– 9 petitions the divine Father-Mother G·
186–13 anthem of one Father-Mother G·,
265–32 we thank our Father-Mother G·.
347– 5 likeness of the Father-Mother G·,
fathers'
My. 185–28 * Our God, our fathers' G·!
fear
Peo. 6–15 Believing . . . we naturally fear G·
find
Mis. 124– 5 cannot find G· in matter,
First Commandment
Mis. 197–28 breaks the First Commandment of G·.
follow
Mis. 236–13 must follow G· in all your ways."
follower after
Pul. 73– 6 * an ardent follower after G·.
forbade
Un. 54–20 G· forbade man to know evil
forbid
'01. 26–17 cast lots for it? G· forbid !
forces of
Mis. 104–32 gives me the forces of G·
foreordained
Mis. 122–10 of him whom G· foreordained

God

forewarned
Mis. 367–23   It was . . . that *G·* forewarned.

found in
Mis. 255–24   may be found in *G·*, the divine Mind.
Un. 10– 4   they are not to be found in *G·*,
'01. 26–11   quality not to be found in *G·* !

fresh from
My. 195–23   deep-drawn breath fresh from *G·*,

fulness of
No. 357– 3   at the spiritual fulness of *G·*,

gave
Mis. 145–12   less than man to whom *G·* gave
373–24   *G·* gave man dominion over all

gift of
Mis. 382–11   this gift of *G·* to the race,
'01. 11– 9   it is the gift of *G·* ;
My. 349–12   a divine largess, a gift of *G·*

give
Mis. 131–22   May *G·* give unto us all that loving
Pul. 87–23   *G·* give you grace.
My. 257– 2   *G·* give to them more of

given to
Pul. 40– 9   * chapter sub-title

gives
Mis. 111–13   Nothing is lost that *G·* gives :
307– 1   *G·* gives you His spiritual ideas,
'01. 31–15   the power that *G·* gives me
'02. 17–23   what *G·* gives, . . . confers happiness :
My. 5–10   man having all that *G·* gives.
20–12   Send her only what *G·* gives
251–25   What *G·* gives, elucidates, armors,

giveth
Mis. 39–14   *G·* giveth to every one this
153–19   *G·* giveth this "new name"— *Rev.* 3 : 12.
213–11   opportunities which *G·* giveth,
317–31   for *G·* giveth not the— *John* 3 : 34.

giving all
My. 5– 9   *G·* giving all and man having all

gleams of
Mis. 377– 3   with gladdening gleams of *G·*,

glorified
No. 39–10   glorified *G·* in secret prayer,
My. 232– 8   mankind blessed, and *G·* glorified.

glorify
Man. 47–11   "Glorify *G·* in your— *I Cor.* 6 : 20.
'02. 1–12   Evil, . . . is made to glorify *G·*.

glory of
My. 206–21   for the glory of *G·* — *Rev.* 21 : 23.

glory to
Mis. 145–29   "Glory to *G·* in the— *Luke* 2 : 14.

good as
Mis. 13–29   then define good as *G·*,

good is
Mis. 24–24   (when good is *G·*, and God is All)
319– 3   good is *G·*, even as God is good,
Ret. 60–13   good is *G·* ever-present,

goodness of
Pul. 6– 9   goodness of *G·* — healing

good or
Un. 2–16   the Mind which is good, or *G·*,
24–22   separate from good or *G·*.

governed by
Mis. 104– 6   Formed and governed by *G·*,
198–16   man as governed by *G·*,

government and
Mis. 59– 1   one government and *G·*.

government of
Hea. 18– 3   yield to the government of *G·*,
Peo. 12– 7   just government of *G·*.

governs
My. 165–10   and by it *G·* governs.

grace from
Mis. 129– 7   through grace from *G·*, forgive

grace of
Un. 7– 3   the impartial grace of *G·*,
Pan. 10–23   accomplished by the grace of *G·*,

grant
Peo. 8–20   *G·* grant that the trembling
My. 165–29   *G·* grant that this church is
176– 7   *G·* grant that such great goodness,
184–19   *G·* grant that this little church
195–28   *G·* grant that this unity remain,
198– 7   May *G·* grant not only the

gratitude to
Mis. xi– 9   one's debt of gratitude to *G·*,
My. 36–19   * pour out our gratitude to *G·*
362–19   * filled with gratitude to *G·*,

guide
My. 282–26   May *G·* guide and prosper

guided by
Mis. 236–21   be guided by *G·* alone ;"

had led me
'02. 15–28   feeling sure that *G·* had led me

God

hand of
Mis. 319–24   in the outstretched hand of *G·*.

hands of
No. 3– 6   better to fall into the hands of *G·*,

harmony with
Hea. 14–27   a mind in harmony with *G·*,

has all power
My. 294– 4   on the basis that *G·* has all power,

has appointed
No. 7–18   *G·* has appointed . . . high tasks,

has blessed
Mis. 155– 6   even as *G·* has blessed you.
My. 158–24   *G·* has blessed and will bless

has called
My. 247–19   *G·* has called you to be a fisher of

has created
Un. 23–20   unless *G·* has created them

has dignified
My. 328– 1   * *G·* has dignified, blessed, and

has fulfilled
Pul. 73–15   * *G·* has fulfilled His promises

has given
Mis. 59–13   *G· has* given all things to
149– 9   what *G·* has given him of experience,
159– 2   *G·* has given to this age "S. and H.

has made
My. 288–30   the best of what *G·* has made.
305–22   All that I am . . . *G·* has made me.

has no bastards
Un. 23– 6   *G·* has no bastards to turn again

has no opposite
No. 5– 6   *G·* has no opposite in Science.

has not forbidden
Un. 4–17   *G·* has not forbidden man to know Him ;

has prepared
Mis. 152–18   heritage that *G·* has prepared for

has provided
'01. 29– 4   *G·* has provided the means for him

has revealed
My. 58–20   * one through whom *G·* has revealed

hath all-power
Mis. 101–21   saith to man, "*G·* hath all-power."

hath created
Hea. 16–23   shall we say that *G·* hath created

hath given
My. 170–15   *G·* hath given it to all mankind.

hath joined
My. 268– 9   What *G·* hath joined together,

hath not joined
Mis. 94– 8   but which *G·* hath not joined together.

hath prepared
My. 184– 5   what *G·* hath prepared for them

hath remembered
My. 126–16   and *G·* hath remembered — *Rev.* 18 : 5.

hath said
Un. 21–10   *Evil.* *G·* hath said,

hath seen
No. 27–24   Who living hath seen *G·*

heals
Pul. 14–26   When *G·* heals the sick or the
My. 348–16   *G·*, heals and saves mankind.

heart of
Mis. 253–22   love touches the heart of *G·*,

heirs of
Mis. 46–24   heirs of *G·*, and joint-heirs — *Rom.* 8 : 17.
255–16   heirs of *G·*, and joint-heirs — *Rom.* 8 : 17.

He is
Mis. 63–20   "that the Lord He is *G·* ; — *Deut.* 4 : 35.
366–11   the Lord He is *G·*, — *Deut.* 4 : 35.
Rud. 13–15   "The Lord, He is *G·* ; — *Deut.* 4 : 35.

her
Pul. 73– 7   * through the mediation of her *G·*.

high calling of
'00. 6– 8   of the high calling of *G·* — *Phil.* 3 : 14.

holds man
No. 26–22   *G·* holds man in the eternal

honoring
My. 225–18   by honoring *G·* and sacredly holding

honors
'02. 1–19   a system that honors *G·*

hope anchors in
'00. 10–21   our hope anchors in *G·* who reigns,

hope thou in
Un. 29–25   Hope thou in *G·* — *Psal.* 42 : 11.
Pan. 4–23   hope thou in *G·* : — *Psal.* 42 : 11.

house of
'01. 15–28   * sat here in the house of *G·*,
My. 37– 7   * heavenward from this house of *G·*.

hues of
'01. 12–21   bring out the entire hues of *G·*.

[human concept] of
Un. 60–15   [human concept] of *G·*. — *Jas.* 3 : 9.

I believe in
Mis. 96– 8   I believe in *G·* as the Supreme

God

ideal of
Ret.	93–10	ideal of *G·* is no longer impersonated
'02.	12– 6	this ideal of *G·* is *now* and *forever*,
Peo.	5–16	our ideal of *G·* has risen

idea of
Mis.	2–20	Christ, the spiritual idea of *G·*,
	78–27	man is the idea of *G·* ;
	165– 8	wholly spiritual idea of *G·*
	166–16	Christ, the incorporeal idea of *G·*,
	176–18	Christ, the true idea of *G·*
	328–23	presence and idea of *G·*.
Ret.	10–15	voicing the idea of *G·* in man's
	70–21	the advancing idea of *G·*,
Un.	51–21	in the idea of *G·*, good,
	61– 7	even the eternal idea of *G·*,
'00.	6– 9	in the true idea of *G·*.
'02.	7– 9	can give man the true idea of *G·*
My.	194– 7	foreshadows the idea of *G·*,
	206–15	not seeing the spiritual idea of *G·* ;

ideas of
No.	20–12	fully conveys the ideas of *G·*,
Peo.	4–16	mysterious ideas of *G·* and man

illustrates
'02.	8– 2	illustrates *G·*, and man as His

image of
Mis.	61–13	created in the image of *G·*,
Un.	32–25	not man (the image of *G·*) who lied,
	39–23	As the image of *G·*, or Life,
Pul.	81– 7	* express image of *G·* for love.
Rud.	13– 9	spiritual image of *G·*.
No.	17–18	therein is no inverted image of *G·*,
Pan.	9–26	chapter sub-title
	11–28	man is the true image of *G·*,

impelled me
Ret.	50– 1	When *G·* impelled me to set a price

in accord with
Mis.	354–19	body and soul in accord with *G.*

in Christian Science
'01.	6–16	is *G·* in C. S. no God

indebtedness to
My.	12–26	increases our indebtedness to *G·*.

indicates
My.	231– 3	purposes only as *G·* indicates.

indites
Mis.	311–27	transcribing what *G·* indites,

individual
Rud.	2–15	the phrase an *individual G·*,

individuality of
Mis.	103–23	presence, and individuality of *G·*
Rud.	2–18	defines the individuality of *G·*
	3–24	*By the individuality of G·, do you*

infinite
Mis.	93–13	the eternal, infinite *G·*, good.
Man.	15– 7	one supreme and infinite *G·*.
Ret.	70–25	reflection, . . . of the infinite *G·*.
No.	37–22	Scriptures teach an infinite *G·*.
'01.	22–20	calculus of the infinite *G·*.
	25–27	as the infinite *G·*, — good,
My.	119– 6	based on one infinite *G·*,
	235–15	Is *G·* infinite? Yes.
	239–20	and likeness of the infinite *G·*,
	281–13	by which the infinite *G·* good,

infinity of
Pan.	7–16	oneness and infinity of *G·*,

in place of
Mis.	175–21	and its methods in place of *G·*,

intended
Pul.	84–25	* as *G·* intended it should be.

interpretation of
Un.	30–17	interpretation of *G·* and His

interprets
Pul.	12–24	interprets *G·* as divine Principle,
No.	10– 8	reveals and interprets *G·* and man ;

is above
My.	360–30	*G·* is above your teacher,

is a consuming fire
Mis.	151– 6	*G·* is a consuming fire.
	326–14	"*G·* is a consuming fire." — *Heb. 12 : 29.*

is All
Mis.	24–24	(when good is God, and *G·* is All)
	26–22	*G·* is All, in all.
	101–26	If *G·* is All, and God is good,
	208– 5	*G·* is All, and by virtue of this
	258– 9	the great truth that *G·* is All,
	293–24	*G·* is All and there is no sickness
	350–16	"*G·* is All ; there is none — *see Deut. 4 : 35.*
Ret.	63– 5	the recognition that *G· is All*,
Un.	7–23	because *G·* is All,
	31– 5	If God is Spirit, and *G·* is All,
	34–11	*G·* is All, and God is Spirit ;
	48–12	To me *G·* is All.
	60– 6	*G·* is All, and there is none beside
No.	38– 6	on the basis that *G·* is All,
Hea.	10–13	*G·* is All, and in all :
Po.	79–17	Life is light, . . . And *G·* is All.

God

is All
My.	109–19	God is one because *G·* is All.
	178–13	Scripture declares that *G·* is All.
	225–12	belongs to God, for *G·* is All ;
	299–19	and that *G·* is *All*

is All-in-all
Mis.	21–18	for *G·* is All-in-all.
	125–20	for *G·* is All-in-all.
	155– 1	Forget not . . . that *G·* is All-in-all
	319– 4	for *G·* is All-in-all.
Un.	3–20	*G·* is All-in-all.
	24– 8	I say unto you, *G·* is All-in-all ;
Rud.	5– 5	Scriptures imply, *G·* is All-in-all,
No.	15–24	*G·* is All-in-all ;
	23–26	*G·* is All-in-all ;
My.	123–31	people whose *G·* is All-in-all,
	127– 4	people whose *G·* is All-in-all,
	181– 3	basis that *G·* is All-in-all ;

is all-power
Mis.	173–21	*G·*, is all-power and all-presence,
Ret.	60–18	*G·* is all-power and all-presence,

is a Person
'01.	11–24	namely, that *G·* is a Person,

is a Spirit
Mis.	219– 8	"*G·* is a Spirit :— *John 4 : 24.*
Un.	31– 1	"*G·* is a Spirit" — *John 4 : 24.*

is blessing
My.	201– 1	*G·* is blessing you, my beloved

is come
'02.	12– 9	Christian idea that *G·* is come,

is commonly called
Un.	15–16	*G·* is commonly called the *sinless*,

is divine
Pan.	4–12	*G·* is divine.

is divine Love
Mis.	186–15	that *G·* is divine Love :
My.	135–30	understand that *G·* is divine Love,

is divine Principle
My.	116–13	for *G·* is divine Principle, Love.
	225–27	stated that *G·* is divine Principle

is egoistic
Un.	27–14	*G·* is *egoistic*, knowing only His own

is eternal
No.	37– 8	evil is temporal and *G·* is eternal,

is ever present
Mis.	27–22	though *G·* is ever present ;
Un.	37–11	Because *G·* is ever present,
	60–21	If *G·* is ever present, He is

is everywhere
Ret.	61–18	*G·* is everywhere.
My.	128–12	*G·* is everywhere.

is Father
My.	279–16	*G·* is Father, infinite, and

is for us
Mis.	157–25	This I know, for *G·* is for us.

is glorified
My.	355–27	*G·* is glorified in His reflection

is God
Po.	72– 3	Till *G·* is God no longer

is good
Mis.	71–31	law of Science, that *G·* is good only,
	93– 5	*G·* is good : in Him dwelleth no evil.
	101–26	If God is All, and *G·* is good,
	153–13	*G·* is good to Israel,
	172–31	*G·* is good ; hence, good is
	184– 2	that *G·* is good, but man is
	199–28	*G·* is good, and goodness is
	206–22	"Good is my God, and my *G·* is good.
	206–25	*G·* is good, and good is the reward
	218– 2	Spirit is God, and *G·* is good.
	319– 3	If good is God, even as *G·* is good·
	389–17	since *G·* is good, and loss is gain
Ret.	63–14	*G·* is good, hence goodness is
Un.	25– 7	Spirit is God, and *G·* is good ;
	39–25	presuppose that *G·* is good
	40–16	Life is God, and *G·* is good.
Rud.	9–27	*G·* is good, and the producer only of
	11– 6	whereby you learn that *G·* is good,
No.	17– 5	*G·* is good, ever-present, and All.
'01.	22– 1	That *G·* is good, that Truth is true.
	23– 6	that *G·* is good and infinite.
Po.	4–16	since *G·* is good, and loss is gain.
	79–11	Our *G·* is good.
My.	299–19	believe that *G·* is good,

is his Father
Ret.	69– 3	*G·* is his Father, and Life is the law
'02.	8–30	conscious that *G·* is his Father,

is individual
Mis.	101–31	*G·* is individual Mind.
No.	19–15	*G·* is individual, and man is His

is infinite
Ret.	73– 4	but *G·* is infinite.
No.	19–11	*G·* is infinite.
Pan.	7– 1	Spirit, *G·*, is infinite,
'01.	5–20	*G·* is infinite Spirit or Person,
My.	239–18	*G·* is *infinite* and so includes *all*

God

is infinite good
Mis. 367–18   *G·* is infinite good,
Pan. 6–15   If *G·* is *infinite* good,
My. 356–26   and this *G·* is infinite good.

is infinite Love
'02. 6–29   wherein *G·* is infinite Love,

is infinite Mind
Rud. 4–15   *G·* is infinite Mind,

is just
Mis. 2– 9   remember that *G·* is just,
Pul. 7– 9   remember also that *G·* is just,

is leading
My. 140–18   *G·* is leading you onward

is Life
Un. 37– 2   *G·* is Life ;
37–13   because *G·* is Life,
37–15   *G·* is Life and All-in-all.

is light
'01. 3–21   * *G·* is light, but light is not God."

is Love
Mis. 96–14   "*G·* is Love," — *I John* 4 : 8.
123–29   Holy Writ declares that *G·* is Love,
125–19   "*G·* is Love ;" — *I John* 4 : 8.
150–24   "*G·* is Love." — *I John* 4 : 8.
206–23   Love is my God, and my *G·* is Love."
250– 2   the *alone G·*, is Love.
399–26   *G·* is Love, and understood
Pul. 13–13   certain sense that *G·* is Love.
16–11   *G·* is Love, and understood
Rud. 10–18   true sense that *G·* is Love.
No. 19–12   *G·* is Love ; and Love is Principle,
'01. 3–16   "*G·* is Love." — *I John* 4 : 8.
3–20   * It is sometimes said : "*G·* is Love,
3–28   logical that because *G·* is Love,
'02. 5–18   "*G·* is Love." — *I John* 4 : 8.
5–25   Since *G·* is Love, and infinite,
8– 1   "*G·* is Love," — *I John* 4 : 8.
8– 7   "*G·* is Love ;" — *I John* 4 : 8.
Hea. 3–24   "*G·* is Love, Truth, and Life,"
Po. 76–10   *G·* is Love, and understood
My. 109–13   "*G·* is Love," — *I John* 4 : 8.
180–21   in mercy, *G·* is Love.
188–15   "*G·* is Love," — *I John* 4 : 8.
278–29   power is God, and *G·* is Love.

is love
Un. 26–16   * God is wisdom, *G·* is love.

is made manifest
Mis. 78– 3   when *G·* is made manifest
'01. 9–16   *G·* is made manifest in the flesh,

is man's origin
Un. 53–25   *G· is* man's origin and loving

is Mind
Mis. 45– 3   understanding that *G·* is Mind,
58–29   if you agree that *G·* is Mind,
105–31   Because *G·* is Mind, and this
173–20   *G·* is Mind and fills all space,
Un. 14–21   As *G·* is Mind, if this Mind is
Pul. 69–18   * idea is that *G·* is Mind,
Rud. 5– 6   since *G·* is Mind.
Pan. 4–17   but *G·* is Mind and one.
My. 349– 1   *G·* is Mind, and divine Mind

is no respecter
'01. 27–20   *G·* is no respecter of persons.

is not finite
'01. 4–19   understand that *G·* is not finite ;

is not in matter
Mis. 75–13   *G·* is not in matter or the

is not mocked
Pul. 7–22   "*G·* is not mocked," — *Gal.* 6 : 7.
My. 6– 5   "*G·* is not mocked : — *Gal.* 6 : 7.

is not part
Mis. 102–14   *G·* is not part, but the whole.

is not personal
Mis. 102– 9   lower sense *G·* is not personal.

is not unable
No. 42– 5   *G·* is not unable or unwilling

is omnipotent
Mis. 63–19   *G·* is omnipotent and omnipresent ;
90– 1   know that *G·* is omnipotent ;
Hea. 5– 3   admitting that *G·* is omnipotent,

is omnipresence
Mis. 229–10   since *G·* is omnipresence,

is One
Mis. 258–14   In divine Science, *G·* is One
'00. 4–24   believe that *G·* is *One* and *All?*

is one
My. 109–19   *G·* is one because God is All.
116–12   If *G·* is one and God is Person,
239–17   *G·* is one, and His idea,

is our Father
Mis. 151–13   *G·* is our Father and our Mother,

is our Life
Mis. 50–24   understanding that *G·* is our Life,

God

is our Shepherd
Mis. 150–31   hence *G·* is our Shepherd.

is over all
Ret. 22–17   *G·* is over all.

is Person
'01. 6–22   *G·* is Person in the infinite
My. 116–12   If God is one and *G·* is Person,

is personal
Rud. 2–10   but *G·* is personal, if by person
'01. 4–17   *G·* is personal in a scientific

is really All
Mis. 27–23   when *G·* is really *All.*

is recognized
Mis. 85– 8   *G·* is recognized as the divine
No. 20–21   *G·* is recognized as the only power,

is regarded
Mis. 234–28   *G·* is regarded more as absolute,

is responsible
Mis. 347–25   *G·* is responsible for the mission of
Un. 64– 2   If . . . *G·* is responsible therefor ;

is seen
Mis. 23–25   *G·* is seen only in that which

is self-existent
'00. 5–12   *G·* is self-existent, the essence

is Spirit
Mis. 55–26   If *G·* is Spirit, as the Scriptures
75–11   synonym of Spirit, and *G·* is Spirit.
113– 4   "*G·* is Spirit," — *see John* 4 : 24.
184– 1   by claiming that *G·* is Spirit,
Un. 31– 2   accurately translated, "*G·* is Spirit"
31– 5   If *G·* is Spirit, and God is All,
34–11   that God is All, and *G·* is Spirit ;
Rud. 4–21   "*G·* is Spirit ;" — *see John* 4 : 24.
13–16   "*G·* is Spirit." — *see John* 4 : 24.
'01. 3–15   "*G·* is Spirit," — *see John* 4 : 24.
22– 5   Mind of God — and *G·* is Spirit.
23– 5   would admit that *G·* is Spirit
Peo. 7–30   Because *G·* is Spirit, our thoughts must
My. 221–16   *G·* is Spirit. Then modes of healing,
266–19   *G·* is Spirit and the origin of all
270–31   *G·* is Spirit,

is supposed
Mis. 72– 9   *G·* is supposed to impart to man

is supreme
Mis. 3–25   *G·* is supreme and omnipotent,
259–17   Science, in which *G·* is supreme,

is the Alpha
Un. 10–19   *G·* is the Alpha and Omega,

is the author
'01. 4–12   *G·* is the author of Science

is the Father
Mis. 164–31   *G·* is the Father of man,

is the fountain
Mis. 117–27   *G·* is the fountain of light,

is the giver
My. 205– 8   and *G·* is the giver.

is the law
Mis. 259– 5   *G·* is the law of Life,

is the only creator
Mis. 286–26   Spirit, *G·*, is the only creator :
No. 6– 6   *G·* is the only creator,

is the only Life
Mis. 16–17   great fact that *G· is the only Life;*
194–28   *know* that *G·* is the only Life.

is the only Mind
Mis. 361–24   *G·* is the only Mind,
No. 35–21   *G·* is the only Mind, Life,

is the Principle
Mis. 78–26   If *G·* is the Principle of man
Hea. 3–21   *G·* is the Principle of Christian healing,

is "the same
Un. 61– 3   *G·* is "the same yesterday, — *Heb.* 13 : 8.

is the temple
Mis. 323– 4   for *G·* is the temple thereof ;

is this Principle
Mis. 194– 4   and *G·* is this Principle.

is Truth
Mis. 25– 8   since *G·* is Truth, and All-in-all.
49–30   *G·* is Truth, the Scriptures aver ;
Un. 35–16   But *G·* is Truth,

is understandable
My. 238–21   *G·* is understandable, knowable,

is understood
Mis. 346– 4   proof that *G·* is understood
Un. 6– 5   selfhood of *G·* is understood,

is universal
Mis. 150–25   *G·* is universal ; confined to no spot,

is upright
Mis. 79–15   *G·* is upright and eternal,

is wisdom
Un. 26–16   * *G·* is wisdom, God is love.

justify
Mis. 374– 3   even the publicans to justify *G·*.

God

kingdom of
(*see* **kingdom**)
knowing
My. 356– 5 privilege of knowing *G·*,
knowledge of
(*see* **knowledge**)
known of
My. 120– 6 know as we are known of *G·*.
known to
No. 7–17 loving sacrifice . . . is known to *G·*,
knows
Mis. 259–12 declares that *G·* knows iniquity!
Un. 1– 3 *G·* knows no such thing as sin.
13–18 If *G·* knows that which is not
15–10 If *G·* knows evil, so must man,
19– 7 If *G·* knows evil at all, He must
22–13 *G·* knows that a knowledge of
54–17 If *G·* knows sin, even as a
No. 16– 7 If *G·* knows evil even as a
17– 2 If *G·* knows the antecedent,
37–27 What *G·* knows, He also predestinates;
'01. 21–24 faith assures me that *G·* knows
Lamb of
Mis. 121–23 "the Lamb of *G·*."— *John* 1 : 29.
law of
(*see* **law**)
laws of
(*see* **laws**)
leadeth me
Mis. 397–20 whereto *G·* leadeth me.
Pul. 19– 4 whereto *G·* leadeth me.
Po. 13– 8 whereto *G·* leadeth me.
lead you to
My. 213–21 whether they lead you to *G·*
leaned on
'02. 15– 5 I leaned on *G·*, and was safe.
learn
Mis. 235–19 learn *G·* aright, and know
Peo. 6–16 but when we learn *G·* aright,
learn that
Peo. 2–10 learn that *G·*, good, is universal,
leave with
Ret. 90–30 leave with *G·* the government
leaving self for
Peo. 9– 6 it is love leaving self for *G·*.
Life and
Un. 37–16 do not testify of Life and *G·*.
Life as
Mis. 189–20 Life in God and Life *as G·*.
Un. 38–23 Life as *G·*, moral and spiritual
My. 273–22 understanding of Life as *G·*,
Life in
Mis. 189–19 Life in *G·* and Life *as* God.
life in
Mis. 64– 8 indestructible eternal life in *G·*.
My. 150–23 raising . . . to life in *G·*.
Life is
(*see* **Life**)
Life, or
Ret. 59–16 antipodes of Life, or *G·*,
Un. 38– 4 a contradiction of Life, or *G·*;
Life that is
Mis. 194–30 naturalness of the Life that is *G·*,
196–21 When the Life that is *G·*, good,
light is not
'01. 3–22 * God is light, but light is not *G·*."
light of
Mis. 340–29 shine with the reflected light of *G·*.
likeness of
Mis. 61–22 image and likeness of *G·*.
97–22 image and likeness of *G·*.
182–20 image and likeness of *G·*,
186– 9 in the image and likeness of *G·*;
188–30 the true likeness of *G·*,
308–31 man in the image and likeness of *G·*.
Rud. 7–10 He is the likeness of *G·*;
No. 25–17 Man is the image and likeness of *G·*,
'02. 8– 5 likeness of *G·*, Spirit, is spiritual,
Hea. 17– 5 present the image and likeness of *G·*.
My. 36–24 * in the image and likeness of *G·*.
119–32 true image and likeness of *G·*.
lives also in
Pul. 4–20 Who lives in good, lives also in *G·*,
lives in
Un. 40–17 abides in good, if he lives in *G·*,
living
Mis. 372–28 character of the living *G·*,
Un. 49–13 consciousness of the only living *G·*
62–22 "I am the living *G·*, and man is My
My. 46–28 * city of the living *G·*,— *Heb.* 12 : 22.
Lord is
Un. 21–15 The Lord is *G·*.
lose with
Mis. 341–19 O learn to lose with *G·*!

God

love
Mis. 10– 7 to them that love *G·*."— *Rom.* 8 : 28.
51–19 educate him to love *G·*, good,
123–25 love *G·*, and keep His commandments,
240–21 Children . . . naturally love *G·*;
311– 1 love *G·* and keep His commandments,
318–11 love *G·* and keep His commandments.
367– 4 and to love *G·* supremely.
'00. 11–11 to them that love *G·*,"— *Rom.* 8 : 28.
'01. 32–20 love *G·* and keep His commandments
My. 4–15 loves all who love *G·*,
6– 3 Do we love *G·* supremely?
143–26 to them that love *G·*,— *Rom.* 8 : 28.
233–29 Do Christian Scientists love *G·* as
276–25 to love *G·* supremely,
286– 7 love *G·* supremely,
love and
Mis. 395– 4 Is out of tune With love and *G·*;
Po. 57–11 Is out of tune With love and *G·*;
Love as
Mis. 234–10 true sense of Love as *G·*;
love for
(*see* **love**)
Love is
'01. 3–21 * this is no argument that Love is *G·*;
love of
Mis. 279– 4 It is the love of *G·*, and not the
No. 7– 8 By the love of *G·* we can cancel
My. 19–10 and the love of *G·*,— *II Cor.* 13 : 14.
46–23 * love of *G·* and our brother,
159–14 perfect love of *G·* and man.
187–16 the grace and love of *G·*
200–17 the love of *G·* and man.
loves
Mis. 100–27 because he loves *G·* most.
'01. 21–16 individual who loves *G·* and man;
love to
Pul. 39– 2 * love to *G·* and love to man
My. 274–24 and love to *G·* and man;
loving
Mis. 328–30 Then, loving *G·* supremely
Rud. 10–20 look up to the loving *G·*,
Po. 43– 4 Loving *G·* and one another,
loyal to
Mis. 277–10 a heart loyal to *G·* is patient
made
Mis. 45–21 If *G· made all that was made,*
50– 1 *G·* made all that was made,
186–14 We learn . . . that *G·* made all;
Un. 14– 6 after *G·* made the universe,
32– 4 saying, . . . *G·* made me, and I make man
'01. 7– 9 *G·* made man in His own image
8–14 more transcendental than *G·* made him?
8–19 As *G·* made man, is he not wholly
'02. 6–12 *G·* made neither evil nor its
Hea. 9–23 *G·* made all that was made,
17– 8 *G·* made all that was made;
My. 107–24 *G·* made all that was made,
124–28 *G·* made "manifest— *I Tim.* 3 : 16.
178–15 all that *G·* made "good;" — *Gen.* 1 : 31.
288–31 all is good because *G·* made all,
made by
Hea. 9–18 man made by *G·* had
made manifest
Mis. 77–10 *G·* made manifest through man,
My. 348– 6 *G·* made manifest in the flesh,
makes
Mis. 111–10 *G·* makes "fishers of men"— *Mark* 1 : 17.
117–30 make their moves before *G·* makes His,
177– 2 *G·* makes to us all, right here,
353–19 *G·* makes *us* pay for tending the
Un. 13– 3 theology makes *G·* tributary to man,
'01. 7– 3 theology makes *G·* manlike;
24– 7 Here he makes *G·* the cause of
My. 205–20 so makes *G·* more supreme
man and
Mis. 77–11 eternal unity of man and *G·*,
332–17 pondered the things of man and *G·*.
Ret. 60–27 or of the real man and *G·*.
Peo. 1– 7 final unity between man and *G·*.
manhood of
Mis. 33–11 as well as in the manhood of *G·*,
Hea. 10– 6 fought the manhood of *G·*,
manifest
My. 109–24 *G·* "manifest in the flesh,"— *I Tim.* 3 : 16.
manifestation of
'00. 10– 3 is some manifestation of *G·*
manlike
Mis. 178– 6 not satisfied with a manlike *G·*,
'01. 7– 3 theology makes *G·* manlike;
man of
Mis. 159–19 as the man of *G·*, the risen Christ,
man or
Ret. 71–19 without the permission of man or *G·*,

God

man to
Un. 51–25　scientific relation of man to G·,

man with
Un. 5–24　marvellous unity of man with G·

men call
'01. 18–26　Truth, Love— whom men call G·

message from
'02. 11–16　new-old message from G·,

methods of
Mis. 270–25　modes and methods of G·.

mighty
Mis. 161– 7　*The mighty G·,* — *Isa.* 9 : 6.
164–18　*The mighty G·,* — *Isa.* 9 : 6.
321– 6　*The mighty G·,* — *Isa.* 9 : 6.

mills of
Ret. 80– 8　* mills of G· grind slowly,

Mind is
(*see* **Mind**)

Mind of
No. 37–27　existed in the Mind of G·.
'01. 22– 5　It is the Mind of G·
27–25　the Mind of G· and not of man

Mind, or
Mis. 69– 6　Mind, or G·, and His attributes.
Ret. 56– 5　the one divine Mind, or G·,
No. 5–20　then Mind, or G·, does not

Mind that is
Mis. 4– 7　Science of the Mind that is G·,
57–31　existed in and of the Mind that is G·,
113– 1　Mind that is G· is not in matter ;
My. 267– 5　law of the Mind that is G·,

Mind which is
Mis. 36– 9　eternal Mind, which is G·,
Un. 44–18　expressive of the Mind which is G·.
56– 6　in the Mind which is G·.

must be One
'01. 6–14　G· must be One although He is three.

must know
Un. 17–20　Error says G· must know evil
18–22　Error says G· must know death

my
Mis. 63–22　"My G·, why hast Thou — Mark 15 : 34.
206–22　"Good is my G·,
206–22　my G· is good.
206–22　Love is my G·,
206–23　my G· is Love."
Un. 29–27　my G· [my Soul, — Psal. 42 : 11.
Pan. 4–24　and my G·. — Psal. 42 : 11.
Po. 33–19　waft me away to my G·.

mysterious
Peo. 3–13　make a mysterious G· and a

name
Mis. 15–24　infinite good that we name G·,
26–28　Scriptures name G· as good,
My. 225–21　to the divine Spirit the name G·.

named
Rud. 2–17　whom mortals have named G·.

named Himself
Mis. 258–18　G· named Himself, I AM

namely
Mis. 189–22　namely G·, the eternal good,
My. 226–14　the infinite, — namely, G·.

name of
'00. 10–14　and this, too, in the name of G·,
My. 190–30　Then, in the name of G·,
233–19　taking the name of G· in vain.

names
My. 225–21　C. S. names G· as divine Principle,

nature of
Mis. 104–12　not in the nature of G·,
217–28　nature of G· must change in order to
218–18　unfolds the real nature of G·
259– 4　partakes not of the nature of G·,
Pan. 5– 9　possessed of the nature of G·,
'01. 3–23　Love expresses the nature of G· ;
3–25　loses the nature of G·, Spirit,
4– 2　both have the nature of G·.
5–26　nature of G· must be seen in man,
10–17　C. S. explains the nature of G·
My. 110– 1　it is the divine nature of G·,
288–11　has no origin in the nature of G·,

nature's
Po. v–15　* through nature, unto nature's G·,"
My. 151–25　"through nature up to nature's G·,"

near enough to
No. 27– 6　get near enough to G· to see this,

nearer to
Mis. 6– 2　to bring man nearer to G·,
Un. 7–25　and brings us nearer to G·,

neither slumbers
Mis. 209–17　G· neither slumbers nor sleeps.

never made
Mis. 122–28　G· never made it,
241–19　"G· never made you sick :
Un. 20–12　First: G· never made evil.

God

never made
Un. 45–11　that G· never made evil.
53– 3　G· never made them ;
'01. 13– 1　and G· never made it.
Hea. 9–17　G· never made a wicked man ;

never said
Un. 14–27　G· never said that man would

noblest work of
Mis. 294– 1　noblest work of G· is man

no cognizance of
Un. 28–19　they take no cognizance of G·.

no other
Mis. 182– 8　no other G·, no other Mind,

nor acknowledged
No. 18– 3　nor acknowledged G· in all His ways.

not asking
No. 39–17　True prayer is not asking G· for

not of
Un. 11– 9　laws of mortal mind, not of G·.
'02. 6–15　something that is not of G·.
My. 4–32　not of G· but originates in the

not ordained of
Ret. 49–15　powers that are not ordained of G·,

noumenon is
My. 347–28　Principle whose noumenon is G·

obedience to
Mis. 12–30　measured by our obedience to G·,
267–28　that action, in obedience to G·,

obey
My. 118– 2　obey G· and steadily go on

of all grace
Mis. 116– 3　The G· of all grace be with you,
159– 7　G· of all grace give you peace.
My. 148– 7　and may the G· of all grace,

of Christian Science
'01. 6– 4　the G· of C. S. is not a person,

of harvest
Mis. 313–21　G· of harvest to send forth more

of harvests
My. 291–28　to pray, that the G· of harvests

of Israel
My. 182–20　the G· of Israel, the divine Love

of my fathers
My. 285–26　G· of my fathers, — Acts 24 : 14.

of nature
My. 349–22　coexist with the G· of nature

of our fathers
My. 192–13　May the G· of our fathers,

of peace
Mis. 128–13　G· of peace shall be — Phil. 4 : 9.
153–30　G· of peace be and abide with this

of spirituality
Un. 49–16　and the G· of spirituality.

of their fathers
My. 43– 7　* revealed the G· of their fathers,

of theology
'01. 6–3　says the G· of theology is a Person,
6–9　Is the G· of theology a finite or an

omnipotence of
Mis. 31–21　faith in the *omnipotence* of G·,

omnipotent
'01. 5– 9　G· omnipotent, omnipresent,

omnipresence of
Ret. 56–17　omnipotence and omnipresence of G·,
Rud. 9–26　omnipotence and omnipresence of G· ;

omnipresent
'02. 12– 8　he has one omnipresent G· :
Po. 23–19　Supreme and omnipresent G·,

One
Pan. 12–22　strictly monotheism, — it has ONE G·.

one
Mis. 22– 1　a theist — believe in one G·,
23–23　synonymous for the one G·,
25– 3　That there is but one G·
36–10　and there is but one G·.
50–29　changed to having but *one* G·
55–24　knows that he can have one G· only,
56–20　one G·, and the brotherhood of man.
75–12　There is but one G·
131–12　one faith, one G·, one baptism.
196– 1　lead to the one G· :
196– 2　for there is but one G·,
196– 5　supposition . . . more than one G·,
252–22　It has one G·.
341– 3　whole human race have one G·,
364–20　nothing apart from this Mind, one G·,
Ret. 69–30　there is and can be but one G·,
Un. 10– 9　utter reliance upon the one G·,
24– 8　assumptions . . . more than the one G· ;
29–12　There is but one G·, one Soul,
37– 3　as there is but one G·,
Pul. 74–27　never can be but one G·,
Rud. 13–12　saith there is more than one G·,
No. 38–16　the interpreter of one G·,
38–19　Having one G·, one Mind.

God

one
Pan.	1–19	know and acknowledge one *G·*
	3–22	In religion, it is a belief in one *G·*, or in
	7– 4	signifies more than one *G·*,
	8–13	chapter sub-title
	8–17	Christianity then had one *G·*
	9– 3	one *G·* and His creation,
	9– 9	one *G·* and the four first rules
	13–22	"one *G·* and Father — *Eph.* 4 : 6.
'00.	4– 4	real and normal as the one *G·*,
	4–10	the perfect worship of one *G·*.
	5–11	they signify one *G·*.
	5–16	whereby to have one *G·*,
'01.	5– 5	lose the nature of one *G·*,
'02.	12–12	the Jew's belief in one *G·*,
Peo.	13– 9	revealing the one *G·* and His
My.	109– 8	we shall have one Mind, one *G·*,
	109–20	there can be but one *G·*,
	116–11	Thou shalt have one *G·*.
	155– 8	May this church have one *G·*,
	191–12	one *G·* and one Christ.
	240– 2	one *G·* and the brotherhood of man
	252– 2	Have one *G·* and you will have no
	281–11	namely, one *G·*, one Mind,
	286– 6	have one *G·*, one Mind ;
	303–18	its pure monotheism — one *G·*,
	339– 6	one *G·*, supreme, infinite,

oneness of
Mis.	93– 9	the allness and oneness of *G·*
	152– 5	the oneness of *G·* includes
My.	342–23	simplicity of the oneness of *G·* ;

oneness with
Mis.	286–10	found to be man's oneness with *G·*,
Un.	54–15	*at-one-ment*, or oneness with *G·*,

one with
Mis.	245–29	* "one with *G·* is a majority."
Pul.	74–25	one with *G·*, in the sense of

only
Mis.	55–24	he can have one *G·* only,
Rud.	4–17	Good is not in evil, but in *G·* only.
'01.	3–26	expresses *G·* only in metaphor,
Peo.	12–12	acknowledge only *G·* in all thy ways,

only waits
Mis.	154–10	*G·* only waits for man's worthiness

opposed to
Mis.	49–27	not only a power opposed to *G·*,
Pul.	13– 5	belief in a power opposed to *G·*.

opposition to
Mis.	197–29	theory that is in opposition to *G·*,
'02.	10–27	opposition to *G·* and His power

oracles of
Mis.	107– 3	mistaken for the oracles of *G·*.

ordains
Ret.	85–17	you do not feel that *G·* ordains you.

or good
Ret.	54–12	believing in *G·*, or good,
Un.	31–23	*G·*, or good, is Spirit alone ;

originates in
Mis.	186– 2	man who originates in *G·*,

origin in
No.	18– 7	proof of its origin in *G·*,

or Life
Mis.	25– 3	there is but one *G·* or Life,
Un.	39–23	As the image of *G·*, or Life,

or man
No.	23–25	cannot understand *G·* or man,
	27–23	personality of *G·* or man is

or Spirit
Un.	10–11	Life is *G·*, or Spirit,
No.	16–13	none beside *G·* or Spirit

other than
'02.	6– 4	apart or other than *G·* — good

our
Mis.	124–13	so great a God as our *G·* !" — *Psal.* 77 : 13.
	129– 9	The law of our *G·*
	206–30	the dwelling-place of our *G·*,
	308–16	Lord our *G·* is one Lord." — *Deut.* 6 : 4.
Pul.	10–18	corner-stone in the house of our *G·*.
	12– 7	kingdom of our *G·*, — *Rev.* 12 : 10.
	12– 9	accused them before our *G·* — *Rev.* 12 : 10.
Po.	79–11	Our *G·* is good.
My.	185–28	* Our *G·*, our fathers' God !
	186–19	May our *G·* make this church
	280–15	chapter sub-title — *Deut.* 6 : 4.

outstretched to
No.	44–18	weak hand outstretched to *G·*.

overrules it
Mis.	41– 6	were it not that *G·* overrules it,

pardoned by
No.	29–19	A mortal pardoned by *G·* is

peace in
Mis.	385– 3	* Above the sod Find peace in *G·*,
Po.	37– 3	* Above the sod Find peace in *G·*,

peace of
No.	8– 8	"the peace of *G·*, — *Phil.* 4 : 7.

God

peace with
Mis.	211–28	and kept peace with *G·*.
'01.	2–20	keeping peace with *G·*.

people of
Mis.	216– 4	Sabbath rest for the people of *G·* ;

perception of
Un.	20–18	perception of *G·* as All-in-all.

perfect in
Mis.	5–27	perfect in *G·*, in Truth, Life, and

personal
Mis.	96– 7	Do I believe in a personal *G·* ?
Rud.	2–16	rather than *a personal G·* ;
'01.	11–25	a sermon from his personal *G·* !
Peo.	3–20	A personal *G·* is based on
	4–13	the error that a personal *G·*

pities
No.	30–13	*G·* pities our woes with the love of a

pitieth
Un.	2– 3	*G·* pitieth them who fear Him ;

possible to
Mis.	183–13	possible to *G·*, is possible to man
Un.	18–27	If such . . . were possible to *G·*,
My.	293– 1	all things are possible to *G·*

power of
		(*see* **power**)

praise
My.	148–18	you have met to praise *G·*.
	207– 4	wrath of men shall praise *G·*,

praise to
My.	323–21	* gratitude and praise to *G·*

praising
My.	245–19	go on *ad infinitum*, praising *G·*,

pray to
Mis.	114–22	cannot . . . pray to *G·* too fervently,

prepares
My.	12–24	*G·* prepares the way for

prerogative of
Un.	32– 3	usurps the prerogative of *G·*,
No.	23– 5	neither grasp the prerogative of *G·*

preserving
My.	344–11	*G·* preserving individuality and

Principle is
Un.	38– 2	immortality, whose Principle is *G·*.
	38–28	being, whose Principle is *G·*.

Principle that is
Peo.	5–20	yea, to the Principle that is *G·*,

proceedeth not from
Mis.	198–14	evil proceedeth not from *G·*,

proceed from
Mis.	76– 1	must proceed from *G·* ;
'00.	4–25	must proceed from *G·*, from Mind,

proceeds from
Mis.	49–29	belief . . . to err proceeds from *G·*.
	58–22	order that proceeds from *G·*.

proceeds not from
Mis.	36–12	harmful and proceeds not from *G·* ;

prophet of
Pan.	8–11	the only prophet of *G·*

providence of
Mis.	80–19	through the providence of *G·*,
	100– 4	left to the providence of *G·*.
	163–15	committed to the providence of *G·*.
Ret.	30–20	providence of *G·*, and the cross of
Pul.	20–12	committed to the providence of *G·*,
My.	148– 3	through the providence of *G·*,
	220– 3	submit to the providence of *G·*,

purpose of
Mis.	366–21	as the purpose of *G·* ;
My.	216–18	purpose of *G·* to youward

quality of
Pan.	5– 2	Can a single quality of *G·*,

reaches others
Mis.	39–26	*by which G· reaches others*

reaches out to
My.	290–12	My soul reaches out to *G·* for your

realities of
No.	5–24	the realities of *G·* and His laws.

reality of
Un.	34–25	What is the reality of *G·*
My.	248–17	reality of *G·*, man, nature,

reconciliation with
No.	35–22	needs no reconciliation with *G·*,

referring to
My.	225–31	Principle, when referring to *G·*,

refer to
Mis.	59–19	Scriptures refer to *G·* as saying,

reflect
'00.	4–27	they reflect *G·* and nothing else.
My.	150–19	enable you to reflect *G·*,

reflecting
No.	21–12	showed man as reflecting *G·*

reflection of
Rud.	7– 9	the manifest reflection of *G·*,

reflects
Mis.	184– 7	only when man reflects *G·*

God

reflects
  Ret. 56–23   *G·* reflects Himself, or Mind,
       57–15   He reflects *G·* as his Mind,
regards
  Mis. 55–25   regards *G·* as the only Mind,
reigns
  Mis. 80–22   *G·* reigns, and will . . . until
relation to
  Mis. 235– 2   recognition of his relation to *G·*.
relying on
  Mis. 115–22   necessity for relying on *G·*
remember
  Mis. 175–32   remember *G·* in all thy ways,
removes
  '01. 13–22   *G·* removes the punishment for sin
render to
  My. 220–11   render 'to *G·* the things — *Mark* 12 : 17.
representatives of
  Mis. 200– 5   better representatives of *G·*
represents
  Mis. 336– 8   that which represents *G·* most,
  Ret. 63–15   represents *G·*, the Life of man.
  No. 26–13   All real being represents *G·*,
requires
  Man. 44–26   *G·* requires our whole heart,
       77–18   *G·* requires wisdom, economy,
  No. 34–20   heathen conception that *G·* requires
resembles
  Mis. 167–9   idea of all that resembles *G·*.
rest in
  Rud. 12–19   and induces rest in *G·*,
  My. 282– 6   my hope must still rest in *G·*,
rests on
  No. 24– 9   which rests on *G·* as One and All,
revealed
  Mis. 179–31   when *G·* revealed to me this risen
  My. v–25   * revealed *G·* to well-nigh countless
reveals
  Mis. 82– 2   and reveals *G·* and man as
       219– 3   neither reveals *G·* in matter,
  Ret. 60–11   C. S. reveals *G·* and
       65–30   reveals *G·* as ever-present Truth and
right hand of
  Mis. 178–13   on the right hand of *G·*'' — *Col.* 3 : 1.
rising to
  Mis. 144–26   our visible lives are rising to *G·*.
robs
  Un. 38–15   material sense of life robs *G·*,
rod of
  Mis. 19– 5   but the rod of *G·*,
saith
  Un. 18–23   *G·* saith, I am ever-conscious Life,
save
  My. 289–17   "*G·* save the Queen"
says
  Mis. 367–15   but *G·* says of this fruit of the tree
  Un. 18– 7   *G·* says, I am too pure to behold
       18–14   *G·*, says you oftenest console others
       18–17   *G·* says, I show My pity
scale of
  Mis. 312– 4   when weighed in the scale of *G·*
scales of
  Mis. 293–12   weighs in the scales of *G·*
      372– 4   weight in the scales of *G·*.
Science of
    (*see* **Science**)
see
  Mis. 15– 8   they shall see *G·*.'' — *Matt.* 5 : 8.
      185– 2   pure in heart shall see *G·*,
  Ret. 26–25   none but the pure in heart can see *G·*,
  Un. 51–24   where we see *G·* as Life,
      55–21   in my flesh shall I see *G·* ;'' — *Job* 19 : 26.
  Pul. 3–20   in my flesh shall I see *G·*.'' — *Job* 19 : 26.
      35–11   'pure in heart' can see *G·*.'' — *Matt.* 5 : 8.
  '01. 26–18   left to such as see *G·*
  My. 132–20   where we may see *G·* and live,
      218– 5   "In my flesh shall I see *G·*.'' — *Job* 19 : 26.
seek
  Mis. 206–26   all who diligently seek *G·*.
seemed
  '01. 32–10   *G·* seemed to shield the whole
sees
  Mis. 361– 2   pure heart that sees *G·*.
  Un. 49–25   something which *G·* sees and knows,
self-existence of
  Pan. 8–10   deny the self-existence of *G·* ?
self-existent
  Pan. 3–19   supreme, holy, self-existent *G·*,
self-same
  Un. 3–27   this self-same *G·* is our helper.
self-sustained by
  Mis. 316– 9   must be self-sustained by *G·*.
sense of
    (*see* **sense**)

God

separate from
  Mis. 36–29   in matter and separate from *G·*,
  Ret. 60– 6   as something separate from *G·*.
      67– 9   yet are separate from *G·*.
serve
  Mis. 237– 8   serve *G·* (or try to) from fear ;
      269– 9   cannot serve *G·* and — *Matt.* 6 : 24.
  01. 20– 4   serve *G·* and benefit mankind.
  '02. 3–28   true ambition is to serve *G·*
  My. 5–29   indulging sin, men cannot serve *G·* ;
      356–24   cannot serve *G·* and — *Matt.* 6 : 24.
shall help her
  Pul. 83–20   * "*G·* shall help her, — *Psal.* 46 : 5.
shall reveal
  Mis. 348–12   *G·* shall reveal His rod,
signet of
  Mis. 121–21   thereby giving the signet of *G·*
smiles of
  Mis. 179–27   to give us these smiles of *G·* !
so clothe
  No. 26–26   "If God so clothe — *Matt.* 6 : 30.
Son of
    (*see* **Son**)
son of
    (*see* **son**)
sonship with
  Mis. 83–23   declared his sonship with *G·* :
      360–11   scientific sonship with *G·*.
sons of
  Mis. 176–13   the liberty of the sons of *G·*.
      180–22   *become the sons of G·*, — *John* 1 : 12.
      181–25   become the sons of *G·*.'' — *John* 1 : 12.
      185–19   become the sons of *G·*.'' — *John* 1 : 12.
      185–26   become the sons of *G·*.'' — *John* 1 : 12.
      251–14   the liberty of the sons of *G·*,
      259–21   sons of *G·* shouted — *Job* 38 : 7.
  Un. 5–20   the liberty of the sons of *G·*,
      42–15   sons of *G·* shouted — *Job* 38 : 7.
  Peo. 11– 1   full liberty of the sons of *G·*
Soul must be
  Un. 28–17   Soul must be *G·* ;
source in
  Pul. 3–22   living waters have their source in *G·*,
speaks
  '00. 8–27   When *G·* speaks to you through
Spirit is
    (*see* **Spirit**)
spirit of
  My. 344–10   "It is not the spirit of *G·*,
Spirit, or
  Rud. 5– 8   made in the image of Spirit, or *G·*.
standeth
  Mis. 368– 9   * Standeth *G·* within the shadow,
stands for
  '01. 4– 2   Principle or Person stands for *G·*
  My. 344– 3   If we say that the sun stands for *G·*,
statutes of
  Peo. 12– 2   these divine statutes of *G·* :
steadfastly in
  Mis. 241– 2   should centre as steadfastly in *G·*
strong in
  Rud. 8–12   thou wilt be strong in *G·*,
substance of
  Mis. 104– 8   yea, the substance of *G·*,
      187–24   Did the substance of *G·*, Spirit,
substantiates
  No. 38– 5   and that *G·* substantiates their
supremacy of
  Hea. 15– 2   rests upon the supremacy of *G·*.
Supreme
  My. 36–31   * proof that our Supreme *G·*,
surrender to
  Mis. 15–15   moments of surrender to *G·*,
symbols of
  Mis. 82–10   cognize the symbols of *G·*,
takes care
  My. 166– 8   *G·* takes care of our life.
      203–19   for *G·* takes care of it.
taught of
  My. 230–27   all taught of *G·*.'' — *John* 6 : 45.
      239–14   *and all are taught of G·*
temporary loss of
  Un. 41– 9   involves a temporary loss of *G·*,
term for
  Mis. 13–28   Seek the Anglo-Saxon term for *G·*,
      26–29   Saxon term for *G·* is also good.
  Pul. 6– 7   Good, the Anglo-Saxon term for *G·*,
  My. 185–14   Love is the generic term for *G·*.
testify of
  Un. 2–14   is ready to testify of *G·*
thank
  Mis. 113–23   Thank *G·* ! this evil can be resisted
      294–22   thank *G·* and take courage,
      331–15   thank *G·* for those redemptive words
  Ret. 16–10   thank *G·*, she is healed !''

God

thank
My. 62– 9 * How can we ever thank G· enough
127–19 thank G· for persecution
159–10 I thank G· who hath sent forth
193– 8 and to thank G· forever
270–21 I thank G· that for the past
341– 4 thank G· that He has emblazoned
thanks to
'00. 2– 4 thanks to G·, the people most
that feedeth
Mis. 322–19 G· that feedeth the hungry heart,
the Father
My. 344– 5 G· the Father is greater than
their
Mis. 10–11 Their G· will not let them be lost ;
10–13 The good cannot lose their G·,
'01. 3– 9 because their G· is not a person.
7–18 call their G· "divine Principle,"
Peo. 7– 1 by their G· and their devil.
theological
'01. 5–28 The theological G· as a Person
the perfect Mind
Mis. 37–18 antidote . . . is G·, the perfect Mind,
the preserver
Pan. 7–10 G·, the preserver of man, declared
the term
Hea. 3–14 the term G· was derived from
the word
Mis. 75–17 where the word G· can be used
Peo. 2– 9 another letter to the word G·
My. 226– 3 substitute the word G·
things of
Mis. 175– 3 takes of the things of G· and
Ret. 24–24 should take the things of G·
'01. 9–23 takes of the things of G·
think of
Un. 18– 2 Rather let us think of G· as
this is
Mis. 173– 6 one Mind, and that this is G·,
this phrase for
'01. 3–17 we use this phrase for G·
this spirit is of
My. 292–27 but this spirit is of G·,
throne of
Ret. 22–13 the throne of G·."— Heb. 12 : 2.
My. 258–16 the throne of G·."— Heb. 12 : 2.
thus crowns
Ret. 71– 4 wisdom that G· thus crowns,
thy
My. 183– 2 love the Lord thy G· — Luke 10 : 27.
184–28 Thy G· reigneth !"— Isa. 52 : 7.
206–19 thy G· thy glory."— Isa. 60 : 19.
229– 7 thy G· doth drive them out — Deut. 18 : 12.
to define
'01. 1–22 As . . . Scientists you seek to define G·
'02. 7–14 Use these words to define G·,
to hide from
Ret. 78–22 or for yourself to hide from G·,
told
Un. 17–21 G· told our first parents
to man
Ret. 31– 5 "the ways of G·'" to man — Job 40 : 19.
68–27 passing from G· to man"
My. 208–17 ministrations of G· to man.
to the rescue
Po. 71–13 G· to the rescue — Liberty, peal!
towards
My. 159–19 the tendency towards G·,
189–23 we are drawn towards G·.
338–20 heart full of love towards G·
to work for
Mis. 116–28 never unready to work for G·,
true
Mis. 333–15 from the only living and true G·,
Ret. 49–25 knowledge of the true G·,
59–19 the only living and true G·,
Un. 4–24 knowledge of the only true G·,
38–14 the living and true G·.
My. 36–21 * dedicated to the only true G·,
187–24 worship of the only true G·.
true perception of
Mis. 15–10 can give the true perception of G·
trust
Mis. 25–26 if the sick cannot trust G· for help
Ret. 14–15 I was willing to trust G·,
My. 129–28 Trust G· to direct your steps.
trust in
My. 161–26 Trust in G·, and "He shall — Prov. 3 : 6.
Truth is
Un. 4– 5 Truth is G·, and in God's law.
truth of
No. 8– 7 utter the truth of G·
'00. 4–19 truth of G·, and of man

God

turns to
Mis. 386–17 a love that steady turns To G· ;
Po. 50– 1 a love that steady turns To G· ;
understand
Mis. 42–24 Only as we understand G·,
77–25 It was to understand G· and man :
94– 6 love good in order to understand G·.
194–21 in following him, you understand G·
194–32 understand G· sufficiently to
No. 23–25 cannot understand G· or man,
Hea. 15–26 because you do not understand G·,
15–28 as we understand G· better.
Peo. 6–23 deemed treason to understand G·,
My. 152–16 Do I understand G· as Love,
understanding of
Mis. 342–11 higher understanding of G·.
Ret. 28–12 understanding of G· in divine Science.
Un. 1–18 closer to the true understanding of G·
3–16 This is the understanding of G·,
38–19 opposite understanding of G·
61–26 the understanding of G· ;
Pul. 35–16 understanding of G· in divine Science.
Rud. 11– 5 understanding of G· and man
11–20 based on a true understanding of G·
Pan. 15–10 life and understanding of G·,
'02. 11–11 spiritual understanding of G·,
Hea. 8– 2 beyond the understanding of G·,
My. 44– 2 * Through the understanding of G·
107–27 knowledge or understanding of G·,
152–10 reached the understanding of G·,
understand that
Mis. 96– 4 I understand that G· is an
Hea. 8–19 When we understand that G· is
understood
Mis. 14–19 that good, G·, understood,
196–27 but Life, G· understood.
Pan. 10–23 the effect of G· understood.
unfolded
My. 348–19 G· unfolded the way,
union with
Mis. 42–12 but by a conscious union with G·.
unity of
Mis. 266–16 inseparable from the unity of G·.
369–10 strong in the unity of G· and man.
'02. 9–18 The unity of G· and man
unity with
Mis. 181– 7 his sonship, or unity with G·,
Man. 15–16 unfolding man's unity with G·
universe of
Mis 217– 6 the universe of G· is spiritual,
unknown
My. 5–20 worship, not an unknown G·, but
192– 2 Ye build not to an unknown G·.
193– 2 not to the unknown G·,
338–12 "The Unknown G· Made Known,"
unlike
Mis. 217–21 a third quality unlike G·.
Un. 38–22 in aught which is unlike G·,
No. 37–16 that what is unlike G·
37–26 whatever is unlike G· ;
My. 64–24 * overcoming all that is unlike G·,
240–17 all that is unlike G·, good
waited on
'02. 15–21 I waited on G· to suggest a name for
waiting on
Mis. 331– 2 mortals looking up, waiting on G·,
wait on
Mis. 81– 8 patiently wait on G· to decide,
'02. 17–17 to be willing to wait on G·,
My. 227–14 turn to . . . and wait on G·.
252–15 wait on G·, the strong deliverer,
wait patiently on
'01. 34–20 brethren, wait patiently on G· ;
waits on
Mis. 130–28 waits on G·, renews his strength,
My. 103– 4 summons the . . . and waits on G·.
306–17 Age, . . . waits on G·.
warned man
Mis. 24–27 G· warned man not to believe the
was manifest
Chr. 53–61 "G· was manifest — I Tim. 3 : 16.
was not outlined
Mis. 103–28 This G· was not outlined.
ways of
Ret. 31– 5 vindicating "the ways of G·'" — Job 40 : 19.
we call
Un. 60– 7 We call G· omnipotent
My. 152–23 good, that we call G·,
we can know
Mis. 79– 8 whereby we can know G·.
weds himself with
Un. 17– 8 man thus weds himself with G·,
we learn
Un. 28–18 only as we learn G·,

God

went forth
Mis. 153– 6   *G·* went forth before His people,
went out to
Mis. 180–14   my heart went out to *G·*,
what is
'02. 5–15   question and wonder, What is *G·*?
where is
Ret. 60–21   Material sense saith, . . . Where is *G·*?
which worketh
My. 300– 5   it is *G·* which worketh— *Phil.* 2 : 13.
who gave
Mis. 388– 1   *G·*, who gave that word of might
'02. 20–10   *G·* who gave that word of might
Po. 7– 1   *G·*, who gave that word of might
who is Love
Mis. 337–11   its Principle, *G·* who is Love.
will bless
My. 197–28   *G·* will bless the work of your
360–21   *G·* will bless and prosper you.
will care for
Pul. 73– 3   * *G·* will care for us, and will send
will confirm
Mis. 153– 3   *G·* will confirm His inheritance.
will give
Mis. 115–26   for *G·* will give the ability to
138–25   *G·* will give to all His soldiers
320– 2   *G·* will give the benediction.
will guide you
Mis. 287–24   *G·* will guide you.
will help
Ret. 86–22   *G·* will help each man who
will make
No. 8–13   knowing that *G·* will make the
will of
Mis. 185– 4   The will of *G·*, or power of Spirit,
will recompense
Mis. 12– 6   *G·* will recompense this wrong,
will reward
My. 128–29   *G·* will reward your enemies
234–11   *G·* will reward their kind motives,
will supply
Pul. 15–17   *G·* will supply the wisdom
wisdom of
Mis. 210–12   wisdom of *G·*, as revealed in C. S.,
359–29   To ask wisdom of *G·*,
My. 261– 5   their elders, who seek wisdom of *G·*,
without
Ret. 61–16   without *G·* in the world.'— *Eph.* 2 : 12.
My. 178–17   if . . . it exists without *G·*.
with us
Mis. 103–28   Immanuel, or "*G·* with us."— *Matt.* 1 : 23.
331–27   "*G·* with us," the I AM.— *Matt.* 1 : 23.
My. 218– 8   proof of "*G·* with us."— *Matt.* 1 : 23.
womanhood of
Hea. 10– 7   fell before the womanhood of *G·*,
My. 346–30   manhood and womanhood of *G·*
Word of
(*see* **Word**)
word of
(*see* **word**)
words of
Mis. 317–31   speaketh the words of *G·* :— *John* 3 : 34.
Word that is
Mis. 363–25   Word that *is G·*, Spirit, and
My. 184–29   Word that is *G·* must at some time
Word was
Mis. 29–12   the Word was *G·*."— *John* 1 : 1.
Pan. 5– 4   "The Word was *G·* ;"— *John* 1 : 1.
My. 117–19   the Word was *G·*'"— *John* 1 : 1.
Word was with
Mis. 29–11   "the Word was with *G·*,— *John* 1 : 1.
My. 117–19   the Word was with *G·*,— *John* 1 : 1.
worketh
Mis. 283–25   *G·* worketh with him,
'01. 10–25   for *G·* worketh with us,
working for
Mis. 343– 7   in working for *G·*.
work of
Ret. 77– 3   * the noblest work of *G·* ;"
work with
Mis. 39–29   work with *G·* in healing the sick,
worship
Ret. 2– 8   seeking "freedom to worship *G·* ;"
My. 151–20   * Go forth, and worship *G·*."
162–23   that in them Christians may worship *G·*,
168– 2   Freedom to worship *G·*
341– 7   * "Freedom to worship *G·*."
worship of
Pul. 40–23   * dedicated to the worship of *G·*.
would forgive
Ret. 9–13   prayed that *G·* would forgive me,
wouldst teach
Mis. 209– 4   and wouldst teach *G·* not to

God

wrath of
No. 35–11   not to appease the wrath of *G·*,
Peo. 3– 8   the wrath of *G·*,
wrought
Mis. 333–26   They believed . . . that *G·* wrought

Mis. 2–19   when *G·*, man's saving Principle,
3–19   The Principle of all cure is *G·*,
11–23   leaving all retribution to *G·*
14–18   as real and eternal as good, *G·* !
16–10   it is indeed *G·* ;
16–12   ability to meet them is from *G·* ;
16–19   *G·* is infinitely more than a person,
16–21   *G·* is a divine *Whole*,
18–23   never separate himself from good, *G·* ;
18–28   to separate Life from *G·*.
18–31   to believe that aught that *G·* sends
19–16   steadfastly flowing on to *G·*,
22–10   C. S. translates Mind, *G·*,
23–18   *G·* is both noumenon and phenomena,
23–22   *G·*, Spirit, . . . are terms synonymous
23–31   *G·*, Spirit, could not change its
26– 2   whatever is of *G·*, hath life
26–24   *G·*, has no antecedent ;
26–30   *G·* is naturally and divinely
27– 4   That *G·*, good, creates evil, or
27–21   evil signifies the absence of good, *G·*,
30–25   There is no *G·*."— *Psal.* 14 : 1.
31–15   *G·*, good, has *all* power.
37– 1   *G·* would not be omnipotent if
37–19   *G·* can and does destroy the
46–10   *Do you teach that you are equal with G·?*
46–26   the Life and Love that are *G·*,
47–20   *G·*, Spirit, is the only substance ;
48–12   animal magnetism is neither of *G·* nor
49–27   presupposes . . . that *G·* is not All-in-all,
50– 3   that *G·* is not its author,
51– 3   and drugs, *G·* does not require.
55–31   *G·* in matter,— which are theories
56– 7   If . . . *G·* is substanceless ;
56–25   *Why did G· command,*
57–18   "*G·* doth know— *Gen.* 3 : 5.
58–23   If *G·* does not govern the action of
63–22   *If Christ was G·, why did Jesus*
72– 6   only living and true origin, *G·*.
73– 1   or that *G·* is conscious of it.
74– 5   enmity of mortal man toward *G·*.
75–13   Soul is one, and is *G·* ;
77–24   the All-Father-Mother *G·*.
78– 1   Life, *G·*, is not buried in matter.
87–22   most reliant on himself and *G·*.
93–18   all cause and effect are in *G·*.
96–16   so worship I *G·*."— *see Acts* 24 : 14.
97–19   there is no *G·* beside me."— *Isa.* 45 : 5.
102–12   *G·* is like Himself
103–32   a *G·* at hand,— *Jer.* 23 : 23.
104–27   *G·* and the real man.
105–32   *G·* is the sum total of the universe.
112–31   There is no *G·*."— *Psal.* 14 : 1.
113–16   commits his way to *G·*,
115–12   May *G·* enable my students to
115–20   since *G·*, good, is All-in-all.
118– 2   cannot obey both *G·*, good, and evil,
124–13   "who is so great a *G·*— *Psal.* 77 : 13.
124–23   stretch out our arms to *G·*.
126–27   *G·* hath indeed smiled on my church
134–13   *G·* will pour you out a blessing
139– 4   *G·* will pour you out a blessing
139–11   *but mighty through G·— II Cor.* 10 : 4.
141–32   *G·* is in the midst of her :
150–21   "If *G·* be for us,— *Rom.* 8 : 31.
151–23   chosen people, whose *G·* is— what?
154–23   Honor thy Father and Mother, *G·*.
155–24   cannot spare time to write to *G·*,
158–22   and *G·* will do the rest.
173–27   Surely not from *G·*,
179– 8   consciousness in matter or in *G·*?
180–24   *but of G·*.— *John* 1 : 13.
181–17   but of *G·*,"— *John* 1 : 13.
184–19   If he says, "I am of *G·*,
184–22   good because it is of *G·*,
186–10   its conception of man from *G·*,
186–20   his perfect Principle, *G·*,
187–22   *G·*,— Life, Truth, Love.
187–23   perfect, and eternal are *G·* ;
192– 2   we do not mean that man is *G·*
196– 8   a separate mind from *G·*
196–13   *G·* was not the author of it ;
197–15   as the Son of God, or as *G·* ;
198– 4   this point of unity of Spirit, *G·*,
198–28   supposition of another . . . than *G·* ;
199– 1   *G·* does not reward . . . with penalties ;
199–27   Life, and intelligence are *G·*.
200– 9   *G·* was the only substance,
200–28   involved in its divine Principle, *G·* :

God

Mis.	204–28	G·, the divine Principle of C. S.,
	206–19	law-abiding Principle, G·.
	212– 2	saith in his heart, ''No G·''— *Psal.* 53 : 1.
	218–10	whence to reason out G·,
	218–32	* purely spiritual personality in G·.''
	226– 5	carried the case on the side of G· ;
	232–25	Principle of all healing is G· ;
	232–28	understood to be of G·,
	244– 8	He further states that G· cannot save
	257– 4	presupposes that G· sleeps in the
	259–27	belongs not to nature nor to G·.
	260–11	Principle of his cure was G·,
	277–24	proof that G·, good, is supreme.
	282– 5	sense of personality in G· or in man,
	317–30	''Whom G· hath sent— *John* 3 : 34.
	321–10	balance . . . more on the side of G·,
	331– 7	cause them to wait patiently on G·
	333–13	denying that G·, good, is supreme,
	346–13	belief . . . opposite intelligence to G·.
	346–15	belief . . . wood or stone is G·.
	352–24	out of himself and into G· so far that
	361–26	G·, the only substance and
	362–11	believing that G·, having made *all*,
	363–16	G· is not chargeable with
	364–11	of the divine Principle, G·.
	367–29	G· is too pure to behold iniquity ;
	396–11	songsters' matin hymns to G·
Ret.	14–25	''Search me, O G·,— *Psal.* 139 : 23.
	15–10	G·, Thou hast taught me— *Psal.* 71 : 17.
	25–11	G· I called *immortal Mind.*
	25–15	G· I characterized as individual
	27–30	old to G·, but new to His
	28– 3	one must acquaint himself with G·,
	48– 9	the one builder and maker, G·,
	50–10	G· has since shown me,
	56–21	not the subdivision, of G·.
	57–11	Soul is the synonym of Spirit, G· ;
	57–22	All must be of G·,
	59–12	mortals apply finite terms to G·,
	68–25	Life and being are of G·.
	69–12	seem to have life as much as G·,
	69–19	that . . . are creations of G·,
	71– 6	and to G· the things — *Mark* 12 : 17.
	73–16	spiritual individuality in G·,
	85–24	''if G· be for us,— *Rom.* 8 : 31.
	91– 1	G· is their sure defense and refuge.
Un.	1–11	*Does G· know or behold sin,*
	2– 6	no refuge from sin, except in G·,
	4–12	G· is all true consciousness ;
	4–16	if G· be conscious of it?
	7–10	has not separated me from G·,
	10–16	G· is their divine Principle.
	10–25	G· was not in the whirlwind.
	13– 8	G· is harmony's selfhood.
	13–13	If G· could be conscious of sin,
	13–15	If G· has any real knowledge of sin,
	14–13	Was it necessary for G· to grow
	14–19	G· is not the shifting vane
	15– 3	more just than G· ?''— *Job.* 4 : 17.
	15– 5	incubus which G· never can throw off?
	15– 6	Do mortals know more than G·,
	15–18	Would G· not of necessity take
	16– 4	sheer nonsense, if G· has, or can
	17– 3	seeks to fasten all error upon G·,
	18– 1	absurdly follow that G· must perish,
	18– 6	Error may say that G· can never
	19– 1	With G·, *knowledge* is necessarily
	25–20	G·, good, is the only creator.
	26– 3	*Evil.* . . . G· is in matter,
	26– 3	*Evil.* . . . matter reproduces G·.
	26– 5	G· is my author,
	26– 9	O evil ! G· is not your authority
	26–21	If G· be *changeless goodness*,
	26–23	there is in G· naught fantastic.
	29– 7	Soul is sinless, and is G·.
	31–22	evil does not obtain in Spirit, G· ;
	35–15	That which was first was G·,
	35–22	is a misstatement of Mind, G·.
	39– 5	sin, and death yield . . . to G·.
	39–15	which opposes itself to G·,
	41– 8	loss of the true sense of good, G· ;
	41–23	G· cannot be the opposite of
	42– 1	Life, G·, being everywhere,
	43– 7	anchorage in infinite good, G·,
	46–24	identical and self-conscious with G·.
	48–17	The Ego is G· Himself,
	51–27	Soul is not in body, but is G·,
	52–16	G· is not the so-called ego of evil ;
	52–23	if G· has no part in them?
	52–26	The senses, not G·, Soul, form the
	53–24	immortal and unerring Mind, G·,
	54–24	representation that G· both knew and
	54–25	G·, who condemned the knowledge
	60–19	If G·, then let them serve Him,
	60–27	material sense, which sees not G·.

God

Un.	62– 3	saith, ''Christ (G·) died for me,
	62– 9	G·, good, is never absent,
	64– 3	G· can no more behold it,
	64–11	even if it were (or could be) G·,
Pul.	2–24	G·, the eternal harmony of
	4– 9	protected by his divine Principle, **G·?**
	7–13	G· has now unsealed their
	30–20	* forgiveness of sin by G·,
	74–15	What I am is for G· to declare
	79–21	* ''If there were no G·, we should
Rud.	1– 6	It is G·, the Supreme Being,
	1–10	*Do you mean by this that G· is a*
	2– 7	In C. S. we learn that G· is
	2–12	We do not conceive rightly of G·,
	3–24	*do you mean that G· has a finite*
	4– 6	*Is G· the Principle of all science,*
	5– 3	''Let G· be true,— *Rom.* 3 : 4.
	14– 2	a portion of their time to G·,
No.	5–14	independent of G·, and dependent on
	9–11	G· will well regenerate
	9–20	G· will ''furnish a table— *Psal.* 78 : 19.
	10–25	turns . . . all hope and faith to G·,
	12–27	G· must be found all
	15–17	presuppose an impotent G·
	16– 1	For G· to know, is to be ;
	17–13	G· is not without an ever-present
	17–22	G· who has no knowledge of sin
	17–24	If G· could know a false claim,
	21–15	philosophy has an undeveloped G·,
	24– 3	to Spinoza's philosophy G· is
	24–11	According to . . . G· is three **persons**
	31– 2	if you admit that G· sends it
	36–21	G·, wherein there is no
	39–12	Prayer can neither change G· nor
	39–24	most of all, it shows us what G· is.
Pan.	2–16	* conceived of as a whole, is G· ;
	2–17	* no G· but the combined forces
	4–14	G· is incapable of evil ;
	4–18	chapter sub-title
	4–20	G·, Spirit, is indeed the preserver
	5– 8	Did G· create evil?
	5–14	not in the truth [G·],
	6– 6	claim that G· is not supreme,
	6–22	For if G·, good, is Mind,
	6–24	if G·, good, is omnipotent,
	7– 8	belief, that after G·, Spirit, had
	7–24	which implies Mind, Spirit, G· ;
	8– 7	belief that Jesus, . . . is G·,
	8– 9	belief that Mary was the mother **of G·**
	12– 5	* ''G·, Spirit, is ever in universal
'00.	5– 7	Jesus said the opposite of G·
	5–12	G·, man, and divine Science.
'01.	3– 7	chapter sub-title
	3– 8	We hear it said the . . . have no G·
	4–22	G· is the infinite One instead of
	5– 3	for if Person is G·,
	6– 5	not a person, hence no G·?
	6–13	We hear that G· is not G· except
	6–16	is God in C. S. no G· because
	6–29	that G· is either inconceivable, or
	7– 8	G· being infinite Mind, He is the
	7–23	The G· whom all Christians now **claim**
	8– 6	who regard Jesus as G·
	8–16	Is G· Spirit? He is.
	9– 4	C. S. shows clearly that G· is the
	9–22	the Holy One of G·.'' — *Mark* 1 : 24.
	18–25	There is no G·.'' — *Psal.* 53 : 1.
	23– 5	yet that G· has an opposite
	25–15	matter minus, and G· all,
	34–13	originating not in G·,
'02.	2–14	G· speed the right !
	5–13	G· must be intelligently considered
	12– 2	that Christ is come and is G·.
	12–13	Jesus Christ is not G·,
Hea.	4– 8	We pray for G· to remember us,
	4–24	G· must be our model,
	5– 9	saying, . . . G· will punish him now
	5–23	relying not on the person of G·
	8– 3	G·,— not a person to whom we should
	9– 3	what is not the person of G·,
	9–17	know that G· never cursed man,
	10– 9	remember that G· — good — is omnipotent ;
	12–13	G·, . . . never made a man sick.
	15–18	You pray for G· to heal you,
	16– 5	no other Life, substance, and . . . but G·.
	16–21	neither see, hear, . . . nor smell G· ;
Peo.	2– 7	we shall learn what G· is,
	4– 3	in hygiene and drugs than in G·.
	4–12	When first good, G·, was named a
	6–19	G· is no longer a mystery
	6–25	thyself with Him [G·],— *Job.* 22 : 21
Po.	40– 4	To G·, to Truth, and you !
	46–13	An offering pure to G·.
	59– 3	songsters' matin hymns to G·
	70– 9	In G· there is no night,

God

Po.	77– 1	*G·* of the rolling year !
	79– 7	*G·* able is To raise up seed
My.	4–30	Thou *G·* most high and nigh.
	6–22	proceedeth out of the mouth of *G·*.
	9–25	will draw on *G·* for the amount
	14– 1	[*G·*, Spirit] sent it." — *Isa.* 55 : 11.
	14– 3	*G·* will pour them out a blessing
	33–10	"Search me, O *G·*, — *Psal.* 139 : 23.
	34– 7	*G·* of his salvation. — *Psal.* 24 : 5.
	37–20	* *G·* is the supreme cause of all
	38– 3	* *G·* is all consolation and comfort,
	52– 9	* to *G·*, for these blessings,
	61–25	* I should be willing to let *G·* work.
	61–27	* "What cannot *G·* do?"
	120– 1	in the Word which *is G·*.
	131–20	Where *G·* is we can meet,
	131–21	where *G·* is we can never part.
	143–28	If *G·* be for us, — *Rom.* 8 : 31.
	151–14	for *G·* is for me" — *Psal.* 56 : 9.
	151–16	"If *G·* be for us, — *Rom.* 8 : 31.
	152–27	*G·*, the divine Principle of nature
	164–29	Man . . . has his being in *G·*, Love.
	183–14	*G·* will multiply thee.
	183–26	*G·* is with thee.
	191– 3	except *G·* be with him." — *John* 3 : 2.
	193–19	*G·* guard and guide you.
	199– 6	May *G·* say this of the church
	200–27	*G·* spare this plunge,
	205– 9	* "*G·* moves in a mysterious way
	205–26	of its divine Principle, *G·* ;
	209– 3	*G·* will abundantly bless
	215– 4	*G·* stretched forth His hand.
	223–29	know that I am *G·*." — *Psal.* 46 : 10.
	226–14	Withdraw *G·*, divine Principle, from
	227–30	fool hath said . . . no *G·*." — *Psal.* 14 : 1.
	231–14	as *G·*, not man, directs.
	235–15	Did *G·* make man?
	235–16	Did *G·* make all that was made?
	235–16	Is *G·* Spirit?
	238– 9	*G·* being Spirit, His language and
	239– 6	acquaint the student with *G·*.
	239–15	for *G·* to be represented by
	241–27	* and had my being in *G·*,
	248–22	to conceive *G·* aright you must be
	260–28	leaves hygiene, medicine, . . . to *G·*
	262–15	Christ conceived of Spirit, of *G·*
	267– 9	remember that *G·* is not the,
	269–13	* and *G·* the Soul.
	269–17	*G·* hath thrust in the sickle,
	271– 1	*G·*, Spirit, is infinite,
	272– 9	no claim that man is equal to *G·*,
	275– 8	know that I am *G·*." — *Psal.* 46 : 10.
	278–29	The Principle of all power is *G·*,
	279–13	*G·* is the divine Mind.
	280–18	in full faith that *G·* does not
	292– 7	May *G·* sanctify our nation's sorrow
	296–20	*G·*, good, omnipotent and infinite.
	299–22	*G·*, the divine Principle of C. S.,
	303– 9	following the divine Principle — *G·*,
	323–24	* if *G·* did not hold you up
	348–13	his divine Principle, *G·*,

(*see also* **All, All-in-all, All-power, Almighty, Almighty God, Arbiter, Being, Blessed, builder, Cause, Comforter, creator, Deity, Ego, Elohim, Esse, Father, Father-Mother, Forever, Giver, Godhead, He, Herself, Him, Himself, His, Holy Father, Holy Ghost, Holy One, Holy Spirit, I, I AM, Immanuel, King, Life, Light, Lord, Lord of Hosts, Love, Maker, Me, Mind, Minister, Most High, Mother, My, One, Only, Parent, Person, Physician, Principle, Providence, Ruler Supreme, Soul, Spirit, Supreme Being, Supreme God, Thee, Thou, Thy, Truth, Unseen, Us, Wonderful**)

god

Mis.	123–13	appease the anger of a so-called *g·*
	123–14	Merodach, or the *g·* of sin,
	123–15	was the "lucky *g·* ;"
	190–29	serpent, liar, the *g·* of this world,
	190–31	"the *g·* of this world ;" — *II Cor.* 4 : 4.
	190–31	and then defines this *g·*
Un.	54–23	would make man a *g·*,
Pan.	2–11	words meaning "all" and "*g·*."
	2–13	His uncapitalized word "*g·*"
	3–26	Pan was the *g·* of shepherds
	8– 3	and the Babylonian sun *g·*,
	8– 4	moon *g·*, and sin *g·*
'00.	3–26	Jehovah, was a *g·* of hate and of
	13–18	Æsculapius, the *g·* of medicine,
'01.	11–28	him whose *g·* is his belly :
	16–14	*the g· of this world;*
	16–14	St. Paul defines this world's *g·*

God-anointed

Mis.	161–24	Jesus Christ, — the *G·* ;

God-bestowed

No.	2– 6	aver that disease is normal, a *G·*
My.	22–22	* nothing less than *G·*

God-blessed

Ret.	11–12	In our *G·* free school.
Po.	60– 9	In our *G·* free school.

God-condemned

My.	109– 5	dream which is mortal and *G·*

God-crowned

Mis.	162– 6	From this dazzling, *G·* summit,
	205–30	lives on, *G·* and blest.
	266– 2	to the *G·* summit of
Ret.	76–23	the *G·* summit of C. S.
Pul.	27–24	* and the woman . . . *G·*.
Po.	22– 1	*G·*, patient century,
My.	133– 6	*G·* summit of divine Science ;

God-driven

Mis.	169– 6	till she was *G·* back to the

God-endowed

My.	188–29	be *G·* for discipleship.

God-endued

My.	190–26	become *G·* with power

God-given

Mis.	117– 7	*G·* intent and volition
	247– 1	demand for man his *G·* heritage,
	394–12	*G·* mandate that speaks from
Peo.	10–12	Discerning the *G·* rights of man,
Po.	45–15	*G·* mandate that speaks from

God-governed

My.	222–25	Mankind will be *G·*

Godhead

Rud.	2– 6	agents, constituting the *G·*.
'01.	5– 4	constitute the *G·*
	7– 4	trinity of the *G·* in C. S.
	8– 7	third *person* in the *G·*
	10–16	enthrall my sense of the *G·*,
Peo.	4–18	*G·* is Life, Truth, and Love,

Godhood

Un.	42–26	true sense of selfhood and *G·* ;

God-idea

Ret.	70–23	scientific ultimate of this *G·*
Po.	29–11	Thou *G·*, Life-crowned,

godless

Mis.	55–30	either a *g·* and material
	212– 3	This *g·* policy never knows
No.	18– 4	*g·* lie that denies Him as All-in-all,
'01.	4–30	merit the epithet "*g·*,"

Godlike

Mis.	122–23	the suffering of the *G·* for
	161–13	Christ-Jesus, the *G·*,
	178– 6	wanted to become a *G·* man.
Un.	46– 1	mortal error, called *mind*, is not *G·*.
No.	20– 7	Truth is moulding a *G·* man.
'01.	7– 4	C. S. makes man *G·*.
'02.	6–26	degree that . . . he becomes *G·*.
	8–24	whereby man *is G·*.
My.	14– 8	*G·* agency of man.
	161–28	the *G·* man said,

Godlikeness

Mis.	213– 2	in the form of *G·*.
Chr.	55–16	Spirit [*G·*] is life — *Rom.* 8 : 10.
Un.	22– 5	eat of the fruit of *G·*,
'02.	16–11	chapter sub-title
	16–23	express the life of *G·*.

godliness

Mis.	53–29	is the mystery of *g·* ;
	53–29	*g·* is simple to the godly ;
	145– 5	Till then, this form of *g·* seems
	328–12	with the mystery of *g·*,
Ret.	37–20	"mystery of *g·*." — *I Tim.* 3 : 16.
	61–27	stated and demonstrated in its *g·*
Un.	5–14	mystery of *g·*," — *I Tim.* 3 : 16.
	62– 8	This is the mystery of *g·*
No.	38–10	This divine mystery of *g·*
'01.	25– 1	spirit or mystery of *g·*.
	34–26	*G·* or Christianity is a
	34–28	nor happiness without *g·*.
'02.	16–27	The mere form of *g·*,
My.	124–28	The mystery of *g·*
	126–11	the mystery of *g·*,

godly

Mis.	53–30	godliness is simple to the *g·* ;
Pul.	3– 1	how can our *g·* temple possibly be
	32–26	* was known as a "*g·* man,"
'01.	25– 2	becomes clear to the *g·*.

God-made

Mis.	49–17	*is it not G·;*
	49–17	*if G·, can it be wrong,*
Un.	53– 8	reality and . . . of man are good and *G·*

God-quality
  Mis. 18–13   in every *G·*, even in substance ;

God's
acres
  Mis. 140–26   Our title to *G·* acres will be safe
action
  Mis. 354–22   pride would regulate *G·* action.
allness
  Mis. 206– 9   can interpret . . . *G·* allness,
all-power
  Mis. 141– 5   *G·* all-power, all-presence,
altar
  Mis. 87–31   help anybody and steady *G·* altar
appointing
  Mis. 208–19   in the way of *G·* appointing.
avenging angel
  Mis. 275– 5   Who — but *G·* avenging angel !
best witnesses
  '02. 10–25   martyrdom of *G·* best witnesses
blessing
  My. 182–15   through *G·* blessing and the
blindness to error
  Un. 6–19   the theory of *G·* blindness to error
business
  Mis. 140–13   but this was *G·* business,
child
  Mis. 181–28   preexistence as *G·* child ;
  Un. 15– 9   Man is *G·* child and image.
  '02. 8–29   He spake of man . . . as *G·* child.
children
  Mis. 170– 9   refreshment of *G·* children
chosen ones
  My. 127–24   garrisoned by *G·* chosen ones,
command
  Mis. 223– 4   according to *G·* command.
       298–17   did not say that it was *G·* command ;
  Peo. 7–18   * Waiting the hour when at *G·* command
commandments
  '00. 6–20   breaks *G·* commandments,
commands
  Mis. 358–28   awaiting, . . . *G·* commands.
  Un. 3–10   have obeyed *G·* commands,
consequent
  Mis. 26–24   *G·* consequent is the spiritual cosmos.
courtesy
  My. 341– 2   breathe it to . . . as *G·* courtesy.
creation
  Mis. 87– 5   to caricature *G·* creation,
       286–13   usher in the dawn of *G·* creation,
  Pan. 6–14   order and harmony of *G·* creation.
dear love
  Mis. 81– 5   by right of *G·* dear love,
  My. 258–27   consciousness of *G·* dear love
direction
  Mis. 127–23   know yourself, under *G·* direction,
  My. 117– 7   helping a leader in *G·* direction,
discipline
  '00. 8–12   till *G·* discipline takes it off
disposal
  My. 281– 6   faith in *G·* disposal of events.
ear
  No. 39– 6   ostensibly to catch *G·* ear,
embrace
  Mis. 400– 2   Slumbers not in *G·* embrace ;
  Pul. 16–14   Slumbers not in *G·* embrace ;
  Po. 76–13   Slumbers not in *G·* embrace ;
essential likeness
  Mis. 61–22   Does *G·* essential likeness sin,
eternal likeness
  Un. 22– 2   made after *G·* eternal likeness,
ever-presence
  Un. 62–27   discern faintly *G·* ever-presence,
eye
  Po. 18–13   *G·* eye is upon him.
       19– 3   *G·* eye is upon me
fatherliness
  Mis. 234–31   *G·* fatherliness as Life, Truth, and
fiat
  '01. 5–17   leave all sin to *G·* fiat
finger
  Ret. 85–18   wait for *G·* finger to point the way.
forgiveness
  Man. 15–10   acknowledge *G·* forgiveness of sin
formations
  No. 6– 5   *G·* formations are spiritual,
frown
  My. 129–10   no night but in *G·* frown ;
gift
  Mis. 140– 2   I knew that to *G·* gift,
glorified
  Po. 79–19   *G·* glorified !
glory
  My. 117– 1   let them alone in, *G·* glory,

God's
government
  Mis. 199– 7   spiritual law, — *G·* government.
  My. 222–26   as *G·* government becomes apparent,
       278– 1   coincide with *G·* government
       283–28   enlightened sense of *G·* government.
great gift
  My. 262–20   reminder of *G·* great gift,
great love
  Mis. 182–24   their place in *G·* great love,
greatness
  Pul. 39– 6   * *G·* greatness flows around our
grooves
  Mis. 104–18   The latter move in *G·* grooves
guidance
  My. 142–12   sought *G·* guidance in doing it,
hand
  '01. 16– 1   * *G·* hand has held you up.''
hands
  My. 278–14   President and . . . are in *G·* hands.
help
  Ret. 86–21   No one . . . without *G·* help,
  My. 197– 4   Attempt nothing without *G·* help.
hour
  Mis. 134–19   In *G·* hour, the powers of
household
  '01. 9–27   He of *G·* household who loveth
idea
  Mis. 261–25   Man as *G·* idea is already saved
       336–14   dislike and hatred of *G·* idea,
  Pul. 75– 3   the Principle of *G·* idea,
  Po. 70–23   Give *G·* idea sway,
ideas
  Mis. 164–30   The limited view of *G·* ideas
image
  (*see* **image**)
impersonality
  My. 117–20   great truth of *G·* impersonality
infinite meaning
  Mis. 25–17   It gives *G·* infinite meaning
interpretation
  Mis. 258–27   *G·* interpretation of Himself
kingdom
  No. 35–26   *G·* kingdom is everywhere
largess
  My. 188–18   a benediction for *G·* largess.
law
  (*see* **law**)
laws
  Mis. 29–27   no infraction of *G·* laws ;
  Ret. 26– 9   in his obedience to *G·* laws,
  No. 11– 5   *G·* laws, and their intelligent and
  My. 203– 8   without mutiny are *G·* laws.
likeness
  (*see* **likeness**)
little ones
  Mis. 130–25   one of *G·* ''little ones.'' -- *Matt. 18 : 6.*
  My. 186– 4   May *G·* little ones cluster around this
love
  (*see* **love**)
man
  Mis. 36– 2   is neither *G·* man nor Mind ;
       167– 2   infantile thought of *G·* man,
  Un. 46– 6   for he is *G·* man ;
mercy
  My. 162– 1   *G·* mercy for mortal ignorance
mere pleasure
  '01. 15–23   * *G·* mere pleasure that keeps you
messages
  Mis. 171–11   spiritual translations of *G·* messages,
methods
  Mis. 135–16   *G·* methods and means of healing,
miracles
  My. 107–22   wouldst thou mock *G·* miracles
most tender mercies
  Mis. 391–17   Share *G·* most tender mercies,
  Po. 38–16   Share *G·* most tender mercies,
nestlings
  Mis. 152–25   you, . . . are *G·* nestlings ;
offspring
  Un. 24–20   Man, as *G·* offspring, must
  No. 37– 1   In human conception *G·* offspring
omnipotence
  No. 20–14   *G·* omnipotence and omnipresence
  My. 293–15   understanding of *G·* omnipotence,
open secret
  My. 289– 2   *G·* open secret is seen through grace,
opposite
  Mis. 181–29   and not of *G·* opposite, — evil,
opposites
  '00. 5–28   in casting out *G·* opposites,
orbits
  Mis. 22–17   true thoughts revolve in *G·* orbits :

God's

own image
Mis. 330–17   man in *G·* own image and likeness,
No. 23–28   is *G·* own image and likeness,
Peo. 14–18   reinstate man in *G·* own image
My. 244–16   man's spiritual state in *G·* own image

own likeness
Mis. 77–27   man, made in *G·* own likeness,

own plan
My. 283–23   *G·* own plan of salvation.

own time
My. 306–19   and that in *G·* own time.

pardon
No. 42– 9   *G·* pardon is the destruction of

paths
Mis. 99–27   "Make straight *G·* paths ;

people
Mis. 117–12   * enduring vivacity among *G·* people."

perfect likeness
Mis. 79– 7   was, and is, *G·* perfect likeness,

perfect ways
Mis. 66–17   *G·* perfect ways and means,

personality
'01. 4–23   able to explain *G·* personality
6–25   *G·* personality must be as infinite

phenomena
My. 249– 6   produce *G·* phenomena.

plan
Peo. 12–18   *G·* plan of redemption,

power
(see **power**)

praise
Pul. 1–11   eloquent in *G·* praise.
No. 44–17   the mouth lisping *G·* praise;

preparations
Mis. 268–22   *G·* preparations for the sick

presence
Mis. 113– 2   *G·* presence gives spiritual light,
345– 1   *G·* presence and providence.
Un. 2– 7   *G·* presence, power, and love,
My. 354–19   Of *G·* presence here.

problems
My. 348–32   the solution of *G·* problems.

providence
Mis. 278–23   necessities and *G·* providence

reflection
Mis. 18–17   spiritual origin, *G·* reflection,
183–13   possible to man *as G· reflection.*
291– 5   true sense of *G·* reflection,

representative
My. 227– 3   spake as *G·* representative

requirement
Man. 77–18   *G·* Requirement.

revelation
Mis. 92–25   substituted for *G·* revelation.
Ret. 84–14   substituted for *G·* revelation.

right hand
Mis. ix–12   the touch of *G·* right hand.
98–19   build up, through *G·* right hand,
364–13   *G·* right hand grasping the
Ret. 27–19   * Touch *G·* right hand in that

servants
Mis. 158–19   All *G·* servants are minute men

service
My. 195–16   use in *G·* service the one talent

side
Mis. 102–31   "one on *G·* side is a majority."
Pul. 4–16   "one on *G·* side is a majority."
No. 45–28   "One on *G·* side is a majority ;"

sight
Mis. 144–22   precious in *G·* sight.
My. 184–22   service acceptable in *G·* sight.

spiritual child
Mis. 18–15   as *G·* spiritual child only,

spiritual idea
My. 120–11   *G·* spiritual idea that takes away all sin,

spiritual ideal
My. 319– 3   *G·* spiritual ideal is the only

supremacy
No. 18– 8   demonstration of *G·* supremacy
Hea. 7– 5   those who understand *G·* supremacy,

temple
Mis. 140–17   to know who owned *G·* temple,

time
Mis. 117–23   *G·* time and mortals' differ.
My. 13– 3   act in *G·* time.

universal kingdom
Mis. 213–28   *G·* universal kingdom will appear,

universe
Mis. 65–13   *G·* universe and man are immortal.

verity
No. 17–16   divine consciousness and *G·* verity.

voice
Mis. 134–27   neither silence nor disarm *G·* voice.

way
My. 293– 8   believed . . . martyrdom was *G·* way.

God's

ways
(see **ways**)

Way-shower
My. 140–22   so soon as *G·* Way-shower, Christ,

whole plan
Peo. 12–21   as *G·* whole plan,

will
Pan. 13–16   till *G·* will be witnessed
My. 18–24   till *G·* will be witnessed
258–12   to know and to do *G·* will,

window
Ret. 90– 2   *G·* window which lets in light,

wisdom
Mis. 362– 5   at rest in *G·* wisdom,
Un. 51–18   in the economy of *G·* wisdom

Word
'01. 31–26   used faithfully *G·* Word,
My. 352–22   hearers and the doers of *G·* Word.

word
My. 47–25   * *G·* word in the wilderness

work
Mis. 317– 3   *Yes, if you are doing G· work.*
My. 231–13   in order to help *G·* work

works
My. 294–21   shown him by *G·* works?

Zion
Mis. 146– 1   remember thee, and *G·* Zion,

Man. 47–12   which are *G·*"— *I Cor.* 6 : 20.
Ret. 71– 6   the things that are *G·*."— *Mark* 12 : 17.
77– 4   * "An honest *G·* the noblest
83–20   to *G·* daily interpretation.
90– 3   or seek to stand in *G·* stead.
'01. 1– 5   can never lack *G·* outstretched arm
'02. 1– 1   *G·* loving providence for His people
My. 128– 8   less than *G·* benign government,
220–11   the things that are *G·*.' "— *Mark* 12 : 17.

Gods

Pan. 6–23   religion has at least two *G·*.
8– 7   imply two *G·*, one the divine,

gods

alias
No. 26– 5   spirits, or souls,— *alias g·*.

are just
Un. 23– 3   * The *g·* are just, and of our

human
Mis. 123–12   human passions and human *g·*,

many
Mis. 333–16   and *g·* many."— *see I Cor.* 8 : 5.
No. 21–21   in the pantheon of many *g·*,
Pan. 2–14   " *g·* many,"— *I Cor.* 8 : 5.
3–22   belief in one God, or in many *g·*.
'00. 4– 5   many minds and many *g·*.

master of the
My. 159–26   Zeus, the master of the *g·*,

material
Mis. 198– 5   turning away from material *g·* ;

more
Un. 38–17   rulership of more *g·* than one.

nectar of the
Mis. 9–17   with the nectar of the *g·*,

no other
Mis. 18–10   no other *g·* before me ;"— *Exod.* 20 : 3.
21– 3   no other *g·* before me."— *Exod.* 20 : 3.
23–13   no other *g·* before me."— *Exod.* 20 : 3.
28–21   no other *g·* before me,"— *Exod.* 20 : 3.
96– 5   and would have no other *g·*,
123– 4   no other *g·* before me :"— *Exod.* 20 : 3.
Pan. 9–10   no other *g·* before me ;"— *Exod.* 20 : 3.
'00. 5–20   no other *g·* before me."— *Exod.* 20 : 3.
'02. 4–20   no other *g·* before me,"— *Exod.* 20 : 3.
5–29   no other *g·* before me,"— *Exod.* 20 : 3.
6–19   no other *g·* before me,"— *Exod.* 20 : 3.
My. 5–14   no other *g·* before me,"— *Exod.* 20 : 3.
64–13   no other *g·* before me,'— *Exod.* 20 : 3.
152–22   and serve no other *g·*,
153–17   no other *g·* before me"— *Exod.* 20 : 3.
221–18   no other *g·* before me,"— *Exod.* 20 : 3.
278– 9   no other *g·* before me,"— *Exod.* 20 : 3.
279–12   no other *g·* before me"— *Exod.* 20 : 3.
364– 8   no other *g·* before me."— *Exod.* 20 : 3.

of medicine
Peo. 4–24   the *g·* of medicine,

of paganism
Pan. 7–12   and hint the *g·* of paganism

other
Mis. 40– 6   thus serve "other *g·*."— *Exod.* 20 : 3.
45–27   "other *g·* before me."— *Exod.* 20 : 3.
174– 4   idolatry, having other *g·* ;
196–15   votaries to "other *g·*"— *Exod.* 20 : 3.
209–21   "other *g·* before me,"— *Exod.* 20 : 3.
No. 42– 6   not compelled to have other *g·*
Pan. 7–25   this error is idolatry — other *g·*.
'00. 3–25   idolatry,— other *g·*.

gods

shall be as
Mis.	57–19	ye shall be as *g·*,'' — *Gen.* 3 : 5.
Ret.	69–10	'Ye shall be as *g·* ;'— *Gen.* 3 : 5.
Un.	44–22	ye shall be as *g·*, — *Gen.* 3 : 5.

Mis.	196– 8	will make you as *g·* ;'' — see *Gen.* 3 : 5.
	255– 1	chapter sub-title
	364–31	this veil of the temple of *g·*,
Pan.	9– 5	in paganism they stand for *g·* ;

Godspeed
My.	99– 9	* and bidden *G·*.''

Godward
Mis.	49–23	that are helping man *G·* :

goes
Mis.	15–14	and *g·* on with years ;
	21– 3	It *g·* on in perfect unity
	254–15	*g·* on to learn that he must
	306– 4	* accompany the bell wherever it *g·*.
	327–31	*g·* back and kindly binds up their
	334–11	away *g·* all its supposed power
	383– 8	it *g·* without saying,
Man.	48–13	Mrs. Eddy's drive when she *g·* out,
	94– 9	*g·* to hear and deride truth,
	94–11	and he who *g·* to seek truth
Ret.	45– 1	spiritually organized Church . . . *g·* on.
Un.	45– 5	and *g·* on saying, ''Am I not myself?
	45–19	*g·* forth into an imaginary sphere
	61–14	retreats, and again *g·* forward ;
	62– 5	that neither comes nor *g·*,
'00.	14– 6	He *g·* on to portray seven churches,
'01.	27–27	* *g·* through three stages.
'02.	8–23	the ego, or I, *g·* to the Father,
Hea.	12– 7	metaphysician *g·* to the fount to
My.	15–12	My heart *g·* out to you
	76–15	* all of which *g·* to show
	96–31	* C. S. just *g·* a little beyond
	97–13	* advantage so far as this *g·*.
	228–30	It *g·* without saying that such
	275–23	the true sense of being *g·* on.
	277–11	The mental animus *g·* on,
	304–25	* *g·* through three stages.

goest
Mis.	327– 4	withersoever thou *g·*.''

goeth
Mis.	118–31	which *g·* into the mouth — *Matt.* 15 : 11.
	156–20	''this kind *g·* not — *Matt.* 17 : 21.
	252–32	*g·* and selleth all that he hath
	328– 5	path that *g·* upward.''
My.	190–17	''This kind *g·* not — *Matt.* 17 : 21.
	222–13	''This kind *g·* not — *Matt.* 17 : 21.
	339–24	''This kind *g·* not — *Matt.* 17 : 21.

going
Mis.	206–28	Way-shower, who, *g·* before you,
	282– 1	You are *g·* out to demonstrate a
Ret.	9– 8	That night, before *g·* to rest,
Un.	28–12	*g·* in or coming out.
	61– 3	Coming and *g·* belong to mortal
Pul.	46–13	* *g·* back to the ancestral tree
	72–27	* *g·* about doing good and healing the
'02.	20– 2	or *g·* down into the deep,
My.	44– 5	* *g·* up to possess the promised land
	54– 2	* hundreds *g·* away who could not
	66– 6	* activity has been *g·* on
	82–29	* their *g·* will not be noticeable
	83– 2	* never *g·* about labelled.
	87– 4	* multitudes *g·* and coming.
	229–13	incentive for *g·* thither.
	239–28	*g·* on since ever time was.
	323–10	* not *g·* to lie about anything

goings
Mis.	245–10	the stately *g·* of C. S.,
Un.	5–26	stately *g·* of this wonderful part

Golconda
My.	175–23	richer than the diamonds of *G·*,

gold
Mis.	126–23	even *g·* is less current.
	151– 7	He separates the dross from the *g·*,
	159–28	devices in embroidery, silver, *g·*,
	205– 8	separates the dross from the *g·*,
	305–21	* *g·*, silver, bronze, copper, and
	346–23	apples of *g·* in pictures of — *Prov.* 25 : 11.
	376–27	*g·*, orange, pink, crimson, violet ;
Ret.	94– 9	As dross is separated from *g·*,
Un.	54– 1	The bright *g·* of Truth
Pul.	26–26	* The mantel is of onyx and *g·*.
	76– 7	* the pale green and *g·* decoration
	76–13	* in white and *g·* tapestry.
	76–14	* Mexican onyx with *g·* decoration
	76–20	* heavily plated with *g·*.''
	77– 4	* a scroll of solid *g·*,
	78– 4	* in the form of a *g·* scroll,

gold
Pul.	78–21	* *g·* key to the church door.
	86– 3	* contains a solid *g·* box,
'00.	10–27	ten five-dollar *g·* pieces
Po.	16– 9	of power, cf glory, or *g·* ;
My.	30–22	* with silver, and with *g·*.
	176– 3	FIFTY DOLLARS IN *G·*
	260–15	may pursue . . . the lure of *g·*,
	283–29	Lured by fame, pride, or *g·*,

golden
Mis.	90–13	This rule is forever *g·* :
	307–25	not intended for a *g·* calf,
	376–25	fairy blue and *g·* flecks
Ret.	79–28	nor its *g·* streets invaded.
	80–20	win the *g·* scholarship
Pul.	26–21	* *g·* letters on a marble tablet,
	39–16	* its flood of *g·* light.
	42–16	* *g·* beehive stamped upon it,
	77– 7	* *g·* key of the church structure.
No.	7– 2	The rule of divinity is *g·* ;
'00.	12– 5	*g·* candlesticks'' — *Rev.* 2 : 1.
Hea.	19–25	*g·* rays in the sunlight
Po.	70– 3	A bright and *g·* shower
My.	86– 4	* *g·* State House dome,
	364– 6	departure from this *g·* rule

Golden Rule
Mis.	31– 6	breaks the *G· R·* and subverts the
	51–19	love God, good, and obey the *G· R·*,
	135–12	or fail to fulfil this *G· R·*,
	266–27	aid each other, and obey the *G· R·*.
	282– 9	practice of C. S. is the *G· R·*,
	287–25	obey the *G· R·* for human life,
	301–26	*Second :* It breaks the *G· R·*,
	334–31	to understand this *G· R·*
	337–10	the *G· R·* and its Principle,
Man.	42–22	practised according to the *G· R·* :
	44– 3	strict adherence to the *G· R·*,
	48–11	The *G· R·*.
'00.	14–16	the more perfect way, or *G· R·* :
'01.	30–11	observing the *G· R·*,
	30–28	to obey the *G· R·*,
My.	4– 2	then he practises the *G· R·*
	5–14	Hebrew Decalogue, . . . and the *G· R·*
	5–28	Forgetting the *G· R·* and
	64–14	Hebrew Decalogue, . . . and the *G· R·*
	160–20	who persist in breaking the *G· R·*
	181–14	demonstrated on the *G· R·*,
	213–24	and the *G· R·* will not rust
	222–26	*G· R·* utilized, and the rights of
	224–16	blind to its loss of the *G· R·*,
	266– 8	trusts in place of the *G· R·*,
	281–16	* chapter sub-title
	282–14	what we already know of the *G· R·*,

Golden Text
My.	33– 9	* *G· T·* : ''Search me, — *Psal.* 139 : 23.

gold-gleaming
Ret.	18– 3	at play with the *g·* fish ;
Po.	63–10	at play with the *g·* fish ;

gold-headed
My.	308–22	handed him a *g·* walking-stick

goldsmith's
Pul.	78– 3	* examples of the *g·* art

Goliath
Mis.	162–31	shepherd boy, to disarm the *G·*.
	195–25	shepherd's sling would slay this *G·*.

Goliaths
My.	125–10	chosen one to meet the *G·*.

gone
Mis.	42– 2	*do we meet those g· before?*
	42–15	existence with those *g·* before,
	48–27	That persons have *g·* away from
	190–12	*when the devil was g· out,* — *Luke* 11 : 14.
	213–19	adherents of Truth have *g·* on
	216–22	* some time after the rest of it had *g·*.''
	234–19	should have *g·* on to establish their
	284–17	*g·* personally to the malpractitioner
	310–12	return of members that have *g·* out
	342–19	our lamps have *g·* out, — see *Matt.* 25 : 8.
	356–25	*g·* down in his own esteem.
Ret.	13–22	The fever was *g·*, and I rose
Un.	9–24	Healing has *g·* on continually ;
	57–13	''virtue had *g·* out of him.''— *Mark* 5 : 30.
Pul.	51–22	* but as time has *g·* on,
Pan.	1– 7	winter winds have come and *g·* ;
'01.	15–27	* why you have not *g·* to hell
	16–10	hatred *g·* mad becomes imbecile
	21–14	after Mrs. Eddy has *g·*.
My.	24–26	* have *g·* away with the conviction
	59–24	* In years *g·* by I have been asked,
	83–18	* realize that the Scientists have *g·*.
	122–16	another Christmas has come and *g·*.
	189–22	last-drawn sigh of a glory *g·*,
	278– 8	and its edict hath *g·* forth :

good (*see also* good's)

abides in
Un. 40–17 abides in man, if man abides in g·,
absence of
Mis. 27–21 evil signifies the absence of g·,
289– 7 It is suppositional absence of g·.
363– 6 supposition that the absence of g· is
Ret. 60–12 evil is the absence of g· ;
absolute
Mis. 299–16 is the only absolute g· ;
364–28 If . . . there is no absolute g·.
accomplished
My. 298– 6 of the g· accomplished therein,
achievement of
Mis. 340–22 work on to the achievement of g· ;
adoption of
Mis. 15–16 childlike trust and joyful adoption of g· ;
aggregation of
My. 99– 8 * aggregation of g· and beneficial
all
Mis. 82– 3 Principle and idea of all g·.
337–18 growing affection for all g·,
No. 24–28 none beside Him, and He is all g·,
My. 15–13 desire that the Giver of all g·
127– 6 We thank the Giver of all g·
292– 3 All g· that ever was written,
356– 2 their present ownership of all g·,
all is
Mis. 105–32 all is g· and all is Mind.
Ret. 63– 6 all is g·, and there is . . . no evil,
My. 288–31 all is g· because God made all,
allness of
My. 364–15 supremacy and allness of g·.
All of
Mis. 250– 1 the infinite All of g·,
all power of
Mis. 14– 4 ever-presence and all-power of g· ;
all that is
Un. 17– 5 all that is g· will aid your journey,
all the
Mis. 38– 2 *all the g· we can do*
89–15 do him all the g· you can ;
273–18 all the g· they are capable of
and evil
Mis. 12–18 in the interest of both g· and evil
24–23 A knowledge of both g· and evil
118– 2 cannot obey both God, g·, and evil,
121– 8 g· and evil, seem to grapple,
197–26 that is both g· and evil ;
198–22 the knowledge of *both g·* and evil ;
319– 3 g· and evil can neither be coeval
333– 3 g· and evil, life and death,
366–21 insists on the unity of g· and evil
367–16 knowledge of *both g·* and evil,
Ret. 56–24 into minds, g· and evil.
57–27 such opposite effects as g· and evil,
59– 7 source of death, and of g· and evil.
Un. 21– 7 In like manner g· and evil talk
44–22 knowing g· and evil — *Gen.* 3 : 5.
46–19 regarded as both g· and evil,
52–10 consciousness of both g· and evil,
Pul. 1– 9 notable for g· and evil.
No. 26– 3 believe . . . that g· and evil blend ;
Pan. 6–20 colloquy between g· and evil,
'00. 4– 2 couples love and hate, g· and evil,
'01. 25–24 as the blending of g· and evil,
Hea. 5– 2 finite sense . . . of g· and evil
18–10 g· and evil never dwelt together.
Peo. 4–11 said . . . of g· and evil,
My. 179–10 both g· and evil, both mind and
and pure
Mis. 368–15 ranks of the g· and pure,
Ret. 68–28 The beautiful, g·, and pure
and Truth
Mis. 36– 4 in contradistinction to g· and Truth,
Peo. 3–16 spiritual idea of g· and Truth
another's
Mis. 127–19 finds one's own in another's g·.
184–27 not her own, but another's g· ;
No. 3–23 not so much thine own as another's g·,
'00. 14–20 not only her own, but another's g·.
'01. 34–19 not her own but another's g·,
My. 18–16 finds one's own in another's g·.''
19–23 ''seeketh . . . another's g·, — *I Cor.* 13 : 5.
appearing of
Mis. 338– 1 appearing of g· in an individual
attendant
Un. 37–19 g· attendant upon spiritual
aught but
Mis. 10–32 belief . . . that aught but g· exists
No. 17–10 to be conscious of aught but g·.
being
Ret. 86– 6 but one way of *being* g·,
being real
Mis. 46– 5 g· being real, evil, . . . is unreal.
346–20 g· being real, its opposite is . . . unreal,

good

cannot lose
Mis. 10–12 The g· cannot lose their God,
capabilities for
Peo. 2– 1 learn our capabilities for g·,
choose only
Mis. 289–32 whence they can choose only g·.
consciousness of
Mis. 9– 1 consciousness of g·, grace, and peace,
259– 9 The consciousness of g· has no
convictions of
Mis. 31–19 against his own convictions of g·
cycle of
My. 270– 3 cycle of g· obliterates the
daily
Mis. 397–17 My prayer, some daily g· to do
Pul. 19– 1 My prayer, some daily g· to do
Po. 13– 5 My prayer, some daily g· to do
defending
My. 207–23 mastering evil and defending g·,
define
Mis. 13–29 then define g· as God,
demonstrates
Mis. 259–25 Truth demonstrates g·,
derivative of
Mis. 14–25 cannot be, the derivative of g·.
destroys evil
'01. 10–23 whereby g· destroys evil,
detract from the
Mis. 302–27 nor detract from the g·
developing
'00. 10– 4 asserting and developing g·.
dies not
Mis. 2–22 for g· dies not
discernment of
Mis. 13–27 clearer discernment of g·.
divine
Mis. 164– 4 idea that represents divine g·,
Ret. 56–17 omnipresence of God, or divine g·.
80– 2 this is the pledge of divine g·
Un. 24– 4 My Mind is divine g·,
does no
My. 122– 8 To cut off the top . . . does no g· ;
doeth
My. 99– 5 * merry heart that doeth g·
doing
Mis. ix– 2 suits my sense of doing g·.
11–24 doing g· to one's enemies
12–30 law of Love, doing g· to all ;
90–18 be sure that your means for doing g·
163– 3 Three years he went about doing g·.
198–29 seems to punish man for doing g·,
198–31 in doing g·, therefore he must
Ret. 29– 4 loving our enemies and doing g· to
86– 5 but one way of *doing g·,*
93– 2 Jesus went about doing g·.
Pul. 21–15 doing g· in all denominations
72–27 * doing g· and healing the sick.
Rud. 14–10 except the bliss of doing g·.
'01. 30–11 too occupied with doing g·,
'02. 10– 1 knowing and doing g·,
17–22 in being and in doing g· ;
Hea. 5– 8 doing g· to his neighbor,
doing of
My. 87–30 * in the cheerful doing of g·.
domain of
My. 278–27 War is not in the domain of g· ;
dominating
Pan. 7–27 hypothesis of . . . evil dominating g·,
domination of
No. 32–22 The domination of g· destroys the
eliminated by
Mis. 259–11 to be known or eliminated by g· :
enemy of
My. 358–10 pray that the enemy of g· cannot
energies of
Mis. 176–12 more of the divine energies of g·,
estimate the
No. 43– 9 * can estimate the g· your books are
eternal
Mis. 189–22 namely God, the eternal g·,
Ret. 22–21 of one parent, the eternal g·.
Un. 60– 3 through ever-present and eternal g·.
Rud. 8–13 strong in God, the eternal g·.
Peo. 3–22 or the quantity of eternal g·.
eternal as
Mis. 14–18 real and eternal as g·, God !
ever-presence of
Rud. 11–23 all-power and ever-presence of g·,
ever-present
Mis. 183– 2 in the ever-present g·,
268–18 omnipotent and ever-present g·.
Un. 62–13 omnipotent and ever-present g·
My. 273–23 Life as God, good, ever-present g·,
evil and
(*see* evil)

good

evil counterfeits
    Mis. 351–20   Evil counterfeits *g·* :

evil from
    Un. 14–28   learning to distinguish evil from *g·*,

evil subordinates
    No. 24–14   evil subordinates *g·* in personality.

evil with
    (*see* **evil**)

existence of
    Mis. 13–17   sense of the existence of *g·*.
          13–23   the existence of *g·* only ;

factor of
    Mis. 13–15   is a factor of *g·*,

faith in
    Mis. 31–12   the lack of faith in *g·*.

falsehood about
    Rud. 8–20   uttering falsehood about *g·*.

flows
    Mis. 185–11   *g·* flows into every avenue of being,

follower of
    Mis. 152–21   the follower of *g·*.

for evil
    Mis. 277–28   and render *g·* for evil.
    Ret. 45–19   returning *g·* for evil,
    My. 204–27   while returning *g·* for evil,
        260–23   returning *g·* for evil,
        270–22   I have returned *g·* for evil,

general
    Mis. 11–26   can do much general *g·*

glory of
    My. 4–28   the glory of *g·*,

God and
    Mis. 27– 3   terms God and *g·*, as Spirit,

God as
    Mis. 26–28   Scriptures name God as *g·*,
    Peo. 3–23   sense of God as *g·*

God calls
    Mis. 110–29   that which God calls *g·*.

God is
    (*see* **God**)

God, or
    Ret. 54–12   Millions are believing in God, or *g·*,
    Un. 31–23   God, or *g·*, is Spirit alone ;

great
    Mis. 292–26   is accomplishing great *g·*,
        338– 3   brings to humanity some great *g·*,
    Peo. 6–26   great *g·* for which we are to leave all

greatest
    Mis. 288– 4   work out the greatest *g·* to the
    Ret. 82–15   greatest *g·* to the greatest number,
    Pul. 54–17   * where the greatest *g·* could be

harmony and
    Mis. 17– 5   law of omnipotent harmony and *g·*,

has all power
    Mis. 31–15   that God, *g·*, has *all* power.

He is
    No. 38– 7   He is *g·*, and good is Spirit ;

higher
    Mis. 227–26   satisfies the mind craving a higher *g·*,

if we regard
    Mis. 3– 4   If we regard *g·* as more natural

immortal
    Mis. 82–29   Mind is God, immortal *g·* ;

immutable
    Un. 51– 2   reflection of immutable *g·*.

impulse for
    My. 10– 6   * this mighty impulse for *g·*

in being
    My. 196–25   The *g·* in being,

inclusive
    Mis. 104– 8   the one inclusive *g·*.

inexhaustible
    Mis. 83– 4   perpetual idea of inexhaustible *g·*.

infinite
    Mis. 15–24   infinite *g·* that we name God,
        26–31   naturally and divinely infinite *g·*.
       100–14   Science . . . unfolds infinite *g·*,
       282– 2   a true sense of the infinite *g·*,
       367–18   If God is infinite *g·*,
    Ret. 56–19   and that one is the infinite *g·*,
    Un. 18– 3   saying, I am infinite *g·* ;
       43– 7   anchorage in infinite *g·*, God,
       61–17   Our highest sense of infinite *g·*
    Pan. 6–16   God is *infinite g·*,
    My. 42–24   * only as infinite *g·* unfolds
       152–17   infinite *g·*, than which there is none else
       204– 3   fact that He is infinite *g·*,
       356–26   and this God is infinite *g·*.

infinity of
    Ret. 68– 8   he reflects the infinity of *g·*.

influence for
    My. 47–12   * touched by its influence for *g·*,

in good
    My. 132–20   see God and live, see *g·* in good,

good

in One
    Mis. 18–21   one in good, and *g·* in One.

inseparable from
    Un. 21–18   is inseparable from *g·*.

intelligent
    Mis. 267–23   governed by Spirit, intelligent *g·*.

in the name of
    Mis. 334–19   evil at work in the name of *g·*,

inverted
    Un. 53– 3   all its forms are inverted *g·*.

is all
    Mis. 279–21   evil is naught and *g·* is all.
    Ret. 60–14   evil is unreal and *g·* is all

is equally one
    Ret. 64–10   teaches that *g·* is equally *one* and *all,*

is forever good
    Mis. 104–12   and *g·* is forever good.

is God
    Mis. 24–24   *g·* is God, and God is All
       319– 3   *g·* is God, even as God is good,
    Ret. 60–13   *g·* is God ever-present,

is great
    No. 32–18   *G·* is great and real.

is infinite
    Mis. 108– 5   *g·* is infinite, All.

is made
    Mis. 339–10   *g·* is made more industrious

is Mind
    Rud. 4–16   *G·* is Mind, but evil is not Mind.
    Pan. 6–22   For if God, *g·*, is Mind,

is more contagious
    Mis. 229– 9   *g·* is more contagious than evil,

is my God
    Mis. 206–22   "*G·* is my God, and my God is good.

is never
    Mis. 340– 3   *G·* is never the reward of evil,
    Un. 62– 9   God, *g·*, is never absent,

is not educed
    Mis. 122–20   *G·* is not educed from its opposite :
    Pan. 12– 2   *g·* is not educed from evil,

is omnipotence
    Mis. 13–30   will find that *g·* is omnipotence,

is omnipotent
    Mis. 172–31   hence, *g·* is omnipotent
    Pan. 6–24   if God, *g·*, is omnipotent,
    Hea. 10– 9   God — *g·* — is omnipotent ;

is one
    Rud. 11– 8   Therefore *g·* is one and All.

is Spirit
    No. 38– 7   He is good, and *g·* is Spirit ;

is supreme
    No. 24–27   truth, that *g·* is supreme.

is the master
    Mis. 209–27   *g·* is the master of evil.

is the only creator
    Un. 25–20   God, *g·*, is the only creator.

is the only substance
    Un. 25– 7   *g·* is the only substance,

is the reward
    Mis. 206–25   *g·* is the reward of all who

it wrought
    No. 33–17   and the *g·* it wrought.

knowledge of
    Mis. 109–23   third stage, — the knowledge of *g·* ;

law of
    Rud. 1– 2   the law of God, the law of *g·*,

leading to
    Mis. 85– 9   thought and act leading to *g·*.

learn it of
    Un. 41– 4   we must learn it of *g·*.

Life and
    Un. 62–16   false sense of Life and *g·*.

Life of
    Un. 62–11   as they reach the Life of *g·*,

likeness of
    Un. 3–18   the image and likeness of *g·*,

lives in
    Pul. 4–20   Who lives in *g·*, lives also in God,

love
    Mis. 94– 6   he must repent, and love *g·*
       206–27   if you love *g·* supremely,
    '00. 11–11   love God," — love *g·*. — *Rom.* 8 : 28.

love of
    Mis. 232–26   sought from the love of *g·*,

marvellous
    Mis. 237–21   marvellous *g·*, and mysterious evil.
    My. 288– 3   Love unfolds marvellous *g·*

may come
    Mis. 122–18   that *g·* may come ! — *Rom.* 3 : 8.
       298– 5   that *g·* may come? — *Rom.* 3 : 8.
       335–29   those who do evil that *g·* may come,

medium of
    Pan. 11–24   evil is not the medium of *g·*,

good

Mind is
Mis. 105–31 and this Mind is g·,
Mind, or
Ret. 56–24 does not subdivide Mind, or g·,
Un. 45–28 in Spirit, immortal Mind, or g·.
modes of
My. 211–14 Reversing the modes of g·,
more
My. 163–15 which I think do them more g·.
much
Mis. 302–14 Much g· has been accomplished
Ret. 82–22 to consummate much g· or else
My. 216–20 by which you can do much g·
mysticism of
My. 167– 3 mysticism of g· is unknown to
none beside
Un. 62–10 and there is none beside g·.
no place in
No. 27– 5 evil finds no place in g·.
not evil
Mis. 4– 9 its power to do g·, not evil.
42–24 learn that g·, not evil, lives
101–23 this power is g·, not evil ;
283–27 to demonstrate g·, not evil,
nothing but
Mis. 367–18 He knows nothing but g· ;
offspring of
Mis. 181–29 offspring of g·, and not of
of others
No. 7–16 sacrifice for the g· of others
omnipotence of
Mis. 121–11 and the omnipotence of g·,
200–27 faith in the omnipotence of g·,
omnipresence of
Ret. 28– 6 understand the omnipresence of g·
omnipresent
Mis. 8–15 Love that is omnipresent g·,
one in
Mis. 18–20 one in g·, and good in One.
oneness of
Mis. 259– 7 infinitude and oneness of g·
one side to
Hea. 10–10 There is but one side to g·,
only
Un. 21– 8 and g· only is reality.
on the side of
Mis. 104–31 gain a balance on the side of g·,
opposed to
Mis. 198–25 law, so-called as opposed to g·,
198–28 belief in . . . evil, opposed to g· ;
opposite to
Mis. 55– 9 Opposite to g·, is the
or evil
Mis. 309– 2 either as g· or evil.
No. 23–24 amount of g· or evil he possesses.
or God
Un. 2–16 Mind which is g·, or God,
24–22 separate from g· or God.
or of evil
No. 22–16 person of g· or of evil.
or Truth
Mis. 196–13 came not from Mind, g·, or Truth.
overcome evil with
(see **evil**, sub-title **overcome**)
overcome with
Ret. 55– 6 it can only be overcome with g·.
over evil
Ret. 26–10 supremacy of g· over evil,
paralyze
My. 213– 4 aim of . . . is to paralyze g·
place of
Rud. 6–11 takes the place of g·.
power and
Mis. 284– 7 this field of limitless power and g·
power is
Mis. 101–23 this power is g·, not evil ;
184–22 learns that all power is g·
power of
Mis. 259–16 moral power of g·, not of evil :
Un. 41–17 presence and power of g·,
Pul. 15– 1 power of g· resident in
power or
Mis. 335–31 seeking power or g· aside from
practical
My. 287–16 love for God, practical g·,
Principle of
My. 152–22 Principle of g·, that we call God,
producing
Mis. 122–15 it is not evil producing g·,
proportions of
Mis. 55–10 seeks the proportions of g·.
quality of
Mis. 78–29 to present the quality of g·.

good

real as
Mis. 49–22 belief . . . that evil is as real as g·,
108–20 wherein evil seems as real as g·,
No. 17–26 If . . . evil would be as real as g·,
24–13 not only as real as g·, but
reality and
My. 164–26 the sum of all reality and g·.
reflects
Mis. 23–26 reflects g·, Life, Truth, Love
reward of
My. 296–17 reward of g· and punishment of evil
Science of
Mis. 27– 2 Science of g· calls evil *nothing*.
352– 7 discern the Science of g·.
No. 24– 2 In the Science of g·,
sense of
Mis. 222– 2 man's proper sense of g·,
341–18 to win the spiritual sense of g·.
Un. 41– 8 loss of the true sense of g·,
some
Mis. 391–20 Some g· ne'er told before,
Po. 38–19 Some g· ne'er told before,
My. 117–16 some g· out of your personality
Spirit and
Ret. 60–10 as real as Spirit and g·.
Spirit or
No. 17– 5 absence of Spirit or g·.
spiritual
Mis. 140– 7 all spiritual g· comes to
Un. 38–23 moral and spiritual g·,
standpoint of
Mis. 289– 8 From a human standpoint of g·,
substance of
Mis. 103–12 for who knoweth the substance of g·?"
Ret. 57–17 the substance of g·.
Un. 61–18 symbol, not the substance of g·.
supersensible
Ret. 73–17 evil is lost in supersensible g·.
supremacy of
Ret. 26–10 supremacy of g· over evil,
64– 5 destroyed by the supremacy of g·.
supreme
Un. 19–12 for if the supreme g· could
Rud. 2–19 supreme g·, Life, Truth, Love.
Pan. 11–24 g· supreme destroys all sense of
the word
Hea. 3–15 derived from the word g·.
to bad
Mis. 345–10 * cannot change from g· to bad."
to conceive of
Mis. 259–12 too evil to conceive of g·
to develop
Mis. 14–10 through which to develop g·.
to harm
Mis. 118–28 Every attempt of evil to harm g·
touch of
'01. 9–19 foams at the touch of g· ;
to understand
Mis. 109–26 To understand g·, one must discern
trinity of
Rud. 3– 8 this trinity of g·
triumph of
Mis. 201–31 demonstrate the triumph of g·
ultimate of
Mis. 14– 7 origin or ultimate of g·
understanding of
Mis. 31–21 with his understanding of g·,
107–17 the understanding of g·.
unity of
(see **unity**)
universal
My. 165–18 identifies man with universal g·.
186– 1 and g· universal.
291–12 universal g· overcoming evil.
unlike
Pan. 14– 1 nature of whatever is unlike g·,
uses of
Mis. 338–16 uses of g·, to abuses from evil ;
utility of
Mis. 60–27 power, wisdom, and utility of g· ;
vacillating
Mis. 268–30 vacillating g· or self-assertive error
wholly
Un. 49–14 cannot be wholly g·.
worketh
'00. 10– 3 All that worketh g· is
work together for
'00. 11–10 work together for g· — *Rom.* 8 : 28.
My. 143–25 work together for g· — *Rom.* 8 : 28.
your
Mis. 89–15 your g· will generally

Mis. 2–28 and into g· that is immortal ;
9–14 doing thee g· far beyond the present **sense**

good

Mis.	9–15	which thou canst entertain of *g·*.
	10– 6	"work together for *g·* — *Rom.* 8 : 28.
	11–20	to do them *g·* whenever
	13– 6	sharp return of evil for *g·*
	14–19	that *g·*, God, understood,
	14–23	*G·* is the primitive Principle of
	18–23	could never separate himself from *g·*,
	26–29	Saxon term for God is also *g·*.
	26–32	changed, to mean that *g·* is evil,
	27– 4	That God, *g·*, creates evil, or
	31–20	power to be or to do *g·*,
	31–21	the *omnipotence* of God, *g·*.
	37– 1	no power besides God, *g·*.
	41– 3	liberated thought to do *g·*,
	51–19	educate him to love God, *g·*,
	71–26	God, *g·*, the all-knowing Mind.
	93–13	the eternal, infinite God, *g·*.
	101–27	it follows that all must be *g·*;
	112–23	* you have brought what will do him *g·*."
	115–20	since God, *g·*, is All-in-all.
	122–16	nor *g·* ultimating in evil.
	127–20	one must do *g·* to others.
	174– 2	than has *g·* to produce evil.
	179– 9	other consciousness than that of *g·*?
	181– 8	unity with God, *g·*.
	182–21	image and likeness of God, *g·*.
	184–19	says, "I am of God, therefore *g·*,"
	192– 3	Hebrew term for Deity was "*g·*,"
	194–30	the Life that is God, *g·*,
	196– 9	a separate mind from God (*g·*),
	196–19	ever-presence and power of God, *g·*.
	196–21	When the Life that is God, *g·*,
	198–14	evil proceedeth not from God, *g·*,
	200– 3	Jesus regarded *g·* as the normal state
	201–11	its powerlessness to destroy *g·*,
	201–14	somethingness of the *g·* we possess,
	205–17	*g·*, whose visible being is
	208– 6	He is cognizant only of *g·*.
	213– 3	taught, or lived, that is *g·*,
	222–27	*g·* should seem more natural than
	228– 5	is to do *g·* to thyself;
	238–17	Yet the *g·* done.
	251–23	the *g·* they would do, that they do,
	259– 6	law . . . of *g·*, not of evil.
	262– 4	power to be good and to do *g·*.
	262–14	for the *g·* you are doing.
	277–24	proof that God, *g·*, is supreme.
	287–13	The *g·* in human affections
	299–15	*g·* which the material senses see not
	319– 6	aught else than *g·*.
	322–26	zealous affection for seeking *g·*,
	333–14	God, *g·*, is supreme, *all* power and
	338–11	hope holding steadfastly to *g·*
	346–10	God created only the *g·*,
	352–11	true consciousness of God, *g·*.
	354–11	error to Truth, and evil to *g·*,
	360– 6	*g·*, because fashioned divinely,
	364–18	it is *g·*, reflects the divine Mind,
	364–23	matter of Spirit and evil of *g·*;
	364–26	*g·* has the same power or modes
	367–21	To *g·*, evil is never present;
	400–20	Father-Mother *g·*,
Man.	41–12	do *g·* unto your enemies
Ret.	67–21	likeness of evil, not of *g·*.
	68– 3	in the name of "the Lord," or *g·*,
	72– 5	one's ability to do *g·*,
Un.	14–22	all cannot be *g·* therein.
	21–15	*G·*. The Lord is God.
	22– 2	*G·*. Because man is made after
	22– 9	*G·*. Thou shalt not admit
	22–13	*Evil.* . . . something besides *g·*.
	22–19	*G·*. Whatever cometh not from
	23–20	*G·*. How can they exist, unless
	24–12	*G·*. All consciousness is Mind;
	25– 1	If you, O *g·*, deny this,
	25– 5	*G·*. Spirit is the only substance.
	25–20	*G·*. Evil is not a creator.
	26– 9	*G·*. You mistake, O evil!
	46–20	even more the ego than was the *g·*.
	47– 3	Nowhere . . . is evil connected with *g·*,
	49–10	reality and substance of being are *g·*,
	51–21	in the idea of God, *g·*,
	53– 6	calling the knowledge of evil *g·*,
Pul.	6– 7	*G·*, the Anglo-Saxon term for God,
	73–13	* to do *g·* and heal the sick,
	81–24	* the true, the beautiful, the *g·*,
Rud.	4–17	*G·* is not in evil, but in God only.
	9–27	and the producer only of *g·*;
	13– 2	that Life is God, *g·*;
No.	36–14	conscious only of God, of *g·*,
	39–20	awakened desire to be and do *g·*.
Pan.	5– 9	possessed of the nature of God, *g·*
	11–22	may believe that evil develops *g·*,
'00.	5– 5	or aught besides God, *g·*.
	5– 8	opposite of God — *g·* — named devil

good

'00.	8–25	not Science for . . . the *g·* to weep.
'01.	23– 8	must either exist in *g·*, or
	25–27	as the infinite God, — *g·*,
	31–25	who held fast to whatever is *g·*,
'02.	6– 4	law, apart or other than God — *g·*
	6– 7	of something besides God, *g·*,
Hea.	18–11	There is in reality but the *g·*:
Peo.	2– 9	and makes it *g·*,
	2–10	learn that God, *g·*, is universal,
	4–11	When first *g·*, God, was named **a**
Po.	28–14	All-merciful and *g·*,
	69– 8	Father-Mother *g·*,
My.	3–20	*g·* which has come into his life,
	4–16	loves all who love God, *g·*;
	12–30	The *g·* they desire to do,
	49– 3	* and we will do thee *g·*,'
	79– 7	* who seem to see no *g·* in C. S.,
	112–28	book that through the *g·* it does
	129– 2	that which is *g·*." — *I Thess.* 5 : 21.
	170–20	"Trust . . . and do *g·*; — *Psal.* 37 : **3.**
	195–16	To do *g·* to all because we love all,
	200–14	Striving to be good, to do *g·*,
	213–12	should be more zealous to do *g·*,
	240–17	all that is unlike God, *g·*
	252– 8	the *g·* you do unto others
	271– 9	the *g·* that a man does
	273–23	understanding of Life as God, *g·*,
	281–13	God, *g·*, the Father-Mother Love,
	283–30	never fastens on the *g·* or the great.
	288– 6	The *g·* done and the *g·* to do
	288– 9	*G·* is divinely natural.
	296–20	God, *g·*, omnipotent and infinite.
	303–29	remains to be proved by the *g·* I **do.**
	310–31	* "Read it, for it will do you *g·*."

good (adj.)

Mis.	13–29	you will find it to be *g·*;
	25–27	If God created drugs *g·*,
	41–12	The *g·* fight must be fought by
	45–21	*all that was made, and it was g·*,
	70–17	He was too *g·* to die;
	71–12	*g·* or bad influences on the unborn
	72– 7	both *g·* and bad traits of the
	118–24	Be of *g·* cheer;
	122–25	*g·* and faithful servant, — *Matt.* 25 : **23.**
	126–20	the silent lesson of a *g·* example.
	128–10	are of *g·* report; — *Phil.* 4 : 8.
	153–14	*g·* to His Israel
	157–18	I am glad that you are in *g·* cheer.
	159–14	are pure and of *g·* report.
	166–31	an honest man, a *g·* carpenter,
	187–28	evil before he can be *g·*;
	204– 8	When the *g·* fight is fought,
	210–14	*G·* deeds are harmless.
	211– 9	by the *g·* judgment of people
	213–27	Christian Scientists, be of *g·* cheer:
	216–26	* nor the laws of reason hold *g·*,
	219–28	a *g·* sense, or conscious goodness,
	220– 2	a *g·* rule works one way,
	221–14	if he denies it, the *g·* effect is lost.
	224–20	beautiful, great, and *g·*,
	233–18	Substituting *g·* words for a *g·* life,
	235–13	that bringeth not forth *g·* fruit;
	236–25	notwithstanding one's *g·* intentions,
	245–19	in all the *g·* tendencies, charities,
	247–29	that God created, He pronounced *g·*.
	252–10	*G·* thoughts are potent;
	257–28	*g·* Samaritan ministering to
	262– 3	confer increased power to be *g·*
	273–17	labor for a *g·* and holy cause.
	278– 6	fight the *g·* fight, and keep the
	283–16	breach of *g·* manners and morals;
	298–17	"It is not *g·* to marry." — *Matt.* 19 : **10.**
	313– 5	It is a digest of *g·* manners,
	318–21	be a *g·* Bible scholar
	327– 9	"thou hast chosen the *g·* part;
	330–18	It is *g·* to talk with our past hours,
	331– 6	obedient, full of *g·* odor,
	340–21	through evil or through *g·* report,
	355– 6	Less teaching and *g·* healing
	357–17	fallen into the *g·* and honest hearts
	358–30	all the *g·* ends of organization,
	362–13	all that He made was *g·*.
	365–16	*G·* health and a more spiritual
	370–27	the *g·* shepherd cares for all
	370–28	*g·* Shepherd does care for all,
	371–19	* "*g·* right, and *g·* wrong,"
	379–23	with phenomenally *g·* results;
	399–24	(Heaven chiselled squarely *g·*)
Man.	30– 3	and *g·* English scholars
	30–20	keep the property in *g·* repair,
	36–21	members thereof in *g·* standing,
	50–17	another member in *g·* standing
	51–11	*g·* and regular standing with
	52–13	previous character has been *g·*.

GOOD   409   GOODNESS

good (adj.)

Man.	73– 8	g· standing with The Mother Church,
	73–13	Also members in g· standing with
	76–17	members of this Church in g· standing.
	83–10	such only as have g· past records
	91–21	and with g· moral records,
	99–13	who is in g· fellowship with
Ret.	15– 1	the g· clergyman's heart also
	45– 3	"bringeth g· tidings,— Isa. 52 : 7.
	47–24	be a g· Bible scholar
	86– 6	and that is to be g· !
	94– 7	whatsoever seems to be g·,
Un.	8–11	All that is beautiful and g·
	15– 8	and pronounced them g·.
	15– 9	Was evil among these g· things?
	15–23	who worship not the g· Deity,
	23–24	a purely g· and spiritual consciousness
	46–16	only as spiritual and g·,
	53– 8	are g· and God-made,
Pul.	3–14	g· fight we have waged is over,
	16– 9	(Heaven chiseled squarely g·)
	21–15	and fellowship for what is g·
	38–29	* g· that each and all shall prosper,
	46–14	* identified with g· and great names
	51–30	* which have done something g·
	69–12	* so fill the mind with g· thoughts
No.	3–22	How g· and pleasant a thing it is
	18–22	G· health and a more spiritual
	42–20	declaring itself both true and g·.
	43– 7	stimulate and sustain a g· sermon.
Pan.	9– 7	a g· Spirit and an evil spirit.
	13–16	to fight the g· fight
'00.	2–28	Well, all that is g·.
	3–11, 12	a g· work or g· workers
	8–11	may steal other people's g· thoughts,
'01.	2–10	to substitute g· words for g· deeds,
	5–24	anything that is real, g·, or true ;
	14–27	it is g· to know that wrong has no
'02.	3–22	on the brow of g· King Edward,
	14–10	* But only great as I am g·."
	20–25	g· people welcome Christian Scientists.
Hea.	1–14	less need of publishing the g· news."
	2–16	"I have fought a g· fight, — II Tim. 4 : 7.
	5–10	reward of his g· deed
	7– 1	"that which is g· for nothing,
	10–12	and that is the g· side.
	10–14	question of a g· and a bad side
Peo.	2–22	has their Deity become g· ;
	13–20	* cannot change . . . from g· to bad."
Po.	22–14	how great, how g· Thou art
	40– 2	G· "Sons," and daughters,
	76– 8	(Heaven chiseled squarely g·)
My.	9– 9	* glory in every g· deed and thought
	11–20	* made g· the pledge.
	12–29	The dear children's g· deeds
	13–23	with g· things ;— Psal. 103: 5.
	14–13	* g· authority for the statement
	18–24	to fight the g· fight
	21–19	* "g· measure, pressed down,— Luke 6 : 38.
	32– 7	* So g· are the acoustic properties
	42– 8	* a g· confession"— I Tim. 6 : 13.
	60– 7	* my uncle, the g· old deacon
	62– 3	* g· and faithful servant ;— Matt. 25 : 23.
	81– 3	* Scientists fairly radiate g· nature
	81– 5	* So ingrained is this g· nature,
	91– 7	* Scientists set a g· example
	99– 2	* g· things that this sect is doing.
	111–19	models of g· morals,
	121–19	external gentility and g· humor
	122–14	in our g· city of Concord.
	129–24	wherein the g· man's heart
	132– 6	be of g· cheer ;— John 16 : 33.
	134–11	Joy over g· achievements
	148– 6	May the g· folk of Concord
	156– 9	abound to every g· work,"— II Cor. 9 : 8.
	162–21	g· and faithful."— Matt. 25 : 23.
	175–11	to the g· folk of Concord
	178–16	all that God made "g· ;"— Gen. 1 : 31.
	184–27	bringeth g· tidings,— Isa. 52 : 7.
	187–13	and of a g· conscience,— I Tim. 1 : 5.
	195–13	We must resign with g· grace
	197– 1	Enjoying g· things is not evil,
	200–14	Striving to be g·, to do good,
	202–13	g· and faithful,"— Matt. 25 : 23.
	203–11	best of everything is not too g·,
	203–13	to be great, — only as g·.
	205–18	* as the thing made is g· or bad,
	207–21	g· and faithful— Matt. 25 : 21.
	210– 7	G· thoughts are an impervious
	219– 6	My g· students have all the
	221–12	so great and g· as Christ Jesus.
	225– 4	g· and faithful,"— Matt. 25 : 23.
	227–10	g· citizens are arrested for
	232–28	exhaustion and no g· results,
	246– 3	in g· and regular standing.
	246– 8	three years with g· success.

good (adj.)

My.	248– 6	* But only great as I am g·."
	248–22	to conceive God aright you must be g·.
	251–19	after three years of g· practice,
	278–17	Follow that which is g·.
	282–26	prosper ever this g· endeavor.
	284–12	issue of your g· paper,
	287–22	bringeth not forth g· fruit ;
	311– 8	my g· housekeeper said to me :
	315–29	g· men and women in our own
	320– 2	* and a g· proofreader.
	322–25	* g· points in the Science,
	330– 1	* criticism of this g· woman
	330–12	* by a Mason of g· standing
	331–16	* the assailant of a g· woman :
		(see also **man, pleasure, will, works**)

good-by

Pul.	34– 8	* came to bid her g·
Po.	22– 6	shall bid old earth g·

good-looking

My.	97–17	* g·, eminently respectable,

goodly

Mis.	276–11	formed a g· assemblage
My.	162–31	towering top of its g· temple

goodman

My.	156–13	say to the g· of the house :
	232–14	g· of the house— Luke 12 : 39.

good-natured

My.	75–19	* They are very patient and g·.

good-naturedly

My.	75–17	* would take it all very g·.

goodness

achievements of

My.	6–26	beauty, and achievements of g·.
	94–30	beauty, and achievements of g·."

affection for

| Mis. | 318– 9 | natural affection for g· |

all the

| Mis. | 347–14 | all the g· of generous natures, |

and benevolence

| My. | 165–24 | G· and benevolence never tire. |

and blessedness

| Mis. | 209–26 | g· and blessedness are one : |

and greatness

| Mis. | 270–24 | pathway of g· and greatness |
| My. | 123– 6 | hearts of men to g· and greatness, |

and happiness

| My. | 267–31 | manifestation of g· and happiness. |

and harmony

| Mis. | 367–11 | reality of being— g· and harmony |

and love

| Po. | 67–22 | fragrance of g· and love ; |

and philanthropy

| My. | 203– 8 | G· and philanthropy begin with work |

and power

| No. | 39–21 | of God, of His g· and power. |
| Pan. | 4– 5 | possesses all wisdom, g·, and power, |

and utility

| Mis. | 365–10 | proof of its g· and utility, |

and virtue

| No. | 13–24 | reason and revelation, g· and virtue. |

beauty and

| Rud. | 6– 7 | All beauty and g· are in and of |
| | 6– 8 | the nature of beauty and g· |

changeless

| Un. | 26–21 | If God be changeless g·, |

conscious

| Mis. | 219–29 | good sense, or conscious g·, |

erect in

| Mis. | 79–16 | man as His likeness is erect in g· |

excludes

| My. | 249–10 | abandon of hating . . . excludes g·. |

faithful to

| Pul. | 5– 8 | Memory, faithful to g·, |

filled with

| My. | 210– 7 | in a mind filled with g·. |

fruits of

| Mis. | 219–29 | the fruits of g· will follow, |
| Ret. | 54–13 | without bearing the fruits of g·, |

genuine

| Ret. | 81–13 | genuine g· become so apparent |

germ of

| No. | 8–15 | rejoice that every germ of g· |

given impulse to

| No. | 12–15 | and given impulse to g·, |

grasp of

| My. | 283–17 | until his grasp of g· grows |

great

| Hea. | 3–20 | great g· and wonderful works |
| My. | 176– 8 | God grant that such great g·, |

greatness and

| No. | 46–22 | health, greatness, and g·, |

goodness

healing-power of
Mis. 199–30 marvellous healing-power of *g·*
hieroglyphs of
My. 205–16 Love and unity are hieroglyphs of *g·*,
His
Mis. 69– 3 at His *g·*, mercy, and might.
No. 39–21 of God, of His *g·* and power.
My. 193– 9 "for His *g·*, — *Psal.* 107 : 8.
his
Mis. 165–22 His *g·* and grace purchased
his own
My. 227– 6 the minifying of his own *g·*
infinite
Rud. 2–25 higher range of infinite *g·*.
in man
Mis. 164– 5 human presentation of *g·* in man.
in others
Pul. 21–17 true sense of *g·* in others,
is greatness
My. 272– 4 *G·* is greatness, and the logic of
is immortal
Mis. 70–17 for *g·* is immortal.
is something
Ret. 63–14 hence *g·* is something,
learned through
Peo. 2–12 is learned through *g·*,
Life and
Ret. 63–17 against man's Life and *g·*.
man's
'00. 3–20 would destroy this man's *g·*.
never fails
My. 165–15 *G·* never fails to receive
not doctrines
Pul. 9–26 *g·*, not doctrines, . . . gain the ear
of God
Pul. 6– 9 *g·* of God — healing and
opposite of
Mis. 49–21 belief in the opposite of *g·*,
Un. 24– 2 sin the opposite of *g·*.
outpouring of
My. 118–10 It is an outpouring of *g·*
peace in
Mis. 219–21 discomfort in sin and peace in *g·*.
perpetual
'02. 8–23 it prompts perpetual *g·*,
power and
No. 13– 1 reflection of His power and *g·*.
preeminent
My. 161–28 his preeminent *g·*,
proceed from
Mis. 155– 5 and proceed from *g·*.
purposes of
Mis. 152– 6 unite in the purposes of *g·*.
reflection of
Rud. 11– 8 the forever reflection of *g·*.
reveals
Mis. 1–19 *G·* reveals another scene
reward of
My. 19–24 reap richly the reward of *g·*.
ripening
My. 155–28 happy hearts and ripening *g·*.
their
Peo. 3–23 thought and action in their *g·*,
time and
My. 306–12 Time and *g·* determine greatness.
to grandeur
My. 163– 5 meekness to might, *g·* to grandeur,
transcendent
Mis. 199–20 his transcendent *g·* is manifest

———

Mis. 15–26 In mortal and material man, *g·* seems
78–28 any more than *g·*, to present
199–29 *g·* is more natural than evil.
250–21 *g·* without activity and power.
294–10 the might and majesty ! — of *g·*.
331–10 *g·* will have its springtide of
333– 5 omnipotence, omnipresence, *g·*,
No. 26–17 Man's real ego, or selfhood, is *g·*.
'00. 8– 5 The good man imparts . . . *g·* ;
My. 123–29 not overlook small things in *g·*
165–16 *g·* makes life a blessing.
165–17 *g·* identifies man with
167– 4 *g·* is "the fruit of the — *Gal.* 5 : 22.
210–13 *G·* involuntarily resists evil.
274– 6 but *g·*, holiness, and love do this,
295–15 and kindness . . . is *g·*.

good's

Mis. 14–24 evil, *g·* opposite, has no Principle,
46– 5 evil, *g·* opposite, is unreal.

goods

Mis. 159–18 Its *g·* commemorate,

Good Templars

Po. 40– 1 "*G· T·*" one and all.

Good-will

Mis. 153–26 * Peace on earth and *G·* !

Gordon, Rev. Dr. A. J.

No. 41–24 Rev. Dr. A. J. *G·*, a Boston Baptist

Gordon's, Dr.

No. 29–11 Dr. *G·* sermon on The Ministry of

gore

Mis. 246–10 purged of that sin by human *g·*,
My. 265– 9 cleanse the earth of human *g·* ;

gorgeous

Mis. 230–28 render it pathetic, tender, *g·*.
373–17 not in soft raiment or *g·* apparel ;
Pul. 48– 9 * in the *g·* October coloring
My. 29–13 * more *g·* church pageantries
193– 7 *g·* skies of the Orient

gorgeously

Mis. 324– 7 *g·* tapestried parlors,

gorging

Peo. 8–27 *g·* his faith with skill

Gospel

Mis. 292– 2 The divinity of St. John's *G·*
Ret. 22– 3 *G·* narratives bear brief testimony
Un. 4–23 John's *G·* declares (xvii. 3) that
My. 222– 1 *G·* according to St. Matthew,

gospel (*see also* **gospel's**)

appeal to the
My. 219–31 and then appeal to the *g·*
expound the
Ret. 36– 3 not expound the *g·* according to
is preached
Mis. 168–12 to the poor . . . the *g·* is preached.
171–20 to the poor the *g·* is preached.
Jesus'
My. 28–24 * Jesus' *g·* was for all time
law and
(*see* **law**)
law and the
(*see* **law**)
new
Mis. 178–22 * found C. S. a new *g·*,
of Christ
Mis. 18– 7 under the law and *g·* of Christ,
'02. 5–20 reiterated in the *g·* of Christ,
of glad tidings
Mis. 369– 4 the *g·* of glad tidings bring
of grace
'02. 2–28 round the *g·* of grace,
of healing
Mis. 67– 3 law and *g·* of healing.
67–18 *g·* of healing demonstrates the
208–21 interprets . . . the *g·* of healing.
Ret. 32– 1 It was the *g·* of healing,
Pul. 7– 7 how the *g·* of healing was
of health
Mis. 241–25 rejoices in the *g·* of health.
of Love
Mis. 135–17 so spreading the *g·* of Love,
of marriage
Mis. 286– 3 *g·* of marriage is not without
of peace
'02. 4–15 new commandment in the *g·* of peace,
of suffering
Ret. 30–20 through the *g·* of suffering,
Un. 57–17 This *g·* of suffering brought life
old
My. 90–19 * reincarnation of the old, old *g·*
or demonstration
Mis. 367– 1 without law, *g·*, or demonstration,
preaching the
Ret. 88–19 C. S. work, . . . preaching the *g·*.
No. 12–19 preaching the *g·* of Truth,
My. 128–21 preaching the *g·* and healing the sick.
preach the
Mis. 325–32 preach the *g·*,— *Mark* 16 : 15.
No. 41–21 preach the *g·* ;" — *Mark* 16 : 15.
My. 46–16 * preach the *g·* of and heal the sick
47–28 * preach the *g·* — *Mark* 16 : 15.
52–18 * heal the sick, and preach the *g·*,
147–16 preach the *g·* which heals
150–28 heal the sick and preach the *g·*,
300–25 preach the *g·* — *Mark* 16 : 15.
saving
My. 24– 9 * this healing and saving *g·*.
this
Un. 57–17 This *g·* of suffering brought life
My. 90–13 * door to this *g·* for many,

———

Mis. 66– 4 *g·* that fulfils the law in
151–11 in the *g·*, He saith of
177–17 establishing the truth, the *g·*,
300–16 thus evade the law, *but not the g·*.
318–17 *g·* work of teaching C. S.,

gospel
Ret.   47–21   student can enter upon the g· work of
     65–11   have no warrant in the g· or
     75–25   no permission in the g· for
Pul.   44–17   * chapter sub-title
'00.   4– 6   the g· of the New Testament
My.   19–31   Wheresoever this g· shall be
     147–11   g· with "signs following," — Mark 16 : 20.
     153– 6   g· ministry of my students
     179– 1   beginning of the g· writings.
     179–18   Old Testament and g· narratives
     227–23   and the g· injunction,

gospel-opposing
Mis.   301–11   law-breaking and g·

gospel's
Mis.   8–29   through the g· benediction.
Pan.   13–13   Love all . . . for the g· sake ;
My.   18–21   Love all . . . for the g· sake ;

Gospels
Mis.   193–11   the authenticity of the G·,
Ret.   65–22   as taught in the four G·.
     89–22   Nowhere in the four G· will
My.   132– 5   go to the G·, and there we hear :

gossip
Mis.   227–12   stuff into the hands of g· !
Man.   81–23   No idle g·, no slander,
'01.   16– 9   supply sacrilegious g· with the

gossiping
Mis.   230– 9   g· mischief, making lingering calls,

got
Mis.   239–10   * chapter sub-title
     239–20   * "I've g· cold, doctor."
     240– 1   "I have not g· cold."
     375–13   * g· quite an idea of what constitutes

gotten
Mis.   63– 5   at first g· up to hinder his
     239–28   must be g· rid of,

Gough, John B.
Mis.   71– 3   John B. G· is said to have

govern
Mis.   10– 5   motives that g· mortal mind
     51–12   g· a child metaphysically?
     51–16   Motives g· acts,
     58–24   If God does not g·
     58–25   if He does g· it,
     59–21   should and does g· man.
     198–20   has no power to g· itself ;
     354–21   to g· His own creation,
Man.   41–25   all mankind, and g· them !
Rud.   10– 9   which g· mortals wrongfully.
Hea.   12– 7   goes to the fount to g·
     15– 9   it enables mind to g· matter,
Peo.   11–18   the laws that g· their bodies,
My.   149–11   that . . . create and g· it ;
     231–18   wisdom must g· charity,
     363–14   that sanity and Science g·

governed
Mis.   34– 6   The body is g· by mind ;
     40–15   All true healing is g· by,
     104– 5   Formed and g· by God,
     146–17   be g· therein by the spirit
     198– 1   wholly g· by the one perfect Mind,
     198–16   recognize man as g· by God,
     206–17   Growth is g· by intelligence ;
     256– 4   The body is g· by Mind,
     257–22   Electricity, g· by this so-called
     259–19   he is g· in the same rhythm
     267–23   g· by Spirit, intelligent good.
     291– 2   they are not g· by the Principle
     291– 3   a mind g· by Principle
     303– 7   unmolested, be g· by divine Love
     353–21   regulator is g· by the principle that
     353–22   and because it is thus g·,
     364–19   is good, . . . is g· by it ;
Ret.   33– 3   g· the action of material medicine.
     78– 7   for it is g· by its Principle,
Pul.   4– 8   g· and protected by his divine
No.   10–28   g· by the immutable and
Pan.   11–10   G· by the divine Principle
Hea.   14–28   a body g· by this mind.
     19– 5   is g· directly and entirely by mind,
My.   247– 4   by the common consent of the g·,
     247– 5   man g· by his creator
     254–25   by the common consent of the g·,
     254–26   man g· by his creator
     265–29   wealth should be g· by honesty,
     303–15   If the individual g· human
     342–25   * "How will it be g·

governing
Mis.   37– 2   g· man or the universe.
     58–28   one human mind g· another ;
     229–14   g· the receptivity of the body,

governing
Mis.   258–14   g· Himself, He governs the universe.
     332– 3   Wisely g·, informing the universe,
     364–16   constituting and g· all identity,
Man.   51–18   By-Law g· the case
Pan.   7–27   hypothesis of . . . matter g· Mind,
'01.   32–30   Love was the g· impulse
My.   287– 9   g· all that really is.
     287–13   g· governments, industries,
     299–21   understand it and the law g· it,

Government
Mis.   80–21   can thrive but feebly under our G·.

government
benign
My.   128– 8   less than God's benign g·,
church
Mis.   284–30   intrusted with the rules of church g·,
Man.   72–18   consolidate under one church g·.
Pul.   20–11   system of ministry and church g·.
My.   vi–13   * devised its church g·,
city
My.   175–19   this favor of our city g· ;
civil arm of
No.   44–22   through the civil arm of g·,
constitutes
Man.   28– 4   Law constitutes g·,
divine
Mis.   56–16   opposed to the divine g·.
form of
Mis.   382–18   originated its form of g·,
Man.   70–15   its own form of g·.
     71–18   The Mother Church's form of g·,
     72–22   shall continue its present form of g·
God's
Mis.   199– 7   spiritual law, — God's g·.
My.   222–26   as God's g· becomes apparent,
     278– 1   To coincide with God's g·
     283–28   enlightened sense of God's g·.
her
Pan.   14–13   continue to characterize her g·,
highest places in
No.   45–17   and the highest places in g·,
His
Mis.   59–16   under His g·,
Rud.   10– 6   His g· is harmonious ;
Hea.   8– 2   and obedience to His g·,
its
Man.   74– 7   democratic in its g·,
My.   247– 3   its g· is administered by
     254–24   its g· is administered by
     342–26   * all now concerned in its g·
     342–28   Its g· will develop as it progresses."
liberal
My.   361–22   * truly democratic and liberal g·.
nature and
'00.   5– 2   nature, and g· of all things
of a nation
My.   282– 1   g· of a nation is its peace maker or
of divine Love
My.   189–15   the g· of divine Love derives its
     278– 7   g· of divine Love is supreme.
of God
Hea.   18– 2   shall yield to the g· of God,
Peo.   12– 7   merciful and just g· of God.
of man
Ret.   90–30   leave with God the g· of man.
one
Mis.   59– 1   one g· and God.
our
'02.   3–14   It is well that our g·,
right
My.   292– 5   Through divine Love the right g· is
righteous
My.   276–24   help support a righteous g· ;
system of
Man.   28– 7   system of g· and form of
this
Hea.   8– 7   and carrying out this g·
wisdom and
Un.   51–19   of God's wisdom and g·.

Mis.   161– 6   g· shall be upon his — Isa. 9 : 6.
     166–11   g· shall be upon his — Isa. 9 : 6.
     167–21   g· shall be upon his — Isa. 9 : 6.
My.   216– 9   regulated by a g· currency,

governmental
My.   220– 4   submit . . . to g· usages.

governments
My.   278–23   G· have no right to
     287–13   governing g·, industries,
     293–32   Human g· maintain the right

Governor
Po.   vi–18   To-day, by order of G· Andrew,
My.   308–20   father was visiting G· Pierce,

Governor

My.	308–21	Franklin Pierce's father, the *G·*
	308–23	My father thanked the *G·*,
	310–14	the *G·* of New Hampshire.
	312–25	The *G·* of the State and his
	331– 7	* and the *G·* of the State,
	340–22	the *G·* of New Hampshire

governor

Un.	26– 5	my author, authority, *g·*,

governs

Mis.	6–18	Mind *g·* all.
	41–27	Principle which *g·* the universe,
	51–16	and Mind *g·* man.
	204–29	*g·* the aims, ambition, and acts
	208– 7	*g·* millions of mortals
	208–10	enters . . . the human heart and *g·* it.
	258–15	He *g·* the universe.
	258–17	infinite Mind *g·* all things.
	287–19	higher nature of man *g·* the lower.
	369– 9	peering into the cause which *g·* all
	380– 5	*g·* the universe, time, space,
Man.	40– 8	divine Love alone *g·* man ;
Un.	10–18	because He is perfect, and *g·* them
	34– 4	declares . . . that non-intelligence *g·*.
Rud.	10– 5	know that God alone *g·*
No.	13–19	voices the infinite, and *g·* the
	35–19	and yet *g·* mankind.
Pan.	3–30	he *g·* the universe ;
Hea.	14–16	to know that mind *g·* the body
Peo.	8–18	Mind, that *g·* the universe,
	8–18	*g·* every action of the body
My.	165–10	and by it God *g·*.
	182–22	created and *g·* the universe
	226–13	*g·* all from the infinitesimal to

gown

'01.	16–23	under sanction of the *g·*,

grace

added
Pul.	81–11	* an added *g·* —a newer charm.

administer
My.	129–21	Then will angels administer *g·*,

all
Mis.	116– 3	God of all *g·* be with you,
	159– 7	God of all *g·* give you peace.
My.	148– 7	God of all *g·*, truth, and love
	156– 7	all *g·* abound toward you ;— *II Cor.* 9 : 8.

and glory
'02.	11– 7	warrant and welcome, *g·* and glory,
My.	339–16	*g·*, and glory of liberty.

and growth
My.	116–22	Every loss in *g·* and growth

and love
My.	187–16	May the *g·* and love of God

and peace
Mis.	9– 1	consciousness of good, *g·*, and peace,

and Truth
Mis.	164–26	full of *g·* and Truth,

and truth
Mis.	292–25	C. S., full of *g·* and truth,

beauty and the
My.	31–17	* for the beauty and the *g·* of

divine
Mis.	360–17	dews of divine *g·*,

fatherly
My.	288–32	evil is not a fatherly *g·*.

foes to
Mis.	118–22	envy, revenge, are foes to *g·*,

from God
Mis.	129– 7	through *g·* from God,

giving
My.	182–23	giving *g·*, health, and immortality

good
My.	195–13	must resign with good *g·* what we

goodness and
Mis.	165–22	His goodness and *g·* purchased

gospel of
'02.	2–28	round the gospel of *g·*,

grace for
Mis.	322–20	that giveth grace for *g·*,

grow in
Un.	14–12	commanded to *grow in g·*.
	14–13	necessary . . . to grow in *g·*,

His
Mis.	154–11	means and measure of His *g·*.
'01.	10–20	"the riches of His *g·*"— *Eph.* 1 : 7.

his
My.	257–19	We own his *g·*,

lightness and
My.	89– 8	* joined lightness and *g·* to

means of
Mis.	115–25	becomes a means of *g·*.
	127–25	Ofttimes the rod is His means of *g·* ;
'01.	19– 2	divinely appointed means of *g·*

grace

miracle of
Mis.	77–30	where the miracle of *g·* appears,
Peo.	4–21	No miracle of *g·* can make

more
Mis.	127–13	more *g·*, obedience, and love.
	354–15	more *g·*, a motive made pure,
'02.	4– 8	Let us all pray . . . for more *g·*,
My.	18– 9	more *g·*, obedience, and love.

nations'
Po.	10–17	Allied by nations' *g·*,
My.	337–18	Allied by nations' *g·*,

of God
Un.	7– 3	impartial *g·* of God,
Pan.	10–23	accomplished by the *g·* of God,

of the Lord
My.	19– 9	"The *g·* of the Lord — *II Cor.* 13 : 14.

pardon and
Po.	32–19	pardon and *g·*, through His Son,

patience, and
My.	209– 7	fidelity, courage, patience, and *g·*.

playful
Po.	9– 4	to his mother's in playful *g·* ;

power of
No.	9–19	point steadfastly to the power of *g·*

spiritual
Un.	57–21	spiritual *g·* was sufficient for him.

startling
My.	9–21	pledged yourselves with startling *g·*

supernal
Ret.	85–16	order prescribed by supernal *g·*.

tender
My.	206– 5	tender *g·* of spiritual understanding,

Mis.	11– 3	it is *g·*, mercy, and justice.
Chr.	53–35	with *g·* towards you and me,
Pul.	87–24	God give you *g·*.
Rud.	15–18	thorough guardianship and *g·*.
'02.	7– 9	neither philosophy, nature, nor *g·*
My.	195–31	fill these spiritual temples with *g·*,
	289– 3	God's open secret is seen through *g·*,

graceful

Pul.	31–26	* singularly *g·* and winning
My.	67–29	* in the *g·* outlines.

gracefully

Ret.	4–14	waving *g·* in the sunlight,
Po.	46– 7	But *g·* it stands

graces

Mis.	149–22	all the rich *g·* of the Spirit.
My.	121–22	adds to these *g·*, and reflects the

gracious

My.	15–16	your *g·* reception of it
	17– 8	the Lord is *g·*.— *I Pet.* 2 : 3.
	283– 8	Your appointment . . . is most *g·*.
	342– 4	* entered with a *g·* smile,

graciously

Mis.	251– 9	welcomed you to Concord most *g·*,
Ret.	80– 3	eternal justice be *g·* gentle,
'01.	31–26	yielded up *g·* what He
My.	171–21	* Mrs. Eddy responded *g·*

graciousness

My.	39–24	* We remember her *g·* and dignity.

gradations

Un.	10–14	Their *g·* are spiritual

grades

Mis.	371–15	but mixing all *g·* of persons

gradual

Mis.	15–27	the *g·* fading out of the
	85–12	regeneration leading thereto is *g·*,
	138–24	at first is more *g·* ;
My.	344–15	must make *g·* approaches to

gradually

Mis.	278–29	I have been *g·* withdrawing
Un.	5– 5	work *g·* and gently up
No.	1– 3	this must be done *g·*,
'00.	7– 3	death-rate to have *g·* diminished.
My.	56– 5	* Attendance . . . *g·* increased,
	307–26	*g·* emerging from *materia medica*,

graduate

Mis.	178– 3	a *g·* of Bowdoin College
	358– 5	*g·* under divine honors,
Ret.	43–11	Ebenezer J. Foster-Eddy, a *g·* of
Un.	6–20	a *g·* of Wellesley College,

graduated

Ret.	6–15	My brother Albert was *g·*
Pul.	32–28	* Albert Baker, *g·* at Dartmouth

graduates

Mis.	143–19	the Normal class *g·*
Man.	73–14	*g·* of said university
	89–10	APPLICANTS AND *g·*.

graduation
   Pan. 10–13 after *g·*, the best students

Grafton S. S.
   My. 315–16 * *G· S. S.* Jan'y, 1902.

grain
   Ret.   4–14 broad fields of bending *g·*
   Un. 12– 4 to the waiting *g·* the curving sickle
   '01. 18– 1 "mother tincture" of one *g·*
   Hea. 13– 5 hundredth part of a *g·* of medicine
        13–10 We have attenuated a *g·* of aconite
   My. 222–10 faith as a *g·* of mustard — *Matt.* 17 : 20.

grammar
   Ret. 10–14 Learning was so illumined, that *g·*
   My. 311–31 * when she finished Smith's *g·*

grammatical
   My. 318–12 defend my *g·* construction,

grand
   Mis.   5–23 do not understand the *g·* reality
        19–31 sense of Life and its *g·* pursuits
        28–27 practical knowledge of this *g·* verity,
        31–15 it denies the *g·* verity of this Science,
        75– 8 fundamental fact and *g·* verity
        79– 5 *g·* verities of Science will sift the
        97– 5 the *g·* verities of being.
      106– 5 parody on Tennyson's *g·* verse,
      116–13 emphasizing its *g·* strains,
      118–25 warfare with one's self is *g·* ;
      124–26 *g·* act crowned and still crowns
      159–17 recollections and rare *g·* collections
      181– 5 Man's knowledge of this *g·* verity
      188– 5 *g·* chorus of harmonious being.
      192–22 *g·* verities of Christian healing
      197–31 placing his trust in this *g·* Truth,
      250–17 *g·* achievements as its results.
      264–27 teacher's mind must be pure, *g·*, true,
      265–31 must stop at the foot of the *g·* ascent,
      273–14 one *g·* family of Christ's followers.
      275–22 at the *g·* meeting in Chicago
      330– 7 join in nature's *g·* harmony,
      333–28 the *g·* realities of Mind,
      337–32 this *g·* verity in Science,
      356–11 give promise of *g·* careers.
      386– 1 "Intensely *g·* and glorious
      393–22 Lessons long and *g·*,
   Ret. 59– 1 C. S. reveals the *g·* verity,
   Un.   6–17 such a *g·* and all-absorbing **verity**
   Pul. vii–17 cradle of this *g·* verity
        9–11 nerved its *g·* fulfilment.
      87–19 to accept your *g·* church edifice.
   No.   5– 2 *g·* verity of Mind-healing.
      24–20 the *g·* verity of C. S. :
      27–15 *g·* and eternal verities of God **and**
      30–26 demonstrates this *g·* verity
   Pan. 11–28 *g·* realism that man is the true
   '00.   1–17 five *g·* divisions of the globe ;
   01. 14–29 apprehension of this *g·* verity.
      29–15 *g·* coworkers for mankind,
      31–28 taught by some *g·* old divines,
   '02.   6–10 demonstrate this *g·* verity,
   Hea. 5–19 obscure the one *g·* truth
      9–28 this *g·* truth of being.
   Peo. 6–21 *g·* realities of Life and Truth
   Po. 39–19 "Social," or *g·*, or great,
      49– 3 *g·* and glorious life's sphere,
      52– 6 Lessons long and *g·*,
   My. 22–10 * this *g·* and noble purpose,
      37–19 * Recognizing the *g·* truth
      43–29 * this *g·* achievement,
      59–19 * in this *g·* amphitheatre ;
      66–30 * never before has such a *g·* **church**
     122– 3 for the world a destiny more *g·*
     136–20 five *g·* divisions of our globe ;
     147– 6 *g·* old elm on North State Street
     165– 5 The *g·* must stoop to the menial.
     180–19 refuses to see this *g·* verity
     188–20 walls of your *g·* cathedral
     194– 8 *g·* man or woman,
     194–13 engraven on your *g·* edifice
     203–12 Be great not as a *g·* obelisk,
     251–27 convince yourselves of this *g·* **verity** :
     283–12 fruits of said *g·* Association,
     285–15 *g·* object embodied in the
     316–15 *g·* defence of our Cause
     321– 1 * your *g·* demonstration in
     351–14 truly Masonic, tender, *g·* in **you**

grandchildren
   Mis. 125–23 *Beloved Brethren, Children, and G· :*
   Pul. 21– 1 Scientists, their children and *g·*

grander
   Mis. 110– 9 What *g·* ambition is there
   Pul. 85–16 * a better and *g·* humanity,

grandest
   Mis. 319–25 opportunity for the *g·* achievement
   Ret. 93–21 this *g·* verity has not been
   Pul. 45–10 * *g·* and most helpful features
      45–25 * succeeded by the *g·* of ministers
      53–25 * Whittier, *g·* of mystic poets,

grandeur
   Mis. x– 1 spiritual glow and *g·* of
      86–22 human conception of beauty, *g·*, **and**
      86–24 divine beauty and the *g·* of Spirit.
      87–13 *g·*, and glory of the immortal Mind."
      99–28 *g·* of the word, the power of Truth,
     354– 6 *g·* of the loyal, self-forgetful,
   Ret. 35–15 glow and *g·* of evangelical religion.
      61–28 demonstrated in its godliness and *g·*,
   Pan. 12– 9 chapter sub-title
   '01. 18–21 the *g·* of our great master
   Peo. 1–12 impart *g·* to the intellectual
   Po. v–13 *Inspired by the g· of this*
   My. 25–24 faith in the *g·* and sublimity of
      29–17 * its *g·* sprang from the
      37– 4 * *g·* of humility and the incense **of**
      50–27 * those few saw the *g·* of its work
      59– 1 * *g·* and magnitude of your work
      67–26 * will in its simple *g·* surpass any
      78–29 * awed by the *g·* of the great room
     124– 8 health, harmony, growth, *g·*,
     163– 5 meekness to might, goodness to *g·*,
     248– 3 its *g·* almost surprises me.

Grandfather
   Ret. 2–26 A relative of my *G·* Baker
      5– 3 *G·* Ambrose was a very

grandfather (*see also* **grandfather's**)
   Pul. 32–26 * Deacon Ambrose, her maternal *g·*

grandfather's
   Ret. 4– 4 he inherited my *g·* farm

Grand Lodge of Massachusetts
   My. 334–29 * Secretary of the *G· L· of M·* :

grandly
   Mis. 392–17 *g·* rising to the heavens above.
   Po. 20–21 *g·* rising to the heavens above.
   My. 63–24 * *G·* does our temple symbolize

Grandmother
   Ret. 2–17 one of my *G·* Baker's books,
      2–30 the line of my *G·* Baker's family

grandmother (*see also* **grandmother's**)
   Mis. 231– 4 The sober-suited *g·*,
   Ret. 1–10 which my *g·* said were **written**
      1–18 so became my paternal *g·*,
      3– 9 A cousin of my *g·* was
      4– 1 *g·* had thirteen children,
      8–15 same room with *g·*,
   Pul. 32–25 * a relative of her *g·*.

grandmother's
   Ret. 2–21 Among *g·* treasures were
      2–28 *g·* stories about General Knox,
      9– 1 returned with me to *g·* room,

grandpa
   Mis. 231–20 *g·* was taken napping.

grandparents
   Ret. 3– 4 *g·* were likewise connected **with**
   Pul. 46–18 * as belonging to her *g·*

Grand Rapids, Mich.
   Pul. 89–31 * *Herald, G· R·, M·*.
   My. 271–11 * *The Evening Press, G· R·, M·*,

Grand Secretary
   My. 333– 1 * with the seal of the *G· S·*,
     334–29 * Charles W. Moore, *G· S·* of the

grandson
   Ret. 4– 8 owned by Uncle James Baker's *g·*,

granite
   Mis. 144– 1 *g·* for this church was taken from
   Pul. 24–22 * church is built of Concord *g·*
      24–23 * pink *g·* of New Hampshire,
      49–21 * return to her native *g·* hills,
      65–16 * beautiful structure of gray *g·*,
      86–1 * corner-stone . . . being of *g·*,
   My. 45–29 * massive pile of New Hampshire *g·*
     157–15 * of the same beautiful Concord *g·*
     158– 2 building a *g·* church edifice
     163–26 friendship, and *g·* character.
     341– 5 engraven on her *g·* rocks,

Granite State (*see also* **New Hampshire**)
   My. 184–16 characteristic of our *G· S·*,
     185–29 sons and daughters of the *G· S·*
     305–14 natives of the *G· S·*.

granitic
   Pul. 80–14 * over its *g·* pebbles.

grant

Mis.	xi–21	*vox populi* is inclined to *g·* us peace,
	272– 3	* *the right to g· degrees*
	272– 6	* Mrs. Eddy's *g·* for a college,
	272–20	* simply an incorporated *g·*,
	319–19	and *g·* me this request,
Pul.	20– 9	refused to *g·* it,
Peo.	8–20	God *g·* that the trembling chords of
My.	165–29	God *g·* that this church is rapidly
	176– 7	God *g·* that such great goodness,
	184–19	God *g·* that this little church
	195–29	God *g·* that this unity remain,
	198– 7	May God *g·* not only the
	256– 8	you must *g·* me my request

granted

Mis.	272– 8	* no charters were *g·* for similar
Ret.	20–23	*g·* me in the city of Salem,
	40– 7	It was *g·*,
	43– 6	No charter was *g·* for similar
	49–20	only one ever *g·* to a *legal college*
My.	314–15	*g·* on the ground of desertion,

granting

My.	173–31	foresight in *g·* permission,
	341–23	* *g·* of interviews is not usual,

grapes

Mis.	27–17	"Do men gather *g·* of — *Matt.* 7 : 16.
	72–14	have eaten sour *g·*, — *Ezek.* 18 : 2.
	336–18	we gather not *g·* of thorns,

graphic

Mis.	xi–11	*g·* guide-book, pointing the path,
	294–27	terse, *g·*, and poetic style

graphically

Ret.	2– 5	so *g·* set forth in the pages of
	32–10	*g·* defined by Calderon,

grapple

Mis.	121– 8	good and evil, seem to *g·*,
Pul.	13– 4	must *g·* with and overcome the
Rud.	15–20	*g·* with this subject,
'01.	23– 4	sects and faculties can *g·*.

grappled

Mis.	284–25	not . . . more real when it is *g·* with.

grapples

Mis.	62–23	the author *g·* with C. S.,

grasp

Mis.	9–18	but it slips from our *g·*,
	82–11	*g·* and gather — in all glory
	100–12	that *g·* neither the meaning nor
	100–17	inadequate to *g·* the word of Truth,
	140–22	rescued from the *g·* of legal power,
Man.	62–21	to *g·* the simpler meanings of
No.	11–24	to *g·* the Principle of C. S.,
	17–21	If mortals could *g·* these two words
	23– 5	Evil can neither *g·* the
My.	122–21	risen to *g·* the spiritual idea
	283–17	his *g·* of goodness grows stronger.

grasped

Mis.	346–21	*g·* in all its divine requirements.
Un.	43–25	"apprehended of [or *g·* — *Phil.* 3 : 12.
No.	21– 8	*g·* in spiritual law the universe,
Po.	26– 8	While Justice *g·* the sword
My.	90–17	* can be readily *g·* by sick or well.
	193–24	have *g·* time and labor,

grasping

Mis.	364–14	right hand *g·* the universe,
My.	189– 2	*g·* the sword of Spirit,
	248– 8	*g·* and defining the demonstrable,

grasps

No.	39–26	photography *g·* the solar light
Peo.	10–15	*g·* the standard of liberty,

grass

Mis.	329–15	weaving the wavy *g·*,
	330–30	*g·*, inhabiting the whole earth,
	331– 5	When downtrodden like the *g·*,
	390–15	The verdant *g·* it weaves ;
Pul.	39–26	* Under the meadow *g·*.
No.	26–26	so clothe the *g·* — *Matt.* 6 : 30.
Po.	53–10	The patient, timid *g·*,
	55–16	The verdant *g·* it weaves ;
	67–16	o'er the dark wavy *g·*.

grateful

Mis.	94– 4	never knew a person who . . . to be *g·* ;
	262–15	I am *g·* to you for
	262–22	more *g·* than words can express,
	273– 9	so *g·* a sense of my labors
	274–12	*g·* acknowledgments to the public
	339–24	and forgettest to be *g·* ?
Man.	75– 9	and she, with *g·* acknowledgments
'00.	1– 9	I am *g·* to say that in the last year
Po.	vii–10	* *With g· acknowledgment,*
	77– 3	holiest hymn in *g·* praise !
My.	42– 1	* truly *g·* to her who has

grateful

My.	63– 5	* we are *g·*.
	125–23	deeply *g·* that the church
	134– 6	we cannot be too *g·* nor too
	199–11	accept my *g·* acknowledgment
	229–29	hence my *g·* joy.
	259– 9	* Loving, *g·* Christmas greetings
	295–12	I am in *g·* receipt of your
	319– 8	in loving, *g·* memory
	326–19	Deeply *g·*, I recognize the
	332– 4	* silent gush of *g·* tears
	332– 8	* tribute of *g·* hearts
	336– 9	* She makes *g·* acknowledgment

gratefully

Mis.	256– 7	While *g·* acknowledging the
	306– 6	* will be *g·* received ;
No.	19–14	*g·* and lovingly conscious of the
'02.	20–23	*g·* appreciating the privilege of
My.	20– 3	*G·* yours in Christ,
	63– 6	* Lovingly and *g·* your students,
	81–19	* spoke simply and *g·*,
	182–19	Humbly, *g·*, trustingly,
	194–23	*g·* accept the spirit of it ;
	207– 3	Your communication is *g·* received.
	362–26	* *G·* yours,

gratification

Mis.	9–27	educated to *g·* in personal
Ret.	65–10	*g·* of appetite and passion,
My.	11–17	* she expressed much *g·*
	76–12	* only feebly expresses the *g·*.

gratified

My.	117– 5	A personal motive *g·* by
	324–22	* was *g·* and pleased in

gratifying

My.	25–11	* and are most *g·* :
	93–12	* *g·* the passions or
	326– 4	* is most *g·* to our people ;
	326– 7	* It is especially *g·* to them
	355– 1	* it was *g·* to them,

gratitude

aglow with

'00.	1– 3	glad faces, aglow with *g·*,

and affection

Mis.	203– 5	mine through *g·* and affection.

and love

(see **love**)

and praise

My.	323–20	* thoughts of *g·* and praise

debt of

Mis.	xi– 9	debt of *g·* to God,
My.	352– 8	* our debt of *g·* to you

debts of

My.	81–18	* debts of *g·* for ills cured,

deep

My.	157– 5	* deep *g·* that your generous gift

everlasting

Ret.	49–22	* everlasting *g·* is due to the

feeling of

My.	331–22	* express the feeling of *g·*

filled with

My.	42–16	* With a heart filled with *g·*
	362–19	* hearts filled with *g·* to God,

forever

My.	176– 6	paved the way to my forever *g·*,

gleam of

Mis.	1–11	kindle all minds with a gleam of *g·*,

glows with

Po.	31– 9	Glad Easter glows with *g·*

great

My.	198– 6	great *g·* to our one Father.

grief and

Pul.	1– 7	redolent with grief and *g·*.

incense of

My.	37– 5	* incense of *g·* and compassionate love

instinctive

My.	9– 7	* instinctive *g·* which not only

joy and

My.	45– 6	* witnessing with joy and *g·*

justice and

Mis.	291–28	station justice and *g·* as sentinels

love and

Man.	75– 9	this Church's love and *g·*,
Pul.	86–22	* testimonial of love and *g·*
My.	58–17	* love and *g·* of a great multitude
	325–16	* With increasing love and *g·*,

loving

My.	323–12	* In loving *g·* for your

my

My.	26–11	You can imagine my *g·*
	120– 7	Accept my *g·* for the chance
	156– 2	You will accept my *g·* for

offering of

Pul.	26–15	* a votive offering of *g·*

gratitude
our
  My. 9–11   * to utter our *g·* to you
        36–18   * pour out our *g·* to God
real
  My. 352–10   * we know that the real *g·* **is**
sense of
  Mis. 131–23   that loving sense of *g·*
tears of
  My. 314–27   with tears of *g·*
tenderest
  My. 37– 8   * from the depths of tenderest *g·*,
thanks and
  My. 51–30   * heartfelt thanks and *g·*
to God
  Mis. xi– 9   one's debt of *g·* to God,
  My. 36–18   * pour out our *g·* to God
       362–19   * hearts filled with *g·* to God,

  Pul. 85– 6   * *g·* to her for her great work,
  My. 30–18   * in *g·* for the epoch-making event.
      164–11   What is *g·* but a powerful

gratuitous
  Mis. 349–27   or to receive my *g·* services,
  Rud. 14–12   in order to do *g·* work.

gratuitously
  Mis. 11– 8   taught indigent students *g·*,
     247–15   unwilling to be taught it, even *g·*.
  My. 122– 1   advice that one *g·* bestows
     204–20   I practised *g·* when starting

grave
  Mis. 12– 5   throughout time and beyond the *g·*.
     74–25   His triumph over the *g·*
     96– 3   robbed the *g·* of victory
     104– 5   to death, or the *g·*.
     146–15   These are matters of *g·* import ;
     163– 6   a *g·* to mortal sense dishonored
     234–22   is matter of *g·* wonderment
     291– 5   but the notion . . . is a *g·* mistake ;
     330– 4   to moan over the new-made *g·*,
     339–29   Change and the *g·* may part us ;
     388–14   *G·* on her monumental pile :
     392–12   A lesson *g·*, of life,
     400– 6   *G·*, silent, steadfast stone,
  Un. 30–20   victorious over death and the *g·*.
     48–11   robs the *g·* of its victory.
  Peo. 5–14   overcome death and the *g·*,
  Po. 15–21   love that outliveth the *g·*,
     20–16   A lesson *g·*, of life,
     21– 1   *G·* on her monumental pile :
     73–15   Pleasant a *g·* By the "Rock"
     76–17   *G·*, silent, steadfast stone,
  My. 5–18   rob the *g·* of its victory.
     125– 4   annual meeting is a *g·* guardian.
     191–23   and the *g·* its victory.
     218–15   absolved from death and the *g·*.
     315–28   from the *cradle* and the *g·*,
     355– 6   *g·* need for more men in C. S.

grave-clothes
  Mis. 370– 8   risen from the *g·* of tradition
  My. 191–17   With *g·* laid aside,

graven
  Mis. 28–23   does not signify a *g·* idol,
     218–25   and matter's *g·* grins
     335– 2   shall you turn . . . to *g·* images?
     346–15   an image *g·* on wood or stone

graves
  Mis. 170– 5   weep over the *g·* of their beloved ;
  Po. 16–20   'Mid *g·* do I hear the glad voices
  My. 36–14   * or withheld from open *g·*

graveyards
  Pul. 30– 7   * but from the *g·* !
     66– 9   * proceeds more from the *g·*

gravitate
  Mis. 267–22   must *g·* from sense to Soul,
  Ret. 76–10   *g·* naturally toward Truth.

gravitating
  My. 154–29   not looking nor *g·* earthward,

gravitation
  Mis. 23– 1   Newton named it *g·*,
     23– 3   what is the power back of *g·*,
     256–22   to speak of *g·* as a law of matter ;
  Un. 35–13   *Force.* What is *g·*?
     35–13   Mortal mind says *g·* is a

gravitations
  Mis. 19–26   of material and spiritual *g·*,

gray
  Mis. 340–14   forsook Blackstone for *g·* stone,
     376–23   softened, grew *g·*, then gay,
  Pul. 24–22   * Concord granite in light *g·*,
     39–11   * angels, on the *g·* church tower,
     65–16   * beautiful structure of *g·* granite,

gray
  Peo. 14– 6   *g·* stones of church-yards
  Po. 53– 2   paint the *g·*, stark trees,
  My. 68–19   * auditorium is of a warm *g·*,
     78– 5   * imposing structure of *g·* stone
     78–11   * an interior done in soft *g·*
     85–30   * its noble dome of pure *g·* tint,

grayest
  My. 87–23   * sunshine on the *g·* day.

gray-haired
  My. 310–23   * her father, a *g·* man of fifty,

grayish
  My. 342–13   * whether blue-gray or *g·* brown,

great
  Mis. 2– 8   causing *g·* obscuration of Spirit.
     4–25   "It must require a *g·* deal of faith
     6–26   *g·* caution is observed in regard to
     7– 7   *G·* charity and humility is necessary
     7–32   enlightened on this *g·* subject.
     9–29   *g·* and only danger
     14–32   he makes a *g·* reality of evil,
     15– 7   *g·* Nazarene Prophet said,
     24– 5   came to me in an hour of *g·* need ;
     30–16   *g·* Way-shower illustrated Life
     38–11   is it a *g·* thing if we— *I Cor.* 9 : 11.
     43–19   qualify students for the *g·* ordeal
     47–22   This *g·* Truth does not destroy
     51– 5   *accompanied by g· mental depression,*
     53–25   their *g·* lack of spirituality.
     54–26   *as g· miracles in healing as Jesus*
     63–17   the *g·* reality that concerns man,
     65–16   Life and its *g·* realities.
     77– 6   *g·* truths asserted by the Messiah :
     77–15   This is the Father's *g·* love
     79–17   If the *g·* cause is perfect,
     107–11   More love is the *g·* need of
     110–28   fleeting is that which men call *g·* ;
     120–12   achieved *g·* guerdons in the
     120–14   a *g·* freedom for the race ;
     120–28   Biblical record of the *g·* Nazarene,
     124–13   "who is so *g·* a God— *Psal.* 77 : 13.
     124–25   Love's *g·* legacy to mortals :
     127–18   *g·* growth in C. S. will follow,
     131–19   *g·* struggles with perplexities
     132–16   the *g·* demand upon my time,
     133–28   affords me *g·* joy to be able to
     143–18   It gives me *g·* pleasure to say
     144–17   shadow of a *g·* rock— *Isa.* 32 : 2.
     150– 3   already you have the *g·* Shepherd
     151–14   our Minister and the *g·* Physician :
     153–12   *g·* was the company of— *Psal.* 68 : 11.
     156–14   no advantage, but *g·* disadvantage,
     157– 2   *g·* thing to be found worthy to
     173–12   Mind is its own *g·* cause and effect.
     176– 6   *g·* theme so deeply and solemnly
     176– 8   chiefly in the *g·* crises of nations
     176–26   *g·* opportunities and responsibilities
     177– 4   *g·* battle of Armageddon is upon us.
     182–24   their place in God's *g·* love,
     183– 3   In the *g·* forever,
     187– 4   The *g·* Metaphysician wrought,
     191–24   original devil was a *g·* talker,
     192–17   his words reveal the *g·* Principle
     201–13   *g·* somethingness of the good
     204–20   *g·* demands of spiritual sense
     205–29   man born of the *g·* Forever,
     222– 7   causes the victim *g·* physical
     224–19   everything beautiful, *g·*, and good,
     228– 9   To be a *g·* man or woman,
     230– 4   A *g·* amount of time is consumed
     238– 8   no sacrifice is too *g·* for the
     241– 9   the *g·* alterative, Truth :
     252–25   rules and practice of the *g·* healer
     253– 3   bought with a price, a *g·* price ;
     253–17   *g·* red dragon that stood ready to
     254–18   Envy, the *g·* red dragon of this hour,
     258– 4   Our *g·* Ensample, Jesus of Nazareth,
     263– 9   shadow of a *g·* rock— *Isa.* 32 : 2.
     269–30   heard the *g·* Red Dragon *whispering*
     275–13   May the *g·* Shepherd that
     278– 8   *g·* joy in this consciousness,
     280–28   *g·* import to the student of C. S.,
     287–31   *G·* mischief comes from attempts **to**
     292–26   *g·* good, both seen and unseen ;
     295–18   statements of the *g·* unknown
     304–13   * any *g·* patriotic celebration
     304–24   * days on which *g·* events have
     312–10   chapter sub-title
     317– 9   *g·* pleasure in instructing,
     321–26   the *g·* wonder of the world,
     322–14   *g·* Shepherd that feedeth my flock,
     338– 3   brings to humanity some *g·* good,
     338–31   * A *g·* and noble creed."
     340–26   lives of *g·* men and women

great

Mis.	357– 7	have lost their *g·* Shepherd
	357–28	true fold and the *g·* Shepherd,
	358–10	his shield and *g·* reward.
	360– 6	*G·* only as good,
	361–17	To this *g·* end, Paul admonished,
	363– 2	*g·* reality of divine Mind and
	371– 6	care of the *g·* Shepherd,
	373–15	One *g·* master clearly delineates
	374– 1	so *g·* a proof of Immanuel
	374–18	To him who brought a *g·* light
	375–12	* old masters and their *g·* works
	379–24	solution of this *g·* question :
Man.	41– 6	*g·* gulf between C. S. and theosophy,
Chr.	53–46	The *g·* I Am,
	55– 8	have seen a *g·* light : — *Isa.* 9 : 2.
Ret.	25– 1	the *g·* curative Principle, — Deity.
	25–29	our *g·* Master's purpose in not
	26– 8	*g·* Way-shower, steadfast to the end
	27– 8	Mind-healing, like all *g·* truths,
	31–12	the one *g·* and ever-present relief
	44–27	a *g·* revival of mutual love,
	49– 8	*g·* need is for more of the spirit
	49–23	for her *g·* and noble work,
	60–15	and there is a *g·* calm.
	68– 8	The *g·* difference between these
	71– 7	*G·* temptations beset an ignorant
	81–22	how *g·* is that darkness !'' — *Matt.* 6 : 23.
	91–13	Where did Jesus deliver this *g·* lesson
	91–14	this series of *g·* lessons
Un.	5–10	personal opinion on so *g·* a matter,
	5–14	''*G·* is the mystery of — *I Tim.* 3 : 16.
	19–15	how *g·* is that darkness !'' — *Matt.* 6 : 23.
Pul.	1–13	*g·* is the value thereof.
	6–18	* turned to the '*g·* Physician.'
	12–14	having *g·* wrath, — *Rev.* 12 : 12.
	12–20	nearer to the *g·* heart of Christ ;
	14–27	*g·* benefit which Mind has wrought.
	14–28	the *g·* delusion of mortal mind,
	20–19	shadow of a *g·* rock — *Isa.* 32 : 2.
	23– 9	* The ''*g·* awakening'' of the time
	26–12	* The *g·* organ comes from Detroit.
	26–26	* Before the *g·* bay window
	27–20	* Another *g·* window tells its
	31–27	* with *g·* claim to personal beauty.
	37– 2	* the *g·* daily that is so fair
	37– 8	* retains in a *g·* degree her energy
	39– 2	* essentials of love to God and
	41–23	* the chimes in the *g·* stone tower,
	46–14	* identified with good and *g·* names
	47– 7	* *g·* circulation with the members of
	51– 4	* a *g·* privilege in these days.
	51–28	* alongside other *g·* demonstrations
	52–20	* The Master was the *g·* healer.
	56–25	* A *g·* C. S. church was dedicated
	62– 7	* *g·* economy of space,
	62–17	* beauties of a *g·* cathedral chime,
	63–19	* *g·* hold she has upon this army
	64–16	* search for the *g·* curative Principle.
	67– 6	* said by a *g·* American writer.
	70–20	* to find the *g·* curative Principle
	72– 1	* inspired in her *g·* task
	72–28	* one *g·* essential that we have faith
	75–22	* in the *g·* New England capital
	81–18	* soars and sings to the *g·* sun.
	82– 2	* brain for its *g·* white throne.
	83–27	* a *g·* wonder in heaven, — *Rev.* 12 : 1.
Rud.	8– 1	confounding the three *g·* kingdoms.
No.	9– 2	have prevented, to a *g·* extent,
	9–15	too *g·* leniency, on my part.
	25– 1	uttering this *g·* thought is not enough !
	25– 3	won through *g·* tribulation
	32–18	Good is *g·* and real.
	32–23	*g·* evil to belie and belittle C. S.,
Pan.	3–15	* envy of the *g·* !
	10– 4	*g·* Nazarene Prophet said,
	14–27	*G·* occasion have we to rejoice
'00.	7–14	This is my *g·* reward for
	9–28	fit others for this *g·* responsibility.
	12–30	phase of a *g·* controversy,
'01.	1–13	*g·* realities of being,
	17–14	and started the *g·* Cause
	18–22	*g·* master Metaphysician's precept
	19–16	*g·* Metaphysician healed the sick,
	24–15	and *g·* was the fall
	25–17	*g·* Metaphysician, Christ Jesus,
	26– 3	The *g·* teacher, preacher, and
	27–14	* ''Every *g·* scientific truth goes
	28– 2	the *g·* naturalist's prophecy.
	30–25	*g·* heart of the unselfed Christian
'02.	5–17	have answered this *g·* question
	11–25	for *g·* is your reward — *Matt.* 5 : 12
	14– 9	* ''*G·* not like Cæsar, stained
	14–10	* But only *g·* as I am good.''
	14–18	beginning of the *g·* battle
	14–24	nor protection in the *g·* struggle.

great

'02.	14–25	prospered preeminently our *g·* Cause,
	15–14	entering upon my *g·* life-work,
	18–22	prophecy of the *g·* Teacher
	20–21	*g·* joy to look into the faces of
Hea.	1–12	the *g·* subject of Christian healing ;
	3–20	*g·* goodness and wonderful works
	11–12	the *g·* pyramid of Egypt,
	14– 9	*G·* caution should be exercised
Peo.	1– 3	*g·* element of reform is not
	6–26	something of that *g·* good
	13– 6	this *g·* impersonal Life, Truth, and
Po.	2–11	*G·* as thou art,
	22–14	how *g·*, how good Thou art
	26–11	Lincoln's own *G·* willing heart
	39–19	''Social,'' or grand, or *g·*,
	43–10	Father, in Thy *g·* heart hold them
My.	6–11	''for *g·* is [our] reward — *see Matt.* 5 : 12.
	18–15	*g·* growth in C. S. will follow,
	25– 2	* there would be *g·* propriety in
	25– 7	* *g·* interest exhibited by the children
	29–20	* dome of the *g·* edifice
	31–11	* first glimpse of the *g·* structure,
	31–31	* the *g·* body of Scientists
	41– 1	* how *g·* no man can number
	42–20	* It affords me *g·* pleasure to
	42–25	* how *g·* is the work that has
	45–13	* The *g·* temple is finished !
	45–28	* The *g·* temple is finished !
	46– 3	* the *g·* structure stands,
	47–10	* has grown to *g·* magnitude,
	47–17	* inception of this *g·* Cause,
	49– 7	* *g·* chance of sweeping the world
	50–18	* trust in the *g·* Father,
	54–21	* desire for services was so *g·*
	57– 5	* of *g·* seating capacity,
	58–17	* gratitude of a *g·* multitude
	60–25	* Now that the *g·* event,
	61–26	* stood under the *g·* dome,
	68– 4	* The *g·* auditorium, with its
	68– 5	* tops of *g·* stone piers,
	68–21	* *g·* organ is placed back of the
	68–26	* plaster work for the *g·* arches
	71–11	* *g·* adornment to the city.
	71–27	* in front of the *g·* organ.
	73–12	* chapter sub-title
	75–13	* of a *g·* number of visitors
	76–26	* first *g·* monument to C. S.,
	77– 1	* because of its *g·* size,
	77– 8	* its dimensions are only half as *g·*.
	78–29	* awed by the grandeur of the *g·* room
	80–25	* to accommodate the *g·* throngs
	81– 3	* prosperity of the *g·* congregation.
	81–23	* song rose tingling to the *g·* dome,
	83– 3	* the holding of a *g·* convention
	84–17	* near to another *g·* demonstration
	85–22	* the *g·* centre of attraction,
	86–15	* building fund of the *g·* temple
	86–28	* *g·* size of the auditorium
	87–13	* a *g·* gathering of people
	88– 4	* opening of their *g·* new temple.
	88–23	* debt to that *g·* and growing cult,
	88–29	* in the building of a *g·* church
	90– 2	* hundreds of *g·* buildings
	90–27	* Founder of a *g·* denomination
	93– 5	* dedication of their *g·* church
	93–28	* by the *g·* meeting of the church
	95–15	* During the *g·* assembly of
	95–19	* faith of these people is certainly *g·*.
	99– 2	* *g·*, and really good things
	99– 7	* with so *g·* an aggregation of
	104– 7	*g·* master of metaphysics,
	106–30	Our *g·* Exemplar, the Nazarene
	113–32	truly *g·* men and women
	123– 5	The *g·* guerdon of divine Love,
	129– 3	I reluctantly foresee *g·* danger
	131–12	signet of the *g·* heart,
	131–30	this *g·*, *g·* blessing ;
	133– 3	in the *g·* light of the present,
	138– 5	a *g·* benefit to me already.
	146–15	heights of the *g·* Nazarene's sayings
	153–16	*g·* and first commandment,
	164–18	A *g·* sanity, a mighty something
	166– 2	efforts to be *g·* will never end in
	176– 8	God grant that such *g·* goodness,
	177–19	the *g·* Shepherd has nurtured
	180–28	in the spirit of our *g·* Exemplar
	183– 5	in this *g·* city of Chicago,
	186–27	gives me *g·* pleasure to know
	190–15	asked their *g·* Teacher,
	194– 2	broad facts over *g·* continents
	197–13	*g·* hearts and ready hands of our
	198– 6	*g·* gratitude to our one Father.
	203–12	Be *g·* not as a grand obelisk,
	203–13	nor by setting up to be *g·*,
	204–21	when starting this *g·* Cause,

great

My.	217–28	Thus it is that our *g·* Exemplar,
	219–19	Bible record of our *g·* Master's life
	219–23	the *g·* demonstrator of C. S.,
	220–25	example of the *g·* Galilean Prophet,
	221–12	so *g·* and good as Christ Jesus.
	222–17	his *g·* demands on the faith of
	234–18	both sides of the *g·* question
	234–21	all our *g·* Master's sayings
	236–28	*g·* importance at this stage
	244–12	the *g·* need of which I daily discern.
	248– 5	* "*G·*, not like Caesar, stained
	248– 6	* But only *g·* as I am good."
	248– 7	You are not setting up to be *g·* ;
	262–20	the reminder of God's *g·* gift,
	267–10	infinite, the *g·* for ever,
	267–28	Our *g·* Teacher hath said :
	272–25	* plays so *g·* a part in the world
	272–27	* and leads . . . her very *g·* following.
	273– 9	* a very *g·* organization
	279–25	God bless that *g·* nation
	284– 1	never fastens on the good or the *g·*.
	285– 9	crowns the *g·* purposes of life
	288–12	The *g·* Galilean Prophet was,
	294–29	passed . . . into the *g·* forever.
	304–25	* "Every *g·* scientific truth
	306– 6	philosophy of a *g·* and good man,
	306–11	than to be thought *g·*.
	308–30	my father was a *g·* reader.
	309–16	slavery he regarded as a *g·* sin.
	317– 9	It is a *g·* mistake to say that I
	322–28	* my *g·* interest in the subject,
	338–26	*g·* Teacher of Christianity
	339– 8	discoursing on the *g·* subject
	347–17	our *g·* Master's first disciples,
	349–17	*g·* Way-shower, invested with glory,
	(see also **fact, Master, truth, work**)	

Great Britain (*see also* **Britain**)

Mis.	295–27	Philosophical Society of *G· B·*,
Man.	94–19	in Canada, in *G· B·* and Ireland.
	97– 9	Canada, *G· B·* and Ireland.
	99– 6	Each county of *G· B·* and Ireland,
	99–23	Committees on Publication for *G· B·*
Pul.	5–24	same in *G· B·*, France, Germany,
Po.	page 10	poem
My.	77–12	* from Canada, from *G· B·*,
	259– 6	From . . . in London, *G· B·*,
	289–15	Victoria, Queen of *G· B·*
	289–29	Victoria, Queen of *G· B·*
	337– 2	poem

greater

Mis.	7–25	*g·* work yet remains to be done.
	65– 9	concerning the *g·* subject of
	111–23	but no *g·* difference existed
	121–28	*g·* than human pity, is divine Love,
	145–11	Am I *g·* for them?
	192–11	*g· works than these— John* 14 : 12.
	251–13	but a *g·* even, the liberty of
	261–21	No *g·* type of divine Love can be
	293–18	brings *g·* torment than ignorance.
	366–23	To a *g·* or less extent, all mortal
	370– 7	*g·* spirit of Christ is also abroad,
Ret.	80–26	no *g·* miracles known to earth
	95– 2	blossom into *g·* freedom,
Un.	6– 1	and the whole is *g·* than its parts.
Pul.	67–10	* show a *g·* number of them
	75– 6	a *g·* degree of this spirit
No.	13–19	No *g·* opposites can be conceived of,
	22–17	than the corporeality we behold.
	33–15	*g·* than the brief agony of the cross ;
Pan.	8–20	"My Father is *g·* than I."— *John* 14 : 28.
'00.	4–12	indicate a renaissance *g·* than
	7– 6	*g·* love of the Scriptures
'01.	2– 4	*g·* power in the perfected Science
	8– 8	"my Father is *g·* than I,"— *John* 14 : 28.
Peo.	9–20	showing our *g·* faith in matter,
My.	21–18	* will receive a *g·* blessing
	52–10	* each and all, will make *g·* efforts
	87– 1	* the attendance was *g·* than
	123– 3	love is the *g·* marvel,
	164–25	into the *g·* and better,
	209– 5	No *g·* hope have we than
	228–13	none *g·* had been born of women
	228–15	is *g·* than he."— *Matt.* 11 : 11.
	253– 5	what *g·* glory can nerve your
	258–18	gifts *g·* than those of Magian kings,
	325–10	* as having a *g·* future
	344– 5	God the Father is *g·* than Christ,

Greater New York (*see also* **New York**)

My.	362–14	* C. S. churches . . . of *G· N· Y·*,
	363–15	C. S. churches in *G· N· Y·*

greatest

Mis.	5–14	not fail in the *g·* emergencies.
	111– 1	proven that the *g·* piety

greatest

Mis.	130–24	*g·* sin that one can commit
	177– 3	*g·* and holiest of all causes.
	268– 4	Who shall be *g·*?
	288–4, 5	the *g·* good to the *g·* number,
	303–12	"who shall be *g·*." — *see Mark* 9 : 34.
	337–14	*g·* in the kingdom of — *Matt.* 18 : 4.
	357–20	*g·* of all stages and states of
	358–25	the *g·* work of the ages,
	363– 7	its *g·* flatterer, identification,
Ret.	75– 3	Who shall be *g·*?
	82–15	the *g·* good to the *g·* number,
	91– 4	and our Master's *g·* utterance
Pul.	20–17	the *g·* moral, physical, civil,
	54–17	* *g·* good could be accomplished."
	73–11	* one of the *g·* Biblical scholars
'00.	10– 5	new birth of the *g·* and best.
'01.	16–25	its *g·* discoverer is a woman
	24–11	* *g·* of all temporal blessings,
	26–20	the *g·* of which is charity
'02.	4– 3	"Who shall be *g·*?" — *see Mark* 9 : 34.
Hea.	9– 8	The *g·* sinner and the most
My.	12–18	lost opportunity is the *g·* of losses.
	45– 7	* *g·* and most important
	89–29	* *g·* religious phenomenon
	159–12	*g·* man or woman on earth
	228–12	Who shall be *g·*?
	228–17	he that hath . . . shall be *g·*.
	240– 2	from the least to the *g·*,
	305–29	"Who shall be *g·*?" — *see Mark* 9 : 34.
	306–12	The *g·* reform, . . . must wait to
	348– 8	*g·* of all questions was solved

great-grandfather

Ret.	1– 2	my *g·*, on my father's side,

great-grandmother

Ret.	1– 4	my *g·*, was Marion Moor,
	1–11	were written by my *g·*.
	1–11	because my *g·* wrote a

greatly

Mis.	35–25	it is *g·* to your advantage
	57–15	*g·* multiply thy sorrow." — *Gen.* 3 : 16.
	127– 7	One thing I have *g·* desired,
	137–14	I *g·* rejoice over the growth of
	139–27	in future be regarded as *g·* wise,
	308– 7	*g·* errs, stops his own progress, and
	327–14	which must *g·* hinder their ascent.
	358– 1	Love is *g·* needed, and must be had
Ret.	8–17	*G·* surprised, my cousin turned
	13– 6	predestination, *g·* troubled me ;
	50– 7	This amount *g·* troubled me.
Un.	53– 6	and *g·* to be desired,
Pul.	38– 7	* *g·* revised and enlarged,
	51–16	* and how *g·* it will affect the
	71–14	* startled and *g·* discomfited
Peo.	11–22	*g·* responsible for all the woes
My.	6–15	*G·* impressed and encouraged
	18– 4	"One thing I have *g·* desired,
	23–23	* We rejoice *g·* that the walls
	139–26	you have been *g·* recompensed.
	174– 5	I *g·* appreciate the courtesy
	175–17	*g·* needs improved streets.
	220–28	*g·* improved human nature
	236–29	it will *g·* aid the students
	328–10	* *g·* pleased at the law

greatness

Mis.	270–25	pathway of goodness and *g·*
	331–11	its springtide of freedom and *g·*.
	340–28	in the constellation of human *g·*,
Pul.	39– 6	* God's *g·* flows around our
No.	8–16	struggle into freedom and *g·*,
	46–22	health, *g·*, and goodness,
'00.	10– 6	*g·* of a cause or of an individual,
My.	118–11	outpouring of goodness and *g·*
	123– 7	hearts of men to goodness and *g·*,
	150– 6	character of true *g·*:
	194–11	Only those men and women gain *g·*
	272– 4	Goodness is *g·*,
	306–12	Time and goodness determine *g·*.

great organ

(*see* **organ**)

Grecian

Mis.	260– 6	Pagan mysticism, *G·* philosophy,
Ret.	86– 9	as said the classic *G·* motto.

Greece

Pul.	5–25	*G·*, Japan, India, and China ;
	5–27	in the Academy of *G·*,

greed

My.	257–20	all human hate, pride, *g·*, lust

Greek

Mis.	1– 2	ancient *G·* looked longingly for
	190–29	in the *G·*, Apollyon, serpent, liar,
Ret.	10–10	Hebrew, *G·*, and Latin.
Pul.	46–26	* Hebrew, *G·*, and Latin.

Greek

Pan.	2–11	derived from two *G·* words
	2–23	*Pan* is a *G·* prefix,
'01.	16–13	In the *G· devil* is named *serpent*
Hea.	6–28	*devil* comes from the *G· diabolos;*
My.	288–14	*G·* philosophy, creed, dogma, or
	305–24	not of the *G·* nor of the Roman

Greeks

Mis.	248– 9	*G·* showed a just estimate of

Greek Testament

Mis.	26–26	is, in the *G· T·*, *character.*

green

Mis.	129–18	for other *g·* eyes to gaze on :
	153–10	*g·* isles of refreshment.
	227–24	mind can rest in *g·* pastures,
	257–27	desolating the *g·* earth.
	329– 8	putting down the *g·* ones,
Ret.	4–19	*g·* pastures bright with berries,
Pul.	26–25	* The room is toned in pale *g·*
	48– 2	* *g·* stretches of lawns,
	76– 7	* pale *g·* and gold decoration
	76–10	* rich hangings of deep *g·* plush,
	78–24	* satin-lined box of rich *g·* velvet.
Po.	25– 9	From your *g·* bowers free,
	41–13	From the *g·* sunny slopes of the
My.	95– 2	* like a *g·* bay-tree,
	129–26	*g·* pastures beside still waters,
	162–26	into "*g·* pastures — *Psal.* 23 : 2.
	173–27	visitors to assemble on the *g·*
	257– 1	*g·* branches of the Christmas-tree.

greenness

Pul.	48– 9	* spring and summer *g·*.

greensward

My.	174– 4	soft *g·* proved an ideal
	193– 6	the *g·* and gorgeous skies

greenwood

Po.	34–17	Unto thy *g·* home

greet

Mis.	251– 6	beloved brethren, . . . I *g·* you ;
	384– 4	And true hearts *g·*,
Pul.	61–15	* Beautiful suggestions *g·* you
Po.	36– 3	And true hearts *g·*,
My.	302–27	members wanted to *g·* me

greeted

Mis.	311– 4	*g·* as brethren endeavoring to
My.	169–20	time and place which *g·* them.
	171–24	* *g·* in behalf of the church

greeting

My.	8–23	* chapter sub-title
	8–26	* send our *g·* to you,
	23–16	* *G·* to *Mrs. Eddy from the*
	86– 1	* the *g·* of admiring eyes,
	163–16	chapter sub-title
	341– 8	chapter sub-title
	341–10	your Leader's Spring *g·*,
	342– 5	* after a kindly *g·* took a seat

greetings

Mis.	319–19	accept my tender *g·*
	387–22	*g·* glorious from high heaven,
Pul.	1– 6	and encumbered with *g·*
Po.	6–17	*g·* glorious from high heaven,
My.	23–20	* their loyal and loving *g·*
	44–26	* convey to you their sincere *g·*
	62–20	* send you loving *g·*
	63–18	* even the *g·* and congratulations
	94–25	* she sent *g·* in which she
	142–17	and merge into a meeting for *g·*.
	171–21	* the silent *g·* of the people
	175–10	chapter sub-title
	207– 9	* unite in loving *g·* to you,
	259– 9	* Christmas *g·* from members
	362–18	* send you their loving *g·*

greets

Mis.	177–29	*g·* with joy a familiar face.

grew

Mis.	164–20	*g·* in the understanding of Christ,
	164–21	it *g·* in favor with them.
	231–12	turkey *g·* beautifully less.
	376–23	softened, *g·* gray, then gay,
Ret.	8–11	until I *g·* discouraged,
	23– 6	pungent lessons . . . *g·* sterner.
	26–13	*g·* divinely natural and
	43– 4	From this seed *g·* the
	73–10	human concept *g·* beautifully less
Un.	59–14	and *g·* to manhood,
My.	56–22	* The Mother Church steadily *g·*,
	343–20	and trust in me *g·*.

grief

Mis.	397–13	From tired joy and *g·* afar,
Ret.	7–19	* with the most poignant *g·*,
Un.	18–13	Error says you must know *g·*

grief

Un.	55– 5	and acquainted with *g·*," — *Isa.* 53 : 3.
Pul.	1– 6	redolent with *g·* and gratitude.
	18–22	From tired joy and *g·* afar,
'00.	11–17	measures himself against deeper *g·*.
Po.	9– 5	unsealed fountains of *g·* and joy
	13– 1	From tired joy and *g·* afar,
	25–16	Whose heart bore its *g·*
	78–13	in the Christ hailowed its *g·*,
My.	258–24	all depths of love, *g·*, death,

grieve

Mis.	325–24	*g·* Him in the desert." — *Psal.* 78 : 40

grim

Mis.	339–16	with finger *g·* and cold it points
Chr.	53– 3	O'er the *g·* night of chaos
Po.	26–13	phantom finger, *g·* and cold,

grin

Mis.	216–21	* and ending with the *g·*,
	216–29	* a *g·* without a cat."
	218–22	"*g·* without a cat ;"
	218–23	a *g·* expresses the nature of a cat,

grind

Ret.	80– 8	* mills of God *g·* slowly,
	80– 9	* Yet they *g·* exceeding small ;

grinds

Ret.	80–11	* With exactness *g·* He all.

grins

Mis.	218–26	matter's graven *g·* are neither

grips

My.	90–11	* *g·* hold of their faith

groan

Mis.	231–10	spiritual *g·* for the unfeasted ones.

grooves

Mis.	104–18	The latter move in God's *g·*
	322–27	laboring in its widening *g·*
My.	107–21	nearer the *g·* of omnipotence.

groped

Mis.	326–29	one who had *g·* his way

groping

Ret.	27–18	* *G·* blindly in the darkness,

Gross, Mr.

My.	42–12	* Mr. *G·*, on assuming office, said :

gross

Po.	47– 7	Ever the *g·* world above ;
My.	48–23	* The scorn of the *g·* and sensual,

Gross, C.S.B.
Willis F.

My.	39–15	* President, Willis F. *G·*, *C.S.B.* ;
	42– 7	* Willis F. *G·*, *C.S.B.*,

grosser

Peo.	2– 6	yields its *g·* elements,

grossly

Mis.	39– 8	*g·* incorrect and false teachers

grot

Ret.	17– 6	soft echoes to kindle the *g·*.
Po.	62– 6	soft echoes to kindle the *g·*.

grotto

Ret.	18– 9	Midst *g·* and songlet
Po.	63–18	Midst *g·* and songlet

grottos

Mis.	323–21	rest in its cool *g·*,
Peo.	14– 5	cool *g·*, smiling fountains,

ground

Mis.	xi–19	intolerance will fall to the *g·*,
	27–15	accept divine Science on this *g·* ?
	127–27	garrulous talk may fall to the *g·*,
	151–12	cumbereth it the *g·*?" — *Luke* 13 : 7.
	195–21	it cannot fall to the *g·*
	234–19	ventured on such unfamiliar *g·*,
	240–15	as it takes the frost out of the *g·*
	349–13	on the *g·* that it was inconsistent
	357–14	They fall on stony *g·*
Man.	64–19	consented on the *g·* that this
Ret.	35–21	too immanent to fall to the *g·*
Pul.	1–16	whereon thou troddest was holy *g·* ;
	24– 9	* on a triangular plot of *g·*,
	39– 1	* that all meet on common *g·*
	49–11	* of most unpromising *g·*
No.	4–11	On the *g·* that harmony is the truth
	27–26	tread lightly, for this is holy *g·*.
Pan.	10– 1	on the *g·* that it takes away
Po.	26– 5	where thou hast trod is holy *g·*.
My.	43–20	* came over this Jordan on dry *g·*.
	55–12	* Mrs. Eddy gave the plot of *g·*
	268– 6	marriage relation is losing *g·*,
	269–25	fruits of your *g·*." — *Mal.* 3 : 11.
	308–17	* regularly beating the *g·* with a
	314–15	on the *g·* of desertion,
	336– 7	* she declined on this *g·*,

grounded
Un. 6–14 Until . . . is firmly *g*·,

groundless
Mis. 266–20 is utterly false and *g*·.

grounds
Mis. 68–28 * regards the ultimate *g*· of being,
Pul. 49–29 * a number of men to keep the *g*·
Rud. 12– 8 on false *g*·,
My. 111– 9 on practically the same *g*·

groundwork
Mis. 264– 6 without the *g*· of right,
Un. 25–23 therefore has no *g*· in Life,

group
Mis. 230–27 It was a beautiful *g*· !
My. 162– 7 A small *g*· of wise thinkers
257–25 I *g*· you in one benison
355–22 the happiest *g*· on earth.
355–26 happy *g*· of Christian Scientists ;

groups
Po. 8– 3 In somber *g*· at the vesper-call,
My. 87–21 * cheerful looking *g*· of people

grove
Mis. 390–13 Through woodland, *g*·, and dell ;
395–15 Written in childhood, in a maple *g*·
Ret. 91–25 The *g*· became his class-room,
Po. vi–28 * (written in a maple *g*·),
34– 8 In what dark leafy *g*·
55–14 Through woodland, *g*·, and dell ;
59– 9 Written in girlhood, in a maple *g*·.

groves
Mis. 330– 2 make melody through dark pine *g*·.
Ret. 4–18 requiems through dark pine *g*·.

grow
Mis. 86–30 we must *g*· out of even this
136– 9 so *g*· upon my vision that I
Un. 14–12 commanded to *g*· in grace.
14–13 Was it necessary for God to *g*·
No. v–12 until you *g*· to apprehend the
37– 2 had to *g*·, develop ;
Hea. 6– 2 and we *g*· more material,
Peo. 3–27 whereby we *g*· out of sin
7–31 our methods *g*· more spiritual
Po. 27– 6 Ere thou *g*· tremulous
27–13 let today *g*· difficult and vast
67– 3 G· cold in this spot as the
My. 11–10 * *g*· into readiness for each step,
17– 7 ye may *g*· thereby :— I Pet. 2 : 2.
91–25 * church has continued to *g*·.
122– 9 the plant will continue to *g*·.
213–23 you will *g*· wiser and better
216–26 As you *g*· older, advance in the

groweth
My. 24–14 * *g*· unto an holy temple — Eph. 2 : 21.

growing
Mis. 239– 8 my shadow is not *g*· less ;
255–11 *g*· into, that altitude of Mind
265–28 *g*· out of the departures from
273–21 *g*· interest in C. S. Mind-healing.
284–19 This *g*· sin must now be dealt with
297–21 *g*· out of this contract,
324–20 *g*· more and more troubled,
337–18 a *g*· affection for all good,
348–17 the *g*· flames of falsehood,
365–24 the *g*· wants of humanity.
Ret. 18–26 alder *g*· from the bent branch
31– 4 solemn certainty in *g*· freedom
48– 7 and the *g*· conviction
71–23 tares *g*· side by side with the
76–27 a *g*· evil in plagiarism ;
Pul. 14– 3 *g*· occultism of this period.
56– 5 * a large and *g*· number
67–19 * and is rapidly *g*·.
No. 19– 6 the *g*· wants of humanity.
Po. 63–24 *g*· from the bent branch
My. 55– 9 * the attendance rapidly *g*·
88–28 * that great and *g*· cult,
224–32 Our Cause is *g*· apace
342–20 It is *g*· wonderfully.

grown
Mis. 138–18 *g*· to know that human strength
159–25 *g*· to behold Thee !
165– 4 he had *g*· beyond the
262–18 encouraging the heart *g*· faint
358–27 who have *g*· to self-sacrifice
Ret. 38–23 *g*· disgusted with my printer,
Un. 2–24 their lives have *g*· so far toward
Pul. 30–27 * within fifteen years it has *g*·
66– 6 * number of believers has *g*·
Peo. 4–26 *g*· out of such false ideals
14– 8 have *g*· more spiritual ;
Po. 71– 4 and guilt, *g*· bold,
My. 47–10 * has *g*· to great magnitude,

grown
My. 99–24 * The denomination has *g*·
172– 5 * *g*· on the farm of Mark Baker,
312–15 * She was a *g*· woman,

grows
Mis. ix–20 youth that never *g*· old ;
16– 6 *g*· into the manhood or womanhood
128– 2 variety of turns, else it *g*· hard
227–28 *g*· into the full stature of wisdom,
254–12 *g*· weak with wickedness
265– 5 He *g*· dark, and cannot regain,
284–26 Evil let alone *g*· more real,
339–15 if it yields not, *g*· stronger.
347–12 theirs *g*· indistinct and ends.
398–13 So, when day *g*· dark and cold,
Ret. 46–19 So, when day *g*· dark and cold,
Un. 3–15 fruit which *g*· on the
Pul. 17–18 So, when day *g*· dark and cold,
Hea. 1– 6 to-morrow *g*· out of to-day.
Po. 14–17 when day *g*· dark and cold,
24–16 night *g*· deeply dark ;
My. 23–29 * the stately structure *g*·,
189–19 and faith *g*· wearisome,
283–18 grasp of goodness *g*· stronger.

growth
and decay
Mis. 362– 3 material birth, *g*·, and decay :
and establishment
My. 220–17 *g*· and establishment of
and experiences
Mis. 165–22 their own *g*· and experiences.
and progress
My. 8– 6 * our own *g*· and progress.
and prosperity
Mis. 291–13 equal *g*· and prosperity of all
'02. 14–13 *g*· and prosperity of C. S.
My. v– 6 * *g*· and prosperity of the Cause
175–12 *g*· and prosperity of our city
and understanding
Mis. 156–28 tests of *g*· and understanding
and vitality
My. 95–25 * religion of *g*· and vitality
consistent
My. 94–10 * consistent *g*· of the sect
continued
My. 56–31 * This continued *g*·, . . . proved
continues
My. 94– 1 * if the *g*· continues
desiring
Ret. 86–17 A student desiring *g*· in the
future
My. 48–13 * future *g*· of her church,
gained through
Mis. 206–12 gained through *g*·, not accretion ;
general
Mis. 138–20 general *g*· in the members
glorious
My. 20–18 glorious *g*· in C. S.
great
Mis. 127–18 great *g*· in C. S. will follow,
My. 18–15 great *g*· in C. S. will follow,
human
Mis. 286– 6 Until time matures human *g*·,
Ret. 49–13 in human *g*· material organization
in Christian Science
Mis. 127–18 great *g*· in C. S. will follow,
Ret. 49–11 principle for *g*· in C. S.
My. 18–15 great *g*· in C. S. will follow,
20–18 glorious *g*· in C. S.
individual
Mis. 98–14 individual *g*· of Christian Scientists,
98–22 it must begin with individual *g*·,
118–15 advance individual *g*·, nor
in love
My. 39–28 * our own *g*· in love and unity
in Science
Ret. 79–14 uproot the germs of *g*· in Science
is governed
Mis. 206–17 G· is governed by intelligence ;
is restricted
Mis. 359–12 G· is restricted by forcing humanity
its
My. 47–14 * epoch-marking stages of its *g*·,
91–25 * Its *g*· in numbers is remarkable,
92–27 * Its *g*· has been wonderfully rapid,
manifest
Mis. 86– 7 manifest *g*· at every experience.
mental
Mis. 357–19 third stage of mental *g*· is
of a faith
Pul. 65–12 * chapter sub-title
of attendance
My. 56–16 * room for *g*· of attendance
of Christian Science
Pul. 50–11 * The *g*· of C. S. is properly

growth

of Christian Scientists
Mis. 98–14 individual *g·* of Christian Scientists,
107–28 the *g·* of Christian Scientists.
of illusion
Mis. 83– 8 "*Sickness is a g· of illusion*,
of its principles
Pul. 51–24 * help on the *g·* of its principles.
of mankind
Mis. 237–23 push on the *g·* of mankind.
of my students
Mis. 137–14 rejoice over the *g·* of my students
of spirituality
Mis. 154–13 as the *g·* of spirituality
of this Cause
My. 58– 8 * magnificent *g·* of this Cause,
58–12 * shows the *g·* of this Cause,
of this cult
My. 85– 4 * *g·* of this cult is the marvel of
origin and
Pul. 67– 4 * SKETCH OF ITS ORIGIN AND *G·*
our
Mis. 267– 5 the best friends to our *g·*.
personal
Mis. 356–28 indispensable to personal *g·*,
physical
No. 13– 4 moral and physical *g·*,
present
My. 47– 7 * church has reached its present *g·*,
prosperous
My. 10–28 * prosperous *g·* of this movement
rapid
Mis. 6–14 as the rapid *g·* of the work shows.
Pul. 52–17 * rapid *g·* of the new movement.
'01. 2–28 explains its rapid *g·*.
My. 52–11 * while we realize the rapid *g·*,
remarkable
My. 94–16 * remarkable *g·* and the apparent
rewarded by
Mis. 84–11 motives were rewarded by *g·*
scientific
Mis. 206–13 scientific *g·* manifests no weakness,
spiritual
(*see* **spiritual**)
stages of
Mis. 355–11 pass through three stages of *g·*.
strength and
My. 83–28 * strength and *g·* of their organization,
strongest
Ret. 82– 9 widest power and strongest *g·*
subject to
Mis. 82–31 Mind, then, is not subject to *g·*,
swift
My. 92–13 * swift *g·* of the new faith
their
Mis. 223–22 no . . . influence can hinder their *g·*
278–25 substitute my own for their *g·*,
this
Pul. 66– 8 * This *g·*, it is said, proceeds
tremendous
My. 93–24 * missed entirely its tremendous *g·*
wonderful
My. 98– 4 * and this is the wonderful *g·*
your
Mis. 206–26 Your *g·* will be rapid, if you
'01. 1–12 most essential to your *g·*

Mis. 138–24 *g·* of these at first is more gradual ;
Un. 50–26 material origin, *g·*, maturity, and
My. 84–18 * *g·* of the C. S. idea
89–27 * The *g·* of this form of religious faith
97–22 * *g·* of the new church
124– 7 health, harmony, *g·*, grandeur, and
148–25 it is a *g·* Christward ;
229–20 beloved students, whose *g·* is
245–10 The *g·* of human inquiry

gruel
Mis. 225–31 * you shall have some *g·*."

grumbling
Mis. 327–29 stumbling and *g·*, and fighting]

Grundmann Studio Building
Pul. 29– 1 * in the new *G· S· B·*

guaranteed
My. 167–25 rights and privileges *g·* to you

guard
Mis. 114–31 how to *g·* against evil
116–27 never off *g·*, never ill-humored,
126– 9 has his own thoughts to *g·*,
134–15 *g·* and guide His own.
281– 5 will-power that you must *g·* against.
307–29 must *g·* against the deification of
312– 1 to *g·* against that temptation.
400–16 *G·* me when I sleep ;
Ret. 81– 5 we should *g·* thought and action,

guard
Ret. 85–13 *G·* yourselves against the
'02. 18– 2 gate of conscience, wakefully *g·* it ;
Po. 43–12 Shield and guide and *g·* them ;
69– 4 *G·* me when I sleep ;
My. 130– 2 Watch and *g·* your own thoughts
193–19 God *g·* and guide you.
194–27 guide and *g·* you and your church
213–19 Be ever on *g·* against this enemy.
213–22 *G·* and strengthen your own citadel
221–30 Truth and Life, can *g·* the entrance
353–13 intended to hold *g·* over Truth,

guarded
Ret. 89–20 *g·* them unto the end,

guardian
Ret. 21– 3 a *g·* was appointed him,
Pan. 3–27 *g·* of flocks and herds.
My. 125– 4 our annual meeting is a grave *g·*.
(*see also* **Eddy**)

guardians
Mis. 347–20 *g·* of His presence go before me.
Peo. 1–11 *g·* of the gloom are the angels of
My. 261– 2 loving parents and *g·* of youth

guardianship
Man. 75– 1 heading
Rud. 15–18 with suitable and thorough *g·*
My. 316–22 under Mr. Flower's able *g·*

guarding
Ret. 18– 8 sentinel hedgerow is *g·* repose,
Po. 63–17 sentinel hedgerow is *g·* repose,
My. 86– 6 * brooding elevation, *g·* as it were,
164–22 guiding, and *g·* your way
182–23 *g·*, guiding, giving grace,
261–11 *g·* and guiding well the

guards
Mis. 150–31 He *g·*, guides, feeds,
331–20 Love that *g·* the nestling's
389– 8 Love that *g·* the nestling's
'01. 14–22 even as one *g·* his door
Po. 4– 5 Love that *g·* the nestling's

guard'st
Mis. 392– 7 *G·* thou the earth,
Po. 20– 9 *G·* thou the earth,

guerdon
Mis. 118–16 *g·* of meritorious faith
Po. 44– 3 With the *g·* of Thy bosom,
My. 123– 5 The great *g·* of divine Love,

guerdons
Mis. 120–12 and achieved great *g·*

guessing
Ret. 33– 6 till I was weary of "scientific *g·*,"
'01. 33–15 or a diploma for scientific *g·*.
Peo. 6– 5 * "Medicine is the science of *g·*."
11–27 Scientific *g·* conspires unwittingly

guesswork
Mis. 355– 7 a healing that is not *g·*,
My. 92–22 * ridiculed by the hostile as mere *g·*,
94– 5 * ridiculed by the hostile as mere *g·*,

guest
Po. 77–18 some dear lost *g·* Bears hence its

guestchamber and guest-chamber
Mis. 342– 9 By entering the *g·* of Truth,
My. 156–15 Where is the *g·*, — *Luke* 22 : 11.

guests
Mis. 225– 6 Among the *g·*, were an orthodox
231–13 to vie with *g·* in the dexterous use of
'00. 14–29 ask who are to be the *g·*.
15– 4 The *g·* are distinguished above human
My. 74–26 * as the *g·* of the city,
296–28 she depicted its rooms, *g·*,
322–15 * when a friend and I were the *g·*

guidance
Mis. 133–27 constantly to divine Love for *g·*,
138–11 *g·* of our common Father
194–24 accept God's power and *g·*,
324–32 receive his heavenly *g·*,
371– 9 *g·* of our common Father,
Man. 40– 3 *g·* OF MEMBERS.
Ret. 13–21 seeking His *g·*.
27–28 under the *g·* of the great Master.
82–11 rest on divine Principle for *g·*,
Un. 5–27 left to the supernal *g·*
Pul. 39– 1 * their best aid and *g·*,
No. 7–26 discriminations and *g·* thereof
My. 45–18 * *g·* of Him who went before
142–12 I sought God's *g·* in doing it,
150– 4 if thou seekest this *g·*,
280– 5 * your watchful care and *g·*
338–18 higher source for wisdom and *g·*.

Guide

(see **Eddy***)*

guide

Mis.	64–17	ethics which *g·* thought spiritually
	134–15	guard and *g·* His own.
	136–21	S. and H. your teacher and *g·*.
	216– 2	to *g·* your own state of combat
	228– 1	safer *g·* than the promptings of
	287–24	God will *g·* you.
	320–11	to cheer, *g·*, and bless man
	327–28	and lose sight of their *g·* ;
	371– 8	Is it that he can *g·* . . . better than
	371– 9	they, . . . can *g·* themselves?
	373–13	should. does, *g·* His children.
	400–17	*G·* my little feet
Man.	15– 4	sufficient *g·* to eternal Life.
Pul.	30–16	* are the *g·* to eternal Life ;
	30–19	* as the teacher and *g·* to salvation ;
No.	20–26	Human reason is a blind *g·*,
Pan.	14–14	*g·* and bless our chief magistrate,
Po.	23–20	*G·* him in wisdom's way !
	43–12	Shield and *g·* and guard them ;
	69– 5	*G·* my little feet
	79– 2	So Love doth *g·* ;
My.	11– 9	* not tried to *g·* us by means of
	104– 1	I have had no other *g·*
	150– 4	will *g·* thee, if thou seekest this
	193–19	God guard and *g·* you.
	194–27	*g·* and guard you and your church
	234–11	*g·* them every step of the way
	282–26	May God *g·* and prosper

(see also **Eddy***)*

guide-book

Mis.	xi–11	a graphic *g·*, pointing the path,

guided

Mis.	147–17	not *g·* merely by affections
	147–19	The upright man is *g·* by
	149–28	*G·* by the pillar and the cloud,
	236–21	be *g·* by God alone ;''
	290–11	*g·* by the divine Principle,
Man.	84–18	pupils shall be *g·* by the BIBLE,
'01.	20– 5	*g·* by no other mind than Truth,
Po.	2– 9	*G·* and led, can never reach to
My.	28–28	* labors of one divinely *g·* woman,
	50–10	* *g·* by their dauntless Leader
	235– 6	tender mother, *g·* by love,

guides

Mis.	77–18	*g·* him by Truth that knows no error,
	81–30	*g·* the understanding,
	118– 6	scientific understanding *g·* man.
	150–31	He guards, *g·*, feeds,
	152–28	which *g·* you safely home.
	373–12	Neither . . . *g·* the infinite Mind
Ret.	83–12	and are their best *g·*.

guides

Un.	3–28	*g·* every event of our careers.
'02.	2– 3	this daystar, and whither it *g·*.
My.	295–18	It *g·* the fisherman.

guiding

Mis.	59–25	*g·* them with Truth.
	303– 8	teaching and *g·* their students.
	321– 1	The wise men follow this *g·* star ;
Ret.	28– 4	*g·* our every thought and action ;
My.	110–10	*g·* the steps of progress
	164–22	*g·*, and guarding your way
	182–23	guarding, *g·*, giving grace, health,
	261–11	guarding and *g·* well the
	273– 8	* *g·* with remarkable skill,

guile

My.	17– 4	all malice, and all *g·*,— *I Pet.* 2 : 1.

guilt

Mis.	115– 9	*g·* as a mental malpractitioner,
	121–11	the *g·* of innocent blood— *Deut.* 19 : 13.
Po.	26–15	dark record of our *g·* unrolled,
	71– 3	and *g·*, grown bold,

guilty

Mis.	66– 3	innocent to suffer for the *g·*.
	112–10	nor detect the *g·*, unless he
	121–15	suffer for the *g·*, is inhuman.
	121–31	punishes the *g·*, not the innocent.
Man.	52–11	If a member is found *g·* of
	53– 5	member *g·* of this offense
Ret.	31–20	he is *g·* of all.'' — *Jas.* 2 : 10.
	80–25	and turns away from it, is *g·*,
My.	160–29	even the fire of a *g·* conscience,
	220–30	suffer for the *g·*,

guise

Pul.	23–14	* under the *g·* of C. S.,
My.	128–31	evil suggestions, in whatever *g·*,

gulf

Man.	41– 6	*g·* between C. S. and theosophy,

Gulf States

Pul.	41– 9	* far-off Pacific coast and the *G· S·*

gulp

Mis.	87– 3	into one *g·* of vacuity

gush

My.	332– 4	* The silent *g·* of grateful tears alone

gushed

Po.	9– 6	fountains of grief and joy That *g·*

gust

My.	297–12	A suppositional *g·* of evil
	297–13	This *g·* blows away the baubles

gustatory

Mis.	209–18	The loss of *g·* enjoyment

H

H——, Mr. C. M.

Mis.	242–26	Also, Mr. C. M. *H·*, of Boston,

habit

Mis.	240–26	the *h·* of smoking is not nice,
	242–24	he is to cure that *h·* in three days,
	243– 2	cured her perfectly of this *h·*,
	319–11	*h·* of mental and audible protest
My.	212–10	alcoholic *h·* is the use of

habitant

Un.	45–18	make mind-matter a *h·* of the

habitation

Mis.	229–17	most High thy *h·* ;— *Psal.* 91 : 9.
	328–18	tarried in the *h·* of the senses,
	344– 9	fit *h·* for the intelligences?''
	389–12	His *h·* high is here,
'00.	10– 2	*h·* of His throne forever.
Po.	4–11	His *h·* high is here,
My.	126–26	become the *h·* of devils, — *Rev.* 18 : 2.

habits

Mis.	119–13	its *h·*, tastes, and indulgences.
Man.	63–24	He or she shall have no bad *h·*,
Pan.	10–26	no pleasure in loathsome *h·*
'01.	27–19	*h·* and appetites of mankind corrected,

habitual

Mis.	18–24	*h·* love for his fellow-man.

habitually

Mis.	315–29	*h·* to study His revealed Word,
Man.	83–21	*h·* to study the Scriptures

hades

Mis.	170–12	*h·*, or hell of Scripture,
'01.	16–10	with the verbiage of *h·*.

Hahnemann Medical College

Ret.	43–11	the *H· M· C·* of Philadelphia,

hail

Mis.	141–10	*h·* with joy this proposed type
Pul.	41–27	* ''All *h·* the power of Jesus' name,''
	81– 2	* ''All *h·* the power of Jesus' name,''
Po.	10– 1	*H·*, brother ! fling thy banner
	70–19	*h·* creation's glorious morn
My.	16–29	*h·* shall sweep away — *Isa.* 28 : 17.
	252–29	All *h·* to this higher hope
	337– 3	*H·*, brother ! fling thy banner

hails

Mis.	393–15	When the buried Master *h·* us
Po.	51–20	When the buried Master *h·* us

hair

Un.	51– 7	never make one *h·* white or black,
Pul.	32– 1	* her face, framed in dark *h·*
	37– 7	* although her *h·* is white,
My.	271–16	* sweet smile and snowy *h·*

half

Mis.	126– 4	I *h·* wish for society again ;
	295–29	for a *h·* century has with such dignity,
	325–18	with eyes *h·* open, the porter starts up
	339– 5	silence for the space of *h·* an hour.
	382–12	latter *h·* of the nineteenth century
Ret.	50–14	or even in *h·* as many lessons.
Pul.	vii– 8	latter *h·* of the nineteenth century,
	2– 4	the *h·* was not told me :— *I Kings* 10 : 7.
	9–19	who, with his better *h·*, is a
	59– 7	* every hour and a *h·*,
	65–23	* gave *h·* of the garment to
No.	29–12	* is not *h·* a man.''
Pan.	3– 4	*h·* goat and *h·* man,

half
Pan. 3– 7 one charm to make it *h·* divine
'01. 22–17 three, or one and a *h·*,
'02. 13–15 about one *h·* the price paid,
Hea. 13–14 at intervals of *h·* an hour
My. 29–28 * *h·* past five in the morning
    30–27 * the service at *h·* past seven,
    30–32 * Before *h·* past seven the chimes
    31– 9 * Promptly at *h·* past six
    38–16 * service at *h·* past twelve
    54– 9 * *h·* an hour before the arrival
    68– 6 * one mile and a *h·* of pews.
    77– 8 * its dimensions are only *h·* as great.
    78–28 * of the *h·* past twelve service ;
    81–13 * up leaped *h·* a dozen Scientists.
    107–15 administers *h·* a dozen or less
    147– 4 Over a *h·* century ago,
    229–12 might cost them a *h·* century.
    243–12 duties of *h·* a dozen or more
          (see also **numbers**)

half-century *and* half century
Mis. 247– 8 professed Christianity a *h·* ;
    295–29 for a *h· c·* has with such dignity
Ret. 13– 3 members of that body for a *h·*.
Un. 6–22 a *h·* ago the assertion
My. 147– 4 Over a *h· c·* ago,
    229–12 might cost them a *h· c·*.

half-days
Ret. 50–14 during twelve *h·*,

half-hostility
'02. 3– 9 the North's *h·* to the South,

halfpenny
My. 215– 1 but nobody . . . gave it a *h·*.

half-persuaded
My. 49– 3 * the hitherto *h·* one
    166– 4 insincerity and a *h·* faith

half-way
My. 260–12 it hath . . . no *h·* stations.

hall
Mis. 178–16 * I strayed into this *h·*,
Man. 96– 7 cost of *h·* shall be paid by
Pul. 29–13 * every seat in the *h·* was filled
'02. 15– 2 contained threats to blow up the *h·*
Po. vi– 6 * poem
  page 39 poem
    39–20 brilliant temperance *h·*
    40– 3 We dedicate this temperance *h·*
My. 54–29 * decided that this *h·* was too large,
    55– 1 * the *h·* was crowded.
    55–21 * *h·* was crowded to overflowing.
    59–17 * little *h·* on Market Street, Lynn,
    75–19 * Crowded as the *h·* was yesterday,
    123–10 we have a modest *h·* in one of
    123–19 I will see you in this *h·*,
    123–21 My little *h·*, which holds
    147– 9 provided for you a modest *h·*,
    147–23 work-rooms and a little *h·*,
    154– 7 to send flowers to this little *h·*
    185–23 audience collected in the *h·*
    214–22 to hire a *h·* in which to speak,
    342–17 * smaller parlor across the *h·*,

hallow
'02. 3–25 *h·* the ring of state.
My. 176– 9 *h·* your Palmetto home with
    226–21 in this you learn to *h·* His name,

hallowed
'02. 15–25 recorded the *h·* suggestion.
Po. 78–13 in the Christ *h·* its grief,
My. 150–11 *h·* by one chord of C. S.
    188– 2 This house is *h·* by His promise :
    188– 3 "I have *h·* this house, — *I Kings* 9 : 3.
    202– 4 him who *h·* this Easter morn.
    225–25 "*H·* be Thy name." — *Matt.* 6 : 9.
    258–26 *h·* by our Lord's blessing.

hallows
Mis. 287–28 *h·* home, — which is woman's world.
My. 257–17 *h·* the close of the nineteenth

halls
Mis. 125–30 rapid transit from *h·* to churches,
    150–18 Convenient houses and *h·*
Ret. 40–23 refused me a hearing in their *h·*
Pul. 62–21 * concert *h·*, and public buildings,
My. 147–25 never stop . . . to dedicate *h·*.
    304–13 lectured in large and crowded *h·*

hallucination
Mis. 3–32 thus to annihilate *h·*.
    94– 5 see himself and the *h·* of sin ;
Hea. 5–16 sleight-of-hand and *h·*

hallways
My. 46– 1 * in generous *h·*, in commodious

halt
Mis. 327–16 travellers *h·* and disagree.
    347–18 take a few steps, then *h·*.

halted
My. 214–25 I therefore *h·* from necessity.

halting
Mis. 168– 5 *h·* between two opinions
Un. 61–16 neither . . . retreating, nor *h·*.

halts
Un. 61–13 *h·*, retreats, and again goes
No. 46– 7 advancing hope . . . *h·* for a reply ;

Hamilton, A. E.
Ret. 95–13 signature

hamlet
My. 134–16 Truth happifies life in the *h·* or
    257–29 the Alpine *h·*,

hammer
My. 69–13 * *h·* and chisel of the sculptor

hammering
Mis. 360– 4 awaiting the *h·*, chiselling, and

Hammond, Dr.
Pul. 69– 1 * Dr. *H·*, the pastor,
    69– 6 * Dr. *H·* says he was converted to

hampered
Mis. 263–24 *h·* by immature demonstrations,
    365–26 Christian metaphysics is *h·* by
No. 11– 9 Christian metaphysics is *h·* by

hand
at
Mis. 61– 3 priceless, eternal, and just at *h·*.
    103–32 "I am a God at *h·*, — see *Jer.* 23 : 23.
Un. 37– 6 heaven is at *h·*." — *Matt.* 10 : 7.
No. 35–25 kingdom of God is at *h·*," — *Mark* 1 : 15.
My. 10–13 * but the time is at *h·*,
    58–22 * heaven is at *h·*," — *Matt.* 3 : 2.
    121–13 helpful, and always at *h·*.
    202– 7 and the day is at *h·*.
    360–30 Your favor . . . is at *h·*.
chisel in
Peo. 7– 8 * "Chisel in *h·* stood a sculptor-boy,
divine
Ret. 27–29 divine *h·* led me into a new world
My. 326–20 I recognize the divine *h·*
every
My. 31–16 * were heard on every *h·*
fanatic
Po. 71– 8 Rescued by the "fanatic" *h·*,
friendly
Mis. 294–17 O friendly *h·* !
gentle
Mis. 250–27 gentle *h·* opening the door
God's
'01. 16– 2 * God's *h·* has held you up."
helping
Pul. 45– 1 * children lent a helping *h·*,
My. 259–19 a true heart, and a helping *h·*
her
Pul. 82– 5 * Her *h·* is tender
    84– 1 * not in her *h·*, but in her soul.
His
Mis. 152–10 o'er the work of His *h·*.
    171– 1 "His *h·* is not shortened — see *Isa.* 59 : 1.
    334– 3 none can stay His *h·*, — *Dan.* 4 : 35.
    347–27 Those who . . . take His *h·*,
    360– 5 transfiguration from His *h·*.
Po. 10–21 His *h·* averts the blow."
My. 200– 7 none can stay His *h·*
    215– 5 God stretched forth His *h·*.
    280–20 none can stay His *h·*
    337–22 His *h·* averts the blow."
his
'02. 11– 1 with a letter in his *h·*
My. 126– 9 has in his *h·* a book open
in hand
Mis. 311– 4 walk with us *h·* in hand,
join in hand
Mis. 281–29 "Though *h·* join in hand, — *Prov.* 11 : 21.
mighty
My. 42–30 * "With a mighty *h·*, — *Deut.* 26 : 8.
my
Mis. 143– 8 I reach out my *h·* to clasp yours,
    151– 5 out of my *h·*." — *John* 10 : 28.
    213–25 out of my *h·*." — *John* 10 : 28.
    251– 6 my *h·* may not touch yours
no
'00. 3– 5 No *h·* that feels not his help,
of God
Mis. 178–13 right *h·* of God" — *Col.* 3 : 1.
    319–24 the outstretched *h·* of God.
of love
'01. 33– 6 *h·* of love must sow the seed.

hand

open
Ret.   6– 7   as one with the open h·.
other
Mis. 241–18   On the other h·, . . . administer this
     279– 1   departures on the other h·.
Pul. 51–20   * it may, on the other h·,
our
Po. 10– 4   With our h·, though not our knees.
My. 337– 6   With our h·, though not our knees.
palsied
Un. 11–13   The palsied h· moved,
right
Mis. ix–12   by the touch of God's right h·.
      98–19   through God's right h·,
     125–11   sit down at the Father's right h· :
     140–14   right h· of His righteousness,
     178–13   right h· of God" — Col. 3 : 1.
     364–14   God's right h· grasping the
     373–28   right h· of the Father. — Matt. 28 : 18.
Ret. 22–13   right h· of the throne — Heb. 12 : 2
      27–19   * Touch God's right h· in that
Pul.   9–28   and right h· of omnipotence.
'00. 12– 4   stars in His right h· — Rev. 2 : 1
My.   v– 8   * right h· of fellowship is being
     258–16   right h· of the throne — Heb. 12 : 2.
     323–25   * right h· of His righteousness,
rung by
Pul. 62–12   * even when rung by h·
same
Chr. 53–51   same h· unfolds His power,
senseless
Un. 11–22   for restoring his senseless h· ;
staff in
Mis. 158–20   with sandals on and staff in h·,
     358–28   awaiting, with staff in h·,
strengthened the
My. 132–17   Divine Love has strengthened the h·
taking by the
Mis. 11–31   taking by the h· all who love me not,
thy
Mis. 370– 3   "Stretch forth thy h·, — Matt. 12 : 13.
     392– 3   skies clasp thy h·,
Po. 20– 4   skies clasp thy h·,
to hand
Mis. 143– 1   heart to heart and h· to hand,
weak
No. 44–18   weak h· outstretched to God.
willing
Mis. xi–9   fervent heart and willing h·
withered
Un. 11–16   "That withered h· looks very real

Mis. vii– 1   * that tak'st my book in h·,
     170–32   "H·," in Bible usage, — Isa. 59 : 1.
     292–21   enjoins taking them by the h· and
     307–13   and many orders on h·,
Man. 76–12   funds which the Church has on h·,
Ret. 38–15   printing the copy he had on h·,
      38–19   printed all the copy on h·,
My. 12– 3   * as soon as the money in h·
      16– 6   * $226,285.73 on h· on that date,
      23–10   * Amount on h· June 1, 1905,
      76– 7   * enough money was on h·

handed

Mis. 373– 8   the following . . . was h· to me,
     376–10   * a small sketch h· down
My. 308–21   h· him a gold-headed walking-stick
     351– 7   letter was h· to me duly.

handful

My. 59–18   * preached to a h· of people
      85– 6   * a mere h· of members

handiwork

Po.   v–13   * masterpiece of nature's h·,

handkerchief

My. 152– 4   the h· of St. Paul

handle

Mis. 24–30   followers should h· serpents ;
     108–21   that which . . . we can h· ;
     211– 5   teaches mortals to h· serpents
     221– 4   opportunity to h· the error,
     299–32   you wished to h· them,
     315–25   shall not silently . . . h· it,
     334–18   then, and only then, do you h· it
     336– 4   h· the serpent and bruise its head ;
'01. 16–23   to h· with garrulity age and
     20–27   laws of our land will h· its thefts,
My. 172– 5   * wood in the h· was grown on the farm
     364– 4   to h· no other mentality

handled

Mis. 350–21   in the mind that h· them.
Un. 36– 7   confirms Truth, when h· by C. S.,

handles

Mis. 203–15   h· it with so-called science,
     210–14   h· it, and takes away its sting.
My. 107–29   homœopathist h· in his practice

handling

Mis. 191– 1   h· the word of God — II Cor. 4 : 2.
     292–29   on this point of h· evil,
'01. 16–15   h· the word of God deceitfully.
My. 75–13   * h· of a great number
     124– 2   h· the word of God — II Cor. 4 : 2.
     338–17   their subjects or the h· thereof,

handmaid

Mis. 261–17   Justice is the h· of mercy,
Man. 69–15   household help or a h·,

handmaiden

Pul. 81–16   * love and her h· duty

hand-painted

Mis. 280–21   containing beautiful h· flowers

hands

and feet
Mis. 375–24   * "The h· and feet of the figures
     375–25   * h· and feet in Angelico's 'Jesus,'
clap their
Mis. 168–20   pure in heart clap their h·.
clasp
Mis. 152– 4   in love continents clasp h·,
Pul. 84– 5   * shall clasp h· with pity,
clasping of
Mis. 306–27   it is not the clasping of h·,
clean
My. 34– 3   He that hath clean h·, — Psal. 24 : 4.
feeble
Ret. 27–17   * But the feeble h· and helpless,
feet and
Pul.   9–14   climbed with feet and h·
God's
My. 278–14   are in God's h·.
hearts and
My. 153– 2   loving hearts and h· of the
     197–28   work of your hearts and h·.
His
Chr. 55–13   operation of His h·. — Isa. 5 : 12.
My. 232– 3   with the helm in His h·.
his
Mis. 224– 9   emperor lifted his h· to his head,
     281–14   that fell into his h·.
Rud. 12– 1   never lays his h· on the patient,
'02. 19– 6   lifting up his h· and blessing them,
human
Mis. 171– 3   to signify human h·.
     302–30   putting . . . into human h·,
little
Pul.   8–17   Little h·, never before devoted to
loving
Pul. 77–12   * loving h· of four thousand members.
      78–10   * loving h· of four thousand members.
made with
Mis. 324– 3   city made with h·.
men's
My.   6–24   above the work of men's h·,
      94–28   above the work of men's h·,
my
Pul.   6–14   * S. and H., was put into my h·.
'02. 13–26   to take the property off my h·,
not made with
Pul.   2–14   "house not made with h·, — II Cor. 5 : 1.
My. 188–13   "house not made with h·, — II Cor. 5 : 1.
     194– 8   "house not made with h·, — II Cor. 5 : 1.
of aspirants
Mis. 351–14   in the h· of aspirants for place
of evil
My. 128–24   betrays Truth into the h· of evil
of God
No.   3– 6   better to fall into the h· of God,
of gossip
Mis. 227–11   weighty stuff into the h· of gossip !
of my students
'01. 17–21   into the h· of my students
of omnipotence
My. 127–29   through the h· of omnipotence.
of others
Mis. 13– 7   endured at the h· of others
of the artisans
Pul. 41– 1   * from the h· of the artisans
of their patients
No.   3–14   in the h· of their patients,
of tyrants
Mis. 99–10   weapon in the h· of tyrants.
on the sick
     (see sick)
our
Mis. 110–19   our h· have wrought steadfastly
outstretched
Un. 26– 6   to be in His outstretched h·,

hands

ready
My. 197–13 the great hearts and ready h·

ruthless
Po. 46– 9 Unplucked by ruthless h·.

strengthened
My. 199–20 of strengthened h·, of unveiled hearts,

swift
My. 124–14 waiting only your swift h·,

their
Mis. 330– 1 the leaves clap their h·,
331– 4 wonders into their h·?

Thy
Mis. 248– 7 works of Thy h·." — Psal. 92 : 4.

thy
My. 199– 5 reward of thy h· is given

use of
Mis. 242– 8 without the use of h·,

willing
My. 124– 9 with glad faces, willing h·,

without
My. 195–28 love that builds without h·,

wrong
Mis. 351–17 never can place it in the wrong h·

Mis. 170–30 putting on of h· . . . she explained as
216–11 means more than "h· off."
216–14 "laying on of h·," — Heb. 6 : 2.
304–32 * have been placed in the h· of
Man. 75–21 remained in the h· of the Directors,
91–16 surplus funds left in the h· of
Hea. 14–12 in the h· of a quack.
My. 331– 5 Mrs. Eddy received at the h· of

handsome
Pul. 63–23 * This h· edifice was paid for
70–14 * a h· fire-proof church
77– 5 * encased in a h· plush casket
My. 87–18 * an edifice so h· architecturally.
171–27 * h· rosewood casket

handsomely
'01. 28–30 usually are h· provided for.

hand-trunk
Mis. 239–14 the ominous h·.

handwriting
Mis. 144–10 names in your own h·,
Man. 26–11 given in her own h·.
81– 4 given in her own h·.
97–12 given in her own h·,
My. 60–18 * on the fly-leaf in your h·,
134–28 * letter is in Mrs. Eddy's own h·,
137– 8 * letter is in Mrs. Eddy's own h·
272–22 * reproduced in her own h·.

hanged
Mis. 61–16 * where a man was said to be 'h·
122–12 were h· about his neck, — Matt. 18 : 6.

hanging
Mis. 347–6 h· like a horoscope in the air,

hangings
Pul. 76– 9 * h· of deep green plush,

hangs
Pul. 26–27 * h· an Athenian lamp

Hankey's, Kate
My. 15–17 Kate H· excellent hymn,

Hanna

Judge
Pul. 28–26 * Judge H·, formerly of Chicago,
29– 3 * Preceding Judge H· were
29–16 * were finely read by Judge H·.
29–19 * In his admirable discourse Judge H· said
30– 3 * remonstrated with Judge H·
43–18 * were read by Judge H· and Dr. Eddy.
45–23 * Judge H· withdrew from the pastorate
46– 1 * Judge H· was so eloquent
60– 6 * Judge H·, who was a Colorado lawyer

Judge and Mrs.
Pul. 36–25 * now occupied by Judge and Mrs. H·,
37–18 * Judge and Mrs. H·, Miss Elsie Lincoln,

Judge Septimus J.
My. 44–15 * Judge Septimus J. H· then advanced

Judge S. J.
Pul. 5– 5 read by Judge S. J. H·,
43– 6 * Judge S. J. H·, editor of
My. 304–18 Judge S. J. H· became editor of

Mrs.
Pul. 37– 2 * remarked Mrs. H·,

haply
Mis. 84– 2 H· he waited for a preparation

happen
Mis. 339– 4 h· very frequently on earth,

happened
Mis. 38–13 How h· you to establish a
Pul. 60– 8 * which h· that day to be

happier
Mis. 229–24 holier, h·, and longer lived.
Pul. 56–16 * makes people better and h·.
'02. 19–15 h· than the conqueror of a world.
My. 150– 8 * rendering the world h·
229–30 The redeemed should be h· than
296–15 healthier and h·, than yesterday.
355–26 Mrs. Eddy is h· because of them ;

happiest
My. 355–22 the h· group on earth.

happifies
Mis. 394– 6 Hope h· life, at the altar
Po. 45– 8 Hope h· life, at the altar
My. 134–16 Truth h· life in the hamlet

happily
Mis. 13– 8 h· wrought out for me
My. 110–29 H·, the misquoting of "S. and H.
177– 3 Most h· would I comply with your

happiness

all
Mis. 118–24 they will uproot all h·.

and heaven
Mis. 308– 8 health, h·, and heaven.
311–17 health, h·, and heaven.

and holiness
Mis. 15–11 health, h·, and holiness.
183– 7 in health, h·, and holiness :
My. 167–20 their health, h·, and holiness
275–22 health, h·, and holiness,

and life
Mis. 212–19 h·, and life flow not into
Un. 22–15 essential to h· and life.

another's
Ret. 72– 2 that hazards another's h·,

confers
'02. 17–24 only what God gives, . . . confers h· :

consists
'02. 17–22 H· consists in being and in doing

constitutes
Mis. 9–31 false sense of what constitutes h·

final
Ret. 78–24 your own success and final h·,

find
Mis. 200–24 find h·, apart from the

forever of
Po. 47–10 Can the forever of h· be

fruition of
Mis. 231– 3 the full fruition of h· ;

gives him
'02. 17– 5 obedience gives him h·.

goodness and
My. 267–31 manifestation of goodness and h·.

health and
Mis. 240–11 promoters of health and h·.
262– 2 bring health and h· to all
My. 165–21 impart truth, health, and h·,

highest
'02. 17– 8 learn that man's highest h·,

hope, nor
'01. 34–28 no intelligence, health, hope, nor h·

human
Ret. 81–27 shifting scenes of human h·

in manhood
My. 274–12 intellectuality, and h· in manhood.

Life and
Un. 37– 8 stepping-stone to Life and h·.

life and
Mis. 209–25 life and h· should still attend it.
341–18 a material sense of life and h·
Ret. 21–19 false sense of life and h·,
Un. 58– 1 a false sense of life and h·.

no
Mis. 324–26 Finding no h· within,

of a fellow-being
Mis. 31– 5 affect the h· of a fellow-being

of her family
Ret. 5–29 * secure the h· of her family.

power and
Mis. 155– 5 All power and h· are spiritual,

procurator of
Mis. 351–26 not the procurator of h·,

rare
Ret. 18–23 those we most love find a h· rare ;
Po. 64–18 those we most love find a h· rare ;

their
Mis. 287–23 questions concerning their h·,

the side of
Hea. 10–21 argue with yourself on the side of h· ;

this
Po. 68– 7 Earth held but this joy, or this h·

happiness

true
Mis. 363– 3   reality of divine Mind and true h·.
welfare and
Ret. 90–22   welfare and h· of her children

Mis. 67–16   indispensable to health, h·, and
212– 4   never knows what h· is,
227–29   by the amount of h· it has
339–21   its all of h· to thy keeping
My. 87–29   * in this doctrine of health, h·,
249–13   mental miasma fatal to health, h·,

happy

Mis. 216–23   a h· hit at idealism,
225– 3   a h· concourse of friends
232– 4   peace, and plenty, and h· households.
385–10   "Joy for thee, h· friend !
388–17   Affection's wreath, a h· home ;
396–10   O h· hours and fleet,
Ret. 94–18   " H· is he that — Rom. 14 : 22.
Pul. 56–18   * Welding . . . was a h· inspiration.
86–17   * We are h· to announce to you
'00. 1– 2   with the tone of your h· hearts,
'02. 16– 7   I am the h· possessor of a copy
Hea. 10–20   If you wish to be h·,
Po. 21– 6   Affection's wreath, a h· home ;
48– 1   Joy for thee, h· friend !
59– 2   O h· hours and fleet,
My. 40–31   * her own blameless and h· life,
63–12   * this h· and holy experience
74–21   * a h· appearing body,
87– 8   * congenial, quietly h·, well-to-do,
87–22   * Their h· faces would make sunshine
93– 1   * h·, gentle, and virtuous.
127– 4   H· are the people whose God is
155–27   h· hearts and ripening goodness.
169–17   I was h· to receive at Concord,
174–11   their reports of the h· occasion.
252–26   gave to the "h· New Year"
256–20   At this h· season
263– 6   wishes you all a h· Christmas,
315– 9   * h· home as one could wish for.
347–12   * Ah h·, h· boughs, that cannot
355–26   h· group of Christian Scientists ;

harbinger

Un. 57–25   Sorrow is the h· of joy.

harbor

'00. 12–14   At the head of the h· was the temple of

harbored

My. 344–19   If I h· that idea

hard

Mis. 128– 2   else it grows h· and uncomfortable
230–14   have become such by h· work ;
233–25   to work h· enough to practise it
234–14   and avoid h· work ;
237–27   dead hero who did the h· work,
261–15   "the way of . . . is h·." — Prov. 13 : 15.
266–18   assertion that I have said h· things
281–19   So, whatever we meet that is h·
338–19   armies of earth press h· upon you.
343–15   cold, h· pebbles of selfishness,
Man. 41– 8   but without h· words.
Un. 1– 4   h· to be understood," — II Pet. 3 : 16.
'00. 2–30   I work h· enough to be so."
'01. 28–29   After a h· and successful career
My. vii– 3   * Strive it ever so h·,
40–30   * H· is the law, nevertheless it is
61–12   * I fought h· with the evidence of
136–24   h· earnings of my pen,
342–12   * shade of which is so h· to catch,

hard-earned

'00. 10–30   send me some of his h· money

harden

Mis. 301–28   All error tends to h· the heart,

hardened

Un. 56–22   suffers least . . . who is a h· sinner.

harder

Rud. 2–27   task, sometimes, may be h· than
My. 145–18   worked even h· than usual,
212– 7   A h· fight will be necessary

hard-headed

My. 81–32   * h· shrewd business men.

hardly

Mis. 224– 5   we can h· afford to be miserable
Ret. 2– 9   h· have crossed the Atlantic
6– 3   * can h· fail to induce them to
Pul. 31–24   * I was h· more than seated
My. 90– 7   * Unaccountable? H· so.
92–12   * h· more than a day's wonder.
98– 9   * as religious annals h· parallel

hardships

My. 52– 3   * many mental h· to endure,

harlequin

Mis. 233– 9   monkey in h· jacket

harlot

My. 126– 2   retaining the heart of the h·

harm

Mis. 12– 1   would not knowingly h· you."
31– 5   h· him morally, physically, or
55–12   to h· rather than to heal,
118–28   Every attempt of evil to h· good
157–27   It cannot h· you ;
221– 3   to h· by a false mental argument ;
263– 2   they will h· myself only,
311–20   as soon h· myself as another ;
335–32   has done himself h·.
350–18   If h· could come from the
351– 9   would not if I could, h· any one
Man. 48– 2   and will not h· them.
Ret. 68–26   In C. S., man can do no h·,
Un. 15–23   who will not h· them,
No. 33– 1   slander loses its power to h· ;
Pan. 9–15   wise enough to do himself no h·,
'01. 20– 7   neither moral right nor might to h·
'02. 19– 9   that would h· him more than
My. 107–14   can be swallowed without h·
210–13   when he would h· others.
232–29   Can watching as Christ demands h·
296–14   Evil has no power to h·,
345– 3   will do the children no h·.

harmful

Mis. 25–28   they cannot be h· ;
34– 1   none of the h· "after effects"
36–11   mortal mind, which is h·

harming

My. 249– 1   without h· any one

harmless

Mis. 210–11   h· as doves." — Matt. 10 : 16.
210–15   Good deeds are h·.
224– 1   mental arrow . . . is practically h·,
374–13   envy, and hatred — earth's h· thunder
Rud. 8– 5   sends forth its own h· likeness.
'01. 33–29   Christian Scientists are h· citizens
Hea. 13–12   single drop of this h· solution,
My. 128–22   Therefore be wise and h·,
150–29   h· as doves." — Matt. 10 : 16.
205– 5   h· as doves." — Matt. 10 : 16.
205–22   friends more faithful, and enemies h·.

harmlessly

Mis. 240–15   or let it remain as h·,

harmonies

Mis. 72– 5   unfolds the eternal h· of
202– 2   whereby the sweet h· of C. S.
329–12   sweet rhythm of unforgotten h·,
333–20   securing the sweet h· of Spirit
390–22   And thou wilt find that h·,
394–18   * Such old-time h· retune,
Pul. 81–21   * all the h· of the universe
No. 11– 3   of life or its h·.
Po. 56– 1   thou wilt find that h·,
57– 4   * Such old-time h· retune,
My. 115– 7   scribe echoing the h· of heaven

harmonious

Mis. 5– 4   reveals man as spiritual, h·, and
34– 8   before the body is renewed and h·,
72–18   Are . . . things real when they are h·,
77 -17   one eternal round of h· being.
104–15   sinless, deathless, h·, eternal.
188– 5   grand chorus of h· being.
220–15   h· thought has the full control
235–21   the real man, h· and eternal.
256– 5   in order to make the body h·.
258–32   nature and man are as h· to-day as
308– 2   be found h· and immortal.
Ret. 59–19   Mind, as h·, immortal, and
Un. 51–18   have none of them lost their h· state
Pul. 54–21   * environment and h· influence that
Rud. 4– 3   perfect beings, h· and eternal,
10– 6   His government is h· ;
No. 4–25   to be eternal, must be h·.
6– 5   God's formations are spiritual, h·,
11– 6   their intelligent and h· action,
26–25   forever individual and forever h·.
'02. 8–10   its h· effects on the sick
Hea. 7– 4   produces the h· effect on the body.
Peo. 10–21   and make it h· or discordant.
My. 39–24   * h· tones of her gentle voice.
44– 6   * land of eternal, h· existence.
119– 4   that which is real, h·, and eternal
146–29   voices the h· and eternal,
226– 6   principle of h· vibration,

harmoniously

Man.	70–19	confer *h·* on individual unity
Pul.	76– 7	* blends *h·* with the pale green
My.	268–27	*h·* ascends the scale of life.
	283–21	unite *h·* on the basis of justice,
	362–15	* to confer *h·* and unitedly

harmonize

'00.	11– 5	*h·*, unify, and unself you.
My.	68–19	* to *h·* with the Bedford stone

harmony (*see also* harmony's)

accentuating
Mis. 206–20 accentuating *h·* in word and deed,
all
Mis. 41–20 produces all *h·* that appears.
No. 13– 5 from the Principle of all *h·*,
and health
Rud. 3–22 upon the body in *h·* and health.
and heaven
No. 34– 2 up to health, *h·*, and heaven.
and holiness
Ret. 65–29 to obtain health, *h·*, and holiness
and immortality
Un. 22– 3 sense of *h·* and immortality,
Peo. 10– 1 of man's *h·* and immortality.
and its Principle
Mis. 14–13 with *h·* and its Principle ;
and Life
Un. 32–19 of holiness, *h·*, and Life."
Rud. 11–24 health, *h·*, and Life eternal.
and prosperity
Ret. 44–15 in its previous *h·* and prosperity.
basis of
Ret. 60–24 C. S. is the only sure basis of *h·*.
brings out
Mis. 337–16 Science brings out *h·* ;
celestial
Pan. 3–29 denotes the celestial *h·* of
conscious
Ret. 64–24 scientific to abide in conscious *h·*,
consciousness of
Rud. 11–15 the absolute consciousness of *h·*
establishes
Mis. 101–14 being which establishes *h·*,
eternal
Mis. 104– 2 at rest in the eternal *h·*.
259–18 In this eternal *h·* of Science,
Un. 52– 5 unbroken and eternal *h·*
Pul. 2–24 eternal *h·* of infinite Soul.
No. 10–27 Eternal *h·*, perpetuity, and
everlasting
My. 253– 4 higher and everlasting *h·*,
goodness and
Mis. 367–11 reality of being — goodness and *h·*
grand
Mis. 330– 7 join in nature's grand *h·*,
health, *alias*
Mis. 41–25 health, *alias h·*, is the normal
health and
Mis. 8– 5 cannot, produce health and *h·*,
59–15 to restore health and *h·*,
187– 6 He established health and *h·*,
heaven is
My. 267–16 Heaven is *h·*, — infinite,
His
Mis. 353–24 Principle carries on His *h·*.
holy
My. 13–26 divine overtures, holy *h·*,
hope, and
Ret. 48–20 restore health, hope, and *h·*
hum of
Pan. 3–11 is voiced with a hum of *h·*,
immortal
Mis. 97– 4 destroy . . . discord with immortal *h·*,
immutable
Ret. 56–15 triumph of Spirit in immutable *h·*.
No. 26–23 immutable *h·* of divine law.
increased
Mis. 204–24 permeates with increased *h·*
infinite
No. 17–23 infinite *h·* would be fathomed.
is heaven
Mis. 337–16 *H·* is heaven.
is perfect
Pul. 62–16 * so that the *h·* is perfect.
is real
Un. 60–10 We say that *h·* is real,
is the real
Rud. 13–19 To aver that *h·* is the real
is the truth
No. 4–11 On the ground that *h·* is the truth of
knowledge of
Un. 18–19 My knowledge of *h·* (not inharmony)

harmony

Life, and
No. 36–14 of good, of eternal Life, and *h·*.
maintain
My. 211– 7 in order to maintain *h·*,
man's
Ret. 61–10 man's *h·* is no more to be invaded
Peo. 10– 1 man's *h·* and immortality.
moral
Mis. 261–32 produce physical and moral *h·*.
365–13 right acting, physical and moral *h·* ;
No. 18–10 right acting, physical and moral *h·*,
moves all in
Mis. 174–11 Principle that moves all in *h·*,
not discord
Mis. 283–28 good, not evil, — *h·*, not discord ;
not in
Mis. 350–22 not in *h·* with Science
obstruct the
No. 40–20 obstruct the *h·* of Mind and body,
of being
Mis. 53– 9 gain heaven, the *h·* of being.
106–28 Music is the *h·* of being ;
116–14 swelling the *h·* of being with
268– 6 way to heaven, the *h·* of being.
Un. 13– 7 fulfil the intended *h·* of being.
of body
Mis. 86–21 *h·* of body and Mind.
of divine Science
Ret. 27–24 so the *h·* of divine Science first
of heaven
My. 274– 7 with the *h·* of heaven ;
of man's being
Un. 53–15 *h·* of man's being is not built on
of Science
Mis. 176– 2 *h·* of Science that declares *Him*,
259–18 In this eternal *h·* of Science,
of Soul
Mis. 85–28 immortality and *h·* of Soul.
omnipotent
Mis. 17– 5 law of omnipotent *h·* and good,
only in
My. 259–30 Soul recognized only in *h·*,
order and
Pan. 6–14 order and *h·* of God's creation.
or discord
Mis. 247–27 reflects *h·* or discord according to
or holiness
Rud. 9–28 health, *h·*, or holiness,
peace and
Mis. 156–11 Let the reign of peace and *h·*
perfect
Pul. 54– 6 * Jesus operated in perfect *h·* with
perpetual
Mis. 72–25 nothing which . . . is in perpetual *h·*.
physical
Un. 6–10 The Science of physical *h·*,
present
My. 129–24 a present *h·* wherein the
Principle and its
Mis. 14–15 lost his Principle and its *h·*,
profound
Mis. 392– 4 Nature divine, in *h·* profound,
Po. 20– 5 Nature divine, in *h·* profound,
real
Mis. 312–17 * the real *h·* between religion and
reign of
Mis. 154–17 reign of *h·* already within us.
344–28 way to heaven and the reign of *h·*.
Ret. 79–30 the reign of *h·* within us,
Un. 52– 7 reign of *h·*, already with us.
represents
Mis. 46–27 sound, in tones, represents *h·* ;
restore
Mis. 236–19 to restore *h·* and prevent dishonor.
rule of
Mis. 187–11 This rule of *h·* must be accepted
scale of
Mis. 290– 6 higher in the scale of *h·*,
Science supports
Mis. 102–23 Science supports *h·*, denies suffering,
sense of
Un. 2–18 gain that spiritual sense of *h·*
22– 3 consists in a sense of *h·*
24– 6 from the supreme sense of *h·*.
'00. 11– 4 Hold . . . the true sense of *h·*,
take hold of
No. 38–18 they take hold of *h·*,
this
Mis. 337–17 this *h·* is not understood unless
No. 45–22 this *h·* would anchor the Church
together in
Ret. 82–25 dwelling together in *h·*,
unity and
My. 270–31 religion and art in unity and *h·*.

harmony
universal
   Mis.   99–28   health, holiness, universal *h·*,
         134–19   the reign of universal *h·*,
   Rud.   1– 4   Principle and rule of universal *h·*.
veil of
   Mis. 352–32   must be covered with the veil of *h·*,
will end in
   My. 296–19   the waking . . . will end in *h·*,
with divine power
   '01.   2– 9   into *h·* with divine power,
with God
   Hea. 14–26   to attain a mind in *h·* with God,
with Life
   Mis. 105–14   in *h·* with Life and its glorious
with the laws
   Pul. 80–28   * into *h·* with the laws of God,

   Mis. 287– 8   To an ill-attuned ear, discord is *h·* ;
   '02.   9–13   Loving chords set discords in *h·*.
   Po. 70–16   Thy discord ne'er in *h·* began !
   My. 118–29   health, *h·*, holiness,
       124– 7   health, *h·*, growth, grandeur, and
       213– 2   *h·*, brotherly love, spiritual growth
       213–21   into *h·* with His true followers.

harmony's
   Un. 13– 9   God is *h·* selfhood.
harms
   Mis.   7–12   although skepticism . . . it *h·* not ;
        8–13   What is it that *h·* you?
      40–32   *h·* himself or another.
     267– 2   wail of evil never *h·* Scientists,
     398–14   Tear or triumph *h·*,
   Ret. 46–20   Tear or triumph *h·*,
   Pul. 17–19   Tear or triumph *h·*,
   Po. 14–18   Tear or triumph *h·*,
harp
   Mis. 394–10   The *h·* of the minstrel,
   Pul. 81–21   * as a perfect *h·*,
   Po. 45–13   The *h·* of the minstrel,
harpstring
   Po. 41–19   *h·*, just breaking, reecho again
harpstrings
   Mis. 106–30   awaken the heart's *h·*.
      396–18   O'er waiting *h·* of the mind
   Pul. 18– 2   O'er waiting *h·* of the mind
   Po. 12– 1   O'er waiting *h·* of the mind
   My. 31– 8   * "O'er waiting *h·* of the mind ;"
Harrisburg, Pa.
   Pul. 88–32   * *Independent, H·, P·.*
Harrison
Mary Hatch
   My. 334–24   * signature
Miss
   My. 329–19   * presented to Mrs. Eddy by Miss *H·.*
Miss Mary Hatch
   My. 327–17   * obtained by Miss Mary Hatch *H·*
Mrs.
   Mis. 306–19   * request of the late Mrs. *H·,*
Harrison's
Miss Mary Hatch
   My. 329–20   * heading
hart
   Hea. 10–26   *h·* panteth for the water brooks,
Hartford, Conn.
   Pul. 88–20   * *Post, H·, C·.*
Harvard College
   Ret. 75–21   If a student at *H· C·*
Harvard Medical School
   Peo.   5–26   in a lecture before the *H· M· S·* :
harvest
   Mis. 214–30   Jesus foretold the *h·* hour
      215–31   not try to gather the *h·* while the
      313–21   pray ye therefore the God of *h·*
      332–10   ripened sheaves, and *h·* songs.
      356–13   the *h·* hour has come ;
   Un. 11–28   and *then* cometh the *h·*,
       12– 1   fields are already white for the *h·* ;
       12– 2   gather the *h·* by mental,
   Po. 47–18   Nevermore reaping the *h·* we deem,
   My. 185– 3   the *h·* bells are ringing.
      269–16   chapter sub-title
      269–19   Its *h·* song is world-wide,
      316– 5   *h·* song of the Redeemer
harvest-home
   Mis. 85– 1   are ripe for the *h·*.
harvests
   Ret. 79– 5   We glean spiritual *h·* from our
   My. 291–28   to pray, that the God of *h·*

hast
   Mis.   9– 9   "Thou *h·* no enemies."
haste
   Mis.   x–11   originally written in *h·*,
   '01. 30– 8   forbids headlong *h·*,
   '02.   2– 9   Truth makes *h·* to meet and to
   My. 16–27   shall not make *h·*.— *Isa.* 28 : 16.
hasten
   Mis. 84– 6   and thereby *h·* or permit it.
      109–22   *h·* through the second to the third
      117–31   then, *h·* to follow
   My. 21– 8   * *h·* the completion of The
hastened
   '02. 19– 3   he *h·* to console his unfaithful
hastens
   Ret. 18–25   This life is a shadow, and *h·* away.
   '02. 11–11   *h·* to help on his fellow-mortals,
   Po. 64–22   This life is a shadow, and *h·* away.
   My. 178– 7   it *h·* hourly to this end.
hastily
   Un.   6–25   if *h·* pushed to the front
hate (*see also* **hate's**)
all
   Un. 20–17   all *h·* and the sense of evil.
animality, and
   Pul. 13–12   mortal beliefs, animality, and *h·*,
annihilates
   Un. 39– 7   Love which annihilates *h·*,
appeared
   Mis. 214– 3   it appeared *h·* to the carnal mind,
envy, and
   Mis. 274–20   impulse to violence, envy, and *h·*,
   '01. 16– 9   its lusts, falsities, envy, and *h·*,
envy, or
   '02. 16–27   pride, self-will, envy, or *h·*.
error and
   Mis. 284–19   against human error and *h·*.
every
   Mis. 389–16   love more for every *h·*,
   Po.   4–15   love more for every *h·*,
filling with
   Mis. 254–23   filling with *h·* its deluded
god of
   '00.   3–27   a god of *h·* and of love,
heat of
   My. 249–12   the heat of *h·* burns the wheat,
human
   My. 257–20   all human *h·*, pride, greed,
individual
   My. 249– 7   raging element of individual *h·*
ingratitude and
   '01. 15–16   their ingratitude and *h·*,
is atheism
   My. 90–15   * teaches that *h·* is atheism,
jaws of
   Mis. 106–11   Into the jaws of *h·*,
jealousy and
   Mis. 250–13   become jealousy and *h·*.
love and
   '00.   4– 2   love and *h·*, good and evil,
Love, not
   My. 239– 2   Truth, not error ; Love, not *h·*.
master of
   Mis. 336– 1   Love is the master of *h·* ;
   My. 214–13   Love to be the master of *h·*.
no
   Mis. 122–27   Divine Love knows no *h·* ;
nothingness of
   No. 35–12   nothingness of *h·*, sin, and death,
or the hater
   Mis. 122–27   for *h·*, or the hater, is nothing :
purposes of
   My. 293–25   overrule the purposes of *h·*
tents of
   Pul. 84– 6   * dwell in the tents of *h·* ;
times of
   Mis. 277–27   Love is . . . near in times of *h·*,

   Mis. 40–28   *h·* that is holding the purpose to
      337–19   evil-speaking, lust, envy, *h·*.
      351–22   it is *h·* instead of Love ;
      356– 6   Envy, rivalry, *h·* need no
   Un. 56–27   ingratitude, lust, malice, *h·*,
   My. 180–17   C. S. meets . . . *h·* with Love,
      249–10   *H·* is a moral idiocy let loose
      252–14   wrong, injustice, envy, *h·* ;
hate (verb)
   Mis. 11–27   good to such as *h·* me,
       12– 2   *H·* no one ; for hatred is a
      32–29   slander, *h·*, or try to injure,
     147–12   manifest love for those that *h·* you
     223–28   * I should make him *h·* somebody."
     238– 3   to believe a lie, and to *h·* reformers.

hate (verb)

Mis. 241–12 Either he will *h·* you, and
269– 7 either he will *h·* the one, — *Matt.* 6 : 24.
278– 5 Error will *h·* more as it
311–18 I *h·* no one ; and love others
336–10 Then you would *h·* Jesus if you saw
Pul. 21– 6 even those that *h·* them.
'00. 13– 5 which I also *h·*."— *Rev.* 2 : 6.
'02. 17–18 to *h·* no man, to love one's enemies,
Hea. 2–20 why should the world *h·* Jesus,
4–14 to drop divinity long enough to *h·*.
My. 356–22 either he will *h·* the one, — *Matt.* 6 : 24.

hated

Mis. 1– 9 perfect Christianity, *h·* by sinners.
9–11 *h·* thee without a cause

hater (*see also* **hater's**)

Mis. 122–27 hate, or the *h·*, is nothing :

hater's

Mis. 122–21 lessens not the *h·* hatred
122–29 The *h·* pleasures are unreal ;

hate's

Po. 79–15 lifteth me, Ayont *h·* thrall :

hates

Mis. 104–30 I will love, if another *h·*.
141–12 *h·* the bonds and methods of Truth,
My. 41–20 * admires friends and *h·* enemies,

hatest

'00. 13– 4 "Thou *h·* the deeds of the— *Rev.* 2 : 6.

hating

Mis. 123– 5 either idolizing . . . or *h·* them :
267– 9 * When they report me as "*h·*
'02. 8– 7 mortals *h·*, or unloving,
My. 249– 9 *h·* even one's enemies
339– 1 charitable towards all, and *h·* none.

hatred

Mis. 10– 4 Whatever envy, *h·*, revenge
12– 2 *h·* is a plague-spot
19– 2 covetousness, lust, *h·*, malice,
114–20 passion, appetites, *h·*,
122–21 lessens not the hater's *h·*
153–15 encompassed not with pride, *h·*,
199–16 cost him the *h·* of the rabbis.
278– 2 fornication, envy, and *h·*
308– 6 by reason of human love or *h·*
324–15 emulation, *h·*, wrath,
336–13 *h·* of God's idea,
374–13 ignorance, envy, and *h·*
Pul. 15–19 human *h·* cannot reach you.
No. 43–27 while envy and *h·* bark and bite
'00. 10– 1 *H·* bites the heel of love
'01. 10– 9 *h·* gone mad becomes imbecile
'02. 8–25 Lust, *h·*, revenge, coincide in
17– 1 worldliness, *h·*, and lust,
My. 41–14 * lawlessness of *h·* he may practise
104– 9 they vented their *h·* of Jesus
213– 6 engenders envy and *h·*,

haunt

Man. 48–12 shall not *h·* Mrs. Eddy's drive

haunted

Mis. 87–29 *h·* by obsequious helpers,
343–26 fill the *h·* chambers of memory,

haunting

Un. 64–13 and the *h·* sense of evil
My. 192– 9 *h·* mystery and gloom

haunts

Ret. 91–26 and nature's *h·* were the
Pul. 82– 3 * into the cold *h·* of sin

have

Mis. vii–16 And nothing *h·* to pray :
vii–20 Wherefor, *h·* much to pay.
2– 3 who *h·* the least wisdom or
2– 5 they *h·* so little of their own.
4–24 is often said, "You must *h·*
5–11 but *h·* not sufficient faith
5–12 that I *h·* the power to heal."
6– 6 C. S. practitioners *h·* plenty to do,
8– 6 and *h·* our being,"— *Acts* 17 : 28.
10– 4 We *h·* no enemies.
10–28 the lesson, "I *h·* no enemies."
10–29 Even in belief you *h·* but one
10–31 belief that you *h·* enemies ;
11–30 I *h·* but two to present.
13–11 what thank *h·* ye? — *Luke* 6 : 32.
18– 9 *h·* no other gods — *Exod.* 20 : 3.
19–20 I should *h·* more faith in an
19–23 or would *h·* in a smooth-tongued
21– 3 *h·* no other gods — *Exod.* 20 : 3.
23–12 *h·* no other gods — *Exod.* 20 : 3.
28–20 *h·* no other gods — *Exod.* 20 : 3.
32–21 But I *h·* not moments enough
34–17 and *h·* them with us ;

have

Mis. 36– 6 *Do animals and beasts h· a mind?*
36–15 beasts that *h·* these propensities
42–19 we shall not *h·* to repeat it ;
44–13 *If I h· the toothache,*
47–26 must *h·* an ending.
47–30 I *h·* no knowledge of mesmerism,
49– 6 *h·* no doubt she could have been
50–25 live thereby, and *h·* being.
51– 2 will *h·* its effect physically as well
51– 9 We *h·* not the particulars of
52–29 Mortals *h·* the sum of being to
55–24 knows that he can *h·* one God **only,**
57– 3 what evidence *h·* you
57–21 or it would *h·* no seeming.
58– 2 *h· any more power over him?*
65– 3 We *h·* no more proof of
65– 4 than we *h·* that the earth's
65–19 I *h·* not ; and this important
69–11 let them *h·* dominion — *Gen.* 1 : 26.
72–16 shall not *h·* occasion — *Ezek.* 18 : 3.
72–20 *knoweth that ye h· need — Matt.* 6 : 32.
73–15 He knoweth that we *h·* need
73–18 We *h·* need of *these* things ;
73–19 *h·* need to know that the so-called
74–31 you may *h·* all that is left of it ;
79– 9 we live, move, and *h·* being.
82–30 and *h·* our being."— *Acts* 17 : 28.
86– 2 these *h·* no fleshly nature.
89–13 attendant and friends *h·* no faith
91–21 *Should not the teacher of C. S. h·*
96– 5 *h·* found Him so ; and would *h·* no **other**
99–22 and they *h·* not.
105–12 would *h·* no conflict with Life
106– 4 Scientists will, *must, h·* a history ;
108–30 they *h·* no intrinsic quality
113–25 We *h·* nothing to fear when Love
114–17 They must always *h·* on armor,
115–32 as you would *h·* them do to you,
118– 4 We shall *h·* no faith in evil
123– 4 *h·* no other gods — *Exod.* 20 : 3.
125– 8 *h·* dominion over his own sinful **sense**
126–24 Scientists *h·* a strong race to run,
126–31 *h·* them in derision." — *Psal.* 2 : 4.
131–24 I, for one, would be pleased to *h·*
131–26 to *h·* them let her state the value
136–19 you *h·* in my last revised edition
150– 3 you *h·* the great Shepherd
151–15 "Whom *h·* I in heaven — *Psal.* 73 : 25.
154–12 You *h·* already proof of the
154–29 *H·* no ambition, affection, nor
158–30 *h·* no record that he used notes
163–20 they *h·* not : they still live ;
170–16 "I *h·* bread to eat — *see John* 4 : 32.
174– 6 Let us *h·* a clearing up of
179– 8 *H·* we any other consciousness
179– 9 If we *h·*, He is saying to us
180–18 *h·* part in his resurrection.
182– 7 and these *h·* no other God,
183–27 will *h·* power to reflect His
184–17 saying, "I *h·* the power to sin
198– 2 will *h·* no desire to sin.
199– 2 we *h·* the right to deny the
208–11 Mortals *h·* only to submit to **the**
209–31 then shall mortals *h·* peace."
210– 9 reptiles because they *h·* stings?
215–24 they *h·* a long warfare with **error**
223– 6 necessarily *h·* pure fountains ;
225–30 * and you shall *h·* some gruel."
228– 9 to *h·* a name whose odor fills **the**
229– 1 that any one is liable to *h·* them
229– 3 prepares one to *h·* any disease
230–18 when they *h·* nothing to say,
235–19 we shall *h·* it,
236–12 you *h·* the rights of conscience,
236–13 as we all *h·*,
239–27 something that she ought not to *h·*,
240–22 *h·* slight sway over the fresh,
241–11 says, "You *h·* no pleasure in sin,"
243– 1 she would *h·* delirium
244– 3 we *h·* the Professor on the
244–24 "And other sheep I *h·*, — *John* 10 : 16.
245– 1 We *h·* no record showing that
245– 2 but we *h·* his words,
245–18 that women *h·* no rights
246–28 we *h·* a spiritual Christianity
249–23 I *h·* proof, but no fear.
262–11 to those who *h·* hearts.
262–27 you *h·* little need of words **of**
263– 2 I shall *h·* the unselfish joy **of**
265– 9 All must *h·* one Principle
265–10 *h·* but one opinion of it.
269–12 *h·* a perpetual freshness
270–18 *h·* full faith in his prophecy,
272–20 *h·* simply an incorporated **grant,**
274– 2 *h·* no Biblical authority for

have

Mis.	276–17	The wise will *h·* their lamps
	276–24	*h·* their lamps trimmed
	285–29	will *h·* no past, present, or
	298–13	*h·* special application to
	299–27	What right *h·* I to do this?
	301– 6	would *h·* others do unto you
	303– 6	should *h·* their own institutes
	305–15	* shall *h·* a part in it.
	307– 4	will *h·* all you need
	307– 8	more we cannot *h·*.
	315–14	*h·* promising proclivities toward
	317– 9	would *h·* great pleasure in
	321–27	I *h·* no desire to see or to
	321–29	I *h·* a world of wisdom and Love
	325– 7	They *h·* small conceptions
	325–10	they *h·* plenty of pelf,
	331–10	goodness will *h·* its springtide of
	334–10	may *h·* the effect of power ;
	335–25	*h·* me get out of a burning
	335–27	I would *h·* you already out,
	341– 2	human race *h·* one God,
	343– 4	all that we *h·* to sacrifice,
	347– 5	*h·* to escape from their houses
	348–18	I *h·* to repeat this,
	348–27	drugs *h·* no beneficial effect
	349– 6	I *h·* students with the degree of
	359–20	from experience ; so *h·* we.
	367– 2	*h·* no place in C. S.
	391–16	*H·* many items more ;
Man.	16–11	as we would *h·* them do
	57–14	must *h·* the consent of this Board
	63–15	shall *h·* a Reading Room,
	63–24	shall *h·* no bad habits,
	70–14	shall *h·* its own form of
	74–12	shall not *h·* their offices or rooms in
	76– 9	to *h·* the books of the Church
	76–26	*h·* the books of the C. S.
	80–13	*h·* the power to declare vacancies
	83–10	such only as *h·* good past records
	84–11	shall *h·* one class triennially,
	85–11	Teachers must *h·* Certificates.
	87–14	must *h·* the necessary moral and
	94–12	should *h·* the opportunity to
Chr.	55–18	such as I *h·* give I thee :— *Acts* 3 : 6.
Ret.	20–26	he should *h·* a home with me.
	23– 8	seemed to *h·* a silver lining ;
	28–11	in order to *h·* the least
	33–12	the less material medicine we *h·*,
	37–24	may *h·* an interest for the reader,
	52– 6	*h·* a small portion of its letter
	59– 4	*h·* no contradictory significations.
	61–16	and *h·* no right to exist,
	61–26	Posterity will *h·* the right to
	65–11	*h·* no warrant in the gospel or
	69–12	shall seem to *h·* life as much as
	93–18	and *h·* our being.''— *Acts* 17 : 28.
Un.	3–24	He can *h·* no consciousness of
	4–18	bids man *h·* the same Mind
	8– 7	can *h·* no other reality than
	9–23	So they *h·*, but in a far different
	16– 4	if God has, or can *h·*,
	18–15	troubles that you *h·* not.
	28–14	hypotheses . . . *h·* less basis ;
	33– 7	we *h·* it on divine authority :
	34–23	so-called mind would *h·* no identity.
	41–13	*h·* part in this resurrection
	42– 7	can *h·* no real existence,
	43–19	*h·* more faith in living than in
	48– 7	I *h·* no faith in any other
	50–19	less consciousness of . . . mortals *h·*,
	53–19	would *h·* one quotient.
Pul.	vii– 6	*h·* not only a record of
	2–23	and *h·* our being''— *Acts* 17 : 28.
	3–22	*h·* their source in God,
	4– 9	*h·* simply to preserve a scientific,
	9–23	*h·* a bounty hidden from the world.
	22– 3	*h·* one bond of unity,
	35–15	in order to *h·* the least
	50– 4	* he deserves to *h·* a home
	51–13	* others who *h·* different methods,
	52– 4	* Christian Scientists *h·* a faith of
	52– 5	* *h·* not a faith approximate to that
	62– 6	* They *h·* the advantage of
	62–16	* They *h·* all the beauties of a
	65– 8	* and may *h·* a future before it.
	67–20	* *h·* strong churches,
	80–10	* *h·* the largest individuality,
	80–17	* we *h·* no opinion to pronounce,
	81–19	* of those who *h·* so much to give
	84–19	* *h·* some measure of understanding
	87–20	*h·* more of earth now, than I desire
Rud.	10– 2	Note this, that if you *h·* power in
	15–16	should *h·* separate departments,
No.	2–21	*h·* large practices and some
	10–22	earth's discords *h·* not the reality of

have

No.	13–26	parts of it *h·* no lustre.
	15–10	*h·* the civil and religious arms
	15–22	matter and mortal mind *h·* neither
	16–20	can *h·* no knowledge or inference but
	17– 7	and *h·* our being ;''— *Acts* 17 : 28.
	23–15	Scriptures *h·* both a literal and a
	23–22	Deity can *h·* no such warfare
	29– 7	mind-quacks *h·* so slight a
	30– 7	sickness and sin *h·* no relapse.
	35– 5	what hope *h·* mortals but
	39–23	what we already *h·* and are ;
	42– 6	not compelled to *h·* other gods
	42–26	* and to *h·* eat beefsteak
	45–24	Let the Word *h·* free course
	46– 3	Shall we *h·* a practical,
	46– 5	or shall we *h·* material medicine
Pan.	4–26	what need *h·* we of drugs,
	9–10	*h·* no other gods — *Exod.* 20 : 3.
	9–25	what reward *h·* ye?''— *Matt.* 5 : 46.
	13–20	and *h·* our being''— *Acts* 17 : 28.
	13–22	*h·* ''one God and — *Eph.* 4 : 6.
	14–27	Great occasion *h·* we to rejoice
'00.	5–15	whereby to *h·* one God,
	5–20	*h·* no other gods — *Exod.* 20 : 3.
	9–26	to *h·* some one take my place
	11– 3	*h·* no discord over music.
	11–10	we *h·* the promise that
	12–18	*h·* somewhat against thee, — *Rev.* 2 : 4.
	15–19	May you *h·* on a wedding garment
'01.	3– 8	said the Christian Scientists *h·* no
	4– 2	both *h·* the nature of God.
	6– 3	*h·* no separate identity
	8–11	we *h·* the authority of Jesus for
	9–20	what *h·* we to do — *Mark* 1 : 24.
	12–14	yet should not *h·* charity, or
	13–12	Sin can *h·* neither entity, verity,
	15–25	* to *h·* you in His sight.
	20– 2	*h·* no moral right and no
	21– 2	they *h·* Science, understanding, and
	25– 3	we *h·* a superstructure eternal in
	26– 7	personal senses can *h·* only a
	26–22	and *h·* not charity, — *I Cor.* 13 : 1.
	30–15	*h·* no craft that is in danger.
	34–12	or must we *h·* a new Bible
'02.	4–19	*h·* no other gods — *Exod.* 20 : 3.
	5–29	*h·* no other gods — *Exod.* 20 : 3.
	6– 2	to *h·* aught unlike the infinite.
	6–19	*h·* no other gods — *Exod.* 20 : 3.
	7–16	we *h·* Scriptural authority for
	8–17	We *h·* no evidence of
	9– 9	we shall *h·* better practitioners,
	12–20	and *h·* our being.''— *Acts* 17 : 28.
	18–23	we shall *h·* more effective healers
	19–23	''Ye *h·* need of — *Matt.* 6 : 32.
Hea.	4–18	become finite, and *h·* an end ;
	4–24	God must be our model, or we *h·* none ;
	5–15	although we *h·* no evidence of
	6–10	abused me . . . and *h·* ever since ;
	9– 2	We should *h·* no anxiety about
	15–25	that you *h·* little or no faith
	16–18	only evidence we *h·* of sin,
Peo.	2–27	*h·* a benign and elevating influence
	12– 2	Let them *h·* ''dominion — *Gen.* 1 : 26.
	13– 1	*h·* a more material deity,
	13– 4	*h·* a lower order of Christianity
Po.	38– 9	*H·* many items more ;
My.	3– 8	*h·* right to the tree of — *Rev.* 22 : 14.
	5–13	*h·* no other gods — *Exod.* 20 : 3.
	8– 9	* ''As we *h·* the best church
	8–10	* *h·* the best expression of the
	8–11	* let us *h·* the best material symbol
	8–20	* should *h·* a seating capacity of
	14–13	* claimed to *h·* good authority for
	16–14	* *h·* the work directly in charge,
	23–27	* we *h·* the privilege of
	32– 9	* did not *h·* to lift their voices
	40– 3	* to *h·* her church able to give
	41– 9	* because they *h·* thoughts adverse to
	43– 5	* that they might *h·* a definite rule
	51–17	* to *h·* our pastor remain
	57– 5	* *h·* the sacred atmosphere of a
	57–31	* Christian Scientists *h·* a faith
	58– 1	* *h·* not a faith approximate to
	60–15	* I *h·* yet the little Bible
	61–19	* never more did I *h·* any doubt.
	64–13	*h·* no other gods — *Exod.* 20 : 3.
	66–14	* necessary to *h·* this property.
	72–14	* chapter sub-title
	72–15	* do not send . . . money — we *h·* enough !''
	82– 1	* they all *h·* the same stories
	83– 2	* the custom Christian Scientists *h·*
	83–14	* will doubtless *h·* fewer questions
	83–16	* *h·* time to rest and sleep,
	87–14	* people we . . . like to *h·* here.
	87–16	* they *h·* their costly church

have

My.	93– 4	* *h·* little of the spirit of bigotry.
	97–12	* *h·* a little the advantage
	106– 9	*h·* not power over and above
	107– 5	you *h·* the correct answer.
	107–11	*h·* not an iota of the drug
	107–12	lower attenuations *h·* so little
	109– 7	we shall *h·* one Mind,
	109–23	and *h·* our being." — *Acts* 17 : 28.
	111– 8	as we *h·* in our time.
	113–21	*h·* a clear perception of it.
	114– 6	as ye would *h·* others do to you.
	115– 5	blush to write . . . as I *h·*, were it
	116–11	Thou shalt *h·* one God.
	123–10	we *h·* a modest hall
	123–27	Seeing that we *h·* to attain to
	126–31	We *h·* it only as we live it.
	130–13	I *h·* neither the time nor the
	130–21	must *h·* the author's name added
	132– 6	ye shall *h·* tribulation ; — *John* 16 : 33.
	133–22	I *h·* a secret to tell you
	136–27	that I may *h·* more peace,
	137–18	to *h·* my property and affairs
	142– 2	we *h·* the mind of Christ.' — *I Cor.* 2 : 16.
	143–12	those with whom I *h·* appointments.
	147–30	You *h·* less need of me
	147–31	less need of me than *h·* they,
	148– 6	May the good folk of Concord *h·*
	149–19	to *h·* a clear perception of divine justice,
	153–17	*h·* no other gods — *Exod.* 20 : 3.
	154–20	* If the poor toil that we *h·* food,
	154–22	* that we *h·* light, freedom,
	155– 8	May this church *h·* one God,
	166– 7	so long as we *h·* the right ideal,
	171– 2	*and h· no other trusts.*
	174–17	I *h·* the pleasure of thanking
	175–28	purporting to *h·* my signature,
	182– 2	it is said to *h·* a majority
	183– 8	* will the world *h·* rest."
	190–24	should *h·* the same opportunity
	195–17	the one talent that we all *h·*,
	203– 3	I *h·* nothing new to communicate ;
	211–11	what *h·* we to do with — *Mark* 1 : 24.
	215–31	we *h·* no hint of his changing
	219– 6	*h·* all the honor of their success
	221–18	*h·* no other gods — *Exod.* 20 : 3.
	221–27	shall we *h·* no faith in God,
	223–12	with whom I *h·* no acquaintance
	223–12	of whom I *h·* no knowledge,
	223–14	because I *h·* not sufficient time
	229– 4	I *h·* no use for such,
	236– 1	*h·* no more of echoing dreams.
	240–29	* *h·* the necessary moral and spiritual
	241–11	* We are glad to *h·* the privilege of
	242– 9	*h·* no Principle to demonstrate
	244–24	What I *h·* to say may not require
	249–22	The report that I prefer to *h·* a
	250–29	*h·* beyond it duties and
	252–2, 3	*H·* one God and you will *h·* no devil.
	253–24	you *h·* His rich blessing already
	254–17	May we *h·* permission to print,
	255– 5	C. S. churches *h·* my consent to
	257–28	Scientists *h·* their record in the
	269–21	beams of right *h·* healing in their
	276–23	politics?'' I *h·* none, in reality,
	278– 9	*h·* no other gods — *Exod.* 20 : 3.
	278–10	Let us *h·* the molecule of faith
	278–24	Governments *h·* no right to
	279–12	*h·* no other gods — *Exod.* 20 : 3.
	286– 6	*h·* one God, one Mind ;
	293–32	and ye shall *h·* them.'' — *Mark* 11 : 24.
	295–26	*h·* cause to lament the demise of
	298–10	*h·* my permission to publish
	299– 6	* *h·* any truth to reveal
	303– 7	Scientists *h·* no quarrel with
	303–26	I *h·* not the inspiration nor
	311– 9	* I shall *h·* to leave ;
	311–24	I *h·* another coat-of-arms,
	319–20	* I *h·* this information.
	323– 7	* I *h·* his little book yet.
	324–13	* to *h·* those very terms
	336– 4	* was afraid to *h·* her brother,
	339–21	*h·* no cause to mourn ;
	339–22	only those who *h·* not the Christ,
	340– 1	*h·* no record of his observing
	341– 1	I *h·* one innate joy,
	351–27	Science is all they need, or can *h·*
	353–26	spiritual *h·* all place and power.
	358–13	I *h·* not the time to do so.
	364– 8	*h·* no other gods — *Exod.* 20 : 3.
		(*see also* **faith**)

haven

Mis.	152–26	Into His *h·* of Soul
	316–18	turn them slowly toward the *h·*.
Ret.	57 –2	we sail into the eternal *h·*

haven

'02.	20– 4	bringeth us into the desired *h·*,
My.	163– 2	to seek the *h·* of hope,

having

Mis.	28– 3	*h·* no sensation of its own.
	45–27	*h·* "other gods before me." — *Exod.* 20 : 3.
	50–29	changed to *h·* but *one* God
	51–20	without your *h·* to resort to
	58–13	"*H·* eyes, see ye not?" — *Mark* 8 : 18.
	59– 1	*H·* no true sense of the
	99– 4	" *H·* eyes ye see not, — *see Mark* 8 : 18.
	125–15	whom, not *h·* seen, we love.
	132–19	*h·* charge of a church,
	168– 7	those who, *h·* ears, hear not,
	170–28	as *h·* any power to see.
	170–29	*H·* eyes, ye see not ;
	174– 4	idolatry, *h·* other gods ;
	174– 4	evil, *h·* presence and power over
	185–22	*h·* no need of statistics
	189–28	as one *h·* authority, — *Matt.* 7 : 29.
	195– 9	*h·* these, every one can prove,
	197–30	omnipotent, *h·* all-power ;
	209–21	for *h·* "other gods — *Exod.* 20 : 3.
	223–13	*h·* the power to heal."
	232–19	will be one *h·* more power,
	232–19	*h·* perfected in Science
	233–27	*h·* a true standard,
	241– 8	one *h·* morals to be healed,
	241– 8	the other *h·* a physical ailment.
	242– 2	*h·* the above caption,
	250–19	*h·* no ring of the true metal.
	262–26	*H·* his word, you have
	285–29	but, *h·* no Truth, it will
	298–11	by *h·* my best friend break troth
	323– 4	*h·* no temple therein,
	327–16	*h·* less baggage, ascend faster
	331–24	filling all space and *h·* all power,
	335–14	as they say, *h·* too much charity ;
	399–22	we depart, *H·* one.
Man.	50–15	be found *h·* the name without
	63–17	may unite in *h·* Reading Rooms,
	91–21	not *h·* the certificate of C.S.D.
	98– 5	for the purpose of *h·* him reply to it.
Chr.	55–20	*h·* neither beginning of — *Heb.* 7 : 3.
Ret.	58–11	as one *h·* authority, — *Matt.* 7 : 29.
Un.	26– 2	*h·* its own innate selfhood
	33– 3	(matter really *h·* no sense)
	42–19	as one *h·* authority, — *Matt.* 7 : 29.
Pul.	12–14	*h·* great wrath, — *Rev.* 12 : 12.
	16– 7	we depart *H·* one.
	23–13	* each *h·* the common identity of
	54–26	* and *h·* thus the most perfect
	60–21	* *h·* an Æolian attachment.
	71–23	* *h·* a divine mission to fulfil,
No.	38–19	*H·* one God, one Mind,
	44– 6	*h·* its best interpretation in
'02.	8–27	*h·* the kingdom of heaven within
	11–10	abuse of him, *h·* a new idea
Hea.	4–26	Or, *h·* faith in it,
	16– 3	*h·* ears, hear and understand.
Peo.	9–11	*H·* one Lord, we shall not
	12–23	*H·* faith in drugs and hygienic
	14–19	*h·* "one Lord, one faith, — *Eph.* 4 : 5.
Po.	76– 6	we depart, *H·* one.
My.	5–10	man *h·* all that God gives.
	12– 6	* those *h·* the work in charge
	53–30	* by *h·* so many different ones
	68– 8	* *h·* a diameter of eighty-two feet
	155– 6	*h·* unfaltering faith in the
	155–18	*h·* a pure peace, a fresh joy,
	156– 7	*h·* all sufficiency — *II Cor.* 9 : 8.
	158–16	*H·* all faith in C. S.,
	163– 9	Not *h·* the time to receive all
	179–29	We are indeed privileged in *h·* the
	215– 9	*h·* charity scholars,
	227–11	*h·* the same disease
	325–10	* as *h·* a greater future

Hawaii

My.	30–16	* from South Africa, from *H·*,

Hawaiian Islands

'00.	1–18	Philippine Islands, *H· I·* ;

hawk

Mis.	145–15	pride is a hooded *h·*

Hawthorne Hall

Mis.	168–27	* *H· H·* was densely packed,

Hawthorne Rooms

My.	53–12	* *H· R·*, at No. 3 Park Street,
	53–19	* as a church in the *H· R·*,
	54– 1	* *H· R·* were inadequate
	54– 7	* *H· R·*, which were crowded
	54–15	* At this time the *H· R·*,
	54–21	* *H· R·* were again secured.
	54–24	* besieged the doors at the *H· R·*,

hazard

Mis. 89–16   h· of casting "pearls — Matt. 7 : 6.

hazards

Ret. 72– 2   that h· another's happiness,

haziness

My. 211–30   mental h· which admits of no

He

Mis. 10– 9   Because H· has called His own,
18– 4   H· chasteneth, — Heb. 12 : 6.
18– 5   whom H· receiveth ;" — Heb. 12 : 6.
18–32   those whom H· commissions
19– 6   carrying out what H· teaches them,
25–28   if H· could create them otherwise,
25–29   and if H· created drugs for healing
26–11   while the Scripture declares H· made
57– 2   which H· had made.
58–24   if H· does govern it, the action is
60– 2   H· sent His Son to save from sin,
63–20   "that the Lord H· is God ; — Deut. 4 : 35.
73– 5   H· chasteneth ;" — Heb. 12 : 6.
73– 5   "H· doth not afflict — Lam. 3 : 33.
73–15   H· knoweth that we have need of
77–15   Love that H· hath bestowed upon us,
78–26   If God is the Principle . . . (and H· is),
81– 8   decide, as surely H· will,
97–23   "H· created man in the
97–24   created H· him."
102–12   H· is universal and primitive.
103–29   H· was too mighty for that.
103–29   H· was eternal Life,
111–13   had H· filled the net, it would not
114–28   H· will deliver us from temptation
117–28   H· illumines one's way when one is
122–28   and H· made all that was made.
125– 4   H· chasteneth." — Heb. 12 : 6.
126–30   "H· that sitteth in the — Psal. 2 : 4.
127– 2   H· has blessed her.
133–26   confidence that H· will reward
134–14   H· who dwelleth in eternal light
142– 1   how hath H· enlarged her borders !
142– 2   H· made her wildernesses to bud and
150– 2   May H· soon give you a pastor ;
150–21   If H· be with us,
150–31   H· guards, guides, feeds,
151– 6   H· separates the dross
151– 8   Those who bear fruit H· purgeth,
151–10   H· speaketh to the unfruitful
151–11   H· saith of the barren fig-tree,
151–14   H· is man's only real relative
152–25   H· will hide you in His feathers
154– 7   H· will dig about this little church,
157– 5   H· that marketh the sparrow's fall
157–15   H· helps us most when
157–16   H· is the ever-present help.
157–23   H· shall bring it to pass. — Psal. 37 : 5.
157–23   And H· shall bring forth — Psal. 37 : 6.
173–27   H· made man in His own likeness.
179– 6   to know where H· is laid.
179–10   H· is saying to us to-day,
179–25   H· made every flower in Mind
186–14   H· is the universal Father and Mother
208– 6   H· is cognizant only of good.
208–19   H· chasteneth." — Heb. 12 : 6.
247–29   that God created, H· pronounced good.
247–30   H· never made sickness.
258–15   H· governs the universe.
263– 7   "H· shall cover thee with — Psal. 91 : 4.
269– 1   H· shall bring it to pass." — Psal. 37 : 5.
287– 4   "It is H· that hath — Psal. 100 : 3.
306–29   "H· shall give His angels — Psal. 91 : 11.
322–22   H· hath given you C. S.,
322–23   H· hath shown you the amplitude of
334– 1   "H· doeth according to — Dan. 4 : 35.
347–25   those whom H· has anointed.
347–27   from the night H· leads to light.
353–20   tending the action that H· adjusts.
361–28   H· elucidates His own idea,
362–13   all that H· made was good.
364– 6   H· will renew your strength." — see Isa. 40 : 31.
364–18   H· made all that was made,
366–11   the Lord H· is God, — Deut. 4 : 35.
366–12   And because H· is All-in-all,
366–13   H· is in nothing unlike Himself ;
367–15   to claim that H· is ignorant of
367–18   H· knows nothing but good ;
367–18   if H· did know aught else,
367–19   H· would not be infinite.
367–23   H· dwelleth in light ;
367–24   and in the light H· sees light,
367–31   H· knoweth that which is,
376–30   H· who fashions forever such forms

Man. 45– 1   H· supplies within the wide channels
Chr. 53–11   The Way in Science H· appoints,
Ret. 22–17   H· alone is our origin, aim, and being.
25–20   conception of God to be that H· was

He

Ret. 28– 4   H· must be ours practically,
60–22   something besides Him, which H·
73– 4   H· is without materiality,
80– 5   H· chasteneth, — Heb. 12 : 6.
80– 6   whom H· receiveth. — Heb. 12 : 6.
80–10   * with patience H· stands waiting,
80–11   * With exactness grinds H· all.
90–30   H· appoints and H· anoints His
Un. 2– 4   H· is "a very present help — Psal. 46 : 1.
3–20   Hence H· is in Himself only,
3–22   H· is all the Life and Mind there is
3–24   If H· is All, H· can have no
3–25   because, if H· is omnipresent,
3–27   H· pities us.
3–28   H· has mercy upon us,
4– 1   H· is near to them who adore
4–25   Jesus Christ, whom H· has sent.
7– 2   as already H· is glorified
10–17   They live, because H· lives ;
10–18   H· is perfect, and governs them
10–25   H· is not the blind force of a
13–16   H· is, in the very fibre of
13–19   it follows that H· knows
13–19   something which H· must
14– 7   held, . . . H· should so gain wisdom
14– 8   that H· could vastly improve upon
14–13   that H· might rectify
17–20   because H· knows all things ;
18– 1   if H· knows evil
18– 7   if H· knows and sees it not ;
19– 4   else H· is not omnipotent,
19– 5   H· foresees events which
19– 6   yet which H· cannot avert.
19– 7   H· must have had foreknowledge
19– 8   and if H· foreknew it,
19– 8   H· must virtually have intended it,
20–13   Second : H· knows it not.
20–21   and believe that H· can see
23–21   And how can H· create anything so
26–10   Neither is H· the author of
30–11   "H· restoreth my soul," — Psal. 23 : 3.
38–15   by declaring that not H· alone is
38–22   or to deny that H· is Life eternal.
39–11   H· loves them from whom divine Science
47– 7   H· sustains my individuality.
48– 8   H· is my individuality
48– 9   Because H· lives, I live.
48– 9   H· heals all my ills,
48–12   H· is best understood as Supreme
48–14   Father and Mother of all H· creates ;
49–26   but which H· straightway commands
53– 4   the lie must say H· made them,
60–19   and H· will be unto them
60–21   H· is neither absent from Himself nor
Pul. 10– 6   H· "who forgiveth all — Psal. 103 : 3.
Rud. 9–26   H· is All, and that there can be
10– 6   H· is too pure to behold iniquity,
10–20   H· afflicteth not willingly the
13–14   "The Lord, H· is God ; — Deut. 4 : 35.
No. 8–14   remainder thereof H· will restrain.
15–25   H· is Spirit ;
15–25   in nothing is H· unlike Himself.
16– 2   what H· knows must truly and
16– 3   If H· knows matter,
16– 4   H· is Mind ;
16– 5   whatever H· knows is made manifest,
16–20   H· who is All, understands all.
16–20   H· can have no knowledge . . . but
17– 3   H· must produce its consequences.
19–11   H· is neither a limited mind nor
23–26   H· is definite and individual,
24– 4   H· is in all things,
24– 4   and therefore H· is in
24– 5   H· is extension, of whatever character.
24–28   and H· is all good,
26–26   shall H· not much more — Matt. 6 : 30.
30– 9   need not know the evil H·
30–16   H· could not destroy our . . . if
30–17   if H· possessed any knowledge of them.
37– 9   H· cannot know beginning or end.
37–28   H· also predestinates ;
38– 7   H· is good, and good is Spirit ;
39–11   H· has rewarded them openly.
39–19   the love wherewith H· loves us.
43– 8   * "Only H· who knows all things
Pan. 4–15   H· is the creator of man,
'01. 4–19   H· is the infinite Person,
4–25   One because H· is infinite ;
4–25   because H· is Life, Truth, Love,
6–10   Is H· one Person, or three
6–13   except H· be a Person,
6–15   God must be One although H· is three.
6–16   because H· is not after this model
6–23   H· can neither be one nor
6–30   In divine Science H· is

He

'01.
7– 8   H· is the all-wise, all-knowing,
7–17   as the Scriptures declare H· will
7–25   H· cannot be apprehended through the
8–17   Is God Spirit? H· is.
15–25 * H· is of purer eyes than to
18–29 remember it is H· who does it
19– 4 and that H· worketh with them
21–25 for did H· not know all things
31–27 and yielded up graciously what H·
35– 1 H· shall direct thy paths;"— Prov. 3 : 6.
35– 2 H· shall bring forth thy — Psal. 37 : 6.
'02.
17– 4 knew that obedience is the test
Hea.
4–11   H· knows deserves to be punished,
5– 4   saying H· is beaten by certain kinds of
9–24   H· never made sin or sickness,
15–20 something H· cannot reach,
19–14 H· made "every plant — Gen. 2 : 5.
Peo.
6–17   H· is found altogether lovely.
12–25 As if Deity would not if H· could,
12–26 or could not if H· would,
Po.
18–13 H· penciled his path
My.
17–30 H· has blessed her.
34–12 h· is the King of glory.— Psal. 24 : 10.
37–21 * recognize that H· has made known
45–24 * "H· took not away the— Exod. 13 : 22.
132–15 begat H· us with the— Jas. 1 : 18.
153– 9 H· that is holy."— Rev. 3 : 7.
156– 5 that H· is able"— II Tim. 1 : 12.
158–25 H· has laid the chief corner-stone
161–26 "H· shall direct thy paths."— Prov. 3 : 6.
162–27 May H· increase its members,
170–22 H· shall give thee— Psal. 37 : 4.
170–24 H· shall bring it to pass.— Psal. 37 : 5.
170–24 H· shall bring forth— Psal. 37 : 6.
178–17 impossible . . . for H· made all
186–13 Rest assured that H· in whom
188–18 H· surely will not shut me out
203–20 H· will if it is ready
204– 2 the fact that H· is infinite
204– 3 H· gives His followers opportunity
205–11 * H· plants His footsteps in the sea
207– 5 remainder thereof H· will restrain.
215– 5 H· it was that bade me
220–19 H· who is overturning will overturn
220–20 H· whose right it is shall reign.
225–19 names of that which H· creates.
235–16 Did God make all . . . H· did.
235–17 Is God Spirit? H· is.
267–10 H· is supreme, infinite,
269–17 H· is separating the tares from
280–19 H· will bless all the inhabitants
280–21 H· must bless all with His
288–11 H· is the Father of all.
341– 4 thank God that H· has emblazoned
355–20 * H· hides a shining face."
356– 7 * "H· plants His footsteps in the sea
357– 1 H· is the only basis of Science ;
360–22 H· has proved it to me
361– 3 H· will direct you into the paths of

head

aching
Mis. 275– 9 bendeth his aching h· ;
and heart
Mis. 160– 9 sweet rhythm of h· and heart,
268–19 heals body and mind, h· and heart ;
at the
Ret. 70–28 virtually stands at the h· of all
'00. 12–13 At the h· of the harbor
her
Pul. 83–29 * upon her h· a crown— Rev. 12 : 1.
his
Mis. 224– 9 lifted his hands to his h·, saying :
Pan. 6– 8 but lifteth his h· above it
hoary
Mis. 231– 1 Age, on whose hoary h·
389– 2 The hoary h· with joy to crown ;
Po. 21–16 The hoary h· with joy to crown ;
hydra
Mis. 246–16 inhumanity lifts its hydra h·
its.
Mis. 336– 5 handle the serpent and bruise its h· ;
'00. 10– 2 that is treading on its h·
man's
My. 188–24 one man's h· lies at another's feet.
my
Mis. 395–19 May rest above my h·.
Po. 58– 4 May rest above my h·.
My. 61–18 * I bowed my h· before the might of
343–18 a shower of abuse upon my h·,
o'erburdened
Mis. 339–22 hast bowed the o'erburdened h·
of his statue
Mis. 224– 8 broken the h· of his statue
of Jesus
Pul. 27–21 * Mary anointing the h· of Jesus,

head

of the church
My. 108–29 the h· of the church :— Eph. 5 : 23.
of the corner
Man. 18– 2 h· of the corner."— Matt. 21 : 42.
Pul. 10–20 h· of the corner."— Matt. 21 : 42.
No. 38–14 h· of the corner."— Matt. 21 : 42.
'00. 5–25 it will become the h· of the corner,
'01. 25– 7 the crown and the h· of the corner.
'02. 2–15 stone at the h· of the corner ;
Hea. 3– 9 again become the h· of the corner.
My. 48– 7 * h· of the corner"— Matt. 21 : 42.
188– 2 made the h· of the corner.
of the gavel
My. 172– 1 * wood of the h· of the gavel
of the serpent
Mis. 210–17 her foot on the h· of the serpent,
of this serpent
Un. 45– 3 Bruise the h· of this serpent,
of this sketch
Pul. 61–18 * stands at the h· of this sketch.
pillow thy
Po. 27–23 Pillow thy h· on time's
plays round the
Po. 2– 5 * "Plays round the h·, but comes not
whole
My. 132–30 body, whose whole h· is sick
willow's
Po. 67–12 winds bow the tall willow's h· !
your
Mis. 355–18 to lift your h· above it,

Mis. 196–24 h· stone of the corner," — Psal. 118 : 22.
(see also Eddy)

headed
Pul. 80– 5 * the revolt was h· by them ;
My. 75–10 * most of them h· straight for

heading
Mis. 132–13 March 18, under the h·,
My. 359–18 appeared under the h·

headless
Mis. 274–25 h· trunks, and quivering hearts

headlines
My. 79–16 * heralded in flaming h·

headlong
Mis. 254–25 laurels of h· human will.
266–13 dashing through space, h· and alone.
327–30 plunge h· over the jagged rocks.
'01. 30– 7 The magnitude . . . forbids h· haste,

headquarters
Mis. 156– 8 All is well at h·,
Pul. 46– 5 at C. S. h· this is denied ;
79–15 * they are held at "h·."
My. 73–18 * The h· was thrown open
75– 7 * a busy day at the h·
173–19 at the denominational h·?

heads
Mis. 240–29 "Battle-Axe Plug" takes off men's h· ;
271– 7 keep out of their h· the notion
Pul. 13–18 not struggling to lift their h·
My. 34–10 Lift up your h·, — Psal. 24 : 9.
59–14 * across that sea of h·,
77–18 * Over the h· of a multitude which
171– 5 joy upon their h· : — Isa. 35 : 10.

heal
Mis.
4–25   said, . . . strong will-power to h·,"
17–14 the power of God to h·
33–15 not proved impossible to h·
38– 4 to h· and elevate man
38–19 h· the sick,
39–26 by which God reaches others to h·
43– 3 enables one to h· cases
44– 9 It cannot fail to h·
45– 6 is able to do more than to h· a
50–17 in order to h·.
51–29 prayer and drugs necessary to h·?
52– 9 to h·, through divine Science,
54–27 they do not h· on the same basis
55–12 to harm rather than to h·,
62–15 mind-cure claims to h· without it?
137–28 h· and teach with increased
151–26 then will you h·, and teach,
163– 4 preparing to h· and teach
193–29 power of Christianity to h·;
194– 9 Christ's command to h· in all ages,
215– 4 saying, "I wound to h·";
220– 5 another would h· mentally.
225–18 * "If you h· my son,
229–22 faith in the power of God to h·
241–27 easier to h· the physical than the
241–28 When divine Truth and Love h·,
241–30 how much more should these h·,
242–20 if he will h· one single case of
260– 5 and found able to h· them.

heal

Mis.	311–26	even as a surgeon who wounds to *h·*.
	333–26	could *h·* and bless ;
	355–26	"Physician, *h·* thyself." — *Luke* 4 : 23.
	380–18	Although *I* could *h·* mentally,
	398–17	Feed the hungry, *h·* the heart,
Man.	47– 5	a patient whom he does not *h·*,
Ret.	46–23	Feed the hungry, *h·* the heart,
	57– 7	in order to *h·* his body.
	60–23	cannot, or does not, *h·*."
	63–11	in order to *h·* them.
	63–21	more difficult to *h·*.
Un.	7–12	*h·* a cancer which had eaten its way
Pul.	17–22	Feed the hungry, *h·* the heart,
Rud.	3– 3	endeavors to *h·* them of bodily ills,
	8–13	*H·* through Truth and Love ;
	8–23	may say the unchristian . . . can *h·* ;
	9–13	To *h·*, in C. S., is to
	17– 7	and its divine efficacy to *h·*.
No.	2– 7	but that you can *h·* it,
	2–24	destroys one's ability to *h·*
	3–15	their patients, whom it will *h·*,
	6–15	trying to *h·* on a material basis.
	15– 1	the sick and sinner, to *h·* them,
	39– 4	potent prayer to *h·* and save.
	40–19	forfeit their ability to *h·* in Science.
	42– 5	not unable or unwilling to *h·*,
	43–28	A man's inability to *h·*,
	44– 7	power of Christianity to *h·*.
Pan.	10–18	Scientists *h·* functional, organic,
	10–19	that M.D.'s have failed to *h·* ;
'01.	12–16	Christ's command to *h·* in all ages,
	19– 7	power of God to *h·* and to save.
	33–20	in order to *h·* them.
'02.	8–11	No person can *h·* . . . unless
Hea.	3– 2	wherewith to *h·* both mind and body ;
	7–15	It begins in mind to *h·* the body,
	15– 5	to *h·* all ills that flesh is heir to.
	15–18	You pray for God to *h·* you,
Peo.	12–15	what a power mind is to *h·*
	14–18	power of divine Life and Love to *h·*
Po.	14–21	Feed the hungry, *h·* the heart,
	22–15	To *h·* humanity's sore heart ;
	27–12	*h·* her wounds too tenderly
My.	24– 4	* is ready to *h·* all who accept its
	117–11	*h·* disease, and make one a
	147–20	able to *h·* both sin and disease.
	150– 3	seeketh to save, to *h·*, and
	152–26	matter, man, or woman can never *h·*
	159–10	sent forth His word to *h·*
	180–18	overcome evil and *h·* disease.
	218–23	teach or *h·* by proxy is a false faith
	221–20	with which to *h·* sin and disease.
	222– 8	why they could not *h·* that case,
	238– 2	*Will the Bible, . . . h·* as *effectually*
	300– 9	and thus *h·* disease
	300–11	*h·* disease, for the reason that the
	328–14	* it gives them a license to *h·*.
	363–27	and practise only to *h·*.

(*see also* **power, sick**)

healed

Mis.	3–14	is man *h·* and saved.
	11–12	if my instructions had *h·* them
	22–25	the deaf, and the blind, *h·* by it,
	33–13	*in order to be h· by it.*
	34– 4	One who has been *h·* by C. S.
	34– 5	is not only *h·* of the disease,
	38–25	*in order to be h· by it*
	39– 5	the understanding of how you are *h·*.
	41–18	*Can all classes of disease be h·*
	54–18	*I was h· of a chronic trouble*
	54–20	When once you are *h·* by Science,
	54–22	disease that you were *h·* of.
	54–24	Science by which you were *h·*.
	63– 3	said of old . . . that Jesus *h·* through
	66–24	not *h·* like the more physical
	69–19	*h·* him of enteritis,
	70– 5	sick man's illusion, and *h·* him.
	71– 8	he *h·* others who were sick.
	93– 7	*have been h· by C. S.*
	133–32	behold the sick who are *h·*,
	162–19	through his stripes we are *h·*.
	163– 9	He *h·* and taught by the
	171–19	the sick are *h·* ;
	187–30	in order to be *h·* and saved,
	198–18	disease also is treated and *h·*.
	210– 4	C. S. never *h·* a patient without
	214–24	mortal mind in being *h·* morally,
	225–20	through the divine power, she *h·* him.
	241– 8	one having morals to be *h·*,
	256– 1	Persons who have been *h·* by C. S.
	260– 2	"stripes we are *h·*." — *Isa.* 53 : 5.
	300–30	patient who pays . . . for being *h·*,
	307–26	look and be *h·*.
	352–14	sickness is *h·* upon the same
	352–15	by the same rule that sin is *h·*.

healed

Mis.	364– 4	whereby the sick are *h·*,
	364– 7	to have *h·*, through Truth,
	372–12	* wonderful book has *h·* my child."
	378– 5	having been *h·*, as he informed the
	382–14	patient *h·* in this age by C. S.
	387–17	Who loved and *h·* mankind
Ret.	15–23	having been *h·* through my preaching.
	15–27	till the persons . . . were *h·*.
	15–29	others present had been *h·*
	16–10	thank God, she is *h·* !"
	16–12	sick to be *h·* by my sermon.
	25– 4	as to how I was *h·* ;
	25–30	not questioning those he *h·*
	34–17	A person *h·* by C. S.
	34–18	is not only *h·* of his disease,
	39– 2	were *h·* simply by reading it,
	40– 1	four successive years I *h·*, preached,
	41– 4	desperate cases I instantly *h·*,
	60–20	and the sick are *h·*.
	92– 4	he *h·* by Truth and Love.
Un.	8–18	basis whereby sickness is *h·*,
	54– 5	To be *h·*, one must lose sight of a
	55– 8	stripes we are *h·*." — *Isa.* 53 : 5.
	61–28	helpless sick are soonest *h·*
Pul.	vii–18	the sick are *h·* and sinners saved,
	6–16	* was *h·* instantaneously
	30– 1	* *h·* by C. S. treatment ;
	54–28	*h·* Mr. Whittier with one visit,
	58– 1	* *h·* by the power of divine Mind,
	72–12	* *h·* a number of years ago
Rud.	7– 2	but that the simplest case, *h·* in Science,
	9–23	oftentimes *h·* inveterate diseases.
	14–25	*h·* by means of my instructions,
	14–28	and were *h·* in the class ;
	15– 3	a student, if *h·* in a class,
No.	2–15	I have *h·* more disease by the
	4–26	can only be — *h·* on this basis.
	6–14	then disease cannot be *h·* by
	31– 4	but has not *h·* mortals ;
	31–18, 19	He *h·* disease as he *h·* sin ;
	42–25	clergyman came to be *h·*.
Pan.	5–28	and thus *h·* sickness and sin.
'01.	11– 8	we are *h·* and saved,
	17–15	It was that I *h·* the deaf, the blind,
	17–28	attenuation in some cases *h·*
	27–14	If any one as yet has *h·* hopeless
	27–19	an equal number of sick *h·*,
Hea.	14– 5	man is *h·* morally and physically.
Po.	6–12	loved and *h·* mankind :
My.	v–24	* *h·* multitudes of disease
	24–11	* have been *h·* through C. S.,
	28–23	* our Master *h·* and reformed them.
	28–27	* *h·* them of their diseases
	44– 3	* the sick are being *h·*,
	58–17	* great multitude that has been *h·*
	63–30	* had been *h·* by Christ, Truth,
	105– 7	I *h·* consumption in its last stages,
	105–11	I *h·* malignant diphtheria
	105–14	I have *h·* at one visit a cancer
	106– 6	The list of cases *h·* by me
	106–13	C. S. has *h·* cases that I assert
	106–30	Nazarene Prophet, *h·* through Mind,
	111–32	They have themselves been *h·*
	112– 1	*h·* others by means of the Principle
	113– 5	and thereby is *h·* of disease.
	127–17	I *h·* ninety-nine to the ten of
	145–13	I *h·* him on the spot.
	153–12	*h·* from the day my flowers
	153–13	Thy faith hath *h·* thee.
	178– 6	sick are *h·* and sinners saved.
	192– 8	thou art being *h·*.
	204–24	sick whom you have not *h·*
	228– 3	thousands are *h·* by learning that
	233–16	"They have *h·* also the hurt — *Jer.* 6 : 14.
	258– 2	and the sick are *h·*.
	339–29	The fact that he *h·* the sick man
	348– 1	*h·* of so-called disease
	348– 8	Then I was *h·*,

(*see also* **sick**)

healer

Mis.	41–21	no other *h·* in the case.
	59–26	That individual is the best *h·* who
	59–29	Mind is the scientific *h·*.
	97–11	by no means a desirable . . . *h·*.
	220– 5	*h·* begins by mental argument.
	252–23	rules and practice of the great *h·*
Ret.	47–17	a better *h·* and teacher
Pul.	52–20	* The Master was the great *h·*.
	53– 9	* the mind of both *h·* and patient,
Rud.	8–14	there is no other *h·*.
	11–25	The lecturer, teacher, or *h·*
	12–21	As power divine is the *h·*,
	13–22	if the *h· realizes* the truth,
No.	6–15	mistaken *h·* is not successful,
'01.	18–27	the Christian Scientists' *h·* ;

healer

My.	36–31	* *h·* of all our diseases
	104–15	the *h·* of men, the Christ,
	328–22	* a prominent *h·* of the church,
	349– 2	*h·* to whom all things are possible.
	360–30	your *h·*, or any earthly friend.

healers

Mis.	40–14	ancient prophets as *h·*.
	40–25	or they cannot be instantaneous *h·*.
	303– 3	as *h·* physical and moral.
	370–26	true fold for Christian *h·*,
Man.	82–18	shall not advertise as *h·*,
Ret.	87–22	*h·* become a law unto themselves.
	88– 2	professional intercourse of C. S. *h·*
Pul.	57–23	* several sects of mental *h·*,
No.	2–12	*h·* who admit that disease is real
'01.	9– 9	seers of men, and Christian *h·*.
'02.	18–23	we shall have more effective *h·*
My.	111–19	become successful *h·* and
	218–25	My published works are teachers and *h·*.
	327–24	* formerly read, ''pretended *h·*,''
	328–13	* the law recognizes them as *h·*,
	328–19	* two C. S. *h·* in this city.
	328–20	* first to be issued to the *h·*
	329– 1	* construed to include the *h·*
	329– 5	* relieved the *h·* of this sect

healest

Mis.	209– 7	*h·* the wounds of my people

healeth

Mis.	173– 6	*h·* all our sickness and sins?
	174– 8	and *h·* all our diseases.
	184–13	*h·* all thy diseases.'' — *Psal.* 103 : 3.
	320–18	''*h·* all our diseases ;'' — *see Psal.* 103 : 3.
	322–21	*h·* the sick and cleanseth
Man.	47–17	*h·* all thy diseases'' — *Psal.* 103 : 3.
Pul.	10– 7	*h·* all thy diseases.'' — *Psal.* 103 : 3.
Pan.	4–25	*h·* all thy diseases.'' — *Psal.* 103 : 3.
'01.	9–30	worketh well and *h·* quickly,
Peo.	12–13	*h·* all thy diseases.'' — *Psal.* 103 : 3.
My.	13–20	*h· all thy diseases;* — *Psal.* 103 : 3.
	119–17	''*h·* all thy diseases'' — *Psal.* 103 : 3.

healing (noun)

aid its
Mis.	58–19	*Does the theology of C. S. aid its h·?*

all
Mis.	232–25	Principle of all *h·* is God ;
	379–15	divine Principle of all *h·*.
Rud.	7– 1	Not that all *h·* is Science,
My.	154– 2	Science of all *h·* is based on Mind

and peace
Mis.	176– 3	*h·*, and peace, and perfect love.

and salvation
Mis.	244–24	way of *h·* and salvation.

and teaching
Ret.	78– 3	In *h·* and teaching the student has not
	83– 1	scientific *h·* and teaching.

art of
My.	327–26	* practise the art of *h·*,''
	328–29	* practise the art of *h·* for pay,

Christian
Mis.	6–15	Christian *h·* will rank far in advance
	88–22	* that Christian *h·* is
	192–22	grand verities of Christian *h·*
	359– 6	in the practice of Christian *h·*
	370–15	the form of Christian *h·*.
Ret.	62– 1	Science of Christian *h·* will again be
'01.	2– 8	new-old cloth of Christian *h·*.
Hea.	1–12	great subject of Christian *h·* ;
	3–22	God is the Principle of Christian *h·*,
	15– 2	Christian *h·*, established upon this
My.	43–21	* Science of Christian *h·* was revealed
	274–23	when beholding Christian *h·*,

Christian Science
Mis.	307–19	proper reception of C. S. *h·*.
Man.	89–14	practised C. S. *h·* acceptably
	89–21	practised C. S. *h·* successfully
Ret.	48– 5	establishment of *genuine* C. S. *h·*
'01.	18– 5	woeful warnings concerning C. S. *h·*
My.	153–27	C. S. *h·* is ''the Spirit and — *Rev.* 22 : 17.
	219–11	chapter sub-title

Christ Jesus'
'01.	18–11	of questioning Christ Jesus' *h·*,

Christ's
Mis.	302– 9	without the Science, of Christ's *h·*.
Ret.	26–15	ignorantly pronounce Christ's *h·*.
Pul.	6– 6	spiritual foundation of Christ's *h·*.
	35– 6	* Christ's *h·* was not miraculous,
'01.	2–12	find the standard of Christ's *h·*
Hea.	12–12	from the Scripture and Christ's *h·*

cross and
Mis.	357–11	Without the cross and *h·*,

demonstrate
Mis.	65–22	in order to demonstrate *h·*,

healing

demonstration of
'01.	18–21	is above a demonstration of *h·*,

department of
Rud.	15–15	the department of *h·*.
My.	90–31	* peculiar department of *h·*,

divine
(*see* **divine**)

divine art of
Pul.	66– 1	* what they term the divine **art of** *h·*,

form of
Rud.	6–25	definite and absolute form of *h·*,

good
Mis.	355– 6	Less teaching and good *h·*

gospel
Pul.	44–17	* chapter sub-title

gospel of
(*see* **gospel**)

has gone on
Un.	9–24	*H·* has gone on continually ;

his
Mis.	200– 2	that made his *h·* easy

in its wings
'02.	9–10	with *h·* in its wings,

Jesus'
Rud.	3–17	Jesus' *h·* was spiritual

last
My.	345–21	* last *h·* that will be vouchsafed

law of
Mis.	65–29	constitute the divine law of *h·*.

lessons on
Mis.	371– 1	among the first lessons on *h·*

lost element of
Man.	17–13	and its lost element of *h·*.
My.	46–13	and its lost element of *h·*.''

means of
Mis.	135–17	God's methods and means of *h·*,
'01.	34– 7	Christ's mode and means of *h·*,

mental
(*see* **mental**)

metaphysical
Mis.	4– 2	Science of metaphysical *h·*,
	4–20	on the subject of metaphysical *h·*,
	45– 6	Principle of metaphysical *h·*,
	50– 6	*entire method of metaphysical h·*,
	54– 9	in the field of metaphysical *h·*,
	68– 8	* *protest against metaphysical h·*
	195– 4	divine Principle of metaphysical *h·*.
	232–21	Metaphysical *h·*, or C. S.,
	233–12	standard of metaphysical *h·*
	234–20	mighty system of metaphysical *h·*,
	241– 7	Test, if you will, metaphysical *h·* on
	369–15	Metaphysical *h·* seeks a wisdom that
	370–24	C. S., a ''metaphysical *h·*''
	380–25	the Science of metaphysical *h·*
Man.	34–16	and practising metaphysical *h·*.
Ret.	24– 5	Science of divine metaphysical *h·*
	25– 9	spiritual Science and metaphysical *h·*,
Pul.	35– 4	spiritual Science and metaphysical *h·*
No.	5–25	Metaphysical *h·* is a lost jewel
'01.	17–12	C. S. or metaphysical *h·*
	26–30	subject of metaphysical *h·* or C. S.
Hea.	11–27	Christianity of metaphysical *h·*,
	13–22	foundations of metaphysical *h·* ?
	14–15	Metaphysical *h·* includes
	16–12	Science of metaphysical *h·*.

method of
Mis.	40–10	the same method of *h·*
	50–11	metaphysical method of *h·*

ministry and
Mis.	138– 8	in your ministry and *h·*.

ministry of
Mis.	195–14	ministry of *h·* at this period.

miracles in
Mis.	54–26	*as great miracles in h·*

modes of
My.	221–16	Then modes of *h·*, other than

of disease
Mis.	63–14	address himself to the *h·* of disease,

of sickness
Mis.	352–29	and the *h·* of sickness is,

of sin
Mis.	352–28	difference between the *h·* of sin and
Rud.	2–26	purpose of C. S. is the *h·* of sin ;

of the sick
Man.	47–13	in regard to the *h·* of the sick
My.	104–32	It was the *h·* of the sick,
	182–16	the *h·* of the sick,

of the wife
Pul.	26–16	* *h·* of the wife of the donor.

on her wings
Mis.	146–2	with *h·* on her wings.

physical
Rud.	3–11	his spiritual than his physical *h·*.

practice of
My.	111–18	establish their practice of *h·*

healing
Principle of
  Mis. 40– 2   scientific Principle of *h·* demands
  Ret. 37–18   the spiritual Principle of *h·*,
  Hea. 14– 7   obscure the divine Principle of *h·*
proof of
  Pul. 13–13   rejoices in the proof of *h·*,
psychic
  Pul. 54–10   * conditions requisite in psychic *h·*
Science of
    (*see* **Science**)
scientific
  Ret. 83– 1   elucidate scientific *h·* and teaching.
  Rud. 16–14   *school of scientific h·?*
silent
  Chr. 53–43   Christ's silent *h·*, heaven heard,
so-called
  Mis. 254–23   hurling its so-called *h·* at random,
spiritual
  Mis. 163–29   demonstrating the spiritual *h·* of
     246–29   Christianity and a spiritual *h·*,
     346– 4   spiritual *h·* as eminent proof that
suppositional
  Mis. 97–11   Such suppositional *h·* I deprecate.
system of
    (*see* **system**)
teaching and
  Mis. 162–13   good will, love, teaching, and *h·*.
  Rud. 15–16   Teaching and *h·* should have
their
  No. 3–13   rules of this practice for their *h·*,
true
  Mis. 40–14   All true *h·* is governed by,
Truth of
  Rud. 9–17   is the Truth of *h·*.
two poles of
  My. 74–29   * of the two poles of *h·*,
work of
  Mis. 7– 8   necessary in this work of *h·*.
     37–27   to her students the work of *h·* ;
  Ret. 54–22   work of *h·*, in the Science of Mind,

  Mis. 6–11   The *h·* of such cases
     80–29   outdoing the *h·* of the old.
     96–24   How is the *h·* done in C. S.?
     104–27   are demonstrated, in *h·*,
     192–26   making *h·* a condition of salvation,
     194–22   turn from matter to Spirit for *h·* ;
     232–20   most important of all arts, — *h·*.
     242– 1   chapter sub-title.
     255–20   I claim for *h·* by C. S.
     270–22   yet follow him in *h·*.
     355– 7   a *h·* that is not guesswork,
  Man. 92– 3   *H·* Better than Teaching.
  Ret. 49–24   will prove a *h·* for the nations,
  Un. 9–24   yet *h·*, as I teach it,
  Pul. 54– 2   * The *h·* of his seamless dress
  My. 59– 9   * as well as of *h·*,
     122–32   see the power of Truth in *h·*.
     153– 6   The *h·* and the gospel ministry
     219– 7   success in teaching or in *h·*.
     219–19   our great Master's life of *h·*,
     269–21   have *h·* in their light.

healing (adj.)
  Mis. 7–24   with *h·*, purifying thought.
     24–12   *h·* Truth dawned upon my sense ;
     59– 2   the *h·* theology of Mind,
     70– 6   *h·* action of Mind upon the body
     222–25   Even the *h·* Principle, whose power
     247–18   *h·* force developed by C. S.
     373–32   Its *h·* and saving power was
  Man. 49– 2   to monopolize the *h·* work
  Ret. 31–30   Love unveiled the *h·* promise
     83– 5   and the *h·* efficacy thereof.
  Pul. 47–20   * definitions of these two *h·* arts.
     53–27   * That *h·* gift he lends to them
  No. 22– 7   on the *h·* properties of tar-water,
     44–19   *h·* balm of Truth and Love
  '01. 2– 6   the *h·* standard of C. S.
  My. 22–27   * touched the *h·* hem of C. S.,
     24– 9   * this *h·* and saving gospel.
     153–14   no intrinsic *h·* qualities from my
     153–15   scientific, *h·* faith is a saving
     180– 7   *h·* Christianity which applies to all
    (*see also* **Christ, power**)

healing (ppr.)
  Mis. ix– 9   *h·* mankind morally, physically,
     19–22   more faith in an honest . . . *h·* me,
     29–21   *h·* the writers of chronic and acute
     33–22   *ordinary methods of h· disease*
     33–23   *H·* by C. S. has the following
     51– 3   spiritually, *h·* disease.
     60– 9   *h·* cases of disease and sin
     74–23   *h·* through Mind, he removed any

healing (ppr.)
  Mis. 88–29   Mind-healing, and *h·* with drugs,
     101– 1   *h·* becomes spontaneous,
     165– 2   casting out evils and *h·*,
     189–29   spiritual power, *h·* sin and sickness,
     300–32   *H·* morally and physically are one.
     352–18   Thus it is in *h·* the moral sickness;
     358– 5   and teaches by *h·*,
     378–13   signally failed in *h·* her case.
  Man. 19– 4   *h·* and saving the world
     83– 6   *h·* and uplifting the race.
  Ret. 34–10   I claim for *h·* scientifically
     63– 3   insist on the need of *h·* sickness
     85–20   or of *h·* on a material basis.
     95– 3   the *h·* of the nations.'' — *Rev.* 22 : 2.
  Pul. 6–10   *h·* and saving mankind.
     10– 2   *h·* both mind and body,
  Rud. 2–23   *H·* physical sickness is the smallest
  No. 2–13   by *h·* one case audibly,
     2–22   marked success in *h·*
     5–27   prevents one from *h·* scientifically,
     32–24   a Cause which is *h·* its thousands
     44–17   instead of *h·*, it palsied
  '01. 9–16   *h·* and saving men,
     17–22   the comparative ease of *h·*
     24–27   *h·* all manner of diseases.
     27–13   C. S. is *h·* and reforming mankind.
     28–21   my demonstration of C. S. in *h·*
     33–21   *h·* them through the might and
     34– 3   *h·* of all manner of diseases.
  '02. 15– 6   *H·* all manner of diseases
  My. 108– 3   *h·* his cases without drugs
     113–16   *h·* sin and sickness,
     190– 8   *h·* the worst forms of contagious
     190–20   and *above matter* in *h·* disease,
     194– 9   *h·* sickness and destroying sin,
     214–20   *h·* all manner of diseases,
     219–17   *h·*, . . . of all manner of diseases.
     239–10   by *h·* all manner of disease,
     257–16   *h·* all sorrow, sickness, and sin.
     257–19   his grace, reviving and *h·*.
     302– 1   all modes of *h·* disease
     345–12   false science — *h·* by drugs.
    (*see also* **sick**)

healing-power
  Mis. 199–30   marvellous *h·* of goodness
healings
  Pul. 54–18   * the accounts of his *h·*,
heals
  Mis. 20– 2   *h·* man spontaneously,
     102–21   and *h·* all our diseases.
     222– 9   reforms him, and so *h·* him :
     241–16   *h·* him of the moral malady.
     260–25   gives out an atmosphere that *h·*
     268–19   *h·* body and mind, head and heart ;
     336–23   Christianity, that *h·* disease and sin
     358– 4   student who *h·* by teaching
     369–21   charity that *h·* and saves ;
     380– 2   if a divine Principle alone *h·*,
  Ret. 26– 3   the divine power which *h·*.
     50– 4   that divine power which *h·* ;
     63– 4   *h·* sin as it *h·* sickness,
  Un. 48– 9   He *h·* all my ills,
  Pul. 82– 5   * which *h·* the stricken soul.
  No. 13– 3   makes disease unreal, and this *h·* it.
     21–26   wherein Principle *h·* and saves.
  '01. 12– 3   *h·* the sinning and the sick.
  Hea. 8– 2   *h·* both mind and body,
  My. 3–15   not a law . . . that *h·* only the sick.
     43–28   * that which *h·* and saves.
     52– 7   * giving . . . the love that *h·*.
     107–29   *h·* the most violent stages of
     132–30   *h·* the poor body,
     154– 4   nor the drug itself that *h·*,
     180–15   *h·* sin, sickness, disease,
     183–12   unfolds, transfigures, *h·*.
     204–30   divine Principle, *h·* all disease.
     206– 6   holiness which *h·* and saves.
     257– 3   that *h·* the wounded heart.
     260– 2   that *h·* and saves mankind.
     300–12   *h·* the most inveterate diseases.
     300–23   the Christianity which *h·*,
     348–13   and that *materia medica h·*
     348–16   but God, *h·* and saves mankind.
     364–16   *h·* all manner of sickness
    (*see also* **sick**)

health
advance
  Mis. 29–26   nor advance *h·* and length of days.
alias **harmony**
  Mis. 41–25   *h·*, *alias* harmony, is the normal
and character
  Peo. 7–28   the *h·* and character of

health

and happiness
Mis. 240–11   promoters of *h·* and happiness.
    262– 1   designed to bring *h·* and happiness
My. 165–20   impart truth, *h·*, and happiness,

and harmony
Mis. 8– 5   produce *h·* and harmony,
    59–15   or to restore *h·* and harmony,
    187– 6   He established *h·* and harmony,

and heaven
Pul. 53–24   * the key to *h·* and heaven,

and holiness
Mis. 179–17   for that of *h·* and holiness?
    194–12   redolent with love, *h·*, and holiness,
Man. 31–12   shall promote *h·* and holiness,
Ret. 59–16   the antipodes . . . of *h·* and holiness,
No. 46– 6   craving *h·* and holiness,
Pan. 10–28   statuesque being, *h·*, and holiness
My. 146–32   scale of being— for *h·* and holiness.
    186–14   dwelleth all life, *h·*, and holiness,
    196–28   work for their *h·* and holiness.
    210–17   can only reflect . . . *h·*, and holiness.
    211–15   allurements to *h·* and holiness,

and immortality
My. 182–23   giving grace, *h·*, and immortality

and Life
Un. 39– 4   yield to holiness, *h·*, and Life,

and life
Rud. 12–27   maintains human *h·* and life.
No. 5–17   destroy both human *h·* and life.
'01. 33–10   * it was not the *h·* and life of religion,
Peo. 8–17   and lean upon it for *h·* and life.
My. 129–22   gives to man *h·* and life

and morals
Mis. 62– 3   individuality, *h·*, and morals ;
Ret. 71–30   end in destroying *h·* and morals.
No. 18–11   need of better *h·* and morals.

and peace
Mis. 169–24   *h·* and peace and hope for all.
My. 350–18   crushing out of *h·* and peace,

and sickness
Ret. 57–27   good and evil, *h·* and sickness,
'00. 4– 2   good and evil *h·* and sickness,

and strength
Mis. 7–29   they think that *h·* and strength
Pul. 52–16   * receive light, *h·*, and strength,

as real as
No. 5–18   If disease is as real as *h·*,

better
Mis. 24–14   and ever after was in better *h·*
    239– 4   I never was in better *h·*.
    365–15   universal need of better *h·*
No. 18–11   universal need of better *h·*

board of
My. 128– 6   A coroner's inquest, a board of *h·*,
    340–13   a simple board of *h·*,

bring
My. 40–18   * its pristine power to bring *h·*

change to
No. 40–26   comes with the change to *h·*,

consciousness of
Mis. 311–17   abiding consciousness of *h·*,
My. 349– 4   consciousness of *h·*, holiness,

demonstrates
My. 274–14   demonstrates *h·*, holiness, and

doctrine of
My. 87–29   * this doctrine of *h·*, happiness,

equivalent for
Mis. 300–32   withholds a slight equivalent for *h·*.

fatal to
My. 249–13   mental miasma fatal to *h·*,

felt in
Mis. 183– 7   felt in *h·*, happiness, and holiness :

found
Mis. 247– 7   I found *h·* in just what I teach.

freedom of
Mis. 101–12   freedom of *h·*, holiness, and

fruits of
Ret. 62– 6   bring forth better fruits of *h·*,

good
Mis. 365–16   Good *h·* and a more spiritual
No. 18–22   Good *h·* and a more spiritual

gospel of
Mis. 241–26   rejoices in the gospel of *h·*.

harmony and
Rud. 3–23   upon the body in harmony and *h·*.

her
Pul. 37– 7   * Her *h·* is excellent,

his
Mis. 308– 4   for his *h·* or holiness,
My. 211–26   undermining his *h·*,

holiness and
Mis. 25– 2   against his holiness and *h·*.

human
Rud. 12–27   maintains human *h·* and life.
No. 5–17   both human *h·* and life.

health

improvement in
Mis. 243– 4   decided improvement in *h·*.

indispensable to
Mis. 67–16   indispensable to *h·*, happiness,

instantaneous
Un. 7–15   raise the dying to instantaneous *h·*.

is catching
Mis. 229– 5   If he believed . . . *h·* is catching

law of
Un. 6–13   Until the heavenly law of *h·*,

laws of
Mis. 6–26   where laws of *h·* are strictly enforced,

life and
    (*see* **life**)

maintain
Mis. 38– 4   ability to gain and maintain *h·*,

moral
Ret. 35– 5   for physical and moral *h·*

nor disease
My. 302– 6   life nor death, *h·* nor disease,

normal condition of
Ret. 13–23   in a normal condition of *h·*.

not disease
My. 239– 1   *h·*, not disease ; Truth, not error ;

not of sickness
Un. 3–18   of *h·*, not of sickness ;

obstacles to
Mis. 309–21   include all obstacles to *h·*,

of my countenance
Un. 29–26   *h·* of my countenance,— *Psal.* 42 : 11.
Pan. 4–23   *h·* of my countenance,— *Psal.* 42 : 11.

of the community
Mis. 43–31   the *h·* of the community.

or existence
Rud. 12–18   *h·* or existence of mankind,

or holiness
Mis. 308– 4   for his *h·* or holiness,

or morals
Mis. 62– 5   improve *h·* or morals,

over sickness
Mis. 321–11   triumphs . . . of *h·* over sickness,

path to
Mis. 308– 8   and loses the path to *h·*,

perfect
Mis. 5– 8   perfect *h·* and perfect morals

physical
My. 93–14   * physical *h·* and spiritual peace.

Principle of
Mis. 163–31   heralding the Principle of *h·*,

promote
Mis. 350–29   promote *h·* and spiritual growth.
Man. 31–12   promote *h·* and holiness,

real as
No. 17–27   would be . . . as real as *h·*,

redolent with
'01. 12–18   redolent with *h·*, holiness, and

regained
Rud. 15– 6   surprise of suddenly regained *h·*

restore
Ret. 48–20   to restore *h·*, hope, and harmony
No. 5–16   restore *h·* and perpetuate life,

restored to
Mis. 180– 6   beholding me restored to *h·*.
Pul. 34–28   by which I was restored to *h·* ;

results in
Mis. 15–11   results in *h·*, happiness, and

saving
My. 274–28   thy saving *h·* among all — *Psal.* 67 : 2.

sickness to
Mis. 220–17   from sickness to *h·*.

state of
Mis. 219–25   a state of *h·* is but a state of
My. 349– 3   A scientific state of *h·* is

tendency to
No. 46–22   this upward tendency to *h·*,

their
My. 167–20   my prayer for their *h·*,

to man
Peo. 12–26   He would, give *h·* to man ;
My. 219–16   giving of life and *h·* to man

to obtain
Ret. 65–29   expect to obtain *h·*, harmony,

to the sick
Mis. 168– 1   *h·* to the sick, salvation from

true
Mis. 298–25   true consciousness is the true *h·*.

undertaken in
No. 4– 4   had better be undertaken in *h·*

will be restored
Mis. 41–25   and *h·* will be restored ;

without
Peo. 12–28   without *h·* there could be no **heaven.**

Mis. 6–31   *h·* is generally the rule ;
    37– 6   toward purity, *h·*, holiness, and

health

Mis.	99–27	make way for *h·*, holiness,
	127–15	bread of heaven, *h·*, holiness,
	172–27	*h·*, holiness, and immortality
	212–19	*h·*, happiness, and life
	238–15	*h·*, virtue, and heaven ;
	245–13	its uplifting influence upon the *h·*,
	259– 6	of *h·*, not of sickness ;
	315–18	prove sound in sentiment, *h·*, and
Chr.	53–36	For *h·* makes room.
Ret.	88– 7	from the tomb to *h·*,
Un.	64– 6	conscious of only *h·*, holiness, and
Rud.	8–26	If by such lower means the *h·* is
	9–28	whatever militates against *h·*,
	11–13	*H·* is the consciousness of
	11–24	*h·*, harmony, and Life eternal.
No.	4– 2	has restored the sick to *h·* ;
	28–12	is found to bring with it *h·*,
	34– 2	leading up to *h·*, harmony, and
'01.	2– 2	demonstrated — *h·*, holiness,
	44–27	no intelligence, *h·*, hope, nor
'02.	9– 3	All-power — giving life, *h·*, holiness ;
Peo.	12–27	heaven not more willingly than *h·* ;
Po.	32–17	That *h·* may my efforts repay ;
My.	18–12	bread of heaven, *h·*, holiness,
	103–21	*h·*, longevity, and morals of men;
	118–28	*h·*, harmony, holiness,
	124– 7	*h·*, harmony, growth, grandeur, and
	153–30	will give thee rest, peace, *h·*,
	155–13	run in joy, *h·*, holiness,
	160–17	for actual being, *h·*, holiness,
	205–18	Hence *h·*, holiness, immortality,
	247– 8	its rules are *h·*, holiness, and
	255– 1	*h·*, holiness, and immortality,
	275–22	and my dear enemies' *h·*,
	300–16	and raise the dying to *h·*?
	300–17	raise the dying to *h·* in Christ's
	344–22	* the *h·* laws of the States
	346– 9	* she is in the flesh and in *h·*.

Heal the Sick

Pul.	28– 7	* "*H· the S·*," — *Matt.* 10 : 8.

healthful

Mis.	170–10	understanding is *h·* life.

health-giving

Mis.	19–32	*h·* and joy-inspiring.
Ret.	64–25	in *h·*, deathless Truth and Love.
	88–14	*h·* and life-bestowing qualities,

healthier

Mis.	229–24	become *h·*, holier, happier, and
My.	296–15	He is wiser to-day, *h·* and happier,

health-seeking

My.	90–13	* while *h·* is the door . . . for many,

healthy

Mis.	229– 6	exposed to contact with *h·* people,
	252–13	*h·* thoughts are reality
Rud.	12–25	free the minds of the *h·* from any
Peo.	5–25	a *h·* mind and body.
My.	14–25	* it is in such a *h·* state that
	81– 4	* *h·* satisfaction with life.
	301– 6	found to be a *h·* fermentation,

heaped

Pul.	45–17	* Much was the ridicule *h·* upon
My.	30–21	* they were *h·* high with bills,

heaps

My.	229–24	*H·* upon *h·* of praise

hear

Mis.	6– 1	We *h·* from the pulpits that
	17– 1	*h·* and record the thunderings
	28– 3	neither see, *h·*, feel, taste,
	35–21	go to church to *h·* it expounded
	81–20	*why does not John* h· *this voice,*
	86–28	What mortals *h·*, see, feel,
	99– 4	and ears ye *h·* not ; — *see Mark* 8 : 18.
	106–25	methinks I *h·* the soft, sweet sigh
	126– 5	to *h·* the soft music of our Sabbath
	132–14	* "like to *h·* from Dr. Cullis ;
	151– 1	"My sheep *h·* my voice, — *John* 10 : 27.
	153–28	* *H·* the first music of this
	168– 3	what things ye shall see and *h·* :
	168– 8	those who, having ears, *h·* not,
	168– 9	how the deaf . . . . *h·* ;
	170–29	and ears, ye *h·* not,
	213–22	"My sheep *h·* my voice, — *John* 10 : 27.
	218– 8	matter can neither see, *h·*, nor feel,
	244–21	the blind to see, the deaf to *h·*,
	248– 3	interpretation they refuse to *h·*.
	269– 5	*H·* the Master on this subject :
	306–23	When angels visit us, we do not *h·* the
	308–16	"*H·*, O Israel : — *Deut.* 6 : 4.
	321–27	no desire to see or to *h·* what
	322– 6	expecting to *h·* me speak
	342–18	*H·* that human cry :
	368– 6	and cause the deaf to *h·*.

hear

Mis.	388–21	First at the tomb to *h·* his word :
Man.	94– 9	goes to *h·* and deride truth,
Chr.	55– 7	*h·* the voice of the — *John* 5 : 25.
	55– 7	they that *h·* shall live. — *John* 5 : 25.
	55–26	if any man *h·* my voice, — *Rev.* 3 : 20.
Ret.	9– 5	if she really did *h·* Mary's name
	16– 6	"Did you *h·* my daughter sing?
	93– 8	*H·* this saying of our Master,
Un.	8– 6	What you see, *h·*, feel, is a
	24–25	see, taste, *h·*, feel, smell.
Pul.	33– 4	* like Jeanne d'Arc, to *h·* "voices,"
	46– 3	* came to *h·* him preach,
	72–30	* "Did you ever *h·* of Jesus' taking
Rud.	5–19	body does not see, *h·*, smell, or taste.
No.	14–18	*H·* the words of our Master :
'00.	3– 3	cannot *h·* himself, unless he
	14–10	*h·* what the Spirit saith unto
'01.	3– 8	We *h·* it said the . . . have no God
	6–13	We *h·* that God is not God
	11–24	willing to *h·* a sermon
	15–21	*h·* the following thunderbolt
Hea.	16– 3	having ears, *h·* and understand.
	16–20	They can neither see, *h·*, feel, taste,
Po.	16–20	'Mid graves do I *h·* the glad voices
	21–10	at the tomb to *h·* his word :
My.	15–29	* To *h·* it like the rest.
	52–26	* interest of the world to *h·* her
	71–25	* can see and *h·* the two Readers
	72– 1	* could *h·* what was said.
	80– 2	* To *h·* prosperous, contented men
	80–26	* or who wanted to *h·* it.
	132– 5	go to the Gospels, and there we *h·* :
	152–21	if ye would *h·* His voice,
	153– 1	I *h·* that the loving hearts
	183–20	the deaf *h·* the words of the Book,
	186–22	yet speaking, I will *h·*." — *Isa.* 65 : 24.
	196– 9	every man be swift to *h·*, — *Jas.* 1 : 19.
	280–15	chapter sub-title — *Deut.* 6 : 4.
	280–18	does not *h·* our prayers only because
	296– 9	chapter sub-title — *Deut.* 6 : 4.
	316– 4	I still *h·* the harvest song

heard

Mis.	81–24	be *h·* divinely and humanly.
	120–17	call of peace will at length be *h·*
	128–12	and *h·*, and seen — *Phil.* 4 : 9.
	171–18	would prove his right to be *h·*.
	206– 6	is *h·* the Father and Mother's welcome,
	237–30	had *h·* the awful story
	246–13	scarcely been *h·* and hushed, when
	246–22	was *h·* crying in the wilderness,
	267– 1	screaming, to make itself *h·* above
	269–30	*h·* the great Red Dragon *whispering*
	277– 6	trying to be *h·* above Truth,
	328–13	Hast not thou *h·* this Christ knock
	329–25	voice of the turtle is *h·* — *Song* 2 : 12.
	342–17	they *h·* the shout,
	360–27	is *h·* as of yore saying
	379–13	I never *h·* him say that
	385– 5	Thou hast *h·* my prayer ;
	398–22	*H·* ye the glad sound?
Chr.	53–43	silent healing, heaven *h·*,
Ret.	8– 4	I repeatedly *h·* a voice,
	8– 9	I *h·* somebody call *Mary,*
	8–16	so loud that Mehitable *h·* it,
	8–24	my cousin had *h·* the voice,
	15–26	I had not *h·* of these cases
	61–19	voice is not *h·* ;" — *Psal.* 19 : 3.
Un.	2– 4	no place where His voice is not *h·* ;
	28–22	nor ear *h·*." — *I Cor.* 2 : 9.
	51– 5	is neither seen, felt, *h·*, nor
Pul.	2– 5	the fame which I *h·*." — *I Kings* 10 : 7.
	12– 5	I *h·* a loud voice — *Rev.* 12 : 10.
	33– 4	* she *h·* her name called
	33– 7	* if she *h·* the voice again
	41–20	* until all who wished had *h·* and
	59– 8	* *h·* these exercises four times
	74–22	not at all as I have *n·* her talk.
No.	39– 5	offered to be *h·* of men,
	39– 7	speaking loud enough to be *h·* ;
	45–13	Let it not be *h·* in Boston
'01.	11–21	nor too transcendental to be *h·*
'02.	9–21	When first I *h·* the life-giving sound
Peo.	1–14	beatings of our heart can be *h·* ;
Po.	37– 5	Oh, Thou hast *h·* my prayer ;
	53–11	Till *h·* at silvery eve
	71–22	Is *h·* your "Cry aloud !" — *Isa.* 58 : 1.
	75– 1	*H·* ye the glad sound?
My.	13– 7	first that I had even *h·* of it.
	31–16	* expressions of surprise . . . were *h·*
	32– 8	* Mrs. Conant could be *h·* perfectly
	59–19	* as I *h·* the sonorous tones of the
	59–27	* I *h·* her talk it before it was
	78–31	* understanding all they *h·*,
	126–14	And a voice was *h·*, saying,
	184– 4	men have not *h·* . . . what God hath

heard

My.	187–14	message that ye *h·* — *I John* 3 : 11.
	245–17	voice of Truth and Love be *h·*
	249– 5	error strives to be *h·* above Truth,
	289–17	is *h·* no more in England,
	319– 5	I *h·* nothing further from him

hearer

Mis.	127–28	on the ear or heart of the *h·*;

hearers

Mis.	302–27	the good that his *h·* received
My.	124–16	hearts of these *h·* and speakers,
	352–21	the *h·* and the doers of God's Word.

hearest

My.	290–25	Thou *h·* me always," — *John* 11 : 42.

heareth

Ret.	9–11	for Thy servant *h·*." — *I Sam.* 3 : 9.
Pul.	33– 9	* for Thy servant *h·*." — *I Sam.* 3 : 9.

hearing

Mis.	155–23	the pleasure of *h·* from you.
	344– 2	*h·* of a Pythagorean professor
Ret.	40–23	refused me a *h·* in their halls
	79– 3	Not by the *h·* of the ear
Rud.	5–13	*h·* in the material ear,
'00.	1–16	C. S. already has a *h·*
My.	105–17	sight to the blind, *h·* to the deaf,
	109–16	by the *h·* of the ear,
	112– 4	where Science gains no *h·*.
	224–25	would not deny their authors a *h·*,

hearken

Peo.	12– 1	*h·* to the higher law of God,
My.	126–14	(*h·* not to her lies),

hearkened

Mis.	268– 8	*h·* to My commandments ! — *Isa.* 48 : 18.

hears

Mis.	81–26	divine Love *h·* and answers
	324– 5	He *h·* the sounds of festivity
Ret.	25–25	matter neither sees, *h·*, nor feels
Un.	25– 8	*h·*, feels, tastes, smells as Mind,

hearsay

Mis.	146– 9	I cannot accept *h·*,

heart (*see also* heart's)

another's		
Mis.	98–28	* another's *h·* would'st reach."
answering to		
'00.	1– 7	*h·* answering to *h·*,
bore its grief		
Po.	25–16	*h·* bore its grief and is still !
change of		
Mis.	50–18	*Do you believe in change of h·?*
	50–26	This change of *h·* would deliver man
	51– 1	This change of *h·* is essential to
Ret.	14–20	experienced a change of *h·* ;
cheer the		
'02.	17–30	cheer the *h·* susceptible of light
clergyman's		
Ret.	15– 2	the good clergyman's *h·* also
contrite		
Un.	61–27	contrite *h·* soonest discerns this
dear		
Po.	24–20	Dear *h·* of Love,
denies it		
Mis.	211–32	when the *h·* denies it,
doubting		
Mis.	241–24	doubting *h·* looks up through faith,
each		
My.	148–22	what is each *h·* in this house
encouraged the		
My.	132–17	encouraged the *h·* of every member
engraven on the		
Mis.	376–13	* living Saviour engraven on the *h·*.
enlightened		
Ret.	81–18	The enlightened *h·* loathes error,
every		
Mis.	213–29	Love will reign in every *h·*,
	231–28	brought sunshine to every *h·*.
Man.	60–16	love should abide in every *h·*
Ret.	95–10	* weight of ill In every *h·* ;
Pul.	10–28	Thy blessing on every *h·*
No.	7– 3	to be . . . true rejoices every *h·*.
My.	132–13	at this time and in every *h·*
falls on the		
Mis.	394– 3	falls on the *h·* like the dew
Po.	45– 3	falls on the *h·* like the dew
fervent		
Mis.	xi– 9	fervent *h·* and willing hand
for any fate		
My.	185– 5	* With a *h·* for any fate ;
full		
My.	201–13	I thank you out of a full *h·*.
	338–19	*h·* full of love towards God

heart

generosity of		
My.	331–27	* the noble generosity of *h·*
good man's		
My.	129–24	good man's *h·* takes hold on heaven,
great		
Pul.	12–20	nearer to the great *h·* of Christ ;
'01.	30–26	great *h·* of the unselfed Christian
Po.	43–10	Father, in Thy great *h·* hold them
My.	131–12	signet of the great *h·*,
grown faint		
Mis.	262–18	*h·* grown faint with hope deferred.
harden the		
Mis.	301–28	error tends to harden the *h·*,
head and		
Mis.	160– 9	sweet rhythm of head and *h·*,
	268–20	body and mind, head and *h·* ;
heal the		
Mis.	398–17	Feed the hungry, heal the *h·*,
Ret.	46–23	Feed the hungry, heal the *h·*,
Pul.	17–22	Feed the hungry, heal the *h·*,
Po.	14–21	Feed the hungry, heal the *h·*,
her		
Mis.	386–11	This hour looks on her *h·*
Po.	49–16	This hour looks on her *h·*
My.	126–19	she saith in her *h·*, — *Rev.* 18 : 7.
	341–13	And in her *h·* is beating
his		
Mis.	30–25	fool hath said in his *h·*, — *Psal.* 14 : 1.
	70– 8	"thinketh in his *h·*, — *Prov.* 23 : 7.
	112–31	fool hath said in his *h·*, — *Psal.* 14 : 1.
	148– 2	meditates evil against us in his *h·*.
	212– 2	a fool that saith in his *h·*,
	335– 3	shall say in his *h·*, — *Matt.* 24 : 48.
'01.	18–24	fool hath said in his *h·*, — *Psal.* 14 : 1.
Peo.	3– 2	"thinketh in his *h·*, — *Prov.* 23 : 7.
My.	33–18	the truth in his *h·*. — *Psal.* 15 : 2.
	201–20	in him who says in his *h·* :
	227–30	fool hath said in his *h·*, — *Psal.* 14 : 1.
	228–17	in the least in his *h·*, — *Matt.* 11 : 11.
	228–25	the truth in his *h·*." — *Psal.* 15 : 2.
his own		
Mis.	324–17	the clearer pane of his own *h·*
homeless		
Po.	28–15	Hover the homeless *h·* !
honest		
Ret.	83–14	this error, in an honest *h·*,
human		
(*see* **human**)		
humble		
My.	188–31	admittance to a humble *h·*,
hungry		
Mis.	127–11	When a hungry *h·* petitions
	322–20	God that feedeth the hungry *h·*,
'02.	17–25	worth satisfies the hungry *h·*,
My.	18– 8	When a hungry *h·* petitions
hushed in the		
Po.	35–11	Hushed in the *h·* whereunto
hushed is the		
Mis.	395–13	Hushed is the *h·*.
Po.	57–20	Hushed is the *h·*.
little		
Po.	24– 5	O little *h·*, To me thou art
lone		
Mis.	392–11	To my lone *h·* thou art a power
Po.	20–15	To my lone *h·* thou art a power
	68– 5	sweet pledge to my lone *h·*
long-hushed		
Mis.	390–20	Ask of its June, the long-hushed *h·*,
Po.	55–21	Ask of its June, the long-hushed *h·*,
loving		
Mis.	149–25	whose altar is a loving *h·*,
	370–18	infinite care from His loving *h·*.
	399–19	Rolled away from loving *h·*
Pul.	16– 4	Rolled away from loving *h·*
Po.	76– 3	Rolled away from loving *h·*
lowly in		
My.	41– 7	* meek and lowly in *h·* are blessed
loyal		
Mis.	277– 9	a *h·* loyal to God is patient and
loyal at		
My.	225– 3	while the loyal at *h·*
man's		
My.	277–10	A bullet in a man's *h·*
many a		
Mis.	340– 3	and repose from many a *h·*.
meeting heart		
My.	124–11	*h·* meeting heart across continents
meets heart		
Mis.	207– 2	*h·* meets heart reciprocally blest,
merry		
My.	99– 5	* merry *h·* that doeth good
mine		
My.	188– 5	mine eyes and mine *h·* — *I Kings* 9 : 3.
music in the		
Mis.	330– 8	make music in the *h·*.

heart

my

Mis.	11– 6	should aim a ball at my *h·*,
	116–12	question, ever nearest to my *h·*,
	145–32	children that my *h·* folds within it,
	153–21	cleansed my *h·* in vain." — *Psal.* 73 : 13.
	159–11	My *h·* has many rooms :
	180–13	then my *h·* went out to God,
	251– 7	but my *h·* will with tenderness
	262–29	to relieve my *h·* of its secrets,
	266–21	I cannot find it in my *h·* not to
	317– 2	my *h·* replies, *Yes*, if you are doing
	321– 7	My *h·* is filled with joy,
	345–19	* "My *h·* has always assured and
	371–14	and my *h·* pleads for them
	393–23	To my *h·* that would be bleaching
	396–13	My *h·* unbidden joins rehearse ;
Ret.	14–26	and know my *h·* : — *Psal.* 139 : 23.
	23–17	My *h·* knew its Redeemer.
	31–23	My *h·* bent low before the
Un.	7– 6	from my *h·* of hearts,
Pan.	13– 5	and nearest my *h·*,
Hea.	10–27	so panteth my *h·* for the true fount
Peo.	13–27	* "My *h·* has assured and reassured me
Po.	3–14	Love divine doth fill my *h·*.
	16– 4	My *h·* hath thy verdure,
	52– 7	To my *h·* that would be bleaching
	59– 5	My *h·* unbidden joins rehearse,
My.	9–27	satisfied with what my *h·* gives
	15–12	My *h·* goes out to you
	33–10	and know my *h·* : — *Psal.* 139 : 23.
	125–11	to dip my pen in my *h·*
	148–20	and my *h·* is asking :
	155– 4	church, nestled so near my *h·*
	170–13	To your home in my *h·* !
	173–20	my *h·* welcomed each and all.
	192–15	My *h·* hovers around your churches
	197–26	in the home of my *h·*,
	229–25	That which I said in my *h·*
	253– 6	My *h·* and hope are with you.
	270–19	Those words . . . fill my *h·* :
	271–30	"nearest and dearest" to my *h·*
	296–26	Clara Barton dipped her pen in my *h·*,
	311–10	It was not in my *h·* to turn the
	323–17	* My *h·* has been too full

my own

Pul.	21– 9	praying for it to inhabit my own *h·*

nation's

Pul.	10–11	they planted a nation's *h·*,

no

'00.	3– 6	no *h·* his comfort.

of a moonbeam

Ret.	31–25	soft as the *h·* of a moonbeam,

of a rock

Mis.	144–15	secret in the *h·* of a rock,

of Christianity

Mis.	25– 5	it is the *h·* of Christianity,

of God

Mis.	253–22	mother's love touches the *h·* of God,

of history

Mis.	93– 4	*h·* of history shall be made glad !

of humanity

Mis.	155–10	find access to the *h·* of humanity.
	294– 8	he inscribes on the *h·* of humanity
Pan.	12–16	from off the *h·* of humanity,
My.	257–11	is winning the *h·* of humanity
	265– 4	at the *h·* of humanity
	268–28	and you see the *h·* of humanity

of man

Mis.	203–10	so the *h·* of man to man." — *Prov.* 27 : 19.
My.	189–16	love it creates in the *h·* of man ;

of millions

My.	289–18	lives on in the *h·* of millions.

of our country

Mis.	303–24	profitable to the *h·* of our country.

of the city

My.	79– 9	* in the *h·* of the city of Boston,

of the harlot

My.	126– 2	retaining the *h·* of the harlot

of the hearer

Mis.	127–28	on the ear or *h·* of the hearer ;

of the leaves

Po.	16–18	To the *h·* of the leaves

of the pink

Ret.	17–12	On the *h·* of the pink
Po.	62–15	On the *h·* of the pink

of Truth

Ret.	75–21	strikes at the *h·* of Truth.

one

Po.	68– 1	So one *h·* is left me
My.	189–12	from one *h·* to another,

one in

Mis.	135– 7	and we shall be one in *h·*,

one's own

'02.	2– 6	on the tablet of one's own *h·*,

heart

or in doctrine

'02.	2–26	either in *h·* or in doctrine ;

our

Peo.	1–14	beatings of our *h·* can be heard ;

overflow of

Mis.	338–24	* It needs the overflow of *h·*,

pierced the

Mis.	339–21	and hast pierced the *h·*

prays

No.	39– 7	when the *h·* prays, and not the lips,

preparation of

Mis.	115–14	need of a proper preparation of *h·*

preparation of the

Rud.	9–15	requires a preparation of the *h·*

pulsates

Mis.	152–13	as a mother whose *h·* pulsates with

pure

Mis.	361– 2	pure *h·* that sees God.
My.	34– 3	and a pure *h·* ; — *Psal.* 24 : 4.
	187–12	charity out of a pure *h·*, — *I Tim.* 1 : 5.

pure in

Mis.	15– 8	pure in *h·* : — *Matt.* 5 : 8.
	168–20	pure in *h·* clap their hands.
	185– 2	None but the pure in *h·* shall see
Ret.	26–25	none but the pure in *h·* can see
Pul.	35–10	'pure in *h·* ' — *Matt.* 5 : 8.

rapture to the

'02.	4–10	music to the ear, rapture to the *h·*

reach not the

'02.	16–25	reach not the *h·* nor renovate it ;

records of the

Mis.	390–25	In records of the *h·*.
Po.	56– 4	In records of the *h·*.

rejoices the

Mis.	12–25	law of Love rejoices the *h·* ;

rosebud

Po.	46– 1	Fair girl, thy rosebud *h·* rests warm

searching the

Mis.	204– 5	Truth, searching the *h·*,

secret

Pul.	83– 4	* In our secret *h·* our better self is

self-forgetful

Mis.	250–24	self-forgetful *h·* that overflows ;

signs of the

Po.	page 24	poem

sings to the

Mis.	204–10	sings to the *h·* a song of angels.

smite the

Ret.	81– 1	smite the *h·* and threaten

softened

Mis.	354–16	a *h·* softened, a character subdued,

sore

Po.	22–15	To heal humanity's sore *h·* ;

speaks

Mis.	262–10	When the *h·* speaks,

stricken to the

Mis.	329–28	stricken to the *h·* with winter's snow,

struggling

Mis.	63–24	Even as the struggling *h·*,

sympathizing

Ret.	5–23	* sympathizing *h·*, and a placid spirit.

tender

My.	158–21	makes the *h·* tender, faithful,

tendril of the

My.	258– 8	bind the tenderest tendril of the *h·*

thankful

My.	332– 5	* emotions of the thankful *h·*,

that

Ret.	81–19	else that *h·* is consciously untrue
Po.	66–10	tell how that *h·* is silent and sad,

that loves

'02.	18–17	*h·* that loves as Jesus loved.

that's hungry

Mis.	391– 3	I hope the *h·* that's hungry
Po.	38– 2	I hope the *h·* that's hungry

thine

Mis.	298– 1	with all thine *h·* ; — *Prov.* 3 : 5.
'01.	34–30	with all thine *h·* ; — *Prov.* 3 : 5.
My.	170–23	desires of thine *h·*. — *Psal.* 37 : 4.

thine own

Mis.	328–14	at the door of thine own *h·*,

this

Mis.	127–13	If this *h·*, humble and trustful,
Ret.	80–14	this *h·* becomes obediently
Po.	24–13	O Love divine, This *h·* of Thine
My.	18–10	If this *h·*, humble and trustful,
	150–12	this *h·* must be honest

thy

Mis.	98–28	* Thy *h·* must overflow,
	400– 8	In thy *h·* Dwell serene,
Pul.	16–20	In thy *h·* Dwell serene,
Po.	23– 6	Come ever o'er thy *h·* ?
	76–19	In thy *h·* Dwell serene,
My.	161–24	say not in thy *h·* : Sickness is possible
	183– 2	with all thy *h·*, — *Luke* 10 : 27.

heart

to heart
Mis. 143– 1   can feel the touch of *h·* to heart
262– 9   chapter sub-title
388–11   life most sweet, as *h·* to heart
Po.   7–11   life most sweet, as *h·* to heart
My. 162–10   spiritual cooperation, *h·* to heart,
touched
My. 150–11   A *h·* touched and hallowed by
touches the
My. 294–24   touches the *h·* and will move the
touch the
My. 186– 9   song and sermon will touch the *h·*,
true
My. 259–19   a true *h·*, and a helping hand
upright in
Mis. 258–17   saveth the upright in *h·*."— *Psal.* 7: 10.
waiting
Mis. 384–14   Be patient, waiting *h·* :
Po.   36–13   Be patient, waiting *h·* :
My. 208–14   dear letter to my waiting *h·*,
weary
Po. vii–15   * a balm to the weary *h·*.
what other
Ret. 90–20   What other *h·* yearns with her
whole
Man. 44–26   God requires our whole *h·*,
My. 132–31   and whose whole *h·* is faint ;
willing
Po. 26–11   Lincoln's own Great willing *h·*
with heart
My. 154–27   Communing *h·* with heart,
without
Po. 42– 6   Without *h·* to define them,
without the
Mis. 302– 8   the skeleton without the *h·*,
wounded
My. 257– 3   love that heals the wounded *h·*.
written on the
Mis. 172–20   which law is written on the *h·*,
yearning of the
Mis. 178– 5   from a yearning of the *h·* ;
young
Po. 66–12   but a young *h·* and glad
your
'00. 14–26   say in your *h·* as the devout
My. 62–13   * fill your *h·* with the joy of
133–29   your *h·* has discovered it.
150–18   This will stir your *h·*.
271–22   * nearest and dearest to your *h·*
327–12   * article will make your *h·* glad,
your heart's
My. 188–18   inner sanctuary, your heart's *h·*,

Mis. ix–19   There is an old age of the *h·*,
50–23   the belief that the *h·* is matter
227–23   speaking the truth in the *h·* ;
230–23   * With a *h·* for any fate ;
320– 6   dear to the *h·* of Christian Scientists;
329–11   even as the *h·* may be ;
336–25   looks in upon the *h·*,
Ret. 81–15   supreme advent of Truth in the *h·*,
Po.   2– 6   * but comes not to the *h·*."
34–18   Bearing no bitter memory at *h·* ;
My. 42–16   * With a *h·* filled with gratitude
88–22   * in the *h·* of all that increasing host
134– 3   a *h·* wholly in protest
160– 4   The *h·* that beats mostly for self is
188–21   where the *h·* of a Southron has

heart-and-hand-fellowship
'01.   1– 1   I extend my *h·*

heart-beats
Chr. 53–16   With fierce *h·* ;
My. 189–11   a diapason of *h·*,

heart-disease *and* heart disease
Mis. 50–26   would deliver man from *h·*,
My. 80– 6   * of *h· d·*, of cancer ;

heartfelt
Mis. 231–29   echo such tones of *h·* joy
My. 32– 6   * *h·* appeal to the creator.
51–29   * *h·* thanks and gratitude
256–10   deep-drawn, *h·* breath of thanks
347– 8   accept my *h·* acknowledgment of

hearth
Pul. 76–15   * before the *h·* is a large rug

heart's
Mis. 106–30   awaken the *h·* harpstrings.
107–10   all the *h·* homage belongs to God.
251–10   loyal to the *h·* core to religion,
276– 9   my *h·* desire met the demand.
Ret. 23–13   *h·* bridal to more spiritual
31–18   *h·* untamed desire which breaketh
Po. 53–17   Come at the sad *h·* call,

heart's
My. 188–17   your inner sanctuary, your *h·* heart,
236– 3   my full *h·* love for them
259–12   I return my *h·* wireless love.

hearts (*see also* hearts')

abides in the
My. 124–16   abides in the *h·* of these hearers
all love
Po.   9–11   reason made right and *h·* all love.
and hands
My. 153– 2   loving *h·* and hands of the
197–28   work of your *h·* and hands.
and lives
Mis. 291–24   fall gently on the *h·* and lives of
are found
Mis. 386– 5   home and peace and *h·* are found
Po. 49– 8   home and peace and *h·* are found
are inspired
Mis. 101– 1   how *h·* are inspired,
bleeding
Mis. 275–15   the wounds of bleeding *h·*,
Po. 27–16   *H·* bleeding ere they break
dear
Mis. 142–17   Because your dear *h·* expressed
filled
My. 362–19   * *h·* filled with gratitude to God,
full
'00. 14–18   hold in your full *h·* fervently
grateful
My. 332– 9   * a tribute of grateful *h·* ?
great
My. 197–13   great *h·* and ready hands of our
happy
'00.   1– 2   the tone of your happy *h·*,
My. 155–27   happy *h·* and ripening goodness.
heart of
Un.   7– 7   and from my heart of *h·*,
heroic
'01.   1–20   characterize heroic *h·* ;
honest
Mis. 357–17   the good and honest *h·*
human
Mis. 294–15   the flowers of human *h·*
303–14   at the door of human *h·*,
hungry
My. 147–29   heavenly homesick or hungry *h·*
kind
My. 153– 4   if these kind *h·* will only
lifted up
My. 81–19   * *h·* lifted up, spoke simply
loving
Pul.   8–24   loving *h·* and deft fingers
My. 13–17   loving *h·*, pledged to this
117–26   their talents and loving *h·*
153– 2   loving *h·* and hands of the
208– 6   mirrored forth by your loving *h·*,
minds and
Mis. 169–17   borne fully to our minds and *h·*.
no separator of
Mis. 150–10   Space is no separator of *h·*.
of all
No.   v– 7   transparent to the *h·* of all
My. 327–12   * made glad the *h·* of all
of Christians
Mis. 383–15   and in the *h·* of Christians.
of Christian Scientists
Mis. 145–26   When the *h·* of Christian Scientists
of men
Mis. 121– 2   inscribed upon the *h·* of men :
My. 123– 6   which moves the *h·* of men
of this people
My. 187–26   has been in the *h·* of this people
our
Mis. 110–18   Our *h·* have kept time together,
135– 4   Principle, . . . is next to our *h·*,
144–21   be this hope in each of our *h·*,
306–26   love they create in our *h·*.
344–24   His words, living in our *h·*,
Pul.   9– 7   never be shattered in our *h·*,
Rud.   3–10   His history is emphatic in our *h·*,
My. 39–25   * Our *h·* were thrilled by her
199–16   C. S., so dear to our *h·*
257–18   our *h·* are kneeling humbly.
our own
No.   7– 9   cancel error in our own *h·*,
overflowing
Mis. 348– 6   with *h·* overflowing with love
pleading
Po. 78–15   Give to the pleading *h·* comfort
quivering
Mis. 274–25   headless trunks, and quivering *h·*
stout
Mis. 222–23   will make stout *h·* quail.
strong
My. 290– 1   the strong *h·* of New England

hearts

swell the
My. 19–27 swell the *h·* of the members
their
Mis. 277– 1 their *h·* are not troubled.
Pul. 85– 6 * turn their *h·* in gratitude
'01. 32–11 shield the whole world in their *h·*,
My. 6–25 even the outcome of their *h·*,
94–29 even the outcome of their *h·*,
160–17 Then they open their *h·* to it
the very
My. 122–31 the very *h·* that rejected it
true
Mis. 384– 4 And true *h·* greet,
Po. 36– 3 And true *h·* greet,
two
Mis. 290– 2 to the compact of two *h·*.
384– 3 When two *h·* meet,
Po. 36– 2 When two *h·* meet,
unveiled
My. 199–20 of strengthened hands, of unveiled *h·*,
waiting
Po. 39–16 And be your waiting *h·* elate,
warm
My. 124– 9 willing hands, and warm *h·*,
weary
My. 93–14 * it has rare lures for weary *h·*,
were thrilled
My. 64– 6 * *h·* were thrilled with tender
your
Mis. 143–10 in each of your *h·* !
156–11 heaven of Love within your *h·*.
Hea. 16–14 come nearer your *h·*
My. 167–12 may fill your *h·*
193– 4 bring to your *h·* so much of heaven
197–28 work of your *h·* and hands.

Mis. 150–12 *h·* to-day are repeating their joy
152– 6 whose *h·* unite in the purposes of
152–17 *h·* of those who worship in this
262–12 acceptable to those who have *h·*.
Ret. 6– 2 * *h·* of those especially entrusted to
'01. 1– 2 to those whose *h·* have been
My. 195–27 in the *h·* of its members
326–20 turning the *h·* of the noble Southrons

hearts'

Mis. 141– 4 of your *h·* offering to her
Pul. 11– 6 rehearse your *h·* holy intents.
Po. 43–14 their pure *h·* off'ring,

heart-stirring

Ret. 2–15 *h·* air, "Scots wha hae wi' Wallace

heart-strings

Mis. 387– 1 the *h·* gently sweep,
Po. 50–18 the *h·* gently sweep
68–15 To sweep o'er the *h·*

hearty

Pul. 44– 6 * I send my *h·* congratulations.
My. 285– 5 accept my *h·* congratulations.
287– 4 enlists my *h·* sympathy.

heat

Mis. 130–18 burden in the *h·* of the day,
134–25 fermenting, and its *h·* hissing at
Ret. 79– 6 In this consuming *h·* false images
Un. 58–12 hypocrite melts in fervent *h·*,
Pul. 25– 3 * *h·* generated by two large boilers
No. 14–14 solar *h·* and light.
28– 4 melt in the fervent *h·* of suffering,
'00. 9–30 *h·* of the day." — *Matt.* 20 : 12.
My. 29–27 * breeze to temper the *h·*,
249–11 Unless withstood, the *h·* of hate
265–28 extremes of *h·* and cold ;

heated

'02. 9–18 is not the dream of a *h·* brain ;

heathen

Un. 15–21 found in *h·* religious history.
No. 34–20 infinitely beyond the *h·* conception
'00. 3–25 In the *h·* conception Yahwah,
3–29 the animus of *h·* religion
13–10 the apostle justly regards as *h·*,
Peo. 4–23 as material as the *h·* deities.
4–25 they inquired of these *h·* deities
My. 103–16 "Why do the *h·* rage, — *Psal.* 2 : 1.
118–25 which rests on a *h·* basis
159–25 Epictetus, a *h·* philosopher
200– 5 Let "the *h·* rage, — *Psal.* 2 : 1.
234–19 introducing C. S. into a *h·* nation,
234–26 prayer in and for a *h·* nation

heathenism

Pul. 75–10 would savor more of *h·* than of
My. 167–30 In our country the day of *h·*.

heating

Pul. 25– 2 * cooling . . . as well as *h·*

heaven (see also heaven's)

and earth
Mis. 86–20 as in the new *h·* and earth,
99–21 "*H·* and earth shall pass — *Matt.* 24 : 35.
111–17 "*H·* and earth shall pass — *Matt.* 24 : 35.
163–18 "*H·* and earth shall pass — *Matt.* 24 : 35.
167–24 Lord of *h·* and earth, — *Luke* 10 : 21.
Un. 59– 6 Principle which made *h·* and earth
No. 44–28 Lord of *h·* and earth, — *Luke* 10 : 21
antipode of
My. 181–30 material earth or antipode of *h·*.
army of
Mis. 334– 2 in the army of *h·*, — *Dan.* 4 : 35.
attainment of
Mis. 101–13 holiness, and the attainment of *h·*.
be praised
My. 200– 4 *H·* be praised for the signs of
bestows
Peo. 12–27 when our Father bestows *h·*
bound in
No. 32– 1 shall be bound in *h·*." — *Matt.* 16 : 19.
bread of
Mis. 127–15 to feed it with the bread of *h·*,
My. 18–12 to feed it with the bread of *h·*,
131– 9 bread of *h·* whereof if a man eat
breath of
Mis. 328–11 with a breath of *h·*,
comes down
Mis. 10–27 *H·* comes down to earth,
consciousness of
My. 118–28 the consciousness of *h·* within
demonstrates
'02. 6–24 points the way, demonstrates *h·*
dew of
Mis. 291–23 The dew of *h·* will fall
dews of
Mis. 154– 9 water it with the dews of *h·*,
My. 208–13 Like the gentle dews of *h·*
diapason of
Mis. 206–21 repeating this diapason of *h·* :
down from
Mis. 149–24 that cometh down from *h·*,
176–22 which came down from *h·*,
254– 7 that cometh down from *h·*,
Un. 59– 9 one who came down from *h·*,
Pan. 14– 8 that cometh down from *h·*,
My. 156–21 that cometh down from *h·*,
earth and
Mis. 30–10 He saw the real earth and *h·*.
86–29 their present earth and *h·* :
228–19 fit for earth and *h·*.
Un. 59– 7 never absent from the earth and *h·* ;
earth and in
Mis. 113–27 to enjoy on earth and in *h·*.
151–15 real relative on earth and in *h·*.
'00. 2– 6 best people on earth and in *h·*.
earth to
(see **earth**)
enough of
Mis. 16– 4 enough of *h·* to come down to
enter
Mis. 241– 5 man will no more enter *h·* sick
Un. 37– 5 inherit eternal life and enter *h·* ?
My. 267–17 enter *h·* in proportion to their
far
Po. 22– 7 lo, the light ! far *h·* is nigh !
fitted for
Mis. 197– 9 fitted for *h·* in the way which
flood-gates of
Mis. 185–11 opens the very flood-gates of *h·* ;
foretaste of
Mis. 100–24 bring to earth a foretaste of *h·*.
gain
Mis. 53– 9 gain *h·*, the harmony of being.
174–26 whereby to gain *h·*.
gates of
Mis. 275–19 throw wide the gates of *h·*.
Ret. 71– 3 to open the gates of *h·*.
God and
Un. 37– 7 God and *h·*, or Life, are present,
happiness, and
Mis. 308– 8 path to health, happiness, and *h·*.
311–17 health, happiness, and *h·*.
harmonies of
My. 115– 7 echoing the harmonies of *h·*
harmony, and
No. 34– 3 up to health, harmony, and *h·*.
harmony is
Mis. 337–16 Harmony is *h·*.
harmony of
My. 274– 7 with the harmony of *h·* ;
health and
Pul. 53–24 * key to health and *h·*,

heaven

high
Mis.	122–25	Neither . . . can win high $h^{\cdot}$,
	387–22	greetings glorious from high $h^{\cdot}$,
Pul.	12–19	reached high $h^{\cdot}$,
Po.	6–17	greetings glorious from high $h^{\cdot}$,
My.	189– 5	that it reaches high $h^{\cdot}$

highway to
| No. | 33–13 | Self-sacrifice is the highway to $h^{\cdot}$. |

holiness and
| Mis. | 309–22 | health, holiness, and $h^{\cdot}$. |
| Un. | 64– 6 | health, holiness, and $h^{\cdot}$, |

home and
| Mis. | 289–18 | compatible with home and $h^{\cdot}$. |
| Pul. | 11– 8 | find within it home, and $h^{\cdot}$. |

homesick for
| Mis. | 177–30 | I am constantly homesick for $h^{\cdot}$. |

hope of
| Mis. | 311–22 | lose my hope of $h^{\cdot}$. |

hosts of
| Po. | 10–18 | cheer the hosts of $h^{\cdot}$; |
| My. | 337–19 | cheer the hosts of $h^{\cdot}$; |

hues of
Mis.	332–10	follow with hues of $h^{\cdot}$,
	377– 1	such forms and hues of $h^{\cdot}$,
'02.	20– 5	hues of $h^{\cdot}$, tipping the dawn

husbands
| '02. | 5–10 | *divine Love*, that $h^{\cdot}$ husbands |

insignia of
| Ret. | 80– 2 | and the insignia of $h^{\cdot}$. |

is afar off
| Mis. | 342–20 | and $h^{\cdot}$ is afar off." |

is harmony
| My. | 267–16 | $H^{\cdot}$ is harmony, |

is spiritual
| My. | 267–16 | $H^{\cdot}$ is spiritual. |

joys of
| Po. | 24– 1 | Come to me, joys of $h^{\cdot}$! |

kingdom of
    (*see* **kingdom**)

less of
| Pul. | 87–20 | more of earth . . . and less of $h^{\cdot}$; |

livery of
| Mis. | 19–18 | But, taking the livery of $h^{\cdot}$ |

Lord of
| Mis. | 167–24 | Lord of $h^{\cdot}$ and earth, — *Luke* 10 : 21. |
| No. | 44–28 | Lord of $h^{\cdot}$ and earth, — *Luke* 10 : 21. |

message from
| Po. | 15– 7 | canst bear A message from $h^{\cdot}$ |

most of
| '02. | 17– 8 | that which has most of $h^{\cdot}$ |

never left
| No. | 36– 7 | conscious being never left $h^{\cdot}$ |

new
| Mis. | 21– 7 | beheld "a new $h^{\cdot}$ — *Rev.* 21 : 1. |
| | 86–20 | as in the new $h^{\cdot}$ and earth, |

of His presence
| Un. | 37–12 | and the $h^{\cdot}$ of His presence ; |

of light
| Po. | 71– 9 | Spans our broad $h^{\cdot}$ of light. |

of Love
| Mis. | 156–10 | $h^{\cdot}$ of Love within your hearts. |

of my youth
| Po. | 8–13 | sketching in light the $h^{\cdot}$ of my youth |

of Soul
Mis.	394– 5	the home, and the $h^{\cdot}$ of Soul.
Po.	45– 6	the home, and the $h^{\cdot}$ of Soul.
My.	163– 2	haven of hope, the $h^{\cdot}$ of Soul,

of Spirit
| My. | 195–28 | eternal in the $h^{\cdot}$ of Spirit. |

of Truth
| Ret. | 85–10 | down from the $h^{\cdot}$ of Truth and Love, |

path to
| '02. | 11– 9 | and point the path to $h^{\cdot}$. |
| My. | 176– 8 | pointing the path to $h^{\cdot}$ |

plan of
| Mis. | 296–14 | and live on the plan of $h^{\cdot}$? |

poetry of
| Po. | 46–14 | Sweet as the poetry of $h^{\cdot}$, |

points to
| Ret. | 31– 2 | loss of . . . points to $h^{\cdot}$. |

point to
| Mis. | 389– 4 | * "To point to $h^{\cdot}$ and lead the way." |
| Po. | 21–18 | * "To point to $h^{\cdot}$ and lead the way." |

rang
| Po. | 70–17 | Immortal Truth, — since $h^{\cdot}$ rang, |

rapid transit to
| Mis. | 206– 1 | take rapid transit to $h^{\cdot}$, |

reaches
| Un. | 57–19 | ladder which reaches $h^{\cdot}$. |
| My. | 194–10 | builds that which reaches $h^{\cdot}$. |

realization of
| My. | 297–17 | and a higher realization of $h^{\cdot}$. |

recorded in
| '02. | 14–22 | achievement . . . recorded in $h^{\cdot}$. |

heaven

reign of
Mis.	384–12	The reign of $h^{\cdot}$ begun,
'00.	15–29	The reign of $h^{\cdot}$ begun,
Po.	36–11	The reign of $h^{\cdot}$ begun,

reward in
| '02. | 11–25 | reward in $h^{\cdot}$: — *Matt.* 5 : 12. |
| My. | 6–12 | reward in $h^{\cdot}$." — *Matt.* 5 : 12. |

ruleth in
| My. | 200– 6 | ruleth in $h^{\cdot}$ and upon earth, |

so much of
| My. | 193– 4 | bring to your hearts so much of $h^{\cdot}$ |

stars of
| Ret. | 28–27 | higher than the stars of $h^{\cdot}$. |

takes hold on
| My. | 129–25 | man's heart takes hold on $h^{\cdot}$, |

this
| Mis. | 30–12 | was not the door to this $h^{\cdot}$. |

to reach
| Mis. | 235– 3 | no longer . . . die to reach $h^{\cdot}$, |
| Hea. | 8–21 | to reach $h^{\cdot}$ through Principle |

under
| Mis. | 185–15 | There is no other way under $h^{\cdot}$ |
| '00. | 5–15 | no other way under $h^{\cdot}$ |

unto
| My. | 126–16 | reached unto $h^{\cdot}$, — *Rev.* 18 : 5. |

verge of
| Mis. | 202– 7 | * Quite on the verge of $h^{\cdot}$." |
| | 357–11 | quite on the verge of $h^{\cdot}$. |

virtue, and
| Mis. | 238–15 | health, virtue, and $h^{\cdot}$; |

vision of
| My. | 155–19 | a clear vision of $h^{\cdot}$ here, |

voice from
| Mis. | 168–15 | voice from $h^{\cdot}$ seems to say, |

way to
| Mis. | 268– 6 | pointing the way to $h^{\cdot}$, |
| | 344–27 | point out the way to $h^{\cdot}$ |

which is in
Mis.	85–15	Father which is in $h^{\cdot}$ — *Matt.* 5 : 48.
	287– 7	Father, which is in $h^{\cdot}$." — *Matt.* 23 : 9.
Chr.	55–23	Father which is in $h^{\cdot}$, — *Matt.* 12 : 50.
Ret.	68–15	Father, which is in $h^{\cdot}$." — *Matt* 23 : 9.
Un.	53–28	Father, which is in $h^{\cdot}$." — *Matt.* 23 : 9.
	59–10	which is in $h^{\cdot}$," — *John* 3 : 13.
Rud.	1– 8	It is our Father which is in $h^{\cdot}$.
No.	36– 9	which is in $h^{\cdot}$," — *John* 3 : 13.
Pan.	8–19	Father, which is in $h^{\cdot}$." — *Matt.* 23 : 9.
	9–12	Father which is in $h^{\cdot}$ — *Matt.* 5 : 48.
'01.	8–16	Father which is in $h^{\cdot}$ — *Matt.* 5 : 48.

windows of
My.	131–27	windows of $h^{\cdot}$, — *Mal.* 3 : 10.
	132– 4	windows of $h^{\cdot}$, — *Mal.* 3 : 10.
	269–22	windows of $h^{\cdot}$ are sending forth
	269–27	windows of $h^{\cdot}$, — *Mal.* 3 : 10.

within us
My.	155–19	$h^{\cdot}$ within us,
	260–21	because of the $h^{\cdot}$ within us.
	303–31	foretasting $h^{\cdot}$ within us.

wonder in
| Mis. | 337– 8 | Wonder in $h^{\cdot}$ and on earth, |
| Pul. | 83–27 | * a great wonder in $h^{\cdot}$, — *Rev.* 12 : 1. |

Mis.	33– 5	they lost, and he won, $h^{\cdot}$.
	67–28	removal of a person to $h^{\cdot}$,
	83–24	lifted up his eyes to $h^{\cdot}$, — *John* 17 : 1.
	151–16	"Whom have I in $h^{\cdot}$ — *Psal.* 73 : 25.
	205–22	with eternal life, holiness, $h^{\cdot}$.
	213–30	*His* will be done on earth as in $h^{\cdot}$.
	251–20	$H^{\cdot}$ right here,
	330–28	violet lifts its blue eye to $h^{\cdot}$,
	339– 4	took place once in $h^{\cdot}$,
	373–27	in $h^{\cdot}$ and in earth," — *Matt.* 28 : 18.
	399–24	($H^{\cdot}$ chiselled squarely good)
Chr.	53–43	silent healing, $h^{\cdot}$ heard,
Ret.	17–20	blossom and branches to $h^{\cdot}$.
Pul.	12– 6	voice saying in $h^{\cdot}$, — *Rev.* 12 : 10.
	16– 9	($H^{\cdot}$ chiselled squarely good)
	22– 8	in earth, as it is in $h^{\cdot}$." — *Matt.* 6 : 10.
	27–14	* from God out of $h^{\cdot}$," — *see Rev.* 3 : 12.
Pan.	3–25	* $h^{\cdot}$, earth, sea, the eternal fire,
	13–17	and done on earth as in $h^{\cdot}$.
Hea.	19–25	up the steep ascent, on to $h^{\cdot}$,
Peo.	12–28	without health there could be no $h^{\cdot}$.
Po.	63– 7	feathery blossom and branches to $h^{\cdot}$.
	68– 8	or this happiness $h^{\cdot}$!
	76– 8	($H^{\cdot}$ chiseled squarely good)
My.	18–25	and done on earth as in $h^{\cdot}$."
	139–11	life-lease of hope, home, $h^{\cdot}$;
	158–13	$h^{\cdot}$ here, the struggle over ;
	201–12	hope repossess us of $h^{\cdot}$.
	203–15	suffering here and of $h^{\cdot}$ hereafter.
	254– 1	$h^{\cdot}$ opens, right reigns,
	267–14	chapter sub-title
	267–15	Is $h^{\cdot}$ spiritual?

heaven
My. 267–19 quality and the quantity of *h.*
    267–23 *H.* is the reign of divine Science.
    278–18 Japanese may believe in a *h.* for
    281– 5 in earth, as it is in *h.*" — *Matt.* 6 : 10.

heaven-appointed
My. 221–19 no other *h.* means than

heaven-born
Mis. 15–17 *h.* hope, and spiritual love.
    374–14 pluck not their *h.* wings.

heaven-crowned
Mis. 328– 7 mountain is *h.* Christianity,
    358–18 *h.* summit of C. S.

heavenly
Mis. 140–28 our title clear" to *h.* mansions.
    324–31 receive his *h.* guidance.
    326–25 Well might this *h.* messenger exclaim,
    343–11 watered by the *h.* dews of Love,
    387–18 Seek holy thoughts and *h.* strain,
    389–25 finds her home and *h.* rest.
Ret. 21–17 *h.* intent of earth's shadows
    80–15 receptive of the *h.* discipline.
Un. 6–13 Until the *h.* law of health,
    51–12 of the *h.* sovereignty.
Pul. 1–13 *h.* assurance ends all warfare,
    27–13 * one representing the *h.* city
'01. 7–12 our *h.* Parent — the divine Mind
    7–15 does not this *h.* Parent know
Hea. 20– 5 * We'd soar and touch the *h.* strings,
Peo. 5–21 Let us then heed this *h.* visitant,
    7–22 * Its *h.* beauty shall be our own,
Po. 5– 6 finds her home and *h.* rest.
    6–13 Seek holy thoughts and *h.* strain,
My. 38– 1 * balm of *h.* joy,
    46–28 the *h.* Jerusalem, — *Heb.* 12 : 22.
    109–12 teaching them the same *h.* lesson.
    147–29 *h.* homesick or hungry hearts
    208– 6 to reflect its *h.* rays over all
    257–13 Christ's *h.* origin and aim.
    (*see also* **Father**)

Heaven's
Hea. 1– 7 *H.* favors are formidable :
    19–16 *H.* signet is Love.

heaven's
Mis. 145–28 float majestically *h.* heraldry,
    312– 9 for the kingdom of *h.* sake.
    389–24 When *h.* aftersmile
Chr. 53–21 For *h.* Christus, earthly Eves,
    53–60 In *h.* hymn.
Ret. 87– 3 * "Order is *h.* first law,"
Peo. 7–14 * With *h.* own light the sculptor
Po. 5– 4 When *h.* aftersmile
    30–22 *h.* lyres and angels' loving lays,
My. 155–24 sing as the angels *h.* symphonies
    167–11 I pray that *h.* messages

heavens
  above
  Mis. 158– 4 higher far than the *h.* above
    392–17 grandly rising to the *h.* above.
  Po. 20–21 grandly rising to the *h.* above.
  build to the
  Mis. 135–13 though you should build to the *h.*,
  My. 165–30 means that build to the *h.*,
  eternal in the
  Pul. 2–15 eternal in the *h.*" — *II Cor.* 5 : 1.
  '01. 25– 4 superstructure eternal in the *h.*,
  My. 188–14 eternal in the *h.*;" — *II Cor.* 5 : 1.
    192–30 "eternal in the *h.*." — *II Cor.* 5 : 1.
  moral 194– 8 eternal in the *h.*," — *II Cor.* 5 : 1.
  Peo. 3–15 spans the moral *h.* with light,
  of divine Science
  Mis. 320–17 fixed in the *h.* of divine Science,
  of Soul
  Mis. 360–13 fixed stars in the *h.* of Soul.
  of thought
  Mis. 355–31 will span thy *h.* of thought.
  our
  Po. 68–22 Be its course through our *h.*,
  our own
  Mis. 170–13 we make our own *h.*
  pointing to the
  My. 162–32 temple . . . pointing to the *h.*,
  signs in the
  Mis. 1– 5 foreshadowed by signs in the *h.*.
  sitteth in the
  Mis. 126–31 "He that sitteth in the *h.* — *Psal.* 2 : 4.
  spiritual
  Mis. 254–20 stars from the spiritual *h.*,
  the very
  Mis. 338–17 But the very *h.* shall laugh
  upon the
  Mis. 333–31 hung his destiny out upon the *h.* ;

Pul. 12–12 Therefore rejoice, ye *h.*, — *Rev.* 12 : 12.

heavenward
Mis. 147–10 worthy to be borne *h.* ?
    316–11 the tide which flows *h.*,
Pul. 11– 1 bear you outward, upward, *h.*.
Po. 19– 4 onward and upward and *h.*
My. 37– 6 * can acceptably ascend *h.*
    154–29 whereby we are looking *h.*,
    204– 7 It is only by looking *h.*
    316– 4 and renews the *h.* impulse ;

heavily
Pul. 76–20 * is all *h.* plated with gold."

heaving
'02. 19–19 *h.* surf of life's troubled sea

heavy
Mis. 20– 4 labor and are *h.* laden, — *Matt.* 11 : 28.
    132– 4 token that *h.* lids are opening,
    262–25 yet were our burdens *h.*
    327–12 had *h.* baggage of their own,
    327–20 lay down a few of the *h.* weights,
Man. 60–11 rest the weary and *h.* laden,
Ret. 2–11 brought to New England a *h.* sword,
    95– 9 * For *h.* is the weight of ill
Pul. 20– 3 Owing to a *h.* loss,
    46–18 * a *h.* sword, encased in a
    62– 6 * *h.* cast bells of old-fashioned
No. 43– 5 labor and are *h.* laden, — *Matt.* 11 : 28.
Hea. 2–18 labor and are *h.* laden, — *Matt.* 11 : 28.
Peo. 11–25 "bind *h.* burdens," — *Matt.* 23 : 4.
Po. vii–14 * *a joy to the h. laden*
My. 44– 3 * *h.* burdens are being laid down,
    84– 3 * *h.* debt, the interest on which
    291– 7 began with *h.* strokes,

heavy-laden
Mis. 208–14 to the weary and *h.*,
'02. 11– 8 earth-weary and *h.* who find

Hebrew
Mis. 8–27 The *H.* law with its
    126–29 penalty of which the *H.* bard spake
    142–23 spiritual strains of the *H.* bard.
    170–26 Spitting was the *H.* method of
    180–26 In the *H.* text, the word "son"
    184–12 brings to remembrance the *H.* strain,
    190–28 In the *H.*, "devil" is — *Luke* 11 : 14.
    191– 2 The *H.* embodies the term
    192– 2 *H.* term for Deity was "good,"
    192–14 The *H.* bard saith,
    193–32 "belief;" the *H.* of which implies
    297–29 The *H.* bard wrote,
    392–13 To love the *H.* figure of a tree.
Ret. 10– 9 ancient tongues, *H.*, Greek, and
    10–10 My brother studied *H.*
Un. 14–15 limited *H.* faith might need
    28– 1 We read in the *H.* Scriptures,
Pul. 46–26 * ancient languages, *H.*, Greek,
Pan. 4–21 words of the *H.* singer,
'00. 12–29 It refers to the *H.* Balaam
'01. 34–29 words of the *H.* writers :
Hea. 6–28 in *H.* it is *belial*,
Peo. 2– 8 The *H.* term that gives
Po. 20–17 love the *H.* figure of a tree.
My. 273–10 King David, the *H.* bard,

Hebrew Decalogue
Mis. 21– 2 First Commandment of the *H. D.*,
    114–14 teach others to practise, the *H. D.*,
'02. 4–14 First Commandment in the *H. D.*,
My. 5–13 First Commandment of the *H. D.*,
    64–12 First Commandment of the *H. D.*,
    268–15 Two commandments of the *H. D.*,
    279–11 First Commandment in the *H. D.*

Hebrews
Mis. 26–26 common version of *H.* i. 3,
Un. 23–10 Scripture, in *H.* xii. 7, 8 :

hedge
Man. 104– 9 *h.* it about with divine Love.
Ret. 52– 4 build a *h.* round about it

hedgerow
Ret. 18– 8 sentinel *h.* is guarding repose,
Po. 63–17 sentinel *h.* is guarding repose,

heed
Mis. 368–11 chapter sub-title
Man. 78– 3 fails to *h.* this admonition,
'02. 15–28 To this, however, I gave no *h.*,
Peo. 5–21 Let us then *h.* this heavenly visitant,
My. 37–31 * pray that we may give *h.*

heeded
Mis. 254– 4 the stern rebuke have been *h.*,
    326–10 slumberers who *h.* them not,
    342– 5 They *h.* not their sloth,
Un. 11–16 He *h.* not the taunt,
No. 9– 2 if it had been *h.* in times past

heed'st
My. 350–14 *h.* Thou not the scalding

heel
Mis. 210–18   as it biteth at the *h·.*
Un.   45– 5   and it stings your *h·,*
Pul. 82–30   * ceased to kiss the iron *h·* of wrong.
'00.   10– 2   Hatred bites the *h·* of love
Hea. 11–15   may not recover from the *h·* of allopathy
Po.   71–11   Feared for an hour the tyrant's *h·* !

heels
No.   43–27   bark and bite at its *h·.*

Hegel
No.   22– 4   Leibnitz, Descartes, Fichte, *H·,*
    22– 7   *H·* was an inveterate snuff-taker.

height
Mis.   8–13   Can *h·,* or depth, or any other
   338– 4   gained its *h·* beforehand,
   379– 8   appearance, *h·,* and complexion
Ret. 48–30   *h·* of prosperity in the institution,
Pul. 24–26   * twenty feet in *h·*
   26–12   * lamps, eight feet in *h·.*
Po.   1–13   from yon cloud-crowned *h·*
   2–14   upon thine exiled *h·* ;
My.   4–29   *h·* of my hope must remain.
   45–29   * Bedford stone, rising to a *h·* of
   67– 8   * *H·* . . . 224 ft.
   68– 9   * a *h·* of fifty-one feet.
   78– 6   * massive dome rising to a *h·* of
   81– 6   * at the very *h·* of fervor,
  117–28   I left Boston in the *h·* of
  281– 7   soaring to the Horeb *h·,*

heightens
Mis.   1–18   *h·* immortal attributes

heights
Mis. 126–11   have gained higher *h·* ;
   369– 8   stand erect on sublime *h·,*
My. 146–15   *h·* of the great Nazarene's sayings

heir
Mis. 33–27   * "the ills that flesh is *h·* to,"
  167–20   Is he *h·* to an estate?
  253–19   "This is the *h·* : — *Luke* 20 : 14.
  254–14   "This is the *h·* : — *Luke* 20 : 14.
No.   42–10   * "the ills that flesh is *h·* to,"
Hea. 15– 6   to heal all ills that flesh is *h·* to.

heirs
Mis. 46–24   if children, then *h·* ; — *Rom.* 8 : 17.
  46–24   *h·* of God, — *Rom.* 8 : 17.
  165–19   makes his followers the *h·* to
  255–15   if children, then *h·* ; — *Rom.* 8 : 17.
  255–16   *h·* of God, — *Rom.* 8 : 17.

held
Mis. 61–15   * the man is *h·* responsible for the crime ;
  61–18   * This 'man' was *h·* responsible
  98– 2   perfect model should be *h·* in mind,
  156–14   the one *h·* at Chicago,
  195– 8   *h·* back by reason of the lack of
  274–25   and quivering hearts are *h·* up
  297–20   is *h·* in C. S. as morally bound
  304–14   * great patriotic celebration is being *h·,*
  315– 5   *h·* on the Sunday following
  365–28   *h·* back by the common ignorance
Man. 26– 8   annual meeting *h·* for this purpose,
  38–13   meetings *h·* for this purpose.
  56–11   *h·* annually, on Monday following
  56–20   *h·* on Monday preceding the
  57– 3   shall be *h·* on the Friday preceding
  57– 6   Special meetings may be *h·*
  70–16   No conference . . . shall be *h·,*
  82–14   meeting *h·* for this purpose
  91–23   which will be *h·* once in three years
Ret.   3– 2   *h·* the position of ambassador to
  14– 3   meeting was *h·* for the examination
Un.   9–22   *h·* by a few spiritual thinkers in
  14– 5   Can it be seriously *h·,* by any
  54–21   Satan *h·* it up before man as
  57–15   he neither *h·* her error by affinity
Pul.   4–28   Parliament of Religions, *h·* in
  28–28   * *h·* its meetings in Chickering Hall,
  29– 9   * service *h·* in Copley Hall.
  30–26   * first meeting *h·* on April 12,
  55–18   * *h·* to be scientific certainty,
  59– 6   * continuous services were *h·*
  68–25   * meeting *h·* at the present location
  79–15   * in most instances they are *h·* at
  87– 2   * services that may be *h·* therein.
No. 11–11   this system is *h·* back by the
  13–17   not . . *h·* as a mere theory.
  25– 6   wherein we were *h·* ; — *Rom.* 7 : 6.
'01. 16– 2   * God's hand has *h·* you up."
  31–25   *h·* fast to whatever is good,
Peo.   2–26   *h·* constantly before the people's
Po. 68– 7   Earth *h·* but this joy,
My. 30– 1   * *h·* large crowds of people,
  38–29   * was *h·* in the extension of The
  39– 2   * second session was *h·* at two

held
My. 42–21   * first annual meeting *h·* in the
  49–16   * meeting of the church was *h·*
  49–20   * August 27 the church *h·* a meeting,
  49–26   * meeting *h·* October 19, 1879,
  50– 2   * *h·* at the home of the pastor,
  53–12   * services were *h·* there until
  54–13   * *h·* at Odd Fellows Hall,
  54–31   * *h·* in Chickering Hall
  55–19   * were *h·* in Chickering Hall,
  55–26   * Sunday services were *h·*
  56– 5   * two services were *h·,*
  56–29   * three services were *h·* each Sunday,
  57–14   * was *h·* in Chickering Hall,
  61–10   * *h·* in the new extension
  65– 4   * largest . . . ever *h·* in Boston
  65– 4   * largest ever *h·* in the
  66–22   * six services will be *h·,*
  78– 3   * were *h·* during the morning,
  80–10   * Meetings were *h·* in the extension
  80–31   * where the largest meeting was *h·,*
  89– 3   * may be *h·* to symbolize that faith
  93–28   * now being *h·* in Boston
  94–21   * *h·* at different hours of the day,
  141– 4   * *h·* annually in The First Church
  141– 8   * the last to be *h·.*
  141–11   * would have been *h·* next year.
  159–25   heathen philosopher who *h·* that
  222–28   liberty of conscience *h·* sacred.
  284–14   *h·* in my church building,
  284–19   been *h·* annually in some church
  289–27   meeting to be *h·* in the capital
  318–20   He *h·* himself well in check
  338– 8   * *h·* and expressed by her.

Helen's
Mis. 374–25   * " *H·* beauty in a brow of Egypt."

hell
Mis. 134–20   earth and *h·* are proven powerless.
  141– 9   "the gates of *h·*" — *Matt.* 16 : 18.
  144–20   the gates of *h·* — *Matt.* 16 : 18.
  170–12   hades, or *h·* of Scripture,
  235– 6   Him who destroys death and *h·.*
  237– 2   olden opinion that *h·* is fire and
Un.   56–24   pangs of *h·* must lay hold of him
No. 38–11   against which the gates of *h·*
'01. 15–18   the old orthodox *h·*
  15–27   * why you have not gone to *h·*
  16– 1   * drop down into *h·,*
'02.   3–29   Envy is the atmosphere of *h·.*
My. 160–19   I am asked, "Is there a *h·* ?"
  160–19   Yes, there is a *h·* for all who
  160–29   this *h·* is mental, not material,
  160–31   makers of *h·* burn in their fire.

hells
Mis. 170–13   our own heavens and our own *h·,*

helm
Mis. 113–26   at the *h·* of thought,
My. 232– 3   with the *h·* in His hands.

help (noun)
affords
'00.   7–27   Christ is found near, affords *h·,*
apply for
Mis. 39– 1   Many who apply for *h·*
call for
Mis. 81–26   answers the human call for *h·* ;
  380–11   imperative call for *h·*
calls for
Mis. 370– 1   feebleness calls for *h·,*
divine
Mis. 39–30   Divine *h·* is as necessary in the
  158–17   a lack of faith in divine *h·,*
  380–15   in faith, turned to divine *h·.*
ever-present
Mis. 96– 4   God is an ever-present *h·*
  157–17   He is the ever-present *h·*
  225–24   spiritual source and ever-present *h·,*
  307– 4   divine Love is an ever-present *h·* ;
My.   3–17   unerring impetus, an ever-present *h·.*
  12–27   supplies the ever-present *h·*
  44– 2   * God as an ever-present *h·,*
  152–23   ever-present *h·* in all things,
  167– 9   ever-present *h·* in trouble,
  240–12   Science . . . an ever-present *h·.*
  254–13   God an ever-present *h·.*
  295–25   Divine Love is your ever-present *h·.*
God's
Ret. 86–22   save himself without God's *h·,*
My. 197– 4   Attempt nothing without God's *h·.*
her
My. 231–15   invalids demanding her *h·*
his
Mis. 268–18   His " *h·* is from — see *Psal.* 121 : 2.
  358–10   God alone is his *h·,*
'00.   3– 6   No hand that feels not his *h·,*

help

household
Man.   69–15   household *h·* or a handmaid,
loss of
My.   195– 6   Adverse circumstances, loss of *h·*,
needed
My.   324–21   * he thought you needed *h·*,
no more
Mis.   197–16   would be of no more *h·*
of others
My.   130–15   I ask the *h·* of others
    138– 1   without the *h·* of others.
of truth-telling
My.   130–19   with the *h·* of truth-telling.
personal
Mis.   283–32   The only personal *h·* required
physical
Mis.   88– 3   feel the need of physical *h·*,
prayer for
Mis.   70–20   poor thief's prayer for *h·*
present
Un.   2– 5   very present *h·* — *Psal. 46 : 1.*
My.   162– 3   "very present *h·* — *Psal. 46 : 1.*
rather than
My.   219– 5   hindrance rather than *h·*.
recognize the
Mis.   33–19   recognize the *h·* they derive
refuse
Mis.   89–17   caused our Master to refuse *h·* to
shriek for
Mis.   326– 7   sufferers shriek for *h·* :
special
Mis.   357–27   and need special *h·*.
spiritual
My.   153–18   spiritual *h·* of divine Love.
their
Mis.   10–13   their *h·* in times of trouble.
to obtain
Ret.   71–27   Secret mental efforts to obtain *h·*
woman's
Pul.   83– 2   * woman's love and woman's *h·*

Mis.   25–26   if the sick cannot trust God for *h·*
    115–24   more unreservedly to Him for *h·*,
    148–16   immediate demand for them as a *h·*
    157–16   when *h·* is most needed,
    353–30   they constantly go to her for *h·*,
Man.   3–13   immediate demand for them as a *h·*
    69–13   *H·*.
    83–23   and S. AND H. . . . as a *h·* thereto.
'01.   26–13   for *h·* in times of need.
Po.   70–11   A *h·* forever near ;
My.   147–30   hearts are calling on me for *h·*,

help (verb)

Mis.   87–30   imagine they can *h·* anybody
    90–15   Then *h·* others to be free ;
    115–26   every effort to hurt one will only *h·*
    129–10   and thereby *h·* him.
    131– 2   can neither *h·* himself nor others ;
    146–22   *h·* him to walk in the footsteps of
    149– 6   to *h·* leaven your loaf
    157–12   They will be glad to *h·* you.
    211– 1   you will *h·* to reform them.
    236–26   in one's efforts to *h·* another,
    237–14   must encounter and *h·* to eradicate.
    267–14   I saw an opportunity really to *h·*
    277–30   I cannot *h·* loathing the
    292–19   enjoins it upon man to *h·* those
    294–23   that you desire to *h·* even such as
    303–17   effort to *h·* them to obey
    311–16   I love my enemies and would *h·* all
    328– 1   and would *h·* them on ;
    348– 6   *h·* on the brotherhood of men.
    357–29   ready and glad to *h·* them
    371– 7   to *h·* them by his own leadership
Ret.   86–22   and God will *h·* each man who
Pul.   4–18   drop of water may *h·* to hide
    7– 2   * I would *h·* that woman."
    14–22   the earth will *h·* the woman ;
    41– 7   * to *h·* erect this beautiful structure,
    51–23   * *h·* on the growth of its principles.
    82–24   * the right to *h·* make the laws,
    82–25   * at least to *h·* enforce the laws
    83–20   * "God shall *h·* her, — *Psal. 46 : 5.*
No.   43–25   reconstruct . . . and *h·* humanity.
Pan.   9–20   to *h·* such a one is to *h·* one's self.
'01.   29– 7   those who want to *h·* them.
    29–17   not to *h·* mother but to recruit
    29–19   attempt to *h·* their parents.
    32– 8   I could not *h·* loving them.
'02.   3–28   to serve God and to *h·* the race.
    11–11   hastens to *h·* on his fellow-mortals,
Po.   28– 3   *H·* us to write a deathless page
    28– 6   *H·* us to humbly bow
My.   47–18   * we cannot *h·* being touched by

help (verb)

My.   165– 8   The best *h·* the worst ;
    166– 1   it can *h·* its neighbor.
    166–19   willing to *h·* and to be helped,
    173–14   to *h·* furnish and beautify our
    190– 3   *h·* to evolve that larger sympathy
    201–18   may *h·* us, not to a start, but to
    216– 4   in order to *h·* mankind with it.
    217– 3   to *h·* your parents,
    229–14   go to *h·* their helper,
    229–15   and thereby *h·* themselves
    231–13   in order to *h·* God's work
    276–24   *h·* support a righteous government ;
    284– 3   to *h·* human purpose and peoples,
    313–15   to *h·* me when I was ill.
    359–30   to *h·* you rise out of it.

helped

Mis.   238– 1   * story that "he *h·* 'niggers'
    382–10   the sick are *h·* thereby,
Man.   18–11   hath the Lord *h·* us." — *I Sam. 7 : 12.*
Ret.   19–15   sympathy *h·* to support me
Pul.   9–14   and *h·* settle the subject.
    11– 7   *h·* erect The Mother Church,
    14–11   *h·* the woman, — *Rev. 12 : 16.*
'02.   11–14   each in turn has *h·* mankind,
    11–15   when the race is *h·* onward
    18– 9   disciples *h·* crown with thorns
My.   116–24   Had the ages *h·* their leaders
    166–20   to help and to be *h·*,
    219– 2   anticipate being *h·* by me
    282–11   nations are *h·* onward
    302– 3   can he be *h·* or be killed
    322–24   * Mr. Wiggin kindly *h·* me
    324–19   * that he had *h·* you
    330–27   sympathy *h·* to support me

helper

Ret.   86–24   To the unwise *h·* our Master
Un.   3–27   this self-same God is our *h·*.
    (see also **Eddy**)

helpers

Mis.   87–29   haunted by obsequious *h·*,

helpful

Ret.   25–11   compassionate, *h·*, and spiritual.
Pul.   29–24   * discourse was able, and *h·*
    45–10   * grandest and most *h·* features
    56–13   * *h·*, and powerful movements
My.   42–10   * one of the *h·* contributors
    121–13   generous, reliable, *h·*,
    224–10   public sentiment is *h·* or

helpfulness

My.   vii–11   * *h·* of consistent and constant
    87–27   * spirit of unselfishness and *h·*,

helping

Mis.   32–19   *h·* those unfortunate seekers
    49–23   are *h·* man Godward :
    50–30   *h·* our brother man.
    98–12   ways and means for *h·*
    327–25   *h·* them on, saying,
    353–29   to think of *h·* others,
    371–10   incapable of *h·* themselves
Pul.   8–12   privileged joy at *h·* to build
    45– 1   * children lent a *h·* hand,
    81–13   * her whole time *h·* others.
My.   117– 7   whereas *h·* a leader
    147–30   calling on me for help, and I am *h·*
    163–28   thank their ancestors for *h·*
    165– 3   *h·* others thus to choose.
    259–19   true heart, and a *h·* hand

helpless

Mis.   72– 8   to their *h·* offspring,
    115–11   *h·* ignorance of the community
    123– 2   butchers the *h·* Armenians,
    221–16   This accounts for many *h·* mental
Ret.   27–17   * But the feeble hands and *h·*,
Un.   61– 5   appeared as a *h·* human babe ;
    61–27   *h·* sick are soonest healed by it.
Peo.   3– 5   *h·* invalids and cripples.
My.   144– 6   lies afloat that I am sick, *h·*, or

helplessness

Mis.   281–20   *h·* without this understanding,
Hea.   3– 3   or, lacking these, to show its *h·*.

helpmeet

Pul.   82–18   * woman as man's proper *h·*.

helps

Mis.   157–16   *h·* us most when help is most **needed,**

hem

Mis.   75– 1   touched the *h·* of the garment
    97–17   touch the *h·* of His garment ;
Ret.   23–23   I had touched the *h·* of C. S.
Pul.   13–11   touches the *h·* of Christ's robe
    53–29   * power that filled his garment's *h·*
No.   22– 2   has certainly not touched the *h·*

hem
'00. 15–20 the touch of the *h·* of this garment
Hea. 16–15 *h·* of Truth's garment.
My. 22–27 * touched the healing *h·* of C. S.,
108–20 slang, and malice touch not the *h·* of
192– 8 Thou hast touched its *h·*,
205–23 touches but the *h·* of C. S.,
351–12 touches the *h·* of his garment

Hemans, Mrs.
Ret. 9–27 signature
My. 185–26 words of Mrs. *H·* :

hemisphere
Mis. 275–26 wonder of the western *h·*.

hence
Mis. 3–30 *H·* the deep demand for the Science
12–19 *h·* the need of watching,
14– 1 *h·*, there is neither place nor power
15– 2 *h·* the sinner must endure the
28–30 *h·* his declaration,
55–30 *h·* it is either a godless and
64– 2 *H·*, the human cry which voiced
66– 4 *H·* the gospel that fulfils the law
68–16 *h·* it is right to know that the works of
71–22 *h·* its mythical origin and
71–30 *h·* the immutable and just law
73–17 *H·* the verdict of experience :
75–13 *h·* Soul is one, and is God ;
76– 1 *h·* it must be sinless, and destitute of
76–13 *h·* these bodies must die
83–16 *h·*, you are the arbiter of your
90– 2 *h·*, that sin is impotent.
97–31 *h·*, it doth not appear
103–31 *H·* the Scripture,
108–12 *h·* the utility of knowing
123–29 *h·* it follows that those who
146–12 *h·* I have hitherto declined
147–21 *h·* we find him ever the same,
148–17 *h·* their simple, scientific basis,
150–31 *h·* God is our Shepherd.
164– 2 *h·* the incorporeal and
172–31 *h·*, good is omnipotent
182– 2 *h·* the impossibility of
187– 9 opposite of man, *h·* the unreality ;
196–13 *h·* the words of our Master :
215– 7 Arise, let us go *h·* ; — *John* 14 : 31.
217– 6 *h·* that the universe of God is
232–18 *h·* a more spiritual Christianity
247–16 *h·* the injustice of their interpretations.
247–30 *H· that* is only an evil belief
264–15 *h·* the aptness to assimilate pure and
268–16 *h·* he suffers no shipwreck in a
272–23 * *H·* to name these institutions,
284–22 *h·* is neither to be *feared* nor
287– 4 *H·* the Scripture : "It is He— *Psal.* 100 : 3.
289– 3 *h·* the only temperance is total
308–31 *H·*, a finite person is not the model
318–11 *H·* the following is
342– 6 *h·* the steady decline of
348–14 *H·*, Solomon's transverse command :
348–26 *H·* I tried several doses of
350–24 *H·* it prevents the normal action,
357–29 *h·* we should be ready and glad to
364–23 *h·* these opposites must
Man. 3–14 *h·* their simple, scientific basis,
28– 9 *h·* the necessity of this By-Law
53–26 *h·* injurious, to C. S.
Ret. 56–18 *H·* there is but one Mind ;
57–11 *H·* there is but one Soul,
63–14 God is good, *h·* goodness is
65–15 *h·* Jesus denounced it.
67– 2 *h·* one's concept of error is
83–18 *H·*, as a rule, the student should
Un. 3– 4 *H·* they awake only to another
3–20 *H·* He is in Himself only,
9– 5 *H·* they must, some time
24–17 and *h·* is the only substance.
25– 7 *h·* good is the only substance,
25–10 *h·*, whatever it appears to say
29– 6 *H·*, as Spirit, Soul is sinless,
30– 8 *h·* this lower sense sins
31–16 *H·* my conscientious position,
32– 2 *H·* the claim of matter usurps
32–24 *H·* it was not man
33–17 *H·* the logical sequence,
35–24 *H·* this spiritual consciousness
36–14 *h·*, that matter is erroneous,
38–24 *H·* the inevitable conclusion
40–16 *H·* Life abides in man,
41–25 *h·* matter neither lives nor dies.
43– 4 *h·* cannot bring out the
49–23 *H·* it is undemonstrable,
51– 4 and *h·* that sin is eternal,
52– 1 *H·* Soul is sinless and immortal,
52– 7 *H·* the need that human
53–26 *h·* that saying of Jesus,

hence
Un. 54–13 *H·* the fact must be denied ;
59– 7 *h·* the phraseology of Jesus,
Pul. vii– 5 Three quarters of a century *h·*,
41–19 * *H·* the service was repeated
Rud. 3– 2 *H·* their comparative acquiescence in
4–15 *h·* there is no other Mind.
9–28 *h·*, that whatever militates against
13– 2 *h·* Life is not functional,
13–10 *h·* it is not the truth of being,
No. 4–13 *h·* error of thought becomes fable
16–18 *h·* their inference of some other
17–19 *H·* the unreality of error,
20–19 *H·* this asking amiss
22–22 *H·* the passage must refer to
23–25 *H·* we cannot understand
26– 8 *H·* it is impossible for those
32–18 *H·* its opposite, named *evil*, must
35–26 *H·* there is no sin,
36–14 *H·* the human Jesus had
38– 7 *h·* there is no intelligent sin,
'00. 8– 6 *h·*, be careful of your company.
12–17 *h·* the Revelator's saying :
'01. 6– 5 says . . . not a person, *h·* no God?
11–11 *h·* the Scripture,
13–25 *h·* the hope of universal salvation.
17–26 *h·* it must be mind that
25– 1 *H·* the mysticism, so called,
28–27 *h·* the inference that he who
'02. 5–22 *H·* our Master's saying,
10– 8 *H·* the footprints of a reformer are
Hea. 11–27 *h·* the Christianity of . . . healing,
Peo. 13– 2 *h·* a lower order of humanity,
Po. 70–15 error, get thee *h·*,
70–25 sin, and death are banished *h·*.
77–19 Bears *h·* its sunlit glow
79–10 darkling sense, arise, go *h·* !
My. 40–29 * rebels against law, *h·* the proverb :
108– 9 *H·* our Master's saying,
108–16 *H·* the divine Mind is the
116–14 *H·* the sin, the danger and
118–13 *h·* I seek to be
130–30 *h·* my request, that you
136– 1 *h·* it is enough for you and me
141–25 *h·* the following :
161– 9 *H·* these words of Christ Jesus :
178–18 *H·* the inevitable revelation
205–28 *H·* health, holiness, immortality,
222–11 Remove *h·* to yonder place ; — *Matt.* 17 : 20.
225–13 *h·* the propriety of giving unto
228– 6 *h·* I am always saying the
229–28 *h·* my disappointed hope
231–14 *H·*, letters from invalids
235–21 *h·* there can be no other creator
237– 9 *H·*, it were wise to accept
238–12 *H·* the revelation, discovery, and
239–23 *H·* mankind . . . a kind of man
242– 9 the child of God, *h·* perfect,
262– 2 *h·* man is the image, idea, or
268– 6 *h·* that some fundamental error
272– 5 *h·* the Scripture, "The law of — *Rom.* 8 : 2.
275– 7 *h·* the Scripture, "Be still, — *Psal.* 46 : 10.
279–14 *H·* the sequence:
288–25 *h·* his saying, "Sin no more,— *John* 5 : 14.
311–15 *H·* a mistake may have occurred
341–23 * *h·* it was a special favor
357– 1 *h·* materiality is wholly apart from
364– 1 *h·* the Scripture, "Judge no — *John* 8 : 15.

henceforth
Mis. 144–18 *h·* to whisper our Master's promise,
188– 3 Man is as perfect now, and *h·*,
Po. 1–14 to look *h·* On insignificance
My. 86– 1 * *H* the greeting of admiring eyes,
148– 8 be and abide with you *h·*.

Herald
The
Pul. 43–26 * as heretofore stated in *The H·*,

Pul. 74– 3 * [By Telegraph to the *H·*]
74– 5 * article published in the *H·*
74–12 * addressed to the editor of the *H·* :
88–31 * *H·*, Rochester, N. Y.
89–31 * *H·*, Grand Rapids, Mich.
89–32 * *H·*, St. Joseph, Mo.
My. 274–19 * sent the following to the *H·* :
341–24 * received the *H·* correspondent.
346– 9 * learn authoritatively from the *H·*

heralded
My. 79–15 * *h·* in flaming headlines

heralding
Mis. 163–31 *h·* the Principle of health,

heraldry
Mis. 145–28 will float majestically heaven's *h·*,
Po. 70–21 A painless *h·* of Soul, not sense,

Herbert

Pul. 28–22 * devotional hymns from *H·*, Faber,

Herculean

Mis. 130–20 such *H·* tasks as they have

herd

Po. 41–11 When the *h·* had forsaken,

herds

Ret. 4–21 with large flocks and *h·*,
Pan. 3–28 guardian of flocks and *h·*.
My. 262– 8 *h·* of a Jewish village.

here

Mis. vii–12 There's nothing *h·* to trust.
2–27 progress *h·* and hereafter out of
16–16 *H·*, then, is the awakening from
16–30 *H·* you stand face to face with
27– 7 *H·* is where C. S. sticks to its
27– 9 *H·* also is found the pith of the
30–14 to be recognized *h·* and now.
68– 6 visible to those beholding him *h·*.
74– 2 are *h·* signified.
77– 4 *H·* the verb *believe* took its
93–28 cannot go unpunished either *h·* or
127– 8 Christian Scientists, *h·* and
127–22 but *h·*, you must so know yourself,
128– 5 Therefore I close *h·*
159–20 *H·* I deposit the gifts that my
159–22 *H·* I talk once a year,
162–11 *H·* the cross became the emblem
168–15 *H·* ends the colloquy ;
174–19 No : it is ever-present *h·*.
174–29 spiritual facts of man's Life *h·*
177– 2 God makes to us all, right *h·*,
178–24 * *to* preach, *h·* or elsewhere.''
179– 1 ''He is not *h·* ;''— *Luke* 24 : 6.
179–13 ''He is not *h·* ;— *Luke* 24 : 6.
180–10 Truth is always *h·*,
180–25 *H·*, the apostle assures us that
191–14 *H·* is an assertion indicating
191–20 The term, being *h·* employed in
203– 4 for *h·*, thine becomes mine through
223– 7 *H·*, divine light, logic, and
244– 3 *H·* we have the Professor on the
251–20 Heaven right *h·*, where
319–10 *H·* Christian Scientists must be most
323–18 ''What do ye *h·* ?
330–13 consciousness thereof is *h·* and now
332– 6 Spring is *h·* ! and doors that
362–22 *H·* revelation must come to the
373–23 it has rich possession *h·*,
384–16 Love divine Is *h·*, and thine ;
385– 8 Thou, *h·* and *everywhere*.
389–12 His habitation high is *h·*,
396– 9 Yet *h·*, upon this faded sod,
Man. 109–15 compare them with the forms *h·* given,
Chr. 53–42 Are *h·*, and now
Ret. 17– 9 *H·* morning peers out,
17–15 *H·* fame-honored hickory rears his
18– 1 *H·* is life ! *H·* is youth !
18– 1 *H·* the poet's world-wish,
19–22 *H·* it is but justice to record,
62– 4 find that the views *h·* set forth
87–14 Let some of these rules be *h·* stated.
94–21 ''lo *h·* ! or lo there !''— *Luke* 17 : 21.
Un. 7–17 views *h·* promulgated on this subject
7–19 and *h·* is one such conviction :
11–26 kingdom of heaven is *h·*,
32–23 *H·* it appears that a *liar* was
34–10 *H·* comes in the summary of the
37– 9 They are now and *h·* ;
37–20 Existing *h·* and now,
46– 5 not see much of the real man *h·*,
46–10 scientific man and his Maker are *h·* ;
53– 9 *h·* to be seen and demonstrated ;
55–22 Now and *h·* shall I behold God,
62–24 He is not *h·*, but is risen.''— *Luke* 24 : 6.
Pul. 13– 3 at some period, *h·* or hereafter,
13–23 *H·* the Scriptures declare that evil
29– 5 * first pastor of the church *h·*
48– 4 * with *h·* and there a fountain
49–10 * ''You have lived *h·* only four years,
49–16 brought *h·* in warm weather,
52– 1 * *H·* is a church whose treasurer has
63–13 brought *h·* in warm weather,
68– 5 * *h·* she taught the principles of the
80–10 * *H·* they have the largest individuality,
80–27 * *h·* to be trained into harmony with
80–28 * what we are *h·* determines where
Rud. 8–10 give you *h·* nothing but an outline
No. 28–26 *H· soul* means sense and organic life ;
36– 8 even while mortals believed it was *h·*.
42–28 *H·* a skeptic might well ask
Pan. 1–10 roseate blush of joyous June is *h·*
13– 7 Lo, *h·* ! or, lo there !— *Luke* 17 : 21.
'00. 2–22 *H·* we add : The doom of such

here

'00. 5– 6 *H·* note the words of our Master
7–28 Thus it is we walk *h·* below,
10–20 *H·* our hope anchors in God
'01. 5– 5 does not Person *h·* lose the nature of
6– 5 *H·* is the departure.
15–27 * since you have sat *h·* in the house
16– 6 punishing itself *h·* and hereafter
24– 7 *H·* he makes God the cause of
32–27 if those venerable Christians were *h·*
'02. 6–13 *H·* all human woe is seen to
6–24 demonstrates heaven *h·*,
7–23 *H·* we proceed to another
12– 3 *H·* C. S. intervenes,
12– 6 *now* and *forever*, *h·* and *everywhere*.
12–21 *H·* allow me to interpolate some
Hea. 6– 1 The more spiritual we become *h·*,
Peo. 1–18 that we are spiritual beings *h·*
9–22 *h·* metaphysics is seen to rise above
Po. 3– 8 watch thy chair, and wish thee *h·* ;
4–11 His habitation high is *h·*, and nigh,
15– 9 *H·* gloom hath enchantment in
15–16 *H·* smileth the blossom and sunshine
16–16 The voice of the night-bird must *h·*
29– 7 Dear Christ, forever *h·* and near,
36–15 Love divine Is *h·*, and thine ;
37– 8 Thou, *h·* and *everywhere*.
41–10 their home is not *h·*
59– 1 Yet *h·*, upon this faded sod,
62– 9 *H·* morning peers out,
62–18 *H·* fame-honored hickory rears his
63– 8 *H·* is life! *H·* is youth!
63– 8 *H·* the poet's world-wish,
68– 4 for this are we *h·*.''
68– 9 *H·* the rock and the sea and the
70–12 For sinless sense is *h·*
My. 7– 4 *H·* allow me to interpolate
8– 6 * The necessity *h·* indicated
18– 5 that Christian Scientists, *h·* and
36–13 * Most of us are *h·* because
44–10 * Christ is *h·*, has come to
47– 4 * gathered *h·* from all parts of
54–23 * should be *h·* stated that
57–29 * *H·* is a church whose Treasurer
71–20 * *h·* are neither nave, aisles,
73–21 * *h·* the visitors will receive
73–23 * There is *h·* also a post-office
74–11 * Christian Scientists are *h·* in force,
74–28 * we have had *h·* the representatives
84–20 * story which the gathering *h·* tells.
85–14 * And *h·* in Boston the zeal
87–14 * people we . . . like to have *h·*.
89–17 * *H·* is an occasion for joy
107– 9 *H·* I speak from experience.
122–23 he is not *h·* :— *Mark* 16 : 6.
126–28 One thing is eternally *h·* ;
132– 9 pass through the waters of Meribah *h·*
134–15 And *h·* let me add :
155– 2 which is effective *h·* and now.
155–19 a clear vision of heaven *h·*,
158–13 heaven *h·*, the struggle over ;
163–22 *H·* let me add that,
164– 1 far from my purpose, when I came *h·*,
170–10 of all present *h·* in Concord.
173–13 would bring thousands *h·* yesterday ;
186–20 *H·* let His promise be verified :
193–23 *H·* I aver that you have grasped
203–15 the summary of suffering *h·*
232–18 *H·* we ask : Are Christ's teachings
236–13 *H·* I have the joy of knowing
248– 7 you are *h·* for the purpose of
253– 8 * ''Thou art not *h·* for ease or pain,
256–17 Again loved Christmas is *h·*,
267– 8 *H·* let us remember that God is
273–18 The ultimatum of life *h·* and
284–23 But *h·* let me say that I
297–20 is *h·* now as veritably as when
297–22 If . . . we should see him *h·*
314–16 Individuals are *h·* to-day
324–17 * and were he *h·* to-day
331– 2 *H·* it is but justice to record,
343–11 * *H·*, then, was the definite statement
345–32 * are *h·* touched upon,
348–17 *H·*, however, was no stopping-place,
354–19 Of God's presence *h·*.

hereafter

Mis. 2–27 progress here and *h·* out of evil,
93–28 either here or *h·*.
120–20 this Association *h·* meet triennially :
136–24 that *h·* you hold three sessions
155–21 will *h·*, as a general rule,
313–27 to be *h·* the only pastor of
317–23 thou shalt know *h·*.''— *John* 13 : 7.
322– 7 I may *h·* notify the Directors
Man. 45– 8 shall not *h·* become members of
69–27 shall *h·* be closed to visitors.

hereafter

Man.	76– 3	h· used for the benefit of
Pul.	13– 3	here or h·, must grapple with
	42–20	* where the organ is to be h· placed,
	45–28	* The sermons h· will consist of
	80–29	* determines where we shall be h·
'01.	16– 6	punishing itself here and h·
Hea.	5–10	reward of his good deed h·.
	6– 2	should this rule fail h·,
Po.	47–12	Will the h· from suffering free
My.	203–15	and of heaven h·.
	246–26	thou shalt know h· ;" — John 13 : 7.
	251– 3	thou shalt know h·." — John 13 : 7.
	273–18	of life here and h·
	353–23	shall h· be closed to visitors.

hereby

Mis.	155–19	she h· requests : First, that you,
	297–16	I h· state, in unmistakable
	313–25	I h· ordain the Bible, and "S. and H.
Ret.	49–30	the same is h· dissolved.
Pul.	77–14	* h· most lovingly invited
	78–13	* You are h· most lovingly invited
	86–21	* we h· present this church to you
My.	27–13	* h· notified that sufficient funds
	44–25	* h· convey to you their sincere
	46–22	* we do h· pledge ourselves
	171–11	I h· invite all my church
	173–25	due and are h· tendered to
	223– 2	I h· notify the public that no
	242–16	I h· announce to the C. S. field
	298–10	and h· say that they have my
	359– 8	I h· publicly declare that I

heredity

Un.	8–21	even the doctrine of h·

herein

Mis.	x–12	a few articles are h· appended.
	xi–15	find h· a "canny" crumb ;
	104–10	H· sin is miraculous
	173– 3	most enlightened sense h·
	190–21	the devil h· referred to
	252– 2	H· the mental medicine of
Man.	51– 1	Rules h· set forth,
Ret.	82–13	orderly methods h· delineated.
Un.	7–16	H· is my evidence,
	29–13	h· lies the discrepancy
Pan.	13– 4	among the questions h·,
My.	138–20	statements h· made by me,
	202–28	"H· is my Father — John 15 : 8.

hereinafter

Man.	99– 7	except as h· specified,

heresy

Mis.	174–21	Shall that be called h·
Ret.	13–17	to win me from dreaded h·.
My.	285–26	which they call h·, — Acts 24 : 14.

heretics

No.	44–25	* " H· of yesterday are martyrs

heretofore

Mis.	x–12	To those h· in print,
	314–30	from the Quarterly, as h·,
	337–31	sensualism, as h·, would hide
Man.	38–18	who have h· been members
Pul.	43–26	* h· stated in The Herald,
My.	135– 8	h· personally attended to
	245– 4	it should be met as h·,
	315–24	dummy h· described?
	356–17	h· presented in S. and H.

herewith

My.	131–26	prove me now h·, — Mal. 3 : 10.
	132– 3	"Prove me now h·, — Mal. 3 : 10.
	269–26	"Prove me now h·, — Mal. 3 : 10.
	289–25	I h· send a few words of
	360–14	I h· cheerfully subscribe

Hering, Prof. Hermann S.

My.	16–17	* Prof. Hermann S. H·, First Reader ;

heritage

Mis.	152–18	h· that God has prepared
	182–25	h· of the Elohim,
	199– 9	into their rightful h·,
	247– 2	demand for man his God-given h·,
	259–15	was the h· of man ;
	331– 7	for man's rich h·,
Pul.	2–26	behooves us to defend our h·.
	3– 9	dispossess you of this h·
My.	128–14	the vital h· of freedom

hero

Mis.	85– 2	battle-worn and weary Christian h·,
	166– 5	philanthropist, h· and Christian.
	237–27	draped in honor of the dead h·
Ret.	11–15	H· and sage arise to show
Pul.	48–29	* as well as the h· who killed the
'00.	9–16	reformer must be a h· at all points,
'01.	30–26	heart of the unselfed Christian h·.
Hea.	2–14	And still another Christian h·

hero

Po.	60–12	H· and sage arise to show
	78– 6	Till molds the h· form?
My.	203–13	A spiritual h· is a mark for
	311–28	John McNeil, the h· of Lundy Lane.

heroes

Mis.	176–14	h· and heroines who counted not
'01.	32–14	They were h· in the strife ;
Po.	78– 8	Shades of our h· !
My.	248– 9	Spiritual h· and prophets

heroic

'01.	1–20	always characterize h· hearts ;

heroines

Mis.	176–15	heroes and h· who counted not

heroism

Ret.	26– 4	Principle of his holy h·

Herold, Der

der Christian Science

Man.	27–15	C. S. Sentinel, Der H· der C. S.,
	81–11	C. S. Sentinel, Der H· der C. S.,
My.	vi–29	* and authorized Der H· der C. S.,
	19– 4	* C. S. Sentinel, Der H· der C. S.,
	353–13	the third, Der H· der C. S.,

Man.	65–12	C. S. Journal, Sentinel, and Der H·,

Herrick

Rev. S. E.

No.	44–24	Rev. S. E. H., a Congregational

Mis.	253–13	signature

herring

Mis.	69–26	eating smoked h·.

Herself

Mis.	367–20	nothing beyond Himself or H·.

hesitate

Mis.	350–11	no transactions . . . which I would h·

hesitated

'00.	3–22	Israelites in Babylon h· not to

hesitation

My.	320–24	* without any h· or restriction.

heterodox

Ret.	64– 9	opposite theory is h·

hiatus

No.	13–11	though the h· be longer still

hickory

Ret.	17–15	h· rears his bold form,
Po.	62–18	h· rears his bold form,

hid

Mis.	149–27	a light that cannot be h·.
	166–22	h· in three measures of meal,
	167–24	h· these things from — Luke 10 : 21.
	171–24	h· in three measures — Matt. 13 : 33.
	174–30	h· in three measures of meal,
	303– 2	lights that cannot be h·,
	348–11	"Nothing is h· — see Matt. 10 : 26.
No.	45– 1	h· these things from — Luke 10 : 21.
'02.	2–16	leaven h· in three measures of meal,

hidden

Mis.	48–21	h· nature of some tragic events
	114–25	and stop their h· influence upon the
	194–16	which scholastic theology has h·.
	223– 1	its h· paths, purpose, and fruits
	343–17	the h· gems of Love,
Ret.	7–13	* however h· and remote.
	85–13	against the subtly h· suggestion
Pul.	9–24	bounty h· from the world.
	15– 3	expose evil's h· mental ways
No.	24–17	the evil that is h· by dogma
'01.	20–25	its h· modus and flagrance
My.	83–10	* h· away in the laces of
	110–13	H· electrical forces annihilating
	124– 1	h· things of dishonesty, — II Cor. 4 : 2.
	130– 5	h· method of committing crime
	160–24	shows that h· unpunished sin
	166–16	they develop h· strength.
	195–11	h· under an appearance of
	204– 4	opportunity to use their h· virtues,
	288– 3	Love . . . uncovers h· evil.

hide

Mis.	63– 5	and to h· his divine power.
	152–25	He will h· you in His feathers
	210–12	wisdom of a serpent is to h·
	323–15	serpents h· among the rocks
	337–31	sensualism, as heretofore, would h·
	337–32	Sin of any sort tends to h·
Ret.	78–22	or for yourself to h· from God,
Un.	10–28	would endeavor to h· from His presence
Pul.	4–18	may help to h· the stars,
No.	7–17	wrath of man cannot h· it
	40– 8	wise to h· from dull and base ears

hides
  Mis. 103–22 *h·* the actual power, presence,
    203–22 veil that *h·* mental deformity.
    210–22 *h·* itself under the false pretense
    294–15 *h·* it in his cell of ingratitude.
  My. 355–20 * "He *h·* a shining face."

hideth
  Mis. 210– 1 pursues the evil that *h·* itself,

hiding
  Mis. 144–16 *h·* place from the wind, — *Isa.* 32 : 2.
  My. 17– 1 overflow the *h·* place." — *Isa.* 28 : 17.
    211– 6 This mistaken way, of *h·* sin

hiding-places
  My. 245–12 have called out of their *h·*

hierarchy
  My. 342–29 * "Will there be a *h·*,

hieroglyphics
  Mis. 331–31 all earth's *h·* of Love,

hieroglyphs
  My. 205–15 Love and unity are *h·* of goodness,

Higdon, Mr. John C.
  My. 351– 4 * addressed to Mr. John C. *H·*

Higgins, Mr. John D.
  My. 283– 5 Mr. John D. *H·*, *Clerk.*

higgles
  Mis. 296–22 * "poises and poses, *h·* and

High
  (*see* **Most High**)

high
  Mis. 19–22 as *h·* a basis as he understands,
    33– 3 The *h·* priests of old caused
    86–26 subjective state of *h·* thoughts.
    116– 4 wickedness in *h·* places." — *Eph.* 6 : 12.
    119–17 scale against man's *h·* destiny.
    126–28 she sitteth in *h·* places ;
    134–28 wickedness is standing in *h·* places ;
    139–12 *and every h· thing that* — *II Cor.* 10 : 5.
    233–22 who think the standard of C. S. too *h·*
    274–21 whose consciences . . . hold *h·* carnival.
    285–11 hold *h·* the banner of Truth and
    287–12 only *h·* and holy joy can satisfy
    295–23 that *h·* and pure ethical tones do
    320–23 *h·* in the zenith of Truth's
    348– 2 towards the mark of a *h·* calling.
    385– 7 This is Thy *h·* behest :
    385–22 "When hope soared *h·*,
    387– 2 divinely fair, the *h·* and deep,
    389–12 His habitation *h·* is here,
    392– 6 majestic oak, from yon *h·* place
  Man. 86–13 ready for this *h·* calling,
  Chr. 53–28 Of his *h·* morn?
  Ret. 2–29 for whom she cherished a *h·* regard.
    48–21 fulfilled its *h·* and noble destiny,
  Un. 7–16 Herein is my evidence, from on *h·*,
  Pul. 10–26 like day-spring from on *h·*.
    33–20 * giving him *h·* counsel and serious
    77–17 * twentieth day of . . . at *h·* noon.
    78–15 * 20th day of February, . . . at *h·* noon.
  No. 7–18 God has appointed . . . *h·* tasks,
    19– 1 regulates the present *h·* premium
  Pan. 12–13 *h·* above the so-called laws of matter,
  '00. 6– 8 the *h·* calling of God in — *Phil.* 3 : 14.
  '01. 2–13 Christ's healing too *h·* for them.
  Hea. 6– 7 opinions of people fly too *h·* or
    11–21 When you have reached this *h·* goal
  Po. 4–11 His habitation *h·* is here,
    19– 1 like the eagle's, oh, still be it *h·*,
    20– 8 majestic oak, from yon *h·* place
    32–14 with strength from on *h·*,
    37– 7 This is Thy *h·* behest :
    39– 6 A temple, whose *h·* dome
    48–16 "When hope soared *h·*,
    50–20 the *h·* and deep,
  My. 4–30 Thou God most *h·* and nigh.
    6–23 *h·* above the work of men's hands,
    30–21 * they were heaped up with bills,
    36–28 * have fulfilled a *h·* resolve
    37– 9 * declare again our *h·* appreciation
    64–18 * constitutes the *h·* standing of C. S.
    64–23 * *h·* and holy task of overcoming
    78–15 * piled *h·* with bank-notes,
    89– 6 * two hundred and twenty feet *h·*,
    94–27 *h·* above the work of men's hands,
    154–21 * must not the *h·* and glorious
    171–23 * and of the *h·* school.
    173–27 green surrounding the *h·* school ;
    201– 2 Press on towards the *h·* calling
    268–28 Look *h·* enough, and you see
    290–23 *h·* and holy call you again to
    320– 9 * *h·* regard for you as a Christian
    331–26 * of the *h·* feeling of honor
  (*see also* **heaven**)

high-domed
  My. 68– 4 * auditorium, with its *h·* ceiling

higher
  Mis. 1– 4 to him, no *h·* destiny dawned
    1–15 stepping-stone to a *h·* recognition
    17–19 a much *h·* and holier conception of
    28–30 by the superiority of the *h·* law ;
    29–31 *h·* rules of Life which Jesus taught
    30– 5 and doubt its *h·* rules,
    52–17 that tends to lift mortals *h·*.
    58–14 through a *h·* than mortal sense.
    63–24 reaching toward a *h·* goal,
    66–19 the *h·* spiritual sense,
    67– 3 *h·* claims of the law and gospel
    98–13 in a *h·* mode of medicine ;
    99–13 called to voice a *h·* order of Science
    126–11 We also have gained *h·* heights ;
    136– 6 broader and *h·* views,
    158– 3 *h·* far than the heavens above
    162– 5 advent of a *h·* Christianity.
    174–13 *h·* than the atmosphere of our planet,
    227–26 satisfies the mind craving a *h·* good,
    228–13 to a capacity for a *h·* life.
    235–23 educate the affections to *h·*
    244–19 by the *h·* law of Spirit,
    270– 8 mankind hath no *h·* ideal
    276–22 a purer, *h·* affection and ideal.
    278–31 This has developed *h·* energies
    287–18 the *h·* nature of man governs
    287–25 they lead to *h·* joys :
    289–26 she may win a *h·*.
    290– 6 *h·* in the scale of harmony,
    330–21 *h·* joys, holier aims,
    342–10 a *h·* understanding of God.
    345–12 pure and strong faith rose *h·*
    346– 3 carries this thought even *h·*,
    354–28 he rests in a liberty *h·*
    355–16 gives scope to *h·* demonstration.
    358–32 a *h·* spiritual unity is won,
    369–16 *h·* than a rhubarb tincture
    383–14 rise *h·* in the estimation of
    399–21 Lifted *h·*, we depart,
  Man. 87–17 *h·* meaning of the Scriptures.
  Ret. 28–27 *h·* than the stars of heaven.
    31–11 a desire for something *h·*
    33–18 disappears in the *h·* attenuations
    48–24 *h·* than physic or drugging ;
    48–29 has led to *h·* ways, means, and
    88– 8 *h·* manifestation of Life.
  Un. 6– 7 *h·* selfhood, derived from God,
    11–12 through the *h·* laws of God.
  Pul. 2– 9 a thought *h·* and deeper than
    15–20 cement of a *h·* humanity will unite
    38–28 * manifestations of a *h·* spirituality
    67–15 * give expression to a *h·* spirituality.
    85–10 * better and *h·* conception of God
  Rud. 2–21 introduces us to *h·* definitions.
    2–25 *h·* range of infinite goodness.
    8–15 from a lower to a *h·* condition
    14–19 No discount . . . made on *h·* classes,
    14–20 their tuition in the *h·* instruction,
    14–24 unprepared to enter *h·* classes.
  No. 36–15 Jesus had a resort to his *h·* self
    36–25 risen from human sense to a *h·*
    44– 4 *h·* demonstration of medicine
    46–17 let us lift their standard *h·*,
  Pan. 2– 7 *h·* than Mt. Ararat above the deluge.
    6–14 *h·* criticism is not satisfied
    10–24 A *h·* manhood is manifest,
  '01. 1–11 to rise *h·* and still *h·*
    3–14 *h·* definition derived from the
    30–17 and the *h·* class of critics
  Hea. 1– 8 they are calls to *h·* duties,
    5–26 lead our lives to *h·* issues ;
    8– 8 results of this *h·* Christianity,
    9–16 Then it is a *h·* duty to know that
    11–28 *h·* attenuations of homœopathy
    12–23 *h·* attenuations prove that
    12–26 admit the *h·* attenuations are
    13– 7 *h·* natures are reached
    13– 8 soonest by the *h·* attenuations,
    16– 9 Christ with a *h·* meaning,
    19–20 bidding man go up *h·*,
  Peo. 5–13 risen *h·* to our mortal sense,
    7– 4 chiselling to *h·* excellence,
    9–27 destroys discord with the *h·* and
    11– 4 struck the keynote of *h·* claims,
    12– 1 hearken to the *h·* law of God,
    14–13 awake to a *h·* and holier love
  Po. 18– 5 Careening in liberty *h·* and *h·*
    18–10 When *h·* he soareth to compass his
    23–17 Life hath a *h·* recompense
    76– 5 Lifted *h·*, we depart, Having one.
  My. 3–19 It is the *h·* criticism,
    46– 5 * *h·* and more spiritual plane of
    48–30 * feed the *h·* nature through the mind,

higher

My.	51–14	* *h·* understanding of Christianity,
	68–12	* *h·* than that of the State House.
	79– 6	* chapter sub-title
	79–21	* upon a far *h·* pedestal
	95–23	* *h·* critics and the men of science
110–17, 18		rising *h·* and forever *h·*
	110–24	*h·* in the altitude of being.
	110–25	Mounting *h·*, mortals will cease to
	112–25	his *h·* life is the result of
	114–26	*h·* meaning of this book
	118–15	embarrass the *h·* criticism.
	136–28	and the *h·* criticism.
	142–19	step *h·* in their passage from sense
	151–27	They were content to look no *h·*
	152– 1	it took a step *h·* ;
	159–17	whereby we reach our *h·* nature.
	191–16	*h·* human sense of Life and
	212–11	*h·* forms of matter,
	216–31	to earn for a purpose even *h·*,
	221– 6	something *h·* than the systems
	237– 2	"*h·* criticism" announced in the
	240– 5	chapter sub-title
	240– 8	* why you call C. S. the *h·* criticism?"
	240– 9	I called C. S. the *h·* criticism
	240–16	C. S. is the *h·* criticism because
	241– 5	* *h·* meaning of the Scriptures.
	246–14	*h·* understanding of the absolute
	250–10	*h·* usefulness in this vast vineyard
	252–26	gave to . . . a *h·* hint.
	253– 3	the *h·* and everlasting harmony,
	277–16	not consonant with the *h·* law
	297–17	a *h·* realization of heaven.
	308– 8	*h·*, nobler, more imperative
	338–18	and they seek a *h·* source
	357–14	desire to build *h·*,
	357–15	demonstrate C. S. to a *h·* extent,
		(*see also* **hope, sense**)

highest

Mis.	15– 9	yea, the *h·* Christianization
	44–12	to demonstrate its *h·* possibilities.
	88–21	* Jesus was the *h·* type of
	145–29	"Glory to God in the *h·*, — *Luke* 2 : 14.
	146–25	*h·* understanding of justice and mercy.
	164–24	*h·* human concept of the man Jesus,
	169–20	to get at the *h·*, or metaphysical,
	247–11	from the *h·* possible ethics.
	260–32	the *h·* attenuation of evil.
	334–19	the *h·* degree of nothingness :
	336– 8	His *h·* idea as seen to-day
	348– 1	But the Scientists aim *h·*.
	365– 6	their *h·* endeavors are to Science
	379–21	*h·* attenuation in homœopathy,
Ret.	7– 8	* *h·* order of intellectual powers,
Un.	7–25	*h·* phenomena of the All-Mind.
	32– 8	not the *h·* Mind,
	50–12	of which evil is the *h·* degree ;
	51–15	Woman is the *h·* species of man,
	61–17	Our *h·* sense of infinite good
Pul.	81–26	* of missions-— the *h·* of all
Rud.	9– 4	not a Christian, in the *h·* sense,
No.	10– 7	former is the *h·* style of man ;
	16–26	its *h·* attenuation is mortal mind ;
	18–15	and their *h·* endeavors are,
	44– 8	swerves not from the *h·* ethics
	45–16	fill the *h·* measure of enlightened
	45–17	the *h·* places in government,
	45–26	urging its *h·* demands on mortals,
Pan.	9–16	demonstrates the *h·* humanity,
	10–25	individual who finds the *h·* joy,
'00.	11–27	*h·* criticism on all human action,
'01.	2– 3	The *h·* spiritual Christianity
	17–25	*h·* attenuations of homœopathy
	28–10	up to his *h·* understanding
'02.	17– 8	learn that man's *h·* happiness,
Hea.	10– 8	presented the *h·* ideal of Love.
	13–15	*h·* attenuation we ever attained
Peo.	6–28	by their *h·* or their lowest ideals,
My.	52– 7	* *h·* type of womanhood,
	96– 4	* *h·* order of intelligence,
	104–25	men and women of the *h·* talents,
	136–17	*h·* fee ever received by
	146–14	altitude of its *h·* propositions
	212–12	*h·* form of mental evil,
	231–13	its *h·* and infinite meanings,
	244–21	In the *h·* sense of a disciple,
	248–29	*h·* inspiration is found nearest the
	283–17	a man's *h·* idea of right

highly

Man.	47–14	Testimony . . . is *h·* important.
Ret.	19–13	He was *h·* esteemed
	83–25	It is also *h·* important
	85–25	*our* Cause, is *h·* prosperous,
Pul.	37–24	* a *h·* gifted personality."
	66–15	* *h·* figurative language.

highly

My.	157–10	* you are so *h·* esteemed,
	208– 4	your *h·* interesting letter.
	330–25	He was *h·* esteemed

high-principled

My.	319– 9	his *h·* character and

highway

Mis.	287–17	find the *h·* of holiness.
No.	33–13	Self-sacrifice is the *h·* to heaven.
My.	3–18	*h·* of hope, faith, understanding.
	240–13	*h·* of hope, faith, understanding."
	308–17	* tramping doggedly along the *h·*,

Hill, Hon. Isaac

Ret.	7– 5	Hon. Isaac *H·*, of Concord,

hill

Mis.	227–22	dwelling upon a holy *h·*,
	232–16	ascend the *h·* of Science,
	323– 2	city set upon a *h·*," — *see Matt.* 5 : 14.
	323–23	up the *h·* it is straight and narrow,
	328–21	ascends the *h·* of C. S.
	344–30	stood on Mars' *h·* at Athens,
Ret.	4–10	situated on the summit of a *h·*,
Pul.	48–16	* on the brow of Bow *h·*,
My.	33–16	dwell in thy holy *h·* — *Psal.* 15 : 1.
	34– 1	into the *h·* of the Lord — *Psal.* 24 : 3.
	133– 6	inhabit His holy *h·*,
	228–23	dwell in Thy holy *h·* — *Psal.* 15 : 1.

hills

Un.	14–20	rock, firmer than everlasting *h·*.
Pul.	49–21	* return to her native granite *h·*,
Po.	30– 2	beckonest from the giant *h·*
My.	155– 5	near my heart and native *h·*,
	185–27	* For the strength of the *h·*,
	186–11	and on to the celestial *h·*,
	341– 6	and lifted to her giant *h·*

Hillsborough

Ret.	6–18	he read law at *H·*,

hillside

Mis.	301–30	the commands of our *h·* Priest,
	397–23	O'er the *h·* steep,
Ret.	46– 4	O'er the *h·* steep,
	91–15	On a *h·*, near the sloping shores
	91–28	What has this *h·* priest,
Pul.	17– 3	O'er the *h·* steep,
'01.	6–19	consistent with Christ's *h·* sermon,
Po.	14– 2	O'er the *h·* steep,
	32– 7	scattered o'er *h·* and dale ;

hilltops and hill-tops

Pul.	53–23	* from the *h·* of Palestine,
'01.	35– 7	asleep upon the *h·* of Zion.

hilt

Mis.	223–18	what we would resist to the *h·*

Him

Mis.	xi–10	nor unrewarded by *H·*.
	8– 5	"in *H·* [Mind] we live, — *Acts* 17 : 28.
	22–18	come from God and return to *H·*,
	22–20	for it dwelleth in *H·*
	41– 7	wrath of man" to praise *H·*. — *Psal.* 76 : 10.
	45–25	Scriptures imply *H·* to be,
	45–28	were made by *H·* ; — *John* 1 : 3.
	45–29	without *H·* was not — *John* 1 : 3.
	46–20	not weighing equally with *H·*,
	49–28	as the Scriptures imply *H·* to be,
	50–30	and loving *H·* supremely,
	55–30	it is in something unlike *H·* ;
	59–13	all things to those who love *H·* ;
	63–20	none else beside *H·*," — *Deut.* 4 : 35.
	71–24	"For of *H·*, — *Rom.* 11 : 36.
	71–24	and through *H·*, — *Rom.* 11 : 36.
	71–24	and to *H·*, — *Rom.* 11 : 36.
	79– 9	In *H·* we live, move, and
	79–10	origin and existence being in *H·*,
	93–10	in *H·* dwelleth no evil.
	96– 5	have found *H·* so ;
	107– 1	your many-throated organ, . . . praises *H·* ;
	107– 2	in and of this temple that praise *H·*,
	115–24	turns us more unreservedly to *H·*
	117–30	or make them too late to follow *H·*.
	118–18	to work alone with God and for *H·*,
	123–30	it follows that those who worship *H·*,
	123–31	must worship *H·* spiritually,
	124– 4	must worship *H·* in spirit.
	124– 7	neither do we love and obey *H·* by
	127–26	cannot avoid . . . if we reflect *H·*.
	150–28	His people are they that reflect *H·*
	151–20	make *H·* thy first acquaintance.
	153–20	who honors *H·* not by positive proof
	155–26	forward their letters to *H·*
	157–22	trust also in *H·* ; — *Psal.* 37 : 5.
	173–25	whence, then, is something besides *H·*
	174– 7	come into the presence of *H·*

Him

Mis.	176– 2	harmony of Science that declares *H·*,
	194– 6	know *H·* better, and love *H·* more.
	196–22	"we shall be like *H·* ;" — *I John* 3 : 2.
	219– 9	they that worship *H·* — *John* 4 : 24.
	219– 9	must worship *H·* in spirit — *John* 4 : 24.
	235– 5	to reflect *H·* who destroys death
	257– 2	or includes *H·* in every mode and
	258–28	only suitable or true idea of *H·* ;
	259– 1	were made by *H·* ; — *John* 1 : 3.
	259– 1	without *H·* was not — *John* 1 : 3.
	260–18	opposite to *H·* who is All.
	269– 1	trust also in *H·* ; — *Psal.* 37 : 5.
	277–25	Though clouds are round about *H·*,
	319– 5	the argument of aught besides *H·*,
	325–23	"provoke *H·* in the — *Psal.* 78 : 40.
	325–24	grieve *H·* in the desert." — *Psal.* 78 : 40.
	331– 3	committing their way unto *H·*
	332–30	that there is something besides *H·* ;
	333–27	that which does not reflect *H·*
	334– 1	the prophet better understood *H·*
	334– 3	or say unto *H·*, — *Dan.* 4 : 35.
	347–28	None can say unto *H·*,
	350–16	none beside *H·*." — *see Deut.* 4 : 35.
	360–27	Jesus, as the true idea of *H·*,
	363– 8	*H·* who compensateth vanity
	366–12	*none beside H·*." — *see Deut.* 4 : 35.
	366–14	nothing that . . . maketh a lie is in *H·*,
Ret.	9–18	* that I may worship *H·*,
	9–26	* won, through clouds, to *H·*,
	13–20	if I went to *H·* in prayer,
	57–23	not our own, separated from *H·*.
	59–19	and all that is made by *H·*,
	60–20	there is nothing beside *H·* ;"
	60–22	saith, . . . is something besides *H·*,
	63– 5	and there is none beside *H·*,
	93–17	in *H·* we live, — *Acts* 17 : 28.
Un.	2– 3	God pitieth them who fear *H·* ;
	3–13	by knowing *H·* in whom they have
	4– 1	He is near to them who adore *H·*.
	4– 2	To understand *H·*, without a single taint
	4–3, 4	approach *H·* and become like *H·*.
	4–14	as we get still nearer *H·*.
	4–18	has not forbidden man to know *H·* ;
	7–11	has so bound me to *H·* as to enable me
	10– 5	this system is built on *H·*
	13–11	To *H·* there is no moral inharmony ;
	15– 6	that they may declare *H·* absolutely
	21–15	With *H·* is no consciousness of evil,
	21–16	because there is nothing beside *H·*
	21–17	or outside of *H·*.
	26– 4	From *H·* come my forms,
	29–26	I shall yet praise *H·*, — *Psal.* 42 : 11.
	31– 3	they that worship *H·* — *John* 4 : 24.
	31– 3	must worship *H·* in spirit — *John* 4 : 24.
	37–12	no . . . can separate us from *H·*
	39–18	power of *H·* who gave and giveth
	41–19	"we shall be like *H·*," — *I John* 3 : 2.
	48– 6	I believe more in *H·* than do most
	60– 6	and there is none beside *H·*,
	60–19	then let them serve *H·*.
	60–22	Without *H·*, the universe would
Pul.	72–23	* faith in *H·* and His teachings.
	73– 6	* She had faith in *H·*,
Rud.	2–12	if we think of *H·* as less than
	4–21	and there is naught beside *H·*.
	4–22	we can only learn and love *H·*
	9–27	there can be none beside *H·* ;
	13–15	none else beside *H·*." — *Deut.* 4 : 35.
	14– 3	give *H·* all their services,
No.	7–17	cannot hide it from *H·*.
	8–14	the wrath of man to praise *H·*,
	16– 8	would manifest evil in *H·*
	16– 8	and proceeding from *H·*.
	16–19	of something unlike *H·*.
	17– 7	"In *H·* we live, — *Acts* 17 : 28.
	17–21	"none beside *H·*." — *see Deut.* 4 : 35.
	18– 4	lie that denies *H·* as All-in-all,
	18– 5	nor does it ascribe to *H·* all presence,
	24–28	As there is none beside *H·*,
	25–18	coexistent and coeternal with *H·*.
	26–13	represents God, and is in *H·*.
	30–23	revealing *H·* and nothing else.
	33– 2	the wrath of man shall praise *H·*.
	35–22	one with *H·* now and forever.
	37–22	infinite God, and none beside *H·* ;
	39–14	uplifting us to *H·*.
	42– 6	to have other gods before *H·*,
Pan.	4–23	for I shall yet praise *H·*, — *Psal.* 42 : 11.
	5– 5	were made by *H·*," — *John* 1 : 3.
	11– 6	after the image of *H·* — *Col.* 3 : 10.
	13–18	Sooner or later all shall know *H·*,
	13–19	and find life in *H·* in whom
'01.	6–22	infinite scientific sense of *H·*,
	6–28	idea of *H·* as a finite Person
	6–30	is not my sense of *H·*.

Him

'01.	7–20	know not where they have laid *H·*.
	8–12	but an impartation of *H·*.
	32–12	willing to renounce all for *H·*.
	35– 1	acknowledge *H·*, and He — *Prov.* 3 : 6.
'02.	12–19	in *H·* we live, — *Acts* 17 : 28.
Hea.	16–25	impossible to approach *H·* ?
Peo.	6–15	more than we love *H·* ;
	6–17	we love *H·*, because
	6–25	"acquaint now thyself with *H·* — *Job* 22 : 21.
	7–31	must spiritualize to approach *H·*,
Po.	43– 5	You in *H·* abide.
	43– 6	Ours through *H·* who gave
My.	5– 9	His idea, coexistent with *H·*
	5–20	not an unknown God, but *H·* whom,
	13–19	to *H·* "who forgiveth — *Psal.* 103 : 3.
	13–29	to *H·* who returns it unto them
	43– 8	* and they learned to know *H·*.
	45–19	* guidance of *H·* who went before
	154–12	"in *H·* was life," — *John* 1 : 4.
	156–10	have committed unto *H·* — *II Tim.* 1 : 12,
	170–24	trust also in *H·* ; — *Psal.* 37 : 5.
	174–27	I know *H·* nearer, love *H·* more,
	174–28	humbly pray to serve *H·*
	184– 6	for them that wait upon *H·*
	187–26	to build a house unto *H·*
	192– 2	Ye worship *H·* whom ye serve.
	193– 2	unto *H·* whom to know aright
	193–17	You are dedicating yours to *H·*.
	196–19	committed himself to *H·* — *I Pet.* 2 : 23.
	206–25	*H·* who hath called you — *I Pet.* 2 : 9.
	209– 5	those that seek and serve *H·*.
	226–23	depend on *H·* for your existence.
	240– 1	till all men shall know *H·*
	267– 7	were made by *H·* ; — *John* 1 : 3.
	267– 7	without *H·* was not — *John* 1 : 3.
	270–23	and that I can appeal to *H·*
	270–32	"they that worship *H·* — *John* 4 : 24.
	270–32	must worship *H·* in spirit — *John* 4 : 24.
	280–21	nor say unto *H·*, What doest Thou?
	290–13	Trust in *H·* whose love enfolds thee.
	295– 6	"In *H·* was life ; — *John* 1 : 4.

Himself

Mis.	72– 2	nothing evil, or unlike *H·*.
	102–12	God is like *H·* and like nothing else.
	258–13	who was a law to *H·*.
	258–14	governing *H·*, He governs the universe.
	258–18	God named we *H·*, I AM.
	258–27	God's interpretation of *H·* furnishes
	366–13	He is in nothing unlike *H·* ;
	367–20	Mind knows nothing beyond *H·*
	367–32	abideth in *H·*, the only Life,
Ret.	56–23	God reflects *H·*, or Mind,
Un.	3–20	Hence He is in *H·* only,
	3–23	Within *H·* is every embodiment of
	3–25	no consciousness of anything unlike *H·* ;
	3–26	there can be nothing outside of *H·*.
	23–22	anything so wholly unlike *H·*
	41–24	God cannot be the opposite of *H·*.
	48–17	The Ego is God *H·*,
	60–21	neither absent from *H·* nor from the
No.	15–25	in nothing is He unlike *H·*.
	17–14	witness, testifying of *H·*.
	21–16	who unfolds *H·* through
	23–22	no such warfare against *H·*.
	26–16	out of *H·* into something below
Pan.	3–19	God, who reveals *H·*
'01.	5–30	God explains *H·* in C. S.
'02.	7– 1	producing nothing unlike *H·*,

hinder

Mis.	63– 5	to *h·* his benign influence
	111–16	the tares cannot *h·* it.
	223–22	no counteracting influence can *h·*
	274– 8	might *h·* the progress of our Cause
	284– 2	and never try to *h·* others
	290– 7	break all bonds that *h·* progress.
	327–14	greatly *h·* their ascent.
No.	45– 8	To *h·* the unfolding truth,
Pan.	9–15	to *h·* not the attainment of
'01.	14–13	so *h·* our way to holiness.
My.	189– 4	who shall *h·* you?
	206– 3	*h·* the divine influx and lose
	296–14	Evil has no power to harm, to *h·*,

hindered

Mis.	154–25	that your prayers be not *h·*.
Un.	11–23	neither . . . *h·* the divine process.
Pan.	9–18	ought to be aided, not *h·*,

hindering

My.	212–27	*h·* in every way conceivable

hinders

Mis.	234–12	What *h·* man's progress is his
	336–14	beam in your own eye that *h·*
No.	23– 1	*h·* the destruction of evil.
My.	296– 4	whatever *h·* the Science of being.

hindrance

Ret. 89– 2 $h\cdot$ opposed to it by material motion,
No. 9– 4 $h\cdot$ of the Cause of Truth.
My. 219– 5 a $h\cdot$ rather than help.

hindrances

My. 294–20 $h\cdot$ previously mentioned,

Hindu

My. 96– 9 * Mecca and the $H\cdot$ shrines,

Hinds, Father

'01. 32– 5 Father $H\cdot$, Methodist Elder.

hinge

Mis. 206– 1 $h\cdot$ on which have turned all

hint

Mis. 278–22 This may be a serviceable $h\cdot$,
Pan. 7–12 and $h\cdot$ the gods of paganism
My. 28– 9 * a $h\cdot$ of the unselfish efforts,
215–31 we have no $h\cdot$ of his changing
252–27 gave to . . . a higher $h\cdot$.

hinted

My. 324–10 * $h\cdot$ that he thought he could give
355– 8 I have not infrequently $h\cdot$ at this.

hints

Mis. 60–29 $h\cdot$ the existence of spiritual
225– 1 chapter sub-title
Ret. 33– 1 aided by $h\cdot$ from homœopathy,
My. 49–24 * useful $h\cdot$ as to the mode of

hire

Pul. 50– 4 * worthy of his $h\cdot$," — Luke 10 : 7.
My. 214–15 chapter sub-title
214–22 $h\cdot$ a hall in which to speak,
215–25 worthy of his $h\cdot$." — Luke 10 : 7.

hired

My. 313–10 being $h\cdot$ to rock me,

hireling

Mis. 213–25 "an $h\cdot$" — John 10 : 13.

hiring

Mis. 300– 1 avoiding the cost of $h\cdot$

His

Mis. 7–15 laborers in $H\cdot$ vineyard.
9– 5 are these uses of $H\cdot$ rod !
9– 6 passes all $H\cdot$ flock under $H\cdot$ rod
9– 7 passes all . . . into $H\cdot$ fold ;
10– 9 He has called $H\cdot$ own,
10–16 and reinstate $H\cdot$ orders,
18–32 bring to you at $H\cdot$ demand
19– 5 demanded of $H\cdot$ servants
23–27 manifests all $H\cdot$ attributes
36–12 $H\cdot$ beast is the lion that
39–15 I have faith in $H\cdot$ promise,
59–16 lost under $H\cdot$ government.
60– 2 He sent $H\cdot$ Son to save from sin,
61–28 Naming these $H\cdot$ embodiment,
69– 2 $H\cdot$ essence, relations, and attributes.
69– 3 at $H\cdot$ goodness, mercy, and might.
69– 6 of Mind, or God, and $H\cdot$ attributes.
78– 5 $H\cdot$ glory encompasseth all being.
97–17 may touch the hem of $H\cdot$ garment ;
101–31 This one Mind and $H\cdot$ individuality
102–10 $H\cdot$ infinity precludes the possibility
102–11 $H\cdot$ being is individual, but not
102–13 $H\cdot$ character admits of no degrees
102–14 In $H\cdot$ individuality I recognize
102–17 $H\cdot$ pity is expressed in modes
102–18 $H\cdot$ chastisements are the manifestations
102–19 sympathy of $H\cdot$ eternal Mind
106–27 and resound $H\cdot$ praise."
114–26 Rest assured that God in $H\cdot$ wisdom
117–30 their moves before God makes $H\cdot$,
118–19 $H\cdot$ rod and $H\cdot$ staff comfort you.
121–21 crucifixion of $H\cdot$ beloved Son,
123–25 and keep $H\cdot$ commandments,
124–21 silence wherein to muse $H\cdot$ praise,
127– 2 smiled on $H\cdot$ "little ones," — Matt. 18 : 6.
127–17 "river of $H\cdot$ pleasure," — see Psal. 36 : 8.
127–24 the rod is $H\cdot$ means of grace ;
134–15 will guard and guide $H\cdot$ own.
138–26 God will give to all $H\cdot$ soldiers
146–23 to walk in the footsteps of $H\cdot$ flock.
151– 1 folds the sheep of $H\cdot$ pasture ;
151– 2 ears are attuned to $H\cdot$ call.
151–22 spoken of you in $H\cdot$ Word.
152–25 He will hide you in $H\cdot$ feathers
152–26 Into $H\cdot$ haven of Soul
152–30 faith in God and $H\cdot$ spiritual means
153– 3 God will confirm $H\cdot$ inheritance.
153– 9 At $H\cdot$ command, the rock became a
153–14 good to $H\cdot$ Israel
154– 6 God's love for $H\cdot$ flock
154– 7 is manifest in $H\cdot$ care.
154–11 means and measure of $H\cdot$ grace.
154–12 proof of the prosperity of $H\cdot$ Zion.
154–19 Abide in $H\cdot$ word.
157–14 safe under the shadow of $H\cdot$ wing.

His

Mis. 158– 4 is $H\cdot$ wisdom above ours.
158– 9 after $H\cdot$ messenger has obeyed
159– 4 to elucidate $H\cdot$ Word.
170– 9 having rightly read $H\cdot$ Word,
173–27 man in $H\cdot$ own likeness.
174–22 God, and $H\cdot$ omnipresence?
175–22 there are other minds than $H\cdot$;
177– 7 the Lord and against $H\cdot$ Christ,
179–25 God does all this through $H\cdot$
182–25 $H\cdot$ sons and daughters.
186– 3 in $H\cdot$ own image and likeness.
186–26 sense of God and $H\cdot$ universe
193–24 our Lord and $H\cdot$ Christ, Truth ;
208–20 $H\cdot$ rod brings to view
209– 5 shut the mouth of $H\cdot$ prophets,
215–16 in the way of $H\cdot$ appointment,
234–32 makes $H\cdot$ sovereignty glorious.
246–24 make $H\cdot$ paths straight." — Matt. 3 : 3.
263– 8 with $H\cdot$ feathers." — Psal. 91 : 4.
263–10 safe in $H\cdot$ strength,
263–10 building on $H\cdot$ foundation,
268–23 potions of $H\cdot$ own qualities.
268–25 $H\cdot$ preparations for the sick
276–20 $H\cdot$ divine Love is found in affliction.
277–29 I thunder $H\cdot$ law to the sinner,
306–29 give $H\cdot$ angels charge — Psal. 91 : 11.
307– 1 God gives you $H\cdot$ spiritual ideas,
311– 1 and keep $H\cdot$ commandments,
315–30 to study $H\cdot$ revealed Word,
318–11 and keep $H\cdot$ commandments.
322–24 the amplitude of $H\cdot$ mercy,
322–24 the justice of $H\cdot$ judgment,
336– 8 $H\cdot$ highest idea as seen to-day
347–26 Those who know no will but $H\cdot$
348–12 when God shall reveal $H\cdot$ rod,
353–24 divine Principle carries on $H\cdot$ harmony.
354–21 to govern $H\cdot$ own creation,
361–12 earth is full of $H\cdot$ glory,
361–24 $H\cdot$ manifestation is the spiritual
361–29 He elucidates $H\cdot$ own idea,
361–32 $H\cdot$ ways are not as our ways.
363–17 $H\cdot$ modes declare the beauty of
363–18 $H\cdot$ manifold wisdom shines through
363–20 the brightness of $H\cdot$ coming.
364–29 God and $H\cdot$ modes,
366–29 according to $H\cdot$ mode of C. S. ;
367–30 $H\cdot$ ignorance of that which is not,
368– 1 $H\cdot$ own image and likeness.
368– 9 * keeping watch above $H\cdot$ own."
368–29 rejoice in $H\cdot$ supreme rule,
370–18 care from $H\cdot$ loving heart.
370–28 $H\cdot$ first care is to separate the
373–14 does, guide $H\cdot$ children.
376–29 the brightness of $H\cdot$ glory.
389– 9 $H\cdot$ habitation high is here,
389–13 $H\cdot$ arm encircles me,
389–18 the shadow of $H\cdot$ mighty wing ;
397– 1 Then $H\cdot$ unveiled, sweet mercies
399–25 Stands $H\cdot$ church,
399–27 and understood By $H\cdot$ flock.
Man. 15– 7 We acknowledge $H\cdot$ Son,
Chr. 53–41 Truth, the Life — $H\cdot$ word
55–13 operation of $H\cdot$ hands. — Isa. 5 : 12.
Ret. 9–23 * learned at last to know $H\cdot$ voice
13–20 seeking $H\cdot$ guidance.
18–18 all $H\cdot$ spirit hath made,
25–16 but $H\cdot$ corporeality I denied.
27–30 new to $H\cdot$ "little one." — see Matt. 10 : 42.
59–24 in $H\cdot$ own image and likeness.
60– 8 sense says that matter, $H\cdot$ antipode,
69–30 keeping $H\cdot$ commandment?' "
91– 1 and He anoints $H\cdot$ Truth-bearers,
Un. 2– 4 no place where $H\cdot$ voice is not heard ;
3–20 in $H\cdot$ own nature and character,
4–12 our sense . . . of $H\cdot$ absence,
7– 1 $H\cdot$ name will be magnified
10–21 the calculation of $H\cdot$ mighty ways,
13– 9 $H\cdot$ universal laws, $H\cdot$ unchangeableness,
13–13 $H\cdot$ infinite power would
13–17 in the very fibre of $H\cdot$ being,
14– 2 do $H\cdot$ work over again,
14– 9 upon $H\cdot$ own previous work,
14–14 rectify $H\cdot$ spiritual universe?
14–16 because $H\cdot$ created children proved
18–28 it would lower $H\cdot$ rank.
19– 5 contrary to $H\cdot$ creative will,
20–22 outside of $H\cdot$ own focal distance.
22–18 Evil. . . . Error, even, is $H\cdot$ offspring.
23–22 unlike Himself and foreign to $H\cdot$ nature?
24– 9 can never be outside of $H\cdot$ oneness.
24–19 God and $H\cdot$ ideas
26– 6 I am proud to be in $H\cdot$ outstretched
26–15 * But $H\cdot$ mercy waneth never,
27–15 knowing only $H\cdot$ own all-presence,
32– 7 universe, is $H\cdot$ spiritual concept.

His

Un.	32–14	the eternal qualities of *H·* being.
	38– 5	not in accordance with *H·* law,
	51–22	and not of *H·* opposite, evil.
	60–28	yield to *H·* eternal presence,
Pul.	3–21	river of *H·* pleasures is a
	7–14	with *H·* outstretched arm.
	9–21	river of *H·* pleasures.'' — *see Psal. 36: 8.*
	10–29	this is *H·* redeemed ; this, *H·* beloved.
	12– 7	the power of *H·* Christ : — *Rev. 12: 10.*
	16–10	Stands *H·* church,
	16–12	and understood By *H·* flock.
	18–10	Then *H·* unveiled, sweet mercies
	30–17	* Supreme Being, and *H·* Son,
	39– 7	* Round our restlessness, *H·* rest.
	72–23	* faith in Him and *H·* teachings.
	73– 4	* *H·* unlimited and divine power.
	73– 9	* meditated over *H·* divine Word.
	73–15	* God has fulfilled *H·* promises to her
	74–16	to declare in *H·* infinite mercy.
Rud.	4–23	love Him through *H·* spirit,
	4–24	by *H·* marvellous light.
	10– 6	*H·* government is harmonious ;
	10–21	disobedience to *H·* spiritual law.
	10–22	*H·* law of Truth, when obeyed,
	10–26	acknowledge God in all *H·* ways.
	17–16	are the paths of *H·* testimony
	17–17	and the footsteps of *H·* flock.
No.	10–26	*H·* omnipotence and omnipresence.
	16–19	God and *H·* true likeness,
	16–21	but *H·* own consciousness,
	17–25	a part of *H·* consciousness.
	18– 3	acknowledged God in all *H·* ways.
	19–16	man is *H·* individualized idea.
	20– 2	*H* person and perfection are
	30–14	the love of a Father for *H·* child,
	30–17	*H·* sympathy is divine, not human.
	34–21	propitiate *H·* justice and bring *H·* mercy
	37–16	demands *H·* continual presence,
	38–20	which includes only *H·* own nature,
	39–12	nor bring *H·* designs into mortal modes ;
	39–21	discoveries of God, of *H·* goodness
'00.	4– 3	makes *H·* opposites as real and
	4–25	and is *H·* reflection and Science.
	5–24	Science of God and *H·* universe,
	8–27	through one of *H·* little ones,
	10–22	habitation of *H·* throne forever.
	12– 4	seven stars in *H·* right hand — *Rev. 2: 1.*
'01.	1– 6	so long as you are in *H·* service.
	5–27	eternal image and likeness.
	5–29	explain both *H·* person and nature,
	7–10	man in *H·* own image and likeness,
	10–20	"the riches of *H·* grace" — *Eph. 1: 7.*
	15–26	* to bear to have you in *H·* sight.
	15–28	* provoking *H·* pure eyes by your sinful,
	15–29	* attending *H·* solemn worship.
	32–20	love God and keep *H·* commandments
'02.	7– 3	*H·* infinite manifestations of love
	8–29	departure from God, or *H·* lost likeness,
	17–24	ourselves and others through *H·* tenure,
Hea.	8– 2	and obedience to *H·* government,
	9–17	man, *H·* own image and likeness.
	12–13	directly or indirectly, through *H·* providence
	19–22	work more earnestly in *H·* vineyard,
Peo.	3– 9	torture of *H·* favorite Son,
	5–17	to declare *H·* omnipotence.''
	13– 9	one God and *H·* all-power
Po.	4–17	shadow of *H·* mighty wing ;
	12–10	*H·* unveiled, sweet mercies show
	32–19	pardon and grace, through *H·* Son,
	64– 9	adore all *H·* spirit hath made,
	76– 9	on this rock . . . Stands *H·* church,
	76–11	understood By *H·* flock.
	79– 9	in thought and deed — To faithful *H·*.
My.	3– 8	that do *H·* commandments, — *Rev. 22: 14.*
	14– 2	their tithes into *H·* storehouse.
	15–14	*H·* own image and likeness.
	17–30	on *H·* 'little ones,' — *Matt. 18: 6.*
	18–14	'river of *H·* pleasure,' — *see Psal. 36: 8.*
	20–12	what God gives to *H·* church.
	20–13	your tithes into *H·* storehouse,
	23– 7	* so long as we follow *H·* commands.
	36–20	* salvation through *H·* divine Christ.
	109–21	but specks in *H·* universe,
	113–20	to perfect *H·* praise.
	129–11	no day but in *H·* smile.
	129–26	These are *H·* green pastures
	132–15	"Of *H·* own will — *Jas. 1: 18.*
	133– 6	inhabit *H·* holy hill,
	143–27	according to *H·* purpose. — *Rom. 8: 31.*
	150–19	*H·* own image and likeness.
	152–21	hear *H·* voice, listen to *H·* Word
	153–31	should be to us *H·* apostles,
	159–10	sent forth *H·* word to heal
	162– 2	*H·* "very present help — *Psal. 46: 1.*
	167–17	one acceptable in *H·* sight,

His

My.	170–16	It is *H·* coin, *H·* currency ;
	182–28	this vine of *H·* husbanding,
	186–15	according to *H·* riches in glory.
	186–21	Here let *H·* promise be verified :
	187–25	light and liberty of *H·* children,
	187–29	majesty of *H·* might
	188– 3	This house is hallowed by *H·* promise :
	190–30	wherefore vilify *H·* prophets
	193– 8	"for *H·* goodness, — *Psal. 107: 8.*
	193– 9	*H·* wonderful works — *Psal. 107: 8.*
	193–16	Nothing dethrones *H·* house.
	198– 7	continuance of *H·* favors,
	202–24	a drop from *H·* ocean of love,
	202–30	God bless this vine of *H·* planting.
	204– 2	faith in God and in *H·* followers
	204– 3	gives *H·* followers opportunity
	205–10	* *H·* wonders to perform ;
	205–11	* plants *H·* footsteps in the sea
	206–26	*H·* marvellous light.'' — *I Pet. 2: 9.*
	206–30	kingdom of *H·* dear Son.'' — *Col. 1: 13.*
	208–25	their confidence in *H·* ways
	213–21	harmony with *H·* true followers.
	221– 8	God in *H·* more infinite meanings,
	225–13	giving unto *H·* holy name
	225–18	sacredly holding *H·* name apart
	225–28	*H·* synonyms are Love, Truth, Life,
	226–21	you learn to hallow *H·* name,
	226–22	*H·* all-power, all-presence,
	232– 3	with the helm in *H·* hands.
	238–10	*H·* language and meaning are
	251–26	armors, and tests in *H·* service,
	251–26	and we are *H·*.
	253–24	you have *H·* rich blessing
	257– 3	*H·* dear love that heals
	260–28	religion to God and *H·* Christ,
	262– 1	eternal in *H·* own image.
	262–21	*H·* spiritual idea, man
	263– 2	alone and without *H·* glory.
	278– 2	If *H·* purpose for peace is to be
	280–21	Out of *H·* allness He must
	280–22	with *H·* own truth and love.
	281–14	we are *H·* in divine Science.
	288–27	*H·* rod is love.
	292–8, 9	*H·* rod and *H·* staff comfort
	300– 6	*H·* good pleasure.'' — *Phil. 2: 13.*
	323–22	* to reveal to us *H·* way.
	347– 2	through . . . *H·* two witnesses.
	355–27	God is glorified in *H·* reflection
	356– 3	in *H·* reflection of love and
	356– 7	* plants *H·* footsteps in the sea

(see also **creation, hand, idea, image, laws, likeness, love, people, power, presence, righteousness, will**)

hisses

Mis.	227– 4	to the *h·* of the multitude,

hissing

Mis.	134–25	fermenting, and its heat *h·*
	323–19	hushing the *h·* serpents,

historians

My.	315–26	thank the enterprising *h·*

historic

Mis.	305–20	* articles of *h·* interest will be
Ret.	21–25	*h·* incidents and personal events
My.	85–25	* this *h·* city is the Mecca of
	90–26	* *h·* place of Mrs. Eddy as the
	148–11	this church becomes *h·*,
	184–20	*h·* gem on the glowing records of

historical

Mis.	197–16	belief in any *h·* event or person.
	306– 2	* send fullest *h·* description.
'00.	12–28	rather than personal or *h·*.
My.	v–13	* recalling the following *h·* facts:
	26–22	This *h·* dedication should
	318–28	ample fund of *h·* knowledge,

historically

Ret.	3– 8	known *h·* as Lovewell's War.
Pul.	8– 2	press has spoken out *h·*,

history

all

My.	89–29	* religious phenomenon of all *h·*.

Biblical

Un.	44–12	according to Biblical *h·*.

Christian

Ret.	45– 8	earliest periods in Christian *h·*.

different

Mis.	224–14	each person has a different *h·*,

divine

Ret.	10–15	Etymology was divine *h·*,

early

Mis.	ix– 6	In the early *h·* of C. S.,
	141–20	stain the early *h·* of C. S.
My.	60– 2	* about the early *h·* of C. S.

history

following
  Mis. 271–28   * following *h·* and statistics
fraught with
  Mis. 253–14   Fraught with *h·*, it repeats the past
heart of
  Mis. 93– 4   heart of *h·* shall be made glad !
his
  Rud. 3–10   His *h·* is emphatic in our hearts,
  My. 291–19   May his *h·* waken a tone of truth
human
    (*see* **human**)
its
  My. 47– 9   * from the pages of its *h·*.
Jesus'
  Mis. 162–11   became the emblem of Jesus' *h·* ;
Major Glover's
  My. 330–14   * concerning Major Glover's *h·*
material
  No. 45–27   material *h·* is drawing to a close.
McClure
  My. 315–21   * the *McClure* "*h·*," so called,
mortal
  Ret. 21–14   mortal *h·* is but the record of
Mrs. Eddy's
  My. 297–26   chapter sub-title
my
  Mis. 247– 6   Those familiar with my *h·*
    278– 9   my *h·* as connected with the Cause
  My. 297–30   circulating regarding my *h·*,
natural
  Mis. 26–20   Natural *h·* shows that neither a
needs
  Mis. 354– 5   *H·* needs it,
no
  Mis. 357–12   no central emblem, no *h·*.
of a seed
  Mis. 26– 9   ponders the *h·* of a seed,
    144–26   As in the *h·* of a seed,
of Christianity
  Peo. 13–25   * "Since ever the *h·* of Christianity
of Christian Science
  Mis. ix– 6   In the early *h·* of C. S.,
    141–20   stain the early *h·* of C. S.
  '01. 2–27   *h·* of C. S. explains its
  '02. 1– 3   marked the *h·* of C. S.
  My. 60– 2   * about the early *h·* of C. S.
    66–27   * an epoch in the *h·* of C. S.
of Europe
  Mis. 170–20   *h·* of Europe and America ;
of its Discoverer
  My. 143–16   the honest *h·* of its Discoverer
of man
  Un. 50–27   as the *h·* of man, disappears,
of Mind-healing
  No. 3–18   *h·* of Mind-healing notes this hour.
of the Church
  Man. 110– 8   recorded in the *h·* of the Church
of the church
  My. 57–18   * largest in the *h·* of the church
    284–15   * first time in the *h·* of the church
of the errors
  Mis. 277–20   * *h·* of the errors of the human mind."
of the spiritual man
  Mis. 186– 1   giving the *h·* of the spiritual man
our
  My. 45– 9   * in the annals of our *h·*.
partial
  Ret. 38– 9   partial *h·* of what I had already
place in
  Mis. 308–10   their proper place in *h·*,
recorded in
  Rud. 16–21   first book, recorded in *h·*, which
records
  '00. 12– 7   *H·* records Ephesus as an
religious
  Un. 15–21   found in heathen religious *h·*.
repeats itself
  No. 41– 3   *H·* repeats itself.
  Hea. 1– 6   *H·* repeats itself ;
  My. 58– 6   * "*H·* repeats itself."
sad
  Mis. 341–23   the sad *h·* of Vesta,
scant
  Mis. 274– 1   From the scant *h·* of Jesus
shows
  Pul. 23–18   * *H·* shows the curious fact that
  '00. 10–17   *H·* shows that error repeats itself
  '01. 28–15   Sacred *h·* shows that those who
society and
  Mis. 296– 6   American society and *h·*,
temporal
  My. 134– 1   spiritual bespeaks our temporal *h·*.
this
  Mis. 57–20   This *h·* of a falsity
  Pul. 8–26   in the fabric of this *h·*,

history

tired tongue of
  Ret. 84–23   tired tongue of *h·* be enriched.
traditional
  Ret. 22– 7   traditional *h·* of the early life of
veritable
  Mis. 312–20   honest utterance of veritable *h·*,
web of
  Mis. 145–27   their names in the web of *h·*,
winds of
  Mis. 79– 5   swept clean by the winds of *h·*.
write the
  Mis. 106– 4   write the *h·* in poor parody on

  Mis. 106– 4   Scientists will, *must*, have a *h·* ;
    238–11   more than *h·* has yet recorded.
    272– 7   * is the first on record in *h·*,
    320– 4   the *h·* of Truth's idea,
  Ret. 44–29   The *h·* of that hour holds this true
  Pul. 33–15   * *h·* not infrequently emphasizes,
  Peo. 7– 3   on the body as well as on *h·*
  My. 89–26   * not to this time alone, but to *h·*.
    90– 5   * in the *h·* of religious expression.
    119– 1   It is convenient for *h·* to record
    125–14   *H·* will record their words,
    236– 1   *h·* of our church buildings.
    292– 2   more than *h·* has yet recorded.
    318–32   I do not find my authority . . . in *h·*,

hit

  Mis. 216–23   a happy *h·* at idealism,
  Hea. 6– 6   The pioneer . . . is never *h·* :

hitch

  Un. 17– 4   * " *H·* your wagon to a star."
  My. 75–15   * not been the slightest *h·*

hither

  Mis. 99–28   come up *h·*."
    326–31   "Wherefore comest thou *h·*?"
    327– 3   I came *h·*, hoping that I
    386–29   *H·* to reap, with all the crowned
  '00. 9–11   art thou come *h·* to — *Matt.* 8 : 29.
  '01. 1–17   have brought you *h·*.
  '02. 10– 6   "Art thou come *h·* to — *Matt.* 8 : 29.
  Po. 16– 7   Ambition, come *h·* !
    50–16   *H·* to reap, with all the crowned
  My. 182–26   turn *h·* with satisfied hope.
    222– 6   bring him *h·* — *Matt.* 17 : 17.
    229– 3   No mesmerist . . . is fit to come *h·*.
    244– 7   You have been invited *h·*

hitherto

  Mis. xi– 7   what they have *h·* achieved
    xi–13   in the *h·* unexplored fields
    125–25   the *h·* untouched problems
    127– 1   *H·*, I have observed that
    146–12   I have *h·* declined to be
  Man. 18–11   "*H·* hath the Lord — *I Sam.* 7 : 12.
  Ret. 15–10   *h·* have I declared — *Psal.* 71 : 17.
    43– 7   the only College, *h·*,
  Pul. 56–17   * Christianity and Science, *h·* divorced
  '01. 35–16   And the working *h·*
  My. 17–29   "*H·*, I have observed that
    49– 3   * the *h·* half-persuaded
    57–20   * the *h·* largest admission,
    195– 7   have *h·* prevented my reply.
    217– 5   your *h·* unselfish toil,
    299–15   *h·* undiscovered in the translations

hits

  Mis. 347–32   whoever *h·* this mark is well paid

hived

  Mis. 294–13   a *h·* bee, with sting ready

hoar

  Po. 10–10   The *h·* fight is forgotten ;
  My. 337–11   The *h·* fight is forgotten ;

hoards

  '00. 3– 7   he *h·* this capital to distribute

hoarse

  Po. 73– 4   *h·* wave revisits thy shore !

hoary

  Mis. 231– 1   on whose *h·* head the almond-blossom
    257–23   and strikes down the *h·* saint.
    336–27   *h·* with eternity, touches time
    389– 2   The *h·* head with joy to crown ;
  No. 13–18   It is *h·* with time.
  Pan. 5–11   answer for all time to this *h·* query.
  Po. 21–16   The *h·* head with joy to crown ;

hobbling

  Mis. 168– 5   or *h·* on crutches,

hobby

  No. 44–10   Error has no *h·*,

Hodgson Hall

  Pul. 74– 7   * meets every Sunday in *H· H·*,

Hogue, Blanche Hersey
My. 237–22 The article . . . by Blanche Hersey *H·*,

hold
Mis. 62–14 *Why do Christian Scientists h·*
    63–17 might lay *h·* of eternal Life,
    97– 3 take *h·* of the eternal energies
    111– 8 losing *h·* of divine Love,
    136–24 *h·* three sessions annually,
    137–30 *h·* these organizations of their own,
    140– 3 could *h·* a wholly material title.
    199– 6 *h·* himself amenable only to
    216–26 * nor the laws of reason *h·* good,
    266–15 *h·* justice and mercy as inseparable
    269– 8 will *h·* to the one, — *Matt.* 6 : 24.
    274–23 those quill-drivers . . . *h·* high carnival.
    276– 5 I did not *h·* interviews with all
    282–18 person with whom you *h·* communion
    285–11 *h·* high the banner of Truth
    290–25 *h·* a place in one's memory,
    315–15 *h·* himself morally obligated to
    333–11 Where do we *h·* intelligence to be?
    350– 1 I *h·* receipts for $1,489.50 paid in,
    351–17 they never can . . . *h·* it there,
    355–28 *H·* thy gaze to the light,
    363–24 *h·* fast to the Principle of C. S.
    374–15 Angels, . . . *h·* charge over both,
Man. 25–12 President shall *h·* office for one year,
    45–20 is not entitled to *h·* office
    46–13 shall *h·* in sacred confidence
    61– 4 shall not *h·* two or more
    76–21 They shall *h·* quarterly meetings
    79–22 *h·* and manage the property
    80– 7 shall *h·* this money subject to
    83–13 *h·* himself morally obligated
Ret. 29– 3 and *h·* to loving our enemies
Un. 43–23 to *apprehend*, or lay *h·* upon,
    49–13 So long as I *h·* evil in consciousness,
    56–24 lay *h·* of him ere he can change
    61– 2 that takes *h·* of eternal Truth.
Pul. 38–24 * They *h·* with strict fidelity to
    63–19 * The great *h·* she has upon this army
    66–13 * They *h·* with strict fidelity to
Rud. 12– 9 until they *h·* stronger than before
No. 8–19 students to *h·* no controversy or
    13–18 It takes *h·* of eternity,
    38–18 they take *h·* of harmony,
'00. 11– 3 *H·* in yourselves the true sense of
    14– 4 *H·* that fast which thou — *Rev.* 3 : 11.
    14–18 *h·* in your full hearts fervently
'01. 13–28 *h·* it invalid, give it the lie,
    14–11 our faith *h·* of the fact that
Hea. 13– 2 *h·* of both horns of the dilemma,
Peo. 11–16 *h·* the children of Israel still in
Po. 26– 8 grasped the sword to *h·* her throne,
    43–10 in Thy great heart *h·* them
My. 53–10 * *h·* its meetings of worship in the
    84–23 * Its *h·* and development are
    85–17 * *h·* place among the architectural
    90–11 * grips *h·* of their faith
    93–27 * its *h·* upon the public,
    126–26 *h·* of every foul spirit, — *Rev.* 18 : 2
    129– 2 "*h·* fast that which is — *I Thess.* 5 : 21.
    129– 7 taking strong *h·* of the public
    129–24 takes *h·* on heaven,
    146–23 Scientists *h·* as a vital point
    234–22 If the Dowager Empress could *h·*
    243–10 *h·* important, responsible offices,
    290–26 *H·* this attitude of mind,
    319– 8 *h·* the late Mr. Wiggin in . . . memory
    323–24 * if God did not *h·* you up
    344–12 I *h·* it absurd to say
    353–12 intended to *h·* guard over Truth,
    356–23 else he will *h·* to the one, — *Matt.* 6 : 24.

holdeth
'00. 12– 3 "*h·* the seven stars — *Rev.* 2 : 1.

holding
Mis. 40–28 If it is hate that is *h·* the purpose
    62– 1 *H·* the *right* idea of man in
    62– 5 *h·* in thought the form of a
    83– 1 *h·* man forever in the
    204–21 *h·* sway over human consciousness.
    308–26 even as *h·* in mind the
    327–27 Obstinately *h·* themselves back,
    338–10 hope *h·* steadfastly to good
    359–13 or by *h·* it in fetters.
Man. 74– 2 C. S. society *h·* public services,
Un. 40–25 *H·* a material sense of Life,
    56– 9 *H·* a quickened sense of
Pul. 25– 9 * capable of *h·* fifteen hundred ;
    41–16 * capacity for *h·* from fourteen hundred
No. 26– 9 *h·* such material and mortal
    30–21 not light *h·* darkness within itself.
    36–17 *h·* the mortal as unreal,
My. 75– 4 * *h·* the centre of the stage
    83– 3 * the *h·* of a great convention

holding
My. 98– 7 * church, *h·* five thousand people,
    121– 3 time for *h·* our semi-annual
    184–25 *h·* unwearied watch over a world.
    222–29 in the *h·* of crime in check,
    225–18 sacredly *h·* His name apart
    306–30 *h·* long conversations with him

holds
Mis. 3–20 mortal thought *h·* in itself all sin,
    77–16 it *h·* man in endless Life
    97– 7 human mind that *h·* within itself
    139–11 *pulling down of strong h·*; — *II Cor.* 10 : 4·
    221–32 *h·* the issues of death to
    260–14 mortal thought *h·* only in itself the
Man. 38– 7 student of . . . who *h·* a degree,
Ret. 44–29 that hour *h·* this true record.
Un. 40–17 who *h·* Life by a spiritual and not by
Pul. 5– 9 Memory, *h·* in her secret chambers
    50–26 * No one . . . *h·* the whole of truth,
    68–17 * now *h·* regular services in the
Rud. 4–11 which *h·* the earth in its orbit.
    15– 7 this *h·* and satisfies the thought
No. 26–22 God *h·* man in the eternal
    42–19 The lie of evil *h·* its own by
My. 84– 6 * *h·* back work that would otherwise
    93–11 * which it *h·* out to its votaries ;
    123–21 My little hall, which *h·* a trifle over
    200–17 What *h·* us to the Christian life
    226–11 *h·* the earth in its orbit
    295– 4 Love *h·* its substance safe

hole
Mis. 210–14 brings the serpent out of its *h·*,
    231–16 made a big *h·*, with two incisors,

holiday
Mis. xi–14 At each recurring *h·*
My. 20– 7 chapter sub-title
    234– 1 and fifty telegrams per *h·*
    339–16 and the observance of the *h·*

holidays
Mis. 319–19 greetings for the forthcoming *h·*,
My. 20– 8 The *h·* are coming,
    121– 6 commotion of the season's *h·*.
    166–21 If all our years were *h·*,
    234– 2 Are the *h·* blest by absorbing
    234– 9 give me the *h·* for this work

holier
Mis. 17–19 much higher and *h·* conception
    229–24 become healthier, *h·*, happier,
    330–22 higher joys, *h·* aims,
Peo. 14–13 higher and *h·* love for God

holiest
Mis. 177– 4 greatest and *h·* of all causes.
Pul. 5– 9 characters of *h·* sort,
Po. 77– 3 A nation's *h·* hymn
My. 258– 8 to all of *h·* worth.

holiness
and health
Mis. 25– 1 against his *h·* and health.
and heaven
Mis. 309–21 health, *h·*, and heaven.
Un. 64– 6 only health, *h·*, and heaven,
and immortality
Mis. 163–32 health, *h·*, and immortality.
    172–27 health, *h·*, and immortality of man.
No. 28–12 health, *h·*, and immortality.
My. 160–11 health, *h·*, and immortality.
    247– 8 health, *h·*, and immortality,
    255– 1 health, *h·*, and immortality,
    274–15 health, *h·*, and immortality.
and Life
Un. 42– 4 outcome of Spirit, *h·*, and Life.
and love
'01. 12–19 redolent with health, *h·*, and love.
My. 274– 6 goodness, *h·*, and love do this,
apart from
Mis. 154–30 nor aim apart from *h·*.
beauty of
    (*see* **beauty**)
happiness, and
Mis. 15–12 health, happiness, and *h·*.
    183– 7 health, happiness, and *h·* :
My. 167–20 their health, happiness, and *h·*
    275–22 health, happiness, and *h·*,
harmony, and
Ret. 65–29 obtain health, harmony, and *h·*
harmony, or
Rud. 10– 1 against health, harmony, or *h·*,
health and
    (*see* **health**)
health or
Mis. 308– 4 for his health or *h·*,
highway of
Mis. 287–17 find the highway of *h·*.

holiness

love-linked
My. 206– 6 love-linked $h\cdot$ which heals
mount of
Mis. 206–30 stands upon the mount of $h\cdot$,
peace, and
Mis. 167–29 He giveth power, peace, and $h\cdot$;
'02. 16–14 To attain peace and $h\cdot$
My. 252–23 into paths of peace and $h\cdot$.
reign of
My. 228–16 kingdom of heaven, the reign of $h\cdot$,
sin to
Un. 37–10 from sin to $h\cdot$,
'02. 10–23 yea, from sin to $h\cdot$
strive after
Mis. 197– 6 to strive after $h\cdot$;
typifies
Mis. 86–15 that beauty typifies $h\cdot$,
way to
'01. 14–14 so hinder our way to $h\cdot$.
yield to
Un. 39– 4 yield to $h\cdot$, health, and Life,

———

Mis. 37– 6 toward purity, health, $h\cdot$, and
99–27 health, $h\cdot$, universal harmony,
101–12 for the freedom of health, $h\cdot$, and
127–15 bread of heaven, health, $h\cdot$,
200– 4 $h\cdot$, life, and health as the better
205–22 with eternal life, $h\cdot$, heaven.
Un. 32–19 the opposite of Spirit, of $h\cdot$,
'01. 2– 2 demonstrated — health, $h\cdot$,
'02. 9– 4 All-power — giving life, health, $h\cdot$;
16–12 $h\cdot$, without which no man — Heb. 12 : 14.
My. 18–12 bread of heaven, health, $h\cdot$,
118–29 harmony, $h\cdot$, entirely apart from
153–30 give thee rest, peace, health, $h\cdot$.
155–13 run in joy, health, $h\cdot$,
158–15 lends a new-born beauty to $h\cdot$,
205–28 Hence health, $h\cdot$, immortality,
349– 4 consciousness of health, $h\cdot$,

Hollis, Allen

My. 138–30 * signature

Holmes

Mr. Marcus
My. 13– 7 presented . . . by Mr. Marcus $H\cdot$.
Oliver Wendell
Peo. 5–26 Oliver Wendell $H\cdot$ said, in a lecture

holy

Mis. 51–28 * transparent like some $h\cdot$ thing."
70–24 body of the $h\cdot$ Spirit of Jesus
122– 8 instrument in this $h\cdot$ (?) alliance
162–28 To carry out his $h\cdot$ purpose,
184–11 presenting our bodies $h\cdot$ and acceptable,
200–25 $h\cdot$ calm of Paul's well-tried hope
227–22 dwelling upon a $h\cdot$ hill,
270–21 cannot depart from his $h\cdot$ example,
273–17 labor for a good and $h\cdot$ cause.
280– 7 messengers of pure and $h\cdot$ thoughts
280– 7 hurt not the $h\cdot$ things of Truth.
287–13 only high and $h\cdot$ joy can satisfy
301–25 injustice standing in a $h\cdot$ place.
321–20 Untiring in your $h\cdot$ fight,
387–18 $h\cdot$ thoughts and heavenly strain,
Man. 49– 5 to enter into this $h\cdot$ work,
Ret. 26– 4 Principle of his $h\cdot$ heroism
86–14 the fellow-saint of a $h\cdot$ household.
91–25 $h\cdot$ messages from the All-Father.
91–30 His $h\cdot$ humility, unworldliness,
Pul. 1–16 spot whereon thou troddest was $h\cdot$
11– 6 rehearse your hearts' $h\cdot$ intents.
82– 6 * steel tempered with $h\cdot$ resolve,
No. 27–26 tread lightly, for this is $h\cdot$ ground.
Pan. 3–19 one supreme, $h\cdot$, self-existent God,
9–19 not hindered, in his $h\cdot$ mission.
15– 7 establish us in the most $h\cdot$ faith,
Po. 6–13 $h\cdot$ thoughts and heavenly strain,
23–13 Yielding a $h\cdot$ strength to right,
26– 5 where thou hast trod is $h\cdot$ ground.
71–17 $h\cdot$ meaning of their song.
My. 13–25 $h\cdot$ harmony, reverberating
17–12 an $h\cdot$ priesthood. — I Pet. 2 : 5.
19–25 words of our $h\cdot$ Way-shower,
24–14 * unto an $h\cdot$ temple — Eph. 2 : 21.
33–16 dwell in thy $h\cdot$ hill? — Psal. 15 : 1.
34– 2 stand in his $h\cdot$ place? — Psal. 24 : 3.
36–11 * to a $h\cdot$ Christian service
63–13 * this happy and $h\cdot$ experience
64–23 * to the high and $h\cdot$ task of
81–22 * $h\cdot$ song rose tingling to the
133– 6 inhabit His $h\cdot$ hill,
153–10 He that is $h\cdot$." — Rev. 3 : 7.
206–13 an $h\cdot$ nation, — I Pet. 2 : 9.
225–13 giving unto His $h\cdot$ name
228–23 dwell in Thy $h\cdot$ hill? — Psal. 15 : 1.

holy

My. 283– 9 To aid in this $h\cdot$ purpose
290–23 the high and $h\cdot$ call you again
291– 2 $h\cdot$ demands rested on the

Holy Bible (see also Bible)

My. 18–29 * The $H\cdot B\cdot$; "S. and H.

Holy Father

Pul. 65– 5 * the $H\cdot F\cdot$ should not overlook
My. 253–16 " $H\cdot F\cdot$, keep through — John 17 : 11.

Holy Ghost

Mis. 55–14 sin against the $H\cdot G\cdot$
174–32 the $H\cdot G\cdot$ that leadeth into
204–12 The baptism of the $H\cdot G\cdot$
Man. 15– 8 the $H\cdot G\cdot$ or divine Comforter ;
Un. 51–23 as Father, Son, and $H\cdot G\cdot$;
52– 4 This Science . . . is the $H\cdot G\cdot$,
Pul. 30–17 * and His Son, and the $H\cdot G\cdot$,
'00. 5–11 Father, Son, and $H\cdot G\cdot$
'01. 8– 3 the $H\cdot G\cdot$, or spiritual idea
8– 6 who regard . . . the $H\cdot G\cdot$ as
12– 6 he baptized with the $H\cdot G\cdot$
'02. 5– 7 it lights the fires of the $H\cdot G\cdot$,
My. 19–10 communion of the $H\cdot G\cdot$, — II Cor. 13 : 14.

Holy of Holies

Mis. 77–29 It was to enter unshod the $H\cdot$ of $H\cdot$,

Holy One

Mis. 268– 7 The $H\cdot O\cdot$ saith,
'01. 9–22 the $H\cdot O\cdot$ of God." — Mark 1 : 24.
My. 168– 4 the $H\cdot O\cdot$ of Israel,

Holy Scriptures

Mis. 132–24 refer you to the $H\cdot S\cdot$,

Holy Spirit

Mis. 161–23 specially endowed with the $H\cdot S\cdot$;
'01. 9–22 The $H\cdot S\cdot$ takes of the things of God

Holy Writ

Mis. 122–17 $H\cdot W\cdot$ denounces him that declares,
123–29 $H\cdot W\cdot$ declares that God is Love,
187–16 set forth in original $H\cdot W\cdot$
199–27 so-called miracles contained in $H\cdot W\cdot$
217–25 According to $H\cdot W\cdot$, it is a
Man. 28–10 the warning of $H\cdot W\cdot$:
Un. 17–21 $H\cdot W\cdot$ declares God told our
30–25 meaning of the declaration of $H\cdot W\cdot$,
Pul. 2– 3 expressive language of $H\cdot W\cdot$,
'01. 8–18 according to $H\cdot W\cdot$
16–17 according to $H\cdot W\cdot$ these qualities
'02. 3–29 According to $H\cdot W\cdot$, the first lie
My. 155– 7 promises, and proofs of $H\cdot W\cdot$.
162–16 We read in $H\cdot W\cdot$:
178– 4 spiritual meaning of $H\cdot W\cdot$
339–17 We read in $H\cdot W\cdot$ that the disciples

homage

Mis. 107–10 heart's $h\cdot$ belongs to God.
226– 9 he loses the $h\cdot$ of fools,
262–24 With all the $h\cdot$ beneath the skies,
374–19 $h\cdot$ is indeed due,
Peo. 9–12 dividing our $h\cdot$ and obedience
My. 26–22 the lie . . . that I claim their $h\cdot$.

home (see also home's)

ancestral
My. 309–28 * the ancestral $h\cdot$ at Bow.
and family
Pul. 50– 4 * deserves to have a $h\cdot$ and family
and heaven
Mis. 289–18 compatible with $h\cdot$ and heaven.
Pul. 11– 8 find within it $h\cdot$, and heaven.
and peace
Mis. 386– 5 $h\cdot$ and peace and hearts are found
Po. 49– 8 $h\cdot$ and peace and hearts are found
at last
My. 155–14 $h\cdot$ at last, it finds the full
beautiful
My. 66–24 * her beautiful $h\cdot$, Pleasant View,
begin at
Mis. 32–24 charity must begin at $h\cdot$.
Boston
Pul. 47–21 * Besides her Boston $h\cdot$, Mrs. Eddy has
call her
Mis. 387– 3 To call her $h\cdot$,
Po. 50–21 To call her $h\cdot$,
childhood's
Ret. 6– 6 My childhood's $h\cdot$ I remember as
Christian Science
My. 214–23 C. S. $h\cdot$ for indigent students,
215–17 C. S. $h\cdot$ for the poor worthy student,
church
'01. 31–19 chapter sub-title
My. 54–16 * been regarded as the church $h\cdot$,
55–18 * plans were made for a church $h\cdot$.
57– 6 * sacred atmosphere of a church $h\cdot$.
157–11 * commodious and beautiful church $h\cdot$
164– 5 to many in this city a church $h\cdot$.

home

country
Pul. 47–22 * has a delightful country h·
  63–12 * her delightful country h· in Concord,
My. 311– 4 at his country h· in North Groton,
desolate
Mis. 231–30 alas! for the desolate h· ;
My. 292–11 mourner at the desolate h· !
every
My. 340–32 light their fires in every h·.
far from
My. 312– 9 * She was far from h·
father's
Pul. 34– 3 * She returned to her father's h·
My. 312–13 * met and taken to her father's h·
  312–28 took me to my father's h· in Tilton,
forest
Mis. 237–19 murmuring winds of their forest h·.
get
Mis. 225–30 * "Wait until we get h·,
greenwood
Po. 34–17 Unto thy greenwood h·
hallows
Mis. 287–28 ruler over one's self and hallows h·,
happy
Mis. 388–17 Affection's wreath, a happy h· ;
Po. 21– 6 Affection's wreath, a happy h· ;
My. 315– 9 * happy h· as one could wish for.
her
Mis. 389–25 And mother finds her h·
Man. 68–18 calls to her h· . . . only those
  69–22 employed by Mrs. Eddy at her h·
Pul. 43–25 * Mrs. Eddy remained at her h·
Po. 5– 6 And mother finds her h·
My. 314–25 kept her a prisoner in her h·,
  326–10 * which Mrs. Eddy has made her h·.
his
Mis. 395– 7 His h· the clod !
Pul. 54–29 at his h· in Amesbury,
Po. 57–14 His h· the clod !
Mrs. Eddy's
My. 53–11 * in the parlors of Mrs. Eddy's h·,
  355–21 Scientists at Mrs. Eddy's h·
my
Ret. 20–11 my h· I regarded as very precious.
My. 189–26 the sunny South —once my h·.
new
My. 31–17 * The new h· for worship
  50– 8 * strangeness of their new h·,
of Love
Mis. 84–24 turn one, . . . to the h· of Love.
of love
Po. 8–21 light of a h· of love and pride ;
of their Leader
Man. 68–26 to the h· of their Leader,
of the pastor
My. 50– 2 * was held at the h· of the pastor,
of the President
My. 112–30 h· of the President of the United
of vice
Un. 52–25 sometimes the h· of vice.
old
'01. 29–17 whenever they return to the old h·
palatial
Pul. 70–26 * She has a palatial h· in Boston
Palmetto
My. 176– 9 hallow your Palmetto h· with palms
provide a
Ret. 52– 8 provide a h· for every true seeker
radiant
Po. 17– 2 O tell of their radiant h·
religious
My. 270– 6 my first religious h·
returned
Mis. 226– 6 clergyman's son returned h· — well.
sackcloth of
Mis. 275– 8 lift the veil on the sackcloth of h·,
stately
Pul. 44–17 * chapter sub-title
substantial
Pul. 49–22 * there to build a substantial h·
summer
My. 314–11 which he fancied, for a summer h·.
their
Po. 41–10 their h· is not here?
thy
Mis. 385–15 Thee to thy h·.
Po. 48– 8 Thee to thy h·.
My. 290–27 remove the sackcloth from thy h·.
your
My. 170–12 To your h· in my heart !

Mis. 100–23 Pure humanity, friendship, h·,
  152–29 which guides you safely h·.
  237–11 cup of gall that conscience strikes h· ;
  251–11 religion, h·, friends, and country.

home

Mis. 304–19 * Washington will be its h·,
  394– 5 the h·, and the heaven of Soul.
Ret. 20–26 he should have a h· with me.
Un. 17–18 into a h· of marvellous light,
Pul. 40–20 * h· for The First Church of Christ,
  58–29 * to make it a h· by day or night.
'01. 14–16 traveller on his way h·.
  17– 9 and to welcome him h·.
Hea. 7–20 he charged h· a crime to mind.
Po. 32– 3 h· where I dwell in the vale,
  45– 6 the h·, and the heaven of Soul.
My. 22– 4 * for the h· of The Mother Church,
  139–11 his is a life-lease of hope, h·,
  145–19 at h· attending to the machinery
  148–19 I, as usual at h· and alone,
  170–12 Beloved Brethren: — Welcome h·!
  197–26 in the h· of my heart,
  216–29 charity begins at h·,
  229–10 Scientists, called to the h· of
  256–23 Parents call h· their loved ones,
  271–13 * modest, pleasantly situated h·
  275–19 demands upon my time at h·,
  276– 6 or a dignified stay at h·,
  323–29 * h· of the late Rev. J. Henry Wiggin
  324– 1 * in Mr. and Mrs. Wiggin's h·.

home (adj.)
Mis. 287–24 Be faithful over h· relations ;
  303– 2 shine from their h· summits
Ret. 19– 5 parting with the dear h· circle
  90– 5 salary for tending the h· flock
Pul. 43– 2 * the choir of the h· church,
  50– 8 * better h· life and citizenship.
'02. 3–12 inauguration of h· rule in Cuba,
My. 157– 9 * the Cause in your h· city,
  174–11 distinguished editors in my h· city
  291–14 His h· relations enfolded a wealth of

home-harmony
Mis. 353–31 interrupt the h·, criticise and

homeless
Mis. 326–17 h· wanderers in a beleaguered city,
Po. 28–15 Hover the h· heart !

homelessness
Mis. 373–21 as h· in a wilderness.

homely
My. 262–10 This h· origin of the babe Jesus

home's
Ret. 18–21 communion with h· magic spell !
Po. 64–14 communion with h· magic spell !

homes
Mis. 7–24 able to reach many h·
  99–32 by the wayside, in humble h·.
  163–10 by the wayside, in humble h· :
  231–28 How many h· echo such tones
  257–24 Floods swallow up h·
  321–25 hospitality of their beautiful h·
  329–28 back to their summer h·.
  337–27 by the wayside, in humble h·,
Pul. 80–25 * the h· of unnumbered invalids.
Pan. 14–19 In your peaceful h· remember
Hea. 16–14 nearer your hearts and into your h·
My. 21– 6 * church h· of their own,
  50– 5 * left their former church h·,
  113– 1 in thousands of h·,
  126–29 We need it in our h·,
  185–13 by the wayside, or in our h·.

homesick
Mis. 177–28 h· traveller in foreign lands
  177–29 I am constantly h· for heaven.
My. 147–29 heavenly h· or hungry hearts

homestead
Ret. 4– 3 who inherited the h·,
  5– 6 In the Baker h· at Bow
Pul. 47–29 * modernized from a primitive h·
My. 309–21 describing the Baker h· at Bow :

homilies
My. 122– 9 Now I am done with h·

homœopathic
Mis. 348–21 h· doses of Natrum muriaticum
Ret. 24–17 Even to the h· physician who
My. 107– 8 namely, the h· system, to which
  107–18 efficiency of the h· system.
  108– 2 the h· physician succeeds as well in

homœopathist
Mis. 49– 8 Her friends employed a h·,
'01. 22– 8 I am a spiritual h· in that
My. 107–14 Yet the h· administers
  107–29 The h· handles in his practice

homœopathists
Hea. 12–25 h· admit the higher attenuations

homœopathy

Mis.	6–16	in advance of allopathy and *h·* ;
	35– 2	practical proof, through *h·*,
	252– 4	allopathy and *h·* differ.
	270–28	*H·* is the last link in
	271– 1	Among the foremost virtues of *h·*
	378–14	Having practised *h·*,
	379–22	the highest attenuation in *h·*,
Ret.	33– 2	aided by hints from *h·*,
	33– 8	allopathy, *h·*, hydropathy,
	33–19	the higher attenuations of *h·*,
Pul.	35–23	* Through *h·*, too, Mrs. Eddy
	47–12	* schools of allopathy, *h·*,
	64–17	* allopathy, *h·*, and electricity,
'01.	17–26	highest attenuations of *h·*
	18– 6	at the medicine of *h·* ;
Hea.	11–15	*H·* may not recover from the
	11–17	*h·* has laid the foundation stone of
	11–24	differing in this from *h·*,
	12– 1	higher attenuations of *h·*
	12–19	on the pharmacy of *h·*,
	13– 4	The pharmacy of *h·* is
My.	107–10	In *h·*, the one thousandth
	108–10	between metaphysics in *h·* and
	345–15	*h·* came like blessed relief

honest

Mis.	19–20	faith in an *h·* drugging-doctor,
	41–10	*h·* student of C. S.
	44– 1	*H·* students speak the truth
	48–17	*h·* declaration as to the animus of
	87–26	to be *h·*, earnest, loving, and
	112– 3	Even *h·* thinkers, not knowing
	116–19	the courage of *h·* convictions,
	128– 7	whatsoever things are *h·*, — *Phil.* 4 : 8.
	166–30	It made him an *h·* man,
	227–18	wider aims of a life made *h·* :
	227–26	sublime summary of an *h·* life
	228–17	and *h·* beyond reproach,
	238– 5	all who dare to be true, *h·*
	247– 3	his *h·* convictions and *proofs* of
	266–14	and *h·* Christian Scientist will
	312–20	*h·* utterance of veritable history,
	357–17	fallen into the good and *h·* hearts
	367– 3	This Science requires man to be *h·*,
Man.	77– 2	by an *h·*, competent accountant.
Ret.	28–10	It must become *h·*,
	29– 3	I esteem all *h·* people,
	52– 8	every true seeker and *h·* worker in
	75–18	and is therefore *h·*.
	77– 3	* *h·* man's the noblest work of God ;"
	77– 4	* *h·* God's the noblest work of man."
	79– 1	*h·* metaphysical theory and
	83–14	error, in an *h·* heart,
Pul.	14– 1	*h·* investigation will bring the hour
	35–14	become *h·*, unselfish, and pure,
Rud.	8–11	Be *h·*, be true to thyself,
No.	2–17	The *h·* student of C. S.
	3–26	becoming odious to *h·* people ;
	39– 3	an *h·* and potent prayer to heal
	40–11	thoughts are our *h·* conviction.
Pan.	10– 7	*h·* verdict of humanity
'00.	10– 8	provided this warfare is *h·*
'01.	30–29	* *h·*, sensible, and well-bred man
	32–16	Their convictions were *h·*,
'02.	2– 1	earnest, *h·* investigator
Hea.	8–22	this will make us *h·* and laborious,
My.	vi– 9	* Scientists are *h·* only as they
	6– 4	Are we *h·*, just, faithful?
	112–15	*h·*, intelligent, and scholarly
	114– 4	be *h·*, just, and pure ;
	120– 9	Forgive, . . . my *h·* position.
	136–25	the fruits of *h·* toil,
	143–16	*h·* history of its Discoverer
	150–13	this heart must be *h·*
	248–11	*h·*, fervid affection for the race
	250– 6	and crowns *h·* endeavors.
	259–18	Do not forget that an *h·*, wise zeal,
	266– 7	insufficient freedom of *h·*
	272– 1	an *h·* man or woman
	284– 2	*h·* efforts . . . to help human purpose
	321–11	* Mr. Wiggin was an *h·* man

honestly

Mis.	62–21	*h·* acknowledges this fact in
	160– 3	unite more *h·* in uttering the word
	283–30	*h·* laboring to learn the principle
Ret.	76– 6	if he writes *h·*,
No.	5– 2	vindicating, fearlessly and *h·*,
'02.	14–27	answered frankly and *h·*,
Hea.	8–25	work to become Christians as *h·*
	13–20	*h·* employed Mind as the only
My.	264– 4	*h·* and not too earnestly,
	305– 5	the defamer will declare as *h·* (?),

honesty

Mis.	88–17	Its manly *h·* follows like a
	118– 6	*H·* in every condition,

honesty

Mis.	126–16	meekness, *h·*, and obedience
	126–26	*h·* always defeats dishonesty.
	252–29	secures the success of *h·*.
	285–28	common sense, and common *h·*,
	341–13	glory of the strife comes of *h·*
Ret.	34– 1	as to the *h·* or utility of using a
My.	4–21	*h·* and justice characterize the
	121–21	No deformity exists in *h·*,
	137–28	as to *h·* and business capacity.
	139–13	Justice, *h·*, cannot be abjured ;
	200–18	seven-fold shield of *h·*,
	265–29	should be governed by *h·*,
	270–10	attest *h·* and valor.
	274–11	*h·*, purity, unselfishness

honey

Mis.	294–14	makes *h·* out of the flowers

Honor

his

Mis.	251– 8	His *H·*, Mayor Woodworth,
My.	173–26	to his *H·*, the Mayor,

honor

Mis.	49– 8	had the skill and *h·* to state,
	154–23	*H·* thy Father and Mother, God.
	158–15	faithful service, thus to *h·* it.
	226–22	even of those who have lost their *h·*
	236–11	"Love and *h·* thy parents,
	237–24	*H·* to faithful merit is delayed,
	237–26	draped in *h·* of the dead hero
	295–15	Has he forgotten how to *h·* his
	308–22	fulfilled its mission, retired with *h·*
Ret.	64–16	Man that is in *h·*, — *Psal.* 49 : 20.
Un.	26– 5	This is my *h·*,
Pul.	49–22	* home that should do *h·* to
	59– 2	* perpetually burning in her *h·* ;
	63– 7	* Was Recently Built in Her *H·*
'01.	29–22	All *h·* and success to those who
	29–23	*h·* their father and mother.
My.	42–15	* for the *h·* conferred upon me.
	118–11	greatness with which you *h·* me.
	125–11	All *h·* to the members of our
	182–31	*h·* the name of C. S.,
	202– 9, 10	*h·* to whom *h·*. — *Rom.* 13 : 7.
	211–21	distrust where *h·* is due,
	219– 6	have all the *h·* of their success
	277–22	if our nation's rights or *h·*
	331–26	* high feeling of *h·* and the noble

honorable

Mis.	136–22	June session of this *h·* body
	139– 1	recommend this *h·* body to adjourn,
	147–20	do nothing but what is *h·*,
My.	277– 5	*h·* and satisfactory to both
	324–18	* he would be too *h·* to
	332–31	* his *h·* record and Christian

honorary

Hea.	3–19	Christ Jesus was an *h·* title ;

honored

Mis.	81–15	*benediction of an h· Father,*
	284–23	neither to be *feared* nor *h·*.
'01.	18– 7	more *h·* and respected to-day
Po.	78– 1	our *h·* dead fought on in gloom !
My.	64–10	* made the name an *h·* one
	289–16	long *h·*, revered, beloved.
	326–16	so signally *h·* his memory,

honoreth

My.	33–23	*h·* them that fear the — *Psal.* 15 : 4.

honoring

My.	225–18	begins in the minds of men by *h·* God

honors

Mis.	153–20	no man who *h·* Him not
	294–11	and *h·* his creator.
	358– 5	will graduate under divine *h·*,
	358– 7	State *h·* perish.
Un.	25–16	*h·* conscious human individuality
'02.	1–19	a system that *h·* God
My.	290– 5	Queen's royal and imperial *h·*
	333–26	* were interred with Masonic *h·*.

hooded

Mis.	145–15	*h·* hawk which flies in darkness.

hoofed

Pan.	3– 4	horned and *h·* animal,

hope (see also hope's)

and comfort

Pul.	56–15	* brought *h·* and comfort to many

and desire

My.	9–15	* modestly renew the *h·* and desire

and faith

Mis.	63–25	appeals to its *h·* and faith,
	207– 2	in *h·* and faith, where heart meets
	330– 7	Human *h·* and faith should join
No.	10–25	turns . . . all *h·* and faith to God,
	35– 1	everything to human *h·* and faith.

hope

and harmony
Ret. 48–20   health, h·, and harmony to man,
and hour
My. 208–15   crowning the h· and hour
and prayer
'02.   6–20   All Christian faith, h·, and prayer,
     15–29   to my waiting h· and prayer.
My. 155–15   fruition of its faith, h·, and prayer.
and tears
Mis. 385– 1   * "Faith, h·, and tears, triune,
Po.   37– 1   * "Faith, h·, and tears, triune,
bare
My. 322–21   * bare h· of a few days' instruction
benediction and
No.   8–25   quietly, with benediction and h·,
bird of
My. 341–11   The bird of h· is singing
cheer me with
Po. 32–21   cheer me with h· when 'tis done ;
common
My. 165–24   a relapse into the common h·.
confidence and
Pul. 21–25   there abide in confidence and h·.
deferred
Mis.   17–29   travail of mortal mind, h· deferred,
    262–19   heart grown faint with h· deferred.
    389–15   h· deferred, ingratitude, disdain !
Po.   4–14   h· deferred, ingratitude, disdain !
disappointed
My. 229–29   hence my disappointed h·
earthly
Ret. 20–20   Star of my earthly h·,
exalted
Mis. 162–32   in the strength of an exalted h·,
exultant
Ret. 32– 8   Exultant h·, if tinged with
faith and
Mis. 246–31   faith and h· of Christianity,
Un.   55–17   Job's faith and h· gained him
My. 201–12   friendship, faith, and h·
fear and
My. 292–30   compound . . . of fear and h·,
for our race
'01.   16–26   Shall the h· for our race
glorious
Pul.   9–21   O glorious h· and blessed
'02.   19–17   O glorious h· !
happifies life
Mis. 394– 6   H· happifies life,
Po.   45– 8   H· happifies life,
haven of
My. 163– 2   seek the haven of h·,
heart and
My. 253– 6   My heart and h· are with you.
heaven-born
Mis. 15–17   heaven-born h·, and spiritual love.
her
Ret. 90–21   waits with her h·, and labors with
higher
'01.   3– 1   higher h·, and increasing virtue,
My.   3–19   higher criticism, the higher h· ;
   199–19   sounded the tocsin of a higher h·,
   246–11   to gain a higher h· for the race,
   252–30   All hail to this higher h·
highway of
My.   3–18   unfolding the highway of h·,
   240–14   unfolding the highway of h·,
human
Mis. 330– 7   Human h· and faith should join in
No.   35– 1   everything to human h· and faith.
Peo.   8–21   trembling chords of human h·
hungry
Mis. 16– 2   These nourish the hungry h·,
life and
Peo. 11–14   gnawing away life and h· ;
life-lease of
My. 139–11   life-lease of h·, home, heaven ;
my
Mis. 311–22   I should lose my h· of heaven.
Pul.   3–29   present realization of my h·
   5–15   was the first to bedew my h·
My.   4–29   The height of my h· must remain.
   282– 6   my h· must still rest in God,
no greater
My. 209– 5   No greater h· have we than in
nor happiness
'01. 34–28   health, h·, nor happiness
of ease
'01. 30–21   by the h· of ease, pleasure,
of ever eluding
Un. 64–12   until the h· of ever eluding their
of our race
Pul.   9– 2   children, . . . the h· of our race !
of relieving
My. 214–18   the h· of relieving the questioners'

hope

of that parent
Mis. 254–10   what of the h· of that parent
of the race
Mis. 163–21   medium of Mind, the h· of the race.
No.   46– 6   The advancing h· of the race,
of universal salvation
'01.   13–25   hence the h· of universal salvation.
our
Mis. 113–24   Divine Love is our h·,
   388– 7   Thou to whose power our h· we give,
'00.   10–21   Here our h· anchors in God
Po.   7– 7   Thou to whose power our h· we give,
peace and
Mis. 169–25   health and peace and h· for all.
perishless
Pul.   9–10   warmed also our perishless h·,
present
Mis. 160–13   It satisfies my present h·.
reason for
Mis.   5–17   no longer any reason for h·."
reason for the
My. 348– 9   to give a reason for the h·
rejoice in
Peo. 14–14   rejoice in h· ;
remained
Mis. 130– 1   so long as a h· remained
rich
My. 201–19   Rich h· have I in him who
satisfied
My. 182–26   turn hither with satisfied h·.
soared high
Mis. 385–22   "When h· soared high,
Po.   48–16   "When h· soared high,
springs
My. 201–29   H· springs exultant on this blest
their
My. 155–21   span the horizon of their h·
   258–22   blossoms that mock their h·
this
Mis. 144–21   be this h· in each of our hearts,
to the disconsolate
Mis. 262–17   giving . . . h· to the disconsolate ;
tower of
Mis. 152–24   sheltered in the strong tower of h·,
upspringing
My. 192–10   Thine is the upspringing h·,
well-tried
Mis. 200–25   holy calm of Paul's well-tried h·
without
Ret. 61–15   without 'h·, and without God — Eph. 2 : 12.
woman's
My. 258– 7   seems illuminated for woman's h·

Mis.   ix–12   joy, sorrow, h·, disappointment,
   ix–13   now h· sits dove-like.
  124–29   to experience, . . . to h·, faith ;
  132–30   those words inspire me with the h·
  136– 6   with the h· that you will follow.
  149–10   h·, faith, and understanding,
  204– 7   doubt, h·, sorrow, joy, defeat, and
  338–10   h· holding steadfastly to good
  386–17   a h· that ever upward yearns,
  394– 1   poem
Ret. 18–16   But h·, as the eaglet
No. 35– 5   and what h· have mortals but
Po. vii–12   * in the h· that these gems
  page 45   poem
  50– 1   h· that ever upward yearns,
  64– 7   h·, as the eaglet that spurneth the
My.   6–28   self-abnegation, h·, faith ;
  124–10   "What a fond fool is h·"
  139– 8   progress, primeval faith, h·, love.
  156–20   with h·, faith, and love ready
  197–20   h· set before us in the Word
  293–14   of trembling faith, h·, and of fear,
  335–19   * h· of allaying the excitement

hope (verb)

Mis. 78–16   We will charitably h·, however,
  78–21   we will h· it is the froth of error
  133–18   I h· I am not wrong in
  143– 6   h· that a closer link hath bound us.
  391– 3   I h· the heart that's hungry
  394–13   but h· thou, and love.
  396–14   I h· it's better made,
Un. 14–25   How then . . . h· to escape,
  29–25   H· thou in God [Soul] :— Psal. 42 : 11.
Pan.   4–22   h· thou in God :— Psal. 42 : 11.
'00.   2–24   than the adversary can h·.
Po.   38– 2   I h· the heart that's hungry
  45–17   but h· thou, and love.
  59– 6   I h· it's better made,
My. 36–11   * all that we are or h· to be
  51–10   * h· she will remain with us.
  120– 4   I h· and trust that you and I may

hope (verb)
  My. 131–18   I *h·* I shall not be found disorderly,
       169– 7   date, which I *h·* soon to name
       259–16   I *h·* that in 1902 the churches
       264– 3   *h·* that those who are kind enough

hoped
  Mis. 27–30   of things *h·* for.'' — *Heb.* 11 : 1.
       47– 8   that which is *h·* for but unseen,
      103– 9   substance of things *not h·* for.
      175–11   of things *h·* for.'' — *Heb.* 11 : 1.
  Rud. 17– 2   Jews whom St. Paul had *h·* to convert
  Pan. 15– 9   of things *h·* for'' — *Heb.* 11 : 1.
  My. 226–18   of things *h·* for ;'' — *Heb.* 11 : 1.
      260–16   substance, the things *h·* for

hopeful
  Mis. 109–11   most *h·* stage of mortal mentality.
      134– 1   sorrowful who are made *h·*,
  Pul. 45–17   * the *h·*, trustful ones,
      80–25   * brought a *h·* spirit into the
  Po. 16– 2   and *h·* though winter appears.

hopefully
  Mis. 5–19   takes up the case *h·*
      324–30   whence he may *h·* look for
  '01. 21–15   my critic, who reckons *h·* on the

hopefulness
  My. 74–30   * one for its *h·* and the other for

hopeless
  Pul. 34– 7   * her case was pronounced *h·*
  '01. 27–14   healed *h·* cases, such as I have
  Hea. 9– 8   sinner and the most *h·* invalid
  My. 106– 7   *h·* organic diseases of almost every

hopelessly
  Mis. 371–28   as *h·* original as is "S. and H.
  Ret. 35– 6   basis . . . was so *h·* original,
  Pul. 41–17   * was *h·* incapable of receiving

hopelessness
  Mis. 169–24   foundation of unbelief and *h·*.

hope's
  Mis. 339– 9   with *h·* rainbow hues.
  Pul. 10–14   the wish to reign in *h·* reality

hopes
  Mis. 341–14   Do human *h·* deceive?
      356–11   chastened affections, and costly *h·*,
  Ret. 7–22   * It blights too many *h·* ;
  Po. 8–15   Its starry *h·* and its waves of truth.
  My. 202–17   endless *h·*, and glad victories
      258–18   *h·* that cannot deceive,

hopeth
  Pan. 1–15   what a man seeth he *h·* not for,
      1–15   *h·* for what he hath not seen,

hoping
  Mis. 327– 3   *h·* that I might follow thee
  Ret. 13–16   *h·* to win me from dreaded heresy.
      20–14   *h·* for a vision of relief
  No. 9– 4   *H·* to pacify repeated complaints
  Pan. 1–11   mortals are *h·* and working,
  My. 164– 4   *h·* thereby to give to many

hordes
  Mis. 325–29   in the midst of murderous *h·*,

Horeb
  My. 281– 7   soaring to the *H·* height,

horizon
  Mis. 376–20   above the *h·*, in the east,
  Pan. 1–18   in the *h·* of Truth
  '02. 17–30   like the sun beneath the *h·*,
  My. 155–21   span the *h·* of their hope

horned
  Pan. 3– 4   a *h·* and hoofed animal,

horns
  Hea. 13– 2   both *h·* of the dilemma,

horoscope
  Mis. 347– 6   hanging like a *h·* in the air,
  My. 350–25   the *h·* of crumbling creeds,

horrible
  Ret. 13–24   "*h·* decree" of predestination

horror
  Un. 6–23   provoked discussion and *h·*,

horrors
  No. 44–22   the *h·* of religious persecution.

hors de combat
  Mis. 285–15   the latter fell *h· de c·* ;

horse-chestnut
  Ret. 17–19   sturdy *h·* for centuries hath given
  Po. 63– 5   sturdy *h·* for centuries hath given

hortatory
  Ret. 89–14   pay this *h·* compliment

Horticultural Hall
  Exhibition Hall
    My. 80–13   * *H· H·* (Exhibition Hall),
  Lecture Hall
    My. 80–13   * *H· H·* (Lecture Hall),

    My. 73–19   * this forenoon in *H· H·*,
        75– 8   * Christian Scientists in *H· H·*.
       75–10   * headed straight for *H· H·*,
       80–23   * *H· H·*, Jordan Hall, Potter Hall,
       83– 1   * leading directly to *H· H·*.
       83– 5   * Up at *H· H·* the one hundred

hospitable
  Pul. 36–14   * met Mrs. Eddy by her *h·* courtesy,
  My. 40– 2   * evidence to us of her *h·* love.

hospitality
  Mis. 321–25   *h·* of their beautiful homes
  Pul. 49– 4   * the air of *h·* that marks its
  My. 40– 7   * will also enlarge their *h·*,
      173– 6   for the generous *h·* extended
      331–14   * such unrestrained *h·*

hospitals
  My. 188–24   in which, like beds in *h·*,

host
  Mis. 231–11   carving of the generous *h·*,
  My. 46–22   * in the presence of this assembled *h·*,
      88–22   * all that increasing *h·* who have
      98– 2   * truly make up a mighty *h·*,

hostess
  Ret. 40– 6   On my arrival my *h·* told me
      40– 8   with my *h·* I went to the invalid's
      (*see also* **Eddy**)

hostile
  My. 92–21   * have been ridiculed by the *h·*
      94– 4   * been ridiculed by the *h·*

Hosts
  My. v– 1   * Lord God of *H·*, be with us yet ;

hosts
  Po. 10–18   cheer the *h·* of heaven ;
  My. 34–12   The Lord of *h·*, — *Psal.* 24 : 10.
      86– 7   * the *h·* of a new religion.
      131–26   saith the Lord of *h·*, — *Mal.* 3 : 10.
      269–26   saith the Lord of *h·*, — *Mal.* 3 : 10.
      337–19   cheer the *h·* of heaven ;

hot
  Un. 34–19   is substantial, is *h·* or cold?

hotel
  My. 83–15   * the *h·* and restaurant keepers,

Hotel Brookline
  My. 66– 2   * which is known as the *H· B·*,

hotels
  My. 73–22   * rooms and board, *h·*, railroads, *etc.*
      75–11   * rooms in *h·* or lodging-houses,
      82– 9   * *H·*, boarding-houses, and private

hothouse
  My. 325– 4   * to leave luscious *h·* fruit.

hounded
  Mis. 358– 9   *h·* footsteps, false laurels.

hour
  adapted to the
    Mis. 313–14   thought, so adapted to the *h·*,
  appointed
    Pul. 29–12   * Before the appointed *h·*
  auspicious
    Pul. 44–10   * It is a most auspicious *h·*
  awful
    Po. 27– 3   oppression in its awful *h·*,
  bridal
    Mis. 276–16   will always be the bridal *h·*,
    Po. 8– 7   waiting alone for the bridal *h·*
  bring the
    Pul. 14– 2   investigation will bring the *h·*
  burdened for an
    Mis. 251–22   burdened for an *h·*, spring into
  changeful
    Po. 31–14   the vassal of the changeful *h·*,
  cometh
    Mis. 321–13   *h·* cometh, and now is, — *John* 4 : 23.
    No. 34– 9   *h·* cometh, and now is, — *John* 4 : 23.
  crucial
    My. 225– 1   This is a crucial *h·*, in which the
  crude
    Un. 4–28   Nevertheless, at the present crude *h·*,
  dark
    My. 297–13   dark *h·* that precedes the dawn.
  demands of the
    Mis. 70–18   not equal to the demands of the *h·* ;
  eventide's
    Mis. 394– 2   on the zephyr at eventide's *h·* ;
    Po. 45– 2   on the zephyr at eventide's *h·* ;

hour

every
Pul.	59– 7	* every *h·* and a half, so long as
Pan.	12–28	every *h·* in time and in eternity
Hea.	19–19	fresh opportunities every *h·* ;
My.	31– 5	* "I need Thee every *h·* ;"
	234– 8	and how I need every *h·*
	340– 4	every day and every *h·*.

evil
Mis.	340– 2	relinquishment of right in an evil *h·*,

exigencies of the
My.	224– 3	to meet the exigencies of the *h·*

feared for an
Po.	71–11	Feared for an *h·* the tyrant's

festive
Po.	77–17	Why from this festive *h·* some

freedom's
Ret.	11– 9	't is freedom's *h·*,
Po.	60– 6	'tis freedom's *h·*,

girt for the
My.	277–23	armed with power girt for the *h·*.

God's
Mis.	134–20	In God's *h·*, the powers of earth

had come
Mis.	83–26	*h·* had come for the avowal of

half an
Mis.	339– 5	silence for the space of half an *h·*.
Hea.	13–14	at intervals of half an *h·*
My.	54– 9	* half an *h·* before the arrival of

harvest
Mis.	214–30	Jesus foretold the harvest *h·*
	356–13	the harvest *h·* has come ;

has passed
Mis.	284–14	*h·* has passed for this evil to

has struck
Mis.	249– 5	The *h·* has struck,
	317– 5	The *h·* has struck for

hope and
My.	208–16	crowning the hope and *h·* of

immortal
My.	257–20	At this immortal *h·*,

is come
Mis.	83–24	Father, the *h·* is come ; — *John* 17 : 1.
	177– 4	The *h·* is come.
My.	125–26	The *h·* is come ;

is coming
Chr.	55– 6	The *h·* is coming, — *John* 5 : 25.

is imminent
My.	223–27	The *h·* is imminent.

memory's
Po.	68–16	o'er the heartstrings in memory's *h·*.

midnight
Mis.	117–26	his lamp at the midnight *h·*
	276–15	In C. S. the midnight *h·* will

miracle of the
Hea.	11–11	it stands and is the miracle of the *h·*,

momentous
My.	45–17	* revealed to you in that momentous *h·*

named
Pul.	31–23	* At the *h·* named I rang the bell

natal
Po.	29– 9	No natal *h·* and mother's tear,
My.	158–10	natal *h·* of my lone earth life ;

next
Mis.	316–22	breaches widened the next *h·* ;

of great need
Mis.	24– 5	came to me in an *h·* of great need ;

of his birth
Mis.	278–15	he cursed the *h·* of his birth ;

of loss
Mis.	179– 4	rightful desire in the *h·* of loss,

of prayer
Po.	65–10	"Sweet *h·* of prayer" !

of trial
Mis.	335–24	and when the *h·* of trial comes

one
Mis.	69–18	In one *h·* he was well,
	136–10	in turning aside for one *h·*
	225–28	In about one *h·* he awoke,
Ret.	16– 8	entered this church one *h·* ago
My.	54– 8	* crowded one *h·* before the service

outweighs an
Mis.	135–19	joy that outweighs an *h·*.

Palestina's
Chr.	53–49	As in blest Palestina's *h·*,

passing
Un.	47– 4	and with every passing *h·*
'02.	17–19	square accounts with each passing *h·*.

pertaining to the
My.	199–13	Christian canon pertaining to the *h·*.

puppets of the
Mis.	368–23	Some of the mere puppets of the *h·*

radiant
Po.	70– 4	At sunset's radiant *h·*,

right
My.	244–13	I have awaited the right *h·*,

hour

same
Man.	61– 5	Sunday services at the same *h·*.
My.	149–29	and forgotten in the same *h·* ;

sunny
My.	194–30	* Ne'er in a sunny *h·* fall off."

that
Ret.	44–29	that *h·* holds this true record.
	73–12	From that *h·* personal corporeality
Pul.	34–18	* From that *h·* dated her conviction
Peo.	10–28	yet that *h·* was a prophecy of
My.	39– 2	* could not gain admittance at that *h·*
	351–16	meet in that *h·* of Soul

thine
Po.	22– 2	Thine *h·* hath come !

this
Mis.	37–28	work of healing ; which, at this *h·*,
	253–21	are type and shadow of this *h·*,
	254–18	the great red dragon of this *h·*,
	317–22	words of our Master explain this *h·* :
	320–10	lends its . . . light to this *h·* :
	386–11	This *h·* looks on her heart
Pul.	7–11	New England metropolis at this *h·*,
No.	3–18	history of Mind-healing notes this *h·*.
'01.	3– 4	benediction . . . rests upon this *h·* :
Po.	49–16	This *h·* looks on her heart
My.	43–26	* has brought us to this *h·*.
	124–15	enough to make this *h·* glad.
	131– 6	For this *h·*, for this period,
	131–22	in this *h·* of the latter days
	131–30	There is with us at this *h·*
	132– 2	is the demand of this *h·*
	132–12	Oh, may this *h·* be prolific,
	185–24	Then and there I foresaw this *h·*,
	269–18	This *h·* is molten in the furnace
	286–10	however, that at this *h·*

until the
Pul.	41–28	* until the *h·* for the dedication

waiting
Mis.	331–19	that owns each waiting *h·* ;
	389– 7	that owns each waiting *h·*,
Po.	4– 4	that owns each waiting *h·*,

waiting the
Peo.	7–18	* Waiting the *h·* when

woman's
Mis.	245–19	This is woman's *h·*,
No.	45–19	This is woman's *h·*,

Mis.	177–23	* the *h·* for the church service
	316–12	the *h·* best for the student.
	335– 8	in an *h·* that he is not — *Matt.* 24 : 50.
Ret.	49– 8	*h·* has come wherein the great need
Po.	71– 1	the *h·* they then foretold
	71– 6	This is the *h·* !
My.	64– 3	* the experiences of the *h·*
	232–15	*h·* the thief would come, — *Luke* 12 : 39.

hourly
Mis.	248–17	or that my *h·* life is prayerless,
Un.	17– 7	*H·*, in C. S., man thus
Po.	33– 6	*h·* seek for deliverance strong
My.	41–22	* into present and *h·* application
	178– 8	it hastens *h·* to this end.

hours

dark
Mis.	276–31	In the dark *h·*, . . . stand firmer
Ret.	20–13	throughout the dark *h·*,

different
My.	94–21	* at different *h·* of the day,

forty-eight
Mis.	243– 2	in forty-eight *h·* cured her

happy
Mis.	396–10	O happy *h·* and fleet,
Po.	59– 2	O happy *h·* and fleet,

her
Ret.	90–23	Mother in Israel give all her *h·*

lagging
Po.	35– 2	the lagging *h·* of weariness

laughing
Mis.	390–12	Looks love unto the laughing *h·*,
Po.	55–13	Looks love unto the laughing *h·*,

long-buried
Po.	67– 6	at work with the long-buried *h·*,

oncoming
Ret.	23–10	The oncoming *h·* were indicated by no

pass into
Mis.	230–15	moments before they pass into *h·*,

past
Mis.	147– 9	Have you improved past *h·*,
	330–19	It is good to talk with our past *h·*,

sacred
Ret.	90–17	in their early and sacred *h·*,

twenty-four
Mis.	243– 1	if . . . without it twenty-four *h·*

vanished
Po.	23– 5	a thought of vanished *h·*

hours
waking
Mis. 47–12   If never in your waking h·,

Mis. 230–16   h· that other people may occupy in
     325–18   dreaming away the h·.
house
big
Pul. 47–28   * big h·, so delightfully remodelled
build a
My. 187–26   build a h· unto Him whose name
burning
Mis. 335–26   have me get out of a burning h·,
enter a
Mis. 282–14   "When ye enter a h·, — see Matt. 10 : 12.
     283– 7   than one has to enter a h·,
entered the
My. 178–23   Christian Scientist entered the h·
Father's
Mis. 326–19   forced to seek the Father's h·,
     369–25   would find our Father's h· again
'01. 17– 4   cause him to return to the Father's h·
My. 133– 1   Father's h· in which are many
father's
My. 309–24   My father's h· had a sloping roof,
    313–31   not welcome in my father's h·.
furnished
My. 342– 1   * ample, richly furnished h·
furnish the
Man. 30–20   suitably furnish the h·,
her
Man. 48–14   continually stroll by her h·,
     69–24   affairs outside of her h·.
His
My. 193–17   Nothing dethrones His h·.
his
My. 231–23   not an empty apartment in his h·,
    232–16   not have suffered his h· — Luke 12 : 39.
    308–30   only book in his h·.
    313– 9   road in front of his h·
invalid's
Ret. 40– 8   I went to the invalid's h·.
is on fire
Mis. 326– 7   that h· is on fire !
master of the
'01. 10– 5   master of the h· — Matt. 10 : 25.
mine
My. 131–25   meat in mine h·, — Mal. 3 : 10.
my
Mis. 249–18   not one has been sent to my h·,
of God
'01. 15–27   * sat here in the h· of God,
My. 37– 7   * heavenward from this h· of God.
of our God
Pul. 10–18   corner-stone in the h· of our God.
of slumberers
Mis. 326–10   spread to the h· of slumberers
of the Pastor
Man. 30–14   the h· of the Pastor Emeritus,
of worship
Pul. 50–12   * visible h· of worship in this city,
My. 182–20   beautiful h· of worship
owned a
My. 314–12   he owned a h· in Franklin, N. H.
publishing
Man. 44–10   publishing h· or bookstore
'02. 13–12   in their publishing h·,
real
Pul.   2–23   The real h· in which
returns to the
Mis. 324–25   So he returns to the h·,
roof of the
Mis. 215–19   summit of the roof of the h·
saw the
Pul.   2– 2   saw the h· Solomon had erected.
spacious
Pul. 31–23   * spacious h· on Columbus Avenue,
spiritual
My. 17–11   built up a spiritual h·, — I Pet. 2 : 5.
this
Mis. 325–23   They in this h· are those that
Pul.   9–10   whose appliances warm this h·,
      10–25   timely shelter of this h·,
      10–28   blessing on every heart in this h·.
My. 37– 7   heavenward from this h· of God.
     61–17   * this h· will be ready for
    148–22   what is each heart in this h·
    187–30   you have built this h·
    188– 2   This h· is hallowed by His
    188– 3   hallowed this h·, — I Kings 9 : 3.
Thy
Pul.   1– 2   fatness of Thy h·; — Psal. 36 : 8.
      3–16   fatness of Thy h·; — Psal. 36 : 8.
      4–27   fatness of Thy h·." — Psal. 36 : 8.
      7–29   fatness of Thy h·; — Psal. 36 : 8.

house
your
Mis. 326–27   Behold, your h· — Matt. 23 : 38.
My. 325– 6   * that you had bought your h·

Mis. 327– 2   When I went back into the h·
Man. 30–21   Mrs. Eddy does not occupy the h·
Pul.   2–13   think . . . of the h· wherewith
       2–14   "h· not made with hands, — II Cor. 5 : 1.
      36–25   * h· is now occupied by
      48– 7   * second story of the h·,
My. 141–23   h· of The Mother Church seats
    145– 7   remodelling of the h·
    156–14   say to the goodman of the h· :
    188–13   "h· not made with hands, — II Cor. 5 : 1.
    192–29   building for you a h·
    194– 7   "h· not made with hands, — II Cor. 5 : 1.
    232–15   goodman of the h· — Luke 12 : 39.
    309–22   * h· itself was a small, square
    310 24   * set the h· in an uproar,"
housed
'01. 29– 1   Have we h·, fed, clothed,
household
Mis. 214– 9   of his own h·." — Matt. 10 : 36.
    239–23   with that of the h· stockholders,
    386–19   o'er thy broken h· band,
Man. 69–15   for h· help or a handmaid,
Ret.   6– 8   accorded special h· privileges.
      86–14   fellow-saint of a holy h·.
'01.   9–27   He of God's h· who loveth
      10– 6   call them of his h· — Matt. 10 : 25.
Po.   50– 3   o'er thy broken h· band,
My. 143–12   by the members of my h·
    257– 2   alas for the broken h· band !
    263– 4   My H·
    308–27   his h· law, constantly enforced,
    355– 1   * members of her h· were with her
households
Mis. 232– 4   peace, and plenty, and happy h·.
    257–24   Floods swallow up homes and h· ;
    262– 2   health and happiness to all h·
housekeeper
My. 311– 8   my good h· said to me :
    311–11   so I lost my h·.
housekeeping
Mis. 353–27   set up h· alone.
houses
Mis. 150–18   Convenient h· and halls
    282–11   Who of us would have our h· broken
    326–17   driven out of their h· of clay
    347– 5   people have to escape from their h·
    373–23   rich possession here, with h· and
'00. 12–26   he labored . . . also in private h·.
My. 31–19   * front rank of the world's h·
     66–29   * many beautiful h· of worship
     82– 9   * boarding-houses, and private h·
    149–26   could not see London for its h·.
housewife
Mis. 329– 6   nature like a thrifty h·
hover
Mis. 388–23   h· o'er the couch of woe ;
Po.   21–12   h· o'er the couch of woe ;
      28–15   H· the homeless heart !
hovers
My. 192–15   My heart h· around your churches
Howe and Woolson Halls
My. 80–14   * H· and W· H·, Chickering Hall.
however
Mis. ix–21   freshness of youth, h·,
       8–20   h· much we suffer in the process.
      29–12   There is, h·, no analogy between
      78–16   We will charitably hope, h·,
      93–24   Bear in mind, h·, that human
     118–12   H· keenly the human affections
     120–16   rejoice, h·, that the clarion call
     121– 6   This, h·, is not the cup to which
     141–11   not so, h·, with error,
     155–18   (h· much she desires thus to do),
     158–27   It is satisfactory to note, h·,
     239–22   H·, her dividend, when compared
     262–10   h· simple the words,
     274– 3   This point, h·, had not impressed me
     287– 2   improved generation, h·,
     291–21   False views, h· engendered,
     294–29   In an issue of January 17, h·,
     340–23   h· slow, thy success is sure :
     355– 4   need, h·, is not of the letter, but
     380–24   Experience, h·, taught me
Man. 41–10   H· despitefully used and
      47–18   testimony, h·, shall not include
Ret.   2–22   Some of these, h·, were not very
       7–13   * h· hidden and remote.

however

Ret.	14–10	H, I was ready for his doleful
	26–22	h, divine Science must be
	61–28	that h little be taught or learned,
	64– 5	This, h, does not annihilate
	68– 5	H, the human concept never was,
Un.	2– 7	must, h, realize God's presence,
	48–20	h faintly able to demonstrate
Pul.	2–12	sublunary views, h enchanting,
	20– 7	not, h, through the State
	21–22	h much this is done to us
	38–26	* h they may differ among
	42– 8	* At 10:30 a. m., h, the scene was
	59–20	* solo singer, h, was a Scientist,
	88– 6	They were, h, too voluminous
No.	44–10	Error has no hobby, h boldly
Pan.	2–25	H, Pan in imagery is preferable to
'00.	2–26	h, I believe in working
	3–29	H, the animus of heathen religion
	6–19	H, to a man who uses tobacco,
'01.	23–11	This departure, h, from the
	32–13	When infidels assailed them, h,
'02.	15–27	To this, h, I gave no heed,
My.	12–10	* must remember, h, that
	28–12	* Suffice it to say, h, that
	39–19	* allow me, h, the privilege
	40–11	* Nothing will be lost, h,
	50–20	* Communion Sunday, h, brought
	55–22	* In March, h, the church was
	97– 5	* physicians, h, ridicule the idea
	121–22	C. S., h, adds
	123– 3	To me, h, love is the greater
	160– 1	The Christian, h, strives for
	175–17	Our picturesque city, h,
	180–19	The obstinate sinner, h, refuses
	192–26	Of this, h, I can sing :
	195– 7	H, it is never too late to
	215–12	H, I returned this money
	244–25	This, h, must depend on results.
	272– 9	presents, h, no claim that man
	284– 2	honest efforts (h meagre)
	286–10	It is unquestionable, h,
	307–32	My idealism, h, limped,
	311– 7	Shortly after, h, my good housekeeper
	312–10	* Glover, h, was a Free Mason,
	340–26	H, Jesus' example in this,
	348–17	Here, h, was no stopping-place,
	355– 8	H, if the occasion demands
	358–12	h much I desire to read all

howl

Mis.	396– 1	winds mutter, h, and moan,
Po.	58–13	winds mutter, h, and moan,

howsoever

My.	41–13	* h far he may stray,

Hub and hub

Pul.	67– 8	* h of the logical universe,
My.	95–17	* described in the newspapers of the H

huddle

Mis.	275–12	little ones, wondering, h together,

Hudson

Pul.	53–15	* H says : "That word, more than
	54–12	* We accept the statement of H :

hue

Mis.	264–29	take its h from the divine Mind.
	326–16	under every h of circumstances,
	372–28	true h and character of the living
	376–26	on a background of cerulean h ;
Po.	3– 2	starlight blends with morning's h,

hues

Mis.	142–19	with bright h of the spiritual,
	194–15	bring out the entire h of Deity,
	332–10	autumn follow with h of heaven,
	339– 9	with hope's rainbow h.
	376–21	one rod of rainbow h,
	377– 1	such forms and h of heaven,
Ret.	4–16	in the mellow h of autumn,
	35–14	brings out the h of Deity.
'01.	12–21	bring out the entire h of God.
'02.	20– 5	h of heaven, tipping the dawn

huge

Pul.	42–21	* a h seven-pointed star was hung
My.	30–11	* In those h congregations
	92–19	* so h and concrete a demonstration
	95–12	* They have built a h church,
	308–18	* with a h walking-stick."

hum

Pan.	3–11	voiced with a h of harmony,

human

abandon

Mis.	250–12	which in their h abandon

human

action

Mis.	268– 3	queries give point to h action :
	288–13	Wisdom in h action begins with
Ret.	93–16	becomes the model for h action.
'00.	11–28	highest criticism on all h action,

affairs

Mis.	204–24	all the minutiæ of h affairs.
	267–22	h affairs should be governed by
	312–14	* divine Providence in h affairs
My.	215–32	wisdom should temper h affairs,

affection

Mis.	287–19	lays the foundations of h affection
My.	234–12	from h affection to spiritual
	268– 8	If the motives of h affection are

affections

Mis.	10–25	tendencies of h affections
	50–20	a change from h affections,
	50–27	h affections need to be changed
	118–12	the h affections yearn to
	287–14	The good in h affections

agencies

Mis.	95–20	understand that no h agencies

agony

Mis.	222–20	cancelled only through h agony :
'01.	35–12	From the h agony !

aims

Mis.	9–24	tasteless and unworthy of h aims.

ambition

My.	202– 3	h ambition, fear, or distrust

anatomy

Rud.	11–26	the subject of h anatomy ;

apprehension

'01.	11– 5	has risen to h apprehension,

babe

Un.	61– 6	appeared as a helpless h babe ;

being

Mis.	345–29	to kill and eat a h being.
Rud.	2– 3	* h being, a corporeal man,
	2–10	especially a finite h being ;
'02.	15–20	never believe that a h being
My.	59–29	* No h being in this generation
	303–11	worshippers of a h being.

beings

Un.	37–17	H beings are physically mortal,
Pul.	51– 7	* inherent right as h beings,
My.	294–28	two hundred and fifty million h beings
	303–14	eschews divine rights in h beings.

belief

Mis.	34–15	speculative opinion and h belief.
	76–11	According to h belief the bodies of
	86–18	pleasant sensations of h belief,
	209–10	h belief fulfils the law of belief,
Rud.	5–20	H belief says that it does :
	11–19	rests on the strength of h belief.
	11–21	takes away every h belief,
	13– 4	Whatever saps, with h belief,
	13–12	h belief which saith there is
No.	26– 7	or the h belief resembles the
My.	118–23	credited only by h belief,
	206–16	but it is seeing a h belief,

beliefs

Mis.	320–25	on the long night of h beliefs,
Rud.	10– 8	material laws are only h beliefs,
My.	44– 1	* out of the wilderness of h beliefs
	206– 8	Schisms, imagination, and h beliefs

birth

Mis.	17–22	h birth is the appearing of a

blood

No.	33–18	h blood was inadequate
	33–20	shedding h blood brought to light
	34–20	conception that God requires h blood

body

My.	218– 7	destruction of the h body,

breast

My.	191–24	Immortal courage fills the h breast

call

Mis.	81–26	answers the h call for help ;
Un.	13– 4	coming at h call ;

capacities

My.	259–26	not that in which h capacities

capacity

Un.	43–23	will interpret . . . to h capacity,

character

Mis.	151– 7	purifies the h character,
Un.	29– 1	hypothesis as to its h character.
'00.	8– 8	so the h character comes forth a
My.	246–18	revealed through the h character.

chords

Mis.	116–16	varied strains of h chords

comprehension

Mis.	79– 6	until it is clear to h comprehension

concept

Mis.	103–26	this h concept of Jesus
	164–24	highest h concept of the man Jesus,

human

concept
Mis. 309–23   h· concept antagonizes the divine.
353– 8   h· concept is always imperfect ;
353– 8   relinquish your h· concept of me,
Ret.   67– 1   before the h· concept of sin
68– 4   in the name of h· concept,
68– 5   However, the h· concept never
68–17   treats of the h· concept,
73–10   h· concept grew beautifully less
93– 5   h· concept of Christ is based on
Un.   60–15   [h· concept] of God. — Jas. 3 : 9.

conception
Mis.   56–15   a h· conception opposed to
86–22   Even the h· conception of beauty,
Ret.   25–20   h· conception of God
Un.   46– 9   not based on a h· conception
No.   37– 1   In h· conception God's offspring

concepts
Mis.   71–28   h· concepts, mortal shadows
351–19   chapter sub-title
353– 3   H· concepts run in extremes ;
My. 293– 2   differing h· concepts as to the

conduct
Mis. 301–27   a divine rule for h· conduct.

consciousness
Mis.   85–27   pain compels h· consciousness to
93–24   h· consciousness does not test sin
107–20   states and stages of h· consciousness
108–17   second stage of h· consciousness,
203–20   stricken state of h· consciousness,
204–21   holding sway over h· consciousness.
205–14   immersion of h· consciousness in
285–18   deep down in h· consciousness,
352–26   argument and the h· consciousness
Ret.   21–18   to rebuke h· consciousness
93– 3   appeared to h· consciousness
Un.   11–14   Jesus stooped not to h· consciousness,
37– 9   a change in h· consciousness,
49– 5   simple appeal to h· consciousness.
50– 5   destroyed to h· consciousness,
52– 8   h· consciousness should become
Pul.   85–10   * built up in h· consciousness
My.   48– 5   * to restore to h· consciousness
113–28   uplifting h· consciousness to
124– 7   assemblage of h· consciousness,
160– 5   keep h· consciousness in constant
303–15   governed h· consciousness,

control
Mis.   97–13   h· control is animal magnetism,

credulity
My.   80– 9   * tax upon frail h· credulity,

crimes
'01.   20–28   darkest and deepest of h· crimes.

cry
Mis.   64– 2   h· cry which voiced that struggle ;
342–18   Hear that h· cry :

débris
Mis. 393– 5   Soul, sublime 'mid h· débris,
Po.   51–10   Soul, sublime 'mid h· débris,

demonstrator
My. 348–27   h· demonstrator of this Science

desire
Mis. 317–20   H· desire is inadequate to
360– 1   Meekness, moderating h· desire,
My.   3– 6   not alone in accord with h· desire
292–21   effect of one h· desire or belief

desires
Pul.   3–23   when all h· desires are quenched,

destiny
Mis. 232–12   right that regulates h· destiny.

devices
Pan.   4–18   chapter sub-title

direction
Mis. 172–17   nor of h· direction.

discord
Mis.   65– 3   no more proof of h· discord,
236–24   remedy for all h· discord.
Ret.   69– 5   parent of all h· discord

displeasure
Pul.   15– 9   risk h· displeasure for the sake of

doctrines
'00.   4–18   beaten path of h· doctrines
My. 262–18   H· doctrines or hypotheses

dreams
Un.   26–25   is a product of h· dreams.

ears
Ret.   91– 6   ever fell upon h· ears

economy
Mis. 286– 5   this verity in h· economy

endeavor
Mis.   41–15   scales the mountain of h· endeavor,
Pul.   53–21   * in every field of h· endeavor.

enjoyment
Mis.   9–22   this cup of selfish h· enjoyment

human

equity
Mis. 289–19   Neither divine justice nor h· equity

error
Mis. 208–17   All states and stages of h· error
284–19   against h· error and hate.
Un.   62–21   undisturbed by h· error,
No.   4– 6   Disease . . . is a h· error,
34– 1   delusion of all h· error,
36–22   no consciousness of h· error,
'02.   10–26   modus operandi of h· error,

ethics
Mis. 340–30   Material philosophy, h· ethics,

events
Mis. 269–13   in relation to h· events

existence
Mis.   52–15   wretched condition of h· existence.
200–14   stage and state of h· existence.
Un.   9–19   perplexing problem of h· existence.
No.   28– 1   would extinguish h· existence.
My. 166–19   seasons and calms of h· existence.

experience
'00.   15–10   of all h· experience is the most

fabrication
Pul.   2–29   true temple is no h· fabrication,

face
Po.   v–12   * resemble the profile of a h· face.

faith
Mis. 182–18   Born of no doctrine, no h· faith,
My. 292– 4   and h· faith in the right.

family
Mis.   18–27   those of the whole h· family,
98–12   helping the whole h· family ;
No.   15– 7   blessings for the whole h· family.
My. 208–20   for the whole h· family.

father
Un.   48–15   than the h· father enters into

fears
Mis. 307– 9   to all h· fears, to suffering

felicity
Pul.   53–16   * law of h· felicity and power

frame
Rud.   11–28   nervous operations of the h· frame.

gods
Mis. 123–12   human passions and h· gods,

gore
Mis. 246–10   purged of that sin by h· gore,
My. 265– 9   cleanse the earth of h· gore ;

governments
My. 293–32   H· governments maintain the

greatness
Mis. 340–28   in the constellation of h· greatness,

growth
Mis. 286– 6   Until time matures h· growth,
Ret.   49–13   in h· growth material organization

hands
Mis. 171– 2   can never . . . signify h· hands.
302–30   evil of putting . . . into h· hands,

happiness
Ret.   81–27   shifting scenes of h· happiness,

hate
My. 257–20   h· hate, pride, greed, lust

hatred
Pul.   15–19   h· hatred cannot reach you.

health
Rud.   12–27   maintains h· health and life.
No.   5–17   destroy both h· health and life.

heart
Mis.   84– 3   a preparation of the h· heart
127–32   h· heart, like a feather bed, needs
208– 9   enters unconsciously the h· heart
245–21   most mischievous to the h· heart,
290–13   its workings in the h· heart.
293–27   rolls on the h· heart a stone :
356–18   uplifted desires of the h· heart,
Chr.   53–32   bud and bloom In h· heart.
Ret.   80–13   it may stir the h· heart to
My.   62– 7   * love that trembled in one h· heart
92–28   * desire in the h· heart for some such
164–12   and all within the h· heart

hearts
Mis. 294–15   out of the flowers of h· hearts
303–14   at the door of h· hearts,

history
Mis.   12–21   former periods in h· history
267–16   Through all h· history, the vital
Ret.   22– 1   h· history needs to be revised,
Un.   57– 9   central emblem of h· history.
My. 256–18   dearest memories in h· history

hope
Mis. 330– 7   H· hope and faith should join
No.   35– 1   everything to h· hope and faith.
Peo.   8–20   trembling chords of h· hope

hopes
Mis. 341–14   Do h· hopes deceive?

human

hypotheses
Mis.   3–15   No . . . *h·* hypotheses enter this
    25–32   No *h·* hypotheses, whether in
    78–29   *H·* hypotheses are always
   361–14   contradiction of *h·* hypotheses ;
   364–22   *H·* hypotheses predicate matter of
   366– 3   attention that *h·* hypotheses consume,
Ret.   35–14   *H·* hypotheses have darkened the
'02.   5–16   by *h·* hypotheses or philosophy.
My. 181– 4   dealing with *h·* hypotheses,
   205–24   apart from *h·* hypotheses,

hypothesis
Mis.   71–17   neither *h·* hypothesis nor matter.
'01.   18–20   teaches that a *h·* hypothesis is
My. 350– 5   minus . . . and plus *h·* hypothesis,

ideal
'02.   2– 7   and my *h·* ideal.
My. 271–12   * chapter sub-title

idolatry
No.   35–17   the shocking *h·* idolatry

ills
Mis.   22–15   impossibility of transmitting *h·* ills,

images
Mis.   96–29   *h·* images of thought

imperfection
Mis. 320–13   dawning upon *h·* imperfection,

indignation
Pul.   14– 6   into *h·* indignation ;

individuality
Un.   25–16   honors conscious *h·* individuality

inquiry
My. 245–10   growth of *h·* inquiry

intellect
Un.   22–21   *h· intellect* and *will-power*,
   25–14   This denial enlarges the *h·* intellect

Jesus
Mis. 199–19   through the *h·* Jesus.
No.   36–14   *h·* Jesus had a resort to his higher

judgment
'00.   9–13   Strong desires bias *h·* judgment

justice
Mis.   11–14   Love metes not out *h·* justice,
   11–21   To mete out *h·* justice
   275– 2   Oh, tardy *h·* justice !

ken
My.   45–22   * marvellous beyond *h·* ken.

kingdom
No.   35–27   *h·* kingdom is nowhere,

knowledge
Mis.   22– 8   far in advance of *h·* knowledge
   288–17   *H·* knowledge inculcates that it is,

language
Un.   30– 3   *H·* language constantly uses the

law
My. 149–19   may know too much of *h·* law
   220– 9   concerning obedience to *h·* law,
   283–26   *H·* law is right only as it

laws
My. 220–27   Jesus obeyed *h·* laws

liberty
Mis. 101–11   for *h·* liberty and rights.

life
Mis.   8–20   sanctifies, and consecrates *h·* life,
   81–30   It gives lessons to *h·* life,
   92– 8   and to spiritualize *h·* life,
   137–22   the sublime ends of *h·* life.
   224–15   *h·* life is the work, the play,
   230–20   all of which drop *h·* life into the
   285– 9   *H·* life is too short for foibles
   287–26   obey the Golden Rule for *h·* life,
   289–10   scientific rules to *h·* life
   330– 3   What is the anthem of *h·* life?
   343– 8   and *h·* life more fruitful,
Ret.   23– 1   The trend of *h·* life was
   84– 5   his own thoughts and *h·* life
No.   33–23   glory of *h·* life is in overcoming
'02.   17–14   curtain of *h·* life should be lifted
My.   6– 8   the wrongs of *h·* life,

likeness
Mis.   23–28   *h·* likeness thrown upon the mirror
   308–30   *h·* likeness is the antipode of man

lives
Mis.   19–11   bring them out in *h·* lives.
   360– 2   *H·* lives are yet uncarved,

love
Mis. 107–13   should swell the lyre of *h·* love.
   290–10   To suppose that *h·* love,
   308– 5   He that by reason of *h·* love

manifestation
Mis.   84–16   *h·* manifestation of the Son of God

means
Mis.   52– 9   beyond all *h·* means and methods.
My. 260–11   no partnership with *h·* means

meekness
Mis. 141–22   nobility of *h·* meekness

human

mentality
My. 106–19   *H·* mentality, expressed in disease,

merit
My. 306–17   *H·* merit or demerit will find its

mind
Mis.   12–22   effects of this so-called *h·* mind
   39–19   to fill the *h·* mind with
   58–28   even one *h·* mind governing another ;
   59–25   away from the *h·* mind or body,
   62–24   rule of *h·* mind, fails, and ends in
   62–29   divine Mind over the *h·* mind
   62–30   notion that the *h·* mind can cure
   97– 6   *h·* mind that holds within itself
   97–10   Erring *h·* mind is by no means
   113–11   mentally manipulating *h·* mind,
   277–21   * history of the errors of the *h·* mind."
   360–32   No advancing modes of *h·* mind
No.   40–26   *h·* mind and body are made better only
'01.   19–23   misuse of the *h·* mind,
   20–12   to mislead the *h·* mind,
'02.   10– 3   capacities of the *h·* mind
   10–12   When the *h·* mind is advancing
My.   61–24   * *h·* mind was giving its consent.
   108–13   pharmacy of the *h·* mind,
   126– 4   the disturbed *h·* mind
   190–19   over the *h·* mind and *above matter*
   265–25   atmosphere of the *h·* mind,
   292–29   the *h·* mind is a compound of
   293–13   conflicting states of the *h·* mind,

mind-cure
Mis.   58–27   leaving it a *h·* "mind-cure,"

misjudgment
Mis.   66– 8   no *h·* misjudgment can pervert it ;

mission
Ret.   32– 2   divinely appointed *h·* mission,

misstatement
Mis. 188– 9   Because of *h·* misstatement

mockeries
Mis.   51–24   * dark pile of *h·* mockeries ;

mockery
My. 262–24   a *h·* mockery in mimicry

modes
Mis. 268– 1   *h·* modes and consciousness,

modus
Mis. 380– 3   what is the *h·* modus for

nature
Mis. 212–18   The currents of *h·* nature
   226–27   disgraces *h·* nature more than
   228– 1   the promptings of *h·* nature.
   237–14   phases of error in *h·* nature
   289–22   *H·* nature has bestowed on a wife
   354– 2   exceeds my conception of *h·* nature.
Un.   6– 6   *h·* nature will be renovated,
'00.   2– 9   three types of *h·* nature
   10–11   Certain elements in *h·* nature
'01.   9–19   The evil in *h·* nature foams
My.   4–21   iron in *h·* nature rusts away ;
   220–28   have greatly improved *h·* nature

necessity
'01.   34–26   Christianity is a *h·* necessity :

need
Mis. 210–22   false pretense of *h·* need,
My.   28– 5   will meet every *h·* need,"
   73–10   will meet every *h·* need."
   214– 6   will meet every *h·* need.
   224– 6   the *h·* need, the divine command,
   238–22   applicable to every *h·* need.

needs
Mis.   25–10   direct application to *h·* needs,
   192–20   its adaptability to *h·* needs,
   263–13   meet all *h·* needs and reflect
No.   42– 8   Spirit supplies all *h·* needs.
'01.   27– 8   * more rationally to *h·* needs."

obligations
Mis. 264– 4   are loyal to . . . *h·* obligations,

obstructions
My.   61– 5   * to remove *h·* obstructions

opinion
Pan.   2–14   of pantheism as a *h·* opinion

opinions
Mis.   17– 9   *h·* opinions and doctrines,
   86–13   indefinite and vague *h·* opinions,
   372– 3   those *h·* opinions had not
Ret.   78– 8   not by *h·* opinions ;
My. 288–13   travesties of *h·* opinions,

organizations
Peo.   1– 4   not . . . from *h·* organizations ;

origin
Mis.   71–27   seems to be of *h·* origin
   172–16   it is neither of *h·* origin nor of
   287– 2   and has no *h·* origin.
Rud.   4– 9   neither is it of *h·* origin.
My. 115– 5   were it of *h·* origin,

human

passions
Mis.	123–12	*h·* passions and human gods,
	236– 1	*h·* passions in their reaction
	237– 9	and the worst of *h·* passions
	294– 3	maëlstrom of *h·* passions,

perception
Un.	61–12	*H·* perception, advancing toward

person
Mis.	75– 4	through a *h·* person,
Rud.	2–13	The *h·* person is finite ;
'01.	5–30	*h·* person, as defined by C. S.,

philosophies
No.	24–16	in *h·* philosophies or creeds :

philosophy
Mis.	361–13	overshadowed all *h·* philosophy,
Un.	9–10	*h·* philosophy, or mystic psychology.
	11– 7	direct opposition to *h·* philosophy
	51– 6	*H·* philosophy and human reason
No.	11–23	Ancient and modern *h·* philosophy
	20–25	veins of all *h·* philosophy.
	21– 2	*H·* philosophy has ninety-nine parts of
	21–12	*H·* philosophy would dethrone
	21–15	*H·* philosophy has an undeveloped God,
My.	262–18	or vague *h·* philosophy
	349–21	natural sciences and *h·* philosophy,

pity
Mis.	102–21	*H·* pity often brings pain.
	121–28	Infinitely greater than *h·* pity,

policy
Mis.	118– 4	selfish motives, and *h·* policy.
	204–17	*h·* policy, ways, and means.
	212– 1	*H·* policy is a fool that saith

possibility
Pul.	45–14	* transcended *h·* possibility.

power
Mis.	138–19	giving to *h·* power, peace.
My.	219– 8	*H·* power is most properly used in
	266– 6	claims of politics and of *h·* power,

praise
Ret.	71– 1	exalts a mortal beyond *h·* praise,

presentation
Mis.	164– 4	*h·* presentation of goodness

pride
Mis.	111– 6	*h·* pride, creeping into its meshes,
	162–25	worldliness, *h·* pride, or self-will,
	183–23	while it shames *h·* pride.
	268–28	*h·* pride forfeits spiritual
	358–13	*H·* pride is human weakness.
Un.	11–18	destroyed *h·* pride by taking away

procreation
Mis.	286–21	*H·* procreation, birth, life,

progress
Mis.	9–31	more disastrous to *h·* progress

propaganda
My.	303–18	no idolatry, no *h·* propaganda

purpose
My.	284– 3	to help *h·* purpose and peoples,

qualities
Mis.	250–11	Love is distorted into *h·* qualities,
Peo.	2–17	out of the worst *h·* qualities,

quality
Mis.	75–19	warped to signify *h·* quality,
	250–21	As a *h·* quality, the glorious

question
'02.	5–14	ever-recurring *h·* question

race
Mis.	176– 8	crises of nations or of the *h·* race.
	194–13	for the whole *h·* race.
	229–23	*h·* race would become healthier,
	259–23	spiritual elevator of the *h·* race,
	278–16	is always a blessing to the *h·* race.
	341– 2	When will the whole *h·* race have
Ret.	79– 1	against the progress of the *h·* race
	91–29	done for the *h·* race?
Un.	6– 4	the whole *h·* race will learn that,
Rud.	2– 4	* an individual of the *h·* race.''
No.	44–19	legitimate to the *h·* race,
My.	136–26	its fruits, — benefiting the *h·* race ;
	152– 9	*h·* race has not yet reached
	154–18	and to clothe the *h·* race.
	189–14	encircle and cement the *h·* race.
	288– 8	is the elevator of the *h·* race ;

reason
Mis.	13–20	and frail *h·* reason accepts.
	100–16	*H·* reason is inaccurate ;
	173– 1	*h·* reason, or man's theorems,
Ret.	34– 9	*H·* reason was not equal to it.
Un.	9–16	upon the sand of *h·* reason.
	51– 6	Human philosophy and *h·* reason
Pul.	47–15	* no *h·* reason has been equal to
No.	20– 4	*h·* reason, imagination, and
	20–26	*H·* reason is a blind guide,
	24–17	hidden by dogma and *h·* reason
My.	161–23	Lest *h·* reason becloud

human

reason
My.	165–23	*H·* reason becomes tired
	260–13	*H·* reason and philosophy may
	283–19	When pride, self, and *h·* reason
	350– 7	revelation, uplifting *h·* reason,

reflection
Un.	28–20	*h·* reflection, reason, or belief

right
Mis.	266– 6	to abridge a single *h·* right

rights
'00.	10–13	*h·* rights, and self-government
Peo.	11– 9	Above the platform of *h·* rights
My.	181–15	religious liberty and *h·* rights.
	287–14	industries, *h·* rights, liberty,
	316–18	It defends *h·* rights and the

sacrifice
My.	125– 1	altars for *h·* sacrifice.

self
Mis.	162–29	he must be oblivious of *h·* self.
My.	194–14	*h·* self lost in divine light,

sense
Mis.	68– 4	disappearance to the *h·* sense ;
	77–32	and resurrecting the *h· sense*
	87– 5	which is unjust to *h·* sense
	164–27	become so magnified to *h·* sense,
	165– 5	had grown beyond the *h·* sense
	212–13	*h·* sense of ways and means
	352– 3	When *h·* sense is quickened
Un.	4– 8	in a certain finite *h·* sense,
	61–20	the earthly acme of *h·* sense.
	63– 9	false *h·* sense of that light
No.	10– 2	in both a divine and *h·* sense ;
	36–25	risen from *h·* sense to a higher
My.	40–29	* *H·* sense often rebels against law,
	191–16	*h·* sense of Life and Love,
	293–19	divine power and poor *h·* sense

senses
My.	189–18	When the *h·* senses wake from

shadows
Mis.	352–11	May the *h·* shadows of thought

sigh
'00.	11–11	The *h·* sigh for peace and love

sight
Mis.	194–17	magnifies the divine power to *h·* sight ;
'01.	12–22	magnifies the divine power to *h·* sight ;

sin
Un.	15–19	and *h·* sin become only an echo of

skill
Mis.	232–12	*H·* skill but foreshadows what is

slavery
Mis.	237–28	fetters of one form of *h·* slavery.

soul
Mis.	76–15	to set a *h·* soul free from its
	76–22	misnamed *h·* soul is material sense,
Un.	51–26	man is reflected not as *h·* soul,
Pul.	53–22	* power of the *h·* soul.

speculation
Mis.	286–31	*h·* speculation will go on,

standpoint
Mis.	289– 8	From a *h·* standpoint of good,

statutes
My.	220–29	human nature and *h·* statutes.

strength
Mis.	138–17	that in unity was *h·* strength ;
	138–18	*h·* strength is weakness,
My.	132–14	no longer to appeal to *h·* strength,

strife
Mis.	388– 8	Free us from *h·* strife.
Po.	7– 8	Free us from *h·* strife.

struggles
No.	35– 7	When *h·* struggles cease,

suffering
Mis.	179– 3	rolled away by *h·* suffering.
Ret.	62– 2	and *h·* suffering will increase.

sympathy
Mis.	253–23	should it not appeal to *h·* sympathy?

system
Mis.	48–16	of any drug, on the *h·* system,
	244– 6	constructing the *h·* system,

systems
Mis.	74– 9	all *h·* systems of etiology and
Ret.	57–24	*H·* systems of philosophy and

theorems
Mis.	312–22	*h·* theorems or hypotheses,

theories
Mis.	365– 5	*H·* theories weighed in the balances
Un.	44–15	*H·* theories call, or miscall,
No.	18–13	*H·* theories, when weighed in the

thought
Mis.	17–28	existence dawns on *h·* thought,
	75–31	or brought forth by *h·* thought,
	166–25	leavening the lump of *h·* thought,
	204–23	By purifying *h·* thought,
	205–10	Truth and Love on the *h·* thought,

human

thought

Mis.	217–31	but spiritualize *h·* thought,
	282–16	personal precincts of *h·* thought,
	307–30	*h·* thought must turn instinctively
	352–22	not sufficient . . . in the *h·* thought
	361– 9	disappear to *h·* thought,
Ret.	67– 3	*h·* thought does not constitute sin,
	93–14	method for uplifting *h·* thought
Un.	61–10	the morning of *h·* thought,
Pul.	15– 3	point out the evil in *h·* thought,
No.	24– 4	in evil in *h·* thought.
	40–15	never to touch the *h·* thought
'02.	9– 9	Truth will arise in *h·* thought
Peo.	3–23	limits *h·* thought and action
My.	114–29	the whole lump of *h·* thought?
	151–21	*h·* thought discerned its idolatrous
	153–28	to all *h·* thought and action,
	191–21	but *h·* thought has risen !
	265–15	has dawned upon *h·* thought
	278–30	Whatever brings into *h·* thought

thoughts

Mis.	393–10	the misty Mine of *h·* thoughts,
Un.	21– 2	processes wherein *h·* thoughts
Po.	51–15	the misty Mine of *h·* thoughts,

title

'00.	15– 4	are distinguished above *h·* title

tone

'00.	11–20	*h·* tone has no melody for me.

tribunals

Mis.	121–29	*H·* tribunals, if just, borrow their

understanding

Mis.	73–28	divine law to *h·* understanding ;
	81–25	desolation of *h·* understanding,
No.	37–24	uplifting the *h·* understanding,
My.	228–19	bathing the *h·* understanding with
	262–14	entrance into *h·* understanding

use

'01.	6–21	impracticable for *h·* use,

vagaries

Mis.	78–30	hypotheses are always *h·* vagaries,

victims

Mis.	123–11	a religion that demands *h·* victims

view

Mis.	282– 3	brings to *h·* view an

views

My.	221– 5	with certain purely *h·* views.

wants

Peo.	12–23	application of . . . to *h·* wants.

weakness

Mis.	292–13	energy that brings to *h·* weakness
	358–14	Human pride is *h·* weakness.
Un.	39–12	divine Science removes *h·* weakness
My.	287– 7	giving to *h·* weakness strength,

weal

Mis.	65– 9	subject of *h·* weal and woe?
My.	36–27	* affection for the cause of *h·* weal,
	213– 9	lurking foe to *h·* weal,

will

Mis.	59– 6	using the power of *h·* will,
	74– 4	the *h·* will, and the unnatural
	118– 1	*H·* will must be subjugated.
	141–21	impulses of *h·* will and pride ;
	181–32	born not of the *h·* will
	201– 5	its original sin, or *h·* will ;
	212–22	*h·* will is lost in the divine ;
	243–22	the basis of matter, or *h·* will,
	254–25	laurels of headlong *h·* will.
Rud.	9–10	malpractice is in erring *h·* will,
No.	11– 1	whereas matter and *h·* will,
'01.	2– 9	magnetic element of *h·* will
	19–26	unbridled individual *h·* will.
My.	5–31	*H·* will may mesmerize and mislead
	159–26	could not control *h·* will,
	349–26	*h·* will divorced from Science.

wills

Mis.	224–12	different *h·* wills, opinions,

wisdom

Mis.	73–14	*H·* wisdom therefore can get no
	204–17	in *h·* wisdom, human policy,
Un.	44–18	*H·* wisdom says of evil,
	54–22	addition to *h·* wisdom,
Peo.	1– 3	is not born of *h·* wisdom ;
My.	224– 2	when *h·* wisdom is inadequate

woe

Mis.	361–22	speculative wisdom and *h·* woe.
Ret.	31–13	relief from *h·* woe.
Un.	58–16	the full compass of *h·* woe,
No.	33–23	physical suffering and *h·* woe.
'02.	6–13	all *h·* woe is seen to obtain in
My.	190– 2	bring the recompense of *h·* woe,

wrong

Mis.	340–32	*H·* wrong, sickness, sin, and death

Mis.	16–11	these claims are divine, not *h·* ;
	58–23	All Science is divine, not *h·*,

human

Mis.	63–26	Jesus as the son of man was *h·* :
	63–28	through the crucifixion of the *h·*,
	64–22	for science is not *h·*.
	100–22	of the divine with the *h·*,
	102–18	expressed in modes above the *h·*.
	103–22	Any inference . . . derived from the *h·*,
	121– 9	*h·* struggles against the divine,
	161–16	both *h·* and divinely endowed,
	163–16	less *h·* and more divine
	184–31	purged of the animal and *h·*,
	187–19	our *h·* and divine Master,
	199–24	but the actor was *h·*.
	246– 7	both *h·* and divine rights,
	247– 2	both *h·* and divine rights ;
	258–29	differs essentially from the *h·*.
	286–22	states of the *h·* erring mind ;
	291– 1	Mistaken or transient views are *h·* :
Ret.	28–26	Its Principle is divine, not *h·*,
	50–20	subordination of the *h·* to the
	56–10	is of *h·* instead of divine origin.
	67– 4	sin constitutes the *h·* or physical
	68– 9	*h·* material concept is *unreal*,
	89–29	and selfish influence is *h·*,
Un.	18–18	through divine law, not through *h·*.
No.	18–18	Thus falsely may the *h·* conceive of
	21–16	wherein the *h·* and divine mingle
	30–14	not by becoming *h·*, and knowing sin,
	30–18	His sympathy is divine, not *h·*,
Pan.	4–11	But reason and will are *h·* ;
	8– 8	the other a *h·* finite personality?
'01.	1–16	*h·* in communion with the Divine,
	10–12	The Christ was not *h·*.
	10–12	Jesus was *h·*.
	10–14	both the divine and the *h·*,
	12– 9	But this is *h·* :
	31– 7	neither personal nor *h·*, but divine.
Peo.	10–16	divine as well as *h·*.
My.	27– 7	for the divine and not the *h·*
	139–22	from the *h·* to the divine.
	244–19	put off the *h·* for the divine.
	262– 7	commemorates the birth of a *h·*,
	265–22	coincidence of the *h·* and divine,
	275– 5	The *h·*, material, so-called senses

humane

Mis.	26– 5	more *h·* and spiritual.
	89–14	it is *h·*, and not unchristian,
	184–32	submerged in the *h·* and divine,
Peo.	10– 9	put her *h·* foot on a tyrannical
My.	175–14	academies, *h·* institutions,
	291–21	renew euphony, emphasize *h·* power,

Human Freedom League

Mis.	305– 6	* the *H· F· L·*,

humanhood

Un.	49– 8	The more I understand true *h·*,

humanitarian

Mis.	284– 6	*h·* at work in this field of
Man.	47– 1	A Christian Scientist is a *h·* ;

humanity (*see also* **humanity's**)

advancing

No.	19– 9	second thought of advancing *h·*.

all

Un.	51–14	Man is the generic term for all *h·*.

and divinity

Ret.	91–14	great lessons — on *h·* and divinity

and equality

Mis.	294–29	true ideas of *h·* and equality.

and sympathy

Mis.	379–18	his rare *h·* and sympathy

benefited

Ret.	85–14	glorified, or *h·* benefited,

brings to

Mis.	338– 3	brings to *h·* some great good,

candor and

Mis.	147–28	full of truth, candor, and *h·*.

consecrated to

Mis.	350–30	My life, consecrated to *h·*

death and

My.	258–24	love, grief, death, and *h·*.

divinity and

My.	179–23	practice of a true divinity and *h·*.

drop of

Pul.	5–15	bedew my hope with a drop of *h·*.

ear of

Peo.	13–12	On the startled ear of *h·*

faith in

Mis.	338–15	faith in *h·* will subject one to

forcing

Mis.	359–12	forcing *h·* out of the proper channels

forearm

My.	273–17	to forewarn and forearm *h·*.

God and
(*see* **God**)

humanity

grander
Pul. 85–16 * a better and grander *h·*,
growing wants of
Mis. 365–25 never met the growing wants of *h·*.
heart of
    (*see* **heart**)
help
No. 43–25 will never . . . help *h·*.
higher
Pul. 15–20 cement of a higher *h·* will
highest
Pan. 9–16 demonstrates the highest *h·*,
his
My. 291–15 His *h·*, weighed in the scales of
imparting to
Mis. 372–31 imparting to *h·* the true sense of
impress
Mis. 207– 4 impress *h·* with the genuine
jaded
Mis. 366–16 At this date, poor jaded *h·* needs
justice, and
'00. 10–15 in the name of God, justice, and *h·*
leading
My. 252–22 leading *h·* into paths of peace
lifts
Mis. 290– 5 Science lifts *h·* higher in the
love for
My. 24– 7 * your unmeasured love for *h·*,
lower order of
Peo. 13– 2 hence a lower order of *h·*,
methods of
Peo. 11–24 mistaken in their methods of *h·*.
models of
Peo. 14–11 form our models of *h·*.
needs of
My. 147–18 moral, and spiritual needs of *h·*,
origin of
Pul. 39– 3 * proof of the divine origin of *h·*
outrages
Mis. 274–19 mocks morality, outrages *h·*,
poor
Mis. 107–15 before poor *h·* is regenerated
     359–17 for poor *h·* to step upon the
problem of
My. 306–18 solves the problem of *h·*,
pure
Mis. 100–22 Pure *h·*, friendship, home,
reaching
Mis. 63–28 reaching *h·* through the crucifixion
rescue of
Mis. 293– 8 will come, . . . to the rescue of *h·*.
reveals itself to
Mis. 95–21 reveals itself to *h·* through
sake of
Pul. 51–30 * something good for the sake of *h·*.
should share
My. 220–30 *h·* should share alike
sorrow-worn
My. 40–18 * pain-racked and sorrow-worn *h·*.
spirit of
My. 129– 5 But the spirit of *h·*, ethics,
suffering
My. 190– 4 sympathy for suffering *h·*
sufferings of
Ret. 30– 8 relieve the sufferings of *h·*
tendency of
'02. 10–15 upward tendency of *h·*
universal
Mis. 29– 6 touches universal *h·*.
My. 37–16 * before the gaze of universal *h·*.
uplifted
No. 34–25 over the steps of uplifted *h·*,
upon
'00. 12– 2 projected from divinity upon *h·*,
verdict of
Pan. 10– 7 the honest verdict of *h·*
victorious
Un. 30–19 made *h·* victorious over death
vitals of
Mis. 131– 4 gnawing at the vitals of *h·*.
wants of
Ret. 52–10 the broader wants of *h·*,
No. 19– 7 the growing wants of *h·*.
was misled
Un. 44–10 *h·* was misled by a false

My. 269– 5 Then shall *h·* have learned

humanity's
Mis. 370–13 according to *h·* needs.
Po. 22–15 To heal *h·* sore heart ;

humanized
Ret. 54– 8 a *h·* conception of His power.

humankind
Un. 59– 3 from what evils . . . to save *h·*?

humanly
Mis. 71–21 Whatever is *h·* conceived is a
     81–25 his voice be heard divinely and *h·*.
Un. 58–11 through what is *h·* called *agony*.
No. 9–26 *h·* construed, and according to

humble
Mis. 99–32 by the wayside, in *h·* homes.
     127–13 If this heart, *h·* and trustful,
     163–10 by the wayside, in *h·* homes :
     204– 3 *h·* before God, he cries,
     331– 5 did it make them *h·*, loving,
     337–14 *h·* himself as this little— *Matt.* 18 : 4.
     337–26 by the wayside, in *h·* homes,
Pul. 87– 5 * with our *h·* benediction.
'01. 14– 4 Publican's wail won his *h·* desire,
Po. 33– 2 make this my *h·* request :
My. 18–10 If this heart, *h·* and trustful,
     134– 6 cannot be too grateful nor too *h·*
     188–31 gains admittance to a *h·* heart,
     334–22 Publican's wail won his *h·* desire,

humbles
Ret. 71– 2 *h·* him with the tax it raises on
My. 131– 4 *h·*, exalts, and commands a man,

humbly
Mis. 313–25 *H·*, and, . . . divinely directed,
Po. 28– 6 Help us to *h·* bow
My. 174–28 *h·* pray to serve Him better.
     182–19 *H·*, gratefully, trustingly.
     257–18 our hearts are kneeling *h·*.
     283–24 and to walk *h·*"— *Mic.* 6 : 8.

humbugs
Ret. 33– 9 and from various *h·*,

Hume, David
Ret. 37–12 David *H·*, Ralph Waldo Emerson, **or**

humiliates
No. 39–15 Such prayer *h·*, purifies, and

humility
Mis. 1–15 *H·* is the stepping-stone to
     7– 7 *h·* is necessary in this work
     158–17 test your *h·* and obedience
     316–28 patterns of *h·*, wisdom, and
     328– 7 that the valley is *h·*,
     341–13 comes of honesty and *h·*.
     354–23 *h·* is the first step in C. S.,
     356–22 The second stage of . . . is *h·*.
     356–25 *H·* is lens and prism to the
     356–30 Cherish *h·*, "watch,"— *Matt.* 26 : 41.
     356–31 *H·* is no busybody :
     358–14 Self-knowledge, *h·*, and love
Ret. 31–25 and a tint of *h·*,
     91–30 His holy *h·*, unworldliness, and
Un. 45–10 come down and learn, in *h·*,
No. 35– 5 through deep *h·* and adoration
My. 36–18 * we are come, in *h·*, to pour out our
     37– 5 * Naught else than the grandeur of *h·*
     262–27 *h·*, benevolence, charity,
     303–29 We need much *h·*, wisdom,

hummed
Pan. 1– 8 shrieked and *h·* their hymns ;

humor
Mis. 117–11 * *h·*, and enduring vivacity
My. 121–19 gentility and good *h·*
     338–23 his comparisons and ready *h·*.

hundred
My. 112–14 ninety-nine out of every *h·*
    (*see also* **dates, numbers, values**)

hundredfold
Mis. 12–17 temptations to sin are increased **a *h·*.**
     50–27 advance Christianity a *h·*.

hundreds
Mis. 54–15 is curing *h·* at this very time ;
Pul. 36– 7 * To this College came *h·* and *h·*
     41–14 * New York sent its *h·*,
     68– 6 * Students came to it in *h·*
My. 30– 8 * many *h·* of other faiths,
     30–28 * *h·* had to be turned away,
     53– 2 * *h·* of dollars were sunk
     54– 2 * going away who could **not**
     59–10 * by the *h·* of thousands
     80–27 * there were many *h·* waiting
     85– 8 * churches have risen by *h·*,
     90– 1 * *h·* of great buildings
     92–17 * number to *h·* of thousands,
     93–31 * number *h·* of thousands,
     99–23 * there are *h·* of such churches.
     112–32 in *h·* of pulpits
     293– 8 *H·*, thousands of others believed
     293– 9 *h·* of thousands who prayed
    (*see also* **numbers**)

hundredth
    (*see* **numbers**)

hung

Mis.	333–30	Chaldee h· his destiny out upon
Pul.	42–21	* a huge seven-pointed star was h·
	49– 5	* h· its walls with reproductions
My.	161– 1	h· around the necks of the wicked.

hunger

Ret.	31– 9	h· and thirst after divine things,
My.	40– 4	* to those who h· and thirst

hungered

Pul.	6–16	* for which I had h· since girlhood,

hungering

Mis.	235–18	H· and thirsting after a better life,
My.	15–28	* Seem h· and thirsting

hungry

Mis.	16– 2	These nourish the h· hope,
	127–11	When a h· heart petitions the
	225–28	he awoke, and was h·.
	322–20	it is God that feedeth the h· heart,
	324–28	Naked, h·, athirst, this time he
	369–20	We are h· for Love,
	391– 3	I hope the heart that's h·
	398–17	Feed the h·, heal the heart,
Ret.	46–23	Feed the h·, heal the heart,
	90– 8	he there taught a few h· ones,
Pul.	17–22	Feed the h·, heal the heart,
'02.	17–25	worth satisfies the h· heart,
Po.	14–21	Feed the h·, heal the heart,
	38– 2	I hope the heart that's h·
My.	18– 8	When a h· heart petitions the
	133–13	crumbs and monads will feed the h·,
	147–29	heavenly homesick or h· hearts

Hunt, Mrs.

My.	31–25	* soloist for the services, Mrs. H·,

hunters

Pan.	3–26	god of shepherds and h·,

Huntington and Massachusetts Avenues

My.	73–19	* corner of H· and M· A·.

Huntington Avenue

Pul.	57–24	* on Back Bay, just off H· A·,

Huntoon

Mehitable

Ret.	8–13	when my cousin, Mehitable H·,
	8–16	so loud that Mehitable heard it,
	8–19	Mehitable then said sharply,
	9– 4	Mother told Mehitable all about this

hurling

Mis.	254–22	h· its so-called healing at random,

hurls

Hea.	2– 6	h· the thunderbolt of truth,

hurried

My.	224– 8	H· conclusions as to the public thought

hurrying

Pul.	39–24	* h· throng before me pass,
My.	66–20	* are h· on with their work

hurt

Mis.	28–32	it shall not h· them ;— Mark 16: 18.
	115–25	every effort to h· one will only
	224– 4	our egotism that feels h· by
	224–10	* I don't feel h· in the least."
	249– 6	it shall not h· them." — Mark 16: 18.
	280– 7	h· not the holy things of Truth.
'01.	20–15	or that they are h·.
Hea.	1– 4	it shall not h· them;— Mark 16: 18.
	7–26	it shall not h· them." — Mark 16: 18.
	15–12	it shall not h· them." — Mark 16: 18.
Peo.	12– 4	it shall not h· them ;— Mark 16: 18.
My.	33–24	swereth to his own h·, — Psal. 15: 4.
	48– 2	* it shall not h· them ;— Mark 16: 18.
	146– 5	it shall not h· them." — Mark 16: 18.
	233–16	healed also the h· of — Jer. 6: 14.

hurting

'01.	20–14	not knowing what is h· them

husband (see also husband's)

Mis.	35–10	the following words of her h·,
	90– 8	to have a h· treated for sin,
	143–21	h· and wife reckoned as one,
	236–15	solicitations of h· or wife
	275–10	where the bereft wife or h·,
	287–22	When asked by a wife or a h·
	287–29	Please your h·, and he will be apt to
	339–20	Art thou a h·, and hast
	339–23	the o'erburdened head of thy h·?
	385– 9	poem
Man.	46– 3	spiritually adopted h· or wife.
	92–12	If both h· and wife are
Ret.	19– 1	I was united to my first h·,
	19–11	My h· was a freemason,
	43– 9	My h·, Asa G. Eddy,
Pul.	6–19	* I went with my h·,
	83– 3	* as h· and office-holder

husband

'02.	15–16	My h·, Colonel Glover,
Po.	page 48	poem
My.	189–26	There my h· died,
	290–19	Thy tender h·, our nation's chief
	312– 5	tragic death of my h·,
	312–18	My first h·, Major . . . Glover,
	314– 2	Dr. . . . . Patterson, my second h·,
	314–19	that a h· was about to
	314–23	letter from me to this self-same h·,
	314–24	When this h· recovered his wife,
	314–27	wife of this h· related these facts
	326–14	my h·, Major George W. Glover,
	329– 9	* reference to the death of her h·,
	330–16	* relating to her h·
	330–23	"My h· was a Free Mason,
	335–29	* save the life of her h·.

husbanding

My.	182–28	this vine of His h·,

husbandman

Mis.	154–15	vine whereof our Father is h·.
Hea.	8–24	by the parable of the h·.
Po.	47–17	Watching the h· fled ;

husbandmen

Mis.	253–18	and the h· that said,
	254–27	come and destroy the h·, — Mark 12: 9.

husband's

Man.	111– 6	Christian name, not her h·,
Ret.	20– 1	I lost all my h· property,
Po.	9– 1	glance of her h· watchful eye
My.	329–14	* notice of her h· death
	334–10	* account of her h· demise
	335–23	* third day of her h· illness,
	335–30	* prayed incessantly for her h·
	336– 5	* come to her after her h· death,
	336– 8	* her h· Masonic brethren,
	336–12	I lost all my h· property,

husbands

Pul.	82–26	* the welfare of their h·,
'02.	5–10	divine Love, that heaven h·

hush

Pan.	3–10	silent as the storm's sudden h· ;

hushed

Mis.	246–14	has scarcely been heard and h·,
	395–13	H· is the heart.
Hea.	17–17	were h· by material sense
Po.	35–11	H· in the heart
	57–20	H· is the heart.

hushing

Mis.	323–19	h· the hissing serpents,

husks

Mis.	369–22	tired of theoretic h·,

Huxley

'01.	24–19	Berkeley, Darwin, or H·.

hyacinth

Po.	67–19	like the blue h·,

hydra

Mis.	246–16	lifts its h· head to forge anew

hydra-headed

No.	2– 3	spurious and h· mind-healing

hydraulics

No.	6–25	optics, acoustics, and h·

hydrology

Mis.	203–14	h· handles it with so-called

hydropathy

Ret.	33– 8	homœopathy, h·, electricity,

Hygeia

My.	205–17	spiritual Æsculapius and H·,

hygiene

Mis.	3–17	H·, manipulation, and mesmerism
	3–26	materia medica, h·, and
	6–23	faith in drugs and material h· ;
	17–11	put off your materia medica and h·
	80–27	pathology, h·, and therapeutics,
	138– 7	time and attention to h·
	240– 5	fattened by metaphysical h·.
Pan.	4–26	what need have we of drugs, h·, and
Hea.	3– 1	requires neither h· nor drugs
	14– 6	physiology, h·, or physics
	15– 6	It places no faith in h· or drugs ;
Peo.	4– 3	more faith in h· and drugs than in
My.	260–27	It leaves h·, medicine, ethics, and
	348– 3	drugs, surgery, h·, electricity,

hygienic

Mis.	40– 5	mingle h· rules, drugs, and prayers
Ret.	26– 2	neither obedience to h· laws, nor
No.	10–14	My h· system rests on Mind,
Peo.	12–23	faith in drugs and h· drills,

Hymn
161
  My. 31–28   * *H·* 161, written by Mrs. Eddy,
        32–13   * *H·* 161, from the Hymnal.
166
  My. 32–20   * *H·* 166, from the Hymnal.

hymn
  Mis. 398–21   poem
  Man. 62– 4   special *h·* selected by the Board
  Chr. 53–60   In heaven's *h·*.
  Un. 26–22   as sings another line of this *h·*,
  Pul. 43–14   * *h·*, "*Laus Deo,* it is done !"
  '01. 31–23   my cradle *h·* and the Lord's Prayer,
  Hea. 20– 1   following *h·* was sung at the close :
  Po. vi– 8   * *as a dedicatory h·.*
    page 75   poem
    page 77   poem
      77– 3   A nation's holiest *h·*
  My. 15–17   Kate Hankey's excellent *h·*,
      77–21   * a first *h·* of thanksgiving

Hymnal
Christian Science
  Pul. 28–21   * compilation called the "C. S. *H·*,"
  My. 19– 2   * C. S. *H·* ;

  My. 32–13   * Hymn 161, from the *H·*.
      32–20   * Hymn 166, from the *H·*.

hymn-books
  Pul. 28–25   * *h·* of the Unitarian churches.

hymning
  Po. 30–21   Echo amid the *h·* spheres of light,

hymns
  Mis. 281– 2   *h·* of victory for triumphs.
    314– 8   reading the *h·*, and chapter
    331–15   remember *their* cradle *h·*,
    396–11   songsters' matin *h·* to God
  Pul. 28–22   * devotional *h·* from Herbert,
    41–27   * Old familiar *h·* . . . were chimed
    59–10   * *h·* and psalms being omitted.
  Pan.   1– 8   shrieked and hummed their *h·* ;
  Po. vi–22   * *the author's best-known h·*
    59– 3   songsters' matin *h·* to God
  My. 31– 2   * succeeded by the following *h·*
    80–17   * *h·*, . . . and selections from

hymn-verse
  Un. 26–12   in the *h·* so often sung

hyperæmia
  My. 107–31   gastritis, *h·*, pneumonia,

hyperbolic
  Mis. 313–14   ill-humor or *h·* tumor.

hypnotism
  Mis.   4– 5   healing on the basis of *h·*,
    112– 6   *H·*, microbes, X-rays,
    233–15   force of mortal mind, termed *h·*,
  Man. 41– 7   *h·*, or spiritualism,
    47–26   *h·*, or spiritualism,
    53–15   Not to Learn *H·*.
    53–16   shall not learn *H·*
  '01. 19–24   such as mesmerism, *h·*,
    20– 1   animal magnetism and *h·* are
  My. 180–12   no element whatever of *h·*
    204–25   the suing for payment, *h·*, and
    364– 9   Animal magnetism, *h·*, etc.,

hypnotists
  '01. 20–30   Christian Scientists are not *h·*,

hypocrisies
  My. 17– 5   all guile, and *h·*, — *I Pet.* 2 : 1.

hypocrisy
  Mis. 123– 7   lust, *h·*, *witchcraft.*
    268– 7   victories of rivalry and *h·*
    319–10   beset with egotism and *h·*.
    326–11   fed by the fat of *h·*
    337–19   *h·*, evil-speaking, lust,
    374– 7   whatever rebuked *h·*
  '02. 16–26   *h·*, pride, self-will, envy,
  Hea. 17– 3   envy, *h·*, or malice,
  My. 228–21   self-righteousness, *h·*, envy,

hypocrite (*see also* hypocrite's)
  Mis. 19–23   in a smooth-tongued *h·*
    163–11   to arrant *h·* and to dull disciples
    226–21   character of a liar and *h·*
  Un. 58–12   ice-bound *h·* melts
  No. 43–16   alarming the *h·*,
  Po. 73–19   No sculptured lie, Or *h·* sigh,
  My. 225– 2   in which the coward and the *h·*

hypocrite's
  Un. 56–22   The *h·* affections must first be
  No. 40–11   pour forth a *h·* prayer ;

hypocrites
  Mis. 133–11   shalt not be as the *h·* — *Matt.* 6 : 5.
    226–12   pretentious praise of *h·*,
    335–11   his portion with the *h·*." — *Matt.* 24 : 51.

hypotheses
  Mis.   3–15   No opinions of mortals nor human *h·*
    25–32   No human *h·*, whether in philosophy,
    78–29   Human *h·* are always human vagaries,
    312–22   human theorems or *h·*,
    361–14   contradiction of human *h·* ;
    364–22   Human *h·* predicate matter of
    366– 3   attention that human *h·* consume,
  Ret. 35–14   Human *h·* have darkened the glow
    56– 2   finite theories, doctrines, and *h·*,
  Un. 28–13   common *h·* about souls
  No. 20–27   a continued series of mortal *h·*,
  '02.   5–16   by human *h·* or philosophy.
  Hea.   5–18   Such *h·* ignore Biblical authority,
  My. 181– 4   dealing with human *h·*,
    205–24   wholly apart from human *h·*,
    262–18   Human doctrines or *h·*
    266–12   of all codes, modes, *h·*,

hypothesis
  Mis. 13–18   This frail *h·* is founded upon
    71–17   neither human *h·* nor matter.
  Un. 29– 1   *h·* as to its human character.
  Pan.   7–26   *h·* of mind in matter,
  '01. 18–20   teaches that a human *h·* is
  My. 349–14   putting off the *h·* of matter
    350– 5   minus divine logic and plus human *h·*,

hypothetical
  Mis. 38–23   too vapory and *h·* for questions of
  Pan.   2– 6   neither *h·* nor dogmatical,
  My. 349–31   Wholly *h·*, inductive reasoning

hypothetically
  Mis. 362–15   Philosophy *h·* regards creation as

hysteria
  My. 310–26   * "*h·* mingled with bad temper."

I

I
  Mis. 39–15   "Lo, *I* am with you alway" — *Matt.* 28 : 20.
    130–15   *I* will repay, saith the — *Rom.* 12 : 19.
    211–13   *I* delivered thee." — *Psal.* 81 : 7.
  Un. 18– 3   saying, *I* am infinite good ;
    18– 3   therefore *I* know not evil.
    18– 4   *I* can see only the brightness of My
    18– 7   God says, *I* am too pure to
    18–11   If . . . *I* could not remedy them,
    18–17   God says, *I* show My pity through
    18–23   God saith, *I* am ever-conscious Life,
    18–24   and thus *I* conquer death ;
    18–25   *I* am All.
    24– 2   *I* am the infinite All.
    24– 8   but verily *I* say unto you,
    25–13   this lie *I* declare an illusion.
  No. 30–11   three words, "*I* am All ;"
  My. 131–26   if *I* will not open you the — *Mal.* 3 : 10.
    132– 3   if *I* will not open you the — *Mal.* 3 : 10.
    132–15   *I* am thy deliverer.
    177–23   '*I* will direct their work — *Isa.* 61 : 8.
    177–24   *I* will make an everlasting — *Isa.* 61 : 8.
    199– 7   *I* have naught against thee.
    223–29   know that *I* am God." — *Psal.* 46 : 10.

I AM
  Mis. 189–20   Life to be the infinite *I A·*,
    258–19   God named Himself, *I A·*.
    258–21   The name, *I A·*, indicated
    331–28   and is . . . the *I A·*.
  Chr. 53–46   brings to view The great *I A·*,
  Un. 63– 2   The *I A·* was neither buried nor
  Rud.   3–27   *I A·*, filling all space,
  '02.   7–15   the forever *I A·*, and All,

ice
  Mis. 88–24   * as imported *i·* was miraculous to
  Un. 64–16   scale the treacherous *i·*,

ice-bound
  Un. 58–12   Even the *i·* hypocrite

ice-cream
  Mis. 240–16   or puts it into the *i·*

ice-creams
  Mis. 226– 6   after eating several *i·*,

Icelandic
  Mis. 97–22   I commend the *I·* translation :

idea

and demonstration
  Ret. 59–16 both in *i·* and demonstration.
and purpose
  Mis. 303–23 *i·* and purpose of a Liberty Bell
any
  My. 324– 5 * any *i·* for your book,
Christian
  '02. 12– 9 Christian *i·* that God is come,
Christian Science
  My. 84–18 * growth of the C. S. *i·*
compound
  Mis. 167– 8 even the compound *i·* of
  My. 269– 2 in the intelligent compound *i·*,
conceivable
  '01. 6–27 lose all conceivable *i·* of Him
concept or
  Ret. 68–10 divine concept or *i·* is spiritually
concise
  Pul. 73–28 * concise *i·* of her belief
conclusive
  Mis. 96–26 give to you any conclusive *i·*
divine
  (see **divine***)*
eternal
  Mis. 79–12 man is the eternal *i·* of Truth,
  Un. 61– 7 even the eternal *i·* of God,
  No. 25–14 eternal *i·* of his divine Principle,
full
  My. 205–26 full *i·* of its divine Principle,
fundamental
  Pul. 69–17 * fundamental *i·* is that God is Mind,
God's
  Mis. 261–25 Man as God's *i·* is already saved
  336–14 dislike and hatred of God's *i·*,
  Pul. 75– 3 the Principle of God's *i·*,
  Po. 70–23 Give God's *i·* sway,
highest
  Mis. 336– 9 His highest *i·* as seen to-day?
  My. 283–17 a man's highest *i·* of right
His
  Mis. 4– 8 of the universe as His *i·*,
  13–24 that is, of God and His *i·*.
  332–29 supposition is, that God and His *i·*
  Ret. 23–23 were God and His *i·*.
  60–11 C. S. reveals God and His *i·*
  63– 1 God and His *i·* are the only
  Un. 47– 6 is God and His *i·*.
  62–28 and that of His *i·*, man ;
  My. 5– 9 His *i·*, coexistent with Him
  119– 6 His *i·*, image, and likeness.
  239–16 *His i· or image and likeness*
  239–17 His *i·*, image, or likeness, man,
his
  My. 139–11 his *i·* is nearing the Way,
His own
  Mis. 361–29 He elucidates His own *i·*,
immortal
  My. 241–21 * immortal *i·* of the one divine Mind.
incorporeal
  Mis. 164– 1 interprets the incorporeal *i·*,
  166–16 the incorporeal *i·* of God,
  My. 218–11 the incorporeal *i·*, came with the
individualized
  No. 19–16 man is His individualized *i·*.
infant
  Mis. 320–12 infant *i·* of divine perfection
infinite
  Mis. 165– 9 This infinite *i·* of infinity will be,
  No. 25–11 even as the infinite *i·* of Truth
its
  Mis. 104–25 and its *i·* represents Love.
  336–17 and not love its *i·* :
its own
  Mis. 41–20 architect that builds its own *i·*,
man, as the
  My. 239–19 Man, as the *i·* or image
Mind's
  No. 27–16 divine Mind and that Mind's *i·*.
"Mother" of the
  Pul. 63– 4 * "MOTHER" OF THE *I·*
My
  Un. 62–22 My *i·*, never in matter,
new
  Mis. 1–12 the new *i·* that comes welling up
  No. 1–10 when thrilled by a new *i·*,
  '02. 11–10 him who, having a new *i·*
  Hea. 18–14 willingly adopt the new *i·*,
  My. 92– 2 * the new *i·* will never have
of being
  Mis. 166– 2 and spiritual *i·* of being.
  188–10 divine Principle and *i·* of being,
of divine Mind
  No. 24– 1 immeasurable *i·* of divine Mind.
of divine Principle
  No. 4–20 not the *i·* of divine Principle,

idea

offspring and
  Mis. 82–15 Man is the offspring and *i·* of
of God
  (see **God***)*
of infinite Mind
  Mis. 5–26 man is the *i·* of infinite Mind,
  247–22 man is the *i·* of infinite Mind,
of man
  Mis. 62– 1 Holding the *right i·* of man
  166–17 the *i·* of man was not understood.
of matter
  Mis. 75– 2 of Jesus' *i·* of matter.
of sound
  Mis. 46–27 even as the *i·* of sound, in tones,
of Spirit
  Mis. 60–27 every creation or *i·* of Spirit
  No. 16–14 Spirit and the *i·* of Spirit.
of the size
  My. 69–26 * chapter sub-title
  69–27 * an *i·* of the size of this building
of Truth
  Mis. 79–12 man is the eternal *i·* of Truth,
  No. 25–11 even as the infinite *i·* of Truth
  Hea. 3–15 Christ is the *i·* of Truth ;
  10– 4 ready to devour the *i·* of Truth.
  Peo. 8– 2 to present the right *i·* of Truth ;
or likeness
  My. 239–21 *i·* or likeness of the infinite *one*,
  262– 2 *i·*, or likeness of perfection
perfect
  Peo. 2–26 This more perfect *i·*,
perpetual
  Mis. 83– 3 perpetual *i·* of inexhaustible good.
prevails
  My. 329– 4 * The *i·* prevails that the last
Principle and
  Mis. 82– 3 Principle and *i·* of all good.
  104–26 Principle and *i·* are demonstrated,
  182–27 of existence as Principle and *i·*,
  188–15 divine Principle and *i·* of being,
  218–15 Science of Principle and *i·* ;
  361–29 Principle and *i·*, God and man,
  374–16 announce their Principle and *i·*.
  No. 13– 6 Principle and *i·* to be divine.
quite an
  Mis. 375–13 * so got quite an *i·* of
repudiated the
  Mis. 97– 9 repudiated the *i·* of casting out
ridicule the
  My. 97– 5 * physicians, however, ridicule the *i·*
right
  Mis. 62– 1 Holding the *right i·* of man
  Hea. 4–22 gain a right *i·* of the Principle
  Peo. 8– 1 to present the right *i·* of Truth ;
spiritual
  (see **spiritual***)*
that
  Hea. 18–14 if that *i·* could be reconciled
  My. 344–19 harbored that *i·* about a disease,
this
  Mis. 78–27 this *i·* cannot fail to express
  163–30 This *i·* or divine essence was,
  360–30 and this *i·* is understood,
  Ret. 93– 6 Science has elevated this *i·*
  No. 10–24 this *i·* . . . turns like the needle
  Peo. 8– 2 then will this *i·* cast out error
true
  Mis. 101–11 a contest for the true *i·*,
  111–13 higher sense of the true *i·*.
  176–18 the true *i·* of God — the supremacy of
  258–28 only suitable or true *i·* of Him ;
  309–16 Son of God, the true *i·*
  360–27 Jesus, as the true *i·* of Him,
  No. 1–14 silent cultivation of the true *i·*
  10–22 C. S. unveil the true *i·*,
  21–25 the true *i·* of the Christ,
  '00. 6– 9 in the true *i·* of God.
  '02. 7– 9 give man the true *i·* of God
  My. 181–11 through the true *i·* of Life,
Truth's
  Mis. 320– 5 the history of Truth's *i·*,
  321– 8 the steady gain of Truth's *i·*
vast
  Mis. 77–20 In adopting all this vast *i·*

  Mis. 186–20 an *i·* cannot be torn apart from its
  Pul. 71– 4 * The *i·* that C. S. has declined in
  No. 3– 3 the *i·* which claims only its

ideal

affection and
  Mis. 276–23 a purer, higher affection and *i·*.
divine
  (see **divine***)*

ideal

his
Mis. 105–21   the individual and his *i*·
human
'02.   2– 7   this is . . . my human *i*·.
My. 271–12   * chapter sub-title
its
Mis. 217– 8   its *i*· or phenomenon must
its own
Mis. 223–10   that mind reaches its own *i*·,
my
Mis. 293– 1   and carried out my *i*·.
374–21   I never looked on my *i*· of
374–31   my *i*· of an angel is a woman
my only
Mis. 105–20   C. S. is my only *i*· ;
no higher
Mis. 270– 8   mankind hath no higher *i*·
of Christianity
My. 40–25   * the *i*· of Christianity,
of God
Ret. 93–10   *i*· of God is no longer impersonated as
'02. 12– 6   this *i*· of God is *now* and *forever*,
Peo.   5–16   our *i*· of God has risen above
of Love
Hea. 10– 8   presented the highest *i*· of Love.
one's
Mis. 374–27   Pictures are portions of one's *i*·,
perfect
My. 179–21   Christianity as the perfect *i*·.
right
Peo.   5–12   The right *i*· is not buried,
My. 166– 7   so long as we have the right *i*·,
spiritual
(see **spiritual**)
that
Hea.   6–17   whether that *i*· is a flower or
this
Mis. 374–27   this *i*· is not one's personality.
'02. 12– 6   this *i*· of God is *now* and *forever*,
true
Mis. 79–21   true *i*· of immortal man's
104–29   or would not gain the true *i*· of
Un. 62–12   true *i*· of omnipotent and
Peo.   6–18   more spiritual and true *i*· of Deity

Mis. 74–15   immortal sense of the *i*· world.
77–15   to support their *i*· man.
102– 2   stature of Christ, the *i*· man.
166– 7   *i*· Christ — or impersonal infancy,
205–21   in Christian metaphysics the *i*· man
217– 7   *i*· world whose cause is the
235–20   and know something of the *i*· man,
Ret. 68– 7   Even the spiritual idea, or *i*· man.
Un. 62–13   an *i*· . . . wherefor there is no evil.
No. 36–16   while the divine and *i*· Christ was
My. 64–21   * the realization of *i*· manhood
174– 5   proved an *i*· meeting place.
192– 7   The *i*· robe of Christ is seamless.
195–21   no miserable piece of *i*· legerdemain,
262– 3   an *i*· which cannot fall from its

idealism
Mis. 216–23   Was this . . . a happy hit at *i*·,
217– 1   True *i*· is a divine Science,
Pul. 23–11   * wave of *i*· that has swept over
38–27   * phases of *i*· and manifestations of
No. 38– 6   He established the only true *i*·
My.   5–16   spiritual *i*· and realism
205–19   This *i*· connects itself with
272–14   demonstration of this *i*·.
307–31   My *i*·, however, limped,

ideals
Ret. 75–10   Life and its *i*· are inseparable,
Hea.   6–15   I saw how the mind's *i*·
Peo.   3– 1   our *i*· form our characters,
3– 3   crudest *i*· of speculative theology
3– 4   the *i*· of *materia medica*
4–26   grown out of such false *i*·
5–10   The *i*· of primitive Christianity
7– 1   their highest or their lowest *i*·,
7– 2   working out our own *i*·,
7– 5   to rot and ruin the mind's *i*·.

ideas
advanced
Mis. 295–25   most advanced *i*· are inscribed
akin to mine
Un.   9–21   *i*· akin to mine have been held by
and principles
'01. 27– 7   * interpret their *i*· and principles
any
Mis. 306– 6   * any *i*· on that subject
author's
Ret. 76– 1   an author's *i*· and their words.
Christian Science
Pul. 80–21   * the spirit of C. S. *i*· has caused

ideas
conveying
Mis. 133– 5   conveying *i*· more opposite to the
different
Pul. 51–14   * and with them bring different *i*·.
God's
Mis. 164–30   The limited view of God's *i*·
His
Un. 24–19   God and His *i*· — that is,
individualized
Mis. 103–14   individualized *i*·, which dwell
its
Mis. 218–10   immortality of Mind and its *i*·.
language and
Ret. 75– 8   appropriating my language and *i*·,
Mind's
Mis. 23–30   All must be Mind and Mind's *i*· ;
my
Mis. 263–28   to appropriate my *i*· and discovery,
new
'02. 10– 3   uncovers new *i*·, unfolds spiritual
of Deity
Ret. 56– 1   The following *i*· of Deity,
Peo. 12–17   As our *i*· of Deity advance
14– 1   As our *i*· of Deity become more
of divinity
Peo. 14–10   our *i*· of divinity form our models
of God
No. 20–12   fully conveys the *i*· of God,
Peo.   4–16   mysterious *i*· of God and man
of Life
Peo. 14– 7   our *i*· of Life have grown
of primitive Christianity
Pul. 69–15   * the *i*· of primitive Christianity.
patchwork
No.   3– 1   not spread abroad patchwork *i*·
pre-Christian
Pul. 66–25   * pre-Christian *i*· of the Asiatics
spiritual
Mis. 82– 1   the mind with spiritual *i*·,
307– 1   gives you His spiritual *i*·,
'00.   3–17   the pioneer of spiritual *i*·,
these
Pul. 80–29   * all these *i*· are Christian.
true
Mis. 294–28   with the true *i*· of humanity
your
My. 324– 6   * you and your *i*· were too much alike

'01. 21– 9   * *i*· about the spiritual world

identical
Mis.   9– 9   *i*· with "Thou hast no enemies."
66–15   sin is *i*· with suffering,
296–16   they are by no means *i*·
375–21   * an almost *i*· resemblance,
Ret. 93–19   in substance *i*· with my own :
Un. 33– 2   which prove matter to be *i*·
33–13   not the Mind that is *i*· with **Truth**.
46–23   equally *i*· and self-conscious
No. 26– 1   believe that mortal man is *i*· with
26– 6   no more *i*· with C. S. than
26– 7   than the babe is *i*· with the **adult**,
'02. 16– 4   pointed out that *i*· phrase,
My. 78– 3   * six services, *i*· in character,
80–17   * introductory services were *i*·,
86–29   * At each of the *i*· services,

identification
Mis. 363– 7   its greatest flatterer, *i*·,
Un. 64–18   nor escape from *i*· with

identified
Mis. 375–29   * *i*· with the old masters,
Pul. 46–14   * *i*· with good and great names
My. 239–24   a kind of man who is *i*· by **sex**
323– 8   * so *i*· yourself with the truth

identifies
Mis. 14–32   *i*· himself with it,
My. 107–19   it *i*· this system with mind,
165–17   *i*· man with universal good.

identify
My. 119–19   could not *i*· Christ spiritually,

identities
Mis. 60–25   *as many i· as mortal bodies?*

identity
Mis. 42– 4   nor does he lose his *i*·,
47–23   substantiates man's *i*·,
60–24   *connection between them and real i·*,
185–10   spiritual *i*· as the child of God,
205–17   man's *i*· or consciousness
362– 7   form, individuality, *i*·.
364–16   constituting and governing all *i*·,
Un. 34–23   so-called mind would have no *i*·.
46–14   In his *i*· there is no evil.
Pul. 23–13   * common *i*· of spiritual demand.

identity

No.	21–11	all phenomena, *i·*, individuality,
	25–22	is not man's eternal *i·*
'01.	6– 3	and have no separate *i·*
My.	239–15	*and see their apparent i·*
	239–23	real and eternal in infinite *i·*.

idiocy

Mis.	107–25	this . . . mental state is moral *i·*.
	112–15	in extreme cases, moral *i·*.
	112–17	mental state called moral *i·*.
	113–23	insanity, dementia, or moral *i·*.
My.	249–10	Hate is a moral *i·*

idiot

Mis.	222–11	in other words, a moral *i·*.
	354– 4	moral *i·*, sanguine of success in

idle

Mis.	357– 2	no time for *i·* words,
Man.	81–23	No *i·* gossip, no slander,
Pul.	67– 6	* This is no *i·* word,
My.	74–23	* would be *i·* to attempt to

idleness

Mis.	206–12	*i·* is the foe of progress.
	230–17	They spend no time in sheer *i·*,
Man.	60–10	Amusement or *i·* is weariness.
'00.	8–16	mental *i·* or apathy is

idler

'00.	2–10	the *i·*, and the intermediate.
	2–16	*i·* earns little and is stingy ;

idlers

'00.	2–21	your *i·* are my busiest workers ;

idol (*see also* idol's)

Mis.	28–23	does not signify a graven *i·*,
'00.	3–10	One's *i·* is by no means his servant,

idolaters

Mis.	324–14	adulterers, fornicators, *i·* ;
Peo.	9–12	we shall not be *i·*,

idolatrous

Un.	31–11	*first i·* claim of sin is,
	38–17	This *i·* and false sense of life
'00.	13– 7	orgies of their *i·* feasts
Peo.	4–28	materialistic and *i·* theory
My.	151–30	discerned its *i·* tendencies,

idolatry

Mis.	45–27	This error of belief is *i·*,
	123– 6	it is the spirit of *i·*,
	174– 4	*i·*, having other gods ;
	196– 4	*I·*, the supposition of the
	307–22	*I·* is an easily-besetting sin
	346–14	This belief is a species of *i·*,
No.	20–20	common *i·* of man-worship.
	35–17	because of the shocking human *i·*
'00.	3–25	sanctioned *i·*, — other gods.
	5– 4	leaves no opportunity for *i·*
	5–18	escape from *i·* of every kind,
	13–23	Æsculapius, *i·* and medicine.
Pan.	7–24	sequence of this error is *i·*
	8–16	*i·*, pantheism, and polytheism.
Peo.	4– 3	*I·* sprang from the belief
Po.	9– 2	Turned to his star of *i·*.
My.	151–29	was *i·* then and is *i·* now.
	152– 2	turned to another form of *i·*,
	220–16	I pray . . . for the end of *i·*
	248–18	No fatal circumstance of *i·*
	303–18	no *i·*, no human propaganda

idolizing

Mis.	123– 5	it is either *i·* something

idol's

My.	192– 1	Ye sit not in the *i·* temple.

idols

Mis.	307–24	keep yourselves from *i·*.'' — *I John* 5 : 21.
	394–13	No place for earth's *i·*,
Po.	45–17	No place for earth's *i·*,

ignoble

'02.	18–25	*i·* conduct of his disciples

ignorance

and charlatanism
Hea.	14–14	*i·* and charlatanism are miserable

and pride
Mis.	92–27	arrogant *i·* and pride,
	354–21	self-conceit, *i·*, and pride

and quackery
No.	19– 6	infidelity, *i·*, and quackery

and self-conceit
Mis.	78–17	*et cetera* of *i·* and self-conceit

and superstition
'02.	9–30	counteracts *i·* and superstition?

and vice
Mis.	81–28	the depths of *i·* and vice.

cave of
Mis.	370–8	tradition and the cave of *i·*.

ignorance

common
Mis.	365–28	held back by the common *i·*
No.	11–12	held back by the common *i·*

culpable
Mis.	115– 5	culpable *i·* of the workings
	283–17	mistaken kindness, a culpable *i·*,

fatal
Ret.	71–23	false convictions and a fatal *i·*.

helpless
Mis.	115–11	helpless *i·* of the community

his
Mis.	53–19	his *i·* of the meaning of the term
	367–30	His *i·* of that which is not,
No.	18–17	child, in his *i·*, may imagine
	44– 1	substantiates his *i·* of its

malice or
Mis.	353–12	through malice or *i·*.

manifested in
My.	245–14	manifested in *i·*, persecution,

man's
Ret.	61– 1	from mortal man's *i·*,

mortal
My.	162– 1	for mortal *i·* and need

mortals'
Mis.	108–16	would remove mortals' *i·*

of American society
Mis.	296– 6	Was it *i·* of American society

of Christian Science
'01.	21–17	a startling *i·* of C. S.,
My.	104–20	A person's *i·* of C. S.
	151– 4	sympathize with their *i·* of C. S. :

of Life
Un.	40–22	comes through our *i·* of Life,

of Science
Ret.	60–16	asks, in its *i·* of Science,

of self
My.	233–19	*I·* of self is the most stubborn

of sin
Un.	6–19	blindness to error and *i·* of sin.

of the cause
Mis.	66–29	*I·* of the cause of disease

or envy
Mis.	383– 8	preeminent over *i·* or envy,

or fanaticism
Mis.	48– 9	whether of *i·* or fanaticism,

present
No.	2–26	present *i·* in relation to C. S.

pride is
Mis.	2– 3	Pride is *i·* ;

sheer
No.	43–26	through the sheer *i·* of people,

spiritual
Mis.	298–10	spiritual *i·* and power of passion,

their
Mis.	171–28	their *i·* or false knowledge
My.	151– 4	sympathize with their *i·* of C. S. :

this
Un.	40–24	is the punishment of this *i·*.

torrents of
My.	316–20	the foaming torrents of *i·*,

Mis.	40–31	*i·* by which one unintentionally
	109–16	*I·* is only blest by reason of its
	109–18	*I·* was the first condition of sin in the
	293–19	brings greater torment than *i·*.
	374–12	*i·*, envy, and hatred
My.	108–20	*I·*, slang, and malice touch not

ignorant

Mis.	51– 8	the *i·*, the fraudulent, or the
	134– 1	and the sinful and *i·* who
	295–23	Nor is the world *i·* of the
	300– 8	it is an *i·* wrong.
	335–20	its supposed power, or *i·* of it.
	363–28	the *i·* man's dictionary,
	365– 8	and is *i·* thereof.
	367–15	to claim that He is *i·* of
Ret.	54–19	this same channel of *i·* belief.
	70– 3	*I·* of the origin and operations
	70– 4	that is, *i·* of itself,
	71– 7	an *i·* or an unprincipled mind-practice
	74– 3	He who does this is *i·* of the
Un.	49– 9	as *i·* of sin as is the perfect
No.	28– 8	Of his intermediate . . . I am *i·*.
Peo.	11–20	but *i·* of the law of belief,
My.	211– 4	they are too cowardly, too *i·*,
	224–22	to those *i·* of this Science
	305–12	* referred to as ''an *i·* woman
	309– 1	* characterizes as ''*i·*, dominating,
	313–11	various stories . . . I am *i·* of.

ignorantly

Mis.	87– 4	*i·* to caricature God's creation,
	261–10	whether intentionally or *i·* ;
Ret.	26–14	uninspired interpreters *i·* pronounce

ignorantly
No. 32–12 *i·* or maliciously misconstrued.
'02. 18– 6 mortals looked *i·*, as now,
Hea. 6–14 produces the manifestations *i·*
My. 146–28 do it *i·* or maliciously.
153–21 therefore ye *i·* worship.'' — *Acts* 17 : 23.

ignore
Pul. 79– 9 * not to *i·* a movement which,
Hea. 5–18 hypotheses *i·* Biblical authority,
My. 99–27 * *i·* them as we may

ignores
My. 153–19 *i·* the power of God,

Ill. (State)
(*see* **Bloomington, Chicago, Peoria**)

ill
Mis. 48– 2 avoid all that works *i·*.
190–23 evil, or whatever worketh *i·*.
225–14 was taken violently *i·*.
265–25 If others, . . . do *i·*,
389–17 No *i·*, — since God is good,
Ret. 61– 7 as when you awaken . . . and feel *i·*,
95– 9 * For heavy is the weight of *i·*
Un. 51–11 whose place is *i·* supplied by
Rud. 10–24 and make you *i·*, is an error
Po. 4–16 No *i·*, — since God is good,
25–19 Wreaths for the triumphs o'er *i·* !
My. 275–12 chapter sub-title
313–15 to help me when I was *i·*.
325– 4 * (he had been *i·*)
348–31 nothing that worketh *i·* can enter

ill-attuned
Mis. 287– 8 To an *i·* ear, discord is harmony ;

ill-concealed
Ret. 75– 2 *i·* question in mortal mind,

ill-done
Mis. 393– 9 Work *i·* within the misty Mine of
Po. 51–14 Work *i·* within the misty Mine of

illegal
Man. 46– 1 *I·* Adoption.

illegitimate
My. 167–28 marred by the *i·* claims of envy,

ill-humor
Mis. 313–14 without *i·* or hyperbolic tumor.

ill-humored
Mis. 116–27 never off guard, never *i·*,

illiberal
My. 167–30 day of heathenism, *i·* views,

illimitable
Pul. 4–24 Wait patiently on *i·* Love,
My. 41–30 * to understand how *i·* is the Love
107–28 nothing beyond *i·* divinity.

illness
Man. 49–25 without previous injury or *i·*,
Ret. 7– 3 after a short *i·*,
My. 307–29 might have caused my *i·*.
331–30 * during his late *i·*,
333–23 * attended him during his *i·*
335–11 * facts regarding . . . his *i·* and
335–23 * third day of her husband's *i·*,
336–16 * no will previous to his last *i·*,

illogical
'01. 3–27 therefore it is *i·* and
My. 111–10 swept away their *i·* syllogisms
225–24 by no *i·* conclusion,

ills
Mis. 22–15 of transmitting human *i·*,
33–27 * ''the *i·* that flesh is heir to,''
37–18 Its antidote for all *i·* is God,
209–18 *i·* of indigestion tend to rebuke
334–27 remedies the *i·* of material beliefs.
Ret. 34–14 all the *i·* which befall mortals.
Un. 48–10 He heals all my *i·*,
Rud. 3– 3 to heal them of bodily *i·*,
10–12 Mortal *i·* are but errors of thought,
No. 42–10 * ''the *i·* that flesh is heir to.''
'01. 24– 7 the cause of all the *i·* of mortals
Hea. 15– 5 all *i·* that flesh is heir to.
My. 81–18 * debts of gratitude for *i·* cured,
99– 4 * above the suffering of petty *i·* ;
166–15 Life's *i·* are its chief recompense ;
268–21 solace the sore *i·* of mankind

ill-starred
Pul. 48–29 * hero who killed the *i·* Paugus.

ill-success
Rud. 14–23 *i·* of itself leaves them unprepared

illumed
Mis. 396–23 angel throng Of thoughts, *i·*
Pul. 18– 7 angel throng Of thoughts, *i·*
Po. 12– 7 angel throng Of thoughts, *i·*

illumes
Mis. 20– 1 *i·* our pathway with the radiance

illuminated
Mis. 75–26 It was evidently an *i·* sense
Ret. 23–16 character of the Christ was *i·*
Pul. 25–27 * *i·* texts from the Bible
My. 258– 6 seems *i·* for woman's hope

illuminates
Pul. 25–18 * seven-pointed star, which *i·* it.

illumination
Mis. 234–30 Christ is clad with a richer *i·*
290–17 * it produced a wonderful *i·*,
342–16 no spiritual *i·* to look upon him
Pul. 34–11 * became aware of a divine *i·*
Rud. 11–22 *i·* of spiritual understanding,
'00. 13– 9 their so-called prophetic *i·*.

illumine
Mis. 276–17 light will *i·* the darkness.
356– 3 *i·* its own atmosphere
Un. 41–16 can *i·* our present being
My. 187– 7 *i·* your faith and understanding,
197–17 *i·* the midnight of the latter,

illumined
Mis. 213–15 chastened and *i·* another's **way**
338– 9 Faith *i·* by works ;
Ret. 10–14 Learning was so *i·*,

illumines
Mis. 117–28 and He *i·* one's way
196–18 *i·* our present existence with
Po. 32–11 *i·* my spiritual eye,

illusion
and delusion
My. 5– 7 this *i·* and delusion of sense,
and error
Mis. 68–17 *i·* and error which Truth casts out.
declare an
Un. 25–14 this lie I declare an *i·*.
delusion and
Pan. 5–19 liar and lie, a delusion and *i·*.
effects of
My. 301–22 baneful effects of *i·* on mortal
evil is
'00. 10– 4 Evil is *i·*, that after a fight
growth of
Mis. 83– 8 ''*Sickness is a growth of i·*,
its own
Mis. 259–27 must have produced its own *i·*,
mere
Ret. 32–14 * What is life? A mere *i·*,
mortal sense is
Mis. 24–22 gained from mortal sense is *i·*,
of matter
Mis. 28–19 he arose above the *i·* of matter.
of mortals
Mis. 50– 2 error is an *i·* of mortals ;
of sin
Ret. 62– 4 *i·* of sin, sickness, and death
of the senses
Mis. 368– 5 dispel this *i·* of the senses,
of time
Mis. 93–13 *i·* of time and mortality.
sick man's
Mis. 70– 4 cast out the sick man's *i·*,
termed sin
Ret. 64–20 in belief an *i·* termed sin,
that death
Un. 59–23 *i·* that death is as real as Life.
undisturbed in the
Ret. 23– 2 undisturbed in the *i·* that this
which calls
Un. 59–20 *i·* which calls sin real,
59–22 *i·* which calls sickness real,

Mis. 36–27 Mortal mind is an *i·* ;
70– 1 must have been an *i·*,
123– 3 Evil was, and is, the *i·* of
Ret. 64–27 in order that the *i·*, error,
Un. 34– 9 material sight is an *i·*, a lie.
'01. 13– 7 a lie from the beginning, — an *i·*,
14–14 We regard evil as a lie, an *i·*,
Hea. 10– 1 he saw it pass away, — an *i·*.

illusions
Mis. 8– 1 is given to material *i·*
24–31 all subtle falsities or *i·*,
68–10 * maintained that . . . are not *i·*
68–11 * to believe they are *i·*.
68–13 pain and sickness are . . . *i·*.
112– 5 look the *i·* in the face.
Ret. 64–22 classify sin, . . . and death as *i·*.
Un. 59–19 to rescue men from these very *i·*
Rud. 11–12 *i·* of the physical senses,
11–13 *i·* are not real, but **unreal**.

illusions
No. 23–21 not as realities, but as *i* ;
My. 278–20 civilization destroys such *i*

illusive
Mis. 206–14 no emasculation, no *i* vision,
Ret. 64–26 *i* forms, methods, and subtlety of
Un. 8–13 That which is not so is *i*
  37–19 physical personality is *i* and
No. 6– 1 If disease is real it is not *i*,
Pan. 6– 6 *i* claim that God is not supreme,
Hea. 19–10 The *i* origin of disease is not

illustrate
Mis. 199–14 *i* the life of Jesus
  203–17 to rebuke the senses and *i* C. S.
  216–23 to *i* the author's following point
  218–27 What can *i* Dr. ——'s views better
  286–12 serve to *i* the superiority of
  286–23 *i* mortal mind and body as *one*,
  292–12 partly *i* the divine energy
  322–13 Life these give, the Truth they *i*,
  341–21 serves to *i* the evil of inaction
  373– 1 *i* the simple nature of art.
Ret. 21–26 unless they *i* the ethics of Truth.
No. 32–23 To *i* : It seems a great evil to
'01. 3–24 last proposition does not *i* the
My. 176– 7 *i* the past by your present love.
  221–11 and *i* the Science of Mind.
  308–19 To *i* : One time when my father
  349–18 *i* "the way, the truth, — *John* 14 : 6.

illustrated
Mis. 30–16 Way-shower *i* Life unconfined,
  33– 1 comments on my *i* poem,
  260– 1 *i* by the life of Jesus
  346– 5 God is understood and *i*.
  371–27 An *I* Poem
Man. 111–15 instructions *i* in Form 1
Ret. 94–26 affection *i* in Jesus' career,
'01. 19–10 he *i* his saying by a parable.
Hea. 8–24 Jesus *i* this by the parable of the
My. 40–26 * She has *i* what the poet perceived
  347–11 *i* by Keats' touching couplet,

illustrates
Mis. 201–32 *i* through the flesh the divine
  337–11 Listen, and he *i* the rule :
Man 47–16 *i* the demonstration of Christ,
'02. 8– 2 *i* God, and man as His likeness,
My. 179–22 *i* the Principle and practice of a
  230– 5 *i* the digestion of spiritual nutriment
  339–16 *i* the joy, grace, and glory of

illustrating
Mis. 374–22 one *i* my poem approximates it.

illustration
Mis. 375–20 * study each *i* thoroughly,
Ret. 6– 5 * living *i* of Christian faith.
No. 34–14 torture affords but a slight *i* of
My. 107– 6 As a pertinent *i* of the

illustrations
Mis. 33– 7 *i* in "Christ and Christmas ;"
  307–25 *i* were not intended for a
  309–27 My Christmas poem and its *i*
  371–28 This poem and its *i*
  372–16 * *i* of your poem are truly
  375– 9 *i* of "Christ and Christmas" :
  375–17 * impressed me in your *i*

illustrative
Pul. 60–10 * with *i* Scripture parallels,
My. 69– 8 * inscriptions *i* of the faith of
  311– 2 as *i* of my disposition :

illustrious
'00. 12– 8 records Ephesus as an *i* city,
Po. 27–24 *I* year, farewell !
My. 85–21 * *i* list for future generations to
  294–26 religious energy of this *i* pontiff

image
and likeness
Mis. 21–21 man is His *i* and likeness.
  23–23 man is His *i* and likeness.
  47–21 His *i* and likeness, is spiritual,
  61–21 man is the *i* and likeness of God.
  79–21 God's *i* and likeness,
  82–18 *i* and likeness of infinite Life,
  97–22 in the *i* and likeness of God.
  97–23 *i* and likeness of Mind,
  97–24 *i* and likeness of Mind
  97–27 *i* and likeness of the infinite.
  182–20 ever was the *i* and likeness of God,
  183–12 Man is God's *i* and likeness ;
  185–14 demonstrating the true *i* and likeness.
  186– 3 in His own *i* and likeness.
  186– 8 in the *i* and likeness of God ;
  235– 5 as *i* and likeness, to reflect Him
  308–30 in the *i* and likeness of God.

image
and likeness
Mis. 330–17 in God's own *i* and likeness,
  368– 1 in his own *i* and likeness.
Man. 15– 9 man in God's *i* and likeness.
Ret. 59–24 made in His own *i* and likeness ;
  64– 8 "*i* and likeness." — *see Gen.* 1 : 26.
  67–20 was the *i* and likeness of evil,
  70–25 "*i* and likeness," — *see Gen.* 1 : 26.
Un. 3–17 in the *i* and likeness of good,
  62– 6 forever His *i* and likeness.
No. 17–11 God's *i* and likeness can never
  19–22 man is in His *i* and likeness.
  23–28 is God's own *i* and likeness,
  25–17 is the *i* and likeness of God,
  26–20 to be His *i* and likeness ;
'00. 5–16 man in His *i* and likeness,
'01. 5–21 man is His *i* and likeness :
  5–27 is His eternal *i* and likeness.
  7–10 in His own *i* and likeness,
  8–17 Then is man His *i* and likeness,
'02. 6–21 the *i* and likeness of divine Love.
Hea. 9–17 man, His own *i* and likeness.
  17– 5 present the *i* and likeness of God.
Peo. 14–18 man in God's own *i* and likeness,
My. 15–14 into His own *i* and likeness.
  36–24 * in the *i* and likeness of God.
  117–21 of man in His *i* and likeness,
  119– 6 His idea, *i*, and likeness.
  119–31 the true *i* and likeness of God.
  150–19 to become His own *i* and likeness,
  235–23 Man is but His *i* and likeness.
  239–16 by His idea or *i* and likeness
  239–20 *i* and likeness of the infinite God,
  244–16 in God's own *i* and likeness,
  261–15 man in His *i* and likeness.
  272–12 that is, God's *i* and likeness ;
  273–30 man in God's *i* and likeness.
  287–17 still rise to His *i* and likeness,
  319– 3 real man in His *i* and likeness."
  347– 4 man in the *i* and likeness of the

child and
Un. 15–10 Man is God's child and *i*.
express
Mis. 26–25 phrase, "express *i*," — *Heb.* 1 : 3.
God's
Mis. 79–21 and never can be, God's *i*
  183–12 Man is God's *i* and likeness ;
  189–13 man as God's *i*, or
Man. 15– 9 man in God's *i* and likeness.
Ret. 64– 8 even God's "*i* and — *see Gen.* 1 : 26.
No. 17–11 God's *i* and likeness can never
My. 5– 9 to reveal man as God's *i*,
  272–12 that is, God's *i* and likeness ;
  273–30 does not awaken man in God's *i*

graven
Mis. 346–14 *i* graven on wood or stone
His
Mis. 21–21 man is His *i* and likeness.
  23–23 man is His *i* and likeness.
  47–21 His *i* and likeness, is spiritual,
Un. 62– 6 forever His *i* and likeness.
Pul. 30–18 * man is made in His *i*.
No. 19–22 man is in His *i* and likeness.
  26–20 to be His *i* and likeness ;
'00. 5–16 man in His *i* and likeness,
'01. 5–21 man is His *i* and likeness :
  8–17 Then is man His *i* and likeness,
My. 117–21 man in His *i* and likeness,
  170–17 His *i* and superscription.
  235–23 Man is but His *i* and likeness.
  261–15 man in His *i* and likeness.
  287–17 rise to His *i* and likeness,
  319– 3 real man in His *i* and likeness."

His own
My. 262– 1 perfect and eternal in His own *i*.
is the reflection
My. 239–22 whose *i* is the reflection of all
likeness and
Mis. 16–13 being His likeness and *i*,
lost
Mis. 97–30 the lost *i* is not this personality,
  97–31 corporeal man is this lost *i* ;
Pan. 11–25 obliterates the lost *i* that
man in the
Mis. 294– 1 man in the *i* of his Maker ;
  308–30 man in the *i* and likeness of God.
My. 347– 4 man in the *i* and likeness of
man is the
Mis. 61–21 man is the *i* and likeness of God.
No. 25–17 Man is the *i* and likeness of God,
My. 262– 2 Hence man is the *i*, idea, or
marred
Un. 15–11 is incomplete, the *i* marred.
Mind's
Un. 14–24 reflected in man, Mind's *i*.

image
molten
Peo.   2–23   no longer . . . a molten *i·*,
no inverted
No.   17–18   therein is no inverted *i·* of God,
of God
    (*see* **God**)
of Him
Pan.   11– 6   after the *i·* of Him that — *Col.* 3 : 10.
of his Maker
Mis.   98– 5   which is the *i·* of his Maker.
   294– 1   man in the *i·* of his Maker ;
of Spirit
Rud.   5– 8   made in the *i·* of Spirit, or God.
'01.   8–20   The reflex *i·* of Spirit is not unlike
of their Father
Mis. 278–18   reflect the *i·* of their Father.
of the soul
Po.   23– 8   An *i·* of the soul,
opposite
Mis.   62– 3   opposite *i·* of man, a sinner,
or likeness
My. 239–17   His idea, *i·*, or likeness,
   269– 2   *i·* or likeness, called man,
our
Mis.   69–11   make man in our *i·*, — *Gen.* 1 : 26.
spiritual
Rud.   13– 9   divine and spiritual *i·* of God.

Mis.   15–24   the *i·* of the infinite good

imagery
Mis. 142–20   *i·* of thought gave place to
Pan.   2–26   Pan in *i·* is preferable to

images
Mis.   96–29   not the transference of human *i·*
   335– 2   shall you turn . . . to graven *i·*?
Ret.   79– 6   false *i·* are effaced from
Un.   34– 5   it sees only material *i·*,
Peo.   10–22   the *i·* that thought reflects
My. 109–21   reflex *i·* of this divine Life,

imaginary
Mis.   65– 5   and her motions *i·*.
   129– 8   an *i·* or an actual wrong,
   268– 6   *i·* victories of rivalry
Un.   38–13   another power, an *i·* life,
   45–20   *i·* sphere of its own creation
Hea.   13–19   we resigned the *i·* medicine
Peo.   12– 8   *i·* laws of matter
My. 106–12   limited to *i·* diseases !
   118– 5   any *i·* benefit they receive

imagination
Mis.   xi–17   be found to surpass *i·*,
   86–10   *exist only in i·?*
   86–24   It is more than *i·*.
   203–13   served the *i·* for centuries.
Ret.   70–12   chimerical wings to his *i·*,
Pul.   32–11   * fascinated the *i·*.
No.   4– 6   Disease is more than *i·*;
   20– 4   human reason, *i·*, and
My.   29–22   * appealed to and fired the *i·*.
   206– 8   Schisms, *i·*, and human beliefs

imaginations
Mis. 139–12   *casting down i·*, — II Cor. 10 : 5.

imagine
Mis.   87–30   *i·* they can help anybody
   280–14   we *i·* all is well if
Pul.   2–16   *I·* yourselves in a poorly
No.   18–17   may *i·* the face of Dante
My.   26–11   *i·* my gratitude and emotion
   103–16   *i·* a vain thing?" — Psal. 2 : 1.
   200– 5   *i·* a vain thing;" — Psal. 2 : 1.
   270–14   rage and *i·* a vain thing.

imagined
My. 303–10   and not *i·* to be unscientific

imagining
My.   59–32   * marvellous beyond all *i·*

imbecile
'01.   16–10   hatred gone mad becomes *i·*

imbedded
Pul.   63–25   * a tablet *i·* in its wall

imbibe
Mis. 303–18   *i·* the spirit of Christ's
My. 239– 8   *i·* the spirit and prove the

imbued
Mis.   4– 1   Thought *i·* with purity,
   194–24   and become *i·* with divine Love
   260–28   Mind, *i·* with this Science
Ret.   47–16   richly *i·* with the spirit of Christ,
Rud.   9–24   be *i·* with a clear conviction
'01.   30– 8   consciousness which is most *i·*
Hea.   11–26   requires mind *i·* with Truth

imbued
Peo.   12–15   when *i·* with the spiritual truth
My.   87–26   * it is certainly *i·* with the spirit
   153–13   *i·* and associated with no intrinsic

imitate
Un.   16– 2   which he is bidden to *i·*.
My. 310–28   for her other children to *i·*,

imitative
Mis. 106–31   organ, in *i·* tones

immaculate
Mis. 337– 9   *i·* Son of the Blessed
'01.   8–26   Jesus, the only *i·*, was born of
'02.   18– 5   the pure sense of the *i·* Jesus

immanent
Ret.   35–21   claim too *i·* to fall to the

Immanuel
Mis. 103–27   individuality that reflected the *I·*,
   374– 1   was so great a proof of *I·*

immaterial
No.   12–26   *i·*, though still individual.

immature
Mis.   87– 6   our *i·* sense of spiritual things,
   263–25   hampered by *i·* demonstrations,

immeasurable
Mis. 369– 8   surveying the *i·* universe of Mind,
No.   24– 1   *i·* idea of divine Mind.
Hea.   16–12   *i·* Life and Love will occupy your

immeasurably
Ret.   31– 6   *i·* paramount to rubric and dogma

immediate
Mis.   24– 8   it wrought my *i·* recovery from
   29– 5   only to his *i·* disciples,
   44– 7   *necessity for i· relief,*
   146–16   will give them *i·* attention,
   148–15   *i·* demand for them as a help
   257–16   and lead to *i·* or ultimate death.
   380–19   save the *i·* recovery of the sick,
Man.   3–12   *i·* demand for them as a help
   51–18   provides for *i·* action.
   78–19   Church bills of *i·* necessity
Ret.   24–12   My *i·* recovery from the effects of
   91–16   spake primarily to his *i·* disciples.
My. 113– 8   follower but not an *i·* disciple
   224–13   Avoid for the *i·* present
   343–12   * Mrs. Eddy's *i·* successor

immediately
Mis. 134– 4   an act which you have *i·* repeated,
   215–21   would fall *i·* if he knew where he
   379– 5   He *i·* presented them.
Man.   28–19   shall *i·* call a meeting
   52–17   the Clerk . . . shall *i·* so inform him.
   53– 4   duty of the Board of Directors *i·* to
   54–22   said member shall *i·* be disciplined,
   68– 1   shall *i·* notify a person who
   69–16   the Board shall *i·* appoint a proper
   69–17   the appointee shall go *i·*
   89– 5   a meeting of . . . shall *i·* be called,
   98– 9   Committee shall *i·* apply for aid to
   100–14   duty of the Directors *i·* to act
Ret.   44–27   was *i·* followed by a great revival of
   52–14   This was *i·* done,
Rud.   15– 4   to *i·* enter upon its practice.
'01.   19– 9   and if not *i·*, continue to ask,
My.   8–15   * something done, and done *i·*,
   22–28   * to get *i·* into the proper
   81– 1   * *i·* struck with the air of
   105–24   On seeing her *i·* restored by
   105–27   he urged me *i·* to write a book
   152– 1   *i·* turned to another form of
   340–17   courts *i·* annulling such bills
   360– 2   Answer this letter *i·*.

immense
Mis.   98–21   This purpose is *i·*,
   223–25   There is *i·* wisdom in the
Un.   43–10   time and *i·* spiritual growth.
Pul.   63– 5   * SHE HAS AN *I·* FOLLOWING
My.   28–15   * has been of *i·* value to them.
   61–30   * in such an *i·* undertaking,
   91– 1   * *i·* membership of the body

immersion
Mis. 205–13   *i·* of human consciousness

imminent
Mis. 113–10   Revelator's vision, . . . is *i·*.
My. 223–27   The hour is *i·*.
   266– 3   *i·* dangers confronting

immobility
No.   10–21   feasibility and *i·* of C. S.

immoral
Mis. 257– 8   a moral or an *i·* force.
   257–11   *i·* force of erring mortal mind,

immoralist
  Mis. 241–10 give to the *i·* a mental dose

immorality
  Mis. 249–22 expelled from my College for *i·*,
       296–18 antagonistic . . . to all *i·*,
  Pan. 10–21 tobacco using, and *i·*, which,

immortal
  and mortal
    Mis. 34–26 *i·* and mortal are . . . opposites
  attributes
    Mis. 1–18 heightens *i·* attributes
  basis
    Hea. 1– 9 builds on less than an *i·* basis,
  being
    Mis. 213– 1 could not behold his *i·* being
    Un. 57–26 forward the birth of *i·* being ;
    No. 27–28 the definition of *i·* being ;
    '02. 16–20 man's *i·* being.
  courage
    My. 191–24 *I·* courage fills the human breast
  cravings
    Mis. 287–13 can satisfy *i·* cravings.
    My. 189–20 satisfies the *i·* cravings
  demands
    Mis. 201– 2 the *i·* demands of Truth.
  facts
    Mis. 14– 4 take in only the *i·* facts
  fruition
    My. 19–21 *i·* fruition of her unselfed love,
  fruits
    My. 182–14 *i·* fruits through God's blessing
  good
    Mis. 82–29 Immortal Mind is God, *i·* good ;
  goodness is
    Mis. 70–17 too good to die ; for goodness is *i·*.
  harmonious and
    Mis. 308– 3 be found harmonious and *i·*.
  harmony
    Mis. 97– 4 *i·* harmony, — the grand verities of
  hour
    My. 257–19 At this *i·* hour, all human hate,
  idea
    My. 241–20 * *i·* idea of the one divine Mind.
  immutable and
    Mis. 79–19 in Science are immutable and *i·*.
  lexicographer
    Mis. 226–13 Shakespeare, the *i·* lexicographer
  Life
    Mis. 56–12 direct opposite of *i·* Life,
  life
    Mis. 170– 2 resurrection and life *i·*
    Pul. 23–24 * intimations of man's *i·* life.
  Love
    Mis. 292–18 unlike the risen, *i·* Love ;
  man
    (*see* **man**)
  man is
    Mis. 34–22 Man is *i·*,
       61–25 A mortal ; but man is *i·*.
       89–24 Man is *i·*.
  Mind
    (*see* **Mind**)
  Mind is
    (*see* **Mind**)
  mode
    No. 25–16 an *i·* mode of the divine Mind.
  model
    My. 261–14 in unfolding the *i·* model,
  modes
    Mis. 363–11 *i·* modes of Mind are spiritual,
  parapets
    Mis. 383–11 the *i·* parapets of this Science.
  part
    No. 29–14 the *i·* part of man a sinner?
  power
    Po. 31–17 solemn splendor of *i·* power,
  Principle
    Mis. 117– 2 Life that unfolds its *i·* Principle.
  saying
    Mis. 76– 7 but this *i·* saying can never
  Science
    Mis. 73– 7 testimony of *i·* Science
  sense
    Mis. 74–15 *i·* sense of the ideal world.
    Un. 52–13 Christ's *i·* sense of Truth,
  Soul
    Un. 51– 4 false . . . that *i·* Soul is sinful,
    No. 11– 3 Man has an *i·* Soul,
       29– 4 Immortal man has *i·* Soul
  Soul is
    '01. 13–26 Soul is *i·*, but sin is mortal.
    My. 273–25 body is mortal, but Soul is *i·* ;
  souls
    Mis. 76–12 belief . . . they contain *i·* souls !

immortal
  Spirit, and
    Mis. 201–15 which is of Spirit, and *i·*.
  status
    Un. 39–21 declare the *i·* status of man,
  strains
    Mis. 345– 5 in *i·* strains of eloquence.
  superstructure
    Hea. 11– 9 The only *i·* superstructure
  teaching
    Ret. 91–22 his *i·* teaching was the bread of
  Truth
    Mis. 21–18 Spirit is *i·* Truth ;
    Ret. 94–16 *i·* Truth be found true,
    No. 40– 6 sense of spiritual and *i·* Truth.
    Po. 70–17 *I·* Truth, — since heaven rang,
  truths
    My. vii– 8 * *i·* truths testified to by Jesus
       203–25 buried *i·* truths in the bosom of
  words
    Mis. 100– 2 *i·* words were articulated
    My. 146–16 his *i·* words and my poor prophecy,
       277–19 *i·* words and deeds of men
  work
    Mis. 237–27 *i·* work, of loosing the fetters

    Mis. 2–28 and into good that is *i·* ;
       24–21 Mind and man are *i·* ;
       36– 5 or the Mind which is *i·*."
       42–25 good, not evil, lives and is *i·*,
       65–14 God's universe and man are *i·*.
       72–28 Mind is not mortal, it is *i·*.
       76–14 to escape and be *i·*.
       79–21 ideal of *i·* man's divine Principle.
      111–20 prove its power to be *i·*.
      186–27 *i·* and true sense of being.
      190– 7 the mortal evolves not the *i·*,
      257– 9 force of *i·* and divine Mind.
      325– 8 few cravings for the *i·*,
    Ret. 59–20 as harmonious, *i·*, and spiritual :
      59–23 Science defines man as *i·*,
    Un. 30–18 man as *i·* instead of mortal
      37–18 physically mortal, but spiritually *i·*.
      37–20 spiritual individuality is *i·*.
      42–13 Man, . . . is as perfect and *i·* now,
      42–27 mortal does not develop the *i·*,
      52– 1 Hence Soul is sinless and *i·*,
      52– 3 supposition that . . . *i·* sinners.
      53–24 *i·* and unerring Mind, God,
      61– 6 to *i·* and spiritual vision he
    Pul. 10–23 your plant is *i·*.
    No. 26– 2 believe . . . that the *i·* is inside
    My. 178–28 contents of "S. and H. . . . remain *i·*.
      179–11 mind and matter, mortal and *i·*,
      194– 6 but the spirit of it is *i·*.
      242– 4 declare yourself to be *i·*
      269–30 Truth is *i·*.

immortality (*see also* **immortality's**)
  against
    Ret. 67–11 the mortal against *i·*,
  and harmony
    Mis. 85–28 *i·* and harmony of Soul.
  certainty of
    My. 295– 5 safe in the certainty of *i·*.
  clad in
    My. 191–18 come forth . . . clad in *i·*.
  concept of
    Un. 41– 2 a feeble concept of *i·*.
  cravings for
    Mis. 16– 2 satisfy more the cravings for *i·*,
  exists
    Mis. 42–25 that *i·* exists only in
  glad
    Po. 70– 5 Like to the soul's glad *i·*,
  glory of
    Peo. 2– 2 is the true glory of *i·*.
  harmony and
    Un. 22– 4 in a sense of harmony and *i·*,
    Peo. 10– 1 man's harmony and *i·*.
  health and
    My. 182–23 giving grace, health, and *i·*
  his
    Mis. 2–22 the necessity of his *i·* ;
      47–24 his *i·* and preexistence,
  holiness and
    (*see* **holiness**)
  Life and
    Un. 38–20 brings to light Life and *i·*.
  life and
    My. 207–14 * life and *i·* brought to light.
  majesty, and
    Mis. 185–16 might, majesty, and *i·*.
  manifests
    Un. 38– 2 which manifests *i·*,

immortality

of his words
Mis. 99–20 his faith in the *i·* of his words.
120–30 *i·* of his words and works.
of his works
My. 246–27 and the *i·* of his works
of man
Mis. 172–27 health, holiness, and *i·* of man.
My. 226–19 evidence of the *i·* of man
of Mind
Mis. 218–10 *i·* of Mind and its ideas.
of Truth
Mis. 163–17 faith in the *i·* of Truth.
proof of
Mis. 186–22 affords self-evident proof of *i·* ;
reason and
Mis. 218–17 comes to the rescue of reason and *i·*,
substance, and
Un. 60–23 space, substance, and *i·*
time, and
'00. 1– 6 filling all space, time, and *i·*
to demonstrate
Ret. 88–15 its power to demonstrate *i·*.
understand
Un. 3– 3 not ready to understand *i·*.

Mis. 364–15 all time, space, *i·*,
380– 6 universe, time, space, *i·*,
Ret. 58– 9 and brought to light *i·*,
Un. 29–27 and my God [my Soul, *i·*]." — *Psal.* 42 : 11.
No. 21– 9 all time, space, *i·*, thought,
'01. 2– 2 demonstrated — health, holiness, *i·*.
Hea. 18– 5 and *i·* be brought to light.
Peo. 8–23 to light our sepulchres with *i·*.
My. 110–26 *i·* will have been brought to light.
119–24 evidence of Soul, *i·*, eternal Life
154–22 * he have light, . . . freedom, *i·* ?"
205–28 Hence health, holiness, *i·*,
349– 4 health, holiness, *i·*

immortality's
Un 58–14 sublime triumph . . . was *i·* goal.
My. 275–25 is *i·* self.

immortalized
Mis. 131–31 last year's records *i·*,

immortelles
Pul. 42–22 * with a centre of white *i·*,
Peo. 14– 9 * are wreaths of *i·*,

immovable
Ret. 89– 1 eternal stillness and *i·* Love.

immovably
Ret. 93–12 *i·* fixed in Principle.

immunity
Mis. 298–28 than *i·* from evil.
320–15 the sweet *i·* these bring

immutable
Mis. 71–30 *i·* and just law of Science,
72–11 The *i·* Word saith,
79–18 cause and effect in Science are *i·*
118–15 this *i·* decree of Love :
172–26 on the side of *i·* right,
Ret. 56–15 of Spirit in *i·* harmony.
Un. 29–13 absolutely *i·* and eternal,
51– 2 the reflection of *i·* good.
No. 4–21 of the *i·* laws of God ;
10–28 *i·* and eternal laws of God ;
26–23 *i·* harmony of divine law.
My. 106– 9 *i·* laws of omnipotent Mind

impanelled
Pul. 25–29 * illuminated texts . . . *i·*.

impart
Mis. 72– 9 God is supposed to *i·* to man
292–11 Could I *i·* to the student
293– 9 should *i·* to his students
Ret. 48–19 to *i·* a thorough understanding of
72– 1 cannot *i·* a mental influence that
Pul. 14–23 ready for the blessing you *i·*
No. 12–11 duty for her to *i·* to others
Peo. 1–12 *i·* grandeur to the intellectual
Po. 23– 3 A look that years *i·* ?
My. 165–20 *i·* truth, health, and happiness,
244–11 designed to *i·* a fresh impulse

impartation
Ret. 48–28 scientific *i·* of Truth,
50– 3 an *i·* of a knowledge of
'01. 8–12 not God, but an *i·* of Him.

imparted
My. 238–12 has *i·* little power to practise

impartial
Mis. 77–19 *i·*, and unquenchable Love.
285–12 *i·* and impersonal in its tenor
Un. 7– 3 in the *i·* grace of God,
Pul. 21– 4 unambitious, *i·*, universal,

impartial
Po. 77– 8 *i·*, blessings spreadst abroad,
My. 218–27 Such labor is *i·*,
230– 9 This church is *i·*.
265–21 divine Love, *i·* and universal,

impartially
Pul. 8– 3 spoken out historically, *i·*.
My. 357–20 open the way, widely and *i·*,

imparting
Mis. 3– 6 *i·* the only power to heal
12–31 *i·*, so far as we reflect them,
372–30 *i·* to humanity the true sense of
Ret. 93–14 and *i·* divine Truth,
Pul. 58– 3 * *i·* this faith to her fellow-beings.

imparts
Mis. 3–21 and *i·* these states to the body ;
38– 3 When teaching *i·* the ability to
74– 6 *i·* a new apprehension of the
No. 46– 8 life-giving understanding C. S. *i·*,
'00. 8– 4 The good man *i·* . . . goodness ;

impassioned
Pul. 32– 4 * she was magnetic, earnest, *i·*.

impatient
Mis. 265–30 If *i·* of the loving rebuke,
No. 1–10 So men, . . . are sometimes *i·* ;
Hea. 19–21 he is *i·* perhaps, or doubts the
My. 203–29 will not be *i·* if you have

impecunious
Rud. 14–22 If the Primary students are still *i·*,

impede
Mis. 115–27 whatever tends to *i·* progress.
Man. 44–25 *i·* their progress in C. S.

impedes
Mis. 308–25 *i·* spiritual growth ;

impediment
Mis. 47–16 accompanies thought with less *i·*
256–16 the old *i·*, lack of time,

impel
Man. 40– 6 *i·* the motives or acts of the

impelled
Mis. 148–12 *i·* by a power not one's own,
380–11 call for help *i·* me to begin this
Man. 3– 9 *i·* by a power not one's own,
Ret. 31– 9 From my very childhood I was *i·*,
50– 1 When God *i·* me to set a price on my
My. 24– 1 * those who pass by are *i·* to ask,

impels
Mis. 80–19 promotes and *i·* all true reform ;
358– 1 Love *i·* good works.
No. 12–20 *i·* a spiritualization of thought
My. 9– 7 * *i·* the Christian to turn
211–15 it *i·* mortal mind into error of
224–12 forward footsteps it *i·*
308– 9 *i·* the impulse of Soul.

impending
Un. 57– 6 it foresees the *i·* doom

impenetrable
Mis. 204– 2 dark, *i·* cloud of error ;

imperative
Mis. 91–13 It is *i·*, at all times
273–32 *i·* call is for my exclusive teaching.
288– 6 Positive and *i·* thoughts
316–18 *I·*, accumulative, sweet demands
380–11 *i·* call for help impelled me
Un. 40–10 *i·* in the divine order
My. 134–12 *i·* demand not yet met.
235– 7 *i·* rules of Science,
245– 4 demand for this . . . is *i·*,
264–18 the Decalogue more *i·*,
268– 5 *i·* nature of the marriage relation
291– 2 *I·*, accumulative, holy demands
308– 8 higher, nobler, more *i·*

imperatively
Mis. 277– 5 more *i·* than ever.
Pul. 20–16 *i·* propelling the greatest moral,

imperfect
Mis. 85–19 infantile and more or less *i·*.
86– 1 material and physical are *i·*.
353– 8 human concept is always *i·* ;
363–16 to make himself *i·*,
Ret. 21–22 The awakening . . . is as yet *i·* ;
Rud. 9– 7 The pupil's *i·* knowledge
16– 8 an *i·* sense of the spiritual
My. 11– 2 * as yet but *i·* followers of the
103– 1 In the midst of the *i·*,

imperfection
Mis. 14– 9 into the *i·* that requires
79–11 by no means the medium of *i·*.
101–20 on mortality, on *i·* ;
320–13 dawning upon human *i·*,

imperfection
Mis.	363–17	God is not chargeable with *i·*.
Un.	4–11	destroys our sense of *i·*,
	40–15	by believing in *i·* and
No.	7–13	every *i·* in the land of Sodom,
	20– 3	nor discerned through *i·* ;
'00.	6– 1	There is no *i·*, no lack
My.	41–17	* with evil, sin, wrong, or *i·*,

imperfectly
Un.	40–15	believing in . . . and living *i·*.

imperial
Mis.	330–29	crown *i·* unveils its regal splendor
My.	290– 5	Queen's royal and *i·* honors

imperialism
My.	129– 4	*i·*, monopoly, and a lax system

imperious
Mis.	177– 1	a more solemn and *i·* call

imperishable
Pul.	10–12	rights of conscience, *i·* glory.
My.	122– 5	That glory only is *i·* which

impersonal
Mis.	161–17	personal and the *i·* Jesus.
	166– 8	*i·* infancy, manhood, and
	178–31	new, living, *i·* Christ-thought
	180–10	Truth . . . the *i·* Saviour."
	190–22	*i·* evil, or whatever worketh ill.
	285–12	*i·* in its tenor and tenets.
	310– 5	Christ, or the *i·* form of Truth,
	322–10	dual and *i·* pastor, the Bible,
Ret.	76–26	sees each mortal in an *i·* depict.
Peo.	13– 6	*i·* Life, Truth, and Love,
My.	139–21	the personal to the *i·*,
	256–14	*i·* presents, pleasures, achievements,

impersonality
My.	117–20	great truth of God's *i·*

impersonalize
Mis.	310– 7	*i·* scientifically the material sense

impersonated
Ret.	93–10	no longer *i·* as a waif

impertinent
Man.	48– 9	uncharitable or *i·* towards religion,

impervious
My.	210– 8	Good thoughts are an *i·* armor ;

impetuosity
Mis.	359–19	Peter's *i·* was rebuked.

impetus
Mis.	245–11	giving it new *i·* and energy ;
Pul.	vii–16	*i·* thereby given to Christianity;
My.	3–16	persuasive animus, an unerring *i·*,
	205–16	their philosophical *i·*,
	239–29	Its *i·*, accelerated by
	248–21	for lack of the divine *i·*.
	252–28	the *i·* comes from above
	283– 9	leading *i·* of my life.

impious
Mis.	122–17	Such an inference were *i·*.
My.	160– 3	laws which it were *i·* to transgress,

implanted
Peo.	3–24	*i·* in our religions

implements
Pul.	51–18	* *i·* of theological warfare,

implication
My.	12– 2	* carried the *i·* that work should be

implicit
Mis.	105– 1	*i·* faith engendered by C. S.,
	341–20	*i·* treason to divine decree.
Ret.	87–12	demands *i·* adherence to fixed rules,
My.	46–24	* more *i·* obedience to the sacred
	137–27	*i·* confidence in each one of them

implicitly
Mis.	120– 4	they must obey *i·*
My.	284–25	believe *i·* in the full efficacy of

implied
Mis.	298–17	*i·* that the period demanded it.
'02.	9–14	condition *i·* by the great Master,
My.	88–29	* *i·* in the building of a great

implies
Mis.	56–29	Your question *i·* that Spirit,
	193–32	Hebrew of which *i·* understanding.
	367–13	*i·* the necessity of knowing evil,
Ret.	88–11	It *i·* such an elevation of
Un.	27– 7	*Egotism i·* vanity and self-conceit.
	41–28	*i·* perpetual disagreement with
	45–14	conscious matter *i·* pantheism.
	50– 1	*i·* the possibility of its
Pan.	7–23	intelligence and law, which *i·* Mind,
	12–25	includes all that the term *i·*,
Hea.	8– 1	it *i·* no necessity beyond the

implies
My.	233–31	*i·* that one is not thinking of
	300–28	If, as he *i·*, C. S. is

implorations
My.	340–28	their *i·* for peace and plenty

implore
Mis.	141–19	Do not, I *i·* you,

imploring
No.	39– 3	silent intercession and unvoiced *i·*
Pan.	14– 7	if daily adoring, *i·*, and living
My.	314–23	*i·* him not to do it.

imply
Mis.	45–25	what the Scriptures *i·* Him to be,
	49–28	as the Scriptures *i·* Him to be,
	72–21	*i· that Spirit takes note of matter*
Rud.	5– 4	If, as the Scriptures *i·*,
Pan.	8– 7	Does not the belief . . . *i·* two Gods,
	9– 6	in spiritualism they *i·* men and
My.	40– 8	* *i·* the subsidence of criticism
	40– 9	* It may even *i·* that some who
	222–24	rather does it *i·* that religion

import
Mis.	38–24	for questions of practical *i·*.
	106–22	long been a question of earnest *i·*,
	146–15	These are matters of grave *i·* ;
	162– 4	wonderful spiritual *i·* to mankind !
	197– 6	full *i·* . . . is not yet recognized.
	275–13	words of strange *i·*.
	280–28	topic of great *i·* to the student of
	317–21	on subjects of such earnest *i·*.
No.	v– 6	the *i·* of this edition is,
'00.	12– 3	the spiritual *i·* whereof
	14–11	divine *i·* of the Revelator's vision
'01.	25–12	because of their more spiritual *i·*
My.	46–27	* Church Manual in its spiritual *i·*,
	208– 5	whole *i·* of C. S.
	270– 4	magnitude of their spiritual *i·*,

importance
Mis.	98– 1	making this . . . of any *i·*,
	192– 6	It is of infinite *i·* to man's
Hea.	10–15	gather the *i·* of this saying,
	16–25	it is of the utmost *i·* that we
My.	10–24	* they recognize the *i·* of
	93–21	* attaching meanwhile no *i·* to
	160– 9	It is of less *i·* that we receive
	224–1	understand the *i·* of that demand
	236–28	*i·* at this stage of the workings
	271– 8	of comparatively little *i·*
	282–23	It is of paramount *i·*

important
Mis.	4–14	questions *i·* to be disposed of
	35–21	Only because both are *i·*.
	65–19	and this *i·* fact must be,
	76–19	on other topics less *i·*.
	92– 1	To omit these *i·* points is
	92–18	*i·* to point out the lesson
	157–10	all questions *i·* for your case,
	170–20	no more *i·* to our well-being
	232–20	most *i·* of all arts, — healing.
	233– 3	*i·* to know that a malpractice
	272–13	* with the following *i·* restrictions :
	287–22	*i·* questions concerning their
Man.	47–14	Testimony . . . is highly *i·*
	78–11	Also *i·* movements of the manager
	100–14	to act upon this *i·* matter
	110– 5	It is *i·* that these seemingly
Ret.	6–27	Among other *i·* bills
	37– 1	edition of my most *i·* work,
	83–25	It is also highly *i·*
Un.	1– 8	reason together on this *i·*
	22–17	be *i·* to our knowledge.
Pul.	4–12	that one is as *i·* a factor
No.	23–16	Which of the two is the more *i·*
Hea.	7–24	*i·* to progress and Christianity.
My.	20–27	* *i·* that the building fund
	45– 8	* most *i·* gatherings
	53– 1	* *i·* missives of inquiry
	91–31	* congregations in every *i·* town
	142–13	most *i·* events are criticized.
	170– 7	the *i·* sentiments uttered
	216–30	Contemplating these *i·* wants,
	231–20	*i·* demands on her time
	241– 2	* to perform this *i·* work.
	241–14	* issue raised is an *i·* one
	243–11	*i·*, responsible offices,
	249–25	perform this *i·* function.
	289– 1	The thing most *i·* is
	319–27	* an *i·* one in my experience,
	355–10	*i·* factors in our field

imported
Mis.	88–24	* *i·* ice was miraculous to

importunate
Peo.	9–22	a desire, fervent, *i·* :

importunately
Mis. 127–10 mentally, meekly, and i·.
My.   18– 7 mentally, meekly, and i·.

importunity
My.   10–21 * as the result of i·

impose
Mis. 148–12 one person might i· on another.
Man.   3– 8 one person might i· on another.

imposed
Mis. 351– 3 burdens i· by students.

imposes
Mis. 256–11 i· on me the severe task

imposing
Mis. 143–15 with quiet, i· ceremony,
My.   68–24 * i· effect of the interior.
      70– 2 * it certainly looks i·.
      71–16 * one of the most i· church edifices
      77–29 * to build the i· edifice
      78– 5 * i· structure of gray stone

imposition
Mis. 366–17 i· in the field of medicine

impositions
Man. 97–17 i· on the public in regard to

impossibility
Mis. 22–15 the i· of transmitting
      43–26 i· for those unacquainted
      60–17 reveals the i· of two
      95–15 i· of intercommunion between
     182– 2 i· of putting him to death,
     380–24 Experience, . . . taught me the i·
Un.   64– 8 To build the . . . is a moral i·.
Rud.   5–17 Matter without Mind is a moral i·.
Hea.   6–11 I saw the i·, in Science,
My. 179–12 Science shows to be an i·.

impossible
Mis. 24–24 knowledge of both good and . . . is i·.
      33–15 has not proved i· to heal those who,
      48–25 Such an occurrence would be i·,
      59–22 copartnership with that Mind is i·;
      75–10 or it is i· to demonstrate the
     191–27 which would be i· if he were
     195–28 abstractions, impractical and i·
     237–12 how i· it is to sin and not suffer.
     261–26 i· to be a Christian Scientist without
     288–19 before it is understood is i·,
     364–25 i· partnership is dissolved.
     375–31 * i· of reproduction.
Ret.   40–16 that it was i· for her to
Un.   18–26 aught beside Myself is i·.
Pul.   45– 8 * seems i· to mortal senses.
Rud.   13– 5 renders it i· to demonstrate the
       15–21 i· to teach thorough C. S. to
No.   17– 8 it is i· for the true man
       17–13 for man to be more . . . is i·.
       22–11 is not stated, and is i·.
       26– 8 Hence it is i· for those
       36– 3 for that would be i·.
       40– 5 they expect also what is i·,
'01.   11–16 that does not make it i· for
       24– 1 * is an i· and unreal concept."
'02.   6– 1 i· to have aught unlike the infinite.
        6–14 an untrue consciousness, an i·
Hea.   16–24 those senses through which it is i· to
My.   61– 7 * seemed i· for the building to be
       81–29 * i· to convey a conception of
      106–14 i· for the surgeon or *materia medica*
      118–22 i· in the Science of God
      119– 2 i· in Science to believe this,
      178–17 But this is i· in reality,
      212–20 i· under other conditions,
      235– 3 as i· as to define truth
      344– 2 to my understanding . . . that is i·.

impostors
Mis. 365–30 i· that come in its name.
Rud. 16–12 some i· are committing this error.

impotence
Mis. 121–10 namely, the i· of evil,

impotent
Mis.   3–26 hygiene, and animal magnetism are i·;
       90– 2 hence, that sin is i·.
      119–10 Evil is i· to turn the righteous
      134–22 nostrums, and knives, are i·
      252–11 evil thoughts are i·,
No.   15–17 presuppose an i· God
Hea.   10–10 therefore evil is i·.

impracticable
Mis. 263–21 i· without a full knowledge of
Rud. 15–10 systematic thinking is i· until
'01.   6–20 regarded as i· for human use,
My. 128–23 without . . . the latter were i·.

impractical
Mis. 195–27 i· and impossible to us;
      311–13 i·, unfruitful, Soul-less.
Pul.   52– 6 * "i·" Christian Scientists.
'02.   4–27 liable to turn from them as i·,
My.   58– 2 * i· Christian Scientists."

impregnable
Mis. 10–10 furnished them defenses i·.
      103– 4 far more i· and solid than matter;

impregnated
Rud.   8–26 mortal mind should not be falsely i·.

impress
Mis. 207– 4 i· humanity with the genuine
Peo.   7– 3 and leaving the i· of mind
My.   84–21 * i· even the man who cannot
       98– 1 * i· the most determined skeptic.

impressed
Mis. 274– 3 This point, however, had not i· me
      313–15 i· by the articles entitled
      375–17 * "The first thing that i· me
Ret.   54–24 i· with the true sense of
Pul.   29–11 * earnestness i· the observer.
       31–25 * i· me as singularly graceful
       50–16 * has i· itself upon a
My.   6–15 Greatly i· and encouraged thereby,
       31–21 * should have i· them as one
       59– 1 * i· with the grandeur
      271–25 * i· by the personality of

impressing
My.   68– 2 * i· the audiences with the beauty

impression
Mis. 142–15 My first i· was to indite a poem;
Pul.   49–27 * first i· given to the visitor
'01.   24– 5 matter is only an i· produced
My.   31–13 * first i· was of vastness,
       87–12 * The i· created is that of
       92–19 * statistics give a feeble i·
      322–31 * the i· he left with me was
      323–11 * nor willingly leave any false i·.
      324–20 * never gave us the i· that
      324–24 * conveyed this i· to us
      334– 1 * forthwith strives to give the i·

impressions
Mis. 133–10 voices my i· of prayer:
      264–21 the bias of their first i·,
Ret.   6– 1 * i· of that sainted spirit,
Pul.   51– 3 * produce the same i· upon all.
My.   188–28 convey all i· to man,
      261–13 the first i· of innocence,

impressive
Pul.   12– 3 i· stillness of the audience
       30–28 * its present i· proportions,
My.   38–23 * no more i· feature of the
       63–26 * even more i· than this
       78–12 * peculiarly rich and i·.
       92– 4 * its beginning has been i·,

impressively
My. 203–25 laid the corner-stone . . . i·,

impressiveness
My.   29–16 * the i· of this lay in its
       78–27 * can convey the peculiar i· of
       90–26 * i· and momentous significance.

imprisonment
Ret.   6–29 abolition of i· for debt.

improve
Mis. 62– 2 i· my own, and other people's
      62– 5 no more i· health or morals, than
      98– 3 whereby to i· his present condition;
     112– 8 given new opportunities, will i·
     176–27 prepared to meet and i· them,
     230– 1 chapter sub-title
     253– 9 may i· our platforms;
     267–11 and failed to i· it;
Ret.   34–20 renovated to i· the body.
Un.   14– 9 i· upon His own previous work,
No.   22– 9 fail to i· the conditions of mortals,
Peo.   7–25 appeal to mind to i· its subjects
My.   10– 3 * C. S. should i· the thought,
       42–14 * I desire to i· this opportunity to
      249– 3 I· every opportunity to correct sin
      294– 3 i· the morals and the lives of men,

improved
Mis. 34– 5 not only healed . . . but is i· morally.
      34– 7 and mortal mind must be i·,
     137–12 such opportunity might have been i·;
     147– 9 Have you i· past hours,
     220–20 and he is i· morally and physically.
     256– 3 they are at the same time i· morally.
     287– 2 The offspring of an i· generation,
Un.   3– 1 having rightly i· the lessons of this
       36–19 i· physically, mentally, morally,

improved

Pul.	1–10	time *i·* is eloquent in God's praise.
'00.	3–27	*i·* on his work of
'01.	21–13	*i·* in its teaching and authorship
'02.	3–14	self-government under *i·* laws.
	3–15	so *i·* her public school system that
Peo.	2–3	*i·* theory and practice of religion
	2–4	due to the people's *i·* views
My.	107–2	Has Christianity *i·* upon its
	175–18	greatly needs *i·* streets.
	217–24	"An *i·* belief is one step out of
	220–28	have greatly *i·* human nature
	307–25	At first my case *i·* wonderfully

improvement

Mis.	230–3	upon the *i·* of moments
	243–3	decided *i·* in health.
	370–23	has discovered an *i·* on

improves

Ret.	55–8	and *i·* the race of Adam.
'00.	3–6	*i·* moments ; to him time is money,
Peo.	6–18	*i·* the race physically and

improving

Mis.	230–15	*i·* moments before they pass into
My.	265–17	*i·* the morals and increasing the

improvise

My.	256–3	allow me to *i·* some new notes,

impulse

Mis.	272–30	intuition and *i·* of love.
	274–20	gives *i·* to violence, envy, and
	288–26	temperance receives a strong *i·* from
Rud.	3–20	all true volition, *i·*, and action ;
	15–11	until this *i·* subsides.
No.	12–14	and given *i·* to goodness.
	13–24	given *i·* to reason and revelation,
'01.	32–30	governing *i·* of every action ;
My.	10–5	* this mighty *i·* for good
	244–11	is designed to impart a fresh *i·* to
	252–31	cold *i·* of a lesser gain !
	308–9	impels the *i·* of Soul.
	316–4	renews the heavenward *i·* ;

impulses

Mis.	141–21	*i·* of human will and pride ;
My.	213–17	for the *i·* of our own thought,

impulsion

Ret.	89–30	incorpóreal *i·* is divine,
My.	10–8	* inevitable that this same *i·*
	250–25	*i·* of this action in The

impure

Mis.	80–1	sellers of *i·* literature,
	223–7	*i·* streams flow from corrupt sources.

impurities

Pul.	6–2	and *i·* are passing off.
'00.	13–8	their *i·* were part of a system

impurity

Mis.	37–21	Intemperance, *i·*, sin of every sort,

impute

No.	29–16	*i·* such doctrines to mortal opinion

imputed

Hea.	6–15	manifestations ignorantly *i·* to
My.	177–11	(already *i·* to me),
	178–32	*Logia,* or *i·* sayings of Jesus

inability

Mis.	112–26	*i·* to see one's own faults,
No.	43–28	A man's *i·* to heal,

inaccuracy

My.	260–8	*i·* of material sense would disappear.

inaccurate

Mis.	100–16	Human reason is *i·* ;

inaction

Mis.	341–22	illustrate the evil of *i·* and delay.

inactive

Pul.	10–3	paralyzed by *i·* faith,

inadequate

Mis.	65–27	*i·* to compensate for the
	100–17	*i·* to grasp the word of Truth,
	317–20	Human desire is *i·* to
Man.	30–6	be found at any time *i·*
Ret.	25–26	therefore *i·* to form any
No.	11–23	*i·* to grasp the Principle
	33–18	human blood was *i·* to
'01.	24–29	*i·* to prove the doctrine
My.	54–1	* were *i·* for the occasion,
	56–8	* was *i·* to meet the need,
	197–10	Words are *i·* to express
	224–2	*i·* to meet the exigencies

inadmissible

Mis.	147–11	learned that sin is *i·*,
My.	130–24	Borrowing from my . . . is *i·*.
	364–6	departure from . . . is *i·*.

inalienable

Mis.	140–6	morally and spiritually *i·*,
	251–14	*i·* rights and radiant reality
No.	45–18	the right of woman . . . is *i·*,
My.	128–11	man's *i·* birthright
	200–16	receives his rights *i·*
	247–2	*i·*, universal rights of men.
	254–23	It stands for the *i·*,

inanimate

Mis.	256–24	inert, *i·*, and non-intelligent.
Rud.	5–9	inert, *i·*, and sensationless,
'01.	19–22	from the use of *i·* drugs

inapt

'01.	29–12	sometimes are *i·* or selfish

inasmuch

Mis.	186–20	*i·* as an idea cannot
	205–19	*i·* as it is the disembodied
	228–22	*i·* as perception, sensation, and
	293–18	*i·* as wilful transgression
Man.	42–21	*i·* as C. S. can only be
No.	28–9	*I·* as these momentous facts
'00.	4–14	*i·* as these are progressive
'01.	14–7	Yes, *i·* as we do know that
'02.	18–14	"*I·* as ye have done it — *Matt.* 25 : 40.
My.	134–7	*i·* as our daily lives serve to

inaudible

Mis.	267–2	audible and *i·* wail of evil
No.	40–13	the *i·* is more effectual.
'01.	20–13	suggestion of the *i·* falsehood,
Hea.	15–27	Prayer will be *i·*
My.	139–24	from the audible to the *i·* prayer ;

inaugurated

Mis.	102–27	*i·* the irrepressible conflict
	382–28	*i·* our denominational form of
Pul.	31–11	* which that meeting *i·* for me.
My.	42–26	* *i·* by our beloved Leader,

inauguration

Mis.	305–29	* anniversary of the *i·* of
'02.	3–11	*i·* of home rule in Cuba,
My.	56–6	* *i·* of two Sunday services

incantations

'00.	13–20	included charms and *i·*.

incapable

Mis.	14–15	*i·* of knowing the facts of
	14–27	a lie that is *i·* of proof
	71–25	man is *i·* of originating :
	209–32	Love, as unconscious as *i·* of error,
	371–10	*i·* of helping themselves thus?
Ret.	85–19	*i·* alike of abusing the practice of
Pul.	41–18	* *i·* of receiving this vast throng,
Pan.	4–14	God is *i·* of evil ;

incapacitates

Mis.	43–24	*i·* one to practise or teach C. S.
No.	44–2	*i·* him for correct comment.

incarnated

Mis.	111–32	or is an *i·* babe,

incarnation

Mis.	77–10	should not only acknowledge the *i·*
My.	303–3	I believe in but one *i·*,

incense

Pul.	83–22	* as if we would pour *i·* upon the
Hea.	2–28	altar of Love with perpetual *i·*.
My.	37–5	* *i·* of gratitude and compassionate

incensed

Un.	46–16	This *i·* the rabbins against Jesus,

incentive

Mis.	238–8	in defense of his own life's *i·*,
	279–5	that is the *i·* in Science.
'00.	3–29	was not the *i·* of the devout Jew
My.	217–4	your early, generous *i·* for action,
	229–13	But this should not be the *i·*
	278–1	proper *i·* to the action of all
	288–5	his life's *i·* and sacrifice need no
	357–8	The only *i·* of a mistaken sense

incentives

Ret.	71–22	selfish motives . . . are dangerous *i·* ;
'02.	13–3	Christ and our Cause my only *i·*,

inception

My.	47–17	* since the *i·* of this great Cause,
	243–6	should be silenced at its *i·*.

incessant

Ret.	7–9	* intense and almost *i·* study
My.	163–19	many years of *i·* labor

incessantly

Mis.	114–7	need to watch *i·* the trend of
My.	335–30	* the young wife prayed *i·*

inch

Pul.	78–5	* an eighth of an *i·* thick.

inches
Pul. 26– 3 * which is twenty-one *i·*
78– 4 * twenty-six *i·* long,
78– 5 * gold scroll, . . . nine *i·* wide,
86– 2 * six *i·* in each dimension,

incident
Mis. 373– 1 One *i·* serves to illustrate
My. 29– 7 * *i·* of the dedicatory services
311– 1 I will relate the following *i·*,

incidental
Mis. 253– 7 the *i·* platform is not broad enough
Man. 48–25 or give *i·* narratives.

incidents
Ret. 21–25 historic *i·* and personal events
My. 97–30 * *i·* witnessed during the week
329–27 * some *i·* of her life in

incipient
Pul. 54–29 *i·* pulmonary consumption.
'01. 21–27 the *i·* touch of divine Love
Hea. 13–14 the *i·* stage of fever.

incision
Peo. 7–13 * With many a sharp *i·*.
7–21 * With many a sharp *i·*,

incisions
Mis. 244– 7 closing the *i·* of the flesh.

incisors
Mis. 231–17 two *i·*, in a big pippin,

incited
Mis. 122–32 was *i·* by the same spirit
296–27 or are they *i·* thereto by

inclement
Mis. 198–30 suffered from *i·* weather,

inclination
Mis. 240–18 with form and *i·* fixed,
Ret. 38–10 contrary to my *i·*,
Pul. vii– 7 *i·* given their own thoughts
'00. 9– 3 obedience is contrary to their *i·*.
My. 130–14 neither the time nor the *i·*

inclinations
Mis. 362–31 the influence of bad *i·*
'00. 8–29 to follow your own *i·*,
My. 211–17 foreign to the natural *i·*.

incline
Mis. 240–19 easier to *i·* the early thought
My. 125– 7 to *i·* the vine towards the parent

inclined
Mis. xi–21 *vox populi* is *i·* to grant us peace,
117–24 *i·* to be too fast or too slow :
129– 3 is *i·* to be uncharitable,
264–18 * "As the twig is bent, the tree's *i·*."
Ret. 78– 2 He is *i·* to do either too much or
My. 97– 1 * almost every one is *i·* to admit.
116– 7 *i·* to cling to the personality of
226– 8 principle of the *i·* plane
322–23 * She and Mrs. Wiggin seemed *i·* to
338–28 *i·* to be, and is instructed to be,

inclining
Mis. 111–28 false beliefs *i·* mortal mind
My. 261–12 germinating and *i·* thought of

include
Mis. 11–25 *i·* them in his general effort to
14– 5 immortal facts which *i·* these,
68– 5 *i·* also man's changed appearance
190–18 these terms will be found to *i·* the
309–21 *i·* all obstacles to health,
358– 8 They *i·* for him at present
Man. 47–18 not *i·* a description of symptoms or
73– 4 *i·* at least one active practitioner
93–11 *i·* in each lecture a true and just
Ret. 30– 9 *i·* all moral and religious reform.
Un. 31–19 *i·* all that denies and defies Spirit,
No. 39–18 *i·* all mankind in one affection.
'01. 7–12 *i·* within this Mind the thoughts
My. 26–18 *i·* enough of their own.
30– 6 * *i·* Scientists from all over the
106– 6 *i·* hopeless organic diseases
129–30 *i·* the spirit and the letter of the
329– 1 * was construed to *i·* the healers of

included
Mis. 24–15 *i·* a glimpse of the great fact
34–10 *Is spiritualism . . . i· in C. S.?*
349– 4 instructions *i·* about twelve lessons,
Un. 11–27 is *i·* in Mind ;
'00. 13–20 Its medical practice *i·* charms
Hea. 14–24 it *i·* more than they understood.
Po. vi–22 * are *i·* in this collection,
My. 16– 7 * *i·* the purchase price of the land
95– 1 * C. S. would soon be *i·* among
122–30 *i·* the very hearts that rejected it
269– 1 universe *i·* in one infinite Mind

includes
Mis. 36–21 Mortal mind *i·* all evil,
75– 9 *i·* a rule that must be understood,
96–10 or what the infinite *i·* ;
96–19 *i·* man's redemption from sickness
96–25 This answer *i·* too much to
113– 5 that which it *i·* is all
152– 5 oneness of God *i·* also His presence
193–30 *i·* the understanding of man's
243–15 *i·* of necessity the Principle,
257– 2 or *i·* Him in every mode and
293–22 *i·* the whole duty of man :
Pul. 26–17 * chime of bells *i·* fifteen,
28–17 * *i·* the use of Mrs. Eddy's book,
30–10 * *i·* those all over the country.
30–15 * The "confession of faith" *i·*
No. 9–24 excludes all error and *i·* all Truth.
38–20 *i·* only His own nature,
Pan. 12– 7 for the universe *i·* man
12–25 *i·* all that the term implies,
'00. 4–28 divine Love *i·* and reflects all
'02. 6–17 mortal concept and all it *i·*
Hea. 14–15 healing *i·* infinitely more than
My. 141–24 membership *i·* forty-eight thousand
225–30 The divine Principle *i·* them all.
239–18 God is *infinite* and so *i· all*
364– 7 *i·* and inculcates the commandment,

including
Mis. 23–20 The universe, *i·* man,
27–11 *i·* all inharmony, sin,
41–27 governs the universe, *i·* man,
56–30 created the universe, *i·* man,
101–24 destroys matter and evil, *i·* sin
272– 3 * (*i· the right to grant degrees*)
333–21 relate to the universe, *i·* man
361–25 spiritual universe, *i·* man
Un. 32– 6 man, *i·* the universe, is His
Pul. 37–27 * by seven persons, *i·* Mrs. Eddy.
Rud. 3–27 *i·* in itself all Mind,
'02. 6–30 *i·* nothing unlovely,
My. 16– 5 * up to and *i·* May 31, 1904,
349–30 the infinite nature, *i·* all law

inclusive
Mis. 104– 8 substance of God, the one *i·* good.

income
Ret. 49– 1 which yields a large *i·*,
'02. 13–10 yield this church a liberal *i·*.
15–10 *i·* from the sale of S. and H.,
15–14 my *i·* from literary sources was
My. 135– 9 my *i·*, investments, deposits,
137–12 my *i·*, investments, deposits,

incoming
My. 39–18 * introduce the *i·* President,

incommunicable
My. 133–25 then my sacred secret is *i·*,

incomparable
Mis. 250– 1 the *i·*, the infinite All

incompetence
My. 236– 8 notwithstanding "*i·*"

incompetency
Peo. 8– 5 *i·* that cannot heal the sick,

incompetent
Mis. 22–26 is *i·* to condemn it ;
Un. 23–17 whereof they are confessedly *i·*
No. 19–20 sinful sense is *i·* to understand

incomplete
Man. 69– 5 *I·* Term of Service.
Un. 15–11 so must man, or the likeness is *i·*,

incompleteness
Pul. 39– 6 * God's greatness flows around our *i·*,

inconceivable
Mis. 102– 5 a theory to me *i·*.
217– 3 effect without a cause is *i·* ;
218–16 they make Deity unreal and *i·*,
234–27 seems to them still more *i·*.
No. 20– 2 Limitless personality is *i·*.
'01. 6–29 That God is either *i·*, or

inconsistency
My. 110–29 to convict the Scriptures of *i·*
235– 1 chapter sub-title

inconsistent
Mis. 349–14 ground that it was *i·* with C. S.,
Hea. 4–28 consistent with our *i·* statement
My. 112–13 is not *i·* in a single instance

incontestable
Un. 7–22 *i·* point in divine Science
No. 21–22 Jesus, whose philosophy is *i·*,

inconvenience
My. 54– 3 * *i·* that comes from crowding,

inconveniences
 My. 29–30 * the *i·* of an oppressive day.
inconvenient
 Mis. 132–21 I find it *i·* to accept
 My. 289–23 It being *i·* for me to attend
incorporated
 Mis. 272–11 * *i·* in Public Statutes, Chapter **115,**
  272–20 * have simply an *i·* grant,
 Man. 102–18 shall be *i·* in all such deeds
incorporates
 Mis. 197– 1 *i·* their lessons into our lives
incorporation
 Man. 25–17 See under "Deed of Trust" for *i·*
incorporeal
 Mis. 102–16 Infinite personality must be *i·.*
  161– 4 *The Corporeal and I· Saviour.*
  162–22 There was no *i·* Jesus of Nazareth.
  163–26 the *i·* Saviour — the Christ
  164– 1 interprets the *i·* idea, or
  164– 2 hence the *i·* and corporeal are
  164– 7 reveals the *i·* Christ ;
  166–15 Christ, the *i·* idea of God,
  205– 4 the *i·* Truth and Love,
 Ret. 70–24 individual, *i·,* and infinite,
  89–30 *i·* impulsion is divine,
  93– 5 the *i·* divine Principle of man,
 '01. 12–26 *I·* evil embodies itself in the
 My. 200–13 upward to the realms of *i·* Life
  218–11 The *spiritual* body, the *i·* idea,
  260–31 Christ is *i·.*
incorrect
 Mis. 39– 8 grossly *i·* and false teachers
  118–10 make *i·* your entire problem,
  263–26 hampered . . . by *i·* teaching ;
  264–22 whether those be correct or *i·.*
  372– 2 *i·,* contradictory, unscientific,
 Man. 43–21 No *I·* Literature.
 No. 23– 1 *i·* concept of the nature of evil
 My. 221–25 correct or *i·* state of thought,
incorrectly
 My. 226– 2 To avoid using this word *i·,*
incorruptible
 My. 41–26 * "*i·* and undefiled" — *I Pet.* 1: 4.
increase
 Mis. 21–14 except by *i·* of spirituality.
  110–24 *i·* rapidly as years glide on.
  175–12 shall *i·* by every spiritual touch,
  229–23 faith in the power of God . . . *i·,*
 Ret. 62– 2 and human suffering will *i·.*
 Un. 5– 6 *i·* their apprehension of God,
 No. 19– 4 and the demand to *i·,*
  42– 3 * manifestations of God's power *i·*
 '02. 1– 5 constantly *i·* in number, unity,
 Po. 33– 3 *I·* Thou my faith
 My. 36–22 * *i·* the measure of our devotion
  55–30 * a steady *i·* in attendance.
  87– 5 * temporary *i·* of the population
  91–26 * even stranger is its *i·* in wealth.
  162–27 May He *i·* its members,
  230–12 *i·* the spirituality of him who obeys
  240– 1 will *i·* till all men shall know Him
increased
 Mis. 12–15 means for sinning . . . have so *i·*
  12–16 one's temptations to sin are *i·*
  29–20 shows that longevity has *i·.*
  42–20 will be proportionally *i·.*
  137–28 heal and teach with *i·* confidence.
  204–24 permeates with *i·* harmony all the
  262– 3 and to confer *i·* power
  289–25 exalted and *i·* affections,
  327– 3 When I went back . . . my misery *i·* ;
 Ret. 15–17 The congregation so *i·* in number
  39– 1 demand for this book *i·,*
  44–11 church *i·* in members,
 No. 8–27 and with *i·* power, patience,
 '00. 7– 4 religious sentiment has *i·* ;
 My. 53–30 * attendants steadily *i·.*
  56– 3 * *i·,* until every seat was filled
  56–18 * number of attendants *i·*
  92–16 * its following had *i·*
  132–19 blessings continue and be *i·* !
  164– 3 But the demand *i·,*
  266–22 have *i·* year by year.
increases
 Mis. 204–18 *i·* the intellectual activities,
  365–22 it continues, and *i·,*
 Ret. 27–27 *i·* in power and perfection
  28–19 which divides, subdivides, *i·,*
  74– 1 *i·* one's sense of corporeality,
 No. 42– 1 * as the faith of the Church *i·,*
 '00. 2– 2 and this interest *i·.*

increases
 '02. 10–22 *i·* the speed of mortals' transit
 My. 12–25 *i·* our indebtedness to God.
  305–17 demand for this book constantly *i·.*
increasing
 Mis. 115–22 *i·* necessity for relying on God
  300–21 and *i·* the record of theft
  302– 2 the reformation begun and *i·*
  307–15 *i·* inquiry of mankind as to
 Man. 18– 9 went steadily on, *i·* in numbers,
 Ret. 44–12 kept pace with its *i·* popularity ;
  47– 8 applicants were rapidly *i·.*
 Pul. 31–18 * by a new and *i·* interest
  37– 4 * *i·* demands of the public
  50–16 * upon a large and *i·* number
 '00. 1–13 with rapidly *i·* numbers,
 '01. 3– 2 *i·* virtue, fervor, and fidelity.
  29–16 parents' *i·* years and needs,
 My. 22– 5 * constantly *i·* attendance
  53–28 * *i·* interest in C. S.
  88–22 * all that *i·* host who have found
  135–11 *i·* demands upon my time
  137–17 *i·* demands upon my time,
  139– 7 *i·,* advancing footsteps
  174–25 An *i·* sense of God's love,
  245–10 *i·* popularity of C. S.,
  265–17 *i·* the longevity of mankind,
  325–16 * With *i·* love and gratitude,
incredible
 No. 15–17 and an *i·* Satan.
incredulity
 Mis. 4–29 with an expression of *i·.*
  7–11 skepticism and *i·* prevail
incriminating
 Mis. 283–23 without *i·* the person
incubus
 Un. 15– 4 May men rid themselves of an *i·*
inculcates
 Mis. 288–17 Human knowledge *i·* that it is,
 My. 364– 7 includes and *i·* the commandment,
incumbents
 Man. 26– 5 *I·* who have served one year
  80–26 *I·* who have served one year
 My. 243–13 or more of the present *i·.*
incumbrance
 No. 38–19 and material *i·* disappears.
incur
 Mis. 126–29 to deride her is to *i·* the penalty
incurable
 Mis. 6–10 cases that are pronounced *i·*
  35– 6 pronounced by the physicians *i·,*
  378– 3 A patient considered *i·*
 Pul. 69– 9 * had pronounced his case *i·.*
 My. 105–10 declared *i·* because the lungs
incurred
 '02. 13– 3 *i·* a sharper fire from enmity.
incurring
 Mis. 300–20 *i·* the penalty of the law,
incurs
 My. 231– 5 *i·* the liability of working in
Ind. (State)
 (*see* **Indianapolis, Lebanon, Terre Haute**)
indebted
 Mis. 228– 3 deemed at least *i·* friends
 Pul. 36–27 * to whose courtesy I am much *i·*
 My. 74–14 * Boston is *i·* to them for
indebtedness
 Man. 76–13 the amount of its *i·*
 My. 12–25 increases our *i·* to God.
  52– 8 * acknowledge our *i·* to her,
  99–17 * was not a cent of *i·* left.
indecision
 Mis. 230– 5 *i·* as to what one should do.
indeed
 Mis. 9– 5 Sweet, *i·,* are these uses of His rod !
  16–10 Principle of Christianity . . . is *i·* God ;
  32– 1 if *i·* he desires success in this
  36–26 neither *i·* can be." — *Rom.* 8: 7.
  125– 1 he will *i·* drink of our Master's cup,
  126–27 God hath *i·* smiled on my church,
  131–27 if, *i·,* it could be estimated.
  147–27 is *i·* what he appears to be,
  203–19 repentance is *i·* a stricken state
  211–26 drink *i·* of my cup." — *Matt.* 20 : 23.
  299–10 glad, *i·,* that this query has
  354–13 are *i·* losing the knowledge of
  374–19 To him . . . homage is *i·* due,
 Ret. 37– 7 "This book is *i·* wholly original,
  68– 6 neither *i·* can be, the father of
  91–10 *I·,* this title really indicates

indeed

Un.	1– 3	*I·*, this may be set down as
	45– 7	"Yes! you are *i·* yourself,
	59– 3	How, *i·*, is he a Saviour, if
Pul.	3–12	*i·* dwellers in Truth and Love,
	45–18	* This is *i·*, then, a scientific
	50– 5	* *I·*, one of her motives in buying
	57–12	* and, *i·*, in all New England.
	79–24	* *i·*, the breath of his soul is a
	80– 9	* socially, *i·* every way.
Rud.	11–25	healer who is *i·* a Christian Scientist,
No.	5–20	Disease becomes *i·* a
Pan.	4–20	is *i·* the preserver of man.
'00.	1– 4	If, *i·*, we may be absent from
'01.	25–27	which, if *i·* Spirit and infinite,
	28–22	is *i·* the way of salvation from
'02.	3–27	*i·*, right is the only real
	10–23	This is *i·* our sole proof
My.	9–11	* this would be scant *i·* if it
	10–27	* *i·*, they know that it is the
	17–10	disallowed *i·* of men, — *I Pet.* 2 : 4.
	46–27	* that we may *i·* reach
	50–25	* This was *i·* the little church
	61– 4	* has been very interesting *i·*,
	103– 9	that C. S. is *i·* Science,
	161–19	shall drink *i·* of my — *Matt.* 20 : 23.
	165–31	that it has *i·* found and felt the
	175–16	if, *i·*, such must remain with us
	179–29	We are *i·* privileged in having
	192–22	It would *i·* give me pleasure
	244–22	students of my books are *i·* my
	315–25	If *i·* it be I, allow me to
	332– 6	* words are *i·* but a meagre tribute
	351–11	is *i·* a divine command,

indefinable

Pan.	3– 9	find an *i·* pleasure in stillness,

indefinite

Mis.	86–12	*i·* and vague human opinions,
Pul.	58–24	* but for an *i·* time
Hea.	4–16	for an *i·* period,

indelibly

My.	48–26	* burned *i·* upon the mind of

Independent

Pul.	88–15	* *I·*, Rockland, Mass.
	88–32	* *I·*, Harrisburg, Pa.
	89– 1	* *I·*, New York City.

independent

Mis.	43– 2	to act of itself, and *i·* of matter,
	289–13	voluntarily surrenders *i·* action
Pul.	55–27	* though each is entirely *i·*
No.	5–13	that life and health are *i·* of
'01.	27– 1	quite *i·* of all other authors except
Hea.	12– 5	to learn what matter is doing *i·* of

independently

Man.	55– 6	*i·* discipline its own members,
Hea.	19– 6	*i·* of material conditions.

indestructibility

Mis.	206– 9	scientific *i·* of the universe

indestructible

Mis.	64– 7	man's *i·* eternal life in God.
My.	127–27	staunch and *i·* on land or sea ;

India

Pul.	5–25	Greece, Japan, *I·*, and China ;
My.	30–15	* from *I·*, from England,
	289–16	Victoria, . . . Empress of *I·*,
	289–29	Victoria, . . . Empress of *I·*.

Indian

Ret.	3– 6	in the *I·* troubles of 1722–1725,

Indianapolis

Ind.

Pul.	90– 5	* *Sentinel, I·*, Ind.

My.	81–15	* "*I·*!" "Des Moines!" "Glasgow !"

indicate

Mis.	245–15	Their movements *i·* fear
Ret.	59–13	*Life* is a term used to *i·* Diety ;
No.	11–10	which must be used to *i·* thoughts
'00.	4–12	*i·* a renaissance greater than
My.	36– 5	* rose as one to *i·* their approval
	187– 2	*i·* that, spiritually as well as
	245–28	They *i·*, respectively, the degrees of
	319–14	* *i·* what he himself thought of

indicated

Mis.	70–20	poor thief's prayer for help *i·*.
	76–22	will find the right meaning *i·*.
	258–22	I AM, *i·* no personality
	314–12	*i·* in the Sunday School Lesson
Man.	47–20	name of the disease may be *i·*.
Ret.	23–11	were *i·* by no floral dial.
Pul.	12– 4	stillness . . . *i·* close attention.
No.	22–26	*i·* his ability to cast it out.

indicated

My.	8– 6	* The necessity here *i·* is
	114–32	steps either written or *i·*
	284–21	Veterans *i·* their desire

indicates

Mis.	100–30	our Father *i·* the different stages of
	147–11	and *i·* a small mind?
	182–22	apostle *i·* no personal plan
	288–18	while Science *i·* that it *is not.*
	290–12	*i·* misapprehension of the divine
Man.	76– 5	*i·* the proper management
Ret.	91–11	*i·* more the Master's mood,
No.	6–13	If, as the error *i·*,
	45–10	Such an attempt *i·* weakness,
Pan.	7–19	*i·*, . . . a lapse in the Mosaic religion,
My.	86–18	* *i·* plainly enough the generosity
	216–19	*i·* another field of work
	231– 3	to bestow . . . only as God *i·*.
	331– 8	* *i·* her irreproachable standing

indicating

Mis.	191–14	*i·* the existence of more than
Pul.	vii–13	*i·* the gain of intellectual

indication

Mis.	56–11	Every *i·* of matter's constituting

indications

Mis.	46–12	no such *i·* in the premises
Ret.	71–12	the *i·* of mental treatment,
My.	82–21	* to-day [June 14] the *i·* were

indifference

My.	195–12	hidden under an appearance of *i·*.
	233–14	can you demonstrate over . . . by *i·*,
	248–28	to challenge universal *i·*,

indifferent

Mis.	146–16	you cannot be *i·* to this,
Pul.	21–19	they are not *i·* to the welfare of

indigenous

Mis.	211–11	are not *i·* to her soil.

indigent

Mis.	ix– 8	Christian Scientists are not *i·* ;
	11– 8	I taught *i·* students gratuitously,
Ret.	50–15	my list of *i·* charity scholars
'02.	15– 7	rooming and boarding *i·* students
My.	214–24	C. S. home for *i·* students,

indigestion

Mis.	209–18	ills of *i·* tend to rebuke

indignation

Mis.	345–21	turn the popular *i·* against
	374– 7	Keen and alert was their *i·*.
Pul.	14– 6	shocked . . . into human *i·* ;

indignity

Un.	11–23	neither red tape nor *i·* hindered
	46–17	an *i·* to their personality ;
My.	165– 6	There is scarcely an *i·* which

indirectly

Mis.	381–23	from directly or *i·* printing,
Hea.	12–13	that God, directly or *i·*,
My.	223–20	coming directly or *i·* from

indiscretion

Mis.	129–16	of another man's *i·*,

indiscretions

Mis.	236– 5	*i·*, and errors of others ;

indiscriminately

Man.	59– 1	revelations of C. S. *i·*,

indispensable

Mis.	v– 5	PRACTICAL TEACHINGS *i·* TO
	38–21	divine metaphysics needful, *i·*.
	67–16	*i·* to health, happiness,
	87–27	*i·* to the demonstration of
	91– 4	It is not *i·* to organize
	91– 8	not as a perpetual or *i·* ceremonial
	108–20	the proper knowledge . . . is *i·* ;
	118– 7	the *i·* rule of obedience.
	122– 6	spoken of what was *i·*
	317–18	*i·* to the progress of every Christian
	318–23	*i·* demands on all those who
	356–27	it is *i·* to personal growth,
No.	6– 9	This refutation is *i·* to the
'00.	14–23	toiled for the spiritually *i·*.
'01.	2– 4	*i·* to the acquiring of
My.	8–27	* the natural and *i·* Leader
	196–26	even the spiritually *i·*,

indisputable

Un.	38– 3	the *i·* realities of being.

indisputably

Mis.	113– 4	If, as is *i·* true,

indissoluble

Mis.	77–12	which is the *i·* bond of union,

indistinct

Mis.	347–12	theirs grows *i·* and ends.

indite

    Mis. 142–15 impression was to *i·* a poem ;

indited

    Mis. 379– 3 if he *i·* anything pathological
    My. 271– 5 I little understood all that I *i·* ;

indites

    Mis. 311–27 transcribing what God *i·*,

individual (*see also* **individual's**)

  another
    Mis. 191–19 cast out of another *i·*
  any other
    My. 363–26 any other *i·* but the patient
  being is
    Mis. 104– 9 In Science all being is *i·* ;
  complexion of the
    Mis. 379– 8 height, and complexion of the *i·*,
  each
    Mis. 119– 8 Each *i·* is responsible for himself.
    Ret. 70–18 Each *i·* must fill his own niche
  good in an
    Mis. 338– 1 the appearing of good in an *i·*
  has met
    '02. 9–28 that an *i·* has met the need of
  hide from an
    Mis. 337–32 tends to hide from an *i·* this grand
  His being is
    Mis. 102–11 His being is *i·*, but not physical.
  interest of the
    '01. 31–16 except in the interest of the *i·*
  knew
    '01. 20–17 if the *i·* knew what was at work
  knowledge of the
    Ret. 71–10 or knowledge of the *i·* treated,
  leaves the
    Mis. 31–17 leaves the *i·* no alternative but to
  mind of the
    Hea. 6–21 mind of the *i·* only can produce a
  misguided
    Mis. 291–31 misguided *i·* who keeps not watch
  nature of the
    Mis. 119–11 nature of the *i·*, more stubborn than
  one
    Mis. 22–16 from one *i·* to another ;
         59–24 success that one *i·* has with another
    My. 267–20 One *i·* may first awaken from
  responsible
    My. 313–18 accompanied by some responsible *i·*
  rights of the
    Ret. 72– 3 nor interfere with the rights of the *i·*.
  single
    Pul. 26–15 * It is the gift of a single *i·*
  that
    Mis. 59–26 That *i·* is the best healer who
    Pan. 10–25 in that *i·* who finds the highest joy,
    My. 188–32 that *i·* ascends the scale of miracles
  this
    Mis. 223–14 This *i·* disbelieves in Mind-healing,
        266–11 this *i·* is doing the work
  unknown
    Mis. 296–29 What manner of man *is* this unknown *i·*
  unknown to the
    Hea. 6–23 may be wholly unknown to the *i·*,

    Mis. 32–26 at present necessary for the *i·*,
        35–14 * I never knew so unselfish an *i·*."
        42– 7 *i·* has but passed through a
        43– 4 without even having seen the *i·*,
        86– 1 The *i·* and spiritual are perfect ;
      105–20 the *i·* and his ideal can never
      107–23 the *i·* may become morally blind,
      108–32 an *i·* believing in that which is
      190–14 Its definition as an *i·* is too
      226– 9 What has an *i·* gained by
      310–27 I as an *i·* would cordially invite
      315–26 except the *i·* needing it asks
      348–28 an *i·* in a proper state of mind.
    Man. 74– 8 no *i·*, and no other church shall
        94– 9 *i·* who goes to hear and deride truth,
    Rud. 2– 4 * an *i·* of the human race."
    No. 23–19 Evil is a quality, not an *i·*.
    '00. 10– 7 greatness of a cause or of an *i·*,
    '01. 16–19 ought not to proceed from the *i·*,
        29–23 *i·* who loves most, does most,
        29–25 is the *i·* who soonest will
    Hea. 8–15 no longer quarrels with the *i·*.
    My. 4–17 such an *i·* subserves the
      206–13 believing that you see an *i·* who has
      218–23 belief that an *i·* can either
      218–28 an *i·* should not enter the
      219–30 I recommend, . . . that an *i·* submit
      249–25 *i·* best fitted to perform this
      303–15 If the *i·* governed
      359–11 can be read by the *i·* who desires
    (*see also* **Eddy**)

individual (adj.)

    Mis. 60–17 *i·* sleepers, in different phases of
      81–22 Every *i·* character,
      81–22 like the *i·* John the Baptist,
      85–17 perpetual, spiritual, *i·* existence.
      98–14 *i·* growth of Christian Scientists,
      98–22 must begin with *i·* growth,
     101–31 God is *i·* Mind.
     104– 1 his *i·* being, the Christ,
     105– 5 our Master's *i·* demonstrations
     105–10 resumed his *i·* spiritual being,
     118–14 can neither . . . advance *i·* growth,
     122– 8 or of the *i·* instrument in
     165–15 *i·* spirituality, perfect and eternal,
     204–18 It develops *i·* capacity,
     205–19 disembodied *i·* Spirit-substance
     267–18 loss from *i·* conceit,
     279– 3 *i·* punishment for sin
     290–27 *i·* blessedness and blessing
     290–28 not so much from *i·* as from
     309–22 Man's *i·* life is infinitely
     350–21 An *i·* state of mind sometimes
     364– 6 In return for *i·* sacrifice,
    Man. 64–17 *i·*, endearing term of Mother.
      70–19 *i·* unity and action of the churches
      72–17 branch churches shall be *i·*,
    Ret. 25–15 God I characterized as *i·* entity.
      67–22 collective as well as *i·*.
      70–14 No person can take the *i·* place
      70–15 fulfil the *i·* mission of Jesus
      70–24 will be, forever *i·*, incorporeal,
      73– 1 man being spiritual, *i·*,
      73–13 fail to appreciate *i·* character.
      74– 5 fails to distinguish the *i·*,
    Un. 5–11 following upward *i·* convictions,
      5–18 or enlighten the *i·* thought.
     25–22 is not *i·*, not actual.
     49– 2 I believe in the *i·* man,
     64– 5 build the *i·* spiritual sense,
    Pul. 4–21 His is an *i·* kingdom,
     74–25 "Christ is *i·*, and one with God,
    Rud. 2– 7 God is definitely *i·*,
     2–15 the phrase *an i·* God,
     2–16 but one infinite *i·* Spirit,
     15–28 to fill anew the *i·* mind.
    No. 1–21 correcting the *i·* thought,
     7–25 the distinctions of *i·* character
     12–26 immaterial, though still *i·*.
     17– 9 a spiritual and *i·* being,
     19–15 God is *i·*,
     19–19 essence of the *i·* infinite.
     23–27 He is definite and *i·*,
     25–19 for he is forever *i·* ;
     26–19 Man's *i·* being must reflect
     26–19 reflect the supreme *i·* Being,
     26–25 *i·* and forever harmonious.
    '01. 2– 3 Christianity in *i·* lives
     7–16 needs of the *i·* mind
     19–25 the unbridled *i·* human will.
    Hea. 8–12 to perceive *i·* advancement ;
    My. 10–30 * *i·* welfare is closely interwoven
     12–11 * his *i·* desires, but as to the
     14– 8 and something from the *i·*,
     111–31 with their *i·* demonstrations.
     117–21 *i·*, but not personal.
     119– 9 and is *i·* in consciousness
     223– 7 to any class of *i·* discords.
     236–30 in their *i·* experiences.
     249– 7 raging element of *i·* hate
    (*see also* **consciousness, rights**)

individualities

    Mis. 102– 1 elements of all forms and *i·*,
    Un. 51–16 not one of all these *i·*

individuality

  all
    Un. 24– 3 all *i·*, all being.
  and Life
    Un. 46–15 *I·* and Life were real to him
  and personality
    My. 344–11 God preserving *i·* and personality.
  and reality
    Un. 46– 7 *i·* and reality of man ;
  constitutes the
    '01. 7– 6 constitutes the *i·* of the infinite
  dwarf
    My. 118–30 dwarf *i·* in personality
  eternal
    Mis. 361–25 man and all eternal *i·*.
  everlasting
    No. 25–20 what this everlasting *i·* is,
  form and
    Mis. 103–13 form and *i·* are never lost,
  His
    Mis. 101–32 This one Mind and His *i·*
      102–15 In His *i·* I recognize

individuality

his
Mis. 104–17 feeble fight with his i,
No. 11– 6 constitute his i in the
his own
Mis. 104–29 and recover his own i
human
Un. 25–16 It honors conscious human i
infinite
'00. 5–14 of eternal, infinite i.
is endless
Mis. 104– 9 i is endless in the calculus of
largest
Pul. 80–10 * Here they have the largest i,
man's
Mis. 104–15 man's i is sinless, deathless,
104–22 man's i reflects the divine law
Un. 53–21 Man's i is not a mortal mind or
No. 23–28 man's i is God's own image and
26–17 If man's i were evil,
Pan. 10– 9 notion that C. S. lessens man's i.
material
Un. 24–10 *Evil.* I am . . . a material i,
mighty
Mis. 258–23 declare a mighty i,
my
Un. 48– 8 He sustains my i.
48– 8 He *is* my i and my Life.
of God
Mis. 103–23 power, presence, and i of God.
Rud. 2–18 Science defines the i of God as
3–24 *By the i of God, do you mean*
of man
Un. 53– 8 reality and i of man are good
Rud. 13– 8 not the actual i of man
other people's
Mis. 62– 2 other people's i, health, and
perpetual
No. 11– 5 Man has perpetual i ;
personality and
'00. 4–29 all personality and i.
spiritual
Mis. 103–27 his spiritual i that reflected the
Ret. 73–15 man's spiritual i in God,
Un. 37–20 spiritual i is immortal.
38– 1 take no cognizance of spiritual i,
their
My. 211–18 The victims lose their i,
this
Mis. 104– 6 this i was safe in the substance of
No. 26–21 this i never originated in molecule,
true
Un. 21–21 consciousness belonging to true i,
53–22 his true i as a perfect child of
unseen
Mis. 104– 3 His unseen i, so superior to
Un. 37–21 this unseen i is real and

Mis. 22–14 absorption, or annihilation of i.
103–30 The i is embraced in Mind,
105– 2 of man's spirituality, i,
145– 6 i to express Soul and substance.
191–11 if devil is an i,
362– 6 reflects all real mode, form, i,
364–16 governing all identity, i, law,
No. 21–11 all phenomena, identity, i, law ;
My. 117–20 God's impersonality and i
344–14 The i of him must make gradual

individualize
My. 160– 7 is to i infinite power :

individualized
Mis. 103–13 i ideas, which dwell forever in
Rud. 3– 9 this trinity of good — was i,
No. 19–16 man is His i idea.

individually
Mis. 137–21 to work out i and alone,
164–28 reveal man collectively, as i,
Man. 76–25 i responsible for said funds.
77–14 Treasurer to be i responsible
Rud. 15–24 persons who cannot be addressed i,
My. 109–20 i but specks in His universe,
134– 9 keep the faith i and collectively,
259–24 either collectively or i

individual's
My. 211–25 spoiling that i disposition,

individuals
Mis. 9–12 those unfortunate i are virtually thy
191–19 can this passage mean several i
230–14 successful i have become such
237– 8 Not a few i serve God
314– 7 One of these i shall open the
347–14 Two i, with all the goodness of
Man. 28– 8 nations, i, and religion
38– 1 i who are known to them to be

individuals
Man. 38–18 I who have heretofore been
63–19 i who take charge of the
68–19 only those i whom she engages
78– 8 not . . . responsible for the debts of i
Pul. 21–22 and close the door on church or i
'00. 8–10 a bane upon i and society.
10–20 sceptre of self and pelf over i,
14–29 they are distinguished i,
'01. 25–10 certain i call aids to
Hea. 3–17 Josephus alludes to several i
Peo. 2–28 nations as well as i,
My. 110– 4 i buried above-ground
116– 6 certain i are inclined to
157–23 a deed of trust to three i
210–19 Certain i entertain the notion
211– 3 unseen wrong to i and society
223–11 Letters and despatches from i
243–11 two i would meet meagrely
265–12 sacred rights of i, peoples,
277– 7 settling difficulties between i
283–21 I, as nations, unite harmoniously
314–16 I are here to-day who were
359– 3 their difficulties with i

indoor
My. 123–21 are bigger than the i.

indorsement
My. 272–32 * gives no editorial i to the

induce
Mis. 243–29 i ulceration, bleeding,
Ret. 6– 3 * can hardly fail to i them
My. 211–20 would i their self-destruction.

induced
My. 40–32 * our Leader has i a multitude
211–32 i by this secret evil influence
348– 3 i a deep research, which
349–28 i by love and deduced from God,

induces
Rud. 12–19 and i rest in God,
My. 9– 9 * i him to glory in every good deed

inductive
My. 349–27 I or deductive reasoning
349–31 i reasoning reckons creation as

indulge
Mis. 93–29 Nothing is more fatal than to i
115–29 if you in any way i in sin ;
348–21 i in homœopathic doses of
369–14 leaders of materialistic schools i
'01. 13–30 So long as we i the presence

indulged
Mis. 12– 3 If i, it masters us ;
94– 3 a person who knowingly i evil,
My. 334–18 * i in while being called unreal.

indulgence
Mis. 354– 1 pleasure seeking, and sense i,
356– 7 rivalry, hate need no temporary i
My. 64–20 * against the i of the sins

indulgences
Mis. 119–13 its habits, tastes, and i.

indulging
My. 5–28 i sin, men cannot serve God ;
5–32 I deceit is like the

industrial
My. 266– 6 human power, i slavery, and
285– 8 i, civic, and national peace.

Industrial Peace Conference
My. 285– 4 to attend the I P C,

industries
My. 287–13 i, human rights, liberty, life.

industrious
Mis. 339–10 good is made more i
Pul. 50– 2 * the welfare of i workmen,

industry
My. 216–16 your sweet i and love
265–29 governed by honesty, i,

inebriate
Po. 71– 2 When earth, i with crime,

ineffable
Mis. 184–25 Oh, for that light and love i,
337–29 The i Life and light
Ret. 13–21 and a soft glow of i joy
25–29 I beheld with i awe
My. 37–28 * its i loving-kindness,
257–11 humanity with i tenderness.

ineligible
Man. 39–16 I for Probation.

inert
Mis.	3–16	Drugs, *i·* matter, never are needed
	256–24	matter in and of itself, is *i·*,
Rud.	5– 9	Matter is *i·*, inanimate,

inestimable
Mis.	114– 2	of *i·* value to all seekers

inevitable
Mis.	127–21	The *i·* condition whereby to
Un.	38–25	*i·* conclusion that Life is not in
Pul.	79–18	* The first is that a revolt was *i·*
	80– 5	* *i·* in the nature of the case.
Pan.	7–28	makes sin, disease, and death *i·*,
'00.	13– 2	* "a controversy was *i·* when the
My.	10– 2	* *i·* that the transforming influence
	10– 5	* *i·* that this mighty impulse
	10– 7	* *i·* that this same impulsion
	178–18	Hence the *i·* revelation of C. S.
	248–14	the needed and the *i·* sponsors

inevitably
Mis.	2–25	he would be *i·* self-annihilated.
	70–21	*i·* separated through Mind.
Ret.	88–17	leads *i·* to a consideration of
Pul.	21– 2	Scientists, . . . *i·* love one another
'02.	10–19	is correct, and *i·* spiritual.
	11– 5	*i·* subject to sin, disease, and
My.	100– 1	* *i·* brought out in connection with

inexhaustible
Mis.	83– 3	perpetual idea of *i·* good.
	92– 4	*i·* topics of that book
Ret.	84– 1	*i·* topics of S. and H.
	84–13	assimilate this *i·* subject — C. S.

inexpedient
Mis.	90–12	sometimes, . . . *i·* to attack evil.

inexplicable
Mis.	222–26	Principle, whose power seems *i·*,
My.	97–16	* audacious, stupendous, *i·* faith

in extremis
My.	45–18	* sense declared you to be *i· e·*.

infallible
Mis.	66– 1	this law is not *i·* in wisdom ;
	84–12	The spiritual Christ was *i·* ;
Ret.	89–30	incorporeal impulsion is divine, *i·*,
Un.	57–15	and rendered this *i·* verdict ;
My.	190–14	regard his sayings as *i·*.
	348–29	law of God — *i·*, eternal.
	364– 1	No mortal is *i·*,

infamous
Hea.	1–18	* At fifty, chides his *i·* delay,

infancy
Mis.	16– 4	In mine *i·*, this is enough of heaven
	166– 8	impersonal *i·*, manhood, and
	231– 3	*i·*, exuberant with joy,
	263–25	by the *i·* of its discovery,

infant
Mis.	15–29	developed into an *i·* Christianity ;
	293– 2	the *i·* thought in C. S.
	320–12	*i·* idea of divine perfection
My.	174–21	offered me to Christ in *i·* baptism.
	312–30	I did open an *i·* school,
	343–28	dangerous in an *i·* church.

infantile
Mis.	85–18	*i·* and more or less imperfect.
	167– 2	*i·* thought of God's man,
	215–17	not according to the *i·* conception
No.	26– 5	This *i·* talk about Mind-healing

infantry
'00.	10–27	lieutenant of the United States *i·*

infants
Mis.	345–23	took their *i·* to a place of worship

infect
Mis.	257–31	may *i·* you with smallpox,

infection
My.	344–29	more dangerous than any material *i·*,

infectious
Mis.	228–30	People believe in *i·* and contagious
My.	219–27	so-called *i·* and contagious diseases
	226–30	decline to doctor *i·* or contagious
	344–21	* heading
	344–23	* of *i·* and contagious diseases.

infer
Mis.	32– 6	I *i·* that some of my students
My.	334– 2	* to *i·* from newspaper reports

inference
Mis.	103–21	Any *i·* of the divine derived from
	122–16	Such an *i·* were impious.
	195–18	in our text, contradicts this *i·*,
	216– 1	and *i·* from his acts,
Ret.	59– 8	Such an *i·* is unscientific.
Pul.	46– 7	* no such *i·* is to be drawn
Rud.	6– 2	equal *i·* that there is no matter.

inference
No.	16–18	*i·* of some other existence
	16–21	He can have no knowledge or *i·* but
'01.	28–27	hence the *i·* that he who would

inferior
Mis.	226–25	Perfidy of an *i·* quality,

inferred
Mis.	379–10	from his remarks I *i·* that

infidel
Mis.	63– 1	is *i·* in the one case,
	248–16	that I am an *i·*, a mesmerist,
	345–14	Methinks the *i·* was blind who said,
No.	43–15	* convicting the *i·*, alarming the
Peo.	13–22	The *i·* was blind who said,

infidelity
Mis.	4–21	confounded with isms, and even *i·*,
	257– 1	that Mind can be in matter is rank *i·*,
	365–24	*i·*, bigotry, or sham has never
Rud.	12–11	fosters *i·*, and is mental quackery,
No.	19– 5	Even doctors will agree that *i·*,
	21–18	This is rank *i·* ;
My.	220–17	the end of idolatry and *i·*,

infidels
Mis.	345–15	but even *i·* may disagree.
'01.	32–12	When *i·* assailed them,
Peo.	13–24	*i·* disagree ; for Bonaparte said :

infinite (noun)
against the
Ret.	67–10	self-arrayed against the *i·*,

apprehend the
Peo.	3–21	wrongly to apprehend the *i·*,

blessings of the
My.	118–21	to supply the blessings of the *i·*,

body of the
Hea.	3–27	person of Truth, the body of the *i·*,

cannot contain the
Hea.	4– 1	finite cannot contain the *i·*,

demonstrated the
No.	36– 1	demonstrated the *i·* as one,

includes
Mis.	96–10	or what the *i·* includes ;

is one
My.	356–25	The *i·* is one, and this one is

likeness of the
Mis.	97–27	image and likeness of the *i·*.

measures the
My.	229–31	measures the *i·* against the finite.

radiation of the
No.	17–19	the focal radiation of the *i·*.

scorner of the
My.	107–21	O petty scorner of the *i·*,

sense of the
'01.	26– 8	only a finite sense of the *i·* :

Spirit and
'01.	25–28	which, if indeed Spirit and *i·*,

unlike the
'02.	6– 2	to have aught unlike the *i·*.

voices the
No.	13–19	voices the *i·*, and governs the

Mis.	75–12	the *i·* is not within the finite ;
	102– 8	and the *i·* forever finite.
	136– 8	The eternal and *i·*,
	153–29	* Far-off, *i·*, Bliss !
	173–15	Can the *i·* be within the finite?
	322–28	from the infinitesimal to the *i·*.
Un.	7– 9	the *i·* recognizes no disease,
No.	1– 2	spiritual idea emanating from the *i·*,
	19–13	person of the *i·* is, we know not ;
	19–20	nature and essence of the individual *i·*.
'01.	6– 7	reckons . . . the *i·* in a finite form,
	23– 6	and that the *i·* is not all ;
	23– 9	or exist outside of the *i·*,
Hea.	4– 2	*i·* can neither go forth from,
My.	159–14	*i·* will not be buried in the finite ;
	159–19	God, the *i·* and eternal
	186–12	Word welling up from the *i·*
	195–26	an edifice in which to worship the *i·*,
	226–14	from the infinitesimal to the *i·*,
	239–21	the infinite *one*, or one *i·*,
	248–17	into the transcendental, the *i·*
	272–10	is not the altitude of the *i·*.
	291– 9	from the infinitesimal to the *i·*.

infinite (adj.)
All
Mis.	250– 1	the *i·* All of good,
Un.	24– 2	I am the *i·* All.

ascent
My.	117– 8	to pursue the *i·* ascent,

Being
Un.	19– 2	must be one, in an *i·* Being.

being
My.	262–17	with the glory of *i·* being.

infinite (adj.)

blessings
(*see* **blessings**)

calculus
Mis. 22–11 *i·* calculus defining the line,
'01. 22–20 *i·* calculus of the infinite God.

calm
'00. 11–25 * With a touch of *i·* calm.

care
Mis. 370–17 *i·* care from His loving heart.

claims
Mis. 16–10 hath *i·* claims on man,

consciousness
Mis. 258–24 *i·* consciousness, ever-presence,
No. 37– 6 eternal God and *i·* consciousness

Deity
Un. 10–14 toward aught but *i·* Deity.

demand
Mis. 77– 7 *i·* demand made upon the eunuch

energies
Ret. 30–14 *i·* energies of Truth and Love,

essence
Mis. 394– 4 *i·* essence from tropic to pole,
Po. 45– 5 *i·* essence from tropic to pole,

faculties
My. 154–19 * deep *i·* faculties of man.''

finite and
Mis. 217–29 or to become both finite and *i·* ;

God
(*see* **God**)

God is
(*see* **God**)

good
(*see* **good**)

good is
Mis. 108– 5 good is *i·*, All.

goodness
Rud. 2–25 higher range of *i·* goodness.

harmony
No. 17–23 *i·* harmony would be fathomed.

idea
Mis. 165– 9 This *i·* idea of infinity will be,
No. 25–11 *i·* idea of Truth is beyond a finite

identity
My. 239–23 real and eternal in *i·* identity.

importance
Mis. 192– 6 of *i·* importance to man's spiritual

individuality
'00. 5–14 of eternal, *i·* individuality.

inquiry
Un. 1–14 to defer this *i·* inquiry,

instructions
Ret. 83–10 *i·* instructions afforded by

law
Mis. 172–19 feeble sense of the *i·* law of God ;

Life
(*see* **Life**)

light
No. 16–15 This infinite logic is the *i·* light,

logic
No. 16–15 This *i·* logic is the infinite light,

Love
(*see* **Love**)

manifestation
Mis. 21–17 Mind and its *i·* manifestation,

manifestations
'02. 7– 3 His *i·* manifestations of love

meaning
(*see* **meaning**)

meanings
Mis. 125–18 learn forever the *i·* meanings of
'02. 4–23 *i·* meanings, applicable to all
My. 202–16 *i·* meanings, endless hopes, and
221– 8 in His more *i·* meanings,
231–13 of its highest and *i·* meanings,
262–31 reveals *i·* meanings and gives

mercy
Pul. 74–16 for God to declare in His *i·* mercy.

Mind
(*see* **Mind**)

mind
Pan. 3–18 *i·* mind of one supreme, holy,

model
Un. 14–22 Our *i·* model would be taken away.

nature
Mis. 284– 6 Its *i·* nature and uses
My. 349–29 makes manifest the *i·* nature,

ocean
Mis. 205–14 in the *i·* ocean of Love,

One
Pul. 4–15 reflects the *i·* One,
'01. 4–22 understand that God is the *i·* One

one
My. 239–21 idea or likeness of the *i·* one,

patience
Hea. 2–17 Jesus, the model of *i·* patience,

infinite (adj.)

penetration
Un. 2–15 in the *i·* penetration of Truth,

perfect and
Mis. 82–16 whose law is perfect and *i·*.

perfection
Un. 16– 1 man bows to the *i·* perfection
My. 103–12 *I·* perfection is unfolded

Person
Pan. 8– 7 one the divine, *i·* Person,
'01. 3– 7 chapter sub-title
4–19 He is the *i·* Person,
6–10 a finite or an *i·* Person?
6–27 We believe in God as the *i·* **Person** ;
7– 6 individuality of the *i·* Person
7–19 as well as *i·* Person,
My. 109–15 This *i·* Person we know not of by
192–13 the *i·* Person whom we worship,
225–22 Principle, Love, the *i·* Person.

personality
Mis. 102–16 *I·* personality must be incorporeal.

power
Un. 13–13 His *i·* power would straightway
My. 160– 7 is to individualize *i·* power ;

Principle
(*see* **Principle**)

progression
Mis. 82–13 *Is there i· progression with man*
82–20 *I·* progression is concrete being,

query
Mis. 337– 8 *I·* query ! Wonder in heaven

reality
Un. 43– 5 cannot bring out the *i·* reality

remedy
Mis. 63– 9 divine trinity is one *i·* remedy

results
Ret. 92– 1 self-abandonment wrought *i·* results.

scope
My. 259–25 give the activity of man *i·* scope ;

sinner
Un. 15–19 precedence as the *i·* sinner,
16– 2 such terms as *divine sin* and *i· sinner*

Soul
Un. 48–13 Ego is God Himself, the *i·* Soul.
Pul. 2–24 the eternal harmony of *i·* Soul.

source
Mis. 287–12 Soul is the *i·* source of bliss :
My. 165–31 *i·* source where is *all*,

Spirit
(*see* **Spirit**)

Spirit is
Pan. 13–19 great truth that Spirit is *i·*,
My. 271– 2 God, Spirit, is *i·*,
357–22 Spirit is *i·* ; therefore *Spirit is all.*

Truth
(*see* **Truth**)

Unseen
Un. 7–21 perfection of the *i·* Unseen

uses
My. 182–32 *i·* uses of Christ's creed,

value
Mis. 232–23 its *i·* value and firm basis.

wisdom
Mis. 18–11 These commands of *i·* wisdom,
Hea. 4–10 We ask *i·* wisdom to possess our

Mis. 16– 9 Principle of Christianity is *i·* :
102– 4 is only an *i·* finite being,
189–20 declare Life to be the *i·* I AM,
252– 2 not necessarily infinitesimal but *i·*.
309–12 *i·* spiritual substance and
330–12 since man's possibilities are *i·*,
367–19 If . . . He would not be *i·*.
386– 2 *i·* appear Life, Love divine,
Ret. 57–11 but one Soul, and that one is *i·*.
70–24 individual, incorporeal, and *i·*,
Un. 19–13 this would be the end of *i·* moral
24–13 an *i·*, and not a finite consciousness.
29–12 Soul, or Mind, and that one is *i·*,
41– 9 the *i·* and only Life.
48–13 as *i·* and conscious Life,
Rud. 1– 6 *i·* and immortal Mind,
2–13 if we think of Him as less than *i·*.
2–16 but one *i·* individual Spirit,
3–26 *i·* and divine Principle of all being,
7– 5 The *i·* and subtler conceptions
No. 36– 2 one *i·* and the other finite ;
36– 4 He knew God as *i·*,
'01. 4–25 One because He is *i·* ;
5– 7 one divine *i·* triune Principle,
6– 8 reckons one as one and this one *i·*.
6–22 in the *i·* scientific sense of Him,
6–23 can neither be one nor *i·* in
6–26 God's personality must be as *i·* as
22–13 Spirit is true and *i·*,
23– 5 God is Spirit and *i·*,

infinite (adj.)

'01.	23– 7	God is good and *i*,
'02.	5–25	Since God is Love, and *i*,
Hea.	4–17	to show itself *i* again.
Peo.	2–25	Love universal, *i*, eternal.
	4– 5	more than an *i* and divine Mind;
	4– 9	Life, which is *i* and eternal,
Po.	49– 4	*i* appear Life, Love divine,
My.	36–10	* with our *i* heavenly Father
	108–16	only lawgiver, omnipotent, *i*, All.
	116–12	God is Person, then Person is *i*;
	135–30	Love, omnipotent, omnipresent, *i*;
	235–21	Because Spirit is God and *i*;
	267–10	supreme, *i*, the great forever,
	267–16	Heaven is harmony, — *i*, boundless
	269– 3	*i* divine Principle, Love,
	279–16	God is Father, *i*,
	296–20	God, good, omnipotent and *i*.
	339– 6	one God, supreme, *i*,
	350–19	Thou all, Thou *i*
	356–28	God being *i*, He is the only basis of

infinitely

Mis.	8–15	blesses *i* one and all
	16–19	God is *i* more than a person,
	121–28	*I* greater than human pity,
	185–21	reveals man *i* blessed,
	309–22	life is *i* above a bodily form
	321–30	*i* beyond all earthly
	332– 4	*I* just, merciful, and wise,
Pul.	62–17	* with *i* less expense.
No.	34–19	*i* beyond the heathen conception
Hea.	14–15	Metaphysical healing includes *i* more
My.	114–24	Truth and Love, *i* above me,
	128– 8	*i* less than God's benign
	146–13	C. S. contains *i* more than

infinites

'01.	6–12	Who can conceive . . . of three *i*?

infinitesimal

Mis.	252– 2	Mind is not necessarily *i*
	322–27	from the *i* to the infinite.
Hea.	12–19	made the *i* dose effectual.
My.	226–13	from the *i* to the infinite,
	291– 8	from the *i* to the infinite.

infinitesimals

Mis.	26–15	Whence came the *i*,

infinitude

Mis.	95–23	C. S. reveals the *i* of divinity
	181–13	if we recognize *i* as personality,
	259– 7	this *i* and oneness of good
Un.	20–20	as you realize the divine *i*
No.	26–16	into something below *i*.
	30–19	Truth's knowledge of its own *i*

infinity

Mis.	15–20	progress is the law of *i*.
	27– 1	What can there be besides *i*?
	72–30	aught material, or outside of *i*.
	79–15	out of the focal distance of *i*.
	102–10	His *i* precludes the possibility of
	165– 9	This infinite idea of *i* will be
	181–15	who can tell what is the form of *i*?
	333– 4	every ray of Truth, of *i*,
Ret.	58– 4	to work out the problem of *i*
	59–12	in demonstration of *i*.
	68– 8	though he reflects the *i* of good.
	70– 7	an attempted infringement on *i*''
Un.	5– 2	a theme involving the All of *i*.
	25–16	from finiteness into *i*.
No.	38–16	the *i* and unity of good.
Pan.	7–16	absolute oneness and *i* of God,
Peo.	4– 7	belief that . . . *i* became finity,
My.	132–10	they embark for *i* and anchor in

infirm

Pul.	4– 2	* "weak and *i* of purpose."

infirmities

Mis.	162–18	The corporeal Jesus bore our *i*,
	199–11	*I take pleasure in i*, — II Cor. 12: 10.
	200–22	"I take pleasure in *i*," — II Cor. 12: 10.
	201–16	Paul took pleasure in *i*,
	201–31	good that has pleasure in *i*;
Un.	55– 4	In his real self he bore no *i*.

infirmity

Mis.	294– 2	last *i* of evil is so-called man,
Un.	57–16	by affinity nor by *i*,
'02.	10–25	is the *i* of evil,
Po.	35– 6	binds to earth — *i* of woe!

inflames

Mis.	222– 3	*i* envy, passion, evil-speaking,

inflammation

Mis.	41–22	action of fear, manifests *i*
	45– 7	power to allay fear, prevent *i*,
	69–25	exciting cause of the *i*
My.	301–27	Drugs cannot remove *i*,

inflammatory

My.	107–30	stages of organic and *i* diseases,

inflate

Mis.	129–17	*i* it, and send it into the atmosphere of
	301–29	All error tends to . . . *i* self;

inflated

Mis.	354–29	genius *i* with worldly desire.

inflection

My.	344–18	* with a prolonged *i*,

inflictions

Mis.	312– 7	bears all burdens, suffers all *i*,

inflow

Pul.	64–13	* the continued *i* of money

influence

adverse

My.	213–26	adverse *i* of animal magnetism.

benign

Mis.	63– 5	to hinder his benign *i*

counteracting

Mis.	223–22	no counteracting *i* can hinder

counteract the

Mis.	291–30	counteract the *i* of envious minds

divine

No.	40–27	made better only by divine *i*.

elevating

Peo.	2–27	a benign and elevating *i*

evil

My.	211–32	induced by this secret evil *i*
	212– 9	effects of this evil *i*,

felt the

Mis.	290–16	* "I felt the *i* of your thought
Un.	57–12	he must have felt the *i* of

harmonious

Pul.	54–21	* environment and harmonious *i*

her

Pul.	23– 7	* MRS. EDDY'S WORK AND HER *I*
	50– 7	* thus add her *i* toward the

hidden

Mis.	114–25	stop their hidden *i* upon the

its

My.	28–14	* its *i* upon the lives of
	47–12	* touched by its *i* for good,
	295– 3	its *i* remains in the minds

mental

Mis.	264–23	mental *i* of their former teacher.
Ret.	72– 2	cannot impart a mental *i* that

money and

Mis.	80– 7	its members to give money and *i*

much

My.	272–31	* much *i* on this generation.

no

No.	9– 9	use no *i* to prevent their

of this Mind

Mis.	279–29	feel the *i* of this Mind;

originating

'01.	33–10	* was never the originating *i*

salutary

Rud.	10– 4	its salutary *i* on yourself

selfish

Ret.	89–29	Corporeal and selfish *i* is human,

silent

No.	1– 6	changed by its silent *i*.

strengthens the

Mis.	362–31	except when it strengthens the *i* of

such an

Ret.	71–15	to be subjected to such an *i*?

their

Peo.	8–10	extend their *i* to others.

transforming

My.	10– 2	* transforming *i* of C. S.

unite the

Un.	43–20	unite the *i* of their own thoughts

uplifting

Mis.	245–13	its uplifting *i* upon . . . mankind.

Man.	52–26	or shall *i* others thus to act,
Ret.	44–30	Adding to its ranks and *i*,
	89–27	endeavoring to *i* other minds to any
'00.	12–21	Under the *i* of St. Paul's preaching
My.	175–28	must fail to *i* the minds of
	281–24	*i* which President Roosevelt

influenced

Mis.	113–15	*i* by any but the divine Mind,
	246– 6	pulpit and press that *i* the people
Man.	40–14	influencing or being *i* erroneously.
My.	137–21	*i* me to select a Board of Trustees
	137–29	No person *i* me to make this
	227–14	*i* by their own judgment

influences

Mis.	71–12	*good or bad i on the unborn child?*
	229–14	faith in Mind over all other *i*
Ret.	52– 6	contaminating *i* of those who

influences
 Rud. 4–12 sweet *i·* of the Pleïades," — *Job* 38 : 31.
 No. 7– 3 evil *i·* waver the scales of justice
   39– 8 no dishonesty or vanity *i·* the

influencing
 Man. 40–14 *i·* or being influenced erroneously.
 '01. 20– 3 no authority in C. S. for *i·* the

influenza
 Mis. 239–21 pride at sharing in a popular *i·*

influx
 My. 114–21 *i·* of divine interpretation
  206– 4 hinder the divine *i·* and lose
  212–20 they would receive a spiritual *i·*

inform
 Mis. 29–21 Daily letters *i·* me that a
  67–21 you shall, *Deo volente, i·* them
  87–15 *i· us, through your Journal,*
  88– 9 I am pleased to *i·* this inquirer,
  97–21 Scriptures *i·* us that man
  240–28 Likewise soberly *i·* them that
  222–10 Clerk of the church can *i·*
 Man. 26–14 shall *i·* the Pastor Emeritus
  29– 1 to *i·* the Board of Directors
  52–17 shall immediately so *i·* him.
  57–11 Clerk to *i·* the Board of Directors
  66– 2 he shall *i·* her of this fact
 No. 23–24 is not sufficient to *i·* us as to
  28–25 The Scriptures *i·* us that
 My. 135–18 I *i·* you of this,
  359–12 to *i·* himself of the facts.

informally
 Ret. 89–12 he did so *i·*,
 My. 352– 4 * *I·* assembled, we, the ushers

informant
 My. 14–13 * *i·* claimed to have good authority

information
 Mis. 69–28 wish to apply to him for *i·*
  89–21 *I ask for i·, not for controversy,*
  132–22 for *i·* as to what I believe
  157–11 that they furnish all *i·* possible.
 Man. 46–15 such *i·* as may come to them
  53–12 without her having requested the *i·*,
 Pul. 37– 1 * "It is a pleasure to give any *i·*
 My. 54–11 * the *i·*, 'No more standing-room.' "
  73–21 * all *i·* concerning rooms and board,
  236–27 I consider the *i·* there given
  242–17 *i·* relating to C. S. practice,
  319–20 * advised that I have this *i·*.

informed
 Mis. 48–15 *i·* his audience that he could
  49– 4 *i·* that, before entering the College,
  91–24 I never dreamed, until *i·* thereof,
  195–32 *i·* by divine Science, the Comforter,
  378– 5 as he *i·* the patients,
 Man. 76–22 *i·* as to the real estate
 Ret. 15–28 agreeably *i·* the congregation
  21– 4 *i·* that my son was lost.
  38– 2 when the printer *i·* me that
  47–13 being *i·* of my intentions,
 No. 3–17 to keep himself well *i·*.
 '01. 27–15 I shall rejoice in being *i·*
 '02. 15– 3 neither *i·* the police of these
 My. 11–23 * *i·* of the purchase of the land
  14–12 * saying that he had just been *i·*
  166–27 I am for the first time *i·* of
  330– 7 * calumniator who *i·* you
  358–12 You have been duly *i·*

informer
 Pul. 15–12 Is the *i·* one who sees the foe?

informing
 Mis. 332– 3 governing, *i·* the universe,
 Ret. 21– 2 *i·* him that his mother was dead
 My. 198– 4 *i·* me of the dedication
  244– 1 before *i·* you of my purpose
  259–30 eternal *i·* Soul recognized only

informs
 Mis. 339– 3 that which St. John *i·* us

infraction
 Mis. 29–27 Miracles are no *i·* of God's laws ;

infrequently
 Ret. 80–29 not *i·* met by envy, ingratitude,
 Pul. 33–15 * which history not *i·* emphasizes,
 My. 355– 8 not *i·* hinted at this.

infringe
 Mis. 348– 5 *i·* neither the books nor the business
 Pan. 8–11 *i·* the sacredness of one
 My. 154– 8 if they can be made to *i·* the

infringed
 Ret. 39– 2 the copyright was *i·*.
 Un. 13–10 are not *i·* in ethics

infringement
 Mis. 300–10 liable to arrest for *i·* of
  302– 4 encourages *i·* of my copyright,
 Ret. 70– 6 attempted *i·* on infinity"
 Peo. 12– 6 *i·* on the merciful and just
 My. 167–25 *i·* of rights and privileges

infringes
 Mis. 56–12 *i·* the rights of Spirit.

infringing
 Mis. 80–17 *i·* individual rights,
  380–30 use of an *i·* pamphlet
  381–27 *i·* books, to the number of

infused
 Mis. 190– 3 nor the outcome of life *i·* into
 Ret. 58–13 it was not *i·* into matter ;

infusion
 Un. 42–22 or of an *i·* of power into matter.

ingenuity
 Mis. 286–16 put *i·* to ludicrous shifts ;

ingenuously
 Pul. 23–15 * *i·* calling out a closer inquiry

Ingersoll's
 Robert
 My. 110–28 Robert *I·* attempt to convict the
    ——
 Ret. 77– 3 *I·* repartee has its moral :

inglorious
 Ret. 10–18 no earthly or *i·* theme.

ingrafting
 Ret. 57–26 *i·* upon one First Cause

ingrained
 My. 81– 5 * So *i·* is this good nature,

ingratitude
 Mis. 13– 5 falsehood, *i·*, misjudgment,
  294–16 hides it in his cell of *i·*.
  389–15 hope deferred, *i·*, disdain !
 Ret. 81– 1 envy, *i·*, and enmity,
 Un. 56–27 *i·*, lust, malice, hate,
 Pul. 84– 4 * bitterness and *i·* of her sting,
 '01. 15–16 mortals, and their *i·* and hate,
 '02. 19– 1 injustice, *i·*, treachery, and
 Po. 4–14 For hope deferred, *i·*, disdain !

ingress
 Mis. 325–28 sees robbers finding ready *i·* to

inhabit
 Pul. 21– 9 praying for it to *i·* my own heart
 '01. 6– 9 infinite Mind *i·* a finite form?
 My. 133– 6 *i·* His holy hill,

inhabitants
 Mis. 334– 2 among the *i·* of the earth :— *Dan.* 4 : 35.
 My. 181–24 to the number of 1,650,000 *i·*.
  280–19 He will bless all the *i·*

inhabiters
 Pul. 12–12 Woe to the *i·* of the earth — *Rev.* 12 : 12.

inhabiting
 Mis. 330–30 modest grass, *i·* the whole earth,
 My. 344–10 not the spirit of God, *i·* clay

inhabits
 Mis. 189–30 extends to all time, *i·* eternity,

inharmonious
 Mis. 58–24 If God does not govern . . . it is *i·* :

inharmony
 Mis. 27–12 all *i·*, sin, disease, death
  98– 4 turn away from *i·*, sickness, and
 Un. 13–11 To Him there is no moral *i·* ;
  18–19 My knowledge of harmony (not *i·*)
  60–10 and *i·* is its opposite.

inherent
 Pul. 51– 7 * liberty which is their *i·* right
 '02. 2–22 It was an *i·* characteristic
 My. 227–22 *I·* justice, constitutional
  262– 3 *i·* unity with divine Love,
  326– 6 * their *i·* rights are recognized

inherit
 Mis. 145–13 "*i·* the earth." — *Psal.* 37 : 11.
  340–22 by patience, they *i·* the promise.
 Ret. 92– 7 *i·* his legacy of love,
 Un. 37– 4 in order to *i·* eternal life
 '01. 26–19 the meek that *i·* the earth ;
 My. 228–18 Who shall *i·* the earth?
  228–21 they shall *i·* the earth,

inheritance
 Mis. 153– 3 God will confirm His *i·*.
  251–20 Think of this *i·* !
  253–19 that the *i·* may be ours," — *Luke* 20 : 14.
  254–14 that the *i·* may be ours," — *Luke* 20 : 14.
  307– 5 What a glorious *i·* is given to us

inheritance
No. 3– 3 idea which claims only its *i·*,
My. 41–26 * and disregard his lawful *i·*,
206–27 partakers of the *i· — Col.* 1 : 12.

inherited
Ret. 1–13 was no sign that she *i·* a
4– 3 Mark Baker, who *i·* the homestead,
4– 4 he *i·* my grandfather's farm
My. 309–18 *i·* his father's real estate,

inhospitable
My. 89– 4 * all facts *i·* to it

inhuman
Mis. 121–15 That the innocent shall . . . is *i·*.
211–10 *I·* medical bills, class legislation,
246– 5 to blot out all *i·* codes.
Peo. 11– 8 not by *i·* warfare, but in divine
12–11 as with an *i·* State law ;

inhumanity
Mis. 246–15 *i·* lifts its hydra head

iniquities
Mis. 102–21 which blots out all our *i·*
174– 7 Him who removeth all *i·*,
Un. 48–10 destroys my *i·*, deprives death of
55– 7 bruised for *our i·* ; — *Isa.* 53 : 5.
Pul. 10– 6 forgiveth all thine *i·* ; — *Psal.* 103 : 3.
Pan. 4–25 forgiveth all thine *i·* ; — *Psal.* 103 : 3.
Peo. 12–13 forgiveth all thine *i·* ; — *Psal.* 103 : 3.
My. 13–20 forgiveth all thine *i·* ; — *Psal.* 103 : 3.
126–17 hath remembered her *i· — Rev.* 18 : 5.

iniquitous
Ret. 67– 9 *i·* manifestation of sin

iniquity
Mis. 19–19 wherewith to cover *i·*,
123–17 and is too pure to behold *i·*.
209–31 egotism and false charity say, . . . cover *i·*
210–29 foolhardiness to cover *i·*.
259–11 while *i·*, too evil to conceive of
259–13 declares that God knows *i·* !
335–21 notion that one is covering *i·* by
348– 8 When God bids one uncover *i·*,
367–30 God is too pure to behold *i·* ;
Ret. 63–19 Whosoever covers *i·* becomes accessory
Un. 2– 2 too pure to behold *i· — see Hab.* 1 : 13.
18– 8 God says, I am too pure to behold *i·*,
Pul. 15– 4 expose evil's . . . ways of accomplishing *i·*.
Rud. 10– 7 He is too pure to behold *i·*,
'01. 14– 3 that clings fast to *i·*.
My. 124–30 and the mystery of *i·*
126–10 kills this mystery of *i·*
161–10 all ye workers of *i·*. — *Luke* 13 : 27.
252–16 reward righteousness and punish *i·*.
334–21 that clings fast to *i·*.

initial
Mis. xi– 3 caused me to retain the *i·* "G"

initials
Man. 46– 7 Use of *I·* "C. S."
46– 8 shall not place the *i·* "C. S."
110–13 *I·* only of first names
111– 4 *I·* alone will not be received.

injunction
Mis. 120– 5 each and every *i·* of the
128– 6 with the apostle's *i·* :
191–31 Let us obey St. Paul's *i·*
302–25 This *i·* did not curtail the
381–21 A writ of *i·* was issued
Ret. 87–19 to obey the celestial *i·*,
Pul. 66–12 * under the *i·* to
My. 227–23 and the gospel *i·*,
282– 7 and the Scriptural *i·*,

injunctions
Pul. 29–20 * while all these *i·* could,
No. 14–21 the *i·* are not confined to

injure
Mis. 12– 8 him who has striven to *i·* you.
32–29 slander, hate, or try to *i·*,
48–30 offered solely to *i·* her
224–29 wilfully attempt to *i·* another,
260–31 whereby it may *i·* the race,
267– 7 whose chief aim is to *i·* me,
267–13 secretly striving to *i·* me.
My. 298– 5 nothing . . . could *i·* me ;
353–17 to *i·* no man, but to bless

injures
My. 210–12 *i·* him when he would harm

injuries
My. 204–26 the resenting of *i·*,
348– 2 healed of so-called disease and *i·*

injuring
Mis. 222– 6 *i·* himself and others.

injurious
Man. 53–26 false or unjust, hence *i·*, to C. S.
My. 128–26 but the result is as *i·*.

injury
Mis. 24– 9 an *i·* caused by an accident,
43–22 does a vast amount of *i·*
Man. 49–25 without previous *i·* or illness,
Ret. 24–12 an *i·* caused by an accident,
24–13 an *i·* that neither medicine nor
40–14 *i·* received from a surgical operation
My. 138– 8 not for my benefit . . . but for my *i·*,

injustice
Mis. 66– 8 No possible *i·* lurks in this
72– 4 were sore *i·*.
80–20 redress wrongs and rectify *i·*.
122–22 nor reconciles justice to *i·* ;
216–17 a big protest against *i·* ;
235–26 chapter sub-title
247–17 *i·* of their interpretations.
301–24 This method is an unseen form of *i·*
317–29 My soul abhors *i·*, and loves mercy.
Pul. 83–15 * wield the ruthless sword of *i·*.
'02. 19– 1 *i·*, ingratitude, treachery, and
Peo. 10–14 *i·* and error enslave him.
Po. 71–12 *I·* to the combat sprang ;
My. 116–23 from *i·* and personal contagion.
151–12 *i·* done by press and pulpit
191– 4 *I·* has not a tithe of the power of
220–14 *I·* denotes the absence of law.
252–14 clouds of wrong, *i·*, envy, hate ;
277–17 whereby wrong and *i·* are righted
283–19 When pride, self, . . . *i·* is rampant.

injustices
Man. 97–18 *i·* done Mrs. Eddy or members

inkling
'02. 16– 6 my first *i·* of Wyclif's use of

inlaid
Mis. 30–13 gates thereof . . . *i·* with pearl,

inmate
Mis. 324–20 this mortal *i·* withdraws ;

inmates
Mis. 283–11 rouse the slumbering *i·*,
325–14 find its *i·* asleep at noontide !

in memoriam
My. 289–28 *i· m·* of the late lamented Victoria,

inmost
My. 133–26 this *i·* something becomes articulate,

innate
Un. 26– 2 having its own *i·* selfhood
My. 341– 1 I have one *i·* joy,

inner
Pul. 32–15 * may translate those *i·* experiences
'01. 30–19 kindles the *i·* genial life
My. 188–17 I enter your *i·* sanctuary,
244–17 *i·* sanctuary of divine Science,

innocence
Mis. 110– 6 it needs your *i·*, unselfishness,
121–20 this sentence passed upon *i·*
Ret. 80–25 while *i·* strayeth yearningly.
My. 261–13 the first impressions of *i·*,
269– 4 pledged to *i·*, purity,

innocent
Mis. 66– 3 may cause the *i·* to suffer
72– 2 For the *i·* babe to be born a
112– 9 can neither defend the *i·* nor
121–15 That the *i·* shall suffer for
121–17 the guilt of *i·* blood — *Deut.* 19 : 13.
121–31 punishes the guilty, not the *i·*.
210–23 *i·* enjoyment, and a medical
227– 6 to offer to the *i·*, security
257–14 It punishes the *i·*,
275–19 console the *i·*, and throw wide the
354– 5 and lead the *i·* to doom?
My. 33–26 reward against the *i·*. — *Psal.* 15 : 5.
220–29 That the *i·* should suffer for the

innocently
Mis. 357–28 sought the true fold . . . and strayed *i·* ;

innocents
Mis. 123– 2 same spirit that . . . slaughters *i·*.

innovations
Mis. 265–16 presume to make *i·* upon

innumerable
Mis. 137–26 one of the *i·* errors that
My. 46–29 * *i·* company of angels, — *Heb.* 12 : 22.

inordinate
Mis. 274–21 reign of *i·*, unprincipled clans.

inorganic
Mis. 56– 4 Life is *i·*, infinite Spirit ;

in propria persona
Pul. 1–19 that I should be present *i· p· p·?*
My. 5–23 I am not with you *i· p· p·*
25–19 I cannot be present *i· p· p·*
143– 1 I will attend . . . but not *i· p· p·.*

inquest
My. 128– 6 A coroner's *i·*, a board of health,

inquire
Mis. 381–10 requested her lawyer to *i·*
Man. 66–19 * if all of the letter has been read,
My. 325– 3 * to *i·* of his welfare

inquired
Pul. 73– 1 * *i·* the speaker.
Peo. 4–24 *i·* of these heathen deities
My. 24–18 * *i·* about the progress of the work

inquirer
Mis. 88– 9 pleased to inform this *i·*,
Un. 20–15 Try this process, dear *i·*,

Inquirer
Pul. 88–32 * *I·*, Philadelphia, Pa.

inquiries
Mis. 132–18 *i·* from all quarters,
193– 1 entertaining the startling *i·*,
My. 223–20 *i·*, coming directly or indirectly
242–17 *i· . . .* relating to C. S. practice,
242–22 not to make *i·* on these subjects,
245–26 *I·* have been made as to the precise
356–13 In reply to *i·*, will you please state

inquiring
'01. 31–14 no vague, fruitless, *i·* wonder.

inquiry
Mis. 28–21 suggests the *i·*, What meaneth
237–19 This is a period of doubt, *i·*,
268–15 His whole *i·* and demonstration
307–16 *i·* of mankind as to Christianity
Man. 52– 9 shall address a letter of *i·* to
Un. 1–14 to defer this infinite *i·*,
27– 1 *i·* as to the meaning of a word
Pul. 23–16 * a closer *i·* into Oriental
33–21 * All *i·* in the neighborhood
No. 46– 9 must answer the constant *i·* :
'01. 17–18 interviews, that started the *i·*,
My. 53– 2 * important missives of *i·*
157–19 * In response to an *i·* from
165–19 oft-repeated *i·*, What am I?
245–10 The growth of human *i·*
292–13 My answer to the *i·*,

Inquisition
Mis. 274–28 car of the modern *I·*

inquisitive
Rud. 15– 9 renders the mind less *i·*, plastic,

inrush
My. 74– 3 * until Saturday night the *i·* will

insane
Mis. 48–23 *Was ever a person made i· by*
48–26 Mind-healing would cure the *i·*.
48–28 * "made *i· . . .* is a baseless fabrication
My. 301–21 committed to *i·* asylums
302–11 insanity is that brain, matter, is *i·*.

insanity
Mis. 49–10 had not produced *i·*."
49–11 into the claim of *i·*
49–13 notable cases of *i·* have been
113–22 if persisted in, will end in *i·*,
My. 222–16 executed (for "*i·*") because of
301–16 Is faith in divine metaphysics *i·?*
301–17 All sin is *i·*,
301–18 a universal *i·* which mistakes
301–23 supposition that we can correct *i·* by
301–24 is in itself a species of *i·*.
302–11 *i·* is that brain, matter, is insane.

inscribed
Mis. 121– 2 *i·* upon the hearts of men :
295–25 advanced ideas are *i·* on tablets
Ret. 2–12 on which was *i·* the name of
5–12 *i·* on the stone memorials
Pul. 46–20 * upon which had been *i·* the name
Po. 73– 1 *i·* to my friends in Lynn.

inscribes
Mis. 294– 7 he *i·* on the heart of humanity
Peo. 3–17 *i·* on the thoughts of men

inscription
Pul. 24–13 * *i·* carved in bold relief :
77– 8 * The *i·* reads thus :
78– 6 * *i·*, cut in script letters :
86– 3 * upon the cover of which is this *i·* :
My. 60–18 * It has this *i·* on the fly-leaf

inscriptions
My. 69– 8 * *i·* illustrative of the faith
inscrutable *Ret.* 79–15 the *i·* problem of being
insects *My.* 178–12 * "counting the legs of *i·*" ?

insensible
Un. 54–10 *i·* to every claim of error.
inseparability
Mis. 189– 9 *i·* of God and man,
inseparable
Mis. 182–28 man and his Maker are *i·*
266–16 *i·* from the unity of God.
361–30 are *i·* as cause and effect.
Ret. 75–10 Life and its ideals are *i·*,
Un. 21–18 man is *i·* from good.
38–10 and is *i·* from it.
My. 23–25 * Spirit, with its *i·* accompaniment,
185–16 spontaneity of Love, *i·* from Love,
300–20 these things, *i·* from C. S.,

insert
Ret. 38– 8 *i·* in my last chapter a partial
inserted
Man. 49–14 may be *i·* in The C. S. Journal
inside
Mis. 344–17 would place Soul wholly *i·* of body,
Pul. 58–13 * *I·* is a basement room, capable of
No. 26– 2 believe . . . the immortal is *i·* the
My. 145– 9 details outside and *i·*
346–13 * She was *i·*, and as she passed me

insidious
Ret. 19– 9 attacked by this *i·* disease,
My. 334– 3 * some *i·* disease was raging

insight
Mis. 169– 5 spiritual *i·* had been darkened
189–10 Spiritual *i·* of Truth and Love
Ret. 32– 4 spiritual *i·*, knowledge, and being.
My. 11–18 * needs no special *i·* to predict
296– 3 his flash of flight and *i·*,

insignia
Ret. 80– 2 and the *i·* of heaven.
No. 9–23 cabalistic *i·* of philosophy ;
My. 83– 9 * no flaunting of badges or *i·*
216–23 drop the *i·* of "Busy Bees,"

insignificance
Po. 1–15 On *i·* that peoples earth,
My. 77– 7 * pales into *i·*,

insignificant
My. 91–13 * no *i·* element in true Christianity.
92–16 * increased from an *i·* number
93–30 * faith had but an *i·* following.

insincerity
My. 166– 3 *i·* and a half-persuaded faith
insinuate
Ret. 36–10 which the evil-minded would *i·*
insist
Mis. 75– 6 *i· that there is but one Soul,*
283–19 I *i·* on the etiquette of C. S.,
336–12 *i·* on the rule and demonstration of
Ret. 63– 2 *i·* on the need of healing sickness
76–28 *i·* upon the strictest observance of
Un. 24– 7 Your assumptions *i·* that there is
43–13 I *i·* only upon the fact,
Pul. 27–11 * members strongly *i·* upon.
No. 10– 3 I *i·* that C. S. is demonstrably as
31–13 I *i·* on the destruction of sin
'01. 22–25 *i·* that the public receive their
My. 13– 1 they *i·* upon doing now.
180–23 *i·* on what we know is right,

insisted
Mis. 88–20 * *i·* that this Science is natural,
158– 6 When I *i·* on your speaking
193–31 The condition *i·* upon is,
327–13 and *i·* upon taking all of it
373– 3 I *i·* upon placing the serpent behind
No. 3– 9 some irresponsible people *i·*
My. 48–10 * *i·* that her students make,

insistence
Un. 8–13 My *i·* upon a proper understanding
My. 48–18 * *i·* upon the constant daily reading
insists
Mis. 200–11 The apostle Paul *i·* on the
241–21 Truth destroys the error that *i·*
346– 3 *i·* on the demonstration of
366–20 evil *i·* on the unity of good and
Ret. 69– 8 serpent, *i·* still upon the

insomnia
Mis. 209–15 *I·* compels mortals to learn
insomuch
Mis. 8–29 *i·* as the consciousness of good,
10–19 *i·* as they thereby have tried
10–20 *i·* as they have found their strength
189–26 *i·* that St. Matthew wrote,
359–15 *i·* as he was able to do this ;
Ret. 58– 9 sense of power . . . *i·* that the people
My. 271–29 *i·* as I know myself, what is

inspected
   My. 24–25   * have recently *i·* the work,
        145– 8   I *i·* the work every day,

inspiration
   Mis. 124–28   it gives to suffering, *i·* ;
        144–27   exudes the *i·* of the wine
   Ret. 30–23   neither can its *i·* be gained without
   Un. 46– 3   All Truth is from *i·*
   Pul. 56–18   * Welding . . . was a happy *i·*.
        83–11   * with the certainty of *i·* she works,
   '02. 8–18   except we possess this *i·*,
   Peo. 7–27   Scientific discovery and the *i·* of
   My. 14–21   * endowed with genius and *i·*,
        48– 5   * one ready to receive the *i·*,
        55–17   * was an *i·* to Christian Scientists,
        131–11   restitution, redemption, and *i·*.
        156–23   the *i·* which giveth victory
        248–29   Your highest *i·* is found
        260–18   its fruits are *i·* and
        297–19   an *i·* to the whole field,
        303–26   I have not the *i·* nor the

inspire
   Mis. 132–30   *i·* me with the hope that you wish
   My. 58–21   * May her example *i·* us to
        134–19   beautify, bless, and *i·* man's power.

inspired
   Mis. 58–13   I read the *i·* page through a higher
        101– 1   how hearts are *i·*,
        169– 6   God-driven back to the *i·* pages.
        169–21   to read what the *i·* writers left
        187–15   *i·* sense of the spiritual man,
        190–19   found to include the *i·* meaning.
        193– 1   Are the Scriptures *i·*?
        312–24   He spake *i·* ;
   Man. 15– 3   we take the *i·* Word of the Bible
   Pul. 72– 1   * *i·* in her great task by
   No. 22–12   Compared with the *i·* wisdom and
   Pan. 12–11   the *i·* Scriptural commands
   '00. 14–12   his *i·* rebuke to all the churches
   '01. 21–28   divine Love which *i·* it.
   '02. 8–15   The spiritually minded are *i·* with
   Po. v–12   * I *i·* by the grandeur of this
   My. 47–21   * *i·* so many of different races
        238–17   law, or *morale* of the *i·* Word
        362–20   * rejoice in your *i·* leadership,

inspires
   Mis. 252–26   *i·* the teacher and preacher ;
        360– 1   *i·* wisdom and procures divine power.
   Po. 32–12   *i·* my pen as I write ;
   My. 24– 8   * *i·* you to welcome all mankind

inspiring
   Mis. 169–29   * beautiful and *i·* are the thoughts
        213–21   *i·* tones from the lips of our Master,
        369–27   We thirst for *i·* wine from the
   My. 50–24   * a very *i·* season to us all,
        363–15   This proof . . . is soul *i·*.

installed
   My. 70–23   * organ which has been *i·*.

instalments
   My. 73–28   * bearing the first *i·* of the crowds

instance
   Mis. 45–19   when Science in a single *i·* decides
        61–14   * For *i·*, the man is held responsible for
        93–31   if you suffer for it in the first *i·*,
        116–29   If in one *i·* obedience be lacking,
        183–16   fulfil the Scriptures in every *i·* ;
        221–19   denial of this fact in one *i·*
        247–10   to furnish a single *i·* of
        247–31   must be met, in every *i·*,
        248– 3   For *i·* : the literal meaning of the
        362– 2   for *i·*, intelligent matter, or
   Ret. 59– 9   means subtraction in one *i·* and
   Pul. 45– 3   * Sacrifices were made in many an *i·*
   '01. 14–25   control it in the first *i·*, or
   Peo. 10–27   in a single *i·* when African slavery
   Po. v– 9   * "Old Man of the Mountain," for *i·*,
   My. 97– 4   * on the part of a sick person, for *i·*,
        112–13   not inconsistent in a single *i·*
        330– 7   * informed you in this *i·*

instances
   Mis. 40–13   In some *i·* the students of
        107–28   in certain morbid *i·*
        301–10   startling *i·* of the above-named
        317–25   already seen in many *i·*
   Ret. 41– 5   in most *i·* without even an
   Pul. 79–15   * in most *i·* they are held at
   My. 28–10   * in many *i·* the loving self-sacrifice,
        67–23   * were spent in other *i·*.
        137–15   except in one or two *i·*
        301–21   only so many well-defined *i·*

instant
   Pul. 44– 8   * willingly pause for an *i·*
   My. 11–16   * the response was *i·*,
        360–29   Your favor of the 10th *i·*

instantaneous
   Mis. 40–11   why do not its students **perform as** *i·*
        40–24   or they cannot be *i·* healers.
        200– 2   made his healing easy and *i·*.
        355– 8   not guesswork, . . . but *i·* cure.
   Un. 7–14   raise the dying to *i·* health.

instantaneously
   Mis. 359– 7   until you can cure without it *i·*,
   Un. 7–11   *i·* to heal a cancer
   Pul. 6–16   * was healed *i·* of an ailment

instantly
   Ret. 41– 4   desperate cases I *i·* healed,
   My. 178–24   *I·* the table sank a charred mass.

instead
   Mis. 16–25   from Soul *i·* of body,
        53–18   below *i·* of above the standard
        54–10   *I·* of losing her power to heal,
        59– 6   *i·* of the divine power understood,
        119– 4   *i·* of aiding other people's
        135– 4   Principle, *i·* of person, is
        175– 8   matter, *i·* of Mind.
        182– 1   began spiritually *i·* of materially
        231–22   *i·* of a real set-to at crying,
        237– 4   thing of mortal mind *i·* of body :
        271– 4   a thought, *i·* of a thing.
        281–20   *i·*, of our poverty and
        300–15   the pulpit, *i·* of the press,
        303–13   Let us serve *i·* of rule,
        303–13   knock *i·* of push at the door
        340–13   agriculture *i·* of litigation,
        340–14   dug into soils *i·* of delving into
        340–15   raised potatoes *i·* of pleas,
        340–16   and drew up logs *i·* of leases.
        351–23   wherefore it is hate *i·* of Love ;
        354–20   *I·* of relying on the Principle
   Ret. 26–15   *i·* of seeing therein the operation of
        33– 3   mortal belief, *i·* of the drug,
        49– 9   more of the spirit *i·* of the letter,
        56–10   is of human *i·* of divine origin.
   Un. 9–16   but have built *i·* upon the sand of
        29–23   by reading *sense i·* of *soul*,
        30–18   man as immortal *i·* of mortal
        35– 9   mortally mental, *i·* of material.
        36–18   (*i·* of acquiescence therein)
   Rud. 12– 7   strengthen . . . disease, *i·* of cure it ;
   No. 3–27   *i·* of possessing the essentials of
        4–13   error . . . becomes fable *i·* of fact.
        12–28   God must be found all *i·* of a part of
        44–17   and *i·* of healing,
   '01. 4–22   the infinite One *i·* of three,
   Hea. 3–12   *i·* of the divine Principle that
        7– 8   language of Soul *i·* of the senses ;
        7–10   gives the spiritual *i·* of the
        7–11   It begins with motive, *i·* of act,
        8–21   through Principle *i·* of a pardon ;
   Peo. 2–13   of Soul *i·* of the senses,
   My. 4–17   will be found that, *i·* of opposing,
        119–14   looked for the person, *i·* of
        120– 3   lose me *i·* of find me.
        152– 2   worshipping person *i·* of Principle,
        233– 8   *i·* of *putting out your watch*
           (*see also* **matter**)

instils
   My. 224–12   or the prejudice it *i·*.

instinct
   Ret. 69– 1   His origin is not, . . . in brute *i·*,
   Pul. 9–11   Woman, true to her *i·*,

instinctive
   My. 9– 7   * *i·* gratitude which not only

instinctively
   Mis. 307–30   human thought must turn *i·* to

instincts
   My. 235– 6   guided by love, faithful to her *i·*,

institute
   Ret. 48– 3   Who else could sustain this *i·*,
        84–30   avoid leaving his own regular *i·*
   '02. 15– 7   keeping a free *i·*,

instituted
   '02. 13–20   legal proceedings were *i·* by
   My. 252–24   *i·* in England on New Year's Day,

institutes
   Mis. 273–17   Their *i·* have not yet
        303– 7   should have their own *i·*
   No. 2–19   *I·* furnished with such teachers

instituting
   Mis. 175–20   *i·* matter and its methods

institution

Mis.	145– 1	more than any other *i·*,
	274– 2	no Biblical authority for a public *i·*.
	295–27	*i·* which names itself after
	378– 4	A patient . . . left that *i·*,
Ret.	6–18	ever connected with that *i·*.
	43–19	judged it best to close the *i·*,
	48–26	in the beginning in this *i·*,
	49– 1	height of prosperity in the *i·*,
My.	84– 4	* all the resources of the *i·*.

institutional

My.	8– 4	* outgrowing the *i·* end thereof.

institutions

Mis.	38–14	*other i· find little interest in*
	98–18	perpetuate our organizations and *i·* ;
	272–24	* Hence to name these *i·*,
Ret.	49– 4	Other *i·* for instruction in
'02.	12–29	When founding the *i·*
My.	104– 5	all sorts of *i·* flourish
	175–14	up-to-date academies, humane *i·*,
	340–31	*I·* of learning and progressive

instruct

Mis.	38–13	*college to i· in metaphysics,*
	114–31	specially *i·* his pupils
	130– 9	Does not the latter *i·* you
	331– 1	construct the stalk, *i·* the ear,
Man.	59–10	shall also *i·* their pupils
	84– 2	Teachers shall *i·* their pupils
	86–23	shall *i·* their pupils from the
Ret.	89–19	Jesus' method was to *i·* his
No.	40–14	I *i·* my students to pursue their
My.	49–23	* proceeded to *i·* those present
	49–30	* it was voted to *i·* the Clerk
	51–16	* It was moved to *i·* the Clerk
	60– 4	* wise to *i·* them on the subject
	142– 1	that he may *i·* him— *I Cor.* 2 : 16.

instructed

Mis.	4– 1	*i·* in the Science of metaphysical
	60–30	if mortals are *i·* in spiritual
	242–17	they shall be *i·* in the Principle
	333–31	Christians, *i·* in divine Science,
Man.	62–20	*i·* according to their understanding
	91–20	Students of C. S., duly *i·*
Ret.	48–22	students *i·* in C. S. Mind-healing,
	68–13	Our Master *i·* his students
My.	221–21	*i·* his followers, saying,
	314–21	the court *i·* the clerk
	338–29	is *i·* to be, charitable

instructing

Mis.	317–10	would have great pleasure in *i·*,
My.	223–16	*i·* persons in regard to that

instruction

Mis.	35–17	*student under your personal i·*
	37–26	Her time is wholly devoted to *i·*,
	39– 2	to take a course of *i·* in C. S.
	61– 4	*i·*, in spiritual Science,
	64–19	philosophy and religion that afford *i·*
	169–21	writers left for our spiritual *i·*.
	256– 9	that protest against receiving *i·*
	265–25	others, who receive the same *i·*,
	273–28	waiting for the same class *i·* ;
	278–24	perpetual *i·* of my students might
	292–23	serves as admonition and *i·*,
	293–10	gained from *i·*, observation, and
	350–13	Christian, and like my public *i·*.
Man.	63– 8	*i·* given by the children's teachers
	85–20	receiving *i·* as above, shall not
	86– 6	personal *i·* of Mrs. Eddy
	87–13	No . . . shall advise against class *i·*.
	89–20	may apply to . . . for *i·* ;
	90–17	Special *I·*.
	91– 8	Tuition of class *i·* . . . shall be $100.00.
Ret.	48–18	give *i·* in scientific methods of
	49– 4	institutions for *i·* in C. S.,
	50– 1	my *i·* in C. S. Mind-healing,
	50–13	any real equivalent for my *i·*
	89–10	*i·* in the Mosaic law.
	90–11	he gave personal *i·*,
Pul.	69– 4	* *i·* of Mrs. Mary Baker Eddy,
Rud.	14–21	their tuition in the higher *i·*,
	14–27	regular course of *i·* from me,
	16– 7	class *i·* in any branch
No.	8–23	who is too blind for *i·*,
My.	62–24	* your wise counsel, timely *i·*,
	218–30	expectation of receiving *i·* from me,
	241–10	* chapter sub-title
	241–16	* fortunate to receive *i·* from
	251– 8	* Primary and Normal class *i·*
	251–17	*i·* in the Board of Education.
	287– 8	serving as admonition, *i·*,
	322–22	* a few days' *i·* by Mrs. Eddy
	361– 4	to give you personal *i·*

instructions

Mis.	11–12	if my *i·* had healed them
	65–17	*Have you changed your i·*
	65–20	those who understand my *i·*
	66–31	I endeavor to accommodate my *i·*
	213– 6	in the proportion that their *i·*
	264–20	Some students leave my *i·*
	292–29	my *i·* on this point of
	293–15	not understand all your *i·* ;
	302– 3	through the *i·* of ''S. and H.
	318–14	Any student, having received *i·* in
	349– 4	*i·* included about twelve lessons,
Man.	92–16	No person shall receive *i·* . . . who is not
	109– 1	heading
	111–15	*i·* illustrated in Form 1 and
Ret.	47–19	received *i·* in a Primary class
	83–11	*i·* afforded by the Bible and my
Rud.	14–25	healed by means of my *i·*,
My.	46–26	* all-inclusive *i·* and admonitions
	49–17	* Clerk, by *i·* received
	51–32	* successful *i·* to heal the sick,
	52– 6	* example, as well as her *i·*,
	220–25	*i·* and example of the great

instructive

Pul.	vii–11	*i·* to turn backward the telescope

instructor (*see also* instructor's)

(*see* Eddy)

instructor's

Mis.	264–28	*i·* mind must take its hue from

instructors

Mis.	38– 9	*i·* and philanthropists in our land
Man.	73– 9	members of the faculty, *i·*, or

instructs

My.	140–23	This *i·* us how to be abased

instrument

Mis.	39–25	*i· by which God reaches others to heal*
	122– 8	*i·* in this holy (?) alliance
My.	70–24	* more musical, or more capable *i·*.

instrumentality

Mis.	260–10	divine Mind was his only *i·*
My.	288–16	divine Mind was his only *i·*

instruments

Mis.	107– 1	in imitative tones of many *i·*,
	244– 6	before surgical *i·* were invented,
Un.	23– 4	* Make *i·* to scourge us.
My.	105–13	*i·* were lying on the table ready
	287– 6	as *i·* of divine Love.

insubordination

Mis.	119–22	*I·* to the law of Love
	206–15	no *i·* to the laws that be,

insufficient

Mis.	95–11	time so kindly allotted me is *i·*
Man.	36–17	for *i·* cause, refuse to endorse
Ret.	33–24	were *i·* to satisfy my doubts
No.	33–16	would have been *i·* to insure the
My.	266– 2	chapter sub-title
	266– 6	*i·* freedom of honest competition ;
	292–15	*I·* faith or spiritual understanding,

insult

Mis.	121–24	shameless *i·* to divine royalty,
Un.	25– 3	*i·* my conscience,
'01.	30–29	* well-bred man will not *i·* me,

insurance

Man.	30–18	the Board shall attend to the *i·*

insure

No.	33–16	insufficient to *i·* the glory
My.	10–26	* in order to *i·* the prosperity of
	52–28	* to *i·* the moral rightness of

insures

Peo.	2– 1	which *i·* man's continuance and
My.	90–12	* *i·* fidelity in pain or death
	287–23	systematizes action, and *i·* success ;

intact

Mis.	173–25	The perfection of man is *i·* ;
	290– 5	the contract is preserved *i·*.
'02.	7– 1	true nature of Love *i·*

intangible

'01.	12– 1	mode of worship may be *i·*,

integrity

Mis.	147–14	The man of *i·* is one who
	270– 4	such as barter *i·* and peace

intellect

Ret.	5–14	father possessed a strong *i·*
	5–23	* She possessed a strong *i·*,
Un.	21–11	your *i·* will be circumscribed
	22–21	*human i· and will-power,*
	25– 3	stultify my *i·*, insult my conscience,
	25–14	enlarges the human *i·* by

intellect

No. 11– 2 *i·*, desire, and fear, are not
11–27 subdue the sophistry of *i·*
Pan. 4– 3 to the reason, *i·*, and will

intellects

Mis. 345–17 * the loftiest *i·* have had
356–10 students, with cultured *i·*,
Peo. 13–26 * the loftiest *i·* have had
My. 48–27 * The *i·* of these people are not

intellectual

Mis. 88–12 *i·* culture, reading, writing,
112–29 *i·*, and spiritual discernment,
113–31 *i·*, moral, and spiritual
204–18 increases the *i·* activities,
339–13 the strain of *i·* wrestlings,
Ret. 7– 8 * highest order of *i·* powers,
Un. 8–16 physical, moral, and *i·*,
Pul. vii–13 gain of *i·* momentum,
80– 6 * the most *i·* city
No. 45–21 Drifting into *i·* wrestlings,
Peo. 1–12 *i·* wrestling and collisions
My. 87– 9 * happy, well-to-do, *i·*,
211–31 admits of no *i·* culture
294–25 *i·*, moral, and religious
309– 2 a well-informed, *i·* man,
309–31 * practically all the *i·* life."

intellectuality

My. 274–12 success, *i·*, and happiness

intelligence

all-pervading
Mis. 16–21 all-pervading *i·* and Love,
and existence
Ret. 59–22 for *i·* and existence.
and law
Pan. 7–23 reality and power, *i·* and law,
and wisdom
My. 79–18 * the *i·* and wisdom of the country
another
Mis. 198–27 supposition of another *i·* than God ;
belief that
Mis. 36–28 belief that *i·*, Truth, and Love, are
centre and
Mis. 308– 1 Mind as its sole centre and *i·*.
divine
Mis. 23– 8 demonstrated a divine *i·*
83– 1 divine *i·*, or Principle,
336–27 Science is the fiat of divine *i·*,
'01. 7– 6 divine *i·* called God.
governed by
Mis. 206–17 Growth is governed by *i* ;
highest order of
My. 96– 5 * of the highest order of *i·*,
his
Mis. 173–23 obstructing his *i·* — pains, fetters,
law, or
Mis. 101–27 no other power, law, or *i·*
Life and
Mis. 199–26 substance, Life, and *i·* are God.
200–10 substance, Life, and *i·* of man.
life and
(*see* **life**)
Life, or
Un. 32–13 as substance, Life, or *i·*,
life, substance, and
Mis. 175– 7 sense of life, substance, and *i·*,
218– 9 life, substance, and *i·*,
Ret. 67– 7 life, substance, and *i·*
manifestations of
Ret. 57–20 supply all manifestations of *i·*.
material
Rud. 4–15 if . . . you mean material *i·*.
matter has no
Mis. 44–28 matter has no *i·* of its own.
Ret. 69–20 matter has no *i·*, life, nor
Mind and
Un. 29–11 only Mind and *i·* in the universe.
no
Mis. 28–25 no *i·* nor life in matter ;
334– 7 has no foundation, — in fact, no *i·* ;
'01. 34–27 no *i·*, health, hope, nor
nor Life
Mis. 74–31 neither substance, *i·*, nor Life,
nor power
Mis. 355–19 neither *i·* nor power,
nor substance
Mis. 21–16 no . . . *i·*, nor substance in matter.
not
'01. 12–28 it is not *i·*, a person or a
obey this
Mis. 23–10 winds, and waves, obey this *i·*.
one
Ret. 30–11 as one *i·*, analyzing,
opposite
Mis. 45–26 an opposite *i·* or mind
346–13 belief . . . opposite *i·* to God.

intelligence

or power
Mis. 260–20 seemeth to be *i·* or power
people of
My. 96–30 * And they were people of *i·*.
personal
Rud. 7–19 neither sensation nor personal *i·*.
power or
Mis. 197–24 believes there is another power or *i·*
reaching
Ret. 69– 2 conditions prior to reaching *i·*.
real
'00. 8–11 wicked man has little real *i·* ;
Soul, and
No. 35–18 Life, substance, Soul, and *i·*
substance and
Mis. 309–13 infinite spiritual substance and *i·*.
Hea. 16– 5 no other Life, substance, and *i·*
substance, nor
Ret. 93–20 no life, truth, substance, nor *i·* in
substance or
My. 235–19 Matter as substance or *i·*

Mis. 23– 4 the *i·* that manifests power
49–25 belief, . . . *i·* in non-intelligence,
68– 1 divine substance, *i·*, Life,
333–11 Where do we hold *i·* to be?
344–18 They would place . . . *i·* in matter ;
Un. 31–13 claim . . . that matter has *i·* ;
Rud. 5–14 or *i·* in non-intelligence?
My. 88– 8 * above the average in *i·*.
95– 6 * *i·* of many communities

intelligences

Mis. 344–10 a fit habitation for the *i·* ?"

intelligent

Mis. 23–16 for matter . . . is not *i·*.
26–17 Matter is not *i·*,
26–19 *i·*, self-creative, and infinite
36–30 there is no *i·* evil,
74–24 supposition that matter is *i·*,
103– 3 *I·* Spirit, Soul, is substance,
260– 1 *i·* Christ-idea illustrated by
267–23 governed by Spirit, *i·* good.
333– 1 that this something is *i·* matter;
362– 2 for instance, *i·* matter, or
Un. 22–21 *will-power,— alias i·* matter.
26– 1 *Evil.* I am *i·* matter ;
42– 8 a divine and *i·* — reality.
Pul. 56– 9 * and, as a rule, are the most *i·*.
60– 7 * manly, and *i·* tones,
63–17 * hundred thousand *i·* people
69–26 * have not done so in an *i·* manner,
No. 11– 6 *i·* and harmonious action,
38– 8 there is no *i·* sin,
Pan. 6–17 how can matter be an *i·* creator
7– 3 plurality of minds, or *i·* matter,
'01. 3–18 fundamental, *i·*, divine Being,
Peo. 4–10 and matter become *i·*
My. vii–12 * *i·* thinking untainted by the
45– 1 * strict and *i·* recognition of
74–21 * an *i·* and a happy appearing body,
92– 5 * numbers of *i·* men and women
93– 9 * the *i·*, and the well-behaved.
96–14 * *i·* and unbiased study
100–15 * a class who are reputable, *i·*,
108– 4 is mind or matter the *i·* cause
112–15 honest, *i·*, and scholarly
175–13 *i·* medical faculty,
226– 4 an *i·* usage of the word
226–10 the one divine *i·* Principle
226–20 *i·* divine Principle, Love.
269– 2 reflected in the *i·* compound idea,

intelligently

Mis. 105– 2 appeals *i·* to the facts
115–18 till you *i·* know and demonstrate,
370–14 more *i·* than ever before,
Un. 6–15 are not prepared to answer *i·*
'02. 5–13 God must be *i·* considered
My. 153–25 Principle of which works *i·*

intelligible

Man. 30– 2 shall select *i·* Readers

intemperance

Mis. 37–16 *Can your Science cure i·?*
37–21 *I·*, impurity, sin of every sort,
210–19 *I·* begets a belief of
210–21 kill this lurking serpent, *i·*,
296–18 C. S., antagonistic to *i·*,
Pan. 10–20 reform desperate cases of *i·*,

intend

Mis. 39–19 they *i·* to fill the human mind with

intended

Mis. 302–28 *i·* to forestall the possible evil
307–25 were not *i·* for a golden calf,

intended
Un. 13– 6 fulfil the *i·* harmony of being.
19– 9 He must virtually have *i·* it,
Pul. 42–13 * *i·* for the sole use of Mrs. Eddy.
56–27 * is *i·* to be a testimonial
84–25 * as God *i·* it should be.
My. 353–12 *i·* to hold guard over Truth,

intense
Ret. 7– 9 * *i·* and almost incessant study
Pul. 23–20 * are years of more *i·* life,

intensely
Mis. 308–24 *i·* contemplating personality
309–28 sometimes take things too *i·*.
386– 1 "*I·* grand and glorious
Po. 49– 3 "*I·* grand and glorious

intent
Mis. 11– 1 to suffer for his evil *i·* ;
117– 7 the God-given *i·* and volition
227–10 to extend their evil *i·*,
310– 2 neither the *i·* of my works nor
Ret. 21–17 heavenly *i·* of earth's shadows
My. 291–17 His public *i·* was uniform,

intention
Man. 57–12 Clerk to inform . . . of his *i·*,
Pul. 74–21 *i·* to be thus understood,
My. 340–25 his *i·* to rule righteously
362–22 * *i·* to take such action

intentional
My. 161– 5 The *i·* destroyer of others

intentionally
Mis. 261–10 whether *i·* or ignorantly ;
264–32 *i·* offers his own thought,
Man. 42–20 will not *i·* or knowingly
Ret. 89–26 trespass not *i·* upon

intentions
Mis. 236–25 notwithstanding one's good *i·*,
Ret. 47–14 informed of my *i·*,
Pul. 87–15 appreciate your kind *i·*.

intents
Pul. 11– 6 your hearts' holy *i·*.

intercedeth
My. 136– 2 and *i·* for us.

intercession
No. 39– 3 *i·* and unvoiced imploring

intercessory
No. 38–24 chapter sub-title
38–25 prayer that is desire is *i·* ;

interchange
Mis. 100–23 home, the *i·* of love,
No. 14– 6 no *i·* of consciousness,

intercommunion
Mis. 95–16 the impossibility of *i·*
Hea. 6–12 impossibility, in Science, of *i·*

intercourse
Ret. 88– 2 in the professional *i·* of

interest
Mis. 4–19 Much *i·* is awakened and expressed
12–18 mutely works in the *i·* of
38–14 *other institutions find little i· in*
98–13 and extend the *i·* already felt
139–29 As with all former efforts in the *i·* of
238–13 utilized in the *i·* of somebody.
273–21 growing *i·* in C. S. Mind-healing.
305–20 * articles of historic *i·* will
306–17 * We would add, as being of *i·*,
Ret. 37–24 may have an *i·* for the reader,
42–11 listened to him with deep *i·*.
83– 6 rather than try to centre their *i·* on
Pul. 27–30 * windows are of still more unique *i·*.
31–18 * new and increasing *i·* in the
50– 2 * in whom she takes a vital *i·*.
50–20 * will awaken some sort of *i·*.
68–21 * adds *i·* to the Baltimore
'00. 2– 2 and this *i·* increases.
'01. 31–16 except in the *i·* of the individual
'02. 13–18 the sum of $4,963.50 and *i·*,
14– 3 only *i·* I retain in this property
My. 25– 7 * great *i·* exhibited by the children
51– 8 * such an *i·* manifested
51–22 * for the *i·* of the Cause,
52– 5 * *i·* of the world to hear her word
53–28 * increasing *i·* in C. S.
84– 3 * heavy debt, the *i·* on which
89–23 * not a matter of *i·* to
92–10 * worthy of perhaps even more *i·*
217–10 This sum is to remain on *i·* till
217–14 will receive his dividend with *i·*
271–23 * reply will be read with deep *i·*
282–22 *i·* you manifest in the success of
297–27 not had sufficient *i·* in the matter
315– 2 is of *i·* in this connection :

interest
My. 319–19 * may *i·* you to be advised that
322–28 * my great *i·* in the subject,
329–10 * gives especial *i·* to the
329–23 * admitting its *i·* in the movement,
334–26 * Of further *i·* in this matter
336–19 * of absorbing *i·* to . . . Scientists
339– 2 subserve the *i·* of mankind,
341–21 * public *i·* centres in the
353–24 nothing . . . of any special *i·*.

interested
Mis. 353–28 being too much *i·* in themselves
Pul. 80–13 * sent us by *i·* friends,
'00. 1–24 my books and those *i·* in them,
2– 1 already *i·* in Christian Science ;
2– 4 *i·* in this old-new theme of
My. 12–10 * Each person *i·* must remember,
49–12 * meeting of those who were *i·*
51– 5 * all others now *i·* in said church,
61–21 * One feature about the work *i·* me.
245– 2 they became deeply *i·* in it.
272–24 * will be *i·* in this communication
272–29 * our readers will be *i·* in
289–27 *i·* in a meeting to be held
313–21 never was especially *i·* in

interesting
Mis. 155–17 all of her *i·* correspondence,
178–10 * delivered an *i·* discourse
320– 4 This *i·* day, crowned with
Pul. vii– 6 it will be *i·* to have not only
31– 6 * a most *i·* personality.
42– 9 * rendered particularly *i·*
65– 8 * undoubtedly an *i·* faith
72– 6 * very *i·* conversations
88– 5 * kind and *i·* articles
My. 13– 8 scanning its *i·* pages,
47–14 * *i·*, and epoch-marking stages
49–21 * *i·* record of this meeting
51–25 * *i·* record relative to this
53–27 * some very *i·* statements,
60–27 * *i·* part I had to perform
61– 3 * has been very *i·* indeed,
74–10 * chapter sub-title
74–12 * *i·* and agreeable visitors,
74–30 * each is *i·*, one for its
86–23 * proved one of the most *i·*
175– 1 this deeply *i·* anniversary,
177– 5 on so *i·* an occasion
231–29 thanks for your *i·* report
273– 3 * *i·* and remarkable proof
329–26 * some *i·* facts concerning
332–21 * in a most *i·* way.
351– 5 * especially *i·* on account of
(see also **letter**)

interests
Mis. 18–26 separate one man's *i·* from
237–20 a period . . . of divided *i·*,
246– 8 subserve the *i·* of wealth,
289–29 Mutual *i·* and affections
Man. 52–22 working against the *i·* of
52–23 *i·* of our Pastor Emeritus
80– 3 promotion of the *i·* of C. S.
Ret. 6–26 he served the public *i·*
Pul. 15–20 will unite all *i·* in the one
68– 9 * the *i·* of her religious work
My. 4–18 subserves the *i·* of both
291–11 uniting the *i·* of all

interfere
Mis. 89–11 or *i·* with *materia medica*.
Man. 74– 8 no other church shall *i·*
Ret. 72– 3 nor *i·* with the rights of
Un. 36–25 must *i·* with its practical
My. 359– 7 not to *i·* in cases of discipline,

interference
Mis. 87–31 this *i·* prolongs the struggle
Man. 73–26 No *I·*.

interferes
Ret. 82–18 This fact *i·* in no way with

interfering
My. 212–24 *i·* with the rights of Mind,

interim
Mis. 241–15 during which *i·*, by constant combat

interior
Pul. 36–24 * *i·* is one of the utmost taste
My. 31–21 * its *i·* should have impressed them
68– 1 * *i·* of this church is carried out
68–20 * enters . . . into the *i·* finish.
68–24 * imposing effect of the *i·*.
68–25 * stone and marble form the *i·*
69–15 * the rich beauty of the *i·*.
71–13 * chapter sub-title
71–17 * For in its *i·* architecture
71–19 * traditions of church *i·* architecture

interior
  My. 72– 3 * traditions of *i·* church architecture.
      78–10 * They looked upon an *i·*
      78–23 * in spite of its vast *i·*,
    147–28 From the *i·* of Africa

interluding
  Mis. xii– 4 meantime *i·* with loving thought

intermediate
  Mis. 188–20 in the *i·* line of thought,
    206– 4 from extremes to *i·*.
    215– 4 Truth comes into the *i·* space,
  No. 28– 6 Of his *i·* conditions
  '00. 2–10 the idler, and the *i·*.
    2–25 *i·* worker works at times.
  My. 181–18 the *i·* line of justice

intermission
  Pul. 42– 5 * Then there was an *i·*,

internal
  Mis. 347– 4 *i·* action of pent-up gas.
  My. 121–20 to disguise *i·* vulgarity
    160–22 *i·* fires of our earth
    160–24 unpunished sin is this *i·* fire,

international
  My. 85– 2 * in its widely *i·* range,
    89–31 * religious movement of *i·* sway ;
    290– 3 this sudden *i·* bereavement,

International Conciliation Committee
  My. 282–19 *I· C· C·*,

***Inter-Ocean,* The** (*see also Daily Inter-Ocean*)
  Pul. 37– 1 * any information for *The I·*,"

interpolate
  '02. 12–21 *i·* some matters of business
  My. 7– 4 *i·* some matters of business

interpolation
  Mis. 194–11 Divine Science is not an *i·* of
  '01. 12–17 Divine Science is not an *i·* of

interpolations
  Ret. 35–11 truths of C. S. are not *i·* of

interposition
  Mis. 312–13 * *i·* of divine Providence

interpret
  Mis. 58–18 I must . . . understand them to *i·*
    71–15 actual causation must *i·* omnipotence,
    100– 4 C. S. was to *i·* them ;
    166–21 than the senses could *i·*.
    206– 8 *i·* man's eternal existence,
  Un. 43–22 This will *i·* the divine power
  Pul. 69–18 * we *i·* the Scriptures wholly from
  '01. 27– 6 * *i·* their ideas and principles
  My. 112– 8 *i·* the Scriptures to fit a doctrine,

Interpretation
  (*see* **Spiritual Interpretation**)

interpretation
  spiritual
    (*see* **spiritual**)

           ————

  Mis. 158–10 But now, . . . comes the *i·* thereof.
    163–12 ripened into *i·* through Science.
    169–10 Truth dawned . . . through right *i·*.
    189– 5 *i·* therein will be found to be
    191–18 By no possible *i·* can this passage
    258–27 God's *i·* of Himself furnishes
  Ret. 37–16 Scriptures gave no direct *i·* of
    83–20 leave S. and H. to God's daily *i·*.
  Un. 30–17 *i·* of God and His creation
  Pul. 29–25 * helpful in its suggestive *i·*.
    59–14 * with its parallel *i·* by Mrs. Eddy.
  No. 44– 6 Truth, having its best *i·* in
  My. 94–13 * in the *i·* of its tenets,
    114–20 in the line of Scriptural *i·*
    114–21 influx of divine *i·* would pour in

interpretations
  Mis. 190–17 contradict the *i·* that the senses
    247–17 hence the injustice of their *i·*.
  Ret. 35–12 but the spiritual *i·* thereof.
  '02. 5– 6 stills all distress over doubtful *i·*
  My. 178– 4 cloud not the . . . by material *i·*,
    340–18 through constitutional *i·*.

interpreted
  Mis. 73– 6 *I·* materially, these passages
    169–15 cannot properly be *i·* in a literal
    170–15 Jesus *i·* all spiritually :
  Un. 63– 1 *i·* this appearing as a risen Christ.
  Pul. 29–21 * *i·* and fulfilled literally,
  No. 27–12 this vision of Truth is fully *i·*
  My. vi– 2 * does not need to be *i·* to those
    220– 5 This statement should be so *i·*

interpreter
  No. 38–16 the *i·* of one God,

interpreters
  Ret. 26–14 though uninspired *i·* ignorantly

interpreting
  Mis. 302–16 mistake in *i·* revealed Truth,
    364– 3 *I·* the Word in the
  Man. 66– 6 *I·* Communications.
  Rud. 1– 2 *i·* and demonstrating the

interprets
  Mis. 164– 1 *i·* the incorporeal idea,
    208–20 *i·* to mortals the gospel
    258–30 It *i·* the law of Spirit,
  Pul. 12–24 This rule clearly *i·* God
  No. 10– 8 the latter reveals and *i·* God
    21– 7 Science that . . . S. and H. *i·*.
  '00. 6–12 *i·* the healing Christ.
  My. 126–10 *i·* the mystery of godliness,

interred
  My. 333–13 * where the body was *i·*
    333–26 * *i·* with Masonic honors.

interrogatory
  Pul. 74–11 * a written answer to the *i·*,

interrupt
  Mis. 353–30 *i·* the home-harmony,

interruption
  My. 14–27 * will be carried on without *i·*

interrupts
  Ret. 56– 8 *i·* the meaning of the omnipotence,
  My. 69–18 * not a single pillar . . . *i·* the view

intersection
  Pul. 24– 8 * *i·* of Norway and Falmouth Streets,
    77–10 * *i·* of Falmouth and Norway Streets,
    78– 9 * *i·* of Falmouth and Norway Streets,

interval
  '01. 27–18 and in this *i·* number one million,
    34– 5 *i·* that detains the patient

intervale
  Pul. 48–11 * *i·* of beautiful meadows and pastures

intervals
  Mis. 256–17 irregular *i·* between my class terms,
  Hea. 13–14 at *i·* of half an hour
  My. 86–30 * services, repeated at *i·*
    105–22 breathing at *i·* in agony.
    181– 5 are aided only at long *i·* with

intervene
  Mis. 92– 4 Centuries will *i·* before the
    319–28 No doubt must *i·* between the
  Ret. 84– 1 Centuries will *i·* before the

intervened
  My. 343–27 I *i·*. Dissensions are dangerous

intervenes
  '02. 12– 3 Here C. S. *i·*, explains

intervening
  Mis. 124– 1 *i·* between God and man,
  Pul. 85– 3 * during the *i·* years

intervention
  My. 278– 4 by the *i·* of the United States,

interview
  Pul. 31–21 * begging the favor of an *i·*
    74–13 calling for an *i·*
  My. 346–19 * recent *i·* which appeared

interviewing
  My. 332–24 * much *i·* with Masonic authorities,

interviews
  Mis. 276– 5 I did not hold *i·* with all
  '01. 17–17 in from one to three *i·*,
    27–14 in one to three *i·*
  My. 341–23 * granting of *i·* is not usual,

interwoven
  My. 10–30 * *i·* with the general welfare of

intimate
  Mis. 249–14 as well as my *i·* acquaintances.

intimately
  Ret. 88–19 a part which concerns us *i·*,

intimates
  No. 6–27 *i·* that the laws of Science are

intimations
  Pul. 23–24 * *i·* of man's immortal life.

intolerance
  Mis. xi–19 The shuttlecock of religious *i·*
    246–26 Shall religious *i·*, arrayed against
  Hea. 11–14 he who has suffered from *i·*

intolerant
  '01. 34–15 material religion, proscriptive, *i·*,
  Hea. 11–14 is the first to be *i·*.

intoxicated
  Mis.   9–20   become *i·* ; become lethargic,
         100– 6   *i·* with pleasure or pain,
         277–30   on the cloud of the *i·* senses.
intoxicates
  Mis. 288–32   Whatever *i·* a man,
intoxicating
  Mis. 288–31   abstinence from *i·* beverages.
intoxication
  My. 212– 1   state induced . . . is a species of *i·*,
         212– 7   sins, and other forms of *i·*.
intrenching
  Pul.   2–28   *i·* ourselves in the knowledge
intrepid
  Mis. 172– 6   *I·*, self-oblivious Protestants
  Hea.   2– 9   Said the *i·* reformer, Martin Luther :
  My. 275–25   *I·*, self-oblivious love fulfils
intricate
  '00. 11–14   besieges you with tones *i·*,
  My. 61–29   * the many *i·* problems which
          71– 2   * some of the most *i·* discoveries
         212– 4   *i·* method of animal magnetism
intrinsic
  Mis. 108–31   they have no *i·* quality
  My. 153–14   with no *i·* healing qualities
         172–12   gift that has no *i·* value
introduce
  Mis. 247–14   statement of the Science I *i·*,
  My. 39–18   * *i·* the incoming President,
          42– 5   * It is my pleasure to *i·*
introduced
  Mis. 177–26   * The pastor *i·* Mr. Easton
         365–32   conscientiously understood and *i·*.
  Ret. 43– 1   *i·* the first purely metaphysical
          86– 7   Then be *i·* to this self.
  Pul.   5–17   *i·* himself to its author
  No.   9– 6   must not be *i·* or established
          11–15   understood and conscientiously *i·*.
introduces
  Rud.   2–21   *i·* us to higher definitions.
          11–26   never *i·* the subject of human
  Pan.   6–11   Mosaic theism *i·* evil,
introducing
  My. 39–17   * In *i·* the new President,
         234–19   question of *i·* C. S. into
introduction
  My. 218–15   *i·* of pure abstractions into C. S.,
introductory
  My. 80–16   * the *i·* services were identical,
intruding
  My. 221–29   wide open to the *i·* disease,
intrusted
  Mis. 284–30   if one is *i·* with the rules of
intuition
  Mis. 152–28   right *i·* which guides you safely
         272–30   *i·* and impulse of love.
invaded
  Ret. 61–10   man's harmony is no more to be *i·* than
          79–29   nor its golden streets *i·*.
  My. 87–10   * multitude that has *i·* the town.
invaders
  Peo. 13–13   iron tread of merciless *i·*,
invalid (*see also* **invalid's**)
  Mis. 27– 7   and prove themselves *i·*.
          83– 7   *every i· the cause of his*
  Un.   59–22   calls sickness real, and man an *i·*,
  Rud.   8–24   *i·* whom he is supposed to cure.
  '01. 13–28   hold it *i·*, give it the lie,
  Hea.   9– 9   sinner and the most hopeless *i·*
  My. 144– 6   that I am sick, helpless, or an *i·*.
invalidism
  Mis. 169– 8   *i·* she endured before Truth dawned
invalid's
  Ret. 40– 8   I went to the *i·* house.
invalids
  Un.   61–28   *I·* say, "I have recovered from
  Pul. 80–25   * into the homes of unnumbered *i·*.
  Rud.   3–16   manipulate *i·*, prescribe drugs, or
          12–16   erases from the minds of *i·*
          14–28   have been *i·* and were healed
          15–13   Few were taken besides *i·*
  Peo.   3– 5   made helpless *i·* and cripples.
  My. 231– 1   chapter sub-title
         231–15   letters from *i·* demanding her help
invaluable
  Mis. 45–10   *i·* in the practice of dentistry.
  '02. 16– 8   copy of Wyclif, the *i·* gift of

invariable
  '01. 24– 6   by means of *i·* rules
invariably
  Mis. 45–16   supply *i·* meets demand,
  My. 59–26   * My answer has *i·* been,
invective
  Mis. 335–13   charge upon me with full-fledged *i·*
  Man. 41–12   in return employ no violent *i·*,
invent
  Pul. 79–21   * we should be obliged to *i·* one."
invented
  Mis. 244– 7   before surgical instruments were *i·*,
  My. 14–22   * could not have *i·* a more subtle lie
invention
  Mis. 232– 7   perfection in art, *i·*, and
inventions
  Mis. 78–14   the *i·* of animal magnetism,
  Un.   60– 1   mortal *i·*, one and all
  Pan. 12–28   philosophy, or by man's *i·*.
  My. 345–25   * pursuit of modern material *i·*?"
inventor
  Pul. 71– 7   * Mrs. Eddy, the *i·* of this cure.
  '02.   9–27   the *i·* of a steam engine?
invert
  Mis. 109– 5   to reverse, *i·*, or controvert,
inverted
  Un.   53– 3   evil and all its forms are *i·* good.
  Rud.   7–11   be lost if *i·* or perverted.
  No.   17–18   therein is no *i·* image of God,
  Pan. 11–29   image of God, not fallen or *i·*,
inverts
  Ret. 70– 1   "Mortal mind *i·* the true likeness,
invested
  My. 217– 8   *i·* in safe municipal bonds
         349–17   Way-shower, *i·* with glory,
investigate
  Mis. 44– 4   ready to *i·* this subject,
investigated
  Pul. 64–17   * *i·* allopathy, homœopathy,
  My. 330–13   * carefully *i·* the points
investigating
  Mis. 222–29   cost of *i·*, for this age,
  Ret.   7–10   * He was fond of *i·* abstruse
investigation
  Mis. 87–20   in the *i·* of C. S.
         247– 9   challenge the world, upon fair *i·*,
  Pul. 14– 1   honest *i·* will bring the hour
investigations
  Hea.   6– 7   From my earliest *i·*
investigator
  '02.   2– 1   the earnest, honest *i·* sees
investments
  My. 135–10   *i·*, deposits, expenditures,
         137–13   *i·*, deposits, expenditures,
         137–14   selected all my *i·*, except
         231–11   uncertain, unfortunate *i·*.
invests
  My. 265– 7   *i·* less in trusts,
inveterate
  Rud.   9–23   oftentimes healed *i·* diseases.
  No.   22– 8   Hegel was an *i·* snuff-taker.
  Hea. 13–17   an *i·* case of dropsy.
  My. 300–13   heals the most *i·* diseases.
invigorate
  My. 230–12   *i·* his capacity to heal the sick,
invigoration
  '01.   1–16   refreshment and *i·* of the human
invincible
  Mis. 171–30   to keep bright their *i·* armor ;
  Ret. 30–14   *i·* and infinite energies of Truth
  My. 178– 5   nor lose the *i·* process and purity of
         189– 1   Clad in *i·* armor,
invincibles
  Pul. 83–17   * Amazons who conquered the *i·*,
inviolate
  Mis. 91–12   bond is wholly spiritual and *i·*.
invisibility
  Ret. 79– 8   pigment beneath fade into *i·*.
invisible
  Mis. 22–31   Mind-force, *i·* to material sense,
         205–18   good, whose visible being is *i·* to
         218– 5   declares the *i·* only by reversion,
         308–29   which is *i·* to corporeal sense.
         329–27   the cuckoo sounds her *i·* lute,
  Pul. 80–26   * that the *i·* is the only real world,
  '01. 13– 5   The visible sin should be *i·* :

invitation

Mis.	132–21	inconvenient to accept your *i·*
	137– 3	my thanks for your card of *i·*,
	148–28	Let the *i·* to this sweet converse
	296– 2	and, by special *i·*,
	311– 6	I would extend a tender *i·* to
Man.	45–22	not entitled . . . except by *i·*.
	85– 3	by *i·* attend each other's
Ret.	15–15	I accepted the *i·*
Pul.	36–10	* by Mrs. Eddy's kind *i·*,
	76–27	* an *i·* formally to accept the
	77– 3	* The *i·* itself is one of the most
	86–26	* *i·* to become the permanent pastor
My.	49–11	* unanimous *i·* to Mrs. Eddy
	49–18	* *i·* to Mrs. Eddy to become pastor
	51–19	* *i·* was extended to Mrs. Eddy
	53–18	* which *i·* she accepted.
	142–26	I thank you for your kind *i·*
	169– 1	chapter sub-title
	174–18	thanking you for your kind *i·*
	177– 4	comply with your cordial *i·*
	183–24	Thanks for *i·* to your dedication.
	191–28	card of *i·* to this feast of soul
	195– 4	acknowledging your card of *i·*
	285– 3	accept my thanks for your kind *i·*,
	324–26	* why he accepted your *i·*

invitations

Mis.	321–24	In reply to all *i·* from Chicago

invite

Mis.	149– 4	*I·* all cordially and freely
	246–18	to *i·* its prey, then turn and
	310–27	would cordially *i·* all persons
	322– 2	*i·* you to its contemplation
Man.	94– 1	The lecturer can *i·* churches
Pul.	87– 1	* cordially *i·* you to be present
Po.	32–10	A loftier life to *i·*
My.	169– 2	I *i·* you, one and all,
	171–11	Therefore I hereby *i·* all my
	173–16	Why not *i·* those who attend

invited

Pul.	77–15	* most lovingly *i·* to visit
	78–13	* most lovingly *i·* to visit
'00.	14–28	When *i·* to a feast you naturally
My.	96–20	* Members were *i·* to contribute
	244– 7	You have been *i·* hither to
	270– 7	*i·* me to its . . . anniversary ;
	304–14	*i·* to lecture in London,
	318–16	I *i·* Mr. Wiggin to visit one of
	322–15	* *i·* to dine with the Wiggin family.

inviting

Pul.	65– 4	* In *i·* the Eastern churches
My.	184–11	*i·* me to be present
	186–26	card *i·* me to be with you
	192–20	*i·* me to be present

invocation

Po.	page 28	poem

invoke

Peo.	9–18	*i·* the divine aid of Spirit

involuntarily

Mis.	290–20	my affections *i·* flow out
My.	210–13	Goodness *i·* resists evil.

involuntary

No.	v– 4	*i·* as well as voluntary error.
Hea.	12–21	without the *i·* thought,

involve

No.	33–10	because they *i·* divine Science,
My.	164– 2	such an effort would *i·* a

involved

Mis.	200–28	*i·* in its divine Principle, God :
Man.	47– 7	on the anatomy *i·*.
Ret.	22–15	*i·* errors are vanquished by
Pul.	35– 3	law *i·* in spiritual Science
'02.	13– 1	to meet the expenses *i·*.
My.	359– 9	not personally *i·* in the affairs

involves

Mis.	76–30	Soul, Spirit, *i·* this appearing,
	338– 2	*i·* the disappearing of evil.
Man.	44– 5	*i·* schisms in our Church
Ret.	47–10	shuns whatever *i·* material means
Un.	5–15	*mystery i·* the unknown.
	41– 7	*i·* a loss of the true sense of good,
	41– 9	*i·* a temporary loss of God,
No.	44– 4	C. S. *i·* a new language,
My.	139–14	*i·* Life, — calm, irresistible,
	261–23	Christmas *i·* an open secret,

involving

Mis.	54–30	to solve a problem *i·* logarithms ;
Man.	52– 1	*i·* The Mother Church discipline.
Un.	5– 1	a theme *i·* the All of infinity.
My.	309– 6	lawsuit *i·* a question of pauperism

inward

My.	159–16	from the *i·* to the outward,

inwardly

Mis.	232– 1	God comfort them all ! we *i·* prayed

iota

'02.	16–26	they never destroy one *i·* of
My.	107–11	have not an *i·* of the drug left
	321–19	* to change my opinion one *i·*

Iowa

(see **Burlington**)

ipecacuanha

Mis.	369–16	rhubarb tincture or an *i·* pill.

ipse dixit

Mis.	65– 6	man's *i· d·* as to the stellar system

ire

Po.	30–17	a patient love above earth's *i·*,

Ireland

Man.	94–19	in Canada, in Great Britain and *I·*.
	97– 9	Canada, Great Britain and *I·*.
	99– 6	Each county of Great Britain and *I·*,
	99–23	for Great Britain and *I·*.

iris

Mis.	355–28	to the light, and the *i·* of faith,

irksome

My.	166–21	sport would be more *i·* than work.

iron

Ret.	5–14	a strong intellect and an *i·* will.
Pul.	25– 6	* The partitions are of *i·* ;
	25–12	* girders are all of *i·*,
	25–14	* window frames are of *i·*,
	25–14	* staircases are of *i·*,
	82–30	* fear has ceased to kiss the *i·* heel
Peo.	13–12	*i·* tread of merciless invaders,
My.	4–21	*i·* in human nature rusts away ;
	68–29	* framed of *i·* and finished with
	160–15	cuts its way through *i·* and sod,

irony

Mis.	291–18	perversion of C. S. is the *i·*
Ret.	23– 4	ultimately yield to the *i·* of fate,

irrefutable

My.	179–27	are, *i·* and eternal.

irregular

Mis.	256–17	has occasioned the *i·* intervals

irreparable

Rud.	16–17	an *i·* loss of Science.
My.	333–29	* to lament this *i·* loss."

irrepressible

Mis.	102–27	the *i·* conflict between

irreproachable

My.	331– 8	* indicates her *i·* standing

irresistible

Mis.	16–31	the *i·* conflict between
	100–15	leads on *i·* forces, and will
	268–28	*i·*, permanent, eternal.
My.	49– 4	* as by an *i·* attraction.
	139–15	Life, — calm, *i·*, eternal.

irrespective

Mis.	357–21	love that is *i·* of self,

irresponsible

No.	3– 9	some *i·* people insisted
My.	316–12	*I·* Attacks on C. S.

irreverent

Man.	41– 3	*i·* reference to Christ Jesus

irrevocable

Pan.	12–26	C. S. is *i·* — unpierced by

irrevocably

Mis.	177–16	give yourselves wholly and *i·* to

irritate

My.	111–27	may *i·* a certain class of

Isaac

My.	161–12	Abraham, and *I·*, — *Luke* 13 : 28.

Isaiah

XI

Po.	43– 1	*picture depictive of I· xi.*

28: 16, 17

My.	16–23	* Scripture reading, *I·* 28 : 16, **17,**

Mis.	145–22	memorial such as *I·* prophesied :
	148–29	in the words of the prophet *I· ·*
	164–17	In our text *I·* foretold,
	301–31	to whom *I·* alluded thus :
Un.	55– 5	as *I·* says of him,
My.	140– 2	* Of this . . . the prophet *I·* said,
	171– 3	is fulfilled the prophecy of *I·* :
	177–22	this prophecy of *I·* is fulfilled
	184–26	*I·* said : "How beautiful — *Isa.* 52 : 7.
	193–26	may the prophecy of *I·* be fulfilled :

Isis
My. 92–12 * new temple to *I·* and Osiris would be

islands
My. 279–26 and those *i·* of the sea
286– 6 on earth and the *i·* of the sea

Isle
Mis. 392–18 poem
392–19 on receiving a painting of the *I·*
392–20 *I·* of beauty, thou art singing
393–21 *I·* of beauty, thou art teaching
Po. page 51 poem
51– 1 On receiving a painting of the *I·.*
51– 2 *I·* of beauty, thou art singing
52– 5 *I·* of beauty, thou art teaching

Isle of Patmos
Pul. 27–28 * representing John on the *I· of P·,*

isles
Mis. 153–10 green *i·* of refreshment.
227–24 on *i·* of sweet refreshment.

ism
Mis. 175–24 *i·* of to-day has nothing to do with
Ret. 28–28 I believe in no *i·.*
My. 119–11 towards Buddhism or any other "*i·.*"

isms
Mis. 4–21 it is confounded with *i·,*
295– 7 * a gamut of *i·* and ists,
No. 43–25 reconstruct the wrecks of "*i·*"

isolate
Pul. 21–16 shun whatever would *i·* us from

isolation
My. 50–13 * felt a peculiar sense of *i·,*

Israel (*see also* **Israel's**)
Mis. 9– 6 Well is it that the Shepherd of *I·*
72–13 concerning the land of *I·,— Ezek.* 18 : 2.
72–17 to use this proverb in *I·.*"— *Ezek.* 18 : 3.
73–26 *the twelve tribes of I·.*"— *Matt.* 19 : 28.
121–17 innocent blood from *I·.*"— *Deut.* 19 : 13.
150– 3 you have the great Shepherd of *I·*
153–13 God is good to *I·,*
153–14 good to His *I·*
162– 2 Jacob was called *I·* ;
308–16 "Hear, O *I·* :— *Deut.* 6 : 4.
360–19 "*I·* after the flesh,"— *I Cor.* 10 : 18.
360–21 "the *I·* according to Spirit"
Man. 17–18 heals the sick, and restores the lost *I·* :
Ret. 79–25 the children of *I·* were saved by
90–23 Thus must the Mother in *I·* give all
Pul. 44–12 * yet the mother in *I·,* alone
Peo. 11–17 children of *I·* still in bondage.
My. 42–31 * were the children of *I·* delivered
43–19 * *I·* came over this Jordan
44– 5 * *I·* is going up to possess the
108– 5 Christ, the Holy One of *I·,*
182–20 house of worship to the God of *I·,*
183–14 light upon the mountain of *I·.*
280–15 chapter sub-title— *Deut.* 6 : 4.
296– 9 chapter sub-title— *Deut.* 6 : 4.

Israelites
'00. 3–22 *I·* in Babylon hesitated not

Israel's
My. 125– 9 with the sling of *I·* chosen one

issue
Mis. xi– 2 copyrighted at the date of its *i·,*
4–11 chapter sub-title
7–23 price at which we shall *i·* it,
80– 4 on the single *i·* of opposition to
105–26 The senses join *i·* with error,
220–14 control . . . on the point at *i·.*
246–28 The question at *i·* with mankind is :
294–29 In an *i·* of January 17,
350–26 I *i·* no arguments, . . . in mental
Un. 46–26 Pharisees fought Jesus on this *i·.*
No. 46– 3 The question now at *i·* is :
My. 27–23 * in this *i·* of the *Sentinel*
73– 2 * to *i·* a similar notice or order,
98–14 * *i·* of the *C. S. Sentinel*
122– 3 *i·* from the brain of a dreamer.
241–14 * *i·* raised is an important one
284–12 In the *i·* of your good paper,
284–17 In your next *i·* please correct

issue
My. 330–18 * as claimed in your *i·*
334– 9 * *i·* of the *C. S. Sentinel,*
352–28 *i·* of *The C. S. Monitor.*
360–11 momentous question at *i·* in

issued
Mis. 372– 1 When the latter was first *i·,*
380–30 pamphlet printed and *i·* by
381–21 A writ of injunction was *i·*
Man. 91– 6 shall be on all certificates *i·.*
Pul. 38– 6 * S. and H., was *i·* in 1875.
Po. vii– 9 * *a popular edition to be i·,*
My. 236–26 which will be *i·* February 29
328–18 * Sheriff Wooten *i·* licenses
328–20 * first to be *i·* to the healers
356–16 nor consent to have my picture *i·,*

issues
Mis. 221–32 holds the *i·* of death
235–15 touches mind to more spiritual *i·,*
No. 27– 2 It *i·* a false claim ;
40–16 never . . . save to *i·* of Truth ;
Hea. 5–26 lead our lives to higher *i·* ;
My. 170– 9 not be confused with other *i·,*
221–24 All *i·* of morality, of Christianity,
287–23 it touches thought to spiritual *i·,*
329–16 * paper in the *i·* of July 3

isthmus-lordling
Mis. 393–17 Art hath bathed this *i·*
Po. 52– 1 Art hath bathed this *i·*

ists
Mis. 295– 7 * a gamut of isms and *i·,*

Italian
Mis. 376– 3 * authentic *I·* school, revived.
Pul. 25–22 * floor is in white *I·* mosaic,
26–21 * by an entrance of *I·* marble,
76– 4 * superb archway of *I·* marble
Rud. 1–13 In Spanish, *I·,* and Latin,

Italian Renaissance
My. 68– 1 * Built in the *I· R·* style,

Italy
Mis. 372–15 masters in France and *I·.*
375–12 * Years ago, while in *I·.*
Pul. 5–25 *I·,* Greece, Japan, India,

itching
Mis. 337–27 to *i·* ears and to dull disciples

Item
Mis. 391– 2 Written to the Editor of the *I·,*
Po. 38– 1 To the editor of the *I·,*

item
Mis. 391– 1 poem
391– 6 An *i·* rich in store ;
391–14 As *i·,* of our life ;
391–22 'T will be an *i·* more.
Po. page 38 poem
38– 5 An *i·* rich in store ;
38–13 As *i·,* of our life ;
38–21 'Twill be an *i·* more.
My. 54– 6 * *Traveler* contained the following *i·* :
145– 3 acquainted with the small *i·*

itemize
Mis. 131–13 prepared to *i·* a report
131–25 *i·* a bill of this church's gifts
131–29 to *i·* or audit their accounts,

itemized
Mis. 131–30 these will be found already *i·,*

items
Mis. 157–20 *i·* relative to Mrs. Stebbin's case.
391–10 Have many *i·* more ;
391–18 Find *i·* at our door.
'00. 12–11 St. Paul's life furnished *i·*
Po. 38– 9 Have many *i·* more ;
38–17 Find *i·* at our door.

iterated
'02. 5–20 *i·* in the law of God,

itinerancy
Ret. 88–27 *I·* should not be allowed to

itinerant
My. 314– 2 * "an *i·* dentist."

J

jacket
Mis. 233– 9 monkey in harlequin *j·*

Jackson, Mich.
Pul. 52– 8 * *Jackson Patriot, J·, M·.,*

Jackson Patriot
Pul. 52– 8 * *J· P·,* Jackson, Mich.,

Jacob (*see also* **Jacob's**)
Mis. 162– 2 *J·* was called Israel ;
My. 34– 9 seek thy face, O *J·.— Psal.* 24 : 6.
161–12 *J·,* and all the prophets,— *Luke* 13 : 28.

Jacob's
'02. 10–15 gain the scope of *J·* vision,

jaded
Mis. 366–16 poor *j·* humanity needs to get
jagged
Mis. 327–30 plunge headlong over the *j·* rocks.
Jahr
Ret. 33–11 remedies enumerated by *J·*,
Hea. 12–15 remedies of the *J·*,
jail
Po. vi–18 *nowhere but in the walls of a j·.*
My. 175–15 well-conducted *j·* and state prison,
jailer
Mis. 112–21 The *j·* thanked me, and said,
Jairus (*see also* Jairus')
Pul. 27–17 * raising of the daughter of *J·*.
Jairus'
Pul. 54–22 * In the case of *J·* daughter
James (*see also* St. James)
Mis. 51–30 The apostle *J·* said,
Pul. 54–25 * Peter, *J·*, and John,
No. 40– 1 The apostle *J·* said :
jammed
My. 99–21 * stuffed and *j·* with money.
January
(*see* months)
Japan
Pul. 2–16 war between China and *J·*.
5–25 Italy, Greece, *J·*, India,
6–22 * leading us to return to *J·*."
My. 279–25 war between Russia and *J·*;
281–19 * peace between Russia and *J·*
Japanese
My. 278–18 A *J·* may believe in a heaven
jarring
'00. 11– 6 *j·* elements among musicians
jaws
Mis. 106–11 Into the *j·* of hate,
294–21 their stings, and *j·*, and claws ;
Pan. 14–25 through the *j·* of death
jealous
Mis. 129–15 If a man is *j·*, envious, or
jealousy
Mis. 123– 6 spirit of idolatry, envy, *j·*,
250–12 which . . . become *j·* and hate.
281– 4 rivalry, *j·*, envy, revenge.
My. 167–29 claims of envy, *j·*, or persecution.
245–13 beasts, superstition and *j·*.
Jeanne d'Arc
Pul. 33– 3 * like *J· d'A·*, to hear "voices,"
jeers
My. 98–11 * must have done with scoffs and *j·*
Jehovah
Mis. 123–15 Babylonian Yawa, or *J·*,
182–23 no personal plan of a personal *J·*,
Ret. 13–15 and in a *J·* merciless
Un. 14–15 The *J·* of limited Hebrew faith
Pan. 7–11 character and sovereignty of *J·*,
'00. 3–23 Yahwah, afterwards transcribed *J·*;
3–26 Yahwah, misnamed *J·*,
Jericho
Mis. 279–16 before the walls of *J·*.
Jerusalem
Mis. 133–23 toward the *J·* of Love and Truth,
326–25 "O *J·*, *J·*, thou that— Matt. 23 : 37.
Ret. 89– 7 assembled in the one temple (at *J·*)
Pul. 7–12 as he wept over *J·* !
My. 13– 9 * "The church at *J·*, like a sun
13–13 church of *J·* seems to prefigure The
46–28 * the heavenly *J·*,— Heb. 12 : 22.
jest
Mis. 353–23 folly of tending it is no mere *j·*.
jester
Mis. 353–17 he said to the *j·*, "You must pay
Jesus (*see also* Jesus')
accepted
Un. 55– 1 *J·* accepted the one fact whereby
according to
Ret. 36– 4 expound the gospel according to *J·*.
achieved
Ret. 88–15 This end *J·* achieved,
action of
Mis. 214–11 This action of *J·* was stimulated by
admonished
Mis. 366–20 even as *J·* admonished.
adult
Mis. 159–20 risen Christ, and the adult *J·*.
against
Un. 46–17 incensed the rabbins against *J·*,

Jesus
and his apostles
Un. 10– 6 *J·* and his apostles, who have thus
and his disciples
Mis. 54–26 *as J· and his disciples did,*
Pul. 52–19 * practised by *J·* and his disciples.
'00. 10–16 and of *J·* and his disciples.
'01. 18–17 *J·* and his disciples would have
and Paul
Mis. 364–32 divine philosophy of *J·* and Paul.
No. 21– 1 life and teachings of *J·* and Paul,
and the apostles
Mis. 23– 7 *J·*, and the apostles, demonstrated
40–10 method . . . *J·* and the apostles used
Pul. 85–13 * of *J·* and the apostles,
Angelico's
Mis. 375–25 * hands and feet in Angelico's '*J·*,'
appeared
Un. 59–14 To mortal thought *J·* appeared as
as a man
Mis. 197–14 concerning *J·* as a man,
ascension of
Mis. 165– 4 because of the ascension of *J·*,
asserted by
Pul. 31– 6 * principles asserted by *J·*,
assumed
Mis. 63–30 *J·* assumed for mortals the
Un. 46–28 *J·* assumed the burden of disproof
as the Son
Mis. 180–30 speak of *J·* as the Son of God
'01. 10–16 and of *J·* as the Son of God
as the son
Mis. 63–26 *J·* as the son of man was human :
atonement of
No. 37–12 vicarious atonement of *J·*,
authority of
'01. 8–11 we have the authority of *J·* for
Peo. 9–21 despite the authority of *J·*
babe
Mis. 164–13 the babe *J·* seemed small to mortals ;
My. 262–10 homely origin of the babe *J·*
baptism of
Ret. 48–26 baptism of *J·*, of which he said,
'02. 5– 8 with the baptism of *J·*.
belief that
Pan. 8– 6 Does not the belief that *J·*,
blood of
No. 35– 1 This blood of *J·* is everything
called
Mis. 337–12 "*J·* called a little child — Matt. 18 : 2.
came
Mis. 60– 4 *J· came healing the sick*
63–15 *J·* came to seek and to save
Un. 59– 5 *J·* came to earth ;
59–19 *J·* came to rescue men from
No. 35–24 *J·* came announcing Truth,
'01. 12– 5 *J·* came neither eating nor drinking,
cast out
Mis. 6– 4 *J·* cast out disease as evil.
68–15 *J·* cast out a devil,
No. 23–13 the diseases *J·* cast out.
31–17 *J·* cast out evils,
My. 288–21 *J·* cast out evil, disease, death,
character of
Mis. 360–11 and the character of *J·*, by his
Ret. 22– 8 summarized the character of *J·*
child
Mis. 166–20 birth to the corporeal child *J·*,
commanded
'02. 9– 5 *J·* commanded, "Follow me ;— Matt. 8 : 22.
commands of
My. 47–27 * founded on the commands of *J·* :
concept of
Mis. 103–26 exchanges this human concept of *J·*
No. 36–27 Mankind's concept of *J·* was
condemned
No. 23– 3 personality that *J·* condemned
corporeal
Mis. 162–18 The corporeal *J·* bore our
crucified
'01. 9–12 the rabbis, who crucified *J·*
14– 5 self-righteousness crucified *J·*."
My. 334–23 self-righteousness crucified *J·*."
crucifixion of
Man. 16– 5 the crucifixion of *J·* and his
declared
Mis. 259– 4 but is what *J·* declared it,
No. 12–17 the Christ, as *J·* declared himself,
32–15 *J·* declared that the devil
My. 122–26 is Truth, even as *J·* declared ;
190–27 *J·* declared that his teaching
declares
Un. 40–12 *J·* declares that they who
defined
No. 22–24 *J·* defined devil as a mortal who

Jesus

defined by
  Ret. 58–12 Life, as defined by *J·*, had no
  Un. 42–21 As defined by *J·*, Life had no
demonstrated
  Mis. 90– 4 *J·* demonstrated sin and death to be
  165– 1 that the personal *J·* demonstrated,
  187– 3 *J·* demonstrated over sin, sickness,
  189–25 This, *J·* demonstrated ;
  No. 21– 5 The Science that *J·* demonstrated,
  My. 218–13 *J·* demonstrated the divine Principle
demonstrated by
  Pul. 70–22 * way of salvation demonstrated by *J·*
  No. 28–18 Has Truth, as demonstrated by *J·*,
demonstration of
  Mis. 244–26 teachings and demonstration of *J·*
demonstrations of
  Un. 31– 8 demonstrations of *J·* annulled the
denounced
  Ret. 65–15 hence *J·* denounced it.
  My. 218–19 ultimates in what *J·* denounced,
dictum of
  Mis. 133–19 following the dictum of *J·* ;
did
  Un. 50– 9 We should subjugate it as *J·* did,
  My. 111–21 Did *J·* mistake his mission
died, and lived
  Un. 62–18 In material sense *J·* died, and lived.
directed
  My. 156–11 When *J·* directed his disciples to
disciples of
  My. 222– 2 even the disciples of *J·* once failed
distinctly taught
  Un. 17–13 *J·* distinctly taught the arrogant
doctrine of
  '01. 24–29 inadequate to prove the doctrine of *J·*,
drapery of
  Mis. 376– 5 * face, figure, and drapery of *J·*,
enunciated
  Pul. 54– 9 * *J·* enunciated and exemplified the
example of
  Ret. 55– 3 Let us follow the example of *J·*,
  No. 14–24 demand and example of *J·*
face of
  Mis. 309– 9 The face of *J·* has uniformly
  No. 18–18 the rapt face of *J·*.
fainting form of
  Mis. 212–31 the fainting form of *J·*,
feet of
  (*see* **feet**)
fleshly
  Un. 62–19 The fleshly *J·* seemed to die,
foretold
  Mis. 214–30 *J·* foretold the harvest hour
forgave
  '02. 19–10 even as *J·* forgave, forgive thou.
formed
  Hea. 7–11 where *J·* formed his estimate ;
fought
  Un. 46–26 Pharisees fought *J·* on this issue.
gave
  My. 190–22 *J·* gave his disciples (students)
had fulfilled
  '01. 10–30 After *J·* had fulfilled his mission
hatred of
  My. 104–10 they vented their hatred of *J·* in
head of
  Pul. 27–22 * Mary anointing the head of *J·*,
healed
  Mis. 63– 3 said . . . *J·* healed through Beelzebub ;
history of
  Mis. 274– 1 history of *J·* and of his disciples,
human
  Mis. 199–19 through the human *J·*.
  No. 36–15 the human *J·* had a resort to his
illustrated this
  Hea. 8–23 *J·* illustrated this by the parable of
immaculate
  '02. 18– 5 pure sense of the immaculate *J·*
impersonal
  Mis. 161–17 the personal and the impersonal *J·*.
interpreted
  Mis. 170–15 *J·* interpreted all spiritually :
is recorded
  Mis. 170–27 *J·* is recorded as having expressed
is the name
  Hea. 3–16 *J·* is the name of a man born in a
knew
  Mis. 260–14 *J·* knew that erring mortal thought
  Hea. 7–22 *J·* knew that adultery is a crime,
life of
  (*see* **life**)
looking unto
  Mis. 361–20 looking unto *J·* the author — *Heb.* 12 : 2.
  My. 258–13 "Looking unto *J·* the author — *Heb.* 12 : 2.
  349–16 "looking unto *J·* the author — *Heb.* 12 : 2.

Jesus

loved
  Mis. 110–10 maintain in yourselves what *J·* **loved,**
  '02. 8– 3 commands man to love as *J·* loved.
  18–18 heart that loves as *J·* loved.
loves you
  Po. 43– 2 *J·* loves you ! so does mother :
made
  Mis. 361– 1 No advancing modes . . . made *J·* ;
  No. 34– 8 sacrifice that *J·* made for us,
man
  (*see* **man**)
marked out
  Mis. 197–10 in the way which *J·* marked out
  358–17 in the way which *J·* marked out,
medicine of
  No. 1 –18 theology and medicine of *J·* were one,
method of
  Mis. 170–22 The method of *J·* was purely
mind of
  Mis. 200– 2 Truth in the mind of *J·*,
miracles of
  Mis. 77–31 where the miracles of *J·* had
mother of
  Pul. 27–21 * great window . . . the mother of *J·*.
name of
  Hea. 3–18 individuals by the name of *J·*.
nativity of
  Mis. 374–18 memorize the nativity of *J·*.
nature of
  '02. 18–30 nature of *J·* made him keenly
never thanked
  Un. 11–22 never thanked *J·* for restoring his
obeyed
  My. 220–26 *J·* obeyed human laws
of Nazareth
  (*see* **Nazareth**)
oneness of
  My. 338–24 recognize the oneness of *J·*
operated
  Pul. 54– 6 * *J·* operated in perfect harmony with
our
  Mis. 376–14 * You have given us back our *J·*,
patience of
  Mis. 7– 8 The loving patience of *J·*,
Paul and
  Mis. 360– 8 colossal characters, Paul and *J·*.
personal
  Mis. 165– 1 the personal *J·* demonstrated,
  166–30 the life of the personal *J·*.
  My. 113–17 not a disciple of the personal *J·* ?
personality of
  Mis. 309–14 the finite personality of *J·*,
phraseology of
  Un. 59– 8 phraseology of *J·*, who spoke of
picture of
  My. 206–13 seeing a person in the picture of *J·*,
portrayed
  Mis. 376– 6 * drapery of that *J·* portrayed by
practice of
  Ret. 65– 4 teaching and practice of *J·*,
practised by
  Mis. 193–12 defined and practised by *J·*,
  Pul. 52–19 * taught and practised by *J·*
prescribed by
  Ret. 87–18 divine order as prescribed by *J·*,
presented
  Mis. 197–18 divinity which *J·* presented
prior to
  '01. 8–25 Christ existed prior to *J·*,
prophecy of
  No. 13– 8 the prophecy of *J·* fulfilled,
proved
  No. 37–28 *J·* proved to perfection,
rebuked
  My. 222– 4 *J·* rebuked them, saying :
received
  Mis. 298–16 *J·* received the material rite
recognized
  Mis. 37– 8 *J·* recognized this relation
recognizes
  Pul. 30–19 * it recognizes *J·* as the teacher
regard
  '01. 8– 6 our brethren, who regard *J·* as God
regarded
  Mis. 200– 3 *J·* regarded good as the normal
rendered
  No. 37–25 *J·* rendered null and void
represented
  Hea. 10– 6 manhood of God, that *J·* represented ;
required
  Un. 11–24 *J·* required neither cycles of
said
  Mis. 8–22 *J·* said : "Blessed are ye, — *Matt.* 5 : 11.
  13–10 *J·* said, "If ye love them — *Luke* 6 : 32.
  57–11 *J·* said of error,

Jesus

said

Mis. 58–13 J· said, "Having eyes, see ye— Mark 8 : 18.
73–22 "And J· said unto them,— Matt. 19 : 28.
76– 4 J· said, "If a man keep— John 8 : 51.
118–31 J· said, "Not that which— Matt. 15 : 11.
174–24 J· said it is within you,
181– 1 J· said to call no man father ;
219– 6 J· said, "Ye do err,— Matt. 22 : 29.
220–29 J· said it would be according to
261–18 J· said, "I came not to— see Matt. 5 : 17.
374– 9 J· said, "Wisdom is justified— Luke 7 : 35.
Ret. 35–16 J· said, "They shall lay hands— Mark 16 : 18.
75–13 J· said, "For there is no man— Mark 9 : 39.
79–27 take it by force !" said J·.— Matt. 11 : 12.
81–21 Said J· : "If the light— see Matt. 6 : 23.
Un. 46–13 J· said, "I and my Father— John 10 : 30.
Pul. 4– 2 J· said, "Be not afraid" !— Mark 6 : 50.
53–12 * J· said to him : "Arise,— Luke 17 : 19.
Rud. 7–17 J· said of personal evil,
12–23 J· said : "Take no thought— Matt. 6 : 25.
No. 23– 7 J· said to Peter,
24–22 J· said, "a murderer— John 8 : 44.
31–25 but J· said to disease :
34– 9 J· said : "The hour cometh,— John 4 : 23.
37– 4 J· said, "Ye do err,— Matt. 22 : 29.
41– 5 J· said, "For which of— John 10 : 32.
42– 8 J· said to the sick,
44–28 J· said : "I thank Thee,— Luke 10 : 21.
Pan. 8–20 J· said, "My Father is— John 14 : 28.
'00. 5– 7 J· said the opposite of God
'01. 7–27 J· said, "Thomas, because— John 20 : 29.
8– 7 J· said, "I and my Father— John 10 : 30.
8–15 J· said, "Be ye therefore— Matt. 5 : 48.
10– 3 J· said, "For all these— see Matt. 10 : 17.
19– 8 J· said, "Ask, and ye— John 16 : 24.
28–23 J· said : "It is enough— Matt. 10 : 25.
31– 9 J· said, "I came not to— Matt. 10 : 34.
'02. 6–11 J· said a lie fathers itself,
16–15 J· said : "I am the way."— John 14 : 6.
17– 3 J· said, "If ye love me,— John 14 : 15.
Hea. 16–27 J· said, "I am the way,— John 14 : 6.
My. 28–19 * doing the works which J· said
150–23 J· said : "If ye abide in me,— John 15 : 7.
161–19 said J·, "Ye shall drink— Matt. 20 : 23.
162– 3 J· said : "Suffer it to be— Matt. 3 : 15.
253–11 J· said : "The world hath— John 17 : 25.
339–24 J· said to his disciples,

saith

'02. 19–16 J· saith : "Come unto me."— Matt. 11 : 28.

saw

Mis. 370– 4 saw J· do such deeds of mercy,

saying of

Un. 53–26 hence that saying of J·,

sayings of

My. 178–32 Logia, or imputed sayings of J·

second appearing of

Ret. 70–20 The second appearing of J· is,

spake

Mis. 83–23 "These words spake J·,— John 17 : 1.

Spirit of

Mis. 70–24 holy Spirit of J· was eternal.

spoke

My. 146– 3 J· spoke the truth.
266–15 of which J· spoke.

stooped not

Un. 11–14 J· stooped not to human

suffered

Un. 56– 3 If J· suffered, . . . it must have
No. 33–24 J· suffered for all mortals
35–13 to show the allness . . . J· suffered.

syllogism of

Mis. 195–20 That perfect syllogism of J·

taught

Mis. 3–10 J· taught them for this very
25– 6 religion that J· taught and
29–32 which J· taught and proved.
53–21 If C. S. is the same as J· taught,
99–32 J· taught by the wayside,
Un. 11– 3 J· taught us to walk over,
No. 35–28 J· taught and demonstrated the
My. 103–14 the Science which J· taught and
303–20 J· taught and proved that

taught by

'01. 33–22 after the manner taught by J·,

teaching of

Pul. 35– 2 meaning of the teaching of J· and

teachings of

(see teachings)

the man

(see man)

turned

Un. 57–11 When J· turned and said,

unreal to

Mis. 200–29 were alike unreal to J· ;

Jesus

walked

Un. 58– 5 J· walked with bleeding feet

was compassionate

'02. 18–12 J· was compassionate, true,

was human

'01. 10–12 J· was human, but the

was questioned

My. 220– 8 When J· was questioned concerning

was the Messiah

Mis. 77– 4 fact that J· was the Messiah.

was the son

Mis. 161– 9 To the senses, J· was the son of man :
'01. 10– 9 J· was the son of Mary,

went about

Ret. 93– 1 J· went about doing good.

we see

Ret. 91–17 we see J· ministering to the

words of

Mis. 37–14 meaning of those words of J·,
198–11 silences . . . with the words of J· :
My. 253–16 my love and these words of J· :

work of

No. 37–19 work of J· would lose its

would hate

Mis. 336–10 Then you would hate J· if you saw him

Mis. 25–30 why did not J· employ them
55– 6 demonstrate to the extent that J· did,
63–11 why did J· come to save sinners?
63–22 why did J· cry out,
70–10 What did J· mean when he said
70–15 paradise of Spirit would come to J·,
70–25 the thief would be with J· only in
74–11 If God does not . . . how did J·,
83–20 Why did J· call himself
84–13 J·, as material manhood, was not
88–21 * that J· was the highest type of
96– 2 as wrought out by J·,
111–24 his doctrines and those of J·,
122– 6 Would J· thus have spoken ∗
158–28 J· was not ordained as our
165–17 truth uttered and lived by J·,
171– 6 To suppose that J· did actually
189–14 plainly declared, through J·,
193– 2 Did J· mean what he said?
193– 4 J· did mean all, and even more
201– 9 When J· reproduced his body
211–27 J· stormed sin in its citadels
212– 6 J· did his work, and left his
215–28 the words, that J· used
292– 6 J·, who so loved the world
359–15 For J· to walk the water was
360–27 J·, as the true idea of Him,
366–32 sophistry and what J· had not,
Ret. 89–15 J· was once asked to exhort,
90– 6 no evidence to show that J·
91–13 Where did J· deliver this great
Un. 9– 8 J· has made the way plain,
37– 1 J· not only declared himself
61– 5 J· first appeared as a
No. 22–21 That J· cast several persons out of
23–10 Out of . . . J· cast seven devils ;
36–22 J· could not have resisted them ;
41– 4 warned the people to beware of J·,
Pan. 5–26 J· treated the lie summarily.
'00. 14–20 cites J· as "he that— Rev. 3 : 7.
'01. 8–26 J·, the only immaculate, was born of
25–28 J· likened such self-contradictions
'02. 18–19 J· laid down his life
Hea. 2–17 J·, the model of infinite patience,
2–21 why should the world hate J·,
My. vii– 8 * truths testified to by J·
15–20 * Of J· and his glory.
15–21 * Of J· and his love.
125–32 of the martyrs of J·,"— Rev. 17 : 6.
222– 8 J·, the master Metaphysician,
222–15 Even in those dark days J· was not
261–27 J·, the Galilean Prophet,
307–15 * and that you are J·."
340– 1 J· attended feasts,

(see also Beloved, Christ Jesus, Ensample, Galilean Prophet, Lamb, Master, Nazarene, Nazarene Prophet, Nazarite, Priest, Prince of Peace, Prophet, Son, Teacher, Watcher, Way, Way-shower)

Jesus'

Mis. 12–13 law of loyalty to J· Sermon
20– 3 aroma of J· own words,
25–22 J· only medicine was omnipotent
30– 3 according to J· example
75– 2 hem of the garment of J· idea
76–16 void by J· divine declaration,
83–27 J· wisdom ofttimes was shown by
91–16 J· character and example.

Jesus'

Mis.	103–24	*J·* personality in the flesh,
	108–25	*J·* definition of sin
	111–18	*J·* faith in Truth must not
	161–11	it was *J·* approximation to
	162–11	emblem of *J·* history ;
	170–24	*J·* proceedings with the blind man
	171– 3	*J·* first effort to realize Truth
	214– 2	*J·* life was full of Love,
	214–21	the personal *J·* labor in the flesh
	260– 7	line of *J·* thought or action.
	373–26	is followed by *J·* declaration,
	388–25	The right to sit at *J·* feet ;
Man.	15–14	We acknowledge *J·* atonement as
Chr.	53–30	that doom Was *J·* part ;
Ret.	25– 7	*J·* teaching and demonstration,
	35–24	perpetuity of *J·* command,
	45–20	in following *J·* command,
	54– 9	drinking *J·* cup,
	75– 4	*J·* Sermon on the Mount,
	89–19	*J·* method was to instruct
	94–26	illustrated in *J·* career,
	94–28	*J·* teachings bore much fruit,
Pul.	41–27	* the power of *J·* name,"
	60– 9	* *J·* miracle of loaves and fishes.
	72–30	* "Did you ever hear of *J·* taking
	81– 2	* the power of *J·* name,"
Rud.	3–17	*J·* healing was spiritual
No.	14–22	not confined to *J·* students
	33–22	*J·* sacrifice stands preeminently
	36– 6	*J·* true and conscious being
	36–11	popular view of *J·* nature.
Pan.	5– 7	chapter sub-title
	5–18	*J·* definition of devil (evil)
'01.	2–21	What *J·* disciples of old experienced,
	8–24	Christ was *J·* spiritual selfhood ;
	11– 3	because of *J·* great work on earth,
	19–15	a flat departure from *J·* practice
	24–25	necessary to follow *J·* teachings,
	26– 1	consistency of *J·* theory and practice
Hea.	18–19	*J·* mission extended to the sick
Po.	21–14	The right to sit at *J·* feet ;
My.	28–24	* *J·* gospel was for all time
	149– 2	divine Principle of *J·* life-work,
	152– 4	the touch of *J·* robe
	190–14	*J·* students, failing to cure a
	190–31	fulfilling *J·* prophecy and verifying
	211–10	even as in *J·* time
	214–11	*J·* three days' work in the sepulchre
	221– 3	*J·* doctrine, now as then,
	232–28	does that . . . accord with *J·* saying?
	340–26	*J·* example in this, as in all else,
		(*see also* **words**)

Jesus Christ

Mis.	77– 2	*J· C·* was the Son of God?
	161–24	new name, Messiah, or *J· C·*,
	196–28	*Believe on the Lord J· C·,* — *Acts* 16 : 31.
Chr.	55–18	In the name of *J· C·* — *Acts* 3 : 6.
Ret.	15– 6	"*J· C·* himself being the — *Eph.* 2 : 20.
Un.	4–24	*J· C·*, whom He has sent.
Pul.	85–19	* prayer and teachings of *J· C·*.
No.	21–24	which is *J· C·*." — *I Cor.* 3 : 11.
'02.	12–12	*J· C·* is not God,
My.	8–10	* of the religion of *J· C·*,
	17–13	acceptable to God by *J· C·*. — *I Pet.* 2 : 5.
	19– 9	grace of the Lord *J· C·*, — *II Cor.* 13 : 14.
	260–30	but one *J· C·* on record.

jet

Po.	74– 5	O blue eyes and *j·*,

Jew (*see also* **Jew's**)

'00.	3–30	not the incentive of the devout *J·*
'02.	11–29	*J·* and Christian can unite in doctrine
	11–30	The *J·* believes that the Messiah
	12– 7	The *J·* who believes in
	12– 9	*J·* unites with the Christian idea

jewel

No.	5–25	a lost *j·* in this misconception of
My.	121–15	plain dealing is a *j·* as beautiful
	357–12	C. S., which is its *j·*.

jewelry

Pul.	78–26	* window of J. C. Derby's *j·* store.

jewels

Mis.	159–29	embroidery, silver, gold, and *j·*,
	201–26	our *j·* have been stolen ;
	201–27	losing those *j·* of character,
	313–13	their *j·* of thought, so adapted to
	395–16	Quickly earth's *j·* disappear ;
Ret.	79–23	*j·* of Love, set in wisdom.
Po.	58– 1	Quickly earth's *j·* disappear ;

Jewish

Mis.	65–30	The *J·* religion demands that
	123–16	was the *J·* tribal deity.
	161–20	*J·* law that none should teach or

Jewish

Mis.	260– 6	*J·* religion, never entered into
Ret.	65–15	*J·* religion was not spiritual ;
Un.	29– 3	*J·* law condemned the sinner
No.	29– 1	this passage refers to the *J·* law,
My.	104– 3	*J·* pagans thought that the
	262– 8	herds of a *J·* village.

Jew's

Mis.	124–10	*J·* or Moslem's misconception of
'02.	12–12	*J·* belief in one God,

Jews (*see also* **Jews'**)

Mis.	186– 6	self-constituted belief of the *J·*
Pul.	82–12	* *J·* claimed to be the conservators
	82–15	* *J·* who never called Abraham "Father,"
	82–16	* *J·* themselves have long acknowledged
Rud.	17– 2	Like certain *J·* whom St. Paul
'02.	11–27	the *J·* put to death the Galilean

Jews'

Mis.	121– 4	Master partook of the *J·* feast

J. H. W.

Pul.	61–18	* signature

Job (*see also* **Job's**)

Mis.	278–14	*J·* sinned not in all he said,
Un.	5–28	Thy ways," says *J·* ; — *see Job* 26 : 14.
Pul.	3–19	with *J·* of old we exclaim,
My.	109–17	we may sometimes say with *J·*,
	218– 4	*J·* said, "In my flesh — *Job* 19 : 26.

Job's

Un.	55–17	*J·* faith and hope gained him

John (*see also* **John's, Revelator, St. John**)

I : 3

Mis.	45–28	In *J·* i. 3 we read,

II : 6

Pul.	27–15	* water-pots referred to in *J·* ii. 6.

IV : 24

Rud.	13–15	In *J·* (iv. 24) we may read :

XVII

Mis.	83–22	In *J·* xvii. he declared his sonship

Mis.	191– 8	The Scripture in *J·*, sixth chapter
Pul.	27–27	* *J·* on the Isle of Patmos,
	54– 5	* followers, Peter, James, and *J·*,
	83–26	* to know what *J·* on Patmos meant
My.	307–14	* and I see that I am *J·*,

I John 3 : 1 – 3

My.	33– 6	* correlative Scripture, 1 *J·* 3 : 1–3.

John

the Baptist

Mis.	81–11	*teachings of J· the Baptist?*
	81–22	like the individual *J·* the Baptist,
	121–23	christened by *J·* the Baptist,
	181–31	*J·* the Baptist had a clear
My.	228–12	Referring to *J·* the Baptist,

Mis.	81–13	*being baptized of J·,*
	81–20	*why does not J· hear this voice,*
	82– 9	Such Christians as *J·* cognize the
	184–29	*J·*, came baptizing with water.

John (McNeil)

Ret.	1–15	*J·* and Marion Moor McNeil

John Bull's

Pul.	67–12	* enumeration of *J· B·* creeds.

Johnism

'01.	12– 8	That is *J·*,

Johnites

'01.	12– 8	only *J·* would be seen in such

John's

Un.	4–23	*J·* Gospel declares

Johnson

Dr. James

Peo.	6– 5	Dr. James *J·*, Surgeon Extraordinary

William B.

Pul.	43– 9	* Stephen A. Chase, and William B. **J**
	86–10	* Ira O. Knapp, William B. *J·*,
	87– 8	* signature
My.	21–30	* signature
	38– 7	* signature
	46–31	* signature
	63– 8	* signature
	280–12	* signature

William Lyman

My.	32–25	* music by William Lyman *J·*.

Johnson C.S.B.

Mr. William B.

My.	289– 7	Mr. William B. *J·*, C.S.B., *Clerk.*

Johnson, C.S.D.

William B.

My.	39–16	* Clerk, William B. *J·*, C.S.D.

join

Mis.	80–11	Anybody . . . can *j·* this league.
	105–26	The senses *j·* issue with error,
	281–30	"Though hand *j·* in hand, — *Prov.* 11 : 21.
	330– 7	should *j·* in nature's grand harmony,
'02.	20–16	brethren, are you ready to *j·* me in
Po.	66– 9	To *j·* with the neighboring choir ;
My.	197–27	*j·* with you in song and sermon.

joined

Mis.	94– 8	which God hath not *j·* together.
	188– 4	creation *j·* in the grand chorus
Pul.	58– 9	* *j·* The Mother Church in Boston,
My.	31–32	* *j·* in the song of praise.
	39–12	* Prayer, in which all *j·*.
	89– 8	* has *j·* lightness and grace
	268– 9	What God hath *j·* together,
	311–13	clerk's book shows that I *j·* the

joining

Mis.	79–29	*j·* any medical league which
Man.	45– 4	*J·* Another Society.
No.	46–11	*j·* the overture of angels.
My.	78–31	* *j·* with their shrill voices
	148–19	*j·* in your rejoicing,

joins

Mis.	396–13	My heart unbidden *j·* rehearse ;
Po.	59– 5	My heart unbidden *j·* rehearse,

joint

My.	199–13	The *j·* resolutions contained
	310–10	*j·* partner with Alexander Tilton,

joint-heirs

Mis.	46–24	*j·* with Christ." — *Rom.* 8 : 17.
	255–16	*j·* with Christ." — *Rom.* 8 : 17.

joints

Un.	7–14	able to replace dislocated *j·*

joker

Mis.	353–14	a practical *j·*, set a man who

Jones (see also Jones')

Elizabeth Earl

My.	326–14	letter from Elizabeth Earl *J·*
	328– 4	* signature

Jones'

Miss

My.	328– 8	* referred to in Miss *J·* letter :

Miss Elizabeth Earl

My.	327–10	* heading

Jonson, Ben

Mis.	vii– 3	BEN *J·* : *Epigram I.*
	vii– 8	BEN *J·* : *Epigram 86.*

Jordan

Mis.	81–19	*the people from beyond J·?*
	206– 5	Above the waves of *J·*,
My.	43–12	* The crossing of the *J·* brought
	43–19	* Israel came over this *J·*

Jordan Hall

My.	80–14	* *J· H·*, Potter Hall,
	80–23	* crowded . . . *J· H·*,

Josephus

Hea.	3–17	*J·* alludes to several individuals

Joshua

Mis.	279–16	The first is that of *J·*
	279–24	in the case of *J·* and his band
My.	43–16	* In obedience to the command of *J·*,

jottings

Ret.	27–14	my first *j·* were but

Journal

Christian Science

Mis.	x– 7	writings published in *The C. S. J·*,
	113–30	Our churches, *The C. S. J·*, and
	126–18	able editors of *The C. S. J·*,
	155–22	editors of *The C. S. J·*
	155–27	and by way of *The C. S. J·* ;
	158–24	April number of *The C. S. J·*
	168–24	* *The C. S. J·* reported as follows :
	177–22	* editor of *The C. S. J·* said
	262– 6	patronage of *The C. S. J·*.
	285–10	*The C. S. J·* will hold high the
	303–21	*Editor of C. S. J·* :
	313– 2	*Editor of The C. S. J·* :
	313–13	contributors to *The C. S. J·*
	347–29	*The C. S. J·* was the oldest
	372–21	*The C. S. J·* gives no uncertain
	382–28	and gave it *The C. S. J·* ;
Man.	27–14	publication of *The C. S. J·*,
	49–15	inserted in *The C. S. J·*.
	65–11	editors of the *C. S. J·*,
	72–16	advertised in *The C. S. J·*.
	73– 6	practitioners in *The C. S. J·*.
	74–16	a card in *The C. S. J·*.
	81–10	editing or publishing *The C. S. J·*,
	81–19	relating to *The C. S. J·*.

Journal

Christian Science

Ret.	53– 2	*The C. S. J·*, as it was now called,
Pul.	9–18	editor of *The C. S. J·*
	36–26	* the editors of *The C. S. J·*,
	43– 7	* editor of *The C. S. J·*,
	84– 9	* [*The C. S. J·*, January, 1895]
My.	vi–18	* founded *The C. S. J·*
	vii– 1	* together with *The C. S. J·*,
	vii–15	* *The C. S. J·*, May, 1906
	19– 3	* current numbers of *The C. S. J·*,
	57–23	* advertised in *The C. S. J·*
	215–20	give my church *The C. S. J·*,
	223–10	cards are in *The C. S. J·*.
	286– 1	[*The C. S. J·*, May, 1908]
	304–16	I started *The C. S. J·*,
	304–19	editor of *The C. S. J·*,
	page 326	* heading
	353–10	The first was *The C. S. J·*,
	363–17	*The C. S. J·*, July, 1895.

C. S.

Mis.	157– 9	find their card in *The C. S. J·*),

of Christian Science

Mis.	139–15	I started the *J·* of C. S.,
Ret.	52–20	was called *J·* of C. S.
Pul.	47– 6	* was called the *J·* of C. S.,

of 1904, page 184

My.	254–20	* in the June *J·* of 1904, page **184** :
Mis.	61–11	* In the October *J·* I read
	87–15	*inform us, through your J·,*
	88– 6	*Please give us, through your J·,*
	156– 8	contributions as usual to our *J·*.
	216– 8	In the May number of our *J·*,
	256–14	October number of the *J·*,
	262– 1	our *J·* is designed to bring health
	262–23	this white-winged messenger, our *J·*.
	303–22	by giving place in your *J·* to
Man.	74–19	and societies advertised in said *J·*,
Pul.	65–10	* *J·*, Kansas City, Mo., January 10,
	89– 2	* *J·*, Lockport, N. Y.
	89–18	* *J·*, Atlanta, Ga.
	89–33	* *J·*, Columbus, Ohio.
	89–34	* *J·*, Topeka, Kans.
My.	57–26	* societies advertised in the *J·*
	97– 9	* The *J·* has kept no books on the
	226–27	*C. S. Sentinel* and *J·*

journalism

Mis.	297–10	Smart *j·* is allowable,
Pul.	31–16	* editorial work in daily *j·*

Journal of Christian Science

(see **Journal**)

journey

Mis.	206–32	As you *j·*, and betimes sigh for
	304–20	* it will *j·* from place to place,
	311– 5	as we *j·* to the celestial city.
	327–15	The *j·* commences.
Ret.	19–22	on her sad *j·* to the North.
Un.	17– 6	will aid your *j·*,
My.	215–24	take no scrip for their *j·*,
	331– 1	on her sad *j·* to the North.

journeying

Mis.	135– 9	sweet sense of *j·* on together,
My.	322–20	* my *j·* from the far South,

journeyings

Mis.	177–30	In my long *j·* I have met

joy

and crown

My.	150– 9	Strive thou for the *j·* and crown

and gladness

My.	171– 6	obtain *j·* and gladness, — *Isa.* 35 : 10.
	194– 3	songs of *j·* and gladness.

and gratitude

My.	45– 6	* witnessing with *j·* and gratitude

and power

Mis.	331–18	peace and *j·* and power ;
	389– 6	peace and *j·* and power ;
Po.	4– 1	peace and *j·* and power ;

and rejoicing

My.	260–18	understanding of *j·* and rejoicing,

and tears

Po.	77–12	giveth *j·* and tears, conflict and

a trembler

Mis.	341–14	is *j·* a trembler?

cause for

'02.	3– 4	It is cause for *j·* that among the

cometh

Hea.	10–18	and *j·* cometh with the light.

distant

Po.	31– 8	tear-filled tones of distant *j·*,

divinely fair

Mis.	387– 2	With *j·* divinely fair,
Po.	50–20	With *j·* divinely fair,

joy

eager
  Mis. 98–14 to watch with eager *j·* the
earthly
  Mis. 81–24 cry in the desert of earthly *j·* ;
eternity of
  Mis. 135–18 an eternity of *j·* that outweighs
everlasting
  My. 171– 5 songs and everlasting *j·* — *Isa.* 35 : 10.
express the
  Mis. 149–19 Lips nor pen can ever express the *j·*
exuberant
  Rud. 15– 8 with exuberant *j·*.
exuberant with
  Mis. 231– 3 infancy, exuberant with *j·*,
filled with
  Mis. 321– 7 My heart is filled with *j·*,
fills me with
  Mis. 281– 7 that fills me with *j·*.
for the captive
  Po. 71–15 *J·* for the captive ! Sound it long !
fresh
  My. 155–19 a pure peace, a fresh *j·*,
giving
  Mis. 262–16 giving *j·* to the suffering
gladdened
  Po. 30–10 Thou gildest gladdened *j·*,
grateful
  My. 229–29 my disappointed hope and grateful *j·*.
great
  Mis. 133–28 affords me great *j·* to be able to
      278– 8 great *j·* in this consciousness,
  '02. 20–21 gives me great *j·* to look into the
greets with
  Mis. 177–29 greets with *j·* a familiar face.
grief and
  Po. 9– 5 fountains of grief and *j·*
hail with
  Mis. 141–10 hail with *j·* this proposed type
harbinger of
  Un. 57–25 Sorrow is the harbinger of *j·*.
heartfelt
  Mis. 231–29 such tones of heartfelt *j·*
heavenly
  My. 38– 2 * the balm of heavenly *j·*,
highest
  Pan. 10–25 who finds the highest *j·*,
holy
  Mis. 287–13 only high and holy *j·*
illustrates the
  My. 339–16 illustrates the *j·*, grace, and glory
in attesting
  My. 96–12 * take *j·* in attesting their faith
ineffable
  Ret. 13–21 a soft glow of ineffable *j·*
innate
  My. 341– 1 I have one innate *j·*,
is real
  '02. 17–16 wherein *j·* is real and fadeless.
is self-sustained
  Mis. 209–26 *J·* is self-sustained ;
juvenile
  My. 261– 7 full supply of juvenile *j·*.
know the
  My. 220–22 know the *j·* and the peace of love.''
leap for
  Mis. 126– 6 in tones that leap for *j·*,
legitimate
  My. 41–25 * postpone his legitimate *j·*,
liberty and
  Mis. 240–10 whereas forecasting liberty and *j·*
light and
  Po. 23– 9 in truth, in light and *j·*,
meet with
  Mis. 326–23 to meet with *j·* his own,
much
  My. 21–23 * who have anticipated much *j·*
      27–21 * much *j·* and thanksgiving
my
  Po. 16–25 waken my *j·*, as in earliest prime.
  My. 253–25 and my *j·* therewith.
occasion for
  My. 89–17 * Here is an occasion for *j·*
of acquiescence
  My. 292– 7 *j·* of acquiescence consummated.
of angels
  Pul. 11– 5 mingle with the *j·* of angels
of divine Science
  Mis. 342– 1 *j·* of divine Science demonstrated.
of knowing
  Mis. 263– 3 unselfish *j·* of knowing that the
      382– 9 *j·* of knowing that the sinner and
  My. 236–13 *j·* of knowing that Christian Scientists
of Love
  No. 8– 7 beauty of holiness, the *j·* of Love

joy

of repentance
  My. 36–16 * the *j·* of repentance and the
of thy Lord
  Mis. 122–26 into the *j·* of thy Lord.'' — *Matt.* 25 : 23.
of thy lord
  My. 62– 3 * into the joy of thy lord.'' — *Matt.* 25 : 23.
      207–22 into the joy of thy lord'' — *Matt.* 25 : 21.
one
  Mis. 281– 9 I have now one ambition and one *j·*.
or woe
  Po. 28– 8 Whate'er the gift of *j·* or woe,
our
  Mis. 386–10 Our *j·* is gathered from
  Po. 49–15 Our *j·* is gathered from
  My. 63–20 * in some degree sharing in our *j·*.
peace and
  Mis. 303–10 peace and *j·*, the fruits of Spirit,
      331–18 peace and *j·* and power ;
      389– 6 peace and *j·* and power ;
  Po. 4– 1 peace and *j·* and power ;
perquisite of
  My. 189– 7 affords even me a perquisite of *j·*.
phantom of
  Po. 65– 7 A phantom of *j·*, it fled with
pride and
  '02. 3–10 the old national family pride and *j·*
privileged
  Mis. 143–29 breathing the donor's privileged *j·*.
  Pul. 8–12 privileged *j·* at helping to build
profound
  My. 157– 4 * profound *j·* and deep gratitude
promised
  '02. 18– 1 light with promised *j·*.
real
  Ret. 18–15 of real *j·* and of visions divine ;
  Po. 64– 6 of real *j·* and of visions divine ;
refinement of
  Mis. 101– 6 blesses . . . by the refinement of *j·*
return in
  My. 170–30 return in *j·*, bearing your sheaves
righteousness and
  My. 41–18 * truth and righteousness and *j·*.
rise with
  Pul. 7–16 They will rise with *j·*,
run in
  My. 155–13 run in *j·*, health, holiness,
secret
  Ret. 15–27 who divulged their secret *j·*
short-lived
  Ret. 32–16 * Short-lived *j·*, that ends in
shouted for
  Mis. 259–21 sons of God shouted for *j·*.'' — *Job* 38 : 7.
  Un. 42–15 sons of God shouted for *j·*.'' — *Job* 38 : 7.
smile of
  Peo. 7–10 * face lit up with a smile of *j·*
special
  Mis. 160–10 special *j·* in knowing that one is
spiritual
  Ret. 21–20 spiritual *j·* and true estimate of
sublunary
  Hea. 11– 3 survey the cost of sublunary *j·*,
tears of
  Ret. 16– 5 tears of *j·* flooding her eyes
  My. 161– 4 with tears of *j·*.
their
  Mis. 150–12 hearts to-day are repeating their *j·*
this
  Po. 68– 7 Earth held but this *j·*,
thrill of
  Mis. 375–27 * thrill of *j·* as no words can
time and
  My. 166–23 let our measure of time and *j·*
tired
  Mis. 397–13 From tired *j·* and grief afar,
  Pul. 18–22 From tired *j·* and grief afar,
  Po. 13– 1 From tired *j·* and grief afar,
to know
  My. 230–22 It is a *j·* to know that
trifle with
  Mis. 257–16 a code whose modes trifle with *j·*,
unprecarious
  My. 201–19 tenure of unprecarious *j·*.
unspeakable
  Mis. 279– 8 sunshine and *j·* unspeakable.
was eagle-plumed
  Mis. 385–22 and *j·* was eagle-plumed,
  Po. 48–15 and *j·* was eagle-plumed,
well-earned
  My. 47–20 * well-earned *j·* that is with us now.
which finds
  Mis. 127–19 *j·* which finds one's own in another's
  My. 18–16 *j·* which finds one's own in another's
wings of
  My. 192–26 My love can fly on wings of *j·*

joy

your
Mis. 155–12 and peace will crown your *j*.

Mis. ix–12 Where *j*, sorrow, hope,
204– 8 hope, sorrow, *j*, defeat, and
351–25 *j* that becomes sorrow.
385–10 "*J* for thee, happy friend !
389– 2 The hoary head with *j* to crown ;
395–22 For *j*, to shun my weary way,
Ret. 22–11 "Who for the *j* that — *Heb.* 12 : 2.
'00. 14–15 to remind you of the *j* you have
'02. 3–24 the *j* of the sainted Queen.
19–11 I say it with *j*,
Hea. 10–23 *to* argue stronger for sorrow than for *j*.
Po. vii–14 * *prove a j to the heavy laden*
21–16 The hoary head with *j* to crown ;
31– 2 *J* — not of time, nor yet by nature
48– 1 *J* for thee, happy friend !
58– 7 For *j*, to shun my weary way,
71–14 *J* is in every belfry bell
My. 47–12 * it is with *j* that those who have
62–13 * with the *j* of Love's victory.
134–10 *J* over good achievements
164–14 Is it not a *j* to compare the
177–21 *j* of many generations awaits it,
258–14 *j* that was set before him — *Heb.* 12 : 2.
273–20 *j*, sorrow, life, and death.
355–28 His reflection of peace, love, *j*.

joyful
Mis. 15–15 *j* adoption of good ;
394– 9 bless, and make *j* again.
Po. 45–12 bless, and make *j* again.

joyfully
'02. 20– 6 hues of heaven, . . . *j* whisper,

joy-giving
Mis. 19–29 spiritual, *j*, and eternal?

joy-inspiring
Mis. 19–32 health-giving and *j*.

joyous
Pul. 16– 6 *J*, risen, we depart
Pan. 1– 9 *j* June is here and ours.
Po. 54– 2 Since *j* spring was there.
My. 131–20 this meeting is very *j* to me.

joys
and sorrows
Mis. 84–26 material *j* and sorrows,
celestial
Mis. 100–25 terrestrial and celestial *j*,
consummate the
Mis. 213– 8 consummate the *j* of acquiescence
departed
Po. 34–22 *j* departed, unforgotten love.
earthly
My. 290–17 earthly *j* seem most afar.
eternal
Mis. xi–16 become footsteps to *j* eternal.
fleeting
Mis. 360–18 blighted flowers of fleeting *j*,
higher
Mis. 287–25 they lead to higher *j* :
330–21 higher *j*, holier aims,
life's
Mis. 10– 2 wherewith to obstruct life's *j*
man of
Mis. 84–14 knew that the man of *j*,
misnamed
Mis. 327– 1 turned my misnamed *j* to sorrow.
mortal
Mis. 385–16 travelled . . . far from mortal *j*,
Po. 48–10 traveled . . . far from mortal *j*,
of heaven
Po. 24– 1 Come to me, *j* of heaven !
supernal
Mis. 387–23 Whence *j* supernal flow,
Po. 6–18 Whence *j* supernal flow,

Mis. 42–19 our *j* and means of advancing
351–27 punishes the *j* of this false sense
My. 158–14 and *j* in the present

jubilant
Po. 27–17 Wrong *j* and right with

jubilee
Mis. 135–15 to the *j* of Spirit?
310–26 receding year of religious *j*,
My. 177– 9 presence at your religious *j*.

Judæo-Christian
'00. 13–27 * authorities of the *J* church."

Judah's
Po. 10–15 To *J* sceptered race,
My. 337–16 To *J* sceptred race,

Judaism
Mis. 162–15 to stem the tide of *J*,
No. 14– 8 Theosophy is a corruption of *J*.
'00. 4– 9 purged by a purer *J*
Peo. 8–11 *J*, enjoining the limited and

Judas
Mis. 212– 3 a caressing *J* that betrays

Judea
Mis. 81–18 *all the cities and towns of J*,
Hea. 3–17 born in a remote province of *J*,
My. 28–27 * preached . . . to the multitudes of *J*

Judean and Judæan
Mis. 82– 1 reconstructs the *J* religion,
166–18 *J* religion even required the

judge
Mis. 90–19 then *j* them by their fruits.
195–24 unfit to *j* in the case ;
239– 2 *j* for yourself whether I can talk
290– 8 chapter sub-title
290–21 cease to *j* of causes from a personal
Pul. 46– 6 * words of the *j* speak to the point,
57–11 * From the description we *j* that
Hea. 7–16 and through which to *j* of it.
My. 148– 5 to *j* our doctrine by its fruits.
296– 2 * able discourse of our "learned *j*,"
314–17 decision was given by the *j*
344– 1 then you can *j* for yourself.
364– 2 "*J* no man." — *John* 8 : 15.

judged
Man. 42– 9 By his works he shall be *j*,
Ret. 43–18 *j* it best to close the institution.
Pan. 10– 7 if the effects . . . be thus *j*,
'01. 33–13 not to be *j* on a doctrinal
33–18 *j* (if at all) by their works.
My. 127– 5 *j* according to their works,
276– 5 to be criticized or *j* by

judges
Mis. 74– 9 *j*, . . . all human systems of etiology
130–21 He who *j* others should know well
Hea. 7–21 as our *j* would not have done

judgeth
My. 126–22 Lord God who *j* her." — *Rev.* 18 : 8.
196–19 that *j* righteously." — *I Pet.* 2 : 23.

judging
Mis. 73–25 *j* the twelve tribes — *Matt.* 19 : 28.
Man. 40–13 prophesying, *j*, condemning,
Pan. 11– 7 Was our Master mistaken in *j* a
'00. 1–23 *J* from the number of the

judgment
Mis. 146–11 to form a proper *j*.
157–24 thy *j* as the noonday." — *Psal.* 37 : 6.
211– 9 by the good *j* of people in
277–26 divine justice and *j* are enthroned.
322–24 the justice of His *j*,
372–14 I sought the *j* of sound critics
381–16 stipulation for a *j* and a decree
'00. 9–13 Strong desires bias human *j*
10–21 justice and *j* are the habitation of
'01. 35– 3 thy *j* as the noonday." — *Psal.* 37 : 6.
My. 16–28 "*J* also will I lay to the — *Isa.* 28 : 17.
41–10 * and so receive *j* without mercy ;
104–18 suspend *j* and sentence on the
170–25 thy *j* as the noonday." — *Psal.* 37 : 6.
222–32 await the end — justice and *j*.
227–15 influenced by their own *j*
316–23 manifesting its unbiased *j* by

judgment-day
Ret. 13–14 belief in a final *j*,

judiciary
Pan. 14–16 and our national *j* ;

jugular
Un. 7–12 had eaten its way to the *j* vein.
My. 105–15 and exposed the *j* vein

juice
Mis. 243–29 secretions of the gastric *j*,

July
(*see* **months**)

juncture
Mis. 161–22 natural to conclude that at this *j*
Ret. 44–23 At this *j* I recommended that
My. 26–14 quite unexpected at this *j*,

June
(*see* **months**)

juniors
Mis. 316–17 My *j* can tell others

jurisdiction
Mis. 227– 8 their crime comes within its *j*.
349–17 I claim no *j* over any students.
Man. 18–15 reorganized, under her *j*,
86– 7 under the *j* of his former teacher.

just

Mis.
2– 9 When we remember that God is *j*·,
11– 4 I used to think it sufficiently *j*·
13– 2 *j*· so far as one and all permit
26–23 this is *j*· what I call matter,
32–28 should be *j*·, merciful ;
61– 3 priceless, eternal, and *j*· at hand.
71–31 immutable and *j*· law of Science,
112– 9 The most *j*· man can neither
112–10 unless he knows *how* to be *j*· ;
121–13 would make this fatal doctrine *j*·
121–29 Human tribunals, if *j*·,
122–19 whose damnation is *j*·." — *Rom.* 3 : 8.
122–32 The murder of the *j*· Nazarite
123–22 whereby the *j*· obtain a pardon
128– 8 whatsoever things are *j*·, — *Phil.* 4 : 8.
131–19 It is but *j*· to consider the
132–29 Even the desire to be *j*· is
132–30 with the hope that you wish to be *j*·.
170–30 he had *j*· told them.
188–20 *J*· there, . . . the present writer found
211–14 drowning man *j*· rescued
228– 7 *j*· amid lawlessness,
228–16 a kind, true, and *j*· person,
239–17 *J*· then a tiny, sweet face appeared
247– 7 I found health in *j*· what I teach.
248– 9 The Greeks showed a *j*· estimate of
262–13 I *j*· want to say, I thank you,
275–15 *j*· comfort, encourage, and bless
277–28 one can be *j*· amid lawlessness,
280–32 *j*· at the moment when you are ready
292–30 as to *j*· how this should be done,
293– 2 *j*· breathing new Life and Love
294–19 *j*· enough to reform and
298– 6 whose damnation is *j*·." — *Rom.* 3 : 8.
332– 4 Infinitely *j*·, merciful, and wise,
334–20 *j*· reduce this falsity to its proper
335–30 "whose damnation is *j*· ;" — *Rom.* 3 : 8.
367– 3 requires man to be honest, *j*·,
Man. 16–12 to be merciful, *j*·, and pure.
93–12 *j*· reply to public topics
Chr. 53–55 *J*· take Me in !
Ret. 5– 1 *j*· across the bridge,
76–19 This *j*· affection serves to
Un. 15– 3 more *j*· than God?" — *Job* 4 : 17.
23– 3 * The gods are *j*·,
54–12 any claim whatever, *j*· or unjust,
Pul. 7– 9 remember also that God is *j*·,
36–21 * *j*· beyond Massachusetts Avenue.
37– 3 * *j*· in its attitude toward all questions."
48– 9 * *j*· then, in the gorgeous October
56–20 * And of the *j*· effect complain ;
57–23 * *j*· off Huntington Avenue.
64–24 * Boston has *j*· dedicated the first
77– 2 * which the church has *j*· erected.
86– 1 * *j*· completed, being of granite,
Rud. 11–16 *j*· so you can awake from
No. 27–13 but it is *j*· as veritable now
'01. 4– 7 *j*· as a departure from the
33–25 *j*· what it was in the first centuries
Peo. 12– 7 merciful and *j*· government of God
Po. 23–18 Than *j*· to please mankind.
41–19 the harpstring, *j*· breaking,
43–21 *J*· the way Thou hast :
72– 4 Quench liberty that's *j*·.
My. 6– 4 Are we honest, *j*·, faithful ?
14–12 * saying that he had *j*· been informed
31– 4 * "*J*· as I am, without one plea ;"
41–21 * love which is *j*· and kind to all
66–11 * *J*· what use the society will make
71–21 * *j*· one vast auditorium
74– 7 * *j*· about in time for the first
83–23 * announcement, which has *j*· been
91–27 * *j*· been dedicated at Boston
96–31 * C. S. *j*· goes a little beyond
97–27 * new temple, *j*· built at a cost of
103–19 *j*· as I have discovered them.
112– 5 did *j*· what he enjoined
114– 4 be honest, *j*·, and pure
132– 3 begin with the law as *j*· announced,
141–21 * has *j*· given out to the press,
163–12 I always try to be *j*·,
184– 3 Have *j*· received your despatch.
208–15 expectation of *j*· such blessedness,
215– 4 *J*· then God stretched forth His hand.
223–28 *J*· now divine Love and wisdom
224–30 Beloved students, *j*· now let us
234–26 is *j*· what is needed.
283–18 It is always safe to be *j*·.
305–29 "Who shall be *j*· ?"
308–10 It becomes my duty to be *j*·
314–28 *j*· as I have stated them.
318–19 *j*· so long as he refrained from
322– 9 * I have *j*· read your statement
345–17 they acted *j*· the same
355– 4 * on which we have *j*· entered.

just

My. 357–28 I have *j*· finished reading your

Justice

Po. 26– 8 While *J*· grasped the sword

justice

and being
'02. 15–12 connection between *j*· and being
and Christianity
Mis. 134– 6 characterize *j*· and Christianity.
and gratitude
Mis. 291–28 station *j*· and gratitude as sentinels
and humanity
'00. 10–14 in the name of God, *j*·, and humanity !
and judgment
Mis. 277–25 *j*· and judgment are enthroned.
'00. 10–21 *j*· and judgment are the habitation
My. 222–31 await the end — *j*· and judgment.
and Love
Ret. 80–17 permeate *j*· and Love,
and mercy
Mis. 146–25 understanding of *j*· and mercy.
266–15 hold *j*· and mercy as inseparable
No. 7– 4 scales of *j*· and mercy.
My. 288– 1 revelation, *j*·, and mercy ;
and truth
Peo. 10–13 *J*· and truth make man free,
My. 316–17 in behalf of common *j*· and truth
basis of
My. 283–22 unite . . . on the basis of *j*·,
chariot-paths of
Pul. 7– 1 from the chariot-paths of *j*·,
common
My. 220– 3 safely submit . . . to common *j*·,
316–17 in behalf of common *j*· and truth
divine
(*see* **divine**)
eternal
Ret. 80– 3 though eternal *j*· be graciously
His
No. 34–21 to propitiate His *j*·
honesty and
My. 4–22 honesty and *j*· characterize the
human
Mis. 11–14 Love metes not out human *j*·,
11–21 To mete out human *j*· to
275– 3 Oh, tardy human *j*· !
industry, and
My. 265–30 honesty, industry, and *j*·,
inherent
My. 227–22 Inherent *j*·, constitutional
is the handmaid
Mis. 261–17 *J*· is the handmaid of mercy,
lack of
Mis. 7–31 not so much from a lack of *j*·,
law of
Mis. 123–23 through the eternal law of *j*· ;
261–16 In this law of *j*·, the atonement
line of
My. 181–18 the intermediate line of *j*·
mercy, and
Mis. 11– 4 it is grace, mercy, and *j*·.
of civil codes
My. 268–13 the *j*· of civil codes,
of the peace
My. 136–22 Josiah E. Fernald, *j*· of the **peace**
309–14 *j*· of the peace at one time.
plea for
My. 305–26 chapter sub-title
power of
My. 191– 5 not a tithe of the power of *j*·.
recompensed by
Mis. 2–12 subdued and recompensed by *j*·,
sense of
Mis. 121–30 borrow their sense of *j*· from
simple
Mis. 112–19 his act as one of simple *j*·,
steadfast
Ret. 50–21 steadfast *j*·, and strict adherence
tardy
Mis. 358– 9 at present naught but tardy *j*·,
the least
Pul. 32– 5 * can do the least *j*· to Mrs. Eddy,
the only
Mis. 13– 1 The only *j*· of which
thrones of
My. 200–22 on crumbling thrones of *j*·
waits
Mis. 277–10 *J*· waits, and is used to waiting ;

———

Mis. 67–19 *J*· uncovers sin of every sort ;
119–24 *J*·, a prominent statute in
122–22 nor reconciles *j*· to injustice ;
154–28 *j*·, meekness, mercy, purity, love.
322–24 the *j*· of His judgment,
Ret. 5–16 to which the pen can never do *j*·.

justice

Ret.	19–23	it is but *j·* to record,
Pul.	9– 8	but *j·*, mercy, and love kindle
Pan.	14–12	that *j·*, mercy, and peace continue
My.	139–13	*J·*, honesty, cannot be abjured ;
	160–10	that we receive from mankind *j·*,
	175–24	*j·*, fraternity, and Christian charity.
	180–20	in *j·*, as well as in mercy,
	220–13	*j·* is the moral signification of law.
	250– 6	quiets mad ambition, satisfies *j·*,
	265–11	and *j·* plead not vainly in behalf of
	272– 3	leavens the loaf of life with *j·*,
	282–12	nations are helped onward towards *j·*,
	331– 2	Here it is but *j·* to record,

Justice of the Peace

My.	138–31	* ALLEN HOLLIS, *J·* of the *P·*.
	315–20	* H. M. MORSE, *J·* of the *P·*.

justifiable

My.	74–20	* pride and satisfaction . . . is *j·*.

justification

Mis.	243–31	in *j·* of material methods,
My.	22–19	* the *j·* of her labors

justified

Mis.	136–10	I cannot feel *j·* in turning
	300–17	you will then be *j·* in it.
	322–17	senses satisfied, or self be *j·*.
	354– 9	"*j·* of her children." — *Matt.* 11 : 19.
	374– 9	*j·* of all her children." — *Luke* 7 : 35.

justified

Man.	42– 9	and *j·* or condemned.
My.	12– 3	* *j·* the letting of contracts.
	228–22	*j·* of her children." — *Matt.* 11 : 19.

justifies

Mis.	216–15	*j·* one in the conclusion
	282–24	and the end *j·* the means ;
Pul.	61–17	* and *j·* the name given

justify

Mis.	299–32	does it *j·* you in appropriating
	374– 3	even the publicans to *j·* God.
My.	12– 9	* sufficient to *j·* the decision

Justin Martyr (*see also* Justin's)

Mis.	344– 2	It is related of *J·* *M·* that,

Justin's

Mis.	344–10	On *J·* confessing that he had

justly

Mis.	119–27	which one *j·* reserves to one's self,
Man.	85– 8	has so strayed as *j·* to be deemed,
Ret.	71–19	is not dealing *j·* and loving mercy,
Un.	1– 9	may *j·* be characterized as
Pul.	75– 7	they can *j·* declare it.
'00.	13–10	the apostle *j·* regards as heathen,
My.	264– 6	speak *j·* of my living.
	283–23	"To do *j·*, and to love — *Mic.* 6 : 8.

juvenile

Man.	63– 6	adapted to a *j·* class,
Pul.	8–30	By *j·* aid, . . . have come $4,460.
My.	261– 7	to the full supply of *j·* joy.

K

Kansas and Kans.

Pul.	59–22	* Joseph Armstrong, formerly of *K·*,
		(*see also* **Topeka**)

Kansas City, Mo.

Pul.	65–10	* *Journal*, *K· C·*, *M·*,
	90– 7	* *Star*, *K· C·*, *M·*.

Kant

Mis.	361–15	*K·*, Locke, Berkeley, Tyndall,
No.	22– 9	cold categories of *K·* fail
My.	349– 9	*K·*, Locke, Berkeley, Tyndall,

Karma

Pul.	38–23	* opposed to the philosophy of *K·*

Keats'

My.	347–11	*K·* touching couplet,

keen

Mis.	224–18	with a *k·* relish for
	374– 6	*K·* and alert was their indignation

keener

Mis.	235–16	gives a *k·* sense of Truth

keenly

Mis.	118–12	However *k·* the human affections
	319– 9	seeing too *k·* their neighbor's.
'02.	18–30	made him *k·* alive to the
My.	139– 4	*k·* alive to the reality of
	275–15	I am well and *k·* alive

Keen's, Dr. W. W.

Ret.	43–13	certificate from Dr. W. W. *K·*

keep

Mis.	38–26	*be healed by it and k· well?*
	41–13	by those who *k·* the faith
	54–17	*to k· well all my life?*
	76– 4	"If a man *k·* my saying, — *John* 8 : 51.
	107–18	cannot *k·* pace with eternity.
	118–15	"*K·* My commandments." — *John* 15 : 10.
	123–25	love God, and *k·* His commandments.
	171–30	*k·* bright their invincible armor ;
	171–30	*k·* their demonstrations modest,
	175–14	shall *k·* the feast of Life,
	271– 6	*k·* out of their heads the notion
	278– 7	fight the good fight, and *k·* the faith.
	294–17	*k·* back thy offerings from asps
	307–23	*k·* yourselves from idols." — *I John* 5 : 21.
	311– 1	love God and *k·* His commandments,
	318–11	love God and *k·* His commandments.
	331–21	*K·* Thou my child on upward wing
	341–32	tended to *k·* aglow the flame
	389– 9	*K·* Thou my child on upward wing
	394–19	* I fain would *k·* the gates ajar,
Man.	30–20	*k·* the property in good repair,
	31–10	*k·* themselves unspotted from the
	76–21	*k·* themselves thoroughly informed
	78–20	*k·* on deposit the sum of
	104–15	shall each *k·* a copy of the
Ret.	31–19	"Whosoever shall *k·* — *Jas.* 2 : 10.
Un.	55–10	must *k·* close to his path,
Pul.	49–29	* a number of men to *k·* the grounds

keep

No.	3–17	to *k·* himself well informed.
	31–27	"If a man *k·* my saying, — *John* 8 : 51.
'01.	32–20	love God and *k·* His commandments
'02.	17– 3	"If ye love me, *k·* my — *John* 14 : 15.
	17–12	Many sleep who should *k·* . . . awake
Hea.	18–16	prevent its effervescing and *k·* it
Po.	4– 7	*K·* Thou my child on upward wing
	57– 5	* I fain would *k·* the gates ajar,
My.	8– 5	* We need to *k·* pace with
	14–30	* *k·* pace with the disbursements.
	51– 1	* so as to *k·* her with us,
	106– 3	or to *k·* silent,
	130– 8	effort . . . to *k·* my works from
	134– 8	*k·* the faith individually and
	145–12	* I do not feel able to *k·* about.
	156– 9	"able to *k·* that which I — *II Tim.* 1 : 12.
	160– 5	to *k·* human consciousness in constant
	191–11	*K·* in mind the foundations of C. S.
	191–12	*K·* personality out of sight,
	210– 2	*k·* your minds so filled with Truth
	215–20	to *k·* . . . from clogging the wheels
	228–29	able to *k·* that which I — *II Tim.* 1 : 12.
	252– 3	*K·* yourselves busy with divine Love.
	253–16	*k·* through Thine own — *John* 17 : 11.
	290–14	*k·* him in perfect peace, — *Isa.* 26 : 3.
	300–18	"If a man *k·* my saying, — *John* 8 : 51.
	324–28	* one . . . who could *k·* to her text.

keepers

My.	83–16	* hotel and restaurant *k·*,

keepeth

Chr.	57– 1	*k·* my works — *Rev.* 2 : 26.
My.	285–18	*k·* my works — *Rev.* 2 : 26.

keeping

Mis.	6–30	in *k·* them clothed and fed,
	339–21	its all of happiness to thy *k·*
	368– 9	* *k·* watch above His own."
Ret.	20–27	A plot . . . for *k·* us apart.
	65–24	*k·* man unspotted from the world,
	69–30	and *k·* His commandment?' "
	81– 6	*k·* them in accord with Christ,
'01.	2–20	and *k·* peace with God.
'02.	15– 6	*k·* a free institute,
My.	223–22	the *k·* or the breaking of

keeps

Mis.	92–11	*k·* his own lamp trimmed
	268–14	*k·* straight to the course.
	291–31	individual who *k·* not watch
Ret.	84– 8	*k·* his own lamp trimmed
Pul.	50–24	* opposition . . . *k·* up a while,
Rud.	12– 3	*k·* unbroken the Ten Commandments,
'01.	15–23	* God's mere pleasure that *k·* you
My.	130–25	him who *k·* the commandments.
	145–20	*k·* the wheels revolving.
	153–16	it *k·* steadfastly the great
	159–28	and *k·* Mind much out of sight.

ken
'*02.*	4–27	or beyond the *k·* of mortals,
Po.	1– 5	Beyond the *k·* of mortal
My.	14– 4	beyond the *k·* of mortals
	45–22	* marvellous beyond human *k·*.

Kennebec Journal
Pul.	88–16	* *K· J·*, Augusta, Me.

kept
Mis.	62– 4	*k·* constantly in mind,
	110–18	Our hearts have *k·* time together,
	208–23	have I *k·* Thy word." — *Psal.* 119 : 67.
	211–27	and *k·* peace with God.
	238–27	*k·* constantly before the public.
Man.	44–21	*k·* abreast of the times.
Ret.	10– 2	*k·* me much out of school,
	44–12	*k·* pace with its increasing popularity ;
	90–14	whom he *k·* near himself
Pul.	26–28	* which will be *k·* always burning
	44–26	* it *k·* coming until the
	54–23	* He *k·* the unbelievers away,
	59– 1	* *k·* perpetually burning in her honor ;
'*00.*	14– 2	and hast *k·* my word, — *Rev.* 3 : 8.
Hea.	2–16	I have *k·* the faith." — *II Tim.* 4 : 7.
My.	97–10	* *k·* no books on the subject,
	314–24	he *k·* her a prisoner
	335–14	* were *k·* by his widow

Key
Mis.	92–30	C. S. textbook is the *K·*.
Ret.	84–18	S. and H. is the *K·*.

key
Mis.	330– 8	if on minor *k·*, make music in
Pul.	47–19	* *k·* words respectively used
	53–24	* the *k·* to health and heaven,
	77– 7	* golden *k·* of the church structure.
	78–21	* gold *k·* to the church door.
'*00.*	14–21	hath the *k·* of David ; — *Rev.* 3 : 7.
My.	256– 4	adapted to the *k·* of my feeling

keyboard
Pul.	62–11	* rung from an electric *k·*,

keynote
Mis.	366– 9	Scriptures give the *k·* of C. S.
Pul.	24– 2	* strikes a *k·* of definite attention.
Peo.	11– 4	struck the *k·* of higher claims,

keys
No.	23– 8	he to whom our Lord gave the *k·*

Keystone State (*see also* Pa.)
My.	196– 4	our denomination in the *K· S·*,

Key to the Scriptures
(*see* Scriptures)

kid
Mis.	145–24	lie down with the *k·* ; — *Isa.* 11 : 6.

kill
Mis.	11– 6	by firing first could *k·* him
	40–28	is holding the purpose to *k·*
	58– 8	consumption did not *k·* him.
	67–10	"Thou shalt not *k·*;" — *Exod.* 20 : 13.
	210–21	and *k·* this lurking serpent,
	238– 1	* helped 'niggers' *k·* the white folks !"
	249–22	combined efforts . . . to *k·* me :
	253–19	come, let us *k·* him, — *Luke* 20 : 14.
	254–14	come, let us *k·* him, — *Luke* 20 : 14.
	254–16	he must at last *k·* this evil
	257–27	Cyclones *k·* and destroy,
	302– 2	a purpose to *k·* the reformation
	325–12	and afterwards try to *k·* him.
	336– 7	*k·* the serpent of a material mind.
	345–29	to *k·* and eat a human being.
'*01.*	33–19	not *k·* people with poisonous drugs,
	33–30	citizens that do not *k·* people
My.	268–16	"Thou shalt not *k·*," — *Exod.* 20 : 13.

killed
Mis.	69–24	had not quite *k·* him.
Pul.	48–29	* *k·* the ill-starred Paugus.
Hea.	18–27	*k·* a man by no other means than
My.	302– 3	can he be helped or be *k·* by a drug ;

killest
Mis.	326–26	thou that *k·* the prophets, — *Matt.* 23 : 37.

killeth
Ret.	65– 8	Pharisaism *k·* ; Spirit giveth Life.

killing
'*01.*	33–20	Is it for not *k·* them thus,
My.	277–15	*K·* men is not consonant with

kills
Mis.	12– 3	spreads its virus and *k·* at last.
	210– 7	the remaining third *k·* itself.
My.	126–10	uncovers and *k·* this mystery
	203–17	a mental malady which *k·* its

Kimball
Edward A.
My.	297–18	My beloved Edward A. *K·*,

Kimball
Mr.
My.	8– 3	* Mr. *K·* said in part :

Mr. Edward A.
My.	36– 4	* Mr. Edward A. *K·* of Chicago,

Kimball, C.S.D.
Edward A.
My.	7–14	* Edward A. *K·*, C.S.D., offered

Mr. E. A.
Mis.	157–19	Mr. E. A. *K·*, C. S. D., of Chicago,

kind
after its
Un.	6– 3	fruit after its *k·*." — see *Gen.* 1 : 11.

any
Pul.	72–17	* medicine or drugs of any *k·*,
My.	83– 9	* badges or insignia of any *k·*.
	305–21	no special merit of any *k·*.

every
No.	20–24	when specimens of every *k·*
'*00.*	5–19	from idolatry of every *k·*,
My.	106– 7	diseases of almost every *k·*.

just and
My.	41–21	* love which is just and *k·* to all

of man
My.	239–24	in other words, a *k·* of man

of men
Mis.	261–24	I mean mortals, or a *k·* of men
'*02.*	14–19	(not by mankind, but by a *k·* of men)

right
No.	40–13	audible prayer of the right *k·* ;

this
Mis.	156–20	"this *k·* goeth not — *Matt.* 17 : 21.
My.	190–16	"This *k·* goeth not — *Matt.* 17 : 21.
	222–13	"This *k·* goeth not — *Matt.* 17 : 21.
	339–24	"This *k·* goeth not — *Matt.* 17 : 21.

unutterably
Mis.	312– 5	self-sacrificing, unutterably *k·* ;

Mis.	88–28	depends upon what *k·* of a doctor
	127–29	a *k·* word spoken, at the right moment,
	137–15	It was *k·* of you to part so gently with
	143– 4	*k·* participants in beautifying this
	227–14	responsible for *k·* (?) endeavors.
	228–16	a *k·*, true, and just person,
	262– 5	*k·* patronage of *The C. S. Journal*,
	294–14	with sting ready for each *k·* touch,
	330–24	Nature's . . . lessons teach man to be *k·*,
	338–12	charity that suffereth long and is *k·*,
Pul.	36–10	* by Mrs. Eddy's *k·* invitation,
	44–22	* the first of its *k·* ;
	87–12	*k·* call to the pastorate of
	87–15	fully appreciate your *k·* intentions.
	88– 5	*k·* and interesting articles
No.	45– 5	and is *k·* ; — *I Cor.* 13 : 4.
'*02.*	2–23	*k·* of birthmark, to love the Church ;
Po.	25–17	Flowers for the *k·*
My.	142–26	I thank you for your *k·* invitation
	153– 4	if these *k·* hearts will only do this in
	172–19	your *k·*, expert call on me."
	174–18	thanking you for your *k·* invitation
	184–11	Your *k·* card, inviting me to
	192–20	Your *k·* letter, inviting me
	231–17	and is *k·*," — *I Cor.* 13 : 4.
	234–11	God will reward their *k·* motives,
	236– 3	for them and their *k·* thoughts.
	239–23	Gender means a *k·*.
	254–10	Responding to your *k·* letter,
	260–23	and is *k·*." — *I Cor.* 13 : 4.
	264– 3	*k·* enough to speak well of me
	285– 3	my thanks for your *k·* invitation
	295–15	It was *k·* of you to give it to me.
	300–20	If, as this *k·* priest claims,
	314–29	he was *k·* to me up to the time of
	319– 7	he wrote a *k·* little pamphlet,
	331–29	* recounting the *k·* attention paid to
	332–11	* or remit his *k·* attention until he
	351– 2	With our Leader's *k·* permission,

kindergarten
My.	147–10	as a sort of C. S. *k·*

kindle
Mis.	1–11	To *k·* all minds with a gleam of
Ret.	17– 6	Muses' soft echoes to *k·* the grot.
Pul.	5– 7	we *k·* in place thereof the glow of
	9– 8	and love *k·* perpetually its fires.
No.	1– 1	*k·* in all minds a common sentiment of
'*02.*	16–15	*K·* the watch-fires of unselfed love,
Po.	62– 6	Muses' soft echoes to *k·* the grot.
My.	125– 1	no longer *k·* altars for

kindled
Mis.	376–26	lower lines of light *k·* into gold,

kindles
Mis.	356– 2	dilates and *k·* into rest.
'*01.*	30–19	*k·* the inner genial life of a man,

kindling

Mis.	313–10	*k·* its glories in the east,
	332– 1	*k·* the stars, rolling the worlds,
No.	22–14	as Stygian night to the *k·* dawn.
	38–25	*k·* desire loses a part of its
My.	164–21	*k·*, guiding, and guarding your way
	350–24	Love divine, whose *k·* mighty rays

kindly

Mis.	95–11	time so *k·* allotted me
	303– 5	*k·* shepherd has his own fold
	327–31	and *k·* binds up their wounds,
	378–16	He answered *k·* and squarely,
	388–12	Speaks *k·* when we meet and part.
Ret.	80–22	The *k·* shepherd of the East
Pul.	6–25	signalled me *k·* as my lone bark
	31–21	* she most *k·* replied,
Po.	7–12	Speaks *k·* when we meet and part.
	33–10	*k·* pass over a wound,
	74– 2	Think *k·* of me,
My.	29–25	* Even the sun smiled *k·* upon
	147– 7	flung its foliage in *k·* shelter
	163–10	who have so *k·* come
	163–16	chapter sub-title
	173–31	*k·* foresight in granting
	270– 7	*k·* invited me to its
	299– 4	*k·* referring to my address
	322–24	* Mr. Wiggin *k·* helped me
	331–23	* *k·* attended him during his
	342– 5	* after a *k·* greeting

kindness

Mis.	117–16	reciprocate *k·* and work wisely,
	283–17	mistaken *k·*, a culpable ignorance,
	322– 1	In return for your *k·*,
Ret.	19–15	whose *k·* and sympathy
My.	42– 4	* the law of *k·*.” — *Prov.* 31 : 26.
	121–21	no vulgarity in *k·*
	281–21	* Will you do us the *k·*
	295–14	*k·* in its largest, profoundest
	330–27	whose *k·* and sympathy

kindnesses

My.	325– 1	* many *k·* you had shown them,

kindred

Mis.	305– 6	* and *k·* organizations.
	317– 4	we are all of one *k·*.
Ret.	6–12	the very dearest of my *k·*.
Pul.	66–23	* and others of *k·* meaning,
Po.	2– 2	Though *k·* rocks,

kinds

Mis.	51– 7	mesmerism is of one of three *k·* ;
	305–18	* They are to be of two *k·* :
Hea.	5– 4	by certain *k·* of food,

kine

Po.	43– 9	Leading *k·* with love.

King

My.	34–11	the *K·* of glory. — *Psal.* 24 : 9.
	34–12	this *K·* of glory? — *Psal.* 24 : 10.
	34–13	the *K·* of glory. — *Psal.* 24 : 10.

King David

My.	273–10	*K· D·*, the Hebrew bard,

kingdom

Christ's

Ret.	94–27	establishment of Christ's *k·*
My.	225–17	The coming of Christ's *k·*

divided

Mis.	56–17	a *k·* divided against itself,
	89– 2	*k·* divided against itself — *Matt.* 12 : 25.
	217–26	a *k·* divided against itself,
Un.	60– 4	Mortal man is a *k·* divided against
No.	5–21	“*k·* divided against itself — *Luke* 11 : 17.
'01.	25–29	a *k·* divided against itself,

floral

'00.	8– 7	As in the floral *k·* odors emit

give you the

Mis.	150– 2	to give you the *k·*.” — *Luke* 12 : 32.
	321–18	to give you the *k·*.” — *Luke* 12 : 32.
Pul.	9–23	to give you the *k·*.” — *Luke* 12 : 32.

God's

No.	35–26	God's *k·* is everywhere

human

No.	35–28	the human *k·* is nowhere,

individual

Pul.	4–21	His is an individual *k·*,

its

Un.	63– 5	Its *k·*, not apparent to material

keys of the

No.	23– 8	our Lord gave the keys of the *k·*

of Christ

No.	33– 7	by advancing the *k·* of Christ.

of God

Mis.	21–10	*k·* of God is within you.” — *Luke* 17 : 21.
	125–10	*k·* of God — the reign of righteousness
	154–17	*k·* of God, the reign of harmony
	251–16	“The *k·* of God cometh — *Luke* 17 : 20.

kingdom

of God

Mis.	251–18	*k·* of God is within you,” — *Luke* 17 : 21.
	254–16	in order to gain the *k·* of God.
	270–14	“Seek ye first the *k·* of God, — *Matt.* 6 : 33.
	344–25	receive the *k·* of God — *Luke* 18 : 17.
Chr.	55– 4	seek ye first the *k·* of God, — *Matt.* 6 : 33.
Pul.	3– 6	*k·* of God is within you.” — *Luke* 17 : 21.
	10–30	*k·* of God within you, — with you alway,
No.	35–25	*k·* of God is at hand,” — *Mark* 1 : 15.
	35–25	*k·* of God is within you.” — *Luke* 17 : 21.
Pan.	13– 7	*k·* of God is within you” — *Luke* 17 : 21.
My.	63–30	* had found the *k·* of God.
	161–12	in the *k·* of God, — *Luke* 13 : 28.
	265–23	*k·* of God is within you ;” — *Luke* 17 : 21.
	267–29	*k·* of God is within you” — *Luke* 17 : 21.

of heaven

Mis.	143– 9	May the *k·* of heaven come
	171–23	*The k· of heaven is like unto* — *Matt.* 13 : 33.
	174–16	What is the *k·* of heaven?
	174–23	The *k·* of heaven is the reign of
	325– 3	for theirs is the *k·* of heaven.” — *Matt.* 5 : 3.
	337–15	greatest in the *k·* of heaven.” — *Matt.* 18 : 4.
Ret.	79–26	“The *k·* of heaven suffereth — *Matt.* 11 : 12.
Un.	11–26	said that the *k·* of heaven is here,
	37– 6	*k·* of heaven is at hand.” — *Matt.* 10 : 7.
	52– 6	It is the *k·* of heaven,
Pul.	85–17	* establish the *k·* of heaven upon earth
'01.	28– 5	working for the *k·* of heaven
	35– 9	the *k·* of heaven within us
'02.	8–27	having the *k·* of heaven within him.
My.	4–27	enter into the *k·* of heaven,” — *Matt.* 18 : 3.
	58–22	* *k·* of heaven is at hand,” — *Matt.* 3 : 2.
	161–14	the *k·* of heaven within himself,
	197–21	is the *k·* of heaven.” — *Matt.* 19 : 14.
	228–14	least in the *k·* of heaven — *Matt.* 11 : 11.
	228–16	*k·* of heaven, the reign of holiness,

of its own

Mis.	197–25	rules over a *k·* of its own,

of our God

Pul.	12– 6	and the *k·* of our God, — *Rev.* 12 : 10.

of Spirit

'02.	20– 4	desired haven, the *k·* of Spirit ;

this

Mis.	174–19	Is this *k·* afar off?
	174–20	first to declare against this *k·* is
Ret.	79–30	We recognize this *k·*,

Thy

Mis.	174–25	“Thy *k·* come ;” — *Matt.* 6 : 10.
	211–31	“Thy *k·* come.” — *Matt.* 6 : 10.
Man.	41–21	“Thy *k·* come ;” — *Matt.* 6 : 10.
Pul.	22– 7	“Thy *k·* come. — *Matt.* 6 : 10.
My.	281– 4	“Thy *k·* come. — *Matt.* 6 : 10.

universal

Mis.	213–28	God's universal *k·* will appear,

Mis.	143– 7	Across lakes, into a *k·*,
	312– 8	and for the *k·* of heaven's sake.
My.	206–30	*k·* of His dear Son.” — *Col.* 1 : 13.

kingdoms

Mis.	217–14	mineral, vegetable, and animal *k·*,
Un.	38–24	mineral, vegetable, or animal *k·*.
	38–25	Life is not in these *k·*,
Rud.	8– 1	confusing . . . the three great *k·*.

King Edward

'02.	3–22	on the brow of good *K· E·*,

King Lear

Un.	22–23	In Shakespeare's tragedy of *K· L·*,

kings

My.	112–29	palaces of emperors and *k·*,
	258–18	greater than those of Magian *k·*,

kings'

Mis.	373–18	living feebly, in *k·* courts.

kinsman

Ret.	2–13	inscribed the name of a *k·*
Pul.	46–20	* inscribed the name of the *k·*

Kinston

My.	328–16	* how this came about in *K·*

Kinston Free Press

My.	328–16	* told in the *K· F· P·*

Kipling's

My.	v– 3	* *K· Recessional*

kiss

Mis.	124–21	to *k·* the feet of Jesus,
	387–21	For faith to *k·*, and know ;
	397– 3	I *k·* the cross, and wake to know
Ret.	17– 7	chords of my lyre, with musical *k·*,
Pul.	18–12	I *k·* the cross, and wake to know
	82–30	* has ceased to *k·* the iron heel
Pan.	9–19	*k·* the feet of such a messenger,
Po.	2–18	waves *k·* the murmuring rill
	6–16	For faith to *k·*, and know ;

kiss
Po. 8–19   ringlets to *k·* my cheek
12–12   I *k·* the cross, and wake to know
62– 7   chords of my lyre, with musical *k·*,

kissed
Mis. 386–22   *k·* my cold brow,
Ret. 15– 1   they came and *k·* me.
Pul. 1– 5   *k·* — and encumbered with greetings
Po. 50– 7   *k·* my cold brow,

kisses
Mis. 204– 9   *k·* the feet of Love,
Pul. 8–18   gave *k·* to earn a few pence

Knapp, Ira O.
Ret. 51– 2   Ira O. *K·* of Roslindale,
Pul. 43– 8   * On the platform . . . Ira O. *K·*,
59–24   * Ira O. *K·*, Edward P. Bates,
86– 9   * Ira O. *K·*, William B. Johnson,
87– 7   * signature
My. 21–29   * signature
65–22   * being taken by Ira O. *K·*

knee
Mis. 127–10   not verbally, nor on bended *k·*,
204– 3   the bended *k·* of prayer,
My. 18– 7   not verbally, nor on bended *k·*,

kneel
Mis. 369–19   we *k·* at our Master's feet,
'00. 15–19   and you *k·* at its altar.
Po. 32–18   *k·* at the altar of mercy
My. 170–27   *k·* with us in sacred silence

kneeling
Peo. 13–15   Galileo *k·* at the feet of priestcraft,
My. 29– 4   * *k·* in silent communion ;
79– 2   * *k·* for silent communion
257–18   our hearts are *k·* humbly.

kneels
Mis. 131– 7   *k·* on a stool in church,

knees
Po. 10– 5   With our hand, though not our *k·*,
My. 337– 6   With our hand, though not our *k·*,

knells
'02. 17– 2   *k·* tolling the burial of Christ.

knelt
Ret. 20–13   I *k·* by his side throughout the
Po. 71– 5   *K·* worshiping at mammon's shrine.
My. 78–19   * *k·* in silent communion,
302–29   *k·* in thanks upon the steps of its
311–26   *k·* in silent prayer

knew
Mis. 35–14   * I never *k·* so unselfish an individual.''
82– 6   He who *k·* the foretelling Truth,
84–14   *k·* that the man of joys,
94– 3   I never *k·* a person who knowingly
140– 1   I *k·* that to God's gift,
158– 7   I little *k·* that so soon another
166–16   *k·* not how to declare its
188–29   she *k·* that the last Adam,
215–21   if he *k·* where he was
231–20   papa *k·* that he could walk,
232–23   she *k·* its infinite value
260–14   *k·* that erring mortal thought
267–12   I *k·* they were secretly striving
290–19   I *k·* that this person was doing well,
292–28   I never *k·* a student who fully
296–31   If he but *k·* whereof he speaks,
336–11   and *k·* your right obligations
Man. 28–11   which *k·* his lord's will, — Luke 12 : 47.
Chr. 53–13   What the Beloved *k·* and taught,
Ret. 5–19   and *k·* my sainted mother
23–17   My heart *k·* its Redeemer.
25–20   I *k·* the human conception of God
Un. 54–24   *k·* and admitted the dignity of
No. 36– 4   He *k·* God as infinite,
'01. 20–17   *k·* what was at work
'02. 9–22   and *k·* not whence it came
17– 4   He *k·* that obedience was the test
Hea. 2–24   they *k·* it was not in the power of
6– 8   I *k·* it was misinterpreted,
7–22   Jesus *k·* that adultery is a crime,
My. 11–15   * She *k·* that we were ready ;
50– 9   * *k·* not the trials before them,
50–26   * and few *k·* of its teachings.
59–32   * *k·* of your early struggles.
137–25   before I *k·* aught about them,
140– 3   a way that they *k·* not ; — Isa. 42 : 16.
215– 3   *k·* well the priceless worth
290–25   *k·* that Thou hearest — John 11 : 42.
304–20   *k·* my ability as an editor.
307–28   drifting whither I *k·* not.
321– 7   *k·* who and what you are,
321–31   * with people who *k·* you
322– 2   * she told me she *k·* you

Knickerbocker (see also **Albany** (**N. Y.**) **Knickerbocker**)
Pul. 89– 3   * *K·*, Albany, N. Y.

knife
Mis. 231–13   dexterous use of *k·* and fork,
381–29   under the edge of the *k·*,
My. 294–17   use of the *k·* or the drug,

knight
Ret. 3– 1   Sir John Macneill, a Scotch *k·*,

knives
Mis. 134–22   poisons, nostrums, and *k·*,

knock
Mis. 303–13   *k·* instead of push
328–13   Christ *k·* at the door of thine
Chr. 55–26   stand at the door, and *k·* : — Rev. 3 : 20.

knocked
My. 311– 4   a girl, totally blind, *k·* at the

knocks
Mis. 83–14   error which *k·* at the door
324– 5   Pausing . . . he *k·* and waits.
326– 6   Once more . . . *k·* loudly.
My. 265– 3   *k·* more loudly than ever

knots
Pul. 67–22   * *k·* of them are to be found.

know
Mis. vii– 4   * WHEN I would *k·* thee
18–30   Not to *k·* what is blessing you,
27–31   can *k·* a stone as substance,
29–24   the people of the Occident *k·*
32– 7   seem not to *k·* in what manner they
48–11   enough for me to *k·* that
52– 5   not so difficult to *k·* that
57–18   "God doth *k·* — Gen. 3 : 5.
58–10   How does Mrs. Eddy k· that
64–25   Is it possible to k· why we are
64–27   It is quite as possible to *k·*
66–25   The beginner in sin-healing must *k·*
67–12   shalt *k·* that by doing thus
68–16   *k·* that the works of Satan are
68–18   *k·* the meaning of divine metaphysics,
73–19   *k·* that the so-called pleasures
77–21   *k·* in whom he believed.
78–10   I *k·* not how to teach either
79– 4   will *k·* them no more forever,
79– 8   reflects all whereby we can *k·* God.
87– 8   *k·*, some time, the spiritual reality
90– 1   *k·* that God is omnipotent ;
90– 2   *k·* that the power of sin is the
96– 8   I *k·* not what the person of
97–17   *k·* that omnipotence has all power.
103–19   Neither does the temporal *k·* the
108–11   Not to *k·* that a false claim is false,
108–22   what we need to *k·* of evil,
108–28   that which we *k·* to be untrue.
110–11   to *k·* that your example,
112– 4   before they *k·* it,
115–19   till you intelligently *k·*
115–27   *K·* this : that you cannot
117– 9   We always *k·* where to look for
117–15   and *k·* as we are known,
120– 7   " *K·* ye not, that — Rom. 6 : 16.
125– 5   to *k·* that there is no sin,
125–15   "to *k·* aright is Life
127–22   you must so *k·* yourself,
130– 4   to those who *k·* her.
130–21   should *k·* well whereof he speaks.
130–27   *K·* ye not that he who exercises
138–18   *k·* that human strength is weakness,
140–17   to *k·* who owned God's temple,
146– 9   need to *k·* the circumstances
157–25   This I *k·*, for God is for us.
170– 4   Those who *k·* not this,
170–16   that ye *k·* not of," — John 4 : 32.
171–26   Few people at present *k·* aught of
179– 5   to *k·* where He is laid.
183– 3   that *k·* no death.
185–24   or to *k·* how much of a man
189–21   For man to *k·* Life as it is,
194– 6   that we may *k·* Him better,
194–27   you *k·* that God is the only Life.
196–10   and make you *k·* evil,
198–13   *k·* that evil proceedeth not from
198–19   We *k·* that man's body,
208– 8   whom the legislators *k·* not,
212–29   before letting another *k·* it.
213–22   and I *k·* them, — John 10 : 27.
220– 7   "You are well, and you *k·* it ;"
220–15   "I am well, and I *k·* it."
228– 2   To *k·* that a deception dark
233– 3   It is important to *k·* that a
235–20   *k·* something of the ideal man,

know

Mis.	247– 7	those who $k\cdot$ me, $k\cdot$ that I
	273– 1	will $k\cdot$ the value of these rebukes.
	282–17	you should $k\cdot$ that the person
	292–20	who $k\cdot$ not what he is doing
	299– 2	To $k\cdot$ the what, when, and how
	302–10	are expected to $k\cdot$ the teaching of
	306–25	we $k\cdot$ their presence by the love
	308–14	even they $k\cdot$ its practicality
	316–17	can tell others what they $k\cdot$,
	317–10	$k\cdot$ that the door to my teaching
	317–23	shalt $k\cdot$ hereafter."— John 13 : 7.
	333–32	$k\cdot$ that the prophet better understood
	335–27	and $k\cdot$ that you are out ;
	341–17	you may $k\cdot$ you are parting with
	347–26	Those who $k\cdot$ no will but His
	348– 3	They $k\cdot$ that whatsoever a man
	352–15	To $k\cdot$ the supposed bodily belief
	355–12	The physician must $k\cdot$ himself
	367–19	if He did $k\cdot$ aught else,
	367–29	would say that . . . must $k\cdot$ sin.
	371–12	They $k\cdot$ far more of C. S.
	379– 3	I had a curiosity to $k\cdot$ if he
	384– 9	Thy will to $k\cdot$, and do.
	386–14	and could not $k\cdot$ the strife
	386–26	I only $k\cdot$ my wife, Thy child, shall
	387–21	For faith to kiss, and $k\cdot$;
	397– 3	I kiss the cross, and wake to $k\cdot$
Man.	49– 6	ye shall $k\cdot$ them."— Matt. 7 : 20.
Ret.	9–23	have learned at last to $k\cdot$
	14–26	and $k\cdot$ my heart :— Psal. 139 : 23.
	14–26	and $k\cdot$ my thoughts :— Psal. 139 : 23.
	21–13	It is well to $k\cdot$, dear reader,
	26–27	$k\cdot$ yet more of the nothingness of
	34– 2	I must $k\cdot$ more of the
	54–16	"I $k\cdot$ whom I have— II Tim. 1 : 12.
	60–18	"K$\cdot$ that God is all-power
	71–12	$k\cdot$ not what is affecting them,
	86– 8	* "K$\cdot$ thyself !" as said the
Un.	1–11	Does God $k\cdot$ or behold sin,
	4–17	God has not forbidden man to $k\cdot$ Him ;
	15– 5	Do mortals $k\cdot$ more than God,
	17–20	Error says God must $k\cdot$ evil
	18– 3	saying, . . . therefore I $k\cdot$ not evil.
	18–13	Error says you must $k\cdot$ grief
	18–22	Error says God must $k\cdot$ death
	19–17	which Truth can $k\cdot$.
	22– 8	Evil. But I would taste and $k\cdot$
	22–10	something to $k\cdot$ or be known,
	41– 8	to $k\cdot$ death, or to believe in it,
	44– 4	$k\cdot$ not what they do."— Luke 23 : 34.
	54–20	God forbade man to $k\cdot$ evil
Pul.	3– 7	K$\cdot$, then, that you possess
	13– 9	we $k\cdot$ that the nothingness of
	14–27	they should $k\cdot$ the great benefit
	14–28	should also $k\cdot$ the great delusion
	15–17	K$\cdot$ thyself, and God will supply
	18–12	I kiss the cross, and wake to $k\cdot$
	40– 1	* Ah, love ! I only $k\cdot$
	81–10	* We all $k\cdot$ her — she is simply
	83–26	* $k\cdot$ what John on Patmos meant
	84–13	* enough for us now to $k\cdot$
Rud.	10– 5	$k\cdot$ that God alone governs man ;
	10–20	and $k\cdot$ that He afflicteth not
No.	14– 4	would $k\cdot$ that between those who have
	15– 2	ye shall $k\cdot$ them."— Matt. 7 : 20.
	16– 1	For God to $k\cdot$, is to be ;
	17–24	If God could $k\cdot$ a false claim,
	19–13	person of the infinite is, we $k\cdot$ not ;
	28–20	$k\cdot$ that Truth has reappeared.
	30– 9	He need not $k\cdot$ the evil He destroys,
	30–10	any more than the legislator need $k\cdot$ the
	36– 5	and we shall $k\cdot$ this truth
	37– 7	to $k\cdot$ both evil and good ;
	37– 9	He cannot $k\cdot$ beginning or end.
Pan.	1–19	$k\cdot$ and acknowledge one God
	2– 4	those who $k\cdot$ whereof they speak
	2– 4	who $k\cdot$ that C. S. is Science,
	7–14	$k\cdot$ of but three theistic religions,
	10– 5	ye shall $k\cdot$ them :"— Matt. 7 : 20.
	11–23	God enables us to $k\cdot$ that
	13–18	Sooner or later all shall $k\cdot$ Him,
'00.	7–20	"I $k\cdot$ not where they have— John 20 : 13.
	8– 1	shall $k\cdot$ and behold more nearly
	9– 1	$k\cdot$ it were best not to do,
	14– 4	$k\cdot$ that I have loved thee.— Rev. 3 : 9.
	15–24	I $k\cdot$ thy works,— Rev. 2 : 19.
'01.	2– 6	We $k\cdot$ the healing standard of C. S.
	7–16	$k\cdot$ and supply the differing needs of
	7–20	$k\cdot$ not where they have laid Him.
	9–21	I $k\cdot$ thee who thou art ;— Mark 1 : 24.
	13– 6	we must $k\cdot$ it is not,
	14– 7	inasmuch as we do $k\cdot$
	14–27	$k\cdot$ that wrong has no divine authority ;
	18–10	$k\cdot$ the danger of questioning
	19– 5	I $k\cdot$ that prayer brings the

know

'01.	19–28	The whole world needs to $k\cdot$
	21–23	Does this critic $k\cdot$ of a better way
	21–25	did He not $k\cdot$ all things
	28–24	well to $k\cdot$ that even Christ Jesus,
'02.	12–24	so far as I $k\cdot$ them,
	18– 2	wilt $k\cdot$ when the thief cometh.
Hea.	3–27	we $k\cdot$ that the Principle is
	9–16	$k\cdot$ that God never cursed man,
	14–16	to $k\cdot$ that mind governs the body
Peo.	5– 5	$k\cdot$ not where they have laid Him ;
	12–14	$k\cdot$ what a power mind is to heal
Po.	6–16	For faith to kiss, and $k\cdot$;
	12–12	I kiss the cross, and wake to $k\cdot$
	33–13	a prayer that His love I may $k\cdot$,
	36– 8	Thy will to $k\cdot$, and do.
	49–21	and could not $k\cdot$ the strife
	50–12	I only $k\cdot$ my wife, Thy child, shall
My.	7– 7	so far as I $k\cdot$ them,
	10–27	* $k\cdot$ that it is the prosperous growth
	10–29	* They $k\cdot$ that their own individual
	11– 4	* we $k\cdot$ that the Leader of
	11– 8	* We $k\cdot$, too, that during these years
	11–11	* we $k\cdot$ that in all this time she
	11–19	* cheered and encouraged to $k\cdot$
	15–23	* Because I $k\cdot$ 'tis true ;
	15–27	* For those who $k\cdot$ it best
	21– 3	* $k\cdot$ of the loving self-sacrifices
	24–11	* we $k\cdot$ that you rejoice in
	33–10	and $k\cdot$ my heart :— Psal. 139 : 23.
	33–10	and $k\cdot$ my thoughts :— Psal. 139 : 23.
	43– 4	* law was given that they might $k\cdot$
	43– 8	* and they learned to $k\cdot$ Him.
	46– 5	* for we $k\cdot$ that without this
	51–13	* we $k\cdot$ of no one who is so able
	87–13	* of people we like to $k\cdot$
	104–19	till they $k\cdot$ of what and of whom
	109–16	This infinite Person we $k\cdot$ not of by
	120– 5	meet in truth and $k\cdot$ each other
	120– 5	$k\cdot$ as we are known of God.
	122–17	Has it enabled us to $k\cdot$ more of the
	122–20	are we satisfied to $k\cdot$ that our
	133–23	Do you $k\cdot$ how much I love you
	133–27	is not all you $k\cdot$ of me.
	135– 8	Perhaps you already $k\cdot$ that I have
	136– 1	enough for you and me to $k\cdot$
	138– 9	I $k\cdot$ it was not needed to
	143–25	"And we $k\cdot$ that all things— Rom. 8 : 28.
	147–27	work . . . "ye $k\cdot$ not of."— John 4 : 32.
	149– 1	men must $k\cdot$ somewhat of the divine
	149– 5	We $k\cdot$ Principle only through
	149–19	may $k\cdot$ too much of human law
	151– 6	Because I $k\cdot$ that no Christian can
	151–14	I $k\cdot$; for God is for me"— Psal. 56 : 9.
	156– 4	"I $k\cdot$ whom I have— II Tim. 1 : 12.
	174–27	Each day I $k\cdot$ Him nearer,
	179–17	Christian Scientists $k\cdot$ that if the
	180–23	insist on what we $k\cdot$ is right,
	180–29	$k\cdot$ not what they do."— Luke 23 : 34.
	186–27	It gives me great pleasure to $k\cdot$
	193– 2	unto Him whom to $k\cdot$ aright is life
	200–19	for you $k\cdot$ the way in C. S.
	203– 5	K$\cdot$ that religion should be distinct
	220–22	the joy and the peace of love."
	223–17	that of which I $k\cdot$ nothing.
	223–29	$k\cdot$ that I am God."— Psal. 46 : 10.
	228– 8	I fail to $k\cdot$ how one can be
	228–28	I $k\cdot$ whom I have— II Tim. 1 : 12.
	230–22	It is a joy to $k\cdot$ that they who
	233– 4	ye shall $k\cdot$ them,"— Matt. 7 : 20.
	233–21	to $k\cdot$ what his errors are ;
	234– 7	$k\cdot$ how much I love them,
	235–10	should $k\cdot$ that it cannot be done
	237–10	teachings that I $k\cdot$ to be correct
	240– 1	till all men shall $k\cdot$ Him
	241–27	* not to $k\cdot$ as real the beliefs of
	241–29	* so that all may $k\cdot$ it."
	246–26	shalt $k\cdot$ hereafter ;"— John 13 : 7.
	248–22	$k\cdot$ that to conceive God aright
	249–19	may $k\cdot$ that I am the Founder
	249–20	I alone $k\cdot$ what that means.
	251– 3	shalt $k\cdot$ hereafter."— John 13 : 7.
	253– 1	rejoices me to $k\cdot$ that you $k\cdot$ that
	258–12	to $k\cdot$ and to do God's will,
	270–20	$k\cdot$ not what they do."— Luke 23 : 34.
	271–30	insomuch as I $k\cdot$ myself,
	275– 8	$k\cdot$ that I am God."— Psal. 46 : 10.
	281– 2	even to $k\cdot$ how to pray
	282–14	we already $k\cdot$ of the Golden Rule,
	288–30	We can $k\cdot$ that all is good
	300– 8	Does he who believes in sickness $k\cdot$
	303– 2	$k\cdot$ of but one Christ.
	303– 4	I $k\cdot$ that I am not that one,
	305–11	People do not $k\cdot$ who is referred to
	306–20	ye shall $k\cdot$ them."— Matt. 7 : 20.
	313–13	I only $k\cdot$ that my father and

know

My.	314–18	and who *k·* the following facts :
	318–25	* "How do you *k·* that there ever was
	319– 2	I should still *k·* that God's
	321–27	* *k·* of my own personal knowledge
	327–11	* I *k·* the enclosed article will make
	352–10	* we *k·* that the real gratitude is
	356– 1	When will mankind awake to *k·*
	357–30	I *k·* that every true follower of
	360–22	This I *k·*, for He has proved it

(*see also* **truth**)

knowable

My.	238–21	God is understandable, *k·*,

knowest (*see also* **know'st**)

Mis.	151–18	*k·* thou thyself,
	317–23	thou *k·* not now ;— *John* 13 : 7.
Po.	28– 9	Knowing Thou *k·* best.
	77– 6	Thou *k·* best !
	77–13	of Thee, who *k·* best !
	77–19	Thou *k·* best !
	78– 6	Thou *k·* best !
	78–12	Thou *k·* best !
My.	229–28	Thou *k·* best what we need
	246–25	thou *k·* not now ;— *John* 13 : 7.
	251– 3	thou *k·* not now ;— *John* 13 : 7.

knoweth

Mis.	72–20	*heavenly Father k·* — *Matt.* 6 : 32.
	73–15	He *k·* that we have need of
	103–12	*k·* the substance of good?''
	253– 4	what man *k·* as did our Master
	367–31	He *k·* that which *is*,
Un.	64–18	can never turn back what Deity *k·*,
Pul.	12– 4	because he *k·* that— *Rev.* 12 : 12.
	13–22	devil *k·* his time is short.
No.	28– 3	How long this . . . no mortal *k·* ;
'01.	34–19	yea, which *k·* *no evil*.
Po.	78–16	benediction which *k·* best !
My.	160–28	but of the time no man *k·*.

knowing

Mis.	14–16	*k·* the facts of existence
	79– 3	the places once *k·* them will
	87–11	*k·* this, I shall be satisfied.
	93–30	*K·* this, obey Christ's Sermon on the
	103–10	lack of *k·* what substance is,
	108–12	hence the utility of *k·* evil aright,
	112– 3	Even honest thinkers, not *k·*
	160–10	joy in *k·* that one is gaining
	168–22	*Ye do err, not k· the*— *Matt.* 22 : 29.
	192–14	*k·* the omnipotence of Truth.
	219– 6	"Ye do err, not *k·* the— *Matt.* 22 : 29.
	221–13	or, *k·* that he is a sinner,
	233– 1	without *k·* its fundamental
	263– 3	*k·* that the wrong motives are not yours,
	265– 3	or, *k·* it, makes the venture from
	269–27	well *k·* the willingness of
	282–22	to treat him without his *k·* it,
	367–13	Error says that *k·* all things
	367–14	implies the necessity of *k·*
	367–22	but against *k·* evil,
	372–13	*K·* that this book would produce a
	382– 9	*k·* that the sinner and the sick
Un.	3–13	by *k·* Him in whom they
	4–26	such an understanding . . . such *k·*,
	9–28	*k· the unreality of disease*,
	23–24	*k·* both evil and good ;
	27–14	*k·* only His own all-presence,
	44–22	*k·* good and evil
No.	8–13	*k·* that God will make the
	9–11	*k·*, as you should, that God
	30–15	not by . . . *k·* sin, or naught,
	37– 4	"Ye do err, not *k·* the— *Matt.* 22 : 29.
	38– 5	by *k·* their claim.
Pan.	5–24	*K·* that evil is a lie,
'01.	20–14	not *k·* what is hurting them
'02.	10– 1	facilities for *k·* and doing good,
Hea.	8– 6	*k·* that Mind can master sickness
	8–22	*k·* that we shall receive only what
Po.	28– 9	*K·* Thou knowest best.
	28–17	In *k·* what Thou art !
My.	38– 2	* *k·* that every perfect gift
	47– 6	* not had the means of *k·* the steps
	164– 1	*k·* that such an effort would
	213–19	wrong direction without *k·* it.
	224– 5	*k·* a little, . . . the human need,
	235– 9	*K·* that she cannot do this
	236–13	joy of *k·* that Christian Scientists
	243–14	not yet had the privilege of *k·*
	244–20	*K·* this, our Master said:
	250–25	in *k·* that the impulsion of this
	295– 2	*k·* our dear God comforts such
	297– 5	*k·* that she can bear the blows
	344–28	*k·* it is not, and that the fear
	356– 5	waken to the privilege of *k·* God,

knowingly

Mis.	11–32	and would not *k·* harm you.''
	94– 3	a person who *k·* indulged evil,
Man.	42–20	or *k·* mentally malpractise,
Ret.	71–17	then he is *k·* transgressing
'00.	8– 4	The good man imparts *k·*

knowledge

and being
Ret.	32– 4	spiritual insight, *k·*, and being.

and power
No.	37–17	His . . . presence, *k·*, and power,

any
No.	30–17	if He possessed any *k·* of them.

demonstrable
Man.	49–10	demonstrable *k·* of C. S. practice,

divine
Un.	4–22	evil is no part of the divine *k·*.

empirical
Mis.	234–16	Empirical *k·* is worse than useless :

false
Mis.	171–28	false *k·* in the name of Science,
No.	17–25	If . . . false *k·* would be a part of
'02.	6– 5	false *k·*, the fruits of the flesh
My.	345– 6	C. S. will overthrow false *k·*

fountain of
My.	79–10	* the supposed fountain of *k·*

full
Mis.	263–22	a full *k·* of the environments.

gained
Mis.	24–21	*k·* gained from mortal sense

general
Mis.	293– 9	general *k·* that he has gained

her
Man.	82– 8	without her *k·* or written consent.

his
Mis.	269–16	he who has fairly proven his *k·*
	283– 6	without his *k·* or consent,
	283–15	to treat another . . . without his *k·*,

historical
My.	318–28	his ample fund of historical *k·*,

human
Mis.	22– 8	so far in advance of human *k·*
	288–17	Human *k·* inculcates that it is,

imperfect
Rud.	9– 7	imperfect *k·* will lead to weakness

I sought
Ret.	33– 7	I sought *k·* from the different

losing the
Mis.	354–13	losing the *k·* of the divine
Un.	20–19	will find yourself losing the *k·* and

man's
Mis.	181– 5	Man's *k·* of this grand verity

mine of
Pul.	51–12	* have worked in the mine of *k·*

My
Un.	18–18	and My *k·* of harmony

my
Mis.	249–17	to my *k·*, not one has been sent
Ret.	21– 3	Without my *k·* a guardian was
My.	138– 6	suit was brought without my *k·*

my own
Pul.	31– 8	* my own *k·* of Mrs. Eddy,

no
Mis.	47–30	I have no *k·* of mesmerism,
	208– 8	God has no *k·* of evil,
Un.	2–16	God, has no *k·* of sin.
No.	16–20	He can have no *k·* or inference but
	17–22	God who has no *k·* of sin
	20– 5	and revelation give us no *k·*.
My.	223–12	and of whom I have no *k·*,
	315–11	* At that time I had no *k·* of

obtained
Mis.	251–17	*k·* obtained from the senses),

of arithmetic
My.	8–18	* with my faint *k·* of arithmetic

of aught
Un.	18–25	A *k·* of aught beside Myself

of both
Mis.	24–23	A *k·* of both good and evil
	198–22	tree of the *k·* of *both*
	367–13	tree of *k·* of *both* good and

of Christ
Mis.	360–15	with the true *k·* of Christ
	360–31	filled with the true *k·* of Christ.
My.	113–15	to aspire to this *k·* of Christ
	239–13	*comes into the k· of Christ*

of Christian Science
Man.	49–10	demonstrable *k·* of C. S.
Rud.	16– 3	a thorough *k·* of C. S.,

of divine law
My.	190–26	power (*k·* of divine law)

of error
Ret.	55– 4	gain sufficient *k·* of error to
My.	232–21	*k·* of error and of its operations

knowledge

of evil
Mis. 107–22   *k·* of evil as evil, so-called.
    108–19   proper *k·* of evil and its subtle
    109–10   *k·* of evil that brings on repentance
    208– 8   God has no *k·* of evil,
    259– 9   no consciousness or *k·* of evil ;
Un. 15–12   destroyed by the *k·* of evil,
    18–27   If such *k·* of evil were possible
    41– 7   *K·* of evil, or belief in it,
    53– 6   by calling the *k·* of evil good,
    54–23   *k·* of evil would make man a
’02. 6– 6   *k·* of evil, of something besides
of God
Mis. 3– 6   understanding — the true *k·* of God
    139–13   *against the k· of God,* — II *Cor.* 10 : 5.
    183–26   As many as do receive a *k·* of God
Ret. 31–12   seek diligently for the *k·* of God
Un. 36– 8   and gains a *k·* of God from
    39–16   as many as receive the *k·* of God
No. 12–12   this new-old *k·* of God.
My. 47–23   * demonstration of the *k·* of God,
    294–12   spiritual *k·* of God.
of good
Mis. 109–23   third stage, — the *k·* of good ;
of his sins
Mis. 107–29   Without a *k·* of his sins,
of life
’02. 6– 3   *k·* of life, substance, or law,
of Mind-healing
Mis. 264–24   Their *k·* of Mind-healing may be
of one’s self
Mis. 108–18   namely, the *k·* of one’s self,
of philosophy
’01. 25– 8   *k·* of philosophy and of medicine,
of salvation
’02. 11–16   *k·* of salvation from sin,
    16– 5   “S. and H.,” . . . “*k·* of salvation.”
of self-support
My. 216–26   in the *k·* of self-support,
of sin
Mis. 109–20   *k·* of sin and its consequences,
Un. 2–16   God, has no *k·* of sin.
    13–15   If God has any real *k·* of sin,
    16– 5   if God has, . . . a real *k·* of sin?
    54–25   condemned the *k·* of sin
No. 17–22   God who has no *k·* of sin
of Soul
No. 29– 8   so slight a *k·* of Soul that they
of the individual
Ret. 71–10   consent or *k·* of the individual
of the true God
Ret. 49–25   to a *k·* of the true God,
of this Science
Mis. 261–29   even a *k·* of this Science,
of this something
Un. 22–14   a *k·* of this something is
of Truth
Mis. 160–11   *k·* of Truth and divine Love,
Ret. 86–17   growth in the *k·* of Truth,
Un. 2–22   a *k·* of Truth and Love
or consent
Mis. 282– 8   without their *k·* or consent?
    283– 6   without his *k·* or consent,
or understanding
My. 107–26   *k·* or understanding of God,
our
Un. 22–17   and be important to our *k·*.
No. 30–15   removing our *k·* of what is not.
peculiar
My. 52–31   * out of his own peculiar *k·*
personal
My. 321–24   * personal *k·* of the authorship
    321–28   * know of my own personal *k·*
practical
Mis. 28–26   The Master’s practical *k·* of
priceless
Mis. 270–13   priceless *k·* of his Principle
real
Un. 13–15   If God has any real *k·* of sin,
    16– 5   if God has, . . . a real *k·* of sin?
renewed in
Pan. 11– 5   which is renewed in *k·*
scientific
Mis. 186–22   This scientific *k·* affords
My. 273–21   scientific *k·* that is portentous ;
sequence of
Mis. 109–24   the valuable sequence of *k·*
sought
Pul. 47–10   * she states that she sought *k·*
stores of
My. 149–11   its radiant stores of *k·*
their
Mis. 264–24   Their *k·* of Mind-healing may
    282– 8   without their *k·* or consent?

knowledge

their
My. 149– 3   prove their *k·* by doing
    321–32   * told me of their *k·* of your work
the very
Un. 15–13   the very *k·* caught from God,
this
Mis. 24– 4   This *k·* came to me in
    24– 7   This *k·* is practical,
    39– 6   this *k·* can be obtained
    112–10   this *k·* demands our time
    125– 7   This *k·* enables him to overcome
    188–31   This *k·* did become to her
Un. 3–14   This *k·* is not the forbidden
    15– 1   that by this *k·*, . . . came
    54–19   and this *k·* would not be
No. 16– 7   this *k·* would manifest evil in
    30–20   This *k·* is light wherein
’02. 6– 9   Love and Truth destroy this *k·*,
My. 113–15   for St. Paul to aspire to this *k·*
thought and
Mis. 68–23   * necessary to thought and *k·* ;
tree of
Mis. 235–13   at the root of the tree of *k·*,
    367–16   this fruit of the tree of *k·*
true
Mis. 3– 5   the true *k·* of God
    189– 8   and true *k·* of preexistence,
    360–15   with the true *k·* of Christ
    360–31   with the true *k·* of Christ.
Un. 41– 3   the true *k·* and consciousness
My. 177–13   the true *k·* and proof of life
Truth’s
No. 30–18   Truth’s *k·* of its own infinitude
uninspired
My. 238–11   Uninspired *k·* of the translations
vain
Mis. 168–13   emptied of vainglory and vain *k·*,
without
Mis. 284– 8   may possess a zeal without *k·*,
your
My. 133–27   your *k·* with its magnitude of meaning

Mis. 24– 2   *k·* of them makes man spiritually
    61– 6   All the *k·* and vain strivings of
    308–23   The *k·* that I have gleaned from
Ret. 10–12   most of the *k·* I had gleaned
    11–11   Where *k·* plants the foot of power
    50– 3   *k·* of that divine power which heals ;
Un. 4–24   in the *k·* of the only true God,
    14–25   a *k·* which is everlasting
    19– 1   With God, *k·* is necessarily
Pul. 2–28   intrenching ourselves in the *k·* that
No. 9–27   * it is “*k·*, duly arranged and
    23–22   *K·* of a man’s physical personality
Po. 60– 8   Where *k·* plants the foot of power
My. 293– 1   *k·* that all things are possible to

Knowles, Frederick Lawrence
My. 48–17   * the late Frederick Lawrence *K·* :

known
Mis. 26– 3   will be *k·* as self-evident truth,
    29–16   Since that date I have *k·* of
    108–24   to be *k·* for what it is not ;
    117–16   and know as we are *k·*,
    143–19   well *k·* physicians, teachers, editors,
    171–19   true disciples of the Master *k·* :
    222–24   for it is not yet *k·*.
    223– 9   the tree is *k·* by its fruit ;
    249–11   *k·* that I am not a spiritualist,
    259–10   not a quality to be *k·* or
    296– 1   system of religion, — widely *k·* ;
    312–16   * *k·* as Christian Scientists,
    350– 3   society *k·* as the P. M.,
    350–12   would hesitate to have *k·*.
    371–21   * “men are *k·* by their enemies.”
Man. 17– 7   were *k·* as “Christian Scientists.”
    18–21   were *k·* as “First Members.”
    29– 5   shall not make *k·* the name of
    38– 2   *k·* to them to be Christians,
    69–26   *k·* as “Mother’s Room”
Ret. 3– 7   *k·* historically as Lovewell’s War.
    44–25   No sooner were my views made *k·*,
    57–12   If that pagan philosopher had *k·*
    80–26   no greater miracles *k·*
    89–28   not first made *k·* to them
    91– 7   *k·* as the Sermon on the Mount,
Un. 5–20   “moderation be *k·* — *Phil.* 4 : 5.
    22–10   something to know or be *k·*,
Pul. 8–14   only the need made *k·*,
    20–18   reform ever *k·* on earth.
    32–26   * was *k·* as a “godly man,”
    42–14   * are *k·* in the church as the
    45– 3   * instance which will never be *k·*
    47– 4   * *k·* to her circle of pupils
    51–19   * is very well *k·*.

known

Pul.	62– 3	* favorably *k·* in the Old Country,
	68– 2	* *k·* as the Rev. Mary Baker Eddy.
	68–15	* It is not generally *k·*
	71–19	* It is well *k·* that Mrs. Eddy
	76– 3	* *k·* as the "Mother's Room,"
No.	7–16	loving sacrifice . . . is *k·* to God,
	37–15	*k·* to the divine Mind,
'01.	20–26	flagrance will finally be *k·*,
	21–26	should not have *k·* C. S.,
	29– 3	or even *k·* of his sore necessities?
	33–17	to be *k·* by their works,
'02.	13–29	trustees, who were to be *k·* as
Po.	vii– 7	* *became k· to her friends,*
My.	37–22	* He has made *k·* through
	64– 8	* *k·* as Christian Scientists,
	66– 1	* *k·* as the Hotel Brookline,
	91–19	* any other country has ever *k·*.
	96–27	* *k·* as The Mother Church
	108–24	to make *k·* the best work of
	111–21	Is not the tree *k·* by its fruit?
	112–24	The tree is *k·* by its fruit.
	120– 6	know as we are *k·* of God.
	136–26	that is *k·* by its fruits,
	140– 4	that they have not *k·* :— *Isa.* 42 : 16.
	142– 1	hath *k·* the mind of — *I Cor.* 2 : 16.
	148– 4	faith be *k·* by your works.
	157–17	* made *k·* in her original deed
	221–11	not *k·* another so great
	227– 7	it is *k·* by its patience
	232–15	had *k·* what hour — *Luke* 12 : 39.
	235–28	*k·* what was being done
	240– 3	shall be *k·* and acknowledged
	253–12	world hath not *k·* — *John* 17 : 25.
	253–12	but I have *k·* Thee, — *John* 17 : 25.
	253–13	and these have *k·* that — *John* 17 : 25.
	274–27	thy way may be *k·* — *Psal.* 67 : 2.
	289–10	first church of C. S. *k·* on earth,
	299– 8	* let them make it *k·* to the world,
	299–11	widely made *k·* to the world,
	300–22	make *k·* his doctrine to the world,
	300–28	tree is *k·* by its fruit."
	305– 6	"I have always *k·* it."
	329–29	* might not have been *k·* but for
	333–20	* *k·* as Major George W. Glover,
	338– 7	* are *k·* to us to be those uniformly
	338–12	"The Unknown God Made *K·*,"
	353–22	formerly *k·* as "Mother's Room"
	359–23	* were *k·* as "the practitioners."

knows

Mis.	41–30	the Principle that he *k·* to be true.
	55–24	Man *k·* that he can have
	77–18	Truth that *k·* no error,
	85– 7	all that he *k·* of Life,
	88–14	*k·* whereof he speaks.
	90– 9	*when she k· he is sinning,*
	100–32	Who *k·* how the feeble lips
	101– 3	He alone *k·* these wonders
	103–17	and *k·* not the temporal.
	112–10	unless he *k·* *how* to be just ;
	122–27	Divine Love *k·* no hate,
	147–28	he *k·* no path but the fair, open,
	179–32	this Life that *k·* no death,
	194–27	sense of Life that *k·* no death,
	201–12	omnipotence of the Mind that *k·* this :
	208–23	He who *k·* the end from the
	212– 4	never *k·* what happiness is,

knows

Mis.	219–16	A third person *k·* that if he
	219–27	*k·* that if he can change this
	220–25	believe that a man is sick and *k·* it,
	220–31	he *k·* that an error of belief
	221–13	and *k·* he is a sinner ;
	265– 2	diverges from Science and *k·* it not,
	367–18	He *k·* nothing but good ;
	367–20	*k·* nothing beyond Himself
	384–21	* But *k·* no ebb and flow.
Ret.	76–18	and *k·* no material limitations.
Un.	13– 8	*k·* nothing of discord.
	13–19	He *k·* something which He must
	17–20	because He *k·* all things ;
	18– 1	must perish, if He *k·* evil
	18– 7	if He *k·* and sees it not ;
	20– 8	*Second :* The Lord *k·* it.
	20–13	*Second :* He *k·* it not.
	23– 8	and Truth *k·* only such.
	39– 8	Life which *k·* no death.
	43–26	Life which *k·* no death,
	43–27	Spirit which *k·* no matter.
	44–19	says of evil, "The Lord *k·* it !"
	49–26	something which God sees and *k·*,
Pul.	82–10	* and to-day she *k·* many things
Rud.	12–28	A Christian Scientist *k·* that,
	13– 3	*k·* that pantheism and theosophy
No.	13–12	Life that *k·* no death,
	16– 2	what He *k·* must truly and eternally
	16– 3	If He *k·* matter, and matter can exist
	16– 5	whatever He *k·* is made manifest,
	18–20	gets things wrong, and *k·* it not ;
	43– 8	* "Only He who *k·* all things
'02.	19– 9	*k·* that that would harm him more
Hea.	1–17	* *K·* it at forty, and reforms his plan ;
	4–11	what He *k·* deserves to be punished,
Po.	36–20	* But *k·* no ebb and flow.
My.	vi– 7	* *k·* anything about C. S.
	6– 2	decision which the defendant *k·* will be
	93– 1	* so far as the writer *k·* them,
	104–23	of which a man *k·* absolutely nothing
	112–18	*k·* that it contains a Science which
	132– 8	Scientist *k·* that spiritual faith
	132–10	he also *k·* they embark for infinity
	155–22	a dawn that *k·* no twilight
	160–29	psychist *k·* that this hell is mental,
	180– 3	Whosoever understands C. S. *k·*
	180–20	for he *k·* not that . . . God is Love.
	271– 9	what a man thinks or believes he *k·* ;
		(see also **God***)*

know'st

Mis.	398–12	And Thou *k·* Thine own ;
Ret.	46–18	And Thou *k·* Thine own.
Pul.	17–17	And Thou *k·* Thine own.
Po.	14–16	And Thou *k·* Thine own ;
My.	350–15	*k·* Thou not the pathway glad

Know Thyself

My.	351–10	"*K· T·*," the title of your gem

Knox

General

Ret.	2–29	stories about General *K·*,
Pul.	48–28	* the McNeils and General *K·*

General Henry

Ret.	2–27	General Henry *K·* of Revolutionary

Ky. (State)

    (see **Louisville***)*

L

La. (State)

    (see **New Orleans***)*

label

Mis.	87– 4	and *l·* beauty nothing,

labelled

Mis.	248–12	the mixture would be *l·* thus :
My.	83– 3	* never going about *l·*.

labor

Mis.	2–13	the outlook demands *l·*,
	20– 4	all ye that *l·* — *Matt.* 11 : 28.
	37–29	the *l·* that C. S. demands.
	120–25	away from their own fields of *l·*.
	133–27	depressing care and *l·*
	137–21	return to his place of *l·*,
	214–21	the personal Jesus' *l·* in the flesh
	230–25	* Learn to *l·* and to wait."
	236– 4	the *l·* of uplifting the race,
	238–14	*l·* for the establishment of
	273–17	in their present line of *l·*
	303– 1	within their own fields of *l·*,
	338–10	which cannot choose but to *l·*.
	340– 5	no excellence without *l·* ;

labor

Ret.	10– 3	less *l·* than is usually requisite.
	79–24	* "Learn to *l·* and to wait."
	84–30	regular institute or place of *l·*,
	84–30	or expending his *l·* where
No.	43– 4	all ye that *l·* — *Matt.* 11 : 28.
	46–22	continue to *l·* and wait.
'00.	3–13	*l·* to awake the slumbering
Hea.	2–18	all ye that *l·* — *Matt.* 11 : 28.
My.	v–20	* nine years of arduous preliminary *l·*,
	50–28	* were willing to *l·* for the Cause.
	52–16	* must use more energy and unselfish *l·*
	57–11	* The *l·* of clearing the land
	58–18	* *l·* and sacrifice of our revered Leader
	135–12	demands upon my time and *l·*,
	136–25	the *l·* that is known by its fruits,
	149–17	richest blessings are obtained by *l·*.
	163–19	from many years of incessant *l·*
	182–15	faithful *l·* of loyal students,
	185– 7	* Learn to *l·* and to wait."
	193–24	you have grasped time and *l·*,
	197–11	appreciation of your *l·* and success
	218–27	Such *l·* is impartial,

labor

My.	231–18	else love's *l·* is lost
	234– 8	to express this love in *l·*
	243–17	remain in their own fields of *l·*
	248–27	philosophy of *l·*, duty, liberty,
	358–17	to relieve me of so much *l·*.

(see also **field***)*

laboratory

My.	178– 9	distilled in the *l·* of infinite Love

labored

'00.	12–25	he *l·* in the synagogue,
My.	22–16	* *l·* for the regeneration of mankind ;
	47–13	* *l·* unceasingly for the work
	50– 5	* in which they had *l·* faithfully
	194–25	sacrificed so much and *l·* so long.
	231– 7	whom she has *l·* much to benefit
	283–10	Many years have I prayed and *l·*

laborer

Pul.	50– 3	* *l·* is worthy of his— *Luke* 10 : 7.
My.	214–15	chapter sub-title
	215–25	*l·* is worthy of his— *Luke* 10 : 7.

laborers

Mis.	2–14	and the *l·* seem few.
	7–15	if faithful *l·* in His vineyard.
	120–11	loyal *l·* are ye that have wrought
	313–22	*l·* of the excellent sort,
	323– 8	where a few *l·* in a valley
Un.	12– 3	*l·* are few in this vineyard
No.	v– 8	*l·* in the realm of Mind-healing.
My.	226–25	*l·* in the field of Science
	291–29	God of harvests send her more *l·*,

laboring

Mis.	155– 7	Forget self in *l·* for mankind ;
	283–30	Whoever is honestly *l·* to learn
	322–26	*l·* in its widening grooves

laborious

Hea.	8–22	this will make us honest and *l·*,

labors

Mis.	7–27	denied the results of our *l·*
	100–11	Love's *l·* are not lost.
	273– 9	so grateful a sense of my *l·*
	278– 9	throughout my *l·*,
	278–19	have shared less of my *l·* than many
	281– 1	to enter on the fruition of your *l·*,
	311–15	My deepest desires and daily *l·*
	322–23	my past poor *l·* and love.
Ret.	30– 7	The motive of my earliest *l·*
	90–21	and *l·* with her love,
Pul.	70–14	* a testimonial to her *l·*,
	72–26	* In our *l·* we take Christ as
	85–26	* the appreciation of her *l·*
	86–22	* love and gratitude for your *l·*
Rud.	14–11	The only pay taken for her *l·*
'00.	2–28	what of the fruits of your *l·*?
My.	22–19	* justification of her *l·* is the
	28–28	* speaks for the successful *l·*
	37–24	* unbroken activity of your *l·*,
	49–28	* their devoted *l·* in the cause
	50–11	* starting out on their *l·*
	51–27	* of Mrs. Eddy's tireless *l·*,
	51–31	* *l·*, and successful instructions
	137–17	my time, *l·*, and thought,
	163–15	time and attention for *l·*
	203–28	You whose *l·* are doing so much
	214–17	taking pay for their *l·*,
	214–20	no remuneration for my *l·*,
	291– 3	rested on the life and *l·*
	295–28	he still lives, loves, *l·*.
	296–12	his *l·* in divine Science ;
	298– 9	*l·* in placing this book

lab'ring

Mis.	398–10	*L·* long and lone,
Ret.	46–16	*L·* long and lone,
Pul.	17–15	*L·* long and lone
Po.	14–14	*L·* long and lone,

lace

My.	259– 4	on either side *l·* and flowers.

laces

My.	83–11	* *l·* of the women's frocks,

lack

Mis.	7–31	not so much from a *l·* of justice,
	31–12	consequently to the *l·* of faith
	53–25	because of their great *l·* of
	103–10	For *l·* of knowing what substance **is**,
	107–25	The *l·* of seeing one's
	158–16	to rebuke a *l·* of faith in divine help,
	195– 8	held back by reason of the *l·* of
	206–15	nor *l·* of what constitutes true manhood.
	256–16	the old impediment, *l·* of time,
	268–27	From *l·* of moral strength empires fall.
	344–16	are spoiled by *l·* of Science.
	356– 8	from *l·* of air and freedom.

lack

Mis.	365–27	hampered by *l·* of proper terms
Ret.	67–17	finally lost for *l·* of witness.
Rud.	10–27	It is only a *l·* of understanding
No.	3– 1	in some vital points *l·* Science.
	37–20	lose its efficacy and *l·* the
	45–11	arise from a spiritual *l·*,
'00.	6– 1	no *l·* in the Principle
'01.	1– 5	never *l·* God's outstretched **arm**
	25–11	regret their *l·* in my books,
Peo.	8– 6	or *l·* of love that will not ;
My.	128–23	A *l·* of wisdom betrays Truth
	213–25	will not rust for *l·* of use
	222– 9	unbelief'' (*l·* of *faith*) ;— *Matt.* 17 : **20.**
	248–21	fall for *l·* of the divine impetus.
	293–14	a *l·* of the absolute understanding
	307–30	its *l·* of science, and the want of

lacked

Mis.	365–10	If C. S. *l·* the proof of its
No.	18– 6	If Science *l·* the proof of its
My.	307–32	for then it *l·* Science.

lacking

Mis.	16– 7	one finds so much *l·*,
	109–25	sequence of knowledge would be *l·*;
	116–30	If in one instance obedience be *l·*,
	291–19	if the spirit thereof be *l·*.
	365–21	effects of divine Science were *l·*,
Un.	40–25	and *l·* the spiritual sense of it,
No.	19– 3	If the . . . effects of C. S. were *l·*,
'00.	11–20	if the divine tone be *l·*,
Hea.	3– 2	*l·* these, to show its helplessness.
My.	299–16	and *l·* in the creeds.

lacks

Mis.	263–23	*l·* the aid and protection of
Un.	45–25	It *l·* the substance of Spirit
Pan.	3– 6	loneness *l·* but one charm

lad

Mis.	225–21	beside the sofa whereon lay the *l·*
Pul.	33–17	* when he was a *l·*, at work in **a**

Ladd, Dr.

My.	310–25	were diagnosed by Dr. *L·*
	310–30	Dr. *L·* said to Alexander Tilton :

ladder

Ret.	85–10	*l·* let down from the heaven of Truth
Un.	57–19	the *l·* which reaches heaven.

laden

Mis.	20– 4	labor and are heavy *l·*,— *Matt.* 11 : 28.
Man.	60–11	rest the weary and heavy *l·*.
No.	43– 5	labor and are heavy *l·*,— *Matt.* 11 : 28.
Hea.	2–18	labor and are heavy *l·*,— *Matt.* 11 : 28.
Po.	vii–14	* *a joy to the heavy l· and a balm to*

ladened

Mis.	147– 9	*l·* them with records worthy to be

ladies

Ret.	16– 3	When the meeting was over, two *l·*
My.	72–10	* lords and *l·* who come to attend

lady

Mis.	49– 1	young *l·* entered the College class
	49– 5	this young *l·* had manifested
	180– 7	A dear old *l·* asked me,
Ret.	90–10	like "the elect *l·*"— *II John* 1 : 1.
Pul.	57–27	* a *l·* born of an old New Hampshire
	72–10	* very pleasant and agreeable *l·*,
No.	43– 8	A *l·* said : "Only He who
My.	322– 1	* not long since I met a *l·*

(see also **Eddy***)*

Lafayette (Ind.) *Journal*

My.	91–15	* [*L· (I·.) J·*]

lagging

Po.	35– 2	Beguile the *l·* hours

laid

Mis.	120–15	with armor on, not *l·* down.
	143–15	is *l·* the corner-stone of
	144– 8	there are *l·* away a copy of
	144–14	*l·* away as a sacred secret
	163–23	yet the foundations he *l·*
	179– 6	to know where He is *l·*.
	250–15	and *l·* on a rose-leaf.
	285– 4	I ordered to be *l·* away
	343– 3	others before us have *l·* upon the
	365– 3	than that is *l·*,''— *I Cor.* 3 : 11.
Man.	52– 7	shall be *l·* before this Board,
Ret.	18–13	but *l·* on the bier.
	27– 3	so *l·* the foundation of my work
	35– 5	basis it *l·* down for physical and
	45–10	and should be *l·* off,
	45–12	mortal existence is finally *l·* off,
	73–18	false personality is *l·* off.
	83– 9	are already *l·* in their minds
Un.	44–13	fable of error, is *l·* bare in C. S.
	64– 9	than that is *l·*.''— *I Cor.* 3 : 11.

laid

Pul.	45–24	* *l·* down his responsibilities
Rud.	15–25	*l·* bare for anatomical examination.
	16–19	Principle and practice *l·* down in
No.	21–24	than that is *l·*, — *I Cor.* 3 : 11.
	46–11	*l·* on the rack, for joining the
'00.	7–21	where they have *l·* him." — *John* 20 : 13.
'01.	7–20	know not where they have *l·* Him.
	23–17	*l·* the axe at the root of all error,
'02.	18–19	Jesus *l·* down his life for mankind ;
Hea.	11–17	*l·* the foundation stone of mental
Peo.	5– 6	we know not where they have *l·* him ;
	14– 3	flowers *l·* upon the bier,
Po.	64– 3	but *l·* on the bier.
My.	16–10	* chapter sub-title
	16–12	* was *l·* Saturday, July 16, 1904.
	18–27	* The corner-stone was then *l·*
	23–29	* and stone is *l·* upon stone,
	44– 4	* heavy burdens are being *l·* down,
	55–32	* corner-stone of The . . . was *l·*,
	57–13	* corner-stone was *l·* July 16, 1904.
	67–16	* Corner-stone of cathedral *l·* . . . 1904
	122–24	place where they *l·* him" — *Mark* 16 : 6.
	127–28	nor *l·* down at the feet of
	158– 6	chapter sub-title
	158–25	has *l·* the chief corner-stone
	187–30	*l·* its foundations on the rock
	191–17	With grave-clothes *l·* aside,
	191–21	Behold the place where they *l·* me ;
	203–24	You have *l·* the corner-stone
	241– 7	* beware the net that is craftily *l·*
	326–17	*l·* on his bier the emblems

lain

Mis.	110–20	while leagues have *l·* between us.

lake

My.	150–15	Stand by the limpid *l·*,

Lake of Galilee

Ret.	91–15	shores of the *L· of G·*,

lakes

Mis.	143– 7	Across *l·*, into a kingdom,

Lamb

Mis.	358–17	the blood of the *L· ;*" — *Rev.* 7 : 14.
Pul.	12–10	the blood of the *L·*, — *Rev.* 12 : 11.
Hea.	10– 5	beast bowed before the *L·* :
Peo.	9–10	white in the blood of the *L·* ;
My.	185–17	"*L·* slain from the — *Rev.* 13 : 8.
	206–22	*L·* is the light thereof." — *Rev.* 21 : 23.
	269– 4	man wedded to the *L·*,

lamb

Mis.	36–13	lion that lieth down with the *l·*.
	145–23	shall dwell with the *l·*, — *Isa.* 11 : 6.
	162–16	lay himself as a *l·* upon the altar
	250– 7	a butcher fattening the *l·*
	275–14	* "tempers the wind to the shorn *l·*,"

lambkin

Po.	41– 3	that fold for the *l·*

lambkins

Mis.	398–15	Lead Thy *l·* to the fold,
Ret.	46–21	Lead Thy *l·* to the fold,
Pul.	17–20	Lead Thy *l·* to the fold,
Po.	14–19	Lead Thy *l·* to the fold,

Lamb of God

Mis.	121–23	"the *L· of G·*." — *John* 1 : 29.

lambs

Mis.	357–27	They are as *l·* that have sought
Ret.	80–22	carries his *l·* in his arms
	90– 4	Does . . . shepherd forsake the *l·*,
Pul.	8–20	*l·* my prayers had christened,

lame

Mis.	22–24	the *l·*, the deaf, and the blind,
	168– 5	the *l·*, those halting between two
	244–21	the deaf to hear, the *l·* to walk,
	362–10	ears to these deaf, feet to these *l·*,
'01.	17–16	the blind, the dumb, the *l·*,
Peo.	11–12	The *l·*, the blind, the sick,
My.	105–18	and have made the *l·* walk.

lament

My.	295–26	have cause to *l·* the demise of
	333–28	* to *l·* this irreparable loss."

lamented

Ret.	19–14	*l·* by a large circle of friends
Pul.	9–16	loss of our late *l·* pastor,
My.	289–15	the late *l·* Victoria,
	289–28	*in memoriam* of the late *l·* Victoria,
	293– 7	Our *l·* President, in his loving
	296–10	The late *l·* Christian Scientist
	330–26	*l·* by a large circle of friends

lamp

Mis.	92–11	keeps his own *l·* trimmed and
	117–26	he would replenish his *l·* at the
	151–24	may the *l·* of your life continually

lamp

Mis.	341–25	if the *l·* she tends is
Ret.	84– 8	keeps his own *l·* trimmed and
Pul.	26–10	* *l·* stand of the Renaissance period
	26–27	* *l·* over two hundred years old,
	59– 1	* behind an antique *l·*,
My.	69– 3	* each *l·* of thirty-two candle-power.

lamps

Mis.	276–17	The wise will have their *l·* aglow,
	276–24	shall have their *l·* trimmed
	342– 3	had no oil in their *l·* :
	342– 8	better-tended *l·* of the faithful.
	342–15	With no oil in their *l·*,
	342–19	our *l·* have gone out, — *see Matt.* 25 : 8.
Pul.	25–26	* silver *l·* of Roman design,
	26–12	* oxidized silver *l·*,
	27–18	* with *l·*, typical of S. and H.
My.	69– 3	* each suspending seventy-two *l·*,
	125–27	Are our *l·* trimmed and burning?

Lancaster Gate, West

My.	295–24	55 *L· G·*, *W·*, London, England.

lance

'01.	33–19	with poisonous drugs, with the *l·*,

Land

Deed Conveying

Man.	136– 1	heading

land

and building

Mis.	139–30	provisions for the *l·* and building

and sea

My.	291–24	waves over *l·* and sea,

and the church

Mis.	140– 3	*l·*, and the church standing on it,

bright

Mis.	386–20	beckoned me to this bright *l·*,
Po.	50– 5	beckoned me to this bright *l·*,

clearing the

My.	57–11	* The labor of clearing the *l·*

dwell in the

Chr.	55– 9	dwell in the *l·* of — *Isa.* 9 : 2.
My.	170–21	dwell in the *l·*, — *Psal.* 37 : 3.

entire

Mis.	150–17	churches are dotting the entire *l·*.

every

Mis.	v– 3	IN THIS AND EVERY *l·*
My.	341– 9	our land and in every *l·*,

exclusive of the

Pul.	28–12	* exclusive of the *l·*

fair

Pul.	82–29	* and in this fair *l·* at least

favored

My.	278–13	Congress of our favored *l·*

for the site

My.	16– 8	* price of the *l·* for the site of

gave back the

Pul.	20– 5	gave back the *l·* to the church.

is reached

'01.	26–15	then when *l·* is reached

laud the

Ret.	11–17	laud the *l·* whose talents
Po.	60–14	laud the *l·* whose talents

laws of the

My.	128–20	abide by . . . the laws of the *l·* ;
	219–22	make void the laws of the *l·*,
	220–12	obeying the laws of the *l·*.

lot of

Mis.	139–18	I gave a lot of *l·* — in Boston,
	140–20	The lot of *l·* which I donated
Ret.	51– 1	I gave a lot of *l·* in Boston

more

'02.	12–25	effort to purchase more *l·*
My.	7– 9	effort to purchase more *l·*
	9–23	towards the purchase of more *l·*

native

Mis.	295–16	to honor his native *l·*

of Israel

Mis.	72–13	concerning the *l·* of Israel, — *Ezek.* 18 : 2.

of promise

Mis.	153–10	and the *l·* of promise,

of Sodom

No.	7–14	imperfection in the *l·* of Sodom,

of the shadow

Chr.	55– 9	*l·* of the shadow — *Isa.* 9 : 2.

or sea

My.	127–27	indestructible on *l·* or sea ;

our

Mis.	38– 9	philanthropists in our *l·*
	141–16	law of God and the laws of our *l·*.
	141–24	law of Love and the laws of our *l·*.
	314– 1	throughout our *l·* and in other lands.
	329–25	is heard in our *l·*." — *Song* 2 : 12.
Man.	46– 6	according to the laws of our *l·*.
	48–10	or the laws of our *l·*.
Pul.	8– 2	throughout our *l·* the press has

land
our
Pul. 10– 9 Our *l·*, more favored, had its
22–11 every Christian church in our *l·*,
No. 2–27 many are flooding our *l·* with
'01. 20–26 laws of our *l·* will handle
My. 341– 9 Beloved brethren all over our *l·*
over
My. 204– 9 Over sea and over *l·*, C. S. unites
291–24 waves over *l·* and sea,
over the
My. 55–11 * was spreading over the *l·*.
parcel of
My. 12– 7 * to secure the large parcel of *l·*
promised
My. 43– 2 * possession of the promised *l·*.
43–13 * into the promised *l·*,
44– 5 * going up to possess the promised *l·*
purchased
Man. 102–16 shall not apply to *l·* purchased for
purchases of
Man. 102–11 deeds of further purchases of *l·*
recover the
Pul. 20– 6 recover the *l·* from the trustees,
redeem the
'02. 13–23 to redeem the *l·* by paying the
regive the
Pul. 20–10 regive the *l·* to the church.
their
'01. 33–17 constitutional laws of their *l·* ;
this
'02. 13–27 This *l·*, now valued at
My. 11–25 * this *l·* has been paid for.
throughout the
Mis. 113–32 is felt throughout the *l·*.
weary
Mis. 144–18 great rock in a weary *l· :"— Isa.* 32 : 2.
263–10 great rock in a weary *l·*,"— *Isa.* 32 : 2.
Pul. 20–20 great rock in a weary *l·*."— *Isa.* 32 : 2.

Mis. 382–19 I donated to this church the *l·*
Man. 75–17 with the *l·* whereon they stand,
Pul. 20– 1 *l·* whereon stands The First Church
'02. 10–30 walking every step over the *l·* route,
13–13 *l·* on which to build The First Church
13–26 *l·* legally conveyed to me,
14– 2 had been paid on the *l·*
14– 5 nor the *l·* whereon it stands.
My. 11–24 * purchase of the *l·* upon which
99–23 * was not a C. S. church in the *l·*.

landlord
My. 231–22 a *l·* who has not an empty

landmark
My. 47–18 * each *l·* of progress
77– 7 * the leading *l·* of Boston,
85–20 * another "*l·*" set in the

landmarks
Mis. x– 9 and reliable as old *l·*.
119–28 should tear up your *l·*,
No. 12–23 departed from the old *l·*.
My. 282–12 the *l·* of prosperity.

lands
Mis. 177–28 homesick traveller in foreign *l·*
314– 2 our land and in other *l·*.
373–24 rich . . . with houses and *l·*.
Ret. 4–12 undulating *l·* of three townships.
48–22 our country, and into foreign *l·*,
Pul. 5–30 literature of our and other *l·*.
22–11 and a few in far-off *l·*,
41– 6 * from many *l·*, the love-offerings
57– 5 * the Union, and from many *l·*.
My. 47–21 * in so many distant *l·*,
112–32 our own and in foreign *l·*,
129– 8 beloved country and in foreign *l·*,
200– 1 in this and in other *l·*.

landscape
Mis. 62– 7 an artist in painting a *l·*.
313–11 dawn, . . . lightens earth's *l·*.
Pul. 48–10 * coloring of the whole *l·*

Langley, **Prof. S. P.**
Rud. 6–13 met a response from Prof. S. P. *L·*,

language
and ideas
Ret. 75– 7 appropriating my *l·* and ideas,
and meaning
My. 238–10 His *l·* and meaning are wholly
any
Mis. 263– 6 to be found in any *l·*
appropriate
Mis. 280–24 in appropriate *l·* and metaphor
decaying
Mis. 100– 3 articulated in a decaying *l·*,
121– 1 written in a decaying *l·*,

language
expressive
Pul. 2– 2 In the expressive *l·* of Holy Writ,
figurative
Pul. 66–16 * poetical and highly figurative *l·*.
gentleman's
Mis. 296–22 in this unknown gentleman's *l·*,
human
Un. 30– 3 Human *l·* constantly uses the
Longfellow's
Ret. 27–16 In Longfellow's *l·*,
modification of the
No. v– 6 By a modification of the *l·*,
new
No. 44– 4 C. S. involves a new *l·*,
new style of
My. 318– 2 constituted a new style of *l·*.
no
Mis. 160– 5 But a mother's love . . . has no *l·* ;
of Soul
Hea. 7– 8 *l·* of Soul instead of the senses ;
of Spirit
My. 180–10 original tongue in the *l·* of Spirit,
one
Mis. 67–26 the sense of words in one *l·* by
original
Hea. 7– 9 into its original *l·*, which is Mind,
Peo. 1– 6 of law back to its original *l·*,
power of
My. 332– 2 * the power of *l·* would be
refers to
Mis. 67–25 If your question refers to *l·*,
speech nor
Ret. 61–18 no speech nor *l·*,— *Psal.* 19 : 3.
unmistakable
Mis. 297–16 I hereby state, in unmistakable *l·*,

Mis. 163–14 in the *l·* of a declining race,
248– 1 "new tongue," the *l·* of — *see Mark* 16 : 17.
262–11 its *l·* is always acceptable to
My. 308–27 attributes to my father *l·* unseemly,

languages
Mis. 64–11 *the study of literature and l·*
64–23 *l·*, to a limited extent, are aids to
Ret. 80– 7 As the poets in different *l·* have
Pul. 46–26 * ancient *l·*, Hebrew, Greek, and

languid
Mis. 395–24 The *l·* brooklets yield their sighs,
Po. 58– 9 The *l·* brooklets yield their sighs,

lap
Ret. 18– 7 In *l·* of the pear-tree,
Po. 63–16 In *l·* of the pear-tree,

lapse
Mis. 79–13 cannot *l·* into a mortal belief
Un. 10–15 they cannot collapse, or *l·* into
Pan. 7–20 a *l·* in the Mosaic religion,
Hea. 4–19 after a temporary *l·*, to begin anew
Peo. 2–25 Truth without a *l·* or error,
My. 273–26 *l·* and relapse, come and go, until

lapses
Pan. 7–27 The hypothesis . . . *l·* into evil

large
Mis. 6–29 *l·* family of children where the
168–27 * drew a *l·* audience.
177– 8 *L·* numbers, in desperate malice,
239– 6 to commence a *l·* class in C. S.
249– 2 some *l·* doses of morphine,
276– 1 the *l·* book of rare flowers,
305–17 * *l·* contributions from a few.
318– 5 a *l·* affection, not alone for
318–27 either too *l·* or too little :
318–27 if too *l·*, we are in the darkness
371– 3 *l·* flocks of metaphysicians
Man. 60–22 No *l·* gathering of people
98–14 shall circulate in *l·* quantities
Ret. 4–20 and flecked with *l·* flocks
7–16 * practice of a very *l·* business.
10– 2 too *l·* for my body
19–14 lamented by a *l·* circle of friends
49– 1 which yields a *l·* income,
50–15 my list of . . . scholars is very *l·*,
82–14 should locate in *l·* cities,
Pul. 1–12 by reason of its *l·* lessons,
25– 4 * *l·* boilers in the basement
26–21 * in *l·* golden letters on a
27– 7 * three *l·* class-rooms and the
27–30 * A *l·* bay window,
32–10 * *l·* and enthusiastic following
41–16 * The *l·* auditorium, with its
42– 1 * had closed the *l·* vestry room
42–28 * *l·* basket of white carnations
50– 6 * in buying so *l·* an estate
50–16 * a *l·* and increasing number
56– 5 * a *l·* and growing number

large

Pul.	63–11	* pointed to a number of *l·* elms
	64–10	* others donating *l·* sums.
	73–26	* *l·* volume which Mrs. Eddy had
	76–15	* *l·* rug composed entirely of
Rud.	1–11	affords a *l·* margin for
	15–23	promiscuous and *l·* assemblies,
No.	2–22	and many . . . have *l·* practices
Pan.	6–13	social prestige, a *l·* following,
'01.	31–13	communicants of my *l·* church,
My.	9– 1	* *l·* accessions to their membership.
	12– 6	* to secure the *l·* parcel of land
	14–29	* necessitates *l·* payments of money,
	20–26	* expenditure of a *l·* amount of money,
	20–29	* the usual *l·* gathering in Boston,
	22– 6	* *l·* gatherings at the annual
	30– 1	* held *l·* crowds of people,
	30–19	* The six collections were *l·*,
	54–26	* a *l·* congregation was present.
	54–30	* decided that this hall was too *l·*,
	69–10	* Two *l·* marble plates with
	74– 2	* from the far West to a *l·* degree
	83–17	* public at *l·* will scarcely realize
	88–14	* its proportions are so *l·*,
	92– 5	* *l·* numbers of intelligent men
	123–26	small beginnings have *l·* endings.
	132–18	every member of this *l·* church.
	148–13	To-day, with the *l·* membership
	156–16	show you a *l·* upper room— *Luke* 22 : 12.
	169–17	and of the world at *l·*,
	173–10	*l·* gathering at this annual meeting
	182–18	*l·* membership and majestic cathedral.
	231– 8	she has given *l·* sums of money,
	243– 8	The Empire City is *l·*,
	294– 2	are yet in a *l·* minority
	304–12	I have lectured in *l·* and crowded
	310–12	*l·* manufacturing establishment
	310–15	carried on a *l·* business in
	330–26	lamented by a *l·* circle of friends
	342– 2	* Seated in the *l·* parlor,
		(*see also* **number**)

large-eyed

My.	343– 3	* looking *l·* into space,

largely

Mis.	47–29	That *l·* depends upon what one
Man.	31– 9	prosperity of C. S. *l·* depends.
Pul.	31–17	* atmosphere was *l·* thrilled and
	48–28	* figure *l·* in her genealogy,
	66–20	* and which is *l·* Oriental
My.	vii–13	* which is *l·* self-glorification
	68–20	* enters so *l·* into the interior finish.
	248–25	I have *l·* committed to you,

largeness

Mis.	276– 5	in its cordiality and *l·*.

larger

Mis.	239– 9	substance is taking *l·* proportions.
	273–27	a *l·* number would be in waiting
Ret.	33–18	not affected by a *l·* dose.
My.	22– 3	* saw the need of a *l·* edifice.
	56–32	* proved the need of a *l·* edifice.
	57– 8	* need of a *l·* church edifice,
	64– 3	* took on a *l·* and truer meaning.
	97– 8	* yet to be shown . . . a *l·* proportion
	190– 4	to evolve that *l·* sympathy
	227–31	cures a *l·* per cent of malignant
	244– 5	if a *l·* class were advantageous

largess

My.	188–18	a benediction for God's *l·*.
	349–12	a divine *l·*, a gift of God

largest

Mis.	130–27	he who exercises the *l·* charity,
	224–18	but with the *l·* patience ;
	252– 5	its *l·* dose is never dangerous,
	305–14	* *l·* number of persons possible
Man.	98–25	three *l·* branch churches in each
	99– 8	its three *l·* branch churches,
Ret.	7– 2	it was the *l·* vote of the State ;
Pul.	80–10	* they have the *l·* individuality,
No.	10– 6	two *l·* words in the vocabulary of
My.	26–12	Your beneficent gift is the *l·* sum
	30–29	* by far the *l·* crowd of the day
	57–18	* *l·* in the history of the church
	57–20	* the hitherto *l·* admission,
	65– 3	* *l·* church business meeting
	65– 4	* perhaps the *l·* ever held in the
	70–29	* *l·* of which is thirty-two feet
	76– 3	* the *l·* of them all.
	77– 3	* one of the *l·* in the world.
	80–30	* where the *l·* meeting was held,
	89– 1	* This church is one of the *l·*
	89– 7	* one of the *l·* organs in the world.
	91–29	* it is the *l·* in New England.
	295–14	kindness in its *l·*, . . . sense is
	309–20	paid the *l·* tax in the colony.

lark (*see also* **lark's**)

Mis.	354–31	gaze on the *l·* in her emerald bower
Pul.	81–18	* as the *l·* who soars and sings
Po.	18– 9	gaze on the *l·* in her emerald bower?
	24–18	With song of morning *l·* ;

lark's

Mis.	390– 6	*l·* shrill song doth wake the dawn :
Po.	55– 7	*l·* shrill song doth wake the dawn :

last

Mis.	42–14	destroyed this *l·* enemy,
	57–26	*the sixth and l· day,*
	59– 9	the *l·* state of patients
	76–32	who overcame the *l·* enemy,
	81–12	*the l· eighteen centuries*
	85–16	The *l·* degree of regeneration
	90–26	the Passover, or *l·* supper,
	110–16	years, since *l·* we met ;
	124–24	The *l·* act of the tragedy
	131–31	*l·* year's records immortalized,
	132– 1	at your *l·* meeting,
	136–19	in my *l·* revised edition
	137–15	within the *l·* few years.
	138–15	the first and *l·* lesson of C. S.
	165– 7	The *l·* appearing of Truth will be
	170– 1	*l·* enemy to be overthrown ;
	185–28	*the l· Adam was made a— I Cor.* 15 : 45.
	186–29	undoubtedly refers to the *l·* Adam
	188– 8	and as *l·*, that which is primal,
	188–29	she knew that the *l·* Adam,
	189– 1	"The *l·* shall be first,— *Matt.* 20 : 16.
	189– 2	and the first *l·*."— *Matt.* 20 : 16.
	192–25	the *l·* chapter of Mark
	205–15	*l·* scene in corporeal sense.
	270–28	*l·* link in material medicine.
	293–17	the *l·* error will be worse than
	294– 2	the *l·* infirmity of evil is
	330–23	Nature's first and *l·* lessons
	350–17	proved to be our *l·* meeting.
	355–14	the *l·* third pierces itself,
	366–20	From first to *l·*, evil insists on
	375–10	* "In my *l·* letter,
Man.	76–14	expenditures for the *l·* year.
	98–12	shall read the *l· proof sheet*
Ret.	15–21	Our *l·* vestry meeting was
	28–12	The first must become *l·*.
	38– 8	insert in my *l·* chapter
	40–15	at the birth of her *l·* babe,
	42– 1	My *l·* marriage was with
	49–12	first, *l·*, and always,
	82–28	my *l·* revision, in 1890,
Un.	30–14	the *l·* Adam was made a— *I Cor.* 15 : 45.
	30–23	I discerned the *l·* Adam as a
	30–25	first shall be *l·*,"— *Matt.* 19 : 30.
Pul.	20–14	From first to *l·* The Mother Church
	23–10	* during the *l·* decade
	23–18	* *l·* quarter of the nineteenth
	29– 8	* *L·* Sunday I gave myself the pleasure
	35–16	The first must become *l·*.
	42– 6	* repeated for the *l·* time.
	43–15	* the corner-stone laying *l·* spring,
	46–27	* Her *l·* marriage was in the spring
	55– 6	* *l·* quarter of preceding centuries
	56–14	* *l·* quarter of the century.
	66–20	* during the *l·* decade,
	68–19	* dedication in Boston *l·* Sunday
	75–19	* ceremonies at Boston *l·* Sunday
Rud.	6–16	* within the *l· few years,*
	9– 1	*l·* state of that man— *Matt.* 12 : 45.
No.	5–28	*l·* state of one's patients
Pan.	1– 5	since *l·* you gathered
'00.	1– 9	in the *l·* year of the
	10–23	Only *l·* week I received a
	15–25	the *l·* to be more than— *Rev.* 2 : 19.
'01.	3– 1	added since *l·* November
	3–24	the *l·* proposition does not
	17–16	the *l·* stages of consumption,
	28– 2	approaching the *l·* stage of the
	33–13	Christian Scientists first and *l·* ask
'02.	2–12	Within the *l·* decade religion
	13– 5	During the *l·* seven years I have
Po.	27–12	heal her wounds too tenderly to *l·*?
My.	8– 3	* "Since the *l·* report, in 1900,
	9–20	at our *l·* annual meeting
	11–27	* The size . . . was decided *l·* June,
	55–21	* during the *l·* year the hall was
	55–31	* the twenty-first of *l·* month,
	57–21	* number admitted during the *l·* year
	58– 4	* *C. S. Sentinel* of *l·* Saturday
	58–30	* at the C. S. church *l·* Sunday
	60–29	* On the twenty-fifth of *l·* March
	65–19	* The *l·* parcel in the block
	66– 8	* *l·* parcel on St. Paul Street
	79– 2	* then, at the *l·*, kneeling
	82– 8	* crowding Boston the *l·* week
	85–25	* *L·* Sunday it was entirely credible

last

My.	89–28	* marvels of the *l·* quarter century.
	97–26	* forty thousand *l·* week to dedicate
	98–14	* *l·* issue of the *C. S. Sentinel*
	105– 8	consumption in its *l·* stages,
	122–11	On the fifth of July *l·*,
	125–21	The students in my *l·* class in 1898
	137–20	I have designated by my *l·* will,
	141– 7	* services attended *l·* Sunday
	141– 8	* were thus the *l·* to be held.
	141–13	* announcement . . . made *l·* night
	170– 8	Message to the church *l·* Sunday
	173–12	a note, sent at the *l·* moment,
	174–10	And *l·* but not least, I thank the
	185–21	destroys the *l·* enemy, death.
	190–31	and verifying his *l·* promise,
	193–25	and the *l·* by love.
	217–17	In the *l·* *Sentinel* [Oct. 12, 1899]
	217–29	does not require the *l·* step to be
	241–19	* "*L·* evening I was catechized by
	264–12	* *l·* Thanksgiving Day of the
	264–15	New England's *l·* Thanksgiving
	300–15	"the *l·* enemy" — *I Cor.* 15 : 26.
	311–25	When I was *l·* in Washington,
	320–29	* *l·* conversation I had with him
	326–19	to their *l·* resting-place.
	327–14	* *l·* winter's term of our Legislature,
	327–19	* on the field until the *l·*.
	328–11	* passed by the *l·* Legislature,
	329– 4	* *l·* General Assembly of North Carolina
	331–23	* attended him during his *l·* sickness,
	333– 7	* paying the *l·* tribute
	335– 1	* on the 27th June *l·*,
	336–16	* previous to his *l·* illness.
	338–11	The contents of the *l·* lecture of
	345–21	the *l·* healing that will be vouchsafed
	356–14	within the *l·* five years
	(see also **cross**)	

last at-

Mis.	9– 8	giving them refuge at *l·*
	10–28	mortals learn at *l·* the lesson,
	12– 3	spreads its virus and kills at *l·*.
	254–15	must at *l·* kill this evil
	385–11	and safely moored at *l·*
Ret.	9–23	* learned at *l·* to know His voice
Pul.	13–21	comes back to him at *l·*
	13–24	at *l·* stung to death
	44– 3	* At *l·* you begin to see the
	83–12	* At *l·* she is becoming
	83–25	* at *l·* we begin to know
No.	8–16	at *l·* struggle into freedom
'00.	8–23	Then, at *l·*, the right will
Po.	43–19	Till they gain at *l·*
	48– 4	and safely moored at *l·*
My.	133– 5	at *l·* come to acknowledge God,
	155–14	at *l·*, it finds the full fruition of
	230–26	realize at *l·* their Master's promise,

last-drawn

My.	189–22	*l·* sigh of a glory gone,

lasted

Pul.	36– 3	* The work . . . *l·* nine years,

lasting

Ret.	50– 7	tuition *l·* barely three weeks.
Rud.	8–27	the restoration is not *l·*,
'00.	2–24	more sudden, severe, and *l·*

lastly

Un.	2–10	*l·*, it removes the pain
'01.	27–30	* *L·*, they say they had always
My.	304–27	* *L·*, they say they have always
	305– 5	*L·*, the defamer will declare

lasts

Mis.	85–24	so long as this temptation *l·*,
	261– 3	and *l·* as long as the evil.
Man.	15–13	punished so long as the belief *l·*.

latchet

Mis.	341–15	unloose the *l·* of thy sandals ;

latchets

Ret.	92– 7	unloose the *l·* of his Christliness,

late

Mis.	10–32	Soon or *l·*, your enemy will wake
	35–10	the *l·* Dr. Asa G. Eddy,
	71– 3	The *l·* John B. Gough is said to have
	117–30	or make them too *l·* to follow
	306–19	* request of the *l·* Mrs. Harrison,
	339–30	the wisdom . . . may come too *l·*.
	351–11	The *l·* much-ado-about-nothing
	379–33	pp. 152, 153 in late editions.
Ret.	3– 1	the *l·* Sir John Macneill,
Pul.	5–12	the *l·* A. Bronson Alcott.
	9–16	loss of our *l·* lamented pastor,
My.	48–16	* the *l·* Frederick Lawrence Knowles :
	105–20	the *l·* Dr. Davis of Manchester,

late

My.	141– 8	* Of *l·* years members of the church
	195– 8	never too *l·* to repent,
	287– 3	the *l·* Baron and Baroness de Hirsch
	289–15	the *l·* lamented Victoria,
	289–28	the *l·* lamented Victoria,
	291– 3	labors of our *l·* beloved President,
	296–10	The *l·* lamented Christian Scientist
	308–12	my *l·* father and his family
	311–27	her *l·* father, General John McNeil,
	319– 8	hold the *l·* Mr. Wiggin in . . . memory
	319–24	* the *l·* J. Henry Wiggin
	323–29	* the *l·* Rev. J. Henry Wiggin
	331–19	* of the *l·* Major George W. Glover
	331–30	* during his *l·* illness,
	334–29	* by the *l·* Charles W. Moore,
	341–20	* has been so much to the fore of *l·*

late-comers

Pul.	29–12	* There was no straggling of *l·*.

latent

Mis.	201–24	tested and developed *l·* power.
	237–10	belch forth their *l·* fires.
Ret.	61– 4	a belief, a *l·* fear,
Hea.	6–24	*l·* cause producing the effect we see.

later

Mis.	57– 2	all was *l·* made which
	115–30	sooner or *l·*, you will
	187–18	*l·* teachings and demonstrations
	381– 9	*L·*, Mrs. Eddy requested
Ret.	6–20	*l·* Albert spent a year in
	19–16	A month *l·* I returned to
	24–20	a miracle which *l·* I found to be
	35– 8	I did not venture . . . until *l·*,
Un.	6– 4	Sooner or *l·* the whole human race
	41–12	must come to all sooner or *l·* ;
Pul.	29– 1	* and *l·* in Copley Hall,
	29– 7	* venture to speak, a little *l·*,
	29–27	* *L·* I was told that almost the
	34–23	*l·* I found it to be in perfect
	46–30	* *l·* he attracted the attention of
	67–28	* charter was obtained two months *l·*.
	83–21	* When we try to praise her *l·* works
No.	7–10	Sooner or *l·* the eyes of sinful
	28– 4	mists of error, sooner or *l·*, will
Pan.	13–18	Sooner or *l·* all shall know Him,
'01.	20–20	agony . . . it must sooner or *l·* cause
	23–27	In *l·* publications he declared
Po.	vii– 4	* *in her l· productions.*
My.	11–16	* *L·* on she expressed
	43–23	* A few years *l·* she gave us our
	45–24	* fulfilment of the *l·* prophecy,
	48–14	* twenty-six years *l·* the following
	63– 4	* advisory capacity in the *l·* days ;
	169– 7	to visit me at a *l·* date,
	311– 1	incident, which occurred *l·*
	315–12	* *L·* on I learned that
	319–22	* A few days *l·*,
	330–28	A month *l·* I returned to

latest

Mis.	318–20	*l·* editions of my works,
Ret.	47–24	*l·* editions of my works,
Pul.	21– 2	grandchildren to the *l·* generations,

Lathrop

Mrs.

Pul.	72–21	* nor did she believe that Mrs. *L·*
	74–20	"I think Mrs. *L·* was not understood.

Mrs. Laura

Pul.	74– 6	* statement made by Mrs. Laura *L·*,

Latin

Mis.	25–23	from the *L·* word meaning *all,*
Ret.	10–10	tongues, Hebrew, Greek, and *L·*.
Pul.	46–26	* Hebrew, Greek, and *L·*.
Rud.	1–13	In Spanish, Italian, and *L·*,
	1–14	The *L·* verb *personare* is
'02.	7–11	*L·* *omni*, which signifies *all,*

latitude

Man.	99– 5	the 36th parallel of *l·*.

latitudes

Ret.	73–11	into more spiritual *l·*
No.	45–23	in more spiritual *l·*,
Peo.	1–14	into more spiritual *l·*.

Latour

Ret.	82– 3	dealing with a simple *L·*

latter (see also **latter's**)

Mis.	42–23	the *l·* is real and eternal.
	53–17	not equal to the *l·*.
	84–22	so far extinguished the *l·*
	104–18	The *l·* move in God's grooves
	112–13	belong to the *l·* days,
	117– 8	arrest the former, and obey the *l·*.
	130– 9	Does not the *l·* instruct you
	164– 4	and the *l·* is the human

latter

Mis.	206– 3	being servant to the *l*,
	285–15	the *l* fell *hors de combat;*
	372– 1	When the *l* was first issued,
	382–12	In the *l* half of the
Ret.	10– 6	the *l* I had to repeat
	24– 9	in the *l* part of 1866
Pul.	vii– 8	*l* half of the nineteenth
	23–23	* *l* part of the present century,
Rud.	5–28	*l* conclusion is the simple
No.	10– 8	*l* reveals and interprets God
'00.	5–13	essence and source of the two *l*,
'01.	25–24	and the *l* superior,
My.	56– 5	* the *l* a repetition of the
	68–29	* *l* framed of iron and finished
	75– 1	* of the value of the *l*,
	108–13	and the *l* couples faith with
	127–21	*l* days of the nineteenth century.
	128–23	the *l* were impracticable.
	130– 2	leave the *l* to propagate.
	131–22	this hour of the *l* days
	180–31	*l* solves the whence and why
	190–11	shows the *l* not only equalling
	197–18	illumine the midnight of the *l*,
	215–30	That he preferred the *l* is evident,
	224–24	not safe to accept the *l*

latter-day

Mis.	113–18	*l* ultimatum of evil,
My.	98–24	* any of the *l* methods

latter's

My.	359–24	* with the *l* unqualified approval.

lattice

Mis.	376–18	morning burst through the *l*

laud

Ret.	11–17	*l* the land whose talents rock
Po.	60–14	*l* the land whose talents rock

laudable

Mis.	281– 1	with *l* ambition are about to chant

lauded

My.	302–21	but I am less *l*, pampered,

laugh

Mis.	126–31	heavens shall *l* :— *Psal.* 2: 4.
	239– 3	whether I can talk— and *l*
	338–18	very heavens shall *l* at them,
Pan.	1– 9	smile of April, the *l* of May,
'01.	18– 9	Those who *l* at or pray against
'02.	9–25	Did the age's thinkers *l* long

laughed

Po.	71– 3	*L* right to scorn,

laughing

Mis.	390–12	Looks love unto the *l* hours,
Ret.	18–11	And ope . . . to the bright, *l* day;
Po.	55–13	Looks love unto the *l* hours,
	63–23	And ope . . . to the bright, *l* day;

laughingly

My.	81– 9	* *l* give precedence to another
	324–26	* He told us *l* why he accepted

laughter

Mis.	324–10	the footfalls abate, the *l* ceases.

launch

Mis.	111–11	they *l* into the depths,

launched

My.	182–21	*l* the earth in its orbit,

launching

My.	29–23	* religion *l* upon a new era,

laureate's

Po.	10– 9	That wakes thy *l* lay.
My.	337–10	That wakes thy *l* lay.

laurel

Mis.	340– 2	torn the *l* from many
Ret.	17–17	bay, and *l*, in classical glee,
Po.	63– 1	bay, and *l*, in classical glee,

laurels

Mis.	254–25	*l* of headlong human will.
	358– 9	hounded footsteps, false *l*.
My.	125–14	they earn their *l*.
	155–12	the low *l* of vainglory,

Laus Deo

Mis.	399–16	poem
	399–18	*L· D·*, it is done !
	399–23	*L· D·*,— on this rock
	400– 1	*L· D·*, night star-lit
	400–11	It has none, *L· D·* !
Pul.	16– 3	*L· D·*, it is done !
	16– 8	*L· D·*,— on this rock
	16–13	*L· D·*, night starlit
	16–23	It has none, *L· D·* !
	43–14	* "*L· D·*, it is done !"
	44– 2	* '*L· D·*, it is done !'

Laus Deo

Po.	page 76	poem
	76– 2	*L· D·*, it is done !
	76– 7	*L· D·*,— on this rock
	76–12	*L· D·*, night star-lit
	76–22	It has none, *L· D·* !

lavatory

Pul.	76–19	* a *l* in which the plumbing

lavender-kid

Mis.	177–14	doff your *l* zeal,

laving

Po.	73–11	*L·* with surges thy silv'ry beach !

law

absence of

My.	220–14	denotes the absence of *l*.

all

Mis.	258–12	all *l* was vested in the Lawgiver,
	258–25	all *l*, Life, Truth, and Love.
'02.	9– 4	All-science— all *l* and gospel.
My.	349–30	infinite nature, including all *l*

all's

My.	40–27	* "All's love, but all's *l*."

and gospel

Mis.	18– 6	the *l* and gospel of Christ,
	65–22	demands both *l* and gospel,
	66–14	The *l* and gospel of Truth
	67– 3	the *l* and gospel of healing.
	121–32	Teacher of both *l* and gospel
'02.	9– 4	All-science— all *l* and gospel.
My.	247– 7	its *l* and gospel are according to
	252– 2	obey the *l* and gospel.
	254–28	its *l* and gospel are according to
	268–12	Principle of *l* and gospel,
	282–25	sunlight of the *l* and gospel.
	350– 1	of Deity and man, *l* and gospel,

and order

Mis.	104–23	divine *l* and order of being.
Ret.	76–29	observance of moral *l* and order
Un.	11–14	sense of physical *l* and order.
	23– 7	are born of *l* and order,
My.	222–30	will maintain *l* and order,
	245– 7	*L* and order characterize its work

and power

Mis.	364–16	individuality, *l*, and power.

and the gospel

Mis.	348– 3	claims of the *l* and the gospel.
'02.	6–29	fulfils the *l* and the gospel.
	8– 4	The *l* and the gospel concur,
	8–13	between the *l* and the gospel,
My.	131–23	of the divine *l* and the gospel.
	216– 6	The *l* and the gospel,

another

No.	30–13	to rebuke any claim of another *l*.

appears to be

Mis.	259– 3	Whatever appears to be *l*,

authority and

Un.	26–10	is not your authority and *l*.

begin with the

My.	132– 2	begin with the *l* as just announced,

ceremonial

No.	34– 4	We shall leave the ceremonial *l*

common

Mis.	11–16	in accordance with common *l*,
	274–20	breaks common *l*, gives impulse to
	285–27	in the face and eyes of common *l*,
Ret.	75–25	no warrant in common *l*

conceive of a

'02.	5–26	why should mortals conceive of a *l*,

construes

Mis.	301– 9	what the *l* construes as crime.

criminal

Un.	29– 4	as does all criminal *l*,

defines

Mis.	300–11	*l* defines and punishes as theft.

deific

Mis.	45–16	deific *l* that supply invariably meets

delivered from the

No.	25– 5	delivered from the *l*,— *Rom.* 7: 6.

demands of the

My.	43– 7	* Obedience to the demands of the *l*

divine

(see **divine**)

doers of the

My.	125– 3	not only sayers but doers of the *l*?

enacted

No.	30–11	is punished by the *l* enacted.

eternal

Mis.	123–23	through the eternal *l* of justice;
No.	30–22	is like the eternal *l* of God,

evade the

Mis.	226–26	such as manages to evade the *l*,
	300–16	thus evade the *l*, *but not the gospel.*

fabulous

Peo.	12–11	Deal, then, with this fabulous *l*

law

first
Ret. 87– 3   * "Order is heaven's first *l*,"

force or
Mis. 257–12   This so-called force, or *l*,
Pan. 6–24   how can matter be force or *l* ;

fulfilled the
My. 202–12   hath fulfilled the *l*." — *Rom.* 13 : 8.

fulfilling of the
Mis. 11– 3   Love is the fulfilling of the *l* :
258– 3   love is the fulfilling of the *l*.
285– 9   Love is the fulfilling of the *l*.

fulfilling the
Mis. 12–30   fulfilling the *l* of Love,
Ret. 65–24   Love, fulfilling the *l*

fulfils the
Mis. 66– 4   fulfils the *l* in righteousness,
117–15   Love . . . fulfils the *l*.
209–10   human belief fulfils the *l* of belief,
Ret. 76–16   This affection, . . . fulfils the *l*
'02. 6–18   fulfils the *l* in righteousness,
6–29   Divine Science fulfils the *l*
My. 275–26   self-oblivious love fulfils the *l*

fulfil the
Mis. 39–24   fulfil the *l* of Christ." — *Gal.* 6 : 2.
Ret. 45–23   fulfil the *l* of Christ
My. 153– 6   fulfil the *l* in righteousness.

God's
Mis. 369– 3   God's *l*, as in divine Science,
Ret. 76– 4   if mortals obeyed God's *l*
Un. 4– 5   Truth is God, and God's *l*.
4– 8   consciousness of God's *l* is
No. 30– 7   God's *l* reaches and destroys evil
30–11   God's *l* is in three words,

governing
My. 299–21   understand it and the *l* governing it,

hard is the
My. 40–30   * *Dura lex, sed lex* (Hard is the *l*,

has found
Mis. 227– 6   *L* has found it necessary to

Hebrew
Mis. 8–27   The Hebrew *l* with its

he read
Ret. 6–18   he read *l* at Hillsborough,

higher
Mis. 28–30   superiority of the higher *l* ;
244–19   by the higher *l* of Spirit,
Peo. 12– 1   hearken to the higher *l* of God,
My. 277–16   not consonant with the higher *l*

His
Mis. 277–29   I thunder His *l* to the sinner,
Un. 38– 5   not in accordance with His *l*,
Rud. 10–22   His *l* of Truth, when obeyed,

household
My. 308–27   his household *l*, constantly

human
My. 149–19   may know too much of human *l*
220– 9   obedience to human *l*,
283–26   Human *l* is right only as it

infinite
Mis. 172–20   the infinite *l* of God ;

in righteousness
Mis. 66– 4   fulfils the *l* in righteousness,
'02. 6–18   fulfils the *l* in righteousness,
My. 153– 6   fulfil the *l* in righteousness.

intelligence and
Pan. 7–23   power, intelligence and *l*,

involved
Pul. 35– 3   Principle and the *l* involved

is perfect
Mis. 82–16   whose *l* is perfect and infinite.

is written
Mis. 172–20   which *l* is written on the heart,

Jewish
Mis. 161–20   Jewish *l* that none should teach
Un. 29– 3   Jewish *l* condemned the sinner
No. 29– 1   passage refers to the Jewish *l*,

lawless
Mis. 257–32   according to this lawless *l*

material
Mis. 17– 3   as opposed to the material *l*
198–24   based on physical material *l*,
200–20   every supposed material *l*.
Rud. 12–27   divine Mind, not material *l*,

mental
Mis. 199– 6   his own erring mental *l*,

moral
Mis. 73–14   The foolish disobey moral *l*,
261–28   without apprehending the moral *l*
Ret. 76–29   observance of moral *l*

Mosaic
Ret. 89–11   instruction in the Mosaic *l*.

name of
Mis. 199– 5   dignify . . . with the name of *l* :

law

natural
Pul. 54– 7   * harmony with natural *l*,
No. 45–15   In natural *l* and in religion

never averts
Mis. 71–14   Science never averts *l*,

not without the
Mis. 286– 3   marriage is not without the *l*,

obedient to
My. 41– 2   * to become gladly obedient to *l*,

obey the
My. 219–31   that he obey the *l*,
252– 2   obey the *l* and gospel.

of being
Mis. 181– 9   blind obedience to the *l* of being,
259–18   the only *l* of being.
No. 2– 8   which is natural and a *l* of being.
My. 217–31   not to destroy the *l* of being,

of belief
Mis. 209–10   fulfils the *l* of belief,
Peo. 11–21   ignorant of the *l* of belief,

of Christ
Mis. 39–24   fulfil the *l* of Christ." — *Gal.* 6 : 2.
Ret. 45–23   fulfil the *l* of Christ
No. 30– 2   Truth is the *l* of Christ,

of creation
Mis. 258–15   This is the *l* of creation :
259–14   was the only *l* of creation,

of death
My. 154– 6   transcending the *l* of death.

of divine Love
Mis. 208–13   the *l* of divine Love gives,

of divine Mind
Mis. 269–22   Science is a *l* of divine Mind.
My. 3–15   Science is a *l* of divine Mind,
108–14   based on the *l* of divine Mind.
240–11   Science is a *l* of divine Mind,

of God
Mis. 22– 4   manifesto of Mind, the *l* of God,
36–26   not subject to the *l* of God, — *Rom.* 8 : 7.
141–15   I vindicate both the *l* of God and
172–20   the infinite *l* of God ;
172–23   This *l* of God is the Science of
208– 8   *l* of God has no knowledge of evil,
208–11   only to submit to the *l* of God,
211–24   risks nothing who obeys the *l* of God,
257– 8   The *l* of God is the law of Spirit,
315–28   unerring wisdom and *l* of God,
Ret. 28–20   according to the *l* of God.
72– 4   is contrary to the *l* of God ;
81– 8   The letter of the *l* of God,
Rud. 1– 2   As the *l* of God, the law of good,
No. 30–22   is like the eternal *l* of God,
'02. 5–20   it is iterated in the *l* of God,
Peo. 12– 1   hearken to the higher *l* of God,
My. 187–10   and the perfect *l* of God.
279– 2   not sanctioned by the *l* of God,
347–24   Science is the *l* of God ;
348–28   Science remains the *l* of God

of good
Rud. 1– 2   As the law of God, the *l* of good,

of health
Un. 6–13   Until the heavenly *l* of health,

of his being
Ret. 69– 4   Life is the *l* of his being"

of infinity
Mis. 15–19   progress is the *l* of infinity.

of justice
Mis. 123–23   through the eternal *l* of justice ;
261–16   In this *l* of justice,

of kindness
My. 42– 4   * the *l* of kindness." — *Prov.* 31 : 26.

of Life
Mis. 17– 2   of the spiritual *l* of Life,
30–19   to demonstrate the *l* of Life,
258–10   supremacy of the *l* of Life
259– 5   God is the *l* of Life,
No. 30– 2   *l* of Life and Truth is the
My. 154– 4   it is the *l* of Life understood

of Love
Mis. 12–25   the *l* of Love rejoices the heart ;
12–30   fulfilling the *l* of Love,
17– 3   the spiritual *l* of Love,
67–18   demonstrates the *l* of Love.
119–22   Insubordination to the *l* of Love
121–14   a divine decree, a *l* of Love !
141–14   even the annihilating *l* of Love.
141–23   in obedience to the *l* of Love
212–20   The *l* of Love saith,
Ret. 76–16   fulfils the *l* of Love
My. 153–23   unmindful of the divine *l* of Love,
154– 8   to infringe the divine *l* of Love
279– 2   not sanctioned by . . . the *l* of Love.

of love
My. 41– 9   * thoughts adverse to the *l* of love.

law

of loving
Mis. 13– 8 the l· of loving mine enemies.
of loyalty
Mis. 12–13 l· of loyalty to Jesus' Sermon on
of matter
Mis. 22– 3 Science is neither a l· of matter nor
173– 4 sees nothing but a l· of matter.
198–31 or violated a l· of matter
256–23 gravitation as a l· of matter;
257–10 The so-called l· of matter is an
My. 3–14 it is not a l· of matter,
of metaphysics
My. 41–11 * l· of metaphysics says,
of Mind
Mis. 173– 9 Science is the l· of Mind
of mortal belief
Peo. 12– 6 is a l· of mortal belief,
of Moses
Mis. 261–20 typified in the l· of Moses,
of nature
Pul. 54–12 * no l· of nature violated
Peo. 10–18 and not a l· of nature,
of omnipotent harmony
Mis. 17– 4 the l· of omnipotent harmony
of opposites
Mis. 14–22 proven by the l· of opposites
57–12 By the l· of opposites,
Un. 52–23 By the l· of opposites.
of our God
Mis. 129– 9 The l· of our God and the rule of
of right thinking
My. 41– 5 * the l· of right thinking,
of Science
Mis. 71–31 immutable and just l· of Science,
of sin
Mis. 17– 6 any supposititious l· of sin.
30–21 the l· of sin and death." — Rom. 8 : 2.
36–23 and the l· of sin and death.
201–19 the l· of sin and death;" — Rom. 8 : 2.
321–16 the l· of sin and death." — Rom. 8 : 2.
326– 3 the l· of sin and death." — Rom. 8 : 2.
Un. 56–17 freeth him from the l· of sin
'02. 9–13 the l· of sin and death." — Rom. 8 : 2.
My. 113–14 the l· of sin and death." — Rom. 8 : 2.
272– 7 the l· of sin and death." — Rom. 8 : 2.
293–29 the l· of sin and death." — Rom. 8 : 2.
of Spirit
Mis. 244–19 by the higher l· of Spirit,
257– 9 law of God is the l· of Spirit,
258–30 It interprets the l· of Spirit,
Un. 56–15 opposes the l· of Spirit;
Rud. 11– 2 contrary to the l· of Spirit.
My. 293–25 l· of Spirit to control matter,
of Spirit's supremacy
Un. 58–10 the l· of Spirit's supremacy;
of the chord
Ret. 82– 2 the l· of the chord remains
of the Spirit
Mis. 201–18 l· of the Spirit of life — Rom. 8 : 2.
321–15 l· of the Spirit of life — Rom. 8 : 2.
326– 2 l· of the Spirit of life — Rom. 8 : 2.
'02. 9–11 l· of the Spirit of life — Rom. 8 : 2.
My. 41–23 * l· of the Spirit of life — Rom. 8 : 2.
113–13 l· of the Spirit of life — Rom. 8 : 2.
272– 5 l· of the Spirit of life — Rom. 8 : 2.
293–28 l· of the Spirit of life — Rom. 8 : 2.
of "the survival
No. 25–13 l· of "the survival of the fittest."
of transmission
Mis. 71–11 set aside the l· of transmission,
of Truth
Mis. 208– 2 This is the l· of Truth to error,
Un. 4– 6 l· of Truth destroys every
Rud. 10–22 His l· of Truth, when obeyed,
old
My. 327–19 * an old l·, or rather a section of an act
one
Pan. 8–17 had one God and one l·,
or intelligence
Mis. 101–27 no other power, l·, or intelligence
penalty of
Mis. 227– 9 to evade the penalty of l·,
penalty of the
Mis. 300–21 incurring the penalty of the l·,
perfect
No. 30–12 this perfect l· is ever present
My. 187–10 and the perfect l· of God.
physical
Mis. 28–29 of physique and of physical l·,
101–15 of mortality, of physical l·,
Un. 11–14 sense of physical l· and order.
power and
My. 36–31 * through His power and l·,
prohibitory
Peo. 10– 9 on a tyrannical prohibitory l·

law

protected by
My. 227–20 are not specially protected by l·.
rebels against
My. 40–29 * Human sense often rebels against l·,
recognizes
My. 328–12 * l· recognizes them as healers,
sacred
Mis. 151– 9 Through the sacred l·, He speaketh
Science is the
My. 267– 5 Science is the l· of the Mind
347–24 Science is the l· of God;
signification of
My. 220–14 the moral signification of l·.
so-called
Mis. 198–24 physical material l·, so-called
257–10 The so-called l· of matter is
257–22 governed by this so-called l·,
Spirit and
Mis. 256–21 chapter sub-title
spiritual
(see **spiritual**)
State
Peo. 12–11 as with an inhuman State l·;
substance, or
'02. 6– 3 knowledge of life, substance, or l·,
suit at
Ret. 39– 3 I entered a suit at l·,
My. 136–16 won a suit at l· in Washington,
this
Mis. 13– 9 This l· I now urge upon the
66– 1 But this l· is not infallible
82–17 In obedience to this l·,
173–10 this l· has no relation to,
208– 3 This l· is a divine energy.
208– 4 the fulfilment of this l·;
257–31 is not exempt from this l·.
Un. 4– 5 This l· declares that Truth is All,
4– 6 This l· of Truth destroys every
My. 221–21 Our Master conformed to this l·,
to destroy the
Mis. 261–19 to destroy the l·," — Matt. 5 : 17.
'02. 5–23 to destroy the l·, — Matt. 5 : 17.
My. 219–24 to destroy the l·, — Matt. 5 : 17.
to Himself
Mis. 258–13 Lawgiver, who was a l· to Himself.
translation of
Peo. 1– 6 translation of l· back to its
understood the
Pul. 54–15 * He understood the l· perfectly,
unto itself
Mis. 260–29 Mind, . . . is a l· unto itself,
unto themselves
Ret. 87–23 become a l· unto themselves.
violates the
Ret. 75– 4 violates the l· given by Moses,
whole
Ret. 31–20 shall keep the whole l·, — Jas. 2 : 10.
Pul. 53–16 * the whole l· of human felicity
My. 153– 8 have come to fulfil the whole l·.
without
Mis. 367– 1 letter without l·, gospel, or

Mis. 12–12 should be to-day a l· to himself,
67– 4 First is the l·, which saith :
71–16 L· brings out Truth, not error ;
73–12 L· is never material :
244–15 * "Has the l· been abrogated
256–25 assertion that matter is a l·,
256–26 Wherever l· is, Mind is ;
257– 7 that which is not l·,
257– 7 L· is either a moral or an
259– 4 not of the nature of God, is not l·,
316– 3 l· not unto others, but themselves.
Man. 28– 3 L· constitutes government,
84– 5 a l·, not unto others, but to
Ret. 30–17 St. Paul declared that the l·
Pul. 35– 8 * a l· as operative in the world to-day
Rud. 1–16 In l·, Blackstone applies the word
4–18 L· is not in matter, but in Mind
No. 21–11 identity, individuality, l·,
'02. 4–20 a l· never to be abrogated
Peo. 12– 5 only l· of sickness or death is
My. 40–31 * nevertheless it is the l·).
41– 4 * l· of Christian metaphysics,
43– 4 * The l· was given that they might
219–30 I recommend, if the l· demand,
220– 8 when the l· so requires.
238–17 man rises above the letter, l·, or
285–27 which are written in the l· — Acts 24 : 14.
328–11 * greatly pleased at the l·

law-abiding

Mis. 206–18 l· Principle, God.
Ret. 87–11 systematic and l· people

law-breaking
  Mis. 301–10 *l·* and gospel-opposing
law-creating
  Mis. 206–18 active, all-wise, *l·*,
law-disciplining
  Mis. 206–18 all-wise, law-creating, *l·*,
lawful
  Un. 23– 5 His *l·* son, Edgar, was to his
  Pul. 48–24 * The natural and *l·* pride
      82–18 * women had few *l·* claims
  My. 41–26 * disregard his *l·* inheritance,
Lawgiver
  Mis. 258–13 all law was vested in the *L·*,
      259–14 When the *L·* was the only
lawgiver
  Mis. 256–25 is a law, or a *l·*,
      364–26 If Spirit is the *l·*
  Peo. 12– 9 matter is not a *l·*
  My. 108–16 this Mind is the only *l·*,
lawless
  Mis. 257–32 according to this *l·* law
      260–30 *l·* mind, with unseen motives,
  My. 349–25 evil, which is *l·* and traceable to
lawlessness
  Mis. 228– 7 just amid *l·*, and pure amid
      277–28 one can be just amid *l·*,
  Ret. 77– 1 and *l·* in literature.
  '00. 11–29 His . . . ethics bravely rebuke *l·*.
  My. 41–14 * whatsoever *l·* of hatred he may
law-maker
  My. 347–25 that matter is not a *l·* ;
lawn
  My. 171–22 * *l·* of the Unitarian church
      174– 1 beautiful *l·* surrounding their
lawns
  Pul. 48– 3 * green stretches of *l·*,
law-office
  Ret. 6–24 he succeeded to the *l·*
Law of Psychic Phenomena
  Pul. 53–14 * book title
Lawrence
  Mis. 154– 2 chapter sub-title
laws
  abortive
  Un. 11–10 this mind and its abortive *l·*.
  broken
  Pul. 56–21 * We tread upon life's broken *l·*,
  church
  My. 203– 7 Church *l·* . . . are God's laws.
  constitutional
  '01. 33–16 constitutional *l·* of their land ;
  divine
  My. 190–19 certainty of the divine *l·* of Mind
  enforce the
  Pul. 82–25 * at least to help enforce the *l·*
  equitable
  My. 277– 9 wholesome tribunals, equitable *l·*,
  forces and
  Pan. 2–17 * forces and *l·* which are manifested
  God's
  Mis. 29–27 are no infraction of God's *l·* ;
  Ret. 26– 9 in his obedience to God's *l·*,
  No. 11– 5 God's *l·*, and their intelligent and
  My. 203– 8 Church laws . . . are God's *l·*.
  health
  My. 344–22 * the health *l·* of the States
  her
  Mis. 219– 4 nor teaches that nature and her *l·*
  Pul. 7– 5 her *l·* have befriended progress.
  His
  Mis. 29–28 on the contrary, they fulfil His *l·* ;
      175–27 perfect Mind and His *l·*.
  No. 5–24 realities of God and His *l·*.
  Hea. 12–14 His providence or His *l·*,
  My. 277–14 shall be according to His *l·*.
  human
  My. 220–27 Jesus obeyed human *l·*
  hygienic
  Ret. 26– 2 neither obedience to hygienic *l·*,
  immutable
  No. 4–21 of the immutable *l·* of God ;
  My. 106– 9 immutable *l·* of omnipotent Mind
  improved
  '02. 3–14 self-government under improved *l·*.
  its
  Mis. 55–27 its *l·* are mortal beliefs.
  legislation and
  Mis. 80–17 coercive legislation and *l·*,
  make
  My. 222–23 shall make *l·* to regulate

laws
  make the
  Pul. 82–25 * right to help make the *l·*,
  Peo. 11–18 make the *l·* that govern their
  making
  My. 340–15 making *l·* for the State
  material
      (*see* **material**)
  medical
  Mis. 80– 5 opposition to unjust medical *l·*.
  obey the
  My. 345– 3 Christian Scientists obey the *l·*,
  of every State
  My. 327–29 * when the *l·* of every State
  of God
  Man. 83–20 with the unerring *l·* of God,
  Un. 11–12 through the higher *l·* of God.
  Pul. 80–28 * harmony with the *l·* of God,
  No. 4–21 of the immutable *l·* of God ;
      11– 1 immutable and eternal *l·* of God ;
  My. 128–19 abide by the *l·* of God
      282– 4 I believe . . . in the *l·* of God.
      349–23 The *l·* of God, or divine Mind,
  of health
  Mis. 6–25 where *l·* of health are
  of infinite Spirit
  Mis. 16–30 with the *l·* of infinite Spirit,
  of limitation
  My. 229–26 namely, *l·* of limitation for a
  of man
  My. 348–23 *l·* of man and the universe,
  of matter
  Mis. 173–30 are these forces *l·* of matter,
      244–18 so-called *l·* of matter
      332– 4 Mind is Truth,— not *l·* of matter.
  Un. 11– 8 He annulled the *l·* of matter,
  Pan. 8–16 annulled the so-called *l·* of matter,
      12–13 high above the so-called *l·* of matter,
  Peo. 11–21 calls its own . . . "*l·* of matter."
      12– 8 spurious, imaginary *l·* of matter
  My. 288–17 so-called *l·* of matter he eschewed ;
  of Mind
  Mis. 173–30 laws of matter, or *l·* of Mind?
  My. 190–19 certainty of the divine *l·* of Mind
  of mortal mind
  Un. 11– 9 *l·* of mortal mind, not of God.
  of my country
  '02. 15– 4 protection of the *l·* of my country.
  of nations
  '00. 10–12 *l·* of nations and peoples,
  of nature
  Mis. 216–26 * neither *l·* of nature nor the
  Pul. 54–14 * obedience to the *l·* of nature.
  '01. 24– 6 rules styled the *l·* of nature.
  of our land
  Mis. 141–15 and the *l·* of our land.
      141–24 law of Love and the *l·* of our land.
  Man. 46– 6 according to the *l·* of our land.
      48–10 the courts, or the *l·* of our land.
  '01. 20–26 *l·* of our land will handle
  of reason
  Mis. 216–26 * neither . . . nor the *l·* of reason
  of Science
  No. 6–27 the *l·* of Science are mental,
  of Spirit
  Mis. 260–11 *l·* of Spirit, not of matter ;
  of the land
  My. 128–20 abide by . . . the *l·* of the land ;
      219–22 nor make void the *l·* of the land,
      220–12 obeying the *l·* of the land.
  of the State
  Man. 45–26 under the *l·* of the *State.*
  Pul. 7– 4 especially the *l·* of the State
  of the universe
  My. 340–30 beneficence of the *l·* of the universe
  other
  Mis. 260–13 these laws annulled all other *l·*.
  our
  Mis. 119– 7 our *l·* punish the dupe as accessory
  My. 222–25 religion shall permeate our *l·*.
  physical
  Po. 32–15 Such physical *l·* to obey,
  prominent
  Mis. 18– 8 The prominent *l·* which forward
  scientific
  Mis. 31– 7 subverts the scientific *l·* of being.
  Pul. 69–22 * certain Christian and scientific *l·*,
  so-called
  Mis. 198– 6 denying material so-called *l·*
      244–18 who annulled the so-called *l·*
  Pan. 8–16 virtually annulled the so-called *l·*
      12–13 high above the so-called *l·*
  My. 288–17 The so-called *l·* of matter
  spiritual
  Mis. 198–26 Principle, and its spiritual *l·*.
  My. 159–23 spiritual *l·* enforcing obedience

laws

State
Mis. 263–24 and protection of State *l*.
My. 204–16 COMPLIANCE WITH THE STATE *L*.
supposed
Mis. 74–21 matter and its supposed *l*.
these
Mis. 260–12 these *l* annulled all other laws.
Pul. 69–23 * understand these *l* aright.
those
My. 220–27 and fell a victim to those *l*.
United States
My. 227–10 State or United States *l*,
universal
Un. 13– 9 universal *l*, His unchangeableness,
your
Po. 39–17 Since temperance makes your *l*.

Mis. 56–14 constituted *l* to that effect,
206–15 no insubordination to the *l*
Man. 28– 5 disobedience to the *l* of The
Pan. 3–20 whose *l* are not reckoned as science.
'01. 34–24 obey strictly the *l* that be,
My. 160– 2 *l* which it were impious to
167–26 by the *l* of my native State.
234–29 and when the *l* are against it,
344–22 * "Then as to the *l*

law-school
Mis. 340–11 That *l* is not at fault

lawsuit
My. 309– 5 acting as counsel in a *l*

lawyer
Mis. 157– 9 that you or your *l* will ask
381–10 requested her *l* to inquire
Ret. 7–15 * As a *l* he was able
Pul. 32–29 * achieved eminence as a *l*.
60– 6 * who was a Colorado *l*
My. 310– 4 Albert was a distinguished *l*.

lawyers
My. 111–10 by many doctors and *l*,
149–18 *L* may know too much of

lax
My. 129– 4 and a *l* system of religion.

laxity
Ret. 77– 1 *l* in discipline and lawlessness in

lay
Mis. 15–23 *l* off the "old man," — Col. 3 : 9.
17– 8 *l* aside your material appendages,
22–31 *l* concealed in the treasure-troves
29– 1 *l* hands on the sick, — Mark 16 : 18.
63–17 might *l* hold of eternal Life,
162–16 *l* himself as a lamb upon the altar
179–28 *l* aside material consciousness,
192–29 *l* hands on the sick, — Mark 16 : 18.
225–21 the sofa whereon *l* the lad
248– 2 "*l* hands on the sick, — Mark 16 : 18.
248– 4 "*l* hands on the sick" — Mark 16 : 18.
319–23 *l* them in the outstretched hand
327–20 *l* down a few of the heavy weights,
335–16 I *l* bare the ability,
348– 9 one should *l* it bare ;
361–11 *l* aside every weight, — Heb. 12 : 1.
365– 3 *l* than that is laid," — I Cor. 3 : 11.
384– 2 Come, in the minstrel's *l* ;
388– 2 Which swelled creation's *l* :
Ret. 17– 4 I bend to thy *l*,
18–24 they darken my *l* :
35–17 *l* hands on the sick, — Mark 16 : 18.
Un. 43–23 *apprehend*, or *l* hold upon,
56–24 *l* hold of him ere he can change
64– 9 *l* than that is laid." — I Cor. 3 : 11.
Pul. 12–22 by which we *l* down all for
85– 1 * began to *l* the foundation
No. 21–24 *l* than that is laid, — I Cor. 3 : 11.
'00. 11–24 * And it *l* on my fevered spirit
14–27 *l* not this sin to their — Acts 7 : 60.
'01. 35– 6 and *l* ourselves upon the altar?
'02. 3–24 and the *l* of angels
20–11 Which swelled creation's *l*,
Hea. 1– 4 *l hands on the sick*, — Mark 16 : 18.
8–10 *l* hands on the sick, — Mark 16 : 18.
19–27 *l* hands on the sick, — Mark 16 : 18.
Peo. 12– 4 *l* hands on the sick, — Mark 16 : 18.
Po. 7– 2 Which swelled creation's *l* :
8– 9 Till vestal pearls that on leaflets *l*,
10– 9 That wakes thy laureate's *l*.
26–11 Great willing heart did *l*.
36– 1 in the minstrel's *l* ;
41– 6 *l* down their woes,
43–14 *l* their pure hearts' off'ring,
53– 5 And soft thy shading *l*
62– 4 I bend to thy *l*,
64–21 they darken my *l* :

lay
Po. 70– 2 In the dim distance, *l*
My. 16–24 Behold, I *l* in Zion — Isa. 28 : 16.
16–28 will I *l* to the line, — Isa. 28 : 17.
17–15 Behold, I *l* in Sion — I Pet. 2 : 6.
29–16 * *l* in its very simplicity ;
48– 2 * *l* hands on the sick, — Mark 16 : 18.
155–11 *l* down the low laurels of vainglory,
178–21 textbook on a table
184–21 *l* upon its altars a sacrifice
337–10 That wakes thy laureate's *l*.
341–12 A lightsome *l*, a cooing call,

laying
Mis. 2–29 thus *l* off the material beliefs
143–13 chapter sub-title
216–13 "*l* on of hands," — Heb. 6 : 2.
285–19 *l* the axe at the root of error.
399–17 Written on *l* the corner-stone
Man. 60–22 *L* a Corner Stone.
60–24 when *l* the Corner Stone of
Pul. 16– 2 poem
43–15 * corner-stone *l* last spring,
Po. 76– 1 *l* of the corner-stone of The
My. 17– 4 *l* aside all malice, — I Pet. 2 : 1.
128– 3 *l* again the foundation of — Heb. 6 : 1.

lays
Mis. 37–17 *l* the axe at the root of the tree.
235–12 *l* the axe at the root of the tree
287–19 This *l* the foundations of
312– 6 that which *l* all upon the altar,
Rud. 12– 1 never *l* his hands on the patient,
'01. 13–15 C. S. *l* the axe at the root of sin,
Po. 30–22 heaven's lyres and angels' loving *l*,
My. 146–30 *l* his whole weight of thought,
268–24 *l* the axe at the root of all evil,
287–21 *l* the axe at the root of the tree
296– 3 *l* the axe "unto the root — Matt. 3 : 10.

lazar-houses
Mis. 296–20 patronize tap-rooms and *l*,

Lazarus
Pul. 27–26 * represents the raising of *L*.
My. 218–11 even the self-same *L*.

lazy
Mis. 342–15 over earth's *l* sleepers.

lead
Mis. 51–18 they will *l* him aright :
61– 7 that *l* to death,
130–30 appoints to *l* the line of
145–25 child shall *l* them." — Isa. 11 : 6.
196– 1 purity, and . . . *l* to the one God :
210–16 special adaptability to *l* on C. S.,
211– 7 else the blind will *l* the blind
257–16 *l* to immediate or ultimate death.
287–25 they *l* to higher joys :
314– 9 *l* in silent prayer,
354– 5 and *l* the innocent to doom?
389– 4 * "To point to heaven and *l* the way."
398–15 *L* Thy lambkins to the fold,
Man. 85–10 not ready to *l* his pupils.
Ret. 14–27 *l* me in the way — Psal. 139 : 24.
46–21 *L* Thy lambkins to the fold,
65– 6 *l* to self-righteousness and
76–14 stairs which *l* up to spiritual love.
Pul. 17–20 *L* Thy lambkins to the fold,
32– 8 * to dominate, to *l*, to control,
Rud. 9– 8 will *l* to weakness in practice,
No. 33– 3 *l* us to bless those who curse,
Hea. 5–25 would *l* our lives to higher issues ;
Po. 14–19 *L* Thy lambkins to the fold,
21–18 * point to heaven and *l* the way."
My. 33–12 and *l* me in the way — Psal. 139 : 24.
45–20 * to *l* you in the way,
51–14 * who is so able as she to *l* us
59–23 * feeble attempts to *l* the singing.
140– 3 I will *l* them — Isa. 42 : 16.
162–25 it gently into
213–20 see whether they *l* you to God
347– 3 What remains to *l* on the centuries

leaden
No. 34–16 falls with its *l* weight

Leader
Man. 33– 5 A Reader not a *L*.
33– 6 Church Reader shall not be a *L*,
65– 3 A Member not a *L*.
65– 6 shall not be called *L* by members
(*see also* **Eddy**)

Leader
Pul. 89–35 * *L*, Bloomington, Ill.
89–36 * *L*, Cleveland, Ohio.

leader
Mis. 295– 4 noted English *l*, whom he quotes
371– 4 wandering about without a *l*,

leader
Pul.	59–13	* *l·* responding with its parallel
Pan.	3–26	*l·* of the nymphs,
'00.	9–27	*l·* of this mighty movement.
My.	31–31	* trained carefully under one *l·*,
	43–12	* obedient to the voice of their *l·*.
	291–27	loss of her renowned *l·* !
		(*see also* **Eddy**)

Leader's
(*see* **Eddy**)

leaders
Mis.	369–14	*l·* of materialistic schools
	370–19	chapter sub-title
Pul.	79–27	* thought of the world's scientific *l·*
'01.	30–14	*l·* of a reform in religion
	32–18	old-fashioned *l·* of religion
Peo.	11–23	*l·* of public thought
My.	40–14	* Through rivalries among *l·*
	116–24	Had the ages helped their *l·*
	340–20	*l·* of our rock-ribbed State.

leadership
Mis.	371– 7	to help them by his own *l·*?
Ret.	3– 6	gallant *l·* and death,
My.	28–19	* consecrated *l·* of Mrs. Eddy,
	44–30	* unerring wisdom of your *l·*,
	64–15	* all the years of her *l·*,
	356– 4	His reflection of love and *l·*
	362–20	* we rejoice in your inspired *l·*,

leadeth
Mis.	163–27	which *l·* into all Truth
	174–32	Holy Ghost that *l·* into all Truth;
	189– 6	Comforter that *i·* into all truth.
	322–14	feedeth my flock, and *l·* them
	397–20	Love, whereto God *l·* me.
Pul.	19– 4	Love, whereto God *l·* me.
Po.	13– 8	Love, whereto God *l·* me.
My.	119–30	Truth that *l·* away from person

leading
Mis.	46– 4	The *l·* self-evident proposition of
	59–24	*l·* his thoughts away from
	66–28	blind *l·* the blind." — *see Matt.* 15 : 14.
	85– 9	every thought and act *l·* to good.
	85–12	regeneration *l·* thereto is
	292–12	*l·* them, if *possible*, to Christ,
	346–19	This *l·*, self-evident proposition of
Man.	98–18	in a *l·* Boston newspaper
Ret.	91–19	*l·* them into the divine order,
Un.	6–15	*l·* questions about God
	42–25	*l·* man into the true sense of
Pul.	6–21	* I feel the truth is *l·* us
	25–19	* *l·* to the auditorium,
	26–28	* *L·* off the "Mother's Room" are
	72– 5	* a few of the *l·* members
	88– 1	chapter sub-title
	88– 4	received *l·* newspapers with
Rud.	11– 3	schoolmaster, *l·* you to Christ;
No.	12– 4	*l·* us to see spirituality
	32– 7	a crime nor the motives *l·* to it.
	34– 2	*l·* up to health, harmony, and
'01.	21– 5	a demonstrable Science *l·* the ages.
Hea.	5–10	One of our *l·* clergymen
Po.	43– 9	*L·* kine with love.
My.	45–23	* we see the earlier *l·*,
	77– 7	* *l·* landmark of Boston,
	77–19	* filled the streets *l·* to the
	79–16	* in the *l·* newspapers of
	82–30	* streets *l·* directly to
	140–19	God is *l·* you onward
	152–19	the blind is *l·* the blind,
	163–24	*l·* people of this pleasant city
	225–15	the *l·* of our Lord's Prayer.
	252–22	*l·* humanity into paths of peace
	270– 8	*l·* editors and newspapers of
	283– 9	*l·* impetus of my life.
	304–10	writing for the *l·* newspapers,
	312– 2	supply the place of his *l·* teacher
	353– 6	Extract from the *l·* Editorial

leadings
Mis.	49–22	opposes the *l·* of the divine Spirit

leads
Mis.	37–20	*l·* to moral or physical death.
	49–19	spirit of Truth *l·* into all truth,
	100–15	*l·* on irresistible forces,
	295– 6	power which in America *l·* women
	344– 7	aught of that which *l·* to bliss,
	347–27	from the night He *l·* to light.
	351–25	life that *l·* unto death,
Ret.	73– 9	great fact *l·* into profound depths.
	88–17	*l·* inevitably to a consideration
Un.	18– 2	necessarily *l·* to extinction
	26–11	belief in which *l·* to such teaching
	55–12	suffering which *l·* out of the flesh.
Rud.	6– 1	*l·* to the equal inference that

leads
Rud.	10–28	*l·* you to believe in the existence
My.	77– 5	* *l·* the Auditorium of Chicago.
	272–26	* *l·* with such conspicuous success
	339– 3	whose every link *l·* upward

leaf
Po.	22–12	'Tis writ on earth, on *l·* and
	53– 3	The bud, the *l·* and wing
My.	149–30	solicit every root and every *l·*
	192–27	and leave a *l·* of olive;

leaflet (*see also* **leaflet's**)
Po.	41– 7	fountain and *l·* are frozen

leaflet's
Po.	31–11	veils the *l·* wondrous birth

leaflets
Man.	46–10	cards, or *l·*, which advertise
Po.	8– 9	vestal pearls that on *l·* lay,

leafy
Po.	34– 8	In what dark *l·* grove

league
Mis.	79–29	Beware of joining any medical *l·*
	80– 6	*l·* which obligates its members
	80–11	everybody, . . . can join this *l·*.
My.	200–24	relinquish its *l·* with evil.

leagued
Mis.	177– 6	*l·* together in secret conspiracy

leagues
Mis.	110–20	*l·* have lain between us.

lean
Mis.	298– 1	*l·* not unto thine own — *Prov.* 3 : 5.
Ret.	13–19	bade me *l·* on God's love,
'01.	34–30	*l·* not unto thine own — *Prov.* 3 : 5.
Peo.	8–17	and *l·* upon it for health and life.
My.	129–28	*L·* not too much on your Leader.
	245–15	persecution, and *l·* glory,

leaned
'02.	15– 5	I *l·* on God, and was safe.

leaner
Mis.	131– 8	let the *l·* sort console this brother's

leaning
Ret.	16–13	went into the church *l·* on crutches

leap
Mis.	126– 6	in tones that *l·* for joy,
Un.	64–15	*l·* the dark fissures,
No.	44–11	no hobby, . . . that can *l·* into the
'02.	3–30	the first lie and *l·* into perdition
My.	129–18	ye who *l·* disdainfully from

leaped
My.	81–13	* up *l·* half a dozen Scientists.
	164–20	has *l·* into living love.

learn
Mis.	xii– 6	"*l·* war no more," — *see Isa.* 2 : 4.
	3– 9	we *l·* in divine Science
	10–28	mortals *l·* at last the lesson,
	14–12	in order to *l·* Science,
	16–19	We must *l·* that God is
	37–13	*l·* the meaning of those words
	42–24	*l·* that good, not evil, lives
	77–23	there *l·*, in divine Science,
	85–31	and to *l·* their way out of both
	125–18	*l·* forever the infinite meanings
	128– 4	to *l·* or to teach briefly;
	129– 6	first lesson is to *l·* one's self;
	176–11	It is then that we *l·*
	183–14	we *l·* this, and receive it:
	183–15	*l·* that man can fulfil the
	185–23	to *l·* his origin and age,
	186–13	We *l·* in the Scriptures.
	199–18	*l·* somewhat of the qualities
	205–31	who on the shores of time *l·*
	205–32	and live what they *l·*,
	207– 1	*L·* its purpose;
	209–15	compels mortals to *l·* that
	230–25	* *L·* to labor and to wait."
	233–31	*l·* that sensation is not in matter,
	235–19	*l·* God aright, and know
	251–25	*l·* a parable of the period,
	252–12	*l·* that sick thoughts are
	254–15	*l·* that he must at last
	278–26	*l·* by the things they suffer,
	279–15	from which we *l·* without study.
	283–30	*l·* the principle of music
	317–13	*l·* by spiritual growth
	328– 2	*l·* from the things they suffer.
	330–19	*l·* what report they bear,
	341–18	O *l·* to lose with God!
	341–29	We *l·* from this parable
	355–21	*L·* what in thine own mentality
	359–19	He had to *l·* from experience;
	366– 5	to *l·* the doctrine of theology,
	378–15	to *l·* his practice,

learn

Mis.	387–20	L·, too, that wisdom's rod is given
	391– 9	And l· that Truth and wisdom
Man.	53–15	Not to L· Hypnotism.
	53–16	shall not l· hypnotism.
Ret.	38–18	to l· that he had printed all
	49–14	Mortals must l· to lose their
	54– 9	and l· the divine way,
	79–24	* "L· to labor and to wait."
Un.	6– 4	whole human race will l· that,
	10–23	to l· the principle of
	10–26	Mortals must l· this;
	13–12	l·, proportionately as we gain
	13–19	He must l· to unknow,
	28–17	l· Soul only as we l· God,
	41– 4	we must l· it of good.
	41– 5	Of evil we can never l· it,
	45–10	egotist must come down and l·,
	55–19	l· how false are the pleasures
	62–11	l· that there is no Life in evil.
Pul.	49–30	* to l· that this rich woman
	81– 3	* l· that the name of Christ
Rud.	2– 7	In C. S. we l· that God
	4–22	we can only l· and love Him
	10–26	must l· to acknowledge God
	11– 6	you l· that God is good,
No.	11–20	than to l· theology, physiology,
	27–28	they may l· the definition of
	42– 1	* more and more l· their duty
	43–22	to l· a system which they
'00.	8–26	L· to obey ;
	8–26	l· first what obedience is.
'01.	31– 8	l· and love the truths of C. S.
'02.	8– 7	When loving, we l· that
	17– 7	When mortals l· to love aright ;
	17– 7	when they l· that man's highest
Hea.	8–21	l· to reach heaven through
	9–27	l· this grand truth
	12– 5	to l· what matter is doing
	14–22	teach them how to l·,
	14–22	together with what they l·
	17–12	l· this as we awake to behold
Peo.	2– 1	l· our capabilities for good,
	2– 7	we shall l· what God is,
	2–10	l· that God, good, is universal,
	6–16	when we l· God aright, we love Him,
	9–25	whereby we l· the great fact
Po.	6–15	L·, too, that wisdom's rod is
	38– 8	And l· that Truth and wisdom
My.	24– 1	* l· that the truth which Christ
	104–28	to l· of her who, thirty years ago,
	119– 7	In Science, we l· that man is
	121– 7	In metaphysics we l· that the
	142–18	l· this and rejoice with me,
	151–23	We l· from the Scriptures that
	181–17	all nations shall speedily l·
	185– 7	* L· to labor and to wait."
	197–16	l· that the translucent atmosphere of
	226–21	in this you l· to hallow His name,
	264– 5	until mankind l· more of my meaning
	278– 5	may l· to make war no more,
	303– 5	It suffices me to l· the Science of
	305–23	to l· definitely more from my
	346– 8	* l· authoritatively from the Herald

learned (adj.)

Mis.	363–28	Bible is the l· man's masterpiece,
Ret.	7–16	* As a lawyer he was able and l·,
Hea.	14–11	be sure he is a l· man and skilful ;
Peo.	6– 2	* "I am sick of l· quackery."
	11–25	The l· quacks of this period
My.	104– 3	thought that the l· St. Paul,
	296– 2	* able discourse of our "l· judge,"

learned (verb)

Mis.	3–20	We have l· that the erring
	14–12	could never be l· ;
	23– 1	having l· so much ;
	24–18	I l· that mortal thought
	41– 3	having l· the power of
	55–11	having l· the power of the
	110–27	l· how fleeting is that
	126– 8	Who hath not l· that when
	126–11	have l· that trials lift us
	128–12	both l·, and received, — Phil. 4 : 9.
	147–10	l· that sin is inadmissible,
	173– 5	l· of the schools that there is
	173– 8	has ever l· from the schools,
	190–14	needs yet to be l·.
	192–19	l· its adaptability to
	234– 7	not l· of the material senses,
	276–29	quickly l· when the door is shut.
	278–15	l· that a curse on sin is always a
	281– 7	I l· long ago that the world
	309–31	more than they have yet l·.
Ret.	9–23	* l· at last to know His voice
	21– 8	had l· that his mother still lived,

learned (verb)

Ret.	25–24	I l· that these material senses
	28– 9	I had l· that thought must be
	28–22	I had l· that Mind reconstructed
	32– 5	l· that whatever is loved materially,
	35– 8	having l· that the merits of C. S.
	45– 5	it was l· that material
	61–28	that however little be taught or l·,
	79– 3	spiritual truth l· and loved ;
Un.	57–21	he l· that spiritual grace was
Pul.	35–13	"I had l· that thought must
	35–21	I had l· that Mind reconstructed
	82–10	* She has long l· with patience,
No.	25–21	remains to be l·.
	28–10	Science of being must be l·
Pan.	12– 2	l· that good is not educed from evil,
'00.	7–15	having suffered, lived, and l·,
	10–25	I have l· it was a private soldier
'01.	17–24	l· that the dynamics of medicine
	22–25	l· its numeration table,
Hea.	6–13	When I l· how mind produces
	6–14	I l· how it produces the
	9–10	having l· that this method
	11–21	reached this high goal you have l·
	12–12	we l· from the Scripture
Peo.	2–12	this Principle is l· through goodness,
Po.	77–15	When we have l· of Truth
My.	vi– 8	* except as he has l· it from her
	21–14	* Christian Scientists have l·
	43– 8	* they l· to know Him.
	43–10	* but they l· from experience
	43–26	* We have l· from experience,
	61– 4	* lessons I have l· of the power of
	124–27	Now what have you l· ?
	125– 1	Have you l· to conquer sin,
	188–26	When it is l· that spiritual sense
	195–20	C. S. is at length l· to be
	269– 6	Then shall humanity have l·
	271– 7	I l· the truth of what I
	315–12	* I l· that Mary Baker G. Eddy,
	332–25	* it was l· that the lodge was
	343–15	I have simply taught as I l·

learner

Mis.	43–15	to the sick and to the l·
	43–30	on the practice of the l·,
	66–32	to the present capability of the l·,
	243–15	Principle, which the l· can

learning (see also learning's)

Mis.	47– 4	By l· that matter is but
	178–20	'Much l'— or something else
	183–17	not by reason of the schools, or l·,
Ret.	10–14	L· was so illumined, that grammar
Un.	14–27	would become better by l· to
Pul.	72– 3	* l· the feeling of Scientists
No.	4– 2	task of l· thoroughly the Science
	11–16	the place in schools of l·
	33– 6	rightful place in schools of l·,
	39–17	True prayer . . . is l· to love,
'02.	2–11	religions, ethics, and l·,
	3–16	her dusky children are l· to read
My.	4–19	l· that Mind-power is good will
	65–13	* L· that a big church was required,
	79–11	* seat of l· of America?
	114–26	l· the higher meaning of this book
	228– 4	by l· that so-called disease is a
	340–31	Institutions of l· and . . . religion

learning's

Ret.	11– 7	On l· lore and wisdom's might,
Po.	60– 3	On l· lore and wisdom's might,

learns

Mis.	58– 4	Waking . . . one l· its unreality ;
	58– 7	l· that consumption did not kill
	85– 6	l· spiritually all that he
	184–21	l· that all power is good
	195– 5	l· the letter of C. S.
	221– 6	l· more of its divine Principle.
Ret.	38–28	l· the letter of this book,
Hea.	14–20	l· the metaphysical treatment
Po.	1–17	to meditate on what it l·.
My.	161–29	l· through meekness and love

leases

Mis.	340–16	drew up logs instead of l·.

least

Mis.	2– 4	who have the l· wisdom or
	7–12	where one would l· expect it,
	12–18	in a manner l· understood ;
	30– 2	we prove it, in a at l· some
	37–28	is in reality the l· difficult
	43–10	is the one l· likely to
	55– 3	and the l· understanding . . . thereof
	59–27	who asserts himself the l·,
	80–30	at l· not until it shall come to
	119–22	Insubordination . . . even in the l·,
	126– 4	for once, at l·, to hear the soft

least

Mis.	224–10	* I don't feel hurt in the *l*."
	228– 3	by those deemed at *l*· indebted
	291–12	or at *l*· it so appears in results.
	356–17	"the *l*· of all seeds," — *Matt.* 13 : 32.
Man.	68– 2	member of this Church at *l*· three
	73– 4	at *l*· one active practitioner
	110–12	one, at *l*·, of the given names
Ret.	28–11	in order to have the *l*· understanding
Un.	56–21	he suffers *l*· from sin who is
Pul.	32– 4	* No photographs can do the *l*· justice
	35–15	in order to have the *l*· understanding
	55– 7	* not the *l*· eventful circumstance is
	80– 8	* sought the line of *l*· resistance.
	82–25	* at *l*· to help enforce the laws
	82–29	* and in this fair land at *l*·
	87–16	If it will comfort you in the *l*·,
No.	21–28	and is, to say the *l*·,
Pan.	6–23	religion has at *l*· two Gods.
'02.	2–25	or at *l*· agree to disagree,
	18–15	unto one of the *l*· — *Matt.* 25 : 40.
My.	88–28	* at *l*· an æsthetic debt to
	91–29	* at *l*· it is the largest in
	174–10	And last but not *l*·,
	182–14	seemed the *l*· among seeds,
	197– 3	*l*· distinct to conscience.
	228–14	"He that is *l*· — *Matt.* 11 : 11.
	228–16	reign of holiness, in the *l*·
	240– 2	from the *l*· to the greatest,

leave

Mis.	37–12	*l*· the animal for the spiritual,
	43–30	the damaging effects these *l*·
	80–13	who *l*· C. S. to rise or fall
	194–22	*how to l*· self, the sense material,
	215– 5	peace I *l*· with thee : — *see John* 14 : 27.
	235–24	*l*· Christianity unbiased by
	249–24	will never *l*· me comfortless,
	264–20	Some students *l*· my instructions
	270–21	we cannot *l*· Christ for the
	274–10	therefore I *l*· all for Christ.
	293– 4	*l*· the righteous unfolding of error
	301–16	must not *l*· persistent plagiarists
	302–17	*not to l*· the Word unspoken
	324–21	seeks to *l*· the odious company
Ret.	23– 1	to *l*· me undisturbed in the
	63–24	and *l*· the subject there.
	79–15	*l*· the inscrutable problem
	83–20	*l*· S. and H. to God's
	90–29	*l*· with God the government
Un.	1–15	better *l*· the subject untouched,
Pul.	69–12	*l*· no room there for the bad,
No.	v–11	*l*· the meat and take the
	7–25	*L*· the distinctions of individual
	34– 4	shall *l*· the ceremonial law
	45–25	*l*· cradle and swaddling-clothes.
'00.	2–21	*l*· a lucrative business to
'01.	5–17	*l*· all sin to God's fiat
'02.	11– 1	to *l*· on a foreign shore.
Hea.	13–16	*l*· the drug out of the question,
	16–16	we will *l*· our abstract subjects
Peo.	6–26	for which we are to *l*· all else.
Po.	27–15	Though thou must *l*· the tear,
My.	6–27	* were obliged to *l*· the church
	114–20	would *l*· me until the rising of the
	117– 6	motive gratified by sense will *l*·
	130– 1	*l*· the latter to propagate
	138–18	except I *l*· all for Christ.
	155–11	*l*· behind those things that
	167–12	*l*· their loving benedictions upon
	192–27	and *l*· a leaf of olive ;
	242–23	*l*· these duties to the Clerk
	311– 9	* I shall have to *l*· ;
	323–10	* nor willingly *l*· any false impression.
	325– 4	* to *l*· luscious hothouse fruit.

leaven

Mis.	39–20	enough of the *l*· of Truth
	39–20	to *l*· the whole lump.
	149– 6	to help *l*· your loaf
	166–22	*l*· that a certain woman hid
	171–23	*is like unto l*·, — *Matt.* 13 : 33.
	174–30	The *l*· which a woman took
	175– 8	spiritual *l*· of divine Science
	175–13	the *l*· expands the loaf.
	175–14	the old *l*· of the scribes
	175–15	"the *l*· of malice — *I Cor.* 5 : 8.
	366–18	the *l*· of the scribes — *see Matt.* 16 : 6.
Pul.	5–28	This book is the *l*· fermenting
'02.	2–16	*l*· hid in three measures
Po.	24– 3	A balm — the long-lost *l*·
My.	4–12	with the *l*· of divine Love
	59– 5	* the little *l*· that should *l*·

leavened

Mis.	166–26	until the whole shall be *l*·
	171–24	*till the whole was l*·. — *Matt.* 13 : 33.
	175– 5	the whole sense of being is *l*·

leavening

Mis.	166–24	C. S., is *l*· the lump
My.	114–28	this book is *l*· the whole lump

leavens

No.	43–11	* "Your book *l*· my sermons."
My.	272– 2	*l*· the loaf of life with justice,

leaves

Mis.	6– 3	*l*· mortals but little time
	31–17	*l*· the individual no alternative
	130– 4	She readily *l*· the answer
	142–18	shaded as autumn *l*·
	165–13	*l*· nothing that is material ;
	188–19	right there he *l*· the subject.
	251–25	falling *l*· of old-time faiths
	251–28	even as dry *l*· fall
	330–1	the *l*· clap their hands,
	331–22	falling *l*· of old-time faiths,
	341– 3	*l*· the unreal material basis
	390–17	The timid, trembling *l*·.
Man.	68– 6	member who *l*· her in less time
	69– 8	*l*· her before the expiration of
Ret.	18– 5	colored softly by blossom and *l*· ;
	75–23	when he *l*· the University,
	94–12	*l*· no flesh, no matter,
	95– 2	and its *l*· will be
Pul.	8– 4	the *l*· of an ancient oak,
	26–24	* with sprays of fig *l*·
Rud.	14–23	*l*· them unprepared to
No.	2– 7	*l*· you to work against that
'00.	4–18	*l*· the beaten path of human
	5– 4	*l*· no opportunity for idolatry
'02.	9–16	that *l*· the minor tones
Peo.	14– 4	evergreen *l*·, fragrant recesses,
Po.	9– 9	*l*· all faded, the fruitage shed,
	16–18	To the heart of the *l*·
	46– 6	Its *l*· have shed
	55–18	The timid, trembling *l*·.
	63–14	softly by blossom and *l*· ;
My.	3–10	*l*· of faith without works,
	89–11	* sect that *l*· such a monument
	99–29	* *l*· no choice but the acceptance
	218–17	*l*· the divine Principle of
	260–27	It *l*· hygiene, medicine,
	347–13	* that cannot shed Your *l*·,

leaving

Mis.	11–22	not *l*· all retribution to God
	34– 1	*l*· none of the harmful "after effects"
	37–27	*l*· to her students the work of
	58–27	*l*· it a human "mind-cure,"
	111–15	*L*· the seed of Truth to its
	240–30	or, *l*· these on,
	242–24	*l*· the patient well.
	242–29	before *l*· the class he took a
	358–31	*l*· the material forms thereof
Ret.	84–29	he should avoid *l*· his own
No.	19–24	*l*· sin, sense rises to the fulness
'01.	26–25	Before *l*· this subject of the
'02.	3–13	*l*· her in the enjoyment of
Peo.	7– 2	*l*· the impress of mind
	7– 4	*l*· to rot and ruin the mind's ideals.
	9– 5	love *l*· self for God.
My.	196–16	*l*· us an example, — *I Pet.* 2 : 21.
	263– 2	*l*· one alone and without His glory.
	301– 7	*l*· a solid Christianity at the
	350– 2	*l*· science at the beck of
	350– 3	*l*· it out of the question.

Lebanon, Ind.

Pul.	70– 1	* *The Reporter, L*·, *I*·.,

Lebanon, Pa.

Pul.	88–29	* *Evening Reporter, L*·, *P*·.

lecture

Mis.	280–19	at close of the *l*· on the fourth
Man.	73–20	may *l*· for said university
	93– 8	The *l*· year shall begin July 1
	93–12	to include in each *l*· a true
	94– 3	unite in their attendance on his *l*·,
	94– 4	for their churches a less *l*· fee ;
	94– 7	after a *l*· on C. S.,
	94–18	shall *l*· in the United States,
	95– 7	to *l*· at such places
	95–15	a member of the Board may *l*·
	95–20	No *l*· shall be given by a
	96– 3	shall not appoint a *l*· for
	96– 4	*L*· Fee.
	96– 4	The *l*· fee shall be left to
	96–10	If a lecturer receive a call to *l*·
Ret.	40–22	my notices for a second *l*·
No.	27–19	Bishop Foster said, in a *l*·
Peo.	5–26	Wendell Holmes said, in a *l*·
My.	296– 1	chapter sub-title
	304–15	invited to *l*· in London,
	304–21	In a *l*· in Chicago,

lecture
My. 338–11 The contents of the last *l·*
338–13 till after the *l·* was delivered
338–19 talented author of this *l·*

lectured
Ret. 42– 9 *l·* so ably on Scriptural topics
My. 304–12 I have *l·* in large and crowded

lecturer (see also lecturer's)
Man. 94– 1 The *l·* can invite churches
96– 5 the discretion of the *l·*.
96– 9 If a *l·* receive a call
Rud. 11–25 The *l·*, teacher, or healer

lecturer's
Man. 96– 6 The *l·* traveling expenses

lecturers
Man. 93–10 Duty of *L·*.

lectures
Mis. 48–13 at one of his recent *l·*
Man. 93–16 shall mail . . . copies of his *l·*
95– 2 CALLS FOR *l·*.
95–16 Annual *L·*.
95–19 for one or more *l·*.
95–20 No *L·* by Readers.
96– 1 No Wednesday Evening *L·*.
Pul. 36– 9 * I was present at the class *l·*
47– 2 * *l·* upon Scriptural topics.
Rud. 15–26 Public *l·* cannot be such
16– 2 public *l·* can take the place of
16– 5 *L·* in public are needed.
My. 125–16 When reading their *l·*,

Lectureship
(see **Board of Lectureship**)

lectureship
Mis. 95– 2 * platform of the Monday *l·*

lecturing
Mis. 239– 6 *L·*, writing, preaching,
266–25 in teaching or *l·* on C. S.,

led
Mis. 85–30 are thereby *l·* to Christ,
225–18 * I may be *l·* to believe."
278–32 *l·* to some startling departures
296– 8 which *l·* the unknown author
301–16 to be long *l·* into temptation ;
326–19 if they would be *l·* to the valley
Ret. 9– 2 *l·* my cousin into an adjoining
24–14 *l·* me to the discovery
27–29 *l·* me into a new world of light
30–19 Even so was I *l·* into
48–29 has *l·* to higher ways, means, and
50– 4 *l·* to name three hundred dollars
50– 8 *l·*, by a strange providence,
81–29 *l·* me to the feet of C. S.,
Pul. 43– 3 * *l·* the singing, under the
Pan. 14–23 *l·* by the dauntless Dewey,
'00. 12–13 *l·* northward and southward.
'02. 15–28 had *l·* me to write that book,
Po. 2– 9 Guided and *l·*, can never reach
My. 110–26 "*l·* captivity captive," — *Psal.* 68 : 18.
212– 1 victim is *l·* to believe
314– 5 * *l·* a roving existence.

lees
My. 301– 6 the *l·* of religion will be lost,

left
Mis. 14– 2 neither place nor power *l·* for evil.
34–18 no more come to those they have *l·*,
65–11 *L·* to the decision of Science,
69–16 and then had *l·* him to die.
75– 1 may have all that is *l·* of it ;
89–18 *l·* this precaution for others.
90–29 *l·* their nets to follow him,
100– 3 *l·* to the providence of God.
106– 8 M. D.'s to *l·* of them,
165–18 *l·* to mortals the rich legacy
169–21 *l·* for our spiritual instruction.
178– 4 He has *l·* his old church,
179–16 Have we *l·* the consciousness of
180– 9 "Christ never *l·*," I replied ;
188–22 And she has *not l·* it,
212– 6 *l·* his glorious career for our
267–19 while the *l·* beats its way downward,
274– 8 if *l·* undone might hinder the
310–28 all persons who have *l·* our fold,
326–27 is *l·* unto you desolate." — *Matt.* 23 : 38.
340– 8 neither to the right nor to the *l·*,
343–24 until no seedling be *l·* to propagate
348–13 Error, *l·* to itself, accumulates.
355–17 To strike out right and *l·*
378– 4 *l·* that institution,
378–10 *l·* the water-cure,
Man. 86–10 whose teacher has *l·* them,
87– 6 Choice of patients is *l·* to the
91–16 Any surplus funds *l·* in the

left
Man. 96– 5 *l·* to the discretion of the
Ret. 5– 2 *l·* bank of the Merrimac River.
8–21 I then *l·* the room,
14–18 *l·* me outside the doors.
16– 7 since she *l·* the choir
38–16 afternoon that he *l·* Boston
90– 9 and then *l·* them to starve
Un. 5–26 *l·* to the supernal guidance.
42– 2 there is no place *l·* for it.
Pul. 42–29 * on its *l·* a vase filled with
47–29 * nothing is *l·* excepting the
59–29 * *l·* by the rear doors,
81–25 * all that the twelve have *l·* **undone.**
83–30 * and he, departing, *l·* his scepter
Rud. 13–27 but *l·* to be fed, clothed, and
15– 3 *l·* it understanding sufficiently the
No. 30– 6 until nothing is *l·* to be forgiven,
36– 6 never *l·* heaven for earth.
'00. 12–18 *l·* thy first love — *Rev.* 2 : 4.
15–23 *l·* thy first love, — *Rev.* 2 : 4.
'01. 10–26 shall be nothing *l·* to perish
23– 3 little *l·* that the sects and
26–18 *l·* to such as see God
26–19 *l·* to them of a sound faith
27–24 and *l·* C. S. as it is,
29– 8 should not be *l·* to the mercy of
'02. 2–26 I never *l·* the Church,
2–27 I but began where the Church *l·* off.
7–14 nothing is *l·* to consciousness but
Po. 41–11 forsaken, and *l·* them to stray
65– 8 And *l·* but a parting in air.
68– 1 So one heart is *l·* me
My. 50– 4 * *l·* their former church homes,
92–18 * would soon be *l·* behind.
94– 2 * every other sect will be *l·* behind
99–17 * not a cent of indebtedness *l·*.
107–12 have not an iota of the drug *l·*
117–28 I *l·* Boston in the height of
126– 8 his *l·* foot on the earth," — *Rev.* 10 : 2.
130–18 A lie *l·* to itself is not
214–22 I had no monetary means *l·*
232–12 Our Lord and Master *l·* to us the
246–13 closed my College . . . *l·* Boston,
257– 7 the Bethlehem babe has *l·* his
303–22 he *l·* his legacy of truth
312– 8 * He *l·* his young wife in a
317–17 *l·* my diction quite out of the
322–31 * the impression he *l·* with me **was**
323– 2 * Before we *l·* that evening,
333–27 * He has *l·* an amiable wife,

legacies
My. 201–11 repeat my *l·* in blossom.

legacy
Mis. 2–11 Adam *l·* must first be seen,
124–25 Love's great *l·* to mortals,
165–18 left to mortals the rich *l·* of
Ret. 92– 7 inherit his *l·* of love,
Pul. 87–25 a *l·* to our race.
My. 303–22 he left his *l·* of truth

legal
Mis. 140–10 over matter or merely *l·* titles.
140–13 I supposed the trustee-deed was *l·* ;
140–22 rescued from the grasp of *l·* power,
141–18 concerned about the *l·* quibble,
141–28 no *l·* authority for obtaining,
Man. 45–23 *L·* Titles.
46– 4, 5 *l·* adoption and *l·* marriage,
49–19 A *L·* Ceremony.
67–10 Unauthorized *L·* Action.
67–12 nor take *l·* action on a case
70–22 the *l·* title of The Mother Church.
Ret. 49–20 granted to a *l· college* for teaching
'02. 13–19 through my *l·* counsel.
13–20 *l·* proceedings were instituted by
My. 217–13 shall have arrived at *l·* age,
327– 6 made it *l·* to practise C. S.
327–28 * *l·* protection and recognition,

legalized
My. 5– 5 synonymous with *l·* lust,

legally
Mis. 226–27 cannot stoop to notice, except *l·*,
249–10 has been met and answered *l·*.
272–25 * but one *l·* chartered college
297– 6 by *l·* coercive measures,
297–23 or this contract is *l·* dissolved.
Man. 49–21 clergyman who is *l·* authorized.
75–17 land whereon they stand, *l·* ;
78– 7 shall not be made *l·* responsible
'02. 13–26 land *l·* conveyed to me,
My. 327– 1 *l·* to protect the practice

legendary
Ret. 22– 7 *l·* and traditional history

legends
    Pul. 28– 7 * emblematic designs, with the *l*·,

legerdemain
    My. 195–21 no miserable piece of ideal *l*·,

legibly
    Man. 109–16 see that names are *l*· written,

legion
    Mis. 366–31 false theories whose names are *l*·,
    Pul. 81–20 * and their name is *l*·.

legislation
    Mis. 80–16 unjust coercive *l*·
    211–10 medical bills, class *l*·,
    274–24 news-dealers shout for class *l*·,
    Peo. 11–20 obedient to the *l*· of mind,
    My. 128– 6 board of health, or class *l*·
    340–12 and her frown on class *l*·.

legislative
    Mis. 208– 6 Like a *l*· bill that governs
    Peo. 11–19 as men pass *l*· acts
    My. 167–24 disposal of the *l*· question

legislator
    No. 30–10 any more than the *l*· need know

legislators
    Mis. 208– 7 mortals whom the *l*· know not,
    Peo. 11–22 *l*· who are greatly responsible

Legislature
    Ret. 6–25 was soon elected to the *L*·
    6–28 were carried through the *L*·
    My. 310– 7 member of the New Hampshire *L*·,
    327– 4 in the *L*· of North Carolina,
    327–14 * last winter's term of our *L*·,
    327–20 * section of an act in the *L*·,
    328–11 * passed by the last *L*·,
    328–23 * machinery act of the *L*·

legislatures
    My. 326– 3 * *l*· and courts are thus

legitimate
    Mis. 287– 9 the *l*· affection of Soul,
    Un. 22–16 though not so *l*· a child of
    54–18 becomes *l*· to mortals,
    No. 9–10 to prevent their *l*· action
    44–18 *l*· to the human race,
    '02. 14–14 are its *l*· fruit.
    My. 37–21 * the activities of *l*· existence,
    41–25 * postpone his *l*· joy,
    159–22 *l*· and eternal demands

legs
    My. 178–12 * "counting the *l*· of insects"?

Leibnitz
    No. 22– 4 *L*·, Descartes, Fichte,
    '01. 24–18 *L*·, Berkeley, Darwin,

lend
    Mis. 146– 6 I cannot conscientiously *l*· my
    342–19 "Oh, *l*· us your oil!— *see Matt.* 25 : 8.
    My. 211–18 *l*· themselves as willing tools

lends
    Mis. 320–10 *l*· its resplendent light
    Pul. 53–27 * healing gift he *l*· to them
    My. 158–14 to-day *l*· a new-born beauty

length
    Mis. x– 4 has at *l*· offered itself for
    xi–17 at *l*· be found to surpass
    29–26 health and *l*· of days.
    67–16 happiness, and *l*· of days.
    120–17 will at *l*· be heard above the din
    223– 4 at *l*· took up the research
    227– 4 must at *l*· be given up
    286–32 stop at *l*· at the spiritual ultimate :
    291–23 at *l*· dissolve into thin air.
    324–29 at *l*· reaches the pleasant path
    326– 9 the flesh at *l*· did feel them ;
    My. 195–20 C. S. is at *l*· learned to be
    273–27 at *l*· they are consigned to dust.

lengthen
    Mis. 352–12 shadows of thought *l*·

lengthened
    My. 52–32 * weeks *l*· into months ;

lengthens
    My. 146–10 "If wisdom *l*· my sum of years
    177–10 if wisdom *l*· my sum of years

length'ning
    Po. 3– 4 noonday's *l*· shadows flee,

leniency
    No. 9–15 too great *l*·, on my part,

lens
    Mis. 129–20 to magnify under the *l*· that
    164–27 by means of the *l*· of Science,
    194–16 The *l*· of Science magnifies the

lens
    Mis. 299– 6 look through the *l*· of C. S.,
    356–25 Humility is *l*· and prism to
    Ret. 87–25 only through the *l*· of their
    '01. 12–22 The *l*· of Science magnifies the
    My. 129–15 seen through the *l*· of Spirit,

lenses
    Pul. vii–12 its *l*· of more spiritual mentality,

lent
    Pul. 45– 1 * *l*· a helping hand,

leopard
    Mis. 145–23 *l*· shall lie down with— *Isa.* 11 : 6.

leper
    Mis. 124–18 healing the sick, cleansing the *l*·,

lepers
    Mis. 168– 7 physical and moral *l*· are cleansed ;
    Pul. 29–18 * cleanse the *l*·,— *Matt.* 10 : 8.
    53–11 * When the ten *l*· were cleansed
    66–12 * cleanse the *l*·,— *Matt.* 10 : 8.
    My. 300–26 cleanse the *l*·,— *Matt.* 10 : 8.

leprosy
    Pul. 29–23 * to cleanse the *l*· of sin,
    53–11 * Can drugs suddenly cure *l*·?

less
    Mis. 17–23 birth is more or *l*· prolonged
    36– 8 they manifest *l*· of Mind.
    38–29 be of *l*· practical value.
    47–16 with *l*· impediment than when
    58–27 "mind-cure," nothing more nor *l*·,
    60– 6 regard sin, . . . with *l*· deference,
    62–13 by that much, *l*· available.
    76–19 on other topics *l*· important.
    85–19 infantile and more or *l*· imperfect.
    88– 4 but the *l*· this is required,
    108–26 This cognomen makes it *l*· dangerous ;
    126–24 even gold is *l*· current.
    145–12 *l*· than man to whom God gave
    145–13 *l*· than the meek who
    155–18 and *l*· wherein to answer it
    163–16 *l*· human and more divine
    186–24 cannot produce a *l*· perfect man
    217– 5 Spirit cannot become *l*· than Spirit ;
    229–21 would thus become beautifully *l*·;
    231–12 turkey grew beautifully *l*·.
    239– 8 my shadow is not growing *l*· ;
    243–11 effected the cure in *l*· than one
    250–10 no sentiment *l*· understood.
    264–22 students are more or *l*· subject to
    271–12 books which are *l*· than the best.
    272–17 * fine not *l*· than five hundred
    278–19 shared *l*· of my labors than many
    282–12 much *l*· would we have our minds
    283–16 nothing *l*· than a mistaken
    289– 9 and of two evils choose the *l*· ;
    302–17 of two evils the *l*· would be
    316–12 Until minds become *l*· worldly-minded,
    318– 8 who are *l*· lovable or Christly.
    319–12 *l*· or more to them than to other
    321– 4 whose birth is *l*· of a miracle than
    327–17 those who, having *l*· baggage,
    355– 6 *L*· teaching and good healing
    366–23 To a greater or *l*· extent,
    370–20 What figure is *l*· favorable than
    370–22 braying donkey . . . is *l*· troublesome.
    374–32 *l*· artistic or less natural
    Man. 44–14 tax of not *l*· than one dollar,
    54– 4 for not *l*· than three years
    68– 6 leaves her in *l*· time without
    73– 1 not be organized with *l*· than sixteen
    79– 4 not *l*· than three loyal members
    87–18 "The *l*· the teacher personally
    90–17 Not *l*· than two thorough lessons
    94– 4 so make . . . a *l*· lecture fee ;
    94–17 shall not be *l*· than three years.
    97–14 not *l*· than four thousand dollars.
    102– 5 not *l*· than three members,
    Ret. 10– 3 *l*· labor than is usually requisite.
    22– 5 Writers *l*· wise than the apostles
    33–12 the *l*· material medicine we have,
    34– 4 Nothing *l*· could solve the
    45–24 withstood *l*· the temptation
    47–18 who partakes *l*· of God's love.
    52– 7 its letter and *l*· of its spirit.
    54– 5 It demands *l*· cross-bearing,
    73–10 human concept grew beautifully *l*·
    73–12 personal corporeality became *l*·
    84–24 The *l*· the teacher personally controls
    87–23 They feel their own burdens *l*·,
    Un. 6–28 *l*· than another fifty years
    28–14 and have *l*· basis ;
    49– 7 I believe *l*· in the sinner,
    50–19 The *l*· consciousness of evil
    Pul. 3– 4 Can Love be *l*· than boundless?

less

Pul.	10–20	If you are *l·* appreciated to-day
	51–11	* Every truth is more or *l·*
	62–18	* with infinitely *l·* expense.
	87–20	more of earth now, . . . and *l·* of heaven ;
Rud.	2–13	if we think of Him as *l·* than
	9– 6	more or *l·* blended with error ;
	15– 9	renders the mind *l·* inquisitive,
No.	17–11	can never be *l·* than a good man ;
	24–15	become both *l·* and more in C. S.,
	24–18	and *l·*, because evil, being thus
	37–18	would make the atonement to be *l·*
Pan.	10– 2	and makes man *l·* than man.
	10–15	With twelve lessons or *l·*,
	11–20	content with something *l·* than
'01.	5– 6	become *l·* coherent than the
	8–19	can man be . . . *l·* than spiritual?
	18– 2	one thousand degrees *l·*
	18– 5	*l·* now than were the sneers
	23– 1	neither more nor *l·* than three ;
	27–22	*l·* of my own personality
'02.	9– 7	pride, and ease concern you *l·*,
	18–24	effective healers and *l·* theorizing ;
Hea.	1– 9	*l·* than an immortal basis,
	1–14	*l·* need of publishing the
	9– 6	The *l·* said or thought of sin,
	11–19	"The *l·* medicine the better,"
	13– 3	accomplish *l·* on either side.
Peo.	6–10	* *l·* sickness and *l·* mortality
	7–29	become more or *l·* perfect as
	7–30	more or *l·* spiritual.
Po.	35– 4	love thee as I love life *l·* !
My.	21–24	* to make no *l·* sacrifice than
	22–22	* nothing *l·* than God-bestowed.
	24–22	* no *l·* than fifteen different trades
	26–14	but not the *l·* appreciated.
	59– 8	* in *l·* than forty years
	66– 6	* no *l·* than ten estates having been
	77–14	* not *l·* than twenty-five thousand
	98– 5	* growth of *l·* than a score of years.
	98–20	* little *l·* than three years.
	99–22	* *L·* than a generation ago
	107–15	administers half a dozen or *l·*
	113– 3	not *l·* the evangel of C. S.
	123–22	is *l·* sufficient to receive a
	128– 7	class legislation is *l·* than the
	128– 8	and infinitely *l·* than God's benign
	147–31	You have *l·* need of me
	160– 9	It is of *l·* importance that we
	178–11	*l·* profitable or scientific
	220–30	seems *l·* divine,
	224–20	more fashionable but *l·* correct.
	224–23	books *l·* correct and therefore *l·*
	259–15	require *l·* attention than packages
	259–20	nothing *l·* is man or woman.
	265– 6	*l·* subordinate to material sight
	265– 7	evil flourishes *l·* invests *l·*
	265–27	*l·* thunderbolts, tornadoes, and
	302–21	*l·* lauded, pampered, provided for,
	363–28	this . . . is more or *l·* dangerous.

lessen

'01.	15– 7	Scientist has enlisted to *l·* sin,
My.	200–27	spare this plunge, *l·* its depths,

lessened

Mis.	60–21	Mind's possibilities are not *l·* by
My.	296–17	mortal dream . . . has been *l·*,

lessening

Mis.	86– 7	though in *l·* degrees
My.	164– 2	would involve a *l·* of the

lessens

Mis.	122–21	*l·* not the hater's hatred
	362–31	*l·* the activities of virtue.
Pan.	10– 9	opposite notion that C. S. *l·*
My.	134–17	Life *l·* all pride — its pomp and

lesser

Un.	33– 1	There are *l·* arguments which prove
Hea.	14– 2	the bigger animal beats the *l·* ;
My.	252–31	cold impulse of a *l·* gain !

Lesson

Mis.	314–30	this *L·* shall be such as is

lesson

Mis.	10–17	The best *l·* of their lives
	10–28	mortals learn at last the *l·*,
	92–19	point out the *l·* to the class,
	125–17	press on to Life's long *l·*,
	126–20	silent *l·* of a good example.
	129– 6	first *l·* is to learn one's self ;
	138–15	first and last *l·* of C. S.
	207– 1	ponder this *l·* of love.
	278–27	the sooner this *l·* is gained
	310– 9	is the *l·* of to-day.
	336– 2	Hath not Science voiced this *l·*

lesson

Mis.	392–12	A *l·* grave, of life, that teacheth
Man.	31– 8	reading of the Sunday *l·*,
	31– 8	a *l·* on which the prosperity
	32–16	made but once during the *l·*.
Ret.	83–26	study each *l·* before the recitation.
	91–13	Where did Jesus deliver this great *l·*
Pul.	29–22	* *l·* was to be taken spiritually
No.	28–11	time for beginning the *l·*.
Po.	20–16	A *l·* grave, of life,
My.	34–29	* S. and H. references in this *l·*
	109–12	teaching them the same heavenly *l·*.
	150– 2	where its tender *l·* is not awaiting
	244–25	may not require more than one *l·*.

lessons

Mis.	3– 9	The *l·* we learn in
	81–30	It gives *l·* to human life,
	84–28	teaches Life's *l·* aright.
	91–31	study the *l·* before recitations.
	128– 3	*l·* of this so-called life
	180–20	chapter sub-title
	197– 1	incorporates their *l·* into our
	264–15	They are taught their first *l·*
	330–24	Nature's first and last *l·*
	349– 2	*l·* outside of my College,
	349– 3	provided he received these *l·* of
	349– 4	included about twelve *l·*,
	371– 1	this is among the first *l·*
	393–22	*L·* long and grand,
Man.	62–24	Subject for *L·*.
	62–25	The first *l·* of the children
	63– 4	The next *l·* consist of
	90–18	Not less than two thorough *l·*
Ret.	10– 9	received *l·* in the ancient tongues,
	21–23	lucid and enduring *l·* of Love
	23– 6	As these pungent *l·* became
	50– 6	course of *l·* at my College,
	50–14	even in half as many *l·*.
	81–30	Though our first *l·* are changed,
	91–14	this series of great *l·*
Un.	3– 1	*l·* of this primary school
Pul.	1–12	by reason of its large *l·*,
Rud.	15–27	cannot be such *l·* in C. S. as
	16– 3	take the place of private *l·* ;
Pan.	10–15	With twelve *l·* or less,
Po.	52– 6	*L·* long and grand,
My.	61– 4	* and the *l·* I have learned
	186– 4	writes in living characters their *l·*
	231–25	chapter sub-title
	231–30	the By-law, "Subject for *L·*"
	244– 8	one or more *l·* on C. S.,
	244–26	*l·* will certainly not exceed three

Lesson-Sermon

Man.	32–21	no remarks explanatory of the *L·*
	58–11	The *L·*.
	58–12	The subject of the *L·*
	58–16	texts in the *L·* shall extend from
My.	32–28	* the specially prepared *L·*.
	32–29	* After the reading of the *L·*,
	33– 8	* subject of the special *L·*
	34–14	* *L·* consisted of the following
	78–17	* At the close of the *L·*,

Lesson-Sermon on Dedication Sunday, June, 1906

My. pages 34, 35 references from Bible and S. and H.

lest

Mis.	109–29	*l·* thereby it master you ;
	210–31	*l·* it should suffer from
	211–19	afraid to do this *l·* he suffer,
	347– 2	*l·* thou also be like — *Prov.* 26 : 4.
	348–15	*l·* he be wise in — *Prov.* 26 : 5.
	398– 2	*L·* my footsteps stray ;
Ret.	46– 8	*L·* my footsteps stray ;
Un.	22– 7	not touch it, *l·* ye die.
	49–27	*l·* it destroy them.
Pul.	17– 7	*L·* my footsteps stray ;
No.	8–24	*l·* it turn and rend you ;
	40– 9	*l·* your pearls be trampled upon.
'01.	11–27	*l·* thou also be like — *Prov.* 26 : 4.
Po.	14– 6	*L·* my footsteps stray ;
My.	v– 2	* *L·* we forget — *l·* we forget !
	161–23	*L·* human reason becloud
	196–21	*l·* ye be wearied and faint — *Heb.* 12 : 3.
	201–22	*L·* my footsteps stray ;
	227–24	*l·* they trample them — *Matt.* 7 : 6.
	288–26	*l·* a worse thing come — *John* 5 : 14.

let

Mis.	3–30	"Satan *l·* loose." — *see Rev.* 20 : 7.
	10–11	God will not *l·* them be lost ;
	47–14	*l·* loose from its own beliefs.
	59–20	*l·* us reason together." — *Isa.* 1 : 18.
	69–10	"*L·* us make man — *Gen.* 1 : 26.
	69–11	*l·* them have dominion — *Gen.* 1 : 26.

let

Mis.	81– 6	*l·* each society of practitioners,
	87– 7	*l·* us say of the beauties of
	91– 7	*l·* it be in concession to the
	111–27	*L·* me specially call the attention
	120–15	*L·* us rejoice, however, that
	121–27	nor *l·* me go." — *Luke* 22 : 68.
	122–17	"*L·* us do evil, that — *Rom.* 3 : 8.
	129– 4	*l·* him put his finger to his lips,
	129–13	"*l·* the dead bury their — *Matt.* 8 : 22.
	129–13	*l·* silence prevail over his remains.
	131– 8	*l·* the leaner sort console this
	131–15	*l·* it do so ;
	131–26	*l·* her state the value thereof,
	134–17	*L·* no consideration bend or
	141–19	*L·* this be speedily done.
	141–21	*l·* the divine will and the
	141–29	and *l·* them, not you, say
	142–13	*L·* me write to the donors,
	145– 9	*l·* him ask himself, and answer
	145–16	*l·* not mortal thought resuscitate too
	145–32	*l·* me say, 'T is sweet to
	148–28	*L·* the invitation to this sweet
	154–28	*L·* your light reflect Light.
	156–11	*L·* the reign of peace and harmony
	158–22	*L·* us be faithful and obedient,
	169–30	"*L·* the dead bury their — *Matt.* 8 : 22.
	172– 4	*l·* us declare the positive
	172– 7	*l·* us meet and defeat the claims of
	174– 6	*L·* us have a clearing up of
	174– 6	*L·* us come into the presence
	174– 8	*L·* us attach our sense of Science to
	174–10	*L·* us open our affections to
	180–18	*L·* us do our work ;
	186–18	*l·* us not lose this Science of man,
	191–31	*L·* us obey St. Paul's injunction
	194– 5	*L·* us, then, seek this Science ;
	197–12	*l·* us see what it is to believe.
	197–20	"*l·* this Mind be in you, — *Phil.* 2 : 5.
	197–29	*L·* man abjure a theory that is
	208–12	and to *l·* His will be done.
	208–15	to do His will or to *l·* it be done?
	211–22	When one protects . . . *l·* him remember,
	211–29	drink it all, and *l·* all drink of it.
	215– 7	Arise, *l·* us go hence ; — *John* 14 : 31.
	215– 7	*l·* us depart from the material
	215–10	*l·* us not seek to climb up some other
	220– 4	*L·* us suppose that there is a
	230– 6	*l·* him make the most of the
	230–22	* "*L·* us, then, be up and doing,
	238–19	*L·* one's life answer
	239– 1	*l·* me say to you, dear reader :
	240–14	*l·* it remain as harmlessly,
	253–19	come, *l·* us kill him, — *Luke* 20 : 14.
	254–14	come, *l·* us kill him, — *Luke* 20 : 14.
	267– 9	*l·* them remember that there never
	268–24	*l·* us not adulterate His
	270– 1	*l·* us take the side of him who
	270–26	*l·* him glory in the Lord." — *I Cor* 1 : 31.
	277–22	*l·* the earth rejoice." — *Psal.* 97 : 1.
	284–25	Evil *l·* alone grows more real,
	289– 5	Drunkenness is sensuality *l·* loose,
	290– 2	*L·* other people's marriage relations
	298– 5	*L·* us do evil, that good may — *Rom.* 3 : 8.
	299– 6	*L·* us look through the lens of C. S.,
	303–13	*L·* us serve instead of rule,
	309–29	*L·* them soberly adhere to the
	310–16	"*L·* all things be done — *I Cor.* 14 : 40.
	319–20	*l·* the present season pass without
	328– 2	"*L·* them alone ; they must learn
	330–15	*l·* mortals bow before the creator,
	343– 1	*L·* us watch and pray
	343– 3	*l·* us not forget that others
	345– 9	* "*L·* them come ;
	346–26	lift the curtain, *l·* in the light,
	355–26	*L·* no clouds of sin gather
	356–19	Now *l·* my faithful students
	357– 4	*L·* Christian Scientists minister **to**
	357– 5	*L·* them seek the lost sheep
	358–26	*L·* Scientists who have grown
	361–17	"*L·* us lay aside — *Heb.* 12 ; 1.
	361–19	*l·* us run with patience — *Heb.* 12 : 1.
	363–14	"*L·* us [Spirit] make man perfect ;"
	368– 3	Even so, Father, *l·* the light
	368–27	*l·* us not forget that the
	370– 9	*L·* the sentinels of Zion's
	388– 3	"*L·* there be light, — *Gen.* 1 : 3.
Man.	41–21	*l·* the reign of divine Truth,
	60–18	"*L·* the dead bury their — *Matt.* 8 : 22.
	60–25	*L·* the ceremony be devout.
Ret.	55– 3	*L·* us follow the example of Jesus,
	61–29	*L·* there be milk for babes,
	61–29	*l·* not the milk be adulterated,
	85–10	*l·* down from the heaven of Truth
	87– 1	*l·* the dead bury their — *Matt.* 8 : 22.
	87–14	*L·* some of these rules be

let

Un.	1– 8	*L·* us then reason together
	5–19	*L·* us respect the rights of
	5–21	*L·* no enmity, no untempered
	5–25	*l·* the stately goings of this
	8– 1	*L·* another query now be
	12– 4	but *l·* them apply to the
	18– 2	*l·* us think of God as saying,
	35– 2	*L·* mortal mind change,
	39–20	*l·* Science declare the immortal
	60–19	then *l·* them serve Him,
Pul.	10–23	*L·* us rejoice that chill vicissitudes
	21–11	*L·* this be our Christian endeavor
Rud.	5– 3	"*L·* God be true, — *Rom.* 3 : 4.
No.	8– 4	*l·* us add one more privilege
	8–26	*l·* the unwise pass by,
	9– 8	*l·* your opponents alone,
	30– 5	will not *l·* sin go until it is
	45–13	*L·* it not be heard in Boston
	45–24	*L·* the Word have free course
	46–17	*l·* us lift their standard higher,
Pan.	6– 5	*l·* us continue to denounce evil
'00.	14– 9	Beloved, *l·* him that hath an ear
	14–17	*l·* no root of bitterness spring up
'01.	3– 9	*L·* us examine this.
	9–20	"*L·* us alone ; — *Mark* 1 : 24.
	16–11	*l·* the dead bury its dead,
	19–16	*L·* us remember that the
	26–17	*L·* it be left to such as
'02.	2– 4	To live and *l·* live,
	4– 7	*L·* us all pray at this Communion
	9– 5	*l·* the dead bury their — *Matt.* 8 : 22.
	9– 6	*L·* the world, popularity, pride,
	10– 8	mortals cry out, . . . *L·* me alone.
	20–12	"*L·* there be light, — *Gen.* 1 : 3.
Hea.	10– 8	*L·* us remember that God
	19–22	*l·* us work more earnestly in
Peo.	3–14	*L·* us rejoice that the bow
	5–21	*L·* us then heed this heavenly
	11– 9	*l·* us build another staging
	12– 2	*L·* them have "dominion — *Gen.* 1 : 26.
	13–18	to *l·* loose the wild beasts upon him,
	13–19	* he replied : "*L·* them come ;
Po.	1–10	"*L·* there be light" — *Gen.* 1 : 3.
	7– 3	"*L·* there be light, — *Gen.* 1 : 3.
	27–13	*l·* today grow difficult and vast
My.	8–11	* *l·* us have the best material symbol
	20–15	*l·* this suffice for her rich portion
	22–10	* *l·* us not be unconsciously blind
	61–25	* should be willing to *l·* God work.
	110–17	luxury of thought *l·* loose,
	116–24	*l·* them alone in, God's glory,
	123–31	*l·* us say with St. Paul
	128– 3	*l·* us go on unto perfection ; — *Heb.* 6 : 1.
	134–15	And here *l·* me add :
	145–11	* "I want to be *l·* off for a
	147–14	*L·* the Bible and the C. S. textbook
	148– 4	*l·* your faith be known by your works.
	150–31	"*l·* your peace — *Matt.* 10 : 13.
	163–22	Here *l·* me add that,
	166–22	*l·* us together sing the
	166–22	*l·* our measure of time and joy
	175–26	*L·* brotherly love continue.
	185– 4	* "*L·* us, then, be up and doing,
	186–21	*l·* His promise be verified :
	191–10	*L·* your light shine.
	196– 9	"*L·* every man be swift — *Jas.* 1 : 19.
	200– 4	*L·* "the heathen rage, — *Psal.* 2 : 1.
	201–15	So *l·* us meekly meet,
	211– 9	All that error asks is to be *l·* alone ;
	211–10	"*L·* us alone ; — *Mark* 1 : 24.
	224–30	*l·* us adopt the classic saying,
	233–30	*L·* us examine it for ourselves.
	236– 1	*L·* us have no more of
	245–16	*l·* Christian Scientists be charitable.
	245–16	*L·* the voice of Truth
	248– 3	*L·* your watchword always be :
	249– 5	*l·* the "still small — *I Kings* 19 : 12.
	249–10	a moral idiocy *l·* loose
	253–28	*L·* the creature become
	254–11	to your kind letter, *l·* me say :
	258–25	To the dear children *l·* me say :
	261– 7	*L·* it continue thus with one
	267– 8	Here *l·* us remember that God
	270–14	*L·* error rage and imagine a
	275–28	*l·* us unite in one *Te Deum*
	278–10	*L·* us have the molecule of faith
	284–23	But here *l·* me say that I am
	299– 8	* *l·* them make it known to the world,
	309–32	*L·* us see what were the fruits
	342–14	* *l·* it not be understood that
	344–30	*l·* your children be vaccinated,
	353–25	"*L·* the dead bury — *Luke* 9 : 60.

lethargic

Mis.	9–20	become *l·*, dreamy objects of

lets

Ret. 90– 2 God's window which *l·* in light,
'02. 6–17 *l·* in the divine sense of being,

letter

above-mentioned
My. 323– 2 * in the above-mentioned *l·*.
above the
My. 238–17 man rises above the *l·*,
all of the
Man. 66–19 inquire if all of the *l·* has
annexed
My. 138–28 * the annexed *l·* directed to
another
Peo. 2– 8 Hebrew term that gives another *l·*
appointment by
My. 223– 3 without previous appointment by *l·*.
by Mrs. Eddy
My. 357–26 chapter sub-title
360– 7 chapter sub-title
360–28 chapter sub-title
Christmas
Mis. 159–10 chapter sub-title
comment on
My. 209– 1 chapter sub-title
commonplace
Mis. 142–24 answer in a commonplace *l·*.
composite
My. 359–19 * quotations from a composite *l·*,
dear
My. 156– 3 my gratitude for your dear *l·*,
208–14 comes your dear *l·* to my
dedicatory
My. 146– 1 In explanation of my dedicatory *l·*
duplicate
Mis. 306–14 * a duplicate *l·* written,
Edward P. Bates'
My. 322–12 * Edward P. Bates' *l·* to you
Elizabeth Earl Jones'
My. 327–10 * heading
entire
My. 137– 7 * entire *l·* is in Mrs. Eddy's own
excellent
My. 118–10 thank you for your most excellent *l·*.
120– 8 to answer your excellent *l·*
extract from a
Mis. 148– 7 chapter sub-title
375– 8 extract from a *l·* reverting to
Man. 3– 1 heading
No. 43–12 following extract from a *l·*
My. 241–12 * extract from a *l·* to Mrs. Eddy,
first
Mis. 191–16 and by omitting the first *l·*,
following
Pul. 43–30 * following *l·* from a former pastor
My. 134–24 * following *l·* from Mrs. Eddy.
144– 1 * Mrs. Eddy also sent the following *l·*
173– 2 * The following *l·* appeared in the
329–11 * following *l·* from Newbern, N. C.,
331–10 * The following *l·* of thanks,
form of a
My. 137– 2 * affidavit, in the form of a *l·*
from a student
My. 355– 6 A *l·* from a student in the field
from Mrs. Eddy
My. 359–16 * chapter sub-title
from our Leader
My. 351– 1 * chapter sub-title
getting the
No. 28–21 getting the *l·* and omitting the
her
My. 351– 3 * publish her *l·* of recent date,
her brother's
My. 329–15 * and of her brother's *l·*,
in his hand
'02. 11– 1 with a *l·* in his hand
instead of the
Ret. 49– 9 of the spirit instead of the *l·*,
interesting
My. 208– 4 your highly interesting *l·*.
326– 2 * the following interesting *l·*
326–13 following deeply interesting *l·*
351– 7 Your interesting *l·* was
357–29 reading your interesting *l·*.
I sent a
Ret. 52–23 June, 1889, I sent a *l·*,
is gained
Mis. 43–17 *l·* is gained sooner than the spirit
its
Ret. 52– 7 have a small portion of its *l·*
kind
My. 192–20 Your kind *l·*, inviting me
last
Mis. 375–10 * "In my last *l·*, I did not utter
learns the
Ret. 38–28 learns the *l·* of this book,

letter

limits of a
Mis. 128– 5 within the limits of a *l·*.
Mary Hatch Harrison's
My. 329–20 * heading
Miss Jones'
My. 328– 9 * referred to in Miss Jones' *l·* :
Mrs. Eddy's
My. 140–17 * following is Mrs. Eddy's *l·* :
326–11 chapter sub-title
my
My. 146– 8 The statement in my *l·* to
not the
Mis. 260–27 The spirit, and not the *l·*,
of Christianity
My. 246–15 teaching and *l·* of Christianity
of Christian Science
Mis. 195– 5 learns the *l·* of C. S.
of dismissal
My. 182– 5 *l·* of dismissal and recommendation
of inquiry
Man. 52– 9 shall address a *l·* of inquiry to
of thanks
My. 295– 9 L· OF THANKS FOR THE GIFT
331–10 * The following *l·* of thanks,
of the law
Ret. 81– 8 The *l·* of the law of God,
of your work
My. 194– 5 The *l·* of your work dies,
oldness of the
No. 25– 7 oldness of the *l·*." — *Rom.* 7 : 6.
or a message
Man. 66–15 When a *l·* or a message from
public
Mis. 95– 6 * to reply to his public *l·*
received a
My. 14–11 * received a *l·* from a friend
reply to a
My. 204–14 REPLY TO A L· Announcing
spirit and the
Mis. 146–18 the spirit and the *l·* of this
195– 9 the spirit and the *l·* are requisite ;
My. 129–30 include the spirit and the *l·*
spirit or
Man. 44– 5 departure from the spirit or *l·*
tender
My. 352–20 for your tender *l·* to me,
this
Mis. 159– 5 read this *l·* to your church,
303–26 will respond to this *l·*
Pul. 74–11 * this *l·*, addressed to the editor
My. 134–24 * In announcing this *l·*, he said :
134–27 * This *l·* is in Mrs. Eddy's own
351– 4 * This *l·* is especially interesting
359–23 * This *l·* was forwarded to Mrs. Eddy
359–25 * Upon receipt of this *l·*
360– 2 Answer this *l·* immediately.
touching
Mis. 143–29 accompanied with a touching *l·*
without law
Mis. 367– 1 *l·* without law, gospel, or
without the
Mis. 195– 7 hath the spirit without the *l·*,
without the spirit
My. 158–19 The *l·* without the spirit
your
Mis. 158– 2 to your *l·* I will say :
My. 202–22 cheer and love in your *l·*.
202–25 From the dear tone of your *l·*,
252–19 Your *l·* and dottings are
253–22 thanks for your *l·* and telegram.
your kind
My. 254–10 Responding to your kind *l·*,

Mis. 135–24 L· read at the meeting of
142–16 my third, a *l·*. Why the *l·* alone?
355– 4 need, however, is not of the *l·*,
Man. 98–19 *l·* sent to the Pastor Emeritus
Ret. 21– 1 *l·* was read to my little son,
My. 118– 8 chapter sub-title
133–21 chapter sub-title
134–20 chapter sub-title
134–27 * to read you a *l·* from her
135– 1 heading
135–24 chapter sub-title
140–12 * *l·* addressed to Christian Scientists
290–11 chapter sub-title
299– 1 L· to the *New York Commercial*
301–14 [L· to the *New York World*]
302–12 [L· to the *New York Herald*]
314–22 *l·* from me to this self-same husband.
362– 9 * chapter sub-title

letterly

Mis. 315– 9 who are *l·* fit

letters

Mis.	29–20	Daily *l·* inform me that a
	132–18	*l·* and inquiries from all quarters,
	155–20	write such excellent *l·* to her,
	155–26	forward their *l·* to Him
	256– 8	in daily *l·* that protest against
	310–11	My answer to manifold *l·*
	364– 5	from the world of *l·*.
	372– 9	*l·* extolling it were pouring in
Man.	66–14	Reading and Attesting *L·*.
	67–20	congratulatory despatches or *l·*
Pul.	26–21	* in large golden *l·* on a
	42–17	* words, "Mother's Room," in gilt *l·*.
	42–23	* in *l·* of red were the words :
	78– 7	* inscription, cut in script *l·* :
'02.	15– 1	anonymous *l·* mailed to me
	15– 4	neither informed . . . of these *l·* nor
My.	58–25	* chapter sub-title
	124–20	is written in luminous *l·*,
	175–27	counterfeit *l·* in circulation,
	198– 3	Your *l·* of May 1 and June 19,
	214–16	In reply to *l·* questioning the
	215–13	*l·* begging me to accept it,
	223– 4	I neither listen . . . read *l·*, nor
	223– 5	*l·* which pertain to church
	223– 7	*L·* from the sick are not read by me
	223–11	*L·* and despatches from individuals
	225– 7	A correct use of capital *l·*
	225–10	where capital *l·* should be
	231–14	*l·* from invalids demanding
	245–27	*l·* of degrees that follow
	305– 9	*l·* in my possession,
	319–11	* heading
	319–12	* following *l·* from students
	336–19	* These *l·* and extracts are

letting

Mis.	176– 1	*l·* the harmony of Science
	212–29	before *l·* another know it.
Un.	5–20	*l·* our "moderation be— *Phil.* 4 : 5.
My.	12– 3	* justified the *l·* of contracts.
	195–10	*l·* the deep love which I cherished
	262–28	*l·* good will towards man,

level

Mis.	143– 2	friendship's "*l·*" and the "square"
Pul.	53–19	* above the *l·* of the brute,
My.	306–18	will find its proper *l·*.

lever

My.	130–13	the *l·* which elevates mankind.

levity

My.	93–19	* approach it in a spirit of *l·*,

lexicographer

Mis.	216–12	*l·*, given to the Anglo-Saxon
	226–13	Shakespeare, the immortal *l·*

lexicographers

Mis.	102– 3	often defined by *l·*
Rud.	2– 9	if our *l·* are right in

lexicography

Mis.	219– 1	According to *l·*, teleology is

lexicons

'01.	3–15	with the literal sense of the *l·* :

Lexington

Pul.	33–18	* on his father's farm at *L·*,

liability

Mis.	92– 3	*l·* of deviating from C. S.
Man.	46–22	*l·* to have his name removed
Ret.	83–29	present *l·* of deviating from
My.	231– 5	*l·* of working in wrong directions.

liable

Mis.	54–21	no reason why you should be *l·* to
	229– 1	that any one is *l·* to have them
	300–10	*l·* to arrest for infringement of
	300–19	Your manuscript copy is *l·*,
Man.	41–16	renders this member *l·* to discipline
Rud.	9– 1	and the patient is *l·* to a relapse,
No.	1–11	are *l·* to be borne on by the
'02.	4–26	we are *l·* to turn from them as

liar

Mis.	24–26	a *l·*, and the father of it."— *John* 8 : 44.
	83–18	"a *l·*, and the father of it— *John* 8 : 44.
	108– 6	his definition of Satan as a *l·*
	190–29	serpent, *l·*, the god of this world,
	192– 4	so, when referring to a *l·*,
	192– 5	defines devil as a "*l·*."— *John* 8 : 44.
	196–14	a *l·*, and the father of it ;"— *John* 8 : 44.
	224–32	of a flatterer, a fool, or a *l·*,
	226–21	character of a *l·* and hypocrite is
	259– 5	"a *l·*, and the father of it."— *John* 8 : 44.
Ret.	67–24	"a *l·*, and the father of it."— *John* 8 : 44.
Un.	32–22	a *l·*, and the father of it."— *John* 8 : 44.
	32–23	Here it appears that a *l·* was
Rud.	5– 4	every man a *l·*."— *Rom.* 3 : 4.
No.	32–16	"a *l·*, and the father of it."— *John* 8 : 44.

liar

Pan.	5–16	a *l·*, and the father of it— *John* 8 : 44.
	5–19	It shows that evil is both *l·* and lie,
'00.	5– 8	a *l·*, and the father of it"— *John* 8 : 44
'01.	16–13	*devil* is named *serpent— l· — the god of*
My.	269–30	lie and the *l·* are self-destroyed.

liberal

Mis.	242– 6	*l·* sum of one thousand dollars
	274–13	to the public for its *l·* patronage,
	308–19	your *l·* patronage and scholarly,
Ret.	49–22	the public for its *l·* patronage.
'02.	13–10	yield this church a *l·* income.
Hea.	14–13	as a physician is enlightened and *l·*
My.	11–17	* because of prompt and *l·* action,
	12– 5	* spontaneous and *l·* donations
	245– 7	on a broad and *l·* basis.
	304–23	* sound education and *l·* culture."
	309–27	* received a *l·* education.
	361–22	* democratic and *l·* government.

liberalism

'02.	2–13	Protestantism to doubtful *l·*.

liberality

Mis.	242–19	to reward his *l·*, I offer him
My.	12–13	* by the *l·* and promptness of

liberally

My.	21–12	* in order to contribute more *l·*

liberals

Mis.	88–11	appreciated by many *l·*.

liberated

Mis.	41– 3	power of *l·* thought to do good,
	67– 1	to support the *l·* thought
Ret.	82–21	Their *l·* capacities of mind

liberator

My.	268–23	Love is the *l·* and gives man the

liberties

My.	326– 3	* courts are thus declaring the *l·* of

liberty

against the

Peo.	11–28	against the *l·* and lives of men.

and glory

My.	356– 5	*l·* and glory of His presence,

and joy

Mis.	240–10	whereas forecasting *l·* and joy does ;

and light

Ret.	81–10	diviner sense of *l·* and light.

and love

My.	236–18	amplitude of *l·* and love
	248–27	labor, duty, *l·*, and love,

and peace

Mis.	304– 5	* by the lovers of *l·* and peace

buoyant with

My.	110–17	buoyant with *l·* and the luxury of

careening in

Po.	18– 5	Careening in *l·* higher and higher

creators of

Mis.	304–27	* birthdays of the "creators of *l·* ;"

divine

Mis.	163–21	are the basis of divine *l·*,

forecasting

Mis.	240–10	whereas forecasting *l·* and joy does ;

full

Peo.	11– 1	full *l·* of the sons of God

giveth

Mis.	167–29	he giveth *l·* to the captive,

giveth him

'01.	10– 1	for the spirit giveth him *l·* :

glorious

Mis.	199– 9	"into the glorious *l·* of— *Rom.* 8 : 21.

glory of

My.	339–16	joy, grace, and glory of *l·*.

higher

Mis.	354–28	As rising he rests in a *l·* higher

human

Mis.	101–11	for human *l·* and rights.

is besieged

Mis.	274–17	press is gagged, *l·* is besieged ;

life and

My.	266– 5	the robbing of people of life and *l·*

light and

Mis.	xii– 8	into light and *l·*.
My.	187–25	light and *l·* of His children,

loving

My.	20–10	loving *l·* of their license.

of conscience

My.	220–31	should share alike *l·* of conscience,
	222–27	*l·* of conscience held sacred.

of Cuba

Pan.	14–29	for the *l·* of Cuba.

outlet to

My.	128– 2	can find no other outlet to *l·*.

progress toward

Mis.	304–25	* the world's progress toward *l·* ;

liberty

Protestant
Ret. 2– 3 devotion to Protestant *l·*
regain his
Mis. 269– 3 using falsehood to regain his *l·*,
regard the
My. 291–30 shall sacredly regard the *l·* of
religious
Mis. 145– 2 bulwark of civil and religious *l·*,
My. 148–14 beheld the omen, — religious *l·*,
181–15 religious *l·* and human rights.
200– 1 Religious *l·* and individual rights
341– 6 the ensign of religious *l·*
spring into
Mis. 251–22 burdened for an hour, spring into *l·*,
standard of
Peo. 10–15 grasps the standard of *l·*,
striking at
'00. 10–13 striking at *l·*, human rights,
that
Pul. 51– 7 * they are enjoying that *l·* which
that's just
Po. 72– 4 ne'er again Quench *l·* that's just.
to lie
Mis. 274–18 when the press assumes the *l·* to lie,

Mis. 176–13 for the *l·* of the sons of God.
251–13 the *l·* of the sons of God,
Man. 96–12 he is at *l·* to supply that need
Un. 5–19 *l·* of the sons of God,
Po. vi– 8 * poem
page 71 poem
71–13 God to the rescue— *L·*, peal !
My. 128–11 man's inalienable birthright — *L·*.
128–12 there is *l·*." — II Cor. 3: 17.
205– 4 *l·* wherewith Christ hath — Gal. 5: 1.
287–14 human rights, *l·*, life.
317–23 The *l·* that I have taken

Liberty and West Streets
Mis. 306–13 * corner *L· and W· S·*, New York,

Liberty Bell
Mis. 303–23 idea and purpose of a *L· B·*

Liberty Island
Mis. 304–11 * it will go to Bunker Hill or *L· I·*,

Liberty National Bank
Mis. 306–12 * sent to the *L· N· B·*,

Librarian
Man. 63–19 *L·*.

libraries
Pul. 5–22 It is in the public *l·*

library
My. 342–17 * the hall, which serves as a *l·*,

license
Mis. 257–13 as a power, prohibition, or *l·*,
260–29 needing neither *l·* nor prohibition ;
No. 37– 6 the *l·* of a short-lived sinner,
'01. 16–23 if now it is permitted *l·*,
My. 20–10 loving liberty of their *l·*.
328–13 * it gives them a *l·* to heal.
328–14 * This *l·* of five dollars annually,
328–24 * application for *l·* was made
328–27 * a *l·* must be obtained
328–29 * a *l·* fee of five dollars."
329– 2 * *l·* was accordingly taken

licensed
My. 211– 7 has *l·* evil, allowing it

licenses
My. 328–18 * Sheriff Wooten issued *l·*

licentious
'00. 6–20 is profane, *l·*, and

licentiousness
Mis. 210–25 shameless brow of *l·*,

licking
Mis. 326–13 *l·* up the blood of martyrs

lids
Mis. 132– 4 token that heavy *l·* are opening,

lie (noun)
and the liar
My. 269–30 *l·* and the liar are self-destroyed.
basis of a
'02. 6– 8 on the basis of a *l·*,
beautiful
Un. 53– 1 which make a beautiful *l·*.
being a
Un. 53– 5 Being a *l·*, it would be truthful to
believe a
Mis. 238– 3 sometimes made to believe a *l·*,
Un. 45– 1 you shall believe a *l·*,
believe the
Pan. 5–20 we should neither believe the *l·*,

lie

bigger
Hea. 14– 1 bigger *l·* occupying the field
biggest
Mis. 123– 9 the serpent's biggest *l·* !
call itself a
Un. 53– 5 would be truthful to call itself a *l·* ;
constitutes the
Un. 53– 7 it constitutes the *l·* an evil.
evil as a
'01. 14–14 We regard evil as a *l·*,
evil is a
Pan. 5–25 Knowing that evil is a *l·*,
exposes the
Mis. 367– 7 exposes the *l·* of suppositional evil,
fathers itself
'02. 6–11 Jesus said a *l·* fathers itself,
first
'02. 3–30 the first *l·* and leap into perdition
give it the
'01. 13–28 hold it invalid, give it the *l·*,
gives the
Mis. 334–15 only as one gives the *l·* to a lie ;
No. 32–14 It gives the *l·* to sin,
giving the
Peo. 13–16 giving the *l·* to science.
godless
No. 18– 4 godless *l·* that denies Him
is never true
Mis. 336– 3 that a *l·* is never true
liar and
Pan. 5–19 that evil is both liar and *l·*,
maketh a
Mis. 137–27 that worketh or maketh a *l·*.
366–14 that worketh or maketh a *l·*
No. 15–26 "worketh or maketh a *l·*" — see Rev. 21: 27.
'01. 28–23 that worketh or maketh a *l·*.
matter is a
Rud. 7–20 matter is a *l·*,
must say
Un. 53– 4 the *l·* must say He made them,
no sculptured
Po. 73–18 No sculptured *l·*, Or hypocrite sigh,
of evil
No. 42–19 The *l·* of evil holds its own by
one
Hea. 13–28 one *l·* getting the better of another,
pursuing a
My. 130–14 to be continually pursuing a *l·*
sin is a
'01. 13– 7 sin is a *l·* from the beginning,
13–14 evil, *alias* devil, sin, is a *l·*
speaketh a
Mis. 24–26 "When he speaketh a *l·*,— John 8: 44.
198–11 "When he speaketh a *l·*,— John 8: 44.
Pan. 5–16 When he speaketh a *l·*,— John 8: 44.
subtle
Mis. 335–12 for opposing the subtle *l·*,
My. 14–22 * subtle *l·* with which to ensnare
takes its pattern
Un. 53– 1 a *l·* takes its pattern from Truth,
this
Un. 25–11 This *l·*, that Mind can be in matter,
25–13 this *l·* I declare an illusion,
36– 4 this *l·* was the false witness
45– 1 this *l·* shall seem truth]."
throttle the
My. 26–21 the time to *throttle the l·*
use of a
Un. 36– 6 The use of a *l·* is that it unwittingly
utter a
Mis. 67–14 thou shalt not utter a *l·*,
veils the truth
Mis. 62– 9 Believing a *l·* veils the truth
victor over a
Mis. 336– 2 Truth, the victor over a *l·*.
worketh a
Mis. 174–18 that maketh or worketh a *l·*.

Mis. 14–27 a *l·* that is incapable of proof
83–19 the father of it [the *l·*]." — John 8: 44.
108– 8 a *l·*, being without foundation
108–26 Jesus' definition of sin as a *l·*.
174– 3 it is a *l·*, claiming to talk
334– 9 does this as a *l·* declaring itself,
334–11 fabrication is found to be a *l·*,
334–15 only as one gives the lie to a *l·* ;
334–16 a *l·*, without one word of Truth in it.
334–19 is a *l·* of the highest degree of
351–21 though it is a *l·* ;
Ret. 67–21 the *l·* was, and *is*, collective
Un. 17– 1 A *l·* has only one chance of
17– 3 and so make the *l·* seem part of
22–12 would be to admit the truth of a *l·*.
22–15 *Evil.* . . . A *l·* is as genuine as Truth,
25–11 whatever it appears to say . . . is a *l·*.

lie

Un.	33– 2	mortal mind, and this mind a *l·*
	34– 9	is an illusion, a *l·*
	36– 1	only as it adds *l·* to *l·*
	44– 9	Of *Satan* and his *l·*
	44–20	[when you, *l·*, get the floor],
No.	32–16	A *l·* is negation,
	42–24	would make a *l·* the author of
	42–24	and so make Truth itself a *l·*
Pan.	5–17	the father of it [a *l·*]." — *John* 8 : 44.
	5–22	we should not believe that a *l·*,
	5–27	Jesus treated the *l·* summarily.
	6– 9	putteth his foot upon a *l·*
'00.	5– 9	its origin is a myth, a *l·*
'02.	6– 5	The curse . . . was pronounced upon a *l·*,
My.	130–18	A *l·* left to itself is not so soon

lie (verb)

Mis.	34–24	*l·* within the realm of mortal thought
	67– 3	Above physical wants, *l·* the
	145–23	leopard shall *l·* down with— *Isa.* 11 : 6.
	268–15	*l·* in the line of Truth ;
	274–18	assumes the liberty to *l·*,
	325–17	*l·* stretched on the floor,
	354–4, 5	can steal, and *l·* and *l·*,
Ret.	44–22	*l·* in Christian warfare.
	79– 9	*l·* in meekness, in unselfish
Pul.	10– 9	pomp and power *l·* low in dust.
	48–15	* does it *l·* on the brow of
Pan.	11– 3	''*L·* not one to another, — *Col.* 3 : 9.
Po.	65–12	'neath thy drap'ry still *l·*.
My.	166–18	the virtues that *l·* concealed
	223–27	*l·* burdens that time will remove.
	323–10	* not going to *l·* about anything

lied

Mis.	23–18	first talker in its behalf, *l·*.
Un.	32–25	it was not man . . . who *l·*,

lies

Mis.	266–28	The spirit of *l·* is abroad.
	365–14	the secret of its success *l·* in
Un.	10– 8	it *l·* in this utter reliance upon
	29–18	herein *l·* the discrepancy
Pul.	41–10	* territory that *l·* between,
	48–10	* landscape that *l·* below,
Rud.	7–21	"the father of *l·* ;" — *see John* 8 : 44.
No.	18–11	*l·* in the universal need of
My.	17– 1	the refuge of *l·*, — *Isa.* 28 : 17.
	112–32	book which *l·* beside the Bible
	122–19	where the young child *l·*,
	126–15	(hearken not to her *l·*),
	144– 5	*l·* afloat that I am sick,
	188–24	man's head *l·* at another's feet.
	204– 5	*l·* concealed in the calm
	211–24	miserable *l·*, poured constantly
	249–24	My preference *l·* with the

lieth

Mis.	36–12	*l·* down with the lamb.

lieu

Mis.	314– 4	Readers in *l·* of pastors.
My.	201–27	in *l·* of my presence

lieutenant

'00.	10–26	the name of a first *l·*

Life (*see also* **Life's**)

abides

Un.	40–16	Hence *L·* abides in man,

all

Pul.	4–20	in all *L·*, through all space.

and being

Ret.	68–24	*L·* and being are of God.

and God

Un.	37–16	not testify of *L·* and God.

and good

Un.	62–16	false sense of *L·* and good.

and goodness

Ret.	63–17	against man's *L·* and goodness.

and happiness

Un.	37– 8	stepping-stone to *L·* and happiness.

and immortality

Un.	38–20	brings to light *L·* and immortality.

and intelligence

Mis.	199–26	all substance, *L·*, and intelligence
	200– 9	substance, *L·*, and intelligence of

and its ideals

Ret.	75–10	*L·* and its ideals are inseparable,

and its manifestation

My.	261–28	thoughts of *L·* and its manifestation.

and light

Mis.	337–29	The ineffable *L·* and light which

and Love

Mis.	16– 1	more spiritual *L·* and Love.
	46–26	the *L·* and Love that are God,
	68– 2	intelligence, *L·*, and Love.
	151–28	everlasting *L·* and Love.
	190–10	infinite *L·* and Love.

Life

and Love

Mis.	258–11	the law of *L·* and Love.
	293– 3	breathing new *L·* and Love
	342–10	the bridal of *L·* and Love,
No.	15–24	from divine *L·* and Love.
	18–14	demonstration of divine *L·* and Love ;
	33–21	efficacy of divine *L·* and Love
Hea.	16–13	immeasurable *L·* and Love
Peo.	5–19	diviner sense of *L·* and Love,
	14–17	power of divine *L·* and Love
My.	52–13	* Mind, Truth, *L·*, and Love,
	153–32	one source, divine *L·* and Love,
	191–16	higher human sense of *L·* and Love,

and Mind

Un.	3–22	He is all the *L·* and Mind there is
	3–23	embodiment of *L·* and Mind.

and substance

Mis.	55–25	only Mind, *L·*, and substance.

and Truth

Mis.	12–26	and Love is *L·* and Truth.
	75– 3	*L·* and Truth were the way
No.	30– 2	The law of *L·* and Truth
Peo.	6–21	grand realities of *L·* and Truth
My.	149– 6	Love, resistless *L·* and Truth.

as defined

Ret.	58–12	*L·*, as defined by Jesus,

as God

Mis.	189–19	Life in God and *L·* as God.
Un.	38–23	*L·* as God, moral and spiritual
My.	273–22	spiritual understanding of *L·* as God,

as it is

Mis.	189–21	For man to know *L·* as it is,

attempt to separate

Mis.	18–28	attempt to separate *L·* from God.

at war with

Mis.	217–23	that death is at war with *L·*,

belief that

Mis.	78– 1	belief that *L·*, God, is not

better views of

Mis.	175–10	giving better views of *L·* ;

Book of

My.	258– 1	Wherever . . . the Book of *L·* is loved,

bread of

Ret.	91–23	his . . . teaching was the bread of *L·*.

conscious

Un.	48–13	as infinite and conscious *L·*,

consciousness of

Un.	41– 4	knowledge and consciousness of *L·*,

conscious of

Un.	18–24	for to be ever conscious of *L·* is

death into

Un.	41–18	portal from death into *L·* ;

deathless

Po.	29–16	living Love, And deathless *L·* !

demonstrated in

No.	13–12	that saying is demonstrated in *L·*

demonstrates

Mis.	189–31	demonstrates *L·* without beginning or
Un.	40–10	demonstrates *L·* as imperative
My.	238–23	it demonstrates *L·*, not death ;

demonstrating

Mis.	270–12	in demonstrating *L·* scientifically,

divine

(*see* **divine**)

endless

Mis.	77–17	it holds man in endless *L·*

eternal

Mis.	63–17	might lay hold of eternal *L·*,
	83–27	proof of his eternal *L·*
	85– 2	*L·* eternal brings blessings.
	103–29	He was eternal *L·*,
	125–15	"to know aright is *L·* eternal,"
	170– 6	with him is *L·* eternal,
	183– 3	omnipotent Love, and eternal *L·*,
	341–19	you find *L·* eternal :
Man.	15– 5	sufficient guide to eternal *L·*.
	16– 7	to understand eternal *L·*,
Un.	38–22	or to deny that He is *L·* eternal.
	39– 3	Eternal *L·* is partially understood ;
Pul.	30–16	* the guide to eternal *L·* ;
Rud.	11–24	health, harmony, and *L·* eternal.
No.	36–14	of eternal *L·*, and harmony.
My.	119–24	eternal *L·* without beginning

ever-conscious

Un.	18–23	God saith, I am ever-conscious *L·*,

everlasting

Mis.	28–13	true sense of reality, everlasting *L·*
	151–28	the ascending scale of everlasting *L·*
Pul.	3–23	and flow into everlasting *L·*.
'01.	10–27	emerge gently into *L·* everlasting.
My.	260– 1	and bounty of *L·* everlasting,
	267–28	environed with everlasting *L·*.

ever-present

Un.	43–26	ever-present *L·* which knows no death,

Life

evidence of
Un. 61– 1 to the true evidence of *L·*,
evidences of
Hea. 16–27 gain our evidences of *L·* from
feast of
Mis. 175–14 Man shall keep the feast of *L·*,
find the
Mis. 211–24 shall find the *L·* that cannot be lost.
giver of
Pul. 4–24 the lord and giver of *L·*.
giveth
Ret. 65– 8 Spirit giveth *L·*.
God is
Un. 37– 2 God is *L·* ;
37–13 because God is *L·*, all Life is
37–15 God is *L·* and All-in-all.
God is our
Mis. 50–24 understanding that God is our *L·*,
God or
Mis. 25– 3 there is but one God or *L·*,
Un. 39–23 As the image of God, or *L·*,
had no beginning
Un. 42–21 *L·* had no beginning ;
harmony, and
Un. 32–19 of holiness, harmony, and *L·*."
He alone is
Un. 38–15 declaring that not He alone is *L·*,
health, and
Un. 39– 4 yield to holiness, health, and *L·*,
higher rules of
Mis. 29–32 higher rules of *L·* which Jesus taught
holds
Un. 40–18 God, who holds *L·* by a spiritual
holiness, and
Un. 42– 4 Spirit, holiness, and *L·*.
ideal of
Mis. 104–29 would not gain the true ideal of *L·*
ideas of
Peo. 14– 7 ideas of *L·* have grown more spiritual ;
ignorance of
Un. 40–22 comes through our ignorance of *L·*,
illustrated
Mis. 30–16 great Way-shower illustrated *L·*
immortal
Mis. 56–12 direct opposite of immortal *L·*,
incorporeal
My. 200–13 to the realms of incorporeal *L·*
individuality and
Un. 46–15 Individuality and *L·* were real
infinite
Mis. 82–18 image and likeness of infinite *L·*,
190– 9 recognized reflection of infinite *L·*
Hea. 4– 6 the compass of infinite *L·*,
4–17 We expect infinite *L·* to become
4–19 as infinite *L·*, without beginning
in God
Mis. 189–19 released sense of *L·* in God
in harmony with
Mis. 105–14 in harmony with *L·* and its glorious
intelligence, nor
Mis. 74–31 substance, intelligence, nor *L·*,
involves
My. 139–14 their vitality involves *L·*,
is a term
Ret. 59–12 *L·* is a term used to indicate Deity ;
is Christ
My. 185–19 *L·* is Christ, and Christ, . . . heals
is eternal
Un. 37–13 all *L·* is eternal.
is God
Mis. 56– 9 *L·* is God, the only creator,
175–10 saying, Man's *L·* is God ;
209–17 man, whose *L·* is God,
Un. 10–11 *L·* is God, or Spirit,
40–16 *L·* is God, and God is good.
Rud. 13– 1 that *L·* is God, good ;
No. 19–21 realities of being,— that *L·* is God,
Peo. 5–16 saying unto us, "*L·* is God ;
8–14 *L·* is God ; but we say that Life is
is immortal Mind
Mis. 56– 9 *L·* is immortal Mind, not matter.
is inorganic
Mis. 56– 4 *L·* is inorganic, infinite Spirit ;
is light
Po. 79–16 *L·* is light, and wisdom might,
is not functional
Rud. 13– 2 hence *L·* is not functional,
is not temporal
Ret. 59– 5 *L·* is not temporal, but eternal,
is real
Un. 38– 9 *L·* is real ; and all is real which
is Spirit
Un. 41–22 All *L·* is Spirit, and Spirit can never
Hea. 9–26 *L·* is Spirit ; and when we waken from

Life

is the Principle
'01. 21–19 *L·* is the Principle of C. S.
its
No. 28–23 nor the practice of its *L·*.
law of
(*see* **law**)
lessens all pride
My. 134–17 *L·* lessens all pride— its pomp and
life in
Pan. 13–21 life in *L·*, all in All.
light and
Ret. 27–30 new world of light and *L·*,
living way to
My. 192–12 lights the living way to *L·*,
Love alone is
Mis. 388–10 For Love alone is *L·* ;
Po. 7–10 For Love alone is *L·* ;
Love, and
My. 185–17 inseparable from Love, and *L·*
Love that is
My. 275–16 Love that is *L·* — is sure
man and
No. 12–26 sense and Soul, man and *L·*,
manifestation of
Ret. 88– 9 a higher manifestation of *L·*.
man's
Mis. 174–29 man's *L·* here and now.
175–10 saying, Man's *L·* is God ;
measure of
Mis. 175–12 The measure of *L·* shall increase
Mind, or
Ret. 57–21 notion of more than one Mind, or *L·*,
Mind which is
Un. 38– 8 that Mind which is *L·*.
my
Un. 48– 9 my individuality and my *L·*.
never fled
Mis. 385–19 thy ever-self ; *L·* never fled ;
Po. 48–13 thy ever-self ; *L·* never fled ;
no conflict with
Mis. 105–12 would have no conflict with *L·*
no groundwork in
Un. 25–23 has no groundwork in *L·*,
no other
Hea. 16– 4 teaches us there is no other *L·*,
no quality of
Un. 38–20 Death has no quality of *L·* ;
not death
Un. 39–24 reflects and embodies *L·*, not death.
My. 238–23 demonstrates *L·*, not death ;
not in matter
My. 181–12 *L·* not in matter but in Mind.
not of death
Un. 3–18 image . . . of *L·*, not of death.
of all being
Mis. 399–12 *L·* of all being divine :
Po. 75–19 *L·* of all being divine :
office of
Un. 40–28 the nature and office of *L·*.
of good
Un. 62–11 only as they reach the *L·* of good,
of man
Mis. 76–26 admit that Soul is the *L·* of man.
Ret. 63–15 represents God, the *L·* of man.
of Spirit
No. 34–22 The real blood or *L·* of Spirit
omniscience of
My. 274– 8 omnipresence, and omniscience of *L·*,
one
Un. 37– 3 there can be but one *L·*.
Rud. 13–13 saith . . . there is more than one *L·*
only
Mis. 16–17 great fact that *God is the only L·*;
28–14 will be found to be the only *L·*.
194–28 you *know* that God is the only *L·*.
367–32 the only *L·*, Truth, and Love,
Ret. 69–13 God, Spirit, who *is* the only *L·*.'
Un. 41–10 the infinite and only *L·*.
43– 6 there is no death, but only *L·*.
or God
Ret. 59–16 antipodes of *L·*, or God,
Un. 38– 4 contradiction of *L·*, or God ;
or intelligence
Un. 32–13 as substance, *L·*, or intelligence,
or Principle
Ret. 28– 2 the *L·*, or Principle, of all being ;
or Spirit
Mis. 56– 4 if *L·*, or Spirit, were organic,
over death
Mis. 61–10 and of *L·* over death.
321–12 triumphs . . . of *L·* over death,
permanence of
My. 177–15 possibilities and permanence of *L·*.
pinnacled in
Pul. 3– 1 and pinnacled in *L·*.

Life

presupposes
No. 35–18 idolatry that presupposes *L·*,
proceeds from
Un. 38–10 all is real which proceeds from *L·*
real as
Un. 60– 1 illusion that death is as real as *L·*.
No. 17–27 Then . . . death as real as *L·* ;
reality of
Mis. 117– 2 progressive life is the reality of *L·*
Un. 43– 5 the infinite reality of *L·*,
reflect the
Un. 30–27 reflect the *L·* of the divine Arbiter.
righteousness and
Ret. 62– 6 health, righteousness, and *L·*,
rule of
Un. 55– 2 rule of *L·* can be demonstrated,
Science of
(*see* **Science**)
Science reveals
Ret. 60– 3 Science reveals *L·* as a complete
sense of
(*see* **sense**)
signification of
Ret. 59–15 has the signification of *L·*.
solution of
Mis. 65–15 to gain the true solution of *L·*
Soul is
Un. 30– 7 Soul is *L·*, and . . . never sins.
space and
Mis. 332– 2 reflecting all space and *L·*,
spiritual
Mis. 16– 1 more spiritual *L·* and Love.
361– 7 spiritual *L·*, whose myriad forms
Un. 30– 7 and being spiritual *L·*, never sins.
30–11 Soul, or spiritual *L·*.
spiritual fact of
Mis. 42–22 and the spiritual fact of *L·* is,
spiritual idea of
My. 139– 6 even the spiritual idea of *L·*,
standard of
Un. 38–27 up to the Christian standard of *L·*,
substance, or
Mis. 367– 9 not Mind, substance, or *L·*.
such
No. 35– 5 demonstrate the Principle of such *L·* ;
supersensible
Mis. 86–31 the glory of supersensible *L·* ;
swallowed up in
Mis. 361– 7 death itself is swallowed up in *L·*,
No. 13– 7 death must be swallowed up in *L·*,
that heals
My. 260– 2 the *L·* that heals and saves
that is God
Mis. 194–29 naturalness of the *L·* that is God,
196–21 When the *L·* that is God, good,
that is Soul
My. 274– 2 even the *L·* that is Soul
that is Truth
My. 214– 8 demonstrating the *L·* that is Truth,
that lives
Po. 24–11 The *L·* that lives in Thee !
the word
Ret. 59– 6 The word *L·* never means that
this
Mis. 24–17 this *L·* being the sole reality
179–32 this *L·* that knows no death,
Un. 41–18 when this *L·* shall appear
Pul. 4–25 *Reflect this L·,* and with it cometh
Rud. 3– 8 This *L·*, Truth, and Love
through
Un. 41–20 not through death, but through *L·* ;
true idea of
My. 181–12 through the true idea of *L·*,
Truth and
(*see* **Truth**)
Truth, and Love
Mis. 2–17 *L·*, Truth, and Love will be found
6–19 conceptions of *L·*, Truth, and Love
77–14 presence, . . . of *L·*, Truth, and Love,
79–16 perpetual in *L·*, Truth, and Love.
82–18 of infinite *L·*, Truth, and Love.
150–27 as divine *L·*, Truth, and Love ;
167–17 divine *L·*, Truth, and Love ;
234–31 fatherliness as *L·*, Truth, and Love,
258–25 all law, *L·*, Truth, and Love.
358–11 He . . . loseth in *L·*, Truth, and Love.
367–32 the only *L·*, Truth, and Love,
Un. 34–27 Spirit, *L·*, Truth, and Love,
51–24 see God as *L·*, Truth, and Love.
55–13 *L·*, Truth, and Love, redeeming us
Pul. 85–11 * God as *L·*, Truth, and Love,
Rud. 1– 8 Spirit, *L·*, Truth, and Love,
3– 8 *L·*, Truth, and Love — this trinity
4– 1 *L·*, Truth, and Love are this trinity
No. 1–19 the trinity, *L·*, Truth, and Love,

Life

Truth, and Love
Hea. 8–20 namely, *L·*, Truth, and Love,
Peo. 2–23 the divine *L·*, Truth, and Love,
4–18 Godhead is *L·*, Truth, and Love,
13– 7 impersonal *L·*, Truth, and Love,
My. 109–22 this divine *L·*, Truth, and Love,
116– 4 omnipotence of *L·*, Truth, and Love,
150–14 the divine *L·*, Truth, and Love.
180–14 Principle, or *L·*, Truth, and Love,
Truth, . . . and Love
(*see* **Truth**)
Truth and the
(*see* **Truth**)
Truth of
Un. 39– 2 Truth of *L·* is rendered practical
truth of
Peo. 9–11 life of Truth and the truth of *L·*.
Truth or
Un. 62–20 Truth or *L·* in divine Science
Truth, or Love
Mis. 67– 6 not adulterate *L·* Truth, or Love,
Truth that is
My. 214– 9 and the Truth that is *L·*.
truth that is
My. 260– 2 in the truth that is *L·*,
understanding
My. 248–23 Christ mode of understanding *L·*
understanding of
My. 273–22 understanding of *L·* as God,
understands
Un. 40–21 who fully understands *L·*.
victory for
Mis. 74–26 an everlasting victory for *L·* ;
volume of
My. 256–13 and open the volume of *L·*
was Spirit
Un. 42–23 To him, *L·* was Spirit.
way of
No. 35–10 He who pointed the way of *L·*
My. 191–25 lights the living way of *L·*.
which is infinite
Peo. 4– 9 *L·*, which is infinite and eternal,
without beginning
Mis. 189–31 demonstrates *L·* without beginning
Hea. 4–19 *L·*, without beginning and without end.
Peo. 2–24 *L·* without beginning or ending,
My. 119–24 *L·* without beginning or end of days.
without birth
Chr. 53–39 *L·*, without birth and without end,
woke to
Mis. 386–13 I woke to *L·*,
Po. 49–20 I woke to *L·*,
words of
Mis. 337–28 him who taught . . . the words of *L·*.

———

Mis. 23–26 reflects good, *L·*, Truth, Love
24–17 *L·* in and of Spirit ;
63– 7 *L·*, Truth, Love are the triune
85– 7 all that he knows of *L·*,
124–14 ever-living *L·*, Truth, Love :
180–16 it speaks to me of *L·*,
187–22 God, — *L·*, Truth, Love.
189–20 declare *L·* to be the infinite
190– 4 infinite Spirit, Truth, *L·*,
196–27 not through death, but *L·*,
322–12 and the *L·* these give,
352– 4 regarding *L·*, Truth, Love as
386– 3 infinite appear *L·*, Love divine,
Chr. 53–41 The Way, the Truth, the *L·*
Ret. 60–29 one Truth, *L·*, Love,
69– 4 *L·* is the law of his being"
69–14 is found to be not *L·*,
Un. 25–25 eternal All, — *L·*, Truth, Love,
29–14 eternal, — Truth, *L·*, Love.
37– 7 God and heaven, or *L·*, are present,
38–25 conclusion that *L·* is not in these
39– 7 that *L·* which knows no death.
41–23 *L·*, therefore, is deathless.
42– 1 *L·*, God, being everywhere,
42–16 With Christ, *L·* was not merely
43– 8 believe in the possibility that *L·*
45–25 Spirit, — Mind, *L·*, Soul.
51– 3 false premises, — that *L·* is
62–11 learn that there is no *L·* in evil.
Pul. 3– 3 Can *L·* die?
13– 1 *L·*, represented by the Father ;
Rud. 2–19 supreme good, *L·*, Truth, Love.
No. 20–10 substance, *L·*, Truth, Love.
35–21 Mind, *L·*, substance, Soul
Pan. 12–24 self-existent *L·*, Truth, Love,
'01. 4–26 because He is *L·*, Truth, Love,
5– 8 named in the Bible *L·*, Truth, Love?
7– 5 *L·*, Truth, Love, constitutes the
Hea. 8– 4 but the *L·*, Love, and Truth that
Peo. 2–11 divine Principle, — *L·*, Truth, Love ;

Life

  Peo. 8–14   but we say that *L·* is carried on
  Po. 49– 5   infinite appear *L·*, Love divine,
     70–13   the *L·*, the Principle of man.
  My. 180–17   C. S. meets death with *L·*,
     185–15   this trinity, Truth, *L·*, Love,
     185–16   *L·* is the spontaneity of Love,
     206–17   fact that portrays *L·*, Truth, Love.
     214–12   He proved *L·* to be deathless
     225–28   His synonyms are Love, Truth, *L·*,

life (*see also* **life's**)

abiding
  Mis. 26– 2   hath *l·* abiding in it,
all
  My. 186–14   in whom dwelleth all *l·*, health, and
and bliss
  Un. 57–17   This gospel . . . brought *l·* and bliss.
and death
  Mis. 286–21   *l·*, and death are subjective states of
     333– 3   good and evil, *l·* and death,
  Ret. 57–28   health and sickness, *l·* and death ;
  Un. 31–14   produces *l·* and death.
  Pan. 8–26   sickness and sin, *l·* and death.
  '00. 4– 2   health and sickness, *l·* and death,
  My. 273–20   joy, sorrow, *l·*, and death.
and happiness
  Mis. 209–25   *l·* and happiness should still attend
     341–17   material sense of *l·* and happiness
  Ret. 21–19   false sense of *l·* and happiness,
  Un. 58– 1   false sense of *l·* and happiness.
and health
  Mis. 200– 4   holiness, *l·*, and health
  Ret. 7–13   * Had *l·* and health been spared
  No. 5–13   namely, that *l·* and health are
  My. 218– 7   its restoration to *l·* and health
     219–16   the giving of *l·* and health to man
and hope
  Peo. 11–13   gnawing away *l·* and hope ;
and immortality
  My. 207–14   * *l·* and immortality brought to light.
and intelligence
  Mis. 53– 5   supposed *l·* and intelligence in
     76– 9   belief . . . *l·* and intelligence are in
  Ret. 69– 7   delusion that *l·* and intelligence
  Hea. 17–23   supposition of *l·* and intelligence in
  My. 161–30   supposititious *l·* and intelligence in
and labors
  My. 291– 3   rested on the *l·* and labors of our
and liberty
  My. 266– 4   *l·* and liberty under the warrant of
and love
  My. 88–21   * *l·*, and love which finds its temple
     113–28   a more spiritual *l·* and love?
     159–21   Truth, *l·*, and love are the only
     268–24   Truth, canonized by *l·* and love,
and peace
  Mis. 24– 4   is *l·* and peace." — *Rom.* 8 : 6.
  '02. 6–28   is *l·* and peace." — *Rom.* 8 : 6.
and religion
  Mis. 374– 8   Christianity in *l·* and religion.
and sacrifice
  My. 323–18   * your wonderful *l·* and sacrifice
and teachings
  Mis. 244–17   *l·* and teachings of Jesus?
  No. 21– 1   *l·* and teachings of Jesus
and the love
  Mis. 398–26   In the *l·* and the love of our Lord.
  Po. 75– 6   In the *l·* and the love of our Lord.
and understanding
  Pan. 15– 9   *l·* and understanding of God,
appreciate a
  '00. 3–13   workers who appreciate a *l·*,
battle of
  Mis. 339–10   In the battle of *l·*, good is
belief of
  Un. 40– 6   belief of *l·* in matter, must perish,
  My. 132–25   destroy the belief of *l·* in matter.
better
  Mis. 235–18   thirsting after a better *l·*,
brim of
  '00. 8–23   will boil over the brim of *l·*
brought back to
  Mis. 211–19   pitied and brought back to *l·*?
busy
  My. 338–17   owing to my busy *l·*,
Christian
  '01. 28–10   a more devout Christian *l·*
  My. 200–18   holds us to the Christian *l·*
Christ Jesus'
  No. 34–27   currents of Christ Jesus' *l·*,
claim to
  Mis. 198–10   claim to *l·*, . . . in matter,
coming to
  Mis. 211–16   cause him to suffer in coming to *l·*?

life

common
  Mis. 202– 6   * beyond the walks of common *l·*,
     357–10   beyond the walks of common *l·*,
common walks of
  My. 189– 6   in the common walks of *l·*,
consciousness and
  Un. 36– 1   evidence of consciousness and *l·*
  My. 203– 6   in our consciousness and *l·*,
consecrated
  Mis. x– 2   grandeur of a consecrated *l·*
     354–17   character subdued, a *l·* consecrated,
constituting
  Mis. 56–11   indication of matter's constituting *l·*
corrected
  Mis. 356– 3   a *l·* corrected illumine its own
country
  Pan. 3–27   patron of country *l·*,
crown of
  '00. 13–15   give thee a crown of *l·*." — *Rev.* 2 : 10.
daily
  My. 36–23   * to the daily *l·* and purpose
     43– 6   * order aright the affairs of daily *l·*.
     233– 4   to watch . . . in your daily *l·*,
defines
  Ret. 60– 1   defines *l·* as something apart from
     60– 4   material sense defines *l·* as a
destroy
  Un. 25–19   *Evil.* . . . I can destroy *l·*.
destroyers of
  No. 11– 3   nor destroyers of *l·* or its
divine
  Po. 70– 6   Making this *l·* divine,
does not dignify
  Mis. 240– 9   Predicting danger does not dignify *l·*,
does not understand
  Mis. 197–23   does not understand *l·* in, Christ.
dream of
  (*see* **dream**)
earth
  My. 158–11   natal hour of my lone earth *l·* ;
earthly
  Mis. 166– 4   the earthly *l·* of a martyr ;
end of
  Chr. 55–21   nor end of *l·* ; — *Heb.* 7 : 3.
eternal
  Mis. 64– 8   indestructible eternal *l·* in God.
     170–22   bears upon our eternal *l·*.
     205–22   forever permeated with eternal *l·*,
     213–23   give unto them eternal *l·* ; — *John* 10 : 28.
  Un. 4–23   "*l·* eternal" consists in — *John* 17 : 3.
     37– 4   in order to inherit eternal *l·*
  Pul. vii–20   vast problem of eternal *l·*,
  My. 273–23   good, and therefore *l·* eternal.
     274– 2   the Principle of *l·* eternal ;
everlasting
  Un. 40–14   no more receive everlasting *l·* by
  My. 129–23   health and *l·* everlasting
     193– 3   to know aright is *l·* everlasting.
every-day
  '02. 17–26   Consult thy every-day *l·* ;
fatal to
  Mis. 380–14   an accident, called fatal to *l·*,
fulfilled
  '02. 4– 8   a more fulfilled *l·* and spiritual
give
  Un. 25–19   *Evil.* . . . I give *l·*, and I can
giving
  '02. 9– 3   the All-power — giving *l·*,
go forth into
  Mis. 224–17   Then, we should go forth into *l·*
good
  Mis. 233–18   good words for a good *l·*,
happifies
  Mis. 394– 6   Hope happifies *l·*, at the altar
  Po. 45– 8   Hope happifies *l·*, at the altar
  My. 134–16   Truth happifies *l·* in the hamlet
happiness and
  Mis. 212–19   happiness, and *l·* flow not into
  Un. 22–15   essential to happiness and *l·*.
happy
  My. 40–31   * her own blameless and happy *l·*,
hath its music
  Po. 65–22   *l·* hath its music in low minor
health and
  (*see* **health**)
healthful
  Mis. 170–10   understanding is healthful *l·*.
her
  Mis. 35–13   * the outgrowths of her *l·*.
     130– 2   her *l·* exemplified long-suffering,
  Ret. 6– 4   * Her *l·* was a living illustration
  Pul. 31–11   * with the work of her *l·* which
     32–14   * She told me the story of her *l·*,
  My. 270–16   Her *l·* is proven under trial,
     329–28   * some incidents of her *l·*

life

here is
  Ret. 18– 1   Here is *l·* !   Here is youth !
  Po. 63– 8   Here is *l·* !   Here is youth !
higher
  Mis. 228–13   capacity for a higher *l·*
  My. 112–29   his higher *l·* is the result of
his
  Mis. 211–23   will save his *l·* — *Matt.* 16 : 25.
    292– 6   so loved the world that he gave his *l·*
    327–26   "He that loseth his *l·* — *Matt.* 10 : 39.
  Ret. 32– 7   will save his *l·* — *Matt.* 16 : 25.
  '02. 18–19   Jesus laid down his *l·* for mankind ;
    19–29   our Saviour in his *l·* of love.
  My. 3–21   good which has come into his *l·*,
    110–29   made his *l·* an abject failure.
    216–11   Either his *l·* must be a miracle
    233–26   he that loseth his *l·* — *Matt.* 10 : 39.
    277–11   the question of his *l·*.
home
  Pul. 50– 8   * better home *l·* and citizenship.
honest
  Mis. 227–26   summary of an honest *l·*
hourly
  Mis. 248–17   or that my hourly *l·* is
human
    (*see* **human**)
imaginary
  Un. 38–13   another power, an imaginary *l·*,
immortal
  Mis. 170– 2   resurrection and *l·* immortal
  Pul. 23–24   * intimations of man's immortal *l·*.
individual
  Mis. 309–22   Man's individual *l·* is infinitely
in God
  Mis. 64– 8   indestructible eternal *l·* in God.
  My. 150–22   raising the . . . to *l·* in God.
in Him
  Pan. 13–19   and find *l·* in Him in whom
in Him was
  My. 295– 6   "In Him was *l·* ; — *John* 1 : 4.
in Life
  Pan. 13–20   *l·* in Life, all in All.
intellectual
  My. 309–31   * practically all the intellectual *l·*."
intelligence nor
  Mis. 28–25   no intelligence nor *l·* in matter ;
intense
  Pul. 23–20   * years of more intense *l·*,
into the world
  '01. 21–22   not . . . death but *l·* into the world.
in truth
  My. 273–20   The truth of life, or *l·* in truth,
is dead
  Ret. 20–19   Oh, *l·* is dead, bereft of all,
is not lost
  My. 295– 3   assurance that *l·* is not lost ;
its
  Ret. 69–14   Its *l·* is found to be not Life,
  '02. 18–24   faith without proof loses its *l·*,
  Peo. 1– 4   draws not its *l·* from human
Jesus'
  Mis. 214– 2   Jesus' *l·* was full of Love,
knowledge of
  '02. 6– 3   knowledge of *l·*, substance, or
later in
  My. 311– 2   which occurred later in *l·*,
line of
  Mis. 38– 5   elevate man in every line of *l·*,
lines of
  Mis. 81– 6   into more spiritual lines of *l·*
loaf of
  My. 272– 3   leavens the loaf of *l·* with justice,
loftier
  Po. 32–10   A loftier *l·* to invite
love for
  My. 90–10   * All the passionate love for *l·*
loyal
  Mis. 386–25   remembrance of her loyal *l·*,
  Po. 50–11   remembrance of her loyal *l·*,
made honest
  Mis. 227–17   wider aims of a *l·* made honest :
man's
  My. 277–12   sublime question as to man's *l·*
Master's
  My. 219–19   our great Master's *l·* of healing,
material
    (*see* **material**)
miscalled
  Mis. 361– 6   its miscalled *l·* ends in death,
mortal
  Mis. 28–10   the phenomena of mortal *l·*
most sweet
  Mis. 388–11   *l·* most sweet, as heart to heart
  Po. 7–11   *l·* most sweet, as heart to heart

life

my
  Mis. 54–18   *to keep well all my l·*
    350–30   My *l·*, consecrated to humanity
    392–14   Faithful and patient be my *l·*
  Pul. 21–10   to be made manifest in my *l·*.
  '01. 24–12   * I owe my *l·* to it."
  Po. 20–18   Faithful and patient be my *l·*
  My. 42–17   * blessings which have come into my *l·*
    133–28   your knowledge . . . uncovers my *l·*,
    283–10   leading impetus of my *l·*.
    306– 3   to narrow my *l·* into a conflict for
my own
  Mis. 11– 7   and save my own *l·*,
no
  Mis. 21–16   "There is no *l·*, . . . in matter.
  Ret. 93–19   "There is no *l·*, . . . in matter."
  Un. 38– 8   Error has no *l·*,
    38–12   matter has no *l·*,
nor death
  My. 302– 6   *l·* nor death, health nor disease,
nor sensation
  Ret. 69–20   matter has no . . . *l·*, nor sensation,
not death
  Mis. 346– 1   *L·*, not death, was and is
of a Christian Scientist
  Man. 50–16   the *l·* of a Christian Scientist,
of a man
  '01. 30–19   the inner genial *l·* of a man,
of Christ
  No. 10–10   *l·* of Christ is the predicate and
    41–13   *l·* of Christ is the perfect example ;
of Christianity
  Mis. 199–30   outflowing *l·* of Christianity,
of Christ Jesus
  '02. 8–16   *l·* of Christ Jesus, his words and
of Godlikeness
  '02. 16–23   express the *l·* of Godlikeness.
of Jesus
  Mis. 199–15   illustrate the *l·* of Jesus
    199–16   The rulers sought the *l·* of Jesus ;
    260– 1   illustrated by the *l·* of Jesus,
    337–22   the *l·* of Jesus was belittled
  Ret. 22– 7   history of the early *l·* of Jesus.
  Un. 9–17   simple teaching and *l·* of Jesus
of Love
  My. 301–11   teach us the *l·* of Love.
of love
  '02. 19–29   our Saviour in his *l·* of love.
  Peo. 5– 6   a deathless *l·* of love ;
of man
  Mis. 187–21   substance, and *l·* of man
    209–16   recuperate the *l·* of man,
  My. 181–10   scientific, sinless *l·* of man
of nations
  My. 277–15   prosperity, and *l·* of nations.
of our Lord
  Mis. 25–15   teachings and *l·* of our Lord.
    83–21   In the *l·* of our Lord,
  '01. 1–10   commemorate . . . the *l·* of our Lord,
  '02. 16–17   agony in the *l·* of our Lord ;
  My. 136– 5   and by the *l·* of our Lord
    179–19   depicted in the *l·* of our Lord,
of spirituality
  My. 352– 9   * for your *l·* of spirituality,
of sympathy
  Ret. 95– 8   * Unto a *l·* of sympathy.
of the author
  Po. v– 2   * in the *l·* of the author,
of the personal Jesus
  Mis. 166–30   of the *l·* of the personal Jesus.
of Truth
  Peo. 9–11   bathes us in the *l·* of Truth
one's
  Mis. 11–15   If one's *l·* were attacked,
    109–27   and consecrate one's *l·* anew.
    238–20   Let one's *l·* answer well
opposite of
  My. 235– 3   suppositional opposite of *l·*,
organic
  Mis. 56– 3   *What is organic l· ?*
    56–21   Organic *l·* is an error of statement
  No. 28–26   *soul* means sense and organic *l·* ;
our
  Mis. 76–28   Christ, who is our *l·*, — *Col.* 3 : 4.
    391–14   As item, of our *l·* ;
  Po. 38–13   As item, of our *l·* ;
  My. 166– 8   and God takes care of our *l·*.
outcome of
  Mis. 190– 3   nor the outcome of *l·* infused into
perfect
  My. 111–13   spiritual status of a perfect *l·*
perfected
  '02. 17–15   on duty done and *l·* perfected,
  Po. 22–17   A *l·* perfected, strong and calm.

life

perpetuate
No. 5–16 restore health and perpetuate *l*,

physical
Un. 39– 6 and the pride of physical *l*

pride of
Mis. 116–18 pleasures and pains and pride of *l* :
     183– 1 pride of *l* will then be quenched
Hea. 17– 2 the pride of *l*, envy, hypocrisy,

private
My. 218–25 My private *l* is given to a servitude

progressive
Mis. 117– 2 progressive *l* is the reality of Life

proof of
My. 177–13 true knowledge and proof of *l*

public
Mis. 249–10 Both in private and public *l*,

purpose in
My. 306–11 quite another purpose in *l*

purposes of
My. 285– 9 crowns the great purposes of *l*

rainbowy
Mis. 231–27 yes, and his little rainbowy *l*

real
Mis. 105–14 Man's real *l* or existence

realities of
Hea. 17–12 they are not the realities of *l* ;

religious
My. 93–25 * our social and religious *l*.

resurrection and
Mis. 170– 2 resurrection and *l* immortal

ruined for
My. 60– 9 * you will be ruined for *l* ;

rush into
Po. 16–10 rush into *l*, and roll on with

satisfaction with
My. 81– 4 * healthy satisfaction with *l*.

save the
My. 292–15 prayers to save the *l* of
     335–28 * nothing could save the *l* of

scale of
My. 268–27 harmoniously ascends the scale of *l*.

science of
Mis. 344–13 such a material science of *l* !

sculptors of
Peo. 7–16 * "Sculptors of *l* are we

sensation and
Mis. 53– 1 claim of sensation and *l* in matter,

sense of
     (*see* **sense**)

short
Ret. 7–10 * throughout his short *l*.

so-called
Mis. 28–11 this so-called *l* is a dream
     128– 3 this so-called *l* in matter
Ret. 23– 2 illusion that this so-called *l*
My. 274– 3 apart from the so-called *l* of matter

soul and
Ret. 59– 3 mortal mind and soul and *l*,

Spirit of
     (*see* **Spirit**)

spiritual
Mis. 351–30 the antipode of spiritual *l* ;
My. 113–28 a more spiritual *l* and love

St. Paul's
'00. 12–10 St. Paul's *l* furnished items

substance, and
Mis. 187–21 substance, and *l* of man are one,

substance, and intelligence
Mis. 175– 6 *l*, substance, and intelligence,
     218– 9 *l*, substance, and intelligence,
Ret. 67– 7 *l*, substance, and intelligence

substance of
Mis. 103–11 senses say . . . "The substance of *l* is

success in
Mis. 230– 2 Success in *l* depends upon

supposed
Mis. 53– 5 supposed *l* and intelligence in
     201–13 nothingness of supposed *l* in matter,

sustains
Mis. 50–23 belief that . . . sustains *l*,

that
Mis. 19–16 never change the current of that *l*
My. 154–13 that *l* "was the light of — *John* 1 : 4.

this
Mis. 52–18 If this *l* is a dream not dispelled,
Ret. 18–25 This *l* is a shadow,
Po. 41–16 And this *l* but one given to suffer
     64–22 This *l* is a shadow,
     70– 6 Making this *l* divine,

thy
Mis. 338–30 * Live truly, and thy *l* shall be
Po. 46–16 Be all thy *l* in music given,
My. 13–21 redeemeth thy *l* from — *Psal.* 103 : 4.

life

tree of
Ret. 95– 1 this "tree of *l*" — *Rev.* 22 : 2.
Un. 3–16 the "tree of *l*." — *Gen.* 2 : 9.
My. 3– 9 right to the tree of *l*, — *Rev.* 22 : 14.

true
No. 12–18 Living a true *l*, casting out evil,

truth, and the
     (*see* **truth**)

truth of
My. 235– 2 To teach the truth of *l*
     273–20 The truth of *l*, or life in truth,

ultimatum of
My. 273–18 The ultimatum of *l* here

vision of
Hea. 9–28 St. John saw the vision of *l*

walks of
Ret. 5–20 in all the walks of *l*.
'00. 7–11 those in all the walks of *l*,

was the light
My. 295– 6 *l* was the light of men." — *John* 1 : 4.

webs of
My. 232– 5 webs of *l* in looms of love

what is
Ret. 32–13 * What is *l* ? 'T is but a madness.
     32–14 * What is *l* ? A mere illusion,

wondrous
Mis. 214–12 closed . . . that wondrous *l*,

your
Mis. 151–25 may the lamp of your *l*
My. 139–29 redeem . . . your *l* from death.
     352– 9 * gratitude to you for your *l*

Mis. 42– 2 *does l continue in thought only*
     51–13 *teach him l in matter?*
     95–17 always attended my *l* phenomena
     227–18 a *l* in which the fresh flowers of
     227–21 a *l* wherein calm, self-respected
     227–23 a *l* wherein the mind can rest
     332– 2 but not *l* in matter.
     351–24 five senses give . . . *l* that leads unto
     392–12 A lesson grave, of *l*,
Man. 55–19 by uniform maintenance of the *l* of
     93–14 *l* of the Pastor Emeritus
Chr. 55–17 Spirit . . . is *l* — *Rom.* 8 : 10.
Ret. 22– 4 *l* of our great Master.
     58– 7 With our Master, *l* was not merely
     69–12 and matter shall seem to have *l*
     69–17 believing that there is *l* in matter,
Un. 37– 2 also "the *l*." — *John* 14 : 6.
     38–16 but that something else also is *l*,
     61–20 *l* which I now live — *Gal.* 2 : 20.
Pul. 33–26 * whose *l* has been destined to more than
     54–27 * he raised the daughter to *l*.
'02. 18– 9 helped crown with thorns the *l* of
Hea. 9–25 *L* in matter is a dream :
Po. 20–16 A lesson grave, of *l*,
     23–17 *L* hath a higher recompense
     31–14 Not *l*, the vassal of the
     35– 4 love thee as I love *l* less!
My. 77–11 * in the *l* of their cult.
     131– 8 for the *l* that we commemorate
     154–12 "in Him was *l*," — *John* 1 : 4.
     165–16 goodness makes *l* a blessing.
     166– 7 *l* is worth living
     229–31 it takes *l* profoundly ;
     287–14 human rights, liberty, *l*.

life (adj.)
Peo. 7–19 * Our *l* dream passes o'er us.

life-battle
Ret. 22–14 It may be that the mortal *l*

life-bestowing
Ret. 88–14 health-giving and *l* qualities,

Life-encrowned
Po. 29–11 Thou God-idea, *L*,

life-experience
Mis. 3–12 his stripes" — his *l* — *Isa.* 53 : 5.

life-giving
Mis. 113–28 are *l* fountains of truth.
     144–29 the *l* Principle of Christianity,
     233–10 onward march of *l* Science,
Un. 55–16 and the *l* way of Truth.
Pul. 10– 1 Master's self-immolation, his *l*
No. v– 9 *l* waters of a true divinity,
     46– 8 *l* understanding C. S. imparts,
'01. 26–11 he endows it with a *l* quality
'02. 9–21 When first I heard the *l* sound
     14– 7 living and *l* spiritual shield
My. 180– 4 its *l* truths were preached

life-lease
My. 139–11 his is a *l* of hope, home,

lifelessness
Mis. 74–27 demonstrated the *l* of matter,

lifelong
Mis. 72– 3 to be born a l· sufferer
life-member
Mis. 296– 3 l· of the Victoria Institute
life-preservers
Pan. 14–21 be unto them l· !
Life-problem
Un. 5–13 to solve every L· in a day.
life-purpose
Mis. 207– 4 of the spirit of my l·,
Life's
Mis. 84–27 teaches L· lessons aright.
125–17 press on to L· long lesson,
397–10 the rock, Upon L· shore,
Pul. 18–19 the rock, Upon L· shore;
Po. 12–19 the rock, Upon L· shore,
My. 290–20 into L· substance.
life's
Mis. 9–16 friends seem to sweeten l cup
10– 2 wherewith to obstruct l· joys
116–13 filling the measures of l· music
116–17 human chords express l· loss or
120– 5 Principle of l· long problem,
238– 8 in defense of his own l· incentive,
316–19 on my retirement from l· bustle.
386– 1 grand and glorious l· sphere,
393–12 Crowns l· Cliff for such as we.
397– 2 sweet mercies show L· burdens light.
Pul. 18–11 sweet mercies show L· burdens light.
54– 4 * We touch him in l· throng and press,
56–21 * We tread upon l· broken laws,
'02. 19–19 heaving surf of l· troubled sea
Po. 12–11 sweet mercies show L· burdens light.
24– 9 From out l· billowy sea,
46– 3 Within l· summer bowers !
49– 3 grand and glorious l· sphere,
51–17 Crowns l· Cliff for such as we.
65– 3 L· pulses move fitful and slow ;
65– 9 enchained to l· dreary night,
65–15 We waken to l· dreary sigh.
67– 1 brief bliss of l· little day
73–17 afar from l· turmoil its goal.
My. 166–15 L· ills are its chief recompense ;
288– 5 his l· incentive and sacrifice
298– 4 occurred in my l· experience
lifetime
No. 12– 9 After a l· of orthodoxy
My. 88– 6 * development of a short l·.
90– 1 * thousands during her l· ;
346– 3 * lived with her subject for a l·,
346– 3 * an ordinary l· ;
life-work
Mis. 29– 6 The purpose of his l·
42–18 our l· proves to have been
'02. 15–14 Before entering upon my great l·,
My. 149– 2 Principle of Jesus' l·,
303–21 His l· subordinated the material
lift
Mis. xii– 7 l· my readers above the smoke of
9–17 We l· this cup to our lips ;
19–10 l· the affections and motives of men
52–16 that tends to l· mortals higher.
126–11 learned that trials l· us to
202– 3 l· man's being into the sunlight of
275– 7 it were well to l· the veil on
338– 4 to be able to l· others toward it.
346–26 l· the curtain, let in the light,
351– 2 so as to l· the burdens imposed by
355–17 but to l· your head above it,
360–19 l· every thought-leaflet Spiritward ;
399– 3 And will l· the shade of gloom,
Ret. 73–14 l· thought above physical personality,
Pul. 13–17 struggling to l· their heads above
No. 46–17 let us l· their standard higher,
Peo. 3– 1 will l· man ultimately to
Po. 30–17 L· Thou a patient love
75–10 will l· the shade of gloom,
My. 32– 9 * did not have to l· their voices
34–10 L· up your heads, — Psal. 24 : 9.
34–10 even l· them up, — Psal. 24 : 9.
200–21 to l· itself on crumbling thrones of
305–31 my purpose was to l· the curtain on
350–13 L· from despair the struggler
lifted
Mis. 83–23 l· up his eyes to heaven, — John 17 : 1.
165–21 until l· to these by their
187–15 were not l· to the inspired sense of
224– 8 l· his hands to his head,
234– 8 what we have not l· ourselves to be,
255– 9 to be thus l· up.
399–21 L· higher, we depart,
Ret. 27–20 * are l· up and strengthened.

lifted
Ret. 88– 6 l· his own body from the sepulchre.
93– 8 "And I, if I be l· up — John 12 : 32.
'02. 17–14 curtain . . . should be l· on reality,
Po. 76– 5 L· higher, we depart,
My. 34– 4 not l· up his soul unto — Psal. 24 : 4.
81–19 * for ills cured, for hearts l· up,
247–13 and you will be l· up
341– 5 l· to her giant hills the ensign of
lifteth
Pan. 6– 8 l· his head above it
12–15 it l· the burden of sharp experience
Po. 79–14 l· me, Ayont hate's thrall :
lifting
Mis. 262–17 l· the fallen and strengthening the
'02. 19– 6 l· up his hands and blessing them,
Hea. 11–16 before l· its foot against its
My. 296–27 l· the curtains of mortal mind,
lifts
Mis. 246–16 inhumanity l· its hydra head
287–15 until progress l· mortals to
290– 5 Science l· humanity higher
330–28 violet l· its blue eye to heaven,
No. 32–13 Mind-healing l· with a steady arm,
'00. 6–22 l· him from the stubborn thrall of
Peo. 12–15 l· man above the demands of matter.
My. 258– 3 What is it that l· a system of
268–25 l· the curtain on the Science of
Light
Mis. 154–29 Let your light reflect L·.
384–15 L·, Love divine Is here,
Po. 36–14 L·, Love divine Is here,
My. 301– 2 rays — from L· emitting light.
light (noun)
 all
'01. 15–17 wickedness against all l·.
 all is
'02. 16–20 there is no darkness, but all is l·,
 and cheerfulness
My. 31–14 * then of l· and cheerfulness,
 and color
Mis. 87– 9 substance of form, l·, and color,
 and darkness
Mis. 34–26 direct opposites as l· and darkness.
 and joy
Po. 23– 9 Mirrored in truth, in l· and joy,
 and liberty
Mis. xii– 8 lift my readers . . . into l· and liberty.
My. 187–25 l· and liberty of His children,
 and Life
Ret. 27–29 new world of l· and Life,
 and love
Mis. 184–25 Oh, for that l· and love ineffable,
235–10 through the l· and love of Truth.
My. 355–23 the reflection of l· and love ;
 and might
My. 246–20 the l· and might of the divine
 and song
Po. 54– 4 With l· and song and prayer !
 and truth
My. 154–24 l· and truth, emanating from the
 approach the
Mis. 352–12 lengthen as they approach the l·,
 borrowed
Ret. 57–15 Man shines by borrowed l·.
 brings the
Mis. 205– 9 brings the l· which dispels darkness.
 brings to
Mis. 189–12 brings to l· the true reflection :
Ret. 64– 7 brings to l·, makes apparent,
Un. 38–19 brings to l· Life and
My. 253– 4 brings to l· the perfect original
 brought to
Mis. 1–21 brought to l· by the evolutions of
82–24 being is brought to l·.
222–23 when brought to l·, will make
Ret. 58– 9 brought to l· immortality,
No. 33–21 brought to l· the efficacy
Hea. 18– 5 immortality be brought to l·.
My. 93–27 * certain statistics brought to l·
110–27 will have been brought to l·.
207–14 * immortality brought to l·.
332–20 * The facts . . . were brought to l·
 cheerful
Ret. 5–24 * gentle dew and cheerful l·,
 children of
Mis. 342–29 children of l· ;" — Luke 16 : 8.
Ret. 90–29 one of the children of l·.
My. 191–10 Children of l·, you are
206–32 as children of l·." — Eph. 5 : 8.
 consciousness of
No. 30–22 The consciousness of l· is like
 darkness for
Mis. 174–27 We do not look into darkness for l·.

light

deliberation and
Ret. 85–18 due deliberation and *l*·,

divine
(*see* **divine**)

dwelleth in
Mis. 367–23 He dwelleth in *l*· ;
367–25 that darkness dwelleth in *l*·,

dwelling in
Un. 18– 4 Dwelling in *l*·, I can see

electric
Pul. 58–30 * electric *l*·, behind an antique

emits
Mis. 290–29 it emits *l*· because it reflects ;

emitting
Chr. 53–40 Life, . . . Emitting *l*· !
My. 282–15 to all mankind a *l*· emitting *l*·.
301– 2 rays — from Light emitting *l*·.

eternal
Mis. 134–14 dwelleth in eternal *l*·
Po. 70–10 Truth is eternal *l*·,

everlasting
My. 206–19 an everlasting *l*·,— *Isa.* 60 : 19.

fled with the
Po. 65– 7 it fled with the *l*·,

focusing
My. 164–12 a thing focusing *l*·

fountain of
Mis. 117–28 God is the fountain of *l*·,

fringed with
Ret. 23– 9 not even fringed with *l*·.

God is
'01. 3–21 * God is *l*·, but light is not God."

golden
Pul. 39–16 * its flood of golden *l*·.

great
Mis. 374–18 brought a great *l*· to all ages,
Chr. 55– 8 have seen a great *l*· :— *Isa.* 9 : 2.
My. 133– 3 in the great *l*· of the present,

heat and
No. 14–15 are to solar heat and *l*·.

heaven of
Po. 71– 9 Spans our broad heaven of *l*·.

heaven's own
Peo. 7–14 * With heaven's own *l*· the sculptor

He sees
Mis. 367–24 and in the light He sees *l*·,

his own
Ret. 83–17 difficult to rekindle his own *l*·

infinite
No. 16–15 infinite logic is the infinite *l*·,

in the Lord
My. 206–31 *l*· in the Lord :— *Eph.* 5 : 8.

into
Mis. 130–32 out of darkness into *l*·.

is not God
'01. 3–21 * God is light, but *l*· is not God."

knowledge is
No. 30–20 This knowledge is *l*· wherein

leads to
Mis. 347–27 from the night He leads to *l*·.

let in the
Mis. 346–26 Then lift the curtain, let in the *l*·,

lets in
Ret. 90– 2 God's window which lets in *l*·,

let there be
Mis. 388– 3 "Let there be *l*·,— *Gen.* 1 : 3.
'02. 20–12 "Let there be *l*·,— *Gen.* 1 : 3.
Po. 1–10 "Let there be *l*·" — *Gen.* 1 : 3.
7– 3 "Let there be *l*·,— *Gen.* 1 : 3.

liberty and
Ret. 81–10 diviner sense of liberty and *l*·.

Life and
Mis. 337–29 The ineffable Life and *l*·

Life is
Po. 79–16 Life is *l*·, and wisdom might,

line of
Mis. 105–19 follow this line of *l*· and battle.
Ret. 42– 7 to follow in this line of *l*·.

lines of
Mis. 376–26 the lower lines of *l*· kindled
My. 155–21 lines of *l*· span the horizon

lost in
Mis. 352–13 until they are lost in *l*·

love and
Mis. 149– 6 what they possess of love and *l*·

manifest
My. 164–13 love, . . . is present to manifest *l*·.

marvellous
Un. 17–18 into a home of marvellous *l*·,
Rud. 4–25 by His marvellous *l*·.
My. 206–26 into His marvellous *l*·." — *I Pet.* 2 : 9.

material
Pul. 2–10 Material *l*· and shade are temporal,

might and
My. 133– 4 might and *l*· of the present

light

more
No. 16–16 forever giving forth more *l*·,

morning
Mis. 222–32 as easily as dawns the morning *l*·
My. 31– 3 * "The morning *l*· is breaking ;"

never a
Un. 28–10 never a *l*· or form was discerned

never see
Ret. 64–16 they shall never see *l*·.— *Psal.* 49 : 19.

new
Ret. 14–23 when the new *l*· dawned
45– 2 A new *l*· broke in upon it,

no
Mis. 276–30 Error giveth no *l*·,
342–20 no *l*· ! earth's fables flee,

of a home
Po. 8–21 The *l*· of a home of love and pride ;

of all ages
Mis. 320–27 is the *l*· of all ages ;

of a single candle
Pul. 28– 3 * by the *l*· of a single candle,

of Christian Science
Mis. 165–11 this appearing is the *l*· of C. S.
253–29 opened their eyes to the *l*· of C. S.
My. 187– 6 May the divine *l*· of C. S.

of divine Science
Mis. 192–17 with the *l*· of divine Science,

of Love
Mis. 132– 5 to the *l*· of Love — and By-laws.
320–28 is the *l*· of Love,

of men
My. 154–13 "was the *l*· of men." — *John* 1 : 4.
295– 6 was the *l*· of men." — *John* 1 : 4.

of modern science
Pul. 54–19 * in the *l*· of modern science,

of one friendship
Pul. 5– 6 *l*· of one friendship after another

of penetration
Mis. 313– 9 throw the *l*· of penetration on

of revelation
Hea. 8–18 becloud the *l*· of revelation,
My. 114–18 *l*· of revelation and solar light.

of Science
Mis. 254–19 would obscure the *l*· of Science,

of the city
No. 27–10 Spirit will be the *l*· of the city,

of the moon
My. 313– 6 * By the *l*· of the moon

of the Science
My. 343–16 the *l*· of the Science came first

of this revelation
Mis. 165–12 The *l*· of this revelation

of Truth
Mis. 320–11 the *l*· of Truth, to cheer,
My. 241–25 * coming to the *l*· of Truth,

one with
'01. 8–10 and it is one with *l*·,

perceived a
Ret. 76–12 which perceived a *l*· beyond

pinions of
Ret. 85–12 on their pinions of *l*·

proper
Un. 20– 2 seeing it in its proper *l*·,

pure white
Pul. 26– 4 * being of pure white *l*·,

ray of
'01. 8– 9 one ray of *l*· is light,
'02. 12–17 a ray of *l*· one with the sun.

rays of
Mis. 333– 9 absorbs all the rays of *l*·.

reflect
Mis. 131– 6 to discern darkness or to reflect *l*·.
154–29 Let your *l*· reflect Light.

reflected
Mis. 340–29 shine with the reflected *l*· of God.
My. 202–23 My work is reflected *l*·,

resplendent
Mis. 320–10 lends its resplendent *l*· to this

seeking
Mis. 276–26 seeking *l*· from matter instead of

seek the
My. 98–11 * critics who seek the *l*·

sends forth
Ret. 56–22 The sun sends forth *l*·,

shined
Chr. 55– 9 hath the *l*· shined. — *Isa.* 9 : 2.

sketching in
Po. 8–13 sketching in *l*· the heaven

solar
No. 39–26 photography grasps the solar *l*·
My. 114–18 light of revelation and solar *l*·.

sons of
Mis. 321–19 Press on, press on! ye sons of *l*·,

spheres of
Po. 30–21 Echo amid the hymning spheres of *l*·,

light

spiritual
Mis. 113– 2 God's presence gives spiritual *l*,
276–28 thus shutting out spiritual *l*.
341–32 the neglect of spiritual *l*,
342– 6 steady decline of spiritual *l*,
susceptible of
'02. 17–30 cheer the heart susceptible of *l*
that illumines
Po. 32–11 *l* that illumines my spiritual eye,
that is in thee
Ret. 81–21 *l* that is in thee — *Matt.* 6 : 23.
that shineth
Mis. 368– 3 *l* that shineth in darkness,
their
My. 269–21 have healing in their *l*.
355–25 and their *l* shines.
thereof
My. 206–22 Lamb is the *l* thereof." — *Rev.* 21 : 23.
there was
Mis. 388– 3 and there was *l*." — *Gen.* 1 : 3.
'02. 20–12 and there was *l*," — *Gen.* 1 : 3.
Po. 7– 3 and there was *l*." — *Gen.* 1 : 3.
this
No. 39–24 Advancing in this *l*, we reflect it ;
39–25 this *l* reveals the pure
throw a
'02. 16–16 and they throw a *l* upon the
Thy
Mis. 275–17 we thank Thee that Thy *l*
thy
Po. 29– 4 Thy *l* was born where storm
My. 183–14 Love be thy *l* upon the mountain
183–27 thy *l* is come, — *Isa.* 60 : 1.
to Love
My. 234–13 from *l* to Love, from sense to Soul.
unconceived
'02. 5– 9 this almost unconceived *l* of
untrue to the
Ret. 81–19 consciously untrue to the *l*,
waves of
Pul. 39–18 * I watch the flow Of waves of *l*.
which shineth
Un. 63–10 *l* which shineth in darkness,
will illumine
Mis. 276–17 *l* will illumine the darkness.
wisdom's
Po. 27– 9 dawn with wisdom's *l*
with darkness
Mis. 333–22 hath *l* with darkness? — *II Cor.* 6 : 14.
your
Mis. 154–29 Let your *l* reflect Light.
My. 191–10 Let your *l* shine.

———

Mis. 149–26 a *l* that cannot be hid.
157–24 righteousness as the *l*, — *Psal.* 37 : 6.
355–28 Hold thy gaze to the *l*,
367–24 and in the *l* He sees light,
Ret. 18– 5 *l* colored softly by blossom
Un. 19–14 the *l* that is in thee — *Matt.* 6 : 23.
Pul. 52–16 * believers receive *l*, health, and
No. 30–21 not *l* holding darkness within
'00. 6–24 is not darkness but *l*.
'01. 3–25 *l*, being matter, loses the nature of
8– 9 one ray of light is *l*,
35– 3 righteousness as the *l*, — *Psal.* 37 : 6.
Hea. 10–18 and joy cometh with the *l*.
Peo. 3–16 spans the moral heavens with *l*,
Po. 22– 7 lo, the *l*! far heaven is nigh!
43–15 *L* with wisdom's ray
53– 8 *L* o'er the rugged steep.
63–13 *l* colored softly by blossom
My. 45–21 * pillar of fire to give you *l*,
140– 5 I will make darkness *l* — *Isa.* 42 : 16.
154–22 * he have *l*, . . . freedom, immortality?"
170–25 righteousness as the *l*, — *Psal.* 37 : 6.
199– 5 *l* hath sprung up.
206–28 of the saints in *l* : — *Col.* 1 : 12

light (adj.)

Mis. 133–29 Love makes all burdens *l*,
262–26 Christ-love that makes them *l*
374–19 and named his burdens *l*,
397– 2 Life's burdens *l*.
Pul. 18–11 Life's burdens *l*.
24–22 * Concord granite in *l* gray,
Po. 12–11 Life's burdens *l*.
My. 89– 5 * The building is of *l* stone,
161–29 "My burden is *l*." — *Matt.* 11 : 30.
342– 5 * uprightly and with *l* step,

light (verb)

Peo. 8–23 to *l* our sepulchres with
My. 340–32 *l* their fires in every home.
345–28 They *l* the way to the Church

lighted

Pul. 32– 1 * *l* by luminous blue eyes,
My. 69– 1 * church is unusually well *l*,

lighten

Mis. 277–29 sharply *l* on the cloud
323– 6 for God doth *l* it.
My. 206–22 glory of God did *l* it, — *Rev.* 21 : 23.

lightens

Mis. 313–10 *l* earth's landscape.

lighter

Mis. 19– 8 healing the sick is far *l* than
66–16 suffering is the *l* affliction.

lighteth

Pan. 12–16 and so *l* the path that he who
My. 187– 6 light of C. S. that *l* every
257–15 *l* every man that — *John* 1 : 9.

lighting

Mis. 250–28 *l* the dark places of earth.
393– 8 *L* up this mortal dream.
Pul. 25– 1 * *l* and cooling of the church
Po. 51–13 *L* up this mortal dream.
My. 68–31 * used in the *l* fixtures,
110–10 daystar will appear, *l*
252–22 *l* and leading humanity

lightly

Mis. 251–21 as men, clothed more *l*,
329–19 her little feet trip *l* on,
Ret. 75–15 that can *l* speak — *Mark* 9 : 39.
No. 27–26 take off thy shoes and tread *l*,

lightness

My. 89– 8 * joined *l* and grace

lightning

Ret. 17–16 brave breast to the *l* and storm,
'00. 9–15 *l*, thunder, and sunshine
Po. 62–20 brave breast to the *l* and storm,

lightnings

Un. 52–20 *l*, earthquakes, poisons,
Po. 18–17 Though *l* be lurid

lights

Mis. 303– 1 they are *l* that cannot be hid,
306–28 spiritual idea that *l* your path !
324–25 only to find the *l* all wasted
Un. 14–17 "the Father of *l*, — *Jas.* 1 : 17.
Pul. 26– 2 * electric *l* in the form of a star,
48– 8 * *l* and shades of spring
76–10 * in certain *l* has a shimmer
'02. 5– 7 *l* the fires of the Holy Ghost,
My. 191–24 *l* the living way of Life.
192–11 *l* the living way to Life,
232–13 living *l* in our darkness :

lightsome

Mis. 142–20 my Muse lost her *l* lyre,
My. 341–12 A *l* lay, a cooing call,

like

Mis. 5–11 "I should *l* to study,
17– 7 *l* the patriarch of old,
21– 6 in the flesh, *l* ourselves,
29–30 *l* students in mathematics,
48–29 *l* a hundred other stories,
51–23 * Shall, *l* a whirlwind, scatter
51–28 * transparent *l* some holy thing."
66–24 *l* the more physical ailment.
81–22 *l* the individual John
84–24 *l* a weary traveller,
88–16 *l* a midnight sun.
88–17 *l* a benediction after prayer,
102–12 *l* Himself and *l* nothing else.
103–25 was *l* that of other men ;
111–11 *l* Peter, they launch into the depths,
127–32 human heart, *l* a feather bed, needs
132–14 * would "*l* to hear from Dr. Cullis ;
134–23 *L* Elisha, look up, and behold :
139–25 *l* all true wisdom,
162–30 *l* him he went forth,
166–22 *L* the leaven that a certain woman
171–23 *is l unto leaven,* — *Matt.* 13 : 33.
196–22 "we shall be *l* Him ;" — *I John* 3 : 2.
208– 6 *L* a legislative bill
221–25 *l* saying that five times ten are
227–19 *l* the camomile, the more trampled
241–24 Then, *l* blind Bartimeus,
264– 8 *l* camera shadows thrown upon the
266–12 is *l* the comet's course,
275– 2 in scenes *l* these,
275– 7 In times *l* these
276– 4 *l* all else, was purely Western
329– 6 nature *l* a thrifty housewife
331– 5 downtrodden *l* the grass,
335–22 zealots, who, *l* Peter, sleep when
340–28 *l* the stars, comes out in the
343–21 reappear, *l* devastating witch-grass,
346–23 *l* apples of gold — *Prov.* 25 : 11.

like

Mis.	347– 2	lest thou also be *l·* — *Prov.* 26 : 4.
	347– 6	hanging *l·* a horoscope
	350–13	*l·* my public instruction.
	353– 3	*l·* the action of sickness,
	355–25	*l·* the dove from the deluge.
	369–25	*L·* him, we would find our
	384–19	* Love, *l·* the sea,
	387–10	*L·* brother birds, that soar
	390–24	*l·* things of earth,
	394– 3	*l·* the dew on the flower,
	400– 4	*L·* this stone, be in thy place :
Chr.	55–21	*l·* unto the Son of God. — *Heb.* 7 : 3.
Ret.	5–24	* *l·* the gentle dew and
	10–13	vanished *l·* a dream.
	25–21	personal being, *l·* unto man ;
	27– 8	*l·* all great truths,
	27–21	*l·* the brooklet in its
	48–26	*l·* the baptism of Jesus,
	57– 7	This would be *l·* correcting the
	58– 4	*l·* trying to compensate for
	59– 8	*l·* saying that addition means
	64–17	is *l·* the beasts — *Psal.* 49 : 20.
	68–29	His origin is not, *l·* that of
	73–23	is *l·* the sick talking sickness.
	78– 1	acts *l·* a diseased physique,
	90– 9	*l·* "the elect lady" — *II John* 1 : 1.
	90–19	the ardent mother?
Un.	4– 4	and become *l·* Him.
	10–23	*l·* commencing with the minus sign,
	19– 4	and, *l·* ourselves, He foresees
	21– 7	In *l·* manner good and evil talk
	23–23	conceive of God only as *l·* itself,
	27–13	fleeing *l·* a shadow at daybreak ;
	41–19	"we shall be *l·* Him," — *I John* 3 : 2.
	44– 5	*l·* the structure raised thereupon,
	50–18	*L·* evil, it is destitute of Mind,
	58–17	*l·* as we are, — *Heb.* 4 : 15.
Pul.	2– 1	*l·* the Queen of Sheba,
	8– 3	*L·* the winds telling tales
	10–25	descended *l·* day-spring
	15– 6	people *l·* you better when
	16–16	*L·* this stone, be in thy place ;
	23–21	* *l·* Prof. Max Muller,
	32–13	* *l·* any abbess of old.
	33– 3	* began, *l·* Jeanne d'Arc, to hear
	46–23	* applied herself, *l·* other girls,
	51– 6	* to a matter *l·* C. S.,
	82– 3	* comes *l·* the south wind
Rud.	17– 1	*L·* certain Jews whom
No.	10–25	*l·* the needle to the pole
	13–25	and sparkle *l·* a diamond,
	21–28	*l·* a cloud without rain,
	30–22	*l·* the eternal law of God,
'00.	7–22	*l·* Peter we believe in
	11–23	* *L·* the close of an angel's psalm,
'01.	11–27	lest thou also be *l·* — *Prov.* 26 : 4.
	19–24	hypnotism, and the *l·*,
	29–13	They are *l·* children that
	30–23	no emperor is obeyed *l·*
	30–24	*l·* the clear, far-seeing vision,
'02.	4–15	ringing *l·* soft vesper chimes
	10–28	is *l·* sentencing a man for
	14– 9	* "Great not *l·* Cæsar,
	17–29	*l·* the sun beneath the horizon,
	18–18	*l·* the summer brook,
Hea.	9–14	*l·* furnishing fuel for the flames.
	11–11	*l·* the great pyramid of Egypt,
Peo.	3–17	*l·* a promise upon the cloud,
Po.	2– 8	*L·* a trained falcon in the
	6– 4	*L·* brother birds, that soar
	10–11	Our eagle, *l·* the dove,
	16– 6	*L·* thee, it endureth
	18– 6	*L·* genius unfolding a quenchless
	19– 1	My course, *l·* the eagle's,
	34– 4	*L·* thee, my voice had stirred
	36–18	* Love, *l·* the sea,
	45– 3	*l·* the dew on the flower,
	47–14	sobbing, *l·* some tired child
	56– 3	Ne'er perish young, *l·* things of
	65–18	darkness and death *l·* mist melt away,
	66– 4	*l·* the thrill of that mountain rill,
	67–19	*l·* the blue hyacinth, change not
	70– 5	*L·* to the soul's glad immortality,
	76–15	*L·* this stone, be in thy place :
My.	5–32	Indulging deceit is *l·* the
	13–10	* *l·* a sun in the centre of its
	13–11	* *l·* so many planets,
	13–24	renewed *l·* the eagle's," — *Psal.* 103 : 5.
	15–29	* To hear it *l·* the rest.
	82–18	* in something *l·* ten minutes.
	87–13	* we *l·* to know and *l·* to have here.
	94– 1	* growth continues in *l·* proportion
	95– 2	* *l·* a green bay-tree,
	99– 5	* doeth good *l·* a medicine,
	105–16	so that it stood out *l·* a cord.

like

My.	121–10	This strength is *l·* the ocean,
	121–14	Peace, *l·* plain dealing,
	122– 7	Sin is *l·* a dock root.
	134–18	*l·* a soft summer shower,
	139– 9	*L·* the verdure and evergreen
	147– 3	past comes forth *l·* a pageant
	149–25	predicament quite *l·* that of
	186– 5	*l·* tender nestlings in the crannies
	188–23	in which, *l·* beds in hospitals,
	208–12	*L·* the gentle dews of heaven
	212–18	Being *l·* the disciples of old,
	221–26	*l·* a watchman forsaking his post,
	248– 5	* not *l·* Caesar, stained with blood,
	252– 4	Then you will be toilers *l·* the bee,
	252– 6	you will not be *l·* the spider,
	302–17	use of the word spread *l·* wildfire.
	307– 1	certainly read *l·* words that I
	337–12	Our eagle, *l·* the dove,
	343–12	* would, *l·* herself, be the ruler.
	345–16	came *l·* blessed relief to me,

likely

Mis.	43–10	least *l·* to pour into other minds
Pul.	50–26	* *l·* to show even some one side
My.	61– 8	* would *l·* be postponed until

likened

Mis.	175– 6	*l·* to the false sense of life,
'01.	25–28	Jesus *l·* such self-contradictions to

likeness

after our
Mis.	69–11	after our *l·* : — *Gen.* 1 : 26.

and image
Mis.	16–13	being His *l·* and image,

divine
Ret.	60– 2	very far from the divine *l·*.
Un.	39–27	losing the divine *l·*.
No.	36– 6	when we awake in the divine *l·*.
My.	121–23	reflects the divine *l·*.

eternal
Un.	22– 2	made after God's eternal *l·*,

God's
Mis.	61–29	logic that man is God's *l·*.
	89–28	Immortal man, in God's *l·*,
	186–32	real man in God's *l·*,
Un.	45– 9	very far from God's *l·*."
Pul.	21–25	a clear expression of God's *l·*,
No.	17–12	more than God's *l·* is impossible.
	25–23	immortal man alone is God's *l·*,

God's essential
Mis.	61–22	Does God's essential *l·* sin,

God's own
Mis.	77–27	man, made in God's own *l·*,

harmless
Rud.	8– 6	sends forth its own harmless *l·*.

His
Mis.	15–22	man awake in His *l·*.
	16–13	being His *l·* and image,
	17–20	and of man as His *l·*,
	30–32	and awake in His *l·*.
	79–15	man as His *l·* is erect
	358–13	"awake in His *l·*," — *see Psal.* 17 : 15.
Rud.	7–11	His *l·* would be lost if inverted
	11– 7	in Science man is His *l·*,
'02.	8– 2	God, and man as His *l·*,
Hea.	17–13	awake to behold His *l·*.
Po.	79–20	doth His will — His *l·* still
My.	194–15	melted into the radiance of His *l·*.
	205–21	makes . . . man more His *l·*,

his
Un.	15–15	for his *l·* to his creator.
'00.	8– 3	till we awake in his *l·*.

His own
Mis.	173–28	made man in His own *l·*.

human
Mis.	23–28	human *l·* thrown upon the
	308–30	human *l·* is the antipode of

idea or
My.	239–21	idea or *l·* of the infinite
	262– 2	idea, or *l·* of perfection

image and
(*see* **image**)

image or
My.	239–17	His idea, image, or *l·*,
	269– 2	compound idea, image or *l·*,

is incomplete
Un.	15–10	or the *l·* is incomplete,

lost
Mis.	184–24	gives back the lost *l·*
'02.	8–29	Adam, . . . or His lost *l·*,

of error
Rud.	13–11	*l·* of error — the human belief

of God
(*see* **God**)

likeness

of his Maker
Mis. 62– 8 the true *l·* of his Maker.
164–23 actual *l·* of his Maker.
My. 232–26 the true *l·* of his Maker"?

of Love
'02. 8– 6 the *l·* of Love is loving

of Spirit
Mis. 61–30 man in the *l·* of Spirit
Rud. 13–10 body is not the *l·* of Spirit ;

original
Mis. 18– 2 original *l·* of perfect man,

perfect
Mis. 79– 8 God's perfect *l·*, that reflects all

this
Un. 22– 3 this *l·* consists in a sense of

to his creator
Un. 15–15 for his *l·* to his creator.

to the portraits
My. 342– 8 * The *l·* to the portraits

true
Mis. 62– 8 the true *l·* of his Maker.
97–29 of him who is the true *l·* :
188–30 the true *l·* of God,
Ret. 70– 1 "Mortal mind inverts the true *l·*,
No. 16–19 God and His true *l·*,
My. 232–26 as the true *l·* of his Maker"

unfallen
Mis. 79–23 that perfect and unfallen *l·*,

likening
Mis. 30–13 *l·* them to the priceless understanding

likewise
Mis. 131– 9 leaner sort console . . . by doing *l·*.
240–28 *L·* soberly inform them that
241–12 and try to make others do *l·*,
338– 8 All must go and do *l·*.
Ret. 3– 4 were *l·* connected with
Pul. 2–21 *L·* should we do as
'00. 7– 4 *L·* the religious sentiment has
'01. 9–15 taught his followers to do *l·*.
23–20 taught his disciples . . . to do *l·* ;
My. 106–31 commanded his followers to do *l·*,
149– 4 "Go, and do thou *l·*."— *Luke* 10 : 37.

lilies
Pul. 42–22 * a star of *l·* resting on palms,
42–26 * palms and ferns and Easter *l·*.
My. 155–27 gathering Easter *l·* of love

limb
Mis. 230–11 travel of *l·* more than mind.

limbs
Peo. 10–19 they alone have fettered free *l·*,
My. 105–12 saving the *l·* when the

lime
My. 108– 2 carbonate and sulphate of *l·* ;

limit
Mis. 60–12 *Does it not l· the power of Mind*
60–15 Does it *l·* the power of Mind
282– 2 a sense that does not *l·* God,
Pul. 62–19 * practically no *l·* to the uses
Hea. 4– 7 Clothing Deity with personality, we *l·*
My. 327–15 * to *l·* or stop the practice of C. S.

limitation
Un. 45–21 sphere of its own creation and *l·*,
My. 229–26 namely, laws of *l·* for a

limitations
Ret. 73– 6 *L·* are put off in proportion as the
76–18 and knows no material *l·*.
My. 118–29 holiness, entirely apart from *l·*,
119– 1 convenient for history to record *l·*
177–14 putting off the *l·*

limited
Mis. 64–23 to a *l·* extent, are aids
85–10 his power is temporarily *l·*.
102– 7 originate in a *l·* body,
102– 9 In this *l·* and lower sense
164–30 The *l·* view of God's ideas
190–14 too *l·* and contradictory.
Un. 14–15 Jehovah of *l·* Hebrew faith
Pul. 6– 4 engendering the *l·* forms of a
30– 9 * not *l·* to the Boston adherents,
Rud. 15–19 a very *l·* number of students
No. 19–11 He is neither a *l·* mind nor
19–12 nor a *l·* body.
Hea. 4– 2 cannot start from a *l·* body.
Peo. 3–22 This *l·* sense of God as good
8–11 the *l·* and definite form of a
My. 106–12 *l·* to imaginary diseases !

limiting
Hea. 5– 3 we shall be *l·* His power

limitless
Mis. 284– 7 in this field of *l·* power
No. 20– 1 *L·* personality is inconceivable.

limits
Mis. 42–30 Mind is not confined to *l·* ;
128– 5 within the *l·* of a letter.
282– 5 sense of personality . . . that *l·* man.
No. 12–27 It removes all *l·* from divine power.
Hea. 4– 3 nor remain for a moment within *l·*.
Peo. 3–23 *l·* human thought and action
My. 106–21 Mind calms and *l·* with a word.

limner's
Mis. 393– 6 Paints the *l·* work, I ween,
Po. 51–11 Paints the *l·* work, I ween,

limp
Mis. 112–20 sank back in his chair, *l·* and pale ;

limped
My. 307–32 My idealism, however, *l·*,

limpid
My. 150–15 Stand by the *l·* lake,

Lincoln, Miss Elsie
Pul. 37–18 * Mrs. Hanna, Miss Elsie *L·*,
43– 5 * Mr. . . . Case and Miss Elsie *L·*.
59–21 * a Scientist, Miss Elsie *L·* ;

Lincoln, Neb.
My. 97–14 * [*Nebraska State Journal, L·, N·.*]

Lincoln's
Po. 26–10 *L·* own Great willing heart

Linden Avenue
1414
Pul. 68–18 * services . . . at 1414 *L· A·*.

Lindley Murray's Grammar
Ret. 10– 5 familiar with *L· M· G·*

line

another
Un. 26–22 as sings another *l·* of this hymn,

defining the
Mis. 22–11 infinite calculus defining the *l·*,

direct
Mis. 212–15 One step away from the direct *l·*
'01. 2–23 a departure from the direct *l·*

dividing
Man. 99– 5 dividing *l·* being the 36th parallel

every
Mis. 38– 4 elevate man in every *l·* of life,
220– 2 in every *l·* of mental healing,

intermediate
Mis. 188–20 in the intermediate *l·* of thought,
My. 181–18 practise the intermediate *l·* of

lead the
Mis. 130–30 and appoints to lead the *l·* of

of Jesus' thought
Mis. 260– 7 *l·* of Jesus' thought or action.

of least resistance
Pul. 80– 8 * sought the *l·* of least resistance.

of life
Mis. 38– 4 elevate man in every *l·* of life,

of light
Mis. 105–19 I must ever follow this *l·* of light
Ret. 42– 7 to follow in this *l·* of light.

of liquids
My. 260–14 the *l·* of liquids, the lure of gold,

of occupation
Mis. 296–25 Do they enter this *l·* of occupation

of the syllogism
Un. 34– 6 What then is the *l·* of the syllogism?

of thought
Mis. 3–16 enter this *l·* of thought or action.
186–28 proceeds in this *l·* of thought,
188–20 in the intermediate *l·* of thought,

of Truth
Mis. 268–15 inquiry . . . in the *l·* of Truth ;

one
'01. 24–21 I had not read one *l·* of

orderly
My. 247–16 came out in orderly *l·*

poet's
Ret. 87– 3 poet's *l·*, "Order is heaven's first

present
Mis. 273–17 in their present *l·* of labor

upon line
Mis. 32–11 *l·* upon line"— *Isa.* 28 : 10.
278–21 *l·* upon line and precept upon precept.

whole
Mis. 265–19 whole *l·* of reciprocal thought.

with progress
Mis. 287–20 human affection in *l·* with progress,

Mis. 264– 2 random thought in *l·* with mine.
Ret. 2–30 In the *l·* of my Grandmother Baker's
My. 16–28 will I lay to the *l·*,— *Isa.* 28 : 17.
114–19 *l·* of Scriptural interpretation
201–27 Please accept a *l·* from me
232– 5 that *l·* the sacred shores.
(*see also* **Science and Health**)

lineage
Mis. 162–30 Of the *l·* of David,
No. 13–15 chapter sub-title

lines
Mis. 81– 6 into more spiritual *l·* of life
291–29 sentinels along the *l·* of thought,
376–26 lower *l·* of light kindled into
Ret. 20–15 The following *l·* are taken from
46– 1 *L·* penned when I was pastor of the
Un. 23– 2 which makes true the *l·* :
Pul. 66–18 * mystical which, along many *l·*, has
87–25 luminous *l·* from your lives linger,
No. 7–21 recommend that Scientists draw no *l·*
Po. page 41 poem
page 67 poem
My. 124–19 between these *l·* of thought
155–21 May long *l·* of light span the
177–19 succeeding years show in livid *l·*
339–12 *l·* of progressive Christendom,
342–10 * no mistaking certain *l·*
354–26 * The above *l·* were written
(*see also* **Science and Health**)

linger
Mis. 218–24 this nature may *l·* in memory :
Pul. 87–25 luminous lines from your lives *l·*,

lingering
Mis. 230– 9 making *l·* calls,
'02. 3– 8 any *l·* sense of the North's

lining
Ret. 23– 8 seemed to have a silver *l·* ;

linings
Pul. 77– 6 * plush casket with white silk *l·*.

link
Mis. 143– 7 a closer *l·* hath bound us.
270–28 Homœopathy is the last *l·* in
My. 339– 3 whose every *l·* leads upward

links
My. 206– 1 Philosophical *l·*, which would

lion
Mis. 36–12 *l·* that lieth down with the lamb.
145–24 calf and the young *l·* — *Isa.* 11 : 6.
Rud. 8– 4 the *l·* of to-day is the *l·* of
Po. 43– 8 Fondling e'en the *l·* furious,

lions
Un. 11– 5 beard the *l·* in their dens.

lip
My. 258–31 a child with finger on her *l·*

lips
Mis. 9–18 We lift this cup to our *l·* ;
51–22 * "When from the *l·* of Truth
100–32 Who knows how the feeble *l·*
129– 4 let him put his finger to his *l·*.
135– 4 on our *l·*, and in our lives.
149– 9 opened his *l·* to discourse
149–18 *L·* nor pen can ever express
213–21 from the *l·* of our Master,
275–13 repeat with quivering *l·*
311–31 never escaped from my *l·*,
331–16 words from a mother's *l·*
338–25 * To give the *l·* full speech.
Ret. 31–27 the tearful *l·* of a babe.
Rud. 9–16 answer of the *l·* from the Lord.
No. 38–26 if the *l·* try to express it.
39– 8 the heart prays, and not the *l·*,
Peo. 13–14 forcing from the *l·* of manhood

liquidate
Mis. xl– 8 While no offering can *l·*
302–31 to subvert or to *l·*.

liquids
My. 260–14 the line of *l·*, the lure of gold,

liquor
'01. 33–20 with the lance, or with *l·*,

lisping
No. 44–16 the mouth *l·* God's praise ;

lispings
'02. 19–14 listens to the *l·* of repentance

list
Mis. 144– 9 subscription *l·* on which appear
Man. 54–15 branch church's *l·* of membership
73– 5 published in the *l·* of practitioners
Ret. 50–15 my *l·* of indigent charity scholars
Pul. 48–27 * long *l·* of worthy ancestors
88– 1 chapter sub-title
'01. 31–20 Among the *l·* of blessings infinite
Po. 10–14 *L·*, brother ! angels whisper
73– 9 *l·* the moan Of the billows' foam,
My. 39–13 * following *l·* of officers for the
85–21 * illustrious *l·* for future generations
106– 6 The *l·* of cases healed by me

list
My. 305–19 eighth in a *l·* of twenty-two
337–15 *L·*, brother ! angels whisper

listen
Mis. 222–13 ready to *l·* complacently to
328– 3 *l·* for the mountain-horn,
337–11 *L·*, and *he* illustrates the rule :
398– 1 I will *l·* for Thy voice,
Man. 59–18 to *l·* to the Sunday sermon
Ret. 46– 7 I will *l·* for Thy voice,
Pul. 15–12 If so, *l·* and be wise.
17– 6 I will *l·* for Thy voice,
41–11 * to *l·* to the Message sent them by
61–22 * to *l·* to the first peal of the chimes
'01. 20–13 People may *l·* complacently to
Po. 14– 5 I will *l·* for Thy voice,
My. 152–21 *l·* to His Word and serve no other
201–21 I will *l·* for Thy voice,
223– 4 I neither *l·* to complaints,
331–28 * yet when we *l·* to Mrs. Glover

listened
Mis. 332–18 supposed to have . . . been *l·* to,
Ret. 9– 3 I *l·* with bated breath.
42–11 *l·* to him with deep interest.
Pul. 61–26 * who *l·* with delight.

listeners
Mis. 100– 1 artless *l·* and dull disciples.
357–14 fall by the wayside, on artless *l·*.
Man. 58–21 To pour into the ears of *l·*
Pul. 46– 2 * that he was attracting *l·*

listening
Mis. 156–24 *l·* to each other amicably,
Man. 56–15 These assemblies shall be for *l·* to
Ret. 2–27 I was fond of *l·*,
Pul. 5– 3 *l·* to an address on C. S.
My. 59–15 * *l·* again to your words

listens
'02. 19–14 *l·* to the lispings of repentance

lit
Peo. 7–10 * face *l·* up with a smile of joy

literal
Mis. 169–15 interpreted in a *l·* way.
169–22 The *l·* rendering of the Scriptures
169–25 The *l·* or material reading
171–12 in *l·* or physical terms,
248– 4 the *l·* meaning of the passage
Pul. 38–25 * the *l·* teachings of Christ.
66–14 * *l·* teachings of the Bible
No. 23–15 a *l·* and a moral meaning.
23–17 the *l·* or the moral sense of
'01. 3–15 the *l·* sense of the lexicons :

literally
Mis. 28–28 He *l·* annulled the claims
108– 9 spiritually, *l·*, it *is nothing.*
133–18 *l·* following the dictum
175–30 is *l·* saying,
204–29 *l·* governs the aims, ambition,
258– 8 *l·* spat upon matter ;
300–15 You *l·* publish my works
333–13 *l·* and practically denying
Pul. 13– 7 is *l·* fulfilled, when we
25– 7 * *l·* fire-proof as is conceivable.
29–21 * interpreted and fulfilled *l·*,
My. 99–20 * *l·* stuffed and jammed with money.
142–14 *l·* a communion of branch church
187– 2 spiritually as well as *l·*,

literary
No. 11– 8 In its *l·* expression, my system
29–23 *l·* driftwood on the ocean
'02. 15–14 my income from *l·* sources
15–26 I showed it to my *l·* friends,
My. 319–30 * that he had done some *l·* work
320– 1 * that he was a fine *l·* student
324–22 * as quite his *l·* equal,
324–23 * among his *l·* friends.

Literary Digest
My. 305–28 scandal in the *L· D·*

literature
Mis. xl–18 to suit and savor all *l·*.
64–10 *the study of l· and languages*
64–22 *L·* and languages, . . . are aids to
80– 1 sellers of impure *l·*,
365–26 As a *l·*, Christian metaphysics is
Man. 27–17 and all other C. S. *l·*
27–24 other *l·* connected therewith.
43–21 No Incorrect *L·*.
43–23 C. S. *l·* which is not correct
44– 1 in which the writer has written his *l·*
44– 3 his *l·* shall not be adjudged C. S.
64– 3 *L·* in Reading Rooms.
64– 4 *l·* sold or exhibited in the
64– 8 also the *l·* published or sold by

literature
Man.	82– 1	books and *l·* it sends forth.
	82– 3	disapproves of certain books or *l·*,
	97–20	by periodicals or circulated *l·*
Ret.	77– 2	lawlessness in *l·*.
Pul.	5–30	*l·* of our and other lands.
'01.	21–18	to criticise it or to compare its *l·*.
	27– 4	* made to the *l·* of C. S.
My.	224–28	to recommend any *l·* as wholly

literatures
Mis.	169– 4	ancient philosophies or pagan *l·*,

litigation
Mis.	340–13	followed agriculture instead of *l·*,

little
Mis.	2– 5	they have so *l·* of their own.
	4–15	but *l·* time has been devoted to
	6– 3	often leaves mortals but *l·* time
	38–14	*other institutions find l· interest in*
	107–32	thinks either too much or too *l·*
	108– 3	Christian asleep, thinks too *l·* of sin.
	127– 2	His "*l·* ones," — *Matt.* 18 : 6.
	130–25	God's "*l·* ones." — *Matt.* 18 : 6.
	142– 8	the *l·* pond at Pleasant View.
	144– 6	a *l·* band called Busy Bees,
	145–25	*l·* child shall lead them." — *Isa.* 11 : 6.
	150– 1	"Fear not, *l·* flock ; — *Luke* 12 : 32.
	158– 5	I *l·* thought of the changes
	158– 7	I *l·* knew that so soon
	176–11	we learn a *l·* more of the
	221–11	The evil-doer can do *l·* at
	231–18	poked into the *l·* mouth
	231–24	soft *l·* palms patting together,
	231–27	and his *l·* rainbowy life
	236– 5	*l·* else than the troubles,
	240– 3	through the cold air the *l·* one
	243–24	"Take a *l·* wine — *see I Tim.* 5 : 23.
	250–26	*l·* feet tripping along the sidewalk ;
	255– 1	chapter sub-title
	262–27	*l·* need of words of approval
	275–12	the motherless *l·* ones, wondering,
	291– 9	Too much and too *l·* is attached
	308–20	This *l·* messenger has done its work,
	318–27	either too large or too *l·* :
	319– 7	If the sense of sin is too *l·*,
	321–16	"Fear not, *l·* flock ; — *Luke* 12 : 32.
	324– 8	But a *l·* while, and the music
	329–18	her *l·* feet trip lightly on,
	337–12	called a *l·* child — *Matt.* 18 : 2.
	337–14	as this *l·* child, — *Matt.* 18 : 4.
	341–23	a *l·* girl of eight years,
	344–26	as a *l·* child, — *Luke* 18 : 17.
	354–15	A *l·* more grace, a motive made pure,
	376–21, 22	*L·* by *l·* this topmost pall,
	400–17	Guide my *l·* feet
Man.	17– 1	*l·* band of earnest seekers
	18– 8	the *l·* Church went steadily on,
Ret.	6–14	than this *l·* book can afford.
	8–14	I sat in a *l·* chair by her side,
	9– 9	Scriptural narrative of *l·* Samuel,
	20– 7	my *l·* son, about four years of age,
	21– 1	letter was read to my *l·* son,
	27–30	new to His "*l·* one." — *see Matt.* 10 : 42.
	35– 3	This *l·* book is converted into
	40–19	never before suffered so *l·*
	61–28	that however *l·* be taught or learned,
	61–29	that *l·* shall be right.
	78– 3	either too much or too *l·*.
Un.	1–12	*l·* apprehended and demonstrated
Pul.	4– 3	"What if the *l·* rain should say,
	4–15	Each of Christ's *l·* ones reflects
	8–17	*L·* hands, never before devoted to
	29– 7	* a *l·* later, in this article.
	33– 9	* the *l·* maid was afraid
	39– 9	a *l·* poem that I consider
	42–11	* the *l·* contributors to the
	48–13	* valley of the *l·* truant river,
	50–25	* after a *l·* skirmishing,
	62–12	* require but *l·* muscular power
	62–22	* *l·* sets of silver bells
	67–22	* *l·* knots of them are to be found.
Rud.	v– 1	THIS *l·* BOOK IS . . . DEDICATED
No.	9–18	first edition of this *l·* work
	21–27	has *l·* resemblance to Science,
	26–27	O ye of *l·* faith?" — *Matt.* 6 : 30.
'00.	2–11	gives *l·* time to society
	2–16	earns *l·* and is stingy ;
	8–10	wicked man has *l·* real intelligence ;
	8–27	through one of His *l·* ones,
	14– 1	"Thou hast a *l·* strength, — *Rev.* 3 : 8.
'01.	15–17	I can conceive of *l·* short of
	23– 3	they have *l·* left that the
	26–26	I have read *l·* of their writings.
'02.	2–16	*l·* leaven hid in three measures
Hea.	15–25	that you have *l·* or no faith in
Po.	v– 1	* *garnered up in this l· volume*

little
Po.	vii–11	* *this l· volume is presented*
	24– 5	O *l·* heart, To me thou art
	53–16	Their downy *l·* breasts.
	67– 2	bliss of life's *l·* day
	69– 5	Guide my *l·* feet
My.	17–30	His '*l·* ones,' — *Matt.* 18 : 6.
	38–19	* *l·* ones were not a whit behind
	50– 6	* *l·* band of prayerful workers,
	50– 9	* so this *l·* band of pioneers,
	52–23	* *L·* cares she, if only
	59– 5	* the *l·* leaven that should leaven
	59–17	* *l·* hall on Market Street, Lynn,
	59–21	* I thought of the *l·* melodeon
	60–15	* I have yet the *l·* Bible
	60–27	* may I ask a *l·* of your time
	60–30	* care to do a *l·* watching
	68–23	* and contributes not a *l·* to the
	79– 3	* *l·* faces turned upward.
	79– 8	* it must stagger their faith not a *l·*
	93– 4	* have *l·* of the spirit of bigotry.
	96–31	* C. S. just goes a *l·* beyond
	97–12	* Scientists have a *l·* the advantage
	98–20	* in a *l·* less than three years.
	107–13	lower attenuations have so *l·*
	123–21	My *l·* hall, which holds
	123–30	"the *l·* foxes — *Song* 2 : 15.
	130–31	that you borrow *l·* else from it,
	131–12	given to me in a *l·* symbol,
	147–13	May this *l·* sanctum be preserved
	147–23	work-rooms and a *l·* hall,
	148–21	singing of this dear *l·* flock,
	154– 7	to send flowers to this *l·* hall
	172–12	to present to you a *l·* gift
	175–16	must remain with us a *l·* longer,
	186– 4	May God's *l·* ones
	224– 6	knowing a *l·*, . . . the human need,
	238–12	has imparted *l·* power to practise
	247–14	*l·* fishes in my fountain
	247–17	these sweet *l·* thoughts
	247–24	Do you come to your *l·* flock
	247–28	The *l·* that I have accomplished
	262–19	afford *l·* divine effulgence,
	271– 5	I *l·* understood all that I indited ;
	271– 8	of comparatively *l·* importance
	288– 4	reformer gives *l·* thought to
	298– 5	not a *l·* is already reported
	313–31	my *l·* boy was not welcome in
	319– 7	*l·* pamphlet, signed "Phare Pleigh."
	323– 7	* I have his *l·* book yet.
	340–13	clad in a *l·* brief authority,
	349–10	Tyndall, and Spencer afford *l·* aid
		(*see also* **children, church**)

Littleton
New Hampshire
My.	315– 4	* with me in *L·*, New Hampshire.

N. H.
My.	314–31	R. D. Rounsevel of *L·*, N. H.,

liturgical
Ret.	89–10	they went for *l·* worship,

live
Mis.	7–18	reflects that it is dangerous to *l·*,
	8– 6	we *l·*, and move, — *Acts* 17 : 28.
	44– 2	speak the truth . . . and *l·* it :
	50–25	we exist in Mind, *l·* thereby,
	72–15	As I *l·*, saith the Lord — *Ezek.* 18 : 3.
	79– 9	we *l·*, move, and have being.
	82–29	"we *l·*, and move, — *Acts* 17 : 28.
	84–20	*to l· is Christ,* — *Phil.* 1 : 21.
	84–25	is to *l·* in Christ, Truth.
	99–24	still *l·*, and to-morrow speak
	106–26	"So *l·*, that your lives attest your
	115–15	practise, teach, and *l·* C. S. !
	140–31	the spiritual idea would *l·*,
	163–20	they still *l·* ; and are the basis of
	180– 1	he lives, I *l·*," — *see John* 14 : 19.
	205–32	and *l·* what they learn,
	216–12	A *l·* lexicographer,
	237–17	few feel and *l·* now as when
	296–13	*l·* on the plan of heaven?
	338–30	* *L·* truly, and thy life shall be
	388– 9	Fed by Thy love divine we *l·*,
Man.	39– 1	*l·* according to its requirements
	51–10	does not *l·* in Christian fellowship
Chr.	55– 7	they that hear shall *l·*. — *John* 5 : 25.
Ret.	11– 8	*l·* to bless mankind.
	93–17	we *l·*, and move, — *Acts* 17 : 28.
Un.	10–16	They *l·*, because He lives ;
	41–26	appears to both *l·* and die,
	48– 9	Because He lives, I *l·*.
	61–20	life which I now *l·* — *Gal.* 2 : 20.
	61–21	I *l·* by the faith of — *Gal.* 2 : 20.
Pul.	2–23	"we *l·*, and move, — *Acts* 17 : 28.
	21– 7	I long, and *l·*, to see this
	50–27	* *l·* down any attempted repression.

live

Pul.	83–24	* *l·* in the reflected royalty
Rud.	12–17	mistaken belief that they *l·* in
No.	17– 7	we *l·*, and move,— *Acts* 17 : 28.
	25– 2	We must *l·* it, until
	35–13	He lived that we also might *l·*.
Pan.	13–20	''*l·*, and move,— *Acts* 17 : 28.
'01.	6– 2	that *l·* in the Father
	34–27	man cannot *l·* without it ;
'02.	2– 4	To *l·* and let *l·*,
	12–19	we *l·*, and move,— *Acts* 17 : 28.
Po.	7– 9	Fed by Thy love divine we *l·*,
	11– 3	Victorious, all who *l·* it,
	15–14	I would *l·* in their empire,
	60– 5	And *l·* to bless mankind.
My.	105–23	declared that she could not *l·*.
	109–22	''we *l·*, and move,— *Acts* 17 : 28.
	126–31	We have it only as we *l·* it.
	127– 5	Happy are the . . . who *l·* to love.
	128–15	to *l·* or to die according to the
	131–10	''he shall *l·* forever,''— *John* 6 : 51.
	132–20	where we may see God and *l·*,
	133–25	then . . . we *l·* apart.
	158– 9	We *l·* in an age of Love's divine
	160– 5	To *l·* so as to keep human
	160–12	a *l·* truth, even though it be a sapling
	164–30	man must *l·*, he cannot die ;
	166–14	will *l·* on and never drift apart.
	195–22	mortals expect to *l·* and die,
	213–11	to *l·* pure and Christian lives,
	216– 2	Till . . . *l·* without eating,
	241–23	* I did not *l·* in my flesh,
	252–12	not only know the truth but *l·* it
	290– 7	Those *l·* on in the affection of
	338– 3	Victorious, all who *l·* it,
	345–14	doctors said I would *l·* if the

lived

Mis.	70–16	Christ Jesus *l·* and reappeared.
	165–17	truth uttered and *l·* by Jesus,
	211–30	He *l·* the spirit of his prayer,
	213– 3	All that I have written, . . . or *l·*,
	229–24	holier, happier, and longer *l·*.
	293–27	Truth talked and not *l·*,
	312– 3	so *l·*, that when weighed in the
	337–24	*l·* according to his precepts,
Ret.	21– 8	learned that his mother still *l·*,
Un.	62–19	Jesus died, and *l·*.
Pul.	34– 2	* who *l·* only a year.
	49–10	* ''You have *l·* here only four years,
	58– 6	* she has *l·* in Concord, N. H.,
No.	35–13	He *l·* that we also might live.
'00.	7–14	reward for having suffered, *l·*,
'01.	28– 9	perhaps none *l·* a more devout
	32–16	were honest, and they *l·* them ;
'02.	18– 6	*l·* when mortals looked ignorantly,
Po.	26–19	chain and charter I have *l·* to see
My.	81–14	* the places where they *l·*.
	89–12	* sect that . . . has not *l·* in vain.
	150– 8	* better for having *l·* in it.''
	241–22	* because I still *l·* in my flesh,
	241–24	* my flesh *l·* or died according to
	241–26	* I *l·* and moved and had my being
	287–11	Love talked and not *l·*
	287–12	Love *l·* in a court or cot
	291–15	not talked but felt and *l·*.
	314– 3	* ''*l·* for a short time at Tilton,
	314–14	I *l·* with Dr. Patterson peaceably,
	322– 1	* I met a lady who *l·* in Lynn,
	325–10	* old part of Boston in which he *l·*
	327–31	* as *l·* by our dear, dear Leader,
	346– 2	* as one who has *l·* with her subject

lively

Ret.	5–29	* *l·* sense of the parental obligation,
My.	17–11	''Ye also, as *l·* stones,— *I Pet.* 2 : 5.
	268–22	a *l·* battle with ''the world,

livery

Mis.	19–18	taking the *l·* of heaven wherewith to

lives (noun)

affections and

My.	156–23	receive into their affections and *l·*

against the

Mis.	177–11	have sworn enmity against the *l·* of

are the embodiment

Peo.	5– 4	whose *l·* are the embodiment of a

better

My.	352–11	* is proved in better *l·*.

characters and

Mis.	357–23	whose Christian characters and *l·*

children's

Mis.	240– 7	out of the children's *l·*

Christian

My.	213–11	to live pure and Christian *l·*,

cleanse our

Mis.	30–30	cleanse our *l·* in Christ's

lives

crown the

Po.	44– 2	Crown the *l·* thus blest

daily

My.	134– 7	our daily *l·* serve to enhance or to

hearts and

Mis.	291–24	fall gently on the hearts and *l·* of

human

Mis.	19–11	bring them out in human *l·*.
	360– 2	Human *l·* are yet uncarved,

individual

'01.	2– 4	Christianity in individual *l·*

mortal

No.	41–15	compare mortal *l·* with this model

noble

My.	112–22	pure morals and noble *l·*,

of Christian Scientists

Pul.	22– 9	*l·* of Christian Scientists attest
My.	114– 9	to the *l·* of Christian Scientists

of great men

Mis.	340–26	The *l·* of great men and women

of his followers

My.	28–21	* mark the *l·* of his followers.

of its professors

My.	107– 3	Compare the *l·* of its professors

of men

Pan.	10– 6	effects of C. S. on the *l·* of men
Peo.	11–28	the liberty and *l·* of men.
My.	277–14	The characters and *l·* of men
	294– 4	the morals and the *l·* of men,

of mortals

Mis.	114–26	influence upon the *l·* of mortals.

of prophets

My.	103–24	the *l·* of prophets and apostles.

of saints

My.	249–15	patience, silence, and *l·* of saints.

our

Mis.	3– 7	demonstrate in our *l·* the power of
	135– 5	on our lips, and in our *l·*.
	160– 8	Thus may our *l·* flow on
	172–22	demonstrated in our *l·*.
	197– 2	incorporates their lessons into our *l·*
'02.	4–28	thoughts of the Bible utter our *l·*
Hea.	5–25	would lead our *l·* to higher issues ;
Peo.	7– 7	to beautify and exalt our *l·*.
	7–17	* With our *l·* uncarved before us,
	7–23	* Our *l·* that angel-vision.''
My.	132– 1	fulfilment of divine Love in our *l·*
	186– 4	writes . . . their lessons on our *l·*.
	215–27	a better example for our *l·*

our own

Peo.	8–10	qualities of character in our own *l·*

their

Mis.	10–17	The best lesson of their *l·*
	84– 8	This cost them their *l·*,
Un.	1–17	able to testify, by their *l·*,
	2–24	because their *l·* have grown so far
Pul.	12–11	loved not their *l·* — *Rev.* 12 : 11.
'01.	32–17	the sermons their *l·* preached
Hea.	9–13	to bring out in their *l·* ?
My.	31–22	* one of the events of their *l·*.
	114–10	book which has moulded their *l·*

their own

Mis.	176–15	counted not their own *l·* dear
	213–16	may perfect their own *l·*

uncontaminated

Mis.	110– 7	it needs . . . uncontaminated *l·*.

visible

Mis.	144–25	our visible *l·* are rising to God.

your

Mis.	106–27	that your *l·* attest your sincerity
Pul.	87–25	luminous lines from your *l·*
My.	143– 2	directs your meetings and your *l·*,
	167–13	loving benedictions upon your *l·*.

Mis.	54– 9	*l·* are worthy testimonials,
	98–23	The *l·* of all reformers
	172– 1	their claims and *l·* steadfast in
'01.	32–18	*l·* of those old-fashioned leaders
My.	28–15	* its influence upon the *l·* of
	28–18	* but in the *l·* of those who,

lives (verb)

Mis.	42–25	learn that good, not evil, *l·*
	86–25	It *l·* with our earth-life,
	115–25	If one *l·* rightly,
	160– 6	*l·* steadily on, through time and
	166– 6	Truth he has taught and spoken *l·*,
	180– 1	''Because he *l·*, I live,'' — *see John* 14 : 19.
	205–30	man born of the great Forever, *l·* on,
	269–10	*L·* there a man who can
	294–10	He *l·* for all mankind,
Man.	97– 6	Scientist who *l·* in Boston,
Ret.	70–26	*l·* the truth he teaches.
Un.	10–17	They live, because He *l·* ;
	40–17	*l·* in God, who holds Life by

lives

Un.	41–25	hence matter neither *l·* nor dies.
	48– 9	Because He *l·*, I live.
	63– 4	This trinity of Love *l·* and reigns
Pul.	4–20	Who *l·* in good, *l·* also in God,
	4–20	*l·* in all Life, through all space.
	47–25	* she *l·* very much retired,
	68–11	* She now *l·* in a beautiful
Rud.	3–11	it *l·* more because of his spiritual
	5–10	*L·* there a man who has ever
Po.	24–11	The Life that *l·* in Thee !
My.	39–26	* and the memory *l·* with us.
	164–29	Man *l·*, moves, and has his being
	165– 9	by this spirit man *l·* and thrives,
	195–23	in whom man *l·*, moves, and has
	271–14	* *l·* at eighty-six years of age
	275– 5	it explains love, it *l·* love,
	289–18	*l·* on in the heart of millions.
	295–28	he still *l·*, loves, labors.

liveth

Chr.	55–28	*l·* and believeth in me — *John* 11 : 26.
No.	13– 8	*l·* and believeth in me — *John* 11 : 26.
Pan.	9–13	*l·* and believeth in me — *John* 11 : 26.
'01.	9–27	*l·* most the things of Spirit,
Po.	16– 6	it endureth and *l·* in love.
My.	136– 2	our "Redeemer *l·*" — *Job* 19 : 25.

livid

My.	177–19	succeeding years show in *l·* lines

living (noun)

Mis.	95–17	between the so-called dead and *l·*.
	325–25	charnel-house of the so-called *l·*,
Man.	60–20	daily Christian endeavors for the *l·*
Chr.	53– 7	rouse the *l·*, wake the dead,
Ret.	81– 3	both for the *l·* and the dead.
Un.	62–23	"Why seek ye the *l·* — *Luke* 24 : 5.
'02.	2– 7	sanity and perfection of *l·*,
Hea.	6–13	between the so-called dead and the *l·*.
Po.	25–13	And breath of the *l·* above.
My.	36–17	* peace of a more righteous *l·*,
	46– 5	* more spiritual plane of *l·*,
	46–19	* fulfil the pledge in righteous *l·*,
	264– 6	can speak justly of my *l·*.
	292– 9	His staff comfort the *l·*
	345–27	more etherealized ways of *l·*.
	352–14	* that our daily *l·* may be a

living (adj.)

Mis.	72– 5	only *l·* and true origin, God.
	83– 3	*l·* witness to and perpetual idea of
	114–32	through Christ, the *l·* Truth,
	150–23	peopled with *l·* witnesses
	178–31	new, *l·*, impersonal Christ-thought
	185–27	made a *l·* soul ; — *I Cor.* 15 : 45.
	207– 3	drink with me the *l·* waters
	294– 9	the *l·*, palpable presence
	323–21	drink from its *l·* fountains?
	333–15	away from the only *l·* and true God,
	357– 7	yearn to find *l·* pastures
	372–28	character of the *l·* God,
	376–11	* handed down from the *l·* *reality.*
	376–13	* *l·* Saviour engraven on the heart.
Chr.	53–19	this *l·* Vine Ye demonstrate.
Ret.	6– 5	* *l·* illustration of Christian faith.
	59–18	only *l·* and true God,
	88–13	apprehend the *l·* beauty of Love,
Un.	14–20	the corner-stone of *l·* rock,
	30–14	made a *l·* soul ; — *I Cor.* 15 : 45.
	30–25	*l·* Soul shall be found a
	38–14	above the *l·* and true God.
	42– 8	because it is not a *l·* . . . reality.
	49–13	*l·* God and the genuine man.
	62–22	"I am the *l·* God,
Pul.	3–21	*l·* waters have their source in God,
Rud.	2– 2	* "a *l·* soul ; a self-conscious being ;
	2– 3	* a *l·* human being,
No.	27–19	* "No man *l·* hath yet seen man."
	27–24	Who *l·* hath seen God
'02.	14– 7	*l·* and life-giving spiritual shield
Po.	29–15	Thou gentle beam of *l·* Love,
My.	12–27	"act in the *l·* present."
	17– 9	unto a *l·* stone, — *I Pet.* 2 : 4.
	46–28	* city of the *l·* God, — *Heb.* 12 : 22.
	64–25	* to be "*l·* stones" — *see I Pet.* 2 : 5.
	70–16	* "Angelus" had *l·* reproductions
	126– 7	such as drink of the *l·* water.
	164–20	has leaped into *l·* love.
	186– 3	that writes in *l·* characters
	191–25	lights the *l·* way of Life.
	192– 5	raise the *l·* dead,
	192–11	lights the *l·* way to Life,
	232–13	as *l·* lights in our darkness :
	268–19	without a *l·* Divina.
	305–19	* of the foremost *l·* authors."
	323–12	* *l·* witness to Truth and Love,
		(*see also* **faith**)

living (ppr.)

Mis.	69–27	The man is *l·* yet ;
	344–24	His words, *l·* in our hearts,
	373–18	as *l·* feebly, in kings' courts.
Ret.	40– 3	*l·* on a small annuity.
Un.	7–15	now *l·* who can bear witness to
	40–15	and *l·* imperfectly.
	43–19	more faith in *l·* than in dying.
Pul.	34– 5	* while *l·* in Lynn, Mass.,
	58–28	* with all conveniences for *l·*,
	84– 7	* all that is worth *l·* for,
No.	12–18	*L·* a true life, casting out evil,
Pan.	8–27	*l·* by reason of it,
	14– 7	*l·* the divine Life, Truth, Love,
Po.	68– 3	"I'm *l·* to bless thee ;
My.	82–30	* those *l·* in the streets leading
	139– 3	*l·*, loving, acting, enjoying.
	139– 5	alive to the reality of *l·*,
	166– 7	life is worth *l·*
	268–26	of wedlock, of *l·* and of loving,
	311– 3	While I was *l·* with Dr. Patterson
	323– 9	* by loving it and *l·* it

loaded

Mis.	7– 4	*l·* down with coverings
	7–18	so *l·* with disease seems the
	327–19	gaining the summit, *l·* as they are,

loaf

Mis.	149– 7	to help leaven your *l·*
	175–13	as the leaven expands the *l·*.
My.	272– 2	one who leavens the *l·* of life

loam

Mis.	26–11	from the seedling and the *l·* ;

loan

Mis.	299–25	did he sell them or *l·* them to you?
Pul.	8–11	nor a *l·* solicited,

loathed

Mis.	222–14	would have resisted and *l·* ;

loathes

Ret.	81–18	The enlightened heart *l·* error,

loathing

Mis.	277–31	*l·* the phenomena of drunkenness
My.	249–14	only to satiate its *l·* of

loathsome

Mis.	240–27	nothing but a *l·* worm
Pan.	10–26	no pleasure in *l·* habits

loaves

Pul.	60– 9	* Jesus' miracle of *l·* and fishes.
My.	123–23	"five *l·* and two fishes" — *Matt.* 14 : 17.

lobbies

Pul.	42– 2	* the spacious *l·* and the sidewalks

local

Man.	55– 4	the members of their *l·* church ;
	59–20	The *L·* Members' Welcome.
	59–21	privilege of the *l·* members
	70–10	*L·* Self-government.
	96–11	and the *l·* church is unable to meet the
Pul.	41–19	* nearly a thousand *l·* believers
My.	19–14	* their *l·* church building funds
	21–20	* *l·* members, who have always
	30– 7	* nearly all the *l·* Scientists,
	83– 6	* members of the *l·* arrangement
	330–10	* *l·* Christian Scientist of your city,

localities

Man.	99·- 2	to serve in their *l·*.
My.	123–11	one of the finest *l·* in the city,
	216–24	work in your own several *l·*,
	237–18	physicians in their respective *l·*.

locality

Man.	49– 3	healing work in any church or *l·*,
	99–10	to serve in its *l·*.
Ret.	91–12	more . . . than the material *l·*.
My.	83–15	* fewer questions as to *l·*

locate

Man.	68–18	or allows to visit or to *l·* therein
Ret.	82–11	who *l·* permanently in one section,
	82–14	students should *l·* in large cities,

located

Man.	27–21	*l·* in the same building,
	63–18	provided these rooms are well *l·*.
	70–17	churches, *l·* in the same State,
Pul.	24– 8	* It is *l·* at the intersection of
	56–26	* *l·* at Norway and Falmouth Streets,
Pan.	4– 9	*l·* in the brain ;
My.	79– 9	* vast temple *l·* in the heart of
	314– 8	was *l·* in Franklin, N. H.

locates

My.	330– 7	* *l·* Mrs. Eddy in Wilmington in 1843,

location
 Man. 68–17 *L·*.
 Pul. 68–26 * meeting held at the present *l·*
 My. 11–25 * The *l·* is, therefore, determined.
   55– 5 * or church, in a suitable *l·*.

Locke
 Mis. 361–15 *L·*, Berkeley, Tyndall, Darwin,
 My. 349– 9 Kant, *L·*, Berkeley, Tyndall,

Lockport, N. Y.
 Pul. 89– 2 * *Journal, L·, N.Y.*

locks
 Mis. 282–12 or our *l·* picked?
 Hea. 18–25 no blind Samson shorn of his *l·*.

Lodge
 My. 334–30 * Grand Secretary of the Grand *L·*
   335– 9 * a member and officer of the *L·*

lodge
 My. 332–22 * to look up the records of this *l·*,
   332–26 * the *l·* was no longer in existence,
   333–15 * procession then returned to the *l·*,

lodged
 Mis. 356–19 have *l·* in its branches.

lodging-houses
 My. 75–11 * assigned rooms in hotels or *l·*,

loftier
 Mis. 235–11 It gives to the race *l·* desires
 Po. 32–10 A *l·* life to invite
 My. 45–30 * *l·* than the Bunker Hill monument,

loftiest
 Mis. 345–17 * the *l·* intellects have had
 Peo. 13–26 * the *l·* intellects have had

lofty
 Mis. 297–12 ventilating his *l·* scorn of
   392– 8 from thy *l·* summit, pouring down
 Peo. 13–16 *l·* faith of the pious Polycarp
 Po. v–11 * this *l·* New Hampshire crag,
   vii– 3 * by the same *l·* trend of thought
   20–11 from thy *l·* summit, pouring down
   39– 2 Gifts, *l·*, pure, and free,
 My. 193–25 *l·* temple, dedicated to God
   287–20 it wakens *l·* desires,

log
 My. 124–24 thy records, time-table, *l·*,

logarithms
 Mis. 54–30 solve a problem involving *l·* ;

Logia
 My. 178–30 *L·* of Papias, written in A.D.
   178–32 *L·*, or imputed sayings of Jesus

logic
 Mis. 27– 9 abandon their own *l·*.
   61–29 the *l·* that man is God's likeness.
   148–15 from necessity, the *l·* of events,
   195–17 The Master's divine *l·*,
   209–29 scientific *l·* and the *l·* of events,
   223– 8 *l·*, and revelation coincide.
   360–26 regenerates philosophy and *l·* ;
   367–26 nor foundation in nature, in *l·*,
 Man. 3–11 from necessity, the *l·* of events,
 Ret. 10– 8 philosophy, *l·*, and moral science.
 Un. 36–24 This error stultifies the *l·* of
   54–28 diabolical and sinuous *l·*?
 Pul. 46–25 * philosophy, *l·*, and moral science,
 No. 16–15 infinite *l·* is the infinite light,
   17– 3 From this *l·* there is no escape.
 '01. 4– 3 In *l·* the major premise must be
   5–25 God and man . . . or the *l·* of Truth,
   6–18 *l·* of divine Science being faultless,
   8–21 *l·* of divine metaphysics
   23– 2 the numeration table and the *l·* of
 My. 224– 4 should wait on the *l·* of events?
   272– 4 the *l·* of events pushes onward
   350– 5 is minus divine *l·* and plus human

logical
 Mis. 26– 5 The only *l·* conclusion is
   26–30 the *l·* conclusion that God is
   93–11 the *l·* conclusion drawn from
   217– 2 which combines in *l·* sequence,
 Un. 33–17 Hence the *l·* sequence,
   53–17 no more *l·*, philosophical, or
 Pul. 67– 8 * the hub of the *l·* universe,
 Pan. 7–24 the *l·* sequence of this error
 '01. 3–28 *l·* that because God is Love,
 '02. 7–19 No other *l·* conclusion can be
 My. 111–17 *l·* in premise and in conclusion.
   111–24 his conclusion was *l·* and divine
   112–13 its *l·* premise and conclusion,

logically
 Mis. 182– 2 to reckon himself *l·* ;
 My. 8–27 * whom we recognize as *l·* the
   45–26 * *l·* followed the preceding one.

logos
 Mis. 362– 8 Christ's *l·* gives sight to

logs
 Mis. 340–16 drew up *l·* instead of leases.

loiter
 My. 11– 3 * may falter or stumble or *l·*

London
 Can.
 Pul. 90–13 * *Free Press, L·*, Can.
 England
 Man. 99–19 in which *L·*, England, is situated
 '02. 16–10 Mrs. F. L. Miller, of *L·*, England.
 My. 13– 5 published in *L·*, England,
   183–10 chapter sub-title
   198– 2 chapter sub-title
   200–10 chapter sub-title
   203–23 chapter sub-title
   205–14 chapter sub-title
   259–10 * from members *L·*, England,
   295–24 Lancaster Gate, West, *L·*, England.
   304–15 invited to lecture in *L·*, England,

 Mis. 295– 3 Mr. Wakeman writes from *L·*,
 '00. 1–22 Montreal, *L·*, Edinburgh,
 My. 149–26 could not see *L·* for its houses.
   252–18 chapter sub-title
   259– 5 First Church of Christ, . . . in *L·*,

Londonderry, Vermont
 Pul. 35–28 * Dr. Asa Gilbert Eddy, of *L·*, *V·*,

lone
 Mis. 159–22 and to their *l·* Leader.
   385–18 Brave wrestler, *l·*.
   386–24 Rears the sad marble . . . In *l·* retreat.
   392–11 To my *l·* heart thou art a power
   398–10 Lab'ring long and *l·*,
 Chr. 53– 4 One *l·*, brave star.
 Ret. 4–16 now the *l·* night-bird cries,
   46–16 Lab'ring long and *l·*,
 Pul. 6–25 as my *l·* bark rose and fell
   17–15 Lab'ring long and *l·*
 Po. 2–12 still art thou drear and *l·*!
   14–14 Lab'ring long and *l·*,
   20–15 To my *l·* heart thou art a power
   48–12 Brave wrestler, *l·*
   50–10 to our memory now, In *l·* retreat.
   68– 5 sweet pledge to my *l·* heart
   73–13 The sea-mew's *l·* cry,
 My. 158–11 natal hour of my *l·* earth life ;
   331–25 * *l·*, feeble, and bereaved widow

lonely
 Mis. 324–27 rushes again into the *l·* streets,
 Po. 53–12 Poor robin's *l·* mass.
 My. 41– 8 * proud are *l·* and uncomforted,
   309–29 * *l·* and unstimulating existence.
   309–32 * "*l·* and unstimulating existence."
   313–16 * long and *l·* wanderings,

loneness
 Pan. 3– 6 that *l·* lacks but one charm
 Po. 31– 8 Deep *l·*, tear-filled tones of

long
 Mis. ix–15 To preserve a *l·* course of years
   x–23 the name would be too *l·*.
   2– 6 a *l·* and strong determination
   13– 7 which I have *l·* endured
   99–17 to stand a *l·* siege,
   106–22 It has *l·* been a question
   120– 5 Principle of life's *l·* problem,
   120–21 *l·* distance from Massachusetts,
   125–17 press on to Life's *l·* lesson,
   126–26 in the *l·* race, honesty always
   169– 8 the *l·* years of invalidism
   177–30 In my *l·* journeyings I have met
   192–16 as *l·* as the sun." — *Psal.* 72 : 17.
   210–28 it may suffer *l·*,
   215–24 a *l·* warfare with error
   241–31 discomforted, and who *l·* for relief !
   261– 3 lasts as *l·* as the evil.
   281– 7 I learned *l·* ago that the world
   301–15 to be *l·* led into temptation ;
   332– 7 * *l·* winter of our discontent,"
   338–12 suffereth *l·* and is kind,
   357– 8 These *l·* for the Christlikeness
   385–16 "You've travelled *l·*, and far
   393–22 teaching Lessons *l·* and grand,
   398–10 Lab'ring *l·* and lone,
 Ret. 46–16 Lab'ring *l·* and lone,
   76–27 I have *l·* remained silent
 Un. 14– 5 *l·* after God made the universe,
 Pul. 17–15 Lab'ring *l·* and lone
   21– 7 I *l·*, and live, to see this
   46–16 * not *l·* before the Revolution.

long

Pul.	48–27	* a *l·* list of worthy ancestors
	49–20	* *l·* wished to get away from
	66–21	* departure from *l·* respected views
	78– 4	* gold scroll, twenty-six inches *l·*,
	79–28	* condition can never *l·* continue.
	82–10	* has *l·* learned with patience,
	82–17	* have *l·* acknowledged woman as
	83– 7	* sunlight cannot *l·* be delayed.
	84–26	* the result of *l·* years of untiring,
No.	28– 2	How *l·* this false sense remains
	41–19	Through *l·* ages people have
	45– 5	"Charity suffereth *l·*,— *I Cor.* 13 : 4.
'01.	1– 5	so *l·* as you are in His service.
	19–22	From . . . to C. S. is a *l·* ascent,
	31–12	After a *l·* acquaintance with the
'02.	9–25	Did the age's thinkers laugh *l·*
	9–26	Did they quarrel *l·* with the
Hea.	4–13	to drop divinity *l·* enough to
Peo.	6– 7	* founded on *l·* observation
	8–26	that man will ere *l·* stop trusting
Po.	14–14	Lab'ring *l·* and lone,
	48– 9	"You've traveled *l·*, and far from
	52– 6	Lessons *l·* and grand,
	65–17	claspeth earth's raptures not *l·*,
	71–15	Sound it *l·* !
My.	15–33	* That I have loved so *l·*.
	38– 1	* recompense your *l·* sacrifice
	41–28	* through *l·* years of consecration
	45–13	* have *l·* prophetically seen
	70–30	* which is thirty-two feet *l·*.
	80–31	* *l·* before seven the auditorium
	123–19	Ere *l·* I will see you in this hall,
	130– 6	will ere *l·* be unearthed and punished
	142– 5	* communicants who come *l·* distances
	155–21	May *l·* lines of light span the
	163– 1	*l·* call the worshipper
	169– 4	if you would enjoy so *l·* a trip
	170–27	have come *l·* distances to kneel
	176– 5	*L·* ago you of the dear South
	181– 5	are aided only at *l·* intervals
	189–18	senses wake from their *l·* slumber
	194–25	sacrificed so much and labored so *l·*.
	204– 1	nor will you be *l·* in doing more.
	204–23	too *l·* treatment of a disease,
	222– 5	how *l·* shall I be with you?— *Matt.* 17 : 17.
	222– 6	how *l·* shall I suffer you?— *Matt.* 17 : 17.
	231–17	"Charity suffereth *l·*— *I Cor.* 13 : 4.
	260–29	love that "suffereth *l·*,— *I Cor.* 13 : 4.
	268–29	Look *l·* enough, and you see
	289–16	Empress of India,— *l·* honored,
	306–30	holding *l·* conversations with him
	311–31	* reached *l·* division in arithmetic,"
	312–26	*l·* procession, followed the remains
	313–16	* *l·* and lonely wanderings,
	318–27	continued with a *l·* argument,
	320–25	* were at times somewhat *l·*
	322– 1	* It is not *l·* since I met a lady
	323– 7	* How *l·* must it be before the
	324–12	* explained how *l·* you had waited
	326–18	in *l·* procession with tender dirge
	(*see also* **night**)	

long so — as

Mis.	85–24	so *l·* as this temptation lasts,
	100–10	so *l·* as there remains a claim
	130– 1	so *l·* as a hope remained
	290– 4	vow is never annulled so *l·* as the
Man.	15–13	so *l·* as the belief lasts.
	30–21	so *l·* as Mrs. Eddy does not occupy
	37–18	so *l·* as both are loyal to
Ret.	68–21	so *l·* as it bases creation on
Un.	49–13	So *l·* as I hold evil
Pul.	7–27	so *l·* as this church is satisfied
	59– 7	* so *l·* as there were attendants ;
'01.	13–30	So *l·* as we indulge the presence
My.	23– 7	* so *l·* as we follow His commands.
	166– 7	so *l·* as we have the right ideal,
	175–25	must remain so *l·* as I remain.
	268– 3	should never be annulled so *l·* as
	318–19	so *l·* as he refrained from questioning
	345– 3	So *l·* as Christian Scientists obey

long-buried

Po.	67– 5	at work with the *l·* hours,

longed

Mis.	142–28	I *l·* to say to the masonic brothers :

longer

Mis.	9–25	wherefore our failure *l·* to relish
	141–26	Delay not *l·* to commence
	229–24	holier, happier, and *l·* lived.
Pul.	82–27	* *l·* remain deaf to their cry?
No.	13–11	and though the hiatus be *l·* still
My.	175–16	must remain with us a little *l·*,

longer no-

Mis.	5–17	There is no *l·* any reason for
	136– 1	this you must no *l·* expect.
	234– 2	then shall matter remain no *l·* to
	235– 2	He is no *l·* obliged to sin,
	354– 8	can no *l·* promote peace
Man.	86– 7	no *l·* under the jurisdiction
Ret.	23– 9	no *l·* spanned with its rainbow
	66– 4	no *l·* buried in materiality.
	93–10	no *l·* impersonated as a waif
Pul.	3–18	No *l·* are we of the church militant,
	82–28	* The date is no *l·* B. C.
	82–29	* Might no *l·* makes right,
No.	8–23	no *l·* cast your pearls before
	32–20	no *l·* be the servants of sin,
	34– 6	no *l·* venture to materialize the
'01.	11– 6	he is no *l·* a material man,
	11– 7	and mind is no *l·* in matter.
Hea.	8–14	no *l·* quarrels with the individual.
	13–11	until it was no *l·* aconite,
Peo.	2–22	no *l·* a personal tyrant
	6–19	God is no *l·* a mystery
	6–23	it should no *l·* be deemed treason
Po.	72– 3	Till God is God no *l·*
My.	90–28	* can no *l·* be questioned,
	124–31	no *l·* kindle altars for
	126–12	no *l·* a mystery or a miracle,
	132–14	no *l·* to appeal to human strength,
	151–14	when it no *l·* blesses
	216–24	and no *l·* contribute to
	226–16	and the universe would no *l·* exist.
	265–20	no *l·* tyrannical and proscriptive ;
	306– 9	question that is no *l·* a question.
	318–23	until he could control himself no *l·*
	332–26	* the lodge was no *l·* in existence,

longevity

Mis.	29–20	shows that *l·* has *increased.*
My.	103–21	health, *l·*, and morals of men ;
	265–17	increasing the *l·* of mankind,

Longfellow

Mis.	271–17	and *L·* is right.

Longfellow's

Ret.	27–15	In *L·* language,

long-hushed

Mis.	390–20	Ask of its June, the *l·* heart,
Po.	55–21	Ask of its June, the *l·* heart,

longingly

Mis.	1– 2	ancient Greek looked *l·* for
	231–30	tear-filled eyes looking *l·*

longings

My.	15–24	* It satisfies my *l·*,

long-kept

My.	134– 2	tell my *l·* secret — evidence a heart

long-lost

Po.	24– 3	A balm — the *l·* leaven

long-suffering

Mis.	130– 2	*l·*, meekness, charity,
Man.	47– 2	benevolent, forgiving, *l·*,
Ret.	45–22	*l·* and temperance, fulfil the
No.	8– 3	We should endeavor to be *l·*,
Pan.	9–17	*l·*, self-surrender, and spiritual

look

Mis.	8–12	*l·* upon the object of your own
	66–20	"we *l·* not at the things— *II Cor.* 4 : 18.
	87–16	to *l·* after the students ;
	112– 5	*l·* the illusions in the face.
	117– 9	We always know where to *l·* for
	134–23	Like Elisha, *l·* up, and behold :
	159–28	I *l·* at the rich devices in
	174–27	We do not *l·* into darkness for light.
	179–26	yet we *l·* into matter and the
	203– 6	as I *l·* on this smile of C. S.,
	228– 6	new standpoint whence to *l·* upward ;
	228–13	We should *l·* with pitying eye on
	228–15	This will bring us also to *l·* on
	231–23	a *l·* of cheer and a toy
	239–18	and tired *l·*, told the story ;
	286– 2	We *l·* to future generations for
	292–15	and *l·* no more into them
	294–21	then, *l·* out for their stings,
	299– 6	*l·* through the lens of C. S.,
	307–26	at which the sick may *l·* and
	315–16	*l·* after the welfare of his students,
	324–30	whence he may hopefully *l·* for
	342–16	to *l·* upon him whom they had
	369– 2	*l·* up with shouts and thanksgiving,
Un.	11–28	I say, *L·* up, not down,
Pul.	49–15	"*L·* at those big elms !
	83–17	* *l·* now to their daughters to
Rud.	10–19	*l·* up to the loving God,
No.	41–12	to *l·* for perfection in churches

look

'01. 27– 5   * I *l·* to see some St. Paul arise
    34–10   where shall we *l·* for the standard
'02. 20–21   great joy to *l·* into the faces
Hea. 10–16   *l·* on the bright side ;
    16–26   that we *l·* into these subjects,
Peo. 5– 8   we *l·* in vain for their more
    14–15   and *l·* upon this dream of life
Po. 1–14   from yon cloud-crowned height **to** *l·*
    23– 3   A *l·* that years impart?
My. 47–13   * *l·* back to the picturesque,
    47–16   * we *l·* back over the years
  119–29   *l·* and wait and watch and pray
  120– 1   We *l·* for the sainted Revelator
  120– 2   Those who *l·* for me in person,
  151–25   sun-worshippers failed to *l·*
  151–27   to *l·* no higher than the symbol.
  234–18   but to *l·* at both sides of the
  247–20   loving *l·* which brings forth
  248–26   to face the foe with loving *l·*
  259– 1   *l·* again at your gift,
  268–27   *L·* high enough, and you see
  268–29   *L·* long enough, and you see
  282– 7   "*L·* unto me, and be— *Isa.* 45 : 22.
  327–28   * *l·* forward to the day, not far
  332–22   * requested to *l·* up the records

looked

Mis. 1– 2   ancient Greek *l·* longingly
  320– 9   star that *l·* lovingly down
  374–20   I never *l·* on my ideal of
  380– 8   it *l·* as if centuries of spiritual
Pul. 43–23   * which was *l·* forward to as the
  71–23   * *l·* upon as having a divine mission
'01. 29– 2   Have we *l·* after or even known
'02. 18– 6   when mortals *l·* ignorantly,
My. 50–16   * and *l·* towards the spiritual,
  78–10   * They *l·* upon an interior done
  82– 6   * this morning it *l·* as though
  119–13   *stooped down* and *l·* into the
  119–14   *l·* for the person, instead of
  221– 5   The prophets of old *l·* for

looketh

Mis. 320–24   *l·* down on the long night
  335– 8   he *l·* not for him,— *Matt.* 24 : 50.

looking

Mis. 7–17   *L·* over the newspapers of
  130– 9   *l·* continually for a fault in
  135–28   You may be *l·* to see me
  225–23   *L·* away from all material aid,
  231–30   *l·* longingly at the portal
  239–19   *l·* up quaintiy, the poor child
  330– 5   *l·* upward, does it patiently pray
  330–16   *l·* through Love's transparency,
  331– 2   *l·* up, waiting on God,
  361–20   *l·* unto Jesus— *Heb.* 12 : 2.
  372–11   * "*L·* at the pictures in your
  374–28   *L·* behind the veil,
Pul. 46–25   * *l·* into the ancient languages,
  49– 8   * *L·* down from the windows
Po. v–14   * *l·* "*up through nature,*
My. 87–20   * cheerful *l·* groups of people
  124– 6   *L·* on this annual assemblage
  125–24   *l·* into the subject of C. S.,
  154–28   whereby we are *l·* heavenward,
  154–29   not *l·* nor gravitating earthward,
  204– 7   only by *l·* heavenward
  258–13   "*L·* unto Jesus— *Heb.* 12 : 2.
  343– 3   * *l·* large-eyed into space,
  346–14   * same expression of *l·* forward,
  349–16   "*l·* unto Jesus— *Heb.* 12 : 2.

look-out

Pul. 48– 5   * straight to her beloved "*l·*"

looks

Mis. vii– 4   * my thought *l·* Upon thy
  23–29   mirror repeats precisely the *l·* and
  241–24   doubting heart *l·* up through faith,
  275–10   *l·* in dull despair at the
  308– 4   Whosoever *l·* to me personally
  324–11   a face *l·* out, anxiously surveying
  324–16   he alone who *l·* from that dwelling,
  325–19   and *l·* at the Stranger,
  336–25   *l·* in upon the heart,
  386–11   This hour *l·* on her heart
  390–12   *L·* love unto the laughing hours,
Un. 11–16   "That withered hand *l·* very real
Po. 2– 1   no soul those *l·* betray ;
  2–13   The moon *l·* down upon
  49–16   This hour *l·* on her heart
  55–13   *L·* love unto the laughing hours,
My. 43–29   * The world *l·* with wonder upon
  70– 1   * and it certainly *l·* imposing.
  110– 5   *l·* down upon the long night of
  119–15   Mary of to-day *l·* up for Christ,
  257–30   child *l·* up in prayer,

looms

Mis. 99– 6   through the *l·* of time,
Pan. 2– 7   *l·* above the mists of pantheism
My. 232– 5   webs of life in *l·* of love

loose

Mis. 3–30   "Satan let *l·*."— *see Rev.* 20 : 7.
  47–14   let *l·* from its own beliefs.
  147–18   a *l·* and unstable character.
  289– 5   Drunkenness is sensuality let *l·*,
Rud. 4–13   "*l·* the bands of Orion."— *Job* 38 : 31.
Peo. 13–18   to let *l·* the wild beasts upon him,
My. 110–17   luxury of thought let *l·*,
  249–10   Hate is a moral idiocy let *l·*

loosed

Ret. 12– 4   Are *l·*, and not effete ;
Po. 61– 2   Are *l·*, and not effete ;

loosening

'02. 3– 3   *l·* cords of non-Christian religions

loosens

Mis. 394– 7   And *l·* the fetters of pride
Po. 45– 9   And *l·* the fetters of pride

looseth

Mis. 262–20   divine Love which *l·* the chains
Po. 79–14   Love *l·* thee, and lifteth me,

loosing

Mis. 237–28   *l·* the fetters of one form of

lopsided

Pul. 79–28   * become materialistically "*l·*,"

loquacious

'01. 16–21   in its origin evil was *l·*,

Lord (*see also* **Lord's**)

and Master
My. 161–17   the cup of their *L·* and Master
  232–12   Our *L·* and Master left to us the
  256–19   nativity of our *L·* and Master.
arm of the
Mis. 183–21   He to whom the arm of the *L·*
Un. 39–10   He to whom the arm of the *L·*
beloved in the
Mis. 151–18   Brother, sister, beloved in the *L·*,
  157– 5   Reign then, my beloved in the *L·*.
blessing from the
My. 34– 6   the blessing from the *L·*,— *Psal.* 24 : 5.
created it
Un. 20– 7   *First:* The *L·* created it.
crucified the
Un. 56– 7   "crucified the *L·*— *I Cor.* 2 : 8.
fear the
My. 33–23   them that fear the *L·*.— *Psal.* 15 : 4.
gave the word
Mis. 153–11   "the *L·* gave the word :— *Psal.* 68 : 11.
glory in the
Mis. 270–26   let him glory in the *L·*."— *I Cor.* 1 : 31.
glory of the
My. 183–27   glory of the *L·* is risen— *Isa.* 60 : 1.
hill of the
My. 34– 1   into the hill of the *L·*— *Psal.* 24 : 3.
is God
Un. 21–15   *Good.* The *L·* is God.
is gracious
My. 17– 8   that the *L·* is gracious.— *I Pet.* 2 : 3.
knows it
Un. 20– 8   *Second:* The *L·* knows it.
  44–19   "The *L·* knows it !"
light in the
My. 206–31   now are ye light in the *L·* :— *Eph.* 5 : 8.
loveth
Mis. 18– 3   "Whom the *L·* loveth— *Heb.* 12 : 6.
  73– 4   "Whom the *L·* loveth— *Heb.* 12 : 6.
  125– 4   "whom the *L·* loveth— *Heb.* 12 : 6.
  208–19   "whom the *L·* loveth— *Heb.* 12 : 6.
Ret. 80– 5   whom the *L·* loveth— *Heb.* 12 : 6.
magnify the
Mis. 75–22   doth magnify the *L·*,"— *Luke* 1 : 46.
  75–23   *spiritual sense* doth magnify the *L·* ;"
Un. 30– 2   doth magnify the *L·*."— *Luke* 1 : 46.
Pul. 12–17   magnify the *L·* of Hosts.
mind of the
My. 142– 1   known the mind of the *L·*,— *I Cor.* 2 : 16.
of heaven
Mis. 167–23   *L·* of heaven and earth,— *Luke* 10 : 21.
No. 44–28   *L·* of heaven and earth,— *Luke* 10 : 21.
of hosts
My. 34–12   The *L·* of hosts,— *Psal.* 24 : 10.
  131–26   the *L·* of hosts,— *Mal.* 3 : 10.
  269–26   the *L·* of hosts,— *Mal.* 3 : 10.
of the vineyard
Mis. 254–26   the *L·* of the vineyard— *Mark* 12 : 9.
one
Mis. 308–17   our Lord is one *L·*."— *Deut.* 6 : 4.
Peo. 1– 1   *One L·, one faith,— Eph.* 4 : 5.
  5– 3   "one *L·*, one faith,— *Eph.* 4 : 5.

Lord

one

Peo.	9– 1	one faith, one *L·*, one baptism ;
	9–11	Having one *L·*, we shall not be
	14–19	"one *L·*, one faith, — *Eph.* 4 : 5.
My.	280–15	chapter sub-title — *Deut.* 6 : 4.

our

Mis.	25–15	teachings and life of our *L·*.
	70–21	dying malefactor and our *L·* were
	70–26	while our *L·* would soon be rising to
	83–21	In the life of our *L·*, meekness was
	120–13	in the vineyard of our *L·* ;
	123–19	from the sepulchre of our *L·* ;
	193–24	who follow the commands of our *L·*
	244–31	especially the children of our *L·*
	276–14	the full coming of our *L·* and Christ.
	276–19	comes the glory of our *L·*,
	311– 8	ready for the table of our *L·* :
	320–10	on the manger of our *L·*,
	398–26	In the life and the love of our *L·*.
Ret.	65–19	follows the example of our *L·*
No.	23– 8	our *L·* gave the keys of the kingdom
Pan.	14– 5	commune at the table of our *L·*
'01.	1–11	in unity the life of our *L·*,
	33– 5	admitted to the vineyard of our *L·*,
'02.	16–17	agony in the life of our *L·* ;
Peo.	3–28	way that our *L·* has appointed ;
	5– 5	have not taken away our *L·*,
Po.	75– 6	In the life and the love of our *L·*.
My.	113– 9	immediate disciple of our *L·*,
	136– 6	and by the life of our *L·*
	179–20	as depicted in the life of our *L·*,
	232–12	Our *L·* and Master left to us the
	250–11	in this vast vineyard of our *L·*.
	256–19	advent and nativity of our *L·*
	330– 4	* noteworthy follower of our *L·*

our blessed

No.	33–14	sacrifice of our blessed *L·*
My.	201–14	bleeding brow of our blessed *L·*,

our loved

My.	159– 5	those words of our loved *L·*,

our loving

Pan.	13–10	the love of our loving *L·*
My.	18–18	the love of our loving *L·*

our risen

Man.	60–21	whereby to exemplify our risen *L·*.

peace of the

Pul.	39– 4	* it finds the peace of the *L·*

present with the

Mis.	344–22	and present with the *L·*." — *II Cor.* 5 : 8.

ransomed of the

My.	171– 4	ransomed of the *L·* — *Isa.* 35 : 10.

redeemed of the

'01.	11–11	and are the redeemed of the *L·*.

reigneth

Mis.	277–22	"The *L·* reigneth ; — *Psal.* 97 : 1

reigns

Mis.	368–28	let us not forget that the *L·* reigns,

rejoice in the

Mis.	330–11	"Rejoice in the *L·* — *Phil.* 4 : 4.

saith the

Mis.	103–32	saith the *L·*." — *Jer.* 23 : 23.
	130–16	will repay, saith the *L·*." — *Rom.* 12 : 19.
	136–16	saith the *L·*." — *II Cor.* 6 : 17.
My.	131–26	saith the *L·* of hosts, — *Mal.* 3 : 10.
	154–12	"my Spirit, saith the *L·* ;" — *Zech.* 4 : 6.
	268–18	"Thus saith the *L·*," — *Exod.* 4 : 22.
	269–26	saith the *L·* of hosts, — *Mal.* 3 : 10.

shall see the

'02.	16–13	shall see the *L·*." — *Heb.* 12 : 14.

Spirit of the

My.	128–12	"Where the Spirit of the *L·* — *II Cor.* 3 : 17.

their

'00.	15– 6	To sit at this table of their *L·*
'01.	7–20	they have not taken away their *L·*,
My.	161–17	cup of their *L·* and Master

thy

Mis.	122–26	into the joy of thy *L·*." — *Matt.* 25 : 23.

trust in the

Mis.	298– 1	"Trust in the *L·* — *Prov.* 3 : 5.
'01.	34–29	"Trust in the *L·* — *Prov.* 3 : 5.
My.	170–20	"Trust in the *L·*, — *Psal.* 37 : 3.

unto the

Mis.	157–22	thy way unto the *L·* ; — *Psal.* 37 : 5.
	269– 1	thy way unto the *L·* ; — *Psal.* 37 : 5.
My.	170–23	thy way unto the *L·* ; — *Psal.* 37 : 5.
	229– 6	abomination unto the *L·* : — *Deut.* 18 : 12.

way of the

Mis.	246–24	the way of the *L·*, — *Matt.* 3 : 3.

word of the

Pul.	7–23	word of the *L·* endureth — *I Pet.* 1 : 25.

work of the

Chr.	55–13	the work of the *L·*, — *Isa.* 5 : 12.

Mis.	63–19	the *L·* He is God ; — *Deut.* 4 : 35.

Lord

Mis.	97–18	"I am the *L·*, — *Isa.* 45 : 5.
	126–31	the *L·* shall have them — *Psal.* 2 : 4.
	177– 7	secret conspiracy against the *L·*
	209–30	and false charity say, " 'Not so, *L·* ;'
	229–16	*L·*, which is my refuge, — *Psal.* 91 : 9.
	245– 5	sought not to the *L·*, — *II Chron.* 16 : 12.
	268–19	"help is from the *L·*," — *see Psal.* 121 : 2.
	308–16	The *L·* our God — *Deut.* 6 : 4.
	364– 5	"Wait . . . on the *L·*, — *see Isa.* 40 : 31.
	366–11	the *L·* He is God, — *Deut.* 4 : 35.
	388–20	Last at the cross to mourn her *L·*,
Man.	18–11	the *L·* helped us." — *I Sam.* 7 : 12.
Ret.	9–11	"Speak, *L·* ; — *I Sam.* 3 : 9.
	68– 3	in the name of "the *L·*," or good,
Un.	2–21	if they die in the *L·*
	3– 7	which die in the *L·*." — *Rev.* 14 : 13.
	6–28	"Wait . . . on the *L·* ;" — *see Psal.* 40 : 1.
Pul.	33– 8	* "Speak, *L·*, — *I Sam.* 3 : 9.
Rud.	9–16	an answer of the lips from the *L·*.
	13–14	"The *L·*, He is God ; — *Deut.* 4 : 35.
'00.	14–27	"*L·*, lay not this sin — *Acts* 7 : 60.
Po.	21– 9	Last at the cross to mourn her *L·*,
My.	24–15	* temple in the *L·*." — *Eph.* 2 : 21.
	33–15	*L·*, who shall abide in — *Psal.* 15 : 1.
	170–22	also in the *L·* ; — *Psal.* 37 : 4.
	183– 2	love the *L·* thy God — *Luke* 10 : 27.
	206–19	"The *L·* shall be unto thee — *Isa.* 60 : 19.
	229– 7	the *L·* thy God doth — *Deut.* 18 : 12.
	280–15	chapter sub-title — *Deut.* 6 : 4.
	324–13	* how long you had waited on the *L·*

lord (*see also* **lord's**)

Mis.	335– 4	*l·* delayeth his coming ; — *Matt.* 24 : 48.
	335– 7	*l·* of that servant — *Matt.* 24 : 50.
Pul.	4–24	the *l·* and giver of Life.
Po.	10– 6	*L·* of the main and manor !
My.	62– 4	* joy of thy *l·*." — *Matt.* 25 : 23.
	207–22	joy of thy *l·*'" — *Matt.* 25 : 21.
	337– 7	*L·* of the main and manor !

Lord God

Mis.	57–20	and the *L· G·* never said it.
	72–15	saith the *L· G·*, — *Ezek.* 18 : 3.
	172–14	"the *L· G·* omnipotent — *Rev.* 19 : 6.
Ret.	15– 8	the strength of the *L· G·* : — *Psal.* 71 : 16.
My.	v– 1	* *L· G·* of Hosts, be with us yet ;
	16–24	* thus saith the *L· G·*, — *Isa.* 28 : 16.
	126–22	*L· G·* who judgeth her." — *Rev.* 18 : 8.

Lord Jesus Christ

Mis.	196–28	*Believe on the L· J· C·*, — *Acts* 16 : 31.
My.	19– 9	grace of the *L· J· C·*, — *II Cor.* 13 : 14.

Lord of Hosts

Pul.	12–17	and magnify the *L·* of *H·*.

Lord's

Mis.	170– 8	drinking of wine at the *L·* supper,
Ret.	88–24	The *L·* command means this,
'02.	11–21	this is thy *L·* benediction
My.	33–28	earth is the *L·*, — *Psal.* 24 : 1.
	258–26	hallowed by our *L·* blessing.

lord's

Man.	28–11	which knew his *l·* will, — *Luke* 12 : 47.

lords

Mis.	333–15	"*l·* many and gods — *see I Cor.* 8 : 5.
My.	72–10	* *l·* and ladies who come to attend

Lord's Prayer

Mis.	211–31	Shall we repeat our *L· P·* when
	314–10	repeat in concert . . . the *L P·*.
	314–18	interpretation of the *L· P·* ;
	331–17	which taught them the *L· P·* ?
Man.	63– 1	the *L· P·* . . . and its Spiritual
Pul.	22– 4	one prayer, — the *L· P·*.
	43–20	* the *L· P·*, with its spiritual
'01.	31–23	my cradle hymn and the *L· P·*,
Hea.	15–28	The *L· P·*, understood in its
My.	17–25	* audible repetition of the *L· P·*
	29– 6	* the words of the *L· P·* !
	32– 4	* began to repeat the *L· P·*,
	32–18	* the *L· P·* with its spiritual
	32–31	* audible repetition of the *L· P·*.
	39–12	* audible repetition of the *L· P·*,
	78–20	* audible repetition of the *L· P·*.
	225–16	the leading of our *L· P·*.
	233– 6	Otherwise, wherefore the *L· P·*,

lore

Mis.	125–18	the eternal *l·* of Love ;
Ret.	11– 7	learning's *l·* and wisdom's might,
Po.	60– 3	learning's *l·* and wisdom's might,

Los Angeles, Cal.

My.	192–19	chapter sub-title

lose

Mis.	10–13	The good cannot *l·* their God,
	42– 4	nor does he *l·* his identity,

lose

Mis.	80– 3	you *l·* much more than can be gained
	84–25	To *l·* error thus, is to live in Christ,
	100–13	may *l·* sight thereof ;
	110– 8	*l·* them not through contact with
	116–30	you *l·* the scientific rule and its
	181–25	Mortals will *l·* their sense of
	182– 9	*l·* their false sense of existence,
	184–16	yield to material sense, and *l·*
	186–18	let us not *l·* this Science of man,
	211– 1	or you will not *l·* them ;
	211–23	save his life shall *l·* it." — *Matt.* 16 : 25.
	221– 2	may *l·* his power to harm
	242–12	he would *l·* his money.
	265– 8	make mistakes and *l·* their way.
	270–12	to *l·* the priceless knowledge of
	287–10	and thereby *l·* it.
	296–31	*his* shame would not *l·* its blush !
	311–22	I should *l·* my hope of heaven.
	319–14	they must not *l·* sight of sin ;
	327–28	and *l·* sight of their guide ;
	341–19	O learn to *l·* with God !
	354–30	nor his pinions *l·* power
Man.	59– 5	is to *l·* some weight in the scale
Ret.	32– 7	save his life shall *l·* it," — *Mark.* 8 : 35.
	49–14	Mortals must learn to *l·* their
	80–28	*l·* them in proportion to our
Un.	1–19	they *l·* all sense of error.
	2–17	the sick *l·* their sense of sickness,
	4–14	*l·* our own consciousness of error.
	4–16	how could we *l·* all consciousness of
	49–19	should appear real . . . or we *l·* the
	54– 5	one must *l·* sight of a false claim.
No.	9–13	err in effort, and *l·* your fruition.
	21–18	because by it we *l·* God's ways
	37–19	*l·* its efficacy and lack the
Pan.	7–11	*l·* the character and sovereignty of
'00.	8–18	We *l·* a percentage due to
'01.	4–10	you *l·* its susceptibility of
	5– 5	*l·* the nature of one God,
	5– 5	*l·* monotheism, and become less
	6–27	*l·* all conceivable idea of
	13–27	To *l·* the sense of sin we must first
Hea.	10–24	win or *l·* according to your plea.
Peo.	10– 4	refinements that *l·* some materiality ;
	12–24	*l·* faith in omnipotence.
Po.	18– 7	tear dim his eye, or pinion *l·* power
My.	120– 3	*l·* me instead of find me.
	134–14	will never *l·* their claim on us.
	142–16	might in time *l·* its sacredness
	149–24	*l·* the Science of Christianity,
	178– 4	nor *l·* the invincible process
	206– 4	*l·* Science, — *l·* the Principle of
	211–17	The victims *l·* their individuality,
	229–14	*l·* all selfishness, as she has
	290– 6	*l·* their lustre in the tomb,

loser

'02.	20–20	I shall be the *l·* by this change,

loses

Mis.	17–31	by which one *l·* himself as matter,
	226–11	he *l·* the homage of fools,
	261–16	atonement of Christ *l·* no efficacy.
	308– 7	*l·* the path to health, happiness,
Un.	2–12	The sinner *l·* his sense of sin,
No.	24– 2	evil *l·* all place, person, and power.
	33– 1	slander *l·* its power to harm ;
	38–26	*l·* a part of its purest spirituality if
'00.	3– 3	he *l·* self in love,
	3– 4	unless he *l·* the chord.
'01.	3–25	*l·* the nature of God, Spirit,
'02.	18–24	faith without proof *l·* its life,
Hea.	13–10	so-called drug *l·* its power.
My.	132–29	and never *l·* a case.
	212–26	*l·* his own power to heal.
	265– 8	*l·* capital, and is bought at par

loseth

Mis.	327–25	*l·* his life for my sake, — *Matt.* 10 : 39.
	358–11	*l·* in Life, Truth, and Love.
My.	233–26	*l·* his life . . . for my sake — *Matt.* 10 : 39.

losing

Mis.	54–11	Instead of *l·* her power
	111– 8	*l·* hold of divine Love,
	113–12	is *l·* in the scale of moral and
	201–26	*l·* those jewels of character,
	226– 9	by *l·* his own self-respect?
	354–13	*l·* the knowledge of the divine
Un.	20–19	You will find yourself *l·* the
	39–26	*l·* the divine likeness.
	47– 4	is *l·* its false claim to existence
No.	41–23	sin is *l·* prestige and power.
'01.	23– 2	*l·* the numeration table
My.	4– 1	*l·* his faith in matter and sin,
	149–22	*L·* the comprehensive in the
	268– 6	marriage relation is *l·* ground,

loss

compensate

Mis.	111–12	compensate *l·*, and gain a higher

error and

Mis.	276–28	error and *l·* will be quickly learned

every

My.	116–22	Every *l·* in grace and growth

gain is

Mis.	358– 7	and their gain is *l·* to the

heavy

Pul.	20– 3	Owing to a heavy *l·*,

his own

My.	212–27	compensate himself for his own *l·*

hour of

Mis.	179– 4	rightful desire in the hour of *l·*,

irreparable

Rud.	16–17	an irreparable *l·* of Science.
My.	333–29	* to lament this irreparable *l·*."

is gain

Mis.	389–17	God is good, and *l·* is gain.
Po.	4–16	God is good, and *l·* is gain.

its

My.	289–14	its *l·* and the world's loss,

marked

Mis.	204–16	marked *l·* of faith in evil,

mourn the

My.	291–26	called to mourn the *l·* of

of funds

'02.	13–15	when a *l·* of funds occurred,

of help

My.	195– 5	Adverse circumstances, *l·* of help,

of material objects

Ret.	31– 1	*l·* of material objects of affection

of self-knowledge

Mis.	112–25	then, in a *l·* of self-knowledge

of suffering

Mis.	219–19	ease and *l·* of suffering ;

of the Golden Rule

My.	224–16	blind to his *l·* of the Golden Rule,

of the true sense

Un.	41– 7	a *l·* of the true sense of good,

or gain

Mis.	116–17	express life's *l·* or gain,

possible

Man.	44– 6	possible *l·*, for a time, of C. S.

shame and

Mis.	267–17	suffered temporary shame and *l·*

sorrow and

Ret.	7–23	* too much of sorrow and *l·*.

temporary

Mis.	99– 8	temporary *l·* of his self-respect.
Un.	41– 9	involves a temporary *l·* of God,

total

Mis.	112–29	total *l·* of moral, intellectual, and

world's

My.	289–14	its loss and the world's *l·*,

Mis.	116–17	*l·* of the pleasures and pains
	206–15	no *l·* nor lack of what constitutes
	209–18	The *l·* of gustatory enjoyment
Pul.	9–16	*l·* of our late lamented pastor.
My.	290– 1	a *l·* felt by the strong hearts of

losses

Mis.	xi–27	sadly to survey . . . the enemy's *l·*.
Ret.	79– 6	from our own material *l·*.
My.	12–19	is the greatest of *l·*.

lost

Mis.	9–22	human enjoyment having *l·* its flavor,
	10–11	God will not let them be *l·* ;
	14–14	if man has *l·* his Principle
	33– 5	and thereby they *l·*, and he won,
	54– 3	*Has Mrs. Eddy l· her power to heal?*
	54– 8	understand . . . what cannot be *l·*.
	59–16	to admit that it has been *l·*
	97–29	the *l·* image is not this
	97–31	corporeal man is this *l·* image ;
	100–11	Love's labors are not *l·*.
	103–13	form and individuality are never *l·*,
	111– 8	*l·* your fishes, and . . . blamed others
	111–13	Nothing is *l·* that God gives :
	113– 8	free moral agency is *l·* ;
	142–19	my Muse *l·* her lightsome lyre,
	149–13	and see that nothing has been *l·*.
	179– 5	believing we have *l·* sight of Truth,
	182–19	man was never *l·* in Adam,
	184–24	gives back the *l·* likeness and
	185– 1	giving back the *l·* sense of
	186–31	the *l·* sense of man's perfection,
	190–26	the wrong power, or the *l·* sense,
	195–12	save that which was *l·*." — *Matt.* 18 : 11.
	211–25	the Life that cannot be *l·*.
	212–22	human will is *l·* in the divine ;
	212–32	*l·* sight of him ;
	221–14	if he denies it, the good effect is *l·*.
	226–10	or what has he *l·* when,

lost

Mis.	226–22	those who have *l·* their honor
	252–25	and restores its *l·* element,
	269– 4	Galileo virtually *l·* it.
	287–12	and restores *l·* Eden.
	295–14	*l·* these sentiments from his
	319– 2	the unreality of evil is *l·*.
	348–25	had *l·* all faith in them.
	352–13	until they are *l·* in light
	357– 5	Let them seek the *l·* sheep
	357– 6	*l·* their great Shepherd
Man.	17–12	and its *l·* element of healing.
	17–18	and restores the *l·* Israel :
Ret.	14– 2	forever *l·* its power over me.
	14– 7	unbelievers in these dogmas *l·*,
	20– 1	*l·* all my husband's property,
	21– 4	informed that my son was *l·*.
	21–30	the *nexus* is *l·*,
	32– 6	whatever is . . . is eventually *l·*.
	54–18	not understood, it may be *l·*,
	62– 1	Unless . . . healing will again be *l·*,
	67–16	false claim called sin is finally *l·*
	73–17	evil is *l·* in supersensible good.
Un.	51–17	They have none of them *l·* their
	53–22	or else he has *l·* his true
	60–24	Without Him, . . . immortality be *l·*.
Rud.	7–11	His likeness would be *l·* if inverted
No.	3–13	not having *l·* the Spirit which
	5–25	*l·* jewel in this misconception of
	10–17	a so-called material sense is *l·*,
	10–17	and Truth restores that *l·* sense,
	43– 1	had *l·* its efficacy for him,
Pan.	5– 1	monotheism is *l·* and
	10–25	never *l·*, in that individual who
	11–25	obliterates the *l·* image
'01.	3–22	is not *l·* by the conclusion,
	13–26	not a sinful soul, that is *l·*.
	34–16	the *l·* chord of Christ ;
'02.	8–29	or His *l·* likeness,
	15– 3	never *l·* my faith in God,
Hea.	3–11	*l·* Christianity and the power to
Peo.	5–11	Truth is not *l·* in the mists
	8– 4	to be saved and others to be *l·*,
Po.	22–20	peace is won, and *l·* is vice :
	77–17	some dear *l·* guest
My.	12–18	*l·* opportunity is the greatest of
	12–21	carelessly *l·* in speaking
	40–11	* Nothing will be *l·*, however,
	46–12	its *l·* element of healing."
	117– 1	the world would not have *l·* the
	117–23	philosophy *l·* to the centuries
	134–12	eclipsed by some *l·* opportunity,
	165–27	*l·* the power of being magnanimous.
	178–14	true sense of life is *l·* to those
	179–14	truths that cannot be *l·*,
	185–19	was *l·*, and is found ;" — *Luke* 15 : 32.
	187– 3	hath not *l·* its saltness.
	191–23	Death has *l·* its sting,
	194–14	human self *l·* in divine light,
	229–15	lose all . . . as she has *l·* it,
	231–18	else love's labor is *l·*
	243– 6	cannot have *l·* sight of the rules
	267–23	bitter sense of *l·* opportunities
	278–22	Nothing is gained . . . but much is *l·*.
	283–22	when self is *l·* in Love
	290– 7	her personal virtues can never be *l·*.
	294–31	the loved and *l·* of many millions.
	295– 3	assurance that life is not *l·* ;
	301– 7	lees of religion will be *l·*,
	311–11	and so I *l·* my housekeeper.
	336–12	*l·* all my husband's property,
	339– 5	C. S. cannot be *l·* sight of,

lot

Mis.	80–24	we should commiserate the *l·* of
	139–18	I gave a *l·* of land
	140–20	The *l·* of land which I donated
Ret.	51– 1	I gave a *l·* of land in Boston
'02.	13–16	purchased the mortgage on the *l·*
Po.	79– 1	matters not what be thy *l·*,

lots

Mis.	302– 5	"cast *l·* for his vesture," — *see Psal.* 22 : 18.
'01.	26–17	and they cast *l·* for it
My.	206–11	divide Truth's garment and cast *l·*

loud

Mis.	238–26	* unable to speak a *l·* word,"
Ret.	8–16	so *l·* that Mehitable heard it,
	16– 9	she could not speak a *l·* word,
Pul.	12– 5	I heard a *l·* voice saying — *Rev.* 12 : 10.
No.	39– 7	*l·* enough to be heard ;
My.	186–12	swelling the *l·* anthem of

louder

Mis.	99–25	speak *l·* than to-day.
	277– 4	Truth is speaking *l·*, clearer,
Pul.	12–18	A *l·* song, sweeter than has

loudest

Mis.	277– 8	Whosoever proclaims Truth *l·*,
Po.	30–19	sacred song and *l·* breath of praise

loudly

Mis.	292–16	It calls *l·* on them to
	326– 6	Once more he . . . knocks *l·*.
'01.	35– 7	appeals *l·* to those asleep
My.	265– 3	knocks more *l·* than ever

Loudon

My.	309– 7	towns of *L·* and Bow,
	309– 9	the counsel for *L·*

Louisville, Ky.

Pul.	89–17	* *Commercial, L·, K·.*

lovable

Mis.	318– 8	less *l·* or Christly.

Love (*see also* Love's)

abiding in
Mis.	135– 8	Abiding in *L·*, not one of you

aflame with
Po.	22– 5	hundred years, aflame with *L·*,

allness of
No.	35–12	but to show the allness of *L·*

alone
Mis.	388–10	For *L·* alone is Life ;
Man.	40– 7	divine *L·* alone governs man ;
Po.	7–10	For *L·* alone is Life ;
My.	247–22	it is *L·* alone that feeds them.

altar of
Hea.	2–27	sprinkled the altar of *L·*

amenities of
Man.	40– 9	reflects the sweet amenities of *L·*,

and Truth
Mis.	133–24	the Jerusalem of *L·* and Truth,
No.	39–14	false sense of Life, *L·*, and Truth,
'02.	6– 4	curse of *L·* and Truth was
	6– 8	*L·* and Truth destroy this knowledge,
Hea.	8– 4	*L·*, and Truth that destroy error
	16–10	and abound in *L·* and Truth,
Po.	77–10	Thou wisdom, *L·*, and Truth,

and wisdom
Po.	44– 1	O tender *L·* and wisdom,
My.	223–28	divine *L·* and wisdom saith,

antipode of
Mis.	351–27	declares itself the antipode of *L·* ;

arms of
Mis.	140–23	put back into the arms of *L·*,

as God
Mis.	234–10	true sense of *L·* as God ;

atones
My.	288–26	*L·* atones for sin

based on
My.	205–27	it is forever based on *L·*,

beauty of
Ret.	88–13	apprehend the living beauty of *L·*,

becomes
Mis.	391–13	*L·* becomes the substance,
Po.	38–12	*L·* becomes the substance,

bonds of
Mis.	135–20	and so cement the bonds of *L·*.

charity is
Mis.	210–29	Charity is *L·* ;

chastisements of
My.	282–11	wholesome chastisements of *L·*,

comes
My.	134–18	*L·* comes to our tears

decree of
Mis.	118–15	this immutable decree of *L·* :

define
'01.	3–16	to define *L·* in divine Science

demands of
Peo.	9– 8	or meet the demands of *L·*.

demonstrate
'01.	4– 9	demonstrate *L·* according to
'02.	8–17	his deeds, demonstrate *L·*.

demonstrates
Mis.	209– 9	this Principle demonstrates *L·*,

demonstration of
Mis.	214– 3	and a demonstration of *L·*,

divine

(*see* **divine**)

door of
Mis.	106–12	Out through the door of *L·*,

doth enter
Po.	22–19	*L·* doth enter in,

doth guide
Po.	79– 2	So *L·* doth guide ;

efficacious
Man.	15–15	of divine, efficacious *L·*,

eternal
Mis.	206–31	baptismal font of eternal *L·*.
	286–10	the unity of eternal *L·*.

eternal lore of
Mis.	125–18	the eternal lore of *L·* ;

Love

ever-present
No. 20–18   Ever-present $L\cdot$ must seem
'00. 1– 6   ever-present $L\cdot$ filling all space,
expresses
'01. 3–23 $L\cdot$ expresses the nature of God ;
faith, and
Mis. 152–25   tower of hope, faith, and $L\cdot$,
feast of
'01. 2–18   death's-head at the feast of $L\cdot$,
feet of
Mis. 204– 9   and kisses the feet of $L\cdot$,
flood-gates of
'01. 32–29   through the flood-gates of $L\cdot$;
forgiving
Mis. 124–26   *$L\cdot$ forgiving its enemies.*
foundation of
Pul. 2–30   reared on the foundation of $L\cdot$,
fruits of
Mis. 100–16   finally show the fruits of $L\cdot$.
Un. 40– 8   and bears the fruits of $L\cdot$,
full of
Mis. 214– 2   Jesus' life was full of $L\cdot$,
gems of
Mis. 343–17   burnishing anew the hidden gems of $L\cdot$,
gives
My. 193–15 $L\cdot$ gives nothing to take away.
God and
'02. 8–14   fact that God and $L\cdot$ are *one*.
God as
'02. 4–18   chapter sub-title
9– 1   consciousness of God as $L\cdot$
My. 152–16   Do I understand God as $L\cdot$,
God is
(see **God**)
God who is
Mis. 337–11   its Principle, God who is $L\cdot$.
gospel of
Mis. 135–18   spreading the gospel of $L\cdot$,
great
Mis. 77–15   This is the Father's great $L\cdot$
hath one race
Po. 22–13 $L\cdot$ hath one race, one realm,
heart of
Po. 24–20   Dear heart of $L\cdot$,
heavenly dews of
Mis. 343–11   by the heavenly dews of $L\cdot$,
heaven of
Mis. 156–10   heaven of $L\cdot$ within your hearts.
hieroglyphics of
Mis. 331–31   hieroglyphics of $L\cdot$, are understood ;
home of
Mis. 84–25   traveller, to the home of $L\cdot$.
hungry for
Mis. 369–20   We are hungry for $L\cdot$,
ideal of
Hea. 10– 8   presented the highest ideal of $L\cdot$.
illimitable
Pul. 4–24   Wait patiently on illimitable $L\cdot$,
immortal
Mis. 292–18   unlike the risen, immortal $L\cdot$;
immovable
Ret. 89– 1   stillness and immovable $L\cdot$.
impels
Mis. 358– 1 $L\cdot$ impels good works.
infinite
Mis. 59–14   pleading with infinite $L\cdot$ to love us,
123– 8   the forever-law of infinite $L\cdot$,
292– 9   rare revelation of infinite $L\cdot$,
Ret. 14–10   the good pleasure of infinite $L\cdot$.
23– 5   merged into the one infinite $L\cdot$.
'01. 7– 1   as the personality of infinite $L\cdot$,
'02. 5–28   an antipode of *infinite $L\cdot$*
6–29   wherein God is infinite $L\cdot$,
14–26   outstretched arm of infinite $L\cdot$
Hea. 4– 6   the effects of infinite $L\cdot$,
4–13   We expect infinite $L\cdot$ to
My. 178– 9   in the laboratory of infinite $L\cdot$
inseparable from
My. 185–17   Life is . . . inseparable from $L\cdot$,
instead of
Mis. 351–23   wherefore it is hate instead of $L\cdot$;
intelligence and
Mis. 16–22   an all-pervading intelligence and $L\cdot$,
is at the helm
Mis. 113–25   when $L\cdot$ is at the helm of thought,
is divine Principle
'01. 3–28   God is Love, $L\cdot$ is divine Principle ;
is God
'01. 3–21   * no argument that $L\cdot$ is God ;
is Life
Mis. 12–26   and $L\cdot$ is Life and Truth.
is my God
Mis. 206–22 $L\cdot$ is my God, and my God is Love."

Love

is our refuge
Mis. 389–10 $L\cdot$ is our refuge ;
Po. 4– 9 $L\cdot$ is our refuge ;
is Principle
No. 19–12 $L\cdot$ is Principle, not person.
is spiritual
Mis. 351–21 $L\cdot$ is spiritual,
is the liberator
My. 268–23   in which $L\cdot$ is the liberator
is the master
Mis. 336– 1 $L\cdot$ is the master of hate ;
is the Principle
Mis. 117–13 $L\cdot$ is the Principle of unity,
234– 6 $L\cdot$ is the Principle of divine
'02. 8–20   and $L\cdot$ is the Principle thereof.
is the way
'01. 35–10 $L\cdot$ is the way alway.
is triumphant
Mis. 153– 4   and $L\cdot$ is triumphant.
jewels of
Ret. 79–23   jewels of $L\cdot$, set in wisdom.
joy of
No. 8– 7   beauty of holiness, the joy of $L\cdot$
justice and
Ret. 80–17   permeate justice and $L\cdot$,
law of
(see **law**)
lessons of
Ret. 21–23   lucid and enduring lessons of $L\cdot$
Life and
(see **Life**)
life of
My. 301–11   Father, teach us the life of $L\cdot$.
Life, Truth, and
(see **Life**)
Life, Truth, or
Mis. 67– 6   not adulterate Life, Truth, or $L\cdot$,
light of
Mis. 132– 5   to the light of $L\cdot$ — and By-laws.
320–28   is the light of $L\cdot$,
light to
My. 234–14   from light to $L\cdot$, from sense to Soul.
likeness of
'02. 8– 6   the likeness of $L\cdot$ is loving
living
Po. 29–15   Thou gentle beam of living $L\cdot$,
looseth
Po. 79–14 $L\cdot$ looseth thee, and lifteth me,
lost in
My. 283–23   when self is lost in $L\cdot$
loved of
Hea. 2–21   loved of the Father, the loved of $L\cdot$
makes
Mis. 133–29 $L\cdot$ makes all burdens light,
Hea. 17– 7 $L\cdot$ makes the spiritual man,
manifestations of
Mis. 102–19   are the manifestations of $L\cdot$.
Mind is
Mis. 332– 5   merciful, and wise, this Mind is $L\cdot$,
Mother
Mis. 159–24   "O glorious Truth ! O Mother $L\cdot$!
nature of
'02. 7– 1   the true nature of $L\cdot$ intact
not hate
My. 239– 1   Truth, not error ; $L\cdot$, not hate.
ocean of
Mis. 205–14   in the infinite ocean of $L\cdot$,
offspring of
Mis. 117–13   Obedience is the offspring of $L\cdot$,
omnipotent
Mis. 183– 3   omnipotent $L\cdot$, and eternal Life,
Un. 39– 7   omnipotent $L\cdot$ which annihilates hate,
omnipresent
Mis. 307– 7   understanding of omnipresent $L\cdot$!
opens the eyes
Mis. 210–29 $L\cdot$ opens the eyes of the blind,
opposed to
My. 279– 1   an element opposed to $L\cdot$,
panoply of
Pul. 15–19   Clad in the panoply of $L\cdot$,
peace in
'02. 19–18   a rest in Christ, a peace in $L\cdot$.
peace of
My. 185– 8   The peace of $L\cdot$ is published,
perfect
Mis. 229–27   the "perfect $L\cdot$" — *I John* 4 : 18.
334–32   the might of perfect $L\cdot$
Ret. 61–17   for 'perfect $L\cdot$ — *I John* 4 : 18.
Un. 20–16   and so reach that perfect $L\cdot$
Peo. 6–16   whereas "perfect $L\cdot$ — *I John* 4 : 18.
power of
No. 9–21   and show the power of $L\cdot$.
prevailing
My. 50–18   * of $L\cdot$ prevailing over the

Love

purpose of
   Mis. 214–15 accomplishing its purpose of *L*·,
purposes of
   Mis. 292–24 works out the purposes of *L*·.
realm of
   Pul. 10–15 hope's reality — the realm of *L*·.
redeeming
   '00. 2– 5 old-new theme of redeeming *L*·
reflect
   Mis. 150–29 that reflect Him — that reflect *L*·.
reflected
   Mis. 293–21 sum total of *L*· reflected is
represents
   Mis. 104–26 and its idea represents *L*·.
righteousness of
   My. 182–31 abound in the righteousness of *L*·,
rules
   My. 278– 7 *L*· rules the universe,
same
   Mis. 214–11 Jesus was stimulated by the same *L*·
sends forth
   Pul. 12–21 *L*· sends forth her primal . . . strain.
significance of
   Mis. 250–11 The divine significance of *L*·
spirit of
   Mis. 288–29 spirit of *L*· that nerves the
   No. v– 4 self-sacrificing spirit of *L*·
spiritual
   Mis. 288– 7 weighed by spiritual *L*·,
spontaneity of
   My. 185–16 Life is the spontaneity of *L*·,
steadfast in
   Mis. 12–16 watchful and steadfast in *L*·,
sunshine of
   My. 252–22 eternal sunshine of *L*·,
that guards
   Mis. 331–20 Thou *L*· that guards the nestling's
   389– 8 Thou *L*· that guards the nestling's
   Po. 4– 5 Thou *L*· that guards the nestling's
that is Life
   My. 275–16 truth of being — the *L*· that is Life
the word
   Pul. 26–22 * over the door, . . . the word "*L*·."
this
   Un. 20–17 then see if this *L*· does not
touch of
   My. 256–21 springs aside at the touch of *L*·.
trespass on
   Pul. 3– 9 nothing can . . . trespass on *L*·.
trinity
   Un. 63– 4 trinity of *L*· lives and reigns
triumphant
   Mis. 124–30 to understanding, *L*· triumphant !
Truth and
   (*see* **Truth**)
Truth, Life, and
   (*see* **Truth**)
truth of
   Mis. 287–11 corrects . . . with the truth of *L*·,
   337– 2 that which reveals the truth of *L*·,
unction of
   '00. 11–18 I want . . . the unction of *L*·.
understanding and
   Pul. 22–18 spiritual understanding and *L*·,
understanding of
   My. 278–12 armed with the understanding of *L*·,
unfolds
   My. 288– 2 *L*· unfolds marvellous good
universal
   Mis. 141–11 proposed type of universal *L*· ;
   Peo. 2–25 *L*· universal, infinite, eternal.
unquenchable
   Mis. 77–19 impartial, and unquenchable *L*·
   328–12 unchanging, unquenchable *L*·
unveiled
   Ret. 31–29 *L*· unveiled the healing promise
which is faithful
   My. 167– 9 in that *L*· which is faithful,
will reign
   Mis. 213–29 *L*· will reign in every heart,
wisdom and
   Mis. 321–29 a world of wisdom and *L*·

   Mis. ix–20 a *L*· that is a boy,
   8–15 *L*· that is omnipresent good,
   11–14 *L*· metes not out human justice,
   12–27 demonstrably is not *L*·.
   23–26 reflects good, Life, Truth, *L*·
   63– 7 Life, Truth, *L*· are the triune
   100–27 He understands this Principle,— *L*·.
   104–24 How shall we . . . Through *L*·.
   104–25 The Principle of C. S. is *L*·,
   124–15 ever-living Life, Truth, *L*· :
   130–29 *L*· is not puffed up;
   186– 2 who originates in God, *L*·,

Love

   Mis. 187–22 God,— Life, Truth, *L*·.
   209– 8 Principle of divine Science being *L*·,
   212–22 and *L*·, the white Christ,
   215–15 *L*·, peace, and good will toward
   234– 6 *L*· is not learned of the material
   249–27 chapter sub-title
   277–26 *L*· is especially near in times of
   290–11 divine Principle, which is *L*·,
   292– 7 *L*· had a new commandment
   292–12 higher sense I entertain of *L*·,
   322–13 the *L*· they demonstrate,
   351–21 it says, "I am *L*·,"
   352– 4 regarding Life, Truth, *L*· **as**
   358– 1 *L*· is greatly needed,
   384–13 And *L*·, the evermore.
   384–19 * *L*·, like the sea,
   387– 7 poem
   387–24 from that *L*·, divinely near,
   388– 5 'T was *L*· whose finger traced
   397–19 An offering pure of *L*·,
   399– 2 *L*· wipes your tears all away,
   Ret. 60–29 one Truth, Life, *L*·,
   61–20 *L*· that casts out fear.
   65–23 *L*·, fulfilling the law and
   Un. 25–25 the eternal All,— Life, Truth, *L*·,
   29–14 eternal,— Truth, Life, *L*·.
   56–25 *L*· which is without dissimulation
   Pul. 3– 4 Can *L*· be less than boundless?
   13– 2 as *L*·, represented by the Mother.
   19– 3 An offering pure of *L*·,
   21– 5 loves only because it *is L*·.
   Rud. 2–19 supreme good, Life, Truth, *L*·.
   10–18 *L*· punishes nothing but sin,
   No. 20–10 substance, Life, Truth, *L*·.
   Pan. 12–24 self-existent Life, Truth, *L*·,
   14– 7 living the divine Life, Truth, *L*·,
   '01. 3–19 called in Scripture, Spirit, *L*·.
   4– 1 *L*· as either divine Principle or
   4–26 because He is Life, Truth, *L*·,
   5– 8 named in the Bible Life, Truth, *L*·
   7– 5 in C. S. being Life, Truth, *L*·,
   8– 4 idea of the divine Principle, *L*·.
   18–26 The divine Life, Truth, *L*·
   32–30 *L*· was the governing impulse of
   '02. 7–14 *L*·, without beginning and without
   20–14 'T was *L*· whose finger traced
   Hea. 19–16 Heaven's signet is *L*·.
   Peo. 2–11 divine Principle,— Life, Truth, *L*· ;
   Po. page 6 poem
   6–19 from that *L*·, divinely near,
   7– 5 'Twas *L*· whose finger traced
   13– 7 An offering pure of *L*·,
   36–12 And *L*·, the evermore.
   36–18 * *L*·, like the sea,
   47– 9 Ever to Truth and to *L*·
   75– 9 *L*· wipes your tears all away,
   My. 40–28 * obeyed the divine Principle, *L*·,
   41–31 * how illimitable is the *L*· which
   116–14 God is divine Principle, *L*·.
   150– 1 where *L*· has not been before thee
   164–30 has his being in God, *L*·.
   164–30 *L*· must necessarily promote and
   180–17 C. S. meets . . . hate with *L*·,
   183–14 *L*· be thy light upon the mountain
   185–14 *L*· is the generic term for God.
   185–14 *L*· formed this trinity,
   185–15 this trinity, Truth, Life, *L*·,
   200–29 with its divine Principle, *L*·.
   206–17 fact that portrays Life, Truth, *L*·.
   214–13 and *L*· to be the master of hate.
   225–22 names God as divine Principle, *L*·,
   225–28 His synonyms are *L*·, Truth, Life,
   226–20 the intelligent divine Principle, *L*·.
   267–26 man's divine Principle, *L*·,
   269– 3 infinite divine Principle, *L*·,
   281–13 the Father-Mother *L*·, is ours
   303–10 divine Principle— God, *L*·
   348–29 *L*· is the basic Principle

love (*see also* **love's**)

abounding in
   My. 155– 6 always abounding in *l*·
affection or
   Ret. 80– 1 an unselfish affection or *l*·,
alight with
   My. 160– 5 is seldom alight with *l*·.
all-conquering
   My. 258–11 Christ's all-conquering *l*·.
all's
   My. 40–27 * "All's *l*·, but all's law."
alone
   Mis. 32–14 *l*· alone is admissible
and God
   Mis. 395– 4 Is out of tune With *l*· and God ;
   Po. 57–11 Is out of tune With *l*· and God ;

love

and good will
'02. 8–12   *l·* and good will towards men.
My. 201– 6   *l·* and good will to man,
and gratitude
Man. 75– 9   this Church's *l·* and gratitude,
Pul. 86–22   * testimonial of *l·* and gratitude
My. 58–16   * *l·* and gratitude of a great multitude
    325–16   increasing *l·* and gratitude,
and hate
'00. 4– 1   misnomer couples *l·* and hate,
and leadership
My. 356– 3   His reflection of *l·* and leadership
and light
Mis. 149– 6   what they possess of *l·* and light
and loyalty
Mis. 275–24   expressions of *l·* and loyalty
and pride
Po. 8–21   light of a home of *l·* and pride ;
and respect
My. 331–11   * *l·* and respect entertained for
and righteousness
My. 292– 1   *l·* and righteousness achieve
and thanks
My. 257–27   two words enwrapped, — *l·* and *thanks.*
and unity
My. 39–28   * our own growth in *l·* and unity
    205–15   *L·* and unity are hieroglyphs
anthems of
Pul. 81–23   * the unwritten anthems of *l·.*
apart from
My. 189–17   no loyalty apart from *l·.*
apostles of
Po. 25–10   Fair floral apostles of *l·,*
benevolence and
Mis. 199– 1   not reward benevolence and *l·* with
betokens a
My. 290– 1   It betokens a *l·* and a loss felt by
bonds of
Mis. 273–14   bonds of *l·* and perfectness,
brotherly
Mis. 149–22   of Christianity, brotherly *l·,*
Man. 77–19   wisdom, economy, and brotherly *l·*
'00. 14–14   signifies "brotherly *l·.*" — *Heb.* 13 : 1.
My. 41–20   * brotherly *l·* which is just and kind
    153– 9   the church of brotherly *l·,*
    175–26   Let brotherly *l·* continue.
    196– 6   called the "city of brotherly *l·.*"
    213– 2   brotherly *l·,* spiritual growth and
bruised
No. 34–23   *L·* bruised and bleeding,
Christian
My. 362–24   * in the bonds of Christian *l·*
circle of
'02. 2–29   in the circle of *l·,* we shall meet
claspeth
Po. 65–17   *l·* claspeth earth's raptures
compassionate
My. 37– 6   * gratitude and compassionate *l·*
constant as
Po. 15–20   constant as *l·* that outliveth
core of
My. 350–17   bitter searing to the core of *l·,*
dear
Mis. 81– 5   by right of God's dear *l·,*
    330–10   springtide of Christ's dear *l·.*
My. 257– 3   more of His dear *l·*
    258–28   consciousness of God's dear *l·*
deep
My. 44–27   * greetings and their deep *l·.*
    195–11   letting the deep *l·* which I cherished
demands on
Mis. 250–16   I make strong demands on *l·,*
demonstrated
Pul. 21– 8   to see this *l·* demonstrated.
demonstrates
My. 275– 5   it demonstrates *l·.*
depths of
My. 258–24   him who sounded all depths of *l·,*
devoted
My. 328– 3   * With devoted *l·,*
diadems of
My. 258–20   coronals of meekness, diadems of *l·*
divine
Mis. 388– 9   Fed by Thy *l·* divine we live,
'00. 11–13   compensated by divine *l·.*
Po. 7– 9   Fed by Thy *l·* divine we live,
early
My. 182– 7   my early *l·* for this church
earthly
Mis. 395–21   Is every earthly *l·* ;
Po. 58– 6   Is every earthly *l·* ;
enfolds thee
My. 290–14   Him whose *l·* enfolds thee.
everlasting
My. 131–13   the covenant of everlasting *l·.*

love

explains
My. 275– 5   it explains *l·,* it lives love,
faith and
Mis. 176–17   steadfast in faith and *l·,*
My. 64–23   * with renewed faith and *l·*
    152–25   God, demands all our faith and *l·* ;
    156–20   with hope, faith, and *l·* ready
fallible
Mis. 332– 5   Mind is Love, — but not fallible *l·.*
fire of
Mis. 176–22   melted away in the fire of *l·*
first
'00. 12–19   left thy first *l·* — *Rev.* 2 : 4.
    15–24   left thy first *l·,* — *Rev.* 2 : 4.
My. 131–14   praise return to its first *l·,*
for all
My. 341–14   in her heart is beating A *l·* for all
for God
Mis. 12–28   should measure our *l·* for God by
    50–28   and *l·* for God and man ;
    126– 6   with *l·* for God and man.
    348– 6   hearts overflowing with *l·* for God,
Peo. 14–13   holier *l·* for God and man ;
Po. 11– 4   The *l·* for God and man.
My. 158–17   manifests *l·* for God and man.
    287–15   only and true sense of *l·* for God,
    338– 4   The *l·* for God and man.
for his enemies
My. 270–19   breathing *l·* for his enemies,
for life
My. 90–10   * All the passionate *l·* for life
for man
Mis. 12–28   our love for God by our *l·* for man ;
    234– 9   In *l·* for man, we gain a
Pan. 8–23   rest on the basis of . . . *l·* for man.
My. 287–15   In *l·* for man we gain the
for mankind
My. 288– 8   *L·* for mankind is the elevator of
for one another
Mis. 91–11   compact is *l·* for one another.
for the sake of
Pul. 81–15   * scorn self for the sake of *l·*
fulfils
My. 106– 4   *l·* fulfils divine law
    275–25   self-oblivious *l·* fulfils the law
full of
My. 167–17   full of *l·,* peace, and good will
    338–19   heart full of *l·* towards God
God is
Un. 26–16   * God is wisdom, God is *l·.*
God's
Mis. 154– 6   God's *l·* for His flock is
    307–17   God's *l·* opening the eyes of
Ret. 13–19   bade me lean on God's *l·,*
    47–18   partakes less of God's *l·.*
My. 174–26   increasing sense of God's *l·,*
    180– 2   man can prove God's *l·,*
goodness and
Po. 67–23   fragrance of goodness and *l·* ;
gratitude and
Mis. 160– 3   gratitude and *l·* unite more
Man. 60–16   Gratitude and *l·* should abide
Pul. 85–15   * is entitled to the gratitude and *l·*
My. 64– 7   * tender gratitude and *l·* for all
    194–22   token of your gratitude and *l·.*
great
Mis. 182–25   their place in God's great *l·,*
growth in
My. 39–28   * our own growth in *l·* and unity
guided by
My. 235– 6   tender mother, guided by *l·,*
habitual
Mis. 18–24   habitual *l·* for his fellow-man.
hand of
'01. 33– 6   hand of *l·* must sow the seed.
heart's
My. 236– 3   accept my full heart's *l·*
hearts all
Po. 9–11   reason made right and hearts all *l·.*
heel of
'00. 10– 2   Hatred bites the heel of *l·*
her
Mis. 127– 4   that in the ratio of her *l·*
Ret. 90–21   labors with her *l·,* to promote
Pul. 82– 7   * whom her *l·* had glorified
My. 18– 1   that in the ratio of her *l·*
His
Mis. 127– 5   hath His *l·* been bestowed upon her ;
    138–27   under the banner of His *l·,*
    154–24   Continue in His *l·.*
    208–20   His rod brings to view His *l·,*
    249–25   in the amplitude of His *l·* ;
    322–25   the omnipotence of His *l·* ;
Po. 33–12   that His *l·* I may know,
My. 18– 2   hath His *l·* been bestowed upon her ;

love

His
My. 187–29 of the riches of His *l·*
292–10 O may His *l·* shield, support,

his
Mis. 84–23 to quench his *l·* for it.
238– 9 silent endurance of his *l·*.
'02. 19– 2 Yet behold his *l·* !
My. 15–21 * Of Jesus and his *l·*.

His rod is
My. 288–28 His rod is *l·*.

holiness and
'01. 12–19 with health, holiness, and *l·*.
My. 274– 6 goodness, holiness, and *l·* do this,

hospitable
My. 40– 2 * evidence to us of her hospitable *l·*.

human
Mis. 107–13 should swell the lyre of human *l·*.
290–11 human *l·*, guided by the divine
308– 5 by reason of human *l·* or hatred

humility and
Mis. 358–15 humility, and *l·* are divine strength.

impulse of
Mis. 272–30 with the intuition and impulse of *l·*.

induced by
My. 349–28 induced by *l·* and deduced from God,

interchange of
Mis. 100–23 home, the interchange of *l·*,

is allegiant
My. 189–16 for *l·* is allegiant,

is consistent
Mis. 312– 4 *L·* is consistent, uniform,

is the fulfilling
Mis. 11– 3 *L·* is the fulfilling of the law :
258– 2 *l·* is the fulfilling of the law.
285– 9 *L·* is the fulfilling of the law.

is universal
No. 8– 1 Father, . . . whose *l·* is universal.

it lives
My. 275– 5 it explains love, it lives *l·*,

labors and
Mis. 322–23 my past poor labors and *l·*.

lack of
Peo. 8– 6 or lack of *l·* that will not ;

law of
My. 41– 9 * thoughts adverse to the law of *l·*.

leaving self
Peo. 9– 5 *l·* leaving self for God.

legacy of
Ret. 92– 7 inherit his legacy of *l·*,

lesson of
Mis. 207– 1 ponder this lesson of *l·*.

liberty and
My. 236–18 amplitude of liberty and *l·*
248–27 labor, duty, liberty, and *l·*,

life and
My. 88–21 * serenity of faith, life, and *l·*
113–29 a more spiritual life and *l·*
159–21 Truth, life, and *l·* are the only
268–24 Truth, canonized by life and *l·*,

life and the
Mis. 398–26 life and the *l·* of our Lord.
Po. 75– 6 life and the *l·* of our Lord.

life-giving
Pul. 10– 2 self-immolation, his life-giving *l·*,

life of
'02. 19–29 our Saviour in his life of *l·*.
Peo. 5– 7 a deathless life of *l·* ;

light and
Mis. 184–25 that light and *l·* ineffable,
235–11 the light and *l·* of Truth.
My. 355–23 the reflection of light and *l·* ;

lilies of
My. 155–27 gathering Easter lilies of *l·*

lived
My. 287–12 *L·* lived in a court or cot

liveth in
Po. 16– 6 endureth and liveth in *l·*.

living
My. 164–20 has leaped into living *l·*.

loathing of
My. 249–15 satiate its loathing of *l·*

looks
Mis. 390–12 Looks *l·* unto the laughing hours,
Po. 55–13 Looks *l·* unto the laughing hours,

looms of
My. 232– 5 webs of life in looms of *l·*

made perfect
Mis. 138–16 *l·* made perfect through the cross.

manifest
Mis. 147–12 manifest *l·* for those that hate

manifestations of
'02. 7– 4 His infinite manifestations of *l·*

manifested in
Mis. 357–19 mental growth is manifested in *l·*,

love

meekness and
My. 161–30 learns through meekness and *l·*

mercy, and
Mis. 152–16 May meekness, mercy, and *l·* dwell
Pul. 9– 8 mercy, and *l·* kindle perpetually its fires.

might of
My. 258–28 give you the might of *l·*,

more
Mis. 107–11 More *l·* is the great need of

Mother's
Mis. 354– 8 When the Mother's *l·* can no longer

mother's
Mis. 160– 4 But a mother's *l·* behind words
253–22 mother's *l·* touches the heart of God,
Po. 8–18 Of a mother's *l·*, that no words

mutual
Ret. 44–28 a great revival of mutual *l·*,

my
My. 163–13 cannot show my *l·* for them in social
167–19 Give to all the dear ones my *l·*,
192–26 My *l·* can fly on wings of joy
253–15 Accept my *l·* and these words

obedience, and
Mis. 127–13 more grace, obedience, and *l·*.
My. 18–10 more grace, obedience, and *l·*.

ocean of
My. 202–24 a drop from His ocean of *l·*,

of a Father
No. 30–13 *l·* of a Father for His child,

of Christ
Mis. 246–10 when the *l·* of Christ would have
Rud. 17– 3 to convert . . . to the *l·* of Christ,

of God
(see **God**)

of good
Mis. 232–26 sought from the *l·* of good,

of pictures
Mis. 365– 7 what a child's *l·* of pictures is to
No. 18–16 what a child's *l·* of pictures is to

of self
Un. 27– 9 passionate *l·* of self,

of the Scriptures
'00. 7– 6 greater *l·* of the Scriptures

on a false basis
Mis. 287–10 may place *l·* on a false basis

one in
Mis. 387–19 make men one in *l·* remain.
Po. 6–14 make men one in *l·* remain.

our
Mis. 12–28 measure our *l·* for God by our *l·* for
My. 37–32 * our rejoicing, and our *l·*
38– 5 * renew the story of our *l·* for you

outpouring
No. 33–19 outpouring *l·* that sustains man's

overflowing
Peo. 9– 4 an overflowing *l·*, washing away the

patient
Po. 30–17 a patient *l·* above earth's ire,

peace and
Mis. 152– 8 thoughts winged with peace and *l·*
Ret. 42–14 with a smile of peace and *l·*
'00. 11–12 The human sigh for peace and *l·*

peace of
My. 220–23 to know the joy and the peace of *l·*."

perfect
Mis. 138–16 perfect *l·*, and love made perfect
176– 3 healing, and peace, and perfect *l·*.
My. 159–14 perfect *l·* of God and man.

perfumed
Mis. 396–25 in raptured song, With *l·* perfumed.
Pul. 18– 9 in raptured song, With *l·* perfumed.
Po. 12– 9 in raptured song, With *l·* perfumed.

power, and
Un. 2– 8 God's presence, power, and *l·*,

present
My. 176– 7 the past by your present *l·*.

prize
My. 123– 4 must continue to prize *l·* even more

proof of
My. 106– 4 and without this proof of *l·*

purity, and
Mis. 195–32 meekness, purity, and *l·*,
Pul. 9–25 purity, and *l·* are treasures

recompense of
No. 3–24 trust Love's recompense of *l·*.

redolent with
Mis. 194–12 redolent with *l·*, health, and

remembrance and
Mis. 91–16 conditions,— remembrance and *l·* ;
My. 166–13 proof of your remembrance and *l·*.

result of the
My. 62– 6 * To me it is the result of the *l·*

sanctuary of
Mis. 159–14 into this sanctuary of *l·*,

love

selfless
Mis. 294– 7 With selfless *l·*, he inscribes on the
selflessness, and
Rud. 17–16 selflessness, and *l·* are the paths of
self-renunciation, and
Ret. 30– 6 toil, self-renunciation, and *l·*,
sense of
Mis. 17– 4 opposed to the material sense of *l·* ;
351–28 this false sense of *l·*
'02. 18–18 It is a false sense of *l·*
My. 287–15 the only and true sense of *l·*
sensuous
Mis. 351–22 sensuous *l·* is material,
shall dwell
Pul. 84– 5 * *l·* shall dwell in the tents of hate ;
shout of
My. 289–18 this shout of *l·* lives on
soil of
Mis. 392–16 deeply rooted in a soil of *l·* ;
Po. 20–20 deeply rooted in a soil of *l·* ;
spirit of
Po. 66– 6 spirit of *l·*, at soft eventide
spiritual
    (*see* **spiritual**)
talked
My. 287–11 *L·* talked and not lived is a poor
test of
'02. 17– 4 obedience is the test of *l·* ;
My. vii–10 * the sound test of *l·* ;
that
Mis. 254– 5 all that *l·* which brooded tireless
254– 6 all that *l·* that hath fed them
Pul. 21– 3 that *l·* wherewith Christ loveth
that destroys sin
My. 288–27 through *l·* that destroys sin.
that foresees
Mis. 238–18 the *l·* that foresees more to do,
that heals
My. 52– 7 * or the *l·* that heals.
that is talked
Mis. 312– 2 may the *l·* that is talked, be *felt!*
that rebukes
My. 162–18 the *l·* that rebukes praises also,
their
Mis. 203– 8 mirror their *l·*, loyalty, and
277– 1 is wedded to their *l·*,
Pan. 14–20 Oh, may their *l·* of country,
'01. 29–13 selfish in showing their *l·*.
My. 85–25 * Mecca of their *l·* and duty.
their Leader's
My. 155–29 their Leader's *l·*, which she sends
this
Pul. 21– 8 live, to see this *l·* demonstrated.
Pan. 9–23 this *l·* benefits its enemies
'00. 11– 7 weaned me from this *l·*
My. 133–24 and the nature of this *l·*
234– 8 to express this *l·* in labor for them,
Thy
Mis. 275–17 that Thy light and Thy *l·* reach earth,
388– 9 Fed by Thy *l·* divine we live,
Po. 7– 9 Fed by Thy *l·* divine we live,
77– 6 Yet wherefore this Thy *l·*?
to God
Pul. 39– 2 * great essentials of *l·* to God
My. 274–24 and *l·* to God and man ;
token of
My. 172–29 as a simple token of *l·*."
to man
Pul. 39– 2 * love to God and *l·* to man
translates
Mis. 124–28 This grand act . . . translates *l·* ;
truth, and
    (*see* **truth**)
unforgotten
Po. 34–22 O'er joys departed, unforgotten *l·*.
union and
My. 343–30 brought all back to union and *l·*
unite in
Pul. 22– 5 rejoicing that we unite in *l·*,
unity, and
My. 6–17 your progress, unity, and *l·*.
universal
Mis. 290–28 from individual as from universal *l·* :
unknown
My. 189– 9 nor talk of unknown *l·*.
unmeasured
My. 24– 7 * your unmeasured *l·* for humanity,
unselfed
Mis. 238– 9 What has not unselfed *l·* achieved
'02. 16–16 watch-fires of unselfed *l·*,
My. 19–22 fruition of her unselfed *l·*,
62–11 * enough for your unselfed *l·*.
195–27 unselfed *l·* that builds without
200–19 seven-fold shield of . . . unselfed *l·*.

love

unselfed
My. 265– 3 It signifies that *l·*, unselfed,
306–16 unselfed *l·*, waits on God.
unselfish
Mis. 100–14 but Science voices unselfish *l·*,
Pul. 21– 3 a *l·* unselfish, unambitious,
My. 157–13 * evidence of your unselfish *l·*."
unutterable in
My. 134– 4 in protest and unutterable in *l·*.
wealth of
'02. 17–21 and the wealth of *l·*.
wireless
My. 259–13 my heart's wireless *l·*.
wisdom and
Mis. 316–22 pounding wisdom and *l·* into sounding
My. 303–30 wisdom, and *l·* to perform
wishes and
My. 358–23 Give my best wishes and *l·* to
with
Mis. 128–14 With *l·*, Mother,
135–21 With *l·*,
142– 4 With *l·*,
143–11 With *l·*,
149–14 With *l·*,
156– 4 With *l·*,
156–29 With *l·*,
157–29 Ever with *l·*,
159– 8 With *l·*,
395– 4 Is out of tune With *l·* and God ;
Man. 48– 5 with *l·* and without fear.
Po. 57–11 Is out of tune With *l·* and God ;
My. 144– 8 With *l·*, ever yours,
169– 9 With *l·*, Mother,
215–13 I returned this money with *l·* ;
289–19 With *l·*,
290–28 With *l·*,
woman's
Pul. 83– 1 * woman's *l·* and woman's help
words of
My. 360–15 subscribe these words of *l·* :
your
Mis. 149–12 full of accessions to your *l·*,
My. 135–26 Your *l·* and fidelity cheer my

Mis. 52–13 occasionally a *l·* affair.
138–15 lesson of C. S. is *l·*,
152– 4 and in *l·* continents clasp hands,
154–28 meekness, mercy, purity, *l·*.
162–13 good will, *l·*, teaching, and healing.
215– 5 I do it all in *l·* :
250–14 *L·* is not something put upon a shelf,
250–20 *L·* cannot be a mere abstraction,
306–25 *l·* they create in our hearts.
330– 4 Has *l·* ceased to moan over the
351–25 *L·* that is not the procurator of
357–20 *l·* that is irrespective of self,
386–16 a *l·* that steady turns To God ;
Pul. 40– 1 * Ah, *l·*! I only know
81– 7 * the express image of God for *l·*.
No. 8–10 to rebuke each other always in *l·*,
39–17 prayer is not asking God for *l·* ;
39–19 the *l·* wherewith He loves us.
Pan. 13–10 the *l·* of our loving Lord
'00. 3– 3 he loses self in *l·*,
3–27 a god of hate and of *l·*,
15–30 And *l·*, the evermore.
'01. 13–19 destroy the fear and the *l·* of it ;
'02. 2–25 or at least agree to disagree, in *l·*,
8–24 *L·*, purity, meekness, co-exist in
Po. 43– 9 Leading kine with *l·*.
49–24 a *l·* that steady turns To God ;
My. 6–28 *l·* catching a glimpse of glory.
14– 5 two millions of *l·* currency
18–18 the *l·* of our loving Lord
123– 3 *l·* is the greater marvel,
139– 8 primeval faith, hope, *l·*.
158–15 holiness, patience, charity, *l·*.
164–12 focusing light where *l·*, memory, and
184–18 a *l·* which stays the shadows of
189–16 *l·* it creates in the heart of man ;
191– 8 and *l·* will cast it out.
191– 9 steadfast in *l·* and good works.
193–25 and the last by *l·*.
202–22 words of cheer and *l·*
216–16 your sweet industry and *l·*
247–29 has all been done through *l·*,
258– 5 save one lowly offering — *l·*.
260–22 basis of Christmas is *l·* loving its
260–23 *l·* that "suffereth long, — *I Cor.* 13 : 4.
290–23 where no partings are for *l·*,
355–28 His reflection of peace, *l·*, joy.

love (verb)
Mis. vii– 6 * Then do I *l·* thee, and behold
8– 8 chapter sub-title

love (verb)

Mis.
- 8– 9 that thou shouldst *l·* him?
- 9– 9 "*L·* thine enemies" — *see Matt.* **5 : 44.**
- 11–17 We must *l·* our enemies
- 11–19 whereby we *l·* our friends ;
- 11–31 all who *l·* me not,
- 11–32 "*I l· you,* and would not knowingly
- 13–11 *l·* them which *l·* you, — *Luke* 6 : 32.
- 13–12 *l·* those that *l·* them." — *Luke* 6 : 32.
- 18–13 Thou shalt *l·* Spirit only,
- 33– 5 I *l·* all ministers and ministries of
- 51–18 and cause him to *l·* them,
- 51–20 he will *l·* and obey you
- 59–13 all things to those who *l·* Him ;
- 59–14 pleading with infinite Love to *l·* us,
- 87– 8 "I *l·* your promise ;
- 94– 6 must repent, and *l·* good
- 104–30 I will *l·,* if another hates.
- 111–25 I *l·* the orthodox church ;
- 111–26 in time, that church will *l·* C. S.
- 116–26 you profess to understand and *l·,*
- 117–17 in proportion as we *l·.*
- 120–23 *l·* to be with you on Sunday,
- 124– 6 neither do we *l·* and obey Him by
- 125–16 not having seen, we *l·.*
- 127–20 To *l·,* and to be loved,
- 129– 8 forgive his brother and *l·* his
- 133–12 they *l·* to pray standing in — *Matt.* 6 : 5.
- 180–16 I *l·* the Easter service :
- 183– 5 *l·* his neighbor as himself,
- 194– 6 know Him better, and *l·* Him
- 206–27 if you *l·* good supremely,
- 210–32 *L·* your enemies,
- 211– 1 if you *l·* them, you will help
- 236–11 "*L·* and honor thy parents,
- 238–23 Are you faithful? Do you *l·?*
- 266–21 cannot find it in my heart not to *l·*
- 267– 9 * as "*hating* those whom I do not *l·,*"
- 269– 7 and *l·* the other ; — *Matt.* 6 : 24.
- 292– 5 That ye *l·* one another." — *John* 13 : 34.
- 294–19 *L·* such specimens of mortality
- 311–16 I *l·* my enemies and would help all to
- 311–18, 19 *l·* others more than they can *l·* me.
- 318– 7 *l·* some of those devoted students
- 336– 8 Do you *l·* that which represents
- 336–17 and not *l·* its idea :
- 338–10 choose but to labor and *l·* ;
- 353–29 They do not *l·* Mother.
- 367– 3 *l·* his neighbor as himself,
- 387–13 from those who watch and *l·.*
- 389–16 *l·* more for every hate,
- 392–13 To *l·* the Hebrew figure of a tree.
- 394–13 but hope thou, and *l·.*
- 397–16 Thine own children are, I *l·* to be.

Ret.
- 18–23 those we most *l·* find a happiness
- 29– 3 *l·* them, and hold to loving our
- 80–27 We *l·* our friends, but ofttimes

Pul.
- 7– 4 I *l·* Boston, and especially the
- 18–25 Thine own children are, I *l·* to be.
- 21– 2 inevitably *l·* one another
- 21– 5 Moreover, they *l·* their enemies,
- 56–19 * "And still we *l·* the evil cause,

Rud.
- 3– 1 while mortals *l·* to sin,
- 3– 2 they do not *l·* to be sick.
- 4–22 we can only learn and *l·* Him

No.
- 7– 7 We must *l·* our enemies,
- 32–21 and shall cease to *l·* it.
- 39–18 prayer . . . is learning to *l·,*

Pan.
- 9–24 *l·* them which *l·* you, — *Matt.* 5 : 46.
- 13–13 *L·* all Christian churches
- 14– 5 *l·* one another ;

'00.
- 3–11 they who *l·* a good work
- 11–11 them that love God," — *l·* good. — *Rom.* 8 : 28.

'01.
- 14–13 make us *l·* it and so hinder our
- 19– 5 I *l·* this doctrine, for I know
- 28–19 I *l·* Christ more than all the
- 31– 8 and *l·* the truths of C. S.
- 32–17 caused me to *l·* their doctrines.

'02.
- 2–23 birthmark, to *l·* the Church ;
- 7–22 chapter sub-title
- 7–25 That ye *l·* one another ; — *John* 13 : 34.
- 8– 3 commands man to *l·* as Jesus loved.
- 9– 7 concern you less, and *l· thou.*
- 17– 3 "If ye *l·* me, — *John* 14 : 15.
- 17– 6 seek and obey what they *l·.*
- 17– 7 When mortals learn to *l·* aright ;
- 17–18 to *l·* one's enemies,
- 18–16 "*L·* one another, — *John* 13 : 34.

Peo.
- 6–15 fear God more than we *l·* Him ;
- 6–17 we *l·* Him, because He is

Po.
- 4–15 Wait, and *l·* more for every hate,
- 6– 8 not from those who watch and *l·.*
- 13– 4 Thine own children are, I *l·* to be.
- 20–17 To *l·* the Hebrew figure of a tree.
- 35– 4 make me *l·* thee as I *l·* life less !
- 45–18 but hope thou, and *l·.*

love (verb)

Po.
- 64–18 And those we most *l·*

My.
- 5–21 he continues to *l·* more
- 15–18 * I *l·* to tell the story,
- 15–22 * I *l·* to tell the story,
- 15–26 * I *l·* to tell the story,
- 18–21 *L·* all Christian churches
- 52–19 * *l·* our neighbor as ourselves."
- 105–50 noble men and women, and I *l·* them ;
- 127– 6 the people . . . who live to *l·.*
- 132–22 may *l·* our neighbor as ourselves,
- 133–23 Do you know how much I *l·* you
- 151– 7 no Christian can . . . and not *l·* it :
- 163–25 I *l·* its people
- 163–26 *l·* their scholarship, friendship,
- 174–27 know Him nearer, *l·* Him more,
- 175– 1 I would *l·* to be with you at
- 175–24 the friendship of those we *l·,*
- 183– 1 "Thou shalt *l·* the Lord — *Luke* 10 : 27.
- 187–15 should *l·* one another." — *I John* 3 : 11.
- 187–28 "that ye *l·* one another." — *John* 15 : 12.
- 195– 8 to *l·* more, to work more,
- 195–16 To do good to all because we *l·* all,
- 200–15 to *l·* our neighbor as ourself,
- 202–10 but to *l·* one another : — *Rom.* 13 : 8.
- 233–29 as much as they *l·* mankind?
- 234– 7 know how much I *l·* them,
- 262–27 *l·* to observe Christmas in quietude,
- 270–24 What we *l·* determines what we are.
- 270–24 I *l·* the prosperity of Zion,
- 283–24 and to *l·* mercy, — *Mic.* 6 : 8.
- 286– 7 *l·* their neighbor as themselves.
- 313– 5 Tell her I *l·* her ;
- 316– 2 those who *l·* Truth ;
- 316– 6 causing man to *l·* his enemies ;
- 341– 1 *l·* to breathe it to the breeze
- 356– 2 *l·* the spot where God dwells
- 356–23 and *l·* the other ; — *Matt.* 6 : 24.

(*see also* **God, neighbor**)

Love-Children's Offering

Pul. 42–23 * "*L· O·* — 1894."

loved

Mis.
- 110–10 maintain in yourselves what Jesus *l·,*
- 127–20 To love, and to be *l·,*
- 231–31 through which the *l·* one comes not,
- 245–23 *l·* the Church and followed it,
- 292– 6 Jesus, who so *l·* the world
- 306–27 nor a *l·* person present ;
- 334–31 you have not *l·* sufficiently
- 386– 7 tidings from our *l·* on earth,
- 387–17 Who *l·* and healed mankind :

Ret.
- 32– 5 whatever is *l·* materially,
- 75–16 is comprehended and *l·,*
- 79– 4 is spiritual truth learned and *l·* ;

Pul.
- 12–11 *l·* not their lives

'00.
- 7–12 *l·* the Bible and appreciated its
- 14– 4 that I have *l·* thee. — *Rev.* 3 : 9.

'01.
- 29–11 not because reformers are not *l·,*
- 32– 7 *l·* Christians of the old sort

'02.
- 2–24 and the Church once *l·* me.
- 7–26 as I have *l·* you." — *John* 13 : 34.
- 8– 3 commands man to love as Jesus *l·.*
- 18–16 as I have *l·* you." — *John* 13 : 34.
- 18–18 the heart that loves as Jesus *l·.*

Hea.
- 2–21 *l·* of the Father, the *l·* of Love?

Po.
- 6–12 Who *l·* and healed mankind :
- 17– 4 My *l·* ones in glory
- 26–10 on her altar our *l·* Lincoln's own
- 49–11 from our *l·* on earth,
- 65– 4 A meeting with *l·* ones

My.
- 15–33 * That I have *l·* so long.
- 86– 4 * *l·* its golden State House
- 159– 5 those words of our *l·* Lord,
- 189–31 Dead is he who *l·* me dearly :
- 256–17 Again *l·* Christmas is here,
- 256–23 Parents call home their *l·* ones,
- 258– 1 or the Book of Life is *l·,*
- 294–31 the *l·* and lost of many millions.
- 302–21 I may be more *l·,*
- 313–27 My oldest sister dearly *l·* me,

loveliness

My. 152–32 my skilful florist has coaxed into *l·*

love-linked

My. 206– 6 *l·* holiness which heals and saves.

love-lorn

Po. 34–11 Or sing thy *l·* note

lovely

Mis.
- 128– 9 whatsoever things are *l·,* — *Phil.* 4 : 8.
- 142–17 expressed in their *l·* gift
- 167– 6 the one altogether *l·.*
- 342–13 One "altogether *l·.*" — *Song* 5 : 16.

Ret. 23–19 One "altogether *l·,*" — *Song* 5 : 16.

lovely
'01.	6–30	He is "altogether *l*," — *Song* 5 : 16.
Peo.	6–17	He is found altogether *l*.
Po.	53– 7	With sunshine's *l*. ray

love-offerings
Pul.	41– 6	* *l*. of the disciples of C. S.
	52–13	* *l*. of the disciples of

lover
Pul.	83– 2	* promise as *l*. and candidate
'01.	32– 6	an eager *l*. and student of

lovers
Mis.	304– 5	* *l*. of liberty and peace
'02.	17–16	Who of the world's *l*. ever found
My.	199–16	loyal *l*. of God and man.

Love's
Mis.	100–11	*L*. labors are not lost
	124–25	unveiled *L*. great legacy to mortals :
	125– 3	then hath he part in *L*. atonement,
	330–16	looking through *L*. transparency,
	387– 1	"When *L*. rapt sense
Ret.	47– 3	wars with *L*. spiritual compact,
No.	3–24	trust *L*. recompense of love.
'00.	15–18	To-day you have come to *L*. feast,
Po.	31– 3	dropped from *L*. throne.
	31–11	*L*. verdure veils the leaflet's
	50–18	"When *L*. rapt sense
My.	62–13	* with the joy of *L*. victory.
	129–13	They come at *L*. call.
	158– 9	We live in an age of *L*. divine

love's
My.	231–18	else *l*. labor is lost

loves
Mis.	100–26	Christian Scientist *l*. man more
	100–27	because he *l*. God most.
	224–13	ambitions, tastes, and *l*. ;
	317–29	abhors injustice, and *l*. mercy.
	395– 2	Who *l*. not June
Un.	39–11	He *l*. them from whom
Pul.	21– 4	*l*. only because it *is* Love.
No.	39–19	the love wherewith He *l*. us.
Pan.	9–21	It *l*. one's neighbor as one's self ;
	9–22	it *l*. its enemies
'00.	3–18	good man *l*. the right thinker
'01.	13–18	because he fears it or *l*. it.
	17– 6	*l*. even the repentant prodigal
	21–15	individual who *l*. God
	29–23	The individual who *l*. most,
'02.	18–18	the heart that *l*. as Jesus loved.
Po.	43– 2	Jesus *l*. you ! so does mother :
	57– 9	Who *l*. not June
My.	4–14	*l*. Protestant and Catholic,
	4–15	*l*. all who love God,
	4–16	and he *l*. his enemies.
	295–28	he still lives, *l*., labors.

loveth
Mis.	18– 4	"Whom the Lord *l*. — *Heb.* 12 : 6.
	73– 5	"Whom the Lord *l*. — *Heb.* 12 : 6.
	125– 4	"whom the Lord *l*. — *Heb.* 12 : 6.
	150–13	and *l*. the gates of Zion.
	208–19	"whom the Lord *l*. — *Heb.* 12 : 6.
Man.	69–18	"He that *l*. father or — *Matt.* 10 : 37.
Ret.	80– 5	whom the Lord *l*. — *Heb.* 12 : 6.
Pul.	21– 3	love wherewith Christ *l*. us ;
'01.	9–27	He of God's household who *l*.
My.	202–11	he that *l*. another — *Rom.* 13 : 8.

love-token
My.	171–26	* as a *l*. for the church

Lovewell, Capt. John
Ret.	3– 5	Capt. John *L*. of Dunstable,

Lovewell's War
Ret.	3– 8	known historically as *L*. *W*.

loving (adj.)
Mis.	xii– 4	interluding with *l*. thought
	7– 8	The *l*. patience of Jesus,
	96–11	as a *l*. Father and Mother ;
	102–15	*l*., divine Father-Mother God.
	131–22	that *l*. sense of gratitude
	138–30	Your *l*. teacher.
	151– 2	In the words of the *l*. disciple,
	238– 2	Father-Mother God, *l*. children are
	254– 3	Should not the *l*. warning,
	265–30	If impatient of the *l*. rebuke,
	292–22	by *l*. words and deeds.
	370–16	that twines its *l*. arms
Un.	53–25	man's origin and *l*. Father,
Pul.	49– 7	* gifts of her *l*. pupils.
	76–18	* tribute of *l*. friends.
	77–12	* *l*. hands of four thousand
	78–10	* *l*. hands of four thousand
	86–20	* In behalf of your *l*. students
	86–23	* your labors and *l*. sacrifice,

loving (adj.)
Rud.	10–19	look up to the *l*. God,
No.	7–16	Every *l*. sacrifice for the good of
Pan.	13–10	the love of our *l*. Lord
'00.	6–23	a meek and *l*. disciple of Christ,
	7–27	the tender, *l*. Christ is found near,
'01.	31–17	would bear *l*. testimony.
'02.	1– 1	God's *l*. providence for His
	8– 6	the likeness of Love is *l*.?
	9–13	*L*. chords set discords in harmony.
	9–15	was *l*. and spiritual,
Po.	8– 5	seek the *l*. rose,
	30–22	heaven's lyres and angels' *l*. lays,
My.	9– 8	* to turn in *l*. thankfulness
	13–30	their *l*. giving has been blessed.
	18–18	the love of our *l*. Lord
	20–10	the *l*. liberty of their license.
	21– 3	* all know of the *l*. self-sacrifices
	23–20	* loyal and *l*. greetings to you,
	28–10	* in many instances the *l*.
	44– 9	* obedient to the *l*. counsel
	62–20	* *l*. greetings and congratulations
	131–10	cup red with *l*. restitution,
	162–25	*l*. Shepherd of this feeble flock
	167–13	*l*. benedictions upon your lives.
	197–26	I send *l*. congratulations,
	207– 9	* unite in *l*. greetings to you,
	207–15	* Yours in *l*. obedience,
	224–27	speak in *l*. terms of their efforts,
	247–20	not a stern but a *l*. look
	248–26	to face the foe with *l*. look
	259– 9	* *L*., grateful Christmas greetings
	261– 2	*l*. parents and guardians
	280– 6	* *l*. solicitude for the welfare of
	280– 9	* a universal, *l*. brotherhood
	287–19	Philanthropy is *l*., ameliorative,
	293– 7	President, in his *l*. acquiescence,
	319– 8	in *l*., grateful memory
	323–12	* In *l*. gratitude for your
	338–22	his broad views and *l*. nature
	362–18	* send you their *l*. greetings.
		(*see also* **heart, hearts**)

loving (ppr.)
Mis.	13– 9	law of *l*. mine enemies.
	50–30	*one* God and *l*. Him supremely,
	87–26	honest, earnest, *l*., and truthful,
	130–29	the meek and *l*., God anoints
	258– 1	for *l*. his neighbor as himself,
	311– 9	*l*. one another, go forth to
	328–30	*l*. God supremely
	331– 5	make them humble, *l*., obedient,
	400–15	Father-Mother God, *l*. me,
Ret.	29– 3	*l*. our enemies and doing good
	49–16	attain the bliss of *l*. unselfishly,
	71–19	not dealing justly and *l*. mercy,
Pul.	85–27	* her labors and *l*. generosity
No.	38–21	*l*. your neighbor as yourself,
'00.	5–16	*l*. another as himself.
'01.	14–21	following it, or *l*. it,
	32– 8	I could not help *l*. them.
'02.	8– 7	When *l*., we learn that
Po.	43– 4	*L*. God and one another,
	69– 3	Father-Mother God, *L*. me,
My.	52– 5	* *l*. them that despitefully use her,
	139– 3	living, *l*., acting, enjoying.
	204–27	good for evil, *l*. one's enemies,
	260–22	love *l*. its enemies,
	268–27	Science of . . . living and of *l*.,
	323– 9	* by *l*. it and living it

loving-cup
My.	347– 6	chapter sub-title
	347– 9	their beautiful gift to me, a *l*.,
	347–20	I shall treasure my *l*.

lovingkindness
My.	13–22	*l*. and tender mercies ; — *Psal.* 103 : 4.
	37–29	* its ineffable *l*., its wise counsel

lovingly
Mis.	v– 4	I *l*. DEDICATE THESE PRACTICAL
	148– 4	*L*. yours,
	155–13	*L*. yours,
	160–16	*L*. yours,
	320– 9	star that looked *l*. down on the
	400–20	Father-Mother good, *l*. Thee I seek,
Pul.	44–13	* "Yours *l*.,
	77–15	* You are hereby most *l*. invited
	78–13	* You are hereby most *l*. invited
	87– 6	* *L*. yours,
No.	19–14	gratefully and *l*. conscious of
	35– 8	yield *l*. to the purpose of
Po.	69– 8	Father-Mother good, *l*. Thee I seek,
My.	5–25	*l*. thanking your generosity
	26–25	*L*. yours,
	63– 6	* *L*. and gratefully your students,
	135–20	*L*. yours in Christ,

lovingly

My. 143– 5 L· yours,
   168– 7 L· yours,
   171–15 L· yours,
   201–16 forgive, wisely ponder, and l·
   263– 8 L· thine,
   284– 6 L· yours,
   351–18 L· yours in Christ,
   358–25 L· your teacher and Leader,
   360– 3 As ever, l· your teacher,
   360–24 L· yours,

low

Mis. 228–15 mad ambition and l· revenge.
   242–21 where the patient is very l·
   396–20 L·, sad, and sweet, whose measures
   400– 7 Dirge and song and shoutings l·
Ret.   4–18 winds sigh l· requiems
   18– 6 alder is whispering l·,
   31–24 My heart bent l· before the
Pul. 10– 9 her pomp and power lie l·
   16–19 Dirge and song and shoutings l·,
   18– 4 L·, sad, and sweet, whose measures
   39–15 * The sunset, burning l·,
Hea.   6– 7 fly too high or too l·.
Po. 12– 3 L·, sad, and sweet, whose measures
   16–15 when the day-god is l·;
   63–15 nestling alder is whispering l·,
   65–22 its music in l· minor tones,
   76–18 Dirge and song and shoutings l·
My. 155–12 the l· laurels of vainglory,

Lowell

Mis. 368–10 signature
Pul. 28–25 * selections from Whittier and L·,

lower

Mis. 36–15 express the l· qualities of the
   84–28 transition from our l· sense of
   102– 9 In this limited and l· sense
   250– 8 What the l· propensities express,
   287–19 higher nature of man governs the l·.
   376–26 l· lines of light kindled into
Un. 18–28 it would l· His rank.
   30– 8 this l· sense sins and suffers,
   32–15 This l·, misnamed mind is a
Pul. 49– 9 * tree-tops on the l· terrace,
Rud.   8–15 from a l· to a higher condition
   8–26 If by such l· means the health
No. 24– 7 through the l· orders of matter
’01. 30–19 destroying all l· considerations.
Peo. 13– 2 hence a l· order of humanity,
   13– 4 a l· order of Christianity than
My. 107–12 l· attenuations have so little
   152– 7 far l· in the scale of thought,
   253– 2 brightening this l· sphere

lowest

Mis. 57–28 beginning with the l· form
No. 32–26 reduce this evil to its l· terms,
Peo.   7– 1 by their highest or their l· ideals,

lowly

Mis. 167–29 he exalteth the l·;
   168–11 the poor — the l· in Christ,
My. 41– 6 * the meek and l· in heart
   258– 5 save one l· offering — love.
   258–29 l· in its majesty.
   259–18 a l·, triumphant trust,

loyal

Mis. v– 2 L· CHRISTIAN SCIENTISTS
   91–24 informed thereof, that a l· student
   120–11 l· laborers are ye that have
   141–10 All l· Christian Scientists
   213–27 L· Christian Scientists, be of
   251–10 l· to the heart's core to
   264– 3 who are l· to Christ, Truth,
   273–16 L· Christian Scientists should
   275–20 chapter sub-title
   276–11 active, earnest, and l·,
   277–10 a heart l· to God is patient
   318–15 from a l· student of C. S.,
   347–31 L· Scientists are targets for envy,
   354– 6 l·, self-forgetful, faithful
   386–25 remembrance of her l· life,
Man. 35–21 l· to the teachings of the
   36–14 L· Christian Scientists whose
   37–19 l· to their Leader and to the
   38– 5 not a l· student of Mrs. Eddy,
   55–16 shall not be counted l· till
   64–15 l· Christian Scientists had given
   71–16 shall be considered l·
   72– 6 l· exemplary Christian Scientist
   73– 1 sixteen l· Christian Scientists,
   79– 4 not less than three l· members
   84–17 the pupils of l· teachers shall
   84–23 A l· teacher of C. S.
   84–25 another l· teacher's pupil,
   85– 5 A l· teacher of C. S. may
   85–19 active and l· Christian Scientists

loyal

Man. 89–11 L· students who have been taught
   89–18 L· Christian Scientists' pupils
   92–25 deemed l· teachers of C. S.
   97– 6 one l· Christian Scientist who
   109– 3 L· members of The Mother Church
   109– 7 l· students of Mrs. Eddy,
Chr. 53– 6 Spirit sped A l· ray
Ret. 47–20 from me, or a l· student,
   53– 1 presenting to its l· members
   85–19 The l· Christian Scientist is
Un. 23– 5 was to his father ever l·.
’01.   3–10 The l· Christian Scientists
’02.   3– 1 ten thousand l· Christian Scientists
Po. 31– 1 l· struggler for the right,
   50–11 remembrance of her l· life,
My. v–11 * earnest and l· Christian Scientists
   14–23 * a generous and l· people.
   23–20 * their l· and loving greetings
   118– 1 the l·, royal natures of the
   125–13 L· to the divine Principle
   130–25 I need not say this to the l·
   199–16 all l· lovers of God and man.
   225– 3 l· at heart and the worker
   229– 9 that l· Christian Scientists,
   251–11 not if you and they are l·
(see also **students***)*

loyalty

Mis. 12–13 law of l· to Jesus' Sermon
   99– 9 His fear overcame his l·;
   203– 8 love, l·, and good works.
   275–24 expressions of love and l·
Man. 35–15 the l· of the applicants.
   55–18 if his l· has been proved
Ret. 50–19 By l· in students I mean this,
My. 19–12 * chapter sub-title
   21–16 * trial and deprivation in our l·
   44–28 * continued l· to your teachings,
   76–15 * show the earnestness and l·
   189–17 no l· apart from love.

lucid

Mis. 50–11 as l· in presentation as can be
Ret. 21–22 l· and enduring lessons

lucidly

No. 39– 1 that we can think more l·

lucky

Mis. 123–14 god of sin, was the "l· god;"

lucrative

’00.   2–22 will leave a l· business

ludicrous

Mis. 286–17 put ingenuity to l· shifts;

luminary

Mis. 340–27 Every l· in the constellation

luminous

Mis. 192–16 L· with the light of
   335–15 made l· by divine Love.
Pul. 32– 2 * lighted by l· blue eyes,
   87–25 l· lines from your lives
My. 124–20 is written in l· letters,

lump

Mis. 39–20 to leaven the whole l·.
   166–25 leavening the l· of human thought,
My. 59– 5 * should leaven the whole l·,
   114–29 is leavening the whole l·

lunacy

Pan.   8– 4 find expression in sun worship, l·,
My. 190–15 to cure a severe case of l·,
   192– 6 cast out fashionable l·.
   222– 4 a violent case of l·.

Lundy Lane

My. 311–28 McNeil, the hero of L· L·.

Lundy's Lane

Ret.   3–10 general who fought at L· L·,

lungs

Pul. 79–24 * much as his l· call for breath;
My. 105–10 l· were mostly consumed.

lure

My. 260–15 the l· of gold,

lured

My. 283–29 L· by fame, pride, or gold,

lures

My. 93–14 * rare l· for weary hearts,

lurid

Po. 18–17 Though lightnings be l·

lurking

Mis. 210–21 uncover and kill this l· serpent,
My. 213– 9 l· foe to human weal,

lurks

Mis. 66– 8 l· in this mandate,
   302– 1 Behind the scenes l· an evil

luscious

My. 325– 4 * to leave *l·* hothouse fruit.

lust

Mis. 19– 2 covetousness, *l·*, hatred, malice,
    118–21 self-will, self-righteousness, *l·*,
    123– 7 *l·*, hypocrisy, *witchcraft.*
    297–27 unmercifulness, tyranny, or *l·*.
    337–19 evil-speaking, *l·*, envy, hate.
    366–27 self-will, envy, and *l·*.
Un. 39– 5 *l·* of the flesh and the pride
    56–27 ingratitude, *l·*, malice, hate,
Rud. 9–20 envy, *l·*, and all fleshly vices.
'02. 8–25 *L·*, hatred, revenge, coincide
    17– 1 worldliness, hatred, and *l·*,
Hea. 7– 1 which is good for nothing, *l·*,"
    17– 7 *l·* makes the material so-called
My. 4– 5 *L·*, dishonesty, sin, disable the
    5– 5 synonymous with legalized *l·*,
    126–25 over the widowhood of *l·*,
    205–25 *l·* of the flesh and the pride
    257–20 pride, greed, *l·* should bow

lustre

No. 13–26 other parts of it have no *l·*.
My. 290– 6 lose their *l·* in the tomb,

lusts

Mis. 52– 1 consume it upon your *l·*." — *Jas.* 4 : 3.
    182–32 *l·* of the flesh and the pride of
Ret. 79–13 "*l·* of the flesh," — *see I John* 2 : 16.
No. 40– 3 consume it on your *l·*." — *see Jas.* 4 : 3.
Pan. 5–13 the *l·* of your father — *John* 8 : 44.
'01. 16– 8 the demon of this world, its *l·*,
Hea. 17– 2 *l·* of the flesh, the pride of life,

lute

Mis. 329–27 cuckoo sounds her invisible *l·*,

Luther (*see also* **Luther's**)

Martin
Hea. 2–10 intrepid reformer, Martin *L·* :

Luther's

Martin
My. 295– 9 Copy of Martin *L·* Translation

luxury

Mis. 326– 8 caught in the dwelling of *l·*,
    326–30 from the dwelling of *l·*,
Pul. 36–24 * of the utmost taste and *l·*,
My. 110–17 *l·* of thought let loose,

Lyceum Club

Ret. 40– 4 speak before the *L· C·*,

Lyceum League of America

Mis. 305– 5 * *L· L· of A·*, the Society of

macadamize

My. 175–19 to *m·* a portion of Warren Street
    175–20 to *m·* North State Street

machinery

Mis. 353–22 makes the *m·* work rightly ;
My. 145–19 at home attending to the *m·*
    328–23 * *m·* act of the Legislature

Macneil, John

Ret. 3– 9 John *M·*, the New Hampshire general
    (*see also* **McNeil**)

Macneill, Sir John

Ret. 3– 1 Sir John *M·*, a Scotch knight,

mad

Mis. 178–21 learning' . . . 'hath made thee *m·*.'
    228–14 *m·* ambition and low revenge.
    254–13 victim of *m·* ambition
    263–27 whose *m·* ambition drives them to
    351–15 repeated attempts of *m·* ambition
    363–27 and drives diviners *m·*.
    369–14 indulge in *m·* antics.
Ret. 79–13 Dishonesty, envy, and *m·* ambition
'01. 16–10 hatred gone *m·* becomes imbecile
My. 129– 9 counteract the trend of *m·* ambition.
    250– 5 promotes wisdom, quiets *m·* ambition,
    262–23 merriment, *m·* ambition, rivalry,

made

Mis. vii– 5 * thy well *m·* choice of friends
    x–25 *m·* out to Mary Baker Eddy,
    10–21 *m·* perfect in weakness,
    26–11 the Scripture declares He *m·*
    26–13 and what *m·* the soil?
    30–20 "hath *m·* me free — *Rom.* 8 : 2.
    34– 9 is simply thought *m·* manifest.

lying

Mis. 273–23 applications *l·* on the desk
Ret. 4– 5 *l·* in the adjoining towns
    67– 7 the *l·* supposition that
'00. 2–19 "By cheating, *l·*, and crime ;
Hea. 6–24 *l·* back in the unconscious thought,
My. 105–13 instruments were *l·* on the table
    227–18 *l·* in wait to catch them

Lynn

Mass.
Mis. 391– 2 Editor of the *Item, L·*, Mass.
Pul. 34– 5 * In 1866, while living in *L·*, Mass.,
    46–28 * at *L·*, Mass., she became
    58– 1 * found herself in *L·*, Mass.,
Po. vi– 6 * in *L·*, Mass., in 1866,
    vi– 9 * *in a L·, Mass., newspaper,*
    vi–25 * *she resided in L·, Mass.,*
    9–12 *L·*, Mass., *September 3, 1866.*
    21–19 *L·*, Mass., *May 6, 1876.*
    23–23 *L·*, Mass., *November 8, 1866.*
    27–25 *L·*, Mass., *January 1, 1866.*
    38– 1 the editor of the *Item, L·*, Mass.
    40– 5 *L·*, Mass., *August 4, 1866.*
    42– 8 *L·*, Mass., *February 19, 1868.*
    46–18 *L·*, Mass., *December 8, 1866.*
    47–23 *L·*, Mass., *September 3, 1871.*
    66–15 *L·*, Mass., *August 25, 1866.*
    68–24 *L·*, Mass., *August 24, 1865.*
    70–26 *L·*, Mass., *April, 1871.*
    72– 5 *L·*, Mass., *February 3, 1865.*
    78–17 *L·*, Mass., *December 7, 1865.*
My. 59– 3 * your *first* class in *L·*, Mass.,
Massachusetts
Ret. 42– 3 solemnized at *L·*, Massachusetts,

Ret. 38–15 started for *L·* to see me.
    38–16 he left Boston for *L·*,
    38–18 at the Eastern depot in *L·*,
'02. 16– 2 Miss Dorcas Rawson of *L·*
Po. 73– 1 inscribed to my friends in *L·*.
My. 59–17 * little hall on Market Street, *L·*,
    60– 8 * First Congregational Church of *L·*,
    322– 1 * I met a lady who lived in *L·*,

lyre

Mis. 107–13 swell the *l·* of human love.
    142–20 my Muse lost her lightsome *l·*,
    329–24 sweep in soft strains her Orphean *l·*.
Ret. 17– 7 Wake chords of my *l·*,
Pul. 9– 6 no Delphian *l·* could break the
Pan. 3–12 and *l·* of bird and brooklet.
Po. 62– 7 Wake chords of my *l·*,
    66– 7 Wake gently the chords of her *l·*,

lyres

Po. 30–22 heaven's *l·* and angels' loving lays,

M

made

Mis. 37– 4 this Mind is *m·* manifest
    43– 4 *m·* acquainted with the mental
    44–19 thought *m·* manifest in the flesh.
    45–21 *If God made all that was m·*,
    45–28 "All things were *m·* by Him ; — *John* 1 : 3.
    45–29 anything *m·* that was *m·*." — *John* 1 : 3.
    48–14 *m·* a man drunk on water,
    48–20 *m·* in season to open the eyes
    48–23 *Was ever a person m· insane by*
    48–28 * "*m·* insane by Mrs. Eddy's teachings,"
    50– 1 God made all that was *m·*,
    57– 2 later *m·* which *He had m·*.
    57– 6 The creative "Us" *m·* all,
    64– 3 way he *m·* for mortals' escape.
    77– 8 demand *m·* upon the eunuch
    77–10 God *m·* manifest through
    77–27 *m·* in God's own likeness,
    78– 3 *m·* manifest in the flesh,
    79–25 all be *m·* alive." — *I Cor.* 15 : 22.
    91–19 that can be *m·* visible.
    93– 4 history shall be *m·* glad !
    97–21 *m·* in the image and likeness
    101– 1 lips are *m·* eloquent,
    114–10 and so *m·* to misteach others.
    117– 1 *m·* "ruler over many — *Matt.* 25 : 23.
    122–28 God never *m·* it,
    122–28, 29 He *m·* all that was *m·*.
    132– 1 A motion was *m·*, and a vote
    134– 1 sorrowful who are *m·* hopeful,
    138–16 *m·* perfect through the cross.
    142– 2 *m·* her wildernesses to bud
    152–19 *m·* ready for the pure in affection,
    154–19 Through the word . . . are you *m·* free.
    154–21 be *m·* manifest in the flesh

made

Mis.	158– 6	changes about to be *m*.
	161–12	that *m*· him the Christ-Jesus,
	166–30	It *m*· him an honest man,
	178–21	'hath *m*· thee mad.'— *see Acts* 26 : 24.
	179–25	He *m*· every flower in Mind
	182–29	When the Word is *m*· flesh,
	184– 6	The Word will be *m*· flesh
	185– 5	is *m*· manifest as Truth,
	185–27	*m*· *a living soul*; — *I Cor.* 15 : 45.
	185–28	*m*· *a quickening spirit.* — *I Cor.* 15 : 45.
	186– 8	the spiritual man *m*· in the image
	189–10	knowledge of . . . *m*· him mighty.
	191–30	sin or disease *m*· manifest.
	200– 2	that *m*· his healing easy and
	201–19	*m*· me free from the law — *Rom.* 8 : 2.
	219–25	*m*· manifest on the body,
	227–17	wider aims of a life *m*· honest :
	229–16	thou hast *m*· the Lord, — *Psal.* 91 : 9.
	231– 7	*m*· busy many appetites ;
	231–16	Why, he *m*· a big hole,
	234–23	she has *m*· some progress,
	236– 4	been *m*· the repository of
	238– 2	sometimes *m*· to believe a lie,
	239–24	*m*· them more serious over it.
	241–19	"God never *m*· you sick ;
	243– 5	not yet *m*· surgery one of the
	247–30	He never *m*· sickness.
	248–10	*m*· the word synonymous with devil.
	248–27	saved me . . . and *m*· me well,
	257– 7	must be *m*· by Mind
	259– 1	were *m*· by Him ; — *John* 1 : 3.
	259– 2	was not any thing *m*·." — *John* 1 : 3.
	262–19	*m*· glad by the divine Love
	266–24	correct mistakes which may be *m*·
	269–17	*m*· his choice between matter and
	280–22	The presentation was *m*·
	280–30	by which so many wrecks are *m*·.
	287– 5	He that hath *m*· us, — *Psal.* 100 : 3.
	289– 5	in whatever form it is *m*· manifest.
	289–16	marriage contract two are *m*· one,
	301– 8	whose substance is *m*· up of my
	303–24	*m*· profitable to the heart of our
	305–19	* can be *m*· a part of the bell ;
	306–18	* having been *m*· such by the
	321–15	hath *m*· me free from — *Rom.* 8 : 2.
	324– 3	streets of a city *m*· with hands.
	326– 3	hath *m*· you free from — *see Rom.* 8 : 2.
	335–15	path *m*· luminous by divine Love.
	339–10	good is *m*· more industrious and
	340–18	Is a musician *m*· by his teacher?
	341– 9	and be *m*· ruler over many things.
	343– 7	Thought must be *m*· better,
	354–15	more grace, a motive *m*· pure,
	360–32	No advancing modes . . . *m*· Jesus ;
	362– 8	Scholastic dogma has *m*· men blind.
	362–12	God, having *m*· all,
	362–12	believing that God, . . . *m*· evil ;
	362–13	all that He *m*· was good.
	364– 8	*m*· the public your friend,
	364–18	He *m*· all that was *m*·,
	396–14	I hope it's better *m*·,
	398–24	'T was the Truth that *m*· us free,
Man.	32–15	announcement shall be *m*· but once
	42– 7	not be *m*· to forget nor to neglect
	46–14	private communications *m*· to them
	50– 1	an autopsy shall be *m*· by
	67– 8	shall not be *m*· public without
	72–13	application, *m*· in accordance with
	78– 7	not be *m*· legally responsible for
	78–10	Donations . . . shall not be *m*· without
	110– 2	that are not correctly *m*· out.
Chr.	55–21	*m*· like unto the Son — *Heb.* 7 : 3.
Ret.	7–14	* he would have *m*· himself one of the
	14–17	*m*· any profession of religion,
	15–21	*m*· memorable by eloquent addresses
	18–18	all His spirit hath *m*·,
	44–24	No sooner were my views *m*· known,
	53– 3	This monthly magazine had been *m*·
	59–19	and all that is *m*· by Him,
	59–24	*m*· in His own image and likeness ;
	61– 4	*m*· manifest on the body
	64–12	the fact is *m*· obvious that the
	67–19	error *m*· its man mortal,
	69–22	*m*· all perfect and eternal.
	80–29	sacrifices *m*· for others are not
	89–28	not first *m*· known to them
	93–16	spiritual ideal is *m*· our own,
Un.	9– 8	Jesus has *m*· the way plain,
	20–12	God never *m*· evil.
	22– 2	*m*· after God's eternal likeness,
	30–14	was *m*· a living soul ; — *I Cor.* 15 : 45.
	30–15	*m*· a quickening spirit." — *I Cor.* 15 : 45.
	30–19	*m*· humanity victorious over
	39– 1	"the Word" is "*m*· flesh" — *John* 1 : 14.

made

Un.	44– 1	Many misrepresentations are *m*·
	45–11	that God never *m*· evil.
	53– 3	God never *m*· them ;
	53– 4	the lie must say He *m*· them,
	56– 1	chaos of mortal mind is *m*· the
	56–23	*m*· to fret in their chains ;
	59– 6	which *m*· heaven and earth
	60–14	*m*· after the similitude — *Jas.* 3 : 9.
Pul.	2–14	not *m*· with hands, — *II Cor.* 5 : 1.
	6–11	*m*· the mistake of thinking she
	7–15	*m*· morals for mankind.
	8–14	only the need *m*· known,
	13–20	*m*· his bosom companion,
	21– 9	be *m*· manifest in my life.
	30–18	* man is *m*· in His image.
	34– 4	* no special record is to be *m*·.
	36–16	* *m*· me feel I could have walked
	45– 3	* Sacrifices were *m*· in many an
	45–28	* result of rules *m*· by Mrs. Eddy.
	53–13	* hath *m*· thee whole." — *Luke* 17 : 19.
	60–16	* organ, *m*· by Farrand & Votey
	61–27	* The chimes were *m*· by the
	63–10	* *m*· recently as she pointed to
	63–15	* *m*· by a remarkable woman,
	65–14	* progress which has been *m*·
	65–20	* *m*· it to be called the Bible of
	73–20	* *m*· a careful and searching study
	74– 6	* *m*· by Mrs. Laura Lathrop,
	80–23	* It has *m*· a myriad of
	85– 3	* *m*· its erection possible.
Rud.	3–21	error *m*· manifest physically,
	5– 8	*m*· in the image of Spirit,
	12–10	first *m*· sick by matter,
	13– 9	*m*· in the divine and spiritual image
	14–18	No discount on tuition was *m*·
No.	2–12	should be *m*· to test the
	3–11	should not be *m*· public ;
	4–10	never *m*· sickness a stubborn
	9–24	More mistakes are *m*· in its name
	16– 5	whatever He knows is *m*· manifest,
	29–20	pardoned by God . . . he is *m*· whole.
	34– 8	sacrifice that Jesus *m*· for us,
	40–27	*m*· better only by divine influence.
Pan.	5– 5	were *m*· by Him," — *John* 1 : 3.
	5–10	who or what hath *m*· evil?
	6–17	Spirit *m*· all that was *m*·,
'00.	6–27	*m*· better physically, morally, and
'01.	7–10	and *m*· them male and female
	9– 9	a sense so pure it *m*· seers of men,
	9–16	*m*· manifest in the flesh, healing and
	11–13	*m*· the Bible, and "S. and H.
	13– 2	and God never *m*· it.
	14–12	evil cannot be *m*· so real as to
	27– 4	* contributions that have been *m*·
'02.	1–11	is *m*· to glorify God.
	9–12	hath *m*· me free from — *Rom.* 8 : 2.
	18– 5	*m*· him a man of sorrows,
	18–30	*m*· him keenly alive to the
Hea.	6–16	evolved and *m*· tangible ;
	8–14	it is willing to be *m*· whole,
	9–18	God never *m*· a wicked man ;
	9–23	God made all that was *m*·,
	9–24	He never *m*· sin or sickness,
	12–14	God, . . . never *m*· a man sick.
	12–19	*m*· the infinitesimal dose effectual.
	17– 9	God made all that was *m*· ;
	19–14	He *m*· "every plant — *Gen.* 2 : 5.
Peo.	3– 4	have *m*· monsters of men ;
	3– 5	have *m*· helpless invalids
	10–18	have *m*· men sinning and sick,
	11–11	*m*· subject to his Maker.
Po.	v–18	* *who m· her acquaintance,*
	9–11	Our reason *m*· right
	59– 6	I hope it's better *m*·,
	64– 9	all His spirit hath *m*·,
	75– 4	the Truth that *m*· us free,
My.	vi–22	* she *m*· over to trustees
	vii– 6	* *m*· to deprive their Leader of
	10–16	* No appeal has ever been *m*·
	10–17	* probable that none will be *m*·
	11–20	* we have also *m*· good the pledge.
	16– 3	* *m*· to the annual meeting.
	21– 4	* self-sacrifices which have been *m*·
	27–22	* announcement *m*· by Mr. Chase
	37–21	* He has *m*· known through your
	48– 7	* and which Mrs. Eddy *m*·
	52–27	* she has *m*· sacrifices from which
	55– 4	* efforts were *m*· to obtain
	55–18	* were *m*· for a church home.
	56–26	* further provision must be *m*·,
	58– 9	* statements that have been *m*·
	64– 9	* *m*· the name an honored one
	66–13	* a number of changes will be *m*·
	76– 9	* formal announcement was *m*·

made

My.	80– 8	* they had been *m·* whole,
	81–26	* If an attempt were *m·* to give
	83–23	* announcement, which has just been *m·*,
	83–29	* *m·* steady gains in recent years.
	92–15	* astonishing revelation was *m·*
	100–12	* C. S. sect *m·* its appearance
	105–18	and have *m·* the lame walk.
	106– 6	could be *m·* to include
	107–24	God made all that was *m·*,
	110–29	*m·* his life an abject failure.
	113–14	hath *m·* me free from — *Rom.* 8 : 2.
	130–11	has been *m·* too many times
	138–20	statements herein *m·* by me,
	138–27	* *m·* oath that the statements
	141–12	* was *m·* last night [June 21]
	149–15	Epictetus *m·* answer,
	152– 6	hath *m·* thee whole." — *Matt.* 9 : 22.
	154– 8	if they can be *m·* to infringe
	157–17	* *m·* known in her original deed of
	157–20	* *m·* the following statement :
	173–10	no preparations would be *m·* for
	178–17, 18	He *m·* all "that was *m·*." — *John* 1 : 3.
	188– 2	you have *m·* the head of the corner.
	188– 7	that is *m·* in this place." — *II Chron.* 7 : 15.
	188–13	"house not *m·* with hands, — *II Cor.* 5 : 1.
	194– 7	"house not *m·* with hands, — *II Cor.* 5 : 1.
	204–18	on the decision you have *m·*
	205– 4	Christ hath *m·* us free." — *Gal.* 5 : 1.
	205–18	* as the thing *m·* is good or bad,
	206–27	hath *m·* us meet to be — *Col.* 1 : 12.
	211–29	Other minds are *m·* dormant by it,
	224–15	or *m·* blind to his loss of
	233–10	are you not *m·* better by watching?
	235–16	Did God make all that was *m·*?
	235–18	Who or what *m·* matter?
	235–19	Matter as substance . . . never was *m·*.
	239–27	God, Spirit, who *m·* all that was *m·*.
	244–27	No charge will be *m·* for my services.
	245–26	Inquiries have been *m·* as to the
	264–17	Truth and Love *m·* more practical ;
	267– 7	"All things were *m·* by Him ; — *John* 1 : 3.
	267– 8	any thing *m·* that was *m·*." — *John* 1 : 3.
	271–18	* has *m·* her famous.
	272– 6	hath *m·* me [man] free — *Rom.* 8 : 2.
	287–17	are *m·* partakers of that Mind
	288–30	can make the best of what God has *m·*.
	293–29	hath *m·* me free from — *Rom.* 8 : 2.
	299–10	C. S. has been widely *m·*
	302– 9	all effect *m·* manifest through
	305–22	All that I am in reality, God has *m·*
	312–16	* Mrs. Glover *m·* only one time at
	315–17	* *m·* oath that the within statement
	315–28	*m·* me the beloved Leader
	317– 4	* *m·* by Mrs. Eddy in refutation
	321–19	* the statements have been *m·*,
	326–10	* in which Mrs. Eddy has *m·* her home.
	327– 5	*m·* it legal to practise C. S.
	327–12	* *m·* glad the hearts of all
	328–25	* application for license was *m·*
	334– 7	* efforts are being *m·* to buy them
	335– 4	* and was *m·* a Mason
	336–15	* Mr. Glover had *m·* no will
	338–12	"The Unknown God *M·* Known,"
	343–23	I *m·* a code of by-laws,
	345–15	could be *m·* to act on me.
	346–11	* *m·* several turns about the
	346–24	* when the statement was *m·*,
	348– 7	God *m·* manifest in the flesh,
	348–20	demonstration thereof was *m·*,
	361–20	* promptly *m·* its demonstration
		(*see also* **God, man**)

Madison

Pul.	56– 3	* Toledo, Milwaukee, *M·*,

madness

Mis.	369–11	"method" in the "*m·*"
	369–12	*m·* it seems to many onlookers.
Ret.	32–13	* What is life? 'T is but a *m·*.
'00.	5–29	Not *m·*, but might and majesty
My.	14– 7	not a *m·* and nothing,

Madonna

Mis.	375–26	* in . . . Botticelli's '*M·*'!

maëlstrom

Mis.	294– 3	the *m·* of human passions,

magazine

Mis.	132–19	editing a *m·*,
	271–10	They should take our *m·*,
Ret.	53– 3	This monthly *m·* had been
My.	215–18	to plant our first *m·*,
	316–11	January number of *The Arena m·*,

magazines

Mis.	271–11	They should eschew all *m·* . . . which
My.	304–11	I wrote for the best *m·*

Magdalen

No.	23–10	Out of the *M·*, Jesus cast

Magian

My.	258–18	greater than those of *M·* kings,

magic

Mis.	29–25	*m·* and Oriental barbarisms
	78–13	occultism, *m·*, alchemy,
Ret.	18–21	communion with home's *m·* spell !
Pul.	81–23	* plays upon *m·* strings
No.	14–11	with its *m·* and enchantments.
Po.	64–14	communion with home's *m·* spell !
My.	61–23	* seemed to move as by *m·* ;

magical

'00.	12–16	*M·* arts prevailed at Ephesus ;
	12–22	*m·* books in that city were

magicians

My.	127–15	rods of the *m·* of Egypt.

magistrate (*see also* **magistrate's**)

Mis.	289–28	fairly stated by a *m·*,
Pan.	14–15	guide and bless our chief *m·*,
My.	290–19	our nation's chief *m·*,

magistrate's

No.	32– 4	A *m·* pardon may encourage a

Magna Charta

My.	246–30	The *M· C·* of C. S. means much,
	254–21	"The *M· C·* of C. S. means much,

magnanimous

My.	165–27	lost the power of being *m·*.

magnetic

Mis.	233–15	*m·* force of mortal mind,
	378–11	proved to be a *m·* practitioner.
Ret.	24– 2	*m·* doctor, Mr. P. P. Quimby,
Pul.	32– 3	* *m·*, earnest, impassioned.
	46– 2	* so eloquent and *m·* that
'01.	2– 9	*m·* element of human will
My.	90– 4	* no eloquence of orator or *m·* ritual,
	307– 6	back of his *m·* treatment and

Magnetism

(*see* **Animal Magnetism**)

magnetism

animal

Mis.	3–26	hygiene, and animal *m·* are
	48–11	animal *m·* is neither of God nor
	48–18	as to the animus of animal *m·*,
	78–15	are the inventions of animal *m·*,
	97–13	human control is animal *m·*,
	175–29	both animal *m·* and divine power,
	280–31	doors of animal *m·* open wide for
	284–14	treat malicious animal *m·*?
	366–22	drugs, electricity, and animal *m·*
'01.	20– 1	animal *m·* and hypnotism are
My.	180–13	hypnotism or animal *m·*.
	211–12	Animal *m·*, in its ascending steps
	211–20	Animal *m·* fosters suspicious
	212– 4	This intricate method of animal *m·*
	212–12	animal *m·* is the highest form of
	212–22	resist the animal *m·* by which
	212–29	saying that animal *m·* never
	212–30	saying that . . . teaches animal *m·* ;
	213– 4	perverted mind-power, or animal *m·*,
	213–26	adverse influence of animal *m·*.
	236–29	of the workings of animal *m·*,
	357– 9	animal *m·*, — the name of all evil,
	358– 6	animal *m·* is the opposite of divine
	359–28	temptation produced by animal *m·*
	364– 9	Animal *m·*, hypnotism, *etc.*,

My.	348– 3	electricity, *m·*, or will-power,

magnetizer

Mis.	156–22	through which the animal *m·* preys,

magnificence

My.	70–19	* chapter sub-title

magnificent

Mis.	275–27	Palmer House, . . . is *m·*
Pul.	25–16	* entrance to this *m·* temple.
	30–29	* its own *m·* church building,
	77– 1	* *m·* new edifice of worship
	77–24	* chapter sub-title
	78– 2	* probably one of the most *m·*
My.	6–14	*m·* temple wherein to enter and
	43–30	* dedication of our *m·* temple,
	45–14	* The *m·* edifice stands a
	58– 7	* *m·* growth of this Cause,
	58–15	* This *m·* structure,
	59–13	* the gallery of that *m·* temple,
	62– 5	* But what of this *m·* structure?
	62–21	* completion of the *m·* extension
	69–14	* sculptor added *m·* carvings to
	77–19	* streets leading to the *m·* temple
	94–18	* *m·* new temple of the cult.

magnificent
 My. 95– 9 * *m·* C. S. church in Boston
  98– 6 * *m·* church, holding five thousand
  194–20 princely gift of your *m·* church
  198– 5 dedication of your *m·* church
  274–21 my thanks for their *m·* gifts,

magnified
 Mis. 164–26 will become so *m·* to human sense,
 Un. 7– 1 His name will be *m·* in the

magnifies
 Mis. 194–16 *m·* the divine power to human sight ;
 '01. 12–22 *m·* the divine power to human sight ;
 Hea. 2–26 *m·* his name who built, on Truth,

magnify
 Mis. 75–22 doth *m·* the Lord,"— Luke 1 : 46.
  75–23 "My *spiritual sense* doth *m·*
  129–20 faults to *m·* under the lens
 Un. 30– 2 doth *m·* the Lord."— Luke 1 : 46.
 Pul. 12–16 give thanks and *m·* the Lord

magnitude
 Mis. 61– 8 when aping the wisdom and *m·* of
  100–13 the *m·* of self-abnegation,
  360–13 these stars of the first *m·*
  380– 7 majesty and *m·* of this query,
 Ret. 65–28 *m·* and distance of the stars,
  71–11 an error of much *m·*.
 '01. 30– 7 The *m·* of its meaning forbids
 My. 47–11 * has grown to great *m·*,
  59– 1 * grandeur and *m·* of your work
  63–22 * new sense of the *m·* of C. S.,
  84–20 * Its very *m·* and the cheerful
  133–28 your knowledge with its *m·* of
  270– 4 *m·* of their spiritual import,

magnolia
 Ret. 17–18 *m·*, and fragrant fringe-tree ;
 Po. 63– 3 *m·*, and fragrant fringe-tree ;

mahogany
 Pul. 76–11 * frames are of white *m·*
 My. 68–32 * pews and . . . woodwork are of *m·*.
  78–;13 * semi-circular sweep of *m·* pews

maid
 Pul. 33– 9 * but the little *m·* was afraid
 Pan. 3–17 * fair wisdom, that celestial *m·*."

maiden
 Mis. x–22 to retain my *m·* name,
  390– 8 Gives back some *m·* melody,
 Po. 55– 9 Gives back some *m·* melody,

mail
 Mis. 171–30 all clad in the shining *m·*
 Man. 93–15 *m·* to the Clerk of this Church
 Pul. 44–28 * checks by *m·* or otherwise.
 My. 73–23 * to which all *m·* may be directed,

mailed
 '02. 15– 1 anonymous letters *m·* to me
 Po. v–22 * *was subsequently m· to them.*
 My. 215–13 but it was again *m·* to me

main
 Pul. 58–15 * *m·* auditorium has wide galleries,
 Po. 10– 6 Lord of the *m·* and manor !
 My. 80–30 * in the *m·* body of the church,
  81–11 * announced at the *m·* meeting
  137– 6 * "in the *m·*, an example of
  337– 7 Lord of the *m·* and manor !

Maine and **Me.** (see also **Pine Tree State**)
 (see **Augusta, Calais, Eastport, Portland**)

mainly
 Mis. 38–22 *m·*, elaborating a man-made
 Un. 25– 1 thus affirms is *m·* correct.
 Peo. 2– 4 *m·* due to the people's improved
 My. 3–20 its effect on man is *m·* this

maintain
 Mis. 27–15 the Scriptures *m·* this fact
  38– 3 ability to gain and *m·* health,
  110–10 *m·* in yourselves what Jesus loved,
  146–13 and still *m·* this position.
  148–17 *m·* the dignity and defense
  205–23 *m·* their obvious correspondence,
  286–16 *m·* morality and generation,
 Man. 3–13 *m·* the dignity and defense
  33– 6 he shall *m·* the Tenets,
  74–20 *m·* toward them an attitude
  93– 5 *m·* a Board of Lectureship,
 Ret. 44–15 able to *m·* the church
 Un. 46– 7 I *m·*, the individuality and reality
 Pul. 3–10 If you *m·* this position,
  74–23 *m·* but one conclusion and statement
 '01. 13– 9 not well to *m·* the position that
 My. 86–20 * *m·* towards their church.
  165–25 They *m·* themselves and others
  211– 7 in order to *m·* harmony,
  222–30 will *m·* law and order,

maintain
 My. 230– 2 will *m·* its rank as in the past,
  294– 1 Human governments *m·* the right of
  358–31 to *m·* them and sustain them.

maintained
 Mis. 68– 9 * *m· that pain and disease are not*
  93–19 neither *m·* by Science nor
 Ret. 14–14 *m·* that I was willing to trust God,
 Pul. 6– 5 *m·* on the spiritual foundation of
  9–17 the church services were *m·* by
 My. 37–17 * has been organized and *m·*,
  216–10 by which each is provided for and *m·*.

maintaining
 My. 279– 9 *m·* its obvious correspondence with

maintains
 Rud. 12–27 *m·* human health and life.
 My. 41–17 * *m·* the perfect standard of truth
  111–15 C. S. *m·* primitive Christianity,

maintenance
 Man. 55–19 by uniform *m·* of the life of a
 My. 220– 4 *m·* of individual rights,
  268–12 *m·* of individual rights,

majestic
 Mis. 123–20 *m·* atonement of divine Love.
  385–26 shed *M·* forms ;
  392– 6 *m·* oak, from yon high place
 Po. 18– 3 eagle's proud wing, His soaring *m·*,
  20– 8 *m·* oak, from yon high place
  49– 1 shed *M·* forms ;
 My. 182–18 large membership and *m·* cathedral.
  245–18 *m·* march of C. S. go on *ad infinitum,*

majestically
 Mis. 145–28 float *m·* heaven's heraldry,
  338–18 move *m·* to your defense

majesty
 Mis. 141–13 freedom, might, and *m·* of Spirit,
  185–16 man be clothed with might, *m·*, and
  191–16 name of his satanic *m·* is found to be
  292–14 to human weakness might and *m·*.
  294–10 might and *m·* !— of goodness.
  380– 7 *m·* and magnitude of this query,
 '00. 2–18 his satanic *m·* is supposed to
  5–30 might and *m·* attend every footstep
 '01. 33–22 might and *m·* of divine power
 My. 58–11 * *m·* and the dignity of this church
  149– 8 More than regal is the *m·* of
  187–29 the *m·* of His might
  188–25 the *m·* of C. S.
  188–26 teaches the *m·* of man.
  258–29 lowly in its *m·*.

Major
 (see **Glover**)

major
 '01. 4– 3 In logic the *m·* premise must be

majority
 Mis. 6– 8 the *m·* of the acute cases
  102–31 "one on God's side is a *m·*."
  130–23 *m·* of one's acts are right,
  245–29 * "one with God is a *m·*."
 Man. 26–23 A *m·* vote or the request of
  30– 8 removed from office by a *m·*
  38–11 elected by *m·* vote
  65–21 supplied by a *m·* vote
  82–12 except by a *m·* vote
  102– 9 supply a vacancy . . . by a *m·* vote.
 Ret. 7– 1 *m·* vote of seven thousand,
 Pul. 4–17 "one on God's side is a *m·*."
  56– 8 * In some churches a *m·* of the
  67–18 * the *m·* of whom are in the
 Rud. 8–17 error has the *m·*.
 No. 46– 1 "One on God's side is a *m·* ;"
 Peo. 3– 7 minority to be saved and the *m·* to be
 My. 182– 2 To-day it is said to have a *m·*
  294– 1 the right of the *m·* to rule.

make
 Mis. 4–26 to *m·* your demonstrations."
  24–16 tried to *m·* plain to others,
  38–27 to *m·* each patient a student
  39–10 risen up in a day to *m·* this claim ;
  43–11 *m·* safe and successful practitioners.
  48–31 trying to *m·* capital out of
  51–16 *m·* clear to the child's thought
  52–23 What progress would a student . . . *m·*,
  53–24 to *m·* the rulers understand,
  60–10 The Nazarene Prophet could *m·* the
  61–28 can neither *m·* them so nor
  69–10 *m·* man in our image,— Gen. 1 : 26.
  75–17 used and *m·* complete sense.
  99–26 "M· straight God's paths ;
  99–27 *m·* way for health, holiness,
  117–29 *m·* their moves before God
  117–30 or *m·* them too late to follow

make

Mis.	118–10	*m·* incorrect your entire problem,
	121–13	would *m·* this fatal doctrine just
	130–13	same power to *m·* you a sinner
	130–14	to *m·* a man sick?
	133– 2	the statement you *m·* at the close
	151–20	*m·* Him thy first acquaintance.
	166–31	it could *m·* him the glorified.
	170–13	we *m·* our own heavens
	196– 7	will *m·* you as gods ;" — *see Gen.* 3 : 5.
	196–10	and *m·* you know evil,
	203– 3	I *m·* no distinction between
	218–15	they *m·* Deity unreal
	222–23	will *m·* stout hearts quail.
	223–28	* should *m·* him hate somebody."
	230– 7	*m·* the most of the present.
	241–10	try to *m·* others do likewise,
	241–23	shall *m·* you free.' " — *John* 8 : 32.
	244–20	*m·* the blind to see,
	246–24	*m·* His paths straight." — *Matt.* 3 : 3.
	250– 5	they *m·* it what it is not,
	250–16	I *m·* strong demands on love,
	253–10	and *m·* amends for the
	256– 5	to *m·* the body harmonious.
	261–30	or else *m·* the claim valid.
	265– 7	*m·* mistakes and lose their way.
	265–16	presume to *m·* innovations
	267– 1	screaming, to *m·* itself heard
	271–22	To *m·* this plain,
	284–10	adhere to the right, and *m·*
	299–20	can I *m·* this right by saying,
	319–12	tends to *m·* sin less or more
	328– 1	*M·* thine own way ;
	330– 2	the winds *m·* melody
	330– 8	*m·* music in the heart.
	331– 5	did it *m·* them humble, loving,
	343– 1	*m·* us wise unto salvation !
	354–18	*m·* manifest the movement of
	362–11	Theologians *m·* the mortal mistake of
	363–16	to *m·* himself imperfect,
	387–19	*m·* men one in love remain.
	389–14	O *m·* me glad for every
	394– 9	bless, and *m·* joyful again.
	398– 7	*M·* self-righteousness be still,
	399– 4	for you *m·* radiant room
Man.	28–15	to watch and *m·* sure that the
	29– 5	shall not *m·* known the name
	32–20	They shall *m·* no remarks
	39– 2	*m·* application for membership
	48–14	or *m·* a summer resort near
	50–18	from Christian motives *m·* this
	70– 2	shall not *m·* a church By-Law,
	94– 4	*m·* . . . a less lecture fee ;
Chr.	53–23	*M·* merriment on Christmas eves,
Ret.	15– 8	I will *m·* mention — *Psal.* 71 : 16.
	24–15	and how to *m·* others so.
	46–13	*M·* self-righteousness be still,
	69–10	saying, . . . I will *m·* error as real
Un.	7– 8	*m·* also the following statement :
	8– 5	Everything as real as you *m·* it,
	17– 3	and so *m·* the lie seem part of
	23– 4	* *M·* instruments to scourge us.
	45–18	Anatomy and physiology *m·*
	49–20	Standing in no basic Truth, we *m·*
	51– 7	human reason can never *m·*
	53– 1	which *m·* a beautiful lie.
	61–19	*m·* the earthly acme of
Pul.	1– 2	*m·* them *drink of the* — *Psal.* 36 : 8.
	3–17	*m·* them drink of the— *Psal.* 36 : 8.
	7–30	*m·* them drink of the— *Psal.* 36 : 8.
	13– 7	I will *m·* thee ruler — *Matt.* 25 : 23.
	17–12	*M·* self-righteousness be still,
	58–29	* to *m·* it a home by day or night.
	82– 1	* *m·* the body not the prison,
	82–24	* to help *m·* the laws,
	87–16	*m·* me your *Pastor Emeritus,* nominally.
Rud.	10–24	belief that matter can . . . *m·* you ill,
No.	5– 9	would be to *m·* it Truth.
	8–13	*m·* the wrath of man to praise Him,
	23– 5	nor *m·* evil omnipotent
	32–15	other theories *m·* sin true.
	37–18	would *m·* the atonement to be
	42–23	would *m·* a lie the author of Truth,
	42–24	and so *m·* Truth itself a lie.
	44– 3	failure should *m·* him modest.
Pan.	3– 7	to *m·* it half divine
	12–10	will *m·* strong claims on religion,
'00.	14– 3	Behold, I will *m·* — *Rev.* 3 : 9.
'01.	10– 2	shall *m·* you free." — *John* 8 : 32.
	11–16	that does not *m·* it impossible
	14–13	*m·* us love it and so hinder our
'02.	6–21	*M·* me the image and likeness
Hea.	3– 4	to *m·* men better, to cast out error,
	8–22	and this will *m·* us honest
	9–20	wherewith to *m·* himself wicked.

make

Peo.	2–15	*m·* a Christian only in theory,
	3–13	that *m·* a mysterious God
	4–22	can *m·* a spiritual mind out of
	8–16	and yet we *m·* more of matter,
	10–21	*m·* it harmonious or discordant
	11–18	*m·* the laws that govern their
Po.	4–13	O *m·* me glad for every
	6–14	*m·* men one in love remain.
	14–11	*M·* self-righteousness be still,
	33– 2	*m·* this my humble request :
	35– 4	To *m·* me love thee as I
	45–12	bless, and *m·* joyful again.
	75–11	for you *m·* radiant room
My.	8–15	* *m·* reasonable accommodation for
	16–27	shall not *m·* haste. — *Isa.* 28 : 16.
	21–24	* have been called upon to *m·*
	28– 1	* to *m·* this announcement
	40–21	* them that *m·* peace." — *Jas.* 3 : 18.
	48–11	* insisted that her students *m·*,
	48–25	* forces that *m·* for righteousness.
	52– 9	* will *m·* greater efforts
	66–11	* what use the society will *m·*
	66–20	* their work to *m·* the spacious
	75–16	* it would not *m·* much difference,
	87–22	* Their happy faces would *m·* sunshine
	98– 2	* *m·* up a mighty host,
	108–24	*m·* known the best work of a
	117–11	*m·* one a Christian Scientist.
	123–29	* "trifles *m·* perfection,"
	124–15	enough to *m·* this hour glad.
	137–29	No person influenced me to *m·*
	140– 4	*m·* darkness light — *Isa.* 42 : 16.
	149–13	*m·* their treasures yours.
	156– 6	*m·* all grace abound — *II Cor.* 9 : 8.
	156–17	there *m·* ready." — *Luke* 22 : 12.
	172– 4	* to *m·* room for Vanderbilt Hall.
	173–23	vied with each other to *m·*
	177–24	will *m·* an everlasting — *Isa.* 61 : 8.
	179–32	as *m·* even God demonstrable,
	186–19	*m·* this church the fold of flocks,
	192– 5	*m·* spotless the blemished,
	203–16	they *m·* us what we are.
	219–22	cannot annul nor *m·* void the
	220–21	*m·* them Thy friends ;
	222–23	*m·* laws to regulate man's
	226– 3	only where you can . . . *m·* sense.
	235–16	Did God *m·* all that was made?
	235–17	Did infinite Spirit *m·* that
	236– 7	to *m·* the *amende honorable*
	237–16	*m·* their charges for treatment
	242–22	not to *m·* inquiries on these subjects,
	252–11	*m·* one not only know the truth
	252–12	*m·* one enjoy doing right,
	252–12	*m·* one . . . work midst clouds of wrong,
	257–22	*m·* man's being pure and blest.
	260– 3	would *m·* matter an alien
	260– 6	to *m·* room for substance,
	278– 5	may learn to *m·* war no more,
	280– 8	* *m·* for the establishment of a
	288–29	*m·* the best of what God has made.
	299– 8	* *m·* it known to the world,
	300–22	that he *m·* known his doctrine
	319– 2	would *m·* no difference to me.
	327–11	* will *m·* your heart glad,
	336–18	* he was unable to *m·* a will.
	344–15	must *m·* gradual approaches to
	345–29	*m·* them our figures of speech.
		(*see also* **man**)

Maker

his

Mis.	46–15	Man is not equal with his *M·* ;
	47–25	coexistence with his *M·*.
	62– 8	the true likeness of his *M·*.
	65–26	man's account with his *M·*.
	98– 5	which is the image of his *M·*.
	164–23	actual likeness of his *M·*.
	182–27	man and his *M·* are inseparable
	183–32	Scriptures declare reflects his *M·*,
	185– 1	and reflecting, his *M·*.
	196–18	man's unity with his *M·*,
	217–24	a rebel against his *M·*.
	255– 5	Man is not equal to his *M·*.
	294– 2	man in the image of his *M·* ;
Un.	41–16	man's unity with his *M·*
	46–10	man and his *M·* are here ;
	52–11	of man separated from his *M·*.
Hea.	9–19	power underived from his *M·*
Peo.	6–14	the victim of his *M·*,
	11–12	is made subject to his *M·*.
My.	232–26	the true likeness of his *M·*"?
Mis.	103–20	neither the pattern nor *M·* of
	184– 1	very opposite of that *M·*,
	363–15	and there is no other *M·* :
Un.	23– 6	turn again and rend their *M·*.

Maker
  Un. 49– 9 as is the perfect *M·*.
        50–23 is without Mind or *M·*.
  My. 219–14 believe that man's *M·* is not equal to

maker
  Ret. 48– 9 one builder and *m·*, God,
  My. 205–18 * is good or bad, so is its *m·*.''
      282– 2 its peace *m·* or breaker.

makers
  My. 160–30 *m·* of hell burn in their fire.

makes
  Mis. 14–32 he *m·* a great reality of evil,
      21–11 *m·* practical all his words
      28– 9 what mortal mind *m·* them ;
      38–20 *m·* divine metaphysics needful,
     108–26 This cognomen *m·* it less dangerous ;
     110–11 *m·* morals for mankind !
     117–30 make their moves before God *m·* His,
     133–13 Love *m·* all burdens light,
     147–14 *m·* it his constant rule
     160–14 *m·* us stronger and firmer
     165–19 *m·* his followers the heirs to
     169–22 *m·* them nothing valuable,
     219–22 that mortal mind *m·* sick,
     219–23 immortal Mind *m·* well ;
     219–24 mortal mind *m·* sinners,
     219–24 immortal Mind *m·* saints ;
     224– 2 *m·* another's criticism rankle,
     224– 3 *m·* another's deed offensive,
     228–28 and it *m·* disease catching.
     234–32 *m·* His sovereignty glorious.
     262–25 Christ-love that *m·* them light
     265– 3 *m·* the venture from vanity,
     287–27 *m·* one ruler over one's self
     293–25 *m·* mortals either saints or sinners.
     294–14 *m·* honey out of the flowers
     316– 3 know the truth that *m·* free,
     324– 2 *m·* his way into the streets
     340–18 *m·* himself a musician by
     353–21 that *m·* the machinery work rightly ;
     355–24 the error . . . that *m·* his body sick,
     363– 7 is mind and *m·* men,
     399– 8 'T is the Spirit that *m·* pure,
  Man. 84– 5 know the truth that *m·* free,
  Chr. 53–36 For health *m·* room.
  Ret. 63– 8 which *m·* him a sinner,
     64– 7 *m·* apparent, the real man,
     78– 7 scientific practice *m·* perfect,
     82–29 *m·* the subject-matter clearer
  Un. 23– 2 which *m·* true the lines :
  Pul. 14–29 when it *m·* them sick or sinful.
     56–16 * It *m·* people better and happier.
     82–29 * Might no longer *m·* right,
  Rud. 8–23 he *m·* morally worse the invalid
  No. 5–28 *m·* the last state of one's patients
     12–25 it *m·* both sense and Soul,
     13– 3 *m·* disease unreal, and this heals it.
     39–20 It *m·* new and scientific discoveries
  Pan. 7–28 *m·* sin, disease, and death
  '00. 4– 3 misnomer . . . *m·* His opposites as real
     11–19 Mind, not matter, *m·* music ;
  '02. 2– 9 Truth *m·* haste to meet and to
  Hea. 7–14 *m·* pure the fountain,
     13–26 Mesmerism *m·* one disease while
     17– 7 Love *m·* the spiritual man,
     17– 8 *m·* the material so-called man,
     19–19 *m·* a more spiritual demand,
  Peo. 2– 9 and *m·* it *good,*
     5–24 *m·* a pure Christianity
     9– 9 *m·* them white in the blood of the
  Po. 39–17 Since temperance *m·* your laws.
     75–15 'Tis the Spirit that *m·* pure,
  My. 24– 3 * the truth which *m·* free
     41–16 * C. S. *m·* no compromise with evil,
     52–31 * statement ''Phare Pleigh'' . . . *m·*
     92– 6 * *m·* it appear that Science cannot
     99– 5 * a religion that *m·* the merry heart
    110–20 if bodily sensation *m·* us captives
    112– 6 what C. S. *m·* practical to-day
    145–21 *m·* me the servant of the race
    154–25 it *m·* the church militant,
    155– 1 *m·* healing the sick and reforming
    157–10 * *m·* necessary the commodious
    158–21 *m·* the heart tender, faithful, true.
    165–16 goodness *m·* life a blessing.
    204–11 which *m·* them one in Christ.
    212– 5 evil, which *m·* mankind drunken.
    336– 9 * She *m·* grateful acknowledgment
    346–29 ''S. and H. *m·* it plain to all
    349–29 *m·* manifest the infinite nature,
        (*see also* **God, man**)

maketh
  Mis. 137–26 that worketh or *m·* a lie.
    174–18 nothing that *m·* or worketh a lie.

maketh
  Mis. 366–14 nothing that worketh or *m·* a lie
    393–13 Students wise, he *m·* now
  No. 15–26 ''worketh or *m·* a lie'' —*see Rev.* 21 : 27.
  '01. 28–23 all that worketh or *m·* a lie.
  Po. 51–18 Students wise, he *m·* now

make-up
  My. 122–6 in one's own moral *m·*.

making
  Mis. vii– 7 * In *m·* thy friends books,
     62–12 *m·* the aggregate positive,
     97–32 The only cause for *m·* this
    133–20 *m·* the following statement :
    192–26 *m·* healing a condition of salvation,
    230– 9 *m·* lingering calls,
    261–25 a kind of men after man's own *m·*.
    294– 4 *m·* place for himself and
    302–26 derived from *m·* his copy,
    305–13 * *m·* the undertaking successful.
    318–26 namely, *m·* sin seem
  Ret. 57–28 *m·* mortality the status
  Pul. 11– 2 *m·* melody more real,
  Pan. 4–16 a creator, *m·* two creators ;
  '01. 24–12 *M·* matter more potent than Mind,
  '02. 1– 8 *m·* total twenty-four thousand
     2–11 *m·* the children our teachers.
    12–25 *m·* another united effort
  Hea. 12–22 *m·* you more powerful,''
    18–28 *m·* him believe he was bleeding
    19–25 *m·* our words golden rays
  Po. v– 5 * *with a view of m· a book,*
    70– 6 *M·* this life divine,
    70– 7 *M·* its waters wine,
  My. 7– 8 before *m·* another united effort
    25– 2 * propriety in *m·* a special effort
    79–25 * *m·* their remarkable statements
    97– 4 * towards *m·* the patient well.
    306–10 purpose of *m·* the true apparent.
    309– 4 *m·* out deeds, settling quarrels,
    340–15 *m·* laws for the State

malady
  Mis. 241–17 Truth heals him of the moral *m·*.
  My. 116– 9 mental *m·*, which must be met
    116–20 not a symptom of this contagious *m·*,
    203–17 Dishonesty is a mental *m·*

male
  Mis. 18–16 ''*m·* and female,'' — *Gen.* 1: 27.
    199– 8 *m·* and female come into their
    314– 6 two Readers : a *m·*, and a female.
  '01. 7–10 made them *m·* and female
    10–11 term for both *m·* and female.
  My. 268–29 you see *m·* and female one
    355–11 *m·* element is a strong

malefactor
  Mis. 70–21 dying *m·* and our Lord

malice
  Mis. 19– 2 hatred, *m·*, are always wrong,
    48–10 prompted by money-making or *m·*.
    54–13 *m·* would fling in her path.
    175–15 ''the leaven of *m·*'' — *I Cor.* 5: 8.
    177– 9 Large numbers, in desperate *m·*,
    227– 9 yet with *m·* aforethought
    228–11 the buffetings of envy or *m·*
    248–15 *m·* aforethought of sinners.''
    277–17 purposes of envy and *m·*
    343–16 weeds of passion, *m·*, envy,
    353–12 through *m·* or ignorance.
    368–14 Charlatanism, fraud, and *m·*
    368–25 Others, from *m·* and envy, are
  Un. 56–27 ingratitude, lust, *m·*, hate,
  Pul. 13–25 stung to death by his own *m·* ;
  No. 36–24 conquered the *m·* of his foes,
    45–10 indicates weakness, fear, or *m·* ;
  '02. 19– 9 more than all the *m·* of his foes.
  Hea. 2–20 beneath the *m·* of the world.
    10– 4 vision of envy, sensuality, and *m·*,
    17– 3 envy, hypocrisy, or *m·*,
    18–22 appetites, passions, envy, and *m·*
  My. 17– 4 laying aside all *m·*, — *I Pet.* 2: 1.
    108–20 slang, and *m·* touch not the hem of
    164–28 against which envy, enmity, or *m·*
    316–20 torrents of ignorance, envy, and *m·*.

malicious
  Mis. 51– 8 *m·* workings of error or mortal mind.
    67–11 shalt not strike . . . with a *m·* aim
    119– 1 If *m·* suggestions whisper evil
    222–15 *m·* mental argument and its action
    274–15 chapter sub-title
    284–14 How shall I treat *m·* animal magnetism ?
    351–12 solely from mental *m·* practice,
    352–19 the *m·* mental operation must

malicious

My. 130– 3 against *m·* mental malpractice,
213– 3 *m·* aim of perverted mind-power,
357– 9 is *m·* animal magnetism,

maliciously

No. 32–12 ignorantly or *m·* misconstrued.
My. 146–28 do it ignorantly or *m·*.

malignant

Mis. 249–21 efforts of some *m·* students,
My. 105–11 I healed *m·* diphtheria
227–15 in taking a case of *m·* disease.
227–31 a larger per cent of *m·* diseases

maligned

Mis. 94– 1 are misjudged and *m·* ;
105–22 If either is misunderstood or *m·*,
'01. 33–24 Is it for . . . that they are *m·* ?
My. 103–12 has been persecuted and *m·*.
330– 4 * not be surprised that . . . be *m·*,

malpractice

mental
(*see* **mental**)

Mis. 233– 3 a *m·* of the best system
249– 1 to test that *m·* I experimented
Man. 42–19 No *M·*.
84– 1 Defense against *M·*.
90–20 of mental practice and *m·*.
Rud. 9–10 *m·* is in erring human will,

malpractise

Man. 42–20 or knowingly mentally *m·*,
My. 363–24 was not to *m·* unwittingly.

malpractises

Man. 42–26 *m·* upon or treats our Leader

malpractitioner

Mis. 19–24 hypocrite or mental *m·*.
115– 9 his own guilt as a mental *m·*,
221– 2 a mental *m·* may lose his
284–17 gone personally to the *m·*
316– 2 never to attack the *m·*,
368–19 address of a mental *m·*
Rud. 9– 9 poor practitioner, if not a *m·*.
'01. 20–10 The mental *m·* is not,
My. 212–24 *m·*, interfering with the

mamma

Mis. 231–23 a toy from *m·*
239–28 and which *m·* thought must be

mammal

Rud. 8– 2 no pine-tree produces a *m·*

mammon *(see also* **mammon's***)*

Mis. 269– 9 cannot serve God and *m·*.''— *Matt.* 6 : 24.
Un. 49–15 serve the *m·* of materiality
Pul. 21–17 we cannot serve *m·*.
My. 356–24 cannot serve God and *m·*. — *Matt.* 6 : 24.

mammon's

Po. 71– 5 worshiping at *m·* shrine.

mammoth

Mis. 231–12 *m·* turkey grew beautifully less.

man *(see also* **man's***)*

abides in
Un. 40–17 Hence Life abides in *m·*,
40–17 if *m·* abides in good,
action of
Mis. 58–24 does not govern the action of *m·*,
activity of
My. 259–25 give the activity of *m·* infinite scope ;
advanced
Mis. 234–17 it never has advanced *m·*
agency of
My. 14– 9 Godlike agency of *m·*.
a kind of
My. 239–24 in other words, a kind of *m·*
allotted years of
My. 273– 7 * far beyond the allotted years of *m·*,
ambitious
Po. 2– 7 Ambitious *m·*, Like a trained falcon
and divine Science
'00. 5–12 God, *m·*, and divine Science.
and God
Mis. 77–11 eternal unity of *m·* and God,
332–17 pondered the things of *m·* and God.
Ret. 60–27 or of the real *m·* and God.
Peo. 1– 7 final unity between *m·* and God.
and his Maker
Mis. 182–27 *m·* and his Maker are inseparable
Un. 46– 9 scientific *m·* and his Maker are here ;
and Life
No. 12–26 both sense and Soul, *m·* and Life,
and the universe
(*see* **universe**)

man

and universe
'01. 5–19 real spiritual *m·* and universe.
My. 253– 4 perfect original *m·* and universe.
and woman
Mis. 12–12 Every *m·* and woman should be
Un. 52–14 spiritual idea, *m·* and *woman.*
Pan. 10–12 were the average *m·* and woman.
'01. 7–14 mentalities of *m·* and woman,
My. 239–13 *until every m· and woman comes into*
animal
Mis. 36–16 qualities of the so-called animal *m·* ;
animus of
Pan. 11– 9 gauge the animus of *m·* ?
annihilate
Mis. 56– 6 would destroy Spirit and annihilate *m·*.
Ret. 64– 6 does not annihilate *m·*,
any
Mis. 151– 4 neither shall any *m·* — *John* 10 : 28.
213–24 neither shall any *m·* — *John* 10 : 28.
226–17 * canst not then be false to any *m·*.
252–15 any *m·* can satisfy himself
Chr. 55–26 if any *m·* hear my — *Rev.* 3 : 20.
Ret. 81–26 * canst not then be false to any *m·*.
'01. 21–25 God knows more than any *m·*
My. 196–12 ''If any *m·* offend not — *Jas.* 3 : 2.
285–22 disputing with any *m·*, — *Acts* 24 : 12.
346–28 did not mean any *m·* to-day on earth.
appeals to
Mis. 252–19 It appeals to *m·* as man ;
applied to
Mis. 180–28 This term, as applied to *m·*,
as God's idea
Mis. 261–25 *M·* as God's idea is already saved
as God's offspring
Un. 24–20 *M·*, as God's offspring, must be
as His likeness
Mis. 17–20 Spirit, and of *m·* as His likeness,
79–15 *m·* as His likeness is erect
'02. 8– 2 God, and *m·* as His likeness,
as the idea
My. 239–19 *M·*, as the idea or image
attains
My. 103–13 as *m·* attains the stature of man
at variance
Mis. 214– 6 set a *m·* at variance — *Matt.* 10 : 35.
average
Pan. 10–12 the average *m·* and woman.
My. 106–24 more than does the average *m·*,
awake
Mis. 15–21 and *m·* awake in His likeness.
awakes
My. 273–28 ''*M·* awakes from the dream of death
became a
Mis. 359–10 when I became a *m·*, — *I Cor.* 13 : 11.
My. 135– 4 when I became a *m·*, — *I Cor.* 13 : 11.
261–17 when I became a *m·*, — *I Cor.* 13 : 11.
becomes
Mis. 235– 6 *m·* becomes the partaker of
'02. 6–25 In the degree that *m·* becomes
10–17 that *m·* becomes finally spiritual.
My. 179– 9 and *m·* becomes both good and
before
Mis. 165–30 before *m·* can truthfully conclude
Un. 54–21 when Satan held it up before *m·*
be found
Mis. 164–22 until *m·* be found in the
No. 28– 6 *m·* be found perfect and eternal.
begins
'00. 8–20 When a *m·* begins to quarrel with
behold
Mis. 330–17 behold *m·* in God's own image
belief that
Mis. 77–26 mortal belief that *m·* has fallen
believe in
Un. 49– 1 *Do you believe in m· ?*
believing that
Peo. 6–14 Believing that *m·* is the victim of his
beneath
My. 350–23 Sunk from beneath *m·*,
better
Mis. 336–26 behold a better *m·*, woman, or
bidding
Hea. 19–20 bidding *m·* go up higher,
bless
Mis. 320–11 to cheer, guide, and bless *m·*
blind
Mis. 170–25 Jesus' proceedings with the blind *m·*
body of
Mis. 25– 1 on the mind and body of *m·*,
born of Spirit
Mis. 184– 9 *m·* born of Spirit is spiritual,
bows
Un. 16– 1 *m·* bows to the infinite perfection
brother
Mis. 50–30 helping our brother *m·*.

man

brotherhood of
Mis. 56–20 one God, and the brotherhood of *m·*.
  318– 4 brotherhood of *m·* is stated and
Peo. 13–10 brotherhood of *m·* in unity of Mind
My. 220–16 I pray for . . . the brotherhood of *m·*,
  240– 3 brotherhood of *m·* shall be known
  265–11 brotherhood of *m·* should be
  279–18 establish the brotherhood of *m·*,
business
Mis. 252–28 and empowers the business *m·*
My. 106–26 politician or business *m·*
call
Pan. 11–26 that mortals are content to call *m·*,
called
Mis. 205–28 mortal molecules, called *m·*,
My. 269– 3 image or likeness, called *m·*,
called a
Mis. 294–13 sometimes called a *m·*,
can do no
Ret. 68–25 In C. S., *m·* can do no harm,
can fulfil
Mis. 183–15 *m·* can fulfil the Scriptures
cannot be separated
Mis. 186–19 see that *m·* cannot be separated from
cannot punish a
My. 128–17 Men cannot punish a *m·* for suicide ;
can prove
My. 180– 1 whereby *m·* can prove God's love,
capability of
'00. 3–14 slumbering capability of *m·*.
causes a
Pan. 8– 2 causes a *m·* to be mentally deranged ;
character of
Peo. 7–29 the health and character of *m·*
claims on
Mis. 16–11 Principle hath infinite claims on *m·*,
colored
Peo. 11– 3 the rights of the colored *m·*
commands
'02. 8– 3 commands *m·* to love as Jesus loved.
commands a
My. 131– 4 exalts, and commands a *m·*,
conception of
Mis. 186–10 separates its conception of *m·*
concerns
Mis. 63–18 great reality that concerns *m·*,
condition of
No. 5–23 normal and real condition of *m·*,
consciousness in
Un. 21–17 Individual consciousness in *m·*
consecrate
Hea. 5–27 elevate, and consecrate *m·* ;
constitute
My. 259–19 true heart, and . . . constitute *m·*,
constitution of
Pul. 79–23 * something in the constitution of *m·*
cooperates
Peo. 11–11 *m·* cooperates with and is made
corporeal
Mis. 97–30 corporeal *m·* is this lost image ;
  163–26 crucifixion of the corporeal *m·*,
Rud. 2– 3 * a corporeal *m·*, woman, or child ;
created
Mis. 56–30 implies that Spirit, . . . created *m·*
  57–22 with *m·* created spiritually.
  97–23 "He created *m·* in the image and
  186– 2 created *m·* in His own image
My. 232–25 *m·* created by and of Spirit,
created after
Pul. 82–14 * because she was created after *m·*,
creator of
Pan. 4–16 that He is the creator of *m·*,
defileth a
Mis. 118–32 "Not that . . . defileth a *m·* ;— *Matt.* 15 : 11.
  119– 1 this defileth a *m·*."— *Matt.* 15 : 11.
defines
Ret. 59–23 Science defines *m·* as immortal,
Deity and
My. 350– 1 draws its conclusions of Deity and *m·*,
deliver
Mis. 50–26 would deliver *m·* from heart-disease,
demanded of
My. 103– 5 faith and works demanded of *m·*
demand for
Mis. 247– 1 demand for *m·* his God-given heritage,
demands upon
My. 159–22 eternal demands upon *m·* ;
deny
Hea. 15–14 why should *m·* deny all might to the
dies not
Un. 43–14 I insist only . . . that *m·* dies not
does
My. 271– 9 good that a *m·* does is the one thing
does not absolve
My. 274– 5 Death alone does not absolve *m·*

man

dooms
Mis. 258– 1 lawless law which dooms *m·*
drowning
Mis. 211–14 drowning *m·* just rescued from
dying
Mis. 187–25 create a sick, sinning, dying *m·*?
each
Ret. 86–22 God will help each *m·*
effect on
My. 3–20 its effect on *m·* is mainly this
elevate
Mis. 38– 4 elevate *m·* in every line of life,
elevates
Pul. 53–18 * elevates *m·* above the level of the
emerges
My. 200–15 *m·* emerges from mortality
enable a
Mis. ix– 5 * enable a *m·* to dispense with
enabled
Mis. 30–19 enabled *m·* to demonstrate the law
enables
Mis. 49–20 enables *m·* to discern between the
enrobe
Mis. 332– 9 enrobe *m·* in righteousness ;
equips
Mis. 183–23 equips *m·* with divine power
every
Mis. 12–12 Every *m·* and woman should be
  232–22 Every *m·* and every woman would
Ret. 86–24 every *m·* cared for and blessed.
Rud. 5– 4 every *m·* a liar."— *Rom.* 3 : 4.
My. 9–10 * thought on the part of every *m·*
  196– 9 every *m·* be swift to hear,— *Jas.* 1 : 19.
  239–13 *until every m· and woman comes into*
  257–11 "which lighteth every *m·* — *John* 1 : 9.
evil
'00. 8– 5 evil *m·* also exhales . . . his evil
faculties of
My. 154–20 * deep infinite faculties of *m·*."
faith in
My. 152– 9 faith in *m·* and in matter,
fallen
Mis. 78–25 *Has m· fallen from a state of*
  181–30 evil, or a fallen *m·*.
Father bids
Un. 4–18 the Father bids *m·* have the same
Father of
Mis. 164–32 God is the Father of *m·*,
father of
Mis. 77–29 or, that man is the father of *m·*.
Ret. 68– 6 never was, . . . the father of *m·*.
findeth
Mis. 252–32 if a *m·* findeth, he goeth and
finite
Peo. 4– 9 could enter finite *m·* through his
first
Mis. 185–27 *The first m· Adam* — *I Cor.* 15 : 45.
  187–14 presuppose . . . to be the first *m·*,
  189–13 "the first *m·*," — *I Cor.* 15 : 45.
Un. 30–14 "The first *m·* Adam — *I Cor.* 15 : 45.
forbade
Un. 54–20 God forbade *m·* to know evil
forbids
Mis. 145–14 vanity forbids *m·* to be vain ;
forever in
'02. 9–21 should abide forever in *m·*.
forever reflects
Un. 39–23 *m·* forever reflects and embodies Life,
furnishes
Mis. 258–27 furnishes *m·* with the only
gains the power
Mis. 182–11 *m·* gains the power to become
gave
Mis. 373–24 God gave *m·* dominion
genuine
Un. 49–13 only living God and the genuine *m·*.
gift to
Mis. 181– 3 sonship a personal gift to *m·*,
give
'02. 7– 9 give *m·* the true idea of God
gives
Mis. 97– 2 gives *m·* ability to rise above
'02. 9– 1 gives *m·* power with untold
My. 268–23 gives *m·* the victory over himself.
gives to
My. 129–22 divine law gives to *m·* health
giveth
Un. 39–18 gave and giveth *m·* dominion
God and
  (*see* **God**)
Godlike
Mis. 178– 7 wanted to become a Godlike *m·*.
No. 20– 7 Truth is moulding a Godlike *m·*.
'01. 7– 4 C. S. makes *m·* Godlike.
My. 161–28 the Godlike *m·* said,

man

godly
Pul. 32–26 * was known as a "godly *m·*,"
God or
No. 23–25 we cannot understand God or *m·*,
27–24 personality of God or *m·*
God's
Mis. 36– 2 mortal man, is neither God's *m·* nor
167– 2 infantile thought of God's *m·*,
Un. 46– 6 for he is God's *m·* ;
God to
Ret. 31– 5 "the ways of God" to *m·*. — *Job* 40 : 19.
68–27 thoughts, passing from God to *m·*"
My. 208–17 ministrations of God to *m·*.
God warned
Mis. 24–27 God warned *m·* not to believe the
good
Mis. 122– 1 substitution of a good *m·* to
166–31 a good carpenter, and a good *m·*,
192– 1 When we speak of a good *m·*,
202– 5 * where the good *m·* meets his fate
257–30 Even the chamber where the good *m·*
No. 17–12 can never be less than a good *m·* ;
'00. 3–18 good *m·* loves the right thinker
8– 4 good *m·* imparts knowingly and
'01. 32–19 explain in a few words a good *m·*.
Hea. 3–19 it signified a "good *m·*," — *John* 7 : 12.
My. 306– 6 philosophy of a great and good *m·*,
333–20 * records that this good *m·*,
goodness in
Mis. 164– 5 presentation of goodness in *m·*.
good will to
My. 201– 6 love and good will to *m·*,
govern
Mis. 59–21 should and does govern *m·*.
governed
My. 247– 5 *m·* governed by his creator is
254–26 *m·* governed by his creator is
governing
Mis. 37– 3 governing *m·* or the universe.
government of
Ret. 90–30 leave with God the government of *m·*.
governs
Man. 40– 8 divine Love alone governs *m·* ;
Rud. 10– 5 know that God alone governs *m·* ;
gray-haired
My. 310–24 * a gray-haired *m·* of fifty,
great
Mis. 312–10 chapter sub-title
guides
Mis. 118– 6 scientific understanding guides *m·*.
half
Pan. 3– 4 animal, half goat and half *m·*,
half a
No. 29–13 * a sick body is not half a *m·*."
has power
Mis. 180–25 assures us that *m·* has power
having all
My. 5–10 *m·* having all that God gives.
heals
Mis. 20– 2 heals *m·* spontaneously,
health to
Peo. 12–26 if He would, give health to *m·* ;
My. 219–17 giving of life and health to *m·*
heart of
Mis. 203–10 so the heart of *m·* — *Prov.* 27 : 19.
My. 189–16 creates in the heart of *m·* ;
helping
Mis. 49–23 that are helping *m·* Godward :
heritage of
Mis. 259–15 and was the heritage of *m·* ;
highest style of
No. 10– 8 is the highest style of *m·* ;
His power in
'02. 10–27 to God and His power in *m·*.
history of
Un. 50–27 as the history of *m·*, disappears,
holding
Mis. 83– 2 holding *m·* forever in the
holds
Mis. 77–16 it holds *m·* in endless Life
No. 26–22 God holds *m·* in the eternal
honest
Mis. 166–30 It made him an honest *m·*,
My. 272– 1 is an honest *m·* or woman
321–11 * Mr. Wiggin was an honest *m·*
ideal
Mis. 77–15 to support their ideal *m·*.
102– 2 stature of Christ, the ideal *m·*.
205–21 in Christian metaphysics the ideal *m·*
235–20 know something of the ideal *m·*,
Ret. 68– 7 spiritual idea, or ideal *m·*,
idea of
Mis. 62– 1 Holding the *right* idea of *m·*
166–17 the idea of *m·* was not understood

man

identifies
My. 165–17 goodness identifies *m·* with
image of
Mis. 62– 4 the opposite image of *m·*,
immortal
Mis. 17–23 a mortal, not the immortal *m·*.
79–12 Immortal *m·* is the eternal idea of
79–20 A mortal . . . is not immortal *m·* ;
89–28 Immortal *m·*, in God's likeness,
103–21 neither the . . . Maker of immortal *m·*.
186–11 the opposite of *immortal m·*,
332–27 the antipode of immortal *m·*.
Ret. 73– 1 immortal *m·* being spiritual,
No. 25–23 immortal *m·* alone is God's likeness,
25–26 the counterfeit of immortal *m·*.
26– 2 believe . . . identical with immortal *m·*,
27–17 the antipode of immortal *m·*,
29– 3 Immortal *m·* has immortal Soul
immortality of
Mis. 172–28 holiness, and immortality of *m·*.
My. 226–19 evidence of the immortality of *m·*
immortal part of
No. 29–14 the immortal part of *m·* a sinner?
impart to
Mis. 72– 9 God is supposed to impart to *m·*
in Christ
Mis. 15–25 stature of *m·* in Christ appears.
No. 19–25 the stature of *m·* in Christ.
My. 103–13 attains the stature of *m·* in Christ
includes
Pan. 12– 8 for the universe includes *m·*
including
Mis. 23–20 The universe, including *m·*,
41–28 governs the universe, including *m·*,
56–30 created the universe, including *m·*,
333–21 to the universe, including *m·*
361–25 spiritual universe, including *m·*
Un. 32– 6 *m·*, including the universe,
individual
Un. 49– 2 I believe in the individual *m·*,
individuality of
Un. 53– 8 reality and individuality of *m·*
Rud. 13– 9 not the actual individuality of *m·*
in God's image
Man. 15– 8 *m·* in God's image and likeness.
My. 273–30 *m·* in God's image and likeness
in His image
'00. 5–16 *m·* in His image and likeness,
My. 117–21 *m·* in His image and likeness,
261–14 *m·* in His image and likeness.
in Science
Mis. 41–26 manifestation of *m·* in Science.
Un. 40– 5 *m·* in Science never dies.
42–13 *M·*, in Science, is as perfect and
'02. 8–26 Christ Jesus reckoned *m·* in Science,
intellectual
My. 309– 2 a well-informed, intellectual *m·*,
intelligence of
Mis. 200–10 Life, and intelligence of *m·*.
in the image
Mis. 294– 1 *m·* in the image of his Maker ;
308–30 *m·* in the image and likeness of God.
My. 347– 4 *m·* in the image and likeness of the
in the likeness
Mis. 61–30 *m·* in the likeness of Spirit
in the moon
My. 206–12 Seeing a *m·* in the moon,
intoxicates a
Mis. 288–32 Whatever intoxicates a *m·*,
is a celestial
No. 26–24 *M·* is a celestial ;
is aroused
My. 308– 6 to say that *m·* is aroused to thought or
is as definite
Un. 49– 5 *m·* is as definite and eternal as God,
is coexistent
Mis. 190– 8 *m·* is coexistent with Mind,
Un. 49– 3 *m·* is coexistent with God,
is dominant
Mis. 297–23 *m·* is dominant over the animal,
is eternal
Mis. 287– 3 forever fact that *m·* is eternal
is foremost
Mis. 57–31 wherein *m·* is foremost.
is forever
Mis. 82–17 *m·* is forever unfolding the
Un. 62– 5 *m·* is forever His image
is found
Mis. 15–23 until *m·* is found to be the image of
Ret. 73– 7 *m·* is found in the reflection of
Un. 3–17 *m·* is found in the image and likeness
is free
My. 119– 8 *M·* is free from the flesh
is free born
Mis. 183–10 *M·* is free born :

man

is Godlike
'02. 8–24 whereby m· *is* Godlike.
is God's child
Un. 15– 9 M· is God's child and image.
is God's image
Mis. 183–12 M· is God's image and likeness ;
is God's likeness
Mis. 61–29 the logic that m· is God's likeness.
is healed
Hea. 14– 5 m· is healed morally and physically.
is His image
Mis. 21–21 m· is His image and likeness.
23–23 m· is His image and likeness.
'01. 5–21 m· is His image and likeness :
is His likeness
Rud. 11– 7 in Science m· is His likeness,
is immortal
Mis. 34–21 M· is im-mortal, and there is not a
61–25 but m· is *immortal.*
89–24 M· is immortal.
is improved
Un. 36–19 m· is improved physically,
is its master
'01. 14–28 therefore m· is its master.
is made
Un. 22– 2 Because m· is made after God's
Pul. 30–18 * m· is made in His image.
is more
No. 25– 9 M· is more than physical personality,
is mortal
No. 5–21 then . . . m· is mortal.
is My idea
Un. 62–22 m· is My idea, never in matter,
is not absorbed
No. 25–19 M· is not absorbed in Deity ;
My. 119– 7 we learn that m· is not absorbed
is not annihilated
Mis. 42– 4 M· is not annihilated,
is not equal
Mis. 46–14 M· is not equal with his Maker ;
255– 5 M· is not equal to his Maker.
is not fallen
Mis. 259–19 In this . . . m· is not fallen :
is not material
Mis. 21–21 Therefore m· is not material ,
is not met
Mis. 173–22 m· is not met by another
is not mortal
Mis. 385–20 M· is not mortal, never of the dead :
Po. 48–14 M· is not mortal, never of the dead :
is perfect
Mis. 46–29 m· is perfect even as the Father,
286–30 m· is perfect even as the Father
Pan. 11–11 Governed by . . . m· is perfect.
is person
'01. 5–11 M· is person ;
is reflected
Un. 51–25 m· is reflected not as human
is saved
Man. 16– 1 that m· is saved through Christ,
is seen
Mis. 62– 8 M· is seen only in the true
Hea. 11– 5 m· is seen wholly apart from
is spiritual
Rud. 5– 7 m· is spiritual and eternal,
is the cause
Po. 65–23 m· is the cause of its tear.
is the climax
No. 17–13 M· is the climax of creation ;
is the idea
Mis. 5–26 m· is the idea of infinite Mind,
78–26 m· is the idea of God ;
247–22 m· is the idea of infinite Mind,
is the image
Mis. 61–21 m· is the image and likeness of God.
No. 25–17 M· is the image and likeness of God,
My. 262– 2 m· is the image, idea, or likeness
is the offspring
Mis. 82–15 M· is the offspring and idea of
181–17 m· is the offspring of Spirit,
Ret. 68–28 "M· is the offspring of Spirit.
is the reflection
Un. 51– 1 wherein m· is the reflection of immutable
is the true image
Pan. 11–28 m· is the true image of God,
is the ultimatum
Mis. 79–10 m· is the ultimatum of perfection,
Jesus
Mis. 164–24 human concept of the m· Jesus,
187– 3 The m· Jesus demonstrated over sin,
Ret. 93– 4 appeared . . . as the m· Jesus.
Rud. 3–10 individualized, . . . in the m· Jesus.
My. 348–12 the belief that the m· Jesus,
Jesus as a
Mis. 197–14 concerning Jesus as a m·,

man

just
Mis. 112– 9 most just m· can neither defend the
keeping
Ret. 65–24 keeping m· unspotted from the
killed a
Hea. 18–27 killed a m· by no other means than
knows
Mis. 55–24 M· knows that he can have
My. 104–23 of which a m· knows absolutely
laws of
My. 348–23 laws of m· and the universe,
leading
Un. 42–25 leading m· into the true sense
learned
Hea. 14–11 he is a learned m· and skilful ;
less than
Mis. 145–12 then is he less than m·
Pan. 10– 2 and makes man less than m·.
let us make
Mis. 69–10 "Let us make m· — Gen. 1: 26.
Life of
Mis. 76–26 Soul is the Life of m·.
Ret. 63–15 represents God, the Life of m·.
life of
Mis. 187–21 substance, and life of m· are one,
209–16 neither . . . recuperate the life of m·,
My. 181–10 scientific, sinless life of m·
life of a
'01. 30–19 the inner genial life of a m·,
lifts
Peo. 12–15 lifts m· above the demands of matter.
like unto
Ret. 25–21 personal being, like unto m· ;
limits
Mis. 282– 5 personality, . . . that limits m·.
lives
My. 164–29 M· lives, moves, and has his being
165– 9 by this spirit m· lives and thrives,
195–23 in whom m· lives, moves, and has
love for
Mis. 12–28 our love for God by our love for m· ;
234– 9 In love for m·, we gain a
Pan. 8–23 on the basis of . . . love for m·.
My. 287–15 In love for m· we gain the only
loves
Mis. 100–26 Christian Scientist loves m· more
'00. 3–18 good m· loves the right thinker
love to
Pul. 39– 2 * love to God and love to m·
made
Mis. 77–27 m·, made in God's own likeness,
173–27 made m· in His own likeness.
'01. 7– 9 God made m· in his own image
8–19 As God made m·, is he not wholly
Hea. 9–18 m· made by God had not a
My. 179– 6 allegory, of . . . m· made of dust.
majesty of
My. 188–26 teaches the majesty of m·.
make
Mis. 57–25 Why does the record make m· a
183–32 material senses would make m·,
363–14 "Let us [Spirit] make m· perfect ;"
Un. 32– 4 make m· and the material universe."
54–23 knowledge of evil would make m· a
Pan. 8–26 They make m· the servant of
Peo. 10–14 Justice and truth make m· free,
My. 235–15 Did God make m·? Yes.
makes
Mis. 24– 2 makes m· spiritually minded.
Pan. 10– 2 makes m· less than man.
'01. 7– 4 C. S. makes m· Godlike.
8–21 makes m· none too transcendental,
13–17 When m· makes something of sin
'02. 8–22 it makes m· active,
8–30 makes m· conscious that God is his
manner of
Mis. 370–22 What manner of m· is it that
man's
Un. 46– 6 while ours is man's m·.
material
(see **material**)
material sense of
Mis. 15–28 mortal and material sense of m·,
matter and
My. 153–32 pointing away from matter and m·
meaning woman
My. 268–31 m· meaning woman as well,
measures
Mis. 172–12 unerring Mind measures m·,
meekest
Mis. 163– 9 the meekest m· on earth.
Mind and
Mis. 24–20 Mind and m· are immortal ;
Mind governs
Mis. 51–16 and Mind governs m·.

man

mislead
My. 5–31 may mesmerize and mislead *m·* ;
misname
No. 27–20 personality, which we misname *m·*,
misnamed
Un. 38– 1 mortal mind which is misnamed *m·*,
model of
Peo. 10–20 marred in mind the model of *m·*.
moral status of the
Mis. 45–14 moral status of the *m·* demands
mortal
 (*see* **mortal**)
must live
My. 164–30 *m·* must live, he cannot die ;
must reflect
Mis. 16–13 *m·* must reflect the full dominion
named
Mis. 186–16 the divine idea named *m·* ;
Un. 49– 7 sinner, wrongly named *m·*.
name of a
Hea. 3–16 Jesus is the name of a *m·*
nature and
Mis. 258–32 and shows that nature and *m·* are
My. 152–28 Principle of nature and *m·*,
nature of
Mis. 287–18 higher nature of *m·* governs
need of
My. 260–27 supplies every need of *m·*.
needs of
Mis. 3–10 applicable to all the needs of *m·*.
 259–29 applicable to all the needs of *m·*.
My. 349–30 supplying all the needs of *m·*.
never cursed
Hea. 9–17 God never cursed *m·*,
new
Pul. 84– 7 * shall stand the new *m·*
Pan. 11– 5 put on the new *m·*, — *Col.* 3 : 10.
no
Mis. 76–17 no *m·* can rationally reject his
 89– 1 "No *m·* can serve two — *Matt.* 6 : 24.
 113– 8 "no *m·* might buy or sell, — *Rev.* 13 : 17.
 153–19 no *m·* who honors Him not
 181– 1 Jesus said to call no *m·* father ;
 197– 9 unless this be so, no *m·* can be
 269– 6 "No *m·* can serve two — *Matt.* 6 : 24.
 269–30 "no *m·* might buy or sell, — *Rev.* 13 : 17.
 287– 6 "Call no *m·* your father — *Matt.* 23 : 9.
 365– 3 can no *m·* lay than that — *I Cor.* 3 : 11.
Ret. 68–13 "call no *m·* your father — *Matt.* 23 : 9.
 75–14 no *m·* which shall do — *Mark* 9 : 39.
Un. 53–26 "Call no *m·* your father — *Matt.* 23 : 9.
 64– 9 can no *m·* lay than that — *I Cor.* 3 : 11.
Rud. 14– 4 "owe no *m·*." — *Rom.* 13 : 8.
No. 21–24 can no *m·* lay than that — *I Cor.* 3 : 11.
 22–16 No *m·* hath seen the person of
 27–19 * "No *m·* living hath yet seen man."
Pan. 8–18 "Call no *m·* your father — *Matt.* 23 : 9.
 12–14 a door that no *m·* can shut ;
'00. 14– 5 no *m·* take thy crown." — *Rev.* 3 : 11.
 14–22 and no *m·* shutteth, — *Rev.* 3 : 7.
 14–22 and no *m·* openeth ;" — *Rev.* 3 : 7.
'01. 30–20 No *m·* or woman is roused to
'02. 16–13 without which no *m·* shall — *Heb.* 12 : 14.
 17–18 to be willing . . . to hate no *m·*,
Hea. 16–28 No *m·* cometh unto the — *John* 14 : 6.
My. 41– 1 * how great no *m·* can number
 114– 3 Owe no *m·* ; be temperate ;
 160–28 but of the time no *m·* knoweth.
 185–15 the trinity no *m·* can sunder.
 191– 2 "No *m·* can do these — *John* 3 : 2.
 202–10 Owe no *m·* — *Rom.* 13 : 8.
 324–30 * no *m·* could have done so any better.
 353–17 to injure no *m·*, but to bless all
 356–22 No *m·* can serve two — *Matt.* 6 : 24.
 364– 2 "Judge no *m·*." — *John* 8 : 15.
no part of
Pan. 10–30 constitute no part of *m·*,
normal state of
Mis. 200– 3 good as the normal state of *m·*,
nor matter
'01. 4–12 neither *m·* nor matter can
not
Mis. 332–26 Not *m·*, but a mortal
Un. 32–25 not *m·* (the image of God)
No. 25–24 that which is mortal is not *m·*
My. 231–14 as God, not *m·*, directs.
obscure
Pan. 10–30 no part of man, but obscure *m·*.
of business
Mis. 147–23 the conscientious *m·* of business,
of Galilee
Pan. 8– 6 Jesus, the *m·* of Galilee,
of God
Mis. 159–19 the *m·* of God, the risen Christ,

man

of himself
Pul. 73–22 * *m·* of himself has no power,
of integrity
Mis. 147–14 The *m·* of integrity is one who
of joys
Mis. 84–14 *m·* of joys, his spiritual self,
of sorrows
Mis. 84–14 "*m·* of sorrows" — *Isa.* 53 : 3.
Un. 55– 4 "a *m·* of sorrows, — *Isa.* 53 : 3.
'02. 18– 5 made him a *m·* of sorrows.
old
Mis. 15–23 lay off the "old *m·*," — *Col.* 3 : 9.
Pul. 33–18 * an old *m·* with a snowy beard
No. 27–21 old *m·* and his deeds," — *see Col.* 3 : 9.
Pan. 11– 4 old *m·* with his deeds ; — *Col.* 3 : 9.
Hea. 18– 4 "the old *m·*" — *Col.* 3 : 9.
Po. v– 9 * poem
 page 1 poem
My. 308–16 * old *m·* tramping doggedly
one
Mis. 295–22 wholly represented by one *m·*.
My. 239–15 one *m·* and one woman
opposite of
Mis. 187– 9 was to him the opposite of *m·*,
or a woman
'01. 13– 1 a *m·* or a woman, a place or a thing,
or beast
'01. 20– 8 to harm either *m·* or beast.
or God
Ret. 71–19 without the permission of *m·* or God,
originated
Mis. 57– 6 *M·* originated not from dust,
origin of
Mis. 75–27 the spiritual origin of *m·*.
 165–32 virgin origin of *m·* according to
Un. 30– 1 Spirit as the sole origin of *m·*,
or the universe
Mis. 37– 3 governing *m·* or the universe.
 164–12 Principle of *m·* or the universe,
or woman
Mis. 123–13 or a miscalled *m·* or woman !
 228– 9 To be a great *m·* or woman,
 297–18 A *m·* or woman, having
'01. 30–20 No *m·* or woman is roused to
My. 152–26 matter, *m·*, or woman can never
 159–12 greatest *m·* or woman on earth
 165–28 The best *m·* or woman is the most
 194– 9 a silent, grand *m·* or woman,
 259–20 and nothing less is *m·* or woman.
 272– 1 is an honest *m·* or woman
outlives
No. 25–12 *M·* outlives finite mortal definitions
perfect
Mis. 18– 2 original likeness of perfect *m·*,
 97–28 I have not seen a perfect *m·*
 186–24 cannot produce a less perfect *m·*
 363–14 "Let us [Spirit] make *m·* perfect ;"
 363–15 a perfect *m·* would not desire to
Ret. 42–15 "Mark the perfect *m·*, — *Psal.* 37 : 37.
No. 20–13 a perfect *m·*, and divine Science.
 27–24 hath seen God or a perfect *m·* ?
My. 187–10 to demonstrate the perfect *m·*
 196–13 the same is a perfect *m·*, — *Jas.* 3 : 2.
 262– 1 God creates *m·* perfect
perfectibility of
Mis. 98–21 the perfectibility of *m·*.
perfecting of
My. 342–23 and the perfecting of *m·*
perfection of
Mis. 173–24 The perfection of *m·* is intact ;
personal
Mis. 97–20 Is there a personal *m·* ?
personality of
Mis. 97–32 the real personality of *m·*.
person of
No. 29–15 a disparagement of the person of *m·*
Hea. 5–23 relying not on the . . . person of *m·*
physical
Ret. 88– 7 Truth called the physical *m·* from
physically
Mis. 252–20 to *m·* physically, as well as
popular
My. 314– 9 was a popular *m·*, and considered a
possible to
Mis. 183–13 possible to *m·* as God's reflection.
predicating
My. 207–24 predicating *m·* upon divine Science.
preserver of
Pan. 4– 6 creator and preserver of *m·*.
 4–19 chapter sub-title
 4–20 is indeed the preserver of *m·*.
 7–10 God, the preserver of *m·*,
prevent a
Mis. ix– 3 * noblest charity is to prevent a *m·*

man

Principle of
(*see* **Principle**)
profane
  Mis. 45–12 *Can an atheist or a profane m·*
prove
  Un. 40– 7 in order to prove *m·* deathless.
punish
  Mis. 198–29 seems to punish *m·* for doing good,
punishes
  Peo. 8– 8 punishes *m·* eternally,
puzzles the
  '00. 6–15 spiritual sense that puzzles the *m·.*
quarrel with a
  My. 270–28 I would no more quarrel with a *m·*
quibbled
  Pul. 9–12 so, when *m·* quibbled over an
real
  Mis. 61–12 real *m·*, who was created in the
        104–27 to be God and the real *m·.*
        186–32 real *m·* in God's likeness,
        235–21 real *m·*, harmonious and
  Ret. 22–18 The real *m·* is not of the dust,
        60–27 or of the real *m·* and God.
        64– 7 makes apparent, the real *m·*,
        74– 6 the individual, or real *m·*
        86–14 that you may behold the real *m·*,
  Un. 46– 5 We do not see much of the real *m·*
  Pan. 11– 2 to perceive the real *m·*,
  My. 272–11 real *m·* was, is, and ever shall be
        319– 3 spiritual ideal is the only real *m·*
reality of
  Mis. 187– 8 as the reality of *m·* ;
  Un. 46– 8 individuality and reality of *m·* ;
recognize
  Mis. 198–16 recognize *m·* as governed by God,
redeems
  Mis. 17–16 redeems *m·* from under the curse
reflected in
  Un. 14–24 Mind must be reflected in *m·*,
reflects
  Mis. 17–20 *m·* reflects the divine power
        184– 7 only when *m·* reflects God in body
  '01. 5–21 *m·* reflects Spirit, not matter.
  My. 124–18 Nature reflects *m·*
reinstate
  Peo. 14–18 reinstate *m·* in God's own image
relative to
  Mis. 187–12 accepted as true relative to *m·.*
religious
  Ret. 5– 3 was a very religious *m·*,
remarkable
  My. 307–22 he was a remarkable *m·.*
represents
  Mis. 46–25 *m·* represents his divine Principle,
requires
  Mis. 367– 3 Science requires *m·* to be honest,
reveal
  Mis. 164–28 reveal *m·* collectively, as individually,
  My. 5– 8 to reveal *m·* as God's image,
        124–19 remains for Science to reveal *m·*
reveals
  Mis. 5– 4 Science reveals *m·* as spiritual,
        185–21 reveals *m·* infinitely blessed,
righteous
  Mis. 119–10 impotent to turn the righteous *m·*
rights of
  (*see* **rights**)
rises
  My. 238–16 *m·* rises above the letter, law, or
save
  Ret. 63–18 and so to save *m·* from it?
  Un. 18– 6 may say that God can never save *m·*
saved
  Mis. 197– 8 *m·* saved from sin, sickness, and
saves
  My. 348–13 divine Principle, God, saves *m·*,
Saviour of
  My. 293–30 And the Saviour of *m·* saith :
Science of
  Mis. 14–11 the Science of *m·* could never
        186–18 let us not lose this Science of *m·*,
  '02. 2– 8 The Science of *m·* and the universe,
  My. 350–10 the cosmos and Science of *m·.*
Science saith to
  Mis. 101–21 but Science saith to *m·*,
scientific
  Un. 46– 9 scientific *m·* and his Maker
seen
  No. 27–19 * "No man living hath yet seen *m·.*"
seen in
  '01. 5–26 nature of God must be seen in *m·*,
sees
  Mis. 228–21 Whatever *m·* sees, feels, or
seeth
  Pan. 1–15 what a *m·* seeth he hopeth not for,

man

sense of
  (*see* **sense**)
sentencing a
  '02. 10–28 is like sentencing a *m·* for
separated
  Un. 52–11 *m·* separated from his Maker.
shall keep
  Mis. 175–13 *M·* shall keep the feast of Life,
shall utilize
  Mis. 69– 8 *m·* shall utilize the divine power.
shines
  Ret. 57–15 *M·* shines by borrowed light.
showed
  No. 21–11 showed *m·* as reflecting God
shows
  My. 41–24 * shows *m·* that his real estate is
sick
  Mis. 69–14 called to visit a sick *m·*
        69–30 Had that sick *m·* dominion over the
        130–14 has to make a *m·* sick?
  Hea. 12–14 never made a *m·* sick.
  My. 339–29 The fact that he healed the sick *m·*
so-called
  Mis. 294– 2 infirmity of evil is so-called *m·*,
  Hea. 17– 8 the material so-called *m·*,
  My. 239–25 so-called *m·* born of the flesh,
Son of
  (*see* **Son**)
son of
  (*see* **son**)
Soul of
  Rud. 1– 7 the Soul of *m·* and the universe.
soul of
  My. 344– 9 * "And the soul of *m·*?"
soweth
  Mis. 66– 7 "Whatsoever a *m·* soweth, — *Gal.* 6 : 7.
        105–29 "Whatsoever a *m·* soweth, — *Gal.* 6 : 7.
        348– 4 whatsoever a *m·* soweth, that shall he
  No. 32– 9 "Whatsoever a *m·* soweth, — *Gal.* 6 : 7.
  Hea. 5–27 "whatsoever a *m·* soweth, — *Gal.* 6 : 7.
  My. 6– 6 whatsoever a *m·* soweth, — *Gal.* 6 : 7.
spake
  Mis. 76–17 who spake as never *m·* spake,
        269–12 as never *m·* spake," — *see John* 7 : 46.
  Un. 17–16 as never *m·* spake," — *see John* 7 : 46.
spake of
  '02. 8–28 He spake of *m·* not as the
species of
  Un. 51–15 the highest species of *m·*,
spiritual
  (*see* **spiritual**)
spiritualizes
  My. 4– 4 obedience . . . spiritualizes *m·*,
standard of
  Pan. 11–21 original standard of *m·*
stature of
  Mis. 15–25 stature of *m·* in Christ appears.
  No. 19–25 of the stature of *m·* in Christ.
  My. 103–13 attains the stature of *m·* in Christ
status of
  Mis. 183–31 arrive at the true status of *m·*
  Un. 39–21 declare the immortal status of *m·*,
strength is in
  My. 162– 6 Strength is in *m·*, not in muscles ;
strong
  Pul. 62–10 * required a strong *m·* to ring them,
subject of
  Mis. 185–29 reasoning on this subject of *m·*
such a
  My. 318–25 * was such a *m·* as Christ Jesus?"
suitable
  Man. 100–26 If a suitable *m·* is not obtainable
suspects
  Hea. 1–16 * *m·* suspects himself a fool :
teach
  Mis. 229–15 would teach *m·* as David taught :
        330–24 lessons teach *m·* to be kind,
tell a
  Pul. 15– 9 to tell a *m·* his faults,
testify that
  Un. 39–22 which testify that *m·* dies.
that
  Mis. 122– 4 but woe to that *m·* — *Matt.* 18 : 7.
        123– 8 That *m·* can break the forever-law
        187–28 That *m·* must be evil before he
        353–18 "You must pay that *m·.*"
  Ret. 36– 3 that *m·* would not expound the
        42–15 end of *that m· is* — *Psal.* 37 : 37.
  Un. 42– 9 That *m·* must be vicious before
  Rud. 9– 1 last state of that *m·* — *Matt.* 12 : 45.
  Pan. 4–16 but that *m·* also is a creator,
  '01. 12– 4 If St. John should tell that *m·* that
the generic term
  My. 347– 5 *m·* the generic term for mankind."

man

the only
Mis. 188–30   was the first, the only *m·*.

the supposer
Mis. 332–25   Is *m·* the supposer, false believer,

thinks
Hea.   6–18   *M·* thinks he is a medium of
My. 271– 9   what a *m·* thinks or believes

this
Mis. 61–18   * This '*m·*' was held responsible
    294–12   The *vice versa* of this *m·*
    312–21   this *m·* must have risen above
Un. 46–11   none other than this *m·*,
My. 162–16   "This *m·* began to build, — *Luke* 14 : 30.

through
Mis. 77–11   God made manifest through *m·*,
'02. 18– 7   power manifested through *m·* ;

thus weds
Un. 17– 8   *m·* thus weds himself with God,

to be Christlike
My. 148–29   summons . . . for *m·* to be Christlike

to God
Un. 51–25   scientific relation of *m·* to God,

to man
Mis. 203–10   so the heart of *m·* to man." — *Prov.* 27 : 19.
My. 124–19   for Science to reveal *m·* to man ;

to show
'02. 17–21   to show *m·* the beauty of holiness

towards
My. 262–28   letting good will towards *m·*,

tributary to
Un. 13– 3   theology makes God tributary to *m·*,

true
Mis. 18–15   true *m·* and true woman,
Un. 2–14   The true *m·*, really *saved*,
No. 17– 8   impossible for the true *m·*

truth of
Mis. 57–12   truth of *m·* had been demonstrated,

uneducated
My. 305– 1   (an obscure, uneducated *m·*),

unfit for
Mis. 25–29   are bad and unfit for *m·* ;

universe and
Mis. 65–13   God's universe and *m·* are immortal.
Un. 10–12   The universe and *m·* are the spiritual

unlimited
Mis. 102– 5   finite being, an unlimited *m·*,

unwary
Mis. 119– 7   If a criminal coax the unwary *m·*

upright
Mis. 147–19   The upright *m·* is guided by a fixed

wake in
Mis. 23– 6   * "sleep in the . . . and wake in *m·*"?

wakes in
Pan. 9– 2   * "sleeps in the . . . and wakes in *m·*."

was made
Mis. 97–21   *m·* was made in the image and likeness

was never lost
Mis. 182–19   *m·* was never lost in Adam,

wedded
My. 269– 4   *m·* wedded to the Lamb,

well-being of
Rud. 12–21   requisite for the well-being of *m·*.

well-bred
'01. 30–29   * honest, sensible, and well-bred *m·*

were begirt
'01. 12–13   Though a *m·* were begirt with the

what manner of
Mis. 296–29   What manner of *m· is* this unknown

who applied
Mis. 353–14   a *m·* who applied for work,

who falls
Pan. 11–19   as the *m·* who falls physically needs

whole
Pul. 9–19   is a very whole *m·*

whole duty of
Mis. 293–22   includes the whole duty of *m·* :
'01. 32–21   is the whole duty of *m·*.

wicked
Mis. 191– 9   refers to a wicked *m·* as the devil :
    257– 5   and wakes in a wicked *m·*.
'00. 8–10   A wicked *m·* has little real
Hea. 9–18   God never made a wicked *m·* ;

will ere long
Peo. 8–26   and that *m·* will ere long stop

will lift
Peo. 3– 1   will lift *m·* ultimately to the

will naturally
My. 188–28   *m·* will naturally seek the Science of

will of
Mis. 180–23   *nor of the will of m·*, — *John* 1 : 13.
    181–17   nor of the will of *m·*, — *John* 1 : 13.
    182–17   "Nor of the will of *m·*." — *John* 1 : 13.

will receive
Un. 6– 6   *m·* will receive a higher selfhood,

will then claim
Mis. 196– 3   *m·* will then claim no mind apart from

wise
Man. 41– 9   The wise *m·* saith,
My. 135– 2   The wise *m·* has said,

with God
Un. 5–24   marvellous unity of *m·* with God

with the smallpox
Mis. 344–15   or to a *m·* with the smallpox?

woman or a
My. 343– 8   a woman or a *m·*.

work of
Ret. 77– 5   * the noblest work of *m·*."

would enable
'00. 5–18   it would enable *m·* to escape from

wrath of
Mis. 41– 6   "the wrath of *m·*" — *Psal.* 76 : 10.
No. 7–17   wrath of *m·* cannot hide it from Him.
    8–13   make the wrath of *m·* to praise Him,
    33– 1   wrath of *m·* shall praise Him.
'02. 1–12   "the wrath of *m·* — *Psal.* 76 : 10.
My. 111– 2   "the wrath of *m·* — *Psal.* 76 : 10.
    151–10   "The wrath of *m·* — *Psal.* 76 : 10.

wrench from
Mis. 246– 7   influenced the people to wrench from *m·*

young
Mis. 201–28   the young *m·* is awakened to
Ret. 7– 7   * young *m·* of uncommon promise.
My. 149–14   a young *m·* vainly boasted,

Mis. 2–24   If *m·* should not progress after
    3–14   is *m·* healed and saved.
    6– 2   bring *m·* nearer to God,
    11– 5   if a *m·* should aim a ball at
    14– 9   It is urged that, . . . *m·* has fallen
    14–14   if *m·* has lost his Principle
    18–22   *m·* could never separate himself from
    22– 3   neither a law of matter nor of *m·*.
    47–21   *m·*, His image and likeness
    48–14   made a *m·* drunk on water,
    51–27   * *M·* in the sunshine of the world's
    57–29   the scale of being up to *m·*.
    61–15   * the *m·* is held responsible for
    61–16   * where a *m·* was said to be 'hanged
    61–24   a sinner, — anything but a *m·* !
    64–27   wherefore *m·* is thus conditioned,
    65–31   by *m·* shall his blood be — *Gen.* 9 : 6.
    67– 8   thou shalt not rob *m·* of money,
    69–26   The *m·* is living yet ;
    70– 7   As a *m·* "thinketh in his — *Prov.* 23 : 7.
    70– 9   the *m·* was well.
    71–25   *m·* is incapable of originating :
    72– 4   Science sets aside *m·* as a creator,
    76– 4   "If a *m·* keep my saying, — *John* 8 : 51.
    77–28   or, that *m·* is the father of man.
    79– 7   *m·* was, and is, God's perfect
    82–13   *Is there infinite progression with m·*
    97–13   we have not seen all of *m·* ;
    123–27   not through the *death* of a *m·*,
    129–15   If a *m·* is jealous, envious, or
    131– 7   *m·* of more than average avoirdupois
    144–15   *m·* shall be as an — *Isa.* 32 : 2.
    153– 1   than in *m·* and his material ways
    161–10   in Science, *m·* is the son of God.
    165– 8   *m·*, without the fetters of the flesh,
    173–14   says that *m·* is both matter and
    173–16   must not *m·* have preexisted
    173–19   to pretend that it is *m·*?
    174–10   religious sentiment within *m·*.
    183– 5   *M·* must love his neighbor as himself,
    184– 2   by claiming that . . . *m·* is matter ;
    184– 2   claiming that . . . *m·* is evil ;
    184– 3   by claiming that . . . *m·* dies.
    184–14   If *m·* should say of the power
    185–15   *m·* be clothed with might,
    185–24   how much of a *m·* he ever has been :
    186–15   universal Father and Mother of *m·* ;
    187–23   *m·* is their reflection and glory.
    188– 3   *M·* is as perfect now,
    189–12   *m·* as God's image, or
    189–21   For *m·* to know Life as it is,
    192– 2   we do not mean that *m·* is God
    194– 7   Though a *m·* were begirt with
    197–29   Let *m·* abjure a theory that is
    198– 2   *m·* has no sinful thoughts
    205–29   *m·* born of the great Forever,
    217–24   and *m·* a rebel against his Maker.
    220–25   people believe that a *m·* is sick
    232–28   of God, and not of *m·* ;
    235– 1   *m·* has a changed recognition of
    241– 4   *m·* will no more enter heaven sick
    245–18   rights that *m·* is bound to respect.
    252–19   It appeals to man as *m·* ;
    253– 4   what *m·* knoweth as did our Master

man

Mis.	255–10	*M·* should be found not claiming
	269–10	Lives there a *m·* who can better
	269–20	*m·* can only be Christianized through
	282– 5	personality in God or in *m·*,
	292–19	Christ enjoins it upon *m·* to help
	308– 2	Until this be done, *m·* will never
	330– 9	And *m·*, more friendly, should
	354–24	not by *m·* or laws material,
	363– 5	molecule and monkey up to *m·*,
	380– 6	time, space, immortality, *m·*
Man.	29–21	shall be a *m·* and a woman,
Chr.	53–48	Mind, mother, *m·*.
	55–14	*M·* that is born of a — *Job* 14 : 1.
Ret.	35–23	Though a *m·* were girt with the
	48–20	health, hope, and harmony to *m·*,
	59– 2	to believe *m·* has a finite and
	60– 2	and *m·* as very far from the
	64–16	*M·* that is in honor, — *Psal.* 49 : 20.
Un.	4–17	God has not forbidden *m·* to know Him ;
	14– 6	earth, *m·*, animals, plants,
	14–24	How then could *m·* escape,
	14–27	God never said that *m·* would
	15–10	If God knows evil, so must *m·*,
	15–12	If *m·* must be destroyed by
	15–16	called . . . *m·* the *sinful* ;
	24–14	*m·*, whose source is infinite Mind.
	26–14	* *M·* decays and ages move ;
	26–19	can it be also true . . . that *m· decays?*
	28– 8	define Soul as something within *m·?*
	37– 4	Must *m·* die, then, in order to
	39–14	*M·* has no underived power.
	39–25	They presuppose . . . that *m·* is evil,
	39–26	that Deity is deathless, but that *m·*
	51–14	*M·* is the generic term for
	59–21	calls sin real, and *m·* a sinner,
	59–22	calls sickness real, and *m·* an invalid,
	62–28	and that of His idea, *m·* ;
Pul.	4– 7	Is not a *m·* metaphysically and
	13–29	brought forth the *m·* child. — *Rev.* 12 : 13.
	16–15	Then, O *m·* ! Like this stone,
	82–15	* was created solely for *m·*.
Rud.	5–11	Lives there a *m·* who has ever
	7– 9	*m·* is the manifest reflection of God.
	7–13	According to . . . *m·* is material,
	8–18	The *m·* who calls himself a
No.	3– 7	hands of God, than of *m·*.
	11– 3	*M·* has an immortal Soul,
	11– 5	*M·* has perpetual individuality ;
	12–28	*m·* the reflection of His power
	17–12	and for *m·* to be more than
	19–15	*m·* is His individualized idea.
	19–21	*m·* is in His image and likeness.
	24– 6	according to Spinoza, *m·* is
	25– 8	chapter sub-title
	25–13	*M·* is the eternal idea of
	26–14	*m·* can no more relapse or collapse
	28–24	chapter sub-title
	31–27	"If a *m·* keep my saying, — *John* 8 : 51.
	45–14	rights which *m·* is bound to respect.
	46–19	*M·* has a noble destiny ;
Pan.	7–10	declared that *m·* should die,
	9–26	chapter sub-title
	10– 3	"If a *m·* think himself to be — *Gal.* 6 : 3.
	11–14	will demonstrate *m·* to be superior
	11–16	If *m·* is spiritually fallen,
'00.	3– 1	"When a *m·* is right,
	4– 3	couples . . . life and death, with *m·*
	6–19	a *m·* who uses tobacco,
'01.	8–13	Is *m·*, according to C. S.,
	8–17	is *m·* His image and likeness,
	8–18	can *m·* be . . . less than spiritual?
	10–11	*m·* is the generic term for
	20– 5	*M·* is properly self-governed,
	27–26	Mind of God and not of *m·*
	30–23	like the *m·* "clouting his own cloak"
	34–27	*m·* cannot live without it ;
'02.	5–12	For *m·* to be thoroughly subordinated
Hea.	5– 8	if a *m·* has taken cold by
	17– 4	Not by the senses . . . does *m·* get nearer
Peo.	3– 2	as a *m·* "thinketh in his — *Prov.* 23 : 7.
	4– 7	became finity, or *m·*,
	13–13	putting *m·* to the rack for his
My.	5– 3	*m·* is supposed to start from dust
	84–22	* *m·* who cannot reconcile himself to
	104–11	what would be thought to-day of a *m·*
	124–20	O *m·*, what art thou?
	129–15	*m·*, seen through the lens of Spirit,
	131– 9	bread of heaven whereof if a *m·* eat
	149–25	*m·* who could not see London for its
	182–24	health, and immortality to *m·*.
	188–23	convey all impressions to *m·*,
	205–20	*m·* more His likeness,
	216–10	What, then, can a *m·* do with
	235–22	*M·* is but His image and likeness.

man

My.	239–17	His idea, image, or likeness, *m·*,
	239–18	*M·* is the generic term for
	248–17	reality of God, *m·*, nature,
	249–22	a *m·*, rather than a woman,
	268– 6	God hath joined . . . *m·* cannot sunder.
	272– 6	hath made me [*m·*] free — *Rom.* 8 : 2.
	272– 9	no claim that *m·* is equal to God,
	300–18	"If a *m·* keep my saying, — *John* 8 : 51.
	308–31	The *m·* whom *McClure's Magazine*
	316– 6	causing *m·* to love his enemies ;
	341–16	* 'Tis meet that *m·* be meek."
	343– 8	It will be a *m·*."
	343– 9	* "Can you name the *m·*?"
	344–13	absurd to say that when a *m·* dies,
	344–13	*m·* will be at once better than
	346–22	* her successor would be a *m·*.
	346–27	"I did say that a *m·* would be
	347–25	*m·* is not the author of Science,
	348–15	neither *m·* nor *materia medica*,

manage

Man.	79–22	shall hold and *m·* the property

managed

Man.	77–12	have not been properly *m·*,

management

Mis.	283– 8	*m·* of another man's property.
Man.	76– 5	indicates the proper *m·* of
Pul.	55–28	* *m·* of its own affairs.

manager

Man.	26– 1	for the editors and the *m·*
	26– 3	*m·* of the general Committee
	27– 4	*m·* of the general Committee
	78–12	the *m·* of the Committee
	80–22	Editors and *M·*.
	80–23	for the editors and the *m·*
	97– 7	*m·* of the Committees
	101– 2	*m·* of the general Committee
	101– 5	appoint an assistant *m·*,
Pul.	59–22	* *m·* of the Publishing Society,

managers

Mis.	296– 4	its constituents and *m·*

manages

Mis.	226–25	*m·* to evade the law,

Manchester, N. H.

Po.	vi– 3	* *published in M·*, *N. H.*,
My.	105–20	Dr. Davis of *M·*, *N. H.*

mandate

Mis.	66– 8	No . . . lurks in this *m·*,
	74– 9	the stern *m·* of Science,
	283–28	Science is the *m·* of Truth
	394–12	*m·* that speaks from above,
'00.	8–28	you obey the *m·* but retain a
Po.	45–15	*m·* that speaks from above,
My.	302– 2	Through the *m·* of mind

man-face

Pan.	3–31	his *m·*, the celestial world.

manfully

Mis.	118–23	they must be met *m·*

manger

Mis.	320– 9	on the *m·* of our Lord,
No.	36–27	Jesus was a babe born in a *m·*,
My.	262– 8	born in a *m·* amidst the flocks

manhood (*see also* **manhood's**)

Mis.	16– 6	*m·* or womanhood of Christianity,
	33–10	*m·* of God, our divine Father
	84–13	Jesus, as material *m·*, was not
	166– 8	*m·*, and womanhood of Truth
	185–23	no need . . . to measure his *m·*,
	206–16	of what constitutes true *m·*.
	257–25	childhood, age, and *m·*
	324– 6	youth, *m·*, and age gayly tread
Un.	2–25	stature of *m·* in Christ Jesus,
	42–28	wherein true *m·* and womanhood
	51– 9	gained through Christ as perfect *m·*.
	59–14	Jesus appeared . . . and grew to *m·*,
No.	37– 3	in Science his divine nature and *m·*
Pan.	10–24	A higher *m·* is manifest,
'00.	10–24	touching token of unselfed *m·*
'01.	9– 3	referring to . . . his temporal *m·*.
Hea.	10– 6	supposed to have fought the *m·* of
Peo.	13–14	forcing from the lips of *m·* shameful
My.	12–30	gems in the settings of *m·*
	64–21	* realization of ideal *m·*
	272–19	* chapter sub-title
	273–17	presented to youth and to *m·*
	274–12	intellectuality, and happiness in *m·*.
	346–30	*m·* and womanhood of God

mankind

awake
My. 356– 1   When will *m·* awake to know their
benedictions for
Mis. 320– 8   with divine benedictions for *m·*.
beneficial to
Ret. 85– 8   and beneficial to *m·*.
benefit
Mis. 227–20   send forth to benefit *m·* ;
     351–18   nor benefit *m·* by such endeavors.
'01. 20– 4   to serve God and benefit *m·*.
My. 203–28   doing so much to benefit *m·*
benefits
'02. 1–19   honors God and benefits *m·*
beset
Mis. 318–26   Two points of danger beset *m·* ;
better for
Hea. 9– 7   better for *m·*, morally and
Peo. 6– 1   * all the better for *m·*
better part of
Mis. 273–13   as well as the better part of *m·*,
bless
Ret. 11– 8   And live to bless *m·*.
Pul. 87–23   states of mind, to bless *m·*.
Po. 60– 5   And live to bless *m·*.
blessed
My. 232– 7   *m·* blessed, and God glorified.
brings forth
My. 247–20   brings forth *m·* to receive your
common walks of
Mis. 125–24   Apart from the common walks of *m·*,
comprehension of
Mis. 200–15   general comprehension of *m·*
Pul. 84–22   * to the comprehension of *m·*.
concerns
Ret. 88–11   The spiritual . . . most concerns *m·*.
confidence of
Mis. 229–20   The confidence of *m·* in
consecrating
Mis. 291–27   refreshing, and consecrating *m·*.
convictions of
'02. 14–17   common convictions of *m·*
coworkers for
'01. 29–15   grand coworkers for *m·*,
delivering
Mis. 235–10   delivering *m·* from all error
determination of
Mis. 2– 7   strong determination of *m·*
dormant in
Pul. 72–24   * dormant in *m·* for ages,''
effects upon
Mis. 12–27   in its effects upon *m·*,
elevates
My. 130–13   lever which elevates *m·*.
enlightened
Mis. 340–31   have not sufficiently enlightened *m·*.
existence of
Rud. 12–19   health or existence of *m·*,
friends of
My. 213–10   truest friends of *m·*,
gave to
Pul. 53–23   * gave to *m·* the key to health
governs
No. 35–20   and yet governs *m·*.
great need of
Mis. 107–11   More love is the great need of *m·*.
growth of
Mis. 237–23   push on the growth of *m·*.
healed
Mis. 387–17   loved and healed *m·* :
Po. 6–12   loved and healed *m·* :
healing
Mis. ix– 9   healing *m·* morally, physically,
helped
'02. 11–14   each in turn has helped *m·*,
ills of
My. 268–21   solace the sore ills of *m·*
inquiry of
Mis. 307–16   inquiry of *m·* as to Christianity
interest of
My. 339– 2   subserve the interest of *m·*,
laboring for
Mis. 155– 7   Forget self in laboring for *m·* ;
longevity of
My. 265–18   increasing the longevity of *m·*,
love
My. 233–30   as much as they love *m·* ?
love for
My. 288– 8   Love for *m·* is the elevator of the
masses of
My. 181–19   classes and masses of *m·*,
message to
'01. 31–11   entrusted me with a message to *m·*
morals for
Mis. 110–12   makes morals for *m·* !
Pul. 7–15   made morals for *m·*.

mankind

morals of
My. 249–14   fatal to . . . the morals of *m·*,
multiplication of
Mis. 244–11   in the multiplication of *m·* ?
must gravitate
Mis. 267–22   *M·* must gravitate from sense to Soul,
need of
'02. 9–29   has met the need of *m·* with
open to
'00. 9– 9   The secret . . . is open to *m·*,
passing out of
Pan. 12– 7   constantly passing out of *m·*
possibilities of
Mis. 251–19   present possibilities of *m·*.
prevent
Mis. 232–28   prevent *m·* from striking out
receive from
My. 160– 9   that we receive from *m·* justice,
reform
'02. 8–11   No person can . . . reform *m·* unless
reforming
'01. 27–13   healing and reforming *m·*.
regenerating
'02. 9–10   regenerating *m·* and fulfilling
regeneration of
My. 22–17   * for the regeneration of *m·* ;
     352–15   * in the regeneration of *m·*.
regulator of
Mis. 353–19   steer the regulator of *m·*.
saves
Mis. 261–24   has saved, and still saves *m·* ;
My. 260– 2   Life that heals and saves *m·*.
     348–16   God, heals and saves *m·*.
saving
Pul. 6–10   healing and saving *m·*.
servant of
Mis. 266–10   unacknowledged servant of *m·*.
spirituality of
Mis. 245–14   morals, and spirituality of *m·*.
struggling with
Mis. 126– 9   when struggling with *m·* his temper,
taught
My. 163– 4   taught *m·* to win through
teach
Un. 59–16   could reach and teach *m·*
telling
Pul. 15–11   telling *m·* of the foe in
term for
My. 347– 5   man the generic term for *m·*.''
to help
My. 216– 4   in order to help *m·* with it.
to please
Po. 23–18   Than just to please *m·*.
to save
Mis. 229–23   to heal and to save *m·*
'02. 11– 6   waits and pleads to save *m·*
unprofitable to
My. 113– 7   such a book be . . . unprofitable to *m·* ?
unwarned
'01. 19–24   subject *m·* unwarned and undefended
uplift
Mis. 3–29   The tendency . . . is to uplift *m·* ;
uplifts
Mis. 260–22   truth of Mind-healing uplifts *m·*,
No. 45– 9   whatever uplifts *m·*,
war with
'00. 8–22   before we can . . . war with *m·*.
woes of
Peo. 11–23   responsible for all the woes of *m·*
wrongs of
No. 40–18   only the wrongs of *m·*.

Mis. vii–10   And *m·* from the dust ;
     25–17   gives God's infinite meaning to *m·*,
     37– 5   draw *m·* toward purity,
     106–23   How shall *m·* worship the
     107–32   *M·* thinks either too much or
     162– 4   wonderful spiritual import to *m·* !
     246–28   question at issue with *m·* is :
     261–24   by *m·* I mean mortals,
     270– 8   than whom *m·* hath no higher ideal
Man. 42– 8   to God, to his Leader, and to *m·*.
Ret. 72– 6   to benefit himself and *m·*.
Pul. 74–18   the blessing it has been to *m·*
'01. 1– 3   through the mental avenues of *m·*
'02. 14–19   (not by *m·*, but by a kind of men)
     18–20   Jesus laid down his life for *m·* ;
My. 45– 5   * of its adherents and of *m·*.
     117–32   is all that I ask of *m·*.
     212– 5   which makes *m·* drunken.
     215–30   effect of both methods on *m·*.
     222–25   *M·* will be God-governed
     225–20   *M·* almost universally gives to
     239– 8   *m·* will, as aforetime,

mankind
My. 239–12 *Must m· wait for the ultimate of*
239–23 m· . . . is the material, so-called man
264– 5 until m· learn more of my meaning
295–26 You, I, and m· have cause to
303–22 his legacy of truth to m·.
344–27 Were . . . I should tremble for m· ;
348– 1 My discovery that m· is absolutely
350–18 m· . . . dost doom above.

mankind's
Mis. 130–30 m· triumphal march out of the
No. 36–27 M· concept of Jesus was a babe

manlike
Mis. 178– 6 not satisfied with a m· God,
No. 20– 6 would fashion Deity in a m· mould,
'01. 6–29 That God is . . . m·, is not my sense of
7– 3 Scholastic theology makes God m· ;

manly
Mis. 88–17 Its m· honesty follows like a
296–19 Do m· Britons patronize taprooms
325–15 Robust forms, with m· brow
Pul. 60– 7 * clear, m·, and intelligent tones,

man-made
Mis. 38–22 elaborating a m· theory,
64–15 M· theories are narrow,
168–11 not the m· rabbi

man-midwife
Peo. 6– 9 * m·, chemist, druggist, or drug

manna
Mis. 153– 7 they were fed with m· :
My. 31– 6 * "Day by day the m· fell ;"

manner
after the
Mis. 96–15 "after the m· of my — see Acts 24 : 14.
140– 7 even after the m· that all
167– 2 after the m· of a mother
315– 3 after the m· of the Sunday service.
Un. 58– 9 saving himself after the m· that
No. 19–26 after the m· of mortal man,
'01. 33–22 after the m· taught by Jesus,
after this
Mis. 126–30 bard spake after this m· :
Ret. 86–23 After this m· and in no other
Pan. 5–23 After this m· our Master cast out
all
Mis. 8–24 all m· of evil — Matt. 5 : 11.
196– 5 in all m· of subtleties
Ret. 60–18 saith to all m· of disease,
'01. 2– 5 healing all m· of diseases.
3– 5 all m· of evil — Matt. 5 : 11.
24–27 healing all m· of diseases.
34– 3 healing of all m· of diseases.
'02. 11–23 all m· of evil — Matt. 5 : 11.
15– 6 Healing all m· of diseases
My. 104–31 all m· of evil — Matt. 5 : 11.
190–22 power over all m· of diseases ;
214–21 healing all m· of diseases,
219–17 all m· of diseases.
239–10 healing all m· of disease,
245– 1 healing all m· of disease,
316– 8 all m· of evil — Matt. 5 : 11.
364–16 heals all m· of sickness
animated
My. 320–32 * spoke in a very animated m·
any
Mis. 351–10 method of Mind-healing, or in any m·.
Pul. 75– 8 or speak of me in any m· as a
My. 223–22 which relate in any m· to the
301–26 in any m· whatever.
authoritative
My. 326– 7 * official and authoritative m·.
bearing and
Pul. 31–26 * winning in bearing and m·,
best possible
Rud. 15–15 to fill in the best possible m· the
Christian
Man. 97–17 to correct in a Christian m·
Christian spirit and
Man. 77–26 in a Christian spirit and m·,
intelligent
Pul. 69–26 * not done so in an intelligent m·,
like
Un. 21– 7 In like m· good and evil talk to
material
Pul. 63–20 * in a very tangible and material m·
no
Man. 81– 8 shall in no m· be connected with
82– 5 are in no m· connected with these
of man
Mis. 296–28 What m· of man is this unknown
370–16 What m· of man is it that has
of Science
No. 35– 3 What m· of Science were C. S. without

manner
same
Un. 2–17 In the same m· the sick lose their
some
Mis. 295–11 * for some m· of notoriety."
striking
Pul. 45–20 * proved, in most striking m·,
suitable
Man. 61–22 dignified and suitable m·.
way or
Mis. 381–24 in any way or m· disposing of,
wicked
'01. 15–29 * wicked m· of attending

———

Mis. 12–18 in a m· least understood ;
31– 4 To mentally argue in a m· that
32– 7 seem not to know in what m· they
171–14 and see what m· they are of.
My. 69–28 * m· in which the dome seems to
280–28 In no way nor m· did I request
321–18 * m· in which the statements have

manners
Mis. 283–16 breach of good m· and morals ;
313– 5 It is a digest of good m·,
'00. 2–12 he gives little time to society m·
My. 309– 3 cultivated in mind and m·.

manor
Po. 10– 6 Lord of the main and m· !
My. 337– 7 Lord of the main and m· !

manright
Ret. 76– 4 God's law of m·.

man's
Mis. 2–19 God, m· saving Principle,
2–21 M· probation after death is the
16–12 m· ability to meet them is from God ;
17–27 m· primitive, sinless, spiritual
18–26 can we . . . separate one m· interests
30–14 understanding of m· real existence,
46–17 It is possible, and it is m· duty,
47–23 substantiates m· identity,
52–21 M· existence is a problem to be
64– 7 m· indestructible eternal life in God.
65– 6 m· ipse dixit as to the stellar system
65–25 balancing m· account with his Maker.
65–31 "whoso sheddeth m· blood, — Gen. 9 : 6.
68– 5 include also m· changed appearance
70– 2 else the Scriptures misstate m· power.
70– 4 cast out the sick m· illusion,
75– 4 m· possible earthly development.
79– 9 M· origin and existence being in Him,
79–22 immortal m· divine Principle.
96– 1 m· salvation from sickness and
96–19 m· redemption from sickness
98– 2 m· perfect model should be
100–31 stages of m· recovery from sin
105– 2 facts of m· spirituality,
105–13 M· real life or existence
119–17 against m· high destiny.
124–19 m· true sense is filled with peace,
124–32 In proportion to a m· spiritual
129–16 an atom of another m· indiscretion,
151–14 He is m· only real relative
154–10 God only waits for m· worthiness
171– 6 annoint the blind m· eyes
173– 2 human reason, or m· theorems,
173–26 the counterfeit of m· creator
174–29 spiritual facts of m· Life here
175–10 M· Life is God;
181– 3 m· spiritual sonship
181– 4 M· knowledge of this grand verity
181–15 understand m· true birthright,
181–27 gain the sense of m· spiritual
182– 6 perceive m· actual existence
182–15 m· primal, spiritual existence,
183–25 is a denial of m· spiritual sonship ;
183–28 m· "dominion over all the — see Gen. 1 : 26.
184–25 as the seal of m· adoption.
186– 7 far below m· original standard,
186–31 lost sense of m· perfection,
192– 6 infinite importance to m· spiritual
192–20 m· ability to prove the truth of
193–30 the understanding of m· capabilities
196–17 m· unity with his Maker.
198–19 We know that m· body, as matter,
199– 5 m· ability to annul his own erring
205–17 m· identity or consciousness
205–25 Mortal m· repentance and
206– 8 interpret m· eternal existence,
214– 9 m· foes shall be they of — Matt. 10 : 36.
220– 9 to refute the sick m· thoughts,
222– 1 takes away a m· proper sense of

man's

Mis.	229– 8	than he does the sick *m·*.
	234–12	What hinders *m·* progress is
	241– 4	are correlated in *m·* salvation ;
	241–21	*m·* bondage to sin and sickness.
	244–22	And he did this for *m·* example ;
	252–30	wise *m·* spiritual dictionary ;
	252–31	the poor *m·* money ;
	261–25	men after *m·* own making.
	267–28	spiritualizes *m·* motives and
	283– 9	management of another *m·* property.
	286– 9	*m·* oneness with God,
	309–16	true idea of *m·* divine Principle.
	309–22	*M·* individual life is infinitely
	320–13	that calms *m·* fears,
	330–11	*m·* possibilities are infinite,
	331– 7	for *m·* rich heritage.
	362– 5	*m·* reason is at rest in God's
	363–28	the learned *m·* masterpiece,
	363–28	the ignorant *m·* dictionary,
	363–29	the wise *m·* directory.
Man.	15–15	unfolding *m·* unity with God
Ret.	9–24	* to know His voice From *m·*
	10–16	*m·* origin and signification.
	21–14	dreams, not of *m·* real existence,
	61– 1	arises . . . from mortal *m·* ignorance,
	61–10	*m·* harmony is no more to be invaded
	63–16	conspiracy against *m·* Life
	73–15	*m·* spiritual individuality in God,
	77– 3	* honest *m·* the noblest work of
Un.	2– 9	takes away *m·* fondness for sin
	4–20	forbid *m·* acquaintance with evil.
	15– 1	by *m·* first disobedience,
	41–15	*m·* unity with his Maker
	46– 6	while ours is *m·* man.
	53–23	*M·* Father is not a mortal mind
	53–25	*m·* origin and loving Father,
	57– 7	*M·* refuge is in spirituality,
Pul.	vii–21	the actual bliss of *m·* existence
	3–12	*m·* eternal mansion.
	23–24	* intimations of *m·* immortal life.
	82–17	* woman as *m·* proper helpmeet.
No.	23–23	Knowledge of a *m·* physical
	25–22	is not *m·* eternal identity.
	26–16	*M·* real ego, or selfhood,
	26–19	*M·* individual being must reflect
	33–19	*m·* at-one-ment with God ;
	43–28	A *m·* inability to heal,
Pan.	4–27	if these are not *m·* preservers?
	10– 1	takes away *m·* personality
	10–29	does not degrade *m·* personality.
	11–23	belittles *m·* personality.
	11–26	*m·* unfallen spiritual perfectibility.
	12–28	unpierced . . . by *m·* inventions.
'00.	3–20	would destroy this *m·* goodness.
'01.	1–21	better side of *m·* nature
	10–19	*m·* salvation comes through
	13–20	*m·* fear, unconquered, conquers him,
'02.	9–30	enlarges *m·* facilities for
	10–18	If such is *m·* ultimate,
	16–20	and *m·* immortal being.
Hea.	5– 7	learn that *m·* highest happiness,
	19–18	bias a *m·* character.
Peo.	2– 1	Tireless Being, patient of *m·*
	9–28	insures *m·* continuance
	10–16	*m·* harmony and immortality.
	12–19	battles for *m·* whole rights,
My.	5– 4	*m·* salvation from sickness
	105– 3	the outcome of *m·* rib,
	124– 4	*m·* only medicine for mind and body.
	128–10	to every *m·* conscience.'' — *II Cor.* 4 : 2.
	128–14	*m·* inalienable birthright — *Liberty.*
	129–24	*m·* right to adopt a religion,
	134–19	good *m·* heart takes hold on heaven,
	188–24	bless, and inspire *m·* power.
	200–15	one *m·* head lies at another's feet.
	219–14	*m·* soul is safe ;
	222–23	to believe that *m·* Maker is
	244–16	make laws to regulate *m·* religion ;
	267–26	is unquestionably *m·* spiritual state
	267–29	*m·* divine Principle, Love,
	277–10	*m·* spiritual understanding of
	277–12	A bullet in a *m·* heart never
	283–17	sublime question as to *m·* life
	302– 3	Wrong may be a *m·* highest idea
	340–31	according to a *m·* belief,
	350–14	which *m·* diligence has utilized.
		the scalding tear *m·* shedding,

(*see also* **being, individuality**)

mansion

Mis.	239–12	before a stately *m·* ;
	324–13	Within this mortal *m·* are
	325– 1	a massive carved stone *m·*,
Un.	52–25	the most beautiful *m·* is sometimes
Pul.	3–12	Truth and Love, man's eternal *m·*.

mansions

Mis.	140–28	title clear'' to heavenly *m·*.
My.	133– 1	house in which are many *m·*,

manslaughter

My.	227–10	citizens are arrested for *m·*

mantel

Pul.	26–26	* *m·* is of onyx and gold.
	48–20	* photograph . . . adorned the *m·*.
	76–13	* superb *m·* of Mexican onyx

mantle

Pul.	65–23	* Roman soldier parted his *m·*

mantled

Ret.	31–25	tint of humility, . . . *m·* the earth.

Manual (*see also* **Church Manual**)

Mis.	148– 8	Rules and By-laws in the *M·*
Man.	3– 3	Rules and By-Laws in the *M·*
	27– 7	named in the *M·* of this Church
	45–10	specified in The Mother Church *M·*,
	71–19	allowed and named in this *M·*.
	72– 1	*M·*.
	72– 2	nor publish the *M·* of
	72–24	with The Mother Church *M·*.
	80–11	By-Laws contained in this *M·*.
	104–10	*M·* shall not be revised without the
My.	230–11	Rule and By-law in this *M·*
	252– 1	S. and H., and our *M·*,

manual

Un.	6–27	drilled in the plainer *m·*
No.	3–10	people insisted that my *m·* of

manuals

(*see* **organ**)

manufacture

Mis.	232– 8	art, invention, and *m·*.
My.	216– 7	*m·*, agriculture, tariff,
	265–28	agriculture, *m·*, commerce,

manufactured

Mis.	299–21	he *m·* them and owns them,

manufacturer

Mis.	353–13	My brother was a *m·* ;

manufacturing

My.	310–12	*m·* establishment in Tilton, N. H.

manumits

Mis.	124–27	it *m·* mortals ;

manuscript

Mis.	300–19	Your *m·* copy is liable,
My.	59–28	* I read it in *m·* before it was
	272–22	* with the corrections on the *m·*
	273– 2	* This *m·* is presented simply as
	322– 3	* that she had seen the *m·*.

manuscripts

Mis.	249– 9	appropriated other people's *m·*
	315– 7	written, and read from *m·*,
	381– 3	*m·* originally composed by
	382– 5	*m·* of mine were in circulation.
Man.	32– 8	not read from copies or *m·*,
Ret.	1– 8	*m·* containing Scriptural sonnets,
	36– 7	writing out my *m·* for students
	36– 9	unpublished *m·* extant,
My.	179– 4	were in two distinct *m·*.
	305– 9	*m·* and letters in my possession,
	306–24	these comprised the *m·* which

man-worship

No.	20–20	the common idolatry of *m·*.

many

Mis.	4–13	*M·* questions important to be
	5–11	*M·* say, ''I should like to study,
	6– 7	and *m·* more are needed for the
	6–13	it surely does, to *m·* thinkers,
	7–15	to *m·*, if faithful laborers in His
	7–24	able to reach *m·* homes with healing,
	39– 1	*M·* who apply for help are
	52–14	susceptible of *m·* definitions.
	60–25	as *m· identities as mortal bodies?*
	71– 5	saved *m·* a drunkard from this
	81–18	*m· of the people from beyond Jordan?*
	88–11	whose thought is appreciated by *m·*
	99–15	How *m·* are there ready to suffer for
	106–31	imitative tones of *m·* instruments,
	112–14	*m·* features and forms of
	117– 1	''ruler over *m·* things.'' — *Matt.* 25 : 23.
	120–21	*m·* of its members reside a long
	150–16	salvation of *m·* people by means of
	159–11	My heart has *m·* rooms :
	159–26	*m·* weary wings sprung upward !
	168–28	* and *m·* had to go away
	171–27	so *m·* are obtruding upon the
	175–31	done *m·* wonderful works?
	180–21	*But as m· as received him,* — *John* 1 : 12.
	181–24	''But as *m·* as received him, — *John* 1 : 12.

many

Mis.	182– 5	"As *m·* as received him ;" — *John* 1 : 12.
	182– 5	as *m·* as perceive man's actual
	183–26	As *m·* as do receive a knowledge of
	185–17	"As *m·* as received him," — *John* 1 : 12.
	185–25	"as *m·* as received him, — *John* 1 : 12.
	194– 1	How *m·* to-day believe that the
	201–21	they were so *m·* proofs that he had
	221–16	This accounts for *m·* helpless
	222– 7	state of false consciousness in *m·*
	231– 7	rich viands made busy *m·* appetites ;
	231–28	How *m·* homes echo such tones of
	244–28	as *m·* as should believe in him.
	247–18	To *m·*, the healing force developed by
	255– 3	on pedestals, as so *m·* petty deities ;
	264–13	*M·* students enter the Normal class
	269–25	*M·* are bidding for it,
	271– 5	(and *m·* who are not students)
	276– 6	so *m·* people and circumstances
	280–30	by which so *m·* wrecks are made.
	299–11	conviction to the minds of *m·*
	303–25	that *m·* Christian Scientists will respond
	305–16	* small contributions from *m·* persons
	307–13	and *m·* orders on hand,
	309–10	that it has turned *m·* from the
	312–18	* to restore the waning faith of *m·*
	317–25	having already seen in *m·* instances
	327–10	*M·* there were who had entered the
	333–16	"lords *m·* — *I Cor.* 8 : 5.
	340– 2	has torn the laurel from *m·* a brow
	340– 3	and repose from *m·* a heart.
	341– 9	and be made ruler over *m·* things.
	369–12	madness it seems to *m·* onlookers.
	375–22	* resemblance, in *m·* things, to
	375–24	* how *m·* times have I seen these
	391–10	Have *m·* items more;
Man.	28–13	beaten with *m·* stripes." — *Luke* 12 : 47.
Ret.	7–22	* It blights too *m·* hopes ;
	8– 1	*M·* peculiar circumstances
	15– 1	To the astonishment of *m·*,
	16–12	*M·* pale cripples went into
	25–22	senses are so *m·* witnesses to
	41– 4	*M·* were the desperate cases
	50–14	or even in half as *m·* lessons.
	50–16	as *m·* as seventeen in one class.
	52– 1	For *m·* successive years I have
	82–17	ample to supply *m·* practitioners,
Un.	8– 2	trouble to *m·* earnest thinkers
	18–10	*M·* fancy that our heavenly Father
	26–19	*M·* ordinary Christians protest
	39–16	as *m·* as receive the knowledge of God
	44– 1	*M·* misrepresentations are made
Pul.	11– 4	as the sound of *m·* waters,
	13– 7	ruler over *m·*," — *Matt.* 25 : 23.
	13–25	how *m·* periods of torture it may
	14–29	*M·* are willing to open the eyes of
	20–22	one of the *m·* dates selected and
	33–25	* certainly true that *m·* and *m·* persons,
	36–18	* met Mrs. Eddy *m·* times since then,
	41– 6	* from *m·* lands, the love-offerings of the
	45– 3	* Sacrifices were made in *m·* an instance
	46–17	* the *m·* souvenirs that Mrs. Eddy
	47– 1	* the attention of *m·* clergymen
	48–26	* *m·* another well-born woman's.
	49– 3	* speaking of her *m·* followers
	50–20	* *m·* who have worn off the novelty
	51– 9	* *m·* pioneers who are searching
	51–12	* *m·* who have worked in the
	51–20	* *m·* a new project in religious
	55–10	* emancipation from *m·* of the
	55–15	* she has revised it *m·* times,
	56–15	* comfort to *m·* weary souls.
	57– 5	* contributions . . . from *m·* lands.
	58– 1	* who, after *m·* vicissitudes,
	60–13	* *m·* having remained over a week
	66–18	* the mystical which, along *m·* lines,
	67–21	* while in *m·* towns and villages
	68– 7	* *m·* are now pastors or in practice.
	68–22	* There are *m·* other church edifices in
	71–21	* faith to which *m·* thousands
	75–17	* *M·* TORONTO SCIENTISTS PRESENT
	80–12	* her book has *m·* a time been sent
	82–11	* *m·* things dear to the soul
	82–15	* *m·* still are Jews who never
	83–22	* It is the proudest boast of *m·*
Rud.	14–26	*M·* students, who have passed through
No.	2–21	and *m·* who are not teachers have
	2–27	*m·* are flooding our land with
	14–23	to as *m·* as shall believe on him.
Pan.	3–25	* are so *m·* members."
	4–15	that there are *m·* so-called minds;
'00.	7– 8	*M·* of our best . . . men and women,
'01.	21– 9	* may be traced *m·* of the ideas
'02.	17–12	*M·* sleep who should keep . . . awake
Peo.	7–13	* With *m·* a sharp incision.
	7–21	* With *m·* a sharp incision,

many

Po.	vi–23	* *m· poems written in girlhood*
	38– 9	Have *m·* items more ;
My.	4– 9	how *m·* are following the
	13–11	* like so *m·* planets, revolving
	13–30	returns it unto them after *m·* days,
	19–13	* To one of the *m·* branch churches
	21– 4	* by *m·* of the branch churches
	21– 9	* the erection of *m·* branch churches.
	21–23	* in meeting very *m·* of them
	24–25	* remarked by the *m·* visitors
	28– 6	* *m·* who have contributed
	28–10	* in *m·* instances the loving
	29–13	* *M·* more gorgeous church pageantries
	30– 8	* *m·* hundreds of other faiths,
	38–13	* *m·* of the visitors showed a
	43–31	* and *m·* are asking,
	47– 5	* *m·* of whom have not had the means
	47–21	* in so *m·* distant lands,
	47–22	* inspired so *m·* of different races
	52– 2	* *m·* obstacles to overcome,
	52– 3	* *m·* mental hardships to endure,
	53–31	* *m·* different ones address them
	56– 4	* *m·* stood in the aisles,
	56–26	* *m·* were obliged to leave
	58–28	* *m·* thousands who attended the
	60– 1	* I have been solicited by *m·*
	61–29	* the *m·* intricate problems which
	62–26	* We acknowledge with *m·* thanks
	66–29	* *m·* beautiful houses of worship
	80–27	* there were *m·* hundreds waiting
	84– 4	* *M·* a clergyman can testify
	84– 9	* experience of *m·* generations
	84–28	* is notable in *m·* ways.
	90– 1	* should number *m·* thousands
	90– 9	* diseases *m·* and diverse.
	90–14	* the door to this gospel for *m·*,
	93–22	* underlie *m·* of the practices
	93–23	* *m·* of us have missed entirely
	94–23	* from *m·* foreign countries
	95– 6	* intelligence of *m·* communities
	96– 5	* *m·* of them prominent figures
	104–25	*m·* professional men and women
	111– 9	by *m·* doctors and lawyers,
	114–12	uncovered to the gaze of *m·* men,
	130–11	has been made too *m·* times
	133– 1	*m·* mansions, *m·* welcomes,
	133– 2	*m·* pardons for the penitent.
	149–15	* have conversed with *m·* wise men,"
	149–16	* "And I with *m·* rich men,
	164– 4	to give to *m·* in this city
	173–13	but as *m·* gifts had come from
	177–21	joy of *m·* generations awaits it,
	198– 5	received with *m·* thanks to you
	236–11	Too *m·* centres may become
	244–20	"*M·* are called, — *Matt.* 22 : 14.
	247–26	after *m·* or a few days it will
	266–25	that *m·* points in theology
	294– 7	"did not *m·* mighty — *Matt.* 13 : 58.
	295– 1	loved and lost of *m·* millions.
	301–21	so *m·* well-defined instances
	305–23	*M·* of the nation's best and
	319–18	* observation of *m·* of your students,
	321–24	* my *m·* conversations with you
	322–25	* *m·* good points in the Science,
	325– 1	* *m·* kindnesses you had shown
	332– 9	* *M·* thanks are due Mr. Cooke.
	332–27	* *m·* Masonic records were transferred
	340–12	In *m·* of the States
	345–31	* We talked on *m·* subjects,
	360–14	as *m·* students think I can,
		(*see also* **gods, minds, others, years**)

many-hued

Mis.	332–15	stately palms, *m·* blossoms,

many-throated

Mis.	106–31	*m·* organ, in imitative tones

maple (*see also* **maple's**)

Mis.	395–15	Written in childhood, in a *m·* grove
Po.	vi–28	* (*written in a m· grove*),
	59– 9	Written in girlhood, in a *m·* grove.

maple's

Mis.	396–16	Beneath the *m·* shade.
Po.	59– 8	Beneath the *m·* shade.

marble

Mis.	316–23	warming *m·* and quenching volcanoes !
	360– 3	rough *m·*, encumbered with
	386–23	Rears the sad *m·* to our memory
Pul.	24–12	* On the front is a *m·* tablet,
	24–27	* The entrances are of *m·*,
	25– 6	* floors of *m·* in mosaic work,
	25–15	* *m·* stairs of rose pink,
	25–15	* and *m·* approaches.
	25–25	* are of pink Tennessee *m·*.

marble
Pul. 26–21 * an entrance of Italian m·,
26–22 * golden letters on a m· tablet,
26–23 * the mosaic m· floor of white
27– 3 * in m· approaches and rich carving,
58–19 * the steps m·, and the walls stone.
76– 5 * superb archway of Italian m·
Peo. 7– 4 as well as on history and m·,
7– 6 turn often from m· to model,
7– 9 * With his m· block before him ;
Po. 50– 9 Rears the sad m·
My. 68–17 * is of a beautiful foreign m·,
68–25 * Bedford stone and m·
68–27 * floors of the first story are of m·.
68–28 * seven broad m· stairways,
68–30 * bronze, m·, and Bedford stone.
69–10 * Two large m· plates
69–13 * pure white m· was used,
291– 9 warming the m· of politics

March
(see months)

march
Mis. xii– 3 With armor on, I continue the m·,
130–31 mankind's triumphal m· out of the
138–25 equal to the m· triumphant,
138–28 for the music of our m·,
138–29 m· on in spiritual organization.
233–10 onward m· of life-giving Science,
Pul. 14– 1 The m· of mind and of honest
83–14 * m· under the black flag of
My. 155–13 in the onward m· of Truth,
245–18 majestic m· of C. S.

marched
Mis. 106–14 M· the one hundred.
153– 7 they m· through the wilderness :

marches
Mis. 136– 6 taking forward m·,
My. 11–10 * not . . . by means of forced m·,

marching
Mis. 135– 1 m· under whatsoever ensign,
Po. 10–20 Is m· under orders ;
My. 337–21 Is m· under orders ;

margin
Rud. 1–11 large m· for misapprehension,

Mark (see also St. Mark)
Mis. 32–13 In M·, ninth chapter,
191–12 In M·, ninth chapter
192–25 last chapter of M· is emphatic

Mark (Baker)
(see Baker)

mark
Mis. 18– 3 efface the m· of the beast.
113– 9 save he that had the m·,— Rev. 13 : 17.
269–31 save he that had the m·,— Rev. 13 : 17.
271–26 * more strongly m· the difference
277– 8 becomes the m· for error's shafts.
279–23 M·, that in the case of Joshua
347–32 whoever hits this m· is well paid
348– 2 towards the m· of a high calling.
358– 2 m· the way in divine Science.
Ret. 42–14 "M· the perfect man,— Psal. 37 : 37.
'00. 6– 7 I press toward the m·— Phil. 3 : 14.
My. 28–14 * qualities which m· the true Christian,
28–21 * m· the lives of his followers.
66–27 * m· an epoch in the history of
203–13 A spiritual hero is a m· for

marked
Mis. 4– 4 m· tendency of mortal mind to
160–12 Your progress, . . . has been m·.
197–10 the way which Jesus m· out
204–16 m· loss of faith in evil,
358–17 way which Jesus m· out,
363–32 show their m· consonance with
Pul. 23–23 * m· by peculiar intimations of
43–13 * simplicity m· the exercises.
50–11 * m· by the erection of a visible
66–22 * m· by the dedication of
No. 2–22 some m· success in healing
'02. 1– 3 m· the history of C. S.
My. 79–29 * m· the close of their visit
181–30 It is a m· coincidence that
239–30 is m·, and will increase till
339–13 New Hampshire's advancement is m·.

market
Mis. 342–29 they watch the m·,

marketh
Mis. 157– 5 He that m· the sparrow's fall

Market Street
My. 59–17 * little hall on M· S·, Lynn,

marking
Mis. 124–16 m· the unwinged bird,
304–25 * m· the world's progress

marks
Pul. 44– 9 * Surely it m· an era in the
49– 4 * air of hospitality that m· its
My. 89–17 * that m· it as different from
226–12 that m· the sparrow's fall,

marred
Un. 15–11 likeness is incomplete, the image m·.
Rud. 6– 9 the beauty is m·, through a
Peo. 10–19 m· in mind the model of man.
My. 167–28 will, I trust, never be m·

Marriage
Pul. 38–12 "M·," "Animal Magnetism,"

marriage
Mis. x–20 first m·, to Colonel Glover
52–11 What do you think of m·?
52–13 M· is susceptible of many
285–20 to write briefly on m·,
285–24 severs the m· covenant.
286– 3 m· is not without the law,
286– 6 m· and progeny will continue
286– 9 when m· shall be found to be
286–14 neither marry nor are given in m·,
286–15 To abolish m· at this period,
288–16 Is m· nearer right than celibacy?
289–15 by the m· contract two are made one,
290– 2 Let other people's m· relations alone :
297–19 claims of the m· covenant,
Man. 46– 5 legal adoption and legal m·,
49–18 m· AND DECEASE.
Ret. 20– 5 before my father's second m·,
20–21 m· was very unfortunate,
20–25 after our m· his stepfather
42– 1 last m· was with Asa Gilbert Eddy,
Pul. 46–27 * Her last m· was in the spring
My. 5– 4 m· synonymous with legalized lust,
268– 4 morale of m· is preserved
268– 5 imperative nature of the m· relation
269– 8 nor are given in m· :— Luke 20 : 35.
312– 4 Regarding my first m·
312– 7 * six months after his m·,
313–30 after my father's second m·
314– 3 It says that after my m·

Marriage of the Lamb
Pul. 6–11 book title

married
Man. 49–20 If a Christian Scientist is to be m·,
111– 5 If the applicant is a m· woman
Ret. 1–17 was m· to an Englishman,
20– 9 our family nurse, who had m·,
Pul. 34– 1 * Miss Baker was m· to Colonel Glover,
35–27 * Mrs. Glover· Dr. Asa Gilbert Eddy,
My. 290– 9 born in 1819, m· in 1840,
314– 7 When I was m· to him,

marrow
My. 48–22 * the m· of their characters.

marry
Mis. 286–14 wherein they neither m· nor
298–14 "It is not good to m·."— Matt. 19 : 10.
My. 269– 8 neither m·, nor are given— Luke 20 : 35.

marrying
Ret. 20–24 dominant thought in m· again

Mars', Gerhardt C.
My. 351–23 have not read Gerhardt C. M· book,

marshal
My. 174– 8 courtesy of the efficient city m·

Mars' Hill and Mars' hill
Mis. 344–29 St. Paul, when he stood on M· h·
My. 104– 4 St. Paul, the M· H· orator,
125–17 the spirit of the M· H· orator,

martyr
Mis. 166– 4 the earthly life of a m· ;
288–23 The selfish rôle of a m·

martyrdom
Mis. 121– 7 even the cup of m· :
'02. 10–25 m· of God's best witnesses
My. 293– 8 believed that his m· was God's way.

martyrs
Mis. 121–12 blood of m· was believed to be the
326–14 licking up the blood of m·
No. 44–25 * are m· to-day."
My. 125–31 with the blood of the m·— Rev. 17 : 6.
177–17 * "The blood of the m· is the seed of

marvel
Mis. 160– 1 m· at the power and permanence of
163– 5 mission was a m· of glory :
294– 6 A real Christian Scientist is a m·,
Pul. 55– 4 * Nature's m· in thy thought."

marvel
My. 67–21   * m· of architectural beauty.
85– 4   * growth of this cult is the m· of
123– 3   love is the greater m·,
126–12   a m·, casting out evil and
249–16   The m· is, that at this enlightened

marvelled
Ret. 13–24   The physician m· ;

marvellous
Mis. 199–23   The Principle of these m· works
199–29   The m· healing-power of goodness
237–20   m· good, and mysterious evil.
354– 4   Sin in its very nature is m· !
Ret. 26– 1   his m· skill in demanding
Un. 5–24   m· unity of man with God
17–18   into a home of m· light,
Rud. 4–24   extinguishes . . . by His m· light.
No. 37–14   this most m· demonstration,
My. 43–14   * this experience was almost as m·
45–22   * m· beyond human ken.
59–32   * m· beyond all imagining
81–27   * account of the m· cures
88–23   * a m· revelation given to this
99– 2   * one of the m·, great, and
127– 6   m· speed of the chariot-wheels of
206–26   into His m· light.” — I Pet. 2 : 9.
288– 3   Love unfolds m· good

marvels
Mis. 376–24   glided into a glory of mottled m·.
My. 89–28   * one of the m· of the

Mary (see also **Mary's**)
Mis. 166–16   and a M· knew not how to declare its
179–29   say with M·, “Rabboni !” — John 20 : 16.
Un. 59–12   divine idea . . . in the son of M·.
62–27   M· had risen to discern faintly God's
Pul. 27–21   * M· anointing the head of Jesus,
27–22   * M· washing the feet of Jesus,
27–22   * M· at the resurrection ;
Pan. 8– 9   belief that M· was the mother of God
'00. 7–20   we say as did M· of old :
'01. 10–10   Jesus was the son of M·,
My. 119–12   M· of old wept because she
258–10   one word, “M·,” — John 20 : 16.
303– 4   one incarnation, one Mother M·.
(see also **Baker, Eddy**)

Mary's
Mis. 75–21   M· exclamation, . . . is rendered
84–18   the Son of man, or M· son.
(see also **Baker**)

Marys
Mis. 337–24   Only the devout M·,
Pul. 27–21   * pictorial story of the four M·

masculine
Un. 32–24   neither m· nor feminine.

mask
Mis. 147–26   He seeks no m· to cover him,
210–24   tears the black m· from the
371–24   What is under the m·,

masked
Mis. 332–20   m· with deformity the glories

Mason
My. 326–18   emblems of a master M·,
330–12   * assisted by a M· of good
333– 5   * one of your own citizens, a M·,
334–25   * heading
335– 4   * a M· in “St. Andrew's Lodge,
351–15   as the widow of a M·.
(see also **Free Mason, Royal Arch Mason**)

Masonic and **masonic**
Mis. 142–10   a number of m· symbols.
142–28   say to the m· brothers :
My. 330–19   * sustained by M· records
332–25   * interviewing with M· authorities,
332–27   * M· records were transferred
333–26   * interred with M· honors.
336– 8   * her husband's M· brethren,
351–14   It was truly M·, tender, grand

Masonry
My. 335– 8   * devotedly attached to M·,

Masons and **masons**
Ret. 19–13   Number 3, of Royal Arch m·.
19–21   directions to his brother m·
My. 312–11   * M· also paid Mrs. Glover's fare
330–25   of Royal Arch M·.
331– 1   directions to his brother M·

masquerades
Un. 49–21   the unreal m· as the real,

mass
Mis. 331– 4   tosses earth's m· of wonders
Chr. 53–56   No m· for Me !

mass
Po. 53–12   Poor robin's lonely m·.
My. 178–25   the table sank a charred m·.

Massachusetts and **Mass.** (see also **Bay State**)
Mis. 120–22   reside a long distance from M·,
Man. 99–15   applies to all States except M·,
Ret. 6–23   two States, M· and New Hampshire.
21– 9   and came to see me in M·.
24– 1   in M·, in February, 1866
Peo. 10– 8   M· succored a fugitive slave
My. 275–18   twice since I came to M·.
334–30   * of the Grand Lodge of M· :
339–13   M· has exchanged Fast Day,
(see also **Arlington, Athol, Attleboro, Boston, Brookline, Cambridge, Charlestown, Chestnut Hill, Lynn, Methuen, Rockland, Salem, Springfield, Swampscott**)

Massachusetts Avenue
Pul. 36–21   * just beyond M· A·,

Massachusetts Metaphysical College
Mis. 38–16   taught by me at the M· M· C·,
39– 7   genuineness at the M· M· C·.
48–27   gone away from the M· M· C·
64–12   a course at the M· M· C·,
110–13   chapter sub-title
116– 8   chapter sub-title
132– 9   M· M· C·, 571 COLUMBUS AVENUE,
135–27   ASSOCIATION OF THE M· M· C·.
239– 2   Call at the M· M· C·, in 1889,
256– 9   instruction in the M· M· C·
271–18   chapter sub-title
271–21   about Mrs. Eddy's M· M· C·
272–27   * and that is the M· M· C·,
273–24   Primary class in the M· M· C·,
279–10   PRIMARY CLASS OF THE M· M· C·,
316–24   Before entering the M· M· C·,
348–29   students of the M· M· C·
358–23   M· M· C·, the first and only
Man. 35–12   students of the M· M· C·
36– 7   Normal Course at the M· M· C·
68–15   the degree of the M· M· C·.
85–15   Normal Course at the M· M· C·
88– 6   President of the M· M· C·,
89– 3   President of the M· M· C·,
90– 9   The term of the M· M· C·
92– 1   M· M· C· Board of Education.
92–17   any class in the M· M· C·,
Ret. 43– 4   the M· M· C· in Boston,
48– 1   M· M· C· drew its
48–16   M· M· C·, chartered in
52–15   Association of the M· M· C·,
Pul. 24–18   * president of the M· M· C·,
64– 3   * president of the M· M· C·,
68– 4   * M· M· C· was founded
70– 8   * president of the M· M· C·,
No. 12– 7   M· M· C· and Church
Pan. 10–11   students of the M· M· C·,
My. 125–20   auspices of the M· M· C·,
218–29   not enter the M· M· C·
240–28   * certificates from the M· M· C·
244–10   degree of C.S.D., of the M· M· C·.
244–28   chapter sub-title
244–29   The M· M· C· of Boston,
245–22   students of the M· M· C·
245–31   or Vice-President of the M· M· C·.
246– 5   Students who enter the M· M· C·
318–17   one of my classes in the M· M· C·,
(see also **Metaphysical College**)

Massachusetts Metaphysical College Association
Mis. 135–24   meeting of the M· M· C· A·,

Massachusetts State House
My. 77– 6   * Beside it the dome of the M· S· H·,
95–14   * famous old M· S· H·.

massacres
Mis. 123– 1   in our time m· our missionaries,

masses
My. 181–18   classes and m· of mankind,

massive
Mis. 325– 1   a m· carved stone mansion,
Pul. 52–11   * erection of a m· temple in Boston
My. 45–28   * m· pile of New Hampshire granite
78– 6   * of gray stone with a m· dome

massiveness
My. 67–28   * its m· is unnoticed

Master (see also **Master's**)
beloved
Man. 60–18   sacred words of our beloved M·,
buried
Mis. 393–15   When the buried M· hails us
Po. 51–20   When the buried M· hails us

Master

commanded
   Ret. 87–16   as the $M\cdot$ commanded.
command of the
   My. 128–21   following the command of the $M\cdot$,
disciples of the
   Mis. 171–19   true disciples of the $M\cdot$
divine
   Mis. 187–19   our human and divine $M\cdot$,
example of the
   Mis. 270– 7   example of the $M\cdot$ in C. S.,
followers of the
   My. 112– 5   followers of the $M\cdot$ in the early
glorified
   '02. 11–18   gave our glorified $M\cdot$ a bitter cup
great
   Mis. 17–14   idea that our great $M\cdot$ gave
       33– 4   crucifixion of even the great $M\cdot$;
       90–25   Our great $M\cdot$ administered
      121–25   drew from the great $M\cdot$ this answer
      150–20   as taught by our great $M\cdot$.
      190–20   that our great $M\cdot$ cast out
      195–11   those words of the great $M\cdot$,
      371– 2   taught by our great $M\cdot$.
   Ret. 22– 4   to the life of our great $M\cdot$.
       27–28   guidance of the great $M\cdot$.
   Pan. 8–15   as taught . . . by our great $M\cdot$,
   '00. 4–17   as taught by our great $M\cdot$;
   '02. 9–14   implied by the great $M\cdot$,
      19–26   great $M\cdot$ triumphed in furnace fires.
   My. 4–25   Our great $M\cdot$ said
      103–24   demonstrations of our great $M\cdot$
      148–30   and the works of our great $M\cdot$.
      153–11   To-day our great $M\cdot$ would say
      172–16   In the words of our great $M\cdot$,
      178–30   the sayings of the great $M\cdot$
      215–23   When the great $M\cdot$ first sent forth
      227– 1   The great $M\cdot$ said,
      251– 2   The great $M\cdot$ saith :
      265–23   fulfils the saying of our great $M\cdot$,
      305–23   more from my great $M\cdot$,
      330– 5   * great $M\cdot$ himself was scandalized,
      339–18   said to the great $M\cdot$,
hear the
   Mis. 269– 5   Hear the $M\cdot$ on this subject :
Lord and
   My. 161–17   cup of their Lord and $M\cdot$
      232–12   Our Lord and $M\cdot$ left to us
      256–20   nativity of our Lord and $M\cdot$.
my
   Mis. 180–12   said, in the words of my $M\cdot$,
of metaphysics
   Hea. 7–17 $M\cdot$ of metaphysics, reading the mind
our
   Mis. 21– 9   Our $M\cdot$ said, "The works — *John* 14 : 12.
      28–15   our $M\cdot$ proved to his doubting
      63– 7   Our $M\cdot$ understood that Life,
      64– 4   Our $M\cdot$ bore the cross
      76– 5   This statement of our $M\cdot$ is true,
      83–18   In the words of our $M\cdot$
      89–17   caused our $M\cdot$ to refuse help to
      97– 8   Our $M\cdot$ said of one of his students,
      108– 6   Our $M\cdot$, in his definition of Satan
      111–16   Our $M\cdot$ said, "Heaven — *Matt.* 24 : 35.
      121– 4   our $M\cdot$ partook of the Jews' feast
      158–28   the example of our $M\cdot$.
      161–18   The only record of our $M\cdot$
      165–28   example, and suffering of our $M\cdot$.
      187–32   such as crucified our $M\cdot$,
      189– 1   those words of our $M\cdot$,
      192–31   This declaration of our $M\cdot$
      196–14   hence the words of our $M\cdot$:
      200–16   so-called miracles of our $M\cdot$,
      211–26   Our $M\cdot$ said, "Ye shall drink — *Matt.* 20 : 23.
      213–21   from the lips of our $M\cdot$,
      245– 1   no record showing that our $M\cdot$
      251–15   whereof our $M\cdot$ said :
      252–32   whereof our $M\cdot$ said,
      253– 4   knoweth as did our $M\cdot$
      257–20   Our $M\cdot$ called it "a murderer — *John* 8 : 44.
      275– 1   Would not our $M\cdot$ say to the
      282–14   Our $M\cdot$ said, "When ye — *Matt.* 10 : 12.
      317–22   These words of our $M\cdot$ explain
      359–21   The methods of our $M\cdot$ were in advance
      370– 2   in the spirit of our $M\cdot$,
      380–23   for thus saith our $M\cdot$
   Man. 17–11   word and works of our $M\cdot$,
      17–17   demonstrated by our $M\cdot$,
   Ret. 44– 2   words and works of our $M\cdot$,
      58– 7   With our $M\cdot$, life was not merely
      67–24   In the words of our $M\cdot$,
      68–13   Our $M\cdot$ instructed his students
      87– 1   our $M\cdot$ said, "Follow me ; — *Matt.* 8 : 22.
      93– 8   Hear this saying of our $M\cdot$,
   Un. 32–21   even as did our $M\cdot$:
      37– 6   Our $M\cdot$ said, "The kingdom — *Matt.* 10 : 7.

Master
our
   Pul. 3– 5   our $M\cdot$ said : "Destroy this — *John* 2 : 19.
      10–19   our $M\cdot$ said : "The stone — *Matt.* 21 : 42.
   No. 2–10   Our $M\cdot$ taught his students to
      14–18   Hear the words of our $M\cdot$:
      43– 4   Our $M\cdot$ said, "Come unto — *Matt.* 11 : 28.
   Pan. 5–10   Our $M\cdot$ gave the proper answer
      5–23   our $M\cdot$ cast out evil,
      11– 1   required the divinity of our $M\cdot$
      11– 7   Was our $M\cdot$ mistaken in judging
   '00. 5– 6   Here note the words of our $M\cdot$
      8–14   Our $M\cdot$ saith to his followers :
      14– 1   approval of this church by our $M\cdot$
   '01. 28– 6   narrow way, whereof our $M\cdot$ said,
   Hea. 3–21   wonderful works of our $M\cdot$
   My. 28–23   * our $M\cdot$ healed and reformed them.
      46–11   word and works of our $M\cdot$,
      108–23   which our $M\cdot$ designated as
      122–30   The mission of our $M\cdot$ was
      147–27   in the words of our $M\cdot$,
      150–26   what our $M\cdot$ said unto his
      152– 5   and our $M\cdot$ declared,
      190–13   accept our $M\cdot$ as authority,
      190–18   This declaration of our $M\cdot$,
      215–27   better . . . than that of our $M\cdot$?
      221–21   Our $M\cdot$ conformed to this law,
      225– 5   spoken by our $M\cdot$
      228–14   Referring to . . . our $M\cdot$ declared :
      233–24   Our $M\cdot$ said, "He that — *Matt.* 10 : 38.
      244–20   Knowing this, our $M\cdot$ said :
      246–25   Our $M\cdot$ said : "What I do — *John* 13 : 7.
our blessed
   Un. 30–17   the Messiah, our blessed $M\cdot$,
   Pul. 15– 9   the spirit of our blessed $M\cdot$
   Peo. 12–20   Our blessed $M\cdot$ demonstrated this
our dear
   Pul. 7–10   were our dear $M\cdot$ in our
pledge of the
   No. 46– 2   is the pledge of the $M\cdot$.
predicted
   My. 63–27   * as the $M\cdot$ predicted,
saith
   My. 156–14   "The $M\cdot$ saith unto thee, — *Luke* 22 : 11.
saying of the
   '01. 8–28   that mystic saying of the $M\cdot$
their
   Mis. 212–10   reiterated warning of their $M\cdot$
   '02. 18–26   ignoble conduct . . . towards their $M\cdot$,
used
   Mis. 270–11   other means than those the $M\cdot$ used
words of the
   Un. 43–15   words of the $M\cdot$ in support of this
   My. 114– 1   In the words of the $M\cdot$,

   Mis. 24–25   of the origin of evil, the $M\cdot$ said :
      179–30   "Rabboni !" — $M\cdot$! — *John* 20 : 16.
      191–13   "$M\cdot$, we saw one — *Mark* 9 : 38.
      393–11   Soon abandoned when the $M\cdot$
   Ret. 32– 7   lose it," saith the $M\cdot$. — *Mark* 8 : 35.
      91– 9   and not by the $M\cdot$ himself
   Pul. 52–20   * The $M\cdot$ was the great healer.
   '01. 26– 4   The great teacher, . . . is the $M\cdot$,
   Po. 51–16   Soon abandoned when the $M\cdot$
   My. 165– 4   in doing this the $M\cdot$ became
      294– 7 $M\cdot$ "did not many mighty — *Matt.* 13 : 58.

master (*see also* **master's**)
great
   Mis. 373–15   One great $m\cdot$ clearly delineates
   '01. 18–22   great $m\cdot$ Metaphysician's precept
   My. 104– 7   great $m\cdot$ of metaphysics,
his
   '00. 3–11   One's idol is . . . his $m\cdot$.
   '01. 28–24   that he be as his $m\cdot$." — *Matt.* 10 : 25.
its
   Mis. 47–18   servant of Mind, not its $m\cdot$:
      108–25   then we are its $m\cdot$, not servant.
   '01. 14–28   therefore man is its $m\cdot$.
Mason
   My. 326–17   the emblems of a $m\cdot$ Mason,
Metaphysician
   Mis. 76–31   prophecy of the $m\cdot$ Metaphysician,
      200– 6   The $m\cdot$ Metaphysician understood
      270–10   is the $m\cdot$ Metaphysician.
   Ret. 55– 3   Jesus, the $m\cdot$ Metaphysician,
   Pul. 20–23   baptism of our $m\cdot$ Metaphysician,
   No. 31–22   with this $m\cdot$ Metaphysician.
   My. 111– 6   Our $m\cdot$ Metaphysician, the Galilean
      222– 8   Jesus, the $m\cdot$ Metaphysician,
of evil
   Mis. 209–27   good is the $m\cdot$ of evil.
of hate
   Mis. 336– 1   Love is the $m\cdot$ of hate ;
   My. 214–13   Love to be the $m\cdot$ of hate.

master

of metaphysics
Mis. 252–23 healer and m· of metaphysics,
My. 104– 7 said of the great m· of metaphysics,
of mind
Un. 34– 3 declares that matter is the m· of mind,
of the gods
My. 159–26 Zeus, the m· of the gods,
of the house
'01. 10– 4 the m· of the house — Matt. 10 : 25.
one
Mis. 52– 6 if he were to serve one m·,

Mis. 40–27 has to m· those elements of evil
45–18 Sin is not the m· of divine Science,
53– 6 only as we m· error with Truth.
109–29 fear not sin, lest thereby it m· you ;
265–13 is m· of the situation.
No. 37–18 power, to meet and m· it
Rud. 10–24 The belief that matter can m· Mind,
'01. 14–13 as to frighten us and so m· us,
Hea. 8– 6 knowing that Mind can m· sickness

mastered

Mis. 208–18 m· by divine Truth's negativing error
284–27 will be m· by Science.
344– 8 without having m· the sciences
Ret. 55– 5 Evil is not m· by evil ;
64–21 which must be met and m·,
My. 134–10 conflicting elements must be m·.

mastering

Mis. 221– 5 m· it one gains in the rules of
My. 207–23 m· evil and defending good,

masterpiece

Mis. 363–28 the learned man's m·,
Po. v–13 * this m· of nature's handiwork,

masterpieces

Mis. 372–27 having seen the painter's m· ;
Pul. 49– 6 * reproductions of some of Europe's m·.

Master's

Mis. 28–26 The M· practical knowledge
105– 5 our M· individual demonstrations
110– 2 poured on our M· feet,
125– 1 indeed drink of our M· cup,
144–18 whisper our M· promise,
195–17 The M· divine logic,
287– 5 and the M· demand,
300–14 spare you our M· condemnation?
369–19 we kneel at our M· feet,
Ret. 25–29 our great M· purpose in not
91– 4 our M· greatest utterance
91–11 indicates more the M· mood,
Un. 44– 3 I can only repeat the M· words :
58–13 The M· sublime triumph
Pul. 10– 1 It was our M· self-immolation,
'01. 23–16 according to the M· teaching
32– 9 busy about their M· business,
35–13 the M· glory won thus,
'02. 5–22 Hence our M· saying,
My. 52–17 * establish these our M· commands
108– 9 Hence our M· saying,
179–16 verification of our M· sayings.
219–19 our great M· life of healing,
222–21 the sandals of thy M· feet.
230–26 realize at last their M· promise,
233– 2 spirit of our M· command?
234–21 M· sayings are practical
258–21 they who drink their M· cup
347–17 our great M· first disciples,

master's

Mis. 373–19 This m· thought presents a sketch

masters

Mis. 12– 3 If indulged, it m· us ;
89– 2 "No man can serve two m· ;" — Matt. 6 : 24.
269– 6 "No man can serve two m· : — Matt. 6 : 24.
270– 5 the skill of the m· in sculpture,
323–14 m· their secret and open attacks
350–28 I cannot serve two m· ;
372–15 m· in France and Italy.
372–18 * delineations from the old m·."
375–12 * I studied the old m·
375–22 * resemblance, . . . to the old m· !
375–29 * identified with the old m·,
376– 7 * by the oldest of the old m·,
Pul. 13–11 and m· his mortal beliefs,
Rud. 3–13 m· in music and painting
14– 1 Neither can they serve two m·,
Peo. 9–21 cannot serve two m·." — see Matt. 6 : 24.
My. 6– 3 We cannot serve two m·.
70–21 * both ancient and modern m·,
138–11 cannot "serve two m·." — Matt. 6 : 24.
302–10 craze is that matter m· mind ;
356–22 No man can serve two m· : — Matt. 6 : 24.

mat

Pul. 42–29 * resting on a m· of palms,

matchless

Hea. 20– 2 * "Oh, could we speak the m· worth,

material (noun)

Mis. 190– 7 nor does the m· ultimate in the
305–19 * M· that can be made a part of
306– 1 * m· to be melted into the bell,
Un. 42–27 nor the m· the spiritual,
Pul. 76– 1 * m· used in its construction
My. 10–10 * design, m·, and situation.

material (adj.)

age
My. 221– 2 medicine in a m· age
aid
Mis. 225–23 Looking away from all m· aid,
My. 105–24 restored by me without m· aid,
appendages
Mis. 17– 9 lay aside your m· appendages,
approach
Mis. 180–13 shuddered at her m· approach ;
atom
Un. 35–26 The m· atom is an outlined falsity
atoms
Mis. 26–14 Was it molecules, or m· atoms?
attraction
Un. 36– 2 This process it names m· attraction,
basis
Mis. 254–22 mental healing on a m· basis
341– 4 leaves the unreal m· basis of things,
Ret. 85–21 of healing on a m· basis.
No. 6–16 trying to heal on a m· basis.
belief
Mis. 60–28 Every m· belief hints the
60–30 it will be seen that m· belief,
186– 7 m· belief has fallen far below
Un. 30– 9 suffers, according to m· belief,
beliefs
Mis. 2–29 m· beliefs that war against Spirit,
5–28 mortal thought with m· beliefs.
334–27 remedies the ills of m· beliefs.
birth
Mis. 362– 2 m· birth, growth, and decay :
bloodgiving
No. 37–14 as a personal and m· bloodgiving
body
Mis. 73– 2 m· body is said to suffer,
105–11 way to escape from the m· body.
Rud. 12– 1 structure of the m· body.
13– 8 A mortal and m· body is not the
13–10 The m· body is not the likeness of
My. 217–19 * deny . . . disease in the m· body
218–14 m· body absolved from death
273–24 the m· body is mortal,
brains
Un. 22–20 physical senses and m· brains,
cause
My. 181– 4 human hypotheses, or m· cause
changes
Un. 26–10 the m· changes, the phantasma,
Christ
My. 122–26 not the m· Christ of creeds,
Christ Jesus
'01. 9– 1 spiritual and m· Christ Jesus,
concept
Ret. 68– 1 m· concept was never a creator,
68– 9 m· concept is unreal,
conceptions
Mis. 375– 1 disordered phases of m· conceptions
Peo. 2– 6 m· conceptions of spiritual being.
8–13 m· conceptions of Deity.
conditions
Mis. 17–25 m· conditions attending it.
Ret. 69– 2 m· conditions prior to reaching
Un. 42–17 ability to subdue m· conditions.
No. 5–14 dependent on m· conditions.
5–16 but that m· conditions can and do
Hea. 19– 7 independently of m· conditions.
conjectures
Un. 28–14 ordinary m· conjectures,
consciousness
Mis. 179–28 must lay aside m· consciousness,
Un. 42– 6 the results of m· consciousness ;
42– 6 m· consciousness can have no
control
Rud. 16– 1 If publicity and m· control
corporeality
Mis. 165–14 The m· corporeality disappears ;
creation
Pan. 7– 9 a m· creation took place,
curative
Ret. 34– 1 using a m· curative.
death
Un. 38–11 transition called m· death,

material

deity
Peo. 13— 1 a more *m·* deity,
development
My. 88–20 * a slight and *m·* development
disease
Rud. 10–12 *m·* disease and mortality.
dream
Mis. 28–12 this mortal and *m·* dream,
ear
Rud. 5–13 hearing in the *m·* ear,
earth
My. 181–30 *m·* earth or antipode of heaven.
ego
Mis. 375– 3 What is the *m·* ego, but the
element
Hea. 3–10 *m·* element stole into religion,
elements
Mis. 3–24 *m·* elements of sin and death.
Ret. 60–17 raging of the *m·* elements cease
Peo. 1– 5 crumbling away of *m·* elements
environments
My. 257– 8 swaddling-clothes (*m·* environments)
error
My. 232–24 *m·* error finally disappears,
evidence
Mis. 380–20 a *m·* evidence wherewith to
Un. 11–18 taking away the *m·* evidence.
Rud. 7–16 *m·* evidence being wholly false.
My. 93– 5 * *m·* evidence of their prosperity ;
existence
Mis. 42–21 a belief of *m·* existence
Ret. 30–15 fables of . . . *m·* existence.
32–10 termed mortal and *m·* existence
eyes
Mis. 170–28 belief of *m·* eyes as having any
falsity
Mis. 201– 7 element of matter, or *m·* falsity,
201–10 myth or *m·* falsity of evil ;
fast
My. 339–30 observance of a *m·* fast
finesse
Mis. 373–12 Neither *m·* finesse, standpoint, nor
flames
Mis. 237– 5 so, in place of *m·* flames
force
Mis. 23–21 not a result of . . . *m·* force or
forces
Peo. 8–16 speculate concerning *m·* forces.
form
Ret. 45– 8 *m·* form of cohesion and fellowship
My. 140–19 a *m·* form of communion
140–21 The *m·* form is a
formation
Mis. 71–18 based on a mortal or *m·* formation ;
forms
Mis. 358–32 by leaving the *m·* forms
No. 42– 7 *m·* forms to meet a mental want.
gifts
My. 262–32 *M·* gifts and pastimes tend to
gods
Mis. 198– 5 turning away from *m·* gods ;
history
No. 45–27 *m·* history is drawing to a close.
hygiene
Mis. 6–22 faith in drugs and *m·* hygiene;
illusions
Mis. 8– 1 thought is given to *m·* illusions
images
Un. 34– 4 it sees only *m·* images,
incumbrance
No. 38–19 *m·* incumbrance disappears.
individuality
Un. 24–10 a *m·* individuality,— a mind in
infection
My. 344–29 more dangerous than any *m·* infection,
intelligence
Rud. 4–15 if . . . you mean *m·* intelligence.
interpretations
My. 178– 4 cloud not the . . . *m·* interpretations,
inventions
My. 345–25 * pursuit of modern *m·* inventions
joys
Mis. 84–26 falsity of *m·* joys and sorrows,
law
Mis. 17– 3 opposed to the *m·* law of death ;
198–24 based on physical *m·* law,
200–19 every supposed *m·* law.
Rud. 12–26 divine Mind, not *m·* law,
laws
Mis. 23– 9 subordinates so-called *m·* laws ;
36–22 relative to the so-called *m·* laws,
104– 5 to laws *m·*, to death, or
181–19 spiritual, and not *m·* laws ;
198–17 governed . . . not by *m·* laws,
354–25 not by man or laws *m·*,

material

laws
Un. 31– 9 and overruled laws *m·*
Rud. 7–25 science, so-called, or *m·* laws,
10– 8 *m·* laws are only human beliefs,
life
Mis. 205–26 dissolves all supposed *m·* life
351–30 *M·* life is the antipode of
Un. 30– 8 sense is the so-called *m·* life.
'02. 9–17 minor tones of so-called *m·* life
Hea. 17–15 explains this dream of *m·* life,
light
Pul. 2–10 *M·* light and shade are
limitations
Ret. 76–18 knows no *m·* limitations.
locality
Ret. 91–11 more . . . than the *m·* locality.
losses
Ret. 79– 6 from our own *m·* losses.
man
Mis. 15–26 In mortal and *m·* man,
185– 8 constitutes a so-called *m·* man,
187–14 presuppose a *m·* man to be
205–16 drops the curtain on *m·* man
Rud. 7– 8 *Is man m· or spiritual?*
No. 19–16 *m·* man and the physical senses
'01. 11– 7 he is no longer a *m·* man,
Hea. 17– 6 *m·* man and the personal senses
17– 9 therefore the so-called *m·* man
Peo. 4–15 a third person, called *m·* man,
manhood
Mis. 84–13 Jesus, as *m·* manhood, was not
manifestations
Mis. 362–19 *m·* manifestations of evil,
manner
Pul. 63–20 * very tangible and *m·* manner
means
Mis. 268–25 not adulterate . . . with *m·* means.
Ret. 47–11 C. S. shuns . . . *m·* means
My. 206– 2 with matter and *m·* means,
medicine
Mis. 96– 6 no remedies in drugs, no *m·* medicine.
255–22 It does away with *m·* medicine,
270–28 the last link in *m·* medicine.
Ret. 33– 4 governed the action of *m·* medicine.
33–12 the less *m·* medicine we have,
No. 46– 5 *m·* medicine and superficial religion
'01. 23–18 He used no *m·* medicine,
My. 110– 7 material religion, *m·* medicine.
medicines
Mis. 33–25 does away with all *m·* medicines,
Ret. 34–11 does away with all *m·* medicines,
method
Ret. 43–15 renounced his *m·* method of practice
My. 106– 2 more certain . . . than any *m·* method.
methods
Mis. 6–24 uselessness of such *m·* methods,
40– 4 if one were to mix *m·* methods with
124– 6 cannot find God in . . . *m·* methods ;
182– 4 through violent means or *m·* methods.
243–31 in justification of *m·* methods,
Ret. 33–23 *m·* methods of medicine,
mind
Mis. 336– 7 to kill the serpent of a *m·* mind.
Un. 23–22 An evil *m·* mind, so-called,
mode
Mis. 363–10 *m·* mode of a suppositional mind ;
modes
Mis. 112– 6 The ages are burdened with *m·* modes.
136– 3 such *m·* modes as society
No. 21–16 *m·* modes, wherein the human
motion
Ret. 89– 3 opposed to it by *m·* motion,
music
'00. 11– 6 passionately fond of *m·* music,
nature
Mis. 119–14 This *m·* nature strives
nerves
Un. 34–16 and the nerves, *m·* nerves,
objects
Mis. 36–23 and all *m·* objects,
86– 9 *Is it correct to say of m· objects,*
Ret. 31– 1 *m·* objects of affection
obliquity
Ret. 31–22 mortal mind's *m·* obliquity
observation
'02. 1–17 wrestling only with *m·* observation,
offering
Pul. 87–21 refusal of that as a *m·* offering.
organism
Rud. 12–18 or that a so-called *m·* organism
organization
Mis. 359– 2 *M·* organization is requisite in
Ret. 45– 6 *m·* organization has its value
47– 2 final outcome of *m·* organization,

material

organization
Ret. 48–25 WHEREAS, The *m·* organization was,
49–13 *m·* organization is first ;

origin
Mis. 361– 3 When the belief in *m·* origin,
Un. 50–26 *m·* origin, growth, maturity,

passover
My. 156–12 to prepare for the *m·* passover,

personality
Mis. 105– 4 discords of this *m·* personality.
308– 6 clings to my *m·* personality,
309– 4 *m·* personality is an error in premise,

phenomena
My. 349–24 obtain not in *m·* phenomena,
350– 2 at the beck of *m·* phenomena,

philosophy
Mis. 340–30 *M·* philosophy, human ethics,

pigment
Ret. 79– 8 the *m·* pigment beneath

portraiture
Mis. 309– 6 *m·* portraiture often fails

power
Un. 35–14 says gravitation is a *m·* power,

prescription
'01. 34– 9 the M. D.'s *m·* prescription.

presents
My. 274–22 an abundance of *m·* presents ;

processes
Un. 12– 2 by mental, not *m·* processes.

questions
Mis. 167– 1 *m·* questions at this age

race
'01. 5–17 the *m·* race of Adam,

reading
Mis. 169–25 The literal or *m·* reading is

record
Mis. 170–19 The *m·* record of the Bible,
Ret. 22– 2 the *m·* record expunged.

religion
Mis. 17–10 *m·* religion with its rites
'01. 34–14 a *m·* religion, proscriptive,
My. 110– 6 *m·* religion, material medicine,

rite
Mis. 298–16 *m·* rite of water baptism,
No. 34– 9 commemorating . . . with a *m·* rite

science
Mis. 344–13 such a *m·* science of life !
Rud. 4–14 There is no *m·* science,

sensation
Mis. 198– 6 so-called laws and *m·* sensation,
331–29 their dream of *m·* sensation,
No. 4– 8 *m·* sensation and mental delusion.

sense
Mis. 15–28 mortal and *m·* sense of man,
17– 4 as opposed to the *m·* sense of love ;
22–31 Mind-force, invisible to *m·* sense,
24– 7 dawned on the night of *m·* sense.
27–28 To erring *m·* sense, No !
37–10 as we oppose the belief in *m·* sense,
42–27 in sin or sense *m·*,
47–19 reverses the evidence of *m·* sense
66–18 the *m·* sense must be controlled by
70–26 finite and *m·* sense of relief ;
72–26 it exists only to *m·* sense.
75–28 mortal man (*alias m·* sense)
76–23 misnamed human soul is *m·* sense,
82–22 *m·* sense of life, is put off,
103–24 so far as *m·* sense could discern it,
120– 3 unclasp the *m·* sense of things
183–29 refute the evidence of *m·* sense
184–16 yield to *m·* sense, and lose his power ;
186–25 *m·* sense of existence is not the
190–24 an error of *m·* sense,
194–23 *how* to leave self, the sense *m·*,
215– 7 *m·* sense of God's ways and means,
217–30 To the *m·* sense, everything is matter ;
218– 6 testimony of *m·* sense in relation to
310– 8 the *m·* sense of existence
341–17 parting with a *m·* sense of life and
341–30 pleasures or pains of *m·* sense
Ret. 59–24 *m·* sense defines life as something
60– 4 *m·* sense defines life as a broken
60– 7 *m·* sense says that matter,
60– 8 *M·* sense adds that the divine
60–16 *M·* sense asks, in its ignorance
60–20 *M·* sense saith, "Oh, when will
60–25 *M·* sense contradicts Science,
66– 4 It raises men from a *m·* sense
79–16 Through the channels of *m·* sense,
Un. 29–17 C. S. defines as *m·* sense ;
29–19 that *m·* sense of a soul which
30– 7 *M·* sense is the so-called
38–14 A *m·* sense of life robs God,
39–28 Science and *m·* sense conflict
40– 4 this dark shadow of *m·* sense,

material

sense
Un. 40– 6 *M·* sense, or the belief of
40–18 not by a *m·* sense of being.
40–25 Holding a *m·* sense of Life,
40–27 A sense *m·* apprehends nothing
55–19 pleasures and pains of *m·* sense,
60–26 *m·* sense, which sees not God.
61– 5 To *m·* sense, Jesus first
62–18 In *m·* sense Jesus died, and lived.
63– 5 not apparent to *m·* sense,
Pul. 45–12 * every evidence of *m·* sense
Rud. 5– 9 There is no *m·* sense.
7–18 because there is no *m·* sense.
No. 5– 9 from a false and *m·* sense,
5–11 this *m·* sense, which is untrue,
5–15 *M·* sense also avers that Spirit,
6–20 To *m·* sense it is plain also
6–24 to *m·* sense and feeling,
10–16 When a so-called *m·* sense is lost,
20–19 ever-present selfishness or *m·* sense.
29–10 not even a *m·* sense.
40– 4 a *m·* sense of approval ;
'00. 6–18 but in the *m·* sense which
'01. 12– 3 and it corrects the *m·* sense
'02. 8–26 coincide in *m·* sense.
Hea. 17–17 were hushed by *m·* sense
My. 110– 4 buried . . . in *m·* sense.
119–21 discharged evidence of *m·* sense
260– 5 The despotism of *m·* sense
260– 8 the inaccuracy of *m·* sense
262– 6 Observed by *m·* sense,
271– 2 matter and *m·* sense are null,
274– 5 a false *m·* sense of life,

senses
Mis. 47– 8 the *m·* senses cannot take in.
73–31 testimony of the so-called *m·* senses.
99– 3 saith to the five *m·* senses,
102–25 thus only to the *m·* senses,
118– 2 *m·* senses, false suggestions,
161–10 *m·* senses could not cognize the
183–31 The *m·* senses would make
185–20 so-called *m·* senses would close,
187–31 declaration of the *m·* senses
188–17 effects of Truth on the *m·* senses ;
204–21 they rebuke the *m·* senses,
218–11 evidence of the *m·* senses
234– 7 not learned of the *m·* senses,
277–23 No evidence before the *m·* senses
299–15 which the *m·* senses see not
362– 1 are not those of the *m·* senses ;
Ret. 9–16 never again to the *m·* senses
25–24 *m·* senses testify falsely,
59–20 the five *m·* senses define
Un. 10–22 evidence before the *m·* senses,
28–16 evidence of the *m·* senses.
29– 9 evidence of the *m·* senses,
30– 6 testimony of the *m·* senses.
35– 8 so-called *m·* senses are found,
37–22 The so-called *m·* senses,
39–22 evidence of the *m·* senses,
39–24 The *m·* senses testify falsely.
57– 3 the design of the *m·* senses
Rud. 4–26 The five *m·* senses testify
5– 2 testimony of the *m·* senses.
5–24 verdict of these *m·* senses,
6–10 to the *m·* senses, evil takes
6–19 *evidence of the m· senses,*
No. 25–10 cognize through the *m·* senses.
38– 3 the evidence of the *m·* senses
42–16 *m·* senses would enthrone error
'01. 7–22 to the personal *m·* senses
7–26 through the *m·* senses,
Peo. 2–15 evidences gained from the *m·* senses,
My. 114–23 as the sunlight on the *m·* senses.
188–27 spiritual sense and not the *m·* senses
217–23 all that the *m·* senses affirm.
274– 4 of matter or the *m·* senses.
301–19 testimony of the *m·* senses.

side
Mis. 140–18 *m·* side of this question.

sight
Un. 34– 9 *m·* sight is an illusion, a lie.
My. 265– 6 subordinate to *m·* sight and sound

signification
Hea. 7–10 instead of the *m·* signification.

standpoint
Pan. 9–27 From a *m·* standpoint,

state
Mis. 64–30 of a *m·* state and universe,

states
Un. 50–16 In reality there are no *m·* states

structure
Un. 34– 1 the so-called *m·* structure,
My. 28–18 * not to be found in the *m·* structure,

material

substance
Un. 24–16 There is no *m·* substance,
superstructure
Mis. 140–29 though the *m·* superstructure should crumble
symbol
My. 8–11 * let us have the best *m·* symbol
172–13 *m·* symbol of my spiritual call
systems
Mis. 232–14 part with *m·* systems and theories,
Peo. 8–25 uncremated fossils of *m·* systems,
tendencies
Mis. 10–25 worldly or *m·* tendencies
terms
No. 11– 9 is hampered by *m·* terms,
theology
'01. 26– 2 my tired sense of . . . *m·* theology
theories
Un. 28–15 *m·* theories are built on the
My. 159–18 *M·* theories tend to check spiritual
things
Mis. 72–18 *Are m· things real when they*
Ret. 28–13 Our reliance upon *m·* things must
31–16 error of faith in things *m·* ;
Pul. 35–17 Our reliance upon *m·* things must
My. 159–28 thought chiefly regards *m·* things,
194– 5 dies, as do all things *m·*,
thought
Mis. 102–26 state of mortal and *m·* thought.
Peo. 3–16 Truth meets the old *m·* thought
My. 267–24 *M·* thought tends to obscure
title
Mis. 140– 3 no one could hold a wholly *m·* title.
token
Mis. 160– 5 it may give no *m·* token,
tonic
My. 152– 8 said, "My *m·* tonic has
type
My. 45–31 * *m·* type of Truth's permanence.
universe
Mis. 72–23 as well as the *m·* universe,
219– 5 nor teaches that . . . are the *m·* universe,
Un. 10–26 not the blind force of a *m·* universe.
32– 5 man and the *m·* universe."
Rud. 4– 4 our *m·* universe and men are
10–11 beliefs of a mortal *m·* universe,
My. 179– 6 allegory, of a *m·* universe
view
Mis. 14– 3 the mortal and *m·* view which
ways
Mis. 153– 1 in man and his *m·* ways
world
Mis. 167–11 substance outweighs the *m·* world.
Ret. 26–18 before the *m·* world saw him.
Un. 52–17 the *m·* world, the flesh, and
Rud. 3– 7 the flesh, — the *m·* world and evil.
'01. 23–26 of an external *m·* world.
My. 74–23 * bondage of the *m·* world,
110– 7 material medicine, a *m·* world ;

Mis. 13–18 basis of *m·* and mortal evidence
17–22 A *m·* or human birth is
19–26 *m·* and spiritual gravitations,
19–29 the sinful, *m·*, and perishable,
21–21 man is not *m·* ; he is spiritual."
30–10 They were spiritual, not *m·* ;
36– 1 termed *m·* or mortal man,
42–10 to awaken with . . . as *m·* as before.
47–22 man, . . . is spiritual, not *m·*.
52– 1 to such as seek the *m·* to aid the
55–31 either a godless and *m·* Mind, or
61– 5 *m·* symbolic counterfeit sciences.
61–30 Mortals seem very *m·* ;
64–22 It is spiritual, and not *m·*.
72–24 nothing which is *m·* is in
72–27 Real sensation is not *m·* ;
72–29 cannot cognize aught *m·*,
73–12 Law is never *m·* :
86– 1 The *m·* and physical are imperfect.
89– 9 under *m·* medical treatment,
102–24 Whatever seems *m·*
165–13 leaves nothing that is *m·* ;
180–11 another person, more *m·*, met me,
180–29 in both a *m·* and a spiritual sense.
181–20 regard him as spiritual, and not *m·*.
184– 9 man . . . is spiritual, not *m·*.
185–31 namely, that creation is *m·* ;
186– 5 *m·* self-constituted belief of
187–29 *m·*, before spiritual ;
188– 7 that which appears second, *m·*, and
196–11 thus become *m·*, sensual, evil.
198– 6 denying *m·* so-called laws
217–17 Sensuous and *m·* realistic views
218–20 things spiritual, and not *m·*.
219– 6 or that . . . is finite or *m·*.
308–29 *m·* human likeness is the antipode of

material

Mis. 342– 4 their way was *m·* ;
351–22 sensuous love is *m·*,
352– 5 error of regarding . . . Love as *m·*
352– 5 or as both *m·* and spiritual,
361– 8 are neither *m·* nor mortal.
Ret. 21–13 our *m·*, mortal history is but
21–19 from a *m·*, false sense of life
67– 8 supposition that . . . are both *m·* and
67–15 testimony of *m·* personal sense
73– 2 his mortal opposite must, be *m·*
73– 9 *m·* human concept grew . . . less
Un. 9– 5 *M·* and sensual consciousness are
25–18 a *m·*, not a spiritual basis.
32–17 mortal mind declares itself *m·*,
33– 6 Now these senses, being *m·*,
35– 9 mortally mental, instead of *m·*.
42–10 *m·* before he can be spiritual,
43– 3 This generation seems too *m·* for
46–16 as spiritual and good, not as *m·* or
51– 3 false premises, — that Life is *m·*,
53–12 To say that Mind is *m·*,
Rud. 4– 8 It is not *m·* ;
5– 6 there is no *m·* mortal man,
6– 5 *are they not tangible and m·?*
7–13 According to . . . man is *m·*,
10– 8 with nothing evil or *m·* ;
No. 6–28 laws of Science are mental, not *m·* ;
10–19 former position, that sense is . . . *m·*,
17– 2 something unreal, *m·*, and mortal.
25–25 A *m·*, sinful mortal is but
26– 9 holding such *m·* and mortal views
27–20 This *m·* sinful personality,
29– 8 believe *m·* and sinning sense to be
31– 2 *M·* and mortal mind-healing
36–19 from *m·* to spiritual selfhood
40– 6 a *m·* and mortal sense of
'01. 8–18 Then can man be *m·*,
10– 9 Christ must be spiritual, not *m·*.
19–12 mixing *m·* and spiritual means,
22– 4 Is Science *m·* ? No !
22– 5 Is Truth *m·* ? No !
Hea. 6– 2 and we grow more *m·*,
7– 7 is the spiritual . . . as opposed to the *m·*.
17– 8 lust makes the *m·* so-called man,
Peo. 1–16 from *m·* to spiritual standpoints.
2–16 shockingly *m·* in practice,
4–22 out of beliefs that are as *m·* as
My. 6–25 giving to the *m·* a spiritual
48–23 * subordination of merely *m·* to
74–29 * the *m·* and the mental,
94–29 giving to the *m·* a spiritual
118–23 by a *m·* and not by the spiritual
139–20 from the *m·* to the spiritual,
139–24 *m·* to the spiritual communion ;
160–29 this hell is mental, not *m·*,
166–24 time and joy be spiritual, not *m·*.
178–15 those who regard being as *m·*.
239–25 is the *m·*, so-called man
260–13 Nothing conditional or *m·* belongs
262– 7 human, *m·*, mortal babe
262–22 which so transcends mortal, *m·*,
273–19 apart from a *m·* or personal sense
275– 6 The human, *m·*, so-called senses
303–21 subordinated the *m·* to the spiritual,
345–11 * are these too *m·* for C. S.?"

materialism

Mis. 17–17 from under the curse of *m·*,
19–27 we go out of *m·* or sin,
30–29 mist of *m·* will vanish
144–31 wake the long night of *m·*,
156–21 It is *m·* through which the
162–17 lamb upon the altar of *m·*,
166–26 and all *m·* disappear.
Pul. 52–21 * wave of *m·* and bigotry
79–19 * crass *m·* of the cruder science
'01. 25–21 metaphysics based on *m·*?
Hea. 8–18 suffocate reason by *m·*.
Peo. 4– 2 *materia medica* nothing but *m·*,
My. 110– 6 upon the long night of *m·*,
221– 3 distance between Christianity and *m·*
254– 7 Released from *m·*,

materialisms

Peo. 5– 7 cold *m·* of dogma and doctrine

materialistic

Mis. 64–16 Man-made theories are . . . always *m·*.
245– 8 *m·* portion of the pulpit
246–29 a *m·* religion and a *materia medica*
369–14 the leaders of *m·* schools
Ret. 78–13 which advocate *m·* systems ;
Peo. 4–28 a *m·* and idolatrous theory

materialistically

Pul. 79–27 * had become *m·* "lopsided,"

materiality

Mis.	28–17	can overbear *m·* and mortality ;
	73–11	and the unreality of *m·*.
	103– 7	*m·*, and destructive forces,
	104–16	His *m·*, clad in a false
	156–19	It is their *m·* that clogs
	162–25	*M·*, worldliness, human pride,
	205– 5	shining through the mists of *m·*
Ret.	66– 4	no longer buried in *m·*.
	68–21	bases creation on *m·*''
	73– 4	He is without *m·*, without finiteness
Un.	49–16	serve the mammon of *m·*
No.	26–21	corpuscle, *m·*, or mortality.
'02.	5– 5	religion parting with its *m·*.
Peo.	10– 4	refinements that lose some *m·* ;
My.	122–22	idea unenvironed by *m·*
	357– 1	*m·* is wholly apart from C. S.,

materialization

Mis. 349– 8	*m·* of a student's thought,

materialize

No. 34– 6	no longer venture to *m·* the

materialized

Peo. 4– 6	belief that Spirit *m·* into

materializes

Mis. 268– 1	*m·* human modes and consciousness,

materially

Mis.	57– 1	created man over again *m·* ;
	57– 7	not from dust, *m·*, but from Spirit,
	57–24	the universe created *m·*.
	73– 6	Interpreted *m·*, these passages
	91– 4	to organize *m·* Christ's church.
	140– 6	but *m·* questionable
	182– 2	began spiritually instead of *m·*
Ret.	32– 5	whatever is loved *m·*,
Rud.	5–22	and we could not see *m·* ;
'01.	5–16	defined spiritually, not *m·*
My.	119–19	not . . . spiritually, but he could *m·*.
	181– 1	defines . . . spiritually, not *m·*.

materia medica

Mis.	3–25	*m· m·*, hygiene, and
	5–15	*M· m·* says, "I can do no more.
	17–11	put off your *m· m·* and hygiene
	81– 2	this is not the basis of *m· m·*,
	89–11	or interfere with *m· m·*,
	134–21	The reeling ranks of *m· m·*,
	246–30	materialistic religion and a *m· m·?*
	379–21	beyond the basis of *m· m·*,
Ret.	33– 5	dim mazes of *m· m·*,
'01.	24–28	*m· m·*, and scholastic theology
	30–18	in theology and *m· m·*,
Peo.	3– 4	and the ideals of *m· m·*
	4– 2	given to all systems of *m· m·*
	5– 9	whose *m· m·* and theology were one.
	5–27	* if the whole *m· m·* could be sunk
My.	106–14	impossible for the surgeon or *m· m·*
	127–13	Comparing . . . with *m· m·*
	127–14	overwhelms *m· m·*, even as
	127–18	ninety-nine to the ten of *m· m·*.
	190– 8	Does C. S. equal *m· m·*
	190–10	both practices— *m· m·* and
	222–23	does not provide that *m· m·*
	227–32	larger per cent . . . than does *m· m·*.
	265–19	that religion and *m· m·* should
	266–26	points in theology and *m· m·*,
	288–15	creed, dogma, or *m· m·*.
	292–23	In the practice of *m· m·*,
	307–27	emerging from *m· m·*,
	307–29	The fallacy of *m· m·*,
	348–13	and that *m· m·* heals him.
	348–15	neither man nor *m· m·*,

maternal

Pul. 32–25	* her *m·* grandfather, was known as

mathematical

Mis.	57–27	is stated in *m·* order,
	210– 5	proving with *m·* certainty

mathematically

Pul. 4– 7	metaphysically and *m·* number one,

mathematician

My. 237– 7	The best *m·* has not attained

mathematics

Mis.	26– 4	truth, as demonstrable as *m·*.
	29–31	Christians, like students in *m·*,
	52–23	if, when tired of *m·* or failing to
	60–16	addition is not subtraction in *m·*
	62–10	even as in *m·*,
	118– 8	To obey the principle of *m·*
	233–23	scientist in *m·* who finds fault
Ret.	87– 6	as in astronomy or *m·*.
Un.	10–24	principle of positive *m·*.
'01.	4– 5	In *m·* four times three is twelve,
	4– 6	To depart from the rule of *m·*
	4– 7	destroys the proof of *m·* ;

mathematics

'01.	23–14	a change of the denominations of *m·* ;
Hea.	8–27	as we do to the rule of *m·*,
My.	235–10	she cannot do this in *m·*,

matin

Mis.	396–11	songsters' *m·* hymns to God
Po.	59– 3	songsters' *m·* hymns to God

matter (*see also* matter's)

above

Ret.	18–17	May soar above *m·*,
Po.	64– 8	May soar above *m·*,
My.	106–10	above *m·* in every mode and form,
	190–20	over the human mind and *above m·*

all

'01.	27–24	taken out of its metaphysics all *m·*
My.	217–18	* "If all *m·* is unreal, why do we

an alien

My.	260– 3	would make *m·* an alien

and evil

Mis.	27–11	*m·* and evil . . . are *unreal.*
	101–24	virtually destroys *m·* and evil,
	367– 5	*M·* and evil are subjective states of
Ret.	60–10	and that *m·* and evil are as real as
Un.	8–14	the unreality of *m·* and evil
	50–24	*M·* and evil cannot be conscious,
	53–11	*M·* and evil are anti-Christian,
No.	21–13	would . . . substitute *m·* and evil for
	24–10	denies . . . both *m·* and evil.
Pan.	7–22	It certainly gives to *m·* and evil
My.	262–16	the gloom of *m·* and evil

and human will

No.	11– 1	whereas *m·* and human will,

and its methods

Mis.	175–21	instituting *m·* and its methods

and man

My.	153–31	pointing away from *m·* and man

and Mind

Mis.	175–28	The attempt to mix *m·* and Mind,
	269–18	his choice between *m·* and Mind,

and mind

Mis.	173–14	says that man is both *m·* and mind,
'01.	25–10	which mix *m·* and mind,
Hea.	13– 1	and divide . . . between *m·* and mind,

and mortal mind

Un.	35–20	*m·* and mortal mind are one ;
No.	15–22	*m·* and mortal mind have neither
	24– 7	lower orders of *m·* and mortal mind.

and Spirit

Mis.	217–11	fallacy . . . *m·* and Spirit are one
No.	26– 3	believe . . . *m·* and Spirit are one ;
Pan.	8–25	admixtures of *m·* and Spirit,
'01.	22– 6	do not try to mix *m·* and Spirit,
Peo.	9–13	between *m·* and Spirit ;

and the earth

Mis.	179–27	yet we look into *m·* and the earth

annihilate

My.	226–16	But annihilate *m·*, and man . . . would

any compromise with

Mis.	53–15	by any compromise with *m·* ;

apart from

'01.	24– 1	* *M·* apart from conscious mind
My.	108– 8	to act apart from *m·*.
	167– 6	which is apart from *m·*,

appears

Un.	41–26	*m·* appears to both live and die,

as its effect

Mis.	218–22	with *m·* as its effect,

as substance

Un.	32–12	all sense of *m·* as substance,
My.	235–18	*M·* as substance or intelligence

as useful

'01.	25–26	to be as real, and *m·* as useful,

basis of

Mis.	243–21	who practise on the basis of *m·*,

because of

Rud.	12–17	that they live in or because of *m·*,

belief in

Mis.	56–19	this false belief in *m·*
Un.	50– 8	pantheistic belief in *m·*

belief of pain in

Mis.	44–18	a belief of pain in *m·* ;

belief that

Rud.	10–24	belief that *m·* can master Mind,
No.	5–10	belief that *m·* has sensation.

believe in

Un.	50– 3	*Do you believe in m·?*
	50– 4	I believe in *m·* only as

belongs to

Mis.	51–15	that sensation belongs to *m·*.

better than

Ret.	31–11	higher and better than *m·*,

brain is

Pan.	4–14	that brain is *m·*,

buried in

Mis.	78– 1	Life, God, is not buried in *m·*.

matter

called
Mis. 173–29 atom or molecule called *m*·?
Un. 33– 5 of a substance called *m*·.
Rud. 5–16 mind which is called *m*·,
'01. 24– 5 which is generally called *m*·

calling on
Mis. 333–18 calling on *m*· to work out the

cannot be, in
Un. 25– 8 Mind is not, cannot be, in *m*·.

cannot cure
Hea. 12– 9 when *m*· cannot cure it,

cannot even talk
Mis. 23–16 *M*· cannot even talk ;

cannot feel
Un. 34–15 that *m*· cannot feel *m*· ;
Rud. 10–14 *m*· cannot feel, see, or report

cannot talk
Un. 25– 9 *M*· cannot talk ;

character of
Un. 31–18 nature and character of *m*·,

claim of
Mis. 258– 5 unrelenting false claim of *m*·
Un. 32– 3 the claim of *m*· usurps the

claims
Mis. 27–22 *m*· claims something besides God,

claims of
Un. 31– 9 annulled the claims of *m*·,
36–18 rejection of the claims of *m*·

conditions of
Pan. 4–10 conditions of *m*·, or brain,

confining itself to
Un. 62–25 Mortal sense, confining itself to *m*·,

conscious
Un. 44–22 [you shall be conscious *m*·],
45–14 conscious *m*· implies pantheism.

control
My. 293–25 law of Spirit to control *m*·,

cords of
Un. 30–22 to break the cords of *m*·,

created
Ret. 60– 9 adds . . . divine Spirit created *m*·,

currents of
Un. 11– 4 currents of *m*·, or mortal mind.

dead
My. 206– 1 would unite dead *m*· with animate,

declaims against
'01. 26–10 he declaims against *m*·,

demands of
No. 18–26 against the so-called demands of *m*·,
Peo. 12–16 lifts man above the demands of *m*·.

denial of
Un. 31–16 position, in the denial of *m*·,

disappearance as
Mis. 271– 3 the point of its disappearance as *m*·

disarrangement of
Pan. 8– 2 the disarrangement of *m*· causes

discovered in
Pan. 5– 3 Can . . . be discovered in *m*·?

does not express
Mis. 218–24 *m*· does not express the nature of

does not recognize
Mis. 74–11 *If God does not recognize m*·,

dream of life in
Mis. 16–17 from the dream of life in *m*·,
Hea. 9–27 from the dream of life in *m*·,
Peo. 14–16 look upon this dream of life in *m*·,
My. 267–21 from his dream of life in *m*·

dweller in
Mis. 189–21 not a dweller in *m*·.

element of
Mis. 201– 7 and death is an element of *m*·,

error or
Mis. 190– 4 Life, defiant of error or *m*·.
Un. 42–24 Truth, defiant of error or *m*·,

evil and
Mis. 27–20 evil and *m*· are negation :
'01. 25–28 excludes evil and *m*·.

evil or
Un. 50–19 consciousness of evil or *m*·

evolve
Mis. 23–32 could not change . . . and evolve *m*·.

evolving
Rud. 7–24 by evolving *m*· from Spirit,

existent in
Un. 46–14 no selfhood as existent in *m*·.

faith in
Mis. 334– 9 mortals' faith in *m*· may have
Peo. 9–20 showing our greater faith in *m*·,
My. 4– 1 losing his faith in *m*· and sin,

finite
Ret. 58– 3 taking the rule of finite *m*·,

forces of
Un. 35–18 the merciless forces of *m*·.
35–19 What then *are* the . . . forces of *m*·?

matter

formed by
Mis. vii– 9 IF worlds were formed by *m*·,

form of
Un. 33–16 that form of *m*· called *brains*,

forms of
My. 212–11 use of higher forms of *m*·,

for rejoicing
Pul. 22– 5 *m*· for rejoicing that we unite
My. 285–13 *m*· for rejoicing that the best,

God is not in
Mis. 75–14 God is not in *m*· or the mortal

has no
Mis. 76–25 *m*· has no sense.
198– 8 understanding that *m*· has no sense ;
Un. 38–12 since *m*· has no life,
My. 109– 2 *M*· has no . . . substance and reality

has no intelligence
Mis. 44–27 *m*· has no intelligence of its own.
Ret. 69–20 *m*· has no intelligence, life, nor

has no sensation
Mis. 44–18 for *m*· has no sensation.
Ret. 61–22 for *m*· has no sensation

hypothesis of
My. 349–15 putting off the hypothesis of *m*·

I challenge
My. 108– 5 I challenge *m*· to act apart from mind ;

idea of
Mis. 75– 2 Jesus' idea of *m*·.

if He knows
No. 16– 3 If He knows *m*·,

illusion of
Mis. 28–19 he arose above the illusion of *m*·.

important
Man. 100–15 to act upon this important *m*·

in and out of
Hea. 4–16 in and out of *m*· for an indefinite

independent of
Mis. 43– 2 act of itself, and independent of *m*·,

inert
Mis. 3–16 Drugs, inert *m*·, never are needed

infused into
Mis. 190– 3 It is neither . . . infused into *m*· :
Ret. 58–13 it was not . . . infused into *m*· ;

instead of
Mis. 35– 3 fact that Mind, instead of *m*·,
190–25 belongs to Mind instead of *m*·,
276–27 from *m*· instead of Spirit,
Hea. 12– 2 Mind instead of *m*· heals
Peo. 2–12 of Mind instead of *m*·,
12–25 to *m*· instead of Spirit.

is a frail conception
Mis. 87–11 *M*· is a frail conception of

is a lie
Rud. 7–20 *m*· is a lie,

is a misstatement
Mis. 174– 2 *M*· is a misstatement of Mind ;

is a phase
Mis. 25– 7 *m*· is a phase of error,

is egoistic
Un. 26– 1 *Evil.* . . . *m*· is egoistic,

is erroneous
Un. 36–14 *m*· is erroneous, transitory,

is inert
Rud. 5– 9 *M*· is inert, inanimate,

is mortal error
Mis. 21–19 *m*· is mortal error.

is mortal mind
Un. 35–10 *m*· is mortal mind ;

is mythology
Mis. 55–27 *m*· is mythology,

is not a lawgiver
Peo. 12– 9 when *m*· is not a lawgiver

is not conscious
My. 221–26 since *m*· is not conscious ;

is not intelligent
Mis. 26–17 *M*· is not intelligent,

is not Mind
No. 27– 4 *M*· is not Mind, to claim aught ;

is not seen
Un. 34– 7 That *m*· is not seen ;

is not sensible
My. 349– 9 and *m*· is not sensible.

is nowhere
Mis. 173–20 *m*· is nowhere and sin is obsolete.

is obsolete
Ret. 34– 4 in which *m*· is obsolete.

is proven powerless
Mis. 29–29 whereby *m*· is proven powerless

is the opposite
Un. 36–12 *m*· is the opposite of Spirit,

is the substratum
No. 16–25 *m*· is the substratum of evil,

is the unreal
Mis. 21–20 *m*· is the unreal and temporal.

matter

is unconscious
  Un. 25– 2 If you say that *m·* is unconscious,
lawgiver to
  Mis. 364–26 If Spirit is the lawgiver to *m·*,
law of
  (*see* **law**)
laws of
  (*see* **laws**)
lifelessness of
  Mis. 74–27 demonstrated the lifelessness of *m·*,
Life not in
  My. 181–12 Life not in *m·* but in Mind.
light, being
  '01. 3–25 light, being *m·*, loses the nature of
manifest as
  Hea. 12–12 before they can become manifest as *m·* ;
man nor
  '01. 4–12 neither man nor *m·* can be.
medicine of
  '01. 18– 8 the old-time medicine of *m·*.
Mind and
  Mis. 56–16 Mind and *m·* mingling in perpetual
    280–12 not two, — Mind *and m·*.
  Ret. 59–21 define Mind and *m·* as distinct,
mind and
  (*see* **mind**)
mind in
  (*see* **mind**)
Mind is not in
  Rud. 7–21 Mind is not in *m·*,
    13– 1 that Mind is not in *m·* ;
Mind, not
  Mis. 56–10 Life is immortal Mind, not *m·*.
    190– 1 Atomic action is Mind, not *m·*.
  '00. 11–19 Mind, not *m·*, makes music ;
mind, not
  My. 107–20 identifies . . . with mind, not *m·*,
    302– 4 mind, not *m·*, produces the result
Mind or
  Mis. 23–10 Was it Mind or *m·* that spake
mind or
  Mis. 103–20 Mortal man, as mind or *m·*,
    218–16 inconceivable, either as mind or *m·* ;
  No. 38– 8 no intelligent sin, evil *mind* or *m·* :
  My. 108– 4 is mind or *m·* the intelligent cause
Mind over
  Mis. 35– 5 supremacy of Mind over *m·*,
  Hea. 7– 6 the power of Mind over *m·*.
mind over
  Pul. 31–19 * dominance of mind over *m·*,
  Hea. 15– 9 the power of mind over *m·*,
  My. 74–14 * triumph of mind over *m·*.
    97– 2 * the power of mind over *m·*.
Mind to
  Mis. 268–11 who departs from Mind to *m·*,
  Rud. 6– 9 when we change . . . from Mind to *m·*,
misnamed
  Mis. 201– 4 resolves the element misnamed *m·*
mists of
  No. 16–23 mists of *m·* — sin, sickness,
molecule, as
  Un. 35–23 molecule, as *m·*, is not formed by
more than
  Mis. 47– 6 substance means more than *m·* :
  Un. 24–23 My mind is more than *m·*.
  No. 25–10 Mind is more than *m·*,
mortal mind or
  No. 16–12 evil, called mortal mind or *m·*,
must be understood
  Mis. 233–30 *M·* must be understood as a false
must disappear
  Mis. 217–29 and *m·* must *dis*appear,
mythical nature of
  Mis. 47–14 the mythical nature of *m·*,
named
  Mis. 27– 6 its opposite, named *m·*,
    361–28 named *m·*, or mortal mind.
  Rud. 7–22 its opposite, named *m·*.
namely
  Mis. 217–12 antipode of Spirit, namely, *m·*.
name of
  Mis. 258–20 and call Mind by the name of *m·*,
names
  Mis. 24–19 subjective state which it names *m·*,
neither in
  No. 15–21 finds Spirit neither in *m·* nor in
neither lives
  Un. 41–25 hence *m·* neither lives nor dies.
neither sees
  Ret. 25–25 *m·* neither sees, hears, nor feels
never appealed to
  My. 288–19 He never appealed to *m·*
never escaped from
  Hea. 18– 9 never escaped from *m·* ;

matter

never in
  Un. 62–22 man is My idea, never in *m·*,
never produced
  Mis. 218– 3 *m·* never produced Mind, and *vice versa.*
no
  Mis. 108–31 and that there is no *m·*
    174–17 No *m·* is there,
    183– 8 there is no *m·* to cope with.
    357–25 no *m·* who has taught them.
  Ret. 94–12 leaves no flesh, no *m·*,
  Un. 31– 6 surely there can be no *m·* ;
    34–13 consequently there is no *m·*.
    41–25 In C. S. there is no *m·* ;
    43–27 Spirit which knows no *m·*.
  Rud. 4–19 *Is there no m·?*
    6– 2 inference that there is no *m·*.
  My. 75–21 * no *m·* how far they had travelled
    357–23 "There is no *m·*"
no easy
  No. 15–14 It is no easy *m·* to believe
no longer in
  '01. 11– 7 and mind is no longer in *m·*.
nor mortal mind
  Un. 33–18 neither *m·* nor mortal mind,
  Rud. 13– 2 neither *m·* nor mortal mind ;
no sense in
  Un. 21–19 no sense in *m·* ;
not by
  Pul. vii–18 not by *m·*, but by Mind ;
  '01. 5–16 by Mind, not by *m·*.
not conscious of
  Un. 36–24 yet is not conscious of *m·*,
not contingent on
  No. 43– 3 Truth is not contingent on *m·*.
nothingness of
  (*see* **nothingness**)
of fact
  My. 14–24 * As a *m·* of fact, the building fund
    310–10 As a *m·* of fact, he was
of interest
  My. 89–23 * *m·* of interest to that city
of the brain
  Mis. 247–21 believe it . . . in *m·* of the brain ;
of wonder
  My. 82–11 * it was a *m·* of wonder
or evil
  Mis. 363–13 changes of *m·*, or evil.
  No. 17– 4 *M·*, or evil, is the absence of Spirit
organizations of
  Un. 33–27 through the organizations of *m·*,
organized
  Ret. 60– 5 as a broken sphere, as organized *m·*,
  Rud. 5–27 the five senses as organized *m·*,
or Mind
  Mis. 334–23 by means of *m·*, or Mind?
or mortals
  Mis. 22– 5 that *m·* or mortals can evolve Science?
or power
  Un. 35–15 Which was first, *m·* or power?
or spirit
  My. 235–20 is he *m·* or spirit?
or the body
  My. 349– 7 *m·*, or the body, cannot cause disease,
or the flesh
  Mis. 124– 7 by means of *m·*, or the flesh,
pains of
  Mis. 73–20 so-called pleasures and pains of *m·*
    209–13 so-called pains of *m·*
passed into
  Ret. 69– 8 delusion that life . . . passed into *m·*.
plane of
  Mis. 143– 6 above the plane of *m·*.
pleasures of
  Mis. 200–29 so-called pains and pleasures of *m·*
points away from
  Peo. 5–18 points away from *m·* and doctrine,
power over
  '01. 23–21 demonstrated his power over *m·*,
  '02. 10– 4 power over *m·*, molecule, space,
predicate
  Mis. 364–22 Human hypotheses predicate *m·* of
problem of
  My. 110–22 solve the blind problem of *m·*.
produce
  Mis. 217–20 and that these . . . produce *m·*,
prove
  Un. 33– 1 which prove *m·* to be identical
qualities of
  Un. 35– 4 the qualities of *m·* are but
quality of
  Mis. 256–23 every quality of *m·*, in and of
recognition of
  Mis. 173–11 no relation to, or recognition of, *m·*
regarded
  Mis. 200–30 regarded *m·* as only a vagary of

matter

saying unto
My. 191–20   Spirit is saying unto *m·* :
schools and
'01. 26–13   to the schools and *m·* for help
self and
Mis. 343–13   the sordid soil of self and *m·*.
self-conscious
Mis. 183–12   and pains of self-conscious *m·*.
Un. 53– 1   supposed modes of self-conscious *m·*,
self-existent
Peo. 5–23   ego is not self-existent *m·*
selfhood in
Ret. 73–15   personality, or selfhood in *m·*,
sense of
Mis. 74–13   Christ Jesus' sense of *m·* was the
187– 5   above every sense of *m·*,
Un. 32–12   destroys all sense of *m·*
sensible
Un. 21–18   There is no sensible *m·*,
sepulchre of
Mis. 180–15   door from this sepulchre of *m·*.
servant of
Pan. 8–27   They make man the servant of *m·*,
shall seem
Ret. 69–12   *m·* shall seem to have life
shows that
No. 16– 9   C. S. shows that *m·*, evil, sin,
so-called
My. 302– 9   manifest through so-called *m·*.
so-called facts of
Mis. 55–20   the so-called facts of *m·* ;
so-called life in
Mis. 128– 3   lessons of this so-called life in *m·*
so-called life of
My. 274– 3   apart from the so-called life of *m·*
so-called power of
My. 293– 4   the so-called power of *m·*,
so great a
Un. 5–10   personal opinion on so great a *m·*,
spat upon
Mis. 258– 8   literally spat upon *m·* ;
Spirit and
    (*see* **Spirit**)
Spirit, not
Mis. 5–19   power of Spirit, not *m·*,
'01. 5–22   man reflects Spirit, not *m·*.
Peo. 9– 2   builds on Spirit, not *m·* ;
Spirit, or
Mis. 28–22   What meaneth this Me, — Spirit, or *m·*?
Spirit over
Mis. 140–10   superiority of . . . Spirit over *m·*
Ret. 26–11   superiority of Spirit over *m·*.
Spirit with
My. 206– 2   would unite . . . Spirit with *m·*
strips
Mis. 185– 6   it strips *m·* of all claims,
subdued
Ret. 58– 9   sense of power that subdued *m·*
subduing
'02. 10–13   subjugating the body, subduing *m·*,
subjugates
'02. 10– 2   and subjugates *m·*,
submerged in
My. 179– 8   In this . . . are submerged in *m·*.
subordinates
Mis. 189–24   spiritual power that subordinates *m·*
suffering
My. 132–27   dreaming of suffering *m·* ;
summary of the
Mis. 35–12   complete, summary of the *m·* :
superiority over
Mis. 379–29   Mind and its superiority over *m·*,
supposed life in
Mis. 201–14   nothingness of supposed life in *m·*,
supposed power of
Mis. 199– 3   deny the supposed power of *m·*
supposition that
Mis. 74–24   supposition that *m·* is intelligent,
supremacy over
Mis. 63–30   Spirit proved its supremacy over *m·*.
take away
Un. 34–21   Take away *m·*, and mortal mind
takes no cognizance
Mis. 28– 8   *M·* takes no cognizance of matter.
teaching that
Un. 45–13   teaching that *m·* can be conscious ;
termed
No. 10–15   What is termed *m·*, or relates to its
testifies
Un. 33–10   *m·* testifies of itself, "I am matter ;"
theory that
Mis. 74–22   theory that *m·* is substance ;
this
Mis. 146–24   you will act, relative to this *m·*,
299– 9   detailed report of this *m·*,

matter

this
My. 130–16   I ask the help of others in this *m·*,
334–26   * Of further interest in this *m·*
through
Mis. 185– 6   not as or through *m·*,
333–26   that God wrought through *m·*
thus affirms
Un. 24–25   Whatever *m·* thus affirms is
to be matter
Mis. 173–32   For *m·* to be matter, it must
to create
Mis. 174– 1   to evolve or to create *m·*
to govern
Hea. 15– 9   it enables mind to govern *m·*,
to Mind
Peo. 7– 6   turn often . . . from *m·* to Mind,
to Spirit
Mis. 194–22   *how* to turn from *m·* to Spirit
'02. 10–22   transit from *m·* to Spirit
My. 163– 6   from *m·* to Spirit.
181–10   departure from *m·* to Spirit,
translates
Mis. 25–12   translates *m·* into Mind,
Hea. 7– 9   translates *m·* into its original
Truth is not in
Mis. 179–14   Truth is not in *m·* ;
unconscious of
No. 36–12   unconscious of *m·*, of sin,
usurpation, by
Un. 51–12   pretentious usurpation, by *m·*,
usurps
Un. 31–17   rests on the fact that *m·* usurps
32– 3   *m·* usurps the prerogative of
vanquished
Mis. 74–21   virtually vanquished *m·* and its
veil of
Mis. 124–25   rent the veil of *m·*,
weary of
Hea. 11– 8   weary of *m·*, it would catch
we name
Mis. 267–24   which we name *m·*, or *non-intelligent*
went out
Hea. 11–22   proportionately as *m·* went out
what made
My. 235–18   Who or what made *m·*?
whole
Un. 34–10   summary of the whole *m·*,
will become vague
Peo. 10– 6   *m·* will become vague,
will be proved
No. 27–11   *m·* will be proved a myth.
within the skull
Un. 33–14   Brain, . . . only *m·* within the skull,
without
Un. 34– 8   mortal mind cannot see without *m·* ;
without Mind
Rud. 5–16   it must be . . . or *m·* without Mind.
5–17   *M·* without Mind is a
with Spirit
'01. 26– 9   combines *m·* with Spirit.
worshipping of
My. 151–28   worshipping of *m·* in the name of

———

Mis. 5–25   but believe it to be brain *m·*.
17–31   by which one loses himself as *m·*,
21–17   "There is no life, . . . in *m·*.
23–15   for *m·* is not the Christian's God,
26–16   from infinite Mind, or from *m·*?
26–16   If from *m·*, how did *m·* originate?
26–23   just what I call *m·*, *nothing*.
28– 2   *M·* can neither see, hear, feel,
28– 8   Matter takes no cognizance of *m·*.
28–25   no intelligence nor life in *m·* ;
30–17   Life . . . untrammelled, by *m·*.
30–28   mist from the earth [*m·*] ;" — *Gen.* 2 : 6.
36–29   in *m·* and separate from God,
44–20   You call this body *m·*,
44–21   That *m·* can report pain,
44–22   or that mind is *in m·*,
45– 3   *m·* is but a belief,
47– 1   *there is no such thing as m·*,
47– 4   *m·* is but manifest mortal mind.
49–25   belief, that Mind is in *m·*,
50–23   the belief that the heart is *m·*
51–13   *teach him life in m·?*
53– 2   false claim of . . . life in *m·*,
53– 6   error of supposed life . . . in *m·*,
55–22   over their opposite, or *m·*,
55–29   If Mind is in *m·*
55–31   or it is God in *m·*,
58–15   As *m·*, the eye cannot see ;
60–28   has its counterfeit in some *m·* belief.
63– 1   and the *sickness of m·*,
68–25   * as distinguished from that of *m·* ;
70–22   The thief's body, as *m·*

matter

Mis.	71–17	neither human hypothesis nor *m*.
	72–22	*that Spirit takes note of m*.?
	72–25	*M*. is manifest mortal mind,
	73– 1	no evidence of the reality of *m*.,
	74–30	*m*. is neither substance, . . . nor Life,
	76–10	belief that . . . are in *m*.
	76–24	false sense of mentality in *m*,
	84–22	Paul's sense of life in *m*,
	85–22	mortal mind which seems to be *m*.
	85–23	suggests pleasure and pain in *m*. ;
	93–19	Fear is a belief of sensation in *m*. :
	101–23	not *m*, but Mind.
	103– 4	more impregnable and solid than *m*. ;
	113– 2	Mind that is God is not in *m*. ;
	124– 5	cannot find God in *m*.,
	173–10	law of Mind and not of *m*,
	173–15	that Mind is in *m*.?
	174–20	first to declare against . . . is *m*.
	175– 8	says, I am sustained by bread, *m*.,
	179– 8	Is our consciousness in *m*. or in God?
	184– 2	by claiming that . . . man is *m*. ;
	189–16	supposition . . . is breathed into *m*.,
	190– 2	It is neither the energy of *m*.,
	196– 2	ego is found not in *m*. but in Mind,
	198–19	man's body, as *m*., has no power to
	199–22	which mortals name *m*.
	200– 8	*m*. was palpably an error of premise
	217–18	presuppose that nature is *m*.,
	217–21	that *m*. is both cause and
	217–29	must change in order to become *m*.,
	217–31	To . . . sense, everything is *m*. ;
	218– 7	*m*. can neither see, hear, nor feel,
	219– 3	neither reveals God in *m*. ;
	228–24	belong to mind and not to *m*.
	233–32	sensation is not in *m*,
	234– 2	then shall *m*. remain no longer to
	234–22	is *m*. of grave wonderment to
	256–25	The assertion that *m*. is a law,
	257– 1	the notion that Mind can be in *m*.
	258–30	the law of Spirit, not of *m*.
	260– 8	His faith partook not of drugs, *m*.,
	260–12	in the laws of Spirit, not of *m*. ;
	280–16	not put into the scales with *m*. ;
	332– 2	but not life in *m*.
	333– 1	that this . . . is intelligent *m*. ;
	333–12	in *m*. as well as Spirit?
	334– 8	simulates power and Truth in *m*,
	334–31	Is *m*. Truth? No!
	336– 7	resort to stones and clubs, — yea, to *m*.,
	344–18	would place . . . intelligence in *m*. ;
	362– 2	for instance, intelligent *m*.,
	362–18	mortal mind, with its phenomenon *m*.,
	379–13	*m*. was not as real as Mind,
	379–25	Is it *m*., or is it Mind,
Man.	66– 4	a clear understanding of the *m*.,
Ret.	23– 9	*M*. was no longer spanned with
	25–19	and *m*., the *unreality*.
	25–23	witnesses to the . . . existence of *m*. ;
	33–19	and *m*. is thereby rarefied
	57–17	*M*. is substance in error,
	60– 8	material sense says that *m*.,
	60–25	*m*. and its so-called organizations
	68–19	"How can *m*. originate or transmit
	69–11	into what I call *m*.,
	69–18	believing that there is life in *m*.,
	69–28	belief that mind is in *m*.,
	93–20	no life, . . . nor intelligence in *m*."
Un.	22–22	*will-power*, — *alias* intelligent *m*.
	24–24	In my mortal mind, *m*. becomes
	25– 9	as Mind, and not as *m*.
	25–11	This lie, that Mind can be in *m*,
	26– 1	*Evil.* I am intelligent *m*. ;
	26– 3	is in *m*., and *m*. reproduces
	31–12	claim of sin is, that *m*. exists ;
	31–12	*second*, that *m*. is substance ;
	31–13	that *m*. has intelligence ;
	31–14	that *m*., being so endowed,
	32– 1	according to belief, obtain in *m*. ;
	32– 7	By *m*. is commonly meant mind,
	33– 3	(*m*. really having no sense)
	33–10	testifies of itself, "I am *m*. ;"
	33–11	but unless *m*. is mind,
	33–26	Mortal mind declares that *m*. sees
	34– 1	or that mind sees by means of *m*.
	34– 3	and declares that *m*. is the master of
	34–14	says . . . nerves, *do* feel *m*.
	34–19	that *m*. is substantial, is hot or
	34–20	Take away . . . and *m*. could not feel
	35–12	is not *m*., but Spirit.
	36–21	deny the existence or reality of *m*.,
	40– 6	or the belief of life in *m*.,
	41–23	Spirit can never dwell in . . . *m*.
	42– 3	*M*., sin, and death are not
	42– 5	What then are *m*., sin, and death?
	42–23	nor . . . power into *m*.

matter

Un.	45–24	the visionary substance of *m*.
	45–28	*M*. is not truly conscious ;
	50–11	*m*. is only a phenomenon of
	50–17	*m*. has neither Mind nor sensation.
	56– 5	comes from mind, not from *m*.,
Pul.	6– 8	not *m*., but Mind ;
	51– 6	* to a *m*. like C. S.,
Rud.	4–17	Spirit is not in *m*.,
	4–18	Law is not in *m*., but in Mind
	5– 1	testify to the existence of *m*.
	5–12	who has ever found Soul in . . . *m*.,
	5–13	who has found sight in *m*.,
	5–15	If there is any such thing as *m*.,
	5–18	Mind in *m*. is pantheism.
	6– 6	they are real, but not as *m*.
	7–18, 19	*M*., as *m*., has neither sensation nor
	10–13	of mortal mind, and not of *m*. ;
	10–28	to believe in the existence of *m*.,
	11– 1	or that *m*. can frame its own
	12–10	belief . . . made sick by *m*.
No.	16– 3	If . . . *m*. can exist in Mind,
	17–15	*M*., or any mode of mortal mind,
	25–15	neither *m*. nor a mode of mortal mind,
	29– 6	believes that Spirit, . . . exists in *m*.
	29–14	statement . . . that Soul is in *m*.
	31–20	not as in or of *m*., but as . . . beliefs
	35–19	*m*., — which is the antipode of God,
Pan.	5– 5	What, then, can *m*. create,
	6–17	can *m*. be an intelligent creator or
	6–24	can *m*. be force or law ;
	7– 4	intelligent *m*., signifies more than
	7–27	hypothesis of . . . *m*. governing Mind,
'01.	22–13	therefore *m*. cannot be a reality.
	24– 3	He denies the existence of *m*.,
	24– 3	and argues that *m*. is not *without*
	24–12	Making *m*. more potent than
	25–15	*m*. minus, and God all,
	25–23	Had he taught the . . . power of *m*.,
	27–26	born of the Spirit and not *m*.
'02.	7– 5	*m*., sin, . . . and death enter not into
Hea.	9–25	Life in *m*. is a dream ;
	10– 1	the vision of life in *m*. ;
	12– 5	to learn what *m*. is doing
	17–24	false supposition of life . . . in *m*.
Peo.	4–10	said . . . and *m*. become intelligent
	8–17	and yet we make more of *m*.,
My.	5–11	Whence, then, came the creation of *m*.,
	75–15	* *m*. of securing accommodations.
	108– 5	If *m*., I challenge matter to
	109– 1	*M*. is but the subjective state of
	119–10	in Mind, not in *m*.
	132–25	destroy the belief of life in *m*.
	151–22	"NOT *M*., BUT SPIRIT"
	152– 9	By reposing faith . . . in *m*.,
	152–26	*m*., man, or woman can never heal
	153–25	as the divine Mind, not as *m*.,
	161–31	supposititious life . . . in *m*.,
	205–24	human hypotheses, *m*., creed and
	228– 5	sensation of mind, not of *m*.
	260– 4	*m*. would reverentially withdraw
	260–10	the things of Spirit, not of *m*.
	261–27	born of Spirit and not of *m*.
	271– 2	*m*. and material sense are null,
	288–18	*m*. was not the auxiliary of Spirit.
	297–27	not had sufficient interest in the *m*.
	302–10	The general craze is that *m*. masters
	302–11	specific insanity is that brain, *m*.,
	307– 8	which had nothing to do with *m*.,
	320– 3	* presented my *m*. for a theme
	345– 5	will be thought to *m*. much.
	347–25	*m*. is not a law-maker ;
	350– 5	with the phenomenon, *m*.,
	357– 6	wherein *m*. has neither part nor
	357– 6	*m*. is the absolute opposite of

matter-agencies
Mis.	244–22	to be raised without *m*.

matter-cure
Mis.	62–20	A "mind-cure" is a *m*.

matter-physician
Hea.	12– 4	*m*. feels the pulse,

matter-physicians
Mis.	81– 6	the *m*. and the metaphysicians,

matter's
Mis.	56–11	indication of *m*. constituting
	218–25	*m*. graven grins are neither
Un.	3– 2	and still believe in *m*. reality,

matters
Mis.	146–15	These are *m*. of grave import ;
	376– 1	* no mean attention to such *m*.,
Pan.	11–16	it *m*. not what he believes ;
'00.	2–12	society manners or *m*.,
'02.	12–21	to interpolate some *m*. of business
Hea.	6–16	*m*. not whether that ideal is a

matters
 Po. 79– 1 *m·* not what be thy lot,
 My. v– 7 * *m·* of general wonderment
    7– 4 to interpolate some *m·* of business
   276–19 * in such *m·* no one should seek to
   320–25 * and went into *m·* of detail

Matthew and **Matt.** (*see also* **St. Matthew**)
 5 : 3–12
 Man. 63– 4 Sermon on the Mount (*M·.* 5 : 3–12)
 6 : 9–13
 Man. 63– 2 Lord's Prayer (*M·.* 6 : 9–13),
 ix. 2
 Mis. 24–11 and opened it at *M·* ix. 2.
 xii. 31, 32
 Mis. 55–14 spoken of in *M·.* xii. 31, 32.
 18 : 15–17
 Man. 51– 3 demand in *M·* 18 : 15–17 ;
    51–16 the requirements . . . in *M·* 18 : 15–17,

mature
 Mis. 85–20 new-born Christian Scientist must *m·*,
 Un. 11–25 to *m·* fitness for perfection
 No. 2–19 to *m·* what he has been taught.
 '02. 3–26 that power must *m·* into

matures
 Mis. 286– 6 Until time *m·* human growth,

maturing
 My. 181– 8 Progress is the *m·* conception of

maturity
 Un. 50–26 material origin, growth, *m·*,

maximum
 Mis. 232–16 *m·* of perfection in all things.
 My. 114– 7 *m·* of these teachings
   165–29 rapidly nearing the *m·* of might,
   181–26 the death-rate was at its *m·*.

May
 (*see* **months**)

mayhap
 Mis. 109– 5 *m·* never have thought of,
   308–22 and *m·* taught me more than

Mayor
 My. 173–26 Special thanks are due . . . the *M·*,

mazes
 Ret. 30–19 *m·* of divine metaphysics
    33– 5 dim *m·* of *materia medica,*

McClure
 My. 315–21 the *M·* "history," so called,

McClure's Magazine
 My. 308– 5 chapter sub-title
   308–12 *M· M·,* January, 1907,
   308–15 *M· M·* refers to my father's
   308–26 Although *M· M·* attributes
   308–28 *M· M·* also declares
   308–31 The man whom *M· M·* characterizes as
   309–21 *M· M·* says, describing the
   309–26 *M· M·* states : "Alone of the
   310– 8 *M· M·* calls my youngest brother,
   310–17 Regarding the allegation by *M· M·*
   310–22 *M· M·* says that "the quarrels
   311–29 Notwithstanding that *M· M·* says,
   312– 5 of my husband, *M· M·* says :
   312–32 rhyme attributed to me by *M· M·*
   313– 8 various stories told by *M· M·*
   313–17 as stated by *M· M·.*
   313–25 as *M· M·* says.
   314– 1 *M· M·* calls Dr. Daniel Patterson,
   314–13 Although, as *M· M·* claims,

McCrackan
 Mr.
 My. 32– 8 * Mr. *M·* and Mrs. Conant
    34–17 * read by Mr. *M·* and Mrs. Conant :
    81–11 * Mr. *M·* announced at the
 Mr. William D.
 My. 134–23 * First Reader, Mr. William D. *M·*,
 William D.
 My. 31–23 * First Reader William D. *M·*,
    35–28 * First Reader William D. *M·*

McKenzie
 Mr.
 My. 39–17 * In introducing . . . Mr. *M·* said :
 Rev. William P.
 My. 39– 4 * the President, Rev. William P. *M·*,

McKinley (*see also* **McKinley's**)
 Mrs.
 My. 290–11 chapter sub-title
   290–12 *My Dear Mrs. M· :*
 President
 My. 291– 1 chapter sub-title
   292–15 to save the life of President *M·*,"
 President, William
 My. 291– 4 beloved President, William *M·*.

McKinley's
 President
 My. 293–22 and President *M·* recovery

McLellan
 Archibald
 My. 21–31 * signature
   136–19 Archibald *M·*, editor-in-chief
 Mr. Archibald
 My. 135–15 Trustees . . . Mr. Archibald *M·*,
   137–23 Trustees . . . Mr. Archibald *M·*,

McNeil
 Fanny
 My. 311–20 Fanny *M·*, President Pierce's niece,
 General John
 My. 311–27 General John *M·*, the hero of
 John
 Ret. 1– 3 John *M·* of Edinburgh.
 Marion
 Ret. 1–17 This second Marion *M·*
    2– 7 Marion *M·*, came to America
 Marion Moor
 Ret. 1–15 Marion Moor *M·* had a daughter,

 My. 311–18 regarding the *M·* coat-of-arms
     (*see also* **Macneil, Macneill**)

McNeils
 Pul. 48–28 * *M·* and General Knox

McRee, Dr.
 My. 335–26 * (Dr. *M·* we think it was),

M. D.
 Mis. 349– 6 students with the degree of M. D.,
 Man. 47– 7 he may consult with an M. D.
    47– 9 to confer with an M. D. on Ontology,
 '01. 34– 1 the early employment of an M. D.
    34– 6 from the attendance of an M. D.,
 My. 4–15 loves . . . D.D. and M. D.,
   105–20 patient of a distinguished M. D.,
   294–16 surgeon or the faithful M. D.

M. D.'s
 Mis. 6– 9 cases are given to the M. D.'s,
    39–16 Unlike the M. D.'s,
   106– 8 M. D.'s to left of them,
 Pan. 10–19 M. D.'s have failed to heal ;
 '00. 14–25 the better class of M. D.'s
 '01. 34– 9 the M. D.'s material prescription.
 My. 105– 8 M. D.'s, by verdict of the stethoscope
   105–29 In the ranks of the M. D.'s are

Me and **me**
 Mis. 18–10 no other gods before *m·* ;"— *Exod.* 20 : 3.
    21– 3 no other gods before *m·*."— *Exod.* 20 : 3.
    23–13 no other gods before *m·*."— *Exod.* 20 : 3.
    23–14 It is plain that the *M·* spoken of
    28–21 no other gods before *m·*,"— *Exod.* 20 : 3.
    28–22 What meaneth this *M·*,
    45–27 "other gods before *m·*."— *Exod.* 20 : 3.
    97–19 no God beside *m·*."— *Isa.* 45 : 5.
   123– 4 no other gods before *m·* :"— *Exod.* 20 : 3.
   209–22 "other gods before *m·*,"— *Exod.* 20 : 3.
 Chr. 53–55 Just take *M·* in !
    53–56 No mass for *M·* !
 Un. 18–19 which alone enable *M·* to rebuke,
    24– 3 From *m·* proceedeth all Mind,
 Pan. 9–10 no other gods before *m·* ;"— *Exod.* 20 : 3.
 '00. 5–20 no other gods before *m·*."— *Exod.* 20 : 3.
 '02. 4–20 no other gods before *m·*,"— *Exod.* 20 : 3.
    5–30 no other gods before *m·*,"— *Exod.* 20 : 3.
    6–20 no other gods before *m·*."— *Exod.* 20 : 3.
 My. 5–14 no other gods before *m·*,"— *Exod.* 20 : 3.
    64–13 no other gods before *m·*,'— *Exod.* 20 : 3.
   131–26 prove *m·* now herewith,— *Mal.* 3 : 10.
   132– 3 "Prove *m·* now herewith,— *Mal.* 3 : 10.
   153–17 no other gods before *m·*."— *Exod.* 20 : 3.
   221–19 no other gods before *m·*."— *Exod.* 20 : 3.
   278– 9 no other gods before *m·*,"— *Exod.* 20 : 3.
   279–12 no other gods before *m·*'"— *Exod.* 20 : 3.
   282– 7 "Look unto *m·*,— *Isa.* 45 : 22.
   364– 8 no other gods before *m·*."— *Exod.* 20 : 3.

meadow
 Mis. 329–14 passes over mountain and *m·*,
 Pul. 39–26 * Under the *m·* grass.

meadows
 Mis. 330– 1 melting murmurs to merry *m·* ;
 Pul. 48–12 * an intervale of beautiful *m·*
 My. 186– 1 rocks, rills, mountains, *m·*,

meagre
 Mis. 137– 5 I gave you a *m·* reception
 My. 284– 2 honest efforts (however *m·*)
   332– 5 * *m·* tribute for so noble an effort

meagrely
 My. 243–12 meet *m·* the duties of half a dozen

meal

Mis. 166–23   hid in three measures of *m·*,
     171–24   *three measures of m·, — Matt.* 13 : 33.
     174–31   hid in three measures of *m·*,
     175– 5   The three measures of *m·*
   '02.   2–16   hid in three measures of *m·*,

mean

Mis. 26–32   to *m·* that good is evil,
     28–23   and must *m·* Spirit.
     38–29   if this is what you *m·*.
     70–10   *What did Jesus m· when he said*
     72–12   "What *m·* ye, — *Ezek.* 18 : 2.
     86–12   They either *m·* formations of
     171–14   This does not *m·* communing with
     191–19   By no . . . can this passage *m·*
     192– 2   we do not *m·* that man is God
     192– 4   we *m·* not that he is a personal devil,
     193– 2   Did Jesus *m·* what he said?
     193– 4   Jesus did *m·* all, and even more
     197–17   But it does *m·* so to understand the
     261–24   by mankind I *m·* mortals,
     375–32   * no *m·* attention to such matters,
   Ret.   8– 8   What do you *m·*?"
     50–19   By loyalty in students I *m·* this,
   Un.   21– 3   "the *m·* while accusing — *Rom.* 2 : 15.
   Rud.   1–10   *Do you m· by this that God is a*
     3–24   *do you m· that God has a finite*
     3–26   I *m·* the infinite and divine
     4–14   if by that term you *m·*
     8–25   By this I *m·* that mortal mind
   '00.   5–12   *m·* God, man, and divine Science.
   '01.   3–18   By this we *m·* Mind,
   My.   30–13   * sacrifices of no *m·* order ;
     43–18   * "What *m·* ye by these — *Josh.* 4 : 6.
     43–31   * "What *m·* ye by these — *Josh.* 4 : 6.
     55– 8   * In the *m·* time,
     55–19   * In the *m·* time Sunday services
     232–31   Then should not "watching out" *m·*,
     233– 2   It must *m·* that.
     242–11   I do not *m·* that mortals are
     255– 7   I do not *m·* that minor officers
     307–14   * "I see now what you *m·*,
     323–25   * should *m·* to your older students much
     342–15   * not be understood that I *m·* weak,
     346–28   did not *m·* any man to-day on earth.

meandering

Ret. 27–22   *m·* midst pebbles and rocks,

meaneth

Mis. 28–21   What *m·* this Me, — Spirit, or matter?

meaning

clears the
  Mis. 75–20   clears the *m·*, and assists one to
dual
  Mis. 169–18   dual *m·* to every Biblical passage,
fullest
  Mis. 169–32   In their fullest *m·*,
her
  My. 334–17   * Nothing could be further from her *m·*
higher
  Hea. 16– 9   name of Christ with a higher *m·*,
  My. 114–26   learning the higher *m·* of this book
     241– 5   * higher *m·* of the Scriptures.
holy
  Po. 71–17   holy *m·* of their song.
infinite
  Mis. 25–17   gives God's infinite *m·* to mankind,
     100– 6   infinite *m·* of those words.
     188–23   up to its infinite *m·*,
  No. 22–12   infinite *m·* of the Word of Truth,
     34– 7   infinite *m·* and efficacy of Truth
inspired
  Mis. 190–19   found to include the inspired *m·*.
interrupts the
  Ret. 56– 9   interrupts the *m·* of the
its
  My. 226– 5   convey its *m·* in C. S.
kindred
  Pul. 66–23   * and others of kindred *m·*,
language and
  My. 238–10   His language and *m·* are wholly
magnitude of
  My. 133–28   knowledge with its magnitude of *m·*
magnitude of its
  '01. 30– 7   The magnitude of its *m·* forbids
mighty
  Pul. 84–21   * tell the story of its mighty *m·*
moral
  Mis. 248– 5   its moral *m·*, found in the
  No. 23–16   a literal and a moral *m·*.
my
  Mis. 66–22   Cynical critics misjudge my *m·*
  Rud. 13–17   elucidate my *m·*.
  No. 32–11   when I touch this subject my *m·* is
  My. 251–16   misapprehension of my *m·*
     264– 6   until mankind learn more of my *m·*

meaning

new
  Ret. 25– 5   a new *m·*, a new tongue.
  Pul. 35– 1   it came to me with a new *m·*,
of a word
  Un. 27– 1   inquiry as to the *m·* of a word
of divine metaphysics
  Mis. 68–19   *m·* of divine metaphysics,
of it all
  Mis. 158–13   The *m·* of it all, as now shown,
of pantheism
  Pan. 2–14   gives the *m·* of pantheism as a
of Spirit
  Hea. 11– 8   it would catch the *m·* of Spirit.
of the context
  Hea. 8– 9   perceive the *m·* of the context,
of the declaration
  Un. 30–24   understood the *m·* of the declaration
of the passage
  Mis. 75–25   bring out the *m·* of the passage.
     248– 4   the literal *m·* of the passage
of the Scriptures
  Mis. 25–14   original *m·* of the Scriptures,
  Man. 87–17   the higher *m·* of the Scriptures.
  Un. 29–22   the deep *m·* of the Scriptures
  My. 241– 5   * higher *m·* of the Scriptures.
of the term
  Mis. 53–19   *m·* of the term and of C. S.
     190–13   The *m·* of the term
     191– 6   changed the *m·* of the term,
of the text
  Mis. 197–12   comprehend the *m·* of the text,
of the word
  Ret. 74– 3   ignorant of the *m·* of the word
of those words
  Mis. 37–13   learn the *m·* of those words
     188–32   beheld the *m·* of those words
original
  Mis. 25–14   original *m·* of the Scriptures,
     74–16   into its original *m·*, Mind.
     77– 5   verb *believe* took its original *m·*,
Paul's
  Mis. 84–19   *Please explain Paul's m·*
right
  Mis. 76–22   you will find the right *m·*
spiritual
     (*see* **spiritual**)
their
  My. 99–28   * their existence points out their *m·*
true
  Mis. 171– 2   be wrested from its true *m·*
truer
  My. 64– 4   * took on a larger and truer *m·*.

           ——

  Mis. 25–23   from the Latin word *m· all*,
     100–12   that grasp neither the *m·* nor
     236–22   *m·* by this, Be not estranged from
  Pan. 2–11   Greek words *m·* "all" and "god."
  '01. 4–28   "divine Principle," *m·* divine Love,
  My. 22–29   * proper perspective of the *m·* of
     268–31   designation *man m·* woman as well,

meaningless

Pan. 7–21   wherein theism seems *m·*,
My. 235–26   *m·* commemoration of birthdays,

meanings

Mis. 125–18   learn forever the infinite *m·*,
Man. 62–22   to grasp the simpler *m·*
'02. 4–23   in a few of their infinite *m·*,
My. 202–16   infinite *m·*, endless hopes,
     221– 9   in His more infinite *m·*,
     231–14   its highest and infinite *m·*,
     262–32   reveals infinite *m·* and gives

means (noun)

and end
  My. 278– 5   this *m·* and end will be
and ends
  No. 21–14   for divine *m·* and ends.
  My. 259–29   merely temporary *m·* and ends.
     260–12   with human *m·* and ends,
and measure
  Mis. 154–11   *m·* and measure of His grace.
and methods
  Mis. 52– 9   beyond all human *m·* and methods.
     152–30   His spiritual *m·* and methods,
  Rud. 13–23   *m· and methods of trustworthy*
  My. 154–23   I welcome the *m·* and methods,
and understanding
  Ret. 48–29   ways, *m·*, and understanding,
better
  Mis. 268–12   better *m·* for healing the sick
by no
  Mis. 6–32   is by no *m·* the exception.
     43– 8   By no *m·* : C. S. is not
     79–11   by no *m·* the medium of imperfection.
     97–10   human mind is by no *m·* a desirable

means

by no
Mis.	296–16	they are by no *m·* identical
	296–18	is by no *m·* associated therewith.
	348–29	I have by no *m·* encouraged
	361–27	is by no *m·* a creative partner
Un.	43–12	by no *m·* spoken of myself,
Rud.	11–18	by no *m·* rests on the strength of
'00.	3–10	One's idol is by no *m·* his servant,
My.	213– 6	is by no *m·* a right of evil
	219– 7	I by no *m·* would pluck their plumes.

comprehensive
My.	45– 2	* comprehensive *m·* by you provided

earned the
My.	215–16	thus that I earned the *m·*

every
Ret.	21– 4	Every *m·* within my power
Pul.	2–20	by every *m·* in your power,

for sinning
Mis.	12–14	*m·* for sinning unseen

heaven-appointed
My.	221–19	no other heaven-appointed *m·*

human
Mis.	52– 9	beyond all human *m·* and methods.
My.	260–12	no partnership with human *m·*

justifies the
Mis.	282–24	and the end justifies the *m·* ;

lower
Rud.	8–26	If by such lower *m·* the health

material
Mis.	268–26	not adulterate . . . with material *m·*.
Ret.	47–11	shuns whatever involves material *m·*
My.	206– 3	with matter and material *m·*,

members and
Mis.	349–25	had sufficient members and *m·*

mental
Mis.	40–29	to kill his patient by mental *m·*,

methods, and
Mis.	135–17	God's methods and *m·* of healing,
	313– 6	manners, morals, methods, and *m·*.

mistaken
My.	234–10	task themselves with mistaken *m·*.

monetary
My.	214–22	no monetary *m·* left wherewith to

no other
'02.	3– 1	used no other *m·* myself ;
Hea.	18–28	killed a man by no other *m·* than

of advancing
Mis.	42–19	our joys and *m·* of advancing

of Christianity
Mis.	269–23	proper *m·* of Christianity,

of Christian Science
Mis.	150–16	by *m·* of C. S.

of grace
Mis.	115–24	thus becomes a *m·* of grace.
	127–25	Ofttimes the rod is His *m·* of grace ;
'01.	19– 2	a divinely appointed *m·* of grace

of healing
Mis.	135–17	God's methods and *m·* of healing,
'01.	34– 7	Christ's mode and *m·* of healing,

of knowing
My.	47– 6	* not had the *m·* of knowing the

of matter
Un.	33–27	or that mind sees by *m·* of matter.

of paying
Rud.	14–20	*m·* of paying for their tuition

of reconciling
My.	314–25	the *m·* of reconciling the couple.

of support
My.	312–15	* without *m·* of support.

of travel
My.	124–26	the rate of speed, the *m·* of travel,

other
Mis.	60– 9	after all other *m·* have failed.
	270–11	other *m·* than those the Master used
	282–25	when other *m·* have failed.
Pan.	6– 2	more effectual than all other *m·* ;

our only
My.	195–17	our only *m·* of adding to that talent

plenty of
'00.	2–17	he has plenty of *m·*,

provided the
'01.	29– 4	God has provided the *m·* for him

purchased the
Mis.	165–23	purchased the *m·* of mortals'

reproachable
Mis.	147–30	than attain it by reproachable *m·*.

some
Mis.	96–27	some *m·* by which it is not done.

spiritual
Mis.	152–30	faith in God and His spiritual *m·*
'01.	19–12	mixing material and spiritual *m·*,
	26–12	from Christ's purely spiritual *m·*
My.	357– 7	absolute opposite of spiritual *m·*,

such
Rud.	16– 5	will never undertake . . . by such *m·*.

means

supplied the
My.	23– 5	* and supplied the *m·* to consummate the

that build
My.	165–30	the *m·* that build to the heavens,

their
My.	30–18	* gave generously of their *m·*

to devise
My.	51– 1	* to devise *m·* to pay our pastor,

to promote
Mis.	288–30	*m·* to promote the ends of temperance ;

used
Mis.	69–22	with the *m·* used in their effort

violent
Mis.	182– 4	violent *m·* or material methods.

ways and
	(*see* **ways**)

your
Mis.	90–18	be sure that your *m·* for doing good
	115–15	Your *m·* of protection and defense

Mis.	45– 5	C. S., by *m·* of its Principle
	124– 7	by *m·* of matter, or the flesh,
	140–25	The diviner claim and *m·* for
	164–27	by *m·* of the lens of Science,
	175–29	by *m·* of both animal magnetism and
	222–30	ways, *m·*, and potency of Truth
	333–27	by *m·* of that which does not
	334–22	by *m·* of matter, or Mind?
Pul.	11– 7	whose *m·*, energies, and prayers
	20– 9	by *m·* of a statute of the State,
Rud.	7– 2	Not that all healing is . . . by any *m·* ;
	14–25	healed by *m·* of my instructions,
'01.	24– 6	by *m·* of invariable rules
My.	11– 9	* not tried to guide us by *m·* of
	38– 8	* By *m·* of a carefully trained corps of
	48–20	* a *m·* of spiritual development
	71– 4	* beautiful effects by *m·* of the bells.
	103–14	by *m·* of the Science which Jesus
	112– 1	by *m·* of the Principle of C. S.
	214–28	where were the *m·* with which to
	216– 7	civil, and educational *m·*,
	267–30	all the divine modes, *m·*, forms,
	277– 8	by *m·* of their wholesome tribunals,
	358– 8	is the *m·* whereby the conflict

means (verb)
Mis.	23–25	what C. S. *m·* by the word
	25–24	omniscience *m·* as well, all-science.
	28–24	the commandment *m·*,
	38–22	metaphysics at other colleges *m·*,
	47– 6	substance *m·* more than matter:
	68– 3	It *m·* more than mere disappearance
	75–28	*m·*, that mortal man . . . shall die;
	76–21	word *m·* the so-called soul
	89–27	This salvation *m·*:
	170–32	often *m·* spiritual power.
	197– 7	It *m·* a *full* salvation,
	197–13	It *m·* more than an opinion
	216–11	*m·* more than "hands off."
	216–15	Whatever his *nom de plume m·*,
	365–27	terms in which to express what it *m·*.
Ret.	59– 6	The word *Life* never *m·*
	59– 9	saying that addition *m·* subtraction
	88–25	The Lord's command *m·* this,
Pul.	84–20	* understanding of what it *m·*.
No.	28–26	*soul m·* sense and organic life;
Pan.	8–13	chapter sub-title
	9– 3	"Infinite Spirit" *m·* one God
	9– 4	term "spirits" *m·* more than
My.	24– 1	* What *m·* this edifice?
	72–24	* This *m·* that nearly two million
	239–23	Gender *m·* a kind.
	246–30	Magna Charta of C. S. *m·* much,
	249–20	I alone know what that *m·*.
	254–21	"The Magna Charta of C. S. *m·* much,
	261–22	chapter sub-title
	323–19	* all that your wonderful life . . . *m·*

meant
Mis.	46–22	significance of what the apostle *m·*
	73–26	*What is m· by regeneration?*
	77– 7	it *m·* to discern and consent to
	214–15	*m·*, all the way through,
	224–26	offended when no wrong is *m·*,
	255–13	what the apostle *m·* when he said :
Man.	64–20	*m·* nothing more than a tender term
Un.	32– 8	By matter is commonly *m·* mind,
Pul.	83–26	* to know what John on Patmos *m·*
Rud.	2–11	if by *person* is *m·* infinite Spirit.
My.	291– 5	*m·* more to him than a mere

meantime
Mis.	xii– 4	*m·* interluding with loving thought
	354– 1	*m·* declaring they "never disobey

meanwhile and mean while
Mis. 283–25 conscious, m·, that God worketh
379–23 m·, assiduously pondering the
Ret. 21–10 M· he had served as a volunteer
Un. 21– 3 m· w· accusing — Rom. 2 : 15.
My. 55– 3 * M· it was felt that the church
93–21 * attaching m· no importance to
222–28 M·, they who name the name of

measurably
'00. 6–12 can m· understand C. S.,
7–25 this attempt m· fails,

measure
Mis. 12–28 We should m· our love for God by
48– 1 save as I m· its demonstrations as
154–11 the means and m· of His grace.
175–12 The m· of Life shall increase
185–23 or to m· his manhood,
222–20 the m· it has meted must be
261–13 m· he has meted is measured to him
298– 8 "With what m· ye mete,— Matt. 7 : 2.
317–31 not the Spirit by m·— John 3 : 34
324–19 Startled beyond m· at beholding
325–21 amazed beyond m· that anybody
Ret. 44–27 This m· was immediately followed
Pul. 28–19 * equal m· to its use of the Bible.
84–20 * have some m· of understanding
85– 8 * In the m· in which she has
No. 45–16 woman to fill the highest m·
'01. 15–16 filling up the m· of wickedness
32–20 They fill the ecclesiastic m·,
My. 21–19 * "good m·, pressed down,— Luke 6 : 38.
36–22 * increase the m· of our devotion
166–23 let our m· of time and joy be
320–17 * but was in a m· in sympathy with

measured
Mis. 12–29 m· by our obedience to God,
261–13 measure he has meted is m· to him
298– 8 m· to you again."— Matt. 7 : 2.
Un. 29–20 can never be seen or m·
My. 85– 6 * handful of members m· its
291– 7 heavy strokes, m· movements,

measureless
'02. 4–17 the m· rounds of eternity.

measures
Mis. 90–16 in your m·, obey the Scriptures,
116–13 the m· of life's music
166–23 hid in three m· of meal,
171–24 three m· of meal,— Matt. 13 : 33.
172–12 unerring Mind m· man,
172–13 until the three m· be
174–31 hid in three m· of meal,
175– 5 The three m· of meal may
297– 7 by legally coercive m·,
396–20 Low, sad, and sweet, whose m· bind
Ret. 44–25 proper m· were adopted
Pul. 18– 4 Low, sad, and sweet, whose m· bind
'00. 11–16 for he m· himself against
'02. 2–16 hid in three m· of meal,
Po. 12– 3 Low, sad, and sweet, whose m· bind
My. 229–31 it m· the infinite against the

measuring
Mis. x–14 mile-stones m· the distance,

meat
No. v–11 leave the m· and take the
43– 2 power of daily m· and drink.
My. 131–25 may be m· in mine house,— Mal. 3 : 10.

Mecca
My. 84–12 * Boston is the M· for . . . Scientists
85–25 * M· of their love and duty.
96– 9 * M· and the Hindu shrines,

mechanical accessories
(see organ)

mechanics
My. 226– 9 the inclined plane in m·,

Mechanics Building
Pul. 57–24 * not far from the big M· B·
My. 57– 3 * and in the M· B·,

mechanism
Mis. 354–18 right action of the mental m·,

meddle
Man. 93–20 not allowed in anywise to m·
No. 5–20 If . . . God, does not m· with it.
40–21 is it right for one mind to m· with

meddlesomeness
Mis. 288– 1 which is virtually m·.

mediæval
'00. 4–13 greater than in the m· period ;

mediating
No. 31–17 m· between what is and is not,

mediation
Pul. 73– 7 * through the m· of her God.
My. 91– 5 * that spiritual and mystic m·

medical
aids
Hea. 14–15 ignorance . . . are miserable m· aids.
attendant
Mis. 89–13 m· attendant and friends
bill
My. 327–15 * when a m· bill was proposed
bills
Mis. 211–10 m· bills, class legislation,
charlatans
Mis. 80– 7 m· charlatans in general,
college
Mis. 382–22 charter for a metaphysical m· college,
discoveries
Mis. 244–31 because of their m· discoveries?
examination
My. 329– 7 * m· examination before a board
examiners
My. 329– 7 * before a board of m· examiners.
faculty
Mis. 80–11 will fight the m· faculty,
243–26 m· faculty will tell you
No. 2– 4 ostracized by the m· faculty,
My. 4–18 both m· faculty and Christianity,
175–13 intelligent m· faculty,
laws
Mis. 80– 5 opposition to unjust m· laws.
league
Mis. 79–29 joining any m· league
men
Mis. 80–13 conscientious m· men,
practice
'00. 13–19 Its m· practice included charms
'01. 17–24 From my m· practice I had learned
My. 107– 7 modern phase of m· practice,
practitioner
Hea. 14–10 If you employ a m· practitioner,
prescription
Mis. 210–23 and a m· prescription.
profession
Mis. 378–19 taught her of his m· profession.
purposes
Ret. 48–17 chartered . . . for m· purposes,
school
Mis. 349–13 feasibility of entering a m· school ;
349–18 He entered the m· school,
schools
Mis. 348–30 to enter m· schools,
Ret. 34– 5 an answer from the m· schools,
skill
Mis. 29–22 that had defied m· skill.
statutes
Mis. 79–28 for violation of m· statutes
system
Mis. 80–31 to understand the m· system
systems
Mis. 252– 3 m· systems of allopathy
therapeutics
Pan. 4–27 drugs, hygiene, and m· therapeutics,
treatment
Mis. 89– 9 under material m· treatment,
use
'01. 18–17 If God created drugs for m· use,

medically
My. 97– 9 * those who were m· treated.

medication
My. 345–17 pellets without any m·

medicinal
Hea. 12– 1 contain no m· properties,

medicine
abjure
My. 97– 8 * of the sick who abjure m·
and religion
No. 44– 5 demonstration of m· and religion.
'02. 2–17 ethics, m·, and religion,
Peo. 5– 1 practice of m· and religion,
and theology
My. 28–32 * aspect of m· and theology.
applies it
Mis. 203–14 m· applies it physically,
art of
Peo. 6–11 * "The art of m· consists in
Christendom and
My. 4–13 put into Christendom and m·.
doses of
Mis. 348–26 I tried several doses of m·,
dynamics of
'01. 17–25 the dynamics of m· is Mind.
elevates
My. 260–24 elevates m· to Mind :

medicine

experimented in
 Mis. 379–20 I had already experimented in *m·*
field of
 Mis. 366–18 imposition in the field of *m·*
god of
 '00. 13–18 Æsculapius, the god of *m·*,
gods of
 Peo. 4–24 Apollo and . . . the gods of *m·*,
grain of
 Hea. 13– 5 one hundredth part of a grain of *m·*
his
 Mis. 268–17 His *m·* is Mind
 '01. 18–10 Scientist's religion or his *m·*,
idolatry and
 '00. 13–23 school of . . . idolatry and *m·*.
imaginary
 Hea. 13–19 we resigned the imaginary *m·*
Jesus' only
 Mis. 25–22 Jesus' only *m·* was . . . Mind.
less
 Hea. 11–19 "The less *m·* the better,"
man's only
 My. 105– 3 man's only *m·* for mind and body
material
   (*see* **material**)
mental
 Mis. 252– 3 mental *m·* of divine metaphysics
 252– 4 Mental *m·* gains no potency by
methods of
 Ret. 33–23 material methods of *m·*,
Mind's
 Mis. 3–18 are not Mind's *m·*.
mode of
 Mis. 98–14 in a higher mode of *m·* ;
modes of
 Mis. 88–30 are opposite modes of *m·*.
 366–23 on drugs, . . . as modes of *m·*.
morals, or
 Mis. 284– 5 religion, morals, or *m·*,
new *régime* **of**
 Mis. 348–23 under this new *régime* of *m·*,
no
 Hea. 11–20 "until you arrive at no *m·*."
 13– 9 they have taken no *m·*,
nor surgery
 Ret. 24–13 neither *m·* nor surgery could reach,
of homœopathy
 '01. 18– 6 sneers . . . at the *m·* of homœopathy ;
of matter
 '01. 18– 8 the old-time *m·* of matter.
of Mind
 Mis. 252– 1 this *m·* of Mind is not necessarily
 348–24 found myself under . . . the *m·* of Mind,
 '01. 18– 7 *m·* of Mind is more honored
or drugs
 Pul. 72–17 * *m·* or drugs of any kind,
or religion
 Mis. 25–32 in philosophy, *m·*, or religion,
practice of
 Peo. 5– 1 theory and practice of *m·*
 10–10 regulating the practice of *m·*
 My. 190–11 metaphysical practice of *m·*
 340–15 on the practice of *m·* !
religion and
 Peo. 8– 1 Religion and *m·* must be dematerialized
 My. 221– 1 spirituality in religion and *m·*
 340–10 progress of religion and *m·*
religion or
 Mis. 260–10 potency, in religion or *m·*.
 My. 288–16 instrumentality in religion or *m·*
schools of
 Ret. 15–26 the popular schools of *m·*,
 Pul. 70–21 * philosophy and schools of *m·*,
 '01. 22–23 the differing schools of *m·*
 My. 245– 2 the approved schools of *m·*,
Science in
 My. 127– 2 Science in *m·*, in physics, and
Science of
 My. 221–14 natural, and divine Science of *m·*,
sure
 Mis. 252–27 with safe and sure *m·* ;
system of
 Mis. 81– 9 is the true system of *m·*.
 243–13 every system of *m·* claims more
 243–19 my system of *m·* is not generally
 My. 105–31 misrepresenting a system of *m·* which
systems of
 No. 4–18 beyond other systems of *m·*,
taking
 Pul. 72–30 * ever hear of Jesus' taking *m·*
their own
 Mis. 39–17 not afraid to take their own *m·*,
theology and
 No. 1–18 theology and *m·* of Jesus were one.

medicine

this
 Mis. 25–24 this *m·* is all-power ;
 39–18 for this *m·* is divine Mind ;
 252– 1 and this *m·* of Mind is
 '01. 24–10 * my having taken this *m·*
 Hea. 13– 7 There is a moral to this *m·* ;
to prepare the
 Hea. 12–20 To prepare the *m·* requires time and
triturations of
 My. 107–11 the same triturations of *m·*
true
 Mis. 233–20 for the practice of true *m·*,
use of
 My. 97– 6 * getting well without the use of *m·*.
worst form of
 Mis. 233– 4 will result in the worst form of *m·*.
your
 Mis. 241– 9 Use as your *m·* the great alterative,

 Mis. 53–11 *Do you sometimes . . . use m·*
 Man. 48– 9 towards religion, *m·*, the courts, or
 '01. 17–10 chapter sub-title
 19–13 either in *m·* or in religion,
 25– 8 A knowledge of philosophy and of *m·*,
 30–14 reform in religion and in *m·*,
 Hea. 14– 3 *M·* will not arrive at the science of
 15–21 He cannot reach, but *m·* can?
 Peo. 2– 4 practice of religion and of *m·*
 4–26 Systems of religion and of *m·*
 6– 4 * "*M·* is the science of guessing."
 My. 99– 6 * that doeth good like a *m·*,
 260–27 leaves hygiene, *m·*, ethics, . . . to God

medicine-man
 My. 152– 7 The *m·*, far lower in the scale of
medicines
 Mis. 33–25 It does away with all material *m·*,
 Ret. 34–11 It does away with all material *m·*,
 Pul. 69– 9 * He says they use no *m·*,
meditate
 Pul. 34–25 * withdrew from the world to *m·*,
 Po. 1–17 to *m·* on what it learns.
meditated
 Pul. 73– 9 * *m·* over His divine Word.
meditates
 Mis. 148– 1 *m·* evil against us in his heart.
 309–12 *m·* most on . . . spiritual substance
meditation
 Pul. 28– 3 * in solitude and *m·*,
 33–16 * certainly offer food for *m·*.
medium
 Mis. 79–11 by no means the *m·* of imperfection.
 132–22 through the *m·* of a newspaper ;
 163–21 *m·* of Mind, the hope of the race.
 248–17 that I am an infidel, . . . a *m·*,
 No. 14– 3 If a spiritualist *m·* understood the
 Pan. 11–24 evil is not the *m·* of good,
 Hea. 6– 4 * "People say you are a *m·*,"
 6–11 they take pleasure in calling me a *m·*.
 6–18 Man thinks he is a *m·* of disease ;
 My. 313–20 I was not a *m·* for spirits.
mediumship
 Mis. 95–19 which spiritualists have miscalled *m·* ;
 No. 13–23 on the subject of *m·*,
 Hea. 6– 8 mental phenomenon named *m·*,
meek
 Mis. 1– 6 The *m·* Nazarene,
 130–29 the *m·* and loving, God anoints
 145–13 *m·* who "inherit the earth." — *Psal.* 37 : 11.
 152–20 pure in affection, the *m·* in spirit,
 189– 8 The *m·* Nazarene's steadfast and true
 393–18 In a beauty strong and *m·*
 400–22 Thee I seek, — Patient, *m·*,
 '00. 6–22 *m·* and loving disciple of Christ,
 '01. 26–19 the *m·* that inherit the earth ;
 '02. 16–21 The *m·* might, sublime patience,
 Po. 52– 2 In a beauty strong and *m·*
 69–10 Thee I seek, — Patient, *m·*,
 My. 41– 6 * It is a forever fact that the *m·* and lowly
 228–18 The *m·*, who sit at the feet of
 341–16 * 'Tis meet that man be *m·*."
meekest
 Mis. 163– 9 the *m·* man on earth.
 Po. 78–14 O *m·* of mourners,
meekly
 Mis. 17–13 *m·* bow before the Christ,
 111– 4 Faithfully, as *m·*, you have toiled
 127–10 mentally, *m·*, and importunately.
 155–10 While pressing *m·* on,
 232–15 *m·* to ascend the hill of Science,
 330–31 stoops *m·* before the blast ;
 369–19 *M·* we kneel at our Master's feet.

meekly

Hea.	19–23	bearing the cross m·
Po.	77–14	to Thee we'll m· bow,
My.	4–11	only as we follow truly, m·,
	18– 7	mentally, m·, and importunately.
	201–15	m· meet, mercifully forgive,

meekness

Mis.	1–18	M· heightens immortal attributes
	83–21	m· was as conspicuous as might.
	126–16	m·, honesty, and obedience of the
	130– 2	long-suffering, m·, charity, purity
	141–22	nobility of human m· rule this
	152–16	May m·, mercy, and love dwell
	154–28	justice, m·, mercy, purity, love.
	195–31	m·, purity, and love, informed by
	360– 1	M·, moderating human desire,
	372–31	true sense of m· and might.
Ret.	79– 9	in m·, in unselfish motives
	79–22	M· and temperance are the jewels of
Un.	5– 6	This m· will increase their
Rud.	17–15	M·, selflessness, and love
'02.	8–24	Love, purity, m·, coexist
	19–12	M· is the armor of a Christian,
My.	149– 9	m· of the Christ-principle ;
	161–30	Only he who learns through m·
	163– 4	to win through m· to might,
	194–15	It stands for m· and might,
	202– 4	faith, m·, and might of
	247–11	Christ is m· and Truth
	258–20	coronals of m·, diadems of love.

meet

Mis.	3–31	to m· sin, and uncover it ;
	4–18	adequate to m· the requirement.
	4–28	we m· with an expression of
	16–12	ability to m· them is from God ;
	39–22	who has more to m· than others
	42– 1	*do we m· those gone before?*
	42–17	If, before the change whereby we m·
	91– 9	it is to m· the demand,
	115–13	and m· the pressing need of a
	120–20	Association hereafter m· triennially :
	130–11	thinking it over, and how to m· it,
	134–10	M· together and m· en masse,
	139– 3	to m· again in three years.
	147– 7	m· in unity, preferring one another,
	160– 9	m· and mingle in bliss supernal.
	172– 7	let us m· and defeat the claims of
	176–27	prepared to m· and improve them,
	256–16	To m· the old impediment,
	263–13	power, and peace m· all human needs
	281–18	So, whatever we m· that is hard
	320–20	It doth m· the antagonism of error ;
	324–24	to go on and to m· the Stranger.
	326–23	first, to m· with joy his own,
	351– 2	and m· the mental malpractice,
	384– 3	When two hearts m·,
	386–21	With thee to m·.
	388–12	Speaks kindly when we m· and part.
Man.	96–12	is unable to m· the expense,
Ret.	48–23	to m· the demand of the age
	52–10	To m· the broader wants of humanity,
	76–14	m· on the stairs which lead up to
Pul.	8–16	vied with their parents to m· the
	39– 1	* that all m· on common ground
No.	37–17	to m· and master it
	39–28	What but silent prayer can m· the
	42– 7	to m· a mental want.
'00.	12–13	elders travelled to m· St. Paul,
'01.	1–10	To-day you m· to commemorate
	17– 8	m· the sad sinner on his way
'02.	2– 9	Truth makes haste to m· and to
	2–29	we shall m· again, never to part.
	13– 1	to m· the expenses involved.
Hea.	5–21	to m· the responsibility of our own
Peo.	9– 8	or m· the demands of Love.
Po.	7–12	Speaks kindly when we m· and part.
	36– 2	When two hearts m·,
	50– 6	With thee to m·.
My.	24–27	* m· the needs of The Mother Church
	28– 5	will m· every human need,"
	47– 3	* It seems m· at this time,
	56– 8	* inadequate to m· the need,
	73–10	will m· every human need."
	85– 9	* its congregations m· in Europe
	120– 5	that you and I may m· in truth
	125–10	chosen one to m· the Goliaths.
	131–20	Where God is we can m·,
	201–16	So let us meekly m·,
	206–27	m· to be partakers— *Col.* 1: 12.
	214– 5	will m· every human need.
	214–25	m· my own current expenses.
	217–22	m· this negation more readily
	224– 3	m· the exigencies of the hour
	243–12	m· meagerly the duties of
	249– 6	M· dispassionately the raging

meet

My.	285– 6	time requisite to m· with you ;
	290–24	holy call you again to m·.
	339–26	not sufficient to m· his demand.
	341–16	* 'Tis m· that man be meek."
	351–16	m· in that hour of Soul

meeting

adjourned

Mis.	156–13	merge the adjourned m·

after the

Ret.	14–30	After the m· was over they came

annual

Mis.	147– 4	annual m· has convened,
Man.	25–11	annual m· of the Church.
	26– 8	annual m· held for this purpose,
	56–18	annual m· of the C. S. Board
	56–21	annual m· of the Church.
	98–20	in annual m· assembled.
My.	9–21	who at our last annual m·
	11–30	* pledge of the annual m·
	16– 4	* report . . . made to the annual m·,
	20–25	* the communion and annual m·
	22– 7	* gatherings at the annual m· ;
	22– 7	* the annual m· in June, 1902,
	23–15	* pledged at the annual m·, 1902,
	27– 6	our annual m· and communion
	38–28	* annual m· of The First Church
	39–22	* to preside at an annual m·
	42–21	* our first annual m· held in the
	44–25	* members . . . in annual m· assembled,
	49–29	* at the annual m·, December 1
	57– 9	* annual m· of the same year
	57–14	* first annual m· of the church
	82–16	* sessions of the annual m·,
	125– 4	annual m· is a grave guardian.
	142–27	annual m· of The Mother Church
	154–16	At this, your first annual m·,
	172–24	* annual m· of The Mother Church
	173–11	annual m· of The Mother Church,
	361–21	* by action at its annual m·

business

My.	8–25	* in annual business m· in Boston,
	23–19	* in annual business m· assembled,
	49–15	* business m· of the church
	65– 3	* largest church business m·

call a

Man.	28–20	shall immediately call a m·
	53– 4	immediately to call a m·,

calling a

Man.	57– 9	calling a m· of the members

Church

Man.	76–11	report at the annual Church m·

church

My.	76–20	* annual church m· in Boston,

dispersed a

Po.	vi–14	* *dispersed a m· of the*

evening

Man.	47–23	at the Wednesday evening m·.
My.	134–21	* At the Wednesday evening m·

every

My.	90– 2	* should be filled at every m·

first

Pul.	30–26	* first m· held on April 12, 1879.
	31– 9	* my first m· with her
My.	49–32	* first m· of this little church

for greetings

My.	142–17	merge into a m· for greetings.

grand

Mis.	275–22	at the grand m· in Chicago

largest

My.	80–30	* where the largest m· was held,

last

Mis.	132– 2	vote passed, at your last m·,
	350–17	This proved to be our last m·.

main

My.	81–11	* announced at the main m·

members

My.	139–18	the Executive Members' m·,

memorial

My.	289–24	to attend the memorial m·

of the Board

Man.	50–18	a m· of the Board of Directors
Ret.	48–12	At a special m· of the Board

of the church
(see **church**)

of this Church

Man.	66– 7	If at a m· of this Church
	66–16	brought before a m· of this Church,

one

Man.	60– 5	One m· on Sunday during the

open the

Mis.	314– 7	open the m· by reading the hymns

places for

My.	54–29	* consideration of places for m·

meeting

previous
My. 49–18 * received at the previous m·,
    49–22 * "The minutes of the previous m·

public
My. 59–16 * first public m· in the little hall

said
Man. 57–16 before he can call said m·.

special
Ret. 48–12 At a special m· of the Board
My. 289–11 special m· of its First Members
    333– 7 * a special m· was convened

that
Mis. 350–15 subject given out at that m· was,
Pul. 31–11 * which that m· inaugurated

their
My. 54– 7 * had their m· Easter Sunday

this
Man. 18–18 At this m· twenty others of
My. 49–21 * An interesting record of this m·
    49–31 * at this m· Mrs. Eddy
    50–13 * "The tone of this m·
    131–19 this m· is very joyous to me.
    148–23 what is being recorded of this m·

vestry
Ret. 15–21 Our last vestry m· was

Mis. 135–24 Letter read at the m· of
    310–22 upon a m· being called,
    385– 9 poem
Man. 17– 8 At a m· of the . . . Association,
    82–14 a m· held for this purpose
    89– 4 m· of the C. S. Board of Directors
Ret. 14– 3 m· was held for the examination of
    16– 3 When the m· was over, two ladies
    43–23 At a m· of the . . . Association,
    47–12 In view of all this, a m· was called
    52–23 at its m· in Cleveland, Ohio,
Pul. 68–25 * m· held at the present location
'02. 20–23 m· you all occasionally
Po. page 48 poem
    65– 4 A m· with loved ones
My. 21–23 * joy in m· very many of them
    39– 3 * m· was opened by the President,
    49–12 * m· of those who were interested
    49–20 * m·, with Mrs. Eddy in the chair.
    49–26 * At a m· held October 19, 1879,
    53–15 * At a m· October 22, 1883,
    83–21 * m· of the Christian Scientists
    124–11 heart m· heart across continents
    143– 1 I will attend the m·,
    174– 5 proved an ideal m· place.
    207–23 m· and mastering evil
    289–27 m· to be held in the capital

Meetings and meetings

Mis. 136–23 close your m· for the summer ;
    148–25 at your Friday evening m·.
    350–11 no transactions at those m· which
Man. 31–18 and the Wednesday evening m·.
    38–13 semi-annual m· held for this
    51–25 shall be present at m· for the
    56– 7 heading
    56– 9 REGULAR AND SPECIAL m·.
    56–10 Annual M·.
    56–11 m· of The Mother Church
    56–17 M· of Board of Directors.
    56–22 m· for electing candidates
    57– 3 properly come before these m·,
    57– 6 Special m· may be held
    61– 3 Overflow M·.
    76–21 shall hold quarterly m·
    84–22 for more frequent m·.
    86–14 m· of their association.
Pul. 28–28 * held its m· in Chickering Hall,
    79–14 * notices of C. S. m·,
My. 53–10 * voted that the church hold its m·
    57– 1 * m· were overcrowded
    69– 6 * m· presenting an oval . . . appearance
    73–16 * June m· of The Mother Church
    79–24 * chapter sub-title
    79–29 * testimony m· that marked the
    80–10 * M· were held in the extension
    80–16 * At each of the m· the introductory
    80–25 * it took ten m· to
    81–27 * at the m· of the Scientists,
    121– 4 holding our semi-annual church m·,
    143– 2 pray that God directs your m·

meets

Mis. 45–16 supply invariably m· demand,
    201– 2 m· the immortal demands of Truth.
    202– 5 * where the good man m· his fate
    207– 2 heart m· heart reciprocally blest,
    323–14 m· and masters their . . . attacks
Pul. 74– 7 * m· every Sunday in Hodgson Hall,
Peo. 3–16 Truth m· the old material thought

meets

My. 180–16 C. S. m· error with Truth,
    188–32 and m· the warmest wish of men

Mehitable (Huntoon)

(see **Huntoon**)

melancholy

Mis. 391– 7 That m· mortals Will count their
Po. 38– 6 That m· mortals Will count their

Melanchthon

Hea. 2–12 Said the more gentle M· :
    2–13 * Adam is too strong for young M·."

mellow

Ret. 4–16 in the m· hues of autumn,
Pul. 62–15 * tone . . . being rich and m·.

mellower

Ret. 18– 4 While cactus a m· glory receives
Po. 63–12 While cactus a m· glory receives

melodeon

My. 59–21 * m· on which my wife played,

melody

Mis. 330– 2 make m· through dark pine groves.
    390– 8 Gives back some maiden m·,
Pul. 11– 3 making m· more real,
'00. 11–20 human tone has no m· for me.
Po. 34– 2 soul of m· by being blest
    55– 9 Gives back some maiden m·,
    66–11 No m· sweeps o'er its strings !

melt

Mis. 145–19 names may m· into one,
    156– 9 when the mist shall m· away
    264– 9 they m· into darkness.
    320–26 to pierce the darkness and m· into dawn.
No. 28– 4 m· in the fervent heat of suffering,
Peo. 10– 6 and m· into nothing under the
Po. 23–22 Bid error m· away !
    65–18 and death like mist m· away,

melted

Mis. 176–21 m· away in the fire of love
    306– 1 * material to be m· into the bell,
    360–16 m· away the cloud of false
Ret. 15– 2 clergyman's heart also m·,
    31–29 philosophy and religion m·,
My. 194–14 m· into the radiance of His

melting

Mis. 205– 5 m· away the shadows called sin,
    329–30 The brooklet sings m· murmurs
    390–16 To m· murmurs ye have stirred
Po. 55–17 To m· murmurs ye have stirred

melts

Un. 58–12 hypocrite m· in fervent heat,

member (see also **member's**)

another
Man. 50–17 another m· in good standing
    51– 9 Pastor Emeritus or another m·,
    52–23 against the interests of another m·,
    54– 1 upon complaint by another m·,
    85– 7 pupils of another m·

any
Man. 28–25 duty of any m· of this Church,
    51– 8 Any m· who shall unjustly
    95– 6 may call on any m· of this

calls a
Man. 48– 3 calls a m· to bear testimony

complaint of a
Man. 53– 2 complaint of a m· for her

dismiss a
Man. 26–24 majority vote . . . shall dismiss a m·.
    52–18 dismiss a m· from the Church.

disqualifies a
Man. 41–14 disqualifies a m· for office

each
Mis. 92–22 require each m· to own a copy
    305–24 * Each m· of the society
Man. 78– 1 demand that each m· thereof
    92– 7 I recommend that each m·
    93–15 Each m· shall mail to the Clerk
Ret. 84–11 each m· should own a copy
My. 165–18 Thus may each m· of this church

every
Mis. 305–12 * circular is sent to every m·
Man. 33– 1 every m· of The Mother Church,
    41–20 every m· of this Church
    42– 5 duty of every m· of this Church
    44–12 Every m· of The Mother Church
    44–17 privilege and duty of every m·,
    59– 6 duty of every m· of this Church,
'01. 31–17 every m· of my church
My. 132–17 every m· of this large church.
    279–22 I request that every m· of

full
Man. 39– 8 A full m· or a probationary

member

name of the
Man. 53– 5 drop forever the name of the *m·*
no
Man. 43– 5 No *m·* shall use written formulas,
    53–18 No *m·* shall enter a complaint
    87–12 No *m·* of this Church shall
My. 98–21 * no *m·* of the church anywhere,
of a branch
Man. 54– 9 *m·* of a branch of this Church
   112– 8 not a *m·* of a branch church,
of another Church
Man. 34–18 receive a *m·* of another Church
of any church
Man. 45–16 not be a *m·* of any church whose
of both
Man. 54–26 *m·* of both The Mother Church and
   74– 3 shall not be a *m·* of both
offending
Man. 65–19 removal of the offending *m·*
of her Church
Man. 67– 8 to a *m·* of her Church
of one branch
Man. 73–27 may be a *m·* of one branch
of the Board
Man. 73–19 *m·* of the Board of Lectureship may
   95–15 *m·* of the Board may lecture for a
of the church
Mis. 129– 2 If a *m·* of the church is inclined
Pul. 73–17 * prominent *m·* of the church.
My. 98–21 * no *m·* of the church anywhere,
of the family
Mis. 89– 4 *to care for a m· of the family,*
of The First Church
Man. 45–14 A *m·* of The First Church
   65– 4 A *m·* of The First Church
   92–19 not a *m·* of The First Church
of The Mother Church
Man. 33– 1 every *m·* of The Mother Church,
   34– 5 become a *m·* of The Mother Church,
   37– 1 *m·* of The Mother Church shall not
   42–25 *m·* of The Mother Church who
   44–12 *m·* of The Mother Church shall pay
   45–19 *m·* of The Mother Church is not
   46– 7 *m·* of The Mother Church shall not
   46–19 *m·* of The Mother Church shall not,
   48–11 *m·* of The Mother Church shall not
   49– 7 *m·* of The Mother Church who
   49–23 If a *m·* of The Mother Church shall
   52– 4 against a *m·* of The Mother Church,
   53–23 If a *m·* of The Mother Church
   54– 8 If a *m·* of The Mother Church
   73–26 *m·* of The Mother Church may be a
My. 223–21 from a *m·* of The Mother Church
   279–22 every *m·* of The Mother Church
of this Board
Man. 95– 6 any *m·* of this Board
   95–11 a *m·* of this Board of Lectureship
of this Church
Man. 28–25 duty of any *m·* of this Church,
   29– 9 a *m·* of this Church
   41–20 duty of every *m·* of this Church
   42– 5 duty of every *m·* of this Church
   43–14 A *m·* of this Church shall not
   43–21 A *m·* of this Church shall neither
   44– 8 A *m·* of this Church shall not
   46– 2 *m·* of this Church who claims
   47– 4 If a *m·* of this Church has a patient
   48– 7 A *m·* of this Church shall not
   50– 8 A *m·* of this Church shall not
   50–14 If a *m·* of this Church shall
   52–21 If a *m·* of this Church shall,
   53– 8 If a *m·* of this Church were
   54–19 If a *m·* of this Church,
   55–21 If a *m·* of this Church is found
   59– 6 duty of every *m·* of this Church,
   67–11 A *m·* of this Church shall not
   68– 2 *m·* of this Church at least three years
   69–16 appoint a proper *m·* of this Church
   72– 4 A *m·* of this Church who obeys its
   85– 7 pupils of another *m·* of this Church
   85–12 A *m·* of this Church shall not
   87– 2 nor a *m·* of this Church
   87–12 No *m·* of this Church shall advise
   92– 7 recommend that each *m·* of this Church
one
My. 230–10 Its rules apply not to one *m·* only,
probationary
Man. 39– 8 A full member or a probationary *m·*,
said
Man. 43– 3 name of said *m·* to be dropped
   50–20 and said *m·* exonerated, . . . or
   52– 5 *if said m· belongs to no branch*
   54–22 said *m·* shall immediately in
   56– 4 if said *m·* persists in this offense,

member

that
Man. 53–10 that *m·* should be excommunicated.
   56– 3 admonish that *m·* according to
this
Man. 41–16 renders this *m·* liable to discipline
weak
Man. 55–15 this weak *m·* shall not be
who leaves her
Man. 68– 5 A *m·* who leaves her in less time

Mis. 306–18 * *m·* of the above organization,
Man. 37– 5 A *m·* who violates this By-Law
   39–17 If a *m·* has been twice notified
   50–22 A *m·* who is found violating any
   52–10 letter of inquiry to the *m·*
   52–11 If a *m·* is found guilty
   53–11 If a *m·*, . . . shall trouble her
   65– 3 A *M·* not a Leader.
   68– 4 shall be the duty of the *m·*
   94–20 A *m·* shall neither resign nor
Ret. 19–11 being a *m·* in Saint Andrew's Lodge,
   89–14 or to a *m·* who had been away
My. 59– 2 * *m·* of your *first* class in Lynn,
   174–23 *m·* of the Congregational Church
   310– 6 *m·* of the New Hampshire Legislature,
   330–23 being a *m·* in St. Andrew's Lodge,
   335– 8 * faithful as a *m·* and officer

member's

Mis. 129–12 drop this *m·* name from the
Man. 46–21 payment for said *m·* practice,

members *(see also* members'*)*

active
Man.
   73–17 vote of, the active *m·* present,
actual
Pul. 55–29 * actual *m·* of different congregations
all
Man. 90– 1 All *m·* of this class must
among the
Man. 66– 8 shall arise among the *m·*
Pul. 56– 6 * among the *m·* of all the churches
assembled
My. 76–20 * pledged by the *m·* assembled
become
Mis. 310–20 and to become *m·* of it,
Man. 45– 9 shall not hereafter become *m·* of
   73–15 become *m·* of the organization
beloved
My. 118– 2 beloved *m·* of my church
Church
Man. 18–14 students and Church *m·* met
   75–18 Church *m·* own the aforesaid
   98–20 Church *m·* in annual meeting
Pul. 29–26 * heading
church
Man. 51–26 complaints against church *m·* ;
My. 74– 6 * numbers of belated church *m·*
   76–11 * church *m·* and their friends
   170– 4 in the request of my church *m·*
dear
My. 122–12 The deportment of its dear *m·*
   171– 1 these dear *m·* of my church :
   254–15 this class and its dear *m·*.
   302–27 dear *m·* wanted to greet me
devout
Mis. 249–13 devout *m·* of evangelical churches
distant
My. 140–15 * need not debar distant *m·*
   140–26 not prevent its distant *m·* from
distinguished
'00. 7–10 distinguished *m·* of the bar
duties of
Man. 64–10 heading
errors of the
Man. 55– 3 errors of the *m·* of their local church ;
five
Man. 26–20 Directors shall consist of five *m·*.
following
My. 136–13 following *m·* constitute the Board
forty thousand
My. 135–18 about forty thousand *m·*,
four thousand
Pul. 30– 8 * numbers now four thousand *m·* ;
   55–25 * now over four thousand *m·*.
   77–12 * loving hands of four thousand *m·*.
   78–11 * loving hands of four thousand *m·*.
greetings from
My. 259– 9 * Christmas greetings from *m·*
handful of
My. 85– 6 * and a mere handful of *m·*
in Mother Church
Man. 52– 3 *M·* in Mother Church Only.
its
Mis. 80– 6 obligates its *m·* to give
   120–21 many of its *m·* reside a long

members

its

Man.	45– 3	occupation for all its *m·*.
	76–18	Its *m·* shall be appointed
	102– 8	supply a vacancy of its *m·*
Ret.	44–22	from the danger to its *m·*
My.	vii– 5	* its *m·* can so protect their
	100–14	* its *m·* are numbered by thousands
	162–27	May He increase its *m·*,
	195–27	in the hearts of its *m·*
	339– 1	The purpose of its *m·* is to

its own

Man.	55– 7	discipline its own *m·*,
	99–11	not . . . confined to its own *m·*

leading

Pul.	72– 5	* a few of the leading *m·*

local

Man.	59–21	local *m·* of The Mother Church
My.	21–20	* The local *m·*, who have always

loyal

Man.	79– 4	not less than three loyal *m·*
	109– 3	Loyal *m·* of The Mother Church are
Ret.	53– 1	presenting to its loyal members

majority of the

Pul.	56– 8	* a majority of the *m·* are

many

Pan.	3–25	* are so many members.''

new

My.	50–25	* two new *m·* were added

number of

Pul.	67–20	* there is a large number of *m·*.

of a church

Mis.	90–23	*m· of a church not organized*

of branch churches

Man.	54–25	*M·* of Branch Churches.
My.	359– 4	with the *m·* of branch churches.

officious

Man.	45–19	Officious *M·*.

of her church

My.	144– 1	* letter to the *m·* of her church
	172– 9	* to the *m·* of her church,

of her household

My.	354–27	* *m·* of her household were with her

of my Church

My.	27– 2	*To the beloved M· of my Church,*

of my church

My.	118– 2	beloved *m·* of my church
	171– 1	these dear *m·* of my church:
	173– 7	to the *m·* of my church,
	280–16	request that the *m·* of my church

of my household

My.	143–11	by the *m·* of my household

of our Board

My.	125–12	All honor to the *m·* of our Board

of that body

Ret.	13– 3	*m·* of that body for a half-century.

of that faith

Pul.	75–20	* by which the *m·* of that faith

of the Board

Man.	29–15	salary of the *m·* of the Board of
My.	125–19	*m·* of the Board of Education,
	338–15	*m·* of the Board of Lectureship

of the Church

Man.	38–19	*m·* of the Church of Christ,
My.	51– 5	* *m·* of the Church of Christ,
	51–28	* *m·* of The Church of Christ,

of the church

(*see* **church**)

of the College

Man.	90–13	teacher and *m·* of the College class

of the Committees

Man.	65–12	*m·* of the Committees on Publication,

of the community

No.	3–21	to be safe *m·* of the community.

of the faculty

Man.	73– 9	*m·* of the faculty, instructors, or

of The Mother Church

Mis.	120–22	they are *m·* of The Mother Church
	251– 2	chapter sub-title
Man.	30– 4	must be *m·* of The Mother Church.
	32–18	shall be *m·* of The Mother Church.
	36– 1	or from *m·* of The Mother Church,
	37–22	*M·* of The Mother Church.
	37–23	Only *m·* of The Mother Church are
	40– 6	acts of the *m·* of The Mother Church.
	45– 5	duty of the *m·* of The Mother Church
	45– 7	*m·* of The Mother Church shall not
	45–18	*m·* of The Mother Church.
	48–18	*m·* of The Mother Church, nor
	51–23	excommunicate *m·* of The Mother Church.
	59–21	local *m·* of The Mother Church
	60–15	*m·* of The Mother Church.
	73– 2	four . . . are *m·* of The Mother Church.
	77–20	of the *m·* of The Mother Church,
	79– 4	loyal *m·* of The Mother Church,
	87– 8	*M·* of The Mother Church who are

members

of The Mother Church

Man.	92–15	Not *M·* of The Mother Church.
	109– 3	Loyal *m·* of The Mother Church
	109– 9	and are *m·* of The Mother Church.
	110– 7	*m·* of The Mother Church will be
My.	9–19	*To the M· of The Mother Church:*
	13–16	that the *m·* of The Mother Church,
	19–28	of the *m·* of The Mother Church,
	20–24	* *m·* of The Mother Church at the
	44–23	* The *m·* of The Mother Church,
	64–26	* *m·* of The Mother Church before men.

of this Board

Man.	51–24	Only the *m·* of this Board shall

of this Church

Man.	18–20	were elected *m·* of this Church,
	29–14	suitable *m·* of this Church to fill
	38–18	been *m·* of this Church,
	40–11	*m·* of this Church should daily
	42–15	*m·* of this Church shall neither
	44–24	*M·* of this Church shall not
	46–12	*M·* of this Church shall hold
	47–24	While *m·* of this Church do not
	53–15	*M·* of this Church shall not
	57– 9	meeting of the *m·* of this Church
	65– 6	by *m·* of this Church,
	66–23	*M·* of this Church shall not report
	67–17	*M·* of this Church who turn their
	76–17	consist of three *m·* of this Church
	82–16	*M·* of this Church who practise
	92–22	persons who are *m·* of this Church
	97–19	injustices done . . . *m·* of this Church

of this Committee

Man.	79– 8	While the *m·* of this Committee

of your church

My.	23–17	* The *m·* of your church,
	36– 8	* The *m·* of your church

older

Mis.	311–11	some of the older *m·* are not

other

Pul.	59–23	* other *m·* of the C. S. Board

privilege of

Man.	73– 7	Privilege of *M·*.

return of

Mis.	310–12	letters relative to the return of *m·*

strayed

Man.	85– 4	Caring for Pupils of Strayed *M·*.

such

Man.	85–18	Such *m·* who have not been

sufficient

Mis.	349–25	When the church had sufficient *m·*

ten thousand

My.	123–23	a church of ten thousand *m·*

thirty thousand

My.	172–15	church of over thirty thousand *m·* ;

those

Man.	68–13	Those *m·* whom she teaches
	82–18	excepting those *m·* who are

three

Man.	36–21	recommendation signed by three *m·*
	76–17	consist of three *m·* of this Church
	88– 7	consisting of three *m·*,
	102– 5	of not less than three *m·*,

twenty-four thousand

My.	8–19	* church of twenty-four thousand *m·*

twenty-six

Man.	18– 4	the *m·*, twenty-six in number,
Ret.	16–17	the *m·*, twenty-six in number,
	44– 6	*m·*, twenty-six in number,
Pul.	30–27	* It opened with twenty-six *m·*,
	38– 1	* was founded with twenty-six *m·*,
	67–28	* founded . . . with twenty-six *m·*,

were asked

My.	96–23	* *m·* were asked to quit giving.

were invited

My.	96–19	* *M·* were invited to contribute

women

My.	30–14	* devoted women *m·*,

Mis.	131–28	*m·* of the C. S. Board of Directors
	135–26	*M·* of the Christian Scientists'
	136–26	*m·* coming from a distance will
	138–21	*m·* of the National . . . Association,
	138–22	*m·* of students' organizations.
Man.	17– 4	*m·* of evangelical churches,
	18–19	*m·* of her former Church were
	26–24	*M·* shall neither report the
	38–17	*M·* who once Withdrew.
	39– 7	*M·* once Dismissed.
	40– 3	GUIDANCE OF *m·*.
	42–19	*M·* will not intentionally or
	51–11	*m·* who are in good . . . standing
	57–14	for which the *m·* are to convene.
	59–10	*M·* shall also instruct their pupils
	68–10	*M·* thus serving the Leader shall
	73– 7	*M·* in good standing

members

Man.	73–13	*m·* in good standing
	93– 5	*m·* of which shall be elected annually
Ret.	44–11	my church increased in *m·*,
Pul.	27–10	* that the *m·* strongly insist upon.
	30– 1	* *m·* of their own families,
	41–13	* *m·* of the denomination
	47– 7	* *m·* of this fast-increasing faith.
	71– 2	* eight hundred of the *m·* are
	76–26	* *m·* of The First Church of Christ,
	77–25	* *M·* of The First Church of Christ,
'02.	1– 6	Two thousand . . . *m·*
	1– 9	twenty-four thousand . . . *m·* ;
My.	16–13	* *m·* of the C. S. Board
	18–27	* by the *m·* of the C. S. Board
	20–30	* ask the *m·* to contribute
	30–10	* devotion of the *m·* to their faith,
	49–10	* *m·* extended a unanimous invitation
	56–23	* *m·* of which had formerly been
	62–27	* *m·* of the business committee,
	65– 5	* *m·* of The First Church of Christ,
	72– 8	* *m·* of the titled aristocracy
	83– 6	* *m·* of the local . . . committee
	83–30	* the readiness of the *m·* to
	95– 6	* by *m·* who represent the
	155–18	the *m·* of this dear church
	157– 3	* *m·* of the Concord church
	164–16	*m·* of which not only possess a
	363–19	chapter sub-title

members'

Man.	59–20	The Local *M·* Welcome.

Membership

(see **Church Membership**)

membership

Mis.	x–25	a certificate of *m·* made out to
	278–30	gradually withdrawing from active *m·*
Man.	34– 3	QUALIFICATIONS FOR *m·*.
	34–21	until that *m·* is dissolved.
	35– 6	may be admitted to *m·* with The
	35– 9	APPLICATIONS for *m·*.
	35–11	Applications for *m·* with The
	35–18	Applicants for *m·* who have not
	36– 5	Applications for *m·* with The
	36–18	endorse their applications for *m·*
	36–23	admit said applicant to *m·*.
	36–25	All applications for *m·*
	37– 3	countersign an application for *m·*
	37– 8	If an application for *m·*
	38– 1	to approve for *m·* individuals who
	38– 9	Applicants for *m·* in this Church,
	38–16	PROBATIONARY *m·*.
	39– 2	make application for *m·*
	39– 5	shall be received into full *m·*,
	39–13	eligible to probationary *m·*
	45–14	Forbidden *M·*.
	46–23	to have his name removed from *m·*.
	51– 6	dropped from the roll of Church *m·*.
	51–22	has power to . . . remove from *m·*,
	53– 6	from the roll of Church *m·*.
	54– 6	suspended . . from Church *m·*.
	54–15	branch church's list of *m·*
	54–24	from *m·* in The Mother Church.
	55–15	repentant . . . and retaining his *m·*,
	56–22	for electing candidates to *m·*
	71– 7	nor written on applications for *m·*
	73– 3	This *m·* shall include
	73–24	shall not confine their *m·* to
Ret.	14– 4	examination of candidates for *m·*,
Pul.	30–23	* entire *m·* of Christian Scientists
	66– 5	* with a *m·* of only twenty-six,
	71– 1	* *m·* of four thousand,
'00.	1–12	a *m·* of over sixteen thousand
My.	9– 2	* large accessions to their *m·*.
	23– 3	* total *m·* of The Mother Church
	49– 7	* the reading of its *m·*,
	56–20	* the *m·* and the attendance
	57–15	* *m·* at that date was 1,545.
	57–16	* *m·* of this church to-day is
	57–24	* show a *m·* of 41,944.
	76–29	* a *m·* of twenty-six persons.
	85– 1	* character of the assembling *m·*,
	91– 1	* immense *m·* of the body
	97–23	* and the zeal of its *m·*.
	141–24	*m·* includes forty-eight thousand
	148–17	*m·* of seventy-four communicants,
	182– 7	a *m·* of thirty years
	182–18	large *m·* and majestic cathedral.
	242–19	relating to . . . Mother Church *m·*,
	311–17	date of my first church *m·*.
	332–19	* facts regarding Major Glover's *m·*
	335– 6	* retained his *m·* in both till

membranes

Mis.	210–20	a belief of disordered brains, *m·*,

membranous

Mis.	44– 7	*for immediate relief, as in m· croup*

Memento

Po.	page 73	poem

memorable

Mis.	144– 8	On this *m·* day there are laid away
Ret.	15–21	last vestry meeting was made *m·* by
	16– 1	One *m·* Sunday afternoon,
My.	5–24	*m·* dedication and communion season,
	55– 1	* This date is *m·* as the one
	81–25	* a fitting close to a *m·* week.
	148–13	*M·* date, all unthought of till
	327– 3	Is it not a *m·* coincidence

memorial

Mis.	145–22	*m·* such as Isaiah prophesied :
Pul.	27– 9	* There are no "*m·*" windows ;
	27–10	* a testimonial, not a *m·*
	71– 6	* a *m·* church for Mrs. Eddy,
My.	20– 2	for a *m·* of her." — *Mark* 14 : 9.
	43–17	* on the other side for a *m·*.
	194–13	tender *m·* engraven on your
	289–23	to attend the *m·* meeting

memorialized

Pul.	65–24	* and so was *m·* in art
	76–23	* REV. MARY BAKER EDDY *M·* BY A

memorials

Ret.	5–12	inscribed on the stone *m·* in
Pul.	77– 4	* one of the most chastely elegant *m·*
'01.	28–13	choicest *m·* of devotion
My.	257–24	your manifold Christmas *m·*,

Memorial service

My.	284–13	*M· s·* of the E. E. Sturtevant Post
	284–19	*M· s·* has been held annually

memories

Po.	3– 7	With evening, *m·* reappear
My.	47–15	* recall *m·* of trials, progress, and
	256–18	dearest *m·* in human history
	258–23	beautiful are the Christmas *m·*

memorize

Mis.	374–17	Scientists *m·* the nativity of Jesus.

memory (see also **memory's**, **mem'ry**)

Mis.	xi–24	thought sometimes walks in *m·*,
	142–27	The symbols . . . wakened *m·*,
	159–12	the *m·* of my students.
	218–24	this nature may linger in *m·* :
	232– 2	but the *m·* was too much ;
	290–25	hold a place in one's *m·*,
	329–11	restoring in *m·* the sweet rhythm
	339–27	will some time flood thy *m·*,
	343–27	fill the haunted chambers of *m·*,
	386–23	Rears the sad marble to our *m·*
	394–16	* The gates of *m·* unbar:
Ret.	5–15	*m·* recalls qualities to which
	6–10	the *m·* of my second brother,
	8– 2	throng the chambers of *m·*.
Pul.	1–12	garner the *m·* of 1894,
	5– 8	*M·*, faithful to goodness,
Po.	25– 7	Around you in *m·* rise !
	34–18	Bearing no bitter *m·* at heart ;
	50– 9	Rears the sad marble to our *m·*
	57– 2	* The gates of *m·* unbar :
	67– 9	*m·* of dear ones deemed dead
	74– 3	those moments to *m·* bestowed?
My.	19–27	fill the *m·* and swell the hearts
	26–12	emotion at the touch of *m·*.
	38–26	* carry with them the *m·* of it.
	39–26	* and the *m·* lives with us.
	125– 5	to report progress, to refresh *m·*,
	147– 3	when at the touch of *m·*
	147–14	sacred to the *m·* of this pure
	164–12	*m·*, and all within the human heart
	258–17	The *m·* of the Bethlehem
	319– 8	in loving, grateful *m·*
	319–27	* very well fixed in my *m·*,
	326–16	so signally honored his *m·*,

memory's

Mis.	159–16	In this chamber is *m·* wardrobe,
Po.	66– 5	songs float in *m·* dream.
	68–15	o'er the heartstrings in *m·* hour.

mem'ry

Mis.	392–22	To my busy *m·* bringing
Po.	33–11	(And *m·* but part us awhile),
	51– 4	To my busy *m·* bringing

men (see also **men's**)

actions of

Mis.	237– 7	a change in the actions of *m·*.
	280– 6	the thoughts and actions of *m·* ;

a kind of

Mis.	261–25	I mean mortals, or a kind of *m·*
'02.	14–19	not by mankind, but by a kind of *m·*

all

Mis.	358–12	All *m·* shall be satisfied when they
Ret.	49–24	bring all *m·* to a knowledge of
	93– 9	draw all *m·* unto me." — *John* 12 : 32.

men

all
Un.   5–21   known to all *m·*." — *see Phil.* 4 : 5.
No.   8– 9   recommending to all *m·* fellowship
'02. 16–12 "Follow peace with all *m·*, — *Heb.* 12 : 14.
My. 28–25   * for all time and for all *m·* ;
     37– 2   * salvation of all *m·* from all evil.
     127–31 adapted to all *m·*, all nations,
     240– 1 till all *m·* shall know Him
     247–13 will draw all *m·* unto you.
     295–20 enriches the being of all *m·*.
among
Ret. 70–27 Preeminent among *m·*, he virtually
'00.   5–15 under heaven and among *m·*
and angels
My. 189– 1 warmest wish of *m·* and angels.
and women
Mis. 99–12 *M·* and women of the nineteenth
     110– 5 as children than as *m·* and women :
     158–19 God's servants are minute *m·* and women.
     340–26 lives of great *m·* and women
Pul. 36–11 * the *m·* and women present
Pan.   9– 6 they imply *m·* and women ;
'00.   7– 9 most scholarly *m·* and women,
My. 54–10   * tide of *m·* and women was turned
     80– 3   * prosperous, contented *m·* and women,
     92– 5   * numbers of intelligent *m·* and women
     104–25 many professional *m·* and women
     105–29 are noble *m·* and women,
     113–32 *m·* and women of this age.
     158–22 Most *m·* and women talk well,
     194–10 *m·* and women gain greatness
     239–19 generic term for *m·* and women.
     285–14 *m·* and women of this period
     305–13 most distinguished *m·* and women
     315–29 millions of the good *m·* and women
     344– 5 each separate ray for *m·* and women.
appetites of
Mis. 296–28 and the bad appetites of *m*?
are known
Mis. 371–20 * "*m·* are known by their enemies."
as angels
Mis. 251–21 and *m·* as angels who,
assembled
Ret. 89– 7 *M·* assembled in the one temple
before
My. 64–27   * worthy members . . . before *m·*.
best
My. 331–13   * by Wilmington's best *m·*,
better
Mis. 365–15 better health and better *m·*.
blind
Mis. 362– 8 dogma has made *m·* blind.
brave
Pan. 14–23 at Manila, where brave *m·*,
brotherhood of
Mis. 348– 7 on the brotherhood of *m·*.
business
My. 30–12   * were business *m·* come from far
     82– 1   * hard-headed shrewd business *m·*.
call God
'01. 18–26 whom *m·* call God
cannot punish
My. 128–17   *M·* cannot punish a man for suicide ;
children of
Rud. 10–21 not willingly the children of *m·*,
My. 90–11   * endows the children of *m·*,
     193–10 the children of *m·*." — *Psal.* 107 : 8.
consist of
Man. 99–25 shall consist of *m·* generally.
count cost
My. 127–26   not costly as *m·* count cost,
covereth
Mis. 153–16 covereth *m·* as a garment,
curse we
Un. 60–14   therewith curse we *m·*, — *Jas.* 3 : 9.
damning
My. 211– 1   error that is damning *m·*.
deeds of
My. 277–20   immortal words and deeds of *m·*
dispraise of
Mis. 245–22 praise or the dispraise of *m·*.
distinguished
Ret.   7–15 * one of the most distinguished *m·*
My. 305–13 most distinguished *m·* and women
doctrines of
Mis. 366–19 doctrines of *m·*, even as
dogmas of
Pan. 11– 9 doctrines, and dogmas of *m·*
draw
Ret. 88–27 spiritual attitude as will draw *m·*
fisher of
My. 247–19   called you to be a fisher of *m·*.
fishers of
Mis. 111–10 "fishers of *m·*" — *Mark* 1 : 17.
My. 295–17 Scientists are fishers of *m·*.

men

give counsel
Mis. 359–28 *M·* give counsel ; but they give not the
have not heard
My. 184– 4   *m·* have not heard with the ear,
healer of
My. 104–15   the healer of *m·*, the Christ,
heard of
No. 39– 5   offered to be heard of *m·*,
hearts of
Mis. 121– 2 inscribed upon the hearts of *m·* :
My. 123– 6 moves the hearts of *m·* to goodness
in our ranks
My. 355– 5   chapter sub-title
killing
My. 277–15   Killing *m·* is not consonant with
learn
Mis. 251–25 *m·* learn a parable of the
light of
My. 154–13   "was the light of *m·*." — *John* 1 : 4.
     295– 6   was the light of *m·*." — *John* 1 : 4.
lives of
Pan. 10– 6 effects of C. S. on the lives of *m·*
Peo. 11–28 liberty and lives of *m·*.
My. 277–14 characters and lives of *m·* determine
     294– 4 morals and the lives of *m·*,
made
Peo. 10–18 mortal beliefs, . . . made *m·* sinning
made monsters of
Peo.   3– 4 have made monsters of *m·* ;
made seers of
'01.   9– 9 a sense so pure it made seers of *m·*,
make
Mis. 387–19 make *m·* one in love remain.
Hea.   3– 4 Christianity was to make *m·* better,
Po.   6–14 make *m·* one in love remain.
makes
Mis. 363– 7 supposition . . . is mind and makes *m·*,
many
My. 114–12   to the gaze of many *m·*,
may revile
My.   6–10   *m·* may revile us and despitefully
medical
Mis. 80–13 cultured and conscientious medical *m·*,
minds of
My. 225–18   begins in the minds of *m·*
     264–16   signifies to the minds of *m·*
     295– 4   remains in the minds of *m·*,
morals of
My. 103–21   longevity, and morals of *m·* ;
more
My. 355– 7   need for more *m·* in C. S.
most
My. 160–15   trenchant truth . . . most *m·* avoid
motives of
Mis. 19–10 the affections and motives of *m·*
My. 268–14 uplifting the motives of *m·*.
must approach
Un. 13– 4   *M·* must approach God reverently,
must know
My. 149– 1   *m·* must know somewhat of
number of
Pul. 49–29 * She employs a number of *m·*
of science
My. 95–23   * higher critics and the *m·* of science
opinions of
Mis. x–16   opinions of *m·* and the progress of
     92–25   opinions of *m·* cannot be substituted
Ret. 84–14 opinions of *m·* cannot be substituted
or women
Un.   4–28   no wise *m·* or women will rudely
other
Mis. 103–25 was like that of other *m·* ;
professional
My. 30–14   * professional *m·*, devoted women
     81–32   * professional *m·*, hard-headed
     104–25   many professional *m·* and women
raises
Ret. 66– 4 It raises *m·* from a material sense
rejected of
'01.   9–18 and yet Christ is rejected of *m·* !
representative
My. 327–22   * representative *m·* of our dear State
rescue
Un. 59–19   Jesus came to rescue *m·*
rich
My. 149–16   * "And I with many rich *m·*,
rights of
My. 247– 2   inalienable, universal rights of *m·*.
     254–23   inalienable, universal rights of *m·*.
save
Un. 60– 2   Christ Jesus came to save *m·*,
saving
'01.   9–17 healing and saving *m·*,
Saviour of
My. 104–15   says that the Saviour of *m·*,

men

seen of
Mis. 133–13   may be seen of *m*·.— *Matt.* 6 : 5.
My. 124–29   seen of *m*·, and spiritually understood ;
sentence
No. 44–14   sentence *m*· to the dungeon
shall revile
Mis. 8–22   when *m*· shall revile— *Matt.* 5 : 11.
'01. 3– 4   when *m*· shall revile— *Matt.* 5 : 11.
'02. 11–22   when *m*· shall revile— *Matt.* 5 : 11.
My. 104–30   when *m*· shall revile— *Matt.* 5 : 11.
316– 7   when *m*· shall revile— *Matt.* 5 : 11.
should do
Mis. 90–14   would that *m*· should do— *Matt.* 7 : 12.
119–32   would that *m*· should do— *Matt.* 7 : 12.
146–18   would that *m*· should do— *Matt.* 7 : 12.
235–28   would that *m*· should do— *Matt.* 7 : 12.
282–10   would that *m*· should do— *Luke* 6 : 31.
Man. 42–23   would that *m*· should do— *Matt.* 7 : 12.
Ret. 87–20   would that *m*· should do— *Matt.* 7 : 12.
'00. 14–17   would that *m*· should do— *Luke* 6 : 31.
My. 266– 9   would that *m*· should do— *Matt.* 7 : 12.
street-car
My. 83–13   * street-car *m*· and policemen,
thoughts of
Peo. 3–18   inscribes on the thoughts of *m*·
tongues of
'01. 26–22   with the tongues of *m*·— *I Cor.* 13 : 1.
toward
Mis. 145–30   good will toward *m*·.”— *Luke* 2 : 14.
215–15   peace, and good will toward *m*·.
369– 5   good will toward *m*·.”— *Luke* 2 : 14.
Man. 45– 7   and good will toward *m*· ;
Pul. 41–26   * good will toward *m*·.”— *Luke* 2 : 14.
No. 44–27   good will toward *m*·'”— *Luke* 2 : 14.
My. 90–20   * good will toward *m*·.”— *Luke* 2 : 14.
127–30   good will toward *m*·,”— *Luke* 2 : 14.
167–12   good will toward *m*·,”— *Luke* 2 : 14.
279–19   good will toward *m*·.”— *Luke* 2 : 14.
281–10   good will toward *m*·.”— *Luke* 2 : 14.
283–12   good will toward *m*·.”— *Luke* 2 : 14.
towards
Pul. 22– 2   peace and good will towards *m*·.
Pan. 15–10   and good will toward *m*·.
'02. 8–12   love and good will towards *m*·.
My. 4–20   is good will towards *m*·.
210–17   reflect peace, good will towards *m*·,
282– 1   purpose is good will towards *m*·.
turned
Mis. 345–31   Christianity turned *m*· away from
universe and
Rud. 4– 4   our material universe and *m*·
unselfs
My. 288– 2   unselfs *m*· and pushes on the ages.
warring
Pul. 83–30   * She brought to warring *m*·
weak
Mis. 345–15   * fit only for women and weak *m*· ;”
weak-minded
Peo. 13–24   * only for women and weak-minded *m*·.”
wise
Mis. 321– 1   wise *m*· follow this guiding star ;
Un. 4–28   no wise *m*· or women will
My. 149–15   * conversed with many wise *m*·,”
wrath of
My. 207– 4   The wrath of *m*· shall praise God,

Mis. 27–16   “Do *m*· gather grapes of— *Matt.* 7 : 16.
36– 7   Beasts, as well as *m*·, express Mind
56–26   if all minds (*m*·) have existed
110–28   how fleeting is that which *m*· call great ;
210– 7   Do *m*· whine over a nest of serpents,
251–21   where angels are as *m*·,
Ret. 35– 6   *m*· were so unfamiliar with the subject
Un. 15– 4   *m*· rid themselves of an incubus
Pul. 45– 1   * *M*·, women, and children
64– 8   * *M*·, women, and children contributed,
No. 1– 9   So when thrilled by a new idea,
'01. 16–25   *m*· go to mock, and go away to pray
Peo. 11–19   as *m*· pass legislative acts
My. 5–28   indulging sin, *m*· cannot serve God ;
17–10   disallowed indeed of *m*·,— *I Pet.* 2 : 4.
83–11   * and the *m*· go entirely unadorned.
94–31   * a few years ago, *m*· there were who
104–17   that *m*· suspend judgment
113–26   *m*· are found casting out the evils
355– 9   *m*· are very important factors

menacing
Mis. 67–20   if you see the danger *m*· others,

mendicant
Mis. 330–26   mere *m*· that boasts and begs,

menial
Pul. 8–17   never before devoted to *m*· services,
My. 165– 5   The grand must stoop to the *m*·.

men's
Mis. 240–29   takes off *m*· heads ;
Pul. 79–20   * taken possession of *m*· minds,
My. 6–24   above the work of *m*· hands,
94–28   above the work of *m*· hands,

mens populi
Mis. 7–31   *m*· *p*· is not sufficiently enlightened

mental

advancement
My. 239–28   and stage of *m*· advancement,
agencies
Pul. 14– 5   active yet unseen *m*· agencies
and moral
Mis. 73–12   it is always *m*· and moral,
anguish
Mis. 237– 5   *m*· anguish is generally accepted as
animus
My. 277–11   The *m*· animus goes on,
argument
Mis. 220– 5   healer begins by *m*· argument.
221– 3   by a false *m*· argument ;
222–15   malicious *m*· argument and its action
359– 5   you continue the *m*· argument
Rud. 9–22   an audible or even a *m*· argument,
arrow
Mis. 223–30   *m*· arrow shot from another's
atmosphere
Mis. 355–27   from thine own *m*· atmosphere.
Man. 31–11   the *m*· atmosphere they exhale
'00. 9–15   till the *m*· atmosphere is clear.
avenues
'01. 1– 3   the *m*· avenues of mankind
bane
'01. 20–15   *m*· bane could not bewilder,
branches
Mis. 243– 5   one of the *m*· branches taught
cause
Ret. 24– 9   physical effects to a *m*· cause ;
collisions
Mis. 339–13   In the *m*· collisions of mortals
condition
Mis. 43– 5   the *m*· condition of the patient.
112–28   Unless this *m*· condition be overcome,
204–15   *m*· condition settles into strength,
281– 6   I find also another *m*· condition
Hea. 17–21   Sin is a supposed *m*· condition ;
conditions
Mis. 91–15   types of these *m*· conditions,
Un. 56–27   Such *m*· conditions as ingratitude,
consciousness
Ret. 94–12   no matter, to the *m*· consciousness.
conviction
My. 121– 8   a true, tried *m*· conviction
darkness
Mis. 355–18   *M*· darkness is senseless error,
deformity
Mis. 203–22   the veil that hides *m*· deformity.
delusion
No. 4– 8   material sensation and *m*· delusion.
denomination
Ret. 28–18   to their own *m*· denomination,
depression
Mis. 51– 5   *accompanied by great m· depression,*
design
Mis. 249–22   of their *m*· design to do this
development
Mis. 264–27   to aid the *m*· development of
356–22   second stage of *m*· development is
digestion
My. 229–19   chapter sub-title
disease
Mis. 112–24   This *m*· disease at first shows
dose
Mis. 241–10   give to the immoralist a *m*· dose
efforts
Ret. 71–27   Secret *m*· efforts to obtain help
error
Rud. 3–20   *m*· error made manifest physically,
evil
My. 212–12   highest form of *m*· evil,
force
Mis. 220– 7   supports this silent *m*· force
forces
Mis. 19–25   centripetal and centrifugal *m*· forces
formation
Mis. 287–16   discern the Science of *m*· formation
growth
Mis. 357–19   The third stage of *m*· growth
hardships
My. 52– 3   * many *m*· hardships to endure,
haziness
My. 211–30   a *m*· haziness which admits of no
healers
Pul. 57–23   * There are several sects of *m*· healers,
No. 2–11   *M*· healers who admit that disease is

mental

healing
Mis. 3–29 The tendency of *m·* healing is to
4– 5 to plant *m·* healing on the basis
34–28 *Who is the Founder of m· healing?*
58–26 the theology of *m·* healing
80– 2 spurious works on *m·* healing.
171–27 the Science of *m·* healing ;
172–23 the Science of *m·* healing,
174–14 the Science of *m·* healing.
175–18 *m·* healing must be understood.
175–25 *m·* healing which acquaints us with
220– 2 in every line of *m·* healing,
223–16 believing in *m·* healing,
254–22 *m·* healing on a material basis
271–27 * false teachers of *m·* healing,
282– 6 chapter sub-title
Ret. 48–18 scientific methods of *m·* healing
No. 31–21 Physical and *m·* healing
Hea. 11–18 foundation stone of *m·* healing ;
idleness
'00. 8–16 *m·* idleness or apathy is always
influence
Mis. 264–23 *m·* influence of their former teacher.
Ret. 72– 2 *m·* influence that hazards another's
law
Mis. 199– 6 to annul his own erring *m·* law,
malady
My. 116– 9 a *m·* malady, which must be met
203–17 Dishonesty is a *m·* malady
malpractice
Mis. 31– 1 *consider to be m· malpractice?*
31– 2 *M·* malpractice is a bland denial
31– 9 and is *m·* malpractice.
41– 5 *m·* malpractice would disgrace
113–21 *m·* malpractice, if persisted in,
115– 4 sin and *m·* malpractice,
222–17 the effects of *m·* malpractice
233– 7 the breath of *m·* malpractice,
233–19 Substituting *m·* malpractice for
248–29 *m·* malpractice of poisoning people
316– 1 defend . . . against *m·* malpractice,
351– 2 and meet the *m·* malpractice.
351– 7 the silent *m·* malpractice.
Man. 52– 6 complaint is not for *m· malpractice,*
53–19 enter a complaint of *m·* malpractice
53–21 the offense of *m·* malpractice,
84– 3 against *m·* malpractice,
Ret. 38– 9 partial history . . . of *m·* malpractice.
'01. 19–20 chapter sub-title
My. 130– 3 against malicious *m·* malpractice.
212–31 to cover his crime of *m·* malpractice,
213–15 to the modes of *m·* malpractice,
malpractitioner
Mis. 19–23 hypocrite or *m·* malpractitioner.
115– 9 guilt as a *m·* malpractitioner,
221– 2 a *m·* malpractitioner may lose his
368–19 silent address of a *m·* malpractitioner
'01. 20– 9 The *m·* malpractitioner is not,
My. 212–24 *m·* malpractitioner, interfering with
means
Mis. 40–29 to kill his patient by *m·* means,
mechanism
Mis. 354–18 right action of the *m·* mechanism,
medicine
Mis. 252– 2 *m·* medicine of divine metaphysics
252– 4 *M·* medicine gains no potency by
method
Mis. 220–21 this *m·* method has power
351– 9 *m·* method of Mind-healing,
methods
Mis. 260–31 silent *m·* methods whereby
miasma
My. 249–13 *m·* miasma fatal to health,
millstone
Mis. 362–23 to remove this *m·* millstone
ministrations
No. 40–14 pursue their *m·* ministrations
monument
My. 6–23 rises to a *m·* monument,
94–27 "rises to a *m·* monument,
mood
Ret. 75–17 the author's own *m·* mood,
mortally
Un. 35– 9 to be mortally *m·*,
operation
Mis. 352–19 *m·* operation must be understood
origin
Hea. 17–26 Then was not sin of *m·* origin,
perfection
Mis. 234–25 physical and *m·* perfection,
period
Mis. 204– 6 *m·* period is sometimes chronic,
phenomenon
Ret. 24–11 every effect a *m·* phenomenon.
Pul. 70–18 every effect a *m·* phenomenon."

mental

phenomenon
Hea. 6– 8 *m·* phenomenon named mediumship,
power
Mis. 115–31 Using *m·* power in the right direction
practice
Mis. 219–11 chapter sub-title
282–20 the above rule of *m·* practice.
283– 1 *m·* practice where there is no
293–10 observation, and *m·* practice.
350–27 none to be used in *m·* practice,
Man. 90–20 *m·* practice and *malpractice.*
Ret. 71–21 motives entering into *m·* practice
'01. 19–21 From ordinary *m·* practice to
Hea. 14–17 the method of a *m·* practice.
My. 106– 5 without . . . *m·* practice were profitless.
364– 3 rule of *m·* practice in C. S.
364– 7 *m·* practice includes and inculcates
practitioner
Mis. 220–16 *m·* practitioner has changed his
220–19 *m·* practitioner undertook to
practitioners
Mis. 221–16 many helpless *m·* practitioners
My. 212–15 dissension among *m·* practitioners
problem
Ret. 34– 5 solve the *m·* problem.
process
Mis. 220–24 if this *m·* process and power
processes
Un. 21– 2 description of *m·* processes
21– 4 If we observe our *m·* processes,
purgation
Mis. 41–13 *M·* purgation must go on :
quackery
Rud. 12–11 *m·* quackery, that denies the
remedy
Mis. 44–28 applying this *m·* remedy
reservations
My. 345– 4 their *m·* reservations will be
Science
Mis. 172–25 *M·* Science, and the five personal
173– 2 misstate *m·* Science,
Peo. 10–15 *M·* Science alone grasps the
science
Mis. 4– 6 calling this method "*m·* science."
58–21 Without . . . there is no *m·* science,
seal
Mis. 269–29 opening of this silent *m·* seal,
sense
Un. 9– 2 Destroy the *m·* sense of the disease,
signs
Mis. 347–10 the *m·* signs of these times,
stages
Mis. 112–12 The *m·* stages of crime,
standpoint
Mis. 379–22 *m·* standpoint not understood,
state
(*see* state)
struggle
My. 307–28 *m·* struggle might have caused my
struggles
Un. 5– 7 their *m·* struggles and pride
suggestion
Man. 42– 6 against aggressive *m·* suggestion,
system
Mis. 35– 8 blessings of this *m·* system
Hea. 13–25 this *m·* system of healing is the
teeth
Pul. 80–14 * fairly broken our *m·* teeth
therapeutics
Pul. 54–20 * practice of *m·* therapeutics,
My. 306–31 my views of *m·* therapeutics.
treatment
Mis. 31– 8 the abuse of *m·* treatment,
315–26 needing it asks for *m·* treatment.
Ret. 71– 9 Promiscuous *m·* treatment,
71–12 indications of *m·* treatment,
My. 363–26 avoid naming, in his *m·* treatment,
unsoundness
Mis. 49– 5 manifested some *m·* unsoundness,
vigor
My. 355– 3 * spiritualized thought and *m·* vigor
virtues
Ret. 33–23 *m·* virtues of the material methods
want
No. 42– 7 material forms to meet a *m·* want.
ways
Pul. 15– 3 evil's hidden *m·* ways
work
Mis. 350–10 no advice given, no *m·* work,

———

Mis. 27–26 must be spiritual and *m·*.
28– 5 Perception by the . . . senses is *m·*,
72–27 Real sensation . . . must be, *m·* :
220– 9 His *m·* and oral arguments aim to

mental

Mis.	244–12	are the conditions of salvation m·,
	269–17	on a Christian, m·, scientific basis ;
	319–11	m· and audible protest against the
	351–12	solely from m· malicious practice,
Un.	12– 2	by m·, not material processes.
Rud.	16–22	a pathological Science purely m·.
No.	6–27	the laws of Science are m·,
'01.	1–14	constitute m· and physical perfection.
My.	74–29	* the material and the m·,
	79–29	* from diseases, physical and m·,
	114–30	each step of m· and spiritual progress,
	134–29	* her usual m· and physical vigor.''
	160–29	this hell is m·, not material,
	294– 9	m· counteracting elements,

mentalities

'01.	7–13	express the different m· of

mentality

Mis.	76–24	false sense of m· in matter,
	104–16	His materiality, clad in a false m·,
	107–26	lack of seeing one's deformed m·,
	109–12	most hopeful stage of mortal m·.
	355–22	what in thine own m· is unlike
Un.	56– 4	from the m· of others ;
	56–10	suffering from m· in opposition to
	56–15	m· which opposes the law of Spirit ;
	58–14	sublime triumph over all mortal m·
Pul.	vii–13	its lenses of more spiritual m·,
My.	106–19	Human m·, expressed in disease,
	364– 4	strictly to handle no other m·

mentally

Mis.	31– 4	To m· argue in a manner
	67– 6	m·, morally, or physically.
	67–14	either m· or audibly,
	113–11	Whoever is m· manipulating
	127–10	m·, meekly, and importunately.
	206–20	accentuating harmony . . . m· and orally,
	220– 5	person whom another would heal m·,
	220– 6	He m· says, ''You are well,
	221–15	stultify the power to heal m·.
	221–24	we must m· struggle against both
	282– 8	treated m· without their knowledge
	282–16	When you enter m· the personal
	293–24	To affirm m· and audibly
	297– 8	m· destroys the appetite for
	315–24	shall not silently m· address
	380–18	Although I could heal m·,
Man.	42–20	will not . . . knowingly m· malpractise,
	42–25	who m· malpractises upon
	52–21	m· or otherwise, persist in
Ret.	38–23	Not a word . . . audibly or m·,
Un.	36–19	m·, morally, spiritually.
Pul.	32–12	* I m· questioned this modern
No.	2–24	destroys one's ability to heal m·.
	40–16	never to trespass m· on individual
Pan.	8– 3	causes a man to be m· deranged ;
Hea.	14– 5	until disease is treated m·
	14–19	You must first m· educate
My.	18– 7	m·, meekly, and importunately.
	146–26	never m· or audibly takes
	222– 2	once failed m· to cure by their faith

mention

Ret.	15– 9	I will make m· of— Psal. 71 : 16.

mentioned

Mis.	68–18	Does the gentleman above m· know
	170–31	The putting on of hands m·,
Man.	69– 9	expiration of the time therein m·
	102–13	m· in the deeds given by
My.	106– 8	I name those m· above
	294–20	hindrances previously m·,
	324–32	* m· many kindnesses

mercantile

My.	53– 2	* inquiry and m· reproach ;

mercenary

Mis.	283– 2	or the motive is m·,
No.	43–18	take it up from m· motives,

mercies

Mis.	391– 8	Will count their m· o'er,
	391–17	Share God's most tender m·,
	397– 1	Then His unveiled, sweet m·
Pul.	18–10	Then His unveiled, sweet m·
Po.	12–10	Then His unveiled, sweet m·
	33–14	Whose m· my sorrows beguile,
	38– 7	Will count their m· o'er,
	38–16	Share God's most tender m·,
My.	13–22	and tender m· ;— Psal. 103 : 4.

merciful

Mis.	32–28	and should be just, m· ;
	332– 4	Infinitely just, m·, and wise,
Man.	16–12	and to be m·, just, and pure.
Peo.	12– 7	m· and just government of God.
My.	41–12	* ''Blessed are the m·,''— Matt. 5 : 7.
	190– 3	m· design of divine Love,

mercifully

My.	201–16	m· forgive, wisely ponder,

merciless

Mis.	211–14	rescued from the m· wave
	257–13	so-called force, . . . is cruel and m·.
Ret.	13–15	m· towards unbelievers ;
Un.	35–18	not the m· forces of matter.
Peo.	13–13	iron tread of m· invaders,

mercilessly

Mis.	335–12	m· assails me for opposing

mercury

Pul.	vii– 9	rise of the m· in the glass

mercy

acme of

Mis.	122–14	divine order is the acme of m· :

altar of

Po.	32–18	To kneel at the altar of m·

and charity

Mis.	13– 2	m· and charity toward every one,

and justice

Mis.	11– 3	it is grace, m·, and justice.

and love

Mis.	152–16	May meekness, m·, and love
Pul.	9– 8	justice, m·, and love kindle

and might

Mis.	69– 4	His goodness, m·, and might.

and peace

Pan.	14–12	justice, m·, and peace continue

and truth

Mis.	151–24	m· and truth go before you :

deeds of

Mis.	370– 4	saw Jesus do such deeds of m·,

demands

Mis.	67–19	m· demands that if you see the

divine

Mis.	11–14	Love metes . . . divine m·.
Ret.	94–11	this purgation of divine m·,
My.	89–20	* constant as petitions for divine m·.

equity and

My.	277–19	equity and m· tips the beam

errand of

Mis.	250–25	stealing on an errand of m·,

God's

My.	162– 1	God's m· for mortal ignorance

handmaid of

Mis.	261–17	Justice is the handmaid of m·,

His

Mis.	322–24	the amplitude of His m·,
Un.	26–15	* But His m· waneth never,
No.	34–21	and bring His m·

infinite

Pul.	74–16	to declare in His infinite m·.

justice and

Mis.	146–25	understanding of justice and m·.
	266–15	hold justice and m· as inseparable
No.	7– 4	scales of justice and m·.
My.	288– 2	revelation, justice, and m· ;

love

My.	283–24	do justly, and to love m·,— Mic. 6 : 8.

loves

Mis.	317–30	abhors injustice, and loves m·,

loving

Ret.	71–20	not dealing justly and loving m·,

showeth

Mis.	261–18	showeth m· by punishing sin.

tender

Chr.	53– 5	In tender m·, Spirit sped

upon us

Un.	3–28	He has m· upon us,

without

My.	41–11	* and so receive judgment without m· ;

Mis.	154–28	meekness, m·, purity, love.
'01.	29– 8	should not be left to the m· of
My.	180–21	in justice, as well as in m·,
	272– 3	with justice, m·, truth, and love.

mere

Mis.	34–14	is a m· speculative opinion
	67– 2	the m· alphabet of Mind-healing.
	68– 4	more than m· disappearance
	80– 4	by m· unity on the single issue
	230–10	and m· motion when at work,
	250–20	Love cannot be a m· abstraction,
	330–26	A m· mendicant that boasts
	353–23	the folly of tending it is no m· jest.
	366–32	m· book-learning,— letter without law,
	368–23	the m· puppets of the hour
Man.	40– 5	nor m· personal attachment
	47–14	a m· rehearsal of blessings,
Ret.	21–25	M· historic incidents and
	32– 6	as m· corporeal personality,
	32–14	* What is life? A m· illusion,
Pul.	9–27	understanding, not m· belief,
	55–12	* not, . . . as a m· coincidence

Messias

Mis. 186–30 last Adam represented by the M·,

met

Mis. 44–25 this demand . . . once m·,
66–27 Error in premise is m· with
74–28 He m· and conquered the
110–16 years, since last we m· ;
118–23 they must be m· manfully
173–22 man is not m· by another power
177–30 In my long journeyings I have m·
180–11 another person, more material, m· me,
200–26 m· no obstacle or circumstances
208–17 are m· and mastered by divine
247–31 must be m·, in every instance,
249– 9 has been m· and answered *legally.*
258– 4 m· and abolished this
263–19 m· in the most effectual way.
276– 9 my heart's desire m· the demand.
279–22 m· together in an upper chamber ;
280–26 m· the class to answer some questions
284–27 m· with Science, it can and will be
345–26 Christians m· in midnight feasts
350– 7 The P. M. . . . Society m: only twice.
350–18 and we have not m· since.
365–30 has never m· the growing wants of
383– 4 m· with the universal approval
Man. 18–14 Church members m· and reorganized,
Ret. 21– 6 We never m· again until he had
38–17 We m· at the Eastern depot in Lynn,
52–17 m· in general convention at New York
64–21 which must be m· and mastered,
80–29 not infrequently m· by envy,
94– 5 the conclusion must be m·
Un. 36–10 m· and solved by C. S.
Pul. 32–19 * At the time I m· her she must have
34– 6 * m· with a severe accident,
36–14 * evening that I first m· Mrs. Eddy
36–18 * m· Mrs. Eddy many times since then,
84–24 * all obstacles . . . m· and overcome,
Rud. 6–12 truth in C. S. m· a response
No. 19– 6 have never m· the growing wants of
'02. 1–17 m· with opposition and detraction ;
9–28 m· the need of mankind with
14–19 every forward step has been m·
Po. 3–11 Since first we m·, in weal or woe
68–18 when *we three m·,*
My. 28– 4 "Divine Love always has m·
43–10 * and m· with disappointments,
50–31 * The business committee m·
51– 8 * she has not m· with the support
55–14 * the members of the church m·,
63–16 * exultation as friend m· friend
73– 9 "Divine Love always has m·
81–28 * two or more of them are m· together,
87–21 * m· in Boston during the
104–28 was m· with the anathema
112– 2 first m· with denunciations.
116– 9 must be m· and overcome.
134–13 imperative demand not yet m·.
148–18 you have m· to praise God.
187–22 You have m· to consecrate
214– 5 Divine Love always has m·
245– 4 it should be m· as heretofore,
312–13 * m· and taken to her father's home
320–31 * I m· him in the vestibule
322– 1 * not long since I m· a lady

metal

Mis. 250–20 having no ring of the true m·.
My. 4–20 unfolding the true m· in character,

metaphor

Mis. 280–24 appropriate language and m·
353–25 turn from the m· of the mill
'01. 3–26 expresses God only in m·,

metaphorically

Mis. 75–18 word *Soul* may sometimes be used m· ;

metaphors

Mis. 253–16 The Scriptural m·,

metaphysical

Mis. 5–22 M· therapeutics can seem a miracle
50–11 m· method of healing is as lucid
50–13 necessity to express the m·
68–19 or of m· theology?
169–20 to get at the highest, or m·,
169–24 The m· rendering is health and
170–22 The method of Jesus was purely m· ;
172– 5 the negative of m· Science ;
182–26 text is a m· statement of existence
184–30 to foreshadow m· purity,
223– 1 the m· mystery of error
237– 3 yielded somewhat to the m· fact
240– 5 painted and fattened by m· hygiene.
272– 6 * a college, for m· purposes *only,*
282–15 Prolonging the m· tone
349– 9 the m· mode of obstetrics

metaphysical

Mis. 378–20 to see that m· therapeutics,
379– 9 not at all m· or scientific ;
379–31 adjusting . . . a m· *practice,*
382–22 for a m· medical college,
Ret. 7–11 * abstruse and m· principles,
43– 1 purely m· system of healing
57–30 demonstration of m·, or C. S.
78–14 right sense of m· Science.
79– 1 *honest m· theory and practice.*
Un. 9–27 difference in my m· system?
Pul. 6–27 * in Mrs. Eddy's m· teachings
69–19 * spiritual or m· standpoint.
Rud. 6–15 * this is not "any m· subtlety,"
No. 22– 6 Berkeley ended his m· theory with
22–10 Such miscalled m· systems are reeds
Hea. 14–18 preparation for a m· practitioner
14–21 learns the m· treatment of disease ;
14–25 M· or divine Science reveals the
16– 4 M· Science teaches us there is no
Peo. 3–18 more m· religion founded upon C. S.
My. 52– 1 * by m· truth or C. S.,
127–12 system of m· therapeutics
190–10 m· practice of medicine
(*see also* **healing**)

Metaphysical College

Mis. 242– 5 as President of the M· C·
Pul. 36– 1 * after her founding of the M· C·
36– 3 * M· C· lasted nine years,
My. 215–18 to establish a M· C·,
322–17 * the day before at the M· C·
(*see also* **Massachusetts Metaphysical College**)

Metaphysical College Corporation

Ret. 48–12 Board of the M· C· C·,

metaphysically

Mis. 51–12 *How can I govern a child m·?*
169–31 one of the passages explained m·.
203–16 M·, baptism serves to rebuke
Pul. 4– 7 Is not a man m· and
No. 11–10 that are to be understood m·.

Metaphysician (*see also* **Metaphysician's**)

Mis. 76–31 prophecy of the master M·,
187– 4 great M· wrought, over and
200– 6 The master M· understood
270–10 He . . . is the master M·.
Ret. 55– 5 example of Jesus, the master M·,
Pul. 20–23 baptism of our master M·,
No. 31–22 the same with this master M·.
'01. 19–16 great M· healed the sick,
25–17 The great M·, Christ Jesus,
My. 111– 6 master M·, the Galilean Prophet,
222– 8 Jesus, the master M·, answered,

metaphysician

Mis. 308–32 is not the model for a m·.
379–12 neither a scholar nor a m·.
'01. 26– 8 m· is sensual that combines
Hea. 12– 7 m· goes to the fount
My. 40–25 * because she is an exact m·.

Metaphysician's

'01. 18–22 great master M· precept

metaphysicians

Mis. 81– 7 the m·, agree to disagree,
233– 6 those who call themselves m·
368–12 to say that all are not m·,
371– 4 large flocks of m·
Pul. 2–22 m· and Christian Scientists.
'01. 26–25 this subject of the old m·,

metaphysics

adds
Hea. 11–19 m· adds, "until you arrive at
Bishop Berkeley's
'01. 24–14 Bishop Berkeley's m· and personality
Christian
Mis. 205–21 in Christian m· the ideal man
365–26 Christian m· is hampered by
No. 11– 8 my system of Christian m·
My. 41– 4 * the law of Christian m·,
classified in
Mis. 112–13 are strictly classified in m·
college of
Mis. 272–26 * legally chartered college of m·,
cured by
Mis. 45–12 *Can an atheist . . . be cured by m·,*
divine
(*see* **divine**)
faith in
My. 301–15 chapter sub-title
his
My. 303–23 His m· is not the sport of philosophy,
in Christian Science
My. 108–11 m· in C. S. consists in
in homœopathy
My. 108–10 difference between m· in homœopathy

metaphysics
instruct in
Mis. 38–14 *college to instruct in m·,*
is seen
Peo. 9–23 *m·* is seen to rise above physics,
is understood
Hea. 18–23 when *m·* is understood ;
its
'01. 27–24 taken out of its *m·* all matter
law of
My. 41–11 * but the law of *m·* says,
Master of
Hea. 7–17 The Master of *m·*, reading the mind of
master of
Mis. 252–23 great healer and master of *m·*,
My. 104– 8 said of the great master of *m·*,
mistake in
Mis. 264–30 A single mistake in *m·*,
modes of
My. 111– 6 crude theories or modes of *m·*.
my
No. 26–10 to demonstrate my *m·*.
my system of
No. 24– 8 at variance with my system of *m·*,
not physics
Mis. 369– 7 *M·*, not physics, enables us to
of Christ
'01. 24–26 Christianity — the *m·* of Christ
physics and
Mis. 126– 3 in physics and *m·*.
power of
Mis. 6–12 power of *m·* over physics ;
7–28 nature and power of *m·*,
questionable
'01. 21– 6 chapter sub-title
requires
Hea. 11–25 *M·* requires mind imbued with Truth
rules of
Mis. 221– 5 one gains in the rules of *m·*,
sneer at
Mis. 69– 3 A sneer at *m·* is a scoff at Deity ;
so-called
Mis. 271– 7 compounded *m·* (so-called)
'01. 25– 9 and the *m·* (so called)
standard of
Mis. 53–18 above the standard of *m·* ;
studying
Mis. 48–23 *made insane by studying m·?*
such
'01. 25–14 alluded to or required in such *m·*,
superiority of
Ret. 34–16 superiority of *m·* over physics.
system of
'01. 26– 5 who founded his system of *m·*
My. 105–28 my curative system of *m·*.
teaching
Mis. 38–21 Teaching *m·* at other colleges
true
Mis. 69– 5 is the unfolding of true *m·* ;
understanding of
Ret. 48–19 a thorough understanding of *m·*,
vulgar
My. 305– 9 * on the subject of "vulgar *m·*,"

Mis. 5–18 *m·* comes in, armed with the power of
34– 2 proving that *m·* is above physics.
38–16 *M·*, as taught by me at the
68–21 According to Webster, *m·* is defined
68–27 calls *m·* "the science which
203–15 *m·* appropriates it topically as
209–11 *M·* also demonstrates this Principle
233–14 the new cloth of *m·* ;
233–18 terming it *m·* !
234–28 In this new departure of *m·*,
255–27 and *m·* is above physics.
'01. 25–20 *m·* based on materialism?
Hea. 6–21 But the fact remains, in *m·*,
11– 7 physics are yielding slowly to *m·* ;
11–16 against its neighbor, *m·*,
11–23 *M·* places all cause and cure as
My. 121– 7 In *m·* we learn that the strength
127– 3 in medicine, in physics, and in *m·*.
235–11 it cannot be done in *m·*,

Metcalf, Albert
Man. 102–14 the deeds given by Albert *M·*
mete
Mis. 11–21 To *m·* out human justice
298– 8 "With what measure ye *m·*, — Matt. 7 : 2.
meted
Mis. 222–21 the measure it has *m·*
261–13 the measure he has *m·*
My. 218–27 *m·* out to one no more than
metes
Mis. 11–14 Love *m·* not out human justice,

methinks
Mis. 106–25 *m·* I hear the soft, sweet sigh
155–29 *M·*, were they to contemplate
345–14 *M·* the infidel was blind
Pul. 1–19 *m·* I should be much like the
'00. 1– 1 *m·* even I am touched with
My. 6–27 *M·* this church is the one edifice
110–20 night thought, *m·*, should unfold
162–18 *m·* the same wisdom which spake
261– 2 *M·* the loving parents and
method
aforenamed
Man. 59–11 aforenamed *m·* for the benefit of
and design
Rud. 3–18 in its nature, *m·*, and design.
best
Mis. 2–32 best *m·* for elevating the race
Christly
Mis. 359– 3 Christly *m·* of teaching and
Ret. 93–13 best spiritual type of Christly *m·*
divine
My. 103–15 Alluding to this divine *m·*,
entire
Mis. 50– 6 *entire m· of metaphysical healing,*
Hebrew
Mis. 170–26 Hebrew *m·* of expressing the
hidden
My. 130– 5 hidden *m·* of committing crime
intricate
My. 212– 4 intricate *m·* of animal magnetism
Jesus'
Ret. 89–19 Jesus' *m·* was to instruct his
material
Ret. 43–15 his material *m·* of practice
My. 106– 2 than any material *m·*.
mental
Mis. 220–21 this mental *m·* has power
351– 9 mental *m·* of Mind-healing,
metaphysical
Mis. 50–11 its metaphysical *m·* of healing
no other
Mis. 170–23 and no other *m·* is C. S.
novel
Pul. 40–11 * Novel *M·* of Enabling
of his religion
Ret. 92– 1 *m·* of his religion was not too simple
of Jesus
Mis. 170–22 The *m·* of Jesus was purely
of perfection
Hea. 14–26 Principle and *m·* of perfection,
operative
Ret. 85– 6 any other organic operative *m·*
same
Mis. 40–10 C. S. is the same *m·* of healing
sanative
Mis. 229–27 any other possible sanative *m·* ;
scientific
Mis. 5–10 by studying this scientific *m·*
this
Mis. 3–30 but this *m·* perverted, is
4– 6 calling this *m·* "mental science."
62–21 An adherent to this *m·*
301–24 This *m·* is an unseen form of
369–12 This *m·* sits serene at the portals of
369–17 This *m·* is devout enough to trust
Ret. 61–30 Unless this *m·* be pursued,
Hea. 9–10 this *m·* has not saved them from either,
thought and
No. 12–21 spiritualization of thought and *m·*,
your
Mis. 41–18 *be healed by your m·*
89–14 no faith in your *m·*,

Mis. 369–11 "*m·*" in the "madness" of this system,
Pan. 13–15 united in purpose, if not in *m·*,
Hea. 14–17 the *m·* of a mental practice.
My. 18–23 united in purpose, if not in *m·*,
137–26 consulted Lawyer . . . about the *m·*.
Methodist Conference Seminary
My. 312– 1 *M· C· S·* at Sanbornton Bridge,
Methodist Elder
'01. 32– 5 Father Hines, *M· E·*.
Methodist Episcopal Church
Pul. 6–21 * under the auspices of the *M· E· C·*.
Methodist Review
My. 48–16 * appeared in the *M· R·*
methods
and means
Mis. 135–16 God's *m·* and means of healing,
313– 5 morals, *m·*, and means.
and power
Mis. 222–30 *m·* and power of error.
and subtlety
Ret. 64–27 *m·*, and subtlety of error,

methods

and tenets
My. 84–23 * m· and tenets of the sect.
both
My. 215–30 to test the effect of both m·
different
Pul. 51–13 * others who have different m·,
its
Mis. 175–21 instituting matter and its m·
latter-day
My. 98–24 * latter-day m· of raising money.
material
(see **material**)
means and
Mis. 52–10 beyond all human means and m·.
153– 1 His spiritual means and m·,
Rud. 13–23 What are the means and m· of
My. 154–24 I welcome the means and m·,
mental
Mis. 260–31 silent mental m· whereby it may
motives and
Mis. 267–28 spiritualizes man's motives and m·,
of divine Love
Mis. 213– 8 in the m· of divine Love.
of God
Mis. 270–25 through the modes and m· of God.
of medicine
Ret. 33–23 material m· of medicine,
of our Master
Mis. 359–20 The m· of our Master were
of Truth
Mis. 141–12 hates the bonds and m· of Truth,
orderly
Ret. 82–13 orderly m· herein delineated.
ordinary
Mis. 33–22 ordinary m· of healing disease?
other
Mis. 97–14 other m· of treating disease.
'01. 17–12 exceeded that of other m·,
our
Peo. 7–31 and our m· grow more spiritual
scientific
Ret. 48–18 give instruction in scientific m·
such
Ret. 57–29 such m· can never reach the
their
Mis. 114–25 uncover their m·, and stop their
Peo. 11–24 mistaken in their m· of humanity.
thoughts and
Rud. 12– 6 Wrong thoughts and m· strengthen the
well-established
Pul. 51–16 * affect the well-established m·.

Methuen, Mass.
Pul. 62– 1 * Bell Company, of M·, M·.,

metropolis
Pul. 7–10 Master in our New England m·
'02. 20–24 in the m· of my native State,
My. 196– 5 a State whose m· is called

Mexican
Pul. 76–13 * superb mantel of M· onyx

Mexican Herald
My. 95– 8 * M· H·, City of Mexico,

miasma
Un. 56–28 constitute the m· of earth.
My. 249–13 sends forth a mental m·

Mich. (State)
(see **Detroit, Grand Rapids, Jackson**)

Mickley, Miss Minnie F.
Mis. 306–16 * Miss Minnie F. M·, Mickleys, Pa.

Mickleys, Pa.
Mis. 306–16 * Miss Minnie F. Mickley, M·, P·

microbe
Mis. 131– 3 a moral nuisance, a fungus, a m·,

microbes
Mis. 112– 6 Hypnotism, m·, X-rays,

microscope
Peo. 10– 7 under the m· of Mind.

'mid
Mis. 393– 5 Soul, sublime 'm· human débris,
Pul. 39–25 * 'm· them all I only see one face,
Po. 16–20 'M· graves do I hear the glad voices
34– 9 chant thy vespers 'm· rich glooms?
51–10 Soul, sublime 'm· human débris,

middle
Mis. 231– 2 m· age, in smiles

Middle States
Pul. 88–24 * heading

midnight
Mis. 88–16 like a m· sun.
117–26 replenish his lamp at the m· hour
226–29 Slander is a m· robber ;

midnight
Mis. 276–15 In C. S. the m· hour will
342– 7 the m· gloom upon them,
342–14 It was m· : darkness profound brooded
345–27 m· feasts in the early days,
Ret. 23–17 the m· torches of Spirit.
Un. 58–20 m· sun shines over the Polar Sea.
Po. 26– 7 Chill was thy m· day,
My. 82–23 * and more . . . by m· to-night.
190– 1 Did that m· shadow,
197–18 illumine the m· of the latter,

midst
Mis. 133–26 In the m· of depressing care
141–32 God is in the m· of her :
152–11 I, as . . . am not in your m· :
166– 6 lives, and moves in our m·
234–26 in the m· of an age so sunken in sin
264– 4 m· of this seething sea of sin.
325–29 in the m· of murderous hordes,
331–22 M· the falling leaves of old-time
332–14 m· the stately palms,
337–13 in the m· of them, — Matt. 18 : 2.
338–11 steadfastly to good in the m· of
399– 5 M· the glories of one endless day."
Ret. 17– 3 m· the zephyrs at play
18– 9 M· grotto and songlet and streamlet
27–22 meandering m· pebbles and rocks,
Pul. 48– 2 * in the m· of green stretches
Pan. 15– 6 m· of our enemies," — see Psal. 23 : 5.
'00. 12– 4 walketh in the m· of — Rev. 2 : 1.
Hea. 11– 6 in the m· of a revolution ;
Po. 30–14 and m· the rod, . . . Lift Thou a
62– 1 m· the zephyrs at play
63–18 M· grotto and songlet and streamlet
75–12 M· the glories of one endless day."
My. 43–16 * taken from the m· of the river
99– 9 * is welcomed within our m·
103– 1 In the m· of the imperfect,
185–25 in the m· of the mountains,
246–12 in the m· of unprecedented
252–14 work m· clouds of wrong,

midwifery
Mis. 349– 5 the surgical part of m·.

might

all
Hea. 15–14 why should man deny all m· to the
and ability
Un. 42–17 a sense of m· and ability to subdue
and light
My. 133– 4 m· and light of the present
and majesty
Mis. 141–13 m·, and majesty of Spirit,
292–13 to human weakness m· and majesty.
294– 9 m· and majesty ! — of goodness.
'00. 5–30 m· and majesty attend every
'01. 33–21 m· and majesty of divine power
clothed with
Mis. 185–16 man be clothed with m·,
divine
Mis. 138–19 unity is divine m·, giving to
162–14 Clad with divine m·, he was ready
My. 3– 4 divine m· of Truth demands
His
My. 187–29 and the majesty of His m·
its
My. 149– 9 its m· is the ever-flowing tides
light and
My. 246–20 the light and m· of the divine
maximum of
My. 165–30 rapidly nearing the maximum of m·,
meek
'02. 16–21 The meek m·, sublime patience,
meekness and
Mis. 372–32 true sense of meekness and m·.
My. 194–16 It stands for meekness and m·,
202– 4 to the faith, meekness, and m· of
mercy and
Mis. 69– 4 His goodness, mercy, and m·.
of divine Love
My. 61–19 * before the m· of divine Love,
of divine power
'02. 18– 6 m· of divine power manifested through
of empires
My. 162– 9 stronger than the m· of empires.
of love
My. 258–28 give you the m· of love,
of perfect Love
Mis 334–32 demonstrate the m· of perfect Love
of Truth
Mis. 52– 8 even the m· of Truth,
100– 8 show the word and m· of Truth
My. 3– 4 m· of Truth demands well-doing
right nor
'01. 20– 7 gives neither moral right nor m· to harm

might

through meekness to
My. 163– 5 to win through meekness to *m·*,
wisdom, and
Mis. 316–28 patterns of humility, wisdom, and *m·*
wisdom's
Ret. 11– 7 On learning's lore and wisdom's *m·*,
Po. 60– 4 On learning's lore and wisdom's *m·*,
word of
Mis. 388– 1 God, who gave that word of *m·*
'*02.* 20–10 God who gave that word of *m·*
Po. 7– 1 God, who gave that word of *m·*

Mis. 83–22 meekness was as conspicuous as *m·*.
Pul. 82–29 * *M·* no longer makes right,
Po. 30–14 fan Thou the flame Of right with *m·* ;
79–16 Life is light, and wisdom *m·*,

mightily
Mis. 119–16 weighs *m·* in the scale against
My. 294–13 He would *m·* rebuke a single doubt

mighty
Mis. 43–27 unacquainted with the *m·* Truth
51–22 * the lips of Truth one *m·* breath
103–29 He was too *m·* for that.
120–13 a *m·* victory is yet to be won,
139–10 *m·* through God — II Cor. 10 : 4.
161– 7 The *m·* God, — Isa. 9 : 6.
164–18 The *m·* God, — Isa. 9 : 6.
189–10 true knowledge . . . made him *m·*.
223–26 better than the *m·*." — Prov. 16 : 32.
234–20 to establish this *m·* system
258–23 did declare a *m·* individuality,
321– 5 The *m·* God, — Isa. 9 : 6.
344–23 the *m·* Nazarene Prophet.
389–18 shadow of His *m·* wing ;
Ret. 11–16 Science the *m·* source,
57– 1 *m·* wrestlings with mortal beliefs,
Un. 10–21 the calculation of His *m·* ways,
Pul. 12–17 *m·* conquest over all sin?
46–21 * Wallace of *m·* Scottish fame.
84–21 * tell the story of its *m·* meaning
'*00.* 9–27 as leader of this *m·* movement.
Po. 2–17 the sun's more genial, *m·* ray ;
4–7 Beneath the shadow of His *m·* wing ;
60–13 Science the *m·* source,
My. 10– 5 * inevitable that this *m·* impulse
42–30 * "With a *m·* hand, — Deut. 26 : 8.
58–14 * the erection of these *m·* walls.
59–20 * *m·* chorus of five thousand voices,
98– 2 * truly make up a *m·* host,
115– 1 *m·* chariot of divine Love,
149–29 a *m·* rush, which waken the
164–18 A great sanity, a *m·* something
196–11 better than the *m·* ; — Prov. 16 : 32.
294– 7 "did not many *m·* works — Matt. 13 : 58.
350–24 Love divine, whose kindling *m·* rays

mild
Mis. 109–12 Even a *m·* mistake must be seen as a
My. 150–17 moon ablaze with her *m·* glory.

milder
'*01.* 19–28 *m·* forms of animal magnetism

mile
Pul. 47–22 * one *m·* from the State House
49–25 * within one *m·* of the "Eton of
My. 68– 6 * one *m·* and a half of pews.

miles
Ret. 5–10 eighteen *m·* from Concord,
Pul. 44– 5 * Across two thousand *m·* of space,
My. 69–30 * in Cambridge, some four *m·* away.
332– 2 * of more than a thousand *m·*,

mile-stones
Mis. x–14 to serve as *m·* measuring the

militant
Pul. 3–18 No longer are we of the church *m·*,
My. 125–23 grateful that the church *m·* is
133– 7 church *m·* rise to the
154–25 it makes the church *m·*,
196– 6 May this dear church *m·* accept

military
'*02.* 3–12 our *m·* forces withdrawing,
My. 310–13 His *m·* title of Colonel came from

militates
Rud. 9–28 whatever *m·* against health,
No. 18–25 *m·* against the so-called demands of

milk
Mis. 15–30 on the *m·* of the Word,
149– 2 come, buy wine and *m·* — Isa. 55 : 1.
Ret. 61–29 Let there be *m·* for babes,
61–30 let not the *m·* be adulterated.
No. v–12 unadulterated *m·* of the Word,
Hea. 13–17 using only the sugar of *m·* ;
My. 17– 6 the sincere *m·* of the word, — I Pet. 2 : 2.

mill
Mis. 353–25 turn from the metaphor of the *m·*
My. 310–10 * "a workman in a Tilton woolen *m·*."

millenial
My. 265–15 full-orbed in *m·* glory ;

millennium
My. 239–12 *ultimate of the m·*
239–27 The *m·* is a state and

Miller, Mrs. F. L.
'*02.* 16–10 Mrs. F. L. *M·*, of London,

Miller, K.C., Mr. W. Nicholas
'*02.* 16– 9 Mr. W. Nicholas *M·*, K.C.,

Millet's "Angelus"
My. 70–15 * *M·* "*A·*" had living reproductions

million
(*see* **numbers, values**)

millions
Mis. 208– 7 bill that governs *m·* of mortals
Ret. 54–12 *M·* are believing in God,
Pul. 14–14 *M·* of unprejudiced minds
Pan. 15– 2 destroying *m·* of her money,
'*00.* 11– 2 gave me more pleasure than *m·*
My. 160–27 may take *m·* of cycles,
249–19 *M·* may know that I am the
289–18 lives on in the heart of *m·*.
294–25 will move the pen of *m·*.
295– 1 the loved and lost of many *m·*.
315–29 the beloved Leader of *m·*
(*see also* **values**)

mills
Mis. 353–14 a workman in his *m·*,
Ret. 80– 8 * *m·* of God grind slowly,

millstone
Mis. 122–11 better for him that a *m·* — Matt. 18 : 6.
362–23 to remove this mental *m·*

millstones
My. 160–32 wrongs done to others, are *m·*

Milwaukee
Wis.
Pul. 90– 6 * *Sentinel*, *M·*, Wis.
My. 207– 2 chapter sub-title

Pul. 56– 3 * Detroit, Toledo, *M·*, Madison,

mimicry
My. 262–25 a human mockery in *m·* of the

Mind (*see also* **Mind's**)
action of
Mis. 70– 6 healing action of *M·* upon the body
all
Ret. 56–20 supplying all *M·* by the reflection,
Un. 24– 3 From me proceedeth all *M·*,
Rud. 4– 1 including in itself all *M·*,
all is
Mis. 26– 6 all is *M·* and its manifestation,
105–32 all is good and all is *M·*.
200–32 statement that all is *M·*,
286–21 All is *M·*.
Rud. 4–20 All is *M·*.
all-knowing
Mis. 71–16 omnipotence, the all-knowing *M·*.
71–26 God, good, the all-knowing *M·*.
all must be
Rud. 5– 5 all must be *M·*, since God is Mind.
allness of
Mis. 253–11 with the allness of *M·*.
alone
Mis. 244– 5 *M·* alone constructing the
No. 18–25 asks for what *M·* alone can supply.
altitude of
Mis. 255–11 that altitude of *M·* which was in
and body
No. 40–20 obstruct the harmony of *M·* and body,
and man
Mis. 24–20 *M·* and man are immortal ;
and matter
Mis. 56–16 *M·* and matter mingling in
280–12 There are not two, — *M·* and matter.
Ret. 59–21 *M·* and matter as distinct,
apart from
Rud. 5–10 considered apart from *M·*.
'*01.* 18–12 administered no remedy apart from *M·*,
based on
My. 154– 2 Science of all healing is based on *M·*
before
My. 260– 5 withdraw itself before *M·*.
belief, that
Mis. 49–25 belief, that *M·* is in matter,
body and
Mis. 86–21 the harmony of body and *M·*.
call
Mis. 258–20 call *M·* by the name of matter,

Mind

came in
　Hea. 11–22　*M·* came in as the remedy,
came not from
　Mis. 196–12　that saying came not from *M·*,
can master
　Hea. 8– 6　*M·* can master sickness as well as
capabilities of
　Mis. 43– 2　recognizing the capabilities of *M·*
casts out
　Mis. 73– 3　when *M·* casts out the suffering.
causation is of
　Pul. 55–20　* all causation is of *M·*,
causation was
　Ret. 24–10　certainty that all causation was *M·*,
　Pul. 70–18　"all causation was *M·*,
coexistent with
　Mis. 190– 9　man is coexistent with *M·*,
conscientious
　Un. 25–21　Evil is not . . . conscientious *M·* ;
consciousness is
　Ret. 56–18　All consciousness is *M·*, and Mind is
　Un. 24–12　*Good.* All consciousness is *M·* ;
　No. 10–18　all consciousness is *M·* and eternal,
consciousness of
　My. 131–31　say with the consciousness of *M·*
consent of
　Pan. 8– 1　or by the consent of *M·* !
controls
　Mis. 5–24　reality that *M·* controls the body.
demonstrates
　Mis. 190– 5　Divine Science demonstrates *M·* as
　Ret. 88–28　*M·* demonstrates omnipresence and
departs from
　Mis. 268–11　who departs from *M·* to matter,
despite of
　Pan. 8– 1　despite of *M·*, or by the consent of
destitute of
　Un. 50–18　Like evil, it is destitute of *M·*,
discredit
　Mis. 223–13　to say, if it must, "I discredit *M·*
divine
　(*see* **divine**)
embraced in
　Mis. 103–30　individuality is embraced in *M·*,
employed
　Hea. 13–20　employed *M·* as the only curative
error is not
　Mis. 367– 8　showing that error is not *M·*,
　Ret. 57–19　Evil, or error, is not *M·* ;
eternal
　Mis. 36– 9　eternal *M·*, which is God,
　　　102–20　The sympathy of His eternal *M·*
　　　103–17　the eternal *M·* is free, unlimited,
　Un. 14–23　eternal *M·* must be reflected in man,
　　　64– 7　on the foundations of an eternal *M·*
　　　64–19　dwelleth in the eternal *M·*.
　No. 15–23　existence in the eternal *M·*.
　My. 267–11　eternal *M·* that hath no beginning
every flower in
　Mis. 179–26　He made every flower in *M·*
evil is not
　Rud. 4–16　Good is Mind, but evil is not *M·*.
exist in
　Mis. 190–27　the right sense, and exist in *M·*.
　Rud. 5–28　or exist in *M·* only ;
　No. 16– 3　If matter can exist in *M·*,
express
　Mis. 36– 7　express *M·* as their origin;
fact that
　Mis. 35– 2　fact that *M·*, . . . is the Principle
faculties of
　Mis. 332–28　are not faculties of *M·*,
faith in
　Mis. 229–14　faith in *M·* over all other influences
forever
　Mis. 218– 3　the fact that Deity was forever *M·*,
God is
　(*see* **God**)
good is
　Rud. 4–16　Good is *M·*, but evil is not Mind.
　Pan. 6–22　For if God, good, is *M·*,
governed by
　Mis. 256– 4　The body is governed by *M·*,
governs all
　Mis. 6–18　*M·* governs all.
governs man
　Mis. 51–16　and *M·* governs man.
has no
　Mis. 174– 1　*M·* has no more power to
heal through
　Mis. 53–14　your power to heal through *M·*,
He is
　No. 16– 4　He is *M·* ; and whatever He knows is
highest
　Un. 32– 8　not the highest *M·*, but a false form

Mind

his
　Ret. 57–16　He reflects God as his *M·*,
his medicine is
　Mis. 268–17　His medicine is *M·* — the omnipotent
imbued with
　Mis. 260–28　*M·*, imbued with this Science
immortal
　Mis. 3–19　unerring and immortal *M·*.
　　　35–27　*What is immortal M·?*
　　　36–18　of mortal mind, — not immortal *M·*.
　　　36–20　*mortal mind and immortal M·?*
　　　37– 4　Immortal *M·* is God ;
　　　37–12　spiritual and immortal *M·*,
　　　56–10　Life is immortal *M·*, not matter.
　　　61– 8　magnitude of immortal *M·*,
　　　82–28　Immortal *M·* is God, immortal good ;
　　　84–16　mortal mind, not the immortal *M·*,
　　　87–14　glory of the immortal *M·*."
　　　102– 6　the unlimited and immortal *M·*
　　　219–23　and immortal *M·* makes well ;
　　　219–23　while immortal *M·* makes saints ;
　　　365–19　immortal *M·* alone can supply.
　Ret. 25–11　God I called immortal *M·*.
　　　33–20　immortal *M·*, the curative Principle,
　　　34–13　antidote . . . in the immortal *M·* ;
　Un. 24– 1　the opposite of immortal *M·*,
　　　34–26　Immortal *M·* is the real substance,
　　　35–16　immortal *M·*, the Parent of *all*.
　　　45–28　Spirit, immortal *M·*, or good,
　　　56– 2　the cosmos of immortal *M·*.
　Rud. 1– 7　infinite and immortal *M·*,
　　　7–10　perfect and immortal *M·*.
　　　9–14　immortal *M·*, the divine Principle
　Hea. 18– 3　government of God, immortal *M·?*
immortality of
　Mis. 218–10　immortality of *M·* and its ideas.
implies
　Pan. 7–23　which implies *M·*, Spirit, God ;
in behalf of
　My. 190–21　a divine decision in behalf of *M·*.
included in
　Un. 11–27　heaven is here, and is included in *M·* ;
individual
　Mis. 101–31　God is individual *M·*.
infinite
　Mis. 5–26　man is the idea of infinite *M·*,
　　　21–17　All is infinite *M·* and its infinite
　　　26–15　from infinite *M·*, or from matter?
　　　26–19　self-creative, and infinite *M·*.
　　　217–19　containing infinite *M·* ;
　　　247–22　man is the idea of infinite *M·*,
　　　258–17　infinite *M·* governs all things.
　　　331–31　and infinite *M·* is seen
　　　367–20　Infinite *M·* knows nothing beyond
　　　373–13　infinite *M·* and spiritual vision
　Ret. 25–12　proper conception of the infinite *M·*.
　　　57–19　infinite *M·* is sufficient to supply all
　Un. 10–13　phenomena of this one infinite *M·*.
　　　24–15　whose source is infinite *M·*.
　　　50– 2　how can infinite *M·* be defiled?
　Rud. 4–15　God is infinite *M·*,
　No. 20–16　or of an infinite *M·* starting from a
　'01. 6– 9　Can the infinite *M·* inhabit a
　　　6–28　with an infinite *M·*.
　　　7– 8　God being infinite *M·*, He is
　My. 64– 4　* the realm of infinite *M·*,
　　　269– 1　included in one infinite *M·*
　　　293– 3　power and purpose of infinite *M·*,
infinite as
　'01. 6–26　must be as infinite as *M·* is.
instead of
　Mis. 175– 8　by bread, matter, instead of *M·*.
　　　190–25　belongs to *M·* instead of matter,
　Hea. 12– 2　*M·* instead of matter heals
　Peo. 2–12　and of *M·* instead of matter,
is All-in-all
　Mis. 183– 8　found that *M·* is All-in-all,
is God
　Mis. 37– 4　Immortal *M·* is God ;
　　　82–28　Immortal *M·* is God,
　　　173–12　*M·* is God, omnipotent and
　Ret. 56–18　consciousness is Mind, and *M·* is God.
　Un. 24–12　consciousness is Mind ; and *M·* is God,
　　　24–18　because *M·* is God.
　　　50–18　destitute of Mind, for *M·* is God.
　No. 27– 5　*M·* is God, and evil finds no place
is immortal
　Mis. 82–25　the one *M·* is immortal.
　　　367– 6　But *M·* is immortal ;
　Un. 32–17　True *M·* is immortal ;
　　　35–11　no mortal mind, for *M·* is immortal,
　No. 16–28　*M·* is immortal.
is Love
　Mis. 332– 5　*M·* is Love, — but not fallible love.

Mind

is made manifest
  Mis. 37– 4   this *M·* is made manifest in
is more
  No. 25–10   *M·* is more than matter,
is not confined
  Mis. 42–30   *M·* is not confined to limits ;
is not in matter
  Rud. 7–21   *M·* is not in matter,
     13– 1   that *M·* is not in matter ;
is not mortal
  Mis. 72–27   *M·* is not mortal, it is immortal.
is supreme
  Mis. 45– 1   prove the fact that *M·* is supreme.
     47–18   *M·* is supreme.
     336– 1   *M·* is supreme :
  Peo. 8–16   *M·* is supreme ; and yet we
is the architect
  Mis. 41–19   *M·* is the architect that builds
is Truth
  Mis. 332– 3   *M·* is Truth,— not laws of matter.
law of
  Mis. 173–10   law of *M·* and not of matter,
laws of
  Mis. 173–31   laws of matter, or laws of *M·*?
  My. 190–19   laws of *M·* over the human mind
Life and
  Un. 3–22   He is all the Life and *M·* there is
     3–23   embodiment of Life and *M·*.
likeness of
  Mis. 97–24   in the image and likeness of *M·*,
     97–24   in the image and likeness of *M·*
made by
  Mis. 257– 7   must be made by *M·* and as Mind.
manifestation of
  Mis. 27–29   it is a small manifestation of *M·*,
manifested
  Rud. 4– 8   Science is *M·* manifested.
manifest less of
  Mis. 36– 8   but they manifest less of *M·*.
manifesto of
  Mis. 22– 4   the unerring manifesto of *M·*,
man nor
  Mis. 36– 2   is neither God's man nor *M·* ;
matter and
  Mis. 175–28   The attempt to mix matter and *M·*,
     269–18   choice between matter and *M·*,
matter is not
  No. 27– 4   Matter is not *M·*, to claim aught ;
matter, or
  Mis. 334–23   by means of matter, or *M·*?
matter to
  Peo. 7– 7   shall turn often . . . from matter to *M·*,
medicine of
  Mis. 252– 1   this medicine of *M·* is . . . infinite.
     348–24   new *régime* . . . the medicine of *M·*,
  '01. 18– 7   the medicine of *M·* is more honored
medium of
  Mis. 163–21   medium of *M·*, the hope of the race.
microscope of
  Peo. 10– 7   under the microscope of *M·*.
misstatement of
  Mis. 174– 3   Matter is a misstatement of *M·* ;
  Un. 35–21   this one is a misstatement of *M·*,
mode of
  Ret. 89– 2   potency of this spiritual mode of *M·*,
modes of
  Mis. 363–12   modes of *M·* are spiritual,
more
  Ret. 33–12   the more *M·*, the better the work is
My
  Un. 24– 4   My *M·* is divine good,
never produced
  Mis. 218– 4   that matter never produced *M·*,
no other
  Mis. 182– 8   no other *M·*, no other origin ;
  Rud. 4–16   hence there is no other *M·*.
nor sensation
  Un. 50–17   matter has neither *M·* nor sensation.
notion that
  Mis. 257– 1   the notion that *M·* can be in matter
not matter
  Mis. 56–10   Life is immortal *M·*, not matter.
     190– 1   Atomic action is *M·*, not matter.
  '00. 11–19   *M·*, not matter, makes music ;
of Christ
  Un. 33–12   it is certainly not the *M·* of Christ,
of God
  No. 37–27   if . . . sin existed in the *M·* of God.
  '01. 22– 4   It is the *M·* of God
     27–25   the *M·* of God and not of man
of Spirit
  Un. 32–11   It is not the *M·* of Spirit ;
omnipotence of the
  Mis. 201–12   omnipotence of the *M·* that knows

Mind

omnipotent
  My. 106– 9   immutable laws of omnipotent *M·*
omniscient
  Mis. 25–23   omnipotent and omniscient *M·*.
  No. 23–27   omnipresent and omniscient *M·* ;
one
  Mis. 82–25   the one *M·* is immortal.
     101–31   This one *M·* and His individuality
     173– 6   that there is but one *M·*,
     196– 3   there is but one God, one *M·* ;
     279–28   enough . . . if we are of one *M·* ;
  Ret. 56–19   Hence there is but one *M·* ;
     57–21   The notion of more than one *M·*,
  Un. 24– 7   assumptions . . . more than the one *M·*,
  Rud. 13–13   one Life and one *M·*.
  No. 20–12   one *M·*, a perfect man, and
     27– 2   supposition . . . more than one *M·*.
     38–20   one *M·*, one consciousness,
  Pan. 6–18   Did one *M·*, or two minds,
     7–27   hypothesis of . . . more than one *M·*,
  My. 109– 8   we shall have one *M·*, one God,
     132–21   one *M·* and that divine ;
     279–14   Had all peoples one *M·*, peace would
     281–11   namely, one God, one *M·*,
     286– 6   have one God, one *M·* ;
only
  Rud. 4–18   not in matter, but in *M·* only.
     5–28   or exist in *M·* only ;
or God
  Mis. 69– 6   *M·*, or God, and His attributes.
  Ret. 56– 5   the one divine *M·*, or God,
  No. 5–19   *M·*, or God, does not meddle with it.
or good
  Ret. 56–24   does not subdivide *M·*, or good,
  Un. 45–28   immortal *M·*, or good.
or Life
  Ret. 57–21   notion of more than one *M·*, or Life,
or matter
  Mis. 23–10   Was it *M·* or matter that spake
over matter
  Hea. 7– 6   the power of *M·* over matter.
perfect
  Mis. 3–22   the supreme and perfect *M·*,
     37–18   God, the perfect *M·*,
     175–26   and reveals the one perfect *M·*
     198– 1   governed by the one perfect *M·*,
  Ret. 28– 7   Science of the perfect *M·*
power of
  Mis. 60–12   *Does it not limit the power of M·*
     60–15   Does it limit the power of *M·* to say
  Hea. 7– 6   power of *M·* over matter.
pretension to be
  Rud. 7–20   As a pretension to be *M·*, matter is
Principle is
  No. 20–10   This Principle is *M·*, substance,
problem of
  Mis. 333–19   to work out the problem of *M·*,
pure
  Mis. 260–16   pure *M·* is the truth of being
     260–23   acknowledging pure *M·* as absolute
     260–25   Pure *M·* gives out an atmosphere that
realities of
  Mis. 333–28   the grand realities of *M·*,
  No. 6– 3   to attempt to destroy the realities of *M·*
reality of
  No. 10–23   discords have not the reality of *M·*
reconstructed
  Ret. 28–22   *M·* reconstructed the body,
  Pul. 35–21   *M·* reconstructed the body,
reign of
  Mis. 51–25   * reign of *M·* commence on earth,
relating to
  Mis. 379–28   momentous facts relating to *M·*
rely on
  Pul. 69–10   * rely on *M·* for cure,
rests on
  No. 10–14   My hygienic system rests on *M·*,
reveals
  Ret. 59–18   reveals *M·*, the only living and true
revolves
  Ret. 88–29   *M·* revolves on a spiritual axis,
right
  Mis. 59–20   There is but one right *M·*,
     104–14   Clothed, and in its right *M·*,
rights of
  My. 212–25   interfering with the rights of *M·*,
same
  Un. 4–19   bids man have the same *M·*
scale of
  Mis. 280–15   into the scale of *M·*,
Science of
     (*see* **Science**)
self-existent
  Ret. 60– 4   as eternal, self-existent *M·* ;

Mind

servant of
Mis. 47–18 body is the servant of M·,
sin is not
No. 27– 1 Sin is not M· ; it is but the
Soul, or
Mis. 189–15 supposition that Soul, or M· is
Un. 29–12 one God, one Soul, or M·,
spake
Mis. 280– 1 M· spake and form appeared.
sphere of
No. 37– 9 and when, as a sphere of M·,
subordinate to
Mis. 29–30 powerless and subordinate to M·.
such a
Un. 64–10 approximate to such a M·,
superiority of
Mis. 30–18 superiority of M· over the flesh,
supremacy of
Mis. 35– 5 supremacy of M· over matter,
that
Mis. 59–22 Any copartnership with that M·
235– 7 becomes the partaker of that M·
Man. 16–10 pray for that M· to be in us
Un. 38– 7 of that M· which is Life.
Pul. 75– 3 that M· which was in Christ Jesus.
My. 287–17 are made partakers of that M·
that governs
Peo. 8–17 M·, that governs the universe,
that is God
Mis. 4– 7 Science of the M· that is God,
57–30 in and of the M· that is God,
113– 1 M· that is God is not in matter ;
My. 267– 5 the law of the M· that is God,
that is identical
Un. 33–13 not the M· that is identical with
theology of
Mis. 59– 2 the healing theology of M·,
the only
Mis. 55–25 regards God as the only M·,
361–24 God is the only M·,
Un. 25– 8 the only substance, the only M·.
29–11 the only M· and intelligence
No. 35–21 God is the only M·,
this
Mis. 82–30 This M·, then, is not subject to
105–31 God is Mind, and this M· is good,
197–21 "let this M· be in you,— Phil. 2: 5.
279–29 will feel the influence of this M· ;
332– 3 this M· is Truth,
332– 5 this M· is Love,
364–20 nothing apart from this M·,
Un. 14–21 if this M· is familiar with evil,
'01. 7–13 include within this M· the thoughts
Hea. 15–16 perpetually at war with this M·,
My. 108–15 this M· is the only lawgiver,
108–18 The more of this M· the better
through
Mis. 70–22 inevitably separated through M·.
74–23 through M·, he removed any
258– 7 through M·, he restored sight
269–20 can only be Christianized through M· ;
368–19 treating disease through M·.
Chr. 53–48 gleaming through M·, mother, man.
Ret. 69–22 God created all through M·,
My. 103–20 demonstrated through M· the effects
106–31 Nazarene Prophet, healed through M·,
to matter
Rud. 6– 9 when we change . . . from M· to matter,
translates
Mis. 22–10 C. S. translates M·, God,
true
Ret. 73–16 in God,— in the true M·,
Un. 32–17 True M· is immortal.
unerring
Mis. 172–12 unerring M· measures man,
Un. 53–24 the immortal and unerring M·,
unfathomable
Un. 28–22 must be the unfathomable M·,
unity of
Peo. 13–11 unity of M· and oneness of Principle.
universe of
Mis. 369– 9 immeasurable universe of M·,
unlimited
Hea. 4– 1 unlimited M· cannot start from
was the creator
Mis. 57– 6 and M· was the creator.
we exist in
Mis. 50–25 we exist in M·, live thereby,
which is God
Un. 44–18 not expressive of the M· which is God.
56– 6 no sin . . . in the M· which is God.
which is good
Un. 2–16 the M· which is good, or God,
which is immortal
Mis. 36– 5 Truth, or the M· which is immortal."

Mind

without
Mis. 269–21 without M· the body is without action ;
Un. 50–23 a consciousness which is without M·
Rud. 5–16 must be . . . or matter without M·.
5–17 Matter without M· is . . . impossibility.
My. 106–15 Without M·, man . . . would collapse ;
would be chained
Mis. 102– 7 If . . . M· would be chained to finity,

———

Mis. 8– 6 "in Him [M·] we live,— Acts 17: 28.
23–15 must be M· ; for matter is not the
23–22 Spirit, M·, are terms synonymous
23–30 All must be M· and Mind's ideas ;
25–12 translates matter into M·,
27–25 being in and of Spirit, M·,
55–29 If M· is in matter
55–31 either a godless and material M·, or
56– 7 If M· is not substance,
74–17 into its original meaning, M·.
101–24 not matter, but M·.
173–12 M· is its own great cause
173–15 that M· is in matter?
173–21 M·, God, is all-power
175–21 and its methods in place of God, M·.
196– 2 found not in matter but in M·,
243–22 or human will, not M·.
256–26 Wherever law is, M· is ;
257– 7 must be made by Mind and as M·.
280–15 M· is not put into the scales with
379–13 matter was not as real as M·,
379–25 Is it matter, or is it M·,
Ret. 28–19 M·, which divides, subdivides,
56– 6 Whatever . . . divides M· into minds,
56–23 God reflects Himself, or M·,
59–19 and all that is made by Him, M·,
60–29 but one Spirit, M·, Soul.
73– 5 without finiteness of form or M·.
76–17 M· "which was also in — Phil. 2: 5.
Un. 25– 8 M· is not, cannot be, in matter.
25– 9 as M·, and not as matter.
25–11 This lie, that M· can be in matter,
45–25 substance of Spirit,— M·, Life, Soul.
50– 1 notion of the destructibility of M·
53–12 To say that M· is material,
53–13 or that evil is M·,
Pul. vii–19 not by matter, but by M· ;
6– 9 not matter, but M· ;
14–27 benefit which M· has wrought.
Rud. 5–17 M· in matter is pantheism.
6– 6 As M· they are real,
6– 7 beauty and goodness are in . . . M·,
10–24 belief that matter can master M·,
Pan. 7–28 hypothesis of . . . matter governing M·,
12–24 Truth, Love, substance, Spirit, M·,
'00. 4–25 must proceed from God, from M·,
'01. 3–18 By this we mean M·,
5–16 by M·, not by matter.
17–25 dynamics of medicine is M·.
24–13 Making matter more potent than M·,
Hea. 7– 9 its original language, which is M·,
13–23 M·, divine Science, the truth of
Peo. 1– 7 back to its original language,— M·,
9–25 of any other power than M· ;
My. 52–13 * M·, Truth, Life, and Love,
119– 9 in M·, not in matter.
159–27 * "What is the essence of God? M·."
160– 1 and keeps M· much out of sight.
181–12 and Life not in matter but in M·.
225–29 M·, Soul, which combine as one.
260–24 elevates medicine to M· ;
350– 4 with the divine noumenon, M·,

mind (see also **mind's**)
action of
(see **action**)
affects
Mis. 247–26 believe that the body affects m·,
affects the
Mis. 5–31 believe that the body affects the m·,
affects the body
Mis. 5–32 that the m· affects the body.
aid of
My. 301–28 cannot . . . without the aid of m·.
already full
My. 210– 5 added to the m· already full.
altitude of
Pan. 6–26 elevating evil to the altitude of m·
and body
Mis. 25– 1 supposed power on the m· and body of
60–29 If mortal m· and body are myths,
62–29 over the human m· and body ;
65–25 the equipoise of m· and body,
187–6 regeneration of both m· and body,
187– 7 the perfection of m· and body,
268–24 ailments of mortal m· and body.

mind

and body
Mis. 286–24   mortal *m·* and body as *one*,
Pul. 10– 2   healing both *m·* and body,
No. 40–26   *m·* and body are made better only by
Hea. 3– 2   to heal both *m·* and body ;
     8– 3   that heals both *m·* and body ;
     8– 6   the truth regarding *m·* and body,
Peo. 5–25   and a healthy *m·* and body.
My. 105– 3   only medicine for *m·* and body.
and character
Mis. 67– 9   his rights of *m·* and character.
and manners
My. 309– 3   cultivated in *m·* and manners.
and matter
Un. 32– 9   so-called *m·* and matter cannot
     45– 6   saying, . . . Am I not *m·* and matter,
Hea. 11–25   supposed to be both *m·* and matter.
My. 179–10   good and evil, both *m·* and matter,
     293– 6   this compound of *m·* and matter
animated by
Peo. 5–23   is not . . . matter animated by *m·*,
another
Mis. 37– 2   if there were in reality another *m·*
     96–28   not one mind acting upon another *m·* ;
No. 40–21   to meddle with another *m·*,
Hea. 15–15   claim another *m·* perpetually at war
another's
Mis. 83–15   If . . . originated in another's *m·*,
apart from
My. 108– 6   challenge matter to act apart from *m·* ;
appeal to
Peo. 7–25   appeal to *m·* to improve its subjects
assent of
Mis. 240–14   without the assent of *m·*,
as something separate
Ret. 60– 5   *m·* as something separate from God.
athletic
Pul. 5–14   his athletic *m·*, scholarly and serene,
attitude of
My. 290–27   Hold this attitude of *m·*, and it will
attribute of
Pul. 53–18   * attribute of *m·* which elevates man
bear in
Mis. 93–24   Bear in *m·*, however, that human
     126–25   bear in *m·* that, in the long race,
     196–11   bear in *m·* that a serpent said that ;
     263–12   bear in *m·* that His presence,
My. 148–24   Bear in *m·* always that Christianity
begins in
Hea. 7–15   begins in *m·* to heal the body,
belief that
Ret. 69–28   belief that *m·* is in matter,
believed to be
Un. 33–15   believed to be *m·* only through error
belong to
Mis. 228–24   belong to *m·* and not to matter.
benefit the
Mis. 241– 3   God . . . to benefit the *m·*.
biased
Mis. 240–20   easier . . . than the biased *m·*.
body and
Mis. 163–29   spiritual healing of body and *m·*.
     241– 3   Body and *m·* are correlated
     268–19   heals body and *m·*, head and heart ;
called
Un. 46– 1   mortal error, called *m·*,
call to
My. 347–17   call to *m·* the number of
came through
Hea. 17–27   If sickness and . . . came through *m·*,
can rest
Mis. 227–23   a life wherein the *m·* can rest
capacities of
Ret. 82–21   Their liberated capacities of *m·*
carnal
Mis. 36–24   says, "The carnal *m·* — *Rom.* 8 : 7.
     54– 1   carnal *m·* cannot discern spiritual
     169–26   carnal *m·*, which is enmity
     214– 3   it appeared hate to the carnal *m·*,
change the
Un. 35– 5   Change the *m·*, and the quality
child's
Mis. 51–15   a declaration to the child's *m·*
claims to be
Ret. 56–21   Whatever else claims to be *m·*,
classified as
Pan. 4– 9   are properly classified as *m·*,
comes from
Un. 56– 5   since all suffering comes from *m·*,
connecting
Mis. 393– 3   Nature, with the *m·* connecting,
Po. 51– 8   Nature, with the *m·* connecting,
conscious
'01. 24– 1   * Matter apart from conscious *m·*
constantly in
Mis. 62– 4   opposite image . . . constantly in *m·*,

mind

disease as
Hea. 12– 8   he diagnoses disease as *m·*,
dishonest
Mis. 288–24   the shift of a dishonest *m·*,
dominance of
Pul. 31–18   * the dominance of *m·* over matter,
enables
Hea. 15– 9   it enables *m·* to govern matter,
erring
Mis. 63– 4   claim that one erring *m·* cures
     199– 4   erring *m·* can claim to do thus,
     286–22   states of the human erring *m·* ;
Ret. 59– 2   a finite and erring *m·*,
error of
Hea. 9–24   an error of *m·* or of body.
evil
Mis. 173–17   Does an evil *m·* exist without space
     362–18   an evil *m·* already doomed,
Un. 24–18   There is, can be, no evil *m·*,
No. 38– 8   no intelligent sin, evil *m·* or matter :
My. 228– 7   The evil *m·* calls it "skulking,"
evil, as
Mis. 261– 1   evil, as *m·*, is doomed,
expression of
Mis. 247–27   body is an expression of *m·*,
faith in
Hea. 15– 7   it reposes all faith in *m·*,
feeblest
Peo. 11– 5   it was found that the feeblest *m·*,
ferocious
Mis. 36–10   ferocious *m·* seen in the beast
fill the
Pul. 69–12   * fill the *m·* with good thoughts
finite
Mis. 162–24   without corporeality or finite *m·*.
Ret. 30–15   finite *m·* and material existence.
Un. 24–15   There is no really finite *m·*,
form of
Un. 32– 9   not . . . but a false form of *m·*.
governed by
Mis. 34– 6   The body is governed by *m·* ;
     291– 3   *m·* governed by Principle
governs
Hea. 14–16   to know that *m·* governs the body
harpstrings of the
Mis. 396–18   O'er waiting harpstrings of the *m·*
Pul. 18– 2   O'er waiting harpstrings of the *m·*
Po. 12– 1   O'er waiting harpstrings of the *m·*
My. 31– 8   * "O'er waiting harpstrings of the *m·*;"
has departed
My. 302– 7   a corpse, whence *m·* has departed.
his
Peo. 9– 8   but it cannot purify his *m·*,
My. 211–25   poured constantly into his *m·*,
his own
Mis. 266– 8   the subjective state of his own *m·*
human
     (*see* **human**)
if it is
Un. 33–12   if it is *m·*, it is certainly not
impress of
Peo. 7– 3   leaving the impress of *m·* on the
independent of
Hea. 12– 6   what . . . is doing independent of *m·*,
individual
Rud. 15–28   to fill anew the individual *m·*.
'01. 7–17   differing needs of the individual *m·*
infinite
Pan. 3–18   infinite *m·* of one supreme, holy,
in harmony
Hea. 14–26   a *m·* in harmony with God,
in matter
Mis. 26–20   belief of *m·* in matter is pantheism.
     113– 1   result of sensuous *m·* in matter.
     179–21   It is the belief of *m·* in matter.
     198– 6   denying . . . *m·* in matter,
     198–10   mortal claim to . . . *m·* in matter,
Ret. 21–22   false sense of . . . *m·* in matter.
Un. 24–11   *Evil.* I am . . . a *m·* in matter,
     54– 2   the doctrine of *m·* in matter.
Pan. 2–15   human opinion of . . . *m·* in matter.
     7–26   hypothesis of *m·* in matter,
'01. 7–26   mortal sense of . . . *m·* in matter
My. 109– 4   Adam-dream of *m·* in matter,
     296–16   mortal dream of . . . *m·* in matter,
instructor's
Mis. 264–28   instructor's *m·* must take its hue from
is stayed
My. 290–15   *m·* is stayed on Thee : — *Isa.* 26 : 3.
is the cause
My. 302– 8   proof that *m·* is the cause of
is the criminal
Hea. 7–22   a crime, and *m·* is the criminal.
keep in
My. 191–11   Keep in *m·* the foundations of

mind

lawless
Mis. 260–30   lawless *m*·, with unseen motives,
legislation of
Peo. 11–20   obedient to the legislation of *m*·,
limited
No. 19–11   He is neither a limited *m*· nor a
mandate of
My. 302– 2   Through the mandate of *m*·
manipulates
Ret. 71–18   He who secretly manipulates *m*·
march of
Pul. 14– 1   march of *m*· and of honest
marred in
Peo. 10–20   fettered free limbs, and marred in *m*·
master of
Un. 34– 3   declares . . . is the master of *m*·,
material
Mis. 336– 7   to kill the serpent of a material *m*·.
Un. 23–22   An evil material *m*·, so-called,
matter and
Mis. 173–15   says that man is both matter and *m*·,
'01. 25–10   which mix matter and *m*·,
Hea. 13– 1   and divide . . . between matter and *m*·,
mind over
Mis. 59–18   *Is not all argument mind over m*·?
      220–28   in this action of mind over *m*·,
misnamed
Un. 32–15   misnamed *m*· is a false claim,
modes of
Mis. 360– 8   Theirs were modes of *m*·
moods of
Pan. 3– 9   Certain moods of *m*· find an
mortal
      (*see* **mortal**)
motive, and
Mis. 195– 3   all action, motive, and *m*·,
moved by
Mis. 106–30   Moved by *m*·, your many-throated
My
Un. 18–11   If pain . . . were not in My *m*·,
my
Mis. 62– 2   the *right* idea of man in my *m*·,
      224–31   it is a question in my *m*·,
      290–16   * influence of your thought on my *m*·,
Un. 24–23   My *m*· is more than matter.
My. 59–16   * my *m*· was carried back to
New England
Pul. 65– 3   * what is called the New England *m*·
no
Mis. 196– 3   will then claim no *m*· apart from
Un. 33–17   and you find no *m*· therein.
no other
'01. 20– 6   guided by no other *m*· than Truth,
not matter
My. 107–20   identifies . . . with *m*·, not matter,
      302– 4   *m*·, not matter, produces the result
obtrude upon the
Mis. 10– 1   obtrude upon the *m*· or engraft upon
of a person
Mis. 283– 5   to enter the *m*· of a person,
of Christ
My. 142– 2   * we have the *m*· of Christ.'— *I Cor.* 2 : 16.
of his pupil
Rud. 9– 7   spring up in the *m*· of his pupil.
of Jesus
Mis. 200– 2   Truth in the *m*· of Jesus,
of the individual
Hea. 6–21   the *m*· of the individual only
of the Lord
My. 142– 1   the *m*· of the Lord, — *I Cor.* 2 : 16.
of the neophyte
My. 48–26   * upon the *m*· of the neophyte
of the perpetrator
Mis. 222–16   action on the *m*· of the perpetrator,
of the pupil
Rud. 15–24   *m*· of the pupil may be dissected
of the reader
My. 218–18   tends to confuse the *m*· of the reader,
of your patient
My. 364– 4   but the *m*· of your patient,
one
Mis. 96–28   not one *m*· acting upon another
      134–12   Be "of one *m*·," — *II Cor.* 13 : 11.
      175–23   that one *m*· controls another ;
      279–23   and they were of one *m*·.
      279–26   disciples, too, were of one *m*·.
No. 40–21   is it right for one *m*· to meddle
or body
Mis. 59–25   away from the human *m*· or body,
      97–28   perfect man in *m*· or body,
      103–22   inference . . . either as *m*· or body,
      341– 2   the right action of *m*· or body.
originate
Hea. 17–26   did not *m*· originate the delusion?

mind

originate in
Hea. 12–11   all physical effects originate in *m*·
or matter
Mis. 103–20   Mortal man, as *m*· or matter,
      218–16   inconceivable, either as *m*· or matter ;
No. 38– 8   no intelligent sin, evil *m*· or matter :
My. 108– 4   is *m*· or matter the intelligent cause
over matter
Hea. 15– 8   the power of *m*· over matter,
My. 74–13   * triumph of *m*· over matter.
      97– 2   * admit the power of *m*· over matter.
patient's
Mis. 220–12   until the patient's *m*· yields,
      355–24   discern the error in thy patient's *m*·
people's
Peo. 2–27   constantly before the people's *m*·,
peoples the
Mis. 82– 1   peoples the *m*· with spiritual ideas,
personality of
Ret. 25–23   physical personality of *m*·
philosophy of
Mis. 68–24   * defines it as "the philosophy of *m*·,
possibilities of
Mis. 47–14   and the possibilities of *m*· when
power of
Hea. 15– 8   the power of *m*· over matter,
      19– 2   test the power of *m*· over body ;
My. 97– 2   * admit the power of *m*· over matter.
produces disease
Hea. 6–13   I learned how *m*· produces disease
public
Mis. 78–19   Misguiding the public *m*· and
purification of
Peo. 9– 3   this baptism is the purification of *m*·,
reaches
Mis. 223–10   that *m*· reaches its own ideal,
reading the
Hea. 7–17   reading the *m*· of the poor woman
reassuring the
My. 293–17   reassuring the *m*· and through the
renders the
Rud. 15– 9   This renders the *m*· less inquisitive,
repeal it in
Peo. 12–12   repeal it in *m*·, and acknowledge only
requires
Hea. 11–26   requires *m*· imbued with Truth
restless
Ret. 11– 6   Go fix thy restless *m*·
Po. 60– 2   Go fix thy restless *m*·
right
'00. 6–23   clothed and in his right *m*·,
satisfies the
Mis. 227–26   honest life satisfies the *m*·
science of
My. 307– 7   and it was the science of *m*·,
science of the
Mis. 68–24   * defined . . . science of the *m*·."
self-satisfied
My. 180–25   the disguised or the self-satisfied *m*·,
sensation of
My. 228– 4   so-called disease is a sensation of *m*·,
sensible
Un. 50– 8   belief in matter as sensible *m*·.
sensuous
Mis. 113– 1   the result of sensuous *m*· in matter.
separate
Mis. 196– 8   a separate *m*· from God (good),
shock to the
Rud. 15– 7   glad surprise . . . is a shock to the *m*· ;
small
Mis. 147–11   and indicates a small *m*·?
so-called
Mis. 41–24   the cause in that so-called *m*·
      196– 9   so-called *m*· shall open your eyes
      233–32   sensation . . . in this so-called *m*· ;
      363– 1   more nearly an erring so-called *m*·
Ret. 70– 4   so-called *m*· puts forth its own
Un. 23–22   An evil material *m*·, so-called,
      32– 9   so-called *m*· and matter cannot be
      34–23   so-called *m*· would have no identity.
spiritual
Peo. 4–22   No . . . can make a spiritual *m*·
state of
      (*see* **state**)
states of
Mis. 221–15   these states of *m*· will stultify
Pul. 87–22   states of *m*·, to bless mankind.
stopped by
Hea. 19– 6   could not have been stopped by *m*·
substance, or
Mis. 198–10   claim to life, substance, or *m*·
My. 296–16   dream of life, substance, or *m*·
suppositional
Mis. 363–11   material mode of a suppositional *m*·
Un. 32–16   a false claim, a suppositional *m*·,

mind

teacher's
Mis. 264–26 teacher's m· must be pure, grand,
this
Mis. 42– 7 this m· is still in a
220–13 has the full control over this m·
Ret. 34–20 this m· must be renovated
Un. 11–10 showed the need of changing this m·
32–11 What is this m·?
33– 2 which prove . . . this m· a lie.
Hea. 14–28 a body governed by this m·,
My. 364– 5 and treat this m· to be Christly.
thy
My. 183– 3 and with all thy m· ; — Luke 10 : 27.
to meditate
Po. 1–17 turns The m· to meditate on
touches
Mis. 235–15 touches m· to more spiritual issues,
transmit
Ret. 68–19 can matter originate or transmit m·?
triumph of
Peo. 13–17 triumph of m· over the body,
My. 74–13 * triumph of m· over matter.
Truth-filled
Peo. 5–24 therefore a Truth-filled m· makes
universal
'01. 23–30 * operations of the universal m·,
with mind
My. 154–27 m· with mind, soul with soul,
without
Mis. 28– 7 muscles cannot move without m·.
without the
'01. 24– 3 not without the m·, but within it,
your
Mis. 271–14 Cleanse your m· of the cobwebs
My. 345– 1 see that your m· is in such a state

Mis. 23– 5 Does m· "sleep in the mineral,
36– 6 Do animals and beasts have a m·?
44–15 has the m·, or extracting, or both,
44–22 or that m· is in matter,
45–26 intelligence or m· termed evil.
98– 2 perfect model should be held in m·,
184– 7 reflects God in body as well as in m·.
228–22 must be caught through m·;
230–12 travel of limb more than m·.
261– 3 As m·, evil finds no escape from
308–26 holding in m· the consciousness of
350–20 in the m· that handled them.
363– 6 supposition that . . . is m·
Ret. 27–23 m· can duly express it to the ear,
69–28 belief . . . that evil is m·,
76–11 m· to which this Science was revealed
Un. 26– 3 and the capacity to evolve m·.
32– 8 By matter is commonly meant m·,
33–11 but unless matter is m·,
33–27 or that m· sees by means of
Pul. 6–30 whose m· never swerved from
53– 9 * in the m· of both healer and patient,
80– 1 * must be a righting-up of the m·
Rud. 5–15 either m· which is called matter, or
No. 5–22 m· that attacks a normal and real
Pan. 6–22 if . . . evil also is m·,
9– 1 that m· "sleeps in the mineral,
'01. 11– 7 and m· is no longer in matter.
17–27 must be m· that controls the effect ;
24– 6 produced by divine power on the m·
Hea. 7–20 he charged home a crime to m·,
11–24 places all cause and cure as m· ;
18– 1 in ruling them out of m·
19– 5 governed . . . entirely by m·,
Peo. 5–24 but in itself is m· ;
12–16 know what a power m· is to heal
My. 48–30 * higher nature through the m·,
108– 6 and if m·, I have proved beyond cavil
210– 7 in a m· filled with goodness.
256–13 close the door of m· on this
272–30 * a m· that has had so much influence
293–17 through the m· resuscitating the
301–29 If m· be absent from the body,
301–30 m· must be, is, the vehicle of
302–10 craze is that matter masters m· ;
334–14 * the woman whom he had in m·
346–23 * had in m· any particular person

mind (verb)

Mis. 13– 4 special care to m· my own business.
283–14 * "M· your own business,"

mind-cure

Mis. 58–27 "m·," nothing more nor less,
59– 5 This is the mortal "m·"
59– 8 there had better be no "m·,"
62–15 when the m· claims to heal
62–20 A "m·" is a matter-cure.
62–30 "m·" rests on the notion that

mind-cure

Mis. 233–16 and naming that "m·,"
243–21 There are charlatans in "m·,"

Mind-cure on a Material Basis

Mis. 62–22 book title

mind-curists

'01. 21– 1 mortal m·, nor faith-curists ;

minded

Mis. 24– 2 makes man spiritually m·.
24– 3 to be carnally m· is death ; — Rom. 8 : 6.
24– 4 to be spiritually m· is — Rom. 8 : 6.
Ret. 76–14 The spiritually m· meet on the
'02. 6–26 degree that man becomes spiritually m·
6–27 to be carnally m· is death ; — Rom. 8 : 6.
6–28 to be spiritually m· is — Rom. 8 : 6.
8–15 The spiritually m· are inspired with

Mind-force

Mis. 22–31 M·, invisible to material sense,
331–23 divine M·, filling all space

Mind-healer

Ret. 76–20 serves to constitute the M·

Mind-healers

No. 3–20 sense which M· specially need ;

Mind-healing

Christian Science
Mis. 78– 7 Can C. S. M· be taught to
80–32 C. S. M· rests demonstrably on
273–22 interest in C. S. M·.
358–24 teaching C. S. M·,
364– 1 the textbook of C. S. M·,
382–15 first student in C. S. M· ;
Ret. 43– 3 teaching one student C. S. M·.
48–23 instructed in C. S. M·,
50– 2 instruction in C. S. M·,
Rud. 7– 1 how much you understand of C. S. M·.
17– 8 understanding of C. S. M·
No. 2–27 in relation to C. S. M·,
3–10 the practice of C. S. M·
12– 1 C. S. M· can only be gained by
32–13 C. S. M· lifts with a steady arm,
43–17 C. S. M· is dishonored by
My. 210–20 notion that C. S. M· should be
212–17 the teaching of C. S. M·,
213– 1 natural fruits of C. S. M·
Science of
(see Science)

Mis. 41– 5 malpractice would disgrace M·,
48–26 study of M· would cure the
66–11 verified in all directions in M·,
67– 2 mere alphabet of M·.
67–22 right practice of M· achieved,
88–28 M·, and healing with drugs,
221–22 baffles the student of M·,
223–14 This individual disbelieves in M·,
255–17 chapter sub-title
260–22 The truth of M· uplifts
264–24 Their knowledge of M· may be
269–23 M· is the proper means of
282–23 believe in the efficacy of M·,
351–10 through the mental method of M·,
356–26 to the understanding of M· ;
Ret. 33–14 to prove the Principle of M·.
35– 2 spiritual, scientific M·,
42–12 remarkably successful in M·,
44– 2 a M· church, without a creed,
52– 3 expansion of scientific M·,
78–15 rules of M· are wholly Christlike
85–20 abusing the practice of M·
89– 4 proven . . . in the practice of M·.
Pul. 35–24 * convinced of the Principle of M·,
Rud. 6–18 basis of M· a destruction of
6–22 this predicate and postulate of M· ;
8–18 not otherwise in the field of M·.
9– 3 The teacher of M· who is not
12–12 denies the Principle of M·.
16– 9 its scientific relation to M·,
16–23 shades of difference in M·
No. v– 8 laborers in the realm of M·.
1–21 the only M· I vindicate ;
3–18 The Nemesis of the history of M·
5– 3 this grand verity of M·.
15–14 far more mystic than M·.
19– 1 high premium on M·.
26– 5 This infantile talk about M·
44– 7 My system of M· swerves not

mind-healing

Mis. 272–19 * "All the m· colleges . . . have simply
No. 2– 3 A spurious and hydra-headed m·
31– 3 Material and mortal m·

minding

My. 276–11 she is m· her own business,

mind-manipulator
Ret. 71–16 Ask the unbridled *m·* if he

mind-matter
Un. 45–18 make *m·* a habitant of the

Mind-medicine
Mis. 270–29 The next step is *M·*.

mind-method
Mis. 277–16 falsehoods, and a secret *m·*,

mind-models
Peo. 7–29 as his *m·* are more or less spiritual.

Mind-pictures
No. 39–25 this light reveals the pure *M·*,

mind-pictures
Un. 64–11 more real those *m·* would become

Mind-power
My. 4–19 *M·* is good will towards men.

mind-power
Mis. 222–22 under this new *régime* of *m·*,
My. 213–3 malicious aim of perverted *m·*,

Mind-practice
Ret. 78–5 achieved the entire wisdom of *M·*.

mind-practice
Ret. 71–8 ignorant or an unprincipled *m·*

mind-quacks
No. 26–1 *m·* believe that mortal man is
   29–7 *m·* have so slight a knowledge of

Mind's
Mis. 3–18 Hygiene, . . . not *M·* medicine.
   23–30 All must be Mind and *M·* ideas ;
   60–20 *M·* possibilities are not lessened by
Un. 12–5 curving sickle of *M·* eternal circle,
   14–24 reflected in man, *M·* image.
No. 27–16 divine Mind and that *M·* idea.

mind's
Mis. 33–28 found in mortal *m·* opposite,
   119–2 through the *m·* tympanum,
   139–28 in advance of the erring *m·* apprehension.
Ret. 31–22 Into mortal *m·* material obliquity
Pul. 2–15 With the *m·* eye glance at the
Hea. 6–15 I saw how the *m·* ideals were
Peo. 7–5 leaving to rot and ruin the *m·* ideals.
   10–24 follow the *m·* freedom from sin ;

minds
all
Mis. 1–11 kindle all *m·* with a gleam of
   6–12 prove to all *m·* the power of
   56–26 *if all m· (men) have existed from the*
   307–18 is fast fitting all *m·* for the
No. 1–1 kindle in all *m·* a common sentiment of
become
Mis. 316–12 Until *m·* become less worldly-minded,
class of
My. 111–7 same class of *m·* to deal with
envious
Mis. 291–30 counteract the influence of envious *m·*
evil
My. 228–5 Evil *m·* signally blunder in divine
influence the
My. 175–29 must fail to influence the *m·* of
many
Mis. 4–21 in many *m·* it is confounded with
   7–20 descriptions carry fears to many *m·*,
   196–4 the supposition of . . . many *m·*
Un. 24–5 To believe in *m·* many is to
'00. 4–4 so unwittingly consents to many *m·*
men's
Pul. 79–20 * had taken possession of men's *m·*,
mortal
Peo. 11–18 Mortals, *alias* mortal *m·*,
My. 301–22 effects of illusion on mortal *m·*
of all present
My. 170–9 in the *m·* of all present
of invalids
Rud. 12–16 erases from the *m·* of invalids their
of men
My. 225–18 begins in the *m·* of men
   264–16 signifies to the *m·* of men
   295–4 remains in the *m·* of men,
of mortals
Mis. 257–11 *alias* the *m·* of mortals.
My. 5–1 originates in the *m·* of mortals.
   294–10 contradicting *m·* of mortals.
of others
Mis. 220–26 put it into the *m·* of others
of the healthy
Rud. 12–24 to free the *m·* of the healthy
of the people
My. 234–28 *m·* of the people are prepared
of thinkers
No. 13–23 a revolution in the *m·* of thinkers

minds
other
Mis. 40–28 evil too common to other *m·*.
   43–11 least likely to pour into other *m·*
   92–10 enlightens other *m·* most readily,
   96–30 not the transference . . . to other *m·* ;
   175–22 that there are other *m·*
Man. 87–19 personally controls other *m·*,
Ret. 84–7 enlightens other *m·* most readily,
   84–24 personally controls other *m·*,
   89–27 endeavoring to influence other *m·*
My. 211–29 Other *m·* are made dormant by it,
our
Mis. 169–17 borne fully to our *m·* and hearts.
   282–12 would we have our *m·* tampered with.
plurality of
Pan. 7–3 shows that a plurality of *m·*,
so-called
Pan. 4–15 there are many so-called *m·* ;
students'
Mis. 93–2 able to empty his students' *m·*,
Ret. 84–21 able to empty his students' *m·*
their
Ret. 83–9 foundations are already laid in their *m·*
Pul. 66–2 * to their *m·*, exists as much to-day
two
Mis. 289–20 *divorced* two *m·* in one.
Pan. 6–19 Did one Mind, or two *m·*, enter
   6–21 if two *m·*, what becomes of theism
unprejudiced
Pul. 14–14 Millions of unprejudiced *m·*
unprepared
Mis. 84–8 on *m·* unprepared for them.
your
My. 196–22 and faint in your *m·*." — *Heb.* 12 : 3.
   210–2 keep your *m·* so filled with Truth

_____

Mis. 265–17 whose *m·* are, . . . disturbed by this
   299–11 conviction to the *m·* of many
Ret. 56–6 or divides Mind into *m·*,
   56–24 does not subdivide Mind, . . . into *m·*,
My. 106–23 Is it because he *m·* his own business

Mind-science
No. 43–24 garbling my statements of *M·*

Mind-sowing
Un. 12–3 few in this vineyard of *M·*

mine (noun)
Mis. 393–10 Work ill-done within the misty *M·*
Pul. 51–12 * worked in the *m·* of knowledge
Po. 51–15 Work ill-done within the misty *M·*

mine (pronoun)
Mis. 130–15 "Vengeance is *m·* ; — *Rom.* 12 : 19.
My. 131–25 meat in *m·* house, — *Mal.* 3 : 10.
   188–4, 5 *m·* eyes and *m·* heart — *I Kings* 9 : 3.
   188–5 *m·* eyes shall be open, — *II Chron.* 7 : 15.
   188–6 *m·* ears attent unto — *II Chron.* 7 : 15.
   193–28 thou art *m·*." — *Isa.* 43 : 1.

mineral
Mis. 23–5 * Does mind "sleep in the *m·*,
   217–13 *m·*, vegetable, and animal kingdoms,
   257–4 sleeps in the *m·*, dreams in the
Un. 38–24 *m·*, vegetable, or animal kingdoms.
Pan. 9–2 * "sleeps in the *m·*, dreams in the

minerals
Rud. 7–26 transforming *m·* into vegetables

Minerva's
Ret. 12–3 *M·* silver sandals still
Po. 61–1 *M·* silver sandals still

mingle
Mis. 40–4 *m·* hygienic rules, drugs, and
   73–7 they *m·* the testimony of
   160–9 meet and *m·* in bliss supernal.
Pul. 11–5 *m·* with the joy of angels
No. 21–17 *m·* in the same realm and consciousness.

mingled
Mis. 81–11 *m· with the teachings of John*
Ret. 80–16 *m·* sternness and gentleness
My. 310–26 * *m·* with bad temper."

mingling
Mis. 56–16 *m·* in perpetual warfare
   396–15 When *m·* with the universe,
Ret. 1–19 thus *m·* in her children.
Po. 59–7 When *m·* with the universe,

minifying
My. 227–5 *m·* of his own goodness by another.

Minister
Mis. 151–13 our *M·* and the great Physician :

minister
Mis. 98–10 to *m·* and to be ministered unto ;
   289–29 by a magistrate, or by a *m·*
   296–11 noble women who *m·* in the sick-room

minister
   Mis. 357– 4 Christian Scientists *m·* to the sick ;
   Ret. 14–19 The *m·* then wished me to tell him
   My. 323– 6 * by some *m·* in the far West.

ministered
   Mis. 98–10 to minister and to be *m·* unto ;

ministering
   Mis. 257–29 Samaritan *m·* to his neighbor's need.
   Ret. 91–18 *m·* to the spiritual needs of all who

ministers
   Mis. 5– 9 and *m·*, to heal the sick
       33– 5 all *m·* and ministries of Christ,
     158–29 as our churches ordain *m·*.
   Pul. 45–25 * succeeded by the grandest of *m·*

ministration
   Ret. 92– 5 His order of *m·* was
   Pul. 34–12 * divine illumination and *m·*.

ministrations
   No. 40–14 pursue their mental *m·* very sacredly,
   My. 130–29 in all your public *m·*,
     208–17 *m·* of God to man.

ministries
   Mis. 33– 6 all ministers and *m·* of Christ,
   My. 230– 3 amid *m·* aggressive and active,

ministry
   Mis. 138– 8 in your *m·* and healing.
     195–14 the *m·* of healing at this period.
   Ret. 88–26 adopt the spirit of the Saviour's *m·*,
   Pul. 20–11 my original system of *m·*
     53– 8 * three years of his *m·* on earth,
   My. 24– 4 * all who accept its divine *m·*.
     28–30 * whose *m·* has revealed the one true
    123–27 to attain to the *m·* of righteousness
    147–17 This *m·*, reaching the physical,
    153– 6 The healing and the gospel *m·*
    327–30 * will dignify the *m·* of Christ
    352– 9 * with its years of tender *m·*,

Ministry of Healing, The
   No. 29–11 Dr. Gordon's sermon on The *M· of H·*,

Minn. (State)
   (*see* **Duluth, Minneapolis, St. Paul**)

Minneapolis, Minn.
   Pul. 90–10 * *Times*, *M·*, *M·*.
     90–11 * *Tribune*, *M·*, *M·*.
   My. 193–14 chapter sub-title

Minneapolis* (Minn.) *News
   My. 275– 1 [*M·* (*M·*.) *N·*]

minor
   Mis. 330– 8 and, if on *m·* key,
   Pul. 42– 7 * scarcely even a *m·* variation
   Rud. 16–23 *M·* shades of difference in
   '01. 4– 4 must be convertible to the *m·*.
   '02. 9–16 *m·* tones of so-called material life
   Po. 65–22 hath its music in low *m·* tones,
   My. 255– 7 I do not mean that *m·* officers

minority
   Mis. 308–13 those are a *m·* of its readers,
   Rud. 8–16 Truth is in the *m·*
   Peo. 3– 7 election of the *m·* to be saved
   My. 294– 2 a large *m·* on the subject

minstrel (*see also* **minstrel's**)
   Mis. 394–10 The harp of the *m·*,
   Po. 45–13 The harp of the *m·*,

minstrel's
   Mis. 384– 2 Come, in the *m·* lay ;
   Po. 36– 1 Come, in the *m·* lay ;

minus
   Un. 10–23 like commencing with the *m·* sign,
   '01. 25–15 demonstration of matter *m·*,
   '02. 7– 7 *M·* this spiritual understanding
   My. 350– 5 is *m·* divine logic

minute
   Mis. 158–19 God's servants are *m·* men

minutes
   Mis. 95– 6 * ten *m·* in which to reply
     353–16 bucket of water every ten *m·*
   Man. 61–24 about eight or nine *m·*
     62– 1 six or seven *m·* for the
   Ret. 40–10 stood by her side about fifteen *m·*
   Pul. 43–19 * A few *m·* of silent prayer came next,
   My. 32– 3 * five *m·* of silent communion
     38–12 * filled . . . in about twenty *m·*,
    49–21 * "The *m·* of the previous meeting
    82–18 * in something like ten *m·*.
    333– 9 * *m·* record this further proceeding :

minutiæ
   Mis. 166–29 entered into the *m·* of the
     204–24 all the *m·* of human affairs.

miracle
   Mis. 5–22 seem a *m·* and a mystery
     77–30 the *m·* of grace appears,
    98–16 Chicago, — the *m·* of the Occident.
    99– 6 To weave . . . is a *m·* in itself.
    294– 6 *m·* in the universe of mortal mind.
    321– 4 whose birth is less of a *m·*
   Ret. 24–20 Spirit had wrought the *m·*
    24–20 a *m·* which later I found
    75–14 do a *m·* in my name, — *Mark* 9 : 39.
   Pul. 8–15 erect this "*m·* in stone."
    34–21 Spirit had wrought a *m·*,"
    60– 9 * *m·* of loaves and fishes.
   Hea. 11–11 is the *m·* of the hour,
    11–12 great pyramid . . . a *m·* in stone.
   Peo. 4–21 No *m·* of grace can make a
   My. 109–25 not alone by *m·* and parable,
    126–12 no longer a mystery or a *m·*,
    216–12 a *m·* that frightens people,

miracles
   Mis. 29–27 *M·* are no infraction of
    54–26 *as great m· in healing as*
    77–30 *m·* of Jesus had their birth,
    199–14 *m·* recorded in the Scriptures
    199–27 The so-called *m·* contained in
    200–16 the so-called *m·* of our Master,
    202– 1 basis of all supposed *m·* ;
    340–26 *m·* of patience and perseverance.
   Ret. 26–12 The *m·* recorded in the Bible,
    80–26 no greater *m·* known to earth
   Hea. 15–13 so-called *m·* recorded in
   My. 80– 2 * back to the age of *m·*.
    95–20 * telling of *m·* performed in this
    107–22 wouldst thou mock God's *m·*
    123–25 Scientist is not frightened at *m·*,
    188–32 ascends the scale of *m·*
    191– 2 *m·* that thou doest, — *John* 3 : 2.

miraculous
   Mis. 88–25 * as imported ice was *m·* to
    104–11 sin is *m·* and supernatural ;
    104–14 perfection is normal, — not *m·*.
   Ret. 26–15 pronounce Christ's healing *m·*,
   Pul. 35– 7 * Christ's healing was not *m·*,
   Rud. 17–12 she needed *m·* vision to
   My. 95–22 * their disbelief in the *m·*.

miraculously
   Pul. 66–11 * rescued from death *m·*

mirage
   '01. 14–15 unreal as a *m·* that misleads

Miriam
   Pul. 82–19 * True, there were *M·* and Esther,

Miriams
   Pul. 82–22 * and *M·* by the million,

mirror
   Mis. 23–28 likeness thrown upon the *m·*
    203– 8 it will always *m·* their love,

mirrored
   Po. 23– 9 *M·* in truth, in light and joy,
   My. 150–16 See therein the *m·* sky
    208– 5 *m·* forth by your loving hearts,

mirrors
   Pul. 27– 2 * with full-length French *m·*
   Po. 25– 1 *M·* of morn

mirth
   Mis. 324– 6 the sounds of festivity and *m·* ;

misapprehending
   Mis. 345–25 distorting or *m·* the purpose

misapprehension
   Mis. 290–12 *m·* of the divine Principle
   Un. 53–13 is a *m·* of being,
   Rud. 1–11 affords a large margin for *m·*,
   No. 7– 6 *m·* as to the motives of others.
   My. 251–16 some *m·* of my meaning

misapprehensive
   Mis. 290–22 conjectural and *m·* !

misbelief
   Un. 38–12 *m·* must enthrone another power,

miscall
   Mis. 250– 5 misrepresent and *m·* affection ;
   Un. 29–17 What the physical senses *m·* soul,
    44–15 Human theories call, or *m·*,

miscalled
   Mis. 95–18 which spiritualists have *m·*
    123–13 or a *m·* man or woman !
    361– 6 its *m·* life ends in death,
   No. 22–10 Such *m·* metaphysical systems

miscellaneous
   Mis. x– 6 to collect my *m·* writings

Miscellaneous Writings
p. 127
    My. 18–16   (*M· W·*, p. 127.)

    Man. 3– 1   heading
    My. 318– 6 proofreader for my book "*M· W·*,"

mischief
    Mis. 230– 9 gossiping *m·*, making lingering calls,
        287–31 Great *m·* comes from attempts to
    Un. 15–24 who seeks to do them *m·*,
    My. 211–27 unless the cause of the *m·* is found

mischief-making
    Man. 81–23 No idle gossip, no slander, no *m·*,

mischievous
    Mis. 245–21 most *m·* to the human heart,

misconceived
    No. 14– 1 It is neither warped nor *m·*,

misconception
    Mis. 46–13 such a *m·* of Truth is not scientific,
        108–21 *m·* of what we need to know of evil,
        124–11 Moslem's *m·* of Deity,
        188– 9 *m·* of God and man,
        350–20 because of the *m·* of those subjects
    Ret. 83–16 communicates, . . . his *m·* of Truth,
    No. 5–25 a lost jewel in this *m·* of reality.

misconceptions
    Ret. 70– 2 names and natures upon its own *m·*.
    No. 8–20 over the *m·* of C. S.,

misconduct
    Mis. 265–23 misstatements or *m·* of this student.

misconstrued
    Mis. 250– 9 No word is more *m·* ;
    No. 32–12 ignorantly or maliciously *m·*.

misconstrues
    My. 180–25 rebels, *m·* our best motives,

misdeeds
    Mis. 264– 6 others stumble over *m·*,

misemployed
    Mis. 312–23 reason too supine or *m·*

miserable
    Mis. 224– 6 to be *m·* for the faults of others.
    Hea. 14–14 ignorance and . . . are *m·* medical aids.
    My. 195–20 no *m·* piece of ideal legerdemain,
        211–24 *m·* lies, poured . . . into his mind,
        312– 8 * in a *m·* plight.

misery
    Mis. 327– 2 my *m·* increased ;

misfortune
    Mis. 119– 5 then whining over *m·*,
    Pul. 37–22 * the *m·* of a church depending on

misguide
    '00. 9–13 bias human judgment and *m·* action,
    '01. 20–16 could not bewilder, darken, or *m·*
    My. 111–22 and unwittingly *m·* his followers?

misguided
    Mis. 114– 9 *m·*, and so made to misteach others.
        268–20 enlightening the *m·* senses,
        291–30 *m·* individual who keeps not watch over
        353–11 attention of the *m·*, fallible sort,
    Ret. 79–17 If beset with *m·* emotions,

misguides
    Mis. 363–23 *m·* reason and affection,
    My. 153–19 *m·* the understanding,

misguiding
    Mis. 78–19 *M·* the public mind and

misinterpret
    Mis. 194–10 *m·* evangelical religion.
    '01. 12–16 *m·* evangelical religion.

misinterpretation
    Mis. 169– 7 through the *m·* of the Word,
    No. 32– 1 The *m·* of such passages has
    My. 238–20 no possibility of *m·*.

misinterpreted
    Hea. 6– 9 I knew it was *m·*,
    My. 213–25 *m·* by the adverse influence

misinterprets
    Ret. 83–15 if he *m·* the text to his pupils,
    My. 304–29 first attack . . . Mrs. Eddy *m·* the

misjudge
    Mis. 66–22 Cynical critics *m·* my meaning
    '01. 4–21 Those who *m·* us because we

misjudged
    Mis. 94– 1 if you . . . are *m·* and maligned ;
        236– 2 human passions . . . have *m·* motives

misjudgment
    Mis. 13– 5 falsehood, ingratitude, *m·*,
        66– 8 no human *m·* can pervert it ;

mislead
    Ret. 83–12 which *m·* no one and are
    '01. 20–12 opportunity to *m·* the human mind,
    My. 5–31 may mesmerize and *m·* man ;
        178– 2 do not *m·* the seeker after Truth.

misleading
    No. 3–28 Plagiarism . . . are tempting and *m·*.
    My. 318–10 as ungrammatical as it was *m·*.

misleads
    '01. 14–15 mirage that *m·* the traveller

misled
    Mis. 222–12 In this state of *m·* consciousness,
        302–13 the temptation to be *m·*.
    Un. 44–10 was *m·* by a false personality,
    My. 212–23 they are being deceived and *m·*.

misname
    No. 27–20 personality, which we *m·* man,

misnamed
    Mis. 76–22 *m·* human soul is material sense,
        201– 4 resolves the element *m·* matter
        327– 1 turned my *m·* joys to sorrow.
    Un. 32–15 *m·* mind is a false claim,
        37–22 mortal mind which is *m·* man,
    '00. 3–26 Yahwah, *m·* Jehovah, was a god of

misnomer
    '00. 4– 1 This seedling *m·* couples love and

misquoting
    My. 110–30 *m·* of "S. *and* H. with Key to the

misread
    '01. 34–11 Have we *m·* the evangelical precepts

misrepresent
    Mis. 109– 2 Beware of those who *m·* facts ;
        250– 5 Mortals *m·* and miscall affection ;
    Ret. 75–13 misunderstand or *m·* the author.

misrepresentation
    Mis. 245– 9 efforts . . . to retard by *m·*

misrepresentations
    Un. 44– 1 *m·* are made concerning my doctrines,
    My. 354– 3 because of alleged *m·* by persons

misrepresented
    Mis. 132–27 * "If we have in any way *m·*
    Man. 41–10 *m·* by the churches and the press,
    My. 139–12 *m·*, belied, and trodden upon.
        363–22 My address . . . has been *m·*

misrepresenting
    My. 105–31 must refrain from persecuting and *m·*

misrepresents
    Mis. 353–12 *m·* one through malice or ignorance.
    My. 306– 1 persistently *m·* my character,

misrule
    Ret. 11–10 No despot bears *m·*,
    Po. 60– 7 No despot bears *m·*,

Miss
    Man. 110–14 Women must sign "*M·*" or " Mrs."
        111– 8 unmarried women must sign "*M·*."

miss
    Mis. 356–31 or you will *m·* the way of Truth
    Po. 3– 3 I *m·* thee as the flower the dew !

missed
    My. 93–23 * many of us have *m·* entirely its

missing
    My. 151–25 thus *m·* the discovery of all cause

mission
divine
    Pul. 71–23 * having a divine *m·* to fulfil,
earthly
    Mis. 74–15 His earthly *m·* was to translate
her
    Pul. 73–12 * Her *m·* was then the mission of a
        85– 5 * who now, in part, understand her *m·*,
his
    '01. 10–30 After Jesus had fulfilled his *m·*
    My. 111–22 Did Jesus mistake his *m·*
        246–27 spirit of his *m·*, the wisdom of his
holy
    Pan. 9–19 aided, not hindered, in his holy *m·*.
human
    Ret. 32– 2 on its divinely appointed human *m·*,
its
    Mis. 304–20 * fulfilling its *m·* throughout the
        308–21 fulfilled its *m·*, retired with honor
Jesus'
    Hea. 18–19 Jesus' *m·* extended to the sick
Messianic
    Mis. 162–12 point of his Messianic *m·* was peace,
    Ret. 70–10 Messianic *m·* of Christ Jesus ;
Mrs. Eddy's
    Pul. 72–25 * it was Mrs. Eddy's *m·* to revive it.

mission
my
  Mis. 278– 6   I shall fulfil my *m·*,
  Ret. 24–23   to ponder my *m·*, to search the
of a Christian
  Pul. 73–12   * *m·* of a Christian, to do good
of Christian Science
  Mis. 4–29   *m·* of C. S. to heal the sick,
of Jesus
  Ret. 70–16   *m·* of Jesus of Nazareth.
of missions
  Pul. 81–26   * Hers is the *m·* of missions
of our Master
  My. 122–29   *m·* of our Master was to all mankind,
spirit and
  Mis. 372–22   concerning the spirit and *m·* of
such a
  My. 150–10   the service of such a *m·*.
their
  Mis. 98–24   attest the authenticity of their *m·*,
three-years
  Mis. 163– 5   his three-years *m·* was a marvel
thy
  Mis. 392–10   Whate'er thy *m·*, mountain sentinel,
  Po. 20–14   Whate'er thy *m·*, mountain sentinel,

  Mis. 347–25   *m·* of those whom He has anointed.
  My. 90–16   * has a *m·* that can be readily
missionaries
  Mis. 123– 1   massacres our *m·*,
missionary
  Mis. 304– 9   * as a *m·* of freedom,
  Pul. 6–19   * a *m·* to China, in 1884.
missions
  Pul. 81–26   * Hers is the mission of *m·*
missives
  My. 53– 1   * important *m·* of inquiry
Missouri and **Mo.**
  My. 207– 8   * societies of C. S. in *M·*,
  207–17   * signature
  (*see also* **Kansas City, St. Joseph, St. Louis**)
misstate
  Mis. 70– 1   or else the Scriptures *m·*
  173– 2   man's theorems, *m·* mental Science,
misstatement
  Mis. 174– 2   Matter is a *m·* of Mind ;
  188– 9   *m·* and misconception of God
  Ret. 56– 7   *m·* of the unerring divine Principle
  Un. 35–21   this one is a *m·* of Mind,
  My. 304– 2   chapter sub-title
misstatements
  Mis. 265–22   not morally responsible for the *m·*
  Un. 20– 5   these three statements, or *m·*,
mist
  Mis. 30–28   "There went up a *m·* — *Gen.* 2 : 6.
  30–29   the *m·* of materialism will vanish
  85–21   Temptation, that *m·* of mortal mind
  156– 9   when the *m·* shall melt away
  355–17   To strike out . . . against the *m·*,
  355–27   fall in *m·* and showers
  Pan. 6– 8   not as one that beateth the *m·*,
  '02. 2– 2   through the *m·* of mortal strife
  Po. 65–18   darkness and death like *m·* melt away,
  My. 290–21   Through a momentary *m·* he beheld
mistake
following
  Mis. 299– 7   look . . . at the following *m·*,
forgive a
  Mis. 118–13   yearn to forgive a *m·*,
grave
  Mis. 291– 5   notion that . . . is a grave *m·* ;
great
  My. 317– 9   It is a great *m·* to say that I
his
  Mis. 265–16   his *m·* is visited upon himself
in physics
  Mis. 264–30   more fatal than a *m·* in physics.
made the
  Pul. 6–12   made the *m·* of thinking she
may have occurred
  My. 311–15   a *m·* may have occurred as to the
mild
  Mis. 109–12   Even a mild *m·* must be seen as a
mortal
  Mis. 339–16   it points to every mortal *m·* ;
  362–11   Theologians make the mortal *m·* of
of believing
  Mis. 223–15   alas ! for the *m·* of believing in
one single
  Mis. 130–20   accomplished, without one single *m·*,
seen as a
  Mis. 109–12   must be seen as a *m·*, in order to

mistake
single
  Mis. 264–29   A single *m·* in metaphysics,
this
  My. 284–17   next issue please correct this *m·*.
to be rectified
  Un. 20– 1   How is a *m·* to be rectified?
which will die
  Un. 53–13   a *m·* which will die of its own delusion ;

  Mis. 10–14   If they *m·* the divine command,
  18–28   This is the *m·* that causes
  87–18   *which is certainly a m·.*
  284– 8   thus *m·* the sphere of his
  298–27   I say, You *m·* ;
  298–29   When unconscious of a *m·*,
  300– 7   We answer, It is a *m·* ;
  302–16   If . . . Scientists occasionally *m·*
  Ret. 83–13   student may *m·* in his conception of
  Un. 26– 9   *Good.* You *m·*, O evil !
  '00. 6– 3   Only the demonstrator can *m·*
  My. 111–21   Did Jesus *m·* his mission
  213–16   working so subtly that we *m·* its
  229– 2   unless I *m·* their calling.
  348–28   demonstrator of this Science may *m·*,
mistaken
  Mis. 66– 2   false testimony or *m·* evidence
  107– 3   *m·* for the oracles of God.
  216–18   the best may be *m·*.
  248–13   *m·* views of Mrs. Eddy's book,
  283–17   nothing less than a *m·* kindness,
  285– 7   *m·* for the corrected edition,
  288– 3   convictions . . . may be *m·* ;
  290– 9   *M·* views ought to be dissolving
  291– 1   *M·* or transient views are human :
  298–29   one thinks he is not *m·*,
  Rud. 12–13   aided in this *m·* fashion,
  12–17   *m·* belief that they live in
  No. 6–15   the *m·* healer is not successful,
  Pan. 11– 7   Was our Master *m·* in judging a
  Hea. 8–17   *m·* views entertained of Deity
  Peo. 11–24   *m·* in their methods of humanity.
  My. 211– 6   This *m·* way, of hiding sin
  234–10   not task themselves with *m·* means.
  357– 8   only incentive of a *m·* sense
mistakenly
  Pul. 7–17   *m·* committed in the name of religion.
mistakes
  Mis. 72– 3   because of his parents' *m·*
  130–24   should avoid referring to past *m·*.
  265– 7   make *m·* and lose their way.
  266– 7   but he *m·* me,
  266–24   If I correct *m·* which may be made
  299– 1   suffering and *m·* recur until
  308– 5   Whosoever looks to . . . *m·*.
  No. 9– 5   It is true that the *m·*, prejudices,
  9–24   More *m·* are made in its name
  28– 1   their present *m·* would extinguish
  My. 301–18   *m·* fable for fact
  322–10   * correcting *m·* widely published
mistaking
  Mis. 284–12   are in no danger of *m·* their way.
  Ret. 57–25   *M·* divine Principle for corporeal
  My. 81–21   * in a way there was no *m·*.
  342– 6   * There was no *m·* that.
  342–10   * There is no *m·* certain lines
  342–11   * there is no *m·* the eyes
mistaught
  Mis. 240–20   Children not *m·*, naturally love
misteach
  Mis. 114–10   and so made to *m·* others.
misteaching
  Man. 55–21   *M·*.
mistiness
  No. 20–23   Adam's *m·* and Satan's reasoning,
mists
  Mis. 107– 9   above the seeming *m·* of sense,
  205– 4   through the *m·* of materiality
  251–30   as the mountain *m·* before the sun.
  264– 8   shadows thrown upon the *m·* of time,
  363–20   Even through the *m·* of mortality
  No. 16–23   *m·* of matter — sin, sickness, and
  28– 3   the *m·* of error, sooner or later,
  Pan. 2– 7   above the *m·* of pantheism
  Peo. 5–11   not lost in the *m·* of remoteness
misty
  Mis. 393– 9   within the *m·* Mine of human thoughts,
  Po. 51–14   within the *m·* Mine of human thoughts,
  My. 341–27   * change from the *m·* air outside
misunderstand
  Ret. 75–12   *m·* or misrepresent the author.

misunderstanding
Man. 64–23 the public *m·* of this name,

misunderstood
Mis. 105–21 If either is *m·* or maligned,
My. 363–22 evidently *m·* by some students.

misuse
'01. 19–23 susceptible *m·* of the human mind,

misused
Mis. 310– 4 teachings of Jesus would be *m·* by

mite
Pul. 45– 2 * some giving a *m·* and some
Hea. 7–18 dropped her *m·* into the treasury,

mitigating
My. 265–18 are *m·* and destroying sin,

mix
Mis. 40– 4 to *m·* material methods with the
   175–28 The attempt to *m·* matter and Mind,
'01. 22– 6 I do not try to *m·* matter and Spirit,
   22– 7 and they will not *m·*.
   25–10 which *m·* matter and mind,
Hea. 4–14 We expect infinite Truth to *m·* with

mixed
Ret. 33–16 *m·* with the faith of ages,
My. 292–23 croton oil is not *m·* with morphine

mixing
Mis. 371–15 *m·* all grades of persons is not
   371–17 he who has self-interest in this *m·*
'01. 19–12 The notion that *m·* material and

mixture
Mis. 248–12 the *m·* would be labelled thus :

moan
Mis. 330– 4 to *m·* over the new-made grave,
   396– 1 The wild winds mutter, howl, and *m·*,
Chr. 53–57 no broken wing, no *m·*,
Po. 58–13 The wild winds mutter, howl, and *m·*,
   73– 9 list the *m·* Of the billows' foam,

moaning
Mis. 225–22 sofa whereon lay the lad . . . *m·*

moans
Po. 15– 3 *m·* from the footsteps of time!

mob
Mis. 224– 7 *m·* had broken the head of his
Po. vi–12 *In 1835 a m· in Boston*

mock
'01. 16–26 go to *m·*, and go away to pray
'02. 18– 7 only to *m·*, wonder, and perish.
Po. 73–20 E'er to *m·* the bright truth
My. 107–22 wouldst thou *m·* God's miracles
   258–22 blossoms that *m·* their hope

mocked
Pul. 7–22 "God is not *m·*," — *Gal.* 6 : 7.
My. 6– 5 "God is not *m·* :— *Gal.* 6 : 7.
   201–14 thorns, which *m·* the bleeding brow

mockeries
Mis. 51–24 * whole dark pile of human *m·* ;

mockery
'02. 14–19 *m·*, envy, rivalry, and
My. 262–24 seem a human *m·*

mocking
Un. 33–23 find them . . . *m·* the Scripture

mockingly
Un. 58– 7 His persecutors said *m·*,

mocks
Mis. 274–19 *m·* morality, outrages humanity,
   351–30 *m·* the bliss of spiritual being ;

mode
Mis. 98–13 felt in a higher *m·* of medicine ;
   165–32 found in the order, *m·*, and
   211– 3 His *m·* is not cowardly,
   257– 3 in every *m·* and form of evil.
   277–14 present *m·* of attempting this
   349– 9 metaphysical *m·* of obstetrics
   361– 9 When every form and *m·* of evil
   362– 6 and reflects all real *m·*, form,
   363–11 material *m·* of a suppositional
   366–29 according to His *m·* of C. S. ;
Ret. 89– 2 divine potency of this spiritual *m·*
Un. 8– 6 is a *m·* of consciousness,
No. 17–15 Matter, or any *m·* of mortal mind,
   25–15 neither matter nor a *m·* of mortal
   25–16 immortal *m·* of the divine Mind.
'01. 12– 1 *m·* of worship may be intangible,
   34– 7 Christ's *m·* and means of healing,
My. 49–25 * *m·* of conducting the church."
   106–10 above matter in every *m·* and form,
   248–23 Christ *m·* of understanding Life
   251–17 as to the *m·* of instruction

Model
Mis. 159–27 how has our *M·*, Christ, been unveiled

model
Mis. 98– 2 perfect *m·* should be held in mind,
   308–31 is not the *m·* for a metaphysician.
Ret. 22– 9 as the *m·* of Christianity,
   93–16 it becomes the *m·* for human action.
Un. 14–11 shortcomings of the Puritan's *m·*
   14–22 Our infinite *m·* would be taken away.
No. 41–15 to compare mortal lives with this *m·*
Pan. 11–13 to turn from clay to Soul for the *m·*
'01. 6–17 because He is not after this *m·*
Hea. 2–17 Jesus, the *m·* of infinite patience,
   4–24 God must be our *m·*, or we have none ;
   4–25 if this *m·* is one thing at one time,
   4–26 can we rely on our *m·*?
   19–23 according to the *m·* on the mount,
Peo. 7– 6 turn often from marble to *m·*,
   9–14 after the *m·* of our Father,
   10–20 marred in mind the *m·* of man.
My. 123– 8 continue to urge the perfect *m·*
   261–14 unfolding the immortal *m·*,
   361– 6 stated in C. S. to be used as a *m·*.

models
Mis. 353– 6 they are neither standards nor *m·*.
Rud. 3–12 *m·* of the masters in music
Peo. 14–11 form our *m·* of humanity.
My. 111–19 healers and *m·* of good morals,

moderately
My. 93– 8 * any class save the *m·* well-to-do,

moderating
Mis. 360– 1 Meekness, *m·* human desire,

moderation
Un. 5–20 letting our "*m·* be known — *Phil.* 4 : 5.

modern
Mis. 173– 1 Ancient and *m·* philosophy,
   225– 9 the seventh *m·* wonder, C. S. ;
   274–28 the car of the *m·* Inquisition
   333–31 ancient or *m·* Christians,
   344–16 Ancient and *m·* philosophies
Ret. 34– 7 Neither ancient nor *m·* philosophy
   57– 4 Neither ancient nor *m·* philosophy
   89– 6 in the *m·* sense of the term.
Pul. 32–12 * questioned this *m·* St. Catherine,
   47–13 * No ancient or *m·* philosophy gave
   54–19 * in the light of *m·* science,
   64–18 * *m·* philosophy gave her no
No. 11–23 Ancient and *m·* human philosophy
'00. 6–28 Some *m·* exegesis on the
'01. 16– 7 scarcely equal the *m·* nondescripts,
   27–16 Or if a *m·* St. Paul could
Peo. 11–16 *m·* Pharaohs that hold the
My. 70–21 * both ancient and *m·* masters,
   98–10 * hardly parallel in *m·* times,
   103–22 * in ancient or in *m·* systems
   107– 7 a *m·* phase of medical practice,
   345–25 * pursuit of *m·* material inventions

modernized
Pul. 47–28 * delightfully remodelled and *m·*

modes
Mis. 71–19 suppositional *m·*, not the factors of
   88–24 * or understand its *m·*
   88–29 are opposite *m·* of medicine.
   102–18 expressed in *m·* above the human.
   112– 6 ages are burdened with material *m·*.
   114–32 to guard against evil and its silent *m·*,
   136– 3 routine of such material *m·* as
   257–15 a code whose *m·* trifle with joy,
   268– 1 materializes human *m·* and
   270–25 through the *m·* and methods of God.
   293– 3 all the claims and *m·* of evil ;
   293– 6 unerring *m·* of divine wisdom.
   360– 8 *m·* of mind cast in the moulds of
   360–32 No advancing *m·* of human mind
   361–32 The divine *m·* and manifestations
   362–19 whose *m·* are material manifestations
   363–12 immortal *m·* of Mind are spiritual,
   363–17 His *m·* declare the beauty of holiness,
   364–27 has the same power or *m·*
   364–29 would either extinguish . . . His *m·*, or
   366–22 as *m·* of medicine.
Un. 52–27 supposed *m·* of self-conscious matter,
No. 15–21 nor in the *m·* of mortal mind.
   21–16 material *m·*, wherein the human
   39–12 nor bring His designs into mortal *m·* ;
   39–13 it can and does change our *m·*
My. 111– 5 crude theories or *m·* of metaphysics.
   211–14 *m·* of good, in their silent
   213–15 *m·* of mental malpractice,
   221–16 Then *m·* of healing, other than
   266–17 all codes, *m·*, hypotheses, of man
   266–27 spiritual *m·* and significations

modes
My.	267–30	of all the divine m·, means, forms,
	302– 1	all m· of healing disease
	349–20	Divine m· or manifestations are

modest
Mis.	145–20	their m· sign be nothingness.
	172– 1	to keep their demonstrations m·,
	243–18	students are proverbially m· :
	330–30	the m· grass, inhabiting the
	372–24	the m· glory of divine Science.
	395–12	Veiled is the m· moon
Ret.	17–10	and the m· Moss-rose ;
No.	2–17	is m· in his claims
	3– 4	m·, generous, and sincere !
	44– 3	failure should make him m·.
Hea.	11–10	her m· tower rises slowly,
Po.	57–19	Veiled is the m· moon
	62–11	and the m· Moss-rose ;
My.	6–17	m· edifice of The Mother Church
	39–18	* my m· task will be ended.
	123–10	in Concord, N. H., we have a m· hall
	147– 9	have provided for you a m· hall,
	271–13	* In a m·, pleasantly situated home

modestly
My.	9–15	* we m· renew the hope

modesty
Ret.	94–25	m· and distinguishing affection
My.	357–12	spiritual m· of C. S.,

modification
Mis.	193–18	a m· of silence on this subject,
No.	v– 6	By a m· of the language,

modifications
Mis.	68–29	* from its phenomenal m·."
'02.	2–19	present m· in ecclesiasticism

modified
Ret.	82– 1	changed, m·, broadened,
My.	266–27	agitated, m·, and disappearing,

modify
Mis.	67–29	I m· my affirmative answer.

modus
Mis.	380– 3	human m· for demonstrating this,
Ret.	24–19	explain the m· of my relief.
'01.	20–25	its hidden m· and flagrance

modus operandi
Mis.	117–19	movements, or m· o·, of other folks.
	156–15	student's opinions or m· o·
Pan.	12– 3	rejection of evil and its m· o·.
'02.	10–26	m· o· of human error,
My.	292–18	against the m· o· of another,

Mohammed
Pan.	8–10	doctrine that M· is the only prophet

Mohammedan
Pan.	7–15	the Christian, and the M·.

moiety
Mis.	317–15	Scarcely a m·, . . . is yet assimilated

molds
Po.	78– 6	Till m· the hero form?

molecule
Mis.	173–28	Whence, then, is the atom or m·
	313– 6	the scientific spiritual m·,
	363– 5	from m· and monkey up to man,
Un.	35–23	m·, as matter, is not formed by
No.	26–21	never originated in m·, corpuscle,
'02.	10– 5	and their power over matter, m·,
My.	110–11	progress from m· and mortals
	278–10	Let us have the m· of faith

molecules
Mis.	26–14	Was it m·, or material atoms?
	205–28	The encumbering mortal m·,

molestation
Ret.	44–21	envy and m· of other churches,

mollusca
My.	271– 3	no vertebrata, m·, or radiata.

mollusk
Mis.	361–10	m· and radiate are spiritual concepts

molten
Peo.	2–23	a personal tyrant or a m· image,
My.	269–18	This hour is m· in the furnace
	303–31	This glory is m· in the furnace of

moment (see also moment's)
Mis.	15–13	not the work of a m·.
	16–27	pause for a m· with me,
	34–22	not a m· when he ceases to
	42– 8	a m· of extreme mortal fear,
	60–11	apparent in a m·.
	85–12	is not won in a m· ;
	93–30	to indulge . . . for even one m·.
	127–29	word spoken, at the right m·,
	154–30	Forget not for a m·, that

moment
Mis.	188–28	At the m· of her discovery,
	280–32	just at the m· when you are
	307– 5	have all you need every m·.
	375–15	* devoting every m· to the study
Ret.	21–26	are frivolous and of no m·,
	23–13	Thus it was when the m· arrived
	72– 9	desolation, as in a m· ! — Psal. 73 : 19.
	89–13	bidden . . . at that particular m·.
Un.	63– 4	were never absent for a m·.
Pul.	2–12	think for a m· with me of the
	30–22	* need of living faith at the m·
Rud.	11–16	In a m· you may awake from
No.	24–25	There was never a m· in which
'01.	15–24	* from being this m· swallowed up
	16– 1	* reason why you do not at this m·
Hea.	4– 3	nor remain for a m· within limits.
Peo.	12– 2	we should think for one m·
My.	173–12	a note, sent at the last m·,
	224– 2	that demand at the m·,
	250–23	can wait for the favored m·
	351– 8	earliest m· in which to answer it.

momentarily
Mis.	283–21	may m· be forgotten ;

momentary
Mis.	42– 6	After the m· belief of dying
	228–14	m· success of all villainies,
My.	290–21	Through a m· mist he beheld

momentous
Mis.	63–29	that m· demonstration of God,
	337– 4	how can you be certain of so m· an
	379–28	m· facts relating to Mind
No.	28– 9	these m· facts in the Science of
My.	42–23	* significance of this m· occasion.
	45–17	* revealed to you in that m· hour
	90–26	* an event of . . . . m· significance.
	360–11	present m· question at issue

moment's
Mis.	342–11	Each m· fair expectancy
My.	144– 5	spare not a m· thought to lies

moments
Mis.	15–14	begins with m·, and goes on with years ;
	15–14	m· of surrender to God,
	15–16	m· of self-abnegation,
	32–21	I have not m· enough in which to
	36–27	as much in our waking m· as
	68– 2	This translation is not the work of m· ;
	230– 3	upon the improvement of m·
	230–15	improving m· before they pass
	356–32	it has no m· for trafficking
'00.	3– 7	He improves m· ; to him time is money,
Po.	65–16	m· most sweet are fleetest alway,
	74– 3	those m· to memory bestowed
My.	17–24	* a few m· of silent prayer
	147– 2	m· when at the touch of memory

momentum
Mis.	110–24	and the m· of C. S.,
Pul.	vii–14	the gain of intellectual m·,

monads
My.	133–13	crumbs and m· will feed the hungry,

monarch (see also monarch's)
Mis.	392– 2	mountain m·, at whose feet I stand,
Po.	20– 1	mountain m·, at whose feet I stand,
	25–15	Be he m· or slave,

monarch's
My.	257–29	have their record in the m· palace,

Monday
Mis.	95– 2	* M· lectureship in Tremont Temple,
	95– 3	* on M·, March 16, 1885,
Man.	25–10	M· preceding the annual meeting
	56–12	M· following the first Sunday in June.
	56–20	M· preceding the annual meeting
	93– 6	M· preceding the Annual Meeting,
My.	171–14	M·, June 13, 1904.

monetary
My.	214–22	no m· means left wherewith to

money
Mis.	67– 8	thou shalt not rob man of m·,
	78–20	taking its m· in exchange for
	80– 6	to give m· and influence
	141–30	what shall be done with their m·.
	144– 2	m· for building "Mother's Room,"
	149– 1	he that hath no m· ; — Isa. 55 : 1.
	149– 3	milk without m· — Isa. 55 : 1.
	242–12	he would lose his m·.
	252–31	the poor man's m· ;
	270– 4	such as barter integrity . . . for m·
	274–26	for m·, place, and power,
	305–23	* m· with which to pay for the bell.
	315–21	shall be no question of m·,
	368–24	are playing only for m·,

money

Man.	80– 7	m· subject to the order of
	83– 6	not be a question of m·,
Ret.	5– 4	gave the m· for erecting the first
	20– 2	except what m· I had brought
	41– 5	"without m· and without— Isa. 55 : 1.
Pul.	8– 8	unemployed in our m· centres,
	8–14	and forth came the m·,
	41– 3	* an appeal, not for more m·,
	42–12	* whose m· was devoted to the
	44–25	* m· has flowed in from all parts
	50– 1	* using her m· to promote the welfare
	59–27	* the m· for the Mother's Room,
	64– 7	* M· came freely from all parts
	64–13	* stop the continued inflow of m·
	71– 7	* m· comes from C. S. believers
	79– 6	* for which the m· was all paid
Pan.	15– 2	destroying millions of her m·,
'00.	2–14	earns his m· and gives it
	2–18	Ask how he gets his m·,
	3– 7	to him time is m·, and he hoards
	10–30	some of his hard-earned m·
	11– 2	more pleasure than millions of m·
'02.	12–30	I furnished the m· from my own
	15– 8	"without m· and without— Isa. 55 : 1.
My.	v–17	* "without m· and without— Isa. 55 : 1.
	10–11	* Some m· has been paid in
	10–21	* not expected to contribute m·
	10–23	* the m· necessary to this end,
	12– 3	* as soon as the m· in hand
	13–18	any part of two millions of m·
	14–29	* necessitates large payments of m·,
	20–26	* of a large amount of m·,
	21– 5	* m· which had been collected
	22– 8	* m· adequate to erect such a
	26–12	gift is the largest sum of m·
	27–16	* requested to send no more m·
	33–25	his m· to usury,— Psal. 15 : 5.
	65–14	* m· to provide it was pledged
	67–20	* m· was used in giving Boston
	67–23	* vaster sums of m· were spent
	72–14	* chapter sub-title
	72–15	* do not send us any more m·
	76– 4	* notices that more m· was needed
	76– 7	* enough m· was on hand
	86–16	* to give no more m·,
	89–19	* petitions for m· are almost as
	96–21	* m· was sent in such quantities that
	98–16	* requested to send no more m·
	98–25	* methods of raising m·.
	99–21	* stuffed and jammed with m·.
	123–15	furnished him the m· to pay for it.
	215– 4	bestowed without m· or price.
	215–12	sent me the full tuition m·.
	215–12	However, I returned this m·
	215–15	* more to me than m· can be."
	216– 3	obtain their m· from a fish's mouth,
	216–29	will want m· for your own uses.
	217– 1	m· that you expend for flowers.
	231– 8	to whom she has given large sums of m·,
	231–10	spend no more time or m·
	312–10	* entirely without m· or friends.
	312–22	amount of m· he would need
	336–13	except what m· I had brought
	358–18	I thank you for the m·

money-bag

Un.	15–26	criminal appeases, with a m·,

moneychangers

Mis.	270– 2	the tables of the m·,— Matt. 21 : 12.

moneyed

Mis.	148–26	collect no m· contributions from

money-making

Mis.	48–10	prompted by m· or malice.

Monitor

Christian Science, The

My.	352–29	first issue of The C. S. M·.
	353– 7	The C. S. M·, November 25, 1908

My.	353–15	the next I named M·,
	353–17	The object of the M· is to

monitor

Mis.	100–20	The spiritual m· understood

monkey

Mis.	233– 9	m· in harlequin jacket
	363– 5	from molecule and m· up to man,

monomania

Mis.	49– 2	had a tendency to m·,

monopolize

Man.	49– 2	shall not endeavor to m·
Un.	9–21	Sometimes it is said, . . . that I m·;

monopoly

Man.	49– 1	No M·.
Un.	10– 8	If there be any m· in my teaching,
My.	129– 4	imperialism, m·, and a lax system of

monotheism

Pan.	4– 1	It is opposed to atheism and m·,
	5– 1	m· is lost and pantheism is found in
	12–21	Christianity is strictly m·,
'00.	4– 9	nearer approach to m·
'01.	5– 5	lose m·, and become less coherent
My.	127–20	purer Protestantism and m·
	303–17	demonstrate Science and its pure m·

monotheist

'02.	12– 8	The Jew who . . . is a m·,
	12–11	The Christian who . . . is a m· :

monotheists

'01.	4–21	Scientists are theists and m·.

Monroe doctrine

My.	282– 3	believe strictly in the M· d·,

monster

Mis.	204– 2	and a mortal seems a m·,

monsters

Peo.	3– 4	ideals of . . . have made m· of men ;

monstrous

Mis.	122– 9	accomplishing such a m· work

Mont Blanc

Un.	64–17	stand on the summit of M· B· ;

month (see also month's)

Mis.	180–27	a m· is called the son of a year.
	314–32	On the first Sunday of each m·,
Man.	18– 4	and the same m· the members,
	40–19	first Sunday of each m·.
	78–24	on the first of the following m·,
Ret.	16–17	and the same m· the members,
	19–16	A m· later I returned to
	44– 6	during the same m· the members,
Pul.	45–11	* one m· before the close of the year
My.	49–10	* in the same m· the members
	55–31	* the twenty-first of last m·,
	272–20	* The Cosmopolitan presents this m·
	290–10	first m· of the new century.
	319–26	* the twentieth of the above-named m·.
	330–28	A m· later I returned to

monthly

Ret.	53– 3	This m· magazine had been made
Pul.	36–26	* The C. S. Journal, a m·

month's

Mis.	54–18	after one m· treatment

months

January

Man.	61–13	on the second Sunday in J·
My.	316–11	article in the J· number

(see also dates, dates — affidavits, dates — chapter sub-titles, dates — newspaper articles)

January 6

Pul.	20–21	church was dedicated on J· 6,
	31– 1	* service on J· 6 shall be

(see also dates — chapter sub-titles, dates — headings, dates — letters to Mrs. Eddy, dates — newspaper articles, dates — telegrams)

January, 6th of

Pul.	56–12	* taking place on the 6th of J·,

January ninth

Mis.	242– 4	came not to my notice until J· n·.

January 17

Mis.	294–29	In an issue of J· 17,

January 29

Pul.	74– 5	* in the Herald on J· 29,

February 3

My.	289–25	on Sunday evening, F· 3,

(see also dates — poems by Mrs. Eddy)

February 22

My.	148–12	completed its organization F· 22

(see also dates)

March

Mis.	279– 9	chapter sub-title
Pan.	1– 7	rushing winds of M· have shrieked
My.	55–22	* In M·, however, the church was

(see also dates, dates — newspaper articles)

March, fifth of

Mis.	280–19	dismissed the f· of M·,

March 18

Mis.	132–13	Zion's Herald, M· 18,

(see also dates)

March, twenty-fifth of last

My.	60–29	* On the t· of l· M·

April

Mis.	158–24	A· number of The C. S. Journal
Pul.	45–16	* could not be completed before A·
Pan.	1– 8	the frown and smile of A·,

(see also dates, dates — newspaper articles)

months

April's
Po. 46– 5 Nor *A·* changeful showers,
April 5
My. 338–14 was delivered in Boston, *A·* 5.
April 30th
Mis. 305–29 * bell shall be cast *A·* 30th,
(see also **dates — interview**)
May
Mis. 216– 8 In the *M·* number of our *Journal*,
384– 5 And all is morn and *M·*.
Pul. 45–16 * before April or *M·* of 1895.
Pan. 1– 9 smile of April, the laugh of *M·*,
Po. 36– 4 And all is morn and *M·*.
My. 254– 4 chapter sub-title
(see also **dates, dates — chapter sub-titles, dates — newspaper articles**)
May 1
My. 198– 3 *Brethren:* — Your letters of *M·* 1
(see also **dates — newspaper articles**)
May first
Man. 77– 4 books are to be audited on *M· f·*.
May 18
My. 137– 5 * was filed . . . *M·* 18.
May 21
My. 284–13 In the issue of . . . the *Patriot*, *M·* 21,
(see also **dates — poems by Mrs. Eddy**)
May 26
My. 51– 3 * *M·* 26 of the same year
(see also **dates — chapter sub-titles**)
June
Mis. 136–22 I recommend that the *J·* session
390– 1 poem
390– 2 Whence are thy wooings, gentle *J·*?
390–20 Ask of its *J·*,
394–15 * "The flowers of *J·*
394–17 * The flowers of *J·*
394–21 * The flowers of *J·*."
395– 2 Who loves not *J·*
395–11 The curtain drops on *J·*;
Man. 56–13 following the first Sunday in *J·*.
57– 4 preceding the first Sunday in *J·*,
Pul. 38– 1 * charter obtained the following *J·*.
Pan. 1– 3 heading
1–10 roseate blush of joyous *J·* is here
Po. page 55 poem
55– 2 Whence are thy wooings, gentle *J·*?
55–21 Ask of its *J·*,
57– 1 * THE flowers of *J·*
57– 3 * The flowers of *J·*
57– 7 * The flowers of *J·*.
57– 9 Who loves not *J·*
57–18 The curtain drops on *J·*;
My. 11–27 * building was decided last *J·*,
25–20 and the dedication in *J·* next
57–24 * *C. S. Journal* of this *J·*
73–16 * *J·* meetings of The Mother Church
254–20 * in the *J· Journal* of 1904,
(see also **dates, dates — addresses, dates — chapter sub-titles**)
June 2
My. 76– 6 * *J·* 2 it became evident to the Board
(see also **dates — notices**)
June 5
My. 57–18 *candidates admitted *J·* 5
(see also **dates — letters from Mrs. Eddy**)
June 10
My. 26–15 My Message for *J·* 10 is ready
61–11 * in the new extension on *J·* 10.
61–18 * ready for the service, *J·* 10."
(see also **dates — chapter sub-titles**)
June 12
My. 38–30 * Tuesday, *J·* 12, at ten o'clock in the
(see also **dates — chapter sub-titles, dates — letters to Mrs. Eddy, dates — telegrams**)
June 13
Mis. 134–18 to be in Chicago on *J·* 13.
(see also **dates — addresses, dates — chapter sub-titles, dates — letters from Mrs. Eddy, dates — letters to Mrs. Eddy**)
June 14
My. 82–21 * at noon to-day [*J·* 14]
141– 7 * attended last Sunday [*J·* 14]
(see also **dates — chapter sub-titles**)
June 19
My. 198– 4 Your letters of May 1 and *J·* 19,
(see also **dates — newspaper articles**)
June 21
My. 141–13 * was made last night [*J·* 21]
(see also **dates — letters from Mrs. Eddy**)
June, 27th
My. 335– 1 * Died . . . on the 27th *J·* last,
June, twenty-seventh of
My. 333–21 * Thursday night, the *t· of J·*.
(see also **dates — letters from Mrs. Eddy**)

months

July
Man. 60– 6 during the months of *J·* and August
61–14 in January and *J·* of each year,
(see also **dates, dates — newspaper articles**)
July 1
Man. 93– 9 shall begin *J·* 1 of each year.
(see also **dates — newspaper articles**)
July 3
My. 329–16 * appear . . . in the issues of *J·* 3
July Fourth
Mis. 176– 4 chapter sub-title
July, Fourth of
Mis. 251– 1 chapter sub-title
(see also **dates, dates — chapter sub-titles**)
July 5
My. 169– 3 I invite you, . . . on *J·* 5,
July, fifth of
My. 122–11 On the *f· of J·* last, my church
July 19
My. 359–19 * a composite letter, dated *J·* 19,
(see also **dates**)
August
Mis. 313– 3 your editorial in the *A·* number
Man. 60– 7 during the months of July and *A·*
(see also **dates, dates — newspaper articles**)
August 22
My. 49–17 * *A·* 22 the Clerk, by instructions
August 27
My. 49–19 * *A·* 27 the church held a meeting,
(see also **dates**)
September
Mis. 88– 7 *critique in the S· number*,
(see also **dates**)
September, first of
My. 54–23 * from the *f· of S·* to our opening,
October
Mis. 61–11 * In the *O· Journal* I read
256–14 *O·* number of the *Journal*,
Pul. 48– 9 * in the gorgeous *O·* coloring
(see also **dates**)
October 11th
Mis. 304–29 * ring at nine o'clock on *O·* 11th,
(see also **dates — letters to Mrs. Eddy**)
October 26
Mis. 168–27 * on the afternoon of *O·* 26,
(see also **dates**)
November
Mis. 376–17 brave splendor of a *N·* sky
Man. 57– 5 first Friday in *N·* of each year.
'01. 3– 1 added since last *N·*
My. 243–19 chapter sub-title
(see also **dates, dates — newspaper articles**)
December
Man. 90–11 first Wednesday of *D·*.
My. 254– 9 chapter sub-title
(see also **dates, dates — chapter sub-titles, dates — newspaper articles**)
December 1
My. 49–29 * *D·* 1 of the same year,
December third
Mis. 242– 3 in *Zion's Herald*, *D· t·*,
December 28
Pul. 23– 8 * Boston, Mass., *D·* 28.
(see also **dates — letters from Mrs. Eddy**)

———

Mis. 110–16 Weeks have passed into *m·*,
110–16 and *m·* into years,
136–25 convening once in four *m·*;
143–23 within about three *m·*,
315–23 as often as once in three *m·*.
Man. 60– 5 continued twelve *m·* each year.
60– 6 *m·* of July and August
Ret. 8– 3 For some twelve *m·*,
19–18 at the end of four *m·*,
20– 5 A few *m·* before my father's
38– 7 After *m·* had passed,
Un. 11–28 There are yet four *m·*,
Pul. 6–13 * "Six *m·* ago your book,
8– 9 Scientists, within fourteen *m·*,
67–28 * charter was obtained two *m·* later.
69– 3 * about eighteen *m·* ago.
Rud. 14–12 often those were put off for *m·*,
'02. 16– 1 Six *m·* thereafter Miss Dorcas Rawson
Po. 54– 1 It may be *m·* or years
My. 52–27 * Within a few *m·* she has
53– 1 * weeks lengthened into *m·*;
55–28 * During the *m·* that
77– 1 * has for *m·* been the cynosure of
145–17 Within the past year and two *m·*,
312– 7 * six *m·* after his marriage,
322–21 * waiting *m·* in Boston
330–29 at the end of four *m·*,
333–28 * brief space of six *m·*,

Montreal
Pul. 67– 4   * The M· Branch
      67–20   * Toronto and M· have strong churches,
'00.   1–22   M·, London, Edinburgh, Dublin,
Montreal (Can.) Gazette
My. 88– 2   *[M· (C·.) G·]
Montreal Daily Herald
Pul. 67– 1   * M· D· H·, Saturday, February 2, 1895
monument
Mis. 141– 2   prophecy fulfilled, the m· upreared,
     166– 3   m· whose finger points upward,
Po.   1–12   Ye rose, a m· of Deity,
My.   6–23   rises to a mental m·,
     36–29   * to stand as an enduring m·,
     45–15   * fitting m· of your obedience
     45–31   * loftier than the Bunker Hill m·,
     74–17   * m· to the sincerity
     76–26   * first great m· to C. S.,
     89–11   * A sect that leaves such a m·
     94–27   "rises to a mental m·,
     287– 2   chapter sub-title
     287– 3   movement to erect a m·
     289– 5   for the De Hirsch m· fund.
monumental
Mis. 388–14   Grave on her m· pile :
Po. 21– 1   Grave on her m· pile :
monuments
Ret. 71– 1   m· which weigh dust,
Peo. 14– 6   smiling fountains, and white m·.
mood
Ret. 75–18   author's own mental m·,
     91–11   indicates more the Master's m·,
Pul. 14– 6   another extreme mortal m·,
moods
Mis. 329– 3   nature in all her m· and forms,
Pan.   3– 8   Certain m· of mind find an
moon
Mis. 323– 6   neither of the m·, for God doth
     395–12   Veiled is the modest m·
Un.   14– 7   m·, and "the stars also," — Gen. 1 : 16.
Pul. 83–28   * the m· under her feet, — Rev. 12 : 1.
Po.   2–13   The m· looks down upon thine
     8–12   O'er the silv'ry m· and ocean flow ;
     57–19   Veiled is the modest m·
My. 150–17   m· ablaze with her mild glory.
     206–12   Seeing a man in the m·,
     206–21   neither of the m·, — Rev. 21 : 23.
     313– 6   By the light of the m·
moonbeam
Ret. 31–25   soft as the heart of a m·,
moonbeams
No. 22–13   they are as m· to the sun,
moon god
Pan.   8– 3   Babylonian sun god, m· g·,
moonlit
Po. 73– 3   I come to thee O'er the m· sea,
Moor, Marion
Ret.   1– 4   my great-grandmother, was Marion M·,
Moore
Charles W.
My. 334–29   * published by the late Charles W. M·,
Mr. George H.
My. 145–15   Mr. George H. M· of Concord,

Po. 41– 2   signature
moored
Mis. 385–11   m· at last — Beyond rough foam.
Po. 48– 4   m· at last — Beyond rough foam.
moral
Mis. 10–23   a m· chemicalization, wherein
     35–22   Why do we read m· science, and then
     37–20   leads to m· or physical death.
     45–14   m· status of the man demands
     45–17   effectual in treating m· ailments.
     73–12   it is always mental and m·,
     73–14   The foolish disobey m· law.
     83–15   you are a free m· agent to reject or
     107–25   this . . . mental state is m· idiocy.
     109– 7   a sure pretext of m· defilement.
     112–15   in extreme cases, m· idiocy.
     112–17   mental state called m· idiocy.
     112–29   total loss of m·, . . . discernment,
     113– 7   free m· agency is lost ;
     113–13   scale of m· and spiritual being,
     113–22   insanity, dementia, or m· idiocy.
     113–32   m·, and spiritual animus is felt
     119–19   a plea for free m· agency,
     131– 3   he will be called a m· nuisance,
     143– 3   the "square" of m· sentiments.
     155–27   fulfilling their m· obligation
     168– 6   m· lepers are cleansed ;

moral
Mis. 199– 7   only to m· and spiritual law,
     204–19   so quickens m· sensibility
     222–11   in other words, a m· idiot.
     240–12   to m· and physical strength
     241–17   Truth heals him of the m· malady.
     241–28   the physical than the m· ailment.
     248– 5   its m· meaning, found in the
     251–26   all error, physical, m·, or
     257– 8   Law is either a m· or an
     257– 9   a m· and spiritual force of
     259–16   m· power of good, not of evil :
     261–28   apprehending the m· law so clearly
     261–32   produced physical and m· harmony.
     264–25   m· and spiritual status of thought
     266– 4   when these sides are m· opposites,
     268–27   From lack of m· strength empires fall.
     284–32   thus it is with all m· obligations.
     297– 4   physical and m· reformation.
     303– 4   as healers physical and m·.
     339–14   m· tension is tested,
     341–27   The m· of the parable is pointed,
     346– 3   m· and spiritual healing
     352–19   in healing the m· sickness ;
     354– 4   m· idiot, sanguine of success in sin,
     365–13   physical and m· harmony ;
     365–17   this want has worked out a m· result ;
     365–19   If the uniform m· and spiritual,
     393– 2   Is the m· that it brings ;
Man. 31– 4   M· Obligations.
     87–15   m· and spiritual qualifications
     91–21   and with good m· records,
Ret. 10– 8   philosophy, logic, and m· science.
     30– 9   include all m· and religious reform.
     35– 5   for physical and m· health
     70–28   civil, m·, and religious reform.
     76–29   strictest observance of m· law
     77– 4   Ingersoll's repartee has its m· :
Un.   8–15   physical, m·, and intellectual,
     13–11   To Him there is no m· inharmony ;
     19–13   would be the end of . . . m· unity.
     35–17   forces of Truth are m· and spiritual,
     36–22   yet admit the reality of m·
     38–23   Life as God, m· and spiritual good,
     60–18   Mortals are free m· agents,
     64– 8   is a m· impossibility.
Pul. 20–17   greatest m·, physical, civil, and
     46–25   * philosophy, logic, and m· science,
     83– 6   * the m· strength and courage
Rud.   2– 2   * person, . . . a m· agent ;
     4–10   a m· and spiritual force,
     5–17   is a m· impossibility.
     8–15   In all m· revolutions,
     17– 6   m· power, and its divine efficacy
No. 13– 4   m· and physical growth,
     18–10   physical and m· harmony,
     18–23   have wrought this m· result,
     19– 1   m· and spiritual, as well as
     23–15   a literal and a m· meaning.
     45–20   its m· and religious reforms.
     46–12   upon free m· agency ;
'01. 20– 2   no m· right and no authority
     20– 7   neither m· right nor might to harm
Hea.   9–11   their m· advisers talk for them
     12–16   the general and m· symptoms
     13– 7   There is a m· to this medicine ;
Peo.   3–15   spans the m· heavens with light,
Po. 51– 7   Is the m· that it brings ;
My. 22–23   * the m· and the physical effects
     52–28   * the m· rightness of her book."
     91–11   * his m· standards debased
     104– 7   That epithet points a m·.
     122– 6   fixed in one's own m· make-up.
     147–18   physical, m·, and spiritual needs
     220–13   the m· signification of law.
     221– 2   and the m· distance between
     221–13   find a better m· philosophy,
     241– 1   * m· and spiritual qualifications
     249– 9   The m· abandon of hating
     249–10   Hate is a m· idiocy let loose
     252–29   it is m·, spiritual, divine.
     294–25   m·, and religious energy
     318–13   m· and spiritual effect upon the age
     364–17   disease, m· or physical.
     (see also **sense**)
morale
Mis. 297–17   statute in the m· of C. S. :
     298–20   the m· of absolute C. S.,
My. 238–17   rises above the letter, law, or m·
     268– 4   the m· of marriage is preserved.
     351–11   m· of Free Masonry is above ethics
moralist
Mis. 265–15   theorist or shallow m· may
Pan. 11–15   the best church-member or m·
My. 297– 2   patriot, philanthropist, m·,

morality

Mis.	274–19	mocks *m·*, outrages humanity,
	286–16	maintain *m·* and generation,
My.	221–24	issues of *m·*, of Christianity,

morally

Mis.	ix– 9	acquired by healing mankind *m·*,
	3– 1	elevating the race physically, *m·*,
	20– 2	heals man . . . *m·* and physically,
	31– 6	harm him *m·*, physically,
	34– 6	but is improved *m·*.
	45–20	better both *m·* and physically.
	67– 7	mentally, *m·*, or physically.
	107–24	may become *m·* blind,
	140– 5	*m·* and spiritually inalienable,
	214–24	mortal mind in being healed *m·*,
	220–20	improved *m·* and physically.
	222–10	he becomes *m·* paralyzed
	222–16	is fatal, *m·* and physically.
	256– 3	at the same time improved *m·*.
	259–24	physically, *m·*, and Christianly,
	265–22	not *m·* responsible for the
	289– 1	degenerate physically and *m·*.
	297–20	*m·* bound to fulfil all the claims
	300–32	Healing *m·* and physically
	301– 9	*m·* responsible for what the
	301–15	too sincere and *m·* statuesque
	315–15	hold himself *m·* obligated to
	357–26	not *m·* responsible for this,
	362–10	physically, *m·*, spiritually.
Man.	83–14	*m·* obligated to promote their
Ret.	34–18	advanced *m·* and spiritually.
Un.	36–19	physically, mentally, *m·*,
Rud.	3–14	will no more deviate *m·*
	8–24	he makes *m·* worse the invalid
No.	13–20	physically, *m·*, and spiritually,
	18–21	the teacher is *m·* responsible.
	22–10	*m·*, spiritually, or physically.
'00.	6–27	are made better physically, *m·*,
'01.	20–16	physically, *m·*, or spiritually,
Hea.	9– 7	the better for mankind, *m·*
	14– 5	is healed *m·* and physically.
My.	130– 6	socially, physically, and *m·*
	130–11	and striven to uplift *m·*
	146–24	tip the scale . . . *m·* and physically,

morals

Mis.	5– 8	perfect *m·* in their children
	62– 3	individuality, health, and *m·* ;
	62– 5	can no more improve health or *m·*,
	110–11	makes *m·* for mankind !
	241– 8	one having *m·* to be healed,
	245–13	influence upon the health, *m·*,
	249–15	whose *m·* are not unquestionable.
	283–16	breach of good manners and *m·* ;
	283–20	its *m·* and Christianity.
	284– 5	of religion, *m·*, or medicine,
	313– 5	of good manners, *m·*, methods,
	315–21	no question of money, but of *m·*
Man.	83– 6	not be a question of money, but of *m·*
Ret.	71–30	end in destroying health and *m·*.
Pul.	7–15	made *m·* for mankind.
	82–13	* conservators of the world's *m·*
No.	18–12	need of better health and *m·*.
My.	103–21	health, longevity, and *m·* of men ;
	111–20	healers and models of good *m·*,
	112–21	pure *m·* and noble lives,
	249–15	fatal to health, happiness, and the *m·*
	265–17	improving the *m·* . . . of mankind,
	294– 3	improve the *m·* and the lives of men,

morbid

Mis.	107–27	in certain *m·* instances stopping,

More, Hannah

Mis.	223–27	Hannah *M·* said, "If I wished to
Ret.	1– 6	in some way related to Hannah *M·*,
	1–13	inherited a spark from Hannah *M·*,
Pul.	32–24	* Hannah *M·* was a relative of

more

Mis.	vii–11	Till time shall end *m·* timely,
	vii–19	Whereof, I've *m·* to glory,
	xii– 6	"learn war no *m·*,"— *see Isa.* 2 : 4.
	2–15	of a *m·* spiritual Christianity,
	2–16	a *m·* rational and divine healing.
	3– 4	If we regard as *m·* natural
	4–28	*m·* than faith is necessary,
	5–15	says, "I can do no *m·*.
	6– 7	many *m·* are needed for the
	7–32	*M·* thought is given to material
	8– 7	we shall have done *m·*.
	9–31	*m·* disastrous to human progress
	10–16	*m·* assured to press on safely.
	12– 7	*m·* severely than you could,
	16– 1	*m·* spiritual Life and Love.
	16– 2	satisfy *m·* the cravings for
	16–20	infinitely *m·* than a person,

more

Mis.	17–10	your *m·* material religion
	17–23	birth is *m·* or less prolonged
	22–28	*m·* than the simple fact
	23– 2	but Science, demanding *m·*,
	25–25	are *m·* deplorably situated
	26– 5	*m·* humane and spiritual.
	26–22	What can be *m·* than All?
	32–16	*m·* than to many others.
	33–30	It is *m·* effectual than drugs ;
	34–17	they can no *m·* come to those
	39–22	who has *m·* to meet than others
	39–28	assumes no *m·* when claiming to
	40–29	it requires *m·* divine understanding
	43–14	far *m·* advantageous to the
	44–26	There is no *m·* pain.
	45– 6	do *m·* than to heal a toothache ;
	45–15	*m·* in this than in most cases ;
	47– 6	substance means *m·* than matter :
	50–19	understand— which is *m·*
	52– 7	he could do vastly *m·*.
	52–25	farther on and *m·* difficult
	53–22	*why is it not m· simple,*
	58– 3	*does that disease have any m· power*
	59– 1	you admit that there is *m·* than
	62– 4	can no *m·* improve health or
	65– 3	no *m·* proof of human discord,
	66–24	like the *m·* physical ailment.
	68– 3	*m·* than mere disappearance
	72–16	have occasion any *m·* — *Ezek.* 18 : 3.
	77– 3	this believing was *m·* than faith
	78– 9	can no *m·* be taught thus,
	78–28	any *m·* than goodness.
	79– 4	know them no *m·* forever,
	80– 3	lose much *m·* than can be gained
	81– 5	into *m·* spiritual lines of life
	84–11	and *m·* spiritual understanding,
	85–19	and *m·* or less imperfect.
	85–26	The pleasures— *m·* than the pains
	85–29	Disease in error, *m·* than ease in it,
	86–16	Earth is *m·* spiritually beautiful
	86–17	*m·* earthly to the eyes of Eve.
	86–23	It is *m·* than imagination.
	93–28	Nothing is *m·* fatal than to
	96–18	atonement becomes *m·* to me
	97–13	*m·* despicable than all other
	97–26	*m·* than personal sense can cognize,
	99–19	Jesus of Nazareth *m·* divine
	100–26	loves man *m·* because he
	103– 4	*m·* impregnable and solid than
	107– 9	we behold *m·* clearly that all
	107–11	*M·* love is the great need
	109–13	how much *m·*, then, should one's sins
	110– 5	*m·* as children than as men and
	111– 9	blamed others *m·* than yourself.
	111–29	inclining mortal mind *m·* deviously :
	115–23	turns us *m·* unreservedly to Him
	117–27	the *m·* provident watcher.
	119–11	*m·* stubborn than the circumstance,
	120–17	come *m·* sweetly to our ear
	124–17	with *m·* than a father's pity ;
	127–13	*m·* grace, obedience, and love.
	131– 7	*m·* than average avoirdupois
	133– 5	ideas *m·* opposite to the fact.
	134–24	*m·* than they that be— *II Kings* 6 : 16.
	135–19	Add one *m·* noble offering to the
	138–24	growth of these at first is *m·*
	142–22	A boat song seemed *m·* Olympian
	144–32	The Church, *m·* than any other
	150–26	Not *m·* to one than to all,
	151– 9	that they may bear *m·* fruit.
	160– 3	unite *m·* honestly in uttering the
	163–16	less human and *m·* divine
	164– 8	continue to be seen *m·* clearly
	165– 2	*m·* than eighteen centuries ago,
	166–13	has evolved a *m·* ready ear
	166–21	Jesus, whose origin was *m·* spiritual
	170–19	no *m·* important to our well-being
	174– 1	has no *m·* power to evolve or to
	176–11	learn a little *m·* of the nothingness of
	176–11	and *m·* of the divine energies of good,
	177– 1	a *m·* solemn and imperious call
	179–15	Truth has become *m·* to us,
	179–15	*m·* true, *m·* spiritual."
	180–11	another person, *m·* material, met me,
	182–21	*m·* than he hath seen the Father.
	182–32	*m·* than eighteen centuries ago.
	188–28	but that we can discern *m·* of them.
	191– 4	"*m·* subtle than — *Gen.* 3 : 1.
	191–12	if . . . there is *m·* than one devil.
	191–15	the existence of *m·* than one
	191–32	*m·* spiritual and practical sense.
	192–28	Nothing can be *m·* conclusive
	193– 4	Jesus did mean all, and even *m·*
	194– 6	know Him better, and love Him *m·*.
	195–29	practice *m·* than theory,

more

Mis.	196– 5	of many minds and $m\cdot$ than one God,
	196–30	require $m\cdot$ than a simple admission
	197– 4	$m\cdot$ frequently used than many others,
	197–13	It means $m\cdot$ than an opinion
	197–15	would be of no $m\cdot$ help to save from
	199–29	goodness is $m\cdot$ natural than evil.
	201–25	protect our dwellings $m\cdot$ securely
	209–13	destroy its $m\cdot$ dangerous pleasures.
	216–11	means $m\cdot$ than "hands off."
	218–22	its effect, is $m\cdot$ ridiculous than the
	221– 6	learns $m\cdot$ of its divine Principle.
	222–25	Error is $m\cdot$ abstract than Truth.
	222–27	good should seem $m\cdot$ natural than
	226–27	disgraces human nature $m\cdot$ than
	227–19	like the camomile, the $m\cdot$ trampled
	229– 9	good is $m\cdot$ contagious than evil,
	229–11	how much $m\cdot$ certain would be the
	230– 3	$m\cdot$ than upon any other one thing.
	230–11	travel of limb $m\cdot$ than mind.
	232– 9	a $m\cdot$ perfect and practical Christianity
	232–18	hence a $m\cdot$ spiritual Christianity
	232–19	will be one having $m\cdot$ power,
	233–16	into a $m\cdot$ fashionable cut
	234–27	seems to them still $m\cdot$ inconceivable.
	234–29	God is regarded $m\cdot$ as absolute,
	235–15	It touches mind $m\cdot$ spiritual
	238–11	$m\cdot$ than history has yet recorded.
	238–18	love that foresees $m\cdot$ to do,
	239–25	made them $m\cdot$ serious over it.
	239–29	saying even $m\cdot$ bravely,
	241– 4	will no $m\cdot$ enter heaven sick than
	241–29	how much $m\cdot$ should these heal,
	242–14	I performed $m\cdot$ difficult tasks
	243–14	claims $m\cdot$ than it practises.
	245–12	directing $m\cdot$ critical observation to
	246–20	A conflict $m\cdot$ terrible than the
	247– 6	Those familiar . . . are $m\cdot$ tolerant ;
	248–19	not $m\cdot$ true than that I am dead,
	248–25	when he could do no $m\cdot$ for me.
	249–25	$m\cdot$ tenderly to save and bless.
	250– 9	No word is $m\cdot$ misconstrued ;
	251–21	as men, clothed $m\cdot$ lightly,
	252– 6	the $m\cdot$ the better in every case.
	255–25	It is $m\cdot$ effectual than drugs,
	262–22	we should be $m\cdot$ grateful
	264–22	$m\cdot$ or less subject to the
	264–30	$m\cdot$ fatal than a mistake in physics.
	271–26	* $m\cdot$ strongly mark the difference
	272–18	* not $m\cdot$ than one thousand dollars.
	273–31	The work is $m\cdot$ than one person can
	274– 9	$m\cdot$ than my teaching would
	277– 5	$m\cdot$ imperatively than ever.
	277–20	* one $m\cdot$ fact to be recorded
	278– 5	will hate $m\cdot$ as it realizes $m\cdot$
	281–26	but it came to me $m\cdot$ clearly
	281–32	*practice* $m\cdot$ than theory.
	283– 4	no $m\cdot$ right to enter the mind
	284– 4	$m\cdot$ than any other system
	284–25	or that becomes $m\cdot$ real
	284–26	Evil let alone grows $m\cdot$ real,
	286–11	$m\cdot$ spiritual conception and
	292–15	look no $m\cdot$ into them as realities.
	297– 6	it has achieved far $m\cdot$ than
	298–27	one no $m\cdot$ gains freedom from
	300–30	is $m\cdot$ apt to recover than
	306–27	it is $m\cdot$ than this :
	307– 7	$M\cdot$ we cannot ask :
	307– 7	$m\cdot$ we do not want :
	307– 8	$m\cdot$ we cannot have.
	308–22	and mayhap taught me $m\cdot$ than
	309–30	$m\cdot$ than they have yet learned.
	311–18	love others $m\cdot$ than they can
	312–13	* "No $m\cdot$ striking manifestation
	313–21	to send forth $m\cdot$ laborers
	319–13	tends to make sin less or $m\cdot$
	321– 9	adjusted $m\cdot$ on the side of God,
	324–20	growing $m\cdot$ and $m\cdot$ troubled,
	326– 5	Once $m\cdot$ he seeks the dwelling-place
	327–21	$m\cdot$ than ever determined not to
	330– 9	man, $m\cdot$ friendly, should call
	330–20	reported $m\cdot$ spiritual growth.
	339–10	good is made $m\cdot$ industrious
	339–12	plants our feet $m\cdot$ firmly.
	342–31	How much $m\cdot$ should we be faithful
	343– 8	and human life $m\cdot$ fruitful,
	346–14	is not $m\cdot$ true or real than
	349–28	I never received $m\cdot$ than this ;
	352–17	to act $m\cdot$ understandingly
	354–15	$m\cdot$ grace, a motive made pure,
	354–33	No vision $m\cdot$ bright than the
	355–29	$m\cdot$ beautiful than the rainbow
	360–21	shall be no $m\cdot$,
	362–32	The $m\cdot$ nearly an erring so-called mind
	363– 1	the $m\cdot$ conscious it becomes of its
	363–31	a $m\cdot$ spiritual apprehension of the
	365–16	and a $m\cdot$ spiritual religion

more

Mis.	365–29	and $m\cdot$ than all else,
	366– 4	True, it requires $m\cdot$ study
	368–16	$m\cdot$ deadly than the upas-tree
	369–17	devout enough to trust Christ $m\cdot$
	370–14	$m\cdot$ intelligently than ever before,
	371–12	They know far $m\cdot$ of C. S. than
	371–15	$m\cdot$ and $m\cdot$ of Truth and Love ;
	373–30	C. S. is $m\cdot$ than a prophet
	375– 6	demands $m\cdot$ than a Raphael to
	382– 7	$m\cdot$ than thirty years of
	389–16	love $m\cdot$ for every hate,
	391–10	Have many items $m\cdot$;
	391–22	'T will be an item $m\cdot$.
	396– 7	$M\cdot$ sorrowful it scarce could seem ;
	397– 4	A world $m\cdot$ bright.
Man.	26– 6	have served one year or $m\cdot$,
	42–17	a belief in $m\cdot$ than one Christ,
	43–18	calls $m\cdot$ serious attention to the
	47–14	$M\cdot$ than a mere rehearsal of
	61– 4	two or $m\cdot$ Sunday services
	61– 8	No $m\cdot$ Communion.
	61–10	observe no $m\cdot$ Communion seasons.
	63–16	two or $m\cdot$ churches may unite
	69–19	$m\cdot$ than me— *Matt.* 10 : 37.
	71– 4	where $m\cdot$ than one church
	72–17	not $m\cdot$ than two small churches
	81– 1	served one year or $m\cdot$
	84– 9	consist of not $m\cdot$ than thirty pupils.
	84–22	or assemble . . . for $m\cdot$ frequent meetings.
	87–19	the $m\cdot$ he trusts them to the divine
	95–19	for one or $m\cdot$ lectures.
Ret.	2– 9	$m\cdot$ than a score of years prior to
	6–13	$m\cdot$ space than this little book can
	7–20	* who expected no $m\cdot$ than they
	8–22	and once $m\cdot$ asked her if she had
	23–14	heart's bridal to $m\cdot$ spiritual
	26–27	know yet $m\cdot$ of the nothingness of
	33–12	the $m\cdot$ Mind, the better the work
	33–21	found to be even $m\cdot$ active.
	34– 2	I must know $m\cdot$ of the unmixed,
	34–14	It is $m\cdot$ effectual than drugs,
	38–20	come to tell me he wanted $m\cdot$,
	45– 2	$m\cdot$ beautiful became the garments
	49– 9	need is for $m\cdot$ of the spirit
	54– 1	sometimes $m\cdot$ speedy than
	57–21	The notion of $m\cdot$ than one Mind,
	61–10	no $m\cdot$ to be invaded than
	63–20	$m\cdot$ dangerous than sickness,
	63–20	$m\cdot$ subtle, $m\cdot$ difficult to heal.
	73–11	into $m\cdot$ spiritual latitudes and purer
	83–17	$m\cdot$ difficult to rekindle his own
	84–25	the $m\cdot$ he trusts them to the divine
	87– 8	$m\cdot$ thoroughly and readily acquired
	91– 5	No purer and $m\cdot$ exalted teachings
	91–11	indicates $m\cdot$ the Master's mood,
Un.	6–22	Not much $m\cdot$ than a half-century ago
	8– 5	as real as you make it, and no $m\cdot$ so.
	13–10	not infringed in ethics any $m\cdot$ than
	15– 3	$m\cdot$ just than God?"— *Job* 4 : 17.
	15– 5	Do mortals know $m\cdot$ grow than God,
	24– 7	insist that there is $m\cdot$ than the one
	24– 7	assumptions . . . $m\cdot$ than the one God ;
	24–23	*Evil.* . . . My mind is $m\cdot$ than matter.
	27– 8	*Egoism* is a $m\cdot$ philosophical word,
	28–13	even $m\cdot$ vague than ordinary
	31– 1	$m\cdot$ accurately translated,
	38–17	rulership of $m\cdot$ gods than
	40–13	therefore mortals can no $m\cdot$
	46–20	To them evil was even $m\cdot$ the
	48– 6	I believe $m\cdot$ in Him than do most
	48– 8	Nay, $m\cdot$ — He *is* my individuality
	48–15	no $m\cdot$ enters into His creation than
	49– 8	The $m\cdot$ I understand true humanhood,
	49– 8	the $m\cdot$ I see it to be sinless,
	53–16	which are no $m\cdot$ logical,
	56–28	$M\cdot$ obnoxious than Chinese stenchpots
	64– 3	for God can no $m\cdot$ behold it,
	64–11	the $m\cdot$ real those mind-pictures
Pul.	vii–12	lenses of $m\cdot$ spiritual mentality,
	2– 3	no $m\cdot$ spirit in her ;" — *I Kings* 10 : 5.
	6–27	* $m\cdot$ than is dreamt of in your
	10– 9	Our land, $m\cdot$ favored, had its
	10–22	devout as they, and $m\cdot$ scientific,
	11– 3	making melody $m\cdot$ real,
	18–13	A world $m\cdot$ bright.
	23–20	* years of $m\cdot$ intense life,
	27–25	* One $m\cdot$ window in the auditorium
	27–29	* of still $m\cdot$ unique interest.
	31–24	* I was hardly $m\cdot$ than seated
	33–26	* to $m\cdot$ than ordinary achievement,
	35–25	* the $m\cdot$ attenuated the drug,
	35–25	* the $m\cdot$ potent its effects.
	41– 2	* not for $m\cdot$ money, but for
	41– 8	* $m\cdot$ than four thousand of these
	51–11	* Every truth is $m\cdot$ or less in a
	53–15	* "That word, $m\cdot$ than any other.

more

Pul.	56– 1	* One or m· organized societies
	62– 8	* not m· than five by eight feet.
	66– 9	* m· from the graveyards than
	73–27	* no m· complete and yet concise
	75–10	would savor m· of heathenism
	80–24	* m· thoughtful and devout ;
	81– 4	* with m· reverence than it was
	82– 8	* you could no m· turn her from
	87–20	m· of earth now, than I desire,
	87–21	M· effectual than the forum
Rud.	3–11	it lives m· because of his
	3–14	will no m· deviate morally
	7–23	Spirit no m· changes its species,
	9– 5	m· or less blended with error ;
	12–14	will return, and be m· stubborn
	13–12	saith there is m· than one God,
	13–13	saith . . . there is m· than one Life
	13–25	not be expected, m· than others,
	15–25	may be dissected m· critically
	16–14	*Is there m· than one school of*
No.	1–17	we can read m· clearly than
	2–15	I have healed m· disease by the
	4– 6	Disease is m· than *imagination ;*
	6–22	m· apparent than the adverse
	8– 5	let us add one m· privilege
	9– 7	clearer and m· conscientious
	9–24	M· mistakes are made in its name
	11–19	it requires m· study
	14–11	Theosophy is no m· allied to
	14–20	perhaps m· than any other
	15–13	m· mystic than Mind-healing.
	16–16	forever giving forth m· light,
	16–22	can take in no m· than all.
	17–12	and for man to be m· than
	18–22	a m· spiritual religion
	22–20	follows that there is m· than one
	23–16	Which of the two is the m· important
	24–13	but much m· real,
	24–15	become both less and m· in C. S.,
	24–16	m·, because the evil that is hidden
	24–27	another and m· glorious truth,
	25– 9	m· than physical personality,
	25–10	Mind is m· than matter,
	26– 6	no m· identical with C. S. than
	26–14	no m· relapse or collapse
	26–27	much m· clothe you, — *Matt. 6 : 30.*
	27– 2	supposition that there is m· than
	27– 9	there will be no m· sea.
	29–21	m· than a fraction of himself.
	30– 3	It does m· than forgive
	30– 9	any m· than the legislator
	31–26	enter no m· into him." — *Mark 9 : 25.*
	35– 9	there will be no m· sickness,
	39– 1	we can think m· lucidly
	39–22	It shows us m· clearly than
	40–13	the inaudible is m· effectual.
	42– 1	* m· and m· learn their duty
	45–23	in m· spiritual latitudes,
Pan.	6– 2	because it was m· effectual
	6–27	belief in m· than one spirit,
	7– 4	signifies m· than one God,
	7–26	hypothesis . . . m· than one Mind,
	9– 4	means m· than one Spirit ;
	13– 1	will witness m· steadfastly to its
	13–11	never m· manifest than in its
	14– 4	Once m· I write, Set your affections
'00.	2–23	and it will be m· sudden,
	6–15	accepts C. S. m· readily
	7– 8	there had been m· Bibles sold
	7–17	Is there m· than one Christ,
	7–23	walk m· closely with Christ ;
	8– 1	know and behold m· nearly
	9–10	a m· convenient season ;
	9–18	Sincerity is m· successful than
	11– 1	it gave me m· pleasure than
	11–13	Music is m· than sound in unison.
	14–16	following the m· perfect way,
	15–25	m· than the first." — *Rev. 2 : 19.*
'01.	1– 7	m· extended, m· rapidly advancing,
	4–29	meaning divine Love, m· frequently
	6– 1	m· transcendental than theology's
	8– 5	m· transcendental than the belief
	8–13	Is man, ... m· transcendental than
	10– 5	how much m· shall they — *Matt. 10 : 25.*
	17–22	m· difficult stage of action
	18– 7	m· honored and respected to-day
	21–24	God knows m· than any man
	23– 1	neither m· or less than three ;
	24–13	Making matter m· potent than
	24–17	m· than two hundred years old.
	25–12	because of their m· spiritual import
	27– 7	will interpret . . . m· clearly,
	27– 8	* apply them m· rationally to
	28– 9	perhaps none lived a m· devout
	28–19	I love Christ m· than all the world,
	33– 8	* in the m· advanced decaying stages

more

'01.	34– 8	is proven to be m· pathological
'02.	2–21	gives place to a m· spiritual
	3– 6	regarded now m· as a philosophy
	4– 8	for m· grace, a m· fulfilled life
	10–20	reformer who finds the m· spiritual way,
	11–10	m· spiritual understanding of God,
	11–15	how much m· is accomplished
	12–25	united effort to purchase m· land
	18–20	what m· could he do?
	18–23	m· effective healers and less theorizing;
	19– 9	m· than all the malice of his foes
Hea.	1–11	m· practical and spiritual religion
	1–21	m· spiritual basis and tendency
	2–11	Said the m· gentle Melanchthon :
	3– 5	proof, m· than a profession thereof ;
	3– 6	demonstration, m· than a doctrine.
	3–21	works of our Master m· than merited.
	5–28	The m· spiritual we become here,
	6– 1	the m· are we separated from
	6– 2	and we grow m· material,
	7–19	m· than they all." — *see Mark 12 : 43.*
	8–28	and do m· than we are now doing,
	9– 4	employed our thoughts m· in
	12–22	making you m· powerful,"
	14–16	includes infinitely m· than
	14–24	included m· than they understood.
	19–20	makes a m· spiritual demand,
	19–22	But let us work m· earnestly
Peo.	1– 2	is a step m· spiritual.
	1–13	into m· spiritual latitudes.
	2–26	This m· perfect idea,
	3–15	and m· spiritual idea of good
	3–18	a m· metaphysical religion
	4– 4	m· than an infinite and divine
	5– 2	the m· spiritual Christianity,
	5– 8	for their m· spiritual ideal,
	6–15	fear God m· than we love Him ;
	6–18	a m· spiritual and true ideal
	7–29	become m· or less perfect
	7–30	mind-models are m· or less spiritual.
	7–32	our methods grow m· spiritual
	8– 2	was not m· the antithesis of
	8–16	and yet we make m· of matter,
	9–28	m· potent evidences in C. S.
	10– 3	steam is m· powerful than water,
	10– 3	because it is m· ethereal.
	12–27	bestows heaven not m· willingly
	13– 1	have a m· material deity,
	13– 5	the Divine Being is m· than a
	14– 1	As our ideas . . . become m· spiritual,
	14– 2	express them by objects m· beautiful.
	14– 8	ideas of Life have grown m· spiritual ;
Po.	2–17	sun's m· genial, mighty ray ;
	4–15	love m· for every hate,
	9–10	wishing this earth m· gifts
	12–13	A world m· bright.
	15–12	as the vision and m· vain
	31– 7	annoy No m· the peace of
	35–15	Written m· than sixty years ago
	38– 9	Have many items m· ;
	38–21	'Twill be an item m·.
	41– 9	the mountains m· friendless,
	53– 9	M· softly warm and weave
	58–19	M· sorrowful it scarce could seem ;
	73– 8	with thee in spirit once m·.
My.	vi– 4	* a simpler or m· pleasing form.
	5–21	to love m· and to serve better.
	7– 9	effort to purchase m· land
	8–20	* m· than nine hundred,
	9–23	the purchase of m· land
	14–22	* invented a m· subtle lie
	18– 9	m· grace, obedience, and love.
	18–19	never m· manifest than in its
	19–20	but I ask for m·, even this :
	21–12	* contribute m· liberally to the
	21–15	* m· than compensates for every
	24–30	* no m· appropriate time for
	27–16	* send no m· money to this fund.
	28– 9	* can give no m· than a hint of
	29–13	* m· gorgeous church pageantries
	29–15	* appealed m· to the eye,
	30– 4	* nobody attended m· than one,
	36–17	* peace of a m· righteous living,
	38–10	* no m· were admitted until
	38–23	* no m· impressive feature of
	39–26	* m· distinctly may we realize
	40– 4	* m· adequate reception to those
	40–17	* may m· widely reassert its
	46– 5	* m· spiritual plane of living,
	46–23	* m· sincere and Christly love
	46–24	* a m· implicit obedience to the
	50–29	* m· than twenty-six years ago,
	52–10	* m· faithfully to sustain her in
	52–16	* m· energy and unselfish labor
	52–24	* M· than once, in her earnestness,
	54–12	* 'No m· standing-room.' "

more

My.
56–22	* and *m·* branch churches were
57–20	* which is 2,194 *m·* than the
58– 4	* no *m·* funds are needed
61–19	* never *m·* did I have any doubt.
63–26	* even *m·* impressive than this
67–24	* never was a *m·* artistic effect
68– 7	* is *m·* than twice the size
70– 5	* has *m·* fine church edifices
70–23	* Nowhere in the world is there a *m·*
70–24	* *m·* musical, or *m·* capable instrument.
71–24	* And what is *m·*, every person
72– 7	* *m·* frequented by members of
72–15	* do not send us any *m·* money
72–19	* to the thirty thousand or *m·*
73– 3	* *m·* than ten thousand dollars
76– 4	* that *m·* money was needed
76– 9	* no *m·* contributions to the
79–20	* must be something *m·* than a fad
81–16	* No *m·* cosmopolitan audience
81–28	* wherever two or *m·* of them are met
82–22	* twenty thousand and *m·* visitors
84– 1	* facts speak *m·* plainly than mere
84– 2	* *m·* of a drag on a church
86–16	* brethren to give no *m·* money,
87–20	* *m·* cheerful looking groups of people
88–12	* ceremonial of far *m·* than usual
92–10	* even *m·* interest than it has evoked
92–12	* hardly *m·* than a day's wonder.
98–16	* requested to send no *m·* money
105– 1	*m·* than the words of Christ,
105–32	*m·* certain and curative in
106–23	minds his own business *m·* than
108–18	The *m·* of this Mind the better
109– 2	no *m·* substance and reality
113–28	*m·* spiritual life and love?
122– 3	a destiny *m·* grand than can issue
122–17	know *m·* of the healing Christ
123– 4	prize love even *m·* than the gifts
124–15	What *m·* abounds and abides in
127–10	*m·* of Christ's teachings and
133–16	one *m·* round of old Sol give birth
135–12	my yearning for *m·* peace
136–27	that I may have *m·* peace,
137–18	and yearning for *m·* peace
141–27	no *m·* communion season in
146–13	*m·* than has been demonstrated,
148– 2	*m·* than ever persistently,
149– 8	*M·* than regal is the majesty of
159– 3	Never *m·* sweet than to-day,
163–15	which I think do them *m·* good.
163–25	all and *m* than I anticipated.
166–21	would be *m·* irksome than work.
174–28	love Him *m·*, and humbly pray
183–13	With you be there no *m·* sea,
191– 1	*m·* of the wisdom of Nicodemus
195– 8	to love *m·*, to work *m·*,
195–14	cannot do *m·* than we are
204– 1	nor will you be long in doing *m·*.
205–20	God *m·* supreme in consciousness,
205–21	man *m·* His likeness,
205–21	friends *m·* faithful,
207–10	* strive *m·* earnestly, day by day,
207–11	* *m·* perfect manifestation of the truth
212– 6	older and *m·* open sins,
213–12	be *m·* zealous to do good,
213–12	*m·* watchful and vigilant.
213–22	strengthen your own citadel *m·*
215–15	* are worth much *m·* to me
216–28	you will feel *m·* than at present
217–22	meet this negation *m·* readily
218–27	to one no *m·* than to another.
219–13	would not be *m·* preposterous than
220–31	seems *m·* divine to-day than
221– 8	in His *m·* infinite meanings,
221–13	*m·* complete, natural, and divine
224–19	*m·* fashionable but less correct
231–10	spend no *m·* time or money in
231–19	*m·* important demands on her time
231–24	to receive *m·* tenants.
234–25	*m·* fatal than the Boxers' rebellion.
236– 1	no *m·* of echoing dreams.
236–20	we can say, the *m·* the better.
240– 7	* to explain *m·* fully why you
243– 9	should be *m·* than one church in it.
243–12	the duties of half a dozen or *m·*
243–15	take charge of three or *m·* churches.
244– 8	one or *m·* lessons on C. S.,
244–24	may not require *m·* than one lesson.
248– 2	I am *m·* than satisfied with your
257– 2	*m·* of His dear love that heals
257–14	Christ is, *m·* than ever before,
259–16	*m·* time to think and work for others.
264– 5	learn *m·* of my meaning
264–17	Truth and Love made *m·* practical ;
264–18	the Decalogue *m·* imperative,
265– 1	*m·* possible and pleasurable.

more

My.
265– 3	knocks *m·* loudly than ever
265– 6	and *m·* apparent to reason ;
266–27	and the *m·* spiritual modes
269– 9	die any *m·* : — *Luke* 20 : 36.
270–28	I would no *m·* quarrel with a man
278– 5	may learn to make war no *m·*,
282–13	In order to apprehend *m·*,
284– 4	may have accorded me *m·* than
286– 4	no *m·* war, no *m·* barbarous
288–26	"Sin no *m·*, — *John* 5 : 14.
289–17	is heard no *m·* in England,
291– 5	*m·* to him than a mere rehearsal
291–29	God of harvests send her *m·* laborers,
292– 2	*m·* than history has yet recorded.
302–21	I may be *m·* loved,
305–23	to learn definitely *m·* from
308– 8	higher, nobler, *m·* imperative
316–22	once *m·* under Mr. Flower's able
317–14	to explain *m·* clearly the points
318–22	manifested *m·* and *m·* agitation,
325– 5	* One thing *m·*, . . . will amuse you :
332– 1	* *m·* than a thousand miles,
344–29	fear of . . . smallpox is *m·* dangerous
345–27	*m·* etherealized ways of living.
355– 7	need for *m·* men in C. S. practice.
363–28	deviation . . . is *m·* or less dangerous.
(see also **faith, nothing, words**)	

moreover

Mis. 233– 4	*M·*, the feverish, disgusting
Pul. 21– 5	*M·*, they love their enemies,
50– 4	* *m·*, that he deserves to have a
No. 5–12	*M·*, this unreal sense substitutes
My. 40– 1	* *M·*, this completed extension of

morn

Mis. 144–24	fresh as a summer *m·*,
384– 5	And all is *m·* and May.
Chr. 53–28	glorious worth Of his high *m·*
Pul. 83–12	* "as fair as the *m·*, — see *Song* 6 : 10.
Pan. 3–12	the gentle murmur of early *m·*,
'02. 5– 1	foretells the dawn and din of *m·* ;
Po. 17– 2	their radiant home and its *m·* !
23–16	In brighter *m·* will find
25– 1	Mirrors of *m·*
page 29	poem
29– 1	Blest Christmas *m·*, though murky clouds
page 30	poem
36– 4	And all is *m·* and May.
70–19	To hail creation's glorious *m·*
My. 31– 5	"Blest Christmas *m·* ;"
155–17	May this glad Easter *m·*
155–30	she sends to them this glad *m·*
202– 1	springs exultant on this blest *m·*.
202– 5	him who hallowed this Easter *m·*.
202–15	the glory of the resurrection *m·*
208–13	the refreshing breeze of *m·*,

morning (*see also* **morning's**)

Mis. 179–20	between us and the resurrection *m·*
222–32	as easily as dawns the *m·* light
239–11	upon the sidewalk one winter *m·*,
259–20	*m·* stars sang together, — *Job* 38 : 7.
280–26	On the *m·* of the fifth,
281–26	it came to me more clearly this *m·*
304–23	* at nine o'clock in the *m·*
376–18	a November sky that this *m·*
Man. 58–12	*m·* service of The Mother Church,
59–24	come to attend the *m·* services.
Chr. 55– 4	bright and *m·* star. — *Rev.* 22 : 16.
57– 4	give him the *M·* STAR. — *Rev.* 2 : 28.
Ret. 17– 9	Here *m·* peers out, from her
Un. 42–14	*m·* stars sang together, — *Job* 38 : 7.
61–10	evening and the *m·* of human thought.
Pul. 34– 8	* a Sunday *m·* when her pastor came
34– 9	* proceeding to his *m·* service,
36–11	* as was given to her *m·* talks
81– 2	* on the *m·* of the dedication.
'00. 7–30	*m·* dawns on eternal day.
Po. 2–16	On wings of *m·* gladly flit away,
24–18	With song of *m·* lark ;
32– 1	rise in the *m·* and drink in the view
62– 9	Here *m·* peers out, from her
My. 29–10	* closing incident . . . yesterday *m·*.
29–28	* half past five in the *m·*
31– 3	* "The *m·* light is breaking ;"
56– 5	* two services were held, *m·* and
56– 6	* repetition of the *m·* service.
56–25	* condition of the *m·* service
77–22	* at six o'clock this *m·*.
78– 4	* *m·*, afternoon, and evening.
82– 6	* For a while this *m·* it looked
82–25	* taxed to the utmost from early *m·*,
86–30	* at intervals from early *m·*
145–14	and the next *m·* noon
147– 5	the *m·* and afternoon services
190– 5	*m·* beams and noonday glory

morning
My. 191–15   glad Easter *m·* witnesseth
354–27   by Mrs. Eddy on New Year's *m·*.

morning's
Mis. 398–18   Till the *m·* beam ;
Ret. 46–24   Till the *m·* beam ;
Pul. 17–23   Till the *m·* beam ;
Po.   3– 1   blends with *m·* hue,
14–22   Till the *m·* beam ;

morphine
Mis. 242–21   is very low and taking *m·*
248–24   physician prescribed *m·*,
249– 2   taking some large doses of *m·*,
My. 292–24   croton oil is not mixed with *m·*

Morrison, Henry K.
My. 174–16   William P. Ballard, Henry K. *M·*,

morrow
Ret. 85–26   *m·* will crown the effort of
My. 13– 3   taking no thought for the *m·*,

Morse (see also Baker)
Mis. x–22   I dropped the name of *M·*

Morse, H. M.
My. 315–19   * signature

morsel
Mis. 130–12   sweet *m·* under your tongue,"

Morse's
'02.   9 -25   *M·* discovery of telegraphy

mortal (see also mortal's)
appearing of a
Mis. 17–22   birth is the appearing of a *m·*,
counsel of a
Mis. 236–20   "Take no counsel of a *m·*,
each
Ret. 76–26   each *m·* in an impersonal depict.
Un. 21– 5   each *m·* is not two personalities,
earthly
My. 241–28   * the beliefs of an earthly *m·*.
every
Pul. 13– 3   Every *m·* at some period, here or
exalts a
Ret. 70–29   exalts a *m·* beyond human praise,
ken of
Po.   1– 5   Beyond the ken of *m·* e'er to tell
no
Mis. 182–21   no *m·* hath seen the spiritual man,
No. 28– 3   no *m·* knoweth ;
My. 364– 1   No *m·* is infallible,
ordinary
My. 65–15   * ordinary *m·* passing out a nickel
pardoned
No. 29–19   A *m·* pardoned by God is not sick,
reformed
Mis. 146–21   every reformed *m·* that desired to
sinful
No. 25–25   sinful *m·* is but the counterfeit of
sinning
Mis. 186–12   in a sick and sinning *m·*.
this
Ret. 67–20   this *m·* was the image and likeness of
vain
Mis. 209– 3   vain *m·*, that usurpest the

Mis. 34–26   the immortal and *m·* are . . . opposites
61–25   A *m·* ; but man is *immortal.*
79–19   A *m·* who is sinning, sick, and
85–25   and the *m·* is not regenerated.
190– 7   the *m·* evolves not the immortal,
204– 1   and a *m·* seems a monster,
332–26   Not man, but a *m·*
333–17   Where art thou, O *m·* !
Ret. 67–11   the *m·* against immortality,
Un. 42–26   *m·* does not develop the immortal,
No. 22–24   devil as a *m·* who is full of evil.
29– 1   that a *m·* should be put to death
Pan. 9–14   What *m·* to-day is wise enough to

mortal (adj.)
admission
Mis. 346–16   *m·* admission of the reality of
anticipations
Ret. 81–28   frailty of *m·* anticipations,
as unreal
No. 36–18   holding the *m·* as unreal,
babe
My. 262– 7   a human, material, *m·* babe
belief
Mis. 59–17   prayer of doubt and *m·* belief
76– 9   *m·* belief that soul is in body,
77–25   sternly to rebuke the *m·* belief
79–13   cannot lapse into a *m·* belief
200–30   only a vagary of *m·* belief,
341– 1   still appear in *m·* belief,
Ret. 33– 3   *m·* belief, instead of the drug,

mortal (adj.)
belief
Pul. 13– 4   *m·* belief in a power opposed to
Peo. 12– 6   death is a law of *m·* belief,
beliefs
Mis. 55–27   its laws are *m·* beliefs.
79– 2   *m·* beliefs will be purged and
Ret. 57– 1   mighty wrestlings with *m·* beliefs,
Pul. 13–12   masters his *m·* beliefs,
No. 31–20   as *m·* beliefs to be exterminated.
Peo. 10–17   *m·* beliefs, and not a law of nature,
My. 182–25   wilderness of *m·* beliefs and fears
bodies
Mis. 60–25   *as many identities as m· bodies?*
body
Mis. 75–14   God is not in matter or the *m·* body.
Ret. 34–19   The *m·* body being but
Un. 28– 3   a reality within the *m·* body?
Hea. 18– 2   mortal mind and *m·* body shall yield to
claim
Mis. 198– 9   the *m·* claim to life, . . . in matter,
clay
Po.   2– 2   to sport at *m·* clay
concept
'02.   6–16   *m·* concept and all it includes
conclusions
Mis. 366–23   *m·* conclusions start from this false
conditions
Un. 59–16   this conformity to *m·* conditions ;
consciousness
Un. 61– 3   belong to *m·* consciousness.
Po. 35– 5   *m·* consciousness Which binds to earth
definitions
No. 25–12   Man outlives finite *m·* definitions
discord
Mis. 97– 4   destroy *m·* discord with immortal
dream
Mis. 393– 8   Lighting up this *m·* dream.
Po. 51–13   Lighting up this *m·* dream.
My.   5– 7   Wholly apart from this *m·* dream,
296–16   The *m·* dream of life, substance, or
element
Mis.   2–28   out of evil, their *m·* element,
environment
Mis. 86–27   constitutes our *m·* environment.
error
Mis. 21–19   matter is *m·* error.
56–14   a *m·* error, a human conception
77–28   could fall into *m·* error ;
Un. 46– 1   *m·* error, called *mind,* is not
evidence
Mis. 13–19   basis of material and *m·* evidence
existence
Mis. 53– 9   wickedness of *m·* existence,
288–11   If the premise of *m·* existence
Ret. 45–12   the first stages of *m·* existence
Un.   3– 2   primary school of *m·* existence,
No.   4– 7   comprise the whole of *m·* existence,
experience
Mis. 205– 7   In *m·* experience, the fire of
fear
Mis. 42– 9   a moment of extreme *m·* fear,
fetters
Peo.   3–24   and assigns them *m·* fetters
history
Ret. 21–13   *m·* history is but the record of
hypotheses
No. 20–27   continued series of *m·* hypotheses,
ignorance
My. 162– 1   God's mercy for *m·* ignorance
ills
Rud. 10–12   *M·* ills are but errors of thought,
inmate
Mis. 324–19   this *m·* inmate withdraws ;
inventions
Un. 60– 1   From such thoughts— *m·* inventions.
joys
Mis. 385–16   and far from *m·* joys,
Po. 48– 9   and far from *m·* joys,
life
Mis. 28–10   and the phenomena of *m·* life
life-battle
Ret. 22–14   the *m·* life-battle still wages,
lives
No. 41–14   compare *m·* lives with this model
man
Mis. 36– 2   termed material or *m·* man,
64–29   the existence of a *m·* man,
74– 5   enmity of *m·* man toward God.
75–28   *m·* man (*alias* material sense)
89–20   If *m· man is unreal, how can he be*
89–24   *M·* man is a false concept
89–29   *M·* man is saved on this divine
103–19   *M·* man, as mind or matter,
140–17   till *m·* man sought to know who
197–23   *M·* man believes in, but does not

mortal (adj.)

man

Mis.	205–27	corporeal or *m·* man disappears
	309– 7	fails to express even *m·* man,
Ret.	67–19	error made its man *m·*,
Un.	15– 3	"Shall *m·* man be— *Job* 4 : 17.
	60– 4	*M·* man is a kingdom divided
Rud.	5– 7	there is no material *m·* man,
No.	19–26	after the manner divided
	26– 1	believe that *m·* man is identical with
	27–17	*M·* man is the antipode of
	29– 4	*M·* man has but a false sense
My.	235–19	Is *m·* man a creator,

man is

No.	5–21	If . . . and man is *m·*.

man's

Mis.	205–25	*M·* man's repentance and
Ret.	61– 1	arises . . . from *m·* man's ignorance,

mansion

Mis.	324–13	Within this *m·* mansion are

mentality

Mis.	109–11	hopeful stage of *m·* mentality.
Un.	58–14	triumph over all *m·* mentality

mind

Mis.	2–10	mortals, *alias m·* mind,
	4– 4	marked tendency of *m·* mind
	5–25	an erring or *m·* mind,
	10– 5	motives that govern *m·* mind
	12–17	*M·* mind at this period mutely works
	15–20	through the sore travail of *m·* mind
	17–29	through the travail of *m·* mind,
	28– 9	only what *m·* mind makes them ;
	33–26	as *m·* mind is the cause of
	34– 6	*m·* mind must be improved,
	36– 3	classify evil and error as *m·* mind,
	36–11	*m·* mind, which is harmful
	36–17	nature and quality of *m·* mind,
	36–19	*distinction between m· mind and*
	36–21	*M·* mind includes all evil,
	36–25	*m·* mind] is enmity— *Rom.* 8 : 7.
	36–26	*M·* mind is an illusion ;
	41–21	*m·* mind, through the action of fear,
	42– 6	belief of dying passes from *m·* mind,
	47– 4	matter is but manifest *m·* mind.
	51– 9	workings of error or *m·* mind.
	58–15	as *m·* mind, it is a belief that sees.
	60–23	*If m· mind and body are myths,*
	61– 6	vain strivings of *m·* mind,
	72–25	Matter is manifest *m·* mind,
	82–14	*after the destruction of m· mind?*
	82–22	*m·* mind, or the material sense of
	82–25	*M·* mind is a myth ;
	84–15	*m·* mind, not the immortal Mind,
	85–22	*m·* mind which seems to be matter
	86–27	The atmosphere of *m·* mind
	87–12	frail conception of *m·* mind ;
	87–12	*m·* mind is a poorer representative of
	103–16	*m·* mind, which must be ever in
	111–29	false beliefs inclining *m·* mind
	127–30	*M·* mind presents phases of
	129–17	into the atmosphere of *m·* mind
	184–31	*m·* mind purged of the animal and
	204–32	and *m·* mind, thus purged,
	214–24	*m·* mind in being healed morally,
	215– 2	The tendency of *m·* mind is
	218– 8	*m·* mind must change all its
	219–22	that *m·* mind makes sick,
	219–23	that *m·* mind makes sinners,
	233–15	*m·* mind, termed hypnotism,
	233–31	belief or product of *m·* mind :
	237– 4	of *m·* mind instead of body :
	247–21	They acknowledge . . . *m·* mind,
	247–31	an evil belief of *m·* mind,
	254–21	it is the *m·* mind sense
	256– 4	*m·* mind must be corrected
	257–11	immoral force of erring *m·* mind,
	260– 9	the travesties of *m·* mind.
	264–18	As *m·* mind is directed, it acts
	268–24	ailments of *m·* mind and body.
	286–24	*m·* mind and body as *one*,
	294– 7	miracle in the universe of *m·* mind.
	343– 6	to find disease in the *m·* mind,
	343–20	The weeds of *m·* mind
	355–10	*m·* mind must pass through
	356– 5	The pent-up elements of *m·* mind
	360–25	When *m·* mind is silenced by the
	361– 3	belief in material origin, *m·* mind,
	361–28	error, named matter, or *m·* mind.
	362– 2	*m·* mind, material birth,
	362–17	whose noumenon is *m·* mind,
	365–18	*m·* mind is calling for what
	367– 5	states of error or *m·* mind.
	367– 7	there being no *m·* mind,
Ret.	23– 7	the cloud of *m·* mind seemed
	25–12	That which sins, . . . I named *m· mind.*
	33–20	its fatal essence, *m·* mind ;

mortal (adj.)

mind

Ret.	34–13	*m·* mind as the source of all the ills
	34–20	objective state of the *m·* mind,
	59– 3	consequently a *m·* mind
	61–22	it is in the *m·* mind only,
	61–25	suffering from *m·* mind,
	68–23	"In reality there is no *m·* mind,
	70– 1	"*M·* mind inverts the true likeness,
	70– 3	origin and operations of *m·* mind,
	75– 2	ill-concealed question in *m·* mind,
	79– 7	effaced from the canvas of *m·* mind ;
Un.	9– 1	*m·* mind is the cause of all disease.
	11– 4	currents of matter, or *m·* mind.
	11– 9	laws of *m·* mind, not of God.
	23–19	*Evil.* But *m·* mind and sin really
	24– 1	*M·* mind is the opposite of
	24–24	In my *m·* mind, matter becomes
	28–20	cannot be taken in by *m·* mind
	32–16	which I prefer to call *m· mind.*
	32–17	*m·* mind declares itself material,
	32–26	which I call *m· mind* ;
	33– 2	identical with *m·* mind,
	33–18	neither matter nor *m·* mind,
	33–26	*M·* mind declares that matter sees
	34– 2	*m·* mind says, "I cannot see ;"
	34– 4	*M·* mind admits that it sees only
	34– 7	that *m·* mind cannot see
	34–14	*M·* mind says that matter cannot
	34–18	What evidence does *m·* mind afford
	34–20	Take away *m·* mind,
	34–21	*m·* mind could not cognize its
	35– 1	*M·* mind says, "I taste ;
	35– 2	Let *m·* mind change, and say
	35– 3	If every *m·* mind believed
	35– 5	are but qualities of *m·* mind.
	35–10	matter is *m·* mind ;
	35–11	there is no *m·* mind,
	35–13	*M·* mind says gravitation
	35–20	the phenomena of *m·* mind,
	35–20	matter and *m·* mind are one ;
	37–22	*m·* mind which is misnamed **man,**
	38– 7	even the unreality of *m·* mind,
	45–25	*M·* mind is self-creative
	50–11	a phenomenon of *m·* mind,
	50–13	no such thing as *m· mind,*
	53–21	is not a *m·* mind or sinner ;
	53–23	Man's Father is not a *m·* mind
	56– 1	The chaos of *m·* mind is made
Pul.	14–28	the great delusion of *m·* mind,
Rud.	8–25	that *m·* mind should not be
	9–11	outcome of what I call *m· mind,*
	10–13	diseases of *m·* mind,
	13– 3	is neither matter nor *m·* mind ;
No.	8–24	before this state of *m·* mind,
	14– 7	subjective states of *m·* mind.
	15–21	nor in the modes of *m·* mind.
	15–22	matter and *m·* mind have neither
	16–12	called *m·* mind or matter,
	16–27	its highest attenuation is *m·* mind ;
	16–27	strictly speaking, *no m·* mind.
	17–15	Matter, or any mode of *m·* mind,
	18–24	the so-called *m·* mind asks for
	24– 7	lower orders of matter and *m·* mind.
	25–15	matter nor a mode of *m·* mind.
Pan.	5–27	denied it, cast it out of *m·* mind,
Hea.	11– 7	*m·* mind rebels at its own boundaries ;
	18– 2	*m·* mind and mortal body shall yield to
My.	109– 1	the subjective state of *m·* mind.
	110–15	*m·* mind pressing to the front,
	201–17	scan the convulsions of *m·* mind,
	211–15	it impels *m·* mind into error of
	296–28	lifting the curtains of *m·* mind,
	349–25	lawless and traceable to *m·* mind

mind-cure

Mis.	59– 5	*m·* "mind-cure" that produces the effect

mind-curists

'01.	21– 1	*m·* mind-curists, nor faith-curists ;

mind-healing

No.	31– 3	Material and *m·* mind-healing

mind's

Mis.	33–28	found in *m·* mind's opposite,
Ret.	31–22	Into *m·* mind's material obliquity

minds

Peo.	11–17	Mortals, *alias m·* minds,
My.	301–22	effects of illusion on *m·* minds

mistake

Mis.	339–16	it points to every *m·* mistake ;
	362–11	Theologians make the *m·* mistake of

modes

No.	39–12	nor bring His designs into *m·* modes ;

molecules

Mis.	205–28	The encumbering *m·* molecules,

mood

Pul.	14– 6	another extreme *m·* mood,

mortal (adj.)

nothingness
My.	245–18	dire din of *m·* nothingness,

opinion
Mis.	7–13	of what can *m·* opinion avail?
No.	29–17	impute such doctrines to *m·* opinion

opposite
Ret.	73– 2	his *m·* opposite must be material,

plane
Mis.	368–26	on the *m·* plane may become the

pride
My.	5–11	*m·* pride and power,

purpose
Mis.	204–26	it unselfs the *m·* purpose,

scoff
Mis.	201– 2	receives the *m·* scoff only because it

self
Ret.	86– 9	Note well the falsity of this *m·* self !

sense
Mis.	24–21	knowledge gained from *m·* sense
	27–32	Take away the *m·* sense of substance,
	58–14	through a higher than *m·* sense.
	73– 8	immortal Science with *m·* sense ;
	81–17	*in order to overcome m· sense,*
	82–26	*m·* sense of existence
	163– 6	a grave to *m·* sense dishonored
	188–26	the unreal or *m·* sense of things ;
	396– 6	Fills *m·* sense with dread ;
Un.	30–22	through a change in the *m·* sense
	43– 6	The present *m·* sense of being
	52–12	redemption of soul, as *m·* sense,
	58–19	revelation that beams on *m·* sense.
	61– 9	The mutations of *m·* sense are the
	62–25	*M·* sense, confining itself to matter,
	62–28	her *m·* sense, reversing Science
Pul.	44– 5	* as *m·* sense puts it,
Rud.	3– 9	to the perception of *m·* sense,
No.	29– 3	*m·* sense, sins and dies.
	40– 6	a material and *m·* sense of
'01.	17– 3	sufferer from the *m·* sense of sin
Peo.	5–13	risen higher to our *m·* sense,
Po.	58–18	Fills *m·* sense with dread ;
	70–14	Away, then, *m·* sense !
My.	45–17	* purblind *m·* sense declared
	61–12	* with the evidence of *m·* sense
	293–20	to *m·* sense the flesh prevailed.
	350–20	Oft *m·* sense is darkened unto death

senses
Mis.	13–20	what the shifting *m·* senses confirm
Pul.	45– 8	* seems impossible to *m·* senses.
	45–21	* the evidence of the *m·* senses

shadows
Mis.	71–28	*m·* shadows flitting across the dial

side
My.	50–15	* turned steadfastly from the *m·* side,

sigh
Po.	30– 7	dayspring ! 'reft of *m·* sigh

sin is
'01.	13–27	Soul is immortal, but sin is *m·*.

sinner
Mis.	268–21	the sin and the *m·* sinner.

sphere
Un.	61–17	infinite good in this *m·* sphere

strife
'02.	2– 2	through the mist of *m·* strife
Po.	29–18	so far above All *m·* strife,

things
Hea.	19–12	origin of all *m·* things.

thought
Mis.	3–20	the erring or *m·* thought
	4–30	to destroy sin in *m·* thought.
	5–28	weighed down as is *m·* thought
	24–18	I learned that *m·* thought evolves
	34–24	within the realm of *m·* thought
	37–19	which corrects *m·* thought,
	44–19	It was a state of *m·* thought
	44–25	this demand of *m·* thought
	70– 8	When the *m·* thought, or belief,
	97– 5	It is not one *m·* thought transmitted
	102–28	*M·* thought wars with this sense
	145–16	*m·* thought resuscitate too soon.
	198–21	the product of *m·* thought
	214– 4	the carnal mind, or *m·* thought,
	228–25	popular current of *m·* thought
	260–14	knew that erring *m·* thought
Ret.	68–24	no transference of *m·* thought
Un.	59–13	To *m·* thought Jesus appeared as a
No.	5– 4	In erring *m·* thought
	37– 5	*M·* thought gives the eternal God
My.	113–27	casting out the evils of *m·* thought,

throes
Un.	57–25	*M·* throes of anguish

views
No.	26– 9	such material and *m·* views

vision
My.	59– 7	* beyond our *m·* vision.

mortal (adj.)

will-power
Mis.	281– 5	the self-asserting *m·* will-power

woes
Po.	8– 6	Her bosom to fill with *m·* woes.

yearnings
Mis.	386– 4	Where *m·* yearnings come not,
Po.	49– 6	Where *m·* yearnings come not,

Mis.	2–23	therefore evil must be *m·*
	14– 3	the *m·* and material view which
	15–26	In *m·* and material man,
	15–28	*m·* and material sense of man,
	28–12	from this *m·* and material dream,
	49–15	*If all that is m· is a dream*
	56–11	Every indication of . . . is *m·*,
	71–18	on a *m·* or material formation ;
	72–28	Mind is not *m·*, it is immortal.
	76–12	the bodies of mortals are *m·*,
	102–26	state of *m·* and material thought.
	104–28	Who wants to be *m·*,
	188– 7	appears second, material, and *m·* ;
	199– 4	only *m·*, erring mind can claim to
	361– 8	neither material nor *m·*.
	385–20	Man is not *m·*, never of the dead :
Ret.	32–10	What is termed *m·* and material
	59–15	Whatever errs is *m·*,
	68– 1	This *m·* material concept was never
Un.	4– 2	our *m·*, finite sense of sin,
	9– 5	Material and sensual . . . are *m·*.
	30–19	man as immortal instead of *m·*
	37–17	Human beings are physically *m·*,
	37–19	personality is illusive and *m·* ;
	60–26	to *m·* and material sense,
Rud.	7–13	fallen, sick, depraved, *m·*.
	10–11	beliefs of a *m·* material universe,
	13– 8	A *m·* and material body is not the
No.	17– 2	unreal, material, and *m·*.
	25–24	that which is *m·* is not man
	26– 3	and that . . . is inside the *m·* ;
Po.	48–14	Man is not *m·*, never of the dead :
My.	109– 5	dream which is *m·* and God-condemned
	110–25	mortals will cease to be *m·*.
	179–10	mind and matter, *m·* and immortal,
	203–18	that its possessor is *m·*.
	232–23	until the entire *m·*, material error
	262–22	*m·*, material, sensual giving
	273–24	that the material body is *m·*,

mortality (see also **mortality's**)

and discord
No.	16– 4	then *m·* and discord must be

condition of
Mis.	64–26	*put into this condition of m·?*

current of
Mis.	234–22	even the entire current of *m·*,

disease and
Rud.	10–12	and of material disease and *m·*.

emerges from
My.	200–16	man emerges from *m·*

evil and
Mis	363–10	mythology of evil and *m·*

foundations of
Mis.	101–16	undermines the foundations of *m·*,

less
Peo.	6–10	* less sickness and less *m·*

man and
Mis.	205–16	on material man and *m·*.

materiality and
Mis.	28–17	can overbear materiality and *m·* ;

materiality, or
No.	26–22	corpuscle, materiality, or *m·*.

mists of
Mis.	363–20	through the mists of *m·*

nothing but
Un.	41– 1	beholds nothing but *m·*,

only
Un.	40– 2	It is *m·* only that dies.

phenomena of
Mis.	286–23	phenomena of *m·*, nothingness,

sense of
Mis.	181–26	will lose their sense of *m·*

shall disappear
Hea.	18– 4	*m·* shall disappear

sin and
Pan.	8– 5	lunacy, sin, and *m·*.
My.	192–11	conquest over sin and *m·*,

sorrow and
Mis.	103–11	is sorrow and *m·* ;

specimens of
Mis.	294–19	Love such specimens of *m·*

state of
Mis.	64–29	as . . . that he *is* in a state of *m·*.

statistics of
My.	181–25	The statistics of *m·* show

time and
Mis.	93–14	illusion of time and *m·*.

mortality

unself
My. 161–18 to unself *m·* and to destroy its
vice, and
Rud. 11–12 disease, vice, and *m·*

Mis. 101–20 bases his conclusions on *m·*,
103– 7 *M·*, materiality, and destructive
Ret. 57–28 making *m·* the status and rule
No. 28– 5 *m·* will burst the barriers of sense,
'02. 10– 5 molecule, space, time, *m·* ;

mortality's
My. 191–22 *M·* thick gloom is pierced.

mortally
Un. 35– 9 *m·* mental, instead of material.

mortal's
Mis. 243–17 a *m·* poor performances.
Pul. 10– 4 sense of *m·* necessities,
My. 181–10 *m·* painless departure from

mortals (*see also* mortals')

all
Mis. 326–16 all *m·*, under every hue of
No. 33–25 Jesus suffered for all *m·*
allow
Pan. 11–12 allow *m·* to turn from clay
among
Un. 39– 1 "made flesh" among *m·*,— *John* 1 : 14.
My. 197–19 will disappear from among *m·*.
appears to
Mis. 14–21 What appears to *m·* from their
apply
Ret. 59–11 even as *m·* apply finite terms
approach Spirit
No. 16–24 in proportion as *m·* approach Spirit,
approximate
No. 38–17 In proportion as *m·* approximate
are content
Pan. 11–26 image that *m·* are content to call
are experiencing
My. 109– 4 *m·* are experiencing the Adam-dream
are hoping
Pan. 1–11 *m·* are hoping and working,
are not compelled
No. 42– 5 *m·* are not compelled to have
are the embodiments
Mis. 61–26 *m·* are the embodiments (or bodies,
assumed for
Mis. 63–30 Jesus assumed for *m·* the
awake
Mis. 331–29 As *m·* awake from their dream
bears to
My. 258–17 Bethlehem babe bears to *m·* gifts
becloud
Ret. 78–22 To becloud *m·*, or for yourself to
become educated
Mis. 9–27 wherewith *m·* become educated to
befall
Ret. 34–14 all the ills which befall *m·*.
beliefs of
My. 146–24 the beliefs of *m·* tip the scale
beliefs that
Mis. 28– 5 on the beliefs that *m·* entertain.
believed
No. 36– 8 while *m·* believed it was here.
bestows on
'01. 15–15 that divine Love bestows on *m·*,
blesses
Mis. 109–18 seeing the need of . . . blesses *m·*.
bodies of
Mis. 76–12 bodies of *m·* are mortal,
cannot prevent
Mis. 208– 3 *M·* cannot prevent the fulfilment of
can understand
Un. 62–10 *M·* can understand this only as
causes
Mis. 292–14 causes *m·* to turn away from
Christianization of
'02. 6–16 The Christianization of *m·*, whereby
cleansing
Mis. 185–12 cleansing *m·* of all uncleanness,
collisions of
Mis. 339–13 In the mental collisions of *m·*
commands
Un. 49–26 commands *m·* to shun
compels
Mis. 209–15 Insomnia compels *m·* to learn that
conceive
'02. 5–25 why should *m·* conceive of a law,
conditions of
No. 22– 9 fail to improve the conditions of *m·*,
cry out
'02. 10– 5 *m·* cry out, "Art thou come— *Matt.* 8 : 29.
dawn on
No. 20–15 omnipresence will dawn on *m·*.

mortals

deification of
Pul. 74–24 the Christ and the deification of *m·*.
deliver
Mis. 81–28 deliver *m·* out of the depths of
My. 233–12 better adapted to deliver *m·* from
demands on
No. 45–26 urging its highest demands on *m·*,
demonstrated by
Un. 1–13 apprehended and demonstrated by *m·*,
demoralize
Ret. 81– 9 tends to demoralize *m·*,
depravity of
Mis. 2–10 depravity of *m·*, *alias* mortal mind,
die
Un. 40–26 lacking . . . *m·* die, in belief,
do not understand
No. 16–17 *M·* do not understand the All ;
dwell among
Mis. 184– 6 made flesh and dwell among *m·*,
dwelling-place of
Mis. 326– 5 he seeks the dwelling-place of *m·*
dying
Peo. 4–21 sinning, sick, and dying *m·*.
earth and
Un. 52–22 Why are earth and *m·* so elaborate in
entertain
Mis. 74–14 opposite of that which *m·* entertain :
environment of
Mis. 85–23 seems to be . . . the environment of *m·*,
estranges
No. 15–24 estranges *m·* from divine Life
even
My. 110–23 show us that even *m·* can mount higher
face of
Mis. 332–21 and shamed the face of *m·*.
finite
Mis. 82–21 finite *m·* see . . . only as abstract
flutterings of
Mis. 85–18 feeble flutterings of *m·* Christward
freedom of
No. 34–28 freedom of *m·* from sin and death.
gain
Mis. 203–20 *m·* gain severe views of themselves ;
give to
Mis. 351–23 five senses give to *m·* pain,
giving
Mis. 204–13 giving *m·* new motives,
govern
Rud. 10– 9 which govern *m·* wrongfully.
great legacy to
Mis. 124–25 Love's great legacy to *m·* :
hating
'02. 8– 7 *m·* hating, or unloving, are
healed
No. 31– 4 but has not healed *m·* ;
hear
Mis. 86–28 What *m·* hear, see, feel, taste,
ills of
'01. 24– 8 all the ills of *m·*
illusion of
Mis. 50– 3 error is an illusion of *m·* ;
ken of
'02. 4–27 or beyond the ken of *m·*,
My. 14– 5 beyond the ken of *m·*
learn
Mis. 10–28 *m·* learn at last the lesson,
'02. 17– 7 When *m·* learn to love aright ;
legitimate to
Un. 54–19 becomes legitimate to *m·*,
lexicographer of
Mis. 226–13 immortal lexicographer of *m·*,
lift
Mis. 52–17 that tends to lift *m·* higher.
lifts
Mis. 287–16 until progress lifts *m·* to
lives of
Mis. 114–26 influence upon the lives of *m·*.
looked
'02. 18– 6 when *m·* looked ignorantly,
love to sin
Rud. 3– 1 while *m·* love to sin,
makes
Mis. 293–25 makes *m·* either saints or
manumits
Mis. 124–27 it manumits *m·* ;
matter or
Mis. 22– 6 Who dare say that matter or *m·*
may climb
Un. 64–15 *M·* may climb the smooth glaciers,
melancholy
Mis. 391– 7 melancholy *m·* Will count their
Po. 38– 6 melancholy *m·* Will count their
millions of
Mis. 208– 7 that governs millions of *m·*

mortals

minds of
Mis. 257–12 *alias* the minds of *m*.
My. 5– 1 originates in the minds of *m*.
    294–10 contradicting minds of *m*.
misrepresent
Mis. 250– 4 *M* misrepresent and miscall affection;
must learn
Ret. 49–14 *M* must learn to lose their
Un. 10–26 *M* must learn this;
must take up
Ret. 65–12 *M* must take up the cross
must work
Mis. 22– 9 *m* must work for the discovery of
no opinions of
Mis. 3–15 No opinions of *m* nor
now believe
Un. 43– 7 *m* now believe in the possibility
obey
Mis. 208–15 *M* obey their own wills,
obeyed
Ret. 76– 3 if *m* obeyed God's law
poor
My. 195–21 by which we poor *m* expect
purify
Mis. 298–18 Trials purify *m* and deliver them
redeem
Mis. 82– 9 to enlighten and redeem *m*.
redemption of
Un. 6– 8 redemption of *m* from sin,
remember
Mis. 331–14 do *m* remember *their* cradle hymns,
rescue of
Mis. 107– 7 these come to the rescue of *m*,
    362–22 must come to the rescue of *m*,
restored to
Mis. 186–30 restored to *m* the lost sense of
rights of
Mis. 283–18 trespass on the rights of *m*.
seek
No. 40– 4 *m* seek, and expect to receive,
seem
Mis. 61–30 *M* seem very material;
sensual
Mis. 328–11 acquaint sensual *m* with the
showing
Mis. 162–20 showing *m* how to escape from
sinful
Mis. 380– 4 how can sinful *m* prove that a
No. 7–10 eyes of sinful *m* must be opened
sinning
Mis. 36–14 animal qualities of sinning *m*;
some
'01. 15–20 Some *m* may even need to hear the
spiritualizing
No. 10–24 dematerializing and spiritualizing *m*
suffer
Mis. 261– 9 *m* suffer from the wrong they commit,
suffering
Ret. 92– 3 for the needs of suffering *m*,
sufferings of
'01. 17– 1 self-inflicted sufferings of *m*
teaches
Mis. 211– 4 it teaches *m* to handle serpents
think
Mis. 219–12 admitted that *m* think wickedly
    219–14 *m* think also after a sickly fashion.
to show
No. 35–14 to show *m* the awful price paid by
turn from
Mis. 28–11 In proportion as *m* turn from
turns
'00. 11– 9 turns *m* away from earth to heaven;
two
Mis. 332–14 two *m*, walking in the cool of
understanding of
Mis. 260– 4 reduced to the understanding of *m*,
vain
Mis. 362–27 O vain *m*! which shall it be?
warn
Un. 57– 4 warn *m* of the approach of danger
who seek
'02. 11– 2 *m* who seek for a better country
wicked
Mis. 187–32 wicked *m* such as crucified our
will become
Ret. 64–28 *m* will become the victims of error.
willingness of
Mis. 269–28 willingness of *m* to buy error at par
will lose
Mis. 181–25 *M* will lose their sense of mortality
yield
No. 35– 7 *m* yield lovingly to the purpose of

Mis. 6– 3 leaves *m* but little time
    15–23 that *m* can lay off the

mortals

Mis. 19–19 most fearful sin that *m* can commit.
    22–11 C. S. translates Mind, God, to *m*.
    27–12 *M* accept natural science,
    27–31 *M* can know a stone as
    52–29 *M* have the sum of being to work out,
    60–29 if *m* are instructed in spiritual
    84–12 which dawns by degrees on *m*.
    103– 8 *m* virtually name *substance*;
    109–22 *m* must hasten through the
    164–13 babe Jesus seemed small to *m*;
    165–18 left to *m* the rich legacy of
    199–21 which *m* name matter.
    205–31 *M* who on the shores of time
    208–11 *M* have only to submit to the law of
    208–21 interprets to *m* the gospel of
    209–31 then shall *m* have peace."
    257–26 churches, schools, and *m*.
    261–24 by mankind I mean *m*,
    289– 8 *m* must first choose between
    292–27 *m*, with the penetration of Soul,
    319– 7 *m* are in danger of not
    328–24 *m* who are striving to enter the
    330–15 let *m* bow before the creator,
    331–'2 then, are *m* looking up,
    358–16 put on only when *m* are
    361–21 So shall *m* soar to final freedom,
Ret. 64–26 *m* must first open their eyes to
    69– 1 His origin is not, like that of *m*,
Un. 15– 5 Do *m* know more than God,
    40– 3 To say that you and I, as *m*,
    40–13 therefore *m* can no more
    50–19 less consciousness of . . . *m* have,
    52–21 beasts, fatal reptiles, and *m*.
    58– 2 *M*, if at ease in so-called existence,
    60–17 *M* are free moral agents,
Rud. 2–17 whom *m* have named God.
    12–22 why should *m* concern themselves
No. 17–21 If *m* could grasp these two words
    23–20 As *m*, we need to discern
    25–21 *M* have not seen it.
    27–27 probation of *m* must go on
    35– 5 what hope have *m* but through
Pan. 11–20 *M*, content with something less than
'01. 29– 5 *m* in the advancing stages of
Peo. 11–17 *M*, *alias* mortal minds,
My. 110–11 progress from molecule and *m*
    110–25 *m* will cease to be mortal.
    161–16 *M* must drink . . . of the cup
    242–11 I do not mean that *m* are
    244–18 *m* do not enter without a struggle

mortals'

Mis. 64– 3 way he made for *m* escape.
    107–19 *M* false senses pass through
    108–15 would remove *m* ignorance
    117–23 God's time and *m* differ.
    165–23 of *m* redemption from sin;
    334– 9 that *m* faith in matter may
'02. 10–22 increases the speed of *m* transit

mortgage

Mis. 140–11 No one could buy, sell, or *m*
    140–21 I redeemed from under *m*.
Pul. 8–10 Not a *m* was given nor a
    20– 4 were unable to pay the *m*;
'02. 13–16 purchased the *m* on the lot
    13–19 After the *m* had expired
    13–24 amount due on the *m*.
    13–26 the *m* was foreclosed,
    14– 4 can neither rent, *m*, nor sell

mortgages

My. 89–15 * not blanketed with debts and *m*.

Mosaic

Ret. 89–10 instruction in the *M* law.
Pan. 6–11 *M* theism introduces evil,
    7–14 the *M*, the Christian, and the
    7–20 a lapse in the *M* religion,

mosaic

Pul. 2– 7 from its *m* flooring to the
    25– 6 * floors of marble in *m* work,
    25–23 * floor is in white Italian *m*,
    26– 9 * *m* work, with richly carved seats
    26–23 * the *m* marble floor of white
    58–18 * The floors are all *m*,
    76– 8 * The floor is of *m*

Mosaic Decalogue

Mis. 248–18 obedience to the *M* *D*,

Moses

Mis. 261–20 typified in the law of *M*,
Ret. 75– 4 the law given by *M*,

Moslem's

Mis. 124–11 *M* misconception of Deity,

Moss-rose

Ret. 17–10   Prairie Queen and the modest $M\cdot$;
Po.   62–12   Prairie Queen and the modest $M\cdot$;

most

Mis.   x–10 $m\cdot$ of these articles were
x–14   where these are $m\cdot$ requisite,
2– 3   those assume $m\cdot$ who have the
4– 3   the $m\cdot$ potent and desirable
6– 6   The $m\cdot$ of our C. S. practitioners
6–28   there is the $m\cdot$ sickness.
10– 5   the $m\cdot$ remorseless motives
13– 8 $m\cdot$ happily wrought out for me
19–19   is the $m\cdot$ fearful sin that
26– 7   in the $m\cdot$ subtle ether,
35–11 $m\cdot$ concise, yet complete, summary
39–26   *what $m\cdot$ obstructs the way?*
45–15   more in this than in $m\cdot$ cases ;
52–14   the $m\cdot$ wretched condition
81– 2   some of the $m\cdot$ skilful and
87–21   who is $m\cdot$ reliant on himself
89–10   advisable in $m\cdot$ cases that Scientists
91–18   should represent the $m\cdot$ spiritual
92–10   He who sees $m\cdot$ clearly and
92–11   enlightens other minds $m\cdot$ readily,
92–31   does $m\cdot$ for his students
92–31   who $m\cdot$ divests himself of pride
100–27   because he loves God $m\cdot$.
106–23 $m\cdot$ adorable, but $m\cdot$ unadored,
108–27 $m\cdot$ of us would not be seen
109–11 $m\cdot$ hopeful stage of mortal mentality.
112– 9   The $m\cdot$ just man can neither
126–22 $M\cdot$ people condemn evil-doing,
157–16   helps us $m\cdot$ when help is $m\cdot$ needed,
169–18   the $m\cdot$ eminent divines of the
173– 3   The $m\cdot$ enlightened sense herein
226–28   disgraces . . . more than do $m\cdot$ vices.
229–17   even the $m\cdot$ High — *Psal.* 91 : 9.
230– 7   make the $m\cdot$ of the present.
232–11   behind . . . in things $m\cdot$ essential,
232–20   that $m\cdot$ important of all arts,
232–26 $m\cdot$ spiritual and unselfish motives.
234–12   things $m\cdot$ essential and divine.
242–22   in its $m\cdot$ concentrated form,
245–21   which may be $m\cdot$ mischievous
246–19   this $m\cdot$ unprecedented warfare.
249–12   The $m\cdot$ devout members of
250– 3   the best become the $m\cdot$ abused,
251– 9   welcomed you . . . $m\cdot$ graciously,
257–19   where there is $m\cdot$ danger.
263–19   be met in the $m\cdot$ effectual way.
267– 6   sacrificed the $m\cdot$ time,
267– 8   caused me to exercise $m\cdot$ patience.
273– 6   where I now seem to be $m\cdot$ needed,
281–24   the $m\cdot$ beautiful and the $m\cdot$ costly,
282–19   exceptions to $m\cdot$ given rules :
287– 1   the $m\cdot$ exalted divine conception.
295–24   The $m\cdot$ advanced ideas are inscribed
304– 6   * in the $m\cdot$ appropriate place
309–11   He advances $m\cdot$ in divine Science
309–12   who meditates $m\cdot$ on infinite
316–26   could have derived $m\cdot$ benefit from
317–17   by the $m\cdot$ faithful seekers ;
319–11   Scientists must be $m\cdot$ watchful.
336– 8   that which represents God $m\cdot$,
341–24   the $m\cdot$ solemn vow of celibacy
353–26   four thousand children, $m\cdot$ of whom,
372–20   and $m\cdot$ distinguished artists.
374– 4   in $m\cdot$ of its varied manifestations.
374–17 $m\cdot$ fitting that Christian Scientists
376– 2   * $m\cdot$ revered, $m\cdot$ authentic
376– 3   * I use the words $m\cdot$ *authentic*
388–11   And life $m\cdot$ sweet, as heart to heart
391–17   Share God's $m\cdot$ tender mercies,
Ret.   6–16   one of the $m\cdot$ talented,
7–14   * one of the $m\cdot$ distinguished men
7–19   * with the $m\cdot$ poignant grief,
10–12 $m\cdot$ of the knowledge I had
18–23   those we $m\cdot$ love find a happiness
19–24   obligations $m\cdot$ faithfully.
32–17   * Whose $m\cdot$ constant substance
37– 1   edition of my $m\cdot$ important work,
41– 5   in $m\cdot$ instances without even
54–22   the $m\cdot$ sacred and salutary
84– 7   enlightens other minds $m\cdot$ readily,
84–19   does $m\cdot$ for his students
84–20   divests himself $m\cdot$ of pride
87–11 $m\cdot$ systematic and law-abiding
88–11 $m\cdot$ concerns mankind.
90– 1   student should be $m\cdot$ careful
Un.   7– 8   When I have $m\cdot$ clearly seen
7– 9   and $m\cdot$ sensibly felt that the
45– 8   need $m\cdot$ of all to be rid of
48– 6   more . . . than do $m\cdot$ Christians,
52–24   The $m\cdot$ beautiful blossom is often
52–25 $m\cdot$ beautiful mansion is sometimes
54–16 $m\cdot$ potent and deadly enemy.

most

Pul.   22–20   her $m\cdot$ beautiful garments,
23– 4   * THE $M\cdot$ UNIQUE STRUCTURE
23–17   * one of the $m\cdot$ potent factors
24– 5   * one of the $m\cdot$ beautiful,
24– 5   * the $m\cdot$ unique structure
28–22   * its songs are for the $m\cdot$ part
31– 6   * a $m\cdot$ interesting personality.
31–21   * she $m\cdot$ kindly replied,
36–23   * one of the $m\cdot$ beautiful residences
37–14   * it is her $m\cdot$ earnest aim to
44–10   * It is a $m\cdot$ auspicious hour
45–10   * grandest and $m\cdot$ helpful
45–19   * proved, in $m\cdot$ striking manner,
47–25   * But for the $m\cdot$ part she
49–11   * of $m\cdot$ unpromising ground
54–26   * $m\cdot$ perfect obtainable environment,
56– 9   * as a rule, are the $m\cdot$ intelligent.
56–13   * one of the $m\cdot$ remarkable,
57–11   * one of the $m\cdot$ beautiful
65–16   * a $m\cdot$ beautiful structure
66–10   * $m\cdot$ of those who embrace the faith
70–11   * $m\cdot$ remarkable women in America.
75– 2   Whoever in any age expresses $m\cdot$
75– 3   has $m\cdot$ of the spirit of Christ,
75–25   * the $m\cdot$ nearly fire-proof church
77– 3   * one of the $m\cdot$ chastely elegant
77–15   * $m\cdot$ lovingly invited to visit
78– 2   * one of the $m\cdot$ magnificent
78–13   * hereby $m\cdot$ lovingly invited
79–15   * in $m\cdot$ instances they are held at
80– 6   * in the $m\cdot$ intellectual city
80–11   * $m\cdot$ recognition, the widest outlook.
82–23   * singing $m\cdot$ for their own sex.
87– 1   * $m\cdot$ cordially invite you to be present
Rud.   7– 3 $m\cdot$ difficult case so treated.
No.   1– 3   is a $m\cdot$ needful work ;
2–23   the $m\cdot$ defiant forms of disease.
23–14   The $m\cdot$ eminent divines,
28–10   the $m\cdot$ acceptable time
37–14 $m\cdot$ marvellous demonstration,
39–23 $m\cdot$ of all, it shows us what God is.
41– 7   work $m\cdot$ derided and envied
41– 7   that is $m\cdot$ acceptable to God?
Pan.   2–13   word "pantheism" is $m\cdot$ suggestive.
15– 7   establish us in the $m\cdot$ holy faith,
'00.   1–18   in $m\cdot$ of the principal cities,
2– 4   the people $m\cdot$ interested
7– 9 $m\cdot$ scholarly men and women,
15–10   which of all . . . is the $m\cdot$ divine ;
'01.   1–12 $m\cdot$ essential to your growth
9–27   who loveth and liveth $m\cdot$
9–28   receiveth them $m\cdot$;
15–14   The $m\cdot$ deplorable sight is to
16–22   to carry a $m\cdot$ vital point.
29–24   loves $m\cdot$, does $m\cdot$, and sacrifices $m\cdot$
30– 8   consciousness which is $m\cdot$ imbued
33–24   The richest and $m\cdot$ positive proof
'02.   17– 8   has $m\cdot$ of heaven in it,
Hea.   9– 8   the $m\cdot$ hopeless invalid
9– 9   think $m\cdot$ of sickness and of sin ;
12–26   attenuations are the $m\cdot$ powerful.
14–18 $m\cdot$ arduous task I ever performed.
16– 7   hath the $m\cdot$ actual substance,
Po.   7–11   life $m\cdot$ sweet, as heart to heart
38–16   God's $m\cdot$ tender mercies,
64–18   Those we $m\cdot$ love find a
65–16   Those moments $m\cdot$ sweet
My.   4–30   Thou God $m\cdot$ high and nigh.
6–28 $m\cdot$ prefigures self-abnegation,
25–11   * and are $m\cdot$ gratifying :
27–26   * to $m\cdot$ of them the fact that he
32– 2   * two of the $m\cdot$ striking features
36–13   * $M\cdot$ of us are here because we
42–13   * $M\cdot$ unexpectedly to me came the
45– 7   * $m\cdot$ important gatherings
50– 4   * $M\cdot$ of those present had left their
51– 6   * $m\cdot$ sincerely regret that our
52–28   * $m\cdot$ authors would have shrunk,
71– 2   * $m\cdot$ intricate discoveries
71– 3   * the $m\cdot$ beautiful effects
71–16   * $m\cdot$ imposing church edifices
75– 9   * $m\cdot$ of them headed straight for
77–10   * the $m\cdot$ notable feature
84–24   * Its hold and . . . are $m\cdot$ notable.
86–23   * one of the $m\cdot$ interesting
86–24   * the $m\cdot$ notable of such occasions.
87– 6   * to the $m\cdot$ casual observer.
91– 2   * $m\cdot$ of whom were already
91–17   * one of the $m\cdot$ remarkable
96–16   * perhaps the $m\cdot$ remarkable,
98– 1   * the $m\cdot$ determined skeptic.
107–30   heals the $m\cdot$ violent stages of
118– 9   your $m\cdot$ excellent letter.
138–21 $m\cdot$ respectfully yours,
142–13 $m\cdot$ important events are criticized.

most

My.	142–21	*M·* truly yours,
	158–22	*M·* men and women talk well,
	160–10	*M·* of us willingly accept
	160–15	*m·* men avoid until compelled
	164–25	unfolds the thought *m·* within
	165–28	is the *m·* unselfed.
	177– 3	*M·* happily would I comply with
	188–10	of the *m·* High,'' — *Psal.* 91 : 1.
	197– 3	That error is *m·* forcible which is
	211–24	where there is *m·* danger ;
	219– 8	Human power is *m·* properly used in
	229–28	Thou knowest best what we need *m·*,
	231– 6	suffered *m·* from those whom she
	233–20	*m·* stubborn belief to overcome,
	240–26	* She *m·* assuredly does,
	249– 7	counteract its *m·* gigantic falsities.
	249–28	student who is *m·* spiritually-minded.
	259–14	*m·* pleasing Christmas presents,
	259–27	*m·* appropriate and proper exercise.
	266– 3	the *m·* imminent dangers
	271–14	* the *m·* discussed woman in
	282–27	*M·* truly yours,
	283– 8	Your appointment . . . is *m·* gracious.
	285–13	*m·* cultured men and women
	285–29	*M·* sincerely yours,
	289– 1	The thing *m·* important is what we do,
	290–18	when all earthly joys seem *m·* afar.
	300–13	heals the *m·* inveterate diseases.
	305–13	*m·* distinguished men and women
	312–25	in my behalf were *m·* tender.
	326– 4	* is *m·* gratifying to our people ;
	331– 3	performed their . . . *m·* faithfully.''
	332–21	* in a *m·* interesting way.
	347–24	*M·* thinkers concede that Science is
	356– 3	where God dwells *m·* conspicuously

Most High *and* most High

Mis.	229–17	even the *m· H·* — *Psal.* 91 : 9.
	277–14	the messages of the *M· H·*.
My.	188–10	of the *m· H·*,'' — *Psalm* 91 : 1.

mostly

Mis.	379– 7	composition was . . . *m·* descriptive of
My.	97–28	* have *m·* departed,
	105–10	the lungs were *m·* consumed.
	160– 4	The heart that beats *m·* for self

mote

Mis.	336–15	*m·* of evil out of other eyes.

moth

Mis.	82–27	is consumed as a *m·*,
Ret.	32– 9	is crushed as the *m·*.
Pul.	81–17	* not as the *m·* to be destroyed
My.	230– 1	the sacrilegious *m·* of time,

Mother (*see also* mother's)

Mis.	18–19	Father, *M·*, and child are the
	33–11	God, our divine Father and *M·*.
	96–12	first, as a loving Father and *M·* ;
	113– 5	Spirit is our Father and *M·*,
	151–13	God is our Father and our *M·*,
	154–23	Honor thy Father and *M·*, God.
	159–24	''O glorious Truth ! O *M·* Love !
	167–17	His Father and *M·* are divine Life,
	186–14	He is the universal Father and *M·*
Pul.	13– 3	as Love, represented by the *M·*.
Un.	48–14	Father and *M·* of all He creates ;
'00.	5–10	Father and *M·* are synonymous terms ;
'01.	10–18	nature of God as both Father and *M·*.
		(*see also* **Eddy**)

mother (*see also* mother's)

and husband

Mis.	385– 9	poem
Po.	page 48	poem

ardent

Ret.	90–19	Who can feel . . . like the ardent *m·*?

become a

Mis.	253–26	until she herself is become a *m·*
	289–24	the right to become a *m·* ;

father and

(*see* **father**)

father or

Man.	69–19	loveth father or *m·* more — *Matt.* 10 : 37.

her

Mis.	214– 8	daughter against her *m·*, — *Matt.* 10 : 35.
Pul.	32–27	* her *m·* was a religious enthusiast,
	33– 5	* would often run to her *m·*
	33–12	* answered as her *m·* had bidden her,

his

Mis.	225– 4	eighty-second birthday of his *m·*
My.	257–12	for himself and for his *m·*,

my

Ret.	5–15	Of my *m·* I cannot speak as
	6–12	next to my *m·*, the very dearest
	8–11	my *m·* was perplexed and
	8–21	left the room, went to my *m·*,
	9– 8	my *m·* read to me

mother

my

Ret.	9–14	as my *m·* had bidden me.
	13–18	My *m·*, as she bathed my
My.	145–13	* an old ailment my *m·* had.''
	310–26	My *m·* often presented my

my sainted

Ret.	5–19	and knew my sainted *m·*

of eight

Mis.	7– 6	often busier than the *m·* of eight.

of Jesus

Pul.	27–21	* the *m·* of Jesus,

of one child

Mis.	7– 5	and the *m·* of one child

related

Pul.	33– 6	* One night the *m·* related to her

saw this

Ret.	13–23	*M·* saw this, and was glad.

sister, and

Chr.	55–24	and sister, and *m·*. — *Matt.* 12 : 50.

stricken

Mis.	275– 9	the faithful, stricken *m·*,

tender

My.	235– 6	tender *m·*, guided by love,

to help

'01.	29–18	go not to help *m·* but to recruit

true

Ret.	90–16	The true *m·* never willingly

virgin

'01.	8–27	was born of a virgin *m·*,

wise

Un.	6–20	No wise *m·*, though a graduate of

without

Chr.	55–20	Without father, without *m·*, — *Heb.* 7 : 3.

worked

'01.	29–21	*m·* worked and won for them

wrote

Mis.	372–10	A *m·* wrote, ''Looking at the pictures

your

Ret.	8–18	''Your *m·* is calling you !''
	8–20	your *m·* is calling you !''

Mis.	6–29	where the *m·* has all that she can
	152–13	but I, as a *m·* whose heart
	167– 3	after the manner of a *m·*
	225–10	whereupon the *m·*, Mrs. Rawson,
	253–23	Can a *m·* tell her child one tithe of
	317– 2	''May I call you *m·* ?''
Ret.	5–28	* As a *m·*, she was untiring in
	8– 9	''*M·*, who *did* call me ?
	8–24	and said that *m·* wanted me.
	9– 4	*M·* told Mehitable all about this
	16– 5	for she was a *m·*
	40–18	The *m·* afterwards wrote to me,
Pan.	8– 9	belief that Mary was the *m·* of God
My.	13–12	* a *m·* and a ruling church.''
		(*see also* **Eddy**)

mother-bird

Mis.	137–16	protecting wings of the *m·*,
	254– 8	as the *m·* tendeth her young

Mother Church

Man.	52– 3	Members in *M· C·* Only.
	71– 9	*M· C·* Unique.
My.	11–15	* need of our *M· C·*.
	88–10	* *M· C·* of the C. S. faith
	89–22	* dedication of the new *M· C·*
	91–29	* *M· C·* is absolutely free from debt.
	97–20	* *M· C·* of the C. S. faith
	242–19	relating to . . . *M· C·* membership,
	320–30	* dedication of the first *M· C·*

Mother Church, The

Building and building

Man.	103– 3	The *M· C·* Building.
My.	15– 5	The *M· C·* Building.
	357–11	have crowned The *M· C·* building

Directors

My.	360–19	supporting The *M· C·* Directors.

Manual

Man.	45–10	specified in The *M· C·* Manual,
	72–23	consonance with The *M· C·* Manual.

member of

(*see* **member**)

members of

(*see* **members**)

Mis.	106–15	chapter sub-title
	125–21	chapter sub-title
	127– 3	connection with The *M· C·*,
	129– 1	chapter sub-title
	143–24	toward building The *M· C·*.
	148–22	chapter sub-title
	311– 2	come and unite with The *M· C·*
	316– 9	The *M· C·* must be self-sustained
	322– 4	chapter sub-title
	322– 6	to hear me speak in The *M· C·*,

Mother Church of Christ, Scientist, The
My. 250– 2 By-law of The *M· C· of C·, S·,*
250–15 By-law of The *M· C· of C·, S·,*
279–23 member of The *M· C· of C·, S·,*
289– 8 proper that The *M· C· of C·, S·,*
347– 7 Members of The *M· C· of C·, S·,*
352–19 *Ushers of The M· C· of C·, S· :*

Mother Church's, The
Man. 71–17 The *M· C·* form of government,

Mother in Israel
(see **Eddy**)

mother-in-law
Mis. 214– 8 against her *m·*.— Matt. 10 : 35.

motherless
Mis. 275–11 and the *m·* little ones,

Mother Mary
My. 303– 3 one incarnation, one *M· M·*.

Mother's
Mis. 206– 6 heard the Father and *M·* welcome,
(see also **Eddy**)

mother's
Mis. 160– 4 a *m·* love behind words
253–22 *m·* love touches the heart of
33⊢16 words from a *m·* lips
Ret. 1–16 perpetuated her *m·* name.
8– 6 thought this was my *m·* voice,
20– 3 until after my *m·* decease.
Po. 8–18 Of a *m·* love, that no words
29– 9 No natal hour and *m·* tear,
My. 311–24 which is of my *m·* ancestry,
336–15 until after my *m·* decease.''
(see also **Eddy**)

mothers
Mis. 5– 7 *M·* should be able to

Mother's Darling
Ret. 20–15 taken from my poem, "*M· D·*,"

Mother's Evening Prayer
(see **Appendix A**)

Mother's Room and room
Mis. 144– 3 The money for building "*M· R·*,"
Man. 69–26 formerly known as "*M· R·*"
Pul. v– 5 *M· R·* IN THE FIRST CHURCH OF
8–27 *M· R·* in The First Church of
25–10 * the "*M· R·*," designed for
25–19 * the auditorium, the "*M· R·*,"
26–19 * heading
26–20 * The "*M· R·*" is approached by
27– 1 * Leading off the "*M· R·*" are
27–29 * In the "*M· R·*" the windows are
42–12 * money was devoted to the "*M· R·*,"
42–17 * words, "*M· R·*," in gilt letters.
49– 2 * or sometimes "*M· r·*,"
58–27 * a room . . . called "*M· R·*,"
59–27 * the money for the *M· R·*,
76– 3 * apartment known as the "*M· R·*,"
76– 5 * The furnishing of the "*M· R·*"
My. 353–22 formerly known as "*M· R·*"

mother tincture
'01. 18– 1 "*m· t·*" of one grain of the drug

motion
Mis. 132– 1 A *m·* was made, and a vote passed,
208–13 unbroken *m·* of the law of divine Love
230–10 and mere *m·* when at work,
Man. 17– 9 on *m·* of Mrs. Eddy, it was voted,
Ret. 31–14 spontaneous *m·* of Truth and Love,
89– 3 opposed to it by material *m·*,
My. 7–15 * offered the following *m·* :
8– 3 * In support of the *m·*, Mr. Kimball
8– 8 * in seconding the *m·*, said :
8–22 * The *m·* was carried unanimously.
22–19 * every purpose she has set in *m·*,
44–18 * The *m·* was carried unanimously
65– 2 * chapter sub-title
65–10 * This astonishing *m·* was passed

motionless
No. 6–17 evidence that the earth is *m·*

motions
Mis. 65– 5 and her *m·* imaginary.

motive
Mis. 117– 6 discern between the thought, *m·*, and
117– 6 superinduced by the wrong *m·* or
130–22 Where the *m·* to do right exists,
135– 7 one in *m·*, purpose, pursuit.
195– 3 all action, *m·*, and mind,
283– 2 or the *m·* is mercenary,
354–15 more grace, a *m·* made pure,
Man. 83– 4 *M·* in Teaching.
Ret. 28–30 no *m·* can cause a surrender of
30– 7 The *m·* of my earliest labors
Hea. 7–11 begins with *m·*, instead of act,

motive
Hea. 7–12 and there correcting the *m·*,
7–13 act that results from the *m·*.
7–16 begins in *m·* to correct the act,
19–17 to spiritualize thought, *m·*, and
My. 117– 5 personal *m·* gratified by sense
128–25 the *m·* is not as wicked,
181–13 the *m·* of true religion,
236–19 far-reaching *m·* and success,

motive-power
Mis. 197– 2 become the *m·* of every act.

motives
affections and
Mis. 19–10 lift the affections and *m·* of men
and acts
Man. 40– 4 A Rule for *M·* and Acts.
Ret. 79–10 in unselfish *m·* and acts,
and aims
My. 125– 2 false affections, *m·*, and aims,
and circumstances
Ret. 38–25 *m·* and circumstances unknown to me.
and methods
Mis. 267–28 spiritualizes man's *m·* and methods,
and object
My. 296–27 traced its emotions, *m·*, and object.
best
My. 180–26 misconstrues our best *m·*,
Christian
Man. 50–18 from Christian *m·* make this evident,
desire, and
No. 12–13 The same affection, desire, and *m·*
for sin
Peo. 9– 5 washing away the *m·* for sin ;
for teaching
Rud. 16– 1 If . . . are the *m·* for teaching,
govern acts
Mis. 51–15 *M·* govern acts, and Mind governs man.
her
Pul. 50– 5 * Indeed, one of her *m·*
his
Mis. 162–26 his *m·* and Christlikeness,
kind
My. 234–11 God will reward their kind *m·*,
leading
No. 32– 7 nor the *m·* leading to it.
mercenary
No. 43–18 take it up from mercenary *m·*,
mere
Rud. 17– 3 from mere *m·* of self-aggrandizement to
misjudged
Mis. 236– 2 human passions . . . have misjudged *m·* ?
my
Mis. 263– 1 if my *m·* are sinister, they will harm
278–11 when my *m·* and acts are understood
new
Mis. 204–14 giving mortals new *m·*,
of human affection
My. 268– 8 If the *m·* of human affection are
of men
Mis. 19–10 lift the affections and *m·* of men
My. 268–14 uplifting the *m·* of men.
of others
No. 7– 7 as to the *m·* of others.
or acts
Man. 40– 6 should impel the *m·* or acts
personal
Mis. 291– 7 demonstrates above personal *m·*,
remorseless
Mis. 10– 5 the most remorseless *m·* that
right
Mis. 51–17 the right *m·* for action,
same
'01. 33–27 the same *m·* which actuate
selfish
Mis. 118– 3 self-will, selfish *m·*, and
Ret. 71–21 selfish *m·* entering into
sinister
Ret. 78– 9 but carnal and sinister *m·*,
their
Mis. 84–10 their *m·* were rewarded
214–23 their *m·*, aims, and tendency.
unseen
Mis. 260–30 lawless mind, with unseen *m·*,
unselfish
Mis. 232–27 spiritual and unselfish *m·*.
Ret. 79–10 in unselfish *m·* and acts,
wrong
Mis. 215–12 or start from wrong *m·*.
263– 3 knowing that the wrong *m·* are not
My. 223–18 superinduced by wrong *m·*
your
Mis. 90–19 are equal to your *m·* ;

'02. 17–26 take its answer as to thy aims, *m·*,

motor
  Pul. 25– 5   * with *m·* electric power.

mottled
  Mis. 376–24   into a glory of *m·* marvels.

motto
  Mis. 139–17   the above Scripture for its *m·*.
       306– 5   * *m·* has not yet been decided upon,
  Ret. 86– 9   as said the classic Grecian *m·*
  '02. 14– 6   a *m·* for every Christian Scientist,
  My. 170–18   it is my sacred *m·*,

mould
  No. 20– 6   would fashion Deity in a manlike *m·*,
  My. 261–12   To *m·* aright the first impressions

moulded
  My. 114–10   book which has *m·* their lives

moulder
  Mis. 293–29   there to *m·* and rot.

moulding
  No. 20– 6   Truth is *m·* a Godlike man.

moulds
  Mis. 360– 8   cast in the *m·* of C. S. :

Moulton, Edward A.
  My. 174–15   Edward A. *M·*, John C. Thorne,

mound
  My. 311–27   knelt in silent prayer on the *m·*

Mount
      (*see* **Sermon on the Mount**)

mount
  Mis. 17– 7   on this *m·* of revelation,
       44– 2   showed to thee in the *m·*," — *Heb.* 8 : 5.
     164–14   from the *m·* of revelation,
     206–29   upon the *m·* of holiness,
     234– 4   attempt to *m·* above error
     326–20   to the valley and up the *m·*.
     328–16   been driven . . . to the foot of the *m·*,
     356–14   from the *m·* of revelation,
     369– 2   foot of the *m·* of revelation,
     387– 4   *m·* upward unto purer skies ;
  No. 1–16   on the *m·* of revelation,
  '01. 10–24   after the pattern of the *m·*.
  Hea. 19–23   to the model on the *m·*,
  Po. 50–22   *m·* upward unto purer skies ;
  My. 110–24   *m·* higher in the altitude of being.
     189– 3   should reach the *m·* of revelation ;

mountain (*see also* **mountain's**)
  Mis. 41–15   the *m·* of human endeavor,
     251–30   *m·* mists before the sun.
     323– 8   at the foot of the *m·*
     323–17   at the foot of the *m·*.
     323–18   Would ye ascend the *m·*,
     324–30   at the foot of the *m·*,
     326–24   and take them up the *m·*.
     327– 6   "Wilt thou climb the *m·*,
     328– 7   *m·* is heaven-crowned Christianity,
     329–14   over *m·* and meadow,
     392– 2   Oh, *m·* monarch, at whose feet
     392–10   Whate'er thy mission, *m·* sentinel,
  No. 7–12   as a bird to your *m·*," — *Psal.* 11 : 1.
  Hea. 10–26   As the *m·* hart panteth for
  Po. v– 9   * poem
    page 1   poem
     20– 1   *m·* monarch, at whose feet
     20–14   Whate'er thy mission, *m·* sentinel,
     66– 4   the thrill of that *m·* rill,
  My. 183–14   upon the *m·* of Israel.
     186–10   up the *m·*, and on to the
     222–11   say unto this *m·*, — *Matt.* 17 : 20.

mountain-horn
  Mis. 328– 4   listen for the *m·*,

mountain's
  Mis. 392– 1   poem
  Po. page 20   poem

mountains
  Un. 11– 1   the *m·* of unholiness
  Pul. 73–16   * If you have faith, you can move *m·*."
  Pan. 3–27   president of the *m·*,
  Po. 41– 9   And the *m·* more friendless,
  My. 184–26   beautiful upon the *m·* — *Isa.* 52 : 7.
     185–22   In 1888 I visited these *m·*
     185–25   to be in the midst of the *m·*,
     185–30   refuge in *m·*, and good universal.
     186– 1   The rocks, rills, *m·*,
     194– 3   fell forests and remove *m·*,
     278–11   molecule of faith that removes *m·*,

mounted
  My. 115– 1   *m·* thought on the swift
     259– 2   *m·* on its pedestal

mounting
  Mis. 1–16   *m·* sense gathers fresh forms
  No. 34–23   *m·* to the throne of glory

mounting
  '02. 20– 1   *m·* the billow or going down into
  My. 110–24   *M·* higher, mortals will cease to

mounts
  My. 129–27   where faith *m·* upward,

mourn
  Mis. 124–15   comforting such as *m·*,
     275–16   encourage, and bless all who *m·*.
     353– 1   it has nothing to *m·* over,
     388–20   Last at the cross to *m·* her Lord,
  Pul. 56–22   * And *m·* our self-inflicted pain."
  Po. 21– 9   Last at the cross to *m·* her Lord,
     67–17   The cypress may *m·* with her
  My. 126–24   and who should *m·* over the
     132–31   comforts such as *m·*,
     230–13   to comfort such as *m·*,
     291–26   called to *m·* the loss of
     291–28   stops to think, to *m·*, yea, to pray,
     295– 1   I sympathize with those who *m·*,
     335–10   * companions, who *m·* his early death.
     339–22   rejoice . . . and have no cause to *m·* ;

mourned
  Mis. 375–30   * true art — that we have . . . *m·*
  My. 12–19   *m·* it as what "might have been."

mourner
  Mis. 399– 1   *M·*, it calls you, — "Come to my bosom,
  Po. 75– 7   *M·*, it calls you, — "Come to my bosom,
  My. 292–11   support, and comfort the chief *m·*

mourners
  Po. 78–14   meekest of *m·*, while yet the chief,

mourning
  My. 126–21   death, and *m·*, and famine ; — *Rev.* 18 : 8 .

mourns
  My. 294–30   The court of the Vatican *m·* him ;

mouse
  Mis. 131– 3   a *m·* gnawing at the vitals of

mouth
  Mis. 118–31   which goeth into the *m·* — *Matt.* 15 : 11.
     118–32   which cometh out of the *m·*, — *Matt.* 15 : 11.
     183–16   if he open his *m·* it shall be filled
     209– 5   wouldst shut the *m·* of His prophets,
     231–18   poked into the little *m·*
     231–25   pucker the rosebud *m·* into saying,
     240–26   with a cigarette in his *m·*
     373–10   the serpent cast out of his *m·*,
  Ret. 81–23   puts this pious counsel into a father's *m·* :
  Un. 33–24   "In the *m·* of two or three — *Matt.* 18 : 16.
     60–15   Out of the same *m·* — *Jas.* 3 : 10.
  Pul. 14– 9   cast out of his *m·* water — *Rev.* 12 : 15.
     14–11   the earth opened her *m·*, — *Rev.* 12 : 16.
     14–13   dragon cast out of his *m·*. — *Rev.* 12 : 16.
  No. 44–16   the *m·* lisping God's praise ;
  '02. 16–22   opening not his *m·* in self-defense
  My. 6–22   proceedeth out of the *m·* of God.
     13–23   satisfieth thy *m·* with — *Psal.* 103 : 5.
     42– 3   * openeth her *m·* with — *Prov.* 31 : 26.
     216– 1   obtain their money from a fish's *m·*,

mouthpiece
  Mis. 277– 9   archers aim at Truth's *m·* ;
  My. 247– 6   The church is the *m·* of C. S.,
     254–27   The church is the *m·* of C. S.,

mouths
  Pul. 8–21   "Out of the *m·* of babes — *Matt.* 21 : 16.

movable
  Pul. 58–15   * by the use of *m·* partitions.

move
  Mis. 8– 6   we live, and *m·*, — *Acts* 17 : 28.
     28– 7   muscles cannot *m·* without mind.
     69–21   even to *m·* his bowels
     79– 9   we live, *m·*, and have being.
     82–30   "we live, and *m·*, — *Acts* 17 : 28.
     104–18   The latter *m·* in God's grooves
     227–13   may give it a forward *m·*,
     338–18   *m·* majestically to your defense
     342–31   and are ready for the next *m·*.
     343– 8   to *m·* it onward and upward.
     377– 1   should *m·* our brush or pen
  Ret. 93–18   we live, and *m·*, — *Acts* 17 : 28.
  Un. 26–14   * Man decays and ages *m·* ;
  Pul. 2–23   "we live, and *m·*, — *Acts* 17 : 28.
     73–16   * have faith, you can *m·* mountains."
  No. 17– 7   we live, and *m·*, — *Acts* 17 : 28.
  Pan. 13–20   we do "live, and *m·*, — *Acts* 17 : 28.
  '02. 12–20   we live, and *m·*, — *Acts* 17 : 28.
  Po. 65– 3   Life's pulses *m·* fitful
  My. 9–11   * *m·* us to utter our gratitude
     61–23   * seemed to *m·* as by magic ;
     69–21   * where . . . people can freely *m·*.
     109–22   "we live, and *m·*, — *Acts* 17 : 28.
     258–29   may you *m·* onward and upward,
     294–24   and will *m·* the pen of millions.

moved

Mis.	106–30	M· by mind, your many-throated organ,
	275–25	m· me to speechless thanks.
Ret.	5–26	* in the circles in which she m·,
	48–10	m· me to close my flourishing
Un.	11–13	The palsied hand m·,
My.	33–27	shall never be m·. — *Psal.* 15 : 5.
	44–17	* m· that it be forwarded at once
	51–16	* m· to instruct the Clerk
	129–25	whose feet can never be m·.
	241–26	* found that I lived and m·
	314– 4	* then m· to Franklin.
	333–11	* m· to the residence of the

movement

Mis.	235–21	This m· of thought must push on
	354–18	the m· of body and soul
Pul.	23–14	* This m·, under the guise of C. S.,
	31–28	* as flexible in m· as that of
	50–19	* Any new m· will awaken some
	51–15	* predict where this m· will go,
	52–17	* rapid growth of the new m·.
	59–26	* connected with the m·.
	69– 2	* to organize this m·.
	69– 5	* the Founder of the m·.
	79–10	* not to ignore a m· which,
'00.	9–27	leader of this mighty m·.
My.	10–28	* prosperous growth of this m·
	11– 4	* the Leader of this m·,
	45–12	* animus and spirit of our m·.
	89–30	* should found a religious m·
	163–28	m· of establishing in this city
	282–17	chapter sub-title
	287– 3	m· to erect a monument
	316–14	Survey of the C. S. M·,"
	320–17	* in sympathy with the m·,
	329–23	* admitting its interest in the m·,

movements

Mis.	117–19	participating in the m·,
	245–15	Their m· indicate fear
Man.	78–11	important m· of the manager
Ret.	82– 6	not allow their m· to be
Pul.	38–26	* Yet each and all these m·,
	56–13	* helpful, and powerful m·
	67–14	* one of those m· which seek to
'02.	12–29	institutions and early m· of
My.	91–18	* religious m· that this country
	291– 8	heavy strokes, measured m·,

moves

Mis.	117–29	The disobedient make their m·
	166– 6	lives, and m· in our midst
	174–11	Principle that m· all in harmony,
	335–14	neither m· me from the path
Peo.	8–19	as directly as it m· a planet
My.	123– 6	which m· the hearts of men
	164–29	m·, and has his being in God,
	195–23	m·, and has deathless being.
	205– 9	* m· in a mysterious way

moving

Mis.	47–10	when m· your body,

Mozart

'00.	11–15	M· rests you.

Mrs.

Man.	110–15	Women must sign " Miss " or "M·."
	111– 7	prefix her signature with "M· ;"

Mrs. ——

Mis.	87–16	*if you sent M· —— to ——.*

Mt. Ararat

Pan.	2– 7	higher than *Mt. A·* above the deluge.

Mt. Auburn

My.	69–30	* Mt. A· cemetery in Cambridge,

much

Mis.	vii–20	Wherefor, have m· to pay.
	4–19	M· interest is awakened
	5–30	It is m· easier for people to
	7–30	not so m· from a lack of justice,
	8– 3	we shall have accomplished m· ;
	8–20	however m· we suffer in
	11–26	Because I can do m· general good
	16– 7	one finds so m· lacking,
	16– 8	and so very m· requisite
	17–19	m· higher and holier conception
	18–29	m· that must be repented of
	23– 1	having learned so m· ;
	36–27	as m· in our waking moments
	52– 3	how m· one can do for himself,
	55– 7	as m· of the divine Spirit
	62–13	by that m·, less available.
	80– 3	m· more than can be gained
	96–25	This answer includes too m·
	107–32	either too m· or too little
	108– 1	sorrowing saint thinks too m·
	108–23	the misconception . . . costs m·.

much

Mis.	109– 8	how m·, sin claims of you ;
	109– 9	how m· of this claim you admit
	109–13	how m· more, then, should
	111– 5	at break of day caught m·.
	114– 3	cannot give too m· time
	130– 6	how m· better it is to be wronged,
	137–23	you must give m· time to
	143–28	sometimes at m· self-sacrifice,
	147–29	would m· rather fail of success
	155–18	(however m· she desires thus to do),
	159–19	not so m· the Bethlehem babe,
	167–10	How m· does he weigh?
	178–20	'M· learning'— or something else
	185–24	how m· of a man he ever has been :
	198–20	a belief of disease is as m·
	229–11	how m· more certain would be
	230–13	is no proof of accomplishing m·.
	232– 2	but the memory was too m· ;
	241–29	how m· more should these heal,
	247–25	It is m· easier for people to
	253–15	portends m· for the future.
	262–29	because I take so m· pleasure in
	271–20	M· is said at this date,
	273– 4	although it will cost him m·,
	282–12	m· less would we have our minds
	287–26	it will spare you m· bitterness.
	290–28	not so m· from individual as
	291– 9	Too m· and too little is attached
	302–14	M· good has been accomplished
	309–30	which contain all and m· more
	335–14	having too m· charity ;
	341– 7	m· slipping and clambering,
	342–31	How m· more should we
	353–11	People give me too m· attention
	353–28	too m· interested in themselves
	357–15	M· of what has been sown
	376–14	* and in a m· better form."
	378– 8	After m· consultation among
Ret.	6– 9	my m· respected parents,
	7–23	* too m· of sorrow and loss.
	9–18	* Is it not m· that I may
	10– 2	kept me m· out of school,
	44–19	m· time and attention
	69–12	seem to have life as m· as God,
	71–11	an error of m· magnitude.
	78– 3	either too m· or too little.
	82–22	m· good or else evil ;
	94–29	Jesus' teachings bore m· fruit,
	95–11	* comforters are needed m·
Un.	1– 2	rouses so m· natural doubt
	6–22	Not m· more than a half-century
	8– 2	gives m· trouble to many
	27– 6	who talks m· of himself.
	46– 5	We do not see m· of the real man
Pul.	2– 1	m· like the Queen of Sheba,
	21–22	however m· this is done to us
	36–27	* I am m· indebted for some of the
	45–16	* M· was the ridicule heaped upon
	46–10	* m· is told of herself in detail
	47–25	* she lives very m· retired,
	58–20	* too m· so for comfortable reading,
	61–21	* M· admiration was expressed
	66– 2	* exists as m· to-day as it did
	72–10	* m· absorbed in the work
	72–11	* given so m· of her attention.
	79–23	* as m· as his lungs call for breath ;
	80–20	* but this m· is true :
	81–12	* she thinks so m· of herself
	81–19	* those who have so m· to give
	87–18	You ask too m· when asking me to
Rud.	6–26	how m· you understand of C. S.
No.	3–22	not so m· thine own as another's good,
	24–13	but m· more real,
	26–27	m· more clothe you, — *Matt.* 6 : 30.
	41– 6	as m· as to ask, Is it the
'01.	10– 5	how m· more shall they — *Matt.* 10 : 25.
'02.	11–15	how m· more is accomplished
	15–18	m· of his property was in slaves,
	18–20	how m· of what he did are we
Hea.	14– 3	in fine, m· ado about nothing.
	16– 5	How m· are you demonstrating
	18–20	as m· as to the sinner :
Po.	2– 4	M· as the chisel of the sculptor's art
My.	11–17	* expressed m· gratification
	21–21	* experienced m· pleasure
	21–23	* have anticipated m· joy
	23– 2	* how m· our neighbor has given,
	27–21	* will read with m· joy
	30–10	* It spoke m· for the devotion
	53–30	* must have been very m· broken
	62–25	* when they were so m· needed.
	75–16	* it would not make m· difference,
	89– 3	* that faith which is so m·
	91–23	* the objects of m· ridicule,
	94–14	* m· to convince the skeptic.

much

My.	111– 7	*m·* the same class of minds
	114–28	Is it too *m·* to say that this book
	129–28	Lean not too *m·* on your Leader.
	131–23	fulfilling *m·* of the divine law
	133–23	Do you know how *m·* I love you
	149–19	may know too *m·* of human law
	160– 1	and keeps Mind *m·* out of sight.
	163–23	retirement I so *m·* coveted,
	164– 3	retirement I so *m·* desired.
	193– 4	will bring to your hearts so *m·*
	194–25	you have sacrificed so *m·*
	202–29	that ye bear *m·* fruit." — *John* 15 : 8.
	203–28	You whose labors are doing so *m·*
	212–14	Why is there so *m·* dissension
	215–14	* "Your teachings are worth *m·*
	216–20	work by which you can do *m·* good
	231– 7	labored *m·* to benefit
	233–29	as *m·* as they love mankind?
	234– 7	know how *m·* I love them,
	236–11	Too *m·* of one thing spoils the
	240– 7	* "Would it be asking too *m·*
	246–30	Magna Charta of C. S. means *m·*,
	247–21	not so *m·* eloquence as
	254–22	Magna Charta of C· S· means *m·*,
	259–28	respects the Christ too *m·* to submerge
	261–10	Too *m·* cannot be done towards
	272–30	* *m·* influence on this generation.
	278–22	Nothing is gained . . . but *m·* is lost.
	280–11	* righteous prayer which availeth *m·*.
	303–29	We need *m·* humility, wisdom,
	309– 4	called upon to do *m·* business
	311– 9	* she troubles me so *m·*.
	320– 5	* He also seemed very *m·* pleased
	323–26	* should mean to your older students *m·*
	324– 7	* ideas were too *m·* alike for
	324– 9	* no one could be of *m·* service to
	325– 6	* Mr. Wiggin was very *m·* troubled
	331–26	* *M·* has often been said of the
	332–24	* *m·* interviewing with Masonic
	341–20	* C. S. has been so *m·* to the fore
	345– 5	will be thought to matter *m·*.
	358–13	however *m·* I desire to read all that
	358–17	to relieve me of so *m·* labor.

much-ado-about-nothing

Mis.	351–11	late *m·* arose solely from

muffled

'02.	3–22	*m·* fear of death and triumph

Muller, Prof. Max

Pul.	23–22	* and scholars . . . like Prof. Max *M·*,

multiplicand

Mis.	221–29	might serve as the *m·*.

multiplication

Mis.	221–27	*m·* of the same two numbers
	244–11	in the *m·* of mankind?

multiplied

My.	236– 7	this name continues to be *m·*,

multiply

Mis.	56–25	*m·*, *and replenish* — *Gen.* 1 : 28.
	57–15	*m·* thy sorrow." — *Gen.* 3 : 16.
Un.	44–16	would *m·* and subdivide
No.	31– 7	They progress and will *m·*
My.	183–15	God will *m·* thee.
	214– 2	as our churches *m·*,

multiplying

'02.	1–10	churches are *m·* everywhere
My.	93– 2	* They are *m·* without efforts

multitude

Mis.	227– 4	to the hisses of the *m·*,
Pul.	42– 3	* filled with a waiting *m·*.
My.	41– 1	* our Leader has induced a *m·*
	58–17	* love and gratitude of a great *m·*
	77–18	* *m·* which began to gather
	78– 8	* *m·* passed through the
	85–24	* *m·* of strangers to whom
	87– 9	* cheerfully contented *m·*
	123–24	to feed the *m·* ;

multitudes

Un.	7– 4	in *m·* of other religious folds.
My.	v–24	* healed *m·* of disease
	28–26	* to the *m·* of Judea
	87– 4	* the *m·* going and coming.
	141–19	* vast *m·* of Christian Scientists

multitudinous

Ret.	50–10	shown me, in *m·* ways,

multum in parvo

Mis.	25– 4	the *m·* in *p·* of C. S.,
My.	247– 1	*m·* in *p·*, — all-in-one and one-in-all.
	254–22	*m·* in *p·*, — all-in-one and one-in-all.

municipal

My.	217– 8	invested in safe *m·* bonds

munificent

Mis.	143–23	*m·* sum of forty-two thousand dollars
Man.	75–11	declined to receive this *m·* gift,
My.	13–29	pledged this *m·* sum
	164– 9	my thanks for your *m·* gift
	166–10	*m·* gift of ten thousand dollars,

murder

Mis.	61–14	* *Or who does m·?*
	61–16	* was said to be 'hanged for *m·*'
	122–32	The *m·* of the just Nazarite
	324–15	emulation, hatred, wrath, *m·*.
	335–17	to *m·*, steal, commit adultery,

murderer

Mis.	257–20	"a *m·* from the beginning." — *John* 8 : 44.
Un.	17–15	was the would-be *m·* of Truth.
	32–21	a *m·* from the beginning. — *John* 8 : 44.
No.	24–23	"a *m·* from the beginning, — *John* 8 : 44.
Pan.	5–13	a *m·* from the beginning, — *John* 8 : 44.

murderers

My.	5– 5	*m·* of their brothers !

murdering

Pan.	15– 1	*m·* her peaceful seamen

murderous

Mis.	325–29	in the midst of *m·* hordes,

murders

No.	3– 5	error *m·* either friend or foe
'01.	20–27	its thefts, adulteries, and *m·*,

murky

Po.	29– 2	Blest Christmas morn, though *m·* clouds

murmur

Pan.	3–11	the gentle *m·* of early morn,
Po.	41–23	to welcome the *m·* it gave
My.	150– 3	Therefore despair not nor *m·*,

murmuring

Mis.	237–18	*m·* winds of their forest home.
Po.	2–18	white waves kiss the *m·* rill
	66– 3	When we walk by that *m·* stream ;

murmurings

No.	9–14	repeated complaints and *m·*

murmurs

Mis.	329–30	The brooklet sings melting *m·*
	390–16	To melting *m·* ye have stirred
Po.	30– 5	wakening *m·* from the drowsy rills
	55–17	To melting *m·* ye have stirred

muscles

Mis.	28– 7	*m·* cannot move without mind.
Peo.	8–19	controls the *m·* of the arm.
My.	162– 6	Strength is in man, not in *m·* ;

muscular

Pul.	62–12	* require but little *m·* power
Rud.	11–27	*m·*, vascular, or nervous operations

Muse

Mis.	142–19	my *M·* lost her lightsome lyre,

muse

Mis.	124–21	silence wherein to *m·* His praise,

Muses'

Ret.	17– 6	*M·* soft echoes to kindle the grot.
Po.	62– 6	*M·* soft echoes to kindle the grot.

music

Mis.	106–28	*M·* is the harmony of being ;
	106–28	the *m·* of Soul affords the only
	116–13	filling the measures of life's *m·*
	116–16	*crescendo* and *diminuendo* accent *m·*,
	126– 5	*m·* of our Sabbath chimes
	138–28	for the *m·* of our march,
	153–28	* Hear the first *m·* of this
	187–10	manifestly the reality of *m·*,
	270– 6	sculpture, *m·*, or painting?
	283–31	learn the principle of *m·*
	324– 9	a little while, and the *m·* is dull,
	324–25	all wasted and the *m·* fled.
	330– 8	make *m·* in the heart.
	344– 5	* have you studied *m·*,
	375–15	* study of *m·* and art.
	385–13	gales celestial, in sweet *m·* bore
Man.	61–17	*m·* IN THE CHURCH.
	61–18	The *m·* in The Mother Church
	61–23	*M·* from the organ alone
Ret.	27–21	As sweet *m·* ripples in one's
	57– 8	correcting the principle of *m·*
Un.	13– 8	principle of *m·* knows nothing of
	13–11	any more than in *m·*.
Pul.	29–14	* The *m·* was spirited,
Rud.	3–13	masters in *m·* and painting
'00.	11– 3	have no discord over *m·*.
	11– 6	passionately fond of material *m·*,
	11– 8	spiritual *m·*, the *m·* of Soul.
	11–13	*M·* is more than sound in unison.
	11–18	*M·* is divine.
	11–19	Mind, not matter, makes *m·* ;

music
'02.   4– 9   *m·* to the ear, rapture to the heart
Po.   41–15   Where the *m·* of waters had fled
   46–16   Be all thy life in *m·* given,
   48– 6   gales celestial, in sweet *m·* bore
   65–22   life hath its *m·* in low minor tones,
My.   32–25   * *m·* by William Lyman Johnson.
   155–23   May those who discourse *m·* to-day,
   267–21   awaken . . . with a sense of *m·* ;

musical
Man.   61–21   standard of *m·* excellence ;
Ret.   17– 7   chords of my lyre, with *m·* kiss,
   18– 7   the pear-tree, with *m·* flow.
Pul.   61–25   * sweet, *m·* tones attracted
Po.   62– 7   chords of my lyre, with *m·* kiss,
   63–16   the pear-tree, with *m·* flow.
My.   70–24   * more beautiful, more *m·*,
   256– 3   not specially *m·* to be sure,

Music Hall
Pul.   57–25   * proposed site of the new *M· H·*,

musician
Mis.   283–31   *m·* to practise for him.
   340–18   Is a *m·* made by his teacher?
   340–19   He makes himself a *m·*

musicians
'00.   11– 7   jarring elements among *m·*

music-tone
Chr.   53–59   Eternal swells Christ's *m·*,

mustard
My.   222–10   grain of *m·* seed,— *Matt.* 17 : 20.

mustard-seed
Pul.   52– 4   * a faith of the *m·* variety.
My.   57–32   * a faith of the *m·* variety.

mutations
Un.   61– 9   *m·* of mortal sense are the

mute
Mis.   390– 9   Too pure for aught so *m·*.
Po.   55–10   Too pure for aught so *m·*.

mutely
Mis.   12–17   Mortal mind at this period *m·* works

mutiny
My.   203– 8   obeyed without *m·* are God's laws.

mutter
Mis.   396– 1   wild winds *m·*, howl, and moan,
Po.   58–13   wild winds *m·*, howl, and moan,

mutual
Mis.   289–22   except by *m·* consent.
   289–25   by *m·* consent,
   289–29   *M·* interests and affections are
   297–22   relinquished by *m·* consent
Ret.   44–28   revival of *m·* love, prosperity, and
My.   155– 2   *m·* aid society, which is effective
   204– 7   *m·* friendships such as ours

mutually
Mis.   98–11   *m·* to aid one another in finding
   266–26   thus we *m·* aid each other,
Ret.   59–21   distinct, but *m·* dependent,

muzzled
No.   44–16   Ecclesiastical tyranny *m·* the

My
Mis.   118–16   "Keep *M·* commandments."— *John* 15 : 10.
   268– 5   to *M·* commandments !— *Isa.* 48 : 18.
Un.   18– 4   brightness of *M·* own glory.
   18–11   were not in *M·* mind,
   18–12   tears from the eyes of *M·* children.
   18–17   show *M·* pity through divine law,
   18–18   It is *M·* sympathy with
   18–18   and *M·* knowledge of harmony
   24– 4   *M·* Mind is divine good,
   62–22   man is *M·* idea, never in matter,

myriad
Mis.   114–19   sin, appearing in its *m·* forms :
   325–27   sensualism in its *m·* forms.
   361– 7   spiritual Life, whose *m·* forms
Pul.   80–23   * *m·* of women more thoughtful

Myself
Un.   18– 9   everything that is unlike *M·*.
   18–26   aught beside *M·* is impossible.

mysteries
My.   149–12   *m·* of exhaustless being.

naiad
Po.   8– 8   *n·* from woodland bower ;

Naiad's and naiad's
Mis.   390– 3   Thou hast a *N·* charm ;
Po.   55– 3   Thou hast a *n·* charm ;

mysterious
Mis.   221–17   mental practitioners and *m·* diseases.
   237–21   marvellous good, and *m·* evil.
Ret.   9– 4   all about this *m·* voice,
   9–16   never again . . . was that *m·* call
Peo.   3–13   a *m·* God and a natural devil.
   4–16   *m·* ideas of God and man
My.   50– 8   * vast gloom of the *m·* forests,
   205– 9   * "God moves in a *m·* way

mysteriously
My.   303– 1   fell *m·* upon my spirit.

mystery
of godliness
Mis.   53–29   is the *m·* of godliness ;
   328–11   with the *m·* of godliness.
Ret.   37–20   this "*m·* of godliness."— *I Tim.* 3 : 16.
Un.   5–14   the *m·* of godliness,"— *I Tim.* 3: 16.
   62– 8   This is the *m·* of godliness
No.   38– 9   This divine *m·* of godliness
'01.   24–30   the spirit or *m·* of godliness.
My.   124–27   The *m·* of godliness
   126–11   interprets the *m·* of godliness,

Mis.   5–23   seem a miracle and a *m·*
   222–24   Its *m·* protects it now,
   223– 1   metaphysical *m·* of error
   247–19   the healing force . . . seems a *m·*,
Ret.   28–24   It was a *m·* to me then,
Un.   5–15   *m·* involves the unknown.
No.   17–22   this *m·* of a God who has no
'00.   6– 9   Any *m·* in C. S. departs
'01.   20–25   At present its *m·* protects it,
Peo.   6–20   God is no longer a *m·*
My.   124–29   and the *m·* of iniquity
   126–10   kills this *m·* of iniquity
   126–12   the second is no longer a *m·*
   192– 9   *m·* and gloom of his glory
   344– 7   *m·* is scientifically explained.

mystic
Un.   9–11   human philosophy, or *m·* psychology.
Pul.   53–25   * Whittier, grandest of *m·* poets,
No.   15–13   far more *m·* than Mind-healing.
'01.   8–27   C. S. explains that *m·* saying
Po.   34–13   Has wooed some *m·* spot,
My.   91– 5   * spiritual and *m·* mediation

mystical
Pul.   66–18   * satisfy a taste for the *m·*

mysticism
Mis.   30–26   any seeming *m·* surrounding realism
   260– 6   Pagan *m·*, Grecian philosophy,
Pan.   13–25   with the *m·* of opposites
'01.   9–11   *m·* complained of by the rabbis,
   10–15   removes the *m·* that used to enthrall
   25– 1   *m·*, so called, of my writings
My.   167– 3   *m·* of good is unknown to the flesh,
   254– 1   *m·* departs, heaven opens,

mysticisms
My.   288–14   pagan *m·*, tribal religion,

mystify
Pan.   7–16   Does not each of these religions *m·*

myth
Mis.   82–25   Mortal mind is a *m·* ;
   201–10   *m·* or material falsity of evil ;
No.   27–11   matter will be proved a *m·*.
'00.   5– 9   its origin is a *m·*, a lie.
Peo.   4– 8   Mythology, or the *m·* of ologies,

mythical
Mis.   47–13   *m·* nature of matter,
   71–22   hence its *m·* origin and certain end.
   82–26   *m·* or mortal sense of existence
Pan.   3– 1   *m·* deity may please the fancy,
'02.   15–13   being approached the *m·*.

mythological
Pan.   2–24   *m·* deity of that name ;

mythology
Mis.   55–27   matter is *m·*, and its laws are
   363–10   *m·* of evil and mortality is but
Pan.   3–23   *m·* (one of my girlhood studies),
Peo.   4– 8   *M·*, or the myth of ologies,

myths
Mis.   60–23   *If mortal mind and body are m·,*

N

nails
My.   119–20   to the prints of the *n·*,

naked
Mis.   324–28   *N·*, hungry, athirst,
Pul.   65–24   * gave half . . . to a *n·* beggar ;
My.   117–14   or *n·*, and clothed thee ?— *Matt.* 25 : 38.

name (noun)
another
　Mis. 336–21　What is it but another *n·* for C. S.,
any
　Ret. 78–18　any *n·* given to it other than
author's
　Mis. 300– 5　announcing the author's *n·*,
　Man. 32–14　and give the author's *n·*.
　　　　58–20　Announcing Author's *N·*.
　My. 130–22　must have the author's *n·* added
blest
　Po. 30–16　cast on Thy blest *n·*,
Christian
　Mis. x–18　changed from my Christian *n·*,
　Man. 111– 6　must sign her own Christian *n·*,
Christian Science
　Pul. 52–18　* The *n·* C. S. alone is new.
　　　　55–17　* she selected the *n·* C. S.
Christ's
　Pul. 14–17　cup of cold water in Christ's *n·*,
　My. 153– 5　will only do this in Christ's *n·*,
　　　　300–17　raise the dying . . . in Christ's *n·*,
divine
　'00. 3–23　to call the divine *n·* Yahwah,
excellent
　Pul. 57–20　* Such is the excellent *n·* given to
first
　My. 236–16　they accepted the first *n·*.
generic
　Man. 47–20　generic *n·* of the disease
having the
　Man. 50–15　having the *n·* without the life
her
　Man. 54–14　her *n·* shall be erased from The
　　　　54–24　remove his or her *n·* from membership
　　　　56– 5　his or her *n·* shall be dropped
　Pul. 33– 4　* heard her *n·* called distinctly,
His
　Un. 7– 1　His *n·* will be magnified
　My. 225–19　sacredly holding His *n·* apart from
　　　　226–21　in this you learn to hallow His *n·*,
his
　Mis. 113–10　number of his *n·*,"— *Rev.* 13 : 17.
　　　　145–10　answer to his *n·* in this
　　　　161– 6　his *n· shall be called* — *Isa.* 9 : 6.
　　　　164–17　"His *n·* shall be called — *Isa.* 9 : 6.
　　　　167–14　What is his *n·*?
　　　　180–22　*believe on his n· :* — *John* 1 : 12.
　　　　192–15　"His *n·* shall endure — *Psal.* 72 : 17.
　　　　192–15　"His *n·* shall be continued — *Psal.* 72 : 17.
　　　　269–32　number of his *n·*." — *Rev.* 13 : 17.
　　　　321– 5　"his *n·* shall be called — *Isa.* 9 : 6.
　Man. 46– 9　after his *n·* on circulars,
　　　　46–23　to have his *n·* removed
　　　　51– 5　his *n·* shall be dropped
　Pul. 22–13　to heal the sick in his *n·*.
　　　　53–28　* Who use it in his *n·* ;
　Hea. 2–26　Past, present, future magnifies his *n·*
holy
　My. 225–13　giving unto His holy *n·* due
I AM
　Mis. 258–21　The *n·*, I AM, indicated
in the
　Mis. 57–21　told in the *n·* of Truth,
　　　　59– 4　in the *n·* of Truth.
　　　　171–29　in the *n·* of Science,
　　　　233– 1　practising in the *n·* of Science
　　　　334–19　evil at work in the *n·* of good,
　Chr. 55–18　In the *n·* of Jesus Christ — *Acts* 3 : 6.
　Ret. 68– 2　claimed to originate in the *n·* of
　　　　68– 3　in the *n·* of human concept,
　Pul. 7–18　in the *n·* of religion.
　No. 42–14　in the *n·* and for the sake of Christ,
　'00. 10–14　in the *n·* of God, justice, and
　　　　10–26　in the *n·* of a first lieutenant
　My. 147–19　in the *n·* of Almighty God,
　　　　151–28　worshipping . . . in the *n·* of nature,
　　　　190–30　in the *n·* of God, wherefore vilify
is legion
　Pul. 81–20　* and their *n·* is legion.
is Wonderful
　Un. 39–13　Messiah, whose *n·* is Wonderful.
its
　Mis. 365–30　impostors that come in its *n·*.
　No. 9–24　More mistakes are made in its *n·*
　　　　11–13　by those who come falsely in its *n·*.
　My. 93–23　* many of the practices in its *n·*.
　　　　228– 1　I call disease by its *n·*
Jesus'
　Pul. 41–28　* "All hail the power of Jesus' *n·*,"
　　　　81– 2　* "All hail the power of Jesus' *n·*,"
justifies the
　Pul. 61–17　* justifies the *n·* given by Mrs. Eddy,
maiden
　Mis. x–22　to retain my maiden *n·*,

name (noun)
Mary's
　Ret. 9– 5　if she really did hear Mary's *n·*
member's
　Mis. 129–12　drop this member's *n·* from the
mother's
　Ret. 1–16　perpetuated her mother's *n·*.
my
　Mis. xi– 2　in my *n·* of Glover,
　Ret. 75– 7　Why withhold my *n·*,
　　　　75–14　do a miracle in my *n·*, — *Mark* 9 : 39.
　'00. 14– 3　hast not denied my *n·*. — *Rev.* 3 : 8.
　Hea. 1– 1　*In my n· shall they* — *Mark* 16 : 17.
　　　　6–27　In my *n·* shall they — *Mark* 16 : 17.
　My. 47–30　* In my *n·* shall they — *Mark* 16 : 17.
　　　　153– 3　send these floral offerings in my *n·*
　　　　188– 4　put my *n·* there forever ; — *I Kings* 9 : 3.
new
　Mis. 153–19　giveth this "new *n·*" — *Rev.* 3 : 12.
　　　　161–24　was given the new *n·*, Messiah,
　　　　320–29　giving to it a new *n·*,
　Pul. 8–21　with his own new *n·*.
　　　　22–14　give to Christianity his new *n·*,
of a candidate
　Man. 100– 4　the *n·* of a candidate for its
of a kinsman
　Ret. 2–13　inscribed the *n·* of a kinsman
of all evil
　My. 357– 9　magnetism, — the *n·* of all evil,
of Almighty God
　My. 147–19　in the *n·* of Almighty God,
of a man
　Hea. 3–16　Jesus is the *n·* of a man
of Christ
　Mis. 19–12　has named the *n·* of Christ,
　　　　223–21　have named the *n·* of Christ
　Pul. 81– 4　* we learn that the *n·* of Christ
　Hea. 16– 9　have named the *n·* of Christ
of Christian Science
　My. 182–31　honor the *n·* of C. S.,
　　　　222–28　name the *n·* of C. S.
of Deity
　Mis. 75–24　*n·* of Deity used in that place
of God
　'00. 10–14　this, too, in the *n·* of God,
　My. 190–30　in the *n·* of God, wherefore vilify
　　　　233–19　taking the *n·* of God in vain.
of its author
　Mis. 314–25　this book, with the *n·* of its author,
of Jesus
　Hea. 3–18　individuals by the *n·* of Jesus.
of law
　Mis. 199– 5　dignify the result with the *n·* of law :
of matter
　Mis. 258–20　and call Mind by the *n·* of matter,
of Morse
　Mis. x–21　I dropped the *n·* of Morse
of religion
　Pul. 7–18　in the *n·* of religion.
　My. 258– 4　worthy the *n·* of religion
of said member
　Man. 43– 3　*n·* of said member to be dropped
of Science
　Mis. 171–29　false knowledge in the *n·* of Science,
　　　　233– 1　practising in the *n·* of Science
of the author
　Mis. 88– 6　the *n·* of the author of
　Man. 59– 9　announce the *n·* of the author.
of the beast
　Mis. 113– 9　*n·* of the beast, — *Rev.* 13 : 17.
　　　　269–31　*n·* of the beast, — *Rev.* 13 : 17.
of the complainant
　Man. 29– 5　the *n·* of the complainant.
of their author
　Man. 71–23　give the *n·* of their author
of the kinsman
　Pul. 46–20　* inscribed the *n·* of the kinsman
of the member
　Man. 5– 5　*n·* of the member guilty of this
of Truth
　Mis. 57–21　told in the *n·* of Truth.
　　　　59– 4　in the *n·* of Truth.
only a
　Po. 42– 7　were only a *n·* !
other
　Ret. 59–13　every other *n·* for the Supreme Being,
present
　My. 236–14　will exchange the present *n·* for
something in a
　My. 353– 8　chapter sub-title
suggest a
　'02. 15–21　waited on God to suggest a *n·* for
suggested the
　My. 236– 6　Because I suggested the *n·* for

name (noun)
that
| Pan. | 2–24 | mythological deity of that n·; |
| '02. | 15–29 | whispered that n· to my waiting hope |

Thine own
| My. | 253–16 | keep through Thine own n· — John 17 : 11. |

this
Man.	64–24	public misunderstanding of this n·,
Ret.	91– 8	this n· has been given it by compilers
My.	236– 6	this n· continues to be multiplied,

Thy
| My. | 225–26 | "Hallowed be Thy n·." — Matt. 6 : 9. |

thy
Mis.	175–30	Have we not in thy n· cast out devils,
	191–14	devils in thy n·." — Mark 9 : 38.
My.	193–28	called thee by thy n·; — Isa. 43 : 1.

whereof
| '00. | 14–13 | Philadelphia — the n· whereof signifies |

without the Spirit
| Mis. | 302– 7 | teaching the n· without the Spirit, |

your
| My. | 236– 9 | adopt generally for your n·, |

Mis.	x–23	the n· would be too long.
	144– 5	and the n· thereof,
	157–19	I enclose you the n· of
	191–16	n· of his satanic majesty is found
	228– 9	a n· whose odor fills the world with
	233– 7	but are such in n· only,
	305–28	* the n· of each contributor.
Man.	100–22	n· the Committee if it so desires,
Ret.	8– 5	calling me distinctly by n·,
My.	64–10	* made the n· an honored one
	104– 6	flourish under the n· of
	187–27	Him whose n· they would glorify
	225–21	to the divine Spirit the n· God.
	302–18	n· is not applicable to me.
	318–10	I availed myself of the n· of
	353– 9	I have given the n· to all

name (verb)
Mis.	15–24	infinite good that we n· God,
	26–28	Scriptures n· God as good,
	96–26	I can n· some means by which
	103– 8	mortals virtually n· substance;
	199–22	which mortals n· matter.
	258–21	error could neither n· nor
	267–24	The antipode . . . which we n· matter,
	272–23	* to n· these institutions,
	314–21	shall n·, at each reading,
Ret.	50– 4	to n· three hundred dollars
Un.	10– 5	to n· any previous teachers,
My.	20–11	and n· your gifts to her,
	81–14	* They had been told to n·,
	106– 7	I n· those mentioned above
	169– 8	date, which I hope soon to n·
	222–28	n· the name of C. S.
	235– 4	not n· its opposite, error.
	235– 9	and never n· a cipher?
	235–12	definitely n· the error,
	257–25	memorials, too numerous to n·,
	302–16	not to n· me thus.
	343– 9	* "Can you n· the man?"

named
Mis.	19–12	has n· the name of Christ,
	23– 1	Newton n· it gravitation,
	27– 6	its opposite, n· matter,
	84–30	through the door n· death,
	166–24	n· in this century C. S.,
	186–16	the divine idea n· man;
	196– 9	separate mind . . . n· evil;
	223–21	n· the name of Christ
	244–10	conditions n· in Genesis
	258–18	God n· Himself, I AM.
	329– 4	what shall this be n·,
	361–28	n· matter, or mortal mind.
	374–19	and n· his burdens light,
	379–29	n· my discovery C. S.
Man.	18–16	and n· it, THE FIRST CHURCH
	27– 7	not n· in the Manual
	71–19	and n· in this Manual.
	92–23	qualifications n· in Sect. 9
	100–23	any Committee so n·
	102–13	n· in them all the trusts
Ret.	1–18	Englishman, n· Joseph Baker,
	24– 6	which I afterwards n· C. S.
	25–10	I n· it Christian,
	25–12	I n· mortal mind.
	63–16	Its opposite, nothing, n· evil,
Un.	49– 7	the sinner, wrongly n· man.
	60– 9	presence n· evil.
Pul.	31–23	* At the hour n· I rang the bell
Rud.	2–17	whom mortals have n· God.
	7–22	its opposite, n· matter.
No.	4–10	error of belief, n· disease,
	23–11	but not one person was n·

named
No.	30– 4	the false sense n· sin,
	32–18	its opposite, n· evil,
'00.	5– 8	good — n· devil — evil
	14– 7	full number of days n·
'01.	5– 7	triune Principle, n· in the Bible
	6–21	its theory even seldom n·.
	16–13	devil is n· serpent
	18–18	used them and n· them
Hea.	6– 8	phenomenon n· mediumship,
	16– 9	n· the name of Christ
Peo.	4–12	When . . . God, was n· a person,
My.	55–15	* n· it The First Church of Christ,
	56–13	* in each of the following n· places :
	56–20	* three foregoing n· churches
	217–15	my request as above n·.
	259– 4	I have n· it my white student.
	353–15	the next I n· Monitor,

nameless
Mis.	166–16	incorporeal idea of God, was n·,
	350–31	through n· suffering and sacrifice,
No.	34–26	N· woe, everlasting victories,

namely
Mis.	x– 5	n·, to collect my miscellaneous
	24–16	n·, Life in and of Spirit ;
	31–15	n·, that God, good, has all power.
	40–16	n·, the action of the divine
	48– 6	n·, that its so-called power
	51– 7	n·, the ignorant
	77– 5	original meaning, n·, to be firm,
	108–18	n·, the knowledge of one's self,
	116–30	n·, to be made "ruler — Matt. 25 : 23.
	121–10	n·, the impotence of evil,
	127– 8	n·, that Christian Scientists,
	172–30	n·, the oft-repeated declaration
	185–31	n·, that creation is material :
	186–11	n·, in a sick and sinning mortal.
	188–29	n·, the true likeness of God,
	189–22	n· God, the eternal good,
	190–25	n·, that speech belongs to Mind
	194–31	set forth in the text, n·, believe ;
	217–12	antipode of Spirit, n·, matter.
	221– 8	n·, that error and sickness
	234– 9	to be, n·, a Christian.
	240–31	belongs to nature, — n·, pure odors.
	247– 2	n·, that his honest convictions
	252–25	n·, healing the sick.
	261– 9	n·, that mortals suffer from
	277–15	n·, by slanderous falsehoods,
	298–13	n·, "It is not good to — Matt. 19 : 10.
	299–27	n·, What right have I to do this?
	307–21	n·, Cast not pearls before
	318–26	n·, making sin seem either
	365–18	n·, that mortal mind is calling
	366–32	n· mere book-learning.
Ret.	33–11	n·, that the less material medicine
	61– 9	n·, that man's harmony is
Un.	8–18	n·, by the establishment,
	43– 5	n·, that there is no death,
	55– 2	n·, that there is no death.
Pul.	55–19	* n·, — that all causation is
Rud.	11–10	n·, that there are no sickness, sin, and
No.	4– 8	n·, material sensation and
	5–13	n·, that life and health are
	8– 5	n·, silence whenever it can
	10–22	n·, that earth's discords have not
	12–17	n·, "the way, the truth, — John 14 : 6.
	24–21	n·, that evil has no claims
	35–20	n·, that God is the only Mind,
Pan.	8–17	one law, n·, divine Science.
	9– 9	rules pertaining thereto, n·,
'01.	2–22	n·, that a departure from the
	11–23	n·, that God is a Person,
	21– 4	n·, students of a demonstrable
'02.	20–17	n·, in 1902 to begin omitting our
Hea.	8–20	n·, Life, Truth, and Love,
Peo.	3–28	n·, by working out our own
	12–19	n·, man's salvation from sickness
My.	18– 5	n·, that Christian Scientists
	46–10	* n·, "To organize a church
	52–18	* n·, heal the sick, and preach the
	107– 8	n·, the homœopathic system,
	135–14	n·, the Hon. Henry M. Baker,
	137–22	n·, the Hon. Henry M. Baker,
	165– 2	n·, of choosing the best,
	172–13	n·, a material symbol of my
	175–19	n·, to macadamize a portion of
	183– 1	uses of Christ's creed, n·,
	218–19	n·, straining at gnats and
	226–14	the infinite, — n·, God.
	229–26	n·, laws of limitation
	240–15	n·, that C. S. is the
	251–28	n·, the unity in C. S.
	281–11	n·, one God, one Mind,

namely
My. 299–21   *n·*, that God, the divine Principle
      339– 5   *n·* — one God, supreme, infinite,

names
Mis. 24–19   state which it *n·* matter,
     144–10   *n·* in your own handwriting,
     145–19   our *n·* may melt into one,
     145–27   their *n·* in the web of history,
     258–19   Error, . . . might give *n·* to itself,
     281–25   because you have signed your *n·*.
     295–27   which *n·* itself after her
     306– 8   * *n·* to be commemorated.
     366–31   theories whose *n·* are legion,
Man. 25– 3   *n·*, ELECTION, AND DUTIES.
      25– 4   *N·*.
      26–15   the *n·* of its candidates
      79–12   *n·* of the persons nominated
    109–15   see that *n·* are legibly written,
    110– 6   the *n·* of the members
    110–10   *n·*, whether of applicants,
    110–12   one, at least, of the given *n·*
    110–13   Initials only of first *n·*
    110–15   "Miss" or "Mrs." before their *n·*
    110–16   *n·* must be written the same in
    111– 3   *n·* must be written in full.
Ret. 5–11   *n·* of both father and mother
     70– 2   confers animal *n·* and natures
Un. 36– 2   it *n·* material attraction,
Pul. 23–13   * and under various *n·*,
     46–14   * identified with good and great *n·*
     88– 8   append only a few of the *n·*
'00. 3–24   also that women's *n·* contained
My. 225–15   distinguishes it from all other *n·*,
    225–19   *n·* of that which He creates.
    225–21   C. S. *n·* God as divine Principle,
    228– 3   My book S. and H. *n·* disease,
    245–27   letters of degrees that follow the *n·*

naming
Mis. 61–28   *N·* these His embodiment,
    233–16   and *n·* that "mind-cure,"
    290–15   *n·* the time of the occurrence,
    295– 4   whom he quotes without *n·*,
Man. 32–10   *N·* Book and Author.
     71– 8   in *n·* such churches.
Pul. 31–22   * *n·* an evening on which
     72–28   * *n·* as one great essential that
My. 363–25   avoid *n·*, in his mental treatment,

napping
Mis. 231–21   but grandpa was taken *n·*.
    295–12   *awake*, and caught *n·*?

narrated
My. 81–27   * cures *n·* at the meetings of
    298– 4   if correctly *n·* and understood,

narrations
Ret. 21–27   such *n·* may be admissible

narrative
Ret. 9– 9   Scriptural *n·* of little Samuel,
    70– 9   Scriptural *n·* of the Virgin-mother

narratives
Man. 48–26   they may . . . give incidental *n·*.
Ret. 22– 3   Gospel *n·* bear brief testimony
My. 179–18   Old Testament and gospel *n·*

narrow
Mis. 32–21   from the straight and *n·* path.
     64–15   Man-made theories are *n·*,
    245–28   the straight and *n·* way ;
    323–23   up the hill it is straight and *n·*,
    347–22   it is always straight and *n·*,
    389–19   sweet secret of the *n·* way,
Ret. 55– 1   enter this strait and *n·* path.
    71– 8   straight and *n·* path of C. S.
'01. 28– 6   enter the strait and *n·* way,
Po. ᴋ–18   sweet secret of the *n·* way,
My. 104– 2   strait and *n·* way of Truth.
    202–27   The way is *n·* at first,
    306– 3   attempts to *n·* my life

natal
Po. 29– 9   No *n·* hour and mother's tear,
My. 129– 9   The nod of Spirit is nature's *n·*.
    158–10   This day is the *n·* hour of

nation (*see also* **nation's**)
Mis. 101–10   have had two in this *n·* ;
    159–30   from all parts of our *n·*,
    176–23   Pilgrims came to establish a *n·*
    237–17   live now as when this *n·* began,
    297–13   sects, or societies, of a *n·*
    304–10   * the capital of the *n·*
Pan. 14–17   and uphold our *n·* with the
    14–27   our *n·*, which fed her starving foe,
'02. 3–18   rejoices with our sister *n·*
My. 89–24   * interest . . . but to the *n·* ;
    89–24   * not to the *n·* alone, but to the

nation
My. 129– 3   danger threatening our *n·*,
    148–15   and the father of our *n·*
    183–11   To-day a *n·* is born.
    200– 2   under the Constitution of our *n·*
    206–24   an holy *n·*, — *I Pet.* 2: 9.
    234–20   introducing C. S. into a heathen *n·*
    234–23   If the . . . Empress could hold her *n·*,
    234–26   Silent prayer in and for a heathen *n·*
    279–26   pray that God bless that great *n·*
    282– 2   government of a *n·* is its peace maker
    289–13   sympathy with the bereaved *n·*,
    291– 4   Presiding over the destinies of a *n·*

national
Mis. 138– 3   to prepare for this *n·* convention
    295–13   Scotchman's *n·* pride and affection,
    370–25   into a "*n·* convention"
Pul. 6– 4   forms of a *n·* or tyrannical religion,
Pan. 14–16   associated with . . . our *n·* judiciary ;
'02. 3– 9   the old *n·* family pride and joy
Peo. 8–12   definite form of a *n·* religion,
Po. page 77   poem
My. 220–15   pacification of all *n·* difficulties,
    285– 8   industrial, civic, and *n·* peace.
    286– 8   *N·* disagreements can

National Association
Mis. 276–12   convention of our *N· A·*,

National Board of Management
Mis. 305– 8   * *N· B· of M·* has placed

National Christian Science Association
Mis. 382–27   by-laws of the *N· C· S· A·* ;
Mis. 98– 9   *N· C· S· A·* has brought us together
    134– 9   chapter sub-title
    134–11   annual session of the *N· C· S· A·*.
    137– 1   chapter sub-title
    137– 6   convention of the *N· C· S· A·*,
    137–19   Disorganize the *N· C· S· A·* !
    138–21   members of the *N· C· S· A·*,
    275–22   meeting in Chicago of the *N· C· S· A·*
Ret. 52–13   forming a *N· C· S· A·*.
    52–22   *N· C· S· A·*, at its meeting in
    (*see also* **Christian Scientist Association**)

National Convention
Mis. 98– 7   Address at the *N· C·* in Chicago,

National Library Building
My. 157–15   * *N· L· B·* in Washington

National Magazine
My. 305–18   I am rated in the *N· M·* (1903) as

National Society
Mis. 305– 9   * representing the *N· S·* of

National State Capital Bank
My. 136–23   *N· S· C· B·*, Concord, N. H.

nation's
Mis. 251–12   our *n·* civil and religious freedom,
Ret. 43–23   Centennial Day of our *n·* freedom.
Pul. 8– 6   condition of our *n·* finances,
    10–11   they planted a *n·* heart,
'02. 3–11   Our *n·* forward step was
Po. 77– 3   A *n·* holiest hymn in grateful
My. 277–21   But if our *n·* rights or honor
    290–19   our *n·* chief magistrate,
    291–23   our *n·* ensign of peace
    292– 8   May God sanctify our *n·* sorrow
    305–13   Many of the *n·* best and

nations (*see also* **nations'**)
affection of
My. 290– 7   Those live on in the affection of *n·*.
all
Pan. 13–21   Then shall all *n·*, peoples,
    14–14   and that they shall rule all *n·*.
My. 127–31   adapted to all men, all *n·*,
    181–17   that all *n·* shall speedily learn
    274–28   health among all *n·*." — *Psal.* 67 : 2.
    278– 2   the action of all *n·*.
    282– 6   in and for all *n·*,
    282–24   all *n·* under the sunlight of
among
My. 286–12   preserving peace among *n·*.
and peoples
My. 284–26   quarrels between *n·* and peoples.
are helped
My. 282–11   *n·* are helped onward
awakening the
My. 316– 5   the Redeemer awakening the *n·*,
both
My. 277– 6   satisfactory to both *n·*?"
character of
Peo. 2–28   the character of *n·* as well as
crises of
Mis. 176– 8   chiefly in the great crises of *n·*
foreign
'02. 10–29   communicating with foreign *n·*

nations
  healing for the
    Ret. 49–24 will prove a healing for the *n·*,
  healing of the
    Ret. 95– 3 the healing of the *n·*.''— *Rev.* 22 : 2.
  individuals and
    My. 277– 8 between individuals and *n·*
  laws of
    '00. 10–12 religious rights and laws of *n·*
  life of
    My. 277–15 prosperity, and life of *n·*.
  peace between
    My. 265–10 civilization, peace between *n·*,
  peace of
    My. 280–17 prayer for the peace of *n·*,
        280–29 praying for the peace of *n·*,
  peoples and
    My. 265–13 rights of individuals, peoples, and *n·*.
  power over the
    Chr. 57– 3 power over the *n·* :— *Rev.* 2 : 26.
    My. 285–19 power over the *n·*.''— *Rev.* 2 : 26.
  welfare of the
    My. 280– 6 * solicitude for the welfare of the *n·*

    Man. 28– 8 *n·*, individuals, and religion
    '02. 4– 2 deceit in councils, dishonor in *n·*,
    My. 281–28 when *n·* are ripe for progress.
        283–21 *n·*, unite harmoniously on the basis of

nations'
    Po. 10–17 Allied by *n·* grace,
    My. 281– 1 spiritual foresight of the *n·* drama
       337–18 Allied by *n·* grace,

native
    Mis. 64– 7 and rose to his *n·* estate,
       70–23 dissolve into its *n·* nothingness ;
     109–15 reduced to their *n·* nothingness !
     144– 2 New Hampshire, my *n·* State.
     251–10 of this city and of my *n·* State
     295–16 to honor his *n·* land
     343–24 away from their *n·* soil,
    Ret. 6–25 Legislature of his *n·* State,
    Un. 58– 3 in their *n·* element of error,
    Pul. 6–30 the *n·* course of whose mind
     24–24 * New Hampshire, Mrs. Eddy's *n·* State.
     43–11 * *n·* of Concord, New Hampshire.
     49–21 * return to her *n·* granite hills,
     68–11 * residence in her *n·* State.
    Pan. 11–17 regain his *n·* spiritual stature
    '01. 26–27 a *n·* or an acquired taste
    '02. 20–24 metropolis of my *n·* State,
    My. 120–12 gives to soul its *n·* freedom.
     136–17 by a *n·* of New Hampshire.
     155– 5 so near my heart and *n·* hills,
     157– 8 * capital city of your *n·* State.
     167–26 by the laws of my *n·* State.
     184– 9 Christian Scientists of my *n·* State
     186– 2 forests of our *n·* State
     270– 9 newspapers of my *n·* State
     289–28 held in the capital of my *n·* State
     327– 4 New Hampshire, my *n·* State,
     341– 2 A *n·* of New Hampshire,

natives
    My. 305–14 *n·* of the Granite State.

nativity
    Mis. 74–14 his *n·* was a spiritual and immortal
     162–17 rise to his *n·* in Spirit.
     320– 5 its earthly advent and *n·*,
     374–18 Scientists memorize the *n·* of Jesus.
    My. 162–29 This church, born in my *n·*,
     256–19 earthly advent and *n·* of our Lord
     262–31 splendor of this *n·* of Christ

Natrum muriaticum
    Mis. 348–21 doses of *N· m·* (common salt).
    Ret. 33–15 thirtieth attenuation of *N· m·*,

natural
    Mis. 3– 4 If we regard good as more *n·*
     26–20 *N·* history shows that neither
     72–19 *disappear only to the n· sense?*
    88–20, 21 * this Science is *n·*, spiritually *n·* ;
     161–22 it is *n·* to conclude that
     183–18 but by the *n·* ability,
     199–29 goodness is more *n·* than evil.
     206– 2 *n·*, civil, or religious,
     222–28 more *n·* than evil.
     247–12 charges . . . are false, but *n·*,
     259–25 demonstrates good, and is *n·* ;
     318– 9 *n·* affection for goodness
     360– 9 *n·* transforming power
     374–32 less artistic or less *n·*?
    Ret. 10– 7 *n·* philosophy, logic, and
     26–13 divinely *n·* and apprehensible ;
     26–17 a *n·* and divine Scientist.
     27–26 Its *n·* manifestation is beautiful
    Un. 1– 2 *n·* doubt and questioning

natural
    Un. 11–20 professor of *n·* philosophy,
    Pul. 35– 7 * *n·* fulfilment of divine law
     48–24 * The *n·* and lawful pride
     54– 6 * harmony with *n·* law,
     54– 8 * The perfectly *n·* is the
     55– 9 * the *n·* outcome of a period
    No. 2– 8 against that which is *n·*
     45–15 In *n·* law and in religion
    Pan. 2–20 deification of *n·* causes,
    Peo. 3–11 would affirm that these are *n·*,
     3–13 mysterious God and a *n·* devil.
    My. 4–31 Whatever is not divinely *n·*
     8–27 * the *n·* and indispensable Leader
     36–31 * *n·* healer of all our diseases
     178–11 is this *n·* Science less profitable
     205–29 health, holiness, . . . are its *n·* effects.
     211–17 foreign to the *n·* inclinations,
     213– 1 *n·* fruits of C. S. Mind-healing
     221–14 *n·*, and divine Science of medicine,
     288–10 Good is divinely *n·*.
     349–13 *n·* to him who sits at the feet of
     349–20 Divine . . . manifestations are *n·*,
     349–21 the so-called *n·* sciences
     (*see also* **science**)

naturalist (*see also* **naturalist's**)
    My. 304–24 Agassiz, the celebrated *n·*

naturalist's
    '01. 28– 2 last stage of the great *n·* prophecy.

naturally
    Mis. 7–17 *n·* reflects that it is dangerous
     7–29 would have returned *n·*
     26–30 *n·* and divinely infinite good.
     33–18 Patients *n·* gain confidence
     129– 7 having done this, one will *n·*,
     240–20 Children not mistaught, *n·* love
     240–28 nothing but a . . . worm *n·* chews tobacco.
     364– 4 *n·* evokes new paraphrase
    Ret. 27–14 *N·*, my first jottings were
     76–10 gravitate *n·* toward Truth.
    No. 2– 3 *n·* glared at by the pulpit,
     3– 3 *n·* modest, generous, and sincere !
    Pan. 12– 6 Then, we *n·* ask, how can Spirit
    '00. 14–28 you *n·* ask who are to be
    '01. 4–30 *n·* conclude that he breaks faith
     12– 6 he would *n·* reply,
    Peo. 6–14 Believing that . . . we *n·* fear God
    My. 83–22 * *n·* takes on a tone of deserved
     178–10 because Science is *n·* divine,
     188–28 man will *n·* seek the Science of
     227–13 we *n·* turn to divine justice

naturalness
    Mis. 194–29 *n·* of the Life that is God,
     200– 1 consummate *n·* of Truth

nature (*see slso* **nature's**)
  all
    Mis. 329–16 rippling all *n·* in ceaseless flow,
  and character
    Un. 1–12 *n·* and character of God is
     3–21 in His own *n·* and character,
     6–18 the divine *n·* and character
     31–18 the *n·* and character of matter,
  and essence
    Mis. 121–18 the *n·* and essence of Deity,
    No. 19–19 drinking in the *n·* and essence of
  and government
    '00. 5– 2 *n·*, and government of all things
  and her laws
    Mis. 219– 4 nor teaches that *n·* and her laws
  and man
    Mis. 258–31 *n·* and man are as harmonious
    My. 152–27 divine Principle of *n·* and man,
  and office
    Un. 40–28 the *n·* and office of Life.
  and power
    Mis. 7–28 *n·* and power of metaphysics,
  and quality
    Mis. 36–17 *n·* and quality of mortal mind,
  and stature
    Mis. 102– 1 the *n·* and stature of Christ,
  and truth
    My. 111– 4 The *n·* and truth of C. S.
  anticipating
    My. 346– 7 * Those who have been anticipating *n·*
  as thought
    Mis. 331–25 divine Science evolved *n·* as thought,
  at work in
    Mis. 257–12 so-called force, . . . at work in *n·*
  becomes Spirit
    Mis. 218– 1 in which *n·* becomes Spirit ;
  belongs to
    Mis. 240–31 sweet something which belongs to *n·*,
  cures the disease
    Peo. 6–12 * while *n·* cures the disease.''

nature

declares
  Mis. 217–13 N· declares, throughout the mineral,
divine
  (*see* **divine**)
dual
  Mis. 161–15 the appearing of this dual n·,
endows
  My. 90–11 * n· endows the children of men,
essential
  Mis. 264–10 Unity is the essential n· of C. S.
evil
  '00. 8– 6 evil man also exhales . . . his evil n·
exact
  Mis. 78–28 exact n· of its Principle,
fleshly
  Ret. 73– 7 as the fleshly n· disappears
foundation in
  Mis. 367–26 neither . . . nor foundation in n·,
God of
  My. 349–23 and coexist with the God of n·
good
  My. 81– 4 * Scientists fairly radiate good n·
      81– 5 * So ingrained is this good n·,
had reproduced
  My. 347–14 suggest that n· had reproduced
hidden
  Mis. 48–21 hidden n· of some tragic events
higher
  Mis. 287–18 the higher n· of man governs
  My. 48–30 * feed the higher n· through the mind,
      159–18 whereby we reach our higher n·.
His
  Un. 23–22 unlike Himself and foreign to His n·
His own
  No. 38–21 includes only His own n·,
human
  (*see* **human**)
imperative
  My. 268– 5 imperative n· of the marriage relation
infinite
  Mis. 284– 6 Its infinite n· and uses
  My. 349–29 makes manifest the infinite n·,
in the name of
  My. 151–28 matter in the name of n·,
is constituted
  Mis. 217–15 and that n· is constituted of
its
  Pul. 3– 1 Such being its n·,
  Rud. 3–18 spiritual in its n·, method,
Jesus'
  No. 36–11 the popular view of Jesus' n·.
law of
  Peo. 10–18 mortal beliefs, and not a law of n·,
laws of
  Mis. 216–26 in which neither laws of n· nor
  Pul. 54–15 * obedience to the laws of n·.
  '01. 24– 7 rules styled the laws of n·.
loving
  My. 338–22 his broad views and loving n·
man's
  '01. 1–21 it is the better side of man's n·
material
  Mis. 119–14 material n· strives to tip the beam
my
  '02. 2–23 inherent characteristic of my n·,
mythical
  Mis. 47–13 or the mythical n· of matter,
no fleshly
  Mis. 86– 3 these have no fleshly n·.
no law of
  Pul. 54–13 * "There was no law of n· violated
nor grace
  '02. 7– 8 neither philosophy, n·, nor grace
of a cat
  Mis. 218–23 grin expresses the n· of a cat,
of all
  '01. 5– 9 possesses the n· of all,
of a revelation
  My. 93–29 * will come in the n· of a revelation.
of beauty
  Rud. 6– 8 when we change the n· of beauty
of Christianity
  My. 179–19 n· of Christianity, as depicted in
of Deity
  Mis. 79– 1 divine order and the n· of Deity.
      192– 9 n· of Deity and devil
of dreams
  Mis. 252–10 possessing the n· of dreams.
of evil
  No. 23– 1 incorrect concept of the n· of evil
of God
  (*see* **God**)
of Jesus
  '02. 18–30 n· of Jesus made him keenly alive to

nature

of man
  Mis. 287–18 higher n· of man governs the lower,
of occultism
  Mis. 78–13 partook of the n· of occultism,
of one God
  '01. 5– 5 lose the n· of one God,
of sin
  Un. 5–24 differ from them as to the n· of sin
of Spirit
  Mis. 218–25 does not express the n· of Spirit,
of the case
  Mis. 379– 9 and the n· of the case :
  Pul. 80– 6 * inevitable in the n· of the case.
of the individual
  Mis. 119–11 The n· of the individual,
of their source
  Mis. 354–14 prove the n· of their source.
of this love
  My. 133–24 and the n· of this love?
penchant for
  Mis. 329– 2 an obstinate *penchant* for n·
person and
  '01. 5–29 to explain both His person and n·,
personified
  Pan. 2–21 conceived as one personified n·,
poetic
  Po. v– 6 * *outpouring of a deeply poetic n·*
presuppose that
  Mis. 217–18 presuppose that n· is matter,
real
  Mis. 88–22 * highest type of real n· ;
      218–18 unfolds the real n· of God
reflects man
  My. 124–18 N· reflects man and art pencils him,
sensuous
  Ret. 25–13 physical senses, or sensuous n·,
simple
  Mis. 373– 1 to illustrate the simple n· of art.
specific
  Mis. 217–14 specific n· of all things
spiritual
  Mis. 119–15 tip the beam against the spiritual n· ;
  My. 188–29 seek the Science of his spiritual n·,
this
  Mis. 208– 5 by virtue of this n· and allness
      218–24 this n· may linger in memory :
through
  Po. v–14 * *through n·, unto nature's God,"*
  My. 151–25 "through n· up to nature's God,"
true
  Mis. 140– 5 the true n· of the gift ;
  '02. 7– 1 the true n· of Love intact
unison with
  Pan. 1–11 In unctuous unison with n·,
universal
  Pan. 3–24 * "universal n· proceeding from
      12– 5 * Spirit, is ever in universal n·."
unsubstantial
  Pan. 14– 1 unsubstantial n· of whatever
very
  Mis. 99– 2 revolutionary in its very n· ;
      354– 3 Sin in its very n· is marvellous !
  '01. 31– 6 from the very n· of Truth,

  Mis. 189– 9 n· and the inseparability of God **and**
      217– 2 n·, reason, and revelation.
      218–30 * recognition of teleology in n·
      240–14 n· would take it out as gently,
      259–27 belongs not to n· nor to God.
      329– 6 n· like a thrifty housewife
      393– 3 N·, with the mind connecting,
  No. 9–18 wrongs of the n· referred to.
  '01. 1–23 n· and practical possibilities of
      23–30 * n· being nothing more than
  Po. 31– 2 nor yet by n· sown,
      51– 8 N·, with the mind connecting,
  My. 248–17 reality of God, man, n·,
      269–13 * Whose body n· is, and God the Soul.

nature's

  Mis. 330– 7 join in n· grand harmony,
      330–23 N· first and last lessons
  Ret. 91–26 n· haunts were the Messiah's
  Pul. 55– 4 * N· marvel in thy thought."
  Pan. 3– 6 My sense of n· rich glooms
      3–10 n· stillness is voiced with a
  Po. v–13 * *masterpiece of n· handiwork,*
      v–14 * *through nature, unto n· God,"*
  My. 129–14 The nod of Spirit is n· natal.
      151–25 * through nature up to n· God,"

natures

  Mis. 226–26 dignified n· cannot stoop to
      228–12 seeking to raise those barren n·
      272–31 If certain n· have not profited
      330–25 sanction what our n· need.

natures
Mis.	347–14	all the goodness of generous *n*·,
Ret.	70– 2	confers animal names and *n*·
No.	1– 5	only as our *n*· are changed
'01.	19–14	That animal *n*· give force to
Hea.	13– 7	higher *n*· are reached soonest by
My.	118– 1	royal *n*· of the beloved members

naught
Mis.	260–24	evil is *n*·, although it seems to be.
	279–20	evil is *n*· and good is all.
	358– 8	*n*· but tardy justice,
Ret.	9–19	* *n*· my spirit's breathings to control,
Un.	21– 8	evil is *n*·, and good only is reality.
	26–24	there is in God *n*· fantastic.
Pul.	4– 1	my strength is *n*·
Rud.	4–21	all is God, and there is *n*· beside
No.	30–15	not by . . . knowing sin, or *n*·,
'02.	7–16	All, than which there is *n*· else.
My.	37– 4	* *N*· else than the grandeur of
	199– 7	I have *n*· against thee.

nave
My.	71–21	* neither *n*·, aisles, nor transept

navies
My.	121–10	like the ocean, able to carry *n*·,
	286–11	armament of *n*· is necessary,

navigation
My.	110–14	wireless telegraphy, *n*· of the air ;

Nazarene (*see also* **Nazarene's**)
Mis.	1– 6	meek *N*·, the scoffed of all scoffers,
	15– 7	The great *N*· Prophet said,
	24–29	The *N*· Prophet declared that
	60–10	The *N*· Prophet could make
	120–28	Biblical record of the great *N*·,
	121–22	His beloved Son, the righteous *N*·,
	162– 6	the *N*· stepped suddenly before the
	344–23	far from the rules of the mighty *N*·
Pul.	6– 5	church established by the *N*· Prophet
Pan.	10– 4	The great *N*· Prophet said,
My.	106–30	Our great Exemplar, the *N*· Prophet,
	179–22	character of the *N*· Prophet

Nazarene's
Mis.	189– 8	*N*· steadfast and true knowledge of
My.	146–15	heights of the great *N*· sayings

Nazareth
Jesus of
Mis.	99–19	seemed Jesus of *N*· more divine
	162–22	no incorporeal Jesus of *N*·.
	252–24	master of metaphysics, Jesus of *N*·.
	258– 4	Our great Ensample, Jesus of *N*·,
	270– 8	Master in C. S., Jesus of *N*·,
Ret.	26–17	Jesus of *N*· was a natural and divine
	70–16	individual mission of Jesus of *N*·.
Pul.	20–24	master Metaphysician, Jesus of *N*·.
	34–20	* when Jesus of *N*· walked the earth.
	53– 7	* condition which Jesus of *N*·,
	53–22	* Jesus of *N*· proclaimed its potency
	75– 1	one Christ, one Jesus of *N*·.
My.	217–28	our great Exemplar, Jesus of *N*·,
Chr.	55–18	name of Jesus Christ of *N*·— *Acts* 3 : 6.
Ret.	89–17	been some time absent from *N*·

Nazarite
Mis.	122–32	murder of the just *N*· was incited by
	374–21	the face of the *N*· Prophet ;

near
Mis.	139–19	*n*· the beautiful Back Bay Park,
	277–26	especially *n*· in times of hate,
	277–27	and never so *n*· as when
	282–28	and no other aid is *n*·.
	377– 4	so *n*· and full of radiant relief
	387–24	that Love, divinely *n*·,
Man.	48–14	make a summer resort *n*·
Ret.	5– 1	town situated *n*· Concord,
	90–14	whom he kept *n*· himself
	91–15	*n*· the sloping shores of the
Un.	4– 1	*n*· to them who adore Him.
	26– 4	my forms, *n*· or remote.
Pul.	58– 6	* Concord, N. H., *n*· her birthplace,
	84– 2	* "The time of times" is *n*·
No.	27– 6	When we get *n*· enough
'00.	7–27	loving Christ is found *n*·,
'01.	31– 7	Every true Christian in the *n*· future
Po.	6–19	that Love, divinely *n*·,
	29– 7	forever here and *n*·,
	68–23	whether *n*· or afar.
	70–11	A help forever *n*· ;
My.	14– 6	discerned in the *n*· future
	21–22	* brethren from far and *n*·,
	82– 3	* one *n*· and dear to them.
	84–17	* Boston is *n*· to another great
	155– 4	nestled so *n*· my heart
	166–20	divine aid is *n*·.
	187– 4	I may at some *n*· future

near
My.	202– 6	may his salvation draw *n*·,
	290– 3	the *n*· seems afar, the distant nigh,
	290–17	Divine Love is never so *n*· as when
	345–23	*n*· a state of spiritual perfection.

nearer
Mis.	6– 2	bring man *n*· to God,
	84–31	a clearer and *n*· sense of Life
	249–25	coming *n*· in my need,
	288–16	Is marriage *n*· right than
	397–14	And *n*· Thee,
Un.	1–16	until they draw *n*· to the
	4–14	as we get still *n*· Him,
	7–24	and brings us *n*· to God,
	64–10	The *n*· we approximate
Pul.	12–20	*n*· to the great heart of Christ ;
	18–23	And *n*· Thee,
'00.	4– 9	*n*· approach to monotheism
'01.	1– 8	*n*· the whole world's acceptance.
Hea.	16–13	come *n*· your hearts
	17– 4	get *n*· his divine nature
Po.	13– 2	tired joy and grief afar, And *n*· Thee,
My.	107–20	*n*· the grooves of omnipotence.
	174–27	Each day I know Him *n*·,
	177–12	*n*· the eternal meridian
	270–11	*n*· my consciousness than before,
	342–32	will advance *n*· perfection."

nearest
Mis.	116–11	This question, ever *n*· to my heart,
	288–13	begins with what is *n*· right
Pan.	13– 4	and *n*· my heart, is this :
Hea.	2– 1	religion *n*· right is that one.
My.	178–29	*n*· approach to the sayings of
	248–29	*n*· the divine Principle
	248–30	*n*· the scientific expression of
	271–22	* "What is *n*· and dearest to your
	271–30	"*n*· and dearest" to my heart

nearing
My.	139–12	his idea is *n*· the Way,
	165–29	*n*· the maximum of might,

nearly
Mis.	362–32	The more *n*· an erring so-called
	381– 8	The time . . . having *n*· expired,
Ret.	90–27	* follow, as *n*· as we can,
Pul.	40–18	* *n*· six thousand persons,
	41–19	* *n*· a thousand local believers
	52–23	* *n*· obliterated all vital belief in
	56– 4	* *n*· every other centre of
	75–25	* the most *n*· fire-proof church
	85– 1	* *n*· thirty years ago.
'00.	8– 1	know and behold more *n*·
My.	30– 7	* *n*· all the local Scientists,
	59– 3	* *n*· forty years ago.
	59–11	* in part by *n*· every religious
	67–25	* begun *n*· two years ago,
	71–19	* In fact, *n*· all the traditions of
	72–24	* *n*· two million dollars
	77–25	* *n*· forty thousand believers
	100– 8	* *n*· all, parts of the country,
	171–10	Concord church is so *n*· completed
	174–22	For *n*· forty years
	272–25	* *n*· eighty-seven years of age,

'neath
Mis.	387– 9	'*N*· which our spirits blend
Po.	6– 3	'*N*· which our spirits blend
	65–12	'*n*· thy drap'ry still lie.
My.	151–19	* '*n*· the temple of uplifted sky

Neb. (State)
(*see* **Lincoln, Norfolk, Omaha**)

Nebraska State Journal
My.	97–14	* [*N*· *S*· *J*·, Lincoln, Neb.]

nebulous
Mis.	378–22	than the *n*· system is from

necessarily
Mis.	18–23	*n*· entertain habitual love
	218–31	* is *n*· the recognition of
	223– 6	*n*· have pure fountains ;
	252– 2	not *n*· infinitesimal but infinite.
	346–20	its opposite is *n*· unreal,
	366–24	*n*· culminate in sickness, sin,
Man.	99–11	Each church is not *n*· confined to
Ret.	50–26	my necessity is not *n*· theirs ;
Un.	18– 1	evil *n*· leads to extinction
	19– 1	*knowledge* is *n*· *foreknowledge* ;
No.	3–19	Dishonesty *n*· stultifies the
My.	61–30	* intricate problems which must *n*·
	165– 1	*n*· promote and pervade all his

necessary
Mis.	4–17	Further enlightenment is *n*·
	4–28	more than faith is *n*·,
	7– 7	charity and humility is *n*·
	14– 6	or find its existence *n*·

necessary

Mis.	32–26	n· for the individual,
	38–25	Is it n· to study your Science
	38–27	It is not n· to make
	39–30	Divine help is as n· in the
	51–29	Are both prayer and drugs n·
	68–23	* n· to thought and knowledge ;
	91– 5	It is not absolutely n·
	169–20	it is n· rightly to read
	177–18	n· to the salvation of
	227– 6	n· to offer to the innocent,
	362–29	except when it is n· to
Man.	41– 6	When it is n· to show
	49–12	wisdom n· in a sick room,
	59–23	give their seats, if n·,
	87–15	must have the n· moral and
Ret.	30–13	Why was this conviction n·
Un.	14–13	Was it n· for God to
Pul.	15– 5	since exposure is n·
	54–11	* n· in apostolic times.
	64–10	* When the n· amount was raised,
	68– 9	* n· for the interests of her
No.	28– 8	n· to effect this end
'01.	24–24	I found it n· to follow
'02.	8– 5	Is it n· to say that the
My.	8– 1	* n· for this purpose."
	10–23	* money n· to this end,
	12– 1	* n· for this purpose,"
	23– 1	not n· for us to delay
	23–14	* n· to complete the sum
	56– 9	* it was found n· to organize
	66–14	* n· to have this property.
	72– 2	* it was n· to set aside
	73– 1	* it was found n· to issue a
	83–31	* the n· expense of church work,
	110–32	torn from their n· contexts,
	123–17	and other n· expenses
	157–11	* makes n· the commodious
	161– 8	the sentence n· to reclaim
	212– 8	A harder fight will be n·
	241– 1	* n· moral and spiritual qualifications
	286–11	armament of navies is n·,
	343–23	authority," . . . "became n·.
	343–23	Rules were n·,

necessitate

Mis.	349– 8	not n· essential materialization

necessitates

Mis.	256–15	n· receiving but a select number
'01.	5–28	God as a Person n· a creed
My.	10–29	* now n· this onward step.
	14–28	* n· large payments of money,

necessities

Mis.	199–11	in reproaches, in n·, — II Cor. 12 : 10.
	201–23	took pleasure in "n·," — II Cor. 12 : 10.
	278–23	n· and God's providence
Pul.	10– 4	quickened sense of mortal's n·,
'01.	29– 3	or even known of his sore n·?

necessity

absolute
My.	22–13	* shown the absolute n· of giving.

all
Mis.	119–20	exemption from all n· to obey a

brother's
Mis.	131– 9	console this brother's n·

case of
Man.	100–25	Case of N·.

consider the
Ret.	83–28	when we consider the n· of

destroy the
Mis.	45– 8	destroy the n· for ether

for understanding
Mis.	92– 2	n· for understanding Science,

halted from
My.	214–26	I therefore halted from n·.

human
'01.	34–26	Christianity is a human n· :

immediate
Man.	78–19	Church bills of immediate n·

implies the
Mis.	367–13	implies the n· of knowing evil,

increasing
Mis.	115–22	increasing n· for relying on God

my
Mis.	311–24	and my n· was to tell it ;
Ret.	50–26	my n· is not necessarily theirs ;

never a
My.	279– 1	never requisite, never a n·,

no
Mis.	241–20	there is no n· for pain ;
	283– 1	there is no n· for it,
Pan.	10–27	no n· for disease and death.
Hea.	8– 1	no n· beyond the understanding of

of his immortality
Mis.	2–21	the n· of his immortality ;

necessity

of this By-Law
Man.	28– 9	hence the n· of this By-Law

recognition of the
My.	9– 2	* In recognition of the n· for

recognizing the
My.	7–16	* "Recognizing the n· for providing

sad
Man.	55– 7	if this sad n· occurs.

sort of
'01.	1–18	All that is true is a sort of n·,

sprang from
Mis.	148–15	They sprang from n·,
Man.	3–11	They sprang from n·,

submitted to
My.	195–10	and so have submitted to n·,

that
Mis.	248–27	saved me from that n·

understand the
Mis.	136–13	you will understand the n· for my

without
Mis.	14–23	for evil, is . . . without n·.

Mis.	4–13	has become a n·.
	14–22	appears to mortals . . . to be the n·
	44– 7	n· for immediate relief,
	50–12	under the n· to express
	241–21	error that insists on the n· of
	243–15	it includes of n· the Principle,
	256–11	of n· this imposes on me the
Ret.	69–23	Where then is the n· for recreation
Un.	15–18	of n· take precedence as
Rud.	14–16	must of n· do better
No.	5–11	which is untrue, is of n· unreal.
My.	8– 6	* n· here indicated is beyond cavil ;
	99– 6	* not a n·, but a pleasure

neck

Mis.	122–12	hanged about his n·, — Matt. 18 : 6.
	370–17	about the n· of omnipotence,
My.	105–15	eaten the flesh of the n·

necks

My.	161– 1	around the n· of the wicked.

necromancy

Mis.	78–13	magic, alchemy, or n·.
	334– 6	N· has no foundation,
'01.	20–24	this new-old régime of n·

nectar

Mis.	9–17	fill it with the n· of the gods.
Pul.	8–25	deft fingers distilled the n·
Po.	66– 1	pure n· our brimming cup fill,

need (noun)

any
Un.	5–13	frightened sense of any n· of

church's
Ret.	44–18	carefully, noting the church's n·,

grave
My.	355– 7	a grave n· for more men

great
Mis.	24– 5	came to me in an hour of great n· ;
	107–11	love is the great n· of mankind.
Ret.	49– 8	great n· is for more of the spirit
My.	244–12	great n· of which I daily discern.

have
Mis.	73–19	we have n· to know that the

human
		(see **human**)

ignorance and
My.	162– 1	mercy for mortal ignorance and n·

is apparent
Man.	95– 4	When the n· is apparent,

less
Hea.	1–14	less n· of publishing the good news."
My.	147–31	You have less n· of me

little
Mis.	262–27	little n· of words of approval

made known
Pul.	8–14	only the n· made known,

meet the
My.	56– 9	* inadequate to meet the n·,

my
Mis.	249–25	coming nearer in my n·,

neighbor's
Mis.	257–29	ministering to his neighbor's n·.

no
Mis.	185–22	no n· of statistics by which to
No.	27–10	no n· of the sun,
My.	71– 8	* no n· of fussing about the
	206–20	no n· of the sun, — Rev. 21 : 23.

nor
Mis.	323– 5	nor n· of the sun

of changing
Un.	11–10	showed the n· of changing this mind

of experience
Mis.	73–16	we have n· of experience.

need (noun)

of living faith
Pul. 30–21 * *n·* of living faith at the moment

of man
My. 260–26 supplies every *n·* of man.

of mankind
Mis. 107–11 love is the great *n·* of mankind.
'02. 9–29 has met the *n·* of mankind

of our Mother Church
My. 11–14 * the *n·* of our Mother Church.

of physical help
Mis. 88– 2 feel the *n·* of physical help,

of these things
Mis. 73–18 We have *n·* of *these* things ;

of watching
Mis. 12–19 hence the *n·* of watching,

present
My. 281– 6 I cited, as our present *n·*,

pressing
Mis. 115–14 and meet the pressing *n·* of a

saw the
My. 22– 3 * saw the *n·* of a larger edifice

seeing the
Mis. 109–17 seeing the *n·* of somethingness

see the
Mis. 371– 5 opened his eyes to see the *n·*
My. 216–27 and see the *n·* of self-culture,

special
Man. 96–11 where he sees there is special *n·*,
My. 177– 8 there seems to be no special *n·*

spiritual
Mis. 245–16 a physical and spiritual *n·*

suggested the
My. 57– 8 * suggested the *n·* of a larger church

supply that
Man. 96–13 he is at liberty to supply that *n·*

times of
'01. 26–13 matter for help in times of *n·*.

universal
Mis. 365–14 universal *n·* of better health
No. 18–11 universal *n·* of better health

urgent
My. 62–31 * when there was urgent *n·* of both.

was felt
My. 57– 4 * *n·* was, felt of an auditorium

what
Pul. 1–18 what *n·* that I should be present
Pan. 4–26 what *n·* have we of drugs, hygiene,

world has
Mis. 110– 4 the world has *n·* of you,

Mis. 72–21 *n·* of all *these things*," — *Matt.* 6 : 32.
263–21 The *n·* of their teacher's counsel,
355– 4 *n·*, however, is not of the letter,
Ret. 63– 2 then insist on the *n·* of healing
Un. 52– 8 *n·* that human consciousness should
'02. 19–23 *n·* of all these things." — *Matt.* 6 : 32.
My. 26–20 as I foresee, the *n·* of it.
56–32 * proved the *n·* of a larger edifice.
217– 2 or, if *n·* be, to help your parents,

need (verb)

Mis. 32–23 time and attention that they *n·*,
50–28 *n·* to be changed from self
86–11 which *n·* correct definition.
87–23 What they *n·* thereafter is to
89–21 *why does he n· to be saved?*
108–22 what we *n·* to know of evil,
110– 7 You *n·* also to watch,
114– 7 teachers of C. S. *n·* to watch
127–31 which *n·* close attention and
145– 4 *n·* no organization to express it.
146– 8 I should *n·* to be with you.
146– 9 *n·* to know the circumstances
157–26 Write me when you *n·* me.
214–19 *n·* to search the Scriptures
214–22 they *n·* to do this even to
270–17 Then you will *n·* no other aid,
281–32 You will *n·*, in future,
303– 2 and *n·* only to shine from
307– 5 you will have all you *n·*
330–25 sanction what our natures *n·*.
344–29 We *n·* the spirit of St. Paul,
345– 7 We *n·* the spirit of the pious
356– 5 *n·* no terrible detonation
356– 6 *n·* no temporary indulgence
357–27 and *n·* special help.
Ret. 64– 8 *N·* it be said that any
65–26 and they *n·* no creed.
Un. 14–15 might *n·* repentance,
20–14 We therefore *n·* not fear it.
45– 8 *n·* most of all to be rid of
45–12 These falsities *n·* a denial.
No. 3–20 which Mind-healers specially *n·* ;
23–20 As mortals, we *n·* to discern
30– 9 He *n·* not know the evil
30–10 than the legislator *n·* know

need (verb)

'01. 15–21 even *n·* to hear the following
29– 6 *n·* the watchful and tender care
30–16 religion and therapeutics *n·*
Hea. 19–16 *n·* it to stamp our religions
Po. 24–14 all I *n·* to comfort mine.
My. vi– 2 * does not *n·* to be interpreted to
8– 5 * We *n·* to keep pace with
31– 4 * " I *n·* Thee every hour ;"
85–11 * One does not *n·* to accept the
126–29 We *n·* it in our homes,
130–24 I *n·* not say this to the loyal
134–10 Defeat *n·* not follow victory.
137–30 able to select the Trustees I *n·*
140–15 * *n·* not debar distant members
200–19 I *n·* not say this to you,
229–28 Thou knowest best what we *n·*
234– 8 and how I *n·* every hour wherein
249–29 What our churches *n·* is that
288– 5 life's incentive and sacrifice *n·* no
303– 8 Scientists *n·* to be understood
303–29 We *n·* much humility,
312–23 amount of money he would *n·*
351–27 divine Science is all they *n·*,
355–12 we *n·* in our ranks . . . the strong,
358– 9 Beloved ! you *n·* to watch and pray

needed

Mis. 3–17 never are *n·* to aid
6– 7 and many more are *n·*
157–16 when help is most *n·*,
273– 6 now seem to be most *n·*,
358– 2 Love is greatly *n·*,
Man. 31–14 *animus* so universally *n·*.
Ret. 26–20 who *n·* no discovery of the
95–11 * comforters are *n·* much
Pul. 41– 4 * amount *n·* was received.
Rud. 16– 6 Lectures in public are *n·*,
17–12 she *n·* miraculous vision
My. 9– 6 * may be *n·* for that purpose.
10–17 * none will be made or ever be *n·*.
55– 3 * *n·* a place of its own,
58– 5 * no more funds are *n·*
59–29 * Now my testimony is not *n·*.
62–25 * when they were so much *n·*.
65– 8 * that might be *n·* to build
65–13 * why the building was *n·*.
72–14 * chapter sub-title
76– 4 * notices that more money was *n·*
76–10 * no more contributions . . . were *n·*.
83–24 * two million dollars *n·* for the
138– 9 not *n·* to protect my person or
229–26 which I said . . . would never be *n·*,
234–27 Silent prayer . . . is just what is *n·*.
248–14 the *n·* and the inevitable sponsors
324–20 * that he thought you *n·* help,

needful

Mis. 38–20 makes divine metaphysics *n·*,
No. 1– 3 is a most *n·* work ;
My. 126–32 that *n·* one thing — divine Science,
271–10 is the one thing *n·*

needing

Mis. 230–27 *n·* but canvas and the touch of an
260–29 *n·* neither license nor prohibition ;
315–26 except the individual *n·* it asks
Un. 59–21 man a sinner, *n·* a Saviour ;
59–23 an invalid, *n·* a physician ;

needle

No. 10–25 turns like the *n·* to the pole

needless

Mis. 31– 9 It is *n·* to say that such a
My. 259–26 merry-making or *n·* gift-giving

needs (noun)

differing
'01. 7–16 supply the differing *n·* of the

further
My. 22–11 * further *n·* of the building fund,

human
(*see* **human**)

humanity's
Mis. 370–13 according to humanity's *n·*.

of man
Mis. 3–10 applicable to all the *n·* of man.
259–29 applicable to all the *n·* of man.
My. 349–30 supplying all the *n·* of man.

of the present
My. 22–21 * discernment of the *n·* of the present

spiritual
Ret. 91–18 ministering to the spiritual *n·* of
My. 147–18 physical, moral, and spiritual *n·*

your
My. 186–15 will supply all your *n·*

Ret. 90–19 comprehend the *n·* of her babe
92– 3 for the *n·* of suffering mortals,

needs (noun)
'01.   29–16   increasing years and n·,
My.   24–27   * that it will meet the n· of

needs (verb)
Mis.   1–12   n· to be understood.
   13–25   only n· to be conceded,
   39–22   n· support at times ;
   46– 6   truism n· only to be tested
   56–22   n· only to be understood ;
   92– 7   n· continually to study this
   108–24   n· only to be known for what
   110– 5   it n· your innocence,
   122– 3   it must n· be that — Matt. 18 : 7.
   127–32   n· often to be stirred,
   163–28   must n· come in C. S.,
   190–13   n· yet to be learned.
   194–13   It only n· the prism of
   274– 7   The work that n· to be done,
   283–26   that he n· no personal aid.
   313– 7   pinnacle, that everybody n·.
   338–24   * It n· the overflow of heart,
   346–21   n· to be grasped in all its
   354– 5   History n· it,
   366–16   jaded humanity n· to get
Man.   101– 3   Committee on Publication n· an
Ret.   22– 1   history n· to be revised,
No.   34–21   atonement . . . n· to be understood.
   35–21   n· no reconciliation with God,
   43– 6   theology n· Truth to stimulate
Pan.   11–19   who falls physically n· to rise
'01.   12–19   It only n· the prism of
   19–28   The whole world n· to know that
   29– 3   Gifts he n· not.
My.   11–18   * n· no special insight to predict
   12–23   Whatever n· to be done
   89– 9   * edifice n· only an open space
   120– 8   Forgive, if it n· forgiveness,
   175–18   greatly n· improved streets.

needy
Ret.   6– 7   The n· were ever welcome,

ne'er
Mis.   390–24   N· perish young, like things of earth,
   391–20   Some good n· told before,
Chr.   53–26   signalize the birth Of him n· born
Ret.   18–19   radiance and glory n· fade.
Pul.   4– 5   Can n· refresh a drooping earth,
Po.   38–19   Some good n· told before,
   56– 3   N· perish young, like things of earth,
   64–10   radiance and glory n· fade.
   70–16   Thy discord n· in harmony began !
   71–10   Righteousness n· — awestruck or dumb
   72– 3   n· again Quench liberty that's just.
My.   194–30   * N· in a sunny hour fall off.''

negation
Mis.   27–21   evil and matter are n· :
   107–17   Evil is a n· :
   334–22   How shall we treat a n·,
Un.   49–24   clearer right to call evil a n·,
No.   32–17   A lie is n·, — alias nothing,
My.   217–22   we can meet this n· more readily

negations
No.   16–10   n· of Spirit, Truth, and Life,

negative
Mis.   62–10   positive and n· quantities,
   62–11   the n· quantity offsets an
   65–12   a n· which the positive Truth destroys ;
   172– 5   the n· of metaphysical Science ;
Un.   45–17   error's affirmative to Truth's n·.
My.   105–26   When answered in the n·,
   217–22   n· all that the material senses affirm.
   232–31   watching against a n· watch,

negatives
No.   16–12   n· destitute of time and space ;

negativing
Mis.   208–18   by divine Truth's n· error

neglect
Mis.   213–10   to n· opportunities which God giveth,
   341–31   the n· of spiritual light,
   351– 5   for want of time, . . . I n· myself.
Man.   42– 7   nor to n· his duty to God,
   51– 3   if he n· to accept such admonition,
   62– 4   not n· to sing any special hymn
Hea.   5– 5   the n· of a bath, and so on.

neglecting
Ret.   89–24   for n· their own students,
My.   163–14   without n· the sacred demands

neglects
Man.   100–10   n· to fulfil the obligations
Ret.   90–16   never willingly n· her children

negotiated
'02.   13–14   The land . . . had been n· for,
   13–23   previously n· for the property

neighbor (see also **neighbor's**)
his
Mis.   183– 5   Man must love his n· as himself,
   258– 1   loving his n· as himself,
   367– 3   to love his n· as himself,
Hea.   5– 8   by doing good to his n·,
My.   33–20   doeth evil to his n·, — Psal. 15 : 3.
   33–21   reproach against his n·. — Psal. 15 : 3.
its
Hea.   11–16   lifting its foot against its n·,
My.   166– 1   from which it can help its n·.
love thy
Mis.   7– 9   love thy n· as thyself'' — Matt. 19 : 19.
   18–10   ''Love thy n· as thyself.'' — Matt. 19 : 19.
   311–21   love thy n· as thyself,'' — Matt. 19 : 19.
Pan.   9–11   ''Love thy n· as thyself ;'' — Matt. 19 : 19.
'00.   5–21   ''Love thy n· as thyself.'' — Matt. 19 : 19.
My.   109– 9   ''Love thy n· as thyself.'' — Matt. 19 : 19.
   196–15   ''Love thy n· as thyself.'' — Matt. 19 : 19.
   265– 1   ''Love thy n· as thyself'' — Matt. 19 : 19.
   278– 9   ''Love thy n· as thyself'' — Matt. 19 : 19.
   281–12   ''Love thy n· as thyself,'' — Matt. 19 : 19.
my
My.   276–25   love God supremely, and my n·
next-door
Ret.   40– 6   her next-door n· was dying.
one's
Pan.   9–22   It loves one's n· as one's self ;
our
My.   23– 2   * how much our n· has given,
   52–19   * love our n· as ourselves.''
   132–22   love our n· as ourselves,
   200–15   to love our n· as ourself,
their
Mis.   2– 5   they steal from their n·,
My.   286– 7   love their n· as themselves.
thy
Mis.   328–30   loving God supremely and thy n·
My.   183– 4   and thy n· as thyself.'' — Luke 10 : 27.
   (see also **love thy**)
your
No.   38–21   loving your n· as yourself,

neighborhood
Ret.   89–15   had been away from the n· ;
Pul.   33–21   * All inquiry in the n·
   48–18   * born and bred in that same n·.
My.   70–17   * on every corner in the n·.

neighboring
Ret.   3–11   n· battle of Chippewa,
Po.   66– 9   To join with the n· choir ;

neighbor's
Mis.   211–22   protects himself at his n· cost,
   257–29   ministering to his n· need.
   319– 9   seeing too keenly their n·.

neighbors
Ret.   87–19   the rights of their n·,

neither
Mis.   14– 1   n· place nor power left for evil.
   14–26   evil is n· a primitive nor
   22– 3   n· a law of matter nor of man.
   25– 8   n· one really exists,
   26–21   n· a genus nor a species
   28– 3   n· see, hear, feel, taste,
   28–25   find n· pleasure nor pain therein.
   29–25   n· flavor Christianity nor
   30–22   * ''is n· Christian nor science !''
   36– 2   is n· God's man nor Mind ;
   36–26   n· indeed can be.'' — Rom. 8 : 7.
   48– 4   should n· be taught nor practised,
   48–11   animal magnetism is n· of God nor
   59– 2   you can n· understand nor
   61–28   can n· make them so nor
   66–29   can n· remove that cause nor
   71–17   n· human hypothesis nor matter.
   74–30   n· substance, intelligence, nor
   93–19   n· maintained by Science nor
   93–21   n· fear nor sin can bring on
   99– 5   n· can you understand.'' — see Mark 8 : 17.
   100–12   that grasp n· the meaning nor
   103–19   N· does the temporal know the
   103–20   n· the pattern nor Maker
   109–20   n· is a knowledge of sin and its
   112– 9   can n· defend the innocent nor
   115–19   evil has n· prestige, power, nor
   118–10   is n· Science nor obedience.
   118–14   sympathy can n· atone for error,
   122–14   it is n· questionable nor assailable :
   122–24   N· spiritual bankruptcy nor a
   123–16   The Christian's God is n·,
   124– 6   n· do we love and obey Him by
   131– 2   can n· help himself nor others by
   134–26   n· silence nor disarm God's voice.
   151– 4   n· shall any man — John 10 : 28.
   165–13   n· darkness, doubt, disease, nor

neither

Mis.	165–20	can *n·* appreciate nor appropriate
	172–16	it is *n·* of human origin nor
	175–15	*n·* with "the leaven of —* I Cor.* 5 : 8.
	182–16	created *n·* from dust nor carnal
	183–10	he is *n·* the slave of sense, nor
	190– 1	It is *n·* the energy of matter,
	192–18	*N·* can we question the
	197–32	*n·* be sick nor forever a sinner.
	199–28	*n·* supernatural nor preternatural ;
	209–15	compels mortals to learn that *n·*
	209–17	for God *n·* slumbers nor sleeps.
	210–28	but has *n·* the cowardice nor the
	213–24	*n·* shall any man — *John* 10 : 28.
	216–25	* in which *n·* laws of nature nor
	217– 3	*n·* philosophy nor reason attempts to
	217–24	This is *n·* Science nor theism.
	218– 8	matter can *n·* see, hear, nor
	218–26	*n·* eliminated nor retained by Spirit.
	219– 3	*n·* reveals God in matter,
	229–18	*n·* shall any plague— *Psal.* 91 : 10.
	249–16	*n·* purchased nor ordered a drug
	258–21	error could *n·* name nor
	260–29	*n·* license nor prohibition ;
	266– 5	is *n·* politic nor scientific ;
	281– 8	*n·* deprive me of something **nor**
	284–21	*n·* an evil claim nor
	284–22	*n·* to be *feared* nor
	286– 5	*n·* be obscured nor throttled.
	286–14	wherein they *n·* marry nor
	286–24	*n·* real nor eternal.
	289–19	*N·* divine justice nor human
	310– 2	*n·* the intent of my works nor
	319– 4	can *n·* be coeval nor coequal,
	323– 5	nor need of the sun, *n·* of the
	335–14	but *n·* moves me from the path
	340– 7	turning *n·* to the right nor to
	341–29	*n·* the cares of this world nor
	348– 5	infringe *n·* the books nor the business
	353– 5	they are *n·* standards nor models.
	355–19	*n·* intelligence nor power,
	359–16	*n·* wisdom nor Science
	361– 8	whose myriad forms are *n·* material
	367–26	has *n·* precedent nor foundation in
	373–11	*N·* material finesse, standpoint, nor
	379–12	*n·* ya scholar nor a metaphysician.
Man.	26–25	*n·* report the discussions of this
	28–12	*n·* did according to — *Luke* 12 : 47.
	37–11	*n·* the Clerk nor the Church shall **be**
	40– 5	*N·* animosity nor mere
	42–16	shall *n·* entertain a belief nor
	43–22	shall *n·* buy, sell, nor circulate
	74– 4	*n·* shall he exercise supervision
	87– 1	*N·* the Pastor Emeritus nor
	94–20	shall *n·* resign nor transfer
	103– 5	shall *n·* be demolished, nor
Chr.	55–13	*n·* consider the— *Isa.* 5 : 12.
	55–20	*n·* beginning of days,— *Heb.* 7 : 3.
Ret.	24–13	that *n·* medicine nor surgery could
	25–25	matter *n·* sees, hears, nor feels Spirit,
	26– 2	*n·* obedience to hygienic laws,
	30–23	*n·* can its inspiration be gained
	34– 6	*N·* ancient nor modern philosophy
	57– 4	*N·* ancient nor modern philosophy
	63– 6	in reality no evil, *n·* sickness nor
	67–18	The sinner created *n·* himself nor
	68– 6	*n·* indeed can be, the father of man.
Un.	2–19	contains *n·* discord nor disease.
	5–17	*n·* will it promote the Cause of
	11–23	*n·* red tape nor indignity
	11–24	Jesus required *n·* cycles of time nor
	14–18	*n·* shadow of turning."— *Jas.* 1 : 17.
	26–10	*N·* is He the author of the material
	32–24	*n·* masculine nor feminine.
	33–18	*n·* matter nor mortal mind,
	41–25	hence matter *n·* lives nor dies.
	46– 2	which *n·* think nor speak.
	50–17	matter has *n·* Mind nor sensation.
	51– 5	reality of being is *n·* seen, felt,
	57–10	*n·* temptation nor glory.
	57–15	but he *n·* held her error by
	60–21	He is *n·* absent from Himself
	61– 8	*n·* young nor old, *n·* dead nor **risen.**
	61–15	*n·* advancing, retreating, nor
	62– 5	ever presence that *n·* comes nor goes,
	63– 2	The I AM was *n·* buried nor
Pul.	14–19	*n·* drown your voice with its roar,
	51– 2	* *N·* does the Christian faith
Rud.	4– 8	*n·* is it of human origin.
	7–19	matter, has *n·* sensation nor
	13– 2	*n·* matter nor mortal mind ;
	14– 1	*N·* can they serve two masters,
No.	14– 1	*n·* warped nor misconceived,
	15–20	finds Spirit *n·* in matter nor **in**
	15–22	*n·* origin nor existence in the
	17–15	*n·* part nor parcel of divine

neither

No.	19–11	He is *n·* a limited mind nor a
	20– 3	*n·* self-created, nor discerned through
	23– 5	Evil can *n·* grasp the prerogative
	25–15	*n·* matter nor a mode of mortal mind,
	28–22	*n·* the comprehension of its Principle
	32– 6	*n·* extinguish a crime nor the
	39–11	Prayer can *n·* change God, nor
Pan.	2– 5	*n·* hypothetical nor dogmatical,
	5–20	should *n·* believe the lie, nor
	13– 6	" *N·* shall they say,— *Luke* 17 : 21.
'01.	4–12	*n·* man nor matter can be.
	6–23	He can *n·* be one nor infinite in the
	12– 5	*n·* eating nor drinking,
	12–27	Evil is *n·* quality nor quantity :
	13–12	Sin can have *n·* entity, verity,
	20– 7	*n·* moral right nor might to harm
	21–21	*n·* the predicate nor postulate
	23– 1	*n·* more nor less than three ;
	31– 6	*n·* personal nor human,
'02.	6–12	God made *n·* evil nor its
	7– 8	*n·* philosophy, nature, nor
	8– 8	*n·* Christians nor Scientists.
	11–12	*n·* Christian nor Science.
	14– 4	*n·* rent, mortgage, nor sell
	14–23	*n·* favor nor protection in the
	15– 3	*n·* informed the police of these
Hea.	3– 1	*n·* hygiene nor drugs
	4– 2	The infinite can *n·* go forth
	16–20	They can *n·* see, hear, feel,
My.	13– 1	They speculate *n·* on the past,
	15– 7	shall *n·* be demolished nor
	71–21	* *n·* nave, aisles, nor transept
	94– 9	* *N·* can we overlook the
	113–18	*N·* is it presumptuous
	121– 9	*n·* tremulous nor relapsing.
	130–13	*n·* the time nor the inclination
	139– 3	*n·* dead nor plucked up by
	166–17	*n·* she nor I would be practising
	184– 5	*n·* hath the eye seen, what God
	186– 8	*n·* dome nor turret tells the tale
	206–20	*n·* of the moon, — *Rev.* 21 : 23.
	218– 5	*N·* the Old nor the New
	223– 4	I *n·* listen to complaints,
	227–19	*n·* should they forget that
	227–23	" *N·* cast ye your pearls — *Matt.* 7 : 6.
	235–20	is he matter or spirit? *N·* one.
	242– 5	it is *n·* behind the point
	250–17	*n·* binds nor compels the
	252–30	*n·* slumbers nor is stilled
	260–31	*N·* the you nor the I in the flesh
	269– 8	*n·* marry, nor are given — *Luke* 20 : 35.
	269– 8	*n·* can they die— *Luke* 20 : 36.
	276– 5	she begs to say, . . . that she is *n·* ;
	285–21	they *n·* found me — *Acts* 24 : 12.
	285–22	*n·* raising up the people, — *Acts* 24 : 12.
	285–22	*n·* in the synagogues, — *Acts* 24 : 12.
	285–23	*n·* can they prove — *Acts* 24 : 13.
	296–12	*n·* does he sleep nor rest from
	302– 6	*N·* life nor death, health nor
	323–19	* *N·* do I now feel at all equal
	324–15	* sure that *n·* Mr. Wiggin nor
	348–15	*n·* man nor *materia medica,*
	357– 6	matter has *n·* part nor portion,
	359– 2	*n·* do they trouble me with

Nemesis

No.	3–18	*N·* of the history of Mind-healing

neophyte

Mis.	117–23	*n·* is inclined to be too fast or
	273– 2	the *n·* will be benefited
Ret.	78– 1	*n·* in C. S. acts like
My.	48–27	* upon the mind of the *n·*

Neoplatonic

No.	14– 9	renewal in the *N·* philosophy ;
'00.	4– 8	Babylonian and *N·* religion,

nerve

Mis.	44–17	thought was pain in the bone or *n·*,
My.	253– 6	what greater glory can *n·* your

nerved

Pul.	9–10	and *n·* its grand fulfilment.
No.	12–15	*n·* her purpose to build on the

nerves

Mis.	210–20	membranes, stomach, and *n· ·*
	288–29	Love that *n·* the struggle.
Un.	34–16	and the *n·*, material *n·*, *do*

nervous

Rud.	11–27	the muscular, vascular, or *n·*
No.	42–26	* suffering from *n·* prostration,

nervousness

Mis.	51– 5	*Is a belief of n·, . . . mesmerism?*

nest
Mis. 210– 7 Do men whine over a n· of serpents,
254– 8 n· of the raven's callow brood !
354–32 Whenever he soareth to fashion his n·,

nestled
My. 155– 4 little church, n· so near my heart

nestles
Mis. 331–13 n· them under her wings,

nestling
Ret. 18– 6 n· alder is whispering low,
Po. 63–15 n· alder is whispering low,

nestling's
Mis. 331–20 guards the n· faltering flight !
389– 8 guards the n· faltering flight !
Po. 4– 5 guards the n· faltering flight !

nestlings
Mis. 152–25 hope, faith, and Love, are God's n· ;
My. 186– 5 like tender n· in the crannies

nests
Mis. 356–20 n· of the raven's callow brood.
Po. 53–14 And build their cozy n·,

net
Mis. 111– 5 At times, your n· has been so full
111–14 had He filled the n·, it would
Man. 80– 4 The n· profits of the business shall
'02. 13– 8 n· profits from the business of The
My. 224–15 not caught in some author's n·,
241– 7 * beware the n· that is craftily laid

nets
Mis. 90–29 left their n· to follow him,
111–11 cast their n· on the right side,
212–11 cast their n· on the right side.

neuter
Un. 32–24 a *liar* was in the n· gender,

neutralize
Mis. 224–25 to n· what is bitter in it,
241–14 big enough apparently to n· your

neutralized
Mis. 69–20 and n· the bad effects of the

neutralizes
Mis. 204– 5 n· and destroys error.
My. 293– 6 mind and matter n· itself.

neutralizing
Pul. 6– 1 when Truth is n· error
My. 292–21 one . . . belief unwittingly n· another,

never (*see also* **ne'er**)
Mis. ix–19 youth that n· grows old ;
3–16 Drugs, inert matter, n· are needed
5–29 That which n· existed, can seem
12– 8 N· return evil for evil ;
14–12 could n· be learned ;
18–22 n· separate himself from good,
19– 6, 7 n· unmerciful, n· unwise.
19–15 can n· change the current
32–28 n· envy, elbow, slander, hate,
35–14 * I n· knew so unselfish an
45–23 It n· originated or existed
47– 9 Have you n· been so preoccupied
47–11 If n· in your waking hours,
49–31 Truth n· created error,
57–20 the Lord God n· said it.
66–26 or he n· can reach the Science
71–14 Science n· averts law,
73–12 Law is n· material :
76– 5 shall n· see death." — *John* 8 : 51.
76– 8 can n· be tested or proven true
76–17 spake as n· man spake,
78–12 n· dreamed that either of these
79–20 n· was, and n· can be,
87–19 I n· commission any one to
88–25 * had n· seen water freeze."
91–24 I n· dreamed, . . . that a loyal
94– 3 n· knew a person who knowingly
95–15 I am not, and n· was.
96–20 adore Christ as n· before.
99–24 n· bear into oblivion his words.
103–13 form and individuality are n· lost,
105–21 individual and his ideal can n·
106–25 praise that shall n· end?
107–18 it n· started with time,
107–27 deep, n· to be repented of,
109– 5 mayhap n· have thought of,
116–26 N· absent from your post,
116–27 n· off guard, n· ill-humored,
116–27 n· unready to work for God,
121– 1 his words can n· pass away :
122–28 God n· made it,
127–30 a kind word . . . is n· wasted.
129–21 lens that he n· turns on himself.
134–13 such as you n· before received.
148– 1 n· shows us a smiling countenance

never
Mis. 148– 2 We shall n· find one part of
154–26 n· desert the post of spiritual
160– 2 N· did gratitude and love
165–16 appears — n· to disappear.
165–24 n· paid the price of sin.
170– 6 which n· changes to death.
171– 2 can n· be wrested from its
174–27 Death can n· usher in the dawn
177– 1 N· was there a more solemn and
180– 9 "Christ n· left," I replied,
182–19 understanding that man was n· lost
187–26 n· extinguished in a night of discord.
195–22 He who n· unsheathed his blade
201– 8 element of matter, . . . n· of Spirit.
210– 4 C. S. n· healed a patient without
210–31 Charity n· flees before error,
212– 4 n· knows what happiness is,
213–24 they shall n· perish, — *John* 10 : 28.
218– 3 that matter n· produced Mind,
232–10 It will n· do to be behind the times
234–15 can n· find a place in Science.
234–16 it n· has advanced man a single step
237–10 Some people n· repent until
239– 4 I n· was in better health.
241–19 "God n· made you sick :
247–30 He n· made sickness.
249–24 will n· leave me comfortless,
252– 6 its largest dose is n· dangerous,
260– 7 n· entered into the line of Jesus'
265–20 can n· bring forth the real fruits of
267– 2 wail of evil n· harms Scientists,
267–10 remember that there n· was a time
269–12 n· man spake," — *John* 7 : 46.
273– 8 My students have n· expressed so
273–10 n· have been so capable of
275–21 Pen can n· portray the satisfaction
277–13 The stake and scaffold have n·
277–17 silence Truth? N·.
277–27 and n· so near as when
278–11 I have n· given occasion
284– 2 n· try to hinder others
290– 4 nuptial vow is n· annulled
292–28 I n· knew a student who
297–14 perhaps he has n· visited.
299– 4 but n· until then.
307– 2 N· ask for tomorrow :
307– 4 if you wait, n· doubting,
308– 2 Until . . . man will n· be found
310–28 together with those who n·
311–30 n· escaped from my lips,
316– 1 but n· to return evil for evil ;
316– 2 n· to attack the malpractitioner,
336– 3 that a lie is n· true?
339– 6 victor, n· the vanquished ;
340– 3 Good is n· the reward of evil,
340–12 who n· brings out a brief.
341– 1 they n· bring out the right action
341–27 so that the flame n· expires.
344–19 Such philosophy can n· demonstrate
346–11 Evil n· did exist as an entity.
346–24 n· to repeat error unless it
349–28 I n· received more than this ;
350– 2 was n· receipted for.
351– 5 I n· have practised by arguments
351–16 n· can place it in the wrong hands
353–10 and n· until then.
354– 1 they "n· disobey Mother" !
355–17 n· clears the vision.
356–24 One can n· go up, until
358–13 they n· should be until then.
360–12 Philosophy n· has produced,
365–24 n· met the growing wants
366–26 n· have abated and n· will
367–21 To good, evil is n· present ;
372–26 n· having seen the painter's
373– 9 I had n· before seen it :
374–20 I n· looked on my ideal of
378–14 n· occurred to the author to learn his
379–13 I n· heard him say that matter was
385–19 Now see thy ever-self ; Life n· fled ;
385–20 Man is not mortal, n· of the dead :
Man. 84– 4 n· to return evil for evil,
Chr. 55–28 shall n· die. — *John* 11 : 26.
Ret. 5–16 to which the pen can n· do justice.
6– 3 * impressions . . . can n· be effaced,
7–11 * and he n· forsook them until
9–15 but n· again to the material senses
14–12 declaring that n· could I unite with
21– 6 We n· met again until he had
27– 5 n· been read by any one but myself,
30– 7 The motive of . . . has n· changed.
37– 8 * but it will n· be read."
40–19 * "I n· before suffered so little
57–29 such methods can n· reach
59– 6 The word *Life* n· means that

never

Ret.	64–16	shall *n·* see light. — *Psal.* 49 : 19.
	64–18	and thoughts have *n·* changed,
	68– 1	material concept was *n·* a creator,
	68– 6	human concept *n·* was, . . . the **father**
	74– 9	I desire *n·* to think of it,
	76–24	*n·* abuses the corporeal personality,
	85–17	*N·* forsake your post without
	87–18	*n·*, in any way, to trespass
	90–16	The true mother *n·* willingly
Un.	10–13	Spiritual phenomena *n·* converge
	11–22	he *n·* thanked Jesus for restoring
	14–27	*n·* said that man would become
	15– 5	which God *n·* can throw off?
	17–16	*n·* man spake,'' — *John* 7 : 46.
	18– 6	Error may say that God can *n·*
	18–25	to be *n·* conscious of death.
	20–12	God *n·* made evil.
	24– 9	you can *n·* be outside of His
	25–25	evil can *n·* take away.
	26–15	* His mercy waneth *n·*,
	26–17	God's power *n· waneth*,
	28– 5	It was *n·* touched by the
	28–10	*n·* a light or form was discerned
	29– 6	Spirit *n·* sins,
	29–20	can *n·* be seen or measured
	30– 7	Soul is Life, and . . . *n·* sins.
	40– 5	man in Science *n·* dies.
	40–13	his sayings will *n·* die ;
	40–20	Death can *n·* alarm or even
	41– 4	Of evil we can *n·* learn it,
	41–22	Spirit can *n·* dwell in its
	43–16	can *n·* ''pass away — *see Matt.* 5 : 18.
	45–11	that God *n·* made evil.
	45–22	But Truth *n·* dies,
	51– 7	human reason can *n·* make
	53– 3	God *n·* made them ;
	59– 7	was *n·* absent from the earth
	59–17	*n·* saw the Saviour come and **go,**
	62– 2	that they *n·* were sick.
	62– 9	good, is *n·* absent,
	62–18	In Science, Christ *n·* died.
	62–22	*n·* in matter, nor resurrected
	63– 4	*n·* absent for a moment.
	63– 6	*n·* disappeared to spiritual **sense,**
	64–17	but they can *n·* turn back
Pul.	6–30	whose mind *n·* swerved
	8–17	Little hands, *n·* before devoted **to**
	9– 7	*n·* be shattered in our hearts,
	14–17	*n·* fear the consequences.
	36–12	* I *n·* saw equalled.
	45– 3	* will *n·* be known in this **world.**
	52– 1	* Wonders will *n·* cease.
	72–20	* that she had *n·* claimed,
	74–27	*n·* can be but one God,
	79– 8	* are not, and *n·* have been,
	79–28	* condition can *n·* long continue.
	80–12	* Mrs. Eddy we have *n·* seen ;
	82–16	* *n·* called Abraham ''Father,''
	83– 3	* what we *n·* fulfil as husband
Rud.	11–26	*n·* introduces the subject of
	11–27	*n·* depicts the muscular,
	11–28	*n·* talks about the structure of
	12– 1	*n·* lays his. hands on the patient,
	14– 8	*n·* sought charitable support,
	14–12	*n·* taught a Primary class without
	16– 3	can *n·* give a thorough knowledge
	16– 4	will *n·* undertake to fit students
	17– 9	Mind-healing *n·* originated in **pride,**
No.	4–10	*n·* made sickness a stubborn **reality.**
	13– 9	shall *n·* die.'' — *John* 11 : 26.
	17–11	can *n·* be less than a good man ;
	18– 2	has *n·* diminished sin
	19– 6	have *n·* met the growing wants
	24–22	and was *n·* a claimant ;
	24–25	There was *n·* a moment in which
	26–21	*n·* originated in molecule,
	28–17	Truth is *n·* understood too soon.
	31– 9	*n·* actual persons or real facts.
	31–27	shall *n·* see death ;'' — *John* 8 : 51.
	36– 6	*n·* left heaven for earth.
	40–15	*n·* to touch the human thought
	40–16	*n·* to trespass mentally on
	40–17	*n·* to take away the rights,
	41–18	*n·* admit such as come to steal
	43–21	can *n·* engraft Truth into error.
	43–24	will *n·* prevent or reconstruct
Pan.	6– 3	*n·* disappear in any other way.
	9–13	shall *n·* die.'' — *John* 11 : 26.
	10–24	is manifest, and *n·* lost.
	13–10	was *n·* more manifest than **in**
'00.	7–11	they *n·* loved the Bible
	7–19	this Christ is *n·* absent.
	10– 8	Such conflict *n·* ends till
	10–24	from a person I *n·* saw.
'01.	1– 5	rest assured you can *n·* lack

never

'01.	11– 2	*n·* suffered and *n·* died.
	13– 2	and God *n·* made it.
	13–23	*n·* punishes it only as it
	13–24	and *n·* afterwards ;
	15–13	or he would *n·* quit sinning.
	20–19	This unseen evil . . . is *n·* forgiven.
	25–19	*n·* recommended drugs, he *n·* used **them.**
	33– 9	* *n·* the originating influence
'02.	2–26	I *n·* left the Church,
	2–29	we shall meet again, *n·* to part.
	4–20	a law *n·* to be abrogated
	5–15	can *n·* be answered satisfactorily
	11– 2	Our heavenly Father *n·* destined
	14–15	could *n·* have been compassed
	15– 3	I *n·* lost my faith in God,
	15–19	I could *n·* believe that a human **being**
	16–26	they *n·* destroy one iota of
Hea.	2– 8	*n·* seen amid the smoke
	6– 6	The pioneer . . . is *n·* hit :
	9–17	God *n·* cursed man,
	9–18	God *n·* made a wicked **man ;**
	9–24	*n·* made sin or sickness,
	12–14	*n·* made a man sick.
	14–11	*n·* trust yourself in the hands **of**
	16– 2	can *n·* be repeated too often
	17–19	*n·* proceeded from Truth,
	18– 9	*n·* entered and it *n·* escaped
	18–10	good and evil *n·* dwelt toge**ther.**
	18–18	*n·* did anything for sickness
Peo.	9–14	who *n·* pardons the sin that
Po.	2– 9	can *n·* reach to thee
	24– 7	A sign that *n·* can depart.
	35– 8	Whose streams will *n·* dry
	42– 1	Oh, there's *n·* a shadow **where**
	42– 3	And *n·* the sunshine without **a**
	47– 6	to gladness and *n·* to tears,
	47– 8	*N·* to toiling and *n·* to fears,
	48–13	Now see thy ever-self ; Life *n·* **fled ;**
	48–14	*n·* of the dead :
My.	vii– 4	* can *n·* do for its Leader **what**
	5–32	divine wisdom, *n·*.
	9–24	I *n·* before felt poor in thanks,
	11–12	* *n·* urged upon us a step **that**
	18–19	*n·* more manifest than in its
	33–27	shall *n·* be moved. — *Psal.* 15 : 5.
	57–29	* ''Wonders will *n·* cease.
	61–19	* *n·* more did I have any doubt.
	61–31	* I appreciated as *n·* before
	66–30	* *n·* before has such a grand **church**
	67- 23	* *n·* was a more artistic effect
	72– 7	*N·* before has the city been
	83– 2	* of *n·* going about labelled.
	92– 2	* Of course the new idea will *n·*
	117–23	There was *n·* a religion or
	121–12	*n·* selfish, stony, nor stormy,
	127–24	can *n·* surrender.
	129–17	*n·* severed from Spirit !
	129–25	whose feet can *n·* be moved.
	130–19	Truth *n·* falters nor fails ;
	131–21	where God is we can *n·* part.
	132–29	Divine Love . . . *n·* loses a **case.**
	134–14	will *n·* lose their claim on us.
	146–26	*n·* mentally or audibly takes
	147–25	*n·* stop ceremoniously to
	150–13	*n·* weary of struggling to
	152–26	can *n·* heal you nor pardon **a**
	159– 3	*N·* more sweet than to-day,
	161– 7	which *n·* remits the sentence
	162–27	may their faith *n·* falter
	165–15	Goodness *n·* fails to receive **its**
	165–25	Goodness and benevolence *n·* **tire.**
	165–26	and *n·* stop from exhaustion.
	166– 2	will *n·* end in anarchy
	166–15	we will live on and *n·* drift **apart.**
	166–16	Had I *n·* suffered for
	167–10	that Love . . . which *n·* deserts **us.**
	167–28	will, I trust, *n·* be marred by
	179–18	narratives had *n·* been written,
	185–13	the victors *n·* to be vanqui**shed.**
	195– 7	it is *n·* too late to repent,
	203– 9	begin with work and *n·* stop
	204– 8	can begin and *n·* end.
	205–30	The . . . may fail, but the Science *n·*.
	212– 2	would *n·*, otherwise, think or do
	212–29	saying that animal magnetism *n·*
	214–29	To desert . . . *n·* occurred to me,
	227– 4	as one who *n·* weakened
	228–31	such a one was *n·* called to
	229–26	said in my heart would *n·* be **needed,**
	235– 9	and *n·* name a cipher?
	235–19	Matter as substance . . . *n·* was made.
	235–30	would *n·* have entered into the
	242– 3	can *n·* demonstrate spirituality **until**
	261–10	deceit or falsehood is *n·* wise.
	262–11, 12	*n·* born and *n·* dying.

never

My. 268– 3   *n·* be annulled so long as
277–10   *n·* settles the question of
279– 1   *n·* requisite, *n·* a necessity,
283–30   *n·* fastens on the good
288–18   He *n·* appealed to matter
290– 7   virtues can *n·* be lost.
290–17   Divine Love is *n·* so near as when
297–23   realize that he *n·* died ;
300–19   shall *n·* see death." — *John* 8 : 51.
303– 4   I have *n·* claimed to be.
308– 2   powers of earth . . . can *n·* prevent
308–19   He *n·* used a walking-stick.
308–24   * "I *n·* use a cane."
310–19   that there was *n·* a death in my
311–23   I *n·* doubted the veracity of
313–16   I was *n·* "given to long and
313–21   I *n·* was especially interested
313–22   *n·* "dabbled in mesmerism,"
313–22   *n·* was "an amateur clairvoyant,"
313–24   I *n·* went into a trance
318–32   If there had *n·* existed such a
324–19   * *n·* gave us the impression that
325– 8   * would *n·* be worth what you
325–13   * my desire has *n·* changed.
333–16   * It has *n·* been claimed by Mrs. Eddy
348–24   *n·* producing an opposite effect,

never-ending

My. 357–20   the way, . . . to their *n·* success,

nevermore

Mis. 397–12   waves can shock, Oh, *n·* !
Pul. 18–21   waves can shock, Oh, *n·* !
Po. 12–22   waves can shock, Oh, *n·* !
    page 47 poem
47– 5   Oh, ever and *n·*?
47–18   *N·* reaping the harvest

nevertheless

Ret. 14–21   *N·*, he persisted in the assertion
50–14   *N·*, my list of indigent
93–22   but it is *n·* true.
Un. 4–28   *N·*, at the present crude hour,
7– 6   *N·*, though I thus speak,
Pul. 2– 9   *N·*, there is a thought higher
No. 13–13   the declaration is *n·* true,
My. 40–30   * *n·* it is the law).
314–15   the cause *n·* was adultery.

New

Mis. 187–20   as spiritual as the *N·*.
292– 1   chapter sub-title
Pan. 7–18   study of the Old and *N·* Testaments
'02. page 1 heading
My. 179–13   The Old and the *N·* Testaments

new

Mis. 10–24   and all things become *n·*.
15– 4   chapter sub-title
16– 1   a *n·* and more spiritual Life
21– 7   *n·* heaven and a *n·* earth," — *Rev.* 21 : 1.
44–26   your belief assumed a *n·* form,
51–27   * sunshine of the world's *n·* spring,
74– 6   imparts a *n·* apprehension of
80–28   now elbowed by a *n·* school
80–30   will not patronize the *n·* school,
80–31   the medical system of the *n·*.
84–29   a *n·* and higher sense thereof,
86–20   the *n·* heaven and earth,
112– 8   error, given *n·* opportunities,
171–17   by which the *n·* teacher would
178–22   * found C. S. a *n·* gospel,
178–29   between the old and the *n·* ;
178–31   the *n·*, living, impersonal
179–13   In the *n·* religion the teaching
204–13   giving mortals *n·* motives,
204–14   *n·* purposes, *n·* affections,
218– 1   spiritual sense takes in *n·* views,
222–22   committed under this *n·* *régime*
228– 6   is to take a *n·* standpoint
233–13   the *n·* cloth of metaphysics ;
234–28   this *n·* departure of metaphysics,
235–11   loftier desires and *n·* possibilities.
239–23   her dividend, . . . was *n·*.
245–11   giving it *n·* impetus and energy ;
262– 7   *n·* and costly spring dress.
292– 4   "A *n·* commandment — *John* 13 : 34.
292– 7   a *n·* commandment even for him.
292–10   *n·* tone on the scale ascending,
293– 2   breathing *n·* Life and Love
299– 3   *n·* patterns which are useful to them ;
348–23   under this *n·* *régime* of medicine,
364– 4   naturally evokes *n·* paraphrase
366–17   to a *n·* style of imposition
375–11   * *n·* book you have given us.
Man. 26– 7   or *n·* officers elected,
81– 1   or *n·* officers elected,
102– 6   until the *n·* church edifice is

new

Man. 105– 1   No *n·* Tenet or By-Law shall be
109–18   *n·* applications will be required,
Ret. 14–23   when the *n·* light dawned within me.
20–18   Awoke *n·* beauty in the surge's roll !
25– 5   Scriptures had to me a *n·* meaning,
26–19   a *n·* date in the Christian era,
27–29   led me into a *n·* world of light
27–30   old to God, but *n·* to His
35– 4   It was so *n·*
45– 2   A *n·* light broke in upon it,
50–27   a *n·* rule of order in divine Science,
52– 2   endeavored to find *n·* ways
Un. 7– 2   in the apprehension of this *n·* subject,
Pul. 1– 4   A *n·* year is a nursling,
14–18   send forth a *n·* flood to drown the
29– 1   * in the *n·* Grundmann Studio Building
31–18   * a *n·* and increasing interest
35– 1   it came to me with a *n·* meaning,
45– 9   * publication of the *n·* denomination :
46– 4   * *n·* rules were formulated.
50–19   * Any *n·* movement will awaken
51–20   * Ere this many a *n·* project
52–17   * growth of the *n·* movement.
52–17   * We call it *n·*. It is not.
52–18   * The name C. S. alone is *n·*.
52–26   * No *n·* doctrine is proclaimed,
53– 6   * no *n·* thing under the — *Eccl.* 1 : 9.
57–20   * given to a *n·* Boston church.
57–25   * site of the *n·* Music Hall,
60– 3   * the *n·* order of service
63–15   * a *n·* phase of religious belief,
65– 7   * which is rather small and *n·*,
67– 5   * "If you would found a *n·* faith,
84– 7   * the *n·* man with the new woman.
No. 8–28   This counsel is not *n·*,
39–21   *n·* and scientific discoveries
41–22   by *n·* discoveries of Truth
44– 4   C. S. involves a *n·* language,
Pan. 11– 5   put on the *n·* man, — *Col.* 3 : 10.
'00. 4–11   *n·* and forward steps in religion,
8–15   things *n·* and old." — *Matt.* 13 : 52.
15– 2   a *n·* one that is up to date.
15–20   a wedding garment *n·* and old,
'01. 1– 6   Our first communion in the *n·* century
21– 3   or *n·* editions of old errors ;
34–12   or must we have a *n·* Bible
34–13   a *n·* system of Christianity,
'02. 4–14   *n·* commandment in the gospel of peace,
7–25   "A *n·* commandment — *John* 13 : 34.
7–27   attention to his *n·* *commandment*.
8– 8   The *n·* commandment of Christ Jesus
8–13   the old and the *n·* commandment,
10– 3   uncovers *n·* ideas, unfolds spiritual
17–10   both the old and the *n·* commandment,
Hea. 1– 2   speak with *n·* tongues ; — *Mark* 16 : 17.
6– 5   pioneer of something *n·* under the sun
Peo. 11– 4   a *n·* abolitionist struck the keynote
11–15   enforce *n·* forms of oppression,
Po. page 22 poem
22– 8   *N·* themes seraphic,
32– 6   fragrance and charms ever *n·*
65–19   rise to a seraph's *n·* song.
My. 8–30   * one hundred and five *n·* churches
11–24   * *n·* building will be erected,
15–31   * I sing the *N·*, *N·* SONG,
16– 8   * site of the *n·* building.
16–11   * corner-stone of the *n·* auditorium
29–22, 23   * *n·* religion launching upon a *n·* era,
31–17   * The *n·* home for worship
32– 7   * acoustic properties of the *n·*
39–17   * In introducing the *n·* President,
47–31   * with *n·* tongues ; — *Mark* 16 : 17.
50– 8   * strangeness of their *n·* home,
50–24   * two *n·* members were added
51–23   * *n·* fields to teach and preach."
59– 8   * *n·* system of faith and worship,
60–26   * dedication of our *n·* church
61–10   * held in the *n·* extension
63–22   * *n·* sense of the magnitude
70–11   * chimes for the *n·* C. S. temple
71–14   * this *n·* cathedral or temple
72–18   * fund of the *n·* C. S. temple,
72–25   * subscribed for the *n·* building,
76– 2   * *n·* two-million-dollar edifice,
76– 5   * *n·* contributions were constantly
76–26   * *n·* two-million-dollar cathedral
76–31   * The *n·* structure, which is now
86– 5   * pleasure in this *n·* symbol,
86– 7   * the hosts of a *n·* religion.
86–11   * *n·* two-million-dollar church,
87–25   * turned to the *n·* religion.
88–10   * *n·* Mother Church of the C. S. faith
89–22   * dedication of the *n·* Mother Church
90– 5   * these things are *n·*, utterly *n·*,
92–13   * swift growth of the *n·* faith
97–20   * opening of the *n·* Mother Church

new
My. 167–16 in our n· church edifice,
171– 9 The n· Concord church is
173–15 n· church building in Concord,
187–27 in a n· commandment
187–28 In this n· recognition of the
195– 6 n· problems to be worked out
201–29 opening of your n· church
203– 3 nothing n· to communicate ;
221– 7 n· dispensation of Truth
228– 2 nothing n· on this score.
231–22 for her to undertake n· tasks,
256– 3 improvise some n· notes,
257– 5 the n· cradle of an old truth.
280– 8 * this n· reminder from you
287–20 lofty desires, n· possibilities,
290–10 first month of the n· century.
307–11 that seemed at first n· to him.
318– 2 constituted a n· style of language.
325–10 * greater future than the n· Back Bay.
(*see also* **birth, church, edifice, idea, name, temple, tongue, wine, woman**)

Newark, N. J.
Pul. 89– 5 * News, N·, N. J.

Newbern, N. C.
My. 329–11 * letter from N·, N. C.,

new-born
Mis. 16–28 this n· spiritual altitude ;
74– 3 This n· sense subdues not only the
85–19 n· Christian Scientist must mature,
254– 1 Cherish these n· children
Pul. 10–28 This is the n· of Spirit,
No. 12–16 n· conception of the Christ,
38–11 built his Church of the n·,
Peo. 14–12 thou of the church of the n· ;
Po. 30– 3 n· beauty in the emerald sky,
My. 17– 6 "As n· babes, — I Pet. 2 : 2.
158–14 lends a n· beauty to holiness,

new-built
Pul. 41–10 * to view the n· temple

New Commandment
Mis. 292– 1 chapter sub-title
'02. page 1 heading

New England (*see also* **New England's**)
Mis. 176–16 sought the N· E· shores,
Ret. 2–11 brought to N· E· a heavy sword,
Pul. 7–10 in our N· E· metropolis
32– 3 * of tint so often seen in N· E·,
41–13 * From all N· E· the members
57–12 * and, indeed, in all N· E·.
65– 5 * what is called the N· E· mind
75–22 * in the great N· E· capital
My. 91–29 * it is the largest in N· E·.
264–10 * to the people of N· E·,
290– 2 by the strong hearts of N· E·

New England's
My. 264–15 N· E· last Thanksgiving Day of this

newer
Pul. 81–11 * an added grace — a n· charm.
My. 345–26 n·, finer, more etherealized ways of

New Hampshire and **N. H.** (*see also* **Granite State, New Hampshire's**)
Mis. 144– 2 the quarries in N· H·,
378– 2 Hydropathic Institute in N· H·,
Ret. 3– 5 John Lovewell of Dunstable, N· H·,
3–10 the N· H· general who fought at
4– 6 Bow, in the State of N· H·.
6–23 Massachusetts and N· H·.
19–17 later I returned to N· H·,
20–10 northern part of N· H·.
Pul. 24–23 * pink granite in N· H·,
48–17 * Congressman Baker from N· H·,
57–27 * born of an old N· H· family,
No. 46–15 among the first settlers of N· H·.
Po. v–11 * this lofty N· H· crag,
My. 45–28 * massive pile of N· H· granite
136–18 received by a native of N· H·.
138–25 * State of N· H·, Merrimack, ss.
167–27 religious rights in N· H·
168– 6 people of my dear old N· H·.
304– 4 Sanbornton Academy, N· H·,
305–12 * "an ignorant woman in N· H·."
310– 6 member of the N· H· Legislature,
310–14 staff of the Governor of N· H·.
312–31 educational system in N· H·.
327– 4 in the Court of N· H·,
330–29 later I returned to N· H·,
339–11 chapter sub-title
340–10 religion and medicine in N· H·,
340–22 the Governor of N· H· has

New Hampshire and **N. H.**
My. 341– 2 A native of N· H·,
(*see also* **Bow, Concord, Fabyans, Franklin, Littleton, Manchester, North Groton, Sanbornton Bridge, Tilton**)

New Hampshire Patriot
Po. 35–15 Written . . . for the N· H· P·.

New Hampshire's
Pul. 47–22 * State House of N· H· quiet capital,
My. 339–12 N· H· advancement is marked.

New Hampshire State Militia
My. 309–12 chaplain of the N· H· S· M·,

New Haven, Conn.
Pul. 88–17 * News, N· H·, C·.

New Jerusalem
Ret. 85–27 diadem of gems from the N· J·.

New London, Conn.
My. 166–26 heading

newly
Mis. 16–23 This n· awakened consciousness

new-made
Mis. 330– 4 to moan over the n· grave,

newness
No. 25– 6 serve in n· of spirit, — Rom. 7 : 6.

new-old
No. 12–12 this n· knowledge of God.
'00. 10–15 n· doctrines of the prophets
'01. 2– 8 n· cloth of Christian healing.
20–23 n· régime of necromancy
30–21 establishment of a n· religion
'02. 9–29 some n· truth that counteracts
11–16 by a n· message from God,
My. 154–17 weaving the n· vesture
182– 8 by establishing a n· church,
248–10 n· birthright is to put an end to
301– 3 C. S. is the n· Christianity,

New Orleans
La.
Pul. 89–20 * Telegram, N· O·, La.
89–21 * Times, N· O·, La.

Mis. 304–12 * to the battle-field of N· O·
Pul. 88– 3 From Canada to N· O·,
'00. 1–20 Atlanta, N· O·, Chicago,

Newport, R. I.
Pul. 88–18 * News, N·, R. I.

News
Pul. 88–17 * N·, New Haven, Conn.
88–18 * N·, Newport, R. I.
89– 4 * N·, Buffalo, N. Y.
89– 5 * N·, Newark, N. J.
89–37 * N·, St. Joseph, Mo.

news
Pul. 71–11 * Surprised at the N·
Hea. 1–14 of publishing the good n·."

news-dealers
Mis. 274–23 n· shout for class legislation,

newspaper
Mis. 4–12 n· edited and published by
132–22 through the medium of a n· ;
Man. 98– 3 corrected a false n· article
98–19 in a leading Boston n·
Po. vi– 9 * in a Lynn, Mass., n·,
My. 151– 1 patient with the n· wares
249–17 that . . . n· should countenance
306– 8 n· controversy over a question
334– 2 * to infer from n· reports
353– 2 and read our daily n·.

newspapers
Mis. 7–17 Looking over the n· of the day,
220–27 publish it in the n· that he
Ret. 2–21 some n·, yellow with age.
2–24 for they were American n·,
Pul. 88– 1 chapter sub-title
88– 4 author has received leading n·
88– 9 prominent n· whose articles
'02. 13–21 advertising . . . in the Boston n·,
My. 79–16 * in the leading n· of the world.
95–17 * described in the n· of the Hub
173– 3 * in the Concord (N. H.) n·
270– 9 the leading editors and n·
304–10 writing for the leading n·,
330–20 * Wilmington n· of that year.

News-Tribune
Pul. 90– 1 * N·, Duluth, Minn.

new-style
Mis. 285–23 a n· conjugality,

New Testament

Mis. 66– 6 these words of the *N· T·* :
195–13 said that the *N· T·* does not
373– 8 translation of the *N· T·*
Un. 14–17 but the *N· T·* tells us of
36–13 referred to in the *N· T·* as the
Pul. 52–15 * with the *N· T·* at the foundation,
'00. 4– 6 gospel of the *N· T·* and the
'02. 16– 3 translation of the *N· T·*,
My. 218– 5 Neither the Old nor the *N· T·*
(see also **Apocryphal New Testament**)

Newton

Benjamin Wills
My. 13– 4 book by Benjamin Wills *N·*,

Mis. 22–28 falling apple suggested to *N·*
23– 1 *N·* named it gravitation,

New Year *(see also* **New Year's**)

Mis. 400–13 MOTHER'S *N· Y·* GIFT
Man. 67–21 Thanksgiving, Christmas, *N· Y·*,
Po. 69– 1 *Mother's N· Y· Gift*
My. 252–26 gave to the "happy *N· Y·*"
354–17 O glad *N· Y·* !
355– 3 * symbol of the glad *N· Y·*

New Year's

My. 354–27 written . . . on *N· Y·* morning.

New Year's Day

My. 252–25 in England on *N· Y· D·*,

New Year's Sunday

Pul. 59– 3 * was dedicated on *N· Y· S·*

New York and N. Y. (State)

(see **Albany, Auburn, Bridgeport, Brooklyn, Buffalo, Lockport, New York, Rochester, Saratoga Springs, Syracuse, Troy***)*

New York *(see also* **Empire City, Greater New York, New York City***)*

N. Y.
My. 193–21 chapter sub-title
201– 9 chapter sub-title
201–26 chapter sub-title
325–19 * *N· Y·*, N. Y., December 7, 1906.
361–25 FIRST CHURCH . . . *N· Y·*, N. Y.,
361–28 * *N· Y·*, N. Y., Januray 19, 1910.
363–11 * *N· Y·*, N. Y., February 5, 1910.

Mis. 266–19 students in Chicago, *N· Y·*,
306–13 * Liberty and West Streets, *N· Y·*,
Ret. 20– 7 George W. Patterson of *N· Y·*,
Pul. 41–14 * *N· Y·* sent its hundreds,
43– 2 * First Church . . . of *N· Y·*,
56– 2 * have sprung up in *N· Y·*,
56–23 * *The Outlook, N· Y·*,
57–18 * *American Art Journal, N· Y·*,
71–15 * announcements in *N· Y·* papers
73–24 * in the reports from *N· Y·*
74– 8 * in Hodgson Hall, *N· Y·*
'00. 1–19 Boston, *N· Y·*, Philadelphia,
My. 74– 6 * church members from *N· Y·*
108–27 the words of the *N· Y·* press
165–11 heading
231–27 SECOND CHURCH OF CHRIST, . . . *N· Y·*
243– 1 chapter sub-title
243–15 students in *N· Y·* and elsewhere
332–10 * to accompany her only to *N· Y·*,
357–13 When my dear brethren in *N· Y·*
359–22 * First Church of Christ, . . . of *N· Y·*,

New York American

My. 267–13 [*N· Y· A·*, February, 1905]
296–25 *N· Y· A·*, January 6, 1908,

New York City

Ret. 52–17 in general convention at *N· Y· C·*,
Pul. 88–25 * *Advertiser, N· Y· C·*.
89– 1 * *Independent, N· Y· C·*.
89– 6 * *Once A Week, N· Y· C·*.
89– 9 * *Press, N· Y· C·*.
89–12 * *Sun, N· Y· C·*.
My. 169–16 Christian Scientists of *N· Y· C·*
194–21 church edifice in *N· Y· C·*,
243– 4 the several churches in *N· Y· C·*
282–20 542 Fifth Avenue, *N· Y· C·*,
283– 4 FIRST CHURCH OF . . . *N· Y· C·*,
304–13 crowded halls in *N· Y· C·*,
312–12 * Mrs. Glover's fare to *N· Y· C·*,
357–27 MRS. AUGUSTA E. STETSON, *N· Y· C·*.
360– 9 FIRST CHURCH OF . . . *N· Y· C·*,
360–12 First Church of . . . *N· Y· C·*,
360–17 First Church of . . . *N· Y· C·*,
362– 3 FIRST CHURCH OF . . . *N· Y· C·*.

New York Commercial Advertiser

My. 299– 1 [Letter to the *N· Y· C· A·*]

New York Herald

Pul. 74– 1 *[*N· Y· H·*, February 6, 1895]
My. 76–23 *[*N· Y· H·*]
275–11 [*N· Y· H·*]
302–12 [Letter to the *N· Y· H·*]
341–17 *[*N· Y· H·*, May 1, 1901]
346–20 * in the columns of the *N· Y· H·*,

New York Journal

'01. 21– 7 published in the *N· Y· J·*,
My. 169–13 [*N· Y· J·*]
169–15 Please say through the *N· Y· J·*,

New York Mail and Express

My. 287– 1 [*N· Y· M· and E·*]

New York Tribune

Pul. 64–22 *[*N· Y· T·*, February 7, 1895]

New York World

My. 77–16 *[*N· Y· W·*]
259–21 [*N· Y· W·*]
266– 1 [*N· Y· W·*, December, 1900]
301–14 [Letter to the *N· Y· W·*]
315–23 whom the *N· Y· W·* declared dying

next

Mis. 69–18 *n·* day he attended to his business.
86–24 It is *n·* to divine beauty
129–11 take the *n·* Scriptural step :
135– 4 *n·* to our hearts, on our lips,
193–22 The *n·* step for ecclesiasticism
232–13 foreshadows what is *n·* to appear
270–29 The *n·* step is Mind-medicine.
304–14 * sent to the *n·* World's Exhibition,
316–22 breaches widened the *n·* hour ;
325–31 *N·* he enters a place of worship,
326–12 they consumed the *n·* dwelling;
342–31 and are ready for the *n·* move.
Man. 63– 4 The *n·* lessons consist of
Ret. 6–11 *n·* to my mother, the very dearest
9–13 resolving to do, *n·* time, as my
Pul. 43–19 * silent prayer came *n·*,
60– 3 * *n·* Sunday the new order of
Rud. 11– 4 *n·* to belief in God as omnipotent ;
11– 9 *n·* proposition in C. S.,
Pan. 8– 1 *N·*, it follows that the disarrangement
'01. 17–22 *n·* more difficult stage of action
26–10 in the *n·* he endows it with
27–29 * *N·*, they say it has been discovered
My. 25–20 the dedication in June *n·*
38–11 * admitted until the *n·* service.
141–11 * *n·* of which would have been held *n·*
145–14 and the *n·* morning said to
184–17 and I treasure it *n·* to your
215–25 *N·*, on the contrary, he bade them
217–26 and aids in taking the *n·* step
240–19 In the *n·* edition of S. and H.
284–17 In your *n·* issue please correct
304–27 * *N·*, they say it has been discovered
322–18 * to enter the *n·* Primary class
353–15 the *n·* I named *Monitor*,

next-door

Ret. 40– 6 that her *n·* neighbor was dying.

nexus

Ret. 21–29 but if . . . the *n·* is lost,

nice

Mis. 227–10 *n·* distinction by which they endeavor
240–27 habit of smoking is not *n·*,

nicely

My. 71–30 * *n·* adjusted acoustic properties

niche

Ret. 70–19 must fill his own *n·* in time

nickel

Mis. 305–21 * silver, bronze, copper, and *n·*
My. 65–16 * passing out a *n·* for carfare.

Nicodemus

My. 191– 1 the wisdom of *N·* of old,

Nicolaitan

'00. 12–29 *N·* church presents the phase of
13–11 so he denounces the *N·* church.

Nicolaitanes

'00. 13– 5 hatest the deeds of the *N·*, — *Rev.* 2 : 6.

niece

My. 311–20 Fanny McNeil, President Pierce's *n·*,

niggers

Mis. 238– 1 * story that "he helped '*n·*'

nigh

Mis. 229–19 *n·* thy dwelling." — *Psal.* 91 : 10.
389–12 His habitation high is here, and *n·*,
Peo. 5–10 are *n·*, even at our door.
Po. 4–11 His habitation high is here, and *n·*,
22– 3 Eternity Draws *n·*
22– 7 lo, the light ! far heaven is *n·* !

nigh
My. 4–30 Thou God most high and n·.
290– 4 the near seems afar, the distant n·,

night (see also **night's**)
all
  Mis. 111– 4 meekly, you have toiled all n· ;
and day
  My. 66–19 * artists are working n· and day
day and
  Mis. 177– 9 engaged day and n· in organizing
341–26 not replenished with oil day and n·,
  Pul. 12– 9 our God day and n·.— Rev. 12 : 10.
26–28 * always burning day and n·.
day or
  Pul. 58–29 * make it a home by day or n·.
dreary
  Po. 65– 9 enchained to life's dreary n·,
every
  My. 61– 2 * every n· since that time.
from the
  Mis. 347–27 from the n· He leads to light.
is far spent
  Mis. 213–27 the n· is far spent, the day dawns ;
  Pan.   1–17 n· is far spent, and day is
  My. 202– 6 n· is far spent and the day is
last
  My. 141–13 * announcement . . . was made last n·
long
  Mis. 144–30 wake the long n· of materialism,
253–28 through the long n·,
320–25 long n· of human beliefs,
  '00.   7–29 till the long n· is past
  Peo.   1–10 a long n· to the traveller ;
  My. 110– 6 upon the long n· of materialism,
no
  Mis. 174–17 No matter is there, no n·
276–16 "no n· is there."— see Rev. 21 : 25.
352–13 and no n· is there !
389–23 No n· drops down upon the
  No. 27– 8 No n· will be there,
  Po.   5– 2 No n· drops down upon the
70– 9 In God there is no n·,
  My. 129–10 There is no n· but in God's frown ;
155–23 knows no twilight and no n·.
183–13 no ebbing faith, no n·.
noon of
  Mis. 276–25 burning at the noon of n·,
of chaos
  Chr. 53– 3 O'er the grim n· of chaos
of discord
  Mis. 187–27 never extinguished in a n· of discord.
of materialism
  Mis. 144–30 wake the long n· of materialism,
  My. 110– 6 upon the long n· of materialism,
of material sense
  Mis. 24– 7 dawned on the n· of material sense.
of physics
  Peo. 10– 5 through the cold n· of physics,
old
  Pul. 14–21 deep waters of chaos and old n·.
one
  Pul. 33– 6 * One n· the mother related to her
Saturday
  My. 74– 3 * From now until Saturday n·
shadowy
  Po. 27– 7 tremulous with shadowy n· !
silence of
  '02. 15–23 came to me in the silence of n·,
silent
  '02.   5– 1 As silent n· foretells the dawn
starless
  Mis. 268–16 no shipwreck in a starless n·
star-lit
  Mis. 400– 1 Laus Deo, n· star-lit
  Pul. 16–13 Laus Deo, n· starlit
  Po. 76–12 Laus Deo, n· star-lit
stillness of the
  My. 61–27 * dark stillness of the n·,
Stygian
  No. 22–14 as Stygian n· to the kindling dawn.
tear-dews of
  Po.   8– 4 Where tear-dews of n· seek the
that
  Ret.   9– 8 That n·, before going to rest,
Thursday
  My. 333–21 * died on Thursday n·,
traversed
  Mis. 320–19 it hath traversed n·,
  My. 257– 6 This truth has traversed n·,

  Mis. 226–16 * must follow, as the n· the day,
  Ret. 20–12 The n· before my child was taken
81–25 * must follow, as the n· the day,
  '00. 12–15 temple was burned on the n· that
  '01. 31–24 Lord's Prayer, repeated at n· ;

night
Hea. 10–17 sorrow endureth but for the n·,
Po. 24–16 And n· grows deeply dark ;
65–11 twin sister of death and of n· !
My. 45–20 * by n· in a pillar of fire
45–26 * pillar of fire by n·,"— Exod. 13 : 22
61–13 * but after a while, in the n·,
74– 5 * n· trains of Saturday will bring
110–20 The n· thought, methinks, should
110–23 The n· thought should show us
313–17 * wanderings, especially at n·,"
333– 9 * on the n· of the twenty-seventh.

night-bird
Ret.   4–16 now the lone n· cries,
Po. 16–16 voice of the n· must here send a

night-dream
Rud. 11–16 In a moment you may awake from a n· ;

night-dreams
Mis. 47–12 you have been in your n· ;
My. 109– 3 than it has in our n·.

nightless
Un. 61–11 n· radiance of divine Life.

night's
Mis. 392– 7 the earth, asleep in n· embrace,
Po. 20– 9 the earth, asleep in n· embrace,
73–12 N· dewy eye, The sea-mew's lone cry,

nights
My. 335–29 * nine days and n· of agony

nine
Mis. 304–23 * at n· o'clock in the morning
304–28 * ring at n· o'clock on October 11th,
Man. 61–24 about eight or n· minutes
Pul. 36– 3 * The work . . . lasted n· years,
59– 6 * services were held from n· to four o'clock,
68– 6 * here she taught . . . for n· years.
78– 4 * n· inches wide,
No. 24–19 exposure is n· points of destruction.
My.   v–19 * in 1875, after n· years of arduous
123–12 a reading-room and n· other rooms
312–21 died in about n· days.
314– 4 * During the following n· years
335–17 * end of n· days he passed away.
335–29 * n· days and nights of agony
  (see also **numbers**)

nineteen
My. 48– 4 * n· centuries had passed
70–26 * seventy-two stops, n· couplers,
70–26 * n· adjustable combination pistons,
220–27 n· centuries have greatly
  (see also **dates, numbers**)

nineteenth
Mis. 99–12 Men and women of the n· century,
382–12 latter half of the n· century
Pul. vii– 8 latter half of the n· century,
23–18 * last quarter of the n· century.
55– 7 * our remarkable n· century
'00.   1– 9 last year of the n· century
My. 127–21 latter days of the n· century.
131–22 latter days of the n· century,
257–18 the close of the n· century,
264–13 * Thanksgiving Day of the n· century

nineteenth-century
Mis. 168–17 The n· prophets repeat,

ninety-first
Pul.   5–21 n· edition of one thousand copies.
38– 8 * it is now in its n· edition.
55–15 * the n· edition is announced.

Ninety-first Psalm
'01. 32–23 N· P·, . . . educated my thought

ninety-five
  (see **dates**)

ninety-four
  (see **dates**)

ninety-nine
Mis. 118– 8 n· times in one hundred
No. 21– 3 has n· parts of error to the
My. 112–14 n· out of every hundred
127–17 n· to the ten of materia medica.

ninety-six
Mis. 231– 5 fall upon n· years.
  (see also **numbers**)

ninth
Mis. 32–13 In Mark, n· chapter,
191–12 In Mark, n· chapter
242– 4 not to my notice until January n·.
332–13 Genesis, third chapter and n· verse,

Nirvana
My. 118–26 a heathen basis for its N·,

noon
Mis.	276–25	burning at the n· of night,
	385– 4	* And one eternal n·."
Pul.	42– 4	* and at n· still another.
	77–17	* twentieth day of . . . at high n·.
	78–15	* 20th day of . . . at high n·.
Po.	37– 4	* And one eternal n·."
My.	38–16	* It was "children's day" at n·,
	82–21	* for at n· to-day [June 14]

noonday (*see also* **noonday's**)
Mis.	157–25	judgment as the n·."— *Psal.* 37 : 6.
	392– 9	her n· glories crown?
'01.	35– 3	judgment as the n·."— *Psal.* 37 : 6.
Po.	20–12	her n· glories crown
My.	170–26	judgment as the n·."— *Psal.* 37 : 6.
	190– 5	morning beams and n· glory

noonday's
Po.	3– 4	n· length'ning shadows flee,

noons
My.	147– 8	my childhood's Sunday n·.

noontide
Mis.	325–14	its inmates asleep at n· !

Norcross
Lanson P.
Pul.	44–14	* signature

Rev. Lanson P.
Mis.	313–16	New Pastor," by Rev. Lanson P. N·,

Rev. L. P.
Pul.	29– 3	* Rev. D. A. Easton and Rev. L. P. N·,

Rev. Mr.
Mis.	149–20	your beloved pastor, Rev. Mr. N·,
	159– 6	and then send it to Rev. Mr. N·,

Norfolk (**Neb.**) *Tribune*
My.	79– 5	* [N· (N·.) T·]

Normal
Mis.	143–19	the N· class graduates of my
	264–13	Many students enter the N· class
	273–30	one Primary and two N·
Man.	37–16	Pupils of N· Students.
	37–17	One N· student cannot recommend
	37–18	the pupil of another N· student,
	84–11	N· class not exceeding thirty
	86–17	teachers of the N· class
	89–11	N· Teachers.
	90– 1	eligible to enter the N· class.
	90–19	given to each N· class
	91–22	may enter the N· class
Ret.	43–16	taught the Primary, N·, and
	47–17	a N· class student who partakes
My.	251– 8	* Primary and N· class instruction
	251–13	eligible to enter the N· class,
	323–31	* N· class in the fall of 1887

normal
Mis.	17–25	n· or abnormal material conditions
	41–26	n· manifestation of man in Science.
	52–15	To be n·, it must be a union of
	104–13	According to C. S., perfection is n·,
	200– 3	Jesus regarded good as the n· state
	350–24	Hence it prevents the n· action,
Ret.	13–23	in a n· condition of health.
No.	4– 6	To aver that disease is n·,
	5–23	a n· and real condition of man,
'00.	4– 3	as real and n· as the one
My.	218– 1	its n· action, functions, and

Normal Course
Man.	36– 7	the Primary or N· C·
	85–15	or has taken a N· C· at the

North (*see also* **North's**)
Ret.	19–22	on her sad journey to the N·.
My.	304–12	best magazines in the South and N·.
	329–28	* her life in N· and South Carolina
	331– 2	on her sad journey to the N·.
	333–18	* never . . . were carried N·.
	336– 6	* to take her back to the N·.

north
My.	63–28	* from the n·, and from the— *Psal.* 107 : 3.

North America
Pul.	75–21	* members . . . all over N· A·

North Carolina and **N. C.**
My.	327– 1	noble Southrons of N· C·
	327– 5	in the Legislature of N· C·,
	327–13	* Christian Scientists in N· C·
	329– 5	* General Assembly of N· C·
		(*see also* **Asheville, Newbern, Raleigh, Wilmington**)

northeast
Mis.	144– 4	tower on the n· corner

Northern
My.	326– 9	* in the Southern and N· States

northern
Ret.	20–10	n· part of New Hampshire.
No.	14–14	coruscations of the n· sky

North Groton
N. H.
My.	311– 4	at his country home in N· G·, N. H.,
My.	314– 6	* from Tilton to N· G·
	314–10	He bought a place in N· G·,

North's
'02.	3– 8	the N· half-hostility to the South,

North State Street
My.	147– 6	grand old elm on N· S· S·
	171–24	* came to a standstill on N· S· S·,
	175–20	to macadamize N· S· S·

northward
'00.	12–13	its gates, . . . led n· and southward.

Norway
'02.	13–17	Falmouth and Caledonia (now N·)

Norway and Falmouth Streets
Pul.	24– 8	* intersection of N· and F· S·,
	40–19	* in Boston at N· and F· S·
	56–26	* located at N· and F· S·,

Norway, and St. Paul Streets
My.	65–20	* Falmouth, N·, and St. P· S·,

nose
Mis.	239–18	red n·, suffused eyes, cough, and

nostrils
Peo.	4–10	enter finite man through his n·,

nostrums
Mis.	134–21	with poisons, n·, and knives,

Nota Bene
My.	139– 1	chapter sub-title
	236– 4	chapter sub-title

notable
Mis.	49–13	n· cases of insanity
Pul.	1– 9	n· for good and evil.
	55–10	* n· for her emancipation from many
	79– 7	* dedication day, is a n· event.
'00.	6–16	This n· fact proves that the
My.	67–12	* N· Dates in C. S.
	77–10	* n· feature in the life of their cult.
	84–24	* Its hold and . . . are most n·.
	84–28	* is n· in many ways.
	86–24	* the most n· of such occasions.

notary public
My.	329–18	* by the certificate of a n· p·

note
Mis.	72–21	*imply that Spirit takes n· of*
	130–14	N· the Scripture on this
	158–27	It is satisfactory to n·,
	168–12	N· this : only such as are pure
	253– 1	N· the scope of that saying,
	296–20	n· or foster a feminine ambition
Ret.	86– 9	N· well the falsity of this mortal
Pul.	vii–15	n· the impetus thereby given
	31–20	* To a n· which I wrote her,
	54–28	N· :— About 1868, the author
Rud.	10– 2	N· this, that if you have power in
'00.	5– 6	n· the words of our Master
	14–12	N· his inspired rebuke to all the
'02.	13–19	the the n· therewith became due,
Po.	vi–10	* A n· from the author,
	34–11	Or sing thy love-lorn n·
My.	172–25	* enclosed n· from Mrs. Eddy was read :
	173–12	a n·, sent at the last moment,
	256– 6	strict observance or n· well.
	266–25	N·, if you please, that many
	272–20	* EDITOR's N·.
	297–28	to read or to n· from others' reading

noted
Mis.	295– 3	n· English leader, whom he quotes
	299–31	the property of a n· firm,
Ret.	7–17	* n· for his boldness and firmness,
My.	94–17	* were n· in the recent dedication

notes
Mis.	158– 7	insisted on your speaking without n·,
	158–16	command, to drop the use of n·,
	158–30	no record that he used n· when
Ret.	27– 5	If these n· and comments,
Pul.	60–22	* C. C. C. to C. 4, 61 n· ;
No.	3–18	Nemesis of the . . . n· this hour.
Hea.	20– 7	* In n· almost divine."
My.	114–14	began with n· on the Scriptures.
	114–19	not write these n· after sunset.
	256– 3	to improvise some new n·,

noteworthy
Ret.	13– 4	some circumstances are n·.
My.	330– 3	* a n· follower of our Lord

nothing
absolutely
My.	104–23	of which a man knows absolutely n·?

nothing

alias
No. 32–17   A lie is negation, — *alias n·*,

and something
Mis. 86–11   *N·* and *something* are words which

antagonistic
My. 87–28   * *n·* antagonistic to it in this

apart
Mis. 364–19   *n·* apart from this Mind,

appears
Mis. 105–24   *N·* appears to the physical senses but

apprehends
Un. 40–27   apprehends *n·* strictly belonging to

beholds
Un. 41– 1   beholds *n·* but mortality,

beside
Ret. 60– 7   that there is *n·* beside God ;
     60–19   there is *n·* beside Him ;''
Un. 21–16   because there is *n·* beside Him

beyond Himself
Mis. 367–20   knows *n·* beyond Himself

but a conspiracy
Ret. 63–16   *evil*, is *n·* but a conspiracy against

but an outline
Rud. 8–10   *n·* but an outline of the practice.

but good
Mis. 367–18   He knows *n·* but good ;

but materialism
Peo. 4– 2   has given . . . *n·* but materialism,

but sin
Rud. 10–18   Love punishes *n·* but sin,

but Spirit
Un. 34–12   there is *n·* but Spirit ;

can be added
My. 210– 4   *n·* can be added to the

can be clearer
Un. 25– 4   *n·* can be clearer than the

can compete
Ret. 31– 2   *N·* can compete with C. S.,

can dispossess you
Pul. 3– 8   *n·* can dispossess you of this

can do
Hea. 12– 6   self-evident it can do *n·*,

can exceed
My. 208–16   than which *n·* can exceed

can substitute
Man. 92– 6   and *n·* can substitute this

circulates
Mis. 126–23   yet *n·* circulates so rapidly :

conditional
My. 260–12   *N·* conditional or material

contrary
Man. 86–22   shall teach *n·* contrary thereto.

could save
My. 335–28   * *n·* could save the life of

count as
Mis. 281–20   we must count as *n·*,

covered
'01. 10– 7   *n·* covered, that shall not — *Matt.* 10 : 26.

dethrones
My. 193–16   *N·* dethrones His house.

doing
Mis. 230– 5   doing *n·*, and indecision as to

else
Mis. 102–12   like Himself and like *n·* else.
     199–15   illustrate . . . as *n·* else can ;
Ret. 28–23   and that *n·* else could.
Un. 7–21   confers a power *n·* else can.
     49–11   are *good*, and *n·* else.
Pul. 35–22   and that *n·* else could.
Rud. 11–15   of harmony and of *n·* else.
No. 12–22   in *n·* else has she departed
     30–23   revealing Him and *n·* else.
'00. 4–27   they reflect God and *n·* else.
'01. 15–30   * *n·* else that is to be given as
'02. 17–25   satisfies . . . and *n·* else can.
My. 15–25   * As *n·* else can do.
     146–30   eternal, and *n·* else.

evil
Mis. 72– 1   *n·* evil, or unlike Himself.
Rud. 10– 7   divides His power with *n·* evil

except sin
Ret. 81– 4   *N·* except sin, in the students

found
My. 103–22   have found *n·* in ancient or

further
My. 319– 5   I heard *n·* further from him

gain
Mis. 227– 1   by which he can gain *n·*.

giving birth to
'01. 30–13   giving birth to *n·* and death to

good for
Hea. 7– 1   ''that which is good for *n·*,

has been lost
Mis. 149–12   and see that *n·* has been lost.

nothing

has occurred
My. 298– 3   *n·* has occurred in my life's

have to pray
Mis. vii–16   And *n·* have to pray :

have we gained
Mis. vii–15   *N·* have we gained therefrom,

here
Mis. vii–12   There's *n·* here to trust.

in Christ
Mis. 155– 4   this world that has *n·* in Christ.
My. 4–25   this world that hath *n·* in Christ.

in this room
My. 353–24   *n·* in this room now of any

is gained
Mis. 298– 2   *N·* is gained by wrong-doing.
My. 278–22   *N·* is gained by fighting,

is hid
Mis. 348–11   ''*N·* is hid — *Matt.* 10 : 26.

is left
Pul. 47–29   * *n·* is left excepting the angles
No. 30– 5   until *n·* is left to be forgiven,
'02. 7–14   *n·* is left to consciousness but

is lost
Mis. 111–13   *N·* is lost that God gives :

is more fatal
Mis. 93–28   *N·* is more fatal than to indulge a

is worthy
My. 258– 4   *N·* is worthy the name of

left
'01. 10–26   shall be *n·* left to perish

less
Mis. 283–16   *n·* less than a mistaken kindness,
Ret. 34– 4   *N·* less could solve the
My. 22–22   * *n·* less than God-bestowed.
     259–20   *n·* less is man or woman.

madness and
My. 14– 7   not a madness and *n·*,

melt into
Peo. 10– 6   become vague, and melt into *n·*

more
Mis. 58–27   ''mind-cure,'' *n·* more nor less,
     136– 4   Rumors are rumors, — *n·* more.
Man. 64–20   meant *n·* more than a tender term
Pul. 74–16   I claim *n·* more than what
'01. 23–30   * nature being *n·* more than
My. 70–22   * *n·* more wonderful than the organ

much ado about
Hea. 14– 3   in fine, much ado about *n·*.

new
My. 203– 3   I have *n·* new to communicate ;
     228– 2   there is *n·* new on this score.

nobody and
Mis. 108–14   proper denominator, — nobody and *n·*.

out of
Mis. 362–16   out of *n·* would create something,

outside
Un. 3–26   can be *n·* outside of Himself.
     20–21   He can see *n·* outside of

profiteth
My. 108– 9   flesh profiteth *n·*.'' — *John* 6 : 63.

promises
My. 93–12   * promises *n·* in the way of

receive
Mis. 342–26   and receive *n·* in return ;

risks
Mis. 211–23   He risks *n·* who obeys the law of God,

saying
My. 210–21   saying *n·*, in particular,

sees
Mis. 173– 4   sees *n·* but a law of matter.

settled
Pul. 51–10   * There is really *n·* settled.

short
Mis. 224–28   *N·* short of our own errors should
     288–24   *n·* short of self-seeking ;

sin can do
Mis. 93–18   Sin can do *n·* :

stops it
Mis. 44–13   and *n·* stops it until

take
Mis. 327– 6   take *n·* of thine own with thee?''

talking
Mis. 230– 5   time is consumed in talking *n·*,

that is material
Mis. 165–13   leaves *n·* that is material ;

that is wrong
Mis. 240–25   teach them *n·* that is wrong.

that worketh
Mis. 366–11   *n·* that worketh or maketh a lie
No. 15–26   *N·* that ''worketh — *Rev.* 21 : 27.
My. 348–31   *n·* that worketh ill can enter

thinking of
Mis. 230–10   thinking of *n·* or planning for

nothing

to do
Mis. 147-20 to do *n·* but what is honorable,
175-24 has *n·* to do with the Science of
My. 307- 8 had *n·* to do with matter,
to fear
Mis. 113-25 *n·* to fear when Love is at the helm
to mourn
Mis. 353- 1 in the sense that it has *n·* to mourn
to say
Mis. 230-18 talking when they have *n·* to say,
Pul. 41-18 * to say *n·* of . . . local believers.
79-13 * to say *n·* of cities
unlike
Mis. 366-13 He is in *n·* unlike Himself ;
Un. 35-25 can form *n·* unlike itself, Spirit,
'02. 6-30 producing *n·* unlike Himself,
unlovely
'02. 6-30 Love, including *n·* unlovely,
will be lost
My. 40-11 *N·* will be lost, however,
would remain
Un. 34-23 *N·* would remain to be seen
written
My. 179-26 being contingent on *n·* written
you pay
Mis. 301- 2 sermon for which you pay *n·*,

Mis. 5-16 There is *n·* to build upon.
15- 8 *N·* aside from the spiritualization
26-22 What can be more than All? *N·* :
26-23 just what I call matter, *n·*.
27- 1 What . . . besides infinity? *N·* !
27- 2 Science of good calls evil *n·*.
42-30 *n·* but our own false admissions
71-25 *n·* can be formed apart from God,
72-24 shows that *n·* which is material is
86- 9 *n·* and exist only in imagination
87- 4 and label beauty *n·*,
108-10 spiritually, literally, it is *n·*.
122-28 for hate, or the hater, is *n·* :
169-22 makes them *n·* valuable,
174-18 *n·* that maketh or worketh a lie.
192-27 *N·* can be more conclusive
240-27 that *n·* but a loathsome worm
280-11 there is *n·* in the opposite scale.
334-17 You must find error to be *n·* :
Ret. 8- 8 "*N·*, child ! What do you mean?"
63-15 Its opposite, *n·*, named *evil*,
Un. 13- 8 principle of music knows *n·* of
42- 5 can be *n·* except the results of
54- 4 it is *n·* but a false claim.
No. 15-25 in *n·* is He unlike Himself.
17-22 these two words *all* and *n·*,
32-26 evil to its lowest terms, *n·*,
Pan. 5-22 not believe that a lie, *n·*, can
10- 4 when he is *n·*, — Gal. 6 : 3.
'01. 13- 8 an illusion, *n·*,
13- 8 assumption that *n·* is something.
13-14 sin, is a lie — therefore is *n·*
15-23 * "It is *n·* but God's mere pleasure
27-10 *n·* has since appeared that is
My. 84- 2 *N·* is more of a drag on a church
92-28 * due apparently to *n·* save
93- 7 * *n·* in them to attract
107-27 *n·* beyond illimitable divinity.
108-17 *n·* in the divine Mind to attenuate.
193-16 Love gives *n·* to take away.
197- 4 Attempt *n·* without God's help.
223-17 of which I know *n·*.
267- 3 *N·* can be correct . . . which
321-17 * *n·* in the circumstances which
334-17 *N·* could be further from her meaning
354- 5 *n·* but what is published or sold by

nothingness

abyss of
Un. 60- 9 from the dark abyss of *n·*,
basis of
'01. 13-16 on the very basis of *n·*.
error and
Mis. 201-13 error and *n·* of supposed life
fact of its
Mis. 93-25 not test sin and the fact of its *n·*,
father of
'01. 13-15 and the father of *n·*.
highest degree of
Mis. 334-20 lie of the highest degree of *n·* :
is thus proven
No. 17- 5 Their *n·* is thus proven ;
its
Mis. 109-16 blest by reason of its *n·* ;
335-22 by asserting its *n·*,
Un. 61-13 the apprehension of its *n·*,
its own
No. 13- 2 rebukes sin with its own *n·*,

nothingness

mortal
My. 245-18 dire din of mortal *n·*,
native
Mis. 70-23 dissolve into its native *n·* ;
109-15 reduced to their native *n·* !
of any other
No. 38-22 *n·* of any other state or stage
of error
Pul. 13- 9 by which the *n·* of error is seen ;
13-10 *n·* of error is in proportion to
of every claim
Un. 8-20 *n·* of every claim of error,
of evil
Mis. 108- 8 powerlessness — yea, *n·* — of evil :
109-27 must discern the *n·* of evil,
176-11 a little more of the *n·* of evil,
Ret. 55- 6 brings out the *n·* of evil
of hate
No. 35-12 allness of Love and the *n·* of hate.
of matter
Mis. 176-19 and the *n·* of matter.
194-18 and the *n·* of matter.
253-10 amends for the *n·* of matter
279-19 to find out the *n·* of matter ;
Man. 16- 8 and the *n·* of matter.
Ret. 26-27 yet more of the *n·* of matter
'01. 12-24 therefore the *n·* of matter.
of sickness
Mis. 64- 6 *n·* of sickness, sin, and death,
of the dream
Mis. 49-24 recognition of the *n·* of the dream,
of wrong
Mis. 267- 3 consciousness of the *n·* of wrong
simply
Ret. 64-13 sinner and . . . are alike simply *n·* ;
to nothingness
No. 26-28 dust . . . to dust, *n·* to nothingness.
utter
Mis. 114-29 evil, — even its utter *n·*.

Mis. 145-20 their modest sign be *n·*.
286-23 phenomena of mortality, *n·*,
333- 7 a palpable falsity, yea, *n·* ;
363- 9 vanity with *n·*, dust with dust !
Ret. 61-15 you are darkness, *n·*.

notice

Mis. 226-27 cannot stoop to *n·*, except legally,
242- 4 came not to my *n·* until January
256-18 send to each applicant a *n·*
302-23 so elect and give suitable *n·*,
303-20 chapter sub-title
303-22 giving place . . . to the following *n·*.
381- 8 gave *n·* through his counsel
Man. 37- 7 *N·* of Rejection.
37-11 shall send to the applicant a *n·* of
Ret. 8-17 though I had ceased to *n·* it.
Po. 18-15 *n·* the frail fledgling hath.
My. 26-19 The enclosed *n·* I submit to you,
26-23 and this *n·* is requisite
27- 1 chapter sub-title
27-10 * chapter sub-title
58- 3 * The fact that a *n·* was published
72-17 * the *n·* which Stephen A. Chase,
73- 2 * to issue a similar *n·* or order,
87-11 * one does not *n·* these unless
173- 9 given *n·* that no preparations would be
236-23 chapter sub-title
237- 4 chapter sub-title
237-12 chapter sub-title
237-20 chapter sub-title
242-15 chapter sub-title
250-13 please send . . . *n·* of their action.
329-14 * the *n·* of her husband's death
351-22 chapter sub-title
358-29 chapter sub-title

noticeable

Mis. 6-25 *n·* fact, that in families where
My. 82-29 * not be *n·* to the residents of

noticed

My. 61-21 * I *n·* that as soon as the workmen
307-10 I *n·* he used that word,

notices

Mis. 308-20 scientific *n·* of my book.
314-11 give out any *n·* from the pulpit,
Man. 32-22 shall read all *n·* and remarks
55- 2 shall not report nor send *n·*
Ret. 40-22 *n·* for a second lecture pulled down,
Pul. 60- 5 * no address of any sort, no *n·*,
79-14 * *n·* of C. S. meetings,
My. 32-21 * Reading of *n·*.
76- 3 * *n·* that more money was needed

noticing

Mis. 169- 2 *n·*, all along the way

notification
Mis. 306–14 * as a n· of the same,

notified
Man. 39–17 twice n· of his excommunication,
68– 4 duty of the member thus n·
109–18 the applicant will be n·,
My. 27–13 * n· that sufficient funds

notifies
Mis. 285–25 coolly n· the public

notify
Mis. 322– 8 n· the Directors when I shall be
Man. 28–20 call a meeting and n· this officer
68– 1 n· a person who has been
100–17 may n· any Church of Christ,
My. 223– 2 I hereby n· the public that

noting
Ret. 44–17 n· the church's need,

notion
Mis. 62–30 "mind-cure" rests on the n· that
218–21 the n· . . . is more ridiculous than
256–26 n· that Mind can be in matter
271– 7 keep out of their heads the n·
280–13 We must get rid of that n·.
291– 3 n· that a mind governed by
335–21 n· that one is covering iniquity
Ret. 57–20 n· of more than one Mind,
Un. 49–27 This n· of the destructibility of
No. 20–15 n· of an everywhere-present body
Pan. 10– 9 n· that C. S. lessens man's
'01. 19–12 n· that mixing material and
My. 91– 5 * It affords refutation of the n·
210–19 individuals entertain the n·

notions
Pul. 6–12 thinking she caught her n· from
No. 15–12 n· of personality to be found in

notoriety
Mis. 295–11 * passion for some manner of n·."
296–26 from a desire for n·
My. 130–10 students seeking only public n·,

notwithstanding
Mis. 236–25 n· one's good intentions,
307–12 N· the rapid sale already
349–16 n· my objection, he should do as
Pul. 8– 6 N· the perplexed condition
84–16 * prognostications to the contrary n·.
My. 11– 1 * N· the fact that as Christian
56–16 * n· the relief that the
67–27 * N· its enormous size,
230– 1 N· the sacrilegious moth of time,
236– 8 amende honorable — n· "incompetence"
311–29 N· that McClure's Magazine says,

noumenon
Mis. 23–19 God is both n· and phenomena,
74– 2 n· and phenomenon understood,
216–28 * phenomenon without a n·
362–17 whose n· is mortal mind,
Ret. 22– 4 spiritual n· and phenomenon
No. 19–23 n· or the phenomena of Spirit ;
Pan. 12–23 Principle, n· and phenomena,
My. 180–32 defines n· and phenomena
287– 9 Love is the n· and phenomenon,
347–28 Principle whose n· is God
350– 4 To begin with the divine n·, Mind,

noun
My. 226– 1 not be written or used as a common n·

nourish
Mis. 16– 1 These n· the hungry hope,
Pul. 63– 8 has the strength to n· trees

nourished
My. 177–20 nurtured and n· this church

novel
Mis. 139–24 in a circuitous, n· way,
252–15 My proof of these n· propositions
Pul. 40–11 * N· Method of Enabling
59– 3 * in a somewhat n· way.

novelty
Pul. 50–21 * who have worn off the n·
62– 2 * something of a n· in this country,
My. 74–31 * and the other for its n·.
77– 2 * and the n· of the cult

November
(see **months**)

novices
Rud. 16–12 some n·, in the truth of Science,

now
Mis. ix– 7 N·, Christian Scientists are not indigent ;
ix–11 n· rejuvenated by the touch
ix–13 n· hope sits dove-like.
x–15 difference between then and n·,
13– 9 This law I n· urge upon the

now
Mis. 16–27 N·, dear reader, pause for a moment
21– 8 C. S. n· bears testimony.
30–15 recognized here and n·.
37–26 She n· does not.
59–19 "Come n·, and let us — Isa. 1 : 18.
69–30 N· comes the question :
76–20 N·, exchange the term soul for sense
76–26 N· if Soul sinned, it would die ;
80–28 n· elbowed by a new school
81–19 N·, if all this be a fair
86–17 beautiful to my gaze n·
87–17 I n· through you discern dimly ;
91–10 "Suffer it to be so n·." — Matt. 3 : 15.
101–11 N· cometh a third struggle ;
134– 3 And n·, dear sir, as you have
137–17 N·, dear ones, if you take my advice
137–29 can n· organize their students
139–19 n· valued at $20,000
140–23 n· it must be put back into
150–18 houses and halls can n· be obtained
158– 9 But n·, after His messenger
158–13 meaning of it all, as n· shown,
158–25 you will find . . . (as I n· think)
174–29 facts of man's Life here and n·.
186–18 N· let us not lose this Science
188– 3 Man is as perfect n·,
188–13 n· no condemnation — Rom. 8 : 1.
193–21 which the people are n· adopting.
208–22 but n· have I kept — Psal. 119 : 67.
216–11 N·, Phare Pleigh evidently means
219– 7 N·, what saith the Scripture ?
220– 1 N·, demonstrate this rule,
220–18 is n· the diametrical opposite
222–24 Its mystery protects it n·,
231–21 N· ! baby has tumbled,
237–17 few feel and live n· as when
238– 4 It is pleasant, n·, to contrast
245–17 The conclusion cannot n· be pushed,
247– 9 n· I calmly challenge the world,
253– 8 speakers that will n· address you
262– 6 n· entering upon its fifth volume,
273– 6 I n· seem to be most needed,
273– 9 my labors with them as n·,
281– 9 I have n· one ambition
284–20 must n· be dealt with as evil,
286–19 The time cometh, and n· is,
295–32 N·, I am a Christian Scientist,
311–19 As I n· understand C. S.,
317–23 thou knowest not n· ; — John 13 : 7.
321–13 cometh, and n· is, — John 4 : 23.
329–26 n· chirps on the breeze ;
330–13 consciousness thereof is here and n·
340– 6 the time to work, is n·.
347–20 I see the way n·.
353–25 N· turn from the metaphor of the
356–19 N· let my faithful students
359–11 n· we see through a — I Cor. 13 : 12.
380–23 "Suffer it to be so n·," — Matt. 3 : 15.
384– 6 Come Thou ! and n·, anew,
385–19 N· see thy ever-self :
386–23 sad marble to our memory n·,
393–13 Students wise, he maketh n·
Man. 75–11 she n· understands the financial
Chr. 53–37 faith's pale star n· blends
53–42 Are here, and n·
55– 6 coming, and n· is, — John 5 : 25.
Ret. 4–16 n· the lone night-bird cries,
4–21 n· the scrub-oak, poplar, and fern
9–25 * N· hath redeemed her birthright
13–16 of these things he n· spoke,
16– 9 n·, oh, thank God, she is healed !"
23– 8 n· it was not even fringed with light.
37–12 n· declare Bishop Berkeley, David Hume,
48–27 "Suffer it to be so n·," — Matt. 3 : 15.
53– 2 The C. S. Journal, as it was n· called,
Un. 3–27 N· this self-same God is our
6–10 as n· presented to the people
7–15 People are n· living who can
8– 1 another query n· be considered,
23– 5 N· God has no bastards
26–17 N· if it be true that
33– 5 N· these senses, being material,
37– 9 They are n· and here ;
37–20 Existing here and n·,
42–13 is as perfect and immortal n·, as
43– 8 n· believe in the possibility that Life
53– 1 N· a lie takes its pattern from
55–22 N· and here shall I behold God,
61–20 life which I n· live — Gal. 2 : 20.
Pul. 7–14 God has n· unsealed their
12– 6 N· is come salvation, — Rev. 12 : 10.
12–19 n· rises clearer and nearer to the
30– 8 * church numbers n· four thousand
30–24 * n· exceeds two hundred thousand
30–28 * has n· its own magnificent church

now

Pul.	36– 9	* at the class lectures n· and then,
	36–25	* n· occupied by Judge and Mrs. Hanna,
	38– 8	* n· in its ninety-first edition.
	49–17	almost as big as they are n·,
	55–25	* n· over four thousand members.
	58– 9	* have n· erected this edifice
	59–22	* and n· the business manager
	63–13	almost as big as they are n·,
	66– 7	* n· there are societies in every
	68– 2	* n· known as the Rev. Mary Baker Eddy.
	68– 7	* and many are n· pastors
	68–10	* She n· lives in a beautiful
	68–17	* n· holds regular services in the
	71–21	* are n· so entirely devoted.
	83–17	* look n· to their daughters to
	84–23	* It is enough for us n· to know
	85– 5	* Those who n·, in part, understand
	87–20	more of earth n·, than I desire,
No.	7–20	must n· fight their own battles.
	9–19	I n· point steadfastly to the power
	25– 4	n· we are delivered— Rom. 7: 6.
	27–14	it is just as veritable n· as it
	28–10	n· is the most acceptable time
	34–10	hour cometh, and n· is,— John 4: 23
	35–23	one with Him n· and forever.
	41–21	n· the Church seems almost
	46– 3	The question n· at issue is :
'00.	3– 1	N·, what saith C. S.?
	12–26	The entire city is n· in ruins.
'01.	2– 1	is n· what Christ Jesus taught
	7–24	n· claim to believe in and worship
	9–26	n·, as aforetime— they cast out evils
	13–18	N·, destroy the conception of sin
	16–22	if n· it is permitted license,
	18– 5	less n· than were the sneers
	21–10	* are n· taught in C. S."
	31– 9	truths . . . that n· seem troublesome.
	33–27	the same reviling . . . it receives n·,
'02.	3– 6	regarded n· more as a philosophy
	3–19	n·, British and Boer may prosper
	12– 6	n· and forever, here and everywhere.
	13–17	Caledonia (n· Norway)
	13–27	n· valued at twenty thousand
	18– 6	mortals looked ignorantly, as n·,
Hea.	5– 9	saying, . . . God will punish him n·
	9– 1	more than we are n· doing,
	9– 1	faster than we are n· progressing.
Peo.	6–11	* less mortality than n· obtains."
	6–24	"acquaint n· thyself — Job 22: 21.
Po.	36– 5	Come Thou ! and n·, anew,
	48–13	N· see thy ever-self ;
	50– 9	sad marble to our memory n·,
	51–18	Students wise, he maketh n·
	77–16	what Thou doest n·
	78– 8	the Union n· is one,
My.	vi–15	* always has been and is n· its guide,
	8–13	* "N· I am sure that I have but
	9–25	I never before felt . . . but I do n·,
	10– 8	* should n· manifest itself in a
	10–13	* but the time is at hand, n·,
	10–29	* n· necessitates this onward step.
	12–16	chapter sub-title
	12–17	n· is the accepted time." — II Cor. 6: 2.
	12–21	we possess only n·.
	12–21	If the reliable n· is carelessly lost
	12–23	which cannot be done n·,
	12–25	while that which can be done n·,
	12–27	supplies the ever-present help and n·,
	13– 1	good . . . they insist upon doing n·.
	14– 1	In the n· they brought their
	15–15	all that you are able to bear n·,
	26–20	N· is the time to throttle the lie
	36–17	* and n· with blessed accord
	40– 5	* sure that n· the branch churches
	45–23	* we n· discern the fulfilment
	47–20	* well-earned joy that is with us n·.
	51– 5	* n· interested in said church,
	53– 6	* This book has n· reached its
	55–12	* The Mother Church n· stands.
	59–29	* N· my testimony is not needed.
	60–25	* N· that the . . . dedication of
	64–22	* and n· it is ours to address
	66– 8	* n· comes the purchase of the
	72– 9	* more frequented by . . . than it is n·.
	74– 3	* From n· until Saturday night
	76–31	* structure, which is n· completed,
	86– 5	* so will it n· find pleasure in
	88– 5	* C. S., as n· before this continent,
	93–28	* n· being held in Boston
	97– 2	* The best physicians n· admit
	109–17	"But n· mine eye — Job 42: 5.
	110– 2	a dispensation n· ended,
	111– 9	n· assumed by many doctors
	113–11	n· no condemnation— Rom. 8: 1.
	122– 9	N· I am done with homilies

now

My.	123–18	n· about twenty thousand dollars.
	124–27	N· what have you learned?
	131–26	prove me n· herewith,— Mal. 3: 10.
	132– 3	"Prove me n· herewith,— Mal. 3: 10.
	140–21	"Suffer it to be so n·," — Matt. 3: 15.
	146–11	may then be even younger than n·."
	147– 8	And n·, at this distant day,
	148– 2	n·, through the providence of God,
	151–29	idolatry then and is idolatry n·.
	153– 4	N·, if these kind hearts will only
	155– 3	is effective here and n·.
	162– 4	"Suffer it to be so n· :— Matt. 3: 15.
	164–15	N· [1904] six dear churches
	176– 6	and n· illustrate the past by your
	177–13	even younger and nearer . . . than n·,
	187–11	"N· the end of the— I Tim. 1: 5.
	188– 5	"N· mine eyes shall be open,— II Chron. 7: 15.
	201– 7	are enthroned n· and forever.
	202– 6	N· may his salvation draw near,
	205– 1	n· no condemnation— Rom. 8: 1.
	206–31	but n· are ye light — Eph. 5: 8.
	216–31	you should begin n· to earn
	218– 3	"Suffer it to be so n· :— Matt. 3: 15.
	221– 4	precludes Jesus' doctrine, n· as then,
	223–28	Just n· divine Love and wisdom
	224–30	n· let us adopt the classic saying,
	240–15	I n· repeat another proof,
	245– 3	N· the wide demand for this
	246–25	thou knowest not n· ;— John 13: 7.
	250–22	But if n· is not the time,
	251– 3	thou knowest not n· ;— John 13: 7.
	266–26	are n· agitated, modified, and
	269–26	"Prove me n· herewith,— Mal. 3: 10.
	273–11	and n· am old ;— Psal. 37: 25.
	280–16	I n· request that the members
	285–24	whereof they n· accuse me.
	294–28	has n· passed through the shadow of
	297– 1	N· if Miss Barton were not
	297–20	is here n· as veritably as when
	307–13	* "I see n· what you mean,
	318–30	"N·, Mr. Wiggin," I said,
	323–19	* Neither do I n· feel at all equal to
	329–21	* At no better time than n·,
	332–17	* paper containing this card is n· in
	333– 2	* is n· in the possession of the chairman
	335–24	* Mrs. Glover (n· Mrs. Eddy)
	342–25	* all n· concerned in its government
	343–10	"I cannot answer that n·."
	353–24	nothing . . . n· of any special
	356–17	ones n· and heretofore presented in
	357– 3	"Suffer it to be so n·'" — Matt. 3: 15.

nowhere

Mis.	173–21	matter is n· and sin is obsolete.
Ret.	89–21	N· in the four Gospels
Un.	42– 2	it must follow that death can be n· ;
	47– 3	N· in Scripture is evil connected with
Pul.	81– 4	* n· spoken with more reverence
No.	35–28	the human kingdom is n·,
Po.	vi–17	n· but in the walls of a jail.
My.	70–23	* N· in the world is there a

noxious

Mis.	343–14	n· weeds of passion, malice, envy,
Peo.	3– 6	eternal roasting amidst n· vapors ;

nucleus

Pul.	22– 4	one n· or point of convergence,

nuisance

Mis.	7–22	counteract . . . this public n· ;
	131– 3	a moral n·, a fungus, a microbe,

null

Mis.	22–19	therefore these are n· and void.
No.	37–25	Jesus rendered n· and void whatever
My.	271– 2	matter and material sense are n·,

nullified

'01.	15– 4	Error uncondemned is not n·.

nullify

Mis.	40–30	than to n· either the disease itself or
	119–29	n· or reverse your rules,

nullity

'01.	13–11	with such a sense of its n·
	18–29	does it and so proves their n·.

numb

Po.	53–15	Where wind nor storm can n·

number (noun)

April

Mis.	158–24	April n· of The C. S. Journal

August

Mis.	313– 3	your editorial in the August n·

en route

My.	124–26	means of travel, and the n· en route.

equal

'01.	27–18	an equal n· of sick healed,

number (noun)

full
'00. 14– 6 full *n·* of days named

great
My. 75–14 * a great *n·* of visitors

greater
Pul. 67–10 * would probably show a greater *n·*

greatest
Mis. 288– 5 greatest good to the greatest *n·*,
Ret. 82–15 greatest good to the greatest *n·*,

growing
Pul. 56– 5 * a large and growing *n·*

increased in
Ret. 15–17 congregation so increased in *n·*

increase in
'02. 1– 5 constantly increase in *n·*,

increasing
Pul. 50–17 * a large and increasing *n·*

insignificant
My. 92–16 * increased from an insignificant *n·*

January
My. 316–11 article in the January *n·*

large
Ret. 7–19 * by a large *n·* of friends,
Pul. 29–13 * and a large *n·* of chairs
67–19 * there is a large *n·* of members.
'02. 12–26 so as to seat the large *n·*
My. 7–10 so as to seat the large *n·*

larger
Mis. 273–27 a larger *n·* would be in waiting

largest
Mis. 305–14 * largest *n·* of persons possible

May
Mis. 216– 8 In the May *n·* of our *Journal*,

October
Mis. 256–14 October *n·* of the *Journal*,

of attendants
My. 53–19 * *n·* of attendants steadily increased.
56–18 * the *n·* of attendants increased

of believers
Pul. 66– 6 * *n·* of believers has grown

of candidates
My. 57–17 * *n·* of candidates admitted June 5

of changes
My. 66–12 * *n·* of changes will be made

of his name
Mis. 113–10 or the *n·* of his name,"— *Rev.* 13 : 17.
269–32 or the *n·* of his name."— *Rev.* 13 : 17.

of large elms
Pul. 63–11 * pointed to a *n·* of large elms

of men
Pul. 49–29 * She employs a *n·* of men

of Pupils
Man. 84– 7 *N·* of Pupils.

of quotations
My. 359–18 * a *n·* of quotations from a

of requests
My. 276–21 * In reply to a *n·* of requests

of societies
My. 57–25 * *n·* of societies advertised in the

of students
Mis. 256–15 a select *n·* of students.
Rud. 15–19 very limited *n·* of students

of the members
Man. 48–18 *n·* of the members of The

of the readers
'00. 1–23 Judging from the *n·* of the readers

of thirty
Pul. 75–18 * Scientists . . . to the *n·* of thirty,

of visitors
My. 75–14 * a great *n·* of visitors
173–19 The *n·* of visitors, . . . exceeded

of years
Pul. 72–13 * healed a *n·* of years ago
My. 335–12 * was for a *n·* of years a resident

one
Pul. 4– 7 Is not a man . . . *n·* one,

plural
Mis. 191–21 here employed in its plural *n·*,
No. 22–19 being used in the plural *n·*.
My. 226– 1 or in the plural *n·*.

selected
Man. 84–21 or assemble a selected *n·* of them,

September
Mis. 88– 8 *genuine critique in the September n·*,

that
Mis. 273–26 class which contains that *n·*.

their
Chr. 55– 2 verses, whereto their *n·* corresponds.

three in
My. 244–26 certainly not exceed three in *n·*.

time or
'00. 14– 8 signifies a complete time or *n·*

total
My. 57–21 * total *n·* admitted during the
57–22 * total *n·* of branch churches

number (noun)

twenty-six in
Man. 18– 5 the members, twenty-six in *n·*,
Ret. 16–18 the members, twenty-six in *n·*,
44– 6 the members, twenty-six in *n·*,

vast
Mis. 156– 3 vast *n·* of earnest readers,
My. 100– 9 * vast *n·* of the followers

whole
Pul. 4– 8 a unit, and therefore whole *n·*,

———

Mis. 142– 9 a *n·* of masonic symbols.
381–27 to the *n·* of thirty-eight hundred
Man. 112– 2 churches are designated by *n·*,
112– 3 *n·* must be written First, Second,
Pul. 51– 5 * *n·* of conscientious followers
72– 6 * *n·* of very interesting
72–14 * *n·* of well-known physicians.
My. 97–26 * to the *n·* of forty thousand
181–24 *n·* of 1,650,000 inhabitants.
226– 7 conservation of *n·* in geometry,
347–17 call to mind the *n·* of

number (verb)

'01. 27–18 in this interval *n·* one million,
My. 41– 1 * how great no man can *n·*
59– 9 * *n·* its adherents by the
85– 7 * adherents *n·* probably a million,
89–31 * *n·* many thousands
93–31 * adherents *n·* hundreds of thousands,

numbered

Ret. 13– 8 *n·* among those who were doomed to
37– 9 edition *n·* one thousand copies.
Pul. 51– 9 * *n·* among the many pioneers
My. 100–14 * members are *n·* by thousands

numbering

Mis. 9– 7 *n·* them, and giving them refuge
Man. 48–16 *N·* the People.
48–21 shall turn away from personality and *n·*
Pul. 43– 3 * *n·* thirty-five singers in all
My. 38– 8 * corps of ushers, *n·* two hundred,
324–23 * *n·* you among his literary friends.

numbers

one thousandth
My. 107–10 the *o· t·* attenuations

one hundredth
No. 21– 3 *o· h·* part of Truth,
Hea. 13– 4 *o· h·* part of a grain

one quarter
My. 294–27 for *o· q·* of a century.

two and a half
Pul. 49–13 she ejaculated ; "*t· and a h·*,
49–14 only *t· and a h·* years."

twenty-one and one half
Pul. 24–26 * *t· and o· h·* feet square.

36th
Man. 99– 5 the 36th parallel of latitude.

a hundred
Mis. 48–29 like *a h·* other stories,
Un. 48– 3 already told *a h·* times,

one hundred
Mis. 106–14 Marched the *o· h·*.
118– 9 ninety-nine times in *o· h·*
Ret. 4– 7 *O· h·* acres of the old farm
Pul. 67–23 * *o· h·* years from the date
'01. 16–27 *o· h·* falsehoods told about it?
Po. 22– 5 *O· h·* years, aflame with Love,
My. 127–17 out of *o· h·* cases I healed

one hundred and five
My. 8–29 * *o· h· and f·* new churches

one hundred and twenty
Pul. 24–25 * tower is *o· h· and t·* feet

one hundred and twenty-six
Pul. 41–24 * rises *o· h· and t·* feet

one hundred and forty-four
Pul. 26– 1 * *o· h· and f·* electric lights

one hundred and fifty
My. 83– 5 * *o· h· and f·* members of the

one hundred and sixty
Mis. 273–23 *o· h· and s·* applications

one hundred and seventy-fifth
My. 174–18 *o· h· and s·* anniversary
270– 7 *o· h· and s·* anniversary ;

two hundred
Mis. 47– 2 *weigh over t· h· pounds*
Pul. 26–27 * lamp over *t· h·* years old,
'01. 24–17 more than *t· h·* years old.
My. 38– 9 * ushers, numbering *t· h·*,
123–21 holds a trifle over *t· h·*

two hundred and twenty
My. 89– 6 * *t· h· and t·* feet high,

220x220x236 ft.
My. 67– 7 * Shape, triangular . . . 220x220x236 ft.

numbers

two hundred and twenty-four
  My.   45–30   * height of *t· h· and t·* feet,
       68–10   * dome is *t· h· and t·* feet
       78– 6   * *t· h· and t·* feet
224 ft.
  My.   67– 8   * Height . . . 224 ft.
two hundred and twenty-five
  My.   53–14   * about *t· h· and t·.*
two hundred and sixty
  Hea.   12–15   *t· h· and s·* remedies
two hundred and sixty-two
  Ret.   33–10   *t· h· and s·* remedies
267
  My.   57–26   * societies advertised . . . is 267.
three hundred
  Ret.   47– 6   over *t· h* applications
four hundred
  Mis. 345– 3   had stood *f· h·* years before,
four hundredth
  My.   53– 7   * reached its *f· h·* edition,
four hundred and sixty-four
  My.   54–30   * seated *f· h· and s·.*
five hundred
  Ret.   4– 4   farm of about *f· h·* acres,
614
  My.   57–24   * 614 of which show a membership
six hundred and twenty-five
  My.   55–25   * capacity of *s· h· and t·,*
682
  My.   57–24   * number of branch churches . . . is 682,
eight hundred
  Pul.   27– 6   * vestry seats *e· h·* people,
       71– 1   * *e· h·* of the members
  My.   54–14   * present about *e· h·* people.
nine hundred
  My.   8–20   * capacity of more than *n· h·,*
several hundred
  Pul.   42–10   * *s· h·* children in the central pews.
a thousand
  Pul.   41–19   * nearly *a t·* local believers.
       58–16   * will seat over *a t·*
       83– 9   * by *a t·* denials
one thousand
  Mis. 276–10   *o· t·* Christian Scientists,
      285– 3   edition of *o· t·* pamphlets
  Ret.   37– 9   numbered *o· t·* copies.
  Pul.   5–21   edition of *o· t·* copies.
  '01.   18– 2   attenuated *o· t·* degrees
  My.   53– 7   * each of *o· t·* copies.
eleven hundred
  Pul.   25– 8   * seating *e· h·* people
twelve hundred
  My.   68–14   * seating capacity of *t· h·,*
fourteen hundred
  Pul.   41–17   * holding from *f· h·* to
fourteen and fifteen hundred
  Pul.   57– 6   * *f· and f· h·,*
fifteen hundred
  Pul.   25– 9   * capable of holding *f· h·* ;
       41–17   * to *f· h·* persons,
1,545
  My.   57–16   * membership at that date was 1,545.
1893
  '00.   7– 8   in all the other 1893 years.
nineteen hundred
  Pul.   35– 9   * *n· h·* years ago.
       53– 2   * *n· h·* years ago,
  My. 109–10   If *n· h·* years ago
two thousand
  Pul.   44– 5   *t· t·* miles of space,
  Hea.   13– 5   reducing the . . . . *t· t·* times,
2,194
  My.   57–19   * which is 2,194 more than
two thousand four hundred and ninety-six
  '01.   2–29   *t· t· f· h· and n·*
2,500
  Mis. 251– 2   chapter sub-title
two thousand and six hundred
  Pul.   v– 2   *t· t· and s· h·* children
two thousand seven hundred and eighty-four
  '02.   1– 5   *T· t· s· h· and e·*
3,000
  My.   67–11   * 3,000 garments
three thousand
  My.   69–23   * *t· t·* wraps.
     169–18   *t· t·* believers
thirty-eight hundred
  Mis. 381–27   number of *t· h·*
four thousand
  Mis. 353–26   *f· t·* children,
  Pul.   30– 8   * numbers now *f· t·* members ·
       41– 8   * *f· t·* of these contributors
       55–25   * now over *f· t·* members.
       71– 1   * membership of *f· t·,*
       77–12   * *f· t·* members.

numbers

four thousand
  Pul.   78–11   * *f· t·* members.
  My. 173–19   about *f· t·,*
four and five thousand
  My.   65–10   * *f· and f· t·* persons.
four or five thousand
  My.   7–17   * *f· or f· t·* persons,
       9– 4   * *f· or f· t·* persons,
forty-five hundred and thirty-eight
  My.   70–29   * *f· h· and t·* pipes,
4,889
  My.   57–19   * and numbers 4,889,
5,000
  My.   67–10   * Seating capacity . . . 5,000
five thousand
  Mis.   29–17   about *f· t·* students.
  My.   24–29   * seating capacity of *f· t·.*
       29– 4   * *F· t·* people kneeling
       36– 4   * the *f· t·* present
       59–21   * chorus of *f· t·* voices,
       69–20   * *f· t·* people
       71–29   * seat *f· t·* people,
       77– 4   * capacity of over *f· t·.*
       78– 1   * capacity . . . is *f· t·,*
       98– 7   * holding *f· t·* people,
       99–15   * seating *f· t·* people,
     141–23   seats only *f· t·* people,
five thousand and twelve
  My.   71–22   * *f· t· and t·* people
six thousand
  Rud.   8– 4   lion of *s· t·* years ago ;
  Pul.   40–11   * Enabling S· T· Believers to
       40–18   * nearly *s· t·* persons,
       64–26   * *s· t·* people
6,181
  My.   57–22   * number admitted . . . is 6,181.
seven thousand
  Ret.   7– 1   majority vote of *s· t·,*
ten thousand
  Ret.   23–20   "among *t· t·.*" — *Song* 5 : 10.
  Pul.   82–22   * *t· t·* Esthers,
  '02.   3– 1   *t· t·* . . . . Scientists
  My.   8–24   * "*T· t·* Christian Scientists
     123–22   a church of *t· t·* members
     141– 7   * *t· t·* persons
fifteen thousand
  My.   80–21   * *F· t·* Scientists
sixteen thousand
  '00.   1–12   over *s· t·* communicants
twenty thousand
  My.   82–22   * *t· t·* and more visitors
       88– 3   * *T· t·* Christian Scientists
twenty-one thousand six hundred and thirty-one
  '01.   2–28   *t· t· s· h· and t·*
twenty-four thousand
  My.   8–19   * *t· t·* members
twenty-four thousand two hundred and seventy-eight
  '02.   1– 8   *t· t· t· h· and s·*
twenty-five thousand
  My.   77–14   * *t· t·* visitors
thirty thousand
  My.   30– 5   * over *t· t·* people
       45– 9   * upwards of *t· t·*
       72–19   * *t· t·* or more
       79–11   * *t· t·* people
       83–27   * The *t· t·* visitors
       92–23   * *t· t·* worshippers
       94– 7   * *t· t·* worshippers
       99–17   * *T· t·* of the faith,
     100– 7   * *t· t·* worshippers
     172–14   *t· t·* members ;
thirty-six thousand
  My. 175– 3   *t· t·* communicants,
forty thousand
  My.   77–25   * nearly *f· t·* believers
       94–21   * *f· t·* Christian Scientists
       95–15   * *f· t·* . . . . Scientists
       96– 1   * *f· t·* . . . . Scientists
       97–26   * to the number of *f· t·*
       98– 1   * *F· t·* people
     135–18   about *f· t·* members,
40,000 sq. ft.
  My.   67– 9   * Area of site . . . 40,000 sq. ft.
40,011
  My.   57–17   * membership is 40,011.
41,944
  My.   57–25   * a membership of 41,944.
forty-eight thousand
  My. 141–24   *f· t·* communicants,
one hundred thousand
  Pul.   55–30   * between *o· h· t·* and
       63–16   * numbers over *o· h· t·*
       70– 5   * *O· H· T·* Followers
       70–12   * *o· h· t·* converts,

numbers

hundreds of thousands
(*see* **hundreds**)
two hundred thousand
   Pul. 30–24 * exceeds *t· h· t·* people.
       55–30 * between . . . and *t· h· t·*.
238,000
   My. 181–23 a population of 238.000
quarter of a million
   Pul. 67–17 * over a *q· of a m·*
four hundred thousand
   My. v–22 * *f· h· t·* copies
a million
   Mis. 35– 7 *a m·* of people acknowledge
   Pul. 83– 9 * *a m·* of broken pledges.
   No. 33–14 it was *a m·* times greater
   '00. 1–24 over *a m·* of people
   Peo. 8–28 proved *a m·* times unskilful.
   My. 85– 7 * adherents number probably *a m·*,
one million
   '01. 27–18 *o· m·*, and an equal number
the million
   Pul. 82–23 * Miriams by *the m·*,
1,650,000
   My. 181–24 number of 1,650,000 inhabitants.
two millions
   My. 14– 5 *t· m·* of love currency
two hundred and fifty million
   My. 294–28 *t· h· and f· m·* human beings
a thousand million
   Mis. 224–12 *a t· m·* different human

   Mis. 55– 2 pupil and the science of *n·*.
       104–10 calculus of forms and *n·*.
       177– 8 Large *n·*, in desperate malice.
       221–27 multiplication of the same two *n·*
       296– 3 *n·* among its constituents and
   Man. 18– 9 went steadily on, increasing in *n·*,
   Ret. 59–11 demonstration of the science of *n·* ;
   Pul. 30– 8 * church *n·* now four thousand
       63–16 * *n·* over one hundred thousand
       67–17 * *n·* over a quarter of a million
   '00. 1–13 with rapidly increasing *n·*,
   My. vi– 1 * to well-nigh countless *n·*
       19– 2 * current *n·* of *The C. S. Journal*,
       57–19 * *n·* 4,889, which is 2,194 more
       74– 6 * *n·* of belated church members
       82–27 * came to Boston in such *n·*
       84–18 * growth of the C. S. idea in *n·*,
       86–27 * unprecedented, as regards *n·*.
       91–25 * growth in *n·* is remarkable,
       92– 5 * *n·* of intelligent men and women
      235– 9 correct numeration of *n·*

oak

   Mis. 240–17 sturdy *o·*, . . . breasts the tornado.
       392– 1 poem
       392– 6 majestic *o·*, from yon high place
   Pul. 8– 4 leaves of an ancient *o·*,
      24–27 * doors of antique *o·* richly carved.
   Po. page 20 poem
      20– 8 majestic *o·*, from yon high place

Oakland, Cal.

   Pul. 89–28 * *Enquirer, O·, C·.*
   My. 202–20 chapter sub-title

Oak on the Mountain's Summit, The

   Mis. 392– 1 poem
   Po. page 20 poem

oasis

   My. 252–20 *o·* in my wilderness.

oath

   My. 138–27 * made *o·* that the statements
      315–17 * made *o·* that the within statement

obduracy

   Pul. 13–26 must depend upon sin's *o·*.

obdurate

   My. 36–15 * redeemed from *o·* sin.

obedience

and love
   Mis. 127–13 more grace, *o·*, and love.
   My. 18–10 more grace, *o·*, and love.
crowns
   Mis. 118–27 *o·* crowns persistent effort
demanded
   Mis. 19– 5 *o·* demanded of His servants
enforcing
   My. 159–23 spiritual laws enforcing *o·*
filial
   Mis. 254– 1 that filial *o·* to which the

numeral

   Mis. 118– 9 and then allow one *n·* to

numeration

   '01. 22–15 *n·* table of C. S.
      22–20 *n·* table of C. S.,
      22–25 have learned its *n·* table,
      22–28 *n·* table of C. S.
      23– 2 losing the *n·* table
   My. 235– 8 the correct *n·* of numbers

numerical

   My. 94– 3 * the race for *n·* supremacy.

numerically

   Pul. 80– 9 * women's paradise, — *n·*, socially,

numerous

   Ret. 5–22 * distinguished for *n·* excellences.
   My. 31– 9 * *n·* doors of the church
      257–25 memorials, too *n·* to name,

nuptial

   Mis. 290– 4 The *n·* vow is never annulled
   My. 268– 3 *n·* vow should never be annulled

Nuremberg

   My. 295–10 PRINTED IN *N·* IN 1733

nurse

   Mis. 388–24 To *n·* the Bethlehem babe
   Man. 49– 7 C. S. *N·*.
      49– 9 C. S. *n·* shall be one who
   Ret. 20– 9 under the care of our family *n·*,
      90–18 to the care of *n·* or stranger.
   Po. 21–13 To *n·* the Bethlehem babe

nursing

   Mis. 329–15 *n·* the timid spray,

nursling

   Pul. 1– 4 A new year is a *n·*,

nurtured

   '01. 29–14 the parents who *n·* them,
   My. 177–19 *n·* and nourished this church

nutriment

   My. 230– 6 digestion of spiritual *n·*

N. Y. Commercial Advertiser

   Pul. 71– 3 * [*N. Y. C· A·*, January 9, 1895]

nymph

   Po. 8– 8 *n·* and naiad from woodland
      34–12 solitude, where *n·* or saint

nymphs

   Pan. 3–27 leader of the *n·*,

O

obedience

final
   Mis. 116–19 final *o·* to spiritual law.
follows
   My. 224– 7 blessing which follows *o·*
gives
   '02. 17– 5 when *o·* gives him happiness.
   My. 131– 4 *o·* gives him courage,
homage and
   Peo. 9–12 dividing our homage and *o·*
honesty, and
   Mis. 126–16 meekness, honesty, and *o·*
humility and
   Mis. 158–17 to test your humility and *o·*
implicit
   My. 46–24 * and a more implicit *o·*
is the test
   '02. 17– 4 *o·* is the test of love ;
loving
   My. 207–15 * Yours in loving *o·*,
of Christ
   Mis. 139–14 to the *o·* of *Christ.* — *II Cor.* 10 : 5.
patience and
   Ret. 80–20 Patience and *o·* win the
perfect
   Pul. 54–14 * perfect *o·* to the laws of nature.
required
   Man. 65– 9 *O·* Required.
reward of
   '02. 17–11 receive the reward of *o·*.
rule of
   Mis. 118– 8 the indispensable rule of *o·*.
spiritual
   '01. 34– 6 in prayer and in spiritual *o·*
strict
   Mis. 119–23 or strict *o·* thereto,
      248–18 not in strict *o·* to the Mosaic

obedience

this
'00.   9– 2 I discern that this *o·* is
My. 220–13 I practise and teach this *o·*,
to divine law
Un. 13– 6 in *o·* to divine law,
to God
Mis. 12–29 measured by our *o·* to God,
        267–27 action, in *o·* to God,
to God's laws
Ret. 26– 8 in his *o·* to God's laws,
to His government
Hea. 8– 2 and *o·* to His government,
to human law
My. 220– 9 concerning *o·* to human law,
to hygienic laws
Ret. 26– 2 neither *o·* to hygienic laws,
to the call
Man. 69–18 go immediately in *o·* to the call.
to the command
My. 43–15 * In *o·* to the command of Joshua,
to the demands
My. 43– 7 * *O·* to the demands of the law
to the law
Mis. 141–23 in *o·* to the law of Love
        181– 8 blind *o·* to the law of being,
to the teachings
My. 43–24 * *O·* to the teachings of this book
to this rule
My. 4– 3 *o·* to this rule spiritualizes man,
understanding and
Mis. 160–15 firmer in understanding and *o·*.
unto righteousness
Mis. 120– 9 *o·* unto righteousness — *Rom.* 6: 16.
yield
Mis. 236–11 and yield *o·* to them
your
My. 37–14 * your *o·* during forty years
        45–15 * fitting monument of your *o·*
        358– 4 you will be blessed in your *o·*.

Mis. 66– 1 *o·* thereto may be found faulty,
        67–15 *O·* to these commandments is
        82–16 In *o·* to this law, man is
        104–22 In *o·* to the divine nature,
        116–10 Subject: *O·*.
        116–28 to work for God, — is *o·* ;
        116–29 If in one instance *o·* be lacking,
        117–13 *O·* is the offspring of Love ;
        118–11 is neither Science nor *o·*.
        156–27 Experience and, above all, *o·*,
'00.   8–26 learn first what *o·* is.
        8–29 that is not *o·*.
Peo. 3–27 *o·* to our Father's demands,
My. 45– 1 * recognition of and *o·* to
        156–18 In *o·* to this command
        189– 5 so due, to God is *o·*,
        360–20 *o·* to The Mother Church,

obedient
Mis. 117–29 when one is *o·*.
        158–22 Let us be faithful and *o·*,
        331– 5 make them humble, loving, *o·*,
Ret. 71– 4 *o·* to the divine command,
Peo. 11–20 *o·* to the legislation of mind,
My. 41– 2 * to become gladly *o·* to law.
        43–11 * *o·* to the voice of their leader.
        44– 8 * *o·* to the loving counsel of our
        46–20 * faithful, *o·*, deserving disciples.
        209– 3 bless this willing and *o·* church
        332–13 * Your friend and *o·* servant,

obediently
Ret. 80–14 *o·* receptive of the heavenly

obelisk
My. 203–12 Be great not as a grand *o·*,

obey
Mis. 23–10 winds, and waves, *o·* this
        46– 3 servants to *o·*, — *Rom.* 6: 16.
        51–19 and *o·* the Golden Rule,
        51–20 he will love and *o·* you without
        90–16 *o·* the Scriptures,
        93–30 *o·* Christ's Sermon on the Mount,
        99–13 Then *o·* this call.
        117– 8 arrest the former, and *o·* the latter.
        118– 1 cannot *o·* both God, good, and evil,
        118– 8 To *o·* the principle of mathematics
        119–20 to *o·* a power that should be
        120– 4 they must *o·* implicitly each
        120– 8 servants to *o·*, — *Rom.* 6: 16.
        120– 9 to whom ye *o·* ; — *Rom.* 6: 16.
        124– 7 neither do we love and *o·* Him by
        158–11 we both had first to *o·*,
        191–31 *o·* St. Paul's injunction
        206–27 and *o·* the Way-shower,
        208–15 Mortals *o·* their own wills,
        266–27 and *o·* the Golden Rule.

obey
Mis. 287–25 *o·* the Golden Rule for human life,
        303–17 to *o·* the Ten Commandments
        346–18 servants to *o·*, — *Rom.* 6: 16.
Man. 68– 7 or who declines to *o·* this call
Ret. 87–19 to *o·* the celestial injunction
'00.   5–19 to *o·* the First Commandment
        8–26 Learn to *o·*;
        8–28 and you *o·* the mandate
        9– 7 therefore, not ready — to *o·*.
'01.   30–28 to *o·* the Golden Rule,
        31–12 I cannot choose but *o·*.
        34–24 *o·* strictly the laws that be,
'02.   17– 6 seek and *o·* what they love.
        17–10 *o·* both the old and the new
Po.   32–15 Such physical laws to *o·*,
My.   37–31 * give heed and ponder and *o·*.
        64–17 * how to *o·* this commandment
        109– 8 we shall *o·* the commandment,
        118– 2 who cheerfully *o·* God and
        219–31 that he *o·* the law,
        241–27 * and to *o·* Christ was not to
        252– 1 and you will *o·* the law and gospel.
        345– 3 Christian Scientists *o·* the laws,

obeyed
Mis. 158– 9 after His messenger has *o·*
        172–24 discerned, understood, and *o·*.
Man. 51–17 have been strictly *o·*,
Ret. 76– 3 if mortals *o·* God's law
Un. 3–10 those who have *o·* God's commands,
Rud. 10–22 His law of Truth, when *o·*,
No. 3–11 I *o·* a diviner rule.
Pan. 11–13 Science . . . understood and *o·*,
'01.   11–18 and *o·* throughout the week,
        19–18 winds and waves, which *o·* him
        30–23 And no emperor is *o·* like
My.   40–27 * She has *o·* the divine Principle,
        41–29 * has *o·* its every demand,
        203– 8 which are *o·* without mutiny
        220–26 Jesus *o·* human laws
        268–16 *o·*, will eliminate divorce and war.
        279–12 The First Commandment . . . *o·*,

obeying
Mis. 116–25 *O·* the divine Principle
        119– 5 instead of aiding . . . by *o·* them,
No. 14–21 *o·* these commands ;
My. 220–12 *o·* the laws of the land.
        225–15 *o·* the leading of our Lord's Prayer.

obeys
Mis. 211–23 He risks nothing who *o·* the law of
Man. 72– 5 member . . . who *o·* its By-Laws
'02.   17– 5 that one gladly *o·* when
My. 230–12 spirituality of him who *o·* it,

obituary
My. 334–27 * extract from an editorial *o·*

object
Mis. 8–12 *o·* of your own conception
        23–29 actions of the *o·* in front of it.
        68–26 * a science of which the *o·* is
        215–14 Principle and *o·* of our work,
        224–29 an *o·* of pity rather than of
        319–24 The *o·* to be won affords ample.
Ret. 5– 7 of their tender solicitude.
Pan. 9–28 the best of people sometimes *o·* to
'01.   23–25 Its *o·* was to deny,
        30– 4 We err in thinking the *o·* of
My. 71–28 * aim and *o·* of the architect :
        285–15 grand *o·* embodied in the
        296–27 its emotions, motives, and *o·*.
        353–17 The *o·* of the *Monitor* is to

objected
Mis. 348–31 and *o·* to their entering
        349–13 to this I *o·* on the ground that
        373– 5 My artist at the easel *o·*,
Man. 64–18 Mrs. Eddy *o·* to being called thus,

objection
Mis. 349–16 notwithstanding my *o·*,
No. 40–12 I have no *o·* to audible prayer
Hea. 12–27 only *o·* to giving the

objectionable
Mis. 64–11 *Do you regard the study . . . as o·?*
Man. 81–20 No *o·* pictures shall be exhibited
'01.   16–18 these qualities are *o·*,

objective
Ret. 34–19 *o·* state of the mortal mind,

object-lesson
Mis. 110–20 wrought steadfastly at the same *o·*,
        372– 8 voices C. S. through song and *o·*.

objects
Mis. 9–21 dreamy *o·* of self-satisfaction ;
        36–23 material laws, and all material *o·*,
        86– 9 *Is it correct to say of material o·*,

objects
Mis.	227–16	these weak, pitifully poor o·
	344– 9	disengage the soul from o· of sense,
Man.	26–16	if she o·, said candidates shall not
Ret.	31– 1	The loss of material o·
Peo.	7–24	To remove those o· of sense
	7–26	its subjects and o· of thought,
	14– 2	express them by o· more beautiful.
My.	91–23	* the o· of much ridicule,

obligated
Mis.	315–16	morally o· to look after
Man.	83–14	morally o· to promote their

obligates
Mis.	79–30	which in any way o· you
	80– 6	o· its members to give

obligation
Mis.	155–28	thus fulfilling their moral o·
Ret.	5–30	* lively sense of the parental o·,
My.	336– 9	* performed their o· to her.
	354– 8	under no o· to buy

obligations
Mis.	176–25	ourselves, and our times and o·?
	264– 4	loyal to . . . human o·,
	284–32	thus it is with all moral o·.
	291– 4	affinities, self-interests, or o·,
	336–11	right o· towards him.
Man.	28–18	all the o· of his office,
	31– 4	Moral O·
	100–10	neglects to fulfil the o· of his
Ret.	19–23	they performed their o·
My.	331– 3	they performed their o·

oblige
Mis.	303–21	You will o· me by giving place

obliged
Mis.	35–17	is one o· to become a student
	35–18	if one is o· to study under you,
	52–27	he would be o· to turn back
	235– 2	He is no longer o· to sin,
	368–12	We regret to be o· to say
Man.	37–12	o· to report the cause
Ret.	44–12	o·, . . . to preach only occasionally,
Pul.	79–21	* should be o· to invent one.''
My.	55–22	* o· to seek other quarters,
	56–26	* o· to leave the church
	251– 7	* o· to take both Primary and Normal
	313–29	o· to be parted from my son,

obliquity
Ret.	31–22	mortal mind's material o·

obliterate
My.	263– 1	tend to o· the spiritual idea

obliterated
Pul.	52–23	* nearly o· all vital belief
'02.	6–17	all it includes is o·,

obliterates
Pan.	11–25	o· the lost image
My.	270– 3	o· the epicycle of evil.

oblivion (see also **oblivion's**)
Mis.	99–24	never bear into o· his words.
	209–15	to learn that neither o· nor dreams
Rud.	5–26	and sinking into o·.
No.	42–16	engulfing error in bottomless o·,
My.	285–12	shall be relegated to o·.

oblivion's
Po.	15–22	cannot quench in o· wave.

oblivious
Mis.	162–28	he must be o· of human self.

obnoxious
Man.	44– 8	O· Books.
	44–10	has for sale o· books.
Un.	56–28	More o· than Chinese stenchpots

obscuration
Mis.	2– 8	causing great o· of Spirit.

obscure
Mis.	181– 9	tend to o· the order of Science,
	222–26	healing Principle, . . . is not so o·;
	254–18	would o· the light of Science,
	337–21	they o· its divine element,
Ret.	22– 1	becomes correspondingly o·.
Un.	53–10	evil belief that renders them o·.
Pan.	10–30	appetites, and passions, . . . o· man.
Hea.	5–18	o· the one grand truth
	14– 7	o· the divine Principle of healing
My.	267–25	Material thought tends to o·
	305– 1	P. P. Quimby (an o·, uneducated

obscured
Mis.	113– 7	and divine light to be o·,
	286– 5	can neither be o· nor throttled.
	333– 6	God cannot be o·,
Ret.	84–16	o· even the power and glory
'01.	12–20	scholastic theology has o·,

obscurity
My.	183–21	the blind see out of o·.

obsequious
Mis.	87–29	If they are haunted by o· helpers,

observance
Ret.	76–28	strictest o· of moral law
My.	256– 5	emphatically phrasing strict o·
	339–15	o· of the holiday illustrates the
	339–30	without the o· of a material fast
	340–23	to recur to a religious o· which

observances
Man.	60–12	Easter O·.
	60–13	there shall be no special o·,
My.	66–22	* elaborate o· of Sunday,
	340– 5	religious o· and precedents

observation
Mis.	88–11	Patience, o·, intellectual culture,
	154–26	never desert the post of spiritual o·
	245–12	directing more critical o· to its
	251–17	cometh not with o·'' — Luke 17 : 20.
	293–10	gained from instruction, o·, and
	308–33	to remove from their o·
Ret.	45–14	From careful o· and experience
'01.	26–30	C. S. is the result of my own o·,
'02.	1–17	wrestling only with material o·,
Peo.	6– 7	* founded on long o· and reflection,
My.	319–17	* o· of many of your students,

observe
Mis.	328–27	o· the apostle's admonition,
Man.	61– 9	shall o· no more Communion seasons.
Un.	21– 4	If we o· our mental processes,
	33–22	o· the foundations of their testimony,
My.	29–21	* opening they had gathered to o·,
	173–21	sweet to o· with what unanimity my
	262–27	I love to o· Christmas in quietude,

observed
Mis.	6–26	caution is o· in regard to diet,
	91– 3	it should be o· at present
	127– 1	Hitherto, I have o· that
	239–11	I o· a carriage draw up
	314–27	This form shall also be o·
Man.	61–12	Communion shall be o·
Ret.	38– 9	of what I had already o·
	88– 1	courtesy should be o·
Pul.	20–22	selected and o· in the East
	54–19	* shows that he o·, in his
My.	17–29	''Hitherto, I have o· that
	226– 4	This rule strictly o·
	244–31	As the people o· the success
	259–24	Certain occasions, . . . o· properly,
	262– 6	O· by material sense, Christmas

observer
Mis.	220–23	Christian Scientist and the o·.
Pul.	29–11	* earnestness impressed the o·.
'00.	2– 8	o· reports three types
My.	48–31	* I am bound as an o· of them
	87– 6	* to the most casual o·.

observers
Ret.	19–20	was remarked by all o·.
My.	330–31	was remarked by all o·.

observing
'01.	30–11	o· the Golden Rule,
My.	340– 2	we have no record of his o·

obsolete
Mis.	173–21	matter is nowhere and sin is o·.
	318– 2	o· terms in absolute C. S.,
Ret.	34– 4	in which matter is o·.
No.	26–28	Sin must be o·,

obstacle
Mis.	200–26	met no o· or circumstances

obstacles
Mis.	54–12	power of C. S. over all o·
	135–11	surmounts all o·,
	309–21	include all o· to health,
Ret.	50–29	such o· as were encountered
Pul.	84–23	* all o· to its completion
My.	52– 3	* had many o· to overcome,
	91–24	* despite the o· put in the way

Obstetric
Ret.	43–17	Primary, Normal, and O·

obstetricians
Mis.	349– 7	students . . . who are skilful o·.

obstetrics
Mis.	349–10	o· taught in my College.
	349–12	above-named course in o·
Man.	88– 9	O· will not be taught.

obstinate
Mis.	329– 2	Mine is an o· penchant
Rud.	3– 4	o· resistance to all efforts
My.	180–19	o· sinner, however, refuses

obstinately
Mis. 327–27 O· holding themselves back,

obstruct
Mis. 10– 2 wherewith to o· life's joys
No. 49–20 o· the harmony of Mind

obstructing
Mis. 173–23 o· his intelligence

obstructions
My. 61– 5 * to remove human o·

obstructs
Mis. 39–27 *and what most o· the way?*
328–23 Whatever o· the way,

obtain
Mis. 123–22 whereby the just o· a pardon
168–29 * had to go away unable to o· seats.
232– 9 and we not o· a more perfect
270–20 if we would o· that promise.
272–21 * may o· for any secular purposes ;
Man. 66– 4 o· a clear understanding of
Ret. 65–28 to o· health, harmony, and
71–27 Secret mental efforts to o· help
86–18 o· it by taking up his cross
Un. 31–22 evil does not o· in Spirit,
32– 1 evil *does,* . . . o· in matter ;
'02. 6–13 human woe is seen to o· in
My. 48–12 * o· the spiritual understanding
54– 2 * could not o· entrance ;
55– 4 * to o· by purchase some building,
171– 6 they shall o· joy — *Isa.* 35 : 10.
216– 3 o· their money from a fish's mouth,
269– 7 worthy to o· that world, — *Luke* 20 : 35.
349–24 o· not in material phenomena,

obtainable
Man. 100–26 If a suitable man is not o·
Pul. 54–27 * the most perfect o· environment,

obtained
Mis. 39– 6 this knowledge can be o·
150–18 halls can now be o· wherein,
212– 5 what happiness is, and how it is o·.
251–17 with knowledge o· from the senses
272– 1 * o· a college charter
382–17 o· the first charter for the first
382–21 o· the first and only charter for a
Man. 18– 3 charter for the Church was o·
Ret. 16–16 was o· June, 1879,
44– 5 charter for this church was o· in June,
Pul. 38– 1 * charter o· the following June.
67–28 * charter was o· two months later.
73–28 * concise idea of her belief could be o·
Peo. 4–15 the error . . . o· expression.
My. 49– 9 * charter . . . was o· August 23, 1879,
54–20 * that some place would be o·,
149–17 blessings are o· by labor.
327–17 * o· by Miss Mary Hatch Harrison
328–25 * application . . . was made and o·.
328–27 * for which a license must be o·

obtaining
Mis. 141–28 no legal authority for o·,
Pan. 6–13 thereby o· social prestige,
My. 55– 7 * thought of o· a church edifice,

obtains
Mis. 205– 1 mind, thus purged, o· peace
220– 1 rule, which o· in every line
368–17 This evil o· in the present
'00. 6–17 o· not in the Science,
Peo. 6–11 * less mortality than now o·."

obtrude
Mis. 9–32 all that an enemy or enmity can o·

obtruding
Mis. 171–27 o· upon the public attention

obtrusive
Mis. 282– 6 chapter sub-title

obviate
Mis. 249– 3 to see if C. S. could not o· its

obvious
Mis. 110–23 o· that the world's acceptance
205–23 maintain their o· correspondence
Ret. 64–12 In C. S. the fact is made o· that
87– 5 its wisdom is as o· in religion
'02. 7–26 It is o· that he called his
My. 279– 9 its o· correspondence with the Scriptures

obviously
Pul. 54–10 * o·, the conditions requisite in

occasion
Mis. 72–16 not have o· any more — *Ezek.* 18 : 3.
91–27 as o· required, read from the book
129–16 he will seek o· to
148–14 written . . . as the o· required.
171– 4 he rose to the o· with the second
274–11 disappointment this will o·,

occasion
Mis. 278–11 never given o· for a single censure,
282–25 o· which may call for aid unsought,
284– 6 Its infinite nature and uses o· this.
315– 3 especially adapted to the o·,
321–28 offered upon this approaching o·.
Man. 3–10 written . . . as the o· required.
76– 4 as the right o· may call for it.
Un. 57– 5 by the pain they feel and o· ;
Pul. 15–18 o· for a victory over evil.
16– 1 and Sung on This O·
43–22 * sermon prepared for the o·
56–11 * o· of the erection of the temple,
60–15 * come to Boston for this . . . o·
Pan. 1– 2 heading
14–27 Great o· have we to rejoice
Po. vi– 7 * *was written for that o·,*
My. 3– 1 chapter sub-title
16–16 * there were present on this o· :
26–17 better to be brief on this rare o·.
39–21 * My thoughts revert to a former o·,
42–23 * significance of this momentous o·.
46–21 * On this solemn o·,
54– 1 * were inadequate for the o·,
64– 1 * the significance of the o·,
77–24 * present to participate in the o·.
79–14 * anywhere in the world on any o· ;
85– 3 * in the significance of the o·.
89–17 * an o· for joy that marks it as
141–18 * Boston church has offered an o· **for**
159– 1 chapter sub-title
170– 2 this was no festal o·, no formal
174– 8 club-house to them on this o· ;
174–11 their reports of the happy o·.
177– 5 on so interesting an o·
201–28 my presence on the auspicious o· of
219– 9 preventing the o· for its use ;
281–19 * to offer an appropriate o·
289–11 should upon this solemn o·
289–26 may be read on that tender o·.
321–12 * with whom he had o· to talk,
355– 9 if the o· demands it,

occasional
Mis. 43–25 The o· temporary success
Ret. 1–12 stray sonnet and an o· riddle,

occasionally
Mis. 52–13 o· a love affair.
88– 3 o· receive it from others ;
302–15 If Christian Scientists o·
Ret. 44–14 to preach only o·,
83–23 o· reading aloud from the
No. 9–16 have opposed o· and strongly
'02. 20–24 privilege of meeting you all o·
My. 81–20 * o· the voices would ring out
140–16 * attending o· The Mother Church.
140–26 o· attending this church.

occasioned
Mis. 256–16 that has o· the irregular
My. 244– 3 the stir that might be o·

occasions
Mis. 148–27 people present on these o·.
250–15 to be taken down on rare o·
261– 4 sin and suffering it o·
350–22 o· effects on patients which
Pul. 53– 8 * on various o· during the
My. 86–25 * the most notable of such o·.
259–23 Certain o·, considered either

Occident
Mis. 29–24 Surely the people of the O·
98–16 the miracle of the O·.
My. 193– 8 dazzling glory in the O·,

occultism
Mis. 78–13 o·, magic, alchemy,
351– 8 I have no skill in o· ;
Pul. 14– 3 growing o· of this period.

occultists
Mis. 80– 1 o·, sellers of impure literature,

occupancy
My. 55–27 * until The . . . was ready for o·,

occupant
Ret. 88–24 stated o· of that pulpit.

occupants
Man. 30–22 o· are satisfactory to her.

occupation
Mis. 296–25 Do they enter this line of o·
Man. 45– 2 sufficient o· for all its members.
'02. 3–15 brief o· of that pearl of the ocean,

occupied
Ret. 6–24 law-office which Mr. Pierce had o·,
Pul. 36–25 * now o· by Judge and Mrs. Hanna,
44– 6 * You are fully o·,
'01. 30–11 too o· with doing good,

occupied

'01.	34– 6	*o·* in prayer and in spiritual
My.	vi–25	* then *o·* by the Publishing Society
	79–22	* than it ever *o·* before.
	184–12	so *o·* that I omitted to wire
	359–21	* who then *o·* offices in the building

occupies

Man.	71–12	*o·* a position that no other church
	85– 1	*o·* only his own field of labor.
No.	11–16	schools . . . that physiology *o·*,

occupy

Mis.	112– 7	*o·* time and thought ;
	173–18	Does . . . exist without space to *o·*,
	230–16	hours that other people may *o·* in
Man.	30–13	*o·*, during his term of Readership,
	30–21	does not *o·* the house herself
Ret.	85–16	Seek to *o·* no position whereto you
Hea.	16–13	Life and Love will *o·* your affections,

occupying

Pul.	62– 8	* *o·* a space not more than
Hea.	14– 1	*o·* the field for a period ;

occur

Mis.	11–24	If special opportunity . . . *o·* not,
	76–15	theory that death must *o·*,
Man.	80–17	Whenever a vacancy shall *o·*,
	94– 8	there may *o·* exceptions.
My.	143–24	cease to bless they will cease to *o·*

occurred

Mis.	49–12	*o·* in a class of Mrs. Eddy's ;
	304–25	* days on which great events have *o·*
	378– 3	About the year 1862, . . . this *o·* :
	378–14	never *o·* to the author to learn his
'02.	13–15	when a loss of funds *o·*,
My.	79–15	* this *o·* in staid old Boston,
	214–29	To desert . . . never *o·* to me,
	284–16	* that such an event has *o·*."
	298– 3	*o·* in my life's experience
	311– 1	incident, which *o·* later
	311–16	Hence a mistake may have *o·*

occurrence

Mis.	48–25	Such an *o·* would be impossible,
	290–15	naming the time of the *o·*,
Ret.	16–11	It was not an uncommon *o·*

occurring

Man.	26–21	a vacancy *o·* on that Board
My.	266–13	consequent vacancies *o·*

occurs

Mis.	11–21	whenever opportunity *o·*.
Man.	41–13	when the opportunity *o·*.
	55– 7	if this sad necessity *o·*.
My.	24–30	* It therefore *o·* to us that

ocean

Mis.	205–14	in the infinite *o·* of Love,
	339–26	sent along the *o·* of events a wave
Ret.	2–23	nor had they crossed the *o·* ;
Pul.	88– 4	from the Atlantic to the Pacific *o·*,
No.	29–23	driftwood on the *o·* of thought ;
'02.	3–15	occupation of that pearl of the *o·*,
	11– 1	swimming the *o·* with a letter
	12–17	drop of water is one with the *o·*,
	20– 1	*o·* of events, mounting the billow
Po.	8–12	the silv'ry moon and *o·* flow ;
	65–20	O'er *o·* or Alps,
My.	121–10	This strength is like the *o·*,
	202–24	a drop from His *o·* of love,

oceans

My.	124–12	across continents and *o·*,

o'clock

(*see* **time**)

Oconto

Mis.	149–17	chapter sub-title

octagonal

Pul.	24–11	* circular front and an *o·* form,

October

(*see* **months**)

Odd Fellows Hall

My.	54–13	* communion was held at *O· F· H·*,

odds

Mis.	234–21	to establish . . . against such *o·*,

odious

Mis.	324–21	seeks to leave the *o·* company
No.	3–26	becoming *o·* to honest people ;

odor

Mis.	227–20	the sweeter the *o·* they send forth
	228–10	name whose *o·* fills the world
	237– 5	in place of material flames and *o·*,
	329–17	"breath all *o·* and cheek all bloom."
	331– 6	obedient, full of good *o·*,
No.	14–12	the *o·* of the upas-tree
My.	184–18	the *o·* of my childhood,

odorous

Mis.	267–15	* *Comparisons are o·*.
Ret.	17–12	the pink — in its *o·* bed ;
Po.	62–15	the pink — in its *o·* bed ;

odors

Mis.	240–32	belongs to nature, — namely, pure *o·*.
Ret.	65– 8	The *o·* of persecution,
'00.	8– 7	*o·* emit characteristics of tree

o'er

Mis.	152–10	*o·* the work of His hand.
	384–10	Stay ! till the storms are *o·*
	386–19	*o·* thy broken household band,
	386–22	She that has wept *o·* thee,
	386–28	cloud not *o·* our ransomed rest
	387– 8	Brood *o·* us with Thy shelt'ring wing,
	388–23	And hover *o·* the couch of woe ;
	391– 8	Will count their mercies *o·*,
	395–25	A requiem *o·* the tomb
	396–18	*O·* waiting harpstrings of the mind
	397– 5	And *o·* earth's troubled, angry sea
	397–23	*O·* the hillside steep,
Chr.	53– 3	*O·* the grim night of chaos shone
	53–24	*O·* babe and crib.
Ret.	20–17	as sunshine *o·* the sea,
	46– 4	*O·* the hillside steep,
Pul.	17– 3	*O·* the hillside steep,
	18– 2	*O·* waiting harpstrings of the mind
	18–14	And *o·* earth's troubled, angry sea
	39–16	* *o·* the Charles its flood of
'00.	15–27	Watch ! till the storms are *o·*
Peo.	7–11	* As an angel dream passed *o·* him.
	7–19	* Our life dream passes *o·* us.
Po.	6– 1	Brood *o·* us with Thy shelt'ring wing,
	8–11	I'm watching alone *o·* the starlit
	8–12	*O·* the silv'ry moon and ocean flow ;
	12– 1	*O·* waiting harpstrings of the mind
	12–14	And *o·* earth's troubled, angry sea
	14– 2	*O·* the hillside steep,
	19– 2	breezes that waft *o·* its sky !
	21–12	And hover *o·* the couch of woe ;
	23– 6	Come ever *o·* thy heart?
	25–19	Wreaths for the triumphs *o·* ill !
	27–10	To brighten *o·* thy bier?
	32– 7	Are scattered *o·* hillside and dale ;
	34–22	*O·* joys departed, unforgotten love.
	36– 9	Stay! till the storms are *o·*
	38– 7	Will count their mercies *o·*,
	50– 3	*o·* thy broken household band,
	50– 7	She that has wept *o·* thee,
	50–14	cloud not *o·* our ransomed rest
	53– 8	Light *o·* the rugged steep.
	58–10	A requiem *o·* the tomb
	65–20	*O·* ocean or Alps,
	66–11	No melody sweeps *o·* its strings !
	67–15	*o·* the dark wavy grass.
	68–15	To sweep *o·* the heartstrings
	73– 3	*O·* the moonlit sea,
My.	31– 7	* "*O·* waiting harpstrings of the mind ;"
	186–13	*o·* all victorious !

o'erarching

Mis.	394–11	rainbow of rapture, *o·*, divine ;
Po.	45–14	rainbow of rapture, *o·*, divine ;

o'erburdened

Mis.	339–22	hast bowed the *o·* head

offal

Un.	17–10	evil ties its wagon load of *o·* to the

offence (*see also* **offense**)

My.	313–29	to a Baker that was a sorry *o·*.

offend

Mis.	224–28	our own errors should *o·* us.
	224–32	to *o·* a whole-souled woman.
Ret.	31–20	yet *o·* in one point, — *Jas.* 2 : 10.
Un.	57– 1	which *o·* the spiritual sense.
My.	196–12	"If any man *o·* not — *Jas.* 3 : 2.

offended

Mis.	224–26	determined not to be *o·*
	235–14	shall not be *o·* in me." — *Matt.* 11 : 6.
My.	307–17	my theological belief was *o·*

offender (*see also* **offender's**)

Mis.	66– 9	for the *o·* alone suffers,
	212–28	speaks plainly to the *o·*
Man.	46–18	subject the *o·* to Church discipline.
	54– 3	the *o·* shall be suspended
	54–16	*o·* shall not be received into

offender's

Man.	50–19	*o·* case shall be tried

offending

Man.	65–19	removal of the *o·* member

offense (*see also* **offence**)

Mis.	115– 2	*o·* against God and humanity.
	122– 4	by whom the *o·* cometh!" — *Matt.* 18 : 7.
	223–24	chapter sub-title

offense

Mis.	224–27	unless the o˙ be against God.
Man.	43– 2	a second o˙ as aforesaid shall
	51– 5	or if he repeat the o˙,
	52–18	second o˙ shall dismiss a member
	53– 5	member guilty of this o˙
	53–14	it shall be considered an o˙.
	53–21	the o˙ of mental malpractice,
	54– 2	that the o˙ has been committed,
	54–19	Special O˙.
	54–23	second similar o˙ shall remove
	56– 4	if said member persists in this o˙,
No.	32– 5	a criminal to repeat the o˙ ;
'02.	19–11	no person can commit an o˙ against

offenses

Mis.	122– 3	because of o˙ ! — Matt. 18 : 7.
	122– 4	that o˙ come ; — Matt. 18 : 7.
	279– 1	"O˙ will come : — Luke 17 : 1.

offensive

Mis.	224– 3	makes another's deed o˙,

offer

Mis.	35–15	o˙ for sale at three dollars,
	159–21	o˙ at the shrine of C. S.,
	227– 4	necessary to o˙ to the innocent,
	242–19	o˙ him three thousand dollars if he
	345–24	to o˙ them in sacrifice,
	349– 1	o˙ of pecuniary assistance
	366– 7	o˙ Science, with fixed Principle,
Ret.	86–16	when we o˙ our gift upon the altar.
Pul.	33–16	* o˙ food for meditation
My.	17–12	to o˙ up spiritual sacrifices,
	281–19	* to o˙ an appropriate occasion

offered

Mis.	x– 4	opportunity has at length o˙ itself
	48–30	o˙ solely to injure her
	242– 5	the Professor o˙ me,
	321–28	to hear what is to be o˙
Man.	42– 2	o˙ for the congregations
Pul.	5– 2	o˙ his audible adoration
No.	39– 5	o˙ to be heard of men,
My.	7–14	* o˙ the following motion :
	141–18	* o˙ an occasion for the gathering
	174–21	o˙ me to Christ in infant baptism.
	293–21	prayer so fervently o˙
	325–12	* Years ago I o˙ my services

offering (see also off'ring)

Mis.	xi– 8	While no o˙ can liquidate
	135–19	Add one more noble o˙
	141– 4	of your hearts' o˙ to her
	397–19	An o˙ pure of Love,
Pul.	19– 3	An o˙ pure of Love,
	26–15	* A votive o˙ of gratitude
	30– 4	* rather than o˙ their strength to
	87– 4	* to accept this o˙, with our
	87–11	For your costly o˙,
	87–21	refusal of that as a material o˙.
'02.	13–24	But no one o˙ the price
Po.	13– 7	An o˙ pure of Love,
	39– 5	An o˙ bring to Thee !
	46–13	An o˙ pure to God.
My.	258– 5	save one lowly o˙ — love.
	354– 3	by persons o˙ Bibles

offerings

Mis.	51– 3	Burnt o˙ and drugs,
	149– 8	presenting the various o˙,
	275–29	floral o˙ sent to my apartments
	294–17	keep back thy o˙ from asps
	319–23	Take thither thy saintly o˙,
My.	24–10	* built by the prayers and o˙ of
	153– 3	floral o˙ in my name

offers

Mis.	265– 1	o˙ his own thought,

offertory

Man.	62– 2	o˙ conforming to the time
My.	78–14	* The o˙ taken at the beginning

office

Mis.	194– 8	Urim and Thummim of priestly o˙,
	194–10	this denial would dishonor that o˙
	366–28	is the o˙ of Christ, Truth,
Man.	25–12	President shall hold o˙ for one year,
	25–16	term of o˙ for the Clerk
	26– 5	from the time of election to o˙.
	28–19	fulfil all the obligations of his o˙,
	28–21	to perform his o˙ faithfully ;
	29–12	shall resign their o˙ or
	30– 8	he or she shall be removed from o˙
	41–15	disqualifies a member for o˙
	45–20	hold o˙ or read in branch churches
	54– 5	his or her o˙ in this Church
	65–20	cause for the removal . . . from o˙.
	78– 4	he may be dismissed from o˙
	79–12	Before being eligible for o˙
	79–13	persons nominated for said o˙

office

Man.	80–23	term of o˙ for the editors
	80–26	from the time of election to the o˙.
	89– 3	or vacate her o˙ of President
	94–16	His term of o˙, if approved,
	94–21	resign nor transfer this sacred o˙.
	100– 9	Removal from O˙.
	100–11	to fulfil the obligations of his o˙
Ret.	6–19	in the o˙ of Franklin Pierce,
	6–21	Albert spent a year in the o˙ of
	35–24	Urim and Thummim of priestly o˙,
	42– 6	symbolic words on his o˙ sign.
Un.	40–28	the nature and o˙ of Life.
Pul.	28–27	* has filled the o˙ of pastor
'00.	5–14	and their o˙ is that of
'01.	4–27	one in essence and in o˙.
	12–14	Urim and Thummim of priestly o˙,
	12–16	he would dishonor that o˙ and
My.	42–12	* Mr. Gross, on assuming o˙, said :
	137– 4	* in the o˙ of the Clerk of the Court,
	172–22	* and my successors in o˙."
	247– 9	rotation in o˙.
	250– 5	Rotation in o˙ promotes wisdom,
	250–29	filled this sacred o˙ many years,
	254–16	* chapter sub-title
	255– 3	rotation in o˙."
	255– 6	By "rotation in o˙" I do not mean

office-holder

Pul.	83– 3	* never fulfil as husband and o˙ ?

officer

Mis.	272–14	* any o˙, agent, or servant
Man.	28–18	If an o˙ fails to fulfil
	28–20	call a meeting and notify this o˙
	28–22	said o˙ shall be dismissed
	29– 3	of any other o˙ in this Church
Un.	15–27	appeases, . . . the venal o˙.
My.	335– 8	* o˙ of the Lodge and Chapter,

Officers and officers

Man.	21– 1	Church O˙.
	25– 1	heading
	25– 4	The Church o˙ shall consist of
	26– 7	re-elected, or new o˙ elected,
	28– 3	Duties of Church O˙,
	28–15	make sure that the o˙ of this Church
	56–13	o˙ are required to be present.
	56–19	for electing o˙ and other business,
	62–15	o˙, teachers, and pupils
	65–10	duty of the o˙ of this Church,
	81– 1	re-elected, or new o˙ elected,
	88– 4	O˙.
	100– 2	for the election of o˙,
My.	39–13	* o˙ for the ensuing year
	49–17	* for the purpose of electing o˙.
	231–26	TO THE O˙ OF THE SUNDAY SCHOOL
	255– 7	minor o˙ who are filling their

offices

Man.	28–17	functions of their several o˙
	74–10	Teachers' and Practitioners' O˙.
	74–12	shall not have their o˙ or rooms in
	77–15	performance of their several o˙
My.	69–22	* and the administration o˙,
	243–11	important, responsible o˙,
	255– 9	or be elevated to o˙
	359–21	* occupied o˙ in the building

official

Man.	29– 4	to perform his o˙ duties.
	65–17	applies to their o˙ functions.
	70–12	assume no general o˙ control
Ret.	52–19	The first o˙ organ of the
Pul.	47– 5	* first o˙ organ of this sect.
'00.	7– 2	United States o˙ statistics
My.	281–18	* "O˙ announcement cf peace
	326– 6	* o˙ and authoritative manner.

officially

Mis.	271–28	* statistics are o˙ submitted :
Man.	82–19	o˙ engaged in the work
Pul.	24– 7	* as it is o˙ called,
	59–25	* gentlemen o˙ connected with

officials

My.	230–21	fidelity . . . in the o˙ of my church

officious

Man.	45–19	O˙ Members.

off'ring

Po.	43–14	lay their pure hearts' o˙,

offset

Ret.	86– 2	to o˙ boastful emptiness,

offsets

Mis.	62–11	o˙ an equal positive quantity,

offspring

Mis.	72– 9	to their helpless o˙,
	82–15	Man is the o˙ and idea of
	117–13	Obedience is the o˙ of Love ;

offspring

Mis.	181–18	man is the *o·* of Spirit,
	181–28	as the *o·* of good, and not of
	286–30	in the *o·* of divine Mind,
	287– 2	*o·* of an improved generation,
Chr.	55– 4	the *o·* of David, — *Rev.* 22 : 16.
Ret.	68– 4	it claimed to beget the *o·* of evil,
	68– 5	*alias* an evil *o·*.
	68–28	"Man is the *o·* of Spirit.
Un.	22–18	*Evil*. . . . Error, even, is His *o·*.
	24–20	Man, as God's *o·*, must be spiritual,
No.	37– 1	In human conception God's *o·* had to
'02.	8–28	not as the *o·* of Adam,
My.	5– 5	*o·* of sense the murderers of
	348– 5	the *o·* of a universal cause.
	357– 5	born of God, the *o·* of Spirit,

oft

Mis.	125–25	revolving *o·* the hitherto untouched
	248–19	that I am dead, as is *o·* reported.
Chr.	53–53	To-day, as *o·*, away from sin
Ret.	18–13	*O·* plucked for the banquet,
'01.	35– 4	The question *o·* presents itself,
Po.	1–16	Recalling *o·* the bitter draft
	64– 3	*O·* plucked for the banquet,
My.	280–19	only because of *o·* speaking,
	339–19	the Pharisees fast *o·*, — *Matt.* 9 : 14.
	350–20	*O·* mortal sense is darkened

often

Mis.	4–24	It is *o·* said, "You must
	6– 3	*o·* leaves mortals but little time
	7– 5	mother of one child is *o·* busier
	40– 9	It is *o·* asked, "If C. S.
	52–12	*o·* convenient, sometimes pleasant,
	59–23	speaking *o·* one to another,
	85–30	the sick *o·* are thereby led to Christ,
	102– 3	A corporeal God, as *o·* defined by
	102–22	Human pity *o·* brings pain.
	120–24	as *o·* as they can afford to
	127–32	needs *o·* to be *stirred*,
	159–14	I *o·* retreat, sit silently,
	169–23	*o·* is the foundation of unbelief
	170–32	*o·* means spiritual power.
	284–13	This question is *o·* proposed,
	291–11	*o·* construed as direct orders,
	309– 7	portraiture *o·* fails to express
	311–30	Being *o·* reported as saying
	315–23	as *o·* as once in three months.
	316– 7	When will you . . . is *o·* asked.
	346– 9	The question is *o·* asked,
	373– 5	objected, as he *o·* did,
Ret.	30–10	It is *o·* asked why C. S.
	54– 1	*o·* asked, Why are faith-cures
	82–27	It is *o·* asked which revision
Un.	26–12	hymn-verse so *o·* sung in church :
	27– 3	two English words, *o·* used as if
	29–22	*O·* we can elucidate the
	52–24	beautiful blossom is *o·* poisonous,
Pul.	32– 3	* tint so *o·* seen in New England,
	33– 5	* would *o·* run to her mother
	43–28	* religious teachers so *o·* receive.
	58–19	* rather dark, *o·* too much so
Rud.	14–11	and *o·* those were put off for
No.	43–26	Science *o·* suffers blame through
'01.	19– 9	because of your *o·* coming
	31–27	was my fair fortune to be *o·*
Hea.	16– 2	can never be repeated too *o·*
Peo.	7– 6	turn *o·* from marble to model,
My.	40–29	* Human sense *o·* rebels against law,
	61–25	* *o·* stood under the great dome,
	86– 2	* *o·* unaccustomed to fine architectural
	93–19	* too *o·* disposed to touch upon it
	93–20	* Too *o·* we see only its ridiculous
	130–12	failed too *o·* for me to fear it.
	138–14	other students *o·* ask me
	142–19	as they so *o·* have done,
	212–14	The question is *o·* asked,
	310–27	My mother *o·* presented my
	317–19	He *o·* dissented from what I
	324– 1	* He *o·* spoke his thoughts
	324– 8	* *o·* said you were so original
	324–10	* *o·* hinted that he thought he
	331–26	* Much has *o·* been said of the
	342– 9	* so *o·* seen in reproductions,
	343– 4	* reaching an answer *o·* unexpectedly

often-coming

Mis.	322–18	my *o·* is unnecessary ;

oftener

Mis.	125–26	*o·*, perhaps, the controversies
	136–25	*o·* is not requisite,
	156– 1	would contribute *o·* to the pages
	204– 6	sometimes chronic, but *o·* acute.

oftenest

Un.	18–14	you *o·* console others

oftentimes

Mis.	7–26	*O·* we are denied the results of
Rud.	9–23	has *o·* healed inveterate diseases.

oft-repeated

Mis.	x– 5	comply with an *o·* request ;
	107–23	*o·* violations of divine law,
	172–30	the *o·* declaration in Scripture
Ret.	6– 1	* The *o·* impressions of
Pul.	45–20	* *o·* declarations of our textbooks,
My.	165–19	the *o·* inquiry, What am I?

ofttimes

Mis.	84– 1	Jesus' wisdom *o·* was shown by his
	117–22	experiments *o·* are costly.
	127–24	*O·* the rod is His means of grace ;
Ret.	80–28	*o·* we lose them in proportion to
'00.	3–17	*o·* to shun him as their tormentor.
	7–25	*o·* this attempt measurably fails,
My.	123–25	*o·* small beginnings have large
	128–32	*O·* examine yourselves,
	133– 3	*O·* I think of this in the
	261– 3	guardians of youth *o·* query :

Ohio

(*see* **Cleveland, Columbus, Sandusky**)

oil

Mis.	69–16	three doses of Croton *o·*,
	69–21	bad effects of the poisonous *o·*.
	117–27	borrow *o·* of the more provident
	151–25	continually be full of *o·*,
	276–26	not . . . be found borrowing *o·*,
	341–26	replenished with *o·* day and night,
	342– 3	The foolish virgins had no *o·*
	342–15	With no *o·* in their lamps,
	342–19	lend us your *o·* ! — *see Matt.* 25 : 8.
	342–22	wise virgins had no *o·* to spare,
My.	292–23	croton *o·* is not mixed with morphine

Old

'02.	page 1	heading
My.	218– 5	Neither the *O·* nor the New Testament

old

Mis.	ix–19	There is an *o·* age of the heart,
	ix–20	a youth that never grows *o·* ;
	x– 9	and reliable as *o·* landmarks.
	xi–25	on to *o·* battlegrounds,
	10–24	wherein *o·* things pass away
	80–29	outdoing the healing of the *o·*.
	80–29	The *o·* will not patronize the new
	93– 6	*Can fear or sin bring back o· beliefs*
	167–19	How *o·* is he?
	175–14	not with the *o·* leaven of the scribes
	178– 4	left his *o·* church, as I did,
	178– 8	could not be put into *o·* bottles
	178–29	wall between the *o·* and the new ;
	178–30	the *o·* religion in which we have
	179– 1	The *o·* churches are saying,
	179–12	This is the *o·* consciousness.
	179–22	*o·* consciousness of Soul in sense.
	180– 7	A dear *o·* lady asked me,
	211–10	people in the *o·* Bay State.
	223–25	wisdom in the *o·* proverb,
	233–13	into the *o·* garment of drugging
	246–16	to forge anew the *o·* fetters ;
	256–16	To meet the *o·* impediment,
	283–15	Any exception to the *o·* wholesome
	329–28	*O·* robin, though stricken to the
	372–18	* delineations from the *o·* masters."
	375–12	* in Italy, I studied the *o·* masters
	375–22	* resemblance, . . . to the *o·* masters !
	375–29	* identified with the *o·* masters,
	376– 7	* oldest of the *o·* masters,
	390– 5	*O·* Time gives thee her palm.
Man.	35– 1	Children when Twelve Years *O·*.
Ret.	4– 7	One hundred acres of the *o·* farm
	8– 4	when I was about eight years *o·*,
	27–30	*o·* to God, but new to His
Un.	23– 1	treatment received by *o·* Gloster
	28– 9	declare some *o·* castle to be peopled
	44– 8	The *o·*, *o·* story,
	61– 8	and is — neither young nor *o·*,
Pul.	1– 8	An *o·* year is time's adult,
	14–18	What if the *o·* dragon should send
	14–21	waters of chaos and *o·* night.
	26–27	* lamp over two hundred years *o·*,
	41–27	* *O·* familiar hymns
	49–24	* She chose the stubbly *o·* farm
	57–27	* born of an *o·* New Hampshire family,
No.	12–22	departed from the *o·* landmarks.
	15– 6	to explain and prop *o·* creeds,
	43–21	"new wine into *o·* bottles ;" — *Matt.* 9 : 17.
'00.	8–15	things new and *o·*." — *Matt.* 13 : 52.
	15– 1	Putting aside the *o·* garment,
	15–20	wedding garment new and *o·*,
'01.	2– 7	trying to put into the *o·* garment
	15–18	little short of the *o·* orthodox hell
	21– 4	new editions of *o·* errors ;

old
'01.	24–17	more than two hundred years o·.
	24–19	It is as o· as God,
	26–25	subject of the o· metaphysicians,
	29–17	whenever they return to the o· home
	31–28	taught by some grand o· divines,
	32– 7	I loved Christians of the o· sort
'02.	3– 9	the o· national family pride and joy
	8–13	the o· and the new commandment,
	10–24	The o· and recurring martyrdom
	17–10	the o· and the new commandment,
Hea.	2–12	* "O· Adam is too strong for young
	18– 6	to put new wine into o· bottles ;
	18–12	new wine into o· bottles.
	18–15	reconciled with the o· belief ;
	18–16	new wine into the o· bottle
Peo.	3–16	Truth meets the o· material thought
Po.	22– 6	shall bid o· earth good-by
	page 26	poem
	39–14	Sons of the o· Bay State,
	55– 6	O· Time gives thee her palm.
My.	15–32	* 'Twill be the O·, O· STORY
	60– 7	* my uncle, the good o· deacon of
	68–13	* The o· church at the corner of
	72– 9	* titled aristocracy of the o· world
	79–15	* this occurred in staid o· Boston,
	80–11	* o· auditorium of The Mother Church,
	80–22	* into the o· church,
	90–19	* reincarnation of the o·, o· gospel
	95–14	* o· Massachusetts State House.
	107– 8	to which the o· school has become
	117–13	Is not the o· question still rampant?
	133–16	one more round of o· Sol
	135– 6	may be applied to o· age,
	145–13	* an o· ailment my mother had."
	147– 6	o· elm on North State Street
	168– 6	people of my dear o· New Hampshire.
	172– 2	* o· Yale College Athenæum,
	225– 8	of the o· "new tongue." — see Mark 16 : 17.
	236–10	An o· axiom says :
	257– 5	the new cradle of an o· truth.
	273– 3	* Mrs. Eddy's ability in o· age
	273–11	and now am o· ; — Psal. 37 : 25.
	310–23	* Mary, a child ten years o·,
	325– 9	* o· part of Boston in which he
	327–19	* an o· law, or rather a section of an
	350–22	o· foundations of an early faith
		(see also man)

old of-
Mis.	17– 8	like the patriarch of o·,
	33– 3	The high priests of o·
	63– 2	said of o· by Truth-traducers,
	158–20	As of o·, I stand with sandals on
Ret.	65–17	of o· ruled Christ out of the
	76–21	as of o·, on the Pentecost Day,
	79–25	Of o· the children of Israel were
Pul.	3–19	with Job of o· we exclaim,
	32–14	* like any abbess of o·.
No.	41– 3	Pharisees of o· warned the people
'00.	7–20	we say as did Mary of o· :
	9–11	or as of o· cry out :
'01.	2–21	disciples of o· experienced,
'02.	11–27	Of o· the Jews put to death the
Hea.	2– 5	synagogues as of o· closed upon it,
My.	104– 7	Of o· the Pharisees said of the
	119–12	Mary of o· wept because she
	191– 2	Nicodemus of o·, who said,
	212–19	Being like the disciples of o·,
	221– 5	prophets of o· looked for

Old and New Testaments
Pan.	7–18	study of the O· and N· T·

Old and the New Testaments
My.	179–13	The O· and the N· T· contain

Old Country
Pul.	62– 3	* favorably known in the O· C·,

olden
Mis.	237– 2	o· opinion that hell is fire
Chr.	53–37	Thus o· faith's pale star
Ret.	2–18	books, printed in o· type
Pul.	82–12	* In o· times the Jews claimed
	83–16	* In o· times it was the Amazons
Po.	47– 3	the o· and dainty refrain,
My.	147–20	truth that to-day, as in o· time,
	162–19	wisdom which spake thus in o· time
	177–17	was allied to that o· axiom :

older
Mis.	187–13	translators of the o· Scriptures
	311–11	some of the o· members are not
Ret.	80–23	the o· sheep pass into the fold
My.	29–14	* and in an o· civilization ;
	212– 6	o· and more open sins,
	216–26	As you grow o·, advance in the
	323–26	* should mean to your o· students
	342– 7	* O· in years, white-haired

oldest
Mis.	347–29	C. S. Journal was the o·
	376– 2	* true art of the o·, most revered,
	376– 7	* the o· of the old masters,
Ret.	14–29	even the o· church-members wept.
My.	310–14	My o· brother, Samuel D. Baker,
	313–27	My o· sister dearly loved me,

old-fashioned
Pul.	62– 6	* cast bells of o· chimes.
	62–10	* the o· chimes required
'01.	32–18	lives of those o· leaders

Old Man of the Mountain
Po.	v– 9	* poem
	page 1	poem

oldness
No.	25– 7	the o· of the letter." — Rom. 7 : 6.

old-new
'00.	2– 5	o· theme of redeeming Love
My.	166–22	the o· song of salvation,

old rose
Pul.	25–22	* upholstered in o· r· plush.
	25–23	* with frieze of the o· r·,
	26–25	* pale green with relief in o· r·.

old-school
Ret.	14– 5	pastor was an o· expounder

Old Testament
Mis.	187–19	the O· T· might have been as
My.	179–17	if the O· T· and gospel

old-time
Mis.	251–25	falling leaves of o· faiths
	331–22	falling leaves of o· faiths,
	394–18	* Such o· harmonies retune,
'01.	18– 8	the o· medicine of matter.
Peo.	1–13	collisions with o· faiths,
Po.	57– 4	* Such o· harmonies retune,

old-wives'
My.	340– 7	o· fables, and endless genealogies.

olive
My.	192–27	and leave a leaf of o· ;

ologies
Peo.	4– 8	Mythology, or the myth of o·,

Olympiad
Mis.	1– 2	looked longingly for the O·.

Olympian
Mis.	142–22	A boat song seemed more O·

Omaha, Neb.
Pul.	89–24	* Bee, O·, N·.

Omega
Mis.	333–10	"Alpha and O·" — Rev. 1 : 8.
Un.	10–19	God is the Alpha and O·,
'02.	2–22	Christ is Alpha and O·.
My.	267– 9	Alpha and O· of man
	267–12	no Alpha and no O·.

omen
Mis.	132– 4	a favorable o·, a fair token
My.	148–14	Then we beheld the o·,

ominous
Mis.	239–13	and take . . . the o· hand-trunk.

omit
Mis.	92– 1	To o· these important points
My.	20–29	* been decided to o· this year the

omits
My.	276– 8	because of . . . she o· her drive,

omitted
Ret.	83–27	That these . . . are ever o·,
Pul.	59–10	* hymns and psalms being o·.
	88– 2	chapter sub-title
	88–10	articles are reluctantly o·.
My.	184–13	I o· to wire an acknowledgment
	275–17	have o· my drive but twice

omitting
Mis.	191–15	and by o· the first letter,
No.	28–21	o· the spirit of this Science
'02.	20–17	begin o· our annual gathering

omni
Mis.	25–23	As o· is from the Latin word
'02.	7–11	Latin o·, which signifies all,

omnipotence
absence of
Ret.	58– 5	for the absence of o·

anchor in
My.	132–11	and anchor in o·.

and omnipresence
Mis.	96– 9	person of o· and omnipresence
Ret.	56–16	o· and omnipresence of God,
Rud.	9–25	o· and omnipresence of God ;
No.	10–26	His o· and omnipresence.
	20–14	God's o· and omnipresence

omnipotence

bow of
   Peo. 3–14 bow of *o·* already spans
definition of
   My. 221–10 establish the definition of *o·*,
faith in
   Peo. 12–24 Having . . . we lose faith in *o·*,
God's
   No. 20–14 God's *o·* and omnipresence
   My. 293–15 understanding of God's *o·*,
good is
   Mis. 13–30 you will find that good is *o·*,
grooves of
   My. 107–21 nearer the grooves of *o·*.
hands of
   My. 127–29 through the hands of *o·*.
has all power
   Mis. 97–17 and know that *o·* has all power.
His
   No. 10–26 His *o·* and omnipresence.
   Peo. 5–17 to declare His *o·*.''
its
   My. 189–15 Love derives its *o·* from
meaning of the
   Ret. 56–9 meaning of the *o·*, omniscience,
must interpret
   Mis. 71–15 causation must interpret *o·*,
neck of
   Mis. 370–17 arms about the neck of *o·*,
of God
   Mis. 31–20 he has no faith in the *o·* of God,
of good
   Mis. 121–10 the *o·* of good, as divinely
   200–27 faith in the *o·* of good,
of His love
   Mis. 322–25 the *o·* of His love ;
of Life
   My. 116–4 *o·* of Life, Truth, and Love,
of Spirit
   Ret. 31–24 bent low before the *o·* of Spirit,
of Truth
   Mis. 61–9 *o·* of Truth over error,
   192–14 knowing the *o·* of Truth.
omnipresence and
   Ret. 88–29 demonstrates omnipresence and *o·*,
   My. 174–26 omnipresence, and *o·* enfolds me.
omniscience of
   My. 188–12 even the omniscience of *o·* ;
proof of the
   Pan. 7–6 gives in proof of the *o·* of
right hand of
   Pul. 9–28 ear and right hand of *o·*,
Science of
   Mis. 101–22 Science of *o·* demonstrates
sense of
   Peo. 14–16 girt with a higher sense of *o·* ;
supremacy and
   No. 18–8 God's supremacy and *o·*.
understanding of
   My. 294–19 conscious understanding of *o·*,
understood
   Mis. 200–6 understood *o·* to be All-power :
unfolds
   Mis. 183–22 Science unfolds *o·*,
vindicates
   Hea. 15–3 vindicates the *o·* of the Supreme

———

   Mis. 174–5 presence and power over *o·* !
   201–11 *o·* of the Mind that knows this :
   258–25 as infinite consciousness, . . . *o·* ;
   333–5 *o·*, omnipresence, goodness,
   Ret. 58–1 Stating the divine Principle, *o·*
   Peo. 9–26 no *o·*, unless *o·* is the *All*-power.
   My. 5–29 demonstrate the *o·* of divine Mind
   274–8 *o·*, omnipresence, and omniscience

omnipotent

   Mis. 3–25 God is supreme and *o·*,
   17–4 the law of *o·* harmony
   25–22 *o·* and omniscient Mind.
   37–1 God would not be *o·* if
   63–19 God is *o·* and omnipresent ;
   90–1 He must know that God is *o·* ;
   134–23 when at war with the *o·* !
   172–14 "the Lord God *o·* — *Rev.* 19 : 6.
   172–31 good is *o·* and omnipresent.
   173–13 Mind is God, *o·*
   183–2 ever-present good, *o·* Love,
   197–30 recognize God as *o·*,
   205–15 This *o·* act drops the curtain
   232–18 Spirit is *o·* ;
   260–19 Truth is supreme and *o·*.
   268–18 *o·* and ever-present good.
   Un. 19–4 else He is not *o·*,
   39–6 *o·* Love which annihilates hate,
   60–7 We call God *o·* and

omnipotent

   Un. 62–12 *o·* and ever-present good
   Rud. 11–4 next to belief in God as *o·* ;
   No. 23–5 nor make evil *o·* and omnipresent.
   42–16 senses would enthrone error as *o·*
   Pan. 6–24 if God, good, is *o·*,
   '01. 5–9 and God *o·*, omnipresent,
   25–4 eternal in the heavens, *o·* on earth,
   Hea. 5–3 admitting that God is *o·*,
   10–9 God — is *o·* ;
   My. 106–9 immutable laws of *o·* Mind
   108–16 lawgiver, *o·*, infinite, All.
   135–30 divine Love, *o·*, omnipresent,
   294–5 God has all power, is *o·*,
   296–20 God, good, *o·* and infinite.

omnipresence

   Mis. 96–9 person of omnipotence and *o·*
   102–32 defines *o·* as universality,
   174–22 the All of God, and His *o·* ?
   229–10 since God is *o·*,
   333–5 omnipotence, *o·*, goodness,
   Ret. 28–6 understand the *o·* of good
   56–10 omniscience, and *o·* of Spirit,
   56–17 omnipotence and *o·* of God,
   88–29 demonstrates *o·* and omnipotence,
   Rud. 9–25 omnipotence and *o·* of God ;
   No. 10–26 His omnipotence and *o·*.
   20–14 God's omnipotence and *o·*
   My. 174–26 *o·*, and omnipotence enfolds me.
   274–8 *o·*, and omniscience of Life,

omnipresent

   Mis. 8–15 Love that is *o·* good,
   14–1 it fills all space, being *o·* ;
   63–19 God is omnipotent and *o·*
   105–18 unknown to the *o·* Truth.
   172–32 good is omnipotent and *o·*.
   173–13 Mind is God, omnipotent and *o·*.
   307–6 understanding of *o·* Love !
   Un. 3–25 because, if He is *o·*,
   43–27 *o·* Spirit which knows no matter.
   60–8 We call God omnipotent and *o·*.
   No. 23–6 nor make evil omnipotent and *o·*.
   23–27 *o·* and omniscient Mind ;
   42–17 would enthrone error as . . . *o·*,
   '01. 5–9 and God omnipotent, *o·*,
   '02. 12–8 he has one *o·* God :
   Po. 23–19 Supreme and *o·* God,
   My. 135–30 divine Love, omnipotent, *o·*,
   294–5 omnipotent, omniscient, *o·*,

omniscience

   Mis. 25–24 *o·* means as well, all-science.
   Ret. 56–9 *o·*, and omnipresence of Spirit,
   My. 188–11 even the *o·* of omnipotence ;
   274–8 omnipresence, and *o·* of Life,

omniscient

   Mis. 25–22 omnipotent and *o·* Mind.
   Chr. 53–47 *O·* power, — gleaming through Mind,
   No. 23–27 omnipotent and *o·* Mind ;
   '01. 5–10 omnipotent, omnipresent, *o·*.
   Po. 18–15 *o·* notice the frail fledgling hath.
   My. 294–5 *o·*, omnipresent, supreme

omnis potens

   Ret. 58–1 Principle, omnipotence (*o· p·*),

once

   Mis. ix–10 *o·* fragmentary and faint
   6–23 *o·* convinced of the uselessness
   44–25 demand of mortal thought *o·* met,
   54–20 When *o·* you are healed by Science,
   61–15 * I went *o·* to a place
   69–14 I was *o·* called to visit a sick man
   73–8 *o·* discern their spiritual meaning,
   79–3 and the places *o·* knowing them
   120–24 *o·* in three years is perhaps as often
   126–4 *o·*, at least, to hear the soft music
   136–25 convening *o·* in four months ;
   138–17 I *o·* thought that in unity
   159–17 grand collections *o·* in each year.
   159–23 Here I talk *o·* a year,
   195–25 I *o·* believed that the practice
   222–13 that *o·* he would have resisted
   278–13 I *o·* wondered at the Scriptural
   315–23 as often as *o·* in three months.
   326–5 *O·* more he seeks the dwelling-place
   339–4 took place *o·* in Heaven,
   348–17 *o·* in about seven years
   370–9 watch-towers shout *o·* again,
   Man. 25–14 but *o·* in three years.
   32–15 but *o·* during the lesson.
   38–17 Members who *o·* Withdrew.
   39–7 Members *o·* Dismissed.
   39–9 who has been excommunicated *o·*,
   52–16 sufficient . . . for forgiveness for *o·*,
   91–23 will be held *o·* in three years
   Ret. 4–13 Where *o·* stretched broad fields

once

Ret.	8–22	o· more asked her if she had
	63–22	St. Augustine o· said,
	89–16	Jesus was o· asked to exhort,
	89–17	o· again entered the synagogue
Pul.	30– 9	* o· when a Boston clergyman
	32– 6	* At o· one would perceive
	49–26	* O· bought, the will of the
	82– 7	* and as one . . . o· said
No.	22– 5	o· clothed with a "brief authority ; "
	36– 8	He o· spoke of himself
Pan.	14– 4	O· more I write, Set your affections
'00.	11– 5	O· I was passionately fond of
'01.	16–20	o· refer to an evil spirit as *dumb*,
'02.	2–24	and the Church o· loved me.
Peo.	14–17	o· again the power of divine Life
Po.	73– 8	with thee in spirit o· more.
My.	44–17	* forwarded at o· to our Leader,
	52–24	* More than o·, in her earnestness,
	108–21	for if they did o· touch it,
	189–26	the sunny South — o· my home.
	222– 2	the disciples of Jesus o· failed
	316–22	o· more under Mr. Flower's able
	338–20	For o· he may have overlooked

once at-

Mis.	177–19	Answer at o· and practically,
	302–22	destroyed the copies at o·
	305–32	* we ask every one . . . *to act at o·*.
.	380–12	to begin this stupendous work at o·,
Ret.	5–27	* at o· pleasing and profitable.
	31–15	banished at o· and forever
Hea.	12–17	saw at o· the concentrated power
Peo.	13–19	* I cannot change at o·
My.	61–11	* I saw at o· that somebody had
	157– 6	* to be used at o· to build a
	344–13	will be at o· better than he was

Once A Week

Pul.	89– 6	* O· A W·, New York City.

oncoming

Ret.	23–10	o· hours were indicated by

One

Mis.	18–21	one in good, and good in O·.
	258–14	In divine Science, God is O·
	264–11	Its Principle is O·,
	264–11	to demonstrate the divine O·,
	268– 8	The Holy O· saith,
	342–12	O· "altogether lovely." — *Song* 5 : 16.
Ret.	23–19	O· "altogether lovely," — *Song* 5 : 16.
Pul.	4–15	reflects the infinite O·,
No.	24– 9	rests on God as O· and All,
Pan.	12–22	monotheism, — it has O· GOD.
'00.	4–24	believe that God is O· and *All?*
'01.	4–22	that God is the infinite O·
	4–25	conceive of God as O·
	5– 3	by the word Person, or as O· ;
	6–14	yet God must be O·
	8– 1	chapter sub-title
	9–22	the Holy O· of God." — *Mark* 1 : 24.

one (see also **one's**)

Mis.	6–32	families of o· or two children,
	7– 5	mother of o· child is often busier
	7–12	where o· would least expect it,
	7–17	o· naturally reflects that
	8–16	that blesses infinitely o· and all?
	10–29	Even in belief you have but o·
	10–30	and this o· enemy is your self
	11–15	and o· could save it only in
	11–17	would o· sooner give up his own?
	11–22	persecute and despitefully use o·,
	11–25	o· can include them in his
	11–29	When smitten on o· cheek,
	12– 2	Hate no o· ; for hatred is
	12–15	unless o· be watchful and steadfast
	13– 2	mercy and charity toward every o·,
	13– 3	just so far as o· and all permit me
	16– 3	so comfort, cheer, and bless o·,
	16– 6	as o· grows into the manhood or
	16– 7	o· finds so much lacking,
	16– 8	o· saith : The Principle . . . is infinite :
	17–31	by which o· loses himself as matter,
	18–18	children of o· common Parent,
	18–20	o· in good, and good in One.
	18–26	can we in belief separate o· man's
	19–21	o· who abides by his statements
	22–15	from o· individual to another ;
	25– 3, 4	o· cause and o· effect,
	25– 5	neither o· really exists,
	34– 4	O· who has been healed by C. S.
	35–17	*is o· obliged to become a student*
	35–18	*if o· is obliged to study under you,*
	37– 9	"I and my Father are o·." — *John* 10 : 30.
	39–14	God giveth to every o· this
	39–21	Christian Scientist who has
	39–23	"o· another's burdens, — *Gal.* 6 : 2.

one

Mis.	40– 1	is as necessary in the o· case as
	40– 3	its power would be arrested if o·
	40–31	or the ignorance by which o·
	41– 2	in the diabolical practice of o· who,
	43– 3	enables o· to heal cases without even
	43–10	is the o· least likely to pour into
	43–12	The simple sense o· gains
	43–21	If o· student tries to undermine
	43–24	incapacitates o· to practise or
	43–26	temporary success of such an o· is
	44–10	when conducted by o· who
	47–27	*What should o· conclude as to*
	47–29	That largely depends upon what o·
	48–13	alleged that at o· of his recent lectures
	50–15	that gives o· the power to heal ;
	51– 7	mesmerism is of o· of three kinds ;
	51–22	* from the lips of Truth o· mighty breath
	52– 4	how much o· can do for himself,
	52– 6	if he were to serve o· master,
	52–19	*if o· gets tired of it, why not*
	52–24	or failing to demonstrate o· rule
	54–18	*after o· month's treatment*
	54–19	*treatment by o· of your students.*
	58– 1	*If o· has died of consumption,*
	58– 4	o· learns its *unreality ;*
	58– 5	then it has no power over o·.
	58–11	*if o· must deny the evidences of*
	58–28	o· human mind governing another ;
	59– 1	o· government and God.
	59–20	There is but o· right Mind,
	59–21	that o· should and does govern man.
	59–23	speaking often o· to another,
	59–24	success that o· individual has with
	60–19	or for o· who sleeps to
	63– 1	which is infidel in the o· case, and
	63– 4	claim that o· erring mind cures
	63– 4	claim that . . . cures another o·
	63– 9	divine trinity is o· infinite remedy
	64–18	must benefit every o· ;
	65–27	proves that strict adherence to o·
	67–25	whereby o· expresses the sense
	67–26	sense of words in o· language by
	69–17	In o· hour he was well,
	69–27	I will send his address to any o·
	71– 6	o· writer thinks that he was
	75– 6	*insist that there is but o· Soul,*
	75–13	hence Soul is o·, and is God ;
	75–20	assists o· to understand C. S.
	77–17	o· eternal round of harmonious being.
	84–24	turn o·, like a weary traveller,
	87– 3	into o· gulp of vacuity
	87–17	*that no o· there was working in*
	87–19	I never commission any o· to
	88–30	As a rule, drop o· of these doctors when
	91–11	Christian compact is love for o· another.
	93–29	for even o· moment.
	94– 7	the twain that are o· flesh,
	97– 5	It is not o· mortal thought
	97– 8	Our Master said of o· of his students,
	98–11	to aid o· another in finding ways
	99– 5	To weave o· thread of Science
	99–26	voice of o· crying in the wilderness,
	101–22	demonstrates but o· power,
	102–29	as o· that beateth the air,
	102–30	"o· on God's side is a majority."
	103– 5	o· is temporal, while the other is
	104– 8	God, the o· inclusive good.
	109–26	To understand good, o· must discern
	112– 1	in other words, the o· evil
	112–18	regarded his act as o· of simple
	115–25	If o· lives rightly,
	115–25	every effort to hurt o·
	115–26	will only help that o· ;
	116–29	If in o· instance obedience be
	117–28	He illumines one's way when o·
	118– 9	allow o· numeral to make incorrect
	118–25	it gives o· plenty of employment,
	119–26	rights which o· justly reserves to
	126– 2	to o· eternal sermon ;
	127–20	o· must do good to others.
	129– 6	having done this, o· will naturally,
	130–20	without o· single mistake,
	130–24	The greatest sin that o· can commit
	130–25	o· of God's "little ones." — *Matt.* 18 : 6.
	131–12	o· faith, — o· baptism.
	131–24	I, for o·, would be pleased to have
	134–12	"in o· place," — *Acts* 2 : 1.
	135– 7	o· in heart, — o· in motive,
	135– 8	not o· of you can be separated from me ;
	135–14	Is it a cross to give o· week's time
	135–19	Add o· more noble offering to
	136–10	in turning aside for o· hour
	137–20	each o· return to his place of labor,
	137–23	each o· of the innumerable errors
	140– 2	no o· could hold a wholly material

one

Mis. 140–11	No *o·* could buy, sell, or mortgage
141– 6	no *o·* can suffer from it,
141– 7	for no *o·* can resist the power
143–22	husband and wife reckoned as *o·*,
143–26	"with *o·* accord — *Acts* 2 : 1.
143–27	in *o·* place." — *Acts* 2 : 1.
145–19	our names may melt into *o·*,
147– 7	in unity, preferring *o·* another,
147–14	The man of integrity is *o·* who
147–29	the fair, open, and direct *o·*,
148– 2	We shall never find *o·* part of
148–29	every *o·* that thirsteth, — *Isa.* 55 : 1.
149– 8	*o·* after another has opened his lips
150–26	Not more to *o·* than to all,
155– 2	but *o·* cause and effect.
155– 6	Sacrifice self to bless *o·* another,
156–13	in the *o·* held at Chicago,
156–15	in *o·* student's opinions
159–11	*o·* of these is sacred to
160–10	joy in knowing that *o·* is gaining
167– 6	the *o·* altogether lovely.
169–31	was *o·* of the passages explained
171–10	When *o·* comes to the age with
175–23	*o·* belief takes the place of another.
175–26	reveals the *o·* perfect Mind
178– 1	have met *o·* who comes from the
178–18	* If any *o·* had said to me that
181– 1	"for *o·* is your Father," — *Matt.* 23 : 9.
181–12	and infinite Spirit must be *o·*.
187–21	substance, and life of man are *o·*,
187–22	and that *o·* is God,
189–28	as *o·* having authority, — *Matt.* 7 : 29.
191–10	*o·* of you is a devil? " — *John* 6 : 70.
191–12	if . . . there is more than *o·* devil.
191–13	"Master, we saw *o·* — *Mark* 9 : 38.
191–15	assertion . . . of more than *o·* devil ;
191–22	supposition of the existence of *o·*
193–25	no *o·* is following . . . without
195–10	every *o·* can prove, in some degree,
195–20	*o·* correct premise and conclusion,
197– 4	*o·* more frequently used than many
198– 1	wholly governed by the *o·* perfect Mind,
198– 4	*o·* must commence by turning away from
209–27	goodness and blessedness are *o·* :
211–21	When *o·* protects himself
212–14	*O·* step away from the direct line
212–19	flow not into *o·* of their channels.
212–24	If, . . . *o·* is at work in a wrong
215– 3	go from *o·* extreme to another :
216–15	justifies *o·* in the conclusion
216–19	*O·* of these extracts is the story of
217– 4	nor reason attempts to find *o·* ;
217–11	fallacy . . . matter and Spirit are *o·*
219–17	in the *o·* he must change his patient's
220– 3	a good rule works *o·* way,
221– 4	gives *o·* opportunity to handle the
221– 5	*o·* gains in the rules of metaphysics,
221– 9	error and sickness are *o·*,
221–19	denial of this fact in *o·* instance
222–12	In this state . . . *o·* is ready to
225–28	In about *o·* hour he awoke,
227–12	Some uncharitable *o·* may give it a
227–13	ere that *o·* himself become aware,
229– 1	believe . . . that any *o·* is liable to
229– 3	This mental state prepares *o·* to
230– 5	indecision as to what *o·* should do.
230– 6	If *o·* would be successful in the future,
230– 8	*o·* of which is contemptible,
231–19	walking ! *o·*, two, three steps,
231–31	through which the loved *o·* comes not,
232–19	will be *o·* having more power,
236–16	to give, to *o·* or the other, advice
236–27	as a general rule, *o·* will be blamed
237–16	is not essentially *o·* of conscience :
237–28	fetters of *o·* form of human slavery.
239–11	upon the sidewalk *o·* winter morning,
240– 3	through the cold air the little *o·*
241– 8	*o·* having morals to be healed,
242– 6	offered me, . . . or *o·* of my students,
242– 9	give sight to *o·* born blind.
242–20	if he will heal *o·* single case of
242–22	at the rate of *o·* ounce in two weeks,
243– 5	I have not yet made surgery *o·* of
243–11	effected the cure in less than *o·* week.
245–27	a thing to be thankful for that *o·* can
245–29	* "*o·* with God is a majority."
247–10	in *o·* of my works
249–18	not *o·* has been sent to my house,
253– 9	*o·* a congressman
253–24	*o·* tithe of the agonies that gave that
256–19	notice from *o·* to two weeks previous to
261–29	*o·* will either abandon his claim
265– 9	All must have *o·* Principle
265–11	have but *o·* opinion of it.
269– 7	either he will hate the *o·*, — *Matt.* 6 : 24.

one

Mis. 269– 8	will hold to the *o·*, — *Matt.* 6 : 24.
270–18, 19	*o·* fold, and *o·* shepherd ; " — *John* 10 : 16.
271– 9	*o·* cause and *o·* effect.
272–25	* but *o·* legally chartered college of
273–14	*o·* grand family of Christ's followers.
273–30	*o·* Primary and two Normal
276–25	not *o·* . . . be found borrowing oil,
277–20	* *o·* more fact to be recorded
277–27	never so near as when *o·* can be just
280– 4	*o·* of the angels presented himself
281– 9	*o·* ambition and *o·* joy.
281–10	if *o·* cherishes ambition unwisely,
281–10	*o·* will be chastened for it.
281–23	yours is *o·* of the most beautiful
282–25	*O·* other occasion which may call for
283– 2	or *o·* can to advantage speak the
283– 4	As a rule, *o·* has no more right to
283– 6	than *o·* has to enter a house,
284– 1	each *o·* to do his own work well,
284–30	if *o·* is intrusted with the rules of
285– 4	and not *o·* of them circulated,
286–24	mortal mind and body as *o·*,
287– 6	for *o·* is your Father, — *Matt.* 23 : 9.
287–27	it makes *o·* ruler over one's self
289–16	marriage contract two are made *o·*,
289–17	"they twain shall be *o·* — *Matt.* 19 : 5.
289–20	*divorced* two minds in *o·*.
290–24	*o·* must benefit those who
291–14	every *o·* has equal opportunity
292– 5	That ye love *o·* another." — *John* 13 : 34.
295–22	not wholly represented by *o·* man.
297– 2	*o·* readily sees that this Science
298–25	*O·* says, "I find relief from pain in
298–27	through unconsciousness *o·* no more
298–29	*o·* thinks he is not mistaken,
299– 1	mistakes recur until *o·* is awake to
300–32	Healing morally and physically are *o·*.
303–15	every *o·* the same rights and
305– 2	* *o·* representative from each Republic
305–24	* asked to contribute *o·* cent to be fused
305–31	* ask every *o·* receiving this circular
309– 1	the personal sense of any *o·*,
310–14	plead for all and every *o·*,
310–19	*o·* must comply with the church rules.
311– 9	so, loving *o·* another,
311–18	I hate no *o·* ;
311–28	ought not that *o·* to take the cup,
314– 6	*O·* of these individuals shall open
317– 4	we are all of *o·* kindred.
319–20	season pass without *o·* gift to me.
325–18	Balancing on *o·* foot,
326–29	Discerning in his path the penitent *o·*
334–15	only as *o·* gives the lie to a lie ;
334–16	without *o·* word of Truth in it.
335–12	*O·* mercilessly assails me
335–21	The notion that *o·* is covering iniquity
336–25	wherever *o·* ray of its effulgence
338–16	will subject *o·* to deception ;
339–19	*o·* furrow to the brow of care?
339–30	*O·* backward step,
340– 1	*o·* relinquishment of right
340– 2	*o·* faithless tarrying,
344– 4	expressed the wish to become *o·* of
347–15	*O·* says, Go this way ;
347–17	premonition of *o·* of them,
348– 8	When God bids *o·* uncover iniquity,
348– 9	*o·* should lay it bare ;
348–25	*o·* who had lost all faith in them.
350–14	convened in about *o·* week
351– 9	would not if I could, harm any *o·*
352–20	in order to enable *o·* to
352–23	Through the divine energies alone *o·*
353– 7	If *o·* asks me, Is my concept of
353– 9	concept of me, or of any *o·*,
353–10	you have gained the right *o·*
353–12	this misrepresents *o·* through
356–24	*O·* can never go up, until *o·*
361–11	testifying to *o·* creator,
361–30	are not *o·*, but are inseparable as
361–31	If *o·*, who could say which
361–31	who could say which that "*o·*" was?
372– 3	had not *o·* feather's weight
373– 1	*O·* incident serves to illustrate
373–15	*O·* great master clearly delineates
374–21	the *o·* illustrating my poem
374–24	*o·* renders not unto Cæsar
375–32	* as *o·* who gives no mean attention
376–20	there rose *o·* rod of rainbow hues,
378– 6	*o·* Mr. P. P. Quimby of Portland,
379–18	*o·* could write a sonnet.
385– 4	* And *o·* eternal noon."
387–19	That make men *o·* in love remain.
399– 5	Midst the glories of *o·* endless day."
399–22	Lifted higher, we depart, Having *o·*.
Man. 15– 6	adore *o·* supreme and infinite God.

one

Man.	28–26	especially of *o·* who has been
	29–22	*o·* to read the BIBLE,
	29–22	*o·* to read S. AND H.
	35– 4	*o·* of Mrs. Eddy's loyal students,
	37–17	*O·* Normal student cannot recommend
	38– 8	must be countersigned by *o·* of these.
	38–22	on *o·* year's probation,
	43–12	by a written text as no *o·* else can.
	49–10	C. S. nurse shall be *o·* who
	50– 4	by *o· of her own sex.*
	60– 5	*O·* meeting on Sunday during
	72–18	under *o·* church government.
	73– 4	include at least *o·* active practitioner
	73–25	the pupils of *o·* teacher.
	73–27	member of *o·* branch Church
	74– 1	or of *o·* C. S. society
	78–20	$200 for any *o·* transaction,
	84– 8	shall teach but *o·* class yearly,
	84–11	shall have *o·* class triennially,
	90–12	will continue not over *o·* week.
	90–20	*O·* student in the class shall prepare
	92–13	either *o·*, not both,
	92–14	should teach yearly *o·* class.
	95–12	*o·* shall be assigned them by the Board.
	95–18	for *o·* or more lectures.
	97– 5	consist of *o·* loyal Christian Scientist
	110–12	*o·*, at least, of the given names
	111– 2	*o·* of the Christian names must be
Chr.	53– 4	*O·* lone, brave star.
	55–25	*o·* fold, and *o·* shepherd. — *John* 10 : 16.
Ret.	2–17	*o·* of my Grandmother Baker's
	2–24	*o·* of which contained a full account
	3– 2	at *o·* time held the position of
	6– 6	*o·* with the open hand.
	6–16	*o·* of the most talented,
	6–29	was *o·* for the abolition of
	7–14	* *o·* of the most distinguished men in
	11– 3	*o·* of my girlhood productions.
	14–16	not *o·* of whom had then made
	16– 1	*O·* memorable Sunday afternoon,
	16– 6	*o·* of them said, "Did you hear
	16– 8	*o·* hour ago she could not speak a
	19– 6	spared to me for only *o·* brief year.
	22–19	father and mother are the *o·* Spirit,
	22–20	*o·* parent, the eternal good.
	23– 5	merged into the *o·* infinite Love.
	26–22	To *o·* "born of the flesh," — *John* 3 : 6.
	27– 6	never been read by any *o·* but myself,
	28– 1	"little *o·*." — *see Matt.* 10 : 42.
	28– 3	*o·* must acquaint himself with God,
	30–11	revealed to me as *o·* intelligence,
	30–21	No *o·* else can drain the cup
	31–12	*o·* great and ever-present relief
	31–20	yet offend in *o·* point, — *Jas.* 2 : 10.
	33–11	*o·* pervading secret ;
	33–14	*O·* drop of the thirtieth attenuation
	33–16	*o·* teaspoonful of the water
	34– 8	give me *o·* distinct statement of
	40– 4	*o·* time I was called to speak before
	43– 3	I began by teaching *o·* student
	43–17	taught the . . . class *o·* term.
	43–18	taught *o·* Primary class, in 1889,
	48– 8	every *o·* should build on his own
	48– 9	subject to the *o·* builder and maker,
	49–20	only *o·* ever granted to a *legal college* for
	49–25	in *o·* common brotherhood.
	50– 5	*o·* course of lessons at my College,
	50–16	as many as seventeen in *o·* class.
	56– 5	diverges from the *o·* divine Mind,
	56–19	and that *o·* is the infinite good,
	57–11	but *o·* Soul, and that *o·* is infinite.
	57–26	ingrafting upon *o·* First Cause
	58–11	as *o·* having authority, — *Matt.* 7 : 29.
	59– 9	means subtraction in *o·* instance and
	60–28	*o·* Truth, Life, Love,
	60–29	but *o·* Spirit, Mind, Soul.
	64– 1	in this sense they are *o·*.
	64–10	good is equally *o·* and *all*,
	64–11	opposite claim of evil is *o·*.
	68–11	*O·* is false, while the other is true.
	68–11	*O·* is temporal, but the other is
	68–14	*o·* is your Father, — *Matt.* 23 : 9.
	71–27	efforts to obtain help from *o·* who
	72– 1	In the practice of C. S. *o·* cannot
	76–22	when the disciples were of *o·* accord.
	76–25	He thinks of every *o·* in his real
	82–12	who locate permanently in *o·* section,
	83–12	mislead no *o·* and are their best guides.
	86– 4	is but *o·* way of *doing* good,
	86– 5	but *o·* way of *being* good,
	86–19	and another *o·* undertakes to
	86–21	No *o·* can save himself without God's
	88– 3	C. S. healers with *o·* another.
	88–22	*O·* would, . . . blush to enter unasked
	89– 6	preaching and teaching were . . . *o·*.

one

Ret.	89– 7	Men assembled in the *o·* temple
	89–11	If *o·* worshipper preached to the others,
	90–10	to whom St. John addressed *o·* of his
	90–14	even though *o·* of the twelve
	90–26	*O·* of my students wrote to me :
	90–29	*o·* of the children of light.
	94–17	and practice be essentially *o·*.
	94–23	since Science is eternally *o·*,
Un.	1– 4	this may be set down as *o·* of the
	5– 9	Every *o·* should be encouraged not to
	7–20	here is *o·* such conviction :
	10–12	phenomena of this *o·* infinite Mind.
	17– 1	has only *o·* chance of successful
	19– 2	must be *o·*, in an infinite Being.
	21– 3	excusing *o·* another." — *Rom.* 2 : 15.
	21– 6	not two personalities, but *o·*.
	21– 7	good and evil talk to *o·* another ;
	21– 8	not two but *o·*, for evil is naught,
	27– 6	An *egotist* is *o·* who talks much of
	27–10	is *o·* uncertain of everything except
	29–12	*o·* Soul, or Mind, and that *o·* is
	35–21	matter and mortal mind are *o·* ;
	35–21	this *o·* is a misstatement of Mind,
	37– 3	there can be but *o·* Life.
	38–17	rulership of more gods than *o·*.
	42–19	as *o·* having authority, — *Matt.* 7 : 29.
	46–13	"I and my Father are *o·*." — *John* 10 : 30.
	48– 1	fair to ask of every *o·* a reason for
	49–18	*O·* should appear real to us,
	51– 7	never make *o·* hair white or black,
	51–16	not *o·* of all these individualities
	53–19	would have *o·* quotient.
	53–27	for *o·* is your Father, — *Matt.* 23 : 9.
	54– 5	*o·* must lose sight of a false claim.
	55– 1	Jesus accepted the *o·* fact whereby
	59– 8	as *o·* who came down from heaven,
	60– 1	mortal inventions, *o·* and all
	61– 7	he was *o·* with the Father,
Pul.	3–26	Perchance some *o·* of you may say,
	4– 8	mathematically number *o·*,
	4–12	will find that *o·* is as important
	4–16	"*o·* on God's side is a majority."
	5– 1	*o·* of the very clergymen who had
	5– 6	light of *o·* friendship after another
	13–20	The sin, which *o·* has made his
	14– 7	*o·* extreme follows another.
	15–12	Is the informer *o·* who sees the foe?
	15–21	unite all interests in the *o·* divinity.
	16– 7	Joyous, risen, we depart Having *o·*.
	20–21	*o·* of the many dates selected
	21– 2	inevitably love *o·* another
	21–20	to the welfare of any *o·*.
	22– 3	Christian churches have *o·* bond
	22– 3	*o·* nucleus or point of convergence,
	22– 4	Christian churches have . . . . *o·* prayer,
	23–17	* *o·* of the most potent factors in
	24– 4	* It is *o·* of the most beautiful,
	26–13	* It is *o·* of vast compass,
	27–12	* *o·* representing the heavenly city
	27–25	* *O·* more window in the auditorium
	32– 7	* At once *o·* would perceive that
	32–28	* *O·* of her brothers, Albert Baker,
	33– 6	* *O·* night the mother related to her
	33–22	* no *o·* else had seen him,
	36–23	* *o·* of the most beautiful residences
	36–24	* *o·* of the utmost taste and luxury,
	37– 5	* *o·* factor in her removal to Concord,
	37–19	* and *o·* or two other friends
	37–22	* depending on any *o·* personality.
	38–30	* in *o·* form of belief or another
	39– 5	* all teach that *o·* great truth,
	39–25	* 'mid them all I only see *o·* face,
	42– 8	* at any *o·* of these services.
	45–10	* "*O·* of the grandest and most helpful
	45–11	* *o·* month before the close of the
	47–22	* *o·* mile from the State House
	48–25	* *o·* of her characteristics,
	49–17	and not *o·* died."
	49–25	* within *o·* mile of the "Eton of
	50– 5	* *o·* of her motives in buying
	50–25	* No *o·* religious body holds the
	52–26	* and C. S. is *o·* result.
	53–10	* is contained in the *o·* word — *faith*.
	53–12	* and *o·* returned to give thanks
	54–15	* as no *o·* before him understood it ;
	54–29	healed Mr. Whittier with *o·* visit,
	56– 1	* *O·* or more organized societies
	56–12	* *o·* of the most remarkable,
	57–11	* *o·* of the most beautiful buildings
	59–13	* congregation repeating *o·* sentence
	59–29	* Before *o·* service was over
	63–14	and not *o·* died."
	65–22	* *o·* bitter winter day,
	67–14	* *o·* of those movements which seek
	70–10	* *o·* of the most remarkable women in

one

Pul.
72– 8   * *o·* of the first to be seen.
72–28   * naming as *o·* great essential
73–11   * *o·* of the greatest Biblical scholars
74–23   maintain but *o·* conclusion
74–25   "Christ is individual, and *o·* with
75– 1   *o·* Jesus of Nazareth.
76–18   * *O·* of the two alcoves is
77– 3   * *o·* of the most chastely elegant
78– 2   * *o·* of the most magnificent examples
79–12   * *o·* cannot take up a daily paper
79–22   * we should be obliged to invent *o·*."
80– 3   * pendulum that has swung to *o·* extreme
81– 9   * chapter sub-title
82– 7   * *o·* whom her love had glorified
82–19   * and no *o·* to urge them.
85–14   * as the *o·* chosen of God

Rud.
2– 5   *o·* of the three subjects, or agents,
2–16   but *o·* infinite individual Spirit,
4– 1   the *o·* Father-Mother God.
9–18   If *o·* is untruthful,
11– 8   Therefore good is *o·* and All.
13–13   *o·* Life and one Mind.
16–14   *Is there more than o· school of*
16–15   but *o·* school of the Science of

No.
1–18   theology and medicine of Jesus were *o·*,
2–13   by healing *o·* case audibly,
5– 5   *o·* of the severe realities of
5–27   prevents *o·* from healing
7–20   strict performance of each *o·*
8– 4   let us add *o·* more privilege
8–23   If *o·* be found who is too blind for
9– 5   prejudices, and errors of *o·* class
10–11   but *o·* standard statement,
10–12   *o·* rule, and *o·* Principle
15– 6   would enable any *o·* to prove
22–20   it follows that there is more than *o·*
22–25   *o·* of you *is a devil?"— John* 6 : 70.
26– 4   believe . . . matter and Spirit are *o·* ;
31–21   Physical and mental healing were *o·*
34–15   *o·* upon whom the world of sense
35–22   *o·* with Him now and forever.
36– 1   demonstrated the infinite as *o·*,
36– 2   *o·* infinite and the other finite ;
38–20   *o·* consciousness,— which includes only
39–18   include all mankind in *o·* affection.
45–28   "*O·* on God's side is a majority ;"

Pan.
1–19   one God and *o·* Christianity.
2–21   conceived as *o·* personified nature,
3– 7   lacks but *o·* charm to make it
3–19   *o·* supreme, holy, self-existent God,
3–23   (*o·* of my girlhood studies),
4–17   but God is Mind and *o·*.
6– 7   but not as *o·* that beateth the mist,
6–27   the belief in more than *o·* spirit,
7– 6   *o·* divine, infinite Principle.
8– 7   *o·* the divine, infinite Person,
8–11   sacredness of *o·* Christ Jesus?
8–17   one God and *o·* law,
8–19   for *o·* is your Father,— *Matt.* 23 : 9.
9– 5   term "spirits" means more than *o·*
9–20   to help such a *o·* is to help one's
11– 3   "Lie not *o·* to another,— *Col.* 3 : 9.
13–12   rebuke and exhort *o·* another,
14– 5   love *o·* another ;
14– 5   at the table of our Lord in *o·* spirit ;

'00.
5–28   enables *o·* to utilize the power of
8–27   When God speaks to you through *o·*
9–23   no *o·* can fight against God, and win.
9–26   have some *o·* take my place
9–29   But no *o·* else has seemed equal to
15– 2   a new *o·* that is up to date.
15– 3   *o·* that for many years has been

'01.
3–12   * "The *o·* Supreme Being,
4–26   these three are *o·* in essence
5– 7   *o·* divine infinite triune Principle,
5–13   by calling *o·* the divine Principle
6– 7   which reckons three as *o·*
6– 8   reckons *o·* as *o·* and this *o· infinite.*
6–10   *o·* Person, or three persons?
6–23   neither be *o·* nor infinite in the
8– 8   "I and my Father are *o·*,"— *John* 10 : 30.
8– 9   in the sense that *o·* ray of light is
8–10   it is *o·* with light, but it is not
12– 1   to such a *o·* our mode of worship
14–21   *o·* must watch and pray
14–22   even as *o·* guards his door against
15–11   in proportion as *o·* understands it
15–18   to waken such a *o·* from his
16–27   commence with *o·* truth told
17–17   in from *o·* to three interviews,
18– 1   "mother tincture" of *o·* grain
22–11   so if *o·* is true, the other is false.
22–16, 17   I do not say that *o·* added to *o·* is
22–17   or *o·* and a half,
22–19   that *o·* and *o·* are two all the way

one

'01.
23– 1   *o·* and two are neither more nor less
24–21   I had not read *o·* line of Berkeley's
26– 9   In *o·* sentence he declaims against
27–13   If any *o·* as yet has healed
27–14   as I have in *o·* to three interviews
33–28   motives which actuate *o·* sect

'02.
3– 2   thousand loyal . . . to *o·* disloyal,
7–22   chapter sub-title
7–25   love *o·* another ;— *John* 13 : 34.
8–15   God and Love are *o·*.
12– 8   he has *o·* omnipresent God :
12–16   "I and my Father are *o·*,"— *John* 10 : 30,
12–16   *o·* in quality, not in quantity.
12–17   drop of water is *o·* with the ocean,
12–17   a ray of light *o·* with the sun,
12–18   Father and son, are *o·* in being.
13–14   about *o·* half the price paid
13–24   no *o·* offering the price I had paid
16–26   they never destroy *o·* iota of
17– 4   *o·* gladly obeys when obedience gives
18–14   unto *o·* of the least — *Matt.* 25 : 40.
18–16   "Love *o·* another,— *John* 13 : 34.
18–29   all his disciples save *o·*.
19– 6   called *o·* a "fool" — *see Luke* 24 : 25.

Hea.
1–20   *o·* religion has a more spiritual basis
2– 1   the religion nearest right is that *o·*.
3–25   not three persons in *o·*,
3–26   three statements of *o·* Principle.
4–25   if this model is one thing at *o·* time,
5–10   *O·* of our leading clergymen
5–14   Does any *o·* think the departed are not
5–19   obscure the *o·* grand truth
5–19   covered, in *o·* way or another,
9–15   Is it a duty for any *o·* to believe
13–13   *o·* teaspoonful of this water
13–26   Mesmerism makes *o·* disease while it
13–27   that *o·* is worse than the first ;
13–28   *o·* lie getting the better of another,
14–20   perceptive faculty by which *o·* learns

Peo.
1– 1   *one faith, o· baptism.— Eph.* 4 : 5.
4–19   three terms for *o·* divine Principle
4–20   three in *o·* that can be understood,
5– 3   one faith, *o·* baptism."— *Eph.* 4 : 5.
5– 9   whose . . . and theology were *o·*.
8– 5   answers the prayer of *o·* and not of
9– 1   one faith, one Lord, *o·* baptism ;
11–26   " with *o·* of their fingers."— *Matt.* 23 : 4.
12– 1   we should think for *o·* moment of
14–19   one faith, *o·* baptism."— *Eph.* 4 : 5.

Po.
6–14   That make men *o·* in love remain.
22–11   And bask in *o·* eternal day.
22–13   hath *o·* race, *o·* realm, *o·* power.
27– 5   *O·* word, receding year,
37– 4   And *o·* eternal noon."
40– 1   "Good Templars" *o·* and all,
41–16   but *o·* given to suffer and be?
42– 4   Yet there's *o·* will be victor,
43– 4   Loving God and *o·* another,
66– 8   whisper of *o·* who sat by her side
68– 1   So *o·* heart is left me
75–12   Midst the glories of *o·* endless day."
76– 6   Lifted higher, we depart, Having *o·*.
78– 8   the Union now is *o·*,

My.
vi– 6   * no *o·* on earth to-day,
4– 1   *o·* finds the spirit of Truth,
6–27   is the *o·* edifice on earth which
10–22   * entreaty on the part of some *o·* else.
11– 7   * She has been the *o·* of all the world who
14–19   * a fabrication of the evil *o·*,
18–21   rebuke and exhort *o·* another.
19–13   * To *o·* of the many branch churches
22– 4   * *o·* that would accommodate the
25–16   *o·* and all of my dear correspondents
28–28   * *o·* divinely guided woman,
28–31   * revealed the *o·* true Science
29–12   * sight which no *o·* who saw it will ever
30– 3   * awaiting admission to *o·*.
30– 4   * nobody attended more than *o·*,
31– 4   * "Just as I am, without *o·* plea ;"
31–22   * *o·* of the events of their lives.
31–31   * trained carefully under *o·* leader,
32– 6   * their voices rose as *o·*
36– 5   * rose as *o·* to indicate their approval
41– 4   * No *o·* can change the law of
41–12   * no *o·* to escape that blessedness,
41–24   * that his real estate is *o·* of blessedness.
41–25   * Why should any *o·* postpone his
42– 7   * *o·* who has for many years
42– 9   * *o·* of the helpful contributors
45– 7   * *o·* of the greatest and most
45–27   * logically followed the preceding *o·*.
45–30   * *o·* foot loftier than the Bunker Hill
49– 4   * half-persuaded *o·* is wholly
51– 2   * no *o·* in the world who could take
51–14   * no *o·* who is so able as she to lead

one

My. 54– 8 * o· hour before the service
55– 2 * date is memorable as the o·
56–12 * o· in each of the following named
57– 5 * o· that would have the sacred
58–30 * doubtful if there was o· so deeply
59–32 * to o· who knew of your early
60–29 * I was asked by o· of the Directors
61–21 * O· feature about the work
62– 7 * love that trembled in o· human heart
64– 1 * As o· thought upon the significance
64–10 * an honored o· before the world.
66–15 * is so well situated . . . as this o·,
68– 6 * about o· mile and a half of pews.
69– 1 * o· of the extraordinary features
69–27 * If o· would get an idea of the size
71– 1 * stationed in o· of the towers,
71–16 * o· of the most imposing church
71–21 * o· vast auditorium
74–14 * Boston is indebted to them for o· of
74–30 * o· for its hopefulness
77– 3 * o· of the largest in the world.
78–20 * O· of the remarkable features
80– 1 * cures that carried o· back to the
81– 1 * Upon entering The Mother Church o· was
81– 8 * o· of them would pause and
81–23 * swelling at o· voice.
82– 3 * o· near and dear to them.
83– 4 * is patent to every o· residing in
85–11 * O· does not need to accept the
85–30 * o· of the few perfect sky-lines
86–18 * o· which indicates plainly enough
86–23 * o· of the most interesting
87–11 * o· does not notice these unless
89– 1 * This church is o· of the largest
89– 7 * o· of the largest organs in the world.
89–10 * o· finds in the English cathedrals,
89–27 * has been o· of the marvels of the
91–17 * serves to call attention to o· of the
91–28 * o· of the finest places of worship
92–22 * but o· cannot sneer away the
94– 6 * "O· cannot sneer away the
96– 8 * in no sense, save o·, be compared
96–10 * The o· point of resemblance is
97– 1 * almost every o· is inclined to
98–25 * record is one of which any church
99– 1 * o· of, the marvellous, great, and
105–14 I have healed at o· visit a cancer
107–23 or scatter the shade of o· who
109–19 God is o· because God is All.
114– 7 Has o· Christian Scientist yet
116–12 If God is o· and God is Person,
117– 6 A personal motive . . . will leave o·
117–11 make o· a Christian Scientist.
117–29 to seek the o· divine Person,
119– 5 based on o· infinite God, and man,
121–25 If o· would follow the advice
122– 1 advice that o· gratuitously bestows
123–10 o· of the finest localities in
125–10 sling of Israel's chosen o·
130–15 the o· evil or the evil o·.
132–21 God all, o·, — one Mind
133– 6 acknowledge God, and be o· ;
133–16 o· more round of old Sol
137–15 except in o· or two instances,
137–28 implicit confidence in each o·
143–10 o· and all of my beloved friends
145– 4 o· of Concord's best builders
150–11 hallowed by o· chord of C. S.,
153–32 up to the o· source, divine Life
155– 8 and that o· the God and Saviour
165–17 portion of o· stupendous whole,
167– 6 and unites us to o· another.
167–17 be o· acceptable in His sight,
169– 2 I invite you, o· and all,
178–26 not o· word in the book was effaced.
181–27 o· expositor of Daniel's dates
186–12 o· Father-Mother God,
187–15 love o· another." — I John 3 : 11.
187–28 "that ye love o· another." — John 15 : 12.
188–24 o· man's head lies at another's feet.
189–11 vibrating from o· pulpit to another
189–12 and from o· heart to another,
189–13 commingling in o· righteous prayer,
195–17 to use . . . the o· talent that we all
198– 6 great gratitude to our o· Father.
202–10 but to love o· another : — Rom. 13 : 8.
204– 0 in o· Principle, divine Love,
204–11 which makes them o· in Christ.
212–19 "with o· accord in o· place," — Acts 2 : 1.
213– 8 o· rancorous and lurking foe
213–27 chapter sub-title
214– 1 select o· only to place on the walls
215–10 dozen or upward in o· class.
217–25 "An improved belief is o· step
218–27 to o· no more than to another.

one

My. 223–23 of o· of the Church By-laws,
224–18 words, and classification of o· author
225–29 Mind, Soul, which combine as o·.
226– 9 are but an effect of o· universal cause,
226–10 the o· divine intelligent Principle
227– 3 as o· who never weakened
227–11 o· out of three of their patients,
228– 9 I fail to know how o· can be
228–31 such a o· was never called to
229– 5 cannot be found at Pleasant View o· of
230–10 apply not to o· member only,
230–10 but to o· and all equally.
231–20 o· woman is sufficient to
233–21 O· should watch to know
233–23 should o· watch against such a result?
233–31 Thinking of person implies that o·
235– 5 Straining at gnats, o· may swallow
235–20 is he matter or spirit? Neither o·.
236– 6 name for o· central Reading Room,
236–14 exchange the present name for the o·
239–15 identity as o· man and o· woman
239–17 God is o·, and His idea, image, or
239–17 image, or likeness, man, is o·.
239–18 and so includes all in o·.
239–21 the infinite o·, or o· infinite,
241–14 * issue raised is an important o·
241–14 * and o· upon which there should be
241–21 * idea of the o· divine Mind.
244– 7 o· or more lessons on C. S.,
244–24 may not require more than o· lesson.
249– 2 without harming any o·
252–11 to make o· not only know the truth
252–12 make o· enjoy doing right,
252–12 make o· not . . . run away in the storm,
253–17 that they may be o·, — John 17 : 11.
254– 1 become o· with his creator,
257–25 I group you in o· benison
258– 5 save o· lowly offering — love.
258–10 o· word, . . . broke the gloom
260–30 but o· Jesus Christ on record.
261– 7 continue thus with o· exception :
263– 2 leaving o· alone and without His glory.
266–15 This flux and flow in o· direction,
266–16 tends in o· ultimate
267– 1 the o· and the only religion
267–20 O· individual may first awaken
268–30 and you see male and female o·
269– 1 universe included in o· infinite Mind
269–12 * parts of o· stupendous whole,
272– 1 o· who steadfastly and actively
272– 2 o· who leavens the loaf of life
273–13 I for o· accept his wise deduction,
274–13 To begin rightly enables o· to end rightly,
274–14 that o· achieves the Science of Life,
275–28 unite in o· Te Deum of praise.
276– 3 as o· watches a criminal
276–19 * no o· should seek to dictate
292–17 prayers in which o· earnest, tender
292–20 effect of o· human desire
293– 5 o· against the other
301–10 unite as brethren in o· prayer :
303– 3 o· incarnation, o· Mother Mary.
303– 4 I know that I am not that o·,
305– 1 from o· P. P. Quimby
307–22 For o· so unlearned, he was
308–20 O· time when my father was visiting
309–14 justice of the peace at o· time.
312–14 * Her position was an embarrassing o·.
312–16 * only o· effort at self-support.
312–27 the remains of my beloved o·
313–19 evening walk, but I seldom took o·.
315–10 * happy home as o· could wish for.
316– 2 uniting in o· body those who
318–16 to visit o· of my classes
319–27 * considered the time an important o·
321– 6 * o· of your devoted and faithful
321– 7 * o· who knew who and what you are,
321–12 * told the same story to every o·
321–19 * to change my opinion o· iota
324– 7 * from any o· but yourself.
324– 9 * no o· could be of much service
324–28 * to see if there was o· woman
325– 2 * spoke of o· especial day
328– 8 * o· referred to in Miss Jones' letter :
333– 5 * found by o· of your own citizens,
334–14 * the woman . . . is some other o·?
335–27 * the case was o· of yellow fever
339– 6 and o· Christ Jesus.
341– 1 I have o· innate joy,
342–21, 22 all the churches, o· by o·,
343–24 each o· was the fruit of experience
343–26 I found at o· time that they had
344– 6 Christ is 'o· with the Father,'
356–22 either he will hate the o·, — Matt. 6 : 24.
356–23 else he will hold to the o·, — Matt. 6 : 24.

one

My.	356–25	infinite is *o·*, and this *o·* is Spirit ;
	362–15	* in *o·* place with *o·* accord,
	363–25	be sure that *o·* is not doing this,

(see also **Christ, church, day, Eddy, faith, God, Lord, Mind, mind, numbers, person, side, thing, values, year**)

one-hundredth

(see **numbers**)

one-in-all

My.	247– 1	all-in-one and *o·*.
	254–22	all-in-one and *o·*.

oneness

Mis.	93– 8	allness and *o·* of God
	131–12	upon the rock of divine *o·*,
	152– 5	the *o·* of God includes also
	259– 7	It is this infinitude and *o·*
	264–12	demands *o·* of thought and action.
	271– 8	C. S., — that rests on *o·* ;
	286– 9	man's *o·* with God,
	289–17	*O·* in spirit is Science,
Un.	24– 9	can never be outside of His *o·*.
	54–15	*at-one-ment*, or *o·* with God,
No.	1–19	in the divine *o·* of the trinity,
Pan.	7–16	absolute *o·* and infinity of God,
Peo.	13–11	unity of Mind and *o·* of Principle.
My.	338–24	recognize the *o·* of Jesus
	342–22	simplicity of the *o·* of God ;
	342–23	the *o·* of Christ and the perfecting
	356–27	This simple statement of *o·*

one's

Mis.	xi– 8	*o·* debt of gratitude to God,
	11–15	If *o·* life were attacked,
	12–16	*o·* temptations to sin are increased
	43–23	To fill *o·* pocket at the expense of
	107–23	*o·* oft-repeated violations of
	107–25	lack of seeing *o·* deformed mentality,
	109–14	*o·* sins be seen and repented of,
	109–27	consecrate *o·* life anew.
	112–26	inability to see *o·* own faults,
	117–28	He illumines *o·* way when one
	118–13	*o·* sympathy can neither atone for
	127–19	finds *o·* own in another's good.
	129– 5	*O·* first lesson is to learn
	130–23	Where . . . *o·* acts are right,
	148–13	impelled by a power not *o·* own,
	221–20	saps *o·* understanding of the
	236–25	notwithstanding *o·* good intentions,
	236–26	in *o·* efforts to help another,
	238–19	Let *o·* life answer well
	290–25	hold a place in *o·* memory,
	310–18	*o·* connection with this church,
	374–27	Pictures are portions of *o·* ideal,
	374–28	this ideal is not *o·* personality.
Man.	3– 9	a power not *o·* own,
Ret.	27–21	ripples in *o·* first thoughts of it
	67– 2	hence *o·* concept of error is
	72– 5	*o·* ability to do good,
	74– 1	*o·* sense of corporeality,
	75–10	*o·* writings on ethics,
	75–16	If *o·* spiritual ideal is comprehended
Rud.	1–17	in distinction from *o·* appearance
No.	2–24	destroys *o·* ability to heal
	5–28	the last state of *o·* patients
Pan.	9–21	It loves *o·* neighbor as
'00.	3–10	*O·* idol is by no means his servant,
'02.	2– 6	on the tablet of *o·* own heart,
Hea.	12–28	dishonest and divide *o·* faith
	15–12	any *o·* perfect satisfaction
Peo.	9– 7	may declare *o·* belief ;
My.	18–16	finds *o·* own in another's good."
	87–27	* whatever *o·* special creed may be,
	105– 6	prove *o·* faith by his works.
	117–10	will break *o·* own dream
	118–19	*O·* voluntary withdrawal from society
	122– 5	in *o·* own moral make-up.
	161–25	because *o·* thought and conduct
	213–15	Unless *o·* eyes are opened to
	234– 3	absorbing *o·* time writing or reading
	249–11	for *o·* own destruction.

(see also **enemies, self**)

ones

Mis.	11–10	teaching the wayward *o·*
	127– 2	His "little *o·*," — *Matt.* 18 : 6.
	130–26	God's "little *o·*." — *Matt.* 18 : 6.
	137–17	dear *o·*, if you take my advice
	231–10	groan for the unfeasted *o·*.
	275–12	the motherless little *o·*,
	317– 9	The dear *o·* whom I would
	329– 8	putting down the green *o·*,
Ret.	90– 8	there taught a few hungry *o·*,
	90– 9	To these selected *o·* . . . he gave
Pul.	4–15	Each of Christ's little *o·*
	45–17	* upon the hopeful, trustful *o·*,

ones

Pul.	81–12	* Some of her dearest *o·*
'00.	8–27	through one of His little *o·*,
Hea.	17–22	are supposed physical *o·*,
Po.	17– 4	My loved *o·* in glory
	65– 4	A meeting with loved *o·*
	67– 9	memory of dear *o·* deemed dead
My.	17–30	His 'little *o·*,' — *Matt.* 18 : 6.
	38–19	* the little *o·* were not a whit behind
	53–31	* by having so many different *o·*
	90–13	* in pain or death for self or dear *o·*.
	127–24	garrisoned by God's chosen *o·*,
	163– 9	beloved *o·* who have so kindly
	166–22	my dear *o·*, let us together sing
	167–19	Give to all the dear *o·* my love,
	186– 4	May God's little *o·*
	256–23	Parents call home their loved *o·*,
	356–16	*o·* . . . presented in S. and H.

onlooker

Pul.	45–15	* predictions of workman and *o·* alike

onlookers

Mis.	369–12	madness it seems to many *o·*.

Only

Mis.	173–17	preexisted in the All and *O·*
Ret.	60–12	God and His idea as the All and *O·*.
No.	25– 2	the All and *O·* of our being.

only

Mis.	1–19	*o·* by removing the dust
	3– 6	imparting the *o·* power to heal
	3–27	their *o·* supposed efficacy is in
	4– 9	Its *o·* power to heal is its power to
	5–23	those *o·* who do not understand
	6– 9	*o·* those cases that are pronounced
	8–28	can *o·* be fulfilled through the gospel's
	9–29	great and *o·* danger in the path
	11–15	and one could save it *o·* in
	13– 1	The *o·* justice of which I feel
	13–19	*o·* upon what the shifting mortal
	13–23	the existence of good *o·* ;
	13–25	Science *o·* needs to be conceded,
	14– 4	take in *o·* the immortal facts
	15–20	*O·* through the sore travail of
	18–13	Thou shalt love Spirit *o·*,
	18–15	as God's spiritual child *o·*,
	18–24	*O·* by admitting evil as a
	23–19	the first and *o·* cause.
	23–26	God is seen *o·* in that which
	25–19	Christianity is Christlike *o·* as it
	25–22	Jesus' *o·* medicine was omnipotent
	26– 5	*o·* logical conclusion is
	27–31	*o·* by first admitting that it is
	28– 1	*o·* to reappear in the spiritual
	28– 9	*o·* what mortal mind makes them ;
	29– 4	Had it been applicable *o·* to his
	29– 8	he prayed, not for the twelve *o·*,
	34– 5	is not *o·* healed of the disease, but
	35–21	*O·* because both are important.
	36– 8	*o·* cause is the eternal Mind,
	41– 1	brute-force that *o·* the cruel and
	42– 2	*does life continue in thought o·*
	42–23	*O·* as we understand God,
	42–25	exists *o·* in spiritual perfection,
	44–18	could *o·* have been a belief of pain
	46– 6	needs *o·* to be tested scientifically
	49–10	*o·* case that could be distorted into
	49–27	This belief presupposes not *o·* a
	52–18	*dream not dispelled, but o· changed,*
	53– 6	*o·* as we master error with Truth.
	53–14	You *o·* weaken your power to heal
	53–26	*o·* the thought educated away from
	55–24	knows that he can have one God *o·*,
	55–25	when he regards God as the *o·* Mind,
	56– 9	Life is God, the *o·* creator,
	56–22	Life needs *o·* to be understood ;
	59–22	*o·* benefit in speaking often
	59–28	divine Mind, who is the *o·* physician ;
	60– 7	*o·* as the woeful unrealities of being,
	60– 7	is the *o·* way to destroy them ;
	60–13	*departed friends — dead o· in belief?*
	62– 8	Man is seen *o·* in the true likeness
	64–18	the *o·* philosophy and religion
	64–29	The *o·* evidence of the existence of
	67–21	*O·* thus is the right practice of
	70– 3	I believe, not *o·*, but I *demonstrated*
	70– 6	*o·* explanation in divine metaphysics.
	70–25	*o·* in a finite and material sense
	71–31	law of Science, that God is good *o·*,
	72– 5	*o·* living and true origin, God.
	72–19	*disappear o· to the natural sense?*
	72–26	it exists *o·* to material sense.
	74– 3	new-born sense subdues not *o·* the
	77– 9	not *o·* acknowledge the incarnation,
	82–21	mortals see and comprehend *o·* as
	86–10	*exist o· in imagination?*

only

Mis.	88–23	* *o·* to those who do not enter into
	89–30	*o·* avail himself of the efficacy of
	93–16	sanctions *o·* what is supported by
	93–20	exists *o·* as fable.
	97–32	*o·* cause for making this question
	102– 4	is *o·* an infinite finite being,
	102–25	seems thus *o·* to the material senses,
	105–20	C. S. is my *o·* ideal ;
	106–20	I can *o·* bring crumbs fallen from
	106–29	affords the *o·* strains that thrill
	108–14	be conceived of *o·* as a delusion.
	108–24	needs *o·* to be known for what
	109–16	Ignorance is *o·* blest by reason of
	109–30	fear not sin, . . . but *o· fear to sin.*
	115– 8	*o·* as the result of sin ;
	115–26	every effort to hurt one will *o·* help
	115–32	mental power in the right direction *o·*,
	134–25	Error is *o·* fermenting,
	140–18	urged *o·* the material side
	151–14	He is man's *o·* real relative
	154–10	God *o·* waits for man's worthiness
	161–18	The *o·* record of our Master as a
	163–22	*O·* three years a personal Saviour !
	164–25	portrayed him as the *o·* Son of God,
	164–25	the *o·* begotten of the Father,
	168–12	*o·* such as are pure in spirit,
	172–26	peace can *o·* be declared on the
	179–21	*o·* come into the spiritual
	182– 3	putting him to death, *o·* in belief,
	184– 7	*o·* when man reflects God in body
	188–30	was the first, the *o·* man.
	191–29	could *o·* be possible as evil beliefs,
	194–13	*o·* needs the prism of this Science
	199– 3	*o·* mortal, erring mind can claim
	199– 7	amenable *o·* to moral and spiritual
	200–30	*o·* a vagary of mortal belief,
	201– 2	receives the mortal scoff *o·* because
	205–17	consciousness reflects *o·* Spirit,
	208– 6	He is cognizant *o·* of good.
	208–11	*o·* to submit to the law of God,
	218– 5	declares the invisible *o·* by
	222–20	cancelled *o·* through human agony :
	228–17	as the *o·* suitable fabric
	229– 9	If *o·* the people would believe
	229–12	if *o·* the pulpit would
	233– 7	but are such in name *o·*,
	233–28	they *o·* who adhere to that standard.
	234– 1	*o·* by reason of our belief in it
	237–21	*o·* work out its own destruction ;
	243–16	*o·* in proportion as he understands
	247–30	*o·* an evil belief of mortal mind,
	248–23	The opium falsehood has *o·* this to it :
	251–12	commemorate not *o·* our nation's
	252–17	C. S. is not *o·* the acme of Science
	256– 2	not *o·* cured of their belief in disease,
	258–20	*o·* suitable or true idea of Him ;
	259–14	the *o·* law of creation,
	259–18	the *o·* law of being.
	260–10	The divine Mind was his *o·*
	260–14	mortal thought holds *o·* in itself
	261– 5	can *o·* be removed by reformation.
	261– 8	C. S. not *o·* elucidates but
	263– 2	they will harm myself *o·*,
	269–19	Mind to be the *o·* physician.
	269–20	man can *o·* be Christianized through
	270–23	the *o·* passport to his power ;
	271–21	*o·* chartered College of Metaphysics.
	272– 7	* for metaphysical purposes *o·*,
	278–17	Those *o·* who are tried in the furnace
	280–16	then *o·* are we working on one side
	283–32	*o·* personal help required
	285– 1	in favor of combating evil *o·*,
	286–26	Spirit, God, is the *o·* creator :
	287–12	*o·* high and holy joy can satisfy
	288– 9	rash conclusion that regards *o·* one
	289– 4	*o·* temperance is total abstinence.
	289–32	whence they can choose *o·* good.
	290– 3	two persons *o·*, should be found
	295–20	should not *o·* be queried, but flatly
	299–15	is the *o·* absolute good ;
	299–17	is the *o·* absolute evil.
	301–14	require *o·* a word to be wise ;
	303– 2	need *o·* to shine from their home
	308–14	know its practicality *o·* by healing
	308–23	*o·* to reappear in due season.
	313–27	hereafter the *o·* pastor of
	315–11	can teach annually three classes *o·*.
	315–14	*o·* of such as have promising
	315–17	not *o·* through class term, but
	324–25	*o·* to find the lights all wasted
	325–14	*o·* to find its inmates asleep
	327–21	*o·* to take them up again,
	333–15	away from the *o·* living and true God,
	334–15	*o·* as one gives the lie to a lie ;
	334–17	*o·* then, do you handle it in Science.

only

Mis.	336–28	touches time *o·* to take away its
	337–24	*O·* the devout Marys,
	338–13	afford the *o·* rule I have found
	340– 6	*O·* by persistent, unremitting,
	345–15	* fit *o·* for women and weak men ;"
	346– 9	God created *o·* the good,
	347–30	*o·* authenticated organ of C. S.
	348–12	*o·* a question of time when God
	350– 8	The P. M. . . . Society met *o·* twice.
	350–29	teach the use of such arguments *o·*
	352–28	*o·* difference between the healing of
	355–15	*o·* stimulates and gives scope to
	358– 6	*o·* appropriate seals for C. S.
	358–16	Christ's vestures are put on *o·* when
	358–24	*o·* College for teaching C. S.
	359–26	*o·* as we rise in the scale of being.
	360– 6	Great *o·* as good,
	361–24	God is the *o·* Mind,
	368–20	can *o·* be portrayed in these words
	368–24	*o·* for money, and at a fearful stake.
	375–28	* the *o·* true art
	382–21	obtained the first and *o·* charter
	382–23	was its first and *o·* president ;
	386–26	I *o·* know my wife, Thy child,
	389–10	Love is our refuge ; *o·* with mine eye
Man.	34–14	*o·* textbooks for self-instruction in
	35–20	can unite with this Church *o·* by
	37–23	*O·* members of The Mother Church
	42–21	C. S. can *o·* be practised according to
	43–18	This By-Law not *o·* calls more
	51–24	*O·* the members of this Board
	52– 3	Members in Mother Church *O·*.
	57– 8	Called *o·* by the Clerk.
	64– 5	literature sold or . . . shall consist *o·* of
	68–19	calls for his home . . . *o·* those
	80– 9	*o·* in accordance with the By-Laws
	81–25	*O·* the Publishing Society
	83–10	such *o·* as have good past records
	83–16	not *o·* during the class term but
	85– 1	occupies *o·* his own field of labor.
	86–24	chapter on "Recapitulation" *o·*.
	91–13	*O·* the President gives free
	92–22	*O·* those persons who are members
	99–17	elected *o·* by the C. S. Board
	104– 3	For The Mother Church *O·*.
	104– 7	is adapted to The Mother Church *o·*.
	110–13	Initials *o·* of first names will not
Ret.	14–24	I could *o·* answer him in the words of
	15– 9	even of Thine *o·*. — *Psal.* 71 : 16.
	19– 6	spared to me for *o·* one brief year.
	21–27	To this end, but *o·* to this end,
	23–20	*o·*, "among ten thousand." — *Song* 5 : 10.
	24–19	I could *o·* assure him that the divine
	34–15	cures when they fail, or *o·* relieve ;
	34–17	A person healed by C. S. is not *o·*
	43– 6	It is the *o·* College, hitherto,
	43–20	the *o·* asisstant teachers in the
	44–14	to preach *o·* occasionally,
	45– 7	requisite *o·* in the earliest periods
	49–20	*o·* one ever granted to a *legal college*
	55– 5	can *o·* be overcome with good.
	59–18	the *o·* living and true God,
	60–24	C. S. is the *o·* sure basis
	61–22	it is in the mortal mind *o·*,
	63– 2	God and His idea are the *o·* realities,
	65–26	constitute the *o·* evangelism,
	69–14	*o·* a transient, false sense of
	73–17	This is the *o·* way whereby
	83–19	should explain *o·* Recapitulation,
	84–27	take charge *o·* of his own pupils
	85–22	awaiting *o·* an opportunity
	87–25	it is *o·* through the lens of
	94–25	I am persuaded that *o·* by the
Un.	3– 4	they awake *o·* to another sphere of
	3–20	Hence He is in Himself *o·*,
	4–24	knowledge of the *o·* true God,
	9–18	as the *o·* true solution of
	15–20	become *o·* an echo of the divine ?
	17– 1	has *o·* one chance of successful
	18– 4	*o·* the brightness of My own glory.
	19–16	evil is *o·* a delusive deception,
	21– 8	and good *o·* is reality.
	21–20	this is the *o·* consciousness
	23– 8	Truth knows *o·* such.
	23–23	conceive of God *o·* as like itself,
	25– 7	only substance, the *o·* Mind.
	25–20	God, good, is the *o·* creator.
	25–23	Life, whose *o·* source is Spirit.
	27–14	knowing *o·* His own all-presence,
	28–17	we learn Soul *o·* as we learn God,
	29–10	the *o·* Mind and intelligence
	32– 6	Spirit is the *o·* creator,
	33– 4	give the *o·* pretended testimony
	33– 6	can *o·* testify from their own
	33–14	is *o·* matter within the skull,

only

Un.	33–15	believed to be mind o· through error
	34– 4	Mortal mind admits that it sees o·
	35–26	Spirit is the o· creator.
	36– 1	o· as it adds lie to lie.
	37– 1	Jesus not o· declared himself
	40– 2	It is mortality o· that dies.
	43–13	I insist o· upon the fact,
	44– 3	I can o· repeat the Master's words :
	46–15	o· as spiritual and good,
	49–12	the o· living God
	50– 4	o· as I believe in evil,
	50–11	matter is o· a phenomenon of
	51–23	full Truth is found o· in
	53–10	o· the evil belief that renders them
	57–28	o· conscious existence in the flesh
	59–16	o· through this conformity to mortal
	61–19	O· faith and a feeble understanding
	62–10	Mortals can understand this o· as
	62–14	Sin exists o· as a sense,
	64– 6	conscious of o· health, holiness, and
Pul.	vii– 7	to have not o· a record of
	8–13	o· the need made known,
	21– 4	that loves o· because it *is* Love.
	21–18	to o· that which is Christlike,
	21–30	O· what feeds and fills the sentiment
	34– 2	* who lived o· a year.
	34–27	"the Bible was my o· textbook.
	35–10	o· the 'pure in heart' — *Matt.* 5 : 8.
	39–25	* 'mid them all I o· see *one* face,
	40– 1	* Ah, love ! I o· know
	45– 5	* Christian Scientists not o· say
	46–10	* can o· be touched upon in this
	49–10	* "You have lived here o· four years,
	49–13	o· two and a half years."
	51–28	* o· aspire to take its place alongside
	54–24	* permitting o· the father and mother,
	58–25	* o· pastor shall be the Bible,
	66– 5	* with a membership of o· twenty-six,
	75– 9	statement would not o· be false,
	75–26	* o· combustible material used in
	80–27	* the invisible is the o· real world,
	84–20	* o· the future will tell the story
	88– 8	append o· a few of the names
Rud.	2–24	It is o· the bugle-call to thought and
	4– 6	o· of *Divine or C. S.?*
	4–17	Good is not in evil, but in God o·.
	4–18	not in matter, but in Spirit o·.
	4–18	not in matter, but in Mind o·.
	4–22	we can o· learn and love Him through
	5–18	Soul is the o· real consciousness
	5–28	exist in Mind o· ;
	7–15	o· true evidence of the being
	8– 9	o· an epitome of the Principle,
	9–27	the producer o· of good,
	10– 8	material laws are o· human beliefs,
	10–27	o· a lack of understanding
	14– 2	giving o· a portion of their time
	14–10	The o· pay taken for her labors
	14–15	o· from those who were able to pay.
	15–19	O· a very limited number of students
No.	1– 5	o· as our natures are changed by its
	1–21	the o· Mind-healing I vindicate ;
	3– 3	at the idea which claims o· its
	4–26	disease must be — and can o· be
	6– 6	that God is the o· creator,
	12– 1	C. S. Mind-healing can o· be
	20–11	Principle is found to be the o· term
	20–22	o· power, presence, and glory.
	24–12	not o· as real as good, but
	31–13	as the o· full proof of its pardon.
	35–21	God is the o· Mind,
	35–24	announcing Truth, and saying not o·
	36–13	was conscious o· of God,
	38– 6	He established the o· true idealism
	38– 8	o· true philosophy and realism.
	38–20	includes o· His own nature,
	40–17	o· the wrongs of mankind.
	40–19	O· when sickness, sin, and fear
	40–27	made better o· by divine influence.
	43– 8	* "O· He who knows all things
Pan.	8–11	the o· prophet of God
	13–26	o· traversed my subject that you may
'00.	3–18	O· the good man loves the right
	4–16	the o· perfect religion is divine Science,
	6– 2	O· the demonstrator can mistake
	6–15	The child not o· accepts C. S.
	10–23	O· last week I received a touching token
	11–17	I want not o· quality, quantity, and
	14–19	charity that seeketh not o· her own,
'01.	2–25	O· a firm foundation in Truth
	3–26	and expresses God o· in metaphor,
	8–26	Jesus, the o· immaculate,
	9– 5	o· generating or regenerating power.
	10–10	son of man o· in the sense that
	12– 8	That is Johnism, and o· Johnites

only

'01.	12–19	o· needs the prism of divine Science,
	13– 4	this is the o· annihilation.
	13– 8	o· an assumption that nothing is
	13–23	o· as the sin is removed
	13–24	o· as it is destroyed,
	14–10	o· departure from ecclesiasticism
	18–15	discerned o· through divine Science.
	23– 4	If Christian Scientists o· would admit
	23–28	* "o· the constant relation between
	24– 5	matter is o· an impression produced
	26– 5	o· on Christ, Truth,
	26– 7	five personal senses can have o· a
	28– 4	It is o· by praying, watching, and
	28–18	my o· apology for trying to follow
	30– 4	o· the bequeathing of itself
	31– 3	The o· opposing element
	34–25	o· so far as she follows Christ.
'02.	1–17	o· with material observation,
	2– 1	o· the earnest, honest investigator
	3–27	right is the o· real potency ;
	3–27	o· true ambition is to serve God
	4– 4	o· so far as she follows Christ.
	13– 3	Christ and our Cause my o· incentives,
	14– 2	o· interest I retain in this property
	14–10	* But o· great as I am good."
	14–11	The o· genuine success possible for any
	14–12	the o· success I have ever achieved
	17–22	o· what God gives,
	18– 7	o· to mock, wonder, and perish.
Hea.	6–21	mind of the individual o· can
	8–23	we shall receive o· what we have
	9–21	o· correct answer to the question,
	11– 9	o· immortal superstructure is built on
	12–27	o· objection to giving the
	13–16	using o· the sugar of milk ;
	13–20	Mind as the o· curative Principle.
	16–17	The o· evidence we have of sin,
Peo.	2–16	make a Christian o· in theory,
	9–16	destroyed o· through suffering.
	12– 5	The o· law of sickness or death
	12–12	acknowledge o· God in all thy ways,
	13–23	* "Christianity is fit o· for women
Po.	4– 9	Love is our refuge ; o· with mine eye
	42– 6	were o· a name !
	50–12	I o· know my wife, Thy child,
My.	vi– 9	* Christian Scientists are honest o· as
	vi–27	* o· a place for the publishing of
	3–15	nor a . . . that heals o· the sick.
	4–10	follow Truth o· as we follow truly,
	9– 7	* gratitude which not o· impels
	12–21	we possess o· *now.*
	13–29	not o· to my church but to Him who
	20–12	o· what God gives to His church.
	21– 7	* course suggested will not o· hasten the
	23–24	* rising, not o· to faith but also to
	30– 6	* Not o· did these include Scientists
	36–21	* dedicated to the o· true God,
	41–27	* not o· discovered C. S., but
	42–23	* an infinite good unfolds in each
	45–10	* represent o· a small part of the
	46–18	* O· as we pledge ourselves anew to
	52–23	* if o· through her work Truth may be
	55– 9	* not o· was the attendance rapidly
	58–12	* not o· shows the growth of this Cause,
	60–10	* o· expressed the thought of all the
	70– 4	* been organized o· thirty years,
	70– 5	* its first church o· twelve years ago,
	74–19	* satisfaction that is not o· evident
	76–11	* o· feebly expresses the gratification.
	77– 8	* as its dimensions are o· half as great.
	86–13	* Not o· was every cent of the
	88–19	* o· a slight and material development
	89– 9	* needs o· an open space about it,
	90–14	* it is not the o· source of appeal.
	93–20	* Too often we see o· its
	96–14	* reached o· through intelligent and
	100–11	* It is o· twenty-five years,
	103–25	Bible has been my o· authority.
	105– 3	man's o· medicine for mind and body
	108–15	Mind is the o· lawgiver,
	112–10	founded . . . o· on the Scriptures.
	115– 7	I was o· a scribe echoing the
	117–26	o· in the right direction !
	118– 4	O· the disobedient
	118–23	credited o· by human belief,
	121–24	not o· polite to all but is
	122– 5	glory o· is imperishable which
	124–14	waiting o· your swift hands,
	125– 3	not o· sayers but doers of the law?
	125–11	I have o· to dip my pen in my heart
	126–31	We have it o· as we live it.
	127– 5	ask o· to be judged according to
	129–29	o· as they include the spirit
	130– 9	seeking o· public notoriety,
	132–28	Divine Love is our o· physician,

only

My. 141–23 seats *o·* five thousand people,
142– 4 * *o·* abolished the disappointment
149– 5 We know Principle *o·* through Science.
152–14 worship *o·* Spirit and spiritually,
153– 4 if these kind hearts will *o·* do this in
159–16 this is the *o·* right activity,
159–21 *o·* legitimate and eternal demands
160–30 *O·* the makers of hell burn in
161–29 *O·* he who learns through meekness
164–17 not *o·* possess a sound faith, but
170–15 *o·* that this gift is already yours.
173–31 not *o·* to use the beautiful lawn
174–25 To-day my soul can *o·* sing and soar.
180–18 *o·* thus, does it overcome evil
181– 5 are aided *o·* at long intervals with
187–23 the worship of the *o·* true God.
190–11 not *o·* equalling but vastly excelling
194– 1 *o·* that which Christianity writes in
194–10 *O·* those men and women
195–17 is our *o·* means of adding to
198– 7 not *o·* the continuance of His favors,
201– 5 Satan is unchained *o·* for a season,
203–13 Be great *o·* as good.
204– 7 It is *o·* by looking heavenward
210–10 not *o·* yourselves are safe, but
210–16 His thoughts can *o·* reflect peace,
210–20 and *o·* denounce error in general,
213–27 chapter sub-title
214– 1 select one *o·* to place on the walls of
224–10 helpful or dangerous *o·* in proportion to
224–31 * "They also serve who *o·* stand and
226– 2 *o·* where you can substitute the
230– 8 digested *o·* when Soul silences the
230–10 Its rules apply not to one member *o·*,
231– 3 for such purposes *o·* as God indicates.
234– 5 they *o·* cloud the clear sky,
234–18 when regarded on one side *o·*,
237–10 wise to accept *o·* my teachings
238– 7 *o·* be determined by personal proof.
248– 6 * But *o·* great as I am good."
248–20 You soar *o·* as uplifted by God's
249–14 all this *o·* to satiate its loathing of
250–19 applies *o·* to C. S. churches
251–15 taught in the Board of Education *o·*.
251–27 *o·* to convince yourselves of this grand
252–11 not *o·* know the truth but live it
259–17 churches will remember me *o·* thus.
259–30 Soul recognized *o·* in harmony,
267– 1 one and first *o·* religion
268–21 I can *o·* solace the sore ills of
272–23 * Not *o·* Mrs. Eddy's own devoted
273–22 *o·* by the spiritual understanding
280–18 *o·* because of oft speaking,
283–26 Human law is right *o·* as it
284–22 *o·* as other churches had done.
287–15 In love for man we gain the *o·*
288–16 Mind was his *o·* instrumentality
301–21 *o·* so many well-defined instances
303–12 of which I have seen *o·* extracts,
306–10 false should be antagonized *o·* for
307–19 I concluded that he *o·* referred to
308– 7 *o·* by ease, pleasure, or recompense.
308–29 Bible was the *o·* book in his house.
309–30 * supplied the *o·* social diversions,
312–16 * made *o·* one effort at self-support.
313–13 I *o·* know that my father
318– 6 for *o·* two of my books.
319– 3 *o·* real man in His image
329– 6 * The board *o·* excused them from
332–10 * accompany her *o·* to New York,
339–22 *o·* those who have not the Christ,
345–12 *o·* false science — healing by drugs.
345–31 * some *o·* of which are
349–27 *o·* as it is spiritual,
349–29 *o·* as it makes manifest the infinite
352–20 I thank you not *o·* for your tender
354–21 Give us not *o·* angels' songs,
356–27 *o·* . . . . correct version of C. S.
357– 1 He is the *o·* basis of Science ;
357– 2 apart from C. S., and is *o·*
357– 8 *o·* incentive of a mistaken sense
357–18 *o·* as they build upon the rock
357–23 not *o·* the axiom of true C. S.,
357–24 *o·* basis upon which this Science
363–27 practise *o·* to heal.
(*see also* **Life, substance**)

Ontario
(*see* **Ottawa**)

Ontology
Man. 47– 9 *O·*, or the Science of being.

onward
Mis. 233– 9 *o·* march of life-giving Science,
343– 9 move it *o·* and upward.
Pul. 7–21 stumble *o·* to their doom ;

onward
Pul. 44– 9 * blessed *o·* work of C. S.
'02. 11–15 helped *o·* by a new-old message
Po. 19– 4 *o·* and upward and heavenward borne.
My. 10–29 * now necessitates this *o·* step.
140–19 God is leading you *o·* and upward.
155–12 *o·* march of Truth,
202–17 *o·* and upward chain of being.
258–29 may you move *o·* and upward,
272– 5 pushes *o·* the centuries ;
282–11 nations are helped *o·* towards
355–24 their way is *o·*, and their light

onyx
Pul. 26–26 * mantel is of *o·* and gold.
76–14 * superb mantel of Mexican *o·*

opal
Mis. 376–28 diamond, topaz, *o·*, garnet,

opaque
Mis. 347–11 peer through the *o·* error.

ope
Ret. 18–11 And *o·* their closed cells
Po. 63–22 And *o·* their closed cells

open
Mis. 92– 9 *o·* fount of Truth and Love.
147–29 no path but the fair, *o·*, and direct
174–10 *o·* our affections to the Principle
180–14 *o·* door from this sepulchre
183–16 if he *o·* his mouth it shall be filled
196– 9 so-called mind shall *o·* your eyes
212–25 *o·* his eyes to see this error?
275–18 *o·* the prison to them that are bound,
280–31 doors of animal magnetism *o·* wide
281– 3 this animal element flings *o·*
282–11 our houses broken *o·* or our locks
283–11 wrong to burst *o·* doors
292–15 away from the *o·* sepulchres of sin,
314– 7 *o·* the meeting by reading the hymns,
317–28 divine Love will *o·* the way
323–14 masters their secret and *o·* attacks
325–18 with eyes half *o·*, the porter starts
326– 6 The door is burst *o·*,
332– 7 doors that closed . . . are *o·* flung.
347– 6 escape from their houses to the *o·*
366–17 humanity needs to get her eyes *o·*
Man. 90– 9 Metaphysical College will *o·*
Chr. 55–26 *o·* the door, — *Rev.* 3 : 20.
Ret. 6– 6 one with the *o·* hand.
64–26 mortals must first *o·* their eyes to
71– 2 *o·* the gates of heaven.
84– 6 *o·* fount of Truth and Love.
Un. 56– 8 "put him to an *o·* shame." — *Heb.* 6 : 6.
'00. 9– 9 secret of C. S. . . . is *o·* to mankind,
'02. 14–29 afford an *o·* field and fair play.
16–17 they *o·* the enigmatical seals
My. 31–10 * doors of the church were thrown *o·*
36–14 * withheld from *o·* graves or
72– 5 * chapter sub-title
72– 6 * gates of Boston are *o·* wide
73–18 * *o·* to visitors this forenoon
77–27 * *o·* its doors absolutely free of
89– 9 * needs only an *o·* space about it,
110–21 *o·* the prison doors
126– 9 has in his hand a book *o·*
131–27 *o·* you the windows — *Mal.* 3 : 10.
132– 4 *o·* you the windows — *Mal.* 3 : 10.
160–16 *o·* their hearts to it for actual
174– 2 throwing *o·* their doors
188– 6 mine eyes shall be *o·*, — *II Chron.* 7 : 15.
212– 6 older and more *o·* sins,
221–29 wide *o·* to the intruding disease,
256–13 *o·* the volume of Life
261–23 Christmas involves an *o·* secret,
269–27 *o·* you the windows — *Mal.* 3 : 10.
289– 2 God's *o·* secret is seen through grace,
312–30 I did *o·* an infant school,
357–19 This will *o·* the way,
(*see also* **eyes**)

opened
Mis. 24–11 *o·* it at Matthew ix. 2.
30–18 *o·* the door to the captive,
57–19 your eyes shall be *o·*, — *Gen.* 3 : 5.
149– 9 one after another has *o·* his lips
253–29 *o·* their eyes to the light of C. S.?
274– 3 when I *o·* my College.
371– 5 *o·* his eyes to see the need of
Ret. 23–14 When the door *o·*, I was waiting
Un. 44–21 your eyes shall be *o·* — *Gen.* 3 : 5.
Pul. 14–11 earth *o·* her mouth, — *Rev.* 12 : 16.
30–26 * *o·* with twenty-six members,
No. 7–10 eyes of sinful mortals must be *o·*
'02. 9–24 *o·* my closed eyes.
Hea. 19–10 a vein had not been opened,
My. 31–18 * *o·* by the Scientists in Boston
39– 3 * meeting was *o·* by the President.

opened
My.	47–26	* o· an era of Christian worship
	54–26	* October 18, . . . the rooms were o·
	94–19	* doors were o· to the public,
	97–21	* o· the eyes of the country
	132–12	Divine Love hath o· the gate
	172–23	* was o· the following day
	213–15	Unless one's eyes are o· to

openeth
Pan.	12–12	The altitude of Christianity o·,
'00.	14–21	o· and no man shutteth,— *Rev.* 3: 7.
	14–22	shutteth and no man o· ;''— *Rev.* 3: 7.
My.	42– 3	* ''she o· her mouth— *Prov.* 31: 26.

opening
Mis.	101–18	o· the doors for them that are
	124–15	o· the prison doors
	132– 4	token that heavy lids are o·,
	250–27	gentle hand o· the door
	256–19	notice . . . previous to the o· term.
	262–20	o· the prison doors
	269–29	o· of this silent mental seal,
	280– 4	o· of the seals,
	307–17	God's love o· the eyes of
Un.	41–17	o· wide the portal from death
Pul.	27– 6	* o· from it are three large
	60–19	* was not ready for the o·.
'02.	16–22	o· not his mouth in self-defense
My.	29–20	* edifice whose formal o·
	29–29	* for the o· of the doors
	30– 6	* people who witnessed the o·.
	31–29	* o· of the dedicatory service.
	54–24	* from the first . . . to our o·,
	88– 4	* o· of their great new temple.
	97–19	* o· of the new Mother Church
	174– 7	o· their spacious club-house
	201–28	o· of your new church
	270–27	o· the eyes of the blind
	300–31	Are the churches o· fire on

openly
Mis.	81– 3	scholarly physicians o· admit.
	133–17	reward thee o·.''— *Matt.* 6: 6.
	133–26	He will reward ''o·.''— *Matt.* 6: 6.
	349–21	students have o· acknowledged this.
No.	39–11	He has rewarded them o·.

opens
Mis.	17–18	o· to the enraptured understanding
	161–19	record . . . o· when he was thirty
	185–11	o· the very flood-gates of heaven ;
	185–19	o· the gates of paradise
	196–20	o· wide the portals of salvation
	210–29	Love o· the eyes of the blind,
Rud.	8–21	o· a way whereby, through
My.	236–18	o· wide on the amplitude of liberty
	254– 2	heaven o·, right reigns,

operated
Pul.	54– 6	* Jesus o· in perfect harmony with

operates
My.	353–16	Science that o· unspent.

operatic
Man.	61–19	The music . . . shall not be o·,

operation
Mis.	205– 9	o· of the spirit of Truth
	244– 4	even a ''surgical o·''
	347–25	diversities of o· by the same spirit.
	352–19	malicious mental o· must be understood
Chr.	55–13	the o· of His hands.— *Isa.* 5: 12.
Ret.	26–16	o· of the divine law.
	40–15	injury received from a surgical o·
Un.	20–19	the knowledge and the o· of sin,
Pul.	60– 4	* new order of service went into o·.

operations
Ret.	70– 3	origin and o· of mortal mind,
Rud.	11–27	nervous o· of the human frame.
'01.	23–29	* by the o· of the universal mind,
My.	11–29	* date for commencing building o·.
	14–25	* building o· have been commenced,
	232–22	''A knowledge of error and of its o·

operative
Mis.	177– 7	Christ, as expressed and o· in C. S.
	207– 5	recognition of practical, o· C. S.
Ret.	85– 6	any other organic o· method
Pul.	35– 8	* a law as o· in the world to-day

opinion
Mis.	7–13	of what can mortal o· avail?
	34–14	speculative o· and human belief.
	49– 9	o· given to her friends,
	197–13	It means more than an o·
	237– 2	olden o· that hell is fire
	265–11	have but one o· of it.
Un.	5– 7	mental struggles and pride of o·
	5–10	not to accept any personal o·
Pul.	vii–10	in the glass of the world's o·.

opinion
Pul.	57–15	* whatever difference of o·
	80–17	* we have no o· to pronounce,
No.	29–17	impute such doctrines to mortal o·
Pan.	2–14	pantheism as a human o·
'01.	21–12	clergyman gives it as his o·
	22–18	to accommodate popular o·
My.	88– 1	* chapter sub-title
	219–26	I have expressed my o· publicly
	316–22	* ''twentieth-century review of o·''
	320–26	* I am of the o· that he
	321–19	* to change my o· one iota

opinions
Mis.	x–16	o· of men and the progress
	3–15	No o· of mortals nor
	17– 9	human o· and doctrines,
	64–20	speculative o· and fables.
	86–13	indefinite and vague human o·,
	92–25	The o· of men cannot be
	148–11	They were not arbitrary o·
	156–15	student's o· or *modus operandi*
	168– 5	halting between two o·
	224–12	o·, ambitions, tastes,
	265– 8	Diverse o· in Science are
	288–30	People will differ in their o·
	372– 3	those human o· had not one
Man.	3– 7	They were not arbitrary o·
Ret.	65– 2	they must rest their o·
	78– 8	and not by human o·;
	84–14	The o· of men cannot be
Pan.	11– 8	the o·, systems, doctrines,
'02.	1–16	systems of religious beliefs and o·
Hea.	6– 6	o· of people fly too high
My.	74–31	* Whatever o· we may entertain
	93– 7	* if their o· seem visionary,
	148–26	nor the o· of a sect
	273– 1	* it has no religious o·
	288–14	the travesties of human o·,

opium
Mis.	242–30	addicted to the use of o·
	248–16	That I take o· ; . . . is not more true
	248–23	The o· falsehood has only this

opium-eating
Mis.	242–20	will heal one single case of o·

opponent
My.	358– 8	this o· is the means whereby

opponents
No.	9– 9	let your o· alone,

opportunities
Mis.	112– 8	given new o·, will improve them.
	176–26	Are we duly aware of our own great o·
	213–10	to neglect o· which God giveth,
Hea.	19–19	affords him fresh o· every hour ;
My.	267–23	bitter sense of lost o·

opportunity
Mis.	x– 4	The o· has at length offered itself
	11–20	but to do them good whenever o· occurs.
	11–24	If special o· for doing good
	13–26	afford o· for proof of its
	131–23	delights in the o· to
	137–12	such o· might have been improved ;
	221– 4	o· to handle the error,
	225–15	Then was the clergyman's o·
	267–10	when I saw an o· really to help
	291–15	each and every one has equal o·
	319–24	o· for the grandest achievement
Man.	41–13	do good unto . . . when the o· occurs.
	67–24	O· for Serving the Leader.
	94–12	o· to depart in quiet *thought*
Ret.	50–27	o· for furnishing a new rule of
	85–22	awaiting only an o·
'00.	5– 4	leaves no o· for idolatry
'01.	20–11	o· to mislead the human mind,
'02.	13–22	giving o· for those who had
My.	11–20	* seized upon this privilege and o·,
	12–18	A lost o· is the greatest of losses
	42–15	* I desire to improve this o· to
	117–31	this o· is all that I ask of mankind.
	119–27	give you the o· of seeing
	134–12	not be eclipsed by some lost o·,
	148– 6	good folk of Concord have this o·,
	151– 8	o· for explaining C. S. :
	163–20	o· in Concord's quiet to revise our
	190–24	o· to become students of the Christ,
	204– 3	o· to use their hidden virtues,
	244– 4	those who wish to share this o·
	244–10	This o· is designed to impart a
	249– 3	Improve every o· to correct sin
	346– 5	* welcomes it as another o· for

oppose
Mis.	37– 9	In proportion as we o· the belief
	201– 5	o· bringing the qualities of Spirit

oppose

My.	345– 8	* Do you *o·* it?''
	345–26	''Oh, we cannot *o·* them.

opposed

Mis.	17– 2	spiritual law of Life, as *o·* to
	17– 4	as *o·* to the material sense of love ;
	17– 5	*o·* to any supposititious law
	48– 8	*o·* to it, as to every form of error,
	49–27	presupposes not only a power *o·* to
	56–15	human conception *o·* to the divine
	62–17	*o·* to which is the error of sickness,
	188– 1	teachings *o·* the doctrines of Christ
	198–25	material law, . . . as *o·* to good,
	198–28	belief in self-existent evil, *o·* to
	199–21	over the qualities *o·* to Spirit
	284–32	I am *o·* to all personal attacks,
Ret.	89– 3	*o·* to it by material motion,
Un.	22– 6	ungodliness, which is *o·* to Truth,
	38– 6	Death, then, is error, *o·* to Truth,
Pul.	13– 5	mortal belief in a power *o·* to God.
	38–22	* *o·* to the philosophy of Karma
No.	9–16	I have *o·* . . . strongly
	36–10	as wholly *o·* to the popular view
Pan.	3–22	It is *o·* to atheism and monotheism,
'01.	31– 4	Truth *o·* to all error,
Hea.	7– 7	spiritual meaning as *o·* to the
	14–27	*o·* to all that is wrong,
My.	279– 1	an element *o·* to Love,
	284–24	religiously *o·* to war,

opposes

Mis.	49–22	*o·* the leadings of the divine **Spirit**
	119–16	whatever or whoever *o·* evil,
Un.	39–15	which *o·* itself to God,
	56–15	which *o·* the law of Spirit ;

opposing

Mis.	335–12	for *o·* the subtle lie,
Rud.	16–24	certain *o·* factions, springing up
'01.	31– 3	The only *o·* element that
My.	4–17	found that, instead of *o·*,
	293–22	possessed no *o·* element,

opposite (noun)

absolute
My.	357– 7	absolute *o·* of spiritual means,

always the
Mis.	374– 6	always the *o·* of what it was.

diametrical
Mis.	220–18	diametrical *o·* of what it was

direct
Mis.	56–12	direct *o·* of immortal Life,

elementary
Mis.	260–18	elementary *o·* to Him

God has no
No.	5– 6	God has no *o·* in Science.

God's
Mis.	181–29	not of God's *o·*, — evil,

good's
Mis.	14–24	good's *o·*, has no Principle,
	46– 5	good's *o·*, is unreal.

His
Un.	51–22	and not of His *o·*, evil.

its
Mis.	18–13	love Spirit only, not its *o·*,
	26–21	neither . . . produces its *o·*.
	27– 5	its *o·*, named matter,
	27–14	no species ever produces its *o·*.
	122–20	not educed from its *o·* :
	346–20	its *o·* is necessarily unreal.
Ret.	63–15	Its *o·*, nothing, named *evil*,
Un.	60–10	inharmony is its *o·*,
Rud.	7–22	cannot originate its *o·*,
No.	32–18	Hence its *o·*, named *evil*,
'01.	22–12	If Truth is true, its *o·*, error,
My.	235– 4	and not name its *o·*, error.

mortal
Ret.	73– 2	his mortal *o·* must be material,

no
'01.	22–13	Spirit is true . . . it hath no *o·* ;

of divine Science
My.	358– 7	is the *o·* of divine Science,

of goodness
Mis.	49–21	belief in the *o·* of goodness,
Un.	24– 2	sin the *o·* of goodness.

of Himself
Un.	41–24	God cannot be the *o·* of Himself.

of immortal man
Mis.	186–10	ultimates in the *o·* of *im*mortal man,

of life
My.	235– 2	the suppositional *o·* of life,

of man
Mis.	187– 9	*o·* of man, hence the unreality ;

of something
No.	32–17	nothing, or the *o·* of something.

opposite (noun)

of Spirit
Mis.	26–18	it is the very *o·* of Spirit,
Un.	32–19	saying, ''I am the *o·* of Spirit,
	36–12	matter is the *o·* of Spirit,

of Truth
Mis.	24–22	error, the *o·* of Truth ;
Ret.	69– 9	insists still upon the *o·* of Truth,
Un.	44–12	pretender taught the *o·* of Truth.

to the fact
Mis.	133– 5	ideas more *o·* to the fact.

very
Mis.	26–18	it is the very *o·* of Spirit,
	184– 1	the very *o·* of that Maker,
Un.	42–11	very *o·* of this error
My.	175–29	very *o·* of my real sentiments.

Mis.	33–29	mortal mind's *o·*, — the divine **Mind**.
	55–22	over their *o·*, or matter,
	188– 2	demonstrated the *o·*, Truth.
Un.	24– 1	is the *o·* of immortal Mind,
'00.	5– 7	*o·* of God — good — named devil — evil
'01.	23– 5	yet that God has an *o·*
Hea.	4–25	and the *o·* of it at another,

opposite (adj.)

Mis.	45–26	*o·* intelligence or mind termed evil.
	55– 9	*O·* to good, is the universal claim of
	57–17	The *o·* error said, ''I am true,''
	62– 3	*o·* image of man, a sinner,
	63– 9	*o·* triad, sickness, sin, and death.
	74–13	*o·* of that which mortals entertain :
	88–29	are *o·* modes of medicine.
	173–13	an *o·* so-called science,
	191–28	*o·* characters ascribed to him
	220– 3	and a false rule the *o·* way.
	280–11	nothing in the *o·* scale.
	292–18	to shut out all *o·* sense.
	293–13	against the *o·* claims of error.
	346–13	belief that there is an *o·* . . . to God.
	347–16	Take the *o·* direction !
	351–29	turns it into the *o·* channels.
	355– 3	presents two *o·* aspects,
	367–25	*o·* conclusion, that darkness
Ret.	57–27	such *o·* effects as good and evil,
	64– 9	any *o·* theory is heterodox
	64–10	even as the *o·* claim of evil is one.
	69–21	*o·* belief is the prolific source
Un.	36– 8	a knowledge of God from *o·* facts,
	38–19	The *o·* understanding of God
	49–17	two *o·* states of existence.
Rud.	3–21	establishes the *o·* manifestation
Pan.	10– 9	prevail over the *o·* notion
Hea.	14– 8	faith in an *o·* direction?
My.	159–20	by an *o·* attraction towards the
	179– 5	the second was an *o·* story,
	292–25	supposed to possess *o·* qualities
	292–26	and so to produce *o·* effects.
	348–24	never producing an *o·* effect,

oppositely

Hea.	15–19	acting *o·* to your prayer,

opposites

compounds and
'01.	22–11	are compounds and *o·* ;

direct
Mis.	34–26	direct *o·* as light and darkness.

excludes
Ret.	75–19	Science of Mind excludes *o·*,

fraught with
My.	258– 6	This period, so fraught with *o·*,

God's
'00.	5–29	in casting out God's *o·*,

His
'00.	4– 3	makes His *o·* as real and

its
Mis.	105–16	common sense of its *o·*

law of
Mis.	14–22	proven by the law of *o·*
	57–12	By the law of *o·*,
Un.	52–24	By the law of *o·*.

moral
Mis.	266– 4	when these sides are moral *o·*,

mysticism of
Pan.	13–25	with the mysticism of *o·*?

no greater
No.	13–19	No greater *o·* can be conceived

their
Un.	10–15	cannot . . . lapse into their *o·*,

these
Mis.	217–19	these *o·*, in suppositional unity
	364–23	these *o·* must either cooperate or
Ret.	68– 9	difference between these *o·*

Hea.	13– 3	work at *o·* and accomplish less

opposition
Mis.	80– 4	*o·* to unjust medical laws.
	135–11	conquers all *o·*, surmounts all
	197–29	a theory that is in *o·* to God,
Ret.	40–24	*o·* which C. S. encountered
	71– 8	in *o·* to the straight and narrow path
Un.	11– 7	in direct *o·* to human philosophy
	56–10	suffering from mentality in *o·* to
Pul.	50–23	* The *o·* against it from
'01.	31– 5	*o·* springs from the very nature of
'02.	1–18	met with *o·* and detraction ;
	10–27	*o·* to God and His power

oppressed
My.	215– 2	Though sorely *o·*, I was above

oppression
Mis.	246–15	another sharp cry of *o·*.
Pul.	83–14	* under the black flag of *o·*
'02.	3–26	mature into *o·* ;
Peo.	11–15	fears, that enforce new forms of *o·*,
Po.	27– 3	Bloated *o·* in its awful hour,
My.	285–10	Bloodshed, war, and *o·*

oppressions
Pul.	55–11	* prejudices, and *o·* of the past.

oppressive
Pul.	7–19	unmerciful, and *o·* priesthood
My.	29–30	* the inconveniences of an *o·* day.

opprobrious
My.	104–10	vented their hatred . . . in *o·* terms.

opprobrium
'01.	12–10	word Christian was anciently an *o·* ;

optics
No.	6–25	Astronomy, *o·*, acoustics, and

optimism
Mis.	119–18	either for pessimism or for *o·*,
My.	84–21	* *o·* and energy of its followers

optimistic
My.	99–11	* remarkably *o·* body of people,

oracle
'02.	17–27	this *o·* of years will put to flight
My.	188–14	your *o·*, under the wings of

oracles
Mis.	107– 3	not be mistaken for the *o·* of God.

oracular
My.	129–11	The *o·* skies, the verdant earth

oral
Mis.	220– 9	His mental and *o·* arguments

orally
Mis.	206–21	in word and deed, mentally and *o·*,

orange
Mis.	376–27	gold, *o·*, pink, crimson, violet ;

orator
My.	90– 4	* wooed by no eloquence of *o·*
	104– 4	St. Paul, the Mars' Hill *o·*,
	125–17	spirit of the Mars' Hill *o·*,

oratories
'01.	28–14	Catholic and Protestant *o·*.

orbit
Rud.	4–11	which holds the earth in its *o·*.
My.	182–22	launched the earth in its *o·*,
	226–11	holds the earth in its *o·*

orbits
Mis.	22–17	true thoughts revolve in God's *o·*:
	104–19	revolve in their own *o·*,

orchards
Ret.	4–15	*o·* of apples, peaches, pears,

ordain
Mis.	91– 5	to *o·* pastors and to dedicate
	158–29	as our churches *o·* ministers.
	313–26	I hereby *o·* the Bible, and
Man.	58– 5	*o·* the BIBLE, and S. AND H.

ordained
Mis.	90–21	*If not o·, shall the pastor*
	90–27	organization and *o·* priesthood.
	158– 5	requested you to be *o·*,
	158–14	you were bidden to be *o·*,
	158–29	Jesus was not *o·* as our
	244– 9	compliance to *o·* conditions.
	382–32	In 1895 I *o·* that the Bible,
Man.	18– 7	and was *o·* A. D. 1881.
Ret.	16–20	and was *o·* A. D. 1881.
	44– 8	and was *o·* in 1881,
	44– 9	five years before being *o·*.
	49–15	powers that are not *o·* of God,
Pul.	7–24	I have *o·* the Bible and the
	38– 3	* before being *o·* in this church,
	58–24	* their prime instructor has *o·*

ordained
Pul.	68– 2	* Mrs. Eddy . . . in 1881 was *o·*,
	86–29	* have already *o·* as our pastor.
My.	37– 1	* *o·* the way of salvation

ordains
Ret.	85–17	whereto you do not feel that God *o·* you.

ordeal
Mis.	1– 9	the *o·* of a perfect Christianity,
	42–13	passed the *o·* called death,
	43–19	the great *o·* of this century.
	126–13	*o·* refines while it chastens.

order
adherent of the
Pul.	59–19	* not an adherent of the *o·*,

and harmony
Pan.	6–14	*o·* and harmony of God's creation.

and truth
Mis.	215–12	C. S. demands *o·* and truth.

decree and
Mis.	380–29	by decree and *o·* of the Court,

divine
		(*see* **divine**)

from Mrs. Eddy
Man.	66–25	an *o·* from Mrs. Eddy

highest
Ret.	7– 8	* highest *o·* of intellectual powers,
My.	96– 5	* highest *o·* of intelligence,

law and
		(*see* **law**)

lower
Peo.	13– 2	hence a lower *o·* of humanity,
	13– 4	a lower *o·* of Christianity

mathematical
Mis.	57–28	stated in mathematical *o·*,

no mean
My.	30–13	* at personal sacrifices of no mean *o·* ;

notice or
My.	73– 2	* to issue a similar notice or *o·*,

of being
Mis.	104–23	divine law and *o·* of being.
Un.	40–11	in the divine *o·* of being.

of divine Science
Mis.	181–22	the *o·* of divine Science.

of ministration
Ret.	92– 5	His *o·* of ministration was

of reading
Man.	32– 1	*O·* of Reading.

of Science
Mis.	99–13	voice a higher *o·* of Science
	181– 9	tend to obscure the *o·* of Science,
	205–22	This *o·* of Science is the chain of
Un.	56–13	In the divine *o·* of Science

of service
Pul.	28–14	* heading
	28–15	* *o·* of service in the C. S. Church
	60– 3	* the new *o·* of service
My.	32–12	* *o·* of service was as follows :

of the services
My.	16–21	* The *o·* of the services,

of wisdom
Mis.	287–18	In the *o·* of wisdom,

perfect
Pul.	49–30	* grounds and farm in perfect *o·*,

prescribed
Ret.	85–15	by any deviation from the *o·* prescribed

rule of
Ret.	50–27	new rule of *o·* in divine Science,

spiritual
Ret.	10–16	Syntax was spiritual *o·* and unity.

their
Mis.	10–15	countermand their *o·*, retrace their

uncommon
Mis.	95–18	phenomena of an uncommon *o·*,

written
Man.	65–16	any written *o·*, signed by

Mis.	21–23	The *o·* of this sentence has been
	58–22	no *o·* that proceeds from
	131– 5	in *o·* rightly to discern darkness
	137– 3	your badge, and *o·* of exercise,
	158–27	*o·* therein given corresponds to
	165–32	*o·*, mode, and virgin origin of man
	276– 8	not big enough to fill the *o·* ;
	310–17	decently and in *o·*." — *I Cor.* 14 : 40.
	329– 7	sets the earth in *o·* ;
Man.	27– 5	shall *o·* no special action to be
	80– 7	hold this money subject to the *o·* of
	80– 9	authorized to *o·* its disposition
Ret.	87– 3	* "*O·* is heaven's first law,"
Pul.	75–16	* TO THE FOUNDER OF THE *O·*
Po.	vi–18	by *o·* of *Governor Andrew*,
My.	43– 6	* *o·* aright the affairs of daily life.
	141– 6	* by *o·* of Mrs. Mary Baker Eddy.

order in — that
Mis.	279–25	in *o·* that the walls might fall ;
	305–28	* In *o·* that the bell
Ret.	64–27	in *o·* that the illusion, error,
'01.	7–22	in *o·* that belief may attend their
My.	78– 2	* in *o·* that all might participate
	190–23	Bible was written in *o·* that

order in — to
Mis.	14–12	in *o·* to learn Science, we begin with
	31–22	in *o·* to retain his faith in evil
	33–12	*in o· to be healed by it*
	38–25	*in o· to be healed by it*
	38–28	in *o·* to cure his present disease,
	50–17	it is essential . . . in *o·* to heal.
	54–17	*in o· to keep well all my life?*
	65–15	in *o·* to gain the true solution of
	65–22	in *o·* to demonstrate healing,
	81–16	*in o· to overcome mortal sense,*
	94– 6	love good in *o·* to understand God.
	109–13	in *o·* to be corrected ;
	181– 7	in *o·* to understand his sonship,
	187–25	Did . . . Spirit, become a clod, in *o·* to
	187–30	in *o·* to be healed and saved,
	197–12	In *o·* to comprehend the
	217–28	in *o·* to become matter,
	246– 8	in *o·* to subserve the interests of
	254–16	in *o·* to gain the kingdom
	256– 5	in *o·* to make the body harmonious.
	265– 3	in *o·* to be thought original,
	273– 5	I close my College in *o·* to work in
	274– 5	in *o·* to do this I must
	345–24	in *o·* to offer them in sacrifice,
	348– 8	in *o·* to exterminate it,
	352–20	in *o·* to enable one to destroy
Man.	74–15	In *o·* to be eligible to
Ret.	26–21	in *o·* to rebuke the evidence.
	28–10	in *o·* to apprehend Spirit.
	28–11	in *o·* to have the least understanding
	34– 2	in *o·* to gain the Science of Mind,
	38–29	in *o·* to demonstrate C. S.
	45–13	in *o·* to gain spiritual freedom
	57– 6	in *o·* to heal his body.
	63– 9	in *o·* to destroy this belief
	63–11	in *o·* to heal them.
	82–15	in *o·* to do the greatest good
	89–25	in *o·* to enlarge their sphere of
Un.	2– 8	in *o·* to be saved from sin.
	11–25	in *o·* to mature fitness for
	18–13	in *o·* to console it.
	18–22	in *o·* to strike at its root ;
	32–27	in *o·* to demonstrate the falsity
	37– 4	in *o·* to inherit eternal life
	40– 7	in *o·* to prove man deathless.
	41– 3	In *o·* to reach the true knowledge
	45–21	dies in *o·* to better itself.
	54– 9	In *o·* to be whole,
Pul.	35–14	in *o·* to apprehend Spirit.
	35–15	in *o·* to have the least understanding
	64–12	* in *o·* to stop the continued inflow
Rud.	14–12	in *o·* to do gratuitous work.
No.	3–21	in *o·* to be safe members of the
	6– 3	in *o·* to heal the sick.
	23–18	in *o·* to cast out this devil?
Pan.	11–18	in *o·* to be in proper shape,
'01.	15– 3	in *o·* to understand and demonstrate
	15– 5	in *o·* to prove it false,
	24–25	in *o·* to demonstrate the divine
	33–20	in *o·* to heal them.
Hea.	7–14	in *o·* to purify the stream.
My.	3– 5	in *o·* to demonstrate truth,
	10–26	* in *o·* to insure the prosperity of
	21–11	* in *o·* to contribute more liberally
	22–12	* in *o·* to complete this great work,
	23– 2	* in *o·* to find out how much
	39– 1	* in *o·* to accommodate those who
	121– 4	in *o·* to separate these sessions
	211– 7	in *o·* to maintain harmony,
	216– 4	in *o·* to help mankind with it.
	231–12	in *o·* to help God's work
	244– 2	in *o·* to avoid the stir
	251– 9	* in *o·* to become teachers of
	273–17	in *o·* to forewarn and forearm
	282–13	In *o·* to apprehend more,
	318– 1	in *o·* to express the
	363–24	In *o·* to be sure that one is

ordered
Mis.	249–16	neither purchased nor *o·* a drug
	285– 3	pamphlets I *o·* to be laid away
	381–18	It was *o·* that the complainant
Un.	19– 9	intended it, or *o·* it aforetime,
No.	46–10	Woman should not be *o·* to the rear,

orderly
Mis.	275–28	is magnificent and *o·*.
Ret.	82–12	*o·* methods herein delineated.
	87–13	in the *o·* demonstration thereof.

orderly
Ret.	87–22	In this *o·*, scientific dispensation
My.	247–15	came out in *o·* line

Order of Communion Services etc.
Present
Man.	125– 1	heading

Order of Exercises
for the Sunday School
Man.	127– 1	heading

Order of Services
Present
Man.	120– 1	heading

orders
Mis.	10–16	reinstate His *o·*, more assured to
	119–30	countermand your *o·*, steal your
	285– 6	gentleman who fills *o·* for my books,
	291–12	often construed as direct *o·*,
	307–13	and many *o·* on hand,
	311–26	I was a scribe under *o·* ;
No.	24– 7	lower *o·* of matter and mortal mind.
Po.	10–20	Is marching under *o·* ;
My.	337–21	Is marching under *o·* ;

ordinance
Mis.	91– 2	This *o·* is significant as a type of
	383– 3	This *o·* took effect the same year,

ordinarily
'02.	12–22	*o·* find no place in my Message.
My.	7– 5	*o·* find no place in my Message.
	83– 3	* *O·* the holding of a great convention

ordinary
Mis.	33–22	*o· methods of healing disease*
Un.	26–19	Many *o·* Christians protest against
	28–14	*o·* material conjectures,
Pul.	33–26	* more than *o·* achievement,
'01.	19–21	From *o·* mental practice to C. S.
'02.	1–16	*o·* systems of religious beliefs
My.	65–15	* *o·* mortal passing out a nickel
	346– 3	* an *o·* lifetime ;

ordination
Man.	58– 4	*O·*.
Pul.	7–28	This is my first *o·*.

Ore. (State)
(see **Portland***)*

O'Rell's, Max
Pul.	67–11	* Max *O·* famous enumeration of

organ (*see also* **organ's**)
choir
Pul.	60–30	* The choir *o·*, enclosed

couplers
Pul.	61– 5	* swell to great ;
	61– 6	* choir to great ;
	61– 6	* swell to choir ;
	61– 6	* swell to great octaves,
	61– 7	* swell to great sub-octaves ;
	61– 7	* choir to great sub-octaves ;
	61– 8	* swell octaves ;
	61– 8	* swell to pedal ;
	61– 8	* great to pedal ;
	61– 9	* choir to pedal.

every
Rud.	13–19	to treat every *o·* in the body.
Hea.	19– 4	every *o·* of the system,

forty-five hundred and thirty-eight pipes
My.	70–29	* forty-five hundred and thirty-eight pipes,

four manuals
My.	70–25	* four manuals, seventy-two stops,

grand crescendo pedal
My.	70–28	* a grand crescendo pedal,

great
Pul.	26–12	* The great *o·* comes from Detroit.
	60–23	* great *o·* has double open diapason
My.	68–21	* The great *o·* is placed back of
	71–27	* in front of the great *o·*.

manual compass
Pul.	60–22	* three-manual compass, C. C. C. to C.

mechanical accessories
Pul.	61– 9	* swell tremulant,
	61–10	* choir tremulant,
	61–10	* bellows signal ;
	61–10	* wind indicator.

nineteen adjustable combination pistons
My.	70–26	* nineteen adjustable combination pistons,

nineteen couplers
My.	70–26	* seventy-two stops, nineteen couplers,

pedal
Pul.	61– 3	* The pedal *o·* has open diapason,

pedal compass
Pul.	60–23	* pedal compass, C. C. C. to F. 30.

pedal movements
Pul.	61–11	* three affecting great and pedal stops,
	61–11	* three affecting swell and pedal stops
	61–12	* great to pedal reversing pedal ;

organ

pedal movements
Pul. 61–13 * crescendo and full organ pedal ;
61–13 * balanced great and choir pedal ;
61–14 * balanced swell pedal.
powerful
My. 59–20 * sonorous tones of the powerful *o·*
seven combination pedals
My. 70–28 * seven combination pedals,
seventy-two stops
My. 70–26 * seventy-two stops, nineteen couplers,
solo
My. 71– 4 * There is also a solo *o·* attached.
swell
Pul. 60–27 * swell *o·* has bourdon, open diapason,
swell-box
Pul. 61– 1 * enclosed in separate swell-box,
three balanced swells
My. 70–27 * three balanced swells,

────

Mis. 106–31 your many-throated *o·*.
155–29 for our denominational *o·*.
243–28 and the *o·* to contract ;
347–30 only authenticated *o·* of C. S.
Man. 61–23 Music from the *o·* alone should
Ret. 52–19 The first official *o·* of
Pul. 26– 6 * *o·* and choir gallery is spacious
42–20 * where the *o·* is to be hereafter
43–14 * After an *o·* voluntary,
47– 5 * first official *o·* of this sect.
60–16 * The *o·*, made by Farrand & Votey
My. 32–11 * Following the *o·* voluntary
38–20 * with the roll of the *o·*
69–11 * placed on the two sides of the *o·*.
70–19 * chapter sub-title
70–22 * *o·* which has been installed.
70–30 * Attached to the *o·* is a set of
71– 2 * discoveries of *o·* builders
166–12 with which to furnish . . . with an *o·*,
(*see also* **organ stops**)

organic
Mis. 56– 3 *What is o· life?*
56– 5 if Life, or Spirit, were *o·*,
56–21 *O·* life is an error of statement
Ret. 85– 6 any other *o·* operative method
No. 10–19 that sense is *o·* and material,
28–26 Here *soul* means sense and *o·* life ;
Pan. 10–18 *o·*, chronic, and acute diseases
My. 106– 1 in functional and *o·* diseases
106– 7 *o·* diseases of almost every kind.
107–30 *o·* and inflammatory diseases,
190– 9 contagious and *o·* diseases

organism
Rud. 12–18 a so-called material *o·*

organist
Man. 61–18 Soloist and *O·*.
My. 71– 3 * enable the *o·* to produce

organization
above
Mis. 306–18 * a member of the above *o·*,
abuses of
Ret. 45–15 uses and abuses of *o·*.
and duties
Man. 93– 3 *o·* AND DUTIES.
Baltimore
Pul. 68–21 * adds interest to the Baltimore *o·*.
Christian Science
Man. 73–11 form and conduct a C. S. *o·*
church
Pul. 66– 4 * first church *o·* of this faith
college
Man. 73–21 for said university or college *o·*.
concerning the
Pul. 57–15 * concerning the *o·* of
continued
Ret. 45– 9 continued *o·* retards spiritual growth,
corporeal
Ret. 45–11 corporeal *o·* deemed requisite
disrupt the
Man. 93–20 to disrupt the *o·* of branch churches.
distinctive
My. 100–13 * its appearance as a distinctive *o·*
functions, and
My. 218– 2 normal action, functions, and *o·*,
good ends of
Mis. 358–31 fulfilled all the good ends of *o·*,
great
My. 273– 9 * a very great *o·*
its
My. 148–12 completed its *o·* February 22
material
(*see* **material**)
members of the
Man. 73–15 may become members of the *o·*

organization
no
Mis. 145– 5 need no *o·* to express it.
of branch churches
Man. 93–20 to disrupt the *o·* of branch churches.
My. 56–17 * the *o·* of branch churches
of churches
Ret. 85– 5 to continue the *o·* of churches,
original
My. 46– 9 * this church in its orginal *o·* ;
parent
Pul. 55–26 * It is regarded as the parent *o·*,
periods of
Ret. 49– 5 working out their periods of *o·*,
result of
Mis. 190– 2 result of *o·*, nor the
Ret. 58–13 not the result of *o·*,
Un. 42–22 nor was it the result of *o·*,
spiritual
Mis. 138–29 march on in spiritual *o·*.
such an
Mis. 295–25 on tablets of such an *o·*
tenets of the
Pul. 58–22 * symbolic of the tenets of the *o·*.
that
Ret. 45–18 when dissolving that *o·*,
their
My. 83–28 * growth of their *o·*,
visible
Mis. 90–27 conferred by a visible *o·*

────

Mis. 304–29 * in recognition of the *o·*
Man. 88– 3 *O·*.
Ret. 45– 7 *o·* is requisite only in the

organizations
Mis. 32–25 social *o·* and societies
98–17 and perpetuate our *o·*
137–30 hold these *o·* of their own,
138–23 members of students' *o·*.
305– 7 * Freedom League, and kindred *o·*.
358–21 to dissolve their *o·*, or to
Man. 44–23 Church *O·* Ample.
44–25 shall not unite with *o·* which
Ret. 60–26 matter and its so-called *o·*
Un. 33–27 through the *o·* of matter,
Peo. 1– 4 draws not its life from human *o·* ;
My. 10–12 * other *o·* have taken steps
175– 4 with the *o·* connected therewith,

organize
Mis. 91– 4 It is not indispensable to *o·*
137–29 can *now o·* their students into
Man. 17–10 To *o·* a church designed to
Ret. 44– 1 voted to *o·* a church
50–24 continue to *o·* churches, schools,
Pul. 69– 2 * came . . . to *o·* this movement.
My. 46–10 "To *o·* a church designed to
56– 9 * necessary to *o·* branch churches

organized
Mis. 23–21 it is not *o·* dust.
90–23 *members of a church not o·*
91– 9 If our church is *o·*,
144– 7 *o·* by Miss Maurine R. Campbell.
300–24 which I had *o·* and of which
350– 3 *o·* a secret society
382–24 *o·* the first Christian Scientist
Man. 38–20 *o·* in 1879 by Mary Baker Eddy,
73– 1 shall not be *o·* with less than
Ret. 43–21 Association was *o·* by myself
44– 4 first such church ever *o·*.
44–30 spiritually *o·* Church of Christ,
49– 8 purpose for which they were *o·*,
60– 5 defines life . . . as *o·* matter,
Pul. 30–25 * was *o·* by Mrs. Eddy,
37–26 * was *o·* on July 4, 1876,
55–24 * was *o·* April 12, 1879,
56– 1 * One or more *o·* societies
58– 5 * she . . . *o·* a church.
67–25 * was *o·* by seven persons,
68–16 * *o·* in this city about a year ago.
68–25 * *o·* at a meeting held at
Rud. 5–27 the five senses as *o·* matter,
My. vi–11 * Mrs. Eddy *o·* The First Church
vi–19 * *o·* . . . The C. S. Publishing Society,
37–17 * Cause of C. S. has been *o·*
56–12 * three branch churches were *o·*,
67–14 * First church *o·* . . . 1879
70– 4 * has been *o·* only thirty years,

organizer
Ret. 42– 7 He was the first *o·* of a
Pul. 46–29 * He was the first *o·* of a
(*see also* **Eddy**)

organizes
Pul. 21–12 which Christ *o·* and blesses.

organizing
Mis.	177– 9	in *o·* action against us.
	358–22	*o·* churches and associations.
Man.	72– 4	*O·* Churches.
	72–25	Requirements for *O·* Branch
My.	343–20	followed it up, teaching and *o·*,

organ's
Pul.	11– 3	*o·* voice, as the sound of many waters,

organs
Man.	44–19	periodicals which are the *o·* of
My.	70–25	* it is a combination of six *o·*,
	89– 7	* one of the largest *o·* in the world.

organ stops
great organ
Pul.	60–24	* double open diapason (stopped bass),
	60–24	* open diapason,
	60–25	* dulciana,
	60–25	* viola di gamba,
	60–25	* doppel flute,
	60–25	* hohl flute,
	60–25	* octave,
	60–26	* octave quint,
	60–26	* superoctave,
	60–26	* trumpet,

swell organ
Pul.	60–27	* bourdon,
	60–27	* open diapason,
	60–27	* salicional,
	60–28	* æoline,
	60–28	* stopped diapason,
	60–28	* gemshorn,
	60–28	* flute harmonique,
	60–29	* flageolet,
	60–29	* cornet — 3 ranks, 183,
	60–29	* cornopean,
	60–29	* oboe,
	60–29	* vox humana

choir organ
Pul.	61– 1	* geigen principal,
	61– 1	* dolce,
	61– 1	* concert flute,
	61– 2	* quintadena,
	61– 2	* fugara,
	61– 2	* flute d'amour,
	61– 2	* piccolo harmonique,
	61– 3	* clarinet,

pedal organ
Pul.	61– 4	* open diapason,
	61– 4	* bourdon,
	61– 4	* lieblich gedeckt (from stop 10),
	61– 5	* violoncello-wood,

orgies
'00.	13– 7	*o·* of their idolatrous feasts

Orient
Mis.	332–16	crystal streams of the *O·*,
'02.	3– 4	non-Christian religions in the *O·*
My.	193– 7	gorgeous skies of the *O·*

Oriental
Mis.	29–25	esoteric magic and *O·* barbarisms
	341–28	and the diction purely *O·*.
Pul.	8–29	which will eclipse *O·* dreams.
	23–16	* inquiry into *O·* philosophy,
	53–12	* to give thanks in *O·* phrase,
	66–20	* largely *O·* in its choice.
No.	14–10	*O·* philosophy of Brahmanism,

origin
and action
Un.	32–10	cannot be separated in *o·* and action.

and aim
My.	257–13	Christ's heavenly *o·* and aim.

and demonstration
Mis.	58–23	not human, in *o·* and demonstration.

and operations
Ret.	70– 3	*o·* and operations of mortal mind,

divine
(*see* **divine**)

his
Mis.	79–14	concerning himself and his *o·* :
	167–23	in admiration of his *o·*,
	185–23	by which to learn his *o·* and age,
Ret.	68–29	His *o·* is not, like that of mortals,
My.	129–16	counterpoised his *o·* from dust,

homely
My.	262–10	homely *o·* of the babe Jesus

human
(*see* **human**)

its
Un.	22–20	has its *o·* in the physical senses
Pul.	55–20	* every effect has its *o·* in desire
	67– 4	* SKETCH OF ITS *O·* AND GROWTH
No.	18– 7	proof of its *o·* in God,
Pan.	4– 3	owes its *o·* and continuity to the
'00.	5– 9	its *o·* is a myth, a lie.
'01.	16–20	in its *o·* evil was loquacious,

origin
man's
Mis.	79– 9	Man's *o·* and existence being in Him,
Ret.	10–16	in man's *o·* and signification.
Un.	53–25	God *is* man's *o·*

material
Mis.	361– 3	belief in material *o·*, mortal mind,
Un.	50–26	material *o·*, growth, maturity,

mental
Hea.	17–26	Then was not sin of mental *o·*,

mythical
Mis.	71–22	its mythical *o·* and certain end.

no
Un.	45–27	has no *o·* or existence in Spirit,
'00.	5– 5	It gives evil no *o·*, no reality.
'02.	7– 2	concedes no *o·* or causation apart from
My.	288–10	it has no *o·* in the nature of God,

no other
Mis.	182– 8	no other Mind, no other *o·* ;

nor existence
No.	15–22	neither *o·* nor existence in the

of all
My.	266–19	*o·* of all that really is,

of disease
Hea.	19–11	The illusive *o·* of disease

of evil
Mis.	24–25	Speaking of the *o·* of evil,
	346– 6	chapter sub-title
	346– 7	*o·* of evil is the problem of ages.

of man
Mis.	75–27	the spiritual *o·* of man.
	165–32	virgin *o·* of man according to
Un.	30– 1	Spirit as the sole *o·* of man,

or existence
Un.	45–27	has no *o·* or existence in Spirit,

or ultimate
Mis.	14– 6	either to the *o·* or ultimate of good

our
Ret.	22–17	He alone is our *o·*, aim, and being.

spiritual
Mis.	18–17	spiritual *o·*, God's reflection,
	75–27	discovered the spiritual *o·* of man.
	166–17	how to declare its spiritual *o·*,

statement of the
'00.	5– 2	This scientific statement of the *o·*,

their
Mis.	36– 7	express Mind as their *o·* ;
Man.	59– 2	without characterizing their *o·*

true
Mis.	72– 6	the only living and true *o·*,

Mis.	166–21	whose *o·* was more spiritual
	187–21	*o·*, substance, and life of man
Hea.	19–11	*o·* of all mortal things.

original
Mis.	14– 8	his *o·* state of perfection,
	18– 2	*o·* likeness of perfect man,
	25–14	*o·* meaning of the Scriptures,
	74–16	into its *o·* meaning, Mind.
	77– 5	*o·* meaning, namely, to be *firm*,
	114–19	arm . . . against *o·* sin,
	186– 7	far below man's *o·* standard,
	187–16	set forth in *o·* Holy Writ.
	188– 6	the translator, not the *o·* Word,
	191–23	*o·* devil was a great talker,
	191–26	the *o·* texts define him as
	192– 5	*o·* text defines devil as a
	201– 4	its *o·* sin, or human will ;
	263–29	or a single *o·* conception,
	265– 4	in order to be thought *o·*,
	295–10	* cause of this "same *o·* evil"
	300–20	printed as your *o·* writings,
	360–11	his *o·* scientific sonship with **God.**
	371–28	are as hopelessly *o·* as
	381– 1	alleging that . . . were not *o·*
Ret.	35– 6	was so hopelessly *o·*,
	37– 7	book is indeed wholly *o·*,
	68– 3	claimed to originate . . . *o·* evil ;
Pul.	20–11	my *o·* system of ministry
	65– 2	* *o·* apostles and promulgators,
Pan.	7–19	in connection with the *o·* text
	11–21	the *o·* standard of man
'01.	16–16	*o·* text defines *devil* as
'01.	33– 2	the *o·* beauty of holiness
Hea.	3–14	In the *o·* text the term *God*
	7– 9	translates matter into its *o·* language,
	13–17	and with this *o·* dose we cured
Peo.	1– 6	back to its *o·* language,
My.	46– 9	* church in its *o·* organization ;
	123–16	The *o·* cost of the estate
	129–17	how he presses to his *o·*,
	157–17	* in her *o·* deed of trust,
	180– 9	restores their *o·* tongue
	253– 4	perfect *o·* man and universe.
	262– 4	spotless purity and *o·* perfection.
	315– 1	*o·* of which is in my possession,

original

My.	317–23	My diction, . . . has been called *o.*
	324– 8	* often said you were so *o.*
	324–25	* as entirely unique and *o.*
	334–10	* *o.* account of her husband's demise

originally

Mis.	x–11	were *o.* written in haste,
	381– 3	manuscripts *o.* composed by
No.	13–10	after those words were *o.* uttered,

originate

Mis.	26–16	how did matter *o.*?
	45–22	*where did evil o.*?
	102– 6	*o.* in a limited body,
Ret.	36–10	would insinuate did not *o.* with me.
	68– 2	it claimed to *o.* in the name of
	68–19	"How can matter *o.*"
Rud.	7–22	Spirit cannot *o.* its opposite,
Hea.	12–11	physical effects *o.* in mind
	17–26	did not mind *o.* the delusion?

originated

Mis.	45–23	It never *o.* or existed
	57– 6	Man *o.* not from dust,
	83–14	*o.* in another's mind
	148– 9	*o.* not in solemn conclave
	382–18	*o.* its form of government,
Man.	3– 5	*o.* not in solemn conclave
Ret.	69– 6	sleep, in which *o.* the delusion
Pul.	32–12	* What had she *o.*?
	63–15	* woman, who has *o.* a
	70–24	* Thus *o.* the divine or spiritual
Rud.	16–23	*o.* with certain opposing factions,
	17– 9	never *o.* in pride, rivalry, or
No.	26–21	individuality never *o.* in molecule
Peo.	4– 5	sickness, and death *o.* in the
My.	vi–13	* *o.* its form of public worship,

originates

Mis.	186– 2	spiritual man who *o.* in God,
Rud.	16–18	*o.* from the Principle and practice
My.	5– 1	*o.* in the minds of mortals.

originating

Mis.	71–25	man is incapable of *o.* :
'01.	33–10	* quackery was never the *o.* influence
	34–13	*o.* not in God, but

originator

My.	267– 6	the *o.* of all that really is.

originators

Ret.	37–14	declare . . . to have been the *o.*

oriole's

Mis.	329–20	rocking the *o.* cradle,

Orion

Rud.	4–13	"loose the bands of *O.*" — *Job* 38 : 31.

orison

My.	281– 8	spirit of this *o.* is the fruit of

orphan

Mis.	388–19	To bless the *o.*, feed the poor ;
Po.	21– 8	To bless the *o.*, feed the poor ;

Orphean

Mis.	329–24	sweep in soft strains her *O.* lyre.

orthodox

Mis.	111–26	I love the *o.* church ;
	225– 6	*o.* clergyman, his wife and child.
Pul.	50–24	* so-called *o.* religious bodies
'01.	15–18	little short of the old *o.* hell
	31–21	Devout *o.* parents ;
My.	307–16	At that date I was a staunch *o.*

orthodoxy

No.	12– 9	After a lifetime of *o.*

Osiris

My.	92–12	* new temple to Isis and *O.*

osseous

My.	342–11	* depend upon the *o.* structure ;

ossification

My.	107–32	pneumonia, diphtheria, and *o.*

ostensibly

No.	39– 5	*o.* to catch God's ear,

ostentation

My.	30–23	* Without *o.* and quite voluntarily

ostracize

No.	45– 8	to *o.* whatever uplifts mankind.
'00.	9–22	Whosoever attempts to *o.* C. S.

ostracized

No.	2– 4	*o.* by the medical faculty,

other (*see also* other's)

Mis.	8–14	or any *o.* creature separate you from
	11–30	I have turned the *o.* :
	21–13	seen to depart from the trend of *o.*
	22–21	"there is none *o.*" — *Mark* 12 : 32.
	25–13	rejects all *o.* theories of causation,

other

Mis.	27– 8	*o.* systems of religion abandon
	33–17	*o.* than to place themselves under **my**
	38–14	*o. institutions find little interest in*
	38–21	metaphysics at *o.* colleges means,
	40– 1	in the one case as in the *o.*
	41–21	There is no *o.* healer in the case.
	48–29	like a hundred *o.* stories,
	57– 5	what evidence . . . of any *o.* creation?
	60– 9	after all *o.* means have failed.
	62– 2	*o.* people's individuality,
	63– 2	and anomalous in the *o.*
	65–28	for the absence of the *o.*,
	76–18	on *o.* topics less important.
	78–10	than can science in any *o.* direction.
	89– 1	when you employ the *o.*
	91–29	my example, and that of *o.* teachers,
	97–14	all *o.* methods of treating disease.
	99–19	In no *o.* one thing seemed
	101–27	no *o.* power, law, or intelligence
	103– 5	while the *o.* is eternal,
	103–25	was like that of *o.* men ;
	105–22	or maligned, it eclipses the *o.*
	112–21	* "*O.* visitors have brought to him
	112–27	exaggerating sense of *o.* people's.
	117–20	*modus operandi*, of *o.* folks.
	119– 4	instead of aiding *o.* people's devices
	129–18	for *o.* green eyes to gaze on :
	142– 9	among *o.* beautiful decorations,
	144–12	*o.* works written by the same author,
	145– 1	more than any *o.* institution,
	170–23	and no *o.* method is C. S.
	179– 9	any *o.* consciousness than that of
	182– 8	no *o.* God, no *o.* Mind, no *o.* origin ;
	193–10	can be established on no *o.* claim
	195– 1	in any *o.* remedy than Christ,
	197–32	working from no *o.* Principle,
	219–19	while in the *o.* he must
	229–14	faith in Mind over all *o.*
	229–26	any *o.* possible sanative method ;
	230– 3	more than upon any *o.* one thing.
	230–16	hours that *o.* people may occupy in
	236–16	to give, to one or the *o.*, advice
	241– 8	the *o.* having a physical ailment.
	241–18	On the *o.* hand,
	244–24	"And *o.* sheep I have, — *John* 10 : 16.
	249– 8	*o.* people's manuscripts
	256–10	from any *o.* than Mrs. Eddy,
	260–12	these laws annulled all *o.* laws.
	264– 1	quote from *o.* authors
	266–19	Chicago, New York, or any *o.* place,
	269– 7	and love the *o.* ; — *Matt.* 6 : 24.
	269– 8	despise the *o.* — *Matt.* 6 : 24.
	270–11	To seek or employ *o.* means than
	270–17	Then you will need no *o.* aid,
	273– 5	in order to work in *o.* directions,
	273– 7	where none *o.* can do the work.
	273–29	the *o.* three classes
	279– 1	startling departures on the *o.* hand.
	282–25	when *o.* means have failed.
	282–25	One *o.* occasion which may
	282–27	and no *o.* aid is near.
	284– 4	C. S., more than any *o.* system
	286–28	shut out all sense of *o.* claims.
	287–31	attempts to steady *o.* people's altars,
	290– 2	Let *o.* people's marriage relations
	291–10	*o.* people's thoughts and actions.
	297– 3	this Science has distanced all *o.*
	304–17	* When not in use in *o.* places,
	308– 6	human love or hatred or any *o.* cause
	314– 2	throughout our land and in *o.* lands.
	317–28	penalty for *o.* people's faults ;
	319–13	more to them than to *o.* people.
	336–16	the mote of evil out of *o.* eyes.
	340– 8	seeking no *o.* pursuit or pleasure
	347–15	the *o.* says, Take the opposite
	357– 1	trafficking in *o.* people's business,
	363–15	and there is no *o.* Maker:
	364–12	and there is no *o.* philosophy.
	365– 2	"*o.* foundation can no man — *I Cor.* 3 : 11.
	374–25	the *o.* sees "Helen's beauty in a
	378– 9	in company with several *o.* patients,
Man.	27–16	all *o.* C. S. literature
	27–24	*o.* literature connected therewith.
	29– 3	any *o.* officer in this Church
	34–13	with S. AND H. and *o.* works by
	34–17	Free from *O.* Denominations.
	45– 9	become members of *o.* societies
	48–25	they may quote from *o.* periodicals
	56–13	No *o.* than its officers are required
	56–20	for electing officers and *o.* business,
	57– 2	such *o.* business as may properly
	58–14	shall be repeated at the *o.* services
	64– 7	*o.* writings by this author ;
	69–23	*o.* affairs outside of her house.
	70–13	it shall be controlled by none *o.*

other

Man.	71–10	In its relation to o· C. S. churches,
	71–13	position that no o· church can fill.
	74– 5	or control over any o· church.
	74– 8	and no o· church shall interfere
	74–18	all o· C. S. churches
	82–16	who practise o· professions or
	82–17	pursue o· vocations,
	98– 4	not been replied to by o· Scientists,
	99–21	he shall, in addition to his o· duties,
	102–17	o· than the erection of a church edifice.
Ret.	1– 9	besides o· verses and enigmas
	6–27	Among o· important bills
	15–23	Among o· diseases cured they specified
	32–18	* But the dream of o· dreams.
	42–10	clergymen of o· denominations
	45–21	turn to him the o· also."— Matt. 5 : 39.
	49– 4	O· institutions for instruction in
	52–16	branch associations in o· States,
	59–13	o· name for the Supreme Being,
	59–22	dependent, each on the o·,
	68–11	One is false, while the o· is true.
	68–12	One is temporal, but the o· is
	71–29	same as o· forms of stealing,
	75– 9	from the works of o· authors?
	78–18	any name given to it o· than C. S.,
	78–20	o· than is stated in S. and H.
	82–24	either excel or fall short of o·
	83–22	same as o· teachers;
	85– 1	o· teachers who should be specially
	85– 6	any o· organic operative method
	88–21	o· vineyards than our own.
	89–26	trespass not . . . upon o· people's
	90–19	What o· heart yearns with
Un.	7– 5	multitudes of o· religious folds.
	8– 7	can have no o· reality than
	8–21	heredity and o· physical causes.
	36– 5	beside which there is no o·
	46–10	none o· than this man,
	48– 7	I have no faith in any o· thing
	49–18	and the o· unreal,
	64– 8	"o· foundation can no man— I Cor. 3 : 11.
Pul.	5–30	literature of our and o· lands.
	21–21	our denomination and o· sects,
	21–26	Our unity with churches of o·
	21–28	It cannot come from any o· source.
	27–16	* The o· rose window represents
	28– 6	* o· panels are decorated with
	28–16	* not differ widely from that of any o·
	28–23	* o· recognized devotional poets,
	37–20	* one or two o· friends
	38– 2	* Mrs. Eddy had preached in o·
	46–23	* applied herself, like o· girls,
	47– 1	* many clergymen of o·
	51–19	* it may, on the o· hand,
	51–28	* alongside o· great demonstrations
	53– 3	* practised in o· countries
	53–16	* "That word, more than any o·
	56– 4	* nearly every o· centre of
	59–23	* o· members of the C. S. Board
	68–22	* Many o· church edifices in
	72–22	* any power o· than that which
	76–19	* the o· a lavatory in which
	80– 4	* one extreme will surely find the o·.
	88– 8	o· prominent newspapers
Rud.	2– 1	O· definitions of person,
	4–16	there is no o· Mind.
	8–13	there is no o· healer.
No.	4–17	beyond o· systems of medicine,
	13–26	o· parts of it have no lustre.
	14–20	more than any o· religious sect,
	16–18	hence their inference of some o·
	21–23	o· foundation can no man— I Cor. 3 : 11.
	32–15	o· theories make sin true.
	36– 3	one infinite and the o· finite ;
	38–23	nothingness of any o· state
Pan.	6– 2	more effectual than all o· means ;
	8– 8	the o· a human finite personality?
	10–22	o· religious teachers are unable to
'00.	7– 8	more Bibles sold than in all the o·
	8–11	steal o· people's good thoughts,
	14–12	seek thou the divine . . . and no o·
'01.	7– 2	than whom there is none o·.
	15–26	* no o· reason to be given
	17–12	exceeded that of o· methods,
	18–13	taught his disciples none o·.
	20– 6	guided by no o· mind than Truth,
	22–11	if one is true, the o· is false.
	23–21	as no o· person has ever
	24–25	Jesus' teachings, and none o·,
	27– 2	all o· authors except the Bible.
	30– 1	are persecuted even as all o·
	30–30	* will not insult me, and no o· can."
'02.	3– 1	used no o· means myself ;
	6– 1	forbids the thought of any o· reality,
	6– 3	law, apart or o· than God

other

'02.	7–18	No o· logical conclusion
	7–20	no o· scientific proposition
	10–29	in o· ways than by walking
	13–12	and desire none o·.
	14–16	on any o· foundation,
Hea.	1–21	more spiritual basis . . . than the o· ;
	6– 3	When I was told the o· day,
	11–28	this excellence above o· systems.
	15– 4	by employing no o· remedy
	16– 4	no o· Life, substance, and
	18–27	killed a man by no o· means than
Peo.	9–24	remove all evidence of any o· power
My.	v– 9	* by o· Christian denominations,
	10–12	* churches and o· organizations
	18–30	* all o· published writings of
	30– 8	* many hundreds of o· faiths,
	43–17	* on the o· side for a memorial.
	55–22	* obliged to seek o· quarters,
	56–22	* were established in o· suburbs,
	62–29	* services of o· members of the church,
	67–23	* vaster sums . . . in o· instances,
	70– 7	* any o· denomination in the world,
	70–15	* chimes were being tested the o· day.
	71–18	* different from any o· church
	73– 5	* in o· countries since that time,
	74–15	* achievements in this or any o· city,
	74–16	* o· denominations might profit by
	74–31	* and the o· for its novelty.
	83–27	* o· evidences of the strength and
	84–14	* o· architectural efforts
	85–29	* Aside from every o· consideration,
	89–18	* all o· of the Christian churches,
	91– 4	* did not find in o· communions.
	91– 7	* good example to o· denominations
	91–18	* that this country or any o· country
	92–17	* every o· sect in the country
	94– 2	* every o· sect will be left behind
	95–21	* clergymen of o· denominations
	96–15	* comparison with o· creeds.
	96–28	* dedication . . . the o· day,
	104– 1	I have had no o· guide
	104–26	in this or any o· country.
	114–15	I consulted no o· authors
	114–16	read no o· book but the Bible
	119–11	Buddhism or any o· "ism."
	123–12	a reading-room and nine o· rooms
	123–17	repairs and o· necessary expenses
	127–11	o· religions since the first century.
	128– 2	no o· outlet to liberty.
	153–18	no o· than the spiritual help
	170– 9	not to be confused with o· issues,
	171– 2	and have no o· trusts.
	182– 3	any o· city in the United States.
	199–21	in this and in o· lands.
	212– 7	o· forms of intoxication.
	212–20	impossible under o· conditions,
	218–30	o· than that which my books afford,
	221–16	modes of healing, o· than the
	221–19	no o· heaven-appointed means
	225–15	distinguishes it from all o· names,
	227–28	turn to him the o· also."— Matt. 5 : 39.
	231–13	in o· of its highest . . . meanings,
	233–14	effects of o· people's sins
	235–22	no o· creator and no o· creation.
	276–24	o· than to help support a
	277– 2	chapter sub-title
	281– 3	o· than the daily prayer of my
	291–30	liberty of o· peoples
	293– 5	one against the o·
	303– 8	Catholics, or any o· sect.
	307–10	o· terms which I employed
	310–27	for her o· children to imitate,
	315–30	in our own and in o· countries,
	324–16	* any o· thought but that you were
	327–18	* o· Scientists who stayed on
	327–25	* "All o· professionals who practise
	328–28	* all o· professionals who practise
	334–14	* whom he had in mind is some o· one?
	340–11	in excess of o· States,
	342–16	* o· and smaller parlor
	348– 2	healed . . . by o· than drugs,
	354– 3	offering Bibles and o· books
	356–16	o· than the ones presented in
	356–23	love the o· ; — Matt. 6 : 24.
	356–24	despise the o·.— Matt. 6 : 24.
	357–17	than which there is no o·,
	363–26	any o· individual but the patient
	364– 4	handle no o· mentality
	364–12	any o· cause or effect

(see also **churches, each, gods, minds, students way, words**)

other's

Man.	85– 2	Pupils may visit each o· churches,
	85– 3	attend each o· associations.

others (*see also* **others'**)

actions of
    My. 276–20 * to dictate the actions of *o*.
advance of
    Ret. 94– 2 perceived, in advance of *o*,
all
    Un. 10– 2 separates my system from all *o*.
    Pul. 55–26 * all *o* being branches,
    My. 51– 5 * and all *o* now interested in
basis for
    Mis. 156–16 becoming the basis for *o* :
before us
    Mis. 343– 3 not forget that *o* before us have
believe
    Mis. 228–27 believe what *o* believe,
best for
    Mis. 288– 3 regarding what is best for *o*
bestowed upon
    Mis. 227–30 happiness it has bestowed upon *o*,
bestows on
    My. 122– 2 gratuitously bestows on *o*,
blamed
    Mis. 111– 9 blamed *o* more than yourself.
bless
    Mis. 127–22 to become blessed, is to bless *o* :
    Pan. 9–18 endeavor to bless *o*,
blessing
    '02. 17– 9 blessing *o*, and self-immolation
business of
    Mis. 348– 5 the books nor the business of *o* ;
concerning
    Mis. 311–31 rehearsing facts concerning *o*
conquer
    '00. 9–18 before he can conquer *o*.
console
    Un. 18–14 you oftenest console *o* in
crowded with
    Pul. 60– 1 * crowded with *o*, waiting for
destroyer of
    My. 161– 5 intentional destroyer of *o*
doing to
    Mis. 115–32 doing to *o* as you would have
doing unto
    Mis. 135–10 doing unto *o* as ye would they should
    223–18 while doing unto *o* what we
    My. 275–24 Doing unto *o* as we would that
do unto
    Mis. 301– 6 as you would have *o* do unto you?
    Man. 16–11 do unto *o* as we would have
    My. 114– 6 Do unto *o* as ye would have
    252– 8 the good you do unto *o*
downfall of
    Mis. 43–24 to build on the downfall of *o*,
errors of
    Mis. 131– 1 challenges the errors of *o*
    236– 6 indiscretions, and errors of *o* ;
experiences of
    Ret. 79– 5 from the experiences of *o*.
eyes of
    Mis. 211– 6 to open the eyes of *o*,
faults of
    Mis. 224– 6 miserable for the faults of *o*.
forgive
    Mis. 129– 5 forgive *o* as he would *be* forgiven.
forsook
    Ret. 90–15 betrayed him, and *o* forsook him.
giving it to
    Pul. 73– 1 * taking . . . or giving it to *o* ?"
God reaches
    Mis. 39–26 *God reaches o to heal them,*
goodness in
    Pul. 21–17 true sense of goodness in *o*,
good of
    No. 7–16 sacrifice for the good of *o*
hands of
    Mis. 13– 8 endured at the hands of *o*
healed
    Mis. 71– 8 he healed *o* who were sick.
    My. 112– 1 healed *o* by means of the Principle
help
    Mis. 90–15 Then help *o* to be free ;
helping
    Mis. 353–29 to think of helping *o*,
    Pul. 81–13 * spends her whole time helping *o*.
    My. 165– 3 helping *o* thus to choose.
help of
    My. 130–16 Therefore I ask the help of *o*
    138– 1 without the help of *o*.
impart to
    No. 12–11 duty for her to impart to *o*
I say to
    Mis. 12– 1 *Because* I thus feel, I say to *o* :
judges
    Mis. 130–21 He who judges *o* should know
lift
    Mis. 338– 4 able to lift *o* toward it.

others

love
    Mis. 311–18 and love *o* more than they
love for
    Mis. 127– 5 in the ratio of her love for *o*,
    My. 18– 2 in the ratio of her love for *o*,
many
    Mis. 32–17 more than to many *o*.
    197– 5 more frequently used than many *o*,
    278–20 shared less of my labors than many *o*,
    Ret. 15–29 many *o* present had been healed
    My. 353– 1 and as many *o* as possible,
means for
    '01. 29– 5 providing ways and means for *o*.
menacing
    Mis. 67–20 if you see the danger menacing *o*,
mentality of
    Un. 56– 4 from the mentality of *o* ;
minds of
    Mis. 220–26 put it into the minds of *o*
misteach
    Mis. 114–10 and so made to misteach *o*.
more than
    Rud. 13–25 not be expected, more than *o*,
motives of
    No. 7– 7 as to the motives of *o*.
ourselves and
    '02. 17–23 and what we give ourselves and *o*
preached to the
    Ret. 89–11 If one worshipper preached to the *o*,
precaution for
    Mis. 89–19 he left this precaution for *o*.
quarrelling with
    '00. 8–21 stops quarrelling with *o*.
recommended
    Mis. 245– 2 or recommended *o* to use, drugs ;
recover
    My. 227–12 dies while the *o* recover,
sacrificed for
    '01. 29–10 even as he has sacrificed for *o*
sake of
    Mis. 312– 8 endures all . . . for the sake of *o*,
saw
    Ret. 76–12 a light beyond what *o* saw.
say
    Mis. 228–27 and say what *o* say.
show
    My. 117–30 show *o* the footsteps from sense to
some
    My. 307–21 understood . . . better than some *o*
success of
    My. 212–28 hindering . . . the success of *o*.
teach
    Mis. 114–14 and teach *o* to practise,
tell
    Mis. 316–17 My juniors can tell *o*
thoughts of
    Un. 56–19 suffered from the thoughts of *o*.
    '01. 20– 4 influencing the thoughts of *o*,
thousands of
    My. 293– 9 thousands of *o* believed the same,
to be lost
    Peo. 8– 4 that elects . . . and *o* to be lost,
to fit
    '00. 9–28 to fit *o* for this great
to hinder
    Mis. 284– 2 and never try to hinder *o*
treat
    Mis. 71– 1 *Is it right for me to treat o, when*
true to
    Rud. 8–11 true to thyself, and true to *o* ;
twenty
    Man. 18–18 twenty *o* of Mrs. Eddy's students
welcome
    Pul. 51–13 * are glad to welcome *o*
welfare of
    Ret. 72– 4 To disregard the welfare of *o*
will approach
    Mis. 233–27 *o* will approach it ;
will attain
    '01. 2–16 *o* will attain it,
work for
    Mis. 138– 2 sustain themselves and work for *o*.
    My. 259–16 time to think and work for *o*.
would harm
    My. 210–13 when he would harm *o*.
yourself and
    Rud. 10– 4 influence on yourself and *o*.
    '00. 8–18 doing rightly by yourself and *o*.

    Mis. 24–16 tried to make plain to *o*,
    39–22 who has more to meet than *o*
    88– 3 occasionally receive it from *o* ;
    119–28 Would you consent that *o* should
    127–20 one must do good to *o*.
    131– 2 can neither help himself nor *o* ;

others

Mis.	137–22	for himself and for *o·*,
	215–25	error in themselves and in *o·*
	222– 6	injuring himself and *o·*.
	226–12	false to themselves as to *o·*?
	228–26	we do what *o·*
	234–14	his effort to steal from *o·*
	241–12	try to make *o·* do likewise,
	244–23	not to teach himself, but *o·*,
	254–28	vineyard unto *o·*." — *Mark* 12:9
	264– 6	*o·* stumble over misdeeds,
	265–25	*o·*, who receive the same instruction,
	291–20	to bestow it upon *o·*,
	298– 7	causing *o·* to go astray,
	305–27	* collect two dollars from *o·*,
	308–23	taught me more than it has *o·*
	316– 4	law not unto *o·*, but themselves.
	335–13	*o·* charge upon me
	368–24	*O·*, from malice and envy,
	391–19	Then if we've done to *o·*
Man.	18–20	*o·* that have since been elected
	49– 3	to the exclusion of *o·*,
	53– 1	influence *o·* thus to act,
	84– 6	law, not unto *o·*, but to themselves.
	87–11	or permit *o·* to solicit,
Ret.	24–16	to be well . . . and how to make *o·* so.
	50–18	for *o·* through them.
	80–29	sacrifices made for *o·*
	81–20	faithless to itself and to *o·*,
	91–21	His power over *o·* was spiritual,
Pul.	27–18	* *o·* with lamps, typical of S. and H.
	27–28	* of *o·* of pictorial significance.
	41–28	* and *o·* such — were chimed
	64–10	* *o·* donating large sums.
	66–22	* *o·* of kindred meaning,
	75– 6	of this spirit than in *o·*,
Rud.	14–18	require *o·* to pay him.
No.	7– 9	and blot it out of *o·*.
	34–13	glory of suffering for *o·*.
'01.	27–23	than *o·* do in proportion,
Peo.	8–10	extend their influence to *o·*.
Po.	38–18	Then if we've done to *o·*
My.	21–25	* no less sacrifice than have *o·*;
	38–22	* service was the same as all the *o·*.
	93–13	* attaining dominion over *o·*,
	114– 6	would have *o·* do to you.
	146–27	*O·* who take the side of error
	160–32	wrongs done to *o·*,
	165–25	maintain themselves and *o·*
	302–22	am less lauded, . . . than *o·*
	343–25	Entrusting their enforcement to *o·*,

others'

Mis.	115–31	your own as well as of *o·* sins.
	223–29	To punish ourselves for *o·* faults,
	291–11	tacit acquiescence with *o·* views
	309– 2	upon their own or *o·* corporeality,
Ret.	71– 3	not the forager on *o·* wisdom
	87–24	bear the weight of *o·* burdens,
My.	297–28	to read or to note from *o·* reading

otherwise

Mis.	x–22	*o·* the name would be too long.
	25–28	if He could create them *o·*,
	41–16	that *o·* could not be reached,
	115– 8	*o·*, his own guilt as a
	131–15	*o·*, I recommend that you
	288–20	believing *o·* would prevent
	350–25	benefit that would *o·* accrue.
Man.	30–12	Unless Mrs. Eddy requests *o·*,
	52–21	If a member . . . mentally or *o·*,
	59–19	and are not *o·* provided with seats.
Ret.	78–23	the blessings *o·* conferred,
Pul.	44–28	* refused . . . checks by mail or *o·*.
	80–16	* to the credit of the book than *o·*.
Rud.	8–17	not *o·* in the field of Mind-healing.
No.	15–23	Thinking *o·* is what estranges mortals
	40–18	*O·* they forfeit their ability
'02.	17– 6	Selfishly, or *o·*, all are ready
My.	83– 8	* *o·* there has been no flaunting of
	84– 7	* work that would *o·* be done.
	111– 1	thus reveal truths which *o·*
	212– 2	would never, *o·*, think or do
	214– 2	*O·*, as our churches multiply,
	219– 9	*o·* its use is abuse.
	229–11	*o·* might cost them a half century.
	233– 5	*O·*, wherefore the Lord's Prayer,
	266–19	How can it be *o·*, since

Ottawa, Ontario

My.	209– 2	chapter sub-title

ought

Mis.	89– 7	*o· the patient to follow the*
	130–18	it *o·* not to be expected that they
	212–14	sense of ways and means *o·* to
	239–27	something that she *o·* not to have,
	290– 9	Mistaken views *o·* to be

ought

Mis.	311–27	*o·* not that one to take the cup,
Ret.	83– 9	which *o·* not to be tampered with.
Un.	60–17	things *o·* not so to be." — *Jas.* 3:10.
Pan.	9–18	*o·* to be aided, not hindered,
'00.	4–13	*o·* not this to be an agreeable
'01.	13– 5	*o·* not to be seen, felt, or acted:
	13– 6	because it *o·* not, we must know
	15–13	A sinner *o·* not to be at ease,
	16–18	*o·* not to proceed from the individual,
'02.	1–18	this *o·* not so to be,
Peo.	7– 5	Recognizing this as we *o·*,
My.	213– 7	they *o·* not to be encouraged in it.
	224– 6	knowing . . . as I *o·*, the human need,
	315– 9	* if he had done as he *o·*,

ounce

Mis.	242–22	at the rate of one *o·* in two weeks,

outcome

Mis.	190– 2	nor the *o·* of life infused into matter:
Ret.	47– 2	final *o·* of material organization,
Un.	9–15	its combinations, phenomena, and *o·*,
	42– 4	not the *o·* of Spirit, holiness, and
Pul.	55– 9	* natural *o·* of a period notable for
Rud.	9–11	*o·* of what I call *mortal mind*,
'01.	13– 2	The *o·* of evil, called sin,
'02.	2–19	an *o·* of progress;
My.	5– 4	supposed . . . woman to be the *o·* of
	6–24	even the *o·* of their hearts,
	94–28	even the *o·* of their hearts,

outcomes

Mis.	267–16	the vital *o·* of Truth

outdoes

'01.	16–11	*o·* itself and commits suicide.

outdoing

Mis.	80–29	*o·* the healing of the old.

outdoor

Mis.	253– 7	not enough . . . for *o·* speaking,
My.	123–19	*o·* accommodations at Pleasant View

outflowing

Mis.	199–30	the *o·* life of Christianity,

outgrowing

My.	8– 4	* *o·* the institutional end thereof.

outgrown

Mis.	309–20	whatever is . . . must be *o·*.
Pan.	1–12	*o·*, wornout, or soiled garments
My.	54–16	* Hawthorne Rooms, . . . were *o·*.
	181– 6	and *o·*, proofless positions.

outgrowth

No.	12– 8	*o·* of the author's religious experience.

outgrowths

Mis.	35–13	* works are the *o·* of her life.

outlet

My.	128– 2	find no other *o·* to liberty.

outline

Rud.	8–10	give you here nothing but an *o·*

outlined

Mis.	103–13	thoughts are *o·*, individualized
	103–28	This God was not *o·*.
Un.	35–26	an *o·* falsity of consciousness,

outlines

Po.	v–11	* *whose rugged o· resemble*
My.	67–29	* unnoticed in the graceful *o·*.

outlives

No.	25–12	*o·* finite mortal definitions of
'02.	17–20	Then thy gain *o·* the sun,

outliveth

Po.	15–20	love that *o·* the grave,

Outlook, The

Pul.	56–23	* *The O·*, New York,

outlook

Mis.	2–13	the *o·* demands labor,
	150–15	The *o·* is cheering.
Pul.	80–11	* most recognition, the widest *o·*.
My.	50–19	* the apparently discouraging *o·*

outmasters

Mis.	102–29	*o·* it, and ends the warfare.

outpouring

No.	33–19	the *o·* love that sustains
Po.	v– 6	* *o· of a deeply poetic nature*
My.	90–24	* *o·* of eager communicants
	118–10	It is an *o·* of goodness

outrages

Mis.	274–19	mocks morality, *o·* humanity,

outrun

Po.	78– 9	star whose destiny none may *o·*;

outset

Mis.	284–16	so dealt with at the *o·*.
Peo.	3–24	assigns them mortal fetters in the *o·*.

outside

Mis. 8–10 thing *o·* thine own creation?
50–14 no . . . secret *o·* of its teachings,
72–30 aught material, or *o·* of infinity.
205– 1 obtains peace and power *o·* of itself.
274– 7 work . . . *o·* of College work,
349– 2 lessons *o·* of my College,
352– 9 facts of Truth *o·* of the error;
Man. 69–24 other affairs *o·* of her house.
84–26 *O·* of this Board each student
Ret. 14–18 even if my creedal doubts left me *o·*
Un. 3–26 can be nothing *o·* of Himself.
18–16 from *o·* and above ourselves?
20–21 *o·* of His own focal distance.
21–17 nothing beside Him or *o·* of Him.
24– 9 never be *o·* of His oneness.
Pul. 50–14 * no additional sums *o·* of the
57–21 * Few people *o·* its own circles
'01. 23– 8 or exist *o·* of the
'02. 16–24 merely *o·* forms of religion,
Po. 47–11 *O·* this ever of pain?
My. 74–22 * even if those *o·* are unable to
141– 9 * members of the church *o·* of Boston
145– 9 details *o·* and inside
223– 6 *o·* of The Mother Church of Christ,
272–28 * *o·* of the C. S. periodicals,
341–27 * change from the misty air *o·*

outstretched

Mis. 319–23 in the *o·* hand of God.
Un. 26– 6 proud to be in His *o·* hands,
Pul. 7–14 with His *o·* arm.
No. 44–18 weak hand *o·* to God.
'01. 1– 5 never lack God's *o·* arm
'02. 14–25 *o·* arm of infinite Love
My. 42–30 * with an *o·* arm" — *Deut.* 26 : 8.
124–11 the world's arms *o·* to us,

outtalk

'01. 16–21 was supposed to *o·* Truth

outtalked

Mis. 191–24 was supposed to have *o·* even Truth,

outward

Mis. 380– 1 *o·* sign of such a practice:
380–25 any *o·* form of practice.
Pul. 11– 1 *o·*, upward, heavenward.
30–13 * not celebrated by *o·* symbols
32–14 * so far as *o·* events may translate
'02. 10–14 taking steps *o·* and upwards.
Hea. 7–20 regardless of any *o·* act,
My. 110–11 *o·* and upward in the scale of being.
127– 1 reaching *o·* and upward to Science
159–16 from the inward to the *o·*,

outweigh

Mis. 134–17 bend or *o·* your purpose

outweighs

Mis. 135–18 joy that *o·* an hour.
167–11 *o·* the material world.
'02. 17–15 on that which *o·* time;

outworn

Un. 13–21 an *o·* theological platform,

oval

My. 69– 6 * presenting an *o·* and dome

over (*see also* **o'er**)

Mis. 6–10 passed *o·* to the Scientist.
6–12 power of metaphysics *o·* physics;
7–17 Looking *o·* the newspapers
16–14 its supremacy *o·* sin, sickness,
30–18 superiority of Mind *o·* the flesh,
33–21 *o· the ordinary methods of healing*
35– 5 supremacy of Mind *o·* matter,
40–24 power *o·* sin in themselves,
47– 2 *weigh o· two hundred pounds*
54–12 power of C. S. *o·* all obstacles
55–21 assert themselves *o·* their opposite,
57– 1 created man *o·* again
58– 3 *have any more power o· him?*
58– 5 then it has no power *o·* one.
59–18 *Is not all argument mind o· mind?*
61– 9 omnipotence of Truth *o·* error,
61–10 and of Life *o·* death.
62–29 divine Mind *o·* the human mind
63–30 proved its supremacy *o·* matter.
64– 4 to show his power *o·* death;
69–12 dominion *o·* the fish — *Gen.* 1 : 26.
69–12 *o·* the fowl of the air." — *Gen.* 1 : 26.
69–31 Had that sick man dominion *o·*
69–32 His want of control *o·*
70– 4 exercised my power *o·* the fish,
74–25 His triumph *o·* the grave
97– 1 it is Truth *o·* error;
105– 5 individual demonstrations *o·* sin,
105– 9 His physical sufferings, . . . were *o·*
107– 4 Art must not prevail *o·* Science.
116–29 "faithful *o·* a few things." — *Matt.* 25 : 21.

over

Mis. 117– 1 "ruler *o·* many things." — *Matt.* 25 : 23.
118–13 pass a friend *o·* it smoothly,
119– 5 then whining *o·* misfortune,
125– 8 dominion *o·* his own sinful sense
129–14 let silence prevail *o·* his remains.
130–11 talking about it, thinking it *o·*,
137–14 rejoice *o·* the growth of my students
140–10 *o·* matter or merely legal titles.
145–13 *o·* all the earth," — *Gen.* 1 : 26.
145–15 *O·* a wounded sense of its own error,
150– 4 Shepherd of Israel watching *o·* you
152– 8 benediction *o·* all the earth,
162– 9 *o·* their fretted, foaming billows.
167–22 dominion *o·* the whole earth;
170– 5 weep *o·* the graves of their beloved;
172–10 white-winged charity, brooding *o·* all,
174– 5 having presence and power *o·*
181–12 What avail, then, to quarrel *o·*
183–28 *o·* all the earth." — *Gen.* 1 : 26.
187– 3 Jesus demonstrated *o·* sin,
187– 4 *o·* and above every sense of matter,
197–25 rules *o·* a kingdom of its own,
199–21 *o·* the qualities opposed to Spirit
201–17 enabled him to triumph *o·* them,
204–21 holding sway *o·* human consciousness.
210– 7 Do men whine *o·* a nest of serpents,
220–13 full control *o·* this mind
220–28 this action of mind *o·* mind,
221– 1 it has no power *o·* him.
225–27 a cool perspiration spread *o·*
229–14 faith in Mind *o·* all other
239–25 made them more serious *o·* it.
240–23 *o·* the fresh, unbiased thought.
249–28 *O·* what worlds on worlds it hath
254– 5 love which brooded tireless *o·* their
261–14 full, pressed down, and running *o·*.
264– 6 others stumble *o·* misdeeds,
270– 9 He who demonstrated his power *o·* sin,
279– 7 but *o·* and above it all
286–12 superiority of spiritual power *o·*
287–14 should preponderate *o·* the evil,
287–15 the spiritual *o·* the animal,
287–24 Be faithful *o·* home relations;
287–28 it makes one ruler *o·* one's self
291–31 keeps not watch *o·* his emotions
297–24 If the man is dominant *o·* the
307– 1 charge *o·* thee." — *Psal.* 91 : 11.
315– 9 Scientists, all *o·* the world,
315–13 consist of not *o·* thirty-three students,
317– 8 *o·* all sin, disease, and death.
321– 2 *o·* the cradle of a great truth,
321–11 triumphs of Truth *o·* error,
321–11 of health *o·* sickness,
321–12 Life *o·* death,
321–12 Soul *o·* sense.
327–30 plunge headlong *o·* the jagged rocks.
329–14 *o·* mountain and meadow,
330– 4 *o·* the new-made grave,
330–14 alders bend *o·* the streams
331– 7 *o·* all the earth" — *Gen.* 1 : 26.
336– 2 Truth, the victor *o·* a lie.
339–17 faithful *o·* a few things." — *Matt.* 25 : 23.
340–16 not been faithful *o·* a few things.
340–24 thou hast been faithful *o·* a few things.
341– 9 be made ruler *o·* many things.
342–14 *o·* earth's lazy sleepers.
342–32 faithful *o·* the few things of Spirit,
349–17 I claim no jurisdiction *o·* any
353– 2 it has nothing to mourn *o·*,
356–23 This virtue triumphs *o·* the flesh;
373–25 God gave man dominion *o·* all
374–15 hold charge *o·* both,
376–22 *o·* a deeply dazzling sunlight,
379–29 Mind and its superiority *o·*
383– 8 preeminent *o·* ignorance or
Man. 17– 2 deliberations *o·* forming a church
58– 7 Pastor *o·* The Mother Church,
74– 5 control *o·* any other church.
80– 5 shall be paid *o·* semi-annually
89– 2 resign *o·* her own signature
90–12 continue not *o·* one week.
91–17 shall be paid *o·* annually to
Chr. 57– 3 power *o·* the nations: — *Rev.* 2 : 26.
Ret. 13–22 ineffable joy came *o·* me.
14– 2 forever lost its power *o·* me.
14–30 After the meeting was *o·*
15–25 treated and given *o·* by physicians
16– 3 When the meeting was *o·*,
22–17 God is *o·* all.
26–10 supremacy of good *o·* evil,
26–11 superiority of Spirit *o·* matter.
34–16 metaphysics *o·* physics.
47– 5 Students from all *o·* our continent,
47– 6 *o·* three hundred applications
57– 2 *o·* the unfathomable sea of

over

Ret.	73–20	or terrifies people *o·* it,
	79–21	victory *o·* self and sin.
	85–26	rapidly spreading *o·* the globe ;
	91–21	His power *o·* others was spiritual,
Un.	11– 3	taught us to walk *o·*, not *into*
	14– 3	do His work *o·* again,
	30–19	made humanity victorious *o·*
	39–18	giveth man dominion *o·* all the
	43– 4	any strong demonstration *o·*
	43–10	complete triumph *o·* death,
	45–19	telegraphs and telephones *o·* its
	58–14	triumph *o·* all mortal mentality
	58–20	midnight sun shines *o·* the Polar Sea.
Pul.	3–14	good fight we have waged is *o·*,
	3–28	so far from victory *o·* the flesh
	7–11	would not weep *o·* it, as he wept *o·*
	9–13	quibbled *o·* an architectural exigency,
	12–16	For victory *o·* a single sin,
	12–18	mighty conquest *o·* all sin?
	13– 6	faithful *o·* a few things, — *Matt.* 25 : 23.
	13– 7	make thee ruler *o·* many,'' *Matt.* 25 : 23.
	15–18	occasion for a victory *o·* evil.
	23–11	* has swept *o·* the country,
	26–21	* *o·* the door, in large golden letters
	26–27	* lamp *o·* two hundred years old,
	30–10	* includes those all *o·* the country.
	30–21	* power of Truth *o·* error.
	30–29	* *o·* two hundred thousand dollars,
	31–18	* dominance of mind *o·* matter,
	43– 7	* presided *o·* the exercises.
	44–20	* shown its power *o·* its students,
	52–12	* *o·* two hundred thousand dollars,
	52–21	* bigotry that swept *o·* the world
	53–19	* dominion *o·* the physical world.
	55–25	* now *o·* four thousand members.
	57– 3	* *o·* two hundred thousand dollars,
	58–10	* *o·* two hundred thousand dollars,
	58–16	* will seat *o·* a thousand
	59–29	* Before one service was *o·*
	60–13	* many having remained *o·* a week
	63–16	* numbers *o·* one hundred thousand
	63–25	* Christian Scientists all *o·* the country,
	67–17	* numbers *o·* a quarter of a million
	68–20	* *o·* two hundred thousand dollars,
	70– 5	* *O·* One Hundred Thousand Followers
	70–12	* *o·* one hundred thousand converts,
	70–16	* Christian Scientists all *o·* the country.
	70–23	* *o·* all error, sin, sickness, and
	71–13	* in fact all *o·* the country,
	71–14	* discomfited *o·* the announcements
	73– 9	* meditated *o·* His divine Word.
	75–21	* members . . . all *o·* North America
	79– 5	* *o·* two hundred thousand dollars,
	80–14	* *o·* its granitic pebbles.
No.	3–17	Every teacher must pore *o·* it
	8–20	enmity *o·* doctrines and traditions,
	8–20	*o·* the misconceptions of C. S.,
	29–24	*o·* the waves of sin, sickness, and
	33–22	Love and its power *o·* death.
	34–24	*o·* the steps of uplifted humanity,
	36–20	recuperated him for triumph *o·* sin,
	41–19	slumbered *o·* Christ's commands,
Pan.	3– 3	supposed to preside *o·* sylvan
	10– 8	prevail *o·* the opposite notion
'00.	1–12	*o·* sixteen thousand communicants
	1–24	*o·* a million of people
	8–23	will boil *o·* the brim of life
	10–20	*o·* individuals, weak provinces, or
	11– 3	have no discord *o·* music.
	12–24	*o·* two years — he labored
	15– 9	passage *o·* a tear-filled sea
'01.	2–28	my church of *o·* twenty-one thousand
	10–23	victory *o·* self, sin, disease,
	11– 4	his demonstration *o·* sin, disease,
	14– 1	it sticks to us and has power *o·* us.
	20–18	and his power *o·* it.
	23–21	demonstrated his power *o·* matter,
'02.	3–18	*o·* the close of the conflict in
	5– 6	*o·* doubtful interpretations of
	6–24	the struggle *o·*, and victory
	9–25	*o·* Morse's discovery of telegraphy?
	10– 4	power *o·* matter, molecule, space,
	10–30	walking every step *o·* the land route,
	15–24	steadfast stars watched *o·* the world,
	20– 1	Christ walketh *o·* the wave ;
Hea.	7– 6	power of Mind *o·* matter.
	8– 7	carrying out this government *o·*
	10–20	even the triumph of Soul *o·* sense.
	15– 9	power of mind *o·* matter,
	19– 2	to test the power of mind *o·* body ;
Peo.	2–20	demoniacal contests *o·* religion.
	11–11	supremacy of Soul *o·* sense,
	12– 3	*o·* all the earth.'' — *Gen.* 1 : 26.
	13–17	triumph of mind *o·* the body,
Po.	33–10	To kindly pass *o·* a wound,

over

Po.	47–15	*O·* the tears it has shed ;
	78– 3	Peace her white wings will spread *o·*
My.	v–22	* *o·* four hundred thousand copies
	vi–22	* she made *o·* to trustees
	21–20	* and running *o·*.'' — *Luke* 6 : 38.
	30– 5	* *o·* thirty thousand people
	30– 7	* Scientists from all *o·* the world,
	31–12	* from *o·* the entire world.
	43–19	* Israel came *o·* this Jordan
	47–11	* people the world *o·* have been
	47–16	* we look back *o·* the years
	49– 4	* one is wholly drawn *o·*,
	50–18	* Love prevailing *o·* the apparently
	55–10	* the Cause itself was spreading *o·*
	60–26	* Now that the great event, . . . is *o·*,
	61–14	* I was climbing *o·* stones and
	63–12	* annual communion and . . . are *o·*,
	65–12	* It was not even talked *o·*,
	72–25	* members of the church all *o·* the
	73– 5	* churches all *o·* this country
	73–13	* from all *o·* the world
	74–14	* their triumph of mind *o·* matter.
	75–18	* They do not get excited *o·* trifles.
	77– 4	* seating capacity of *o·* five thousand.
	77– 9	* From all *o·* the world
	77–18	* *O·* the heads of a multitude
	82–19	* when the entertainment is *o·*
	84–12	* Christian Scientists all *o·* the world.
	89– 6	* *o·* two hundred and twenty feet high,
	90–25	* from all *o·* the civilized world,
	93–13	* or attaining dominion *o·*
	97– 2	* power of mind *o·* matter.
	106–10	power *o·* and above matter
	119–18	gives dominion *o·* all the earth.
	123–21	*o·* two hundred people,
	126–25	*o·* the widowhood of lust,
	134–10	Joy *o·* good achievements
	137–11	It is *o·* forty years that I have
	142–19	*o·* a step higher in their passage
	147– 4	*O·* a half century ago,
	147– 7	*o·* my childhood's Sunday noons.
	148–27	to gain power *o·* contending
	154– 3	power of Truth *o·* error.
	156–23	which giveth victory *o·* sin, disease,
	158–13	heaven here, the struggle *o·* ;
	161–31	can triumph *o·* their ultimatum,
	162–11	Christian Scientists all *o·* the field,
	172–14	church of *o·* thirty thousand
	182– 3	*o·* any other city in the
	184–25	unwearied watch *o·* a world.
	185–10	reign triumphant *o·* all the earth.
	190–19	Mind *o·* the human mind
	190–22	power *o·* all manner of diseases ;
	192–11	conquest *o·* sin and mortality,
	194– 2	in broad facts *o·* great continents
	196–28	*O·* the glaciers of winter
204–	8, 9	*O·* sea and *o·* land, C. S. unites
	208– 6	its heavenly rays *o·* all the earth.
	219–29	''Rather than quarrel *o·* vaccination,
	229–23	messages of rejoicing *o·* the
	230–23	faithful *o·* foundational trusts,
	232– 3	sailing *o·* rough seas
	233–14	*o·* the effects of other people's
	245– 1	*o·* and above the approved schools
	257– 4	*o·* the new cradle of an old truth.
	258–21	repine *o·* blossoms that mock
	268–24	gives man the victory *o·* himself.
	275–27	white-winged charity brooding *o·* all,
	276– 9	or swallow camels *o·* it,
	285–19	power *o·* the nations.'' — *Rev.* 2 : 26.
	291– 4	*o·* the destinies of a nation
	291–24	prosperity waves *o·* land and sea,
	294– 6	omnipresent, supreme *o·* all.
	299– 3	*O·* the signature ''A Priest of
	306– 8	newspaper controversy *o·* a question
	323–22	* Your crowning triumph *o·* error
	341– 9	Beloved brethren all *o·* our land
	353–13	intended to hold guard *o·* Truth,
	361– 9	not seen Mrs. Stetson for *o·* a year,
	362– 5	right *o·* wrong, of Truth *o·* error.

overbalance

Mis.	354– 7	to *o·* this foul stuff.

overbear

Mis.	28–16	Science alone can *o·* materiality

overcame

Mis.	76–32	*o·* the last enemy, death.
	99– 9	His fear *o·* his loyalty ;
Pul.	12– 9	they *o·* him by the — *Rev.* 12 : 11.

overcome

Mis.	6–22	*o·* the patient's faith in drugs
	18–29	must be repented of and *o·*.
	55– 8	utilizes its power to *o·* sin.
	66–27	''*o·* evil with good.'' — *Rom.* 12 : 21.

overcome
Mis.	81–16	*in order to o· mortal sense,*
	89–27	saved from error, or error o·.
	104–32	wherewith to o· all error.
	112–28	Unless this mental condition be o·,
	115–27	God will give the ability to o·
	115–28	o· the baneful effects of sin
	116– 1	will o· evil with good,
	118–23	must be met manfully and o·,
	125– 7	enables him to o· the world,
	131–22	which they have o·.
	236–17	the best way to o· them,
	334–29	"Be not o· of evil, — *Rom.* 12 : 21.
	334–30	o· evil with good," — *Rom.* 12 : 21.
	352–27	through argument . . . o· evil.
Man.	47– 2	seeks to o· evil with good.
	55– 5	strive to o· these errors.
Ret.	55– 6	it can only be o· with good.
Pul.	13– 4	o· the mortal belief in a
	15–16	o· evil with good.
	83–18	* o· our own allied armies of evil
	84–24	* all obstacles . . . met and o·,
No.	9–20	power of grace to o· evil
	33– 4	thus we may o· evil with good.
'01.	14–25	To o· all wrong,
	15– 9	teaching him that they cannot o· us.
	17–19	o· a difficult stage of the work,
	34–21	be not o· of evil,
	34–21	but o· evil with good ;
'02.	2–30	to o· evil with good,
Peo.	5–14	having o· death and the grave,
My.	6–10	When we have o· sin
	52– 3	* she had many obstacles to o·,
	116– 9	must be met and o·.
	128–27	"o· evil with good." — *Rom.* 12 : 21.
	132– 7	I have o· the world." — *John* 16 : 33.
	180–18	o· evil and heal disease.
	228– 8	"o· evil with good." — *Rom.* 12 : 21.
	233–20	most stubborn belief to o·,
	278–21	should o· evil with good.
	300– 3	o· sin according to the Scripture,
	300–15	o· "the last enemy" — *I Cor.* 15 : 26.

overcomes
'01.	15– 8	he o· them through Christ,
My.	106–16	o· the evidence of diseased sensation.

overcometh
Mis.	168– 2	and o· the world !
Chr.	57– 1	he that o·, — *Rev.* 2 : 26.
My.	285–18	he that o·, — *Rev.* 2 : 26.

overcoming
Mis.	53– 7	by o· temptation and sin
	319–14	o· sin in themselves,
Man.	16– 3	healing the sick and o· sin
No.	33–24	o· sickness, sin, and death.
My.	64–24	* o· all that is unlike God,
	204–28	o· evil with good,
	239–10	by o· sin and death.
	291–12	universal good o· evil.

overcrowded
My.	56–11	* relieve the o· condition of
	56–24	* o· condition of
	57– 1	* annual meetings were o·
	57– 2	* o· in Tremont Temple,

overcrowding
My.	56–31	* continued o·, proved the need of

overcrowned
My.	201–14	was o· with a diadem of duties done.

overflow
Mis.	98–28	* Thy heart must o·, if thou
	296– 9	o· in shallow sarcasm,
	338–22	* Thy soul must o·, if thou
	338–24	* It needs the o· of heart,
Man.	61– 3	O· Meetings.
My.	17– 1	o· the hiding place." — *Isa.* 28 : 17.

overflowing
Mis.	310–25	chapter sub-title
	348– 6	hearts o· with love for God,
Pul.	29–14	* chairs . . . for the o· throng.
Peo.	9– 4	tears of repentance, an o· love,
My.	55–21	* hall was crowded to o·.
	96–22	* the fund was full to o·

overflows
Mis.	250–24	self-forgetful heart that o· ;

overlook
Pul.	65– 6	* should not o· the Boston sect of
My.	94– 9	* Neither can we o· the
	123–28	we must not o· small things
	227–17	they should not o· the fact that

overlooked
My.	93–26	* have o· these essentials of
	338–20	For once he may have o· the

overmuch
Rud.	16–10	attempt o· in their translation of

overrule
My.	293–24	to o· the purposes of hate

overruled
Un.	31– 9	and o· laws material

overrules
Mis.	41– 6	were it not that God o· it,

overseer's
Mis.	353–15	in the o· absence,

overshadow
My.	202– 1	May its white wings o· this

overshadowed
Mis.	361–12	C. S. has o· all human philosophy,

overshadowing
Mis.	84–21	o· Paul's sense of life in matter,
My.	46– 3	* in towering, o· dome,

overshadows
My.	127–14	o· and overwhelms *materia medica,*

oversubscribed
My.	73– 3	* which had been o·.

overthrew
Mis.	270– 2	"o· the tables of the — *Matt.* 21 : 12.

overthrow
Mis.	61–29	nor o· the logic that man is
	119– 6	rise and o· both.
Pul.	2–25	would o· this sublime fortress,
My.	345– 6	Science will o· false knowledge

overthrown
Mis.	170– 1	the last enemy to be o· ;

overture
Mis.	78– 2	o· of the angels.
	166–14	ready ear for the o· of angels
No.	46–11	joining the o· of angels.

overtures
Mis.	374–14	Angels, with o·, hold charge over
My.	13–25	reach the stars with divine o·,

overturn
Mis.	80–22	"turn and o·" — *see Ezek.* 21 : 27.
My.	220–20	o· until He whose right it is shall

overturned
Peo.	2–19	Such a theory has o· empires

overturning
My.	220–20	He who is o· will overturn

overturns
Mis.	13–21	o· the testimony of the

overwhelming
Mis.	273– 7	I withdraw from an o· prosperity.
	292– 2	o· tides of revelation,
Ret.	81–16	o· sense of error's vacuity,
No.	1– 9	demolishing bridges and o· cities.

overwhelms
My.	127–14	overshadows and o· *materia medica,*

overworked
Mis.	198–30	by saying he has o·,

owe
Mis.	126–16	sensible of what we o· to the
Ret.	94– 2	we o· to ourselves and to the world
Rud.	14– 4	"o· no man." — *Rom.* 13 : 8.
'01.	24–12	* under Providence I o· my life to it."
My.	9–26	draw on God for the amount I o· you,
	73– 6	* very few of them o· a cent.
	114– 3	O· no man ; be temperate ;
	202–10	O· no man any thing, — *Rom.* 13 : 8.
	331–22	* express the feeling of gratitude we o·

owes
Pan.	4– 2	o· its origin and continuity to
My.	37–23	* this church o· itself and its prosperity to

owing
Mis.	x– 9	O· to the manifold demands on my
	43–26	success of such an one is o·, in part,
	161–20	o· in part, perhaps, to the Jewish law
Man.	64–23	o· to the public misunderstanding
Pul.	20– 3	O· to a heavy loss, they were unable
My.	25–17	O· to the time consumed
	338–17	o· to my busy life,

owl
Peo.	14– 8	* "bat and o· on the bending stones,

own
Mis.	2– 5	they have so little of their o·.
	7–21	A periodical of our o· will
	8–10	thing outside thine o· creation?
	8–12	object of your o· conception?
	10– 9	Because He has called His o·,
	11– 7	and save my o· life,
	11–17	would one sooner give up his o·?
	13– 4	special care to mind my o· business.

own

Mis.	20– 3	aroma of Jesus' *o·* words,
	22–30	by reason of its *o·* ponderosity ;
	24–26	he speaketh of his *o·* : — *John* 8 : **44.**
	27– 9	abandon their *o·* logic.
	28– 4	having no sensation of its *o·*.
	31–18	argue against his *o·* convictions
	32–22	give to my *o·* flock all the
	33– 3	wrong will receive its *o·* reward.
	39–17	to take their *o·* medicine,
	41– 8	destroys their *o·* possibility of
	41–20	architect that builds its *o·* idea,
	42–31	our *o·* false admissions prevent us
	44–28	matter has no intelligence of its *o·*.
	47–15	loose from its *o·* beliefs.
	62– 2	improve my *o·*, and other people's
	62–31	can cure its *o·* disease,
	67–12	by doing thus thine *o·* sense of Life
	74–20	stone from the door of his *o·* tomb.
	77–27	made in God's *o·* likeness,
	80–14	rise or fall on its *o·* merit or
	82–27	treacherous glare of its *o·* flame
	83– 7	*cause of his o· sufferings."*
	83– 9	*your o· thought or another's."*
	83–13	with the consent of his *o·* belief.
	83–14	at the door of your *o·* thought
	83–17	arbiter of your *o·* fate,
	85–20	work out his *o·* salvation.
	92–11	his *o·* lamp trimmed and burning.
	92–22	*o·* a copy of the above-named **book**
	92–32	spiritualizes his *o·* thought,
	104–19	revolve in their *o·* orbits,
	104–29	recover his *o·* individuality?
	105–25	*o·* subjective state of thought.
	111–15	seed of Truth to its *o·* vitality,
	112–27	inability to see one's *o·* faults,
	113–14	depths of perdition by his *o·*
	114– 8	trend of their *o·* thoughts ;
	115– 6	even the teacher's *o·* deficiency
	115– 8	his *o·* guilt as a mental
	115–30	your *o·* as well as of others' sins.
	116– 2	destroy your *o·* sensitiveness to
	120–25	away from their *o·* fields of labor.
	122– 2	foretelling his *o·* crucifixion,
	123–24	sinners suffer for their *o·* sins,
	125– 8	dominion over his *o·* sinful sense
	126– 9	has his *o·* thoughts to guard,
	127–19	finds one's *o·* in another's good.
	131– 2	and cherishes his *o·*,
	134–16	guard and guide His *o·*.
	134–28	blind to its *o·* fate,
	137–17	spread your *o·* so bravely.
	138– 1	organizations of their *o·*,
	144–10	names in your *o·* handwriting,
	145–16	wounded sense of its *o·* error,
	148–13	impelled by a power not one's *o·*,
	154–13	beneath your *o·* vine and fig-tree
	155–24	If my *o·* students cannot spare time
	165–21	lifted to these by their *o·* growth
	170–13	make our *o·* heavens and our *o·* hells,
	173–12	Mind is its *o·* great cause and
	173–27	made man in His *o·* likeness.
	176–15	counted not their *o·* lives dear
	176–26	our *o·* great opportunities
	178– 1	place of my *o·* sojourning
	182– 1	antedated his *o·* existence,
	184–27	not her *o·*, but another's good ;
	186– 3	in His *o·* image and likeness.
	197–25	rules over a kingdom of its *o·*,
	198–12	he speaketh of his *o·*." — *John* 8 : **44.**
	199– 6	annul his *o·* erring mental law,
	208–15	Mortals obey their *o·* wills,
	209–10	and dies of its *o·* physics.
	209–23	Evil passions die in their *o·* flames
	211– 5	Our *o·* vision must be clear
	212–27	cast the beam out of his *o·* eye,
	213–16	may perfect their *o·* lives by
	214– 9	his *o·* household." — *Matt.* 10 : 36.
	216– 2	your *o·* state of combat with error.
	223–10	that mind reaches its *o·* ideal,
	224– 1	unless our *o·* thought barbs it.
	224– 5	wounded by our *o·* faults ;
	224–28	Nothing short of our *o·* errors **should**
	226– 9	by losing his *o·* self-respect?
	226–10	retaining his *o·*, he loses the
	226–15	* To thine *o·* self be true,
	227–22	abide in tabernacles of their *o·*,
	227–29	reckoning its *o·* by the
	237–22	work out its *o·* destruction ;
	238– 8	his *o·* life's incentive.
	242–15	C. S. that furnishes its *o·* **proof.**
	259–26	produced its *o·* illusion,
	261–25	kind of men after man's *o·* making.
	264– 6	their *o·* unsubstantiality,
	265– 1	offers his *o·* thought,
	266– 8	subjective state of his *o·* mind

Mis.	266–23	in unison with my *o·* endeavors
	268–23	potions of His *o·* qualities.
	268–30	error dies of its *o·* elements.
	278–25	substitute my *o·* for their growth,
	283–14	* "Mind your *o·* business,"
	283–24	work out his *o·* problem
	284– 1	each one to do his *o·* work well,
	288–22	as well as thine *o·*,
	294– 4	elbowing the concepts of his *o·*
	295–15	sentiments from his *o·* breast?
	296–28	by their *o·* poverty
	297–25	consequences of his *o·* conduct ;
	298– 2	thine *o·* understanding." — *Prov.* 3 : **5.**
	300– 6	reading it publicly as your *o·*
	302– 6	preserves in his *o·* consciousness
	302–32	within their *o·* fields of labor,
	303– 5	kindly shepherd has his *o·* fold
	303– 6	and tends his *o·* flock.
	303– 6	should have their *o·* institutes
	308– 7	stops his *o·* progress,
	309– 2	their *o·* or others' corporeality,
	312–20	his *o·* spiritual discernment,
	317– 6	Scientists to do their *o·* work ;
	319– 8	not seeing their *o·* belief in sin,
	324–17	his *o·* heart tired of sin,
	326–23	to meet with joy his *o·*,
	327– 6	take nothing of thine *o·* with thee?"
	327–13	heavy baggage of their *o·*,
	327–18	burden them with their *o·*.
	328– 3	Make thine *o·* way
	328–13	door of thine *o·* heart,
	330–17	God's *o·* image and likeness,
	336–13	first cast out your *o·* dislike and
	336–14	beam in your *o·* eye that hinders
	348–16	wise in his *o·* conceit." — *Prov.* 26 : 5.
	350– 1	of my *o·* contributions.
	350–32	its *o·* proof of my practice.
	354–21	to govern His *o·* creation,
	355–21	out of thine *o·* eye." — *Matt.* 7 : 5.
	355–22	in thine *o·* mentality
	355–27	thine *o·* mental atmosphere.
	356– 3	life corrected illumine its *o·*
	356–25	gone down in his *o·* esteem.
	360–20	who partaketh of its *o·* altars,
	361–29	He elucidates His *o·* idea,
	362–15	regards creation as its *o·* creator,
	363– 2	of its *o·* unreality,
	368– 1	His *o·* image and likeness.
	368– 9	* keeping watch above His *o·*."
	371– 7	help them by his *o·* leadership?
	379–16	had advanced views of his *o·*,
	387– 6	Our spirits' *o·* !"
	397–15	where Thine *o·* children are,
	398–12	And Thou know'st Thine *o·* ;
Man.	3– 9	impelled by a power not one's *o·*,
	26–11	given in her *o·* handwriting,
	50– 4	by *one of her o· sex.*
	55– 6	discipline its *o·* members,
	70–15	its *o·* form of government.
	75–18	*o·* the aforesaid premises
	81– 4	given in her *o·* handwriting.
	85– 1	occupies only his *o·* field of labor.
	89– 2	resign over her *o·* signature
	97–12	given in her *o·* handwriting,
	99–11	not . . . confined to its *o·* members
	111– 6	sign her *o·* Christian name,
Ret.	9–26	* her *o·* unfettered way !
	14– 2	rightly called his *o·* tenet
	15– 5	till I founded a church of my *o·*,
	16–11	occurrence in my *o·* church
	28–18	their *o·* mental denomination,
	46–18	And Thou know'st Thine *o·*.
	48– 8	every one should build on his *o·*
	57–22	must be of God, and not our *o·*,
	59–24	in His *o·* image and likeness ;
	70– 2	upon its *o·* misconceptions.
	70– 5	puts forth its *o·* qualities,
	70–19	his *o·* niche in time and eternity.
	73–21	victim of his *o·* corporeality.
	74– 4	by his *o· corpus sine pectore*
	74– 8	My *o·* corporeal personality
	75–17	author's *o·* mental mood,
	75–24	write out as his *o·* the substance of
	78–24	your *o·* success and final happiness,
	79– 6	from our *o·* material losses.
	81–24	* To thine *o·* self be true ;
	83–17	more difficult to rekindle his *o·*
	84– 5	spiritualize his *o·* thoughts
	84– 8	keeps his *o·* lamp trimmed
	84–11	should *o·* a copy of S. and H.,
	84–27	take charge only of his *o·* pupils
	84–29	avoid leaving his *o·* regular
	85– 2	doing his *o·* work well.
	86–22	each man who performs his *o·* part.
	87–23	They feel their *o·* burdens less,

own

Ret.	88– 6	his o· body from the sepulchre.
	88–22	other vineyards than our o·.
	89–19	to instruct his o· students ;
	89–24	neglecting their o· students,
	91–20	his o· perfect understanding.
	93–16	spiritual ideal is made our o·,
	93–19	identical with my o· :
Un.	1– 7	their o· destruction.'' — *II Pet.* 3 : 16.
	3–21	in His o· nature and character,
	4–14	lose our o· consciousness of error.
	10–28	under their o· falsities,
	13– 5	doing their o· work in obedience to
	14– 9	improve upon His o· previous work,
	18– 5	only the brightness of My o· glory.
	20–22	outside of His o· focal distance.
	26– 2	having its o· innate selfhood
	27–10	doubts all existence except its o·.
	27–11	everything except his o· existence.
	27–15	knowing only His o· all-presence,
	29–16	any standpoint of their o·.
	33– 6	only testify from their o· evidence,
	34–22	its o· so-called substance.
	43–21	influence of their o· thoughts
	45–19	telephones over its o· body,
	45–20	imaginary sphere of its o· creation
	53–14	will die of its o· delusion ;
	55– 6	''in his o· body — *I Pet.* 2 : 24.
	56– 7	Not his o· sins, but the sins of the
Pul.	vii– 7	inclination given their o· thoughts
	3–30	Because of my o· unfitness
	5–20	with a beauty all its o·
	8–21	rechristen them with his o· new name.
	13–24	stung to death by his o· malice ;
	17–17	And Thou know'st Thine o·.
	18–24	where Thine o· children are,
	21– 9	to inhabit my o· heart
	30– 1	* members of their o· families,
	30–28	* its o· magnificent church
	31– 8	* my o· knowledge of Mrs. Eddy,
	35–29	* sympathy with her o· views,
	48–14	* pleased her to point out her o·
	50– 5	* home and family of his o·.
	55–28	* management of its o· affairs.
	57–21	* Few people outside its o· circles realize
	81–22	* her o· soul plays upon magic strings
	82–24	* by singing most for their o· sex.
	83–18	* our o· allied armies of evil
Rud.	8– 5	in Science, Spirit sends forth its o·
	11– 1	can frame its o· conditions,
	13–21	according to their o· belief
	14–22	it is their o· fault,
No.	3–23	seek not so much thine o·
	6– 8	take cognizance of their o· phenomena,
	7– 9	cancel error in our o· hearts,
	7–21	must now fight their o· battles.
	8–12	work out his o· salvation,
	9–10	their o· standpoint of experience,
	13– 2	rebukes sin with its o· nothingness,
	16–21	His o· consciousness,
	23–28	is God's o· image and likeness,
	26–11	brings forth its o· sensuous conception.
	29– 2	put to death for his o· sin,
	30–18	Truth's knowledge of its o·
	38–20	includes only His o· nature,
	42–19	The lie of evil holds its o· by
	42–22	cleaving to their o· vices.
	43–19	build a baseless fabric of their o·
Pan.	5–16	he speaketh of his o· : — *John* 8 : 44.
'00.	8–12	purloined garment as his o·,
	8–29	desire to follow your o·
	14–19	not only her o·, but another's good.
'01.	1–23	you seek to define God to your o·
	7–10	God made man in His o· image
	10–25	working out our o· salvation,
	13– 3	annihilates its o· embodiment :
	20– 9	alone with his o· being
	26–30	result of my o· observation,
	27–22	less of my o· personality
	29–26	a tithe of my o· difficulties,
	30–24	* man ''clouting his o· cloak''
	34–19	not her o· but another's good,
	34–30	thine o· understanding. — *Prov.* 3 : 5.
'02.	2– 6	on the tablet of one's o· heart,
	13– 1	from my o· private earnings
Hea.	5– 1	our o· erring finite sense of God,
	5–21	work out our o· salvation,
	5–22	responsibility of our o· thought
	9–17	His o· image and likeness.
	11– 7	rebels at its o· boundaries ;
Peo.	4– 1	by working out our o· salvation.
	7– 2	working out our o· ideals,
	7–14	* With heaven's o· light the sculptor
	7–22	* Its heavenly beauty shall be our o·,
	8–10	these qualities . . . in our o· lives
	9–13	work out our o· salvation,

own

Peo.	10–21	We possess our o· body,
	11–21	calls its o· enactments ''laws
	14–18	reinstate man in God's o· image
Po.	13– 3	where Thine o· children are,
	14–16	Thou know'st Thine o· ;
	26–10	on her altar our loved Lincoln's o·
	41– 1	* my o· stricken deer.
	50–24	Our spirits' o· !''
My.	vii– 6	* can so protect their o· thoughts
	8– 5	* our o· growth and progress.
	10–30	* their o· individual welfare
	12–13	* promptness of his o· contribution.
	12–20	We o· no past, no future,
	15–14	transform you into His o· image
	18–16	finds one's o· in another's good.''
	19–23	''seeketh not her o·'' — *I Cor.* 13 : 5.
	21– 6	* building church homes of their o·,
	26–18	include enough of their o·.
	33–24	sweareth to his o· hurt, — *Psal.* 15 : 4.
	39–28	* our o· growth in love and unity
	40–31	* her o· blameless and happy life,
	41–30	* for our sakes as well as for her o· ;
	48–19	* Bible and her o· writings,
	52–31	* his o· peculiar knowledge of the
	55– 4	* needed a place of its o·,
	59–22	* my o· feeble attempts
	83– 7	* for their o· self-identification,
	84– 5	* testify from his o· experience
	103–23	on which to found my o·,
	106–23	because he minds his o· business
	108–29	will close with his o· words :
	112–31	our o· and in foreign lands,
	117–10	one's o· dream of personal sense,
	122– 6	fixed in one's o· moral make-up.
	124–31	they consume in their o· fires
	128–16	his o· rational conscience
	130– 2	Watch and guard your o· thoughts
	132–15	''Of His o· will — *Jas.* 1 : 18.
	134–28	* Mrs. Eddy's o· handwriting,
	136–14	Trustees who o· my property :
	137– 8	* in Mrs. Eddy's o· handwriting
	150–19	become His o· image and likeness,
	161–15	within his o· consciousness,
	174–23	until I had a church of my o·,
	212–26	loses his o· power to heal.
	212–27	compensate himself for his o· loss
	213–17	impulses of our o· thought,
	213–22	strengthen your o· citadel
	214–25	even to meet my o· current expenses.
	216–23	work in your o· several localities,
	216–29	will want money for your o· uses.
	217– 2	for your o· school education,
	227– 4	in his o· personal sense of
	227– 6	minifying of his o· goodness by
	227–15	influenced by their o· judgment
	243–17	remain in their o· fields of labor
	243–18	caring for their o· flocks.
	244–16	God's o· image and likeness,
	249– 2	or your o· moral sense,
	249– 4	through your o· perfectness.
	249–11	let loose for one's o· destruction.
	253–16	through Thine o· name — *John* 17 : 11.
	257–19	We o· his grace,
	262– 1	perfect and eternal in His o· image.
	272–22	* reproduced in her o· handwriting.
	272–23	* Mrs. Eddy's o· devoted followers,
	273– 4	* to vindicate in her o· person
	275–12	chapter sub-title
	276– 4	begs to say, in her o· behalf,
	276–11	is minding her o· business,
	278–28	pierced by its o· sword.
	280–22	with His o· truth and love.
	283–15	Sin is its o· enemy.
	283–23	God's o· plan of salvation.
	291–30	work for their o· country,
	300– 4	your o· salvation — *Phil.* 2 : 12.
	300–31	fire on their o· religious ranks,
	306–19	and that in God's o· time.
	306–29	purporting to be Dr. Quimby's o·
	311–22	her o· family coat-of-arms.
	315–30	in our o· and in other countries,
	321–28	* my o· personal knowledge
	330– 8	* contradicting his o· statement,
	333– 5	* found by one of your o· citizens,
	334–16	* quote her o· words.
	343– 2	* in Mrs. Eddy's o· spirit.
	343– 4	* in her o· way,
	349–32	reckons creation as its o·
	359– 4	individuals in their o· church
	364–10	excludes from his o· consciousness,

owned

Mis.	140–17	to know who o· God's temple,
Man.	76–22	real estate o· by this Church
Ret.	4– 8	o· by Uncle James Baker's grandson,
Pul.	68–23	* o· by Christian Scientists.

owned
  My. 310–11 and together they *o·* a large
        314–12 *o·* a house in Franklin, N. H.

ownership
  My. 65–21 * has passed to the *o·* of the
      66– 3 * the *o·* of the entire block.
     66–10 * the *o·* of the entire block.
    356– 1 their present *o·* of all good,

owning
  Pul. 58– 7 * *o·* a beautiful estate

owns
  Mis. 299–22 manufactured them and *o·* them,

owns
  Mis. 331–19 that *o·* each waiting hour ;
     389– 7 that *o·* each waiting hour,
  Man. 75–16 *o·* the church edifices,
   Po. 4– 3 that *o·* each waiting hour,

Oxford
  Hea. 18–27 The *O·* students proved this :

Oxford University
  Pul. 5–25 *O· U·* and the Victoria Institute,

oxidized
  Pul. 25–25 * *o·* silver lamps of Roman design,
     26–11 * six richly wrought *o·* silver lamps,

P

Pa. *(see also* **Keystone State***)*
  (see **Harrisburg, Lebanon, Mickleys, Philadelphia, Pittsburg, York***)*

pace
  Mis. 107–18 cannot keep *p·* with eternity.
  Ret. 44–12 spiritual growth kept *p·* with
  My. 8– 5 * We need to keep *p·* with our
    14–30 * keep *p·* with the disbursements.

Pacific
  Mis. 251– 5 from the *P·* to the Atlantic
  Pul. 41– 9 * from the far-off *P·* coast
    88– 4 from the Atlantic to the *P·*
  My. 85–10 * from the Atlantic to the *P·*

pacification
  My. 220–15 *p·* of all national difficulties,

pacified
  Pul. 14–24 The waters will be *p·*,

pacify
  No. 9–14 Hoping to *p·* repeated complaints

packages
  My. 259–15 they require less attention than *p·*

packed
  Mis. 168–28 * Hawthorne Hall was densely *p·*,

paddling
  Mis. 329–19 *p·* the watercresses,

pæan
  My. 167–23 send forth a *p·* of praise
   355–18 chapter sub-title

pagan
  Mis. 111–23 Plato was a *p·* ;
    123–10 *p·* priests bloated with crime ;
    124–10 *p·* Jew's or Moslem's misconception
    169– 4 philosophies or *p·* literatures,
    173– 8 *p·* philosophy, or scholastic
    187–31 transcribed by *p·* religionists,
    260– 6 *P·* mysticism, Grecian philosophy,
    345–22 *p·* slanderers affirmed that Christians
  Ret. 57–12 If that *p·* philosopher had known
  Pul. 65–22 * the spot where, in *p·* times,
  '00. 13–26 * amalgamation of different *p·* religions
  '02. 5– 3 *p·* philosophies and tribal religions
  Peo. 4–23 The *p·* priests appointed Apollo
  My. 288–14 *p·* mysticisms, tribal religion,

paganism
  Pan. 7–12 and hint the gods of *p·* ?
    8–25 pantheism, polytheism, and *p·*
    9– 5 in *p·* they stand for gods ;

pagans
  My. 104– 3 Jewish *p·* thought that the

page
  Mis. 58–14 I read the inspired *p·* through a
    280–22 hand-painted flowers on each *p·*,
    294– 8 transcribes on the *p·* of reality
    313– 9 light of penetration on the *p·* ;
    314–27 unnecessary to repeat the title or *p·*.
    318–12 the paragraph on *p·* 47
  Man. 87–22 Retrospection . . . *p·* 84.
    112– 4 as shown on *p·* 118.
    112–11 according to the form on *p·* 114.
  Chr. 53–52 And writes the *p·*.
  Pul. 39– 9 on the following *p·* a little poem
  '00. 10–25 since publishing this *p·* I have
  Po. 28– 4 Help us to write a deathless *p·*
  My. 146– 2 dedicatory letter . . . *p·* 177
    254–20 * *Journal* of 1904, *p·* 184 :
    (see also **Science and Health***)*

pageant
  My. 147– 3 the past comes forth like a *p·*

pageantries
  My. 29–13 Many more gorgeous church *p·*

pageantry
  My. 189–22 twilight of the world's *p·*,

pages
  Mis. xi– 5 These *p·*, although a reproduction
    156– 2 contribute oftener to the *p·*
    169– 1 Within Bible *p·* she had found all
    169– 6 God-driven back to the inspired *p·*.
  Man. 111–16 on *p·* 114 and 118.
  Ret. 2– 5 in the *p·* of Sir Walter Scott
  Pul. 6–15 * I had not read three *p·* before I
    88– 7 too voluminous for these *p·*.
  My. 13– 8 When scanning its interesting *p·*,
    47– 8 * from the *p·* of its history.
    256–14 pure *p·* of impersonal presents,
    (see also **Science and Health***)*

paid
  Mis. 165–24 they never *p·* the price of sin.
    239–24 familiarity with what the stock *p·*,
    253– 5 the price that he *p·* for it?
    347–32 is well *p·* by the umpire.
    350– 1 $1,489.50 *p·* in,
  Man. 68–10 shall be *p·* semi-annually
    76– 2 spared after the debts are *p·*,
    79–11 be *p·* from the Church funds.
    80– 5 shall be *p·* over semi-annually
    91–17 shall be *p·* over annually to the
    96– 7 cost of hall shall be *p·* by
    97–13 an annual salary, *p·* quarterly,
  Ret. 38– 3 *p·* him seven hundred dollars,
    49–29 debts of the corporation have been *p·*,
  Pul. 20– 4 therefore I *p·* it,
    30–30 * and entirely *p·* for when its
    41– 2 * with every stone *p·* for
    57– 4 * It is entirely *p·* for,
    58–11 * every bill being *p·*.
    63–23 * was *p·* for before it was begun,
    70–16 * *p·* for by Christian Scientists
    79– 6 * for which the money was all *p·* in
  No. 35–14 the awful price *p·* by sin,
  '02. 13–15 about one half the price *p·*,
    13–25 no one offering the price I had *p·*
    14– 2 five thousand dollars had been *p·*
    15–11 *p·* me not one dollar of royalty
  My. 10–11 * Some money has been *p·* in
    11–25 * this land has been *p·* for.
    14–15 * entire amount . . . had been *p·* in ;
    70– 8 * and they are all *p·* for.
    72–26 * every cent of it was *p·* in
    75–24 * chapter sub-title
    87–16 * their costly church fully *p·* for,
    89–16 * Everything, . . . is *p·* for,
    91– 8 * church edifices to be fully *p·* for
    136–17 *p·* the highest fee ever received by
    137–15 and have *p·* for the same.
    161– 2 Christ Jesus *p·* our debt
    232– 7 whereby all our debts are *p·*,
    309–20 *p·* the largest tax in the colony.
    312–11 * *p·* Mrs. Glover's fare to New York
    325– 9 * what you then *p·* for it.
    331–29 * kind attention *p·* to the

paid-up
  My. 90–23 * *p·* cost of two million dollars

pain
  all
    Po. 41–18 call them to banish all *p·*,
  and disease
    Mis. 68– 9 * *maintained that p· and disease*
      68–14 penalty . . . the very *p·* and disease.
    Rud. 11–14 unreality of *p·* and disease ;
  and pleasure
    Mis. 74–25 recognize or express *p·* and pleasure.
  and sickness
    Mis. 68–12 *p·* and sickness are . . . illusions.
  and sin
    Po. 22–18 dark domain of *p·* and sin
  and sorrow
    Un. 18–11 *p·* and sorrow were not in My mind,

pain

bedside of
Mis. 201–30 Go to the bedside of *p*',
beds of
Pul. 54– 3 * Is by our beds of *p*' ;
belief in
Mis. 44–27 When your belief in *p*' ceases,
belief of
Mis. 44–18 a belief of *p*' in matter ;
brings
Mis. 102–22 Human pity often brings *p*'.
caused the
Mis. 44–15 *caused the p*' *to cease?*
ceases
Mis. 44–14 *and then the p*' *ceases,*
compels
Mis. 85–27 *p*' compels human consciousness to
ease or
My. 253– 8 * art not here for ease or *p*',
ever of
Po. 47–11 Outside this ever of *p*'?
foretells the
Un. 57– 7 foresees . . . and foretells the *p*'.
freedom from
Mis. 298–28 no more gains freedom from *p*' than
in the bone
Mis. 44–17 What you thought was *p*' in the bone
moaning in
Mis. 225–22 the lad . . . moaning in *p*'.
no
'02. 20– 7 "No drunkards . . no sorrow, no *p*' ;
My. 80– 6 * felt no *p*' when having
351–17 where are no partings, no *p*'.
no more
Mis. 44–26 There is no more *p*'.
no necessity for
Mis. 241-20 there is no necessity for *p*' ;
or death
My. 90–12 * insures fidelity in *p*' or death
or disease
Rud. 10–14 cannot . . . report *p*' or disease.
or power
No. 32– 8 its pleasure, *p*', or power
pestilence or
Mis. 389–22 no fowler, pestilence or *p*' ;
Po. 5– 1 no fowler, pestilence or *p*' ;
pillow of
Mis. 257–31 Smoothing the pillow of *p*'
pleasure and
Mis. 85–23 suggests pleasure and *p*' in matter ;
198– 7 varied forms of pleasure and *p*'.
333– 2 pleasure and *p*', good and evil,
Un. 3– 3 matter's reality, pleasure, and *p*',
pleasure nor
Mis. 28–26 neither pleasure nor *p*' therein.
pleasure or
Mis. 100– 6 intoxicated with pleasure or *p*',
relief from
Mis. 262–16 giving to the sick relief from *p*' ;
298–26 "I find relief from *p*' in
removes the
Un. 2–10 and, lastly, it removes the *p*'
self-inflicted
Pul. 56–22 * And mourn our self-inflicted *p*'."
to control
Mis. 45– 4 enables you to control *p*'.
without
Mis. 30–11 without *p*', sin, or death.
would cease
Mis. 44–24 extracted, the *p*' would cease :

Mis. 44–22 That matter can report *p*',
44–27 belief . . . ceases, the *p*' stops :
200–22 the touch of weakness, *p*',
351–23 five senses give to mortals *p*',
396–21 whose measures bind The power of *p*',
Un. 57– 5 by the *p*' they feel and occasion ;
58– 1 sin, *p*', death, — a false sense of
Pul. 1–10 Time past . . . may *p*' us,
18– 5 whose measures bind The power of *p*'.
Po. 12– 5 whose measures bind The power of *p*',
31–22 sting of death — sin, *p*'.
My. 221–25 of pleasure, or of *p*'
273–19 personal sense of pleasure, *p*',

painful

Mis. 17–24 more or less prolonged and *p*',
Ret. 38–11 to fulfil this *p*' task,

painless

Po. 70–21 A *p*' heraldry of Soul,
My. 181–10 mortal's *p*' departure from matter

pain-racked

My. 40–18 * *p*' and sorrow-worn humanity.

pains

pleasures and
(*see* **pleasures**)

pains

Mis. 17–30 accumulating *p*' of sense,
85–26 The pleasures — more than the *p*'
173–24 *p*', fetters, and befools him.
185– 7 disabilities, *p*' or pleasures.
200–28 so-called *p*' and pleasures of matter
209–13 admits the so-called *p*' of matter
341–30 pleasures or *p*' of material sense
395– 6 The stars reject his *p*',
Hea. 17– 3 *p*' of the personal senses
Po. 57–13 The stars reject his *p*',

paint

Mis. 329–23 *p*' in pink the petals of arbutus,
377– 2 brush or pen to *p*' frail fairness
Po. 34–14 Divinely desolate the shrine to *p*'
53– 2 And *p*' the gray, stark trees,

painted

Mis. 240– 5 ruby cheeks *p*' and fattened by
Pul. 8–25 *p*' the finest flowers in the

painter's

Mis. 372–27 the *p*' masterpieces ;

painting

Mis. 62– 6 an artist in *p*' a landscape.
270– 6 in sculpture, music, or *p*'
392–19 on receiving a *p*' of the Isle
Rud. 3–13 models . . . in music and *p*'
Po. 51– 1 On receiving a *p*' of the Isle.

paintings

Pul. 65–20 * arrangement of statuary and *p*'

paints

Mis. 393– 6 *P*' the limner's work, I ween,
Po. 51–11 *P*' the limner's work, I ween,

palace

Pul. 82– 1 * but the *p*' of the soul,
My. 257–29 their record in the monarch's *p*',

palaces

My. 112–29 *p*' of emperors and kings,

palatial

Mis. 324– 4 at the threshold of a *p*' dwelling,
Pul. 70–26 * She has a *p*' home in Boston

pale

Mis. 112–20 sank back in his chair, limp and *p*' ;
Chr. 53–37 Thus olden faith's *p*' star
53–44 Crowns the *p*' brow.
Ret. 16–12 *p*' cripples went into the church
Pul. 26–25 * The room is toned in *p*' green
76– 7 * *p*' green and gold decoration
My. 200–21 *P*', sinful sense, at work to

pales

My. 77– 7 * *p*' into insignificance,

Palestina's

Chr. 53–49 As in blest *P*' hour,

Palestine

Pul. 53–23 * from the hilltops of *P*',

pall

Mis. 376–22 Little by little this topmost *p*',

palm

Mis. 390– 5 Old Time gives thee her *p*'.
Ret. 17–17 *p*', bay, and laurel, in classical glee,
Po. 10– 7 Thy *p*', in ancient day,
55– 6 Old Time gives thee her *p*'.
63– 1 *p*', bay, and laurel, in classical glee,
My. 337– 8 Thy *p*', in ancient day,

Palmer House

Mis. 275–27 The *P*' *H*', where we stopped,
276– 3 spacious rooms of the *P*' *H*',

Palmetto

Mis. 251– 5 from the *P*' to the Pine Tree
My. 176– 9 hallow your *P*' home

palms

Mis. 231–24 soft little *p*' patting together,
332–15 stately *p*', many-hued blossoms,
Pul. 27–17 * windows bearing *p*' of victory,
42–22 * a star of lilies resting on *p*',
42–26 * *p*' and ferns and Easter lilies.
42–29 * resting on a mat of *p*',
My. 176– 9 *p*' of victory and songs of glory.

palpable

Mis. 294– 9 the living, *p*' presence
333– 7 renders error a *p*' falsity,

palpably

Mis. 200– 8 *p*' an error of premise
Pul. 5–29 *p*' working in the sermons,
My. 8– 4 * denomination is *p*' outgrowing

palpitating

Mis. 376–13 * a *p*', living Saviour

palsied

Un. 11–13 The *p*' hand moved,
No. 44–17 it *p*' the weak hand

palsy
Mis. 238–26 or that I died of *p*·,
paltering
My. 340–19 *p*·, timid, or dastardly policy,
pampered
My. 302–21 but I am less lauded, *p*·,
pamphlet
Mis. 380–30 use of an infringing *p*·
  381–25 disposing of, the enjoined *p*·,
No. v– 1 each edition of this *p*·
My. 319– 7 *p*·, signed "Phare Pleigh."
  323– 3 * Mr. Wiggin gave me a *p*·
pamphlets
Mis. 285– 3 edition of one thousand *p*·
  285– 7 some of these *p*· were mistaken for
  301– 7 authors and editors of *p*·
Pan
Pan. 2–26 *P*· in imagery is preferable to
  3– 2 *P*·, as a deity, is supposed to
  3–23 *P*· stood for "universal nature
  3–26 *P*· was the god of shepherds
pan
Pan. 2–23 *P*· is a Greek prefix,
panacea
Mis. 355–18 is a sovereign *p*·.
pane
Mis. 324–17 clearer *p*· of his own heart
panel
Pul. 28– 2 * The central *p*· represents
  28– 5 * *p*· containing the C. S. seal,
panelled
Pul. 26– 5 * The galleries are richly *p*·
My. 69– 8 * curved and *p*· surface,
panels
Pul. 28– 1 * composed of three separate *p*·,
  28– 6 * other *p*· are decorated with
pang
Po. 15–18 Flowers fresh as the *p*· in the bosom
pangs
Un. 56–23 *p*· of hell must lay hold of him
No. 34–15 *p*· which come to one upon whom
Peo. 1–17 Even the *p*· of death disappear,
panoplied
Mis. 162–31 *P*· in the strength of
panoply
Mis. 374– 3 clad in *p*· of power,
Pul. 15–19 Clad in the *p*· of Love,
panteth
Hea. 10–26 hart *p*· for the water brooks,
  10–27 so *p*· my heart for the true fount
pantheism
Mis. 23– 4 Is *p*· true?
  26–20 belief of mind in matter is *p*·.
  56– 1 theories of agnosticism and *p*·,
  76–11 is not theism, but *p*·.
  257– 3 *P*· presupposes that God
Ret. 23–21 *p*·, and theosophy were void.
Un. 45–14 conscious matter implies *p*·.
  45–14 This *p*· I unveil.
  51–10 In *p*· the world is bereft of
Rud. 5–18 Mind in matter is *p*·
  13– 3 *p*· and theosophy are not
No. 15–20 C. S. refutes *p*·,
  29– 6 This is *p*·, and is not the
Pan. 1– 4 SUBJECT: *Not P*·, *but C. S.*
  2– 1 chapter sub-title
  2– 3 that C. S. is *p*· is anomalous
  2– 7 looms above the mists of *p*·
  2– 9 chapter sub-title
  2–10 the word "*p*·" is derived from
  2–12 word "*p*·" is most suggestive.
  2–14 gives the meaning of *p*·
  2–19 *p*· is the doctrine of
  2–24 might stand, in the term *p*·,
  2–26 preferable to *p*· in theology.
  3– 1 *p*· suits not at all the
  4– 1 agrees with certain forms of *p*·
  5– 1 *p*· is found in scholastic theology.
  8–16 idolatry, *p*·, and polytheism.
  8–24 *p*·, polytheism, and paganism
  9– 1 reiterate the belief of *p*·,
  13– 2 And Science is not *p*·,
pantheist
Mis. 133– 6 In refutation . . . that I am a *p*·,
  248–17 a mesmerist, a medium, a "*p*·;"
  249–12 I am not a spiritualist, a *p*·,
pantheistic
Mis. 133– 3 * "the *p*· and prayerless Mrs. Eddy,
  189–16 *p*· doctrine that presents a

pantheistic
Ret. 69– 8 *p*· error, or so-called *serpent*,
Un. 50– 7 the temptation of *p*· belief
No. 15–19 chapter sub-title
  29–13 Is this *p*· statement sound theology,
pantheon
No. 21–20 in the *p*· of many gods,
papa
Mis. 231–20 *p*· knew that he could walk,
paper
Mis. 7–22 through our *p*·, . . . we shall be able
  294–26 I have read the daily *p*·,
Man. 90–21 prepare a *p*· on said subject
  90–23 this *p*· shall be given to the teacher,
  91– 3 but shall destroy this *p*·.
Pul. 36–28 * for some of the data of this *p*·.
  79–13 * a daily *p*· in town or village
My. 60–16 * a reward for the best *p*·
  157–20 * inquiry from the editor of that *p*·,
  173– 5 Allow me through your *p*·
  284–12 In the issue of your good *p*·,
  329–16 * as they appear in that *p*·
  330– 1 * was published in your *p*·
  331–18 * Through the columns of your *p*·,
  332–17 * The *p*· containing this card
papers
Man. 98–15 *p*· containing such an article,
Pul. 27– 5 * safe preservation of *p*·.
  71–15 * announcements in New York *p*·
My. 332–29 * roll of *p*· recording the death
Papias
My. 178–30 *Logia* of *P*·, written in A.D. 145,
  179– 1 ancient *Logia*, . . . by *P*·,
par at
Mis. 269–28 to buy error at *p*· value.
My. 265– 8 and is bought at *p*· value;
parable
Mis. 27–16 maintain this fact by *p*·
  251–26 learn a *p*· of the period,
  341–21 *p*· of "the ten virgins" — *see Matt.* 25 : 1
  341–22 This *p*· is drawn from the
  341–27 moral of the *p*· is pointed,
  341–29 We learn from this *p*· that
Ret. 91– 3 *p*· of "the prodigal son"
'01. 19–11 illustrated his saying by a *p*·.
Hea. 8–24 the *p*· of the husbandman.
My. 109–25 not alone by miracle and *p*·,
  347–18 *P*· of the priceless pearl
parables
Ret. 91– 4 rightly called "the pearl of *p*·,"
'01. 25–13 No Christly axioms, practises, or *p*·
paradisaical
Mis. 70–12 *P*· rest from physical agony
paradise
Mis. 70–11 *shalt thou be with me in p*·'" — *Luke* 23 : 43.
  70–14 *p*· of Spirit would come
  185–20 opens the gates of *p*·
Pul. 80– 9 * emphatically the women's *p*·,
My. 118–27 finds its *p*· in Spirit,
paragons
Mis. 316–27 there would be on earth *p*·
paragraph
Mis. 88–15 following *p*·, glows in the shadow
  318–12 an amendment of the *p*·
Pul. 60–10 * Each *p*· he supplemented
My. 236–25 universally to read the *p*·
  305– 7 S. and H., page 68, third *p*·,
paragraphs
Mis. 309–25 page 229, third and fourth *p*·,
Pul. 59–15 * Antiphonal *p*· were read
My. 110–31 quoting sentences or *p*·
parallel
36th
Man. 99– 5 being the 36th *p*· of latitude.

———

Mis. 66–12 supported in the Scripture by *p*· proof.
Pul. 59–14 * *p*· interpretation by Mrs. Eddy.
My. 98– 9 * such as religious annals hardly *p*·
paralleled
Mis. 258–22 no personality that could be *p*·
Pul. 23–10 * *p*· during the last decade
Po. 2–11 Great as thou art, and *p*· by none,
parallels
Pul. 60–11 * illustrative Scripture *p*·,
paralyze
Ret. 81– 2 threaten to *p*· its beneficence.
My. 213– 4 malicious aim of . . . is to *p*· good

paralyzed
Mis. 222–10 he becomes morally *p·*
Pul. 10– 3 *p·* by inactive faith,
My. 48–29 * *p·* by sentimental fiction.

paramount
Mis. 160– 7 as part and *p·* portion of her being.
200–26 no obstacle or circumstances *p·* to
Ret. 31– 7 *p·* to rubric and dogma
My. 282–23 It is of *p·* importance

parapets
Mis. 383–11 beat in vain against the immortal *p·*

paraphrase
Mis. 364– 4 naturally evokes new *p·*
My. 313– 1 a *p·* of a silly song

paraphrased
Un. 44– 7 popular couplet may be so *p·*

paraphrases
'00. 12– 2 *p·* projected from divinity

paraphrasing
Pul. 5–18 Then eloquently *p·* it.

parcel
Mis. 336–24 Part and *p·* of Truth and Love,
362–13 was evil part and *p·* of His creation?
No. 17–16 is neither part nor *p·* of divine
My. 12– 7 * to secure the large *p·* of land
65–19 * The last *p·* in the block
66– 1 * The purchase of this *p·*,
66– 9 * purchase of the last *p·*

pardon
Mis. xi–22 *p·* for the preliminary battles
123–22 whereby the just obtain a *p·* for
261– 7 cancelled by repentance or *p·*.
Pul. 87–21 *p·* my refusal of that as a material
No. 31–11 To me *divine p·* is that
31–14 as the only full proof of its *p·*.
32– 4 A magistrate's *p·* may encourage
42– 9 God's *p·* is the destruction of
Hea. 6– 4 *p·* me if I smiled.
8–21 through Principle instead of a *p·*;
Peo. 3–26 dependence on personal *p·*
Po. 32–19 *p·* and grace, through His Son,
My. 152–26 nor *p·* a single sin;
195– 3 You will *p·* my delay
299–18 those who claim to *p·* sin,

pardonable
Man. 46–20 shall not, under *p·* circumstances,
My. 64– 8 * If to-day we feel a *p·* pride

pardoned
Mis. 93–26 believing that sin is *p·* without
No. 29–19 A mortal *p·* by God is not sick,
Hea. 2– 8 afterwards *p·* and adopted,

pardons
Peo. 9–14 who never *p·* the sin that
My. 133– 2 many *p·* for the penitent.

Parent
Mis. 18–18 as children of one common *P·*,
155–26 to Him as our common *P·*,
Un. 35–16 immortal Mind, the *P·* of *all*.
48–15 *P·* no more enters into His creation
'01. 7–12 then does not our heavenly *P·*
7–16 does not this heavenly *P·* know

parent
Mis. 254–10 what of the hope of that *p·*
Ret. 22–20 are all the children of one *p·*,
68– 7 is not a *p·*, though he reflects
69– 5 "The *p·* of all human discord
Pul. 55–26 * regarded as the *p·* organization,
My. 10–26 * must be a prosperous *p·* church,
125– 8 vine towards the *p·* trunk.

parental
Ret. 5–30 * lively sense of the *p·* obligation,

parents (*see also* **parents'**)
Mis. 72– 8 good and bad traits of the *p·*
167–16 his *p·*, brothers, and sisters?
184– 9 has the formation of his *p·*;
225–29 The *p·* said :— "Wait until we
236–10 child complaining of his *p·*
236–11 "Love and honor thy *p·*,
240– 6 *P·* and doctors must not take
Ret. 5– 9 my *p·* removed to Tilton,
6–10 *p·*, brothers, and sisters,
13– 2 my *p·* having been members
20– 3 remained with my *p·* until after
Un. 17–21 God told our first *p·*
Pul. 8–16 children vied with their *p·* to
'01. 29–14 *p·* who nurtured them,
29–19 if they attempt to help their *p·*,
31–21 Devout orthodox *p·*;
My. 174–21 where my *p·* first offered
217– 3 your *p·*, brothers, or sisters.

parents
My. 256–23 *P·* call home their loved ones,
261– 2 loving *p·* and guardians of youth
336–14 remained with my *p·* until

parents'
Mis. 72– 3 because of his *p·* mistakes or sins,
Ret. 5– 7 youngest of my *p·* six children
'01. 29–16 forget their *p·* increasing years

par excellence
Mis. 313– 3 your editorial . . . is *p· e·*.

Paris
France
Mis. 304–15 * takes place at *P·*, France.

Mis. 375–15 * I spent two years in *P·*,
'00. 1–22 London, Edinburgh, Dublin, *P·*,

parishes
Pul. 38– 2 * preached in other *p·* for five years

Park Cemetery
Ret. 5–12 stone memorials in the *P· C·*

Parker
Mr.
Pul. 33–23 * and Mr. *P·* always believed,
Theodore
Pul. 33–16 * Theodore *P·* related that when

Park Street, No. 3
My. 53–13 * Hawthorne Rooms, at No. 3 *P· S·*,

parlance
Mis. 219–15 In common *p·*, one person feels sick,
300– 7 in common *p·*, it is an *ignorant*

parlor
Pul. 68–17 * holds regular services in the *p·* of
My. 342– 2 * Seated in the large *p·*,
342–17 * smaller *p·* across the hall,

parlors
Mis. 324– 7 the gorgeously tapestried *p·*,
My. 53–10 * in the *p·* of Mrs. Eddy's home,

parody
Mis. 62–25 and ends in a *p·* on this Science
106– 5 *p·* on Tennyson's grand verse,
122–30 his existence is a *p·*,

parsimonious
My. 149–27 Clouds *p·* of rain,

part (noun)
and parcel
Mis. 336–24 *P·* and parcel of Truth and Love,
362–13 was evil *p·* and parcel of His creation?
another
Ret. 88–18 another *p·* of C. S. work,
any
My. 9–22 any *p·* of two millions of dollars
13–18 any *p·* of two millions of money
57–10 * any *p·* of two millions of dollars
65– 7 * any *p·* of two million dollars
75–28 * with any *p·* of the expense
better
Mis. 273–12 as well as the better *p·* of mankind,
constituent
No. 4– 7 error, a constituent *p·* of what
demonstrate in
Peo. 13– 6 can demonstrate in *p·* this great
early
Mis. 373–20 early *p·* of the Christian era,
even in
Ret. 28– 7 to demonstrate, even in *p·*,
My. 5–21 understanding even in *p·*,
every
Pul. 61–15 * in every *p·* of this unique church,
66– 8 * in every *p·* of the country.
79–11 * adherents in every *p·* of
No. 14– 1 is sound in every *p·*.
My. 32– 9 * heard perfectly in every *p·*
good
Mis. 327– 9 "thou hast chosen the good *p·*;
his
My. 315– 8 * being wholly on his *p·*;
his own
Ret. 86–23 man who performs his own *p·*.
immortal
No. 29–14 the immortal *p·* of man a sinner?
interesting
My. 60–28 * to tell you of the interesting *p·*
in this resurrection
Un. 41–13 have *p·* in this resurrection
Jesus'
Chr. 53–30 that doom Was Jesus' *p·*;
latter
Ret. 24– 9 and in the latter *p·* of 1866
Pul. 23–23 * as is the latter *p·* of
loses a
No. 38–26 loses a *p·* of its purest spirituality

part
  most
    Pul. 28–22   * its songs are for the most *p·*
         47–25   * for the most *p·* she lives very
  my
    No. 9–15   too great leniency, on my *p·*,
    My. 170–7   due to a desire on my *p·*
        244–14   to contribute my *p·* towards
  no
    Un. 4–21   evil is no *p·* of the divine
        52–23   if God has no *p·* in them
    Pan. 10–30   constitute no *p·* of man,
    My. 160–30   that the Christian has no *p·* in it.
  nor parcel
    No. 17–15   neither *p·* nor parcel of divine
  nor portion
    My. 357–6   matter has neither *p·* nor portion,
  northern
    Ret. 20–10   northern *p·* of New Hampshire.
  no studied
    Mis. 147–26   for he acts no studied *p·* ;
  of a grain
    Hea. 13–5   one hundredth *p·* of a grain of
  of a system
    ’00. 13–8   *p·* of a system supported by their
  of being
    No. 12–28   all instead of a *p·* of being,
  of Christian worship
    Mis. 345–29   a *p·* of Christian worship
  of eternal Truth
    Un. 17–3   the lie seem *p·* of eternal Truth.
  of every night
    My. 61–2   * *p·* of every night since that time.
  of His consciousness
    No. 17–25   would be a *p·* of His consciousness.
  of the bell
    Mis. 305–19   * that can be made a *p·* of the bell ;
  of the city
    My. 66–16   * being in a fine *p·* of the city.
  of their duties
    My. 358–16   It is *p·* of their duties
  of the preamble
    My. 254–18   * *p·* of the preamble to our By-laws,
  of this transfer
    ’02. 13–9   (which was a *p·* of this transfer)
  of true followers
    Mis. 278–31   on the *p·* of true followers,
  of Truth
    Un. 5–26   this wonderful *p·* of Truth
    No. 21–4   to the one-hundredth *p·* of Truth,
  old
    My. 325–9   * old *p·* of Boston in which he lived
  one
    Mis. 148–2   one *p·* of his character at variance
  our
    My. 224–26   not against us is on our *p·*.” — *Mark* 9 : 40.
  principal
    Man. 31–17   principal *p·* of the Sunday services,
  shall have
    Mis. 180–18   shall have *p·* in his resurrection.
  small
    My. 45–11   * small *p·* of the entire body
  smallest
    Rud. 2–23   the smallest *p·* of C. S.
  Soul hath
    Mis. 390–23   In which the Soul hath *p·*,
    Po. 56–2   In which the Soul hath *p·*,
  surgical
    Mis. 349–5   the surgical *p·* of midwifery.
  take
    My. 86–12   * take *p·* in the subsequent ceremonies
  third
    Mis. 254–19   take away a third *p·* of the stars
  took
    Pul. 75–19   * took *p·* in the ceremonies at Boston
  understood in
    Peo. 6–21   divine Principle, understood in *p·*,
  your
    My. 148–3   called to do your *p·* wisely

    Mis. 43–26   is owing, in *p·*, to the
        102–14   God is not *p·*, but the whole.
        125–3   hath he *p·* in Love’s atonement,
        132–17   consisting in *p·* of dictating
        160–7   as *p·* and paramount portion of
        161–20   owing in *p·*, perhaps, to the Jewish
        305–15   * shall have a *p·* in it.
        381–5   taken on the *p·* of Mrs. Eddy,
        381–7   on the *p·* of the defendant
        395–10   When sweet *rondeau* Doth play a *p·*,
    Man. 31–20   as a *p·* of the Wednesday evening
        110–8   and become a *p·* thereof.
    Ret. 88–18   a *p·* which concerns us intimately,
    Pul. 84–27   * on the *p·* of our beloved teacher
        85–5   * who now, in *p·*, understand
    Hea. 3–22   we must understand in *p·* this divine

part
    Hea. 3–23   or we cannot demonstrate it in *p·*.
        19–3   not in *p·*, but as a whole ;
    Po. 57–17   When sweet *rondeau* Doth play a *p·*,
    My. 8–3   * Mr. Kimball said in *p·* :
        9–10   * on the *p·* of every man
        10–19   * sacrifice on the *p·* of its people.
        10–22   * on the *p·* of some one else.
        51–13   * on the *p·* of the people,
        59–11   * accepted wholly or in *p·* by
        63–13   * has become a *p·* of our expanding
        93–24   * *p·* it has come to play in the
        97–3   * faith on the *p·* of a sick person,
        110–21   unfold in *p·* the facts of day,
        219–4   such an anticipation on the *p·* of
        272–26   * plays so great a *p·* in the world

part (verb)
    Mis. 137–15   kind of you to *p·* so gently with
        232–14   as we *p·* with material systems
        286–4   * “until death do us *p·* ;”
        291–19   would *p·* with a blessing myself to
        327–22   determined not to *p·* with their
        339–29   Change and the grave may *p·* us ;
        384–17   You therefore cannot *p·*.
        388–12   Speaks kindly when we meet and *p·*.
    ’00. 10–29   to *p·* with his soap,
    ’02. 2–25   remains friends, or . . . *p·* fair foes.
        2–29   shall meet again, never to *p·*.
    Po. 3–13   Till bursting bonds our spirits *p·*
        7–12   Speaks kindly when we meet and *p·*.
        33–11   (And mem’ry but *p·* us awhile),
        36–16   You therefore cannot *p·*.
    My. 131–21   where God is we can never *p·*.

partake
    Mis. 170–18   strength, we also may all *p·* of.
        387–16   Pray that his spirit you *p·*,
    Un. 17–22   *p·* of the fruit of evil,
    Pan. 14–8   *p·* of the bread that cometh down
    ’00. 15–6   *p·* of what divine Love hath prepared
    Po. 6–11   Pray that his spirit you *p·*,
    My. 156–21   *p·* of the bread that cometh down
        267–19   to *p·* of the quality . . . of heaven.

partaker
    Mis. 235–6   man becomes the *p·* of that Mind

partakers
    Mis. 291–16   If any are not *p·* thereof,
    Un. 23–13   whereof all are *p·*, — *Heb.* 12 : 8.
    My. 206–27   *p·* of the inheritance of — *Col.* 1 : 12.
        287–17   *p·* of that Mind whence springs the

partakes
    Mis. 259–3   *p·* not of the nature of God,
    Ret. 47–18   *p·* less of God’s love.

partaketh
    Mis. 360–20   *p·* of its own altars,

parted
    Ret. 15–19   we *p·* in Christian fellowship,
    Pul. 65–22   * *p·* his mantle with his sword
    My. 313–29   I was obliged to be *p·* from my son,

partial
    Mis. 182–23   a personal Jehovah, *p·* and finite ;
        290–12   *p·*, unmerciful, or unjust,
    Ret. 38–8   in my last chapter a *p·* history of

partiality
    Peo. 8–3   *p·* that elects some to be saved

partially
    Un. 5–23   Christians who wholly or *p·* differ
        9–7   That time has *p·* come,
        39–3   Eternal Life is *p·* understood ;

participants
    Mis. 143–4   explained to the kind *p·*
        335–19   either willing *p·* . . . or ignorant
    My. 86–29   * accommodate the throng of *p·*.

participate
    Pul. 64–27   * to *p·* in the ceremonies,
    My. 77–10   * to *p·* in the most notable
        77–15   * will *p·* in the dedication.
        77–24   * present to *p·* in the occasion.
        78–2   * that all might *p·* in the dedication,
        96–2   * to *p·* in the dedication

participating
    Mis. 117–19   while *p·* in the movements,
    My. 23–27   * *p·* in the work of its erection.

particular
    Ret. 89–13   duty at that *p·* moment.
    Pul. 50–15   * *p·* phase of religious belief
    My. 10–18   * could prosper, in any *p·*,
        83–29   * But of this *p·* example
        210–21   saying nothing, in *p·*, of error
        346–23   * whether she had in mind any *p·*

particularly
Mis. 305–14   * p· desired that the largest number
    305–20   * will be p· appreciated
Pul. 42– 9   * was rendered p· interesting
    47–18   * dwelling p· upon the terms
    76– 6   * is described as "p· beautiful,

particulars
Mis. 51– 9   We have not the p· of the case

parties
Mis. 141–17   spirit of Christ actuating all the p·
    297–23   by mutual consent of both p·,
Pul. 41–15   * came p· of forty and fifty.
My. 281–23   * effect on the two p· to the treaty

parting
Mis. 149–19   p· so promptly with your beloved pastor,
    341–17   p· with a material sense of life
    386–10   gathered from her p· sigh :
    386–26   her loyal life, And p· prayer,
Ret. 19– 5   p· with the dear home circle
    19–20   With his p· breath he gave
'02. 5– 5   religion p· with its materiality.
Hea. 2–11   * the p· will be easy."
Po. 8–19   p· the ringlets to kiss my cheek.
    49–15   gathered from her p· sigh :
    50–12   her loyal life, And p· prayer,
    65– 8   And left me a p· in air.
    74– 6   blue eyes and jet, Soft as when p·
My. 170–30   In p· I repeat to these
    330–32   With his p· breath he gave

partings
Po. 15– 7   "No p· are there."
My. 290–23   where no p· are for love,
    351–16   where are no p·, no pain.

partition
Mis. 178–29   we are as a p· wall

partitions
Pul. 25– 5   * The p· are of iron ;
    58–15   * by the use of movable p·.

partizanship
My. 291–11   quenching the volcanoes of p·,

partly
Mis. 292–12   p· illustrate the divine energy

partner
Mis. 242–26   formerly p· of George T. Brown,
    361–27   p· in the firm of error,
My. 310–11   joint p· with Alexander Tilton,

partners
Pul. 84– 6   * equal p· in all that is worth

partnership
Mis. 364–25   this impossible p· is dissolved.
Peo. 4–14   error that . . . entered into p·
My. 260–11   hath no p· with human means

partnerships
Mis. 289–12   All p· are formed on agreements

partook
Mis. 78–12   p· of the nature of occultism,
    121– 4   our Master p· of the Jews' feast
    260– 8   His faith p· not of drugs,
My. 288–13   His piety p· not of the travesties of

parts
Mis. 31–21   He p· with his understanding of good,
    159–30   Scientists from all p· of our nation,
Ret. 48–21   sent to all p· of our country,
Un. 5–28   but p· of Thy ways," — see Job 26 : 14.
    6– 1   the whole is greater than its p·.
Pul. 44–25   * money has flowed in from all p· of
    60–15   * from all p· of the country.
    64– 8   * from all p· of the United States.
    68– 7   * from all p· of the world,
Rud. 12– 2   p· of the body supposed to be ailing.
No. 13–26   other p· of it have no lustre.
    21– 3   has ninety-nine p· of error to the
My. 47– 5   * from all p· of the world,
    88– 7   * It shows strength in all p·,
    95– 7   * in different p· of the world.
    96– 2   * Scientists from all p· of the world
    96–29   * from all p· of the United States.
    99–18   * coming from all p· of the world,
    100– 9   * nearly all, p· of the country,
    141–19   * Scientists from all p· of the world.
    147–28   to the utmost p· of the earth,
    206– 9   human beliefs are not p· of C. S. ;
    269–12   * p· of one stupendous whole,

party
Mis. 289–13   each p· voluntarily surrenders
    290– 1   is not a p· to the compact of
My. 300–32   attacking a peaceable p·

pass
Mis. 10–24   wherein old things p· away
    34–20   p· on to their state of existence,

pass
Mis. 99–21   earth shall p· away, — Matt. 24 : 35.
    99–22   my words shall not p· — Matt. 24 : 35.
    107–19   Mortals' false senses p· through
    111–17   earth shall p· away, — Matt. 24 : 35.
    111–18   my words shall not p· — Matt. 24 : 35.
    118–13   yearn to . . . p· a friend over it
    121– 1   his words can never p· away :
    157–23   shall bring it to p·. — Psal. 37 : 5.
    163–19   earth shall p· away, — Matt. 24 : 35.
    163–19   my words shall not p· — Matt. 24 : 35.
    190–12   it came to p·, — Luke 11 : 14.
    213–18   p· through a baptism of fire.
    230–15   improving moments before they p·
    269– 2   shall bring it to p·." — Psal. 37 : 5.
    304– 8   * bell will p· from place to place
    319–20   season p· without one gift to me.
    355–10   mortal mind must p· through
    363–12   p· through none of the changes of
    385–24   To p· away.
Ret. 24– 7   discovery came to p· in this way.
    69– 1   p· through material conditions
    80–23   older sheep p· into the fold
Un. 3– 5   p· through another probationary
    43–16   words which can never "p· — Matt. 5 : 18.
Pul. 1–14   P· on, returnless year !
    1–17   P· proudly to thy bier !
    39–24   * hurrying throng before me p·,
No. 8–26   let the unwise p· by,
    27–11   Until centuries p·,
Pan. 12–18   p· gently on without
'01. 20–28   p· sentence on the darkest and
Hea. 10– 1   saw it p· away, — an illusion.
Peo. 1– 8   footsteps of thought, as they p·
    11–19   directly as men p· legislative acts
Po. 26– 1   P· on, returnless year !
    26– 6   P· proudly to thy bier !
    33–10   To kindly p· over a wound,
    48–20   To p· away.
    67–14   p· From your sight as the
My. 23–29   * those who p· by are impelled to
    132– 9   p· through the waters of Meribah here
    151–17   * "P· ye the proud fane by,
    170–24   shall bring it to p·. — Psal. 37 : 5.
    225– 2   come to the surface to p· off,
    301– 7   dogma and creed will p· off

passage
Mis. 72–31   p· quoted affords no evidence of
    75–25   bring out the meaning of the p·.
    169–18   dual meaning to every Biblical p·,
    170–24   p· recording Jesus' proceedings
    182–15   This p· refers to man's primal,
    191–18   By no . . . interpretation can this p·
    248– 4   literal meaning of the p·
No. 22–22   p· must refer to the evils which
    29– 1   this p· refers to the Jewish law,
'00. 15– 9   p· over a tear-filled sea
'01. 10–21   Love spans the dark p· of sin,
'02. 7–23   p· which serves to confirm C. S.
My. 43–14   * p· of the Red Sea
    135– 5   this p· of Scripture
    142–19   in their p· from sense to Soul.
    170–18   This gift is a p· of Scripture ;
    182–27   May the birds of p· rest their

passages
Mis. 73– 6   materially, these p· conflict ;
    169–28   * Taking several Bible p·,
    169–31   was one of the p· explained
    300–26   p· giving the spiritual meaning
Pul. 45–29   * p· read from the two books
    60–11   * and then by p· selected for him
    73–10   * She delved deep into the Biblical p·.
No. 32– 1   misinterpretation of such p·

passed
Mis. 6–10   are p· over to the Scientist.
    42– 8   individual has but p· through
    42–13   p· the ordeal called death,
    110–15   Weeks have p· into months,
    121–20   sentence p· upon innocence?
    132– 1   vote p·, at your last meeting,
    137–13   but that time has p·.
    152–26   till the storm p·
    153– 8   p· through the Red Sea, untouched
    165–17   p· on and left to mortals the rich
    284–14   hour has p· for this evil to be
    343– 4   have p· to their reward.
    356–12   remember that the seedtime is p·,
    386–19   "Years had p· o'er thy
Man. 36–10   p· an examination by the Board of
Ret. 7– 3   p· away at the age of thirty-one,
    38– 7   After months had p·,
    38–22   Not a word had p· between us,
    42–13   In 1882 he p· away,
    48–11   following resolutions were p· :
    48–14   presented and p· unanimously :

passed

Ret.	69– 7	and p· into matter.
Pul.	38–18	* p· the change of death
Rud.	14–27	p· through a regular course
No.	13– 9	centuries p· after those words were
	14– 5	not p· the transition called death,
'01.	26–14	I have p· through deep waters to
	28– 1	p· through the first two stages,
'02.	2–13	p· from stern Protestantism to
Hea.	2–14	ere he p· from his execution to
	11– 5	when the dream has p·,
Peo.	7–11	* As an angel dream p· o'er him.
Po.	50– 3	"Years had p· o'er thy
My.	47–17	* back over the years that have p·
	47–23	* years that have p· since
	48– 4	* Not until nineteen centuries had p·
	51– 4	* following resolutions were p· :
	65–11	* This astonishing motion was p·
	65–21	* p· to the ownership of the
	78– 8	* p· through the twelve entrances
	99–20	* contribution baskets when p·
	148–13	unthought of till the day had p· !
	168– 1	uncultivated understanding has p·.
	206–14	p· through the shadow called death,
	230– 4	when those have p· to rest.
	257– 9	p· from a corporeal to the
	290–20	has p· earth's shadow
	294–29	p· through the shadow of death
	309–28	* Mary Baker p· her first fifteen years
	326–15	George W. Glover, p· on
	327–19	* amendment had been p·,
	328–11	* p· by the last Legislature,
	335–18	* at the end of nine days he p· away.
	340–29	The dark days of . . . have p·,
	342–26	* all now concerned . . . have p· on?"
	346–13	* and as she p· me

passes

Mis.	9– 6	p· all His flock under His rod
	42– 6	momentary belief of dying p·
	329–14	Spring p· over mountain
	363– 4	p· from molecule and monkey
Pul.	5– 6	p· from earth to heaven,
Peo.	7–19	* Our life dream p· o'er us.

passeth

Mis.	125–14	Love that p· all understanding ;
	133–30	peace that p· understanding,
No.	8– 8	p· all understanding," — Phil. 4 : 7.

passing

Mis.	42– 5	p· through the belief called death.
	78–21	froth of error p· off ;
	224–22	so settled that no p· breath
Ret.	44–26	p· without a dissenting voice.
	68–26	thoughts, p· from God to man"
Un.	47– 4	with every p· hour
Pul.	6– 2	and impurities are p· off.
Pan.	12– 6	how can Spirit be constantly p·
'02.	17–19	square accounts with each p· hour.
Po.	v–18	* Some tourists who were p·,
	vi–19	p· of a resolution in Congress
My.	46– 6	* it were but a p· dream.
	65–15	* p· out a nickel for carfare.

passion

Mis.	114–19	p·, appetites, hatred, revenge,
	137–25	p·, pride, envy, evil-speaking,
	222– 3	It inflames envy, p·, evil-speaking,
	295–10	* p· for some manner of notoriety."
	298–11	spiritual ignorance and power of p·,
	343–14	noxious weeds of p·, malice,
	374–11	fogs of sense and storms of p·,
Ret.	65–11	gratification of appetite and p·,
My.	339–28	appetites, p·, and all that wars

passionate

Un.	27– 9	signifying a p· love of self,
My.	90–10	* All the p· love for life
	309– 1	* dominating, p·, fearless,"

passionately

'00.	11– 5	p· fond of material music,

passionless

Po.	2– 1	Stern, p·, no soul those looks betray ;

passions

Mis.	36–13	Appetites, p·, anger, revenge,
	123–12	human p· and human gods,
	209–22	Evil p· die in their own flames,
	236– 1	human p· in their reaction
	237– 9	the worst of human p·
	240–22	P·, appetites, pride, selfishness,
	294– 3	by the maëlstrom of human p·,
	324–15	p· have so dimmed their sight
Pan.	10–29	Sin, sickness, appetites, and p·,
'01.	30–22	stress of the appetites and p·.
Hea.	18–22	Pride, appetites, p·, envy, and malice
My.	93–13	* gratifying the p· or

Passover

Mis.	90–26	P·, or last supper,
	121– 5	partook of the Jews' feast of the P·,
Pan.	1– 6	gathered at the feast of our P·,
'00.	15– 5	and this feast is a P·.
	15– 8	P·, spiritually discerned, is a
	15–11	after this P· cometh victory,

passover

My.	156–12	to prepare for the material p·,
	156–12	p· from sense to Soul,
	156–15	eat the p· — Luke 22 : 11.

passport

Mis.	270–23	the only p· to his power ;

past (noun)

Mis.	100– 8	P·, present, future, will show the
	253–15	it repeats the p· and portends much
	285–29	having no Truth, it will have no p·,
	311– 9	so, bury the dead p· ;
	339–15	The p· admonishes us :
	339–30	wisdom that might have blessed the p·
	375–31	* a thing of the p·, impossible of
Un.	46–27	furnished the battle-ground of the p·,
Pul.	7– 7	Yet when I recall the p·,
	7–20	prophets in the present as in the p·
	55–11	* and oppressions of the p·.
	69–25	* than the Church has had in the p·.
	81–10	* woman of the p· with an added grace
'02.	2–20	dogmatism, relegated to the p·,
	4–23	all periods — p·, present, and future.
Hea.	2–25	P·, present, future magnifies his
Po.	27–11	Or we the p· forget,
	68–17	Of the p· 'tis the talisman,
My.	12–20	We own no p·, no future,
	13– 2	on the p·, present, nor future,
	147– 3	p· comes forth like a pageant
	153–22	in the p· as in the present,
	158–14	it profits by the p·.
	176– 7	illustrate the p· by your present
	191–18	come forth from the tomb of the p·,
	230– 3	will maintain its rank as in the p·,
	340–24	virtually belongs to the p·,

past (adj., adv., etc.)

Mis.	125–29	within the p· few years :
	130–24	avoid referring to p· mistakes.
	131–31	perils p· and victories won.
	147– 9	Have you improved p· hours,
	295– 7	* leads . . . p· a score of reforms,
	322–23	my p· poor labors and love.
	330–19	good to talk with our p· hours,
	385–10	happy friend ! thy bark is p·
Man.	83–10	such only as have good p· records
Un.	14– 8	power from p· experience
Pul.	1– 9	Time p· and time present,
	58– 6	* For several years p· she has
	72–16	* "And for the p· eleven years,"
'00.	7– 7	that during the p· three years
	7–29	till the long night is p·
'02.	4–27	and p· finding out.
Po.	48– 2	happy friend ! thy bark is p·
My.	29–28	* half p· five in the morning
	30–28	* service at half p· seven,
	30–32	* Before half p· seven the chimes
	31– 9	* Promptly at half p· six
	38–17	* the service at half p· twelve
	66– 5	* During the p· two weeks
	73–15	* have been for several days p·
	78–28	* of the half p· twelve service ;
	86–10	* into Boston in the p· few days
	87–22	* in Boston during the p· few days.
	220–24	P·, present, or future philosophy
	270–21	for the p· forty years I have
	321–29	during the p· twenty years.
		(see also times, year)

pastime

My.	119–26	pleasant p· of seeing your
	261– 9	aught to do with this p·.

pastimes

Mis.	xi–16	p· become footsteps to joys
My.	263– 1	p· tend to obliterate the spiritual

Pastor and pastor (see also pastor's)

Mis.	90–21	shall the p· of the Church
	149–20	p·, Rev. Mr. Norcross,
	150– 2	May He soon give you a p· ;
	152– 3	Beloved P· and Brethren :
	313–27	to be hereafter the only p·
	322–11	dual and impersonal p·,
	383– 2	C. S. textbook, be the p·,
	383– 7	p· is the Bible and my book.
Man.	58– 3	THE CHRISTIAN SCIENCE p·.
	58– 6	P· over The Mother Church,
Ret.	14– 5	p· was an old-school expounder of
	15–15	by the p· of this church.
Pul.	7–26	p· of The First Church of Christ,

Pastor and pastor
Pul.	7–28	is satisfied with this *p·*.
	9–16	loss of our late lamented *p·*,
	28–27	* *p·* to the church in this city,
	34– 8	* her *p·* came to bid her goodby
	43–30	* letter from a former *p·*
	58–25	* only *p·* shall be the Bible, with
	68–18	* parlor of the residence of the *p·*,
	69– 1	* Dr. Hammond, the *p·*,
	74– 6	* *p·* of the C. S. congregation
	86–29	* already ordained as our *p·*.
'01.	11–12	chapter sub-title
	11–14	*p·* for all the churches of the
	11–16	not make it impossible for this *p·*
My.	174–14	*P·* of the First Congregational Church,
	178– 1	*p·* and ethical tenets,

(*see also* **Eddy**)

pastorate
Pul.	45–23	* withdrew from the *p·* of the church,
	87–12	kind call to the *p·* of
My.	49–31	* call Mrs. Eddy to the *p·*
	51–20	* the *p·* for the ensuing year ;

Pastor Emeritus
My.	174–13	Rev. Franklin D. Ayer, D.D., *P· E·* ;

(*see also* **Eddy**)

pastor's
Pul.	27– 7	* class-rooms and the *p·* study.
	58–23	* Adjoining the chancel is a *p·* study ;

(*see also* **Eddy**)

pastors
Mis.	91– 5	not absolutely necessary to ordain *p·*
	143–20	editors, and *p·* of churches,
	314– 4	by Readers in lieu of *p·*.
Pul.	68– 7	* many are now *p·* or in practice.

pastorship
Pul.	68– 1	* Mrs. Eddy assumed the *p·*

pasture
Mis.	151– 1	folds the sheep of His *p·* ;

pastures
Mis.	227–24	mind can rest in green *p·*,
	357– 1	yearn to find living *p·*
Ret.	4–19	green *p·* bright with berries,
Pul.	48–12	* beautiful meadows and *p·*
My.	129–26	These are His green *p·*
	162–26	into "green *p·* — *Psal.* 23 : 2.
	252–20	They point to verdant *p·*,

patching
Mis.	316–21	*p·* breaches widened the next hour ;

patchwork
No.	3– 1	should not spread abroad *p·* ideas

patent
Mis.	79–31	vendors of *p·* pills,
	220–22	is *p·* both to the conscientious
Pan.	4–12	it is *p·* that will is capable of
My.	83– 4	* holding of a great convention is *p·* to

paternal
Ret.	1–18	so became my *p·* grandmother,
	19– 3	under the *p·* roof in Tilton.
	20– 1	After returning to the *p·* roof
My.	336–12	"After returning to the *p·* roof

Pater Noster
Pul.	59–11	* The *P· N·* was repeated

path
back to the
Mis.	328– 5	will call thee back to the *p·*

beaten
'00.	4–18	beaten *p·* of human doctrines

behind thee
Pul.	1–15	*p·* behind thee is with glory crowned ;

entered the
Mis.	206–24	you have entered the *p·*.

enter the
Mis.	328–25	are striving to enter the *p·*,
	347–21	I enter the *p·*.

her
Mis.	54–13	malice would fling in her *p·*.

his
Mis.	326–29	Discerning in his *p·* the penitent
Un.	55–11	must keep close to his *p·*,
Po.	18–14	He penciled his *p·*

lighteth the
Pan.	12–17	and so lighteth the *p·*

made luminous
Mis.	335–15	*p·* made luminous by divine Love.

narrow
Mis.	32–21	from the straight and narrow *p·*.
Ret.	55– 1	enter this strait and narrow *p·*,
	71– 9	straight and narrow *p·* of C. S.

no
Mis.	147–28	he knows no *p·* but the fair, open,

path
of Christian Science
Ret.	71– 9	narrow *p·* of C. S.
No.	42–20	*p·* of C. S. is beset with

perfect
My.	187– 9	perfect *p·* wherein to walk,

pleasant
Mis.	324–29	reaches the pleasant *p·* of the valley

pointing the
Mis.	xi–12	guide-book, pointing the *p·*,
My.	176– 8	pointing the *p·* to heaven within you,
	202– 2	pointing the *p·* from earth to heaven

points the
Pan.	12–20	way-seeker gains and points the *p·*.

point the
'02.	11– 8	find and point the *p·* to heaven.
My.	186–10	point the *p·* above the valley,

prowl in the
Mis.	323–12	beasts of prey prowl in the *p·*,

this
No.	28–14	none too soon for entering this *p·*.

thy
'02.	19–24	A danger besets thy *p·* ?

to health
Mis.	308– 8	loses the *p·* to health,

to heaven
'02.	11– 8	find and point the *p·* to heaven.
My.	176– 8	pointing the *p·* to heaven within you,

your
Mis.	306–28	spiritual idea that lights your *p·* !

Mis.	9–29	in the *p·* that winds upward.
Ret.	90–28	* in the *p·* you have pursued !"
Un.	9–10	this way is not the *p·* of physical

pathetic
Mis.	230–28	to render it *p·*, tender, gorgeous.
Ret.	19–21	gave *p·* directions to his
My.	330–32	gave *p·* directions to his

pathological
Mis.	297– 4	other religious and *p·* systems
	379– 3	if he indited anything *p·*
Rud.	16–21	elucidates a *p·* Science
'01.	34– 8	proven to be more *p·* than

pathology
Mis.	35– 3	the Principle of *p·* ;
	80–27	what they deem *p·*, hygiene,
Ret.	43– 7	the *p·* of spiritual power,
My.	108– 5	the intelligent cause in *p·* ?
	230– 5	Scientific *p·* illustrates the

pathos
Mis.	295–17	with his ready pen and *p·*

paths
Mis.	99–27	"Make straight God's *p·* ;
	223– 1	its hidden *p·*, purpose, and fruits
	246–24	make His *p·* straight." — *Matt.* 3 : 3.
Rud.	17–16	are the *p·* of His testimony
'01.	35– 2	He shall direct thy *p·* ;" — *Prov.* 3 : 6.
My.	140– 4	I will lead them in *p·* — *Isa.* 42 : 16.
	161–27	"He shall direct thy *p·*." — *Prov.* 3 : 6.
	252–22	into *p·* of peace and holiness.
	260–14	philosophy may pursue *p·* devious,
	361– 3	will direct you into the *p·* of peace.

pathway
Mis.	20– 1	illumes our *p·* with the radiance
	270–24	*p·* of goodness and greatness
Ret.	30– 6	have cleared its *p·*.
Pul.	vii–15	the *p·* of this generation ;
My.	62–12	* brightest beams on your *p·*,
	350–15	the *p·* glad and free?

patience
Mis.	7– 8	The loving *p·* of Jesus,
	88–11	*P·*, observation, intellectual culture,
	100–29	*p·*, forgiveness, abiding faith,
	124–29	gives . . . to *p·*, experience ,
	224–18	but with the largest *p·* ;
	228–11	bear with *p·* the buffetings
	267– 8	caused me to exercise most *p·*.
	268–31	Through *p·* we must possess
	340–22	by *p·*, they inherit the promise.
	340–26	miracles of *p·* and perseverance.
	361–19	run with *p·* the race — *Heb.* 12 : 1.
Ret.	80–10	* Though with *p·* He stands
	80–20	*P·* and obedience win the
	90–20	endures with her *p·*,
Pul.	82–10	* has long learned with *p·*,
	83–11	* with the *p·* of genius
No.	8–27	power, *p·*, and understanding,
'00.	15–25	thy *p·*, and thy works ; — *Rev.* 2 : 19.
'02.	16–21	meek might, sublime *p·*,
	17–28	*P·* and resignation are the
Hea.	2–17	Jesus, the model of infinite *p·*,
My.	158–15	holiness, *p·*, charity, love.
	209– 7	fidelity, courage, *p·*, and grace.

patience
My.	227– 8	known by its *p·* and endurance.
	249–15	*p·*, silence, and lives of saints.
	306–16	Age, with experience-acquired *p·*

patient (*see also* **patient's**)
amusing the
| *Peo.* | 6–12 | * amusing the *p·* while nature cures |

attend the
| *My.* | 105–19 | I was wired to attend the *p·* |

belief of the
| *Mis.* | 352–16 | supposed bodily belief of the *p·* |

condition of the
| *Mis.* | 43– 5 | mental condition of the *p·*. |

each
| *Mis.* | 38–27 | to make each *p·* a student |

first
| *Mis.* | 382–14 | first *p·* healed in this age by C. S. |

friends of a
| *Mis.* | 282–21 | If the friends of a *p·* desire you to |

healer and
| *Pul.* | 53–10 | * in the mind of both healer and *p·*, |

his
Mis.	40–29	to kill his *p·* by mental means,
	355–13	the mental state of his *p·*.
Man.	46–20	shall not, . . . sue his *p·* for
Un.	11–19	If his *p·* was a theologian of
Rud.	13–22	it will free his *p·*.
My.	306–30	while I was his *p·* in Portland

is better
| *Mis.* | 45–20 | *p·* is better both morally and |

is liable
| *Rud.* | 8–27 | and the *p·* is liable to a relapse, |

may gain
| *Pul.* | 69–24 | * *p·* may gain a better understanding |

physician and
| *My.* | 108–19 | better for both physician and *p·*. |

practitioner to
| *Man.* | 46–17 | relation of practitioner to *p·*. |

receive a
| *Ret.* | 87–29 | not receive a *p·* who is under the |

says
| *Mis.* | 220–14 | *p·* says and feels, "I am well, |

this
| *Mis.* | 89– 6 | *would it be right to treat this p·* |

treating a
| *Rud.* | 13–18 | When treating a *p·*, |

who pays
| *Mis.* | 300–29 | *p·* who pays whatever he is able |

would have died
| *My.* | 336– 1 | * but for . . . the *p·* would have died |

your
| *Mis.* | 241–25 | your *p·* rejoices in the gospel of |
| *My.* | 364– 5 | the mind of your *p·*, |

Mis.	89– 7	ought the *p·* to follow the
	89–11	If the *p·* is in peril,
	210– 4	C. S. never healed a *p·* without
	242–21	where the *p·* is very low
	242–24	leaving the *p·* well.
	242–29	*p·* . . . addicted to the use of opium
	378– 3	A *p·* considered incurable
Man.	47– 5	a *p·* whom he does not heal,
Rud.	10–19	the *p·* can then look up to
	12– 2	He never lays his hands on the *p·*,
No.	40–25	religious views of the *p·*
'01.	34– 5	interval that detains the *p·* from
	34– 8	cannot be fatal to the *p·*,
Po.	47–22	Or to the *p·* who sow?
My.	97– 4	* go far towards making the *p·* well.
	97– 6	* *p·* getting well without the use of
	105–21	The *p·* was pronounced dying
	293–18	resuscitating the body of the *p·*.
	293–26	and the *p·* would have recovered.
	363–27	*p·* whom he is treating,

patient (adj.)
Mis.	277–10	heart loyal to God is *p·* and strong.
	323–17	He saith unto the *p·* toilers
	330–31	when the *p·* corn waits
	384–14	Be *p·*, waiting heart :
	392–14	Faithful and *p·* be my life
	400–22	Thee I seek, *P·*, meek,
Ret.	79–25	were saved by *p·* waiting.
	86– 3	to crown *p·* toil,
'01.	35–18	do we walk in *P·* faith
Hea.	19–18	*p·* of man's procrastination,
Peo.	14–14	be *p·* in tribulation,
Po.	20–18	Faithful and *p·* be my life
	22– 1	God-crowned, *p·* century,
	30–17	*p·* love above earth's ire,
	36–13	Be *p·*, waiting heart :
	53–10	The *p·*, timid grass,
	69–10	Thee I seek, *P·*, meek,
My.	75–18	* very *p·* and good-natured.
	151– 1	*p·* with the newspaper wares
	191– 4	Be *p·* towards persecution.

patient (adj.)
| *My.* | 222–19 | Be *p·*, O Christian Scientist ! |
| | 247–29 | *p·*, unfaltering tenderness. |

patiently
Mis.	81– 8	*p·* wait on God to decide,
	118–18	suffer *p·* for error until
	206–25	Press *p·* on ;
	315–27	*p·* strive to educate their
	325–13	*p·* seeks another dwelling,
	330– 5	does it *p·* pray for the
	331– 6	cause them to wait *p·*
	364– 5	"Wait *p·* on the Lord— *see Isa.* 40 : 31.
Man.	83–19	and *p·* counsel his pupils
Ret.	49–16	loving unselfishly, working *p·*,
Un.	6–28	"Wait *p·* on the Lord ;"— *see Psal.* 37 : 7.
Pul.	4–23	Wait *p·* on illimitable Love,
Pan.	1–16	waiteth *p·* the appearing
'01.	34–20	brethren, wait *p·* on God ;
My.	4–11	meekly, *p·*, spiritually,
	29–29	* were able to wait *p·* for the
	185– 2	waited *p·* for the appearing

patient's
Mis.	6–22	the *p·* faith in drugs
	53–13	*to start the p· recovery?*
	219–17	must change his *p·* consciousness
	219–20	*p·* sense of sinning at ease
	220–12	until the *p·* mind yields,
	220–16	changed his *p·* consciousness
	220–17	The *p·* mental state is now
	355–23	discern the error in thy *p·* mind

patients
Mis.	33–18	*P·* naturally gain confidence
	37–25	*Does Mrs. Eddy take p·?*
	59– 9	in which the last state of *p·*
	89– 9	When *p·* are under material
	171– 9	seances with their *p·*,
	241– 7	metaphysical healing on two *p·* :
	350–22	sometimes occasions effects on *p·*
	378– 6	as he informed the *p·*,
	378–10	with several other *p·*,
	379– 1	After treating his *p·*,
	379– 4	relative to his *p·*,
	380–20	my students' *p·*,
Man.	43– 6	nor permit his *p·* or pupils to use
	46–12	Practitioners and *P·*.
	46–15	made to them by their *p·* ;
	47– 4	Duty to *P·*.
	87– 5	Choice of *p·* is left to the wisdom of
Ret.	33–17	would cure *p·* not affected by a
	83– 4	commend . . . *p·* to the teachings of
	84–28	only of his own pupils and *p·*,
No.	3–15	in the hands of their *p·*,
	5–28	makes the last state of one's *p·*
'01.	17–17	restored the *p·* in from one to three
	17–20	put *p·* into the hands of my students
	27–15	interviews with the *p·*,
My.	219– 2	Nor should *p·* anticipate
	227–11	one out of three of their *p·*,
	306–23	were descriptions of his *p·*,
	307– 6	treatment and manipulation of *p·*,
	364–11	his own . . . and that of his *p·*,

Patmos
| *Pul.* | 83–26 | * to know what John on *P·* meant |

patriarch
| *Mis.* | 17– 8 | like the *p·* of old, |

Patriot
| *My.* | 284–13 | your good paper, the *P·*, |

patriot
| *My.* | 297– 2 | *p·*, philanthropist, moralist, |

patriotic
| *Mis.* | 304–13 | * any great *p·* celebration |
| | 305– 3 | * from the *p·* societies, |

patriotism
| *Ret.* | 2–14 | from whose *p·* and bravery |

Patriots' Day
| *My.* | 339–15 | exchanged Fast Day, . . . for *P· D·*, |

patron
| *Pan.* | 3–27 | Pan was the . . . *p·* of country life, |

patronage
Mis.	262– 6	*p·* of *The C. S. Journal*,
	274–13	to the public for its liberal *p·*,
	296–23	Why fall into such *p·*,
	308–19	I thank you, . . . for your liberal *p·*
Ret.	49–22	we thank the public for its liberal *p·*.

patronize
Mis.	80–29	The old will not *p·* the new school,
	296–19	Do manly Britons *p·* tap-rooms
Man.	44– 9	member of this Church shall not *p·* a

Pat's
| *Mis.* | 218–27 | better than *P·* echo, |

pattern
Mis.	44– 2	''according to the *p·* — *Heb.* 8 : 5.
	103–20	is neither the *p·* nor Maker
	197–20	compel us to *p·* after both;
Un.	53– 2	lie takes its *p·* from Truth,
'01.	10–24	after the *p·* of the mount.

patterns
Mis.	299–29	gives to the public new *p·*
	316–28	*p·* of humility, wisdom,
My.	283–26	only as it *p·* the divine.

Patterson (*see also* Patterson's)
Dr.
My.	311– 3	living with Dr. *P·* at his
	313–12	Dr. *P·* driving into Franklin,
	314–14	my divorce from Dr. *P·*
	314–20	about to have Dr. *P·* arrested
	314–29	lived with Dr. *P·* peaceably,
	315– 3	* About the year 1874, Dr. *P·*,

Dr. Daniel
My.	314– 1	Dr. Daniel *P·*, my second husband,
	314– 8	Dr. Daniel *P·* was located

Lieutenant-Governor George W.
Ret.	20– 7	Lieutenant-Governor George W. *P·*

Patterson's
Dr.
My.	314–22	prevented Dr. *P·* arrest

Pattersons
My.	314– 5	* the following nine years the *P·*

patting
Mis.	231–24	little palms *p·* together,

Paugus
Pul.	48–30	* killed the ill-starred *P·*.

Paul (*see also* Paul's, St. Paul)
admonished
Mis.	361–17	To this great end, *P·* admonished,

and Jesus
Mis.	360– 7	characters, *P·* and Jesus.

apostle
Mis.	200–11	The apostle *P·* insists on

asked
Mis.	333–22	*P·* asked: "What communion — *II Cor.* 6 : 14.

declares
My.	113– 9	*P·* declares the truth of the

enjoined
Ret.	76–16	fulfils the law of Love which *P·* enjoined

Jesus and
Mis.	364–32	divine philosophy of Jesus and *P·*.
No.	21– 2	life and teachings of Jesus and *P·*,

refers
Mis.	184–10	*P·* refers to this when speaking of
	190–30	*P·* refers to this personality

said
Mis.	157– 3	*P·* said, "If we suffer, — *II Tim.* 2 : 12.
Peo.	10–13	*P·* said, "I was free born." — *Acts* 22 : 28.

says
Un.	5–14	of godliness," says *P·* ; — *I Tim.* 3 : 16.
	43–24	as *P·* says in the third chapter of

termed
My.	41–18	* what *P·* termed "the law of — *Rom.* 8 : 2.

understood
Mis.	344–21	Science which *P·* understood when he

words of
Hea.	18– 3	In the words of *P·*,

writes
Un.	30–13	*P·* writes : "The first man — *I Cor.* 15 : 45.

Mis.	71– 5	*P·* had a thorn in the flesh :
	162– 2	was called Israel ; and Saul, *P·*.
	201–16	*P·* took pleasure in infirmities,
Un.	1– 6	were taught by his fellow-apostle *P·*,
No.	46–17	rejoicing, as *P·* did, that we

Paul's
Mis.	84–19	*Please explain P· meaning*
	84–21	overshadowing *P·* sense of life in
	200–25	The holy calm of *P·* well-tried hope
	201– 3	The Science of *P·* declaration
	243–23	alludes to *P·* advice to Timothy.
	360– 9	*P·*, by the supremely natural
Un.	57–20	confirmation of *P·* faith.

pauperism
My.	309– 6	involving a question of *p·*

pause
Mis.	16–27	dear reader, *p·* for a moment
Pul.	44– 7	* willingly *p·* for an instant to
My.	81– 8	* *p·* and laughingly give precedence to
	280–29	simply to *p·* in special prayer for

paused
Pul.	48–16	* she *p·* and reminded the reporter

pausing
Mis.	324– 4	*P·* at the threshold of a

paved
My.	176– 6	*p·* the way to my forever gratitude,

pay
Mis.	vii–20	Wherefor, have much to *p·*.
	165–25	cost, none but the sinner can *p·* ;
	269–26	but are not willing to *p·* the price.
	299–22	*p·* me, not him, for this exhibit
	300–30	pays whatever he is able to *p·*
	301– 2	sermon for which you *p·* nothing,
	301– 3	and receive *p·* therefor,
	305–23	* money with which to *p·* for the bell.
	305–26	* twenty-five cents to *p·* for it.
	317–27	should not *p·* the penalty for
	342–25	you are willing to *p·* for error
	342–26	if you *p·* the price of Truth,
	349–26	and means to *p·* a salary,
	349–30	accepted no *p·* from my church
	353–18	"You must *p·* that man."
	353–20	God makes *us* p· for
Man.	30–16	Board of Directors shall *p·* from
	44–13	*p·* annually a per capita tax
	69–10	student shall *p·* to Mrs. Eddy
	78–18	may *p·* from the funds of the
Ret.	40– 3	refusing to take any *p·*
	89–13	It was the custom to *p·* this
Pul.	20– 4	were unable to *p·* the mortgage ;
Rud.	14–10	The only *p·* taken for her labors
	14–16	from those who were able to *p·*.
	14–17	better than he who does not *p·*
	14–18	expect and require others to *p·* him.
My.	vi–22	* *p·* all future profits to her church ;
	27–25	* *p·* all bills in connection with the
	51– 1	* to devise means to *p·* our pastor,
	96–20	* what they could to *p·* for it.
	123–15	the money to *p·* for it.
	161– 2	by enabling us to *p·* it ;
	214–17	taking *p·* for their labors
	306–25	I would *p·* for having published.
	328–29	* practise the art of healing for *p·*,
	328–29	* shall *p·* a license fee

payable
Man.	77–10	shall render them *p·*.

paying
Man.	77– 5	Prior to *p·* bills against the
Rud.	14–20	means of *p·* for their tuition
No.	35–15	how to avoid *p·* it.
'02.	13–18	*p·* for it the sum of $4,963.50
	13–23	to redeem the land by *p·* the
My.	16– 7	* *p·* out the sum of $199,607.93,
	74–17	* *p·* for their church before dedicating
	329– 5	* relieved . . . from *p·* this fee,
	333– 7	* *p·* the last tribute of respect

payment
Man.	46–21	recovery of *p·* for said
	78–22	for the *p·* of such bills.
My.	10–15	* amount and date of *p·*.
	204–25	the suing for *p·*, hypnotism,

payments
Man.	78–23	Such *p·* shall be reported,
My.	14–16	* further *p·* or subscriptions
	14–29	* necessitates large *p·* of money,

pays
Mis.	261–12	*p·* his full debt to divine law,
	300–30	*p·* whatever he is able to pay
Rud.	14–16	student who *p·* must of necessity

Peabody, D.D., Rev. A. P.
My.	53–23	* Rev. A. P. *P·*, D.D., of Cambridge,

peace
and good will
Mis.	215–15	*p·*, and good will toward men.
Pul.	22– 1	*p·* and good will towards men.
My.	167–18	full of love, *p·*, and good will

and harmony
Mis.	156–11	Let the reign of *p·* and harmony

and holiness
Mis.	167–28	He giveth power, *p·*, and holiness ;
'02.	16–14	To attain *p·* and holiness
My.	252–22	into paths of *p·* and holiness.

and joy
Mis.	303–10	*p·* and joy, the fruits of Spirit,
	331–18	O gentle presence, *p·* and joy
	389– 6	O gentle presence, *p·* and joy
Po.	4– 1	O gentle presence, *p·* and joy

and love
Mis.	152– 7	thoughts winged with *p·* and love
Ret.	42–13	with a smile of *p·* and love
'00.	11–12	human sigh for *p·* and love

and perfect love
Mis.	176– 3	healing, and *p·*, and perfect love.

and plenty
Mis.	232– 3	*p·*, and plenty, and happy households.
My.	340–28	their implorations for *p·* and plenty

and power
Mis.	124–19	is filled with *p·*, and power;
	205– 1	obtains *p·* and power outside of

peace

and progress
Mis. 118–22   foes to grace, *p*·, and progress ;
and prosperity
My. 279–26   God bless . . . with *p*· and prosperity.
   291–23   ensign of *p*· and prosperity
and understanding
Mis. 290–17   * *p*·, and understanding ;"
announcement of
My. 281–18   * "Official announcement of *p*·
armaments of
Mis. xii– 2   privileged armaments of *p*·.
at
Mis. 209–21   it has no right to be at *p*·.
   211–18   if a criminal is at *p*·,
Ret. 28– 4   if he would be at *p*·.
Peo. 6–25   and be at *p*· ;" — *Job* 22 : 21.
be declared
Ret. 56–14   must go on until *p*· be declared
be still
Mis. 307– 9   "*P*·, be still" — *Mark* 4 : 39.
between nations
My. 265–10   civilization, *p*· between nations,
bonds of
Pul. 22–17   bonds of *p*· are cemented by
break his
Mis. 211–16   Why, then, do you break his *p*·
bring
Mis. 7–15   if you cannot bring *p*· to all,
brings the
Mis. 82– 5   brings the *p*· symbolized by
call of
Mis. 120–16   clarion call of *p*· will at length
compassionate in
Pan. 15– 4   has been compassionate in *p*·.
consolation and
My. 283–27   Consolation and *p*· are based on
convenient
My. 211– 2   a false, convenient *p*·,
curtailed in
My. 127–27   it is not curtailed in *p*·,
demonstrates
My. 279– 7   C. S. demonstrates *p*·.
destroy the
Mis. 209–19   destroy the *p*· of a false sense.
divine
Peo. 11– 8   victory is achieved, . . . in divine *p*·.
dove of
My. 192–16   the dove of *p*· sits smilingly
dwelleth
Mis. x– 2   life wherein dwelleth *p*·,
fathomless
'02. 4–10   fathomless *p*· between Soul and
follow
'02. 16–12   "Follow *p*· with all men, — *Heb.* 12 : 14.
giveth a
Mis. 133–30   it giveth a *p*· that passeth
give you
Mis. 159– 7   May the God of all grace give you *p*·.
God of
Mis. 128–13   God of *p*· shall be with you." — *Phil.* 4 : 9.
   153–30   God of *p*· be and abide with
gospel of
'02. 4–15   commandment in the gospel of *p*·,
grace, and
Mis. 9– 1   grace, and *p*·, comes through affliction
grant us
Mis. xi–21   *vox populi* is inclined to grant us *p*·,
have
Mis. 209–32   then shall mortals have *p*·."
health and
Mis. 169–25   health and *p*· and hope for all.
My. 350–18   * crushing out of health and *p*·,
home and
Mis. 386– 5   home and *p*· and hearts are found
Po. 49– 8   home and *p*· and hearts are found
in error
My. 233–22   destroys his *p*· in error,
in God
Mis. 385– 3   * Find *p*· in God,
Po. 37– 3   * Find *p*· in God,
in goodness
Mis. 219–21   discomfort in sin and *p*· in goodness.
in Love
'02. 19–18   a rest in Christ, a *p*· in Love.
integrity and
Mis. 270– 4   such as barter integrity and *p*· for
is desirable
My. 121–15   *p*· is desirable, and plain dealing is
is the promise
My. 278–23   *P*· is the promise and reward of
is won
Po. 22–20   Love doth enter in, And *p*· is won,
justice of the
My. 136–22   Josiah E. Fernald, justice of the *p*·
   309–14   justice of the *p*· at one time.

peace

liberty and
Mis. 304– 5   * by the lovers of liberty and *p*·
life and
Mis. 24– 4   is life and *p*·." — *Rom.* 8 : 6.
'02. 6–28   is life and *p*·." — *Rom.* 8 : 6.
make
My. 40–21   * them that make *p*·." — *Jas.* 3 : 18.
mercy, and
Pan. 14–12   justice, mercy, and *p*·
more
My. 135–12   my yearning for more *p*·
   136–27   that I may have more *p*·,
   137–18   yearning for more *p*·
my
Mis. 215– 5   my *p*· I leave with thee :
   278– 4   my *p*· returns unto me.
My. 279– 4   "My *p*· I give unto you : — *John* 14 : 27.
national
My. 285– 8   industrial, civic, and national *p*·.
no
Mis. 209– 6   when there is no *p*·," — *Jer.* 6 : 14.
My. 233–18   when there is no *p*·" — *Jer.* 6 : 14.
not power
My. 341–15   * "'Tis *p*· not power I seek,
of a desert
Mis. 246–22   yield its prey the *p*· of a desert,
of God
No. 8– 8   "the *p*· of God, — *Phil.* 4 : 7.
of Love
My. 185– 8   The *p*· of Love is published,
of love
My. 220–23   the joy and the *p*· of love."
of nations
My. 280–17   special prayer for the *p*· of nations,
   280–29   praying for the *p*· of nations,
of the Lord
Pul. 39– 4   * until it finds the *p*· of the Lord
on earth
Mis. 145–30   on earth *p*·, — *Luke* 2 : 14.
   153–26   * *P*· on earth and Good-will !
   214– 5   to send *p*· on earth : — *Matt.* 10 : 34.
   227–27   cool waters of *p*· on earth ;
   369– 5   "on earth *p*·, — *Luke* 2 : 14.
Man. 45– 6   to promote *p*· on earth
Pul. 41–25   * "On earth *p*·, — *Luke* 2 : 14.
No. 44–26   "On earth *p*·, — *Luke* 2 : 14.
Po. 24– 8   Come to me, *p*· on earth !
My. 90–19   * "on earth *p*·, — *Luke* 2 : 14.
   127–30   "on earth *p*·, — *Luke* 2 : 14.
   167–11   "on earth *p*·, — *Luke* 2 : 14.
   279–19   "on earth *p*·, — *Luke* 2 : 14.
   281– 9   "on earth *p*·, — *Luke* 2 : 14.
   283–11   "on earth *p*·, — *Luke* 2 : 14.
paths of
My. 361– 3   direct you into the paths of *p*·.
perfect
My. 290–15   keep him in perfect peace, — *Isa.* 26 : 3.
permanence and
Mis. 352– 2   bereft of permanence and *p*·.
pillars of
'02. 17–29   are the pillars of *p*·
plenty and
Po. 77– 5   Plenty and *p*· abound
power, and
Mis. 263–13   power, and *p*· meet all human
prayer for
My. 279–21   chapter sub-title
   280–30   to pause in special prayer for *p*·.
pregnant with
My. 283–13   Association, pregnant with *p*·,
preserving
My. 286–12   preserving *p*· among nations.
promote
Mis. 354– 8   can no longer promote *p*·
Man. 45– 6   its branches to promote *p*·
prosper in
'02. 3–20   British and Boer may prosper in *p*·,
publisheth
Ret. 45– 4   that publisheth *p*·." — *Isa.* 52 : 7.
pure
Po. 79– 3   storm or shine, pure *p*· is thine,
My. 155–18   this dear church having a pure *p*·,
purer
Mis. 330–22   holier aims, a purer *p*·
purity and
No. 34–24   throne of glory in purity and *p*·,
reflect
My. 210–16   His thoughts can only reflect *p*·,
reflection of
My. 355–28   His reflection of *p*·, love, joy.
righteousness, and
My. 282–12   justice, righteousness, and *p*·,
sacrificed
'02. 13– 2   self was forgotten, *p*· sacrificed,

peace

seeking
Mis. 324–27   seeking *p·* but finding none.

silly
Mis. 254–24   resting in silly *p·* upon the

sown in
My. 40–21   * is sown in *p·* — *Jas.* 3 : 18.

spiritual
My. 93–15   * physical health and spiritual *p·*.

strength of
My. 121– 7   we learn that the strength of *p·*

this
Mis. 82– 5   this *p·* floweth as a river
My. 121–11   This *p·* is spiritual ;

thy
Mis. 268– 9   thy *p·* been as a river." — *Isa.* 48 : 18.

to send
Mis. 214– 6   I came not to send *p·*, — *Matt.* 10 : 34.
'01. 31–10   "I came not to send *p·* — *Matt.* 10 : 34.

treacherous
Mis. 9–23   trained in treacherous *p·*

weapons of
Pul. 84– 3   * with the weapons of *p·*.

white-winged
Mis. 204–10   white-winged *p·* sings to the heart

with God
Mis. 211–27   and kept *p·* with God.
'01. 2–20   keeping *p·* with God.

would reign
My. 279–14   one Mind, *p·* would reign.

your
My. 150–31   your *p·* return to you." — *Matt.* 10 : 13.

Mis. 124–11   turn, with sickened sense, . . . for *p·*;
133–31   As to the *p·*, it is unutterable ;
138–19   divine might, giving . . . *p·*.
155–11   and *p·* will crown your joy.
162–12   *p·*, good will, love, teaching, and
172–26   *p·* can only be . . . on the side of
209– 6   and cry, "*P·*, *p·* ; — *Jer.* 6 : 14.
209–23   *P·* has no foothold on the false
Ret. 42–16   end of *that man is p·*." — *Psal.* 37 : 37.
'01. 23– 9   be in *p·* with the schools.
Po. 31– 7   *p·* of Soul's sweet solitude !
78– 3   *P·* her white wings will spread
My. 36–17   * *p·* of a more righteous living,
121–14   *P·*, like plain dealing,
153–30   will give thee rest, *p·*, health,
233–17, 18   saying, *P·*, *p·* ; — *Jer.* 6 : 14.
277–15   *p·*, prosperity, and life of nations.
278– 3   If His purpose for *p·* is to be
281–25   * influence . . . exerted for *p·*,
282– 2   is its *p·* maker or breaker.
282–17   chapter sub-title

peaceable
My. 40–20   * first pure, then *p·*, — *Jas.* 3 : 17.
300–32   are they attacking a *p·* party

peaceably
My. 314–29   I lived with Dr. Patterson *p·*,

peacebreakers
My. 40–10   * some who have been *p·*

peaceful
Mis. 392– 5   With *p·* presence hath begirt
Pan. 14–19   In your *p·* homes remember
15– 1   murdering her *p·* seamen
Po. 20– 6   With *p·* presence hath begirt
23–21   Give *p·* triumph to the
My. 280– 7   * *p·* tranquillity of the race.
333–22   * "His end was calm and *p·*,

peacefully
My. 250–25   I rest *p·* in knowing that the
277– 4   settled *p·* by statesmanship

peacemakers
My. 40–11   * into the blessedness of *p·*.
40–22   * "Blessed are the *p·* : — *Matt.* 5 : 9.

peacemaking
My. 40–16   * demand of this age is for *p·*,

peaches
Ret. 4–15   orchards of apples, *p·*,

peal
Pul. 61–22   * the first *p·* of the chimes
Po. 71–13   God to the rescue — Liberty, *p·* !

pealed
My. 77–21   * *p·* from the chimes a first hymn

pearl
Mis. 30–13   he declared were inlaid with *p·*,
252–31   yea, it is the *p·* priceless
313– 7   spiritual molecule, *p·*, and pinnacle,
Ret. 91– 4   "the *p·* of parables,"
'02. 3–15   occupation of that *p·* of the ocean,
My. 347–18   parable of the priceless *p·*

pearls
Mis. 7–14   Cast not your *p·* before swine ;
89–16   "*p·* before swine" — *Matt.* 7 : 6.
127–24   though your *p·* be downtrodden,
211–20   trample on your *p·* of thought,
247– 4   not as *p·* trampled upon.
307–21   Cast not *p·* before the unprepared
325–11   seize his *p·*, throw them away,
No. 8–24   no longer cast your *p·* before
40– 9   *p·* of awakened consciousness,
40– 9   lest your *p·* be trampled upon.
Po. 8– 9   vestal *p·* that on leaflets lay,
My. 215–21   preying upon my *p·*,
227–24   *p·* before swine, — *Matt.* 7 : 6.
347–16   *p·* that crown this cup

pears
Ret. 4–15   orchards of apples, peaches, *p·*,

Pears' soap
'00. 10–28   gold pieces snuggled in *P· s·*.

pear-tree
Ret. 18– 7   In lap of the *p·*, with musical flow.
18–26   from the bent branch of a *p·*.
Po. 63–16   In lap of the *p·*, with musical flow.
63–24   from the bent branch of a *p·*.

pebbles
Mis. 343–15   cold, hard *p·* of selfishness,
Ret. 27–22   meandering midst *p·* and rocks,
Pul. 80–14   * over its granitic *p·*.

peculiar
Ret. 8– 1   *p·* circumstances and events
Pul. 23–23   * marked by *p·* intimations of
57–13   * *p·* tenets of the . . . Scientists,
59–12   * way *p·* to Christian Scientists,
My. 50–12   * felt a *p·* sense of isolation,
52–31   * *p·* knowledge of the circumstances.
78–27   * convey the *p·* impressiveness
90–30   * *p·* department of healing,
123–31   *p·* people whose God is All-in-all,
206–24   holy nation, a *p·* people ; — *I Pet.* 2 : 9.
352– 6   * *p·* privileges we enjoy

peculiarities
Hea. 12–16   characteristic *p·* and . . . symptoms

peculiarly
Pul. 36–15   * I went to her *p·* fatigued.
My. 78–11   * carvings *p·* rich and impressive.

pecuniarily
Mis. 11– 9   afterwards assisting them *p·*,
My. 130–10   whom I have assisted *p·*

pecuniary
Mis. 349– 1   even the offer of *p·* assistance

pedal
Pul. 60–23   * *p·* compass, C. C. C. to F. 30.
    (*see also* **organ**)

pedal movements
    (*see* **organ**)

pedal organ
    (*see* **organ**)

pedals
    (*see* **organ**)

pedestal
My. 79– 6   * chapter sub-title
79–21   * placed upon a far higher *p·*
259– 3   mounted on its *p·*

pedestals
Mis. 255– 3   set themselves on *p·*,

peel
Mis. 231–18   to arrest the *p·* !

peep
Po. 73– 7   And the stars *p·* out,
My. 173–17   to take a *p·* at this church
258–32   take a *p·* into my studio ;

peer
Mis. 22–19   It hath no *p·*, no competitor,
347–10   *p·* through the opaque error.

peering
Mis. 369– 9   *p·* into the cause which

peers
Ret. 17– 9   morning *p·* out, from her
Po. 62– 9   morning *p·* out, from her

Pekin
'00. 1–23   Paris, Berlin, Rome, *P·*.

pelf
Mis. 325–10   they have plenty of *p·*,
'00. 10–20   the sceptre of self and *p·*

pellets
My. 107–13   that a vial full of the *p·* can
107–17   tells you, . . . with these *p·* he heals
345–17   *p·* without any medication

Pembroke

Ret.	4–24	Nathaniel Ambrose of *P·*,
	5– 5	Congregational Church in *P·*.
'01.	32– 1	Abraham Burnham of *P·*,

pen

Mis.	xii– 6	take my *p·* and pruning-hook,
	149–18	lips nor *p·* can ever express
	227–15	Would that my *p·* or pity could
	275–21	*P·* can never portray the satisfaction
	295–17	with his ready *p·* and pathos?
	377– 2	*p·* to paint frail fairness
Ret.	5–16	the *p·* can never do justice.
Pul.	5– 4	address on C. S. from my *p·*,
	87–23	This wish stops not with my *p·*
'00.	12– 1	beyond the power of the *p·*.
Po.	32–12	inspires my *p·* as I write ;
My.	48–16	* *Methodist Review* from the *p·* of
	124–17	*p·* may not tell.
	125–11	to dip my *p·* in my heart,
	136–25	hard earnings of my *p·*,
	146–31	weight of thought, tongue, and *p·*
	148–23	as with the *p·* of an angel
	294–24	will move the *p·* of millions.
	296–26	dipped her *p·* in my heart,

penal

Peo.	11–19	and enact *p·* codes ;

penalties

Mis.	199– 1	God does not reward . . . love with *p·* ;
	209– 1	attaches to sin due *p·*

penalty

Mis.	68–14	*p·* for believing in their reality
	119–31	and escape the *p·* therefor?
	126–29	*p·* of which the Hebrew bard spake
	222–19	suffer its full *p·* after death.
	227– 9	Thus, to evade the *p·* of law,
	237– 6	accepted as the *p·* for sin.
	300–20	incurring the *p·* of the law,
	317–27	Such students should not pay the *p·*
	381–25	on *p·* of ten thousand dollars.
Man.	46–22	on *p·* of discipline and liability to
	53–17	on *p·* of being excommunicated
Un.	11– 2	from the *p·* of error.
My.	248–24	sin and suffering and their *p·*, death

penance

Mis.	244–12	are they bodily *p·* and torture, or
'02.	16–24	Fasting, feasting, or *p·*,
My.	228–31	for *p·* or for reformation ;

pence

Pul.	8–19	to earn a few *p·* toward

penchant

Mis.	329– 2	Mine is an obstinate *p·* for nature

penciled

Po.	18–13	He *p·* his path

pencils

My.	124–18	Nature reflects man and art *p·* him,

pendulum

Pul.	80– 3	* *p·* that has swung to one extreme

penetrated

Pul.	65– 2	* it has *p·* what is called the

penetration

Mis.	292–27	with the *p·* of Soul,
	313– 9	throw the light of *p·* on the page ;
Un.	2–15	in the infinite *p·* of Truth,

penitent

Mis.	326–29	*p·* one who had groped his way
'01.	17– 4	cause him to return . . . *p·* and saved ;
My.	133– 2	many pardons for the *p·*.

penmanship

My.	137– 9	* in both substance and *p·* :

Penna. Ave., 1505

Mis.	304– 2	* 1505 *P· A·*, Washington, D. C.
	306–15	* 1505 *P· A·*, Washington, D. C.,

penned

Ret.	46– 1	Lines *p·* when I was pastor of

pennies

Mis.	305–27	* in *p·*, if possible,

pennings

Mis.	379– 4	asked if I could see his *p·*

penny

My.	77–28	* every *p·* of the two million dollars

Pentecost Day

Ret.	76–21	as of old, on the *P· D·*,

pent-up

Mis.	347– 4	the internal action of *p·* gas.
	356– 5	*p·* elements of mortal mind

people (*see also* people's)
accuse

Ret.	73–22	or accuse *p·* of being unduly personal,

people
all

Mis.	32–27	all *p·* can and should be just,
Pan.	1–18	day when all *p·* shall know

among the

My.	53–29	* C. S. among the *p·*,

any

My.	148– 5	All that we ask of any *p·*

are being healed

Rud.	14–25	*P·* are being healed by means of

are surprised

'00.	4–11	*p·* are surprised at the new

attended by

My.	96–29	* attended by *p·* from all parts

before the

Mis.	162– 7	before the *p·* and their schools
'01.	22–22	rules, are before the *p·*,
My.	323– 8	* before the *p·* find out

believe

Mis.	220–25	*p·* believe that a man is sick
	228–30	*P·* believe in infectious and

best

'00.	2– 5	best *p·* on earth and in heaven.

blinding the

Rud.	17– 5	blinding the *p·* to the true

body of

Mis.	312–16	* body of *p·* known as . . . Scientists,
My.	95–18	* well-dressed body of *p·*.
	99–12	* optimistic body of *p·*,

chosen

Mis.	151–23	Ye are a chosen *p·*,

Christian

Pul.	50–17	* number of Christian *p·*,

Christian(?)

My.	60–11	* all the Christian (?) *p·* at that time.

Christian Science

My.	328–10	* The C. S. *p·*, greatly pleased at

clamor

No.	45–25	The *p·* clamor to leave cradle and

coming

Mis.	322– 5	*P·* coming from a distance

consign

Mis.	350–27	which consign *p·* to suffering.

crowds of

My.	30– 1	* held large crowds of *p·*,

dear

My.	175–29	influence the minds of this dear *p·*
	197– 5	be upon this dear *p·*,

dependent

No.	3–12	*P·* dependent on the rules of this

devourer of the

'00.	12–29	as the devourer of the *p·*.

diseased

Rud.	15–13	advising diseased *p·* not to enter

disinterested

Ret.	50–11	I beg disinterested *p·* to ask

do not kill

'01.	33–19	We admit that they do not kill *p·*
	33–30	citizens that do not kill *p·*

do not know

My.	305–11	*P·* do not know who is referred to as

do not understand

Mis.	7–27	because *p·* do not understand

easier for

Mis.	5–30	It is much easier for *p·* to believe
	247–25	It is much easier for *p·* to believe

eight hundred

Pul.	27– 6	* The vestry seats eight hundred *p·*,
My.	54–15	* about eight hundred *p·*.

eleven hundred

Pul.	25– 9	* seating eleven hundred *p·*

exhort

Mis.	197– 5	exhort *p·* to turn from sin

eyes of the

Mis.	48–20	to open the eyes of the *p·*
Pul.	15– 1	to open the eyes of the *p·*

few

Mis.	171–26	Few *p·* at present know aught of
Pul.	57–21	* Few *p·* outside its own circles

five thousand

My.	29– 4	* Five thousand *p·* kneeling
	69–21	* where five thousand *p·* can
	71–29	* would seat five thousand *p·*,
	98– 7	* holding five thousand *p·*,
	99–15	* seating five thousand *p·*,
	141–24	seats only five thousand *p·*,

five thousand and twelve

My.	71–23	* five thousand and twelve *p·*

forty thousand

My.	98– 2	* Forty thousand *p·* truly make

frightens

My.	160–14	a live truth, . . . frightens *p·*.
	216–12	a miracle that frightens *p·*,

gathering of

Man.	60–23	No large gathering of *p·*
My.	87–13	* a great gathering of *p·*

people

generally
 Mis. 380–20 p· generally, called for a sign
God's
 Mis. 117–12 * vivacity among God's p·."
good
 '02. 20–25 whose good p· welcome
groups of
 My. 87–21 * cheerful looking groups of p·
handful of
 My. 59–18 * preached to a handful of p·
have slumbered
 No. 41–19 long ages p· have slumbered
healthy
 Mis. 229– 6 contact with healthy p·,
His
 Mis. 144–22 the assembling of His p·
   150–28 His p· are they that reflect Him
   152–19 God has prepared for His p·,
   153– 6 went forth before His p·,
 '02. 1– 2 loving providence for His p·
honest
 Ret. 29– 3 I esteem all honest p·,
 No. 3–26 odious to honest p· ;
ignorance of
 No. 43–27 sheer ignorance of p·,
imagine
 My. 103–16 p· imagine a vain — *Psal.* 2 : 1.
   200– 5 p· imagine a vain — *Psal.* 2 : 1.
influenced the
 Mis. 246– 7 press that influenced the p· to
intelligent
 Pul. 63–17 * intelligent p· among her devoted
irresponsible
 No. 3– 9 irresponsible p· insisted
its
 My. 10–20 * sacrifice on the part of its p·.
   163–25 I love its p·
law-abiding
 Ret. 87–12 most systematic and law-abiding p·
leading
 My. 163–24 the leading p· of this pleasant city
loyal
 My. 14–23 * to ensnare a generous and loyal p·.
many
 Mis. 150–16 seen the salvation of many p·
   276– 6 solely because so many p·
many of the
 Mis. 81–18 *many of the p· from beyond Jordan*
may listen
 '01. 20–12 P· may listen complacently to
million of
 Mis. 35– 7 a million of p· acknowledge and
 '00. 2– 1 over a million of p·
minds of the
 My. 234–28 before the minds of the p· are
most
 Mis. 126–22 Most p· condemn evil-doing,
my
 Mis. 209– 7 the wounds of my p·
 My. 126–14 "Come out of her, my p·" — *Rev.* 18 : 4.
   233–17 the daughter of my p· — *Jer.* 6 : 14.
   270–13 shall be my p·" — *Ruth* 1 : 16.
non-church-going
 Pul. 56– 7 * churches and non-church-going p·.
numbering the
 Man. 48–16 Numbering the P·.
   48–21 turn away from . . . numbering the p·.
observed
 My. 244–30 As the p· observed the success
of common sense
 No. 2– 5 scorned by p· of common sense.
of God
 Mis. 216– 4 rest for the p· of God ;
of intelligence
 My. 96–30 * And they were p· of intelligence.
of New England
 My. 264–10 * to the p· of New England,
of standing
 My. 81–31 * p· of standing and of substance,
of substance
 My. 80– 3 * p· of substance and of standing,
of the Occident
 Mis. 29–24 the p· of the Occident know
of the South
 My. 331–28 * characterized the p· of the South,
opinions of
 Hea. 6– 6 opinions of p· fly too high or
other
 Mis. 230–16 hours that other p· may occupy in
   319–13 or more to them than to other p·.
our
 My. 326– 4 * is most gratifying to our p· ;
peculiar
 My. 123–31 peculiar p· whose God is All-in-all,
   206–24 a peculiar p· ; — *I Pet.* 2 : 9.

people

poisoning
 Mis. 248–29 mental malpractice of poisoning p·
prepare
 Mis. 347– 8 p· prepare shelter in caves of the
present
 Mis. 148–26 contributions from the p· present
presented to the
 Un. 6–11 presented to the p· in divine light,
privileges of the
 My. 168– 5 forever the privileges of the p·
raising up the
 My. 285–22 raising up the p·, — *Acts* 24 : 12.
robbing of
 My. 266–4 the robbing of p· of life and
say
 Mis. 335–25 Such p· say, "Would you
 '01. 27–28 * First, p· say it conflicts with
 Hea. 6– 4 * "P· say you are a medium,"
 My. 49– 2 * when these smiling p· say,
   304–26 * First, p· say it conflicts with
six thousand
 Pul. 64–27 * six thousand p· to participate in
some
 Mis. 78–17 some p· employ the *et cetera* of
   237–10 Some p· never repent until
   317–12 not absolutely requisite for some p·
   353–18 Some p· try to tend folks,
 Pul. 59– 8 * some p· heard these exercises four
sometimes object
 Pan. 9–27 the best of p· sometimes object to
stirred the
 My. 105– 2 stirred the p· to search the
stirreth up the
 My. 104– 8 stirreth up the p·." — *Luke* 23 : 5.
   104–16 "stirreth up the p·" — *Luke* 23 : 5.
   222–19 stirreth up the p·." — *Luke* 23 : 5.
teach
 Mis. 44– 4 may profitably teach p·,
terrifies
 Ret. 73–20 wrongs it, or terrifies p· over it,
that walked
 Chr. 55– 8 p· that walked in darkness — *Isa.* 9 : 2.
their
 Pul. 82–20 * sang and sacrificed for their p·,
these
 Rud. 13–25 These p· should not be expected,
 My. 48–28 * The intellects of these p·
   71–19 * When these p· enter this new
   75–17 * these p· would take it
   95–19 * The faith of these p· is certainly
   96– 4 * These p· were of the highest
thirty thousand
 My. 30– 5 * well over thirty thousand p·
   79–12 * thirty thousand p· assembling
this
 My. v– 9 * extended to this p· by
   187–26 in the hearts of this p·
   202–16 the spiritual sense of this p·
those
 My. 81–21 * In those p· was the depth of
throng of
 Pul. 61–25 * attracted quite a throng of p·,
thy
 My. 270–12 "thy p· shall be — *Ruth* 1 : 16.
two hundred
 My. 123–22 a trifle over two hundred p·,
two hundred thousand
 Pul. 30–24 * exceeds two hundred thousand p·.
unaware
 Ret. 71–11 P· unaware of the indications
unfamiliar
 My. 338–21 that p· unfamiliar with his
unfortunate
 My. 301–20 Those unfortunate p· who are
warned the
 No. 41– 4 warned the p· to beware of Jesus,
warning
 Mis. 210– 8 warning p· not to stir up
well-meaning
 Pul. 80–22 * an army of well-meaning p·
 '01. 29–12 well-meaning p· sometimes are
were astonished
 Mis. 189–26 "The p· were astonished — *Matt.* 7 : 28.
 Ret. 58–10 the p· "were astonished — *Matt.* 7 : 28.
 Un. 42–18 "p· were astonished — *Matt.* 7 : 28.
were healed
 Ret. 39– 1 p· were healed simply by reading
what sort of
 Mis. 178–16 * wondered what sort of p· you were,
whose God
 My. 127– 4 the p· whose God is All-in-all,
will chain
 Pul. 14– 2 the hour when the p· will chain,
will differ
 Mis. 288–29 P· will differ in their opinions

people
wrong class of
Mis. 80–15   with a wrong class of *p·*.

Mis. 193–20   which the *p·* are now adopting.
    211– 9   by the good judgment of *p·* in
    229– 9   If only the *p·* would believe
    245–24   allows the *p·* to go no further
    282– 7   Shall *p·* be treated mentally
    301–32   of the *p·* there was none— *Isa. 63 : 3.*
    339– 2   If *p·* would confine their talk to
    347– 5   *p·* have to escape from their houses
    353–10   *P·* give me too much attention
Ret. 73–13   less to me than it is to *p·* who
Un. 7–15   *P·* are now living who can
Pul. 15– 6   *p·* like you better when you
    56–16   * It makes *p·* better and happier.
'00. 2– 4   *p·* most interested in this old-new
Hea. 18– 5   *P·* are willing to put new wine into
My. 47–11   * *p·* the world over have been
    51–13   * on the part of the *p·*,
    114– 9   why point the *p·* to the lives of
    171–21   * *p·* who were assembled on the **lawn**
    321–31   * *p·* who knew you years before

People and Patriot
Pul. 77–23   * *P· and P·*, Concord, N. H.,

peopled
Mis. 150–23   *p·* with living witnesses
Ret. 91–24   *p·* with holy messages from **the**
Un. 28– 9   *p·* with demons or angels,
Rud. 4– 3   *p·* with perfect beings,

people's
Mis. 62– 2   other *p·* individuality, health,
    112–27   exaggerating sense of other *p·*.
    119– 4   aiding other *p·* devices
    249– 8   appropriated other *p·* manuscripts
    287–32   attempts to steady other *p·* altars,
    290– 2   Let other *p·* marriage relations *alone :*
    291–10   other *p·* thoughts and actions.
    317–28   penalty for other *p·* faults ;
    357– 1   trafficking in other *p·* business,
Ret. 89–26   upon other *p·* thoughts,
'00. 8–11   he may steal other *p·* good
Peo. 2– 4   due to the *p·* improved views
    2–20   Proportionately as the *p·* belief
    2–26   constantly before the *p·* mind,
My. 147–16   the *p·* sense of C. S.
    233–14   the effects of other *p·* sins

peoples
Mis. 81–30   *p·* the mind with spiritual
    244–27   for all *p·* and for all time ;
    307–22   easily-besetting sin of all *p·*.
Ret. 26– 9   demonstrated for all time and *p·*
Pan. 12–14   it showeth to all *p·* the way
    13–21   Then shall all nations, *p·*,
'00. 10–13   laws of nations and *p·*,
    10–20   weak provinces, or *p·*.
'02. 2–10   It is purifying all *p·*,
Peo. 6–28   *p·* are characterized by
Po. 1 –15   insignificance that *p·* earth,
My. 178–10   and prepared for all *p·*.
    190–24   in order that all *p·*, in all **ages,**
    265–12   individuals, *p·*, and nations.
    265–30   reaching out to all classes and *p·*.
    279–14   Had all *p·* one Mind,
    281–10   brotherhood of all *p·*
    284– 3   to help human purpose and *p·*,
    284–27   quarrels between nations and *p·*.
    286– 5   prayed that all the *p·* on earth
    291–12   uniting the interests of all *p·* ;
    291–31   liberty of other *p·*

Peoria
Pul. 56– 4   * Scranton, *P·*, Atlanta, Toronto,
My. 81–16   * "Dresden !" "*P·* !" they cried.

Peoria (**Ill.**) *Journal*
My. 96–24   *[P· (I·.) J·]*

pepper
Mis. 348–20   capsicum (red *p·*) ;

per
Rud. 1–15   *p·* (through) and *sonare* (to sound).
My. 234– 1   fifty telegrams *p·* holiday

Per Capita Tax
Man. 44–12   *P· C· T·*.
    44–13   shall pay annually a *p· c· t·*

perceive
Mis. 53–28   abstract or difficult to *p·*.
    179–29   then we can *p·* Truth,
    182– 5   as many as *p·* man's actual existence
Pul. 32– 7   * *p·* that she had the temperament
    35– 6   * Mrs. Eddy came to *p·* that Christ's
Rud. 6–21   so far as you *p·* and understand
Pan. 11– 1   to *p·* the real man,

perceive
Hea. 8– 9   *p·* the meaning of the context,
    8–12   slow to *p·* individual advancement ;
    13–24   You can readily *p·* this
My. 242– 8   Unless you fully *p·* that you are
    275– 6   so-called senses do not *p·* this fact

perceived
Ret. 76–12   *p·* a light beyond what others saw.
    94– 1   Having *p·*, in advance of others,
My. 40–26   * She has illustrated what the poet *p·*

perceives
Mis. 374–29   *p·* a semblance between the thinker

per cent
My. 227–31   C. S. cures a larger *p· c·* of

percentage
No. 32–25   diminishing the *p·* of sin.
'00. 8–18   We lose a *p·* due to our activity
'01. 29–28   * "With this *p·*," students wrote me,

perception
Mis. 15–10   give the true *p·* of God
    28– 4   *P·* by the five personal senses
    139–25   but to my spiritual *p·*,
    228–23   *p·*, sensation, and consciousness
Ret. 28–14   a *p·* of and dependence on
Un. 20–18   awake to the *p·* of God
    61–12   Human *p·*, advancing toward
Pul. 35–18   a *p·* of and dependence on
Rud. 3– 9   to the *p·* of mortal sense,
My. 37–22   * through your spiritual *p·*
    113–22   and have a clear *p·* of it.
    149–19   to have a clear *p·* of divine **justice,**

perceptions
Un. 46–11   subordinate the fleshly *p·*

perceptive
Hea. 14–20   the spiritual sense or *p·* faculty

perchance
Mis. 9–19   *P·*, having tasted its tempting **wine,**
Pul. 3–26   *P·* some one of you may say,
Po. 66–14   Might cheer it, *p·*, when she sings.

per contra
Mis. 24–20   *P· c·*, Mind and man are immortal ;
    254–21   *P· c·*, it is the mortal mind sense
My. 119–11   *P· c·*, C. S. destroys such tendency.

perdition
Mis. 113–14   carried to the depths of *p·*
Ret. 14– 8   converted and rescued from *p·* ;
'02. 3–30   the first lie and leap into *p·*

perfect
Mis. 1– 9   ordeal of a *p·* Christianity,
    5– 8   produce *p·* health and *p·* **morals**
    5–26   always *p·* in God, in Truth,
    6–18   we exist in God, *p·*,
    6–20   Truth, and Love must be *p·* ;
    10–21   strength made *p·* in weakness,
    21– 4   *p·* unity with Christ's Sermon
    46–29   man is *p·* even as the Father,
    46–30   his divine Principle, is *p·*.
    50–22   "Be ye therefore *p·* ;"— *Matt. 5 : 48.*
    66–17   to discern God's *p·* ways
    79– 7   man was, and is, God's *p·* likeness,
    79–17   If the great cause is *p·*,
    79–17   its effect is *p·* also ;
    79–22   *p·* and unfallen likeness,
    82–16   whose law is *p·* and infinite.
    85–14   "Be ye therefore *p·*,— *Matt. 5 : 48.*
    85–15   which is in heaven is *p·*." — *Matt. 5 : 48.*
    86– 2   individual and spiritual are *p·* ;
    98– 2   *p·* model should be held in mind,
    138–15   lesson of C. S. is love, *p·* love,
    138–16   love made *p·* through the cross.
    176– 3   healing, and peace, and *p·* love.
    184–14   power to be *p·* which he possesses,
    186–20   his *p·* Principle, God,
    188– 3   Man is as *p·* now,
    195–19   That *p·* syllogism of Jesus
    213–16   may *p·* their own lives
    232– 6   *p·* Principle of things ;
    232– 9   *p·* and practical Christianity
    286–30, 31   man is *p·* even as the Father is *p·*,
    362– 5   wherein God and man are *p·*,
    375–23   * In other words, the art is *p·*.
    376– 1   * the art is *p·*.
Ret. 24–21   in *p·* scientific accord with divine
    78– 7   scientific practice makes *p·*,
    91–20   his own *p·* understanding.
Un. 3–21   is *p·* being, or consciousness.
    5– 5   toward the *p·* thought divine.
    10–17, 18   eternally *p·*, because He is *p·*,
    24–21   must be spiritual, *p·*, eternal.
    40–15   than they can become *p·* by
    42–13   is as *p·* and immortal now,
    49– 9   ignorant of sin as is the *p·* Maker.

perfect

Un.	51– 9	gained through Christ as *p·* manhood.
	53–22	as a *p·* child of God.
Pul.	26–18	* of fine range and *p·* tone.
	34–23	in *p·* scientific accord with the divine
	49–30	* grounds and farm in *p·* order,
	54– 6	* *p·* harmony with natural law,
	54–14	* *p·* obedience to the laws of
	54–26	* most *p·* obtainable environment,
	62–16	* so that the harmony is *p·*.
	81–21	* as a *p·* harp,
Rud.	4– 3	peopled with *p·* beings,
	7– 9	*p·* and immortal Mind.
No.	30–12	this *p·* law is ever present
	31–18	*p·* consciousness is attained.
	41–14	life of Christ is the *p·* example ;
Pan.	9–11	" Be ye therefore *p·*,— *Matt.* 5 : 48.
	9–12	which is in heaven is *p·* ;"— *Matt.* 5 : 48.
	11–11	Governed by . . . man is *p·*.
	12– 1	"Be ye therefore *p·*,"— *Matt.* 5 : 48.
'00.	4–10	*p·* worship of one God.
	4–16	only *p·* religion is divine Science,
	14–16	following the more *p·* way,
'01.	8–15	"Be ye therefore *p·*,— *Matt.* 5 : 48.
	8–16	which is in heaven is *p·*."— *Matt.* 5 : 48.
Hea.	15–12	to any one's *p·* satisfaction
Peo.	2–26	This more *p·* idea,
	7–29	become more or less *p·* as
My.	11– 2	* followers of the *p·* Christ,
	38– 2	* every *p·* gift cometh from above,
	38–21	* in almost *p·* time.
	41–18	* maintains the *p·* standard of truth
	75–12	* So *p·* have been all the
	78–22	* congregation singing in *p·* unison.
	78–24	* were found to be *p·*.
	85–31	* one of the few *p·* sky-lines
	111–13	spiritual status of a *p·* life
	113–19	to *p·* His praise.
	123– 8	continue to urge the *p·* model
	150–14	never weary of struggling to be *p·*
	159–14	*p·* love of God and man.
	179–21	Christianity as the *p·* ideal.
	187– 9	*p·* path wherein to walk,
	187– 9	the *p·* Principle whereby
	187–10	*p·* law of God.
	205–27	demonstrated *p·* rules ;
	207–11	* more *p·* manifestation of the truth
	242– 9	you are the child of God, hence *p·*,
	253– 4	brings to light the *p·* original man
	290–14	keep him in perfect peace,— *Isa.* 26 : 3.
		(see also **eternal, Love, man, Mind**)

perfected

Mis.	232–19	having *p·* in Science that
Pul.	8–22	Thou has *p·* praise."— *Matt.* 21 : 16.
'01.	2– 5	the *p·* Science of healing
'02.	17–15	duty done and life *p·*,
Po.	22–17	A life *p·*, strong and calm.

perfectibility

Mis.	98–21	God and the *p·* of man.
Pan.	11–27	man's unfallen spiritual *p·*.
'00.	7–15	the Science of *p·*

perfecting

My.	342–23	*p·* of man stated scientifically."

perfection

and demonstration
Ret.	57–29	*p·* and demonstration of metaphysical,

cannot force
My.	344–26	cannot force *p·* on the world.

collapse from
No.	26–15	no more relapse or collapse from *p·*,

divine
Mis.	320–12	infant idea of divine *p·*

fitness for
Un.	11–25	in order to mature fitness for *p·*

in art
Mis.	232– 7	pushing towards *p·* in art,

in churches
No.	41–13	to look for *p·* in churches

infinite
Un.	16– 1	man bows to the infinite *p·*
My.	103–12	Infinite *p·* is unfolded

is normal
Mis.	104–13	According to C. S., *p·* is normal,

less than
Pan.	11–20	with something less than *p·*

likeness of
My.	262– 2	image, idea, or likeness of *p·*

man's
Mis.	186–31	the lost sense of man's *p·*,

maximum of
Mis.	232–17	maximum of *p·* in all things.

mental
Mis.	234–25	physical and mental *p·*,

perfection

method of
Hea.	14–26	Principle and method of *p·*,

nearer
My.	342–32	will advance nearer *p·*."

of all things
My.	52–15	* does bring out the *p·* of all things,

of living
'02.	2– 7	sanity and *p·* of living,

of man
Mis.	173–24	The *p·* of man is intact ;

of the rule
Mis.	233–25	*p·* of the rule of C. S.

original
My.	262– 5	its spotless purity and original *p·*.

person and
No.	20– 2	His person and *p·* are

physical
'01.	1–15	mental and physical *p·*.

point of
My.	242– 6	neither behind the point of *p·* nor

power and
Mis.	189–18	power and *p·* of a released sense of
Ret.	27–27	increases in power and *p·*

practicality of
My.	182–32	prove the practicality of *p·*,

proved to
No.	38– 1	Jesus proved to *p·*,

pure
Mis.	343–17	their pure *p·* shall appear

Soul's
My.	344–15	gradual approaches to Soul's *p·*."

spiritual
Mis.	42–26	exists only in spiritual *p·*,
My.	345–23	near a state of spiritual *p·*.

state of
Mis.	14– 8	his original state of *p·*,
	78–25	*Has man fallen from a state of **p·**?*

strives for
My.	272– 2	actively strives for *p·*,

trifles make
My.	123–29	* "trifles make *p·*,"

ultimatum of
Mis.	79–10	man is the ultimatum of *p·*,

unto
My.	128–3	let us go on unto *p·* ;— *Heb.* 6 : 1.

would dethrone
No.	21–13	philosophy would dethrone *p·*,

Mis.	85–11	*P·*, the goal of existence,
	187– 7	the *p·* of mind and body,
Ret.	80–26	*p·* and an unbroken friendship.
Un.	7–20	an acknowledgment of the *p·* of
No.	10–27	harmony, perpetuity, and *p·*,
My.	103– 1	*p·* is reluctantly seen
	269– 5	pledged to innocence, purity, *p·*.

perfections

Ret.	52– 5	should shelter its *p·* from the
Un.	43– 1	eternal being and its *p·*,

perfectly

Mis.	243– 2	cured her *p·* of this habit,
Pul.	54– 8	* The *p·* natural is the *p·* spiritual.
	54–15	* He understood the law *p·*,
	72–18	* and yet have been *p·* well."
	73–21	* *p·* versed in all their beliefs
My.	32– 9	* Mrs. Conant could be heard *p·*

perfectness

Mis.	273–14	in the bonds of love and *p·*,
Ret.	76–19	unity of good and bond of *p·*.
My.	164–23	It is *unity*, the bond of *p·*,
	249– 4	correct sin through your own *p·*.

perfidy

Mis.	226– 8	chapter sub-title
	226–25	*P·* of an inferior quality,

perform

Mis.	40–11	*p·* as instantaneous cures
	54–25	*to p· as great miracles*
Man.	28–16	*p·* the functions of their
	28–21	to *p·* his office faithfully ;
	29– 4	to *p·* his official duties.
	29–12	or *p·* their functions faithfully.
My.	42–18	* endeavor to *p·* this service
	60–28	* the interesting part I had to *p·*
	205–10	* His wonders to *p·* ;
	241– 1	* to *p·* this important work.
	249–25	to *p·* this important function.
	288–19	to *p·* the functions of Spirit,
	303–30	*p·* the functions of foreshadowing

performance

Man.	77–14	*p·* of their several offices
No.	7–19	strict *p·* of each one of them.
My.	42–28	* in the *p·* of her daily tasks.

performances
Mis. 243–17 unbecoming a mortal's poor *p·*.
performed
Mis. 242–14 I *p·* more difficult tasks
244– 5 *p·* by divine power,
Man. 49–21 ceremony shall be *p·* by a clergyman
Ret. 19–23 *p·* their obligations most faithfully.
Pul. 73–14 * and this duty she faithfully *p·*.
Hea. 14–19 the most arduous task I ever *p·*.
My. 95–20 * telling of miracles *p·*
331– 2 *p·* their obligations
336– 9 * faithfully *p·* their obligation
performs
Mis. 260–27 *p·* the vital functions of Truth
Ret. 86–22 each man who *p·* his own part.
perfume
Ret. 18–10 beauty and *p·* from buds burst away,
'00. 8– 8 a *p·* or a poison,
Po. 46–12 And yield its beauty and *p·*
63–20 beauty and *p·* from buds burst away,
perfumed
Mis. 396–25 in raptured song, With love *p·*.
Pul. 18– 9 in raptured song, With love *p·*.
Po. 12– 9 in raptured song, With love *p·*.
perfume-laden
Mis. 332–15 many-hued blossoms, *p·* breezes,
Pergamene
'00. 13–22 The *P·* church consisted of the
Pergamos
'00. 13–17 city of *P·* was devoted to a sensual
perhaps
Mis. 35– 9 *P·* the following words
120–24 once in three years is *p·* as often as
125–26 oftener, *p·*, the controversies
126–15 *P·* our church is not yet quite
161–20 owing in part, *p·*, to the Jewish law
197– 5 than many others, *p·*,
262–28 *P·* it is even selfish in me
297–13 that *p·* he has never visited.
Un. 1– 1 *P·* no doctrine of C. S.
Pul. 28–18 * in *p·* equal measure to its use of
46–24 * though *p·* with an unusual zest,
48–25 * is *p·* one of her characteristics,
No. 14–20 *p·* more than any other religious sect,
'01. 28– 9 *p·* none lived a more devout
Hea. 19–21 he is impatient *p·*, or doubts
My. 65– 4 * *p·* the largest ever held in the
82–30 * except *p·* those living in the
92–10 * worthy of *p·* even more interest
96–16 * *p·* the most remarkable,
135– 8 *P·* you already know that I have
319–17 some facts which *p·* have
343– 7 You would ask, *p·*, whether my
peril
Mis. 89–12 If the patient is in *p·*,
323–10 descent and ascent are beset with *p·*,
Ret. 45– 6 organization has its value and *p·*,
periled
Po. 71– 7 *p·* right, Rescued by the
perilous
Mis. 110–26 dared the *p·* defense of Truth,
perils
Mis. 131–31 with *p·* past and victories won.
period
advance of the
Mis. 359–21 were in advance of the *p·*
concession to the
Mis. 91– 7 let it be in concession to the *p·*,
demanded it
Mis. 298–18 implied that the *p·* demanded it.
end of the
Pul. 73–10 * at the end of the *p·* came from
enlightened
My. 249–16 that at this enlightened *p·*
eventful
Mis. 162– 3 third event of this eventful *p·*,
every
Mis. 192–23 belongs to every *p·* ;
Ret. 35–16 his true followers in every *p·*,
indefinite
Hea. 4–16 for an indefinite *p·*,
mediæval
'00. 4–13 greater than in the mediæval *p·* ;
mental
Mis. 204– 6 This mental *p·* is sometimes chronic,
notable
Pul. 55–10 * *p·* notable for her emancipation
of captivity
'00. 3–21 during the *p·* of captivity
of doubt
Mis. 237–19 This is a *p·* of doubt, inquiry,

period
parable of the
Mis. 251–26 learn a parable of the *p·*,
religious
Mis. 307–15 this revolutionary religious *p·*,
Renaissance
Pul. 26–10 * lamp stand of the Renaissance *p·*
restricted
Mis. 244–28 a privileged class or a restricted *p·*,
Revolutionary
Ret. 2–10 prior to the Revolutionary *p·*.
senior
Mis. 235–25 superstitions of a senior *p·*.
some
Ret. 94– 4 At some *p·* and in some way
Pul. 13–3 Every mortal at some *p·*,
successive
Mis. 26– 4 Each successive *p·* of progress
that
My. 152– 3 At that *p·*, the touch of Jesus'
this
Mis. 4– 4 At this *p·* there is a marked
12–17 Mortal mind at this *p·* mutely works
48–22 sudden deaths at this *p·*.
195–14 ministry of healing at this *p·*.
237–16 This *p·* is not essentially one of
253–14 This *p·* is big with events.
253–27 Do the children of this *p·* dream of
274–22 At this *p·*, 1888, those quill-drivers
286–15 To abolish marriage at this *p·*,
317– 8 to demonstrate, as this *p·* demands,
337– 1 I discovered and founded at this *p·*
Ret. 27– 1 I wrote also, at this *p·*,
82–14 At this *p·* my students should
94–30 In this *p·* and the forthcoming
Pul. 14– 3 growing occultism of this *p·*.
No. 9–25 More . . . than this *p·* comprehends.
Pan. 2– 2 At this *p·* of enlightenment,
Peo. 3–18 on the thoughts of men at this *p·*
11–25 learned quacks of this *p·*
My. 54–22 * A record of this *p·* reads,
131– 6 For this hour, for this *p·*,
136– 3 At this *p·* my demonstration of
159–12 At this *p·*, the greatest man or
258– 6 This *p·*, so fraught with opposites,
285–14 men and women of this *p·*
woman of the
Mis. 253– 6 not enough the new woman of the *p·*

Mis. 26– 5 is a *p·* more humane and spiritual.
162– 3 a *p·* of such wonderful spiritual
Hea. 14– 1 occupying the field for a *p·* ;
periodical
Mis. 4–17 a *p·* devoted to this work
7–21 A *p·* of our own will counteract
382–24 proprietor of the first C. S. *p·* ;
Man. 98– 8 promptly published by the *p·*
My. 304–18 sole editor of that *p·*.
333–32 * This *p·* then forthwith strives to
periodicals
Mis. 301– 7 editors of pamphlets and *p·*
Man. 44–16 Church *P·*.
44–18 *p·* which are the organs of this
44–20 these *p·* are ably edited
47–22 testimonials which appear in the *p·*
48–22 The *p·* of our denomination
48–25 they may quote from other *p·*
65– 2 already used in our *p·*.
81–14 *P·*.
81–14 *P·* which shall at any time be
82–11 removed from our *p·*
97–20 by *p·* or circulated literature
My. 42–10 * helpful contributors to our *p·*,
136–20 editor-in-chief of the C. S. *p·*,
173– 9 C. S. *p·* had given notice
250–13 send to the Editor of our *p·* notice of
272–29 * outside of the C. S. *p·*,
326–12 I send for publication in our *p·*
353–10 given the name to all the C. S. *p·*.
periods
Mis. 12–21 at former *p·* in human history
205–24 unites all *p·* in the divine
Ret. 45– 7 requisite only in the earliest *p·*
49– 5 working out their *p·* of organization,
Pul. 13–25 but how many *p·* of torture
'02. 4–23 applicable to all *p·*
Peo. 6–28 *P·* and peoples are characterized
Po. v– 2 * *were written at different p·*
My. 279–10 uniting all *p·* in the design of
perish
Mis. 204– 4 cries, "Save, or I *p·*." — *see Matt.* 8 : 25.
213–24 they shall never *p·*, — *John* 10 : 28.
358– 7 State honors *p·*,
390–24 Ne'er *p·* young, like things of earth,

perish
Ret. 64–17 like the beasts that *p*·."— *Psal.* 49 : 20.
Un. 18– 1 God must *p*·, if He knows evil
40– 6 belief of life in matter, must *p*·,
Pul. 7–20 oppressive priesthood must *p*·,
'00. 7–26 we cry, "Save, or I *p*·!"— *see Matt.* 8 : 25.
'01. 10–26 shall be nothing left to *p*·
'02. 18– 8 only to mock, wonder, and *p*·.
Po. 56– 3 Ne'er *p*· young, like things of earth,

perishable
Mis. 19–29 sinful, material, and *p*·,
103– 3 which say that . . . substance is *p*·.
My. 273–26 five personal senses are *p*· :

perishing
Mis. 17–29 *p*· pleasure and accumulating pains

perishless
Pul. 9–10 warmed also our *p*· hope,

permanence
Mis. 47– 7 glory and *p*· of Spirit :
74–27 power and *p*· of Spirit.
126– 1 from unsettled questions to *p*·,
160– 1 power and *p*· of affection
194– 9 *p*· of Christ's command
196–17 sweet, sacred sense and *p*·
206– 3 from flux to *p*·, from foul to pure,
287–21 giving them strength and *p*·.
320–30 in token of purity and *p*·.
352– 1 it is bereft of *p*· and peace.
Un. 41–15 sacred sense of the *p*· of
'01. 12–15 *p*· of Christ's command
My. 45–32 * material type of Truth's *p*·.
177–15 possibilities and *p*· of Life.

permanency
My. 94–16 * the apparent *p*· of C. S.

permanent
Mis. 110–28 how *p*· that which God calls good.
268–28 Right alone is irresistible, *p*·,
Un. 8–12 All that is beautiful . . . is *p*·.
13–18 that which is not *p*·,
Pul. 86–27 * the *p*· pastor of this church,
'01. 3–18 Mind, a *p*·, fundamental,

permanently
Ret. 82–12 locate *p*· in one section,
My. 51–18 * for a few Sundays if not *p*·."

permeate
Mis. 223–20 May divine Love so *p*· the
Ret. 80–17 *p*· justice and Love,
My. 222–24 religion shall *p*· our laws.

permeated
Mis. 205–21 *p*· with eternal life, holiness, heaven.
My. 265–25 *p*· with divine Love,

permeates
Mis. 204–23 *p*· with increased harmony all the

permission
Mis. 299–24 Did he give you *p*· to do this,
300– 1 I gave *p*· to cite, . . . from my work
302–18 till this *p*· was *withdrawn*,
Man. 43–16 quotations . . . without her *p*·,
71–24 her *p*· to publish them as
Ret. 40– 7 I asked *p*· to see her.
71–19 without the *p*· of man or God,
75–25 no *p*· in the gospel for
Po. vii–10 * *acknowledgment*, . . . of this *p*·,
My. 134–26 * "*P*·" has been secured from
173–31 foresight in granting *p*·,
254–17 * May we have *p*· to print,
298–10 my *p*· to publish . . . this work.
322–18 * *p*· to enter the next Primary class
335–21 * refused *p*· to take the remains to
351– 2 * With our Leader's kind *p*·,

permit
Mis. 11–28 since they *p*· me no other way,
13– 3 *p*· me to exercise these sentiments
84– 6 thereby hasten or *p*· it.
313– 2 *p*· me to say that your editorial
Man. 43– 6 nor *p*· his patients . . . to use them,
73–12 provided its rules so *p*·,
73–18 if the rules . . . so *p*·.
87–11 or cause or *p*· others to solicit,
Pul. 87–14 *p*· me, respectfully, to decline their
My. 154–16 *p*· me to congratulate this little
172–11 *P*· me to present to you
236– 7 *p*· me to make the *amende honorable*
271–29 to your question *p*· me to say
275–13 *P*· me to say, the report . . . is dead,
331–18 * will you *p*· me, in behalf of

permitted
Mis. 249–14 None are *p*· to remain in my
262– 2 wherein it is *p*· to enter,
Pul. 58–12 * pictures we are *p*· to publish,
'01. 16–22 if now it is *p*· license,

permitted
My. 69–12 * within . . . where conditions *p*· it
256– 8 that I be *p*· total exemption

permitting
Pul. 54–24 * *p*· only the father and mother,

permits
'02. 19–30 cup that our Father *p*· us.

perpetrator
Mis. 222–16 action on the mind of the *p*·,
'01. 20–21 sooner or later cause the *p*·,

perpetual
Mis. x– 1 coloring glory of *p*· bloom ;
29– 4 that his promise is *p*·.
56–16 mingling in *p*· warfare
72–25 is in *p*· harmony.
79–16 *p*· in Life, Truth, and Love.
83– 3 *p*· idea of inexhaustible good.
85–17 *p*·, spiritual, individual existence.
91– 7 not as a *p*· or indispensable
140–31 a *p*· type of the divine
269–13 *p*· freshness in relation to
278–24 *p*· instruction of my students might
330– 5 *p*· springtide wherein no arrow
Ret. 13– 8 *p*· banishment from God.
Un. 41–28 *p*· disagreement with Spirit.
No. 11– 5 Man has *p*· individuality ;
'02. 8–22 it prompts *p*· goodness,
Hea. 2–28 sprinkled . . . with *p*· incense.

perpetually
Mis. 206–21 *p*· repeating this diapason
Ret. 73–19 *p*· warns you of "personality,"
74– 2 *p*· egotistical sensibility.
Un. 21– 5 *p*· arguing with ourselves ;
Pul. 9– 8 kindle *p*· its fires.
59– 1 * lamp, kept *p*· burning
Hea. 15–15 *p*· at war with this Mind,
My. 188– 5 shall be there *p*·."— *I Kings* 9 : 3.

perpetuate
Mis. 91–14 *p*· no ceremonials except
98–17 We come to strengthen and *p*· our
Pul. 21–20 To *p*· a cold distance between
No. 5–16 restore health and *p*· life,
21–19 *p*· the supposed power and reality of

perpetuated
Mis. 244–10 have those conditions . . . been *p*·
Ret. 1–16 who *p*· her mother's name.

perpetuates
Mis. 46– 1 *p*· the belief or faith in evil.
346–16 *p*· faith in evil ;

perpetuating
My. 261–13 aids in *p*· purity

perpetuity
Ret. 35–24 *p*· of Jesus' command,
No. 10–27 Eternal harmony, *p*·, and
My. 45– 3 * will result in its *p*·

perplexed
Ret. 8–11 my mother was *p*· and anxious.
Pul. 8– 6 *p*· condition of our nation's

perplexing
Un. 9–18 true solution of the *p*· problem

perplexities
Mis. 131–20 *p*· and difficulties which the

perplexity
My. 214–18 relieving the questioners' *p*·,

perquisite
My. 189– 7 affords even me a *p*· of joy.

per se
Mis. 109–21 Their mental state . . . *p*· *s*·;

persecute
Mis. 8–23 revile you, and *p*· you,— *Matt.* 5 : 11.
11–21 who *p*· and despitefully use one,
Ret. 29– 5 and *p*· you."— *Matt.* 5 : 44.
No. 32–24 great evil to . . . *p*· a Cause
'01. 3– 4 revile you, and *p*· you,— *Matt.* 5 : 11.
33–28 to *p*· another in advance of it.
'02. 11–22 revile you, and *p*· you,— *Matt.* 5 : 11.
My. 104–30 revile you, and *p*· you,— *Matt.* 5 : 11.
300–30 why *p*· it?
316– 7 revile you, and *p*· you,— *Matt.* 5 : 11.

persecuted
Mis. 8–25 so *p*· they the prophets— *Matt.* 5 : 12.
Pul. 7– 8 praised and *p*· in Boston,
13–28 *p*· the woman— *Rev.* 12 : 13.
'01. 9–13 healing power . . . that is *p*· to-day,
28–17 *p*· from city to city.
30– 1 Christian Scientists are *p*· even as
'02. 11–25 so *p*· they the prophets— *Matt.* 5 : 12.
My. 103–12 Science, until understood, has been *p*·
270– 2 so *p*· they the prophets— *Matt.* 5 : 12.

persecuting
  '02. 10–28 *P·* a reformer is like sentencing a
  My. 105–30 but they must refrain from *p·*

persecution
  Ret. 45–25 Christianity has withstood . . . *p·.*
          54–11 gaining the end through *p·*
          65– 8 *p·,* tobacco, and alcohol
  No.   14–25 frozen dogmas, persistent *p·,*
          34–12 baptized in the purification of *p·*
          41– 9 on account of *p·,*
          44–23 the horrors of religious *p·.*
  '00. 10– 5 Conflict and *p·* are the truest signs
  '02.   1– 2 for His people in times of *p·*
  My.   v–10 * threatens to supersede *p·,*
          127–19 should thank God for *p·*
          167–29 claims of envy, jealousy, or *p·.*
          191– 4 Be patient towards *p·.*
          191– 7 *P·* is the weakness of tyrants
          221– 2 price . . . in a material age is *p·,*
          224–32 under the present *p·*
          245–14 manifested in ignorance, *p·,*

persecutions
  Mis. 199–12 *in necessities, in* *p·,* — *II Cor.* 12 : 10.
          201–20 "reproaches" and "*p·,*" — *II Cor.* 12 : 10.

persecutors
  Un.   58– 6 His *p·* said mockingly,

perseverance
  Mis. 340–27 are miracles of patience and *p·.*

Persia
  Ret.   3– 3 position of ambassador to *P·.*

persist
  Mis. 220–28 and *p·* in this action of mind
  Man. 52–22 If a member . . . *p·* in working against
  My. 160–20 a hell for all who *p·* in

persisted
  Mis. 113–22 mental malpractice, if *p·* in,
  Ret. 14–22 he *p·* in the assertion that I

persistent
  Mis. 118–27 obedience crowns *p·* effort
          230– 2 depends upon *p·* effort,
          301–16 must not leave *p·* plagiarists
          339–11 made more industrious and *p·*
          340– 6 Only by *p·,* unremitting,
  Ret.   6–28 by his *p·* energy
  No.   14–25 frozen dogmas, *p·* persecution,
  My. 116–20 *p·* pursuit of his or her person

persistently
  Mis. 326–22 those who *p·* rejected him,
  Man. 83–18 *p·* and patiently counsel
  Ret. 75–12 those who *p·* misunderstand
  My. 148– 2 Faithfully and more than ever *p·,*
          306– 1 *p·* misrepresents my character,

persisting
  Mis. 184–18 *p·* in believing that he is sick

persists
  Mis. 184–20 yet *p·* in evil,
          220–11 He *p·* in this course until
  Man. 55– 4 if said member *p·* in this offense,

Person
  Pan.   8– 7 one the divine, infinite *P·,*
  '01.   3– 7 chapter sub-title
           4– 1 Principle or *P·* stands for God
           4–19 He is the infinite *P·,*
           4–29 Love, more frequently than *P·,*
           5– 3 defined strictly by the word *P·,*
           5– 3 for if *P·* is God,
           5– 4 does not *P·* here lose the nature of
           5– 7 Christian Scientist's sense of *P·*
           5–20 God is infinite Spirit or *P·,*
           5–28 The theological God as a *P·*
           6– 4 Who says the God of theology is a *P·,*
           6–10 a finite or an infinite *P·?*
           6–11 Is He one *P·,* or three
           6–13 except He be a *P·,*
           6–14 this *P·* contains three persons :
           6–22 God is *P·* in the . . . scientific sense
           6–27 God as the infinite *P·* ;
           6–28 idea of Him as a finite *P·*
           7– 6 individuality of the infinite *P·*
           7–19 as well as infinite *P·,*
          11–24 namely, that God is a *P·,*
  My. 109–14 operative divine Principle (or *P·,*
          109–15 This infinite *P·* we know not of by
          116–12 If God is one and God is *P·,*
          116–12 then *P·* is infinite ;
          117–29 to seek the one divine *P·,*
          192–13 the infinite *P·* whom
          225–22 Principle, Love, the infinite *P·.*

person (*see also* **person's**)
  and power
    No. 24– 2 evil loses all place, *p·,* and power.

person
  and thing
    Un. 45– 6 mind and matter, *p·* and thing?"
  another
    Mis. 180–11 another *p·,* more material,
            190–21 cast out of another *p·* ;
    No.   15–16 cast out of another *p·.*
            22–21 out of another *p·,*
    Peo.   4–12 and evil another *p·,*
    My. 123–14 by the courtesy of another *p·*
  any particular
    My. 346–24 * had in mind any particular *p·*
  assailed the
    Po.   vi–15 *and assailed the p· of*
  away from
    My. 119–30 Truth that leadeth away from *p·*
  corporeal
    Mis. 152–11 I, as a corporeal *p·,* am not in
  defining
    Rud.   2–10 right in defining *p·* as
  definitions of
    Rud.   2– 1 definitions of *p·,* as given by
  demoralizes the
    Ret. 71–28 demoralizes the *p·* who does this,
  each
    Mis. 224–13 each *p·* has a different history,
    My.   12–10 * Each *p·* interested must remember,
            72– 1 * each *p·* could hear what was said.
  event or
    Mis. 197–17 any historical event or *p·.*
  every
    My.   71–24 * every *p·* seated in the auditorium,
  evil
    Mis. 284–22 neither an evil claim nor an evil *p·*
  finite
    Mis. 217–18 and that Deity is a finite *p·*
            308–31 a finite *p·* is not the model
  God as a
    No.   20– 4 and of God as a *p·,*
    Hea.   3–12 the qualities of God as a *p·,*
  God is not a
    '01.   3– 9 their God is not a *p·.*
  healed
    Ret. 34–17 A *p·* healed by C. S. is
  her own
    My. 273– 4 * vindicate in her own *p·* the value
  His
    No.   20– 2 His *p·* and perfection are
    '01.   5–29 explain both His *p·* and nature,
  his or her
    My. 116–21 pursuit of his or her *p·* is.
  human
    Mis. 75– 4 gave us, through a human *p·,*
    Rud.   2–13 The human *p·* is finite ;
    '01.   5–30 Is the human *p·,* as defined by
  incriminating the
    Mis. 283–23 without incriminating the *p·*
  instead of
    Mis. 135– 4 Principle, instead of *p·,*
    My. 119–14 *p·,* instead of the Principle
            152– 2 *p·* instead of Principle,
  is defined
    '01.   6– 5 *P·* is defined differently
  is formed
    No.   19–26 *P·* is formed after the manner of
  is man a
    No.   25– 8 chapter sub-title
  is meant
    Rud.   2–11 if by *p·* is meant infinite Spirit.
  is not corporeal
    My. 109–15 whose *p·* is not corporeal,
  just
    Mis. 228–16 a kind, true, and just *p·,*
  loved
    Mis. 306–27 it is not . . . a loved *p·* present ;
  man is
    '01.   5–11 Man is *p·* ;
  mind of a
    Mis. 283– 5 to enter the mind of a *p·,*
  more than a
    Mis. 16–20 God is infinitely more than a *p·,*
    Peo. 13– 6 Divine Being is more than a *p·,*
  my
    My. 118–12 In a call upon my *p·,*
            138– 9 not needed to protect my *p·*
  my father's
    My. 308–18 My father's *p·* was erect
  no
    Mis. 83–12 No *p·* can accept another's belief,
            107–30 no *p·* is or can be a
    Man. 46– 1 No *p·* shall be a member . . . who
            92–16 No *p·* shall receive instructions in
    Ret. 70–14 No *p·* can take the individual place of
            70–15 No *p·* can compass or fulfil the
            70–16 No *p·* can take the place of

person

no
'02.	8–11	No p· can heal or reform mankind
	19–11	no p· can commit an offense against
My.	137–29	No p· influenced me to make this

no other
'01.	23–22	no other p· has ever

notify a
Man.	68– 1	notify a p· who has been a

not the
Hea.	3–28	the Principle is not the p·,
	9– 3	is not the p· of God,
My.	154– 3	not the p· who gives the drug

of either
No.	23–26	through the p· of either.

of God
Hea.	5–23	relying not on the p· of God
	9– 3	is not the p· of God,

of good
No.	22–16	No man hath seen the p· of good

of man
No.	29–15	a disparagement of the p· of man
Hea.	5–23	relying not on . . . the p· of man

of omnipotence
Mis.	96– 9	p· of omnipotence and omnipresence

of Spirit
Mis.	181–13	over what is the p· of Spirit,

of the infinite
No.	19–13	What the p· of the infinite is,

of Truth
Hea.	3–27	cannot tell what is the p· of Truth,

one
Mis.	148–12	such as one p· might impose on
	219–15	one p· feels sick, another feels
	219–26	while one p· feels wickedly
	273–31	The work is more than one p· can
Man.	3– 8	such as one p· might impose on
No.	7–22	between one p· and another,
	15–15	three persons in one p·,
	15–15	that one p· is cast out of
	23–11	not one p· was named among them.
	24–12	three persons in one p·.
'01.	4–20	not three persons in one p·.
	6–12	of three persons as one p·,

or a Principle
My.	117– 3	A p·, or a Principle?

or a principle
'01.	12–28	a p· or a principle,

Principle, not
No.	19–13	Love is Principle, not p·.

Principle or
My.	233–28	chapter sub-title

removal of a
Mis.	67–28	the removal of a p· to heaven,

same
Man.	25–13	same p· is eligible for election

seeing a
My.	206–12	seeing a p· in the picture of Jesus,

sick
Mis.	220– 4	suppose that there is a sick p·
My.	97– 3	* faith on the part of a sick p·,
	276– 4	watches a criminal or a sick p·,

such a
My.	319– 1	such a p· as the Galilean Prophet,

that
Mis.	145– 9	when that p· shall possess these,

the word
Rud.	1–11	The word p· affords a large margin

thinking of
My.	233–31	Thinking of p· implies that
	234– 2	signalize the thinking of p·.

third
Mis.	219–16	A third p· knows that if he would
	290– 1	A third p· is not a party to the
'01.	8– 7	as the third p· in the Godhead?
Peo.	4–14	a third p·, called material man,

this
Mis.	290–19	knew that this p· was doing well,

turned to the
My.	119–20	He turned to the p·, . . . to prove

vile
My.	33–22	vile p· is contemned ;— Psal. 15: 4.

worshippers of a
Peo.	13– 4	worshippers of a p· have a lower

Mis.	48–23	Was ever a p· made insane by
	94– 3	a p· who knowingly indulged evil,
	135– 2	p· is not in the question of C. S.
	190–20	It could not have been a p·
	226–18	was asked what a p· could gain by
	248– 9	of the p· they called slanderer,
	282–17	the p· with whom you hold communion
	285– 2	combating evil only, rather than p·.
	290–15	A p· wrote to me,
Man.	67–14	if said case relates to the p· or
	81– 5	A p· who is not accepted by

person

Rud.	1–10	*Do you mean by this that God is a p· ?*
	2– 8	we learn that God is . . . not a p·,
'00.	10–24	from a p· I never saw.
'01.	6– 5	God of C. S. is not a p·,
Hea.	4– 9	even as we ask a p·
	8– 3	not a p· to whom we should pray
Peo.	4–12	God, was named a p·,
My.	118–18	A saving faith comes not of a p·,
	120– 3	Those who look for me in p·,

persona

Rud.	1–14	In Spanish, . . . it is p·.

personal

Mis.	9–28	gratification in p· pleasure
	35–17	*under your p· instruction?*
	97–20	Is there a p· man ?
	102– 9	God is not p·.
	161–16	the p· and the impersonal Jesus.
	161–19	public benefactor, or p· Saviour,
	163–22	Only three years a p· Saviour !
	165– 1	idea that the p· Jesus demonstrated.
	166–30	minutiæ of the life of the p· Jesus.
	181– 3	Is man's spiritual sonship a p· gift
	181– 8	p· requirement of blind obedience
	181–22	it is not, then, a p· gift,
	182–23	no p· plan of a p· Jehovah,
	191–22	supposition of one p· devil.
	192– 4	we mean not that he is a p· devil,
	214–21	p· Jesus' labor in the flesh for
	232–15	p· doctrines and dogmas,
	236– 8	giving advice on p· topics.
	268– 3	Two p· queries give point to
	282–16	p· precincts of human thought,
	283–26	he needs no p· aid.
	283–32	only p· help required
	284–29	I deprecate p· animosities
	284–32	I am opposed to all p· attacks,
	285– 5	had been p· in condemnation.
	291– 4	into p· channels, affinities,
	291– 7	demonstrates above p· motives,
	305–12	* asking for her p· cooperation
	308– 9	p· revelators will take their
	322–15	p· presence, or word of mine,
	356–28	indispensable to p· growth,
Man.	40– 5	animosity nor mere p· attachment
	83–12	shall not assume p· control of,
	84–20	not by their teachers' p· views.
	86– 6	p· instruction of Mrs. Eddy,
Ret.	21–25	historic incidents and p· events
	25–21	physically p· being, like unto man ;
	73–12	p· corporeality became less to me
	73–23	or accuse people of being unduly p·,
	76–15	so far from being p· worship,
	90–11	he gave p· instruction.
Un.	5– 9	not to accept any p· opinion
Pul.	31–27	* with great claim to p· beauty.
	43–28	* that sort of p· worship which
	46– 8	* In Mrs. Eddy's p· reminiscences,
Rud.	1–16	Blackstone applies the word p· to
	2–11	God is p·, if by *person* is meant
	7–17	Jesus said of p· evil,
	7–19	sensation nor p· intelligence.
No.	7– 4	No p· considerations should
	19–10	chapter sub-title
	22–15	chapter sub-title
	37–14	as a p· and material
'00.	12–28	symbolic, rather than p·
'01.	4–17	God is p· in a scientific sense,
	7–22	tangible to the p· material senses
	11–22	no sermon without p· preaching,
	11–25	his personal God !
	31– 6	neither p· nor human, but divine.
'02.	9–28	Is it cause for . . . p· abuse
	13– 6	of my p· property and funds,
	13–10	I receive no p· benefit
Hea.	3–10	proportion as the p· and material
Peo.	2–22	no longer a p· tyrant
	3–26	such as dependence on p· pardon
	4–13	error that . . . a p· devil entered
	13– 3	who believe that God is a p· Spirit.
My.	v–12	* mesmerism of p· pride
	30–13	* p· sacrifices of no mean order ;
	105–32	from p· experience I have proved
	113–17	not a disciple of the p· Jesus?
	116– 1	chapter sub-title
	116–13	there is no p· worship,
	116–15	darkness of p· contagion.
	116–17	based upon p· sight or sense.
	116–23	from injustice and p· contagion.
	117– 5	A p· motive gratified by sense
	117–22	individual, but not p·,
	118– 4	the disobedient spread p· contagion,
	119–27	of seeing your p· self,
	138–11	My p· reputation is assailed
	138–12	my students and trusted p· friends
	139–20	the p· to the impersonal,

personal

My	177– 8	no special need of my *p·* presence
	234– 6	*p·* worship which C. S. annuls.
	238– 7	be determined by *p·* proof.
	290– 6	her *p·* virtues can never be lost.
	321–24	* my *p·* knowledge of the authorship
	321–28	* know of my own *p·* knowledge
	361– 4	to give you *p·* instruction as to your
	361– 7	do not bring . . . into a *p·* conflict.

(see also **God, sense, senses**)

personalities

Mis.	337–23	belittled and belied by *p·*
Un.	21– 6	is not two *p·*, but one.

personality

absolute

No.	27–23	the absolute *p·* of God

all

'00.	4–29	all *p·* and individuality.
My.	205–23	C. S., shorn of all *p·*,

and presence

My.	143–15	*p·* and presence of Mary Baker Eddy,

belief in the

Pan.	3–18	Theism is the belief in the *p·* and

believe in

'01.	5–14	Do Christian Scientists believe in *p·*?

blind

Mis.	375– 2	*p·* blind with animality,

centres in the

My.	341–21	* public interest centres in the *p·* of

claim to

Un.	32–26	the false claim to *p·*,

clings to

Ret.	73–19	He who clings to *p·*, or

cling to

Mis.	310– 8	rather than cling to *p·*

cling to the

My.	116– 7	inclined to cling to the *p·* of

conceive of

No.	20– 1	so far as he can conceive of *p·*.

contemplating

Mis.	308–25	contemplating *p·* impedes spiritual

corporeal

Mis.	102–10	precludes . . . corporeal *p·*.
Ret.	32– 6	as mere corporeal *p·*,
	57–26	Mistaking . . . for corporeal *p·*,
	67–13	rising above corporeal *p·*,
	74– 8	My own corporeal *p·* afflicteth me not
	76–24	never abuses the corporeal *p·*,

dual

'01.	8–28	his dual *p·*, or the spiritual

egotistical

Ret.	73–24	violent and egotistical *p·*,

element of

Pul.	37–15	* to eliminate the element of *p·*

evil-doer or

Mis.	284–20	not as an evil-doer or *p·*.

false

Ret.	73–18	whereby the false *p·* is laid off.
Un.	44–11	humanity was misled by a false *p·*,

finite

Mis.	307–29	against the deification of finite *p·*.
	309–14	finite *p·* of Jesus,
Pan.	8– 8	a human finite *p·*?

gifted

Pul.	37–24	* a highly gifted *p·*."

God's

'01.	4–23	should be able to explain God's *p·*
	6–26	God's *p·* must be as infinite as

his

Mis.	104– 1	Even while his *p·* was on earth

infinite

Mis.	102–16	Infinite *p·* must be incorporeal.

interesting

Pul.	31– 6	* is a most interesting *p·*.

Jesus'

Mis.	103–24	Jesus' *p·* in the flesh,

limitless

No.	20– 1	Limitless *p·* is inconceivable.

man's

Pan.	10– 1	takes away man's *p·*
	10–29	does not degrade man's *p·*.
	11–23	belittles man's *p·*.

material

Mis.	105– 4	discords of this material *p·*,
	308– 6	clings to my material *p·*,
	309– 4	material *p·* is an error in premise,

model

'01.	6–17	not after this model of *p·*

Mrs. Eddy's

Pul.	36–13	* heading

my

Mis.	276– 7	my *p·* was not big enough to
My.	307–23	Had his remark related to my *p·*,

my own

'01.	27–22	I have put less of my own *p·* into

personality

no

Mis.	258–22	indicated no *p·* that could

notions of

No.	15–12	notions of *p·* to be found in creeds

of infinite Love

'01.	7– 1	as the *p·* of infinite Love,

of infinite Spirit

Mis.	219– 5	the *p·* of infinite Spirit

one

Pul.	37–23	* depending on any one *p·*.

one's

Mis.	374–28	this ideal is not one's *p·*.

or form

No.	23– 2	in *p·*, or form

physical

(see **physical**)

poor

My.	153–15	from my poor *p·*.

question of

Mis.	98– 1	making this question of *p·* a point,

real

Mis.	97–32	the real *p·* of man.

seeks

My.	153–23	seeks *p·* for support,

sense of

Mis.	282– 4	sense of *p·* in God or in man,

sinful

No.	27–20	sinful *p·*, which we misname man,

spiritual

Mis.	218–31	* recognition of purely spiritual *p·*

subdivide

Un.	44–16	would multiply and subdivide *p·*

substituting

Mis.	310– 5	misused by substituting *p·*

such a

Pul.	32– 9	* such a *p·*, . . . fascinated the

their

Un.	46–18	an indignity to their *p·*;
'01.	5–15	their *p·* is defined spiritually,

theological

'01.	6–25	departure from theological *p·*

the word

Ret.	74– 4	meaning of the word *p·*,

this

Mis.	97–30	lost image is not this *p·*,
	190–30	Paul refers to this *p·* of evil
Un.	46–18	this *p·* they regarded as

turn away from

Man.	48–20	they shall turn away from *p·*

unity and

Mis.	217–20	suppositional unity and *p·*,

warns you of

Ret.	73–20	perpetually warns you of "*p·*,"

wrong

No.	7–24	reference to right or wrong *p·*

your

My.	117–17	to get some good out of your *p·*?

Mis.	33– 9	or that these refer not to *p·*,
	97–29	such must be the *p·* of him who
	181–14	if we recognize infinitude as *p·*,
	282– 4	it is *p·*, . . . that limits man.
	307–11	chapter sub-title
Ret.	73–	chapter sub-title
Man.	67–19	from the divine Principle . . . to *p·*,
No.	23– 3	*p·* that Jesus condemned as devilish,
	24–14	since evil subordinates good in *p·*.
'01.	24–14	Bishop Berkeley's metaphysics and *p·*
Hea.	4– 7	Clothing Deity with *p·*, we limit
My.	117–24	except by sinking . . . in *p·*.
	118–30	would dwarf individuality in *p·*
	191–12	Keep *p·* out of sight,
	271–25	* *p·* of this remarkable woman.
	344–12	preserving individuality and *p·*

personally

Mis.	132–18	answering *p·* manifold letters
	284–15	for this evil to be treated *p·*,
	284–17	gone *p·* to the malpractitioner
	308– 4	Whosoever looks to me *p·* for
	336–10	if you saw him *p·*,
	359–21	period in which he *p·* appeared;
	381– 6	defendant being present *p·*
Man.	67–15	*p·* conferred with her
	78–16	*p·*, or through the Clerk of
	87–18	"The less the teacher *p·* controls
Ret.	84–24	The less the teacher *p·* controls
Pul.	37–10	* She *p·* attends to a vast
My.	135– 8	*p·* attended to my secular affairs,
	137–12	attended *p·* to my secular affairs,
	137–14	*p·* selected all my investments,
	138–26	* *p·* appeared Mary Baker Eddy
	147–26	I shall be with you *p·* very seldom.
	219– 1	unless I am *p·* present.
	294–11	if he were *p·* with us to-day,
	315–16	* *p·* appeared R. D. Rounsevel

personally
My. 325– 2   * you *p·* called to inquire of
    359– 9   not *p·* involved in the affairs of the

personare
Rud. 1–14   Latin verb *p·* is compounded of

personified
Pan. 2–21   conceived as one *p·* nature,
    6–10   chapter sub-title

personne
Rud. 1–13   In French the equivalent word is *p·*.

person's
My. 91–10   * no *p·* spiritual aspirations were
    104–20   A *p·* ignorance of C. S.

persons
actual
No. 31– 9   never actual *p·* or real facts.
all
Mis. 310–27   would cordially invite all *p·*
all grades of
Mis. 371–16   mixing all grades of *p·* is not
and purposes
My. 137–20   *p·* and purposes I have designated
applications from
Ret. 47– 7   applications from *p·* desiring to
composed of
Pul. 29–28   * composed of *p·* who had either been
divine
'01. 6– 2   theology's three divine *p·*,
few
Mis. 139–24   wisdom whereof a few *p·* have since
few thousand
My. 91–21   * The few thousand *p·* who followed
fifteen hundred
Pul. 41–17   * to fifteen hundred *p·*,
five thousand
My. 7–18   * will seat four or five thousand *p* ,
    9– 4   * will seat four or five thousand *p·*,
    65–10   * between four and five thousand *p·*.
instructing
My. 223–16   capable of instructing *p·*
many
Mis. 305–16   * contributions from many *p·*
Pul. 33–25   * true that many and many *p·*,
nominated
Man. 79–13   *p·* nominated for said office
no respecter of
'01. 27–21   God is no respecter of *p·*.
My. 128– 9   "no respecter of *p·*." — *Acts* 10 : 34.
number of
Mis. 305–15   * largest number of *p·* possible
of all sects
Man. 59–17   *p·* of all sects and denominations
representative
My. 281–21   views by representative *p·*.
seven
Pul. 37–27   * seven *p·*, including Mrs. Eddy.
    67–26   * was organized by seven *p·*,
several
No. 22–21   That Jesus cast several *p·* out of
six thousand
Pul. 40–18   * aggregating nearly six thousand *p·*,
such
Man. 49–14   The cards of such *p·* may be
ten thousand
My. 141– 7   * attended . . . by ten thousand *p·*
these
My. 91– 2   * that it supplies these *p·*,
three
No. 15–15   believe there are three *p·* in one
    24–12   three *p·* in one person.
'01. 4–20   not three *p·* in one person.
    5– 2   who believes that three *p·* are
    5– 4   he believes three *p·* constitute the
    6–11   Is He one Person, or three *p·*?
    6–12   of three *p·* as one person,
    6–14   and this Person contains three *p·* :
Hea. 3–25   not three *p·* in one,
to receive
My. 138–15   ask me to receive *p·* whom I
twenty-six
My. 76–30   * a membership of twenty-six *p·*.
two
Mis. 290– 3   two *p·* only, should be found within
who are members
Man. 92–22   Only those *p·* who are members

Mis. 48–27   That *p·* have gone away from
    64–12   *P·* contemplating a course at
    79–27   *p· brought before the courts*
    256– 1   *P·* who have been healed by C. S.
Man. 109– 6   No *p·* are eligible to countersign
Ret. 15–22   from *p·* who feelingly testified
    15–27   *p·* who divulged their secret joy
Rud. 15–23   or to *p·* who cannot be addressed

persons
My. 249– 2   but condemn *p·* seldom, if ever.
    313–10   and about *p·* being hired to
    354– 3   alleged misrepresentations by *p·*

perspective
Mis. 373–12   Neither . . . standpoint, nor *p·*
My. 22–26   * appear in their proper *p·*.
    22–29   * proper *p·* of the meaning

perspiration
Mis. 225–26   a cool *p·* spread over it,

perspire
Mis. 7– 3   when they *p·*, they must be

persuade
Ret. 38– 5   All efforts to *p·* him to finish

persuaded
Ret. 94–25   *p·* that only by the modesty
My. 156– 4   *p·* that He is able" — *II Tim.* 1 : 12.
    228–28   *p·* that he is able — *II Tim.* 1 : 12.

persuasion
My. 247–22   not so much eloquence as *tender p·*

persuasive
My. 3–16   *p·* animus, an unerring impetus,

pertain
Mis. 167– 3   *p·* to the spiritual idea,
My. 223– 5   which *p·* to church difficulties

pertaining
Mis. 272– 2   * privileges *p·* thereunto
Man. 18–26   *p·* to "Executive Members"
    93–14   the facts *p·* to the life of
Pan. 9– 9   four first rules *p·* thereto,
My. 199–13   Christian canon *p·* to the hour.

pertinent
My. 107– 6   As a *p·* illustration of the

perturbed
Ret. 13– 9   So *p·* was I by the thoughts

perusal
Mis. 29–21   a *p·* of my volume is healing
Pul. 73–28   * than by a *p·* of it.

pervade
My. 165– 1   promote and *p·* all his success.

pervaded
Pul. 31–17   * was largely thrilled and *p·* by

pervading
Ret. 33–11   I found, in . . . one *p·* secret ;

perverse
My. 222– 5   "O faithless and *p·* — *Matt.* 17 : 17.

perversion
Mis. 291–17   the possible *p·* of C. S.

perversity
Mis. 250– 3   By what strange *p·* is the

pervert
Mis. 66– 9   no human misjudgment can *p·* it ;
    293–16   he will *p·* the rules of C. S.,

perverted
Mis. 3–30   but this method *p·*, is
    293–22   Truth *p·*, in belief, becomes the
    351– 6   arguments which, *p·*, are the
    368–26   *p·*, . . . may become the worst,
Rud. 7–11   would be lost if inverted or *p·*.
My. 213– 3   malicious aim of *p·* mind-power,

perverter
Mis. 302– 6   *p·* preserves in his own consciousness

perverts
Mis. 41– 3   *p·* it, and uses it to accomplish an

pessimism
Mis. 119–18   not an argument either for *p·* or

pessimistic
My. 81– 4   * No *p·* faces there !

pest
My. 104–12   call St. Paul a "*p·*," — *see Acts* 24 : 5.
    104–13   Scientist a "*p·*"? — *see Acts* 24 : 5.
    106–22   Scientist a "*p·*"? — *see Acts* 24 : 5.

pestilence
Mis. 389–22   no fowler, *p·* or pain ;
Po. 5– 1   no fowler, *p·* or pain ;

pestilent
My. 104– 4   a "*p·* fellow," — *Acts* 24 : 5.
    104– 6   this "*p·* fellow." — *Acts* 24 : 5.

pests
Mis. 227–7   slanderers — those *p·* of society

petals
Mis. 329–23   paint in pink the *p·* of arbutus,

Peter (*see also* Peter's)
Mis. 111–11   like *P·*, they launch into the depths,
    335–22   zealots, who, like *P·*, sleep when the
Un. 1– 5   such as the apostle *P·* declared

Peter
 Un. 57–23 P· rejoiced that he was found worthy
 Pul. 54–25 * followers, P·, James, and John,
 No. 23– 7 Jesus said to P·,
 '00. 7–22 like P· we believe in the

I Peter 2 : 1–6
 My. 17– 3 * Also, 1 P· 2 : 1–6,

Peter's
 Mis. 359–19 P· impetuosity was rebuked.

petition
 Mis. 212– 1 fulfil the conditions of our p·?
 Pul. 22– 6 and in this sacred p· with every
 No. 39– 9 vanity influences the p·.
 '02. 6–21 all devout desire, virtually p·,

petitions
 Mis 127–11 When a hungry heart p· the divine
 263–18 constant p· for the same,
 310–21 send in their p· to this effect
 '01. 7–23 attend their p· to divine Love.
 My. 18– 8 When a hungry heart p· the divine
 89–19 * where p· for money are
 89–20 * p· for divine mercy.
 231– 4 solicitations or p· from strangers,

petty
 Mis. 255– 3 on pedestals, as so many p· deities ;
 Man. 78–21 p· cash fund, to be used by him for
 My. 99– 4 * above the suffering of p· ills ;
 107–21 O p· scorner of the infinite,

pews
 Ret. 15–17 p· were not sufficient to seat the
 16– 2 floating up from the p·,
 Pul. 25–21 * with p· of curly birch,
 42–11 * children in the central p·.
 58–17 * its exceedingly comfortable p·.
 76– 2 * used in the doors and p·.
 My. 59–19 * that would scarce fill a couple of p·
 68– 6 * about one mile and a half of p·.
 68–31 * p· and principal woodwork are of
 78–13 * semi-circular sweep of mahogany p·
 79– 2 * before the p·, in absolute stillness,

phantasm
 My. 148–26 a philosophical p·,

phantasma
 Un. 26–11 p·, a belief in which leads to

phantasmagoria
 Un. 26–24 p· is a product of human dreams.

phantom
 Po. 26–13 thy p· finger, grim and cold,
 65– 7 A p· of joy,

Pharaohs
 Peo. 11–16 are the modern P·

Phare Pleigh
 Mis. 216–10 "Scientific Theism," by P· P·.
 216–11 P· P· evidently means more than
 My. 52–29 * "P· P·" [the *nom de plume* of
 319– 7 little pamphlet, signed "P· P·,"
 323– 4 * "C. S. and the Bible," by "P· P·,"

Pharisaism
 Ret. 65– 7 P· killeth ; Spirit giveth Life.

Phariseeism
 Mis. 234–13 the P· of the times,

Pharisee's
 '01. 14– 4 P· self-righteousness crucified Jesus.
 My. 334–22 P· self-righteousness crucified Jesus."

Pharisees
 Mis. 175–15 old leaven of the scribes and P·,
 366–19 scribes and P·," — see Matt. 16 : 6.
 370– 4 P· saw Jesus do such deeds of mercy,
 374– 4 P· scorned the spirit of Christ
 Un. 17–13 distinctly taught the arrogant P·
 46–26 P· fought Jesus on this issue.
 No. 41– 3 P· of old warned the people to
 My. 104– 7 P· said of the great master
 339–19 we and the P· fast oft, — Matt. 9 : 14.

pharmacist
 Mis. 242–27 partner of George T. Brown, p·,

pharmacy
 Mis. 271– 2 exclusion of compounds from its p·,
 Hea. 12–18 on the p· of homœopathy,
 13– 4 p· of homœopathy is reducing the
 My. 108–12 faith in the p· of the human mind,

phase
 Mis. 25– 7 matter is a p· of error,
 Un. 4– 7 Truth destroys every p· of error.
 Pul. 50–15 * particular p· of religious belief
 63–16 * a new p· of religious belief,
 Pan. 3– 5 poetical p· of the genii of forests.
 '00. 12–30 the p· of a great controversy,
 '01. 15– 5 condemn the claim of error in every p·

phase
 My. 107– 7 a modern p· of medical practice,
 281–22 * on some p· of the subject,

phases
 Mis. 60–18 in different p· of thought,
 127–30 Mortal mind presents p· of character
 191–30 p· of sin or disease made manifest.
 237–13 p· of error in human nature
 375– 1 p· of material conceptions
 Pul. 38–27 * p· of idealism and manifestations of
 My. 93–21 * we see only its ridiculous p·,

phenomena
 Mis. 23–19 God is both noumenon and p·,
 28– 9 the p· of mortal life are as
 73–31 The p· of Spirit in C. S.,
 95–17 p· of an uncommon order,
 105–15 Life and its glorious p·.
 218–14 cognizance of Spirit or of its p·.
 277–31 the p· of drunkenness produced by
 286–23 p· of mortality, nothingness,
 Un. 7–25 bringing out the highest p·
 9–15 combinations, p·, and outcome,
 10–12 p· of this one infinite Mind.
 10–13 Spiritual p· never converge toward
 35–20 They are the p· of mortal mind,
 36– 9 from opposite facts, or p·.
 41–27 p· appear to go on *ad infinitum* ;
 No. 4–20 not the p· of the immutable laws
 6– 8 take cognizance of their own p·,
 10–28 constitute the p· of being,
 14– 6 all sensible p· are merely
 19–23 noumenon or the p· of Spirit ;
 21–10 the Principle of all p·, identity,
 Pan. 12–23 noumenon and p·, is demonstrably
 '01. 23–28 * constant relation between p·
 My. 180–32 defines noumenon and p·
 249– 6 let the . . . produce God's p·.
 349–24 obtain not in material p·,
 350– 2 at the beck of material p·,

phenomenal
 Mis. 68–29 * from its p· modifications."
 My. 349–24 p· evil, which is lawless

phenomenally
 Mis. 379–23 with p· good results ;

phenomenism
 Mis. 216–27 * attempt of p· to conceive the

phenomenon
 Mis. 74– 2 noumenon and p· understood,
 216–28 * a p· *without a noumenon*
 217– 8 p· must correspond in quality
 217–11 p· of Spirit is the antipode of
 362–18 mortal mind, with its p·
 Ret. 22– 5 His spiritual noumenon and p·
 24–11 every effect a mental p·.
 Un. 50–11 only a p· of mortal mind,
 Pul. 70–18 every effect a mental p·."
 Hea. 6– 8 p· named mediumship,
 My. 89–29 * greatest religious p· of all
 98–12 * if they would deal with the p·
 260– 4 matter an alien save as p·,
 287–10 Love is the noumenon and p·,
 347–26 and that a p· is chimerical,
 347–28 and whose p· is Science.
 350– 4 to end with the p·, matter,

Philadelphia
 Pa.
 Pul. 88–32 * *Inquirer*, P·, Pa.
 89–10 * *Press*, P·, Pa.
 89–13 * *Telegram*, P·, Pa.
 My. 199– 2 chapter sub-title

 Ret. 43–12 Hahnemann Medical College of P·,
 Pul. 56– 3 * P·, Detroit, Toledo, Milwaukee,
 '00. 1–19 Boston, New York, P·,
 13–30 angel of the church in P·
 14–13 except the church in P·
 My. 153– 8 angel of the church in P·," — Rev. 3 : 7.
 199– 7 May God say this of the church in P· :

Philadelphia School of Anatomy and Surgery
 Ret. 43–13 P· S· of A· and S·,

philanthropist
 Mis. 166– 5 p·, hero, and Christian.
 My. 288– 4 p· . . . gives little thought to
 297– 2 soldier, patriot, p·, moralist,

philanthropists
 Mis. 38– 9 instructors and p· in our land
 '01. 30–17 P·, and the higher class of critics

philanthropy
 Mis. 238–19 stimulate p· and are an ever-present
 '00. 14–24 p· of the better class of M.D.'s

philanthropy
  My. 203– 9 Goodness and *p·* begin with work
       287–19 *P·* is loving, ameliorative,

Philip (*see also* **Philip's**)
  Pul. 83– 5 * appeals from *P·* drunk to *P·* sober,

Philippians
  Un. 43–25 in the third chapter of *P·*,

Philippine Islands
  '00. 1–18 *P· I·*, Hawaiian Islands ;
      10–27 in the *P· I·*,

Philip's
  Mis. 77– 9 *P·* requirement was, that he should

Phillips, Wendell
  Mis. 245–29 in the words of Wendell *P·*,
  Pul. 6–30 apostle of anti-slavery, Wendell *P·*,

philosopher
  Mis. ix– 1 apothegm of a Talmudical *p·*
      363–26 This Word corrects the *p·*,
  Ret. 57–12 If that pagan *p·* had known
  '02. 1–21 engaging the attention of *p·* and
  My. 159–25 Even Epictetus, a heathen *p·*

philosophers
  Mis. 296– 5 profound *p·*, brilliant scholars.
  Ret. 37–13 Emerson, or certain German *p·*,

philosophical
  Un. 27– 8 *Egoism* is a more *p·* word,
      53–17 no more logical, *p·*, or
  My. 148–26 it is not . . . a *p·* phantasm,
      205–16 and their *p·* impetus,
      206– 1 *P·* links, which would unite

Philosophical Society of Great Britain
  Mis. 295–26 *P· S· of G· B·*, an institution which

philosophies
  Mis. 169– 4 the bypaths of ancient *p·*
      344–16 Ancient and modern *p·* are
  No. 24–16 than in human *p·* or creeds :
  '02. 5– 3 pagan *p·* and tribal religions
      14–22 popular *p·* and religions

philosophy
  and logic
    Mis. 360–26 regenerates *p·* and logic ;
  and religion
    Mis. 64–18 the only *p·* and religion that
    Ret. 31–29 systems of *p·* and religion
      57–24 Human systems of *p·* and religion
  and schools
    Pul. 70–21 * *p·* and schools of medicine,
  bald
    Pan. 12–27 by bald *p·*, or by man's inventions.
  broader
    Mis. 2–16 embraces a deeper and broader *p·*
  concerned with
    My. 351–26 are not concerned with *p·* ;
  delighting in
    Pul. 46–24 * delighting in *p·*, logic, and
  divine
    Mis. 364–12 It is the soul of divine *p·*,
      364–32 reproduces the divine *p·* of Jesus
    No. 21–25 Divine *p·* is demonstrably the
  dogma and
    No. 42–12 vain power of dogma and *p·*
  Emerson's
    My. 305– 4 resorted to Ralph Waldo Emerson's *p·*
  false
    No. 24–11 false *p·* and scholastic theology,
    '01. 26– 2 my tired sense of false *p·*
    My. 112– 3 false *p·* flourishes for a time
  Grecian
    Mis. 260– 6 Pagan mysticism, Grecian *p·*,
  Greek
    My. 288–14 tribal religion, Greek *p·*,
  his
    Ret. 57–13 his *p·* would have yielded to Science.
  human
      (*see* **human**)
  hypotheses or
    '02. 5–16 human hypotheses or *p·*.
  insignia of
    No. 9–23 cabalistic insignia of *p·* ;
  knowledge of
    '01. 25– 8 A knowledge of *p·* and of medicine,
  material
    Mis. 340–30 Material *p·*, human ethics,
  modern
    Mis. 173– 1 Ancient and modern *p·*,
    Ret. 34– 7 Neither ancient nor modern *p·* could
      57– 4 Neither ancient nor modern *p·*
    Pul. 47–14 * No ancient or modern *p·* gave her any
      64–18 * and modern *p·* gave her no
  moral
    My. 221–13 can we find a better moral *p·*,

philosophy
  natural
    Ret. 10– 7 natural *p·*, logic, and moral science.
    Un. 11–20 or a professor of natural *p·*,
  Neoplatonic
    No. 14– 9 a renewal in the Neoplatonic *p·* ;
  no other
    Mis. 364–12 and there is no other *p·*.
  nor reason
    Mis. 217– 3 neither *p·* nor reason attempts
  of Christian Science
    Pan. 9–28 sometimes object to the *p·* of C. S..
  of Karma
    Pul. 38–22 * opposed to the *p·* of Karma
  of mind
    Mis. 68–24 * defines it as "the *p·* of mind,
  of the ages
    My. 37–18 * *p·* of the ages transformed.
  Oriental
    Pul. 23–16 * inquiry into Oriental *p·*,
    No. 14–10 Oriental *p·* of Brahmanism,
  or physics
    Mis. 366– 6 theology, *p·*, or physics,
  or religion
    My. 4–32 in ethics, *p·*, or religion,
      220–24 present, or future *p·* or religion,
  pagan
    Mis. 173– 8 pagan *p·*, or scholastic theology,
  principles of
    '01. 23–26 on received principles of *p·*,
  reason and
    My. 260–13 Human reason and *p·* may
  religion and
    My. 248–27 religion and *p·* of labor, duty,
  religion or
    Mis. 363–23 shoals of a sensual religion or *p·*
    My. 117–23 never a religion or *p·* lost
  schools of
    Mis. 162– 8 people and their schools of *p·* ;
  Science and
    Mis. 359–27 chapter sub-title
  Spinoza's
    No. 24– 3 According to Spinoza's *p·*
  sport of
    My. 303–23 metaphysics is not the sport of *p·*,
  such
    Mis. 344–19 Such *p·* can never demonstrate
      344–23 Such *p·* is far from the rules of
    No. 22– 1 Such *p·* has certainly not
  theology and
    Un. 45–16 forms of theology and *p·*,
  this
    Mis. 365– 1 This *p·* alone will bear the strain
  true
    Mis. 344– 1 chapter sub-title
    No. 38– 9 true *p·* and realism.
  which cannot heal
    No. 21–26 A *p·* which cannot heal the sick
  your
    Pul. 6–28 * more than is dreamt of in your *p·*."

  Mis. 25–32 in *p·*, medicine, or religion,
      216–25 * "When *p·* becomes fairy-land,
      360–11 *P·* never has produced,
      362–15 *P·* hypothetically regards creation
  Un. 44–16 *P·* would multiply and subdivide
  No. 21–22 whose *p·* is incontestable,
  '01. 24–27 *P·*, *materia medica*, and
  '02. 3– 6 more as a *p·* than as a religion.
      7– 8 neither *p·*, nature, nor grace
  My. 181– 3 *p·* and so-called natural science,
     306– 6 *p·* of a great and good man,

phœnix
  Mis. 285–26 nondescript *p·*, . . . may appear
  My. 164–21 this *p·* fire, this pillar by day,

photograph
  Pul. 48–19 * *p·* of Hon. Hoke Smith,

photographed
  My. 329–13 * has in her possession *p·* copies

photographs
  Pul. 32– 4 * No *p·* can do the least justice
  My. 329–17 * The *p·* are verified by the

photography
  No. 39–26 as *p·* grasps the solar light

phrase
  Mis. 26–25 The *p·*, "express image," — *Heb.* 1 : 3.
  Man. 102–19 *p·*, "Mary Baker Eddy's Church,
  Un. 50–14 we are compelled to use the *p·*
  Pul. 53–12 * to give thanks in Oriental *p·*,
  Rud. 2–15 the *p· an individual* God,
  '01. 3–17 we use this *p·* for God
  '02. 16– 4 that identical *p·*, "S. and H.,"

phraseology
  Ret.   2–19   replete with the *p·* current in the
  Un.   59– 8   hence the *p·* of Jesus,
  No.   31–11   Our *p·* varies.

phrases
  My.   308–28   no profanity and no slang *p·*.

phrasing
  My.   256– 5   emphatically *p·* strict observance

phrenology
  Hea.   5– 6   *P·* will be saying the developments of

phylacteries
  My.   357–14   to enlarge their *p·* and

physic
  Ret.   48–24   higher than *p·* or drugging ;

physical
  agony
    Mis.   70–12   Paradisaical rest from *p·* agony
  ailment
    Mis.   66–24   like the more *p·* ailment.
      241– 8   the other having a *p·* ailment.
    Pul.   69– 7   * cured by Mrs. Eddy of a *p·* ailment
  ailments
    Mis.   168–10   buried in dogmas and *p·* ailments,
  causes
    Un.   8–21   heredity and other *p·* causes.
  cleanliness
    Mis.   184–30   a type of *p·* cleanliness
  concept
    Ret.   67– 5   the human or *p·* concept.
  death
    Mis.   37–21   leads to moral or *p·* death.
  effects
    Mis.   365–20   spiritual, as well as *p·*, effects of
    Ret.   24– 8   all *p·* effects to a mental cause ;
    No.   19– 2   spiritual, as well as *p·*, effects of
    Hea.   12–10   all *p·* effects originate in mind
    My.   22–23   * *p·* effects produced by The
  growth
    No.   13– 4   demonstration of moral and *p·* growth,
  harmony
    Un.   6–10   The Science of *p·* harmony,
  healing
    Rud.   3–11   more . . . than his *p·* healing.
  health
    My.   93–14   * *p·* health and spiritual peace.
  help
    Mis.   88– 3   feel the need of *p·* help,
  law
    Mis.   28–29   claims of physique and of *p·* law,
      101–17   It undermines . . . *p·* law,
    Un.   11–14   boastful sense of *p·* law
  laws
    Po.   32–15   Such *p·* laws to obey,
  life
    Un.   39– 5   pride of *p·* life must be quenched
  man
    Ret.   88– 7   called the *p·* man from the tomb
  moral or
    My.   364–17   sickness and disease, moral or *p·*.
  ones
    Hea.   17–22   are supposed *p·* ones,
  perfection
    '01.   1–14   constitute mental and *p·* perfection.
  personality
    Ret.   25–22   the *p·* personality of mind
      73– 3   *P·* personality is finite ;
      73–14   lift thought above *p·* personality,
      73–22   to scrutinize *p·* personality,
    Un.   37–18   evil accompanying *p·* personality
    No.   23–23   Knowledge of a man's *p·* personality
      25– 9   Man is more than *p·* personality,
  rejuvenation
    Mis.   169–11   With . . . had come *p·* rejuvenation.
  results
    My.   220– 1   save him from bad *p·* results.
  science
    Un.   9–10   is not the path of *p·* science,
    My.   160–21   *P·* science has sometimes argued
  sensation
    Mis.   123–31   far apart from *p·* sensation
      205–26   material life or *p·* sensation,
  sense
    Ret.   57–12   *p·* sense, not Soul, causes
  senses
    Mis.   104–17   his *p·* senses with his spiritual
      105–24   Nothing appears to the *p·* senses but
      205–18   invisible to the *p·* senses :
    Ret.   25–13   *p·* senses, or sensuous nature,
      25–22   *p·* senses are so many witnesses to
      30–12   false testimony of the *p·* senses.
      56–13   evidences of the five *p·* senses ;
      65– 3   evidences of the *p·* senses,
    Un.   8– 4   *of which the p· senses are cognizant*
      22–20   has its origin in the *p·* senses

physical
  senses
    Un.   28– 6   five *p·* senses do not cognize it.
      29–16   What the *p·* senses miscall soul,
      33– 3   The *p·* senses . . . give the only
      33–19   self-testimony of the *p·* senses
    Rud.   5–22   with each of the *p·* senses.
      7–12   evidence of the so-called *p·* senses,
      11–12   illusions of the *p·* senses.
    No.   6–26   testimony of the *p·* senses.
      19–17   *p·* senses receive no spiritual idea,
  sickness
    Rud.   2–23   Healing *p·* sickness is the smallest
  side
    Ret.   33– 1   *p·* side of this research was aided by
    Pul.   47–11   * knowledge concerning the *p·* side
  strength
    Mis.   240–12   contribute to moral and *p·* strength
  substance
    '01.   23–27   declared *p·* substance to be "only
  suffering
    Mis.   222– 7   causes the victim great *p·* suffering ;
    No.   33–23   amidst *p·* suffering and human woe.
  sufferings
    Mis.   105– 8   His *p·* sufferings, which came from
      221– 7   Error produces *p·* sufferings,
  terms
    Mis.   50–13   the metaphysical in *p·* terms.
      171–12   expressed in literal or *p·* terms,
  torture
    No.   34–14   *P·* torture affords but a slight
  vigor
    My.   134–30   * her usual mental and *p·* vigor."
  wants
    Mis.   67– 2   Above *p·* wants, lie the higher claims
  world
    Pul.   53–20   * dominion over the *p·* world.

    Mis.   86– 1   The material and *p·* are imperfect.
      102–11   His being is individual, but not *p·*.
      168– 6   *p·* and moral lepers are cleansed ;
      198–24   bad deed, based on *p·* material law,
      234–25   *p·* and mental perfection,
      241–27   easier to heal the *p·* than the
      244–12   are the conditions . . . mental, or *p·*;
      245–15   a *p·* and spiritual need
      251–26   all error, *p·*, moral, or religious,
      261–31   must produce *p·* and moral harmony.
      297– 4   for *p·* and moral reformation.
      303– 3   as healers *p·* and moral.
      365–13   *p·* and moral harmony ;
    Ret.   35– 5   for *p·* and moral health
      58– 5   *p·*, false, and finite substitute.
    Un.   8–15   deleterious effects, *p·*, moral, and
      35–17   moral and spiritual, not *p·*.
    Pul.   20–17   *p·*, civil, and religious reform
    Rud.   10–23   erroneous *p·* and mental state.
    No.   18– 9   *p·* and moral harmony,
      31–21   *P·* and mental healing were one
    My.   79–28   * from diseases, *p·* and mental,
      111–13   *p·* and spiritual status of a perfect
      147–18   *p·*, moral, and spiritual needs

physicality
  Un.   29–21   can never be . . . touched by *p·*.
    56–20   *p·* and the sense of sin.

physically
  Mis.   ix– 9   healing mankind morally, *p·*,
    3– 1   elevating the race *p·*, morally,
    20– 3   heals man . . . morally and *p·*,
    31– 6   morally, *p·*, or spiritually
    45–20   is better both morally and *p·*.
    51– 2   *p·* as well as spiritually,
    67– 7   mentally, morally, or *p·*.
    138–14   ethically, *p·*, and spiritually.
    168– 4   the blind, spiritually and *p·*,
    203–14   medicine applies it *p·*,
    214–25   is the same as its attitude *p·*.
    220–20   he is improved morally and *p·*.
    222–17   is fatal, morally and *p·*.
    252–20   to man *p·*, as well as spiritually,
    259–23   *p·*, morally, and Christianly,
    289– 1   degenerate *p·* and morally.
    300–32   Healing morally and *p·* are one.
    362–10   *p·*, morally, spiritually.
  Ret.   25–21   a *p·* personal being, like unto
  Un.   36–19   man is improved *p·*, mentally,
    37–17   Human beings are *p·* mortal,
  Rud.   3–21   mental error made manifest *p·*,
  No.   13–20   *p·*, morally, and spiritually,
    22–10   morally, spiritually, or *p·*.
  Pan.   11–19   man who falls *p·* needs to rise again.
  '00.   6–27   better *p·*, morally, and spiritually.
  '01.   20–16   *p·*, morally, or spiritually,
  Hea.   9– 8   better for mankind, morally and *p·*.
    14– 5   man is healed morally and *p·*.

physically
Peo. 6–19 improves the race p· and spiritually.
My. 45–10 * p· present at the dedication
105–16 p· restored sight to the blind,
130– 6 socially, p·, and morally
146–24 scale of being, morally and p·,

Physician
Mis. 151–14 our Minister and the great P·:
Pul. 6–19 * and turned to the 'great P·.'

physician
Mis. 59–28 divine Mind, who is the only p·;
89– 6 *employing a regular p·,*
248–24 my regular p· prescribed morphine,
269–19 divine Mind to be the only p·.
349– 3 a certain regular-school p·,
355–12 p· must know himself and understand
355–26 "P·, heal thyself." — *Luke* 4 : 23.
Ret. 13–24 The p· marvelled;
24–11 homœopathic p· who attended me,
87–30 under the care of a regular p·,
Un. 11–20 a p·, or a professor of natural
59–23 and man an invalid, needing a p·;
Pul. 35–28 * a p· who had come into sympathy with
Hea. 14–12 In proportion as a p· is enlightened
Peo. 6– 8 * p·, surgeon, apothecary,
My. 105–22 Her p·, who stood by her bedside,
108– 2 homœopathic p· succeeds as well
108–19 better for both p· and patient.
128–15 man's right . . . to employ a p·,
132–28 Divine Love is our only p·,
310–20 by p· or post-mortem examination
335–24 * sent for the distinguished p· who
335–31 * told by the expert p· that

physicians
Mis. 24–10 pronounced fatal by the p·.
35– 6 pronounced by the p· incurable,
69–15 p· had given three doses
69–21 p· had failed even to move his
81– 3 scholarly p· openly admit.
143–20 well known p·, teachers,
245– 5 but to the p·.— *II Chron.* 16 : 12.
Ret. 15–25 by p· of the popular schools
40– 9 The p· had given up the case
40–13 told me that her p· had said
Pul. 34– 7 * pronounced hopeless by the p·.
72–15 * by a number of well-known p·.
Hea. 14–10 exercised in the choice of p·.
My. 97– 2 * best p· now admit the
97– 5 * p·, however, ridicule the idea of
237–17 equal to those of reputable p·
293–11 Even the p· may have feared this.
328–15 * license . . . required of p·,

physicists
Rud. 6–17 * universally accepted, . . . by p·."

physics
Mis. 6–13 power of metaphysics over p·;
34– 3 metaphysics is above p·.
53–17 He that resorts to p·,
126– 3 from darkness to daylight, in p·
209–11 and dies of its own p·.
209–12 Short-sighted p· admits the so-called
255–27 metaphysics is above p·.
264–31 more fatal than a mistake in p·.
340–31 theology, and p· have not
366– 6 theology, philosophy, or p·,
369– 7 Metaphysics, not p·, enables us
Ret. 34–16 superiority of metaphysics over p·.
No. 11–20 theology, physiology, or p·;
Pan. 4– 7 may agree with p· and anatomy
Hea. 11– 6 p· are yielding slowly to
14– 6 physiology, hygiene, or p·
Peo. 9–23 metaphysics is seen to rise above p·,
10– 5 through the cold night of p·,
My. 127– 2 in p·, and in metaphysics.
307– 9 matter, electricity, or p·.

Physiology
Pul. 38–10 "P·," "Footsteps of Truth,"

physiology
Un. 45–17 Anatomy and p· make mind-matter a
No. 11–16 place . . . that p· occupies,
11–20 learn theology, p·, or physics;
Hea. 5– 7 P· will be saying,
14– 6 p·, hygiene, or physics

physique
Mis. 28–29 claims of p· and of physical
34– 8 since the p· is simply
Ret. 78– 2 acts like a diseased p·,

piazza
Pul. 48– 6 * broad p· on the south side
48–15 * Straight . . . from her p·,

pick
Mis. 357–15 fowls of the air p· them up.

picked
Mis. 282–12 houses broken open or our locks p·?

picking
Mis. 343–15 p· away the cold, hard pebbles

pictorial
Pul. 25– 1 * are very rich in p· effect.
27–20 * great window tells its p· story
27–28 * and others of p· significance.

picture
Mis. 279–22 second p· is of the disciples
323– 2 P· to yourself "a city— *Matt.* 5 : 14.
373– 4 in the p· "Seeking and Finding."
Po. 43– 1 p· *depictive of Isaiah xi.*
My. 58–16 * speaks more than words can p·
206–13 seeing a person in the p· of Jesus,
356–16 nor consent to have my p· issued,

pictured
Un. 34– 5 images, p· on the eye's retina.

picture-lesson
Mis. 280– 3 third p· is from Revelation,

pictures
Mis. ix–10 easel of time presents p·
279–14 p· from which we learn
346–23 in p· of silver." — *Prov.* 25 : 11.
365– 7 what a child's love of p· is
372–11 * p· in your wonderful book
374–27 P· are portions of one's ideal,
375– 1 P· which present disordered
Man. 81–21 No objectionable p· shall be
Pul. 58–12 * appearance is shown in the p·
58–21 * p· symbolic of the tenets
76–16 * P· and bric-a-brac everywhere
No. 18–16 what a child's love of p· is
27– 8 similitude of the Apocalyptic p·.
My. 308–16 p· "the old man tramping

picturesque
Ret. 4–11 p· view of the Merrimac River
Pul. 47–26 * is so p· all about Concord
My. 47–13 * look back to the p·, interesting,
175–17 Our p· city, however,

picturesqueness
Ret. 2– 4 poetic daring and pious p·

picture-stories
Mis. 279–13 three p· from the Bible

picturing
Po. 9– 3 I'm p· alone a glad young face,

pie
Mis. 231–14 delicious p·, pudding, and fruit

piece
My. 71–10 * a stunning p· of architecture
195–21 no miserable p· of ideal legerdemain,

pieces
'00. 10–28 ten five-dollar gold p·

Pierce (see also **Pierce's**)
Franklin
Ret. 6–19 in the office of Franklin P·,
My. 309– 7 Franklin P·, afterwards President of
Governor
My. 308–20 my father was visiting Governor P·,
Mr.
Ret. 6–24 law-office which Mr. P· had occupied,
My. 309–11 Mr. P· bowed to my father

pierce
Mis. 320–25 p· the darkness and melt into dawn.
'00. 12– 1 His types of purity p· corruption

pierced
Mis. 339–20 hast p· the heart venturing its all
342–17 him whom they had p·,
My. 191–22 Mortality's thick gloom is p·.
278–28 p· by its own sword.

Pierce's
President
My. 311–20 Fanny McNeil, President P· niece,
President Franklin
My. 308–21 President Franklin P· father,

pierces
Mis. 355–15 and the last third p· itself,

piercing
Mis. 312– 8 endures all p· for the sake of others,
Po. 30–18 P· the clouds with its triumphal

piers
My. 68– 6 * tops of great stone p·,

piety
Mis. 111– 1 proven that the greatest p· is
'01. 33– 1 their p· was the all-important
My. 288–13 His p· partook not of the

pigment
Ret. 79– 8 p· beneath fade into invisibility.

Pilate
Un. 59–15 to suffer before *P·* and on Calvary,

pile
Mis. 51–24 * dark *p·* of human mockeries ;
388–14 Grave on her monumental *p·* :
Po. 21– 1 Grave on her monumental *p·* :
My. 45–28 * massive *p·* of New Hampshire granite

piled
My. 78–15 * basket *p·* high with bank-notes,

pilgrim
Mis. 155– 9 win the *p·* and stranger
341–15 weary *p·*, unloose the latchet

pilgrimage
'02. 20–20 sacrament in our church and a *p·* to
My. 150– 9 joy and crown of such a *p·*

pilgrimages
Ret. 90–13 depart on their united *p·*.

Pilgrim Fathers
Pul. 10–10 Our land, . . . had its *P· F·*.
My. 183– 6 wrote in 1620 to our *P· F·* :

Pilgrims
Mis. 176–20 When first the *P·* planted their
176–23 *P·* came to establish a nation
My. 50– 7 * *P·* felt the strangeness of

pilgrims
Pul. 51–24 * *P·* from everywhere will go there
My. 77–13 * *p·* are pouring into Boston,

pill
Mis. 369–16 tincture or an ipecacuanha *p·*.

pillar
Mis. 149–28 Guided by the *p·* and the cloud,
My. 45–19 * by day in a *p·* of cloud
45–20 * by night in a *p·* of fire
45–25 * *p·* of cloud by day, — see Exod. 13 : 22.
45–25 * *p·* of fire by night,'' — Exod. 13 : 22.
69–17 * not a single *p·* or post anywhere
164–21 this phœnix fire, this *p·* by day,

pillars
'02. 17–29 Patience and resignation are the *p·* of

pillow
Mis. 257–31 Smoothing the *p·* of pain
Un. 57–18 earth's Bethel in stone, — its *p·*,
Po. 27–23 *P·* thy head on time's untired

pillows
Mis. 144–25 from earth's *p·* of stone,

pills
Mis. 79–31 vendors of patent *p·*, mesmerists,

pin
My. 83–10 * Scientists frequently wear a small *p·*,
192–25 demands . . . *p·* me to my post.

pine
Mis. 330– 2 make melody through dark *p·* groves.
Ret. 4–18 requiems through dark *p·* groves.
Po. 68–10 the sea and the tall waving *p·*

Pine Grove Cemetery
Po. page 67 poem

pinest
Po. 34–21 Nor *p·* thou in vain

pine-tree
Rud. 8– 2 no *p·* produces a mammal

Pine Tree State (see also **Maine**)
Mis. 251– 6 from the Palmetto to the *P· T· S·*,

pining
Po. 35– 7 Or *p·* tenderness

pinion
Po. 18– 7 or *p·* lose power

pinions
Mis. 354–30 nor his *p·* lose power
385–23 ''When . . . Thy *p·* drooped ;
Ret. 85–12 bearing on their *p·* of light
Po. 33–16 faith spreads her *p·* abroad,
48–18 ''When . . . Thy *p·* drooped ;
My. 238–16 swift *p·* of spiritual thought

pink
Mis. 329–23 paint in *p·* the petals of arbutus,
376–27 orange, *p·*, crimson, violet ;
Ret. 17–12 On the heart of the *p·*
Pul. 24–23 * with trimmings of the *p·* granite
25–15 * with marble stairs of rose *p·*,
25–24 * of *p·* Tennessee marble.
42–30 * filled with beautiful *p·* roses.
Po. 62–15 On the heart of the *p·*

pinnacle
Mis. 313– 7 molecule, pearl, and *p·*,
358–26 at the *p·* of prosperity,
Man. 47–15 scales the *p·* of praise

pinnacled
Pul. 2–30 *p·* in Life.

pinnacles
Ret. 47–10 being placed on earthly *p·*,

pinned
'01. 26–16 shall the word popularity be *p·* to

pioneer
Mis. x–10 in the early *p·* days,
xii– 1 *p·* signs and ensigns of war,
213–17 In every age, the *p·* reformer
Ret. 30– 1 As the *p·* of C. S. I stood alone
50–30 in the beginning of *p·* work.
Pul. 47– 9 * her experiences as the *p·* of C. S.,
'00. 3–16 not apt to worship the *p·* of
Hea. 6– 5 *p·* of something new under the sun
Po. vi–13 *Boston has since been the p· of*
My. 148– 1 to do your *p·* work in this city.

Pioneer-Press
Pul. 90– 2 * *P·*, St. Paul, Minn.

pioneers
Pul. 51– 9 * many *p·* who are searching after
My. 50–10 * so this little band of *p·*,
104–18 on the *p·* of Christianity
104–20 of whom these *p·* speak.

pious
Mis. 147–24 *p·* worker, the public-spirited citizen.
345– 7 need the spirit of the *p·* Polycarp,
Ret. 1– 6 the *p·* and popular English authoress
2– 4 the poetic daring and *p·*
81–22 Shakespeare puts this *p·* counsel
Peo. 13–17 lofty faith of the *p·* Polycarp

pipe
Chr. 55–12 tabret, and *p·*, and wine, — Isa. 5 : 12.
Pan. 3–28 His *p·* of seven reeds denotes the

pipes
Pul. 60–26 * 61 *p·* each.
60–30 * 61 *p·* each.
61– 3 * 61 *p·* each.
61– 5 * 30 *p·* each.
(see also **organ**)

pippin
Mis. 231–17 made a big hole, . . . in a big *p·*,

piqued
Mis. 363– 8 flatterer, identification, is *p·*

pistons
(see **organ**)

pit
Mis. 389–11 the snare, the *p·*, the fall :
Po. 4–10 the snare, the *p·*, the fall :

pitch
Pul. 47–30 * angles and *p·* of the roof,

pith
Mis. 27–10 *p·* of the basal statement,
My. 303–24 *p·* and finale of them all.

pitiable
Mis. 115–12 ignorance . . . on this subject is *p·*,

pitied
Mis. 105–27 has no right either to be *p·* or to
211–18 is he not to be *p·* and brought back

pities
Un. 3–27 God is our helper. He *p·* us.
4– 9 that God comes to us and *p·* us ;
No. 30–13 God *p·* our woes with the love of a

pitieth
Un. 2– 3 God *p·* them who fear Him ;

pitifully
Mis. 227–16 these weak, *p·* poor objects from

pitiless
Mis. 257–28 This *p·* power smites with disease

pittance
Pul. 64– 9 * some giving a *p·*,

Pittsburgh, Pa.
Pul. 89– 7 * Post, *P·*, *P·*.
My. 196– 2 chapter sub-title

pity
Mis. 102–17 His *p·* is expressed in modes above
102–22 Human *p·* often brings pain.
105–26 and *p·* what has no right either to
121–28 Infinitely greater than human *p·*,
124–17 with more than a father's *p·* ;
224–30 is an object of *p·* rather than of
227–15 Would that my pen or *p·* could
Un. 18–17 show My *p·* through divine law,
Pul. 52– 5 * What a *p·* some of our practical
84– 5 * revenge shall clasp hands with *p·*,
'01. 16–12 surviving defamers share our *p·*.
'02. 18–12 nor spared through false *p·*

pity
My. 57–32   * What a *p·* some of our practical
     189–29   why throng in *p·* round me?

pitying
Mis. 124–16   *p·* with more than a father's pity ;
     212–30   *P·* friends took down from the cross
     228–13   We should look with *p·* eye
     386–11   looks on her heart with *p·* eye,
Po. 49–16   looks on her heart with *p·* eye,

placards
Mis. 210– 8   *p·* warning people not to stir up

place (noun)
accustomed
Mis. 135–29   to see me in my accustomed *p·*
all
No. 24– 2   evil loses all *p·*, person, and
My. 353–26   and the spiritual have all *p·*
and power
Mis. 274–26   exchange for money, *p·*, and power,
     351–15   aspirants for *p·* and power.
My. 353–26   the spiritual have all *p·* and power.
appropriate
Mis. 304– 6   * in the most appropriate *p·*
behold the
My. 122–24   behold the *p·* where— *Mark* 16 : 6.
     191–21   Behold the *p·* where they laid me ;
each
My. 330–19   * Masonic records in each *p·*
for himself
Mis. 294– 4   making *p·* for himself
from the
Mis. 178– 1   from the *p·* of my own sojourning
gave
Mis. 142–20   gave *p·* to chords of feeling
gives
'02. 2–21   gives *p·* to a more spiritual
giving
Mis. 303–22   giving *p·* in your *Journal* to the
her
Man. 72–20   her *p·* as the head or Leader
My. 51– 2   * no one . . . who could take her *p·*
hiding
Mis. 144–16   an hiding *p·* from the— *Isa.* 32 : 2.
My. 17– 2   overflow the hiding *p·*." — *Isa.* 28 : 17.
high
Mis. 392– 6   majestic oak, from yon high *p·*
Po. 20– 8   majestic oak, from yon high *p·*
his
Mis. 137–20   each one return to his *p·*
Man. 28–21   either to resign his *p·* or
'00. 12–20   candlestick out of his *p·*,— *Rev.* 2 : 5.
historic
My. 90–27   * The historic *p·* of Mrs. Eddy as the
hold a
Mis. 290–25   hold a *p·* in one's memory,
holy
Mis. 301–25   injustice standing in a holy *p·*.
My. 34– 2   stand in his holy *p·*? — *Psal.* 24 : 3.
individual
Ret. 70–14   the individual *p·* of the Virgin
in North Groton
My. 314–10   bought a *p·* in North Groton,
in schools
No. 11–16   the *p·* in schools of learning
in Science
Mis. 234–15   can never find a *p·* in Science.
its
Mis. 334– 5   Astrology is well in its *p·*,
Pul. 51–28   * aspire to take its *p·* alongside
meeting
My. 174– 5   proved an ideal meeting *p·*.
my
'00. 9–27   to have some one take my *p·*
needed a
My. 55– 3   * church needed a *p·* of its own,
no
Mis. 31–13   Such false faith finds no *p·* in,
     357– 1   no *p·* for envy, no time for
     367– 2   have no *p·* in C. S.
     394–13   No *p·* for earth's idols,
Ret. 21–15   dream has no *p·* in the Science of being.
Un. 2– 3   no *p·* where His voice is not heard ;
     42– 2   because there is no *p·* left for it.
No. 27– 5   evil finds no *p·* in good.
'02. 12–22   ordinarily find no *p·* in my Message.
Po. 45–17   No *p·* for earth's idols,
My. 7– 5   ordinarily find no *p·* in my Message.
     54–18   * no *p·* suitable could be found
nor power
Mis. 14– 1   neither *p·* nor power left for evil.
of a virtue
Mis. 227– 3   may stand in the *p·* of a virtue ;
of darkness
My. 199– 4   In *p·* of darkness, light hath

place
of good
Rud. 6–11   takes the *p·* of good.
of labor
Mis. 137–20   return to his *p·* of labor,
Ret. 84–30   regular institute or *p·* of labor,
of the author
Ret. 70–17   No person can take the *p·* of the author of
of the Golden Rule
My. 266– 8   in *p·* of the Golden Rule,
of worship
Mis. 325–31   Next he enters a *p·* of worship,
     345–23   took their infants to a *p·* of worship
one
Mis. 134–12   "in one *p·*," — *Acts* 2 : 1.
     143–27   in one *p·*." — *Acts* 2 : 1.
My. 212–19   in one *p·*," — *Acts* 2 : 1.
     362–15   * in one *p·* with one accord,
or a thing
'01. 13– 1   a man or a woman, a *p·* or a thing,
or power
My. 4–24   The pride of *p·* or power
other
Mis. 266–19   Chicago, New York, or any other *p·*,
pleasant
My. 147–22   I have purchased a pleasant *p·*
proper
Mis. 308–10   take their proper *p·* in history,
rightful
No. 33– 6   rightful *p·* in schools of learning,
My. vii– 7   * her rightful *p·* as the revelator
same
Mis. 27–18   send forth at the same *p·* — *Jas.* 3 : 11.
Man. 71– 5   established in the same *p·* ;
secret
My. 188–10   secret *p·* of the most High," — *Psal.* 91 : 1.
     244–15   "secret *p·*," whereof — *Psal.* 91 : 1.
some
My. 54–20   * expectation that some *p·* would
supply the
My. 312– 2   supply the *p·* of his leading teacher
take
My. 84–28   * to take *p·* on Sunday,
     217–12   This disbursal will take *p·* when
take a
My. 31–19   * take a *p·* in the front rank of
takes
Mis. 42– 1   *change called death takes p·*,
     304–15   * takes *p·* at Paris, France.
takes the
Mis. 175–24   one belief takes the *p·* of another.
Pul. 25–30   * takes the *p·* of chandeliers.
take the
Rud. 16– 2   take the *p·* of private lessons ;
taking
Ret. 19– 3   taking *p·* under the paternal roof
Pul. 56–12   * taking *p·* on the 6th of January,
taking the
My. 212– 6   In this era it is taking the *p·* of
that
Mis. 75–24   name of Deity used in that *p·*
My. 55–26   * in that *p·* Sunday services were held
their
Mis. 182–24   finding their *p·* in God's great love,
thereof
Mis. 189–18   revealing, in *p·* thereof, the power
this
Mis. 334– 5   but this *p·* is secondary.
My. 188– 7   made in this *p·*." — *II Chron.* 7 : 15.
thy
Mis. 400– 4   Like this stone, be in thy *p·* :
Pul. 16–16   Like this stone, be in thy *p·* ;
Po. 76–15   Like this stone, be in thy *p·* :
time and
My. 169–20   beauty of time and *p·*
took
Mis. 339– 3   took *p·* once in heaven,
Pul. 38– 4   * which ceremony took *p·* in 1881.
Pan. 7–10   belief, . . . a material creation took *p·*,
to place
Mis. 304– 8   * will pass from *p·* to place
     304–20   * journey from *p·* to place,
where Demosthenes
Mis. 345– 4   in the *p·* where Demosthenes had
will hold
My. 85–17   * structure which will hold *p·* among
yonder
My. 222–12   Remove hence to yonder *p·* ; — *Matt.* 17 : 20.

Mis. 61–16   * a *p·* where a man was said to
     175–21   and its methods in *p·* of God,
     237– 4   in *p·* of material flames and odor,
     304–13   * *p·* where any great patriotic
     341–16   *p·* whereon thou standest is sacred.
Man. 96–10   a *p·* where he sees there is
Un. 26–22   what *p·* has *chance* in the divine

place

Un.	51–11	whose *p·* is ill supplied by
Pul.	5– 7	we kindle in *p·* thereof the glow of
	60–12	* The *p·* was again crowded,
Peo.	14– 8	in *p·* of "bat and owl on the
My.	vi–27	* *p·* for the publishing of her works ;
	37– 3	* no pride of circumstances has *p·*
	53–14	* seating capacity of which *p·* was
	188–23	C. S. has a *p·* in its court,

place (verb)

Mis.	33–17	*p·* themselves under my care,
	117– 8	will *p·* him on the safe side
	287–10	may *p·* love on a false basis
	296–10	*p·* the barmaids of English alehouses
	344–17	would *p·* Soul wholly inside of body,
	351–16	never can *p·* it in the wrong hands
Man.	46– 8	shall not *p·* the initials "C. S."
	51–21	to discipline, *p·* on probation,
Ret.	42– 5	and *p·* these symbolic words on
	84–28	*p·* themselves under his direction ;
Pul.	35–30	* *p·* "Christian Scientist" on the sign
My.	214– 1	one only to *p·* on the walls
	321– 6	* *p·* him as one of your devoted and

placed

Mis.	134– 5	you are *p·* in this dilemma :
	304– 5	* *p·* by the lovers of liberty
	304–32	* *p·* in the hands of a committee
	305– 8	* *p·* upon me the responsibility
Man.	51– 4	he shall be *p·* on probation,
Ret.	47– 9	being *p·* on earthly pinnacles,
	91–18	*p·* themselves under his care,
Pul.	42–21	* where the organ is to be . . . *p·*,
	48– 1	* well *p·* upon a terrace
	62–23	* *p·* on a small centre table.
	73–23	* She *p·* no credit whatever in the
My.	68–21	* *p·* back of the Readers' platform
	69– 8	* whereon are *p·* inscriptions
	69–11	* *p·* on the two sides of the organ.
	79–21	* *p·* upon a far higher pedestal
	166–29	cabinet, . . . *p·* in my room

places

Mis.	7–11	*p·* where one would least expect it,
	79– 3	the *p·* once knowing them
	116– 4	wickedness in high *p·*." — *Eph.* 6 : 12.
	126–28	she sitteth in high *p·* ;
	127– 6	watering her waste *p·*,
	134–28	wickedness is standing in high *p·* ;
	250–29	lighting the dark *p·* of earth.
	304–17	* When not in use in other *p·*,
Man.	95– 7	at such *p·* and at such times
	110–17	*p·* where they are required.
Pul.	22–21	her waste *p·* budded
No.	45–17	highest *p·* in government,
Hea.	11–23	*p·* all cause and cure as mind ;
	15– 6	*p·* no faith in hygiene or drugs ;
My.	3–11	scattered abroad in Zion's waste *p·*,
	18– 3	watering her waste *p·*,
	54–17	* different *p·* were considered,
	54–29	* consideration of *p·* for meeting
	55– 5	* Several *p·* were considered,
	56–13	* each of the following named *p·* :
	80–27	* when these *p·* had all been filled,
	81–14	* the *p·* where they lived.
	91–28	* one of the finest *p·* of worship
	107–20	*p·* it nearer the grooves of
	310– 4	at various times and *p·*.
	334–12	* *p·* certain circumstances in 1843,

placid

Ret.	5–23	* sympathizing heart, and a *p·* spirit.

placing

Mis.	197–31	*p·* his trust in this grand Truth,
	351–14	*p·* C. S. in the hands of
	373– 3	*p·* the serpent behind the woman
My.	298– 9	*p·* this book before the public,

plagiarism

Ret.	76–27	a growing evil in *p·* ;
No.	3–25	*P·* from my writings is so common

plagiarists

Mis.	301–17	must not leave persistent *p·*

plagiarize

Man.	43–17	shall not *p·* her writings.

plagiarizing

Ret.	76– 1	for *p·* an author's ideas

plague

Mis.	229–18	neither shall any *p·* — *Psal.* 91 : 10.

plagues

My.	126–15	receive not of her *p·*. — *Rev.* 18 : 4.
	126–20	*p·* come in one day, — *Rev.* 18 : 8.

plague-spot

Mis.	12– 2	hatred is a *p·* that spreads

plain

Mis.	23–14	It is *p·* that the Me spoken of
	24–16	since tried to make *p·* to others,
	115–12	is pitiable, and *p·* to be seen.
	121–17	This is *p·* : that whatever belittles,
	124– 1	*p·* that aught unspiritual,
	124– 4	It is also *p·*, that we should not
	271–22	To make this *p·*,
Ret.	30–17	The answer is *p·*.
	90–11	and gave in *p·* words,
Un.	9– 8	Jesus has made the way *p·*,
	9– 9	so *p·* that all are without excuse who
No.	6–20	To material sense it is *p·* also that
Pan.	6–26	It is *p·* that elevating evil to the
'01.	13–22	In C. S. it is *p·* that God removes the
My.	121–14	Peace, like *p·* dealing,
	121–15	and *p·* dealing is a jewel
	210– 4	*p·* that nothing can be added to
	343– 1	* *p·* that the answers to questions
	346–29	"S. and H. makes it *p·* to all

plainer

Un.	6–27	drilled in the *p·* manual

plainly

Mis.	93– 8	The Scriptures *p·* declare the allness
	189–13	Christ *p·* declared, through Jesus,
	192–23	as the above Scripture *p·* declares,
	212–27	speaks *p·* to the offender
Man.	110–11	must be *p·* written,
Pan.	5– 3	The Scriptures *p·* declare,
My.	84– 1	* facts speak more *p·* than mere
	86–18	* one which indicates *p·* enough
	216– 1	is *p·* set forth in the Scriptures.
	319–29	* I also recall very *p·* the

plain-speaking

My.	137– 7	* crisp, clear, *p·* English."

plaintiff

My.	6– 1	arguing for the *p·* in favor of

plan

Mis.	182–23	apostle indicates no personal *p·* of
	296–14	live on the *p·* of heaven
	348–13	show the *p·* of battle.
Hea.	1–17	* Knows it at forty, and reforms his *p·* ;
Peo.	12–18	God's *p·* of redemption,
	12–22	as God's whole *p·*,
My.	145– 4	*p·* for C. S. Hall in Concord,
	145– 6	He drew the *p·*, showed it to me,
	269–11	Christ's *p·* of salvation from divorce.
	278– 3	to be subserved by the battle's *p·*
	283–23	or God's own *p·* of salvation.

plane

Mis.	22–12	defining the line, *p·*, space,
	34–24	on this present *p·* of existence,
	42–14	same *p·* of conscious existence
	143– 6	above the *p·* of matter.
	368–27	perverted, on the mortal *p·*
	393–20	Points the *p·* of power to seek.
Pul.	38–19	* different a *p·* of consciousness
Po.	52– 4	Points the *p·* of power to seek.
My.	46– 5	* more spiritual *p·* of living,
	226– 8	inclined *p·* in mechanics,

planet

Mis.	174–14	the atmosphere of our *p·*,
	383– 2	textbook, be the pastor, on this *p·*,
No.	6–18	revolves around our *p·*,
Peo.	8–19	as directly as it moves a *p·*
My.	160–23	will eventually consume this *p·*.
	267– 2	the only . . . therapeutics on this *p·*.

planets

Mis.	54– 4	and the *p·* to revolve around it?
Pan.	3–29	celestial harmony of the seven *p·* ;
My.	13–11	* other churches, like so many *p·*,

plank

Mis.	21–15	My first *p·* in the platform of

planks

Un.	14– 1	such *p·* as the divine repentance,
My.	61–14	* over stones and *p·* and plaster,

planning

Mis.	230–11	or *p·* for some amusement,

plans

My.	55–17	* *p·* were made for a church home.
	352–28	thanks for your successful *p·*

plant

Mis.	4– 5	to *p·* mental healing on the
	26–12	"every *p·* of the field — *Gen.* 2 : 5.
	107– 7	*p·* the feet steadfastly in Christ.
Pul.	10–23	your *p·* is immortal,
Pan.	15– 7	*p·* our feet firmly on Truth,
'01.	33– 4	To *p·* for eternity,
Hea.	19–14	"every *p·* of the field — *Gen.* 2 : 5.
My.	122– 7	To cut off the top of a *p·*
	122– 8	or the *p·* will continue to grow.
	129–19	*p·* thy steps in Christ,

plant
My. 154–19 * "Wouldst thou *p·* for eternity,
   154–19 * *p·* into the deep infinite faculties
   186–20 those that *p·* the vineyard
   215–18 to *p·* our first magazine,

planted
Mis. 80–26 have *p·* and sown and reaped
   176–20 *p·* their feet on Plymouth Rock,
Pul. vii–15 C. S. as *p·* in the pathway of
   10–11 they *p·* a nation's heart,
   10–16 you have *p·* your standard

planting
My. 202–30 God bless this vine of His *p·*.

plants
Mis. 339–12 *p·* our feet more firmly.
Ret. 11–11 knowledge *p·* the foot of power
Un. 14– 6 earth, man, animals, *p·*,
Rud. 7–27 or *p·* into animals,
Po. 60– 8 knowledge *p·* the foot of power
My. 205–11 * He *p·* His footsteps in the sea
  356– 7 * "He *p·* His footsteps in the sea

plaster
Pul. 25–13 * galleries are in *p·* relief,
  25–14 * iron, coated with *p·*;
My. 61–14 * stones and planks and *p·*,
  68–26 * *p·* work for the great arches

plastic
Rud. 15– 9 renders the mind less inquisitive, *p·*,

plated
Pul. 76–20 * heavily *p·* with gold."

plates
My. 30–20 * when the *p·* were returned
  69–10 * Two large marble *p·*

Platform
(*see* **Christian Science Platform**)

platform
Mis. 21–15 plank in the *p·* of C. S.
  95– 2 * *p·* of the Monday lectureship
  177–26 * came on the *p·*.
  244– 3 on the *p·* of C. S. !
  253– 7 *p·* is not broad enough for me,
  364–17 It stands on this Scriptural *p·* :
Man. 34– 9 according to the *p·* and teaching
Ret. 16– 4 two ladies . . . reached the *p·*.
Un. 14– 1 an outworn theological *p·*,
Pul. 12– 3 were read from the *p·*.
  26– 7 * *p·* — corresponding to the chancel of
  42–20 * choir gallery above the *p·*,
  42–25 * choir and the steps of the *p·*
  43– 7 * On the *p·* with him were
  59–21 * on the *p·* sat Joseph Armstrong,
  60–19 * recess behind the spacious *p·*,
No. 12–10 on the *p·* of doctrines, rites, and
'01. 33–14 not to be judged on a doctrinal *p·*,
Peo. 11– 9 Above the *p·* of human rights
My. 31–26 * was on the Readers' *p·*.
  31–26 * Stepping to the front of the *p·*,
  32–10 * above the usual *p·* tone.
  44–16 * advanced to the front of the *p·*,
  68–17 * *p·* is of a beautiful foreign marble,
  68–21 * placed back of the Readers' *p·*
  69–19 * view of the *p·* from any seat.
  71–26 * *p·* in front of the great organ.
  145–18 I cannot go upon the *p·*

platforms
Mis. 253–10 may improve our *p·* ;

Plato
Mis. 111–23 *P·* was a pagan,
  361–14 Socrates, *P·*, Kant, Locke,
Ret. 57– 5 *P·* believed he had a soul,
No. 21– 6 Confucius and *P·* but dimly discerned,
Hea. 8–15 *P·* did better ; he said,

platoons
Un. 6–25 while the *p·* of C. S. are not

play
Mis. 224–15 human life is the work, the *p·*,
  395–10 Doth *p·* a part,
Ret. 17– 3 midst the zephyrs at *p·*
  18– 3 Cool waters at *p·* with the
'02. 14–29 an open field and fair *p·*.
Hea. 11– 1 fountains *p·* in borrowed sunbeams,
Po. 57–17 Doth *p·* a part,
  62– 2 midst the zephyrs at *p·*
  63–10 Cool waters at *p·* with the
My. 31– 1 * chimes . . . began to *p·*,
  93–25 * and the part it has come to *p·*

played
Man. 61–22 shall be *p·* in a dignified and
Pul. 81– 2 * *p·* "All hail the power of
My. 59–22 * melodeon on which my wife *p·*,

playful
Po. 9– 4 Upturned . . . in *p·* grace ;

playing
Mis. 368–23 puppets of the hour are *p·*

plays
Pul. 81–23 * her own soul *p·* upon magic strings
Po. 2– 5 * "*P·* round the head,
My. 272–25 * *p·* so great a part

plea
Mis. 119–19 a *p·* for free moral agency,
Hea. 10–25 win or lose according to your *p·*
My. 31– 4 * "Just as I am, without one *p·* ;"
  305–26 chapter sub-title

plead
Mis. 310–14 my affections *p·* for all
  341–31 nor . . . adequate to *p·* for the
My. 265–11 *p·* not vainly in behalf of the

pleaded
Mis. 345– 5 *p·* for freedom in immortal strains

pleading
Mis. 59–14 *p·* with infinite Love to love us,
Po. 78–15 Give to the *p·* hearts comfort

pleads
Mis. 174–21 *p·* for Spirit — the All of God,
  371–14 my heart *p·* for them to
Chr. 53–55 Truth *p·* to-night :
'02. 11– 6 Love waits and *p·* to save mankind

pleas
Mis. 340–15 raised potatoes instead of *p·*,
My. 309–10 Both entered their *p·*,

pleasant
Mis. 52–12 often convenient, sometimes *p·*,
  86–18 *p·* sensations of human belief,
  238– 3 It is *p·*, now, to contrast with
  324–29 reaches the *p·* path of the valley
Un. 23– 3 * and of our *p·* vices
Pul. 72– 9 * very *p·* and agreeable lady,
No. 3–22 How good and *p·* a thing it is
  39–27 portray the face of *p·* thought.
Po. 73–15 *P·* a grave By the "Rock" or
My. 39–22 * my *p·* duty to preside at an
  87– 8 * *p·*, congenial, quietly happy,
  119–26 *p·* pastime of seeing your
  121–25 *p·* to those who practise it.
  147–22 I have purchased a *p·* place
  163–24 leading people of this *p·* city
  173–24 Scientists' short stay so *p·*.
  315– 9 * as *p·* and happy home
  341–27 * *p·* warmth within the

pleasanter
Mis. 287–27 *p·* to do right than wrong ;

pleasantly
Man. 27–20 *p·* located in the same building,
No. 46–12 descant *p·* upon free moral agency ;
My. 271–13 * In a modest, *p·* situated home

Pleasant View
Mis. 116– 5 *P· V·*, Concord, N. H.,
  142– 8 for the little pond at *P· V·*.
  203– 2 pretty pond contributed to *P· V·*,
  251– 1 chapter sub-title
  376–16 chapter sub-title
Pul. 37– 6 * beautiful residence, called *P· V·*.
  49–28 * as he approaches *P· V·*.
  58– 7 * beautiful estate called *P· V·* ;
'02. 20–18 our *annual* gathering at *P· V·*,
Po. 22–22 *P· V·*, Concord, N. H.,
  24–22 *P· V·*, Concord, N. H.,
  25–20 *P· V·*, Concord, N. H.,
  31–23 *P· V·*, Concord, N. H.,
  44– 5 *P· V·*, Concord, N. H.,
  79–22 *P· V·*, Concord, N. H.,
My. 9–29 *P· V·*, Concord, N. H.,
  20– 5 *P· V·*, Concord, N. H.,
  20–20 *P· V·*, Concord, N. H.,
  25–29 *P· V·*, Concord, N. H.,
  26–27 *P· V·*, Concord, N. H.,
  44–22 * *P· V·*, Concord, N. H.
  58–27 * *P· V·*, Concord, N. H.
  60–24 * *P· V·*, Concord, N. H.
  62–18 * *P· V·*, Concord, N. H.
  66–24 * *P· V·*, in Concord, N. H.,
  123–20 accommodations at *P· V·*
  133–19 *P· V·*, Concord, N. H.,
  135–22 *P· V·*, Concord, N. H.,
  136–10 *P· V·*, Concord, N. H.,
  136–30 *P· V·*, Concord, N. H.,
  138–23 *P· V·*, Concord, N. H.,
  155–31 flowers and the cross from *P· V·*,
  169– 3 *P· V·*, Concord, N. H.,
  169–11 *P· V·*, Concord, N. H.,
  170–11 chapter sub-title
  170–13 Welcome to *P· V·*,

Pleasant View

My.	171–17	*P· V·*, Concord, N. H.,
	175– 8	*P· V·*, Concord, N. H.,
	187–18	*P· V·*, Concord, N. H.,
	193–11	*P· V·*, Concord, N. H.,
	197–29	*P· V·*, Concord, N. H.,
	223– 3	received at *P· V·*
	228–26	Who shall be called to *P· V·*?
	228–31	never called to *P· V·* for penance
	229– 4	there cannot be found at *P· V·* one
	230–28	*P· V·*, Concord, N. H.,
	236–21	*P· V·*, Concord, N. H.,
	259– 7	* *P· V·*, Concord, N. H.
	261–19	*P· V·*, Concord, N. H.
	272–17	*P· V·*, Concord, N. H.
	279–29	*P· V·*, Concord, N. H.,
	280– 2	* *P· V·*, Concord, N. H.
	280–24	*P· V·*, Concord, N. H.,
	282–29	*P· V·*, Concord, N. H.,
	284– 8	*P· V·*, Concord, N. H.,
	284–29	*P· V·*, Concord, N. H.,
	285–31	*P· V·*, Concord, N. H.
	289–21	*P· V·*, Concord, N. H.,
	290–30	*P· V·*, Concord, N. H.,
	295–30	*P· V·*, Concord, N. H.,
	296– 7	*P· V·*, Concord, N. H.,
	296–22	*P· V·*, Concord, N. H.,
	297– 9	*P· V·*, Concord, N. H.,
	301–12	*P· V·*, Concord, N. H.,
	327– 8	*P· V·*, Concord, N. H.,
	346–10	* on my return from *P· V·*,
	351–20	*P· V·*, Concord, N. H.,

please

Mis.	61–27	(or bodies, if you *p·*)
	83–10	*Will you p· explain this seeming*
	84–19	*P· explain Paul's meaning*
	87–15	*P· inform us, through your Journal,*
	88– 6	*P· give us, through your Journal,*
	156– 7	*P·* send in your contributions
	287–29	*P·* your husband,
	287–29	and he will be apt to *p·* you ;
	306– 1	* *p·* send fullest historical
Pan.	3– 1	mythical deity may *p·* the fancy,
Po.	23–18	Than just to *p·* mankind.
My.	20–14	*p·* add to your givings to The
	72–15	* "*P·* do not send us any more
	109–14	Principle (or Person, if you *p·*)
	169–15	*P·* say through the *New York Journal,*
	172–18	You will *p·* accept my thanks
	172–27	You will *p·* accept from me
	175– 6	*P·* accept the enclosed check
	199–11	will *p·* accept my grateful
	201–27	*P·* accept a line from me
	236– 9	and to say, *p·* adopt generally
	241–28	* *P·* give the truth in the *Sentinel,*
	250–12	will *p·* send to the Editor
	264–10	* *p·* send through the *Globe*
	266–25	Note, if you *p·*, that many points
	284–17	In your next issue *p·* correct this
	285– 2	*P·* accept my thanks
	347– 8	will *p·* accept my heartfelt
	356–14	will you *p·* state that within the
	361– 6	*P·* find it there,

pleased

Mis.	88– 9	am *p·* to inform this inquirer,
	131–24	I, for one, would be *p·* to have the
	328–19	hast thou tarried . . . *p·* and stupefied,
Pul.	48–14	* It *p·* her to point out her
Po.	v–20	* *They were so p· with it*
My.	136–13	I am *p·* to say that the
	184–15	The beautiful birch bark . . . *p·* me ;
	302–26	My first visit to . . . *p·* me,
	316–21	I am *p·* to find this
	320– 5	* He also seemed very much *p·*
	321–30	* I am also *p·* to have had
	324–23	* *p·* in numbering you among
	328–10	* greatly *p·* at the law
	328–12	* *p·* with the fact that the law

pleasing

Mis.	86–30	even this *p·* thraldom,
	303–23	purpose of a Liberty Bell, is *p·*,
Ret.	5–27	* themes at once *p·* and profitable.
Pul.	3–24	what is *p·* to the divine Mind.
	49–30	* it was *p·* to learn that this
My.	vi– 4	* in a simpler or more *p·* form.
	259–14	most *p·* Christmas presents,

pleasurable

My.	265– 2	more possible and *p·*.

pleasure

and pain
Mis.	85–23	suggests *p·* and pain in matter ;
	198– 7	its varied forms of *p·* and pain.
	333– 2	*p·* and pain, good and evil,
Un.	3– 3	believe in matter's . . . *p·*, and pain,

pleasure

childish
Mis.	310– 1	prohibit ourselves the childish *p·* of

false
Mis.	209–20	False *p·* will be, is, chastened ;

find
My.	86– 5	* find *p·* in this new symbol,

fleeting
Ret.	32–15	* Fleeting *p·*, fond delusion,

give me
My.	192–22	It would indeed give me *p·* to

good
Mis.	150– 1	your Father's good *p·* — *Luke* 12 : 32.
	321–17	your Father's good *p·* — *Luke* 12 : 32.
Ret.	14–10	good *p·* of infinite Love.
Pul.	9–22	your Father's good *p·* — *Luke* 12 : 32.
My.	300– 7	to do of His good *p·*." — *Phil.* 2 : 13.

great
Mis.	143–18	It gives me great *p·* to say
	317–10	would have great *p·* in instructing,
My.	42–20	* affords me great *p·* to welcome you
	186–27	It gives me great *p·* to know

he finds
Mis.	15– 1	fancies he finds *p·* in it,

His
Mis.	127–17	"river of His *p·*," — *see Psal.* 36 : 8.
My.	18–14	'river of His *p·*,' — *see Psal.* 36 : 8.

his
Un.	2–10	sin and his *p·* in it ;

indefinable
Pan.	3– 9	indefinable *p·* in stillness,

in infirmities
Mis.	201–16	Paul took *p·* in infirmities,
	201–31	good that has *p·* in infirmities ;

in sin
Mis.	90– 3	power of sin is the *p·* in sin.
	241–11	"You have no *p·* in sin,"
My.	132–26	sinner, dreaming of *p·* in sin ;

is no crime
Mis.	362–30	*p·* is no crime except when it

its
No.	32– 7	belief in sin — its *p·*, pain, or power

mere
'01.	15–23	* nothing but God's mere *p·*

more
'00.	11– 1	and it gave me more *p·* than

much
Mis.	263– 1	because I take so much *p·* in
My.	21–21	* always experienced much *p·* in

my
My.	42– 5	* It is my *p·* to introduce to you

no
Pan.	10–26	no *p·* in loathsome habits

nor pain
Mis.	28–25	neither *p·* nor pain therein.

of attending
Pul.	29– 8	* *p·* of attending the service

of hearing
Mis.	155–23	the *p·* of hearing from you.

of sin
Ret.	63– 7	sinner's belief in the *p·* of sin,

of thanking
My.	174–17	I have the *p·* of thanking you

or pain
Mis.	100– 6	intoxicated with *p·* or pain,

or recompense
'01.	30–21	the hope of ease, *p·*, or recompense,
My.	308– 7	by ease, *p·*, or recompense.

pain and
Mis.	74–25	or express pain and *p·*.

perishing
Mis.	17–30	perishing *p·* and accumulating pains

personal
Mis.	9–28	gratification in personal *p·*

pursuit of
Mis.	230–17	occupy in the pursuit of *p·*.

pursuit or
Mis.	340– 8	seeking no other pursuit or *p·*

read with
My.	230–18	read with *p·* your approval

sense of
My.	273–19	personal sense of *p·*, pain, joy,

slaves to
My.	197– 2	but becoming slaves to *p·*

take
Mis.	199–11	*take p· in infirmities*, — *II Cor.* 12 : 10.
	200–21	take *p·* in infirmities," — *II Cor.* 12 : 10.
Hea.	6–10	they take *p·* in calling me a medium.

takes
My.	26– 3	* takes *p·* in announcing

that is false
Mis.	351–24	senses give . . . *p·* that is false,

this
Mis.	90– 4	Take away this *p·*, and you

thrill of
Mis.	132–26	It was with a thrill of *p·* that

pleasure

took

Mis.	201–20	he took p· in
	201–23	he took p· in
Ret.	37– 6	critics took p· in saying,

Mis.	353–32	world worship, p· seeking, and
Pul.	36–28	* a p· to give any information
My.	99– 6	* but a p· and an essential ;
	143– 9	I have the p· to report
	163–11	must not allow myself the p· of
	221–24	All issues of morality, . . . of p·,

pleasures

and pains

Mis.	73–19	so-called p· and pains of matter
	84–27	joys and sorrows, p· and pains,
	116–17	loss of the p· and pains
	183–11	the so-called p· and pains of
Un.	55–19	how false are the p· and pains of
Pan.	1–13	the p· and pains of sensation

corporeal

My.	260–20	tradition, usage, or corporeal p·,

dangerous

Mis.	209–14	destroy its more dangerous p·.

deny

Po.	32–16	with appetite, p· deny,

earth's

'02.	19–21	Are earth's p·, its ties and

hater's

Mis.	122–29	The hater's p· are unreal ;

His

Pul.	3–21	The river of His p·
	9–21	river of His p·.'' — see Psal. 36 : 8.

or pains

Mis.	341–30	nor the so-called p· or pains of

or the pains

Hea.	17– 3	p· or the pains of the personal

pains and

Mis.	200–29	so-called pains and p· of matter

pains or

Mis.	185– 7	abilities or disabilities, pains or p·.

Thy

Pul.	1– 2	river of Thy p·. — Psal. 36 : 8.
	3–18	river of Thy p·.'' — Psal. 36 : 8.
	7–30	river of Thy p·.'' — Psal. 36 : 8.

Mis.	85–25	The p· — more than the pains
My.	256–14	p·, achievements, and aid.

pledge

Ret.	80– 2	this is the p· of divine good
No.	46– 2	the p· of the Master.
Po.	68– 5	sweet p· to my lone heart
My.	11–21	* we have also made good the p·.
	11–29	* The p· of the annual meeting was
	46–18	* Only as we p· ourselves anew
	46–19	* fulfil the p· in righteous living,
	46–22	* we do hereby p· ourselves to a
	207–10	* p· themselves to strive more

pledged

My.	7–13	chapter sub-title
	9–21	p· yourselves with startling grace
	13–17	p· to this church in Boston
	13–28	virtually p· this munificent sum
	22– 9	* sum of money adequate . . . was p·.
	23–15	* $2,000,000 p· at the annual meeting,
	65–14	* money to provide it was p·.
	76–19	* was p· by the members assembled
	269– 4	p· to innocence, purity, perfection.

pledges

Pul.	83– 9	* or a million of broken p·.
My.	93–10	* prospers according to the p·

Pleiades

Rud.	4–12	influences of the P·,'' — Job 38 : 31.

plenitude

Pul.	54–16	* and in the p· of his power

plenty

Mis.	6– 7	C. S. practitioners have p· to do,
	118–25	it gives one p· of employment,
	232– 3	drank to peace, and p·,
	325–10	they have p· of pelf,
'00.	2–17	he has p· of means,
Po.	77– 5	P· and peace abound at Thy behest,
My.	340–28	their implorations for peace and p·

plight

My.	312– 9	* in a miserable p·.

Pliny

My.	150– 5	P· gives the following description of

plot

Ret.	20–26	A p· was consummated for
Pul.	24– 9	* on a triangular p· of ground,
My.	55–11	* Mrs. Eddy gave the p· of ground

pluck

Mis.	151– 4	neither shall any man p· — John 10 : 28.
	213–24	neither shall any man p· — John 10 : 28.
	374–13	p· not their heaven-born wings.
My.	219– 7	I by no means would p· their plumes.

plucked

Ret.	18–13	Oft p· for the banquet,
Hea.	11– 1	p· from the wings of vanity.
Po.	64– 3	Oft p· for the banquet,
My.	139– 4	neither dead nor p· up by the roots,

plucking

My.	340–17	annulling such bills and p· their

plucks

'01.	35–11	Love divine that p· us From the

plumbing

Pul.	76–19	* p· is all heavily plated

plumed

Mis.	267–21	p· for rarefied atmospheres

plumes

Mis.	371–25	error in borrowed p·?
Ret.	11– 5	If fancy p· aerial flight,
Un.	17–17	despoil error of its borrowed p·,
Hea.	11– 1	p· are plucked from the wings
Po.	34– 7	airy wing, and fold thy p·?
	60– 1	If fancy p· aerial flight,
My.	219– 8	I by no means would pluck their p·.
	340–18	and plucking their p· through

plummet

My.	16–29	righteousness to the p· :— Isa. 28 : 17.

plunge

Mis.	327–30	they p· headlong over the
My.	200–27	God spare this p·,

plural

Mis.	191–21	employed in its p· number,
No.	22–19	used in the p· number.
My.	226– 1	not be written . . . in the p· number.

plurality

Pan.	7– 3	Science shows that a p· of minds,

plus

My.	350– 5	and p· human hypothesis,

plush

Pul.	25–22	* upholstered in old rose p·.
	76–10	* hangings of deep green p·,
	77– 5	* in a handsome p· casket
	86–12	* encased in an elegant p· box.

Plymouth Rock

Mis.	176–20	planted their feet on P· R·,
Ret.	11–19	wreaths are twined round P· R·,
Pul.	10–11	shores of solitude, at P· R·,
Po.	60–16	wreaths are twined round P· R·,

P. M.

Mis.	350– 4	secret society known as the P. M.,
	350– 7	The P. M. (Private Meeting) Society met
	350–14	The second P. M. convened in

pneumatic

Pul.	60–20	* p· wind-chests throughout,

pneumonia

'01.	17–16	last stages of consumption, p·,
My.	105–21	pronounced dying of p·,
	107–32	gastritis, hyperæmia, p·,

pocket

Mis.	43–23	fill one's p· at the expense of

pockets

Mis.	274–23	whose consciences are in their p·

poem

Mis.	33– 1	comments on my illustrated p·,
	142–12	beautiful boat and presentation p·.
	142–15	first impression was to indite a p· ;
	309–27	Christmas p· and its illustrations
	313–17	''The Temptation,'' a p· by J. J. Rome,
	371–27	An illustrated P·
	371–28	This p· and its illustrations
	372–16	* ''The illustrations of your p· are
	374–22	the one illustrating my p·
Ret.	20–15	my p·, ''Mother's Darling,''
Pul.	39– 9	p· that I consider superbly sweet
	54– 1	* in a p· entitled ''The Master,''
Po.	v– 5	* each p· being the spontaneous
	v–15	* the p· began to take form
	v–20	* she replied by reading the p·
	vi– 1	* p· finally found its way into print,
	vi– 5	* p· on the ''Dedication of a
	vi–11	* was published with the p·,
My.	189–28	a p· written in 1844,

poems

Man.	59– 8	books or p· of our Pastor Emeritus,
Po.	v– 1	* p· garnered up in this little volume
	vi–23	* many p· written in girlhood
	vi–26	* Among her earliest p·

poems
Po. vii– 6 * *bound volumes of her p·,*
My. 358–16 shall publish your *p·.*

poet (*see also* **poet's**)
Ret. 32–11 Calderon, the famous Spanish *p·,*
My. 40–26 * illustrated what the *p·* perceived

poetic
Mis. 294–27 terse, graphic, and *p·* style
Ret. 2– 4 *p·* daring and pious picturesqueness
Pul. 61–16 * is practical as well as *p·,*
Po. v– 6 * *outpouring of a deeply p· nature*

poetical
Pul. 66–15 * *p·* and highly figurative language.
Pan. 3– 5 *p·* phase of the genii of forests.

poet-patriarch
Un. 15– 4 more just . . . asks the *p·.—Job* 4 : 17.

poetry
Ret. 11– 1 *P·* suited my emotions better
Po. 46–14 Sweet as the *p·* of heaven,

poet's
Ret. 18– 1 Here the *p·* world-wish,
87– 3 *p·* line, "Order is heaven's first
Po. 63– 8 Here the *p·* world-wish,

poets
Mis. 372–10 letters . . . from artists and *p·.*
Ret. 80– 7 *p·* in different languages have
Pul. 28–24 * other recognized devotional *p·,*
53–26 * Whittier, grandest of mystic *p·,*

poignant
Ret. 7–19 * deplored, with the most *p·* grief,
'01. 16– 5 *p·* present sense of sin

point (noun)
achieved the
Mis. 316–25 had my students achieved the *p·*
at issue
Mis. 220–13 over this mind on the *p·* at issue.
cardinal
Mis. 27–10 cardinal *p·* in C. S.,
Un. 9 –27 cardinal *p·* of the difference
No. 25– 4 this cardinal *p·* of divine Science,
'01. 8– 2 I reiterate this cardinal *p·* :
central
Mis. 162–12 central *p·* of his Messianic mission
every
Mis. 46–20 but comprehending at every *p·,*
Hea. 5– 4 His power at every *p·,*
My. 304–22 * "Mrs. Eddy is from every *p·* of view
following
Mis. 216–24 illustrate the author's following *p·*
give
Mis. 268– 3 Two personal queries give *p·* to
incontestable
Un. 7–22 incontestable *p·* in divine Science
of convergence
Pul. 22– 4 one nucleus or *p·* of convergence,
of departure
Pul. 31– 9 * and take, as the *p·* of departure,
of discovery
Mis. 121– 9 up to a *p·* of discovery ;
of its disappearance
Mis. 271– 3 up to the *p·* of its disappearance
of perfection
My. 242– 6 is neither behind the *p·* of perfection
of view
Mis. 241– 1 From a religious *p·* of view,
Pul. 81– 9 * chapter sub-title
My. 69–29 * best *p·* of view is on top of the
304–22 * "Mrs. Eddy is from every *p·* of view
one
Ret. 31–20 and yet offend in one *p·, — Jas.* 2 : 10.
Pul. 81– 9 * chapter sub-title
My. 96–10 * The one *p·* of resemblance is
sharp
Pan. 12–27 bold conjecture's sharp *p·,*
sneering
My. 96–27 * will soon be beyond the sneering *p·.*
speak to the
Pul. 46– 6 * words of the judge speak to the *p·,*
this
Mis. 186– 1 he was not at this *p·* giving the
198– 4 To arrive at this *p·* of unity
274– 3 This *p·,* however, had not impressed
292–29 my instructions on this *p·*
Pul. 37–15 * "On this *p·,* Mrs. Eddy feels
My. 69–31 * From this *p·* the building
241–17 * receive instruction . . . on this *p·.*
242– 7 it is at this *p·* and must be
to point
Pul. 26– 3 * twenty-one inches from *p·* to point,
vital
'01. 16–22 and to carry a most vital *p·.*
My. 146–23 Scientists hold as a vital *p·*

point
Mis. 98– 1 question of personality a *p·,*
Pul. 27–10 * a *p·* that the members

point (verb)
Mis. 92–18 *p·* out the lesson to the class,
117–20 To *p·* out every step to a student
147–16 voice of his conscience *p·* it out
213– 7 *p·* the way, shorten the process,
344–27 *p·* out the way to heaven
357–30 help them and *p·* the way.
389– 4 * *p·* to heaven and lead the way."
Chr. 53– 8 wake the dead, And *p·* the Way
Ret. 85–19 wait for God's finger to *p·* the way.
Pul. 15– 2 *p·* out the evil in human thought,
48–14 * *p·* out her own birthplace.
No. 9–19 *p·* steadfastly to the power of grace
'02. 11– 8 *p·* the path to heaven.
Po. 21–18 * "To *p·* to heaven and lead the way."
My. 114– 8 why *p·* the people to the lives of
186–10 *p·* the path above the valley,
252–20 They *p·* to verdant pastures,
273– 6 * fortunate in being able to *p·* to

pointed
Mis. 341–27 The moral of the parable is *p·,*
Pul. 63–11 * *p·* to a number of large elms
No. 35– 9 He who *p·* the way of Life
'02. 16– 3 *p·* out that identical phrase,
My. 87–12 * unless they are *p·* out.
292– 6 the way *p·* out, the process shortened,

pointing
Mis. xi–12 guide-book, *p·* the path,
204–14 new affections, all *p·* upward.
268– 5 *p·* the way to heaven,
327–23 the Stranger is *p·* the way,
Pul. 49–15 * touching my sleeve and *p·,*
No. 28–11 If Science is *p·* the way,
Peo. 14–10 * white fingers *p·* upward."
My. 124–23 with finger *p·* upward,
153–31 *p·* away from matter and man
162–32 towering top . . . *p·* to the heavens,
176– 8 *p·* the path to heaven
202– 2 *p·* the path from earth to heaven

points
all
Un. 39–28 Science and . . . conflict at all *p·,*
58–16 "in all *p·* tempted like— *Heb.* 4: 15.
'00. 9–17 reformer must be a hero at all *p·,*
My. 181– 2 to settle all *p·* beyond cavil,
cardinal
Mis. 107–14 Three cardinal *p·* must be gained
My. 339– 4 cardinal *p·* of C. S.
chief
Man. 111–14 chief *p·* of these instructions
disputed
Mis. 84– 7 prophets thrust disputed *p·* on
distant
My. 30–13 * come from far distant *p·*
doctrinal
'02. 12– 4 explains these doctrinal *p·,*
essential
Ret. 83–27 That these essential *p·* are ever
good
My. 322–25 * advancing many good *p·*
important
Mis. 92– 1 To omit these important *p·* is
many
My. 266–25 that many *p·* in theology
nine
No. 24–19 exposure is nine *p·* of destruction.
of action
Hea. 13– 1 so weaken both *p·* of action ;
spiritual
Mis. 143– 5 spiritual *p·,* above the plane of
two
Mis. 318–26 Two *p·* of danger beset mankind ;
vital
No. 3– 1 in some vital *p·* lack Science.

Mis. 166– 3 whose finger *p·* upward,
211– 3 Christ *p·* the way of salvation.
254– 2 *p·* with promise of prosperity
313– 6 *p·* to the scientific spiritual
339–16 it *p·* to every mortal mistake ;
356–28 *p·* out the chart of its divine
393–20 *P·* the plane of power to seek.
Ret. 31– 2 and *p·* to heaven.
Pan. 12–20 way-seeker gains and *p·* the path.
'02. 6–23 divine metaphysics *p·* the way,
Peo. 5–18 thought *p·* away from matter
Po. 52– 4 *P·* the plane of power to seek.
My. 99–28 * *p·* out their meaning
104– 6 That epithet *p·* a moral.
140–23 Christ, *p·* the advanced step.
158–12 it *p·* to the new birth,

points
My. 266–14   *p·* unmistakably to the
317–14   *p·* that might seem ambiguous
330–13   * *p·* concerning Major Glover's

point'st
Po. 26–13   Thou *p·* thy phantom finger,

poise
Mis. 263–20   *p·* the wavering balance

poises
Mis. 296–22   * which, "*p·* and poses,

poison
Mis. 248–21   have said that I died of *p·*,
368–15   sending forth a *p·* more deadly
368–21   "the *p·* of asps— *Rom.* 3: 13.
'00. 8– 8   emit . . . a perfume or a *p·*,
My. 126– 6   to *p·* such as drink of the

poisoning
Mis. 248–29   mental malpractice of *p·* people

poisonous
Mis. 69–20   effects of the *p·* oil.
Un. 52–24   beautiful blossom is often *p·*,
'01. 33–19   with *p·* drugs, with the lance,
My. 90–15   * that discord is *p·*,
245–12   *p·* reptiles and devouring beasts,

poisons
Mis. 134–21   with *p·*, nostrums, and knives,
Un. 52–20   lightnings, earthquakes, *p·*,

poked
Mis. 231–18   finger . . . *p·* into the little mouth

polar
Mis. 320–17   *p·* star, fixed in the heavens

Polar Sea
Un. 58–20   sun shines over the *P· S·*.

pole
Mis. 394– 4   An infinite essence from tropic to *p·*,
No. 10–25   turns like the needle to the *p·*
Po. 45– 5   An infinite essence from tropic to *p·*,

poles
My. 74–29   * representatives of the two *p·*

police
'02. 15– 3   neither informed the *p·*
My. 174– 9   marshal and his staff of *p·*

policemen
My. 83–14   * street-car men and *p·*,

policy
Mis. 118– 4   selfish motives, and human *p·*.
204–17   human wisdom, human *p·*,
212– 1   Human *p·* is a fool
212– 4   This godless *p·* never knows
212– 8   reminded . . . of their worldly *p·*.
327–11   worldly *p·*, religion, politics,
Ret. 78–16   adoption of a worldly *p·*
79–16   worldly *p·*, pomp, and pride,
My. 340–20   timid, or dastardly *p·*,

polite
My. 121–24   not only *p·* to all but is

politic
Mis. 266– 5   is neither *p·* nor scientific;

political
Mis. 246– 9   religious caste, civil and *p·* power.
Ret. 6–30   received further *p·* preferment,
7– 4   His noble *p·* antagonist,
My. 276–22   * an expression of her *p·* views,

politician
My. 106–26   nor a dishonest *p·*

politics
Mis. 327–11   religion, *p·*, finance,
Ret. 3– 2   prominent in British *p·*,
My. 266– 6   claims of *p·* and of human power,
276–16   * chapter sub-title
276–23   I am asked, "What are your *p·*?"
291– 9   warming the marble of *p·*
355–12   to religion as well as to *p·*,

Polycarp
Mis. 345– 7   need the spirit of the pious *P·*,
Peo. 13–17   *P·* proved the triumph of mind over

polytheism
Pan. 4– 2   forms of pantheism and *p·*.
8–16   idolatry, pantheism, and *p·*.
8–24   doctrines that embrace pantheism, *p·*,

pomp
Mis. 144–14   without *p·* or pride,
Ret. 79–16   worldly policy, *p·*, and pride,
Pul. 10– 9   her *p·* and power lie low in dust.
Po. 16–11   toil for its *p·* and its pride.
27– 2   *p·* and tinsel of unrighteous power;
My. 134–17   pride— its *p·* and its frown

pond
Mis. 142– 8   little *p·* at Pleasant View.
203   chapter title
203– 2   your gift of the pretty *p·*

ponder
Mis. 159–15   sit silently, and *p·*.
207– 1   *p·* this lesson of love.
Ret. 24–23   to *p·* my mission,
Po. 33–17   I *p·* the days may be few
My. 37–31   * give heed and *p·* and obey.
117–25   Christian Scientists *p·* this fact,
201–16   mercifully forgive, wisely *p·*,

pondered
Mis. 332–16   *p·* the things of man and God.

pondering
Mis. 309–14   *P·* on the finite personality of
379–24   assiduously *p·* the solution of

ponderosity
Mis. 22–30   by reason of its own *p·*;

ponderous
My. 188–20   *p·* walls of your grand cathedral

ponders
Mis. 26– 9   *p·* the history of a seed,

pontiff
My. 294–26   energy of this illustrious *p·*

poor
Mis. 70–20   *p·* thief's prayer for help
106– 4   *p·* parody on Tennyson's grand verse,
107–14   before *p·* humanity is regenerated
137– 8   the privilege, *p·* as it was,
142–24   *P·* return, is it not?
168–10   *p·*— the lowly in Christ,
171–19   to the *p·* the gospel is preached.
227–16   these weak, pitifully *p·* objects
231– 8   but, what of the *p·*!
233–20   a *p·* shift for the weak and worldly
239–19   the *p·* child said,
243–17   a mortal's *p·* performances.
252–31   the *p·* man's money;
322–23   my past *p·* labors and love.
325– 3   "Blessed are the *p·*— *Matt.* 5: 3.
344–14   *p·* sinner struggling with temptation,
359–17   nor Science for *p·* humanity to
366–16   *p·* jaded humanity needs to
388–19   bless the orphan, feed the *p·*;
Ret. 26–26   "*p·* in spirit"— *Matt.* 5: 3.
Rud. 9– 9   and he will be a *p·* practitioner,
No. 35– 2   Without it, how *p·* the precedents of
'01. 2–19   blessing the *p·* in spirit
'02. 15–16   I became *p·* for Christ's sake.
Hea. 7–17   reading the mind of the *p·* woman
12–21   cannot shake the *p·* drug without the
Po. 21– 8   bless the orphan, feed the *p·*;
28–10   Aid our *p·* soul to sing
53–12   *P·* robin's lonely mass.
My. 9–24   I never before felt *p·* in thanks,
132–30   heals the *p·* body,
146–17   and my *p·* prophecy,
153–15   from my *p·* personality.
154–20   *"If the *p·* . . . toil that we have food,
195–21   by which we *p·* mortals expect to
196–27   The *p·* toil for our bread,
215–17   home for the *p·* worthy student,
231– 8   undeserving *p·* to whom she has given
287–11   a *p·* shift for the weak and worldly.
293–19   divine power and *p·* human sense

poorer
Mis. 87–12   mortal mind is a *p·* representative

poorly
Pul. 2–17   in a *p·* barricaded fort,
Pan. 3– 5   *p·* presents the poetical phase of

Pope (*see also* **Pope's**)
Ret. 77– 2   *P·* was right in saying,
My. 269–14   * signature

pope
My. 343–13   * heading
343–14   "I have been called a *p·*,
343–21   term *p·* is used figuratively.
343–30   If that is to be a *p·*,

Pope Leo XIII
My. 294–22   chapter sub-title
294–23   decease of *P· L·* XIII,

Pope's
'01. 30–28   and to adopt *P·* axiom:

poplar
Ret. 4–22   scrub-oak, *p·*, and fern flourish.

popping
Hea. 18–17   keep it from *p·* out

poppy
Ret. 26– 6   a preparation of *p·*, or aconite,

popular

Mis.	228–24	p· current of mortal thought
	239–21	sharing in a p· influenza
	345–21	To turn the p· indignation
Ret.	1– 6	pious and p· English authoress
	15–25	physicians of the p· schools
Un.	13– 3	P· theology makes God tributary
	38–26	p· views to this effect
	44– 7	p· couplet may be so paraphrased
No.	32– 5	*forgiveness,* in the p· sense of
	36–10	p· view of Jesus' nature.
'01.	18–28	destroys the p· triad
	22–18	to accommodate p· opinion as to
	28–25	Jesus, who was not p· among the
	28–26	not p· with them in this age ;
	28–27	he who would be p· if he could,
'02.	14–22	p· philosophies and religions
Hea.	18–17	until it became p·.
Po.	vii– 8	* *to allow a p· edition to be issued,*
My.	302–23	Because C. S. is not yet p·,
	314– 9	He . . . was a p· man,

popularity

Mis.	295–19	for whose ability and p·
	330–25	P·, — what is it?
Ret.	44–12	kept pace with its increasing p· ;
	45–24	withstood less the temptation of p·
	47– 4	unprecedented p· of my College.
Pul.	21–28	P·, self-aggrandizement,
	71– 4	* idea that C. S. has declined in p·
'01.	26–16	shall the word p· be pinned to the
'02.	9– 6	Let the world, p·, pride, and
My.	v– 9	* when p· threatens to supersede
	245–10	the increasing p· of C. S.,

population

Ret.	82–16	The p· of our principal cities
Pul.	56– 5	* nearly every other centre of p·,
My.	87– 5	* temporary increase of the p·
	181–23	Chicago has gained from a p· of

pore

No.	3–17	teacher must p· over it in secret,

portal

Mis.	180– 5	dark shadow and p· of death,
	231–31	looking longingly at the p·
Un.	41–18	opening wide a p· from death

portals

Mis.	196–20	opens wide the p· of salvation
	369–13	p· of the temple of thought,
	391– 5	Will find within its p·
Po.	38– 4	Will find within its p·
My.	92–24	* who entered its p· Sunday.
	94– 8	* who entered its p· Sunday,"

portend

Mis.	2– 6	signs of these times p· a

portending

Peo.	1–10	p· a long night to the traveller ;

portends

Mis.	253–15	p· much for the future.

portent

My.	92–10	* p· worthy of perhaps even more

portentous

My.	273–21	scientific knowledge that is p· ;

porter

Mis.	325–19	p· starts up in blank amazement

porticos

Pul.	24–11	* accented by stone p·

portion

Mis.	22–10	discovery of even a p· of it
	139–16	p· of the above Scripture for its
	160– 7	paramount p· of her being.
	245– 8	materialistic p· of the pulpit
	252–19	to the whole and not to a p· ;
	314– 8	chapter (or p· of the chapter)
	335–10	appoint him his p· — *Matt.* 24 : 51.
Man.	31– 6	devote a suitable p· of their time
Ret.	52– 6	have a small p· of its letter
Rud.	14– 2	giving only a p· of their time
'01.	1–18	p· of the primal reality of things.
My.	8– 1	* any p· of two million dollars
	9– 5	* any p· of two million dollars
	11–30	* "any p· of two million dollars
	20–16	let this suffice for her rich p·
	151– 2	attacks of a p· of Christendom :
	165–16	active p· of one stupendous whole,
	175–20	macadamize a p· of Warren Street
	357– 6	matter has neither part nor p·,

portions

Mis.	374–27	Pictures are p· of one's ideal,
My.	209–12	also whatever p· of truth

Portland

Maine

Mis.	378– 6	Mr. P. P. Quimby of P·, Maine.

Portland

Me.

My.	306–22	Dr. Quimby of P·, Me.,
Mis.	378–11	*en route* for the aforesaid doctor in P·.
My.	304–13	Chicago, Boston, P·,
	306–30	while I was his patient in P·

Portland (**Me.**) *Advertiser*

My.	98–27	*[P· (M·.) A·]*

Portland, Ore.

Pul.	90– 8	* Telegram, P·, O·.

Portland (**Ore.**) *Telegram*

My.	98–13	*[P· (O·.) T·]*

portly

Mis.	239–12	a p· gentleman alight,

portrait

Pul.	58–30	* Therein is a p· of

portraits

My.	342– 8	* p· of twenty years ago,

portraiture

Mis.	309–15	material p· often fails to express
Ret.	22– 5	noumenon and phenomenon silenced p·.

portray

Mis.	275–21	Pen can never p· the satisfaction
No.	39–26	to p· the face of pleasant thought.
'00.	14– 6	He goes on to p· seven churches,

portrayed

Mis.	164–24	p· him as the only Son of God,
	368–20	p· in these words of the apostle,
	376– 6	* p· by the oldest of the

portrays

Ret.	72– 7	p· the result of secret faults,
My.	206–16	fact that p· Life, Truth, Love.

Portsmouth

My.	281–23	* two parties to the treaty of P·,
	281–29	treaty of P· is not an executive

poses

Mis.	296–22	* "poises and p·, higgles and wriggles"

position

Mis.	146–14	and still maintain this p·.
Man.	71–12	a p· that no other church can fill.
	71–14	such p· would be disastrous
Ret.	3– 2	p· of ambassador to Persia.
	85–16	Seek to occupy no p· whereto
Un.	31–16	Hence my conscientious p·,
Pul.	3–10	If you maintain this p·,
No.	10–19	former p·, that sense is organic
'01.	13– 9	It is not well to maintain the p·
My.	22–25	* p· taken by our Pastor Emeritus
	92– 2	* its real p· in the doctrines of
	120– 9	Forgive, ... my honest p·.
	206– 3	power and pride of p·,
	312–14	* Her p· was an embarrassing one.
	321– 8	* also your p· as regards your
	321–10	* he always gave you that p·
	343–22	"A p· of authority," she went on,

positions

My.	181– 7	and outgrown, proofless p·.
	255– 8	filling their p· satisfactorily

positive

Mis.	44– 8	power of C. S. is p·,
	62–10	p· and negative quantities,
	62–11	offsets an equal p· quantity,
	62–12	making the aggregate p·, . . . less
	65–12	which the p· Truth destroys ;
	153–20	by p· proof of trustworthiness.
	172– 4	let us declare the p·
	288– 6	P· and imperative thoughts
Un.	10–24	principle of p· mathematics.
Pul.	4–10	scientific, p· sense of unity
'01.	33–24	richest and most p· proof
My.	91– 2	* proof p· that it supplies these
	166–13	p· proof of your remembrance

positives

No.	16–11	p· that cannot be gainsaid.

possess

Mis.	40–20	does not in every case p·
	40–22	p· the spirit of Truth and Love,
	145– 9	when that person shall p· these,
	149– 6	what they p· of love and light
	201–14	somethingness of the good we p·,
	268–31	we must p· the sense of Truth ;
	284– 8	may p· a zeal without knowledge,
	371–14	to p· more and more of Truth
Pul.	3– 7	you p· sovereign power to
No.	3–20	which they must p·, in order to
	7–11	to see every error they p·,
'02.	8–18	except we p· this inspiration,
Hea.	4–11	We ask infinite wisdom to p·
Peo.	10–21	We p· our own body,

possess

My.	12–20	we *p·* only *now.*
	44– 5	* going up to *p·* the promised land
	164–17	not only *p·* a sound faith, but
	292–25	supposed to *p·* opposite qualities

possessed

Man.	92–23	*p·* of the qualifications named
Ret.	5–14	My father *p·* a strong intellect
	5–22	* She *p·* a strong intellect,
Un.	2–23	Love beyond what they *p·* before ;
No.	30–17	if He *p·* any knowledge of them.
Pan.	5– 9	*p·* of the nature of God,
'01.	9–14	and Christ Jesus *p·* it,
My.	181–13	*p·* the motive of true religion,
	293–21	Had prayer so fervently offered *p·* no

possesses

Mis.	55– 6	when the student *p·* as much of the
	184–15	power to be perfect which he *p·*,
	195– 6	but *p·* not its spirit,
No.	23–24	amount of good or evil he *p·*.
Pan.	4– 4	*p·* all wisdom, goodness, and
'01.	5– 8	each of these *p·* the nature of all,
My.	127–10	C. S. *p·* more of Christ's teachings
	164–17	but that faith also *p·* them.

possessing

Mis.	252–10	*p·* the nature of dreams.
	337–23	personalities *p·* these defacing
No.	3–27	*p·* the essentials of C. S.,

possession

Mis.	373–23	it has rich *p·* here,
Pul.	79–19	* that had taken *p·* of men's minds,
'01.	13–10	can take *p·* of us and
	13–11	take *p·* of sin with such a sense of
My.	43– 2	* in *p·* of the promised land.
	192– 4	unto the *p·* of unburdened bliss.
	273–28	in *p·* of the five personal senses,
	305–10	manuscripts and letters in my *p·*,
	315– 1	original of which is in my *p·*,
	329–13	* has in her *p·* photographed copies
	333– 2	* now in the *p·* of the chairman

possessions

Mis.	119–30	that others should . . . steal your *p·*,

possessor

Mis.	12– 4	brings suffering . . . to its *p·*,
Pan.	9–24	and rewards its *p·* ;
'02.	16– 8	happy *p·* of a copy of Wyclif,
My.	203–17	malady which kills its *p·* ;
	203–18	precursor that its *p·* is mortal

possibilities

Mis.	30– 7	all the *p·* of Christianity?
	44–12	demonstrate its highest *p·*.
	47–14	*p·* of mind when let loose
	55– 5	prove all its *p·*.
	60–20	Mind's *p·* are not lessened by
	187– 6	proper sense of the *p·* of Spirit.
	235–12	loftier desires and new *p·*.
	251–19	the present *p·* of mankind.
	330–12	man's *p·* are infinite,
Ret.	32– 3	*p·* of spiritual insight,
	57– 3	unfathomable sea of *p·*.
Un.	11–25	fitness for perfection and its *p·*.
Pul.	30–22	* *p·* of the divine Life.
	81–20	* She is as full of beautiful *p·* as
'01.	1–24	practical *p·* of divine Love.
My.	177–14	the *p·* and permanence of Life.
	287–20	lofty desires, new *p·*,

possibility

Mis.	41– 8	destroys their own *p·* of progressing.
	54–27	*does it not suggest the p·*
	60–12	*deny the p· of communion with*
	102–10	His infinity precludes the *p·* of
	182–24	but the *p·* of all finding
	214–28	*p·* of destroying the tares :
Un.	43– 8	mortals now believe in the *p·*
	50– 1	the *p·* of its defilement ;
Pul.	38–21	* no *p·* of communication.
	45–14	* transcended human *p·*.
My.	238–20	no *p·* of misinterpretation.

possible

Mis.	46–16	It is *p·*, and it is man's duty,
	48–18	*p·* purpose to which it can be
	50–12	as can be *p·*, under the
	64–25	*Is it p· to know why we are*
	64–27	*p·* to know wherefore man
	66– 7	No *p·* injustice lurks in this
	67–30	believe in this removal being *p·*
	75– 4	man's *p·* earthly development.
	78–15	deceive, if *p·*, the very elect.
	157–11	furnish all information *p·*.
	175–20	if it were *p·*, — *Matt.* 24 : 24.
	183–13	whatever is *p·* to God,
	183–13	*p·* to man *as God's reflection.*
	191–18	By no *p·* interpretation can this

possible

Mis.	191–29	could only be *p·* as evil beliefs,
	229–26	any other *p·* sanative method ;
	247–11	the highest *p·* ethics.
	255– 7	it is *p·*, and dutiful,
	286–17	yet this is *p·* in *Science,*
	291–17	*p·* perversion of C. S.
	292–22	leading them, if *p·*, to Christ,
	294–20	transform them, — if it be *p·*,
	302–28	intended to forestall the *p·* evil of
	305–15	* largest number of persons *p·*
	305–27	* in pennies, if *p·*,
	310– 2	neither the intent of my works nor *p·*
	344– 6	do you think it *p·* for you to
Man.	44– 6	*p·* loss, for a time, of C. S.
	50– 2	When it is *p·* the body
	77–24	any *p·* future deviation from duty,
Ret.	52– 4	if *p·*, to build a hedge round about
Un.	15–17	if the thought of sin could be *p·* in
	18–27	If such knowledge of evil were *p·*
Pul.	85– 4	* made its erection *p·*.
	85–17	* who believe it to be *p·* to
Rud.	15–15	to fill in the best *p·* manner
No.	2–14	if this is *p·*.
Pan.	12– 1	it will be found *p·* to fulfil it.
'01.	5– 1	has no *p·* conception of ours,
'02.	14–11	The only genuine success *p·*
My.	vi– 3	* not *p·* to state . . . in a simpler
	20–28	be completed as early as *p·*,
	62–29	* to assist us in every way *p·* ;
	63–16	* scarcely *p·* to repress a feeling of
	126– 6	and if *p·*, to poison such as drink
	161–25	Sickness is *p·* because one's
	180–15	to whom all things are *p·* ;
	243–17	give all *p·* time and attention to
	265– 1	more *p·* and pleasurable.
	293– 1	all things are *p·* to God
	349– 3	to whom all things are *p·*.
	353– 1	and as many others as *p·*,
	356–27	only *p·* correct version of C. S.

possibly

Mis.	80– 8	and *p·* to aid individual rights
	111– 8	*p·* blamed others more than
Man.	41–17	discipline and, *p·*, dismissal
Un.	22– 4	in which no evil can *p·* dwell.
Pul.	3– 2	how can our godly temple *p·* be
My.	60– 6	* *p·* you may remember the words
	93–18	* *p·* too prone to approach it

Post

Pul.	72– 4	* a *P·* reporter called upon
	88–19	* *P·*, Boston, Mass.
	88–20	* *P·*, Hartford, Conn.
	89– 7	* *P·*, Pittsburgh, Pa.
	89–19	* *P·*, Washington, D. C.

Post, The

Pul.	71– 9	* *The P·*, Syracuse, New York,

post

Mis.	116–27	Never absent from your *p·*,
	154–26	never desert the *p·* of spiritual
	210– 8	*p·* around it placards warning people
Ret.	70–29	*p·* of duty, unpierced by vanity,
	85–17	Never forsake your *p·* without due
My.	11– 5	* constantly at her *p·* during all the
	69–17	* not a single pillar or *p·* anywhere
	192–25	pin me to my *p·*.
	221–27	like a watchman forsaking his *p·*,

postal

'02.	11–13	If a *p·* service, a steam engine,

posterity

Mis.	93– 3	so teach that *p·* shall
	364– 9	and *p·* your familiar !
Ret.	61–26	*P·* will have the right to demand
	84–22	*p·* will call him blessed,

posterns

Mis.	383–13	down the dim *p·* of time unharmed,

Post-Intelligencer

Pul.	90– 3	* *P·*, Seattle, Wash.

postlude

Man.	62– 1	six or seven minutes for the *p·*,

post mortem

Rud.	16–27	or else *p· m·* evidence.

post-mortem

My.	310–20	by physician or *p·* examination

post-office

My.	73–23	* There is here also a *p·*

postpone

My.	41–25	* Why should any one *p·*

postponed

My.	54–19	* Sunday services were *p·*.
	61– 9	* communion would likely be *p·*

postulate
Mis.	13–25	This *p·* of divine Science only needs to
	57–13	the *p·* of error must
	364–11	not a *p·* of the divine Principle,
Rud.	6–22	predicate and *p·* of Mind-healing ;
No.	10–10	predicate and *p·* of all that I teach,
'01.	21–21	neither the predicate nor *p·* of Truth,
My.	224–17	C. S. is the predicate and *p·*,

potatoes
Mis. 340–15 raised *p·* instead of pleas,

potato-patch
Mis. 26– 7 from the rolling of . . . to a *p·*.

potence
'02, 7–12 words *p·*, *presence, science.*

potency
Mis.	222–31	ways, means, and *p·* of Truth
	252– 5	gains no *p·* by attenuation,
	260–10	his only instrumentality and *p·*,
Ret.	31–30	the healing promise and *p·*
	89– 2	divine *p·* of this spiritual mode
Pul.	53–23	* proclaimed its *p·* from the hilltops
'02.	3–27	right is the only real *p·* ;
Hea.	11–23	as matter went out and . . . was its *p·*.

potent
Mis.	4– 3	is the most *p·* and desirable
	126–20	No reproof is so *p·* as the silent
	252–11	Good thoughts are *p·* ;
Un.	54–16	most *p·* and deadly enemy.
Pul.	23–17	* as one of the most *p·* factors
	35–25	* the more *p·* was its effects.
No.	39– 3	an honest and *p·* prayer
'01.	24–13	Making matter more *p·* than
Peo.	9–28	more *p·* evidences in C. S.
My.	108– 8	*p·* in proportion as it is seen to act

potential
Mis.	331–26	supreme *p·* Principle reigns
	379–14	not as *p·* or remedial,

potentially
My. 349– 2 is first *p·*, and is the healer

potion
Mis. 239–16 and what may the *p·* be?"

potions
Mis. 268–22 are *p·* of His own qualities.

potted
Pul. 42–25 * *p·* palms and ferns

Potter, Mrs. Judge
My.	311–21	Mrs. Judge *P·*, presented me my
	311–26	Mrs. Judge *P·* and myself knelt

Potter Hall
My.	80–14	* held in . . . *P. H·*,
	80–23	* Jordan Hall, *P. H·*,

pounding
Mis. 316–22 *p·* wisdom and love into

pounds
Mis.	47– 2	*weigh over two hundred p·*
Ret.	40–18	babe . . . weighed twelve *p·*.

pour
Mis.	43–10	least likely to *p·* into other minds
	134–13	God will *p·* you out a blessing
	139– 5	God will *p·* you out a blessing
	339–28	*p·* forth the unavailing tear.
	353–15	to *p·* a bucket of water
Man.	58–21	*p·* into the ears of listeners
Un.	7–18	*p·* into my waiting thought
Pul.	83–21	* *p·* incense upon the rose.
No.	40–10	and *p·* forth a hypocrite's prayer ;
Po.	22–16	probe the wound, then *p·* the balm
My.	14– 3	God will *p·* them out a blessing
	36–18	* *p·* out our gratitude to God
	114–21	would *p·* in upon my spiritual sense
	126– 3	*p·* wormwood into the waters
	131–27	*p·* you out a blessing, — *Mal.* 3 : 10.
	132– 4	*p·* you out a blessing," — *Mal.* 3 : 10.
	269–27	*p·* you out a blessing, — *Mal.* 3 : 10.

poured
Mis.	110– 2	*p·* on our Master's feet,
	140–16	generously *p·* into the treasury.
	144–28	*p·* into the cup of Christ.
	396–12	Are *p·* in strains so sweet,
Po.	31–19	*P·* on the sense which deems no
	59– 4	Are *p·* in strains so sweet,
	78–10	Tears of the bleeding slave *p·* on
My.	75– 8	* They *p·* into the city
	81–18	* *p·* out their debts of gratitude
	211–24	lies, *p·* constantly into his mind,

pouring
Mis.	172– 9	clans *p·* in their fire upon us ;
	372–10	letters extolling it were *p·* in
	392– 8	from thy lofty summit, *p·* down
Po.	20–11	from thy lofty summit, *p·* down

pouring
My.	77–13	* pilgrims are *p·* into Boston,
	86– 9	* have been *p·* into Boston
	269–23	*p·* out blessing for cursing,

pours
No. 44–19 *p·* the healing balm of Truth

poverty
Mis.	281–20	our *p·* and helplessness without this
	296–28	incited thereto by their own *p·*
'00.	8–13	takes it off for his *p·* to appear.

poverty-stricken
Ret.	86–10	this *p·* "stranger — *Deut.* 5 : 14.
My.	100– 6	* property of no *p·* sect.

powder
Mis. 242–21 and taking morphine *p·*

power
accumulation of
Ret. 82–20 an accumulation of *p·* on his side
activity and
Mis. 250–21 goodness without activity and *p·*.
actual
Mis. 103–23 hides the actual *p·*, presence, and
all
Mis.	13–30	omnipotence, has all *p·* ;
	14–30	deprives evil of all *p·*,
	31–16	God, good, has *all p·* ;
	97–18	omnipotence has all *p·*.
	155– 4	All *p·* and happiness are spiritual,
	184–21	learns that all *p·* is good
	331–24	filling all space and having all *p·*,
	333–14	good, is supreme, *all p·*
	373–26	"All *p·* is given unto — *Matt.* 28 : 18.
No.	42–11	All *p·* belongs to God ;
My.	278–29	The Principle of all *p·* is God,
	294– 5	basis that God has all *p·*,
and glory
Mis.	92–28	*p·* and glory of the Scriptures,
Ret.	84–16	*p·* and glory of the Scriptures,
No.	18– 5	all presence, *p·*, and glory.
and good
Mis. 284– 7 field of limitless *p·* and good
and goodness
No. 13– 1 reflection of His *p·* and goodness.
and love
Un. 2– 8 God's presence, *p·*, and love,
and peace
Mis. 263–13 His presence, *p·*, and peace
and perfection
Mis.	189–18	the *p·* and perfection of a
Ret.	27–27	increases in *p·* and perfection
and permanence
Mis.	74–27	the *p·* and permanence of Spirit.
	160– 1	*p·* and permanence of affection
and prerogative
My.	179– 7	*p·* and prerogative of Spirit
	218– 9	*p·* and prerogative of Truth
and presence
Mis.	77–13	*p·* and presence, in divine Science,
	173–22	not met by another *p·* and presence,
	333–14	is supreme, *all p·* and presence,
and pride
My. 206– 3 with *p·* and pride of position,
and purpose
Pul.	10– 5	God's *p·* and purpose to supply them.
My.	293– 3	*p·* and purpose of infinite Mind,
and spell
Mis.	392–11	thou art a *p·* and spell ;
Po.	20–15	thou art a *p·* and spell ;
and Truth
Mis. 334– 8 Whatever simulates *p·* and Truth
another
Un. 38–13 must enthrone another *p·*,
any
Mis.	170–29	eyes as having any *p·* to see.
Pul.	72–22	* that Mrs. Eddy had any *p·* other than
any more
Mis. 58– 3 *have any more p· over him?*
any other
Peo. 9–24 remove all evidence of any other *p·*
armed with
My. 277–23 armed with *p·* girt for the hour.
assumed
Un. 45–12 An evil ego, and his assumed *p·*,
attributed
Mis. 48– 3 If mesmerism has the *p·* attributed
attributes and
Mis. 23–27 manifests all His attributes and *p·*,
authority and
Mis. 333–25 believed that . . . had authority and *p·*,
belief in the
Mis. 58– 8 belief in the *p·* of disease
Christ's
My. 257–21 should bow and declare Christ's *p·*,

power

circumstance or
Mis. 155– 3   pride of circumstance or *p·*
claimed the
Mis. 60–26   Evil in the beginning claimed the *p·*,
claim to
Mis. 31–11   Its claim to *p·* is in proportion to
confers a
Un. 7–21   confers a *p·* nothing else can.
deific
Un. 17– 5   Be allied to the deific *p·*,
destroy the
Mis. 97– 1   to destroy the *p·* of the flesh ;
divine
(*see* **divine**)
effect of
Mis. 334–10   may have the effect of *p·* ;
electric
Pul. 25– 5   * with motor electric *p·*.
embodiment or
Pan. 5–21   that it hath embodiment or *p·* ;
energy and
Pul. 37– 8   * retains . . . her energy and *p·* ;
ever-present
My. 294–14   ever-present *p·* of divine Spirit
evil
Mis. 103– 2   which say that sin is an evil *p·*,
executive
My. 281–29   is not an executive *p·*,
faculty or
Hea. 9–19   not a faculty or *p·* underived from
fame and
Mis. 145– 8   burn for fame and *p·*?
fatal
Mis. 72–10   supposed to impart . . . this fatal *p·*.
foot of
Ret. 11–11   knowledge plants the foot of *p·*
Po. 60– 8   knowledge plants the foot of *p·*
gives it
Pan. 6–27   altitude of mind gives it *p·*,
gives man
'02. 9– 1   God as Love gives man *p·*
giveth
Mis. 167–28   He giveth *p·*, peace,
God-endued with
My. 190–26   thus become God-endued with *p·*
God's
Mis. 52– 3   to support God's *p·* to heal
52– 8   has no doubt of God's *p·*,
194–24   *how* to accept God's *p·*
Un. 26–17   true that God's *p·* never *waneth*,
Pul. 10– 5   God's *p·* and purpose to supply them.
No. 29–16   a denial of God's *p·*?
42– 3   * manifestations of God's *p·* increase
My. 248–21   only as uplifted by God's *p·*,
goodness and
No. 39–22   of His goodness and *p·*.
Pan. 4– 5   possesses all wisdom, goodness, and *p·*,
greater
'01. 2– 4   to the acquiring of greater *p·*
healing
Mis. 5–13   healing *p·* is Truth and Love,
258–10   he demonstrated the healing *p·*
373–16   and his healing *p·*,
Pul. 22–19   healing *p·* of Christ will prevail.
Rud. 9–19   weighs against his healing *p·* ;
No. 42–13   to dispossess the . . . of healing *p·*,
46– 4   Christianity, with its healing *p·*,
'01. 9–13   it is the healing *p·* of Truth
'02. 9–23   its divine origin, and healing *p·*,
Peo. 12–24   and give the healing *p·* to matter
My. 81– 8   * healing *p·* of the faith,
her
Ret. 11–18   The cradle of her *p·*,
Po. 60–15   The cradle of her *p·*,
My. 90–28   * and the sources of her *p·*
His
Mis. 183–27   have power to reflect His *p·*,
Chr. 53–51   same hand unfolds His *p·*,
Ret. 54– 8   humanized conception of His *p·*,
Rud. 10– 7   divides His *p·* with nothing evil
No. 13– 1   reflection of His *p·* and goodness.
'02. 10–27   God and His *p·* in man.
Hea. 5– 3   we shall be limiting His *p·*
My. 36–31   * God, through His *p·* and law,
his
Mis. 31–19   destroy his *p·* to be or to do good,
64– 4   to show his *p·* over death ;
85–10   his *p·* is temporarily limited.
162–15   prove his *p·*, derived from Spirit,
162–27   would have dethroned his *p·*
184–16   he would . . . lose his *p·* ;
197–19   his *p·* to heal and to save,
221– 3   may lose his *p·* to harm
270– 9   demonstrated his *p·* over sin,
270–24   the only passport to his *p·* ;

power

his
Ret. 91–21   His *p·* over others was spiritual,
92– 2   nor was his *p·* so exalted as to
Pul. 54–16   * in the plenitude of his *p·*
'01. 20–17   if the individual knew . . . his *p·*
23–21   demonstrated his *p·* over matter,
human
Mis. 138–19   giving to human *p·*, peace.
My. 219– 8   Human *p·* is most properly
266– 6   claims of politics and of human *p·*,
humane
My. 291·21   emphasize humane *p·*,
immortal
Po. 31–17   splendor of immortal *p·*,
increased
Mis. 262– 3   increased *p·* to be good
No. 8–27   in equanimity, and with increased *p·*,
in criticism
Mis. 216–16   he is a *p·* in criticism,
infinite
Un. 13–14   His infinite *p·* would straightway
My. 160– 7   to individualize infinite *p·* ;
infusion of
Un. 42–22   infusion of *p·* into matter.
intelligence nor
Mis. 355–19   error, neither intelligence nor *p·*,
intelligence or
Mis. 260–20   seemeth to be intelligence or *p·*
in this world
Pul. 53–17   * human felicity and *p·* in this world,
is good
Mis. 101–23   this *p·* is good, not evil ;
184–21   learns that all *p·* is good
its
Mis. 4– 9   its *p·* to do good, not evil.
40– 3   its *p·* would be arrested if one
40–21   Christ-spirit and its *p·*
45– 7   its *p·* to allay fear,
48– 8   If such be its *p·*, I am opposed
55– 8   utilizes its *p·* to overcome sin.
90– 4   all reality from its *p·*.
111–19   prove its *p·* to be immortal.
Ret. 14– 2   forever lost its *p·* over me.
88–15   its *p·* to demonstrate immortality.
88–30   and its *p·* is displayed
Pul. 44–20   * C. S. has shown its *p·*
No. 33– 1   slander loses its *p·* to harm ;
33–21   Love and its *p·* over death.
'00. 6– 3   in proving its *p·* and divinity.
'02. 8–19   its *p·* to heal and to save.
Hea. 13–14   so-called drug loses its *p·*.
joy and
Mis. 331–18   peace and joy and *p·* ;
389– 6   peace and joy and *p·* ;
Po. 4– 2   peace and joy and *p·* ;
knowledge, and
No. 37–17   presence, knowledge, and *p·*,
latent
Mis. 201–24   tested and developed latent *p·*.
law, and
Mis. 364–17   individuality, law, and *p·*.
learned the
Mis. 41– 3   having learned the *p·* of liberated
55–11   having learned the *p·* of the
legal
Mis. 140–22   rescued from the grasp of legal *p·*,
Life and
Mis. 70–16   spiritual sense of Life and *p·*.
little
My. 238–12   has imparted little *p·* to practise
lose
Mis. 354–30   nor his pinions lose *p·*
Po. 18– 8   or pinion lose *p·*
lost the
My. 165–27   lost the *p·* of being magnanimous.
manifests
Mis. 23– 4   intelligence that manifests *p·*?
man's
Mis. 70– 2   else the Scriptures misstate man's *p·*.
My. 134–19   bless, and inspire man's *p·*.
material
Un. 35–14   says gravitation is a material *p·*,
matter or
Un. 35–15   Which was first, matter or *p·*?
mental
Mis. 115–31   Using mental *p·* in the right direction
methods and
Mis. 222–30   the methods and *p·* of error.
moral
Mis. 259–16   freedom was the moral *p·* of good,
Rud. 17– 6   its moral *p·*, and its divine efficacy
more
Mis. 232–19   will be one having more *p·*,
muscular
Pul. 62–13   * require but little muscular *p·*

power

my
Mis. 70– 4   exercised my p· over the fish,
Ret. 21– 5   Every means within my p·

no
Mis. 2–26   second death hath no p·'' — *Rev.* 20 : 6.
36–30   and no p· besides God, good.
46–16   has no p· underived from
58– 5   then it has no p· over one.
93–15   This being true, sin has no p· ;
157–26   Error has no p· but to destroy itself.
198–19   has no p· to govern itself ;
221– 1   it has no p· over him.
Un. 3– 9   second death, . . . hath no p·,
41–14   the second death has no p·.
Pul. 73–14   * She of herself had no p·.
73–22   * man of himself has no p·,
My. 296–14   Evil has no p· to harm,

no more
Mis. 174– 1   no more p· to evolve or to create

no other
Mis. 101–27   no other p·, law, or intelligence

nor existence
Mis. 115–20   neither prestige, p·, nor existence,

no underived
Mis. 255– 6   and has no underived p·.
Un. 39–14   Man has no underived p·.

of absolute Truth
My. 293–16   the p· of absolute Truth

of a drug
Mis. 194– 2   equals even the p· of a drug

of any doctrine
Mis. 46– 8   beyond the p· of any doctrine

of being
Pul. 4–25   cometh the full p· of being.

of Christ
Mis. 225–11   testimony to the p· of Christ,
Ret. 65–22   demonstrates the p· of Christ
Pul. 22–19   healing p· of Christ will prevail.
72–24   * p· of Christ has been dormant in
No. 11–18   through the p· of Christ.

of Christianity
Mis. 193–26   the spirit and p· of Christianity.
193–29   p· of Christianity to heal ;
No. 44– 7   p· of Christianity to heal.
My. 239– 9   redemptive p· of Christianity

of Christian Science
Mis. 44– 8   remedial p· of C. S.
54–12   p· of C. S. over all
Ret. 86– 3   spirit and p· of C. S.,

of civilization
My. 278–20   elevating p· of civilization

of darkness
My. 206–29   the p· of darkness, — *Col.* 1 : 13.

of divine Life
Peo. 14–17   p· of divine Life and Love

of divine Love
'00. 5–28   utilize the p· of divine Love
My. 293–24   p· of divine Love to overrule

of divine Mind
Pul. 58– 2   * healed by the p· of divine Mind,
My. 61– 5   * learned of the p· of divine Mind

of eloquence
Hea. 2–24   knew it was not in the p· of eloquence

of faith
Pul. 80–22   * believe in God and the p· of faith,

of God
Mis. 17–14   p· of God to heal and to save.
168–22   p· of God.'' — *Matt.* 22 : 29.
184–24   p· of God as the seal of man's
194– 1   believe that the p· of God equals
196–19   ever-presence and p· of God, good.
219– 7   p· of God.'' — *Matt.* 22 : 29.
222–27   for this is the p· of God,
229–22   faith in the p· of God to heal
259–28   Truth is the p· of God
Pul. 81– 6   * set forth as the p· of God
No. 37– 5   p· of God.'' — *Matt.* 22 : 29.
'01. 19– 7   p· of God to heal and to save.
My. 153–19   ignores the p· of God,
293–23   contingent on the p· of God,

of good
Mis. 259–16   freedom was the moral p· of good,
Un. 41–17   presence and p· of good,
Pul. 15– 1   p· of good resident in divine Mind,

of grace
No. 9–19   point steadfastly to the p· of grace

of Him
Un. 39–18   reflect, . . . the p· of Him

of His Christ
Pul. 12– 7   p· of His Christ :— *Rev.* 12 : 10.

of his teachings
Un. 43–21   with the p· of his teachings,

of infinite Truth
Hea. 4– 6   the p· of infinite Truth.

power

of Jesus' name
Pul. 41–27   * "All hail the p· of Jesus' name,"
81– 2   * "All hail the p· of Jesus' name,"

of justice
My. 191– 5   has not a tithe of the p· of justice.

of language
My. 332– 2   * p· of language would be but beggared

of Love
No. 9–21   and show the p· of Love.

of metaphysics
Mis. 6–12   p· of metaphysics over physics ;
7–28   nature and p· of metaphysics,

of Mind
Mis. 60–12   *Does it not limit the p· of Mind*
60–15   Does it limit the p· of Mind to **say**
Hea. 7– 6   the p· of Mind over matter.

of mind
Hea. 15– 8   the p· of mind over matter,
19– 2   p· of mind over body ;
My. 97– 2   * admit the p· of mind over **matter.**

of passion
Mis. 298–10   ignorance and p· of passion,

of prayer
My. 292–12   chapter-sub-title

of Spirit
Mis. 5–18   armed with the p· of Spirit,
52– 7   understands the p· of Spirit,
185– 4   The will of God, or p· of Spirit,
188–23   explanation of the p· of Spirit
201–32   the divine p· of Spirit,
258– 6   righteous scorn and p· of Spirit.
Un. 30–21   I discovered the p· of Spirit to
'01. 25–22   he taught the p· of Spirit,

of the human soul
Pul. 53–21   * It constitutes the p· of the human **soul.**

of the pen
'00. 12– 1   beyond the p· of the pen.

of the Word
Mis. 398–23   Felt ye the p· of the Word?
Po. 75– 3   Felt ye the p· of the Word?

of thought
Hea. 12–18   the concentrated p· of thought

of Truth
Mis. 2– 1   whereby we discern the p· of Truth
3– 8   in our lives the p· of Truth
40–17   p· of Truth to destroy error,
99–29   p· of Truth, . . . casting out evils
183– 6   p· of Truth must be seen and felt
184–20   he has denied the p· of Truth,
220–32   belief has not the p· of Truth,
293–13   p· of Truth against the opposite
333–29   exemplify the p· of Truth and Love.
360–10   transforming p· of Truth ;
Pul. vii–21   absolute p· of Truth
30–20   * affirms the p· of Truth over **error,**
70–23   * p· of Truth over all error, sin,
No. 43– 3   p· of Truth is not contingent on
'01. 9–13   p· of Truth that is persecuted
Hea. 7– 2   manifestations of the p· of Truth
My. 114–23   divine p· of Truth and Love,
122–31   p· of Truth in healing.
153– 5   the p· of Truth and Love
154– 2   p· of Truth over error.
268–13   p· of Truth uplifting the motives **of**

of words
Pul. 26– 7   * beyond the p· of words to depict.

omniscient
Chr. 53–47   The great I Am, — Omniscient p·,

one
Mis. 101–23   demonstrates but one p·,
Po. 22–13   one race, one realm, one p·.

only
Mis. 3– 6   imparting the only p· to heal
4– 9   Its only p· to heal is
No. 20–22   the only p·, presence, and glory.

opposed to God
Mis. 49–27   presupposes . . . p· opposed to God,
Pul. 13– 5   belief in a p· opposed to God.

or good
Mis. 335–31   seeking p· or good aside from God,

or intelligence
Mis. 197–24   another p· or intelligence

over death
Mis. 64– 4   to show his p· over death ;
No. 33–21   Love and its p· over death.

over matter
'01. 23–21   demonstrated his p· over matter,
'02. 10– 4   p· over matter, molecule, space,

over sin
Mis. 40–23   must gain the p· over sin
270– 9   demonstrated his p· over sin,

over the nations
Chr. 57– 3   p· over the nations :— *Rev.* 2 : 26.
My. 285–19   p· over the nations." — *Rev.* 2 : 26.

power

pain, or
  No. 32– 8 its pleasure, pain, or *p*·
panoply of
  Mis. 374– 3 Although clad in panoply of *p*·,
peace and
  Mis. 124–19 is filled with peace, and *p*· ;
  205– 1 peace and *p*· outside of itself.
peace not
  My. 341–15 * "'Tis peace not *p*· I seek,
person, and
  No. 24– 2 evil loses all place, person, and *p*·.
pitiless
  Mis. 257–28 This pitiless *p*· smites with disease
place and
  Mis. 274–27 exchange for money, place, and *p*·,
  351–15 aspirants for place and *p*·.
  My. 353–26 the spiritual have all place and *p*·
place nor
  Mis. 14– 2 neither place nor *p*· left for evil.
place or
  My. 4–24 pride of place or *p*· is the prince of
political
  Mis. 246– 9 civil and political *p*·.
pomp and
  Pul. 10– 9 her pomp and *p*· lie low
presence and
    (*see* **presence**)
presence or
  My. 262–20 deific presence or *p*·.
prestige and
  No. 41–23 sin is losing prestige and *p*·.
pride and
  My. 5–12 mortal pride and *p*·, prestige or
pride and of
  Mis. 394– 7 fetters of pride and of *p*· ;
  Po. 45– 9 fetters of pride and of *p*· ;
pride of
  My. 205–25 of the flesh and the pride of *p*·.
pride, or
  My. 252–28 allurements of wealth, pride, or *p*· ;
pristine
  My. 40–17 * its pristine *p*· to bring health
process and
  Mis. 220–24 mental process and *p*· be reversed,
reality and
  Mis. 252– 9 Right thoughts are reality and *p*· ;
  364–30 or give reality and *p*· to evil
  Pan. 7–23 reality and *p*·, intelligence and
redemptive
  Mis. 107– 5 Its redemptive *p*· is seen in
  My. 239– 9 redemptive *p*· of Christianity
regenerating
  '01. 9– 5 only generating or regenerating *p*·.
remains
  Hea. 12–25 drug disappears . . . the *p*· remains,
remedial
  Mis. 44– 8 remedial *p*· of C. S.
right and
  Mis. 193–29 the right and *p*· of Christianity
salutary
  Ret. 54–23 most sacred and salutary *p*·
same
  Mis. 130–12 has the same *p*· to make you a
  295– 6 same *p*· which in America
  364–26 If . . . good has the same *p*· or modes
saving
  Mis. 374– 1 Its healing and saving *p*·
seeming
  Mis. 298–22 delivers you from the seeming *p*· of
sense of
  Mis. 184–23 destroys his self-deceived sense of *p*·
  Ret. 58– 8 sense of *p*· that subdued matter
sequel of
  Po. 16– 9 sequel of *p*·, of glory, or gold ;
show of
  Pul. 55– 3 * Not for show of *p*·,
so-called
  Mis. 48– 6 its so-called *p*· is despotic,
  My. 293– 4 so-called *p*· of matter,
sovereign
  Pul. 3– 8 sovereign *p*· to think and act rightly,
spirit and
  Mis. 193–26 spirit and *p*· of Christianity.
  Ret. 86– 3 rejoice in the spirit and *p*· of C. S.,
spiritual
    (*see* **spiritual**)
stationary
  Ret. 93–15 stationary *p*·, stillness, and
strange
  Po. 35– 3 strain which hath strange *p*·
supernatural
  Mis. 3– 4 shall claim . . . no supernatural *p*·.
  Pul. 72– 2 * inspired . . . by supernatural *p*·.

power

supposed
  Mis. 24–32 claims exercising their supposed *p*·
  199– 3 to deny the supposed *p*· of matter
  334–11 away goes all its supposed *p*·
  335–20 afraid of its supposed *p*·,
  No. 21–19 supposed *p*· and reality of evil
sustains
  Po. 1– 6 What *p*· sustains thee
that
  Mis. 55–13 and who are using that *p*· against
that saved
  Pan. 14–24 shielded by the *p*· that saved them,
that Truth bestows
  Rud. 10– 3 you forfeit the *p*· that Truth bestows,
this
  Mis. 101–23 this *p*· is good, not evil ;
  188–24 recognition of this *p*· came to her
  194– 3 reveals the Principle of this *p*·,
to act
  Mis. 173–18 without space to occupy, *p*· to act,
  My. 12–27 *p*· to "act in the living present."
to become
  Mis. 180–21 *p*· to become the sons of — *John* 1: 12.
  180–25 *p*· to become the son of God.
  181–24 *p*· to become the sons of — *John* 1: 12.
  182–12 *p*· to become the son of God,
  185– 8 *p*· to become the sons of — *John* 1: 12.
  185–25 *p*· to become the sons of — *John* 1: 12.
to be perfect
  Mis. 184–14 say of the *p*· to be perfect
to declare vacancies
  Man. 80–14 have the *p*· to declare vacancies
to demonstrate
  Mis. 181– 5 *p*· to demonstrate his divine Principle,
  Ret. 88–15 its *p*· to demonstrate immortality.
  No. 35– 4 without the *p*· to demonstrate
to determine
  No. 42–17 with *p*· to determine the fact
to discipline
  Man. 51–21 Board of Directors has *p*· to discipline,
to escape
  Mis. 109–25 even the *p*· to escape from the
to gain
  My. 148–27 sect struggling to gain *p*·
to heal
  Mis. 4– 9 Its only *p*· to heal is
  5–12 faith that I have the *p*· to heal."
  41– 8 deprives those . . . of the *p*· to heal,
  50–15 that gives one the *p*· to heal ;
  52– 3 God's *p*· to heal them.
  53–14 your *p*· to heal through Mind,
  54– 3 *Has Mrs. Eddy lost her p*· *to heal?*
  54–11 Instead of losing her *p*· to heal,
  197–19 his *p*· to heal and to save,
  221–15 stultify the *p*· to heal mentally.
  223–13 having the *p*· to heal."
  No. 43– 1 if Christ's *p*· to heal was not
  '02. 8–19 its *p*· to heal and to save.
  Hea. 3–11 Christianity and the *p*· to heal ;
  My. 212–26 loses his own *p*· to heal.
to prayer
  Po. 30–12 Give risen *p*· to prayer ;
to reflect
  Mis. 183–27 will have *p*· to reflect His power,
to sin
  Mis. 184–17 saying, "I have the *p*· to sin
to wash away
  Pul. 7–16 with *p*· to wash away, . . . every crime,
unity and
  My. 162– 6 unity and *p*· are not in atom
unknown
  My. 153–21 appeals to an unknown *p*·
unrighteous
  Po. 27– 2 pomp and tinsel of unrighteous *p*· ;
uplifting
  Pan. 10– 8 humanity will attest its uplifting *p*·,
use the
  '01. 31–15 I can use the *p*· that God gives
using the
  Mis. 59– 6 It is using the *p*· of human will,
vain
  No. 42–12 vain *p*· of dogma and philosophy
verity, nor
  '01. 13–12 neither entity, verity, nor *p*·
war weakens
  My. 278–27 war weakens *p*· and must finally fall,
was the thought
  Hea. 12–24 prove that the *p*· was the thought,
widest
  Ret. 82– 9 widest *p*· and strongest growth
wisdom and
  Mis. 204–26 foresight, wisdom, and *p*· ;
  Un. 14– 8 He should so gain wisdom and *p*·
world
  My. 85–13 * this wonderful woman is a world *p*·.

power

wrong
Mis. 190-26 the wrong *p*·, or the lost sense,
your
Pul. 2-20 by every means in your *p*·,

Mis. 23- 3 *p*· back of gravitation,
90- 3 *p*· of sin is the pleasure in sin.
116- 2 sensitiveness to the *p*· of evil.
119-20 to obey a *p*· that should be
141- 7 the *p*· that is behind it ;
148-13 impelled by a *p*· not one's own,
170-31 explained as the putting forth of *p*·.
184-15 If man should say . . . "I am the *p*·,"
199-19 *p*· of his transcendent goodness
220-21 That this mental method has *p*·
222-26 whose *p*· seems inexplicable,
257-13 as a *p*·, prohibition, or license,
388- 7 Thou to whose *p*· our hope we give,
393-20 Points the plane of *p*· to seek.
396-21 whose measures bind The *p*· of pain,
Man. 3- 9 impelled by a *p*· not one's own,
Pul. 18- 5 whose measures bind The *p*· of pain.
53-29 * *p*· that filled his garment's hem
69-20 * *p*· fully developed to heal
Rud. 10- 3 if you have *p*· in error, you forfeit
No. v- 4 *p*· and self-sacrificing spirit of
43- 2 equal to the *p*· of daily meat and
Pan. 6-25 what *p*· hath evil?
'01. 14- 1 or believe in the *p*· of sin,
14- 1 sticks to us and has *p*· over us.
25-23 Had he taught . . . *p*· of matter,
'02. 3-26 not follow that *p*· must mature into
Peo. 12-14 who know what a *p*· mind is
Po. 7- 7 Thou to whose *p*· our hope we give,
12- 5 whose measures bind The *p*· of pain,
52- 4 Points the plane of *p*· to seek.
68-14 is the spell that hath *p*·
My. 106-10 *p*· over and above matter
190-22 *p*· over all manner of diseases ;
204- 4 *p*· which lies concealed in the calm

powerful
Ret. 7-17 * and for his *p*· advocacy of the
Un. 60- 9 and then conjure up, . . . a *p*· presence
Pul. 56-13 * helpful, and *p*· movements of
'01. 11-20 Word of God is a *p*· preacher,
Hea. 12-22 "I am making you more *p*·,"
12-26 higher attenuations are the most *p*·.
Peo. 10- 3 steam is more *p*· than water,
My. 59-20 * sonorous tones of the *p*· organ
164-11 a *p*· camera obscura,

powerless
Mis. 29-29 matter is proven *p*·
90- 5 sin and death to be *p*·.
119-21 and is found *p*· in C. S.
134-20 earth and hell are proven *p*·.
252-10 wrong thoughts are . . . *p*·,
336- 3 that evil is *p*·,
My. 128-29 shaft aimed at you . . . will fall *p*·,
296-19 will end in harmony, — evil *p*·,

powerlessness
Mis. 108- 7 attested the absolute *p*·
114-29 show us the *p*· of evil,
201-10 its *p*· to destroy good,

powers
Mis. 134-20 *p*· of earth and hell
177- 5 *p*· of evil are leagued together
272-26 * with *p*· to confer diplomas
Ret. 7- 8 * highest order of intellectual *p*·,
49-15 *p*· that are not ordained of
'02. 14- 7 against the *p*· of darkness,
My. 308- 1 all the *p*· of earth combined

practicability
Mis. 192-18 *p*· of the divine Word.

practical
Mis. v- 4 DEDICATE THESE *p*· TEACHINGS
21-11 makes *p*· all his words and works.
24- 8 This knowledge is *p*·,
28-26 Master's *p*· knowledge of this
35- 1 Years of *p*· proof.
38-18 *p*· application to benefit the race,
38-24 questions of *p*· import.
39- 1 would be of less *p*· value.
90- 6 This *p*· Truth saves from sin,
182-30 rendered *p*·, — this eternal Truth
192- 1 more spiritual and *p*· sense.
205- 3 *p*· C. S. is the divine Mind,
207- 5 *p*·, operative C. S.
232- 9 more perfect and *p*· Christianity?
246-32 earnest seeking after *p*· truth
315-19 health, and *p*· C. S.
345-18 * had a *p*· faith in God."
353-14 workman in his mills, a *p*· joker,
Man. 49-12 *p*· wisdom necessary in a sick room,

practical
Man. 83-18 sound in sentiment and *p*· in C. S.
Ret. 35-20 was and is demonstrated as *p*·,
48-19 mental healing on a purely *p*· basis,
65-25 *p*· manifestations of Christianity
Un. 36-25 interfere with its *p*· demonstration.
39- 2 is rendered *p*· on the body.
Pul. 52- 5 * some of our *p*· Christian folk
61-16 * which is *p*· as well as poetic,
Rud. 6-23 best understood in *p*· demonstration.
No. 46- 3 a *p*·, spiritual Christianity,
Pan. 13- 2 will witness . . . to its *p*· truth.
'01. 1-24 *p*· possibilities of divine Love :
11-20 not too spiritual to be *p*·,
Hea. 1-11 more *p*· and spiritual religion
Peo. 13-26 * had a *p*· faith in God ;"
My. 40- 5 * thirst after *p*· righteousness ;
58- 1 * some of our *p*· Christian folk
81-24 * It was a *p*· demonstration of
112- 6 what C. S. makes *p*· to-day
121-24 Self-denial is *p*·,
168- 3 *p*· religion in agreement with
180- 1 make . . . the divine Love *p*·,
234-21 our great Master's sayings are *p*·
237-22 is *p*· and scientific,
264-17 Truth and Love made more *p*· ;
287-16 love for God, *p*· good,
306-14 to be transfused into the *p*·
362-24 * demonstrating *p*· Christianity.

practicality
Mis. 193- 8 *p*· of all Christ's teachings
308-14 know its *p*· only by healing
Ret. 88-13 living beauty of Love, its *p*·,
My. 103- 7 proof of the *p*· of this faith
180- 6 by him who proved their *p*·,
182-32 prove the *p*· of perfection,
239- 9 *p*·, validity, and redemptive power

practically
Mis. 48- 1 *p*· or theoretically,
177-19 Answer at once and *p*·,
224- 1 *p*· harmless, unless our own thought
333-13 literally and *p*· denying that God,
Ret. 28- 4 He must be ours *p*·,
79-19 and *p*· come short of the
Un. 1-17 *p*· able to testify, by their lives,
Pul. 62-19 * *p*· no limit to the uses to which
67-16 * *p*· unknown a decade since,
72-14 * *p*· been given up by a number of
'01. 10-19 Theoretically and *p*· man's
30-10 Christian Scientists are *p*·
My. 77-12 * *p*· every civilized country,
84- 3 * calls for *p*· all the resources
111- 9 on *p*· the same grounds as are
273- 9 * covers *p*· the civilized world.
309-31 * *p*· all the intellectual life."

practice

and proof
'01. 19-16 departure from Jesus' *p*· and proof.
and teachings
Mis. 195-26 the *p*· and teachings of Jesus
ceased
My. 231-12 has ceased *p*· herself in order to
character and
Ret. 28-30 character and *p*· of the anointed ;
Christian
Ret. 54-20 whose Christian *p*· is far in advance of
'01. 11-19 would be enough for Christian *p*·.
Christian Science
Man. 49-11 knowledge of C. S. *p*·,
My. 242-18 information relating to C. S. *p*·,
355- 7 need for more men in C. S. *p*·.
diabolical
Mis. 41- 2 given vent in the diabolical *p*· of
error in
Mis. 66-28 is met with error in *p*· ;
faithful
Man. 82-21 devote ample time for faithful *p*·.
false
Mis. 368-18 false teaching and false *p*· of
fit students for
Rud. 16- 5 undertake to fit students for *p*·
form of
Mis. 380-26 by any outward form of *p*·.
genuine
No. 3-14 sustains the genuine *p*·,
good
My. 251-20 and after three years of good *p*·,
her
Man. 92- 8 to demonstrate by his or her *p*·,
his
Mis. 378-15 to learn his *p*·,
Pul. 54-20 * in his *p*· of mental therapeutics,
My. 107-29 homœopathist handles in his *p*·
its
Rud. 15- 5 to immediately enter upon its *p*·.

practice

malicious
Mis. 351–12   solely from mental malicious *p*·,
material in
Peo.   2–16   shockingly material in *p*·,
medical
'00.   13–20   Its medical *p*· included charms
'01.   17–24   From my medical *p*· I had learned
My. 107– 7   a modern phase of medical *p*·,
member's
Man. 46–22   payment for said member's *p*·,
mental
     (*see* **mental**)
metaphysical
Mis. 379–31   adjusting . . . a metaphysical *p*·,
My. 190–11   metaphysical *p*· of medicine
method of
Ret. 43–15   his material method of *p*·
more than theory
Mis. 195–28   and *p*· more than theory,
    281–32   will need, . . . *p*· more than theory.
my
Mis. 350–32   its own proof of my *p*·.
not profession
Pul.   9–26   *P*·, not profession,— goodness, not
of Christian healing
Mis. 359– 5   in the *p*· of Christian healing
of Christian Science
Mis. 282– 9   direct rule for *p*· of C. S.
Ret. 72– 1   In the *p*· of C. S. one cannot
No.   3–10   manual of the *p*· of C. S.
My. 42– 8   * in the *p*· of C. S.
    204–18   *p*· of C. S. in your State,
    251–18   can teach pupils the *p*· of C. S.,
    327– 1   protect the *p*· of C. S.
    327–16   * or stop the *p*· of C. S.
of dentistry
Mis. 45–10   invaluable in the *p*· of dentistry.
of divine metaphysics
'01.   2–13   certainty in the *p*· of divine metaphysics
of its Life
No. 28–23   its Principle nor the *p*· of its Life.
of *materia medica*
My. 292–23   In the *p*· of *materia medica*,
of medicine
Peo. 10–10   regulating the *p*· of medicine in 1880.
My. 190–11   metaphysical *p*· of medicine
    340–15   laws . . . on the *p*· of medicine !
of Mind-healing
Mis. 67–22   right *p*· of Mind-healing achieved,
Ret. 85–20   of abusing the *p*· of Mind-healing
    89– 4   in the *p*· of Mind-healing.
of the learner
Mis. 43–30   on the *p*· of the learner,
outline of the
Rud.   8–10   nothing but an outline of the *p*·.
preaching, and
Ret. 94–17   teaching, preaching, and *p*·
precepts and
Mis. 270–23   Fidelity to his precepts and *p*·
Principle and
     (*see* **Principle**)
Principle or
Ret. 64–19   either in Principle or *p*·.
put into
Pul. 53– 2   * a Principle that was put into *p*· by
My. 204– 4   to put into *p*· the power which
quiet
No.   1–14   the quiet *p*· of its virtues.
right
Mis. 67–22   right *p*· of Mind-healing achieved,
rule of
Mis. 356–29   Principle and rule of *p*·.
rules and
Mis. 252–23   rules and *p*· of the great healer
My. 239– 5   rules, and *p*· of Christianity
safe side of
Mis. 117– 9   place him on the safe side of *p*·.
same
My. 76– 1   * same *p*· would be followed
scientific
Ret. 78– 7   scientific *p*· makes perfect,
successful
Ret.   7–16   * in the successful *p*· of
such
My. 219– 3   Such *p*· would be erroneous,
such a
Mis. 380– 2   outward sign of such a *p*·:
teaching and
Ret. 65– 4   teaching and *p*· of Jesus,
My. 190–28   Jesus declared that his teaching and *p*·
teachings and
Pul. 10– 1   Christ's teachings and *p*·.

practice

their
'01. 33–30   by their *p*· or by preventing the
My. 111–18   establish their *p*· of healing
    227–19   in their *p*·, whether successful **or**
theories and
No.   2–28   conflicting theories and *p*·.
theory and
     (*see* **theory**)
this
Ret. 78– 6   textual explanation of this *p*·
    78– 9   entering into this *p*·,
No.   3–12   dependent on the rules of this *p*·
weakness in
Rud.   9– 8   will lead to weakness in *p*·,
wrong
Mis. 67–22   and the wrong *p*· discerned,
your
Rud.   9–13   base your *p*· on immortal Mind,
My. 128–28   shaft aimed at you or your *p*·

Mis. 233–20   for the *p*· of true medicine,
Ret.   57– 9   it is *p*· that is wrong.
Pul. 68– 8   * many are now pastors or in *p*·.
'02. 11–30   unite in doctrine and in *p*·
My.   4– 6   they preclude the *p*· . . . of C. S.,
    127–16   declare that when I was in *p*·,
    245– 9   preparation of the student for *p*·.

practices

No.   2–22   many . . . have large *p*·
'01. 25–13   No Christly axioms, *p*·, or
My. 93–23   * many of the *p*· in its name.
    190–10   My experience in both *p*·
    221– 6   systems and *p*· of their times.

practise

Mis. 41– 7   It deprives those who *p*· it of
    43–25   incapacitates one to *p*· or
    59– 3   *p*· your belief of it
    114–13   They must themselves *p*·,
    114–14   and teach others to *p*·,
    115–14   *p*·, teach, and live C. S. !
    233–25   to work hard enough to *p*· it?
    243–21   who *p*· on the basis of matter,
    283–31   learn the principle . . . and *p*· it,
    283–32   teacher or musician to *p*· for him.
Man. 55–22   trying to *p*· or to teach
    82–16   Members . . . who *p*· other professions
No.   6–12   as all understand who *p*· the
    28–19   Study C. S. and *p*· it,
'00.   6–27   accept it, understand and *p*· it,
'01. 33–23   enjoined his students to teach and *p*·,
My. 41–14   * whatsoever lawlessness . . . he may *p*·
    121–25   pleasant to those who *p*· it.
    158–22   and some *p*· what they say.
    181–17   nations shall speedily learn and *p*·
    204–15   TO *P*· WITHOUT FEES
    212–16   Because they do not *p*· in strict
    220–12   I *p*· and teach this obedience,
    238– 8   to read and to *p*· the Scriptures,
    238–12   has imparted little power to *p*·
    281–16   * chapter sub-title
    282–14   we must *p*· what we already know
    327– 6   made it legal to *p*· C. S.
    327–25   * who *p*· the art of healing,"
    328–29   * who *p*· the art of healing for pay,
    363–27   and *p*· only to heal.

practised

Mis. 29–10   Christ-healing was *p*· even before
    48– 4   should neither be taught nor *p*·,
    193–12   as defined and *p*· by Jesus,
    228– 3   has been *p*· upon thee,
    351– 6   never have *p*· by arguments which,
    378–14   Having *p*· homœopathy,
    380–17   My students at first *p*· in
Man. 42–21   *p*· according to the Golden Rule :
    89–13   *p*· C. S. healing acceptably
    89–21   *p*· C. S. healing successfully
Un.   9–25   not been *p*· since the days of Christ.
Pul. 52–19   * *p*· by Jesus and his disciples.
    53– 3   * though *p*· in other countries
'01.   9–14   Christ Jesus possessed it, *p*· it,
My. 103–15   which Jesus taught and *p*·.
    180– 5   truths were preached and *p*·
    204–20   *p*· gratuitously when starting
    238– 2   *the Bible, if read and p*·,
    238–20   When the Bible is thus read and *p*·,
    242– 7   and must be *p*· therefrom.
    246– 8   *p*· C. S. three years
    271– 6   when I *p*· its precepts,
    314– 6   * *p*· in several towns,
    327–30   * as taught and *p*· in C. S.,

practises

Mis. 243–14   medicine claims more than it *p*·.
Rud. 12– 4   *p*· Christ's Sermon on the Mount.

practises
'00.	6–16	not only accepts . . . but he p· it.
My.	4– 2	then he p· the Golden Rule
	113– 4	p· the teachings of this book

practising
Mis.	4–15	and to the p· students,
	5–10	scientific method of p· Christianity.
	62–27	she is p· this Science,
	232–29	p· in the name of Science
	340–19	by p· what he was taught.
	349–15	which he claimed to be p· ;
	382–30	teaching and p· C. S.
Man.	34–15	teaching and p· metaphysical healing.
Rud.	14– 6	strictly p· Divine Science,
'01.	20–22	till he . . . stops p· it.
My.	166–17	neither she nor I would be p·
	242–12	In p· C. S. you must state its

practitioner
Mis.	40–26	p· has to master those elements
	41–29	p· may not always prove equal to
	220–16	p· has changed his patient's
	220–19	p· undertook to transform it,
	352–17	enables the p· to act
	378–11	He proved to be a magnetic p·.
Man.	46–11	except as a C. S. p·.
	46–16	relation of p· to patient.
	73– 4	include at least one active p·
	87– 6	left to the wisdom of the p·,
Pul.	69–23	* p· must understand these laws
Rud.	8–23	sense may say the unchristian p·
	9– 9	he will be a poor p·,
	9–24	thoughts of the p· should be imbued
	12–24	p· should also endeavor to
Hea.	14–10	If you employ a medical p·,
	14–18	preparation for a metaphysical p·
My.	154– 5	Life understood by the p·
	205–29	p· may fail, but the Science never.
	212–28	You will find this p· saying
	241–20	* catechized by a C. S. p·
	241–21	* p· said that my statement was wrong,
	364–10	are disarmed by the p· who

practitioners (see also **practitioners'**)
Mis.	6– 6	C. S. p· have plenty to do,
	43–12	make safe and successful p·.
	80–28	by a new school of p·,
	81– 6	let each society of p·,
	221–16	accounts for many helpless mental p·
Man.	46–12	P· and Patients.
	73– 5	list of p· in The C. S. Journal.
	74–11	Teachers and p· of C. S.
Ret.	82– 7	p· of the same blessed faith.
	82–17	to supply many p·, teachers, and
Rud.	15–14	until there were enough p· to
'02.	9– 9	we shall have better p·,
My.	212–15	dissension among mental p·?
	223– 9	should be sent to the C. S. p·
	237–16	C. S. p· should make their
	246– 3	continue for three years as p·
	359–23	* were known as "the p·."

practitioners'
Man.	74–10	Teachers' and P· Offices.
My.	237–15	chapter sub-title

Prairie Queen
Ret.	17–10	P· Q· and the modest Moss-rose ;
Po.	62–11	P· Q· and the modest Moss-rose ;

praise (noun)
Mis.	48– 7	Mr. Carpenter deserves p· for his
	106–24	begin that p· that shall never end?
	106–27	and resound His p·."
	124–21	silence wherein to muse His p·,
	128–11	if there be any p·,— Phil. 4 : 8.
	146– 3	and her gates with p· !
	226–11	pretentious p· of hypocrites,
	245–22	p· or the dispraise of men.
	331– 9	sunlight of prayer and p·
Man.	47–16	it scales the pinnacle of p·
Ret.	71– 1	exalts a mortal beyond human p·,
Pul.	1–11	eloquent in God's p·.
	8– 1	All p· to the press of America's
	8–22	Thou hast perfected p·."— Matt. 21 : 16.
No.	44–17	mouth lisping God's p· ;
Po.	30–20	sacred song and loudest breath of p·
	77– 4	nation's holiest hymn in grateful p· !
My.	6–21	evidencing the p· of babes
	27– 8	sacred season of prayer and p·.
	31–32	* joined in the song of p·.
	113–20	to perfect His p·.
	116–19	rendering p· to whom p· is due,
	131–14	apostate p· return to its first love,
	167–24	send forth a pæan of p·
	170–29	faith, understanding, prayer, and p·
	208–19	wherein to gather in p·
	229–24	heaps of p· confront me,
	262–29	eloquent silence, prayer, and p·

praise (noun)
My.	275–28	unite in one Te Deum of p·.
	297– 3	shrink from such salient p·.
	323–20	* gratitude and p· to God
	355–18	chapter sub-title

praise (verb)
Mis.	41– 7	wrath of man" to p· Him.— Psal. 76 : 10.
	107– 2	sweetness and beauty . . . that p· Him,
Un.	29–26	I shall yet p· Him.— Psal. 42 : 11.
Pul.	80–20	* either to p· or blame,
	83–21	* When we try to p· her
No.	8–14	make the wrath of man to p· Him,
	33– 2	wrath of man shall p· Him.
Pan.	4–23	I shall yet p· Him,— Psal. 42 : 11.
'02.	1–13	wrath of man shall p·— Psal. 76 : 10.
My.	111– 3	wrath of man shall p·— Psal. 76 : 10.
	148–18	you have met to p· God.
	151–11	wrath of man shall p·— Psal. 76 : 10.
	163– 3	to p· him who won the way
	207– 4	The wrath of men shall p· God,
	356– 2	and p· and love the spot

praised
Pul.	7– 8	p· and persecuted in Boston,
My.	200– 4	Heaven be p· for the signs of

praises
Mis.	107– 1	organ, . . . p· Him ;
My.	162–18	love that rebukes p· also,
	206–25	show forth the p·— I Pet. 2 : 9.
	332–30	p· to his honorable record

praiseworthy
My.	195–24	p· success of this church,

praising
Mis.	295–13	p· the Scotchman's national pride
My.	149–31	while those . . . ask no p·.
	245–19	go on ad infinitum, p· God,

pray
Mis.	vii– 1	* P· thee, take care, that tak'st my book
	vii–16	And nothing have to p· :
	59–11	to p· for the recovery of the sick ?
	59–12	Not if we p· Scripturally,
	87–26	To watch and p·, to be honest,
	109–30	Watch and p· for self-knowledge ;
	110– 7	p· that you preserve these virtues
	114–22	cannot . . . p· to God too fervently,
	127– 9	p· daily for themselves ;
	133–12	love to p· standing in— Matt. 6 : 5.
	133–15	p· to thy Father which— Matt. 6 : 6.
	144–29	To-day I p· that divine Love,
	151–20	I p· thee as a Christian Scientist,
	154–25	P· without ceasing.
	174–25	and taught us to p·,
	174–26	did not teach us to p· for death
	276–24	I p· that all my students
	313–20	p· ye therefore the God of harvest
	330– 5	p· for the perpetual springtide
	343– 1	Let us watch and p· that we
	356–30	"p· without ceasing,"— I Thess. 5 : 17.
	387–16	P· that his spirit you partake,
	389– 3	the right to work and p·,
	389–21	watch and p·.
Man.	16– 9	promise to watch, and p·
	40–12	watch and p· to be delivered from
	41–20	every member of this Church to p·
Un.	50– 7	We should watch and p· that we
Pul.	34–25	* to p·, to search the Scriptures.
No.	8–22	p· for the amelioration of sin,
	39–28	"P· without ceasing"— I Thess. 5 : 17.
Pan.	14–11	P· for the prosperity of our country,
	14–14	P· that the divine presence may
'00.	2– 8	work — work — watch and p·."
'01.	14–21	one must watch and p· that he
	16–26	men go to mock, and go away to p·
	18– 9	Those who laugh at or p· against
	18–30	clergymen p· for sinners ;
'02.	4– 7	p· at this Communion season
Hea.	4– 8	We p· for God to remember us,
	8– 4	not a person to whom we should p·
	15–17	You p· for God to heal you,
	15–24	is it not asking amiss to p· for
Po.	4–21	watch and p·.
	6–11	P· that his spirit you partake,
	21–17	the right to work and p·,
	32–18	kneel at the altar of mercy and p·
My.	6–15	temple wherein to enter and p·.
	18– 6	p· daily for themselves ;
	37–30	* With sacred resolution do we p·
	119–29	watch and p· for the spirit of Truth
	128–30	Watch, and p· daily
	143– 1	p· that God directs your meetings
	167–11	I p· that heaven's messages of
	174–28	humbly p· to serve Him better.
	180–28	in the spirit of our great Exemplar p· ;
	189–30	Wherefore, p·, the bell did toll?
	195– 9	to work more, to watch and p· ;

pray

My.	196–27	Work and *p·* for it.
	200–30	For this I shall continue to *p·*.
	203– 4	*P·* aright and demonstrate your
	220–15	Each day I *p·* for the pacification of
	220–21	I *p·* : "God bless my enemies ;
	234– 4	I cannot watch and *p·* while
	254– 6	Watch, *p·*, demonstrate.
	279–23	*p·* each day for the amicable
	279–25	that God bless that great nation
	281– 3	even to know how to *p·*
	291–28	to think, to mourn, yea, to *p·*,
	293–31	when ye *p·*, believe— *Mark* 11 : 24.
	340– 4	"*P·* without ceasing."— *I Thess.* 5 : 17.
	358– 5	"Watch and *p·*,— *Matt.* 26 : 41.
	358–10	Beloved ! you need to watch and *p·*

prayed

Mis.	29– 7	At another time he *p·*,
	232– 1	God comfort them all ! we inwardly *p·*
Ret.	9–13	*p·* that God would forgive me,
	13–21	I *p·* ; and a soft glow of
Pul.	33–11	* she *p·* for forgiveness,
	44– 4	* worked, toiled, *p·* for.
	69–25	* have *p·* for the cure of disease,
My.	283–10	Many years have I *p·* and labored
	286– 3	*p·* daily that there be no more war,
	286– 5	*p·* that all the peoples on earth
	293–10	thousands who *p·* for him
	335–30	* the young wife *p·* incessantly

Prayer

Lord's

(*see* **Lord's Prayer**)

| *Pul.* | 38–13 | "*P·*," "Atonement and Eucharist," |

prayer

after

| *Mis.* | 88–18 | like a benediction after *p·*, |

all

| *No.* | 38–25 | All *p·* that is desire is intercessory ; |

and drugs

| *Mis.* | 51–29 | *Are both p· and drugs necessary* |

and fasting

Mis.	156–21	but by *p·* and fasting."— *Matt.* 17 : 21.
My.	190–17	but by *p·* and fasting."— *Matt.* 17 : 21.
	222–13	but by *p·* and fasting"— *Matt.* 17 : 21.
	339–25	but by *p·* and fasting,"— *Matt.* 17 : 21.

and praise

Mis.	331– 9	sunlight of *p·* and praise
My.	27– 8	sacred season of *p·* and praise.
	170–29	understanding, *p·*, and praise
	262–29	eloquent silence, *p·*, and praise

and teachings

| *Pul.* | 85–18 | * *p·* and teachings of Jesus Christ. |

and watchfulness

| *No.* | 33– 8 | struggle, *p·*, and watchfulness |

audible

| *No.* | 39– 4 | audible *p·* may be offered to |
| | 40–12 | I have no objection to audible *p·* |

bended knee of

| *Mis.* | 204– 3 | on the bended knee of *p·*, |

brings

| *'01.* | 19– 5 | *p·* brings the seeker into |

cannon's

| *Po.* | 26–20 | Purged by the cannon's *p·* ; |

ceaseless

| *Mis.* | 250–24 | the silent, ceaseless *p·* ; |

daily

| *Man.* | 41–19 | Daily *P·*. |
| *My.* | 281– 3 | daily *p·* of my church, |

days for

| *My.* | 340– 3 | St. Paul's days for *p·* were |

earnest

| *My.* | 352–12 | * It is our earnest *p·* that we |

effect of

| *'01.* | 34– 2 | effect of *p·*, whereby Christendom |

evening

| *Mis.* | 389– 5 | poem |
| *Po.* | page 4 | poem |

family

| *'01.* | 31–23 | Bible reading and family *p·* ; |

for peace

| *My.* | 279–21 | chapter sub-title |
| | 280–30 | to pause in special *p·* for peace. |

hope and

'02.	6–20	Christian faith, hope, and *p·*,
	15–30	my waiting hope and *p·*.
My.	155–15	its faith, hope, and *p·*.

hour of

| *Po.* | 65–10 | "Sweet hour of *p·*" ! |

hypocrite's

| *No.* | 40–11 | and pour forth a hypocrite's *p·* ; |

inaudible

| *My.* | 139–24 | from the audible to the inaudible *p·* ; |

in church

| *Man.* | 42– 1 | *P·* in Church. |

prayer

in stone

Mis.	141– 1	The First Church . . . our *p·* in stone,
	320– 1	push upward our *p·* in stone,
Pul.	23– 4	* "Our *P·* in Stone"
	24– 8	* is termed . . . "Our *p·* in stone."
	44– 4	* The '*p·* in stone' is accomplished.
	57–19	* chapter sub-title
	65–17	* call it their "*p·* in stone,"
	84–15	* completion of "our *p·* in stone,"

intercessory

| *No.* | 38–24 | chapter sub-title |

is the utilization

| *No.* | 39–18 | *P·* is the utilization of the love |

looks up in

| *My.* | 258– 1 | Wherever the child looks up in *p·*, |

my

Mis.	385– 5	Oh, Thou hast heard my *p·* ;
	397–17	My *p·*, some daily good to do
Pul.	19– 1	My *p·*, some daily good to do
Po.	13– 5	My *p·*, some daily good to do
	37– 5	Oh, Thou hast heard my *p·* ;
My.	167–20	my *p·* for their health, happiness,
	183–26	blending with thine my *p·*
	220–19	faith that my *p·* availeth,

my form of

| *Pul.* | 4–29 | used, . . . my form of *p·* |

my impressions of

| *Mis.* | 133–10 | voices my impressions of *p·* : |

not fatigued by

| *Man.* | 60– 8 | Scientist is not fatigued by *p·*, |

occupied in

| *'01.* | 34– 6 | The interval . . . occupied in *p·* |

of doubt

| *Mis.* | 59–16 | *p·* of doubt and mortal belief |

of faith

| *No.* | 41–25 | * *p·* of faith shall save— *Jas.* 5 : 15. |
| *My.* | 221–32 | *p·* of faith shall save— *Jas.* 5 : 15. |

of one

| *Peo.* | 8– 5 | or that answers the *p·* of one |

one

| *Pul.* | 22– 4 | Christian churches have . . . one *p·*, |
| *My.* | 301–10 | unite as brethren in one *p·* : |

parting

| *Mis.* | 386–26 | her loyal life, And parting *p·*, |
| *Po.* | 50–12 | her loyal life, And parting *p·*, |

potent

| *No.* | 39– 4 | an honest and potent *p·* |

power of

| *My.* | 292–12 | chapter sub-title |

power to

| *Po.* | 30–12 | Give risen power to *p·* ; |

praise and

| *My.* | 208–19 | to gather in praise and *p·* |

result of

| *My.* | 343–25 | each one was . . . the result of *p·*. |

righteous

Mis.	33– 2	righteous *p·* that avails with God.
My.	189–13	commingling in one righteous *p·*,
	280–10	* righteous *p·* which availeth much.

ripe in

| *My.* | 350–27 | Science ripe in *p·*, in word, and |

secret

| *No.* | 39–10 | glorified God in secret *p·*, |

sentence or

| *Pul.* | 59– 5 | * sentence or *p·* of consecration, |

silent

Mis.	133–24	in silent *p·* to the Father
	314– 9	lead in silent *p·*,
Pul.	30–14	* by uniting in silent *p·*.
	43–19	* A few minutes of silent *p·*
No.	39–26	pure Mind-pictures, in silent *p·*,
	39–28	silent *p·* can meet the demand,
Peo.	9–22	Silent *p·* is a desire,
My.	17–24	* a few moments of silent *p·*
	32–17	* Silent *p·*, followed by the audible
	39–11	* Then followed a short silent *p·*
	234–26	Silent *p·* in and for a heathen nation
	311–26	knelt in silent *p·* on the mound

song and

| *Po.* | 54– 4 | With light and song and *p·* ! |

special

| *My.* | 280–17 | special *p·* for the peace of nations, |
| | 280–30 | to pause in special *p·* for peace. |

speechless

| *My.* | 150–18 | in speechless *p·*, ask God to |

spirit of his

| *Mis.* | 211–30 | He lived the spirit of his *p·*, |

spirit of the

| *My.* | 292–26 | spirit of the *p·* of the righteous |

such

| *No.* | 39–14 | Such *p·* humiliates, purifies, |

their

| *My.* | 225–25 | to forget their *p·*, |

thief's

| *Mis.* | 70–20 | poor thief's *p·* for help |

prayer
 true
    No. 39–17   True *p·* is not asking God for love ;
 unto the
    My. 188– 6   attent unto the *p·* — *II Chron.* 7 : 15.
 watchfulness and
    Mis. 115–17   constant watchfulness and *p·*
 your
    Hea. 15–19   acting oppositely to your *p·,*
    My. 203– 5   Pray aright and demonstrate your *p·* ;

    Mis. 116–23   fruits of watchfulness, *p·,*
         132– 8   chapter sub-title
         242– 1   chapter sub-title
    Ret. 13–20   if I went to Him in *p·,*
    No. 39–11   *P·* can neither change God, nor
         39–19   *P·* begets an awakened desire to
    Pan. 14–10   chapter sub-title
    '01. 19– 1   *p·* is a divinely appointed means of
    Hea. 15–27   *P·* will be inaudible,
    Po. 33–12   a *p·* that His love I may know,
    My. 205– 7   won through faith, *p·,* experience ;
         206– 3   *p·* with power and pride of
         293–21   *p·* so fervently offered

"Prayer and Healing; supplemental"
    Mis. 132–13   the heading, "*P·* and *H·* ; *s·,*"
prayerful
    My. 48–11   * a *p·* study of the Bible,
        50– 6   * a little band of *p·* workers.
prayerfully
    Ret. 44–17   Examining the situation *p·*
prayerless
    Mis. 133– 3   * "the pantheistic and *p·* Mrs. Eddy,
        133– 8   As to being "*p·,*" I call your
        248–17   or that my hourly life is *p·,*
        249–12   well known that I am not . . . *p·.*
    Pul. 5– 2   * "the *p·* Mrs. Eddy,"
prayers
    Mis. 40– 5   hygienic rules, drugs, and *p·*
        154–25   that your *p·* be not hindered.
        237–18   forefathers' *p·* blended with the
        266–23   my own endeavors and *p·.*
    Man. 42– 1   *p·* in C. S. churches
    Un. 15–25   they wish to bribe with *p·*
    Pul. 8–20   lambs my *p·* had christened,
        9–25   constant *p·,* prophecies,
        11– 7   means, energies, and *p·*
    '01. 19– 1   God answers their *p·,*
    My. 24–10   * builded by the *p·* and offerings
        37–32   * We would be glad if our *p·,*
        189– 9   silent *p·* of our churches,
        192–28   ever-presence, answering your *p·,*
        280–18   does not hear our *p·* only because
        292–14   fail in their *p·* to save the life of
        292–17   a compound of *p·* in which
        336– 1   but for her *p·* the patient
        345– 2   that by your *p·* vaccination will
prayest
    Mis. 133–11   "When thou *p·,* — *Matt.* 6 : 5.
        133–14   when thou *p·,* — *Matt.* 6 : 6.
praying
    Pul. 21– 8   I am seeking and *p·* for it
        22– 6   every *p·* assembly on earth,
    '01. 28– 4   It is only by *p·,* watching,
    My. 254–12   sure reward . . . of watching and *p·,*
        275–21   Working and *p·* for my dear
        280–29   *p·* for the peace of nations,
prays
    Pul. 83–10   * With the assurance of faith she *p·,*
    No. 39– 8   but when the heart *p·,*
preach
    Mis. 151–27   heal, and teach, and *p·,*
        161–21   that none should teach or *p·* in
        177–25   * was announced to *p·* the sermon,
        178–19   * to *p·* a sermon on C. S.,
        178–24   * could not have stood up again *to p·,*
        325–32   *p·* the gospel, — *Mark* 16 : 15.
    Man. 58– 9   continue to *p·* for this Church
    Ret. 15–13   I was called to *p·* in Boston
        44–13   to *p·* only occasionally,
        88–23   and *p·* without the consent of the
    Pul. 46– 3   * came to hear him *p·,*
    No. 41–20   *p·* the gospel ;" — *Mark* 16 : 15.
    '01. 11–16   for this pastor of ours to *p·* !
    My. 46–16   * To *p·* the gospel and heal the
        47–28   * *p·* the gospel — *Mark* 16 : 15.
        51–24   * go into new fields to teach and *p·.*"
        52–18   * heal the sick, and *p·* the gospel,
        53–17   * to ascertain if she would *p·*
        53–21   * when she could give the time to *p·,*
        147–15   *p·* the gospel which heals
        150–28   heal the sick and *p·* the gospel,
        300–25   *p·* the gospel — *Mark* 16 : 15.

preached
    Mis. 168–12   to the poor . . . the gospel is *p·.*
        171–20   to the poor the gospel is *p·.*
        315– 1   shall be *p·* to the children,
        349–23   state that I *p·* four years,
        349–28   each Sunday when I *p·.*
        349–29   the contributions, when I *p·,*
    Ret. 40– 1   I healed, *p·,* and taught
        44– 8   *p·* five years before
        89–11   If one worshipper *p·* to the
    Pul. 38– 2   * had *p·* in other parishes
    '01. 32–17   sermons their lives *p·*
    '02. 15– 2   the hall where I *p·* ;
    My. 19–31   gospel shall be *p·* — *Mark* 14 : 9.
        28–26   * he *p·* the Word of God
        50–30   * *p·* her farewell sermon
        53–32   * When our pastor *p·* for us
        54–32   * Mrs. Eddy *p·* at this service
        59–17   * *p·* to a handful of people
        180– 4   its life-giving truths were *p·*
preacher
    Mis. 176– 7   solemnly expounded by the *p·,*
        252–26   inspires the teacher and *p·* ;
    '01. 11–20   The Word of God is a powerful *p·,*
        26– 3   great teacher, *p·,* and demonstrator
preachers
    Ret. 82–17   many practitioners, teachers, and *p·*
    My. 178– 3   These unpretentious *p·* cloud not the
preaches
    Mis. 169– 2   the divine Science she *p·* ;
preaching
    Mis. 158–30   no record that he used notes when *p·.*
        239– 7   Lecturing, writing, *p·,* teaching,
        301– 4   the *precedent* for *p·* C. S.,
        359– 4   Christly method of teaching and *p·*
    Ret. 15–23   healed through my *p·.*
        15–30   healed under my *p·,*
        88–19   *p·* the gospel.
        89– 5   In those days *p·* and teaching were
        89– 6   no church *p·,* in the modern sense
        94–17   scientific teaching, *p·,* and practice
    No. 12–19   *p·* the gospel of Truth,
        43–14   * *p·* deliverance to the captive,
    '00. 12–21   Under the influence of St. Paul's *p·*
    '01. 11–23   sermon without personal *p·,*
    My. 58–21   * inspire us to follow her in *p·,*
        91–23   * during the first years of her *p·*
        128–21   *p·* the gospel and healing the sick.
preamble
    My. 254–18   * part of the *p·* to our By-laws,
precaution
    Mis. 89–18   he left this *p·* for others.
        285–20   We have taken the *p·* to
precautions
    My. 219–26   *p·* against the spread of
precede
    Man. 32– 6   The readings from the Scriptures shall *p·*
    Ret. 63–12   denunciation must *p·* its destruction.
    My. 232–22   must *p·* that understanding of Truth
precedence
    Un. 15–19   Would God not of necessity take *p·*
    My. 81– 9   laughingly give *p·* to another
precedent
    Mis. 220– 8   explanation, attestation, and *p·,*
        301– 3   *p·* for preaching C. S.,
        367–26   neither *p·* nor foundation in nature,
    Ret. 89–22   Nowhere . . . find any *p·* for
    '00. 4– 5   *p·* that would commingle Christianity,
    My. 237– 6   I do not consider a *p·* for
precedents
    No. 35– 2   Without it, how poor the *p·* of
    My. 340– 6   religious observances and *p·*
precedes
    My. 297–13   dark hour that *p·* the dawn.
precedeth
    Un. 61–11   *p·* the nightless radiance
preceding
    Man. 25–11   *p·* the annual meeting of the
        56–20   *p·* the annual meeting of the
        57– 4   *p·* the first Sunday in June,
        93– 6   Monday *p·* the Annual Meeting,
    Pul. 29– 2   * *P·* Judge Hanna were
        55– 6   * last quarter of *p·* centuries.
    My. 45–27   * logically followed the *p·* one.
precept
    Mis. 11–11   followed them with *p·* upon *p·* ;
        32–10   "*p·* upon *p·* ; line upon — *Isa.* 28 : 10.
        66–11   This sacred, solid *p·* is
        235–27   tried to follow the divine *p·,*
        278–22   line upon line and *p·* upon *p·.*
        289–17   according to the divine *p·,*

precept
   Ret. 88–16 both by example and *p·*.
   '01. 18–22 Metaphysician's *p·* and example,
   My. 64–16 * teaching . . . both by *p·* and example

precepts
   Mis. 129–22 your Leader's *p·* and example!
      269–12 whose *p·* and example have a
      270–23 Fidelity to his *p·* and practice
      337–25 lived according to his *p·*,
   '01. 34–11 misread the evangelical *p·*
   My. 271– 6 when I practised its *p·*,

pre-Christian
   Pul. 66–25 * *p·* ideas of the Asiatics

precinct
   Pul. 49–23 * do honor to that *p·* of Concord.

precincts
   Mis. 282–16 personal *p·* of human thought,
      290– 3 found within their *p·*.

precious
   Mis. 144–21 *p·* in God's sight
      320– 7 Christ's appearing . . . is so *p·*,
   Ret. 20–12 I regarded as very *p·*.
      37– chapter sub-title
   Un. 52–12 *p·* redemption of soul,
   Pul. 8–24 *p·* children, your loving hearts
   My. 16–25 a *p·* corner stone, — *Isa.* 28 : 16.
      17–10 chosen of God, and *p·*, — *I Pet.* 2 : 4.
      17–15 corner stone, elect, — *I Pet.* 2 : 6.
      47–16 * victories that are *p·* each and all.
      61– 6 * the lessons . . . have been very *p·*.
      62– 8 * may I not take this *p·* truth
      169– 6 My *p·* Busy Bees,
      184–24 *p·* in the sight of divine Love,

precipitately
   No. 1– 7 Small streams are noisy and rush *p·*;

precise
   Ret. 14–21 I could not designate any *p·* time.
   My. 245–26 *p·* signification of the letters of

precisely
   Mis. 23–29 mirror repeats *p·* the looks and
      242–25 I cured *p·* such a case in 1869.
   My. 30– 3 * all the services were *p·* the same

preclude
   My. 4– 5 *p·* the practice or efficient teaching of

precludes
   Mis. 102–10 His infinity *p·* the possibility of
      103– 1 *p·* the presence of evil.
   My. 221– 3 materialism *p·* Jesus' doctrine,

precursor
   '01. 33–11 * *p·* that they were about to die."
   My. 203–18 sure *p·* that its possessor is mortal.

predestinates
   No. 37–28 What God knows, He also *p·*;

predestination
   Ret. 13– 6 doctrine of . . . election, or *p·*,
      14– 1 "horrible decree" of *p·*

predestine
   Un. 19–12 if . . . could *p·* or foreknow evil,

predestined
   Mis. 122–10 whom God foreordained and *p·*
   Un. 17– 9 union *p·* from all eternity;

predicament
   My. 149–25 a *p·* quite like that of the man who

predicate
   Mis. 103– 6 the ultimate and *p·* of being.
      364–22 Human hypotheses *p·* matter of Spirit
   Rud. 6–21 this *p·* and postulate of Mind-healing;
   No. 10–10 life of Christ is the *p·* and postulate of
   '01. 21–21 Death is neither the *p·* nor postulate
   '02. 10–18 his *p·* tending thereto is correct,
   My. 224–17 of which C. S. is the *p·* and
      272– 8 *p·* and ultimate of scientific being

predicated
   '01. 4–13 *p·* of Principle and demonstrated as
   My. 219–20 *p·* of what Christ Jesus taught

predicating
   My. 207–24 *p·* man upon divine Science.

predict
   Pul. 22–10 I *p·* that in the twentieth century
      51–15 * It is too early to *p·*
   My. 11–18 * to *p·* that she will be cheered

predicted
   My. 63–27 * had come, as the Master *p·*,
      94–31 * men there were who *p·*

predicting
   Mis. 240– 9 *P·* danger does not dignify life,

predictions
   Pul. 45–14 * *p·* of workman and onlooker
      84–15 * all *p·* and prognostications
   My. 95– 3 * Those *p·* have not been verified.

predilections
   My. 273– 1 * has no religious opinions or *p·*

predisposes
   Mis. 265– 7 *p·* his students to make mistakes

predisposing
   Mis. 229– 2 certain *p·* or exciting causes.
      267–25 *p·* and exciting cause of all
   Ret. 44–18 *p·* and exciting cause of its
   My. 152–29 remote, *p·*, and present cause

predominate
   Mis. 113– 6 evil seems to *p·*

preeminent
   Mis. 383– 8 *p·* over ignorance or envy,
   Ret. 70–27 *P·* among men, he virtually
   My. 161–28 his *p·* goodness, the Godlike man

preeminently
   No. 33–22 Jesus' sacrifice stands *p·*
   '02. 14–25 prospered *p·* our great Cause,

preen
   My. 186– 6 *p·* their thoughts for upward flight.

preexisted
   Mis. 173–16 And must not man have *p·*

preexistence
   Mis. 47–24 with his immortality and *p·*,
      181–28 man's spiritual *p·* as God's child ;
      189– 9 true knowledge of *p·*,

prefaced
   Mis. 178–13 * which he *p·* by saying :

prefer
   Un. 32–16 which I *p·* to call *mortal mind*.
   Rud. 2–14 I *p·* to retain the proper sense of
   My. 233–11 Which should we *p·*, ease or
      249–22 report that I *p·* to have a
      249–27 I should *p·* that student who

preferable
   Pan. 2–26 Pan in imagery is *p·* to pantheism

preference
   My. 249–24 My *p·* lies with the individual
      276– 8 a *p·* to remain within doors

preferment
   Ret. 6–30 received further political *p·*,

preferred
   Mis. 354–10 When depraved reason is *p·* to
   Man. 99–12 if *p·*, can appoint a Committee on
   Pul. 74–10 * Mrs. Eddy *p·* to prepare a
   My. 215–30 That he *p·* the latter is evident,

preferring
   Mis. 147– 7 meet in unity, *p·* one another,

prefers
   Ret. 65–19 and *p·* Christ to creed.

prefigure
   My. 13–13 seems to *p·* The Mother Church

prefigures
   Pul. 23–16 * *p·* itself to us as one of the
   My. 6–28 *p·* self-abnegation, hope, faith ;

prefix
   Man. 111– 7 *p·* her signature with "Mrs ;"
   Rud. 1–15 *p· per* (through) and *sonare*
   Pan. 2–23 *Pan* is a Greek *p·*,
   '02. 7–12 English *p·* to the words *potence,*

pregnant
   '02. 14–26 This *p·* question, answered frankly
   My. 283–12 grand Association, *p·* with peace,

prejudice
   No. 15– 4 Reading my books, without *p·*,
   My. 224–12 or the *p·* it instils.
      224–12 This *p·* the future must disclose

prejudices
   Pul. 55–11 * *p·*, and oppressions of the past.
   No. 9– 5 *p·*, and errors of one class of
   Hea. 2– 4 factions and *p·* arrayed against it,

preliminary
   Mis. xi–22 *p·* battles that purchased it.
      64–10 *take for p·* studies ?
   Man. 51–14 *P·* Requirement.
   My. v–19 * nine years of arduous *p·* labor,
      75–13 * So perfect have been all the *p·*

prematurely
   Mis. 293– 1 It is safe not to teach *p·* the
   Un. 5– 1 rudely or *p·* agitate a theme

premise

Mis.	26–29	From this *p·* comes the logical
	27– 7	conclusions that destroy their *p·*
	66–27	Error in *p·* is met
	76– 8	never be tested . . . upon a false *p·*,
	101–28	On this proof rest *p·* and
	195–20	but one correct *p·* and conclusion,
	200– 8	an error of *p·* and conclusion,
	265–20	An error in *p·* can never
	288–11	If the *p·* of mortal existence
	309– 5	personality is an error in *p·*,
	344–18	and from error of *p·* would seek a
	366–24	start from this false *p·*,
'01.	3–26	deserts its *p·*,
	4– 3	In logic the major *p·* must be
My.	111–17	is logical in *p·* and in conclusion.
	111–24	in adhering to his *p·*
	112–13	with its logical *p·* and conclusion,

premises

Mis.	46–12	in the *p·* or conclusions of C. S.,
	93– 9	to be the *p·* of Truth,
	195–16	*p·* whereof are not to be found
Man.	75–19	aforesaid *p·* and buildings,
Ret.	21–29	are separated from their *p·*,
	51– 5	the *p·* thereby conveyed,
Un.	51– 3	Reasoning from false *p·*,
'02.	7–19	can be drawn from the *p·*,
Peo.	3–20	personal God is based on finite *p·*,

premium

No.	19– 1	present high *p·* on Mind-healing.
	19– 3	the *p·* would go down.

premonition

Mis.	347–17	accepting the *p·* of one of them,

prenatal

Mis.	71–12	*law of transmission, p· desires,*

preoccupied

Mis.	47– 9	Have you never been so *p·*

preparation

Mis.	x–11	written in haste, without due *p·*.
	84– 3	a *p·* of the human heart
	114– 5	in the *p·* of the *Quarterly*
	115–14	a proper *p·* of heart
	322– 3	and to *p·* to behold it.
Man.	31– 7	*p·* for the reading of the
Ret.	26– 6	a *p·* of poppy, or aconite,
Rud.	9–15	requires a *p·* of the heart
'01.	32–25	all the way up to its *p·*
Hea.	13– 6	shaking the *p·* thirty times
	14–17	*p·* for a metaphysical practitioner is
My.	245– 8	thorough *p·* of the student
	319–23	* about the *p·* of a theme,

preparations

Mis.	268–22	God's *p·* for the sick are potions of
	268–25	let us not adulterate His *p·* for
My.	173–10	notice that no *p·* would be made for

prepare

Mis.	64–13	*p·* for it through no books except
	138– 3	to *p·* for this national convention
	246–24	"*P·* ye the way of — *Matt.* 3 : 3.
	347– 8	*p·* shelter in caves of the earth.
Man.	90–21	*p·* a paper on said subject
Pul.	74–10	* Mrs. Eddy preferred to *p·* a
'00.	14–30	*p·* accordingly for the festivity.
Hea.	12–20	To *p·* the medicine requires time and
Po.	vii– 6	* *to p· a few bound volumes of*
My.	156–11	to *p·* for the material passover,

prepared

Mis.	39– 2	*p·* to take a course of instruction
	90–28	His spiritually *p·* breakfast,
	131–13	If our Board of Directors is *p·* to
	152–18	receive the heritage that God has *p·*
	176–27	Are we *p·* to meet and improve them,
Man.	18–23	By-Laws, as *p·* by Mrs Eddy,
	28–11	and *p·* not himself, — *Luke* 12 : 47.
	38–11	whose applications are correctly *p·*,
	50– 3	shall be *p·* for burial by
Ret.	40–12	clothes already *p·* for her burial ;
	83–10	Also, they are *p·* to receive the
Un.	6–15	not *p·* to answer intelligently
Pul.	43–22	* sermon *p·* for the occasion by
	57– 8	* The sermon, *p·* by Mrs. Eddy,
	59–17	* The sermon, *p·* by Mrs. Eddy,
	77– 4	* elegant memorials ever *p·*,
'00.	15– 6	partake of what divine Love hath *p·*
My.	32–28	* the specially *p·* Lesson-Sermon.
	147–22	and *p·* for your use work-rooms
	156–19	*p·* for the reception of Truth
	178– 9	and *p·* for all peoples.
	184– 5	what God hath *p·* for them that wait
	234–28	before the minds . . . are *p·* for it,

prepares

Mis.	229– 2	This mental state *p·* one to
My.	12–24	God *p·* the way for doing ;

preparing

Mis.	163– 4	*p·* to heal and teach divinely ;
'00.	15–17	Love has been *p·* a feast for
My.	345–30	They are *p·* the way for us."

preponderate

Mis.	287–14	should *p·* over the evil,

preposterous

My.	219–13	not be more *p·* than to believe

prerogative

Mis.	90–26	without this *p·* being conferred by
	209– 3	usurpest the *p·* of divine wisdom,
Un.	32– 3	usurps the *p·* of God, saying,
No.	23– 5	neither grasp the *p·* of God nor
My.	179– 7	power and *p·* of Spirit
	218– 9	The power and *p·* of Truth
	340–14	the *p·* of making laws for the State

prerogatives

Ret.	70– 6	usurps the deific *p·*

presage

Ret.	18–24	clouds are a *p·*, — they darken my lay :
Po.	64–20	clouds are a *p·*, — they darken my lay :

Presbyterian

Ret.	14– 5	of the strictest *P·* doctrines.

prescribe

Rud.	3–16	*p·* drugs, or deny God.
Peo.	4–25	inquired of . . . what drugs to *p·*.

prescribed

Mis.	248–24	my regular physician *p·* morphine,
Ret.	85–15	order *p·* by supernal grace.
	87–17	divine order as *p·* by Jesus,
My.	345–16	*p·* pellets without any medication

prescribing

Ret.	26– 2	nor *p·* drugs to support the

prescription

Mis.	210–23	and a medical *p·*.
	243–26	Even doctors disagree on that *p·* :
'01.	34– 9	the M. D.'s material *p·*.

presence

all

No.	18– 5	all *p·*, power, and glory.

all-pervading

Un.	45–15	I try to show its all-pervading *p·*

and glory

No.	20–22	only power, *p·*, and glory.

and power

Mis.	71–19	factors of divine *p·* and power.
	174– 4	claiming . . . *p·* and power over
	175– 1	breathes His *p·* and power,
Un.	41–17	continual *p·* and power of good,
My.	118–18	of Truth's *p·* and power.

bodily

Rud.	1–17	the word *personal* to *bodily p·*,

continual

No.	37–17	His continual *p·*, knowledge, and

divine

(see **divine**)

dread

Un.	64–13	hope of ever eluding their dread *p·*

eternal

Un.	60–28	must yield to His eternal *p·*,

gentle

Mis.	331–18	O gentle *p·*, peace and joy
	389– 6	O gentle *p·*, peace and joy
Po.	4– 1	O gentle *p·*, peace and joy

God's

Mis.	113– 2	God's *p·* gives spiritual light,
	345– 2	God's *p·* and providence.
Un.	2– 7	realize God's *p·*, power, and
My.	354–19	sign and substance Of God's *p·*

her

Ret.	5–24	* Her *p·*, like the gentle dew
My.	39–27	* realize her *p·* with us to-day.

His

Mis.	152– 5	includes also His *p·*
	175– 1	breathes His *p·* and power,
	263–13	His *p·*, power, and peace
	347–20	guardians of His *p·* go before me.
Ret.	9–20	* feel His *p·* in the vast and dim
Un.	4–10	the understanding of His *p·*,
	10–28	to hide from His *p·* under their
	37–12	and the heaven of His *p·* ;
'01.	7–27	any evidence of His *p·* thereby.
Peo.	1–11	the angels of His *p·*,
My.	177–21	glory of His *p·* rests upon it,
	188– 8	but in recognition of His *p·* ;
	193– 3	His *p·* with you will bring
	356– 5	liberty and glory of His *p·*,

his

Mis.	379– 6	I read the copy in his *p·*,

its

Ret.	88–30	and its *p·* felt in eternal stillness
No.	18–11	the secret of its *p·* lies in the

presence

its
My.	3–17	Its *p·* is felt, for it acts
	240–12	Its *p·* is felt, for it acts

my
Po.	73–14	Witness my *p·* and utter my
My.	201–28	a line from me in lieu of my *p·*
	321–16	* talked so freely in my *p·*.

of evil
Mis.	103– 1	precludes the *p·* of evil.

of Him
Mis.	174– 7	come into the *p·* of Him

of its tormentor
Mis.	278– 5	the *p·* of its tormentor.

of Mary Baker Eddy
My.	143–15	personality and *p·* of Mary Baker Eddy,

of the thousands
My.	63–26	* *p·* of the thousands who had come,

or power
My.	262–19	effulgence, deific *p·* or power.

palpable
Mis.	294– 9	transcribes . . . the living, palpable *p·*

peaceful
Mis.	392– 5	With peaceful *p·* hath begirt thee
Po.	20– 6	With peaceful *p·* hath begirt thee

personal
Mis.	322–15	By any personal *p·*, or word
My.	177– 8	no special need of my personal *p·*

power and
Mis.	77–13	bond of union, the power and *p·*,
	173–23	not met by another power and *p·*,
	333–14	good, is supreme, *all* power and *p·*,

powerful
Un.	60– 9	then conjure up, . . . a powerful *p·*

primal
My.	347–15	had reproduced her primal *p·*,

prompt
My.	243–20	Your prompt *p·* in Concord

spiritual
Mis.	328–22	spiritual *p·* and idea of God.

supposititious
Mis.	355–20	responsible for its supposititious *p·*.

their
Mis.	306–25	we know their *p·* by the love
'02.	12–27	annually favor us with their *p·*
My.	7–11	annually favor us with their *p·*
	63–29	* to tell by their *p·* that they

your
My.	188–19	will not shut me out from your *p·*.

Mis.	103–23	*p·*, and individuality of God.
Pul.	40–17	* *p·* of four different congregations,
	42–10	* *p·* of several hundred children
No.	27–25	In *p·* of such thoughts
'01.	13–30	So long as we indulge the *p·*
'02.	7–12	prefix to the words *potence, p·*,
My.	46–21	* in the *p·* of this assembled host,

present (noun)
Mis.	12–11	The *p·* is ours ;
	84–31	those who have utilized the *p·*,
	100– 8	Past, *p·*, future, will show
	230– 7	make the most of the *p·*.
	285–22	In the *p·* or future,
	285–30	will have no past, *p·*, or future.
Un.	46–27	as it does of the *p·*.
Pul.	7–20	false prophets in the *p·*
No.	28–16	*p·*, as well as the future,
Pan.	10–15	*p·* and future of those students
Hea.	2–25	Past, *p·*, future magnifies his name
My.	12–28	power to "act in the living *p·*."
	13– 2	on the past, *p·*, nor future,
	22–21	* needs of the *p·* and of the future
	133– 3	in the great light of the *p·*,
	147– 4	the *p·* is prophetic.
	153–22	in the past as in the *p·*,
	158–14	and joys in the *p·*
	224–14	Avoid for the . . . *p·* public debating

present (adj., adv.)
Mis.	9–14	good far beyond the *p·* sense
	34–18	in our *p·* state of existence,
	34–24	mortal thought on this *p·* plane
	38–28	in order to cure his *p·* disease,
	42–29	*Can I be treated without being p·*
	56–28	*of existence to the p· time?*
	66–32	*p·* capability of the learner,
	86–29	constitutes their *p·* earth and
	92– 3	*p·* liability of deviating from
	95– 8	* shorthand reporter who was *p·*,
	98– 3	to improve his *p·* condition ;
	146–12	This is not my *p·* province ;
	148–26	contributions from the people *p·*
	152–12	I, as a dictator, . . . am not *p·* ;
	152–14	am *p·*, and rejoice with them
	160–13	It satisfies my *p·* hope.
	188–21	where the *p·* writer found it,
	196–18	illumines our *p·* existence

present (adj., adv.)
Mis.	251–19	*p·* possibilities of mankind.
	273–16	in their *p·* line of labor
	277–14	Then can the *p·* mode
	284– 9	sphere of his *p·* usefulness.
	299– 8	which demands our *p·* attention.
	306–27	nor a loved person *p·* ;
	316–14	profited up to their *p·* capacity
	319–20	let the *p·* season pass without
	322– 8	*p·* to address this congregation,
	322–19	though I be *p·* or absent,
	344–22	*p·* with the Lord." — *II Cor.* 5 : 8.
	352– 7	error of its *p·* erroneous course,
	355– 2	*p·* stage of progress in C. S.
	357– 9	is above the *p·* status of religion
	358–28	Let Scientists . . . do their *p·* work,
	367–21	To good, evil is never *p·* ;
	368–17	This evil obtains in the *p·* false
	381– 6	defendant being *p·* personally
Man.	51–24	shall be *p·* at meetings
	56–14	its officers are required to be *p·*.
	72–22	continue its *p·* form of government
	73–17	vote of, the active members *p·*,
	90–14	shall be *p·* at the sessions,
Chr.	53–33	Forever *p·*, bounteous, free,
Ret.	14– 4	I was of course *p·*.
	15–29	many others *p·* had been healed
	31–30	potency of a *p·* spiritual *afflatus*.
	41– 2	as contrasted with its *p·* welcome
	83–29	*p·* liability of deviating
	93– 4	At the *p·* epoch
Un.	2– 4	"a very *p·* help — *Psal.* 46 : 1.
	4–28	at the *p·* crude hour,
	6– 1	Our *p·* understanding is
	37– 7	God and heaven, or Life, are *p·*,
	41–16	illumine our *p·* being with
	43– 6	The *p·* mortal sense of being
	54– 6	If the claim be *p·* to the thought,
	59–18	divine idea is always *p·*.
Pul.	1–10	Time past and time *p·*,
	1–19	be *p·* *in propria persona?*
	1–19	Were I *p·*, methinks I should
	3–29	to reach out for a *p·* realization
	14– 4	*p·* apathy as to the tendency of
	23–23	* latter part of the *p·* century,
	30–28	* grown to its *p·* impressive
	31– 5	* *p·* application of the principles
	36– 9	* I was *p·* at the class lectures
	36–11	* by the men and women *p·*
	55–24	* The *p·* Boston congregation
	68–25	* meeting held at the *p·* location
	75–17	* MANY TORONTO SCIENTISTS *P·*
	87– 1	* cordially invite you to be *p·*
	87– 3	* We especially desire you to be *p·*
No.	2–26	*p·* ignorance in relation to C. S.
	18–26	regulates the *p·* high premium on
	28– 1	else their *p·* mistakes would
'00.	1– 5	*p·* with the ever-present Love
'01.	16– 5	poignant *p·* sense of sin
	17– 1	The *p·* self-inflicted sufferings of
'02.	2–19	*p·* modifications in ecclesiasticism
	4–23	all periods — past, *p·*, and future.
My.	16–15	* there were *p·* on this occasion :
	23– 6	* erection of the *p·* edifice in 1894,
	24–21	* *p·* time there are no less than
	25– 1	* the *p·* Thanksgiving season ;
	25–18	I cannot be *p·* *in propria persona*
	36– 5	* five thousand *p·* rose as one
	39–23	* Mrs. Eddy, was *p·*.
	41–22	* into *p·* and hourly application
	45–10	* physically *p·* at the dedication
	47– 7	* church has reached its *p·* growth,
	49–23	* instruct those *p·* as to their duties
	50– 4	* Most of those *p·* had left their
	54– 3	* those *p·* enduring the
	54–14	* there were *p·* about eight hundred
	54–27	* large congregation was *p·*.
	63–24	* has come to the *p·* age.
	74–25	* Our *p·* relations with them are
	77–24	* *p·* to participate in the occasion.
	86–10	* to be *p·* at the dedication
	100– 8	* were *p·* in the building,
	110– 5	At the *p·* time this Bethlehem star
	129–23	*p·* harmony wherein the good man's
	133– 4	light of the *p·* fulfilment.
	137–24	before the *p·* proceedings were
	138–10	*p·* proceedings test my trust
	142–27	your kind invitation to be *p·*
	146–19	their *p·* application to mankind,
	151– 2	*p·* schoolboy epithets and attacks
	152–29	remote, predisposing, and *p·* cause
	162– 3	"very *p·* help — *Psal.* 46 : 1.
	164–13	is *p·* to manifest light.
	164–15	with its *p·* prosperity?
	170–10	all *p·* here in Concord.
	176– 7	illustrate the past by your *p·* love.

present (adj., adv.)

My.	184–12	inviting me to be *p·*
	192–21	to be *p·* at the dedication
	204–18	*p·* practice of C. S. in your State,
	216–21	adapted to your *p·* unfolding
	219– 1	unless I am personally *p·.*
	220–24	Past, *p·*, or future philosophy
	224–32	under the *p·* persecution
	236–14	exchange the *p·* name for
	237– 6	for a *p·* student of this Science.
	237–11	adapted to the *p·* demand.
	243–13	dozen or more of the *p·* incumbents.
	281– 6	I cited, as our *p·* need,
	301– 5	*p·* flux in religious faith
	314–17	*p·* in court when the decision was
	339–21	rejoice in their *p·* Christianity
	342–31	*p·* rules of service and *p·* rulership
	343– 6	"No *p·* change is contemplated
	356– 1	know their *p·* ownership of all good,
	360–10	*p·* momentous question at issue

present at—

Mis.	6– 8	At *p·* the majority of the acute
	13– 1	of which I feel at *p·* capable,
	32–26	at *p·* necessary for the individual,
	43– 6	*Do all who at p· claim to be*
	91– 3	it should be observed at *p·*
	145– 1	at *p·* is the cement of society,
	171–26	Few people at *p·* know aught of
	242–15	At *p·*, I am in another department
	256–12	remaining at *p·* a public servant:
	272–11	* this Act is at *p·* incorporated
	273–11	of relieving my tasks as at *p·.*
	273–20	should continue, as at *p·*,
	274– 6	I must stop teaching at *p·.*
	286–10	At *p·*, more spiritual conception
	289–10	at *p·* the application of scientific
	358– 8	They include for him at *p·*
Man.	29–16	salary . . . shall be at *p·*
Ret.	50–24	at *p·*, continue to organize
	85– 5	at *p·* they can employ any other
Rud.	14– 4	must at *p·* ask a suitable price
'01.	20–25	At *p·* its mystery protects it,
My.	187– 5	too busy to think of doing so at *p·.*
	216–28	you will feel more than at *p·*
	251–14	which at *p·* is taught in the
	345–23	At *p·* I am conservative about

present ever—

Mis.	27–22	though God is ever *p·*;
Un.	37–11	Because God is ever *p·*,
	60–21	If God is ever *p·*,
No.	30–12	this perfect law is ever *p·*
'02.	12–10	that God is come, and is ever *p·.*
My.	110– 2	is ever *p·*, casting out evils,

present (verb)

Mis.	11–30	I have but two to *p·.*
	33– 9	*p·* the type and shadow of Truth's
	46–11	would not *p·* this question.
	78–29	to *p·* the quality of good.
	164–15	*p·* a wonderful manifestation of
	196–31	acceptance of the truths they *p·*;
	279–13	*p·* themselves to my thought;
	282– 7	The question will *p·* itself:
	375– 1	Pictures which *p·* disordered phases
	381–11	why he did not *p·* evidence to
	381–15	"There is no evidence to *p·.*"
Man.	36–20	*p·* to him a recommendation
	89–14	*p·* such credentials as are required
Pul.	86–21	* we hereby *p·* this church to you
'02.	14–17	truths . . . to *p·* to the world.
Hea.	17– 5	*p·* the image and likeness of God.
Peo.	8– 1	to *p·* the right idea of Truth;
My.	47– 7	* *p·* in this report a few
	61–30	* problems which . . . *p·* themselves
	170–14	I would *p·* a gift to you to-day,
	172–11	Permit me to *p·* to you
	194–19	you *p·* to me the princely gift
	216–19	which I *p·* to your thought,

presentation

Mis.	50–11	as lucid in *p·* as can be possible,
	142–12	beautiful boat and *p·* poem.
	164– 5	human *p·* of goodness in man.
	280–22	*p·* was made in a brief address by
Man.	91–12	on *p·* of the card to the teacher.
Pul.	56–10	* does not admit of an elaborate *p·*
My.	238–13	discovery, and *p·* of C. S.
	272–30	* interested in this *p·* of the

presented

Mis.	95– 5	* was *p·* to Mr. Cook's audience,
	142– 7	boat *p·* by Christian Scientists
	148–24	*p·* at your Friday evening meetings.
	153–23	to whom I *p·* a copy of . . . "S. and H.
	197–19	divinity which Jesus *p·*

presented

Mis.	261–22	No greater type of . . . Love can be *p·*
	280– 4	one of the angels *p·* himself
	280–19	*p·* their teacher with an elegant
	379– 5	He immediately *p·* them.
	379–11	vein of thought *p·* by these.
Man.	75– 7	*p·* to Rev. Mary Baker Eddy
	79–13	names . . . shall be *p·* to Mrs. Eddy
Ret.	48–14	*p·* and passed unanimously:
Un.	6–10	as now *p·* to the people
Pul.	28– 9	* crown and the star are *p·* in
Hea.	10– 8	*p·* the highest ideal of Love.
Po.	vii–11	* *volume is p· to the public,*
My.	vi–24	* *p·* to her church the property
	13– 6	was *p·* to me in 1903 by
	40–24	* Mrs. Eddy, has *p·* to the world
	95– 5	* built upon the tenets first *p·* by
	121–16	Christmas ring *p·* to me
	165–13	*p·* to me for First Church
	171–26	* *p·* as a love-token for the church
	218–14	*p·* his *material* body absolved from
	273– 2	* This manuscript is *p·* simply as an
	273–16	should be early *p·* to youth
	281– 1	*p·* itself and awakened a wiser want,
	310–27	* my disposition as exemplary
	311–21	*p·* me my coat-of-arms,
	320– 3	* I *p·* my matter for a theme
	329–18	* *p·* to Mrs Eddy by Miss Harrison.
	347– 9	a loving-cup, *p·* July 16, 1903.
	356–17	now and heretofore *p·* in S. and H.

presenting

Mis.	149– 8	after *p·* the various offerings,
	184–10	*p·* our bodies holy and acceptable,
Man.	66– 3	before *p·* it to the Church
Ret.	53– 1	*p·* to its loyal members
Pul.	43–29	* Before *p·* the sermon,
My.	69– 6	* *p·* an oval and dome appearance
	172– 8	* In *p·* this gavel to President Bates,
	315–21	what is the *McClure* "history," . . . *p·*?
	346– 5	* *p·* another view of her religion.

Present Order of Communion Services
in Branch Churches

Man.	125– 1	heading

Present Order of Services, etc.

Man.	120– 1	heading

presents

Mis.	ix–10	easel of time *p·* pictures
	52–14	sometimes *p·* the most wretched
	127–30	Mortal mind *p·* phases of character
	172–19	*p·* but a finite, feeble sense of
	188– 6	*p·* as being first that which
	189–16	*p·* a false sense of existence,
	355– 2	stage of progress in C. S. *p·*
	373–19	This master's thought *p·* a sketch
	373–31	it *p·* not words alone, but works,
Un.	52–13	*p·* Truth's spiritual idea,
Pul.	6– 8	It *p·* to the understanding,
No.	27–14	*p·* the grand and eternal verities
Pan.	3– 5	poorly *p·* the poetical phase of
'00.	12–30	Nicolaitan church *p·* the phase of
'01.	35– 4	The question oft *p·* itself,
My.	20–14	what you would expend for *p·* to her,
	256–14	the pure pages of impersonal *p·*,
	259–14	most pleasing Christmas *p·*,
	272– 8	*p·*, . . . no claim that man is equal to
	272–20	* The *Cosmopolitan p·* this month
	274–22	an abundance of material *p·*;
	299–14	*p·* the demonstrable divine Principle

preservation

Pul.	27– 5	* vault for the safe *p·* of papers.

preserve

Mis.	ix–15	To *p·* a long course of years
	110– 8	pray that you *p·* these virtues
	131– 9	Christian Scientists *p·* unity,
	287–30	*p·* affection on both sides.
Pul.	4–10	to *p·* a scientific, positive sense of
'01.	26–14	to *p·* Christ's vesture unrent;
My.	226– 4	*p·* an intelligent usage of the word

preserved

Mis.	290– 5	animus of the contract is *p·* intact.
My.	147–13	May this little sanctum be *p·* sacred
	268– 4	so long as the *morale* . . . is *p·.*

preserver

Pan.	4– 5	the creator and *p·* of man.
	4–18	chapter sub-title
	4–20	Spirit, is indeed the *p·* of man.
	7–10	God, the *p·* of man, declared

preservers

Pan.	4–27	if these are not man's *p·*?

preserves

Mis.	302– 6	*p·* in his own consciousness

preserving
- *My.* 286–12 *p·* peace among nations.
- 344–11 *p·* individuality and personality

preside
- *Pan.* 3– 3 supposed to *p·* over sylvan
- *My.* 39–22 * pleasant duty to *p·* at an annual

presided
- *Pul.* 43– 7 * *p·* over the exercises.
- 60– 7 * Judge Hanna, . . . *p·*, reading in clear,

presidency
- *Man.* 89– 1 *P·* of College.

President
- *Mis.* 305–30 * first *P·* of the United States,
- 306–20 * who was at that time the *P·*
- 312–11 *P·* of the World's Congress
- *Man.* 25– 6 *P·*, a Clerk, a Treasurer, and
- 25– 8 *P·*.
- 25– 8 *P·* shall be elected, subject to
- 25–12 *P·* shall hold office for one year,
- 33– 8 A Reader shall not be a *P·*
- *Ret.* 6–19 afterwards *P·* of the United States ;
- '02. 3– 7 I rejoice that the *P·* of
- *My.* 16–16 * *P·* of The Mother Church ;
- 39– 4 * meeting was opened by the *P·*,
- 39–15 * *P·*, Willis F. Gross, C.S.B. ;
- 39–17 * In introducing the new *P·*,
- 39–18 * When I introduce the incoming *P·*,
- 42– 6 * *P·* for the coming year,
- 112–30 home of the *P·* of the United States,
- 171–25 * by the *P·*, Mr. E. P. Bates,
- 172– 1 * *P·* of The Mother Church.
- 278–13 The revered *P·* and Congress
- 293– 7 Our lamented *P·*, in his loving
- 309– 8 afterwards *P·* of the United States,
- (*see also* **Eddy, Garfield, McKinley, Pierce's, Roosevelt**)

president
- *Pan.* 3–27 *p·* of the mountains,
- *My.* 136–22 justice of the peace and *p·* of
- (*see also* **Eddy**)

presiding
- *My.* 291– 4 *P·* over the destinies of

Press
- *Pul.* 89– 8 * *P·*, Albany, N. Y.
- 89– 9 * *P·*, New York City.
- 89–10 * *P·*, Philadelphia, Pa.

press
- *Mis.* 10–16 more assured to *p·* on safely.
- 125–17 *p·* on to Life's long lesson,
- 206–24 *P·* patiently on; God is good,
- 245– 9 combined efforts of . . . pulpit and *p·*
- 246– 1 It is the pulpit and *p·*,
- 246– 6 It was the Southern pulpit and *p·*
- 274–17 *p·* is gagged, liberty is besieged ;
- 274–18 when the *p·* assumes the liberty to
- 300–16 the pulpit, instead of the *p·*,
- 321–19 *P·* on, *p·* on ! ye sons of light,
- 338–19 armies of earth *p·* hard upon you.
- 348– 1 They *p·* forward towards the mark
- *Man.* 41–11 by the churches or the *p·*,
- 97–19 by the daily *p·*, by periodicals or
- *Pul.* vii– 1 scintillations from *p·* and pulpit
- 5–16 *p·* and pulpit cannonaded this book,
- 8– 1 All praise to the *p·* of
- 8– 2 the *p·* has spoken out historically,
- 8– 5 chimes repeat my thanks to the *p·*.
- 31–21 * favor of an interview for *p·* use,
- 54– 4 * touch him in life's throng and *p·*,
- '00. 6– 7 I *p·* toward the mark — *Phil.* 3 : 14.
- 7–10 bar and bench, *p·* and pulpit,
- '01. 16–19 individual, the pulpit, or the *p·*.
- *Po.* 39– 9 May we *p·* on and up !
- *My.* 95–11 * *p·* gallery of commentators.
- 99–19 * *p·* reports state that the
- 108–27 words of the New York *p·*
- 114–31 from pulpit and *p·*,
- 141–21 * has just given out to the *p·*,
- 151–12 injustice done by *p·* and pulpit
- 154–25 emanating from the pulpit and *p·*.
- 182–32 *p·* on to the infinite uses of
- 192– 3 *p·* on unto the possession of
- 195–14 *p·* on with what we are,
- 201– 2 *P·* on towards the high calling
- 202–27 *P·* on. The way is narrow at first,
- 207– 4 *P·* on ! The wrath of men shall
- 253– 6 *P·* on ! My heart and hope
- 297– 1 gave her discovery to the *p·*.
- 316–17 eloquent appeal to the *p·*
- 317– 5 * allegations in the public *p·*
- 329–24 * fair attitude of the *p·*

pressed
- *Mis.* 261–14 full, *p·* down, and running over.
- *Pul.* 29–13 * number of chairs *p·* into service
- *My.* 21–19 * "good measure, *p·* down, — *Luke* 6 : 38.

presses
- *My.* 129–17 he *p·* to his original,

pressing
- *Mis.* 115–14 *p·* need of a proper preparation of
- 155–10 *p·* meekly on, be faithful,
- *My.* 110–15 mortal mind *p·* to the front,
- 155–12 *p·* forward in the onward march of

prestige
- *Mis.* 115–20 evil has neither *p·*, power, nor
- 334–12 all its supposed power and *p·*.
- *No.* 41–23 sin is losing *p·* and power.
- *Pan.* 6–13 social *p·*, a large following,
- *My.* 5–12 mortal pride and power, *p·* or

presume
- *Mis.* 265–15 shallow moralist may *p·* to
- *My.* 330– 3 * I *p·* we should not be surprised
- 361– 4 I do not *p·* to give you

presumption
- *My.* 228–27 who has the divine *p·* to say :

presumptuous
- *Ret.* 72– 8 result of secret faults, *p·* sins,
- *My.* 113–18 Neither is it *p·* or unscriptural

presumptuously
- *Mis.* 231–17 finger *p·* poked into the little mouth

presuppose
- *Mis.* 187–13 *p·* a material man to be the first
- 217–17 *p·* that nature is matter,
- *Un.* 39–25 They *p·* that . . . man is evil,
- *No.* 15–17 *p·* an impotent God and an incredible

presupposes
- *Mis.* 49–26 *p·* . . . a power opposed to God,
- 257– 3 Pantheism *p·* that God sleeps
- *No.* 35–13 *p·* Life, substance, . . . in matter,

pretence
- *Mis.* 210–22 under the false *p·* of human need,

pretend
- *Mis.* 173–18 without . . . power to act, or vanity to *p·*
- 353–30 They do not love Mother, but *p·* to ;

pretended
- *Un.* 33– 4 give the only *p·* testimony
- *My.* 327–24 * section formerly read, "*p·* healers,"

pretender
- *Un.* 44–12 *p·* taught the opposite of Truth.
- *No.* 31– 4 has for ages been a *p·*,

pretense
- *Un.* 64– 1 If sin has any *p·* of existence,

pretension
- *Rud.* 7–20 As a *p·* to be Mind,

pretentious
- *Mis.* 226–11 *p·* praise of hypocrites,
- *Un.* 51–11 supplied by the *p·* usurpation,

preternatural
- *Mis.* 199–28 neither supernatural nor *p·* ;
- *Peo.* 3–12 would affirm that . . . are *p·* ;

pretext
- *Mis.* 109– 6 sure *p·* of moral defilement.
- *My.* 37–25 * *p·* for our confident and favorable

pretty
- *Mis.* 203– 2 your gift of the *p·* pond
- 218–29 "*P·* well, I thank you !"
- 231–25 into saying, "Oh, *p·* !"

prevail
- *Mis.* 7–11 skepticism and incredulity *p·*
- 107– 4 Art must not *p·* over Science.
- 129–14 let silence *p·* over his remains.
- 141– 9 gates of hell" cannot *p·*. — *Matt.* 16 : 18.
- 144–20 gates of hell shall not *p·* — *Matt.* 16 : 18.
- *Pul.* 22–19 healing power of Christ will *p·*.
- *No.* 38–12 gates of hell cannot *p·*.
- *Pan.* 10– 8 *p·* over the opposite notion

prevailed
- *Mis.* 140–16 Unity *p·*, — till mortal man sought
- '00. 12–16 Magical arts *p·* at Ephesus
- *My.* 293–20 to mortal sense the flesh *p·*.

prevailing
- *Pul.* 66–24 * encroachment upon *p·* faiths,
- *My.* 50–18 * Love *p·* over the apparently
- 309–24 *p·* style of architecture

prevails
- *My.* 329– 4 * idea *p·* that the last

prevalent
- *Un.* 11–21 the ruder sort then *p·*,

prevent
Mis.	ix –3	* *p·* a man from accepting charity ;
	19– 4	and *p·* its demonstration ;
	42–31	our own false admissions *p·* us from
	45– 7	allay fear, *p·* inflammation, and
	81– 4	*p·* all unpleasant and unchristian
	208– 4	Mortals cannot *p·* the fulfilment of
	214–28	This would *p·* the possibility of
	232–28	this will *p·* mankind from
	236–19	restore harmony and *p·* dishonor.
	243–28	will *p·* the secretions of
	256–12	*p·* my classes from forming
	279– 4	*p·* the wrong action?
	288–20	would *p·* scientific demonstration.
	302– 1	an evil which you can *p·* :
	362–29	*p·* sin or reform the sinner.
Man.	43–19	*p·* C. S. from being *adulterated*.
	110– 3	*p·* applications being duplicated
Ret.	78– 9	will *p·* the demonstration of C. S.
No.	9– 9	to *p·* their legitimate action
	43–24	will never *p·* or reconstruct
Hea.	18–16	if it could *p·* its effervescing
My.	64–21	* sins which would *p·* the realization
	140–26	does not *p·* its distant members
	188–20	cannot *p·* me from entering
	241– 8	* concealed to *p·* their advancement
	292–19	would *p·* the result desired.
	308– 2	can never *p·* being accomplished

prevented
No.	9– 2	would have *p·*, to a great extent,
My.	195– 7	have hitherto *p·* my reply.
	235–29	in time to have *p·* it,
	293–15	and thus they *p·* the power of
	314–22	*p·* Dr. Patterson's arrest

preventing
'01.	33–30	by *p·* the early employment of an M.D.
My.	219– 9	*p·* the occasion for its use ;
	286–12	for the purpose of *p·* war

prevention
My.	268– 2	chapter sub-title

preventive
Mis.	229–25	a better *p·* of contagion

prevents
Mis.	49–23	it *p·* a recognition of the
	308–26	consciousness of disease *p·* the
	350–24	Hence it *p·* the normal action,
No.	5–27	*p·* one from healing scientifically,
Pan.	7– 4	and thus *p·* the demonstration
My.	233– 5	which *p·* an effective watch?
	275–20	all that *p·* my daily drive.

previous
Mis.	52–28	work out the *p·* example,
	256–19	*p·* to the opening term.
Man.	49–25	without *p·* injury or illness,
	52–12	his *p·* character has been good,
Ret.	44–15	*p·* harmony and prosperity.
	82–29	clearer than any *p·* edition,
Un.	10– 6	to name any *p·* teachers,
	14– 9	improve upon His own *p·* work,
Pul.	55– 5	* In a *p·* article we have referred
My.	49–18	* received at the *p·* meeting
	49–22	* minutes of the *p·* meeting were
	54–28	* *p·* consideration of places for
	223– 3	without *p·* appointment
	336–16	* had made no will *p·* to his

previously
Mis.	46– 8	any doctrine *p·* entertained.
Ret.	23– 7	*P·* the cloud of mortal mind
'02.	13–22	*p·* negotiated for the property
My.	9– 1	* those *p·* established have had
	294–20	hindrances *p·* mentioned,

prey
Mis.	156–23	and in turn becomes a *p·*.
	246–18	to invite its *p·*, then turn and
	246–22	refused to yield its *p·*
	323–12	beasts of *p·* prowl in the path,
	323–20	taming the beasts of *p·*,

preying
My.	215–21	*p·* upon my pearls,

preys
Mis.	156–22	the animal magnetizer *p·*,

price
Mis.	7–23	*p·* at which we shall issue it,
	99– 8	awful *p·* : the temporary loss of his
	149– 3	and without *p·*." — *Isa.* 55 : 1.
	165–24	but, they never paid the *p·* of sin.
	253– 3, 4	bought with a *p·*, a great *p·* ;
	253– 5	the *p·* that he paid for it?
	269–26	not willing to pay the *p·*.
	342–26	if you pay the *p·* of Truth,
Man.	46–24	reduce his *p·* in chronic cases
	84–13	student's *p·* for teaching C. S.

price
Ret.	41– 5	and without *p·*," — *Isa.* 55 : 1.
	50– 1	God impelled me to set a *p·* on my
	50– 5	*p·* for each pupil in one course
Rud.	14– 5	suitable *p·* for their services,
	14–15	to take the full *p·* of tuition
No.	35–14	the awful *p·* paid by sin,
'00.	15– 1	you purchase, at whatever *p·*,
'02.	13–15	about one half the *p·* paid,
	13–25	the *p·* I had paid for it,
	15– 8	and without *p·*," — *Isa.* 55 : 1.
Po.	22–21	blood was not its *p·*.
My.	v–18	* and without *p·*." — *Isa.* 55 : 1.
	16– 8	* the purchase *p·* of the land
	127–26	but it is rich beyond *p·*,
	215– 4	bestowed without money or *p·*.
	221– 1	The earthly *p·* of spirituality

priceless
Mis.	30–13	*p·* understanding of man's real
	61– 2	*p·*, eternal, and just at hand.
	252–31	yea, it is the pearl *p·*
	270–13	*p·* knowledge of his Principle
My.	215– 3	knew well the *p·* worth of
	347–18	parable of the *p·* pearl

pride
all
My.	134–17	Life lessens all *p·*

and affection
Mis.	295–13	Scotchman's national *p·* and affection,

and ease
'02.	9– 7	*p·* and ease concern you less,

and joy
'02.	3–10	the old national family *p·* and joy

and satisfaction
My.	74–18	* *p·* and satisfaction that is

and self
Mis.	92–32	divests himself of *p·* and self,
Ret.	84–20	divests himself most of *p·* and self,

apparent
Mis.	239–21	Her apparent *p·* at sharing in

arrogant
Ret.	84–15	In times past, arrogant *p·*,

burdened by
Mis.	328–17	burdened by *p·*, sin, and self,

chastens
Mis.	387–25	chastens *p·* and earth-born fear,
Po.	6–20	chastens *p·* and earth-born fear,

cheek of
Ret.	31–23	Blanched was the cheek of *p·*.

come from
Rud.	9–19	similar effects come from *p·*,

disgusting
Mis.	233– 5	the feverish, disgusting *p·* of

fetters of
Mis.	394– 7	loosens the fetters of *p·*
Po.	45– 9	loosens the fetters of *p·*

her
My.	313–28	wounded her *p·* when I adopted C. S.,

human
(see **human**)

ignorance and
Mis.	92–27	arrogant ignorance and *p·*,
	354–22	self-conceit, ignorance, and *p·*

is ignorance
Mis.	2– 3	*P·* is ignorance ;

lawful
Pul.	48–24	* The natural and lawful *p·*

love and
Po.	8–21	a home of love and *p·* ;

mortal
My.	5–12	mortal *p·* and power, prestige or

of circumstance
Mis.	155– 3	*p·* of circumstance or power

of circumstances
My.	37– 3	* no *p·* of circumstances has place

of life
Mis.	116–18	pleasures and pains and *p·* of life :
	183– 1	*p·* of life will then be quenched
Hea.	17– 2	lusts of the flesh, the *p·* of life,

of opinion
Un.	5– 7	mental struggles and *p·* of opinion

of physical life
Un.	39– 5	and the *p·* of physical life

of place
My.	4–24	The *p·* of place or power

of power
My.	205–25	lust of the flesh and the *p·* of power

of sects
'01.	2–17	feverish *p·* of sects and systems

or gold
My.	283–29	Lured by fame, *p·*, or gold,

or power
My.	252–28	allurements of wealth, *p·*, or power ;

our
Mis.	224– 2	our *p·* that makes another's criticism

pride

pardonable
My. 64– 8   * If to-day we feel a pardonable *p·*
personal
My. v–12   * the mesmerism of personal *p·*
pomp and
Ret. 79–17   worldly policy, pomp, and *p·*,
pomp and its
Po. 16–11   toil for its pomp and its *p·*.
pomp or
Mis. 144–14   without pomp or *p·*,
power and
My. 206– 3   with power and *p·* of position,
rebels
Mis. 204– 1   agony struggles, *p·* rebels,
self-seeking
My. 210–12   self-seeking *p·* of the evil thinker
should sanction
Mis. 330–24   even *p·* should sanction
struggle with
Mis. 378– 9   After . . . a struggle with *p·*,
their
Mis. 226–24   should be restrained by their *p·*.
       327–24   rebuking their *p·*, consoling their
will and
Mis. 141–21   impulses of human will and *p·* ;

Mis. 9– 3   *p·*, self-ignorance, self-will,
     137–25   must control appetite, passion, *p·*,
     145–15   *p·* is a hooded hawk which flies in
     153–15   encompassed not with *p·*, hatred,
     240–22   Passions, appetites, *p·*, selfishness,
Rud. 17– 9   never originated in *p·*, rivalry, or
'02. 16–26   *p·*, self-will, envy, or hate.
Hea. 18–22   *P·*, appetites, passions, envy, and
My. 41– 9   * *P·*, arrogance, and self-will are
     82–16   * *p·* of the Church Directors that
     257–20   all human hate, *p·*, greed, lust
     283–19   When *p·*, self, and human reason

Priest *and* priest

Mis. 301–30   the commands of our hillside *P·*,
Ret. 91–28   this hillside *p·*, this seaside teacher,
My. 300–20   If, as this kind *p·* claims,

priestcraft

Mis. 106– 9   *P·* in front of them,
Peo. 13–15   Galileo kneeling at the feet of *p·*,

priesthood

Mis. 90–27   organization and ordained *p·*.
     105– 6   rested the anathema of *p·*
Pul. 7–19   unmerciful, and oppressive *p·*
My. 17–12   an holy *p·*,— I *Pet.* 2: 5.
     206–23   a royal *p·*,— I *Pet.* 2: 9.

priestly

Mis. 194– 8   Urim and Thummim of *p·* office,
Ret. 35–24   Urim and Thummim of *p·* office,
'01. 12–14   Urim and Thummim of *p·* office,

priests

Mis. 33– 3   high *p·* of old caused the crucifixion
     123–10   pagan *p·* bloated with crime ;
Peo. 4–23   pagan *p·* appointed Apollo

primal

Mis. 22–30   the *p·* cause, or Mind-force,
     182–15   man's *p·*, spiritual existence,
     187–26   *p·* facts of being are eternal ;
     188– 8   that which is *p·*, spiritual, and
Pul. 12–21   her *p·* and everlasting strain.
'01. 1–19   the *p·* reality of things.
My. 347–15   reproduced her *p·* presence,

primarily

Mis. 9–13   *P·* and ultimately,
Ret. 91–16   spake *p·* to his immediate

Primary

Mis. 264–14   not fitted for it by the *P·* course.
     273–24   applications . . . for the *P·* class
     273–29   if I should teach that *P·* class,
     273–30   one *P·* and two Normal
     280–18   students of this *P·* class,
     318–14   received instructions in a *P·* class
Man. 36– 7   taken the *P·* or Normal Course
     86–23   teachers of the *P·* class shall
     89–12   taught in a *P·* class by Mrs. Eddy
     90–14   no *P·* classes shall be taught under
     91–19   *P·* Students.
Ret. 43–16   taught the *P·*, Normal, and
     43–18   taught one *P·* class, in 1889,
     47–16   *P·* class student, richly imbued with
     47–19   received instructions in a *P·* class
Rud. 14–13   never taught a *P·* class without
     14–22   If the *P·* students are
My. 245–32   given to students of the *P·* class ;
     251– 8   * *P·* and Normal class instruction
     251– 9   * to become teachers of *P·* classes?"
     251–18   A *P·* student of mine can teach

Primary

My. 251–20   my *P·* student can himself be
     319–21   * I entered your *P·* class at Boston.
     320–21   * while I was in your *P·* class
     322–19   * to enter the next *P·* class

primary

Un. 3– 1   *p·* school of mortal existence,
My. 46– 9   * *p·* declaration of this church

Primary Class

Mis. 279– 9   chapter sub-title
     279–10   To THE *P· C·* OF

prime

Ret. 88– 4   his *p·* command, was that his
Pul. 58–24   * their *p·* instructor has ordained
Po. 16–25   waken my joy, as in earliest *p·*.

primeval

Po. 1– 3   *P·* dweller where the wild winds rest,
My. 139– 8   *p·* faith, hope, love.

primitive

Mis. 14–23   Good is the *p·* Principle of man ;
     14–26   evil is neither a *p·* nor a
     17–27   man's *p·*, sinless, spiritual
     102–13   He is universal and *p·*.
     192–24   as *p·* Christianity confirms.
Man. 17–12   should reinstate *p·* Christianity
Ret. 69– 3   *p·* and ultimate source of being ;
Pul. 47–29   * modernized from a *p·* homestead
     69–15   * ideas of *p·* Christianity.
'01. 30– 2   since ever the *p·* Christians,
Hea. 3– 3   *p·* privilege of Christianity
Peo. 5–10   ideals of *p·* Christianity are nigh,
My. 46–12   reinstate *p·* Christianity
     95–28   * days of the *p·* Christians,
     111–15   maintains *p·* Christianity,
     239– 4   relegates Christianity to its *p·*
     245–20   doing the works of *p·* Christianity,

primitives

Mis. 316–13   depart farther from the *p·* of the

primordial

My. 180–10   that *p·* standard of Truth.

prince

Mis. 155– 3   *p·* of this world that has nothing in
My. 4–24   *p·* of this world that hath nothing in

princely

My. 194–20   *p·* gift of your magnificent church

Prince of Peace

Mis. 161– 8   The *P·* of *P·*.— *Isa.* 9: 6.
     164–19   The *P·* of *P·*."— *Isa.* 9: 6.
     321– 6   The *P·* of *P·*."— *Isa.* 9: 6.
Pul. 83–30   * brought to warring men the *P·* of *P·*,

Principal

My. 311–32   Rev. R. S. Rust, D.D., *P·* of the

principal

Man. 31–17   *p·* part of the Sunday services,
Ret. 82–16   population of our *p·* cities
Pul. 5–22   public libraries of the *p·* cities,
     25– 8   * The *p·* features are
Rud. 15–12   This was the *p·* reason for
'00. 1–19   in most of the *p·* cities,
     13–24   *p·* deity in the city of Thyatira
Peo. 8–15   carried on through *p·* processes,
My. vi–19   * *p·* contributor to its columns ;
     68–32   * pews and *p·* woodwork are of
     304– 4   *p·* of Sanbornton Academy,

principally

Mis. 143–18   *p·* the Normal class graduates

Principle

and demonstration
Mis. 69– 7   Science rests on *P·* and demonstration.
and idea
    (*see* **idea**)
and practice
Mis. 173– 2   Science, its *P·* and practice.
     270–13   knowledge of his *P·* and practice.
Rud. 16–18   *P·* and practice laid down in S. and H.,
No. 44– 1   ignorance of its *P·* and practice,
My. 179–22   illustrates the *P·* and practice of
     287–10   *P·* and practice of divine metaphysics.
and rule
Mis. 265–10   all *who follow the P· and rule*
     337– 7   *P·* and rule of C. S.
     356–29   its divine *P·* and rule of practice.
Man. 87–16   *P·* and rule of C. S.,
Ret. 25– 8   *P·* and rule of spiritual Science
Rud. 1– 3   *P·* and rule of universal harmony.
'01. 2–15   demonstrable *P·* and rule
     4– 8   *P·* and rule of divine Science
My. 113–25   in proportion as this *P·* and rule are
     241– 4   * *P·* and rule of C. S.

Principle

and rules
Mis. 19– 9 *P.* and rules of C. S.
354–14 *P.* and rules of C. S.,
Man. 43–24 statement of the divine *P.* and rules
'00. 4–20 *P.* and rules of this Christianity
6– 2 no lack in the *P.* and rules
'01. 22–21 C. S., its divine *P.* and rules,
22–24 if they understood its *P.* and rules
My. 299–14 divine *P.* and rules of the Bible,
basic
My. 348–30 Love is the basic *P.* of all Science,
changing
Hea. 4–27 can we demonstrate a changing *P.*?
curative
Ret. 25– 2 reveal the great curative *P.*,
33–21 the curative *P.*, remains,
Pul. 64–16 * a search for the great curative *P.*.
64–21 * curative *P.* was the Deity.
70–20 * to find the great curative *P.*
Hea. 13–21 Mind as the only curative *P.*.
deific
Pul. 4–14 thus demonstrating deific *P.*.
Rud. 1– 9 these are the deific *P.*.
demonstrable
'01. 2–15 demonstrable *P.* and rule
My. 348–26 demonstrable *P.* and given rule.
demonstrate the
Mis. 215–16 Then we shall demonstrate the *P.*
266–14 demonstrate the *P.* of C. S.
336–16 demonstrate the *P.* of C. S.
Rud. 13– 6 demonstrate the *P.* of this Science,
No. 35– 4 demonstrate the *P.* of such Life ;
destitute of
Un. 49–22 destitute of *P.*, it is devoid of
devotion to
Mis. 176– 9 supreme devotion to *P.*
discerned the
Ret. 26– 4 Adoringly I discerned the *P.*
divine
(see **divine**)
epitome of the
Rud. 8– 9 only an epitome of the *P.*,
eternal
Mis. 369–26 perfect and eternal *P.* of man.
Pul. 4–23 ever unfolding its eternal *P.*.
exemplified the
Pul. 54– 9 * enunciated and exemplified the *P.* ;
fixed
Mis. 147–19 upright man is guided by a fixed *P.*,
232–24 fixed *P.* of all healing is God ;
366– 7 with fixed *P.*, given rule,
No. 11–21 divine Science, with fixed *P.*,
33–10 with fixed *P.*, a given rule,
'01. 23–15 its fixed *P.* and given rule,
My. 106–18 on the basis of fixed *P.*,
113–24 demonstrated on a fixed *P.*
347–27 manifestation of a fixed *P.*
fixed in
Ret. 93–12 immovably fixed in *P.*.
fundamental
Mis. 233– 2 without knowing its fundamental *P.*.
God is the
Mis. 78–26 If God is the *P.* of man
Hea. 3–21 God is the *P.* of Christian healing,
governed by
Mis. 291– 3 a mind governed by *P.*
great
Mis. 192–17 great *P.* of a full salvation.
healing
Mis. 222–25 healing *P.*, . . . is not so obscure ;
heals
No. 21–26 wherein *P.* heals and saves.
My. 180–15 and this *P.* heals sin,
his
Mis. 14–14 if man has lost his *P.*
270–13 priceless knowledge of his *P.*
immortal
Mis. 117– 2 unfolds its immortal *P.*.
infinite
Mis. 16–10 infinite *P.* hath infinite claims
16–22 Love, a divine, infinite *P.* ;
150–29 infinite *P.*, with its universal
181–11 Infinite *P.* and infinite Spirit
258–18 this infinite *P.* of freedom,
Pan. 7– 7 one divine, infinite *P.*.
12–22 infinite *P.*, noumenon and phenomena,
Hea. 4– 5 results of an infinite *P.*,
instead of
Mis. 135– 5 *P.*, instead of person,
Hea. 8–21 through *P.* instead of a pardon ;
My. 152– 2 worshipping person instead of *P.*,
intelligent
My. 226–10 the one divine intelligent *P.*
is found
No. 20–11 *P.* is found to be the only term

Principle

is God
Un. 38– 2 individuality, . . . whose *P.* is God.
38–28 being, whose *P.* is God.
is One
Mis. 264–11 Its *P.* is One,
is right
Ret. 57– 8 *P.* is right ;
its
Mis. 14–14 with harmony and its *P.* ;
45– 5 its *P.* of metaphysical healing,
78–28 exact nature of its *P.*,
173– 2 Science, its *P.* and practice.
264–11 Its *P.* is One,
265–13 demonstrates its *P.* according to
337–10 the Golden Rule and its *P.*,
338– 7 proved . . . that its *P.* is divine.
Ret. 28–26 Its *P.* is divine, not human,
78– 7 for it is governed by its *P.*,
No. 28–23 neither the comprehension of its *P.*
44– 1 substantiates his ignorance of its *P.*
'01. 22–24 understood its *P.* and rules
Peo. 12–22 proved the application of its *P.*
My. 242–13 state its *P.* correctly,
law-abiding
Mis. 206–18 law-abiding *P.*, God.
Life, or
Ret. 28– 2 Life, or *P.*, of all being ;
lose the
My. 206– 4 lose the *P.* of divine metaphysics
Love is
No. 19–12 God is Love ; and Love is *P.*,
Love is the
Mis. 117–14 Love is the *P.* of unity,
234– 6 Love is the *P.* of divine Science ;
'02. 8–21 and Love is the *P.* thereof.
Mind or
My. 246–17 divine Mind or *P.* of man's being
no
Mis. 14–24 evil, good's opposite, has no *P.*,
My. 242– 9 Unless . . . you have no *P.*
no other
Mis. 197–32 and working from no other *P.*,
of all
Mis. 354–20 relying on the *P.* of all
'01. 5–13 calling one the divine *P.* of all.
Hea. 4–22 *P.* of all that is right,
My. 152–16 divine *P.* of all that really is,
of all being
Ret. 28– 2 Life, or *P.*, of all being ;
of all cure
Mis. 3–18 The *P.* of all cure is God,
of all harmony
No. 13– 5 deduction from the *P.* of all harmony,
of all phenomena
No. 21–10 demonstrated the *P.* of all phenomena
of all power
My. 278–29 The *P.* of all power is God,
of all Science
My. 348–30 Love is the basic *P.* of all Science,
of all science
Rud. 4– 6 *Is God the P. of all science,*
of all things
Ret. 26–25 the *P.* of all things pure ;
of being
Mis. 93–17 the unerring *P.* of being.
269–11 elucidate the *P.* of being,
Man. 67–19 the divine *P.* of being
of Christ
My. 149– 5 The *P.* of Christ is divine Love,
of Christianity
Mis. 16– 9 *P.* of Christianity is infinite :
144–29 life-giving *P.* of Christianity,
of Christian Science
Mis. 69– 7 *P.* of C. S. is divine.
104–24 The *P.* of C. S. is Love,
147– 8 divine *P.* of C. S.
221– 8 fundamental *P.* of C. S. ;
242–17 instructed in the *P.* of C. S.
266–14 demonstrate the *P.* of C. S.,
336–16 demonstrate the *P.* of C. S.
363–24 hold fast to the *P.* of C. S.
Rud. 1– 5 *What is the P. of C. S.?*
No. 11–24 grasp the *P.* of C. S.,
43–28 on the *P.* of C. S.,
'01. 21–20 Life is the *P.* of C. S.
My. 112– 1 by means of the *P.* of C. S.
118– 3 promoting the true *P.* of C. S.
218–13 the divine *P.* of C. S.
270–29 *P.* of C. S. will ultimately
279– 7 *P.* of C. S. demonstrates peace.
299–22 God, the divine *P.* of C. S.,
300–12 *P.* of C. S., demonstrated,

Principle

of divine healing
Pul. 34–17   * heading
34–18   * the *P·* of divine healing,
67–13   * C. S., or the *P·* of divine healing,

of divine Science
Mis. 209– 8   *P·* of divine Science being Love,
234– 6   Love is the *P·* of divine Science ;
291– 2   by the *P·* of divine Science :

of God's idea
Pul. 75– 2   Love, the *P·* of God's idea,

of good
My. 152–22   Then the divine *P·* of good,

of healing
Mis. 40– 1   *P·* of healing demands
Ret. 37–17   the spiritual *P·* of healing,
Hea. 14– 7   obscure the divine *P·* of healing

of health
Mis. 163–31   heralding the *P·* of health,

of his cure
Mis. 260–11   *P·* of his cure was God,

of law
My. 268–12   the *P·* of law and gospel,

of life
My. 274– 2   demonstrates the *P·* of life

of man
Mis. 14–23   Good is the primitive *P·* of man ;
78–26   If God is the *P·* of man
164–12   *P·* of man or the universe,
186–23   *P·* of man cannot produce a
369–26   perfect and eternal *P·* of man.
Ret. 93– 6   incorporeal divine *P·* of man,
Un. 51–27   the divine *P·* of man.
Po. 70–13   Life, the *P·* of man.

of Mind-healing
Ret. 33–14   prove the *P·* of Mind-healing.
Pul. 35–24   * convinced of the *P·* of Mind-healing,
Rud. 12–12   denies the *P·* of Mind-healing.

of pathology
Mis. 35– 3   is the *P·* of pathology ;

of Science
Rud. 8–21   the Truth and the *P·* of Science,

of this proof
Hea. 15–26   God, the *P·* of this proof?

of unity
Mis. 117–14   Love is the *P·* of unity,

one
Mis. 265– 9   All must have *one P·*
No. 10–12   one *P·* for all scientific truth.
Hea. 3–26   three statements of one *P·*.
My. 204–10   unites its true followers in one *P·*,

oneness of
Peo. 13–11   unity of Mind and oneness of *P·*.

or person
My. 233–28   chapter sub-title

or practice
Ret. 64–19   either in *P·* or practice.

perfect
Mis. 186–20   his perfect *P·*, God,
232– 6   towards the perfect *P·* of things ;
My. 187– 9   perfect *P·* whereby to demonstrate

person, or a
My. 117– 3   A person, or a *P·*?

potential
Mis. 331–26   This supreme potential *P·*

predicated of
'01. 4–14   predicated of *P·* and demonstrated as

primitive
Mis. 14–23   Good is the primitive *P·* of man ;

reveals the
Mis. 194– 3   Divine Science reveals the *P·*
Hea. 14–25   reveals the *P·* and method of

same
Mis. 40–15   demonstrated on, the same *P·*
352–14   sickness is healed upon the same *P·*

saving
Mis. 2–19   God, man's saving *P·*,

Science of the
My. 149– 7   Science of the *P·* must be

self-created
Mis. 217– 7   whose cause is the self-created *P·*,

spiritual
Mis. 186–17   spiritual *P·* of spiritual man.
Ret. 37–17   demonstrating the spiritual *P·*

that is God
Peo. 5–20   yea, to the *P·* that is God,

that moves
Mis. 174–10   *P·* that moves all in harmony,

that reveals
My. 119–14   the *P·* that reveals Christ.

their
Ret. 93– 7   in consonance with their *P·*.

thinking of
My. 234– 1   implies that one is not thinking of *P·*,

Principle

this
Mis. 100–27   He understands this *P·*, — Love.
194– 5   God is this *P·*.
198–18   On this *P·*, disease also is treated
209– 9   rule of this *P·* demonstrates Love,
209–11   demonstrates this *P·* of cure
232–25   this *P·* should be sought from
Ret. 26–27   could first state this *P·*,
No. 11–25   Revelation shows this *P·*,
20–10   This *P·* is Mind, substance, Life,
35– 7   to reach the understanding of this *P·* !
Hea. 8–27   adhere to the rule of this *P·*
15– 3   established upon this *P·*,
Peo. 2–11   this *P·* is learned through goodness,
My. 113–25   in proportion as this *P·* and rule are
180–15   this *P·* heals sin, sickness,

triune
Mis. 63– 8   triune *P·* of all pure theology ;
'01. 5– 7   as one divine infinite triune *P·*,

understand the
Mis. 215–14   understand the *P·* and object of

understood the
Hea. 9– 4   if we understood the *P·* better

we know
My. 149– 5   We know *P·* only through Science.

without
Un. 49–22   Evil is without *P·*.

word
My. 225–30   The word *P·*, when referring to God,

———

Mis. 31–14   *P·* or the rules of C. S. ;
41–30   the result of the *P·*
83– 1   *P·*, of all real being ;
199–23   *P·* of these marvellous works
243–15   includes of necessity the *P·*,
Ret. 94–24   unchanging, in *P·*, rule, and
Pul. 35– 3   *P·* and the law involved in
53– 1   * fresh development of a *P·* that
No. 5– 2   *P·* of this grand verity
Hea. 3–28   know that the *P·* is not the person,
My. 149–23   Losing . . . the *P·* in its accessories,
153–24   *P·* of which works intelligently as the

principle

Mis. 118– 8   To obey the *p·* of mathematics
283–30   laboring to learn the *p·* of music
353–21   regulator is governed by the *p·*
359– 5   On the same *p·*, you continue the
Ret. 49–11   The fundamental *p·* for growth
57– 1   like correcting the *p·* of music for
Un. 10–23   *p·* of positive mathematics.
13– 2   same *p·* that it does in astronomy.
13– 8   The *p·* of music knows nothing of
'01. 13– 1   not intelligence, a person or a *p·*,
My. 226– 6   the *p·* of harmonious vibration,
226– 7   the *p·* of conservation and
226– 8   the *p·* of the inclined plane
237– 8   the full understanding of the *p·*

principles

Mis. 68–26   * *p·* and causes of all things existing,"
Ret. 7–11   * abstruse and metaphysical *p·*,
Pul. 31– 5   * *p·* asserted by Jesus,
32–22   * due to the *p·* of C. S.
50–18   * tempted to examine its *p·*,
51–24   * help on the growth of its *p·*.
68– 5   * taught the *p·* of the faith
No. 9–28   * referred to general truths and *p·*
'01. 23–25   on received *p·* of philosophy,
27– 7   * interpret their ideas and *p·*

print

Mis. x–12   those heretofore in *p·*,
300– 9   If you should *p·* and publish
Man. 72– 2   *p·*, nor publish the Manual
Po. vi– 1   * *poem finally found its way into p·*,
My. 254–17   * May we have permission to *p·*,

printed

Mis. 300–20   *p·* as your original writings,
380–30   *p·* and issued by a student of C. S.
Man. 32–23   *p·* in the C. S. QUARTERLY.
Ret. 2–18   *p·* in olden type and replete with
37– 6   When it was first *p·*,
38–19   he had *p·* all the copy on hand,
Pul. 59– 9   * *p·* program was for some
My. 26–16   too short to be *p·* in book form,
59–29   * before it was ever *p·*."
295–10   *p·* IN NUREMBERG IN 1733

printer (see also printer's)

Ret. 38– 2   *p·* informed me that he could not
38–13   my *p·* resumed his work
38–24   I had grown disgusted with my *p·*,
My. 53– 5   * would she allow *p·* and binder to

printer's

Mis. 300–13   and spares you the *p·* bill,

printing
Mis. 381–23	*p*·, publishing, selling, giving
Ret. 38–14	finished *p*· the copy he had on hand,

prints
My. 119–20	to the person, to the *p*· of the nails,

prior
Mis. 382– 4	*p*· to my discovery of this Science.
Man. 77– 5	P· to paying bills against the
100– 1	If *p*· to the meeting of the church
Ret. 2–10	*p*· to the Revolutionary period.
24– 7	twenty years *p*· to my discovery
69– 2	*p*· to reaching intelligence.
'01. 8–25	Christ existed *p*· to Jesus,
My. 244– 8	*p*· to conferring . . . the degree of C.S.D.,

prism
Mis. 194–14	needs the *p*· of this Science
356–26	Humility is lens and *p*·
Ret. 35–13	Science is the *p*· of Truth,
'01. 12–19	needs the *p*· of divine Science,

prisms
Pul. 26– 4	* *p*· which reflect the rainbow tints.

prison
Mis. 124–15	opening the *p*· doors to the
262–21	opening the *p*· doors to such
275–18	open the *p*· to them that are bound,
Pul. 82– 1	* make the body not the *p*·,
My. 110–22	open the *p*· doors and solve
117–15	sick, or in *p*·,— *Matt.* 25 : 39.
175–15	well-conducted jail and state *p*·,

prisoner
My. 314–25	kept her a *p*· in her home,

pristine
My. 40–17	* widely reassert its *p*· power

private
Mis. 249–10	Both in *p*· and public life,
275–24	public and *p*· expressions of love
301–18	since my *p*· counsel they disregard.
315– 7	either in *p*· or in public assemblies.
Man. 46–14	all *p*· communications made to them
67– 6	P· Communications.
67– 7	strictly *p*· communication from
Rud. 16– 2	can take the place of *p*· lessons ;
'00. 10–25	I have learned it was a *p*· soldier
12–26	and also in *p*· houses.
'02. 13– 1	money from my own *p*· earnings
14–28	forever silence all *p*· criticisms.
Po. vii– 7	* *her poems, for p· distribution.*
My. 49– 1	* both in public and *p*·,
82– 9	* boarding-houses, and *p*· houses
218–25	My *p*· life is given to a servitude

privately
My. 310– 5	I was *p*· tutored by him.

Private Meeting
Mis. 350– 7	The P. M. (*P· M·*) Society

privation
Mis. 323–10	peril, *p*·, temptation,

privilege
Mis. 137– 7	simply to give you the *p*·,
266– 6	a single human right or *p*·
289–24	if the wife esteems not this *p*·,
300–28	this was a special *p*·,
302–20	*p*· of copying and reading my works
369–28	*p*· of saying to the sick,
Man. 44–17	*p*· and duty of every member,
47– 8	*p*· of a Christian Scientist
59–21	duty and *p*· of the local members
73– 7	P· of Members.
100–21	shall be the *p*· of this Board to
Pul. 51– 4	* Freedom to believe . . . is a great *p*·
No. 8– 5	let us add one more *p*·
'02. 12–22	It is a *p*· to acquaint communicants
13–11	*p*· of publishing my books
20–23	the *p*· of meeting you all
Hea. 3– 3	The primitive *p*· of Christianity
My. 5–12	pride and power, prestige or *p*·?
7– 6	*p*· to acquaint communicants with
11–20	* having seized upon this *p*·
23–27	* *p*· of participating in the work
39–20	* *p*· of saying a few words
193– 5	*p*· remains mine to watch
241–11	* *p*· of publishing an extract
243–13	*p*· of knowing two students
276–12	recommends this surprising *p*·
298– 1	request the *p*· of buying,
356– 4	the *p*· of knowing God,

privileged
Mis. xii– 2	*p*· armaments of peace.
143–29	breathing the donor's *p*· joy.
202– 6	* *p*· beyond the walks of common life,
244–27	not for a *p*· class
Man. 49– 5	*p*· to enter into this holy work,

privileged
Ret. 89–12	bidden to this *p*· duty
Pul. 8–12	*p*· joy at helping to build
My. 179–29	*p*· in having the untranslated
184– 8	To-day I am *p*· to congratulate
351– 3	* *p*· to publish her letter

privileges
Mis. 272– 2	* with all the rights and *p*·
303–15	*p*· that we claim for ourselves.
Ret. 6– 8	accorded special household *p*·.
My. 24– 8	* welcome all mankind to the *p*·
167–25	infringement of rights and *p*·
168– 5	forever the *p*· of the people
195– 9	*p*· I have not had time to express,
247– 9	its rules . . . equal rights and *p*·,
255– 2	its rules . . . equal rights and *p*·,
352– 6	* *p*· we enjoy in this church work.

prize
Un. 55–11	that they may win the *p*·.
'00. 6– 8	*p*· of the high calling — *Phil.* 3 : 14.
My. 123– 4	continue to *p*· love even more

probability
Pul. 34–10	* no *p*· that she would be alive

probable
My. 10–16	* *p*· that none will be made

probably
Pul. 67–10	* would *p*· show a greater number
78– 2	* *p*· one of the most magnificent
My. 85– 7	* adherents number *p*· a million,
86–27	* attendance . . . *p*· unprecedented,
328–19	* *p*· the first to be issued

probation
Mis. 2–21	Man's *p*· after death
Man. 38–23	received . . . on one year's *p*·,
39–16	Ineligible for P·.
50–21	exonerated, put on *p*·, or
51– 4	he shall be placed on *p*·, or
51–22	power to discipline, place on *p*·,
55–10	P·.
No. 27–26	*p*· of mortals must go on

probationary
Man. 38–16	*p*· MEMBERSHIP.
39– 8	A full member or a *p*· member,
39–13	eligible to *p*· membership
Un. 3– 5	pass through another *p*· state

probe
Po. 22–16	*p*· the wound, then pour the balm

problem
of being
Mis. 201–21	that he had wrought the *p*· of being
283–24	work out his own *p*· of being ;
Ret. 79–15	the inscrutable *p*· of being
Rud. 6– 1	solution of the *p*· of being,
My. 348–30	it solves the *p*· of being ;

Mis. 52–21	*p*· to be wrought in divine Science.
52–29	before solving the advanced *p*·.
54–30	to solve a *p*· involving logarithms ;
55– 2	simplest *p*· in C. S. is
118–10	make incorrect your entire *p*·,
120– 6	divine Principle of life's long *p*·,
291–29	would aid the solution of this *p*·,
333–19	to work out the *p*· of Mind,
346– 7	The origin of evil is the *p*· of ages.
Ret. 34– 5	could solve the mental *p*·.
58– 4	work out the *p*· of infinity or
Un. 9–18	perplexing *p*· of human existence.
Pul. vii–20	vast *p*· of eternal life,
My. 110–22	solve the blind *p*· of matter.
181–15	the *p*· of religious liberty
306–18	alone solves the *p*· of humanity,

problematic
Mis. 286–18	although it is to-day *p*·.
'01. 26–28	*p*· and self-contradictory.

problematical
Mis. 14–28	therefore, wholly *p*·.

problems
Mis. 125–25	hitherto untouched *p*· of being,
Un. 6–21	about the *p*· of Euclid.
'02. 4–26	by abstruse *p*· of Scripture,
My. 12– 9	* decision of these remaining *p*·.
61–29	* As I discovered the many intricate *p*·
181– 6	and ultimate in unsolved *p*·
195– 6	*p*· to be worked out for the field,
348–32	solution of God's *p*·.

Probst, Arthur O.
My. 361–27	* signature

proceed
Mis. 76– 1	and must *p*· from God ;
155– 5	spiritual, and *p*· from goodness.
232–11	*p*· from the standard of right

proceed
Ret.	71–22	they p· from false convictions
'00.	4–25	whatever is real must p· from God,
'01.	16–18	ought not to p· from the individual,
'02.	7–23	p· to another Scriptural passage
My.	300–15	understand . . . and p· to overcome

proceeded
Ret.	69– 7	delusion that life . . . p· from
Hea.	17–19	never p· from Truth, Life, and Love.
My.	49–23	* Mrs. Eddy p· to instruct those
	318–21	As I p·, Mr. Wiggin manifested more

proceedeth
Mis.	198–13	evil p· not from God,
Un.	24– 3	From me p· all Mind,
	60–16	p· blessing and cursing. — Jas. 3 : 10.
My.	6–21	p· out of the mouth of God.

proceeding
Pul.	34– 9	* before p· to his morning service,
No.	16– 8	and p· from Him.
Pan.	3–24	* "universal nature p· from
My.	24–20	* erection of the building is p·
	333–10	* minutes record this further p· :

proceedings
Mis.	170–24	Jesus' p· with the blind man
Man.	77–20	characterize all the p· of
'02.	13–20	legal p· were instituted by
My.	137–24	the present p· were brought
	138–10	present p· test my trust in

proceeds
Mis.	36–11	is harmful and p· not from God ;
	49–29	that the capacity to err p· from
	58–22	no order that p· from
	186–28	As the apostle p· in this line
Un.	38– 9	all is real which p· from Life
Pul.	66– 8	* p· more from the graveyards

process
Mis.	8–21	however much we suffer in the p·.
	40– 5	mingle . . . in the same p·,
	213– 7	point the way, shorten the p·,
	215– 1	through this very p·,
	220–24	if this mental p· and power be
	221–32	belief in evil and in the p· of evil,
Un.	8–22	You demonstrate the p· of Science,
	11–24	neither . . . hindered the divine p·.
	20–10	By a reverse p· of argument
	20–15	Try this p·, dear inquirer,
	36– 2	p· it names material attraction,
Pul.	34–28	p· by which I was restored to health ;
Hea.	12–25	when the drug disappears by your p·
My.	71–15	* has been in p· of construction,
	178– 5	nor lose the invincible p·
	219–30	an individual submit to this p·,
	292– 6	way pointed out, the p· shortened,

processes
Un.	12– 2	by mental, not material p·.
	21– 2	description of mental p·
	21– 4	If we observe our mental p·,
No.	28– 7	p· and terrible revolutions
Peo.	8–15	carried on through principal p·,

procession
My.	312–26	his staff, with a long p·,
	326–18	long p· with tender dirge
	333–11	* p· was formed, which moved to
	333–14	* The p· then returned to the

proclaim
My.	248–11	p· Truth so winningly that
	353–14	p· the universal activity

proclaimed
Pul.	5– 2	clergymen who had publicly p·
	52–26	* No new doctrine is p·,
	53–22	* When Jesus of Nazareth p·

proclaims
Mis.	277– 7	Whosoever p· Truth loudest,
My.	28–24	* p· to the world that Jesus' gospel
	58–12	* p· the trust, the willingness

proclivities
Mis.	315–14	such as have promising p·
Man.	83–11	promising p· toward C. S.

proconsul
Mis.	345– 8	when the p· said to him,

procrastination
Hea.	19–18	patient of man's p·,

procreation
Mis.	286–21	Human p·, birth, life, and
Ret.	69–24	for recreation or p·?"

Proctor, Adelaide A.
'00.	11–21	Adelaide A. P· breathes my thought :

procurator
Mis.	351–26	is not the p· of happiness,
Rud.	10–16	fear is the p· of the thought which

procures
Mis.	360– 2	and p· divine power.

prodigal
Mis.	369–22	as tired as was the p· son
Ret.	91– 3	The parable of "the p· son"
'01.	17– 7	who so loves even the repentant p·

prodigious
My.	92– 9	* p· convention of Christian Scientists

prodigy
Pul.	51– 2	* If it did, it would be a p·.

produce
Mis.	5– 8	able to p· perfect health and
	8– 5	drugs do not, cannot, p· health
	48–15	could p· the effect of alcohol,
	174– 2	than has good to p· evil.
	186–23	cannot p· a less perfect man
	217–20	that these opposites, . . . p· matter,
	221– 1	does not, p· the slightest effect,
	229– 4	which he believes p· it.
	261–31	must p· physical and moral harmony.
	352–17	and what has claimed to p· it,
	372–13	Knowing that this book would p· a
Pul.	51– 3	* Neither . . . p· the same impressions
No.	17– 3	He must p· its consequences.
Hea.	6–22	can p· a result upon his body.
My.	71– 3	* p· the most beautiful effects
	124–23	Then p· thy records, time-table,
	249– 5	p· God's phenomena.
	275– 3	does p· universal fellowship.
	292–25	to p· opposite effects.
	301–29	drugs can p· no curative effect

produced
Mis.	49–10	had not p· insanity."
	186–24	than it p· in the beginning.
	218– 4	matter never p· Mind,
	221–12	believes that sin has p· the effect
	259–26	must have p· its own illusion,
	277–31	drunkenness p· by animality.
	290–17	* p· a wonderful illumination,
	360–12	Philosophy never has p·,
	375–28	* to see p· to-day that art
Pul.	6– 1	upheaval p· when Truth is
	51–17	* p· a sensation in religious
'01.	24– 5	impression p· by divine power
Hea.	8–13	the thought that has p· this,
	17–25	sickness and death were p· by sin.
	18–26	death has been p· by a belief alone.
Peo.	3–10	beliefs that have p· sin, sickness,
My.	22–24	* moral and the physical effects p· by
	97–29	* p· by that stupendous gathering.
	238– 6	effects p· by reading the
	302– 6	Neither life nor . . . can be p· on
	359–28	temptation p· by animal magnetism

producer
Rud.	9–27	God is good, and the p· only of

produces
Mis.	26–21	neither . . . p· its opposite.
	27–13	no species ever p· its opposite.
	41–20	p· all harmony that appears.
	59– 5	p· the effect of mesmerism.
	221– 6	Error p· physical sufferings,
	337–17	p· a growing affection for all good,
Un.	31–14	fourth, that matter, . . . p· life
Rud.	8– 2	no pine-tree p· a mammal
Hea.	6–13	When I learned how mind p· disease
	6–14	I learned how it p· the
	6–22	The belief that p· this result
	7– 4	p· the harmonious effect on the body.
My.	232–27	If so-called watching p· fear
	302– 4	mind, not matter, p· the result

producing
Mis.	53–12	to assist in p· a cure,
	122–15	it is not evil p· good,
Rud.	10–10	p· the beliefs of a mortal material
'02.	6–30	p· nothing unlike Himself,
Hea.	6–25	a latent cause p· the effect we see.
My.	302– 2	of healing disease and of p· disease.
	348–24	never p· an opposite effect,

product
Mis.	198–20	as much the p· of mortal thought
	221–28	would not yield the same p·
	233–32	belief or p· of mortal mind :
Un.	26–25	The phantasmagoria is a p· of

production
Mis.	304–31	* The responsibility of its p·,

productions
Mis.	376–11	* Their p· are expressionless copies of
Ret.	11– 3	following is one of my girlhood p·.
Po.	vii– 4	* reached its fulness in her later p·.

productive
Mis.	371–16	is not p· of the better sort,

profane
    Mis. 45–12   *Can an atheist or a p· man*
    '00. 6–20   a man who . . . is *p·*, licentious,
    My. 106–25 a tobacco user, a *p·* swearer,
        113–15 Was it *p·* for St. Paul to aspire to
        307–24 I should still think that it was *p·*.

profanely
    No. 5–23 is *p·* tampering with the

profanity
    My. 308–28 no *p·* and no slang phrases.

profess
    Mis. 116–25 you *p·* to understand and love,
        311–10 exemplifying what we *p·*.

professed
    Mis. 247– 8 *p·* Christianity a half-century ;
        301–12 a few *p·* Christian Scientists.

profession
    Mis. 378–19 taught her of his medical *p·*.
    Man. 46–10 which advertise his business or *p·*,
    Ret. 14–17 made any *p·* of religion,
    Pul. 9–26 Practice, not *p·*, . . . gain the
    Hea. 3– 5 a proof, more than a *p·*

professional
    Ret. 88– 2 observed in the *p·* intercourse
    Pul. 59–18 * read by a *p·* elocutionist,
    My. 30–13 * *p·* men, devoted women
        81–32 * *p·* men, hard-headed shrewd
       104–25 *p·* men and women of the highest

professionally
    Mis. 51–11 cannot answer your question *p·*.

professionals
    My. 111–27 irritate a certain class of *p·*
       327–25 * other *p·* who practise the art
       328–28 * all other *p·* who practise the art

professions
    Man. 82–17 who practise other *p·*
    '01. 31– 3 sects or *p·* can encounter
    My. 328–26 * enumerating the different *p·*

Professor
    Mis. 47–27 *P· Carpenter's exhibitions of*
       242– 2 The article of *P· T——*,
       242– 4 In it the *P·* offered me,
       243–13 I agree with the *P·*,
       243–23 The *P·* alludes to Paul's advice
       243–31 Again, the *P·* quotes,
       244– 3 we have the *P·* on the platform
    '01. 27–27 *P·* Agassiz said :

professor
    Mis. 344– 3 a Pythagorean *p·* of ethics,
       344–12 he was dismissed by the *p·*.
    Un. 11–20 a *p·* of natural philosophy,

professors
    Mis. 120– 1 The *p·* of C. S. must
    My. 89– 4 * deemed by its *p·* not to exist
       107– 4 Compare the lives of its *p·* with

proffer
    Po. 10– 3 We *p·* thee warm welcome
    My. 337– 5 We *p·* thee warm welcome

proffering
    My. 78–16 * and none *p·* small change.

profile
    Po.   v–12 * *resemble the p· of a human face.*

profit
    Mis. 213–14 May my friends and my enemies so *p·*
       359–29 give not the wisdom to *p·* by it.
    My. 74–16 * might *p·* by their example
       261– 4 How shall we . . . *p·* them withal?

profitable
    Mis. 64–21 Works on science are *p·* ;
       303–24 *p·* to the heart of our country.
       339– 3 subjects that are *p·*,
    Ret. 5–27 * themes at once pleasing and *p·*.
    My. 178–11 less *p·* or scientific

profitably
    Mis. 44– 3 and may *p·* teach people,
    Ret. 35–10 before . . . could be *p·* published.

profited
    Mis. 272–31 have not *p·* by my rebukes,
       316–14 *p·* up to their present capacity

profiteth
    My. 108– 9 "The flesh *p·* nothing." — *John* 6 : 63.

profitless
    My. 106– 5 mental practice were *p·*.

profits
    Man. 80– 4 The net *p·* of the business
    '02. 13– 8 net *p·* from the business of
    My. vi–23 * to pay all future *p·* to her church ;
       158–13 it *p·* by the past

profound
    Mis. 234–23 wonderment to *p·* thinkers.
       296– 5 *p·* philosophers, brilliant scholars.
       342–14 darkness *p·* brooded over
       392– 4 Nature divine, in harmony *p·*,
    Ret. 73– 9 great fact leads into *p·* depths.
    Un. 43–18 Because of these *p·* reasons I
    Pul. 87–13 accept my *p·* thanks.
    No. 13–14 *p·* deduction from C. S.
    '00. 11–14 tones intricate, *p·*, commanding.
    Po. 20– 5 Nature divine, in harmony *p·*,
    My. 29– 5 * a stillness *p·* ;
       157– 4 * with *p·* joy and deep gratitude
       224–23 less correct and therefore less *p·*.
       229–22 accept *p·* thanks for
       250– 4 has received *p·* attention.
       253–21 accept my *p·* thanks

profoundest
    My. 295–14 in its largest, *p·* sense

profoundly
    No. 39– 2 can think more lucidly and *p·*
    My. 194–22 *p·* thank you for it,
       229–31 it takes life *p·* ;

profuse
    Man. 43–15 shall not publish *p·* quotations

progeny
    Mis. 286– 6 marriage and *p·* will continue
       297–26 effects, on himself and his *p·*,

prognostications
    Pul. 84–15 * *p·* to the contrary

program
    Pul. 59– 9 * *p·* was for some reason

progress
  and Christianity
    Hea. 7–24 important to *p·* and Christianity.
  and victories
    My. 47–15 * trials, *p·*, and victories
  befriended
    Pul. 7– 6 her laws have befriended *p·*.
  continued
    Mis. 110–22 thanksgiving for the continued *p·*
  every step of
    Peo. 1– 2 Every step of *p·* is a step more
  feet of
    My. 127–29 nor laid down at the feet of *p·*
  foe of
    Mis. 206–13 idleness is the foe of *p·*.
  footsteps of
    My. 139– 8 advancing footsteps of *p·*,
  growth and
    My. 8– 6 * pace with our own growth and *p·*.
  hinder
    Mis. 290– 7 break all bonds that hinder *p·*.
  his own
    Mis. 308– 7 greatly errs, stops his own *p·*,
  human
    Mis. 9–31 more disastrous to human *p·*
  in Christian Science
    Mis. 355– 5 present stage of *p·* in C. S.
    Man. 44–25 which impede their *p·* in C. S.
  indispensable to the
    Mis. 317–18 indispensable to the *p·* of every
  is demonstration
    Mis. 235– 8 In C. S., *p·* is demonstration,
  is spiritual
    My. 181– 8 *P·* is spiritual.
  is the law
    Mis. 15–19 *p·* is the law of infinity.
  is the maturing
    My. 181– 8 *p·* is the maturing conception
  its
    Pul. vii– 3 its *p·* during the ensuing
    My. 47– 8 * a few of the stages of its *p·*,
  landmark of
    My. 47–19 * touched by each landmark of *p·*
  lifts mortals
    Mis. 287–15 *p·* lifts mortals to discern the
  line with
    Mis. 287–20 affection in line with *p·*,
  man's
    Mis. 234–13 What hinders man's *p·*
  of Christianity
    No. 32– 2 retarded the *p·* of Christianity
  of Christian Science
    My. 134– 5 unprecedented *p·* of C. S.
       329–22 * recognizing the steady *p·* of C. S.
  of our Cause
    Mis. x–16 *p·* of our Cause.
       274– 8 might hinder the *p·* of our Cause
    My. 21–13 * aid the *p·* of our Cause
  of religion
    My. 340– 9 the *p·* of religion and medicine
  of students
    Mis. 156–20 clogs the *p·* of students,
  of the human race
    Ret. 78–24 against the *p·* of the human race

progress

of the work
My. 24–18   * inquired about the p· of the work
our
My. 44– 7   * our p· may be fast or it
outcome of
'02. 2–20   are an outcome of p· ;
peace, and
Mis. 118–23   foes to grace, peace, and p· ;
period of
Mis. 26– 4   Each successive period of p·
promote their
Man. 83–14   obligated to promote their p·
report
My. 125– 5   It requires you to report p·,
ripe for
My. 281–28   when nations are ripe for p·.
rise and
Ret. 80–20   unceasing spiritual rise and p·.
some
Mis. 234–24   she has made some p·,
spiritual
Mis. 124–32   In proportion to a man's spiritual p·,
192– 6   importance to man's spiritual p·,
My. 114–30   each step of mental and spiritual p·,
stage of
Mis. 355– 2   stage of p· in C. S.
steps of
My. 110–11   guiding the steps of p·
their
Man. 44–25   impede their p· in C. S.
88–21   subjects essential to their p·.
My. 267–18   in proportion to their p·,
to impede
Mis. 115–27   whatever tends to impede p·.
unity and
My. 123– 1   Our unity and p· are proverbial,
waymarks of
Ret. 27–11   valuable to me as waymarks of p·,
wheels of
Mis. 234– 3   and clog the wheels of p·.
Rud. 17– 4   clogging the wheels of p· by
world's
Mis. 304–25   * marking the world's p· toward liberty ;
your
Mis. 160–12   Your p·, the past year,
My. 6–17   I thank you for this proof of your p·,

Mis. 2–24   If man should not p· after death,
2–27   those who p· here and hereafter
52–22   What p· would a student of science
98–15   p· of our common Cause in Chicago,
Pul. 10–22   as p· certainly demands,
65–13   * Attention is directed to the p·
No. 31– 7   They p· and will multiply into
44–18   P·, legitimate to the human race,
Hea. 9– 1   and p· faster than we are now
My. 35–27   * During the p· of each service,
181– 8   P· is the maturing conception of

progresses
My. 342–28   government will develop as it p·."

progressing
Mis. 41– 9   destroys their own possibility of p·.
Hea. 9– 1   faster than we are now p·.

progression
Mis. 82–13   *Is there infinite p· with man*
82–20   Infinite p· is concrete being,

progressive
Mis. 117– 1   A p· life is the reality of Life
Rud. 16–26   snatch at whatever is p·,
'00. 4–14   these are p· signs of the times
My. 65–18   * chapter sub-title
114–32   and find these p· steps
339–12   Along the lines of p· Christendom,
340–32   of learning and p· religion

prohibit
Mis. 309–31   p· ourselves the childish pleasure of

prohibited
Man. 41– 5   is abnormal . . . and is p·.

prohibiting
Mis. 246– 1   and the p· of free speech,
Po. vi–20   p· *slavery in the United States.*"

prohibition
Mis. 257–13   as a power, p·, or license,
260–30   needing neither license nor p· ;

prohibitory
Peo. 10– 9   p· law regulating the practice of

project
Pul. 51–20   * Ere this many a new p·

projected
'00. 12– 2   paraphrases p· from divinity

prolific
Mis. 113–31   p· sources of spiritual power
Ret. 69–21   opposite belief is the p· source of
My. 132–12   Oh, may this hour be p·,

prolong
Po. 31– 5   P· the strain "Christ risen !"

prolonged
Mis. 17–24   This birth is more or less p·
89–25   concept that is not spared or p·
366–10   and this is the p· tone :
Ret. 3– 7   caused that p· contest to be known
My. 343– 5   * unexpectedly after a p· exordium.
344–18   * "Oh," with a p· inflection,

prolonging
Mis. 282–15   P· the metaphysical tone of his

prolongs
Mis. 87–31   this interference p· the struggle
274–21   p· the reign of . . . unprincipled clans.

prominent
Mis. 18– 8   p· laws which forward birth in
119–25   a p· statute in the divine law,
Ret. 3– 1   p· in British politics,
15–28   p· churchman agreeably informed the
Pul. 73–17   * a very p· member of the church.
88– 9   names of other p· newspapers
My. 90–29   * P· among these is the
96– 5   * many of them p· figures in
328–22   * Upon the request of a p· healer

promiscuous
Mis. 282–29   p· and unannounced mental practice
Ret. 71– 9   P· mental treatment,
Rud. 15–22   to p· and large assemblies,
My. 214– 2   p· selections would write your

promiscuously
Mis. 232–29   prevent mankind from striking out p·,

promise
Mis. 29– 3   his p· is perpetual.
39–15   I have faith in His p·,
87– 8   "I love your p· ;
144–19   to whisper our Master's p·,
153–10   and the land of p·,
254– 2   points with p· of prosperity?
270–20   if we would obtain that p·.
319–28   between the p· and event ;
340–22   by patience, they inherit the p·.
355– 3   a full-orbed p·, and a gaunt want.
356–11   give p· of grand careers.
373–27   his p· that the Christlike shall
388– 6   A bow of p· on the cloud.
394– 5   p·, the home, and the heaven of
Man. 16– 9   we solemnly p· to watch,
Ret. 7– 7   * young man of uncommon p·.
23–10   spanned with its rainbow of p·.
31–30   Love unveiled the healing p·
89–21   even according to his p·,
92– 8   reach the fruition of his p· :
Un. 43–20   I exhort them to accept Christ's p·,
Pul. 1– 5   p· clad in white raiment,
83– 2   * p· as lover and candidate
'00. 11–10   we have the p· that
13–16   A glad p· to such as wait
'02. 9–15   every p· fulfilled,
20–15   A bow of p· on the cloud.
Peo. 3–17   like a p· upon the cloud,
Po. 7– 6   A bow of p· on the cloud.
45– 6   The p·, the home, and the heaven
My. 12– 8   * p· of the speedy accumulation of
25–27   divinity appears in all its p·.
125– 9   your flocks, big with p· ;
186–21   Here let His p· be verified :
188– 3   This house is hallowed by His p· :
190–32   verifying his last p·,
230–26   realize at last their Master's p·,
278–23   the p· and reward of rightness.

promised
Pul. 33–11   * p· to reply if the call came
'02. 17–30   susceptible of light with p· joy.
Po. 33– 5   bless me with Christ's p· rest :
My. 43– 2   * in possession of the p· land.
43–13   * brought them into the p· land,
44– 5   * going up to possess the p· land

promises
Pul. 73–15   * God has fulfilled His p· to her
My. 48–13   * spiritual understanding of its p·.
92–29   * for some such comfort as it p·.
93–12   * C. S. p· nothing in the way of
155– 7   p·, and proofs of Holy Writ.
201– 4   is fast fulfilling the p·.

promising
Mis. 315–14   p· proclivities toward C. S.
Man. 83–10   p· proclivities toward C. S.

promote
Mis.	273–21	*p·* the growing interest in C. S.
	288–30	to *p·* the ends of temperance ;
	296–26	wish to *p·* female suffrage?
	350–29	*p·* health and spiritual growth.
	354– 8	can no longer *p·* peace
Man.	31–12	shall *p·* health and holiness,
	45– 6	*p·* peace on earth and good will
	45–11	strive to *p·* the welfare of all
	83–14	obligated to *p·* their progress
Ret.	90–21	*p·* the welfare and happiness
Un.	5–17	neither will it *p·* the Cause of
	6–11	is radical enough to *p·*
Pul.	50– 1	* using her money to *p·* the welfare
My.	99– 7	* cult able to *p·* its faith with
	165– 1	*p·* and pervade all his success.

promoted
Mis.	228– 4	whose welfare thou hast *p·*,
My.	270–25	be it *p·* by Catholic, by Protestant,

promoters
Mis.	240–10	*p·* of health and happiness.

promotes
Mis.	41–14	it *p·* spiritual growth,
	80–19	*p·* and impels all true reform ;
Ret.	82–20	*p·* the ease and welfare of
Pan.	10–27	Whatever *p·* statuesque being,
My.	250– 5	*p·* wisdom, quiets mad ambition,

promoting
My.	118– 3	*p·* the true Principle of
	362–16	* *p·* and enlarging the activities

promotion
Man.	80– 2	*p·* of the interests of C. S.
Ret.	47–11	for the *p·* of spiritual ends.
	52– 2	*p·* and expansion of scientific

prompt
Mis.	317–19	These considerations *p·* my answers
My.	11–17	* because of *p·* and liberal action,
	243–20	Your *p·* presence in Concord

prompted
Mis.	48–10	*p·* by money-making or malice.
My.	23– 5	* Love that *p·* the desire,
	24–17	* We are *p·* to state,
	352– 7	* We are *p·* to acknowledge

promptings
Mis.	228– 1	the *p·* of human nature.

promptly
Mis.	143–27	Each donation came *p·* ;
	149–19	parting so *p·* with your
Man.	28–17	perform the functions of . . . *p·*
	65–15	*p·* to comply with any written
	79– 6	shall transact *p·* and efficiently
	98– 7	If the correction . . . is not *p·*
My.	14–18	* Our friend very *p·*
	31– 9	* *P·* at half past six
	361–20	* *p·* made its demonstration

promptness
My.	12–13	* *p·* of his own contribution.

prompts
'02.	8–22	it *p·* perpetual goodness,

promulgated
Un.	7–17	that the views here *p·*
My.	316– 1	the truth I have *p·* has

promulgators
Pul.	65– 2	* original apostles and *p·*,

prone
My.	93–18	* possibly too *p·* to approach it

pronoun
Mis.	29– 5	the *p·* would be *you*, not *them*.

pronounce
Mis.	314–13	shall *p·* the benediction.
Ret.	26–15	*p·* Christ's healing miraculous,
Pul.	80–17	* we have no opinion to *p·*,
My.	111–28	they may *p·* it absurd,

pronounced
Mis.	6–10	cases that are *p·* incurable
	24– 9	*p·* fatal by the physicians.
	35– 5	*p·* by the physicians incurable,
	247–29	Everything . . . He *p·* good.
Ret.	9– 5	*p·* in audible tones.
	13–11	*p·* me stricken with fever.
Un.	15– 8	and *p·* them good.
Pul.	34– 7	* *p·* hopeless by the physicians.
	69– 8	* *p·* his case incurable.
'02.	6– 5	The curse . . . was *p·* upon a lie,
My.	14–18	* *p·* the story a fabrication
	105–21	*p·* dying of pneumonia,

pronouncement
My.	46–14	* this early *p·* is the work of

pronounces
My.	178–15	Scripture *p·* all that God made

proof

absolute
Ret.	31– 6	absolute *p·* and self-evident

another
My.	240–15	I now repeat another *p·*,

any
No.	10– 4	as any *p·* that can be given

convincing
Ret.	93–24	convincing *p·* of the validity of

demand a
Mis.	225–15	opportunity to demand a *p·*

denies in
Hea.	15–17	admits . . . what he denies in *p·* ?

eminent
Mis.	346– 4	spiritual healing as eminent *p·*

fair
Mis.	239– 7	give fair *p·* that my shadow is

full
No.	31–13	as the only full *p·* of its pardon.

further
Un.	36–16	A further *p·* of this is the

incapable of
Mis.	14–28	a lie that is incapable of *p·*

its own
Mis.	242–18	C. S. that furnishes its own *p·*.
	350–32	furnishes its own *p·* of my practice.

lacked the
Mis.	365–10	If C. S. lacked the *p·* of its
No.	18– 6	If Science lacked the *p·* of its

my
Mis.	68–13	My *p·* of this is, that the penalty
	252–14	My *p·* of these novel propositions

no
Mis.	230–12	Rushing around smartly is no *p·* of
	338– 6	these afford no *p·*,

of Christianity
Hea.	2–23	and gave this *p·* of Christianity

of divine power
Hea.	15–25	to pray for a *p·* of divine power,

of healing
Pul.	13–12	rejoices in the *p·* of healing,

of Immanuel
Mis.	374– 1	was so great a *p·* of Immanuel

of life
My.	177–13	true knowledge and *p·* of life

of mathematics
'01.	4– 7	destroys the *p·* of mathematics ;

of the omnipotence
Pan.	7– 6	*p·* of the omnipotence of one divine,

of the prosperity
Mis.	154–12	*p·* of the prosperity of His Zion.

opportunity for
Mis.	13–26	to afford opportunity for *p·* of its

parable and
Mis.	27–16	maintain this fact by parable and *p·*,

parallel
Mis.	66–13	supported . . . by parallel *p·*.

personal
My.	238– 7	be determined by personal *p·*.

positive
Mis.	153–20	by positive *p·* of trustworthiness.
'01.	33–25	richest and most positive *p·*
My.	91– 2	* *p·* positive that it supplies these
	166–13	positive *p·* of your remembrance

practical
Mis.	35– 1	Years of practical *p·*,

practice and
'01.	19–16	from Jesus' practice and *p·*.

primitive
My.	239– 4	relegates . . . to its primitive *p·*,

rational
My.	348–18	Science demanded a rational *p·*

real
My.	119–22	gave the real *p·* of his Saviour,

remarkable
My.	273– 3	* interesting and remarkable *p·* of

scientific
Mis.	277–24	the scientific *p·* that God,
'01.	4–11	its susceptibility of scientific *p·*.
My.	218– 8	restoration . . . as the scientific *p·*

sealed that
Mis.	35– 6	sealed that *p·* with the signet of

self-evident
Mis.	186–22	self-evident *p·* of immortality ;

signal
Pul.	39– 3	* a signal *p·* of the divine origin of

simple
Mis.	265–16	innovations upon simple *p·* ;

sole
'02.	10–24	This is indeed our sole *p·*
My.	271–10	and the sole *p·* of rightness.

susceptible of
Mis.	27–26	and is susceptible of *p·*.
	200–13	a rule that is susceptible of *p·*,

teaching and
'01.	23–16	to the Master's teaching and *p·*.

proof

that Christian Science
Mis. 193–11 *p·* that C. S., . . . heals the sick,
No. 28–14 The *p·* that C. S. is the way
My. 158–18 burden of *p·* that C. S. is Science
238–22 *p·* that C. S. is Science,

this
Mis. 101–28 On this *p·* rest premise and
Hea. 2–23 gave this *p·* of Christianity
15–27 God, the Principle of this *p·*
My. 6–16 this *p·* of your progress, unity,
106– 4 and without this *p·* of love
363–14 This *p·* that sanity and Science

unmistakable
Mis. 366– 8 given rule, and unmistakable *p·*.
No. 11–22 given rule, and unmistakable *p·*.
33–11 a given rule, and unmistakable *p·*.

without
Un. 49–24 Hence it is undemonstrable, without *p·*.
'02. 18–24 faith without *p·* loses its life,

Mis. 65– 3 We have no more *p·* of
83–27 *p·* of his eternal Life and sonship.
183–27 in *p·* of man's "dominion — *Gen.* 1 : 26.
186–23 *p·*, also, that the Principle of man
249–23 of their mental design . . . I have *p·*,
Man. 98–12 shall read the *last p· sheet*
Rud. 6–24 The *p·* of what you apprehend,
No. 37–15 or as a *p·* that sin is known to
'02. 9–23 was the *p·* of its divine origin,
Hea. 3– 5 a *p·*, more than a profession thereof ;
My. 36–30 * *p·* that our Supreme God, through
103– 7 *p·* of the practicality of this faith
109–25 not alone by miracle . . . but by *p·* ;
302– 8 is *p·* that mind is the cause of all

proofless
My. 181– 7 outgrown, *p·* positions.

proofreader
My. 318– 5 Mr. Wiggin was not my *p·* for
318–11 name of the former *p·* for
320– 2 * student and a good *p·*.

proofs
Mis. 65– 2 by repeated *p·* of its falsity.
201–21 because they were so many *p·*
247– 3 convictions and *p·* of advancing truth
My. 155– 7 promises, and *p·* of Holy Writ.

prop
No. 15– 9 to explain and *p·* old creeds,

propaganda
My. 303–18 no idolatry, no human *p·*

propagate
Mis. 343–24 until no seedling be left to *p·*
My. 130– 2 then leave the latter to *p·*.

propagates
Mis. 111–15 Leaving the seed of . . . it *p·* :

propagation
'01. 30– 7 are essential to its *p·*.
My. 344–17 * theory of the *p·* of disease?"

propelling
Pul. 20–17 *p·* the greatest moral, physical,

propensities
Mis. 36–15 beasts that have these *p·*
250– 8 What the lower *p·* express,

proper
Mis. 48–26 *p·* study of Mind-healing would cure
89–23 *p·* answer to this question
107–16 (1) A *p·* sense of sin ;
108–13 reducing its claim to its *p·*
108–18 *p·* knowledge of evil
115–14 *p·* preparation of heart to practise,
138–26 God will give . . . the *p·* command,
146–11 to form a *p·* judgment.
177–23 * hour for the church service *p·*,
187– 5 *p·* sense of the possibilities of
222– 1 man's *p·* sense of good,
269–23 correct Mind-healing is the *p·* means
307–18 *p·* reception of C. S. healing.
308–10 take their *p·* place in history,
334–20 to its *p·* denomination,
348–28 individual in a *p·* state of mind.
359–13 *p·* channels for development,
365–27 lack of *p·* terms in which to express
373–18 forced out of its *p·* channel,
Man. 28– 7 *p·* system of government
49–13 who can take *p·* care of the sick.
69–16 appoint a *p·* member of this Church
72–12 Upon *p·* application,
76– 5 *p·* management of the Church funds :
77–16 *p·* distribution of the funds
Ret. 25–26 any *p·* conception of the infinite
44–25 *p·* measures were adopted to
90–26 * *p·* thing for us to do is to follow,

proper
Un. 8–14 *p·* understanding of the unreality
20– 2 by seeing it in its *p·* light,
35–10 Reduced to its *p·* denomination,
40–19 *p·* or true sense of Life,
Pul. 82–17 * woman as man's *p·* helpmeet.
Rud. 2–14 retain the *p·* sense of Deity by
Pan. 4–11 for their *p·* exercise.
5–11 Our Master gave the *p·* answer
11–18 in order to be in *p·* shape,
Hea. 4–21 *p·* conception of the divine character,
My. 22–26 * appear in their *p·* perspective.
22–28 * *p·* perspective of the meaning of
162–21 Our *p·* reason for church edifices is,
220– 7 reporting . . . to the *p·* authorities
232– 1 recognizing the *p·* course,
259–27 appropriate and *p·* exercise.
278– 1 *p·* incentive to the action
289– 8 I deem it *p·* that The Mother
306–17 will find its *p·* level.

properly
Mis. 112–14 of what is *p·* denominated,
169–14 cannot *p·* be interpreted in a
193–23 *p·* called Scientists who follow the
Man. 37– 4 *p·* filled out by an applicant.
57– 2 such other business as may *p·*
77–12 have not been *p·* managed,
Ret. 59–14 *p·* employed, has the signification
Pul. 50–11 * *p·* marked by the erection of a
No. 14– 2 when *p·* demonstrated.
Pan. 4– 8 are *p·* classified as mind,
'01. 3–27 the conclusion is not *p·* drawn.
20– 5 Man is *p·* self-governed, and he
My. 219– 8 most *p·* used in preventing the
259–24 Certain occasions, . . . observed *p·*,

properties
No. 22– 7 treatise on the healing *p·* of
Hea. 12– 1 contain no medicinal *p·*,
My. 32– 7 * acoustic *p·* of the new structure
72– 1 * nicely adjusted acoustic *p·*
78–22 * acoustic *p·* of the temple,
293– 4 the different *p·* of drugs

property
Mis. 248–22 bequeathed my *p·* to
283– 9 management of another man's *p·*.
299–31 *p·* of a noted firm,
Man. 30–18 taxes and rent on this *p·* ;
30–20 keep the *p·* in good repair,
67–14 or to the *p·* of Mary Baker Eddy
79–22 shall hold and manage the *p·*
Ret. 20– 2 lost all my husband's *p·*,
'02. 13– 6 my personal *p·* and funds,
13–21 advertising the *p·* in the
13–23 previously negotiated for the *p·*
13–25 nor to take the *p·* off my hands,
14– 3 only interest I retain in this *p·*
15–18 much of his *p·* was in slaves,
15–20 never believe that . . . was my *p·*.
My. vi–24 * presented to her church the *p·*
vii– 2 * *p·* of the Publishing Society.
66– 6 * in *p·* on these streets,
66–11 * use the society will make of the *p·*
66–14 * it was necessary to have this *p·*.
100– 6 * *p·* of no poverty-stricken sect.
123–13 I had the *p·* bought by
135–14 to take the charge of my *p·* ;
136–14 Board of Trustees who own my *p·* :
137–19 have my *p·* . . . carefully taken care of
137–22 to take charge of my *p·* ;
138– 1 I gave them my *p·* to take care of
138– 4 agreed . . . to take care of my *p·*
138–10 to protect my person or *p·*.
325– 8 * Back Bay *p·* would never
336–13 lost all my husband's *p·*,

prophecies
Mis. 84– 9 the *p·* were fulfilled,
Pul. 9–25 prayers, *p·*, and anointings.
My. 155– 7 *p·*, promises, and proofs

prophecy
Mis. 76–31 glorious *p·* of the master
141– 2 will be the *p·* fulfilled,
144–15 there to typify the *p·*,
192–21 man's ability to prove the . . . *p·*.
270–18 have full faith in his *p·*,
286– 1 above *p·*, written years ago,
373–30 more than a prophet or a *p·* :
Pul. 1– 4 *p·* and promise clad in white
5–20 *That p· is fulfilled.*
No. 13– 8 *p·* of Jesus fulfilled,
27–13 this *p·* will be scoffed at ;
'00. 12–20 This *p·* has been fulfilled.
'01. 28– 3 great naturalist's *p·*.
'02. 18–22 *p·* of the great Teacher
Peo. 11– 1 that hour was a *p·* of

prophecy
My. 39–20   * words of reminder and *p*·.
      44–11   * rejoices in *p*· fulfilled,
      45–24   * fulfilment of the later *p*·,
   146–17   his immortal words and my poor *p*·,
   171– 3   fulfilled the *p*· of Isaiah :
   177–22   *p*· of Isaiah is fulfilled
   190–31   who are fulfilling Jesus' *p*·
   193–26   may the *p*· of Isaiah be fulfilled :
   258–19   hopes . . . that waken *p*·,

prophesied
Mis. 145–22   such as Isaiah *p*· :
   161–15   *p*· the appearing of this
My. 238–15   of which St. Mark *p*·
   330– 5   * he *p*· that his followers

prophesies
Mis. 329–29   *p*· of fair earth and sunny skies.
'02.   5– 2   *p*· renewed energy for to-morrow,
My. 147–12   of which St. Mark *p*·

prophesy
Mis. 84– 5   did not *p*· his death,
   102– 1   *p*· the nature and stature
Ret. 23–12   could not *p*· sunrise

prophesying
Man. 40–13   from *p*·, judging, condemning,
Pul.   5–19   and *p*· its prosperity,

Prophet
Galilean
Man. 16– 3   demonstrated by the Galilean *P*·
'02. 11–27   put to death the Galilean *P*·,
My. 111– 7   Metaphysician, the Galilean *P*·,
   220–26   example of the great Galilean *P*·,
   261–27   Galilean *P*·, was born of the
   288–12   The great Galilean *P*· was, is,
   319– 1   such a person as the Galilean *P*·,
Nazarene
Mis. 15– 7   great Nazarene *P*· said,
   24–29   Nazarene *P*· declared that his
   60–10   Nazarene *P*· could make the
   344–24   rules of the mighty Nazarene *P*·.
Pul.   6– 5   established by the Nazarene *P*·
Pan. 10– 5   great Nazarene *P*· said,
My. 106–30   Nazarene *P*·, healed through Mind,
   179–22   character of the Nazarene *P*·

Mis. 374–21   face of the Nazarite *P*· ;

prophet (*see also* **prophet's**)
Mis. 72–12   saith, through the *p*· Ezekiel,
   121–16   The *p*· declared,
   148–29   in the words of the *p*· Isaiah :
   161–14   *p*· whose words we have chosen
   164–14   *p*· beheld it from the beginning
   308–16   In the words of the *p*·,
   333–32   the *p*· better understood Him
   373–30   C. S. is more than a *p*·
Pul. 20–19   In the words of the *p*· :
No. 37–23   Messiah and *p*· saved the sinner
   39–10   *P*· and apostle have glorified God
Pan.   8–11   doctrine that Mohammed is the only *p*·
My. 5–27   saying virtually what the *p*· said :
   140– 2   Of this . . . the *p*· Isaiah said,

prophetic
'00. 6–28   modern exegesis on the *p*· Scriptures
   13– 9   their so-called *p*· illumination.
My. 46– 8   * it stands in *p*· verity of the
   147– 4   and the present is *p*·.
   186– 3   should be *p*· of the finger divine

prophetically
My. 45–14   * which you have long *p*· seen

prophet's
Mis. 245– 3   we have his words, and the *p*·,

prophets
Mis. 8–25   persecuted they the *p*· — Matt. 5 : 12.
   23– 7   The *p*·, Jesus, and the apostles,
   40–14   equal the ancient *p*· as healers.
   84– 7   *p*· thrust disputed points on
   168–17   nineteenth-century *p*· repeat,
   209– 5   shut the mouth of His *p*·,
   326–26   thou that killest the *p*·, — Matt. 23 : 37.
Un. 56–18   *P*· . . . suffered from the thoughts of
Pul.   7–20   false *p*· in the present
No. 39– 6   after the fashion of Baal's *p*·,
'00. 10–16   new-old doctrines of the *p*·
'02. 5–24   law, or the *p*· : — Matt. 5 : 17.
   11–26   persecuted they the *p*· — Matt. 5 : 12.
Peo. 5– 3   The *p*· and apostles,
My. vii– 9   * testified to by Jesus and the *p*·.
   103–25   the lives of *p*· and apostles.
   106–32   *p*· and apostles and the Christians
   161–12   Jacob, and all the *p*· — Luke 13 : 28.
   190–30   wherefore vilify His *p*· to-day
   219–24   law, or the *p*· : — Matt. 5 :17.

prophets
My. 221– 5   *p*· of old looked for something higher
   248– 9   Spiritual heroes and *p*· are they
   270– 2   persecuted they the *p*· — Matt. 5 : 12.
   285–28   in the law and in the *p*·." — Acts 24 : 14.

propitiate
No. 34–21   to *p*· His justice

proportion
as a physician
Hea. 14–12   In *p*· as a physician is enlightened
as he understands
Mis. 243–16   only in *p*· as he understands it.
as mortals
Mis. 28–11   In *p*· as mortals turn from this
No. 16–24   in *p*· as mortals approach Spirit,
   38–17   In *p*· as mortals approximate
as one understands
'01. 15–10   in *p*· as one understands it
as this church
Mis. 127– 1   in *p*· as this church has
My. 17–29   in *p*· as this church has
as we love
Mis. 117–17   work wisely, in *p*· as we love.
as we oppose
Mis. 37– 9   In *p*· as we oppose the belief
larger
My. 97– 8   * a larger *p*· have died than
like
My. 94– 1   * growth continues in like *p*·
prospers in
Mis. 288–28   and their cause prospers in *p*·
same
Mis. 229–21   in the same *p*· would faith in
that Science
Mis. 367–10   in the *p*· that Science is understood,
that they gain
Mis. 181–27   in the *p*· that they gain the sense of
to its right
My. 224–10   only in *p*· to its right or its wrong concept,
to its wickedness
Pul. 13–10   in *p*· to its wickedness.
to its worth
Mis. 273– 4   and in *p*· to its worth.
to our affection
Ret. 80–28   lose them in *p*· to our affection.
to the faith
Mis. 31–11   in *p*· to the faith in evil,
to their fitness
My. 267–18   in *p*· to their fitness to partake of
to their progress
My. 267–18   enter heaven in *p*· to their progress,

Mis. 124–32   In *p*· to a man's spiritual progress,
   213– 6   in the *p*· that their instructions
Ret. 73– 6   Limitations are put off in *p*·
Un. 6– 5   in *p*· as the spotless selfhood
'01. 27–23   than others do in *p*·,
Hea. 3–10   In *p*· as the personal and
My. 108– 8   is salutary and potent in *p*· as
   113–25   in *p*· as this Principle and rule
   222–25   in *p*· as God's government becomes

proportionably
Un. 20–20   *p*· as you realize the divine
My. 357–17   *p*· estimate their success

proportionately
Mis. 42–20   joys . . . will be *p*· increased.
   232–14   *P*· as we part with material
Un. 5– 8   pride of opinion will *p*· diminish.
   13–12   *p*· as we gain the true understanding
Hea. 11–21   *p*· as matter went out
Peo. 2–20   *P*· as the people's belief of God,
My. 67–28   * it is so *p*· built
   213–13   Then they will be *p*· successful

proportions
Mis. 55–10   seeks the *p*· of good.
   239– 9   substance is taking larger *p*·.
Pul. 30–28   * its present impressive *p*·,
My. 88–14   * its *p*· are so large,

propose
Mis. 137–10   if you had any questions to *p*·,
   371–17   although he . . . is apt to *p*· it.
My. 300–22   we *p*· that he make known

proposed
Mis. 141–10   *p*· type of universal Love ;
   156–13   I *p*· to merge the
   284–13   This question is often *p*·,
   304–22   * *p*· use of the bell :
Pul. 57–25   * *p*· site of the new Music Hall,
My. 145– 4   *p*· to one of Concord's best builders
   327–15   * when a medical bill was *p*·

proposition

Mis.	13–14	theology elaborates the *p·*
	13–21	Science of Soul reverses this *p·*,
	14–11	Were we to admit this vague *p·*,
	46– 4	The leading self-evident *p·*
	346–19	self-evident *p·* of C. S.,
Rud.	11– 9	next *p·* in C. S.,
No.	4–15	self-evident *p·*, in the Science
'01.	3–22	The first *p·* is correct,
	3–24	last *p·* does not illustrate
'02.	7–20	no other scientific *p·* can be
	20–16	ready to join me in this *p·*,

propositions

Mis.	193– 6	they form *p·* of self-evident
	252–15	My proof of these novel *p·*
	269–19	These are self-evident *p·* :
Ret.	31– 6	self-evident *p·* of Truth
Un.	7–18	Certain self-proved *p·*
Rud.	13–16	These *p·*, understood in their Science,
'01.	22– 3	demonstrates the truth of these *p·*
My.	146–14	altitude of its highest *p·*

propound

'02.	5–26	*p·* a question, formulate a doctrine,

proprietor

My.	314–32	*p·* of the White Mountain House,
		(*see also* **Eddy**)

propriety

Mis.	255– 4	no fairness or *p·* in the aspersion.
Ret.	52–12	the *p·* of forming a National
My.	25– 2	* *p·* in making a special effort
	138–19	not exceeded the bounds of *p·*
	225–13	God is All ; hence the *p·* of

prosaics

My.	122–10	Now I am done with . . . tedious *p·*.

proscription

Hea.	11–13	fires of ancient *p·* burn upon the

proscriptive

'01.	34–14	material religion, *p·*, intolerant,
My.	265–20	no longer tyrannical and *p·* ;

prose

Ret.	11– 2	suited my emotions better than *p·*.

prosecute

Pul.	83– 6	* courage to *p·* the appeal.

prosecution

My.	127–19	for persecution and for *p·*,

proselytizing

My.	93– 3	* without efforts at *p·* ;

prosody

Ret.	10–17	*P·*, the song of angels,

prospect

Mis.	262– 5	will aid our *p·* of fulfilling it
My.	208–18	I congratulate you on the *p·* of

prospective

Mis.	64– 9	*p· students of the College*

Prospectus

Mis.	1– 1	chapter sub-title

prosper

Mis.	213– 9	shall not *p·*."— *Prov.* 28 : 13.
Pul.	38–29	* It is good that each and all shall *p·*,
'02.	3–20	British and Boer may *p·* in peace,
My.	10–18	* It is doubtful if . . . could *p·*,
	13–32	"*p·* in the thing whereto— *Isa.* 55 : 11.
	282–26	May God guide and *p·*
	360–22	God will bless and *p·* you.

prospered

Mis.	140–14	church was *p·* by the right hand of
	140–26	diviner claim and means . . . were *p·*.
'02.	14–25	*p·* preeminently our great Cause,
My.	37–18	* its followers have been *p·*,
	215– 6	and it *p·* at every step.
	328– 2	* dignified, blessed, and *p·* it,

prospering

My.	143–20	The Cause of C. S. is *p·*

prosperity

Mis.	110–22	progress and unprecedented *p·* of
	154–12	proof of the *p·* of His Zion
	254– 2	points with promise of *p·*?
	273– 8	I withdraw from an overwhelming *p·*.
	291–13	equal growth and *p·* of all
	358–26	at the pinnacle of *p·*,
Man.	31– 8	*p·* of C. S. largely depends.
Ret.	44–16	previous harmony and *p·*.
	44–28	love, *p·*, and spiritual power.
	45– 5	the *p·* of my church,
	48–30	at the height of *p·* in the institution,
	82–18	with the *p·* of each worker ;
Pul.	2– 5	thy wisdom and *p·*— *I Kings* 10 : 7.
	5–19	and prophesying its *p·*,
	20–13	*p·* of this church is unsurpassed.
	36– 4	* in the very zenith of its *p·*,

prosperity

Pan.	14–11	Pray for the *p·* of our country,
'00.	1–12	crowned with unprecedented *p·* ;
'02.	14–14	remarkable growth and *p·* of C. S.
My.	v– 6	* growth and *p·* of the Cause
	10–26	* *p·* of the branch churches ;
	37–24	* church owes itself and its *p·* to
	81– 2	* air of well-being and of *p·*
	93– 6	* material evidence of their *p·* ;
	116– 6	In time of religious or scientific *p·*,
	117–28	I left Boston in the height of *p·*
	157– 8	* rejoice that the *p·* of the Cause
	164–15	with its present *p·*?
	175–12	growth and *p·* of our city
	184–24	The *p·* of Zion is very precious
	192–23	to visit you, to witness your *p·*,
	246–12	in the midst of unprecedented *p·*,
	270–25	I love the *p·* of Zion,
	277–15	peace, *p·*, and life of nations.
	279–27	with peace and *p·*.
	282–13	which are the landmarks of *p·*.
	291–23	ensign of peace and *p·* waves

prosperous

Ret.	53– 4	*p·* under difficult circumstances,
	85–25	The Cause, *our* Cause, is highly *p·*,
My.	10–26	* must be a *p·* parent church,
	10–28	* *p·* growth of this movement
	80– 2	* *p·*, contented men and women,
	95–10	* cheerful and *p·* body of believers

prospers

Mis.	288–28	and their cause *p·* in proportion
My.	93–10	* religion *p·* according to the pledges

prostration

No.	42–26	* suffering from nervous *p·*,

protect

Mis.	115– 1	to *p·* themselves therefrom,
	201–25	We *p·* our dwellings more securely
Pan.	14–22	May the divine Love succor and *p·*
Po.	vi–17	*authorities could p· him nowhere*
My.	vii– 5	* so *p·* their own thoughts
	138– 9	not needed to *p·* my person
	245–22	To *p·* the public,
	327– 1	to *p·* the practice of C. S.

protected

Ret.	39– 4	and my copyright was *p·*.
Pul.	4– 9	*p·* by his divine Principle, God
My.	138– 2	because I wanted it *p·*
	227–20	*they are not specially p· by law.*

protecting

Mis.	137–16	*p·* wings of the mother-bird,

protection

Mis.	115–16	means of *p·* and defense from sin
	263–12	by divine *p·* and affection.
	263–24	lacks the aid and *p·* of State laws.
Ret.	76– 2	nor would *p·* by copyright be
'01.	33–16	*p·* of the constitutional laws
'02.	14–23	afforded me neither favor nor *p·*
	15– 4	*p·* of the laws of my country.
My.	227– 9	*p·* of State or United States laws,
	327–28	* dignified legal *p·* and recognition,

protects

Mis.	211–21	*p·* himself at his neighbor's cost,
	222–24	Its mystery *p·* it now,
'01.	20–25	At present its mystery *p·* it,

protest

Mis.	68– 8	* *A true Christian would p· against*
	216–17	a big *p·* against injustice ;
	256– 8	in daily letters that *p·* against
	319–12	*p·* against the reality of sin,
Ret.	15– 3	and my *p·* along with me,
Un.	26–20	*p·* against this stanza of Bowring's,
My.	134– 3	evidence a heart wholly in *p·*

Protestant

Mis.	111–25	between the Catholic and *P·* sects.
Ret.	2– 3	Calvinistic devotion to *P·* liberty
'01.	28–13	in Catholic and *P·* oratories.
My.	4–14	loves *P·* and Catholic, D.D. and M.D.,
	270–25	be it promoted by Catholic, by *P·*, or

Protestantism

Mis.	281–13	was converted to *P·* through a
No.	44–13	In Queen Elizabeth's time *P·* could
'02.	2–13	from stern *P·* to doubtful liberalism.
My.	127–20	purer *P·* and monotheism

Protestants

Mis.	172– 6	*P·* in a higher sense than ever before,
My.	303– 7	Scientists have no quarrel with *P·*,

protestations

My.	358– 3	if you are sincere in your *p·*

protesting

My.	193–17	*P·* against error, you unite with

proud
Ret.	17–10	p· Prairie Queen and the modest
Un.	26– 6	p· to be in His outstretched hands,
Po.	1–13	P· from yon cloud-crowned height
	18– 2	the eagle's p· wing,
	62–11	On p· Prairie Queen
My.	41– 8	* If the p· are lonely
	84–13	* temple is something to be p· of.
	98–26	* any church might well be p·.
	122–12	tempted me tenderly to be p· !
	151–17	* "Pass ye the p· fane by,
	210–14	evil thinker is the p· talker
	320–13	* quite p· of his having had
	320–27	* p· of his acquaintance with you.
	321– 2	* He seemed very p· to think that

proudest
Pul.	83–22	* the p· boast of many

proudly
Un.	45– 5	rears its crest p·,
Pul.	1–17	Pass p· to thy bier !
Po.	26– 6	Pass p· to thy bier !

prove
Mis.	6–12	should certainly p· to all minds
	27– 7	p· themselves invalid.
	30– 2	understand . . . before we p· it,
	41–29	may not always p· equal to
	45– 1	p· the fact that Mind is supreme.
	55– 4	p· all its possibilities.
	111–19	who p· its power to be immortal.
	138–13	especially should he p· his faith by
	162–15	p· his power, derived from Spirit,
	167–28	His works thus p· him.
	171–17	p· his right to be heard.
	192–20	man's ability to p· the truth of
	195–10	every one can p·, in some degree,
	250–17	active witnesses to p· it,
	311–15	p· that I love my enemies
	315–18	p· sound in sentiment, health, and
	354–14	whose fruits p· the nature of their
	380– 4	p· that a divine Principle heals
	382– 2	contradict it and p· an exception.
Man.	83–17	p· sound in sentiment and practical
Ret.	33–13	p· the Principle of Mind-healing.
	49–24	p· a healing for the nations,
Un.	28– 4	Who can p· that?
	33– 1	arguments which p· matter to be
	40– 7	in order to p· man deathless.
No.	15– 6	would enable any one to p·
Pan.	5–23	deny it and p· its falsity.
	13–27	you may p· for yourselves the
'01.	2–22	his followers of to-day will p·,
	15– 6	p· it false, therefore unreal.
	24–29	to p· the doctrine of Jesus,
Hea.	12–23	p· that the power was the thought,
Po.	vii–13	* p· a joy to the heavy laden
My.	vi– 1	* p·, (1) that S. and H. does not
	64–24	* thus p· our worthiness
	98– 6	* anything that its foes try to p· it
	105– 6	p· one's faith by his works.
	119–21	He turned to . . . to p· Christ,
	124–25	p· fairly the facts
	131–26	p· me now herewith, — Mal. 3 : 10.
	132– 3	"P· me now herewith, — Mal. 3 : 10.
	149– 2	must p· their knowledge by
	180– 1	whereby man can p· God's love,
	182–31	p· the practicality of perfection,
	184–20	shall p· a historic gem
	239– 9	imbibe the spirit and p· the
	269–26	"P· me now herewith, — Mal. 3 : 10.
	285–24	neither can they p·— Acts 24 : 13.
	293–11	that the bullet would p· fatal.

proved
Mis.	28–15	Master p· to his doubting disciple,
	29–32	which Jesus taught and p·.
	30–17	He p· the superiority of Mind
	33–15	not p· impossible to heal those who,
	63–29	Spirit p· its supremacy over matter.
	74–22	he p· the fallacy of the theory
	338– 5	I first p· to myself,
	348–27	so p· to myself that drugs have no
	350–17	This p· to be our last meeting.
	378–11	p· to be a magnetic practitioner.
Man.	55–19	decide if his loyalty has been p·
Ret.	19–10	which in his case p· fatal.
	69–13	This error has p· itself to be error.
Un.	14–16	created children p· sinful ;
	40– 5	is to assert what we have not p· ;
Pul.	45–19	* p·, in most striking manner,
	57–17	* p· their faith by their works.
No.	27–11	matter will be p· a myth.
	38– 1	Jesus p· to perfection,
Hea.	18–27	Oxford students p· this :
	19– 2	they did test it, and p· it.
	19– 3	p· it not in part, but as a whole ;

proved
Hea.	19– 4	p· that every organ of the system,
Peo.	8–28	skill p· a million times unskilful.
	12–22	p· the application of its Principle
	13–17	p· the triumph of mind over
My.	28– 5	* this has been p· true
	56–32	* p· the need of a larger edifice.
	86–23	* p· one of the most interesting
	105–32	p· to be more certain
	106–17	p· that C. S. rests on the
	108– 6	I have p· beyond cavil
	174– 5	p· an ideal meeting place.
	180– 5	by him who p· their practicality,
	214–12	He p· Life to be deathless
	303–20	Jesus taught and p· that
	303–28	What I am remains to be p·
	348– 4	p· conclusively that all effect
	348–25	demonstrated Christianity and p·
	352–10	what is p· in better lives.
	360–22	He has p· it to me

proven
Mis.	10–20	tried their strength and p· it ;
	14–22	p· by the law of opposites to be
	22–25	have p· to a waiting world.
	29–29	whereby matter is p· powerless
	73– 3	this supposition is p· erroneous
	76– 8	or p· true upon a false premise,
	111– 1	p· that the greatest piety is
	134–20	powers of earth . . . are p· powerless.
	269–16	he who has fairly p· his knowledge
	269–18	p· the divine Mind to be
	278–10	it can be p· that I have never
Ret.	35– 9	merits of C. S. must be p·
	83– 2	already been p· that this volume is
	89– 3	p· beyond a doubt in the practice of
No.	10–19	the former position, . . . is p·
	17– 5	Their nothingness is thus p· ;
'00.	6–26	the Science of God is p· when,
'01.	13–30	and its unreality is p·.
	19–14	The notion . . . is p· false.
	28–21	p· to me beyond a doubt
	34– 8	and is p· to be more pathological
My.	24– 3	* is to-day being p· and is ready
	270–16	Her life is p· under trial,

proverb
Mis.	72–13	that ye use this p·— Ezek. 18 : 2.
	72–16	to use this p·— Ezek. 18 : 3.
	223–25	wisdom in the old p·,
My.	40–29	* often rebels . . . hence the p· :

proverbial
Ret.	75–20	p· that dishonesty retards
	80– 3	This also is p·,
My.	123– 1	Our unity and progress are p·,
	134– 5	progress of C. S. is p·,

proverbially
Mis.	243–18	students are p· modest :

proves
Mis.	42–18	life-work p· to have been well done,
	56–23	p· the correctness of my statements,
	58– 6	p· to him who thought he died that
	65–26	p· that strict adherence to one is
	102–30	p· daily that "one on God's side
	209– 9	p· that human belief fulfils the
	212–21	C. S. p· that human will is lost
	223– 9	Science p·, beyond cavil,
	309–13	Experience p· this true.
	336–30	the sequence p·.
Un.	8–22	it p· my view conclusively,
'00.	6–17	fact p· that the so-called fog of
'01.	18–29	and so p· their nullity.
Hea.	12–23	and the sequel p· it ;
My.	58– 6	* p· the truth of the axiom,

provide
Man.	27–13	to p· a suitable building for the
	27–20	to p· suitable rooms,
Ret.	52– 8	to p· a home for every true seeker
	52–10	p· folds for the sheep that were
My.	10–23	* They will p· the money necessary
	65–14	* money to p· it was pledged
	76– 7	* to p· for the entire cost of
	222–22	does not p· that materia medica shall

provided
Mis.	302–21	p·, they each and all
	349– 2	p· he received these lessons of
Man.	36– 2	as p· in Article VI, Sect. 2,
	36–12	except in such cases as are p· for
	37–20	except as p· for in Article V,
	38–23	p· they are willing and anxious to
	59–19	not otherwise p· with seats.
	63–17	p· these rooms are well located.
	67–12	on a case not p· for in its By-Laws
	73–12	p· its rules so permit.

provided

Man.	91–24	p· their diplomas are for
'00.	10– 7	p· this warfare is honest
'01.	28–30	usually are handsomely p· for.
	29– 4	God has p· the means for him
My.	6–13	wisely p· for The Mother Church
	45– 2	* p· for the furtherance of our Cause,
	75–12	* if they had not already been p· for.
	147– 9	have p· for you a modest hall,
	216– 9	by which each is p· for
	217–14	p· he has complied with my request
	261– 5	seems to have amply p· for this,
	302–21	less lauded, pampered, p· for,

Providence

Mis.	312–14	* divine P· in human affairs
	320– 1	trust the divine P·,
'01.	24–12	* under P· I owe my life to it.''

providence

Mis.	80–18	through the p· of God,
	100– 3	left to the p· of God.
	163–15	committed to the p· of God.
	278–23	since necessities and God's p· are
	345– 2	God's presence and p·.
Ret.	21– 8	by a strange p· had learned
	30–20	p· of God, and the cross of Christ.
	50– 9	finally led, by a strange p·,
Pul.	20–12	Thus committed to the p· of God,
Pan.	3–24	* from the divine Mind and p·,
	3–30	care and p· by which he governs
'02.	1– 2	God's loving p· for His people
Hea.	12–13	through His p· or His laws,
My.	148– 3	through the p· of God,
	220– 3	submit to the p· of God,
	355–19	* ''Behind a frowning p·

provident

Mis.	117–27	oil of the more p· watcher.

provides

Man.	51–18	p· for immediate action.
Rud.	8– 2	or p· breast-milk for babes.

providing

'01.	29– 4	p· ways and means for others.
My.	7–16	* necessity for p· an auditorium
	9– 3	* necessity for p· an audience-room

province

Mis.	146–12	This is not my present p· ;
	336– 4	your p· to wrestle with error,
Hea.	3–17	in a remote p· of Judea,
My.	359– 6	My p· as a Leader

provinces

'00.	10–20	sways . . . weak p·, or peoples.

proving

Mis.	34– 2	thus p· that metaphysics
	60– 8	is p· this by healing
	210– 4	never healed . . . without p·
	337– 5	By p· its effect on yourself
Man.	92–10	thus p· this Science to be
Ret.	31– 7	paramount . . . in p· the Christ.
	34–16	thus p· the superiority of
No.	38– 2	what C. S. is to-day p·
Pan.	10–17	thus p· the utility of what they
'00.	6– 3	p· its power and divinity.
My.	111–24	p· that his conclusion was

provision

Man.	77–23	P· for the Future.
My.	56– 8	* this p· was inadequate
	56–26	* still further p· must be made,
	215–28	p· for their expenses?

provisions

Mis.	139–30	that the p· for the land
Man.	81–17	conducted according to the p·
	85– 9	p· of Article XII,
My.	175–14	p· for the army,
	312–24	and their p· in my behalf

provoke

Mis.	325–23	''p· Him in the wilderness, — Psal. 78 : 40.

provoked

Un.	6–23	p· discussion and horror,

provoking

'01.	15–28	* p· His pure eyes by your sinful,

prowl

Mis.	323–12	beasts of prey p· in the path,

proximity

'01.	19– 6	closer p· with divine Love,

proxy

Rud.	1–18	one's appearance . . . by deputy or p·.
My.	218–23	either teach or heal by p·

prudence

Mis.	204–30	divine ruling gives p· and energy ;

prudent

Mis.	167–25	the wise and p·, — Luke 10 : 21.
No.	45– 2	the wise and p·, — Luke 10 : 21.
Pan.	3–15	* Choice of the p· ! envy of the great !
Hea.	1–19	* Pushes his p· purpose to resolve.''

prudential

My.	173–29	chairman of the p· committee

prune

Mis.	154– 8	p· its encumbering branches,

pruning-hook

Mis.	xii– 6	I take my pen and p·,

psalm

Mis.	142–16	my second, a p· ; my third, a letter.
	142–22	seemed more Olympian than the p·
'00.	11–23	* Like the close of an angel's p·,

Psalmist

Mis.	153–11	In the words of the P·,
	306–29	The P· saith :
Ret.	14–25	answer him in the words of the P· :
	64–14	where the P· saith :
	72– 7	The P· vividly portrays the result of
Pul.	10– 6	in the words of the P·,
My.	103–15	Alluding to this . . . the P· said :
	188–11	whereof the P· sang,
	274–27	The P· sang,

Psalms 15 : 1-5 ; 24 : 1-6, 9, 10

My.	33–13	* P· 15 : 1-5 ; 24 : 1-6, 9, 10.

psalms

Pul.	59–10	* hymns and p· being omitted.

Psyche

Mis.	ix–20	a P· who is ever a girl.

psychic

Pul.	54–10	* conditions requisite in p· healing

psychics

My.	111– 5	cannot be destroyed by false p·,

psychist

My.	160–29	p· knows that this hell is mental,

psychology

Mis.	3–31	demand for the Science of p·
Un.	9–11	human philosophy, or mystic p·.

public (noun)

Mis.	161–21	teach or preach in p·
	238–28	kept constantly before the p·.
	274–12	grateful acknowledgments to the p·
	285–25	notifies the p· of broken vows.
	297–11	p· cannot swallow reports of
	299–29	gives to the p· new patterns
	301–17	without this word of warning in p·,
	364– 8	made the p· your friend,
Man.	50– 6	DEBATING IN p·.
	58–19	READING IN p·.
	97–17	impositions on the p·.
Ret.	15–30	were too timid to testify in p·.
	37–21	My reluctance to give the p·,
	49–21	we thank the p· for its liberal
Pul.	37– 4	* increasing demands of the p·
Rud.	16– 6	Lectures in p· are needed,
'01.	22–26	and insist that the p· receive
Po.	vii–11	* volume is presented to the p·,
My.	31–10	* p· had its first glimpse of the
	49– 1	* both in p· and private.
	83–16	* p· at large will scarcely realize
	92–13	* p· has in a general way
	93–27	* essentials of its hold upon the p·,
	94–19	* the doors were opened to the p·,
	175–18	May I ask in behalf of the p·
	223– 2	I hereby notify the p· that
	245–22	To protect the p·, students of the
	272–23	* the p· generally, will be interested
	298– 3	recommending it to the p·.
	298–10	placing this book before the p·,
	338– 5	* chapter sub-title

public (adj.)

Mis.	7–22	counteract . . . this p· nuisance ;
	48– 7	for his p· exposure of it.
	78–19	Misguiding the p· mind and
	78–23	purification of p· thought
	95– 6	* to reply to his p· letter
	161–18	our Master as a p· benefactor,
	171–28	obtruding upon the p· attention
	221–31	or call p· attention to that crime?
	238–25	The frequent p· allegement
	249–10	Both in private and p· life,
	256– 7	acknowledging the p· confidence
	256–12	at present a p· servant :
	274– 2	for a p· institution.
	275–23	p· and private expressions
	299–14	* read them for our p· services?''
	301–20	read them for our p· services?''
	315– 7	in private or in p· assemblies,
	335–16	In my p· works I lay bare the

public (adj.)
Mis. 350–13   and like my *p·* instruction.
Man. 50– 9   in *p·* debating assemblies,
        64–23   owing to the *p·* misunderstanding
        67– 9   shall not be made *p·* without
        74– 2   C. S. society holding *p·* services,
        93–12   reply to *p·* topics condemning C. S.,
Ret.   6–26   served the *p·* interests faithfully
         7–23   * It is a *p·* calamity.
Pul.   4–29   used, in all its *p·* sessions,
         5–22   It is in the *p·* libraries of the
        31–15   * that close contact with *p·* feeling
        62–21   * concert halls, and *p·* buildings,
        79– 9   * as students of *p·* questions
Rud. 15–26   *P·* lectures cannot be such lessons in
        16– 2   *p·* lectures can take the place of
No.   1–11   when *p·* sentiment is aroused,
         3–11   should not be made *p·* ;
'01. 17–13   would not have arrested *p·* attention
        17–19   when the *p·* sentiment would allow
'02.   3–16   so improved her *p·* school system
        14–28   all unjust *p·* aspersions,
My.   vi–13   * originated its form of *p·* worship,
        51–11   * to have the *p·* services discontinued
        59–16   * that first *p·* meeting in the little hall
        88–17   * which must arrest *p·* attention.
       129–32   Refrain from *p·* controversy ;
       130– 9   to keep my works from *p·* recognition
       130– 9   students seeking only *p·* notoriety,
       130–29   in all your *p·* ministrations,
       144– 6   The *p·* report that I am in
       224–10   *p·* sentiment is helpful or dangerous
       224–14   Avoid . . . *p·* debating clubs.
       291–17   His *p·* intent was uniform,
       316–18   demands *p·* attention.
       317– 5   * allegations in the *p·* press
       341–21   * unusual *p·* interest centres in
                (*see also* **thought**)

Publican's
'01. 14– 4   *P·* wail won his humble desire,
My. 334–21   *P·* wail won his humble desire,

publicans
Mis. 374– 2   caused even the *p·* to justify God.

Publication
        (*see* **Committee on Publication, Committees on
         Publication**)

publication
Mis. 29–18   date of the first *p·* of my work,
       155–22   send them to the . . . *Journal* for *p·*,
       307–14   thought best to stop its *p·*.
       372– 9   two weeks from the date of its *p·*
       382– 4   Before the *p·* of my first work
Man. 27–14   suitable building for the *p·* of
        27–21   *p·* and sale of the books of the
        48–17   not report for *p·* the number of
Ret. 35– 1   I copyrighted the first *p·* on
        35– 7   not venture upon its *p·* until later,
Pul.   5–13   After the *p·* of "S. and H.
        36–27   * *C. S. Journal*, a monthly *p·*,
        45– 9   * from a *p·* of the new denomination :
My. 141–13   * Alfred Farlow of the *p·* committee
       242–18   *p·* committee work, reading-room work,
       326–12   for *p·* in our periodicals
       333– 3   * the C. S. *p·* committee.

Publication Committee
'02.   4– 6   congratulate our . . . *P· C·*,

publications
Mis. 132–24   refer you . . . to my various *p·*,
       133– 7   to read my sermons and *p·*.
       300–12   from copies of my *p·*
       301– 8   made up of my *p·*,
Man. 48– 6   Uncharitable *P·*.
        53–23   *P·* Unjust.
'01. 23–27   In later *p·* he declared
Po.   vi–26   * *in various p· of that day.*
My. 272–28   * for any *p·* outside of the

publicity
Mis. 296–23   wriggles" itself into *p·*?
Rud. 16– 1   If *p·* and material control

publicly
Mis. 136– 2   socially, *p·*, and finally,
       300– 6   then reading it *p·* as your own
       301–22   read it *p· without my consent.*
Man. 59– 7   when *p·* reading or quoting from
        72–11   shall be acknowledged *p·* as a
Ret. 42– 4   first student *p·* to announce
Pul.   5– 1   clergymen who had *p·* proclaimed
'00. 12–22   in that city were *p·* burned.
My. 219–26   expressed my opinion *p·*
       359– 8   I hereby *p·* declare that

public-spirited
Mis. 147–24   the pious worker, the *p·* citizen.

Public Statutes
    Chapter 115, Section 2
Mis. 272–12   * in *P· S·*, Chapter 115, Section 2,

publish
Mis. 220–27   *p·* it in the newspapers
       300– 9   If you should print and *p·* your copy
       300–15   You literally *p·* my works through
Man. 43–14   shall not *p·* profuse quotations from
        48– 7   member of this Church shall not *p·*,
        48–23   do not *p·* descriptions of our
        71–24   her permission to *p·* them
        72– 2   not adopt, print, nor *p·* the Manual
        82– 4   the Society will not *p·* them.
Pul. 58–13   * pictures we are permitted to *p·*.
My. 237– 3   I have since decided not to *p·*.
       255– 5   my consent to *p·* the foregoing
       298–11   my permission to *p·* . . . this work.
       326– 1   * glad to *p·* the following
       351– 3   * to *p·* her letter of recent date,
       358–16   whether or not they shall *p·* your

published
Mis.   x– 6   writings *p·* in *The C. S. Journal*,
         x–27   in connection with my *p·* works.
         4–12   *p·* by the Christian Scientists
        89–24   proper answer . . . in my *p·* works.
       153–12   those that *p·* it." — *Psal.* 68 : 11.
       242– 3   *p·* in *Zion's Herald*,
       271–24   *p·* in the *Boston Traveler*
       300– 3   Copying my *p·* works *verbatim*,
Man. 27–17   *p·* by The C. S. Publishing Society.
        48– 8   nor cause to be *p·*, an article that
        53–25   publishes, or causes to be *p·*,
        64– 8   also the literature *p·* or sold by
        73– 5   *p·* in the list of practitioners
        81–15   *p·* by The C. S. Publishing Society,
        81–22   C. S. textbook is *p·* or sold.
        81–25   Books to be *P·*.
        82– 7   not be *p·* . . . without her knowledge
        98– 7   not promptly *p·* by the periodical
        98–13   see that it is *p·* according to copy ;
        98–18   have *p·* each year in a leading
Ret. 27– 4   S. and H., *p·* in 1875.
        27– 6   If these notes . . . were *p·*,
        35–10   could be profitably *p·*.
        36– 8   This will account for certain *p·*
        37– 4   was *p·* in 1875.
Pul. 46– 8   * which are *p·* under the title of
        55–14   * should have been *p·* in 1875.
        74– 4   * article *p·* in the *Herald*
Rud. 16–20   a work which I *p·* in 1875.
'00.   7– 2   "S. and H. was . . . first *p·*.
'01. 21– 7   *p·* in the *New York Journal*,
        23–23   Bishop Berkeley *p·* a book
        24–22   when I *p·* my work S. and H.,
        27– 9   first ever *p·* on C. S.
'02. 13–30   is *p·* in our Church Manual.
Po.   vi– 3   * *p· in Manchester, N. H.,*
        vi–11   * *which was p· with the poem,*
My.   v–20   * wrote and *p·* the C. S. textbook,
        13– 5   *p·* in London, England, in 1853,
        18–30   * all other *p·* writings of
        58– 3   * was *p·* in the *C. S. Sentinel*
        76–13   * *p·* at the time of the dedication
       130–21   All *p·* quotations from my works
       185– 8   peace of Love is *p·*,
       218–24   My *p·* works are teachers
       243– 7   as *p·* in our Church Manual.
       266–24   "S. and H. . . . . was *p·* in 1875.
       306–25   that I would pay for having *p·*.
       306–27   Dr. Quimby had tried to get them *p·*
       306–28   Quotations have been *p·*,
       310–30   first edition of S. and H. was *p·*,
       317– 1   * which was *p·* in the *Sentinel*
       321– 9   * as regards your *p·* works
       321–14   * your relations to your *p·* works
       322–10   * correcting mistakes widely *p·*
       330– 1   * which was *p·* in your paper
       334–28   * *p·* by the late Charles W. Moore,
       354– 6   nothing but what is *p·* or sold by
       359–10   through my written and *p·* rules,

publisher
'02. 15–10   my *p·* paid me not one dollar
Po. vii– 5   * *Mrs. Eddy requested her p· to prepare*
My. 296–11   the *p·* of my books,
                (*see also* **Eddy**)

publishers
Man. 49–16   rules established by the *p·*.

publishes
Man. 53–24   *p·*, or causes to be published,
        82– 1   *p·* the books and literature

publisheth
Ret. 45– 3   that *p·* peace." — *Isa.* 52 : **7.**

pupils

Mis.	91–30	require their *p·* to study the
	114–31	specially instruct his *p·*
Man.	36– 4	Students' *P·*.
	36– 6	from *p·* of loyal students
	36– 9	or from *p·* of those who have
	37–16	*P·* of Normal Students.
	43– 7	nor permit his patients or *p·* to
	59–10	instruct their *p·* to adopt the
	62– 8	*P·* may be received in the
	62–16	officers, teachers, and *p·* should
	73–24	to the *p·* of one teacher.
	83– 8	Care of *P·*.
	83– 9	select for *p·* such only
	83–13	or attempt to dominate his *p·*,
	83–19	patiently counsel his *p·* in
	84– 2	Teachers shall instruct their *p·*
	84– 7	Number of *P·*.
	84–10	consist of not more than thirty *p·*.
	84–12	class not exceeding thirty *p·*.
	84–17	associations of the *p·* of loyal
	84–18	*p·* shall be guided by the BIBLE,
	84–21	shall not call their *p·* together, or
	85– 2	*P·* may visit each other's churches,
	85– 4	*P·* of Strayed Members.
	85– 7	the *p·* of another member of
	85–10	not ready to lead his *p·*.
	85–12	shall not teach *p·* C. S. unless
	86– 2	*P·*.
	86–23	shall instruct their *p·* from the
	87–11	shall not solicit, . . . *p·* for their classes.
	89–19	Loyal Christian Scientists' *p·*
Ret.	83–15	if he misinterprets the text to his *p·*,
	83–25	highly important that their *p·* study
	84–27	take charge only of his own *p·*
Pul.	47– 4	* her circle of *p·* and admirers
	49– 7	* gifts of her loving *p·*.
My.	251–13	if, . . . your *p·* are found eligible
	251–18	teach *p·* the practice of C. S.,

puppets

Mis.	368–23	Some of the mere *p·* of the hour

purblind

My.	45–17	* when *p·* mortal sense declared

purchase

'00.	15– 1	you *p·*, at whatever price,
'02.	12–25	united effort to *p·* more land
My.	7– 9	united effort to *p·* more land
	9–23	*p·* of more land for its site,
	11–23	* informed of the *p·* of the land
	16– 8	* included the *p·* price of the land
	55– 4	* *p·* some building, or church,
	66– 1	* The *p·* of this parcel,
	66– 8	* now comes the *p·* of the last parcel
	215–19	to *p·* the site for a church edifice,

purchased

Mis.	xi–23	preliminary battles that *p·* it.
	165–22	*p·* the means of mortals' redemption
	249–16	I have neither *p·* nor ordered
Man.	102–16	rule shall not apply to land *p·* for
Pul.	20– 2	*p·* by the church and society.
'02.	13–16	*p·* the mortgage on the lot
My.	147–22	I have *p·* a pleasant place for you,

purchases

Man.	102–11	All deeds of further *p·* of land
My.	347–18	priceless pearl which *p·* our

purchasing

Mis.	299–28	saves your *p·* these garments,
	300– 2	avoiding the cost of hiring or *p·*
No.	34–27	*p·* the freedom of mortals from sin
My.	123–15	responsibility of *p·* it,

pure

Mis.	63– 8	triune Principle of all *p·* theology ;
	98–19	*p·* and undefiled religion
	100–22	*P·* humanity, friendship, home,
	107–11	A *p·* affection, concentric,
	123–17	is too *p·* to behold iniquity.
	128– 8	whatsoever things are *p·*, — *Phil.* 4 : 8.
	152–19	made ready for the *p·* in affection,
	159– 3	where all things are *p·*
	168–12	only such as are *p·* in spirit,
	185–22	infinitely blessed, upright, *p·*, and free ;
	206– 4	from foul to *p·*, from torpid to serene,
	223– 6	necessarily have *p·* fountains ;
	228– 7	and *p·* amid corruption.
	240–31	namely, *p·* odors.
	260–16	*p·* Mind is the truth of being
	260–23	acknowledging *p·* Mind as absolute
	260–25	*P·* Mind gives out an atmosphere that
	262– 4	wish to brighten so *p·* a purpose,
	264–16	to assimilate *p·* and abstract Science
	264–27	teacher's mind must be *p·*, grand,
	266– 3	unselfish, *p·* aims and
	270–16	Gain a *p·* Christianity ;
	280– 6	messengers of *p·* and holy thoughts

pure

Mis.	295–23	high and *p·* ethical tones
	338–15	a *p·* faith in humanity will
	343–17	their *p·* perfection shall appear?
	345–12	his *p·* and strong faith rose higher
	354–15	a motive made *p·*,
	367– 3	requires man to be honest, just, *p·* ;
	367–29	God is too *p·* to behold iniquity ;
	368–15	the ranks of the good and *p·*,
	388–18	The right to worship deep and *p·*,
	390– 9	Too *p·* for aught so mute.
	397–19	An offering *p·* of Love,
	399– 8	'T is the Spirit that makes *p·*,
Man.	16–12	to be merciful, just, and *p·*.
Ret.	26–25	Principle of all things *p·* ;
	28–11	honest, unselfish, and *p·*,
	65–20	C. S. is the *p·* evangelic truth.
	68–29	The beautiful, good, and *p·*
	71–20	*p·* and undefiled religion.
Un.	2– 1	God is too *p·* to — *see* Hab. 1 : 13.
	18– 7	too *p·* to behold iniquity,
	57–14	His *p·* consciousness was
Pul.	19– 3	An offering *p·* of Love,
	21–10	unite with me in this *p·* purpose,
	26– 3	* the centre being of *p·* white light,
	35–15	become honest, unselfish, and *p·*,
	42–27	* with ferns and *p·* white roses
Rud.	10– 6	He is too *p·* to behold iniquity,
No.	v–13	the *p·* spirituality of Truth.
	39–25	reveals the *p·* Mind-pictures,
	40– 9	*p·* pearls of awakened consciousness,
Pan.	3–16	* By thy *p·* stream,
'01.	6–15	Is this *p·*, specific Christianity?
	9– 8	submerged them in a sense so *p·*
	15–28	* provoking His *p·* eyes by your
	26–18	to the *p·* in spirit, and the meek
'02.	18– 4	*p·* sense of the immaculate Jesus
Hea.	7–14	makes *p·* the fountain,
Peo.	5–14	wrapped in a *p·* winding-sheet,
	5–25	makes a *p·* Christianity
	13–21	his *p·* faith went up through
Po.	13– 7	An offering *p·* of Love,
	21– 7	right to worship deep and *p·*,
	39– 2	Gifts, lofty, *p·*, and free,
	43–14	their *p·* hearts' off'ring,
	46–13	An offering *p·* to God.
	55–10	Too *p·* for aught so mute.
	66– 1	*p·* nectar our brimming cup fill,
	68–21	*p·* as its rising, and bright
	75–15	'Tis the Spirit that makes *p·*,
	79– 3	*p·* peace is thine,
My.	40–20	* first *p·*, then peaceable, — *Jas.* 3 : 17.
	69–13	* *p·* white marble was used,
	85–30	* noble dome of *p·* gray tint,
	112–21	their uniformly *p·* morals
	114– 5	be honest, just, and *p·* ;
	147–14	memory of this *p·* purpose,
	152–12	The restoration of *p·* Christianity
	155–18	a *p·* peace, a fresh joy,
	213–11	to live *p·* and Christian lives,
	218–15	introduction of *p·* abstractions into
	256–14	*p·* pages of impersonal presents,
	257–22	make man's being *p·* and blest.
	303–17	Science and its *p·* monotheism
	315– 7	* a *p·* and Christian woman,
		(*see also* **heart**)

purely

Mis.	170–22	method of Jesus was *p·* metaphysical ;
	218–31	* *p·* spiritual personality in God."
	276– 4	was *p·* Western in its cordiality
	341–28	and the diction *p·* Oriental.
	359– 3	*p·* Christly method of teaching
Ret.	43– 1	first *p·* metaphysical system of
	48–18	on a *p·* practical basis,
	48–27	*p·* spiritual and scientific impartation
Un.	23–24	*p·* good and spiritual consciousness
Rud.	16–22	pathological Science *p·* mental.
No.	12– 2	from a *p·* Christian standpoint.
'01.	26–12	from Christ's *p·* spiritual means
	27–25	left C. S. as it is, *p·* spiritual,
My.	221– 5	with certain *p·* human views.

pure-minded

Mis.	240–21	*p·*, affectionate, and generally brave.

purer

Mis.	276–22	a *p·*, higher affection and ideal.
	330–22	a *p·* peace and diviner energy,
	387– 4	mount upward unto *p·* skies ;
Ret.	73–11	and *p·* realms of thought.
'00.	4– 9	No *p·* and more exalted teachings
		is being purged by a *p·* Judaism
'01.	15–25	* He is of *p·* eyes than to bear to
Po.	50–22	mount upward unto *p·* skies ;
My.	127–20	a *p·* Protestantism and monotheism
	300– 1	"of *p·* eyes than to behold — *Hab.* 1 : 13.

purest
　　No. 38–26　loses a part of its *p·* spirituality
　　Po. vii–12　* *these gems of p· thought*

purgation
　　Mis. 41–14　Mental *p·* must go on :
　　Ret. 94–11　this *p·* of divine mercy,

purge
　　'00. 12–23　to *p·* our cities of charlatanism.

purged
　　Mis. 41–10　is *p·* through Christ, Truth,
　　　　79– 2　beliefs will be *p·* and dissolved
　　　184–31　mortal mind *p·* of the animal
　　　205– 1　mortal mind, thus *p·*, obtains peace
　　　246–10　*p·* of that sin by human gore,
　　'00. 4– 8　*p·* by a purer Judaism
　　Po. 26–20　*P·* by the cannon's prayer ;

purgeth
　　Mis. 151– 8　Those who bear fruit He *p·*,

purification
　　Mis. 9– 3　*p·* it brings to the flesh,
　　　 18– 1　The *p·* or baptismals that come from
　　　 78–23　for the *p·* of the public thought
　　Ret. 79–12　*p·* of the affections and desires.
　　　 94–10　his *p·* through suffering,
　　No. 34–12　baptized in the *p·* of persecution
　　Peo. 9– 3　this baptism is the *p·* of mind,

purified
　　Mis. 125– 2　*p·* as by fire, — the fires of suffering ;
　　　166–19　to go to the temple and be *p·*,
　　My. 58–18　* *p·* through the labor and sacrifice of
　　　265–26　reflect this *p·* subjective state

purifies
　　Mis. 8–19　*p·*, sanctifies, and consecrates
　　　151– 7　*p·* the human character,
　　　351–28　chastens its affection, *p·* it,
　　No. 39–15　Such prayer humiliates, *p·*, and
　　'00. 8–24　fire that *p·* sense with Soul
　　My. 131– 1　that which *p·* the affections

purify
　　Mis. 5– 1　will elevate and *p·* the race.
　　　223– 6　Streams which *p·*,
　　　298–18　Trials *p·* mortals and deliver them
　　　341– 6　First *p·* thought,
　　Hea. 5–26　*p·*, elevate, and consecrate man ;
　　　 7–14　in order to *p·* the stream.
　　Peo. 9– 8　*p·* his mind, or meet the demands of

purifying
　　Mis. 7–24　with healing, *p·* thought.
　　　204–23　By *p·* human thought,
　　No. 28– 7　*p·* processes and terrible revolutions
　　'02. 2–10　*p·* all peoples, religions, ethics,

Puritan (*see also* Puritan's)
　　No. 46–15　*P·* standard of undefiled religion.

Puritan's
　　Un. 14–11　shortcomings of the *P·* model

Puritans
　　No. 46–16　As dutiful descendants of *P·*,
　　My. 181–13　The *P·* possessed the motive of

purity
　　and love
　　Mis. 195–31　when meekness, *p·*, and love,
　　Pul. 9–24　*p·*, and love are treasures
　　and peace
　　No. 34–24　yet mounting . . . in *p·* and peace,
　　and permanence
　　Mis. 320–30　in token of *p·* and permanence.
　　and sweetness
　　Pul. 62–13　* *p·* and sweetness of their tones.
　　approaches
　　Mis. 363– 1　The more nearly . . . approaches *p·*,
　　christened
　　Un. 17–11　its vileness may be christened *p·*,
　　faith and
　　'00. 6–14　through his simple faith and *p·*,
　　imbued with
　　Mis. 4– 1　Thought imbued with *p·*,
　　its
　　My. 63–25　* its *p·*, stateliness, and vastness ;
　　metaphysical
　　Mis. 184–30　to foreshadow metaphysical *p·*,
　　of Christianity
　　My. 178– 5　process and *p·* of Christianity
　　perpetuating
　　My. 261–14　aids in perpetuating *p·*
　　persecution and
　　Ret. 54–11　gaining . . . through persecution and *p·*.
　　self-abnegation and
　　Mis. 298–21　self-abnegation and *p·* ;
　　spotless
　　My. 262– 4　spotless *p·* and original perfection.

purity
　　types of
　　'00. 11–29　His types of *p·* pierce corruption
　　unity and the
　　'00. 13– 1　to destroy the unity and the *p·* of

　　Mis. 37– 6　toward *p·*, health, holiness, and
　　　130– 3　long-suffering, meekness, charity, *p·*
　　　154–28　meekness, mercy, *p·*, love.
　　Ret. 28–17　*P·*, self-renunciation, faith, and
　　'02. 8–24　Love, *p·*, meekness, co-exist in
　　My. 200–18　seven-fold shield of honesty, *p·*, **and**
　　　269– 5　pledged to innocence, *p·*,
　　　274–11　honesty, *p·*, unselfishness

purloined
　　'00. 8–12　and wear the *p·* garment

purporting
　　My. 175–28　*p·* to have my signature,
　　　306–28　*p·* to be Dr. Quimby's own words,

purpose
　　and fruits
　　Mis. 223– 2　its hidden paths, *p·*, and fruits
　　animated with a
　　Mis. 325–21　that anybody is animated with a *p·*,
　　another
　　My. 306–11　I have quite another *p·* in life
　　any
　　Man. 102–16　for any *p·* other than the
　　charitable
　　My. 358–20　a worthy and charitable *p·*.
　　definition of
　　Mis. 371–23　to unite, in a definition of *p·*,
　　divine
　　Ret. 37–23　divine *p·* that this should be done,
　　　 83– 3　accomplishing the divine *p·*
　　entire
　　My. 252–10　entire *p·* of true education
　　every
　　My. 22–18　* every *p·* she has set in motion,
　　evil
　　Mis. 41– 4　uses it to accomplish an evil *p·*.
　　exalted
　　Mis. 341–10　finds . . . its strength in exalted *p·*.
　　Pul. 10–13　No dream . . . broke their exalted *p·*,
　　feeling and
　　Mis. 177–10　Their feeling and *p·* are deadly,
　　her
　　No. 12–15　nerved her *p·* to build on the
　　His
　　My. 143–27　according to His *p·*.
　　　278– 2　If His *p·* for peace is to be
　　his
　　Mis. 85– 9　His *p·* must be right,
　　Un. 59– 2　his *p·* to save humankind
　　No. 33–25　his *p·* was to show them that the
　　holy
　　Mis. 162–28　To carry out his holy *p·*,
　　My. 283– 9　To aid in this holy *p·* is
　　human
　　My. 284– 3　to help human *p·* and peoples,
　　idea and
　　Mis. 303–23　idea and *p·* of a Liberty Bell
　　infirm of
　　Pul. 4– 2　* "weak and infirm of *p·*."
　　its
　　Pul. 59–17　* was well adapted for its *p·*,
　　My. 282– 1　its *p·* is good will towards men.
　　learn its
　　Mis. 207– 1　Learn its *p·* ;
　　life and
　　My. 36–23　* devotion to the daily life and *p·*
　　Master's
　　Ret. 25–29　our great Master's *p·*
　　misapprehending the
　　Mis. 345–26　distorting or misapprehending the *p·*
　　mortal
　　Mis. 204–26　it unselfs the mortal *p·*,
　　my
　　My. 164– 1　my *p·*, when I came here,
　　　244– 2　my *p·* in sending for you,
　　　305–31　my *p·* was to lift the curtain
　　noble
　　My. 22–10　* for this grand and noble *p·*,
　　no such
　　My. 317–11　It was for no such *p·*.
　　of blessing
　　Mis. 351– 4　for the *p·* of blessing even my
　　of building
　　My. 21– 6　* for the *p·* of building church homes
　　　 57–10　* for the *p·* of building a suitable
　　of Christian Science
　　Rud. 2–26　The emphatic *p·* of C. S.
　　of divine Love
　　Mis. 154–16　It is the *p·* of divine Love
　　No. 35– 8　yield . . . to the *p·* of divine Love,

purpose

  of electing
    My. 49–16 * for the *p·* of electing officers.
  of God
    Mis. 366–21 as the *p·* of God ;
    My. 216–18 The *p·* of God to youward
  of its members
    My. 339– 1 The *p·* of its members is to
  of learning
    Pul. 72– 3 * *p·* of learning the feeling of
  of Love
    Mis. 214–15 accomplishing its *p·* of Love,
  of preventing
    My. 286–11 for the *p·* of preventing war
  possible
    Mis. 48–19 possible *p·* to which it can be
  power and
    Pul. 10– 5 power and *p·* to supply them.
    My. 293– 3 power and *p·* of infinite Mind,
  prudent
    Hea. 1–19 * Pushes his prudent *p·* to resolve."
  pure
    Pul. 21–10 unite with me in this pure *p·*,
    My. 147–14 memory of this pure *p·*,
  right
    My. 160– 2 he abides in a right *p·*,
  sacred
    My. 289–12 convene for the sacred *p·* of
  singleness of
    Mis. 317–26 singleness of *p·* to uplift
  sinister
    Man. 53–19 a complaint . . . for a sinister *p·*.
  strong of
    Mis. 238– 6 honest . . . and strong of *p·*.
  stubborn
    Un. 5–15 No stubborn *p·* to force conclusions
  such a
    Man. 48–15 near her for such a *p·*.
  that
    Mis. 25–31 recommend them for that *p·*?
    '01. 18–19 would have used them . . . for that *p·*,
    29– 2 or visited a reformer for that *p·*?
    My. 9– 6 * that may be needed for that *p·*.
  their
    No. 15– 5 convince all that their *p·* is right.
  this
    Mis. 98–21 This *p·* is immense,
    315–22 form associations for this *p·* ;
    Man. 26– 8 meeting held for this *p·*,
    38–14 meetings held for this *p·*.
    82–14 a meeting held for this *p·*
    No. 31–14 "For this *p·* the Son— *I John* 3 : 8.
    My. 8– 2 * may be necessary for this *p·*."
    12– 1 * may be necessary for this *p·*,"
  this very
    Mis. 3–11 Jesus taught them for this very *p·* ;
  thought and
    My. 24–12 * unity of thought and *p·*
  thy
    Po. 26–12 Thy *p·* hath been won !
  to kill
    Mis. 40–28 holding the *p·* to kill
    302– 2 a *p·* to kill the reformation
  to restore
    Mis. 236–18 with the *p·* to restore harmony
  vital
    Ret. 48– 4 was aimed at its vital *p·*,
  worthy
    Ret. 49– 7 having accomplished the **worthy** *p·*
  your
    Mis. 134–17 your *p·* to be in Chicago

    Mis. 29– 6 *p·* of his life-work touches
    135– 7 one in motive, *p·*, pursuit.
    139–20 for the *p·* of having erected thereon
    203 chapter title
    261–22 effecting so glorious a *p·*.
    262– 4 If you wish to brighten so pure a *p·*,
    351–13 for the *p·* of placing C. S. in
    Man. 57–13 state definitely the *p·* for which
    98– 5 for the *p·* of having him reply
    Ret. 57– 8 for the *p·* of destroying discord.
    No. v– 1 of each edition of this pamphlet
    Pan. 13–15 united in *p·*, if not in method,
    My. 18–23 united in *p·*, if not in method,
    29–18 * unanimity of thought and of *p·*.
    126– 2 *p·* of the destroying angel,
    139–18 *p·* of my request was sacred.
    169– 5 so long a trip for so small a *p·*
    204–14 P· of the Christian Scientists to
    216–31 for a *p·* even higher,
    248– 8 *p·* of grasping and defining the
    306–10 *p·* of making the true apparent.
    312–30 for the *p·* of starting that
    333– 7 * *p·* of paying the last tribute

purposes

    Mis. 10– 1 or engraft upon its *p·*
    152– 6 unite in the *p·* of goodness.
    204–14 new *p·*, new affections,
    227–17 nobler *p·* and wider aims
    272– 7 * for metaphysical *p·* only,
    272–22 * obtain for any secular *p·* ;
    277–16 the *p·* of envy and malice
    292–24 works out the *p·* of Love.
    Man. 99– 2 For the *p·* of this By-Law, the
    Ret. 43– 6 granted for similar *p·*
    48–17 for medical *p·*,
    '02. 17–27 aims, motives, fondest *p·*,
    My. 63–15 * work out the *p·* of divine Love.
    66–15 * well situated for church *p·*
    137–20 persons and *p·* I have designated
    231– 3 charities for such *p·*
    285– 9 crowns the great *p·* of life
    293–24 to overrule the *p·* of hate

pursue

    Mis. 197–11 and bade his followers *p·*.
    342–24 Seek Truth, and *p·* it.
    Man. 82–17 or *p·* other vocations,
    No. 40–14 I instruct my students to *p·* their
    Po. 29– 3 though murky clouds *P·* thy way,
    My. 117– 8 to *p·* the infinite ascent,
    260–14 may *p·* paths devious,

pursued

    Ret. 61–30 Unless this method be *p·*,
    90–28 * in the path you have *p·* !"
    Un. 10–27 unless, *p·* by their fears,
    My. 19–20 shall be *p·* by her *substance,*
    340–20 is *p·* by the leaders of our

pursues

    Mis. 210– 1 *p·* the evil that hideth itself,
    No. 30– 4 for it *p·* and punishes it,

pursuing

    Mis. 230–24 * Still achieving, still *p·*,
    250– 7 The so-called affection *p·* its
    My. 130–14 to be continually *p·* a lie
    185– 6 * Still achieving, still *p·*,

pursuit

    Mis. 135– 7 one in motive, purpose, *p·*.
    230–16 in the *p·* of pleasure.
    268–12 in *p·* of better means
    340– 8 no other *p·* or pleasure
    My. 116–20 *p·* of his or her person
    345–25 * the *p·* of modern material

pursuits

    Mis. 10–26 human affections and *p·*
    19–31 Life and its grand *p·*
    147–28 In all his *p·*, he knows no

push

    Mis. 129–19 and try to *p·* him aside ;
    235–22 thought must *p·* on the ages :
    237–22 *p·* on the growth of mankind.
    303–14 knock instead of *p·* at the door of
    320– 1 *p·* upward our prayer in stone,

pushed

    Mis. 245–18 The conclusion cannot now be *p·*,
    Un. 6–25 if hastily *p·* to the front
    54–27 serpent, who *p·* that claim
    My. 14–28 * the work will be *p·* forward
    24–20 * being *p·* with the utmost energy,

pushes

    Mis. 23– 2 *p·* the question :
    Hea. 1–19 * *P·* his prudent purpose to resolve."
    My. 272– 4 logic of events *p·* onward the
    288– 2 it unselfs men and *p·* on the ages.

pushing

    Mis. 232– 7 is *p·* towards perfection in art,
    Ret. 16– 3 *p·* their way through the crowd

pussy-willow

    Mis. 329–22 put the fur cap on *p·*,

put

    Mis. 17–11 *p·* off your *materia medica* and
    24–30 *p·* down all subtle falsities
    64–25 *p· into this condition of mortality?*
    82–22 material sense of life, is *p·* off,
    121–16 "Thou shalt *p·* away— *Deut.* 19 : 13.
    129– 4 let him *p·* his finger to his lips,
    140–23 *p·* back into the arms of Love,
    178– 8 could not be *p·* into old bottles
    214– 1 chapter sub-title— *John* 18 : 11.
    214–14 "*P·* up thy sword."— *John* 18 : 11.
    214–16 "*P·* up thy sword ;"— *John* 18 : 11.
    220–26 *p·* it into the minds of others
    233–13 *p·* into the old garment of drugging
    243– 8 doctor had *p·* on splints
    250–14 Love is not something *p·* upon a shelf,
    280–15 Mind is not *p·* into the scales with
    286–16 *p·* ingenuity to ludicrous shifts ;

put

Mis.	288– 8	before being *p·* into action.
	299–19	*p·* myself and them on exhibition,
	329–22	*p·* the fur cap on pussy-willow,
	330–32	to *p·* forth its slender blade,
	341– 6	then *p·* thought into words,
	349–32	I have *p·* into the church-fund
	358–15	Christ's vestures are *p·* on only
	359–10	I *p·* away childish things. — *I Cor.* 13 : 11.
	381– 9	he should not *p·* in testimony.
	381–28	*p·* under the edge of the knife,
Man.	50–21	*p·* on probation, or
Ret.	20– 9	*p·* under the care of our family nurse,
	69–11	saying, . . . 'I will *p·* spirit into
	73– 6	Limitations are *p·* off in proportion
Un.	34–15	yet *p·* your finger on a burning
	56– 8	"*p·* him to an open shame." — *Heb.* 6 : 6.
Pul.	6–14	*S. and H., was *p·* into my hands.
	22–20	*p·* on her most beautiful garments,
	53– 1	* Principle that was *p·* into practice
	54–23	*"*p·* them all out," — *Luke* 8 : 54.
	62–20	* to which these bells may be *p·*.
Rud.	14–11	often those were *p·* off for months,
No.	3–14	will *p·* that book in the hands of
	27–22	to be "*p·* off." — *Col.* 3 : 9.
	29– 2	*p·* to death for his own sin,
	43–20	cannot *p·* the "new wine — *Matt.* 9 : 17.
Pan.	11– 4	*p·* off the old man with — *Col.* 3 : 9.
	11– 4	*p·* on the new man, — *Col.* 3 : 10.
'00.	8– 1	Then, if sin and flesh are *p·* off,
'01.	2– 7	by trying to *p·* into the *old* garment
	17–20	*p·* patients into the hands of my
	27–22	I have *p·* less of my own
'02.	3– 7	*p·* an end, at Charleston, to
	11–27	*p·* to death the Galilean Prophet,
	17–27	will *p·* to flight all care
Hea.	18– 4	shall be "*p·* off," — *Col.* 3 : 9.
	18– 6	to *p·* new wine into old bottles ;
	18–12	cannot *p·* the new wine into old bottles.
	18–15	it would *p·* the new wine into
Peo.	10– 8	and *p·* her humane foot on a
	14–13	*p·* on the whole armor of Truth ;
My.	4–21	woman has *p·* into Christendom
	22–17	* and time has *p·* its seal
	43– 1	* did not *p·* them in possession of
	91–24	* despite the obstacles *p·* in the way
	125–25	*p·* on her beautiful garments
	130–27	has an enormous strain *p·* upon it,
	135– 4	I *p·* away childish things." — *I Cor.* 13 : 11.
	188– 4	*p·* my name there forever ; — *I Kings* 9 : 3.

put

My.	204– 4	to *p·* into practice the power which
	212– 9	*p·* down the evil effects of alcohol.
	233– 8	should you not *p·* that out
	244–19	*p·* off the human for the divine.
	247–12	*P·* on the robes of Christ,
	248–10	*p·* an end to falsities in a wise way
	261–17	I *p·* away childish things." — *I Cor.* 13 : 11.
	273– 2	* to *p·* before its readers.
	329–26	* *p·* before them some interesting
	338–22	construction that people . . . might *p·*
	353–11	to *p·* on record the divine Science

puts

Mis.	120–29	*p·* to flight every doubt as to the
	210–17	*p·* her foot on the head of the
	240–16	or *p·* it into the ice-cream
	285–24	*p·* virtue in the shambles,
	362–16	Philosophy . . . *p·* cause into effect,
Ret.	70– 4	so-called mind *p·* forth its own
	81–22	Shakespeare *p·* this pious counsel
Pul.	44– 5	* as mortal sense *p·* it,

putteth

Pan.	6– 8	*p·* his foot upon a lie.
My.	33–25	*p·* not out his money to — *Psal.* 15 : 5.

putting

Mis.	2–30	*p·* on the spiritual elements
	170–30	The *p·* on of hands mentioned,
	170–31	explained as the *p·* forth of power.
	182– 3	impossibility of *p·* him to death,
	302–28	forestall the possible evil of *p·* the
	329– 8	and *p·* down the green ones,
Pan.	1–12	*p·* off outgrown, wornout, or soiled
'00.	14–30	*P·* aside the old garment,
Peo.	13–13	*p·* man to the rack for his conscience,
My.	177–14	*p·* off the limitations
	177–14	and *p·* on the possibilities
	233– 8	instead of *p·* *out your watch?*
	349–14	*p·* off the hypothesis of matter

puzzled

My.	346– 4	* far from being *p·* by any question,

puzzles

'00.	6–14	spiritual sense that *p·* the man.

pyramid

Hea.	11–12	like the great *p·* of Egypt,

Pythagorean

Mis.	344– 2	*P·* professor of ethics,

Q

quack

Hea.	14–12	in the hands of a *q·*.

quackery

Rud.	12–12	*q·*, that denies the Principle of
No.	19– 6	infidelity, ignorance, and *q·*
'01.	33– 7	* "*Q·* and dupery do abound
	33– 9	* *q·* was never the originating
Peo.	6– 3	* "I am sick of learned *q·*."

quacks

'01.	30–12	Christian Scientists . . . are not *q·*,
Peo.	11–25	The learned *q·* of this period

quail

Mis.	222–23	will make stout hearts *q·*.

quaintly

Mis.	239–19	looking up *q·*, the poor child

qualifications

Man.	34– 3	*q·* FOR MEMBERSHIP.
	87–15	moral and spiritual *q·*
	89–18	*Q·*.
	92–23	*q·* named in Sect. 9
My.	241– 1	* moral and spiritual *q·*

qualified

Man.	37–23	*q·* to approve for membership
	50– 2	made by *q·* experts.
	90– 5	if found *q·* to receive them.
	90–18	lessons by a well *q·* teacher
	92–12	found duly *q·* to teach C. S.,
My.	231–11	*q·* students for healing
	240–27	* by those who are duly *q·*,
	255–10	for which they are not *q·*.

qualify

Mis.	43–19	thoroughly to *q·* students

qualities

Mis.	36–14	animal *q·* of sinning mortals ;
	36–16	express the lower *q·* of
	199–18	*q·* of the divine Mind
	199–21	over the *q·* opposed to Spirit

qualities

Mis.	201– 6	bringing the *q·* of Spirit into
	250–11	distorted into human *q·*,
	268–23	are potions of His own *q·*.
	332–28	but *q·* of error.
Ret.	5–16	*q·* to which the pen can never
	70– 5	puts forth its own *q·*,
	88–14	health-giving and life-bestowing *q·*,
Un.	32–14	the eternal *q·* of His being.
	35– 4	for the *q·* of matter
	35– 5	are but *q·* of mortal mind.
'01.	16–18	these *q·* are objectionable,
Hea.	3–12	*q·* of God as a person,
Peo.	2–17	out of the worst human *q·*,
	8– 9	we shall bring out these *q·*
My.	28–14	* stimulated those gentle *q·*
	153–14	with no intrinsic healing *q·*
	292–25	supposed to possess opposite *q·*

quality

and quantity
Mis.	217– 9	correspond in *q·* and quantity.

begets the
Hea.	3–13	Principle that begets the *q·*,

changes
Un.	35– 6	Change the mind, and the *q·* changes.

disappears
Un.	35– 6	and the *q·* disappears.

evil is a
No.	23–18	Evil is a *q·*, not an individual.

evil is not a
Mis.	259–10	evil is not a *q·* to be known

human
Mis.	75–19	warped to signify human *q·*,
	250–21	As a human *q·*, the glorious

inferior
Mis.	226–25	Perfidy of an inferior *q·*,

life-giving
'01.	26–11	endows it with a life-giving *q·*

nature and
Mis.	36–17	nature and *q·* of mortal mind,

quality

no
Un. 38–20 Death has no *q·* of Life ;
no intrinsic
Mis. 108–31 they have no intrinsic *q·*
nor quantity
'01. 12–28 Evil is neither *q·* nor quantity :
of God
Pan. 5– 2 Can a single *q·* of God,
of good
Mis. 78–29 to present the *q·* of good.
of matter
Mis. 256–23 while every *q·* of matter
of tone
Pul. 62–14 * The *q·* of tone is something superb,
one in
'02. 12–16 one in *q·*, not in quantity.
or quantity
Mis. 333–28 in a single *q·* or quantity !
or the quantity
Peo. 3–21 *q·* or the quantity of eternal good.
quantity or
Un. 31–20 defies Spirit, in quantity or *q·*.
real
Ret. 76–25 every one in his real *q·*,
third
Mis. 217–21 a third *q·* unlike God.
unselfed
My. 249–29 unselfed *q·* of thought

Mis. 250– 4 either as a *q·* or as an entity
'00. 11–17 *q·*, quantity, and variation in tone,
My. 267–19 *q·* and the quantity of heaven.

quantities

Mis. 62–11 positive and negative *q·*,
Man. 98–14 shall circulate in large *q·* the papers
My. 96–21 * money was sent in such *q·*

quantity

Mis. 62–11 the negative *q·* offsets an equal
62–12 offsets an equal positive *q·*,
62–12 aggregate positive, or true *q·*,
217– 9 must correspond in quality and *q·*.
333–28 in a single quality or *q·* !
Un. 31–20 in *q·* or quality.
'00. 11–17 quality, *q·*, and variation in tone,
'01. 12–28 Evil is neither quality nor *q·* :
'02. 12–16 one in quality, not in *q·*.
Peo. 3–22 quality or the *q·* of eternal good.
My. 267–19 quality and the *q·* of heaven.

quarrel

Mis. 181–12 What avail, then, to *q·* over
364–24 must either cooperate or *q·*
'00. 8–20 When a man begins to *q·* with himself
'02. 9–26 Did they *q·* long with the inventor
My. 219–24 "Rather than *q·* over vaccination,
270–28 would no more *q·* with a man because
303– 7 Scientists have no *q·* with

quarrelling

'00. 8–21 he stops *q·* with others.

quarrels

Mis. 284–29 personal animosities and *q·*.
Hea. 8–14 and no longer *q·* with the individual.
My. 284–26 *q·* between nations and peoples.
309– 5 making out deeds, settling *q·*,
310–22 * says that "the *q·* between

quarries

Mis. 144– 1 taken from the *q·* in New Hampshire,

quarter

Pul. 23–18 * last *q·* of the nineteenth century.
55– 6 * last *q·* of preceding centuries.
56–14 * the last *q·* of the century.
My. 53– 1 * from every *q·* came important
78– 8 * from every *q·* of the city.
89–28 * marvels of the last *q·* century.
(see also **numbers, values***)*

quarter-century

Ret. 41– 1 which C. S. encountered a *q·* ago,
My. 89–28 marvels of the last *q·*.

Quarterly

Christian Science
Mis. 113–30 *Journal,* and the C. S. *Q·*,
300–26 permission to cite, in the *C. S. Q·*,
314–13 Lesson of the *C. S. Q·*.
Man. 32–23 printed in the C. S. *Q·*.
63– 7 found in the *C. S. Q·* Lessons,
My. 19– 5 current numbers of . . . *C. S. Q·*.

Mis. 114– 5 in the preparation of the *Q·*
314–30 shall be taken from the *Q·*,
Pul. 60– 8 * reading . . . the *Q·* Bible Lesson,

quarterly

Man. 76–21 They shall hold *q·* meetings
97–13 an annual salary, paid *q·*,

quarters

Mis. 132–19 letters and inquiries from all *q·*,
Pul. vii– 4 Three *q·* of a century hence,
My. 55–23 * was obliged to seek other *q·*,
77–23 * Scientists from all *q·* of the globe

Queen *(see also* **Queen's***)*

'02. 3–24 the joy of the sainted *Q·*,
My. 289–17 "God save the *Q·*"

queen

Mis. 295–28 unquestionably the best *q·* on earth ;

Queen Elizabeth's

No. 44–13 In *Q· E·* time Protestantism

Queen of Great Britain

My. 289–15 lamented Victoria, *Q· of G· B·*
289–29 lamented Victoria, *Q· of G· B·*

Queen of Sheba

Pul. 2– 1 I should be much like the *Q· of S·*,

Queen's

My. 290– 5 *Q·* royal and imperial honors

Queen Victoria *(see also* **Victoria***)*

My. 289– 6 chapter sub-title

quench

Mis. 84–23 forever to *q·* his love for it.
348–17 To *q·* the growing flames of
Po. 15–22 cannot *q·* in oblivion's wave.
72– 4 *Q·* liberty that's just.
My. 127–32 cannot *q·* my desire to say
128–13 nor rulers rampant can *q·* the

quenched

Mis. 183– 1 pride of life will then be *q·*
Un. 39– 6 *q·* in the divine essence,
Pul. 3–24 all human desires are *q·*,
'02. 18–10 *q·* not the smoking flax,

quenching

Mis. 316–23 warming marble and *q·* volcanoes !
'02. 9– 3 the All-presence — *q·* sin ;
My. 291–10 *q·* the volcanoes of partizanship,

quenchless

Po. 18– 6 genius unfolding a *q·* desire.

queried

Mis. 295–20 should not only be *q·*, but

queries

Mis. 268– 3 Two personal *q·* give point to
303–12 therefore no *q·* should arise as to

query

Mis. 32–10 The *q·* is abnormal,
32–31 To the *q·* in regard to some
65–12 your *q·* concerns a negative
299–10 glad, indeed, that this *q·* has finally
337– 8 Infinite *q·* !
380– 8 majesty and magnitude of this *q·*,
Un. 8– 1 Let another *q·* now be considered
Pan. 5–11 proper answer . . . to this hoary *q·*.
'01. 5–14 This suggests another *q·* :
My. 261– 3 guardians of youth ofttimes *q·* :
299–17 I *q·* : Do Christians, who believe

querying

Ret. 35–18 There is no authority for *q·* the

quest

My. 181– 1 The specific *q·* of C. S. is

question

ancient
Hea. 19–12 the ancient *q·*, Which is first,
answer to a
Mis. 349–22 In answer to a *q·* on the
answer to the
Hea. 9–21 only correct answer to the *q·*,
answer your
Mis. 51–11 cannot answer your *q·* professionally.
any
My. 346– 4 * far from being puzzled by any *q·*,
as to religion
'00. 4–22 The *q·* as to religion is :
at issue
Mis. 246–27 The *q·* at issue with mankind is :
My. 360–11 momentous *q·* at issue in First Church
brings up the
Mis. 350– 6 student who brings up the *q·* of
carried the
Mis. 191–25 and carried the *q·* with Eve.
conjugal
Mis. 289–26 Science touches the conjugal *q·*
dodge the
Mis. 53– 4 Committing suicide to dodge the *q·*
every
Mis. 65–10 Every *q·* between Truth and error,

question

fervid
My. 25–17 my answer to their fervid *q*:
finishes the
Hea. 10–13 that finishes the *q* of
following
Mis. 299– 9 simply answer the following *q*
My. 217–18 In the . . . was the following *q*:
251– 5 I reply to the following *q*
great
Mis. 379–25 solution of this great *q*:
'02. 5–17 have answered this great *q*
My. 234–19 both sides of the great *q*
human
'02. 5–14 ever-recurring human *q*
ill-concealed
Ret. 75– 2 spring from this ill-concealed *q*
legislative
My. 167–24 noble disposal of the legislative *q*
no
Mis. 315–20 shall be no *q* of money,
Pul. 57–16 * there can be no *q* but that the
now at issue
No. 46– 3 The *q* now at issue is :
of applying
Man. 88–18 on the *q* of applying for admission
of Christian Science
Mis. 135– 3 person is not in the *q* of C. S.
of money
Mis. 315–20 shall be no *q* of money,
Man. 83– 5 shall not be a *q* of money,
of pauperism
My. 309– 6 involving a *q* of pauperism
of time
Mis. 348–12 It is only a *q* of time when
of unity
My. 236–17 seals the *q* of unity,
old
My. 117–13 Is not the old *q* still rampant?
one side of a
Mis. 288– 9 regards only one side of a *q*,
out of the
No. 45– 9 is of course out of the *q*.
Hea. 13–16 leave the drug out of the *q*,
My. 317–18 left my diction quite out of the *q*,
350– 3 or leaving it out of the *q*.
pregnant
'02. 14–26 This pregnant *q*, answered frankly
propound a
'02. 5–26 conceive of a law, propound a *q*,
pushes the
Mis. 23– 2 but Science, . . . pushes the *q*:
settles the
Mis. 192–31 declaration of . . . settles the *q*;
My. 277–10 never settles the *q* of his life.
settle the
My. 358–15 Publishing Society will settle the *q*
settling the
Mis. 380– 1 settling the *q*, What shall be the
shocks me
Pul. 74–15 "Even the *q* shocks me.
sublime
My. 277–12 sublime *q* as to man's life
this
Mis. 23– 7 Christianity answers this *q*.
32– 6 From this *q*, I infer that some
46–11 would not present this *q*.
65–21 my instructions on this *q*.
81–20 *fair or correct view of this q*,
89–23 answer to this *q* in my . . . works.
98– 1 making this *q* of personality
116–11 This *q*, ever nearest to my heart,
133–20 to set you right on this *q*,
140–19 material side of this *q*.
284–13 This *q* is often proposed,
299–26 have you asked yourself this *q*
333–11 C. S. voices this *q*:
346–11 To this *q* C. S. replies :
381–14 asked the defendant's counsel this *q*,
Un. 5–11 divine Science of this *q* of Truth
Rud. 6–26 this *q* of how much you understand of
My. 190– 7 The age is fast answering this *q*:
271–21 * addressed this *q*,
vexed
Man. 66–12 to report to her the vexed *q*
whole
'02. 12– 4 settles the whole *q* on the basis
without
No. 41–16 Without *q*, the subtlest forms of sin
wrong side of the
Hea. 9– 6 talking on the wrong side of the *q*.
your
Mis. 56–29 Your *q* implies that Spirit,
67–25 If your *q* refers to language,
My. 271–29 to your *q* permit me to say

question

your
My. 277– 3 In reply to your *q*,

Mis. 33–14 *q* that is being asked every day.
69–30 Now comes the *q* :
88–10 author of the article in *q*
106–22 long been a *q* of earnest import,
192–18 Neither can we *q* the
224–30 while it is a *q* in my mind,
270– 5 What artist would *q* the skill of
282– 7 The *q* will present itself :
301–19 To the *q* of my true-hearted
337– 3 Have I discovered . . . is the *q*.
346– 9 The *q* is often asked,
Ret. 48– 3 The *q* was, Who else could
70– 8 We do not *q* the authenticity of
Pul. 47–16 * no . . . has been equal to the *q*.
'01. 35– 4 The *q* oft presents itself,
Hea. 5–12 * the *q* chiefly is concerning
My. 133– 9 chapter sub-title
133–23 secret to tell you and a *q* to ask.
162– 2 *q* our want of more faith
212–14 The *q* is often asked,
218–21 chapter sub-title
233–30 Aye, that's the *q*.
240–24 * *q*, Does Mrs. Eddy approve of class
241–17 * The *q* and Mrs. Eddy's reply follow.
305–28 My recent reply . . . was not a *q* of
306– 8, 9 a *q* that is no longer a *q*.
318–19 I agreed not to *q* him
343– 4 * and works around a *q*
344–23 * *q* of infectious and contagious
questionable
Mis. 122–15 is neither *q* nor assailable :
140– 6 a type . . . materially *q*
243–24 Did he refer to that *q* counsel,
'01. 21– 6 chapter sub-title
questioned
Pul. 32–12 * I mentally *q* this modern
My. 90–28 * can no longer be *q*,
220– 8 When Jesus was *q* concerning
330–14 * are *q* by this critic,
342–18 * Mrs. Eddy sat back to be *q*.
questioners (*see also* **questioners'**)
My. 251– 5 question from unknown *q* :
questioners'
My. 214–14 relieving the *q* perplexity,
questioning
Mis. 228–25 without *q* the reliability of
Ret. 25–30 not *q* those he healed as to
Un. 1– 2 much natural doubt and *q*
Pul. 33– 5 * often run to her mother *q*
'01. 18–11 *q* Christ Jesus' healing,
My. 190–21 remains beyond *q* a divine
214–16 letters *q* the consistency of
318–20 so long as he refrained from *q* me.
questions
Mis. 4–14 *q* important to be disposed of
38–24 for *q* of practical import.
91–26 take his textbook . . . ask *q* from it,
92–13 repeat the *q* in the chapter on
92–16 adhere to the *q* and answers
95–13 I shall confine myself to *q* and
114–27 will test all mankind on all *q* ;
121–25 to the *q* of the rabbinical rabble :
126– 1 from unsettled *q* to permanence,
137–10 if you had any *q* to propose,
157–10 all *q* important for your case,
167– 1 The material *q* at this age
179– 7 resolves itself into these *q* :
238–20 Let one's life answer . . . these *q*,
265–27 constantly called to settle *q*
280–27 I met the class to answer some *q*
287–22 *q* concerning their happiness,
317–20 prompt my answers to the above *q*.
Man. 63– 5 *q* and answers as are adapted to
Ret. 14–11 I was ready for his doleful *q*,
25– 3 It answered my *q*
83–23 they should ask *q* from it,
Un. 6–15 *q* about God and sin,
Pul. 34–26 * in reply to my *q*,
34–27 It answered my *q*
37– 3 * just in its attitude toward all *q*."
79– 9 * as students of public *q*
Pan. 13– 4 Chief among the *q* herein,
'02. 5–30 silences all *q* on this subject,
My. 83–14 * fewer *q* as to locality
223–13 *q* about secular affairs,
223–17 such *q* are superinduced by
228–11 chapter sub-title
238– 1 chapter sub-title
277–20 can settle all *q* amicably

questions

My.	318–18	not ask him any *q·*.
	319–18	* *q·* which have recently appeared,
	343– 1	* plain that the answers to *q·* would
	348– 8	greatest of all *q·* was solved

quibble

Mis. 141–18 concerned about the legal *q·*,

quibbled

Pul. 9–13 *q·* over an architectural exigency,

Quibus

Mis. 88– 8 * *"What Q· Thinks."*

quicken

Mis.	98–12	to *q·* and extend the interest
	145–21	to *q·* even dust into sweet memorial

quickened

Mis.	352– 3	When human sense is *q·*
Un.	56– 9	Holding a *q·* sense of
Pul.	10– 4	a *q·* sense of mortal's

quickening

Mis.	185–28	*was made a q· spirit.— I Cor.* 15 : 45.
	188–31	to her *"a q· spirit ;"— I Cor.* 15 : 45.
	189–17	*q·* spirit takes it away :
Un.	30–15	was made a *q·* spirit." *— I Cor.* 15 : 45.
	30–23	last Adam as a *q·* Spirit,
	30–26	shall be found a *q·* Spirit ;
No.	43–16	* and *q·* the Christian."

quickens

Mis.	204–19	so *q·* moral sensibility
	352–10	*q·* the true consciousness of
No.	39–15	purifies, and *q·* activity,

quickly

Mis.	49– 2	I *q·* saw, had a tendency to
	57–11	"That thou doest, do *q·*."*— John* 13 : 27.
	74– 5	It *q·* imparts a new
	276–29	*q·* learned when the door is shut.
	325–26	the Stranger turns *q·*,
	395–16	*Q·* earth's jewels disappear ;
Man.	92– 9	C. S. heals the sick *q·*
Ret.	9– 6	My cousin answered *q·*,
No.	13– 2	destroys sin *q·* and utterly.
'01.	9–30	he worketh well and healeth *q·*,
	17– 5	*q·* to return to divine Love,
	29–29	* "quite *q·* we have regained
	32–14	they armed *q·*, aimed deadly,
Po.	58– 1	*Q·* earth's jewels disappear ;
My.	v–16	* and reforming the sinner *q·*
	331–15	* as *q·* as it would have punished

quicksands

Ret. 79–18 *q·* of worldly commotion,

quiescence

Un. 15–25 to bribe with prayers into *q·*,

quiet

Mis.	143–15	with *q·*, imposing ceremony,
	143–25	*q·* call from me for this extra
Man.	94–12	to depart in *q· thought*
Pul.	47–23	* of New Hampshire's *q·* capital,
Rud.	12– 7	or else *q·* the fear of the sick
No.	1–14	*q·* practice of its virtues.
My.	163–21	opportunity in Concord's *q·*
	291– 6	a *q·* assent or dissent.

quieted

My. 317–20 I *q·* him by quoting . . . texts

quietly

No.	8–25	*q·*, with benediction and hope,
My.	11–14	* *q·* alluded to the need
	79–25	* *Q·*, without a trace of fanaticism,
	87– 8	* congenial, *q·* happy, well-to-do,

quiets

My. 250– 5 promotes wisdom, *q·* mad ambition,

quietude

My. 262–27 I love to observe Christmas in *q·*,

quill-drivers

Mis. 274–22 *q·* whose consciences are in

Quimby (*see also* Quimby's)

Dr.
Mis.	381–12	claim that Dr. *Q·* was the author
My.	306–22	when I first visited Dr. *Q·*
	306–26	Dr. *Q·* had tried to get them published

Dr. P. P.
Mis. 381– 4 composed by Dr. P. P. *Q·*.

Mr.
Mis.	379– 1	Mr. *Q·* would retire to an anteroom
My.	324– 5	* scorned the suggestion that Mr. *Q·*

Mr. P. P.
Mis.	378– 6	one Mr. P. P. *Q·* of Portland,
Ret.	24– 2	magnetic doctor, Mr. P. P. *Q·*,

Quimby

P. P.
My. 305– 1 P. P. *Q·* (an obscure, uneducated

Quimby's

Dr.
My. 306–29 purporting to be Dr. *Q·* own words,

Mr.
Mis. 379–27 It was after Mr. *Q·* death

quinine

Mis. 244–30 discoverers of *q·*, cocaine, etc.,

quintessence

Mis. 336–22 the *q·* of Christianity,

quit

'01.	15–13	or he would never *q·* sinning.
My.	96–23	* members were asked to *q·* giving.

quite

Mis.	48– 6	One thing is *q·* apparent ;
	64–27	It is *q·* as possible to know
	69–24	had not *q·* killed him.
	126–15	church is not yet *q·* sensible of
	200–15	this rule is *q·* as remote from
	202– 7	* *Q·* on the verge of heaven."
	216–20	* which "vanished *q·* slowly,
	229– 7	*q·* as surely and with better effect
	264–20	before they are *q·* free from
	311–11	not *q·* ready to take this advanced
	357–10	*q·* on the verge of heaven.
	372–17	* artist seems *q·* familiar with
	375–13	* *q·* an idea of what constitutes
Ret.	93–20	It is *q·* clear that as yet
Pul.	61–25	* attracted *q·* a throng
'01.	27– 1	*q·* independent of all other
	29–29	* "*q·* quickly we have regained
	34– 2	*q·* as salutary in the healing of
My.	26–13	*q·* unexpected at this juncture,
	30–23	* *q·* voluntarily the Scientists
	70–13	* The effect . . . is *q·* remarkable.
	149–25	predicament *q·* like that of the man
	177– 9	I am *q·* able to take the trip
	184–23	success *q·* sacred in its results.
	227– 6	Charity is *q·* as rare as wisdom,
	234–20	gives the subject *q·* another aspect.
	300–32	peaceable party *q·* their antipode?
	306–11	I have *q·* another purpose in life
	307–20	in some respects he was *q·* a seer
	317–17	left my diction *q·* out of the
	320–12	* and seemed *q·* proud of his
	324–22	* as *q·* his literary equal,

quitting

Mis. 179–22 by *q·* the old consciousness of

quivering

Mis.	274–25	headless trunks, and *q·* hearts
	275–13	and repeat with *q·* lips
	347– 3	rumbling and *q·* of the earth

quotation

My.	73– 8	* in the form of a *q·* from S. and **H.**
	213–27	chapter sub-title
	227–21	above *q·* by the editor-in-chief

quotation-marks

My.	130–22	*Q·* are not sufficient.
	224–18	one author without *q·*,

quotations

Man.	43–15	shall not publish profuse *q·*
My.	69–10	* marble plates with Scripture *q·*
	130–21	published *q·* from my works
	213–28	three *q·* from "S. and H.
	306–28	*Q·* have been published,
	307– 1	these *q·* certainly read like
	359–18	* *q·* from a composite letter,

quote

Mis.	264– 1	while they *q·* from other authors
Man.	48–25	may *q·* from other periodicals
My.	334–16	* to *q·* her own words.

quoted

Mis.	72–31	The Scriptural passage *q·*
	83–28	* *Q·* from the sixteenth edition.
Ret.	76– 8	is cited, and *q·* deferentially.
My.	146– 9	has been *q·* and criticized :
	313– 2	Correctly *q·*, it is as follows,
	351–10	the title of your gem *q·*,

quotes

Mis.	243–31	Professor *q·*, in justification of
	295– 4	whom he *q·* without naming.

quotient

Un. 53–20 would have one *q·*.

quoting

Man.	59– 7	*q·* from the books or poems
My.	110–31	or *q·* sentences or paragraphs
	317–20	*q·* corroborative texts of Scripture.

R

rabbi
Mis. 168–11 lowly in Christ, not the man-made *r·*
rabbinical
Mis. 121–26 the questions of the *r·* rabble :
rabbins
Un. 46–17 incensed the *r·* against Jesus,
rabbis
Mis. 199–16 cost him the hatred of the *r·*.
'01. 9–11 mysticism complained of by the *r·*,
rabble
Mis. 121–26 questions of the rabbinical *r·* :
274–26 are held up before the *r·*
Rabboni
Mis. 179–29 "*R·* !"—Master! — *John* 20 : 16.
rabid
Un. 52–20 *r·* beasts, fatal reptiles,
race
achieved for the
Mis. xi– 8 hitherto achieved for the *r·*.
238–10 unselfed love achieved for the *r·*
achieve for the
My. 292– 2 righteousness achieve for the *r·*
affection for the
My. 248–12 honest, fervid affection for the *r·*
benefit the
Mis. 11–26 general effort to benefit the *r·*.
38–19 application to benefit the *r·*,
'01. 21–24 whereby to benefit the *r·*
declining
Mis. 163–15 language of a declining *r·*,
elevating the
Mis. 3– 1 elevating the *r·* physically, morally,
emancipation of the
My. 248–13 for the emancipation of the *r·*.
exalts the
No. 12– 3 heals the sick and exalts the *r·*.
freedom for the
Mis. 120–14 great freedom for the *r·* ;
gives to the
Mis. 235–11 It gives to the *r·* loftier desires
help the
'02. 3–28 to serve God and to help the *r·*.
his
Mis. 330– 9 should call his *r·* as gently
hope for the
My. 246–11 to gain a higher hope for the *r·*,
hope of our
Pul. 9– 3 the hope of our *r·* !
hope of the
Mis. 163–21 the basis . . . the hope of the *r·*.
No. 46– 6 The advancing hope of the *r·*,
human
   (see **human**)
improves the
Peo. 6–19 improves the *r·* physically
injure the
Mis. 260–32 it may injure the *r·*,
is helped
'02. 11–15 when the *r·* is helped onward
long
Mis. 126–26 in the long *r·*, honesty always
of Adam
Ret. 55– 8 improves the *r·* of Adam.
'01. 5–17 the material *r·* of Adam,
of the centuries
My. 126–30 win we the *r·* of the centuries.
one
Po. 22–13 one *r·*, one realm, one power.
our
Un. 13–20 for the benefit of our *r·*.
Pul. 15–11 doing right and benefiting our *r·*.
87–26 a legacy to our *r·*.
'01. 16–27 Shall the hope for our *r·*
primitives of the
Mis. 316–14 the primitives of the *r·*,
purify the
Mis. 5– 2 elevate and purify the *r·*.
sceptered
Po. 10–15 To Judah's sceptered *r·*,
sceptred
My. 337–16 To Judah's sceptred *r·*,
servant of the
My. 145–21 makes me the servant of the *r·*
spiritualization of the
No. 32– 3 and the spiritualization of the *r·*
strong
Mis. 126–24 have a strong *r·* to run,
suffering
Mis. 156– 1 in behalf of a suffering *r·*,

race
this
My. 37–11 * everlasting advantage of this *r·*.
tranquillity of the
My. 280– 7 * peaceful tranquillity of the *r·*.
uplifting the
Mis. 236– 4 labor of uplifting the *r·*,
315–21 of morals and of uplifting the *r·*.
Man. 83– 7 healing and uplifting the *r·*.
uplift the
Mis. 317–27 purpose to uplift the *r·*.
upon the
Un. 8–16 deleterious effects, . . . upon the *r·*.
value to the
No. 19– 5 shows its real value to the *r·*.
My. 348–21 value to the *r·* firmly established.
work for the
Mis. 303– 1 to work for the *r·* ;
———
Mis. 148–20 which will do for the *r·*
329–21 streams to *r·* for the sea.
361–19 *r·* that is set before us, — *Heb.* 12 : 1.
365–23 value of C. S. to the *r·*.
382–11 this gift of God to the *r·*,
Man. 3–17 which will do for the *r·* what
No. 21– 5 an unsafe decoction for the *r·*.
My. 94– 2 * *r·* for numerical supremacy.
155–14 the *r·* set before it,
167–19 your flock, and the *r·*.
races
My. 47–22 * inspired so many of different *r·*
127–32 all times, climes, and *r·*.
rack
No. 46–11 or laid on the *r·*,
Peo. 13–13 putting man to the *r·* for his
radiance
Mis. 20– 1 with the *r·* of divine Love ;
Ret. 18–19 *r·* and glory ne'er fade.
Un. 42–28 go forth in the *r·* of eternal being
61–11 nightless *r·* of divine Life.
'00. 12– 5 the *r·* of glorified Being.
Po. 64–10 *r·* and glory ne'er fade.
My. 194–15 *r·* of His likeness.
radiant
Mis. 251–14 *r·* reality of Christianity,
356– 1 *r·* sunset, beautiful as blessings
377– 4 so near and full of *r·* relief
385–26 *r·* glory sped The dawning day.
399– 4 for you make *r·* room
Po. 17– 2 their *r·* home and its morn !
49– 1 *r·* glory sped The dawning day.
70– 4 At sunset's *r·* hour,
75–11 for you make *r·* room
My. 149–11 its *r·* stores of knowledge
150–20 *r·* reflection of Christ's glory,
radiata
My. 271– 3 no vertebrata, mollusca, or *r·*.
radiate
Mis. 361–10 mollusk and *r·* are spiritual concepts
My. 81– 3 * Scientists fairly *r·* good nature
radiating
Un. 51–20 *r·* throughout all space
radiation
Mis. 290–26 share the benefit of that *r·*.
No. 17–19 focal *r·* of the infinite.
radical
Mis. 193–28 *r·* and unmistakable declaration
226–30 red-tongued assassin of *r·* worth ;
Un. 6–11 is *r·* enough to promote as forcible
Pul. 66–24 * wonder as to how *r·* is to be
radically
Man. 39–12 and of being *r·* reformed,
radius
Mis. 12–32 *r·* of our atmosphere of thought.
rage
My. 103–16 "Why do the heathen *r·*, — *Psal.* 2 : 1.
200– 5 Let "the heathen *r·*, — *Psal.* 2 : 1.
270–14 Let error *r·* and imagine a
raged
Ret. 19– 8 yellow-fever *r·* in that city,
ragged
Mis. 391–15 That every *r·* urchin,
Po. 38–14 That every *r·* urchin,

raging
Ret.	60–17	r· of the material elements
My.	249– 6	r· element of individual hate
	334– 4	* disease was r· at that time.

railroads
My.	73–22	* rooms and board, hotels, r·,

railways
Mis.	296–10	English alehouses and r·

raiment
Mis.	373–17	soft r· or gorgeous apparel ;
Pul.	1– 5	clad in white r·,
No.	29–22	though clad in soft r·,

rain
Mis.	394– 8	as the soft summer r·,
Pul.	4– 3	"What if the little r· should say,
No.	21–28	like a cloud without r·,
Po.	45–11	as the soft summer r·,
My.	149–27	Clouds parsimonious of r·,
	149–31	with the treasures of r·,

rainbow
Mis.	339– 9	robes the future with hope's r·
	355–29	r· seen from my window
	376–20	one rod of r· hues,
	394–11	A r· of rapture, o'erarching,
Ret.	17–13	Flora has stolen the r· and sky,
	23– 9	spanned with its r·
Pul.	26– 4	* which reflect the r· tints.
Po.	25– 3	Soft tints of the r·
	45–14	A r· of rapture, o'erarching,
	62–16	Flora has stolen the r· and sky,

rainbows
Po.	8–17	r· of rapture floated by !

rainbowy
Mis.	231–27	his little r· life

raining
My.	341–26	* It had been r· all day

raise
Mis.	227–15	that my pen or pity could r·
	228–12	to r· those barren natures
	326– 1	cast out devils, r· the dead ;
Ret.	88– 5	"r· the dead." — *Matt.* 10 : 8.
	88–10	"R· the dead," — *Matt.* 10 : 8.
Un.	7–14	r· the dying to instantaneous
Pul.	3– 6	I will r· it up." — *John* 2 : 19.
	29–18	* r· the dead, — *Matt.* 10 : 8.
	66–22	* r· the dead, — *Matt.* 10 : 8.
Po.	77– 2	to Thee we r· A nation's
	79– 8	To r· up seed — in thought
My.	57–10	* to r· any part of two millions
	65– 7	* to r· any part of two million
	99– 3	* "A faith which is able to r·
	192– 5	r· the living dead
	218–10	and to r· the dead
	300–15	r· the dying to health?
	300–16	Christian Scientists r· the dying
	300–26	r· the dead, — *Matt.* 10 : 8.

raised
Mis.	28–28	healed the sick and r· the dead.
	74–18	he r· the dead,
	168–10	how the dead, . . . are r· ;
	244–22	and the dead to be r·
	340–15	r· potatoes instead of pleas,
Un.	44– 6	like the structure r· thereupon,
	60–24	if Christ be not r·, — *I Cor.* 15 : 17.
Pul.	10– 2	r· the deadened conscience,
	54–27	* he r· the daughter to life.
	64–11	* necessary amount was r·,
No.	37–23	Messiah . . . r· the dead,
'01.	19–17	healed the sick, r· the dead,
My.	61–15	* I r· my eyes, and the
	83–25	* the new temple has been r·
	98–19	* r· in a little less than
	241–14	* issue r· is an important one

raises
Ret.	66– 4	It r· men from a material sense
	71– 2	tax it r· on calamity
My.	67– 1	* r· its dome above the city
	219–16	Christ, . . . who r· the dead,
	260–25	r· the dormant faculties,

Raise the Dead
Pul.	28– 7	* "R· the D·," — *Matt.* 10 : 8.

raising
Mis.	25–18	r· the spiritually dead.
	124–18	r· the dead, saving sinners.
	187– 2	*healing the sick,* and r· the dead.
	312–15	* shown in the r· up of the
Ret.	66– 2	in casting out error, in r· the dead.
Pul.	27–16	* r· of the daughter of Jairus.
	27–26	r· represents the r· of Lazarus.
Peo.	12–21	healing the sick and r· the dead
My.	98–24	* latter-day methods of r· money.

raising
My.	110– 3	healing the sick, and r· the dead
	150–22	r· the spiritually dead
	285–22	neither r· up the people, — *Acts* 24 : 12.

Raleigh* (N. C.) *News and Observer
My.	328– 7	* copied from the R· (N. C.) N· and O·,

rampant
My.	117–13	Is not the old question still r· ?
	128–13	nor rulers r· can quench the
	283–20	When . . . injustice is r·.

ran
Mis.	379–11	usually r· in the vein of thought
Po.	1– 9	And far the universal fiat r·,

rancorous
My.	213– 8	one r· and lurking foe

random
Mis.	254–23	its so-called healing at r·,
	264– 2	r· thought in line with mine.
Man.	59– 4	who think at r· on this subject,

rang
Pul.	31–23	* r· the bell at a spacious house
	61–20	* chapter sub-title
Po.	70–17	Immortal Truth, — since heaven r·,

range
Mis.	249–29	it hath r· and is sovereign !
Pul.	26–17	* of fine r· and perfect tone.
	62–21	* as they r· in all sizes,
Rud.	2–25	higher r· of infinite goodness.
My.	85– 2	* in its widely international r·,

ranged
Mis.	231– 3	r· side by side.

rank
Mis.	6–15	will r· far in advance of allopathy
	99–17	take the front r·, face the foe,
	257– 1	notion that Mind . . . is r· infidelity,
	357–21	irrespective of self, r·, or
Un.	18–28	it would lower His r·.
No.	21–18	This is r· infidelity ;
My.	31–19	* take a place in the front r· of
	230– 3	maintain its r· as in the past,

rankle
Mis.	224– 2	that makes another's criticism r·,

ranks
Mis.	29–17	but fourteen deaths in the r·
	134–21	reeling r· of *materia medica,*
	135– 2	come into the r· !
	368–15	r· of the good and pure,
Ret.	44–30	Adding to its r· and influence,
	85–23	to divide the r· of C. S.
My.	105–29	In the r· of the M.D.'s
	127– 8	calm coherence in the r· of C. S.
	300–32	on their own religious r·,
	355– 5	chapter sub-title
	355–12	in our r· of divine energy,

ransomed
Mis.	386–28	cloud not o'er our r· rest
Po.	50–14	cloud not o'er our r· rest
My.	171– 4	r· of the Lord shall — *Isa.* 35 : 10.
	192– 3	thou r· of divine Love,

Raphael
Mis.	375– 6	it demands more than a R·

rapid
Mis.	6–14	r· growth of the work shows.
	6–24	once convinced . . . the gain is r·.
	125–30	r· transit from halls to churches,
	205–32	take r· transit to heaven,
	206–26	Your growth will be r·,
	307–12	Notwithstanding the r· sale already
Pul.	52–16	* r· growth of the new movement.
	66–21	* Such a r· departure
'01.	2–27	history of C. S. explains its r·
My.	52–11	* while we realize the r· growth,
	92–27	* Its growth has been wonderfully r·,
	113–30	in the r· and steady advancement of

rapidity
Pul.	66– 7	* has grown with remarkable r·,
My.	14–27	* The r· with which the work
	99–25	* grown with a r· that is startling,

rapidly
Mis.	110–24	increase r· as years glide on.
	126–23	yet nothing circulates so r· :
Ret.	47– 8	applicants were r· increasing.
	85–25	r· spreading over the globe ;
Pul.	67–18	* and is r· growing.
No.	32–25	r· diminishing the percentage of sin.
'00.	1–13	with r· increasing numbers,
'01.	1– 7	more extended, more r· advancing,
'02.	2–17	little leaven . . . is r· fermenting,
My.	24–20	* building is proceeding r· ;
	55– 9	* the attendance r· growing

rapidly
My. 77– 9 * are *r·* gathering in this city
165–29 *r·* nearing the maximum of might,
200– 2 individual rights . . . *r·* advancing,
336– 3 * The disease spread so *r·*

rapt
Mis. 387– 1 "When Love's *r·* sense
No. 18–17 to be the *r·* face of Jesus.
Po. 50–18 "When Love's *r·* sense
My. 343– 2 * She has a *r·* way of talking,

rapture
Mis. 394–11 A rainbow of *r·*, o'erarching,
Ret. 18–19 *r·* and radiance and glory
'02. 4–10 music to the ear, *r·* to the heart
Po. 8–17 What rainbows of *r·*
45–14 A rainbow of *r·*, o'erarching,
64–10 *r·* and radiance and glory
My. 163– 1 bursting into the *r·* of song

raptured
Mis. 396–24 breathed in *r·* song,
Pul. 18– 8 breathed in *r·* song,
Po. 12– 8 breathed in *r·* song,

raptures
Po. 65–17 claspeth earth's *r·* not long,

rare
Mis. 159–17 recollections and *r·* grand collections
200–11 Paul insists on the *r·* rule
250–15 to be taken down on *r·* occasions
276– 1 the large book of *r·* flowers,
283–14 Any exception to . . . is *r·*.
292– 9 It must have been a *r·* revelation
379–18 his *r·* humanity and sympathy
Ret. 18–23 And those . . . find a happiness *r·* ;
30– 3 *r·* bequests of C. S. are costly,
82– 8 exception to this rule should be very *r·*.
Po. 31–13 *r·* footprints on the dust of earth.
64–19 And those . . . find a happiness *r·* ;
My. 26–17 to be brief on this *r·* occasion.
70–20 * replete with *r·* bits of art,
93–14 * yet it has *r·* lures for weary hearts,
227– 7 Charity is quite as *r·* as wisdom,

rarefied
Mis. 267–21 plumed for *r·* atmospheres
Ret. 33–19 thereby *r·* to its fatal essence,

rarely
My. 272–28 * Mrs. Eddy writes very *r·* for
314–10 considered a *r·* skilful dentist.

rash
Mis. 288– 9 *r·* conclusion that regards only

rate
Mis. 242–22 *r·* of one ounce in two weeks,
Man. 68–11 *r·* of one thousand dollars yearly
My. 92–17 * a *r·* at which every other sect
124–26 *r·* of speed, the means of travel,

rated
My. 305–18 *r·* in the *National Magazine*

rather
Mis. 24–28 *r·* the allegory describing it.
55–12 to harm *r·* than to heal,
81–12 *r·*, *Are not the last eighteen*
127–28 *r·* than on the ear or heart
147–29 *r·* fail of success than
224–30 pity *r·* than of resentment ;
285– 1 evil only, *r·* than person.
305–17 * *r·* than large contributions
310– 8 *r·* than cling to personality
361– 1 *r·* was it their subjugation,
Ret. 65– 3 *r·* than on the teaching
82–19 *r·* does it represent an accumulation
83– 6 *r·* than try to centre their interest
91–13 *r·*, this series of great lessons
91–29 Ask, *r·*, what has he *not* done.
Un. 5– 3 *R·* will they rejoice in the
5–25 *R·* let the stately goings
17– 8 *r·* he ratifies a union predestined
18– 2 *R·* let us think of God as saying,
30–26 or, *r·*, shall reflect the Life of
Pul. 2–19 would you not *r·* strengthen
30– 4 * *r·* than offering their strength to
46– 3 * *r·* than in search of the truth
47–25 * driving *r·* into the country,
58–19 * It is *r·* dark, often too much so
65– 7 * which is *r·* small and new,
80–15 * *r·* to the credit of the book
Rud. 2–15 *r·* than *a personal* God ;
11–14 *r·*, the absolute consciousness
'00. 12–28 *r·* than personal or historical.
Peo. 1– 5 *r·* is it the crumbling away of
3–26 *r·* than obedience to
My. 50–14 * "The tone . . . was *r·* sorrowful ;"
97–15 * a *r·* bitter critic of Mrs. Eddy
98–15 * a *r·* remarkable announcement

rather
My. 219– 5 a hindrance *r·* than help.
219–29 "*R·* than quarrel over vaccination,
222–24 *r·* does it imply that religion
249–22 a man, *r·* than a woman,
303–24 *r·* is it the pith and finale
327–20 * an old law, or *r·* a section of
345–22 or *r·* attained by us, as we
348–12 *r·* than his divine Principle,

ratifies
Un. 17– 8 or rather he *r·* a union

ratio
Mis. 127– 4 in the *r·* of her love for others,
Ret. 67–14 In the *r·* that the testimony of
My. 18– 1 in the *r·* of her love for others,
239– 7 In the *r·* that C. S. is

rational
Mis. 2–16 a more *r·* and divine healing.
'00. 4–16 *r·* that the only perfect religion
My. 128–16 dictates of his own *r·* conscience
348–18 Science demanded a *r·* proof

rationally
Mis. 76–17 no man can *r·* reject his authority
'01. 4–23 to explain God's personality *r·*.
27– 3 * apply them more *r·* to human needs."
My. 350– 8 calmly and *r·*, though faintly,

ravening
Mis. 294–18 from wolves . . . and all *r·* beasts.

raven's
Mis. 254– 9 nest of the *r·* callow brood !
356–21 nests of the *r·* callow brood.

ravished
Po. 8–10 *R·* with beauty the eye of day.

Rawson
Miss Dorcas
'02. 16– 2 Six months thereafter Miss Dorcas *R·*
Mr.
Mis. 225– 2 At the residence of Mr. *R·*,
Mrs.
Mis. 225–10 whereupon the mother, Mrs. *R·*,
225–20 Mrs. *R·* then rose from her seat,
226– 1 But Mrs. *R·* said :— "Give the child

ray
Mis. 333– 4 every *r·* of Truth, of infinity,
336–25 wherever one *r·* of its effulgence
Chr. 53– 6 Spirit sped A loyal *r·*
Pul. 26– 4 * each *r·* under prisms which reflect
'01. 8– 9 in the sense that one *r·* of light is
'02. 12–17 a *r·* of light one with the sun,
Po. 2–17 sun's more genial, mighty *r·* ;
43–15 Light with wisdom's *r·*
53– 7 With sunshine's lovely *r·*
My. 282–10 no uncertain *r·* of dawn.
344– 4 and each separate *r·* for men and

rays
Mis. 194–14 to divide the *r·* of Truth,
333– 8 it absorbs all the *r·* of light.
Ret. 35–13 prism of Truth, which divides its *r·*
'01. 12–21 to divide the *r·* of Truth,
Hea. 19–25 making our words golden *r·*
Po. 31–13 Rich *r·*, rare footprints
My. 208– 6 heavenly *r·* over all the earth.
252–21 *r·* from the eternal sunshine of Love,
269–22 sending forth their *r·* of reality
301– 2 it shines with borrowed *r·*
344– 4 all his *r·* collectively stand for
350–24 whose kindling mighty *r·*

razed
My. 172– 4 * built in 1761, and *r·* in 1893

reach
Mis. 7–24 *r·* many homes with healing,
66–16 To *r·* the summit of Science,
66–26 *r·* the Science of Mind-healing,
82–10 *r·* the sure foundations of time,
86–31 *r·* the glory of supersensible Life ;
98–29 * another's heart would'st *r·*."
104–24 How shall we *r·* our true selves?
143– 8 I *r·* out my hand to clasp yours,
194–29 *r·* the consummate naturalness of
218–10 *r·* the immortality of Mind and
232–16 *r·* the maximum of perfection
234–11 *r·* this spiritual sense, and rise
235– 3 no longer . . . die to *r·* heaven,
275–18 Thy light and Thy love *r·* earth,
309–15 through which we *r·* the Christ,
338–23 * Another's soul wouldst *r·* ;
358–18 *r·* the heaven-crowned summit
Ret. 24–14 neither medicine nor . . . could *r·*,
57–29 such methods can never *r·* the
92– 8 *r·* the fruition of his promise :
Un. 2–28 Those who *r·* this transition,
20–15 *r·* that perfect Love which

reach

Un.	41– 3	In order to *r·* the true knowledge
	49–12	I *r·*, in thought, a glorified
	59–15	*r·* and teach mankind only through
	62–10	only as they *r·* the Life of good,
Pul.	3–28	to *r·* out for a present realization
	15–19	human hatred cannot *r·* you.
No.	35– 6	*r·* the understanding of this
'02.	16–25	*r·* not the heart nor renovate it ;
Hea.	8–21	we shall learn to *r·* heaven
	14–23	student to *r·* the ability to teach ;
	15–21	cannot *r·*, but medicine can?
	18–19	or claimed to *r·* that woe ;
Po.	v–23	* *requests continued to r· the author*
	2– 9	can never *r·* to thee
My.	13–25	*r·* the stars with divine overtures,
	46–27	* *r·* "unto the city of — *Heb.* 12: 22.
	159–17	whereby we *r·* our higher nature.
	189– 3	*r·* the mount of revelation ;
	231–15	letters from . . . do not *r·* her.
	254– 6	you must *r·* its meridian.
	300–17	to *r·* the summit of Jesus' words,

reached

Mis.	41–16	that otherwise could not be *r·*,
	81–21	*has not Truth yet r· the shore?*
Ret.	16– 4	two ladies . . . *r·* the platform.
	21– 6	he had *r·* the age of thirty-four,
	37–10	it had *r·* sixty-two editions.
	54–13	not having *r·* its Science.
Un.	3–12	Thus they have *r·* the goal
Pul.	12–19	ever before *r·* high heaven,
'01.	26–15	when land is *r·* and the world
Hea.	11–21	When you have *r·* this high goal
	13– 8	*r·* soonest by the higher
Po.	vii– 3	* *r· its fulness in her later*
My.	47– 7	* church has *r·* its present growth,
	52–25	* has *r·* her bottom dollar,
	53– 7	* *r·* its four hundredth edition,
	67–24	* never was a more artistic effect *r·*.
	76–13	* A similar decision was *r·*
	96–14	* *r·* only through intelligent and
	114– 7	*r·* the maximum of these teachings?
	126–16	have *r·* unto heaven, — *Rev.* 18: 5.
	146–15	altitude . . . has not yet been *r·*.
	152–10	human race has not yet *r·* the
	238–18	whereby the Science is *r·*
	311–31	* *r·* long division in arithmetic,"
	346–10	* Soon after I *r·* Concord

reaches

Mis.	39–26	*by which God r· others to heal*
	67– 1	until its altitude *r·* beyond
	156– 3	it *r·* a vast number of earnest
	202– 1	*r·* the basis of all supposed
	223–10	that mind *r·* its own ideal,
	320–12	*r·* forth for the infant idea of
	324–29	at length *r·* the pleasant path
	348–10	and those whom it *r·*.
Un.	57–19	the ladder which *r·* heaven.
No.	30– 8	God's law *r·* and destroys evil
Hea.	8–13	but when it *r·* the thought that
My.	68–11	* *r·* an altitude twenty-nine feet
	189– 5	that it *r·* high heaven
	194–10	builds that which *r·* heaven.
	290–12	My soul *r·* out to God

reaching

Mis.	30– 6	or despair of ultimately *r·* them,
	63–24	toward a higher goal,
	63–27	*r·* humanity through the crucifixion
	154– 4	fast *r·* out their broad shelter
	232– 6	This age is *r·* out towards
	328–29	*r·* forth unto those — *Phil* 3 : 13.
Man.	62–14	after *r·* the age of twenty.
Ret.	28–26	*r·* higher than the stars of heaven.
	69– 2	conditions prior to *r·* intelligence.
'00.	6– 6	*r·* forth to those — *see Phil.* 3 : 13.
My.	127– 1	*r·* outward and upward to Science
	147–17	*r·* the physical, moral, and
	208–26	*r·* the very acme of C. S.
	248–15	*r·* deep down into the universal
	265–30	*r·* out to all classes and peoples.
	291– 8	*r·* from the infinitesimal
	343– 4	* *r·* an answer often unexpectedly

react

Mis.	263– 4	not yours, to *r·* on yourselves.

reaction

Mis.	224–16	action and *r·* upon each other
	236– 2	human passions in their *r·*

read

Mis.	vii– 2	* *r·* it well ; that is, to understand.
	24–12	As I *r·*, the healing Truth dawned
	35–20	Why do we *r·* the Bible, and then
	35–22	Why do we *r·* moral science,
	45–28	In John i. 3 we *r·*,
	58–10	*she has r· and studied correctly,*

read

Mis.	58–12	*She had to use her eyes to r·.*
	58–13	I *r·* the inspired page through
	58–16	I may *r·* the Scriptures through a
	61–11	* In the October *Journal* I *r·*
	69–10	In Genesis i. 26, we *r·* :
	91–27	*r·* from the book as authority for
	106– 5	it would *r·* thus :
	132–26	I *r·* in your article these words :
	133– 7	I request you to *r·* my sermons
	135–24	Letter *r·* at the meeting of
	140–27	* when we can "*r·* our title clear"
	155–17	not the time even to *r·* all of
	156–16	*r·* "Retrospection" on this subject.
	159– 5	*r·* this letter to your church,
	169–20	it is necessary rightly to *r·*
	170– 9	having rightly *r·* His Word,
	271–11	write for it, and *r·* it.
	294–25	I have *r·* the daily paper,
	299–13	* *r·* them for our public services?"
	301–13	*r·* copies of my works in the pulpit
	301–20	*r·* them for our public services?"
	301–22	*r·* it publicly *without my consent.*
	314–12	shall *r·* the Scriptures indicated
	314–15	First Reader shall *r·* from my book,
	314–18	*r·* all the selections from S. and H.
	315– 3	*r·* after the manner of the Sunday
	315– 7	and *r·* from manuscripts,
	373–24	In Genesis we *r·* that God gave
	379– 5	I *r·* the copy in his presence,
Man.	29–22	one to *r·* the BIBLE,
	29–22	one to *r·* S. AND H.
	31–20	The First Readers shall *r·*,
	32– 2	*r·* the correlative texts in S. AND H.
	32– 5	Second Readers shall *r·* the BIBLE texts.
	32– 8	Readers shall not *r·* from copies or
	32–12	before commencing to *r·* from
	32–19	They shall *r·* understandingly
	32–22	shall *r·* all notices and remarks
	40–16	To be *R·* in Church.
	40–17	above Church Rule shall be *r·*
	40–21	Church Tenets are to be *r·*.
	45–21	not entitled to hold office or *r·* in
	61–15	the Tenets . . . are to be *r·*.
	63– 8	Lessons, *r·* in Church services.
	66–19	inquire if . . . letter has been *r·*,
	66–20	require all of it to be *r·* ;
	90–22	shall be *r·* to the class,
	98–12	shall *r·* the *last proof sheet*
Ret.	6–18	he *r·* law at Hillsborough,
	9– 8	That night, . . . my mother *r·* to me
	21– 1	letter was *r·* to my little son,
	27– 6	never been *r·* by any one but myself,
	37– 8	original, but it will never be *r·*."
	78–11	not to *r·* so-called scientific
Un.	3– 8	second death, of which we *r·*
	21– 1	we *r·* the apostle's description of
	28– 1	We *r·* in the Hebrew Scriptures,
Pul.	5– 4	*r·* by Judge S. J. Hanna,
	6–14	* I had not *r·* three pages before
	12– 2	were *r·* from the platform.
	29–16	* were finely *r·* by Judge Hanna.
	43–18	* *r·* by Judge Hanna and Dr. Eddy.
	43–24	* sermon . . . was then *r·* by Mrs. Bemis.
	43–29	* Mrs. Bemis *r·* the following letter
	45– 8	* *R·* the following,
	45–29	* passages *r·* from the two books by
	57– 8	* was *r·* by Mrs. Bemis.
	59–15	* *r·* from the book of Revelation
	59–18	* *r·* by a professional elocutionist,
Rud.	13–14	In Deuteronomy (iv. 35) we *r·* :
	13–16	In John (iv. 24) we may *r·* :
No.	1–17	*r·* more clearly the tablets of Truth.
'01.	11–17	*r·* each Sunday without comment
	18–23	should *r·* this Scripture :
	24–21	I had not *r·* one line of Berkeley's
	26–26	I have *r·* little of their writings.
'02.	3–17	learning to *r·* and write.
Po.	vi–11	* *r· as follows :*
My.	15– 4	* has been amended to *r·* as follows :
	17–28	* following extracts . . . were *r·* :
	27–21	Scientists will *r·* with much joy
	34–17	* *r·* by Mr. McCrackan and Mrs. Conant :
	35–28	* *r·* to the congregation the
	36– 3	* telegram . . . to Mrs. Eddy was *r·*
	37–27	* We have *r·* your annual Message
	39– 4	* *r·* from the Bible and S. and H.
	39–13	* list of officers . . . was *r·* by
	44–16	* *r·* the following despatch,
	49–22	* minutes . . . were *r·* and approved.
	59–28	* I *r·* it in manuscript
	79– 8	* to *r·* the account of the dedication
	114–15	*r·* no other book but the Bible
	126– 9	a book open (ready to be *r·*),
	134–23	* *r·* the following letter from
	134–27	* to *r·* you a letter from her

read

My.	149–20	deeply r· in scholastic theology
	150– 7	* writing what deserves to be r· ;
	162–16	We r· in Holy Writ :
	172–26	* note from Mrs. Eddy was r· :
	205– 1	We r· in the Scriptures :
	222– 7	we r· that even the disciples of Jesus
	223– 4	I neither . . . r· letters, nor
	223– 8	not r· by me or by my secretaries.
	230–18	I r· with pleasure your approval
	232–21	r· on page 252, ''A knowledge of
	236–24	universally to r· the paragraph
	238– 2	*Bible, if r· and practised,*
	238– 7	Rightly to r· and to practise the
	238–19	When the Bible is thus r·
	271–23	* will be r· with deep interest
	284–15	it r·, ''It is said to be the first
	289–26	r· on that tender occasion.
	297–27	r· or to note from others' reading
	297–30	have r· Sibyl Wilbur's book,
	307– 1	certainly r· like words that I
	310–31	* ''R· it, for it will do you good.
	322– 9	* have just r· your statement
	327–24	* The section formerly r·,
	327–24	* changed to r· as follows :
	339–17	r· in Holy Writ that the disciples
	351–23	have not r· Gerhardt C. Mars' book,
	353– 2	r· our daily newspaper.
	358–13	however much I desire to r·
	359–11	can be r· by the individual

Reader (*see also* Reader's)

Mis.	314–21	The R· of the Scriptures
	314–22	The R· of ''S. and H.
Man.	30– 5	If a R· in The Mother Church
	33– 4	the church in which he is R·.
	33– 5	A R· not a Leader,
	33– 6	Church R· shall not be a Leader,
	33– 8	A R· shall not be a President of
	55– 1	a R·, shall not report nor send
	55–12	not to be fit for the work of a R·
	95–21	No lecture shall be given by a R·
	95–22	The duties alone of a R· are ample.

(*see also* **First Reader, Second Reader**)

reader

Mis.	xi–11	May this volume be to the r·
	16–27	dear r·, pause for a moment
	30–26	Take courage, dear r·,
	46–11	A r· of my writings would not
	239– 1	let me say to you, dear r· :
	328– 6	Dear r·, dost thou suspect
Ret.	21–13	It is well to know, dear r·,
	37–24	may have an interest for the r·,
My.	111– 2	the r· would not have sought.
	218–18	confuse the mind of the r·,
	225– 9	the r· who does not comprehend
	274–10	Dear r·, right thinking,
	308–31	my father was a great r·.
	317–15	seem ambiguous to the r·.

Reader's

My.	81–10	* the first to catch the R· eye.

Readers (*see also* Readers')

Mis.	314– 4	conducted by R· in lieu of pastors.
	314– 6	shall elect two R· :
Man.	25– 7	Clerk, a Treasurer, and two R·.
	26–12	R·.
	26–12	Every third year R· shall be elected
	26–18	shall fix the salaries of the R·
	29–19	r· OF THE MOTHER CHURCH.
	29–20	The R· for The Mother Church
	30– 2	Directors shall select intelligible R·
	31– 2	DUTIES OF r· OF THE MOTHER CHURCH
	31– 4	The R· of The Mother Church
	32– 7	R· shall not read from copies or
	32–11	The R· of S. AND H.
	32–17	R· in Branch Churches.
	32–18	These R· shall be members of
	32–24	R· in all the branch churches.
	45–17	whose R· are not Christian Scientists
	95–20	No Lectures by R·.
	98–24	R· of the three largest branch
	99– 7	through the R· of its three largest
	100– 5	R· shall appoint said candidate.
Pul.	45–29	* read from the two books by R·,
My.	71–26	* see and hear the two R·
	71–30	* each of whom could see the R·,
	243–10	The R· of The Church of Christ,
	249–21	chapter sub-title
	250– 3	three years' term for church R·,
	250– 8	their R· will retire *ex officio,*
	250–10	acceptable service as church R·,
	250–17	three years as the term for its R·,
	250–28	R· who have filled this sacred office
	362–13	* The Trustees and R· of

readers

Mis.	xii– 7	lift my r· above the smoke of
	35–16	*teach its r· to heal the sick,*
	62–26	amusing to astute r·,
	156– 3	vast number of earnest r·,
	262– 1	Dear r·, our *Journal* is designed to
	308–13	but those are a minority of its r·,
	313– 8	May the . . . rest on the dear r·,
	378–20	r· of my books cannot fail to see
'00.	1–24	number of the r· of my books
My.	11–23	* Our r· have been informed of the
	25– 2	* it is suggested to our r· that
	112–15	its r· — honest, intelligent, and
	272–21	* presents this month to its r·
	272–29	our r· will be interested in this
	273– 2	* to put before its r·.
	329–25	* to give your r· the following

Readers'

My.	31–25	* Mrs. Hunt, was on the R· platform.
	68–17	* The R· platform is of a beautiful
	68–21	* placed back of the R· platform
	68–22	* above the R· special rooms.

Readership

Man.	30–14	shall occupy, during his term of R·,
	95–22	during his term of R·.

readily

Mis.	52–24	failing to demonstrate one rule r·,
	53–22	*so that all can r· understand it?*
	53–26	r· understood by the children ;
	92–11	enlightens other minds most r·,
	130– 4	She r· leaves the answer to
	297– 2	one r· sees that this Science has
Ret.	84– 8	enlightens other minds most r·,
	87– 8	more thoroughly and r· acquired by
'00.	6–16	accepts C. S. more r· than the
Hea.	13–24	You can r· perceive this
My.	75– 9	* chapter sub-title
	90–16	* can be r· grasped by sick or well.
	90–29	* can be r· apprehended.
	217–22	we can meet this negation more r·
	320– 4	* he r· consented to assist me,

readiness

My.	11–10	* grow into r· for each step,
	65–15	* r· and despatch of an ordinary mortal
	83–30	* example of the r· of the members

reading (noun)

Mis.	43–14	contemplative r· of my books,
	54–13	r· of her book, ''S. and H.
	88–12	r·, writing, extensive travel, and
	169–25	The literal or material r· is
	169–26	r· of the carnal mind,
	302–27	his hearers received from his r·
	314–22	shall name, at each r·,
Man.	31– 7	r· of the Sunday lesson,
	32– 1	Order of R·.
Pul.	28–19	* r· is from the two alternately ;
	54–18	* careful r· of the accounts of
	58–20	* too much so for comfortable r·,
'01.	31–22	daily Bible r· and family prayer ;
My.	16–23	* Scripture r·, Isaiah 28 : 16, 17,
	17–17	* r· of selections from ''S. and H.
	32–15	* R· from the Scriptures :
	32–21	* R· of notices.
	32–22	* R· of Tenets
	32–26	* R· of annual Message
	32–28	* R· the . . . Lesson-Sermon.
	32–29	* r· of the Lesson-Sermon,
	33– 2	* R· of a despatch from the members
	33– 4	* R· of ''the scientific statement
	33–13	* responsive r· was from Psalms
	48– 9	* With the r· of her textbook,
	48–19	* constant daily r· of the Bible
	48–27	* every day through its r·.
	49– 7	* the r· of its membership,
	79– 1	* singing and responsive r·,
	80–17	* appropriate r· from the Bible,
	297–28	to note from others' r· what the

reading (ppr.)

Mis.	35–24	You are benefited by r· S. and H.,
	159– 1	r· the Scriptures and expounding
	300– 5	r· it publicly as your own
	300–11	R· in the pulpit from copies of
	302–20	r· my works for Sunday service ;
	314– 7	open the meeting by r· the hymns,
Man.	58–19	r· IN PUBLIC.
	59– 7	r· or quoting from the books or
	60– 8	not fatigued . . . by r· the Scriptures
	66–14	R· and Attesting Letters.
	72– 9	by r· the SCRIPTURES and the
Ret.	1– 8	I remember r·, in my childhood,
	39– 2	were healed simply by r· it,
	83–24	occasionally r· aloud from the book
Un.	29–23	by r· *sense* instead of *soul,*
Pul.	60– 7	* r· in clear, manly, and intelligent
No.	4– 1	R· S. and H. has restored the sick

reading (ppr.)
No.	15– 4	R· my books, without prejudice,
'00.	7–13	after *r·* "S. and H.
Hea.	7–17	*r·* the mind of the poor woman
Po.	v–20	* by *r· the poem to them.*
My.	125–16	When *r·* their lectures,
	234– 3	writing or *r·* congratulations?
	234– 4	while *r·* telegrams ;
	238– 6	*r·* the above-named books
	258–31	a child with finger on her lip *r·*
	357–28	*r·* your interesting letter.

reading-matter
Mis.	155–28	obligation to furnish some *r·*

Reading Room
Man.	63–16	church . . . shall have a *R· R·,*
My.	236– 6	name for one central *R· R·,*
	236–10	for your name, C. S. *R· R·.*

reading-room
My.	123–11	*r·* and nine other rooms
	242–18	publication committee work, r· work,

Reading Rooms
Man.	63–12	heading
	63–17	may unite in having *R· R·,*
	63–20	take charge of the *R· R·*
	64– 3	Literature in *R· R·.*
	64– 4	exhibited in the *R· R·*
	74–13	in the *R· R·,* nor in rooms connected

readings
Man.	32– 5	*r·* from the Scriptures shall
	32– 6	precede the *r·* from S. and H.

reads
Mis.	ix– 2	*r·* thus : "The noblest charity is
	191–13	it *r·* : "Master, we saw one — *Mark* 9 : 38.
Pul.	77– 8	* The inscription *r·* thus :
'02.	12–19	Scripture *r·* : "For in Him — *Acts* 17 : 28.
My.	4– 7	Scripture *r·* : "He that — *Matt.* 10 : 38.
	49–21	* record of this meeting *r·* :
	51–27	* interesting record . . . which *r·,*
	54–22	* A record of this period *r·,*
	118–16	Scripture *r·* : "Blessed are they — *John* 20 : 29.
	170–19	my sacred motto, and it *r·* thus :
	267– 6	Scripture *r·* : "All things — *John* 1 : 3.

ready
Mis.	41–11	*r·* for victory in the ennobling
	44– 4	*r·* to investigate this subject,
	99–16	*r·* to suffer for a righteous cause,
	152–19	made *r·* for the pure in affection,
	162–14	*r·* to stem the tide of Judaism,
	165–26	*r·* to avail himself of the rich
	166–13	has evolved a more *r·* ear
	222–12	In this state . . . one is *r·* to
	253–17	dragon that stood *r·* to devour the
	280–32	just at the moment when you are *r·*
	294–14	a hived bee, with sting *r·*
	295–17	with his *r·* pen and pathos?
	308–12	*r·* for "Christ and Christmas ;"
	311– 7	*r·* for the table of our Lord :
	311–11	not quite *r·* to take this advanced
	313–20	the storehouse is *r·* :
	316–15	they are not *r·* for the word
	323–13	wolves . . . are *r·* to devour ;
	325–28	sees robbers finding *r·* ingress to
	342–31	are *r·* for the next move.
	357–29	we should be *r·* and glad to help
Man.	85– 9	not *r·* to lead his pupils.
	86–13	*r·* for this high calling,
Ret.	14–11	I was *r·* for his doleful questions,
Un.	2–14	is *r·* to testify of God
	2–25	*r·* for a spiritual transfiguration,
	3– 3	not *r·* to understand immortality.
	6–16	the world is far from *r·* to
Pul.	14–23	Those *r·* for the blessing you impart
	60–18	* was not *r·* for the opening.
	72–10	* *r·* to converse,
	80– 2	* under stress of storm it is *r·* to
'00.	9– 7	therefore, not *r·* — to obey.
	12–30	*r·* to destroy the unity
'02.	17– 6	*r·* to seek and obey what they love.
	18–13	faithful to rebuke, and *r·* to forgive.
	20–16	are you *r·* to join me in this
Hea.	10– 2	wroth with the woman, and stood *r·*
	10– 4	*r·* to devour the idea of Truth.
My.	11–15	* She knew that we were *r·* ;
	24– 3	* *r·* to heal all who accept its
	26–15	My Message for June 10 is *r·*
	48– 5	* one *r·* to receive the inspiration,
	55–27	* The Mother Church edifice was *r·*
	61–17	* this house will be *r·*
	62–28	* ever *r·* to assist us in every way
	81–12	* *r·* to receive testimony,
	105–13	*r·* for their amputation.
	126– 9	book open (*r·* to be read),
	156–17	there make *r·.*" — *Luke* 22 : 12.
	156–20	*r·* to partake of the bread

ready
My.	180–25	not *r·* to be uplifted, rebels,
	197–13	great hearts and *r·* hands of our
	203–21	if it is *r·* for the blessing.
	241– 6	* Students who are *r·* for this step
	244– 9	any or all of you who are *r·* for it,
	338–23	his comparisons and *r·* humor.

real

affection
Mis.	91–16	a *r·* affection for Jesus' character

all is
Un.	26–24	All is *r·,* all is serious.
	38– 9	all is *r·* which proceeds from Life

All that is
Mis.	125–20	All that is *r·* is divine,

and eternal
Mis.	14–17	to him evil is as *r·* and eternal as
	21–19	Spirit is the *r·* and eternal ;
	42–23	the latter is *r·* and eternal.
	113– 6	all that is *r·* and eternal,
	164–32	of all that is *r·* and eternal.
Ret.	69–10	as *r·* and eternal as Truth.
Un.	37–21	individuality is *r·* and eternal.
Pan.	12–25	is all that is *r·* and eternal.
My.	239–22	of all that is *r·* and eternal

and normal
'00.	4– 3	makes . . . as *r·* and normal as

and the unreal
Mis.	49–20	discern between the *r·* and the unreal.
	119–24	the *r·* and the unreal Scientist.

appear
Un.	49–18	One should appear *r·* to us,

appears
No.	6–24	appears *r·,* to material sense

as good
Mis.	49–22	belief . . . that evil is as *r·* as good,
	108–20	wherein evil seems as *r·* as good,
No.	17–26	Then evil would be as *r·* as good,
	24–13	By the same token, . . . as *r·* as good,

as health
No.	5–18	If disease is as *r·* as health,
	17–26	would be . . . as *r·* as health,

as Life
Un.	59–23	illusion that death is as *r·* as Life.
No.	17–27	Then evil would be . . . as *r·* as Life ;

as Mind
Mis.	379–13	not as *r·* as Mind,

as Spirit
Ret.	60–10	as *r·* as Spirit and good.

atonement
No.	34–19	*r·* atonement — so infinitely beyond

being
Mis.	46– 5	good being *r·,* evil, . . . is unreal.
	83– 1	Principle, of all *r·* being ;
	346–20	good being *r·,* its opposite is
No.	26–13	All *r·* being represents God,

blood
No.	34–22	The *r·* blood or Life of Spirit

Christ
No.	36–12	*r·* Christ was unconscious of

Christian compact
Mis.	91–10	*r·* Christian compact is love for

Christian Scientist
Mis.	206–19	The *r·* Christian Scientist is
	294– 6	*r·* Christian Scientist is a marvel,
My.	122–24	*r·* Christian Scientist can say
	122–27	the *r·* Christian Scientist is

condition
No.	5–23	a normal and *r·* condition

consciousness
Rud.	5–18	Soul is the only *r·* consciousness

earth
Mis.	30– 9	He saw the *r·* earth and heaven.

ego
No.	26–17	Man's *r·* ego, or selfhood,

equivalent
Ret.	50–13	any *r·* equivalent for my instruction

estate
My.	41–24	* his *r·* estate is one of blessedness.

everything is as
Un.	8– 5	Everything is as *r·* as you make it,

existence
Mis.	30–14	understanding of man's *r·* existence,
Ret.	21–14	not of man's *r·* existence,
	25–23	many witnesses to . . . the *r·* existence of
Un.	42– 7	can have no *r·* existence,

facts
No.	31–10	never actual persons or *r·* facts.

fruits
Mis.	265–20	never . . . the *r·* fruits of Truth.

gratitude
My.	352–10	* we know that the *r·* gratitude

great and
No.	32–18	Good is great and *r·.*

harmony
Mis.	312–17	* to declare the *r·* harmony

real

harmony is
Un. 60–10   harmony is *r*·, . . . yet we descant upon

harmony is the
Rud. 13–19   To aver that harmony is the *r*·

house
Pul. 2–22   The *r*· house in which

identity
Mis. 60–24   *between them and r*· *identity*,

intelligence
'00. 8–10   wicked man has little *r*· intelligence ;

joy
Ret. 18–15   of *r*· joy and of visions divine ;
Po. 64– 6   of *r*· joy and of visions divine ;

joy is
'02. 17–16   wherein joy is *r*· and fadeless.

knowledge
Un. 13–15   If God has any *r*· knowledge of sin,
16– 5   a *r*· knowledge of sin?

life
Mis. 105–13   Man's *r*· life or existence

Life is
Un. 38– 9   Life is *r*· ; and all is real which

man
    (*see* **man**)

mode
Mis. 362– 6   and reflects all *r*· mode,

more
Mis. 284–25   or that becomes more *r*· when
284–26   Evil let alone grows more *r*·,
Un. 64–11   the more *r*· those mind-pictures
Pul. 11– 3   making melody more *r*·,
No. 24–13   but much more *r*·,

nature
Mis. 88–22   * highest type of *r*· nature ;
218–18   unfolds the *r*· nature of God

nor eternal
Mis. 286–24   and neither *r*· nor eternal.

personality
Mis. 97–31   *r*· personality of man.

position
My. 92– 2   * have determined its *r*· position

potency
'02. 3–27   right is the only *r*· potency ;

proof
My. 119–22   gave the *r*· proof of his Saviour,

quality
Ret. 76–25   of every one in his *r*· quality,

realm of the
Mis. 174–17   the realm of the *r*·.
331–27   reigns in the realm of the *r*·,

relative
Mis. 151–14   He is man's only *r*· relative

right or
'01. 14–19   as either right or *r*·

satisfaction
Pul. 47–13   * without receiving any *r*· satisfaction.

Scientist
Mis. 117–10   where to look for the *r*· Scientist,

self
Un. 55– 4   In his *r*· self he bore no infirmities.

sensation
Mis. 72–26   *R*· sensation is not material ;

sense
Un. 41– 5   sin shuts out the *r*· sense of

sensible and
No. 6–18   is as sensible and *r*· as the

sentiments
My. 175–30   the very opposite of my *r*· sentiments.

set-to
Mis. 231–22   instead of a *r*· set-to at crying,

something
Mis. 108–23   conception of . . . as something *r*·,

spiritually
Ret. 68–11   concept or idea is spiritually *r*·.

stepping-stone
Un. 37– 8   not the *r*· stepping-stone to Life

substance
Un. 34–26   Immortal Mind is the *r*· substance,

suffering
Mis. 288–24   *r*· suffering would stop the farce.

this faith is
My. 90– 8   * Whatever else it is, this faith is *r*·

true or
Mis. 346–14   and is not more true or *r*· than

Truth is the
Hea. 10–14   Truth is the *r*· ;
18–11   Truth is the *r*· ;

unreal and the
Mis. 86–14   of the unreal and the *r*·.

value
Mis. 365–22   shows the *r*· value of C. S.
No. 19– 5   shows its *r*· value to the race.

very
Un. 11–17   looks very *r*· and feels very *r*· ;"
My. 90– 8   * and is given very *r*· tests.

real

whatever is
'00. 4–24   whatever is *r*· must proceed from God,

world
Pul. 80–27   * invisible is the only *r*· world,

worship
My. 262–25   in mimicry of the *r*· worship

wrongs
Mis. 13– 6   *r*· wrongs (if wrong can be **real**)

Mis. 10–31   belief . . . that evil is *r*· ;
13– 7   (if wrong can be *r*·)
49–16   *is not our capacity . . . r*·;
50– 4   it cannot be *r*·.
71–30   Whatever is *r*· is right
72–18   *Are material things r*· *when they*
125– 6   all that is *r*· is *right*.
177–15   *r*· and consecrated warriors?
188–25   through a spiritual sense of the *r*·,
267–25   is no *r*· aid to being.
284–22   neither an evil claim nor . . . is *r*·,
341– 5   superstructure that is *r*·, right,
Ret. 23– 3   could be a *r*· and abiding rest.
25–16   The *r*· I claimed as eternal ;
28–18   reduce all things *r*· to their own
60–14   good is all that is *r*·.
Un. 8– 4   *Is anything r*· *of which the physical*
8–10   not absolute, and therefore not *r*·,
46–15   *r*· to him only as spiritual
49–21   the unreal masquerades as the *r*·,
59–21   illusion which calls sin *r*·,
59–22   illusion which calls sickness *r*·,
60– 7   talk of sin and sinners as *r*·.
Rud. 6– 6   As Mind they are *r*·,
11–13   illusions are not *r*·, but unreal.
No. 2–12   healers who admit that disease is *r*·
5– 8   As Truth alone is *r*·,
5– 8   to declare error *r*· would be to
6– 1   If disease is *r*· it is not illusive,
24–25   never a moment in which evil was *r*·.
36–18   and the divine as *r*·.
'01. 5–19   *r*· spiritual man and universe.
5–24   anything that is *r*·, good, or true ;
14–10   enjoys, suffers, or is *r*·.
14–12   evil cannot be made so *r*· as to
23– 7   yet that evil exists and is *r*·,
25–26   been avowed to be as *r*·,
My. 110–19   if waking to bodily sensation is *r*·
111–30   C. S. is valid, simple, *r*·, and
119– 2   and to regard evil as *r*·,
119– 4   divine Principle of that which is *r*·,
241–28   * not to know as *r*· the beliefs of
260– 9   Christmas stands for the *r*·,
296–14   or to destroy the *r*· spiritual man.

real estate

Man. 76–22   *r*· *e*· owned by this Church
My. 309–18   inherited his father's *r*· *e*·,

realism

Mis. xi–17   *R*· will at length be found to
30–27   seeming mysticism surrounding *r*·
87– 6   unjust . . . to the divine *r*·.
374– 2   a proof of Immanuel and the *r*· of
No. 38– 9   only true philosophy and *r*·.
Pan. 11–28   *r*· that man is the true image of God,
My. 5–16   the spiritual idealism and *r*·
364–11   excludes . . . all sense of the *r*· of

realistic

Mis. 217–17   Sensuous and material *r*· views
218–14   False *r*· views sap the Science of

realities

forever-existing
Mis. 362– 4   forever-existing *r*· of divine Science ;

grand
Peo. 6–21   grand *r*· of Life and Truth

great
Mis. 65–16   solution of Life and its great *r*·.
'01. 1–14   the great *r*· of being,

not as
No. 23–21   not as *r*·, but as illusions ;

of being
Mis. 188–27   in the *r*· of being,
Un. 38– 3   the indisputable *r*· of being.
49–17   not two *r*· of being,
No. 19–21   to understand the *r*· of being,
'01. 1–14   the great *r*· of being,

of God
No. 5–24   tampering with the *r*· of God

of life
Hea. 17–11   they are not the *r*· of life ;

of Mind
Mis. 333–28   the grand *r*· of Mind,
No. 6– 3   attempt to destroy the *r*· of Mind

severe
No. 5– 6   one of the severe *r*· of this error.

realities

spiritual
  Mis. 53– 2   spiritual *r·* of existence,
the only
  Ret. 63– 2   God and His idea are the only *r·*,

  Mis. 68–10   * *are not illusions but r·;*
     292–16   look no more into them as *r·.*
  Un. 60–12   yet we descant upon . . . as *r·.*

reality

admit the
  Un. 36–22   yet admit the *r·* of moral evil,
all
  Mis. 90– 4   and you remove all *r·* from its power.
  No. 2– 9   scientific to rob disease of all *r·* ;
  My. 164–26   the sum of all *r·* and good.
and individuality
  Un. 53– 8   The *r·* and individuality of man
and omnipotence
  Mis. 61– 9   *r·* and omnipotence of Truth
and power
  Mis. 252– 9   Right thoughts are *r·* and power ;
    364–30   or give *r·* and power to evil
  Pan. 7–22   *r·* and power, intelligence and
and Soul
  Peo. 1– 9   *r·* and Soul of all things,
and strength
  Mis. 252–14   healthy thoughts are *r·* and strength.
and substance
  Un. 49–10   *r·* and substance of being are *good,*
any
  Un. 54– 7   becomes as tangible as any *r·.*
any other
  '02. 6– 1   forbids the thought of any other *r·,*
believe in the
  Mis. 13–15   to believe in the *r·* of evil
    63–16   such as believe in the *r·* of the
  My. 300–10   do not believe in the *r·* of disease,
conscious
  No. 36–17   conscious *r·* and royalty of his
contending for the
  Hea. 9–13   Contending for the *r·* of
deathless
  Pul. 5– 8   glow of some deathless *r·.*
divine
  Mis. 345–20   * Christianity must be a divine *r·.*"
  Peo. 13–28   * Christianity must be a divine *r·.*"
establishes the
  Mis. 73–10   establishes the *r·* of what is
eternal
  Un. 36–12   Spirit is Truth and eternal *r·* ;
    49–11   the eternal *r·* of existence
existence or
  Un. 36–21   To deny the existence or *r·* of
gleam of
  My. 14– 7   discerned . . . as a gleam of *r·* ;
good only is
  Un. 21– 9   good only is *r·.*
grand
  Mis. 5–24   grand *r·* that Mind controls
great
  Mis. 14–32   he makes a great *r·* of evil,
    63–17   the great *r·* that concerns man,
    363– 2   the great *r·* of divine Mind
hope's
  Pul. 10–14   the wish to reign in hope's *r·*
impossible in
  My. 178–17   But this is impossible in *r·,*
intelligent
  Un. 42– 8   a divine and intelligent — *r·.*
its
  No. 2–10   cannot begin by admitting its *r·.*
lifted on
  '02. 17–14   the curtain . . . should be lifted on *r·,*
living
  Mis. 376–11   * handed down from the *living r·.*
misconception of
  No. 5–26   jewel in this misconception of *r·.*
no
  Mis. 63–12   If there is no *r·* in sickness,
  Un. 59– 1   If there is no *r·* in evil,
    64– 3   but there is no *r·* in sin,
  Pan. 9– 4   no *r·* in aught else.
  '00. 5– 6   It gives evil no origin, no *r·.*
  '01. 12–25   chapter sub-title
    14– 2   To assume there is no *r·* in sin
  My. 334–20   "To assume there is no *r·* in sin,
no other
  Un. 8– 7   can have no other *r·* than the
of being
  Mis. 367–11   *r·* of being — goodness and harmony
  Un. 38–27   *r·* of being, whose Principle is God.
    51– 5   *r·* of being is neither seen, felt,
  No. 16–25   Spirit, which is the *r·* of being.

reality

of God
  Un. 34–25   *r·* of God and the universe
  My. 248–17   to the *r·* of God, man, nature,
of his being
  Mis. 181– 4   *r·* of his being, in divine Science
of Life
  Mis. 117– 2   A progressive life is the *r·* of Life
  Un. 43– 5   the infinite *r·* of Life,
of living
  My. 139– 5   keenly alive to the *r·* of living,
of man
  Mis. 187– 7   health and harmony, . . . the *r·* of man ;
  Un. 46– 7   individuality and *r·* of man ;
of Mind
  No. 10–23   *r·* of Mind in the Science of being ;
of music
  Mis. 187–10   chord is manifestly the *r·* of music,
of sin
  Ret. 63– 8   pleasure of sin, *alias* the *r·* of sin,
of that Mind
  Un. 38– 7   *r·* of that Mind which is Life.
of things
  '01. 1–19   portion of the primal *r·* of things.
    20– 9   and with the *r·* of things.
of Truth
  No. 4–14   Science demonstrates the *r·* of Truth
    5– 4   the *r·* of Truth has an antipode,
one side to
  Hea. 10–11   there is but one side to *r·,*
page of
  Mis. 294– 9   transcribes on the page of *r·*
power and
  No. 21–19   supposed power and *r·* of evil
radiant
  Mis. 251–14   radiant *r·* of Christianity,
rays of
  My. 269–22   sending forth their rays of *r·*
realm of
  Mis. 30–30   spirituality, the realm of *r·* ;
sole
  Mis. 24–17   Life being the sole *r·* of existence.
spiritual
  Mis. 60–29   hints the existence of spiritual *r·* ;
    87– 9   spiritual *r·* and substance of form,
stubborn
  No. 2– 6   a God-bestowed and stubborn *r·,*
    4–11   never made sickness a stubborn *r·.*
    5–21   becomes indeed a stubborn *r·,*
substance and
  My. 109– 2   no more substance and *r·* in
such
  My. 260– 6   flesh would flee before such *r·,*
tangible
  My. 98–10   * magnificent church, . . . is a tangible *r·,*
their
  Mis. 68–14   penalty for believing in their *r·*
  Ret. 62– 6   better . . . than *a belief in their r·*
  Hea. 5–14   * and not the doubt of their *r·.*"
true sense of
  Mis. 28–13   turn . . . to the true sense of *r·,*
within
  Un. 28– 3   Is it a *r·* within the mortal body?

  Mis. 10–29   (that, not in *r*),
    18–25   Only by admitting evil as a *r·,*
    37– 2   if there were in *r·* another mind
    37–28   in *r·* the least difficult of the
    46– 1   The admission of the *r·* of
    73– 1   no evidence of the *r·* of matter,
    93–12   is in *r·* none besides the eternal,
    93–23   since there is in *r·* no disease.
    155– 1   in *r·* there is but one cause
    170–11   This is the *r·* behind the symbol.
    319–12   protest against the *r·* of sin,
    346–16   mortal admission of the *r·* of
  Ret. 25–18   Spirit I called the *r·;*
    63– 6   there is in *r·* no evil,
    63–10   belief of the sick in the *r·* of
    68–23   "In *r·* there is no *mortal* mind,
  Un. 3– 2   still believe in matter's *r·,*
    10– 3   *r·* of these so-called existences
    33–18   in *r·* neither matter nor mortal mind,
    50–16   In *r·* there are no material states
  Rud. 16–15   In *r·* there is, and can be, but one
  No. 5– 5   antipode, — the *r·* of error ;
    27– 3   is in *r·* no claim whatever.
  Pan. 5–15   no truth [*r·*] in him — *John* 8 : 44.
  '01. 13–19   conception of sin as . . . a *r·,*
    22–14   therefore matter cannot be a *r·.*
    23–26   to deny, . . . the *r·* of an external
  Hea. 10–19   and your waking the *r·,*
    18–10   There is in *r·* but the good :
  My. 70–25   * In *r·* it is a combination of six
    110–19   And what of *r·,* if waking
    276–24   I have none, in *r·,*

reality
My.	297–14	for there is in *r·* no evil,
	305–22	All that I am in *r·*, God has made me.
	351–27	all they need, or can have in *r·*.

realization
Ret.	81–27	A *r·* of the shifting scenes of
Un.	2– 9	*r·* takes away man's fondness for sin
	7–23	*r·* of this fact dispels even
	61–24	demonstration and *r·* of this Science !
Pul.	3–29	present *r·* of my hope
My.	64–21	* would prevent the *r·* of ideal
	297–17	and a higher *r·* of heaven.

realize
Mis.	171– 3	Jesus' first effort to *r·* Truth
	237–12	then they are brought to *r·*
	280–15	we must *r·* that Mind is not
Ret.	61– 8	whose existence you do not *r·* ;
Un.	2– 7	*r·* God's presence, power, and
	20–20	as you *r·* the divine infinitude
Pul.	30–22	* to *r·* the possibilities of the
	57–21	* *r·* how extensive is the belief in
My.	10–25	* *r·* that there must be a prosperous
	39–27	* *r·* her presence with us to-day.
	42–23	* I *r·* that only as infinite good
	52–11	* while we *r·* the rapid growth,
	52–16	* *r·* we must use more energy
	83–17	* scarcely *r·* that the Scientists
	230–26	*r·* at last their Master's promise,
	297–22	and *r·* that he never died ;

realized
Mis.	137–11	*r·* that such opportunity
	281–27	*r·* what a responsibility you
Ret.	7–20	* expected no more than they *r·*
Pul.	6–15	* *r·* I had found that for which
My.	5–16	idealism and realism which, when *r·*,
	116– 5	this great fact in C. S. *r·*

realizes
Mis.	278– 5	as it *r·* more the presence
Pul.	81–21	* *r·* that all the harmonies
Rud.	13–22	if the *healer* *r·* the truth,

really
Mis.	25– 8	neither one *r·* exists,
	27–23	when God is *r·* *All.*
	27–25	all that *r·* is,— must be spiritual
	30– 1	Do we *r·* understand
	57–29	all that *r·* is, always was
	112– 5	*r·* look the illusions in the face.
	150–30	is all that *r·* is or can be ;
	259–26	evil, is *r·* non-existent,
	267–11	when I saw an opportunity *r·* to help
	345–31	*R·*, Christianity turned men . . . from
	354–20	Principle of all that *r·* exists,
Ret.	9– 5	if she *r·* did hear Mary's name
	91–10	Indeed, this title *r·* indicates
	94– 8	and yet errs, . . . is *r·* evil.
Un.	2–14	true man, *r·* *saved*, is ready to
	23–19	*Evil.* . . . mortal mind and sin *r·* exist !
	24–15	There is no *r·* finite mind,
	27– 4	*r·* have a shade of difference
	33– 3	(matter *r·* having no sense)
	50–12	*r·* there is no such thing as
	62– 1	fact *r·* remains, in divine Science,
Pul.	21–18	*r·* united to only that which is
	51–10	* There is *r·* nothing settled.
	69–15	* *r·* is a return to the ideas of
	85–12	* all things which *r·* exist,
'00.	4–28	reflects all that *r·* is,
My.	8–17	* and I believe *r·*,
	14–20	* If the devil were *r·* an entity,
	59–25	* "Did Mrs. Eddy *r·* write S. and H.?
	99– 2	* great, and *r·* good things
	152–17	divine Principle of all that *r·* is,
	266–20	origin of all that *r·* is,
	267– 6	originator of all that *r·* is.
	287– 9	governing all that *r·* is.
	297– 4	all that Miss Barton *r·* is,
	334–13	* which records show *r·* existed in 1844,
	345– 9	"Not,". . . "if it is *r·* science."

realm
Mis.	30–30	spirituality, the *r·* of reality ;
	34–24	lie within the *r·* of mortal thought
	174–17	abode of Spirit, the *r·* of the real.
	331–27	reigns in the *r·* of the real,
Pul.	10–14	hope's reality — the *r·* of Love.
No.	v– 8	laborers in the *r·* of Mind-healing.
	21–17	in the same *r·* and consciousness.
Po.	22–13	Love hath one race, one *r·*,
My.	64– 4	* glories of the *r·* of infinite Mind,

realms
Ret.	73–11	and purer *r·* of thought.
My.	200–13	upward to the *r·* of incorporeal Life

realness
No.	17– 1	false assumption of the *r·* of

reap
Mis.	15– 2	will *r·* what he sows ;
	38–11	*r·* your carnal things?" — *I Cor.* 9 : 11.
	66– 7	that shall he also *r·*." — *Gal.* 6 : 7.
	105–30	that shall he also *r·*." — *Gal.* 6 : 7.
	348– 4	man soweth, that shall he *r·*.
	386–29	Hither to *r·*, with all the crowned
No.	32– 9	that shall he also *r·*." — *Gal.* 6 : 7.
Hea.	5–28	that shall he also *r·*." — *Gal.* 6 : 7.
Po.	50–16	Hither to *r·*, with all the crowned
My.	6– 6	that shall he also *r·*." — *Gal.* 6 : 7.
	19–23	*r·* richly the reward of goodness,
	185– 1	for he that soweth shall *r·*.
	230–24	will *r·* the reward of rightness,
	254–11	*r·* the sure reward of right thinking

reaped
Mis.	80–26	have planted and sown and *r·*

reapers
Mis.	313–19	*r·* are strong, the rich sheaves are
My.	291–24	while her *r·* are strong,

reaping
Un.	12– 4	vineyard of Mind-sowing and *r·* ;
Po.	47–18	Nevermore *r·* the harvest we deem,

reappear
Mis.	28– 2	only to *r·* in the spiritual sense
	308–23	only to *r·* in due season.
	343–21	*r·*, like devastating witch-grass,
Po.	3– 7	With evening, memories *r·*

reappearance
Mis.	324–31	look for the *r·* of the Stranger,

reappeared
Mis.	70–16	Christ Jesus lived and *r·*.
No.	28–18	Has Truth, . . . *r·*?
	28–20	you will know that Truth has *r·*.

reappearing
Mis.	167– 1	*r·* of the infantile thought
	343–23	stupid gardener ! watch their *r·*,
Un.	63– 8	so-called . . . *r·* of ever-presence,
No.	13–10	before this *r·* of Truth,
	46– 7	the *r·* Christ, whose life-giving
My.	279– 8	scientific being *r·* in all ages,

reappears
Peo.	1–18	as the understanding . . . *r·*,

rear
Pul.	59–30	* auditors left by the *r·* doors,
No.	46–10	Woman should not be ordered to the *r·*,

reared
Ret.	2– 1	Mrs. . . . Baker was *r·* among
Pul.	2–30	*r·* on the foundation of Love,
	65–21	* Frankish church was *r·* upon the
No.	46–15	*r·* there the Puritan standard
My.	59–14	* temple, which has been *r·* by you,

rears
Mis.	386–23	*R·* the sad marble to our memory
Ret.	17–15	hickory *r·* his bold form,
Un.	45– 5	*r·* its crest proudly,
Po.	50– 9	*R·* the sad marble to our memory
	62–18	hickory *r·* his bold form,

reascending
Pul.	11– 1	*r·*, bear you outward,

reason (noun)
and affection
Mis.	363–23	that misguides *r·* and affection,

and immortality
Mis.	218–17	to the rescue of *r·* and immortality,

and philosophy
My.	260–13	*r·* and philosophy may pursue

and revelation
Mis.	23–18	*R·* and revelation declare that
	27–20	According to *r·* and revelation,
	217– 2	nature, *r·*, and revelation.
No.	13–24	impulse to *r·* and revelation,

and will
Pan.	4– 8	*r·* and will are properly classified
	4–11	But *r·* and will are human ;

any
Mis.	5–17	There is no longer any *r·* for

based upon
My.	96–13	* It is a faith based upon *r·*,

better
Un.	49–20	* "the worse appear the better *r·*,"

deluding
Mis.	3–28	apparently deluding *r·*,
	260–21	deluding *r·* and denying revelation,

depraved
Mis.	354–10	When depraved *r·* is preferred

erring
Mis.	362–24	refute erring *r·* with the

eyes of
Mis.	332–20	blinded the eyes of *r·*,

reason (noun)

for his faith
My. 294–20 r· for his faith in what
for the faith
Un. 48– 1 a r· for the faith within.
for the hope
My. 348– 9 to give a r· for the hope
given as a
'01. 15–30 * to be given as a r· why you
human
  (*see* **human**)
laws of
Mis. 216–26 * nor the laws of r· hold good,
man's
Mis. 362– 5 man's r· is at rest in God's
my
My. 165–21 this is . . . my r· for existing.
no
Mis. 54–20 there is no r· why you should be
no other
'01. 15–26 * no other r· to be given
or belief
Un. 28–21 human reflection, r·, or belief
our
Po. 9–11 Our r· made right
philosophy nor
Mis. 217– 4 neither philosophy nor r·
principal
Rud. 15–12 This was the principal r·
proper
My. 162–22 proper r· for church edifices
right
My. 288– 1 starts the wheels of right r·,
sole
Mis. 200–17 sole r· that it is their basis.
some
Pul. 59– 9 * for some r· not followed,
sufficient
My. 104–21 sufficient r· for his silence
suffocate
Hea. 8–18 suffocate r· by materialism.
supporting
Peo. 2–14 revelation supporting r·.
this
Mis. 51–10 for this r· cannot answer
  305–15 * For this r· small contributions
to expect
My. 51– 9 * should have r· to expect,
wheels of
Mis. 235–22 it must start the wheels of r·
will rescue
No. 11–26 will rescue r· from the thrall

Mis. xi–20 It is r· for rejoicing
  22–30 by r· of its own ponderosity ;
  40–18 r· that the same results follow not
  59–20 let us r· together."— *Isa.* 1 : 18.
  93– 1 by r· thereof is able to
  109–16 by r· of its nothingness ;
  183–17 not by r· of the schools,
  195– 8 by r· of the lack of understanding.
  234– 1 only by r· of our belief in it :
  308– 5 by r· of human love or hatred
  312–23 r· too supine or misemployed
Man. 46–16 by r· of their relation of
Ret. 84–20 by r· thereof is able to
Un. 8–19 through r·, revelation, and Science,
Pul. 1–12 wiser by r· of its large lessons,
Pan. 4– 3 to the r·, intellect, and will of
  8–27 living by r· of it,
Peo. 1– 6 of material elements from r·,
Po. 32–16 As r· with appetite,
My. 37–16 * By r· of your spiritual achievement
  56–27 * for the r· that there was not
  239– 5 proof, wherein r·, revelation,
  265– 7 more apparent to r· ;
  300–11 for the r· that the divine Principle

reason (verb)
Mis. 218–12 whence to r· out God,
Un. 1– 8 Let us then r· together

reasonable
Mis. 184–11 which is our r· service ;
  200–27 triumph of a r· faith
My. vii–13 * is a r· service which all
  8–15 * r· accommodation for
  130–32 request, . . . should seem r·.
  334– 2 * It is r· to infer

reasonably
Man. 46–24 shall r· reduce his price
Pul. 66–23 * may r· excite wonder

reasoning
Mis. 185–29 When r· on this subject
Un. 34–14 Take another train of r·.
  51– 3 R· from false premises,
No. 20–23 Adam's mistiness and Satan's r·,

reasoning
My. 349–27 r· is correct only as it
  349–31 inductive r· reckons creation

reasons
Mis. 188–16 St. Paul first r· upon the basis of
  301–22 My r· are as follows :
Man. 55–10 For sufficient r· it may be decided
  80–15 for such r· as to the Board may seem
Un. 18–10 fancy that our . . . Father r· thus :
  43–18 Because of these profound r·
Pul. 79–16 * believe there are two r· for this
Hea. 2– 5 while it r· with the storm,
My. 218– 6 furnishes r· or examples for the

reassert
My. 40–17 * widely r· its pristine power

reassured
Mis. 345–19 * r· me that Christianity must be
Pul. 5–20 his conversation . . . r· me.
Peo. 13–27 * r· me that Christianity must be

reassures
No. 44–20 It r· us that no Reign of Terror

reassuring
My. 293–16 r· the mind and through the mind

rebel
Mis. 217–24 and man a r· against his Maker.

rebellion
My. 234–25 more fatal than the Boxers' r·.

rebels
Mis. 204– 1 agony struggles, pride r·,
Hea. 11– 7 mortal mind r· at its own boundaries ;
My. 40–29 * Human sense often r· against law,
  180–25 r·, misconstrues our best motives,

rebound
My. 252–10 must, will, r· upon you.

rebuild
My. 195–30 continue to build, r·, adorn,

rebuke
Mis. 77–25 sternly to r· the mortal belief
  158–16 r· a lack of faith in divine help,
  203–17 baptism serves to r· the senses
  204–21 they r· the material senses,
  209–19 tend to r· appetite
  254– 4 gentle entreaty, the stern r·
  265–30 If impatient of the loving r·,
  277–32 I r· it wherever I see it.
Ret. 21–18 to r· human consciousness
  26–21 in order to r· the evidence.
  80–12 divine r· is effectual
  86– 1 to r· vainglory,
Un. 18–20 which alone enable Me to r·,
No. v– 3 "reprove, r·, exhort,"— *II Tim.* 4 : 2.
  8–10 to r· each other always in love,
  30–12 r· any claim of another law.
Pan. 13–12 r· and exhort one another.
'00. 11–29 bravely r· lawlessness.
  14–12 r· to all the churches
'02. 18–13 faithful to r·, ready to forgive.
Po. 23–14 A stern r· to wrong !
My. 18–20 r· and exhort one another.
  130–17 reprove, r·, and exhort.
  132–24 Divine Love will also r·
  269–24 r· the devourer — *Mal.* 3 : 11.
  294–11 r· whatever accords not
  294–13 He would mightily r·
  343–29 in exhortation, and in r·,

rebuked
Mis. 359–19 Peter's impetuosity was r·.
  374– 7 whatever r· hypocrisy
No. 8–11 as I have r· them.
02. 19– 5 he r· them on the eve of his
Hea. 2–22 r· their carnality,
My. 222– 4 Jesus r· them, saying :
  307–18 demurrer which r· him.

rebukes
Mis. 210–30 r· error, and casts it out.
  272–31 not profited by my r·,
  273– 2 the value of these r·.
No. 13– 1 This Science r· sin
  18– 3 Blasphemy r· not the
  43– 5 Truth r· error ;
My. 162–18 the love that r· praises

rebuking
Mis. 327–24 r· their pride,
Man. 40– 9 r· sin, in true brotherliness,

recall
Ret. 14–14 Distinctly do I r· what followed.
Pul. 7– 7 Yet when I r· the past,
My. 39–24 * We r· the harmonious tones
  47–15 * and r· memories of trials,
  59– 2 * whom you will r· as a member

recall
  My. 319–28   * *r·* very plainly the conversation
       322–31   * The exact words I do not *r·*,

recalling
  Po. 1–16   *R·* oft the bitter draft
  My. v–13   * *r·* the following historical facts :

recalls
  Ret. 5–16   for memory *r·* qualities

Recapitulation
  Mis. 92–13   in the chapter on *R·*,
  Man. 86–18   shall teach from the chapter "*R·*"
       86–24   from the said chapter on "*R·*"
  Ret. 35– 4   chapter on *R·* in S. and H.
       83–19   should explain only *R·*,
       84–10   in the chapter on *R·*.
  Pul. 38–15   "*R·*."   Key to the Scriptures,

recapitulation
  Mis. 316–20   What, then, of continual *r·*

receding
  Mis. 206– 5   dashing against the *r·* shore,
      310–26   *r·* year of religious jubilee,
      321– 7   each *r·* year sees the steady gain of
  Po. 27– 5   One word, *r·* year,

receipt
  Mis. 142– 7   Written on *r·* of a beautiful boat
  My. 199–12   acknowledgment of the *r·* of their
      280– 4   * the *r·* of your message,
      295–12   grateful *r·* of your time-worn Bible
      359–25   * Upon *r·* of this letter Mrs Eddy wrote

receipted
  Mis. 350– 2   balance was never *r·* for.

receipts
  Mis. 350– 1   I hold *r·* for $1,489.50 paid in,
  My. 23–12   * total *r·* June 19, 1902 to June 1, 1905,

receive
  Mis. 33– 3   wrong will *r·* its own reward.
      51–30   "Ye ask, and *r·* not, — *Jas.* 4 : 3.
      81–15   *to r· the benediction of*
      84– 3   *r·* startling announcements.
      88– 3   occasionally *r·* it from others ;
      90–23   *r· the communion?*
     123–26   *r·* the reward of righteousness :
     127–16   a fitness to *r·* the answer
     152–18   then will they *r·* the heritage
     168– 4   spiritually and physically, *r·* sight ;
     168–13   pure in spirit, . . . *r·* Truth.
     182– 7   *r·* the Truth of existence ;
     183–15   we learn this, and *r·* it :
     183–26   *r·* a knowledge of God
     194–26   *r·* the sense of Life that knows no
     265–25   who *r·* the same instruction,
     301– 3   and *r·* pay therefor,
     324–31   *r·* his heavenly guidance.
     342–26   and *r·* nothing in return ;
     342–27   you shall *r·* all.
     344–25   *r·* the kingdom of God — *Luke* 18 : 17.
     349–26   or to *r·* my gratuitous services,
     357–24   should *r·* full fellowship from us,
  Man. 34–18   This Church will *r·* a member of
     65–26   If the Clerk of this Church shall *r·*
     68–15   *r·* the degree of the
     75–10   declined to *r·* this munificent gift,
     85– 6   teach and *r·* into his association
     89–16   eligible to *r·* the degree of C.S.D.
     90– 5   if found qualified to *r·* them.
     92–16   No person shall *r·* instructions in
     92–18   *r·* the degree of C.S.B. or C.S.D.,
     96–10   If a lecturer *r·* a call to lecture
     97–13   shall *r·* an annual salary,
    101– 6   who shall *r·* an adequate salary
  Ret. 83–10   *r·* the infinite instructions
     87–29   not *r·* a patient who is under the
  Un. 6– 6   man will *r·* a higher selfhood,
     39–16   as many as *r·* the knowledge of God
     40–13   therefore mortals can no more *r·*
  Pul. 31–22   * evening on which she would *r·* me.
     43–28   * which religious teachers so often *r·*.
     44– 8   * to *r·* this brief message of
     52–16   * *r·* light, health, and strength,
  No. 19–17   physical senses *r·* no spiritual idea,
     40– 2   "Ye ask, and *r·* not, — *Jas.* 4 : 3.
     40– 4   mortals seek, and expect to *r·*,
  '01. 19– 8   "Ask, and ye shall *r·* ;" — *John* 16 : 24.
     22–26   public *r·* their sense of the Science,
     22–26   *r·* no sense whatever of it.
  '02. 13–10   I *r·* no personal benefit therefrom
     17–10   *r·* the reward of obedience
  Hea. 8–23   *r·* only what we have earned.
     15–23   "Ye ask, and *r·* not, — *Jas.* 4 : 3.
  Peo. 9–17   We ask and *r·* not, because we
  My. 18–13   a fitness to *r·* the answer to its
     21–18   * will *r·* a greater blessing
     34– 6   shall *r·* the blessing — *Psal.* 24 : 5.

receive
  My. 41–10   * so *r·* judgment without mercy ;
     48– 5   * one ready to *r·* the inspiration,
     73–21   * visitors will *r·* all information
     81–12   * ready to *r·* testimony,
     118– 5   any imaginary benefit they *r·* is
     123–22   is less sufficient to *r·* a church of
     126–15   *r·* not of her plagues. — *Rev.* 18 : 4.
     131–29   enough to *r·* it." — *Mal.* 3 : 10.
     133–10   will not *r·* a Message from me
     138–15   often ask me to *r·* persons whom
     138–16   decline to *r·* solely because I
     156–22   to *r·* into their affections and lives
     160– 9   of less importance that we *r·*
     163– 9   Not having the time to *r·* all
     165–15   Goodness never fails to *r·* its
     169–17   was happy to *r·* at Concord,
     194–24   but I must decline to *r·* that
     212–20   would *r·* a spiritual influx
     217–13   each contributor will *r·* his
     231–23   to *r·* more tenants.
     241–16   * to *r·* instruction from their **Leader**
     244– 7   to *r·* from me one or more lessons
     247–21   brings forth mankind to *r·* your
     251–21   *r·* a certificate of the degree C.S.D.
     269–29   enough to *r·* it." — *Mal.* 3 : 10.
     293–31   believe that ye *r·* them, — *Mark* 11 : 24.

received
  Mis. x–24   I *r·* from the Daughters of the
     128–12   both learned, and *r·*, — *Phil.* 4 : 9.
     134–14   such as you never before *r·*.
     137–11   I *r·* no reply.
     139– 6   such as you even yet have not *r·*.
     172–20   *r·* through the affections,
     180–21   *But as many as r· him,* — *John* 1 : 12.
     181–24   "But as many as *r·* him, — *John* 1 : 12.
     182– 5   "As many as *r·* him ;" — *John* 1 : 12.
     185–17   "As many as *r·* him," — *John* 1 : 12.
     185–25   "as many as *r·* him, — *John* 1 : 12.
     212–12   they *r·* the blessing.
     298–16   Jesus *r·* the material rite of
     299– 4   error, has *r·* its death-blow ;
     302–27   good that his hearers *r·* from his
     306– 6   * will be gratefully *r·* ;
     318–14   *r·* instructions in a Primary class
     349– 1   *r·* my consent and even the offer of
     349– 3   provided he *r·* these lessons of
     349–28   I never *r·* more than this ;
  Man. 38–22   may be *r·* into this Church
     39– 4   *r·* into full membership,
     39–18   not again be *r·* into this Church.
     45–25   *r·* these titles under the *laws*
     54–16   offender shall not be *r·* into
     62– 9   *r·* in the Sunday School classes
     76–23   amount of funds *r·* by the Treasurer
    110–14   Initials only . . . will not be *r·*.
    111– 4   Initials alone will not be *r·*.
  Ret. 6–30   *r·* further political preferment,
     10– 9   I *r·* lessons in the ancient tongues,
     15– 2   *r·* me into their communion,
     40–14   injury *r·* from a surgical operation
     43–12   who also *r·* a certificate from
     47–19   *r·* instructions in a Primary class
  Un. 23– 1   cruel treatment *r·* by old Gloster
  Pul. 41– 5   * amount needed was *r·*.
     52– 3   * already subscribed can be *r·* !
     76–26   * has *r·* from the members of
     85–24   * Rev. Mary Baker Eddy *r·* **Friday,**
     88– 4   author has *r·* leading newspapers
  No. 43–13   specimen of those *r·* daily :
  '00. 10–23   I *r·* a touching token of
  '01. 23–25   on *r·* principles of philosophy,
     33–26   the same reviling it *r·* then
  '02. 19– 2   brutality that he *r·*.
  My. 14–11   * we *r·* a letter from a friend in
     16– 5   * total of $425,893.66 had been *r·*
     26–10   Your generous check . . . is duly *r·*.
     26–13   ever *r·* from my church,
     27–14   sufficient funds have been *r·*
     27–24   * sufficient funds have been *r·*
     28– 9   * dollars and cents *r·* by him,
     49–18   * *r·* at the previous meeting,
     57–31   * those already subscribed can be *r·*.
     76– 5   * were constantly being *r·* ;
     76–10   * it was *r·* with rejoicing by
    136–17   highest fee ever *r·* by a native of
    163–24   also *r·* from the leading people of
    172–17   'Freely ye have *r·*, — *Matt.* 10 : 8.
    182– 4   I *r·* from the Congregational
    184– 3   Have just *r·* your despatch.
    191–30   card of invitation . . . was duly *r·*.
    192–22   Your kind letter, . . . was duly *r·*.
    198– 5   been *r·* with many thanks to you
    207– 4   communication is gratefully *r·*.
    223– 2   no comers are *r·* . . . without
    240–27   * who have *r·* certificates from

received
My. 242–23 nor to reply to any r,
245–23 students . . . have r certificates,
250– 4 has r profound attention.
259– 6 I r the following cabled message :
309–27 * r a liberal education.
312–11 * thus r a decent burial.
322–18 * r your permission to
326– 2 * enclosures r from our Leader.
331– 4 * r at the hands of
341–24 * r the *Herald* correspondent.

receivers
Pul. 56– 6 * r of the faith among the

receives
Mis. 31–13 and r no aid from,
201– 1 r the mortal scoff only because it
288–26 r a strong impulse from the cause of
Ret. 18– 4 While cactus a mellower glory r
'01. 14–30 evil-doer r no encouragement from
33–27 same reviling . . . it r now,
Po. 63–12 While cactus a mellower glory r
My. 118–19 Soul, not sense, r and gives it.
200–16 and r his rights inalienable

receiveth
Mis. 18– 5 every son whom He r ;" — Heb. 12 : 6.
Ret. 80– 6 every son whom He r. — Heb. 12 : 6.
'01. 9–28 who loveth . . . r them most ;

receiving
Mis. 132–20 teaching C. S., r calls, etc.,
146– 7 on r or dismissing candidates.
256– 8 letters that protest against r
256–15 r but a select number of students.
305–31 * we ask every one r this circular
392–19 on r a painting of the Isle
Man. 27– 9 r the written consent of
85–20 since r instruction as above,
89– 7 found worthy, on r her approval
Ret. 33– 9 but without r satisfaction.
Pul. 41–18 * incapable of r this vast throng,
47–13 * without r any real satisfaction.
Rud. 13–26 r no wages in return,
No. 20–20 asking amiss and r not,
Po. 51– 1 On r a painting of the Isle.
My. 163–11 the pleasure of r any of them.
218–30 r instruction from me,
231–19 Mrs. Eddy is constantly r
246– 2 after r the first degree,

recent
Mis. 48–13 at one of his r lectures
312–15 * has come in r years,
Ret. 48– 6 r experience of the church
Po. v– 4 * *girlhood* up to r *years.*
My. 83–29 * made steady gains in r years.
94–17 * in the r dedication in Boston
99–30 * r dedication of a C. S. temple
305–27 My r reply to the reprint
316–12 R Reckless . . . Attacks on
346–19 * r interview which appeared
351– 3 * to publish her letter of r date,

recently
Mis. 148–23 Until r, I was not aware
Pul. 52–24 * R a revived belief in what he
63– 6 * R BUILT IN HER HONOR
63–10 * remark . . . made r as she
63–20 * tangible and material manner r,
70–13 * r saw completed in Boston,
My. 24–25 * have r inspected the work,
98–17 * church which was r dedicated
99–14 * built a splendid cathedral
100– 4 * temple r dedicated
282– 9 Douma r adopted in Russia
319–19 * which have r appeared,
321–18 * which have arisen r,
323–23 * which we have so r witnessed,

receptacle
Pul. 7–14 now unsealed their r

reception
Mis. 137– 5 gave you a meagre r
276– 3 r in the spacious rooms
307–18 proper r of C. S.
'01. 32–25 r of the Science of Christianity.
My. 15–16 for your gracious r of it
40– 4 * able to give more adequate r
156–20 prepared for the r of Truth

receptions
Man. 94– 6 R.
94– 7 no r nor festivities

receptive
Mis. 189– 3 as little children, we are r,
290–29 all who are r share this
Ret. 80–14 becomes obediently r

receptivity
Mis. 229–15 governing the r of the body,

recess
Pul. 60–19 * r behind the spacious platform,

recesses
Peo. 14– 5 fragrant r, cool grottos,

Recessional
My. v– 3 * Kipling's R

rechristen
Pul. 8–20 r them with his own new name.

reciprocal
Mis. 265–19 whole line of r thought.

reciprocally
Mis. 207– 3 where heart meets heart r blest,

reciprocate
Mis. 117–16 r kindness and work wisely,

recitation
Ret. 83–26 study each lesson before the r.
Pul. 43–20 * followed by the r of the Lord's Prayer,

recitations
Mis. 91–31 study the lessons before r.
92–20 to study it before the r ;

reckless
My. 316–12 R and Irresponsible Attacks

recklessly
Pul. 83– 2 * r promise as lover and candidate

reckon
Mis. 182– 2 to r himself logically ;
288–21 To r the universal cost and gain,

reckoned
Mis. 143–22 husband and wife r as one,
Un. 9– 6 in some way, be r unreal.
9–13 talent and genius . . . have wrongly r.
Pan. 3–21 whose laws are not r as science.
'01. 20–24 The crimes . . . are not easily r.
'02. 8–26 Christ Jesus r man in Science,

reckoning
Mis. 227–28 r its own by the amount of
My. 203–10 All that is worth r is what we do,

reckons
'01. 6– 6 by theology, which r three as one
6– 8 C. S., which r one as one
21–15 critic, who r hopefully on the death
My. 349–31 r creation as its own creator,

reclaim
My. 161– 8 necessary to r the sinner.

reclaimed
My. 36–14 * withheld from open graves or r from

reclaiming
Mis. 100– 9 Truth . . . r the sinner

reclaims
My. 113– 2 heals the sick and r sinners

reclines
Ret. 17–11 vesper r — when the dewdrop
Po. 62–13 vesper r — when the dewdrop

recognition
Mis. 1–15 a higher r of Deity.
18–22 With this r man could
49–24 a r of the nothingness of
173–11 no relation to, or r of, matter?
188–24 The r of this power
196–26 arise to spiritual r of being,
207– 5 r of practical, operative C. S.
214–27 r or approbation of it.
218–30 * "The r of teleology
218–31 * the r of purely spiritual
235– 1 r of his relation to God.
255–13 r of what the apostle meant
304–29 * r of the organization
Man. 74–15 R.
Ret. 63– 4 establishing the r that God *is All,*
Pul. 80–11 * most r, the widest outlook.
No. 1– 5 which comes to our r
'02. 2– 5 for distinction or r ;
My. 9– 2 * In r of the necessity for
45– 1 * r of and obedience to
130– 9 to keep . . . from public r
187–20 r of the riches of His love
188– 8 in r of His presence ;
297–22 If we would awaken to this r,
326– 8 * declaration of this r
327–28 * legal protection and r,
352– 1 * chapter sub-title
352– 5 * r of the blessings

recognize
Mis. 18–14 thou shalt r thyself as
28–24 r no intelligence nor life in
33–19 as they r the help they derive
37–11 r ourselves under the control
42–16 to communicate with and to r
42–27 r a better state of existence.

recognize
Mis.	43–28	to *r*·, as such, the barefaced errors
	60– 2	*God does not r· any,*
	74–11	*If God does not r· matter,*
	74–24	or can *r*· or express pain
	89–30	if he will . . . *r*· his Saviour.
	102–15	In His individuality I *r*·
	113–21	*r*· that mental malpractice,
	181–13	if we *r*· infinitude as personality,
	181–18	*r*· him through spiritual, . . . laws ;
	182–12	*r*· his perfect and eternal estate.
	197–30	*r*· God as omnipotent,
	198–16	*r*· man as governed by God,
	286–27	should *r*· this verity of being,
	348– 2	They *r*· the claims of the law
Ret.	79–30	We *r*· this kingdom,
	80–16	If the Christian Scientist *r*· the
Pul.	21–24	*r*· a clear expression of God's
Pan.	13–18	*r*· the great truth that Spirit is
'01.	30–18	*r*· that C. S. kindles the
'02.	16–14	*r*· the divine presence and allness.
My.	8–26	* whom we *r*· as logically the
	10–24	* *r*· the importance of The
	37–21	* we also *r*· that He has made
	85–12	* to *r*· the fact that this wonderful
	212–21	*r*· and resist the animal magnetism
	326–20	I *r*· the divine hand
	338–24	*r*· the oneness of Jesus

recognized
Mis.	30–14	to be *r*· here and now.
	37– 8	Jesus *r*· this relation so clearly
	85– 8	God is *r*· as the divine Principle
	190– 9	the *r*· reflection of infinite Life
	197– 7	full import . . . is not yet *r*·.
	204–20	demands of spiritual sense are *r*·,
	286–20	*r*· and understood in Science.
Man.	61–21	*r*· standard of musical excellence ;
Ret.	71–24	must be *r*·, and uprooted,
Pul.	25– 2	* cooling is a *r*· feature as well as
	28–23	* and other *r*· devotional poets,
	37–13	* *r*· head of the C. S. Church.
	55–28	* Truth is the sole *r*· authority.
No.	20–21	God is *r*· as the only power,
My.	232–25	*r*· as the true likeness of his Maker"
	259–30	Soul *r*· only in harmony,
	326– 6	* *r*· in an official and authoritative

recognizes
Mis.	33–26	*r*· the fact that, as mortal mind
	255–22	*r*· the fact that the antidote for
Ret.	34–12	*r*· the antidote for all sickness,
Un.	7– 9	the infinite *r*· no disease,
	54–16	sin *r*· as its most potent . . . enemy.
Pul.	30–19	* *r*· Jesus as the teacher and guide
My.	108–15	C. S. *r*· that this Mind is the
	328–12	* the law *r*· them as healers,

recognizing
Mis.	43– 1	C. S., *r*· the capabilities of Mind
Peo.	7– 5	*R*· this as we ought, we shall turn
My.	7–16	* "*R*· the necessity for providing an
	37–19	* *R*· the grand truth that God is the
	232– 1	It rejoices me that you are *r*·
	329–22	* *r*· the steady progress of C. S.
	364–15	*r*· the supremacy and allness of good.

recollect
Ret.	63–23	*r*· that it encourages sin to say,
My.	309–13	as I *r*· it, he was justice of the

recollection
Pul.	65–18	* suggests to *r*· the story of

recollections
Mis.	159–16	where I deposit certain *r*·
My.	321– 6	* My *r*· of Mr. Wiggin

recommend
Mis.	25–31	and *r*· them for that purpose?
	120–20	I *r*· that this Association
	131–16	I *r*· that you waive the
	136–22	I *r*· that the June session
	139– 1	I *r*· this honorable body
	302–32	I *r*· that students stay within
	357–24	characters and lives *r*· them,
Man.	37–17	One Normal student cannot *r*· the
	92– 7	I *r*· that each member of this
Ret.	78–11	I *r*· students not to read so-called
No.	3–15	and *r*· it to their students,
	7–21	I *r*· that Scientists draw no
My.	204–19	*r*· it under the circumstances.
	219–29	I *r*·, if the law demand,
	224–28	we cannot afford to *r*·
	237–23	I *r*· its careful study
	354– 5	to state that I *r*· nothing but

recommendation
Man.	36–20	present to him a *r*·
	37–15	*r*· AND ELECTION.
My.	182– 5	*r*· to evangelical churches

recommended
Mis.	245– 2	or *r*· others to use, drugs ;
Ret.	44–23	I *r*· that the church be dissolved.
'01.	23–19	used no material medicine, nor *r*· it,
	25–19	He never *r*· drugs,

recommending
No.	8– 8	*r*· to all men fellowship
My.	298– 2	*r*· it to the public.

recommends
Peo.	5– 2	devoutly *r*· the more spiritual
My.	276–11	*r*· this surprising privilege to all

recompense
Mis.	12– 6	God will *r*· this wrong,
	364– 7	what a *r*· to have healed,
No.	3–24	trust Love's *r*· of love.
'01.	30–22	hope of ease, pleasure, or *r*·,
Po.	23–17	Life hath a higher *r*·
My.	37–32	* *r*· your long sacrifice
	166–15	Life's ills are its chief *r*· ;
	190– 2	bring the *r*· of human woe,
	283–16	Right has its *r*·,
	308– 8	by ease, pleasure, or *r*·.

recompensed
Mis.	2–12	subdued and *r*· by justice,
My.	139–26	and you have been greatly *r*·.

reconcile
My.	84–22	* cannot *r*· himself to the methods

reconciled
Mis.	124– 8	will not be *r*· thereto.
Hea.	18–14	if that idea could be *r*· with
My.	107– 9	old school has become *r*·.

reconciles
Mis.	122–22	nor *r*· justice to injustice ;

reconciliation
No.	35–22	needs no *r*· with God,

reconciling
My.	314–25	the means of *r*· the couple.

reconstruct
No.	43–24	will never prevent or *r*·

reconstructed
Ret.	28–22	I had learned that Mind *r*· the body,
Pul.	20–10	I *r*· my original system of ministry
	35–21	learned that Mind *r*· the body,

reconstructs
Mis.	82– 1	*r*· the Judean religion,

record
Bible
My.	219–19	Bible *r*· of our great Master's life

Biblical
Mis.	120–27	Biblical *r*· of the great Nazarene,

court
My.	314–14	the court *r*· may state that my divorce

dark
Po.	26–15	dark *r*· of our guilt unrolled,

first
Mis.	57– 2	If the first *r*· is true,

first on
Mis.	272– 7	* the first on *r*· in history,

honorable
My.	332–31	* his honorable *r*· and Christian

interesting
My.	49–21	* interesting *r*· of this meeting reads :
	51–25	* An interesting *r*· relative to this

Major Glover's
My.	334–25	* heading

material
Mis.	170–19	The material *r*· of the Bible,
Ret.	22– 2	and the material *r*· expunged.

no
Mis.	158–30	no *r*· that he used notes
	245– 1	no *r*· showing that our Master ever
My.	340– 1	no *r*· of his observing

of dreams
Ret.	21–14	history is but the *r*· of dreams,

of theft
Mis.	300–21	increasing the *r*· of theft

of this period
My.	54–22	* A *r*· of this period reads,

only
Mis.	161–18	The only *r*· of our Master

put on
My.	353–11	put on *r*· the divine Science of

said
My.	333– 1	* said *r*·, with the seal of the

special
Pul.	34– 4	* no special *r*· is to be made.

their
My.	257–28	Christian Scientists have their *r*·

this
No.	22–18	This *r*· shows that the term devil
Po.	26–17	"This *r*· I will bear

record

true
Ret. 44–29 that hour holds this true *r.*
unparalleled
My. v–23 * unparalleled *r.* for a work of

Mis. 17– 1 *r.* the thunderings of the spiritual
57–25 *Why does the r. make man a*
390–21 What hath the *r.* been?
Ret. 19–23 Here it is but justice to *r.*,
Pul. vii– 7 to have not only a *r.* of
Po. 55–22 What hath the *r.* been?
My. 30–25 * some of the *r.* collections
50–29 * The *r.* of May 23, 1880,
98–25 * *r.* is one of which any church
119– 1 for history to *r.* limitations
125–15 History will *r.* their words,
260–30 but one Jesus Christ on *r.*
309–19 on *r.* that Mark Baker's father
314–21 to *r.* the divorce in my favor.
331– 2 Here it is but justice to *r.*,
333–10 * The minutes *r.* this

recorded

Mis. 170–27 So Jesus is *r.* as having
199–14 miracles *r.* in the Scriptures
238–11 more than history has yet *r.*
277–20 * "It is one more fact to be *r.*
Man. 110– 7 *r.* in the history of the Church
Ret. 26–12 miracles *r.* in the Bible.
Rud. 16–20 first book, *r.* in history, which
'02. 14–22 achievement has been . . . *r.* in heaven.
15–25 *r.* the hallowed suggestion.
Hea. 15–13 miracles *r.* in the Bible.
My. 148–22 and what is being *r.*
292– 3 more than history has yet *r.*

recording

Mis. 141–31 O *r.* angel ! write :
170–24 passage *r.* Jesus' proceedings
My. 126– 7 the *r.* angel, standing with
332–29 * roll of papers *r.* the death of

records

Mis. 131–31 last year's *r.* immortalized,
147– 9 ladened them with *r.* worthy to be
390–25 In *r.* of the heart.
Man. 28–24 shall be written on the Church *r.*
83–10 as have good past *r.*
91–21 with good moral *r.*,
Pul. 1–13 and *r.* deeply engraven,
'00. 12– 8 History *r.* Ephesus as an illustrious
Po. 56– 4 In *r.* of the heart.
My. 50–13 * for their *r.* state,
50–16 * as the *r.* further relate,
50–21 * the *r.* contain these simple
51–21 * but, as the *r.* state,
107– 3 improved upon its earlier *r.*,
124–24 produce thy *r.*, time-table, log,
184–21 glowing *r.* of Christianity,
270–10 *r.* of my ancestry attest honesty
330–19 * sustained by Masonic *r.*
332–22 * to look up the *r.* of this lodge,
332–27 * Masonic *r.* were transferred to
333– 4 * In the *r.* of St. John's Lodge,
333–19 * *Chronicle* of July 3, 1844, *r.* that
334–13 * *r.* show really existed in 1844,

recounting

Pul. 47– 9 * *r.* her experiences as the pioneer
My. 331–29 * *r.* the kind attention paid to

recover

Mis. 10–14 they will *r.* it, countermand their
29– 1 and they shall *r.*" — *Mark* 16 : 18.
104–29 and *r.* his own individuality
192–30 and they shall *r.*" — *Mark* 16 : 18.
248– 2 and they shall *r.*" — *Mark* 16 : 18.
300–31 is more apt to *r.* than he who
381–19 *r.* of the defendant her cost of suit,
Ret. 35–18 and they shall *r.*" — *Mark* 16 : 18.
Pul. 20– 6 In 1892 I had to *r.* the land
Hea. 1– 4 *and they shall r.* — *Mark* 16 : 18.
8–11 and they shall *r.*" — *Mark* 16 : 18.
11–15 may not *r.* from the heel of
19–28 and they shall *r.*" — *Mark* 16 : 18.
Peo. 12– 5 and they shall *r.*" — *Mark* 16 : 18.
My. 48– 3 * and they shall *r.*" — *Mark* 16 : 18.
200–28 to *r.* its connection with its divine
227–12 one . . . dies while the others *r.*,

recovered

Un. 62– 1 Invalids say, "I have *r.*"
My. 97–28 * Boston has not yet *r.* from
293–27 and the patient would have *r.*
314–24 When this husband *r.* his wife,

recovery

Mis. 24– 8 wrought my immediate *r.*
35– 4 and subsequently her *r.*,

recovery

Mis. 53–13 *to start the patient's r.?*
59–11 *to pray for the r. of the sick ?*
100–31 man's *r.* from sin and his
308–27 prevents the *r.* of the sick.
355– 8 chronic *r.* ebbing and flowing,
380–19 immediate *r.* of the sick,
Man. 46–21 for *r.* of payment
46–25 chronic cases of *r.*,
Ret. 24–12 My immediate *r.* from the effects
24–18 and rejoiced in my *r.*,
My. 293–22 President McKinley's *r.*
335–31 * for her husband's *r.*,

recreation

Ret. 69–23 for *r.* or procreation?"

recruit

Pul. 30– 7 * did not *r.* itself from other
'01. 29–18 but to *r.* themselves.

rectified

Un. 20– 1 How is a mistake to be *r.*?

rectify

Mis. 80–20 redress wrongs and *r.* injustice.
371–22 To sympathize . . . is not to *r.*
Un. 14–13 that He might *r.* His

recuperate

Mis. 209–16 can *r.* the life of man,

recuperated

No. 36–19 which *r.* him for triumph

recur

Mis. 299– 1 suffering and mistakes *r.* until
My. 340–23 to *r.* to a religious observance

recurrence

Ret. 70–13 the *r.* of such events.

recurring

Mis. xi–14 At each *r.* holiday the
321– 9 each *r.* year witnesses
'02. 10–25 old and *r.* martyrdom
My. 192–24 constant *r.* demands upon

red

Mis. 239–18 *r.* nose, suffused eyes, cough,
253–17 *r.* dragon that stood ready
254–18 the great *r.* dragon of this hour,
348–20 capsicum (*r.* pepper) ;
Un. 11–23 neither *r.* tape nor indignity
Pul. 42–23 * in letters of *r.* were the words :
My. 131–10 cup *r.* with loving restitution,

Red Dragon

Mis. 269–30 heard the great *R. D.*

redeem

Mis. 82– 9 to enlighten and *r.* mortals.
Rud. 3– 6 Truth and Love, which *r.* them,
'02. 13–23 *r.* the land by paying the amount
My. 139–27 so doth the divine Love *r.* your body

redeemed

Mis. 140–20 I *r.* from under mortgage.
310–15 my desire is that all shall be *r.*,
Ret. 9–25 * *r.* her birthright of the day,
Pul. 10–29 this is His *r.* ; this, His beloved.
'01. 11–11 and are the *r.* of the Lord.
'02. 14– 2 paid on the land when I *r.* it.
My. 36– 5 * *r.* from obdurate sin.
229–29 The *r.* should be happier than

Redeemer

Mis. 123–28 divine *Life*, which is our *R.*
164–15 from the beginning as the *R.*,
Ret. 23–17 My heart knew its *R.*
My. 136– 2 know that our "*R.* liveth" — *Job* 19 : 25.
192–12 and sings of our *R.*
316– 5 the harvest song of the *R.*
333–25 * on the merits of a crucified *R.*

redeemeth

My. 13–21 *r.* thy life — *Psal.* 103 : 4.

redeeming

Un. 55–14 *r.* us from the false sense of
'00. 2– 5 this old-new theme of *r.* Love

redeems

Mis. 17–16 divine Principle that *r.* man

redemption

Mis. 15– 6 the *r.* of our body." — *Rom.* 8 : 23.
95–22 the *r.* of our body." — *Rom.* 8 : 23.
96–19 includes man's *r.* from sickness
165–23 the means of mortals' *r.* from sin ;
182–10 to wit, the *r.* of the body.
Un. 6– 7 *r.* of mortals from sin, sickness, and
52–12 This is the precious *r.* of soul,
Peo. 10–26 the *r.* of our body." — *Rom.* 8 : 23.
12–19 of God's plan of *r.*,
My. 131–11 restitution, *r.*, and inspiration,

redemptive
 Mis. 107– 5 Its *r·* power is seen in sore trials,
     331–16 thank God for those *r·* words
 '01. 11– 8 Through this *r·* Christ, Truth,
 My. 239– 9 *r·* power of Christianity

rediscovery
 My. 284– 1 Because of my *r·* of C. S.,

redolent
 Mis. 194–12 *r·* with love, health, and holiness,
 Pul. 1– 6 *r·* with grief and gratitude.
 '01. 12–18 *r·* with health, holiness, and love.

redress
 Mis. 80–20 *r·* wrongs and rectify injustice.
 '01. 30–12 too occupied with . . . to seek *r·* ;

Red Sea
 Mis. 153– 8 they passed through the *R· S·*,
 My. 43–14 * the passage of the *R· S·*

red-tongued
 Mis. 226–29 *r·* assassin of radical worth ;

reduce
 Mis. 334–20 just *r·* this falsity to its
 Man. 46–24 shall reasonably *r·* his price
 Ret. 26–29 *r·* the demonstration of being,
     28–18 must *r·* all things real to their
 Un. 13–14 *r·* the universe to chaos.
 No. 32–26 *r·* this evil to its lowest terms,

reduced
 Mis. 109–15 *r·* to their native nothingness !
     260– 4 C. S. has been *r·* to
 Un. 35– 9 *R·* to its proper denomination,

reducing
 Mis. 108–13 *r·* its claim to its proper
 Hea. 13– 4 *r·* the one hundredth part of a grain

reduction
 Un. 36–17 by the *r·* and the rejection of
 No. 33– 2 The *r·* of evil, in Science,

redundant
 '02. 19–29 no *r·* drop in the cup

reecho
 Po. 41–19 harpstring, just breaking, *r·* again

reechoing
 '02. 4–16 echoing and *r·* through

Reed, Rev. George H.
 My. 174–14 Rev. George H. *R·*, Pastor of

reed
 Mis. 387–14 If thou the bending *r·* wouldst break
 '02. 18–10 broke not the bruised *r·*
 Po. 6– 9 If thou the bending *r·* wouldst break
 My. 117– 6 *r·* shaken with the— *Matt.* 11 : 7.

reeds
 No. 22–11 are *r·* shaken by the wind.
 Pan. 3–28 His pipe of seven *r·* denotes

re-elected
 Man. 26– 6 *r·*, or new officers elected,
     81– 1 can be *r·*, or new officers elected,

reeling
 Mis. 134–21 The *r·* ranks of *materia medica*,

reenact
 No. 44–21 or *r·*, . . . the horrors of

reenunciated
 Pul. 57–10 * *r·* the truths which

reestablished
 Hea. 3– 8 *r·* on its former basis.

refer
 Mis. 33– 8 these *r·* not to personality,
     35–28 we *r·* you to "S. and H.
     51–10 the case to which you may *r·*,
     52– 1 text may *r·* to such as seek
     59–19 Scriptures *r·* to God as saying,
     67–27 If you *r·* to the removal of a person
     132–23 would *r·* you to the Holy Scriptures,
     243–24 Did he *r·* to that questionable
 No. 22–22 passage must *r·* to the *evils*
 '01. 16–20 *r·* to an evil spirit as *dumb*,
 My. 240–20 I shall *r·* to this.
     292–20 I *r·* to the effect of one human

reference
 Mis. x– 8 in book form, — accessible as *r·*,
     243–11 *R·*, Mrs. M. A. F——,
 Man. 41– 4 irreverent *r·* to Christ Jesus
 Pul. 34–22 * in *r·* to this experience.
 No. 7–24 without *r·* to right or wrong
 My. 237– 1 contemplated *r·* in S. and H.
     249–27 then without *r·* to sex
     329– 9 * *r·* to the death of her husband,
     338– 8 * A *r·* to her writings

references
 Mis. 295– 1 certain *r·* to American women
 My. 34–29 * S. and H. *r·* in this lesson

referred
 Mis. 48– 4 by the gentleman *r·* to,
     181–20 His sonship, *r·* to in the **text,**
     186– 6 as *r·* to by St. Paul.
     190–22 devil herein *r·* to
     314–19 *r·* to in the Sunday Lessons.
 Man. 66–17 or she is *r·* to as authority
 Un. 36–13 *r·* to in the New Testament
 Pul. 27–15 * six water-pots *r·* to in John
     55– 5 * we have *r·* to cyclic changes
     73–25 * She *r·* the reporter to the
 No. 9–18 wrongs of the nature *r·* to.
     9–28 * *r·* to general truths
 Hea. 7– 2 signs *r·* to are the manifestations
 My. 125–29 woman, *r·* to in Revelation,
     241–20 * because I *r·* to myself
     305–12 People do not know who is *r·* to
     307–19 *r·* to the *coming* anew of Truth,
     320–21 * at the time above *r·* to,
     320–22 * *r·* to you as the author of
     321– 4 * always *r·* to you as the one **who**
     328– 8 * *r·* to in Miss Jones' letter :

referring
 Mis. 130–24 we should avoid *r·* to past mistakes.
     133– 2 *r·* to me, "the pantheistic and
     163–18 *R·* to this, he said,
     192– 3 so, when *r·* to a liar,
     193–14 *R·* to The Church of Christ, Scientist,
 Pul. 3– 4 *R·* to this temple, our Master said :
 '01. 9– 2 *r·* to his eternal spiritual selfhood
 My. 137– 5 * The *Boston Globe*, *r·* to this
     225–31 The word Principle, when *r·* to **God,**
     228–12 *R·* to John the Baptist,
     284–13 *r·* to the Memorial service
     299– 4 kindly *r·* to my address to

refers
 Mis. 67–25 If your question *r·* to language,
     182–15 *r·* to man's primal, spiritual
     184–10 Paul *r·* to this when speaking of
     186–29 undoubtedly *r·* to the last Adam
     190–30 Paul *r·* to this personality of **evil**
     191– 9 *r·* to a wicked man as the devil :
     191–23 our text *r·* to the devil as dumb ;
 Un. 30–15 apostle *r·* to the second Adam as
 No. 29– 1 this passage *r·* to the Jewish law,
 Pan. 14–28 This *r·* to the war between
 '00. 11–26 In Revelation St. John *r·* to
     12–28 It *r·* to the Hebrew Balaam as the
     13–21 The Revelator *r·* to the church in
 My. 308–15 *McClure's Magazine r·* to my **father's**

refilled
 My. 149–18 must be emptied before it can be *r·*.

refinement
 Mis. 101– 6 blesses . . . by the *r·* of joy

refinements
 Peo. 10– 4 *r·* that lose some materiality ;

refines
 Mis. 126–13 the ordeal *r·* while it chastens
 My. 131– 3 that which *r·* character

reflect
 Mis. 8–19 Christ-image that you should *r·*.
     12–31 imparting, so far as we *r·* them,
     16–13 *r·* the full dominion of Spirit
     127–26 it must be ours, . . . if we *r·* Him.
     131– 6 to discern darkness or to *r·* light.
     150–28 His people are they that *r·* Him
     150–30 His people are they . . . that *r·* **Love.**
     154–29 Let your light *r·* Light.
     183–27 will have power to *r·* His power,
     235– 5 *r·* Him who destroys death and hell.
     263–14 meet all human needs and *r·* all bliss.
     278–17 *r·* the image of their Father.
     333–27 by means of that which does not *r·* **Him**
 Man. 19– 5 to *r·* in some degree the Church
 Un. 30–26 *r·* the Life of the divine Arbiter.
     39–17 must *r·*, in some degree, the power of
 Pul. 4–24 *R· this* Life,
     26– 4 * prisms which *r·* the rainbow tints.
 No. 26–19 Man's individual being must *r·* the
     39–24 Advancing in this light, we *r·* it ;
 '00. 4–27 they *r·* God and nothing else.
 My. 150–14 *r·* the divine Life, Truth, and
     150–19 ask God to enable you to *r·* God,
     208– 6 to *r·* its heavenly rays over all
     210–16 His thoughts can only *r·* peace,
     265–26 *r·* this purified subjective state
     352–12 * may so *r·* in our thoughts

reflected
 Mis. 103–27 individuality that *r·* the Immanuel,
     293–21 sum total of Love *r·*

reflected

Mis.	337–29	Life and light which he *r·*
	340–29	to shine with the *r·* light of God.
	368– 1	and is *r·* by a universe
Un.	14–23	must be *r·* in man, Mind's image.
	24–14	*r·* in individual consciousness,
	51–26	*r·* not as human soul,
Pul.	83–24	* we live in the *r·* royalty
My.	74–20	* *r·* in their faces,
	202–23	My work is *r·* light,
	269– 1	*r·* in the intelligent compound idea,
	301– 1	C. S. is a *r·* glory ;

reflecting

Mis.	77–27	in God's own likeness, and *r·* Truth,
	185– 1	in unity with, and *r·*, his Maker.
	332– 1	*r·* all space and Life,
	393– 1	Chief, the charm of thy *r·*,
No.	21–11	showed man as *r·* God
Po.	51– 6	Chief, the charm of thy *r·*,

reflection

and glory
Mis.	187–23	man is their *r·* and glory.

divine
'00.	1– 8	in the glow of divine *r·*.
My.	129–13	richly fraught with divine *r·*.

forever
Rud.	11– 7	the forever *r·* of goodness.

God's
Mis.	18–17	of spiritual origin, God's *r·*,
	183–14	possible to man *as God's r·*.
	291– 6	dims the true sense of God's *r·*,

His
'00.	4–25	and is His *r·* and Science.
My.	355–27	God is glorified in His *r·*
	356– 3	in His *r·* of love and leadership

human
Un.	28–21	human *r·*, reason, or belief

image is the
My.	239–22	whose image is the *r·* of all

is creation
Mis.	23–23	God, whose *r·* is creation,

man is the
Un.	51– 1	man is the *r·* of immutable good.

no
Peo.	4–20	find no *r·* in sinning, sick, and

observation and
Peo.	6– 7	* founded on long observation and *r·*,

of God
Rud.	7– 9	man is the manifest *r·* of God,

of His power
No.	12–28	man the *r·* of His power and goodness.

of light
My.	355–23	the *r·* of light and love ;

of Spirit
Ret.	73– 7	man is found in the *r·* of Spirit.

of the divine
Mis.	352–25	his consciousness is the *r·* of the divine,

of the Ego
Un.	48–17	not the Ego, but the *r·* of the Ego.

radiant
My.	150–20	radiant *r·* of Christ's glory,

recognized
Mis.	190– 9	recognized *r·* of infinite Life

shocking
No.	29–18	such a statement is a shocking *r·*

this
Mis.	235– 6	By this *r·*, man becomes the
Ret.	57–16	and this *r·* is substance,

true
Mis.	189–12	brings to light the true *r·* :

Mis.	23–25	what C. S. means by the word *r·*.
	183–18	that *r·* already has bestowed
Ret.	56–20	supplying all Mind by the *r·*,
	70–25	the *r·*, . . . of the infinite God.

reflects

Mis.	7–18	*r·* that it is dangerous to live,
	17–20	man *r·* the divine power to heal
	23–26	*r·* good, Life, Truth, Love
	79– 8	*r·* all whereby we can know God.
	104–23	*r·* the divine law and order of being.
	140–32	type of the divine Principle it *r·*.
	183–32	Scriptures declare *r·* his Maker,
	184– 7	only when man *r·* God in body
	205–17	man's identity . . . *r·* only Spirit,
	247–27	*r·* harmony or discord according to
	290–29	it emits light because it *r·* ;
	313– 8	May the Christlikeness it *r·* rest on
	362– 6	comprehends and *r·* all real mode, form,
	364–18	*r·* the divine Mind,
Man.	40– 9	*r·* the sweet amenities of Love,
Ret.	56–23	God *r·* Himself, or Mind,
	57–15	He *r·* God as his Mind,
	68– 8	he *r·* the infinity of good.
Un.	39–23	man forever *r·* and embodies

reflects

Pul.	4–14	A dewdrop *r·* the sun.
	4–15	Each of Christ's little ones *r·*
'00.	4–28	divine Love includes and *r·*
'01.	5–21	man *r·* Spirit, not matter.
Peo.	10–22	the images that thought *r·*
My.	121–23	and *r·* the divine likeness.
	124–18	Nature *r·* man and art pencils him,
	288– 9	demonstrates Truth and *r·* divine Love.

reflex

'01.	8–20	The *r·* image of Spirit is not
My.	109–21	*r·* images of this divine Life,

reform

Mis.	38–20	enlighten and *r·* the sinner,
	80–19	promotes and impels all true *r·* ;
	211– 1	you will help to *r·* them.
	215– 5	saying, . . . I punish to *r·* ;
	222– 9	failing of conviction and *r·*,
	237–22	*r·* does and must push on
	244–13	repentance and *r·*, which are
	246– 5	through civil and religious *r·*,
	294–20	*r·* and transform them,
	362–29	prevent sin or *r·* the sinner.
Ret.	30– 9	all moral and religious *r·*.
	70–28	civil, moral, and religious *r·*.
Pul.	20–18	physical, civil, and religious *r·*
No.	11–17	revolutionize and *r·* the world,
Pan.	10–20	they *r·* desperate cases
'01.	30–14	they are leaders of a *r·*
'02.	8–11	No person can . . . *r·* mankind unless
Peo.	1– 3	The great element of *r·*
My.	5–17	heal the sick, *r·* the sinner,
	9–15	* the effort for righteous *r·*,
	26–23	date some special *r·*,
	51–16	* heal the sick and *r·* the sinner.
	51–32	* heal the sick, and *r·* the sinner,
	306–13	The greatest *r·*, . . . must wait

reformation

Mis.	93–26	without repentance and *r·*.
	205– 8	*r·* brings the light which
	261– 5	can only be removed by *r·*.
	297– 4	physical and moral *r·*.
	302– 2	it is a purpose to kill the *r·*
My.	229– 1	for penance or for *r·* ;

reformatory

'01.	9–25	they are revolutionary, *r·*,

reformed

Mis.	146–21	I would gather every *r·* mortal
	219–30	and he has *r·* the sinner.
Man.	39–12	and of being radically *r·*,
'01.	27–19	sick healed, also sinners *r·*
My.	28–23	* our Master healed and *r·* them.
	258– 2	there the sinner is *r·*
	348–26	healed the sick and *r·* the sinner

reformer

Mis.	213–17	pioneer *r·* must pass through a
	237–14	*r·* must encounter and help
	238– 7	The *r·* has no time to
	238–11	*r·* works on unmentioned,
'00.	9–14	*r·* continues his lightning,
	9–16	*r·* must be a hero
'01.	23–17	He was ultra ; he was a *r·* ;
	29– 2	visited a *r·* for that purpose?
	29– 8	aged *r·* should not be left to
	29–24	sacrifices most for the *r·*,
'02.	10– 9	footprints of a *r·* are
	10–20	Wherefore, then, smite the *r·*
	10–28	Persecuting a *r·* is like
Hea.	2– 9	intrepid *r·*, Martin Luther :
My.	288– 4	*r·* gives little thought to
	288–12	Galilean Prophet was, is, the *r·*

reformers

Mis.	98–23	lives of all *r·* attest the
	237– 1	chapter sub-title
	238– 3	to believe a lie, and to hate *r·*.
'01.	28–29	After a hard . . . *r·* usually are
	29–11	not because *r·* are not loved,
	30– 6	successive utterances of *r·*
My.	3–11	Zion's waste places, appeal to *r·*,
	288–12	was, is, the reformer of *r·*.

reforming

'01.	27–13	healing and *r·* mankind.
My.	v–16	* healing the sick and *r·* the sinner
	58–23	* healing the sick and *r·* the sinful,
	155– 1	healing the sick and *r·* the sinner
	182–16	the *r·* of the sinner,
	271– 6	healing the sick and *r·* the sinner,

reforms

Mis.	222– 8	*r·* him, and so heals him :
	245–20	charities, and *r·* of to-day.
	295– 8	* past a score of years
Ret.	67–14	*r·* the sinner and destroys sin.
No.	45–20	its moral and religious *r·*.

reforms
Hea.	1–17	* Knows it at forty, and *r·* his plan ;
My.	28–22	* heals the sick and *r·* the sinful
	161– 6	were it not that his suffering *r·* him,
	287– 7	Divine Love *r·*, regenerates,

refrain
Mis.	311–27	and who can *r·* from transcribing
	392–21	singing To my sense a sweet *r·* ;
Po.	47– 3	Singing the olden and dainty *r·*,
	51– 3	singing To my sense a sweet *r·* ;
My.	105–30	they must *r·* from persecuting
	129–32	*R·* from public controversy ;

refrained
My.	318–19	just so long as he *r·* from

refraining
My.	222–14	*r·* from admitting the claims of

refresh
Pul.	4– 5	Can ne'er *r·* a drooping earth,
Peo.	9– 6	The cool bath may *r·* the body,
My.	125– 5	to report progress, to *r·* memory,

refreshing
Mis.	149–21	a *r·* demonstration of Christianity,
	291–26	*r·*, and consecrating mankind.
My.	208–13	and the *r·* breeze of morn,
	259–14	*r·* and most pleasing . . . presents,

refreshment
Mis.	153–10	land of promise, green isles of *r·*.
	170– 8	spiritual *r·* of God's children
	170–17	was *r·* of divine strength,
	227–25	on isles of sweet *r·*.
Pul.	1–11	For due *r·* garner the memory of
'01.	1–15	*r·* and invigoration of the human

'reft
Po.	30– 7	dayspring ! *'r·* of mortal sigh

refuge
Mis.	9– 8	*r·* at last from the elements of earth.
	229–11	my *r·*, even the most High — *Psal.* 91 : 9.
	389–10	Love is our *r·* ;
	396–17	poem
Ret.	91– 2	God is their sure defense and *r·*.
Un.	2– 6	no *r·* from sin, except in God,
	57– 7	Man's *r·* is in spirituality,
Pul.	18– 1	poem
No.	7–14	rescue and *r·* in Truth and Love.
Po.	4– 9	Love is our *r·* ;
	page 12	poem
My.	17– 1	sweep away the *r·* of lies, — *Isa.* 28 : 17.
	185–30	sermons in stones, *r·* in mountains,

refusal
Pul.	87–21	*r·* of that as a material offering.

refuse
Mis.	89–17	caused our Master to *r·* help to some
	246–18	and *r·* the victim a solitary vindication
	248– 3	interpretation they *r·* to hear.
Man.	36–17	*r·* to endorse their applications
	111–18	*r·*, without sufficient cause, to sign
Ret.	64–30	If evangelical churches *r·* fellowship
Pul.	64–12	* to *r·* further contributions,
My.	302–24	and I *r·* adulation.
	311– 7	I could not *r·* her.

refused
Mis.	196–24	which the builders *r·* — *Psal.* 118 : 22.
	246–21	*r·* to yield its prey
	349–26	and *r·* to give me up
Ret.	26– 5	when he *r·* to drink the
	40–23	*r·* me a hearing in their halls
Pul.	20– 8	Commissioner, who *r·* to grant it,
	44–28	* *r·* to accept any further checks
My.	122–31	*r·* to see the power of Truth
	335–21	* but they *r·* permission

refuses
Mis.	113–15	*r·* to be influenced by any but
	211–32	*r·* to bear the cross
My.	180–19	*r·* to see this grand verity

refusing
Ret.	40– 2	*r·* to take any pay

refutation
Mis.	133– 6	In *r·* of your statement
No.	6– 9	This *r·* is indispensable to the
My.	58– 8	* *r·* of the statements
	91– 4	* affords *r·* of the notion that
	317– 4	* in *r·* of allegations

refute
Mis.	183–29	dares at this date *r·* the evidence
	220– 9	to *r·* the sick man's thoughts,
	362–24	*r·* erring reason with the

refutes
Mis.	22–13	absolutely *r·* the amalgamation,
	364–10	*r·* everything that is not a
No.	6– 7	C. S. *r·* the validity of
	15–20	C. S. *r·* pantheism,

regain
Mis.	265– 5	He grows dark, and cannot *r·*,
	269– 3	By using falsehood to *r·* his
	310–19	to *r·* it, one must comply with
Pan.	11–17	*r·* his native spiritual stature

regained
Rud.	15– 6	surprise of suddenly *r·* health
'01.	29–29	* we have *r·* our tuition

regal
Mis.	330–29	unveils its *r·* splendor
My.	149– 8	More than *r·* is the majesty

regard
Mis.	3– 4	If we *r·* good as more natural
	6–27	caution is observed in *r·* to
	32–31	To the query in *r·* to some
	60– 6	To *r·* sin, disease, and death
	64–10	*Do you r· the study of literature*
	79–26	*in r· to aiding persons*
	181–19	and *r·* him as spiritual,
Man.	47–13	Testimony in *r·* to the healing
	97–17	impositions on the public in *r·* to
Chr.	55–12	they *r·* not the work — *Isa.* 5 : 12.
Ret.	2–29	for whom she cherished a high *r·*.
	5–30	* in *r·* to the education of her
Un.	40–26	*r·* all things as temporal.
	54– 7	To *r·* sickness as a false claim,
Pul.	55–12	* *r·* it as a mere coincidence
	72–19	* In *r·* to Mrs. Eddy,
No.	1– 1	*r·* for the spiritual idea
	37–13	but to *r·* this wonder of glory,
'01.	8– 6	who *r·* Jesus as God
	14–14	We *r·* evil as a lie,
	31–13	they *r·* me with no vague, fruitless,
My.	119– 2	and to *r·* evil as real,
	141–12	* announcement in *r·* to the services
	143–22	I do not *r·* this attack upon
	157– 9	* without *r·* to class or creed,
	178–14	those who *r·* being as material.
	190–13	*r·* his sayings as infallible.
	223–16	in *r·* to that of which
	244–23	have come so to *r·* them.
	291–30	shall sacredly *r·* the liberty of
	302–20	I *r·* self-deification as blasphemous.
	320– 9	* as to his high *r·* for you

regarded
Mis.	112–18	*r·* his act as one of simple justice,
	139–26	will in future be *r·* as
	200– 3	Jesus *r·* good as the normal
	200–30	*r·* matter as only a vagary of
	234–28	God is *r·* more as absolute,
Ret.	20–11	my home I *r·* as very precious.
	20–29	was then *r·* as the Far West.
Un.	46–18	personality they *r·* as both good and
Pul.	55–26	* *r·* as the parent organization,
'01.	6–20	* as impracticable for human use,
	13–13	Sin can have neither . . . thus *r·*,
'02.	3– 6	*r·* now more as a philosophy
My.	54–16	* had been *r·* as the church home,
	86–17	* *r·* as an extraordinary achievement,
	234–17	when *r·* on one side only,
	293–23	*r·* as wholly contingent on the
	309–15	slavery he *r·* as a great sin.
	324–21	* Mr. Wiggin *r·* you as quite
	324–25	* he *r·* you as entirely unique
	325– 9	* *r·* the old part of Boston

regarding
Mis.	98– 4	his contemplation *r·* himself
	130–13	acting thus *r·* disease
	146–10	facts *r·* both sides of the subject,
	288– 2	convictions *r·* what is best for
	352– 4	error of *r·* Life, Truth, Love as
Man.	109– 2	*R· Applications for Church Membership.*
Pul.	74– 5	* *r·* a statement made by
Hea.	8– 5	truth *r·* mind and body,
My.	116–18	truth *r·* an individual
	227– 2	*r·* that which he spake
	231–29	interesting report *r·* the By-law,
	297–29	are said to be circulating *r·* my
	310–17	*R·* the allegation by *McClure's*
	311–18	*r·* the McNeil coat-of-arms
	312– 4	*R·* my first marriage
	319–13	* confirm her statement *r·* the work
	320–26	* matters of detail *r·* your work,
	332–19	* *r·* Major Glover's membership
	335–11	* Additional facts *r·* Major Glover,

regardless
Mis.	172– 8	*r·* of the bans or clans
Hea.	7–20	*r·* of any outward act,

regards
Mis.	55–25	he *r·* God as the only Mind,
	68–28	* *r·* the ultimate grounds of being,
	288– 9	*r·* only one side of a question,
	362–15	*r·* creation as its own creator,
'00.	13–10	the apostle justly *r·* as heathen,
My.	86–27	* unprecedented, as *r·* numbers.
	159–28	thought chiefly *r·* material things,
	250–21	as *r·* its adaptability to their
	319–29	* as *r·* Mr. Wiggin.
	321– 8	* as *r·* your published works ;

regenerate
No.	9–12	that God will well *r·*

regenerated
Mis.	85– 5	*has he who is sick been r·?*
	85–25	and the mortal is not *r·.*
	107–15	before poor humanity is *r·*
Ret.	14–22	that I *had* been truly *r·,*

regenerates
Mis.	360–26	Truth that *r·* philosophy and logic ;
My.	287– 7	Divine Love reforms, *r·,*

regenerating
'01.	9– 5	only generating or *r·* power.
	30–16	religion and therapeutics need *r·.*
'02.	9–10	*r·* mankind and fulfilling the

regeneration
Mis.	73–23	*in the r· when the Son — Matt.* 19 : 28.
	73–27	*What is meant by r·?*
	85–12	*r·* leading thereto is gradual,
	85–16	last degree of *r·* rises into the
	85–26	pleasures . . . of sense, retard *r·* ;
	86– 3	This final degree of *r·* is saving,
	187– 1	spiritual *r·* of both mind and body,
My.	22–17	* has labored for the *r·* of mankind ;
	45– 4	* ultimate *r·* of its adherents
	352–15	* in the *r·* of mankind.

regenerative
Mis.	235– 9	This Science is ameliorative and *r·,*

régime
Mis.	160– 2	under the *r·* of C. S. !
	222–22	under this new *r·* of mind-power,
	348–23	this new *r·* of medicine,
'01.	20–23	this new-old *r·* of necromancy

regions
Pul.	76–16	* brought from the Arctic *r·.*

registered
Mis.	395–23	Is *r·* above.
Po.	58– 8	Is *r·* above.

registry
Pul.	vii– 9	*r·* of the rise of the mercury

regive
Pul.	20–10	*r·* the land to the church.

regret
Mis.	137– 9	I remember my *r·,* when,
	368–12	We *r·* to be obliged to say
Pan.	10–21	immorality, which, we *r·* to say,
'01.	25–11	*r·* their lack in my books,
My.	51– 6	* sincerely *r·* that our pastor,
	245–11	The growth of . . . I *r·* to say,

regrets
My.	40–28	* without *r·* and without resistance.

regretting
Mis.	274–11	Deeply *r·* the disappointment

regular
Mis.	69–15	to whom the *r·* physicians
	80–25	the lot of *r·* doctors,
	89– 6	*employing a r· physician,*
	243– 8	*r·* doctor had put on splints
	248–24	*r·* physician prescribed morphine,
Man.	51–11	are in good and *r·* standing
	56– 9	*r·* AND SPECIAL MEETINGS.
	56–10	*r·* meetings of The Mother Church
	56–21	*R·* meetings for electing
	57–10	(excepting its *r·* sessions)
	111– 9	There are two *r·* forms
Ret.	84–29	*r·* institute or place of labor,
	87–29	under the care of a *r·* physician,
Pul.	68–17	* now holds *r·* services
Rud.	14–27	a *r·* course of instruction
My.	8–16	* accommodation for the *r·* business
	171–20	* on her *r·* afternoon drive
	246– 3	in good and *r·* standing.

regularly
Ret.	87– 9	*r·* settled and systematic
My.	308–17	* *r·* beating the ground

regular-school
Mis.	349– 3	a certain *r·* physician,

regulate
Mis.	354–22	would *r·* God's action.
My.	222–23	laws to *r·* man's religion ;

regulated
My.	216– 8	*r·* by a government currency,

regulates
Mis.	232–12	standard of right that *r·* human
No.	18–26	*r·* the present high premium on

regulating
Peo.	10– 9	law *r·* the practice of medicine
My.	327–20	* act in the Legislature *r·* taxes,

regulator
Mis.	353–16	pour a bucket of water . . . on the *r·.*
	353–19	should steer the *r·* of mankind.
	353–21	*r·* is governed by the principle
	354–12	the children are tending the *r·* ;

rehearsal
Man.	47–15	More than a mere *r·* of blessings,
My.	291– 5	more to him than a mere *r·* of

rehearse
Mis.	396–13	My heart unbidden joins *r·* ;
Chr.	53–27	What can *r·* the glorious worth
Pul.	11– 6	*r·* your hearts' holy intents.
Po.	59– 5	My heart unbidden joins *r·,*

rehearsed
Pul.	57– 9	* It *r·* the significance of the

rehearsing
Mis.	311–31	*r·* facts concerning others
My.	269–24	*r·* : "I will rebuke the— *Mal.* 3 : 11.

reign
of Christianity
Mis.	345–17	* since the *r·* of Christianity began

of difficulties
Mis.	212–16	return under the *r·* of difficulties,

of divine Science
Mis.	174–23	heaven is the *r·* of divine Science :
My.	267–24	Heaven is the *r·* of divine Science.

of divine Truth
Man.	41–21	*r·* of divine Truth, Life, and Love

of harmony
Mis.	154–17	*r·* of harmony already within us.
	344–28	way to heaven and the *r·* of harmony.
Ret.	79–30	*r·* of harmony within us,
Un.	52– 7	the ever-present *r·* of harmony,

of heaven
Mis.	384–12	The *r·* of heaven begun,
'00.	15–29	The *r·* of heaven begun,
Po.	36–11	The *r·* of heaven begun,

of holiness
My.	228–16	kingdom of heaven, the *r·* of holiness,

of Mind
Mis.	51–25	* *r·* of Mind commence on earth,

of peace
Mis.	156–11	*r·* of peace and harmony

of righteousness
Mis.	125–10	*r·* of righteousness— within him ;
'01.	35– 8	call to the *r·* of righteousness,
My.	4–27	*r·* of righteousness, the glory of

of the Christ
My.	64–22	* the *r·* of the Christ

of Truth
My.	257–21	the *r·* of Truth and Life

of universal harmony
Mis.	134–19	the *r·* of universal harmony,

peace would
My.	279–15	one Mind, peace would *r·.*

prolongs the
Mis.	274–21	prolongs the *r·* of inordinate,

Mis.	94– 2	in the second, you will *r·* with him.
	125– 4	Then shall he also *r·* with him :
	157– 4	shall also *r·* with him." — *II Tim.* 2 : 12.
	157– 4	*R·* then, my beloved in the Lord.
	213–29	Love will *r·* in every heart,
Un.	57–24	to suffer with him is to *r·* with him.
Pul.	10–14	the wish to *r·* in hope's reality
My.	185–10	till Truth shall *r·* triumphant
	220–21	He whose right it is shall *r·.*
	283–19	When pride, self, and . . . *r·,*

reigned
Mis.	259–15	freedom reigned, and was the heritage

reigneth
Mis.	172–15	God omnipotent *r·.*" — *Rev.* 19 : 6.
	277–22	"The Lord *r·* ; — *Psal.* 97 : 1.
My.	184–28	Thy God *r·* !" — *Isa.* 52 : 7.
	278–12	divine Science, where right *r·.*

Reign of Terror
No.	44–20	It reassures us that no *R· of T·*

reigns
Mis.	80–22	God *r·*, and will
	331–27	*r·* in the realm of the real,
	368–28	not forget that the Lord *r·*,
	395– 5	The rose his rival *r·*,
Un.	63– 5	Love lives and *r·* forever.
'00.	10–21	hope anchors in God who *r·*,
Po.	22–21	Right *r·*, and blood was not
	57–12	The rose his rival *r·*,
My.	126–28	*r·* supreme to-day, to-morrow,
	182–21	Love that *r·* above the shadow,
	183– 7	* "When Christ *r·*, and not till then,
	254– 2	heaven opens, right *r·*,

reincarnation
Pul.	38–23	* philosophy of Karma and of *r·*,
My.	90–18	* *r·* of the old, old gospel

reinforces
My.	279– 6	C. S. *r·* Christ's sayings

reinstate
Mis.	10–16	and *r·* His orders,
Man.	17–12	should *r·* primitive Christianity
Peo.	14–18	*r·* man in God's own image
My.	46–12	should *r·* primitive Christianity

reinstated
My.	46–17	* requirement of a *r·* Christianity.

reinstating
'02.	3– 9	*r·* the old national family' pride

reiterate
Mis.	134– 5	*r·* such words of apology
Pan.	9– 1	*r·* the belief of pantheism,
'01.	8– 2	I *r·* this cardinal point :
'02.	10– 8	and *r·*, Let me alone.

reiterated
Mis.	212–10	remember the *r·* warning
'02.	5–20	*r·* in the gospel of Christ,

reiterates
Mis.	25–19	only as it *r·* the word,
Ret.	93–23	If C. S. *r·* St. Paul's teaching,

reject
Mis.	76–17	no man can rationally *r·*
	83–15	to *r·* or to accept this error ;
	191–31	St. Paul's injunction to *r·* fables,
	352–31	aroused to *r·* the sense of error ;
	395– 6	The stars *r·* his pains,
'00.	5–23	the builders *r·* for a season ;
'01.	25– 6	stone which the builders *r·*
	25– 6	The stone . . . which they *r·*
Po.	57–13	The stars *r·* his pains,
My.	344–16	* "Do you *r·* utterly the

rejected
Mis.	5–20	stone that the builders have *r·*,
	326–22	those who persistently *r·* him,
Man.	18– 1	which the builders *r·*,— *Matt.* 21 : 42.
	37– 9	If an application . . . is *r·*,
Pul.	10–19	which the builders *r·*,— *Matt.* 21 : 42.
No.	38–13	rock which the builders *r·* ;
'01.	9–18	yet Christ is *r·* of men !
Hea.	3– 9	stone which the builders *r·*
My.	48– 6	* the stone that had been *r·*,
	60–12	* which the builders *r·*'' — *Matt.* 21 : 42.
	122–31	the very hearts that *r·* it
	129–20	which the builders *r·*'' !— *Matt.* 21 : 42.
	188– 1	stone which the builders *r·*

rejection
Man.	37– 7	Notice of *R·*.
	37–11	notice of such *r·* ;
	37–13	report the cause for *r·*.
Un.	36–17	*r·* of the claims of matter
Pan.	12– 3	comes from the *r·* of evil

rejects
Mis.	25–13	*r·* all other theories of causation,
	245–26	*r·* apostolic Christianity,

rejoice
Mis.	18– 5	therefore *r·* in tribulation,
	120–16	*r·*, however, that the clarion call
	137–14	*r·* over the growth of my students
	152–14, 15	and *r·* with them that *r·*.
	277–22	let the earth *r·*." — *Psal.* 97 : 1.
	279– 6	I *r·* with those who *r·*,
	330–11	"*R·* in the Lord — *Phil.* 4 : 4.
	353– 1	consciousness be allowed to *r·* in
	368–28	*r·* in His supreme rule,
	370– 1	We *r·* to say, in the spirit of our
	398– 3	I will follow and *r·*
Ret.	9–22	* Shall I not *r·* That I have learned
	9–24	* I will *r·* !
	46– 9	I will follow and *r·*
	86– 3	*r·* in the spirit and power of C. S.,
Un.	5– 3	Rather will they *r·* in the
Pul.	9–23	Christians *r·* in secret,
	10–23	Let us *r·* that chill vicissitudes

rejoice
Pul.	12–11	Therefore *r·*, ye heavens, — *Rev.* 12 : 12.
	17– 8	I will follow and *r·*
	44–11	* we all *r·*, yet the mother in Israel,
	83–25	* We *r·* with her that at last
No.	8–15	*r·* that every germ of goodness
Pan.	14–27	Great occasion have we to *r·*
'01.	14–28	*r·* in the scientific apprehension of
	27–15	shall *r·* in being informed thereof.
	34–18	rejoicing with them that *r·* ;
'02.	3– 7	I *r·* that the President of the
	11–24	*R·*, and be exceeding glad : — *Matt.* 5 : 12.
Peo.	3–14	*r·* that the bow of omnipotence
	14–14	*r·* in hope ; be patient in tribulation,
Po.	14– 7	I will follow and *r·*
My.	6–11	*r·*, "for great is — *Matt.* 5 : 12.
	21–26	* *r·* in the glad reunion
	23–23	* We *r·* greatly that the walls of
	24–12	* *r·* in the unity of thought
	43–27	* *r·* that we have found in C. S.
	139–26	*R·* and be exceedingly glad,
	142–18	learn this and *r·* with me,
	157– 8	* *r·* that the prosperity of the Cause
	174–30	*r·* in the church triumphant
	183–18	*Brethren :* — I *r·* with you ;
	192–23, 24	"*r·* with them that do *r·*," — *Rom.* 12 : 15.
	199– 3	*Brethren :* — I *r·* with thee.
	201–23	I will follow and *r·*
	270– 1	"*R·*, and be exceeding glad : — *Matt.* 5 : 12.
	280– 7	* We *r·* also in this new reminder
	285– 7	I *r·* with you in all your wise
	295– 2	*r·* in knowing our dear God comforts
	339–21	*r·* in their present Christianity
	361–19	* We *r·* that our church has
	362– 4	I *r·* with you in the victory of
	362–19	* *r·* in your inspired leadership,

rejoiced
Ret.	24–18	and *r·* in my recovery,
Un.	57–23	*r·* that he was found worthy
My.	169–19	*r·* at the appropriate beauty

rejoices
Mis.	12–25	law of Love *r·* the heart ;
	241–25	*r·* in the gospel of health.
Pul.	13–12	*r·* in the proof of healing,
No.	7– 2	to be wise and true *r·* every
'02.	3–18	*r·* with our sister nation
My.	44–11	* *r·* in prophecy fulfilled,
	232– 1	*r·* me that you are recognizing
	253– 1	*r·* me to know that you

rejoiceth
No.	45– 6	*r·* in the truth." — *I Cor.* 13 : 6.
My.	159– 6	Christ *r·* and comforteth us.

rejoicing
Mis.	xi–21	reason for *r·* that the *vox populi*
	72–10	It is cause for *r·* that this belief
	213–19	But the faithful . . . have gone on *r·*.
Pul.	22– 5	It is matter for *r·* that we
No.	46–17	*r·*, as Paul did,
'01.	34–17	*r·* with them that rejoice ;
My.	37–32	* our *r·*, and our love
	63–17	* at every turn with words of *r·* ;
	76–10	* That it was received with *r·*
	125–22	stars in my crown of *r·*.
	148–20	joining in your *r·*,
	183–26	blending with thine my prayer and *r·*.
	229–23	their swift messages of *r·*
	260–19	understanding of joy and *r·*,
	274–25	this is my crown of *r·*,
	280– 3	* We acknowledge with *r·* the
	285–13	It is a matter for *r·* that the

rejuvenate
My.	125– 6	to *r·* the branches

rejuvenated
Mis.	ix–11	*r·* by the touch of God's

rejuvenation
Mis.	169–12	With . . . had come physical *r·*.

rekindle
Ret.	83–17	difficult to *r·* his own light

relapse
Rud.	9– 1	patient is liable to a *r·*,
No.	26–14	can no more *r·* or collapse
	30– 7	sickness and sin have no *r·*.
My.	165–24	a *r·* into the common hope.
	273–26	they lapse and *r·*, come and go,

relapsed
My.	307–26	case improved . . . but it *r·*.

relapsing
My.	121– 9	is neither tremulous nor *r·*.

relate
Mis.	333–20	harmonies of Spirit that *r·* to the
	350– 5	* "terrible and too shocking to *r·*."

relate

My.	50–17	* as the records further *r*·,
	223–22	which *r*· in any manner to the
	311– 1	I will *r*· the following incident,

related

Mis.	344– 2	It is *r*· of Justin Martyr that,
Ret.	1– 5	in some way *r*· to Hannah More,
Pul.	33– 6	* *r*· to her the story of Samuel,
	33–16	* Theodore Parker *r*· that when he was
My.	307–23	Had his remark *r*· to my personality,
	314–27	*r*· these facts to her just as I have

relates

Man.	67–13	if said case *r*· to the person
No.	10–15	What is termed matter, or *r*· to its

relating

Mis.	131–17	By-law *r*· to finances
	379–28	facts *r*· to Mind and its
Man.	81–18	*r*· to *The C. S. Journal.*
My.	124–25	facts *r*· to the thitherward,
	242–17	information *r*· to C. S. practice,
	330–15	* Mrs. Eddy's statements, *r*· to

relation

Mis.	4– 8	and their *r*· to each other.
	37– 8	Jesus recognized this *r*· so clearly
	173–10	this law has no *r*· to,
	181–21	his spiritual *r*· to Deity :
	218– 7	testimony of material sense in *r*· to
	235– 2	recognition of his *r*· to God.
	269–13	in *r*· to human events
	285–21	showing his *r*· to C. S.
Man.	46–16	*r*· of practitioner to patient.
	64–10	heading
	71–10	In its *r*· to other C. S. churches,
Un.	29– 1	Soul stands in this *r*· to
	51–25	scientific *r*· of man to God,
Rud.	16– 9	its scientific *r*· to Mind-healing,
No.	2–26	present ignorance in *r*· to C. S.
	36–15	his higher self and *r*· to the Father,
'01.	23–28	* "only the constant *r*· between
My.	64– 2	* our beloved Leader and her *r*· to
	70– 1	* in their *r*· to the city itself,
	160– 6	in constant *r*· with the divine,
	268– 6	marriage *r*· is losing ground,
	302–18	I stand in *r*· to this century as

relations

Mis.	68–22	* science of the conceptions and *r*·
	69– 2	His essence, *r*·, and attributes.
	287–24	Be faithful over home *r*·;
	290– 2	Let other people's marriage *r*· *alone:*
My.	74–25	* Our present *r*· with them are
	291–14	His home *r*· enfolded a wealth
	317– 3	* exactly defining her *r*· with
	321–14	* your *r*· to your published works
	361– 5	your *r*· with other students.

relationship

My.	8–18	* arithmetic and the *r*· of figures,
	114–17	strange coincidence or *r*· with

relative

Mis.	9–10	Wherein is this conclusion *r*· to
	36–22	all beliefs *r*· to the so-called
	146–24	will act, *r*· to this matter,
	147–23	the trusty friend, the affectionate *r*·,
	151–14	He is man's only real *r*·
	157–20	*r*· to Mrs. Stebbin's case.
	187–12	accepted as true *r*· to man.
	195–26	teachings of Jesus *r*· to healing
	291–21	*r*· to the true and unswerving
	310–11	*r*· to the return of members
	379– 3	anything pathological *r*· to
Ret.	1–14	no sign that she . . . was her *r*·.
	2–26	*r*· of my Grandfather Baker
Pul.	32–25	* Hannah More was a *r*· of
	48–20	* another distinguished *r*·,
No.	10– 4	*r*· to the unseen verities of being,
My.	51–25	* *r*· to this very early work
	190–18	as to the *r*· value, skill, and
	250– 3	*r*· to a three years' term
	303– 6	Scriptures *r*· to this subject.
	338–16	not allowed to consult me *r*· to

relatives

My.	294–30	his *r*· shed "the unavailing tear."
	331–19	* in behalf of the *r*· and friends

release

No.	7–19	will not *r*· them from the strict

released

Mis.	189–19	a *r*· sense of Life in God
My.	254– 7	*R*· from materialism, you shall run

relegated

'02.	2–20	dogmatism, *r*· to the past,
My.	285–11	shall be *r*· to oblivion.

relegates

My.	239– 4	*r*· Christianity to its primitive

relentless

Ret.	13–13	My father's *r*· theology

reliability

Mis.	228–25	without questioning the *r*· of its

reliable

Mis.	x– 8	and *r*· as old landmarks.
Hea.	16–21	shall we call that *r*· evidence
My.	12–21	If the *r*· *now* is carelessly lost
	121–12	*r*·, helpful, and always at hand.
	175–13	dear churches, *r*· editors,

reliance

Mis.	257–18	*r*· where there should be avoidance,
Ret.	28–13	Our *r*· upon material things
Un.	10– 9	utter *r*· upon the one God,
Pul.	35–17	Our *r*· upon material things
My.	211–22	*r*· where there should be avoidance,
	333–25	* and of his full *r*· for salvation

reliant

Mis.	87–21	who is most *r*· on himself

relief

Mis.	44– 7	*necessity for immediate r*·,
	70–26	and material sense of *r*· ;
	241–31	and who long for *r*· !
	262–16	giving to the sick *r*· from pain ;
	298–26	One says, "I find *r*· from
	377– 4	yet so near and full of radiant *r*·
Ret.	20–14	a vision of *r*· from this trial.
	24–19	explain the *modus* of my *r*·.
	31–13	ever-present *r*· from human woe.
	54– 7	and appeal to God for *r*·
Pul.	24–13	* inscription carved in bold *r*· :
	25–13	* galleries are in plaster *r*·,
	26– 5	* richly panelled in *r*· work.
	26–25	* pale green with *r*· in old rose.
Rud.	12–14	because the *r*· is unchristian
My.	56–17	* notwithstanding the *r*· that the
	267–22	*r*· from fear or suffering,
	345–16	homœopathy came like blessed *r*·

relieve

Mis.	262–29	*r*· my heart of its secrets,
	378–12	seemed at first to *r*· her,
Ret.	30– 8	It was to *r*· the sufferings of
	34–15	cures when they fail, or only *r*· ;
My.	20–10	May I *r*· you of selecting,
	56–10	* would *r*· the overcrowded condition
	358–16	to *r*· me of so much labor.

relieved

My.	138– 3	*r*· of the burden of doing this.
	329– 5	* *r*· the healers of this sect from

relieving

Mis.	273–10	so capable of *r*· my tasks
My.	214–18	*r*· the questioners' perplexity,

religion (*see also* religion's)

abound in
'01.	33– 7	* "Quackery and dupery do abound in *r*· ;

adopt a
My.	128–14	man's right to adopt a *r*·,

and art
My.	270–31	*r*· and art in unity and harmony.

and ethics
My.	114–31	pulpit and press, in *r*· and ethics,

and *materia medica*
My.	265–19	*r*· and *materia medica* should be

and medicine
Peo.	7–32	*R*· and medicine must be dematerialized
My.	221– 1	spirituality in *r*· and medicine
	340– 9	progress of *r*· and medicine

and philosophy
My.	248–27	*r*· and philosophy of labor, duty,

and scholarship
Ret.	87– 5	as obvious in *r*· and scholarship

and Science
Mis.	312–17	* harmony between *r*· and Science,

and therapeutics
'01.	30–16	Even *r*· and therapeutics need
My.	267– 1	the only *r*· and therapeutics

at the sick-bed
Hea.	18–24	and *r*· at the sick-bed will be

better
My.	221–15	or a better *r*· than his?

Christian
Pan.	6–23	if . . . the Christian *r*· has at least two
My.	220–18	Christian *r*· — Christ's Christianity.

Christian Scientist's
'01.	18–10	Christian Scientist's *r*· or his

claims on
Pan.	12–11	will make strong claims on *r*·,

contests over
Peo.	2–20	demoniacal contests over *r*·.

denominations of
Pul.	21–15	in all denominations of *r*·,

religion

devotees of a
   My. 76–28   * by the devotees of a *r·* which
essence of
   My. 178– 8   This Science is the essence of *r·*,
ethics, and
   My. 260–27   It leaves . . . ethics, and *r·* to God
evangelical
   Mis. 193– 9   evangelical *r·* can be established
          194–11   and misinterpret evangelical *r·*.
   Ret. 35–15   glow and grandeur of evangelical *r·*.
   '01. 12–17   and misinterpret evangelical *r·*.
form of
   Mis. 345–22   an advanced form of *r·*,
   My. 99–13   * whenever their form of *r·* is
forms of
   '02. 16–24   merely outside forms of *r·*,
forward steps in
   '00. 4–12   new and forward steps in *r·*,
heathen
   '00. 3–29   animus of heathen *r·* was not the
her
   My. 346– 6   * presenting another view of her *r·*.
his
   Ret. 92– 1   method of his *r·* was not too simple to
   My. 270–28   quarrel with a man because of his *r·*
in this century
   '01. 33–25   proof that a *r·* in this century is
Jewish
   Mis. 65–30   The Jewish *r·* demands that
        260– 6   Grecian philosophy, or Jewish *r·*,
   Ret. 65–15   Jewish *r·* was not spiritual ;
Judean
   Mis. 82– 2   reconstructs the Judean *r·*,
       166–18   The Judæan *r·* even required
leaders of
   '01. 32–18   those old-fashioned leaders of *r·*
lees of
   My. 301– 6   by which the lees of *r·* will
life and
   Mis. 374– 8   demanded Christianity in life and *r·*.
life of
   '01. 33–11   * not the health and life of *r·*,
man's
   My. 222–24   make laws to regulate man's *r·* ;
material
   Mis. 17–10   more material *r·* with its rites and
   '01. 34–14   material *r·*, proscriptive, intolerant,
   My. 110– 6   material *r·*, material medicine,
materialistic
   No. 246–29   spiritual . . . or a materialistic *r·*
medicine and
   No. 44– 5   demonstration of medicine and *r·*.
   '02. 2–17   ethics, medicine, and *r·*,
   Peo. 5– 1   practice of medicine and *r·*,
medicine, or
   Mis. 26– 1   philosophy, medicine, or *r·*,
metaphysical
   Peo. 3–19   metaphysical *r·* founded upon C. S.
morals and
   Man. 83– 6   of morals and *r·*, healing and
Mosaic
   Pan. 7–20   a lapse in the Mosaic *r·*,
name of
   Pul. 7–18   committed in the name of *r·*.
   My. 258– 4   Nothing is worthy the name of *r·* save
national
   Peo. 8–12   definite form of a national *r·*,
nearest right
   Hea. 2– 1   *r·* nearest right is that one.
Neoplatonic
   '00. 4– 8   Babylonian and Neoplatonic *r·*,
new
   Mis. 179–13   In the new *r·* the teaching is,
   My. 29–22   * A comparatively new *r·*
        86– 7   * the hosts of a new *r·*.
       87–25   * world turned to the new *r·*.
new-old
   '01. 30–21   establishment of a new-old *r·*
of growth
   My. 95–24   * no *r·* of growth and vitality
of Jesus Christ
   My. 8–10   * expression of the *r·* of Jesus Christ,
of pagan priests
   Mis. 123–10   ultimates in a *r·* of pagan priests
of to-day
   Ret. 65–16   If the *r·* of to-day is constituted
old
   Mis. 178–30   old *r·* in which we have been
one
   Hea. 1–20   one *r·* has a more spiritual basis
or medicine
   Mis. 260–10   potency, in *r·* or medicine.
   My. 288–16   instrumentality in *r·* or medicine.

religion

or philosophy
   Mis. 363–22   sensual *r·* or philosophy
   My. 117–23   never a *r·* or philosophy lost
or science
   My. 303–24   not the sport of . . . *r·*, or science ;
perfect
   '00. 4–16   rational that the only perfect *r·* is
philosophy and
   Mis. 64–18   the only philosophy and *r·* that
   Ret. 31–29   philosophy and *r·* melted,
       57–24   systems of philosophy and *r·*
philosophy, or
   My. 4–32   true, in ethics, philosophy, or *r·*,
      220–24   future philosophy or *r·*,
practical
   My. 168– 3   practical *r·* in agreement
practice of
   Peo. 2– 3   theory and practice of *r·*
profession of
   Ret. 14–17   made any profession of *r·*,
progressive
   My. 340–32   learning and progressive *r·*
prospers
   My. 93–10   * *r·* prospers according to
question as to
   '00. 4–22   The question as to *r·* is:
reform in
   '01. 30–14   reform in *r·* and in medicine,
scientific
   My. 265–16   that scientific *r·* and
sense of
   Pan. 3– 2   the Christian sense of *r·*.
shall permeate
   My. 222–24   *r·* shall permeate our laws.
spiritual
   Mis. 365–16   a more spiritual *r·*
   No. 18–22   a more spiritual *r·*
   Hea. 1–11   more practical and spiritual *r·*
spiritualizes
   Mis. 252–24   spiritualizes *r·* and restores its
stages of
   '01. 33– 8   * decaying stages of *r·*,
status of
   Mis. 357– 9   above the present status of *r·*
stole into
   Hea. 3–11   material element stole into *r·*,
such a
   My. 348–14   writer's departure from such a *r·*
superficial
   No. 46– 5   material medicine and superficial *r·*?
system of
   Mis. 284– 5   than any other system of *r·*, morals,
      296– 1   Founder of this system of *r·*,
   My. 129– 4   and a lax system of *r·*.
      258– 3   lifts a system of *r·* to deserved fame
systems of
   Mis. 27– 9   other systems of *r·* abandon their
   '00. 5–26   foundation of all systems of *r·*.
   Peo. 4–26   Systems of *r·* and of medicine
   My. 216– 5   All systems of *r·* stand on
their
   Ret. 87–12   their *r·* demands implicit
   No. 44–14   dungeon or stake for their *r·*,
tribal
   My. 288–14   pagan mysticisms, tribal *r·*,
true
   Mis. 336–22   cognomen of all true *r·*,
   My. 181–13   possessed the motive of true *r·*,
tyrannical
   Pul. 6– 4   a national or tyrannical *r·*,
undefiled
   Mis. 98–20   pure and undefiled *r·*
      320–28   to-day christening *r·* undefiled,
   Ret. 71–20   according to pure and undefiled *r·*.
   No. 46–16   Puritan standard of undefiled *r·*.
unhealing
   Ret. 65–30   an unspiritual and unhealing *r·*.
vitality to
   Ret. 66– 3   C. S. gives vitality to *r·*,
war on
   My. 234–24   But a war on *r·* in China would be
which heals
   My. 28–22   * a *r·* which heals the sick
your
   Mis. 345– 9   * unless you yield your *r·*,"

   Mis. 25– 6   the *r·* that Jesus taught
      123–10   a *r·* that demands human victims
      232– 8   Why, then, should *r·* be stereotyped,
      251–11   loyal to the heart's core to *r·*,
      327–11   in worldly policy, *r·*, politics,
      366–18   in the field of medicine and of *r·*,
   Man. 28– 8   nations, individuals, and *r·* are
      48– 9   towards *r·*, medicine, the courts, or

religion

Pul.	5–28	is the leaven fermenting *r·* ;
No.	45–15	In natural law and in *r·*
Pan.	3–21	In *r·*, it is a belief in one God,
	4–12	In academics and in *r·*
	9– 8	Is there a *r·* under the sun that
'01.	19–13	either in medicine or in *r·*,
'02.	2–12	*r·* in the United States has
	3– 6	more as a philosophy than as a *r·*.
	5– 5	*r·* parting with its materiality.
My.	70– 3	* a *r·* which has been organized only
	99– 4	* a *r·* that makes the merry heart
	203– 5	*r·* should be distinct in our
	355–12	a strong supporting arm to *r·*

religionists (*see also* **religionists'**)

Mis.	187–31	transcribed by pagan *r·*,
Ret.	2– 4	gave those *r·* the poetic
	82–24	fall short of other *r·* ;
'00.	4–23	Do *r·* believe that God

religionists'

Mis.	248–13	"*R·* mistaken views of

religion's

Mis.	25–15	It is *r·* "new tongue," — *see Mark* 16 : 17.

religions

Pan.	7–13	chapter sub-title
	7–14	We know of but three theistic *r·*,
	7–16	Does not each of these *r·*
'00.	13–26	* amalgamation of different pagan *r·*
'02.	2–10	purifying all peoples, *r·*, ethics,
	3– 3	cords of non-Christian *r·*
	5– 3	tribal *r·* of yesterday
	10–17	*R·* in general admit that man
	14–22	popular philosophies and *r·*
Hea.	1–20	difference between *r·* is,
	2–23	this proof . . . that *r·* had not given.
	19–17	We need it to stamp our *r·*
Peo.	3–25	It has implanted in our *r·*
My.	127–11	*r·* since the first century.
	166– 6	*R·* may waste away,

religious

Mis.	xi–19	shuttlecock of *r·* intolerance
	4–22	so that its *r·* specialty
	38– 8	education, secular and *r·*,
	122–24	Neither . . . nor a *r·* chancery
	145– 3	*r·* element, or Church of Christ,
	174– 9	touches the *r·* sentiment
	206– 2	revolutions, natural, civil, or *r·*,
	241– 1	From a *r·* point of view,
	246– 5	through civil and *r·* reform,
	246– 8	interests of wealth, *r·* caste,
	246–26	Shall *r·* intolerance,
	251–13	civil and *r·* freedom,
	251–27	all error, physical, moral, or *r·*,
	297– 3	*r·* and pathological systems
	307–15	In this revolutionary *r·* period,
	310–26	receding year of *r·* jubilee,
Man.	61–20	of an appropriate *r·* character
Ret.	5– 3	was a very *r·* man,
	15– 4	My connection with this *r·* body
	30– 9	include all moral and *r·* reform.
	70–28	civil, moral, and *r·* reform.
Un.	7– 5	in multitudes of other *r·* folds.
	15–21	found in heathen *r·* history.
Pul.	20–18	moral, physical, civil, and *r·*
	32–27	* her mother was a *r·* enthusiast,
	36– 6	* deeper foundation of her *r·* work
	43–28	* personal worship which *r·* teachers
	50–16	* This particular phase of *r·* belief
	50–24	* so-called orthodox *r·* bodies
	50–25	* No one *r·* body holds the whole of
	51–10	* searching after *r·* truth.
	51–17	* produced a sensation in *r·* circles,
	51–21	* many a new project in *r·* belief
	51–29	* demonstrations of *r·* belief
	63–16	* a new phase of *r·* belief,
	67– 9	* census of the *r·* faiths
	68– 9	* for the interests of her *r·* work
	79–23	* that requires the *r·* sentiment
	80– 4	* *r·* sentiment in women is so strong
No.	12– 9	the author's *r·* experience.
	14–20	more than any other *r·* sect,
	15–10	civil and *r·* arms in their defense ;
	40–25	change in the *r·* views of the patient
	44–23	horrors of *r·* persecution.
	45–20	its moral and *r·* reforms.
Pan.	2–21	to which the *r·* sentiment is
	10–22	other *r·* teachers are unable to
'00.	3–30	has it not tainted the *r·* sects?
	7– 4	Likewise the *r·* sentiment has
	10–12	*r·* rights and laws of nations
'01.	22–22	the different *r·* sects
	30– 2	even as all other *r·* denominations
'02.	1–16	systems of *r·* beliefs and opinions
Hea.	2– 3	*r·* factions and prejudices arrayed

religious

Peo.	9– 7	as compliance with a *r·* rite
My.	8–28	* Leader of our *r·* denomination
	49– 5	* The *r·* body which can direct,
	59–11	* nearly every *r·* and scientific body
	89–27	* growth of this form of *r·* faith
	89–29	* the greatest *r·* phenomenon
	89–30	* *r·* movement of international sway ;
	90– 5	* in the history of *r·* expression.
	91–18	* most remarkable *r·* movements
	93–25	* economy of our social and *r·* life.
	95–30	* demonstration of *r·* faith
	98– 9	* such as *r·* annals hardly parallel
	100–13	* organization among *r·* bodies,
	112– 8	Our *r·* denominations interpret
	116– 6	In time of *r·* or scientific prosperity,
	163–27	I respect their *r·* beliefs,
	167–22	chapter sub-title
	167–27	*r·* rights in New Hampshire
	177– 9	presence at your *r·* jubilee.
	270– 6	my first *r·* home in this capital
	271–24	* who, whatever their *r·* beliefs,
	273– 1	* it has no *r·* opinions
	294–25	*r·* energy of this illustrious pontiff
	300–31	opening fire on their own *r·* ranks,
	301– 5	The present flux in *r·* faith
	311–14	my *r·* experience seemed to
	340– 5	seasons for *r·* observances
	340–23	to recur to a *r·* observance
	348–11	*r·* departure from divine Science
		(*see also* **liberty**)

religiously

Mis.	203–13	Theology *r·* bathes in water,
My.	284–24	*r·* opposed to war,

relinquish

Mis.	31–17	to *r·* his faith in evil,
	353– 8	*r·* your human concept of me,
Man.	72–20	If . . . Mrs. Eddy, should *r·* her
Un.	49–27	commands mortals to shun or *r·*,
My.	40–12	* *r·* their cherished resentments,
	200–24	*r·* its league with evil.

relinquished

Mis.	64– 5	*r·* his earth-task of teaching
	297–22	unless such claims are *r·* by
'01.	24–29	I *r·* the form to attain the

relinquishing

My.	140–19	*R·* a material form of

relinquishment

Mis.	340– 1	*r·* of right in an evil hour,

relish

Mis.	9–25	our failure longer to *r·* this
	224–19	keen *r·* for and appreciation of

relishes

Mis.	226– 2	* "Give the child what he *r·*,

reluctance

Ret.	37–21	My *r·* to give the public,

reluctant

My.	10–19	* basis of fretful or *r·* sacrifice

reluctantly

Pul.	34–13	* and *r·* they did so,
	88– 9	articles are *r·* omitted.
My.	103– 1	perfection is *r·* seen
	129– 3	I *r·* foresee great danger

rely

Pul.	69–10	* *r·* on Mind for cure,
Hea.	4–26	can we *r·* on our model?
	16–19	how can we *r·* on their testimony

relying

Mis.	115–22	necessity for *r·* on God
	354–20	Instead of *r·* on the Principle
Hea.	5–22	*r·* not on the person of God

remain

Mis.	2–24	but should *r·* in error,
	234– 2	*r·* no longer to blind us
	240–14	let it *r·* as harmlessly,
	243– 9	bandages to *r·* six weeks,
	249–14	None are permitted to *r·*
	265–32	*r·* until suffering compels the
	387–19	make men one in love *r·*.
Man.	62–13	no pupil shall *r·* in the
	68– 4	notified to *r·* with Mrs. Eddy
	68–14	Those . . . who *r·* with her
	69– 2	a signed agreement to *r·*
	76– 2	should *r·* on safe deposit,
	91– 2	not allow it or a copy of it to *r·*,
Un.	34–23	Nothing would *r·* to be seen
Pul.	2–20	*r·* within the walls
	82–28	* *r·* deaf to their cry?
'02.	2–24	Then why not *r·* friends,
Hea.	4– 3	nor *r·* for a moment within limits.
Po.	6–14	make men one in love *r·*.

remain

My.	4–29	The height of my hope must *r·*.
	51–10	* hope she will *r·* with us.
	51–17	* *r·* with us for a few Sundays
	68–15	* church . . . will *r·* as it was,
	108–28	I *r·* steadfast in St. Paul's faith,
	138–21	I *r·* most respectfully
	175–16	*r·* with us a little longer,
	175–25	must *r·* so long as I *r·*.
	178–28	would *r·* immortal.
	190–28	would *r·*, even as it did,
	195–29	grant that this unity *r·*,
	217–10	This sum is to *r·* on interest
	226–17	would *r·* the forever fact,
	243–16	*r·* in their own fields
	276– 8	a preference to *r·* within doors
	311– 6	begged to be allowed to *r·*

remained

Mis.	130– 1	so long as a hope *r·*
	216–21	* which *r·* some time after the
	379–30	there *r·* the difficulty of
Man.	75–21	*r·* in the hands of the Directors,
Ret.	5–10	and there the family *r·*
	20– 3	*r·* with my parents until
	76–27	I have long *r·* silent
Un.	63– 6	*r·* forever in the Science of being.
Pul.	43–25	* *r·* at her home in Concord,
	60–13	* many having *r·* over a week
My.	11–27	* still *r·* for definite decision
	145–14	He *r·* at work, and the next
	336–14	*r·* with my parents until

remainder

Mis.	355–15	for the *r·* only stimulates
No.	8–14	*r·* thereof He will restrain.
'02.	1–13	*r·* of wrath shalt Thou — *Psal.* 76 : 10.
My.	151–11	*r·* of wrath shalt Thou — *Psal.* 76 : 10.
	207– 5	*r·* thereof He will restrain.

remaineth

Mis.	144–23	rest that *r·* for the righteous,
	216– 3	There *r·*, it is true, a
	357–16	what *r·* has fallen into the good and
'02.	19–17	*r·* a rest for the righteous,

remaining

Mis.	210– 6	and the *r·* third kills itself.
	256–11	*r·* at present a public servant :
Man.	80–20	*r·* trustees shall fill the vacancy,
Peo.	12–18	we shall take in the *r·* two thirds
My.	12– 9	* decision of these *r·* problems.
	75–29	* expense . . . *r·* unprovided for,

remains

Mis.	7–26	greater work yet *r·* to be done.
	23–12	and the command *r·*,
	76– 6	and *r·* to be demonstrated;
	100–10	so long as there *r·* a claim of
	129–14	let silence prevail over his *r·*.
	145–21	visible unity of spirit *r·*,
	372– 4	fact *r·*, that the textbook of
Ret.	33–21	Mind, the curative Principle, *r·*,
	82– 2	law of the chord *r·* unchanged,
Un.	62– 1	when the fact really *r·*,
No.	13–13	*r·* a clear and profound deduction
	25–20	*r·* to be learned.
	28– 2	How long this false sense *r·*
Hea.	6–20	But the fact *r·*, in metaphysics,
	12–25	when the drug disappears . . . power *r·*,
My.	6–20	The room of your Leader *r·*
	124–18	but it *r·* for Science to reveal
	190–20	*r·* beyond questioning a divine
	193– 5	privilege *r·* mine to watch
	295– 4	*r·* in the minds of men,
	303–28	What I am *r·* to be proved
	312–26	long procession, followed the *r·*
	326–19	bore his *r·* to their last
	333–17	* Major Glover's *r·* were carried North.
	333–26	* *r·* were interred with Masonic
	335–22	* to take the *r·* to Charleston.
	347– 3	What *r·* to lead on the centuries
	348–28	Science *r·* the law of God

remake

My.	288–29	We cannot *r·* ourselves,

remark

Pul.	63– 9	* *r·* Rev. Mary Baker Eddy, . . . made
My.	307–23	Had his *r·* related to my

remarkable

Mis.	125–28	*r·* achievements that have been ours
Ret.	83– 3	accomplishing . . . to a *r·* degree.
Pul.	27– 8	* windows are a *r·* feature of
	29–10	* whose *r·* earnestness impressed the
	31– 2	* certainly a very *r·* retrospect.
	55– 7	* Of our *r·* nineteenth century
	56–13	* one of the most *r·*, helpful,
	63–14	* This is a *r·* statement,
	63–15	* but it is made by a *r·* woman,

remarkable

Pul.	66– 7	* has grown with *r·* rapidity,
	70– 4	* R· Career of Rev. Mary Baker Eddy,
	70–11	* most *r·* women in America.
	79–16	* two reasons for this *r·* development,
No.	36–10	*r·* words, as wholly opposed to
'02.	14–13	*r·* growth and prosperity of C. S.
My.	70–13	* The effect on all . . . is quite *r·*.
	78–21	* One of the *r·* features of the
	79–26	* making their *r·* statements
	82–28	* departing with such *r·* expedition,
	84–19	* It is a *r·* story
	85– 1	* *r·* in the character of the
	86–26	* The attendance . . . was *r·*,
	88–16	* *r·* external manifestations
	89–13	* A *r·* thing in this building is
	91–17	* one of the most *r·* religious
	91–25	* Its growth in numbers is *r·*,
	94–16	* *r·* growth and the apparent
	96–16	* *r·* feature, perhaps the most *r·*,
	98–15	* a rather *r·* announcement
	100– 3	* as *r·* in their aggregate
	271–25	* personality of this *r·* woman.
	273– 3	* *r·* proof of Mrs. Eddy's ability
	273– 8	* guiding with *r·* skill,
	287– 5	used in a *r·* degree
	307–22	he was a *r·* man.

remarkably

Ret.	42–11	*r·* successful in Mind-healing,
Pul.	47–30	* *r·* well placed upon a terrace
My.	99–11	* a *r·* optimistic body of people,

remarked

Ret.	19–20	was *r·* by all observers.
Pul.	37– 1	* *r·* Mrs. Hanna,
My.	24–24	* have been *r·* by the many visitors
	330–31	was *r·* by all observers.

remarks

Mis.	32– 5	*r·* on "*Christ and Christmas*"
	176– 5	Extempore R·
	312–12	in his *r·* before that body,
	379–10	from his *r·* I inferred that
Man.	32–20	shall make no *r·* explanatory of
	32–22	shall read all notices and *r·*
My.	170– 6	The brevity of my *r·* was due to
	185–26	closing my *r·* with the words of

remeasured

Mis.	222–21	measure . . . must be *r·* to it.

remedial

Mis.	4– 3	potent and desirable *r·* agent
	44– 8	*r·* power of C. S.
	379–14	was not as potential or *r·*,

remedies

Mis.	96– 6	no other gods, no *r·* in drugs,
	209– 2	as its antidotes and *r·*.
	334–27	Science *r·* the ills of
Ret.	33–10	*r·* enumerated by Jahr,
Un.	14–10	as Burgess, the boatbuilder, *r·*
Hea.	12–15	two hundred and sixty *r·*
My.	283–14	*r·* for all earth's woe.

remedy

Mis.	2–18	found alone the *r·* for sin,
	44–29	By applying this mental *r·*
	45–14	demands the *r·* of Truth
	63– 9	*r·* for the opposite triad
	97–15	is not a *r·* of faith alone,
	195– 1	any other *r·* than Christ,
	200–24	to seek the *r·* for it,
	221–10	Truth is their *r·*.
	236–24	*r·* for all human discord.
	371– 7	behold the *r·*, to help them
Un.	18–12	I could not *r·* them,
Pul.	6–18	* false *r·* I had vainly used,
'01.	18–12	no *r·* apart from Mind,
Hea.	11–22	Mind came in as the *r·*,
	12–17	symptoms requiring the *r·*,
	15– 4	no other *r·* than Truth,
My.	118– 6	*r·* is worse than the disease.
	292–24	not mixed with morphine to *r·*

remember

Mis.	2– 9	*r·* that God is just,
	108–25	R·, and act on, Jesus' definition
	137– 9	I *r·* my regret, when,
	138–14	R· that the first and last
	146– 1	'T is sweet to *r·* thee,
	175–32	*r·* God in all thy ways,
	211–22	let him *r·*,
	212–10	*r·* the reiterated warning
	224–11	*r·* that the world is wide ;
	237–29	I *r·*, when a girl,
	267– 9	*r·* that there never was a time
	268–28	R· that human pride forfeits
	281–29	*r·* the words of Solomon,
	282– 4	R·, it is personality, and the

remember
Mis.	331–15	*r· their* cradle hymns,
	335– 2	*R·* the Scripture :
	335–28	*r·* the Scripture concerning
	338–15	*r·*, a pure faith in humanity
	339–24	*R·*, that for all this thou alone
	356–12	*r·* that the seedtime is passed,
	359–24	*r·* that Science is demonstrated by
Ret.	1– 8	I *r·* reading, in my childhood,
	6– 6	I *r·* as one with the open hand.
	86–10	Behold its vileness, and *r·*
Pul.	7– 9	*r·* also that God is just,
Pan.	14–19	*r·* our brave soldiers,
'00.	8–15	*r·* that sensitiveness is sometimes
'01.	18–28	*r·* it is He who does it
	19–16	*r·* that the great Metaphysician
	29–21	*r·* that mother worked and won
Hea.	4– 8	We pray for God to *r·* us,
	10– 8	*r·* that God — good — is omnipotent ;
Po.	33– 1	To daily *r·* my blessings
My.	12–10	* Each person interested must *r·*,
	39–23	* We *r·* her graciousness and dignity.
	60– 6	* Possibly you may *r·* the words of
	149–31	*R·*, thou canst be brought into no
	154–10	*r·* it is not he who gives the
	194– 6	*R·* that a temple but foreshadows the
	259–17	churches will *r·* me only thus.
	267– 8	Here let us *r·* that God is
	313–11	Nor do I *r·* any such stuff
	323–28	* I wonder if you will *r·*
	324–11	* I *r·* telling you of this,
	351–14	grand in you to *r·* me as the

remembered
Mis.	91–17	Be it *r·*, that all types employed
	284–21	It must also be *r·* that neither
My.	126–16	hath *r·* her iniquities — *Rev.* 18 : 5.
	284– 5	but 'tis sweet to be *r·*.

remembers
Mis.	100–28	Who *r·* that patience, forgiveness,
Pul.	46–18	* souvenirs that Mrs. Eddy *r·*
My.	331–15	* she *r·* the Rev. Mr. Reperton,

remembrance
Mis.	58– 1	*no r· of that disease or dream,*
	91–15	mental conditions, — *r·* and love ;
	184–12	brings to *r·* the Hebrew strain,
	386–25	"By the *r·* of her loyal life,
Po.	34– 5	Some dear *r·* in a weary breast.
	50–11	"By the *r·* of her loyal life,
My.	166–13	proof of your *r·* and love.

remind
'00.	14–15	to *r·* you of the joy you have had
My.	110–15	*r·* me of my early dreams of flying

reminded
Mis.	212– 7	*r·* his students of their worldly
Pul.	48–16	* she paused and *r·* the reporter

reminder
My.	39–20	* a few words of *r·* and prophecy.
	262–20	Christmas to me is the *r·* of God's
	280– 8	* We rejoice also in this new *r·*

reminds
Mis.	176–14	*r·* us of the heroes and heroines
My.	322–13	* *r·* me of a conversation I had with

reminiscences
Ret.	6– 9	Among the treasured *r·*
Pul.	46– 8	* In Mrs. Eddy's personal *r·*,
My.	306–21	chapter sub-title

remit
My.	332–11	* or *r·* his kind attention until

remits
My.	161– 8	never *r·* the sentence necessary

remodelled
Pul.	47–28	* delightfully *r·* and modernized
My.	55–23	* Chickering Hall was to be *r·*.

remodelling
My.	145– 7	*r·* of the house was finished,

remonstrated
Pul.	30– 3	* when a Boston clergyman *r·*

remorse
Pul.	33–10	* This caused her tears of *r·*
My.	267–23	lost opportunities and *r·*.

remorseless
Mis.	10– 5	the most *r·* motives
	72–11	as false as it is *r·*.

remorselessly
Mis.	339–25	Carelessly or *r·* thou mayest

remote
Mis.	200–15	*r·* from the general comprehension
Ret.	7–13	* corner, however hidden and *r·*.
Un.	26– 4	my forms, near or *r·*.

remote
Hea.	3–16	a *r·* province of Judea,
My.	152–29	*r·*, predisposing, and present cause

remoteness
Peo.	5–11	not lost in the mists of *r·*

removal
Mis.	67–27	If you refer to the *r·* of a person
	67–30	this *r·* being possible
Man.	30– 5	*R·*.
	65–19	*r·* of the offending member
	82–10	*R·* of Cards.
	100– 9	*R·* from Office.
Ret.	21– 1	After his *r·* a letter was read
Pul.	37– 5	* factor in her *r·* to Concord,

remove
Mis.	xii– 1	to *r·* the pioneer signs
	66–30	can neither *r·* that cause nor
	90– 4	*r·* all reality from its power.
	108–15	would *r·* mortals' ignorance
	219–16	if he would *r·* this feeling
	237– 8	but *r·* that fear,
	245–16	should *r·* with glorious results.
	249–19	something to *r·* stains or vermin.
	308–33	to *r·* from their observation
	328–25	Whatever obstructs . . . Love will *r·* ;
	355–24	discern the error . . . and *r·* it,
	362–23	to *r·* this mental millstone
	370– 5	how they might *r·* him.
Man.	51–22	power to . . . *r·* from membership,
	54–23	shall *r·* his or her name
	100–17	to *r·* its Committee on Publication
Pul.	13–26	torture it may take to *r·* all sin,
Rud.	10–17	*R·* this fear by the true sense
'00.	12–19	*r·* thy candlestick — *Rev.* 2 : 5.
Peo.	7–24	To *r·* those objects of sense
	9–24	*r·* all evidence of any other
My.	61– 5	* to *r·* human obstructions
	194– 3	fell forests and *r·* mountains,
	222–11	*R·* hence — *Matt.* 17 : 20.
	222–12	and it shall *r·*." — *Matt.* 17 : 20.
	223–28	burdens that time will *r·*.
	290–27	will *r·* the sackcloth from thy home.
	301–27	Drugs cannot *r·* inflammation,

removed
Mis.	69–19	I *r·* the stoppage,
	70– 9	When the . . . belief, was *r·*,
	74–23	he *r·* any supposition that
	243–10	*r·* these appliances the same day
	261– 5	can only be *r·* by reformation.
	378–22	are farther *r·* from such thoughts
Man.	30– 7	he or she shall be *r·*
	46–23	liability to have his name *r·*
	82–11	*r·* from our periodicals
	103– 6	nor *r·* from the site
Ret.	5– 9	my parents *r·* to Tilton,
	20–28	The family . . . very soon *r·* to
	94–15	every spot and blemish . . . is *r·*,
Pul.	36–20	* Several years ago Mrs. Eddy *r·*
'01.	13–23	only as the sin is *r·*
Hea.	19– 8	*r·* the bandage from his eyes,
My.	15– 8	nor *r·* from the site
	55–24	* church *r·* to Copley Hall
	163–17	When I *r·* from Boston
	255– 8	I do not mean that . . . should be *r·*

removes
Un.	2–10	and, lastly, it *r·* the pain
	39–11	divine Science *r·* human weakness
Rud.	10–22	*r·* every erroneous physical and
No.	12–26	It *r·* all limits from divine power.
'01.	10–15	metaphysics *r·* the mysticism
	13–22	*r·* the punishment for sin only as
My.	107–31	stops decomposition, *r·* enteritis,
	131– 2	*r·* fear, subdues sin,
	278–11	faith that *r·* mountains,

removeth
Mis.	174– 7	Him who *r·* all iniquities,

removing
Mis.	1–19	by *r·* the dust that dims them.
	41–23	*r·* the cause in that so-called mind
	221–11	*r·* the effect of sin on himself,
Un.	25–15	*r·* its evidence from sense to Soul,
No.	30–15	*r·* our knowledge of what is not.

remuneration
Mis.	349–24	before I would accept the slightest *r·*.
Man.	91– 7	*R·* and Free Scholarship.
Rud.	14– 9	seven-eighths of her time without *r·*,
My.	214–20	taking no *r·* for my labors,

remunerator
Mis.	212–23	Love, the white Christ, is the *r·*.

Renaissance
Pul.	26–10	* lamp stand of the *R·* period
My.	68– 1	* Built in the Italian *R·* style,

renaissance
'00.   4–12   indicate a r· greater than
rend
  Mis. 211–20   and turn on you and r· you?
  Un.   23– 6   to turn again and r· their Maker.
  No.   8–25   lest it turn and r· you ;
  My. 227–25   turn again and r· you."— *Matt.* 7 : 6.
render
  Mis. 45–10   r· this Science invaluable in the
      230–28   to r· it pathetic, tender, gorgeous.
      277–28   be just . . . and r· good for evil.
  Man. 77– 9   shall r· them payable.
  Ret. 71– 5   "*R·* to Cæsar the things— *Mark* 12 : 17.
  My. vii–14   * service which all . . . can r·
      202– 8   "*R·* therefore to all their — *Rom.* 13 : 7.
      220– 9   '*R·* to Cæsar the things — *Mark* 12 : 17.
      220–11   r· 'to God the things that — *Mark* 12 : 17.
      344–25   '*R·* to Caesar the things — *Mark* 12 : 17.
rendered
  Mis. 75–22   r· in Science, "My *spiritual sense*
      76–16   r· void by Jesus' divine declaration,
    182–29   made flesh,— that is, r· practical,
  Un.   39– 2   Truth of Life is r· practical
     57–14   and r· this infallible verdict ;
  Pul. 42– 9   * was r· particularly interesting
  No. 37–25   Jesus r· null and void whatever
  '*02.* 16– 4   r· in the Authorized Version
  My. 62–27   * valuable services r· to this Board
rendering
  Mis. 80– 2   By r· error such a service,
    169–22   The literal r· of the Scriptures
    169–24   The metaphysical r· is health and
    344– 9   so r· it a fit habitation for
  '*02.* 16– 7   combination of words, or of their r·.
  My. 116–19   r· praise to whom praise is due,
    150– 7   * r· the world happier and better
renderings
  My. 179–24   different r· or translations
renders
  Mis. 262–26   and r· the yoke easy.
    333– 6   r· error a palpable falsity,
    374–24   one r· not unto Cæsar
  Man. 41–16   r· this member liable to
  Un. 53–10   belief that r· them obscure.
  Rud. 13– 5   r· it impossible to demonstrate
    15– 9   r· the mind less inquisitive,
rends
  Mis. 165–12   Science which r· the veil
    203–21   state of mind which r· the veil
    364–31   C. S. r· this veil
  No. 21–20   C. S. r· this veil
renew
  Mis. 312–25   and r· its emphasis
    364– 6   will r· your strength."— *see Isa.* 40 : 31.
  My.   9–15   * we modestly r· the hope
    38– 5   * r· the story of our love for you
    291–20   shall reverberate, r· euphony,
renewal
  No. 14– 9   r· in the Neoplatonic philosophy ;
renewed
  Mis. 34– 7   body is r· and harmonious,
  Ret. 82– 2   yet their core is constantly r· ;
  Pan. 11– 5   r· in knowledge— *Col.* 3 : 10.
  '*02.*   5– 2   r· energy for to-morrow,
  My. 13–23   r· like the eagle's,"— *Psal.* 103 : 5.
    64–23   * address ourselves with r· faith
    157–13   * r· evidence of your unselfish
    202–16   r· vision, infinite meanings,
renews
  Mis. 130–28   r· his strength, and is exalted
  My. 316– 4   r· the heavenward impulse ;
renounce
  Pul.   5–10   firmest to suffer, soonest to r·.
  '*01.* 32–12   willing to r· all for Him.
renounced
  Mis. 238–22   Have you r· self?
  Ret. 43–14   having r· his material method
  My. 123–32   r· the hidden things — *II Cor.* 4 : 2.
renovate
  '*02.* 16–25   they reach not the heart nor r· it ;
renovated
  Ret. 34–20   this mind must be r·
  Un.   6– 6   human nature will be r·,
renown
  My. 271–20   * aged woman of world-wide r·
renowned
  Pul.   6–29   r· apostle of anti-slavery,
  My. 177–16   In your r· city, the genesis of
    291–26   mourn the loss of her r· leader !

rent
  Mis. 124–24   r· the veil of matter,
  Man. 30–17   taxes and r· on this property ;
    68–12   in addition to r· and board.
  '*02.* 14– 4   can neither r·, mortgage, nor sell
  Po. 72– 1   O not too soon is r· the chain
reobtain
  Pul. 20– 7   and r· its charter
reorganize
  Pul. 20– 6   r· the church, and
reorganized
  Man. 18–14   Church members met and r·,
  My. 55–15   * r· the church, and named it The
repair
  Man. 30–20   keep the property in good r·,
repairing
  My. 175– 7   to aid in r· your church
repairs
  My. 123–17   r· and other necessary expenses
repartee
  Ret. 77– 4   Ingersoll's r· has its moral :
repay
  Mis. 130–15   will r·, saith the Lord."— *Rom.* 12 : 19.
  Po. 32–17   That health may my efforts r· ;
repays
  Mis. 257–14   r· our best deeds with sacrifice
repeal
  Peo. 12–11   r· it in mind, and acknowledge only
repealed
  Mis. 272– 5   * "This Act was r· from
  Man. 18–27   By-Laws pertaining to . . . were r·
repealing
  Mis. 272– 9   * r· of said Act in January, 1882.
repeat
  Mis. 42–19   we shall not have to r· it ;
    92–13   r· the questions in the chapter on
    120– 6   or r· their work in tears.
    135– 2   Again I r·, person is not in the
    168–17   nineteenth-century prophets r·,
    211–31   Shall we r· our Lord's Prayer when
    275–12   r· with quivering lips words of
    314– 9   r· in concert with the congregation
    314–27   unnecessary to r· the title or page.
    346–24   rule in C. S. never to r· error
    348–18   r· this,— that I use no drugs
    391–21   When angels shall r· it,
  Man. 51– 5   if he r· the offense,
  Ret. 10– 6   latter I had to r· every Sunday.
  Un. 44– 3   I can only r· the Master's words :
    48– 2   to r· my twice-told tale,
  Pul.   8– 5   church chimes r· my thanks
  No. 32– 5   pardon may encourage a criminal to r·
    41– 9   r· his work to the best advantage for
  '*02.*   4– 3   I again r·, Follow your Leader,
  Po. 38–20   When angels shall r· it,
  My. 32– 4   * began to r· the Lord's Prayer,
    171– 1   In parting I r· to these
    201–11   r· my legacies in blossom.
    240–15   I now r· another proof,
    270– 5   we r· the signs of these times.
    285–20   In the words of St. Paul, I r· :
    355– 9   I will r· that men are very important
repeated
  Mis. 65– 2   by r· proofs of its falsity.
    134– 4   an act which you have immediately r·,
    196– 5   has r· itself in all manner of
    351–15   r· attempts of mad ambition
  Man. 58–14   r· at the other services on Sunday.
  Ret. 8–19   the same call was thrice r·.
    9–17   never . . . was that mysterious call r·.
  Pul. 36–19   * always with this experience r·
    40–12   * THE SERVICE *R·* FOUR TIMES
    40–16   * simple ceremonies, four times r·,
    41–20   * Hence the service was r·
    42– 5   * service was r· for the last time.
    59– 8   * these exercises four times r·.
    59–12   * The *Pater Noster* was r·
  No.   9–14   Hoping to pacify r· complaints
  '*01.* 31–23   Lord's Prayer, r· at night ;
  Hea. 16– 2   can never be r· too often
  My. 29–11   * r· six times during the day.
    86–30   * services, r· at intervals
    332–28   * but on r· search a roll of papers
    333–24   * r· assurance of his willingness to
repeatedly
  Ret. 8– 4   I r· heard a voice,
  Pul. 45–18   * r· asseverated to the contrary.

repeating
Mis. 150–12 to-day are r· their joy
206–21 r· this diapason of heaven :
Un. 44– 6 are vain shadows, r·
Pul. 59–13 * congregation r· one sentence
My. 148–22 what is each heart in this house r·,

repeats
Mis. 23–28 r· precisely the looks and actions of
25–20 reiterates the word, r· the works,
253–15 r· the past and portends much
Chr. 53–14 What the Beloved knew . . . Science r·,
Pul. 25–24 * wainscoting r· the same tints.
39–20 * splendor of the sky R· its glory
No. 41– 3 History r· itself.
'00. 10–17 History shows that error r· itself
Hea. 1– 6 History r· itself ;
My. 58– 6 * "History r· itself."

repent
Mis. 94– 6 must r·, and love good
123–24 r·, forsake sin, love God,
237–10 Some people never r· until
'00. 12–20 except thou r·." — Rev. 2 : 5.
'01. 15– 2 r· and forsake it,
My. 195– 8 it is never too late to r·,

repentance
Mis. 93–26 without r· and reformation.
107–16 (1) A proper sense of sin ; (2) r· ;
107–26 and of r· therefor,
107–29 r· so severe that it destroys them,
108–17 advance the second stage . . . r·.
109–11 r· is the most hopeful stage
109–21 and its consequences, r·,
109–31 and thus, cometh r·,
110– 1 R· is better than sacrifice.
203–19 The baptism of r· is
205– 7 fire of r· first separates the dross
205–25 r· and absolute abandonment
244–13 bodily penance and torture, or r·
261– 7 are not cancelled by r·
Un. 14– 1 such planks as the divine r·,
14–16 might need r·, because
'00. 15– 9 over a tear-filled sea of r·
'02. 19–14 listens to the lispings of r·
Peo. 9– 4 tears of r·, an overflowing love,
My. 36–16 * joy of r· and the peace of
128– 4 r· from dead works." — Heb. 6 : 1.
150–21 bringing the sinner to r·,
228–20 with tears of r·

repentant
Man. 55–14 Although r· and forgiven
'01. 17– 6 loves even the r· prodigal

repented
Mis. 18–29 causes much that must be r· of
107–27 deep, never to be r· of,
109–14 one's sins be seen and r· of,
Man. 39–12 evidence of having genuinely r·
'00. 3–27 r· himself, improved on his work

repenteth
Peo. 8– 3 If changeableness that r· itself ;

Reperton, Rev. Mr.
My. 331– 6 * Rev. Mr. R·, a Baptist clergyman,

repetition
My. 17–25 * audible r· of the Lord's Prayer
19– 6 * r· of "the scientific statement of
32– 1 * unanimity and r· in unison
32–17 * audible r· of the Lord's Prayer
32–30 * audible r· of the Lord's Prayer.
39–12 * audible r· of the Lord's Prayer,
56– 5 * a r· of the morning service.
78–20 * audible r· of the Lord's Prayer.

repetitions
My. 56–30 * being r· of the first service.

repine
My. 258–21 r· over blossoms that mock

replace
Un. 7–13 able to r· dislocated joints and

replenish
Mis. 56–26 and r· the earth," — Gen. 1 : 28.
92– 8 His work is to r· thought,
117–26 r· his lamp at the midnight hour
149– 7 and r· your scanty store.

replenished
Mis. 341–26 if the lamp she tends is not r·

replete
Ret. 2–18 printed in olden type and r· with
Po. 29–13 Beloved, r·, by flesh embound
My. 70–14 * church is r· with rare bits of art,

repletion
Pul. 41–22 * filled the church to r·.

replied
Mis. 178–20 * I should have r·, 'Much learning'
180– 9 "Christ never left," I r· ;
226–19 he r·, "Not to be credited
281–14 He r· to his wife, who urged him
344– 5 "Very well," the teacher r· ;
345– 9 r· : "Let them come ;
381–14 and he r·, in substance,
Man. 98– 3 not been r· to by other Scientists,
Ret. 14–24 I r· that I could only answer
Pul. 30– 6 * he r· that the C. S. Church
31–21 * she most kindly r·, naming an
Peo. 13–19 he r· : "Let them come ;
Po. v–19 * she r· by reading the poem
My. 60– 3 * I have r· that if Mrs. Eddy
220– 9 questioned . . . he r· :
241–23 * I r· that I did not live in
324–30 * When we asked him . . . he r·

replies
Mis. 317– 2 my heart r·, Yes,
346–11 To this question C. S. r· :
367–29 r· that God is too pure to
372–16 such r· as the following :
My. 223– 5 r· to letters which pertain to
240–23 * r·, through her student,

reply (noun)
in
Mis. 35–28 In r·, we refer you to "S. and H.
158– 2 In r· to your letter I will say :
321–24 In r· to all invitations
Pul. 34–26 * said, in r· to my questions,
My. 172–20 * In r· Mr. Bates said,
204–14 IN R· TO A LETTER ANNOUNCING
214–16 In r· to letters questioning
276–21 * In r· to a number of requests
277– 3 * In r· to your question,
356–13 In r· to inquiries,
just
Man. 93–12 just r· to public topics
Mrs. Eddy's
Pul. 87–10 * heading
My. 142– 7 chapter sub-title
207– 6 * chapter sub-title
207–20 heading
241–13 * and Mrs. Eddy's r· thereto.
241–18 * The question and Mrs. Eddy's r·
242– 1 heading
255– 4 heading
271–23 * Mrs. Eddy's r· will be read
281–26 heading
352–18 heading
361–15 * chapter sub-title
362– 1 heading
362– 9 * chapter sub-title
363–13 heading
my
Mis. 244–17 Will he accept my r·
287–23 the substance of my r· is :
My. 195– 7 have hitherto prevented my r·.
311–12 My r· to the statement that the
no
Mis. 137–11 I received no r·.
recent
My. 305–27 My recent r· to the reprint
to Mark Twain
My. 302–13 chapter sub-title
to McClure's
My. 308– 5 chapter sub-title

Mis. 95– 7 * which r· was taken in full by
Ret. 34– 6 the r· was dark and contradictory.
No. 46– 7 halts for a r· ;
My. 73– 8 * the r· will be in the form of
271–21 * requesting the courtesy of a r· :

reply (verb)
Mis. 95– 6 * ten minutes in which to r·
193– 3 we r· in the affirmative
353– 7 I r·, The human concept
Man. 98– 6 purpose of having him r· to it.
Ret. 9–10 to r· as he did,
Pul. 33– 8 * to r· as he did :
33–10 * was afraid and did not r·.
33–11 * promised to r· if the call came
'01. 12– 7 he would naturally r·,
Po. 35–11 heart whereunto none r·,
My. 156– 3 to r· in words of the Scripture :
242–22 nor to r· to any received,
251– 5 I r· to the following question

report
Mis. 44–21 That matter can r· pain,
128–10 things are of good r· :— Phil. 4 : 8.
131–13 is prepared to itemize a r·
159–14 are pure and of good r·,
171– 7 according to the r· of some,

report

Mis.	183–20	hath believed our *r·*?"— *Isa.* 53 : 1.
	249– 8	false *r·* that I have appropriated
	249–20	The *r·* that I was dead
	267– 8	When they *r·* me as *"hating*
	277–19	truth of Benjamin Franklin's *r·*
	299– 8	I have no time for detailed *r·*
	330–19	learn what *r·* they bear,
	340–21	through evil or through good *r·*,
Man.	26–25	shall neither *r·* the discussions
	37–12	to *r·* the cause for rejection.
	48–17	shall not *r·* for publication
	55– 2	shall not *r·* nor send notices
	66–11	duty of the Clerk to *r·* to her
	66–24	shall not *r·* on authority
	76– 7	*R·* of Directors.
	76–10	*r·* at the annual Church meeting
Un.	39– 9	hath believed our *r·*?"— *Isa.* 53 : 1.
Rud.	10–14	cannot feel, see, or *r·* pain
My.	8–29	* "Since the last *r·*, in 1900,
	16– 1	* chapter sub-title
	16– 2	* *r·* of Mr. Stephen A. Chase,
	22– 2	* *Extract from the Clerk's R·*
	23– 9	* *Extract from the Treasurer's R·*
	25–10	* taken from the *r·* of the secretary
	47– 1	* heading
	47– 7	* to present in this *r·* a few of the
	53–25	* annual *r·* of the business committee
	125– 5	It requires you to *r·* progress,
	143–10	I have the pleasure to *r·* to
	144– 6	public *r·* that I am in either of the
	231–29	interesting *r·* regarding the By-law,
	234–16	The *r·* of the success of C. S. in
	249–22	The *r·* that I prefer to have a
	275–13	Permit me to say, the *r·*

reported

Mis.	168–24	* *The C. S. J. r·* as follows :
	248–19	that I am dead, as is oft *r·*.
	248–20	alleged to have *r·* my demise,
	298– 4	as we be slanderously *r·*,
	311–30	Being often *r·* as saying
	330–20	*r·* more spiritual growth.
Man.	78–23	Such payments shall be *r·*,
Pul.	72– 4	* *r·* deification of Mrs. Eddy,
My.	178–31	all else *r·* as his sayings are
	298– 5	not a little is already *r·* of the
	310–20	*r·* by physician or post-mortem

Reporter, The

Pul.	70– 1	* *The R·*, Lebanon, Ind.,

reporter

Mis.	95– 8	* shorthand *r·* who was present,
Pul.	48–16	* she paused and reminded the *r·*
	49– 9	* the *r·* exclaimed :
	72– 5	* a *Post r·* called upon a few of
	73–26	* She referred the *r·* to the

reporting

Mis.	44–22	or that mind is . . . *r·* sensations,
	311–32	others who were *r·* false charges,
My.	220– 7	*r·* of a contagious case to the

reports

Mis.	274–15	chapter sub-title
	297–11	the public cannot swallow *r·* of
Man.	56–15	*r·* of Treasurer, Clerk, and
	56–16	general *r·* from the Field.
	66–23	Unauthorized *R·*.
Pul.	73–24	* in the *r·* from New York
'00.	2– 8	close observer *r·* three types of
My.	99–19	* press *r·* state that the
	174–11	for their *r·* of the happy occasion.
	243– 2	According to *r·*, the belief is
	333–31	* "We are assured that *r·* of
	334– 3	* newspaper *r·* of that date

repose

Mis.	128– 2	uncomfortable whereon to *r·*.
	340– 3	*r·* from many a heart.
Ret.	17– 9	peers out, from her crimson *r·*,
	18– 8	sentinel hedgerow is guarding *r·*,
Po.	41– 4	the lambkin soft virtue's *r·*,
	62–10	peers out, from her crimson *r·*,
	63–17	sentinel hedgerow is guarding *r·*,

reposes

Hea.	15– 7	it *r·* all faith in mind,

reposing

My.	152– 8	By *r·* faith in man

repository

Mis.	236– 4	*r·* of little else than

repossess

My.	201–12	hope *r·* us of heaven.

represent

Mis.	91–18	*r·* the most spiritual forms
	266– 7	may *r·* me as doing it ;
Ret.	82–19	*r·* an accumulation of power

represent

No.	33–18	was inadequate to *r·* the
My.	45–10	* *r·* only a small part of the
	95– 6	* *r·* the intelligence of many

representation

Un.	54–23	a *r·* that God both knew

representations

Mis.	55–19	Spirit and its forms and *r·*,

representative

Mis.	61– 2	*r·* of verities priceless,
	87–13	mortal mind is a poorer *r·*
	305– 2	* *r·* from each Republic
	305– 3	* *r·* from the patriotic
My.	30–30	* *r·* of the entire body
	227– 3	he spake as God's *r·*
	281–20	* views by *r·* persons.
	327–21	* *r·* men of our dear State

representatives

Mis.	200– 5	the better *r·* of God
My.	74–28	* *r·* of the two poles of healing,
	112–22	better *r·* of C. S. than
	207– 7	* *r·* of churches and societies

represented

Mis.	186–29	Adam *r·* by the Messias,
	295–22	not wholly *r·* by one man.
Pul.	13– 1	Life, *r·* by the Father ;
	13– 2	Truth, *r·* by the Son ;
	13– 2	Love, *r·* by the Mother.
'01.	10–13	*r·* both the divine and the
Hea.	10– 7	manhood of God, that Jesus *r·* ;
My.	24–22	* fifteen different trades *r·*.
	239–16	*r· by His idea or image*

representing

Mis.	140– 5	*r·* the true nature of the gift ;
	305– 1	* women *r·* each State
	305– 9	* *r·* the National Society
Pul.	27–12	* *r·* the heavenly city
	27–27	* *r·* John on the Isle of Patmos,
My.	100– 9	* *r·* a vast number of the followers

represents

Mis.	46–25	man *r·* his divine Principle,
	46–27	sound, in tones, *r·* harmony ;
	104–25	and its idea *r·* Love.
	164– 4	idea that *r·* divine good,
	336– 8	Do you love that which *r·* God
Man.	49– 8	member of The Mother Church who *r·*
	54–20	*r·* falsely to or of the Leader
Ret.	63–14	*r·* God, the Life of man.
Pul.	27–16	* other rose window *r·* the
	27–25	* *r·* the raising of Lazarus.
	28– 2	* central panel *r·* her in solitude
	81–14	* She *r·* the composite beauty,
Rud.	4–10	All true Science *r·* a moral
No.	26–13	All real being *r·* God,
My.	23–25	* the worship of Spirit,
	24– 6	* vastness of the truth it *r·*,
	77– 3	* novelty of the cult which it *r·*.
	118–26	*r·* not the divinity of C. S.,
	172–13	save that which it *r·*
	259–29	*r·* the eternal informing Soul

repress

My.	63–16	* to *r·* a feeling of exultation

repressed

Mis.	250– 9	should be *r·* by the sentiments.

repression

Pul.	50–28	* and live down any attempted *r·*.

reprint

My.	305–27	My recent reply to the *r·*

reprinted

My.	29– 1	* *R·* from *Boston Herald*
	363–17	*R·* in *C. S. Sentinel,*

reproach

Mis.	228–17	and honest beyond *r·*,
My.	33–20	nor taketh up a *r·*— *Psal.* 15 : 3.
	53– 2	* inquiry and mercantile *r·* ;

reproachable

Mis.	147–30	than attain it by *r·* means.

reproaches

Mis.	199–11	*in infirmities, in r·,— II Cor.* 12 : 10.
	201–20	pleasure in "*r·*"— *II Cor.* 12 : 10.

reproduce

Mis.	360–12	nor can it *r·*, these stars of the
	372–24	to *r·*, with reverent touch,

reproduced

Mis.	165–30	treasures *r·* and given to the world,
	201– 9	Jesus *r·* his body after its burial,
	337–30	is again *r·* in the character which
Pul.	32– 6	* expression cannot thus be *r·*.
My.	272–22	* *r·* in her own handwriting.
	347–14	*r·* her primal presence,

reproduces
Mis. 364–32   r· the divine philosophy of Jesus
Un. 26– 3   *Evil. . . . and matter r·* God.
No. 21–21   r· the teachings of Jesus,

reproduction
Mis. xi– 5   r· of what has been written,
375–31   * thing of the past, impossible of r·.

reproductions
Pul. 49– 5   * has hung its walls with r of
My. 70–16   * Millet's "Angelus" had living r·
342– 9   * so often seen in r·,

reproof
Mis. 126–20   No r· is so potent as the silent
Ret. 80–17   he will not scorn the timely r·,

reprove
No. v– 3   "r·, rebuke, exhort,"— *II Tim.* 4 : 2.
My. 130–17   my students r·, rebuke, and

reptiles
Mis. 210– 9   warning people not to stir up these r·
Un. 52–21   rabid beasts, fatal r·, and
My. 245–12   poisonous r· and devouring beasts,

Republic
Mis. 305– 2   * one representative from each R·
My. 341– 3   child of the R·, a Daughter of

Republic, The
Pul. 63– 1   * The R·, Washington, D. C.,

Republican
Pul. 88–21   * R·, Springfield, Mass.

republish
Mis. x– 7   and r· them in book form,

republished
Man. 82– 8   published nor r· by this Society

repudiated
Mis. 97– 9   r· the idea of casting out

repudiates
Hea. 15– 1   r· the evidences of the senses

reputable
My. 100–15   * a class who are r·, intelligent,
237–17   equal to those of r· physicians

reputation
My. 52–22   * Mrs. Eddy's future r·,
138–11   My personal r· is assailed

reputations
Mis. 274–24   legislation, and decapitated r·,

reputed
Ret. 6–16   r· one of the most talented,

request
Mis. x– 5   comply with an oft-repeated r· ;
127– 8   and again earnestly r·,
133– 7   I r· you to read my sermons
306–19   * r· of the late Mrs. Harrison,
319–20   and grant me this r·,
Man. 18–13   r· of Rev. Mary Baker Eddy,
26–23   A majority vote or the r· of
67–25   r· of the Pastor Emeritus,
82–11   without the r· of the advertiser,
94–15   written r· of Mrs. Eddy,
100– 6   if she shall send a special r·
100– 7   r· shall be carried out
100–21   to comply with this r·.
Ret. 45–16   in accord with my special r·,
Po. 33– 2   And make this my humble r· :
My. 18– 5   and again earnestly r·,
130–31   r·, that you borrow little else
139–19   purpose of my r· was sacred.
170– 3   r· of my church members
182– 4   at my r· I received from the
216–22   r· that from this date you disband
217–15   my r· as above named.
236–24   I r· the Christian Scientists
256– 8   my r· that I be permitted
279–22   I r· that every member of
280–16   I now r· that the members
280–28   In no way nor manner did I r·
298– 1   r· the privilege of buying,
307– 2   which I, at his r·, had added
328–22   * r· of a prominent healer

requested
Mis. 49– 2   r· her to withdraw
157–10   r· that they furnish
158– 5   r· you to be ordained,
381–10   r· her lawyer to inquire
Man. 53–11   without her having r· the
Pul. 34–12   * r· those with her to withdraw,
Po. v–21   * each r· a copy,
vii– 5   * r· her publisher to prepare a few
My. 27–15   * r· to send no more money
98–16   * r· to send no more money
169– 7   are r· to visit me at a later
242–21   I have r· my secretary not to

requested
My. 332–22   * r· to look up the records
339– 7   specially r· to be wise

requesting
My. 271–21   * r· the courtesy of a reply :

requests
Mis. 155–19   she hereby r· : First, that you,
Man. 30–12   Unless Mrs. Eddy r· otherwise,
Po. v–22   * Similar r· continued to reach the
My. 276–21   * In reply to a number of r·

requiem
Mis. 395–25   A r· o'er the tomb
Po. 58–10   A r· o'er the tomb

requiems
Ret. 4–18   wandering winds sigh low r·

require
Mis. 4–25   "It must r· a great deal of faith
39– 4   would r· the understanding of how you
51– 4   drugs, God does not r·.
54–23   r· an understanding of the Science
91–30   r· their pupils to study the lessons
92–19   r· the students thoroughly to study it
92–22   teacher should r· each member to
196–30   Scriptures r· more than a simple
197– 1   they r· a living faith,
301–14   r· only a word to be wise ;
358–20   Be it understood that I do not r·
Man. 66–20   r· all of it to be read ;
Ret. 6–13   would r· more space than
Pul. 62–12   * r· but little muscular power
Rud. 14–17   expect and r· others to pay him.
My. 177– 7   daily duties r· attention elsewhere,
217–29   not r· the last step to be . . . first.
244–24   may not r· more than one lesson.
259–15   r· less attention than packages
358–31   r· the C. S. Board of Directors

required
Mis. 4–27   there is no will-power r·,
43–18   time is r· thoroughly to qualify
88– 4   the less this is r·, the better
91–27   as occasion r·, read from the book
148–14   and as the occasion r·.
166–18   The Judæan religion even r·
235– 3   r· and empowered to conquer sin,
283–32   The only personal help r·
334–25   understanding is r· to do this.
Man. 3–10   and as the occasion r·.
56–13   its officers are r· to be present.
62– 2   offertory conforming to the time r·
65– 9   Obedience R·.
68–23   Agreement R·.
74–17   churches and societies are r· to
89–15   such credentials as are r·
109–13   as r· by Article V, Sect. 6,
110– 1   new applications will be r·,
110–17   in all places where they are r·.
Un. 11–24   Jesus r· neither cycles of time nor
Pul. 62–10   * r· a strong man to ring them,
Rud. 15–27   as are r· to empty and to fill anew the
Pan. 11– 1   r· the divinity of our Master
'01. 25–14   or r· in such metaphysics,
My. 14–14   * entire amount r· to complete
43– 5   * might know what was r· of them,
65–14   * Learning that a big church was r·,
77–28   * the two million dollars r·
98–19   * all of the funds r· to build it
212– 9   than has been r· to put down
245–24   these credentials are still r·
328–14   * license . . . r· of physicians,
328–15   * has been r· of them,

requirement
Mis. 4–19   adequate to meet the r·.
77– 9   Philip's r· was, that he should
181– 8   personal r· of blind obedience
181–10   unless that r· should express
Man. 51–14   Preliminary R·.
77–18   God's R·.
110– 2   This r· is to prevent
My. 46–17   * r· of a reinstated Christianity.

requirements
Mis. 261–19   divine r· typified in the law
346–21   grasped in all its divine r·.
Man. 29– 8   fulfil the r· of this By-Law,
39– 1   to live according to its r·
51–15   r· according to the Scriptures,
72–25   R· for Organizing Branch Churches.
Pul. 50–22   * thoroughly carried away with the r·,

requires
Mis. ix–17   r· strength from above,
6–21   r· time to overcome the patient's
14– 9   imperfection that r· evil
40–29   it r· more divine understanding
68– 3   it r· both time and eternity.

requires
Mis.	246– 4	r· the enlightenment of these
	366– 4	it r· more study to understand
	367– 2	This Science r· man to be honest,
Man.	44–26	God r· our whole heart,
	77–18	God r· wisdom, economy,
Un.	43–10	r· time and immense spiritual
Pul.	15– 8	r· the spirit of our blessed Master
	79–23	* r· the religious sentiment
Rud.	9–15	r· a preparation of the heart
No.	11–18	it r· more study to understand
	33– 8	r· sacrifice, struggle, prayer,
	34–20	heathen conception that God r·
Hea.	3– 1	Christianity r· neither hygiene nor
	11–26	r· mind imbued with Truth
	12–20	To prepare the medicine r· time
My.	125– 5	r· you to report progress,
	175– 4	r· my constant attention and time,
	220– 8	when the law so r·.
	276– 7	When accumulating work r· it,

requiring
Hea.	12–17	moral symptoms r· the remedy,
My.	91– 8	* r· their church edifices to be fully

requisite
Mis.	x–14	where these are most r·,
	16– 8	r· to become wholly Christlike,
	67–30	after all the footsteps r·
	136–25	oftener is not r·,
	145– 6	r· to manifest its spirit,
	148–18	r· to demonstrate genuine C. S.,
	181– 6	r· in order to understand
	195– 9	spirit and the letter are r· ;
	257–18	fear where courage is r·,
	270–16	r· for healing the sick.
	317–12	is not absolutely r·
	346–25	unless it becomes r·
	359– 2	is r· in the beginning ;
	380– 9	were r· to enable me
Man.	3–15	r· to demonstrate genuine C. S.,
	43– 9	Whatever is r· for either
Ret.	10– 4	less labor than is usually r·.
	45– 7	r· only in the earliest periods
	45–11	r· in the first stages
	76– 3	nor . . . copyright be r·,
	79–20	wisdom r· for teaching
	81–29	r· at every stage of advancement.
Un.	40–19	A sense of death is not r·
Pul.	54–10	* conditions r· in psychic healing
Rud.	12–20	r· for the well-being of man.
My.	26–23	this notice is r· to give
	238–15	became r· in the divine order.
	279– 1	never r·, never a necessity,
	285– 6	cannot spare the time r·

requisition
Pul.	62–20	* They can be called into r·

rescue
Mis.	107– 7	come to the r· of mortals,
	134–19	Firm in your . . . go to its r·.
	218–17	Truth comes to the r·
	293– 8	will come, . . . to the r·
	362–22	must come to the r· of mortals,
Un.	59–19	Jesus came to r· men from
Pul.	9–12	came to the r· as sunshine
No.	7–14	find r· and refuge in Truth
	11–25	r· reason from the thrall of
'02.	13–16	and I came to the r·,
Po.	71–13	God to the r·
My.	350– 8	came to the writer's r·,

rescued
Mis.	140–22	had to be r· from the grasp
	211–14	r· from the merciless wave
Ret.	14– 8	converted and r· from perdition ;
Pul.	66–11	* r· from death miraculously
Po.	71– 8	R· by the "fanatic" hand,

research
Mis.	114– 5	should spare no r·
	116–20	scientific r· and attainment
	223– 4	at length took up the r·
Ret.	33– 1	physical side of this r· was
Pul.	23–21	* scholars of special r·,
	47–11	* physical side in this r·
My.	348– 4	induced a deep r·,

researches
Mis.	169– 2	all along the way of her r·

resemblance
Mis.	375–21	* I find an almost identical r·,
No.	21–27	has little r· to Science,
My.	96–10	* The one point of r· is that the

resemble
Mis.	376– 5	* very closely r· in detail the
Po.	v–12	* r· *the profile of a human face.*

resembles
Mis.	167– 9	compound idea of all that r· God.
No.	26– 8	or the human belief r· the
My.	310–32	* it so r· the author."

resembling
No.	23– 2	To conceive of God as r·

resenting
My.	204–25	hypnotism, and the r· of injuries,

resentment
Mis.	137–25	pride, envy, evil-speaking, r·,
	224–30	an object of pity rather than of r· ;
'02.	19– 8	Christian Scientist cherishes no r· ;

resentments
My.	40–12	* relinquish their cherished r·,

reservations
My.	345– 4	do not suppose their mental r·

reserved
My.	38–17	* was specially r· for them.
	159–30	All rights r·.
	164–27	This unity is r· wisdom and strength.

reserves
Mis.	119–27	individual rights which one justly r·
Man.	80–18	Pastor Emeritus r· the right to

reserving
My.	vi–26	* r· for herself only a place for

reset
Mis.	242– 7	if either would r· certain dislocations

reside
Mis.	120–21	r· a long distance from Massachusetts,
	247–21	believe it to r· in matter of the brain ;

resided
Ret.	5–18	for many years had r· in Tilton
	20–10	r· in the northern part of
Po.	vi–24	* *during the years she* r· *in Lynn,*
My.	312–18	r· in Charleston, S. C.
	335– 3	* Brother Glover r· in Charleston,

residence
Mis.	225– 2	At the r· of Mr. Rawson,
	249–17	since my r· in Boston ;
	294–25	Since my r· in Concord,
Man.	30–11	First Reader's R·.
Pul.	37– 6	* where she has a beautiful r·,
	68–11	* r· in her native State.
	68–17	* the r· of the pastor,
My.	27– 4	Assemble not at the r· of
	284–18	Since my r· in Concord,
	333–11	* the r· of the deceased,

residences
Pul.	36–23	* one of the most beautiful r·

resident
Pul.	8–23	r· youthful workers were called
	15– 1	good r· in divine Mind,
My.	330– 9	* not then a r· of Wilmington.
	335–12	* a r· of Charleston, S. C.,

residents
My.	82–29	* not be noticeable to the r·

residing
My.	83– 4	* r· in the convention city.

resign
Man.	28–21	notify this officer either to r·
	29–11	Directors shall r· their office or
	89– 2	Should the President r·
	94–20	A member shall neither r· nor
My.	167–27	teaches us to r· what we are not
	195–13	r· with good grace what we are denied,

resignation
'02.	17–28	Patience and r· are the pillars of
My.	51– 7	* feels it her duty to tender her r·,

resigned
Pul.	71–19	* Mrs. Eddy has r· herself
Hea.	13–19	we r· the imaginary medicine
My.	276–10	try to be composed and r·

resist
Mis.	64–20	r· speculative opinions and fables.
	114–17	r· the foe within and without.
	141– 7	for no one can r· the power
	223–18	what we would r· to the hilt
	278–20	seem stronger to r· temptation
Ret.	80–14	it may stir the human heart to r·
My.	212–21	r· the animal magnetism

resistance
Mis.	74–28	conquered the r· of the world.
Pul.	80– 8	* sought the line of least r·.
Rud.	3– 4	r· to all efforts to save them
'01.	15–10	r· to C. S. weakens in proportion
My.	8– 7	* beyond r· in your thought."
	40–28	* without regrets and without r·.

resisted

Mis. 113–23   evil can be *r·* by true Christianity.
    222–14   would have *r·* and loathed ;
No. 36–23   could not have *r·* them ;

resistless

My. 149– 6   divine Love, *r·* Life and Truth.

resists

My. 210–14   Goodness involuntarily *r·* evil.

resolution

Po. vi–20   *r·* in Congress prohibiting
My. 37–30   * With sacred *r·* do we pray

resolutions

Ret. 48–11   following *r·* were passed :
    48–14   *r·* which were presented
Po. vi–27   * poem
  page 32   poem
    32–13   form *r·*, with strength from on high,
    33–15   If these *r·* are acted up to,
My. 51– 4   * the following *r·* were passed :
   199–13   joint *r·* contained therein
   364–23   preamble and *r·*

Resolutions for the Day

Po. vi–27   * poem
  page 32   poem

resolve

Mis. 204–27   gives steadiness to *r·*, and success to
   319–29   faith and *r·* are friends to Truth ;
Pul. 82– 6   * steel tempered with holy *r·*,
Hea. 1–19   * Pushes his prudent purpose to *r·*.''
My. 36–28   * have fulfilled a high *r·*

resolved

Ret. 49–19   *R·*, That we thank the State
My. 52– 2   * *R·* : That while she had many
    52–11   * *R·* : That while we realize the
   231– 9   *r·* to spend no more time

resolves

Mis. 179– 6   *r·* itself into these questions :
   201– 3   Science of Paul's declaration *r·* the

resolving

Ret. 9–13   *r·* to do, next time, as my mother

resort

Mis. 51–21   to *r·* to corporeal punishment.
   336– 6   you cannot, . . . *r·* to stones and clubs,
Man. 48–14   or make a summer *r·* near
Ret. 78–17   or a *r·* to subterfuge in the
No. 36–15   Jesus had a *r·* to his higher self
My. 98–23   * No *r·* was had to any of the latter-day

resorted

My. 305– 3   the calumniator has *r·* to

resorts

Mis. 53–17   He that *r·* to physics,

resound

Mis. 106–27   and *r·* His praise.''
   295–24   *r·* from Albion's shores.

resounding

My. 189– 9   *r·* through the dim corridors of time,

resources

Mis. 235–23   educate the affections to higher *r·*,
Un. 9–14   source and *r·* of being,
My. 84– 4   * the *r·* of the institution.

respect

Mis. 223–11   I *r·* that moral sense which
   245–19   rights that man is bound to *r·*.
Man. 112–10   fill out his application in this *r·*
Un. 5–19   Let us *r·* the rights of conscience
Pul. 21–14   entertain due *r·* and fellowship
   80–13   * and out of *r·* to them we have
No. 45–15   rights which man is bound to *r·*.
'00. 14–24   *r·* the character and philanthropy of
'01. 17–14   commands the *r·* of our best thinkers.
My. 30– 4   * precisely the same in every *r·*
   37– 8   * tenderest gratitude, *r·*, and
   38–21   * In every *r·* their service was
   77– 5   * In this *r·* it leads the Auditorium
   88–25   * to whom they rightfully turn with *r·*
  122–13   such as to command *r·* everywhere.
  163–27   I *r·* their religious beliefs,
  321–20   * to change my opinion . . . in this *r·*.
  331–12   * testifies to the love and *r·*
  333– 8   * paying the last tribute of *r·*

respectable

My. 97–18   * *r·*, evidently wealthy congregation
  249–17   that at this . . . period a *r·* newspaper

respected

Ret. 6– 9   reminiscences of my much *r·* parents,
Pul. 66–21   * departure from long *r·* views
'01. 18– 7   more honored and *r·* to-day
My. 137–11   *R· Sir* : — It is over forty years

respecter

'01. 27–21   God is no *r·* of persons.
My. 128– 9   "no *r·* of persons." — *Acts* 10 : 34.

respectful

My. 75– 2   * our *r·* acknowledgment of its

respectfully

Pul. 86–26   * *r·* extend to you the invitation
   87–14   permit me, *r·*, to decline their
Rud. v– 3   TENDERLY AND *r·* DEDICATED
Po. 73– 1   *R·* inscribed to my friends in Lynn.
My. 60–20   * *R·* and faithfully yours,
  138–21   I remain most *r·* yours,
  224– 5   I *r·* call your attention to this

respective

My. 237–18   physicians in their *r·* localities.

respectively

Pul. 43– 4   * under the direction, *r·*, of
   47–19   * key words *r·* used in the
   59–16   * read from . . . and her work *r·*.
My. 16–19   * *r·* the architect and the builder
  245–28   indicate, *r·*, the degrees of
  329–17   * of July 3 and August 21, 1844, *r·*.

respects

My. 89–29   * in some *r·*, the greatest religious
  259–28   Christmas *r·* the Christ too much to
  307–20   in some *r·* he was quite a seer

resplendent

Mis. 320–10   lends its *r·* light to this hour :

respond

Mis. 303–25   *r·* to this letter by contributions.
Ret. 14–20   I had to *r·* that I could not

responded

Pul. 8– 9   *r·* to the call for this church
My. 171–20   * Mrs. Eddy *r·* graciously to the

responding

Mis. 95–10   * Mrs. Eddy *r·*, said :
Pul. 59–13   * *r·* with its parallel interpretation
My. 254–10   *R·* to your kind letter,

responds

Un. 32–20   To this declaration C. S. *r·*,

response

Mis. 314–17   in *r·* to the congregation,
Rud. 6–12   met a *r·* from Prof. S. P. Langley,
My. 11–15   * *r·* was instant, spontaneous.
  157–19   * In *r·* to an inquiry from the
  165–20   rise above . . . to the scientific *r·* :
  264–14   heading

responsibilities

Mis. 176–27   our own great opportunities and *r·*
Pul. 45–24   * gladly laid down his *r·*

responsibility

Mis. 281–27   I realized what a *r·* you assume
  304–31   * The *r·* of its production,
  305– 9   * *r·* of representing the National
Un. 26– 7   I shirk all *r·* for myself as evil,
'00. 9–28   to fit others for this great *r·*.
Hea. 5–21   *r·* of our own thoughts and acts ;
My. 123–14   to be rid of the care and *r·* of

responsible

Mis. 61–15   * man is held *r·* for the crime :
   61–18   * This 'man' was held *r·*
  119– 3   *r·* for our thoughts and acts;
  119– 8   Each individual is *r·* for himself.
  227–14   *r·* for kind (?) endeavors.
  263–20   *r·* for supplying this want,
  265–22   I am not morally *r·* for
  301– 9   are morally *r·* for what
  347–25   God is *r·* for the mission
  355–20   its victim is *r·* for its
  357–26   not morally *r·* for this,
Man. 76–25   individually *r·* for said funds.
  77–14   *r·* for the performance
  78– 7   shall not be made legally *r·*
  98– 1   shall be *r·* for correcting
Ret. 77– 1   I become *r·*, as a teacher,
  85– 1   should be specially *r·*
Un. 64– 2   If . . . God is *r·* therefor ;
No. 18–21   the teacher is morally *r·*.
Peo. 11–22   legislators who are greatly *r·*
My. 243–11   hold important, *r·* offices,
  313–18   accompanied by some *r·* individual

responsive

My. 33–13   * The *r·* reading was from
  79– 1   * singing and *r·* reading,

rest (noun)

abiding
Ret. 23– 3   could be a real and abiding *r·*.
all the
Mis. 224–15   different . . . from all the *r·* ;
and drink
Pul. 14–16   watching for *r·* and drink.
at
Mis. 104– 2   at *r·* in the eternal harmony.
  362– 5   reason is at *r·* in God's wisdom,

rest (noun)
  calls for
    My. 165–23 becomes tired and calls for *r*.
  comfort and
    Po. 78–15 Give . . . comfort and *r*,
  compass his
    Po. 18–10 he soareth to compass his *r*,
  conflict and
    Po. 77–12 joy and tears, conflict and *r*,
  day of
    Mis. 279–20 the seventh is the day of *r*,
  find
    Mis. 124–12 find *r* in the spiritual ideal,
         133–28 I turn . . . and find *r*.
    No. 36–16 could find *r* from unreal trials
  for the righteous
    '02. 19–17 remaineth a *r* for the righteous,
  heavenly
    Mis. 389–25 finds her home and heavenly *r*.
    Po.   5– 7 finds her home and heav'nly *r*.
  His
    Pul. 39– 7 * Round our restlessness, His *r*.
  in Christ
    '02. 19–18 a *r* in Christ, a peace in Love.
  in God
    Rud. 12–19 induces *r* in God, divine Love,
    My. 282– 6 my hope must still *r* in God,
  kindles into
    Mis. 356– 2 dilates and kindles into *r*.
  like the
    My. 15–29 * To hear it like the *r*.
  no
    Pul. 39– 3 * no *r* until it finds the peace of the
    Pan. 13–26 Truly there is no *r* in them,
  of righteousness
    Pan. 14– 2 rise into the *r* of righteousness
  our
    Mis. 216– 5 and entered into our *r*,
  paradisaical
    Mis. 70–12 Paradisaical *r* from physical agony
  passed to
    My. 230– 4 when those have passed to *r*.
  promised
    Po. 33– 5 bless me with Christ's promised *r* ;
  ransomed
    Mis. 386–28 cloud not o'er our ransomed *r*
    Po. 50–15 cloud not o'er our ransomed *r*
  Sabbath
    Mis. 216– 3 a Sabbath *r* for the people of God ;
  sigh for
    Mis. 206–32 journey, and betimes sigh for *r*
  stupid
    Mis. 398– 8 Break earth's stupid *r*.
    Ret. 46–14 Break earth's stupid *r*.
    Pul. 17–13 Break earth's stupid *r*.
    Po.   14–12 Break earth's stupid *r*.
  such a
    Pul.   9– 6 break the full chords of such a *r*.
  take thy
    Po. 27–22 and may take thy *r*,
  that remaineth
    Mis. 144–23 sweet as the *r* that remaineth
  triumph and
    Po. 78– 5 waited their reward, triumph and *r*,
  will give thee
    My. 153–30 will give thee *r*, peace, health,
  will give you
    Mis. 20– 5 and I will give you *r*."— *Matt.* 11 : 28.
    No.   43– 5 and I will give you *r*."— *Matt.* 11 : 28.
    Hea.   2–19 and I will give you *r*."— *Matt.* 11 : 28.
  would give me
    Ret. 13–19 God's love, which would give me *r*,

    Mis. 85–16 the *r* of perpetual, . . . existence.
         158–23 and God will do the *r*.
         208–14 to the weary and heavy-laden, *r*.
         216–22 * after the *r* of it had gone.''
         313– 8 reflects *r* on the dear readers,
    '01. 26– 3 give my tired sense . . . .*r*.
    My. 183– 8 * will the world have *r*.''

rest (verb)
    Mis. 101–28 On this proof *r* premise and
         114–26 *R* assured that God in His wisdom
         125–12 *r* on the bosom of God ;
         125–13 *r*, in the understanding of divine
         125–14 *r*, in that which ''to know aright
         160–13 Of this we *r* assured,
         227–24 a life wherein the mind can *r*
         276– 8 *r* assured my heart's desire met the
         289–11 seems to *r* on this basis.
         303–10 fruits of Spirit, will *r* upon us
         316–19 *r* on my retirement from
         323–21 *r* in its cool grottos,
         355–24 *r* like the dove from the deluge.
         357– 8 *r* beside still waters.

rest (verb)
    Mis. 361–21 and *r* from the subtlety of
         395–19 May *r* above my head.
    Man. 60–10 *r* the weary and heavy laden.
    Ret.   9– 8 That night, before going to *r*,
          65– 2 *r* their opinions of Truth . . . on
          82–10 *r* on divine Principle for guidance,
          85– 9 Of this also *r* assured,
    Un.   8– 9 *r* upon the evidence of the senses,
    Pul. 21–27 must *r* on the spirit of Christ
    Pan.   8–22 must ever *r* on the basis of the
    '01.   1– 4 *r* assured you can never lack
    Peo.   9–23 and *r* all faith in Spirit,
    Po.   1– 4 where the wild winds *r*,
          17– 3 I'll think of its glory, and *r*
          41– 1 * Come, *r* in this bosom,
          44– 4 Whereon they may *r* !
          58– 4 May *r* above my head.
    My.   38– 4 * *r* in this satisfying assurance,
          83–16 * who will have time to *r*
         139– 2 *R* assured that your Leader
         151–12 *R* assured that the injustice
         182–27 *r* their weary wings amid the
         186–13 *R* assured that He in whom
         192–15 blessing of divine Love *r* with you.
         202–14 *r* worthily on the builders of
         210–10 all whom your thoughts *r* upon
         250–25 I *r* peacefully in knowing
         252– 8 *R* assured that the good you do
         296–12 nor *r* from his labors

restaurant
    My. 83–15 * hotel and *r* keepers,
rested
    Mis. 105– 6 *r* the anathema of priesthood
         140–12 Thus the case *r*,
    My. 85–27 * *r* on this structure,
         291– 2 *r* on the life and labors of
restful
    Mis. 153– 4 Truth is *r*, and Love is triumphant.
resting
    Mis. 254–24 *r* in silly peace upon the
         325–16 their feet *r* on footstools,
    Ret. 42–14 *r* on his serene countenance.
    Pul. 42–22 * a star of lilies *r* on palms,
          42–29 * white carnations *r* on a mat of palms,
resting-place
    Mis. 118– 5 when faith finds a *r*
         150–23 and the desert a *r*
    My. 257–30 the Christian traveller's *r*.
         326–19 bore his remains to their last *r*.
restitution
    My. 131–10 loving *r*, redemption, and inspiration,
restless
    Ret. 11– 6 Go fix thy *r* mind
    Po.   60– 2 Go fix thy *r* mind
restlessness
    Pul. 39– 7 * Round our *r*, His rest.
restoration
    Rud.   6–19 *r* of the true evidence of
           8–27 If by such . . . the *r* is not lasting,
    My. 152–12 The *r* of pure Christianity
         218– 7 its *r* to life and health
restore
    Mis. 59–14 or to *r* health and harmony,
         236–19 *r* harmony and prevent dishonor.
         312–18 * to *r* the waning faith of many
         354–17 *r* the right action of the mental
    Ret. 48–20 *r* health, hope, and harmony to man,
    No.   5–16 *r* health and perpetuate life,
    Pan.   6– 1 Science will *r* and establish,
    My.   48– 5 * to *r* to human consciousness
         301–27 *r* disordered functions, or
         332– 1 * to *r* her to her friends
restored
    Mis. 41–25 and health will be *r* ;
          49– 6 *r* by C. S. treatment.
         180– 6 beholding me *r* to health.
         180– 8 * ''How is it that you are *r* to us ?
         186–30 *r* to mortals the lost sense of
         186–32 *r* this sense by the spiritual
         258– 7 he *r* sight to the blind,
         282–24 he is *r* through C. S.
         382–13 *r* the first patient healed in this
    Pul. 34–28 process by which I was *r* to health ;
    Rud.   8–27 the health is seemingly *r*,
          12–10 and then *r* through its agency.
    No.   4– 1 Reading S. and H. has *r* the sick to
    '01. 17–17 *r* the patients in from one to three
    My. 105–16 I have physically *r* sight to the blind,
         105–24 On seeing her immediately *r* by me
         218– 1 He *r* the diseased body to

restores

Mis.	25–13	r· the spiritual . . . meaning
	252–25	r· its lost element, namely,
	287–11	and r· lost Eden.
Man.	17–18	and r· the lost Israel :
Un.	30–10	r· Soul, or spiritual Life.
No.	10–17	Truth r· that lost sense,
My.	180– 9	r· their original tongue

restoreth

Un.	30–11	"He r· my soul," — *Psal.* 23 : 3.

restoring

Mis.	65–24	r· the equipoise of mind
	329–11	r· in memory the sweet rhythm
Un.	11–22	for r· his senseless hand ;
	30–18	r· the spiritual sense of man

restrain

Mis.	380–28	a bill in equity . . . to r·,
Ret.	79–24	R· untempered zeal.
No.	8–15	remainder thereof He will r·.
'02.	1–14	wrath shalt Thou r·." — *Psal.* 76 : 10.
My.	151–11	wrath shalt Thou r·." — *Psal.* 76 : 10.
	207– 5	remainder thereof He will r·.

restrained

Mis.	226–24	should be r· by their pride.

restraining

Mis.	381–22	r· the defendant from directly

restricted

Mis.	244–28	not for a . . . r· period,
	359–12	Growth is r· by forcing

restriction

My.	320–24	* without any hesitation or r·.
	321–10	* position without any r·.

restrictions

Mis.	272–13	* the following important r· :

rests

Mis.	62–30	"mind-cure" r· on the notion that
	69– 6	Science r· on Principle
	80–32	Mind-healing r· demonstrably on
	104–32	On this r· the implicit faith
	118–17	trustworthiness r· on being willing
	267–27	r· on this scientific basis :
	271– 8	that r· on oneness ;
	336–29	r· on everlasting foundations,
	354–28	he r· in a liberty higher
	365–11	it r· alone on demonstration.
Ret.	75–19	and r· on unity.
Un.	31–17	r· on the fact that matter usurps
Rud.	11–19	Mind-healing by no means r· on
No.	4–24	r· on the exclusive truth
	10–14	My hygienic system r· on Mind,
	18– 7	r· alone on the demonstration of
	24– 9	r· on God as One and All,
'00.	11–15	Mozart r· you.
'01.	3– 3	benediction . . . r· upon this hour :
Hea.	15– 2	r· upon the supremacy of God.
Po.	18–19	rides on the whirlwind or r· on the
	46– 1	thy rosebud heart r· warm
My.	106–17	r· on the basis of fixed Principle,
	118–25	r· on a heathen basis for its
	152–12	r· solely on spiritual understanding,
	158–18	r· on Christian Scientists.
	177–21	glory of His presence r· upon it,
	204– 2	r· in the fact that He is infinite
	258–27	A transmitted charm r· on them.

result (noun)

await the
Mis.	241–15	else he will doubtingly await the r· ;

bringing out the
Mis.	41–30	bringing out the r· of the Principle

desired
My.	292–19	would prevent the r· desired.

dignify the
Mis.	199– 5	dignify the r· with the name of law :

moral
Mis.	365–18	has worked out a moral r· ;
No.	18–24	have wrought this moral r·,

of importunity
My.	10–21	* as the r· of importunity or entreaty

of organization
Mis.	190– 2	neither . . . r· of organization, nor
Ret.	58–13	it was not the r· of organization,
Un.	42–22	nor was it the r· of organization,

of prayer
My.	343–25	and the r· of prayer.

of rules
Pul.	45–27	* r· of rules made by Mrs. Eddy.

of secret faults
Ret.	72– 7	portrays the r· of secret faults,

of sin
Mis.	115– 8	only as the r· of sin ;

of the love
My.	62– 6	* To me it is the r· of the love that

result (noun)

of the work
My.	327–13	* This is the r· of the work done

one
Pul.	52–26	* and C. S. is one r·.

produce a
Hea.	6–22	produce a r· upon his body.

produces the
My.	302– 4	mind, not matter, produces the r·

scientific
Mis.	172–28	To gain this scientific r·,

such a
Ret.	38–13	I had not thought of such a r·,
My.	233–23	watch against such a r·

this
Mis.	69–23	effort to accomplish this r·,
Ret.	21–23	which tend to this r·,
	49–10	adapted to work this r· ;
'02.	1– 4	effort to achieve this r·,
Hea.	6–23	The belief that produces this r·
My.	244–14	my part towards this r·.

Mis.	23–20	not a r· of atomic action,
	24–13	r· was that I rose, dressed myself,
	112–32	r· of sensuous mind in matter.
	210– 2	behold the r· : evil, uncovered.
Pul.	84–26	* r· of long years of untiring,
'01.	26–30	* r· of my own observation,
My.	48–32	* the r· is already manifest
	112–25	r· of his conscientious study of
	128–26	but the r· is as injurious.
	246–22	r· is an auxiliary to the College
	293–26	r· would have been scientific,

result (verb)

Mis.	27– 5	or aught that can r· in evil,
	233– 4	r· in the worst form of medicine.
	309– 5	r· in erroneous conclusions.
Man.	110– 4	confusion that might r·
My.	11–12	* that did not r· in our welfare.
	45– 3	* will r· in its perpetuity

resulting

Pul.	31–15	* r· from editorial work

results

appears in
Mis.	291–12	at least it so appears in r·.

bad
Mis.	243– 3	with no bad r·,

calculating the
Hea.	4– 5	before calculating the r· of an

denied the
Mis.	7–27	denied the r· of our labors

depend on
My.	244–25	This, however, must depend on r·.

fatal
Mis.	45– 9	avoiding the fatal r· that frequently

glorious
Mis.	245–17	remove with glorious r·.
My.	213–14	and bring out glorious r·.

good
Mis.	379–23	with phenomenally good r· ;
My.	232–28	exhaustion and no good r·,

infinite
Ret.	92– 1	His . . . wrought infinite r·.

its
Mis.	19–28	choose our course and its r·.
	250–18	grand achievements as its r·.
	299– 1	not change the fact, or its r· ;
'01.	21–20	Principle of C. S. and of its r·.
My.	184–24	quite sacred in its r·.

of error
Mis.	288–10	works out the r· of error.

of Science
Mis.	341–11	to arrive at the r· of Science :

physical
My.	220– 1	save him from bad physical r·.

same
Mis.	40–18	same r· follow not in every case,

their
My.	143– 4	are blessed in their r·.

things and
'01.	21–26	did He not know all things and r·

witness
Pul.	8–29	are destined to witness r·

Un.	42– 6	r· of material consciousness ;
Hea.	8– 8	r· of this higher Christianity,
My.	45–21	* r· of such following have been

results (verb)

Mis.	15–11	r· in health, happiness, and
'01.	23–13	r· as would a change of
Hea.	7–13	corrects the act that r· from

resumed

Mis.	105–10	r· his individual spiritual being,
Ret.	38–13	my printer r· his work

resurrect
   Mis. 154–16   to *r·* the understanding,

resurrected
   Un. 62–23   never in matter, nor *r·* from it."
       62–26   all that can be buried or *r·*.
       63– 3   neither buried nor *r·*.
   Peo. 5– 6   *r·* a deathless life of love ;

resurrecting
   Mis. 77–32   *r·* the human *sense*
   My. 110– 3   *r·* individuals buried

resurrection
   Mis. 90–29   breakfast, after his *r·*,
       170– 2   *r·* and life immortal are
       179–20   between us and the *r·* morning?
       179–22   come into the spiritual *r·*
       180–19   shall have part in his *r·*.
   Man. 16– 6   *r·* served to uplift faith
   Un. 41–11   *R·* from the dead
       41–13   have part in this *r·*
       61– 1   the *r·* that takes hold of
   Pul. 27–22   * window . . . Mary at the *r·* ;
   My. 164–19   has wrought a *r·* among you,
       202–15   the glory of the *r·* morn
       258–11   her *r·* and task of glory,
       269– 7   *r·* from the dead, — *Luke* 20 : 35.

resuscitate
   Mis. 145–17   let not mortal thought *r·* too soon.

resuscitated
   Hea. 19–10   he would have *r·*.

resuscitating
   My. 293–17   mind *r·* the body of the patient.

retain
   Mis. x–22   to *r·* my maiden name,
       xi– 3   caused me to *r·* the initial "G"
       xii– 2   to *r·* at this date the privileged
       31–22   in order to *r·* his faith in evil
   Rud. 2–14   I prefer to *r·* the proper sense of
   '00. 8–28   *r·* a desire to follow your own
   '02. 14– 3   only interest I *r·* in this property

retained
   Mis. 218–26   neither eliminated nor *r·* by Spirit.
   Ret. 15– 4   *r·* till I founded a church of my own,
   My. 335– 6   * *r·* his membership in both till

retaining
   Mis. 226–10   when, *r·* his own, he loses the
   Man. 55–15   *r·* his membership, this weak member
   Ret. 90– 4   *r·* his salary for tending the
   My. 126– 2   *r·* the heart of the harlot

retains
   Pul. 37– 8   * *r·* . . . her energy and power ;

retaken
   Mis. 289–21   must not be *r·* by the contractors,

retaliate
   '01. 30–12   to *r·* or to seek redress ;

retard
   Mis. 85–26   pleasures . . . of sense, *r·*
       233– 9   *r·* the onward march of life-giving
       245– 9   to *r·* by misrepresentation
       351–16   mad ambition may *r·* our Cause,

retarded
   No. 32– 2   *r·* the progress of Christianity

retarding
   Mis. 107–27   *r·*, and in . . . instances stopping,

retards
   Ret. 45–10   organization *r·* spiritual growth,
       75–20   dishonesty *r·* spiritual growth
   My. 84– 6   * *r·* and holds back work

retina
   Un. 34– 5   pictured on the eye's *r·*.

retire
   Mis. 133–22   I *r·* to seek the divine blessing
       227– 2   *r·* for forgiveness to no fraternity
       379– 1   Mr. Quimby would *r·* to an anteroom
   Pul. 36– 6   * to *r·* from active contact with
       68–10   * to *r·* from active contact with
   '01. 17–21   *r·* from the comparative ease of
   My. 250– 9   their Readers will *r· ex officio*,

retired
   Mis. 136– 1   When I *r·* from the field
       308–21   *r·* with honor
   Ret. 40– 9   given up the case and *r·*.
   Pul. 47–25   * she lives very much *r·*,

retirement
   Mis. 316–19   my *r·* from life's bustle.
   Ret. 48– 2   but I was yearning for *r·*.
   My. 117– 8   time and *r·* to pursue
       163–19   that I might find *r·*
       163–23   *r·* I so much coveted,
       164– 2   the *r·* I so much desired.

retiring-room
   Pul. 76–18   * One of the two alcoves is a *r·*

retrace
   Mis. 10–15   they will . . . *r·* their steps,

retreat
   Mis. 159–15   *r·*, sit silently, and ponder.
       386–24   In lone *r·*.
   No. 36–19   It was this *r·* from material
   Pan. 3–14   * sacred solitude ! divine *r·* !
   Po. 50–10   In lone *r·*.
   My. 117–28   to *r·* from the *world*,

retreating
   Un. 61–16   neither advancing, *r·*, nor

retreats
   Un. 61–13   *r·*, and again goes forward ;

retribution
   Mis. 11–22   is not leaving all *r·* to God

retrograded
   My. 107– 3   improved . . . or has it *r·*?

retrospect
   Pul. 31– 2   * certainly a very remarkable *r·*.
   My. 45–23   * in *r·* we see the earlier leading,
       145– 1   chapter sub-title

"Retrospection"
   Mis. 156–16   read "*R·*" on this subject.

Retrospection and Introspection
   p. 19
   My. 330–20   * In "*R·* and *I·*" (p. 19)
   p. 20
   My. 336–10   * "*R·* and *I·*." . . . (p. 20)
   page 47
   Mis. 318–13   page 47 . . . "*R·* and *I·*":
   page 84
   Man. 87–21   *R·* and *I·*, page 84.

   Pul. 46– 9   * under the title of "*R·* and *I·*,"
   My. 334– 5   * Mrs. Eddy's book, "*R·* and *I·*,"
       336–21   * by Mrs. Eddy in "*R·* and *I·*."

retune
   Mis. 394–18   * Such old-time harmonies *r·*,
   Po. 57– 4   * Such old-time harmonies *r·*,

return (noun)
   in
   Mis. 38– 6   expect in *r·* something to
       254– 4   in *r·* for all that love
       322– 1   In *r·* for your kindness,
       342–26   and receive nothing in *r·* ;
       364– 6   In *r·* for individual sacrifice,
   Man. 41–11   in *r·* employ no violent invective,
   Rud. 13–27   receiving no wages in *r·*,
   My. 154–21   * in *r·*, that he have light, . . . freedom,
   my
   My. 346–10   * on my *r·* from Pleasant View,
   of Christ
   My. 181–29   for the *r·* of Christ
   of members
   Mis. 310–11   relative to the *r·* of members
   of the disease
   Mis. 54–21   be liable to a *r·* of the disease
   sharp
   Mis. 13– 6   sharp *r·* of evil for good
   speedy
   Mis. 212–15   A speedy *r·* under the reign of
   under difficulties
   '01. 2–23   costs a *r·* under difficulties ;

   Mis. 142–24   Poor *r·*, is it not?
   Pul. 69–15   * C. S. really is a *r·* to
   My. 181–29   the *r·* of the spiritual idea

return (verb)
   Mis. 12– 8   Never *r·* evil for evil ;
       22–17   come from God and *r·* to Him,
       34–19   *r·* to his boyhood.
       34–21   they cannot *r·* to ours.
       58– 9   destroyed, disease cannot *r·*.
       137–20   *r·* to his place of labor,
       141–27   or else *r·* every dollar
       304–17   * will *r·* to Washington
       316– 1   never to *r·* evil for evil ;
       353–31   "*r·* to their vomit," — *see Prov.* 26 : 11.
   Man. 84– 4   never to *r·* evil for evil,
   Pul. 6–12   * leading us to *r·* to Japan."
       49–21   * *r·* to her native granite hills,
   Rud. 12–14   will *r·*, and be more stubborn
   '01. 17– 4   *r·* to the Father's house
       17– 5   quickly to *r·* to divine Love,
       17– 8   and struggling to *r·*
       29–17   whenever they *r·* to the old home
       34–20   *r·* blessing for cursing;
   Hea. 4– 3   neither go forth from, *r·* to, nor
   My. 73– 2   * *r·* more than ten thousand dollars

return (verb)
My. 128–26 R· not evil for evil,
129–19 r· and plant thy steps in Christ,
131–14 r· to its first love,
150–32 "let your peace r·— Matt. 10 : 13.
170–29 r· in joy, bearing your sheaves
171– 4 r·, and come to Zion— Isa. 35 : 10.
184–14 and to r· my cordial thanks
247–26 it will r· to you.
259–12 I r· my heart's wireless love.
331–21 * to r· our thanks and express

returned
Mis. 7–29 r· naturally without any assistance.
214–17 r· into the scabbard.
226– 6 clergyman's son r· home— well.
326–22 the Stranger r· to the valley ;
353–17 When my brother r· and saw it,
378– 4 in a few weeks r· apparently well,
379– 6 I read the copy . . . and r· it to him.
Man. 109–12 should have applications r· to them
110– 1 as none will be r· that are
Ret. 9– 1 r· with me to grandmother's room,
19–17 I r· to New Hampshire,
Pul. 34– 3 * r· to her father's home— in 1844
53–12 * and one r· to give thanks
No. 31–24 r·, to be again forgiven ;
My. 30–20 * plates were r· after having been
165– 7 I r· blessing for cursing.
215–12 However, I r· this money
270–22 I have r· good for evil,
330–28 I r· to New Hampshire,
333–14 * procession then r· to the lodge,

returning
Mis. 11–23 r· blessing for cursing.
330–21 With each r· year, higher joys,
Ret. 20– 1 After r· to the paternal roof
45–19 forgiving enemies, r· good for evil,
No. 20–17 starting from . . . and r· to it
26–28 dust r· to dust, nothingness to
'01. 2–24 beset all their r· footsteps.
My. 204–27 while r· good for evil,
260–22 r· good for evil,
336–12 "After r· to the paternal roof
346–12 * made several turns . . . before r·.

returnless
Pul. 1–14 Pass on, r· year !
Po. 26– 1 Pass on, r· year !

returns
Mis. 278– 4 my peace r· unto me.
324–24 So he r· to the house,
Po. 10–12 R· to bless a bridal
My. 13–30 r· it unto them after many days,
337–13 R· to bless a bridal

reunion
My. 21–27 * rejoice in the glad r·

Rev. ——
Mis. 68– 7 The R· said in a sermon :
'01. 21– 8 R· writes : " To the famous Bishop

reveal
Mis. 164–28 r· man collectively, as individually,
192–17 his words r· the great Principle
308– 9 Scriptures and C. S. r·
348–13 God shall r· His rod,
Ret. 25– 1 r· the great curative Principle,
28–24 Science of Mind must r·.
Un. 37–10 would r· this wonder of being.
My. 5– 8 r· man as God's image,
111– 1 r· truths which otherwise the
124–19 for Science to r· man to man ;
299– 6 * have any truth to r·
323–22 * to r· to us His way.
347– 3 and r· my successor,

revealed
Mis. 2–20 spiritual idea of God will be r·.
30– 8 spiritually discerned and r·
35– 2 r· to her the fact that Mind,
141– 5 r· to you God's all-power,
167–25 r· them unto babes "— Luke 10 : 21.
179–31 when God r· to me this
183–21 arm of the Lord is r· ;— Isa. 53 : 1.
201–10 r· the myth or material falsity
210–13 wisdom of God, as r· in C. S.,
302–16 in interpreting r· Truth,
315–30 to study His r· Word,
348–11 that shall not be r·."— Matt. 10 : 26.
Ret. 30–10 asked why C. S. was r· to me
76–11 mind to which this Science was r·
Un. 39–10 arm of the Lord is r·.
51–22 Ego is r· as Father, Son,
58–19 unreality of sin, sickness, . . . was r·,
Pul. 77–13 * Truth, as r· by divine Love
78–12 * Truth, as r· by divine Love
No. 45– 2 r· them unto babes."— Luke 10 : 21.

revealed
'01. 10– 7 that shall not be r·."— Matt. 10 : 26.
My. v–25 * r· God to well-nigh countless numbers
24– 2 * truth which Christ Jesus r·
28–30 * has r· the one true Science
37–12 * r· the verity and rule of
43– 7 * r· the God of their fathers,
43–22 * r· to our beloved Leader,
44– 1 * The way . . . has been r·.
45–16 * divine Principle r· to you
58–20 * r· a demonstrable way of salvation.
64– 5 * realm of infinite Mind, r· to us
246–17 r· through the human character.
299– 7 * has not been r· by the church
324–14 * to have those very terms r·
347– 1 have already been r· in a degree

revealing
Mis. 189–18 r·, in place thereof,
No. 30–23 r· Him and nothing else.
Peo. 13– 9 r· the one God and His all-power

revealings
Mis. 15–30 it drinks in the sweet r· of

reveals
Mis. 1–20 Goodness r· another scene
5– 4 Science r· man as spiritual,
13–22 r· in clearer divinity the existence
60–17 Science . . . r· the impossibility of
82– 2 r· God and man as the Principle and
95–21 Mind r· itself to humanity
95–23 C. S. r· the infinitude of divinity
164– 6 r· the incorporeal Christ ;
174–28 Science that r· the spiritual facts of
175–26 r· the one perfect Mind and His laws.
185–21 r· man infinitely blessed, upright,
194– 3 Divine Science r· the Principle of
219– 3 neither r· God in matter,
337– 2 that which r· the truth of Love,
Ret. 59– 1 C. S. r· the grand verity,
59–18 r· Mind, the only living and true
60– 3 Science r· Life as a complete sphere,
60– 6 Science r· Spirit as All,
60–11 C. S. r· God and His idea as
61–21 C. S. r· the fact that,
65–30 Christianity r· God as ever-present
Un. 29–15 Science r· Soul as that which the
52– 5 r· and sustains the unbroken
55–15 r· the self-destroying ways of error
Rud. 11–22 r· the all-power and ever-presence
No. 10– 8 the latter r· and interprets God
28–16 r· the fact that Truth is never
39–25 this light r· the pure Mind-pictures,
Pan. 3–19 self-existent God, who r· Himself
Hea. 14–25 Science r· the Principle and method
My. 119–15 Principle that r· Christ.
262–31 r· infinite meanings and gives
272–13 C. S. r· the divine Principle,

Revelation
Mis. 21– 5 culminates in the R· of St. John,
280– 3 third picture-lesson is from R·,
366–10 keynote of C. S. from Genesis to R·,
Man. 58–17 shall extend from Genesis to R·.
Pul. 59–16 * read from the book of R·
No. 20–27 antagonistic to R· and Science,
37–21 From Genesis to R· the Scriptures
'00. 11–26 In R· St. John refers to
12– 6 In R·, second chapter,
12–27 R· of St. John in the apostolic age
'01. 32–24 St. John's R·, educated my thought
My. 125–29 Babylonish woman, referred to in R·,
285–17 In R· 2 : 26, St. John says :

revelation
and Science
Un. 8–19 through reason, r·, and Science,
astonishing
My. 92–15 * astonishing r· was made that since
based upon
Un. 9–13 have not based upon r· their
denying
Mis. 3–28 denying r·, and dethroning Deity.
260–21 denying r·, and seeking to dethrone
glories of
Mis. 332–21 masked . . . the glories of r·,
God's
Mis. 92–26 cannot be substituted for God's r·.
Ret. 84–15 cannot be substituted for God's r·.
imagination and
No. 20– 5 human reason, imagination, and r·
inevitable
My. 178–18 Hence the inevitable r· of C. S.
inspiration and
Un. 46– 3 Truth is from inspiration and r·,
light of
Hea. 8–18 becloud the light of r·,
My. 114–18 light of r· and solar light.

revelation

logic, and
Mis. 223– 8   divine light, logic, and *r·*

marvellous
My. 88–23   * marvellous *r·* given to this

mount of
Mis. 17– 7   died away on this mount of *r·*,
     164–14   but from the mount of *r·*,
     356–14   ascend from the mount of *r·*,
     369– 2   at the foot of the mount of *r·*,
No. 1–16   die away on the mount of *r·*,
My. 189– 3   should reach the mount of *r·* ;

must come
Mis. 362–22   *r·* must come to the rescue

must subdue
No. 11–26   *R·* must subdue the sophistry of

nature of a
My. 93–29   * will come in the nature of a *r·*.

of divine Love
My. 301– 4   was and is the *r·* of divine Love.

of divinity
My. 63–23   * *r·* of divinity which has come to

of Spirit
Mis. 56–19   at the full *r·* of Spirit,

rare
Mis. 292– 9   a rare *r·* of infinite Love,

reason and
Mis. 23–18   Reason and *r·* declare that God
     27–20   According to reason and *r·*,
     217– 2   nature, reason, and *r·*.
No. 13–24   given impulse to reason and *r·*,

Science is a
Ret. 28–26   All Science is a *r·*.
Pul. 35–22   All Science is a *r·*.''

shows
No. 11–25   *R·* shows this Principle,

spiritual
Mis. 75– 4   spiritual *r·* of man's possible

this
Mis. 165–13   light of this *r·* leaves
My. 63–25   * Grandly . . . symbolize this *r·*,

tides of
Mis. 292– 3   overwhelming tides of *r·*,

Mis. 158–21   *r·* of what, how, whither.
     354–10   When . . . reason is preferred to *r·*,
Un. 58–19   a *r·* that beams on mortal sense
Peo. 2–13   by *r·* supporting reason.
My. 238–13   *r·*, . . . and presentation of C. S.
     239– 5   primitive proof, wherein reason, *r·*,
     265– 5   *r·*, spiritual voice and vision,
     288– 1   reason, *r·*, justice, and mercy ;
     318–32   not . . . in history, but in *r·*.
     350– 7   *r·*, uplifting human reason,

revelations
Mis. 248–26   glorious *r·* of C. S.
Man. 59– 1   sacred *r·* of C. S.
My. 179–30   untranslated *r·* of C. S.

Revelator (*see also* **John, Revelator's, St. John**)
Mis. 269–28   *R·* beheld the opening of
     278– 1   vision of the *R·* is before me.
'00. 13– 3   *R·* commends the church at Ephesus
     13–13   *R·* writes of this church
     13–20   *R·* refers to the church
     13–29   *R·* speaks of the angel
My. 120– 1   We look for the sainted *R·*
     126–22   *R·* saw in spiritual vision
     201– 5   for a season, as the *R·* foresaw,

revelator
(*see* **Eddy**)

Revelator's
Mis. 113– 8   and the *R·* vision, that
'00. 12–17   hence the *R·* saying :
     14–11   import of the *R·* vision

revelators
Mis. 308–10   *r·* will take their proper place

revelling
Pul. 48– 8   * *r·* in the lights and shades of

revenge
Mis. 10– 4   Whatever envy, hatred, *r·*,
     36–13   Appetites, passions, anger, *r·*,
     114–20   passion, appetites, hatred, *r·*,
     118–22   lust, covetousness, envy, *r·*,
     228–15   mad ambition and low *r·*.
     281– 4   rivalry, jealousy, envy, *r·*,
Pul. 84– 5   * *r·* shall clasp hands with pity,
'02. 8–25   Lust, hatred, *r·*, coincide in
My. 249–15   its loathing of love and its *r·*

revenged
'00. 3–28   and *r·* himself upon his enemies.

revengeful
Mis. 129–15   If a man is jealous, envious, or *r·*,

revenue
My. 216– 8   and *r·* subsist on demand and supply,

reverberate
Mis. 312–25   *r·* and renew its emphasis
My. 291–20   waken a tone of truth that shall *r·*,

reverberating
My. 13–26   harmony, *r·* through all cycles of

revere
Pul. 41–12   * sent them by the teacher they *r·*.
My. 362–21   * *r·* and cherish your friendship,

revered
Mis. 376– 2   * true art of the oldest, most *r·*,
My. 58–18   * labor and sacrifice of our *r·* Leader
     278–13   The *r·* President and Congress
     289–16   long honored, *r·*, beloved.
     290– 8   as venerable, *r·*, and beloved
     362–12   * *R· Leader, Counsellor, and Friend:*

reverence
Mis. 96–20   I *r·* and adore Christ as never before.
     238– 4   *r·* of my riper years for all who
Pul. 81– 5   * is nowhere spoken with more *r·*
My. 63–21   * and of *r·* beyond words,
     85–21   * for future generations to *r·*
     98– 8   * an enthusiasm and *r·* of worship

Reverend
Man. 45–24   drop the titles of *R·* and Doctor,

reverent
Mis. 372–24   aimed to reproduce, with *r·* touch,

reverentially
My. 260– 4   *r·* withdraw itself before Mind.

reverently
Un. 13– 5   Men must approach God *r·*,

reversal
Un. 20– 1   By *r·* or revision,

reverse
Mis. 109– 5   and try to *r·*, invert, or controvert,
     119–29   nullify or *r·* your rules,
Un. 13– 4   whereas the *r·* is true in Science.
     20–10   By a *r·* process of argument
     30– 5   delusion that the senses can *r·* the

reversed
Mis. 61– 1   in all its manifestations, *r·*,
     220–24   if this mental process . . . be *r·*,

reverses
Mis. 13–21   Science of Soul *r·* this
     47–19   Science *r·* the evidence of
     222– 4   It *r·* C. S. in all things.
Un. 13– 1   Science *r·* the evidence of
     30– 5   Science *r·* the testimony of
     36– 7   Science, which *r·* false testimony

reversing
Un. 20– 4   undo the statements of error by *r·*
     53– 2   lie takes its pattern . . . by *r·* Truth.
     62–28   mortal sense, *r·* Science
My. 211–13   *R·* the modes of good,

reversion
Mis. 218– 5   declares the invisible only by *r·*,
'02. 19–24   a spiritual behest, in *r·*,

revert
Mis. 261–11   wrong will *r·* to the wrong-doer,
My. 39–21   * My thoughts *r·* to a former occasion,
     288–24   wrong will *r·* to the wrong-doer ;

reverting
Mis. 375– 8   letter *r·* to the illustrations of

review
Mis. 216– 9   there appeared a *r·* of,
My. 316–21   * "twentieth-century *r·* of opinion"

revile
Mis. 8–23   men shall *r·* you, — *Matt.* 5 : 11.
'01. 3– 4   men shall *r·* you, — *Matt.* 5 : 11.
'02. 11–22   men shall *r·* you, — *Matt.* 5 : 11.
My. 6–10   men may *r·* us and despitefully
     104–30   men shall *r·* you, — *Matt.* 5 : 11.
     316– 7   men shall *r·* you, — *Matt.* 5 : 11.

reviled
My. 196–18   was *r·*, *r·* not again ;— *I Pet.* 2 : 23.

reviling
'01. 33–26   the same *r·* it received then

revise
Mis. 274– 4   I desire to *r·* my book
My. 163–21   in Concord's quiet to *r·* our textbook,

revised
Mis. 136–19   my last *r·* edition of S. and H.
     309–32   See the *r·* edition of 1890,
     379–32   S. and H., p. 47, *r·* edition of 1890,
Man. 86–21   page 330 of the *r·* editions
     104–10   This Manual shall not be *r·*

revised
 Man. 104–17 appears in any *r·* edition,
 Ret. 22– 2 human history needs to be *r·*,
 Pul. 38– 7 * has been greatly *r·* and enlarged,
  55–14 * she has *r·* it many times,
 No. 3– 8 When I *r·* "S. and H.
 My. 15– 3 * Article XLI (XXXIV in *r·* edition)

revising
 My. 246–19 While *r·* "S. and H. with Key to the

revision
 Ret. 82–27 often asked which *r·* of S. and H.
  82–28 The arrangement of my last *r·*,
 Un. 20– 1 By reversal or *r·*,

revisions
 My. 318– 4 I have erased them in my *r·*.

revisits
 Po. 73– 4 hoarse wave *r·* thy shore !

revival
 Ret. 44–27 *r·* of mutual love, prosperity,

revive
 Pul. 72–26 * it was Mrs. Eddy's mission to *r·* it.

revived
 Mis. 355– 9 demonstration of Science must be *r·*.
  376– 3 * most authentic Italian school, *r·*.
 Pul. 52–25 * *r·* belief in what he taught is manifest,

reviver
 Pul. 52–13 * *r·* of the ancient faith and author of

reviving
 My. 257–19 We own his grace, *r·* and healing.

revolt
 Pul. 79–18 * a *r·* was inevitable
  80– 5 * the *r·* was headed by them ;

Revolution
 Pul. 46–17 * not long before the *R·*.
 My. 341– 3 a Daughter of the *R·*,

revolution
 Un. 40– 1 from the *r·* of the earth to the
 No. 6–21 error of the *r·* of the sun
  13–22 S. and H. has effected a *r·*
 Hea. 11– 6 We are in the midst of a *r·* ;

Revolutionary
 Ret. 2–10 score of years prior to the *R·* period.
  2–27 General Henry Knox of *R·* fame.
 Pul. 48–27 * in Colonial and *R·* days,

revolutionary
 Mis. 99– 1 It is *r·* in its very nature ;
  101– 9 It is a *r·* struggle.
  307–15 In this *r·* religious period,
 '01. 9–25 they are *r·*, reformatory, and
 My. 287–19 is loving, ameliorative, *r·* ;

revolutionize
 No. 11–17 *r·* and reform the world,
  33– 6 they would *r·* the world

revolutions
 Mis. 206– 1 *r·*, natural, civil, or religious,
 Rud. 8–15 *r·*, from a lower to a higher
 No. 28– 7 *r·* necessary to effect this end

revolve
 Mis. 22–16 all true thoughts *r·* in
  54– 5 the planets to *r·* around it?
  104–19 *r·* in their own orbits,

revolves
 Ret. 88–29 Mind *r·* on a spiritual axis,
 No. 6–18 *r·* around our planet,

revolving
 Mis. 125–24 *r·* oft the hitherto untouched
  184– 4 from the *r·* of worlds to the
 My. 13–11 * like so many planets, *r·* around
  145–20 keeps the wheels *r·*.

reward
 ever-present
  Mis. 238–19 and are an ever-present *r·*.
  My. 288– 7 are his ever-present *r·*.
 good is the
  Mis. 206–25 good is the *r·* of all who
 great
  Mis. 358–10 his shield and great *r·*.
  '00. 7–14 great *r·* for having suffered,
 in heaven
  '02. 11–25 *r·* in heaven :— *Matt.* 5 : 12.
  My. 6–12 *r·* in heaven." — *Matt.* 5 : 12.
 its
  Mis. 116–30 scientific rule and its *r·* :
   341–10 Fidelity finds its *r·*
  My. 165–15 never fails to receive its *r·*,
   273–15 feeling, and acting, and its *r·*.
 its own
  Mis. 33– 3 wrong will receive its own *r·*.

reward
 no
  Mis. 362–28 suffering has no *r·*, except
 of evil
  Mis. 340– 4 Good is never the *r·* of evil,
 of good
  My. 296–17 *r·* of good and punishment of evil
 of goodness
  My. 19–23 reap richly the *r·* of goodness.
 of obedience
  '02. 17–11 receive the *r·* of obedience.
 of righteousness
  Mis. 123–26 receive the *r·* of righteousness :
 of rightness
  My. 230–25 will reap the *r·* of rightness,
   278–23 promise and *r·* of rightness.
 of thy hands
  My. 199– 5 *r·* of thy hands is given thee
 rich
  My. 209– 4 with the rich *r·* of those that
 sure
  '01. 2–26 a fearless wing and a sure *r·*.
  My. 254–11 sure *r·* of right thinking
 taketh
  My. 33–26 nor taketh *r·* against — *Psal.* 15 : 5.
 their
  Mis. 343– 5 and have passed to their *r·*.
  Po. 78– 5 Why waited their *r·*,
 won the
  My. 62– 2 * in the battle, and won the *r·*,

  Mis. 133–17 *r·* thee openly." — *Matt.* 6 : 6.
   133–26 He will *r·* "openly." — *Matt.* 6 : 6.
   158–14 in *r·* for your faithful service,
   199– 1 does not *r· . . .* love with penalties ;
   242–19 to *r·* his liberality,
  Pan. 9–25 what *r·* have ye?" — *Matt.* 5 : 46.
  Hea. 5–10 the *r·* of his good deed
  My. 60–16 * as a *r·* for the best paper on
   123– 7 will *r·* these givers,
   128–29 will *r·* your enemies according to
   194–26 *r·* you according to your works,
   217– 5 to *r·* your hitherto unselfish toil,
   234–11 God will *r·* their kind motives,
   252–15 who will *r·* righteousness

rewarded
 Mis. xi– 7 *r·* by what they have hitherto
  84–10 their motives were *r·*
 No. 39–11 and He has *r·* them openly.

rewarding
 '02. 20– 8 *r·*, satisfying, glorifying
 My. 270–12 I am *r·* your waiting,

rewards
 Pan. 9–24 and *r·* its possessor ;

rhetoric
 Ret. 79–11 in shuffling off scholastic *r·*,

rheumatism
 Mis. 71– 7 he was troubled with *r·*,

Rhine
 Mis. 120–19 vintage bells to villagers on the *R·*.

Rhode Island and **R. I.**
 (*see* **Newport, Westerly**)

rhubarb
 Mis. 369–16 is higher than a *r·* tincture

rhyme
 My. 312–32 The *r·* attributed to me by

rhythm
 Mis. 160– 8 same sweet *r·* of head and heart,
  259–19 same *r·* that the Scripture describes,
  329–12 *r·* of unforgotten harmonies,
 Ret. 61–10 no more to be invaded than the *r·* of

rhythmic
 Mis. 83– 2 *r·* round of unfolding bliss,

rib
 My. 5– 4 the outcome of man's *r·*,

ribbon
 Pul. 42–28 * fastened with a broad *r·* bow.
  78–21 * Attached by a white *r·* to the scroll

rich
 Mis. 149–22 and all the *r·* graces of the Spirit.
  159–28 *r·* devices in embroidery, silver,
  165–18 *r·* legacy of what he said and did,
  165–27 to avail himself of the *r·* blessings
  231– 4 grandmother, *r·* in experience,
  231– 7 *r·* viands made busy many appetites ;
  313–20 the *r·* sheaves are ripe,
  331– 7 wait . . . on God for man's *r·* heritage,
  373–23 it has *r·* possession here,
  391– 6 An item *r·* in store ;
 Ret. 4–21 covered areas of *r·* acres,

rich

Pul.	24–28	* very *r·* in pictorial effect.
	26– 6	* choir gallery is spacious and *r·*
	27– 4	* marble approaches and *r·* carving,
	42–18	* *r·* with the adornment of flowers.
	50– 1	* *r·* woman is using her money to
	62–15	* superb, being *r·* and mellow.
	76– 9	* *r·* hangings of deep green plush,
	78–24	* satin-lined box of *r·* green velvet.
Pan.	3– 6	My sense of nature's *r·* glooms is,
'00.	1–13	*r·* spiritual attainments,
Po.	31–13	*R·* rays, rare footprints on the
	34– 9	chant thy vespers 'mid *r·* glooms
	38– 5	An item *r·* in store ;
My.	20–16	suffice for her *r·* portion
	69–15	* *r·* beauty of the interior.
	78–11	* peculiarly *r·* and impressive.
	88–13	* *r·* in the architectural symbolisms of
	127–26	but it is *r·* beyond price,
	132–18	may these *r·* blessings continue
	149–16	* with many *r·* men, but I am not *r·.*''
	159– 9	*r·* fruit of this branch of his vine,
	160–13	a sapling within *r·* soil
	185–29	*r·* in signs and symbols,
	201–19	*R·* hope have I in him who says
	209– 4	*r·* reward of those that seek
	252–21	*r·* rays from the eternal sunshine of
	253–24	you have His *r·* blessing already
	297–16	*r·* blessing of disbelief in death,

richer

Mis.	234–30	Christ is clad with a *r·* illumination
My.	90–18	* The world is enormously *r·* for this
	175–22	*r·* than the diamonds of Golconda,

riches

Mis.	325– 8	small conceptions of spiritual *r·*,
'01.	10–20	''the *r·* of His grace'' — *Eph.* 1 : 7.
My.	186–15	according to His *r·* in glory.
	187–29	the *r·* of His love
	203–11	but is economy and *r·*.

richest

Mis.	166–28	seen as diffusing *r·* blessings.
'01.	33–24	*r·* and most positive proof
My.	149–17	*r·* blessings are obtained by labor.

richly

Mis.	xi– 7	*r·* rewarded by what they have hitherto
	294–28	*r·* flavored with the true ideas
Ret.	4–16	pears, and cherries shone *r·*
	47–16	*r·* imbued with the spirit
Pul.	24–27	* doors of antique oak *r·* carved.
	26– 5	* *r·* panelled in relief work.
	26– 9	* with *r·* carved seats
	26–11	* *r·* wrought oxidized silver lamps,
My.	19–23	reap *r·* the reward of goodness.
	129–12	*r·* fraught with divine reflection.
	342– 1	* ample, *r·* furnished house

rid

Mis.	239–28	thought must be gotten *r·* of,
	280–13	must get *r·* of that notion.
Un.	15– 4	May men *r·* themselves of an incubus
	45– 8	to be *r·* of this self,
My.	123–14	*r·* of the care and responsibility of

ridden

No.	44–10	no hobby, however boldly *r·*

ridding

Ret.	79–11	*r·* the thought of effete doctrines,

riddle

Ret.	1–12	stray sonnet and an occasional *r·*,

ride

My.	74– 4	* within two or three days' *r·*,
	219–12	To say that it is sin to *r·* to church

rides

Po.	18–19	He *r·* on the whirlwind
My.	205–12	* And *r·* upon the storm.''
	356– 8	* And *r·* upon the storm.''

ridicule

Pul.	45–16	* *r·* heaped upon the hopeful,
My.	91–23	* were the objects of much *r·*,
	92– 7	* cannot be brushed aside by *r·*
	97– 5	* physicians, however, *r·* the idea

ridiculed

My.	92–21	* The statistics have been *r·*
	94– 4	* The figures . . . have been *r·*

ridiculous

Mis.	218–22	is more *r·* than the ''grin
My.	93–20	* we see only its *r·* phases,

right (noun)

adhere to the

Mis.	284–10	strictly adhere to the *r·*,

and power

Mis.	193–28	*r·* and power of Christianity

right (noun)

beams of

My.	269–21	beams of *r·* have healing in their

clearer

Un.	49–24	This gives me a clearer *r·*

determines the

My.	117– 4	determines the *r·* or the wrong

doing

Pul.	4–13	in being and doing *r·*,
	15–10	for the sake of doing *r·*
My.	252–12	to make one enjoy doing *r·*,

faith in the

Mis.	213– 5	and my faith in the *r·*.
My.	292– 5	and human faith in the *r·*.

flame of

Po.	30–14	fan Thou the flame Of *r·*

God speed the

'02.	2–14	God speed the *r·* !

good

Mis.	371–19	* ''good *r·*, and good wrong,''

groundwork of

Mis.	264– 7	without the groundwork of *r·*,

highest idea of

My.	283–17	a man's highest idea of *r·*

his

Mis.	171–18	prove his *r·* to be heard.

human

Mis.	266– 6	to abridge a single human *r·*

immutable

Mis.	172–27	on the side of immutable *r·*,

in dust

Po.	72– 2	charter, trampling *r·* in dust !

inherent

Pul.	51– 7	* which is their inherent *r·*

moral

'01.	20– 7	neither moral *r·* nor might

no

Mis.	105–26	no *r·* either to be pitied or
	209–21	it has no *r·* to be at peace.
Ret.	61–17	and have no *r·* to exist,
My.	278–24	Governments have no *r·* to

no moral

'01.	20– 2	no moral *r·* and no authority

no more

Mis.	283– 4	one has no more *r·* to enter

of the majority

My.	294– 1	*r·* of the majority to rule.

of way

My.	232– 6	right way wins the *r·* of way,

of woman

No.	45–16	*r·* of woman to fill the highest

over wrong

My.	362– 5	victory of *r·* over wrong,

periled

Po.	71– 7	periled *r·*, Rescued by the

reigneth

My.	278–12	in divine Science, where *r·* reigneth.

reigns

Po.	22–21	*R·* reigns, and blood was not its
My.	254– 2	heaven opens, *r·* reigns,

relinquishment of

Mis.	340– 1	relinquishment of *r·* in an evil hour,

reserves the

Man.	80–18	reserves the *r·* to fill the same by

side of

Mis.	255– 8	thought and action on the side of *r·*,

standard of

Mis.	232–12	proceed from the standard of *r·*

struggler for the

Po.	31– 1	loyal struggler for the *r·*,

subversion of

Mis.	31–10	subversion of *r·* is not scientific.

supremacy of

Mis.	267– 4	and the supremacy of *r·*.

this

Man.	80–20	not elect to exercise this *r·*,

to adopt

My.	128–14	man's *r·* to adopt a religion,

to demand

Ret.	61–26	the *r·* to demand that C. S. be stated

to deny

Mis.	199– 2	the *r·* to deny the supposed power of

to expose error

Mis.	335–19	my wisdom or *r·* to expose error,

to grant

Mis.	272– 3	* *(including the r· to grant degrees)*

to help

Pul.	82–24	* They are demanding the *r·* to help

to sit

Mis.	388–25	The *r·* to sit at Jesus' feet :
Po.	21–14	The *r·* to sit at Jesus' feet ;

to work

Mis.	389– 3	the *r·* to work and pray,
Po.	21–17	the *r·* to work and pray,

right (noun)

to worship
Mis.	388–18	The *r·* to worship deep and pure,
Po.	21– 7	The *r·* to worship deep and pure,

unconquerable
'00.	10– 9	unconquerable *r·* is begun anew,

wins
Mis.	277–11	*r·* wins the everlasting victory.

Mis.	71– 9	unquestionably right to do *r·* ;
	80–23	until *r·* is found supreme.
	81– 5	by *r·* of God's dear love,
	130–22	Where the motive to do *r·* exists,
	287–27	It is pleasanter to do *r·*
	289–23	the *r·* to become a mother ;
	299–27	What *r·* have I to do this?
Pul.	82–29	* Might no longer makes *r·*,
'00.	8–23	*r·* will boil over the brim of life
'01.	31– 2	of truth, of *r·*, and of wrong.
'02.	3–27	*r·* is the only real potency ;
Po.	23–13	Yielding a holy strength to *r·*,
	27–17	and *r·* with bright eye wet,
	71– 3	Laughed *r·* to scorn,
My.	3– 9	*r·* to the tree of life, — *Rev.* 22 : 14.
	213– 6	is by no means a *r·* of evil
	213–11	in their desire to do *r·*
	220–20	He whose *r·* it is shall reign.
	283–15	*R·* has its recompense,

right (adj.)

Mis.	11– 7	I used to think . . . this was *r·*.
	39–23	*r·* to bear "one another's — *Gal.* 6 : 2.
	51–17	*r·* motives for action,
	55– 1	failed to get the *r·* answer,
	59–20	There is but one *r·* Mind,
	62– 1	Holding the *r·* idea of man
	65–17	*instructions as to the r· way*
	67–21	Only thus is the *r·* practice of
	68–16	hence it is *r·* to know that the
	71– 1	*Is it r· for me to treat others, when*
	71– 9	It is unquestionably *r·* to do right ;
	71–10	is a very *r·* thing to do.
	71–30	Whatever is real is *r·*,
	76–22	will find the *r·* meaning indicated.
	85–10	His purpose must be *r·*,
	88–27	*Is it r· for a Scientist to treat*
	89– 6	*would it be r· to treat this patient*
	90–11	It is always *r·* to act rightly ;
	104–14	Clothed, and in its *r·* Mind,
	106– 7	Traitors to *r·* of them,
	111–19	cast their nets on the *r·* side,
	115–31	mental power in the *r·* direction
	117–14	basis of all *r·* thinking and acting ;
	125– 6	all that is *real* is *r·*.
	127–29	kind word spoken, at the *r·* moment,
	130–23	and the majority of one's acts are *r·*,
	133–20	because of my desire to set you *r·*
	152–28	to silence the *r·* intuition
	153– 7	If *r·* yourself, God will confirm
	169–10	through *r·* interpretation.
	170–14	by *r·* and wise, . . . conceptions
	171–12	our *r·* action is not to condemn
	177– 2	makes to us all, *r·* here,
	188–19	and *r·* there he leaves the subject.
	190–20	must yield to the *r·* sense,
	212–11	cast their nets on the *r·* side.
	212–18	rush in against the *r·* course ;
	236–12	obedience to them in all that is *r·* ;
	236–27	blamed for all that is not *r·* :
	251–20	Heaven *r·* here, where angels
	252– 8	*R·* thoughts are reality and **power** ;
	263–21	balance on the *r·* side,
	264–24	may be *r·* theoretically,
	264–26	status of thought must be *r·*
	267–19	The bird whose *r·* wing
	268–27	*R·* alone is irresistible.
	271–17	and Longfellow is *r·*.
	283–10	It would be *r·* to break into a
	288– 4	be demonstratively *r·* yourself,
	288–12	is not absolutely *r·*.
	288–14	begins with what is nearest *r·*
	288–16	Is marriage nearer *r·* than celibacy?
	288–22	is *r·* in every state and stage
	299–13	* "Is it *r·* to copy your works
	299–20	can I make this *r·* by saying,
	301–20	"Is it *r·* to copy my book . . . *without*
	301–21	not *r·* to copy my book . . . *without*
	336–11	*r·* obligations towards him.
	340– 7	turning neither to the *r·* nor to
	341– 1	they never bring out the *r·* action
	341– 5	that is real, *r·*, and eternal?
	353– 7	Is my concept of you *r·*?
	353–10	you have gained the *r·* one
	354–17	would restore the *r·* action
	355–16	To strike out *r·* and left
	359–22	but his example was *r·*,

right (adj.)

Mis.	359–23	available at the *r·* time.
	365–12	*r·* thinking and *r·* acting,
Man.	59– 5	in the scale of *r·* thinking.
	76– 4	*r·* occasion may call for it.
Ret.	7–18	* the side he deemed *r·*.
	30–13	*r·* apprehension of the invincible
	45–21	on thy *r·* cheek, — *Matt.* 5 : 39.
	57– 9	Principle is *r·* ;
	57– 9	Soul is *r·* ;
	61–29	that little shall be *r·*.
	70–26	The *r·* teacher of C. S.
	77– 2	Pope was *r·* in saying,
	78–14	*r·* sense of metaphysical Science.
Un.	17–15	*r·* apprehension of the wonderful
	54–25	Which is *r·*, — God, . . . or
Pul.	42–28	* On its *r·* was a large basket
	83–20	* and that *r·* early." — *Psal.* 46 : 5.
Rud.	2– 9	if our lexicographers are *r·*
	9–21	power of a scientific, *r·* thought,
No.	7–24	without reference to *r·* or wrong
	12– 4	*r·* thinking and *r·* acting
	15– 5	convince all that their purpose is *r·*.
	18– 9	*R·* thinking and *r·* acting,
	40–13	audible prayer of the *r·* kind ;
	40–20	is it *r·* for one mind to meddle
Pan.	4–13	capable . . . of *r·* and wrong action,
	14–17	*r·* arm of His righteousness.
'00.	1–14	and *r·* convictions fast forming
	2– 9	the *r·* thinker and worker,
	2–11	The *r·* thinker works ;
	3– 2	"When a man is *r·*,
	3– 2	his thoughts are *r·*, active, and
	3– 4	*r·* thinker and worker does his best,
	3– 9	If the *r·* thinker and worker's
	3–18	good man loves the *r·* thinker
	6–23	clothed and in his *r·* mind,
	9– 8	secret of C. S. in *r·* thinking
'01.	2–11	a fair seeming for *r·* being,
	14–19	as either *r·* or real
Hea.	2– 1	religion nearest *r·* is that one.
	3– 7	foundation of *r·* thinking and *r·* acting,
	4–22	gain a *r·* idea of the Principle
	4–23	Principle of all that is *r·*,
	12–10	showing he was *r·*.
	14–27	in sympathy with all that is *r·*
	17–28	are we not *r·* in ruling them out
Peo.	5–12	The *r·* ideal is not buried,
	8– 1	to present the *r·* idea of Truth ;
Po.	9–11	reason made *r·* and hearts all love.
My.	vii–11	* consistent and constant *r·* thinking
	14–20	* he was entirely *r·* in doing so.
	21–17	* but *r·* to expect that those who
	41– 5	* the law of *r·* thinking,
	117–27	free scope only in the *r·* direction !
	126– 8	"*r·* foot upon the sea, — *Rev.* 10 : 2.
	146–25	in the *r·* or in the wrong direction.
	159–17	this is the only *r·* activity,
	160– 2	he abides in a *r·* purpose,
	166– 7	so long as we have the *r·* ideal,
	180–24	insist on what we know is *r·*,
	193–23	* if it succeeds, it is a *r·* thing."
	209–5, 6	in *r·* thinking and *r·* acting,
	210–15	The *r·* thinker abides under the shadow of
	224–11	to its *r·* or its wrong concept,
	225–23	In this, as in all that is *r·*,
	227–27	smite thee on thy *r·* cheek, — *Matt.* 5 : 39.
	232– 6	The *r·* way wins the right of way,
	244–13	I have awaited the *r·* hour,
	254–11	sure reward of *r·* thinking
	268– 8	If the motives of . . . are *r·*,
	274–10	Dear reader, *r·* thinking,
	274–10	*r·* feeling, and *r·* acting
	277–19	mercy tips the beam on the *r·* side,
	283–14	*R·* thoughts and deeds are the
	283–26	Human law is *r·* only as it patterns
	288– 1	it starts the wheels of *r·* reason,
	292– 5	Through divine Love the *r·* government
	316–25	and of all that is *r·*.

(*see also* **hand**)

righted

My.	277–17	whereby wrong and injustice are *r·*

righteous

Mis.	33– 1	*r·* prayer that avails with God.
	99–16	ready to suffer for a *r·* cause,
	119–10	Evil is impotent to turn the *r·* man
	121–22	His beloved Son, the *r·* Nazarene,
	144–24	rest that remaineth for the *r·*
	258– 6	*r·* scorn and power of Spirit.
	281–31	seed of the *r·* — *Prov.* 11 : 21.
	293– 4	*r·* unfolding of error
'00.	4– 7	teaching of the *r·* Galilean,
'02.	19–17	there remaineth a rest for the *r·*,
My.	9–15	* forefront of the effort for *r·* reform,
	36–17	* the peace of a more *r·* living,

righteous

My. 46–19 * then fulfil the pledge in r· living,
165– 8 the r· suffer for the unrighteous;
189–13 commingling in one r· prayer,
273–11 not seen the r· forsaken,— *Psal.* 37 : 25.
276–24 to help support a r· government ;
280–10 * r· prayer which availeth much.
292–26 prayer of the r· heals the sick,

righteously

My. 41– 3 * they think rightly or r·.
196–19 Him that judgeth r·."— *I Pet.* 2 : 23.
340–25 rule r· the affairs of state.

righteousness

all
My. 162– 5 to fulfil all r·."— *Matt.* 3 : 15.
218– 4 to fulfil all r·."— *Matt.* 3 : 15.
and joy
My. 41–18 * standard of truth and r· and joy.
and Life
Ret. 62– 6 fruits of health, r·, and Life,
and peace
My. 282–12 towards justice, r·, and peace,
because of
Chr. 55–17 life because of r·.— *Rom.* 8 : 10.
Christ's
Mis. 30–31 cleanse our lives in Christ's r· ;
'01. 10–22 Love spans the . . . with Christ's r·,
fruit of
My. 40–20 * the fruit of r·— *Jas.* 3 : 18.
His
Mis. 140–15 by the right hand of His r·,
270–14 kingdom of God, and His r· ;— *Matt.* 6 : 33.
Chr. 55–10 kingdom of God, and His r· ;— *Matt.* 6 : 33.
Pan. 14–18 with the right arm of His r·.
My. 323–25 * by the right hand of His r·,
law in
Mis. 66– 4 gospel that fulfils the law in r·,
'02. 6–18 fulfils the law in r·,
My. 153– 6 Love will fulfil the law in r·.
love and
My. 292– 1 What cannot love and r· achieve
ministry of
My. 123–27 ministry of r· in all things,
of Love
My. 182–30 abound in the r· of Love,
practical
My. 40– 5 * thirst after practical r· ;
reign of
Mis. 125–10 in the . . . reign of r·
'01. 35– 8 call to the reign of r·,
My. 4–27 reign of r·, the glory of good,
rest of
Pan. 14– 2 rise into the rest of r·
reward
My. 252–15 reward r· and punish iniquity.
reward of
Mis. 123–26 receive the reward of r· :
sense of
My. 227– 4 personal sense of r·
suffer for
Mis. 291–25 worthy to suffer for r·,
Thy
Ret. 15– 9 make mention of Thy r·,— *Psal.* 71 : 16.
thy
Mis. 157–24 bring forth thy r·— *Psal.* 37 : 6.
'01. 35– 2 bring forth thy r·— *Psal.* 37 : 6.
My. 170–25 bring forth thy r·— *Psal.* 37 : 6.
vested in
Mis. 298–22 faith vested in r· triumphs !
work
My. 184– 6 wait upon Him and work r·.
worketh
My. 33–17 and worketh r·,— *Psal.* 15 : 2.
228–24 and worketh r·,— *Psal.* 15 : 2.

Mis. 120–10 *obedience* unto r·— *Rom.* 6 : 16.
185– 5 manifest as Truth, and through r·,
261–20 fulfil it" in r·,— *see Matt.* 5 : 17.
332– 9 and enrobe man in r· ;
Ret. 45–23 fulfil the law of Christ in r·.
Pul. 81– 6 * power of God for r·
Po. 71–10 R· ne'er — awestruck or dumb
My. 16–28 and r· to the plummet :— *Isa.* 28 : 17.
34– 7 r· from the God of his— *Psal.* 24 : 5.
48–25 * are all forces that make for r·.
217–31 but to fulfil it in r·.
274– 1 true sense of life and of r·,

rightful

Mis. 179– 4 r· desire in the hour of loss,
199– 9 come into their r· heritage,
Ret. 21–30 argument, with its r· conclusions,
No. 33– 6 r· place in schools of learning,
My. vii– 7 * r· place as the revelator

rightfully

My. 88–25 * r· turn with respect

righting-up

Pul. 80– 1 * must be a r· of the mind

rightly

Mis. 9– 2 through affliction r· understood,
90–11 It is always right to act r· ;
115–25 If one lives r·,
131– 5 r· to discern darkness or
169–20 it is necessary r· to read
169–29 * thoughts when r· understood.
170– 9 having r· read His Word,
240–19 incline the early thought r·,
353–22 makes the machinery work r· ;
Ret. 14– 1 as John Calvin r· called his own tenet
91– 3 r· called "the pearl of parables,"
Un. 3– 1 r· improved the lessons
Pul. 3– 8 power to think and act r·,
Rud. 2–12 We do not conceive r· of God,
'00. 8–18 doing r· by yourself and others.
Hea. 15– 8 r· understanding the power
My. 41– 2 * they think r· or righteously.
152–30 cause of all that is r· done.
238– 7 R· to read and to practise
274–13 begin r· enables one to end r·,

rightness

My. 52–29 * the moral r· of her book."
230–25 reap the reward of r·,
271–10 the sole proof of r·.
273–15 This sense of r· acquired by
278–23 promise and reward of r·.
281– 9 is the fruit of r·,

rights

all
My. 159–29 All r· reserved.
and privileges
Mis. 272– 2 * with all the r· and privileges
303–15 the same r· and privileges
My. 167–25 r· and privileges guaranteed
247– 8 equal r· and privileges,
255– 2 equal r· and privileges,
bill of
Mis. 289–27 on the basis of a bill of r·.
conjugal
Mis. 289–28 Can the bill of conjugal r· be
divine
Mis. 246– 7 both human and divine r·,
247– 2 both human and divine r· ;
My. 303–14 C. S. eschews divine r· in
human
(*see* **human**)
inalienable
Mis. 251–14 inalienable r· and radiant reality
My. 200–16 and receives his r· inalienable
individual
Mis. 80– 8 individual r· in a wrong direction
80–17 laws, infringing individual r·,
119–26 individual r· which one justly reserves
274–27 individual r· are trodden under foot,
Ret. 71–14 robbed of their individual r·,
No. 40–17 never to trespass . . . on individual r· ;
46–13 begin by admitting individual r·.
My. 200– 1 Religious liberty and individual r·
220– 4 the maintenance of individual r·,
227–22 constitutional individual r·,
268–13 maintenance of individual r·,
inherent
My. 326– 6 * their inherent r· are recognized
liberty and
Mis. 101–11 for human liberty and r·.
nation's
My. 277–21 if our nation's r· or honor were
no
Mis. 245–18 no r· that man is bound to respect.
272–23 * bestow no r· to *confer degrees.*
No. 45–14 no r· which man is bound to respect.
of Christian Scientists
My. 316–24 the r· of Christian Scientists
of conscience
Mis. 176–24 freedom, in the r· of conscience.
236–12 you have the r· of conscience,
Un. 5–19 Let us respect the r· of conscience
Pul. 10–12 r· of conscience, imperishable glory.
No. 44–15 abrogate the r· of conscience
'01. 33–15 to be allowed the r· of conscience
of freedom
Mis. 297–29 belongs to the r· of freedom.
of individuals
My. 265–12 in behalf of the sacred r· of individuals,
of man
Mis. 246–26 arrayed against the r· of man,
Peo. 10–13 Discerning the God-given r· of man,
10–26 The r· of man were vindicated
My. 222–27 r· of man and the liberty of
291–31 sacredly regard . . . the r· of man.

rights

of men
   My. 247– 2 inalienable, universal *r·* of men.
       254–23 inalienable, universal *r·* of men.
of Mind
   My. 212–25 interfering with the *r·* of Mind,
of mind
   Mis. 67– 9 his *r·* of mind and character.
of mortals
   Mis. 283–18 trespass on the *r·* of mortals.
of Spirit
   Mis. 56–13 and infringes the *r·* of Spirit.
of the individual
   Ret. 72– 3 with the *r·* of the individual.
of their neighbors
   Ret. 87–19 the *r·* of their neighbors,
religious
   ’00. 10–12 religious *r·* and laws of nations
   My. 167–27 religious *!·* in New Hampshire
States’
   My. 309–15 strong believer in States’ *r·*,
these
   Mis. 289–30 the spirit of these *r·*,
   No. 45–18 these *r·* are ably vindicated
universal
   My. 247– 2 universal *r·* of men.
       254–23 inalienable, universal *r·* of men.
whole
   Peo. 10–16 battles for man’s whole *r·*,
woman’s
   Mis. 388–13 poem
   Po. page 21 poem

   Mis. 289–21 *R·* that are bargained away
   No. 40–17 never to take away the *r·*,
   Peo. 11– 2 *r·* of the colored man were

rill
   Po. 2–18 waves kiss the murmuring *r·*
     66– 4 the thrill of that mountain *r·*,

rills
   Po. 30– 6 murmurs from the drowsy *r·*
   My. 186– 1 rocks, *r·*, mountains, meadows,

rim
   My. 247–16 to the *r·* where I stood.

ring
   Mis. 250–19 having no *r·* of the true metal.
     304–23 * It shall *r·* at sunrise and sunset ;
     304–28 * It will always *r·* at nine o’clock
   Pul. 62–11 * required a strong man to *r·* them,
   ’02. 3–25 hallow the *r·* of state.
   My. 81–20 * occasionally the voices would *r·* out
     121–16 gems that adorn the Christmas *r·*
     256– 2 Before the Christmas bells shall *r·*,

ringing
   ’02. 4–15 *r·* like soft vesper chimes
   Po. vi–19 *r·* to celebrate the passing of a
   My. 185– 3 and the harvest bells are *r·*.
     302–28 with escort and the *r·* of bells,

ringlets
   Po. 8–19 parting the *r·* to kiss my cheek.

rings
   Peo. 13–12 *r·* out the iron tread of merciless

ripe
   Mis. 85– 1 are *r·* for the harvest-home.
     313–20 the rich sheaves are *r·*,
   My. 281–28 when nations are *r·* for progress.
     350–27 Science *r·* in prayer, in word, and

ripen
   Mis. 331–10 understanding will *r·* the fruits of Spirit,
   Po. 46–10 Thus may it *r·* into bloom,

ripened
   Mis. 163–12 *r·* into interpretation through
     332–10 *r·* sheaves, and harvest songs.
   My. 198– 8 their abundant and *r·* fruit.

ripeness
   Mis. 164– 6 has appeared in the *r·* of time,

ripening
   My. 155–27 happy hearts and *r·* goodness.
     159– 9 *r·* and rich fruit of this branch
     195–15 nor understand what is not *r·*

riper
   Mis. 238– 5 the reverence of my *r·* years

ripples
   Ret. 27–21 As sweet music *r·* in one’s first

rippling
   Mis. 329–16 *r·* all nature in ceaseless flow,

rise
   Mis. 10–12 if they fall they shall *r·* again,
     80–13 to *r·* or fall on its own merit
     97– 2 gives man ability to *r·* above the
     107– 8 As we *r·* above the seeming mists of

rise
   Mis. 119– 6 *r·* and overthrow both.
     125– 5 *r·* to know that there is no sin,
     162–17 *r·* to his nativity in Spirit.
     234–11 reach this spiritual sense, and *r·*
     234–11 *r·* — to things most essential
     254–11 whose children *r·* up against her ;
     289–31 *r·* to the spiritual altitude whence they
     359–26 only as we *r·* in the scale of being.
     370– 1 “*R·* and walk.” — *see John 5 : 8.*
     374–12 its art will *r·* triumphant ;
     383–14 *r·* higher in the estimation of
   Chr. 55–19 *r·* up and walk. — *Acts 3 : 6.*
   Ret. 80–19 spiritual *r·* and progress.
   Pul. vii– 9 a registry of the *r·* of the mercury
     7–16 They will *r·* with joy,
   No. 1– 8 fill the rivers till they *r·* in floods,
     19– 4 it continues to *r·*, and the demand to
     42– 9 *r·* up and walk !” — *Luke 5 : 23.*
   Pan. 11–19 physically needs to *r·* again.
     14– 2 *r·* into the rest of righteousness
   ’01. 1–11 to *r·* higher and still higher
   ’02. 10–16 *r·* from sense to Soul, from earth to
   Peo. 9–23 metaphysics is seen to *r·* above physics,
   Po. 25– 7 Around you in memory *r·* !
     32– 1 *r·* in the morning and drink in
     65–19 *r·* to a seraph’s new song.
   My. 41–19 * *r·* from sentimental affection
     46–13 * *r·* to the demands of this
     116– 3 *r·* in consciousness to the true
     133– 7 *r·* to the church triumphant,
     165–19 *r·* above the oft-repeated inquiry,
     230–25 *r·* in the scale of being,
     287–16 so *r·* and still *r·* to His image
     359–30 get your students to help you *r·*

risen
   Mis. 39–10 They have *r·* up in a day
     123–19 *r·* to the awakened thought
     178–11 *r·* with Christ, — *Col. 3 : 1.*
     179–14 he is *r·* ; — *Matt. 28 : 6.*
     292–18 unlike the *r·*, immortal Love ;
     312–21 this man must have *r·* above
     370– 7 *r·* from the grave-clothes
   Man. 60–21 to exemplify our *r·* Lord.
   Ret. 76–11 *r·* to the altitude which
   Un. 61– 9 neither dead nor *r·*.
     62–24 not here, but is *r·*.” — *Luke 24 : 6.*
     62–27 Mary had *r·* to discern faintly
   Pul. 16– 6 Joyous, *r·*, we depart
   No. 36–25 *r·* from human sense
   ’01. 11– 5 *r·* to human apprehension,
   ’02. 20– 7 glory of earth’s woes is *r·*
   Peo. 5–13 *r·* higher to our mortal sense,
     5–17 *r·* above the sod to declare
   Po. 30–12 Give *r·* power to prayer ;
   My. 85– 8 * churches have *r·* by hundreds,
     119–29 have *r·* to look and wait
     122–21 *r·* to grasp the spiritual idea
     122–21 “He is *r·* ; he is not here : — *Mark 16 : 6.*
     122–25 can say his Christ is *r·*
     183–28 is *r·* upon thee.” — *Isa. 60 : 1.*
     191–15 witnesseth a *r·* Saviour,
     191–21 but human thought has *r·* !
   (see also **Christ***)*

rises
   Mis. 85–16 *r·* into the rest of perpetual,
     113–16 *r·* superior to suggestions from
     359–25 only as we rise
   Pul. 12–19 now *r·* clearer and nearer to
     41–24 * *r·* one hundred and twenty-six feet
   No. 19–24 *r·* to the fulness of the stature of
   Hea. 11–10 her modest tower *r·* slowly,
     15– 9 *r·* to that supreme sense
   My. 6–23 *r·* to a mental monument,
     94–27 “*r·* to a mental monument,
     200–12 *r·* upward to the realms of
     238–17 man *r·* above the letter,

rising
   Mis. 70–27 *r·* to the supremacy of Spirit,
     139–20 valued at $20,000 and *r·* in value
     144–25 our visible lives are *r·* to God.
     162– 9 stem these *r·* angry elements,
     354–28 As *r·* he rests in a liberty higher
     392–17 grandly *r·* to the heavens above.
   Ret. 51– 3 twenty thousand dollars, and *r·* in value,
     67–13 *r·* above corporeal personality,
   Un. 60–28 *R·* above the false, to the true
   Po. 20–21 grandly *r·* to the heavens above.
     68–21 pure as its *r·*, and bright as the star,
   My. 23–24 * walls of our new edifice are *r·*,
     29– 5 * *r·* in unison from the
     38–20 * *r·* with the roll of the organ
     44–19 * carried unanimously by a *r·* vote.
     45–29 * massive pile . . . *r·* to a height of
     78– 6 * massive dome *r·* to a height of

rising
My. 110–17	*r·* higher and forever higher
114–20	would leave me until the *r·* of the sun.
225– 4	*r·* to the zenith of success,
248–16	*r·* above theorems into the

risk
Mis. 99– 7	The *r·* is stupendous.
213–10	No *r·* is so stupendous as to
Pul. 15– 9	and so *r·* human displeasure
31– 7	* At the *r·* of colloquialism,

risks
Mis. 211–23	He *r·* nothing who obeys the law of

rite
Mis. 298–16	material *r·* of water baptism,
No. 34– 9	commemorating . . . with a material *r·*.
Hea. 2–25	not in the power of . . . a dead *r·*
Peo. 9– 7	compliance with a religious *r·*

rites
Mis. 17–10	material religion with its *r·* and
No. 12–10	doctrines, *r·*, and ceremonies,

ritual
Mis. 176–21	frozen *r·* and creed
No. 12–22	beyond doctrine and *r·* ;
My. 90– 4	* eloquence of orator or magnetic *r·*,
262–24	*r·* of our common Christmas
266– 7	*r·*, creed, and trusts in place of

ritualism
Ret. 65– 6	*R·* and dogma lead to

ritualistic
Mis. 81–14	*ceremonial (or r·) waters*

rival
Mis. 395– 5	The rose his *r·* reigns,
Po. 57–12	The rose his *r·* reigns,

rivalries
My. 40–14	* Through *r·* among leaders

rivalry
Mis. 43–22	such sinister *r·* does . . . injury
204–31	all envy, *r·*, evil thinking,
268– 7	imaginary victories of *r·*
281– 4	*r·*, jealousy, envy, revenge.
347–31	targets for envy, *r·*, slander ;
356– 6	Envy, *r·*, hate need no temporary
Rud. 17– 9	never originated in pride, *r·*,
'02. 14–20	envy, *r·*, and falsehood
My. 40–14	* their strongholds of *r·*.
262–23	merriment, mad ambition, *r·*,

rivals
My. 95–14	* a dome which *r·* that of

river (*see also* **river's**)
Mis. 82– 6	peace floweth as a *r·*
127–17	"*r·* of His pleasure,"— *see Psal.* 36 : 8.
268– 9	peace been as a *r·*."— *Isa.* 48 : 18.
373–11	cast out . . . water as a *r·*,
Pul. 1– 2	*r·* of Thy pleasures.— *Psal.* 36 : 8.
3–17	*r·* of Thy pleasures."— *Psal.* 36 : 8.
3–20	The *r·* of His pleasures is a
3–23	We drink of this *r·* when all
7–30	*r·* of Thy pleasures."— *Psal.* 36 : 8.
9–21	*r·* of His pleasures."— *see Psal.* 36 : 8.
48–13	* *r·*, as it wanders eastward.
My. 18–14	'*r·* of His pleasure,'— *see Psal.* 36 : 8.
43–16	* taken from the midst of the *r·*

river-borne
Mis. 373–11	might cause her to be *r·*."

river's
Pul. 39–20	* Repeats its glory in the *r·* flow ;

rivers
No. 1– 8	fill the *r·* till they rise in floods,

road
Mis. 32– 2	broad *r·* to destruction.
147–15	to follow the *r·* of duty,
Pul. 49–24	* on the *r·* from Concord,
My. 313– 9	the *r·* in front of his house

roads
'00. 12–12	Corresponding to its *r·*, its gates,

roadside
Pan. 12–18	and walk, not wait by the *r·*,
Po. v–17	* *seated herself by the r·*

roam
Mis. 396– 3	to *r·* Where ghosts and goblins stalk.
Po. 58–15	to *r·* Where ghosts and goblins stalk.

roams
Po. 65–20	the stranger who *r·*

roar
Pul. 14–20	drown your voice with its *r·*,

roasting
Peo. 3– 6	eternal *r·* amidst noxious vapors ;

rob
Mis. 67– 8	thou shalt not *r·* man of money,
No. 2– 8	to *r·* disease of all reality ;
41–19	such as come to steal and to *r·*.
My. 5–18	*r·* the grave of its victory.
165– 2	Of two things fate cannot *r·* us ;

robbed
Mis. 96– 2	*r·* the grave of victory
114– 9	watch that these be not secretly *r·*,
Ret. 71–13	*r·* of their individual rights,
Pul. 84– 4	* wrong be *r·* of her bitterness

robber
Mis. 226–29	Slander is a midnight *r·* ;

robberies
Mis. 201–29	to bar his door against further *r·*.

robbers
Mis. 325–28	he sees *r·* finding ready ingress

robbery
Mis. 201–25	protect . . . more securely after a *r·*,

robbing
My. 266– 4	*r·* of people of life and liberty

robe
Pul. 13–11	He that touches the hem of Christ's *r·*
'01. 26–17	pinned to the seamless *r·*,
My. 152– 4	the touch of Jesus' *r·*
192– 7	The ideal *r·* of Christ is seamless.

Robertson
G. D.
My. 73–21	* It is in charge of G. D. *R·*,

Pul. 28–23	* Faber, *R·*, Wesley, Bowring,

robes
Mis. 246– 1	pulpit and press, clerical *r·* and
339– 8	*r·* the future with hope's rainbow
Un. 3–11	washed their *r·* white through
Peo. 9– 9	baptism of Spirit that washes our *r·*
Po. 65– 6	*r·* were as spotless as snow :
My. 125–25	beautiful garments — her bridal *r·*.
247–12	Put on the *r·* of Christ,

robin (*see also* **robin's**)
Mis. 329–28	Old *r·*, though stricken to the heart

robin's
Po. 53–12	Poor *r·* lonely mass.

Robinson, John
My. 183– 6	verify what John *R·* wrote

robs
Un. 38–14	A material sense of life *r·* God,
48–11	*r·* the grave of its victory.

robust
Mis. 325–15	*R·* forms, with manly brow
My. 308–19	My father's person was erect and *r·*.

Rochester, N. Y.
Pul. 88–31	* Herald, *R·*, N. Y.

Rochester* (N. Y.) *Post Express
My. 92–25	* [*R·* (*N. Y.*) *P· E·*]

Rock
Man. 19– 2	to be built on the *R·*, Christ;
Po. 73–16	By the "*R·*" or wave,

rock
and feathers
Mis. 263– 6	in any language— *r·* and *feathers:*

and the sea
Po. 68– 9	Here the *r·* and the sea

built on the
Mis. 140–28	Built on the *r·*, our church

great
Mis. 144–17	shadow of a great *r·*— *Isa.* 32 : 2.
263– 9	shadow of a great *r·*— *Isa.* 32 : 2.
Pul. 20–19	shadow of a great *r·*— *Isa.* 32 : 2.

heart of a
Mis. 144–15	in the heart of a *r·*,

living
Un. 14–20	corner-stone of living *r·*,

of Christ
Mis. 152–22	founded upon the *r·* of Christ,
176–18	to build upon the *r·* of Christ,
383–10	built upon the *r·* of Christ.
Pul. 10–17	your standard on the *r·* of Christ,
Pan. 15– 8	Truth, the *r·* of Christ,
My. 187–30	its foundations on the *r·* of Christ,
357–18	build upon the *r·* of Christ,

of Christ's teachings
'01. 25– 3	on the *r·* of Christ's teachings,

of divine oneness
Mis. 131–11	upon the *r·* of divine oneness,

of salvation
My. 165–21	this is my *r·* of salvation

of Truth
No. 38–10	*r·* of Truth, on which he built his

rock

rests on the
Po. 18–20 or rests on the r·.
sea-beaten
My. 295–18 The Bible is our sea-beaten r·.
this
Mis. 144–19 "Upon this r· I will build — *Matt.* 16 : 18.
263– 7 "Upon this r· I will build — *Matt.* 16 : 18.
399–23 *Laus Deo,* — on this r·
Pul. 16– 8 *Laus Deo,* — on this r·
'00. 5–22 On this r· C. S. is built.
Po. 76– 7 *Laus Deo,* — on this r·
My. 129–18 leap disdainfully from this r·
Truth is the
No. 38–13 Truth is the r· which the builders
upon the
My. 139– 6 soulfully founded upon the r·, Christ Jesus,
162–30 may it build upon the r· of ages
164–28 It builds upon the r·,

Mis. 153– 9 the r· became a fountain ;
393–19 As the r·, whose upward tending
397– 9 Truth engrounds me on the r·,
Ret. 11–17 r· The cradle of her power,
Pul. 18–18 Truth engrounds me on the r·,
Rud. 8– 1 No r· brings forth an apple ;
'00. 5–23 r· which the builders reject
Po. 10– 8 Didst r· the country's cradle
12–18 Truth engrounds me on the r·,
52– 3 r·, whose upward tending
60–14 r· The cradle of her power,
My. 260–17 basis of Christmas is the r·,
313–10 persons being hired to r· me,
337– 9 Didst r· the country's cradle

rock-bound
Mis. 145–18 In our r· friendship,
Po. 1– 6 sustains thee in thy r· cell.

Rockies
My. 77–11 * From beyond the R·,

rocking
Mis. 329–20 r· the oriole's cradle ;

Rockland, Mass.
Pul. 88–15 * *Independent,* R·, M·.

rock-ribbed
Mis. 254– 8 her young in the r· nest
356–20 r· nests of the raven's callow
My. 186– 5 cluster around this r· church
340–20 leaders of our r· State.

rocks
Mis. 280–29 r· and sirens in their course,
323–12 serpents hide among the r·,
327–30 plunge headlong over the jagged r·.
Ret. 27–22 meandering midst pebbles and r·,
Po. 2– 2 Though kindred r·, to sport at
My. 186– 1 r·, rills, mountains, meadows,
186– 6 nestlings in the crannies of the r·,
341– 5 engraven on her granite r·,

rod
Mis. 9– 5 these uses of His r· !
9– 6 passes all His flock under His r·
19– 4 but the r· of God, and the
51–13 *Doesn't the use of the r· teach*
51–14 The use of the r· is virtually
118–19 His r· and His staff comfort you.
127–24 Ofttimes the r· is His means of grace ;
208–20 His r· brings to view His love,
348–19 when God shall reveal His r·,
376–20 there rose one r· of rainbow hues,
387–20 Learn, too, that wisdom's r· is given
Ret. 80–24 under his compelling r·.
Po. 6–15 Learn, too, that wisdom's r·
30–14 and midst the r·,
My. 127–15 even as Aaron's r· swallowed up the
288–27 His r· is love.
292– 8 His r· and His staff comfort the

rode
Pul. 6–25 rose and fell and r· the rough sea.

rods
My. 127–15 r· of the magicians of Egypt.

rôle
Mis. 285–28 in the r· of a superfine conjugality ;
288–23 The selfish r· of a martyr

roll
Mis. 179– 2 r· away the stone?" — *see Mark* 16 : 3.
275– 4 r· away the stone from the door
Man. 51– 6 name shall be dropped from the r·
53– 6 the r· of Church membership.
56– 5 name shall be dropped from the r·
Ret. 9–21 * where dying thunders r·
20–18 Awoke new beauty in the surge's r· !
Po. 16–10 rush into life, and r· on with its tide.

roll
My. 38–20 * rising with the r· of the organ
332–29 r· of papers recording the death of

rolled
Mis. 1–20 and another self seemingly r· up in
74–19 r· away the stone from the door of
123–18 Divine Science has r· away the stone
147– 3 Another year has r· on,
179– 3 r· away by human suffering.
399–19 R· away from loving heart
Pul. 16– 4 R· away from loving heart
No. 36–24 r· away the stone from the sepulchre,
Po. 76– 3 R· away from loving heart
My. 191–22 The stone is r· away.

rolling
Mis. 26– 7 r· of worlds, in the most subtle
130–11 "r· sin as a sweet morsel
174–12 from . . . to the r· of a world.
332– 1 kindling the stars, r· the worlds,
Po. 28– 2 Of every r· sphere,
77– 1 God of the r· year !

rolls
Mis. 274–29 r· along the streets besmeared with
293–27 r· on the human heart a stone ;
384–20 * like the sea, R· on with thee,
Po. 36–19 * like the sea, R· on with thee,

Roman
Pul. 25–26 * silver lamps of R· design,
65–22 * a R· soldier parted his mantle
Pan. 3–23 R· mythology (one of my girlhood studies),
'00. 12–10 time of the R· Emperor Augustus.
My. 305–24 not of the Greek nor of the R·

Roman Catholics
Man. 87– 3 Neither . . . shall teach R· C·

Romanesque
Pul. 24–10 * the design a R· tower
24–24 * architecture is R· throughout.
26–23 * has a R· border

Romans
Un. 21– 1 In R· (ii. 15) we read

Rome (*see also* Rome's)
Pul. 5–27 and the Vatican at R·.
65– 5 * inviting . . . to unity with R·,
65– 9 * whatever attitude R· may assume
'00. 1–23 Paris, Berlin, R·, Pekin.

Rome
James J.
My. 62–15 * signature
J. J.
Mis. 313–18 "The Temptation," a poem by J. J. R·,

Rome's
Pul. 10– 8 R· fallen fanes and silent Aventine

rondeau
Mis. 395– 9 And yet I trow, When sweet r·
Po. 57–16 And yet I trow, When sweet r·

Rondelet
Mis. 394–14 * poem
Po. page 57 * poem

roof
Mis. 215–19 summit of the r· of the house
Ret. 19– 3 under the paternal r· in Tilton.
20– 1 After returning to the paternal r·
Pul. 25–12 * the r· is of terra cotta tiles,
47–30 * angles and pitch of the r·,
My. 69– 5 * ceiling or r· and side walls
309–24 father's house had a sloping r·,
336–12 "After returning to the paternal r·

room
Mis. 399– 4 And for you make radiant r·
Man. 49–13 wisdom necessary in a sick r·,
69–25 Mrs. Eddy's R·
69–25 The r· in The Mother Church
Chr. 53–36 For health makes r·.
Ret. 8–15 in the same r· with grandmother,
8–21 I then left the r·,
9– 2 returned with me to grandmother's r·,
Pul. 25–11 * the "directors' r·," and the vestry.
25–20 * and the directors' r·.
26–22 * In this r· the mosaic marble
26–25 * The r· is toned in pale green
27– 3 * The directors' r· is very beautiful
31–25 * Mrs. Eddy entered the r·.
34–15 * walked into the adjoining r·,
40–14 * R· WHICH THE CHILDREN BUILT
42– 1 * had closed the large vestry r·
49– 1 * sunny r· which Mrs. Eddy
58–14 * Inside is a basement r·,
58–27 * a r· devoted to her,
69–12 * to leave no r· there for the bad,
Po. 75–11 And for you make radiant r·

room

My.	6–19	The *r·* of your Leader remains
	56–15	* *r·* for growth of attendance
	68–16	* famous *r·* will be undisturbed.
	78–29	* *r·* in which they were seated,
	131–28	shall not be *r·* enough — *Mal.* 3 : 10.
	156–16	upper *r·* furnished : — *Luke* 22 : 12.
	166–29	cabinet, . . . placed in my *r·*
	172– 4	* *r·* for Vanderbilt Hall.
	216–16	the *r·* of the Pastor Emeritus
	217– 9	the *r·* of the Pastor Emeritus.
	260– 7	to make *r·* for substance,
	269–28	shall not be *r·* enough — *Mal.* 3 : 10.
	353–21	Mrs. Eddy's *R·*.
	353–21	The *r·* in The Mother Church
	353–24	nothing in this *r·* now

rooming

'02.	15– 7	*r·* and boarding indigent students

rooms

Mis.	159–11	My heart has many *r·* :
	276– 3	*r·* of the Palmer House,
Man.	27–20	Directors to provide suitable *r·*,
	63–18	these *r·* are well located.
	74–12	not have their offices or *r·* in
	74–13	nor in *r·* connected therewith.
	81–21	*r·* where the C. S. textbook
My.	54–26	* the *r·* were opened and a large
	68–22	* the Readers' special *r·*.
	73–22	* information concerning *r*
	75–11	* were assigned *r·* in hotels
	123–12	*r·* in the same building.
	296–28	she depicted its *r·*,

Roosevelt, President

My.	281–24	* influence which President *R·* has

root

Mis.	37–17	the axe at the *r·* of the tree.
	235–12	the axe at the *r·* of the tree
	285–19	laying the axe at the *r·* of error.
Chr.	55– 4	I am the *r·* and the — *Rev.* 22 : 16.
Un.	18–23	in order to strike at its *r·* ;
No.	7– 5	any *r·* of bitterness to spring up
'00.	14–17	Let no *r·* of bitterness spring up
'01.	13–15	lays the axe at the *r·* of sin,
	23–17	axe at the *r·* of all error,
My.	122– 7	Sin is like a dock *r·*.
	128–31	take no *r·* in your thought
	149–30	solicit every *r·* and every leaf
	268–25	lays the axe at the *r·* of all evil,
	287–21	lays the axe at the *r·* of the tree
	296– 3	"unto the *r·* of the trees," — *Matt.* 3 : 10.

rooted

Mis.	392–16	deeply *r·* in a soil of love ;
Po.	20–20	deeply *r·* in a soil of love ;
My.	47–21	* *r·* itself in so many distant lands,

roots

Mis.	154– 9	enrich its *r·*, and enlarge its borders
My.	122– 8	the *r·* must be eradicated
	139– 4	nor plucked up by the *r·*,

rope

Mis.	61–18	* dangling at the end of a *r·*.
	61–23	or dangle at the end of a *r·*

rose (see also rose's)

Mis.	24–13	I *r·*, dressed myself,
	64– 7	and *r·* to his native estate,
	142– 3	to bud and blossom as the *r·* !
	171– 4	*r·* to the occasion with the second
	225–20	Mrs. Rawson then *r·* from her seat,
	345–12	his pure and strong faith *r·* higher
	376–20	there *r·* one rod of rainbow hues,
	395– 5	The *r·* his rival reigns,
Chr.	53–31	Sharon's *r·* must bud and bloom
Ret.	13–22	and I *r·* and dressed myself,
	40–11	sick woman *r·* from her bed,
Pul.	6–25	*r·* and fell and rode the rough sea.
	22–15	budded and blossomed as the *r·*.
	25–15	* marble stairs of *r·* pink,
	27–12	* In the auditorium are two *r·* windows
	27–16	* The other *r·* window represents
	83–22	* pour incense upon the *r·*.
Rud.	6–14	* "color is in *us*," not "in the *r·* ;"
'01.	11– 1	*r·* to the fulness of his stature in
'02.	1–10	and blossoming as the *r·*.
	15–24	I *r·* and recorded the hallowed
	19– 7	he *r·* from earth to heaven.
Po.	1–12	Ye *r·*, a monument of Deity,
	8– 5	seek the loving *r·*,
	39– 7	*R·* from a water-cup ;
	57–12	The *r·* his rival reigns,
My.	32– 5	* and their voices *r·* as one
	36– 5	* the five thousand present *r·* as one
	81–23	* *r·* tingling to the great dome,

roseate

Pan.	1– 9	*r·* blush of joyous June is here

rosebud

Mis.	231–24	pucker the *r·* mouth into saying,
Po.	46– 1	thy *r·* heart rests warm

rose-flush

Pul.	32– 2	* transparency and *r·* of tint

rose-leaf

Mis.	250–16	and laid on a *r·*.

rose's

Mis.	390– 4	Thy breezes scent the *r·* breath ;
Po.	55– 4	Thy breezes scent the *r·* breath ;

roses

Pul.	42–27	* with ferns and pure white *r·*.
	42–30	* filled with beautiful pink *r·*.

rosewood

My.	171–27	* *r·* casket beautifully bound with

Roslindale

Ret.	51– 2	Mr. Ira O. Knapp of *R·*,

rosy

Pul.	83– 7	* But the east is *r·*,

rot

Mis.	293–30	there to moulder and *r·*.
	343–25	left to propagate — and *r·*.
Pul.	7–22	tabernacles crumble with dry *r·*.
Peo.	7– 4	to *r·* and ruin the mind's ideals.

rotation

My.	247– 9	equality of the sexes, *r·* in office.
	250– 4	*R·* in office promotes wisdom,
	254–16	* chapter sub-title
	255– 2	equality of the sexes, *r·* in office."
	255– 6	By "*r·* in office" I do not mean

Rotherham's

Mis.	373– 7	the following from *R·* translation

rough

Mis.	323–19	climbing its *r·* cliffs,
	360– 3	in the *r·* marble, encumbered .
	385–12	moored at last — Beyond *r·* foam.
Pul.	6–25	and rode the *r·* sea.
Po.	43–17	*R·* or treacherous way.
	48– 5	moored at last — Beyond *r·* foam.
My.	194–29	* stood the storm when seas were *r·*,
	232– 3	sailing over *r·* seas

roughly

Mis.	128– 1	needs often to be *stirred*, sometimes *r·*,

round

Mis.	77–17	eternal *r·* of harmonious being.
	83– 2	rhythmic *r·* of unfolding bliss,
	237–30	fear clustered *r·* his coming.
	277–25	Though clouds are *r·* about Him,
	385–25	triumphant *r·* thy death-couch
	392– 5	peaceful presence hath begirt thee *r·*.
Ret.	11–19	wreaths are twined *r·* Plymouth Rock,
	52– 4	to build a hedge *r·* about it
Pul.	39– 7	* *R·* our restlessness, His rest.
'02.	2–28	*r·* the gospel of grace,
Po.	2– 5	* "Plays *r·* the head,
	20– 7	peaceful presence hath begirt thee *r·*.
	25–12	Fragrance fresh *r·* the dead,
	48–21	faith triumphant *r·* thy
	60–16	wreaths are twined *r·* Plymouth Rock,
My.	133–16	one more *r·* of old Sol
	189–29	why throng in pity *r·* me?

rounded

Mis.	13–16	*r·* sense of the existence of good.

rounds

'02.	4–17	through the measureless *r·* of eternity.

Rounsevel, R. D.

My.	314–31	following affidavit by R. D. *R·*
	315–15	* signature
	315–17	* personally appeared R. D. *R·*

rouse

Mis.	283–11	*r·* the slumbering inmates,
Chr.	53– 7	*r·* the living, wake the dead,

roused

Ret.	31–15	acting . . . on my *r·* consciousness,
'01.	30–20	*r·* to the establishment of a new-old

rouses

Un.	1– 1	*r·* so much natural doubt

route

'02.	10–30	walking every step over the land *r·*,

routine

Mis.	136– 3	*r·* of such material modes

rove

Po.	34– 6	But whither wouldst thou *r·*,

roving

My.	314– 5	* the Pattersons led a *r·* existence.

Roxbury

My.	56–14	* Cambridge, Chelsea, and *R·*.

royal

My.	3–13	not a dweller apart in *r·* solitude ;
	118– 1	My soul thanks the loyal, *r·* natures
	206–23	a *r·* priesthood, — *I Pet. 2 : 9.*
	290– 5	Queen's *r·* and imperial honors

Royal Arch Mason

My. 335– 5 * degree of a *R· A· M·*

Royal Arch Masons and masons

Ret. 19–13 Number 3, of *R· A· m·*.
My. 330–25 No. 3, of *R· A· M·*.

Royal College of Physicians

Peo. 6– 3 Fellow of the *R· C· of P·*

royalty

Mis.	121–24	insult to divine *r·*,
Pul.	83–24	* we live in the reflected *r·*
No.	36–17	reality and *r·* of his being,
'02.	3–21	dazzling diadem of *r·*
	15–11	paid me not one dollar of *r·*

rubric

Ret. 31– 7 paramount to *r·* and dogma

rubs

Mis. 325–20 calls out, *r·* his eyes,

ruby

Mis. 240– 4 sparkling eyes, and *r·* cheeks

rude

Mis. 360– 4 with crude, *r·* fragments,

rudely

Un. 5– 1 will *r·* or prematurely agitate

ruder

Un. 11–21 the *r·* sort then prevalent,

rudimentary

My. 309–23 * building of *r·* architecture.''

rudiments

Mis. 44– 5 teach . . . the *r·* of C. S.,

ruffle

Mis. 224–23 no . . . shall agitate or *r·* it ;

rug

Pul. 76–15 * *r·* composed entirely of skins of

rugged

Mis.	347–21	may be smooth, or it may be *r·* ;
	398– 4	All the *r·* way.
Ret.	46–10	All the *r·* way.
Pul.	17– 9	All the *r·* way.
Hea.	19–24	along the *r·* way, into the
Po.	v–11	* *whose r· outlines resemble*
	14– 8	All the *r·* way.
	53– 8	Light o'er the *r·* steep.
My.	201–24	All the *r·* way.

ruin

Peo. 7– 5 leaving to rot and *r·* the

ruined

My. 60– 9 * you will be *r·* for life ;

ruins

Mis. 326–14 wrapping their altars in *r·*.
'00. 12–26 The entire city is now in *r·*.

Rule

My. 230–11 each *R·* and By-law in this Manual

rule (noun)

above
Mis. 282–20 above *r·* of mental practice.
according to
Mis. 265–13 demonstrates . . . according to *r·*,
and demonstration
Mis. 336–12 insist on the *r·* and demonstration
Ret. 94–24 Principle, *r·*, and demonstration.
apostle's
Hea. 5–24 but on the apostle's *r·*,
as a

Mis.	88–30	As a *r·*, drop one of these doctors
	283– 4	As a *r·*, one has no more right to
Man.	94– 6	As a *r·* there should be no receptions
Ret.	83–18	as a *r·*, the student should explain
Pul.	56– 9	* as a *r·* are the most intelligent.
'00.	3–16	As a *r·* the Adam-race are not apt to
My.	231– 6	As a *r·*, she has suffered most from

commandment and
My. 64–17 * obey this commandment and *r·*,
constant
Mis. 147–15 makes it his constant *r·*
definite
My. 43– 5 * they might have a definite *r·*
direct
Mis. 282– 9 direct *r·* for practice of C. S.
My. 363–28 this direct *r·* is more or less
divine
Mis. 85–13 this divine *r·* in Science :
| | 209– 9 | the divine *r·* of this Principle |
| | 301–26 | divine *r·* for human conduct. |

rule (noun)

diviner
No. 3–12 but I obeyed a diviner *r·*.
emphatic
My. 12–17 an emphatic *r·* of St. Paul :
false
Mis. 220– 3 a false *r·* the opposite way.
first
Mis. 52–26 because the first *r·* was not
for motives
Man. 40– 4 A *R·* for Motives and Acts.
general
Mis. 155–21 will hereafter, as a general *r·*,
| | 236–27 | as a general *r·*, one will be |
| | 293– 5 | (as a general *r·*) |
Ret. 82– 5 general *r·* is, that my students
given

Mis.	366– 7	fixed Principle, given *r·*,
No.	11–22	fixed Principle, given *r·*,
	33–11	fixed Principle, a given *r·*,
'01.	23–15	fixed Principle and given *r·*,
My.	113–25	fixed Principle and a given *r·*,
	348–27	demonstrable Principle and given *r·*.

golden
My. 364– 6 departure from this golden *r·*
good
Mis. 220– 2 you will find that a good *r·*
home
'02. 3–12 inauguration of home *r·* in Cuba,
illustrates the
Mis. 337–11 and he illustrates the *r·* :
in Christian Science
Mis. 200–11 Paul insists on the rare *r·* in C. S.
| | 346–24 | It is a *r·* in C. S. |
Pul. 12–23 Self-abnegation, . . . a *r·* in C. S.
includes a
Mis. 75– 9 includes a *r·* that must be understood,
indispensable
Mis. 118– 7 the indispensable *r·* of obedience.
in Science
Mis. 85–13 this divine *r·* in Science :
| | 265–12 | understands a single *r·* in Science, |
no
My. 242–10 and no *r·* for its demonstration.
of addition
Un. 53–18 assertion that the *r·* of addition
of being
Mis. 189– 4 divine Principle and *r·* of being,
of Christian Science
Mis. 19– 3 will break the *r·* of C. S.
| | 233–26 | perfection of the *r·* of C. S. |
| | 337– 7 | Principle and *r·* of C. S. |
Man. 87–16 Principle and *r·* of C. S.,
My. 241– 5 * Principle and *r·* of C. S.
of conduct
Man. 81–20 *R·* of Conduct.
of divinity
Ret. 57–28 the status and *r·* of divinity,
No. 7– 2 The *r·* of divinity is golden ;
of error
No. 44–21 no Reign of Terror or *r·* of error
of finite matter
Ret. 58– 3 taking the *r·* of finite matter,
of human mind
Mis. 62–24 to solve . . . by the *r·* of human mind,
of Life
Un. 55– 1 *r·* of Life can be demonstrated,
of mathematics
'01. 4– 6 To depart from the *r·* of mathematics
Hea. 8–27 as we do to the *r·* of mathematics,
of mental practice
My. 364– 3 *r·* of mental practice in C. S.
of order
Ret. 50–27 for furnishing a new *r·* of order
of our church
Mis. 129– 9 and the *r·* of our church
of Science
Mis. 172–29 first and fundamental *r·* of Science
Un. 50–25 Adopt this *r·* of Science,
of spiritual love
'02. 8–22 works out the *r·* of spiritual love ;
of subtraction
Un. 53–18 assertion that . . . is the *r·* of subtraction,
of this Church
Man. 67–22 break a *r·* of this Church and are
of this Principle
Hea. 8–26 adhere to the *r·* of this Principle
one
Mis. 52–24 or failing to demonstrate one *r·*
No. 10–12 one *r·*, and one Principle for all
or demonstration
'01. 23–12 *r·*, or demonstration of C. S.,
Principle and
(*see* **Principle**)

rule (noun)

same
Mis. 265–10 *one* Principle and the same *r·* ;
352–15 by the same *r·* that sin is healed.
Un. 2–20 According to this same *r·*,
scientific
Mis. 116–30 lose the scientific *r·* and its reward :
Scriptural
Mis. 283–20 The Scriptural *r·* of this Science
second
Mis. 341– 9 up the scale of Science to the second *r·*,
supreme
Mis. 368–29 rejoice in His supreme *r·*,
the only
Mis. 338–13 these afford the only *r·* I have found
this
Mis. 90–13 This *r·* is forever golden :
129–11 If this *r·* fails in effect,
187–11 This *r·* of harmony must be accepted
200–14 The divine Science of this *r·*
220– 1 demonstrate this *r·*, which obtains
Man. 41–14 departure from this *r·* disqualifies a
102–15 but this *r·* shall not apply to
Ret. 59–10 applying this *r·* to a demonstration of
82– 8 exception to this *r·* should be very rare.
Un. 50–25 Adopt this *r·* of Science,
Pul. 12–24 This *r·* clearly interprets God as
Hea. 6– 2 should this *r·* fail hereafter,
My. 4– 3 obedience to this *r·* spiritualizes
226– 3 This *r·* strictly observed will preserve
227–28 I abide by this *r·* and triumph by it.
verity and
My. 37–12 * verity and *r·* of the Christianity of
wholesome
Mis. 283–13 Any exception to the old wholesome *r·*,

Mis. 6–31 health is generally the *r·* ;
52–25 *r·* farther on and more difficult
69– 8 Its *r·* is, that man shall utilize
194– 3 and the *r·* whereby sin, sickness,
200–12 a *r·* that is susceptible of proof,
233–24 with the exactness of the *r·*
382– 1 were either a truism or a *r·*,
My. 84– 7 * It is a *r·* in some denominations
272–13 the *r·*, and the demonstration of

rule (verb)

Mis. 141–22 *r·* this business transaction,
303–13 Let us serve instead of *r·*,
Man. 41–23 and *r·* out of me all sin ;
Ret. 61–24 *r·* out every sense of disease
Pan. 14–13 they shall *r·* all nations.
My. 192–10 gloom of his glory *r·* not
294– 1 right of the majority to *r·*.
340–25 intention to *r·* righteously

ruled

Ret. 65–17 *r·* Christ out of the synagogues,

ruler

Mis. 117– 1 "*r·* over many things." — *Matt.* 25 : 23.
152–12 dictator, arbiter, or *r·*,
287–28 makes one *r·* over one's self
341– 9 be made *r·* over many things.
Pul. 13– 7 *r·* over many," — *Matt.* 25 : 23.
My. 294–27 *r·* . . . has now passed through
342–30 * directed by a single earthly *r·*?"
343–12 * would, like herself, be the *r·*.

rulers

Mis. 53–24 to make the *r·* understand,
199–16 The *r·* sought the life of Jesus ;
My. 128–13 No crown nor sceptre nor *r·*

rulership

Un. 38–17 *r·* of more gods than one.
My. 342–31 present *r·* will advance
343– 6 * is contemplated in the *r·*.

Ruler Supreme

Po. 77–14 *R· S·* ! to Thee we'll

Rules

Mis. 148– 8 *R·* and By-laws in the Manual
Man. 3– 3 *R·* and By-Laws in the Manual
18–22 Tenets, *R·*, and By-Laws,
33– 7 maintain the Tenets, *R·*,
51– 1 *R·* herein set forth,
52–15 compliance with our Church *R·*

rules

and by-laws
My. 49–14 * formulate the *r·* and by-laws,
and divine Principle
Mis. 32– 9 *r·* and divine Principle of C. S.
195– 3 *r·* and divine Principle of
and practice
Mis. 252–23 divine Principle, *r·*, and practice
My. 239– 5 divine Principle, *r·*, and practice
both
Un. 53–19 sums done under both *r·*

rules

church
Mis. 310–19 comply with the church *r·*.
contrary to the
My. 359– 2 do not act contrary to the *r·*
definite
My. 358– 1 C. S. abides by the definite *r·*
demonstrated
My. 105– 5 *r·* demonstrated prove one's faith
divine Principle and
Mis. 19– 9 divine Principle and *r·* of C. S.
87–23 taught the divine Principle and *r·*
307–28 adhere to the divine Principle and *r·*
established
Man. 49–15 *r·* established by the publishers.
fixed
Ret. 87–13 implicit adherence to fixed *r·*,
for branch churches
My. 243– 7 *r·* for branch churches as published
four first
Pan. 9– 9 four first *r·* pertaining thereto,
furnish
My. 180– 1 furnish *r·* whereby man can prove
given
Mis. 282–19 exceptions to most given *r·* :
higher
Mis. 29–32 working up to those higher *r·*
30– 5 and doubt its higher *r·*,
hygienic
Mis. 40– 5 to mingle hygienic *r·*, drugs,
in Christian Science
Ret. 56– 3 demonstrable *r·* in C. S.,
invariable
'01. 24– 6 by means of invariable *r·*
its
Man. 73–12 provided its *r·* so permit.
Ret. 93– 7 established its *r·* in consonance
My. 230– 9 Its *r·* apply not to one member only,
247– 7 its *r·* are health, holiness, and
255– 1 its *r·* are health, holiness, and
new
Pul. 46– 4 * new *r·* were formulated.
of Christian Science
Mis. 19– 9 Principle and *r·* of C. S.
31–14 Principle or the *r·* of C. S. ;
293–16 will pervert the *r·* of C. S.,
354–14 Principle and *r·* of C. S.,
Ret. 87– 7 the *r·* of C. S. can be
of church government
Mis. 284–30 the *r·* of church government,
of conduct
My. 223– 1 chapter sub-title
of divine Love
Man. 45–12 demonstrating the *r·* of divine Love.
of divine Science
Mis. 114–11 *r·* of divine Science announced in
of its divine Principle
Mis. 22–23 the *r·* of its divine Principle,
of its Tenets
Man. 54–10 break the *r·* of its Tenets
of metaphysics
Mis. 221– 5 one gains in the *r·* of metaphysics,
of Mind-healing
Ret. 78–15 *r·* of Mind-healing are wholly
of Science
My. 235– 7 imperative *r·* of Science,
of service
My. 342–31 "In time its present *r·* of service
of the university
Man. 73–17 if the *r·* of the university or
of this practice
No. 3–12 dependent on the *r·* of this practice
perfect
My. 205–28 demonstrated by perfect *r·* ;
Principle and
(*see* **Principle**)
published
My. 359–11 my written and published *r·*,
result of
Pul. 45–27 * result of *r·* made by Mrs. Eddy.
scientific
Mis. 289–10 the application of scientific *r·*
these
Ret. 87–14 Let some of these *r·* be here stated.
those
Mis. 284–31 those *r·* must be carried out ;
were necessary
My. 343–23 *R·* were necessary, and I made a code
your
Mis. 119–29 nullify or reverse your *r·*,

Mis. 197–25 *r·* over a kingdom of its own,
344–23 *r·* of the mighty Nazarene Prophet.
Man. 72–13 *r·* of The C. S. Publishing Society,
My. 278– 7 Love *r·* the universe,

Rules and By-Laws
Mis. 148– 8   *R·* and *B·* in the Manual
Man.   3– 3   *R·* and *B·* in the Manual

ruleth
My. 196–11   he that *r·* his spirit — *Prov.* 16 : 32.
    200– 6   *r·* in heaven and upon earth,

ruling
Mis. 204–30   divine *r·* gives prudence and energy ;
Hea. 17–28   are we not right in *r·* them out
My. 13–12   * a *mother* and a *r·* church.''

rumbling
Mis. 347– 3   *r·* and quivering of the earth

Rumney
My. 314– 7   * to North Groton and then to *R·*.''

rumor
Mis. 266–17   chapter sub-title
    345–28   *r·* that it was a part of Christian
My. 334– 2   * impression that the *r·* is not true.

rumors
Mis. 136– 4   *R·* are *r·*, — nothing more.

run
Mis. 126–25   Scientists have a strong race to *r·*,
    203–11   waters that *r·* among the valleys,
    353– 3   Human concepts *r·* in extremes ;
    361–19   *r·* with patience the race — *Heb.* 12 : 1.
Pul. 33– 5   * would often *r·* to her mother
No. 20–25   *r·* through the veins of all human
Pan. 12–17   may *r·* and not weary,
My. 155–13   *r·* in joy, health, holiness,
    189– 4   if ye would *r·*, who shall hinder you?
    252–13   not . . . *r·* away in the storm,
    254– 7   you shall *r·* and not be weary,

rung
Pul. 41–25   * *r·* out their message of
    62–11   * *r·* from an electric keyboard,
    62–12   * and even when *r·* by hand

running
Mis. 261–14   pressed down, and *r·* over.
    266–29   *r·* to and fro in the earth,
My. 21–20   * and *r·* over.'' — *Luke* 6 : 38.

runs
Mis. 270–25   *r·* through the modes and methods of

Sabbath
Mis. 126– 5   music of our *S·* chimes
    216– 3   *S·* rest for the people of God ;

Sabbath School
Man. 62–19   *S· S·* children shall be taught

sackcloth
Mis. 275– 8   veil on the *s·* of home,
Pan.   1–14   and the *s·* of waiting
'00. 15–15   it sits in *s·* — it waits in the
My. 290–27   it will remove the *s·* from thy
    339–23   only those . . . should wear *s·*.

sacked
'00. 13–13   it was taken and *s·*.

sacrament
'02. 20–19   the *s·* in our church
My. 131– 6   for spiritual *s·*, sacrifice,

sacraments
Mis. 345–26   purpose of Christian *s·*.

sacred
Mis.   x– 2   *s·* and sincere in trial
    66–10   *s·*, solid precept is verified
    144–14   laid away as a *s·* secret
    151– 9   Through the *s·* law, He speaketh
    159–12   *s·* to the memory of my students.
    196–17   *s·* sense and permanence of
    312–19   * verities of the *s·* Scriptures.''
    318–19   Before entering this *s·* field
    323– 6   Then from this *s·* summit
    331–25   In *s·* solitude divine Science
    341–16   whereon thou standest is *s·*.
Man. 46–13   shall hold in *s·* confidence
    58–21   the *s·* revelations of C. S.
    60–17   *s·* words of our beloved Master,
    94–21   nor transfer this *s·* office.
Ret. 18–21   In *s·* communion with home's
    54–23   most *s·* and salutary power
    90–17   in their early and *s·* hours,
    90–23   to those first *s·* tasks,
Un. 41–15   The sweet and *s·* sense of the
Pul.   7–13   Those *s·* drops were but
    11– 4   Word spoken in this *s·* temple
    22– 6   in this *s·* petition with every
No. 12–11   a *s·* duty for her to impart
Pan.   3–14   * ''O *s·* solitude ! divine retreat !

rural
My. 184–23   Your *r·* chapel is a social success

rush
Mis. 212–18   currents of human nature *r·* in against
Pul.   2–18   Would you *r·* forth single-handed
No.   1– 7   are noisy and *r·* precipitately ;
Po. 16–10   *r·* into life, and roll on with its
My. 149–29   a mighty *r·*, which waken the

rushes
Mis. 324–26   he *r·* again into the lonely streets,

rushing
Mis. 230–12   *R·* around smartly is no proof of
Pan.   1– 7   *r·* winds of March have shrieked

Russia
Pul.   5–24   France, Germany, *R·*,
My. 279–25   war between *R·* and Japan ;
    281–18   * peace between *R·* and Japan
    282– 9   Douma recently adopted in *R·*

Russia's
My. 127–25   Unlike *R·* armament,

Rust, D.D.
Rev. Richard S.
Ret.   5–18   eulogy of the Rev. Richard S. *R·*, D.D.,
Rev. R. S.
My. 311–32   called by the Rev. R. S. *R·*, D.D.,

rust
My. 213–24   will not *r·* for lack of use

rustic
My. 184–17   *r·* scroll brought back to me

rustle
Mis. 306–23   we do not hear the *r·* of wings,

rusts
My.   4–21   iron in human nature *r·* away ;

ruthless
Pul. 83–15   * the *r·* sword of injustice.
Po. 46– 9   Unplucked by *r·* hands.

ruthlessly
My. 308–11   tread not *r·* on their ashes.

S

sacred
'01. 28–15   *S·* history shows that those who
'02.   5–29   *s·* command, ''Thou shalt — *Exod.* 20 : 3.
Po. 30–19   *s·* song and loudest breath of praise
    64–14   In *s·* communion with home's magic
My. 27– 7   *s·* season of prayer and praise
    36– 9   * assembled at this *s·* time to
    37– 3   * *s·* confines of this sanctuary.
    37–30   * With *s·* resolution do we pray
    46–24   * obedience to the *s·* teachings of
    57– 6   * *s·* atmosphere of a church home.
    63–20   * within our *s·* edifice
    133–24   No : then my *s·* secret is
    139–19   purpose of my request was *s·*.
    147–13   *s·* to the memory of this pure
    163–14   *s·* demands on my time and
    170–18   it is my *s·* motto,
    170–28   to kneel with us in *s·* silence
    184–23   a social success quite *s·* in its
    193–28   Within its *s·* walls may song and
    204–10   that *s·* *ave* and essence of Soul
    222–28   liberty of conscience held *s·*.
    232– 5   looms of love that line the *s·* shores.
    250–29   filled this *s·* office many years,
    265–12   *s·* rights of individuals,
    289–12   convene for the *s·* purpose of

sacredly
No. 40–15   pursue their . . . ministrations very *s·*,
My. 19–29   gift which you so *s·* bestowed
    225–18   *s·* holding His name apart
    291–30   shall *s·* regard the liberty of

sacredness
Pan.   8–11   infringe the *s·* of one Christ Jesus ?
My. 142–16   lose its *s·* and merge into

sacrifice
and ascension
My. 131– 6   sacrament, *s·*, and ascension,
and suffering
Mis. 257–15   repays . . . with *s·* and suffering.
and torture
Peo.   3– 8   *s·* and torture of His favorite Son,
better than
Mis. 110– 1   Repentance is better than *s·*.
fleshly
Mis. 345–32   away from the thought of fleshly *s·*,

sacrifice
his
No. 33–16   to insure the glory his *s·* brought
human
My. 125– 1   kindle altars for human *s·*.
incentive and
My. 288– 5   his life's incentive and *s·*
individual
Mis. 364– 7   In return for individual *s·*,
Jesus'
No. 33–22   Jesus' *s·* stands preeminently
labor and
My. 58–18   * through the labor and *s·* of our
life and
My. 323–18   * your wonderful life and *s·*
long
My. 38– 1   * could recompense your long *s·*
loving
Pul. 86–23   * your labors and loving *s·*,
No. 7–16   Every loving *s·* for the good of
no
Mis. 238– 8   since no *s·* is too great for
no less
My. 21–25   * no less *s·* than have others ;
offer them in
Mis. 345–24   in order to offer them in *s·*,
reluctant
My. 10–19   * fretful or reluctant *s·*
requires
No. 33– 8   requires *s·*, struggle, prayer,
spirit of
Mis. 261–23   spirit of *s·* always has saved,
suffering and
Mis. 350–31   nameless suffering and *s·*,
that Jesus made
No. 34– 7   the *s·* that Jesus made for us,
this
Mis. 149–23   May this *s·* bring to your

Mis. 155– 6   *S·* self to bless one another,
343– 4   all that we have to *s·*,
Ret. 49– 2   to *s·* all for the advancement of
No. 33–13   The *s·* of our blessed Lord
'01. 29– 9   *s·* for him even as he has sacrificed
35– 4   Are we willing to *s·* self for
My. 184–21   a *s·* and service acceptable in God's
sacrificed
Mis. 123–11   human victims to be *s·* to
267– 6   I have *s·* the most time,
Pul. 82–20   * sang and *s·* for their people,
'01. 29– 9   as he has *s·* for others
'02. 13– 2   self was forgotten, peace *s·*,
My. 194–25   that for which you have *s·*
sacrifices
Mis. 250–17   *s·* and grand achievements
Ret. 80–29   *s·* made for others are not
Pul. 45– 2   * *S·* were made in many an instance
'01. 29–24   does most, and *s·* most for
My. 17–12   to offer up spiritual *s·*,
30–13   * personal *s·* of no mean order ;
52–27   * she has made *s·* from which
sacrificial
Ret. 89– 8   for *s·* ceremonies, not for sermons.
No. 33–12   chapter sub-title
sacrilegious
Pul. 75– 8   or speak of me . . . as a Christ, is *s·*.
'01. 16– 9   envy, and hate, supply *s·* gossip with
My. 230– 1   Notwithstanding the *s·* moth of time,
sad
Mis. 43–17   *s·* fact at this early writing is,
329–10   whose voices are *s·* or glad,
341–23   the *s·* history of Vesta,
386–23   Rears the *s·* marble to our memory
396–20   a strain, Low, *s·*, and sweet,
Man. 55– 7   if this *s·* necessity occurs.
Ret. 7–21   * This *s·* event will not be
19–22   her *s·* journey to the North.
Pul. 18– 4   a strain, Low, *s·*, and sweet,
No. 3– 3   How *s·* it is that envy will
'01. 17– 8   meet the *s·* sinner on his way
'02. 18– 8   *S·* to say, the cowardice and
Po. 12– 3   a strain, Low, *s·*, and sweet,
31– 5   *S·* sense, annoy No more the peace of
50– 9   Rears the *s·* marble to our memory
53–17   Come at the *s·* heart's call,
65– 2   My spirit is *s·*,
66–10   that heart is silent and *s·*,
My. 294–23   The *s·*, sudden announcement of
331– 1   her *s·* journey to the North.
sadly
Mis. xi–26   *s·* to survey the fields of the slain
sadness
Ret. 32–16   * Short-lived joy, that ends in *s·*,

safe
Mis. 43–11   *s·* and successful practitioners.
89–28   is *s·* in divine Science.
104– 6   *s·* in the substance of Soul,
111– 7   extended it beyond *s·* expansion ;
117– 9   This will place him on the *s·* side of
140–27   Our title to God's acres will be *s·*
157–14   *s·* under the shadow of His wing.
193– 5   deemed it *s·* to say at that time.
252–27   with *s·* and sure medicine ;
263–10   *s·* in His strength,
293– 1   *s·* not to teach prematurely the
Man. 76– 2   should remain on *s·* deposit,
Ret. 90–29   It is *s·* to leave with God the
Pul. 27– 5   * *s·* preservation of papers.
No. 3–21   *s·* members of the community.
'02. 15– 5   I leaned on God, and was *s·*.
Po. 43–20   *S·* in Science, bright with glory
My. 200–15   man's soul is *s·* ;
203–26   in the bosom of earth *s·* from
210–10   not only yourselves are *s·*,
217– 8   invested in *s·* municipal bonds
224–24   not *s·* to accept the latter as
283–18   It is always *s·* to be just.
295– 5   divine Love holds its substance *s·*
safely
Mis. 10–16   more assured to press on *s·*.
152–24   *s·* sheltered in the strong tower of
152–28   right intuition which guides you *s·*
328–31   wilt *s·* bear thy cross up to the
385–11   *s·* moored at last — Beyond rough foam.
Ret. 40–17   her babe was *s·* born,
Po. 48– 3   *s·* moored at last — Beyond rough foam.
My. 139– 5   *s·*, soulfully founded upon
220– 2   *s·* submit to the providence of God,
safer
Mis. 228– 1   a *s·* guide than the promptings of
safety
Mis. 257–19   a belief in *s·* where there is
Ret. 14–16   and take my chance of spiritual *s·*
My. 211–23   a belief in *s·* where there is
sage
Mis. 1–14   The seer of this age should be a *s·*.
Ret. 11–15   Hero and *s·* arise to show
'02. 1–21   attention of philosopher and *s·*,
Po. 60–12   Hero and *s·* arise to show
said
Mis. ix–18   Truly may it be *s·* :
1– 7   the scoffed of all scoffers, *s·*,
4–24   often *s·*, "You must have
15– 7   The great Nazarene Prophet *s·*,
21– 9   Our Master *s·*, "The works — *John 14 : 12.*
24–25   *s·* : "When he speaketh — *John 8 : 44.*
30–25   fool hath *s·* in his heart, — *Psal. 14 : 1.*
37– 8   he *s·*, "I and my Father — *John 10 : 30.*
44–26   *s·*, There is no more pain.
51–30   The apostle James *s·*,
57–15   God, denounced it, and *s·* :
57–17   error *s·*, "I am true,"
57–20   and the Lord God never *s·* it.
61–16   * a man was *s·* to be 'hanged
63– 2   It was *s·* of old by Truth-traducers,
68– 7   *The Rev. —— s· in a sermon:*
70–10   *What did Jesus mean when he s·*
71– 3   John B. Gough is *s·* to have
73– 2   material body is *s·* to suffer,
83–24   and *s·*, Father, the hour is come ;
87–16   *She s· that you sent her there*
95–10   * Mrs. Eddy responding, *s·* :
97– 8   Our Master *s·* of one of his students,
99–21   He *s·*, "Heaven and earth — *Matt. 24 : 35.*
111–16   *s·*, "Heaven and earth — *Matt. 24 : 35.*
112–21   The jailer thanked me, and *s·*,
112–31   fool hath *s·* in his heart, — *Psal. 14 : 1.*
122– 2   he *s·*, "Woe unto the — *Matt. 18 : 7.*
122– 9   *s·* of him whom God foreordained
142–13   Each day since they arrived I have *s·*,
157– 3   Paul *s·*, "If we suffer, — *II Tim. 2 : 12.*
159–23   a bit of what I *s·* in 1890 ;
163–18   he *s·*, "Heaven and earth — *Matt. 24 : 35.*
165–18   legacy of what he *s·* and did,
170–17   ye know not of," he *s·*. — *John 4 : 32.*
170–19   record of the Bible, she *s·*,
170–25   he is *s·* to have spat upon the dust,
177–22   * editor of *The C. S. Journal s·*
178–18   * If any one had *s·* to me
180–12   I *s·*, in the words of
193– 2   Did Jesus mean what he *s·*?
193– 5   all, and even more than he *s·*
193–19   *s·* when critics attacked me for
195–13   It has been *s·* that the New Testament
196–12   bear in mind that a serpent *s·* that ;
208–21   David *s·*, "Before I was — *Psal. 119 : 67,*
210– 9   Christ *s·*, "They shall — *Mark 16 : 18.*

said

Mis.	211–26	Our Master s·, "Ye shall— *Matt.* 20 : 23.
	211–28	and he s· to his followers,
	214– 4	He s·, "Think not that I — *Matt.* 10 : 34.
	218–28	when he s· "How do you do?"
	223–27	Hannah More s·, "If I wished
	225–16	he s· to this venerable Christian :
	225–29	The parents s· : — "Wait until we
	226– 1	s· : — "Give the child what he relishes,
	236–10	we have s·, "Love and honor thy
	236–20	In such cases we have s·,
	236–23	by anything that is s· to you,
	239–19	the poor child s·, — "I've got cold,
	244–24	He s·, "And other sheep — *John* 10 : 16.
	248–21	have s· that I died of poison,
	251–15	s· : "The works that I do — *John* 14 : 12.
	252–32	our Master s·, if a man findeth,
	253–18	and the husbandmen that s·,
	255– 2	It is sometimes s·, cynically,
	255–13	what the apostle meant when he s· :
	258– 2	Christ has s· that love is the
	266–18	assertion that I have s· hard things
	270–14	He s·, "Seek ye first the— *Matt.* 6 : 33.
	271–20	Much is s· at this date, 1889,
	272– 9	* till the repealing of s· Act
	278–14	that Job sinned not in all he s·,
	282–14	Our Master s·, "When ye — *Matt.* 10 : 12.
	302–22	at once after s· service.
	312–13	s·, "No more striking manifestation
	334– 1	s· : "He doeth according to — *Dan.* 4 : 35.
	337–13	in the midst of them, and s·, —*Matt.* 18 : 2, 3.
	342–23	and they s· to the foolish,
	345– 8	the proconsul s· to him,
	345–14	s·, "Christianity is fit only for
	345–18	Webster s·, "My heart has always
	349–15	I was willing, and s· so,
	353–17	he s· to the jester, "You must pay
	363–13	Truth s·, and s· from the beginning,
	376– 7	* and s· to have been authentic ;
	380–22	s·, "Suffer it to be so — *Matt.* 3 : 15.
	381–22	under the seal of the s· Court,
Man.	26–16	s· candidates shall not be chosen.
	27– 6	to be taken by s· Committee
	27–10	written consent of s· Board.
	28–22	s· officer shall be dismissed
	36–23	may admit s· applicant
	39– 3	expiration of s· one year,
	43– 3	name of s· member to be dropped
	46–21	for s· member's practice,
	50–20	and s· member exonerated,
	52– 5	*if s· member belongs to no*
	54–22	s· member shall immediately be
	56– 4	if s· member persists in this
	57–16	before he can call s· meeting.
	67–13	if s· case relates to the person
	67–16	conferred with her on s· subject.
	69– 1	s· student shall come under a
	70– 5	consulting her on s· subject
	70–18	confer on a statute of s· State,
	70–20	the churches in s· State.
	73–14	graduates of *s· university*
	73–20	may lecture for s· university
	74–19	advertised in s· *Journal,*
	75–13	situation between . . . and s· Church
	76–25	responsible for s· funds.
	77– 7	submit them all to s· committee
	79–13	persons nominated for s· office
	80–14	vacancies in s· trusteeship,
	86–24	instruct . . . from the s· chapter
	88–13	elected every third year by s· Board,
	90–22	prepare a paper on s· subject
	100– 1	employing s· Committee.
	100– 5	shall appoint s· candidate.
	100–15	in accordance with s· By-Laws.
Ret.	1– 5	her family is s· to have been
	1–10	my grandmother s· were written
	8–18	my cousin turned to me and s·,
	8–20	Mehitable then s· sharply,
	8–24	s· that mother wanted me.
	14–29	This was so earnestly s·,
	16– 6	s·, "Did you hear my daughter
	40–13	that her physicians had s·
	48–26	baptism of Jesus, of which he s·,
	63–22	St. Augustine once s·,
	64– 8	Need it be s· that any
	86– 8	s· the classic Grecian motto.
	87– 1	Master s·, "Follow me ; — *Matt.* 8 : 22.
	93–17	St. Paul s· to the Athenians,
Un.	3– 6	before it can be truly s·
	9–20	Sometimes it is s·, by those who
	9–21	and this is s· because ideas
	11–26	s· that the kingdom of heaven
	14–27	God never s· that man
	21–21	*Evil.* God hath s·,
	37– 6	Our Master s·, "The kingdom— *Matt.* 10 : 7.
	57–11	When Jesus turned and s·,

said

Un.	58– 6	His persecutors s· mockingly,
Pul.	2– 4	s·, "Behold, the half — *I Kings* 10 : 7.
	3– 5	Master s· : "Destroy this— *John* 2 : 19.
	3– 6	s· : "The kingdom of God — *Luke* 17 : 21.
	6–26	At a *conversazione* in Boston, he s·,
	7– 2	s· : "Had I young blood in my veins,
	10–19	Master s· : "The stone— *Matt.* 21 : 42.
	29–20	* Judge Hanna s· that while all these
	34–16	* that it was my apparition," she s·.
	34–21	* s·, in reference to this experience.
	34–26	* she s·, in reply to my questions,
	35–12	* Mrs. Eddy has s· : — "I had learned
	37–16	* s· a gentleman to me on Christmas eve,
	57– 6	* The auditorium is s· to seat
	66– 8	* This growth, it is s·, proceeds
	67– 6	* s· by a great American writer.
	72–16	* past eleven years," s· Mrs. Copeland,
	72–19	* Mrs. Copeland s· that she was the
	73–27	* and s· that no more complete
	74–20	If she s· aught with intention to
	79–21	* wicked but witty writer has s·,
	82– 7	* s· — she is soft and gentle,
	82–14	* s· that because she was created after
Rud.	16–17	Whatever is s· and written correctly
No.	25– 4	St. Paul s·, "But now we are — *Rom.* 7 : 6.
	27–18	Bishop Foster s·, in a lecture
	29–12	he s·, "The forgiven soul in a
	31–26	He s· also : "If a man— *John* 8 : 5·.
	40– 1	The apostle James s· :
	41–25	Baptist clergyman, s· in a sermon :
	42–18	It is s· that the devil is the ape
	42–25	He s· : "I am suffering from
	43– 4	Master s·, "Come unto me, — *Matt.* 11 : 28.
	43– 8	A lady s· : "Only He who knows
	43–10	distinguished Doctor of Divinity s· :
	45– 3	St. Paul s· that without charity
Pan.	5–12	He s· of evil :
	8–18	It s·, "Call no man your— *Matt.* 23 : 9.
	10– 5	The great Nazarene Prophet s·,
'00.	3–14	thinker and worker has s·
	13– 1	It is s· "a controversy was
	14–26	as the devout St. Stephen s· :
'01.	3– 8	We hear it s· the Christian Scientists
	3–20	It is sometimes s· : "God is Love,
	8– 9	was s· in the sense that one ray of
	8–25	Christ existed prior to Jesus, who s·,
	16–24	Shall it be s· of this century
	18–24	fool hath s· in his heart, — *Psal.* 14 : 1.
	26–21	St. Paul s· : "Though I speak — *I Cor.* 13 : 1.
	27–27	Agassiz s· : "Every great scientific
	28– 6	narrow way, whereof our Master s·,
'02.	3– 5	Buddhism and Shintoism are s· to
	11–28	for the truths he s· and did :
	18–14	He s·, "Inasmuch as ye — *Matt.* 25 : 40.
	18–21	s·, "The works that I do— *John* 14 : 12.
Hea.	2– 9	S· the intrepid reformer,
	2–11	S· . . . gentle Melanchthon :
	2–17	model of infinite patience, s· :
	2–19	s· this when bending beneath
	6– 9	misinterpreted, and I s· it.
	7–18	the poor woman . . . s·,
	8–15	Plato did better ; he s·,
	9– 6	The less s· or thought of sin, sickness,
Peo.	4– 8	s· that Life, which is infinite
	4–11	because a serpent s· it.
	5–26	Oliver Wendell Holmes s·,
	10–13	Discerning the . . . Paul s·,
	13–23	The infidel was blind who s·,
	13–25	for Bonaparte s· :
	13–27	and Daniel Webster s· :
My.	4–25	Our great Master s· :
	5–27	virtually what the prophet s· :
	8– 3	* Mr. Kimball s· in part :
	8– 8	* in seconding the motion, s· :
	15–15	I have s· to you all
	28– 3	* Our Leader has s· in S. and H.
	38–24	* s· after the service that
	39–17	* Mr. McKenzie s· :
	40–27	* poet perceived when he s·,
	42–12	* on assuming office, s· :
	51– 6	* now interested in s· church,
	57–28	* *Transcript* s· :
	61–16	* so clearly, I s· aloud,
	66–12	* s· that a number of changes
	72– 2	* could hear what was s·.
	83–19	* chapter sub-title
	91– 9	* It is to be s· for C. S.
	92–26	* two things to be s· in favor of
	93– 6	* it may be s· that if their opinions
	93– 9	* It has been s· cynically
	99–12	* s· in their behalf that they
	103–16	the Psalmist s· :
	104– 7	Of old the Pharisees s·
	104–14	what shall be s· of him
	131–24	The divine law has s· to us :

said

My. 134–25   * In announcing this letter, he *s·* :
     135– 2   The wise man has *s·*,
     137–27   I selected *s·* Trustees
     140– 2   the prophet Isaiah *s·*,
     145–11   carpenters' foreman *s·* to me :
     145–15   *s·* to Mr. George H. Moore
     146– 3   *s·* : "They shall take up — *Mark* **16 : 18.**
     150–26   what our Master *s·*
     152– 7   The medicine-man, . . . *s·*,
     161–29   the Godlike man *s·*,
     172–20   * In reply Mr. Bates *s·*,
     173–30   his colaborers on *s·* committee
     178–29   *s·* that the nearest approach
     181–27   It is authentically *s·* that one
     182– 2   To-day it is *s·* to have a majority
     184–26   Isaiah *s·* : "How beautiful — *Isa.* **52 : 7.**
     191– 2   Nicodemus of old, who *s·*,
     218– 3   *s·*, "Suffer it to be so — *Matt.* **3 : 15.**
     218– 4   Job *s·*, "In my flesh — *Job* **19 : 26.**
     219–23   *s·*, "Think not that I am — *Matt.* **5 : 17.**
     222–18   he was arrested because, as was *s·*,
     227– 1   The great Master *s·*,
     227– 2   He *s·* this to satisfy himself
     227–30   fool hath *s·* in his heart, — *Psal.* **14 : 1.**
     228–13   John the Baptist, of whom he *s·*
     229–25   That which I *s·* in my heart
     233–24   Master *s·*, "He that taketh — *Matt.* **10 : 38.**
     240–11   I *s·*, "This Science is a law of
     241–21   * *s·* that my statement was wrong,
     244–20   Knowing this, our Master *s·* :
     246–25   Master *s·* : "What I do — *John* **13 : 7.**
     267–28   Our great Teacher hath *s·* :
     279– 3   The Founder of Christianity *s·* :
     283–12   fruits of *s·* grand Association,
     284–15   * "It is *s·* to be the first time
     297– 6   *s·* description of her soul-visit,
     297–29   what the enemies of C. S. are *s·* to
     304–21   In a lecture in Chicago, he *s·* :
     304–25   *s·* : "Every great scientific truth
     307– 1   words that I *s·* to him,
     307–21   understood what I *s·* better than
     310–30   Dr. Ladd *s·* to Alexander Tilton :
     311– 8   my good housekeeper *s·* to me :
     318–30   "Now, Mr. Wiggin," I *s·*,
     321–13   * cannot believe that he has ever *s·*
     323– 5   * he *s·* he had written in answer to
     324– 6   * as he *s·* you and your ideas
     324– 8   * *s·* you were so original
     324–24   * Everything he *s·* conveyed this
     324–27   * He *s·* he wanted to see if
     324–30   * and *s·* that no man could have
     331–26   * Much has often been *s·* of the
     333– 1   * *s·* record, with the seal of the
     339–18   disciples of St. John the Baptist *s·*
     340– 4   *s·*, "Pray without ceasing." — *I Thess.* **5 : 17.**
     342–20   * she *s·*, in her clear voice,
     345–14   The doctors *s·* I would live if
     (*see also* **Jesus**)

sail

Ret. 57– 2   we *s·* into the eternal haven

sailed

Pan. 14–24   *s·* victoriously through the jaws of

sailing

My. 232– 2   *s·* over rough seas

saint

Mis. 108– 1   sorrowing *s·* thinks too much of it :
     257–23   strikes down the hoary *s·*.
Pul. 65–26   * exemplar afterward became a *s·*,
Po. 29–21   be thou our *s·*, Our stay,
     34–12   solitude, where nymph or *s·*
My. 4–11   spiritually, blessing *s·* and sinner
     104– 4   Mars' Hill orator, the canonized *s·*,

Saint and St. Andrew's Lodge, Number 10

Ret. 19–11   member in *S· A· L·*, *N·* 10,
My. 330–23   member in *St. A· L·*, No. 10,
     332–20   * membership in *St. A· L·*, No. 10,
     335– 4   * Mason in "*St. A· L·*, No. 10."

sainted

Ret. 5–19   and knew my *s·* mother
     6– 2   * impressions of that *s·* spirit,
'02. 3–24   the joy of the *s·* Queen,
My. 120– 1   We look for the *s·* Revelator

saintly

Mis. 319–23   Take thither thy *s·* offerings,
Pul. 32–27   * a *s·* and consecrated character.

saints

Mis. 149–26   fellowship with *s·* and angels.
     219–24   immortal Mind makes *s·* ;
     293–25   makes mortals either *s·* or
'00. 8– 2   with *s·* and angels shall be satisfied
My. 125–31   blood of the *s·*, — *Rev.* **17 : 6.**

saints

My. 206–28   inheritance of the *s·* — *Col.* **1 : 12.**
     249–16   patience, silence, and lives of *s·*.

saith

Mis. 16– 3   *s·* : In mine infancy, this is enough of
     16– 9   *s·* : The Principle of Christianity
     67– 4   First is the law, which *s·* :
     72–12   The immutable Word *s·*,
     72–15   As I live, *s·* the Lord — *Ezek.* **18 : 3.**
     99– 3   *s·* to the five material senses,
     101–20   but Science *s·* to man,
     109–28   Christ, Truth, *s·* unto you,
     151–11   He *s·* of the barren fig-tree,
     179–32   Life that knows no death, that *s·*,
     184–27   *s·* Abba, Father, and *is* born of
     192–15   The Hebrew bard *s·*,
     203– 9   Solomon *s·*, "As in water — *Prov.* **27 : 19.**
     212– 2   Human policy is a fool that *s·*
     212–20   The law of Love *s·*,
     219– 8   Now, what *s·* the Scripture?
     254–13   victim of mad ambition that *s·*,
     268– 8   The Holy One *s·*,
     306–29   The Psalmist *s·* :
     307–23   *s·*, "Little children, — *I John* **5 : 21.**
     321– 3   *s·*, "Unto us a child — *Isa.* **9 : 6.**
     323–17   He *s·* unto the patient toilers
     325– 2   *s·* unto the dwellers therein,
     325–31   enters a place of worship, and *s·*
     326–30   the Stranger *s·* unto him,
     327– 5   And the Stranger *s·* unto him,
     327– 8   "Then," *s·* the Stranger,
     334–29   divine Science, which *s·*,
     339–17   *s·*, "Thou hast been faithful — *Matt.* **25 : 23.**
     380–23   for thus *s·* our Master.
Man. 41– 9   The wise man *s·*,
Ret. 32– 7   *s·* the Master.
     60–14   C. S. *s·* to the wave
     60–18   *s·* to all manner of disease,
     60–20   Material sense *s·*,
     61–13   Science *s·* to fear,
     64–15   where the Psalmist *s·* :
Un. 18–23   *s·*, I am ever-conscious Life,
     62– 3   The Christian *s·*,
     62–21   Truth or Life . . . *s·* forever,
Rud. 13–12   human belief which *s·*
No. v–10   *s·* tenderly, "Come and drink ;"
Pan. 10– 2   But what *s·* the apostle?
'00. 3– 1   Now, what *s·* C. S.?
     8–14   *s·* to his followers :
     11–26   "the Spirit *s·* — *Rev.* **2 : 7.**
     14– 1   The Revelator . . . *s·* :
     14–10   hear what the Spirit *s·*
     15–12   *s·* "there is no sin,"
'01. 11–22   Whosoever *s·* there is no
'02. 7–24   *s·*, "A new commandment — *John* **13 : 34.**
     19–16   *s·* : "Come unto me." — *Matt.* **11 : 28.**
     20– 3   him who stilled the tempest *s·*,
My. 16–24   thus *s·* the Lord God, — *Isa.* **28 : 16.**
     126–19   *s·* in her heart, — *Rev.* **18 : 7.**
     153– 9   *s·* He that is holy." — *Rev.* **3 : 7.**
     156–14   Master *s·* unto thee, — *Luke* **22 : 11.**
     184–28   that *s·* unto Zion, — *Isa.* **52 : 7.**
     205–17   Æsculapius and Hygeia, *s·*,
     223–29   divine Love and wisdom *s·*,
     251– 2   The great Master *s·* :
     270–11   Divine Love, . . . *s·* :
     293–30   the Saviour of man *s·* :
     (*see also* **Lord, Scripture**)

sake

Mis. 8–24   *falsely*, for my *s·* ; — *Matt.* **5 : 11.**
     199–12   *for Christ's s·*. — *II Cor.* **12 : 10.**
     243–25   for thy stomach's *s·*"? — *I Tim.* **5 : 23.**
     261–28   for conscience' *s·*, one will either
     312– 8   endures all piercing for the *s·* of
     312– 9   for the kingdom of heaven's *s·*.
     327–26   loseth his life for my *s·*, — *Matt.* **10 : 39.**
Pul. 15–10   for the *s·* of doing right
     51–30   * for the *s·* of humanity.
     81–15   * scorn self for the *s·* of love
No. 42–14   and for the *s·* of Christ,
Pan. 13–14   Love all . . . for the gospel's *s·* ;
'01. 3– 6   falsely, for my *s·*." — *Matt.* **5 : 11.**
'02. 11–24   falsely, for my *s·*. — *Matt.* **5 : 11.**
     15–16   I became poor for Christ's *s·*.
My. 18–22   Love all . . . for the gospel's *s·* ;
     54– 4   * for the *s·* of the eternal truth
     104–31   falsely, for my *s·*"? — *Matt.* **5 : 11.**
     233–26   for my *s·* shall find — *Matt.* **10 : 39.**
     316– 8   falsely, for my *s·*." — *Matt.* **5 : 11.**

sakes

My. 41–29   * for our *s·* as well as for her own ;
     269–24   for your *s·*, — *Mal.* **3 : 11.**

salaries

Man. 26–18   fix the *s·* of the Readers.

salary

Mis.	300–13	gives you the clergyman's *s·*
	349–26	church had . . . means to pay a *s·*,
Man.	29–15	*s·* of the members of the Board
	97–13	shall receive an annual *s·*,
	101– 6	shall receive an adequate *s·*
Ret.	90– 5	his *s·* for tending the home flock
My.	312–29	My *s·* for writing gave me

sale

Mis.	35–15	*S· and H·, that you offer for s·*
	299–19	garments that are on *s·*,
	307–12	rapid *s·* already of two editions
Man.	27–22	publication and *s·* of the books of
	44–10	that has for *s·* obnoxious books.
'02.	15–10	income from the *s·* of S. and H.,
My.	354– 4	Bibles and other books for *s·*

Salem

Massachusetts

Ret.	20–23	in the city of *S·*, Massachusetts.

Mis.	211–11	class legislation, and *S·* witchcraft,

salient

My.	297– 3	shrink from such *s·* praise.

sallies

My.	201–18	that its sudden *s·* may help us,

salt

Mis.	348–22	*Natrum muriaticum* (common *s·*).

Salt Lake City

Utah

Pul.	90– 4	* *Salt Lake Herald, S· L·.C·*, Utah.
	90–12	* *Tribune, S· L· C·*, Utah.
My.	186–24	chapter sub-title

'00.	1–21	St. Louis, Denver, *S· L· C·*,
My.	187– 3	church in *S· L· C·* hath not lost its

Salt Lake Herald

Pul.	90– 4	* *S· L· H·*, Salt Lake City, Utah.

saltness

My.	187– 3	hath not lost its *s·*.

salts

My.	108– 1	the effects of calcareous *s·*

salutary

Ret.	54–23	most sacred and *s·* power
Rud.	10– 4	*s·* influence on yourself and others.
'01.	34– 3	*s·* in the healing of all manner of
Hea.	14–14	and his efforts are *s·* ;
My.	108– 7	the action of the divine Mind is *s·*
	252– 5	will be *s·* as Soul ;

salute

Mis.	282–14	enter a house, *s·* it." — *see Matt.* 10 : 12.
My.	347–15	bough, bird, and song, to *s·* me.

saluting

Mis.	126– 5	*s·* the ear in tones that leap for joy,

salvation

abundance of

My.	36–19	* bear witness to the abundance of *s·*

and strength

Pul.	12– 6	*s·*, and strength, — *Rev.* 12 : 10.

condition of

Mis.	192–26	making healing a condition of *s·*,

conditions of

Mis.	244–12	are the conditions of *s·* mental, or

cup of

Pan.	14– 9	drink of the cup of *s·*,

everlasting

Mis.	261–26	saved with an everlasting *s·*.

from divorce

My.	269–11	Christ's plan of *s·* from divorce.

from sin

Mis.	123–26	*s·* from sin, . . . through a divine
	168– 1	*s·* from sin to the sinner
	196–20	the portals of *s·* from sin,
'02.	11–17	*s·* from sin, disease, and death.
My.	154– 1	*s·* from sin, disease, and death.

full

Mis.	192–18	great Principle of a full *s·*.
	197– 7	It means a *full s·*,

grace and

'01.	19– 2	means of grace and *s·*.

guide to

Pul.	30–19	* as the teacher and guide to *s·* ;

healing and

Mis.	244–24	the way of healing and *s·*.

his

Un.	2– 7	except in God, who is his *s·*.
My.	34– 7	from the God of his *s·*. — *Psal.* 24 : 5.
	202– 6	Now may his *s·* draw near,

his own

Mis.	85–20	and work out his own *s·*.
No.	8–12	to work out his own *s·*,

is as eternal

Un.	59–13	*S·* is as eternal as God.

salvation

knowledge of

'02.	11–17	knowledge of *s·* from sin,
	16– 5	Authorized Version "knowledge of *s·*."

man's

Mis.	96– 1	man's *s·* from sickness and death,
	241– 4	correlated in man's *s·* ;
'01.	10–19	man's *s·* comes through
Peo.	12–19	man's *s·* from sickness and death.

of a world

Mis.	122– 7	*s·* of a world of sinners,

of many people

Mis.	150–16	*s·* of many people by means of

of the eunuch

Mis.	77– 1	*Did the s· of the eunuch*

of the world

Mis.	177–18	necessary to the *s·* of the world

our own

'01.	10–25	working out our own *s·*,
Hea.	5–21	to work out our own *s·*,
Peo.	4– 1	working out our own *s·*.
	9–14	shall work out our own *s·*,

pardon for

Peo.	3–26	personal pardon for *s·*,

plan of

My.	283–23	God's own plan of *s·*.

rock of

My.	165–21	and this is my rock of *s·*

song of

My.	166–23	sing the old-new song of *s·*,

their

Mis.	214–21	labor in the flesh for their *s·* :

this

Mis.	89–26	This *s·* means : saved from error,

universal

Un.	6–23	assertion of universal *s·*
'01.	13–25	hence the hope of universal *s·*.

vocal with

Mis.	146– 2	May her walls be vocal with *s·* ;

way of

(*see* **way**)

whole

Mis.	96–23	It brings . . . a *whole s·*.

wise unto

Mis.	134– 2	"wise unto *s·*" ! — *II Tim.* 3 : 15.
	343– 1	to make us wise unto *s·* !

your own

My.	300– 5	"Work out your own *s·* — *Phil.* 2 : 12.

Mis.	169–32	*s·* from the belief of death,
Ret.	14– 9	both *s·* and condemnation depended.
Pul.	53–17	* *s·* in the world to come.
My.	333–25	* reliance for *s·* on the merits of
	357–21	to *s·* and eternal C. S.

Samaritan

Mis.	257–28	smites with disease the good *S·*

same

Mis.	27–18	send forth at the *s·* place — *Jas.* 3 : 11.
	40– 5	in the *s·* process,
	40– 9	asked, "If C. S. is the *s·* method
	40–15	the *s·* Principle as theirs ;
	40–18	*s·* results follow not in every case,
	42–14	*s·* plane of conscious existence
	53–21	*If C· S· is the s· as Jesus taught,*
	54–28	*they do not heal on the s· basis*
	92–14	answer them from the *s·* source.
	110–19	steadfastly at the *s·* object-lesson,
	123– 1	incited by the *s·* spirit
	130–12	*s·* power to make you a
	144–12	written by the *s·* author,
	147–22	hence we find him ever the *s·*,
	160– 8	flow on in the *s·* sweet rhythm
	214–11	was stimulated by the *s·* Love
	214–25	*s·* as its attitude physically.
	221–27	multiplication of the *s·* two numbers
	221–28	would not yield the *s·* product
	229–21	in the *s·* proportion would faith
	243–10	removed these appliances the *s·* day
	259–19	governed in the *s·* rhythm
	263–19	constant petitions for the *s·*,
	265– 9	*one* Principle and the *s·* rule ;
	265–25	who receive the *s·* instruction,
	273–28	waiting for the *s·* class instruction ;
	295– 6	*s·* power which in America
	295–10	* cause of this "*s·* original evil"
	296–11	in the *s·* category with noble women
	296–30	barmaid and . . . in the *s·* breath?
	298– 9	Under the *s·* circumstances,
	298–10	in the *s·* spiritual ignorance
	303–15	the *s·* rights and privileges
	306–14	* as a notification of the *s·*,
	337–14	the *s·* is greatest — *Matt.* 18 : 4.
	347–10	operation by the *s·* spirit.
	349–20	the *s·* as the foregoing,
	352–14	healed upon the *s·* Principle

same

Mis. 352–15 and by the s· rule
359– 4 On the s· principle,
364–26 s· power or modes
364–27 the s· consciousness,
381–32 * founder and discoverer of the s·
387–11 And on the s· branch bend.
Man. 18– 1 s· is become the head — Matt. 21 : 42.
18– 4 the s· month the members,
25–13 s· person is eligible for election
27–21 located in the s· building,
61– 5 services at the s· hour.
70–17 located in the s· State,
71– 5 established in the s· place ;
80–18 reserves the right to fill the s·
110–16 names must be written the s·
Chr. 53–51 s· hand unfolds His power,
55–23 the s· is my brother, — Matt. 12 : 50.
Ret. 8–15 in the s· room with grandmother,
8–19 s· call was thrice repeated.
16–17 the s· month the members,
44– 5 during the s· month the members,
49–30 and the s· is hereby dissolved.
54–19 s· channel of ignorant belief.
71–29 the s· as other forms of stealing,
82– 7 practitioners of the s· blessed faith.
83–22 the s· as other teachers ;
88– 1 s· courtesy should be observed
94–22 "the s· yesterday, — Heb. 13 : 8.
Un. 2–17 In the s· manner the sick lose
2–20 According to this s· rule,
4–19 bids man have the s· Mind
7–13 In the s· spiritual condition
8–17 s· basis whereby sickness is healed,
13– 2 on the s· principle that it does in
60– 5 With the s· breath he articulates
60–15 Out of the s· mouth — Jas. 3 : 10.
61– 3 "the s· yesterday, — Heb. 13 : 8.
Pul. 5–24 the s· in Great Britain, France,
10–20 s· is become the head — Matt. 21 : 42.
25–24 * repeats the s· tints.
48–18 * bred in that s· neighborhood.
51– 3 * the s· impressions upon all.
53–30 * Is evermore the s·.
54–11 * are the s· as were necessary
73–19 * of the s· theory as Mrs. Copeland.
No. 12–13 s· affection, desire, and motives
13–15 chapter sub-title
21–17 in the s· realm and consciousness.
24–12 By the s· token, evil is not only
31–22 were one and the s· with this
38–14 s· is become the head — Matt. 21 : 42.
'01. 33–26 the s· reviling it received
33–27 and from the s· motives
Hea. 7–15 the s· as it begins in motive
Po. vii– 3 * s· lofty trend of thought
6– 6 And on the s· branch bend.
My. 10– 8 * this s· impulse should now
30– 3 * services were precisely the s·
38–22 * the s· as all the others.
49–10 * in the s· month the members
76– 1 * the s· practice would be
82– 1 * all have the s· stories
97– 5 * These s· physicians, however,
107–11 s· triturations of medicine
107–15 dozen or less of these s· globules,
109–12 the s· heavenly lesson.
109–12 "the s· yesterday, — Heb. 13 : 8.
111– 7 s· class of minds to deal with
111– 9 on practically the s· grounds
123–12 other rooms in the s· building.
137–16 and have paid for the s·.
149–28 seen and forgotten in the s· hour ;
157–14 * s· beautiful Concord granite
162–19 s· wisdom which spake thus in
182– 9 foundations of which are the s·,
190–24 s· opportunity to become students
196–12 the s· is a perfect man, — Jas. 3 : 2.
227–11 having the s· disease
227–12 and in the s· family,
246–28 his works are the s· to-day as
292–28 Mind is the s· yesterday, to-day, and
293– 9 thousands of others believed the s·,
321–11 * told the s· story to every one
322–13 * letter to you on the s· subject;
345–18 they acted just the s·
346–13 * s· expression of looking forward,
(see also **time, year**)

Samson

Hea. 18–25 no blind S· shorn of his locks.

Samuel

Ret. 9– 9 Scriptural narrative of little S·,
9–15 I did answer, in the words of S·,
Pul. 33– 7 * related to her the story of S·,

sanative

Mis. 229–26 any other possible s· method ;

Sanborn, Professor Dyer H.

My. 304– 6 studies under Professor Dyer H. S·,

Sanborn's Grammar

My. 304– 6 book title

Sanbornton Academy

My. 304– 4 principal of S· A·,

Sanbornton Bridge
N. H.

My. 332–15 * S· B·, N. H., August 12, 1844.

My. 312– 1 Seminary at S· B·,

sanctified

Mis. 9– 2 s· by the purification it brings
'01. 32–27 their s· souls would take in the

sanctifies

Mis. 8–19 purifies, s·, and consecrates

sanctify

My. 292– 8 s· our nation's sorrow

sanction

Mis. 330–25 s· what our natures need.
'01. 16–23 under s· of the gown,

sanctioned

Man. 78–13 s· by the Board of Directors
'00. 3–25 and so s· idolatry,
My. 279– 2 not s· by the law of God,

sanctions

Mis. 93–16 Science s· only what is

sanctuary

Mis. 77–22 to enter the spiritual s·
150–22 the wayside is a s·,
159–14 into this s· of love,
Ret. 91–24 a fishing-boat became a s·,
No. 41–18 s· will never admit such
My. 37– 4 * sacred confines of this s·.
188–17 I enter your inner s·,
244–17 inner s· of divine Science,

sanctum

No. 44–11 leap into the s· of C. S.
My. 147–13 May this little s· be preserved

sand

Mis. 135–13 you would build on s·.
298–15 is to build on s·.
Un. 9–16 the s· of human reason.
Hea. 1– 9 whoso . . . hath built on s·.

sandals

Mis. 158–20 with s· on and staff in hand,
341–15 unloose the latchet of thy s· ;
Ret. 12– 3 Minerva's silver s·
Po. 61– 1 Minerva's silver s·
My. 222–20 s· of thy Master's feet.
338–27 whose s· none may unloose.

Sandusky (Ohio) Star-Journal

My. 95–27 * [S· (O·) S·]

sane

My. 49– 6 * direct, . . . through s· counsel,

saneness

My. 93–22 * s· and common sense which

San Francisco
Cal.

Pul. 89–25 * Bulletin, S· F·, Cal.
89–26 * Chronicle, S· F·, Cal.

Mis. 304–12 * Then it will go to . . . S· F·,
'00. 1–21 S· F·, Montreal, London,
My. 285– 3 Civic League of S· F·,

sang

Mis. 151–15 David s·, "Whom have I — Psal. 73 : 25.
188– 4 when the stars first s· together,
259–21 stars s· together, — Job 38 : 7.
Un. 42–14 stars s· together, — Job 38 : 7.
Pul. 82–20 * s· and sacrificed for their people,
83–19 * will succeed, for as David s·
Po. 70–18 while the glad stars s·
My. 81–22 * when they s·, the volume of
188–11 whereof the Psalmist s·,
244–15 whereof David s·,
273–10 King David, the Hebrew bard, s·,
274–27 s·, "That thy way may be — Psal. 67 : 2.

sanguine

Mis. 354– 4 s· of success in sin,

Sanhedrim

Mis. 148–10 as in ancient S·.
Man. 3– 6 as in ancient S·.

sanitary

Ret. 30– 8 a s· system that should include all
70–28 s·, civil, moral, and religious

sanity
'02.   2– 6   s· and perfection of living,
My.   14– 7   a s· something
    164–18   A great s·, a mighty something
    363–14   proof that s· and Science govern

San José, Cal.
My.   197– 9   chapter sub-title

sank
Mis.   112–20   s· back in his chair, limp and pale ;
My.   178–24   the table s· a charred mass.

Santa Claus
My.   261– 9   that S· C· has aught to do with

sap
Mis.   218–14   realistic views s· the Science of
Ret.   63–12   When we deny . . . we begin to s· it ;

sapling
Mis.   240–17   The s· bends to the breeze,
My.   160–12   even though it be a s·

sapphire
Mis.   376–28   opal, garnet, turquoise, and s·
Pul.   40– 4   * Beyond the s· sea?

saps
Mis.   221–20   s· one's understanding of the
Rud.   13– 4   Whatever s·, with human belief,

Saratoga Springs, N. Y.
Pul.   89–11   * Saratogian, S· S·, N. Y.

Saratogian
Pul.   89–11   * S·, Saratoga Springs, N. Y.

sarcasm
Mis.   296– 9   to overflow in shallow s·,

sat
Mis.   225–20   s· down beside the sofa
    231– 6   s· at that dinner-table.
Ret.   8–14   s· in a little chair by her side,
Pul.   37–17   * s· in the beautiful drawing-room,
    59–21   * on the platform s· Joseph Armstrong,
'01.   15–27   * since you have s· here in the house
Po.   66– 8   of one who s· by her side
My.   81–17   * audience ever s· in Boston.
    342–18   * s· back to be questioned.

Satan (see also **Satan's**)
Mis.   3–30   is "S· let loose." — see Rev. 20 : 7.
    23–17   S·, the first talker in its behalf,
    68–16   the works of S· are the
    108– 6   in his definition of S·
Un.   44– 9   Of S· and his lie.
    54–21   S· held it up before man
No.   15–18   and an incredible S·.
    23– 7   "Get thee behind me, S· ;" — Matt. 16 : 23.
'00.   14– 4   the synagogue of S· — Rev. 3 : 9.
'01.   25–25   S· demanded in the beginning,
My.   201– 5   S· is unchained only for a

satanic
Mis.   191–16   name of his s· majesty
'00.   2–18   his s· majesty is supposed

Satan's
No.   20–23   Adam's mistiness and S· reasoning,
'00.   13–22   "where S· seat is." — Rev. 2 : 13.

satiate
My.   249–14   only to s· its loathing

satin
Pul.   42–15   * wore a white s· badge

satin-lined
Pul.   78–23   * encased in a white s· box

satisfaction
Mis.   141–18   corrected to the s· of all.
    240–16   to the s· of all.
    275–21   Pen can never portray the s·
    329– 3   a s· with whatever is hers.
Ret.   33– 9   but without receiving s·.
Pul.   47–13   * without receiving any real s·.
Hea.   15–13   explains to any one's perfect s·
My.   74–19   * pride and s· that is not only
    74–24   * s· that springs from a belief in
    81– 4   * and healthy s· with life.
    83–22   * takes on a tone of deserved s·,
    152–31   I have the sweet s· of
    207–22   s· of meeting and mastering evil

satisfactorily
Man.   66–21   supposed to come . . . s· attested.
    77–15   their several offices s·,
'02.   5–15   can never be answered s· by
My.   255– 8   filling their positions s·
    277–21   settle all questions amicably and s·.

satisfactory
Mis.   158–27   It is s· to note, however,
Man.   30–22   occupants are s· to her.
My.   55– 6   * but were not s· :

satisfactory
My.   277– 6   honorable and s· to both nations
    302–26   and the situation was s·.

satisfied
Mis.   15–21   shall soul as sense be s·,
    87–11   knowing this, I shall be s·.
    178– 5   not s· with a manlike God,
    322–17   senses s·, or self be justified.
    358–12   All men shall be s· when
Pul.   1– 1   shall be abundantly s· — Psal. 36 : 8.
    2–13   shall be abundantly s·," — Psal. 36 : 8.
    3–16   shall be abundantly s· — Psal. 36 : 8.
    3–24   s· with what is pleasing to
    4–26   shall be abundantly s· — Psal. 36 : 8.
    7–27   so long as this church is s·
    7–29   shall be abundantly s· — Psal. 36 : 8.
    51–25   * some may be s· and some will not.
Pan.   6–15   is not s· with this theism,
'00.   8– 3   s· to go on till we awake in
Po. page 79   poem
    79–21   Who doth His will . . . Is s·.
My.   9–26   s· with what my heart gives
    40– 8   * seekers everywhere may be s·.
    53– 4   * not until the authoress was s·
    122–19   are we s· to know that our sense of
    132–27   slothful, s· to sleep and dream.
    182–26   fears turn hither with s· hope.
    248– 2   I am more than s· with your work :

satisfies
Mis.   160–12   It s· my present hope.
    227–26   s· the mind craving a
Rud.   15– 7   s· the thought with
'02.   17–24   s· the hungry heart,
My.   15–24   * It s· my longings,
    189–20   s· the immortal cravings
    250– 5   s· justice, and crowns

satisfieth
My.   13–22   s· thy mouth with — Psal. 103 : 5.

satisfy
Mis.   16– 2   s· more the cravings for
    252–16   can s· himself of their verity.
    287–13   can s· immortal cravings
    348–24   I wanted to s· my curiosity
    380–21   wherewith to s· the sick
Ret.   33–24   insufficient to s· my doubts
Pul.   66–18   * s· a taste for the mystical
My.   227– 2   to s· himself regarding

satisfying
'02.   20– 8   rewarding, s·, glorifying
My.   38– 4   * rest in this s· assurance,

Saturday
Pul.   67– 1   * S·, February 2, 1895
My.   16–12   * S·, July 16, 1904,
    58– 4   * Sentinel of last S·
    74– 3   * From now until S· night
    74– 5   * the night trains of S·
    137– 5   * filed in the office . . . S·,

Saul
Mis.   162– 2   called . . . S·, Paul.

save
Mis.   11– 6   and s· my own life,
    11–15   s· it only in accordance with
    17–15   to heal and to s·.
    48– 1   s· as I measure its demonstrations
    60– 2   when He sent His Son to s·
    63–11   why did Jesus come to s·
    63–15   Jesus came to seek and to s·
    63–16   s· them from this false belief ;
    89–12   you s· him or alleviate his
    90– 6   s· all who understand it.
    113– 9   s· he that had the mark, — Rev. 13 : 17.
    116– 3   be with you, and s· you from
    129–23   Were they to s· the sinner,
    171– 1   that it cannot s·," — Isa. 59 : 1.
    195–12   s· that which was lost." — Matt. 18 : 11.
    197–16   of no more help to s· from sin,
    197–19   to heal and to s·,
    204– 4   "S·, or I perish." — see Matt. 8 : 25.
    210–26   s· him from his destroyer.
    211–17   wish to s· him from death.
    211–23   "Whosoever will s· — Matt. 16 : 25.
    229–22   to heal and to s· mankind
    238–12   s· when he is abused
    244– 8   states that God cannot s·
    249–26   more tenderly to s· and bless.
    269–31   s· he that had the mark, — Rev. 13 : 17.
    380–19   s· the immediate recovery of
Ret.   32– 7   whosoever will s· — Matt. 16 : 25.
    63– 9   in order to . . . s· him
    63–18   and so to s· man from it?
    86–21   No one can s· himself
Un.   10– 6   s· Jesus and his apostles,
    18– 6   can never s· man from sin,

save

Un.	58– 7	"*S*· thyself, — *Mark* 15 : 30.
	59– 3	his purpose to *s*· humankind?
	60– 2	Christ Jesus came to *s*· men,
	62– 4	and came to *s*· me ;"
Pul.	28–16	* *s*· that its service includes
	83–18	* and to *s*· us from ourselves.
Rud.	3– 4	all efforts to *s*· them from sin
No.	39– 4	potent prayer to heal and *s*·.
	40–16	*s*· to issues of Truth ;
	41–25	* shall *s*· the sick, — *Jas.* 5 : 15.
'00.	7–26	"*S*·, or I perish !" — *see Matt.* 8 : 25.
'01.	19– 4	worketh with them to *s*· sinners.
	19– 8	to heal and to *s*·.
'02.	8–19	its power to heal and to *s*·.
	11– 6	waits and pleads to *s*· mankind
	14– 3	is to *s*· it for my church.
	18–28	of all his disciples *s*· one.
My.	92–28	* *s*· the desire in the human heart
	93– 8	* *s*· the moderately well-to-do,
	96– 8	* gathering can in no sense, *s*· one,
	150– 3	for that which seeketh to *s*·,
	159–11	to heal and to *s*·.
	172–12	*s*· that which it represents
	200–27	*s*· sinners and fit their being to
	220– 1	*s*· him from bad physical results.
	221–32	shall *s*· the sick"? — *Jas.* 5 : 15.
	258– 5	*s*· one lowly offering — love.
	260– 4	an alien *s*· as phenomenon,
	289–17	"God *s*· the Queen"
	292–14	fail in their prayers to *s*·
	335–28	* nothing could *s*· the life of
	364–12	*s*· that which cometh from God.

saved

Mis.	3–14	is man healed and *s*·.
	71– 5	yet he *s*· many a drunkard
	89–20	*how can he be s*·,
	89–21	*does he need to be s*·?
	89–26	being *s*· from itself,
	89–27	*s*· from error, or error overcome.
	89–29	*s*· on this divine Principle,
	185–15	whereby we can be *s*·,
	187–30	in order to be healed and *s*·,
	196–28	*and thou shalt be s*·. — *Acts.* **16** : 31.
	197– 8	man *s*· from sin, sickness, and
	248–26	*s*· me from that necessity
	261–23	spirit of sacrifice always has *s*·,
	261–26	*s*· with an everlasting salvation.
Man.	16– 1	man is *s*· through Christ,
Ret.	13– 7	unwilling to be *s*·, if my brothers
	79–25	were *s*· by patient waiting.
Un.	2– 8	in order to be *s*· from sin.
	2–14	The true man, really *s*·,
Pul.	vii–18	the sick are healed and sinners *s*·,
No.	37–23	*s*· the sinner and raised the dead,
Pan.	5–24	healed the sick, and *s*· sinners.
	14–24	shielded by the power that *s*· them,
'00.	7–27	we are *s*· from our fears.
'01.	11– 8	we are healed and *s*·,
	11–10	*s*· from the sins and sufferings
	17– 5	to return . . . penitent and *s*· ;
Hea.	9–10	this method has not *s*· them from
Peo.	3– 7	the election of the minority to be *s*·
	8– 4	partiality that elects some to be *s*·
My.	161–16	is *s*· through Christ, Truth,
	178– 6	the sick are healed and sinners *s*·.
	282– 7	and be ye *s*·, — *Isa.* 45 : 22.

saves

Mis.	90– 6	practical Truth *s*· from sin,
	260–26	an atmosphere that heals and *s*·.
	261–23	has saved, and still *s*· mankind ;
	299–28	*s*· your purchasing these garments,
	367–28	whatever *s*· from sin,
	369–21	charity that heals and *s*· ;
Un.	59– 4	evils from which he *s*·
No.	21–26	wherein Principle heals and *s*·.
'01.	34– 2	whereby Christendom *s*· sinners,
'02.	8–20	The energy that *s*· sinners
My.	43–28	* that which heals and *s*·.
	122–18	healing Christ that *s*· from sickness
	185–20	heals the sick, *s*· sinners,
	206– 7	holiness which heals and *s*·.
	260– 2	Life that heals and *s*· mankind.
	348–13	his divine Principle, God, *s*· man,
	348–16	God, heals and *s*· mankind.
	348–19	heals the sick and *s*· the sinner.

saveth

Mis.	258–16	*s*· the upright in heart." — *Psal.* 7 : 10.

saving

Mis.	2–19	God, man's *s*· Principle,
	39–18	this *s*·, exhaustless source
	86– 3	final degree of regeneration is *s*·,
	124–18	raising the dead, *s*· sinners.
	373–32	Its healing and *s*· power

saving

Man.	19– 4	healing and *s*· the world
Un.	58– 9	*s*· himself after the manner
Pul.	6–10	healing and *s*· mankind.
'01.	9–16	healing and *s*· men,
'02.	6–10	*s*· the sinner and healing
My.	4–28	healing the sick and *s*· the sinner.
	24– 9	* this healing and *s*· gospel.
	104–32	healing of the sick, the *s*· of sinners,
	105–12	*s*· the limbs when the surgeon's
	118–17	A *s*· faith comes not of
	122–29	healing the sick and *s*· sinners.
	153–15	healing faith is a *s*· faith ;
	274–28	thy *s*· health among — *Psal.* 67 : 2.

Saviour (*see also* Saviour's)

Mis.	90– 1	and recognize his *S*·.
	161– 4	*Corporeal and Incorporeal S*·.
	161–19	benefactor, or personal *S*·,
	163–22	three years a personal *S*· !
	163–26	the incorporeal *S*· — the Christ
	164– 9	the *S*·, which is Truth,
	180–10	always here, — the impersonal *S*·."
	234–30	as our *S*· from sickness, sin,
	345–28	talked of the crucified *S*· ;
	376–13	* *Yours* is a palpitating, living *S*·
	398–22	Saw ye my *S*·?
Un.	59– 3	How, indeed, is he a *S*·,
	59–17	never saw the *S*· come and go,
	59–21	a sinner, needing a *S*· ;
Rud.	3– 6	and become their *S*·,
'02.	19–29	our *S*· in his life of love.
Hea.	20– 4	* Which in our *S*· shine,
Po.	75– 1	Saw ye my *S*·?
My.	104–14	*S*· of men, the healer of men,
	119–22	gave the real proof of his *S*·,
	155– 9	*S*· whom the Scriptures declare.
	191–15	witnesseth a risen *S*·,
	270–18	words of our dear, departing *S*·,
	293–30	And the *S*· of man saith :

saviour

My.	108–30	the *s*· of the body." — *Eph.* 5 : 23.

Saviour of the World

Pul.	53–25	* earned the title of *S*· *of the W*·."

Saviour's

Ret.	88–26	spirit of the *S*· ministry,

savor

Mis.	xi–18	to suit and *s*· all literature.
Ret.	65– 9	sweet-smelling *s*· of Truth
Pul.	75–10	would *s*· more of heathenism

savors

Pul.	3–29	present realization of my hope *s*· of

saw

Mis.	30– 9	He *s*· the real earth and heaven.
	49– 2	I quickly *s*·, had a tendency to
	61–17	* certainly I *s*· him, or his effigy,
	156–14	because I *s*· no advantage,
	171– 5	and the blind *s*· clearly.
	191–13	*s*· one casting out devils — *Mark* 9 : 38.
	267–10	when I *s*· an opportunity
	292– 7	*s*· that Love had a new commandment
	326– 8	the blind *s*· them not,
	336–10	Then you would hate Jesus if you *s*· him
	353–17	When my brother returned and *s*· it,
	370– 4	Pharisees *s*· Jesus do such deeds of
	398–22	*S*· ye my Saviour?
Ret.	13–23	Mother *s*· this, and was glad.
	26–18	before the material world *s*· him.
	37–18	until our heavenly Father *s*· fit,
	44–19	I *s*· that the crisis had come
	45–21	I *s*· these fruits of Spirit,
	45–23	I also *s*· that Christianity has
	76–13	a light beyond what others *s*·.
Un.	59–17	never *s*· the Saviour come and go,
Pul.	2– 1	*s*· the house Solomon had erected.
	13–27	when the dragon *s*· that — *Rev.* 12 : 13.
	33– 2	* As a child Mary Baker *s*· visions
	36–12	* I never *s*· equalled.
	53–26	* Whittier, . . . *s*· the truth :
	70–13	* very recently *s*· completed
No.	39–22	more clearly than we *s*· before,
'00.	10–24	from a person I never *s*·.
Hea.	6–11	I *s*· the impossibility, in Science, of
	6–15	I *s*· how the mind's ideals
	9–28	St. John *s*· the vision of life in
	10– 1	he *s*· it pass away, — an illusion.
	12–17	we *s*· at once the concentrated
Po.	75– 1	*S*· ye my Saviour?
My.	22– 3	* *s*· the need of a larger edifice
	29–12	* no one who *s*· it will ever
	50–27	* few *s*· the grandeur of its work
	61–11	* I *s*· at once that somebody had to
	78– 5	* worshippers *s*· an imposing structure
	117–13	"When *s*· we thee a — *Matt.* 25 : 38.

saw

My.	117–15	Or when *s·* we thee sick, — *Matt.* 25 : 39.
	126–23	That which the Revelator *s·*
	145–10	and *s·* them carried out.
	320–28	* *s·* Mr. Wiggin several times
	321–21	* twenty years since I first *s·* you
	332–11	* until he *s·* her in the fond

Saxon

Mis.	26–28	*S·* term for God is also good.

say

Mis.	vii–14	to evolution's Geology, we *s·*,
	5–11	Many *s·*, "I should like to study,
	8–23	shall *s·* all manner of evil — *Matt.* 5 : 11.
	12– 1	*Because* I thus feel, I *s·* to others :
	22– 5	Who dare *s·* that matter or
	27–27	But, *s·* you, is a stone spiritual?
	31–10	It is needless to *s·* that
	33– 1	I will *s·* : It is the righteous prayer
	50– 8	*is there a secret . . . as some s·?*
	52– 3	It is difficult to *s·* how much
	60–15	to *s·* that addition is not subtraction
	73–15	can get no farther than to *s·*,
	73–22	*Verily I s· unto you, — Matt.* 19 : 28.
	83– 6	*you s·:* "*Every sin is the*
	83– 8	*you s·:* "*Sickness is a growth of*
	86– 9	*Is it correct to s· of material objects,*
	87– 7	let us *s·* of the beauties of the
	103– 2	which *s·* that sin is an evil power,
	103–10	the senses *s·* vaguely :
	124–20	we *s·*, It is well that C. S. has
	141–29	let them, not you, *s·* what shall be
	142–28	to *s·* to the masonic brothers :
	143–18	gives me great pleasure to *s·*
	146– 1	let me *s·*, 'T is sweet to
	153–21	May you be able to *s·*,
	158– 3	In reply to your letter I will *s·* :
	168–16	voice from heaven seems to *s·*,
	179–16	Can we *s·* this to-day?
	179–29	perceive Truth, and *s·* with Mary,
	184–14	If man should *s·* of the power
	193– 5	deemed it safe to *s·* at that time.
	200–20	Christians to-day should be able to *s·*,
	209–30	egotism and false charity *s·*,
	223–12	and to *s·*, if it must,
	228–27	and *s·*, what others say.
	230–18	when they have nothing to *s·*,
	238–17	It is enough, *s·* they,
	239– 1	let me *s·* to you, dear reader :
	245–21	It is difficult to *s·* which
	249– 4	I *s·* with tearful thanks,
	249–13	members of . . . churches will *s·*
	262–13	I just want to *s·*,
	275– 1	Would not our Master *s·* to the
	280– 7	pure and holy thoughts that *s·*,
	282–15	I *s·*, When you enter mentally
	298– 5	some affirm that we *s·*, — *Rom.* 3 : 8.
	298–17	not *s·* that it was God's command ;
	298–26	I *s·*, You mistake ;
	313– 3	Permit me to *s·* that
	321–26	I *s·*, Do not expect me.
	334– 3	or *s·* unto Him, — *Dan.* 4 : 35.
	335– 3	shall *s·* in his heart, — *Matt.* 24 : 48.
	335–14	they *s·*, having too much charity ;
	335–25	Such people *s·*, "Would you
	337– 9	who shall *s·*?
	347–28	None can *s·* unto Him,
	361–31	who could *s·* which that "one" was?
	367–28	The senses would *s·* that whatever
	368–12	We regret to be obliged to *s·*
	370– 2	to *s·*, in the spirit of our Master,
	371–12	I as their teacher can *s·*,
	371–19	to *s·*, "good right, and good wrong,"
	375–32	* "All that I can *s·* to you,
	379–13	I never heard him *s·* that matter
Chr.	55– 6	verily, I *s·* unto you, — *John* 5 : 25.
Ret.	8– 9	would *s·*, "Mother, who *did* call me?
	14–23	asked me to *s·* how I felt when
	15– 7	I could *s·* in David's words,
	54–15	Blind belief cannot *s·* when
	63– 1	Scientists *s·* God and His idea
	63–24	it encourages sin to *s·*,
Un.	11–27	ye *s·*, There are yet four months,
	11–28	I *s·*, Look up, not down,
	17– 4	I *s·*, Be allied to the deific power,
	18– 6	Error may *s·* that God can never
	24– 8	I *s·* unto you, God is All-in-all ;
	25– 2	If you *s·* that matter is unconscious,
	25–10	hence, whatever it appears to *s·*
	35– 2	and *s·* that sour is sweet,
	36–22	or to *s·* that the divine Mind is
	40– 3	To *s·* that you and I, as mortals,
	42– 8	that is to *s·*, a divine and
	51–14	*What s· you of woman?*
	52–15	*What s· you of evil?*
	53– 4	the lie must *s·* He made them,

Un.	53–12	To *s·* that Mind is material,
	54– 3	*s·* there *is* a false claim,
	60– 5	We *s·* that God is All,
	60–10	We *s·* that harmony is real,
	61–28	Invalids *s·*, "I have recovered
Pul.	3–26	Perchance some one of you may *s·*,
	4– 3	"What if the little rain should *s·*,
	12–17	What shall we *s·* of the mighty
	41–18	* to *s·* nothing of nearly a thousand
	45– 5	* Christian Scientists not only *s·*
	69–17	* I may *s·* that the fundamental idea
	79–13	* to *s·* nothing of cities
	80– 7	* that is to *s·*, it sought the line of
Rud.	8–22	sense may *s·* the unchristian
No.	2–13	test the feasibility of what they *s·*
	16–25	not enough to *s·* that matter is the
	21–28	is, to *s·* the least, like a cloud
	27–23	Who can *s·* what the absolute
Pan.	10–21	immorality, which, we regret to *s·*,
	13– 7	"Neither shall they *s·*, — *Luke* 17 : 21.
'00.	1– 9	I am grateful to *s·* that in
	7–20	we *s·* as did Mary of old :
	9– 4	withdraw that advice and *s·* :
	9– 5	But I *s·* this not because it is
	14–26	*s·* in your heart as the devout St. Stephen
'01.	3– 5	shall *s·* all manner of evil — *Matt.* 5 : 11.
	7–14	whereby we may consistently *s·*,
	22–16	I do not *s·* that one added to
	22–17	nor *s·* this to accommodate
	27–28	* First, people *s·* it conflicts
	27–29	* they *s·* it has been discovered before.
	27–30	* they *s·* they had always believed
	29–11	I *s·* this not because reformers
'02.	8– 5	Is it necessary to *s·* that in
	11–23	shall *s·* all manner of evil — *Matt.* 5 : 11.
	18– 8	Sad to *s·*, the cowardice and
	19–11	I *s·* it with joy,
Hea.	6– 4	* "People *s·* you are a medium,"
	16–23	Again, shall we *s·* that God
Peo.	8–14	but we *s·* that Life is carried on
	8–22	I *s·* unto thee, arise." — *Mark* 5 : 41.
Po.	27– 8	*S·*, will the young year dawn
	47–20	*S·*, are the sheaves and the
My.	19–30	"Verily I *s·* unto you, — *Mark* 14 : 9.
	27– 4	Divine Love bids me *s·* :
	28–12	* Suffice it to *s·*, however,
	48–31	* bound as an observer of them to *s·*,
	49– 2	* when these smiling people *s·*,
	59–25	* Some *s·* she did not."
	59–26	* "Send those who *s·* she did not
	60– 2	* to *s·* something about the early
	63–19	* seemed to *s·* that all the world was
	70–13	* They *s·* that workingmen stopped
	104–30	shall *s·* all manner of evil — *Matt.* 5 : 11.
	109–17	may sometimes *s·* with Job,
	114–28	Is it too much to *s·* that this book
	122–22	Can we *s·* with the angels
	122–25	can *s·* his Christ is risen
	123–31	let us *s·* with St. Paul :
	124– 9	who would *s·* to-day,
	125–11	to *s·*, All honor to the members of our
	128– 1	cannot quench my desire to *s·*
	130–24	I need not *s·* this to the loyal
	131–19	but I wish to *s·* briefly that
	131–31	I *s·* with the consciousness of Mind
	136–13	I am pleased to *s·* that the
	143–27	What shall we then *s·* — *Rom.* 8 : 31.
	146– 2	I will *s·* : It is understood by all
	150–28	I *s·* unto you :
	153–11	To-day our great Master would *s·*
	156–13	he bade them *s·* to the goodman
	158–23	and some practise what they *s·*.
	161–24	*s·* not in thy heart :
	162–19	would *s·* to the builder of the
	169–15	*s·* through the *New York Journal,*
	175–11	Allow me to *s·* to the good folk
	177– 7	I am glad to *s·* that
	199– 6	May God *s·* this of the church
	200– 7	none can stay His hand or *s·*,
	200–19	I need not *s·* this to you,
	214–18	with the hope of . . . I will *s·* :
	216–18	on behalf of . . . I *s·* :
	219–12	To *s·* that it is sin to ride to church
	219–21	but I do *s·* that C. S.
	222–11	*s·* unto this mountain, — *Matt.* 17 : 20.
	228–27	has the divine presumption to *s·* :
	232–13	"What I *s·* unto you — *Mark* 13 : 37.
	232–13	I *s·* unto all, — *Mark* 13 : 37.
	233–16	*s·*, "They have healed also — *Jer.* 6 : 14.
	236– 9	to *s·*, please adopt generally
	236–19	we can *s·*, the more the better.
	244–24	What I have to *s·*
	245–11	I regret to *s·*,
	251– 2	What these are I cannot yet *s·*.
	254–11	to your kind letter, let me *s·* :

say

My. 258–25 To the dear children let me s :
270–15 those who s that she is
271–29 permit me to s that, insomuch as I
273–27 But s you, "Man awakes from
274–21 allow me to s that I am not fond of
275–13 Permit me to s , the report
276– 4 to s , in her own behalf,
277– 6 I will s I can see no other way
280–20 none can stay His hand nor s
284–23 But here let me s that I am
289– 2 what we do, not what we s .
297– 6 I will s , Amen, so be it.
298–10 hereby s that they have my
304–26 * s it conflicts with the Bible.
304–27 * s it has been discovered before.
304–28 * s they have always believed it."
308– 6 It is calumny on C. S. to s
310–19 I will s that there was never
316– 8 shall s all manner of evil — Matt. 5 : 11.
317– 9 It is a great mistake to s that I
342–14 * And when I s frail,
344– 3 If we s that the sun stands for God,
344–12 I hold it absurd to s that when
344–25 "I s , 'Render to Caesar — Mark 12 : 17.
344–30 I s : Where vaccination
346–27 "I did s that a man
358– 4 doing as you s you are,
358– 5 s , "Watch and pray, — Matt. 26 : 41.
360–12 I am constrained to s ,
361– 5 All I s is stated in C. S.

sayers

My. 125– 3 not only s but doers of the law

sayeth

'02. 19–23 Love that doeth it, and s ,

saying (noun)

apostle's
'02. 9–11 fulfilling the apostle's s :
classic
My. 224–31 let us adopt the classic s ,
fulfils the
My. 265–23 fulfils the s of our great Master,
his
Mis. 312–10 chapter sub-title
325– 4 they understand not his s .
'01. 19–11 and he illustrated his s
My. 288–25 his s , "Sin no more, — John 5 : 14.
307–17 was offended by his s
339–27 animus of his s was :
immortal
Mis. 76– 7 this immortal s can never
Jesus'
My. 232–28 does that watch accord with Jesus' s ?
Master's
'02. 5–22 Hence our Master's s ,
My. 108– 9 Hence our Master's s ,
my
Mis. 76– 4 "If a man keep my s , — John 8 : 51.
No. 31–27 "If a man keep my s , — John 8 : 51.
My. 300–18 "If a man keep my s , — John 8 : 51.
319– 5 My s touched him,
mystic
'01. 8–28 mystic s of the Master
Revelator's
'00. 12–17 hence the Revelator's s :
stale
Mis. 30–22 The stale s that C. S.
that
Mis. 196–12 that s came not from Mind,
253– 2 Note the scope of that s ,
Un. 53–26 hence that s of Jesus,
No. 13–12 before that s is demonstrated
this
Ret. 93– 8 Hear this s of our Master,
'02. 9– 8 the full significance of this s
Hea. 10–16 gather the importance of this s ,
My. 146– 5 I believe this s because I
146–12 Few believe this s .
229–16 according to this s of Christ Jesus :
wise
Mis. 371–20 It is a wise s that

Mis. 383– 8 In 1896 it goes without s ,
My. 76– 1 * it went without s that the same
228–30 It goes without s that such a one

saying (verb)

Mis. 11–32 s to them, "I love you,
59–19 Scriptures refer to God as s ,
72–13 s , The fathers have eaten — Ezek. 18 : 2.
116–21 it is not merely s , but doing,
168–30 * speaker began by s
170–13 s , that we make our own heavens
175–15 s , Man's Life is God
175–30 s , Have we not in thy name
178–14 * which he prefaced by s :

saying (verb)

Mis. 179– 1 The old churches are s ,
179–10 He is s to us to-day,
184–17 s , "I have the power to sin
196– 6 s as in the beginning,
198–30 by s he has overworked,
206– 6 s forever to the baptized
215– 4 s , "I wound to heal ;
221–25 s that five times ten are fifty
223– 2 I was s all the time,
223–17 s , "I am a Christian Scientist,"
224– 9 lifted his hands to his head, s :
231–25 s , "Oh, pretty !"
239–29 taught the saying s
245– 4 "Take no thought, s , — Matt. 6 : 31.
299–21 can I make this right by s ,
311–30 often reported as s
327–25 and helping them on, s ,
360–27 s to sensitive ears
369–28 privilege of s to the sick,
Man. 18–10 at every epoch s ,
Ret. 37– 7 critics took pleasure in s ,
59– 8 s that addition means subtraction
69– 9 serpent, insists . . . s ,
77– 2 Pope was right in s ,
Un. 18– 3 let us think of God as s ,
32– 3 s , "I am a creator.
32–18 s , "I am the opposite of
45– 5 s , "Am I not myself ?
Pul. 5–17 s , "I have come to comfort you."
12– 5 heard a loud voice s — Rev. 12 : 10.
45–24 * s he gladly laid down his
No. 35–24 announcing Truth, and s
'00. 3–15 not far from s and doing.
13– 4 commends the church . . . s :
'01. 8–11 authority of Jesus for s
Hea. 5– 4 s He is beaten by certain
5– 6 Phrenology will be s ,
5– 7 Physiology will be s ,
5–11 startles us by s that
Peo. 5–16 s unto us, "Life is God ;
My. 5–26 s virtually what the prophet
14–12 * s that he had just been
39–20 * privilege of s a few words
108–23 designated as his best work, s ,
126–14 And a voice was heard, s ,
148–20 What are the angels s
191–19 Spirit is s unto matter :
210–21 s nothing, in particular,
212–29 s that animal magnetism never
215–14 begging me to accept it, s ,
215–24 s , "The laborer is — Luke 10 : 7.
221–22 s , "He that believeth — John 14 : 12.
222– 4 Jesus rebuked them, s :
228– 6 always s the unexpected
233–17 s , Peace, peace ; — Jer. 6 : 14.
307–13 s what I cannot forget
308–24 s , "I never use a cane."
310–28 s , "When do you ever see
311–21 presented me my coat-of-arms, s
317–18 s , "I wouldn't express it that way."

sayings

Mis. 84– 5 which characterized his s ,
127–27 Wise s and garrulous talk
183–21 Who understands these s ?
Un. 39–10 Who understands these s ?
40–12 they who believe his s
'02. 12–15 with another of his s :
My. 146–16 heights of the great Nazarene's s
146–19 absolute truth of his s
178–29 s of the great Master
178–31 all else reported as his s are
178–32 Logia, or imputed s of Jesus
179–16 verification of our Master's s .
190–14 regard his s as infallible.
227–18 to catch them in their s ;
232–12 left to us the following s
234–21 our great Master's s are practical
279– 6 C. S. reinforces Christ's s

says

Mis. 5–15 Materia medica s ,
36–24 s , "The carnal mind — Rom. 8 : 7.
173–14 so-called science, which s
175– 7 s , I am sustained by bread,
184–19 If he s , "I am of God,
188–12 but the apostle s ,
218–30 Dr. —— s : "The recognition of
220– 6 He mentally s , "You are well,
220–14 patient s and feels, "I am well,
241–10 a mental dose that s ,
244– 4 "surgical operation" that he s was
298–25 One s , "I find relief from pain in
347–15 One s , Go this way ;
347–16 the other s , Take the opposite
351–20 Evil counterfeits good : it s ,

says

Mis.	351–21	it *s·*, "I am Love,"
	359– 8	St. Paul *s·* : "When I was — *I Cor.* 13 : 11.
	367–13	Error *s·* that knowing all things
	367–15	God *s·* of this fruit of the tree
Ret.	31–19	As *s·* St. James :
	60– 7	material sense *s·* that matter,
Un.	5–14	of godliness," *s·* Paul ; — *I Tim.* 3 : 16.
	5–28	of Thy ways," *s·* Job ; — *see Job* 26 : 14.
	17– 4	Emerson *s·*, "Hitch your wagon to a
	17–20	Error *s·* God must know evil
	18– 7	God *s·*, I am too pure to
	18–13	Error *s·* you must know grief
	18–14	God, *s·* you oftenest console others
	18–17	God *s·*, I show My pity through
	18–22	Error *s·* God must know death
	30–11	restoreth my soul," *s·* David. — *Psal.* 23 : 3.
	34– 2	and then mortal mind *s·*,
	34–15	*s·* that matter cannot feel matter ;
	35– 1	Mortal mind *s·*, "I taste ;
	35–13	Mortal mind *s·* gravitation is a
	43–24	as Paul *s·* in the third chapter of
	44–18	Human wisdom *s·* of evil,
	55– 5	as Isaiah *s·* of him,
	60–24	St. Paul *s·*, "And if Christ — *I Cor.* 15 : 17.
Pul.	35–10	* is begotten of spirituality," she *s·*,
	46– 6	* Mrs. Eddy *s·* the words of the judge
	53–15	* Hudson *s·* : "That word, more than
	64–14	* Mrs. Eddy *s·* she discovered C. S.
	69– 6	* Dr. Hammond *s·* he was converted to
	69– 9	* He *s·* they use no medicines,
Rud.	5– 3	Bible *s·* : "Let God be true, — *Rom.* 3 : 4.
	5–20	Human belief *s·* that it does ;
	6–14	He *s·* that "color is in *us*,"
No.	44–25	*s·* : "Heretics of yesterday are
'00.	2–25	He *s·* : "It is my duty to take
'01.	6– 3	Who *s·* the God of theology is a
Hea.	15–23	Scripture *s·*, "Ye ask, and — *Jas.* 4 : 3.
Peo.	6– 6	*s·* : "I declare my conscientious belief,
	6–11	Voltaire *s·* : "The art of medicine
My.	41–11	* the law of metaphysics *s·*,
	64–12	* Mrs. Eddy *s·*, "The First Commandment
	94– 8	* *s·* the *Springfield Republican.*
	99– 3	* It *s·* : "A faith which is able to
	104–14	*s·* that the Saviour of men,
	153–29	*s·* : Come, and I will give thee rest,
	187–14	*s·* : "For this is the message — *I John* 3 : 11.
	201–19	in him who *s·* in his heart :
	210– 1	chapter sub-title
	212–31	he *s·* this to cover his crime
	236–10	An old axiom *s·* :
	285–17	In Revelation 2 : 26, St. John *s·* :
	309–21	*McClure's Magazine s·*, describing
	310–22	*McClure's Magazine s·* that
	311–29	*McClure's Magazine s·*, "Mary Baker
	312– 5	*McClure's Magazine s·* : "He
	313–26	as *McClure's Magazine s·*.
	314– 2	It *s·* that after my marriage
	328–28	* *s·*, "and all other professionals
	330–21	* Mrs. Eddy *s·* of this circumstance :
	355– 6	*s·* there is a grave need for

say'st

Po.	26–16	smiling, *s·*, "'Tis done !

scabbard

Mis.	214–18	could be returned into the *s·*.
Ret.	2–12	sword, encased in a brass *s·*,
Pul.	46–19	* sword, encased in a brass *s·*,

scaffold

Mis.	99–14	to the dungeon or the *s·*,
	277–13	stake and *s·* have never silenced
	368– 7	* "Truth forever on the *s·*,
	368– 8	* Yet that *s·* sways the future,

scalding

Mis.	389–14	O make me glad for every *s·* tear,
Po.	4–13	O make me glad for every *s·* tear,
My.	350–14	heed'st Thou not the *s·* tear

scale

of being

Mis.	57–29	ascending the *s·* of being
	96–12	as thought ascends the *s·* of being
	234–17	a single step in the *s·* of being.
	359–26	only as we rise in the *s·* of being.
My.	110–12	upward in the *s·* of being.
	146–24	tip the *s·* of being, morally and
	146–31	in the divine *s·* of being
	230–25	rise in the *s·* of being,

Mis.	46–19	in the *s· with* his creator ;
	113–13	*s·* of moral and spiritual being,
	119–17	weighs mightily in the *s·* against
	151–27	ascending *s·* of everlasting Life
	280–12	nothing in the opposite *s·*.
	280–14	into the *s·* of Mind,
	290– 6	higher in the *s·* of harmony,

scale

Mis.	292–10	a new tone on the *s·* ascending,
	312– 3	weighed in the *s·* of God
	341– 8	you will go up the *s·* of Science
	379–31	adjusting in the *s·* of Science
Man.	59– 5	in the *s·* of right thinking.
Ret.	8– 5	three times, in an ascending *s·*.
Un.	64–16	*s·* the treacherous ice,
My.	150–12	can accomplish the full *s·* ;
	152– 7	far lower in the *s·* of thought,
	188–32	ascends the *s·* of miracles
	268–27	ascends the *s·* of life.
	277–18	weighs in the eternal *s·* of equity

scaled

Mis.	206–28	*s·* the steep ascent of C. S.,
My.	146–16	The heights . . . are not fully *s·*.

scales

Mis.	41–15	*s·* the mountain of human endeavor,
	280–16	Mind is not put into the *s·* with
	293–12	Experience weighs in the *s·* of God
	372– 4	weight in the *s·* of God.
Man.	47–15	it *s·* the pinnacle of praise
No.	7– 3	*s·* of justice and mercy.
My.	291–16	weighed in the *s·* of divinity,

scaling

My.	229–21	*s·* the steep ascent of Christ's Sermon

scalpel

Un.	28– 5	It was never touched by the *s·*

scan

Pul.	vii–19	to *s·* further the features of
My.	201–17	*s·* the convulsions of mortal mind,

scandal

My.	48–28	* are not drugged by *s·*,
	305–27	*s·* in the *Literary Digest*

scandalized

My.	330– 5	* great Master himself was *s·*,

scanning

My.	13– 8	*s·* its interesting pages,

scant

Mis.	274– 1	the *s·* history of Jesus
My.	9–10	* this would be *s·* indeed

scanty

Mis.	120–29	The Biblical record . . . is *s·* ;
	149– 7	replenish your *s·* store.

scarce

Mis.	396– 7	More sorrowful it *s·* could seem ;
Po.	58–19	More sorrowful it *s·* could seem ;
My.	59–18	* would *s·* fill a couple of pews

scarcely

Mis.	111– 1	*s·* sufficient to demonstrate
	222–18	*s·* awakes in time,
	246–13	*s·* been heard and hushed,
	317–14	*S·* a moiety, compared with
Pul.	42– 7	* *s·* even a minor variation
	58–17	* *S·* any woodwork is to be found.
'01.	16– 7	St. John's types of sin *s·* equal
Peo.	11– 3	*s·* done with their battles
My.	63–15	* *s·* possible to repress a
	83–17	* *s·* realize that the Scientists
	154– 7	*s·* venture to send flowers
	165– 5	*s·* an indignity which I have not
	173–11	I *s·* supposed that a note,

scare

Mis.	396– 2	To *s·* my woodland walk,
Po.	58–14	To *s·* my woodland walk,

scatter

Mis.	51–23	* *s·* in its breeze
Ret.	85–23	*s·* the sheep abroad ;
My.	107–22	or *s·* the shade of one who

scattered

Ret.	89– 9	*s·* about in cities
Po.	32– 7	*s·* o'er hillside and dale ;
My.	3–11	*s·* abroad in Zion's waste

scene

Mis.	1–20	Goodness reveals another *s·*
	205–15	last *s·* in corporeal sense.
Pul.	42– 9	* *s·* was rendered . . . interesting
My.	29–10	* *s·* repeated six times
	80–28	* A few were upon the *s·*

scenes

Mis.	275– 1	chief actors in *s·* like these,
	302– 1	Behind the *s·* lurks an evil
	392–23	*S·* that I would see again.
Ret.	81–27	shifting *s·* of human happiness,
Pul.	2–16	direful *s·* of the war
'02.	17–13	Earth's actors change earth's *s·* ;
Po.	51– 5	*S·* that I would see again.
My.	15–30	* And when, in *s·* of glory,
	313–25	to describe *s·* far away,

scent
  Mis. 390– 4   Thy breezes *s·* the rose's breath ;
  Po. 55– 4   Thy breezes *s·* the rose's breath ;

scents
  My. 155–28   sweet *s·* and beautiful blossoms

scepter (*see also* **sceptre**)
  Pul. 83–30   * and he, departing, left his *s·*

sceptered (*see also* **sceptred**)
  Po. 10–15   To Judah's *s·* race,
  21– 4   Her dazzling crown, her *s·* throne,

sceptre (*see also* **scepter**)
  Mis. 295–31   English crown and . . . English *s·*.
  '00. 10–19   sways the *s·* of self and pelf
  My. 128–13   No crown nor *s·* nor rulers
  201– 7   good will to man, sweeter than a *s·*,

sceptred (*see also* **sceptered**)
  Mis. 388–16   Her dazzling crown, her *s·* throne,
  My. 337–16   To Judah's *s·* race,

scheme
  My. 68–18   * color *s·* for all the auditorium
  200–23   will tumble from this *s·* into

schemes
  Mis. 312–22   risen above worldly *s·*,

schisms
  Man. 44– 6   involves *s·* in our Church
  My. 206– 8   *S·*, imagination, and human beliefs

scholar
  Mis. 318–21   and be a good Bible *s·*
  379–12   neither a *s·* nor a metaphysician.
  Ret. 47–25   Bible *s·* and a consecrated Christian.
  Rud. 15– 1   has shown that this defrauds the *s·*,

scholarly
  Mis. 81– 3   skilful and *s·* physicians
  308–19   *s·*, artistic, and scientific notices
  Pul. 5–14   his athletic mind, *s·* and serene,
  Pan. 12– 4   *s·* expositor of the Scriptures,
  '00. 7– 9   most *s·* men and women,
  My. 112–15   honest, intelligent, and *s·*
  113–31   among the *s·* and titled,
  316–15   *s·* editor, Mr. B. O. Flower,

scholars
  Mis. 296– 5   profound philosophers, brilliant *s·*.
  Man. 30– 3   Christians and good English *s·*.
  90– 2   must be thorough English *s·*.
  Ret. 6–17   one of the most . . . thorough *s·*
  50–15   my list of indigent charity *s·*,
  Pul. 23–21   * *s·* of special research,
  73–11   * one of the greatest Biblical *s·*
  My. 215– 9   without having charity *s·*,

scholarship
  Man. 91– 7   Remuneration and Free *S·*.
  91–10   bearer of a card of free *s·*
  Ret. 80–20   win the golden *s·* of
  87– 5   is as obvious in religion and *s·*
  My. 104–26   talents, *s·*, and character
  163–26   love their *s·*, friendship,
  319–10   and well-equipped *s·*.

scholastic
  Mis. 13–14   *S·* theology elaborates the
  102– 4   lexicographers and *s·* theologians,
  173– 9   pagan philosophy, or *s·* theology,
  194–15   which *s·* theology has hidden.
  340–30   human ethics, *s·* theology,
  362– 8   *S·* dogma has made men blind.
  Ret. 79–10   in shuffling off *s·* rhetoric,
  No. 24–11   false philosophy and *s·* theology,
  Pan. 5– 2   pantheism is found in *s·* theology.
  '01. 7– 3   *S·* theology makes God manlike ;
  12–20   which *s·* theology has obscured,
  24–28   *materia medica*, and *s·* theology
  My. 149–21   too deeply read in *s·* theology
  205–22   *S·* theology at its best
  307–30   want of divinity in *s·* theology,

scholasticism
  '01. 25– 8   the *s·* of a bishop,

school
  church and
  Mis. 313–24   chapter sub-title
  district
  My. 309–30   * district *s·* practically all the
  flooding the
  Ret. 47– 6   Students . . . were flooding the *s·*.
  flourishing
  Ret. 48–10   to close my flourishing *s·*,
  free
  Ret. 11–12   In our God-blessed free *s·*.
  Po. 60– 9   In our God-blessed free *s·*.
  her
  Mis. 48–30   to injure her or her *s·*.

school
  high
  My. 171–23   * on the lawn . . . of the high *s·*.
  173–28   green surrounding the high *s·* ;
  infant
  My. 312–30   I did open an infant *s·*,
  Italian
  Mis. 376– 3   * most authentic Italian *s·*,
  medical
  Mis. 349–13   of entering a medical *s·* ;
  349–18   He entered the medical *s·*,
  new
  Mis. 80–28   a new *s·* of practitioners,
  80–30   will not patronize the new *s·*,
  of Balaam
  '00. 13–23   *s·* of Balaam and Æsculapius,
  of Tyrannus
  '00. 12–25   labored . . . in the *s·* of Tyrannus,
  old
  My. 107– 8   old *s·* has become reconciled.
  one
  Rud. 16–14   *Is there more than one s· of*
  16–15   but one *s·* of the Science of
  out of
  Ret. 10– 3   kept me much out of *s·*,
  primary
  Un. 3– 1   lessons of this primary *s·*
  taught
  My. 310– 3   all taught *s·* acceptably
  312–17   * a brief season she taught *s·*."
  Mis. 365– 7   *s·* whose schoolmaster is not Christ,
  Ret. 47–14   voted that the *s·* be discontinued.
  No. 18–19   If . . . the *s·* gets things wrong,
  '02. 3–16   improved her public *s·* system
  My. 217– 2   for your own *s·* education,

schoolbooks
  Ret. 10–13   knowledge I had gleaned from *s·*

schoolboy
  My. 151– 2   the present *s·* epithets

schooled
  Ret. 7– 9   * trained and *s·* them

schoolmaster
  Mis. 365– 8   whose *s·* is not Christ,
  Ret. 30–18   the law was the *s·*,
  Rud. 11– 3   Sickness is the *s·*,
  No. 18–19   If the *s·* is not Christ,

schoolroom
  Mis. 91–23   *have our textbook, . . . in his s·*
  357– 4   *s·* is the *dernier ressort*.
  Ret. 83–22   take their textbook into the *s·*

schools
  Mis. 162– 7   before the people and their *s·*
  173– 5   learned of the *s·* that there is
  173– 8   the *s·*, pagan philosophy, or
  183–17   not by reason of the *s·*, or learning,
  257–26   cities, churches, *s·*, and mortals.
  270–22   we cannot leave Christ for the *s·*
  348–30   to enter medical *s·*,
  348–32   objected to their entering those *s·*.
  366– 2   had in our *s·* the time or attention
  369–14   leaders of materialistic *s·*
  Ret. 15–26   by physicians of the popular *s·*
  33– 7   knowledge from the different *s·*,
  34– 6   an answer from the medical *s·*,
  50–24   churches, *s·*, and associations
  Pul. 47–12   * *s·* of allopathy, homœopathy,
  70–21   * philosophy and *s·* of medicine,
  Rud. 17– 4   so-called *s·* are clogging the wheels of
  No. 11–16   had the place in *s·* of learning
  33– 6   rightful place in *s·* of learning.
  Pan. 11–12   When will the *s·* allow mortals to
  '01. 22–23   the differing *s·* of medicine
  23–10   would be in peace with the *s·*.
  26–12   turns away . . . to the *s·* and matter
  34–14   a creation of the *s·*
  My. 105– 9   of the stethoscope and the *s·*,
  245– 2   the approved *s·* of medicine,
  305–24   of the Greek nor of the Roman *s·*
  340–11   as witness her *s·*, her churches,

Science
  absolute
  Mis. 286– 9   to comply with absolute *S·*,
  286–29   Until this absolute *S·* of being is
  Ret. 27– 7   absolute *S·* of Mind-healing.
  My. 349–23   God of nature in absolute *S·*.
  abstract
  Mis. 264–16   to assimilate pure and abstract *S·*
  acme of
  Mis. 252–17   C. S. is not only the acme of *S·*
  action is
  Mis. 58–25   the action is *S·*.
  affirmations of
  Mis. 65– 9   submit to the affirmations of *S·*

Science

affords the evidence
Mis. 164–31   *S·* affords the evidence that God is the

all
Mis.   4– 6   All *S·* is *C. S.* ;
         58–22   All *S·* is divine, not human,
        219– 3   (and all *S·* is divine)
      261–30   All *S·* is divine.
Ret.   28–25   All *S·* is a revelation.
Pul.   35–22   All *S·* is a revelation.''
My.   348–30   basic Principle of all *S·*,

and Christianity
Peo.   2– 9   unites *S·* and Christianity,

and material sense
Un.   39–28   *S·* and material sense conflict

and philosophy
Mis. 359–27   chapter sub-title

and sense
Mis. 184– 3   *S·* and sense conflict,

and spiritual sense
Rud.   7–14   *S·* and spiritual sense contradict this,

answers it
Un.   8– 2   before *S·* answers it.

antipodes of
Un.   53–12   anti-Christian, the antipodes of *S·*.

any departure from
Rud. 16–16   Any departure from *S·* is an

art and
Mis. 393– 7   Art and *S·*, all unweary,
Po.   51–12   Art and *S·*, all unweary,

author of
'01.   4–12   God is the author of *S·*
My. 347–26   man is not the author of *S·*,

basis of
My. 357– 1   He is the only basis of *S·* ;

bonds of
No. 26–23   in the eternal bonds of *S·*,

brings out
Mis. 337–16   *S·* brings out harmony ;

certainty of
Mis. 220–31   with the certainty of *S·* he knows

Christ
Mis. 167–15   What is his name? Christ *S·*.
My. 238–14   presentation of C. S. — the Christ *S·*,

Christian
Mis.   v– 8   DEMONSTRATE THE ETHICS OF *C· S·*
         4– 7   All *Science* is *C· S·* ;
       4–30   the mission of *C· S·* to heal the sick,
       6– 6   The most of our *C· S·* practitioners
     12–25   In *C· S·*, the law of Love rejoices the
     16–26   the new birth begun in *C· S·*.
     21– 1   *C· S·* begins with the First Commandment
     21– 8   whereof *C· S·* now bears testimony.
     21–12   *C· S·* will be seen to depart from the
     21–15   My first plank in the platform of *C· S·*
     22–10   *C· S·* translates Mind, God, to mortals.
     22–22   That *C· S·* is Christian,
     23–25   what *C· S·* means by the word
     25– 4   is the *multum in parvo* of *C· S·* ;
     27– 8   Here is where *C· S·* sticks to its text,
     27–11   the cardinal point in *C· S·*,
     29–13   no analogy between *C· S·* and
     29–15   I taught the first student in *C· S·*.
     30– 5   adopt the "simple addition" in *C· S·*
     30–22   The stale saying that *C· S·* "is
     31– 3   and is the antipode of *C· S·*.
     32– 9   rules and divine Principle of *C· S·*.
     33–12   *Must I have faith in C· S· in order*
     33–19   naturally gain confidence in *C· S·*
     33–23   Healing by *C· S·* has the following
     34– 4   One who has been healed by *C· S·*
     34–11   *Is spiritualism . . . included in C· S·?*
     34–12   *C· S·* is based on divine Principle ;
     34–25   and are the antipodes of *C· S·* ;
     35– 7   sealed that proof with the signet of *C· S·*.
     37–17   *C· S·* lays the axe at the root of
     37–29   the labor that *C· S·* demands.
     38– 1   *Why do you charge for teaching C· S·*,
     39– 3   to take a course of instruction in *C· S·*.
     39– 9   false teachers of what they term *C· S·* ;
     39–11   the Founder of genuine *C· S·*
     40– 9   It is often asked, "If *C· S·* is
     40–22   The Founder of *C· S·* teaches her
     41–10   The honest student of *C· S·* is
     43– 1   *C· S·*, recognizing the capabilities of
     43– 7   *Do all who . . . claim to be teaching C· S·*,
     43– 8   *C· S·* is not sufficiently understood for
     43–18   gained sooner than the spirit of *C· S·* :
     43–25   incapacitates one to practise . . . *C· S·*.
     43–28   the mighty Truth of *C· S·*
     44– 5   investigate . . . the rudiments of *C· S·*.
     44– 6   *Can C· S· cure acute cases where*
     44– 8   The remedial power of *C· S·* is
     45– 5   *C· S·*, by means of its Principle

Science

Christian
Mis. 45–13   *be cured by metaphysics or C· S·?*
     46– 4   self-evident proposition of *C· S·*
     46–13   in the premises or conclusions of *C· S·*,
     49– 7   been restored by *C· S·* treatment.
     53–20   the meaning of the term and of *C· S·*.
     53–21   *If C· S· is the same as Jesus taught,*
     53–25   *C· S·* is simple, and readily understood
     54– 6   demonstrated, and teaches *C· S·?*
     54–12   power of *C· S·* over all obstacles
     55– 3   The simplest problem in *C· S·*
     55–16   *Is C· S· based on the facts of*
     55–18   *C· S·* is based on the facts of Spirit
     56– 2   the very antipodes of *C· S·*.
     58–19   *Does the theology of C· S· aid its*
     59– 7   divine power understood, as in *C· S·* ;
     60– 8   *C· S·* is proving this by healing
     62–17   The theology of *C· S·* is Truth ;
     62–23   the author grapples with *C· S·*,
     62–28   The theology of *C· S·* is based on the
     64–24   a student of the Bible and of *C· S·*.
     65–21   *C· S·* demands both law and gospel,
     68– 9   * *metaphysical healing being called C· S·.*
     69– 5   *C· S·* is the unfolding of true
     71–11   *Does C· S· set aside the law of*
     74– 1   The phenomena of Spirit in *C· S·*,
     75– 9   fact and grand verity of *C· S·*,
     75–21   assists one to understand *C· S·*.
     76– 7   it is the ultimatum of *C· S·* ;
     78–22   and that *C· S·* will some time appear
     80– 9   A league . . . which *C· S·* eschews
     80–13   leave *C· S·* to rise or fall on its
     82– 4   Understanding this fact in *C· S·*,
     87–21   in the investigation of *C· S·*
     88–15   His allusion to *C· S·* in the
     91–18   employed in the service of *C· S·*
     92– 3   liability of deviating from *C· S·*.
     93– 7   *that have been healed by C· S·*
     93–10   *C· S·* authorizes the logical
     95– 1   chapter sub-title
     95–12   for even a synopsis of *C· S·*,
     95–23   *C· S·* reveals the infinitude of
     96–24   How is the healing done in *C· S·?*
     97–15   *C· S·* is not a remedy of faith alone,
   100– 4   *C· S·* was to interpret them ;
   100–22   the acme of *C· S·*.
   101– 8   *C· S·* and the senses are at war.
   104–13   According to *C· S·*, perfection is
   105– 1   implicit faith engendered by *C· S·*,
   105– 8   is the foundation of *C· S·*.
   105–17   *C· S·* is an everlasting victor,
   105–20   *C· S·* is my only ideal ;
   106– 3   *C· S·* and Christian Scientists will,
   107–15   before . . . *C· S·* is demonstrated :
   110–24   and the momentum of *C· S·*,
   111–27   in time, that church will love *C· S·.*
   113–17   *C· S·* shows that there is a way
   113–28   systematized centres of *C· S·*
   114–30   The teacher in *C· S·* who does not
   115–15   teach, and live *C· S·* !
   119–21   is found powerless in *C· S·*,
   120– 1   The professors of *C· S·* must
   120– 4   at the very threshold of *C· S·* :
   124–20   It is well that *C· S·* has taken
   127–18   growth in *C· S·* will follow,
   132–20   teaching *C· S·*, receiving calls,
   135– 3   is not in the question of *C· S·*.
   136–18   absolute demonstration of *C· S·*.
   138–15   first and last lesson of *C· S·* is love,
   139–30   in the interest of *C· S·*,
   141– 3   the monument upreared, of *C· S·*.
   142–30   nor you with me in *C· S·*,
   144–13   Discoverer and Founder of *C· S·* ;
   148–19   demonstrate genuine *C· S·*,
   149– 5   to this banquet of *C· S·*,
   149–29   first temple for *C· S·* worship
   150–16   salvation . . . by means of *C· S·.*
   153– 2   establishing the Cause of *C· S·*.
   156–26   in acquiring solid *C· S·*.
   159–22   offer at the shrine of *C· S·*,
   160– 2   under the *régime* of *C· S·* !
   163–28   must needs come in *C· S·*,
   165–11   The daystar . . . is the light of *C· S·*
   166–24   idea, named in this century *C· S·*,
   167– 4   the spiritual idea, as in *C· S·* :
   170–23   and no other method is *C· S·*.
   177– 8   expressed and operative in *C· S·*.
   178– 9   * to preach a sermon on *C· S·*,
   178–22   * *If I had not found C· S· a new gospel,*
   185– 4   the divine Principle of *C· S·*.
   188–22   when she discovered *C· S·*
   193–12   *C· S·*, as defined and practised
   195– 5   Whosoever learns the letter of *C· S·*
   195–23   to try the edge of truth in *C· S·*,
   199–25   divine Principle is discerned in *C· S·*,

Science
Christian

Mis. 200–12	insists on the rare rule in *C· S·*
200–18	The foundational facts of *C· S·*
202– 2	the sweet harmonies of *C· S·*
203– 7	as I look on this smile of *C· S·*,
203–18	serves to . . . illustrate *C· S·*.
204–29	the divine Principle of *C· S·*,
205– 3	This practical *C· S·* is the
205–32	learn *C· S·*, and live what they learn,
206–11	The advancing stages of *C· S·* are
206–29	scaled the steep ascent of *C· S·*,
207– 6	practical, operative *C· S·*.
210– 4	*C· S·* never healed a patient without
210–13	as revealed in *C· S·*,
210–16	adaptability to lead on *C· S·*,
212–21	*C· S·* proves that human will is lost in
213–19	*C· S·* gives a fearless wing
215–12	*C· S·* demands order and truth.
219–22	This is *C· S·* :
222– 4	It reverses *C· S·* in all things.
225– 9	seventh modern wonder, *C· S·* ;
232– 5	chapter sub-title
232–21	Metaphysical healing, or *C· S·*,
233–22	who think the standard of *C· S·* too high
234–21	metaphysical healing, called *C· S·*,
235– 8	In *C· S·*, progress is demonstration,
239– 6	to commence a large class in *C· S·*.
244– 4	on the platform of *C· S·* !
245–10	the stately goings of *C· S·*
245–16	spiritual need that *C· S·* should
246–12	washed it divinely away in *C· S·* !
247–19	healing force developed by *C· S·*
248–26	glorious revelations of *C· S·*
249– 3	to see if *C· S·* could not
252– 8	*C· S·* classifies thought thus :
252–17	*C· S·* is not only the acme
253–29	opened their eyes to the light of *C· S·*?
255–20	I claim for healing by *C· S·*
256– 2	have been healed by *C· S·*
260– 3	*C· S·* has been reduced to the
261– 7	*C· S·* not only elucidates
263–23	educational system of *C· S·*
264–10	the essential nature of *C· S·*.
265–28	disaffections toward *C· S·*
266–25	in teaching or lecturing on *C· S·*,
269–25	*C· S·* may be sold in the shambles.
270– 7	example of the Master in *C· S·*,
271– 8	notion that . . . is, or can be, *C· S·*,
276–15	In *C· S·* the midnight hour will
278–10	connected with the Cause of *C· S·*,
281–28	assume when subscribing to *C· S·*.
282–25	he is restored through *C· S·*
283–19	I insist on the etiquette of *C· S·*,
283–27	It is the genius of *C· S·* to
284– 4	*C· S·*, more than any other system
285–21	showing its relation to *C· S·*,
286– 2	It is seen in *C· S·* that the
286– 7	will continue unprohibited in *C· S·*.
288–27	impulse from the cause of *C· S·* :
291–18	the possible perversion of *C· S·*
292–25	*C· S·*, full of grace and truth,
293– 2	the infant thought in *C· S·*
295– 8	* past a score of reforms, to *C· S·*."
296–15	This writer classes *C· S·* with
296–17	*C· S·*, antagonistic to intemperance,
297– 2	since the discovery of *C· S·*,
297–15	chapter sub-title
297–17	statute in the *morale* of *C· S·* :
297–20	held in *C· S·* as morally bound
298–20	the *morale* of absolute *C· S·*,
299– 6	look through the lens of *C· S·*,
300–29	*C· S·* demonstrates that the
301– 4	the *precedent* for preaching *C· S·*,
302–10	to know the teaching of *C· S·*
302–15	through *C· S·* Sunday services.
303– 9	these strongholds of *C· S·*,
307–21	absolute basis of *C· S·* ;
308– 9	The Scriptures and *C· S·*
308–28	*C· S·* is taught through its
309– 4	According to *C· S·*,
310– 7	by the discovery of *C· S·*.
311–19	As I now understand *C· S·*, I would
311–23	The works I have written on *C· S·*
315–15	proclivities toward *C· S·*.
315–19	health, and practical *C· S·*.
315–20	Teaching *C· S·* shall be no
316– 6	When will you take a class in *C· S·*
316–10	The date of a class in *C· S·* should
318– 3	obsolete terms in absolute *C· S·*,
318–18	gospel work of teaching *C· S·*,
321– 8	gain of Truth's idea in *C· S·* ;
322–22	He hath given you *C· S·*,
328–21	ascends the hill of *C· S·*
332– 7	doors that closed on *C· S·*
333–10	*C· S·* voices this question :

Science
Christian

Mis. 336–21	another name for *C· S·*,
337– 2	founded at this period *C· S·*,
337–20	Where these exist, *C· S·* has no
338–14	which demonstrates *C· S·*.
343–11	fruits of *C· S·* spring upward,
346– 2	*C· S·* carries this thought
346– 8	It confronts *C· S·*.
346–11	To this question *C· S·* replies :
346–20	self-evident proposition of *C· S·*,
346–24	It is a rule in *C· S·* never to
347–30	only authenticated organ of *C· S·*
349–14	it was inconsistent with *C· S·*,
351–14	placing *C· S·* in the hands of
354–24	humility is the first step in *C· S·*,
355– 2	present stage of progress in *C· S·*
356–16	The seed of *C· S·*, which
356–24	it is the genius of *C· S·*.
357–31	Divine Love is the substance of *C· S·*,
358– 6	the only appropriate seals for *C· S·*.
358–19	the heaven-crowned summit of *C· S·*.
360– 9	cast in the moulds of *C· S·* :
360–16	When *C· S·* has melted away the
361–12	and *C· S·* has overshadowed all
364–10	*C· S·* refutes everything that is not
364–31	*C· S·* rends this veil of the temple of
365–10	If *C· S·* lacked the proof of
365–23	the real value of *C· S·* to the race.
366– 9	give the keynote of *C· S·*
366–29	according to His mode of *C· S·* ;
367– 2	have no place in *C· S·*.
370–23	*C· S·*, a "metaphysical healing"
371–13	They know far more of *C· S·* than
372– 7	voices *C· S·* through song and
372–28	the *art* of *C· S·*, with true hue
373–30	*C· S·* is more than a prophet
374–12	*C· S·* and its art will rise
375– 5	The truest art of *C· S·* is to be a
378–21	metaphysical therapeutics, as in *C· S·*,
379–30	and named my discovery *C· S·*.
380–13	the first student in *C· S·*.
382– 3	No works on the subject of *C· S·*
382– 7	discovery and founding of *C· S·*
382–14	patient healed in this age by *C· S·*.
382–24	the first *C· S·* periodical ;
382–31	teaching and practising *C· S·*.
383– 3	churches of the *C· S·* denomination.
383– 6	a church of *C· S·* is established,
383– 9	*C· S· is founded by its discoverer*,
Man. 3–16	to demonstrate genuine *C· S·*,
17– 6	and students . . . in *C· S·*,
17–16	*C· S·*, as taught and demonstrated
27–16	and all other *C· S·* literature
31– 9	the prosperity of *C· S·*
34– 4	Believe in *C· S·*.
34– 8	believer in the doctrines of *C· S·*,
34–15	for self-instruction in *C· S·*,
35–18	who have not studied *C· S·*
41– 3	is the Ensample in *C· S·*.
41– 7	gulf between *C· S·* and theosophy,
42–12	In accordance with the *C· S·* textbooks,
42–21	inasmuch as *C· S·* can only
43– 8	auxiliaries to teaching *C· S·*
43–11	Discoverer and Founder of *C· S·*.
43–13	No Adulterating *C· S·*.
43–20	tends to prevent *C· S·* from
43–23	nor circulate *C· S·* literature which
44– 4	shall not be adjudged *C· S·*.
44– 7	possible loss, for a time, of *C· S·*.
44–26	impede their progress in *C· S·*.
46–11	except as a *C· S·* practitioner.
49– 7	*C· S·* Nurse.
49– 9	represents himself . . . as a *C· S·* nurse
49–11	demonstrable knowledge of *C· S·*
50– 9	shall not debate on *C· S·* in public
52–26	and to the Cause of *C· S·*,
53–26	hence injurious, to *C· S·*
55–23	trying to practise or to teach *C· S·*
58– 3	THE *C· S·* PASTOR.
59– 1	sacred revelations of *C· S·*
63–10	*C· S·* contained in their textbook.
63–15	church of the *C· S·* denomination
64–16	the Founder of *C· S·*.
65– 8	used in connection with *C· S·*.
71–15	would be disastrous to *C· S·*.
73–11	conduct a *C· S·* organization
74– 2	*C· S·* society holding public services,
74– 6	In *C· S·* each branch church
74–11	Teachers and practitioners of *C· S·*
80– 3	of the interests of *C· S·*.
82–20	engaged in the work of *C· S·*,
83– 1	heading
83– 5	Teaching *C· S·* shall not be a
83–11	proclivities toward *C· S·*.
83–18	and practical in *C· S·*.

Science
Christian

Science

Christian

My. 315–13	* Discoverer and Founder of *C· S·*,
315–27	of the divine power of *C· S·*,
316–13	Attacks on *C· S·* and its Founder,
316–14	Survey of the *C· S·* Movement,''
317–13	criticisms of my statement of *C· S·*,
317–22	diction, as used in explaining *C· S·*,
318–32	find my authority for *C· S·*
322–22	* instruction by Mrs. Eddy in *C· S·*.
327– 6	made it legal to practise *C· S·*
327–31	* taught and practised in *C· S·*,
328–10	* *C· S·* people, greatly pleased
328–19	* two *C· S·* healers in this city.
329–23	* the steady progress of *C· S·*
333– 3	* *C· S·* publication committee.
339– 5	cardinal points of *C· S·*
339– 9	on the great subject of *C· S·*.
341–20	* *C· S·* has been so much to the fore
344–24	* How does *C· S·* stand as to them?''
345– 6	*C· S·* will overthrow false knowledge
345–11	* are these too material for *C· S·*?''
346– 1	* from the standpoint of *C· S·*,
346–21	* Discoverer and Founder of *C· S·*,
347– 2	* through Christ Jesus and *C· S·*,
347–23	chapter sub-title
349–12	*C· S·* is a divine largess,
352–29	first issue of *The C· S· Monitor.*
353– 7	*C· S· Monitor,* November 25, 1908
353– 9	given the name to all the *C· S·*
355– 7	need for more men in *C· S·* practice.
355–11	in our field of labor for *C· S·*.
356–28	correct version of *C· S·*.
357– 2	wholly apart from *C· S·*,
357– 4	even the divine idea of *C· S·*,
357–12	spiritual modesty of *C· S·*,
357–15	demonstrate *C· S·* to a higher extent,
357–21	to salvation and eternal *C· S·*.
357–23	the axiom of true *C· S·*,
358– 1	*C· S·* abides by the definite rules
359– 7	Discoverer and Founder of *C· S·*
361– 2	directions . . . as simplified in *C· S·*,
361– 6	stated in *C· S·* to be used as
362–17	* Cause of *C· S·* in this community,
364– 3	rule of mental practice in *C· S·*

(*see also* **Board of Directors, Church, church, Churches** and **churches, demonstration, healing,** *Herald,* **history,** *Journal,* **Mind-healing, practice, Principle, Publishing Society,** *Quarterly,* **rule, rules,** *Sentinel,* **student, students, teacher, teachers, teachings, temple, text-book, understanding**)

Christianity and

Pul. 56–17	* Welding Christianity and *S·*,
My. 179–25	Christianity and *S·*, being

come with

No. 18–10	Right thinking and . . . come with *S·*,

completeness of

No. 10– 5	proof . . . of the completeness of *S·*.

consciousness in

My. 117–10	order and consciousness in *S·*,

contains a

My. 112–18	contains a *S·* which is demonstrable

contradicts

Mis. 96–31	*S·* contradicts this evidence;
Ret. 60–25	Material sense contradicts *S·*,

corrects

Mis. 287–10	*S·* corrects this error

dawn of

Mis. 174–28	the dawn of *S·* that reveals

decision of

Mis. 65–12	Left to the decision of *S·*,

declare

Un. 39–20	let *S·* declare the immortal

declares

Un. 29–10	*S·* declares God to be the Soul

defines

Mis. 102–32	*S·* defines *omnipresence* as
Rud. 2–18	*S·* defines the individuality

defines man

Ret. 59–22	*S·* defines man as immortal,

demanded

My. 348–17	*S·* demanded a rational proof

demonstrable

'01. 21– 5	demonstrable *S·* leading the ages.
My. 143–22	an eternal and demonstrable *S·*,

demonstrate

My. 303–17	demonstrate *S·* and its pure

demonstrate, in

Mis. 115–19	demonstrate, in *S·*, that evil has

demonstrate its

Mis. 59– 3	understand nor demonstrate its *S·*,

demonstrates

Mis. 98–20	religion whose *S·* demonstrates God
No. 4–14	*S·* demonstrates the reality of

Science

demonstrate the

Mis. 75–10	to demonstrate the *S·*.
344–20	demonstrate the *S·* of Life,

demonstration of

Mis. 355– 9	absolute demonstration of *S·*

departures from

Mis. 265–29	out of the departures from *S·*

devoid of

Un. 49–23	it is devoid of *S·*.

discernment of

My. 206–10	darken the discernment of *S·*;

discern the

Mis. 287–16	lifts mortals to discern the *S·* of

discovered the

Ret. 24– 5	I discovered the *S·* of

diverges from

Mis. 265– 2	diverges from *S·* and knows it not,

Divine

Mis. 174–31	The leaven . . . is Divine *S·*;
336–20	chapter sub-title
Rud. 14– 6	strictly practising Divine *S·*,

divine

Mis. 2–31	spiritual elements in divine *S·*.
3– 9	lessons we learn in divine *S·*
3–13	his life-experience — and divine *S·*,
13–25	This postulate of divine *S·*
15–11	divine *S·*, that results in health,
16–23	Christianity is a divine *S·*.
19–14	Truth and Love in divine *S·*,
25– 7	In divine *S·* it is found that
27– 3	In divine *S·* the terms God and good,
27–14	accept divine *S·* on this ground?
28–16	he demonstrated that divine *S·* alone
45–18	Sin is not the master of divine *S·*,
46–21	at every point, in divine *S·*,
52– 9	to heal, through divine *S·*,
52–22	problem to be wrought in divine *S·*.
59–17	belief that is unavailing in divine *S·*.
66–15	teach, through divine *S·*,
77–14	power and presence, in divine *S·*,
77–23	there learn, in divine *S·*,
89–28	God's likeness, is safe in divine *S·*.
102–20	fully expressed in divine *S·*,
114–11	rules of divine *S·* announced
116–21	divine *S·* is not an argument;
123–18	Divine *S·* has rolled away the stone
166– 1	according to divine *S·*,
169– 1	found all the divine *S·* she preaches;
174–23	heaven is the reign of divine *S·*:
175– 9	divine *S·* changes this false sense,
181– 4	reality of his being, in divine *S·*?
181–22	but is the order of divine *S·*.
181–32	clear discernment of divine *S·*:
182–11	Through divine *S·* man gains
183– 2	in the divine *S·* of being;
183–22	divine *S·* unfolds omnipotence,
184–16	he would trespass upon divine *S·*,
186–13	in the Scriptures, as in divine *S·*,
189– 5	as unfolded in divine *S·*,
190– 4	Divine *S·* demonstrates Mind
192–17	Luminous with the light of divine *S,*
194– 2	Divine *S·* reveals the Principle
194–11	Divine *S·* is not an interpolation
195–32	informed by divine *S·*,
200–14	The divine *S·* of this rule is quite as
206– 8	What but divine *S·* can interpret
209– 8	Principle of divine *S·* being Love
212–15	One step away from . . . divine *S·*
217– 1	True idealism is a divine *S·*,
219– 2	divine *S·* . . . neither reveals God in
222–19	This sin against divine *S·* is
234– 6	Love is the Principle of divine *S·*;
255–12	He should comprehend, in divine *S·*,
258–14	In divine *S·*, God is One and All;
259–17	divine *S·*, in which God is supreme,
291– 2	by the Principle of divine *S·*:
309–12	He advances most in divine *S·* who
320–17	fixed in the heavens of divine *S·*,
320–29	religion undefiled, divine *S·*;
331–25	divine *S·* evolved nature as thought,
333–32	Christians, instructed in divine *S·*,
334–29	dis-covered for you divine *S·*,
335–30	whoso departeth from divine *S·*,
336–12	rule and demonstration of divine *S·*:
337–30	which he reflected through divine *S·*
342– 1	joy of divine *S·* demonstrated.
358– 3	to mark the way in divine *S·*.
359–24	The *way* is absolute divine *S·*:
362– 4	realities of divine *S·*;
365–20	If the uniform . . . effects of divine *S·*
369– 1	God's law, as in divine *S·*,
372–25	modest glory of divine *S·*.
Ret. 26–23	divine *S·* must be a discovery.
27–24	so the harmony of divine *S·*
28–12	understanding of God in divine *S·*.

Science

divine

Ret.	50–28	new rule of order in divine *S*·,
	54– 6	self-renunciation, and divine *S*·
	56–15	Divine *S*· disclaims sin, sickness,
	56–24	Divine *S*· demands mighty wrestlings
	61– 2	enmity to God and divine *S*·
	64– 9	divine *S*·, which teaches that good is
	79– 9	signs for the wayfarer in divine *S*·
	88–28	the wings of divine *S*·.
	94– 6	whatsoever . . . contradicts divine *S*·
	94–21	There is no . . . in divine *S*·;
	95– 1	watered by dews of divine *S*·,
Un.	2–20	this same rule, in divine *S*·,
	3–13	reached the goal in divine *S*·,
	5–11	but to seek the divine *S*·
	6– 2	for it, is divine *S*·,
	7–22	An incontestable point in divine *S*·
	10–19	in the Truth of divine *S*·,
	36–25	stultifies the logic of divine *S*·,
	39–11	divine *S*· removes human weakness
	43–14	the fact, as it exists in divine *S*·,
	51–24	full Truth is found only in divine *S*·,
	57–26	divine *S*· wipes away all tears.
	61–25	Truth, in divine *S*·, is the
	62– 2	fact really remains, in divine *S*·,
	62–20	The Truth or Life in divine *S*·
Pul.	13–14	those who break faith with divine *S*·
	35– 9	"Divine *S*· is begotten of spirituality,"
	35–16	understanding of God in divine *S*·.
Rud.	5– 6	in divine *S*· there is no material
	7–23	According to divine *S*·, Spirit
	11–21	understanding of God and divine *S*·,
No.	11–21	because they teach divine *S*·,
	18–15	highest endeavors are, to divine *S*·,
	20–13	perfect man, and divine *S*·.
	20–21	In divine *S*·, God is recognized as
	25– 4	this cardinal point of divine *S*·,
	27–12	fully interpreted by divine *S*·,
	27–14	divine *S*·, presents the grand and
	33–10	divine *S*·, with fixed Principle,
Pan.	8–18	one law, namely, divine *S*·.
'00.	4–17	the only perfect religion is divine *S*·,
	4–28	In divine *S*·, divine Love includes
	5–12	God, man, and divine *S*·.
	5–17	the divine *S*· of divine Love,
'01.	3–17	Then, to define Love in divine *S*·
	4– 8	Principle and rule of divine *S*·
	4–15	Christianity is divine *S*·,
	5–25	God and man in divine *S*·,
	6–18	logic of divine *S*· being faultless,
	6–30	In divine *S*· He is
	11– 6	we see the Son of man in divine *S*·;
	12–17	Divine *S*· is not an interpolation of
	12–20	only needs the prism of divine *S*·,
	18–16	discerned only through divine *S*·.
	24–26	divine *S*· of Christianity
'02.	6–28	Divine *S*· fulfils the law and the
	8–25	coexist in divine *S*·.
	19–28	divine *S*· glorifies the cross
Hea.	13–23	divine *S*·, the truth of being
	14–25	divine *S*· reveals the Principle and
My.	112–10	doctrines taught by divine *S*·
	126–32	that needful one thing — divine *S*·,
	133– 7	God-crowned summit of divine *S*·;
	179–11	all of which divine *S*· shows to be
	207–24	thus predicating man upon divine *S*·.
	208–16	hope and hour of divine *S*·,
	221–14	natural, and divine *S*· of medicine,
	225–12	In divine *S*· all belongs to God,
	244–17	inner sanctuary of divine *S*·,
	265–21	as understood in divine *S*·,
	267– 3	demonstrated to be divine *S*·
	267–24	Heaven is the reign of divine *S*·.
	273–31	divine *S*· of Life alone gives
	278–12	in divine *S*·, where right reigneth.
	281–14	and we are His in divine *S*·.
	283–13	find their birthright in divine *S*·.
	296–13	nor rest from his labors in divine *S*·;
	308– 4	divine healing and its divine *S*·.
	348– 8	understood through divine *S*·.
	348–11	religious departure from divine *S*·
	351–26	divine *S*· is all they need,
	353–11	put on record the divine *S*·
	358– 7	the opposite of divine *S*·,

divine order of

Mis.	18– 9	in the divine order of *S*·,

divine Principle of

Ret.	56– 8	unerring divine Principle of *S*·,

divorced from

My.	349–26	human will divorced from *S*·.

doors of

No.	41–17	to force the doors of *S*·

entrance into

Mis.	100–32	man's . . . entrance into *S*·?

Science

evolve

Mis.	22– 6	that matter . . . can evolve *S*·?

exchanges

Mis.	103–25	*S*· exchanges this human concept

existence in

Pul.	vii–22	man's existence in *S*·.

facts of

Mis.	183–30	refute . . . with the facts of *S*·,
Un.	30– 5	reverse the spiritual facts of *S*·,

fatal in

Rud.	17– 1	divergence is fatal in *S*·.

field of

My.	226–25	laborers in the field of *S*·

fields of

Mis.	xi–14	hitherto unexplored fields of *S*·.

finale in

Un.	2–12	this, as the *finale* in *S*· :

foundation of

Mis.	81– 1	broad and sure foundation of *S*· ;

grand verities of

Mis.	79– 5	grand verities of *S*· will sift

grooves of

Mis.	104–19	move in God's grooves of *S*· :

growth in

Ret.	79–14	uproot the germs of growth in *S*·

handle it in

Mis.	334–18	do you handle it in *S*·.

harmony of

Mis.	176– 2	harmony of *S*· that declares
	259–18	this eternal harmony of *S*·,

has dethroned

Mis.	65– 2	delusive evidence, *S*· has dethroned

has elevated

Ret.	93– 6	and *S*· has elevated this idea

have

'01.	21– 2	they have *S*·, understanding,

healed by

Mis.	54–20	When once you are healed by *S*·,

healed in

Rud.	7– 2	the simplest case, healed in *S*·,

higher order of

Mis.	99–13	voice a higher order of *S*·

hill of

Mis.	232–16	meekly to ascend the hill of *S*·,

ignorance of

Ret.	60–16	sense asks, in its ignorance of *S*·,

immortal

Mis.	73– 8	testimony of immortal *S*·

incentive in

Mis.	279– 5	that is the incentive in *S*·.

in Christianity

My.	127– 1	upward to *S*· in Christianity,

indicates

Mis.	288–17	while *S*· indicates that it *is not*.

in medicine

My.	127– 2	*S*· in medicine, in physics,

is absolute

Mis.	99– 1	*S*· is absolute and final.
	156–17	*S*· is absolute,

is a law

Mis.	269–21	*S*· is a law of divine Mind.

is demonstrated

Mis.	359–24	*S*· is demonstrated by degrees,

is divine

(*see* **divine**)

is eternally one

Ret.	94–23	*S*· is eternally one, and unchanging,

is Mind

Rud.	4– 8	*S*· is Mind manifested.

is not pantheism

Pan.	13– 2	*S*· is not pantheism, but *C*· *S*·

is pointing

No.	28–11	If *S*· is pointing the way,

is reached

My.	238–18	whereby the *S*· is reached

is Science

'01.	22– 1	Truth is true, and *S*· is Science,

is the law

Mis.	173– 9	*S*· is the law of Mind
My.	267– 5	*S*· is the law of the Mind
	347–24	concede that *S*· is the law of God ;

is the mandate

Mis.	283–28	*S*· is the mandate of Truth

is the prism

Ret.	35–13	*S*· is the prism of Truth,

is true

Mis.	65– 7	this is because *S*· is true,

is understood

Mis.	367–10	proportion that *S*· is understood

is unimpeachable

My.	103– 2	Because *S*· is unimpeachable,

its

Mis.	35–25	taught its *S*· by the author of
	372–29	the *art* . . . is akin to its *S*· :
Ret.	54–13	not having reached its *S*·.

Science

lack
No.   3– 1   in some vital points lack S·.
lacked
My. 307–32   for then it lacked S·.
lack of
Mis. 344–17   spoiled by lack of S·.
law of
Mis. 71–31   immutable and just law of S·,
laws of
No.   6–27   the laws of S· are mental,
lens of
Mis. 164–27   by means of the lens of S·,
    194–16   The lens of S· magnifies
'01.   12–22   The lens of S· magnifies
life-giving
Mis. 233–10   onward march of life-giving S·,
lifts humanity
Mis. 290– 5   S· lifts humanity higher in the
light of
Mis. 254–19   would obscure the light of S·,
light of the
My. 343–17   It was in 1866 that the light of the S·
lose
My. 206– 4   and lose S·, — lose the Principle
loss of
Rud. 16–17   an irreparable loss of S·.
mandate of
Mis. 74– 9   through the stern mandate of S·,
man in
Mis. 41–26   manifestation of man in S·.
Un. 40– 5   but man in S· never dies.
    42–13   Man, in S·, is as perfect
'02.   8–26   Jesus reckoned man in S·,
mastered by
Mis. 284–28   and will be mastered by S·.
mental
Mis. 172–25   Mental S·, and the five personal
    173– 2   theorems, misstate mental S·,
Peo. 10–15   Mental S· alone grasps the
metaphysical
Mis. 172– 5   the negative of metaphysical S· ;
Ret. 78–14   right sense of metaphysical S·.
Hea. 16– 4   Metaphysical S· teaches us
met with
Mis. 284–27   met with S·, it can . . . be mastered
must be understood
No. 11–14   S· must be understood
name of
Mis. 171–29   false knowledge in the name of S·,
    233– 1   practising in the *name* of S·
natural
My. 178–11   is this natural S· less profitable
no
'01.   4–15   else there is no S· and no
no opposite in
No.   5– 7   God has no opposite in S·.
nor theism
Mis. 217–25   This is neither S· nor theism.
of all healing
My. 154– 2   S· of all healing is based on Mind
of being
Mis. 46–28   S· of being, wherein man is perfect
    60–22   conformed to the S· of being.
    82–23   S· of being is brought to light.
    183– 2   quenched in the divine S· of being ;
    184–23   S· of being gives back the
    286–29   Until this absolute S· of being
Man. 47–10   Ontology, or the S· of being.
Ret. 21–15   dream has no place in the S· of being.
    26–21   discovery of the S· of being
Un. 42–12   opposite . . . is the genuine S· of being.
    43–22   his teachings, in the S· of being.
    49–19   or we lose the S· of being.
    63– 7   forever in the S· of being.
No. 10–23   reality of Mind in the S· of being ;
    17–10   created in the eternal S· of being
    26–14   In this S· of being,
    28– 9   facts in the S· of being
Pan. 11–13   S· of being, understood and obeyed,
My. 268–26   lifts the curtain on the S· of being,
    285–10   demonstrates the S· of being.
    296– 4   whatever hinders the S· of being.
    (*see also* **Science of Being**)
of Christ
My. 103– 9   S· of Christ, the Science of God
of Christian healing
Ret. 62– 1   S· of Christian healing will again be
My. 43–21   * S· of Christian healing was revealed to
of Christianity
Mis. 164– 5   S· of Christianity, that has appeared
    382–13   I discovered the S· of Christianity,
Pan. 12–21   S· of Christianity is strictly monotheism,
'01. 15–11   demonstrates the S· of Christianity.
    22–18   as to the S· of Christianity.
    24–26   demonstrate the divine S· of Christianity
    32–26   reception of the S· of Christianity.

Science

of Christianity
Hea.   7–13   S· of Christianity makes pure the
My. 117– 1   not have lost the S· of Christianity.
    149–24   lose the S· of Christianity,
    178– 6   S· of Christianity is not generally
    265–14   It signifies that the S· of Christianity
of creation
Mis. 57–22   S· of creation is the universe with
    57–27   In its genesis, the S· of creation is
of divine Love
'00.   5–17   being the divine S· of divine Love,
offer
Mis. 366– 7   because they contain and offer S·,
of God
Mis. 96–22   understanding of the S· of God,
    166–23   S· of God and the spiritual idea,
Un.   4–11   through the S· of God,
    52– 4   This S· of God and man
'00.   5–24   S· of God and His universe,
    6–25   C. S. is the S· of God
'01.   4–13   S· of God must be, is, *divine*,
My. 103– 9   S· of God and man,
    118–22   impossible in the S· of God
of good
Mis. 27– 2   S· of good calls evil *nothing*.
    352– 6   to discern the S· of good.
No. 24– 2   In the S· of good,
of healing
Mis. 34–30   discovered the S· of healing
    260–28   Mind, imbued with this S· of healing,
Rud. 9–17   S· of healing is the Truth of
    15– 4   understanding . . . the S· of healing
'01.   2– 5   in the perfected S· of healing
of Life
Mis. 56–22   S· of Life needs only to be
    84–21   S· of Life, overshadowing Paul's
    344–20   demonstrate the S· of Life,
    380–14   to discover the S· of Life,
My. 51– 3   * in teaching us the S· of Life.''
    273–31   S· of Life alone gives the true sense of
    274–14   one achieves the S· of Life,
of man
Mis. 14–11   the S· of man could never
    186–18   let us not lose this S· of man,
'02.   2– 7   S· of man and the universe,
My. 350–10   the cosmos and S· of man.
of mental healing
Mis. 171–26   of the S· of mental healing ;
    172–23   is the S· of mental healing.
    174–14   is the S· of mental healing.
    175–18   S· of mental healing must be
    175–25   with the S· of mental healing
of metaphysical healing
Mis.   4– 2   in the S· of metaphysical healing,
    380–25   the S· of metaphysical healing
Hea. 16–12   the S· of metaphysical healing.
of Mind
Mis. 60–16   The S· of Mind reveals the
    72–23   The S· of Mind, . . . shows that
    78–11   either Euclid or the S· of Mind
Ret. 24–24   to find the S· of Mind
    28–24   S· of Mind must reveal.
    34– 3   in order to gain the S· of Mind,
    54–22   healing, in the S· of Mind,
    75–18   The S· of Mind excludes opposites,
My. 221–11   and illustrate the S· of Mind.
of Mind-healing
Mis. 66–26   reach the S· of Mind-healing,
    78– 9   S· of Mind-healing can no more be
    87–23   rules of the S· of Mind-healing.
    221–21   understanding of the S· of Mind-healing.
    269–15   the actual S· of Mind-healing
Ret. 27– 7   the absolute S· of Mind-healing,
    34– 8   the spiritual S· of Mind-healing.
    36– 6   I taught the S· of Mind-healing,
    37– 4   spiritual, S· of Mind-healing,
    37–14   originators of the S· of Mind-healing
    43– 8   *alias* the S· of Mind-healing.
    49–21   teaching the S· of Mind-healing ;
    57– 5   basis for the S· of Mind-healing,
    78–17   statement of the S· of Mind-healing,
    78–21   departure from the S· of Mind-healing.
Pul. 47–14   * statement of the S· of Mind-healing.
    64–19   * statement of the S· of Mind-healing.
    70–24   * spiritual S· of Mind-healing,
Rud. v– 7   OF THE S· OF MIND-HEALING
    6–22   S· of Mind-healing is best understood
    11–15   S· of Mind-healing by no means
    16–16   school of the S· of Mind-healing.
No.   4– 2   learning . . . the S· of Mind-healing
    4–12   S· of Mind-healing destroys the
    4–16   in the S· of Mind-healing,
    6– 2   contradict the S· of Mind-healing
    6–12   the true S· of Mind-healing.
    7– 1   chapter sub-title
    14– 3   understood the S· of Mind-healing,

Science

this
My. 240–11   "This *S·* is a law of divine Mind,
   348–27   human demonstrator of this *S·*
   357–24   basis upon which this *S·* can be
to learn
Mis. 14–12   for in order to learn *S·*, we
touches
Mis. 289–26   *S·* touches the conjugal question
transparency of
Mis. 183–14   Through the transparency of *S·*
treasure-troves of
Mis. 22–32   in the treasure-troves of *S·*.
true
Un. 29–19   between the true *S·* of Soul and
Rud. 4–10   All true *S·* represents a moral
No. 6–12   practise the true *S·* of Mind-healing.
   6–22   true *S·* of the stellar universe.
My. 28–31   * has revealed the one true *S·*
true in
Un. 13– 4   whereas the reverse is true in *S·*.
truth of
Rud. 16–12   some novices, in the truth of *S·*,
ultimatum of
Un. 43– 9   achievement of this ultimatum of *S·*,
uncovered by
No. 24–18   human reason is uncovered by *S·* ;
understanding
Mis. 92– 2   necessity for understanding *S·*,
Ret. 83–29   thoroughly understanding *S·*,
understanding of
Un. 4–26   from such an understanding of *S·*,
understanding of the
Mis. 54–24   require an understanding of the *S·*
   221–21   saps one's understanding of the *S·*
understood in
Mis. 286–20   recognized and understood in *S·*.
unfolds
Mis. 218– 2   *S·* unfolds the fact that Deity was
uprooted in
Un. 8–17   All forms of error are uprooted in *S·*,
vast
My. 354–22   *S·* vast, to which belongs
verity in
Mis. 338– 1   this grand verity in *S·*,
victory-bringing
Ret. 22–16   Vanquished by victory-bringing *S·* ;
voiced
Mis. 336– 2   Hath not *S·* voiced this lesson to you,
voices
Mis. 100–14   *S·* voices unselfish love,
Way in
Chr. 53–11   The Way in *S·* He appoints,
what manner of
No. 35– 3   What manner of *S·* were C. S. without
whole of
Rud. 2–22   * *Is healing the sick the whole of S·?*
will restore
Pan. 6– 1   *S·* will restore and establish,
wisdom nor
Mis. 359–17   but it is neither wisdom nor *S·*
working in
Mis. 87–18   *that no one there was working in S·,*
works on
Ret. 76– 5   voluminous works on *S·*
yielded to
Ret. 57–14   would have yielded to *S·*.
yields to
Mis. 37–23   appetite for alcohol yields to *S·*
your
Mis. 37–16   *Can your S· cure intemperance?*
   38–25   *Is it necessary to study your S·*
   54–17   *Must I study your S· in order to*

Mis. 4– 7   the *S·* of the Mind that is God,
   10–32   that aught good exists in *S·*.
   22– 3   *S·* is neither a law of matter nor
   23– 2   but *S·*, demanding more,
   25–12   *S·*, understood, translates matter
   27–26   is *S·*, and is susceptible of proof.
   33–16   had no faith whatever in the *S·*,
   38–18   *S·* that has the animus of Truth.
   38–29   Were it so, the *S·* would be of
   45– 2   for that is not *S·* but mesmerism.
   45–19   and when *S·* in a single instance
   46–25   In *S·*, man represents his divine
   47–17   In *S·*, body is the servant of Mind,
   48–12   magnetism is neither of God nor *S·*.
   65–11   *S·* must and will decide.
   71–14   *S·* never averts law, but supports it.
   72– 4   *S·* sets aside man as a creator,
   79–18   cause and effect in *S·* are immutable
   93–20   is neither maintained by *S·* nor
   98– 6   chapter sub-title
   99–31   "This is *S·*."
   101–29   premise and conclusion in *S·*,

Science

Mis. 102–23   *S·* supports harmony,
   102–27   *S·* has inaugurated the
   102–29   *S·* outmasters it, and ends the
   103–12   In *S·*, form and individuality are
   104– 9   In *S·* all being is individual ;
   105–12   *S·* would have no conflict with Life
   105–28   does not exist in *S·*.
   107– 4   Art must not prevail over *S·*.
   118–10   is neither *S·* nor obedience.
   161– 9   in *S·*, man is the son of God.
   163–13   interpretation through *S·*.
   165–11   *S·* which rends the veil of the flesh
   177–17   the truth, the gospel, and the *S·*
   183–27   knowledge of God through *S·*,
   185–10   *S·* that opens the very flood-gates
   187–10   even as in *S·* a chord is manifestly
   193–20   for supplying the word *S·* to
   196–18   man's unity with his Maker, in *S·*,
   198–26   which is corrected alone by *S·*,
   201– 3   The *S·* of Paul's declaration
   221–23   divorces his work from *S·*.
   243–14   If the system is *S·*, it includes
   254–21   This is not *S·*.
   261–31   to be *S·*, it must produce
   263–24   The *S·* is hampered by
   265– 8   Diverse opinions in *S·* are
   269–24   correct Mind-healing . . . is *S·*.
   280–17   then only are we working . . . in *S·*.
   289–18   Oneness in spirit is *S·*,
   336–27   *S·* is the fiat of divine intelligence,
   344–20   the *S·* which Paul understood
   350–23   not in harmony with *S·*
   352–14   In *S·*, sickness is healed
   365– 6   their highest endeavors are to *S·*
   365–28   As a *S·*, it is held back by the
   379–17   and were not *S·*.
Man. 40– 7   In *S·*, divine Love alone governs
Ret. 11–16   *S·* the mighty source,
   26–29   demonstration of being, in *S·*,
   28– 7   *S·* of the perfect Mind
   59– 5   In *S·*, Life is not temporal,
   90 - 2   careful not to thrust aside *S·*,
Un. 39–17   receive the knowledge of God in *S·*
   42–24   *S·*, dispelling a false sense
   62–18   In *S·*, Christ never died.
Pul. 6– 7   unites *S·* to Christianity.
Rud. 3–15   from that divine digest of *S·*
   7– 1   Not that all healing is *S·*,
   7– 9   In *S·*, man is the manifest
   8– 5   in *S·*, Spirit sends forth its own
   11– 7   in *S·* man is His likeness,
   12–28   in *S·*, disease is unreal ;
   13– 4   pantheism and theosophy are not *S·*.
   13–18   not *S·* to treat every organ in the
No. 6–19   *S·* determines the evidence
   9–22   *S·* is not the shibboleth of a sect
   9–25   *S·* is the atmosphere of God ;
   10– 7   "Christian" and "*S·*."
   11–11   As a *S·*, this system is held back by
   13–17   *S·* is not susceptible of being
   17–17   In *S·* there is no fallen state
   18– 6   If *S·* lacked the proof of its
   21– 5   The *S·* that Jesus demonstrated,
   21–27   has little resemblance to *S·*,
   27–14   *S·*, . . . presents the grand and
   30–26   In *S·*, the cure of the sick
   33– 2   The reduction of evil, in *S·*,
   37– 2   in *S·* his divine nature and
   40–19   forfeit their ability to heal in *S·*.
   42–15   While *S·* is engulfing error in
   43–26   *S·* often suffers blame through the
Pan. 2– 5   who know that C. S. *is S·*,
'00. 4–26   is His reflection and *S·*.
   4–27   coexist with God in *S·*,
   6–18   obtains not in the *S·*, but in
   8–25   not *S·* for the wicked to wallow
'01. 10–14   *S·* of divine metaphysics removes the
   22– 4   Is *S·* material? No !
   22– 7   I do not try . . . since *S·* does not
'02. 11–12   is neither Christian nor *S·*.
Hea. 6–11   I saw the impossibility, in *S·*, of
   19–19   *S·* makes a more spiritual demand,
Po. 60–13   *S·* the mighty source,
My. 85–22   * *S·* church has become the great
   92– 6   * *S·* cannot be brushed aside by
   103– 9   C. S. is indeed *S·*,
   103–11   *S·*, until . . . has been persecuted
   103–14   *S·* which Jesus taught and practised.
   112– 2   *S·* has always been first met with
   112– 4   where *S·* gains no hearing.
   119– 3   impossible in *S·* to believe this,
   119– 7   In *S·*, we learn that man is
   124–19   it remains for *S·* to reveal man
   149– 5   We know Principle only through *S·*.
   158–18   proof that C. S. is *S·*

Science

My.	178–10	because $S^.$ is naturally divine,
	205–30	The . . . may fail, but the $S^.$ never.
	229–11	$S^.$ that otherwise might cost them
	238–23	proof that C. S. is $S^.$,
	322–25	* many good points in the $S^.$,
	350–27	$S^.$ ripe in prayer, in word, and
	353–16	$S^.$ that operates unspent.

science

all
Rud. 4– 6 Is God the Principle of all $s^.$,
cruder
Pul. 79–19 * materialism of the cruder $s^.$
false
My. 345–12 false $s^.$ — healing by drugs.
in general
My. 345– 7 * attitude to $s^.$ in general?
lack of
My. 307–30 its lack of $s^.$, and the want of
leaving
My. 350– 2 leaving $s^.$ at the beck of
material
Mis. 344–13 a material $s^.$ of life !
Rud. 4–14 There is no material $s^.$,
men of
My. 95–23 * the men of $s^.$ may think
mental
Mis. 4– 6 calling this method "mental $s^.$."
58–21 Without . . . there is no mental $s^.$,
modern
Pul. 54–19 * in the light of modern $s^.$,
moral
Mis. 35–22 Why do we read moral $s^.$,
Ret. 10– 8 philosophy, logic, and moral $s^.$.
Pul. 46–25 * philosophy, logic, and moral $s^.$,
natural
Mis. 23–31 according to natural $s^.$,
27–13 Mortals accept natural $s^.$,
172–17 which is termed "natural $s^.$,"
Un. 11– 8 so-called natural $s^.$.
Rud. 7–25 no more . . . than natural $s^.$,
My. 181– 4 and so-called natural $s^.$,
not reckoned as
Pan. 3–21 laws are not reckoned as $s^.$.
of guessing
Peo. 6– 5 * "Medicine is the $s^.$ of guessing."
of mind
My. 307– 7 it was the $s^.$ of mind,
of numbers
Mis. 55– 2 condemn . . . the $s^.$ of numbers.
Ret. 59–11 demonstration of the $s^.$ of numbers ;
of the mind
Mis. 68–23 * metaphysics . . . $s^.$ of the mind."
of treating disease
Hea. 14– 4 the $s^.$ of treating disease
physical
Un. 9–10 not the path of physical $s^.$,
My. 160–21 Physical $s^.$ has sometimes
religion, or
My. 303–24 philosophy, religion, or $s^.$;
so-called
Mis. 173–14 an opposite so-called $s^.$,
203–15 handles it with so-called $s^.$,
Rud. 7–25 natural $s^.$, so-called, or material
speculative
Mis. 68–30 * speculative $s^.$, which soars
student of
Mis. 52–22 What progress would a student of $s^.$
truth or
My. 107–26 classification as truth or $s^.$
word
My. 307– 4 word $s^.$ was not used at all,
works on
Mis. 64–21 Works on $s^.$ are profitable ;

Mis. 30–23 * "is neither Christian nor $s^.$!"
58–26 and you take away its $s^.$,
64–21 for $s^.$ is not human.
68–22 * $s^.$ of the conceptions and relations
68–25 * a $s^.$ of which the object is to
68–28 * $s^.$ which regards the ultimate
78–10 than can $s^.$ in any other direction.
219– 1 $s^.$ of the final cause of things ;
'02. 7–12 to the words *potence, presence, $s^.$*,
Peo. 13–16 and giving the lie to $s^.$.
My. 307– 7 I declared . . . there was a $s^.$,
345– 9 "Not," . . . "if it is really $s^.$."
345–19 could I believe in a $s^.$ of drugs?"

Science and Health

page 35, lines 20-25
My. 17–23 " 35, " 20–25
p. 47, revised edition of 1890
Mis. 379–32 $S^.$ and $H^.$, p. 47, revised edition of 1890,
p. 63
Ret. 69– 4 quotation from

Science and Health

page 68
My. 305– 7 In $S^.$ and $H^.$, page 68,
pp. 103, 104
Ret. 68–27 quotation from
p. 135
My. 61–27 * ($S^.$ and $H^.$, p. 135.)
page 136, lines 1-5, 9-14
My. 17–20 " 136, " 1–5, 9–14
page 137, lines 16-5
My. 17–21 " 137, "16–5
page 140
Man. 61– 2 (See $S^.$ AND $H^.$, page 140.)
pp. 152, 153
Mis. 379–33 pp. 152, 153 in late editions.
page 181
Mis. 83– 5 In your book, $S^.$ and $H^.$, page 181,
page 182
Mis. 83– 7 On page 182 you say :
p. 205
Ret. 69–24 quotation from
p. 227
My. 207–24 (See $S^.$ and $H^.$, p. 227.)
page 229
Mis. 309–25 on page 229, third and fourth paragraphs,
page 241, lines 13-30
My. 17–19 Page 241, lines 13–30
page 252
My. 232–21 read on page 252, "A knowledge
p. 296
My. 217–27 (p. 296).
pp. 306, 307
Ret. 69–15 quotation from
pp. 307, 308
Ret. 69–30 quotation from
page 330
Man. 86–20 beginning on page 330
page 442, line 30
My. 237–13 $S^.$ and $H^.$, page 442, line 30,
line 30 of page 442
My. 236–25 beginning at line 30 of page 442
page 468
My. 19– 7 * from $S^.$ and $H^.$ (p. 468),
33– 4 * ($S^.$ and $H^.$, p. 468),
111–26 ($S^.$ and $H^.$, p. 468)
(p. 494)
My. 28– 3 * has said in $S^.$ and $H^.$ (p. 494),
73– 8 * quotation from $S^.$ and $H^.$ (p. 494),
p. 495
My. 60–14 * ($S^.$ and $H^.$, p. 495.)
pp. 512, 513
Ret. 70– 7 quotation from
p. 551
Ret. 68–22 quotation from
pages 568-571
Pul. 12– 2 pages 568–571, were read
page 583, lines 12-19
My. 17–22 "583, "12–19
Vol. I. page 14
Mis. 35–29 Vol. I. page 14 :
(*see also* **Lesson-Sermon on Dedication Sunday,** and **Selections read on June 12, 1906**)

Mis. xi– 1 The first edition of $S^.$ and $H^.$
21–24 1908 edition of $S^.$ and $H^.$
29–19 publication of my work, "$S^.$ and $H^.$
34–29 The author of "$S^.$ and $H^.$
35–15 Will the book $S^.$ and $H^.$, . . . heal the sick,
35–24 You are benefited by reading $S^.$ and $H^.$,
35–28 In reply, we refer you to "$S^.$ and $H^.$
42–10 $S^.$ and $H^.$ clearly states
50– 5 "$S^.$ and $H^.$ with Key to the Scriptures"
50– 9 "$S^.$ and $H^.$ with Key to the Scriptures,"
54–14 "$S^.$ and $H^.$ with Key to the Scriptures,"
64–14 except the Bible, and "$S^.$ and $H^.$
87–25 "$S^.$ and $H^.$ with Key to the Scriptures."
91–22 "$S^.$ and $H^.$ with Key to the Scriptures,"
92–17 contained in that chapter of "$S^.$ and $H^.$
106–18 its correlative in "$S^.$ and $H^.$
115– 2 With $S^.$ and $H^.$ for their textbook,
136–20 my last revised edition of $S^.$ and $H^.$
153–24 copy of my first edition of "$S^.$ and $H^.$
159– 2 God has given to this age "$S^.$ and $H^.$
214–19 search the Scriptures and "$S^.$ and $H^.$
248–13 views of Mrs. Eddy's book, '$S^.$ and $H^.$
274– 4 I desire to revise my book "$S^.$ and $H^.$
284–11 make the Bible and $S^.$ and $H^.$ a study,
285–14 about the year 1875 that $S^.$ and $H^.$
285–17 $S^.$ and $H^.$, the book that cast the first
300–26 from my work $S^.$ and $H^.$,
302– 3 through the instructions of "$S^.$ and $H^.$
302–29 divine teachings contained in "$S^.$ and $H^.$
309–24 "$S^.$ and $H^.$ with Key to the Scriptures,"
309–29 adhere to the Bible and $S^.$ and $H^.$,
313–26 ordain the Bible, and "$S^.$ and $H^.$
314–15 shall read from my book, "$S^.$ and $H^.$
314–19 read all the selections from $S^.$ and $H^.$

scientific

Pul.	2–27	How can we do this Christianly *s·*
	4–10	a *s·*, positive sense of unity
	10–22	are as devout as they, and more *s·*,
	34–23	*s·* accord with the divine law."
	45–19	* a *s·* demonstration.
	55–19	* held to be *s·* certainty,
	69–22	* certain Christian and *s·* laws,
	79–27	* the thought of the world's *s·*
Rud.	7– 3	demonstrably *s·*, in a small degree,
	9–21	power of a *s·*, right thought,
	13–21	that harmony is the real . . . is scientific ;
	16– 9	*s·* relation to Mind-healing,
	16–14	*more than one school of s· healing?*
No.	2– 8	*s·* to rob disease of all reality ;
	4–19	Sin and disease are not *s·*,
	10–12	one Principle for all *s·* truth.
	13– 5	*s·* deduction from the Principle
	39–21	new and *s·* discoveries of God,
Pan.	8–13	chapter sub-title
	9–15	attainment of *s·* Christianity
'01.	4–11	lose its susceptibility of *s·* proof.
	14–28	*s·* apprehension of this grand verity.
	27–27	* "Every great *s·* truth
	33–14	a diploma for *s·* guessing.
'02.	7–20	no other *s·* proposition
	8–21	*S·* Christianity works out the rule
Peo.	7–27	*S·* discovery and the inspiration
	11–27	*S·* guessing conspires unwittingly
My.	59–12	* by nearly every . . . *s·* body in the
	109– 7	When this *s·* classification is
	116– 6	religious or scientific prosperity,
	127–12	*s·* system of metaphysical
	153–15	*s·*, healing faith is a saving faith ;
	165–20	rise . . . to the *s·* response :
	178–11	is this natural Science less . . . *s·*
	181– 9	demonstrates the *s·*, sinless life
	190–10	*s·* metaphysical practice of
	218– 8	*s·* proof of "God with us." — *Matt. 1 : 23.*
	230– 5	*S·* pathology illustrates the
	234–22	great Master's sayings are . . . *s·*.
	237–23	is practical and *s·*,
	246–14	*s·* unity which must exist
	248–30	the *s·* expression of Truth.
	265–16	*s·* religion and *s·* therapeutics
	267– 4	Nothing . . . which is not divinely *s·*,
	272– 8	predicate and ultimate of *s·* being
	273–21	*s·* knowledge that is portentous ;
	279– 8	*s·* being reappearing in all ages,
	293–26	result would have been *s·*,
	304–25	* "Every great *s·* truth goes through
	349– 3	A *s·* state of health is a

(*see also* **basis, sense, statement**)

scientifically

Mis.	44–29	you *s·* prove the fact that Mind is
	46– 6	truism needs only to be tested *s·*
	270–12	in demonstrating Life *s·*,
	310– 7	impersonalize *s·* the material sense
Ret.	34–10	I claim for healing *s·* the following
No.	5–28	prevents one from healing *s·*,
My.	105– 5	This Æsculapius, . . . demonstrated *s·*,
	135–29	spiritually and *s·* understand
	235–13	and teach truth *s·*.
	242– 2	*s·* correct in your statement
	245– 5	cautiously, systematically, *s·*.
	342–24	the perfecting of man stated *s·*."
	342–27	"It will evolve *s·*.
	344– 7	so the mystery is *s·* explained.

Scientific Theism

Mis.	216– 7	chapter sub-title
	216– 9	some extracts from, "*S· T·*,"

Scientist (*see also* **Scientist's**)

acts of the

Mis.	204–30	aims, ambition, and acts of the *S·*.

Christian

Mis.	xi–15	the Christian *S·* will find herein
	39–22	Christian *S·* who has more to meet
	39–25	*In what way is a Christian S· an*
	39–28	a Christian *S·*, assumes no more when
	63–13	why does a Christian *S·* go to the
	85– 4	*Is a Christian S· ever sick,*
	85– 6	The Christian *S·* learns spiritually
	85–20	The new-born Christian *S·* must mature,
	86– 5	Until this be attained, the Christian *S·*
	100–26	The Christian *S·* loves man more
	107–31	is or can be a Christian *S·*.
	108–19	What would be thought of a Christian *S·*
	134– 9	chapter sub-title
	137– 1	chapter sub-title
	151–12	pray thee as a Christian *S·*, delay not
	157–12	Every true Christian *S·* will feel
	206–19	The real Christian *S·* is constantly
	212–26	He who *is* a Christian *S·*,
	214–26	The Christian *S·* cannot
	220–22	to the conscientious Christian *S·*

Scientist

Christian

Mis.	223–17	saying, "I am a Christian *S·*,"
	225– 5	a friend of mine, and a Christian *S·*.
	225–16	a proof of what the Christian *S·* had
	261–27	impossible to be a Christian *S·* without
	266–14	clear-headed and honest Christian *S·*
	268–14	Christian *S·* keeps straight to the
	291–22	unswerving course of a Christian *S·*,
	294– 6	A real Christian *S·* is a marvel,
	295–32	Now, I am a Christian *S·*,
	296–30	bar-maid and Christian *S·*
	317–18	progress of every Christian *S·*.
	336– 6	but you cannot, as a Christian *S·*,
	358– 8	gain is loss to the Christian *S·*.
	369– 1	and the true Christian *S·*
	375– 6	truest art . . . is to be a Christian *S·* ;
Man.	40– 8	a Christian *S·* reflects the sweet
	41– 5	is abnormal in a Christian *S·*,
	46–26	A Christian *S·* is a humanitarian ;
	47– 9	the privilege of a Christian *S·*
	49–20	If a Christian *S·* is to be married,
	50–16	the life of a Christian *S·*,
	55–20	consistent, consecrated Christian *S·*.
	60– 7	A Christian *S·* is not fatigued by
	64– 2	and a devout Christian *S·*.
	70– 4	Christian *S·* in the employ of
	72– 6	loyal exemplary Christian *S·*
	86–11	elect an experienced Christian *S·*,
	97– 6	consist of one loyal Christian *S·*
Ret.	26–20	a Christian *S·*, who needed no
	42– 5	to announce himself a Christian *S·*,
	70–11	in our time no Christian *S·* will
	80–15	If the Christian *S·* recognize the
	83– 4	wise Christian *S·* will commend
	85–19	The loyal Christian *S·* is
Pul.	35–30	* "Christian *S·*" on the sign at his
Rud.	8–19	man who calls himself a Christian *S·*,
	11–26	healer who is indeed a Christian *S·*,
	12–28	Christian *S·* knows that, in Science,
	16– 4	a Christian *S·* will never undertake to
'01.	15– 7	Christian *S·* has enlisted to lessen sin,
	20– 8	The Christian *S·* is alone with his
	20–10	cannot be, a Christian *S·* ;
	22– 4	is to some extent a Christian *S·*.
	27–17	years ago without a Christian *S·*
'02.	14– 6	a motto for every Christian *S·*,
	19– 8	Christian *S·* cherishes no resentment ;
Peo.	6–20	God is . . . to the Christian *S·*,
	14–11	O Christian *S·*, thou of the church
My.	3–22	A Christian *S·* verifies his calling.
	4–14	Christian *S·* loves Protestant and
	5–17	constitute a Christian *S·*,
	52–21	* who was not a Christian *S·*,
	73– 7	* If you ask a Christian *S·* how they
	97–11	* and is not a Christian *S·*,
	104–13	who shall call a Christian *S·* a
	106–22	In what sense is the Christian *S·* a
	106–28	is the Christian *S·* a charlatan?
	108–25	the best work of a Christian *S·*.
	111–12	genuine Christian *S·* will tell you
	114– 7	Has one Christian *S·* yet reached
	117–12	make one a Christian *S·*.
	122–25	the real Christian *S·* can say
	122–28	of the real Christian *S·*
	123–25	Christian *S·* is not frightened at
	130–25	to the loyal Christian *S·*
	132– 8	Christian *S·* knows that spiritual
	138–17	cannot be a Christian *S·* except
	139–10	Christian *S·* thrives in adversity ;
	142–10	*Beloved Christian S· :*— Accept my
	146–26	Christian *S·* never mentally or
	146–29	The Christian *S·* voices the harmonious
	178–22	A Christian *S·* entered the house
	222–19	Be patient, O Christian *S·* !
	229– 3	No mesmerist nor disloyal Christian *S·*
	229–27	laws of limitation for a Christian *S·*.
	235–24	Are you a Christian *S·*?
	241–12	* from a Christian *S·* in the West,
	254– 3	have begun to be a Christian *S·*.
	294–18	the Christian *S·* with his conscious
	295–27	Christian *S·*, the servant of God
	296–10	late lamented Christian *S·* brother
	297–17	Christian *S·* who believes that he dies,
	314–26	A Christian *S·* has told me that
	320–16	* did not claim to be a Christian *S·*,
	322–27	* told me he was not a Christian *S·*,
	330–10	* A local Christian *S·* of your city,
	330–12	* a Christian *S·* of Charleston, S. C.,
	332–21	* A Christian *S·* in Charleston
	353– 1	My desire is that every Christian *S·*,

devout

My.	5–20	enables the devout *S·* to worship,

divine

Ret.	26–17	a natural and divine *S·*.

Scientists
Christian

My. 21–14	* Christian S· have learned from
22– 9	* Christian S· have contributed
27–21	* Christian S· will read with much joy
36–26	* the Christian S· of the world,
45– 8	* important gatherings of Christian S·
46–15	* the work of true Christian S·.
47– 4	* thousands of Christian S· have
55–17	* inspiration to Christian S·,
57–31	* Christian S· have a faith
58– 2	* these impractical Christian S·."
64– 9	* being known as Christian S·,
72–12	* new church for Christian S·.
72–14	* chapter sub-title
72–20	* thirty thousand or more Christian S·
72–28	* the way the Christian S· began
73–13	* Christian S· are flocking
73–29	* the crowds of Christian S· from
74–11	* The Christian S· are here in force,
75– 8	* headquarters of the Christian S·
75–25	* the custom of the Christian S·.
76–16	* loyalty which Christian S· manifest
77– 9	* From all over the world Christian S·
77–23	* Christian S· from all quarters of
79–28	* scores of Christian S· told of cures
82– 7	* looked as though all the Christian S·
82–20	* characteristic of Christian S·,
83– 2	* custom Christian S· have of never
83– 9	* Christian S· frequently wear
83–21	* The meeting of the Christian S·
84–12	* Boston is the Mecca for Christian S·
84–26	* gathering of Christian S· for the
86– 9	* Thousands of Christian S· have
86–19	* the devotion that the Christian S·
86–22	* the edifice of the Christian S·
88– 3	* Twenty thousand Christian S·
89–23	* Mother Church of the Christian S·
91– 7	* Christian S· set a good example
92– 9	* convention of Christian S·
92–29	* Christian S·, . . . are happy,
94–22	* Christian S· from every State
95–16	* forty thousand Christian S·
96– 1	* Christian S· from all parts of
96–11	* Christian S· are thoroughly in
97–25	* Christian S· who descended upon
98–29	* church of the Christian S·
99–11	* Christian S· are a remarkably
106– 2	I admonish Christian S· either to
108–21	the garment of Christian S·,
112–20	Christian S·, because of their
114– 9	point . . . to the lives of Christian S·
116– 2	Christian S· endeavor to rise in
117–25	May all Christian S· ponder this fact,
128–19	Christian S· abide by the laws of God
135–12	As Christian S· you understand the
140–12	* letter addressed to Christian S·
140–18	*Beloved Christian S· :—* Take courage.
141–19	* vast multitudes of Christian S·
146–23	Christian S· hold as a vital point
147–24	since Christian S· never
153– 2	Christian S· in Concord
158–19	proof . . . rests on Christian S·.
162–11	Christian S· all over the field,
169–16	Christian S· of New York City
173– 3	* visit of the Christian S· in 1904 :
173–14	gifts had come from Christian S·
174– 3	convenience of the Christian S·
179–17	Christians and Christian S· know that
184– 9	Christian S· of my native State
197–14	ready hands of . . . the Christian S·.
204–15	PURPOSE OF THE CHRISTIAN S· TO
208–12	*Beloved Christian S· :—* Like the
210– 2	Christian S·, keep your minds so
214–17	Christian S· taking pay for
216– 2	Till Christian S· give all their time
224– 1	Do all Christian S· see or
225–23	Christian S· are expected to
226–29	that Christian S· decline to
227–14	Christian S· should be influenced by
229– 2	I call none but genuine Christian S·,
229– 9	true that loyal Christian S·,
229–14	Christian S· go to help their helper,
233–29	Do Christian S· love God as
236– 5	*Beloved Christian S· :—* Because I
236–13	joy of knowing that Christian S· will
236–24	request the Christian S· universally
237–13	*Christian S· :—* See S. and H., page 442,
237–24	its careful study to all Christian S·.
241–16	Christian S· are fortunate to receive
243–20	*Beloved Christian S· :—* Your prompt
245–16	let Christian S· be charitable.
245–28	that follow the names of Christian S·.
250– 7	Christian S· will be the first to
251–11	are loyal Christian S·,
256– 7	This year, my beloved Christian S·,

Scientists
Christian

My. 257–28	Christian S· have their record in the
273– 5	* Christian S·, enthusiastic in their belief,
274–20	Will the dear Christian S· accept my
294– 2	Christian S· are yet in
295–17	Christian S· are fishers of men.
299– 6	* "If they [Christian S·] have any
299–20	Christian S· firmly subscribe to this
300–10	Christian S·, who do not believe in
300–16	Christian S· raise the dying
303– 7	Christian S· have no quarrel with
303– 8	Christian S· need to be understood as
316–24	the rights of Christian S·
326– 4	* the liberties of Christian S·
327–13	* Christian S· in North Carolina.
327–23	* "discourteous to the Christian S·."
333–17	* nor by any Christian S·
336–20	* of . . . interest to Christian S·
338–23	But all Christian S· deeply
345– 3	So long as Christian S· obey the
346–30	makes it plain to all Christian S·
351–25	Christian S· are not concerned with
352–27	*Beloved Christian S· :—* Accept my
354– 7	Christian S· are under no
355–21	Christian S· at Mrs. Eddy's
355–26	happy group of Christian S·;

devout
My. 38–24	* Devout S· said after the service

feeling of
Pul. 72– 3	* the feeling of S· in this city

fifteen thousand
My. 80–21	* Fifteen thousand S· crowded into

local
My. 30– 7	* nearly all the local S·,

loyal
Mis. 347–31	Loyal S· are targets for envy,

other
Man. 98– 4	has not been replied to by other S·,
My. 327–18	* other S· who stayed on the field

Toronto
Pul. 75–17	* TORONTO S· PRESENT

true
Mis. 135– 1	Christians, and all *true* S·,

will silence
Mis. 114–24	S· will silence evil suggestions,

Mis. 89– 4	*If S· are called upon to care for*
89–10	advisable in most cases that S·
233– 6	who call themselves . . . S·,
267– 2	wail of evil never harms S·,
309–28	S· sometimes take things too intensely.
348– 1	But the S· aim highest.
358–27	S· who have grown to self-sacrifice
No. 7–21	I recommend that S· draw no lines
'02. 8– 8	are neither Christians nor S·.
My. 30– 6	* S· from all over the world,
30–24	* S· gave a sum surpassing some of
31–18	* by the S· in Boston
31–31	* great body of S· joined
76–24	* chapter sub-title
81– 3	* S· fairly radiate good nature
81–13	* up leaped half a dozen S·.
81–27	* at the meetings of the S·,
82–27	* S· came to Boston in such numbers
83–17	* scarcely realize that the S·
97–12	* S· have a little the advantage
111–17	Can S· adhere to it,

Scientists'
Christian

Mis. 311– 7	invitation to Christian S· students,
Man. 89–19	Christian S· pupils who so desire
'01. 11–12	chapter sub-title
18–27	the Christian S· healer ;
My. 162–20	the Christian S· church edifice
173–23	to make the Christian S·

scintillations
Un. 17–12	consolation from borrowed s·.
Pul. vii– 1	s· from press and pulpit

scoff
Mis. 69– 3	sneer at metaphysics is a s· at Deity ;
201– 2	receives the mortal s·
My. 204–22	was then the s· of the age.

scoffed
Mis. 1– 6	the s· of all scoffers,
No. 27–13	this prophecy will be s· at ;
My. 109–24	metaphysics is not to be s· at ;

scoffers
Mis. 1– 6	meek Nazarene, the scoffed of all s·,

scoffs
My. 98–11	* must have done with s· and jeers

scope
Mis. 100–16 the s· of the senses is inadequate to
253– 2 Note the s· of that saying,
355–16 gives s· to higher demonstration.
'02. 10–15 gain the s· of Jacob's vision,
My. 117–26 free s· only in the right direction !
259–25 give the activity of man infinite s· ;

scopes
Mis. 372–30 S. and H. gives s· and shades to

score
Mis. 295– 8 * past a s· of reforms, to C. S."
Ret. 2–10 more than a s· of years prior to
My. 98– 5 * growth of less than a s· of years.
228– 2 there is nothing new on this s·.

scores
My. 79–27 * s· of . . . Scientists told of cures

scorn
Mis. 258– 6 righteous s· and power of Spirit.
297–12 his lofty s· of the sects,
Ret. 80–17 he will not s· the timely reproof,
Pul. 81–15 * nobility of all those who s· self
Po. 71– 3 Laughed right to s·,
My. 48–22 * The s· of the gross and sensual,

scorned
Mis. 374– 4 Pharisees s· the spirit of Christ
No. 2– 5 s· by people of common sense.
My. 324– 4 * and he s· the suggestion
331–13 * Southern chivalry would have s·

scorner
My. 107–21 O petty s· of the infinite,

Scotch
Ret. 1–19 S· and English elements thus mingling
3– 1 Sir John Macneill, a S· knight,
Pul. 32–24 * S· and English ancestry,

Scotch Covenanters
Ret. 2– 2 reared among the S· C·,

Scotchman's
Mis. 295–13 S· national pride and affection,

Scotland
Ret. 1– 2 were from both S· and England,
Pul. 46–15 * both in S· and England.
(see also **Edinburgh**)

Scots
Ret. 2–15 "S· wha hae wi' Wallace bled."

Scott, Sir Walter
Ret. 2– 6 set forth in the pages of Sir Walter S·

Scottish
Pul. 46–22 * Wallace of mighty S· fame.

scourge
Un. 23– 4 * Make instruments to s· us.

scourged
'01. 28–16 have been s· in the synagogues
Hea. 2– 7 s· and condemned at every

scourgeth
Mis. 18– 4 and s· every son — Heb. 12 : 6.
Ret. 80– 6 And s· every son — Heb. 12 : 6.

scourging
My. 148–28 s· the sect in advance of it.

Scranton
Mis. 150– 9 chapter sub-title
Pul. 56– 4 * S·, Peoria, Atlanta, Toronto,

scream
Mis. 396– 5 cricket's sharp, discordant s·
Po. 58–17 cricket's sharp, discordant s·

screaming
Mis. 266–29 s·, to make itself heard

screen
My. 68–23 * It has an architectural stone s·

scribblings
My. 306–23 his s· were descriptions of
307– 4 in his s·, the word science

scribe
(see **Eddy**)

scribes
Mis. 175–15 leaven of the s· and Pharisees,
189–28 and not as the s·." — Matt. 7 : 29.
366–19 the s· and Pharisees," — see Matt. 16 : 6.
Ret. 58–11 and not as the s·." — Matt. 7 : 29.
Un. 42–20 and not as the s·." — Matt. 7 : 29.

scrip
My. 215–24 take no s· for their journey,
215–26 he bade them take s·.

script
Pul. 78– 7 * inscription, cut in s· letters :

Scriptural
Mis. 50– 1 that God made all . . . is again S· ;
72–31 The S· passage quoted
129–11 then take the next S· step :
194–19 the foregoing S· text
253–16 S· metaphors, — of the woman
278–13 S· declaration that Job sinned **not**
283–20 S· rule of this Science
364–17 stands on this S· platform :
Man. 51– 2 the S· demand in Matthew
Chr. 55– 1 These S· texts are the basis
Ret. 1– 9 containing S· sonnets,
9– 9 S· narrative of little Samuel,
42–10 he lectured so ably on S· topics
70– 8 authenticity of the S· narrative
Pul. 47– 2 * lectures upon S· topics.
Pan. 6–19 enter into the S· allegory,
12–11 S· commands be fulfilled.
'02. 7–17 we have S· authority for
7–23 another S· passage which
My. 5– 2 according to the S· allegory,
114–19 in the line of S· interpretation
240–18 on a S· basis,
282– 6 and the S· injunction,

Scripturally
Mis. 59–12 Not if we pray S·,

Scripture
above
Mis. 139–16 with a portion of the above S·
192–23 above S· plainly
according to
Un. 36–11 solved by C. S. according to S·.
according to the
Mis. 191–11 According to the S·, if devil is
Man. 48–20 According to the S· they shall
My. 300– 4 overcome sin according to the S·,
another
Mis. 248– 6 as, in another S·,
answered by the
Hea. 19–14 is answered by the S·,
believe the
My. 221–31 Shall we not believe the S·,
called in
'01. 3–19 called in S·, Spirit, Love.
9– 1 called in S· the Son of God
composed of
Mis. 106–18 Lesson, composed of S· and
correlative
My. 33– 5 * and the correlative S·,
countermand the
Mis. 124– 3 and countermand the S·
declaration in
Mis. 172–30 oft-repeated declaration in S·
declares
Mis. 26–11 even while the S· declares He made
Pan. 5–25 and, as the S· declares,
'02. 1–12 S· declares, "The wrath of — Psal. 76 : 10.
My. 107–24 If, as S· declares, God made all
178–12 The S· declares that God is All.
224–25 since the S· declares,
declares the
Un. 31– 2 declares the S· (John iv. 24),
describes
Mis. 259–20 same rhythm that the S· describes,
explained in the
Mis. 30–27 is explained in the S·,
following
Mis. 133– 9 consideration to the following S·,
is true
Mis. 193– 4 that the S· is true ;
learned from the
Hea. 12–12 we learned from the S·
mocking the
Un. 33–23 divided in evidence, mocking the S·
nowhere
Un. 47– 3 Nowhere in S· is evil connected with
on this subject
Mis. 130–14 Note the S· on this subject :
passage of
My. 135– 5 this passage of S· and its
170–18 This gift is a passage of S· ;
problems of
'02. 4–26 abstruse problems of S·,
pronounces
My. 178–15 S· pronounces all that God made
reads
'02. 12–19 S· reads : "For in Him — Acts 17 : 28.
My. 4– 7 S· reads : "He that taketh — Matt. 10 : 38.
118–16 S· reads : "Blessed are they — John 20 : 29.
267– 6 S· reads : "All things were — John 1 : 3.
remember the
Mis. 335– 2 Remember the S· :
335–28 remember the S· concerning those who

Scripture

saith
Mis. 73– 4 *S·* saith, "Whom the Lord — *Heb.* 12 : 6.
76–27 *S·* saith, "When Christ, — *Col.* 3 : 4.
82–29 in whom the *S·* saith
89– 1 *S·* saith, "No man can — *Matt.* 6 : 24.
213– 9 *S·* saith, "He that — *Prov.* 28 : 13.
326– 1 *S·* saith the law of the Spirit
'01. 11–26 *S·* saith "Answer not a — *Prov.* 26 : 4.
saith the
Mis. 219– 8 Now, what saith the *S·*?
says
Mis. 36–24 *S·* says, "The carnal mind — *Rom.* 8 : 7.
Hea. 15–23 *S·* says, "Ye ask, and — *Jas.* 4 : 3.
spoken of in
My. 104–29 anathema spoken of in *S·* :
supported by the
Ret. 64–14 this view is supported by the *S·*,
supported in the
Mis. 66–12 is supported in the *S·*
texts of
My. 317–21 corroborative texts of *S·*.
this
Mis. 72–20 *this S·,* " *Your heavenly* — *Matt.* 6 : 32.
112–30 is characterized in this *S·* :
146–18 and the letter of this *S·* :
'01. 18–24 should read this *S·* :
translations of
My. 179–24 renderings or translations of *S·*
truth of the
No. 17–20 and the truth of the *S·*,
understanding of
'02. 7– 7 spiritual understanding of *S·*,
understand the
My. 135–28 you understand the *S·*,
word of
Un. 23–10 agrees with the word of *S·*,
words of the
My. 156– 4 to reply in words of the *S·* :
196– 7 in these words of the *S·*,

Mis. 103–31 *S·*, "I am a God at hand, — *see Jer.* 23 : 23.
170–12 hades, or hell of *S·*,
190–15 When the *S·* is understood,
191– 8 The *S·* in John, sixth chapter
263– 5 These two words in *S·* suggest
287– 4 Hence the *S·* : "It is He — *Psal.* 100 : 3.
Man. 42–18 whereof *S·* beareth testimony.
Ret. 91–10 or by the *S·* authors.
Pul. 13– 6 The *S·*, "Thou hast been — *Matt.* 25 : 23.
60–11 * with illustrative *S·* parallels,
'01. 12–11 the *S·*, "When the Son of — *Luke* 18 : 8.
My. 16–23 * *S·* reading, Isaiah 28 : 16, 17,
69–10 * marble plates with *S·* quotations
272– 5 the *S·*, "The law of — *Rom.* 8 : 2.
275– 7 hence the *S·*, "Be still, — *Psal.* 46 : 10.
364– 1 the *S·*, "Judge no man." — *John* 8 : 15.

scripture
My. 17–14 contained in the *s·*, — *I Pet.* 2 : 6.

Scripture-meanings
Mis. 169–11 With the understanding of *S·*,

Scriptures

accept the
Mis. 191–32 reject fables, and accept the *S·*
according to the
Mis. 71–23 According to the *S·*,
Man. 51–16 requirements according to the *S·*,
Rud. 4–20 According to the *S·* and C. S.,
'01. 5–20 We believe, according to the *S·*,
My. 130–17 I ask that according to the *S·*
apprehension of the
Mis. 363–32 spiritual apprehension of the *S·*,
are criticized
My. 179–15 the *S·* are criticized.
are the guide
Pul. 30–16 * *S·* are the guide to eternal Life ;
aver
Mis. 49–30 God is Truth, the *S·* aver ;
comments on the
Ret. 27– 1 wrote . . . comments on the *S·*,
declare
Mis. 46– 2 *S·* declare, "To whom ye — *Rom.* 6 : 16.
55–26 God is Spirit, as the *S·* declare,
63–20 as the *S·* declare.
183–32 *S·* declare reflects his Maker,
189–20 The *S·* declare Life to be
346–17 and the *S·* declare that
362–12 but the *S·* declare that
Un. 2– 1 The *S·* declare that God is
56– 3 suffered, as the *S·* declare,
Pul. 13–23 Here the *S·* declare that
'01. 7–11 made them . . . as the *S·* declare ;
7–17 even as the *S·* declare

Scriptures

declare
Hea. 3–24 The *S·* declare that
My. 155– 9 whom the *S·* declare.
271– 1 If, as the *S·* declare,
demand
'01. 10–28 This is what the *S·* demand
drawn from the
Mis. 93–11 conclusion drawn from the *S·*,
enjoin
Mis. 310–15 not unmindful that the *S·* enjoin,
Peo. 6–24 when the *S·* enjoin us to
explaining the
My. 59–15 * your words explaining the *S·*,
expositor of the
Pan. 12– 4 scholarly expositor of the *S·*,
found in the
Mis. 32–11 are to be found in the *S·*,
195–16 are not to be found in the *S·*.
fulfil the
Mis. 183–15 man can fulfil the *S·*
gave no
Ret. 37–16 *S·* gave no direct interpretation of
give the keynote
Mis. 366– 9 *S·* give the keynote of C. S.
glory of the
Mis. 92–29 power and glory of the *S·*,
Ret. 84–17 power and glory of the *S·*,
have declared
Hea. 8–19 God is what the *S·* have declared,
Hebrew
Un. 28– 1 We read in the Hebrew *S·*,
Holy
Mis. 132–24 refer you to the Holy *S·*,
imply
Mis. 45–25 what the *S·* imply Him to be,
49–28 as the *S·* imply Him to be,
Rud. 5– 4 If, as the *S·* imply,
inform us
Mis. 97–21 *S·* inform us that man
No. 28–25 The *S·* inform us that
inspired
Mis. 193– 1 Are the *S·* inspired?
interpolation of the
'01. 12–18 not an interpolation of the *S·*,
interpret the
Pul. 69–18 * we interpret the *S·* wholly from
My. 112– 9 denominations interpret the *S·*
Key to the
Mis. 29–19 "S. and H. with Key to the *S·*"
34–30 "S. and H. with Key to the *S·*,"
35–29 "S. and H. with Key to the *S·*,"
50– 5 "*S. and H. with Key to the S·*"
50– 9 "S. and H. with Key to the *S·*"
54–14 "S. and H. with Key to the *S·*,"
64–15 "S. and H. with Key to the *S·*,"
87–25 "S. and H. with Key to the *S·*,"
91–22 "*S. and H. with Key to the S·*,"
92–18 "S. and H. with Key to the *S·*,"
106–19 "S. and H. with Key to the *S·*,"
114–13 "S. and H. with Key to the *S·*,"
144–11 "S. and H. with Key to the *S·*,"
153–25 "S. and H. with Key to the *S·*,"
159– 3 "S. and H. with Key to the *S·*,"
214–20 "S. and H. with Key to the *S·*,"
248–14 'S. and H. with Key to the *S·*,'
274– 5 "S. and H. with Key to the *S·*,"
302– 4 "S. and H. with Key to the *S·*,"
302–30 "S. and H. with Key to the *S·*"
309–25 "S. and H. with Key to the *S·*,"
313–27 "S. and H. with Key to the *S·*,"
314–16 "S. and H. with Key to the *S·*,"
314–23 "S. and H. with Key to the *S·*"
315–31 "S. and H. with Key to the *S·*,"
318–17 "S. and H. with Key to the *S·*,"
322–12 "S. and H. with Key to the *S·*,"
364– 2 "S. and H. with Key to the *S·*,"
366– 2 "S. and H. with Key to the *S·*"
371–29 "S. and H. with Key to the *S·*,"
383– 1 "S. and H. with Key to the *S·*,"
Man. 29–23 S. AND H. WITH KEY TO THE *S·*.
31–23 S. AND H. WITH KEY TO THE *S·*.
32– 4 S. AND H. WITH KEY TO THE *S·* ;
32–12 S. AND H. WITH KEY TO THE *S·*,
34–11 S. AND H. WITH KEY TO THE *S·*,
36– 1 S. AND H. WITH KEY TO THE *S·*,
38– 4 S. AND H. WITH KEY TO THE *S·*,
42–14 S. AND H. WITH KEY TO THE *S·*,
56– 1 S. AND H. WITH KEY TO THE *S·*,
58– 6 S. AND H. WITH KEY TO THE *S·*,
64– 6 *S. and H. with Key to the S·*,
71–26 S. AND H. WITH KEY TO THE *S·*,
83–23 S. AND H. WITH KEY TO THE *S·*
86–19 S. AND H. WITH KEY TO THE *S·*,
Ret. 37–19 Key to the *S·*, in S. and H.,

Scriptures

Key to the

Pul.	5–14	"S. and H. with Key to the *S·*,"
	7–25	"S. and H. with Key to the *S·*,"
	12– 2	"S. and H. with Key to the *S·*,"
	24–18	* "S. and H. with Key to the *S·* ;"
	25–28	* "S. and H. with Key to the *S·*,"
	28–18	* "S. and H. with Key to the *S·*,"
	38–15	"Recapitulation." Key to the *S·*,
	43–18	* "S. and H. with Key to the *S·*,"
	45–26	* "S. and H. with Key to the *S·*,"
	55–23	* "S. and H. with Key to the *S·*,"
	58–26	* "S. and H. with Key to the *S·*,"
	64– 2	* 'S. and H. with Key to the *S·*,'
	70– 8	* "S. and H. with Key to the *S·*,"
	86–25	* "S. and H. with Key to the *S·*."
No.	3– 9	"S. and H. with Key to the *S·*,"
	42–23	"S. and H. with Key to the *S·*"
'00.	7– 1	"S. and H. with Key to the *S·*,"
	7–13	"S. and H. with Key to the *S·*."
'01.	11–14	"S. and H. with Key to the *S·*,"
My.	v–22	* "S. and H. with Key to the *S·* ;"
	17–18	* "S. and H. with Key to the *S·*"
	18–30	* "S. and H. with Key to the *S·*"
	34–16	* "S. and H. with Key to the *S·*"
	43–24	* "S. and H. with Key to the *S·*,"
	48–10	* "S. and H. with Key to the *S·*,"
	80–19	* "S. and H. with Key to the *S·*"
	103– 7	"S. and H. with Key to the *S·*,"
	110–31	"S. and H. with Key to the *S·*"
	112–12	"S. and H. with Key to the *S·*"
	114–25	"S. and H. with Key to the *S·*"
	115– 5	"S. and H. with Key to the *S·*"
	130–27	"S. and H. with Key to the *S·*"
	136– 8	"S. and H. with Key to the *S·*,"
	163–22	"S. and H. with Key to the *S·*"
	178–28	"S. and H. with Key to the *S·*"
	213–29	"S. and H. with Key to the *S·*"
	215– 7	"S. and H. with Key to the *S·*,"
	217–24	"S. and H. with Key to the *S·*" ;
	232–21	"S. and H. with Key to the *S·*,"
	238– 4	*"S. and H. with Key to the S·*"
	239– 3	"S. and H. with Key to the *S·*"
	246–20	"S. and H. with Key to the *S·*,"
	266–24	"S. and H. with Key to the *S·*,"
	271– 5	"S. and H. with Key to the *S·*,"
	304–31	"S. and H. with Key to the *S·*,"
	305–16	"S. and H. with Key to the *S·*"
	317– 7	* "S. and H. with Key to the *S·*."
	318– 8	"S. and H. with Key to the *S·*,"
	318–15	"S. and H. with Key to the *S·*,"
	320–11	* "S. and H. with Key to the *S·*"

learn from the
My. 151–23 We learn from the *S·* that the

love of the
'00. 7– 6 greater love of the *S·* manifested.

maintain
Mis. 27–15 since the *S·* maintain this fact

meaning of the
Mis. 25–14 original meaning of the *S·*,
Man. 87–17 higher meaning of the *S·*.
Un. 29–22 deep meaning of the *S·*
My. 241– 6 * higher meaning of the *S·*.

misinterprets the
My. 304–30 misinterprets the *S·* ;

notes on the
My. 114–15 began with notes on the *S·*.

not knowing the
Mis. 168–22 *not knowing the S·, — Matt.* 22 : 29.
219– 7 not knowing the *S·, — Matt.* 22 : 29.
No. 37– 5 not knowing the *S· — Matt.* 22 : 29.

obey the
Mis. 90–16 in your measures, obey the *S·*,

older
Mis. 187–13 translators of the older *S·*

once refer
'01. 16–19 The *S·* once refer to an evil

plainly declare
Mis. 93– 8 *S·* plainly declare the allness
Pan. 5– 3 The *S·* plainly declare,

practise the
My. 238– 8 to read and to practise the *S·*,

prophetic
'00. 6–29 exegesis on the prophetic *S·*

Reader of the
Mis. 314–21 Reader of the *S·* shall name,

reading the
Mis. 159– 1 reading the *S·* and expounding
Man. 60– 8 reading the *S·* or the C. S. textbook.
72–10 reading the *S·* and the C. S. textbook

read the
Mis. 58–16 I may read the *S·* through a
314–12 shall read the *S·* indicated in

recorded in the
Mis. 199–14 miracles recorded in the *S·*

Scriptures

require
Mis. 196–30 The *S·* require more than a

sacred
Mis. 312–19 * verities of the sacred *S·*."

say
My. 233–16 *S·* say, "They have healed — *Jer.* 6 : 14.
358– 5 *S·* say, "Watch and pray, — *Matt.* 26 : 41.

Science of the
My. 239– 2 Science of the *S·* coexists with God ;
303– 6 Science of the *S·* relative to this

searching the
Pul. 28– 3 * searching the *S·* by the light of

search the
Mis. 214–19 My students need to search the *S·*
Ret. 24–23 to search the *S·*,
Pul. 34–25 * to pray, to search the *S·*.
My. 105– 2 stirred the people to search the *S·*

selections from the
Pul. 43–17 * Selections from the *S·* and from

sense of the
'00. 5–27 The spiritual sense of the *S·*
6–11 spiritual sense of the *S·*

speak
Mis. 180–29 *S·* speak of Jesus as the Son of God

studied the
Pul. 64–15 * studied the *S·* and the sciences,

study the
Man. 83–21 to study the *S·* and S. AND H.

synoptic
My. 179– 2 synoptic *S·*, as set forth in the

taught the
Man. 62–20 children shall be taught the *S·*,

teach
No. 37–21 *S·* teach an infinite God,

translation of the
Rud. 16–11 in their translation of the *S·*

translations of the
My. 238–11 the translations of the *S·*

truth in the
My. 179–20 and the truth in the *S·*,

truth of the
My. 299–12 the entire truth of the *S·*,

understanding of the
My. 28–30 * spiritual understanding of the *S·*,
180– 9 A spiritual understanding of the *S·*

warrant of the
My. 266– 5 under the warrant of the *S·* ;

whole of the
Mis. 317–15 compared with the whole of the *S·*

words of the
My. 206–18 words of the *S·* comfort you :

written in the
No. 42– 2 * all things written in the *S·*,

Mis.	26–28	The *S·* name God as good,
	59–19	The *S·* refer to God as saying,
	70– 1	else the *S·* misstate man's power.
	87–24	study thoroughly the *S·*
	169–14	She affirmed that the *S·*
	169–22	literal rendering of the *S·*
	186–13	in the *S·*, as in divine Science,
	194–12	not an interpolation of the *S·*,
	216– 5	as the *S·* give example.
	281–14	through a stray copy of the *S·*
	300– 4	in connection with the *S·*,
	308– 8	The *S·* and C. S. reveal
	315– 2	taken from the *S·* and S. and H.,
	315–30	study His revealed Word, the *S·*,
Man.	31–21	from the *S·*, and from S. AND H.
	32– 6	readings from the *S·* shall precede the
Ret.	25– 4	the *S·* had to me a new meaning,
	35–12	not interpolations of the *S·*,
No.	23–15	*S·* have both a literal and a moral
'00.	14– 8	of whatever is spoken of in the *S·*.
My.	32–15	* Reading from the *S·* :
	110–28	attempt to convict the *S·* of
	112–11	founded squarely . . . on the *S·*.
	112–24	not in accordance with the *S·*.
	205– 1	We read in the *S·* :
	216– 1	plainly set forth in the *S·*.
	279–10	obvious correspondence with the *S·*

scroll

Pul. 77– 4 *s·* of solid gold, suitably engraved,
77– 6 * Attached to the *s·* is a golden key
78– 4 * in the form of a gold *s·*,
78–21 * Attached . . . to the *s·* is a gold
78–25 * The *s·* is on exhibition in
My. 184–17 That rustic *s·* brought back to me

scrub-oak

Ret. 4–21 *s·*, poplar, and fern flourish.

scrupled

Mis. 139–25 whereof a few persons have since *s·* ;

scruples
  Ret. 48– 6   conscientious *s·* about diplomas,
scrutinize
  Ret. 73–22   to *s·* physical personality,
scrutiny
  No. 41–15   is to subject them to severe *s·*.
sculptor (*see also* **sculptor's**)
  Peo. 7–14   * With heaven's own light the *s·* shone,
  My. 69–14   * hammer and chisel of the *s·*
sculptor-boy
  Peo. 7– 8   * "Chisel in hand stood a *s·*,
sculptor's
  Po. 2– 4   Much as the chisel of the *s·* art
sculptors
  Peo. 7– 2   *s·*, working out our own ideals,
  7–16   * "*S·* of life are we as we stand
sculpture
  Mis. 270– 6   skill of the masters in *s·*, music,
sculptured
  Pul. 39–21   * *s·* angels, on the gray church
  Po. 73–18   No *s·* lie, Or hypocrite sigh,
  My. 259– 2   sweetest *s·* face and form
scum
  My. 301– 7   creed will pass off in *s·*,
sea
  across the
    My. 183–11   *Beloved Brethren across the S·:*
    200–12   stretches across the *s·* and rises
    259–12   To this church across the *s·*
  angry
    Mis. 397– 5   o'er earth's troubled, angry *s·*
    Pul. 18–14   o'er earth's troubled, angry *s·*
    Po. 12–14   o'er earth's troubled, angry *s·*
  billowy
    Po. 24– 9   From out life's billowy *s·*,
  bottomless
    My. 53– 3   * bottomless *s·* of corrections;
  bottom of the
    Peo. 5–28   * sunk to the bottom of the *s·*,
  dangerous
    Mis. 385–11   is past The dangerous *s·*,
    Po. 48– 3   is past The dangerous *s·*,
  depth of the
    Mis. 122–13   in the depth of the *s·*"? — *Matt.* 18 : 6.
  fish of the
    Mis. 69–12   over the fish of the *s·*, — *Gen.* 1 : 26.
    69–32   over "the fish of the *s·*" — *Gen.* 1 : 26.
  fled to the
    Po. 41–10   waters had fled to the *s·*,
  islands of the
    My. 279–26   and those islands of the *s·*
    286– 6   and the islands of the *s·* have one
  land and
    My. 291–24   prosperity waves over land and *s·*,
  land or
    My. 127–27   indestructible on land or *s·* ;
  like the
    Mis. 384–19   * Love, like the *s·*,
    Po. 36–18   * Love, like the *s·*,
  moonlit
    Po. 73– 3   O'er the moonlit *s·*,
  no more
    No. 27– 9   there will be no more *s·*.
    My. 183–13   With you be there no more *s·*,
  of heads
    My. 59–14   * gazing across that *s·* of heads,
  of repentance
    '00. 15– 9   a tear-filled *s·* of repentance
  of sin
    Mis. 264– 5   of this seething *s·* of sin.
  over
    My. 204– 8   Over *s·* and over land,
  race for the
    Mis. 329–22   streams to race for the *s·*.
  rock and the
    Po. 68– 9   rock and the *s·* and the tall waving
  rough
    Pul. 6–26   and rode the rough *s·*.
  sapphire
    Pul. 40– 4   * Beyond the sapphire *s·*
  surging
    Pul. 13–17   They are in the surging *s·* of error,
  troubled
    '00. 7–22   the wave of earth's troubled *s·*,
    '02. 19–19   heaving surf of life's troubled *s·*
  unfathomable
    Ret. 57– 3   unfathomable *s·* of possibilities.
  upon the
    My. 126– 8   "right foot upon the *s·*, — *Rev.* 10 : 2.

  Ret. 20–17   as sunshine o'er the *s·*,
  Pul. 12–13   earth and of the *s·* ! — *Rev.* 12 : 12.

sea
  Pan. 3–25   * of which heaven, earth, *s·*,
  My. 205–11   * He plants His footsteps in the *s·*
  350–13   the struggler with the *s·*
  356– 7   * "He plants His footsteps in the *s·*
sea-beaten
  My. 295–18   The Bible is our *s·* rock.
seal
  Mis. 184–24   as the *s·* of man's adoption.
  269–29   opening of this silent mental *s·*,
  381–21   under the *s·* of the said Court,
  Pul. 28– 5   * panel containing the C. S. *s·*,
  My. 22–18   * time has put its *s·* of affirmation
  191–13   will *s·* your apostleship.
  214–11   set the *s·* of eternity on time.
  333– 1   * with the *s·* of the Grand Secretary,
sealed
  Mis. 35– 6   *s·* that proof with the signet of
  Pul. 52–24   * The Bible was a *s·* book.
sealing
  My. 211–26   and *s·* his doom,
seals
  Mis. 280– 4   at the opening of the *s·*,
  358– 6   the only appropriate *s·* for C. S.
  '02. 16–18   enigmatical *s·* of the angel,
  My. 131–13   *s·* the covenant of everlasting love.
  236–17   *s·* the question of unity,
seamen
  Pan. 15– 2   murdering her peaceful *s·*
sea-mew's
  Po. 73–13   The *s·* lone cry,
seamless
  Pul. 54– 2   * healing of his *s·* dress
  '01. 26–16   pinned to the *s·* robe,
  My. 192– 7   ideal robe of Christ is *s·*.
seances
  Mis. 171– 9   sit in back-to-back *s·*
sear
  My. 3–10   *s·* leaves of faith without works,
search
  Mis. 214–19   need to *s·* the Scriptures
  327–12   *s·* for wealth and fame.
  364–13   is not a *s·* after wisdom,
  Ret. 14–25   "*S·* me, O God, — *Psal.* 139 : 23.
  24–23   to *s·* the Scriptures, to find
  Pul. 34–25   * to pray, to *s·* the Scriptures.
  46– 3   * in *s·* of the truth as taught.
  51–25   * will go there in *s·* of truth,
  64–16   * a *s·* for the great curative
  No. 21– 7   was not a *s·* after wisdom ;
  My. 33– 9   "*S·* me, O God, — *Psal.* 139 : 23.
  105– 2   the people to *s·* the Scriptures
  332–29   * on repeated *s·* a roll of papers
searched
  Mis. 292–27   *s·* the secret chambers of sense?
searching
  Mis. 204– 4   Truth, *s·* the heart,
  Pul. 28– 3   * *s·* the Scriptures by the light of
  51– 9   * *s·* after religious truth.
  73–20   * a careful and *s·* study
  My. 122–18   Are we still *s·* diligently
searchings
  My. 332–24   * After frequent *s·* and much
searing
  My. 350–17   bitter *s·* to the core of love ;
seas
  My. 33–30   founded it upon the *s·* — *Psal.* 24 : 2.
  194–29   * stood the storm when *s·* were rough,
  232– 3   sailing over rough *s·*
seaside
  Ret. 91–28   hillside priest, this *s·* teacher,
season (*see also* **season's**)
  Mis. 48–20   in *s·* to open the eyes of
  117–25   and, sometimes out of *s·*,
  160– 4   than ours at this *s·*.
  264–19   directed, it acts for a *s·*.
  308–23   only to reappear in due *s·*.
  319–20   let the present *s·* pass
  Man. 60–14   nor gifts at the Easter *s·*
  '00. 5–23   the builders reject for a *s·* ;
  9–11   a more convenient *s·* ;
  '02. 4– 8   pray at this Communion *s·* for more
  Hea. 4–15   become finite for a *s·* ;
  My. 5–24   dedication and communion *s·*,
  20–16   for her rich portion in due *s·*.
  20–17   Send no gifts to her the ensuing *s·*,
  25– 1   * the present Thanksgiving *s·* ;
  27– 8   sacred *s·* of prayer and praise.
  50–24   * a very inspiring *s·* to us all,

season
My. 141– 2   * chapter sub-title
    141–17   * annual communion s· of the
    141–27   no more communion s· in The
    142–11   communion s· of The Mother Church.
    142–14   The Mother Church communion s·
    197–25   At this dedicatory s·
    201– 5   Satan is unchained only for a s·,
    256–20   At this happy s· the veil of time
    312–17   * For a brief s· she taught school.''

season's
My. 121– 5   commotion of the s· holidays.

seasons
Mis. 384–18   * ''The s· come and go :
Man. 61–10   no more Communion s·.
Pul. 40– 3   * I wonder how the s· come and go
Po. 36–17   * ''The s· come and go :
My. 141–10   * to attend the communion s·
    141–16   · its famous communion s·.
    141–26   continue their communion s·,
    166–18   lie concealed in the smooth s·
    340– 5   usage of special days and s·

seat
Mis. 225–20   Mrs. Rawson then rose from her s·,
    231–32   vacant s· at fireside and board
    275–11   looks . . . at the vacant s·,
Ret. 15–18   not sufficient to s· the audience
Pul. 29–12   * every s· in the hall was filled
    57– 6   * s· . . . fourteen and fifteen hundred,
    58–16   * will s· over a thousand
'00. 13–22   ''where Satan's s· is.'' — Rev. 2 : 13.
'02. 12–26   so as to s· the large number
My. 7–10   so as to s· the large number
    7–17   * will s· four or five thousand
    9– 4   * will s· four or five thousand
    56– 3   * until every s· was filled
    69–19   * view of the platform from any s·.
    71–22   * s· . . . five thousand and twelve
    71–23   * and s· them comfortably.
    71–29   * auditorium that would s· five thousand
    79–11   * s· of learning of America ;
    342– 5   * after a kindly greeting took a s·

seated
Pul. 25–21   * s· with pews of curly birch,
    31–24   * I was hardly more than s· before
Po. v–16   * she s· herself by the roadside
My. 31–15   * thousands had been s·,
    54–30   * s· four hundred and sixty-four.
    59–13   * S· in the gallery of that magnificent
    71–24   * every person s· in the
    78–29   * great room in which they were s·,
    342– 2   * S· in the large parlor.
    342–16   * When we were snugly s·

seating
Pul. 25– 8   * s· eleven hundred people
My. 8–20   * have a s· capacity of more than
    24–29   * s· capacity of five thousand.
    38–10   * when all s· space had been filled
    53–13   * s· capacity of which place
    55–25   * a s· capacity of six hundred
    56– 1   * thought the s· capacity would be
    57– 5   * would be of great s· capacity,
    65– 9   * church edifice capable of s·
    67–10   * S· capacity . . . 5,000
    67–22   * exceeds it in s· capacity,
    68–14   * s· capacity of twelve hundred,
    77– 4   * s· capacity of over five thousand.
    78– 1   * s· capacity of the temple
    78–12   * The s· is accomplished in a
    99–15   * s· five thousand people,
    296–29   standing and s· capacity,

seats
Mis. 168–29   * go away unable to obtain s·.
    270– 3   s· of them that could — Matt. 21 : 12.
Man. 59–16   welcomes her s· in the church,
    59–19   not otherwise provided with s·.
    59–22   give their s·, if necessary,
Pul. 26– 9   * with richly carved s·
    27– 6   * vestry s· eight hundred people,
    59–27   * s· were especially set apart
My. 31–27   * congregation had taken their s·,
    38–10   * no confusion in finding s·,
    38–18   * They filled all the s·
    80–29   * s· in the main body of the church,
    141–23   s· only five thousand people,
    142– 6   * and then find no s· in

Seattle, Wash.
Pul. 90– 3   * Post-Intelligencer, S·, W·.

secluded
Pul. 73– 8   * s· herself from the world

seclusion
Mis. 136–14   necessity for my s·,
Pul. 73–11   * came from her s· one of the

Second
Man. 112– 3   must be written First, S·,

second
Mis. 2–26   s· death hath no power'' — Rev. 20 : 6.
    33–30   S· : It is more effectual than drugs ;
    51–26   * starting fresh, as from a s· birth,
    75–15   S· : Because Soul is a term for
    94– 1   in the s·, you will reign
    108–16   s· stage of human consciousness,
    109–23   through the s· to the third stage,
    142–15   my s·, a psalm ; my third, a letter.
    144– 3   in the s· story of the tower
    158–15   s· command, to drop the use of notes,
    171– 4   rose to the occasion with the s·
    188– 7   that which appears s·, material, and
    204–12   S· : The baptism of the Holy Ghost
    255–25   S· : It is more effectual than drugs,
    279–22   s· picture is of the disciples
    301–26   S· : It breaks the Golden Rule,
    305–33   * S· : Of money with which to pay
    318– 6   students of the s· generation.
    332–23   s·, a false belief ;
    341– 9   up the scale . . . to the s· rule,
    350–14   s· P. M. convened in about one week
    356–22   s· stage of mental development
Man. 43– 2   and a s· offense as aforesaid
    52–18   s· offense shall dismiss a member
    54–23   a s· similar offense shall remove
    61–13   on the s· Sunday in January
Ret. 1–16   This s· Marion McNeil
    6–11   my s· brother, Albert Baker.
    20– 5   before my father's s· marriage,
    20–21   My s· marriage was very unfortunate,
    34–14   S· : It is more effectual than drugs,
    40–22   my notices for a s· lecture
    68– 3   s·, in the name of human concept,
    70–20   The s· appearing of Jesus
    88– 4   S· : Another command of the Christ,
Un. 3– 8   the s· death, of which we read
    20– 8   S· : The Lord knows it.
    20–13   S· : He knows it not.
    30–16   The apostle refers to the s· Adam as
    31–12   the s·, that matter is substance ;
    41–14   the s· death has no power.
Pul. 48– 6   s· story of the house,
    59–28   * at the s· dedicatory service.
    74–14   'Am I the s· Christ?'
No. 19– 8   it is the sober s· thought of
Pan. 6– 3   s·, because evil and disease
'00. 6–29   as the year of the s· coming of
    7–17   hath Christ a s· appearing?
    7–23   we believe in the s· coming,
    12– 6   In Revelation, s· chapter,
'01. 14–25   or it will control you in the s·.
My. 39– 2   * s· session was held at two o'clock
    56–29   * s· and third being repetitions
    126–12   s· is no longer a mystery or a
    147– 1   chapter sub-title
    179– 3   first and s· chapters of Genesis,
    179– 5   the s· was an opposite story,
    223–15   s·, because I do not consider
    246– 1   s· degree (C.S.D.) is given
    303–27   a first or s· Virgin-mother
    304–30   s·, she has stolen the contents
    313–30   after my father's s· marriage
    314– 2   Daniel Patterson, my s· husband,
    323–30   * studying in the s· class
    335–18   * This was the s· case of
    353–12   the s· I entitled Sentinel,

secondary
Mis. 334– 5   but this place is s·.

Second Church
Man. 112– 2   as First Church, S· C·, etc.,

Second Church of Christ, Scientist
Chicago, Ill.
My. 191–26   chapter sub-title
Minneapolis, Minn.
My. 193–13   chapter sub-title
New York
My. 201–25   chapter sub-title
    231–26   S· C· of C·, S·, NEW YORK

Man. 71– 3   S· C· of C·, S·, and so on,
My. 362–28   * signature

seconding
My. 8– 8   * Judge . . . Ewing in s· the motion,

Second Reader
My. 16–18   * Mrs. Ella E. Williams, S· R· ;
    31–24   * S· R· Mrs. Laura Carey Conant,

Second Readers
Man. 32– 4   S· R· shall read the BIBLE texts.
    99–27   appointed by the First and S· R·
My. 249–26   If both the First and S· R·

secret
Mis.	50– 7	*is there a s· back of*
	50–14	no additional s· outside of its
	133–16	thy Father which is in s· ; — *Matt.* 6 : 6.
	133–16	seeth in s· — *Matt.* 6 : 6.
	133–25	"seeth in s·," — *Matt.* 6 : 6.
	144–14	laid away as a sacred s·
	165–29	s· stores of wisdom
	177– 6	leagued together in s· conspiracy
	223– 3	into the s·" — *see Gen.* 49 : 6.
	250–23	unselfish deed done in s· ;
	277–16	falsehoods, and a s· mind-method,
	292–27	searched the s· chambers of sense
	323–14	masters their s· and open attacks
	339– 7	out of defeat comes the s· of
	350– 3	organized a s· society
	365–13	the s· of its success lies in
	389–19	sweet·s· of the narrow way,
Ret.	15–27	who divulged their s· joy
	33–11	I found, . . . one pervading s· ;
	71–27	S· mental efforts to obtain help
	72– 7	portrays the result of s· faults,
Pul.	5– 9	holds in her s· chambers
	9–23	Christians rejoice in s·,
	83– 4	* In our s· heart our better self
No.	3–17	must pore over it in s·,
	18–10	the s· of its presence lies in the
	39–10	glorified God in s· prayer,
'00.	9– 8	s· of C. S. in right thinking
Po.	4–18	sweet s· of the narrow way,
My.	133–22	I have a s· to tell you
	133–24	then my sacred s· is incommunicable,
	134– 3	tell my long kept s·
	188–10	"the s· place of the — *Psal.* 91 : 1.
	211–32	induced by this s· evil influence
	244–15	The "s· place," — *Psal.* 91 : 1.
	261–23	involves an open s·,
	289– 2	God's open s· is seen through grace,

secretaries
My.	223– 8	not read by me or by my s·.
	231–16	to the waste-basket by her s·.

Secretary
My.	63– 8	* WILLIAM B. JOHNSON, S·.

secretary
Mis.	132–17	answers through my s·,
	157– 7	caused fny s· to write,
My.	25–10	* from the report of the s·
	242–21	I have requested my s· not to
	358–21	Mr. Adam Dickey is my s·,

secretions
Mis.	243–29	s· of the gastric juice,

secretly
Mis.	114– 9	that these be not s· robbed,
	267–12	s· striving to injure me.
Ret.	71–18	He who s· manipulates mind

secrets
Mis.	262–29	relieve my heart of its s·,
	343–16	uncovering the s· of sin

sect
Mis.	150–26	appropriated by no s·.
	325– 5	of different s·, and of no sect ;
Un.	11–20	theologian of some bigoted s·,
Pul.	28–16	* from that of any other s·,
	47– 6	* official organ of this s·.
	64–26	* of the Founder of that s·,
	65– 6	* Boston s· of Christian Scientists,
	70–12	* founded a s· that has
No.	9–22	not the shibboleth of a s·
	14–20	more than any other religious s·,
'01.	33–28	one s· to persecute another
My.	84–23	* methods and tenets of the s·.
	89–11	* A s· that leaves such a monument
	92–17	* every other s· in the country
	94– 2	* every other s· will be left behind
	94–10	* consistent growth of the s·
	99– 3	* good things that this s· is doing.
	100– 6	* property of no poverty-stricken s·.
	100–12	* C. S. s· made its appearance
	148–27	opinions of a s· struggling to
	148–28	scourging the s· in advance of it.
	292–14	"Why did Christians of every s·
	303– 8	Catholics, or any other s·.
	316– 3	Truth divides between s· and Science
	328–20	* issued to the healers of this s·
	329– 5	* relieved the healers of this s· from

Section
2		
Mis.	272–12	* Public Statutes, Chapter 115, S· 2,
3		
My.	15– 3	* S· 3 of Article XLI
4		
Mis.	272– 4	* Act of 1874, Chapter 375, S· 4.

section
Ret.	82–12	locate permanently in one s·,
My.	84–15	* in that s· of the Back Bay.
	327–20	* s· of an act in the Legislature
	327–23	* The s· formerly read,
	328–23	* the s· of the machinery act
	328–26	* The s·, after enumerating

Section 1.

Article I.
Man.	25– 4	Names.

Article II.
Man.	29–20	Election.

Article III.
Man.	31– 4	Moral Obligations.

Article IV.
Man.	34– 4	Believe in C. S.

Article V.
Man.	35–10	Students of the College.

Article VI.
Man.	37–16	Pupils of Normal Students.

Article VII.
Man.	38–17	Members who once Withdrew.

Article VIII.
Man.	40– 4	A Rule for Motives and Acts.

Article IX.
Man.	49–19	A Legal Ceremony.

Article X.
Man.	50– 7	No Unauthorized Debating.

Article XI.
Man.	50–13	Departure from Tenets.

Article XII.
Man.	55–10	Probation.
	85– 9	provisions of Article XII, S· 1,

Article XIII.
Man.	56–10	Annual Meetings.

Article XIV.
Man.	58– 4	Ordination.

Article XV.
Man.	58–20	Announcing Author's Name.

Article XVI.
Man.	59–15	The Leader's Welcome.

Article XVII.
Man.	60– 3	Continued Throughout the Year.

Article XVIII.
Man.	61– 8	No more Communion.

Article XIX.
Man.	61–18	Soloist and Organist.

Article XX.
Man.	62– 8	The Sunday School.

Article XXI.
Man.	63–14	Establishment.

Article XXII.
Man.	64–13	The Title of Mother Changed.

Article XXIII.
Man.	70–10	Local Self-government.

Article XXIV.
Man.	75– 3	Church Edifice a Testimonial.

Article XXV.
Man.	79–18	Board of Trustees.

Article XXVI.
Man.	83– 4	Motive in Teaching.

Article XXVII.
Man.	86– 3	Authorized to Teach.

Article XXVIII.
Man.	88– 4	Officers.

Article XXIX.
Man.	89–11	Normal Teachers.

Article XXX.
Man.	90– 8	Sessions.

Article XXXI.
Man.	93– 4	Election.

Article XXXII.
Man.	95– 3	From the Directors.

Article XXXIII.
Man.	97– 3	In The Mother Church.

Article XXXIV.
Man.	102– 3	Building Committee.

Article XXXV.
Man.	72– 3	See Article XXXV, S· 1.
	104– 3	For The Mother Church Only.

Sect. 2.

Article I.
Man.	25– 8	President.

Article II.
Man.	30– 1	Eligibility.

Article III.
Man.	31–15	First Readers' Duties.

Article IV.
Man.	34–17	Free from Other Denominations.

Article V.
Man.	35–17	Other Students.

Article VI.
Man.	36– 2	as provided in Article VI, S· 2,
	37–22	Members of The Mother Church.

Sect. 25.
  Article VIII.
  Man. 47–24 Charity to All.
Sect. 26.
  Article VIII.
  Man. 48– 6 Uncharitable Publications.
Sect. 27.
  Article VIII.
  Man. 48–11 The Golden Rule.
Sect. 28.
  Article VIII.
  Man. 48–16 Numbering the People.
Sect. 29.
  Article VIII.
  Man. 48–22 Our Church Edifices.
Sect. 30.
  Article VIII.
  Man. 49– 1 No Monopoly.
Sect. 31.
  Article VIII.
  Man. 49– 7 C. S. Nurse.

sections
  My. 73–27 * extra s· of trains are due
       74– 1 * western s· of this country.
       74– 4 * s· within two or three days' ride,
       82–26 * trains . . . in double s·.

sects
  Mis. 111–21 Christianity that is merely of s·,
       111–25 Catholic and Protestant s·.
       297–13 his lofty scorn of the s·,
       325– 5 believers of different s·,
  Man. 59–17 of all s· and denominations
  Pul. 21–21 our denomination and other s·,
        57–22 * several s· of mental healers,
  '00.   4– 1 has it not tainted the religious s·?
  '01.   2–17 feverish pride of s· and systems
        22–23 and the different religious s·
        23– 3 little left that the s· and faculties
        31– 3 only opposing element that s· or
  My.   40–15 * divided into warring s·;
       148–27 power over contending s·

secular
  Mis. 38– 8 education, s· and religious,
       272–22 * for any s· purposes;
  My. 135– 9 attended to my s· affairs,
       137–12 to my s· affairs, to my income,
       223–13 questions about s· affairs,

secure
  Ret.   5–28 * untiring in her efforts to s· the
  My.   12– 6 * to s· the large parcel of land
        63– 2 * to s· the services of Mr. Whitcomb
        80–29 * to s· seats in the main body of the
       245– 8 s· a thorough preparation of

secured
  My.   30–25 * collections s· by evangelists
        54–22 * Rooms were again s·.
        77–30 * s· by voluntary subscription.
        82–12 * s· express wagons enough to
       134–26 * "Permission has been s· from

securely
  Mis. 201–25 protect our dwellings more s·

secures
  Mis. 135–11 conquers . . . and s· success.
       252–28 s· the success of honesty.

securing
  Mis. 333–20 s· the sweet harmonies of
  Pul. 64– 5 * s· sufficient funds for the
  My.   75–15 * matter of s· accommodations.

security
  Mis. 227– 7 s· from slanderers

sedentary
  Mis. 329–20 challenging the s· shadows

sedulously
  Mis. 114–21 Scientists cannot watch too s·,

see
  Mis.   8–11 Can you s· an enemy,
        14– 5 where will you s· or feel evil,
        28– 3 Matter can neither s·, hear,
        34–16 s· them as they were before death,
        35–30 * S· the sixth edition.
        58–13 "Having eyes, s· ye not?" — Mark. 8 : 18.
        58–15 As matter, the eye cannot s·;
        67–20 if you s· the danger menacing
        76– 5 shall never s· death." — John 8 : 51.
        81–10 Do we not s· in the commonly accepted
        81–18 or s· many of the people from
        81–20 hear this voice, or s· the dove,
        82–21 which finite mortals s·
        86–28 What mortals hear, s·, feel,

see
  Mis. 94– 5 s· himself and the hallucination of
        99–.4 "Having eyes ye s· not, — see Mark 8 : 18.
       109– 8 s· what, and how much, sin claims
       112–26 inability to s· one's own faults,
       117–15 We s· eye to eye and know as we
       129–20 s· somebody's faults to magnify
       135–28 You may be looking to s· me
       149–12 s· that nothing has been lost.
       156– 9 s· clearly the signs of Truth
       158–11 you s· we both had first to obey,
       168– 3 tell what things ye shall s·
       168–16 "Come and s·." — Rev. 6 : 1.
       170–29 as having any power to s·.
       170–29 Having eyes, ye s· not;
       171–13 and s· what manner they are of.
       186– 5 we s· the material self-constituted
       186–19 we shall s· that man cannot
       194–17 we then s· the supremacy of Spirit
       197–13 let us s· what it is to believe.
       212–26 open his eyes to s· this error?
       218– 8 matter can neither s·, hear,
       233–32 we s· and feel disease only by
       240–25 If they s· their father with a cigarette
       241–27 you s·, it is easier to heal the physical
       244–20 the blind to s·, the deaf to hear,
       249– 3 to s· if C. S. could not obviate its
       277–32 I rebuke it wherever I s· it.
       280– 7 S· thou hurt not the holy things
       299–15 good which the material senses s· not
       299–16 evil which these senses s· not
       309–32 S· the revised edition of 1890,
       318–28 S· edition of 1909.
       321–27 I have no desire to s· or to
       324–18 tired of sin, can s· the Stranger.
       347–19 I s· the way now.
       352– 7 But it must first s· the error
       359–11 we s· through a glass, — I Cor. 13 : 12.
       367–24 He sees light, and cannot s· darkness.
       371– 5 opened his eyes to s· the need
       375–28 * to s· produced to-day that art
       378–20 cannot fail to s· that metaphysical
       379– 4 asked if I could s· his pennings
       379–32 S· S. and H., p. 47,
       385–19 Now s· thy ever-self;
       392–23 Scenes that I would s· again.
       393–10 we s· Soon abandoned
       397– 6 I s· Christ walk,
  Man. 25–17 S· under "Deed of Trust"
        44–20 to s· that these periodicals are ably
        61– 1 (S· S. and H., page 140.)
        64–25 S· also Article XXV, Sect. 7.
        72– 3 S· Article XXXV, Sect. I.
        78–15 (S· Article I, Sect. 6.)
        98–13 s· that it is published according to copy;
       109–15 s· that names are legibly written,
       111–19 (s· Art. V, Sect. 4),
       112– 6 S· Article XXIII, Sect. 2.
  Ret. 14–27 s· if there be any wicked — Psal. 139 : 24.
        21– 9 came to s· me in Massachusetts.
        38–15 started for Lynn to s· me.
        40– 7 I asked permission to s· her.
        50–23 I s· clearly that students in C. S.
        64–16 shall never s· light. — Psal. 49 : 19.
        91–17 we s· Jesus ministering to the
  Un.   8– 6 What you s·, hear, feel, is a
        18– 4 Dwelling in light, I can s· only
        20–16 then s· if this Love does not
        20–21 He can s· nothing outside of
        22–10 to eat or be eaten, to s· or be seen,
        24–24 and is able to s·, taste, hear,
        34– 2 mortal mind says, "I cannot s· ;"
        34– 7 that mortal mind cannot s·
        36–11 Thus we s· that Spirit is Truth
        46– 5 We do not s· much of the real man
        49– 8 I s· it to be sinless,
  Pul. 18–15 I s· Christ walk,
        21– 7 to s· this love demonstrated.
        39–24 * I s· the hurrying throng
        39–25 * 'mid them all I only s· one face,
        44– 3 * At last you begin to s· the fruition
        85– 8 * s· and acknowledge it.
  Rud.   5–19 The body does not s·, hear,
         5–22 we could not s· materially;
        10–14 matter cannot feel, s·, or
        16–11 I s· that some novices,
  No.   7–11 to s· every error they possess,
        12– 5 leading us to s· spirituality
        27– 6 get near enough to God to s· this,
        31–27 shall never s· death;" — John 8 : 51.
  '00.   1– 2 * your glad faces, aglow with
         5–14 I s· no other way under heaven
         9– 9 few, comparatively, s· it;
        15–13 to s· through sin's disguise
        15–14 to s· that sin has no claim,
  '01. 11– 6 s· the Son of man in divine Science;

see

'01.	12–23	we then *s·* the allness of Spirit,
	27– 5	* I look to *s·* some St. Paul arise
'02.	16–13	no man shall *s·* the—*Heb.* 12 : 14.
Hea.	6–20	whatever manifestation we *s·*.
	6–25	producing the effect we *s·*.
	11– 3	gladly waken to *s·* it was unreal.
	16– 8	*S·* to it, O Christian Scientists,
	16–20	They can neither *s·*, hear, feel,
Po.	12–15	I *s·* Christ walk,
	17– 3	rest till I *s·* My loved ones
	26–19	charter I have lived to *s·* Purged
	48–13	Now *s·* thy ever-self ;
	51– 5	Scenes that I would *s·* again.
	51–15	we *s·* Soon abandoned
	70– 8	the glory that eye cannot *s·*.
My.	26–20	trust that you will *s·*,
	33–11	*s·* if there be any wicked — *Psal.* 139 : 24.
	41–16	* So we *s·* that C. S.
	45–23	* as in retrospect we *s·* the
	71–25	* *s·* and hear the two Readers
	71–30	* each of whom could *s·* the Readers,
	79– 7	* those who seem to *s·* no good in
	93–20	* *s·* only its ridiculous phases,
	117– 3	went ye out for to *s·*?" — *Matt.* 11 : 8.
	117–16	But when may we *s·* you,
	118–12	you would not *s·* me,
	119–28	you would not *s·* me thus,
	122–31	refused to *s·* the power of Truth
	123–19	Ere long I will *s·* you in this hall,
	129– 1	*s·* if there be found anywhere a
	132–20	see God and live, *s·* good in good,
	138–15	persons whom I desire to *s·*
	146– 2	(*s·* page 177),
	149–26	could not *s·* London for its houses.
	150–16	*S·* therein the mirrored sky
	161–11	ye shall *s·* Abraham, — *Luke* 13 : 28.
	170– 4	that they might *s·* the Leader of C. S.
	180–19	refuses to *s·* this grand verity
	183–20	blind *s·* out of obscurity.
	189–18	to *s·* how soon earth's fables flee
	206–13	or believing that you *s·* an individual
	207–24	(*S·* S. and H., p. 227.)
	213–20	*s·* whether they lead you to God
	216–27	and *s·* the need of self-culture,
	216–30	I *s·* that you should begin now
	224– 1	*s·* or understand the importance of
	237–13	*S·* S. and H., page 442, line 30,
	239–14	*and s· their apparent identity*
	243–16	will *s·* that it is wise to remain
	256–22	and *s·* whence they came
	259– 1	will *s·* the sweetest sculptured face
	268–28	and you *s·* the heart of humanity
	268–29	you *s·* male and female one
	268–30	you *s·* the designation *man*
	268–31	you *s·* the whole universe included
	277– 6	I will say I can *s·* no other way
	297–22	we should *s·* him here
	300–19	shall never *s·* death." — *John* 8 : 51.
	307–13	* "I *s·* now what you mean,
	307–14	* and I *s·* that I am John,
	309–32	Let us *s·* what were the fruits
	310–28	* "When do you ever *s·* Mary angry?"
	324–27	* he wanted to *s·* if there was one
	345– 1	*s·* that your mind is in such a state
	355– 2	to *s·* in her spiritualized thought
		(*see also* **God**)

seed

Mis.	26– 9	ponders the history of a *s·*,
	26–13	Whence came the first *s·*,
	83– 9	*springing from a s· of thought,*
	111–15	Leaving the *s·* of Truth
	121–12	believed to be the *s·* of the Church.
	144–26	As in the history of a *s·*,
	281–31	*s·* of the righteous shall — *Prov.* 11 : 21.
	338–29	* Shall be a fruitful *s·* ;
	356–16	*s·* of C. S., which when sown
Ret.	43– 4	From this *s·* grew the
Un.	6– 2	*s·* within itself," — *see Gen.* 1 : 11.
'01.	33– 6	hand of love must sow the *s·*.
Po.	31– 3	celestial *s·* dropped from Love's
	79– 8	God able is To raise up *s·*
My.	177–18	* the *s·* of the Church ;"
	182–13	small sowing of the *s·* of Truth,
	222–11	a grain of mustard *s·*, — *Matt.* 17 : 20.
	273– 8	nor his *s·* begging bread." — *Psal.* 37 : 25.

seedling

Mis.	26–10	that his crops come from the *s·*
	343–24	until no *s·* be left to propagate
'00.	4– 1	This *s·* misnomer couples love and

seeds

Mis.	356–17	"the least of all *s·*," — *Matt.* 13 : 32.
	357–13	*s·* of Truth fall by the wayside,
Rud.	9– 4	*s·* of discord and disease.
My.	182–14	seemed the least among *s·*,

seedtime

Mis.	332– 8	Its *s·* has come to enrich earth
	356–12	remember that the *s·* is passed,

seeing

Mis.	107–25	lack of *s·* one's deformed mentality,
	109–17	*s·* the need of somethingness
	225–13	* *s·*, I may be led to believe."
	319– 8	not *s·* their own belief in sin,
	319– 8	*s·* too keenly their neighbor's.
	326–21	*S·* the wisdom of withdrawing
	336–15	*s·* clearly how to cast the mote of
Ret.	26–15	*s·* therein the operation of the
Un.	20– 2	by *s·* it in its proper light,
Pul.	79–14	* *s·* notices of C. S. meetings,
Rud.	5–21	this belief of *s·* with the eye,
Pan.	11– 3	*s·* that ye have put off — *Col.* 3 : 9.
'00.	9–10	or, *s·* it, shut their eyes
My.	105–24	*s·* her immediately restored by me
	119–26	*s·* your personal self,
	119–27	give you the opportunity of *s·*
	120–10	bliss of *s·* the risen Christ,
	123–27	*S·* that we have to attain to the
	169– 5	as simply *s·* Mother.
	171–10	I think you would enjoy *s·* it.
	206–12	*S·* a man in the moon,
	206–12	or *s·* a person in the picture of
	206–15	not *s·* the spiritual idea of God ;
	206–15	it is *s·* a human belief,
	322–28	* *S·* my great interest in the subject,

seek

Mis.	13–28	*S·* the Anglo-Saxon term for God,
	52– 1	refer to such as *s·* the material
	63–15	Jesus came to *s·* and to save
	124– 5	*s·* and cannot find God in matter,
	129–15	*s·* occasion to balloon an atom
	133–22	to *s·* the divine blessing
	138–11	Each student should *s·*
	178–11	*s·* those things which are — *Col.* 3 : 1.
	194– 5	Let us, then, *s·* this Science ;
	200–23	compels me to *s·* the remedy
	206–26	all who diligently *s·* God.
	215–10	not *s·* to climb up some other way,
	236–23	*s·* in divine Love the remedy
	270–11	To *s·* or employ other means
	270–14	"*S·* ye first the kingdom — *Matt.* 6 : 33.
	326–18	forced to *s·* the Father's house,
	342–24	*S·* Truth, and pursue it.
	344–19	would *s·* a correct conclusion.
	348– 7	It is not *mine* but *Thine* they *s·*.
	357– 5	Let them *s·* the lost sheep
	387–18	*S·* holy thoughts and heavenly
	393–20	Points the plane of power to *s·*.
	400–21	Thee I *s·*, Patient, meek,
Man.	94–11	he who goes to *s·* truth
Chr.	55–10	*s·* ye first the kingdom — *Matt* 6 : 33.
Ret.	31–12	*s·* diligently for the knowledge
	85–16	*S·* to occupy no position whereto
	90– 3	or *s·* to stand in God's stead.
Un.	5–10	to *s·* the divine Science of this
	62–23	*s·* ye the living among — *Luke* 24 : 5.
Pul.	67–14	* which *s·* to give expression
	81–16	* all those who *s·* the brightness
No.	3–22	*s·* not so much thine own as
	40– 4	mortals *s·*, and expect to receive,
'00.	14–11	*s·* thou the divine import of
'01.	1–22	you *s·* to define God to your
	30–12	to retaliate or to *s·* redress ;
'02.	11– 2	who *s·* for a better country
	17– 6	*s·* and obey what they love.
Po.	6–13	*S·* holy thoughts and heavenly
	8– 4	*s·* the loving rose,
	33– 6	*s·* for deliverance strong
	52– 4	Points the plane of power to *s·*.
	69– 9	Thee I *s·*, Patient, meek,
My.	34– 8	of them that *s·* him, — *Psal.* 24 : 6.
	34– 9	*s·* thy face, O Jacob. — *Psal.* 24 : 6.
	55–22	* obliged to *s·* other quarters,
	98–11	* critics who *s·* the light
	117–29	to *s·* the one divine Person,
	118–13	hence I *s·* to be
	149–12	*S·* ye these til you make
	163– 2	to *s·* the haven of hope,
	188–28	man will naturally *s·* the Science
	209– 4	those that *s·* and serve Him.
	261– 5	who *s·* wisdom of God,
	276–19	* no one should *s·* to dictate
	313–24	nor did . . . *s·* my advice.
	338–17	they *s·* a higher source
	341–15	* "'Tis peace not power I *s·*,
	345–27	They *s·* the finer essences.

seeker

Mis.	89–22	for I am a *s·* after Truth.
Ret.	52– 8	a home for every true *s·*
Pul.	6–23	*s·*, and servant of Truth,

seeker

'01.	19– 6	prayer brings the s· into
My.	4–22	s· and finder of C. S.
	178– 2	do not mislead the s· after Truth.

seekers

Mis.	32–20	unfortunate s· after Truth
	114– 2	value to all s· after Truth.
	156– 3	number of earnest readers, and s·
	317–17	by the most faithful s· ;
Man.	17– 2	earnest s· after Truth
Pul.	14–14	simple s· for Truth,
My.	40– 7	* s· everywhere may be satisfied.

seekest

My.	150– 4	if thou s· this guidance.

seeketh

Mis.	184–27	that s· not her own,
	358–11	s· aught besides God,
'00.	14–19	that s· not only her own,
'01.	34–18	which s· not her own
My.	19–22	"s· not her own" — I Cor. 13 : 5.
	150– 3	that which s· to save,

seeking

Mis.	171–16	s· out of the basis upon which
	228–12	s· to raise those barren natures
	245–26	s· to stereotype infinite Truth,
	246–32	s· after practical truth
	260–21	s· to dethrone Deity.
	276–26	s· light from matter instead of
	322–26	zealous affection for s· good,
	324–27	s· peace but finding none.
	335–31	s· power or good aside from God,
	340– 8	s· no other pursuit
	341–10	S· is not sufficient
	353–32	world worship, pleasure s·,
	389–20	S· and finding,
Ret.	2– 8	s· "freedom to worship
	13–20	s· His guidance.
	52– 3	s· to broaden its channels
Pul.	21– 8	s· and praying for it
	38–28	* spirituality s· expression.
Po.	4–19	S· and finding,
My.	vi– 3	* are earnestly s· Truth ;
	130– 9	s· only public notoriety,
	174–29	Thus s· and finding

Seeking and Finding

Mis.	373– 4	picture "S· and F·."

seeks

Mis.	53–17	s· what is below instead of
	55–10	s· the proportions of good.
	147–25	He s· no mask to cover him,
	302– 5	s· again to "cast lots — Matt. 27 : 35.
	324–21	s· to leave the odious company
	325–13	patiently s· another dwelling,
	326– 5	s· the dwelling-place of mortals
	369–15	s· a wisdom that is higher
Man.	47– 2	s· to overcome evil with good.
Un.	15–24	who s· to do them mischief,
	17– 2	s· to fasten all error upon
	17–10	or s· so to do,
	45–23	not the goal which Truth s·.
'01.	19– 7	thus he finds what he s·,
My.	153–23	s· personality for support,
	349–32	s· cause in effect,

seem

Mis.	2–14	and the laborers s· few.
	5–22	s· a miracle and a mystery
	5–29	can s· solid substance to
	9–16	friends s· to sweeten life's cup
	32– 7	s· not to know in what manner they
	61–30	Mortals s· very material ;
	112–12	s· to belong to the latter days,
	121– 8	good and evil, s· to grapple,
	136–12	verities of being s· to you as to me,
	222–27	good should s· more natural than
	234– 8	attempt to s· . . . a Christian.
	273– 6	where I now s· to be most needed,
	278–20	s· stronger to resist temptation
	318–27	making sin s· either too large or
	337–21	and thus s· to extinguish it.
	396– 7	More sorrowful it scarce could s· ;
Man.	80–15	such reasons as . . . s· expedient.
Ret.	69–12	matter shall s· to have life
	80– 4	yet it may s· severe.
Un.	17– 3	and so make the lie s· part of
	45– 1	this lie shall s· truth]."
Rud.	11–11	s· to be disease, vice, and
No.	20– 9	it may s· distant or cold, until
	20–18	Love must s· ever absent to
'00.	4–16	It should s· rational
'01.	31– 9	that now s· troublesome.
Hea.	11–11	though it may s· to the age like the
Po.	58–19	More sorrowful it scarce could s· ;
My.	15–28	* S· hungering and thirsting

seem

My.	47–24	* s· but a short time.
	79– 7	* who s· to see no good in C. S.,
	82–18	* It would s· that this ability
	93– 7	* if their opinions s· visionary,
	130–32	should s· reasonable.
	159– 4	s· to me, and must s· to thee,
	208– 4	s· as if the whole import of C. S.
	262–24	s· a human mockery in mimicry
	290– 4	and the tried and true s· few.
	290–17	earthly joys s· most afar.
	317–14	s· ambiguous to the reader.

seemed

Mis.	22–29	s· to fall by reason of its own
	99–19	In no other one thing s·
	142–22	A boat song s· more Olympian
	163–16	In no one thing s· he less human
	164–13	babe Jesus s· small to mortals ;
	378–12	His treatment s· at first to
Ret.	23– 7	cloud of mortal mind s· to
	26–13	s· to me supernatural,
Un.	59–20	to which he s· to conform :
	62–19	The fleshly Jesus s· to die,
Pul.	20–14	s· type and shadow of the warfare
'00.	9–29	no one else has s· equal to
'01.	32–10	s· to shield the whole world
My.	56–15	* s· that there would be ample room
	61– 7	* it s· impossible for the building to
	61–23	* s· to move as by magic ;
	63–19	* s· to say that all the world
	182–14	s· the least among seeds,
	307–11	that s· at first new to him.
	311–14	s· to culminate at twelve years
	320– 5	*He also s· very much pleased
	320–12	* s· quite proud of his having had
	321– 2	* He s· very proud to think that he
	322–23	* s· inclined to banter me

seemeth

Mis.	260–20	whatever else s· to be intelligence

seeming

Mis.	30–26	s· mysticism surrounding realism
	53–28	Its s· abstraction is the
	57–22	or it would have no s·.
	83–10	explain this s· contradiction?
	107– 8	above the s· mists of sense,
	298–22	the s· power of error,
'01.	2–11	a fair s· for right being,
'02.	20–18	thus breaking any s· connection
My.	21–15	* compensates for every s· trial

seemingly

Mis.	1–20	s· rolled up in shades,
Man.	110– 5	these s· strict conditions
Rud.	8–26	the health is s· restored,

seemliest

My.	89– 1	* one of the largest and s· in

seems

Mis.	4–18	periodical . . . s· alone adequate to
	7–19	so loaded with disease s· the very air.
	15–26	goodness s· in embryo.
	71–27	What s· to be of human origin
	85–22	mind which s· to be matter
	102–24	Whatever s· material,
	102–25	s· thus only to the material senses,
	108–20	wherein evil s· as real as good,
	113– 6	when evil s· to predominate
	145– 6	form of godliness s· as requisite
	168–15	voice from heaven s· to say,
	179–19	What is it that s· a stone
	188–11	s· to be a war between the
	198–29	whatever s· to punish man
	204– 1	a mortal s· a monster,
	222–15	because the false s· true.
	222–26	whose power s· inexplicable,
	234–26	s· to them still more inconceivable.
	247–19	C. S. s· a mystery,
	247–24	s·, to the common estimate, solid
	260–24	evil is naught, although it s· to be.
	289–11	s· to rest on this basis.
	354–11	and sense s· sounder than
	369–12	madness it s· to many onlookers.
	372–17	* the artist s· quite familiar with
Ret.	32–17	* Whose most constant substance s·
	33–13	s· to prove the Principle
	81–29	s· to be requisite at every
	94– 5	that whatsoever s· true,
	94– 7	whatsoever s· to be good,
Un.	43– 3	s· too material for any
Pul.	45– 8	* s· impossible to mortal senses.
No.	32–23	It s· a great evil to belie
	41–22	Church s· almost chagrined
Pan.	7–21	wherein theism s· meaningless,
'00.	13–26	* s· not to have been wholly
'01.	18–13	C. S. s· transcendental

seems

01.	33– 2	that to-day s· to be fading
'02.	1–15	s· calculated to displace
Hea.	10–16	when sorrow s· to come,
My.	13–13	Jerusalem s· to prefigure
	47– 3	* It s· meet at this time,
	69–28	* the dome s· to dominate
	177– 8	s· to be no special need of
	220–30	s· less divine,
	220–31	s· more divine to-day
	258– 6	s· illuminated for woman's hope
	261– 5	s· to have amply provided for
	281–19	* s· to offer an appropriate occasion
	290– 4	the near s· afar,

seen

Mis.	2–11	Adam legacy must first be s·,
	3–23	as s· in the truth of being,
	21–12	C. S. will be seen to
	23–25	God is s· only in that which
	36–10	ferocious mind s· in the beast
	43– 3	without even having s· the individual,
	57–14	s· when Truth, God, denounced it,
	60–30	it will be s· that material belief,
	62– 8	s· only in the true likeness
	66–20	things which are s·, — *II Cor.* 4 : 18.
	66–21	which are not s·." — *II Cor.* 4 : 18.
	82–12	what eye hath not s·.
	88–26	* had never s· water freeze."
	95– 4	* will be s· by what follows,
	97–25	we have not s· all of man ;
	97–27	I have not s· a perfect man
	104– 4	superior to that which was s·,
	107– 5	Its redemptive power is s·
	108–27	not be s· believing in,
	109–12	must be s· as a mistake,
	109–14	sins be s· and repented of,
	115–12	pitiable, and plain to be s·.
	125–15	whom, not having s·, we love.
	127– 4	I have s·, that in the ratio
	128–12	heard, and s· in me, — *Phil.* 4 : 9.
	133–13	may be s· of men. — *Matt.* 6 : 5.
	150–15	already s· the salvation of
	164– 8	s· more clearly until it
	165– 4	was s· that he had grown beyond
	166–28	s· as diffusing richest blessings.
	175–18	Thus it can be s· that the Science of
	182–21	no mortal hath s· the spiritual man,
	182–22	than he hath s· the Father.
	183– 6	the power of Truth must be s·
	187– 8	discord, as s· in disease and death,
	188–17	upon the basis of what is s·,
	195–17	divine logic, as s· in our text,
	205–19	eye hath not s· it,
	212– 9	had suffered, and s· their error.
	213–12	if s·, can be destroyed
	219–13	beginning to be s· by thinkers,
	231– 5	had s· sunshine and shadow
	234–24	has s· far into the spiritual facts of
	278–10	and s· as my Father seeth them.
	286– 2	It is s· in C. S. that the
	286–29	Science of being is s·, understood,
	292–26	good, both s· and unseen ;
	299– 3	error that is s· aright as error,
	317– 1	students whom I have not s·
	317–25	s· in many instances their talents,
	325–22	and s· working for it !
	332– 1	Mind is s· kindling the stars,
	336– 9	His highest idea as s· to-day ?
	355–29	rainbow s· from my window
	363–20	is s· the brightness of His coming.
	372–26	having s· the painter's masterpieces ;
	373– 9	I had never before s· it :
	375–25	* many times have I s· these
	390–19	As smiles through teardrops s·,
Chr.	55– 5	have s· a great light : — *Isa.* 9 : 2.
Ret.	37–24	s· in the following circumstances.
Un.	7– 9	clearly s· and most sensibly felt
	22–10	to see or be s·,
	28–11	not a spectre had ever been s·
	28–22	"eye hath not s·, — *I Cor.* 2 : 9.
	29–20	sense declares can never be s·
	34– 7	That matter is not s· ;
	34–24	Nothing would remain to be s·
	38–23	not s· in the mineral, vegetable, or
	51– 5	is neither s·, felt, heard, nor
	53– 9	here to be s· and demonstrated ;
	62– 6	"The things which are s· — *II Cor.* 4 : 18.
	62– 7	things which are not s· — *II Cor.* 4 : 18.
Pul.	13– 9	nothingness of error is s· ;
	15–14	stewards who have s· the danger
	30– 1	* s· members of their own families,
	32– 3	* so often s· in New England,
	33–23	* no one else had s· him,
	41–20	* all who wished had heard and s· ;
	72– 9	* was one of the first to be s·.
	73–18	* When s· yesterday she emphasized

seen

Pul.	80–12	* Mrs. Eddy we have never s· ;
Rud.	5–12	who has ever s· spiritual substance
No.	22–16	No man hath s· the person of good
	25–21	Mortals have not s· it.
	27–19	* "No man living hath yet s· man."
	27–24	Who living hath s· God
Pan.	1–16	hopeth for what he hath not s·,
'01.	5–26	nature of God must be s· in man,
	7–28	because thou hast s· — *John* 20 : 29.
	7–29	they that have not s·, — *John* 20 : 29.
	12– 9	would be s· in such company."
	13– 5	ought not to be s·, felt, or
	32–13	courage of their convictions was s·.
'02.	6–13	human woe is s· to obtain in
	19–14	repentance s· in a tear
Hea.	2– 8	never s· amid the smoke of battle.
	11– 5	s· wholly apart from the dream.
	19– 9	had s· that a vein had not been
Peo.	9–23	is s· to rise above physics,
Po.	55–20	smiles through teardrops s·,
My.	18– 1	I have s·, that in the ratio
	21– 7	* it will thus be s· that
	29–14	* have been s· in this country
	45–14	* have long prophetically s·
	69–31	* building and dome can be s·
	87–20	* I do not think I have ever s·
	103– 2	reluctantly s· and acknowledged.
	108– 8	in proportion as it is s· to act apart
	118–17	they that have not s·, — *John* 20 : 29.
	124–28	s· of men, and spiritually
	129–15	s· through the lens of Spirit,
	143–11	am s· daily by the members of my
	149–28	s· and forgotten in the same hour ;
	152–25	It will also be s· that this
	184– 5	neither hath the eye s·,
	270–30	C. S. will ultimately be s· to
	273–11	yet have I not s· the — *Psal.* 37 : 25.
	289– 2	God's open secret is s·
	303–12	I have s· only extracts,
	322– 3	* she had s· the manuscript.
	322–17	* I had s· you the day before
	342– 9	* often s· in reproductions,
	361– 9	I have not s· Mrs. Stetson

seer (*see also* seer's)

Mis.	1–13	The s· of this age should be
My.	307–20	he was quite a s· and understood

seer's

Pul.	4–16	is the s· declaration true,

seers

'01.	9– 9	so pure it made s· of men,

sees

Mis.	58–16	eye cannot . . . it is a belief that s·.
	92–10	He who s· most clearly
	173– 3	s· nothing but a law of matter.
	228–21	Whatever man s·, feels, or
	297– 2	one readily s· that this Science
	321– 7	s· the steady gain of Truth's idea
	325–28	s· robbers finding ready ingress
	361– 2	pure heart that s· God.
	367–24	and in the light He s· light,
	374–15	the other s· "Helen's beauty in a
Man.	96–10	where he s· there is special need,
Ret.	25–25	neither s·, hears, nor feels Spirit,
	76–26	s· each mortal in an impersonal
	80–24	He who s· the door and turns away
	84– 7	He who s· clearly and enlightens
Un.	18– 7	if He knows and s· it not ;
	25– 8	It s·, hears, feels, tastes, smells
	33–26	Mortal mind declares that matter s·
	33–27	or that mind s· by means of
	34– 4	Mortal mind admits that it s· only
	49–25	be to something which God s·
	60–27	material sense, which s· not God.
Pul.	15–12	one who s· the foe?
No.	31– 2	admit that God sends it or s· it.
'02.	2– 1	s· through the mist of mortal strife

seest

Hea.	8–16	* "What thou s·, that thou beest."

seeth

Mis.	133–16	Father which s· in secret — *Matt.* 6 : 6.
	133–25	Father which "s· in secret," — *Matt.* 6 : 6.
	213–26	he s· the wolf coming.
	278–13	seen as my Father s· them.
Pan.	1–15	what a man s· he hopeth not for,
My.	109–18	now mine eye . . . s· Thee." — *Job* 42 : 5.

seething

Mis.	264– 5	midst of this s· sea of sin.
	338–11	in the midst of s· evil ;

seize

Mis.	319–29	s· them, trust the divine Providence,
	325–11	s· his pearls, throw them away,
My.	131–14	above the symbol s· the spirit,

seized

My.	11–19	* having *s·* upon this privilege and
	277–22	if our nation's rights . . . were *s·*,
	312–20	*s·* with yellow fever

seizure

My.	336–16	* *s·* of disease was so sudden

seldom

Mis.	75–16	this term should *s·* be employed
	283–22	*s·* the case with loyal students,
	283–31	*s·* calls on his teacher or musician to
	316– 5	speak to my dear church . . . very *s·*.
Ret.	83– 7	*s·* benefited by the teachings of
Rud.	15– 3	*s·* that a student, if healed in a class,
'01.	6–21	its theory even *s·* named.
My.	79–13	* *s·* witnessed anywhere
	147–26	be with you personally very *s·*.
	160– 4	is *s·* alight with love.
	215– 8	I *s·* taught without
	249– 3	condemn persons *s·*, if ever.
	264– 5	and this *s·*, until mankind learn more
	313–19	but I *s·* took one.

select

Mis.	256–15	*s·* number of students.
Man.	30– 2	shall *s·* intelligible Readers
	83– 9	shall carefully *s·* for pupils
My.	135–13	*s·* a Board of Trustees to
	137–21	*s·* a Board of Trustees to
	137–30	able to *s·* the Trustees I need
	214– 1	*s·* one only to place on the walls

selected

Mis.	315–13	thirty-three students, carefully *s·*,
Man.	62– 4	any special hymn *s·* by the Board
	84–21	assemble a *s·* number of them,
Ret.	90– 9	To these *s·* ones
Pul.	20–22	*s·* and observed in the East as the
	55–17	* Afterward she *s·* the name C. S.
	60–12	* *s·* for him from Mrs. Eddy's book.
My.	137–14	personally *s·* all my investments,
	137–27	I *s·* said Trustees because I
	312–27	The Free Masons *s·* my escort,

selecting

Man.	99–11	in *s·* this Committee,
My.	20–11	May I relieve you of *s·*,

selection

My.	137–29	to make this *s·*.

selections

Mis.	314–18	read all the *s·* from S. and H.
	314–28	*s·* from both the Bible and the
	315– 1	*s·* taken from the Scriptures and
Man.	31–19	Suitable S·.
	31–21	*s·* from the SCRIPTURES, and from
Pul.	12– 1	following *s·* from "S. and H.
	28–24	* *s·* from Whittier and Lowell,
	29–15	* *s·* from the Bible and from S. and H.
	43–16	* S· from the Scriptures and from
My.	17–17	* reading of *s·* from "S. and H.
	80–18	* *s·* from "S· and H.
	214– 3	promiscuous *s·* would write your

Selections read on June 12, 1906

My.	39– 7 to 10	references from Bible and S. and H.

selects

Man.	81–26	Publishing Society of The . . . *s·*,

self (see also self's)

and matter

Mis.	343–12	sordid soil of *s·* and matter.

and sin

Ret.	79–21	victory over *s·* and sin.

another

Mis.	1–20	reveals another scene and another *s·*

better

Pul.	83– 4	* our better *s·* is shamed and
'01.	17– 7	departed from his better *s·*
My.	6– 7	To abide in our unselfed better *s·*

cleansed of

My.	265–25	cleansed of *s·* and permeated with

deification of

Rud.	17–10	rivalry, or the deification of *s·*.

deny

No.	2–11	taught his students to deny *s·*,

dissolving

Mis.	1–17	from the ashes of dissolving *s·*,

egotistic

Ret.	74– 7	corporeality, or egotistic *s·*.

evil in

Mis.	254–16	kill this evil in "*s·*" in order to

exterminate

'00.	8–21	We must exterminate *s·* before we

forget

Mis.	155– 7	Forget *s·* in laboring for mankind ;

forgetting

Mis.	107–12	forgetting *s·*, forgiving wrongs

self

higher

No.	36–15	Jesus had a resort to his higher *s·*

how to leave

Mis.	194–22	*how* to leave *s·*, the sense material,

human

Mis.	162–29	he must be oblivious of human *s·*.
My.	194–14	human *s·* lost in divine light,

ignorance of

My.	233–19	Ignorance of *s·* is the most stubborn

immortality's

My.	275–25	is immortality's *s·*.

inflate

Mis.	301–30	stop the ears of . . . and inflate *s·* ;

irrespective of

Mis.	357–21	love that is irrespective of *s·*,

is lost

My.	283–22	when *s·* is lost in Love

leaving

Peo.	9– 5	love leaving *s·* for God.

loses

'00.	3– 3	he loses *s·* in love,

love of

Un.	27– 9	a passionate love of *s·*,

mortal

Ret.	86– 9	the falsity of this mortal *s·* !

one's

Mis.	38– 7	support one's *s·* and a Cause?
	108–18	namely, the knowledge of one's *s·*,
	118–25	warfare with one's *s·* is grand ;
	119–27	justly reserves to one's *s·*,
	129– 6	first lesson is to learn one's *s·* ;
	131– 5	The darkness in one's *s·* must
	227–31	Not to avenge one's *s·* upon
	283– 8	suit one's *s·* in the arrangement
	287–28	makes one ruler over one's *s·*
Pan.	9–20	to help such a one is to help one's *s·*.
	9–22	loves one's neighbor as one's *s·* ;
My.	122– 2	for one's *s·* and for the world

personal

My.	119–27	pastime of seeing your personal *s·*,

pride and

Mis.	92–32	divests himself of pride and *s·*,
Ret.	84–20	divests himself most of pride and *s·*,

real

Un.	55– 4	In his real *s·* he bore no infirmities.

renounced

Mis.	238–22	Have you renounced *s·*?

sacrifice

Mis.	155– 6	Sacrifice *s·* to bless one another,
'01.	35– 5	to sacrifice *s·* for the Cause

sceptre of

'00.	10–19	the sceptre of *s·* and pelf

scorn

Pul.	81–15	* scorn *s·* for the sake of love

selfish

Pul.	82–27	* Why should our selfish *s·*

sense and

Mis.	125– 9	his own sinful sense and *s·*.

silencing

Ret.	67–13	Silencing *s·*, *alias* rising above

sin, and

Mis.	328–17	burdened by pride, sin, and *s·*,

spiritual

Mis.	84–15	his spiritual *s·*, or Christ,

subordination of

My.	194–12	complete subordination of *s·*.

thine own

Mis.	226–15	* To thine own *s·* be true,
Ret.	81–24	* To thine own *s·* be true ;

this

Ret.	86– 8	be introduced to this *s·*.
Un.	45– 8	most of all to be rid of this *s·*,

victory over

Ret.	79–21	victory over *s·* and sin.
'01.	10–23	victory over *s·*, sin, disease,

was forgotten

'02.	13– 2	In this endeavor *s·* was forgotten,

Mis.	50–28	from *s·* to benevolence and love
	299– 7	lens of C. S., not of "*s·*,"
	322–17	senses satisfied, or *s·* be justified.
My.	90–12	* for *s·* or dear ones.
	160– 4	The heart that beats mostly for *s·*
	283–19	When pride, *s·*, and human reason

self-abandonment

Ret.	91–30	humility, unworldliness, and *s·*

self-abnegation

Mis.	15–16	moments of *s·*, self-consecration,
	100–13	meaning nor the magnitude of *s·*,
	154–27	Strive for *s·*, justice, meekness,
	298–21	absolute C. S.,— *s·* and purity ;
Pul.	12–22	S·, by which we lay down all
My.	6–28	prefigures *s·*, hope, faith,
	81– 6	* so complete this *s·*,

self-adulation
  My. v–12 * mesmerism of personal pride and *s*·

self-aggrandizement
  Pul. 21–28 Popularity, *s*·, aught that can darken
  Rud. 17– 3 to convert from mere motives of *s*·

self-annihilated
  Mis. 2–25 he would be inevitably *s*·.

self-arrayed
  Ret. 67–10 finite was *s*· against the infinite,

self-asserting
  Mis. 281– 4 It is the *s*· mortal will-power

self-assertion
  Mis. 224– 4 feels hurt by another's *s*·.
  Pul. 32– 8 * to control, not by any crude *s*·,

self-assertive
  Mis. 268–30 *s*· error dies of its own elements.

self-conceit
  Mis. 78–17 *et cetera* of ignorance and *s*·
    265–32 compels the downfall of his *s*·.
    354–21 *s*·, ignorance, and pride
  Un. 27– 7 *Egotism* implies vanity and *s*·.

self-condemnation
  Mis. 112–26 loss of self-knowledge and of *s*·,

self-conscious
  Mis. 183–11 pleasures and pains of *s*· matter.
  Un. 46–23 equally identical and *s*·
    52–27 supposed modes of *s*· matter,
  Rud. 2– 2 * "a living soul ; a *s*· being ;

self-consecration
  Mis. 15–16 moments of self-abnegation, *s*·,

self-constituted
  Mis. 186– 5 material *s*· belief of the Jews
  Ret. 61–14 saith . . . you are a *s*· falsity,

self-contradictions
  '01. 25–29 Jesus likened such *s*· to

self-contradictory
  Un. 53–14 for being *s*·, it is also
  '01. 26–28 was problematic and *s*·.
  My. 113– 6 *s*·, or unprofitable to

self-control
  My. 161–14 who gains self-knowledge, *s*·,

self-created
  Mis. 76– 2 *s*· or derived capacity
    173–32 it must have been *s*·.
    217– 7 cause is the *s*· Principle,
    364–20 *s*· or evolves the universe.
  Ret. 67–23 but supposititiously *s*·.
  No. 20– 3 are neither *s*·, nor

self-creative
  Mis. 26–19 *s*·, and infinite Mind.
  Un. 45–26 is *s*· and self-sustained,

self-culture
  My. 216–27 and see the need of *s*·,

self-damnation
  My. 200–24 bottomless abyss of *s*·,

self-deceived
  Mis. 184–22 destroys his *s*· sense of power in
    319–15 they are *s*· sinners

self-deception
  Ret. 72– 8 presumptuous sins, and *s*·,

self-defence
  My. 288– 4 gives little thought to *s*· ;

self-defense
  '02. 16–22 opening not his mouth in *s*·

self-degradation
  Mis. 227–16 from their choice of *s*·

self-deification
  My. 302–20 I regard *s*· as blasphemous.

self-denial
  My. 121–24 *S*· is practical, and is not only

self-denials
  Mis. 107– 6 is seen in sore trials, *s*·,

self-destroyed
  Mis. 2–23 evil must be mortal and *s*·.
    104–20 must stand . . . until *s*·.
    209–12 demonstrates . . . when sin is *s*·.
    210– 3 evil, uncovered, is *s*·.
  No. 32– 8 must suffer, until it is *s*·.
  My. 269–30 The lie and the liar are *s*·.

self-destroying
  Un. 52–19 *s*· elements of this world,
    55–15 reveals the *s*· ways of error
  No. 10–16 matter, . . . is a *s*· error.
    26–18 would be annihilated, for evil is *s*·.

self-destruction
  My. 211–20 would induce their *s*·.

self-destructive
  Mis. 2–22 good dies not and evil is *s*·,
  Un. 53–15 self-contradictory, it is also *s*·.
  No. 18– 7 If Science . . . it would be *s*·,

self-distrust
  Rud. 17–11 could tell you of timidity, of *s*·,

self-evident
  Mis. 23–11 The answer is *s*·,
    26– 3 will be known as *s*· truth,
    46– 4 The leading *s*· proposition of
    49–31 Truth never created . . . is *s*· ;
    186–22 *s*· proof of immortality ;
    193– 7 *s*· demonstrable truth.
    269–19 These are *s*· propositions :
    346–19 *s*· proposition of C. S.,
  Ret. 31– 6 *s*· propositions of Truth
  Un. 25– 4 and dispute *s*· facts ;
  No. 4–15 *s*· proposition, in the Science
  Pan. 4–28 By admitting *s*· affirmations
  '00. 5– 7 corroborating this as *s*·.
  '01. 14–17 *s*· that error is not Truth ;
  Hea. 4–23 with such *s*· contradictions
    12– 6 *s*· it can do nothing,
  My. 111–30 valid, simple, real, and *s*·,
    143–17 It is *s*· that the discoverer of
    179–13 Testaments contain *s*· truths
    302– 8 *s*· fact is proof that mind
    349– 6 *s*· that matter, or the body,

self-examination
  Mis. 137–23 must give much time to *s*·
    154–27 spiritual observation and *s*·.

self-existence
  Pan. 8– 9 deny the *s*· of God?

self-existent
  Mis. 26–17 Was it *s*·?
    187–22 The *s*·, perfect, and eternal
    198–28 a belief in *s*· evil,
  Ret. 60– 3 as eternal, *s*· Mind ;
  Pan. 3–19 supreme, holy, *s*· God,
    4– 4 will of a *s*· divine Being,
    5– 8 or is evil *s*·,
    12–23 demonstrably the *s*· Life,
  '00. 5–12 God is *s*·, the essence
  '01. 3–13 * Supreme Being, *s*· and eternal."
  Peo. 5–23 The ego is not *s*· matter

self-extinction
  '01. 5–18 leave all sin to God's fiat — *s*·,

self-extinguished
  Mis. 362–20 until *s*· by suffering !

self-forgetful
  Mis. 234–19 and, *s*·, should have gone on to
    250–24 the *s*· heart that overflows
    354– 6 *s*·, faithful Christian Scientists
  My. 247–29 *s*·, patient, unfaltering

self-forgetfulness
  Mis. 213– 4 flowed through cross-bearing, *s*·,
  Pul. 9–24 *S*·, purity, and love are treasures

self-glorification
  My. vii–13 * emotionalism which is largely *s*·

self-governed
  '01. 20– 5 Man is properly *s*·, and
  My. 247– 5 man governed by his creator is *s*·.
    254–26 man governed by his creator is *s*·.

self-government
  Mis. 240–24 Teach the children early *s*·,
    317– 7 demonstrate self-knowledge and *s*· ;
  Man. 70–10 Local *S*·.
    71–11 in its By-Laws and *s*·,
  Ret. 71–14 freedom of choice and *s*·.
  '00. 10–13 liberty, human rights, and *s*·
  '02. 3–13 *s*· under improved laws.

selfhood
  Mis. 104–20 must stand the friction of false *s*·
    183–24 Asserting a *s*· apart from God,
    333– 1 that sin — yea, *s*· — is apart from God,
    363– 4 "ego" that claims *s*· in error,
  Ret. 73–15 above physical personality, or *s*·
  Un. 6– 5 spotless *s*· of God
    6– 7 higher *s*·, derived from God,
    13– 9 God is harmony's *s*·.
    26– 2 having its own innate *s*·
    39–14 That *s*· is false which opposes
    42–25 true sense of *s*· and Godhood ;
    46–14 taught no *s*· as existent in matter.
  No. 26–17 Man's real ego, or *s*·, is goodness.
    36–19 retreat from material to spiritual *s*·
  '01. 8–24 Christ was Jesus' spiritual *s*· ;
    9– 3 referring to his eternal spiritual *s*·

self-identification
  My. 83– 7 * buttons, for their own *s*·,

self-ignorance
  Mis. 9– 3 pride, *s*·, self-will, self-love,
  118–21 S·, self-will, self-righteousness,
self-immolated
  Mis. 10–22 and their fear is *s*·.
self-immolation
  Pul. 10– 1 It was our Master's *s*·,
  '*02.* 17– 9 in blessing others, and *s*·
self-imposed
  Mis. 122–30 his sufferings, *s*· ;
  361– 4 through *s*· suffering,
self-inflicted
  Mis. 209–27 suffering is *s*·, and good is the
  Pul. 56–22 * mourn our *s*· pain.''
  '*01.* 17– 1 *s*· sufferings of mortals
self-instruction
  Man. 34–14 * textbooks for *s*· in C. S.,
self-interest
  Mis. 371–17 has *s*· in this mixing
self-interests
  Mis. 291– 4 affinities, *s*·, or obligations,
selfish
  Mis. 9–22 this cup of *s*· human enjoyment
  118– 3 *s*· motives, and human policy.
  262–28 *s*· in me sometimes to relieve my
  288–23 The *s*· rôle of a martyr
  Ret. 71–21 Sinister and *s*· motives entering
  89–29 Corporeal and *s*· influence
  Pul. 81–12 * call her "*s*·" because she
  82–27 * Why should our *s*· self
  '*01.* 29–12 *s*· in showing their love.
  My. 121–12 never *s*·, stony, nor stormy,
selfishly
  '*02.* 17– 5 S·, or otherwise, all are ready
selfishness
  Mis. 211–21 Cowardice is *s*·.
  237–20 inquiry, speculation, *s*· ;
  240–22 appetites, pride, *s*·,
  297–26 *s*·, unmercifulness, tyranny,
  298–15 To build on *s*· is to build on sand.
  343–16 cold, hard pebbles of *s*·,
  No. 20–19 absent to ever-present *s*·
  '*00.* 8–16 sensitiveness is sometimes *s*·,
  '*02.* 17– 1 *s*·, worldliness, hatred,
  Hea. 1–10 We have asked, in our *s*·,
  Po. 33– 7 *s*·, sinfulness, dearth,
  My. 229–14 and thus lose all *s*·,
self-justification
  Mis. 9– 4 self-will, self-love, *s*·.
  153–15 hatred, self-will, and *s*· ;
  293–29 sensuality, ease, self-love, *s*·,
self-knowledge
  Mis. 109–30 Watch and pray for *s*· ;
  112–25 of *s*· and of self-condemnation,
  317– 7 *s*· and self-government ;
  355–12 First, *s*·.
  358–14 S·, humility, and love
  My. 161–14 He who gains *s*·, self-control,
selfless
  Mis. 294– 7 With *s*· love, he inscribes on the
  My. 41–31 * supports such *s*· devotion,
selflessness
  Rud. 17–16 Meekness, *s*·, and love
self-love
  Mis. 9– 4 self-will, *s*·, self-justification.
  293–29 ease, *s*·, self-justification,
self-made
  Pan. 5–10 Since evil is not *s*·,
self-mesmerism
  My. 118– 6 *s*·, wherein the remedy is worse
self-oblivious
  Mis. 172– 6 Intrepid, *s*· Protestants
  My. 275–25 Intrepid, *s*· love fulfils the
self-preservation
  My. 227–22 individual rights, *s*·,
self-proved
  Un. 7–18 Certain *s*· propositions
self-renunciation
  Mis. 185– 7 S· of all that constitutes
  Ret. 28–17 Purity, *s*·, faith, and
  30– 5 Ceaseless toil, *s*·, and love,
  54– 5 It demands less cross-bearing, *s*·,
self-respect
  Mis. 99– 8 temporary loss of his *s*·.
  226– 9 losing his own *s*·?
self-respected
  Mis. 227–21 calm, *s*· thoughts abide in

self-righteousness
  Mis. 118–21 Self-ignorance, self-will, *s*·,
  398– 7 Make *s*· be still,
  Ret. 46–13 Make *s*· be still,
  65– 6 lead to *s*· and bigotry,
  Pul. 17–12 Make *s*· be still,
  No. 40– 3 Because of vanity and *s*·,
  '*01.* 14– 5 *s*· crucified Jesus.
  Po. 14–11 Make *s*· be still,
  My. 228–21 taints of *s*·, hypocrisy, envy,
  334–23 *s*· crucified Jesus.''
self's
  My. 133–15 free from *s*· sordid sequela ;
self-sacrifice
  Mis. 143–28 sometimes at much *s*·,
  358–27 Scientists who have grown to *s*·
  No. 33–13 S· is the highway to heaven.
  My. 28–11 * loving *s*·, of those who have
  167– 2 especially for the *s*· it may have
  298– 6 *s*·, *etc.*, that has distinguished all my
self-sacrifices
  My. 21– 3 * *s*· which have been made
self-sacrificing
  Mis. 312– 5 *s*·, unutterably kind ;
  No. v– 4 *s*· spirit of Love
self-same
  Un. 3–27 this *s*· God is our helper.
  Po. 10–16 "Thou of the *s*· spirit,
  My. 218–10 even the *s*· Lazarus.
  314–23 letter from me to this *s*· husband,
  337–17 "Thou of the *s*· spirit,
self-satisfaction
  Mis. 9–21 dreamy objects of *s*· ;
self-satisfied
  Mis. 265–29 *s*·, unprincipled students.
  My. 180–24 the disguised or the *s*· mind,
self-seeking
  Mis. 288–24 nothing short of *s*· ;
  '*02.* 18– 8 cowardice and *s*· of his disciples
  My. 210–12 *s*· pride of the evil thinker
self-support
  Ret. 20–11 had no training for *s*·,
  My. 216–26 in the knowledge of *s*·,
  312–17 * only one effort at *s*·.
self-surrender
  Pan. 9–17 *s*·, and spiritual endeavor
self-sustained
  Mis. 209–26 Joy is *s*· ;
  316– 9 Mother Church must be *s*·
  Un. 45–26 Mortal mind is self-creative and *s*·,
self-sustaining
  My. 275–26 love . . . is *s*· and eternal.
self-testimony
  Un. 33–19 *s*· of the physical senses is false.
self-will
  Mis. 9– 4 *s*·, self-love, self-justification.
  118– 3 false suggestions, *s*·, selfish motives,
  118–21 Self-ignorance, *s*·, self-righteousness,
  153–15 hatred, *s*·, and self-justification ;
  162–25 worldliness, human pride, or *s*·,
  224– 3 *s*· that makes another's deed
  366–27 dishonesty, *s*·, envy, and lust.
  '*02.* 16–27 pride, *s*·, envy, or hate.
  My. 41–10 * arrogance, and *s*· are unmerciful,
sell
  Mis. 113– 9 "no man might buy or *s*·,— *Rev.* 13 : 17.
  140–11 No one could buy, *s*·, or mortgage
  269–31 "no man might buy or *s*·,— *Rev.* 13 : 17.
  299–25 *s*· them or loan them to you?
  342–23 "Go to them that *s*·,— *see Matt.* 25 : 9.
  Man. 43–22 shall neither buy, *s*·, nor
  '*02.* 14– 4 can neither rent, mortgage, nor *s*·
  15–18 I declined to *s*· them
sellers
  Mis. 80– 1 *s*· of impure literature,
selleth
  Mis. 252–32 he goeth and *s*· all that he hath
selling
  Mis. 381–23 publishing, *s*·, giving away,
sells
  Mis. 227– 1 *s*· himself in a traffic by which he
selves
  Mis. 104–24 How shall we reach our true *s*·?
  '*01.* 11– 9 saved, and that not of our *s*·,
semblance
  Mis. 374–29 perceives a *s*· between the

semi-annual
   Man. 38–13   *s·* meetings held for this purpose.
   My. 121– 3   holding our *s·* church meetings,

semi-annually
   Man. 68–11   shall be paid *s·* at the rate of
       76–10   to have the books . . . audited *s·*,
       80– 5   be paid over *s·* to the Treasurer

semi-circular
   My. 78–12   * *s·* sweep of mahogany pews

semi-individuality
   My. 211–30   victim is in a state of *s·*,

seminaries
   My. 266–12   decrease of students in the *s·*

send
   Mis. 27–18   "Doth a fountain *s·* forth— *Jas.* 3 : 11.
       41– 1   that only the cruel and evil can *s·*
       69–27   I will *s·* his address to any one
       129–17   *s·* it into the atmosphere of mortal
       142–23   So I *s·* my answer in a
       149–20   to *s·* him to aid me.
       155–21   *s·* them to the editors of *The*
       156– 7   *s·* in your contributions as usual
       159– 6   then *s·* it to Rev. Mr. Norcross,
       214– 5   that I am come to *s·* peace— *Matt.* 10 : 34.
       214– 5   I came not to *s·* peace, — *Matt.* 10 : 34.
       227–20   the sweeter the odor they *s·* forth
       256–18   *s·* to each applicant a notice
       273–20   *s·* out students from these sources of
       305–27   * *s·* with the amount the name of
       306– 2   * *s·* fullest historical description.
       310–21   *s·* in their petitions to this effect
       313–21   to *s·* forth more laborers
   Man. 37–10   shall *s·* to the applicant a notice
       55– 2   nor *s·* notices to The Mother Church,
       100– 3   *s·* to the First Reader of the church
       100– 6   Or if she shall *s·* a special request
   Pul. 14–18   What if the old dragon should *s·* forth
       44– 6   * I *s·* my hearty congratulations.
       52– 2   * treasurer has to *s·* out word
       73– 3   * will *s·* to us those who have faith,
   '00. 10–30   *s·* me some of his hard-earned money
   '01. 31–10   "I came not to *s·* peace— *Matt.* 10 : 34.
   Po. 16–16   voice of the night-bird must here *s·*
       24–21   *S·* us thy white-winged dove.
       31– 1   *S·* to the loyal struggler
   My. 8–26   * *s·* our greeting to you,
       20–12   *S·* her only what God gives
       20–16   *S·* no gifts to her
       23– 4   * what amount each shall *s·*
       23–20   * *s·* their loyal and loving greetings
       27–15   * requested to *s·* no more money
       53– 6   * to *s·* forth her book
       59–26   * "*S·* those who say
       62–20   * *s·* you loving greetings
       72–15   * do not *s·* us any more money
       98–16   * requested to *s·* no more money
       153– 3   *s·* these floral offerings
       154– 7   to *s·* flowers to this little hall
       154– 9   *S·* flowers and all things fair
       159– 7   I *s·* to you the throbbing of
       167–23   *s·* forth a pæan of praise
       197–26   I *s·* loving congratulations,
       215–27   *s·* forth his students
       250–12   *s·* to the Editor of our periodicals
       253–23   I *s·* with this a store of wisdom
       256– 9   I beg to *s·* to you all a
       256–12   to *s·* to your Leader.
       257–26   and *s·* you my Christmas gift,
       264–10   * *s·* through the *Globe* to the people
       289–25   *s·* a few words of condolence,
       291–29   *s·* her more laborers,
       300–23   *s·* out students according to
       326–12   I *s·* for publication in our
       358–13   to read all that you *s·* to me,
       358–18   thank you for the money you *s·*
       362–18   * *s·* you their loving greetings.

sending
   Mis. 135–16   *S·* forth currents of Truth,
       368–15   *s·* forth a poison more deadly
   Man. 67–19   *s·* gifts, congratulatory despatches
       98–15   *s·* a copy to the Clerk
       109–16   *s·* them to the Clerk
   My. 152–31   *s·* to you weekly flowers
       244– 2   my purpose in *s·* for you,
       269–22   *s·* forth their rays of reality

sends
   Mis. 18–31   to believe that aught that God *s·*
       340–11   which *s·* forth a barrister
   Man. 82– 2   books and literature it *s·* forth.
   Ret. 56–22   The sun *s·* forth light,
   Pul. 12–21   Love *s·* forth her primal and
   Rud. 8– 5   Spirit *s·* forth its own harmless
   No. 31– 2   if you admit that God *s·* it

sends
   My. 155–29   Leader's love, which she *s·* to them
       249–12   *s·* forth a mental miasma
       274–17   * chapter sub-title

senior
   Mis. 235–25   superstitions of a *s·* period.

sensation
   and consciousness
    Mis. 228–23   perception, *s·*, and consciousness
       360–23   spiritual *s·* and consciousness.
   and life
    Mis. 53– 1   false claim of *s·* and life
   belief of
    Mis. 93–19   belief of *s·* in matter :
   bodily
    My. 110–19   if waking to bodily *s·* is real
       110–20   if bodily *s·* makes us captives?
   diseased
    My. 106–19   the evidence of diseased *s·*.
   false
    Mis. 73–20   subjective states of false *s·*
   has no
    Mis. 44–19   for matter has no *s·*.
   having no
    Mis. 28– 3   having no *s·* of its own.
   is not in matter
    Mis. 233–31   learn that *s·* is not in matter,
   life, nor
    Ret. 69–20   has no intelligence, life, nor *s·*,
   material
    Mis. 198– 6   so-called laws and material *s·*,
       331–29   their dream of material *s·*,
    No. 4– 8   material *s·* and mental delusion.
   Mind nor
    Un. 50–17   matter has neither Mind nor *s·*.
   no
    Ret. 61–22   for matter has no *s·*
    No. 19–17   and feel no *s·* of divine Love,
   of mind
    My. 228– 4   so-called disease is a *s·* of mind,
   pains of
    Pan. 1–13   pleasures and pains of *s·*
   physical
    Mis. 123–31   far apart from physical *s·*
       205–27   material life or physical *s·*,
   produced a
    Pul. 51–17   * produced a *s·* in religious circles,
   real
    Mis. 72–26   Real *s·* is not material ;
    Mis. 51–15   declaration . . . that *s·* belongs to
    Rud. 7–19   Matter, . . . has neither *s·* nor
    No. 5–10   the belief that matter has *s·*.

sensationless
   Rud. 5–10   Matter is inert, inanimate, and *s·*,

sensations
   Mis. 44–22   or that mind is . . . reporting *s·*,
       86–18   pleasant *s·* of human belief,

sense
   accepted
    No. 31–24   in the generally accepted *s·*,
   all
    Mis. 78– 4   all *s·* of sin, sickness, and death,
       286–28   shut out all *s·* of other claims.
    Un. 1–19   they lose all *s·* of error.
       32–12   destroys all *s·* of matter
    No. 30– 3   destroying all *s·* of sin and death.
    Pan. 11–25   destroys all *s·* of evil,
    My. 364–11   all *s·* of the realism
   and power
    Mis. 293–12   the *s·* and power of Truth
   and self
    Mis. 125– 9   over his own sinful *s·* and self.
   and sin
    Mis. 172– 8   defeat the claims of *s·* and sin,
   and Soul
    Mis. 102–28   conflict between *s·* and Soul.
    No. 12–25   both *s·* and Soul, man and Life,
   anthropomorphic
    '01. 6–24   in the corporeal or anthropomorphic *s·*.
   any
    Rud. 12–25   from any *s·* of subordination to
   arbitrary
    My. 49– 6   * and control, in no arbitrary *s·*,
   awakened
    My. 155–20   awakened *s·* of the risen Christ.
   barriers of
    No. 28– 5   will burst the barriers of *s·*,
   best
    My. 46– 8   * In the best *s·* it stands in prophetic
   bitter
    My. 267–23   with a bitter *s·* of lost opportunities
   bitter to
    My. 252– 5   sweet things which, if bitter to *s·*,

sense

boastful
  Un.   11–13   boastful *s·* of physical law
captive
  My. 133–15   set the captive *s·* free
certain
  Mis. 80–24   In a certain *s·*, we should
  Pul. 13–13   sweet and certain *s·* that God
chambers of
  Mis. 292–28   searched the secret chambers of *s·*
chastened
  Ret. 31–27   spoke to my chastened *s·*
Christian Scientist's
  '01.   5– 6   Christian Scientist's *s·* of Person
common
  Mis. 105–13   no conflict with Life or common *s·*,
        105–16   the too common *s·* of its opposites
        285–27   common *s·*, and common honesty,
  No.   2– 5   scorned by people of common *s·*.
  My.   93–22   * saneness and common *s·* which underlie
complete
  Mis. 75–17   can be used and make complete *s·*
corporeal
  Mis. 205–15   last scene in corporeal *s·*.
        308–29   invisible to corporeal *s·*.
darkling
  Po. 79–10   darkling *s·*, arise, go hence !
deluded
  Mis. 107–21   deluded *s·* must first be shown its
  '01. 15–19   waken such a one from his deluded *s·* ;
       15–19   for all sin is a deluded *s·*,
delusion of
  My.   5– 8   this illusion and delusion of *s·*,
discords of
  Mis. 202– 3   to correct the discords of *s·*,
divine
  Un. 21–21   or a divine *s·* of being.
  '02.   6–17   lets in the divine *s·* of being,
diviner
  Mis. 385–17   diviner *s·*, that spurns such toys,
  Ret. 81–10   diviner *s·* of liberty and light.
  Un.   4–12   diviner *s·* that God is all
  Peo.   5–19   diviner *s·* of Life and Love,
  Po. 48–11   diviner *s·*, that spurns such toys,
doubtful
  My. 260–15   doubtful *s·* that falls short of
dream of
  Mis. 176– 1   truth that breaks the dream of *s·*,
dyspepsia of
  My. 230– 9   silences the dyspepsia of *s·*.
enlarged
  Mis. 193–26   this enlarged *s·* of the spirit
       282– 3   an enlarged *s·* of Deity.
enlightened
  Mis. 173– 3   most enlightened *s·* herein sees
  My. 283–27   enlightened *s·* of God's government.
escape from
  Mis. 85–28   to escape from *s·* into the
every
  Mis. 187– 5   above every *s·* of matter,
  Ret. 61–24   If you rule out every *s·* of disease
  Pul. 37–12   * In every *s·* she is the recognized
evil
  Mis. 219–28   if he can change this evil *s·*
       332–19   an evil *s·* that blinded the eyes of
exaggerating
  Mis. 112–27   an exaggerating *s·* of other people's.
ex-common
  Mis. 112– 7   microbes, X-rays, and ex-common *s·*,
fallibility of
  Ret. 60–30   arises from the fallibility of *s·*,
false
  Mis.   9–30   false *s·* of what constitutes
       42–26   we drop our false *s·* of Life
       57–23   false *s·* and error of creation
       73– 9   separates the false *s·* from the true,
       74– 4   subdues not only the false *s·*
       76–24   an error or false *s·* of mentality
      175– 6   likened to the false *s·* of life,
      175– 9   Science changes this false *s·*,
      182– 9   lose their false *s·* of existence,
      189–17   presents a false *s·* of existence,
      190– 5   Mind as dispelling a false *s·*
      209–20   destroy the peace of a false *s·*.
      222– 2   gives him a false *s·* of both
      276–21   When a false *s·* suffers,
      351–28   punishes the joys of this false *s·*
  Ret. 21–19   false *s·* of life and happiness,
       21–21   awakening from a false *s·* of life,
       69–15   transient, false *s·* of an existence
       74– 6   from the false *s·* of corporeality,
  Un. 38–18   idolatrous and false *s·* of life
      42–25   Science, dispelling a false *s·*
      55–14   from the false *s·* of the flesh
      58– 1   false *s·* of life and happiness.
      60–27   false *s·* of substance must yield

sense

false
  Un. 62–16   false *s·* of Life and good.
  No. 28– 2   How long this false *s·* remains
      29– 5   a false *s·* of Soul and body.
      30– 4   does more than forgive the false *s·*
      37–25   buried in a false *s·* of being.
      39–13   false *s·* of Life, Love, and Truth,
  '02. 18–18   It is a false *s·* of love
  My. 119–23   Truth, which destroys the false *s·*
      233–26   [his false *s·* of life]
famine of
  My. 263– 7   a feast of Soul and a famine of *s·*.
feeble
  Mis. 172–19   presents but a finite, feeble *s·*
finite
  Un.   4– 2   finite *s·* of sin, sickness, or death,
  '01. 26– 7   only a finite *s·* of the infinite :
  Hea.   4–11   to possess our finite *s·*,
      5– 1   our own erring finite *s·* of God,
  Peo.   2– 5   As the finite *s·* of Deity, based on
fleeting
  Mis.   9–26   failure . . . to relish this fleeting *s·*,
fogs of
  Mis. 374–11   Above the fogs of *s·*
following
  Mis. 376– 4   * *most authentic* in the following *s·* :
frightened
  Un.   5–12   undisturbed by the frightened *s·* of
fuller
  Mis. 320– 7   Christ's appearing in a fuller *s·*
fullest
  Mis. 223–21   name of Christ in its fullest *s·*,
      303–11   brethren in the fullest *s·*
good
  Mis. 219–29   good *s·*, or conscious goodness,
grateful a
  Mis. 273– 9   so grateful a *s·* of my labors
gratified by
  My. 117– 6   A personal motive gratified by *s·*
higher
  Mis. 16–18   we must entertain a higher *s·* of
      84–29   to a new and higher *s·* thereof,
     111–12   higher *s·* of the true idea.
     113–12   not gaining a higher *s·* of Truth
     172– 7   a higher *s·* than ever before,
     195–29   higher *s·* of Christianity.
     292–12   higher *s·* I entertain of Love,
  Un.   2–13   gains a higher *s·* of God,
      5–17   unfold in us a higher *s·* of Deity ;
  Peo. 13–22   to a higher *s·* of Life.
     14–16   higher *s·* of omnipotence ;
highest
  Un. 61–17   Our highest *s·* of infinite good
  Rud.   9– 4   not a Christian, in the highest *s·*,
  My. 244–21   In the highest *s·* of a disciple,
human
      (*see* **human**)
illuminated
  Mis. 75–26   It was evidently an illuminated *s·*
immature
  Mis. 87– 6   immature *s·* of spiritual things,
immortal
  Mis. 74–15   immortal *s·* of the ideal world.
  Un. 52–13   Christ's immortal *s·* of Truth,
imperfect
  Rud. 16– 8   an imperfect *s·* of the spiritual
increasing
  My. 174–26   An increasing *s·* of God's love,
inspired
  Mis. 187–15   not lifted to the inspired *s·* of the
instead of soul
  Un. 29–23   reading *s·* instead of *soul*,
lingering
  '02.   3– 8   any lingering *s·* of the North's
literal
  '01.   3–15   literal *s·* of the lexicons :
lively
  Ret.   5–29   * lively *s·* of the parental obligation,
lost
  Mis. 185– 1   lost *s·* of man in unity with,
     186–31   the lost *s·* of man's perfection,
     190–26   the lost *s·*, must yield to the right
  No. 10–17   Truth restores that lost *s·*,
lower
  Mis. 102– 9   In this limited and lower *s·*
  Un. 30– 9   Hence this lower *s·* sins and suffers,
make
  My. 226– 3   only where you can . . . make *s·*.
material
      (*see* **material**)
may say
  Rud.   8–22   *s·* may say the unchristian
mental
  Un.   9– 2   the mental *s·* of the disease,

sense

mistaken
My. 357– 8   only incentive of a mistaken *s·*

mists of
Mis. 107– 9   above the seeming mists of *s·*,

modern
Ret. 89– 6   modern *s·* of the term.

moral
Mis. 223–11   I respect that moral *s·* which
    269– 5   commits his moral *s·* to a dungeon.
    352–30   moral *s·* be aroused to reject the
No. 23–17   moral *s·* of the word *devil*,
My. 249– 2   without harming . . . your own moral *s·*,

mortal
    (*see* **mortal**)

mortal mind
Mis. 254–22   *Per contra*, it is the mortal mind *s·*

mounting
Mis. 1–16   The mounting *s·* gathers fresh forms

my
Mis. ix– 2   suits my *s·* of doing good.
    24–12   healing Truth dawned upon my *s·* ;
    86–14   My *s·* of the beauty of the universe is,
    96–21   It brings to my *s·*,
    97–25   To my *s·*, we have not seen all of
    373– 5   my *s·* of Soul's expression
    392–21   To my *s·* a sweet refrain ;
Ret. 27–24   first broke upon my *s·*,
No. 29–18   To my *s·*, such a statement is
Pan. 3– 6   My *s·* of nature's rich glooms is,
'01. 6–29   is not my *s·* of Him.
    10–15   enthrall my *s·* of the Godhead,
    11–17   To my *s·* the Sermon on the Mount,
Po. 51– 3   To my *s·* a sweet refrain ;
My. 262–11   my *s·* of the eternal Christ, Truth,
    266– 3   To my *s·*, the most imminent dangers

natural
Mis. 72–19   *disappear only to the natural s·*

new
My. 63–22   * new *s·* of the magnitude of C. S.,

new-born
Mis. 74– 3   new-born *s·* subdues not only the

no
Mis. 76–25   and matter has no *s·*.
    112–14   He had no *s·* of his crime ;
    198– 9   understanding that matter has no *s·* ;
Un. 21–19   no *s·* in matter ;
    23–25   has no *s·* whereby to cognize
    33– 3   (matter really having no *s·*)
'01. 22–27   receive no *s·* whatever of it.
My. 96– 8   * can in no *s·*, save one, be compared

objects of
Mis. 344– 9   disengage the soul from objects of *s·*,
Peo. 7–24   objects of *s·* called sickness and

of being
Mis. 47–17   which is the truer *s·* of being.
    101–14   scientific *s·* of being which establishes
    175– 4   whole *s·* of being is leavened
    186–27   immortal and true *s·* of being.
Un. 21–21   or a divine *s·* of being.
    40–18   not by a material *s·* of being.
    43– 6   mortal *s·* of being is too finite for
No. 29– 4   and a deathless *s·* of being.
    37–25   buried in a false *s·* of being.
'02. 6–17   lets in the divine *s·* of being,
My. 275–22   the true *s·* of being goes on.

of Christian Science
My. 147–17   enlightens the people's *s·* of C. S.

of death
Un. 2–21   awake from a *s·* of death
    40–19   A *s·* of death is not requisite

of Deity
Mis. 282– 3   enlarged *s·* of Deity.
Un. 5–17   unfold in us a higher *s·* of Deity ;
Rud. 2–14   to retain the proper *s·* of Deity
    2–19   enlarges our *s·* of Deity,
Peo. 2– 5   As the finite *s·* of Deity, based on

of discomfort
Mis. 219–20   a *s·* of discomfort in sin

of disease
Ret. 61–24   If you rule out every *s·* of disease
Rud. 12– 6   Wrong . . . strengthen the *s·* of disease,

of divine Love
Pul. 74–25   in the *s·* of divine Love

of error
Mis. 352–31   aroused to reject the *s·* of error ;
Un. 1–19   they lose all *s·* of error.

of evil
Mis. 332–18   A *s·* of evil is supposed to have
Un. 20–17   all hate and the *s·* of evil.
    64–13   and the haunting *s·* of evil
No. 32–22   good destroys the *s·* of evil.
Pan. 11–25   destroys all *s·* of evil,

of existence
Mis. 82–26   mythical or mortal *s·* of existence
    182– 9   lose their false *s·* of existence,

of existence
Mis. 186–25   material *s·* of existence is not **the**
    189–17   presents a false *s·* of existence,
    189–23   not merely a *s·* of existence,
    310– 8   the material *s·* of existence
Ret. 58– 7   not merely a *s·* of existence,
Un. 42–16   not merely a *s·* of existence,
No. 4– 9   But an erring *s·* of existence,

offspring of
My. 5– 5   offspring of *s·* the murderers **of**

of God
Mis. 186–26   spiritual *s·* of God and His
Un. 2–13   and gains a higher *s·* of God,
No. 12–25   so enlarges our *s·* of God
Hea. 5– 1   our own erring finite *s·* of God,
Peo. 3–22   This limited *s·* of God as good

of good
Mis. 222– 2   a man's proper *s·* of good,
    341–18   to win the spiritual *s·* of good.
Un. 41– 8   a loss of the true *s·* of good,

of gratitude
Mis. 131–23   that loving *s·* of gratitude

of harmony
Un. 2–18   gain that spiritual *s·* of harmony
    22– 3   in a *s·* of harmony and immortality,
    24– 6   the supreme *s·* of harmony.
'00. 11– 4   the true *s·* of harmony,

of imperfection
Un. 4–11   destroys our *s·* of imperfection,

of its nullity
'01. 13–11   with such a *s·* of its nullity

of justice
Mis. 121–30   borrow their *s·* of justice from

of Life
Mis. 19–31   spiritual *s·* of Life and its
    20– 1   *s·* of Life illumes our pathway
    42–26   false *s·* of Life in sin
    67–11   strike at the eternal *s·* of Life
    67–12   thine own *s·* of Life shall be
    70–15   in a spiritual *s·* of Life
    84–28   from our lower *s·* of Life to a
    84–31   a clearer and nearer *s·* of Life
    189–19   a released *s·* of Life in God
    194–27   *s·* of Life that knows no death,
Un. 2–22   to a *s·* of Life in Christ,
    40–20   proper or true *s·* of Life,
    40–25   Holding a material *s·* of Life,
    41– 5   shuts out the real *s·* of Life,
    62–16   death is a false *s·* of Life
No. 39–13   our false *s·* of Life
Peo. 5–19   diviner *s·* of Life and Love,
    13–22   to a higher *s·* of Life.
My. 191–16   human *s·* of Life and Love,

of life
Mis. 82–22   material *s·* of life, is put off,
    84–21   Paul's *s·* of life in matter,
    175– 6   likened to the false *s·* of life,
    341–17   parting with a material *s·* of life
Ret. 21–19   from a material, false *s·* of life
    21–21   awakening from a false *s·* of life,
Un. 38–14   A material *s·* of life robs God,
    38–18   false *s·* of life is all that dies,
    58– 1   false *s·* of life and happiness.
My. 178–14   true *s·* of life is lost to
    233–26   [his false *s·* of life]
    274– 1   true *s·* of life and of righteousness,
    274– 6   a false material *s·* of life,

of love
Mis. 17– 4   opposed to the material *s·* of love ;
    351–28   punishes . . . this false *s·* of love,
'02. 18–18   It is a false *s·* of love that,
My. 287–15   true *s·* of love for God,

of man
Mis. 57–24   *s·* of man and the universe
    185– 1   lost *s·* of man in unity with,
    185–19   spiritualization of our *s·* of man
Un. 30–18   spiritual *s·* of man as immortal
My. 118–24   not by the spiritual *s·* of man,

of matter
Mis. 74–13   Christ Jesus' *s·* of matter
    187– 5   over and above every *s·* of matter,
Un. 32–12   destroys all *s·* of matter as substance

of might
Un. 42–17   a *s·* of might and ability to subdue

of mortality
Mis. 181–25   lose their *s·* of mortality

of music
My. 267–21   awaken . . . with a *s·* of music ;

of personality
Mis. 282– 4   *s·* of personality in God

of power
Mis. 184–23   self-deceived *s·* of power in evil.
Ret. 58– 8   *s·* of power that subdued matter

of religion
Pan. 3– 2   not at all the Christian *s·* of religion.

sense

of Science
Mis. 12–29   our s· of Science will be measured by
174– 8   attach our s· of Science to
My. 212–25   destroys the true s· of Science,

of sickness
Un. 2–17   the sick lose their s· of sickness,

of sin
Mis. 78– 4   thus it destroys all s· of sin,
107–16   (1) A proper s· of sin ;
319– 7   If the s· of sin is too little,
Un. 2–12   The sinner loses his s· of sin,
4– 2   our mortal, finite s· of sin,
9– 3   Destroy the s· of sin,
56–20   physicality and the s· of sin.
62–15   Destroy this s· of sin,
No. 30– 3   destroying all s· of sin
'01. 13–25   s· of sin, and not a sinful soul,
13–27   To lose the s· of sin we must first
16– 5   poignant present s· of sin
17– 3   mortal s· of sin and mind in matter

of sinning
Mis. 219–20   change the patient's s· of sinning

of Spirit
Mis. 17–31   gains a truer s· of Spirit
24–20   shutting out the true s· of Spirit.
Un. 21–19   s· of Spirit, and this is the only

of substance
Mis. 86–20   gain the glorified s· of substance
Un. 60–27   This false s· of substance must yield

of the body
Mis. 47–15   In sleep, a s· of the body

of the existence
Mis. 13–16   s· of the existence of good.

of the word
Un. 8–11   not real, in our s· of the word.
No. 23–17   moral s· of the word devil,
32– 6   in the popular s· of the word,

of Truth
Mis. 113–12   not gaining a higher s· of Truth
235–16   gives a keener s· of Truth
268–31   we must possess the s· of Truth ;
Un. 52–13   Christ's immortal s· of Truth,
Rud. 9–12   false and temporal s· of Truth,
My. 122–20   our s· of Truth is not demoralized,
122–27   s· of Truth of the real Christian

of unity
Pul. 4–10   a scientific, positive s· of unity

of words
Mis. 67–26   s· of words in one language

of worship
My. 139–19   turn your s· of worship from the

one's
Ret. 74– 1   increases one's s· of corporeality,

only as a
Un. 62–14   Sin exists only as a s·,

opposite
Mis. 292–19   to shut out all opposite s·.

or consciousness
Mis. 93–29   a sinning s· or consciousness
Un. 7–24   s· or consciousness of sin,

overwhelming
Ret. 81–16   overwhelming s· of error's vacuity,

pains of
Mis. 17–30   accumulating pains of s·,
85–26   pleasures— more than the pains— of s·,

peculiar
My. 50–12   * felt a peculiar s· of isolation,

personal
Mis. 97–26   more than personal s· can cognize,
287– 9   personal s·, discerning not the
290–22   personal s· of things, conjectural and
309– 1   the personal s· of any one,
357– 3   ways and means of personal s·.
Ret. 67–15   testimony of material personal s·
My. 117–11   one's own dream of personal s·,
227– 4   his own personal s· of righteousness
273–19   material or personal s· of pleasure,

physical
Ret. 57–12   had known that physical s·, not Soul,

poured on the
Po. 31–19   Poured on the s· which deems

practical
Mis. 192– 1   more spiritual and practical s·.

present
Mis. 9–14   far beyond the present s·
'01. 16– 5   poignant present s· of sin

profoundest
My. 295–15   in its largest, profoundest s·

proper
Mis. 107–16   A proper s· of sin ;
187– 5   proper s· of the possibilities of
222– 2   a man's proper s· of good,
Rud. 2–14   the proper s· of Deity

pure
'02. 18– 4   thrust upon the pure s· of the

sense

purifies
'00. 8–24   fire that purifies s· with Soul

quickened
Un. 56– 9   Holding a quickened s· of
Pul. 10– 4   raised . . . to a quickened s· of

rapt
Mis. 387– 1   rapt s· the heart-strings gently sweep,
Po. 50–18   rapt s· the heartstrings gently sweep

right
Mis. 190–27   must yield to the right s·,
Ret. 78–14   right s· of metaphysical Science.

rises
No. 19–24   s· rises to the fulness of the

sacred
Mis. 196–17   sacred s· and permanence of
Un. 41–15   The sweet and sacred s· of

sad
Po. 31– 5   Sad s·, annoy No more

Science and
Mis. 184– 4   Science and s· conflict,

scientific
Mis. 101–14   The scientific s· of being
No. 25–24   in a spiritually scientific s·.
'00. 6–11   the scientific s· which interprets
'01. 4–18   personal in a scientific s·,
6–22   in the infinite scientific s·

seems
Mis. 354–11   s· seems sounder than Soul,

sickened
Mis. 124–10   We turn, with sickened s·,

sight and
Un. 47– 2   destroying . . . to sight and s·.

sight or
My. 116–17   based upon personal sight or s·.

simple
Mis. 43–12   The simple s· one gains of this

sinful
Mis. 125– 9   over his own sinful s· and self.
No. 19–20   A sinful s· is incompetent to
My. 200–21   Pale, sinful s·, at work to

sinless
Po. 70–12   For sinless s· is here

sinning
Mis. 93–29   a sinning s· or consciousness
No. 7–13   the enemy of sinning s·,
29– 9   they believe . . . sinning s· to be soul ;

slave of
Mis. 183–10   he is neither the slave of s·, nor

Soul and
'02. 4–11   peace between Soul and s·

soul as
Mis. 15–21   shall soul as s· be satisfied,

soul for
Mis. 76–20   exchange the term soul for s·
Un. 30– 4   uses the word soul for s·.

soul from
My. 139–28   redeem . . . your soul from s· ;

soul means
No. 28–26   Here soul means s· and organic life ;

Soul, not
Po. 70–21   heraldry of Soul, not s·,
My. 118–19   Soul, not s·, receives and gives

Soul over
Mis. 321–12   triumphs . . . of Soul over s·.
Hea. 10–20   the triumph of Soul over s·.
Peo. 11–11   supremacy of Soul over s·,

spiritual
(see **spiritual**)

supreme
Hea. 15–10   as it rises to that supreme s·

sweet
Mis. 135– 9   sweet s· of journeying on together,
My. 163– 2   sweet s· of angelic song

that very
Un. 29–20   soul which that very s· declares

their
Mis. 121–30   borrow their s· of justice from
181–25   will lose their s· of mortality
191– 7   meaning of the term, to their s·,
Un. 2–17   sick lose their s· of sickness,
'01. 22–26   receive their s· of the Science,

this
Mis. 102–29   Mortal thought wars with this s·
105–13   if this s· were consistently sensible.
186–32   restored . . . by the spiritual
332–22   What was this s·?
Ret. 64– 1   and in this s· they are one.
Un. 57– 5   but as this s· disappears
62–15   Destroy this s· of sin,
No. 32–19   When this s· is attained,
'00. 11– 4   this s· will harmonize, unify,
My. 273–15   This s· of rightness acquired

tired
'01. 26– 2   my tired s· of false philosophy

sense

to Soul
Mis. 267–22 must gravitate from *s·* to Soul,
Un. 25–15 removing its evidence from *s·* to Soul,
'02. 10–16 and rise from *s·* to Soul,
My. 117–30 footsteps from *s·* to Soul.
142–20 their passage from *s·* to Soul.
156–13 the passover from *s·* to Soul,
163– 6 from *s·* to Soul, from gleam to glory,
234–14 from light to Love, from *s* to Soul.

trifling
Mis. 43–11 into other minds a trifling *s·* of it

true
Mis. 24–20 shutting out the true *s·* of Spirit.
28–12 to the true *s·* of reality,
59– 2 no true *s·* of the healing theology
84–26 true *s·* of the falsity of material
124–19 man's true *s·* is filled with peace,
186–27 immortal and true *s·* of being.
190– 6 giving the true *s·* of itself,
234–10 true *s·* of Love as God ;
276–21 the true *s·* comes out,
282– 2 a true *s·* of the infinite good,
291– 5 it dims the true *s·* of God's reflection,
319– 1 true *s·* of the unity of good
347–19 A true *s·* not unfamiliar
372–31 true *s·* of meekness and might.
Ret. 54–24 impressed with the true *s·* of the
Un. 40–20 proper or true *s·* of Life,
41– 8 a loss of the true *s·* of good,
42–25 leading man into the true *s·* of
Pul. 3–15 gives us the true *s·* of victory,
21–16 a true *s·* of goodness in others,
Rud. 10–18 true *s·* that God is Love,
'00. 11– 4 the true *s·* of harmony,
My. 116– 3 true *s·* of the omnipotence of Life,
160–25 waking to a true *s·* of itself,
178–14 true *s·* of life is lost to those who
212–25 destroys the true *s·* of Science,
274– 1 gives the true *s·* of life
275–22 the true *s·* of being goes on.
287–15 true *s·* of love for God,

truer
Mis. 17–31 gains a truer *s·* of Spirit
47–17 is the truer *s·* of being.
No. 34– 5 truer *s·* of following Christ
'01. 9– 7 their truer *s·* of Christ baptized them

unreal
Un. 41– 6 unreal *s·* of suffering and death.
No. 5–12 this unreal *s·* substitutes for Truth an

Virgin-mother's
Un. 29–28 Virgin-mother's *s·* being uplifted to

whatever
My. 154–30 take it in whatever *s·* you may.

wings of
Mis. 230–19 floating off on the wings of *s·* :

without the Science
Mis. 302– 9 *s·* without the Science, of Christ's

wounded
Mis. 145–16 a wounded *s·* of its own error,

―――

Mis. 75–20 substitution of *s·* for *soul*
96–21 to the *s·* of all who entertain this
107–22 Without a *s·* of one's
159–24 *s·* of Thy children grown to
179–23 old consciousness of Soul in *s·*.
181–27 *s·* of man's spiritual preexistence
186–31 even the *s·* of the real man
282– 2 a *s·* that does not limit God,
353– 1 allowed to rejoice in the *s·* that
354– 1 pleasure seeking, and *s·* indulgence,
Un. 8– 7 than the *s·* you entertain of it.
29–25 O my soul [*s·*] — *Psal.* 42 : 11.
Rud. 8– 4 To *s·*, the lion of to-day
No. 2–11 to deny self, *s·*, and take up the
10–19 former position, that *s·* is organic
34–15 one upon whom the world of *s·*
'01. 8– 9 in the *s·* that one ray of light is
9– 8 a *s·* so pure it made seers of men,
10–11 son of man only in the *s·* that
My. 106–22 In what *s·* is the . . . Scientist a
106–28 In what *s·* is the . . . a charlatan?
349– 8 disease is in a *s·* susceptible of

senseless
Mis. 355–19 Mental darkness is *s·* error,
Un. 11–22 for restoring his *s·* hand ;

senses (*see also* senses')

afford no evidence
Hea. 16–19 *s·* afford no evidence of Truth?

cannot define
Un. 29–15 that which the *s·* cannot define

claims of the
My. 222–14 admitting the claims of the *s·*

cognized by the
Mis. 22–29 simple fact cognized by the *s·*,

senses

corporeal
Ret. 54– 7 claims of the corporeal *s·*

could not prophesy
Ret. 23–11 *s·* could not prophesy sunrise

delusion that the
Un. 30– 4 delusion that the *s·* can reverse

doubleminded
Mis. 198–23 adherence to the "doubleminded" *s·*,

dull
Mis. 100– 5 was to awaken the dull *s·*,

erring
Mis. 13–22 testimony of the five erring *s·*,

error of the
Un. 42–11 is an error of the *s·* ;

evidence of the
(*see* **evidence**)

evidences of the
Mis. 58–11 *deny the evidences of the s·?*
Hea. 15– 1 repudiates the evidences of the *s·*

false
Mis. 107–19 false *s·* pass through three states

fear of the
Ret. 74– 2 begets a fear of the *s·*

feasting the
Ret. 65–10 Feasting the *s·*, gratification of

finite
Hea. 4– 8 we limit . . . to the finite *s·*.

five
Mis. 351–23 the five *s·* give to mortals pain,
Un. 25– 5 the testimony of the five *s·*.
28–18 the five *s·* take no cognizance of
Rud. 5–26 the five *s·* as organized matter,

foul
Mis. 399– 7 Cleanse the foul *s·* within ;
Po. 75–14 Cleanse the foul *s·* within ;

habitation of the
Mis. 328–19 tarried in the habitation of the *s·*,

human
My. 189–18 When the human *s·* wake

illusion of the
Mis. 368– 5 dispel this illusion of the *s·*,

instead of the
Hea. 7– 8 language of Soul instead of the *s·* ;
Peo. 2–13 of Soul instead of the *s·*,

intoxicated
Mis. 277–30 the cloud of the intoxicated *s·*.

join issue
Mis. 105–26 *s·* join issue with error,

material
(*see* **material**)

misguided
Mis. 268–21 enlightening the misguided *s·*,

mortal
Mis. 13–20 the shifting mortal *s·* confirm
Pul. 45– 8 * seems impossible to mortal *s·*.
45–21 * evidence of the mortal *s·* is

obtained from the
Mis. 251–18 knowledge obtained from the *s·*

personal
Mis. 28– 4 Perception by the five personal *s·*
65– 1 from the five personal *s·*.
96–31 evidence before the personal *s·*,
100–12 The five personal *s·*,
172–19 taken in by the five personal *s·*,
172–25 Science, and the five personal *s·*,
198–15 false belief of the personal *s·* ;
200–25 apart from the personal *s·*.
218–13 the five personal *s·* can take no
Un. 21–12 the evidence of your personal *s·*
'01. 18–15 evidence of the five personal *s·*,
26– 7 The five personal *s·* can have
Hea. 16–16 A word about the five personal *s·*,
17– 4 or the pains of the personal *s·*
17– 6 material man and the personal *s·*
17–10 material man and these personal *s·*,
My. 273–25 personal *s·* are perishable :
273–29 in possession of the five personal *s·*,

physical
(*see* **physical**)

rebuke the
Mis. 203–17 baptism serves to rebuke the *s·*

satisfied
Mis. 322–17 *s·* satisfied, or self be justified.

say
Mis. 103–10 the *s·* say vaguely :

scope of the
Mis. 100–17 scope of the *s·* is inadequate

so-called
My. 275– 6 so-called *s·* do not perceive this

spiritual
Mis. 104–18 physical senses with his spiritual *s·*.
Rud. 5– 1 spiritual *s·* afford no such evidence,
No. 19–19 spiritual *s·* are drinking in the
Hea. 17–17 when the spiritual *s·* were hushed

senses

testimony of the
Mis. 103– 2 annuls the testimony of the *s*,
    105– 9 came from the testimony of the *s*,
    164–31 arose from the testimony of the *s*.
No.   6– 8 validity of the testimony of the *s*,

these
Mis. 198–15 if we deny the claims of these *s*
    299–16 the evil which these *s* see not
Un. 33– 5 Now these *s*, being material,
Hea. 16–18 is furnished by these *s* ;

those
Hea. 16–24 those *s* through which it is impossible to

thraldom of the
Mis. 101– 5 departing from the thraldom of the *s*

would say
Mis. 367–28 *s* would say that whatever saves from

————

Mis. 98– 6 chapter sub-title
   100–19 Science speaks when the *s* are
   101– 8 C. S. and the *s* are at war.
   105– 7 anathema of priesthood and the *s* ;
   161– 9 To the *s*, Jesus was the son of man :
   166–21 more spiritual than the *s* could
   190–17 interpretations that the *s* give
   191– 3 which the *s* are supposed to
   214–12 closed — to the *s* — that wondrous life,
   310– 1 studying Truth through the *s*,
Un. 41–26 To the *s*, matter appears to
   52–26 The *s*, not God, Soul, form the
Hea. 17– 2 Not by the *s* — the lusts of the
Po. 68–11 Enchant deep the *s*,

senses'

My. 230– 7 during the *s* assimilation thereof,

sensibilities

Mis. 224–21 shall not wear upon our *s* ;

sensibility

Mis. 204–19 and so quickens moral *s*
   293–28 consigns *s* to the charnel-house
Ret. 74– 2 perpetually egotistical *s*.

sensible

Mis. 105–13 if this sense were consistently *s*.
   126–15 not yet quite *s* of what we owe
Ret. 73–16 true Mind, where *s* evil is lost
Un. 21–18 There is no *s* matter,
   50– 8 belief in matter as *s* mind.
No. 6–18 is as *s* and real as the
   14– 6 all *s* phenomena are
   38– 4 falsity of . . . are *s* claims,
'01. 30–29 * *s*, and well-bred man will not
My. 349– 9 and matter is not *s*.

sensibly

Un. 7– 9 clearly seen and most *s* felt
'01. 33– 3 fading so *s* from our sight.

sensitive

Mis. 108– 1 The *s*, sorrowing saint
   360–28 to *s* ears and dark disciples,

sensitiveness

Mis. 112–25 shows itself in extreme *s* ;
   116– 2 destroy your own *s* to the
'00. 8–15 remember that *s* is sometimes

sensual

Mis. 196–11 become material, *s*, evil.
   328–11 acquaint *s* mortals with the
   361– 3 mortal mind, *s* conception,
   363–22 avoid the shoals of a *s* religion
Un. 9– 5 Material and *s* consciousness
'00. 13–17 was devoted to a *s* worship.
'01. 26– 8 metaphysician is *s* that combines
Peo. 1– 8 as they pass from the *s* side
   11–12 the sick, the *s*, are slaves,
My. 48–23 * The scorn of the gross and *s*,
   262–22 mortal, material, *s* giving

sensualism

Mis. 325–27 as a testimony against *s*
   337–31 *s*, as heretofore, would hide
No. 21– 1 forbidden by-paths of *s*,

sensualist

'01. 30–30 The *s* and world-worshipper

sensuality

Mis. 234–26 so sunken in sin and *s*,
   285–16 the whole warfare of *s*
   289– 5 Drunkenness is *s* let loose,
   293–28 the charnel-house of *s*,
   298–19 all the claims of *s*.
Hea. 10– 4 vision of envy, *s*, and malice,
My. 139–28 redeem . . . your being from *s* ;

sensuous

Mis. 87– 7 of the beauties of the *s* universe :
   113– 1 result of *s* mind in matter.
   217–17 *S* and material realistic views

sensuous

Mis. 286–13 of spiritual power over *s*,
   351–22 and *s* love is material,
Ret. 25–13 physical senses, or *s* nature,
No. 26–10 Theirs is the *s* thought,
   26–11 brings forth its own *s* conception.

sent

Mis. 6– 1 that sickness is *s* as a discipline
   60– 2 *He s His Son to save from*
   87–15 *inform us, . . . if you s*
   87–16 *She said that you s her there to*
   158–26 divine directions *s* out to the
   249–18 not one has been *s* to my house,
   275–29 floral offerings *s* to my apartments
   299–10 following question *s* to me ;
   304–14 * *s* to the next World's Exhibition,
   305–11 * circular is *s* to every member
   306–12 * Contributions should be *s* to the
   317–30 "Whom God hath *s* — *John* 3 : 34.
   326–27 stonest them which are *s* — *Matt.* 23 : 37.
   339–26 *s* along the ocean of events a wave
Man. 66–25 an order . . . that she has not *s*,
   98–19 letter *s* to the Pastor Emeritus
Ret. 20– 8 was *s* away from me,
   48–21 *s* to all parts of our country,
   52–23 June, 1889, I *s* a letter,
   90– 7 towns whither he *s* his disciples ;
Un. 4–25 Jesus Christ, whom He has *s*.
Pul. 41–11 * listen to the Message *s* them by
   41–14 * New York *s* its hundreds,
   80–12 * us by interested friends,
'00. 10–25 * to me, in the name of a
Po. 43– 1 *s me the picture depictive of*
My. 14– 1 whereto [God, Spirit] *s* it." — *see Isa.* 55 : 11.
   49–18 * *s* an invitation to Mrs. Eddy
   57–29 * Treasurer has *s* out word
   72–19 * *s* forth to the thirty thousand
   94–25 * *s* greetings in which she declared
   96–21 * money was *s* in such quantities
   144– 1 * Mrs. Eddy also *s* the following
   150–27 when he *s* them forth to heal
   159–10 hath *s* forth His word to heal
   173–12 a note, *s* at the last moment,
   215–11 *s* me the full tuition money.
   215–23 When the great Master first *s* forth his
   223– 9 *s* to the C. S. practitioners
   242–19 *s* to the C. S. Board of Directors
   253–13 that Thou hast *s* me." — *John* 17 : 25.
   258–30 *s* me that beautiful statuette
   272–21 * an article *s* to us by Mrs. Eddy,
   274–18 * *s* the following to the *Herald :*
   335–24 * *s* for the distinguished physician

sentence

Mis. 8–28 *s*, can only be fulfilled
   21–23 order of this *s* has been conformed
   121–20 this *s* passed upon innocence
   133– 4 to build a *s* of so few words
Pul. 59– 5 * There was no special *s* or prayer
   59–13 congregation repeating one *s*
No. 44–13 could *s* men to the dungeon or stake
'01. 20–28 and will pass *s* on the
   26– 9 In one *s* he declaims against
My. 104–18 suspend judgment and *s*
   161– 8 never remits the *s* necessary

sentenced

Mis. 261– 1 doomed, already *s*, punished ;
Hea. 7–21 *s* it as our judges would not

sentences

Mis. 125–19 meanings of these short *s* :
My. 110–31 *s* or paragraphs torn from
   113–10 Paul declares . . . in these brief *s* :

sentencing

'02. 10–28 *s* a man for communicating

sentiment

Mis. 127–29 tender *s* felt, or a kind word
   174– 9 what touches the religious *s*
   250–10 no *s* less understood.
   295–21 English *s* is not wholly
   315–18 that they prove sound in *s*,
Man. 83–17 that they prove sound in *s*
Un. 26–20 its *s* is foreign to C. S.
Pul. 21–30 Only what feeds and fills the *s*
   79–23 * requires the religious *s*
   80– 4 * religious *s* in women is so strong
No. 1– 1 kindle in all minds a common *s*
   1–11 when public *s* is aroused.
Pan. 2–21 to which the religious *s* is directed.
'00. 7– 4 religious *s* has increased ;
'01. 17–19 when the public *s* would allow it,
My. 224–10 public *s* is helpful or dangerous
   264–12 * will you please send . . . a *s* on
   281–21 * a *s* on some phase of the subject,

sentimental
My. 41–19 * teaches us to rise from s· affection
     48–29 * or paralyzed by s· fiction.

sentiments
Mis. 13– 3 permit me to exercise these s·
     143– 3 and the "square" of moral s·.
     250– 9 should be repressed by the s·.
     295–14 lost these s· from his
Chr. 55– 1 basis of the s· in the verses,
No.   1–15 stir of contending s· cease,
      42– 4 Such s· are wholesome
Hea. 18–13 world would accept our s· ;
My. 170– 7 s· uttered in my annual
    175–30 very opposite of my real s·.
    316–19 freedom of Christian s·,

Sentinel
Christian Science
Man. 27–15 The C. S. Journal, C. S. S·,
     81–11 The C. S. Journal, C. S. S·,
My. vi–28 * she established the C. S. S·
     10– 1 * [C. S. S·, May 16, 1903]
     11–22 * Editorial in C. S. S·,
     12–15 * Mrs. Eddy in C. S. S·,
     14–10 * [Editorial in C. S. S·,
     15– 1 * [C. S. S·, March 5, 1904]
     19– 3 * The C. S. Journal, C. S. S·,
     24–16 * Editorial in C. S. S·,
     25– 5 * [C. S. S·, March 17, 1906]
     26– 1 * [C. S. S·, April 14, 1906]
     26– 7 * [C. S. S·, April 28, 1906]
     27–20 * Editorial in C. S. S·,
     29– 1 * C. S. S·, June 16, 1906.
     58– 4 * notice was published in the C. S. S·
     63–10 * Editorial in C. S. S·,
     72–22 also through the C. S. S·
     98–14 * last issue of the C. S. S·
    226–27 editor-in-chief of the C. S. S·
    232–11 which Appeared in the C. S. S·,
    276– 1 [C. S. May 16, 1908]
    279–20 [C. S. S·, June 17, 1905]
    280–14 [C. S. S·, July 1, 1905]
    280–26 [C. S. S·, July 22, 1905]
    316– 9 [C. S. S·, January 19, 1907]
    334– 9 * weekly issue of the C. S. S·,
    356–13 Editor C. S. S· :
    363–18 Reprinted in C. S. S·,

Man. 65–11 editors of the C. S. Journal, S·,
Pul. 88–22 * S·, Eastport, Me.
     90– 5 * S·, Indianapolis, Ind.
     90– 6 * S·, Milwaukee, Wis.
My. 27–23 * in this issue of the S·
    142– 6 * Editor S·.
    217–17 In the last S· [Oct. 12, 1899]
    237– 2 in the S· a few weeks ago,
    237–22 in the S· of September 10 [1910]
    241–29 * Please give the truth in the S·,
    317– 2 * S· of December 1, 1906,
    338–10 * Editor S·.
    351– 2 * the S· is privileged to publish
    353–12 the second I entitled S·,
    355– 4 * Editor S·.]
    359–17 * In the S· of July 31, 1909,

sentinel
Mis. 392–10 Whate'er thy mission, mountain s·,
Ret. 18– 8 s· hedgerow is guarding repose,
Po.   20–14 Whate'er thy mission, mountain s·,
      63–17 s· hedgerow is guarding repose,

sentinels
Mis. 291–28 as s· along the lines of thought,
     370– 9 Let the s· of Zion's watch-towers

separate
Mis. 8–14 s· you from the Love
     18–22 could never s· himself from
     18–26 can we in belief s· one man's
     18–28 to s· Life from God.
     36–29 in matter and s· from God,
    110–18 time and space, . . . do not s· us.
    117– 4 s· the tares from the wheat ;
    136–15 and be ye s·, — II Cor. 6 : 17.
    196– 8 s· mind from God
    370–29 s· the sheep from the goats ;
Ret. 60– 5 mind as something s· from God.
      64– 2 cannot s· sin from the sinner,
      67– 8 and yet are s· from God.
      81– 5 Nothing except sin, . . . can s·
Un.   24–22 Evil. I am something s·
      37–12 no boundary of time can s· us
Pul. 27–30 * composed of three s· panels,
      30– 4 * enticing a s· congregation
      61– 1 * enclosed in s· swell-box,
Rud. 15–16 should have s· departments,
No.   9–12 regenerate and s· wisely

separate
'01.   6– 3 and have no s· identity?
My. 121– 4 in order to s· these sessions
     124–30 to s· the tares from the wheat,
     344– 4 and each s· ray for
     358–10 cannot s· you from your Leader

separated
Mis. 70–21 inevitably s· through Mind.
     135– 8 not one of you can be s· from
     186–19 man cannot be s· from
     214–29 must be s· from the wheat
     223–11 cannot be s· from it.
Ret. 21–29 are s· from their premises,
      57–23 not our own, s· from Him.
      81– 8 law of God, s· from its spirit,
      94– 9 As dross is s· from gold,
Un.   7–10 this has not s· me from God,
      32– 9 cannot be s· in origin and action.
      52–11 man s· from his Maker.
Pul. 76– 9 * are s· from the apartment
Hea.   6– 1 the more are we s· from the
My. 111–11 chaff is s· from the wheat.
     315– 6 * wife, from whom he was s·.
     316– 1 has s· the tares from the wheat,

separately
Man. 55– 6 shall s· and independently discipline

separates
Mis. 73– 9 it s· the false sense from
     151– 6 He s· the dross from the gold,
     186– 9 s· its conception of man from
     205– 7 s· the dross from the gold,
Un.   10– 2 s· my system from all others.
My. 167– 5 s· us from the spiritual world,

separating
Mis. 172– 3 s· the tares from the wheat,
My. 269–17 s· the tares from the wheat.

separation
Ret. 20–16 poem, . . . written after this s· :
My. 315– 7 * cause of the s· being wholly

separator
Mis. 150–10 Space is no s· of hearts.

September
(see **months**)

sepulchre
Mis. 123–18 stone from the s· of our Lord ;
     180–14 I found the open door from this s·
     275– 5 stone from the door of this s·
Ret. 88– 6 lifted his own body from the s·.
No.   36–25 rolled away the stone from the s·,
      45–14 "last at the cross and first at the s·,"
Peo.   5–15 it sitteth beside the s·
My. 119–13 stooped down and looked into the s·
     214–11 Jesus' three days' work in the s·
     258– 9 To the woman at the s·,

sepulchres
Mis. 292–15 turn away from the open s· of sin,
'01. 25–18 denounced all such gilded s·
Peo.   8–23 to light our s· with immortality.
My. 191–19 The s· give up their dead.

sequel
Hea. 12–23 and the s· proves it ;
Po.   16– 9 s· of power, of glory, or gold ;

sequela
My. 133–16 free from self's sordid s· ;

sequence
Mis. 65–26 s· proves that strict adherence to
     109–24 s· of knowledge would be lacking,
     217– 2 in logical s·, nature, reason, and
     336–29 the s· proves.
     366–28 To destroy sin and its s·,
Un.   33–17 Hence the logical s·,
Pan.   7–24 logical s· of this error is idolatry
My. 275– 4 As the s· of divine Love
     279–14 Hence the s· : Had all peoples

seraphic
Po.   22– 8 New themes s·, Life divine,

seraph's
Po.   65–19 rise to a s· new song.

seraphs
Po.   16–22 call to my spirit with s· to dwell ;

sere
Po.   41– 8 fountain and . . . are frozen and s·,

serene
Mis. 206– 4 from foul to pure, from torpid to s·,
     323– 3 in s· azure and unfathomable glory :
     323–15 masters their . . . attacks with s·
     369–13 This method sits s· at the portals
     400– 9 In thy heart Dwell s·,
Ret. 42–14 resting on his s· countenance.

serene
Pul.	5–14	his athletic mind, scholarly and *s*,
	16–21	In thy heart Dwell *s*,
Po.	76–20	In thy heart Dwell *s*,
My.	87–24	* such *s*, beautiful expressions,

serenely
Mis.	162– 9	walk *s* over their fretted, foaming

serenity
My.	88–21	* *s* of faith, life, and love

series
Ret.	91–14	this *s* of great lessons
No.	20–26	a continued *s* of mortal hypotheses,
'00.	13–13	after a *s* of wars it was taken
My.	78– 9	* beneath a *s* of arches

serious
Mis.	239–25	made them more *s* over it.
Man.	43–18	calls more *s* attention to the
Un.	26–24	All is real, all is *s*.
Pul.	33–20	* high counsel and *s* thought.
My.	51–11	* a *s* blow to her Cause

seriously
Un.	14– 5	Can it be *s* held, by any thinker,

sermon
Mis.	68– 7	*The Rev. —— said in a s:*
	126– 2	to one eternal *s*;
	161– 1	chapter sub-title
	168–21	chapter sub-title
	171–21	chapter sub-title
	177–26	* was announced to preach the *s*,
	178–19	* to preach a *s* on C. S.,
	178–25	* At the conclusion of the *s*,
	301– 1	compiling and delivering that *s*
	314–32	*s* shall be preached to the children,
Man.	59–18	to listen to the Sunday *s*
Ret.	16–12	for the sick to be healed by my *s*.
	91– 5	well be called "the diamond *s*."
Pul.	29–17	* *s*, which dealt directly with the
	40–13	* S· BY REV. MARY BAKER EDDY,
	43–22	* *s* prepared for the occasion by
	43–29	* Before presenting the *s*,
	57– 8	* *s*, prepared by Mrs. Eddy,
	59–16	* The *s*, prepared by Mrs. Eddy,
No.	29–11	*s* on The Ministry of Healing,
	41–25	Baptist clergyman, said in a *s*:
	42–28	* to support me through a *s*."
	43– 7	stimulate and sustain a good *s*.
'01.	6–19	consistent with Christ's hillside *s*,
	11–22	saith there is no *s* without personal
	11–25	a *s* from his personal God!
My.	50–31	* her farewell *s* to the church.
	186– 9	its song and *s* will touch the heart,
	194– 1	may song and *s* generate only
	197–27	join with you in song and *s*.

Sermon on the Mount
Mis.	12–13	loyalty to Jesus' *S· on the M·*,
	21– 4	unity with Christ's *S· on the M·*,
	25– 9	Christ's *S· on the M·*, in its direct
	93–30	obey Christ's *S· on the M·*,
	114–14	Decalogue, the *S· on the M·*,
Man.	63– 3	*S· on the M·*
Ret.	75– 4	tramples upon Jesus' *S· on the M·*,
	91– 7	known as the *S· on the M·*,
Rud.	3–15	called the *S· on the M·*,
	12– 4	practises Christ's *S· on the M·*.
'01.	11–17	*S· on the M·*, read each Sunday
	32–23	Ninety-first Psalm, the *S· on the M·*,
'02.	5–22	breathed in the *S· on the M·*.
My.	180– 6	uttered Christ's *S· on the M·*,
	229–22	ascent of Christ's *S· on the M·*,

sermons
Mis.	133– 7	to read my *s* and publications.
Ret.	89– 8	for . . . ceremonies, not for *s*.
Pul.	5–29	palpably working in the *s*,
	9–18	excellent *s* from the editor
	45–28	* *s* hereafter will consist of
No.	29–22	Such *s*, though clad in soft
	43–11	* "Your book leavens my *s*."
'01.	32–16	the *s* their lives preached
My.	185–30	*s* in stones, refuge in mountains,
	194– 2	*s* that fell forests

serpent (*see also* serpent's)
cast out
Mis.	373– 9	*s* cast out of his mouth,
Pul.	14– 8	*s* cast out of his mouth — *Rev. 12 : 15.*

handle the
Mis.	336– 5	to handle the *s* and bruise its

head of the
Mis.	210–17	puts her foot on the head of the *s*,

kill the
Mis.	336– 7	to kill the *s* of a material mind.

lurking
Mis.	210–21	kill this lurking *s*, intemperance,

serpent
named
'01.	16–13	*devil* is named *s* — *liar*

of sin
Pul.	13–15	and fail to strangle the *s* of sin

placing the
Mis.	373– 3	placing the *s* behind the woman

said
Mis.	196–11	bear in mind that a *s* said that ;
Peo.	4–11	because a *s* said it.

so-called
Ret.	69– 8	pantheistic error, or so-called *s*,

talking
Mis.	24–28	not to believe the talking *s*,
Pan.	6–12	in the form of a talking *s*,

this
Mis.	191– 4	and then defines this *s* as
Un.	45– 3	Bruise the head of this *s*,

was the emblem
'00.	13–19	*s* was the emblem of Æsculapius.

wisdom of a
Mis.	210–12	wisdom of a *s* is to hide itself.

Mis.	23–17	and the *s*, Satan,
	190–29	*s*, liar, the god of this world,
	191– 3	in another term, *s*,
	191– 7	*s* became a symbol of wisdom.
	210–13	brings the *s* out of its hole,
Ret.	68– 2	although as a *s* it claimed to
Un.	54–26	*s*, who pushed that claim
Pan.	6–10	chapter sub-title
	6–20	between good and evil, God and a *s*?
Hea.	17–18	claimed audience with a *s*.

serpent's
Mis.	123– 9	the *s* biggest lie !
Un.	44–19	carrying out the *s* assurance :

serpents
Mis.	24–30	his followers should handle *s* ;
	90–17	wise as *s*." — *Matt. 10 : 16.*
	210– 7	Do men whine over a nest of *s*,
	210–10	"They shall take up *s* ;" — *Mark 16 : 18.*
	210–11	wise as *s* and harmless as — *Matt. 10 : 16.*
	211– 5	it teaches mortals to handle *s*
	323–11	Venomous *s* hide among the rocks,
	323–20	hushing the hissing *s*,
'02.	17–18	and to be wiser than *s*,
Hea.	1– 3	*they shall take up s·*; — *Mark 16 : 18.*
	7–25	"They shall take up *s* ; — *Mark 16 : 18.*
	15–10	"take up *s*'" — *Mark 16 : 18.*
My.	47–31	* they shall take up *s* ; — *Mark 16 : 18.*
	146– 4	"They shall take up *s* ; — *Mark 16 : 18.*
	150–29	wise as *s*, and harmless as — *Matt. 10 : 16.*
	205– 5	wise as *s*, and harmless as — *Matt. 10 : 16.*

servant
Mis.	47–18	body is the *s* of Mind,
	108–25	then we are its master, not *s*.
	122–26	good and faithful *s*, — *Matt. 25 : 23.*
	206– 2	the former being *s* to the latter,
	256–12	remaining at present a public *s* :
	266–10	unacknowledged *s* of mankind.
	272–14	* any officer, agent, or *s* of
	335– 3	if that evil *s* say — *Matt. 24 : 48.*
	335– 7	"The lord of that *s* shall — *Matt. 24 : 50.*
Man.	28–10	"That *s*, which knew — *Luke 12 : 47.*
Ret.	9–11	for Thy *s* heareth." — *I Sam. 3 : 9.*
Pul.	6–23	seeker, and *s* of Truth,
	33– 8	* for Thy *s* heareth." — *I Sam. 3 : 9.*
Pan.	8–27	make man the *s* of matter,
'00.	3–11	by no means his *s*, but his master.
My.	62– 3	* good and faithful *s* ; — *Matt. 25 : 23.*
	145–21	makes me the *s* of the race
	165– 4	the Master became the *s*.
	207–21	good and faithful *s* : — *Matt. 25 : 21.*
	295–27	the *s* of God and man,
	332–13	* Your friend and obedient *s*,

servants
Mis.	19– 5	obedience demanded of His *s*
	46– 3	*s* to obey, — *Rom. 6 : 16.*
	46– 3	his *s* ye are." — *Rom. 6 : 16.*
	120– 8	*s* to obey, — *Rom. 6 : 16.*
	120– 8	his *s* ye are." — *Rom. 6 : 16.*
	158–19	God's *s* are minute men
	275–28	The *s* are well-mannered,
	346–18	*s* to obey, — *Rom. 6 : 16.*
	346–18	his *s* ye are." — *Rom. 6 : 16.*
No.	32–20	no longer be the *s* of sin,

serve
Mis.	x–14	*s* as mile-stones measuring
	40– 6	*s* "other gods." — *Exod. 20 : 3.*
	52– 6	if he were to *s* one master,
	89– 2	"No man can *s* two — *Matt. 6 : 24.*
	221–28	might *s* as the multiplicand.
	237– 8	Not a few individuals *s* God
	269– 6	"No man can *s* two — *Matt. 6 : 24.*

serve

Mis.	269– 9	cannot *s·* God and — *Matt.* 6 : 24.
	271–13	whom ye will *s·*." — *Josh.* 24 : 15.
	286–12	will *s·* to illustrate the
	303–13	Let us *s·* instead of rule,
	350–28	I cannot *s·* two masters.
Man.	69– 6	has been called to *s·* our Leader
	99– 2	to *s·* in their localities.
	99–10	to *s·* in its locality.
Un.	49–15	You cannot simultaneously *s·*
	60–18	to choose whom they would *s·*.
	60–19	If God, then let them *s·* Him,
Pul.	21–17	we cannot *s·* mammon.
Rud.	14– 1	Neither can they *s·* two masters,
No.	25– 6	*s·* in newness of spirit, — *Rom.* 7 : 6.
'01.	20– 4	to *s·* God and benefit mankind.
'02.	3–28	to *s·* God and to help the race.
Peo.	9–21	cannot *s·* two masters." — *see Matt.* 6 : 24.
My.	5–22	to love more and to *s·* better.
	5–27	to choose whom ye will *s·*.
	5–29	indulging sin, men cannot *s·* God ;
	6– 3	We cannot *s·* two masters.
	42–14	* to *s·* you in this capacity,
	110–32	may *s·* to call attention to
	134– 7	daily lives *s·* to enhance
	138–16	"*s·* two masters." — *Matt.* 6 : 24.
	145–22	if in this way I can *s·* equally
	152–21	and *s·* no other gods.
	174–28	pray to *s·* Him better.
	192– 2	Ye worship Him whom ye *s·*.
	209– 4	those that seek and *s·* Him.
	224–31	* "They also *s·* who only stand
	325–13	* in which I could *s·* you,
	356–22	*s·* two masters : — *Matt.* 6 : 24.
	356–24	cannot *s·* God and— *Matt.* 6 : 24.

served

Mis.	203–13	*s·* the imagination for centuries.
Man.	16– 6	his resurrection *s·* to uplift faith
	26– 6	who have *s·* one year or more,
	80–26	who have *s·* one year or more
Ret.	6–26	*s·* the public interests faithfully
	21–10	he had *s·* as a volunteer
Pul.	8–15	*s·* to erect this "miracle in

serves

Mis.	203–17	baptism *s·* to rebuke the senses
	210–20	*s·* to uncover and kill this lurking
	292–23	Charity thus *s·* as admonition
	341–21	*s·* to illustrate the evil of
	373– 1	One incident *s·* to illustrate the
Ret.	76–20	*s·* to constitute the Mind-healer a
'02.	7–24	passage which *s·* to confirm C. S.
My.	91–17	* *s·* to call attention to one of the
	342–17	* which *s·* as a library,

service

acceptable
My.	184–22	*s·* acceptable in God's sight.
	250– 9	three years of acceptable *s·* as

after the
My.	38–25	* Scientists said after the *s·*

another
Pul.	42– 4	* At 10 : 30 o'clock another *s·* began,

before the
My.	54– 8	* crowded one hour before the *s·*

charity, and
'00.	15–24	charity, and *s·*, and faith, — *Rev.* 2 : 19.

children's
Mis.	315– 4	The children's *s·* shall be held
My.	78–26	* chapter sub-title

Christian
My.	36–11	* holy Christian *s·* that shall be

Christ's
My.	147–24	already dedicated to Christ's *s·*,

church
Mis.	177–23	* the hour for the church *s·*

Communion
Mis.	314–28	observed at the Communion *s·* ;

communion
My.	27– 6	annual meeting and communion *s·*,
	29– 3	* chapter sub-title
	140–14	* dropping the annual communion *s·* of
	141– 3	* The general communion *s·* of

consecration
Pul.	31– 1	* its consecration *s·* on January 6

dedication
Pul.	41–29	* until the hour for the dedication *s·*

dedicatory
Pul.	59–29	* at the second dedicatory *s·*.
My.	31–30	* as the opening of the dedicatory *s·*.

each
My.	35–27	* During the progress of each *s·*,
	38–12	* church was filled for each *s·*

Easter
Mis.	180–16	I *love* the Easter *s·* :

end of the
My.	32– 4	* at the end of the *s·*,

service

evening
My.	29–31	* until the close of the evening *s·*,

faithful
Mis.	158–15	reward for your faithful *s·*,
Pan.	14–21	and their faithful *s·* thereof,

first
My.	56–30	* repetitions of the first *s·*.

God's
My.	195–16	use in God's *s·* the one talent

half past twelve
My.	78–28	* of the half past twelve *s·* ;

His
'01.	1– 6	so long as you are in His *s·*.
My.	251–26	armors, and tests in His *s·*,

its
Pul.	28–17	* save that its *s·* includes

Memorial
My.	284–13	referring to the Memorial *s·*
	284–19	the aforesaid Memorial *s·*

morning
Man.	58–12	Lesson-Sermon in the morning *s·*
Pul.	34– 9	* before proceeding to his morning *s·*,
My.	56– 6	* repetition of the morning *s·*.
	56–25	* crowded condition of the morning *s·*

much
My.	324– 9	* no one could be of much *s·*

next
My.	38–11	* admitted until the next *s·*.

of Christian Science
Mis.	91–17	employed in the *s·* of C. S.

one
Pul.	59–29	* Before one *s·* was over and the

order of
Pul.	28–14	* heading
	28–15	* order of *s·* in the C. S. Church
	60– 3	* new order of *s·* went into operation.
My.	32–12	* order of *s·* was as follows :

postal
'02.	11–13	postal *s·*, a steam engine,

reasonable
Mis.	184–11	which is our reasonable *s·* ;
My.	vii–13	* a reasonable *s·* which all

repeated
Pul.	40–12	* *S·* REPEATED FOUR TIMES

rules of
My.	342–31	its present rules of *s·*

said
Mis.	302–22	destroyed . . . after said *s·*.

such
Man.	69–12	during the time of such *s·*.

such a
Mis.	80– 3	By rendering error such a *s·*,

Sunday
Mis.	302–21	reading my works for Sunday *s·* ;
	315– 4	after the manner of the Sunday *s·*.
My.	54–31	* Sunday *s·* held in Chickering Hall
	56– 3	* Attendance at the Sunday *s·*
	74– 8	* in time for the first Sunday *s·*.
	147– 1	chapter sub-title

telephone
My.	73–24	* telegraph and telephone *s·*.

ten o'clock
My.	30–30	* admission at the ten o'clock *s·*,

term of
Man.	69– 5	Incomplete Term of *S·*.

that
Mis.	314–31	such as is adapted to that *s·*.

their
My.	38–21	* their *s·* was the same as all

this
Man.	61–14	at this *s·* the Tenets
Pul.	42– 1	* Before this *s·* had closed
My.	42–18	* endeavor to perform this *s·*
	54–32	* Mrs. Eddy preached at this *s·*

was repeated
Pul.	41–19	* Hence the *s·* was repeated until
	42– 5	* at 3 p. m. the *s·* was repeated

Pul.	29– 9	* *s·* held in Copley Hall.
	29–14	* pressed into *s·* for the
	66–17	* belief and *s·* are well suited to
My.	30– 2	* either coming from a *s·* or
	30–27	* for the *s·* at half past seven,
	38–16	* for the *s·* at half past twelve
	61–18	* ready for the *s·*, June 10."
	150– 9	* the *s·* of such a mission.

serviceable

Mis.	278–22	This may be a *s·* hint,

services

afternoon
My.	147– 5	morning and afternoon *s·*

after the
My.	50–32	* committee met after the *s·*

services
all the
   My. 22– 6   * attendance at all the *s*,
        30– 3   * As all the *s* were . . . the same
any
   Pul. 87– 2   * any *s* that may be held therein.
attended
   My. 141– 6   * *s* attended last Sunday [June 14] by
Church
   Man. 63– 8   Quarterly Lessons, read in Church *s*.
church
   Man. 72– 9   church *s* conducted by reading the
   Pul. 9–17   church *s* were maintained by
communion
   My. 56–32   * Our communion *s* and annual
conduct the
   My. 71–26   Readers who conduct the *s*
continuous
   Pul. 59– 6   * continuous *s* were held
dedicatory
   My. 29– 7   * incident of the dedicatory *s*
        58–29   * attended the dedicatory *s*
        82–14   * At the dedicatory *s* of
        94–20   * dedicatory *s* were being held
      195– 5   invitation to the dedicatory *s*
desire for
   My. 54–21   * desire for *s* was so great
Easter
   Mis. 177–21   chapter sub-title
four
   Pul. 57– 7   * at the four *s* on the day of
gratuitous
   Mis. 349–27   to receive my gratuitous *s*,
identical
   My. 86–30   * At each of the identical *s*,
introductory
   My. 80–16   * introductory *s* were identical,
menial
   Pul. 8–18   never before devoted to menial *s*,
morning
   Man. 59–24   come to attend the morning *s*.
my
   Ret. 40– 3   refusing to take any pay for my *s*
   My. 244–27   No charge will be made for my *s*.
      325–12   * Years ago I offered my *s*
of Sunday
   My. 66–27   * *s* of Sunday will mark an epoch
order of the
   My. 16–21   * The order of the *s*,
other
   Man. 58–15   shall be repeated at the other *s*
public
   Mis. 299–14   * and read them for our public *s*?"
      301–21   and read them for our public *s*?"
   Man. 74– 2   C. S. society holding public *s*,
   My. 51–11   * to have the public *s* discontinued
regular
   Pul. 68–17   * It now holds regular *s*
secure the
   My. 63– 2   * secure the *s* of Mr. Whitcomb
six
   My. 66–22   * when six *s* will be held,
       78– 3   * six *s*, identical in character,
Sunday
   Mis. 176– 4   chapter sub-title
      302–15   through C. S. Sunday *s*.
      314– 3   From this date the Sunday *s*
      382–29   denominational form of Sunday *s*,
   Man. 31–17   principal part of the Sunday *s*,
       61– 5   not hold two or more Sunday *s*
   My. 54–19   * the Sunday *s* was postponed.
      55–19   * In the mean time Sunday *s*
      55–26   * in that place Sunday *s* were held
      56– 7   * inauguration of two Sunday *s*
their
   Rud. 14– 3   must give Him all their *s*,
       14– 5   suitable price for their *s*,
these
   Pul. 42– 8   * exercises at any one of these *s*.
those
   Pul. 81– 5   * than it was during those *s*,
three
   My. 56–29   * three *s* were held each Sunday,
two
   My. 56– 4   * in consequence two *s* were held,
uninterrupted
   Man. 60– 2   *s* UNINTERRUPTED.
valuable
   My. 62–26   * valuable *s* rendered to this Board
      63– 5   * and for their valuable *s*,
Wednesday evening
   Man. 31–21   of the Wednesday evening *s*,

   Man. 60– 4   *s* of The Mother Church
      72–14   *s* of such a church may be
   My. 31–25   * soloist for the *s*, Mrs. Hunt,

services
   My. 32– 2   * striking features of the *s*.
      51–30   * all who have attended the *s*,
      53–11   * The *s* were held there until
      61–10   * announcement that the *s* would
      62–29   * also the *s* of other members
      78–14   * at the beginning of the *s*
      78–21   * remarkable features of the *s*
     141–12   * announcement in regard to the *s*
serving
   Mis. 7–12   if *s* Christ, Truth,
      303–16   If ever I wear out from *s* students,
   Man. 67–24   Opportunity for *S* the Leader.
       68–10   Members thus *s* the Leader
   Ret. 90– 5   while he is *s* another fold?
   Pul. 38–29   * *s* those who find in one form
   '00. 10–29   for a soldier *s* his country
   My. 287– 8   *s* as admonition, instruction, and
servitude
   '00. 3– 9   worker's *s* is duly valued,
   My. 218–25   My private life is given to a *s*
session
   Mis. 134–11   at the annual *s* of the National
      136–22   I recommend that the June *s*
   My. 39– 2   * a second *s* was held at two o'clock
sessions
   Mis. 136–24   hold three *s* annually,
   Man. 57–10   (excepting its regular *s*)
      90– 8   *S*.
      90–11   *s* will continue not over one week.
      90–14   shall be present at the *s*,
   Pul. 4–29   used, in all its public *s*,
   My. 82–15   * at the *s* of the annual meeting,
     121– 4   in order to separate these *s* from
set
   Mis. 9–23   *s* it aside as tasteless
      71–11   Does C. S. *s aside the law of*
      72–15   teeth are *s* on edge— *Ezek.* 18 : 2.
      76–15   to *s* a human soul free from its
     133–19   to *s* you right on this question,
     187–16   as *s* forth in original Holy Writ.
     194–31   *s* forth in the text,
     214– 6   to *s* a man at variance— *Matt.* 10 : 35.
     255– 3   *s* themselves on pedestals,
     323– 2   "a city *s* upon a hill,"— *see Matt.* 5 : 14.
     337–12   *s* him in the midst of— *Matt.* 18 : 2.
     345– 8   * "I will *s* the beasts upon you,
     345–11   *s* fire to the fagots,
     353–14   *s* a man who applied for work,
     353–27   *s* up housekeeping alone.
     361–19   race that is *s* before us,— *Heb.* 12 : 1.
   Man. 51– 1   By-Laws or Rules herein *s* forth,
   Ret. 2– 5   *s* forth in the pages of
      22–11   joy that was *s* before him— *Heb.* 12 : 2.
      22–12   *s* down at the right hand of— *Heb.* 12 : 2.
      38–10   I *s* to work, contrary to my
      50– 1   impelled me to *s* a price on
      62– 4   find that the views here *s* forth
      79–23   jewels of Love, *s* in wisdom.
      95– 7   * And *s* apart Unto a life of
   Un. 1– 3   may be *s* down as one of the
   Pul. 16– 1   *S* to the Church Chimes
      21–30   Popularity, . . . must be *s* aside.
      49–26   * the will of the woman *s* at work,
      54–22   * they are fully *s* forth.
      58–13   * In the belfry is a *s* of
      59–28   * seats were especially *s* apart
      60–11   * Scripture parallels, as *s* down
      76– 5   * superb archway . . . *s* in the wall.
      81– 6   * *s* forth as the power of God
   Rud. 7– 6   *s* forth in my work S. and H.
   Pan. 14– 4   *S* your affections on things above ;
   '01. 6–20   which is *s* aside to some degree,
   '02. 9–13   Loving chords *s* discords in harmony.
   Peo. 13–21   *s* fire to the fagots,
   Po. 1–10   from chaos dark *s* free,
      68–20   star of our friendship arose not to *s* ;
   My. 22–18   * every purpose she has *s* in motion,
      36–28   * and *s* up this tabernacle,
      43–17   * were *s* up on the other side
      67–18   * Two million dollars was *s* aside
      71– 1   * a *s* of cathedral chimes,
      71–20   * traditions . . . have been *s* aside
      72– 2   * necessary to *s* aside the traditions
      80– 7   * when having broken bones *s* ;
      85–20   * another "landmark" *s* in the illustrious
      91– 7   * Christian Scientists *s* a good example
      96–22   * before the day *s* for the dedication
     103–18   I have *s* forth C. S.
     133–15   *s* the captive sense free
     155–14   the race *s* before it,
     161– 2   paid our debt and *s* us free
     179– 2   synoptic Scriptures, as *s* forth in
     197–20   for the hope *s* before us

set
My. 214–11	*s·* the seal of eternity on time.
216– 1	plainly *s·* forth in the Scriptures.
258–14	for the joy that was *s·* before him
258–16	and is *s·* down at the right hand of
310–24	* *s·* the house in an uproar,''

sets
Mis. 72– 4	Science *s·* aside man as a creator,
101–17	and *s·* the captive free,
329– 6	*s·* the earth in order ;
Pul. 62–22	* little *s·* of silver bells
80–19	* speak of the system it *s·* forth,
Po. 3– 9	Till sleep *s·* drooping fancy free

setting
Ret. 27– 2	*s·* forth their spiritual
My. 203–12	nor by *s·* up to be great,
248– 7	You are not *s·* up to be great ;

settings
My. 12–29	gems in the *s·* of manhood

settle
Mis. 265–27	constantly called to *s·* questions
Pul. 9–15	and helped *s·* the subject.
My. 181– 2	to *s·* all points beyond cavil,
277–20	can *s·* all questions amicably
358–15	will *s·* the question whether or not
360–13	if I can *s·* this church difficulty

settled
Mis. 165–25	accordingly as this account is *s·*
224–22	with an equanimity so *s·*
Ret. 87– 9	*s·* and systematic workers,
Pul. 51–10	* There is really nothing *s·*.
My. 277– 4	*s·* peacefully by statesmanship
286– 9	wisely, fairly ; and fully *s·*.

settlement
My. 279–24	amicable *s·* of the war

settlers
No. 46–14	first *s·* of New Hampshire.

settles
Mis. 192–31	This declaration . . . *s·* the question ;
204–15	This mental condition *s·* into strength,
'02. 12– 4	*s·* the whole question on the basis that
My. 277–10	never *s·* the question of his life.

settling
Mis. 380– 1	and *s·* the question,
My. 277– 7	no other way of *s·* difficulties
309– 5	making out deeds, *s·* quarrels,

set-to
Mis. 231–22	instead of a real *s·* at crying,

seven
Mis. 279–17	*s·* times around these walls,
279–17	the *s·* times corresponding to
279–18	the *s·* days of creation :
348–18	once in about *s·* years
Man. 62– 1	six or *s·* minutes for the postlude,
Pul. 6–17	* an ailment of *s·* years' standing.
37–27	* was organized . . . by *s·* persons,
58–14	* *s·* excellent class-rooms,
67–26	* was organized by *s·* persons,
No. 23–11	Out of . . . Jesus cast *s·* devils ;
Pan. 3–28	His pipe of *s·* reeds denotes
3–29	harmony of the *s·* planets ;
'00. 12– 3	''holdeth the *s·* stars — *Rev.* 2 : 1.
12– 4	*s·* golden candlesticks'' — *Rev.* 2 : 1.
14– 6	He goes on to portray *s·* churches,
'02. 13– 5	During the last *s·* years
My. 30–28	* for the service at half past *s·*,
30–32	* Before half past *s·* the chimes
68–28	* *s·* broad marble stairways,
69–16	* auditorium contains *s·* galleries,
70–28	* *s·* combination pedals,
80–31	* long before *s·* the auditorium
	(*see also* **numbers, values**)

seven-eighths
Rud. 14– 9	gave fully *s·* of her time

seven-fold
My. 200–18	*s·* shield of honesty, purity,

seven-hued
Chr. 53–38	now blends In *s·* white !

seven-pointed
Pul. 25–17	* sunburst with a *s·* star,
42–21	* a huge *s·* star was hung

seventeen
Ret. 50–16	as many as *s·* in one class.
Rud. 14–14	sometimes *s·*, free students
My. 311–14	at the age of *s·*

seventeenth
Ret. 2–19	*s·* and eighteenth centuries.
My. 221–32	In the *s·* chapter of the Gospel

seventh
Mis. 225– 9	*s·* modern wonder, C. S. ;
279–19	the *s·* is the day of rest,
My. 336– 2	* would have died on the *s·* day.

seventieth
Mis. 191– 8	John, sixth chapter and *s·* verse,

seventy-eight
(*see* **numbers**)

seventy-fifth
(*see* **numbers**)

seventy-five
(*see* **values**)

seventy-four
My. 148–17	membership of *s·* communicants,

Seventy-third Edition
Man. 104–12	*S·* Edition the Authority.
104–15	keep a copy of the *S·* Edition

seventy-two
My. 69– 3	* each suspending *s·* lamps,
70–26	* *s·* stops, nineteen couplers,

several
Mis. 141–29	return . . . to the *s·* contributors,
144–10	on which appear your *s·* names
169–28	* Taking *s·* Bible passages,
191–19	*s·* individuals cast out of
226– 6	after eating *s·* ice-creams,
348–26	Hence I tried *s·* doses of
349–18	and *s·* other students with him.
378– 9	in company with *s·* other patients,
Man. 28–17	the functions of their *s·* offices
77–15	performance of their *s·* offices
Pul. 23–12	* under *s·* different aspects
42–10	* presence of *s·* hundred children
57–22	* *s·* sects of mental healers,
69– 8	* after *s·* doctors had pronounced
Rud. 14–13	without *s·*, . . . free students in it ;
No. 22–21	That Jesus cast *s·* persons out of
Hea. 3–17	Josephus alludes to *s·* individuals
My. 55– 5	* *S·* places were considered,
73–14	* as they have been for *s·* days past
73–15	* and will be for *s·* days to come,
78– 9	* series of arches in the *s·* facades.
216–23	work in your own *s·* localities,
243– 3	the *s·* churches in New York City
314– 6	* doctor practised in *s·* towns,
320–20	* I called on Mr. Wiggin *s·* times
320–21	* *s·* times subsequent thereto,
320–28	* I saw Mr. Wiggin *s·* times
346–12	* made *s·* turns about the court-house
	(*see also* **years**)

severe
Mis. 35– 5	*s·* casualty pronounced . . . incurable,
107–29	and repentance so *s·* that it
203–21	gain *s·* views of themselves ;
256–11	this imposes on me the *s·* task of
Ret. 80– 4	gentle, yet it may seem *s·*.
Pul. 34– 6	* met with a *s·* accident,
No. 5– 6	*s·* realities of this error.
41–15	is to subject them to *s·* scrutiny.
'00. 2–24	more sudden, *s·*, and lasting
My. 80– 8	* *s·* tax upon frail human credulity,
149–32	no condition, be it ever so *s·*,
190–15	failing to cure a *s·* case of lunacy,

severed
Mis. 105–21	his ideal can never be *s·*.
386–13	''When, *s·* by death's dream,
Po. 49–19	''When, *s·* by death's dream,
My. 129–17	never *s·* from Spirit !

severely
Mis. 12– 7	punish, more *s·* than you could,

severest
My. 103– 3	summons the *s·* conflicts of the ages

severs
Mis. 285–23	*s·* the marriage covenant,

sex
Man. 50– 4	by *one of her own s·*.
Pul. 82–21	* for their people, not for their *s·*.
82–24	* singing most for their own *s·*.
My. 239–25	a kind of man who is identified by *s·*
249–27	without reference to *s·* I should
268–30	*s·* or gender eliminated ;

sexes
No. 45–19	vindicated by the noblest of both *s·*.
My. 247– 9	equality of the *s·*, rotation in office.
255– 2	equality of the *s·*, rotation in office.''

shackle
Mis. 246–17	to *s·* conscience, stop free speech,

shackles
My. 44– 3	* the *s·* of sin are being broken,

shade
Mis.	392– 9	Thy sheltering *s·*,
	396–16	Beneath the maple's *s·*.
	399– 3	will lift the *s·* of gloom,
Ret.	90– 2	*s·* God's window which lets in light,
Un.	27– 4	really have a *s·* of difference
Pul.	2–10	Material light and *s·* are temporal,
	63–11	* *s·* her delightful country home
Pan.	3–16	* or in thy evening *s·*,
Po.	20–12	Thy sheltering *s·*,
	29–14	Was but thy *s·* !
	59– 8	Beneath the maple's *s·*.
	67–15	*s·* o'er the dark wavy grass.
	75–10	will lift the *s·* of gloom,
My.	107–22	or scatter the *s·* of one who
	166–14	Days of *s·* and shine
	342–12	* *s·* of which is so hard to catch,

shaded
Mis.	142–18	*s·* as autumn leaves

shades
Mis.	1–21	seemingly rolled up in *s·*,
	372–30	gives scopes and *s·* to the
Pul.	48– 8	* in the lights and *s·* of spring
Rud.	16–23	Minor *s·* of difference in
Po.	78– 8	*S·* of our heroes !

shading
Po.	53– 5	And soft thy *s·* lay

shadow
Mis.	33– 9	*s·* of Truth's appearing
	88–16	in the *s·* of darkling criticism
	105–22	the *s·* cast by this error.
	131–10	so *s·* forth the substance
	134–15	is bigger than the *s·*,
	144–17	*s·* of a great rock — *Isa.* 32 : 2.
	157–14	under the *s·* of His wing.
	180– 5	dark *s·* and portal of death,
	203–16	topically as type and *s·*.
	231– 5	had seen sunshine and *s·*
	239– 8	my *s·* is not growing less ;
	253–20	type and *s·* of this hour.
	263– 9	*s·* of a great rock — *Isa.* 32 : 2.
	368– 9	* Standeth God within the *s·*,
	386– 2	Beyond the *s·*, infinite appear
	389–18	Beneath the *s·* of His mighty wing ;
Chr.	55– 9	the *s·* of death, — *Isa.* 9 : 2.
Ret.	18–25	This life is a *s·*, and hastens
	21–16	"as the *s·* when it — *see Psal.* 102 : 11.
	25–14	I called *error* and *s·*.
Un.	14–18	neither *s·* of turning." — *Jas.* 1 : 17.
	27–14	fleeing like a *s·* at daybreak ;
	40– 4	this dark *s·* of material sense,
	57– 7	*s·* of the Almighty." — *Psal.* 91 : 1.
	63– 9	no variableness or *s·* of turning,
Pul.	20–15	type and *s·* of the warfare
	20–16	*s·* whose substance is the
	20–19	*s·* of a great rock — *Isa.* 32 : 2.
Po.	4–17	*s·* of His mighty wing ;
	23– 1	a *s·* on thy brow
	42– 1	there's never a *s·* where
	49– 4	Beyond the *s·*, infinite appear
	64–22	This life is a *s·*,
My.	107–23	*s·* of the Almighty"? — *Psal.* 91 : 1.
	182–21	Love that reigns above the *s·*,
	190– 1	Did that midnight *s·*,
	206–14	through the *s·* called death,
	210–15	under the *s·* of the Almighty.
	260– 7	and the *s·* of frivolity,
	268–21	flutters . . . as an unreal *s·*,
	290–20	has passed earth's *s·*
	294–29	through the *s·* of death
	350–21	Stygian *s·* of a world of glee

shadowed
Un.	5–25	*s·* forth in scientific thought.

shadows
Mis.	71–28	human concepts, mortal *s·*
	205– 5	melting away the *s·* called sin,
	222–32	dawns the morning light and *s·* flee,
	264– 8	*s·* thrown upon the mists of time,
	329–21	challenging the sedentary *s·* to
	352–11	human *s·* of thought lengthen
	372–30	shades to the *s·* of divinity,
Ret.	21–17	heavenly intent of earth's *s·*
Un.	44– 6	are vain *s·*, repeating
Po.	3– 4	When noonday's length'ning *s·* flee,
	8– 1	sitting alone where the *s·* fall
	24–15	Come when the *s·* fall,
	30–15	dark *s·* cast on Thy blest name,
My.	19–18	our *s·* follow us in the sunlight
	184–19	a love which stays the *s·* of years.

shadowy
Un.	46– 2	These are the *s·* and false,
Po.	25– 6	*s·* throng Around you in memory rise !
	27– 6	grow tremulous with *s·* night !

shaft
My.	128–28	*s·* aimed at you or your practice

shafts
Mis.	277– 8	becomes the mark for error's *s·*.

shake
Mis.	330–14	to *s·* out their tresses
Hea.	12–21	cannot *s·* the poor drug without

shaken
No.	22–11	reeds *s·* by the wind.
My.	21–19	* pressed down, and *s·* — *Luke* 6 : 38.
	108–27	* "Mrs. Eddy not *s·*"
	117– 6	"a reed *s·* with the wind," — *Matt.* 11 : 7.

Shakers
My.	313–22	interested in the *S·*,

Shakespeare (*see also* Shakespeare's)
Mis.	8–21	*S·* writes : "Sweet are the uses of
	226–13	*S·*, the immortal lexicographer
	267–15	signature
Ret.	81–22	*S·* puts this pious counsel into

Shakespearean
Un.	23– 9	How well the *S·* tale agrees with

Shakespeare's
Un.	22–23	In *S·* tragedy of King Lear,

shaking
Hea.	13– 6	*s·* the preparation thirty times

shallow
Mis.	265–15	egotistical theorist or *s·* moralist
	296– 9	to overflow in *s·* sarcasm,
	357–14	on stony ground and *s·* soil.

sham
Mis.	250–19	cast aside the word as a *s·* and
	365–24	infidelity, bigotry, or *s·* has never

shambles
Mis.	269–25	C. S. may be sold in the *s·*.
	285–24	puts virtue in the *s·*,

shame
Mis.	267–17	suffered temporary *s·* and loss
	296–31	his *s·* would not lose its blush !
Ret.	22–12	despising the *s·*, — *Heb.* 12 : 2.
Un.	56– 8	"put him to an open *s·*." — *Heb.* 6 : 6.
My.	258–15	despising the *s·*, — *Heb.* 12 : 2.

shamed
Mis.	332–21	*s·* the face of mortals.
Pul.	83– 4	* our better self is *s·* and

shameful
Peo.	13–14	forcing from the lips of manhood *s·*

shameless
Mis.	121–24	*s·* insult to divine royalty,
	210–25	*s·* brow of licentiousness,

shamelessness
My.	340–16	shorn of some of its *s·*

shames
Mis.	183–23	while it *s·* human pride.

shape
Pan.	11–18	in order to be in proper *s·*,
My.	65–20	* in the *s·* of a triangle,
	66– 3	* in the *s·* of a triangle,
	67– 7	* *S·*, triangular . . . 220x220x236 ft.

shapeless
Peo.	7–12	* carved the dream on that *s·* stone

share
Mis.	290–26	*s·* the benefit of that radiation.
	290–30	all who are receptive *s·* this
	321–24	to *s·* the hospitality of their
	391–17	*S·* God's most tender mercies,
Pul.	51–27	* *s·* of attention it deserves,
'01.	16–12	surviving defamers *s·* our pity.
	35–17	the working hitherto — Shall we *s·* it
Po.	38–16	*S·* God's most tender mercies,
My.	83–31	* *s·* of the necessary expense
	120–10	*s·* with me the bliss of seeing the
	218–26	fruit of which all mankind may *s·*.
	220–30	*s·* alike liberty of conscience,
	244– 4	wish to *s·* this opportunity
	317– 6	* that Mr. Wiggin had a *s·* in the

shared
Mis.	55– 7	as much . . . as he *s·*,
	278–19	have *s·* less of my labors
	369–23	which he *s·* with the swine,
My.	51–30	* gratitude *s·* by all who

shares
Un.	56–14	*s·* his cup of sorrows.
My.	217–11	equal *s·* to each contributor.

sharing
Mis.	239–21	Her apparent pride at *s·*
My.	63–19	* *s·* in our joy.

Sharon's
Chr.	53–31	*S·* rose must bud and bloom

sharp
Mis.	13– 5	s· return of evil for good
	246–15	another s· cry of oppression.
	396– 5	cricket's s·, discordant scream
Pan.	12–15	the burden of s· experience
	12–27	by bold conjecture's s· point,
'00.	15–15	it yields to s· conviction
Peo.	7–13	* With many a s· incision.
	7–21	* With many a s· incision,
Po.	58–17	cricket's s·, discordant scream
My.	69– 6	* no s· angles are visible,
	244–18	a struggle or s· experience,

sharper
'02.	13– 4	incurred a s· fire from enmity.

sharply
Mis.	277–29	and s· lighten on the cloud of
Ret.	8–20	Mehitable then said s·,

shattered
Pul.	9– 7	never be s· in our hearts,

shatters
My.	296– 4	and s· whatever hinders the

sheathed
Ret.	11– 9	The sword is s·,
Po.	60– 6	The sword is s·,
My.	185– 9	nor will it be s· till Truth

sheaves
Mis.	313–20	the rich s· are ripe,
	332–10	hues of heaven, ripened s·,
Po.	47–20	are the s· and the gladness
My.	170–30	bearing your s· with you.
	202–26	bringing your s· into the
	291–25	her s· garnered, her treasury filled,

shed
Mis.	65–31	shall his blood be s·."— Gen. 9 : 6.
	385–25	faith . . . . s· Majestic forms ;
Ret.	17–11	when the dewdrop is s·
	81– 3	The unavailing tear is s·
Po.	9– 9	leaves all faded, the fruitage s·,
	25–11	Sweetly to s· Fragrance fresh
	46– 6	Its leaves have s· or bowed the
	47–15	Over the tears it has s· ;
	48–22	faith . . . s· Majestic forms ;
	62–14	when the dewdrop is s·
My.	62–12	* s· its brightest beams on your
	91–12	* and s· sunshine about them
	294–31	s· "the unavailing tear."
	347–12	* boughs, that cannot s· Your leaves,

sheddeth
Mis.	65–30	"whoso s· man's blood,— Gen. 9 : 6.

shedding
No.	33–20	though s· human blood
My.	350–14	the scalding tear man's s·,

sheep (see also sheep's)
Mis.	151– 1	folds the s· of His pasture ;
	151– 3	"My s· hear my voice,— John 10 : 27.
	213–22	"My s· hear my voice,— John 10 : 27.
	244–24	"And other s· I have,— John 10 : 16.
	357– 5	Let them seek the lost s·
	370–29	separate the s· from the goats ;
	397–21	poem — John 21 : 16.
	397–25	How to feed Thy s· ;
Ret.	page 46	poem — John 21 : 16.
	46– 6	How to feed Thy s· ;
	52–11	provide folds for the s·
	80–23	the older s· pass into the fold
	85–24	scatter the s· abroad ;
Pul.	17– 1	poem — John 21 : 16.
	17– 5	How to feed Thy s· ;
Po.	page 14	poem — John 21 : 16.
	14– 4	How to feed Thy s· ;

sheepcot
Ret.	80–23	carries his lambs . . . to the s·,

sheep's
Mis.	294–18	from wolves in s· clothing
	323–13	wolves in s· clothing are ready to
	325– 6	Christian Scientists in s· clothing ;
	370–20	a wolf in s· clothing?
My.	215–21	wolves in s· clothing,"— see Matt. 7 : 15.

sheer
Mis.	230–17	spend no time in s· idleness,
Un.	16– 4	would they be s· nonsense,
No.	43–26	through the s· ignorance of people,

sheet
Man.	98–12	shall read the last proof s·

shelf
Mis.	250–14	not something put upon a s·,

shelter
Mis.	154– 5	reaching out their broad s·
	347– 8	people prepare s· in caves
	362–25	find s· from the storm

shelter
Ret.	52– 5	should s· its perfections
Pul.	10–24	s· of this house,
My.	147– 7	flung its foliage in kindly s·
	182–28	find s· from the storm

sheltered
Mis.	14–31	But the sinner is not s·
	152–24	s· in the strong tower
Rud.	13–27	to be fed, clothed, and s·

sheltering (see also shelt'ring)
Mis.	392– 9	pouring down Thy s· shade,
Po.	20–12	pouring down Thy s· shade,
My.	36–25	* by this s· dome ;

shelt'ring
Mis.	387– 8	Brood o'er us with Thy s· wing,
Po.	6– 1	Brood o'er us with Thy s· wing,

Shepherd
Mis.	9– 6	Well is it that the S· of Israel
	150– 3	you have the great S· of Israel
	150–31	hence God is our S·.
	275–14	May the great S· that
	322–14	S· that feedeth my flock,
	357– 7	have lost their great S·
	357–28	the true fold and the great S·,
	370–28	good S· does care for all,
	371– 6	the care of the great S·,
	397–22	S·, show me how to go
	398–20	S·, wash them clean.
Ret.	46– 3	S·, show me how to go
	46–26	S·, wash them clean.
Pul.	17– 2	S·, show me how to go
	17–25	S·, wash them clean.
Po.	14– 1	S·, show me how to go
	14–24	S·, wash them clean.
My.	31– 3	"S·, show me how to go ;"
	162–25	S· of this feeble flock
	177–19	the great S· has nurtured

shepherd (see also shepherd's)
Mis.	162–31	simple as the s· boy,
	270–19	one fold, and one s· ;"— John 10 : 16.
	303– 5	kindly s· has his own fold
	321– 2	watchful s· chants his welcome
	370–27	the good s· cares for all
Chr.	55–25	one fold, and one s·.— John 10 : 16.
Ret.	80–22	The kindly s· of the East
	90– 4	Does the faithful s· forsake
My.	257– 4	To-day the watchful s·

Shepherd of Israel
Mis.	150– 3	S· of I· watching over you.

shepherd's
Mis.	195–25	s· sling would slay this Goliath.
Pan.	3–29	his s· crook, that care and

shepherds
Mis.	168–19	s· shout, "We behold the
Ret.	52–11	sheep that were without s·,
Pan.	3–26	Pan was the god of s·

shibboleth
No.	9–22	Science is not the s· of a sect

shield
Mis.	113–25	our hope, strength, and s·.
	358–10	his s· and great reward.
Un.	11– 1	to s· them from the penalty
'01.	32–11	s· the whole world in their hearts,
'02.	14– 7	life-giving spiritual s·
	19–13	his s· and his buckler.
Po.	43–12	S· and guide and guard them ;
My.	200–18	the seven-fold s· of honesty,
	292–10	O may His love s , support,

shielded
Pan.	14–24	s· by the power that saved
'02.	14–24	What has s· and prospered
My.	210– 9	s· from the attacks of error

shift
Mis.	233–20	a poor s· for the weak
	288–23	the s· of a dishonest mind,
My.	287–11	a poor s· for the weak

shifting
Mis.	13–19	the s· mortal senses confirm
Ret.	81–27	s· scenes of human happiness,
Un.	14–19	the s· vane on the spire

shifts
Mis.	286–17	put ingenuity to ludicrous s· ;
'01.	29–20	waiting till the wind s·.
Peo.	3–25	certain unspiritual s·, such as

shimmer
Pul.	2– 7	soft s· of its starlit dome.
	76–10	* which in certain lights has a s·

shine
Mis.	54– 4	Has the sun forgotten to s·,
	303– 2	s· from their home summits

shine
Mis. 340–29 s· with the reflected light of God.
Hea. 20– 4 * Which in our Saviour s·,
Po.   70–22 S· on our 'wildered way,
      79– 3 storm or s·, pure peace is thine,
My. 166–14 Days of shade and s· may come
     183–27 "Arise, s· ; for thy light is— *Isa.* 60 : 1.
     191–11 Let your light s·.
     206–21 neither of the moon, to s·— *Rev.* 21 : 23.
     355–22 s· with the reflection of light

shined
Chr. 55– 9 upon them hath the light s·.— *Isa.* 9 : 2.

shines
Mis. 363–18 His manifold wisdom s· through the
Ret. 57–15 Man s· by borrowed light.
Un.   58–20 midnight sun s· over the Polar Sea.
Pul. 28– 4 * star of Bethlehem s· down
      83–25 * royalty which s· from her brow.
'02. 17–20 sun s· but to show man the
My. 110– 7 and it s· as of yore,
     301– 2 it s· with borrowed rays
     355–25 and their light s·.

shineth
Mis. 368– 3 light that s· in darkness,
Un.   63–10 light which s· in darkness,
My. 110– 8 "s· in darkness ; — *John* 1 : 5.

shining
Mis. 171–29 all clad in the s· mail
     205– 4 s· through the mists of materiality
My. 355–20 * He hides a s· face."

Shintoism
'02.   3– 5 Buddhism and S· are said to

ship
Pul. 80– 2 * s· when under stress of storm

shipwreck
Mis. 268–16 suffers no s· in a starless night

shirk
Un.   26– 7 I s· all responsibility for myself

shoals
Mis. 268–17 on the s· of vainglory.
     363–22 avoid the s· of a sensual religion

shock
Mis. 397–11 waves can s·, Oh, nevermore !
Pul. 18–20 waves can s·, Oh, nevermore !
Rud. 15– 6 is a s· to the mind ;
Po.   12–21 waves can s·, Oh, nevermore !
      18–18 and earthquakes may s·,

shocked
Mis. 210–16 will not be s· when she
Pul. 14– 5 s· into another extreme mortal mood,
      74– 2 * chapter sub-title

shocking
Mis. 112–26 s· inability to see one's own faults,
     350– 5 * not "terrible and too s· to relate."
No.   29–18 such a statement is a s· reflection
      35–17 s· human idolatry that presupposes
My. 276–10 s· fact that she is minding her own

shockingly
Peo.   2–16 s· material in practice,

shocks
Pul. 74–15 "Even the question s· me.

shoes
Mis. 17– 8 you take off your s·
     120– 2 take off their s· at our altars ;
No.   27–25 take off thy s· and tread lightly,

shone
Chr. 53– 3 s· One lone, brave star.
Ret.   4–15 peaches, pears, and cherries s·
Peo.   7–14 * With . . . light the sculptor s·,

shoot
No.   3– 2 envy will bend its bow and s·

shore
Mis. 81–21 *has not Truth yet reached the s·?*
      82–11 stand upon the s· of eternity,
     111–10 will not pull for the s· ;
     206– 6 dashing against the receding s·,
     212– 7 On the s· of Gennesaret
     251– 5 from the Pacific to the Atlantic s·,
     385–14 Spirit emancipate for this far s·
     397–10 Life's s·, 'Gainst which the winds
     398– 9 Strangers on a barren s·,
Ret. 46–15 Strangers on a barren s·,
Pul. 17–14 Strangers on a barren s·,
      18–19 Life's s· ; 'Gainst which the winds
'02. 11– 1 to leave on a foreign s·.
Po.   12–19 Life's s·, 'Gainst which the winds
      14–13 Strangers on a barren s·,
      48– 7 Spirit emancipate for this far s·
      73– 5 hoarse wave revisits thy s· !
My. 126– 5 swimmer struggling for the s·,

shoreless
Mis. 82– 6 floweth . . . into a s· eternity.

shores
Mis. 176–16 sought the New England s·,
     205–31 Mortals who on the s· of time
     295–24 resound from Albion's s·.
     393–16 From the s· afar, complete.
Ret. 91–15 s· of the Lake of Galilee,
Pul. 10–10 On s· of solitude, at Plymouth Rock,
No.   2–21 along the s· of erudition ;
'02. 11– 3 to wander on the s· of time
Po.   51–21 From the s· afar, complete.
My. 232– 5 looms of love that line the sacred s·.

shorn
Mis. 275–14 * "tempers the wind to the s· lamb,"
Hea. 18–25 no blind Samson s· of his locks.
My. 205–23 C. S., s· of all personality,
     340–16 s· of some of its shamelessness by

short
Mis. 24–15 That s· experience included a
     125–19 meanings of these s· sentences :
     224–28 Nothing s· of our own errors
     233–27 if some fall s·, others will
     285–10 Human life is too s· for foibles
     288–24 nothing s· of self-seeking ;
     297– 1 Taking into account the s· time
     380– 4 in s·, how can sinful mortals
     389– 3 In s·, the right to work
Ret.   7– 3 after a s· illness,
       7–10 * throughout his s· life.
      79–19 s· of the wisdom requisite for
      82–23 or fall s· of other religionists ;
Pul. 12–15 he hath but a s· time.— *Rev.* 12 : 12.
      13–22 devil knoweth his time is s·.
'01.   2–15 if some fall s· of Truth,
      15–17 s· of the old orthodox hell
Po.   21–17 In s·, the right to work
My.   26–16 too s· to be printed in book form,
      39–11 * Then followed a s· silent prayer
      47–24 * the years . . . seem but a s· time.
      88– 6 * the development of a s· lifetime.
     114– 5 in s·, Do unto others
     173–23 Scientists' s· stay so pleasant.
     260–15 sense that falls s· of substance,
     262–10 falls far s· of my sense of the
     314– 3 * "lived for a s· time at Tilton,

shortcomings
Un.   14–11 s· of the Puritan's model?
My. 195–19 discontent with our s·.

shorten
Mis. 213– 7 point the way, s· the process,

shortened
Mis. 171– 1 "His hand is not s·— *see Isa.* 59 : 1.
My. 292– 6 way pointed out, the process s·,

shortens
'02. 10–21 reformer . . . s· the distance,

shorthand
Mis. 95– 8 * s· reporter who was present,

short-lived
Ret. 32–16 * S· joy, that ends in sadness,
No.   37– 7 license of a s· sinner,

shortly
My.   57–27 * S· before the dedication of
     311– 7 S· after, . . . my good housekeeper

short-sighted
Mis. 209–12 S· physics admits the

shot
Mis. 223–30 arrow s· from another's bow

shoulder
Mis. 161– 6 *shall be upon his s· :— Isa.* 9 : 6.
     166–12 shall be upon his s·."— *Isa.* 9 : 6.
     167–21 shall be upon his s· !"— *Isa.* 9 : 6.

shoulders
Ret. 16–14 carrying them on their s·.

shout
Mis. 168–19 shepherds s·, "We behold the appearing
     274–24 s· for class legislation,
     279–25 they had all to s· *together*
     342–17 they heard the s·,
     370– 9 sentinels of Zion's watch-towers s·
Po.   73– 6 waters s·, And the stars peep out,
My. 289–18 s· of love lives on in the heart

shouted
Mis. 259–21 sons of God s· for joy."— *Job* 38 : 7.
Un.   42–15 sons of God s· for joy."— *Job* 38 : 7.

shoutings
Mis. 400– 7 Dirge and song and s· low
Pul. 16–19 Dirge and song and s· low
Po.   76–18 Dirge and song and s· low

shouts
Mis.	328– 1	Stranger *s*, "Let them alone ;
	369– 2	look up with *s* and thanksgiving,
My.	257– 4	watchful shepherd *s* his welcome

shoveled
Pul.	8–18	Little hands, . . . *s* snow,

show
Mis.	ix– 4	* the best alms are to *s* and
	64– 4	to *s* his power over death ;
	100– 8	*s* the word and might of Truth
	100–15	finally *s* the fruits of Love.
	114–28	*s* us the powerlessness of evil,
	205–11	*s* it unto you." — *John* 16 : 15.
	212–28	and tries to *s* his errors to him
	221– 7	*s* the fundamental Principle of
	348–13	and *s* the plan of battle.
	363–32	*s* their marked consonance with
	397– 1	*s* Life's burdens light.
	397–22	Shepherd, *s* me how to go
Man.	41– 6	*s* the great gulf between C. S. and
	44– 2	writings must *s* strict adherence to
	85–14	unless he has a certificate to *s*
Ret.	11–15	Hero and sage arise to *s*
	25– 1	take the things of God and *s* them
	27– 7	*s* that after my discovery of
	40–24	simply to *s* the opposition
	46– 3	Shepherd, *s* me how to go
	90– 6	There is no evidence to *s*
Un.	18–17	*s* My pity through divine law,
	45–15	to *s* its all-pervading presence
Pul.	17– 2	Shepherd, *s* me how to go
	18–10	his unveiled, sweet mercies *s*
	50–27	* to *s* even some one side of it
	55– 3	* Not for *s* of power,
	67–10	* probably *s* a greater number
No.	9–21	and *s* the power of Love.
	33–26	his purpose was to *s* them
	35–11	to *s* the allness of Love
	35–14	to *s* mortals the awful price
'00.	7– 3	*s* the annual death-rate
'02.	17–21	*s* man the beauty of holiness
Hea.	3– 3	to *s* its helplessness.
	4–17	to *s* itself infinite again.
	5–24	"I will *s* thee my faith — *Jas.* 2 : 18.
Po.	12–10	*s* Life's burdens light.
	14– 1	Shepherd, *s* me how to go
	60–12	Hero and sage arise to *s*
My.	3–12	"*S* me thy faith — *Jas.* 2 : 18.
	28– 8	* will *s* the dollars and cents
	31– 3	"Shepherd, *s* me how to go ;"
	52–23	* reputation, time will *s*.
	57–24	*s* a membership of 41,944.
	76–15	* all of which goes to *s*
	97–12	* might *s* that the Scientists
	103– 8	*s* conclusively that C. S.
	106– 8	to *s* the folly of believing that
	110–23	should *s* us that even mortals
	117–30	to *s* others the footsteps
	156–16	*s* you a large upper room — *Luke* 22 : 12.
	163–13	cannot *s* my love for them
	177–18	*s* in livid lines that the
	181–25	*s* that thirty years ago
	199–14	*s* explicitly the attitude of
	206–24	*s* forth the praises — *I Pet.* 2 : 9.
	227–30	Statistics *s* that C. S.
	334–13	* which records *s* really existed

showed
Mis.	44– 2	pattern *s* to thee — *Heb.* 8 : 5.
	169–28	* Mrs. Eddy *s* how beautiful
	201–12	he also *s* forth the error
	248– 9	Greeks *s* a just estimate
Ret.	40–12	they *s* me the clothes
Un.	11– 9	He *s* the need of changing this mind
No.	21–11	*s* man as reflecting God
'02.	15–26	I *s* it to my literary friends,
My.	16– 4	* report . . . *s* that a total of
	38–14	* the visitors *s* a tendency to
	47–19	* *s* a forward effort
	56–25	* *s* that still further provision
	145– 6	He drew the plan, *s* it to me,
	288–23	*s* that every effect or amplification

shower
Mis.	390–18	When sunshine beautifies the *s*,
Po.	55–19	When sunshine beautifies the *s*,
	70– 3	A bright and golden *s*
My.	134–18	like a soft summer *s*,
	343–18	a *s* of abuse upon my head,

showers
Mis.	355–27	fall in mist and *s* from
Po.	46– 5	Nor April's changeful *s*,

showeth
Mis.	175– 3	*s* them unto the creature,
	261–17	*s* mercy by punishing sin.

showeth
Pan.	12–14	*s* to all peoples the way of escape
'01.	9–23	*s* them unto the creature ;

showing
Mis.	53–19	*s* his ignorance of the meaning of
	105–10	after *s* us the way to escape
	162–20	*s* mortals how to escape from
	245– 1	no record *s* that our Master ever
	285–21	*s* its relation to C. S.
	327–23	*s* them their folly,
	367– 8	*s* that error is not Mind,
Ret.	31– 4	*s* this solemn certainty in
Un.	11– 8	*s* them to be laws of mortal mind,
	25–17	by *s* God as its source.
Pul.	64–27	* *s* that belief in that curious
'01.	29–13	inapt or selfish in *s* their love.
'02.	6–12	a lie fathers itself, thereby *s*
	18–26	*s* their unfitness to follow him,
Hea.	12– 9	*s* he was right.
Peo.	9–20	*s* our greater faith in matter,
My.	24–13	* *s* that The Mother Church
	269– 3	*s* forth the infinite divine
	288–21	*s* that all suffering

shown
Mis.	11–12	*s* them the sure way of salvation,
	28–17	this great truth was *s* by
	70– 5	Thus it was *s* that the healing
	84– 1	Jesus' wisdom ofttimes was *s* by
	107–21	sense must first be *s* its falsity
	158–13	meaning of it all, as now *s*,
	312–15	* *s* in the raising up of the
	321–10	as *s* by the triumphs of Truth
	322–23	hath *s* you the amplitude of His mercy,
Man.	112– 4	as *s* on page 118.
Ret.	47– 9	Example had *s* the dangers
	50–10	God has since *s* me,
Un.	7– 4	*s* by the changes at Andover Seminary
	31–14	It can be *s*, in detail,
Pul.	44–20	* has *s* its power over its students,
	58–12	* Its appearance is *s* in the
	66–19	* has *s* an uncommon development
	74– 8	* was *s* to Mrs. Mary Baker Eddy,
	79–17	* has *s* a vitality so unexpected.
Rud.	15– 1	experience has *s* that this defrauds
No.	6–23	Copernicus has *s* that what
My.	22–13	* *s* the absolute necessity of giving.
	22–20	* she has *s* wisdom, faith, and
	25– 8	* by their contributions to the
	97– 7	* It has yet to be *s* that of the
	152–20	even as the ages have *s*.
	294–21	in what is *s* him by God's works
	325– 1	* kindnesses you had *s* them,
	328–24	* machinery act . . . was *s*,
	329–24	* *s* by the fair attitude of the press
	333– 5	* *s* that on the twenty-eighth day of

shows
Mis.	6–14	rapid growth of the work *s*.
	22–14	It *s* the impossibility of
	26–20	Natural history *s* that
	29–20	*s* that longevity has *increased.*
	72–24	*s* that nothing which is material
	112–24	*s* itself in extreme sensitiveness ;
	113–17	*s* that there is a way of escape
	148– 1	never *s* us a smiling countenance
	258–31	*s* that nature and man are as
	354–23	*s* that humility is the first step
	365–22	*s* the real value of C. S.
Pul.	23–19	* History *s* the curious fact that
	54–19	* *s* that he observed, in his practice
Rud.	8–23	*s* that he makes morally worse the
No.	11–25	Revelation *s* this Principle,
	15–21	*s* that matter and mortal mind
	16– 9	C. S. *s* that matter, evil,
	19– 4	*s* its real value to the race.
	22–18	*s* that the term devil is generic,
	39–22	*s* us more clearly than we saw
	39–23	it *s* us what God is.
Pan.	5–18	It *s* that evil is both liar and
	7– 3	Science *s* that a plurality of minds,
'00.	10–17	History *s* that error repeats itself
'01.	9– 4	C. S. *s* clearly that God is
	28–15	Sacred history *s* that those who
'02.	8– 9	*s* what true spirituality is,
My.	41–24	* *s* man that his real estate is one of
	58–12	* *s* the growth of this Cause,
	79–13	* *s* an enthusiasm for C. S.
	88– 6	* It *s* strength in all parts,
	111–16	*s* how to demonstrate it,
	134–29	* *s* her usual mental and physical
	160–24	*s* that hidden unpunished sin
	179–11	Science *s* to be an impossibility.
	190–11	*s* the latter not only equalling but
	268– 5	The frequency of divorce *s* that
	311–12	statement that the clerk's book *s*

shrank
Ret. 50– 8   I s' from asking it,

shrewd
My. 81–32   * hard-headed s' business men.

shriek
Mis. 326– 7   sufferers s' for help :

shrieked
Pan. 1– 7   winds of March have s'

shrill
Mis. 390– 6   The lark's s' song doth wake
Po. 55– 7   The lark's s' song doth wake
My. 38–35   * their s' trebles rising with
78–31   * joining with their s' voices

shrine
Mis. 159–21   offer at the s' of C. S.,
Ret. 18–14   as the s' Or fount of real joy
Po. 34–14   Divinely desolate the s' to paint?
43–13   when At some siren s'
64– 5   as the s' Or fount of real joy
71– 5   Knelt worshiping at mammon's s'.

shrines
My. 96– 9   * Mecca and the Hindu s',

shrink
My. 297– 3   s' from such salient praise.

shrubs
Pul. 48– 3   * dotted with beds of flowering s',

shrunk
Mis. 236– 6   until thought has s' from
My. 52–28   * authors would have s',

shuddered
Mis. 180–13   s' at her material approach ;

shudders
Mis. 141–13   s' at the freedom, might, and

shuffling
Ret. 79–10   in s' off scholastic rhetoric,

shun
Mis. 395–22   For joy, to s' my weary way,
Un. 49–27   commands mortals to s' or
Pul. 21–16   s' whatever would isolate us from
'00. 3–17   to s' him as their tormentor.
Po. 58– 7   to s' my weary way,

shuns
Ret. 47–10   C. S. s' whatever involves material

shut
Mis. 133–15   when thou hast s' thy door, — Matt. 6 : 6.
209– 5   wouldst s' the mouth of His prophets,
276–29   learned when the door is s'.
286–28   s' out all sense of other claims.
292–18   to s' out all opposite sense.
317–11   door to my teaching was s'
324– 5   The door is s'.
342–22   The door is s'.
Pan. 12–14   a door that no man can s' ;
'00. 9–10   s' their eyes and wait for a more
My. 188–19   s' me out from your presence,

shuts
Un. 41– 5   sin s' out the real sense of Life,
Rud. 8–20   This falsity s' against him the Truth

shutteth
'00. 14–22   openeth and no man s', — Rev. 3 : 7.
14–22   s' and no man openeth ;" — Rev. 3 : 7.

shutting
Mis. 24–19   s' out the true sense of Spirit.
276–28   thus s' out spiritual light.

shuttlecock
Mis. xi–18   s' of religious intolerance

sick (noun)
and sinful
Mis. 364– 8   to have healed, . . . the s' and sinful,
and sinner
No. 15– 1   falling on the s' and sinner,
and sorrowing
Mis. 133–23   divine blessing on the s' and sorrowing,
and suffering
My. 153– 3   in my name to the s' and suffering.
and the sinner
Mis. 3– 7   power to heal the s' and the sinner,
74–18   he healed the s' and the sinner ;
259–28   which heals the s' and the sinner,
Man. 92– 4   Healing the s' and the sinner with Truth
'00. 15–21   heal the s' and the sinner !
'02. 8–10   effects on the s' and the sinner.
My. 5–30   that heals the s' and the sinner.
158–20   heals the s' and the sinner
180– 2   healing the s' and the sinner.
are aided
Rud. 12–13   If the s' are aided in this mistaken
are being healed
My. 44– 2   * the s' are being healed,

sick (noun)
are healed
Mis. 171–19   By these signs . . . the s' are healed ;
364– 4   whereby the s' are healed,
Ret. 60–20   and the s' are healed.
Pul. vii–18   s' are healed and sinners saved,
My. 178– 6   s' are healed and sinners saved.
258– 2   is reformed and the s' are healed.
belief of the
Ret. 63–10   belief of the s' in the reality of
benefit the
Mis. 378–16   ask him how . . . could benefit the s'.
care of the
Man. 49–13   can take proper care of the s'.
cure of the
No. 6–11   consequent cure of the s',
30–26   cure of the s' demonstrates this
extended to the
Hea. 18–20   Jesus' mission extended to the s'
fear of the
Rud. 12– 8   or else quiet the fear of the s'
giving to the
Mis. 262–16   giving to the s' relief from pain ;
hands on the
Mis. 29– 1   lay hands on the s', — Mark 16 : 18.
192–30   lay hands on the s', — Mark 16 : 18.
248– 2   "lay hands on the s', — Mark 16 : 18.
248– 4   "lay hands on the s'" — Mark 16 : 18.
Ret. 35–17   lay hands on the s', — Mark 16 : 18.
Hea. 1– 4   lay hands on the s', — Mark 16 : 18.
8–10   lay hands on the s', — Mark 16 : 18.
19–27   lay hands on the s', — Mark 16 : 18.
Peo. 12– 5   lay hands on the s', — Mark 16 : 18.
My. 48– 2   * lay hands on the s', — Mark 16 : 18.
healed the
Mis. 28–28   healed the s' and raised the dead.
74–18   healed the s' and the sinner ;
Un. 11– 6   he healed the s',
Pul. 66– 3   * as it did when Christ healed the s'.
No. 1–20   Truth, and Love, which healed the s'
Pan. 5–24   healed the s', and saved sinners.
'01. 19–17   great Metaphysician healed the s',
My. 37–13   * Christ which has ever healed the s'.
107– 1   healed the s' as a token of their
288–23   cast out devils and healed the s'.
345–18   and healed the s'.
348–26   healed the s' and reformed the sinner
healeth the
Mis. 322–21   healeth the s' and cleanseth the
healing of the
Man. 47–14   in regard to the healing of the s'
My. 104–32   healing of the s', the saving of
182–16   healing of the s', the reforming of
healing the
Mis. 19– 8   healing the s' is far lighter than
25–18   healing the s', casting out evil,
25–30   drugs for healing the s',
30– 4   Jesus' example in healing the s'
39–29   work with God in healing the s',
55– 3   simplest problem . . . is healing the s',
60– 5   Jesus came healing the s'
71– 9   healing the s' is a very right thing
77–31   healing the s', casting out evils,
99–30   casting out evils and healing the s' ;
100– 9   healing the s' and reclaiming the
124–17   healing the s', cleansing the leper,
175– 2   casting out error and healing the s'.
187– 2   casting out evils, healing the s',
195–27   relative to healing the s',
247–16   demonstrate . . . by healing the s' ;
252–25   lost element, namely, healing the s'.
268–12   healing the s' and casting out error.
270–17   requisite for healing the s'.
308–15   only by healing the s'
Man. 16– 3   healing the s' and overcoming sin
43– 8   or for healing the s'.
92– 4   Healing the s' and the sinner
Ret. 65–23   casting out evils and healing the s' ;
66– 1   to be utilized in healing the s',
Pul. 72–27   * doing good and healing the s'.
Rud. 2–22   Is healing the s' the whole of Science?
8– 8   demonstrate C. S. in healing the s'?
14– 7   practising . . . healing the s'.
No. 12–19   casting out evil, healing the s',
43–14   * S. and H. is healing the s',
'00. 5–29   casting out . . . and in healing the s'.
'01. 4–10   Love . . . healing the s' ;
'02. 6–11   saving the sinner and healing the s'.
Peo. 5–21   demonstration . . . in healing the s'.
12–21   healing the s' and raising the dead
13– 8   casting out error and healing the s'.
My. v–16   * healing the s' and reforming the
4–28   healing the s' and saving the sinner.
58–23   * healing the s' and reforming the sinful,
110– 3   casting out evils, healing the s',
113–27   healing the s', and uplifting

sick (noun)

healing the

My.	122–29	healing the *s*· and saving sinners.
	126–13	casting out evil and healing the *s*·.
	128–22	preaching the gospel and healing the *s*·.
	150–21	healing the *s*·, bringing the
	153–26	casting out evil and healing the *s*·.
	155– 1	healing the *s*· and reforming
	180– 2	healing the *s*· and the sinner.
	231–12	qualified students for healing the *s*·,
	253– 2	healing the *s*·, soothing sorrow,
	270–27	anoints with Truth, . . . healing the *s*·.
	271– 6	healing the *s*· and reforming the
	301–17	but healing the *s*· is *not* sin.
	343–16	as I learned while healing the *s*·.

heals the

Mis.	193–13	heals the *s*·, casts out error,
	259–28	power of God which heals the *s*·
	379–26	Mind, that heals the *s*·
	380– 5	divine Principle heals the *s*·,
Man.	17–18	casts out error, heals the *s*·,
	92– 9	C. S. heals the *s*· quickly
Pul.	14–26	When God heals the *s*·
Rud.	15– 2	though it heals the *s*·.
No.	12– 3	heals the *s*· and exalts the race.
	15–12	Christianity that heals the *s*·
'02.	8–20	saves sinners and heals the *s*·
Hea.	12– 3	Mind instead of matter heals the *s*·.
	13–24	casts out error and thus heals the *s*·.
	18–22	Christ, Truth, heals the *s*·
My.	5–30	divine Mind that heals the *s*·
	28–22	* a religion which heals the *s*·
	106–29	he heals the *s*· without drugs
	107–17	that with these . . . he heals the *s*·.
	113– 2	heals the *s*· and reclaims sinners
	147–16	heals the *s*· and enlightens the
	158–20	it is the Spirit that heals the *s*·
	185–20	Christ, as aforetime, heals the *s*·,
	260–25	casts out evils, heals the *s*·,
	292–27	prayer of the righteous heals the *s*·,
	348–19	divine Mind heals the *s*·

heal the

Mis.	2– 2	power of . . . Love to heal the *s*·.
	3– 7	power to heal the *s*·
	4–30	mission of C. S. to heal the *s*·,
	5– 9	and ministers, to heal the *s*·
	17–21	divine power to heal the *s*·.
	35–16	*teach its readers to heal the s*·,
	37–15	heal the *s*·." — *Matt.* 10 : 8.
	38–19	to benefit the race, heal the *s*·,
	62–15	*essential to heal the s*·,
	194– 2	power of a drug to heal the *s*· !
	214–26	cannot heal the *s*·, and take
	225–12	power of Christ, . . . to heal the *s*·.
	247– 1	cast out error and heal the *s*·,
	326– 1	heal the *s*·, — *Matt.* 10 : 8.
	352–22	to heal the *s*· or the sinful.
Chr.	55–22	Heal the *s*·. — *Matt.* 10 : 8.
Ret.	36– 1	"Heal the *s*·," — *Matt.* 10 : 8.
	87–15	"heal the *s*·" — *Matt.* 10 : 8.
Pul.	22–13	to heal the *s*· in his name.
	29–18	* "heal the *s*·, — *Matt.* 10 : 8.
	66–12	* "heal the *s*·, — *Matt.* 10 : 8.
	69–21	* power to heal the *s*·.
	73–13	* to do good and heal the *s*·,
No.	6– 4	in order to heal the *s*·.
	14–19	"Heal the *s*·, — *Matt.* 10 : 8.
	21–27	A philosophy which cannot heal the *s*·
	40–23	cast out fear and heal the *s*·,
	41–21	"Heal the *s*·, — *Matt.* 10 : 8.
	42–15	and so heal the *s*·.
'00.	15–21	heal the *s*· and the sinner !
'01.	9–26	they cast out evils and heal the *s*·.
	25–13	which because of . . . heal the *s*· !
Hea.	2–25	to cast out error and heal the *s*·.
	3– 5	to cast out error, and heal the *s*·.
	7–28	and ability of Christians to heal the *s*· ;
	8– 4	pray to heal the *s*· ;
	11–26	imbued with Truth to heal the *s*· ;
Peo.	4–27	false ideals . . . cannot heal the *s*·
	8– 3	cast out error and heal the *s*·.
	8– 6	incompetency that cannot heal the *s*·,
	9–18	divine aid of Spirit to heal the *s*·,
My.	5–17	heal the *s*·, reform the sinner,
	46–16	* preach the gospel and heal the *s*·
	51–15	* to heal the *s*· and reform the sinner.
	51–32	* to heal the *s*·, and reform the sinner,
	52–14	* Life, and Love, . . . does heal the *s*·,
	52–18	* heal the *s*·, and preach the gospel,
	109–11	taught his followers to heal the *s*·,
	114– 5	cast out evil and heal the *s*·
	150–27	sent them forth to heal the *s*·
	152– 5	were supposed to heal the *s*·,
	172–16	'heal the *s*·,' — *Matt.* 10 : 8.
	192– 4	Heal the *s*·, make spotless the
	230–13	his capacity to heal the *s*·,

sick (noun)

heal the

My.	270–21	My writings heal the *s*·,
	294– 4	they heal the *s*· on the basis that
	300–26	"Heal the *s*·, — *Matt.* 10 : 8.
	364–14	and to heal the *s*·, by

health to the

Mis.	168– 1	health to the *s*·, salvation from

helpless

Un.	61–28	helpless *s*· are soonest healed

letters from the

My.	223– 8	Letters from the *s*· are not read

lose

Un.	2–17	*s*· lose their sense of sickness,

may look

Mis.	307–26	at which the *s*· may look

preparations for the

Mis.	268–22	God's preparations for the *s*·
	268–25	His preparations for the *s*·

recovery of the

Mis.	59–11	*to pray for the recovery of the s*·?
	308–27	prevents the recovery of the *s*·.
	380–19	the immediate recovery of the *s*·,

restored the

No.	4– 1	has restored the *s*· to health ;

said to the

No.	42– 8	Jesus said to the *s*·,

satisfy the

Mis.	380–21	wherewith to satisfy the *s*· that

save the

No.	41–26	* prayer of faith shall save the *s*·,
My.	221–32	shall save the *s*·"? — *Jas.* 5 : 15.

saying to the

Mis.	369–28	privilege of saying to the *s*·,

sinner and the

Mis.	382– 9	the sinner and the *s*· are helped

the dear

My.	154–10	comforting to the dear *s*·,

tonic for the

Mis.	252– 1	Truth is the tonic for the *s*·,

treatment of the

Mis.	66–23	scientific treatment of the *s*·.

who are dis-eased

Mis.	241–30	the *s*· who are dis-eased,

who are healed

Mis.	133–32	behold the *s*· who are healed,

———

Mis.	22–24	with the *s*·, the lame, the deaf,
	25–25	*s*· are more deplorably situated
	25–26	if the *s*· cannot trust God for help
	43–15	far more advantageous to the *s*·
	54–15	the *s*·, . . . are testifying thereto.
	85–30	*s*· often are thereby led to Christ,
	357– 4	Scientists minister to the *s*· ;
Ret.	16–12	for the *s*· to be healed by my
	73–23	is like the *s*· talking sickness.
'01.	12– 4	heals the sinning and the *s*·,
	27–18	an equal number of *s*· healed,
Peo.	11–12	The lame, the blind, the *s*·,
My.	3–15	nor a . . . that heals only the *s*·.
	90–17	* readily grasped by *s*· or well.
	97– 7	* of the *s*· who abjure medicine
	132–26	*s*·, dreaming of suffering matter ;
	147–29	the *s*· and the heavenly homesick
	204–24	the *s*· whom you have not healed
	219– 4	anticipation on the part of the *s*·

sick (adj.)

Mis.	36– 1	is erring, sinful, *s*·, and dying,
	70– 4	cast out the *s*· man's illusion,
	71– 9	he healed others who were *s*·.
	79–19	A mortal who is sinning, *s*·, and
	85– 4	*Is a Christian Scientist ever s*·,
	85– 5	*has he who is s*· *been regenerated ?*
	184–18	to sin and be *s*·,"
	184–18	believing that he is *s*· and a
	186–11	in a *s*· and sinning mortal.
	187–25	create a *s*·, sinning, dying man?
	187–29	*s*· and a sinner in order to be
	197–32	he can neither be *s*· nor forever a
	219–15	one person feels *s*·, another feels
	219–23	mortal mind makes *s*·,
	220– 4	suppose that there is a *s*· person
	220– 9	aim to refute the *s*· man's thoughts,
	220–25	people believe that a man is *s*·
	220–26	speak of him as being *s*·,
	220–27	minds of others that he is *s*·,
	220–29	he will believe that he is *s*·,
	229– 8	than he does the *s*· man's.
	235– 3	no longer obliged to sin, be *s*·,
	238–24	chapter sub-title
	238–25	* public allegement that I am "*s*·,
	241– 5	man will no more enter heaven *s*· than
	241–19	"God never made you *s*· :
	252–13	*s*· thoughts are unreality
	355–24	mind that makes his body *s*·,

sick (adj.)

Man.	49–12	wisdom necessary in a s· room,
Ret.	40–10	s· woman rose from her bed,
Un.	62– 2	that they never were s·.
Pul.	14–29	it makes them s· or sinful.
	73– 3	* If we become s·, God will
Rud.	3– 2	they do not love to be s·.
	7–13	fallen, s·, depraved, mortal.
	12–10	that they are first made s· by
No.	29–12	* "The forgiven soul in a s· body
	29–20	A mortal pardoned by God is not s·,
	31– 5	and they are yet s· and sinful.
Hea.	6–19	Man thinks . . . that when he is s·,
Peo.	4–21	sinning, s·, and dying mortals.
	6– 2	* "I am s· of learned quackery."
	10–18	have made men sinning and s·,
My.	97– 3	* faith on the part of a s· person,
	117–15	when saw we thee s·, — Matt. 25 : 39.
	132–30	whose whole head is s·
	144– 5	to lies afloat that I am s·,
	275–13	the report that I am s·
	276– 4	a criminal or a s· person,

(see also **man**)

sick-bed

Hea.	18–24	religion at the s· will be

sick-bound

No.	46–20	has dawned on the s· and

sickened

Mis.	124–10	We turn, with s· sense,

sickle

Un.	12– 5	s· of Mind's eternal circle,
My.	269–17	God hath thrust in the s·,

sickly

Mis.	211– 7	s· charity that supplies criminals
	219–14	think also after a s· fashion.
My.	116– 8	This state of mind is s· ;
	345–13	I was a s· child.

sickness

action of
Mis.	353– 4	they are like the action of s·,

all
Ret.	34–12	the antidote for all s·,
	61–13	"You are the cause of all s· ;

all our
Mis.	173– 6	healeth all our s· and sins

and death
Mis.	96– 2	salvation from s· and death,
Hea.	17–22	s· and death are supposed physical
	17–25	s· and death were produced by sin.
	17–27	If s· and death came through
Peo.	12–19	salvation from s· and death.

and disease
Pul.	73– 2	* worry . . . about s· and disease?
Peo.	7–24	objects . . . called s· and disease,
My.	364–16	all manner of s· and disease,

and of sin
Hea.	9– 9	think most of s· and of sin ;

and sin
Mis.	37–23	as do s· and sin.
	85–31	way out of both s· and sin.
	98– 4	from inharmony, s·, and sin,
	179–17	the consciousness of s· and sin
	262–20	looseth the chains of s· and sin,
	399–10	sorrow and s· and sin."
Ret.	63– 3	need of healing s· and sin
No.	30– 7	s· and sin have no relapse.
Pan.	5–28	and thus healed s· and sin.
	8–26	s· and sin, life and death.
Po.	75–17	sorrow and s· and sin."
My.	50–12	* dogma, creed, s·, and sin,
	122–18	saves from s· and sin
	257–16	all sorrow, s·, and sin.

and sorrow
Mis.	250–28	want and woe, s· and sorrow

and suffering
Rud.	10–17	which causes s· and suffering.

antidote for
Mis.	33–27	antidote for s·, as well as for sin,
	255–23	antidote for s·, as well as for sin,

beds of
My.	36–14	* delivered from beds of s·

believes in
My.	300– 8	Does he who believes in s·

believe that
Hea.	15–20	and believe that s· is something

called
Un.	54– 3	a false claim, called s·,

calls
Un.	59–22	illusion which calls s· real,

can master
Hea.	8– 6	Mind can master s· as well as

casts out
Mis.	241– 6	Christianity casts out s·

sickness

culminate in
Mis.	366–25	culminate in s·, sin,

destroying
Mis.	40– 7	effectual in destroying s·

disease, and death
Mis.	14–30	sin, s·, disease, and death.
	187– 3	sin, s·, disease, and death.
	194– 4	sin, s·, disease, and death.
No.	6– 9	phenomena, — s·, disease, and **death.**
My.	180–15	sin, s·, disease, and death.

disease, or death
Mis.	65– 4	sin, s·, disease, or death,

dream of
Rud.	11–17	awake from the dream of s· ;

error and
Mis.	221– 9	that error and s· are one,

healing
Ret.	63– 3	need of healing s· and sin?
My.	194– 9	healing s· and destroying sin,

healing of
Mis.	352–29	and the healing of s·

heals
Ret.	63– 4	heals sin as it heals s·,

health and
Ret.	57–27	health and s·, life and death ;
'00.	4– 2	good and evil, health and s·,

health, not of
Un.	3–18	of health, not of s· ;

health over
Mis.	321–11	triumphs . . . of health over s·,

is a belief
Ret.	61– 3	declares that s· is a belief,

is healed
Mis.	352–14	In Science, s· is healed
Un.	8–18	same basis whereby s· is healed,

is the schoolmaster
Rud.	11– 3	S· is the schoolmaster,

last
My.	331–24	* during his last s·,

less
Peo.	6–10	* there would be less s· and

moral
Mis.	352–19	in healing the moral s· ;

more dangerous than
Ret.	63–20	is more dangerous than s·,

must be covered
Mis.	352–31	s· must be covered with the

never made
Mis.	247–30	He never made s·.
No.	4–10	never made s· a stubborn reality.

no
Mis.	293–25	and there is no s·
Rud.	11–10	no s·, sin, and death in the divine
My.	300– 9	there is no s· or disease,

no more
No.	35– 9	there will be no more s·,

no reality in
Mis.	63–12	If there is no reality in s·,

nor sin
Ret.	63– 6	no evil neither s· nor sin.

or death
Peo.	12– 5	s· or death is a law of mortal belief,

or disease
My.	300– 9	declare that there is no s· or disease,

pain and
Mis.	68–12	to believe that pain and s· are

physical
Rud.	2–23	Healing physical s· is the smallest

recovered from
Un.	62– 1	"I have recovered from s· ;"

redemption from
Mis.	96–19	man's redemption from s·

sense of
Un.	2–17	the sick lose their sense of s·,

sin and
(see **sin**)

sin, and death
Mis.	6–21	we conquer s·, sin, and death.
	37–10	belief . . . in s·, sin, and death.
	61–27	of error, . . . of s·, sin, and death.
	62–18	error of s·, sin, and death,
	63– 9	opposite triad, — s·, sin, and death.
	64– 6	nothingness of s·, sin, and death,
	86– 6	to strive with s·, sin, and death
	181–26	disease, s·, sin, and death
	182–31	s·, sin, and death will yield to it,
	234–30	our Saviour from s·, sin, and death
	340–32	Human wrong, s·, sin, and death
	351–24	pain, s·, sin, and death,
Un.	39– 3	s·, sin, and death yield to holiness,
	60–11	descant upon s·, sin, and death as
	64– 7	conscious of s·, sin, and death,
Rud.	11–10	no s·, sin, and death in the divine
No.	17–27	s·, sin, and death would be as

sickness

sin, and death
No. 33–24 in overcoming s·, sin, and death.
Po. 70–24 s·, sin, and death are banished hence.
sin, . . . and death
(see sin)
sin, . . . and disease
Mis. 251–29 Sin, s·, and disease flee before the
sin or
Hea. 9–24 He never made sin or s·,
sin, or death
Un. 62–15 S·, sin, or death is a false sense
sin, . . . or death
Mis. 17– 6 opposed to . . . sin, s·, or death.
Un. 4– 3 finite sense of sin, s·, or death,
Hea. 9– 7 less said . . . of sin, s·, or death,
16–18 only evidence . . . of sin, s·, or death
sorrow and
Mis. 399–10 thy sorrow and s· and sin.''
No. 30–24 Sympathy with sin, sorrow, and s·
Po. 75–17 thy sorrow and s· and sin.
talking
Ret. 73–23 is like the sick talking s·.
the most
Mis. 6–28 there is the most s·.
there is no
Mis. 60– 4 believe there is no s·,
to health
Mis. 220–17 consciousness from s· to health.
to regard
Un. 54– 7 To regard s· as a false claim,
unusual
My. 333–32 * reports of unusual s·
worse than
Ret. 63–23 Sin is worse than s· ;

Mis. 6– 1 We hear from the pulpits that s· is
6– 3 s· often leaves mortals but little
6–32 s· is by no means the exception.
63– 1 and the s· of matter,
83– 8 "S· is a growth of illusion,
89– 5 to care for . . . a friend in s·,
105–28 Destroy the thought of sin, s·,
192– 8 s·, sin, disease, and death,
241–30 much more should these heal, of s·,
259– 6 of health, not of s· ;
Ret. 60–22 S· is something besides
63–10 belief . . . in the reality of s·,
Un. 54– 4 is to admit all there is of s· ;
54–11 As with s·, so is it with sin.
Pul. 13–15 serpent of sin as well as of s· !
No. 4– 4 be undertaken in health than s·.
17–26 Then . . . s· as real as health,
40–19 Only when s·, sin, and fear
Pan. 10–29 Sin, s·, appetites, and passions,
Hea. 18–18 never did anything for s·
Peo. 10–23 The emancipation . . . from s·
My. 161–24 S· is possible because one's

sick-producing
Pul. 69–11 * evil and s· thoughts,

sick-room
Mis. 296–12 who minister in the s·,
Ret. 41– 2 welcome into the s·.

side (noun)
bad
Hea. 10–14 a good and a bad s· to existence.
better
'01. 1–21 it is the better s· of man's nature
bright
Hea. 10–17 if you will look on the bright s· ;
either
Hea. 13– 3 and accomplish less on either s·.
My. 69–17 * galleries, two on either s·
259– 4 on either s· lace and flowers.
evil
Hea. 10–11 it has no evil s· ;
father's
Ret. 1– 3 great-grandfather, on my father's s·,
Pul. 32–23 * On her father's s· Mrs. Eddy came
God's
Mis. 102–31 "one on God's s· is a majority.''
Pul. 4–16 "one on God's s· is a majority.''
No. 46– 1 "One on God's s· is a majority ;''
good
Hea. 10–12 and that is the good s·.
her
Ret. 8–14 I sat in a little chair by her s·,
40–10 I had stood by her s·
Po. 66– 8 whisper of one who sat by her s·
his
Ret. 20–13 * I knelt by his s· throughout
82–20 accumulation of power on his s·
Pul. 33–19 * suddenly appeared at his s·,
material
Mis. 140–18 material s· of this question.

side (noun)
mortal
My. 50–16 * steadfastly from the mortal s·,
of Adam
Mis. 244– 1 from the s· of Adam, — see Gen. 2 : 21.
of error
My. 146–28 Others who take the s· of error
of existence
Mis. 65–14 not consider the false s· of existence
Peo. 1– 9 the sensual s· of existence
of God
Mis. 226– 5 carried the case on the s· of God ;
321–10 adjusted more on the s· of God,
of good
Mis. 104–30 gain a balance on the s· of good,
of happiness
Hea. 10–21 on the s· of happiness ;
of right
Mis. 255– 8 action on the s· of right,
of sin
My. 146–27 audibly takes the s· of sin,
of Spirit
Mis. 180– 2 so far as to take the s· of Spirit,
of Truth
Mis. 46–18 acts on the s· of Truth,
'02. 6–25 victory on the s· of Truth.
one
Mis. 280–16 working on one s· and in Science.
288– 9 regards only one s· of a question,
Pul. 50–27 * to show even some one s· of it
Hea. 10–10 There is but one s· to good,
10–11 there is but one s· to reality,
My. 234–17 when regarded on one s· only,
other
My. 43–17 * set up on the other s· for a
physical
Ret. 33– 1 physical s· of this research was aided by
Pul. 47–11 * knowledge concerning the physical s·
right
Mis. 111–12 cast their nets on the right s·,
212–11 cast their nets on the right s·.
263–21 wavering balance on the right s·,
My. 277–19 tips the beam on the right s·,
safe
Mis. 117– 9 place him on the safe s· of practice.
side by
Mis. 231– 4 exuberant with joy, — ranged side by s·.
Ret. 71–24 growing side by s· with the wheat,
Pul. 84– 6 * side by s·, equal partners in
My. 227–26 side by s· with Christ's command,
south
Pul. 48– 6 * broad piazza on the south s·
under
Pul. 86– 8 * On the under s· of the cover
wrong
Hea. 9– 6 talking on the wrong s· of the question.

Mis. 172–26 on the s· of immutable right,
270– 2 let us take the s· of him who
Ret. 7–18 * of the s· he deemed right.
Hea. 10–21 take the s· you wish to carry,

side (adj.)
Mis. 250–26 out of a s· door ;
My. 69– 5 * ceiling or roof and s· walls

sides
Mis. 146–10 regarding both s· of the subject,
266– 4 these s· are moral opposites,
287–30 preserve affection on both s·.
Rud. 15–17 should be fortified on all s·
Hea. 10–22 be careful not to talk on both s·,
My. 69–11 * placed on the two s· of the organ.
234–18 both s· of the great question of

sidewalk
Mis. 239–11 upon the s· one winter morning,
250–26 little feet tripping along the s· ;

sidewalks
Pul. 42– 2 * the s· around the church

siege
Mis. 99–17 to stand a long s·,
My. 127–22 A s· of the combined centuries,

sieges
My. 124–12 bloodless s· and tearless triumphs,

sift
Mis. 79– 6 will s· the chaff from the wheat,

sifted
'00. 7– 5 creeds and dogmas have been s·,

sifting
Mis. 215– 2 the s· and the fire.

sigh
Mis. ix–13 s·, and smile commingled,
106–26 s· of angels answering,
206–32 and betimes s· for rest

sigh

Mis.	386–10	gathered from her parting s· :
Ret.	4–18	winds s· low requiems
Pan.	14– 1	weigh a s·, and rise into
'00.	11–11	The human s· for peace
Po.	30– 7	dayspring ! 'reft of mortal s·
	49–15	gathered from her parting s·.
	65–15	We waken to life's dreary s·.
	73–19	Or hypocrite s·,
My.	189–22	last-drawn s· of a glory gone,

sighing

Po.	15– 1	soft s· zephyrs through foliage
My.	171– 6	s· shall flee away.'' — *Isa.* 35 : 10.

sighs

Mis.	386– 4	yearnings come not, s· are stilled,
	395–15	languid brooklets yield their s·,
Po.	49– 6	yearnings come not, s· are stilled,
	58– 9	languid brooklets yield their s·,

sight

and sense
Un.	47– 2	by destroying . . . to s· and sense.

deplorable
'01.	15–14	The most deplorable s· is

faith in
My.	149–24	cause in effect, and faith in s·,

faith, not
Mis.	158–12	through faith, not s·.

first
My.	31–20	* first s· which the visitors caught

give
Mis.	242– 9	give s· to one born blind.

gives
Mis.	362– 9	gives s· to these blind,

God's
Mis.	144–22	precious in God's s·
My.	184–22	service acceptable in God's s·.

His
'01.	15–26	* to have you in His s·.
My.	167–17	acceptable in His s·,

human
Mis.	194–17	the divine power to human s· ;
'01.	12–23	magnifies the divine power to human s·;

lose
Mis.	100–13	may lose s· thereof ;
	319–15	they must not lose s· of sin ;
	327–28	and lose s· of their guide ;
Un.	54– 5	one must lose s· of a false claim.

lost
Mis.	179– 5	believing we have lost s· of Truth,
	212–32	His disciples, . . . lost s· of him ;
My.	243– 7	You cannot have lost s· of the rules
	339– 5	C. S. cannot be lost s· of,

material
Un.	34– 9	material s· is an illusion, a lie.
My.	265– 6	less subordinate to material s·

of thee
Mis.	326–32	"The s· of thee unveiled my sins,

or sense
My.	116–17	based upon personal s· or sense.

our
'01.	33– 3	fading so sensibly from our s·.
Hea.	5–20	constantly covered, . . . from our s·.

out of
Mis.	292–17	to bury the dead out of s· ;
My.	160– 1	and keeps Mind much out of s·.
	191–13	Keep personality out of s·,

receive
Mis.	168– 4	how the blind, . . . receive s· ;

restored
Mis.	258– 7	he restored s· to the blind,
My.	105–17	physically restored s· to the blind,

their
Mis.	212–31	buried it out of their s·.
	324–16	passions have so dimmed their s·

your
Po.	67–15	pass From your s· as the shade

Un.	33–26	S·. Mortal mind declares that
Rud.	5–13	who has found s· in matter,
My.	23–24	* not only to faith but also to s· ;
	29–12	* s· which no one who saw
	184–25	precious in the s· of divine Love,

sign

Mis.	145–20	modest s· be nothingness.
	320–18	shall be the s· of his appearing
	380–18	outward s· of such a practice
	380–18	without a s· save the . . . recovery of
	380–20	and people generally, called for a s·
Man.	110–14	Women must s· "Miss." or "Mrs."
	111– 6	must s· her own Christian name,
	111– 8	unmarried women must s· "Miss."
	111–19	whose teachers refuse, . . . to s·
Ret.	1–13	no s· that she inherited a spark from
	42– 6	symbolic words on his office s·.

sign

Un.	10–23	like commencing with the minus s·,
	61–18	is but the s· and symbol,
Pul.	30–11	* s· a brief "confession of faith,"
	35–30	* on the s· at his door.
Po.	24– 7	A s· that never can depart.
My.	36–29	* a s· of your understanding
	354–18	Sweet s· and substance

signal

Pul.	39– 2	* s· proof of the divine origin
My.	187– 8	and s· the perfect path

signalize

Chr.	53–25	wherefore s· the birth
My.	234– 1	s· the thinking of person.

signalled

Pul.	6–24	William R. Alger of Boston, s· me

signally

Mis.	378–13	s· failed in healing her case.
'00.	9–23	attempts to . . . will s· fail ;
My.	228– 5	Evil minds s· blunder
	326–16	s· honored his memory,

signature

Mis.	x–17	My s· has been slightly changed
	x–26	adopted that form of s·,
Man.	36–11	approval and s· of their teachers,
	89– 2	resign over her own s·
	91– 4	The s· of the teacher
	111– 7	prefix her s· with "Mrs ;"
My.	175–28	purporting to have my s·,
	299– 3	s· "A Priest of the Church,"

signatures

Armstrong
Pul.	87– 7	* JOSEPH A·,
My.	21–29	* JOSEPH A·,

Baker
My.	332–14	* GEORGE S. B·.

Bancroft
My.	60–21	* S. P. B·.

Bates
Pul.	77–19	* EDWARD P. B·,
	77–20	* CAROLINE S. B·.
	78–17	* EDWARD P. B·.
	78–18	* CAROLINE S. B·.
My.	322– 7	* EDWARD P. B·.

Board of Directors
Pul.	87– 9	* The C. S. B· of D·.
My.	21–32	* The C. S. B· of D·.
	63– 7	* THE C. S. B· of D·,

Chase
Pul.	87– 8	* STEPHEN A. C·,
My.	21–30	* STEPHEN A. C·,
	27–13	* STEPHEN A. C·,

Churches and Societies in New York
My.	361–24	* FIRST CHURCH OF CHRIST, SCIENTIST,
	362–27	* FIRST CHURCH OF CHRIST, SCIENTIST,
	362–28	* SECOND CHURCH OF CHRIST, SCIENTIST,
	363– 1	* THIRD CHURCH OF CHRIST, SCIENTIST,
	363– 2	* FOURTH CHURCH OF CHRIST, SCIENTIST,
	363– 3	* FIFTH CHURCH OF CHRIST, SCIENTIST,
	363– 4	* SIXTH CHURCH OF CHRIST, SCIENTIST,
	363– 5	* FIRST CHURCH OF CHRIST, SCIENTIST, Brooklyn,
	363– 6	* FOURTH CHURCH OF CHRIST, SCIENTIST, Brooklyn,
	363– 7	* FIRST CHURCH OF CHRIST, SCIENTIST, Staten Island,
	363– 8	* C. S. SOCIETY, Bronx,
	363– 9	* C. S. SOCIETY, Flushing, L. I.,

Churches . . . in Missouri
My.	207–16	* CHURCHES AND SOCIETIES OF C. S. IN MISSOURI.

Dean
My.	361–26	* CHARLES D·, *Chairman,*

Desha
Mis.	306–10	* MARY D·,

Dickey
Po.	vii–16	* ADAM H. D·.

Eddy

(*see* **Eddy-signatures**)

Frye
Ret.	49–31	C. A. F·, *Clerk.*

Harrison
My.	334–24	* MARY HATCH H·.

Hollis
My.	138–30	* ALLEN H·, *Justice of the Peace.*

Johnson
Pul.	87– 8	* WILLIAM B. J·,
My.	21–30	* WILLIAM B. J·,
	38– 7	* WILLIAM B. J·, *Clerk.*
	46–31	* WILLIAM B. J·, *Clerk.*
	63– 8	* WILLIAM B. J·, *Secretary.*
	280–12	* WILLIAM B. J·, *Clerk.*

signatures

Knapp
Pul. 87– 7   * Ira O. K·,
My. 21–29   * Ira O. K·,
McLellan
My. 21–31   * Archibald M·,
Morse
My. 315–19   * H. M. M·, *Justice of the Peace.*
Norcross
Pul. 44–14   * "Lanson P. N·."
Probst
My. 361–27   * Arthur O. P·, *Clerk.*
Rome
My. 62–15   * James J. R·.
Rounsevel
My. 315–15   * R. D. R·.
Snider
My. 325–18   * Carrie Harvey S·.
White
Mis. 394–22   * James T. W·.
Po. 57– 8   * *James T. W·.*
Whiteside
My. 323–14   * Florence W·.
Whiting
Pul. 40– 5   * Lilian W·.

Man. 91– 4   S·.
Pul. 86– 8   * facsimile s· of the Directors,

signed

Mis. 281–25   have s· your names.
      381–17   drawn up and s· by counsel.
Man. 15– 1   *To be s· by those uniting with*
      35–14   s· by the C. S. Board of Directors
      36–20   a recommendation s· by three members
      65–16   order, s· by Mary Baker Eddy,
      69– 2   s· agreement to remain with Mrs. Eddy
My. 315–15   * (S·) R. D. Rounsevel.
      315–18   * statement by him s· is true.
      315–19   * (S·) H. M. Morse,
      319– 7   little pamphlet, s· "Phare Pleigh."
      332–14   * (S·) George S. Baker.

signet

Mis. 35– 7   with the s· of C. S.
      121–21   thereby giving the s· of God to
Hea. 19–16   Heaven's s· is Love.
My. 131–12   The s· of the great heart,

significance

Mis. 46–21   s· of what the apostle meant
      250–11   divine s· of Love
      250–22   glorious s· of affection
Ret. 38–29   must also gain its spiritual s·,
      88–10   spiritual s· of this command,
Pul. 27–28   * and others of pictorial s·.
      44–12   * comprehends its full s·.
      57– 9   * rehearsed the s· of the building,
      84–17   * Of the s· of this achievement
No. 34–25   deep s· of the blood of Christ.
      46–19   full-orbed s· of this destiny
'02. 9– 8   When the full s· of this saying is
My. 6–25   giving to the material spiritual s·
      28–17   * The s· of this building is
      42–22   * s· of this momentous occasion.
      46– 6   * without this spiritual s· it were
      60–16   * spiritual s· of the first chapter of
      64– 1   * As one thought upon the s· of
      85– 3   * in the s· of the occasion.
      88–12   * more than usual ecclesiastic s·.
      90–26   * event of . . . momentous s·.
      94–29   giving . . . a spiritual s·
      259–22   chapter sub-title

significant

Mis. 91– 2   s· as a type of the true worship,
Un. 56–10   s· of that state of mind which
Pul. 32–16   * experiences which alone are s·.
      79–12   * it is a s· fact that one
My. 28– 3   * announcement will be deeply s·.
      45– 6   * s· events associated with this,
      228–11   chapter sub-title

signification

Mis. 190–16   spiritual s· of its terms
Man. 66– 9   s· of the communications
Ret. 10–16   man's origin and s·.
      25– 5   Their spiritual s· appeared ;
      59–14   has the s· of Life.
Rud. 16– 8   spiritual s· of the Bible,
No. 12–24   spiritual s· of the Word
Hea. 7–10   spiritual instead of the material s·.
My. 220–13   the moral s· of law.
      245–26   s· of the letters of

significations

Ret. 59– 4   terms have no contradictory s·.
My. 266–28   modes and s· are adopted.

signified

Mis. 74– 2   correspondence of . . . are here s·.
Hea. 3–19   s· a "good man," — *John* 7: 12.
My. 339–15   and all that it formerly s·,

signifies

Mis. 27–21   evil s· the absence of good,
Pan. 7– 4   s· more than one God,
'00. 14– 7   which s· a complete time
      14–14   the name whereof s·
'02. 7–11   Latin *omni*, which s· *all*,
      7–12   s· all-power, all-presence,
Hea. 7– 1   in Hebrew it is *belial*, and s·
      7– 5   s· those who understand
My. 264–16   s· to the minds of men
      265– 3   It s· that love, unselfed,
      265–14   It s· that the Science of

signify

Mis. 18–12   commands of infinite wisdom, . . . s· :
      28–23   does not s· a graven idol,
      75–19   warped to s· human quality,
      171– 2   to s· human hands.
Man. 42–16   nor s· a belief in more than one
Ret. 88–21   should not be so warped as to s·
No. 20– 8   Principle is used to s· Deity
Pan. 9– 7   s· a good Spirit and an evil spirit.
'00. 5–11   they s· one God.
My. 264–13   * should s· to all mankind?

signifying

Un. 27– 8   s· a passionate love of self,

signs

and symbols
My. 185–30   are rich in s· and symbols,
following
Mis. 25–16   with "s· following," — *Mark* 16: 20.
      29–28   the s· following Christianity,
      65–24   and with s· following.
      133–31   with "s· following." — *Mark* 16: 20.
      154–24   "s· following" — *Mark* 16: 20.
No. 37–20   "s· following." — *Mark* 16: 20.
My. 147–11   with "s· following," — *Mark* 16: 20.
      190–27   with "s· following." — *Mark* 16: 20.
      258– 2   "s· following." — *Mark* 16: 20.
foreshadowed by
Mis. 1– 5   foreshadowed by s· in the
for the wayfarer
Ret. 79– 9   s· for the wayfarer in divine Science
no
Mis. 242–16   "where there shall no s· — *see Matt.* 12: 39.
of the heart
Po. page 24   poem
of these times
Mis. 2– 6   The s· of these times portend
      278– 3   and are the s· of these times ;
      347–10   the mental s· of these times,
My. 270– 5   repeat the s· of these times.
of the times
Mis. 1– 8   discern the s· of the times?" — *Matt.* 16: 3.
      317– 6   to appreciate the s· of the times ;
'00. 4–14   are progressive s· of the times
My. 113–29   The s· of the times emphasize
      114– 1   discern the s· of the times?" — *Matt.* 16: 3.
      200– 4   praised for the s· of the times.
      235–14   chapter sub-title
      265–31   For these s· of the times we thank
      266–14   to the "s· of the times" — *Matt.* 16: 3.
      266–22   special "s· of the times" — *Matt.* 16: 3.
of Truth
Mis. 156–10   will see clearly the s· of Truth
pioneer
Mis. xii– 1   pioneer s· and ensigns of war,
referred to
Hea. 7– 2   s· referred to are the manifestations
spiritual
Mis. 18– 6   these spiritual s· of the new birth
these
Mis. 28–31   "These s· shall follow — *Mark* 16: 17.
      171–18   By these s· are the true disciples
      192–28   these s· shall follow — *Mark* 16: 17.
Ret. 16–14   these s· shall follow — *Mark* 16: 17.
Hea. 1– 1   *these s· shall follow* — *Mark* 16: 17.
      6–26   these s· shall follow — *Mark* 16: 17.
      19–26   "these s· shall follow — *Mark* 16: 17.
My. 47–29   * these s· shall follow — *Mark* 16: 17.
      265–31   For these s· of the times we thank
truest
'00. 10– 6   Conflict and . . . are the truest s· that

Mis. 133–32   as to "s·," behold the — *Mark* 16: 20.

silence

Mis. 114–24   Scientists will s· evil suggestions,
      124–21   s· wherein to muse His praise,
      129–13   let s· prevail over his remains.

silence
Mis.	134–26	neither s· nor disarm God's voice.
	152–28	to s· the right intuition which
	193–18	a modification of s· on this subject,
	212–14	The ultimatum . . . ought to s· ours.
	277–17	s· Truth? Never.
	299–30	does this s· your conscience?
	339– 5	s· for the space of half an hour.
No.	8– 5	s· whenever it can substitute censure.
'02.	14–27	s· all private criticisms,
	15–23	came to me in the s· of night,
Po.	2–19	thy deep s· is unbroken still.
	15– 5	Break not on the s·,
	27–16	Hearts bleeding ere they break in s·
My.	104–21	sufficient reason for his s·
	124–22	s·, or with finger pointing upward,
	170–26	sacred s· in blest communion
	195–18	best way to s· a deep discontent
	246–13	and sought in solitude and s·
	249–15	patience, s·, and lives of saints.
	262–29	eloquent s·, prayer and praise
	339–27	S· . . . all that wars against Spirit

silenced
Mis.	277–13	stake and scaffold have never s· the
	360–25	When mortal mind is s· by
Ret.	22– 5	spiritual noumenon s· portraiture.
My.	243– 6	should be s· at its inception.

silences
Mis.	198– 9	s· the mortal claim to life,
	259– 8	s· the supposition that evil is a
'02.	5–30	s· all questions on this subject,
My.	230– 8	Soul s· the dyspepsia of sense.

silencing
Ret.	67–13	S· self, *alias* rising above

silent
Mis.	12–22	human mind in its s· arguments,
	70–28	working out, even in the s· tomb,
	100–19	speaks when the senses are s·,
	114–32	against evil and its s· modes,
	126–20	s· lesson of a good example.
	143– 8	with this s· benediction :
	152– 8	breathe a s· benediction
	220– 7	supports this s· mental force
	238– 9	s· endurance of his love.
	250–23	the s·, ceaseless prayer ;
	260–31	s· mental methods whereby
	269–29	opening of this s· mental seal,
	275–10	wife or husband, s· and alone,
	351– 7	weapons of the s· mental malpractice.
	368–19	The s· address of a mental
	400– 6	Grave, s·, steadfast stone,
Chr.	53–43	s· healing, heaven heard,
Ret.	38–24	disgusted . . . and become s·.
	61– 6	unconsciously in the s· thought,
	76–27	I have long remained s·
Pul.	10– 8	fallen fanes and s· Aventine
	16–18	Cold, s·, stately stone,
No.	1– 5	changed by its s· influence.
	1–13	for the s· cultivation of the
	39– 2	s· intercession and unvoiced
Pan.	3–10	s· as the storm's sudden hush ;
'02.	5– 1	As s· night foretells the dawn
Po.	66–10	that heart is s· and sad,
	76–17	Grave, s·, steadfast stone,
My.	29– 4	* kneeling in s· communion ;
	32– 3	* five minutes of s· communion
	32–29	* s· communion, which concluded with
	38–24	* than the s· communion
	70–14	* stood in s· admiration
	78–19	* knelt in s· communion,
	79– 2	* kneeling for s· communion
	106– 3	speak charitably . . . or to keep s·,
	171–21	* s· greetings of the people
	189– 9	s· prayers of our churches,
	194– 8	a s·, grand man or woman,
	211–13	by unseen, s· arguments.
	211–14	in their s· allurements to
	268–18	as s· as the dumb centuries
	332– 4	* The s· gush of grateful tears alone
		(*see also* **prayer**)

silently
Mis.	78–12	I know not how to teach . . . s· ;
	159–15	sit s·, and ponder.
	225–24	s·, through the divine power,
	231–32	gazing s· on the vacant seat
	315–24	Teachers shall not s· mentally
My.	46– 4	* s· but eloquently beckoning
	247–15	I stood s· beside it,

silk
Pul.	77– 6	* casket with white s· linings.

silly
Mis.	183–11	nor a s· ambler to the
	254–24	resting in s· peace upon the
My.	313– 1	a paraphrase of a s· song

silver
Mis.	159–28	embroidery, s·, gold, and jewels,
	305–21	* gold, s·, bronze, copper, and
	346–24	in pictures of s·." — *Prov.* 25 : 11.
Ret.	12– 3	Minerva's s· sandals still
	23– 8	seemed to have a s· lining ;
Pul.	25–26	* s· lamps of Roman design,
	26–11	* s· lamps eight feet in height.
	62–23	* down to little sets of s· bells
	76–11	* in certain lights has a shimmer of s·.
Po.	61– 1	Minerva's s· sandals still
My.	30–22	* with bills, with s·, and with gold.

silver-throated
Pul.	11– 2	sweet song of s· singers,

silvery (*see also* silv'ry)
Po.	53–11	Till heard at s· eve

silv'ry
Po.	8–12	O'er the s· moon and ocean
	73–11	Laving with surges thy s· beach !

similar
Mis.	272– 8	* were granted for s· colleges,
	296–17	by no means identical — nor even s·.
Man.	54–23	a second s· offense shall remove
Ret.	43– 6	granted for s· purposes after
Un.	6–24	discussion and horror, s· to
Rud.	9–19	s· effects come from pride,
Po.	v–22	* S· *requests continued to reach*
My.	73– 3	* necessary to issue a s· notice
	76–13	* A s· decision was reached

similarly
Pul.	65–27	* s· expresses the faith of

similes
Mis.	263– 6	sweetest s· to be found

similitude
Mis.	162–23	after the s· of the Father,
Un.	60–14	after the s· . . . of God. — *Jas.* 3 : 9.
No.	27– 8	s· of the Apocalyptic pictures.

simple
Mis.	22–29	s· fact cognized by the senses,
	30– 4	adopt the "s· addition" in C. S.
	43–12	s· sense one gains of this Science
	53–22	*why is it not more s·*,
	53–23	The teachings of Jesus were s· ;
	53–26	C. S. is s·, and readily understood
	53–29	godliness is s· to the godly ;
	54–29	the pupil in s· equations
	112–18	regarded his act as . . . s· justice,
	148–18	hence their s·, scientific basis,
	162–30	s· as the shepherd boy,
	196–30	require more than a s· admission
	248–11	s· falsehoods uttered about me
	262–10	however s· the words,
	265–16	innovations upon s· proof ;
	373– 1	the s· nature of art.
Man.	3–14	hence their s·, scientific basis,
Ret.	82– 3	dealing with a s· Latour exercise
	92– 2	not too s· to be sublime,
Un.	9–17	s· teaching and life of Jesus
	49– 5	s· appeal to human consciousness.
Pul.	14–14	s· seekers for Truth,
	40–16	* s· ceremonies, four times repeated,
	50–22	* s· and direct as they are,
Rud.	6– 1	s· solution of the problem of being,
'00.	6–13	through his s· faith and purity,
'01.	22–30	s· statement as to Spirit and
My.	50–21	* s· but suggestive words,
	67–26	* will in its s· grandeur surpass
	111–30	C. S. is valid, s·, real,
	172–28	as a s· token of love."
	340–13	a s· board of health,
	356–27	This s· statement of oneness

simpler
Man.	62–22	to grasp the s· meanings
My.	vi– 4	* to state truth absolutely in a s·

simplest
Mis.	55– 2	The s· problem in C. S.
Rud.	6–24	in the s· . . . form of healing,
	7– 2	s· case, healed in Science,

simplicity
Ret.	91–17	In this s·, and with such fidelity,
Pul.	43–13	* utmost s· marked the exercises.
My.	29–17	* impressiveness . . . in its very s· ;
	79–26	* a s· which sprang from the
	342–22	s· of the oneness of God ;

simplified
My.	361– 1	directions of God as s· in C. S.,

simply
Mis.	8–17	S· count your enemy to be that
	9–11	S·, in that those unfortunate
	34– 8	physique is s· thought made manifest.
	43– 4	or s· after having been

simply

Mis. 137– 7	it was *s·* to give you the privilege,
272–20	* have *s·* an incorporated grant,
299– 9	*s·* answer the following question
363– 6	*s·* the supposition that the absence
Ret. 39– 2	were healed *s·* by reading it,
40–24	*s·* to show the opposition
64–13	are alike *s·* nothingness ;
Pul. 4–10	*s·* to preserve a scientific,
35– 7	* was *s·* a natural fulfilment of
80–17	* but *s·* state the fact.
81–10	* *s·* the woman of the past
No. 25– 1	*S·* uttering this great thought
Peo. 10– 3	*s·* because it is more ethereal.
My. 31–28	* announced *s·* that they would sing
81–19	* spoke *s·* and gratefully,
106– 8	*s·* to show the folly of believing
114–10	*S·* because the treasures of this
169– 5	as *s·* seeing Mother.
170– 3	*s·* my acquiescence in the request
273– 2	* This manuscript is presented *s·* as
280–29	*s·* to pause in special prayer
305–24	*s·* how to do his works.
343–15	I have *s·* taught as I learned

simulates

Mis. 334– 8	Whatever *s·* power and Truth

simultaneously

Un. 49–15	You cannot *s·* serve the
Pul. 7– 8	*s·* praised and persecuted

sin *(see also* sin's*)*

abandonment of
Mis. 205–26	absolute abandonment of *s·*

all
Mis. 3–21	holds in itself all *s·*,
184–26	all *s·*, sickness, and death ;
204–13	Truth cleansing from all *s·* ;
208– 4	it covers all *s·* and its effects.
317– 8	over all *s·*, disease, and death.
Man. 41–23	and rule out of me all *s·* ;
Pul. 12–18	mighty conquest over all *s·*
13–26	to remove all *s·*, must depend upon
'01. 5–17	leave all *s·* to God's fiat
15–19	all *s·* is a deluded sense,
My. 120–11	takes away all *s·*, disease, and death,
301–17	All *s·* is insanity,

and death
Mis. 3–24	elements of *s·* and death.
30–21	law of *s·* and death." — *Rom.* 8 : 2.
36–23	and the law of *s·* and death.
49–26	non-intelligence, *s·*, and death.
90– 5	*s·* and death to be powerless.
201–19	law of *s·* and death ;" — *Rom.* 8 : 2.
321–16	law of *s·* and death." — *Rom.* 8 : 2.
326– 3	law of *s·* and death." — *Rom.* 8 : 2.
Man. 16– 4	overcoming *s·* and death.
19– 5	saving the world from *s·* and death ;
Un. 42– 3	*s·*, and death are not the outcome of
42– 5	What then are matter, *s·*, and death?
56–17	from the law of *s·* and death.
62–21	human error, *s·*, and death
No. 30– 3	all sense of *s·* and death.
34–28	freedom . . . from *s·* and death.
35– 9	sickness, sorrow, and death.
35–12	nothingness of hate, *s·*, and death,
'02. 9–13	law of *s·* and death." — *Rom.* 8 : 2.
My. 5–11	creation of matter, *s·*, and death,
113–14	law of *s·* and death." — *Rom.* 8 : 2.
239–11	by overcoming *s·* and death.
272– 7	law of *s·* and death." — *Rom.* 8 : 2.
293–29	law of *s·* and death." — *Rom.* 8 : 2.

and Deity
Un. 6–24	declarations about *s·* and Deity

and disease
Mis. 101–25	including *s·* and disease.
No. 4–18	*S·* and disease are not scientific,
My. 147–20	to heal both *s·* and disease.
221–20	with which to heal *s·* and disease.

and fear
No. 40–19	when sickness, *s·*, and fear

and flesh
'00. 7–30	if *s·* and flesh are put off,

and mortality
Pan. 8– 5	lunacy, *s·*, and mortality.
My. 192–11	conquest over *s·* and mortality,

and self
Mis. 328–17	burdened by pride, *s·*, and self,

and sensuality
Mis. 234–26	sunken in *s·* and sensuality,

and sickness
Mis. 189–29	healing *s·* and sickness,
241–22	bondage to *s·* and sickness.
No. 18– 2	never diminished *s·* and sickness,
My. 113–16	healing *s·* and sickness,
207–13	* *s·* and sickness are destroyed

sin

and sinners
Un. 60– 7	talk of *s·* and sinners as real.
My. 180–22	struggles with *s·* and sinners,

and sorrow
Pul. 82– 4	* cold haunts of *s·* and sorrow,

and suffering
Mis. 261– 4	*s·* and suffering it occasions
261– 6	*s·* and suffering are not cancelled **by**
My. 248–24	exterminating *s·* and suffering

annihilated
Un. 31–10	overruled . . . as they annihilated *s·*.

as a claim
Ret. 63–19	*S·*, as a claim, is more dangerous

as well as
Ret. 34–12	all sickness, as well as *s·*,
Hea. 8– 7	can master sickness as well as *s·*,
Peo. 11– 7	from disease as well as *s·* ;

at ease in
Mis. 241–29	the sinner who is at ease in *s·*,

atones for
My. 288–27	Love atones for *s·*

attaches to
Mis. 209– 1	attaches to *s·* due penalties

authority of
Ret. 63–12	When we deny the authority of *s·*,

author of
Mis. 83–17	sin is the author of *s·*.

away from
Chr. 53–53	away from *s·* Christ summons thee !

because of
Chr. 55–16	body is dead because of *s·* ; — *Rom.* 8 : 10.

belief in
	(see belief*)*

believe in
My. 299–17	Do Christians, who believe in *s·*,

blotted-out
'01. 35–15	the bliss of blotted-out *s·*

brought death
Mis. 201– 6	*S·* brought death ; and death is an

called
Mis. 205– 5	melting away the shadows called *s·*,
Ret. 67–16	the false claim called *s·*
No. 31–23	If the evils called *s·*, sickness, and
'01. 13– 2	The outcome of evil, called *s·*,

calls
Un. 59–21	illusion which calls *s·* real,

cancels not
Mis. 338–13	cancels not *s·* until it be destroyed,

can do nothing
Mis. 93–17	*S·* can do nothing :

claim of
Un. 31–12	*first* idolatrous claim of *s·* is,
'00. 15–14	to see . . . the claim of *s·*,
'01. 13–28	first detect the claim of *s·* ;

claims
Mis. 109– 8	and see what, . . . *s·* claims of you ;

claims of
Mis. 109–26	to escape from the false claims of *s·*.

cleaves
No. 32–13	cleaves *s·* with a broad battle-axe.

clouds of
Mis. 355–26	Let no clouds of *s·* gather

cognizant of
Un. 15– 7	declare Him absolutely cognizant of *s·*?

commensurate with
My. 288–22	suffering is commensurate with *s·* ;

conception of
'01. 13–18	destroy the conception of *s·*

condition of
Mis. 109–18	Ignorance was the first condition of *s·*

conquer
Mis. 235– 4	empowered to conquer *s·*,
My. 125– 2	Have you learned to conquer *s·*,

conquer this
Mis. 40–30	requires more . . . to conquer this *s·*

consciousness of
Un. 7–24	the sense or consciousness of *s·*,

conscious of
Un. 13–13	If God could be conscious of *s·*,

constitutes
Ret. 67– 4	*s·* constitutes the human or physical

correct
My. 249– 4	opportunity to correct *s·*

defense from
Mis. 115–16	protection and defense from *s·*

definition of
Mis. 108–26	Jesus' definition of *s·* as a *lie*.

departure of
My. 197– 1	comes with the departure of *s·*.

destroy
Mis. 4–30	to destroy *s·* in mortal thought.
366–28	To destroy *s·* and its sequence,
My. 221– 9	which was to destroy *s·*,

sin

destroying
Un. 47– 1   burden of disproof by destroying *s·*,
Peo. 6–22   are found destroying *s·*, sickness, and
My. 194– 9   healing sickness and destroying *s·*,
     265–18   destroying *s·*, disease, and death ;

destroys
Mis. 189–25   subordinates matter and destroys *s·*,
Ret. 67–14   reforms the sinner and destroys *s·*.
Un. 54–14   then *s·* destroys the *at-one-ment*,
No. 13– 2   and thus destroys *s·* quickly
My. 288–27   through love that destroys *s·*.

destruction of
Mis. 40– 8   as in the destruction of *s·*.
Man. 15–11   in the destruction of *s·*
No. 31–12   which is the sure destruction of *s·* ;
     31–13   I insist on the destruction of *s·*

diminishes
Ret. 67–15   personal sense ceases, *s·* diminishes,

diminishing
Mis. 8– 2   abating suffering and diminishing *s·*,

disappears
Un. 62–15   Destroy this . . . and *s·* disappears.
'01. 13–20   destroy . . . and *s·* disappears.
     13–29   we get the victory, *s·* disappears,

discomfort from
My. 233–12   Is not discomfort from *s·* better

discomfort in
Mis. 219–21   a sense of discomfort in *s·*

disease and
     (*see* **disease**)

disease, and death
Mis. 17–17   materialism, — *s·*, disease, and death.
     60– 6   To regard *s·*, disease, and death
     103– 8   such as *s·*, disease, and death,
     177–19   error, *s·*, disease, and death?
     189–25   destroys *s·*, disease, and death.
     192– 8   sickness, *s·*, disease, and death.
     200– 5   than *s·*, disease, and death.
     205– 5   called *s·*, disease, and death.
     270– 9   power over *s·*, disease, and death,
     317– 8   over all *s·*, disease, and death.
     366–25   in sickness, *s·*, disease, and death.
No. 4–24   unreality of *s·*, disease, and death,
     29–20   He in whom *s·*, disease, and death
     36–12   of matter, of *s·*, disease, and death,
Pan. 7–28   makes *s·*, disease, and death inevitable,
     12–15   escape from *s·*, disease, and death ;
'01. 10–21   dark passage of *s·*, disease, and death
     10–23   over self, *s·*, disease, and death,
     11– 4   over *s·*, disease, and death,
     15– 7   to lessen *s·*, disease, and death,
     17– 1   from *s·*, disease, and death
     23–21   matter, *s·*, disease, and death,
'02. 7– 5   *s·*, disease, and death enter not
     11– 5   subject to *s·*, disease, and death.
     11–17   from *s·*, disease, and death.
My. 120–11   takes away all *s·*, disease, and death,
     154– 1   from *s·*, disease, and death.
     156–23   victory over *s·*, disease, and death.
     210– 3   *s·*, disease, and death cannot enter
     221– 9   to destroy *s·*, disease, and death,
     265–18   destroying *s·*, disease, and death ;
     350– 6   its effects, *s·*, disease, and death.

disease, . . . and death
Un. 10– 1   *unreality of disease, s·, and death,*
My. 106–19   expressed in disease, *s·*, and death,

dis-ease in
'01. 15–20   dis-ease in *s·* is better than ease.
My. 233–11   prefer, ease or dis-ease in *s·* ?

disease, or death
My. 146–27   takes the side of *s·*, disease, or death.

divine
Un. 16– 2   In Truth, such terms as *divine s·*

does not commit
Mis. 61–13   image of God, does not commit *s·*.'

does not constitute
Ret. 67– 4   human thought does not constitute *s·*,

does not test
Mis. 93–25   does not test *s·* and the fact of

ease in
Mis. 343– 2   the temptation of ease in *s·* ;
My. 233–13   better . . . than ease in *s·* ?

easily-besetting
Mis. 307–22   Idolatry is an easily-besetting *s·*

effect of
Mis. 221–11   the effect of *s·* on himself,

effects of
Mis. 115–29   effects of *s·* on yourself,

encourages
Ret. 63–24   it encourages *s·* to say,

error and
No. 37–27   if error and *s·* existed in
My. 323–23   * triumph over error and *s·*,

sin

every
Mis. 83– 6   "*Every s· is the author of itself,*
No. 8–16   every *s·* will so punish itself

evil or
'01. 12–25   chapter sub-title

except
Ret. 81– 4   Nothing except *s·*, in the students

expiate their
Pul. 13–20   expiate their *s·* through suffering.

fear nor
Mis. 93–21   neither fear nor *s·* can bring on

fear not
Mis. 109–29   fear not *s·*, lest thereby it

fear or
Mis. 93– 6   *Can fear or s· bring back old*

fear to
Mis. 109–30   but only *fear to s·*.

fondness for
Un. 2– 9   takes away man's fondness for *s·*

forgiven
No. 30– 1   chapter sub-title

forgiveness of
Man. 15–10   acknowledge God's forgiveness of *s·*
Pul. 80–20   * the forgiveness of *s·* by God,

forms of
No. 41–16   sublest forms of *s·* are trying to

forsake
Mis. 123–25   repent, forsake *s·*, love God,

freed from
Mis. 90–15   Do you desire to be freed from *s·* ?

freedom from
Peo. 10–24   the mind's freedom from *s·* ;

from the sinner
Ret. 64– 2   cannot separate *s·* from the sinner,

giant
Mis. 55–13   This giant *s·* is the sin against

gloom is
My. 90–16   * teaches . . . that gloom is *s·*,

God and
Un. 6–16   questions about God and *s·*,

god of
Mis. 123–14   Merodach, or the god of *s·*,

great
My. 309–16   slavery he regarded as a great *s·*.

greatest
Mis. 130–24   greatest *s·* that one can commit

growing
Mis. 284–19   This growing *s·* must now be dealt with

grow out of
Peo. 3–28   whereby we grow out of *s·*

hallucination of
Mis. 94– 5   see . . . the hallucination of *s·* ;

has no claim
'00. 15–14   thence to see that *s·* has no claim,

has no power
Mis. 93–15   This being true, *s·* has no power ;

has produced
Mis. 221–12   believes that *s·* has produced the

healed
No. 31–19   healed disease as he healed *s·* ;

healing of
Mis. 352–28   healing of *s·* and the healing of
Rud. 2–27   purpose of . . . is the healing of *s·* ;

heal, of
Mis. 241–29   Truth and Love heal, of *s·*,

heals
Ret. 63– 4   C. S. heals *s·* as it heals sickness,
My. 180–15   this Principle heals *s·*,

hiding
My. 211– 6   This mistaken way, of hiding *s·*

his own
No. 29– 2   put to death for his own *s·*,

human
Un. 15–19   human *s·* become only an echo of

human concept of
Ret. 67– 2   before the human concept of *s·*

ignorance of
Un. 6–19   blindness . . . and ignorance of *s·*.

ignorant of
Un. 49– 9   as ignorant of *s·* as is the perfect

indulge in
Mis. 115–29   if you in any way indulge in *s·* ;

indulging
My. 5–28   indulging *s·*, men cannot serve God ;

in its citadels
Mis. 211–27   Jesus stormed *s·* in its citadels

in itself
'01. 14–19   to conceive of . . . is *s·* in itself.

is a lie
'01. 13– 7   *s·* is a lie from the beginning,
     13–14   evil, *alias* devil, *s·*, is a lie

is destroyed
'01. 16– 6   till the *s·* is destroyed.

is healed
Mis. 352–15   by the same rule that *s·* is healed.

sin

is impotent
  Mis. 90– 2 hence, that *s·* is impotent.
is inadmissible
  Mis. 147–11 learned that *s·* is inadmissible,
is losing
  No. 41–23 *s·* is losing prestige and power.
is mortal
  '01. 13–27 Soul is immortal, but *s·* is mortal.
is not Mind
  No. 27– 1 *S·* is not Mind ;
is obsolete
  Mis. 173–21 matter is nowhere and *s·* is obsolete.
is removed
  '01. 13–23 only as the *s·* is removed
is self-destroyed
  Mis. 209–12 when *s·* is self-destroyed.
is sin
  '01. 13– 9 the position that *s·* is sin
is the sinner
  Ret. 64– 3 *s·* is the sinner, and *vice versa,*
is worse
  Ret. 63–23 *S·* is worse than sickness ;
itself
  Un. 9– 3 and *s·* itself disappears.
  '01. 14– 3 *s·* itself, that clings fast to iniquity.
  My. 334–21 *s·* itself, that clings fast to iniquity.
knowing
  No. 30–15 becoming human, and knowing *s·,*
knowledge of
  (*see* **knowledge**)
knows
  Un. 54–17 If God knows *s·,*
law of
  (*see* **law**)
leaving
  No. 19–24 leaving *s·,* sense rises to the
leprosy of
  Pul. 29–23 * to cleanse the leprosy of *s·,*
lose sight of
  Mis. 319–15 or they must not lose sight of *s· ;*
makes something of
  '01. 13–17 When man makes something of *s·*
manifestation of
  Ret. 67– 9 first iniquitous manifestation of *s·*
materialism or
  Mis. 19–27 out of materialism or *s·,*
matter and
  My. 4– 1 losing his faith in matter and *s·,*
most fearful
  Mis. 19–19 most fearful *s·* that mortals can
motives for
  Peo. 9– 5 washing away the motives for *s· ;*
must be obsolete
  No. 26–28 *S·* must be obsolete,
must be *uncovered*
  Mis. 352–29 *s·* must be *uncovered* before it
named
  No. 30– 4 the false sense named *s·,*
nature of
  Un. 5–24 as to the nature of *s·*
never pardons the
  Peo. 9–15 never pardons the *s·* that deserves to
no
  Mis. 63–11 *If there is no s·, why did Jesus*
  125– 5 rise to know that there is no *s·,*
  293–25 there is no sickness and no *s·,*
  Ret. 63–24 to say, "There is no *s·,*"
  Un. 56– 6 no *s·* or suffering in the Mind which
  No. 35–26 Hence there is no *s·,*
no intelligent
  No. 38– 8 no intelligent *s·,* evil *mind* or
no knowledge of
  Un. 2–16 God, has no knowledge of *s·.*
  No. 17–22 God who has no knowledge of *s·*
no reality in
  Un. 64– 3 there is no reality in *s·,*
  '01. 14– 2 To assume there is no reality in *s·,*
  My. 334–20 "To assume there is no reality in *s·,*
no refuge from
  Un. 2– 6 The sinner has no refuge from *s·,*
not
  My. 301–17 but healing the sick is *not s·.*
nothing but
  Rud. 10–19 Love punishes nothing but *s·,*
obdurate
  My. 36–15 * redeemed from obdurate *s·.*
of any sort
  Mis. 108– 4 To allow *s·* of any sort
  337–31 *S·* of any sort tends to hide from
of every sort
  Mis. 37–21 *s·* of every sort, is destroyed by
  67–19 Justice uncovers *s·* of every sort ;
  241– 6 sickness as well as *s·* of every sort.
of sins
  '01. 20–19 This unseen evil is the *s·* of sins ;

sin

of the world
  '01. 9–18 the *s·* of the world ;" — *John* 1 : 29.
operation of
  Un. 20–20 knowledge and the operation of *s·,*
or death
  Mis. 30–11 without pain, *s·,* or death.
  Un. 62–16 *s·,* or death is a false sense of
or disease
  Mis. 191–30 *s·* or disease made manifest.
original
  Mis. 114–19 original *s·,* appearing in its myriad
  201– 4 its original *s·,* or human will
or sense
  Mis. 42–27 sense of Life in *s·* or sense material,
or sickness
  Hea. 9–24 He never made *s·* or sickness,
or suffering
  Un. 56– 6 no *s·* or suffering in the Mind which
or suicide
  Mis. 53– 7 Not through *s·* or suicide,
overcome
  Mis. 55– 8 utilizes its power to overcome *s·.*
  My. 6–10 When we have overcome *s·*
  300– 4 enabling the sinner to overcome *s·*
overcoming
  Mis. 319–14 overcoming *s·* in themselves,
  Man. 16– 4 healing the sick and overcoming *s·*
  My. 239–11 by overcoming *s·* and death.
paid by
  No. 35–14 the awful price paid by *s·,*
pain and
  Po. 22–18 dark domain of pain and *s·*
pardon
  My. 299–18 those who claim to pardon *s·,*
penalty for
  Mis. 237– 6 accepted as the penalty for *s·.*
percentage of
  No. 32–25 diminishing the percentage of *s·.*
pleasure in
  Mis. 90– 3 power of sin is the pleasure in *s·.*
  241–11 "You have no pleasure in *s·,*"
  My. 132–26 sinner, dreaming of pleasure in *s· ;*
pleasure of
  Ret. 63– 8 belief in the pleasure of *s·,*
power over
  Mis. 40–24 must gain the power over *s·*
  270– 9 demonstrated his power over *s·,*
prevent
  Mis. 362–29 when it is necessary to prevent *s·*
price of
  Mis. 165–24 they never paid the price of *s·.*
produced by
  Hea. 17–25 sickness and . . . produced by *s·.*
proof that
  No. 37–15 or as a proof that *s·* is known to
punish
  Mis. 209– 5 wouldst teach God not to punish *s· ?*
punishes itself
  Mis. 93–27 *S·* punishes itself, because it cannot
  My. 288–25 that *s·* punishes itself ;
punishing
  Mis. 261–18 showeth mercy by punishing *s·.*
punishing of
  Mis. 293– 7 This uncovering and punishing of *s·*
punishment for
  Mis. 279– 4 individual punishment for *s·*
  '01. 13–23 removes the punishment for *s·*
punishment of
  '01. 16– 3 chapter sub-title
quenching
  '02. 9– 3 the All-presence — quenching *s· ;*
reality of
  Ret. 63– 8 *alias* the reality of *s·,* which makes
rebukes
  No. 13– 1 This Science rebukes *s·*
rebuking
  Man. 40–10 amenities of Love, in rebuking *s·,*
recognizes
  Un. 54–15 unity which *s·* recognizes as its
recovery from
  Mis. 100–31 of man's recovery from *s·*
redemption from
  Mis. 165–23 of mortals' redemption from *s· ;*
result of
  Mis. 115– 8 only as the result of *s· ;*
rolling
  Mis. 130–11 "rolling *s·* as a sweet morsel
root of
  '01. 13–16 lays the axe at the root of *s·,*
salvation from
  (*see* **salvation**)
saved from
  Mis. 197– 8 man saved from *s·,* sickness,
  Un. 2– 8 in order to be saved from *s·.*

sin

save from
Mis. 60– 3   sent His Son to save from s·,
197–16   no more help to save from s·, than
save him from
Ret. 63– 9   and save him from s· ;
save man from
Un. 18– 6   can never save man from s·, if
saves from
Mis. 90– 6   practical Truth saves from s·,
367–28   that whatever saves from s·,
save them from
Rud. 3– 5   all efforts to save them from s·
sea of
Mis. 264– 5   midst of this seething sea of s·.
secrets of
Mis. 343–16   uncovering the secrets of s·
self and
Ret. 79–21   the victory over self and s·.
sense and
Mis. 172– 8   defeat the claims of sense and s·,
sense of
(see **sense**)
sepulchres of
Mis. 292–15   from the open sepulchres of s·,
serpent of
Pul. 13–15   fail to strangle the serpent of s·
servants of
No. 32–20   no longer be the servants of s·,
shackles of
My. 44– 3   * shackles of s· are being broken,
shuts out
Un. 41– 5   s· shuts out the real sense of Life,
sickness and
(see **sickness**)
sickness, and death
Mis. 2–18   remedy for s·, sickness, and death ;
3–21   all s·, sickness, and death,
16–14   over s·, sickness, and death.
78– 4   sense of s·, sickness, and death,
105– 5   over s·, sickness, and death,
106– 1   where are s·, sickness, and death?
179–11   is in s·, sickness, and death.
184–26   all s·, sickness, and death ;
196–20   from s·, sickness, and death.
197– 8   saved from s·, sickness, and death ;
235– 4   to conquer s·, sickness, and death ;
260–15   s·, sickness, and death are its
320–15   from s·, sickness, and death.
Ret. 56–16   disclaims s·, sickness, and death,
62– 5   illusion of s·, sickness, and death
64–21   classify s·, sickness, and death as
69–18   that s·, sickness, and death are
Un. 1–11   behold s·, sickness, and death ?
3–15   fruit of s·, sickness, and death,
6– 8   from s·, sickness, and death
13–15   knowledge of s·, sickness, and death,
32–18   material, in s·, sickness, and death,
46–21   S·, sickness, and death were evil's
47– 1   destroying s·, sickness, and death,
50–20   evade s·, sickness, and death,
58–18   unreality of s·, sickness, and death
Pul. 70–23   * all error, s·, sickness, and death.
No. 8–22   of s·, sickness, and death.
16– 9   evil, s·, sickness, and death
16–23   of matter— s·, sickness, and death
29–24   waves of s·, sickness, and death.
31–23   called s·, sickness, and death
36–20   over s·, sickness, and death.
38– 4   that s·, sickness, and death are
Pan. 5–26   brought s·, sickness, and death
'01. 18–28   triad— s·, sickness, and death
Hea. 9–25   s·, sickness, and death are this
17–10   evidences of s·, sickness, and death,
17–18   S·, sickness, and death never
17–19   S·, sickness, and death are error ;
Peo. 3–10   produced s·, sickness, and death
4– 5   s·, sickness, and death originated in
6–22   destroying s·, sickness, and death ;
sickness, . . . and death
(see **sickness**)
sickness, and disease
Mis. 251–29   S·, sickness, and disease flee
sickness and of
Hea. 9– 9   think most of sickness and of s· ;
sickness nor
Ret. 63– 7   no evil, neither sickness nor s·.
sickness, or death
Mis. 17– 6   law of s·, sickness, or death.
Un. 4– 3   finite sense of s·, sickness, or death,
Hea. 9– 7   thought of s·, sickness, or death,
16–18   evidence we have of s·, sickness, or death
single
Pul. 12–16   For victory over a single s·,
My. 152–27   nor pardon a single s· ;

sin

sinner and
Ret. 64– 4   sinner and s· will be destroyed by
sinner and the
Mis. 94– 7   sinner and the s· are the twain
Ret. 64–13   the sinner and the s· are alike
sinner from his
Ret. 64– 3   nor the sinner from his s·.
spectacle of
'02. 18– 4   The constant spectacle of s·
storming
'01. 2–19   storming s· in its citadels,
struggle with
Mis. 41–17   struggle with s· is forever done.
subdues
My. 131– 2   removes fear, subdues s·,
subject of
Mis. 115– 4   subject of s· and mental malpractice,
subtleties of
Mis. 112– 2   with the subtleties of s· !
success in
Mis. 354– 4   sanguine of success in s·,
'00. 10– 1   Success in s· is downright defeat.
suffering due to
Mis. 122–23   for the suffering due to s·.
suffering for
Mis. 15–27   By suffering for s·, and the
suffering from
Mis. 14–32   not sheltered from suffering from s· :
sum total of
My. 212–13   to complete the sum total of s·.
superinduced by
Mis. 66–24   Disease that is superinduced by s·
sympathy with
No. 30–24   Sympathy with s·, sorrow, and sickness
take possession of
'01. 13–11   take possession of s· with such a sense
temptation and
Mis. 53– 8   by overcoming temptation and s·,
termed
Ret. 64–20   in belief an illusion termed s·,
that
Mis. 246–10   purged of that s· by human gore,
there is no
Mis. 60– 1   you believe there is no s·,
Un. 2–13   of God, in whom there is no s·.
'00. 15–13   that saith "there is no s·,"
this
Mis. 40–30   requires more . . . to conquer this s·
222–19   This s· against divine Science
'00. 14–27   lay not this s· to their— Acts 7 : 60.
thought of
Mis. 105–28   Destroy the thought of s·,
Un. 15–17   if the thought of s· could be
Hea. 9– 7   The less said or thought of s·,
thrall of
'00. 6–22   from the stubborn thrall of s· to a
tired of
Mis. 324–18   his own heart tired of s·,
to efface
Ret. 64– 6   to efface s·, alias the sinner,
to holiness
Un. 37–10   a change . . . from s· to holiness,
'02. 10–23   yea, from s· to holiness
to meet
Mis. 3–31   to meet s·, and uncover it ;
treated for
Mis. 90– 9   to have a husband treated for s·,
turn from
Mis. 197– 5   exhort people to turn from s·
types of
'01. 16– 7   St. John's types of s·
ultimates
Ret. 64– 1   S· ultimates in sinner,
unless it be a
Un. 37–15   Not unless it be a s· to believe that
unpunished
My. 160–24   unpunished s· is this internal fire,
unreality of
Un. 58–18   the absolute unreality of s·,
No. 4–24   unreality of s·, disease, and death,
unseen
Mis. 318–25   chapter sub-title
Ret. 31–17   the unseen s·, the unknown foe,
unto death
Mis. 120– 9   whether of s· unto death, or of
visible
'01. 13– 5   The visible s· should be invisible :
vision of
Un. 4–26   the vision of s· is wholly excluded.
wages of
Mis. 76–27   wages of s· is death."— Rom. 6 : 23.
'00. 2–20   his stock in trade, the wages of s· ;
was first
Hea. 17–24   S· was first in the allegory,

sin

whatsoever is of
Ret. 94–11 consumes whatsoever is of s·.
without
Un. 58–17 yet without s·." — Heb. 4 : 15.
Mis. 14–30 destroys all error, s·, sickness,
27–12 s·, disease, death) are *unreal.*
33–28 for sickness, as well as for s·,
45–17 S· is not the master of
55–14 is the s· against the Holy Ghost
61–19 * held responsible for the 's·.'"
65– 3 s·, sickness, disease, or death,
66–15 s· is identical with suffering,
70–18 s· was destroying itself,
83–17 s· is the author of sin.
90– 3 power of s· is the pleasure in sin.
93–26 believing that s· is pardoned
96–20 from sickness as well as from s·.
103– 2 say that s· is an evil power,
104–11 Herein s· is miraculous and
107–32 too much or too little of s·.
108– 3 thinks too little of s·.
108–14 S· should be conceived of only as
108–23 S· needs only to be known
187– 3 Jesus demonstrated over s·,
194– 4 s·, sickness, disease, and death are
198–21 product of mortal thought as s· is.
237–21 s· can only work out its own
255–24 for sickness, as well as for s·,
268– 2 curing alike the s· and the
278–16 a curse on s· is always
318–27 making s· seem either too large or
319–12 protest against the reality of s·,
319–12 tends to make s· less or more
333– 1 s· . . . is apart from God,
354– 3 S· in its very nature is
361–18 s· which doth so easily — Heb. 12 : 1.
367–29 would say that . . . must know s·.
Ret. 67– 1 S· existed as a false claim before
67– 6 S· is both concrete and abstract.
67– 6 S· was, and *is,* the lying supposition
67–18 created neither himself nor s·,
67–18 but s· created the sinner ;
94–20 not of faith is s·." — Rom. 14 : 23.
Un. 1– 3 God knows no such thing as s·.
19–13 there would be s· in Deity,
23–19 But mortal mind and s·
24– 2 s· the opposite of goodness.
36–22 and yet admit the reality of . . . s·,
51– 4 and hence that s· is eternal,
54–11 As with sickness, so is it with s·.
54–11 To admit that s· has any claim
56–22 he suffers least from s· who is
58– 1 s·, pain, death, — a false sense of
62–14 S· exists only as a sense,
64– 1 If s· has any pretense of
Pul. 13–20 The s·, which one has made his
No. 30– 5 will not let s· go until it is
32–10 chapter sub-title
32–14 It gives the lie to s·,
32–15 other theories make s· true.
Pan. 10–26 in loathsome habits or in s·,
10–29 S·, sickness, appetites, and
'01. 13–12 S· can have neither entity, verity,
14– 1 or believe in the power of s·,
14– 3 To assume . . . and yet commit s·,
Hea. 17–21 S· is a supposed mental condition ;
17–26 Then was not s· of mental origin;
Po. 31–21 sting of death — s·, pain.
My. 4– 5 Lust, dishonesty, s·, disable the
41–17 * makes no compromise with evil, s·,
116–14 Hence the s·, the danger and
122– 7 S· is like a dock root.
161–32 s·, suffering, and death.
219–12 To say that it is s· to ride to
233–21 apathy, dishonesty, s·.
283–15 S· is its own enemy.
334–21 "To assume . . . and yet commit s·,

sin (verb)
Mis. 12–16 temptations to s· are increased
61–13 *What then does s·?*
61–22 Does God's essential likeness s·,
76– 3 derived capacity to s·.
184–17 saying, "I have the power to s·
198– 3 will have no desire to s·.
198–13 When tempted to s·, we should
235– 2 no longer obliged to s·,
237–13 impossible . . . to s· and not **suffer.**
Pul. 3–10 what can cause you to s·
Rud. 3–5 while mortals love to s·,
My. 288–25 "S· no more, — John 5 : 14.

Sinai
Mis. 17– 1 awful detonations of S·.
151–10 speaketh . . . in tones of S· :
'02. 5–21 voiced in the thunder of S·,

since
Mis. x– 7 published . . . s· April, 1883,
8– 5 cannot, produce health . . . s·
11–27 s· they permit me no other way,
23–30 s·, according to natural science,
24–16 I have s· tried to make plain
25– 8 s· God is Truth, and All-in-all.
27–15 s· the Scriptures maintain
29–16 S· that date I have known
29–18 The census s· 1875
34– 8 s· the physique is simply
65–28 s· both constitute the divine law
66– 2 s· false testimony or mistaken
75– 3 s· Life and Truth were the way
93–22 s· there is in reality no disease.
96–18 atonement becomes more to me s· it
108– 8 s· a lie, being without foundation
108–20 s· that which is truly conceived of,
109–31 s· then, . . . cometh repentance,
110–16 months into years, s· last we met ;
115–20 s· God, good, is All-in-all.
125– 6 s· all that is *real* is *right.*
131–14 s· the erection of the edifice of
136–19 well afford to give me up, s· you
137–11 S· then you have doubtless
139–25 wisdom whereof a few persons have s·
142–13 Each day s· they arrived
163–12 has s· ripened into interpretation
182–20 s· he is and ever was the image
229–10 s· God is omnipresence,
236– 3 s· undertaking the labor of
238– 8 s· no sacrifice is too great for the
243–19 s· my system of medicine is
247–13 s· those bringing them do not
248–27 s· which time I have not
249–17 s· my residence in Boston ;
278–23 s· necessities and God's providence
290– 9 s· whatever is false should disappear.
294–25 S· my residence in Concord,
297– 2 s· the discovery of C. S.,
301–17 s· my private counsel they disregard.
311–20 s· by breaking Christ's command,
330–11 s· man's possibilities are infinite,
334–14 s· there is no disease
345–16 * s· the reign of Christianity began
350–18 and we have not met s·.
369–11 s· madness it seems to many
370–27 s· the good shepherd cares for all
389–17 s· God is good, and loss is gain.
Man. 18–21 others that have s· been elected
85–19 s· receiving instruction as above,
86–21 revised editions s· 1902.
Ret. 16– 7 s· she left the choir
26–24 s· none but the pure in heart
28–25 but I have s· understood it.
43– 2 of healing s· the apostolic days.
50–10 God has s· shown me,
64–20 S· there is in belief an illusion
87–24 s· it is only through the lens of
94–23 s· Science is eternally one,
Un. 9–25 s· the days of Christ.
13–16 s· He is, in the very fibre of His
28–17 s· we learn Soul only as we learn
38–12 s· matter has no life,
56– 4 s· all suffering comes from mind,
Pul. 5– 1 used, . . . my form of prayer s· 1866 ;
6–16 * for which I had hungered s· girlhood,
15– 5 s· exposure is necessary to
35–10 "s· only the 'pure in — Matt. 5 : 8.
36–18 * met Mrs. Eddy many times s·
55–14 * S· then she has revised it
66– 6 * s· then the number of believers
67–16 * unknown a decade s·,
Rud. 5– 5 s· God is Mind.
No. 20–23 ever s· the flood,
24–13 s· evil subordinates good
Pan. 1– 5 s· last you gathered at the
5– 9 S· evil is not self-made,
'00. 10–24 s· publishing this page I have
'01. 2–14 s· it has a divine . . . Principle
2–30 added s· last November
8–15 Can he be too spiritual, s· Jesus said,
15–27 * s· you have sat here in the house
22– 6 not try to mix matter and Spirit, s·
25–26 which has s· been avowed to be
27–10 nothing has s· appeared that
28– 8 writers s· the first century
30– 2 s· ever the primitive Christians,
'02. 5–25 S· God is Love, and infinite,
6– 1 s· it is impossible to have aught
6– 6 S· knowledge of evil, . . . brought
6–10 abused me . . . and have ever s· ;
Hea. 13–25 * "S· ever the history of Christianity
Peo. vi–13 *Boston has s· been the pioneer of*
Po. 3–11 S· first we met, in weal or woe

since

Po.	4–16	*s·* God is good
	39–17	*S·* temperance makes your laws.
	54– 2	*S·* joyous spring was there.
	70–17	Immortal Truth, — *s·* heaven rang,
My.	8–29	* "*S·* the last report, in 1900,
	22–14	* *S·* 1866, almost forty years ago,
	47–17	* *s·* the inception of this great
	47–23	* the years that have passed *s·*
	61– 2	* every night *s·* that time.
	61– 6	* *s·* it seemed impossible
	66–28	* *S·* the discovery by Mrs. Eddy,
	73– 5	* in other countries *s·* that time,
	86–16	* *s·* he had enough.
	91–19	* *s·* C. S. was announced
	92–15	* *s·* 1890 its following had
	95–28	* It is doubtful if, *s·* the days of
	100–11	* *s·* the C. S. sect
	114–26	meaning of this book *s·* writing it.
	116–22	Every loss . . . *s·* time began,
	127–11	religions *s·* the first century.
	146– 7	*s·* the third century.
	147–24	*s·* Christian Scientists never
	181–26	*S·* that time it has steadily
	184– 4	*S·* the world was, men have
	187–24	*S·* the day in which you were
	215–31	*s·* we have no hint of his changing
	219–19	*s·* Christianity must be
	219–22	*s·* Christ, the great demonstrator
	220–13	*s·* justice is the moral signification
	221–26	*s·* matter is not conscious ;
	224–25	*s·* the Scripture declares,
	233– 4	in your daily life, *s·*
	235–26	*s·* there are none
	237– 3	I have *s·* decided not to publish.
	239–29	going on *s·* ever time was.
	266–19	*s·* God is Spirit
	266–20	*s·* this great fact is to be
	266–22	*S·* 1877, these special "signs — *Matt.* 16 : 3.
	267– 2	why not, *s·* Christianity is
	275–18	twice *s·* I came to Massachusetts.
	276– 3	*S·* Mrs. Eddy is watched,
	284–18	*S·* my residence in Concord,
	321–21	* twenty years *s·* I first saw you
	322– 1	* It is not long *s·* I met a
	330– 4	* *s·* the great Master himself
	330– 9	* *s·* Mrs. Eddy was not then a
	334–12	* *s·* this critic places certain
	348–17	*s·* Science demanded a rational
	349– 8	cannot cause disease, *s·* disease
	361–10	not written to her *s·* August 30,

sincere

Mis.	x– 3	sacred and *s·* in trial
	288– 1	your *s·* and courageous convictions
	301–15	too *s·* and morally statuesque
No.	3– 4	modest, generous, and *s·* !
My.	17– 6	the *s·* milk of the word, — *I Pet.* 2 : 2.
	44–26	* convey to you their *s·* greetings
	46–23	* a more *s·* and Christly love
	62–14	* Your *s·* follower,
	86– 3	* will be constant and *s·*.
	292–22	though both are equally *s·*.
	358– 3	if you are *s·* in your protestations

sincerely

Mis.	229– 5	If he believed as *s·* that health
Ret.	19–14	*s·* lamented by a large circle
My.	51– 6	* most *s·* regret that our pastor,
	52– 8	* *s·* acknowledge our indebtedness
	272–15	*S·* yours,
	285–29	Most *s·* yours,
	330–25	*s·* lamented by a large circle
	361–11	*S·* yours,

sincerity

Mis.	106–27	"So live, that your lives attest your *s·*
	175–16	unleavened bread of *s·* — *I Cor.* 5 : 8.
	200–21	sweet *s·* of the apostle,
Man.	39–11	thoroughly to test his *s·*,
'00.	9–18	*S·* is more successful than genius
'01.	1–19	Truth comes from a deep *s·*
My.	74–18	* monument to the *s·* of their faith ;
	81–22	* was the depth of *s·*,
	203–19	A deep *s·* is sure of success,

sin-enslaved

No.	46–20	the sick-bound and *s·*.

sinful

Mis.	19–28	*s·*, material, and perishable,
	25–26	more deplorably situated than the *s·*,
	25–27	and the *s·* can.
	36– 1	erring, *s·*, sick, and dying,
	49–17	*can it be wrong, s·, or*
	125– 8	dominion over his own *s·*
	134– 1	the *s·* and ignorant who
	198– 2	man has no *s·* thoughts
	352–22	to heal the sick or the *s·*.

sinful

Mis.	364– 8	healed, through Truth, the . . . *s·*,
	380– 4	how can *s·* mortals prove that
Un.	14–16	created children proved *s·* ;
	15–16	called . . . man the *s·* ;
	51– 4	that immortal Soul is *s·*,
	52– 2	that there can be *s·* souls
Pul.	14–29	when it makes them sick or *s·*.
No.	1–20	and cleansed the *s·*.
	7–10	eyes of *s·* mortals must be opened
	19–20	A *s·* sense is incompetent to
	25–25	*s·* mortal is but the counterfeit of
	27–20	This material *s·* personality,
	31– 5	they are yet sick and *s·*
'01.	13–26	sense of sin, and not a *s·* soul,
	15–28	* your *s·*, wicked manner of
My.	28–23	* heals the sick and reforms the *s·*
	58–23	* healing the sick and reforming the *s,·*
	200–21	Pale, *s·* sense, at work to

sinfulness

Po.	33– 7	From selfishness, *s·*, dearth,

sing

Mis.	387–10	brother birds, that soar and *s·*,
	389–20	with the angels *s·* :
Man.	62– 4	not neglect to *s·* any special hymn
Ret.	16– 6	"Did you hear my daughter *s·*?
Pul.	82–23	* who *s·* best by singing most
Po.	4–19	with the angels *s·* :
	6– 5	brother birds, that soar and *s·*,
	28–10	Aid our poor soul to *s·*
	34–11	Or *s·* thy love-lorn note
	page 65	poem
	65– 1	O *S·* me that song !
	65–10	O *s·* me "Sweet hour of prayer" !
My.	15–31	* I *s·* the NEW, NEW SONG,
	31–28	* would *s·* Hymn 161,
	155–24	*s·* as the angels heaven's symphonies
	166–22	*s·* the old-new song of salvation,
	174–25	my soul can only *s·* and soar.
	192–26	Of this, however, I can *s·* :
	203– 5	*s·* in faith.

singer

Man.	62– 3	solo *s·* shall not neglect to sing
Pul.	59–20	* solo *s·*, however, was a Scientist,
Pan.	4–21	in the words of the Hebrew *s·*,

singers

Pul.	11– 2	song of silver-throated *s·*,
	43– 3	* thirty-five *s·* in all

singing

Mis.	392–20	Isle of beauty, thou art *s·*
Ret.	4–19	*s·* brooklets, beautiful wild flowers,
Pul.	28–20	* *s·* is from a compilation called
	43– 3	* led the *s·*,
	59–10	* *s·* by a choir and
	82–23	* *s·* most for their own sex.
Po.	47– 3	*S·* the olden and dainty refrain,
	51– 2	Isle of beauty, thou art *s·*
My.	31–30	* And what *s·* it was !
	33– 1	* *S·* the Communion Doxology.
	38–19	* when it came to the *s·*,
	59–23	* attempts to lead the *s·*.
	78–22	* *s·* in perfect unison.
	79– 1	* in the *s·* and responsive reading,
	148–21	*s·* of this dear little flock,
	341–11	The bird of hope is *s·*

single

Mis.	45–19	Science in a *s·* instance decides
	80– 4	on the *s·* issue of opposition to
	110– 3	had not the value of a *s· tear*.
	130–20	without one *s·* mistake,
	145– 8	Does a *s·* bosom burn for fame
	234–17	it never has advanced man a *s·* step
	242–20	if he will heal one *s·* case of
	247–10	to furnish a *s·* instance of
	263–29	a *s·* original conception,
	264–29	A *s·* mistake in metaphysics,
	265–12	Whosoever understands a *s·* rule
	266– 6	to abridge a *s·* human right
	278–11	occasion for a *s·* censure,
	333–27	in a *s·* quality or quantity !
Man.	84–23	A *S·* Field of Labor.
Un.	4– 2	without a *s·* taint of our mortal,
Pul.	4–18	A *s·* drop of water may help to
	12–16	For victory over a *s·* sin,
	26–15	* the gift of a *s·* individual
	28– 3	* by the light of a *s·* candle,
	67–21	* *s·* believers or little knots of them
Pan.	5– 2	Can a *s·* quality of God,
Hea.	13–12	a *s·* drop of this harmless
Peo.	6– 8	* if there was not a *s·* physician,
	10–27	but in a *s·* instance when
My.	69–17	* not a *s·* pillar or post
	112–13	not inconsistent in a *s·* instance
	152–27	nor pardon a *s·* sin ;

single
  My. 294–13   mightily rebuke a *s·* doubt
       342–30   * directed by a *s·* earthly ruler?''

single-handed
  Pul.   2–18   *s·* to combat the foe?

singleness
  Mis. 317–26   *s·* of purpose to uplift the race.

sin god
  Pan.   8– 4   sun god, moon god, and *s· g·*

sings
  Mis. 204–10   while white-winged peace *s·*
       329–30   brooklet *s* melting murmurs
  Un.   26–22   as *s·* another line of this hymn,
  Pul.   81–18   * the lark who soars and *s·*
  Hea.   20– 6   * vie with Gabriel, while he *s·*,
  Po.   66–14   cheer it, perchance, when she *s·*.
  My. 192–17   and *s·* of our Redeemer.

singularly
  Pul.   31–26   * *s·* graceful and winning

sin-healing
  Mis.   66–25   beginner in *s·* must know this,

sinister
  Mis.   43–21   such *s·* rivalry does a vast amount of
       263– 1   but if my motives are *s·*,
  Man.   53–19   a complaint . . . for a *s·* purpose.
  Ret.   71–21   *S·* and selfish motives
       78– 8   carnal and *s·* motives,

sink
  Pul.   14–20   nor again *s·* the world into the

sinking
  Rud.   5–26   and *s·* into oblivion.
  My. 117–24   except by *s·* its divine

sinks
  Ret.   81–20   and so *s·* into deeper darkness.

sinless
  Mis.   17–27   primitive, *s·*, spiritual existence
       76– 2   hence it must be *s·*,
       104–15   *s·*, deathless, harmonious, eternal.
  Un.   15–16   God is commonly called the *s·*,
       15–18   would Deity then be *s·*?
       29– 7   Soul is *s·*, and is God.
       49– 9   the more I see it to be *s·*,
       52– 1   Soul is *s·* and immortal,
  Po.   70–12   For *s·* sense is here
  My. 181– 9   scientific, *s·* life of man

sinned
  Mis.   76–26   if Soul *s·*, it would die ;
       278–14   Job *s·* not in all he said,

sinner (*see also* **sinner's**)
  and sin
    Ret.   64– 4   both *s·* and sin will be destroyed
  and the sick
    Mis. 382– 9   *s·* and the sick are helped thereby,
  and the sin
    Mis.   94– 7   *s·* and the sin are the twain that are
    Ret.   64–13   obvious that the *s·* and the sin are
  awaken the
    My. 230–14   and to awaken the *s·*.
  cleanseth the
    Mis. 322–21   healeth . . . and cleanseth the *s·*.
  condemned the
    Un.   29– 4   Jewish law condemned the *s·*
  converting the
    Mis.   39–30   than in converting the *s·*.
  created the
    Ret.   67–19   sin created the *s·* ;
  from his sin
    Ret.   64– 2   nor the *s·* from his sin.
  greatest
    Hea.   9– 8   The greatest *s·* and the most hopeless
  hardened
    Un.   56–22   suffers least . . . who is a hardened *s·*.
  has no refuge
    Un.   2– 6   The *s·* has no refuge from sin,
  infinite
    Un.   15–19   precedence as the infinite *s·*,
       16– 3   such terms as . . . and *infinite s·*
  is consumed
    My. 160–26   *s·* is consumed, — his sins destroyed.
  is not sheltered
    Mis.   14–31   But the *s·* is not sheltered from
  is reformed
    My. 258– 1   *s·* is reformed and the sick are
  loses
    Un.   2–12   The *s·* loses his sense of sin,
  makes him a
    Ret.   63– 8   which makes him a *s·*,
  mortal
    Mis. 268–22   curing . . . sin and the mortal *s·*.
  must endure
    Mis.   15– 2   *s·* must endure the effects of his

sinner
  none but the
    Mis. 165–25   This cost, none but the *s·* can pay ;
  obstinate
    My. 180–19   The obstinate *s·*, however,
  poor
    Mis. 344–14   poor *s·* struggling with temptation,
  reclaiming the
    Mis. 100– 9   healing . . . and reclaiming the *s·*
  reclaim the
    My. 161– 8   necessary to reclaim the *s·*.
  reformed the
    Mis. 219–30   and he has reformed the *s·*.
    My. 348–26   healed the sick and reformed the *s·*
  reforming of the
    My. 182–17   the reforming of the *s·*,
  reforming the
    My.   v–16   * reforming the *s·* quickly
       155– 2   healing the sick and reforming the *s·*
       271– 7   healing the sick and reforming the *s·*,
  reforms the
    Ret.   67–14   reforms the *s·* and destroys sin.
  reform the
    Mis.   38–20   enlighten and reform the *s·*,
       362–30   to prevent sin or reform the *s·*.
    My.   5–17   heal the sick, reform the *s·*,
       51–16   * heal the sick and reform the *s·*.
       52– 1   * heal the sick, and reform the *s·*,
  sad
    '01.   17– 8   meet the sad *s·* on his way
  saint and
    My.   4–11   blessing saint and *s·* with the leaven of
  saved the
    No.   37–23   saved the *s·* and raised the dead,
  saves the
    My. 348–19   heals the sick and saves the *s·*.
  save the
    Mis. 129–23   Were they to save the *s·*,
  saving the
    '02.   6–11   saving the *s·* and healing the sick.
    My.   4–29   healing the sick and saving the *s·*.
  short-lived
    No.   37– 7   the license of a short-lived *s·*,
  sick and
    No.   15– 1   falling on the sick and *s·*,
  sick and the
    (*see* **sick**)
  sin from the
    Ret.   64– 2   cannot separate sin from the *s·*,
  sin is the
    Ret.   64– 3   sin is the *s·*, and *vice versa*.
  sordid
    Mis. 108– 2   sordid *s·*, . . . thinks too little of sin.
  ultimates in
    Ret.   64– 1   Sin ultimates in *s·*,
  veriest
    Mis. 172–11   shall cover . . . the veriest *s·*.
  was the antipode
    Ret.   67–11   a *s·* was the antipode of God.
  willing
    Mis.   22–27   he who is a willing *s·*,

           —————

  Mis.   61–23   a *s·*, — anything but a man !
       61–24   Then, what is a *s·*?
       62– 4   opposite image of man, a *s·*,
       130–13   same power to make you a *s·*
       165–26   is the *s·* ready to avail himself of
       168– 2   salvation from sin to the *s·*
       184–19   believing that he is sick and a *s·*.
       187–30   sick and a *s·* in order to be
       198– 1   neither be sick nor forever a *s·*.
       221–13   and knows he is a *s·* ;
       221–14   or, knowing that he is a *s·*,
       241– 5   man will no more enter . . . as a *s·*,
       241–29   the *s·* who is at ease in sin,
       277–29   I thunder His law to the *s·*,
       399– 6   *S·*, it calls you,
  Ret.   64– 7   to efface sin, *alias* the *s·*,
       67–18   *s·* created neither himself nor sin,
  Un.   29– 3   If Soul sins, it is a *s·*,
       49– 7   the *s·*, wrongly named *man*.
       53–21   is not a mortal mind or *s·* ;
       53–23   not a mortal mind and a *s·* ;
       59–21   calls sin real, and man a *s·*,
  No.   19–22   A *s·* can take no cognizance of
       29–14   the immortal part of man a *s·*?
  '01.   15–13   A *s·* ought not to be at ease,
  Hea.   18–20   to the sick as much as to the *s·* :
  Po.   75–13   *S·*, it calls you,
  My. 132–26   the *s·*, dreaming of pleasure in sin ;
       150–21   bringing the *s·* to repentance,
       227–29   The *s·* may sneer at this beatitude,
       300– 3   enabling the *s·* to overcome sin

sinner's
  Ret.   63– 7   We attack the *s·* belief in

sinners

addressed to
Mis. 60– 3 *Bible is addressed to s·*
also love
Mis. 13–12 s· also love those that — *Luke* 6 : 32.
apprehension of
Mis. 201–22 beyond the common apprehension of s· ;
contradiction of
Ret. 22–10 such contradiction of s· — *Heb.* 12 : 3.
My. 196–21 such contradiction of s· — *Heb.* 12 : 3.
conversion of
Mis. 229–12 clergyman's conversion of s·.
death of
Un. 50–27 growth, maturity, and death of s·,
hated by
Mis. 1–10 Christianity, hated by s·.
in all societies
No. 41–12 There are s· in all societies,
makes
Mis. 219–24 that mortal mind makes s·,
pray for
'01. 18–30 clergymen pray for s· ;
reclaims
My. 113– 2 reclaims s· in court and in
reformed
'01. 27–19 sick healed, also s· reformed
saints or
Mis. 293–26 makes mortals either saints or s·.
save
Mis. 63–11 *why did Jesus come to save s·?*
'01. 19– 4 He worketh with them to save s·.
My. 200–27 lessen its depths, save s·
saved
Pul. vii–18 sick are healed and s· saved,
Pan. 5–24 healed the sick, and saved s·.
My. 178– 6 sick are healed and s· saved.
saves
'01. 34– 2 whereby Christendom saves s·,
'02. 8–20 The energy that saves s·
My. 185–21 heals the sick, saves s·,
saving
Mis. 124–18 raising the dead, saving s·.
My. 122–29 healing the sick and saving s·.
saving of
My. 104–32 healing of . . . the saving of s·,
sin and
Un. 60– 7 then talk of sin and s· as real.
My. 180–22 In our struggles with sin and s·,
suffer
Mis. 123–24 s· suffer for their own sins,
world of
Mis. 122– 7 salvation of a world of s·,

Mis. 248–15 malice aforethought of s·."
319–15 self-deceived s· of the worst sort.
Un. 52– 3 sinful souls or immortal s·.

sinneth

Mis. 75–27 "The soul that s·, — *Ezek.* 18 : 20.
75–29 material sense) that s·, shall die ;
76–23 sense, which s· and shall die ;
Un. 28– 2 "The soul that s·, — *Ezek.* 18 : 20.
No. 28–25 "the soul that s·, — *Ezek.* 18 : 20.

sinning

Mis. 12–14 s· unseen and unpunished
36–14 animal qualities of s· mortals ;
79–19 A mortal who is s·, sick, and
90– 9 *when she knows he is s·,*
93–29 to indulge a s· sense
186–11 in a sick and s· mortal.
187–25 to create a sick, s·, dying man?
219–20 change the . . . sense of s· at ease
Pul. 14–26 When God heals the sick or the s·,
No. 7–13 away from the enemy of s· sense,
29– 9 believe . . . s· sense to be soul ;
'01. 12– 3 heals the s· and the sick.
15–14 or he would never quit s·.
Peo. 4–21 s·, sick, and dying mortals.
10–18 beliefs, . . . made men s· and sick,

sin's

Ret. 80–13 pulling down of s· strongholds,
Un. 54–13 if s· claim be allowed
Pul. 13–26 must depend upon s· obduracy.
'00. 15–13 to see through s· disguise

sins

her
My. 126–16 her s· have reached unto — *Rev.* 18 : 5.
his
Mis. 107–29 Without a knowledge of his s·,
213– 9 "He that covereth his s· — *Prov.* 28 : 13.
Un. 55– 6 he bore not *his* s·, but *ours*,
My. 160–27 sinner is consumed, — his s· destroyed.
his own
Un. 56– 7 Not his own s·, but the sins of

sins

indulgence of the
My. 64–21 * against the indulgence of the s·
mistakes or
Mis. 72– 3 because of his parent's mistakes or s·,
my
Mis. 326–32 "The sight of thee unveiled my s·,
of a few
Peo. 8– 7 for the s· of a few tired years
of the flesh
Mis. 162–21 to escape from the s· of the flesh.
My. 6– 7 done forever with the s· of the flesh,
of the world
Mis. 246– 2 covers the s· of the world,
Un. 56– 7 but the s· of the world,
one's
Mis. 109–14 should one's s· be seen
open
My. 212– 7 older and more open s·,
other people's
My. 233–14 the effects of other people's s·
others'
Mis. 115–31 of your own as well as of others' s·.
presumptuous
Ret. 72– 8 presumptuous s·, and self-deception,
saved from the
'01. 11–10 saved from the s· and sufferings
sickness and
Mis. 173– 7 healeth all our sickness and s·?
sin of
'01. 20–19 This unseen evil is the sin of s· ;
their
My. 28–27 * of their diseases and their s·,
their own
Mis. 123–24 sinners suffer for their own s·,
thy
No. 42– 9 "Thy s· are forgiven — *see Luke* 5 : 23.
trespasses and
My. 133–15 "dead in trespasses and s·," — *Eph.* 2 : 1.
150–22 dead in trespasses and s·
your
Un. 60–25 are yet in your s·." — *I Cor.* 15 : 17.

Mis. 61–20 *What s·?*
Ret. 25–12 That which s·, suffers, and dies,
Un. 29– 3 If Soul s·, it is a sinner,
29– 6 Spirit never s·,
30– 7 Soul is Life, and . . . never s·.
30– 9 Hence this lower sense s·
No. 29– 3 Not Soul, but mortal sense, s·

sinuous

Un. 54–28 diabolical and s· logic?

Sion

My. 17–15 Behold, I lay in S· a — *I Pet.* 2 : 6.

sir

Mis. 132–12 *Dear S· :* — In your communication
134– 3 dear s·, as you have expressed
My. 118– 9 *My Dear S· :* — I beg to thank you
137–11 *Respected S· :* — It is over forty years

sire

Po. 1– 1 s·, unfallen still thy crest !

siren

Po. 43–13 and, when At some s· shrine

sirens

Mis. 280–29 rocks and s· in their course,

Sisera

Un. 17– 7 fought against S·. — *Judges* 5 : 20.

sister

Mis. 151–18 Brother, s·, beloved in the Lord,
Man. 64–21 such as s· or brother.
Chr. 55–24 my brother, and s·, — *Matt.* 12 : 50.
Ret. 20– 6 s· of Lieutenant-Governor
'02. 3–18 rejoices with our s· nation
Peo. 10–10 It were well if the s· States
Po. 65–11 Ah, sleep, twin s· of death
My. 313–27 My oldest s· dearly loved me,
(see also **Eddy**)

sisterhood

'02. 3–10 joy in the s· of States.

sisters

Mis. 167–16 his parents, brothers, and s·?
Ret. 6–10 parents, brothers, and s·,
13– 7 if my brothers and s· were to be
14–16 safety with my brothers and s·,
Po. 25– 5 S· of song,
My. 62– 9 * give it to my brothers and s·?"
217– 3 your parents, brothers, or s·.

sit

Mis. 17–12 to s· at the feet of Jesus.
73–24 *shall s· in the throne* — *Matt.* 19 : 28.
73–25 *s· upon twelve thrones,* — *Matt.* 19 : 28.
125–11 s· down at the Father's right hand :

sit

Mis.	125–12	s· *down ;* not stand waiting
	154–13	s· beneath your own vine
	159–15	s· silently, and ponder.
	171– 8	that Christian Scientists s· in
	361–16	s· at the feet of Jesus.
	373–28	s· down at the right hand of the
	388–15	The right to s· at Jesus' feet ;
	400– 5	be in thy place : Stand, not s·.
Pul.	16–17	be in thy place ; Stand, not s·.
	48– 7	* can s· in her swinging chair,
'00.	15– 5	To s· at this table of their
'02.	3–21	will s· easier on the brow of
Po.	21–14	The right to s· at Jesus' feet ;
	76–16	be in thy place : Stand, not s·.
My.	192– 1	Ye s· not in the idol's temple.
	228–18	who s· at the feet of Truth,
	324–27	* to s· through your class.

site

Mis.	139–23	had this desirable s· transferred
Man.	103– 6	nor removed from the s·
Pul.	57–25	* s· of the new Music Hall,
My.	9–23	purchase of more land for its s·,
	15– 8	nor removed from the s·
	16– 8	the s· of the new building.
	67– 9	* Area of s· . . . 40,000 sq. ft.
	215–19	to purchase the s· for a church

sits

Mis.	ix–13	now hope s· dove-like.
	369–12	This method s· serene at the portals
'00.	15–15	it s· in sackcloth
My.	192–16	s· smilingly on these branches
	349–13	s· at the feet of Jesus

sitteth

Mis.	126–28	she s· in high places ;
	126–30	"He that s· in the heavens— *Psal.* 2 : 4.
	178–12	s· on the right hand of God"— *Col.* 3 : 1.
Peo.	5–15	it s· beside the sepulchre

sitting

Po.	page 8	poem
	8– 1	s· alone where the shadows fall
My.	159– 7	S· at his feet,

sitting-at-table

Mis.	231–26	his first s· on Thanksgiving

situated

Mis.	25–25	The sick are more deplorably s·
	139–19	s· near the beautiful Back Bay Park,
	144– 3	s· in the second story of the
Man.	99–19	in which London, England, is s·
Ret.	4–10	s· on the summit of a hill,
	5– 1	small town s· near Concord,
My.	66–15	* so well s· for church purposes
	271–13	* modest, pleasantly s· home
	309–18	an extensive farm s· in Bow

situation

Mis.	236– 1	has not suffered from the s·
	265–14	is master of the s·.
	298– 3	St. Paul's words take in the s· :
Man.	75–12	now understands the financial s·
	75–15	Financial S·.
Ret.	44–17	Examining the s· prayerfully
My.	10–10	* best of design, material, and s·.
	217–26	understanding the s· in C. S."
	302–26	and the s· was satisfactory.

six

Mis.	243– 9	bandages to remain s· weeks,
	279–18	the s· days are to find out the
Man.	62– 1	s· or seven minutes for the postlude,
Ret.	5– 7	youngest of my parents' s· children
	43–22	by myself and s· of my students
Pul.	6–13	* "S· months ago your book, S. and H.,
	26–11	* bearing s· . . . silver lamps,
	27–14	* with s· small windows beneath,
	27–15	* the s· water-pots referred to
	86– 2	* s· inches in each dimension,
'02.	15–21	S· weeks I waited on God to
	16– 1	S· months there after Miss Dorcas
My.	30–19	* repeated s· times during the day.
	31– 9	* The s· collections were large,
	66–22	* Promptly at half past s·
	70–25	* when s· services will be held,
	77–22	* it is a combination of s· organs,
	78– 3	* at s· o'clock this morning.
	164–16	* s· services, identical in character,
	312– 7	s· dear churches are there,
	333–28	* s· months after his marriage,
		* brief space of s· months,
		(*see also* **numbers**)

sixteen

Man.	73– 1	organized with less than s·
My.	304– 9	At s· years of age,
		(*see also* **numbers;**

sixteenth

Mis.	83–28	* Quoted from the s· edition.
My.	138–26	* On this s· day of May,

sixth

Mis.	35–30	* See the s· edition.
	57–25	of the s· and last day,
	191– 8	in John. s· chapter

Sixth Church of Christ, Scientist

My.	363– 4	* signature

sixty

Pul.	32–20	* must have been some s· years of age,
Po.	35–15	Written more than s· years ago
		(*see also* **numbers**)

sixty-five

Mis.	279–12	AN ATTENDANCE OF S· STUDENTS.

sixty-four

(*see* **numbers**)

sixty-two

Ret.	37–10	it had reached s· editions.
		(*see also* **numbers**)

size

My.	11–26	* The s· of the building was decided
	67–27	* Notwithstanding its enormous s·,
	68– 8	* twice the s· of the dome on the
	69–26	* chapter sub-title
	69–27	* an idea of the s· of this building
	77– 2	* its great s·, beautiful architecture,
	86–28	* the great s· of the auditorium
	89– 2	* in its s·, if not in its aspect,

sizes

Pul.	62–22	* as they range in all s·,

skeleton

Mis.	302– 7	the s· without the heart,

skeptic

No.	42–28	Here a s· might well ask if the
My.	94–14	* much to convince the s·.
	98– 1	* impress the most determined s·.

skepticism

Mis.	7–11	s· and incredulity prevail in
My.	179–15	Some dangerous s· exists

sketch

Mis.	373–19	master's thought presents a s· of
	376–10	* small s· handed down from
Pul.	46–11	* touched upon in this brief s·.
	61–18	* which stands at the head of this s·.
	67– 4	* S· OF ITS ORIGIN AND GROWTH

sketches

Ret.	2– 6	in John Wilson's s·.

sketching

Po.	8–13	s· in light the heaven of my youth

skies

Mis.	262–24	With all the homage beneath the s·,
	329–30	of fair earth and sunny s·.
	347– 9	discern the face of the s·
	387– 4	mount upward unto purer s· ;
	392– 3	s· clasp thy hand,
	395–26	Of sunny days and cloudless s·,
Po.	20– 3	s· clasp thy hand,
	25– 4	Soft tints of the rainbow and s·
	50–22	mount upward unto purer s· ;
	58–11	Of sunny days and cloudless s·,
My.	129–11	The oracular s·, the verdant earth
	193– 7	gorgeous s· of the Orient
	265–27	clearer s·, less thunderbolts,

skilful

Mis.	81– 2	s· and scholarly physicians
	231–11	s· carving of the generous host,
	349– 6	who are s· obstetricians.
Hea.	14–11	be sure he is a learned man and s· ;
My.	152–32	flowers that my s· florist has
	294–16	s· surgeon or the faithful M.D.
	314–10	considered a rarely s· dentist.

skill

Mis.	29–23	diseases that had defied medical s·.
	49– 8	had the s· and honor to state,
	232–13	Human s· but foreshadows
	270– 5	What artist would question the s· of
	351– 7	I have no s· in occultism ;
Ret.	26– 1	and his marvellous s· in
	95– 4	* Ask God to give thee s·
Pul.	55– 2	Not in cunning sleight of s·,
Peo.	8–28	s· proved a million times unskilful.
My.	190–18	as to the relative value, s·, and
	273– 8	* s·, determination, and energy

skin

Pan.	3–30	his spotted s·, the stars ;

skins

Pul.	76–15	* of s· of the eider-down duck,

skirmishing

Pul.	50–25	* after a little s·, finally subsides.

skirt

Pul.	48–12	* woods that *s·* the valley

skulking

My.	228– 7	The evil mind calls it "*s·*,"

skull

Mis.	55–29	If Mind is . . . beneath a *s·* bone,
Un.	33–15	is only matter within the *s·*,

sky

Mis.	1– 7	discern the face of the *s·* ; — *Matt.* 16 : 3.
	87– 2	clear ether of the blue temporal *s·*.
	376–18	splendor of a November *s·*.
Ret.	17–13	has stolen the rainbow and *s·*,
Pul.	4– 6	I'll tarry in the *s·*.' "
	39–19	* The splendor of the *s·*
Rud.	6– 3	*glories of earth and s·*,
No.	14–14	coruscations of the northern *s·*
Po.	8–16	dreaming alone of its changeful *s·*
	19– 2	breezes that waft o'er its *s·* !
	30– 4	new-born beauty in the emerald *s·*,
	32– 9	sunbeams enkindling the *s·*
	35–14	Bird, bear me through the *s·* !
	62–16	has stolen the rainbow and *s·*,
My.	149–27	Clouds . . . that swing in the *s·*
	150–16	See therein the mirrored *s·*
	151–19	* 'neath the temple of uplifted *s·*
	234– 5	they only cloud the clear *s·*,

sky-lines

My.	85–31	* one of the few perfect *s·*

slain

Mis.	xi–26	sadly to survey the fields of the *s·*
My.	185–17	Life is the "Lamb *s·* — *Rev.* 13 : 8.

slander

Mis.	32–28	should never envy, elbow, *s·*,
	226– 8	chapter sub-title
	226–29	*S·* is a midnight robber ;
	246–17	stop free speech, *s·*, vilify ;
	347–32	targets for envy, rivalry, *s·* ;
Man.	81–23	No idle gossip, no *s·*,
No.	32–26	*s·* loses its power to harm ;

slanderer

Mis.	248–10	estimate of the person they called *s·*,

slanderers

Mis.	227– 7	*s·* —those pests of society
	345–22	pagan *s·* affirmed that Christians

slanderous

Mis.	277–15	namely, by *s·* falsehoods

slanderously

Mis.	298– 4	as we be *s·* reported, — *Rom.* 3 : 8.

slang

My.	108–20	Ignorance, *s·*, and malice
	308–28	no profanity and no *s·* phrases.

slaughtering

My.	286– 4	no more barbarous *s·* of

slaughters

Mis.	123– 2	same spirit that . . . *s·* innocents.

slave

Mis.	183–10	he is neither the *s·* of sense, nor
	246–13	The cry of the colored *s·*
Peo.	10– 8	succored a fugitive *s·* in 1853,
Po.	25–15	Be he monarch or *s·*,
	78–10	Tears of the bleeding *s·*

slavery

Mis.	237–28	fetters of one form of human *s·*.
Peo.	10–27	when African *s·* was abolished
Po.	vi–20	*prohibiting s· in the United States.*"
My.	266– 6	industrial *s·*, and insufficient freedom
	309–15	*s·* he regarded as a great sin.

slaves

'02.	15–18	much of his property was in *s·*,
Peo.	11–13	the sick, the sensual, are *s·*,
My.	197– 2	becoming *s·* to pleasure

slay

Mis.	195–25	sling would *s·* this Goliath.
	250– 8	fattening the lamb to *s·* it.

slays

Mis.	254–11	when brother *s·* brother,

sleep

Mis.	23– 5	* Does mind "*s·* in the mineral,
	36–28	as in the dreams of *s·*.
	47–15	In *s·*, a sense of the body
	215–16	as when a child in *s·* walks on the
	298–26	relief from pain in . . . *s·*."
	335–23	zealots, who, like Peter, *s·* when
	400–16	Guard me when I *s·*.
Ret.	61– 6	as when you awaken from *s·*
	69– 6	deep *s·*, in which originated the
'02.	17–12	Many *s·* who should keep themselves
Hea.	17–16	the "deep *s·*" — *Gen.* 2 : 21.
Po.	3– 9	*s·* sets drooping fancy free

sleep

Po.	65–11	*s·*, twin sister of death
	69– 4	Guard me when I *s·* ;
My.	83–16	* will have time to rest and *s·*,
	132–28	satisfied to *s·* and dream.
	296–12	neither does he *s·* nor rest from

sleeper

My.	133–14	should waken the *s·*,

sleepers

Mis.	60–17	*s·*, in different phases of thought,
	325–29	ingress to that dwelling of *s·*
	342–15	brooded over earth's lazy *s·*.

sleeping

My.	150–15	*s·* amid willowy banks

sleeps

Mis.	60–19	or for one who *s·* to communicate
	209–17	God neither slumbers nor *s·*.
	257– 4	presupposes that God *s·*
Pan.	9– 1	* "*s·* in the mineral,

sleeve

Pul.	49–14	* touching my *s·* and pointing,

sleight

Pul.	55– 2	* Not in cunning *s·* of skill,

sleight-of-hand

Hea.	5–16	except *s·* and hallucination

slender

Mis.	330–32	to put forth its *s·* blade,
Pul.	31–28	* Her figure was tall, *s·*, and

slept

Mis.	225–27	deep flush faded . . . and he *s·*.
	245– 6	Asa *s·* with his fathers." — *II Chron.* 16 : 13.

slight

Mis.	240–23	*s·* sway over the fresh, unbiased
	300–31	he who withholds a *s·* equivalent
Rud.	17– 1	A *s·* divergence is fatal
No.	29– 8	mind-quacks have so *s·* a knowledge
	34–14	Physical torture affords but a *s·*
My.	88–19	* a *s·* and material development

slightest

Mis.	221– 1	does not, produce the *s·* effect,
	289– 3	its *s·* use is abuse ;
	349–24	before I would accept the *s·*
My.	75–14	* has not been the *s·* hitch
	75–20	* not the *s·* evidence of temper,
	96– 7	* none . . . with the *s·* trace of

slightly

Mis.	x–17	My signature has been *s·* changed
	209– 7	healest the wounds of my people *s·*
	380–17	practised in *s·* differing forms.
My.	233–17	healed . . . my people *s·*, — *Jer.* 6 : 14.

sling

Mis.	195–25	*s·* would slay this Goliath.
My.	125– 9	the *s·* of Israel's chosen one

slipping

Mis.	341– 7	after much *s·* and clambering,

slips

Mis.	9–18	but it *s·* from our grasp,

slopes

Pul.	48– 1	* well placed upon a terrace that *s·*
Po.	41–13	green sunny *s·* of the woodland

sloping

Ret.	91–15	near the *s·* shores of the Lake of
My.	309–24	My father's house had a *s·* roof,

sloth

Mis.	342– 5	They heeded not their *s·*,

slothful

My.	132–27	*s·*, satisfied to sleep and dream.

slow

Mis.	117–24	inclined to be too fast or too *s·* :
	223–26	"He that is *s·* to anger — *Prov.* 16 : 32.
	340–23	however *s·*, thy success is sure :
	400–24	Be it *s·* or fast,
Ret.	78– 2	being too fast or too *s·*.
Hea.	8–12	The world is *s·* to perceive
Peo.	1–10	footsteps of thought, . . . are *s·*,
Po.	65– 3	Life's pulses move fitful and *s·* ;
	69–12	Be it *s·* or fast,
My.	44– 7	* may be fast or it may be *s·*,
	196– 9	*s·* to speak, *s·* to wrath." — *Jas.* 1 : 19.
	196–10	"He that is *s·* to anger — *Prov.* 16 : 32.

slowly

Mis.	216–20	* "vanished quite *s·*,
	316–18	turn them *s·* toward the haven.
Ret.	80– 8	* mills of God grind *s·*
Hea.	11– 7	yielding *s·* to metaphysics ;
	11–10	her modest tower rises *s·*,
My.	342– 3	* *s·* descending the stairs.

slumber
'02. 15–24 when s· had fled,
My. 189–18 senses wake from their long s·

slumbered
No. 41–19 Through long ages people have s·

slumberers
Mis. 326–10 thence they spread to the house of s·

slumbering
Mis. 283–11 rouse the s· inmates,
'00. 3–13 the s· capability of man.

slumbers
Mis. 209–17 God neither s· nor sleeps.
400– 2 S· not in God's embrace ;
Pul. 16–14 S· not in God's embrace ;
Po. 76–13 S· not in God's embrace ;
My. 252–30 that neither s· nor is stilled by

small
Mis. 6–31 s· families of one or two children,
27–29 it is a s· manifestation of Mind,
134–26 "still, s· voice" — I Kings 19 : 12.
138–27 "still, s· voice" — I Kings 19 : 12.
147–11 and indicates a s· mind?
164–13 babe Jesus seemed s· to mortals ;
175– 1 "still, s· voice" — I Kings 19 : 12.
294–13 but he is a s· animal :
305–16 * s· contributions from many persons
325– 7 s· conceptions of spiritual riches,
360–25 "still, s· voice" — I Kings 19 : 12.
376–10 * s· sketch handed down from
Man. 72–17 not more than two s· churches
112– 5 capitalized (The), or s· (the),
Ret. 5– 1 s· town situated near Concord,
40– 3 and living on a s· annuity.
52– 6 have a s· portion of its letter
80– 9 * Yet they grind exceeding s· ;
Un. 5– 3 rejoice in the s· understanding
Pul. 3–27 so s· that I am afraid.
4– 4 'So s· a drop as I
27–14 * with six s· windows beneath,
27–17 * Beneath are two s· windows
62–23 * placed on a s· centre table.
65– 7 * which is rather s· and new,
69–16 * It would take a s· book to explain
Rud. 7– 3 scientific, in a s· degree,
No. 1– 4 still, s· voice," — I Kings 19 : 12.
1– 7 S· streams are noisy
8– 4 To this s· effort let us add
32–19 evil, must be s· and unreal.
38– 2 is to-day proving in a s· degree,
'00. 7–15 learned, in a s· degree, the Science
'02. 15–30 "still, s· voice" — I Kings 19 : 12.
My. 42–25 * to comprehend, even in s· degree,
45–11 * represent only a s· part of the
78–16 * and none proffering s· change.
83–10 * Scientists frequently wear a s· pin,
123–25 s· beginnings have large endings.
123–28 we must not overlook s· things
145– 3 acquainted with the s· item
162– 7 A s· group of wise thinkers
169– 4 so long a trip for so s· a purpose
182–13 s· sowing of the seed of Truth,
249– 5 "still s· voice" — I Kings 19 : 12.
309–22 * a s·, square box building

smaller
My. 82–10 * and s· articles of baggage
342–16 * in the other and s· parlor

smallest
Mis. 224–17 into life with the s· expectations,
Rud. 2–23 Healing . . . sickness is the s· part
13– 7 even in the s· degree.
My. 88–17 * constitute the s· feature of the

smallpox
Mis. 257–32 may infect you with s·,
344–15 or to a man with the s·
My. 344–28 the fear of catching s· is

smart
Mis. 297–10 S· journalism is allowable,

smartly
Mis. 230–12 Rushing around s· is no proof of

smell
Mis. 28– 3 Matter can neither see, . . . nor s· ;
86–28 What mortals hear, see, . . . s·,
Un. 24–25 to see, taste, hear, feel, s·.
Rud. 5–20 The body does not see, hear, s·,
Hea. 16–21 can neither see, . . . nor s· God ;

smells
Un. 25– 9 s· as Mind, and not as matter.

smile
Mis. ix–13 hope, disappointment, sigh, and s·
203– 6 as I look on this s· of C. S.,
388–15 won from vice, by virtue's s·,

smile
Ret. 20–17 Thy s· through tears,
42–13 with a s· of peace and love
Pan. 1– 8 frown and s· of April,
Peo. 7–10 * his face lit up with a s· of joy
Po. 21– 3 won from vice, by virtue's s·,
74– 4 S· on me yet, O blue eyes and jet,
My. 6– 9 s· and deceit of damnation.
129–11 there is no day but in His s·.
271–16 * This lady with sweet s·
342– 4 * She entered with a gracious s·,
345– 9 * "Not," with a s·, "if it is really

smiled
Mis. 126–27 hath indeed s· on my church,
127– 2 s· on His "little ones," — Matt. 18 : 6.
Hea. 6– 5 pardon me if I s·.
My. 17–30 s· on His 'little ones,' — Matt. 18 : 6.
29–25 * Even the sun s· kindly upon the

smiles
Mis. 179–27 to give us these s· of God !
231– 2 middle age, in s· and the
390–19 As s· through teardrops seen,
Pul. 82– 4 * her words are s·
82– 4 * her s· are the sunlight
Po. 55–20 As s· through teardrops seen,

smileth
Po. 15–16 Here s· the blossom

smiling
Mis. 148– 1 never shows us a s· countenance
339–17 s· saith, "Thou hast — Matt. 25 : 23.
Peo. 14– 5 cool grottos, s· fountains,
Po. 26–16 And s·, say'st, " 'Tis done !
My. 49– 2 * when these s· people say,
155–31 flowers . . . s· upon them.

smilingly
'00. 2–19 is supposed to answer s· :
My. 192–16 dove of peace sits s·

smite
Mis. 335– 5 shall begin to s· — Matt. 24 : 49.
Ret. 30– 2 endeavoring to s· error with the
45–20 "Whosoever shall s· — Matt. 5 : 39.
81– 1 which s· the heart and threaten
'02. 10–20 s· the reformer who finds the
My. 227–27 "Whosoever shall s· — Matt. 5 : 39.

smites
Mis. 257–28 pitiless power s· with disease

Smith (see also Smith's)
Hon. Hoke
Pul. 48–19 * photograph of Hon. Hoke S·,

'00. 13–25 S· writes : "In this city

Smith, LL.B., C. S. B.,
Judge Clifford P.
My. 142– 8 Judge Clifford P. S·, LL.B., C.S.B.,

Smith's
Mr.
Mis. 299–18 If I enter Mr. S· store
299–21 These garments are Mr. S· ;

Smith's grammar
My. 311–30 * finished S· grammar and

smitten
Mis. 11–29 When s· on one cheek,

smoke
Mis. xii– 7 above the s· of conflict
Hea. 2– 9 amid the s· of battle.

smoked
Mis. 69–26 was — eating s· herring.

smoking
Mis. 90–10 or for drinking and s·?
240–27 habit of s· is not nice,
'02. 18–11 quenched not the s· flax,

smooth
Mis. 347–21 It may be s·, or it may be rugged ;
Un. 64–15 Mortals may climb the s· glaciers,
My. 166–18 in the s· seasons and calms

smoothing
Mis. 257–31 S· the pillow of pain

smoothly
Mis. 118–13 and pass a friend over it s·,

smooth-tongued
Mis. 19–23 or would have in a s· hypocrite

smoulder
My. 211– 8 allowing it first to s·,

Smyrna
'00. 13–12 founded the city of S·,
13–14 writes of this church of S· :

snake
Un. 44–11 a false personality, — a talking s·,

snare
Mis. 389–11 Can I behold the s·,
 389–22 No s·, no fowler, pestilence or
Po.   4–10 Can I behold the s·,
 5– 1 No s·, no fowler, pestilence or

snares
Mis. 307–27 should beware of unseen s·,

snatch
Rud. 16–26 s· at whatever is progressive,

snatched
My. 178–23 s· this book from the flames.
 315–28 s· me from the *cradle* and

sneer
Mis. 69– 3 A s· at metaphysics is a scoff at
 86–23 is something that defies a s·.
My. 92–22 * cannot s· away the two-million-dollar
 94– 6 * cannot s· away the two-million-dollar
 96–25 * It is the custom to s· at C. S.,
 227–29 sinner may s· at this beatitude,

sneered
Ret. 37–11 Those who formerly s· at it,

sneering
My. 96–26 * will soon be beyond the s· point.

sneers
'01. 18– 6 the s· forty years ago

Snider
 Carrie Harvey
My. 325–18 * signature
 Mr.
My. 323–28 * Mr. S· and myself boarded in the

snow
Mis. 329–29 stricken . . . with winter's s·,
Pul. 8–18 Little hands, . . . shoveled s·,
Po. 65– 6 robes were as spotless as s· :

snow-bird
Mis. 329–25 The s· that tarried

snows
My. 153– 1 despite our winter s·.

snowstorm
Pul. 60– 1 * (despite the s·) were crowded

snowy
Pul. 33–18 * an old man with a s· beard
My. 271–16 * with sweet smile and s· hair

snuff-taker
No. 22– 8 an inveterate s·.

snuggled
'00. 10–28 gold pieces s· in Pears' soap.

snugly
My. 342–16 * When we were s· seated

soap
'00. 10–28 gold pieces snuggled in Pears' s·.
 10–30 to part with his s·,

soar
Mis. 87– 1 s· above, as the bird in the
 267–19 whose right wing flutters to s·,
 277– 4 but Truth will s· above it.
 361–21 mortals s· to final freedom,
 387–10 brother birds, that s· and sing,
Ret. 18–17 May s· above matter,
Hea. 20– 5 * s· and touch the heavenly strings,
Po. 6– 4 brother birds, that s· and sing,
 28–13 The dove's to s· to Thee !
 34–20 in azure bright s· far above ;
 64– 8 May s· above matter,
My. 131–15 and may thought s·
 174–25 my soul can only sing and s·.
 202– 2 s· above it, pointing the path
 248–20 You s· only as uplifted by

soared
Mis. 385–22 "When hope s· high,
Po. 48–16 "When hope s· high,

soareth
Mis. 354–32 he s· to fashion his nest,
Po. 18–10 he s· to compass his rest,

soaring
Ret. 9–24 * My s· soul Now hath redeemed her
Po. 18– 3 His s· majestic, and feathersome fling
My. 281– 7 s· to the Horeb height,
 290–22 where no arrow wounds the eagle s·,

soars
Mis. 68–30 * which s· beyond the bounds of
Pul. 81–18 * the lark who s· and sings

sobbing
Po. 47–14 Weary of s·, like some tired child

sober
Mis. 384– 8 To thought and deed Give s· speed,
Pul. 83– 5 * from Philip drunk to Philip s·,
No. 19– 8 it is the s· second thought of
Po. 36– 7 To thought and deed Give s· speed,

soberly
Mis. 240–28 s· inform them that "Battle-Axe Plug"
 309–29 Let them s· adhere to the Bible

sober-suited
Mis. 231– 4 The s· grandmother,
 332– 9 may its s· autumn follow

so-called
Mis. 12–22 effects of this s· human mind
 23– 8 subordinates s· material laws ;
 28–10 this s· life is a dream soon told.
 36–16 qualities of the s· animal man ;
 36–22 relative to the s· material laws,
 48– 6 its s· power is despotic,
 55–20 antipodes of the s· facts of
 73– 2 s· material body is said to suffer,
 73–19 s· pleasures and pains of matter
 73–30 s· material senses.
 76–21 the s· soul in the body,
 95–16 between the s· dead and living.
 107–22 knowledge of evil as evil, s·.
 108– 2 or the s· Christian asleep,
 123–13 to appease the anger of a s· god
 128– 3 The lessons of this s· life
 173–14 an opposite s· science,
 183–11 s· pleasures and pains of
 185– 8 constitutes a s· material man,
 185–20 that the s· material senses would
 193–16 "the s· Christian Scientists."
 198–25 based on physical material law s·
 199–27 s· miracles contained in Holy Writ
 200–16 s· miracles of our Master,
 200–28 the s· pains and pleasures of matter
 203–15 hydrology handles it with s· science,
 209–13 physics admits the s· pains of matter
 250– 6 s· affection pursuing its victim
 254–23 hurling its s· healing at random,
 257–10 The s· law of matter is an
 257–12 This s· force, or law,
 257–22 governed by this s· law,
 271– 7 compounded metaphysics (s·)
 272–22 * these s· charters bestow no rights to
 294– 2 last infirmity of evil is s· man,
 325– 6 some, s· Christian Scientists
 325–25 charnel-house of the s· living,
 341–30 the s· pleasures or pains
Ret. 23– 2 illusion that this s· life
 60–26 matter and its s· organizations
 69– 8 pantheistic error, or s· *serpent,*
 78–11 not to read s· scientific works,
 88– 8 the s· dead forthwith emerged
Un. 10– 3 these s· existences I deny,
 11– 7 and s· natural science.
 30– 8 is the s· material life.
 34– 1 the s· material structure,
 34–22 its own s· substance,
 35– 8 s· material senses are found,
 35–19 *are* the s· forces of matter?
 37–21 The s· material senses,
 52–16 God is not the s· ego of evil ;
 54– 9 the s· fact of the *claim.*
 55–18 the s· sufferings of the flesh
 58– 2 if at ease in s· existence,
 63– 7 s· appearing, disappearing,
Pul. 50–24 * s· orthodox religious bodies
Rud. 7–12 s· physical senses,
 7–25 than natural science, s·,
 10–11 mortal material universe, — s·,
 12–18 a s· material organism
 17– 4 these s· schools are clogging
No. 10–15 relates to its s· attributes,
 10–16 When a s· material sense is lost,
 18–24 the s· mortal mind asks for
 18–26 militates against the s· demands of
 31– 3 mortal mind-healing (s·) has
Pan. 4–15 that there are many s· minds ;
'00. 6–17 fact proves that the s· fog of
 13– 9 s· prophetic illumination.
'01. 12–26 embodies itself in the s· corporeal,
 25– 1 Hence the mysticism, s·,
 25– 9 metaphysics (s·) which mix
'02. 9–16 tones of s· material life
Hea. 6–12 intercommunion between the s· dead
 13– 9 s· drug loses its power.
 15–13 the s· miracles recorded in
 17– 8 makes the material s· man,
 17– 9 therefore the s· material man
My. 91– 6 * in this s· commercial age.
 181– 3 and s· natural science,
 219–27 spread of s· infectious
 228– 4 s· disease is a sensation of mind,

so-called

My. 232–27 If *s·* watching produces **fear**
239–25 is the material, *s·* man
274– 3 apart from the *s·* life of matter
275– 6 human, material, *s·* senses
293– 3 and the *s·* power of matter.
302– 9 manifest through *s·* matter.
315–21 what is the *McClure* "history," *s·*,
348– 1 absolutely healed of *s·* disease
349–21 beyond the *s·* natural sciences
(*see also* **laws, mind**)

Social

Po. 39–19 "*S·*," or grand, or great,

social

Mis. 32–25 denominational and *s·* organizations
Pul. 23–17 * potent factors in the *s·* evolution
Pan. 6–13 thereby obtaining *s·* prestige,
'00. 10–12 civic, *s·*, and religious rights
My. 93–25 * economy of our *s·* and religious life.
96– 6 * figures in the *s·* and business world,
163–13 show my love for them in *s·* ways
184–23 rural chapel is a *s·* success
309–30 * supplied the only *s·* diversions,

socially

Mis. 136– 2 it was a departure, *s·*, publicly,
Pul. 80– 9 * women's paradise, — numerically, *s·*,
My. 130– 6 *s·*, physically, and morally

Societies

Man. 95–14 From *S·*.
My. 207–16 * signature

societies

Mis. 32–26 social organizations and *s·*
136– 4 as society and our *s·* demand.
297–13 lofty scorn of the sects, or *s·*,
305– 3 * representative from the patriotic *s·*,
Man. 45– 9 members of other *s·*
74–17 churches and *s·* are required to
74–19 *s·* advertised in said *Journal,*
Pul. 56– 1 * One or more organized *s·*
66– 7 * until now there are *s·* in every
No. 41–12 There are sinners in all *s·*,
My. 57–25 * The number of *s·* advertised
207– 8 * representatives of churches and *s·*
362–14 * churches and *s·* of Greater New York,
362–23 * churches and *s·* in this field

Society

Mis. 350– 7 P. M. (Private Meeting) *S·*
Man. 82– 3 the *S·* will not publish them.
82– 8 nor republished by this *S·*
95–15 may lecture for a *S·*.
Pul. 48–22 * *S·* of the Daughters of the Revolution.

society

above
My. 66– 3 * gives to the above *s·* the ownership
66– 9 * purchase of . . . by the above *s·*,
American
Mis. 296– 6 Was it ignorance of American *s·*
benefits
'00. 2–12 benefits *s·* by his example
cement of
Mis. 145– 1 at present is the cement of *s·*,
Pul. 9– 2 the cement of *s·*, the hope of
Christian endeavor
Pul. 21–12 Let this be our Christian endeavor *s·*,
Christian Science
Man. 74– 2 C. S. *s·* holding public services,
church and
Pul. 20– 3 purchased by the church and *s·*.
church or
Mis. 314– 5 Each church, or *s·* formed for
conforming to
Mis. 138– 6 The detail of conforming to *s·*,
dissolved the
Mis. 350–17 I dissolved the *s·*,
each
Mis. 81– 6 let each *s·* of practitioners,
effect on
Ret. 62– 3 Test C. S. by its effect on *s·*,
fashionable
Mis. 111–22 the pulpit, and fashionable *s·*,
individuals and
'00. 8–10 or a bane upon individuals and *s·*.
My. 211– 4 unseen wrong to individuals and *s·*
member of the
Mis. 305–12 * sent to every member of the *s·*,
305–24 * Each member of the *s·* is asked to
mutual aid
My. 155– 2 mutual aid *s·*, which is effective
our
Mis. 304–10 * under the care of our *s·*.
pests of
Mis. 227– 7 slanderers — those pests of *s·*

society

secret
Mis. 350– 3 I temporarily organized a secret *s·*
sweet
Pul. 8–24 Sweet *s·*, precious children,
thanks of the
My. 49–28 * merited the thanks of the *s·*
this
Mis. 350– 6 brings up the question of this *s·*,
wish for
Mis. 126– 4 Truly, I half wish for *s·* again ;
withdrawal from
My. 118–20 One's voluntary withdrawal from *s·*,
withdrew from
Ret. 24–22 I then withdrew from *s·*

Mis. 126–10 and in *s·* his tongue?
136– 3 as *s·* and our societies demand.
Man. 45– 4 Joining Another *S·*.
74– 4 a branch church and a *s·* ;
'00. 2–11 he gives little time to *s·* manners
My. 53–17 * if she would preach for the *s·*
66–11 * use the *s·* will make of the
93– 4 * in no wise at war with *s·* ;
216–22 request that . . . you disband as a *s·*,

Society of German Patriots

Mis. 305– 5 * the *S· of G· P·*,

Socrates

Mis. 345– 2 St. Paul stood where *S·* had stood
361–14 *S·*, Plato, Kant, Locke,
'01. 24–18 It dates beyond *S·*,

sod

Mis. 385– 2 * triune, Above the *s·*
396– 9 Yet here, upon this faded *s·*,
Ret. 18–16 the eaglet that spurneth the *s·*,
Peo. 5–17 has risen above the *s·* to declare
Po. 37– 2 * triune, Above the *s·*
46–11 Fresh as the fragrant *s·*,
59– 1 Yet here, upon this faded *s·*,
64– 7 eaglet that spurneth the *s·*,
My. 160–15 cuts its way through iron and *s·*,

Sodom

No. 7–14 imperfection in the land of *S·*,

soever

My. 293–31 "What things *s·* ye — *Mark* 11 : 24.

sofa

Mis. 225–21 sat down beside the *s·*.
My. 342– 6 * took a seat on a *s·*.

soft

Mis. 106–26 the *s·*, sweet sigh of angels
126– 5 to hear the *s·* music of our Sabbath
231–21 *s·* as thistle-down, on the floor ;
231–23 *s·* little palms patting together,
329–16 stirring the *s·* breeze ;
329–23 and sweep in *s·* strains her
343–26 Among the manifold *s·* chimes
373–17 as clad not in *s·* raiment
385–13 *S·* gales celestial, in sweet music
390–14 And *s·* thy footstep falls upon
394– 8 tears, as the *s·* summer rain,
Man. 41– 9 "A *s·* answer turneth — *Prov.* 15 : 1.
Ret. 13–21 *s·* glow of ineffable joy
17– 6 Muses' *s·* echoes to kindle the grot.
31–25 *s·* as the heart of a moonbeam,
Pul. 2– 7 *s·* shimmer of its starlit dome.
82– 7 * she is *s·* and gentle,
No. 29–22 though clad in *s·* raiment,
Pan. 3– 9 in stillness, *s·*, silent as the
'02. 4–15 ringing like *s·* vesper chimes
17–28 world's *s·* flattery or its frown.
Po. 15– 1 *s·* sighing zephyrs through foliage
15–12 Their wooings are *s·*
25– 3 *S·* tints of the rainbow
41– 3 Was that fold . . . *s·* virtue's **repose,**
45–10 as the *s·* summer rain,
48– 6 *S·* gales celestial, in sweet music
53– 5 And *s·* thy shading lay
55–15 And *s·* thy footstep falls upon
62– 6 Muses' *s·* echoes to kindle the grot.
66– 6 spirit of love, at *s·* eventide
74– 6 *S·* as when parting
My. 78–10 * an interior done in *s·* gray
134–18 tears like a *s·* summer shower,
174– 4 *s·* greensward proved an ideal

softened

Mis. 354–16 a heart *s·*, a character subdued,
376–23 *s·*, grew gray, then gay,

softening

Hea. 4– 9 a person with *s·* of the brain

softly

Ret.	18– 5	colored *s·* by blossom and leaves ;
Po.	53– 9	More *s·* warm and weave
	63–13	colored *s·* by blossom and leaves ;

soil

Mis.	26–14	and what made the *s·*?
	211–12	are not indigenous to her *s·*.
	251–28	to enrich the *s·* for fruitage.
	265–26	is not in the culture but the *s·*.
	343–12	away from the sordid *s·* of self
	343–24	tear them away from their native *s·*,
	357–14	stony ground and shallow *s·*.
	392–16	deeply rooted in a *s·* of love ;
Po.	20–20	deeply rooted in a *s·* of love ;
My.	160–13	a sapling within rich *s·*

soiled

Mis.	391–16	With bare feet *s·* or sore,
Ret.	86–12	this wanderer's *s·* garments,
Pan.	1–12	wornout, or *s·* garments
Po.	38–15	With bare feet *s·* or sore,

soils

Mis.	340–14	dug into *s·* instead of delving into

sojourn

My.	43– 9	* During their *s·* in the wilderness

sojourning

Mis.	178– 1	the place of my own *s·*

Sol

My.	133–16	and one more round of old *S·*

solace

'01.	34–17	*s·* us with the song of angels
My.	135– 7	applied to old age, is a *s·*.
	268–21	*s·* the sore ills of mankind

solar

Mis.	174–13	broader than the *s·* system
No.	14–14	to *s·* heat and light.
	39–26	as photography grasps the *s·* light
My.	114–18	light of revelation and *s·* light.

sold

Mis.	269–25	C. S. may be *s·* in the shambles.
	270– 3	of them that *s·* doves,''—*Matt.* 21 : 12.
	285– 8	were mistaken for . . . and *s·*.
Man.	64– 4	The literature *s·* or exhibited
	64– 9	literature published or *s·* by
	81–22	C. S. textbook is published or *s·*.
'00.	7– 8	more Bibles *s·* than in all the
'01.	29–25	every book of mine that they *s·*.
My.	v–23	* four hundred thousand copies . . . *s·*
	354– 6	nothing but what is published or *s·* by

soldier

Pul.	65–22	* a Roman *s·* parted his mantle
'00.	10–25	a private *s·* who sent to me,
	10–29	Surely it is enough for a *s·*
My.	277–22	every citizen would be a *s·*
	297– 2	*s·*, patriot, philanthropist,

soldiers

Mis.	138–26	God will give to all His *s·*
Un.	39–20	As *s·* of the cross we must be brave,
Pan.	14–19	remember our brave *s·*,

soldier–shroud

Po.	71–20	O war-rent flag ! O *s·* !

sole

Mis.	24–17	this Life being the *s·* reality
	200–17	*s·* reason that it is their basis.
	308– 1	divine Mind as its *s·* centre
Un.	10– 5	built on Him as the *s·* cause.
	30– 1	Spirit as the *s·* origin of man,
Pul.	42–13	* for the *s·* use of Mrs. Eddy.
	55–28	* Truth is the *s·* recognized authority.
'02.	10–24	*s·* proof that Christ, . . . is the way.
My.	271–10	the *s·* proof of rightness.
	304–17	*s·* editor of that periodical.

solely

Mis.	48–30	*s·* to injure her or her school.
	187–14	*s·* because their transcribing thoughts
	276– 6	*s·* because so many people
	351–11	*s·* from mental malicious practice,
Man.	75–22	and not *s·* to the Directors.
Pul.	82–15	* created *s·* for man.
My.	138–11	but decline to receive *s·* because
	152–12	rests *s·* on spiritual understanding,

solemn

Mis.	13–10	the *s·* consideration of all
	148–10	originated not in *s·* conclave
	177– 1	Never was there a more *s·*
	286– 3	the *s·* vow of fidelity,
	341–24	takes the most *s·* vow of celibacy
Man.	3– 5	originated not in *s·* conclave
Ret.	31– 4	in showing this *s·* certainty
'01.	15–29	* of attending His *s·* worship.
Po.	31–17	*s·* splendor of immortal power,

solemn

My.	46–21	* On this *s·* occasion,
	79– 3	* *s·* little faces turned upward.
	289–11	should upon this *s·* occasion

solemnized

Ret.	42– 2	*s·* at Lynn, Massachusetts,

solemnly

Mis.	176– 6	deeply and *s·* expounded
Man.	16– 9	*s·* promise to watch, and pray

solicit

Man.	87–10	shall not *s·*, or cause or permit
	87–11	or permit others to *s·*,
My.	149–30	*s·* every root and every leaf

solicitations

Mis.	236–15	*s·* of husband or wife
My.	231– 4	in compliance with *s·*

solicited

Pul.	8–11	nor a loan *s·*,
My.	60– 1	* I have been *s·* by many
	89–16	* and subscriptions are not *s·*.

solicitude

Ret.	5– 8	object of their tender *s·*.
	90–20	What other heart yearns with her *s·*,
My.	280– 6	* loving *s·* for the welfare of
	331- 4	* Such watchful *s·* as Mrs. Eddy

solid

Mis.	5–29	seem *s·* substance to this thought.
	66–11	This sacred, *s·* precept
	103– 4	more impregnable and *s·* than matter ;
	156–26	students in acquiring *s·* C. S.
	247–24	seems, . . . *s·* and substantial.
Pul.	77– 4	* a scroll of *s·* gold,
	86– 2	* contains a *s·* gold box,
'02.	14–13	accomplished on this *s·* basis.
My.	45–32	* In *s·* foundation, in symmetrical
	301– 8	leaving a *s·* Christianity at the

solidity

Pan.	3–31	the *s·* of the earth ;
My.	89– 8	* joined lightness and grace to *s·*,

solitary

Mis.	246–18	refuse the victim a *s·* vindication
	282–18	There are *s·* exceptions to

solitude

Mis.	331–25	In sacred *s·* divine Science evolved
Ret.	91–24	*s·* was peopled with holy messages
Pul.	10–10	On shores of *s·*, at Plymouth Rock,
	28– 2	* panel represents her in *s·*
Pan.	3– 3	to preside over sylvan *s·*,
	3– 8	to whisper, "*S·* is sweet.''
	3–14	* "O sacred *s·* ! divine retreat !
Po.	31– 7	peace of Soul's sweet *s·* !
	34–12	In deeper *s·*, where nymph or saint
My.	3–13	not a dweller apart in royal *s·* ;
	230–22	give my *s·* sweet surcease.
	246–13	sought in *s·* and silence

solo

Man.	62– 3	*s·* singer shall not neglect to
Pul.	59–20	* *s·* singer, however, was a Scientist,
My.	32–24	* *S·*, "Communion Hymn," words by
	71– 4	* There is also a *s·* organ attached.

soloist

Man.	61–18	*S·* and Organist.
My.	31–25	* *s·* for the services, Mrs. Hunt,

Solomon (see also Solomon's)

Mis.	203– 9	*S·* saith, "As in water— *Prov.* 27 : 19.
	281–29	remember the words of *S·*,
	347– 1	this first command of *S·*,
Pul.	2– 2	saw the house *S·* had erected.
My.	133–17	give birth to the sowing of *S·*.

Solomon's

Mis.	348–14	Hence, *S·* transverse command :

solution

Mis.	65–15	to gain the true *s·* of Life
	291–29	would aid the *s·* of this problem,
	379–24	assiduously pondering the *s·* of
Un.	9–18	true *s·* of the perplexing problem
Rud.	6– 1	simple *s·* of the problem of being,
Hea.	13–12	single drop of this harmless *s·*,
My.	348–31	nothing . . . ill can enter into the *s·* of

solve

Mis.	54–30	to *s·* a problem involving logarithms ;
	62–24	attempts to *s·* its divine Principle by
Ret.	34– 4	could *s·* the mental problem.
Un.	5–13	attempting to *s·* every Life-problem
My.	110–22	*s·* the blind problem of matter.

solved

Un.	36–10	met and *s·* by C. S.
My.	181–15	would have *s·* ere this the problem of
	348– 9	*s·* sufficiently to give a reason for

solves

My. 180–31 the latter s· the whence and why
306–18 Divinity alone s· the problem of
348–30 it s· the problem of being ;

solving

Mis. 52–28 before s· the advanced problem.

somber

Po. 8– 3 In s· groups at the vesper-call,

some

Mis. x–13 To s· articles are affixed data,
7–20 to be depicted in s· future time
7–22 will counteract to s· extent
30– 2 s· feeble demonstration thereof,
32– 6 I infer that s· of my students
32–31 query in regard to s· clergyman's
38–23 s· speculative view too vapory
39– 8 s· grossly incorrect and false
40–13 In s· instances the students
48–21 hidden nature of s· tragic events
49– 5 manifested s· mental unsoundness,
50– 8 is there a secret . . . as s· say ?
51–28 * transparent like s· holy thing.''
60–28 its counterfeit in s· matter belief.
81– 2 as s· of the most skilful
81–23 Every individual . . . at s· date
89–17 to refuse help to s· who sought
96–26 I can name s· means by which
112–14 s· of the many features and forms
115– 4 apathy of s· students on the subject
155–28 to furnish s· reading-matter
159–30 and s· from abroad,
171– 8 according to the report of s·,
198–23 of adherence . . . to s· belief,
215–10 not seek to climb up s· other way,
216– 9 review of, and s· extracts from,
225–30 * you shall have s· gruel.''
227–12 S· uncharitable one may give
230–11 planning for s· amusement,
233–27 if s· fall short, others will
234–24 she has made s· progress,
236–26 at s· step in one's efforts
243–26 s· of the medical faculty
249– 2 s· large doses of morphine,
249–21 s· malignant students,
264–19 S· students leave my instructions
278–21 than s· of those who have had
278–32 led to s· startling departures
280–27 to answer s· questions
285– 7 s· of these pamphlets were
285–22 s· extra throe of error
293– 7 will come, at s· date,
295–10 * for s· manner of notoriety.''
298– 4 as s· affirm that we say, — Rom. 3 : 8.
311–11 s· of the older members are not
318– 7 s· of those devoted students
318– 8 better than s· of mine who are
325– 6 s·, so-called Christian Scientists
338– 3 brings to humanity s· great good,
349–20 s· of these students have
368–23 S· of the mere puppets of the hour
390– 8 Gives back s· maiden melody,
391–20 S· good ne'er told before,
397–17 My prayer, s· daily good to do
Man. 59– 5 lose s· weight in the scale of
Ret. 2–21 s· newspapers, yellow with age.
2–22 S· of these, however, were not very
8– 3 For s· twelve months,
13– 4 s· circumstances are noteworthy.
48–13 following are s· of the resolutions
54– 2 s· of the cures wrought through
87–14 Let s· of these rules be here stated.
94– 4 At s· period and in some way
Un. 11–19 a theologian of s· bigoted sect,
28– 9 declare s· old castle to be peopled with
44– 2 s· of which are as unkind and unjust
57–28 existence in the flesh is error of s· sort,
Pul. 3–26 Perchance s· one of you may say,
5– 8 glow of s· deathless reality.
8–19 S· of these lambs my prayers had
13– 3 Every mortal at s· period,
14– 3 with fetters of s· sort,
19– 1 My prayer, s· daily good to do
28–13 * valued at s· forty thousand dollars.
31–14 * during s· year in the early '80's
32–20 * s· sixty years of age,
36–28 * s· of the data of this paper.
45– 1 * s· giving a mite
45– 2 * and s· substantial sums.
49– 5 * reproductions of s· of Europe's
50–20 * will awaken s· sort of interest.
50–27 * to show even s· one side of it
51–25 * s· may be satisfied and s· will not.
52– 5 * What a pity s· of our practical
56– 7 * In s· churches a majority of

some

Pul. 59– 9 * program was for s· reason not
64– 9 * s· giving a pittance,
66–25 * s· of the pre-Christian ideas
69– 8 * s· twelve years ago, after several
81–11 * S· of her dearest ones
84–19 * s· measure of understanding
Rud. 16–12 I see that s· novices,
16–12 s· impostors are committing
No. 2–22 s· marked success in healing
3– 1 in s· vital points lack Science.
3– 9 in 1878, s· irresponsible people
9–15 towards s· of my students
16–18 inference of s· other existence
44– 9 To climb up by s· other way
'00. 6–28 S· modern exegesis on the
9–26 to have s· one take my place
10– 3 is s· manifestation of God
10–30 s· of his hard-earned money
'01. 2–15 if s· fall short of Truth,
15–20 S· mortals may even need
17–28 this attenuation in s· cases
22– 3 to s· extent a Christian Scientist.
25–15 ends in s· specious folly.
27– 5 * I look to see s· St. Paul arise
27–11 cannot be traced to s· of those
28–11 S· of his writings have been
31–28 taught by s· grand old divines,
'02. 9–29 s· new-old truth that counteracts
12–21 s· matters of business that
Peo. 3– 9 s· of the false beliefs that
8– 4 partiality that elects s· to
10– 4 that lose s· materiality ;
Po. v– 7 * s· experience that claimed
v–17 * S· tourists who were passing,
13– 5 My prayer, s· daily good to do
34– 5 S· dear remembrance in a
34–13 Has wooed s· mystic spot,
38–19 S· good ne'er told before,
43–13 At s· siren shrine
47–14 sobbing, like s· tired child
55– 9 Gives back s· maiden melody,
77–17 s· dear lost guest
My. 7– 4 s· matters of business that
10–11 * S· money has been paid in
10–12 * s· of the churches and other
10–22 * on the part of s· one else.
26–23 should date s· special reform,
30–22 * S· of these contributions were
30–24 * gave a sum surpassing s· of
40– 9 * It may even imply that s· who
49–24 * giving s· useful hints as to
53–27 * s· very interesting statements,
54–20 * that s· place would be obtained,
55– 4 * purchase s· building, or church,
57–32 * What a pity s· of our practical
59– 6 * in s· far distant day beyond our
59–25 * S· say she did not.''
69–30 * Cambridge, s· four miles away.
71– 2 * and s· of the most intricate
84– 7 * a rule in s· denominations
86–24 * s· of its aspects the most notable
89–28 * It is, in s· respects, the greatest
90–31 * the efficacy of which to s· extent
92–29 * s· such comfort as it promises.
94– 5 * s· of the evidence appears in
100– 2 * s· of the facts and figures
117–16 to get s· good out of your
134–12 eclipsed by s· lost opportunity,
134–12 * s· imperative demand not yet met.
138–12 s· of my students and trusted
152–15 or do I climb up s· other way?
155–28 may they find s· sweet scents
158–22 s· practise what they say.
170–27 Beloved, s· of you have come
179–15 S· dangerous skepticism exists
187– 4 I may at s· near future
219– 3 through s· favored student.
224–15 not caught in s· author's net,
237– 5 wrote . . . s· twenty-five years ago
251–16 evidently s· misapprehension
256– 3 to improvise s· new notes,
268– 6 s· fundamental error is engrafted
281–22 * on s· phase of the subject,
284–19 in s· church in Concord, N. H.
306–31 S· words in these quotations
307–20 in s· respects he was quite
307–21 better than s· others did.
313–18 by s· responsible individual
318– 8 because at that date s· critics
319–16 * conversant with s· facts
319–30 * had done s· literary work
320–13 * something to do with s· editions.
323– 6 * s· minister in the far West.
323–32 * We were at that time s· eight days
329–26 * s· interesting facts concerning

some

My. 329–27   * s· incidents of her life
    334– 3   * s· insidious disease was raging
    334–14   * May it not be, . . . s· other one?
    340–16   shorn of s· of its shamelessness
    345–31   * many subjects, s· only of which
    363–23   misunderstood by s· students.
    (see also **degree, people, time, way**)

somebody (see also **somebody's**)

Mis. 111–30   belief . . . that s· in the flesh is
    123– 5   idolizing something and s·, or
    129–19   he will always find s· in his way,
    130–10   for a fault in s· else,
    223–28   * I should make him hate s·."
    238–13   utilized in the interest of s·.
    239–15   "Ah !" thought I, "s· has to take it ;
    265– 4   original, or wiser than s· else,
Ret.   8– 9   I heard s· call Mary,
My. 61–11   * I saw at once that s· had to
    299– 4   s·, kindly referring to my address

somebody's

Mis. 129–20   will see s· faults to magnify
    335–24   would cut off s· ears.

Some Objections Answered

Pul. 38–12   "S· O· A·,"

something

and somebody
Mis. 123– 5   idolizing s· and somebody, or
apart
Ret. 60– 1   sense defines life as s· apart from
below
No. 26–16   into s· below infinitude.
beside God
Un. 25–12   claiming to be s· beside God,
besides God
Mis. 27–22   claims s· besides God,
    333–25   They believed that s· besides God
Ret. 60– 8   says that . . . is s· besides God.
'02.   6– 7   knowledge of evil, of s· besides God,
besides Him
Mis. 173–25   whence, then, is s· besides Him
    332–30   that there is s· besides Him ;
Ret. 60–22   saith, . . . is s· besides Him,
cast
Mis. 280–14   cast s· into the scale of Mind,
create
Mis. 362–17   out of nothing would create s·,
desirable
Un. 54–21   held it up before man as s· desirable
else
Mis. 178–20   * 'Much learning' — or s· else
Un. 38–15   that s· else also is life,
evil is not
Mis. 284–24   Evil is not s· to fear
for the toilers
Pul. 50– 6   * do s· for the toilers,
good
Pul. 51–29   * have done s· good for the sake of
goodness is
Ret. 63–14   God is good, hence goodness is s·,
higher
Ret. 31–10   s· higher and better
    48–24   s· higher than physic or
My. 221– 6   looked for s· higher
    308– 8   S· higher, nobler, more imperative
impossible
My. 118–22   s· impossible in the Science of
in a name
My. 353– 8   chapter sub-title
inmost
My. 133–26   inmost s· becomes articulate,
in the constitution
Pul. 79–22   * s· in the constitution of
knows
Un. 13–19   that He knows s· which
less
Pan. 11–20   s· less than perfection
makes
'01. 13–17   When man makes s· of sin
matter claims
Mis. 27–22   matter claims s· besides God,
mighty
My. 164–18   A great sanity, a mighty s·
more
Mis.   4–27   s· more than faith is necessary,
My. 79–20   * must be s· more than a fad
new
Hea.   6– 5   pioneer of s· new under the sun
nothing and
Mis. 86–11   Nothing and s· are words which
of a novelty
Pul. 62– 1   s· of a novelty in this country,
opposite of
No. 32–17   nothing, or the opposite of s·.

something

real
Mis. 108–23   conception of it at all as s· real,
sanity and
My. 14– 8   a sanity and s· from the
separate
Ret. 60– 5   as s· separate from God.
Un. 24–22   Evil. I am s· separate from
suggestive
My. 131–21   There is s· suggestive to me in
superb
Pul. 62–15   * quality of tone is s· superb,
sweet
Mis. 240–31   takes from their bodies a sweet s·
tangible
'01.   7–21   not believe there must be s· tangible
that defies
Mis. 86–23   s· that defies a sneer.
that enjoys
'01. 14– 9   and No, as s· that enjoys,
this
Mis. 333– 1   that this s· is intelligent
Un. 22–14   that a knowledge of this s· is
My. 164–21   this s·, this phœnix fire,
    233– 7   if this s·, . . . frightens you,
to be denied
Un. 50– 5   it is s· to be denied
to be desired
Mis. 86–15   and is s· to be desired.
to be proud of
My. 84–13   * temple is s· to be proud of.
to do
My. 320–13   * having had s· to do with
to forget
Mis. 353– 2   but s· to forget.
to know
Un. 22– 9   not admit that error is s· to know
to watch
My. 233– 3   Is there not s· to watch in
understand
Mis. 54– 7   understand s· of what cannot be lost.
Peo.   6–26   we should understand s· of
unlike Him
Mis. 55–30   it is in s· unlike Him ;
No. 16–19   of s· unlike Him
unreal
No. 17– 1   s· unreal, material, and

Mis.   5–27   is s· not easily accepted,
    38– 6   s· to support one's self and
    235–20   and know s· of the ideal man,
    239–27   s· that she ought not to have,
    249–18   unless it was s· to remove stains or
    250–14   Love is not s· put upon a shelf,
    281– 8   could neither deprive me of s· nor
    327– 2   to take s· out of it,
    342–25   It should cost you s· :
    380–21   that s· was being done for them ;
Un. 22–13   Evil. But there is s· besides
    28– 8   define Soul as s· within man?
    49–25   s· which God sees and knows,
Pul. 49–19   * s· of her domestic arrangements,
Pan.   5–22   not believe that . . . can be s·,
    10– 3   think himself to be s·, — Gal. 6: 3.
'01. 13– 8   assumption that nothing is s·.
    13–18   conception of sin as s·,
'02.   6–15   false claim, . . . s· that is not of
Hea. 15–20   believe that sickness is s·
My.   8–14   * that there should be s· done,
    24– 6   * s· of the vastness of the truth it
    29–18   * There was s· emanating from
    60– 2   * s· about the early history of
    82–17   * in s· like ten minutes.
    91– 3   * s· they did not find in other

somethingness

Mis. 109–17   seeing the need of s· in its stead,
    201–14   great s· of the good we possess,
Ret. 55– 7   brings out . . . the eternal s·,

sometimes

Mis. xi–24   thought s· walks in memory,
    52–12   often convenient, s· pleasant,
    52–14   It s· presents the most wretched
    53–11   Do you s· find it advisable to
    75–18   may s· be used metaphorically ;
    88– 2   s· feel the need of physical help,
    90–11   s·, under circumstances exceptional,
    117–25   and, s· out of season,
    128– 1   needs often to be stirred, s· roughly,
    138–10   but s· to coelbow !
    143–28   s· at much self-sacrifice,
    204– 6   This mental period is s· chronic,
    238– 2   are s· made to believe a lie,
    255– 2   It is s· said, cynically,
    255–18   s· asked, What are the advantages of
    262–28   s· to relieve my heart of its

sometimes
Mis.	280–31	*s·* just at the moment when you
	282–23	it is *s·* wise to do so,
	294–12	*vice versa* of this man is *s·* called
	309–28	*s·* take things too intensely.
	350–21	An individual state of mind *s·*
	351– 1	I have *s·* called on students to
Man.	43–11	*S·* she may strengthen the faith by
Ret.	8– 6	*s·* went to her, beseeching her
	54– 1	Why are faith-cures *s·* more speedy
Un.	9–20	*S·* it is said, by those who fail to
	52–25	is *s·* the home of vice.
Pul.	49– 2	* or *s·* "Mother's room,"
Rud.	2–27	this task, *s·*, may be harder than
	14–13	*s·* seventeen, free students
No.	1–10	thrilled by a new idea, are *s·*
	40– 8	*s·* wise to hide . . . pure pearls of
Pan.	9–27	*s·* object to the philosophy of C. S.,
'00.	8–16	sensitiveness is *s·* selfishness,
	8–29	I *s·* advise students not to
	9– 3	I *s·* withdraw that advice and say :
'01.	3–20	It is *s·* said : "God is Love,
	29–12	well-meaning people *s·* are inapt or
My.	109–17	yet we may *s·* say with Job,
	160–22	Physical science has *s·* argued
	206–30	"Ye were *s·* darkness,— *Eph.* 5 : 8.
	215– 9	*s·* a dozen or upward in one class.
	317–18	*s·* saying, "I wouldn't express it

somewhat
Mis.	77–23	learn, in divine Science, *s·* of
	117–25	he works *s·* in the dark ;
	199–18	We learn *s·* of the qualities of
	237– 3	has yielded *s·* to the
	264–17	abstract Science is *s·* untested.
	325–13	*S·* disheartened, he patiently
Pul.	59– 3	* in a *s·* novel way.
'00.	12–18	have *s·* against thee,— *Rev.* 2 : 4.
My.	121–14	is *s·* out of fashion.
	149– 1	must know *s·* of the divine Principle
	320–25	* were at times *s·* long
	324– 3	* Mr. Wiggin had *s·* of a

somewhere
Pul.	32–18	* *s·* in the early decade of

somnambulist
Mis.	215–19	because he is a *s·*,

Son
and Holy Ghost
Un.	51–22	revealed as Father, *S·*, and Holy Ghost ;
'00.	5–11	Father, *S·*, and Holy Ghost mean

beloved
Mis.	121–22	crucifixion of His beloved *S·*,
	206– 8	"This is my beloved *S·*." — *Matt.* 17 : 5.

dear
My.	206–30	kingdom of His dear *S·*." — *Col.* 1 : 13.

His
Mis.	60– 2	*when He sent His S·* to save
Man.	15– 7	We acknowledge His *S·*, one Christ ;
Pul.	30–17	* His *S·*, and the Holy Ghost,
Po.	32–19	pardon and grace, through His *S·*,

His favorite
Peo.	3– 9	torture of His favorite *S·*,

of God
Mis.	63–27	Christ as the *S·* of God was divine.
	77– 2	*Jesus Christ was the S· of God*
	84–15	Christ, was the *S·* of God ;
	84–17	manifestation of the *S·* of God
	161–11	the Christ, or *S·* of God :
	164– 2	incorporeal idea, or *S·* of God ;
	164–25	as the only *S·* of God,
	180–30	*S·* of God and the Son of man ;
	197–14	as a man, as the *S·* of God,
	309–16	we reach the Christ, or *S·* of God,
Chr.	55– 7	voice of the *S·* of God :— *John* 5 : 25.
	55–21	unto the *S·* of God.— *Heb.* 7 : 3.
Un.	61–21	faith of the *S·* of God." — *Gal.* 2 : 20.
No.	31–14	*S·* of God was manifested,— *I John* 3 : 8.
	36–28	ideal Christ was the *S·* of God,
'01.	9– 2	*S·* of God and the Son of man
	10– 8	Christ being the *S·* of God,
	10–16	and of Jesus as the *S·* of God
	11– 2	Christ, the eternal *S·* of God,
'02.	12–13	but is the *S·* of God.

of man
Mis.	73–24	the *S· of man shall* — *Matt.* 19 : 28.
	74– 8	which enthrone the *S·* of man
	83–20	"*the S· of man*" — *Matt.* 16 : 13.
	84–17	was called the *S·* of man,
	180–30	Son of God and the *S·* of man ;
	195–11	*S·* of man is come— *Matt.* 18 : 11.
Ret.	85–14	the *S·* of man will be glorified,
Un.	59– 9	*S·* of man *which is in* — *John* 3 : 13.
No.	36– 9	*S·* of man which is in — *John* 3 : 13.
'01.	9– 2	Son of God and the *S·* of man
	11– 1	his mission . . . as the *S·* of man,

Son
of man
'01.	11– 6	*S·* of man in divine Science ;
	12–11	the *S·* of man cometh, — *Luke* 18 : 8.

of the Blessed
Mis.	337– 9	immaculate *S·* of the Blessed

represented by the
Pul.	13– 2	Truth, represented by the *S·* ;

Thy
Mis.	83–25	glorify Thy *S·*, — *John* 17 : 1.
	83–25	that Thy *S·* also may — *John* 17 : 1.

son
adopted
Ret.	43–10	adopted *s·*, Ebenezer J. Foster-Eddy,

and daughter
Mis.	167– 8	Both *s·* and daughter :
My.	282–24	*s·* and daughter of all nations

bastard
Un.	23– 2	from his bastard *s·* Edmund

clergyman's
Mis.	225–13	clergyman's *s·* was taken violently ill.
	226– 6	clergyman's *s·* returned home— well.

every
Mis.	18– 4	and scourgeth every *s·* — *Heb.* 12 : 6.
Ret.	80– 6	And scourgeth every *s·* — *Heb.* 12 : 6.
My.	282–24	importance to every *s·* and daughter

Father and
'02.	12–18	Father and *s·*, are one in being.

is given
Mis.	161– 5	*unto us a s· is given :* — *Isa.* 9 : 6.
	166–11	unto us a *s· is given :* — *Isa.* 9 : 6.
	168–18	"Unto us a *s· is given.*" — *Isa.* 9 : 6.
	370–10	unto us a *s· is given.*" — *Isa.* 9 : 6.

lawful
Un.	23– 5	His lawful *s·*, Edgar,

Mary's
Mis.	84–18	Son of man, or Mary's *s·*.

my
Mis.	225–18	* "If you heal my *s·*,
Ret.	21– 4	informed that my *s·* was lost.
My.	313–30	obliged to be parted from my *s·*,

my little
Ret.	20– 8	my little *s·*, about four years of age,
	21– 1	letter was read to my little *s·*,

of a year
Mis.	180–27	month is called the *s·* of a year.

of God
Mis.	111–31	that somebody . . . is the *s·* of God,
	161–10	in Science, man is the *s·* of God.
	164–28	reveal man . . . to be the *s·* of God.
	180–26	power to become the *s·* of God.
	182–12	power to become the *s·* of God,

of man
Mis.	63–26	Jesus as the *s·* of man was human :
	161– 9	Jesus was the *s·* of man :
	309–14	personality of Jesus, the *s·* of man,
'01.	10–10	*s·* of man only in the sense that
	10–16	Son of God and the *s·* of man.

of Mary
Un.	59–11	divine idea . . . in the *s·* of Mary.
'01.	10–10	Jesus was the *s·* of Mary,

or daughter
Mis.	167– 7	Is the babe a *s·*, or daughter?

prodigal
Mis.	369–23	as tired as was the prodigal *s·* of the
Ret.	91– 3	The parable of "the prodigal *s·*"

the word
Mis.	180–27	In the Hebrew text, the word "*s·*"

Un.	23–11	what *s·* is he whom — *Heb.* 12 : 7.

sonare
Rud.	1–15	*per* (through) and *s·* (to sound).

song
Mis.	142–22	A boat *s·* seemed more Olympian
	145–28	and echo the *s·* of angels :
	204–10	sings to the heart a *s·* of angels.
	372– 8	through *s·* and object-lesson.
	390– 6	lark's shrill *s·* doth wake the dawn :
	396–24	and breathed in raptured *s·*,
	400– 7	Dirge and *s·* and shoutings low
Ret.	10–17	Prosody, the *s·* of angels,
	17– 3	spirit of *s·*, — midst the zephyrs
Pul.	11– 2	sweet *s·* of silver-throated singers,
	12–18	A louder *s·*, sweeter than has
	16–19	Dirge and *s·* and shoutings low,
	18– 8	and breathed in raptured *s·*,
'00.	2– 7	The *s·* of C. S. is, "Work— work
'01.	34–17	solace us with the *s·* of angels
Po.	12– 8	and breathed in raptured *s·*,
	24–18	With *s·* of morning lark ;
	25– 5	Sisters of *s·*, What a shadowy throng
	29– 8	No cradle *s·*, No natal hour
	30–19	sacred *s·* and loudest breath of
	39– 3	Temperance and truth in *s·* sublime

song
Po.	54– 4	With light and *s·* and prayer !
	55– 7	lark's shrill *s·* doth wake the dawn :
	62– 1	spirit of *s·*, — midst the zephyrs
	page 65	poem
	65– 1	O sing me that *s·* !
	65–19	To rise to a seraph's new *s·*.
	71–17	holy meaning of their *s·*.
	76–18	Dirge and *s·* and shoutings low
My.	14– 4	above the *s·* of angels,
	15–31	* I sing the NEW, NEW *S·*,
	31–32	* joined in the *s·* of praise.
	81–22	* holy *s·* rose tingling
	163– 1	bursting into the rapture of *s·*
	163– 3	sweet sense of angelic *s·*
	166–22	the old-new *s·* of salvation,
	175–25	The *s·* of my soul must remain
	186– 9	its *s·* and sermon will touch
	189–27	the *s·* and the dirge, surging
	194– 1	*s·* and sermon generate only
	197–27	join with you in *s·* and sermon.
	201–10	Your Soul-full words and *s·*
	269–19	Its harvest *s·* is world-wide,
	313– 2	paraphrase of a silly *s·*
	316– 5	harvest *s·* of the Redeemer
	347–15	bird, and *s·*, to salute me.
	354–24	And the *s·* of songs.

songlet
Ret.	18– 9	grotto and *s·* and streamlet
Po.	63–18	grotto and *s·* and streamlet

songs
Mis.	332–11	sheaves, and harvest *s·*.
	356–13	*s·* should ascend from the mount
Pul.	28–21	* its *s·* are for the most part
Po.	53–20	The vernal *s·* and flowers.
	66– 5	*s·* float in memory's dream.
My.	171– 5	with *s·* and everlasting joy
	176–10	palms of victory and *s·* of glory.
	194– 3	*s·* of joy and gladness.
	354–21	Give us not only angels' *s·*,
	354–24	And the song of *s·*.

songsters'
Mis.	396–11	*s·* matin hymns to God
Po.	59– 3	*s·* matin hymns to God

sonnet
Mis.	379–19	one could write a *s·*.
Ret.	1–12	wrote a stray *s·* and an

sonnets
Ret.	1– 9	containing Scriptural *s·*,

Son of God
(see **Son**)

Son of man
(see **Son**)

sonorous
My.	59–19	* as I heard the *s·* tones

Sons
Po.	40– 2	Good "*S·*," and daughters, too,

sons
Mis.	174–12	Above Arcturus and his *s·*,
	176–13	liberty of the *s·* of God.
	180–22	*to become the s· of God,* — *John* 1 : 12.
	181–25	to become the *s·* of God." — *John* 1 : 12.
	182–25	His *s·* and daughters.
	185–18	to become the *s·* of God." — *John* 1 : 12.
	185–26	to become the *s·* of God." — *John* 1 : 12.
	251–14	the liberty of the *s·* of God,
	259–21	all the *s·* of God — *Job* 38 : 7.
	321–19	Press on, press on ! ye *s·* of light,
Un.	5–20	the liberty of the *s·* of God,
	23–11	with you as with *s·* ; — *Heb.* 12 : 7.
	23–14	bastards, and not *s·*" — *Heb.* 12 : 8.
	42–14	all the *s·* of God — *Job* 38 : 7.
Peo.	11– 1	full liberty of the *s·* of God
Po.	39–14	*S·* of the old Bay State,
My.	185–29	*s·* and daughters of the Granite State

sonship
Mis.	83–22	he declared his *s·* with God :
	83–27	his eternal Life and *s·*.
	181– 3	Is man's spiritual *s·* a personal
	181– 7	in order to understand his *s·*,
	181–20	His *s·*, referred to in the text,
	183–25	denial of man's spiritual *s·* ;
	360–11	scientific *s·* with God.
Un.	39–16	and denies spiritual *s·* ;

soon
Mis.	10–32	*S·* or late, your enemy will
	28–11	so-called life is a dream *s·* told.
	70–27	our Lord would *s·* be rising
	145–17	let not . . . resuscitate too *s·*.
	150– 2	May He *s·* give you a pastor ;
	158– 8	I little knew that so *s·*

soon
Mis.	225–13	*S·* after this conversation,
	253–18	as *s·* as it was born,
	311–20	as *s·* harm myself as another ;
	343– 5	Too *s·* we cannot turn from
	393–11	*S·* abandoned when the Master
Ret.	6–25	was *s·* elected to the Legislature
	7–21	* sad event will not be *s·* forgotten.
	20–28	The family . . . very *s·* removed
Pul.	34–14	* *S·*, to their bewilderment and fright,
No.	28–13	none too *s·* for entering this path.
	28–17	is never understood too *s·*.
'02.	18–19	summer brook, *s·* gets dry.
	19– 2	So *s·* as he burst the bonds of
Hea.	10– 3	as *s·* as it was born," — *Rev.* 12 : 4.
Po.	51–16	*S·* abandoned when the Master
	71–21	nor too *s·* Is heard your
	72– 1	O not too *s·* is rent the chain
My.	12– 3	* as *s·* as the money in hand
	56– 7	* It was *s·* evident that
	61–22	* as *s·* as the workmen began to admit
	92–18	* country would *s·* be left behind.
	95– 1	* C. S. would *s·* be included among
	96–26	* cult will *s·* be beyond the
	130–18	left to itself is not so *s·* destroyed
	140–22	abandoned so *s·* as God's Way-shower,
	169– 8	which I hope *s·* to name to them.
	189–19	how *s·* earth's fables flee
	291– 6	a uniting of breaches *s·* to widen,
	321–21	* will *s·* be twenty years since I
	335– 5	* He was *s·* exalted to the
	346– 9	* *S·* after I reached Concord

sooner
Mis.	11–17	would one *s·* give up his own?
	43–18	letter is gained *s·* than the spirit
	115–30	if . . . *s·* or later, you will fall
	278–27	*s·* this lesson is gained the better.
Ret.	44–24	No *s·* were my views made known,
Un.	6– 4	*S·* or later the whole human race
	41–12	must come to all *s·* or later ;
No.	7–10	*S·* or later the eyes of . . . mortals
	28– 4	mists of error, *s·* or later, will melt
Pan.	13–18	*S·* or later all shall know Him,
'01.	20–20	agony . . . it must *s·* or later cause

soonest
Un.	61–27	contrite heart *s·* discerns this truth,
	61–28	helpless sick are *s·* healed
Pul.	5–10	firmest to suffer, *s·* to renounce.
'01.	29–25	who *s·* will walk in his footsteps.
Hea.	13– 8	higher natures are reached *s·* by

soothing
My.	253– 2	healing the sick, *s·* sorrow,

sophist
Mis.	363–27	exposes the subtle *s·*,

sophistry
Mis.	366–32	false theories . . . gilded with *s·*
	370–26	*s·* that such is the true fold for
No.	11–27	Revelation must subdue the *s·* of

soprano
Ret.	16– 1	a *s·*, — clear, strong, sympathetic,
Pul.	37–19	* Miss Elsie Lincoln, the *s·* for the choir

sordid
Mis.	108– 2	*s·* sinner, . . . thinks too little of sin.
	343–12	*s·* soil of self and matter.
My.	133–16	from self's *s·* sequela ;

sore
Mis.	15–20	*s·* travail of mortal mind
	71– 7	that he had *s·* eyes ;
	72– 4	were *s·* injustice.
	107– 5	in *s·* trials, self-denials, and
	253–28	the spiritual Mother's *s·* travail,
	391–16	With bare feet soiled or *s·*,
'01.	29– 3	known of his *s·* necessities?
Po.	22–15	To heal humanity's *s·* heart ;
	38–15	With bare feet soiled or *s·*,
My.	268–21	solace the *s·* ills of mankind

sore-footed
Mis.	327–27	*s·*, they fall behind

sorely
My.	215– 2	Though *s·* oppressed,

sorrow
all
My.	257–16	all *s·*, sickness, and sin.

and loss
Ret.	7–23	* too much of *s·* and loss.

and mortality
Mis.	103–11	say . . . life is *s·* and mortality ;

and sickness
Mis.	399–10	thy *s·* and sickness and sin."
No.	30–24	Sympathy with sin, *s·*, and sickness
Po.	75–17	thy *s·* and sickness and sin."

sorrow

and sighing
My. 171– 6   s· and sighing shall — *Isa.* 35 : 10.
becomes
Mis. 351–25   joy that becomes s·.
dismissal of
Mis. 101– 7   and the dismissal of s·.
endureth
Hea. 10–17   s· endureth but for the night,
is the harbinger
Un. 57–25   S· is the harbinger of joy.
multiply thy
Mis. 57–16   multiply thy s·." — *Gen.* 3 : 16.
nation's
My. 292– 8   sanctify our nation's s·
no
'02. 20– 7   no s·, no pain ;
pain and
Un. 18–11   If pain and s· were not in
seems to come
Hea. 10–16   when s· seems to come, if you will
sickness and
Mis. 250–28   want and woe, sickness and s·
sin and
Pul. 82– 4   * cold haunts of sin and s·,
soothing
My. 253– 2   healing the sick, soothing s·,
subdued
My. 290–26   him who suffered and subdued s·.
tears of
My. 36–16   * exchanged the tears of s· for
your
Hea. 10–18   Then will your s· be a dream,

Mis. ix–12   joy, s·, hope, disappointment,
204– 7   hope, s·, joy, defeat, and
327– 1   turned my misnamed joys to s·.
400– 9   and s·?   No, It has none,
Pul. 16–21   and s·?   No, It has none,
No. 35– 9   no more sickness, s·, sin, and
Hea. 10–23   or to argue stronger for s· than
Po. 76–20   and s·?   No, It has none,
My. 273–20   joy, s·, life, and death.

sorrowful
Mis. 133–32   the s· who are made hopeful,
396– 7   More s· it scarce could seem ;
Po. 58–19   More s· it scarce could seem ;
My. 50–15   * this meeting . . . was rather s· ;"

sorrowing
Mis. 108– 1   s· saint thinks too much of it :
133–23   blessing on the sick and s·,

sorrows
Mis. 10– 2   and enhance its s·.
84–14   "man of s·" — *Isa.* 53 : 3.
84–26   falsity of material joys and s·,
Un. 55– 5   "a man of s·, — *Isa.* 53 : 3.
56–14   shares his cup of s·.
'02. 18– 5   made him a man of s·.
Po. 33–14   Whose mercies my s· beguile,

sorrow-worn
My. 40–18   * pain-racked and s· humanity.

sorry
Mis. 132–28   * "If we have . . . we are s·."
311–32   I have been s· that I spoke at all,
'01. 21–14   I am s· for my critic,
My. 313–29   that was a s· offence.

sort
Mis. 37–22   impurity, sin of every s·,
40–18   error, discord of whatever s·.
67–19   Justice uncovers sin of every s· ;
108– 4   To allow sin of any s·
131– 8   let the leaner s· console this
178–16   * wondered what s· of people you were,
241– 6   as well as sin of every s·.
307–10   to suffering of every s·.
313–22   laborers of the excellent s·,
319–16   sinners of the worst s·.
337–32   Sin of any s· tends to hide from
353–11   of the misguided, fallible s·,
371–16   not productive of the better s·,
Man. 97–20   or circulated literature of any s·.
Ret. 61–12   fear or suffering of any s·.
Un. 11–21   the ruder s· then prevalent,
58– 1   error of some s·, — sin, pain,
Pul. 5–10   those characters of holiest s·,
14– 3   will chain, with fetters of some s·,
43–27   * that s· of personal worship
50–20   * will awaken some s· of interest.
60– 4   * There was no address of any s·,
'01. 1–18   All that is true is a s· of necessity,
32– 7   I loved Christians of the old s·
My. 147–10   a s· of C. S. kindergarten
210– 9   attacks of error of every s·.
229– 5   cannot be found . . . one of *this* s·.

sorts
Mis. 370–25   would gather all s· into a
My. 104– 5   all s· of institutions flourish

sought
Mis. 89–18   to some who s· his aid ;
140–17   till mortal man s· to know
163– 1   he s· to conquer the
176–16   s· the New England shores,
199–16   rulers s· the life of Jesus ;
232–26   s· from the love of good,
245– 5   s· not to the Lord, — II *Chron.* 16 : 12.
303– 3   s· and found as healers
357–27   have s· the true fold
372–13   I s· the judgment of sound
Chr. 53–15   Through understanding, dearly s·,
Ret. 23–18   my affections had diligently s·
33– 7   I s· knowledge from the different
34– 5   If I s· an answer from the
88– 1   and different aid is s·.
89–28   not . . . known to them or s· by them.
Pul. 47–10   * she states that she s· knowledge
80– 8   * s· the line of least resistance.
Rud. 14– 8   never s· charitable support,
'02. 15– 4   nor s· the protection of the laws
My. 111– 2   the reader would not have s·.
142–12   I s· God's guidance in doing
189–21   that which defies decay . . . is s·
246–13   s· in solitude and silence
247–17   s· their food of me.
343–14   s· no such distinction.
348– 5   I s· this cause,

Soul (*see also* Soul's)

allness of
Man. 16– 7   even the allness of S·, Spirit,
alone
Ret. 25–14   S· alone is truly substantial.
and body
No. 29– 5   a false sense of S· and body.
and intelligence
No. 35–18   presupposes . . . S·, and intelligence
and sense
'02. 4–11   peace between S· and sense
and substance
Mis. 145– 7   to express S· and substance.
bands of
Un. 12– 6   bind it with bands of S·.
cannot be formed
Mis. 75–31   S· cannot be formed . . . by
consciousness of
Mis. 179–23   old consciousness of S· in sense.
define
Un. 28– 8   define S· as something within man?
described
Un. 28– 5   has not descried nor described S·.
dignity of
Mis. 126–12   lift us to that dignity of S·
emanates from
Mis. 16–25   emanates from S· instead of body,
essence of
My. 204–11   sacred *ave* and essence of S·
evergreen of
Mis. ix–22   is not the evergreen of S· ;
evidence of
My. 119–24   with the evidence of S·,
feast of
My. 263– 6   feast of S· and a famine of sense.
flow of
Mis. 149– 5   this feast and flow of S·.
from clay to
Pan. 11–12   turn from clay to S· for the model
furnace of
My. 269–19   is molten in the furnace of S·.
harmony of
Mis. 85–28   immortality and harmony of S·.
has man a
No. 28–24   chapter sub-title
hath part
Mis. 390–23   In which the S· hath part,
Po. 56– 2   In which the S· hath part,
haven of
Mis. 152–27   Into His haven of S·
heaven of
Mis. 394– 5   the home, and the heaven of S·.
Po. 45– 7   the home, and the heaven of S·.
My. 163– 2   the haven of hope, the heaven of S·,
heavens of
Mis. 360–14   stars in the heavens of S·.
heraldry of
Po. 70–21   A painless heraldry of S·,
immortal
Un. 51– 4   that immortal S· is sinful,
No. 11– 4   Man has an immortal S·,
29– 4   Immortal man has immortal S·
impulse of
My. 308– 9   impels the impulse of S·.

Soul

infinite
Un. 48–18 The Ego is God . . . infinite *S·*
Pul. 2–24 eternal harmony of infinite *S·.*
informing
My. 259–30 represents the eternal informing *S·*
instead of
Peo. 2–13 of *S·* instead of the senses,
is a synonym
Mis. 75–11 *S·* is a synonym of Spirit,
is immortal
'01. 13–26 *S·* is immortal, but sin is mortal.
My. 273–25 body is mortal, but *S·* is immortal ;
is Life
Un. 30– 7 *S·* is Life, and . . . never sins.
is not in body
Un. 51–27 *S·* is not in body, but is God,
is one
Mis. 75–13 hence *S·* is one, and is God ;
is right
Ret. 57– 9 *S·* is right ;
is sinless
Un. 29– 7 *S·* is sinless, and is God.
52– 1 *S·* is sinless and immortal,
is substance
Mis. 103– 3 Spirit, *S·,* is substance,
is the divine Mind
Mis. 75–30 *S·* is the divine Mind,
is the Life
Mis. 76–25 *S·* is the Life of man.
is the synonym
Ret. 57–10 *S·* is the synonym of Spirit,
knowledge of
No. 29– 8 so slight a knowledge of *S·*
language of
Hea. 7– 8 language of *S·* instead of the senses ;
legitimate affection of
Mis. 287– 9 not the legitimate affection of *S·,*
Life that is
My. 274– 3 even the Life that is *S·* apart from
living
Un. 30–25 living *S·* shall be found a
music of
Mis. 106–28 music of *S·* affords the only
'00. 11– 8 spiritual music, the music of *S·.*
must be God
Un. 28–17 *S·* must be God ;
my
Un. 29–27 [my *S·,* immortality].
never saw
Un. 59–17 *S·* never saw the Saviour come
no cognizance of
Un. 28–19 senses take no cognizance of *S·,*
not sense
Po. 70–21 heraldry of *S·,* not sense,
My. 118–19 *S·,* not sense, receives and gives it.
of all being
Un. 29–10 declares God to be the *S·* of all being,
of man
Rud. 1– 7 the *S·* of man and the universe.
one
Mis. 75– 6 *there is but one S·,*
Ret. 57–11 hence there is but one *S·,*
Un. 29–12 There is but one God, one *S·,*
or Mind
Mis. 189–15 supposition that *S·,* or Mind,
Un. 29–12 There is but one God, one *S·,* or Mind,
or Spirit
No. 26– 4 and that *S·,* or Spirit, is subdivided
over sense
Mis. 321–12 of Life over death, and of *S·* over sense.
Hea. 10–20 even the triumph of *S·* over sense.
Peo. 11–10 supremacy of *S·* over sense,
penetration of
Mis. 292–27 with the penetration of *S·,*
purifies sense with
'00. 8–24 fire that purifies sense with *S·*
reality and
Peo. 1– 9 reality and *S·* of all things,
restores
Un. 30–11 restores *S·,* or spiritual Life.
Science of
(*see* **Science**)
Science reveals
Un. 29–15 Science reveals *S·* as that which
sense and
Mis. 102–28 conflict between sense and *S·.*
No. 12–25 it makes both sense and *S·,*
sense to
(*see* **sense**)
silences
My. 230– 8 digested only when *S·* silences
soul to
My. 129–23 divine law . . . gives a soul to *S·,*
Spirit, or
No. 29– 6 He believes that Spirit, or *S·,*

Soul

springtide of
Pan. 1–14 waiting — for the springtide of *S·.*
stands
Un. 28–22 *S·* stands in this relation to
sublime
Mis. 393– 5 *S·,* sublime 'mid human *débris,*
Po. 51–10 *S·,* sublime 'mid human *débris,*
substance of
Mis. 104– 7 safe in the substance of *S·,*
sunlight of
Mis. 202– 4 into the sunlight of *S·.*
supremacy of
Peo. 11–10 even the supremacy of *S·*
the word
Mis. 75–18 The word *S·* may sometimes
we learn
Un. 28–17 we learn *S·* only as we learn God,
what is
Un. 28– 3 What is *S·*?
would place
Mis. 344–17 They would place *S·* wholly inside

Mis. 75– 7 *S· is not in the body*
75–15 *S·* is a term for Deity,
76–26 if *S·* sinned, it would die ;
186– 4 in which *S·* is supposed to
287–12 *S·* is the infinite source of bliss :
354–12 and sense seems sounder than *S·.*
Ret. 25–14 *S·* I denominated *substance,*
56– 6 or divides . . . *S·* into souls,
57–13 sense, not *S·,* causes . . . ailments,
60–29 but one Spirit, Mind, *S·.*
Un. 29– 3 If *S·* sins, it is a sinner,
29–25 Hope thou in God [*S·*] :—*Psal.* 42 : 11.
42– 3 *S·,* Spirit, is deathless.
45–25 substance of Spirit, . . . *S·,*
52–26 The senses, not God, *S·,*
62–14 only as a sense, and not as *S·.*
Rud. 5–11 who has ever found *S·* in the body
5–18 *S·* is the only real consciousness
No. 29– 3 Not *S·,* but mortal sense, sins
29–14 statement . . . that *S·* is in matter,
35–21 the only Mind, Life, substance, *S·*
My. 119–31 Truth that leadeth . . . from body to *S·,*
131–16 may thought soar and *S·* be.
225–29 Truth, Life, Spirit, Mind, *S·,*
252– 6 will be salutary as *S·* ;
269–13 * and God the *S·.*
351–16 meet in that hour of *S·* where are no

soul (*see also* **soul's**)

alone in
My. 189–32 Am I not alone in *s·*?
and life
Ret. 59– 3 a mortal mind and *s·* and life,
another's
Mis. 338–23 * Another's *s·* wouldst reach ;
as sense
Mis. 15–21 shall *s·* as sense be satisfied,
belief that
Mis. 76– 9 mortal belief that *s·* is in body,
body and
Mis. 354–19 body and *s·* in accord with God.
dear to the
Pul. 82–11 * many things dear to the *s·*
disengage the
Mis. 344– 8 disengage the *s·* from objects of
feast of
My. 191–29 invitation to this feast of *s·*
forgiven
No. 29–12 * "The forgiven *s·* in a sick body
for sense
Mis. 76–20 exchange the term *s·* for *sense*
Un. 30– 3 uses the word *s·* for *sense.*
from sense
My. 139–28 redeem . . . your *s·* from sense ;
gives to
My. 120–12 gives to *s·* its native freedom.
her
Pul. 84– 1 * not in her hand, but in her *s·.*
her own
Pul. 81–22 * her own *s·* plays upon magic strings
his
Pul. 79–24 * breath of his *s·* is a belief in
My. 34– 4 not lifted up his *s·* unto — *Psal.* 24 : 4.
human
Mis. 76–15 to set a human *s·* free from its
76–23 misnamed human *s·* is material sense,
Un. 51–26 man is reflected not as human *s·,*
Pul. 53–22 * the power of the human *s·.*
image of the
Po. 23– 8 An image of the *s·,*
is deathless
Mis. 75–30 that *s·* is deathless.

soul

is emancipate
My. 267–27   whereby *s·* is emancipate
living
Mis. 185–27   *was made a living s· ;* — *I Cor.* 15 : 45.
Un. 30–14   was made a living *s· ;* — *I Cor.* 15 : 45.
Rud. 2– 2   * *person,* . . . "a living *s· ;*
man's
My. 200–15   man's *s·* is safe ;
means sense
No. 28–26   Here *s·* means sense
miscall
Un. 29–17   the physical senses miscall *s·,*
must overflow
Mis. 338–22   * Thy *s·* must overflow,
my
Mis. 75–22   "My *s·* doth magnify — *Luke* 1 : 46.
    317–29   My *s·* abhors injustice,
Ret. 20– 2   earthly hope, babe of my *s·*.
Un. 29–24   cast down, O my *s·* — *Psal.* 42 : 11.
    30– 1   "My *s·* . . . doth magnify — *Luke* 1 : 46.
    30–11   "He restoreth my *s·*," — *Psal.* 23 : 3.
Pan. 4–22   cast down, O my *s·* ? — *Psal.* 42 : 11
Po. 32–20   comfort my *s·* all the wearisome day,
    65– 9   My *s·* is enchained to life's
My. 118– 1   My *s·* thanks the loyal,
    174–25   my *s·* can only sing and soar.
    175–25   The song of my *s·* must remain
    262–12   celebrate Christmas with my *s·,*
    290–12   My *s·* reaches out to God
    360–17   I advise you with all my *s·*
no
Po. 2– 1   no *s·* those looks betray ;
of divine philosophy
Mis. 364–11   It is the *s·* of divine philosophy,
of man
My. 344– 9   * "And the *s·* of man?"
of melody
Po. 34– 2   *s·* of melody by being blest
palace of the
Pul. 82– 1   * the body . . . the palace of the *s·,*
poor
Po. 28–10   Aid our poor *s·* to sing
redemption of
Un. 52–12   precious·redemption of *s·,*
save the
Mis. 244– 8   states that God cannot save the *s·*
sense instead of
Un. 29–23   by reading *sense* instead of *s·,*
sense of a
Un. 29–19   that material sense of a *s·* which
sinful
'01. 13–26   a sense of sin, and not a sinful *s·,*
soaring
Ret. 9–24   * My soaring *s·* Now hath
so-called
Mis. 76–21   the so-called *s·* in the body,
stricken
Pul. 82– 5   * which heals the stricken *s·.*
that sinneth
Mis. 75–27   "The *s·* that sinneth, — *Ezek.* 18 : 4.
Un. 28– 1   "The *s·* that sinneth, — *Ezek.* 18 : 4.
No. 28–25   "the *s·* that sinneth, — *Ezek.* 18 : 4.
the word
Un. 30– 3   the word *s·* for *sense.*
this
No. 29–10   and then they doctor this *s·*
thrills the
My. 125–18   which always thrills the *s·.*
thy
My. 183– 2   and with all thy *s·,* — *Luke.* 10 : 27.
to Soul
My. 129–23   gives a *s·* to Soul,
truth of the
Po. 73–20   mock the bright truth of the *s·.*
upborne
Po. 23–15   *s·,* upborne on wisdom's wings,
with soul
My. 154–28   mind with mind, *s·* with soul,

Mis. 75–20   a substitution of *sense* for *s·*
Ret. 57– 6   Plato believed he had a *s·,*
Pul. 10–28   Speak out, O *s·* !
No. 29– 9   believe material . . . sense to be *s·* ;
My. 179– 9   In other words, *s·* enters
    363–15   This proof that . . . is *s·* inspiring.

Soul-full
My. 201–10   Your *S·* words and song

soulfully
My. 139– 5   *s·* founded upon the rock,

Soul-less
Mis. 311–14   impractical, unfruitful, *S·.*

soulless
Ret. 23–20   *S·* famine had fled.
    74– 5   *corpus sine pectore* (*s·* body),

Soul's
Mis. 373– 5   *S·* expression through the brush ;
    385–17   To *S·* diviner sense,
Hea. 10–27   the true fount and *S·* baptism.
Po. 31– 7   peace of *S·* sweet solitude !
    48–11   To *S·* diviner sense,
My. 344–15   approaches to *S·* perfection."

soul's
Po. 70– 5   the *s·* glad immortality,

souls
Mis. 76–13   belief the . . . contain immortal *s·* !
    76–13   for these *s·* to escape
    153–27   * *S·* that are gentle and still
Ret. 56– 7   Soul into *s·,* . . . is a misstatement
Un. 28–13   common hypotheses about *s·*
    52– 2   sinful *s·* or immortal sinners.
Pul. 56–15   * comfort to many weary *s·.*
    63– 9   nourish trees as well as *s·,*"
No. 26– 5   spirits, or *s·,* — *alias* gods.
'01. 32–28   sanctified *s·* would take in the

soul-visit
My. 297– 6   description of her *s·,*

sound
Mis. 46–27   even as the idea of *s·,* in tones,
    120–18   *s·* of vintage bells to villagers
    140–27   Our title . . . will be safe and *s·*
    315–18   prove *s·* in sentiment, health, and
    356–14   sweeter than the *s·* of vintage bells.
    372–14   sought the judgment of *s·* critics
    398–22   Heard ye the glad *s·* ?
Man. 83–17   *s·* in sentiment and practical
Pul. 11– 3   organ's voice, as the *s·* of many waters,
Rud. 1–15   *per* (through) and *sonare* (to *s·*)
No. 13–15   A theory may be *s·* in spots,
    14– 1   C. S. is *s·* in every part.
    29–13   Is this . . . statement *s·* theology,
'00. 11–13   Music is more than *s·* in unison.
'01. 26–20   *s·* faith and charity,
'02. 9–21   When first I heard the life-giving *s·*
Hea. 20– 3   * Oh, could we *s·* the glories forth,
Po. 71–15   Joy for the captive !   *S·* it long !
    75– 2   Heard ye the glad *s·* ?
My. v–15   * established the Cause on a *s·* basis
    vii–10   * Deeds, . . . are the *s·* test of love ;
    164–17   not only possess a *s·* faith, but
    189–11   go forth in waves of *s·,*
    265– 6   subordinate to material sight and *s·*
    277– 9   and *s·,* well-kept treaties.
    304–22   * a woman of *s·* education
    316–23   *s·* appreciation of the rights of

sounded
My. 199–19   *s·* the tocsin of a higher hope,
    258–23   memories of him who *s·* all depths of

sounder
Mis. 354–11   sense seems *s·* than Soul,

sounding
Mis. 292–11   such as eternity is ever *s·.*
    316–23   pounding . . . love into *s·* brass ;
No. 45– 3   "as *s·* brass, — *I Cor.* 13 : 1.
'01. 26–23   as *s·* brass, — *I Cor.* 13 : 1.

soundness
Mis. 350–23   *s·* of the argument used.

sounds
Mis. 324– 6   *s·* of festivity and mirth ;
    329–26   *s·* her invisible lute,
Rud. 6– 3   *sweet s· and glories of earth*

sour
Mis. 72–14   have eaten *s·* grapes, — *Ezek.* 18 : 2.
Un. 35– 2   this is sweet, this is *s·.*"
    35– 2   and say that *s·* is sweet,
    35– 4   believed sweet to be *s·,*

source

any other
Pul. 21–28   cannot come from any other *s·.*
correct
Hea. 16–27   evidences . . . from the correct *s·.*
divine
Mis. 19–17   God, its divine *s·.*
    22– 7   if not from the divine *s·,*
    333–18   from the divine *s·* of being,
Pul. 4–11   unity with your divine *s·,*
essence and
'00. 5–13   essence and *s·* of the two latter,
evil
Mis. 113–17   suggestions from an evil *s·.*
exhaustless
Mis. 39–19   this saving, exhaustless *s·*
higher
My. 338–18   they seek a higher *s·*
infinite
Mis. 287–12   Soul is the infinite *s·* of bliss :
My. 165–31   found and felt the infinite *s·*

source

is infinite Mind
Un. 24–15   man, whose *s·* is infinite Mind.

is Spirit
Un. 25–23   whose only *s·* is Spirit.

its
Un. 25–17   by showing God as its *s·*.

mighty
Ret. 11–16   Science the mighty *s·*,
Po. 60–13   Science the mighty *s·*,

of appeal
My. 90–14   * not the only *s·* of appeal.

of being
Mis. 333–18   from the divine *s·* of being,
Ret. 69– 3   and ultimate *s·* of being ;
Un. 46–12   spiritual sense and *s·* of being.

of death
Ret. 59– 7   that which is the *s·* of death,

one
My. 153–32   up to the one *s·*, divine Life

prolific
Ret. 69–21   prolific *s·* of all suffering?

same
Mis. 92–15   from the same *s·*.

spiritual
Mis. 225–24   spiritual *s·* and ever-present help,

their
Mis. 354–15   prove the nature of their *s·*.
Pul. 3–22   have their *s·* in God,

this
Mis. 347– 5   To avoid danger from this *s·*

unerring
Ret. 34– 2   unmixed, unerring *s·*,

Ret. 34–13   mortal mind as the *s·* of all the ills
Un. 9–14   conclusions as to the *s·* and

sources
Mis. 113–31   prolific *s·* of spiritual power
    223– 7   flow from corrupt *s·*.
    273–21   from these *s·* of education, to
'02. 15–14   my income from literary *s·*
My. 90–28   * *s·* of her power and following

South
Ret. 19– 6   I went with him to the *S·* ;
'02. 3– 9   half-hostility to the *S·*,
My. 176– 6   you of the dear *S·*
    189–26   erected in the sunny *S·*
    304–12   magazines in the *S·* and North.
    322–20   * journeying from the far *S·*,
    331–28   * characterized the people of the *S·*,

south
Pul. 48– 6   * broad piazza on the *s·* side
    76–14   * gold decoration adorns the *s·* wall,
    82– 3   * When she comes like the *s·* wind
My. 63–29   * and from the *s·*,'' — *Psal.* 107 : 3.

South Africa
'02. 3–19   close of the conflict in *S· A·* ;
My. 30–16   * from Switzerland, from *S· A·*,

South Carolina and S. C.
My. 312– 6   * took his bride to Wilmington, *S· C·*,
    329–28   * her life in North and *S· C·*
    (*see also* **Charleston**)

South Congregational church
My. 289–24   meeting in the *S· C· c·*

Southern
Mis. 246– 6   It was the *S·* pulpit and press
My. 326– 9   * in the *S·* and Northern States
    331–13   * whose *S·* chivalry would have

Southern States
Pul. 89–16   * heading

Southron
My. 188–21   heart of a *S·* has welcomed

Southrons
My. 327– 1   turning the hearts of the noble *S·*

southward
'00. 12–13   its gates, . . . led northward and *s·*.

souvenir
Pul. 76–22   * chapter sub-title
    86–11   * beautiful *s·* is encased in

souvenirs
Pul. 46–17   * Among the many *s·*

sovereign
Mis. 121–14   would make this . . . just and *s·*,
    249–29   it hath range and is *s·* !
    355–18   to lift . . . is a *s·* panacea.
Pul. 3– 7   *s·* power to think and act rightly,
Pan. 6–23   If Spirit is *s·*, how can matter be
My. 108–17   divine Mind is the *s·* appeal,
    283–14   *s·* remedies for all earth's woe.

sovereigns
My. 290– 8   Few *s·* have been as venerable,

sovereignty
Mis. 234–32   makes His *s·* glorious.
Un. 51–12   usurpation, . . . of the heavenly *s·*.
Pan. 7–11   lose the character and *s·* of

sow
Mis. 397–24   How to gather, how to *s·*,
Ret. 46– 5   How to gather, how to *s·*,
Pul. 17– 4   How to gather, how to *s·*,
No. 3–23   to *s·* by the wayside for the way-weary,
'01. 33– 6   hand of love must *s·* the seed.
Po. 14– 3   How to gather, how to *s·*,
    47–22   Or to the patient who *s·*

soweth
Mis. 66– 7   "Whatsoever a man *s·*, — *Gal.* 6 : 7.
    105–29   "Whatsoever a man *s·*, — *Gal.* 6 : 7.
    348– 4   whatsoever a man *s·*, that shall he
No. 32– 9   "Whatsoever a man *s·*, — *Gal.* 6 : 7.
Hea. 5–27   "whatsoever a man *s·*, — *Gal.* 6 : 7.
My. 6– 6   whatsoever a man *s·*, — *Gal.* 6 : 7.
    185– 1   he that *s·* shall reap.

sowing
Mis. 144–27   may our earthly *s·* bear fruit that
Rud. 9– 4   *s·* the seeds of discord and disease.
Po. 47–16   Weary of *s·* the wayside
My. 133–17   give birth to the *s·* of Solomon.
    182–13   small *s·* of the seed of Truth,

sown
Mis. 38–10   "If we have *s·* unto you — *I Cor.* 9 : 11.
    80–26   have planted and *s·* and reaped
    356–16   seed of C. S., which when *s·* was
    357–16   Much of what has been *s·*
Po. 31– 2   nor yet by nature *s·*,
My. 40–21   * fruit of righteousness is *s·* — *Jas.* 3 : 18.
    129– 6   and Christianity *s·* broadcast
    182–14   seed of Truth, which, when *s·*,

sows
Mis. 15– 2   will reap what he *s·* ;

space

airy
My. 110–16   dreams of flying in airy *s·*,

all
Mis. 14– 1   it fills all *s·*, being omnipresent ;
    173–20   If God is Mind and fills all *s·*,
    331–24   Mind-force, filling all *s·*
    332– 2   reflecting all *s·* and Life,
Un. 51–21   radiating throughout all *s·*
Pul. 4–21   lives in all Life, through all *s·*.
Rud. 3–27   ever-present I AM, filling all *s·*,
'00. 1– 6   ever-present Love filling all *s·*,

brief
My. 333–28   * brief *s·* of six months,

celestial
Mis. 376–29   spangled the gloom in celestial *s·*

dashing through
Mis. 266–13   comet's course, dashing through *s·*

economy of
Pul. 62– 7   * advantage of great economy of *s·*,

intermediate
Mis. 215– 4   Truth comes into the intermediate *s·*,

miles of
Pul. 44– 5   * Across two thousand miles of *s·*,

more
Ret. 6–14   would require more *s·* than

no
My. 210– 6   and no *s·* for evil to fill

occupying a
Pul. 62– 8   * occupying a *s·* not more than

of time
Mis. 147– 4   another *s·* of time has been given us,

open
Mis. 347– 6   from their houses to the open *s·*.
My. 89– 9   * needs only an open *s·* about it,

seating
My. 38–10   * when all seating *s·* had been filled

time and
Mis. 110–17   time and *s·*, when encompassed by
No. 16–13   destitute of time and *s·* ;
My. 110–13   forces annihilating time and *s·*,

vast
My. 69–18   * anywhere in the vast *s·*

without
Mis. 173–18   Does an evil mind exist without *s·*

Mis. 22–12   defining the line, plane, *s·*, and
    150–10   *S·* is no separator of hearts.
    339– 5   silence for the *s·* of half an hour.
    364–14   all time, *s·*, immortality,
    380– 6   governs the universe, time, *s·*,
Un. 60–23   *s·*, substance, and immortality
Pul. 56–10   * *S·* does not admit of an elaborate
No. 21– 9   all time, *s·*, immortality,
'02. 10– 5   power over matter, molecule, *s·*,
My. 343– 3   * looking large-eyed into *s·*,

spacious
Mis.	276– 3	s' rooms of the Palmer House,
Pul.	26– 6	* organ and choir gallery is s'
	29– 9	* s' apartment was thronged
	31–23	* I rang the bell at a s' house
	42– 1	* the s' lobbies and the sidewalks
	60–19	* recess behind the s' platform,
My.	66–21	* s' and elegant edifice
	174– 7	opening their s' club-house

Spain
Pan.	14–28	war between United States and *S·*
My.	277– 4	between the United States and *S·*

spake
Mis.	23–10	Was it Mind or matter that s'
	68–15	cast out a devil, and the dumb s' ;
	76–16, 17	who s' as never man s',
	83–23	"These words s' Jesus,—*John* 17 : 1.
	100– 1	He s' of Truth and Love
	126–30	s' after this manner :
	159– 1	s' in their synagogues,
	185–30	first s' from their standpoint
	190–12	*the dumb s'.—Luke* 11 : 14.
	192–13	words of him who s' divinely,
	269–11, 12	"s' as never man s',"— see *John* 7 : 46.
	280– 1	Mind s' and form appeared.
Mis.	312–24	He s' inspired ;
	359– 8	I s' as a child,— *I Cor.* 13 : 11.
Ret.	91–16	Lake of Galilee, where he s'
Un.	17–16	"s' as never man s',"— see *John* 7 : 46.
'00.	14–20	angel that s' unto the churches
'02.	8–27	He s' of man not as the
My.	135– 3	I s' as a child,— *I Cor.* 13 : 11.
	162–19	which s' in olden time
	227– 3	he s' as God's representative
	261–16	I s' as a child,— *I Cor.* 13 : 11.
	351–13	his garment who s' divinely.

span
Mis.	355–30	will s' thy heavens of thought
My.	155–21	s' the horizon of their hope

spangled
Mis.	376–28	s' the gloom in celestial space

Spanish
Ret.	32–11	Calderon, the famous *S·* poet,
Rud.	1–13	In *S·*, Italian, and Latin,
Pan.	14–26	blotted out the *S·* squadron.

spanned
Mis.	163– 8	dated time, . . . and s' eternity,
Ret.	23– 9	Matter was no longer s' with

spans
'01.	10–21	Love s' the dark passage of sin,
Peo.	3–15	s' the moral heavens with light,
Po.	71– 9	*S·* our broad heaven of light.

spare
Mis.	114– 4	and should s' no research
	129–23	to save the sinner and to s' his
	155–24	If my own students cannot s' time
	287–26	it will s' you much bitterness.
	300–14	does it s' you our Master's
	342–22	The wise virgins had no oil to s',
My.	144– 5	s' not a moment's thought to lies
	200–27	God s' this plunge,
	285– 6	I cannot s' the time requisite

spared
Mis.	89–25	false concept that is not s'
Man.	76– 1	funds, which can be s'
Ret.	7–13	* Had life and health been s'
	19– 6	s' to me for only one brief year.
'01.	32–15	and s' no denunciation
'02.	18–12	nor s' through false pity

spares
Mis.	300–13	and s' you the printer's bill,
My.	249–12	burns the wheat, s' the tares,

sparing
Mis.	302–12	thus s' their teacher a task

spark
Mis.	132–29	desire to be just is a vital s' of
Ret.	1–13	no sign that she inherited a s' from

sparkle
No.	13–25	and s' like a diamond,

sparkles
Mis.	257–22	Electricity, . . . s' on the cloud,

sparkling
Mis.	240– 4	s' eyes, and ruby cheeks

sparrow (*see also* **sparrow's**)
Mis.	174–11	from the falling of a s' to
	184– 5	from . . . to the death of a s'.
Un.	40– 1	from . . . to the fall of a s'.

sparrow's
Mis.	157– 5	He that marketh the s' fall
My.	226–13	that marks the s' fall,

sparse
Mis.	119–26	s' individual rights which one

spasmodic
Ret.	87–10	unsettled and s' efforts.

spat
Mis.	170–25	he is said to have s' upon the dust.
	258– 8	literally s' upon matter ;

speak
Mis.	44– 1	Honest students s' the truth
	84– 1	shown by his forbearing to s',
	99–25	s' louder than to-day.
	141– 3	It will s' to you of the
	168–26	* would s' before the Scientist
	180–29	The Scriptures s' of Jesus as the
	192– 1	When we s' of a good man,
	220–26	and s' of him as being sick,
	238–26	* unable to s' a loud word,"
	256–22	to s' of gravitation as a law
	266–20	I s' of them as I feel,
	283– 3	s' the truth audibly ;
	316– 7	s' to your church in Boston?
	316– 8	I shall s' to my dear church
	322– 6	expecting to hear me s'
	338–28	* *S·* truly, and each word
Ret.	5–15	I cannot s' as I would,
	6–12	To s' of his beautiful character
	9–10	"*S·*, Lord ; for Thy servant — *I Sam.* 3 : 9.
	16– 9	she could not s' a loud word,
	40– 4	I was called to s' before the
	50–17	students s' with delight of
	75–15	lightly s' evil of me."— *Mark* 9 : 39.
Un.	7– 6	Nevertheless, though I thus s',
	23–18	incompetent to s'.
	43–12	of myself I *cannot* s'
	46– 2	which neither think nor s'.
Pul.	10–28	*S·* out, O soul !
	29– 7	* I shall venture to s',
	33– 8	* "*S·*, Lord, for Thy servant — *I Sam.* 3 : 9.
	46– 6	* the words of the judge s'
	75– 7	But to think or s' of me
	80–19	* s' of the system it sets forth,
	84–18	* we shall not undertake to s'
	87–18	* s' to you each Sunday.
No.	7–23	s', teach, and write the truth
	39– 2	than we can write or s'.
Pan.	2– 4	who know whereof they s'
'01.	26–21	"Though I s' with — *I Cor.* 13 : 1.
Hea.	1– 2	s' *with new tongues ; — Mark* 16 : 17.
	20– 2	* s' the matchless worth,
Po.	8–18	love, that no words could s'
My.	42–22	* I shall not attempt to s' of
	47–31	* s' with new tongues ; — *Mark* 16 : 17.
	84– 1	* the facts s' more plainly than
	104–20	of whom these pioneers s'.
	106– 3	either to s' charitably of all
	107– 9	Here I s' from experience.
	131–15	s' the "new tongue" — see *Mark* 16 : 17.
	147–19	s' the truth that to-day,
	175–16	s' for themselves.
	196– 9	slow to s', — *Jas.* 1 : 19.
	214–23	a hall in which to s',
	224–27	also s' in loving terms of
	264– 4	kind enough to s' well of
	264– 6	can s' justly of my living.
	308–14	compels me . . . to s'.

speaker
Mis.	168–29	* distinguished s' began by saying :
Man.	95–12	may apply . . . for a s',
Pul.	72–25	* added the s',
	73– 1	* inquired the s'.

speakers
Mis.	253– 8	s' that will now address you
'00.	9–21	challenge the thinkers, s', and
My.	124–16	hearts of these hearers and s',

speaketh
Mis.	24–26	"When he s' a lie, — *John* 8 : 44.
	24–26	he s' of his own : — *John* 8 : 44.
	151–10	He s' to the unfruitful in tones of
	198–11	"When he s' a lie, — *John* 8 : 44.
	198–11	he s' of his own." — *John* 8 : 44.
	317–30	s' the words of God : — *John* 3 : 34.
No.	34–18	blood of Christ s' better things
Pan.	5–15	When he s' a lie, — *John* 8 : 44.
	5–16	he s' of his own : — *John* 8 : 44.
'01.	9–28	he s' wisely, for the spirit of
	9–29	his Father s' through him ;
My.	33–18	s' the truth in his heart. — *Psal.* 15 : 2.
	228–24	s' the truth in his heart." — *Psal.* 15 : 2.

speaking
Mis.	19– 2	Envy, evil thinking, evil s',
	24–24	*S·* of the origin of evil,
	59–23	benefit in s' often one to another,
	84– 2	by s', the whole truth.

speaking

Mis.	137– 8	*s·* a few words aside to your teacher.
	158– 7	I insisted on your *s·* without notes,
	178–27	I wished to be excused from *s·*
	184–10	Paul refers to this when *s·* of
	204–32	evil thinking, evil *s·* and acting ;
	227–22	*s·* the truth in the heart ;
	253– 7	not enough . . . for outdoor *s·*,
	277– 4	Truth is *s·* louder, clearer,
Man.	81–24	no evil *s·* shall be allowed.
Ret.	35–16	When *s·* of his true followers
Un.	35–11	strictly *s·*, there is no mortal mind,
Pul.	7– 1	*s·* of my work, said :
	49– 2	* *s·* of her many followers
No.	16–27	strictly *s·*, *no* mortal mind.
	39– 7	*s·* loud enough to be heard ;
Pan.	8–20	*S·* of himself, Jesus said,
My.	12–22	lost in *s·* or in acting,
	156–12	spiritually *s·* is the passover from
	186–22	while they are yet *s·*,— *Isa.* 65 : 24.
	225–25	either in *s·* or in writing,
	257–12	The Christ is *s·* for himself
	280–19	only because of oft *s·*,

speakings

My.	17– 5	and all evil *s·*,— *I Pet.* 2 : 1.

speaks

Mis.	15– 5	St. Paul *s·* of the new birth
	88–14	critic who knows whereof he *s·*.
	100–19	*s·* when the senses are silent,
	130–22	know well whereof he *s·*.
	180–16	it *s·* to me of Life,
	212–27	*s·* plainly to the offender
	262–10	When the heart *s·*,
	296–31	but knew whereof he *s·*,
	388–12	*S·* kindly when we meet and part.
	394–12	mandate that *s·* from above,
Rud.	9– 5	Even the truth he *s·*
'00.	8–27	When God *s·* to you
	13–29	Revelator *s·* of the angel
Po.	7–12	*S·* kindly when we meet and part.
	45–15	mandate that *s·* from above,
My.	28–28	* It *s·* for the successful labors
	58–16	* *s·* more than words can picture
	97–16	* *s·* of "the audacious,
	137– 6	* *Boston Globe,* . . . *s·* of it as,

special

Mis.	11–23	If *s·* opportunity for doing good
	11–27	I do it with earnest, *s·* care
	13– 4	taking *s·* care to mind my
	160–10	There is a *s·* joy in knowing
	162– 1	at times of *s·* enlightenment,
	210–15	woman's *s·* adaptability to lead
	293– 5	to the *s·* care of the unerring
	296– 1	by *s·* invitation, have allowed
	298–13	*s·* application to Christian Scientists ;
	300–28	but this was a *s·* privilege,
	306–19	* *s·* request of the late Mrs. Harrison,
	357–27	and need *s·* help.
Man.	27– 5	shall order no *s·* action
	54–19	*S·* Offense.
	56– 9	REGULAR AND *S·* MEETINGS.
	57– 5	*S·* meetings may be held
	60–13	shall be no *s·* observances,
	61– 1	No *s·* trowel should be used.
	62– 4	shall not neglect to sing any *s·*
	90–17	*S·* Instruction.
	96–11	where he sees there is *s·* need,
	100– 6	if she shall send a *s·* request
	109– 1	heading
	111–20	will be furnished *s·* forms
Ret.	6– 8	accorded *s·* household privileges.
	42– 9	also taught a *s·* Bible-class ;
	45–16	in accord with my *s·* request,
	48–12	At a *s·* meeting of the Board
Pul.	23–21	* scholars of *s·* research,
	29–22	* *s·* lesson was to be taken
	34– 4	* no *s·* record is to be made.
	44–26	* without any *s·* appeal,
	59– 5	* There was no *s·* sentence
	76–12	* mahogany in *s·* designs,
Rud.	13–20	then give *s·* attention to
'01.	3– 2	The *s·* benediction of our
'02.	1– 3	With no *s·* effort to achieve
	7–27	called his disciples' *s·* attention
My.	11–18	* it needs no *s·* insight
	25– 3	* in making a *s·* effort
	26–23	should date some *s·* reform,
	33– 8	* the *s·* Lesson-Sermon was
	68–22	* above the Readers' *s·* rooms.
	73–26	* chapter sub-title
	73–27	* *S·* trains and extra sections
	87–27	* whatever one's *s·* creed
	132– 2	is . . . the *s·* demand.
	173–25	*S·* thanks are due
	177– 8	no *s·* need of my personal

special

My.	266–22	Since 1877, these *s·*
	280–17	cease *s·* prayer for the peace
	280–30	in *s·* prayer for peace.
	289–11	*s·* meeting of its First Members
	305–21	I claim no *s·* merit
	333– 6	* a *s·* meeting was convened
	340– 5	*s·* days and seasons for
	341–24	* it was a *s·* favor
	347–22	*S·* contribution to "Bohemia."
	353–24	nothing . . . of any *s·* interest.

Special Correspondence

Pul.	23– 8	* *S· C·*.

specially

Mis.	111–27	*s·* call the attention of
	114–30	who does not *s·* instruct
	148–25	*s·* desire that you collect no
	161–23	he was *s·* endowed
	315–10	*s·* spiritually fitted for
Man.	71–19	*s·* allowed and named
Ret.	85– 1	*s·* responsible for
No.	3–20	which Mind-healers *s·* need ;
My.	32–28	* *s·* prepared Lesson-Sermon.
	38–17	* *s·* reserved for them.
	227–20	*not s· protected by law.*
	256– 3	notes, not *s·* musical
	339– 7	*s·* requested to be wise

specialty

Mis.	4–22	so that its religious *s·*

species

Mis.	23–31	could not change its *s·*
	26–21	neither a genus nor a *s·*
	27–13	no *s·* ever produces its opposite.
	346–13	This belief is a *s·* of idolatry,
Un.	51–15	Woman is the highest *s·* of
Rud.	7–24	Spirit no more changes its *s·*,
	7–26	bring about alteration of *s·*
My.	212– 1	is a *s·* of intoxication,
	301–24	is in itself a *s·* of insanity.

specific

Mis.	217–14	the *s·* nature of all things
	244–16	* visible agencies for *s·* ends?"
'01.	6–15	Is this pure, *s·* Christianity?
	31– 5	all error, *s·* or universal.
My.	181– 1	The *s·* quest of C. S.
	302–10	*s·* insanity is that brain, matter,

specifically

My.	10–14	* donation to be *s·* subscribed

specifications

My.	335–14	* *s·* of which were kept by

specified

Man.	45–10	*s·* in The Mother Church Manual,
	69– 3	during the time *s·* in the
	78– 8	such debts as are *s·* in
	99– 7	except as hereinafter *s·*,
Ret.	15–24	Among . . . they *s·* cancers.

specimen

No.	43–12	a *s·* of those received daily :

specimens

Mis.	294–19	Love such *s·* of mortality
No.	20–24	*s·* of every kind emerged

specious

'01.	25–16	ends in some *s·* folly.

specks

My.	109–21	but *s·* in His universe,

spectacle

'02.	18– 4	The constant *s·* of sin
My.	79–11	* *s·* of thirty thousand people

spectators

Mis.	299–24	The *s·* may ask,

spectre

Un.	28–11	not a *s·* had ever been seen

speculate

Mis.	327–10	to *s·* in worldly policy,
'02.	5–27	or *s·* on the existence of
Peo.	8–15	and *s·* concerning material forces.
My.	13– 1	They *s·* neither on the past,

speculation

Mis.	237–20	period of doubt, inquiry, *s·*,
	286–31	human *s·* will go on,

speculative

Mis.	29–13	between it and any *s·* theory.
	34–14	*s·* opinion and human belief.
	38–23	*s·* view too vapory and hypothetical
	64–20	resist *s·* opinions and fables.
	68–30	* "A *s·* science, which
	234– 4	by *s·* views of Truth.
	361–22	subtlety of *s·* wisdom
Ret.	70–12	*s·* theories as to the recurrence of
Peo.	3– 3	crudest ideals of *s·* theology

sped
Mis. 385–26 radiant glory s· The dawning day.
Chr. 53– 5 Spirit s· A loyal ray
Po. 49– 1 radiant glory s· The dawning day.

speech
Mis. 190–25 s· belongs to Mind instead of
246– 2 the prohibiting of free s·,
246–17 to shackle conscience, stop free s·,
338–25 * To give the lips full s·.
Ret. 61–18 no s· nor language, — Psal. 19 : 3.
Po. 73–14 Witness my presence and utter my s·.
My. 105–17 hearing to the deaf, s· to the dumb,
226– 6 termed in common s· the principle
345–29 make them our figures of s·.

speechless
Mis. 191–28 would be impossible if he were s·.
275–25 They moved me to s· thanks.
312– 6 s· and alone, bears all burdens,
My. 150–18 in s· prayer, ask God to enable you to

speed
Mis. 384– 8 To thought and deed Give sober s·,
'02. 2–14 God s· the right!
10–22 increases the s· of mortals' transit
Po. 36– 7 To thought and deed Give sober s·,
My. 6–26 s·, beauty, and achievements of
94–30 s·, beauty, and achievements of
124–26 rate of s·, the means of travel,
127– 7 s· of the chariot-wheels of Truth

speedily
Mis. 141–19 Let this be s· done.
144–30 s· wake the long night of
My. 181–17 that all nations shall s· learn

speedy
Mis. 212–15 s· return under the reign of
Ret. 54– 2 sometimes more s· than some of the
My. 12– 8 * s· accumulation of a sum sufficient

spell
Mis. 390–11 Enraptured by thy s·,
392–11 thou art a power and s·;
Ret. 18–21 communion with home's magic s·!
Po. 20–15 thou art a power and s·;
55–12 Enraptured by thy s·,
64–15 communion with home's magic s·!
68–13 stronger than these is the s· that hath

Spencer
Mis. 361–15 Tyndall, Darwin, and S·
My. 349–10 Berkeley, Tyndall, and S·

spend
Mis. 230–17 s· no time in sheer idleness,
My. 231–10 s· no more time or money in

spends
Pul. 81–13 * s· her whole time helping

spent
Mis. 213–28 the night is far s·,
375–14 * I s· two years in Paris,
Ret. 6–20 but later Albert s· a year
Pan. 1–17 The night is far s·,
My. 67–23 * sums of money were s· in
202– 7 the night is far s·

sphere
Mis. 284– 9 s· of his present usefulness.
386– 1 glorious life's s·,
Ret. 60– 3 Life as a complete s·,
60– 5 life as a broken s·,
89–25 enlarge their s· of action.
Un. 3– 4 another s· of experience,
45–20 into an imaginary s·
61–17 good in this mortal s·
No. 37– 9 and when, as a s· of Mind,
Po. 28– 2 Of every rolling s·,
49– 3 glorious life's s·,
My. 253– 2 brightening this lower s·

spheres
Po. 30–21 the hymning s· of light,
My. 13–27 cycles of systems and s·.

spider
My. 252– 6 will not be like the s·,

spilled
Hea. 18– 7 break and the wine be s·.

spilling
No. 33–17 s· of human blood

Spinoza (see also **Spinoza's**)
No. 22– 4 Fichte, Hegel, S·,
24– 6 according to S·,

Spinoza's
No. 24– 3 According to S· philosophy

spire
Mis. 144–32 the s· of this temple.
Un. 14–19 shifting vane on the s·,
Po. 30–18 with its triumphal s·.
My. 13–24 the spiritual s· of which

Spirit (see also **Spirit's**)
abode of
Mis. 174–16 abode of S·, the realm of the real.
absence of
No. 17– 4 evil, is the absence of S·
according to
Mis. 360–21 "the Israel according to S·"
after the
Mis. 188–15 but after the S·." — Rom. 8 : 1.
My. 113–13 but after the S·. — Rom. 8 : 1.
205– 3 but after the S·." — Rom. 8 : 1.
aid of
Peo. 9–18 invoke the divine aid of S·
All-in-all of
Ret. 34– 3 Science of Mind, the All-in-all of S·,
all is
My. 178–13 Then all is S· and spiritual.
All must be
Un. 31– 6 for the divine All must be S·.
allness of
Ret. 26– 28 and the allness of S·,
'01. 12–23 and we then see the allness of S·,
alone
Mis. 359– 7 instantaneously, and through S· alone.
Un. 31–23 God, or good, is S· alone;
and flesh
Mis. 85–21 S· and flesh antagonize.
and good
Ret. 60–10 as real as S· and good.
and immortal
Mis. 201–14 which is of S·, and immortal.
and infinite
'01. 25–27 if indeed S· and infinite,
and law
Mis. 256–21 chapter sub-title
and matter
Mis. 55–16 the facts of both S· and matter?
121– 7 S· and matter, good and evil,
'01. 22–10 Truth and error, S· and matter,
22–30 statement as to S· and matter,
Hea. 18– 8 no connection between S· and matter.
and Spirit
'01. 22– 9 S· and Spirit is not:
and the bride
My. 153–27 "the S· and the bride," — Rev. 22 : 17.
and Truth
Mis. 363–25 Word that is God, S·, and Truth.
and Word
Ret. 76– 9 touched with the S· and Word
antipode of
Mis. 217–12 antipode of S·, namely, matter.
267–24 antipode of S·, which we name matter,
Un. 31–19 matter, the antipode of S·,
approach
No. 16–24 in proportion as mortals approach S·,
as well as
Mis. 333–12 in matter as well as S·?
at war with
Un. 36–14 flesh at war with S·;
baptism of
Mis. 30–31 bathe in the baptism of S·,
82– 8 out of the baptism of S·,
205–13 The baptism of S·,
Peo. 9– 9 It is the baptism of S· that
baptism of the
'01. 1–15 The baptism of the S·,
baptized in
Pan. 14– 9 and be baptized in S·.
baptized of
Mis. 206– 7 to the baptized of S·:
baptized them in
'01. 9– 8 Christ baptized them in S·
becomes
Mis. 218– 1 in which nature becomes S·;
behold
Un. 30– 1 uplifted to behold S· as the
belief that
Peo. 4– 6 belief that S· materialized into
bestows
Mis. 345– 1 S· bestows spiritual gifts,
blind us to
Mis. 234– 2 no longer to blind us to S·,
born of
Mis. 184– 9 man born of S· is spiritual,
My. 261–26 born of S· and not of matter.
born of the
'01. 27–26 born of the S· and not matter.

Spirit

can never
    Un. 41–22   *S·* can never dwell in its
claims of
    Mis. 140–10   the claims of *S·* over matter
conceived of
    My. 262–14   conceived of *S·,* of God
conception of
    My. 152–11   conception of *S·* and its all-power.
concerning
    Un. 23–17   they testify concerning *S·,*
constitutes
    Mis. 56–13   to conclude that *S·* constitutes
controls body
    Mis. 247–20   that *S·* controls body.
could not change
    Mis. 23–31   God, *S·,* could not change
creates
    Mis. 27– 5   or that *S·* creates its opposite,
defies
    Un. 31–19   all that denies and defies *S·,*
demonstrate
    Mis. 258–21   neither name nor demonstrate *S·.*
demonstration of
    Mis. 74–20   His demonstration of *S·* virtually
departure from
    My. 151–28   This departure from *S·,*
derived from
    Mis. 162–15   his power, derived from *S·,*
disagreement with
    Un. 41–28   perpetual disagreement with *S·.*
divine
    (*see* **divine**)
dominion of
    Mis. 16–14   reflect the full dominion of *S·*
dream of
    Mis. 180– 1   the dream of *S·* in the flesh
eternal
    Un. 22–19   cometh not from the eternal *S·,*
evidences of
    Ret. 56–12   between the evidences of *S·* and
existence in
    Un. 45–27   no origin or existence in *S·,*
facts of
    Mis. 55–18   C. S. is based on the facts of *S·*
faith in
    Peo. 9–24   and rest all faith in *S·,*
false conceptions of
    Peo. 2–14   false conceptions of *S·,* based on
finds
    No. 15–20   finds *S·* neither in matter nor in
flesh and
    (*see* **flesh**)
flesh not
    '02. 6– 6   fruits of the flesh not *S·.*
flesh to
    Un. 56–25   ere he can change from flesh to *S·,*
fourth dimension of
    Mis. 22–12   and fourth dimension of *S·.*
from matter to
    Mis. 194–22   turn from matter to *S·* for healing ;
fruit of the
    My. 167– 4   "the fruit of the *S·*."— *Gal.* 5 : 22.
fruits of
    (*see* **fruits**)
functions of
    My. 288–19   to perform the functions of *S·,*
giveth Life
    Ret. 65– 8   Pharisaism killeth ; *S·* giveth Life.
God is
    (*see* **God**)
God is a
    Mis. 219– 8   "God is a *S·* :— *John* 4 : 24.
    Un. 31– 1   "God is a *S·*"— *John* 4 : 24.
God, or
    Un. 10–11   Life is God, or *S·,*
    No. 16–14   there is none beside God or *S·*
good
    Pan. 9– 7   a good *S·* and an evil spirit.
good is
    No. 38– 7   He is good, and good is *S·* ;
governed by
    Mis. 267–23   should be governed by *S·,*
graces of the
    Mis. 149–22   all the rich graces of the *S·.*
grandeur of
    Mis. 86–25   divine beauty and the grandeur of *S·.*
harmonies of
    Mis. 333–20   securing the sweet harmonies of *S·*
heaven of
    My. 195–28   eternal in the heaven of *S·.*
He is
    No. 15–25   He is *S·* ;
Holy
    Mis. 161–23   endowed with the Holy *S·* ;
    '01. 9–22   Holy *S·* takes of the things of God

Spirit

holy
    Mis. 70–24   body of the holy *S·* of Jesus
idea of
    Mis. 60–27   every creation or idea of *S·*
    No. 16–14   God or Spirit and the idea of *S·.*
image of
    Rud. 5– 8   in the image of *S·,* or God.
    '01. 8–20   The reflex image of *S·* is not
individual
    Rud. 2–17   but one infinite individual *S·,*
infinite
    Mis. 16–31   with the laws of infinite *S·,*
        56– 4   Life is inorganic, infinite *S·* ;
        72–29   Being is God, infinite *S·* ;
       181–12   Infinite Principle and infinite *S·*
       190– 3   it is infinite *S·,* Truth, Life,
       219– 5   the personality of infinite *S·*
    Rud. 2–11   if by *person* is meant infinite *S·.*
    Pan. 9– 3   "Infinite *S·*" means one God
    '01. 5–20   God is infinite *S·* or Person,
        7– 2   infinite Love, infinite *S·,*
    Hea. 4–16   and, after infinite *S·* is forced in
    My. 235–17   Did infinite *S·* make that
infinity or
    Ret. 58– 4   the problem of infinity or *S·,*
instead of
    Mis. 276–27   from matter instead of *S·,*
    Peo. 12–25   power to matter instead of *S·.*
intelligent
    Mis. 103– 3   Intelligent *S·,* Soul, is substance,
is All and **is all**
    Un. 36– 5   against the fact that *S·* is All,
    My. 357–22   Spirit is infinite ; therefore *S· is all.*
is causation
    Hea. 19–12   *S·* is causation,
is deathless
    Un. 42– 3   Soul, *S·,* is deathless.
is God
    Mis. 21–20   *S·* is God, and man is His image
       218– 2   *S·* is God, and God is good.
    Un. 25– 6   *S·* is God, and God is good ;
       29– 6   Spirit never sins, because *S·* is God.
    My. 235–21   Because *S·* is God and *infinite;*
       356–25   *S·* is God, and this God is infinite
is immortal Truth
    Mis. 21–18   *S·* is immortal Truth ;
is infinite
    Pan. 13–19   great truth that *S·* is infinite,
    My. 271– 1   God, *S·,* is infinite,
       357–22   *S·* is infinite ; therefore *Spirit is all.*
is omnipotent
    Mis. 232–18   *S·* is omnipotent ;
is sovereign
    Pan. 6–23   If *S·* is sovereign, how can matter
is substance
    Ret. 57–17   *S·* is substance in Truth.
is the lawgiver
    Mis. 364–25   If *S·* is the lawgiver to matter,
is the only creator
    Un. 32– 6   *S·* is the only creator,
       35–26   *S·* is the only creator.
is the only substance
    Mis. 47–20   God, *S·,* is the only substance ;
    Un. 25– 6   *Good.* *S·* is the only substance.
is the real
    Mis. 21–19   *S·* is the real and eternal ;
is true
    '01. 22–12   *S·* is true and infinite,
is Truth
    Un. 36–11   Thus we see that *S·* is Truth
itself
    Mis. 46–22   *S·* itself beareth witness— *Rom.* 8 : 16.
       255–14   *S·* itself beareth witness— *Rom.* 8 : 16.
jubilee of
    Mis. 135–15   to the jubilee of *S·*
kingdom of
    '02. 20– 5   desired haven, the kingdom of *S·* ;
language of
    My. 180–10   in the language of *S·,*
law of
    (*see* **law**)
law of the
    (*see* **law**)
laws of
    Mis. 260–12   laws of *S·,* not of matter ;
leavened with
    Mis. 175– 5   sense of being is leavened with *S·.*
lens of
    My. 129–15   seen through the lens of *S·,*
less than
    Mis. 217– 6   cannot become less than *S·* ;
Life is
    Un. 41–22   All Life is *S·,*
    Hea. 9–26   Life is *S·* ; and when we

Spirit

Life of
No. 34–22 The real blood or Life of S·
Life, or
Mis. 56– 4 if Life, or S·, were organic,
Life was
Un. 42–23 To him, Life was S·.
likeness of
Mis. 62– 1 man in the likeness of S· is spiritual.
Rud. 13–10 body is not the likeness of S· ;
love
Mis. 18–13 Thou shalt love S· only,
made all
Pan. 6–16 if S· made all that was made,
majesty of
Mis. 141–13 might, and majesty of S·,
matter and
    (see **matter**)
matter to
'02. 10–23 transit from matter to S·
My. 163– 7 from matter to S·.
    181–11 departure from matter to S·,
matter with
'01. 26– 9 that combines matter with S·.
meaning of
Hea. 11– 9 would catch the meaning of S·.
might be found
Mis. 64– 1 S· might be found "All-in-all."
Mind of
Un. 32–11 It is not the Mind of S· ;
my
My. 154–12 "my S·, saith the Lord ;" — Zech. 4 : 6.
name without the
Mis. 302– 7 teaching the name without the S·,
nativity in
Mis. 162–17 therefrom rise to his nativity in S·.
nature of
Mis. 218–25 not express the nature of S·,
negations of
No. 16–10 are but negations of S·, Truth,
never entered
Hea. 18– 9 S· never entered . . . matter ;
never sins
Un. 29– 6 S· never sins, because
new-born of
Pul. 10–29 This is the new-born of S·,
no cognizance of
Mis. 218–14 take no cognizance of S·
nod of
My. 129–14 The nod of S· is nature's natal.
not formed by
Un. 35–23 molecule, . . . is not formed by S· ;
nothing but
Un. 34–12 therefore there is nothing but S· ;
notion of
Mis. 218–21 notion of S· as cause and end, with
not matter
Mis. 5–18 power of S·, not matter,
'01. 5–22 man reflects S·, not matter.
Peo. 9– 2 this faith builds on S·, not matter ;
obscuration of
Mis. 2– 8 causing great obscuration of S·.
offspring of
Mis. 181–18 offspring of S·, and not of the flesh ;
Ret. 68–28 "Man is the offspring of S·.
My. 357– 5 Christ, . . . the offspring of S·,
of life
Mis. 201–18 S· of life in Christ Jesus — Rom. 8 : 2.
    321–15 S· of life in Christ Jesus — Rom. 8 : 2.
    326– 2 S· of life in Christ Jesus — Rom. 8 : 2.
'01. 9–10 "S· of life in Christ Jesus," — Rom. 8 : 2.
'02. 9–12 S· of life in Christ Jesus — Rom. 8 : 2.
My. 41–23 * S· of life in Christ Jesus," — Rom. 8 : 2.
    113–13 S· of life in Christ Jesus — Rom. 8 : 2.
    272– 6 S· of life in Christ Jesus — Rom. 8 : 2.
    293–28 S· of life in Christ Jesus — Rom. 8 : 2.
of the Lord
My. 128–11 "Where the S· of the Lord — II Cor. 3 : 17.
omnipotence of
Ret. 31–24 before the omnipotence of S·,
omnipresence of
Ret. 56–10 omniscience, and omnipresence of S·,
omnipresent
Un. 43–27 omnipresent S· which knows no matter.
one
Ret. 22–20 his father and mother are the one S·,
    60–29 but one S·, Mind, Soul.
Pan. 9– 5 "spirits" means more than one S· ;
only
Mis. 18–13 Thou shalt love S· only,
Rud. 4–18 not in matter, but in S· only.
My. 152–15 worship only S· and spiritually,
opposed to
Mis. 199–21 the qualities opposed to S·

Spirit

opposite of
Mis. 26–18 it is the very opposite of S·,
Un. 32–19 saying, "I am the opposite of S·,
    36–13 that matter is the opposite of S·;
or God
Rud. 5– 8 in the image of S·, or God.
or good
No. 17– 4 evil, is the absence of S· or good.
or matter
Mis. 28–22 What meaneth this Me, — S·, or matter?
or Soul
No. 29– 6 He believes that S·, or Soul,
or Truth
No. 5–15 sense also avers that S·, or Truth,
outcome of
Un. 42– 4 not the outcome of S·, holiness,
over matter
Ret. 26–11 superiority of S· over matter.
paradise in
My. 118–28 finds its paradise in S·,
paradise of
Mis. 70–14 paradise of S· would come to
permanence of
Mis. 47– 7 glory and permanence of S· :
    74–28 and the power and permanence of S·.
personal
Peo. 13– 3 believe that God is a personal S·,
phenomena of
Mis. 73–31 phenomena of S· in C. S.,
No. 19–23 noumenon or the phenomena of S· ;
phenomenon of
Mis. 217–12 or, that the phenomenon of S·
pleads for
Mis. 174–21 Shall that . . . which pleads for S·
possibilities of
Mis. 187– 6 sense of the possibilities of S·.
power of
    (see **power**)
prerogative of
My. 179– 8 the power and prerogative of S·
Principle and
Un. 61–14 but the divine Principle and S·
proved
Mis. 63–29 in which S· proved its supremacy
qualities of
Mis. 201– 6 bringing the qualities of S·
quickening
Un. 30–24 last Adam as a quickening S·,
    30–26 shall be found a quickening S· ;
reflection of
Ret. 73– 8 is found in the reflection of S·.
reflects only
Mis. 205–17 consciousness reflects only S·,
retained by
Mis. 218–26 neither eliminated nor retained by S·.
reveals
Ret. 60– 6 Science reveals S· as All,
revelation of
Mis. 56–20 at the full revelation of S·,
rights of
Mis. 56–13 and infringes the rights of S·.
saith
'00. 11–26 S· saith unto the— Rev. 2 : 7.
    14–10 hear what the S· saith unto the
sends forth
Rud. 8– 5 S· sends forth its own
sense of
Mis. 17–32 gains a truer sense of S·
    24–20 shutting out the true sense of S·.
Un. 21–20 spiritual sense, a sense of S·,
side of
Mis. 180– 2 so far as to take the side of S·,
Soul, or
No. 26– 4 and that Soul, or S·, is subdivided
source is
Un. 25–24 whose only source is S·.
sprung from
Mis. vii–17 My world has sprung from S·,
strives against
Mis. 119–15 flesh strives against S·,
subjection to
Mis. 201– 6 bringing . . . into subjection to S·.
substance of
Mis. 56– 8 substance of S· is divine Mind.
    104– 7 was safe in . . . the substance of S·,
Un. 45–25 It lacks the substance of S·,
supremacy of
    (see **supremacy**)
sword of
Mis. 215–26 at this stage use the sword of S·.
My. 189– 2 grasping the sword of S·,
sword of the
My. 185– 9 sword of the S· is drawn ;

Spirit

synonym of
Mis. 75–11 Soul is a synonym of *S*·,
Ret. 57–10 Soul is the synonym of *S*·,
tabernacle of
Mis. 362–26 in the tabernacle of *S*·.
teaches
My. 167– 7 *S*· teaches us to resign what we
temple of
My. 64–26 * in the universal temple of *S*·,
that heals
My. 158–20 it is the *S*· that heals the sick
"the way" in
Un. 55–13 "The way," in *S*·, is — *John* 14 : 6.
things of
Mis. 342–32 faithful over the few things of *S*·,
'01. 9–28 liveth most the things of *S*·,
My. 260–10 the things of *S*·, not of matter.
this force is
Rud. 4–11 This force is *S*·,
this one is
My. 356–25 and this one is *S*· ;
to apprehend
Ret. 28–10 in order to apprehend *S*·.
Pul. 35–14 in order to apprehend *S*·.
torches of
Ret. 23–17 the midnight torches of *S*·.
triumph of
Ret. 56–15 triumph of *S*· in immutable harmony.
triumphs of
Un. 3–12 through . . . the triumphs of *S*·.
understanding of
Un. 50–10 by a dominant understanding of *S*·.
unity of
Mis. 198– 4 arrive at this point of unity of *S*·,
My. 167– 8 what we are in the unity of *S*·
unlike
Mis. 55–23 destruction of all that is unlike *S*·,
'01. 8–21 image of Spirit is not unlike *S*·.
verities of
Mis. 55–21 verities of *S*· assert themselves over
war against
Mis. 2–30 beliefs that war against *S*·,
warreth against
Mis. 124– 8 which warreth against *S*·,
wars against
My. 339–28 and all that wars against *S*·
with matter
My. 206– 2 would unite . . . *S*· with matter
works of the
Ret. 65– 5 or the works of the *S*·.
worship of
My. 23–25 * represents the worship of *S*·,
would destroy
Mis. 56– 5 would destroy *S*· and annihilate man.

Mis. 18– 1 baptismals that come from *S*·,
23–22 God, *S*·, Mind, are terms synonymous
24–17 Life in and of *S*· ;
26–23 *S*·, God, has no antecedent ;
27– 3 terms God and good, as *S*·, are
27–24 being in and of *S*·, Mind,
28–23 and must mean *S*·.
56–29 Your question implies that *S*·,
57– 7 not from dust, . . . but from *S*·,
72–21 *imply that S· takes note of matter ?*
76–29 The Science of Soul, *S*·,
96–32 not of the flesh, but of the *S*·.
113– 4 *S*· is our Father and Mother,
123–29 God is Love, is *S*· ;
169–27 which is enmity toward God, *S*·.
181–13 over what is the person of *S*·,
187–24 Did the substance of God, *S*·,
198–16 man as governed by God, *S*·,
200– 7 because *S*· was to him All-in-all,
201– 8 element of matter, . . . never of *S*·.
217– 5 *S*· cannot become less than
217–16 nature is constituted of and by *S*·.
217–30 matter must . . . for *S*· to appear.
218– 3 Deity was forever Mind, *S*· ;
286–26 *S*·, God, is the only creator :
317–31 God giveth not the *S*· by — *John* 3 : 34.
363–14 "Let us [*S*·] make man perfect ;"
364–22 hypotheses predicate matter of *S*·
399– 8 'T is the *S*· that makes pure,
Man. 16– 7 even the allness of Soul, *S*·,
Chr. 53– 5 *S*· sped A loyal ray
55–16 *S*· [God-likeness] is life — *Rom.* 8 : 10.
Ret. 25–18 *S*· I called the *reality* ;
25–25 neither sees, hears, nor feels *S*·,
28–15 For *S*· to be supreme
56– 6 or divides . . . *S*· into spirits,
58–14 not the result of . . . it was *S*·.
69– 2 *S*· is his primitive . . . source
69–12 God, *S*·, who *is* the only Life.'
Un. 24–17 *S*· is all that endureth,

Spirit

Un. 29– 7 as *S*·, Soul is sinless, and is God.
31–18 usurps the authority of God, *S*· ;
31–22 evil does not obtain in *S*·,
34–26 *S*·, Life, Truth, and Love.
35–12 is not matter, but *S*·.
35–24 *S*· is *spiritual* consciousness
35–25 can form nothing unlike itself, *S*·,
46– 4 from *S*·, not from flesh.
Pul. 2–24 *S*·, God, the eternal harmony
35–19 For *S*· to be supreme
Rud. 1– 8 It is substance, *S*·, Life, Truth,
4–17 *S*· is not in matter,
7–21 *S*· cannot originate its opposite,
7–23 According to divine Science, *S*·
7–24 by evolving matter from *S*·,
No. 3–13 not having lost the *S*· which
27–10 *S*· will be the light of the city,
Pan. 4–20 *S*·, is indeed the preserver of man.
5– 3 *S*·, be discovered in matter?
7– 1 *S*·, God, is infinite,
7– 8 belief, that after God, *S*·, had
7–17 infinity of God, *S*·
7–24 which implies Mind, *S*·, God ;
12– 5 * *S*·, is ever in universal nature."
12– 6 we naturally ask, how can *S*· be
12–24 Life, Truth, Love, substance, *S*·,
'01. 3–19 called in Scripture, *S*·, Love,
3–25 loses the nature of God, *S*·,
8–17 Is God *S*·? He is.
'02. 7– 3 It accords all to God, *S*·,
8– 5 likeness of God, *S*·, is spiritual,
Po. 75–15 'Tis the *S*· that makes pure,
My. 14– 1 whereto [God, *S*·] sent it." — see *Isa.* 55 : 11.
129–18 never severed from *S*· !
151–22 SUBJECT : "NOT MATTER, BUT *S*·"
191–19 *S*· is saying unto matter :
225–29 Truth, Life, *S*·, Mind, Soul,
232–25 man created by and of *S*·,
235–17 Is God *S*·? He is.
238–10 God being *S*·, His language and
239–27 spiritual man, created by God, *S*·,
288–18 matter was not the auxiliary of *S*·.
349–29 and deduced from God, *S*· ;
357– 4 spiritual fulness of God, *S*·,

spirit (*see also* spirit's)

and in truth
Mis. 150–20 "in *s*· and in truth," — *John* 4 : 23.
219– 9 in *s*· and in truth." — *John* 4 : 24.
321–14 in *s*· and in truth." — *John* 4 : 23.
Ret. 65–13 "in *s*· and in truth." — *John* 4 : 23.
Un. 31– 4 in *s*· and in truth." — *John* 4 : 24.
Pul. 21– 7 Scientists in *s*· and in truth.
No. 34–11 in *s*· and in truth." — *John* 4 : 23.
Pan. 14– 6 worship in *s*· and in truth ;
My. 5–25 "in *s*· and in truth." — *John* 4 : 23.
25–22 "in *s*· and in truth." — *John* 4 : 24.
270–32 in *s*· and in truth." — *John* 4 : 24.
and mission
Mis. 372–22 concerning the *s*· and mission of
and power
Mis. 193–26 *s*· and power of Christianity.
Ret. 86– 3 *s*· and power of C. S.,
and the flesh
My. 293–19 yea, the *s*· and the flesh
and the letter
Mis. 146–17 *s*· and the letter of this Scripture :
195– 9 *s*· and the letter are requisite ;
My. 129–30 they include the *s*· and the letter
and the Word
My. 246–21 *s*· and the Word appeared,
and understanding
'01. 32–28 *s*· and understanding of C. S.
animus and
My. 45–12 * animus and *s*· of our movement.
Christian
Man. 77–26 in a Christian *s*· and manner,
Christly
Ret. 48–29 whose Christly *s*· has led to higher ways,
divine
Pul. 65–25 * was called the divine *s*· of giving,
evil
Pan. 9– 7 a good Spirit and an evil *s*·.
'01. 16–20 refer to an evil *s*· as *dumb*,
fevered
'00. 11–24 * it lay on my fevered *s*·
following Christ in
No. 34– 5 following Christ in *s*·,
foul
My. 126–26 hold of every foul *s*·, — *Rev.* 18 : 2.
full
Mis. 311–12 the full *s*· of that charity
His
Ret. 18–18 adore all His *s*· hath made,
Rud. 4–23 love Him through His *s*·,
Po. 64– 9 adore all His *s*· hath made,

spirit

his
Mis. 387–16   Pray that his s· you partake,
Po.   6–11   Pray that his s· you partake,
My. 196–11   and he that ruleth his s·— Prov. 16 : 32.

hopeful
Pul. 80–25   * it has brought a hopeful s·

imbibe the
Mis. 303–18   imbibe the s· of Christ's Beatitudes.
My. 239– 8   imbibe the s· and prove the

its
Mis. 145– 6   as requisite to manifest its s·,
195– 6   but possesses not its s·,
292– 3   and its s· is baptismal ;
Ret. 52– 7   and less of its s·.
81– 8   The letter . . . separated from its s·,

letter without the
My. 158–19   The letter without the s· is dead :

matter or
My. 235–20   Is mortal man . . . matter or s·?

meek in
Mis. 152–20   pure in affection, the meek in s·,

more of the
Ret. 49– 9   more of the s· instead of the letter,

my
Po. 16–22   call to my s· with seraphs to dwell ;
65– 1   Sing me that song !   My s· is sad,
My. 303– 1   mysteriously upon my s·.

need the
Mis. 345– 7   need the s· of the pious Polycarp,

newness of
No. 25– 6   serve in newness of s·, — Rom. 7 : 6.

of beauty
Pul. 2– 6   s· of beauty dominates The

of bigotry
My. 93– 4   * have little of the s· of bigotry.

of Christ
Mis. 25–21   manifests the s· of Christ.
141–17   s· of Christ actuating all the parties
370– 7   greater s· of Christ is also abroad,
374– 4   Pharisees scorned the s· of Christ
Ret. 47–16   richly imbued with the s· of Christ,
Pul. 21–27   rest on the s· of Christ
75– 3   has most of the s· of Christ,

of Christianity
My. 246–16   s· of Christianity, dwelling forever

of Christian Science
Mis. 43–18   gained sooner than the s· of C. S. :
Pul. 80–20   * the s· of C. S. ideas has caused

of Christmas
My. 260–24   true s· of Christmas elevates

of divine Love
'01. 9–14   the s· of divine Love,

of evil
Mis. 370– 6   antagonistic s· of evil is still abroad ;
My. 212– 5   essence, or s·, of evil,

of faith
My. 85–26   * s· of faith and brotherhood

of God
'01. 9–16   s· of God is made manifest
My. 344–10   "It is not the s· of God,

of his Father
'01. 9–29   s· of his Father speaketh

of his mission
My. 246–26   and the s· of his mission,

of his prayer
Mis. 211–30   lived the s· of his prayer,

of humanity
My. 129– 5   the s· of humanity, ethics, and

of idolatry
Mis. 123– 6   the s· of idolatry, envy,

of levity
My. 93–18   * to approach it in a s· of levity,

of lies
Mis. 266–28   The s· of lies is abroad.

of Love
Mis. 288–29   s· of Love that nerves the struggle.
No. v– 4   self-sacrificing s· of Love

of love
Po. 66– 6   s· of love, at soft eventide

of our Master
Mis. 370– 2   say, in the s· of our Master,

of sacrifice
Mis. 261–23   This s· of sacrifice always has

of song
Ret. 17– 3   s· of song, — midst the zephyrs
Po. 62– 1   s· of song, — midst the zephyrs

of St. Paul
Mis. 344–29   We need the s· of St. Paul,

of the prayer
My. 292–26   s· of the prayer of the righteous

of these rights
Mis. 289–29   are the s· of these rights,

of this orison
My. 281– 8   s· of this orison is the fruit of

spirit

of true watching
My. 233– 1   the s· of true watching,

of Truth
Mis. 40–23   must possess the s· of Truth
49–19   s· of Truth leads into all truth,
204–12   s· of Truth cleansing from
205–10   s· of Truth and Love on
Ret. 81–10   s· of Truth extinguishes
Pul. 75– 2   the s· of Truth and Love,
No. 32–14   in the s· of Truth ;
My. 4– 2   one finds the s· of Truth,
119–30   s· of Truth that leadeth away
130–12   s· of Truth is the lever
225– 3   worker in the s· of Truth
238–18   the s· of Truth, whereby the

of unselfishness
My. 87–26   * imbued with the s· of unselfishness

omitting the
No. 28–22   omitting the s· of this Science

one
Pan. 6–27   belief in more than one s·,
14– 6   at the table of our Lord in one s· ;

oneness in
Mis. 289–18   Oneness in s· is Science,

or letter
Man. 44– 5   s· or letter of this By-Law

our
Mis. 46–23   witness with our s·, — Rom. 8 : 16.
255–14   witness with our s·, — Rom. 8 : 16.

placid
Ret. 5–23   * sympathizing heart, and a placid s·.

poor in
Mis. 325– 3   the poor in s· : — Matt. 5 : 3.
Ret. 26–26   none but the "poor in s·" — Matt. 5 : 3.
'01. 2–19   blessing the poor in s·

pure in
Mis. 168–13   only such as are pure in s·,
'01. 26–18   the pure in s·, and the meek

quickening
Mis. 185–28   made a quickening s·. — I Cor. 15 : 45.
188–32   "a quickening s· ;" — I Cor. 15 : 45.
189–17   quickening s· takes it away :
Un. 30–15   made a quickening s·." — I Cor. 15 : 45.

requires the
Pul. 15– 8   requires the s· of our blessed Master

sainted
Ret. 6– 2   * impressions of that sainted s·,

same
Mis. 123– 1   same s· that in our time massacres
347–13   operation by the same s·.

self-same
Po. 10–16   "Thou of the self-same s·,
My. 337–17   "Thou of the self-same s·,

thereof
Mis. 291–19   if the s· thereof be lacking.

this
Pul. 75– 6   a greater degree of this s·
'01. 9–16   This s· of God is made manifest
My. 165– 9   and by this s· man lives
292–27   but this s· is of God,

underlying
My. 71– 8   * fussing about the underlying s·

unity of
Mis. 145–21   the visible unity of s· remains,
Pul. 22–18   there will be unity of s·,

uplifting of
Mis. 169–12   The uplifting of s· was the

with thee in
Po. 73– 8   I am with thee in s· once more.

with you in
Pul. 1–18   being with you in s·,
My. 148–19   am with you in s·,

wounded
Mis. 258– 9   anointing the wounded s·

your
Man. 47–12   and in your s·, — I Cor. 6 : 20.

Mis. 124– 4   must worship Him in s·.
195– 7   hath the s· without the letter,
207– 4   s· of my life-purpose,
260–27   The s·, and not the letter,
355– 5   not of the letter, but the s·.
385–14   S· emancipate for this far shore
Man. 43–26   s· in which the writer has written
Ret. 69–11   saying, . . . 'I will put s· into
88–25   s· of the Saviour's ministry,
Pul. 2– 3   no more s· in her ;" — I Kings 10 : 5.
'01. 9–30   s· giveth him liberty :
24–30   to attain the s· or mystery of
'02. 9–19   s· of the healing Christ,
Po. 48– 7   S· emancipate for this far shore
My. 125–17   s· of the Mars' Hill orator,
131–15   above the symbol seize the s·,
180–28   in the s· of our great Exemplar
188–17   In s· I enter your inner sanctuary,

spirit
My. 194– 6 but the *s·* of it is immortal.
194–23 gratefully accept the *s·* of it ;
233– 2 *s·* of our Master's command
343– 2 * in Mrs. Eddy's own *s·*.

spirited
Pul. 29–14 * The music was *s·*,

spiritless
No. 29–22 Such sermons, . . . are *s·* waifs,
Peo. 5–12 barbarisms of *s·* codes.
Po. 67– 3 Grow cold in this spot as the *s·* clay,

spirit-rappings
Mis. 231– 9 though I take no stock in *s·*

Spirit-revelator
Mis. 3–14 through Christ, the *S·*,

Spirit's
Un. 58–10 by the law of *S·* supremacy ;

spirit's
Ret. 9–19 * naught my *s·* breathings to control,

spirits (*see also* spirits')
Mis. 34–23 are called "communications from *s·*,"
171–13 "try the *s·*"— *I John* 4 : 1.
171–15 *s·* supposed to have departed
278– 2 the distilled *s·* of evil,
387– 9 'Neath which our *s·* blend
Ret. 56– 6 Spirit into *s·*, . . . is a misstatement
No. 26– 4 *s·*, or souls,— *alias* gods.
Pan. 9– 4 term "*s·*" means more than one
Hea. 6–15 ignorantly imputed to *s·*.
Po. 3–13 Till bursting bonds our *s·* part
6– 3 'Neath which our *s·* blend
My. 211–10 the unclean *s·* cried out,
313–21 I was not a medium for *s·*.

spirits'
Mis. 387– 6 in what glad surprise, Our *s·* own !"
Po. 50–24 in what glad surprise, Our *s·* own !"

Spirit-substance
Mis. 205–20 disembodied individual *S·*

spiritual
abstractions
Mis. 195–27 *s·* abstractions, impractical and
achievement
My. 37–16 * By reason of your *s·* achievement
advent
Ret. 70–21 *s·* advent of the advancing idea
Æsculapius
My. 205–16 *s·* Æsculapius and Hygeia,
afflatus
Ret. 31–30 potency of a present *s·* afflatus.
altitude
Mis. 16–28 this new-born *s·* altitude ;
289–31 allowed to rise to the *s·* altitude
and eternal
(*see* eternal)
animus
Mis. 113–32 moral, and *s·* animus is felt
Man. 31–13 *s·* animus so universally needed.
Pul. 3–30 unfitness for such a *s·* animus
32– 9 * but a *s·* animus.
application
Mis. 170–21 *s·* application bears upon our
apprehension
Mis. 363–31 *s·* apprehension of the Scriptures,
My. 183–12 *S·* apprehension unfolds,
armament
Un. 6–27 manual of their *s·* armament.
My. 355–14 the untiring *s·* armament.
ascendency
'01. 19–19 through *s·* ascendency alone.
aspirations
My. 91–10 * no person's *s·* aspirations were
attainments
Mis. 345–32 directed them to *s·* attainments.
'00. 1–14 rich *s·* attainments,
My. 64– 5 * through her *s·* attainments,
244–11 impulse to our *s·* attainments,
attitude
Ret. 88–26 abide in such a *s·* attitude
attraction
My. 159–18 tend to check *s·* attraction
axis
Ret. 88–30 Mind revolves on a *s·* axis,
bankruptcy
Mis. 122–24 Neither *s·* bankruptcy nor
basis
Un. 25–19 a material, not a *s·* basis.
Hea. 1–21 more *s·* basis and tendency
beauty
My. 141–28 blossomed into *s·* beauty,
behest
'02. 19–24 a *s·* behest, in reversion,

spiritual
being
Mis. 105–10 his individual *s·* being,
113–13 scale of moral and *s·* being,
352– 1 the bliss of *s·* being ;
Peo. 2– 6 material conceptions of *s·* being,
beings
Peo. 1–18 understanding that we are *s·* beings
birth
Mis. 17–18 This *s·* birth opens to the
17–27 With the *s·* birth, man's
body
My. 218–11 The *s·* body, the incorporeal
call
My. 172–13 symbol of my *s·* call
chemicalization
Pul. 5–30 This *s·* chemicalization is the
child
Mis. 18–15 as God's *s·* child only,
Christ
Mis. 84–12 *s·* Christ was infallible ;
Christianity
Mis. 2–15 view of a more *s·* Christianity,
232–18 a more *s·* Christianity will be
246–28 Shall we have a *s·* Christianity
No. 46– 4 a practical, *s·* Christianity,
'01. 2– 3 The highest *s·* Christianity
Peo. 5– 2 recommends the more *s·* Christianity,
coexistence
Mis. 47–24 *s·* coexistence with his Maker.
communion
Mis. 90–30 is the *s·* communion which
My. 139–24 the material to the *s·* communion ;
compact
Ret. 47– 3 wars with Love's *s·* compact,
concept
Un. 32– 7 man . . . is His *s·* concept.
conception
Mis. 286–11 more *s·* conception and education of
concepts
Mis. 361–10 *s·* concepts testifying to one
conclusions
Ret. 21–28 if *s·* conclusions are separated from
condition
Un. 7–13 In the same *s·* condition
consciousness
Un. 23–25 a purely good and *s·* consciousness
35–24 Spirit is *s·* consciousness alone.
35–24 Hence this *s·* consciousness
cooperation
My. 162– 9 Unity is *s·* cooperation,
cosmos
Mis. 26–25 God's consequent is the *s·* cosmos.
362–24 *s·* cosmos and Science of Soul.
creation
My. 179– 5 gave an account of the *s·* creation,
danger
No. 23– 4 is fraught with *s·* danger.
dawn
Mis. 78– 1 *s·* dawn of the Messiah,
'02. 5– 4 *s·* dawn of the twentieth century
death
Un. 29– 8 there can be, no *s·* death.
demand
Pul. 23–14 * common identity of *s·* demand.
Hea. 19–20 Science makes a more *s·* demand,
development
My. 48–20 * a means of *s·* development
dictionary
Mis. 252–30 the wise man's *s·* dictionary ;
discernment
Mis. 112–29 intellectual, and *s·* discernment,
215–32 a wise *s·* discernment must be used
312–21 his own *s·* discernment,
My. 22–21 * a *s·* discernment of the needs of
effect
My. 318–13 declare the moral and *s·* effect
element
Ret. 65– 7 freeze out the *s·* element.
elements
Mis. 2–30 putting on the *s·* elements
elevator
Mis. 259–23 *s·* elevator of the human race,
endeavor
Pan. 9–17 *s·* endeavor to bless others,
ends
Ret. 47–11 means for the promotion of *s·* ends.
existence
Mis. 17–28 primitive, sinless, *s·* existence
182–15 man's primal, *s·* existence,
Ret. 23–14 heart's bridal to more *s·* existence.
eye
Po. 32–11 illumines my *s·* eye,
fact
Mis. 42–22 the *s·* fact of Life is,
My. 109– 6 not the *s·* fact of being.

spiritual

facts
Mis.   8– 1   More . . . than to *s·* facts.
      37– 6   the *s·* facts of being.
   174–28   that reveals the *s·* facts
   234–24   has seen far into the *s·* facts
Ret. 60–26   the *s·* facts of the universe,
Un.   30– 5   can reverse the *s·* facts

faith
My. 132– 8   *s·* faith and understanding

famine
Mis. 246–23   the *s·* famine of 1866,

force
Mis. 257– 9   a moral and *s·* force
Rud.   4–10   represents a moral and *s·* force,

forces
'02. 10– 3   unfolds *s·* forces,

foresight
My. 281– 1   Because a *s·* foresight of

form
Pul. 33–24   * his visitor was a *s·* form from

formation
Ret. 49–12   *s·* formation first, last, and always,

forms
Mis. 91–18   most *s·* forms of thought

foundation
Mis. 74– 7   *s·* foundation for the affections
   341– 4   *s·* foundation and superstructure
Pul.   6– 6   *s·* foundation of Christ's healing.
My. 357–16   on a wholly *s·* foundation,
   357–19   Christ, the *s·* foundation.

freedom
Ret. 45–13   in order to gain *s·* freedom

fulness
My. 357– 3   until we arrive at the *s·* fulness

gates
Ret. 79–28   its *s·* gates not captured,

Genesis
Mis. 258–12   the *s·* Genesis of creation,

gifts
Mis. 345– 1   Spirit bestows *s·* gifts,

glow
Mis.   x– 1   *s·* glow and grandeur of
   356– 3   *s·* glow and understanding.

goal
No. 44– 8   swerves not . . . from the *s·* goal.

good
Mis. 140– 7   all *s·* good comes to
Un.   38–23   *s·* good, is not seen in

grace
Un.   57–21   *s·* grace was sufficient

gravitations
Mis. 19–26   material and *s·* gravitations,

groan
Mis. 231–10   table give a *s·* groan

growth
Mis. 41–14   it promotes *s·* growth,
   308–25   impedes *s·* growth ;
   317–13   by *s·* growth and by the study
   330–20   reported more *s·* growth.
   350–30   promote health and *s·* growth.
   380– 8   as if centuries of *s·* growth
Ret. 44–11   and its *s·* growth kept pace with
   45–10   retards *s·* growth,
   75–20   dishonesty retards *s·* growth
Un. 43–11   time and immense *s·* growth.
My. 116–22   loss in grace and growth *s·*,
   211–31   intellectual culture or *s·* growth.
   213– 2   brotherly love, *s·* growth

harvests
Ret. 79– 5   We glean *s·* harvests from our

healing
Mis. 163–28   *s·* healing of body and mind.
   246–29   a *s·* healing, or a materialistic
   346– 4   demonstration of moral and *s·* healing

heaven is
My. 267–16   Heaven is *s·*.

heavens
Mis. 254–20   stars from the *s·* heavens,

help
My. 153–18   *s·* help of divine Love.

hero
My. 203–13   A *s·* hero is a mark for gamesters,

heroes
My. 248– 9   *S·* heroes and prophets

homœopathist
'01. 22– 7   I am a *s·* homœopathist

house
My. 17–11   built up a *s·* house, — *I Pet. 2 : 5.*

idea
Mis.   2–20   Christ, the *s·* idea of God,
   17–13   before the Christ, the *s·* idea
   77–12   divine Principle and *s·* idea ;
  140–31   the *s·* idea would live,
  151–26   wedded to the *s·* idea, Christ ;
  163–27   *s·* idea which leadeth into

spiritual

idea
Mis. 164– 3   the former is the *s·* idea
  164–11   *s·* idea of the Principle of man
  164–21   understanding of Christ, the *s·* idea,
  164–32   This *s·* idea that the personal
  165– 7   *s·* idea of God and of man,
  166– 2   Principle and *s·* idea of being.
  166–13   This child, or *s·* idea,
  166–23   *s·* idea, named in this century
  166–29   This *s·* idea, or Christ,
  167– 4   pertain to the *s·* idea,
  175– 3   woman, the *s·* idea,
  306–28   it is a *s·* idea that lights
  328– 8   Christ, the *s·* idea which
Ret. 68– 7   the *s·* idea, or ideal man
  93– 3   the *s·* idea, appeared to
Un. 52–14   *s·* idea, *man and woman.*
Pul. 10–17   Christ, the true, the *s·* idea,
  14–22   *s·* idea will be understood.
No.   1– 2   *s·* idea emanating from
  19–17   senses receive no *s·* idea,
  26–12   *s·* idea which transfigures
'01.   8– 3   Holy Ghost, or *s·* idea of
'02. 12– 5   Messiah, the true *s·* idea,
  16–19   a glorified *s·* idea
Peo.   3–16   *s·* idea of good and Truth
My. 120–11   *s·* idea that takes away all sin,
  122–22   to grasp the *s·* idea
  139– 6   even the *s·* idea of Life,
  181–29   return of the *s·* idea to
  206–15   not seeing the *s·* idea
  219–15   the ever-present *s·* idea,
  262–21   His *s·* idea, man
  263– 1   to obliterate the *s·* idea
  303–10   to understand the *s·* idea.

ideal
Mis. 124–12   find rest in the *s·* ideal,
Ret. 75–16   If one's *s·* ideal is comprehended
  93–15   *s·* ideal is made our own,
Peo.   5– 8   for their more *s·* ideal,
My. 319– 3   *s·* ideal is the only real man

idealism
My.   5–15   *s·* idealism and realism

ideas
Mis. 82– 1   peoples the mind with *s·* ideas,
  307– 1   gives you His *s·* ideas,
'00.   3–17   the pioneer of *s·* ideas,

identity
Mis. 185–10   *s·* identity as the child of God,

ignorance
Mis. 298–10   in the same *s·* ignorance

illumination
Mis. 342–16   With no . . . *s·* illumination

image
Rud. 13– 9   divine and *s·* image of God.

import
Mis. 162– 4   *s·* import to mankind !
'00. 12– 3   the *s·* import whereof
'01. 25–12   because of their more *s·* import
My. 46–27   * Manual in its *s·* import,
  270– 4   magnitude of their *s·* import,

individuality
Mis. 103–27   *s·* individuality that reflected the
Ret. 73–15   man's *s·* individuality in God,
Un. 37–19   *s·* individuality is immortal.
  38– 1   no cognizance of *s·* individuality,

influx
My. 212–20   *s·* influx impossible under other

insight
Mis. 169– 5   her *s·* insight had been darkened
  189–10   *S·* insight of Truth and Love
Ret. 32– 4   *s·* insight, knowledge, and being.

instruction
Mis. 169–21   left for our *s·* instruction.

interpretation
Mis. 248– 3   *s·* interpretation they refuse to
  314–17   *s·* interpretation of the
Ret. 27– 2   setting forth their *s·* interpretation,
Pul. 43–20   * with its *s·* interpretation
No. 37–11   *s·* interpretation of the vicarious
My. 17–26   * its *s·* interpretation, as given in
  32–18   * its *s·* interpretation as given in

interpretations
Ret. 35–12   but the *s·* interpretations thereof.

issues
Mis. 235–15   touches mind to more *s·* issues,
My. 287–23   touches thought to *s·* issues,

joy
Ret. 21–20   *s·* joy and true estimate of being.

knowledge
My. 294–12   *s·* knowledge of God.

lack
No. 45–11   such efforts arise from a *s·* lack,

spiritual

latitudes
Ret.   73–11   floated into more *s·* latitudes
No.   45–23   anchor . . . in more *s·* latitudes,
Peo.   1–13   drift into more *s·* latitudes.

law
Mis.   17– 2   thunderings of the *s·* law of Life,
     17– 3   *s·* law of Love, as opposed to
     95–21   reveals itself . . . through *s·* law.
     116–19   final obedience to *s·* law.
     199– 7   amenable only to moral and *s·* law,
     200–19   the supremacy of *s·* law
Rud.   10–22   disobedience to His *s·* law.
No.   21– 8   it grasped in *s·* law the universe,

laws
Mis.   198–26   divine Principle, and its *s·* laws.
My.   159–23   *s·* laws enforcing obedience

Leader
Pul.   49– 3   * consider her their *s·* Leader

leaven
Mis.   175– 8   *s·* leaven of divine Science

Life
Mis.   16– 1   new and more *s·* Life and Love.
     361– 7   *s·* Life, whose myriad forms
Un.   30– 7   Soul is Life, and being *s·* Life,
     30–11   restores Soul, or *s·* Life.

life
Mis.   351–30   the antipode of *s·* life ;
My.   113–28   more *s·* life and love?

light
Mis.   113– 2   God's presence gives *s·* light,
     276–28   thus shutting out *s·* light.
     341–31   for the neglect of *s·* light,
     342– 6   decline of *s·* light, until,

lines
Mis.   81– 5   into more *s·* lines of life

Love
Mis.   288– 7   and weighed by *s·* Love,

love
Mis.   15–17   heaven-born hope, and *s·* love.
Ret.   76–15   which lead up to *s·* love.
'01.   26–21   charity — *s·* love.
'02.   8–22   the rule of *s·* love ;
     8–29   *S·* love makes man conscious that

man
Mis.   17–32   truer sense of Spirit and *s·* man.
     79–22   *s·* man is that perfect and unfallen
     162–23   The *s·* man, or Christ,
     182–21   no mortal hath seen the *s·* man,
     186– 1   history of the *s·* man
     186– 8   *s·* man made in the image
     186–17   spiritual Principle of *s·* man.
     187–16   inspired sense of the *s·* man,
Un.   61–15   Spirit and *s·* man are
No.   19–18   *s·* man and his spiritual senses
'01.   5–19   real *s·* man and universe
'02.   7–17   *s·* man and the universe
Hea.   17– 7   Love makes the *s·* man,
My.   239–26   and is not the *s·* man,
     296–14   to destroy the real *s·* man.

manifestation
'02.   2–21   to a more *s·* manifestation,

meaning
Mis.   18–12   new tongue, their *s·* meaning,
     73– 9   discern their *s·* meaning,
     300–27   *s·* meaning of Bible texts ;
Ret.   25– 7   in their *s·* meaning,
Pul.   35– 2   I apprehended the *s·* meaning
'00.   6–10   dawns the *s·* meaning thereof ;
Hea.   7– 7   *s·* meaning as opposed to
My.   178– 3   *s·* meaning of Holy Writ

means
Mis.   152–30   His *s·* means and methods,
'01.   19–12   mixing material and *s·* means,
     26–12   from Christ's purely *s·* means
My.   357– 7   *s·* means, manifestation,

mentality
Pul.   vii–13   lenses of more *s·* mentality,

mind
Peo.   4–22   No . . . can make a *s·* mind out of

mode
Ret.   89– 2   potency of this *s·* mode of Mind,

modes
My.   266–27   more *s·* modes and significations

modesty
My.   357–12   *s·* modesty of C. S.,

molecule
Mis.   313– 6   points to the scientific *s·* molecule,

monitor
Mis.   100–20   *s·* monitor understood is coincidence

music
'00.   11– 8   *s·* music, the music of Soul.

nature
Mis.   119–14   strives . . . against the *s·* nature ;
My.   188–29   seek the Science of his *s·* nature,

need
Mis.   245–16   *s·* need that C. S. should remove

needs
Ret.   91–18   ministering to the *s·* needs of all
My.   147–18   moral, and *s·* needs of humanity,

noumenon
Ret.   22– 4   His *s·* noumenon and phenomenon

nutriment
My.   230– 5   digestion of *s·* nutriment

obedience
'01.   34– 6   in *s·* obedience to Christ's mode

observation
Mis.   154–26   post of *s·* observation and self-examination.

order
Ret.   10–16   Syntax was *s·* order and unity.

organization
Mis.   138–29   march on in *s·* organization.

origin
Mis.   18–17   of *s·* origin, God's reflection,
     75–27   discovered the *s·* origin of man.
     166–17   how to declare its *s·* origin,

peace
My.   93–14   * physical health and *s·* peace.

perception
Mis.   139–25   but to my *s·* perception,
My.   37–22   * known through your *s·* perception

perfectibility
Pan.   11–27   man's unfallen *s·* perfectibility.

perfection
Mis.   42–26   exists only in *s·* perfection,
My.   345–23   as we near a state of *s·* perfection.

perfectly
Pul.   54– 8   * The . . . is the perfectly *s·*.

personality
Mis.   218–31   * purely *s·* personality in God."

phenomena
Un.   10–12   *s·* phenomena of this one infinite
     10–13   *S·* phenomena never converge toward

plane
My.   46– 5   * more *s·* plane of living,

points
Mis.   143– 5   our *s·* points, above the plane of

power
Mis.   3–17   never are needed to aid *s·* power.
     113–31   prolific sources of *s·* power
     170–32   in Bible usage, often means *s·* power.
     189–24   *s·* power that subordinates matter
     189–29   *s·* power, healing sin and sickness,
     193–31   man's capabilities and *s·* power.
     248– 6   its moral meaning, . . . is *s·* power,
     268–29   human pride forfeits *s·* power,
     286–12   superiority of *s·* power over sensuous,
     352–21   not sufficient *s·* power in the
Ret.   43– 7   teaching the pathology of *s·* power,
     44–28   love, prosperity, and *s·* power.
Rud.   9–21   *s·* power of a scientific, right thought,
Hea.   15– 7   in *s·* power divinely directed.
My.   3– 7   not . . . but with *s·* power.
     152–13   spiritual worship, *s·* power.
     226–11   by evolved *s·* power,
     339–29   wars against Spirit and *s·* power.

preexistence
Mis.   181–27   man's *s·* preexistence as God's child ;

presence
Mis.   328–22   *s·* presence and idea of God.

Principle
Mis.   186–17   *s·* Principle of spiritual man.
Ret.   37–17   demonstrating the *s·* Principle

progress
Mis.   124–32   proportion to a man's *s·* progress,
     192– 6   importance to man's *s·* progress,
My.   114–30   each step of mental and *s·* progress,

qualifications
Man.   87–15   moral and *s·* qualifications
My.   241– 1   * moral and *s·* qualifications

realities
Mis.   53– 2   up to the *s·* realities of existence,

reality
Mis.   60–29   hints the existence of *s·* reality ;
     87– 9   *s·* reality and substance of form,

recognition
Mis.   196–26   arise to *s·* recognition of being,

refreshment
Mis.   170– 8   symbolize the *s·* refreshment of

regeneration
Mis.   187– 1   *s·* regeneration of both mind and

relation
Mis.   181–21   his *s·* relation to Deity :

religion
Mis.   365–16   Good health and a more *s·* religion
No.   18–22   Good health and a more *s·* religion
Hea.   1–11   more practical and *s·* religion

resurrection
Mis.   179–22   come into the *s·* resurrection by

spiritual

revelation
Mis. 75– 4   s· revelation of man's possible
riches
Mis. 325– 8   small conceptions of s· riches,
rise
Ret. 80–19   unceasing s· rise and progress.
sacrament
My. 131– 6   s· sacrament, sacrifice, and
sacrifices
My. 17–12   to offer up s· sacrifices, — I Pet. 2 : 5.
safety
Ret. 14–16   take my chance of s· safety with my
sanctuary
Mis. 77–22   to enter the s· sanctuary of Truth,
Science
Mis. 57– 9   its s· Science is alluded to in
      61– 4   will be instruction, in s· Science,
Ret. 25– 8   Principle and rule of s· Science
      27– 8   s· Science developed itself to me
      28–23   s· Science of Mind must reveal.
      34– 8   s· Science of Mind-healing.
      37– 4   s·, Science of Mind-healing,
Pul. 35– 3   law involved in s· Science
      70–24   * s· Science of Mind-healing,
self
Mis. 84–14   his s· self, or Christ, was the Son of
selfhood
No. 36–19   retreat from material to s· selfhood
'01. 8–24   Christ was Jesus' s· selfhood ;
      9– 3   his eternal s· selfhood
sensation
Mis. 360–23   ever-flowing tides of s· sensation
sense
Mis. 19–31   s· sense of Life and its grand
      27–28   to unerring s· sense, it is
      28– 2   to reappear in the s· sense
      47–20   s· sense that God, Spirit, is the only
      66–19   controlled by the higher s· sense,
      68– 1   s· sense and fact of divine substance,
      70–15   s· sense of Life and power.
      73–29   that comes from s· sense
      75–23   "My s· sense doth magnify
      82–23   s· sense and Science of being
      180–29   in both a material and a s· sense.
      186–26   s· sense of God and His universe
      188–18   the testimony of s· sense ;
      188–25   through a s· sense of the real,
      194–23   how to leave self, . . . for the sense s· ;
      204–20   great demands of s· sense
      217–32   s· sense takes in new views,
      218–18   unfolds . . . the universe to the s· sense,
      234–11   reach this s· sense, and rise
      293–14   If s· sense is not dominant
      341–18   to win the s· sense of good.
Ret. 81–12   s· sense, affectional consciousness,
Un. 2–18   that s· sense of harmony
      21–19   but there is a s· sense,
      30– 2   "My soul [s· sense] — Luke 1 : 46.
      30–18   by restoring the s· sense of
      40–25   lacking the s· sense of it,
      46–12   s· sense and source of being.
      57– 2   which offend the s· sense.
      63– 6   never disappeared to s· sense,
      64– 5   the individual s· sense,
Rud. 6–20   true evidence of s· sense ?
      7–14   Science and s· sense contradict this,
No. 3–19   stultifies the s· sense
'00. 5–27   s· sense of the Scriptures
      6–11   s· sense of the Scriptures
      6–14   he takes in its s· sense
'01. 12– 2   s· sense drinks it in,
Hea. 14–20   s· sense or perceptive faculty
      16– 1   understood in its s· sense,
My. 109–17   mine eye [s· sense] — Job 42 : 5.
      114–22   pour in upon my s· sense
      118–13   s· sense demands and commands
      118–24   not by the s· sense
      188–27   s· sense and not the material
      202–15   s· sense of this people
      238– 8   their s· sense must be discerned,
      257–10   to the s· sense of Christ
      262–13   with my soul, my s· sense,
      273–14   s· sense of thinking, feeling,
senses
Mis. 104–18   with his s· senses.
Rud. 5– 1   s· senses afford no such evidence,
No. 19–18   his s· senses are drinking in the
Hea. 17–16   when the s· senses were hushed
shield
'02. 14– 7   s· shield against the powers of
significance
Ret. 38–29   gain its s· significance,
      88–10   s· significance of this command,
My. 6–25   giving . . . a s· significance
      46– 6   * without this s· significance

spiritual

significance
My. 60–16   * on the s· significance of the
      94–29   giving . . . a s· significance
signification
Mis. 190–16   s· signification of its terms
Ret. 25– 5   Their s· signification appeared ;
Rud. 16– 8   s· signification of the Bible,
No. 12–24   s· signification of the Word
signs
Mis. 18– 6   s· signs of the new birth
sonship
Mis. 181– 3   Is man's s· sonship a
      183–25   denial of man's s· sonship ;
Un. 39–16   and denies s· sonship ;
source
Mis. 225–23   s· source and ever-present help,
spire
My. 13–24   temple the s· spire of which
standpoint
Mis. 52–30   up, to its s· standpoint.
standpoints
Peo. 1–16   from material to s· standpoints.
state
My. 244–16   is unquestionably man's s· state
stature
Pan. 11–18   regain his native s· stature
status
Mis. 264–25   moral and s· status of thought
No. 45–26   s· status is urging its highest
My. 111–13   s· status of a perfect life
strains
Mis. 142–23   s· strains of the Hebrew bard.
substance
Mis. 27–29   a type of s· substance,
      309–12   s· substance and intelligence.
Rud. 5–12   who has ever seen s· substance
My. 226–18   s· "substance of things — Heb. 11 : 1.
temples
My. 195–30   fill these s· temples with grace,
things
Mis. 38–11   sown unto you s· things, — I Cor. 9 : 11.
      54– 1   cannot discern s· things.
      57– 4   cannot discern s· things
      60–30   are instructed in s· things,
      87– 6   immature sense of s· things,
      218–19   beareth witness of things s·,
Ret. 28–14   and dependence on s· things.
Pul. 35–18   and dependence on s· things.
My. 216– 2   give all their time to s· things,
thinkers
Un. 9–22   held by a few s· thinkers
thought
My. 136–28   and time for s· thought
      238–16   swift pinions of s· thought
thoughts
My. 261–28   Virgin Mary's s· thoughts
touch
Mis. 175–12   increase by every s· touch,
transfiguration
Un. 2–25   ready for a s· transfiguration,
translations
Mis. 171–11   s· translations of God's messages,
Truth
Mis. 265–21   s· Truth and its ethics
Ret. 54– 5   to understand s· Truth.
Rud. 3– 5   Christ, s· Truth and Love,
truth
Mis. 101– 5   and accepting s· truth,
      190–24   by the s· truth of being ;
Ret. 79– 3   s· truth learned and loved ;
Peo. 12–15   s· truth that lifts man
type
Ret. 93–13   s· type of Christly method
ultimate
Mis. 286–32   stop at length at the s· ultimate :
understanding
Mis. 3– 5   If we regard . . . s· understanding
      50–16   gain the s· understanding of
      84–11   growth and more s· understanding,
      199–25   advance in the s· understanding
      215– 8   gain a s· understanding of them."
      338– 9   s· understanding which cannot
Man. 15–11   s· understanding that casts out
Ret. 66– 5   into the s· understanding
Un. 63– 1   reversing Science and s· understanding,
Pul. 9–27   s· understanding, not mere belief,
      22–17   cemented by s· understanding
Rud. 11–22   illumination of s· understanding,
'02. 4– 9   life and s· understanding,
      7– 7   Minus this s· understanding
      11–11   s· understanding of God,
My. 5–18   s· understanding which
      28–29   * s· understanding of the Scriptures,
      48–12   * obtain the s· understanding
      108–13   couples faith with s· understanding

spiritual

understanding

My.	140– 1	abiding *s·* understanding
	152–13	rests solely on *s·* understanding,
	161–24	becloud *s·* understanding,
	180– 8	*s·* understanding of the Scriptures
	205–19	with *s·* understanding,
	206– 5	tender grace of *s·* understanding,
	234–12	from . . . to *s·* understanding,
	260–18	*s·* understanding of joy
	267–25	obscure *s·* understanding,
	267–29	within man's *s·* understanding
	273–22	*s·* understanding of Life
	292–16	faith or *s·* understanding,

union

Ret.	42– 2	a blessed and *s·* union,

unity

Mis.	358–32	a higher *s·* unity is won,
My.	243–22	*s·* unity with your Leader.

universe

Mis.	21– 7	the *s·* universe, whereof
	361–25	*s·* universe, including man
Un.	14–14	rectify His *s·* universe?
No.	26–24	in the *s·* universe he is

values

My.	48–24	* subordination . . . to *s·* values,

verity

Pul.	3–27	evidence of *s·* verity

version

Hea.	16– 2	and given its *s·* version,

vision

Mis.	373–13	*s·* vision that should, does, guide
Un.	61– 6	to immortal and *s·* vision he was
My.	126–23	which the Revelator saw in *s·* vision

voice

My.	265– 5	revelation, *s·* voice and vision,

warfare

Ret.	86– 1	energize wholesome *s·* warfare,

way

'02.	10–20	reformer who finds the more *s·* way,

wholly

Mis.	16–24	awakened consciousness is wholly *s·*;
	91–11	This bond is wholly *s·* and inviolate.
My.	238–10	His language and . . . are wholly *s·*.

wickedness

Mis.	116– 4	"*s·* wickedness in high — *Eph.* 6:12.
	134–27	*S·* wickedness is standing in

world

'01.	21–10	* ideas about the *s·* world
My.	167– 5	*s·* world, which is apart from matter,

worship

My.	152–13	*s·* worship, spiritual power.

Mis.	5– 4	Science reveals man as *s·*,
	19–29	*s·*, joy-giving, and eternal
	21–22	man is not material; he is *s·*."
	25–13	*s·* and original meaning of the
	26– 5	period more humane and *s·*.
	27–25	must be *s·* and mental.
	27–27	But, say you, is a stone *s·*?
	30–10	They were *s·*, not material;
	37–12	*s·* and immortal Mind,
	37–13	leave the animal for the *s·*,
	40– 4	material methods with the *s·*,
	47–22	man, . . . is *s·*, not material.
	52– 2	to such as seek . . . to aid the *s·*,
	62– 1	man in the likeness of Spirit is *s·*.
	64–22	It is *s·*, and not material.
	73–10	reality of what is *s·*,
	74–14	his nativity was a *s·* and immortal
	85–17	*s·*, individual existence.
	86– 2	The individual and *s·* are perfect;
	142–19	with bright hues of the *s·*,
	155– 5	All power and happiness are *s·*,
	166–21	whose origin was more *s·*
	179–15	more true, more *s·*"
	181–19	*s·*, and not material laws;
	181–20	as *s·*, and not material.
	184– 9	man . . . is *s·*, not material.
	187–20	might have been as *s·* as the New.
	187–29	material, before *s·*;
	190– 8	nor does . . . ultimate in the *s·*;
	191–32	more *s·* and practical sense.
	217– 6	the universe of God is *s·*,
	232–26	most *s·* and unselfish motives.
	253–27	the *s·* Mother's sore travail,
	287–15	the *s·* over the animal,
	351–21	Love is *s·*,
	352– 5	as material and not *s·*,
	352– 5	or as both material and *s·*,
	363–12	the immortal modes of Mind are *s·*,
	365–20	moral and *s·*, as well as physical,
	375– 4	the counterfeit of the *s·*
Ret.	25–11	compassionate, helpful, and *s·*.
	35– 1	*s·*, scientific Mind-healing,
	48–28	*s·* and scientific impartation of
	59–20	harmonious, immortal, and *s·*:
	65–15	Jewish religion was not *s·*;

spiritual

Ret.	67– 8	both material and *s·*,
	73– 1	immortal man being *s·*,
	78–16	wholly Christlike and *s·*.
	91–21	His power over others was *s·*,
Un.	10–14	Their gradations are *s·* and divine;
	24–21	Man, as God's offspring, must be *s·*,
	25–22	Evil is not *s·*,
	35–17	forces of Truth are moral and *s·*,
	40–18	by a *s·* and not by a material sense
	42–11	material before he can be *s·*,
	42–27	nor the material the *s·*,
	46–16	were real to him only as *s·*
Pul.	69–19	* *s·* or metaphysical standpoint.
Rud.	3–11	more because of his *s·* than
	3–17	Jesus' healing was *s·* in its nature,
	4– 3	universe is *s·*, peopled with
	7– 8	*Is man material or s·?*
No.	6– 5	God's formations are *s·*,
	12– 5	leading us . . . to be *s·*,
	17– 9	a *s·* and individual being,
	19– 2	moral and *s·*, as well as physical,
	25–22	*S·* . . . man alone is God's likeness,
	34– 6	*s·* and infinite meaning
	40– 6	*s·* and immortal Truth.
'01.	8–14	Can he be too *s·*, since Jesus said,
	8–19	can man be . . . less than *s·*
	8–20	is he not wholly *s·*?
	8–28	*s·* and material Christ Jesus,
	9–24	and these things being *s·*,
	10– 8	a *s·*, divine emanation.
	10– 9	Christ must be *s·*, not material.
	11–20	not too *s·* to be practical,
	27–25	left C. S. as it is, purely *s·*,
'02.	8– 6	likeness of God, Spirit, is *s·*,
	9–15	was loving and *s·*,
	10–18	man becomes finally *s·*.
	10–19	correct, and inevitably *s·*.
Hea.	5–28	The more *s·* we become here,
	7–10	*s·* instead of the material
Peo.	1– 2	is a step more *s·*.
	6–18	more *s·* and true ideal of Deity
	7–30	his mind-models are more or less *s·*.
	7–32	and our methods grow more *s·*
	14– 1	As our ideas of Deity become more *s·*,
	14– 8	ideas of Life have grown more *s·*;
My.	50–16	* and looked towards the *s·*,
	91– 5	* *s·* and mystic mediation
	121–11	This peace is *s·*; never selfish,
	133–29	*s·* bespeaks our temporal history.
	139–20	from the material to the *s·*,
	160– 2	Christian, . . . strives for the *s·*;
	160– 6	relation with the divine, the *s·*,
	166–23	measure of time and joy be *s·*,
	178–13	Then all is Spirit and *s·*.
	181– 8	Progress is *s·*.
	193–15	The *s·* dominates the temporal.
	221–17	other than the *s·* and divine,
	221–20	no other . . . means than the *s·*
	235–18	that which is not *s·*?
	252–29	it is moral, *s·*, divine.
	267–15	Is heaven *s·*?
	303–22	the material to the *s·*,
	349–22	because they are *s·*,
	349–28	is correct only as it is *s·*,
	353–25	*s·* have all place and power.

Spiritual Interpretation

Man.	63– 2	*S· I·* by Mary Baker Eddy,

spiritualism

Mis.	29–13	between C. S. and *s·*,
	34–10	*Is s· or mesmerism included*
	34–13	with *s·*, so far as I understand it,
	296–16	with theosophy and *s·*;
Man.	41– 7	theosophy, hypnotism, or *s·*,
	47–26	theosophy, hypnotism, or *s·*,
Ret.	28–28	Am I a believer in *s·*?
	29– 2	*s·* is the antipode of C. S.
Pul.	38–18	* not accept the belief we call *s·*.
No.	13–16	chapter sub-title
	13–21	C. S., *s·*, and theosophy.
Pan.	9– 6	in *s·* they imply men and
Hea.	5–12	* "between Christianity and *s·*,
	5–25	*s·* would lead our lives to

spiritualist

Mis.	95–14	Am I a *s·*?
	249–12	well known that I am not a *s·*,
No.	14– 2	If a *s·* medium understood

spiritualists

Mis.	95–18	which *s·* have miscalled
Ret.	24– 3	*s·* would associate therewith,
Hea.	6– 9	*s·* abused me for it then,

spirituality

accession of

Mis.	204–28	Through the accession of *s·*,

spirituality
  advance in
    Mis. 21–12   As the ages advance in *s·*,
  begotten of
    Ret. 26–24   It must be begotten of *s·*,
    Pul. 35–10   "Divine Science is begotten of *s·*,"
  demonstrate
    My. 242– 3   You can never demonstrate *s·* until
  God of
    Un. 49–16   and the God of *s·*.
  growth of
    Mis. 154–14   as the growth of *s·*
  higher
    Pul. 38–28   * a higher *s·* seeking expression.
    67–15   * to give expression to a higher *s·*.
  his
    Hea. 2–22   his *s·* rebuked their carnality,
  increase of
    Mis. 21–14   in no wise except by increase of *s·*.
  increase the
    My. 230–12   increase the *s·* of him who obeys it,
  individual
    Mis. 165–15   individual *s·*, perfect and eternal,
  is the basis
    Mis. 156–23   *S·* is the basis of all true thought
  lack of
    Mis. 53–25   because of their great lack of *s·*.
  life of
    My. 352– 9   * for your life of *s·*,
  man's
    Mis. 105– 2   facts of man's *s·*, individuality,
  morals, and
    Mis. 245–13   morals, and *s·* of mankind.
  of Truth
    No. v–13   apprehend the pure *s·* of Truth.
  our
    Pul. 21–29   aught that can darken . . . our *s·*,
  price of
    My. 221– 1   earthly price of *s·* in religion
  purest
    No. 38–26   loses a part of its purest *s·*
  refuge is in
    Un. 57– 7   Man's refuge is in *s·*,
  to see
    No. 12– 5   leading us to see *s·*
  true
    '02. 8– 9   shows what true *s·* is,
  we approach
    Mis. 30–29   will vanish as we approach *s·*,
    Pul. 39– 4   * the peace of the Lord in *s·*.

spiritualization
  Mis. 10–27   this is the advent of *s·*.
    15– 9   Nothing aside from the *s·*
    42–11   states that *s·* of thought is
    73–29   the *s·* that comes from
    185–19   The *s·* of our sense of man
  Un. 28–18   we learn Soul only . . . by *s·*.
    32–12   *s·* of thought destroys
  No. 12–20   impels a *s·* of thought
    32– 2   and the *s·* of the race.
  My. 266–17   final *s·* of all things,
    266–19   verified by the *s·* of all?

spiritualize
  Mis. 92– 8   and to *s·* human life,
    217–31   but *s·* human thought,
  Ret. 82–30   better adapted to *s·* thought
    84– 5   to *s·* his own thoughts
  Un. 31– 7   to *s·* thought and action.
  No. 11–27   and *s·* consciousness with the
  Hea. 19–17   to *s·* thought, motive, and
  Peo. 7–31   our thoughts must *s·* to

spiritualized
  Mis. 86–19   sensations . . . must be *s·*, until we
  Ret. 28– 9   learned that thought must be *s·*,
  Pul. 35–13   learned that thought must be *s·*
  Peo. 11– 6   feeblest mind, enlightened and *s·*,
  My. 122–28   *s·* to behold this Christ,
    127– 1   Science, whereby thought is *s·*,
    355– 2   to see in her *s·* thought

spiritualizes
  Mis. 92–20   this *s·* their thoughts.
    92–32   *s·* his own thought,
    252–24   It *s·* religion
    267–28   *s·* man's motives and methods,
  My. 4– 3   obedience to this rule *s·* man,
    249–30   which *s·* the congregation.

spiritualizing
  No. 10–24   dematerializing and *s·* mortals

spiritually
  Mis. ix–10   morally, physically, *s·*.
    3– 1   physically, morally, and *s·*,
    24– 2   makes man *s·* minded.
    24– 4   but to be *s·* minded — *Rom.* 8 : 6.
    25–18   and raising the *s·* dead.
    30– 8   St. John *s·* discerned

spiritually
  Mis. 31– 6   morally, physically, or *s·*
    43–16   those who are *s·* unqualified.
    51– 2   its effect physically as well as *s·*,
    56–29   first *s·* created the universe,
    57– 7   but from Spirit, *s·*.
    57–23   universe with man created *s·*.
    58–17   but I must *s·* understand them
    64–17   ethics which guide thought *s·*
    85– 6   learns *s·* all that he knows
    86–16   Earth is more *s·* beautiful
    88–21   * Science is natural, *s·* natural;
    90–28   *s·* prepared breakfast,
    108– 9   *s·*, literally, it *is nothing*.
    111–31   or is a *s·* adopted child,
    123–31   must worship Him *s·*,
    138–14   ethically, physically, and *s·*.
    140– 6   morally and *s·* inalienable,
    150–11   *S·*, I am with all who
    168– 4   the blind, *s·* and physically,
    169–16   must be *s·* discerned,
    170–15   Jesus interpreted all *s·*:
    172–21   affections, *s·* understood,
    172–24   *s·* discerned, understood,
    182– 1   *s·* instead of materially
    252–20   physically, as well as *s·*,
    315–10   *s·* fitted for teachers,
    317–16   is yet assimilated *s·*
    362–10   physically, morally, *s·*.
  Man. 46– 2   a *s·* adopted child
    46– 3   a *s·* adopted husband
  Ret. 34–19   advanced morally and *s·*.
    44–30   this *s·* organized Church
    68–10   idea is *s·* real.
    76–14   The *s·* minded meet on the
  Un. 36–20   mentally, morally, *s·*
    37–17   physically mortal, but *s·* immortal.
  Pul. 29–22   * lesson was to be taken *s·*
  No. 13–20   physically, morally, and *s·*,
    22–10   morally, *s·*, or physically.
    25–24   in a *s·* scientific sense.
  Pan. 7– 9   had created all things *s·*,
    11–16   If man is *s·* fallen,
  '00. 6–28   physically, morally, and *s·*.
    14– 9   let him . . . (that discerneth *s·*)
    14–23   toiled for the *s·* indispensable.
    15– 8   Passover, *s·* discerned,
  '01. 5–15   their personality is defined *s·*,
    20–16   physically, morally, or *s·*,
  '02. 6–26   that man becomes *s·* minded
    6–28   to be *s·* minded — *Rom.* 8 : 6.
    8–15   *s·* minded are inspired with
  Hea. 17–14   when *s·* understood,
  Peo. 6–19   improves the race physically and *s·*,
  My. 4–11   meekly, patiently, *s·*,
    119–19   could not identify Christ *s·*,
    124–29   seen of men, and *s·* understood;
    135–29   *s·* and scientifically understand
    140–20   Relinquishing . . . advances it *s·*.
    150–22   *s·* dead in trespasses
    152–15   worship only Spirit and *s·*,
    156–12   *s·* speaking is the passover
    180–32   defines noumenon . . . *s·*,
    187– 2   *s·* as well as literally,
    196–26   even the *s·* indispensable,
    275–27   *s·* understood and demonstrated,
    350– 9   she *s·* discerned the divine idea

spiritually-minded
  Po. vii–13   * *gems . . . from this s· author*
  My. 249–28   student who is most *s·*.

Spiritward
  Mis. 360–19   lift every thought-leaflet *S·*;

spite
  My. 38–13   * in *s·* of the fact that many
    78–23   * in *s·* of its vast interior,
    294–19   in *s·* of the constant stress

spitting
  Mis. 170–26   *S·* was the Hebrew method of

spittle
  Mis. 171– 7   anoint the . . . eyes with his *s·*,

splendid
  My. 48–15   * *s·* appreciation of her efforts
    99–14   * recently built a *s·* cathedral

splendor
  Mis. 330–29   unveils its regal *s·* to the sun;
    376–19   brave *s·* of a November sky
  Pul. 39–19   * *s·* of the sky Repeats its glory
  Po. 31–17   solemn *s·* of immortal power,
  My. 262–31   The *s·* of this nativity of Christ

splints
  Mis. 243– 8   regular doctor had put on *s·*

spoil
  My. 123–30   *s·* the vines." — *Song* 2 : 15.

spoiled
Mis. 344–16   are *s·* by lack of Science.

spoiling
My. 211–25   *s·* that individual's disposition,

spoils
My. 236–11   Too much of one thing *s·* the whole.

spoke
Mis. 170–12   she *s·* of the hades, or hell of
     312– 1   sorry that I *s·* at all,
     344–21   which Paul understood when he *s·* of
Ret. 13–16   of these things he now *s·*,
     31–27   *s·* to my chastened sense as by
Un. 59– 8   Jesus, who *s·* of the Christ as
No. 36– 8   He once *s·* of himself . . . as
My. 30–10   * It *s·* much for the devotion of
     81–19   * *s·* simply and gratefully,
     146– 3   Jesus *s·* the truth.
     172– 9   * Mrs. Eddy *s·* as follows
     185–22   *s·* to an attentive audience
     185–24   I foresaw this hour, and *s·* of
     266–15   of which Jesus *s·*.
     315– 6   * He *s·* of her being a
     320–11   * Mr. Wiggin *s·* of ''*S·* and *H·*
     320–14   * always *s·* of you as the author
     320–23   * and *s·* of your ability
     320–32   * *s·* in a very animated manner
     322–20   * *s·* of my journeying from
     322–29   * *s·* earnestly and beautifully of you
     324– 1   * often *s·* his thoughts freely
     325– 1   * and *s·* of one especial day

spoken
Mis. 23–14   It is plain that the Me *s·* of
     25–16   *s·* of by St. Mark.
     55–14   *s·* of in Matt. xii. 31, 32.
     89–16   ''be evil *s·* of.'' — *Rom.* 14 : 16.
     122– 6   Would Jesus thus have *s·*
     127–29   word *s·*, at the right moment,
     151–22   Glorious things are *s·* of
     154–19   word that is *s·* unto you,
     166– 6   Truth he has taught and *s·*
     266–28   Because Truth has *s·* aloud,
     316–16   the word *s·* at this date.
     332–18   evil is supposed to have *s·*,
     337–10   *s·* of them as the Golden Rule
     346–23   ''A word fitly *s·* — *Prov.* 25 : 11,
Un. 9– 8   words would not have been *s·*.
     43–12   I have by no means *s·* of myself,
Pul. 8– 2   press has *s·* out historically,
     11– 4   Word *s·* in this sacred temple
     27–23   * woman *s·* of in the Apocalypse,
     81– 4   * nowhere *s·* with more reverence
No. 2–15   by the *s·* than the unspoken word.
'00. 14– 8   *s·* of in the Scriptures.
'01. 9–10   *s·* of by St. Paul.
My. 20– 2   *s·* of for a memorial — *Mark* 14 : 9.
     104–29   anathema *s·* of in Scripture :
     162–17   This was *s·* derisively.
     185–11   wherever thought, felt, *s·*,
     225– 5   *s·* by our Master.
     344– 1   even been *s·* of as a Christ,

sponsors
My. 248–14   the inevitable *s·* for the

spontaneity
My. 185–16   Life is the *s·* of Love,

spontaneous
Mis. 101– 2   healing becomes *s·*,
Ret. 31–13   first *s·* motion of Truth
Po. v– 5   * the *s·* outpouring of a
My. 11–16   * response was instant, *s·*,
     12– 5   * *s·* and liberal donations
     32– 1   * *S·* unanimity and repetition

spontaneously
Mis. 20– 2   heals man *s·*, morally and
'01. 3– 1   spring *s·* the higher hope,
My. 4– 3   practises the Golden Rule *s·* ;
     128–10   Truth crushed . . . springs *s·* upward,

sport
Po. 2– 2   to *s·* at mortal clay
My. 166–21   *s·* would be more irksome than work.
     303–23   His metaphysics is not the *s·* of

spot
Mis. 150–25   God is universal ; confined to no *s·*,
Ret. 17– 5   while I worship in deep sylvan *s·*,
     18–20   *s·* where affection may dwell
     94–14   *s·* and blemish on the disk of
Pul. 1–16   This *s·* whereon thou troddest
     65–21   * Frankish church was reared upon the *s·*
Po. 34–13   Has wooed some mystic *s·*,
     42– 3   sunshine without a dark *s·* ;
     62– 5   while I worship in deep sylvan *s·*,
     64–12   *s·* where affection may dwell
     67– 3   Grow cold in this *s·* as the

spot
My. 145–14   I healed him on the *s·*.
     197– 6   without *s·* or blemish.
     356– 2   praise and love the *s·* where God

spotless
Un. 6– 5   the *s·* selfhood of God
Po. 65– 6   robes were as *s·* as snow :
My. 192– 5   make *s·* the blemished,
     262– 4   *s·* purity and original perfection.

spots
No. 13–25   A theory may be sound in *s·*,

spotted
Pan. 3–30   his *s·* skin, the stars ;

sprain
Mis. 243– 7   In the case of *s·* of the wrist-joint,

sprains
Mis. 243– 6   although students treat *s·*,

sprang
Mis. 148–14   They *s·* from necessity,
     163– 7   from which *s·* a sublime and
     179–26   before it *s·* from the earth :
     235– 7   Mind whence *s·* the universe.
Man. 3–11   They *s·* from necessity,
No. 14– 9   *s·* from the Oriental philosophy of
Peo. 4– 4   Idolatry *s·* from the belief that
Po. 71–12   Injustice to the combat *s·* ;
My. 29–17   * its grandeur *s·* from the
     79–26   * which *s·* from the conviction that
     182–14   From this . . . *s·* immortal fruits
     195–26   *s·* from the temples erected first in
     348–11   *s·* from the belief that the man Jesus,

spray
Mis. 329–16   nursing the timid *s·*,

sprays
Pul. 26–24   * *s·* of fig leaves bearing fruit.

spread
Mis. 137–16   to *s·* your own so bravely.
     225–27   a cool perspiration *s·* over it,
     234– 3   We *s·* our wings in vain when
     326– 9   thence they *s·* to the house of
No. 2–28   We should not *s·* abroad
Pan. 15– 6   hath *s·* for us a table
Po. 78– 3   will *s·* over their tomb ;
My. 118– 4   Only . . . *s·* personal contagion,
     219–27   the *s·* of so-called infectious
     256–24   the festive boards are *s·*,
     302–17   the word *s·* like wildfire.
     336– 3   * The disease *s·* so rapidly
     353–16   to *s·* undivided the Science

spreading
Mis. 135–17   and so *s·* the gospel
     154– 3   The *s·* branches of The Church
Ret. 85–26   rapidly *s·* over the globe ;
My. 52–12   * *s·* world wide of this great truth,
     55–10   * the Cause itself was *s·*
     191– 6   C. S. is *s·* steadily
     313– 9   *s·* the road in front of

spreads
Mis. 12– 2   *s·* its virus and kills
Po. 33–16   *s·* her pinions abroad,

spreadst
Po. 77– 8   impartial, blessings *s·* abroad,

Spring and **spring**
Mis. 51–27   * sunshine of the world's new *s·*,
     251–22   burdened for an hour, *s·* into liberty,
     262– 8   new and costly *s·* dress.
     329– 1   chapter sub-title
     329– 6   In *s·*, nature like a thrifty
     329–10   *S·* is my sweetheart,
     329–14   *S·* passes over mountain and
     329–18   Whatever else droops, *s·* is gay :
     332– 6   *S·* is here !
     343–12   fruits of C. S. *s·* upward,
Man. 17– 1   In the *s·* of 1879,
Ret. 75– 2   *s·* from this ill-concealed
     80–19   will be within him a *s·*,
Un. 5–22   Let no enmity, . . . *s·* up
Pul. 43–16   * corner-stone laying last *s·*,
     46–27   * Her last marriage was in the *s·* of
     48– 8   * lights and shades of *s·*
     82– 9   * stop the coming of *s·*
Rud. 9– 6   and this error will *s·* up
No. 7– 5   root of bitterness to *s·* up
'00. 14–18   Let no root of bitterness *s·* up
'01. 3– 1   *s·* spontaneously the higher hope,
Po. page 53   poem
     53– 1   Come to thy bowers, sweet *s·*,
     54– 2   Since joyous *s·* was there.
My. 56–24   * In the *s·* of 1905
     341– 8   chapter sub-title
     341–10   accept your Leader's *S·* greeting,
     347–13   * nor ever bid the *S·* adieu !

Springfield, Mass.
Pul. 88–21 * *Republican, S·, M·.*

Springfield (Mass.) *Republican*
My. 92– 8 *[S· (M·.) R·]*

Springfield *Republican*
My. 94– 9 * says the *S· R·.*

springing
Mis.	83– 8	*s· from a seed of thought,*
	285–25	S· up from the ashes of
Rud.	16–24	s· up among unchristian students,
'00.	2– 3	s· up in the above-named cities,
My.	68– 5	* s· from the tops of great stone piers,
	243– 3	belief is s· up among you

springs
'01.	31– 5	s· from the very nature of Truth,
My.	74–24	* the satisfaction that s· from
	128– 9	s· spontaneously upward,
	201–29	Hope s· exultant on this blest morn.
	256–21	s· aside at the touch of Love.
	287–18	Mind whence s· the universe.

springtide
Mis.	330– 6	pray for the perpetual s·
	330–10	s· of Christ's dear love.
	331–10	s· of freedom and greatness.
No.	14–13	to the sweet breath of s·,
	27– 6	s· of Truth in C. S.
Pan.	1–14	for the s· of Soul.

springtime
Po.	16–24	breath from the verdant s·,

sprinkle
Ret.	17–14	s· the flowers with exquisite dye.
Po.	62–17	s· the flowers with exquisite dye.

sprinkled
Hea.	2–27	s· the altar of Love

sprung
Mis.	vii–17	My world has s· from Spirit,
	159–26	many weary wings s· upward !
	196–16	gods" which s· from it. — *Exod.* 20 : 3.
	356–17	has s· up, borne fruit,
Pul.	56– 1	* organized societies have s· up
No.	9– 3	the factions which have s· up
My.	199– 5	light hath s· up.

spurious
Mis.	43–15	s· teaching of those who are
	80– 2	s· works on mental healing.
	271–14	cobwebs which s· "compounds"
Un.	23–15	s· evidence of the senses
No.	2– 3	s· and hydra-headed mind-healing
Peo.	12– 8	s·, imaginary laws of matter

spurned
Mis.	122–21	Love divine s·, lessens not the

spurneth
Ret.	18–16	eaglet that s· the sod,
Po.	64– 7	eaglet that s· the sod,

spurns
Mis.	385–17	diviner sense, that s· such toys,
Po.	48–11	diviner sense, that s· such toys,

squadron
Pan.	14–26	blotted out the Spanish s·.

square
Mis.	143– 3	"s·" of moral sentiments.
Pul.	24–26	* twenty-one and one half feet s·.
'02.	17–19	s· accounts with each passing hour.
My.	309–22	* a small, s· box building

squarely
Mis.	378–17	He answered kindly and s·,
	399–24	(Heaven chiselled s· good)
Pul.	16– 9	(Heaven chiselled s· good)
Po.	76– 8	(Heaven chiselled s· good)
My.	112–10	founded s· and only on the

squills
Mis.	240– 2	doctor's s· and bills

staff
Mis.	118–20	His rod and His s· comfort you.
	158–20	with sandals on and s· in hand,
	358–28	awaiting, with s· in hand,
Man.	43– 1	or treats our Leader or her s·
My.	174– 9	city marshal and his s·
	292– 9	His rod and His s· comfort the
	310–14	s· of the Governor of New Hampshire.
	312–25	Governor of the State and his s·,

stage
Mis.	108–17	second s· of human consciousness,
	109–11	most hopeful s· of mortal mentality.
	109–23	through the second to the third s·,
	200–13	applicable to every s· and state of
	215–25	at this s· use the sword of Spirit.
	288–22	in every state and s· of being.
	355– 2	present s· of progress in C. S.

stage
Mis.	356–22	second s· of mental development
	357–19	third s· of mental growth
Ret.	81–30	at every s· of advancement.
No.	38–23	of any other state or s· of being.
'01.	17–20	had overcome a difficult s·
	17–22	next more difficult s· of action
	28– 2	last s· of the great naturalist's
Hea.	13–14	cured the incipient s· of fever.
My.	75– 4	* holding the centre of the s·
	236–28	of great importance at this s· of
	239–28	state and s· of mental

stages
Mis.	56–27	*successive s· of existence*
	100–31	indicates the different s· of
	107–20	three states and s· of human
	112–12	The mental s· of crime,
	206–11	advancing s· of C. S.
	208–17	states and s· of human error
	355–11	pass through three s· of growth.
	357–20	all s· and states of being ;
Ret.	45–12	first s· of mortal existence
Un.	50–16	no material states or s· of
'01.	17–16	the last s· of consumption,
	27–28	* goes through three s·.
	28– 1	passed through the first two s·,
	29– 6	advancing s· of their careers
'01.	33– 8	* decaying s· of religion,
My.	47– 8	* a few of the s· of its progress,
	47–14	* epoch-marking s· of its growth,
	80– 5	* of consumption in its advanced s·,
	105– 8	healed consumption in its last s·,
	107–30	s· of organic and inflammatory
	304–26	* goes through three s·.

stagger
My.	79– 8	* must s· their faith not a little

staging
Peo.	11–10	another s· for diviner claims,

stagnant
My.	149–30	waken the s· waters

staid
My.	79–15	* this occurred in s· old Boston,

stain
Mis.	141–20	s· the early history of C. S.
Ret.	86–11	Cleanse every s· from this wanderer's

stained
Pul.	24–28	* The windows of s· glass
	58–30	* portrait of her in s· glass ;
'02.	10– 9	footprints . . . are s· with blood.
	14– 9	* not like Cæsar, s· with blood,
My.	248– 5	* not like Caesar, s· with blood,

stains
Mis.	249–19	to remove s· or vermin.
	327–32	wipes away the blood s·,

staircases
Pul.	25–14	* the s· are of iron,

stairs
Ret.	76–14	meet on the s· which lead
Pul.	25–15	marble s· of rose pink,
My.	342– 3	* lady slowly descending the s·.

stairways
My.	46– 2	* commodious foyer and broad s·,
	68–28	* seven broad marble s·,

stake
Mis.	277–13	The s· and scaffold have never
	345–11	bound him to the s·,
	368–24	and at a fearful s·.
No.	44–14	sentence men to the dungeon or s·
Peo.	13–20	they bound him to the s·,

stale
Mis.	30–22	The s· saying that C. S.

stalk
Mis.	331– 1	construct the s·, instruct the ear,
	396– 4	Where ghosts and goblins s·.
Po.	58–16	Where ghosts and goblins s·.

stalled
Mis.	121–13	S· theocracy would make this

stall-fed
No.	43– 6	whether s· or famishing,

stamp
Hea.	19–16	We need it to s· our religions

stamped
Pul.	42–16	* golden beehive s· upon it,

stand
Mis.	16–30	Here you s· face to face with
	16–32	You s· before the awful detonations
	82–10	s· upon the shore of eternity,
	99–16	to s· a long siege,
	104–20	s· the friction of false self-hood

stand

Mis.	125–12	not s· waiting and weary ;
	140–29	church will s· the storms of ages :
	158–20	I s· with sandals on
	178–18	* s· before you to preach a sermon
	197–27	and therefore cannot s·.
	227– 3	may s· in the place of a virtue ;
	276–31	Scientists s· firmer than ever
	307–20	I must s· on this absolute basis
	347–17	Between the two I s· still ;
	369– 7	to s· erect on sublime heights,
	392– 2	monarch, at whose feet I s·,
	400– 5	be in thy place : S·, not sit.
Man.	75–17	with the land whereon they s·,
Chr.	55–26	Behold, I s· at the door, — *Rev.* 3 : 20.
Ret.	90– 3	or seek to s· in God's stead.
Un.	64–16	s· on the summit of Mont Blanc ;
Pul.	16–17	be in thy place ; S·, not sit.
	26–10	* lamp s· of the Renaissance period
	84– 7	* shall s· the new man with
Pan.	2–23	s·, in the term pantheism, for the
	9– 5	in paganism they s· for gods ;
'01.	25–30	a kingdom . . . that cannot s·.
Peo.	7–16	* "Sculptors of life are we as we s·
Po.	20– 2	monarch, at whose feet I s·,
	76–16	be in thy place : S·, not sit.
My.	34– 2	s· in his holy place? — *Psal.* 24 : 3.
	36–29	* to s· as an enduring monument,
	106–16	would weary, and the world s· still.
	150–15	S· by the limpid lake,
	158–28	s· through all time for
	205– 3	"S· fast therefore in the — *Gal.* 5 : 1.
	216– 5	All systems of religion s· on this
	224–31	* "They also serve who only s· and
	230– 4	s· when those have passed to rest.
	302–18	I s· in relation to this century as
	305–11	manuscripts . . . s· in evidence.
	322– 5	* facts . . . and they must s·.
	344– 4	rays collectively s· for Christ,
	344–24	* How does C. S. as to

standard

Mis.	50–21	a change . . . to the divine s·,
	53–18	the s· of metaphysics ;
	186– 8	far below man's original s·,
	232–12	s· of right that regulates human
	233–12	s· of metaphysical healing
	233–21	think the s· of C. S. too high
	233–27	having a true s·,
	233–29	they only who adhere to that s·.
Man.	61–21	s· of musical excellence ;
Ret.	53– 5	s· of genuine C. S.
Un.	38–27	not up to the Christian s· of Life,
Pul.	10–16	planted your s· on the rock
No.	2– 1	on its s· have emblazoned
	10–11	but one s· statement, one rule,
	46–15	Puritan s· of undefiled religion.
	46–17	let us lift their s· higher,
Pan.	11–21	the original s· of man
'01.	2– 6	the healing s· of C. S.
	2–12	the s· of Christ's healing
	34–10	look for the s· of Christianity
Peo.	10–15	alone grasps the s· of liberty,
My.	41–18	* maintains the perfect s· of truth
	180–11	primordial s· of Truth.
	283–24	is the s· of C. S.

standard-bearers

Mis.	177–11	against the lives of our s·.

Standard Dictionary

Pan.	2–19	S· D· has it that pantheism

Standard dictionary's

'01.	3–11	S· d· definition of God,

standards

Mis.	353– 6	are neither s· nor models.
My.	91–11	* or his moral s· debased
	224–24	to accept the latter as s·.

standest

Mis.	341–16	place whereon thou s·

standeth

Mis.	368– 9	* S· God within the shadow,

standing

Mis.	133–12	they love to pray s· in — *Matt.* 6 : 5.
	134–27	wickedness is s· in high places ;
	140– 4	and the church s· on it,
	178–22	* I should not be s· before you :
	301–25	injustice s· in a holy place.
Man.	36–21	members thereof in good s·,
	50–17	another member in good s·
	51–11	are in good and regular s·
	73– 8	Members in good s· with The
	73–13	Also members in good s·
	76–17	members of this Church in good s·.
Un.	49–19	S· in no basic Truth,
Pul.	6–17	* ailment of seven years' s·.

standing

'02.	16–18	angel, s· in the sun,
My.	9–14	* you, who are s· in the forefront
	64–18	* high s· of C. S. before the world.
	80– 3	* people of substance and of s·,
	81–31	* people of s· and of substance,
	126– 7	the recording angel, s· with
	199–18	This year, s· on the verge of the
	246– 4	in good and regular s·.
	296–28	s· and seating capacity,
	305–18	* "s· eighth in a list of twenty-two
	330–12	* by a Mason of good s·
	331– 9	* indicates her irreproachable s·

standing-room

My.	54–12	* "'No more s·.' "
	56–28	* there was not even s·.

standpoint

Mis.	14–21	appears to mortals from their s·
	52–30	up, to its spiritual s·.
	185–30	first spake from their s·
	228– 6	is to take a new s·
	289– 8	From a human s· of good,
	373–12	Neither material finesse, s·, nor
	379–22	a mental s· not understood,
Un.	29–16	from any s· of their own.
Pul.	69–19	* spiritual or metaphysical s·.
No.	9–10	their own s· of experience,
	12– 2	from a purely Christian s·.
Pan.	9–27	From a material s·,
My.	346– 1	* from the s· of C. S.,

standpoints

Peo.	1–16	from material to spiritual s·.

stands

Mis.	206–29	s· upon the mount of holiness,
	323–16	eventually s· in the valley
	364–17	s· on this Scriptural platform :
	399–25	on this rock . . . S· His church,
Man.	71–12	The Mother Church s· alone ;
	104– 7	It s· alone, uniquely
Ret.	70–27	he virtually s· at the head of
	80–10	* with patience He s· waiting,
Un.	29– 1	Soul s· in this relation to
Pul.	16–10	on this rock . . . S· His church,
	20– 1	The land whereon s· The
	61–17	* s· at the head of this sketch.
Rud.	2– 5	s· for one of the three subjects,
No.	3– 5	foe who s· in its way.
	33–22	Jesus' sacrifice s· preeminently
'01.	4– 2	then Love . . . s· for God
'02.	14– 5	the land whereon it s·.
Hea.	11–10	it s· and is the miracle of
Po.	46– 7	But gracefully it s·
	76– 9	on this rock . . . S· His church,
My.	28–21	* It s· as the visible symbol
	45–15	* edifice s· a fitting monument
	45–31	* as a material type of
	46– 4	* the great structure s·, silently
	46– 8	* In the best sense it s·
	49– 7	* a great chance of sweeping
	55–12	* The Mother Church now s·.
	143–15	s· the eternal fact of C. S.
	143–21	s· forever as an eternal
	159–13	s· at the vestibule of C. S.,
	194–14	s· for human self lost in
	194–15	s· for meekness and might,
	227–21	above quotation . . . s· for this :
	227–26	it s· side by side with
	247– 1	It s· for the inalienable,
	254–23	It s· for the inalienable,
	260– 9	Christmas s· for the real,
	295–18	It s· the storm.
	338–24	s· alone in word and deed,
	344– 3	If we say that the sun s· for God,

standstill

Ret.	38–25	He had come to a s·
My.	171–23	* Her carriage came to a s·

stanza

Un.	26–20	protest against this s· of Bowring's,

Star

Pul.	90– 7	* S·, Kansas City, Mo.

star

Mis.	1– 4	watched the appearing of a s· ;
	164–12	spiritual idea . . . appeared as a s·.
	168–20	behold the appearing of the s· !"
	276– 2	and the crescent with a s·.
	320– 9	s· that looked lovingly down
	320–17	polar s·, fixed in the heavens
	320–23	The s· of Bethlehem
	320–25	is the s· of Boston,
	320–27	s· of Bethlehem is the light of
	321– 1	wise men follow this guiding s· ;
Chr.	53– 4	One lone, brave s·.

star

Chr.	53–37	faith's pale *s·* now blends
	55– 4	bright and morning *s·*.— *Rev.* 22 : 16.
	57– 4	give him the MORNING *S·*.— *Rev.* 2 : 28.
Ret.	20–20	*S·* of my earthly hope,
Un.	17– 4	* "Hitch your wagon to a *s·*."
Pul.	25–18	* sunburst with a seven-pointed *s·*,
	26– 2	* electric lights in the form of a *s·*,
	28– 4	* *s·* of Bethlehem shines down from
	28– 9	* the crown and the *s·* are presented
	42–21	* a huge seven-pointed *s·*
	42–21	* a *s·* of lilies resting on palms,
Po.	9– 2	Turned to his *s·* of idolatry.
	46–15	Bright as her evening *s·*,
	68–19	*s·* of our friendship arose
	68–21	and bright as the *s·*,
	78– 9	*s·* whose destiny none may outrun ;
My.	110– 5	this Bethlehem *s·* looks down

stark

Po.	53– 2	paint the gray, *s·* trees,

starless

Mis.	268–16	no shipwreck in a *s·* night

starlight

Ret.	23–12	could not prophesy sunrise or *s·*.
Po.	3– 1	*s·* blends with morning's hue,

star-lit and starlit

Mis.	400– 1	*Laus Deo*, night *s·*
Pul.	2– 8	soft shimmer of its *s·* dome.
	16–13	*Laus Deo*, night *s·*
Po.	8–11	watching alone o'er the *s·* glow,
	76–12	*Laus Deo*, night *s·*

starry

Po.	8–15	Its *s·* hopes and its waves

stars

Mis.	188– 4	when the *s·* first sang together,
	254–19	*s·* from the spiritual heavens,
	259–20	morning *s·* sang together,— *Job* 38 : 7.
	319–27	feel themselves alone among the *s·*.
	332– 5	Mind is seen kindling the *s·*,
	340–28	like the *s·*, comes out in
	360–13	*s·* of the first magnitude
	360–13	fixed *s·* in the heavens of Soul.
	395– 6	The *s·* reject his pains,
Ret.	28–27	higher than the *s·* of heaven.
	65–28	magnitude and distance of the *s·*,
Un.	14– 7	"the *s·* also,"— *Gen.* 1 : 16.
	17– 6	*s·* in their courses— *Judg.* 5 : 20.
	42–14	morning *s·* sang together,— *Job* 38 : 7.
Pul.	4–18	water may help to hide the *s·*,
	83–29	* a crown of twelve *s·*."— *Rev.* 12 : 1.
Pan.	3–31	his spotted skin, the *s·* ;
'00.	12– 3	"holdeth the seven *s·*— *Rev.* 2 : 1.
'02.	15–23	steadfast *s·* watched over the world,
Po.	2–15	*s·*, so cold, so glitteringly bright,
	57–13	The *s·* reject his pains,
	70–18	The while the glad *s·* sang
	73– 7	And the *s·* peep out,
My.	13–25	reach the *s·* with divine overtures,
	125–22	are *s·* in my crown of rejoicing.

start

Mis.	53–12	to *s·* the patient's recovery ?
	215–11	or *s·* from wrong motives.
	235–22	*s·* the wheels of reason aright,
	366–24	*s·* from this false premise,
'00.	15– 7	*s·* forward with true ambition.
'01.	27–16	*s·* thirty years ago without a
Hea.	4– 1	unlimited Mind cannot *s·* from
My.	5– 3	man is supposed to *s·* from dust
	201–18	not to a *s·*, but to a tenure of
	215–16	I earned the means with which to *s·* a
	308–23	as they were about to *s·* for church.

started

Mis.	107–18	it never *s·* with time,
	139–15	I *s·* the *Journal* of C. S.,
Ret.	38–15	*s·* for Lynn to see me.
	38–16	*s·* for Boston with my finished
	52–20	I *s·* it, April, 1883, as editor and
Un.	34–11	wherewith we *s·*
'01.	17–13	and *s·* the Great Cause
	17–18	that *s·* the inquiry, What is it ?
My.	189– 2	*s·* in this sublime ascent,
	304–16	I *s·* *The C. S. Journal*,

starting

Mis.	51–26	* *s·* fresh, as from a second birth,
Pul.	79–10	* which, *s·* fifteen years ago,
No.	20–16	of an infinite Mind *s·* from
'01.	29–26	To aid my students in *s·*
My.	50–11	* *s·* out on their labors
	204–21	when *s·* this great Cause,
	312–31	*s·* that educational system

startle

Mis.	70–13	should *s·* him from the dream

startled

Mis.	324–19	*S·* beyond measure at beholding
Pul.	71–14	* *s·* and greatly discomfited
Peo.	13–12	On the *s·* ear of humanity
My.	294– 9	the *s·* or the unrighteous
	307–12	*s·* me by saying what I cannot forget

startles

Hea.	5–11	clergymen *s·* us by saying

startling

Mis.	84– 3	to receive *s·* announcements.
	193– 1	entertaining the *s·* inquiries,
	278–32	led to some *s·* departures
	301–10	There are *s·* instances of
	361–13	understood in *s·* contradiction of
Ret.	50– 6	a *s·* sum for tuition
'01.	21–17	*s·* ignorance of C. S.,
My.	9–21	pledged yourselves with *s·* grace
	99–25	* with a rapidity that is *s·*,

starts

Mis.	325–19	*s·* up in blank amazement
	339– 8	to-morrow *s·* from to-day
My.	213– 5	It *s·* factions and engenders
	288– 1	it *s·* the wheels of right reason,

starve

Ret.	90– 9	left them to *s·* or to stray.

starving

Pan.	15– 1	fed her *s·* foe,

State

Mis.	11– 5	abide by our *S·* statutes ;
	144– 2	New Hampshire, my native *S·*.
	251–10	of this city and of my native *S·*
	263–24	aid and protection of *S·* laws.
	305– 1	* women representing each *S·*
Man.	45–26	under the *laws* of the *S·*
	70–17	located in the same *S·*,
	70–18	on a statute of said *S·*,
	70–20	of the churches in said *S·*.
	98–21	*S·* Committees on Publication
	98–25	in each *S·* of the United States
	99– 3	the *S·* of California shall be
Ret.	4– 6	in the *S·* of New Hampshire.
	6–25	Legislature of his native *S·*,
	7– 2	the largest vote of the *S·* ;
	49–19	thank the *S·* for its charter,
Pul.	7– 4	especially the laws of the *S·*
	20– 9	by means of a statute of the *S·*,
	24–24	* Mrs. Eddy's native *S·*.
	41– 5	* From every *S·* in the Union,
	57– 5	* from every *S·* in the Union,
	68–11	* residence in her native *S·*.
No.	44–21	will again unite Church and *S·*,
'02.	20–25	metropolis of my native *S·*,
Peo.	12–11	as with an inhuman *S·* law ;
My.	94–22	* from every *S·* in the Union
	138–25	* *S·* OF NEW HAMPSHIRE,
	157– 8	* capital city of your native *S·*.
	167–26	the laws of my native *S·*.
	184– 9	Scientists in your native *S·*
	186– 2	forests of our native *S·*
	196– 5	a *S·* whose metropolis is called the
	196– 8	engrafted in church and *S·* :
	204–16	IN COMPLIANCE WITH THE *S·* LAWS
	204–19	practice of C. S. in your *S·*,
	227– 9	under the protection of *S·*
	270– 9	newspapers of my native *S·*
	289–28	the capital of my native *S·*
	312–25	The Governor of the *S·*
	326–14	the *S·* where my husband,
	326–15	the *S·* that so signally honored
	327– 2	practice of C. S. in that *S·*.
	327– 4	New Hampshire, my native *S·*,
	327–16	* practice of C. S. in our *S·*.
	327–22	* representative men of our dear *S·*
	327–29	* when the laws of every *S·*
	328–21	* healers of this sect in the *S·*.
	328–28	* to carry them on in this *S·*,
	331– 7	* the Governor of the *S·*,
	340–15	of making laws for the *S·*
	340–21	leaders of our rock-ribbed *S·*.
	341– 5	on the escutcheon of this *S·*,

state (noun)

affairs of

My.	340–26	to rule . . . the affairs of *s·*.

and stage

Mis.	288–22	in every *s·* and stage of being.
My.	239–28	The millennium is a *s·* and stage of

any other

No.	38–23	any other *s·* or stage of being.

Christian

Mis.	229–25	A calm, Christian *s·* of mind

Christianity's

Mis.	373–20	a sketch of Christianity's *s·*,

first

Mis.	108–18	The first *s·*, namely, the knowledge of

state (noun)

harmonious
    Un. 51–18   none . . . lost their harmonious *s·*,
healthy
    My. 14–25   * but it is in such a healthy *s·*
induced
    My. 211–32   *s·* induced by this secret evil
last
    Mis. 59– 9   in which the last *s·* of patients
    Rud. 9– 1   last *s·* of that man — *Matt.* 12 : 45.
    No. 5–28   makes the last *s·* of one's patients
material
    Mis. 64–30   or of a material *s·* and universe,
mental
    Mis. 107–25   this deplorable mental *s·* is
    109–20   Their mental *s·* is not desirable,
    112–17   the mental *s·* called moral idiocy.
    174–24   kingdom of heaven . . . is a mental *s·*.
    220–18   The patient's mental *s·* is now the
    229– 2   This mental *s·* prepares one to
    355–13   the mental *s·* of his patient.
    Ret. 54–17   this mental *s·* called belief ;
    Rud. 9–18   his mental *s·* weighs against his
    10–23   erroneous physical and mental *s·*.
    My. 349– 6   disease is a mental *s·* or error
normal
    Mis. 200– 3   regarded good as the normal *s·*
objective
    Ret. 34–19   objective *s·* of the mortal mind,
of agitation
    Pul. 51–11   * more or less in a *s·* of agitation.
of being
    Mis. 161–12   approximation to this *s·* of being
    No. 5–18   and is itself a *s·* of being,
    17–17   there is no fallen *s·* of being ;
of combat
    Mis. 216– 2   your own *s·* of combat with error.
of consciousness
    Mis. 219–25   *s·* of consciousness made manifest
    367–21   evil is a different *s·* of consciousness.
    '02. 9–16   urging a *s·* of consciousness
of evil thoughts
    Mis. 18–25   entering into a *s·* of evil thoughts,
of exhilaration
    Pul. 36–16   * a *s·* of exhilaration and energy
of existence
    Mis. 34–18   in our present *s·* of existence,
    34–20   pass on to their *s·* of existence,
    42– 7   still in a conscious *s·* of existence ;
    42–27   recognize a better *s·* of existence.
of false consciousness
    Mis. 222– 6   This *s·* of false consciousness
of feeling
    Mis. 222– 8   conviction of his wrong *s·* of feeling
    229– 6   would catch their *s·* of feeling
of health
    Mis. 219–25   a *s·* of health is but a
    My. 349– 3   A scientific *s·* of health
of human existence
    Mis. 200–14   stage and *s·* of human existence.
of mind
    Mis. 112–31   This *s·* of mind is the
    115– 7   this *s·* of mind in the teacher
    203–21   a *s·* of mind which rends the veil
    204–23   this *s·* of mind permeates with
    229–25   calm, Christian *s·* of mind
    348–28   in a proper *s·* of mind.
    350–21   An individual *s·* of mind
    Un. 56–11   are significant of that *s·* of mind
    My. 116– 8   This *s·* of mind is sickly ;
of misled consciousness
    Mis. 222–12   In this *s·* of misled consciousness,
of mortality
    Mis. 64–28   that he *is* in a *s·* of mortality.
of mortal mind
    No. 8–24   this *s·* of mortal mind,
    My. 109– 1   subjective *s·* of mortal mind.
of mortal thought
    Mis. 44–19   *s·* of mortal thought made manifest
of perfection
    Mis. 14– 8   his original *s·* of perfection,
    78–25   *fallen from a s· of perfection ?*
of spiritual perfection
    My. 345–23   a *s·* of spiritual perfection.
of thought
    Mis. 105–25   their own subjective *s·* of thought.
    My. 221–25   correct or incorrect *s·* of thought,
probationary
    Un. 3– 6   pass through another probationary *s·*
ring of
    '02. 3–25   hallow the ring of *s·*.
spiritual
    My. 244–16   man's spiritual *s·* in God's own
stricken
    Mis. 203–20   stricken *s·* of human consciousness,

state (noun)

subjective
    Mis. 24–19   subjective *s·* which it names matter,
    86–26   subjective *s·* of high thoughts.
    102–26   subjective *s·* of mortal and material
    105–25   their own subjective *s·* of thought.
    266– 8   subjective *s·* of his own mind
    My. 109– 1   subjective *s·* of mortal mind.
    265–26   reflect this purified subjective *s·*
such a
    My. 345– 1   see that your mind is in such a *s·*
———
    Mis. 138–20   to the *s·* of general growth
    358– 6   *S·* honors perish,
    My. 211–30   in a *s·* of semi-individuality,

state (verb)

    Mis. 49– 8   had the skill and honor to *s·*,
    131–27   let her *s·* the value thereof,
    132–14   you *s·* that you would "like to
    297–16   *s·*, in unmistakable language,
    349–23   will *s·* that I preached four years,
    Man. 57–13   to *s·* definitely the purpose
    Ret. 26–26   could first *s·* this Principle,
    Pul. 80–17   * but simply *s·* the fact.
    My. vi– 4   * to *s·* truth absolutely in a simpler
    24–17   * We are prompted to *s·*,
    50–13   * for their records *s·*,
    51–21   * but, as the records *s·*,
    99–19   * *s·* that the contribution baskets
    224–21   My books *s·* C. S. correctly.
    242–13   you must *s·* its Principle correctly,
    314–14   the court record may *s·* that
    334–15   * We can *s·* Mrs. Eddy's teaching
    354– 5   it is due the field to *s·* that I
    356–14   will you please *s·* that within

State Commissioner

    Pul. 20– 8   not, however, through the *S· C·*,

State Committee

    Man. 99–26   *S· C·* shall be appointed by

stated

    Mis. 57–27   *s·* in mathematical order,
    289–28   fairly *s·* by a magistrate
    318– 4   brotherhood of man is *s·*
    Ret. 37–15   Mind-healing as therein *s·*.
    61–27   demand that C. S. be *s·*
    78–20   other than is *s·* in S. and H.
    87–14   Let some of these rules be here *s·*.
    88–24   *s·* occupant of that pulpit.
    Pul. 43–26   * heretofore *s·* in *The Herald*,
    73–22   * She *s·* that man of himself
    No. 22–22   is not *s·*, and is impossible.
    My. 54–23   * "It should be here *s·*
    66–12   * what use . . . has not been *s·*,
    225–27   In their textbook it is clearly *s·*
    313–17   as *s·* by *McClure's Magazine.*
    314–28   just as I have *s·* them.
    322–26   * so clearly *s·* that I was surprised
    342–24   perfecting of man *s·* scientifically."
    346–21   * *s·* that her successor would be
    361– 5   All I say is *s·* in C. S.

State House

    Pul. 47–22   * one mile from the *S· H·*
    My. 68– 8   * size of the dome on the *S· H·*,
    68–12   * higher than that of the *S· H·*.
    86– 4   * loved its golden *S· H·* dome,
    (*see also* **Massachusetts State House**)

stateliness

    My. 63–25   * its purity, *s·*, and vastness ;

stately

    Mis. 239–12   draw up before a *s·* mansion ;
    245–10   *s·* goings of C. S.,
    332–15   midst the *s·* palms,
    Un. 5–26   *s·* goings of this wonderful part
    Pul. 16–18   Cold, silent, *s·* stone,
    44–17   * chapter sub-title
    My. 23–28   * As the *s·* structure grows
    36–25   * By these *s·* walls ;
    84–14   * *s·* cupola is a fitting crown

statement

abstract
    Mis. 200–32   abstract *s·* that all is Mind,
admits in
    Hea. 15–17   admits in *s·* what he denies in proof?
basal
    Mis. 27–10   the pith of the basal *s·*,
by Mrs. Eddy
    My. 356–12   chapter sub-title
complete
    Ret. 37– 2   the complete *s·* of C. S.,
correct
    Mis. 14–13   begin with the correct *s·*,
corrections of the
    Mis. 133– 1   not delay corrections of the *s·*

statement

definite
My. 343–11 * Here, then, was the definite *s·*
distinct
Ret. 34– 8 or give me one distinct *s·*
Pul. 47–14 * any distinct *s·* of the Science
64–19 * gave her no distinct *s·* of
error of
Mis. 56–21 Organic life is an error of *s·*
following
Mis. 133–21 in making the following *s·* :
Un. 7– 8 to make also the following *s·* :
My. 141–20 * According to the following *s·*,
157–21 * Mrs. Eddy made the following *s·* :
317– 1 * following *s·*, which was published
her
My. 319–13 * confirm her *s·* regarding the
his
My. 320– 7 * his *s·* of what he had done
his own
My. 330– 8 * contradicting his own *s·*,
in Christian Science
Un. 1– 9 whose *s·* in C. S.
in my letter
My. 146– 8 The *s·* in my letter
its
Man. 43–24 not correct in its *s·*
Mrs. Eddy's
My. 317– 8 chapter sub-title
my
Mis. 247–13 understand my *s·* of the Science
My. 241–22 * said that my *s·* was wrong,
303–16 my *s·* of C. S. would be
317–12 criticisms of my *s·* of C. S.,
of being
Ret. 94– 1 this scientific *s·* of being.
My. 19– 7 * "the scientific *s·* of being,"
33– 4 * "the scientific *s·* of being"
111–26 "The scientific *s·* of being"
of Deity
Hea. 4–28 our inconsistent *s·* of Deity,
of existence
Mis. 182–26 metaphysical *s·* of existence
of Hudson
Pul. 54–12 * We accept the *s·* of Hudson :
of the Christ
Pul. 74–24 one conclusion and *s·* of the Christ
of the Science
Mis. 247–13 my *s·* of the Science
Ret. 78–17 *s·* of the Science of Mind-healing,
Pul. 47–14 * *s·* of the Science of Mind-healing.
64–19 * *s·* of the Science of Mind-healing.
pantheistic
No. 29–13 Is this pantheistic *s·* sound
regarding a
Pul. 74– 5 * regarding a *s·* made by
remarkable
Pul. 63–14 * This is a remarkable *s·*,
scientific
Ret. 94– 1 this scientific *s·* of being.
'00. 5– 2 This scientific *s·* of the origin,
'01. 8– 4 Is this scientific *s·* more
23–11 scientific *s·*, the divine Principle,
Hea. 9–22 scientific *s·* that evil is unreal ;
My. 19– 7 * "the scientific *s·* of being,"
33– 4 * "the scientific *s·* of being"
111–26 "The scientific *s·* of being"
simple
'01. 22–30 its absolute simple *s·* as to
My. 356–27 This simple *s·* of oneness
such a
Pul. 75– 8 Such a *s·* would not only be false,
No. 29–18 such a *s·* is a shocking reflection
that
No. 4–18 vouches for the validity of that *s·*.
thereof
Man. 55–23 contrary to the *s·* thereof
the within
My. 315–17 * made oath that the within *s·*
this
Mis. 16–29 this *s·* demands demonstration.
76– 5 This *s·* of our Master
201– 1 this *s·* receives the
Ret. 58– 2 then departing from this *s·*
93–18 This *s·* is in substance identical
Hea. 16– 6 demonstrating of this *s·* ?
My. 52–29 * This *s·* "Phare Pleigh"
220– 5 This *s·* should be so interpreted
270–23 to the truth of this *s·*.
276–22 * she has given out this *s·* :
299–20 subscribe to this *s·* ;
338– 9 * fully corroborate this *s·*.
unqualified
Hea. 7–27 unqualified *s·* of the duty
unscientific
Mis. 217–10 fallacy of an unscientific *s·*

statement

was made
My. 346–24 * when the *s·* was made,
your
Mis. 133– 6 In refutation of your *s·*
My. 242– 2 scientifically correct in your *s·*
322– 9 * I have just read your *s·*

Mis. 92– 4 *s·* of the inexhaustible topics
Ret. 84– 1 *s·* of the inexhaustible topics
No. 10–12 there is but one standard *s·*,
My. 14–14 * good authority for the *s·*
311–12 My reply to the *s·* that

statements

Mis. 19–21 one who abides by his *s·*
56–23 the correctness of my *s·*,
78–19 false *s·* and claims.
295–18 flaunting and floundering *s·*
Un. 20– 4 We undo the *s·* of error by
20– 5 Through these three *s·*,
No. 43–23 Stealing or garbling my *s·*
Hea. 3–26 three *s·* of one Principle.
16–10 abide by your *s·*, and
My. 53–27 * some very interesting *s·*,
58– 9 * *s·* that have been made
79–26 * making their remarkable *s·*
112–18 demonstrates . . . its *s·*,
138–20 *s·* herein made by me
138–27 * *s·* contained in the annexed
143– 8 chapter sub-title
235–25 adopt as truth the above *s·* ?
320–18 * did not endorse all the *s·*
321–18 * the manner in which the *s·*
330–15 * *s·*, relating to her husband

State Militia
My. 309–13 New Hampshire *S· M·*,

Staten Island
My. 363– 7 First Church . . . *S· I·*,

state prison
My. 175–15 well-conducted jail and *s· p·*,

States *(see also States')*
Man. 99– 4 as though it were two *S·*,
99–15 This By-Law applies to all *S·*
Ret. 6–22 admitted to the bar in two *S·*,
52–16 branch associations in other *S·*,
Pul. 41–15 * and even from the distant *S·*
'02. 3–10 and joy in the sisterhood of *S·*.
Peo. 10–11 It were well if the sister *S·*
My. 30–17 * from Hawaii, from the coast *S·*,
326– 9 * in the Southern and Northern *S·*
327– 6 to practise C. S. in these *S·*
340–11 in excess of other *S·*,
340–12 In many of the *S·* in our Union
344–22 * the health laws of the *S·*

states

all
Mis. 208–17 All *s·* and stages of human error
conflicting
My. 293–13 conflicting *s·* of the human mind,
material
Un. 50–16 In reality there are no material *s·*
of being
Mis. 357–20 all stages and *s·* of being ;
of existence
Un. 49–17 not . . . two opposite *s·* of existence.
of false belief
Un. 50–21 but *s·* of false belief,
of mind
Mis. 221–15 these *s·* of mind will stultify the
Pul. 87–22 More effectual . . . are our *s·* of mind,
subjective
Mis. 73–20 subjective *s·* of false sensation
260–16 are its subjective *s·* ;
286–22 subjective *s·* of the human erring
367– 5 subjective *s·* of error or
Rud. 10–10 the subjective *s·* of thought,
No. 14– 7 subjective *s·* of mortal mind.
16–12 subjective *s·* of evil, called
these
Mis. 3–22 imparts these *s·* to the body ;
221–15 these *s·* of mind will stultify the
three
Mis. 107–19 three *s·* and stages of human

Mis. 42–10 *s·* that spiritualization of thought,
244– 8 He further *s·* that God cannot
371– 3 the gentleman aforesaid *s·*,
Pul. 47–10 * *s·* that she sought knowledge
My. 50–30 * The record of May 23, . . . *s·* :
309–26 *McClure's Magazine s·* :
330–16 * who she is *s·* was of Charleston,
333–22 * The *Chronicle s·* :
336–11 * In this book (p. 20) she also *s·*,

States'
  My. 309–15   strong believer in *S·* rights,
statesmanship
  My. 277– 5   settled peacefully by *s·*
stateswoman
  My. 297– 2   philanthropist, moralist, and *s·*,
stating
  Ret. 58– 1   *S·* the divine Principle,
station
  Mis. 291–28   *s·* justice and gratitude as
stationary
  Mis. 266–10   *S·* in the background,
  Ret. 93–14   *s·* power, stillness, and strength ;
stationed
  My. 71– 1   * chimes, *s·* in one of the towers,
stations
  My. 82–24   * *s·* were taxed to the utmost
  260–12   it hath . . . no half-way *s·*.
statistics
  Mis. 185–22   having no need of *s·* by which to
  271–28   * following history and *s·*
  '00.   7– 3   *s·* show the annual death-rate
  My. 92–18   * mere *s·* give a feeble impression
  92–21   * The *s·* have been ridiculed by
  93–27   * certain *s·* brought to light
  181–25   The *s·* of mortality show that
  227–30   *S·* show that C. S. cures
statuary
  Pul. 65–19   * arrangement of *s·* and paintings
statue
  Mis. 224– 8   mob had broken the head of his *s·*
statuesque
  Mis. 301–15   sincere and morally *s·*
  Pan. 10–28   Whatever promotes *s·* being,
statuette
  My. 258–30   beautiful *s·* in alabaster
stature
  Mis. 15–25   fulness of the *s·* of man in Christ
  102– 1   nature and *s·* of Christ,
  172–14   and he arrives at fulness of *s·* ;
  227–28   grows into the full *s·* of wisdom,
  Un.   2–24   *s·* of manhood in Christ Jesus,
  No. 19–24   fulness of the *s·* of man in Christ.
  Pan. 11– 9   his *s·* in Christ, Truth,
  11–18   regain his native spiritual *s·*
  '01. 11– 1   fulness of his *s·* in Christ,
  My. 103–13   the *s·* of man in Christ
status
  Mis. 45–14   The moral *s·* of the man
  183–31   arrive at the true *s·* of man
  264–25   moral and spiritual *s·* of thought
  357– 9   above the present *s·* of religion
  Ret. 57–28   making mortality the *s·* and rule of
  Un. 39–21   the immortal *s·* of man,
  No. 45–26   spiritual *s·* is urging its highest
  My. 29–24   * different *s·* before the world !
  111–13   spiritual *s·* of a perfect life
statute
  Mis. 119–25   prominent *s·* in the divine law,
  297–15   chapter sub-title
  297–17   *s·* in the *morale* of C. S. :
  Man. 70–18   confer on a *s·* of said State,
  Pul. 20– 9   but by means of a *s·* of the State,
  '02.   4–21   a divine *s·* for yesterday, and
statutes
  Mis. 11– 5   to abide by our State *s·* ;
  79–28   *for violation of medical s·*
  Peo. 12– 2   these divine *s·* of God :
  My. 220–29   human nature and human *s·*.
Statutes of 1883
  Chapter 268
  Mis. 272–13   * *S·* of 1883, Chapter 268,
St. Augustine
  Ret. 63–22   *St. A·* once said,
  '01. 28–10   none lived a more . . . than *St. A·*.
staunch
  My. 127–26   it is rich beyond price, *s·* and
  307–16   At that date I was a *s·* orthodox,
stay
  Mis. 302–32   *s·* within their own fields
  334– 3   none can *s·* His hand, — *Dan.* 4 : 35.
  335–26   get out of a burning house, or *s·*
  384–10   *S·* ! till the storms are o'er
  '00. 12–24   During St. Paul's *s·* in that city
  Po. 29–22   our saint, Our *s·*, alway.
  36– 9   *S·* ! till the storms are o'er
  My. 134– 8   to enhance or to *s·* its glory.
  173–23   short *s·* so pleasant.
  200– 7   none can *s·* His hand — *Dan.* 4 : 35.

stay
  My. 276– 6   or a dignified *s·* at home,
  280–20   none can *s·* His hand nor say
  315– 4   * During his *s·*, at different times,
stayed
  My. 290–15   mind is *s·* on Thee : — *Isa.* 26 : 3.
  327–18   * Scientists who *s·* on the field
stays
  My. 184–19   *s·* the shadows of years.
  311– 8   * "If this blind girl *s·*
St. Catherine
  (*see* **Eddy**)
stead
  Mis. 109–17   need of somethingness in its *s·*,
  Ret. 90– 3   or seek to stand in God's *s·*.
steadfast
  Mis. 12–15   watchful and *s·* in Love,
  172– 2   their claims and lives *s·* in Truth.
  176–17   *s·* in faith and love,
  189– 8   Nazarene's *s·* and true knowledge of
  267– 3   *s·* in their consciousness of
  400– 6   Grave, silent, *s·* stone,
  Ret. 26– 8   *s·* to the end in his obedience to
  50–20   *s·* justice, and strict adherence to
  '01. 34–22   be *s·*, abide and abound in faith,
  '02. 15–23   *s·* stars watched over the world,
  Hea.   2– 2   a calm and *s·* communion with God ;
  Po. 76–17   Grave, silent, *s·* stone,
  My. 108–28   I remain *s·* in St. Paul's faith,
  127– 7   *s·*, calm coherence in the ranks of
  155– 5   *s·* in Christ, always abounding in
  191– 9   *s·* in Love and good works.
  275–16   Love that is Life — is sure and *s·*.
steadfastly
  Mis. 19–16   *s·* flowing on to God,
  107– 8   plant the feet *s·* in Christ.
  110–19   wrought *s·* at the same
  149–30   abide *s·* in the faith of Jesus' words :
  241– 2   should centre as *s·* in God
  338–11   hope holding *s·* to good
  Ret. 90–24   walk *s·* in wisdom's ways.
  No.   9–19   point *s·* to the power of grace
  Pan. 13– 1   witness more *s·* to its practical
  My. 50–15   * turned *s·* from the mortal side,
  153–16   it keeps *s·* the great and first
  251–28   Cherish *s·* this fact.
  272– 1   *s·* and actively strives for
steadfastness
  '02.   1– 5   increase in number, unity, *s·*.
steadily
  Mis. 160– 6   lives *s·* on, through time and
  315–27   shall *s·* and patiently strive to
  Man. 18– 8   little Church went *s·* on,
  My. 53–20   * number of attendants *s·* increased.
  53–28   * *s·* increasing interest in C. S.
  56–21   * attendance . . . *s·* grew,
  118– 3   *s·* go on promoting the true Principle
  181–27   Since that time it has *s·* decreased.
  191– 6   C. S. is spreading *s·*
steadiness
  Mis. 204–26   gives *s·* to resolve,
steady
  Mis. 87–30   imagine they can . . . *s·* God's altar
  92–27   attempting to *s·* the ark of Truth,
  287–31   attempts to *s·* other people's altars,
  321– 8   sees the *s·* gain of Truth's idea
  342– 6   *s·* decline of spiritual light,
  386–16   a love that *s·* turns To God ;
  Ret. 84–16   attempting to *s·* the ark of Truth,
  No. 32–13   Mind-healing lifts with a *s·* arm,
  Po. 49–24   a love that *s·* turns
  My. 55–29   * *s·* increase in attendance.
  83–29   * made *s·* gains in recent years.
  94–10   * *s·*, consistent growth of the sect
  113–30   rapid and *s·* advancement of
  329–22   * recognizing the *s·* progress
steadying
  My. 278–19   *s·*, elevating power of
steal
  Mis.   2– 4   they *s·* from their neighbor,
  67– 7   "Thou shalt not *s·* ;" — *Ex.* 20 : 15.
  119–30   that others . . . *s·* your possessions,
  234–14   his effort to *s·* from others
  335–17   to murder, *s·*, commit adultery,
  354– 4   can *s·*, and lie and lie,
  No. 41–18   never admit such as come to *s·*
  '00.   8–11   may *s·* other people's good thoughts,
stealing
  Mis. 250–25   *s·* on an errand of mercy,
  324–22   *S·* cautiously away from
  Ret. 71–29   same as other forms of *s·*,
  No. 43–23   *S·* or garbling my statements

steam
Peo. 10– 2 steam is more powerful
steam engine
'02. 9–27 with the inventor of a *s· e·*?
11–13 a *s· e·*, a submarine cable,
My. 345–10 * the telephone, the *s· e·*
Stebbin's, Mrs.
Mis. 157–20 relative to Mrs. *S·* case.
steel
Pul. 82– 6 * *s·* tempered with holy resolve,
steep
Mis. 206–28 the *s·* ascent of C. S.,
397–23 O'er the hillside *s·*,
Ret. 46– 4 O'er the hillside *s·*,
Pul. 17– 3 O'er the hillside *s·*,
Hea. 19–24 up the *s·* ascent, on to heaven,
Po. 14– 2 O'er the hillside *s·*,
53– 8 Light o'er the rugged *s·*.
My. 229–21 scaling the *s·* ascent of
steepeth
Po. 16–14 *s·* the trees when the day-god
steer
Mis. 353–19 *s·* the regulator of mankind.
steering
My. 232– 3 *S·* thus, the waiting waves
stellar
Mis. 65– 6 *ipse dixit* as to the *s·* system
No. 6–23 Science of the *s·* universe.
stem
Mis. 162– 9 *s·* these rising angry elements,
162–14 *s·* the tide of Judaism,
Po. 46– 6 leaves have shed or bowed the *s·* ;
stenchpots
Un. 57– 1 More obnoxious than Chinese *s·*
step
advanced
Mis. 311–12 to take this advanced *s·*
My. 140–23 points the advanced *s·*.
advancing
My. 45–26 * for each advancing *s·*
backward
Mis. 340– 1 One backward *s·*, . . . has torn the
each
Mis. 117–21 watch that each *s·* be taken,
My. 11–11 * grow into readiness for each *s·*,
114–30 trace its teachings in each *s·*
every
Mis. 117–20 To point out every *s·* to a student
'02. 10–30 walking every *s·* over the land route,
Peo. 1– 2 Every *s·* of progress is a step more
My. 215– 6 it prospered at every *s·*.
234–12 guide them every *s·* of the way
first
Mis. 354–23 humility is the first *s·* in C. S.,
forward
Mis. 212–25 who will *s·* forward and
'02. 3–11 Our nation's forward *s·* was
14–18 every forward *s·* has been
higher
My. 142–19 a *s·* higher in their passage from
151–30 it took a *s·* higher ;
in advance
My. 252–25 was a *s·* in advance.
last
My. 217–30 does not require the last *s·* to be
light
My. 342– 5 * walking . . . with light *s·*,
next
Mis. 193–22 next *s·* for ecclesiasticism to take,
270–29 The next *s·* is Mind-medicine.
My. 217–26 aids in taking the next *s·*
one
Mis. 212–14 one *s·* away from the direct line
My. 217–25 "An improved belief is one *s·* out
onward
My. 10–29 * necessitates this onward *s·*.
Scriptural
Mis. 129–12 then take the next Scriptural *s·* :
single
Mis. 234–17 never has advanced man a single *s·*
some
Mis. 236–26 in some way or at some *s·*
step by
Mis. 18– 2 develop, step by *s·*, the original
take
Mis. 138–28 we all shall take *s·*
My. 155–10 take *s·* with the twentieth century,
this
Ret. 13– 5 Before this *s·* was taken,
My. 241– 7 * Students who are ready for this *s·*

Mis. 359–17 to *s·* upon the Atlantic

step
'00. 9–26 I have desired to *s·* aside
Peo. 1– 2 is a *s·* more spiritual.
My. 11–12 * never urged upon us a *s·* that
stepfather
Ret. 20–25 his *s·* was not willing
stepped
Mis. 162– 7 *s·* suddenly before the people
stepping
My. 31–26 *S·* to the front of the platform,
stepping-stone
Mis. 1–15 Humility is the *s·* to
Un. 37– 8 *s·* to Life and happiness.
56– 1 *s·* to the cosmos of
61–25 *s·* to the understanding
steps
Mis. 10–15 retrace their *s·*, and reinstate His
231–19 one, two, three *s·*,
347–18 take a few *s·*, then halt.
Pul. 42–25 * the *s·* of the platform were
58–18 * the *s·* marble,
No. 34–24 *s·* of uplifted humanity,
'00. 4–12 forward *s·* in religion,
'02. 10–14 taking *s·* outward and upwards.
My. 10–13 * taken *s·* in this direction,
47– 6 * the *s·* by which this church
65–18 * chapter sub-title
110–11 guiding the *s·* of progress
114–32 find these progressive *s·*
129–19 plant thy *s·* in Christ,
129–29 Trust God to direct your *s·*.
141–16 * has taken *s·* to abolish
196–17 should follow his *s·* :— *I Pet.* 2 : 21.
211–12 its ascending *s·* of evil,
302–30 upon the *s·* of its altar.
stereotype
Mis. 245–26 seeking to *s·* infinite Truth,
stereotyped
Mis. 232– 9 should religion be *s·*,
No. 45–28 Truth cannot be *s·* ;
stern
Mis. 74– 9 through the *s·* mandate of Science,
254– 4 gentle entreaty, the *s·* rebuke
Pan. 13–11 its *s·* condemnation of all error,
'02. 2–13 has passed from *s·* Protestantism
Po. 2– 1 *S·*, passionless, no soul
23–14 A *s·* rebuke to wrong !
30–15 *s·*, dark shadows cast on Thy
My. 18–19 its *s·* condemnation of all error,
247–20 not a *s·* but a loving look
sterner
Ret. 23– 7 became clearer, they grew *s·*.
sternly
Mis. 77–25 *s·* to rebuke the mortal belief
sternness
Ret. 80–16 mingled *s·* and gentleness
stethoscope
My. 105– 9 by verdict of the *s·*
Stetson
Mrs.
My. 359–24 * letter was forwarded . . . by Mrs. *S·*
359–26 * Mrs. Eddy wrote to Mrs. *S·*
361– 9 not seen Mrs. *S·* for over a year,
Mrs. Augusta E.
My. 357–27 Mrs. Augusta E. *S·*, New York
359–20 * written to Mrs. Augusta E. *S·*
stewards
Pul. 15–14 designate those as unfaithful *s·*
Stewart
Mr. and Mrs.
Mis. 157– 8 to write, to Mr. and Mrs. *S·*,
Rev. Samuel Barrett
Ret. 42– 3 by the Rev. Samuel Barrett *S·*,
stick
Mis. 370–21 braying donkey whose ears *s·* out
My. 225–23 expected to *s·* to their text,
308–24 declined to accept the *s·*,
sticklers
My. 211– 1 *s·* for a false, convenient peace,
sticks
Mis. 27– 8 C. S. *s·* to its text,
'01. 14– 1 So long as we indulge . . . it *s·* to us
stifled
Mis. 356– 8 they should be *s·* from lack of air
still
Mis. ix–15 course of years *s·* and uniform,
xi– 6 *s·* in advance of their time ;
42– 7 is *s·* in a conscious state of
99–24 *s·* live, and to-morrow speak

still

Mis.	124–27	and s· crowns Christianity :
	134–26	"s·, small voice" — I Kings 19 : 12.
	136– 5	I am s· with you on the field of
	138–27	"s·, small voice" — I Kings 19 : 12.
	146–13	and s· maintain this position.
	153–27	* Souls that are gentle and s·
	163–20	they s· live ; and are the basis
	166– 9	ideal Christ . . . is s· with us.
	170– 4	may s· believe in death
	174–32	"s·, small voice" — I Kings 19 : 12.
	209–25	happiness should s· attend it.
	230–24	* S· achieving, s· pursuing,
	233–17	s· worse in the eyes of Truth
	234–11	and rise — and s· rise
	234–27	to them s· more inconceivable.
	261–23	and s· saves mankind ;
	285–18	s· at work, deep down in
	307– 9	"Peace, be s·" — Mark 4 : 39.
	321–21	S· treading each temptation down,
	340–32	sin, and death s· appear
	347–17	Between the two I stand s· ;
	360–25	"s·, small voice" — I Kings 19 : 12.
	370– 6	spirit of evil is s· abroad ;
	398– 7	Make self-righteousness be s·,
Ret.	4– 7	s· cultivated and owned by
	12– 3	Minerva's silver sandals s·
	12– 5	echoes s· my day-dreams thrill,
	21– 8	learned that his mother s· lived,
	22–14	mortal life-battle s· wages,
	45– 1	Church of Christ, . . . s· goes on.
	46–13	Make self-righteousness be s·,
	60–15	"Be s·," — Mark 4 : 39.
	69– 9	insists s· upon the opposite
	69–26	voice of Truth s· calls :
	86– 7	Art thou s· unacquainted with thyself?
Un.	3– 2	and s· believe in matter's reality,
	4–14	as we get s· nearer Him,
	46–19	is s· claimed by the worldly-wise.
Pul.	13–16	They are dwellers s· in the
	17–12	Make self-righteousness be s·,
	27–29	* the windows are of s· more unique
	42– 4	* and at noon s· another.
	56–19	* "And s· we love the evil cause,
	67–16	* it was s· practically unknown
	82–15	* Too many s· are Jews who
Rud.	14– 2	and s· be Christian Scientists.
	14–22	If . . . are s· impecunious,
No.	1– 4	s·, small voice," — I Kings 19 : 12.
	11–13	and (worse s·) by those who
	12–26	immaterial, though s· individual.
	13–11	though the hiatus be longer s·
Pan.	10–20	better s·, they reform desperate
	14–14	s· guide and bless our
'01.	1–11	rise higher and s· higher
'02.	15–30	"s·, small voice" — I Kings 19 : 12.
Hea.	2–14	s· another Christian hero,
Peo.	11–17	hold . . . s· in bondage.
Po.	1– 1	unfallen s· thy crest !
	2–12	s· art thou drear and lone !
	2–19	thy deep silence is unbroken s·.
	14–11	Make self-righteousness be s·,
	16–19	when the winds are all s·.
	17– 4	in glory s· waiting for me.
	19– 1	oh, s· be it high,
	25–16	heart bore its grief and is s· !
	30– 9	thy s· fathomless Christ-majesty.
	53–19	s· and dead are all The vernal songs
	61– 1	Minerva's silver sandals s·
	61– 3	echoes s· my day-dreams thrill,
	65–12	'neath thy drap'ry s· lie.
	79– 9	His likeness s· — Is satisfied.
My.	11–27	* s· remained for definite decision
	23– 7	* is s· with us, and will bless us
	31– 7	* "S·, s· with Thee ;"
	37–25	* will s· be the pretext for our
	56–26	* s· further provision must be made,
	106–16	and the world stand s·.
	117–13	the old question s· rampant?
	122–18	Are we s· searching diligently
	145–19	and s· be at home attending to
	161– 3	for which we are s· his debtors,
	185– 6	* S· achieving, s· pursuing,
	223–29	"Be s·, and know that I — Psal. 46 : 10.
	241–22	* I s· lived in my flesh.
	245–24	these credentials are s· required
	249– 5	"s· small voice" — I Kings 19 : 12.
	267–22	s· another with a bitter sense of
	275– 8	"Be s·, and know that I — Psal. 46 : 10.
	279–13	is sufficient to s· all strife.
	282– 6	my hope must s· rest in God,
	287–16	so rise and s· rise to His image
	295–28	he s· lives, loves, labors.
	302–17	I s· must think the name is not
	305–22	I s· wait at the cross to
	307–23	s· think that it was profane.

still

My.	316– 4	I s· hear the harvest song
	319– 2	I should s· know that God's
	319–28	* and do so s·.
	331–24	* who s· extended their care and
	334–10	* s· contain the original account
		(see also **waters**)

stilled

Mis.	386– 4	yearnings come not, sighs are s·,
'02.	20– 3	voice of him who s· the tempest
Po.	49– 7	yearnings come not, sighs are s·,
My.	252–30	neither slumbers nor is s·
	278–16	chapter sub-title

stillness

Ret.	89– 1	eternal s· and immovable Love.
	93–15	stationary power, s·, and strength ;
Pul.	12– 3	impressive s· of the audience
Pan.	3– 9	find an indefinable pleasure in s·,
	3–10	nature's s· is voiced with
My.	29– 5	* a s· profound ;
	61–26	* in the dark s· of the night,
	79– 3	* in absolute s·, their eyes closed

stills

Chr.	53–12	That s· all strife.
'02.	5– 6	C. S. s· all distress over
	19–18	The thought of it s· complaint ;
Hea.	2– 6	s· the tempest of error ;

stimulate

Mis.	238–18	s· philanthropy and
No.	43– 7	to s· and sustain a good sermon.

stimulated

Mis.	214–11	This action of Jesus was s· by
No.	12–13	s· true Christianity in all ages,
My.	28–13	* has s· those gentle qualities

stimulates

Mis.	355–15	for the remainder only s·

sting

Mis.	96– 3	robbed . . . death of its s·.
	210–14	handles it, and takes away its s·.
	294–13	with s· ready for each kind touch,
Un.	48–10	deprives death of its s·,
Pul.	84– 4	* ingratitude of her s·,
Po.	31–21	wipes away the s· of death
My.	191–23	Death has lost its s·,

stings

Mis.	210– 9	because they have s·
	294–21	their s·, and jaws, and claws ;
Un.	45– 4	and it s· your heel,

stingy

'00.	2–16	idler earns little and is s· ;

stipulating

My.	250–16	s· three years as the term for its

stipulation

Mis.	381–16	s· for a judgment and a decree

stir

Mis.	210– 8	not to s· up these reptiles
	283– 5	s·, upset, and adjust his thoughts
	351–13	falsehood designed to s· up strife
	372–13	this book would produce a s·,
Ret.	80–13	it may s· the human heart
No.	1–15	s· of contending sentiments cease,
My.	150–17	This will s· your heart.
	244– 3	in order to avoid the s·

stirred

Mis.	127–32	needs often to be s·,
	390–16	To melting murmurs ye have s·
Ret.	40–21	demonstration so s· the doctors
Pul.	51–21	* belief has s· up feeling,
Po.	34– 4	Like thee, my voice had s·
	55–17	To melting murmurs ye have s·
My.	105– 2	had of a verity s· the people

stirreth

My.	104– 8	s· up the people." — Luke 23 : 5.
	104–15	"s· up the people" — Luke 23 : 5.
	222–18	s· up the people." — Luke 23 : 5.

stirring

Mis.	329–16	s· the soft breeze ;
My.	v– 4	* In these s· times

stirs

Mis.	391–12	It s· no thought of strife ;
Po.	38–11	It s· no thought of strife ;

St. James (see also **James**)

Ret.	31–19	As says St. J· : "Whosoever — Jas. 2 : 10.

St. John (see also **John, Revelator, St. John's**)

Mis.	21– 5	in the Revelation of St. J·,
	30– 8	St. J· spiritually discerned and
	205–11	in the words of St. J·,
	317–30	St. J· writes : "Whom God — John 3 : 34.
	339– 3	that which St. J· informs us
Ret.	90–10	to whom St. J· addressed one of

St. John

'00. 11–26 In Revelation *St. J·* refers to
12–27 The Revelation of *St. J·*
15–22 In the words of *St. J·*,
'01. 12– 4 If *St. J·* should tell that man
'02. 5–17 Divine metaphysics and *St. J·* have
Hea. 9–28 *St. J·* saw the vision of life in
My. 3– 7 *St. J·* writes : "Blessed are— *Rev.* 22 : 14.
119–32 *St. J·* found Christ, Truth, in the
187–13 *St. J·* says : "For this is— *I John* 3 : 11.
285–17 In Revelation 2 : 26, *St. J·* says :
339–17 disciples of *St. J·* the Baptist said

St. John's

Mis. 292– 2 divinity of *St. J·* Gospel
'01. 16– 6 *St. J·* types of sin
32–24 Sermon on . . . and *St. J·* Revelation,

St. John's Lodge

My. 333– 4 * records of *St. J. L·*, Wilmington,

St. Joseph, Missouri and Mo.

Pul. 89–32 * *Herald, St. J·*, *M·*.
89–37 * *News, St. J·*, *M·*.
My. 207–18 * *St. J·*, *M·*, January 5, 1909.

St. Louis

Mo.

My. 196–24 chapter sub-title
351– 4 * Mr. John C. Higdon of *St. L·*, Mo.

'00. 1–21 *St. L·*, Denver, Salt Lake City,

St. Louis Democrat

Mis. 248–20 The *St. L· D·* is alleged to have

St. Mark (see also **Mark**)

Mis. 25–17 spoken of by *St. M·*.
373–22 and, as *St. M·* writes,
My. 147–12 of which *St. M·* prophesies
238–15 of which *St. M·* prophesied

St. Matthew (see also **Matthew**)

Mis. 189–26 insomuch that *St. M·* wrote,
298–12 These words of *St. M·*
My. 222– 1 Gospel according to *St. M·*,

stock

Mis. 231– 8 though I take no *s·* in spirit-rappings
239–24 familiarity with what the *s·* paid,
272–21 * such as any *s·* company may
'00. 2–20 his *s·* in trade, the wages of sin ;

stockholders

Mis. 239–23 with that of the household *s·*,

Stoic

Mis. 162– 8 Gnostic, Epicurean, and *S·*.

stole

Hea. 3–11 material element *s·* into religion,

stolen

Mis. 201–26 our jewels have been *s·* ;
Ret. 17–13 Flora has *s·* the rainbow and sky,
76– 7 The Bible is not *s·*,
Po. 62–16 Flora has *s·* the rainbow and sky,
My. 304–30 second, she has *s·* the contents of

stomach (see also **stomach's**)

Mis. 69–31 dominion over the fish in his *s·*?
210–20 membranes, *s·*, and nerves ;
243–27 cause the coats of the *s·* to thicken

stomach's

Mis. 243–25 for thy *s·* sake"— *I Tim.* 5 : 23.

Stone

(see **Corner Stone**)

stone (noun)

art and

Pul. 65–25 * memorialized in art and *s·*

as substance

Mis. 27–31 Mortals can know a *s·* as substance,

Bedford

My. 45–29 * New Hampshire granite and Bedford *s·*,
68–19 * harmonize with the Bedford *s·*
68–25 * Bedford *s·* and marble form the
68–30 * bronze, marble, and Bedford *s·*.

corner

My. 16–26 precious corner *s·*,— *Isa.* 28 : 16.
17–15 a chief corner *s·*,— *I Pet.* 2 : 6.

cut in a

Mis. 376–12 * engraving cut in a *s·*.

every

Pul. 41– 2 * with every *s·* paid for

first

Mis. 285–18 book that cast the first *s·*,

foundation

Hea. 2–27 eternity's foundation *s·*,
11–18 foundation *s·* of mental healing ;

gray

Mis. 340–14 forsook Blackstone for gray *s·*,
My. 78– 6 * imposing structure of gray *s·*

stone (noun)

head

Mis. 196–24 head *s·* of the corner,"— *Psal.* 118 : 22.

is rolled away

My. 191–22 The *s·* is rolled away.

light

My. 89– 5 * The building is of light *s·*,

living

My. 17– 9 as unto a living *s·*,— *I Pet.* 2 : 4.

miracle in

Pul. 8–15 erect this "miracle in *s·*."
Hea. 11–12 pyramid . . . a miracle in *s·*.

pillows of

Mis. 144–25 from earth's pillows of *s·*,

prayer in

(see **prayer**)

roll away the

Mis. 179– 2 roll away the *s·*?"— see *Mark* 16 : 3.
275– 5 Who can roll away the *s·*

rolled away the

Mis. 74–19 rolled away the *s·* from the
123–18 rolled away the *s·* from the
No. 36–24 rolled away the *s·* from the

shapeless

Peo. 7–12 * the dream on that shapeless *s·*

stately

Pul. 16–18 Cold, silent, stately *s·*,

steadfast

Mis. 400– 6 Grave, silent, steadfast *s·*,
Po. 76–17 Grave, silent, steadfast *s·*,

testimonial in

My. 58–16 * this fitting testimonial in *s·*,

this

Mis. 400– 4 Like this *s·*, be in thy place :
Pul. 16–16 Like this *s·*, be in thy place :
Po. 76–15 Like this *s·*, be in thy place :

tried

My. 16–25 a tried *s·*,— *Isa.* 28 : 16.

white

Mis. 320–29 white *s·* in token of purity

wood and

Peo. 13– 1 worshippers of wood and *s·*

wood or

Mis. 346–15 an image graven on wood or *s·*
Peo. 2–18 form its Deity . . . of wood or *s·*.

yielding

Peo. 7–20 * carve it then on the yielding *s·*

Mis. 5–20 *s·* that the builders have rejected,
27–27 But, say you, is a *s·* spiritual?
28– 1 the *s·* itself would disappear,
127–12 it is not given a *s·*,
179– 3 The *s·* has been rolled away
179–19 What is it that seems a *s·*
196–23 *s·* which the builders— *Psal.* 118 : 22.
293–28 rolls on the human heart a *s·*
399–20 Rolled away from loving heart Is a *s·*.
Man. 18– 1 *s·* which the builders— *Matt.* 21 : 42.
Un. 57–18 This is earth's Bethel in *s·*,
Pul. 10–19 *s·* which the builders— *Matt* 21 : 42.
16– 5 Rolled away from loving heart Is a *s·*.
'01. 25– 5 The *s·* which the builders reject
'02. 2–15 *s·* at the head of the corner ;
Hea. 3– 8 The *s·* which the builders rejected
Po. 76– 4 Rolled away from loving heart Is a *s·*.
My. 16–25 for a foundation a *s·*,— *Isa.* 28 : 16.
18– 9 it is not given a *s·*,
23–29 * and *s·* is laid upon *s·*,
48– 6 * the *s·* that had been rejected,
60–12 * *s·* which the builders— *Matt.* 21 : 42.
129–20 *s·* which the builders— *Matt.* 21 : 42.
188– 1 the *s·* which the builders rejected

stone (adj.)

Mis. 325– 1 enters a massive carved *s·* mansion,
Ret. 5–12 inscribed on the *s·* memorials in
Pul. 24–11 * *s·* porticos and turreted corners,
41–23 * chimes in the great *s·* tower,
58–19 * the steps marble, and the walls *s·*.
86–13 * Accompanying the *s·* testimonial
My. 68– 6 * from the tops of great *s·* piers,
68–23 * It has an architectural *s·* screen
92–23 * two-million-dollar *s·* edifice
94– 7 * two-million-dollar *s·* edifice

stone (verb)

No. 41– 6 do ye *s·* me?"— *John* 10 : 32.
My. 108–24 do ye *s·* me,"— *John* 10 : 32.
227– 2 do ye *s·* me?"— *John* 10 : 32.

stoned

'00. 14–25 if you are *s·* from the pulpit,
My. 108–22 To be *s·* for that which our Master

stones

Mis. 224– 8 broken the head of his statue with *s·*
336– 6 cannot, . . . resort to *s·* and clubs,
Peo. 14– 6 dismal gray *s·* of churchyards

stones
Peo.	14– 9	* "bat and owl on the bending *s*·,
Po.	79– 6	of these *s*·, or tyrants' thrones,
My.	17–11	"Ye also, as lively *s*·, — *I Pet.* 2 : 5.
	43–16	* twelve *s*· taken from the midst of
	43–19	* "What mean ye by these *s*·?" — *Josh.* 4 : 6.
	43–32	* "What mean ye by these *s*·?" — *Josh.* 4 : 6.
	61–14	* climbing over *s*· and planks
	64–25	* "living *s*·" — see *I Pet.* 2 : 5.
	185–30	signs and symbols, sermons in *s*·,

stonest
Mis.	326–26	*s*· them which are sent — *Matt.* 23 : 37.

stony
Mis.	357–14	on *s*· ground and shallow soil.
My.	121–12	never selfish, *s*·, nor stormy,

stood
Mis.	178–23	* could not have *s*· up again *to* preach,
	253–17	*s*· ready to devour the child
	344–29	*s*· on Mars' hill at Athens,
	345– 2	St. Paul *s*· where Socrates
	345– 3	*s*· four hundred years before,
Ret.	30– 1	I *s*· alone in this conflict,
	31–22	I gazed, and *s*· abashed.
	40–10	*s*· by her side about fifteen minutes
Pan.	3–23	Pan *s*· for "universal nature
Hea.	10– 2	dragon that . . . *s*· ready
Peo.	7– 8	* "Chisel in hand *s*· a sculptor-boy,
My.	56– 4	* many *s*· in the aisles,
	61–26	* *s*· under the great dome,
	62– 1	* *s*· at the breast-works
	70–14	* and *s*· in silent admiration
	92– 3	* *s*· the test of time.
	105–16	so that it *s*· out like a cord.
	105–23	physician, who *s*· by her bedside,
	194–29	* *s*· the storm when seas were rough,
	247–15	I *s*· silently beside it,
	247–16	to the rim where I *s*·.

stool
Mis.	131– 8	kneels on a *s*· in church,

stoop
Mis.	226–26	dignified natures cannot *s*· to
My.	165– 5	The grand must *s*· to the menial.

stooped
Un.	11–14	Jesus *s*· not to human
My.	119–13	*s*· *down* and looked into the sepulchre

stoops
Mis.	330–30	*s*· meekly before the blast ;

stop
Mis.	114–25	and *s*· their hidden influence
	157–27	it cannot *s*· the eternal currents
	246–17	to shackle conscience, *s*· free speech,
	265–31	student must *s*· at the foot of the
	274– 6	I must *s*· teaching at present.
	286–32	*s*· at length at the spiritual
	288–25	real suffering would *s*· the farce.
	301–29	blind the eyes, *s*· the ears
	307–14	thought best to *s*· its publication.
	327–20	Despairing . . . they conclude to *s*·
	358–21	to *s*· teaching, to dissolve their
Pul.	64–12	* in order to *s*· the continued inflow of
	82– 9	* no more . . . than winter could *s*· the
Peo.	8–26	*s*· trusting where there is no trust,
My.	116– 5	C. S. realized will *s*· a contagion.
	147–25	never *s*· ceremoniously to dedicate
	165–26	and never *s*· from exhaustion.
	203– 9	and never *s*· working.
	327–16	* or *s*· the practice of C. S.

stoppage
Mis.	69–19	I removed the *s*·, healed him
	69–26	cause of the inflammation and *s*·

stopped
Mis.	275–27	Palmer House, where we *s*·,
Ret.	38– 4	and yet he *s*· my work.
Hea.	19– 6	could not have been *s*· by mind
My.	70–13	* workingmen *s*· in the street
	318–29	would have continued . . . but I *s*· him.

stopping
Mis.	107–28	*s*·, the growth of Christian Scientists.

stopping-place
My.	348–17	Here, however, was no *s*·,

stops
Mis.	44–13	*and nothing s*· *it until I*
	44–27	belief in pain ceases, the pain *s*· ;
	308– 7	greatly errs, *s*· his own progress,
Pul.	87–23	This wish *s*· not with my pen
'00.	8–21	he *s*· quarrelling with others.
'01.	20–22	till he . . . *s*· practising it.
My.	107–31	*s*· decomposition, removes enteritis,
	291–27	She *s*· to think, to mourn,
		(*see also* **organ**)

store
Mis.	149– 7	and replenish your scanty *s*·.
	299–18	If I enter Mr. Smith's *s*·
	391– 6	An item rich in *s*· ;
Pul.	78–26	* window of J. C. Derby's jewelry *s*·.
Po.	38– 5	An item rich in *s*· ;
My.	253–23	I send with this a *s*· of wisdom

storehouse
Mis.	139– 4	bring your tithes into the *s*·.
	159–18	This is my Christmas *s*·.
	313–20	the *s*· is ready :
My.	14– 2	brought their tithes into His *s*·.
	20–13	your tithes into His *s*·,
	131–25	tithes into the *s*·, — *Mal.* 3 : 10.
	202–26	sheaves into the *s*·.

stores
Mis.	165–29	secret *s*· of wisdom must be
My.	149–11	its radiant *s*· of knowledge

storied
'00.	1– 4	chinked within the *s*· walls

stories
Mis.	48–29	like a hundred other *s*·,
Ret.	2–28	*s*· about General Knox,
My.	82– 1	* all have the same *s*·
	313– 8	*s*· told by *McClure's Magazine*

storm (*see also* storm's)
Mis.	ix–16	darkness of *s*· and cloud
	152–22	when *s*· and tempest beat
	152–26	till the *s*· has passed.
	329–26	that tarried through the *s*·,
	362–26	shelter from the *s*· and tempest
Ret.	17–16	to the lightning and *s*·,
	60–15	saith to the wave and *s*·,
Pul.	80– 2	* ship when under stress of *s*·
Hea.	2– 5	while it reasons with the *s*·,
Po.	29– 4	born where *s*· enshrouds
	46– 4	Nor blasts of winter's angry *s*·,
	53–15	Where wind nor *s*· can numb
	62–21	to the lightning and *s*·,
	79– 3	*s*· or shine, pure peace is thine,
My.	182–28	find shelter from the *s*·
	194–29	* stood the *s*· when seas were rough,
	205–12	* And rides upon the *s*·."
	252–13	and run away in the *s*·,
	295–19	It stands the *s*·.
	356– 8	* And rides upon the *s*·."

stormed
Mis.	211–27	Jesus *s*· sin in its citadels

storming
'01.	2–19	ever *s*· sin in its citadels,

storm's
Pan.	3–10	silent as the *s*· sudden hush ;

storms
Mis.	140–29	will stand the *s*· of ages :
	374–11	Above the . . . *s*· of passion,
	384–10	Stay ! till the *s*· are o'er
	392–15	wrestle with the *s*· of time.
'00.	15–27	Watch ! till the *s*· are o'er
'01.	24–13	when the *s*· of disease beat
Po.	20–19	to wrestle with the *s*· of time ;
	36– 9	Stay ! till the *s*· are o'er
My.	11– 6	* *s*· that have surged against her
	204– 5	which *s*· awaken to vigor

stormy
My.	121–12	never selfish, stony, nor *s*·,

story
Mis.	144– 4	situated in the second *s*·
	216–19	*s*· of the Cheshire Cat,
	238– 1	I had heard the awful *s*·
	239–19	tired look, told the *s*· ;
Un.	44– 8	The old, old *s*·,
Pul.	vii– 2	*s*· of the birth of C. S.,
	27–20	* window tells its pictorial *s*·
	32–14	* She told me the *s*· of her life,
	33– 7	* related to her the *s*· of Samuel,
	46– 1	* A *s*· has been abroad that
	48– 7	* the second *s*· of the house,
	65–18	* *s*· of the cathedral of Amiens,
	84–21	* the *s*· of its mighty meaning
My.	14–19	* pronounced the *s*· a fabrication
	15–18	* I love to tell the *s*·
	15–22	* I love to tell the *s*·,
	15–26	* I love to tell the *s*·
	15–32	* 'Twill be the OLD, OLD *S*·
	38– 5	* the *s*· of our love for you
	68–27	* floors of the first *s*· are of marble.
	84–19	* It is a remarkable *s*·
	179– 5	the second was an opposite *s*·,
	321–12	* told the same *s*· to every one

stout
Mis.	222–23	will make *s*· hearts quail.

stoutest
    My. 88–27 * *s·* enemies of C. S.
stoutly
    Mis. 327–16 They *s·* belay those who,
    Ret. 14–14 I *s·* maintained that I was willing
St. Paul (*see also* **Paul, St. Paul's**)
  admonishes
    Peo. 10–24 as St. *P·* admonishes, we should
  avers
    Mis. 253– 3 not merely a gift, as *St. P·* avers,
  complains
    '01. 11–28 *St. P·* complains of him whose
  declared
    Ret. 30–17 *St. P·* declared that the law
  declares
    Mis. 30–20 law of Life, which *St. P·* declares
    71–23 *St. P·* declares astutely,
  defines
    '01. 16–14 *St. P·* defines this world's god as
  handkerchief of
    My. 152– 4 and the handkerchief of *St. P·*
  learned
    My. 104– 3 thought that the learned *St. P·*,
  modern
    '01. 27–16 Or if a modern *St. P·* could start
  rule of
    My. 12–17 This was an emphatic rule of *St. P·* :
  said
    Ret. 93–17 *St. P·* said to the Athenians,
    No. 25– 4 *St. P·* said, "But now — *Rom.* 7 : 6.
    45– 3 *St. P·* said that without charity
    '01. 26–21 *St. P·* said : "Though I — *I Cor.* 13 : 1.
  says
    Mis. 359– 8 *St. P·* says : "When I was — *I Cor.* 13 : 11.
    Un. 60–24 *St. P·* says, "And if Christ — *I Cor.* 15 : 17.
  speaks
    Mis. 15– 5 *St. P·* speaks of the new birth
  spirit of
    Mis. 344–29 We need the spirit of *St. P·*,
  stood
    Mis. 345– 2 *St. P·* stood where Socrates
  summarized
    Ret. 22– 8 *St. P·* summarized the character of
  terms
    No. 27–21 *St. P·* terms "the old man — *Col.* 3 : 9.
  words of
    (*see* **words**)
  writes
    Mis. 24– 2 *St. P·* writes : "For to be — *Rom.* 8 : 6.
    '02. 6–26 *St. P·* writes : "For to be — *Rom.* 8 : 6.
    16–12 *St. P·* writes : "Follow peace — *Heb.* 12 : 14.
    My. 293–28 *St. P·* writes : "For the law — *Rom.* 8 : 2.
  wrote
    Mis. 330–10 *St. P·* wrote, "Rejoice in — *Phil.* 4 : 4.
    My. 261–15 *St. P·* wrote, "When I was — *I Cor.* 13 : 11.

    Mis. 186– 6 as referred to by *St. P·*.
    188–16 *St. P·* first reasons upon the basis
    Man. 47–13 which are God's" (*St. P·*). — *I Cor.* 6 : 20.
    Rud. 17– 2 Jews whom *St. P·* had hoped to convert
    Pan. 11– 3 It caused *St. P·* to write,
    '00. 4–29 *St. P·* beautifully enunciates this
    12–13 travelled to meet *St. P·*,
    12–23 It were well if we had a *St. P·*
    '01. 9–10 spoken of by *St. P·*.
    27– 5 * I look to see some *St. P·* arise
    My. 104–11 call *St. P·* a "pest," — *see Acts* 24 : 5.
    113– 8 *St. P·* was a follower but not
    113–15 Was it profane for *St. P·* to
    123–32 let us say with *St. P·* :
    228–30 against that day" (*St. P·*). — *II Tim.* 1 : 12.

St. Paul, Minn.
    Pul. 90– 2 * *Pioneer-Press, St. P·, M·*.

St. Paul's
    Mis. 191–31 Let us obey *St. P·* injunction
    298– 3 *St. P·* words take in the situation :
    Ret. 93–23 If C. S. reiterates *St. P·* teaching,
    94– 6 divine Science and *St. P·* text,
    '00. 12–10 *St. P·* life furnished items
    12–21 influence of *St. P·* preaching
    12–24 During *St. P·* stay in that city
    My. 108–28 I remain steadfast in *St. P·* faith,
    340– 3 *St. P·* days for prayer were

St. Paul's School
    Pul. 49–25 * "Eton of America," *St. P· S·*.

St. Paul Street
    My. 66– 9 * the last parcel on *St. P· S·*

straggling
    Pul. 29–11 * no *s·* of late-comers.

straight
    Mis. 32–21 from the *s·* and narrow path.
    99–27 "Make *s·* God's paths ;
    245–28 the *s·* and narrow way ;

straight
    Mis. 246–25 make His paths *s·*." — *Matt.* 3 : 3.
    268–14 Scientist keeps *s·* to the course.
    323–23 up the hill it is *s·* and narrow,
    347–22 but it is always *s·* and narrow ;
    Ret. 71– 8 *s·* and narrow path of C. S.
    Pul. 48– 5 * Mrs. Eddy took the writer *s·* to
    48–14 * *S·* as the crow flies,
    My. 75–10 * headed *s·* for Horticultural Hall,
    140– 5 and crooked things *s·* — *Isa.* 42 : 16.
straightforward
    Mis. 233–19 fair-seeming for *s·* character,
    340– 6 unremitting, *s·* toil ;
straightway
    Mis. 81–14 *coming up s· out of the*
    Un. 13–14 would *s·* reduce the universe to
    49–26 He *s·* commands mortals
strain
    Mis. 184–12 brings to remembrance the Hebrew *s·*,
    339–13 the *s·* of intellectual wrestlings,
    365– 1 will bear the *s·* of time and
    387–18 Seek holy thoughts and heavenly *s·*,
    396–19 There sweeps a *s·*,
    Pul. 12–22 her primal and everlasting *s·*.
    18– 3 There sweeps a *s·*,
    No. 21–22 bears the *s·* of time,
    Po. 6–13 holy thoughts and heavenly *s·*,
    12– 2 There sweeps a *s·*,
    31– 5 Prolong the *s·* "Christ risen !"
    35– 3 *s·* which hath strange power
    41–21 *s·* of enchantment that flowed
    My. 130–27 enormous *s·* put upon it,
    276– 9 do not *s·* at gnats
strained
    My. 87– 3 * have been *s·* to their utmost
straining
    My. 211– 2 sticklers . . . *s·* at gnats
    218–19 namely, *s·* at gnats
    235– 5 *S·* at gnats, one may swallow camels.
strains
    Mis. 106–29 affords the only *s·* that thrill
    116–14 emphasizing its grand *s·*,
    116–16 varied *s·* of human chords
    142–23 the psalm in spiritual *s·*
    329–24 sweep in soft *s·* her Orphean
    345– 5 in immortal *s·* of eloquence.
    396–12 Are poured in *s·* so sweet,
    Ret. 12– 1 *S·* nobler far than clarion call
    Po. 59– 4 Are poured in *s·* so sweet,
    60–21 *S·* nobler far than clarion call
strait
    Ret. 55– 1 this *s·* and narrow path,
    '01. 28– 6 the *s·* and narrow way,
    My. 104– 1 the *s·* and narrow way
stranded
    Ret. 79–18 *s·* on the quicksands of
strange
    Mis. 1–17 *s·* fire from the ashes of
    250– 3 By what *s·* perversity is the
    275–13 words of *s·* import.
    Ret. 21– 8 by a *s·* providence had learned
    50– 9 led, by a *s·* providence,
    Po. 35– 3 strain which hath *s·* power
    My. 114–17 *s·* coincidence or relationship
strangeness
    My. 50– 7 * Pilgrims felt the *s·* of their
Stranger
    Mis. 323– 7 *S·* wending his way downward,
    323–13 but the *S·* meets and
    323–16 *S·* eventually stands in the
    324–18 he alone . . . can see the *S·*.
    324–22 he seeks . . . to find the *S·*.
    324–24 to go on and to meet the *S·*.
    324–31 the reappearance of the *S·*,
    325– 1 The *S·* enters a massive
    325–10 fear not to fall upon the *S·*,
    325–20 and looks at the *S·*,
    325–25 the *S·* turns quickly,
    326–22 the *S·* returned to the valley ;
    326–30 the *S·* saith unto him,
    327– 5 the *S·* saith unto him,
    327– 8 saith the *S·*, "thou hast chosen
    327–23 the *S·* is pointing the way,
    328– 1 suddenly the *S·* shouts,
    328– 8 the *S·* the ever-present Christ,
stranger
    Mis. 155– 9 win the pilgrim and *s·* to your
    178–16 * I strayed into this hall, a *s·*,
    Ret. 86–11 "*s·* that is within — *Deut.* 5 : 14.
    89–14 hortatory compliment to a *s·*,
    90–18 to the care of nurse or *s·*.
    Pul. 33–21 * as to whence the *s·* came

stranger
Po.	65–20	the s· who roams
My.	91–26	* even s· is its increase in wealth.
	117–14	"When saw we thee a s·,— Matt. 25 : 38.

strangers
Mis.	308–18	Friends, s·, and Christian Scientists,
	398– 9	S· on a barren shore,
Man.	59–14	WELCOMING S·.
	59–23	s· who may come to attend
Ret.	46–15	S· on a barren shore,
Pul.	17–14	S· on a barren shore,
Po.	14–13	S· on a barren shore,
My.	85–24	* but for a multitude of s·
	231– 4	solicitations or petitions from s·,

strangle
Pul.	13–15	to s· the serpent of sin

strangled
Mis.	233–11	and so s· in its attempts.

straw
My.	313–10	with tan-bark and s·,

stray
Mis.	281–13	a s· copy of the Scriptures
	398– 2	Lest my footsteps s· ;
Ret.	1–12	wrote a s· sonnet
	46– 8	Lest my footsteps s· ;
	90– 9	left them to starve or to s·.
Pul.	17– 7	Lest my footsteps s· ;
Po.	14– 6	Lest my footsteps s· ;
	41–12	and left them to s·
My.	41–13	* howsoever far he may s·,
	201–22	Lest my footsteps s· ;

strayed
Mis.	32– 8	or such as have s· from
	178–15	* I s· into this hall, a stranger,
	357– 6	having s· from the true fold,
	357–28	lambs that have . . . s· innocently ;
Man.	55–12	decided that a teacher has so s·
	85– 4	Caring for Pupils of S· Members.
	85– 8	member of this Church who has so s·

strayest
Mis.	328– 3	and if thou s·, listen for the

strayeth
Ret.	80–25	while innocence s· yearningly.

straying
Mis.	32–20	s· from the straight and narrow path.
No.	20–28	s· into forbidden by-paths

stream
Pan.	3–16	* By thy pure s·,
Hea.	7–14	in order to purify the s·.
Po.	66– 3	walk by that murmuring s· ;

streaming
My.	72–10	* there are s· into town

streamlet
Ret.	18– 9	songlet and s· that flows
Po.	63–18	songlet and s· that flows

streamlets
Ret.	11–13	from this fount the s· flow,
Po.	60–10	from this fount the s· flow,

streams
Mis.	223– 6	S· which purify, necessarily have
	223– 7	impure s· flow from corrupt
	323–21	and bathe in its s·,
	329–21	the s· to race for the sea.
	330–14	The alders bend over the s·
	332–16	crystal s· of the Orient,
No.	1– 7	Small s· are noisy
Hea.	10– 2	Earth's fading dreams are empty s·,
	12– 7	goes to the fount to govern the s· ;
Po.	35– 8	s· will never dry or cease to flow;

street
Mis.	274–16	Truth is fallen in the s·,— Isa. 59 : 14.
Pul.	59–30	* the front vestibule and s·
My.	68–11	* the dome . . . above the s·,
	70–14	* workingmen stopped in the s·

street-car
My.	83–13	* s· men and policemen,

Streeter, Lawyer
My.	137–26	* I had consulted Lawyer S·

Street Fund
My.	176– 4	THE CONCORD (N. H.) S· F·

Streets
'02.	13–17	Falmouth and Caledonia . . . . S· ;

streets
Mis.	133–13	in the corners of the s·,— Matt. 6 : 5.
	237–25	s· through which Garrison
	274–29	s· besmeared with blood.
	324– 2	s· of a city made with hands.
	324–27	rushes again into the lonely s·,
Ret.	79–28	nor its golden s· invaded,

streets
My.	66– 6	* property on these s·,
	77–19	* filled the s· leading to the
	80–28	* waiting vainly in the s·.
	82–30	* living in the s· leading directly to
	175–18	greatly needs improved s·.

strength

and beauty
My.	39–29	* s· and beauty of her character.

and growth
My.	83–28	* s· and growth of their

and permanence
Mis.	287–20	giving them s· and permanence.

and shield
Mis.	113–24	Love is our hope, s·, and shield.

beauty and
My.	68– 3	* beauty and s· of the design.

calm
Mis.	338–17	calm s· will enrage evil.

divine
Mis.	170–18	refreshment of divine s·,
	358–15	humility, and love are divine s·.
Un.	39–12	removes . . . weakness by divine s·,

from on high
Po.	32–13	resolutions, with s· from on high,

gathering
Mis.	354–27	gathering s· for a flight well begun,

health and
Mis.	7–29	think that health and s· would have
Pul.	52–16	* receive light, health, and s·,

hidden
My.	166–16	they develop hidden s·.

His
Mis.	263–10	safe in His s·, building on His

his
Mis.	130–28	renews his s·, and is exalted

holy
Po.	23–13	Yielding a holy s· to right,

human
Mis.	138–17	I once thought . . . was human s· ;
	138–18	know that human s· is weakness,
My.	132–14	no longer to appeal to human s·,

in union
Mis.	98–18	and to find s· in union,

is in man
My.	162– 6	S· is in man, not in muscles ;

its
Mis.	341–10	its s· in exalted purpose.

little
'00.	14– 2	"Thou hast a little s·,— Rev. 3 : 8.

moral
Mis.	268–27	From lack of moral s·
Pul.	83– 6	* has not yet the moral s·

of human belief
Rud.	11–19	on the s· of human belief.

of peace
My.	121– 7	we learn that the s· of peace

of the hills
My.	185–27	* For the s· of the hills, we bless

of the Lord God
Ret.	15– 8	s· of the Lord God :— Psal. 71 : 16.

of union
Mis.	254–12	the s· of union grows weak with

of weakness
Po.	2–10	With all the s· of weakness

physical
Mis.	240–12	physical s· and freedom.

reality and
Mis.	252–14	healthy thoughts are reality and s·.

requires
Mis.	ix–17	requires s· from above,

salvation and
Pul.	12– 6	salvation, and s·,— Rev. 12 : 10.

settles into
Mis.	204–15	settles into s·, freedom,

shows
My.	88– 7	* It shows s· in all parts,

stillness, and
Ret.	93–15	power, stillness, and s· ;

their
Mis.	10–20	tried their s· and proven it ;
	10–21	their s· made perfect in weakness,
Pul.	30– 5	* offering their s· to unite with

this
My.	121–10	This s· is like the ocean,

thy
My.	183– 3	and with all thy s·,— Luke 10 : 27.
	252–17	so shall thy s· be."— Deut. 33 : 25.
	270–17	so shall thy s· be."— Deut. 33 : 25.

time and
Mis.	296–12	give their time and s· to

to bear
Un.	6–12	as the age has s· to bear.

to build
Mis.	98–18	s· to build up,

strength

to nourish
Pul. 63– 8 * has the s· to nourish trees
wisdom and
My. 164–27 is reserved wisdom and s·.
your
Mis. 364– 6 renew your s·." — see Isa. 40 : 31.

Mis. 126–16 s·, meekness, honesty, and
162–32 in the s· of an exalted hope,
Pul. 4– 1 may say, . . . my s· is naught
My. 287– 8 giving to human weakness s·,

strengthen

Mis. 98–17 s· and perpetuate our organizations
328–26 lift the fallen and s· the weak.
Man. 43–11 s· the faith by a written text
Pul. 2–19 s· your citadel by every means
Rud. 12– 6 Wrong thoughts . . . s· the sense of
My. 213–22 s· your own citadel

strengthened

Mis. 298–11 would I be s· by having my
Ret. 27–20 * are lifted up and s·.
Pul. 50–19 * comforted and s· by them.
My. 95– 5 * constantly s· by members
132–16 Divine Love has s· the hand
152– 8 said, . . . tonic has s· you."
199–19 a higher hope, of s· hands,

strengthening

Mis. 262–17 lifting the fallen and s· the

strengthens

Mis. 362–31 no crime except when it s·
My. 129–27 expatiates, s·, and exults.
131– 1 s· them, removes fear,

stress

Pul. 80– 2 * a ship when under s· of storm
'01. 30–22 or by the s· of the appetites
My. 294–19 in spite of the constant s·

stretch

Mis. 124–22 s· out our arms to God.
370– 2 "S· forth thy hand, — see Matt. 12 : 13.

stretched

Mis. 325–17 lie s· on the floor,
Ret. 4–13 Where once s· broad fields
My. 215– 4 God s· forth His hand.

stretches

Pul. 48– 3 * green s· of lawns, dotted with
48–11 * s· on through an intervale
My. 200–12 unbroken, s· across the sea

stricken

Mis. 203–19 s· state of human consciousness,
275– 8 the faithful, s· mother,
329–28 robin, though s· to the heart
Ret. 13–11 pronounced me s· with fever.
Pul. 82– 5 * which heals the s· soul.
Po. 41– 1 * rest in this bosom, my own s· deer.
My. 291–26 suddenly s·, — called to mourn

strict

Mis. 65–26 proves that s· adherence to one is
119–23 s· obedience thereto, tests and
248–18 s· obedience to the Mosiac Decalogue,
Man. 44– 2 s· adherence to the Golden Rule,
110– 5 these seemingly s· conditions
Ret. 50–21 s· adherence to divine Truth
Pul. 38–24 * s· fidelity to what they believe
66–13 * s· fidelity to what they
No. 7–19 will not release them from the s·
My. 45– 1 * s· and intelligent recognition of
212–16 s· accordance with the teaching of
256– 5 phrasing s· observance

strictest

Ret. 14– 5 the s· Presbyterian doctrines.
76–28 s· observance of moral law

strictly

Mis. 6–26 where laws of health are s·
22–1 I am s· a theist
92–16 the teacher should s· adhere to
112–13 s· classified in metaphysics as
114–11 Teachers must conform s· to the
284–10 Students who s· adhere to the right,
Man. 51–17 requirements . . . s· obeyed,
67– 6 A s· private communication
70– 6 adhering s· to her advice
80– 2 on a s· Christian basis,
Ret. 84– 9 s· adheres to the teachings in
Un. 35–11 s· speaking, there is no mortal mind,
40–27 s· belonging to the nature and
Pul. 73– 5 * s· an ardent follower after God.
Rud. 14– 6 s· practising Divine Science,
No. 16–27 s· speaking, no mortal mind.
Pan. 12–21 The Science of Christianity is s·

strictly

'01. 5– 2 defined s· by the word Person,
34–24 obey s· the laws that be,
My. 13–12 * s· a mother and a ruling church."
226– 3 This rule s· observed will
282– 3 I believe s· in the Monroe doctrine,
345–32 * her views, s· and always
364– 4 s· to handle no other mentality

strife

Mis. 41–12 victory in the ennobling s·.
222– 4 passion, evil-speaking, and s·.
333– 4 commingle, and are forever at s· ;
341–12 glory of the s· comes of honesty
343–15 malice, envy, and s·
351–13 to stir up s· between brethren,
386–14 and could not know the s·
388– 8 Free us from human s·.
391–12 It stirs no thought of s· ;
Chr. 53–12 That stills all s·.
'01. 32–14 They were heroes in the s· ;
'02. 2– 2 through the mist of mortal s·
Po. 7– 8 Free us from human s·,
29–18 far above All mortal s·,
38–11 It stirs no thought of s· ;
49–22 and could not know the s·
My. 278–16 chapter sub-title
279–13 is sufficient to still all s·.

strike

Mis. 67–10 thou shalt not s· at the
355–16 To s· out right and left
Un. 18–22 in order to s· at its root ;
Pul. 51– 1 * C. S. does not s· all as a

strikes

Mis. 237–11 that conscience s· home ;
257–23 s· down the hoary saint.
Ret. 75–21 s· at the heart of Truth.
Pul. 24– 2 * strikes a keynote of definite

striking

Mis. 232–29 from s· out promiscuously,
312–13 * "No more s· manifestation
Pul. 45–20 * proved, in most s· manner,
76– 2 * A s· feature of the church
'00. 10–13 s· at liberty, human rights,
My. 32– 2 * two of the most s· features
88–19 * s· as are its beauties,

strikingly

Pul. 49–27 * a s· well-kept estate

strings

Pul. 81–23 * her own soul plays upon magic s·
Hea. 20– 5 * soar and touch the heavenly s·,
Po. 66–11 No melody sweeps o'er its s· !

stripes

Mis. 3–12 "through his s·" — see Isa. 53 : 5.
162–19 through his s· we are healed.
260– 2 "s· we are healed." — Isa. 53 : 5.
Man. 28–13 beaten with many s·." — Luke 12 : 47.
Un. 55– 8 s· we are healed." — Isa. 53 : 5.

strips

Mis. 185– 6 s· matter of all claims,
210– 1 s· off its disguises,
Pan. 11–22 whatever s· off evil's disguise

strive

Mis. 7– 9 we must s· to emulate.
86– 6 Scientist must continue to s·
154–27 S· for self-abnegation, justice,
176–12 s· valiantly for the liberty of the
180– 2 and s· to cease my warfare.
197– 6 and to s· after holiness ;
315–27 s· to educate their students
341–12 Seeking is not . . . you must s· ;
Man. 45–11 s· to promote the welfare of all
55– 4 shall s· to overcome these errors.
92– 8 shall s· to demonstrate by
My. vii– 3 * S· it ever so hard, The Church
132–14 to s· with agony ;
150– 8 S· thou for the joy and crown
207–10 * pledge themselves to s· more

striven

Mis. 11–28 though with tears have I s· for it.
12– 8 him who has s· to injure you.
My. 130–10 and s· to uplift morally

strives

Mis. 119–14 s· to tip the beam against the
119–15 the flesh s· against Spirit,
371–23 but error always s· to
My. 160– 1 s· for the spiritual ;
228–26 He who s·, and attains ;
249– 4 error s· to be heard above Truth,
272– 2 actively s· for perfection,
334– 1 * s· to give the impression that

striving

Mis. 267–12	secretly s· to injure me.
328–24	mortals who are s· to enter the
My. 200–14	S· to be good, to do good,
300–17	s· to reach the summit of

strivings

Mis. 61– 6	vain s· of mortal mind,

stroke

Mis. 195–22	s· of unskilled swordsmen.
Ret. 35–21	beneath the s· of artless workmen.

strokes

My. 291– 7	His work began with heavy s·,

stroll

Man. 48–13	continually s· by her house,

strong

Mis. xii– 7	with s· wing to lift my readers
2– 6	s· determination of mankind to
4–24	a very s· will-power
126–24	Scientists have a s· race to run
139–11	*pulling down of s· holds;— II Cor.* 10 : 4.
152–24	s· tower of hope, faith, and
223–12	is sufficiently s· to discern
238– 6	honest . . . and s· of purpose.
240–10	s· promotors of health and
250–16	I make s· demands on love,
252–30	children's toy and s· tower ;
277–10	heart loyal to God is patient and s·.
288–26	a s· impulse from the cause of
289– 2	S· drink is unquestionably an evil,
313–19	the reapers are s·,
345–12	his pure and s· faith rose higher
369–10	s· in the unity of God and man.
392–15	s· to wrestle with the storms of
393–18	In a beauty s· and meek
Ret. 5–14	a s· intellect and an iron will.
5–22	* She possessed a s· intellect,
16– 2	a soprano, — clear, s·, sympathetic,
Un. 43– 3	too material for any s· demonstration
Pul. 62–10	* required a s· man to ring them,
67–20	* Toronto and . . . have s· churches,
80– 4	* religious sentiment in women is so s·
Rud. 8–12	thou wilt be s· in God,
No. 42–27	* He said : . . . drink s· coffee to
Pan. 12–10	will make s· claims on religion,
'00. 9–13	S· desires bias human judgment
Hea. 2–12	* "Old Adam is too s· for
6–18	if the belief is s· enough
Po. 20–19	s· to wrestle with the storms
22–17	life perfected, s· and calm.
23–12	With utterance deep and s·,
33– 6	hourly seek for deliverance s·
52– 2	In a beauty s· and meek
My. 126– 5	to drown the s· swimmer
126–21	s· is the Lord God — *Rev.* 18 : 8.
129– 7	is taking s· hold of the public
229–30	Truth is s· with destiny ;
252–15	wait on God, the s· deliverer,
258– 9	bowed in s· affection's anguish,
290– 1	felt by the s· hearts of New England
291–24	while her reapers are s·,
309–15	s· believer in States' rights,
355–11	a s· supporting arm to religion
355–13	the s·, the faithful, the untiring

stronger

Mis. 10–12	rise again, s· than before
160–14	trial of our faith in God makes us s·
235–17	and a s· desire for it.
278–20	seem s· to resist temptation
339–15	if it yields not, grows s·.
Rud. 12– 9	until they hold s· than before
Pan. 10–14	s· and better than before it.
Hea. 10–23	or to argue s· for sorrow
Peo. 10– 2	and the s· element of action ;
Po. 68–13	s· than these is the spell
My. 162– 8	s· than the might cf empires.
283–18	his grasp of goodness grows s·.

strongest

Mis. 399–11	S· deliverer, friend of the
Ret. 82– 9	widest power and s· growth
Po. 75–18	S· deliverer, friend of the
My. 211–22	where courage should be s·,

strongholds

Mis. 303– 9	garrisons these s· of C. S.,
Ret. 80–13	pulling down of sin's s·,
My. 40–13	* abandon their s· of rivalry.
127–23	cannot demolish our s·.

strongly

Mis. 271–26	* more s· mark the difference
295–20	for whose ability . . . Mr. Wakeman s·
Pul. 27–11	* members s· insist upon.
37–16	* Mrs. Eddy feels very s·,"
37–21	* "Mother feels very s·,"

strongly

No. 9–17	opposed occasionally and s·
My. 213–22	strengthen your own citadel more s·.

strove

'00. 9–28	s· earnestly to fit others for this

struck

Mis. 249– 5	The hour has s·,
317– 5	The hour has s· for . . . Scientists
Peo. 11– 4	s· the keynote of higher claims,
My. 81– 2	* s· with the air of well-being

structure

Un. 34– 1	the so-called material s·,
44– 5	like the s· raised thereupon,
Pul. 23– 5	* Most Unique S· in Any City
24– 5	* most unique s· in any city.
41– 1	* s· came forth from the hands of
41– 7	* to help erect this beautiful s·,
65–16	* beautiful s· of gray granite,
75–26	* most nearly fire-proof church s·
77– 7	* golden key of the church s·.
Rud. 12– 1	s· of the material body.
My. 23–28	* As the stately s· grows,
24–26	* the s· is worthy of our Cause
28–18	* not . . . in the material s·,
31–11	* first glimpse of the great s·,
32– 7	* acoustic properties of the new s·
46– 3	* the great s· stands,
58–15	* This magnificent s·, this fitting
62– 5	* But what of this magnificent s·?
62–12	* crowns the completion of this s·
66–26	* giving her blessing to the s·.
76–31	* s·, which is now completed,
78– 5	* imposing s· of gray stone
84–27	* dedication of the beautiful s·
85–16	* in the building of a church s·
85–27	* rested on this s·,
94–19	* the s· was free from debt.
98–18	* s· cost about two million dollars,
171–13	view this beautiful s·,
342–11	* depend upon the osseous s· ;

struggle

Mis. 41–17	s· with sin is forever done.
64– 2	human cry which voiced that s· ;
87–31	this interference prolongs the s·
101– 9	It is a revolutionary s·.
101–12	Now cometh a third s· ;
163–25	After his brief brave s·,
221–25	s· against both evil and disease,
266– 1	that student must s· up,
288–29	spirit of Love that nerves the s·.
378– 8	and a s· with pride,
Ret. 94– 3	a s· for its demonstration.
Pul. 21–11	faithfully s· till it be accomplished
No. 8–16	s· into freedom and greatness,
33– 8	It requires sacrifice, s·, prayer,
'00. 8–15	In this s· remember that
10– 8	and a world-imposed s·.
'02. 6–24	heaven here, — the s· over,
14–24	nor protection in the great s·.
Peo. 10– 5	as we s· through the cold night
My. 158–13	heaven here, the s· over ;
244–18	mortals do not enter without a s·
307–28	mental s· might have caused

struggled

'02. 15– 8	I s· on through many years ;
My. 293–20	spirit and the flesh — s·,

struggler

Po. 31– 1	the loyal s· for the right,
My. 350–13	Lift from despair the s·

struggles

Mis. 116–23	watchfulness, prayer, s·, tears,
121– 9	human s· against the divine,
131–20	to consider the great s·
204– 1	agony s·, pride rebels,
241–16	constant combat and direful s·,
324–28	this time he s· on,
Un. 5– 7	mental s· and pride of opinion
No. 35– 7	When human s· cease,
'01. 30– 9	s· to articulate itself.
My. 60– 1	* one who knew of your early s·.
180–22	In our s· with sin and sinners,

struggling

Mis. 63–24	Even as the s· heart,
126– 9	when s· with mankind
344–14	poor sinner s· with temptation,
Pul. 13–17	not s· to lift their heads
No. 40–22	thought s· for freedom.
'01. 17– 7	repentant prodigal . . . s· to return
My. 126– 5	swimmer s· for the shore,
148–27	a sect s· to gain power
150–13	and never weary of s·
159–13	s· to enter into the perfect love

St. Stephen
'00. 14–26 as the devout *St. S·* said :

stubbly
Pul. 49–24 * She chose the *s·* old farm

stubborn
Mis. 119–11 more *s·* than the circumstance,
398– 5 Thou wilt bind the *s·* will,
Ret. 46–11 Thou wilt bind the *s·* will,
Un. 5–15 No *s·* purpose to force
Pul. 17–10 Thou wilt bind the *s·* will,
Rud. 12–14 will return, and be more *s·*
No. 2– 6 To aver that disease is . . . *s·* reality,
4–10 never made sickness a *s·* reality,
5–21 becomes indeed a *s·* reality,
7–13 sinning sense, *s·* will,
'00. 6–22 from the *s·* thrall of sin
Po. 14– 9 Thou wilt bind the *s·* will,
My. 99–27 * Facts and figures are *s·* things,
233–20 most *s·* belief to overcome,

student (*see also* student's)
affectionate
My. 322– 6 * Your affectionate *s·*,
another
Mis. 283–15 to treat another *s·* without his
Ret. 89–23 employing another *s·* to take charge
any
Mis. 318–14 Any *s·*, having received instructions
at Harvard College
Ret. 75–21 If a *s·* at Harvard College
become a
Mis. 35–17 *is one obliged to become a s·*
beloved
Mis. 158– 2 *My Beloved S· :* — In reply
My. 135– 2 *Beloved S· :* — The wise man has
234–16 *Beloved S· :* — The report of the
247–11 *Beloved S· :* — Christ is meekness
289– 8 *Beloved S· :* — I deem it proper that
351– 7 *Beloved S· :* — Your interesting
357–28 *Beloved S· :* — I have just finished
calls a
Man. 68–24 calls a *s·* in accordance with
can enter
Ret. 47–21 *s·* can enter upon the gospel work
can write
Ret. 76– 4 *A s·* can write voluminous works
class
Ret. 47–16 A Primary class *s·*,
47–18 a Normal class *s·*
dear
Mis. 157– 2 *My Dear S· :* — It is a great thing
My. 285– 2 *Dear S· :* — Please accept
295–12 *Dear S· :* — I am in grateful receipt
359–27 *My Dear S· :* — Awake and arise
360–29 *My Dear S· :* — Your favor of the
derived
Mis. 302–26 benefit which the *s·* derived
desiring growth
Ret. 86–17 *A s·* desiring growth in the
disable the
My. 4– 5 dishonesty, sin, disable the *s·* ;
each
Mis. 138–10 Each *s·* should seek alone the
283–24 Each *s·* should, must, work out his
Man. 85– 1 Outside of this Board each *s·*
earnest
My. 112–16 The earnest *s·* of this book,
240– 6 An earnest *s·* writes to me :
faithful
Mis. 88– 2 A faithful *s·* may even
favored
My. 219– 3 through some favored *s·*.
first
Mis. 29–15 taught the first *s·* in C. S.
380–12 teach the first *s·* in C. S.
382–15 first *s·* in C. S. Mind-healing ;
Ret. 42– 4 first *s·* publicly to announce
her
My. 240–23 * replies, through her *s·*,
impart to the
Mis. 292–11 Could I impart to the *s·* the
is not willing
'00. 9– 6 because the *s·* is not willing
letter from a
My. 355– 6 letter from a *s·* in the field
literary
My. 320– 1 * that he was a fine literary *s·*
lover and
'01. 32– 6 lover and *s·* of vital Christianity.
loyal
Mis. 91–25 never dreamed, . . . that a loyal *s·*
318–15 from a loyal *s·* of C. S.,
Man. 38– 5 If the approver is not a loyal *s·* of
Ret. 47–20 from me, or a loyal *s·*,
may mistake
Ret. 83–13 *s·* may mistake in his conception of

student
must have studied
Mis. 318–20 *s·* must have studied faithfully
must stop
Mis. 265–30 If impatient . . . the *s·* must stop
my
Mis. 157–15 Yes, my *s·*, my Father is your
242–28 he was my *s·* in December, 1884 ;
Ret. 51– 2 my *s·*, Mr. Ira O. Knapp
no
Ret. 44–14 no *s·*, at that time, was found able
Normal
Man. 37–17 One Normal *s·* cannot recommend
37–18 pupil of another Normal *s·*,
of Christian Science
Mis. 41–10 The honest *s·* of C. S.
117– 4 The *s·* of C. S. must first
280–28 import to the *s·* of C. S.,
318–15 a loyal *s·* of C. S.,
380–30 issued by a *s·* of C. S.
No. 2–17 honest *s·* of C. S. is modest
of Christ Jesus
'01. 28–28 is not a *s·* of Christ Jesus.
of Mind-healing
Mis. 221–22 baffles the *s·* of Mind-healing,
of mine
Mis. 243– 9 a *s·* of mine removed these
283–14 For a *s·* of mine to treat
My. 251–18 Primary *s·* of mine can teach
of science
Mis. 52–22 What progress would a *s·* of science
of the Bible
Mis. 64–23 aids to a *s·* of the Bible
of this book
My. 112–24 *s·* of this book will tell you
of this Science
Mis. 43– 9 *s·* of this Science who understands
My. 237– 7 a present *s·* of this Science.
one
Mis. 43–21 If one *s·* tries to undermine
Man. 90–21 One *s·* in the class shall
Ret. 43– 3 I began by teaching one *s·*
possesses
Mis. 55– 6 will come when the *s·* possesses
preparation of the
My. 245– 8 thorough preparation of the *s·*
Primary
My. 251–18 A Primary *s·* of mine can teach
251–20 Primary *s·* can himself be examined
said
Man. 69– 1 said *s·* shall come under a
should explain
Ret. 83–18 the *s·* should explain only
success of a
Mis. v– 6 CONSTITUTE THE SUCCESS OF A *S·*
such
Man. 69– 9 such *s·* shall pay to Mrs. Eddy
such a
Ret. 90–29 gladdening to find, in such a *s·*,
taught the
'02. 2–30 taught the *s·* to overcome evil
teacher and
Man. 87–21 better . . . for both teacher and *s·*."
Ret. 84–26 better . . . for both teacher and *s·*.
that
Mis. 88– 5 the better it is for that *s·*.
266– 1 Then that *s·* must struggle up,
My. 249–28 I should prefer that *s·* who
the very
Mis. 350– 6 with advice of the very *s·* who
this
Mis. 265–23 misconduct of this *s·*.
349–11 This *s·* had taken the above-named
white
My. 259– 4 I have named it my *white s·*.
who heals
Mis. 358– 4 *s·* who heals by teaching
who pays
Rud. 14–16 *s·* who pays must of necessity
worthy
My. 215–17 home for the poor worthy *s·*,
your
My. 325–17 * ever faithfully your *s·*,

Mis. 38–27 to make each patient a *s·*
40–19 the *s·* does not in every case
40–26 *s·* or practitioner has to master
50–15 essential that the *s·* gain the
117–20 To point out every step to a *s·*
157– 1 chapter sub-title
158– 1 chapter sub-title
264–28 mental development of the *s·* ;
265–22 Truth and its ethics to a *s·*,
292–28 I never knew a *s·* who fully
293–14 If . . . is not dominant in a *s·*,
316–12 hour best for the *s·*.

student

Mis.	348–32	A *s·* who consulted me
Man.	35– 5	by a *s·* of the Board of Education,
	38– 6	or a *s·* of the Board of Education
	69– 6	*s·* who has been called to serve our
Ret.	78– 4	In healing . . . the *s·* has not yet
	90– 1	*s·* should be most careful not to
Rud.	15– 3	a *s·*, if healed in a class,
Hea.	14–23	I waited many years for a *s·* to
My.	239– 6	acquaint the *s·* with God.
	285– 1	chapter sub-title
		(*see also* **Eddy**)

student's

Mis.	156–15	one *s·* opinions or *modus*
	349– 8	materialization of a *s·* thought,
Man.	84–13	*s·* price for teaching C. S.
	86– 4	After a *s·* pupil has been duly

students (*see also* students')

advise
No.	8–10	Advise *s·* to rebuke each other
'00.	8–30	I sometimes advise *s·*

affectionate
Pul.	86– 6	* from her affectionate *S·*,

all
Mis.	32–18	to talk with all *s·* of C. S.,
	272–29	to act toward all *s·* of C. S.

and patients
Ret.	83– 4	will commend *s·* and patients

any
Mis.	349–17	no jurisdiction over any *s·*.

are examined
Man.	90– 3	*S·* are examined and given

association of
Man.	86–13	in charge of an association of *s·*
Pul.	58– 5	* gathered an association of *s·*,

beloved
Mis.	93– 3	Beloved *s·*, *so* teach that
	110–15	*Beloved S·* :— Weeks have passed
	116–11	*Beloved S·* :— This question,
	120–11	Beloved *s·*, loyal laborers
	134–10	*Beloved S·* :— Meet together
	135–28	*Beloved S·* :— You may be looking
	142–11	*Beloved S· and Friends* :
	143–14	*Beloved S·* :— On the 21st day
	146– 6	*Beloved S·* :— I cannot conscientiously
	147– 3	*Beloved S·* :— Another year
	155–16	*Beloved S·* :— Because Mother
	159–11	*Beloved S·* :— My heart has
	203– 1	*Beloved S·* :— In thanking you
	206–24	Beloved *s·*, you have entered
	278–18	beloved *s·*, who are absent
My.	20– 8	*Beloved S·* :— The holidays are
	26– 9	*Beloved S·* :— Your generous
	139– 2	*Beloved S·* :— Rest assured
	142–26	*Beloved S·* :— I thank you
	167–15	*Beloved S·* :— May this, your first
	171– 9	*Beloved S·* :— The new Concord church
	183–24	*Beloved S· and Church:* — Thanks for
	192–20	*Beloved S·* :— Your kind letter,
	194–19	*Beloved S·* :— Your telegram,
	197–10	*Beloved S·* :— Words are inadequate
	198– 3	*Beloved S· and Brethren* : —Your letters
	199– 3	BELOVED *S·* AND BRETHREN : — I rejoice
	201– 1	God is blessing you, my beloved *s·*
	203–24	*Beloved S·* :— You have laid the
	224–30	Beloved *s·*, just now let
	226–21	Beloved *s·*, in this you learn
	229–20	Will those beloved *s·*, whose growth
	230–18	*Beloved S·* :— I read with pleasure
	236– 2	Will the beloved *s·* accept
	243– 2	BELOVED *S·* :— According to reports,
	248– 2	*Beloved S·* :— I am more than
	250–15	*Beloved S·* :— The By-law of
	251–24	*Beloved S·* :— I call you mine,
	252–19	*Beloved S·* :— Your letter and
	253–21	*Beloved S·* :— You will accept
	254–10	*Beloved S·* :— Responding to
	257–24	*Beloved S·* :— For your manifold

best
Pan.	10–13	best *s·* in the class averred

called on
Mis.	351– 1	called on *s·* to test their ability

came
Pul.	68– 6	* *S·* came to it in hundreds

can confer
Man.	88–20	*s·* can confer with their teachers

certain
Mis.	353–28	Certain *s·*, being too much

charity
Mis.	267– 6	Charity *s·*, for whom I have

Christian
Mis.	132–25	and to my Christian *s·*.
	243–18	My Christian *s·* are . . . modest :
	301–13	My Christian *s·* who have read copies
	303– 6	Christian *s·* should have their own

students

Christian
Ret.	54–24	My Christian *s·*, impressed with the
No.	9– 1	as my Christian *s·* can testify ;

Christian Science
Un.	5–22	C. S. *s·* and Christians who

class of
Mis.	32–16	to the above-named class of *s·*

crowded with
Mis.	5– 6	crowded with *s·* who are willing to

dear
Mis.	137– 2	*My Dear S· and Friends* :
	143– 4	My dear *s·* may have explained
	159–21	gifts that my dear *s·* offer
	262–13	I thank you, my dear *s·*,
My.	234– 7	Did the dear *s·* know how much I
	358–23	love to your dear *s·* and church.

decrease of
My.	266–12	decrease of *s·* in the seminaries

devoted
Mis.	318– 7	love some of those devoted *s·*

disloyal
Mis.	32– 4	*students of disloyal s·*
My.	130– 8	effort of disloyal *s·* to blacken me

early
My.	321–27	* that I was among your early *s·*

employed
Man.	69–21	*S·* employed by Mrs. Eddy

faithful
Mis.	356–20	Now let my faithful *s·*

five thousand
Mis.	29–17	about five thousand *s·*.

free
Rud.	14–14	sometimes seventeen, free *s·* in it ;

good
My.	219– 6	My good *s·* have all the honor of

her
Mis.	37–27	leaving to her *s·* the work of
	40–22	Founder of C. S. teaches her *s·*
	54–10	Thousands . . . are her *s·*,
Man.	18–14	twelve of her *s·*
My.	48–11	* insisted that her *s·* make,
	53–22	* pulpit was supplied . . . by her *s·*
	359–21	* by twenty-four of her *s·*

his
Mis.	92–14	and his *s·* will answer them
	92–31	teacher does most for his *s·*
	97– 8	Master said of one of his *s·*,
	212– 8	tersely reminded his *s·*
	265– 7	also predisposes his *s·* to
	265–17	visited upon himself and his *s·*,
	293– 9	should impart to his *s·* the
	315–16	look after the welfare of his *s·*,
Ret.	68–13	Our Master instructed his *s·*
	84–19	teacher does most for his *s·* who
No.	2–11	Our Master taught his *s·* to
'01.	33–23	which he enjoined his *s·* to teach
My.	215–23	Master first sent forth his *s·*,
	215–28	Why did he send forth his *s·*
	364–13	should teach his *s·* to defend

his own
Ret.	89–19	method was to instruct his own *s·* ;

honest
Mis.	44– 1	Honest *s·* speak the truth

hundreds of
Pul.	36– 8	* hundreds and hundreds of *s·*,

imposed by
Mis.	351– 3	to lift the burdens imposed by *s·*.

in Christian Science
Ret.	50–23	I see clearly that *s·* in C. S.

indigent
Mis.	11– 8	taught indigent *s·* gratuitously,
'02.	15– 7	rooming and boarding indigent *s·*
My.	214–24	C. S. home for indigent *s·*,

in mathematics
Mis.	29–30	Christians, like *s·* in mathematics,

in New York
My.	243–15	*s·* in New York and elsewhere

its
Mis.	40–11	why do not its *s·* perform as
Pul.	44–20	* has shown its power over its *s*,

I warn
Mis.	309–18	I warn *s·* against falling into

Jesus'
No.	14–22	are not confined to Jesus' *s·*
My.	190–14	Jesus' *s·*, failing to cure a severe

letters from
My.	319–11	* heading
	319–12	* following letters from *s·*

loving
Pul.	86–20	* In behalf of your loving *s·*

loyal
Mis.	266–19	my loyal *s·* in Chicago,
	283–22	is seldom the case with loyal *s·*,
Man.	35– 4	by one of Mrs. Eddy's loyal *s·*,
	36– 6	coming from pupils of loyal *s·*

students

loyal
Man. 38– 3 loyal *s·* of the textbook,
89–11 Loyal *s·* who have been taught
109– 7 except loyal *s·* of Mrs. Eddy,
Ret. 50–12 ask my loyal *s·* if they
50–17 Loyal *s·* speak with delight
82–10 attained by those loyal *s·*
Rud. v– 5 LOYAL *S·*, WORKING and WAITING
'00. 9–25 loyal *s·* will tell you that
My. 182–16 faithful labor of loyal *s·*,
244–21 all loyal *s·* of my books
loyalty in
Ret. 50–19 By loyalty in *s·* I mean this,
malignant
Mis. 249–21 efforts of some malignant *s·*,
many
Mis. 264–13 Many *s·* enter the Normal class
299–12 to the minds of many *s·*.
Rud. 14–26 Many *s·*, who have passed through
My. 360–14 as many *s·* think I can,
Mrs. Eddy's
Man. 18–19 Mrs. Eddy's *s·* and members of
my
Mis. 32– 6 some of my *s·* seem not
87–22 My *s·* are taught the divine
88– 1 to blight the fruits of my *s·*.
115–13 May God enable my *s·*
137–14 rejoice over the growth of my *s·*
137–29 My *s·* can *now* organize
159–12 to the memory of my *s·*.
203– 4 my *s·* and your students ;
203– 7 this gift from my *s·*
214–19 My *s·* need to search the
215–23 My *s·* are at the beginning
242– 6 offered me, . . . or one of my *s·*,
264–15 taught their first lessons by my *s·* ;
273– 8 My *s·* have never expressed
273–13 gather all my *s·*, in the
276–10 My *s·*, our delegates,
276–24 I pray that all my *s·*
278–25 perpetual instruction of my *s·*
279–13 My *s·*, three picture-stories
281–23 Among the gifts of my *s·*,
302– 9 My *s·* are expected to know
316–25 had my *s·* achieved the point
318– 1 chapter sub-title
318– 5 not alone for my *s·*,
356–10 My *s·*, with cultured intellects,
380–17 My *s·* at first practised
Ret. 43–22 six of my *s·* in 1876,
52–12 I suggested to my *s·*,
82– 5 my *s·* should not allow
82–14 my *s·* should locate in
90–26 One of my *s·* wrote to me :
Un. 1–14 I counsel my *s·* to defer
No. 8–19 my *s·* to hold no controversy
9–16 my *s·* who fall into error,
40–14 I instruct my *s·* to pursue
'01. 17–21 into the hands of my *s·*
29–26 To aid my *s·* in starting
My. 121–17 presented to me by my *s·*
130–17 my *s·* reprove, rebuke,
138–12 my *s·* and trusted personal friends
153– 7 gospel ministry of my *s·*
244–22 are indeed my *s·*,
249–27 If both . . . Readers are my *s·*,
my own
Mis. 155–24 If my own *s·* cannot spare time
no aid to
Mis. 156–26 no aid to *s·* in acquiring
noble
Mis. 264– 3 My noble *s·*, who are loyal to
Normal
Man. 37–16 Pupils of Normal *S·*.
not
Mis. 271– 6 (and many who are not *s·*)
number of
Mis. 256–15 but a select number of *s·*.
Rud. 15–19 very limited number of *s·*
of Christian Science
Mis. 32–18 to talk with all *s·* of C. S.,
40–13 In some instances the *s·* of C. S.
271– 5 *S·* of C. S. (and many who
272–29 to act toward all *s·* of C. S.
357–22 those *s·* of C. S. whose
Man. 45–23 *S·* of C. S. must drop the titles of
91–19 *S·* of C. S., duly instructed
of mine
Mis. 87–19 to teach *s·* of mine.
Ret. 43–19 These *s·* of mine were the only
of Mrs. Eddy
Man. 35–20 *s·* of Mrs. Eddy, loyal to the
109– 7 except loyal *s·* of Mrs. Eddy,
My. 319–12 * letters from *s·* of Mrs. Eddy

students

of students
Mis. 317–24 enlisted for the *s·* of students ;
of the Christ
My. 190–25 become *s·* of the Christ,
of the College
Mis. 64– 9 *prospective s· of the College*
Man. 35–10 *S·* of the College.
older
My. 323–26 * should mean to your older *s·*
other
Mis. 349–19 several other *s·* with him.
Man. 35–17 Other *S·*.
Ret. 82– 6 to be controlled by other *s·*,
83– 8 by the teachings of other *s·*,
My. 138–14 Mr. Calvin A. Frye and other *s·*
361– 5 your relations with other *s·*.
Oxford
Hea. 18–27 Oxford *s·* proved this :
practising
Mis. 4–15 and to the practising *s·*,
Primary
Man. 91–19 Primary *S·*.
Rud. 14–22 If the Primary *s·* are
progress of
Mis. 156–20 clogs the progress of *s·*,
prospective
Mis. 64– 9 *What can prospective s· of the College*
qualified
My. 231–11 She has qualified *s·* for healing
scientific
Mis. 308–12 scientific *s·* are ready for
send out
Mis. 273–20 to send out *s·* from these sources
My. 300–24 send out *s·* according to Christ's
serving
Mis. 303–17 If ever I wear out from serving *s·*,
sixty-five
Mis. 279–12 ATTENDANCE OF SIXTY-FIVE *S·*.
some
Mis. 115– 4 the apathy of some *s·*
264–19 Some *s·* leave my instructions
My. 363–23 misunderstood by some *s·*.
students'
Mis. 155–20 First, that you, her students' *s·*,
316– 5 chapter sub-title
such
Mis. 264–22 Such *s·* are more or less subject
317–27 Such *s·* should not pay the
No. 43–22 Such *s·* come to my College
My. 197–15 Comparing such *s·* with those
taught
My. 215– 7 taught *s·* for a tuition of
their
Mis. 137–29 organize their *s·* into associations,
138– 1 their *s·* will sustain themselves
203– 8 from my students and their *s·*,
303– 8 teaching and guiding their *s·*.
315–25 nor allow their *s·* to do thus,
315–28 strive to educate their *s·*
315–32 They shall teach their *s·*
Ret. 85– 4 band together their *s·* into
89–24 to take charge of their *s·*,
No. 3–16 and recommend it to their *s·*,
their own
Ret. 89–24 or for neglecting their own *s·*,
these
Mis. 349–21 some of these *s·* have openly
Ret. 43–19 These *s·* of mine were the only
thirty-three
Mis. 315–13 consist of not over thirty-three *s·*,
those
Mis. 357–22 those *s·* of C. S.
Pan. 10–15 present and future of those *s·*
those very
My. 215–11 those very *s·* sent me the
thy
Mis. 318– 1 chapter sub-title
318– 6 not alone for . . . but for thy *s·*,
to fit
Rud. 16– 5 will never undertake to fit *s·* for
to qualify
Mis. 43–19 to qualify *s·* for the great ordeal
treat
Mis. 243– 6 although *s·* treat sprains,
true-hearted
Mis. 301–19 question of my true-hearted *s·*,
two
My. 243–14 two *s·* who are adequate to
unchristian
Rud. 16–25 among unchristian *s·*,
unprincipled
Mis. 265–30 self-satisfied, unprincipled *s·*.
Western
My. 197–13 of our far Western *s·*,

students

wise
Mis.	393–13	S· wise, he maketh now
Po.	51–18	S· wise, he maketh now

with Mrs. Eddy
Man.	69–21	S· with Mrs. Eddy.

with the degree
Mis.	349– 6	s· with the degree of M. D.,

your
Mis.	54–19	*treatment by one of your s·.*
	54–25	*Because none of your s· have*
	119–29	manipulate your s·, . . . No !
	203– 4	between my students and your s· ;
My.	63– 6	* gratefully your s·,
	319–18	* observation of many of your s·,
	358–19	was given you by your s·.
	359–29	allowing your s· to deify you
	359–30	get your s· to help you

Mis.	ix– 7	among my thousands of s·
	11–13	my whole duty to s·.
	32– 3	*s· of disloyal students*
	32– 8	the s· of false teachers,
	87–17	*to look after the s·;*
	91–28	I supposed that s· had
	92–19	require the s· . . . to study it
	138– 9	For s· to work together
	156– 6	chapter sub-title
	263–16	The need of . . . felt by s·,
	280–18	s· of this Primary class,
	284–10	S· who strictly adhere to the right,
	298–24	chapter sub-title
	302–19	s· working faithfully for Christ's
	302–32	I recommend that s· stay
	311– 7	to Christian Scientists' s·,
	317– 1	To the s· whom I have not seen
	318– 6	for s· of the second generation.
	348–29	have by no means encouraged s· of
	358–30	When s· have fulfilled all the
Man.	17– 5	s· of Mrs. Mary Baker Eddy
	35–12	s· of the Massachusetts Metaphysical
	73– 9	or s· in any university
	88–17	is not to be consulted by s·
	109– 8	s· of the Board of Education
Ret.	36– 7	writing out my manuscripts for s·
	47– 4	S· from all over our continent,
	48–22	s· instructed in C. S. Mind-healing,
	50–29	S· are not environed with such
	78–11	I recommend s· not to
	81– 4	Nothing except sin, in the s·
	83– 7	S· whom I have taught,
	91–22	s· whom he had chosen,
Pul.	79– 9	* as s· of public questions
Rud.	14–19	furnished s· with the means of
	15–14	besides invalids for s·,
No.	7–20	s· must now fight their own battles.
Pan.	10–11	s· at the Massachusetts Metaphysical
'01.	21– 4	s· of a demonstrable Science
	29–29	this percentage," s· wrote me,
My.	26–21	*the lie that s· worship me*
	125–21	s· in my last class in 1898
	130– 9	s· seeking only public notoriety,
	190–22	gave his disciples (s·) power over
	236–29	it will greatly aid the s·
	241– 6	* S· who are ready for this step
	244– 6	if . . . were advantageous to the s·.
	245–22	s· . . . have received certificates,
	245–32	to s· of the Primary class,
	246– 5	* S· who enter the . . . College,
	251– 7	* s·, whom I have taught,
	253–19	chapter sub-title
	302–14	I begged the s· who first

students'
Mis.	93– 1	able to empty his s· minds,
	138–23	members of s· organizations.
	155–20	her s· students, who write such
	266–26	in accordance with my s· desires,
	316– 5	chapter sub-title
	380–19	my s· patients, and people generally,
Man.	36– 4	S· Pupils.
Ret.	84–21	to empty his s· minds of error,

studied
Mis.	58–10	*that she has read and s· correctly,*
	147–26	for he acts no s· part ;
	318–16	s· thoroughly "S. and H.
	318–20	student must have s· faithfully
	344– 5	have you s· music, astronomy, and
	344–11	had not s· those branches,
	375–12	* s· the old masters and their great
Man.	35–13	s· with Rev. Mary Baker Eddy,
	35–18	who have not s· C. S. with
	111–10	s· C. S. with an authorized teacher ;
	111–12	not s· C. S. with a teacher.
Ret.	10–10	My brother s· Hebrew
	47–20	s· thoroughly S. and H.,

studied
Ret.	47–24	s· the latest editions of my works,
	75–22	s· a textbook written by
Pul.	64–15	* She s· the Scriptures and
	73– 9	* s· and meditated over His
My.	60– 8	* told that I had s· with you.
	239– 7	In the ratio that C. S. is s·

studies
Mis.	64–10	*take for preliminary s·?*
Ret.	10– 7	My favorite s· were
Pul.	46–23	* applied herself, . . . to her s·,
Pan.	3–23	(one of my girlhood s·),
My.	113– 5	s· it and thereby is healed
	237– 9	his earliest s· or discoveries.
	304– 5	finished my course of s·
	304– 7	Among my early s· were

studio
My.	259– 1	take a peep into my s· ;

study (noun)

and foundation
Pul.	71–20	* the s· and foundation of the faith

careful
Pul.	64–20	* After careful s· she became
My.	237–23	I recommend its careful s·

close
Pan.	7–18	close s· of the Old and New

continue the
Mis.	92–23	continue the s· of this textbook.

incessant
Ret.	7– 9	* intense and almost incessant s·

more
Mis.	366– 4	requires more s· to understand
No.	11–19	requires more s· to understand

observation or
Mis.	308–33	from their observation or s·

of literature
Mis.	64–10	*s· of literature and languages*

of music
Mis.	375–15	* s· of music and art.

of Science and Health
My.	112–26	conscientious s· of S. and H.

pastor's
Pul.	27– 7	* class-rooms and the pastor's s·.
	58–23	* Adjoining . . . is a pastor's s· ;

prayerful
My.	48–11	* prayerful s· of the Bible,

proper
Mis.	48–26	proper s· of Mind-healing would

searching
Pul.	73–20	* a careful and searching s·

unbiased
My.	96–15	* intelligent and unbiased s·

weary with
Mis.	236– 8	and become weary with s·

without
Mis.	279–15	from which we learn without s·.

Mis.	156–18	through the s· of my works
	284–11	make the Bible and S. and H. a s·,
	317–14	by the s· of what is written.

study (verb)
Mis.	5–11	Many say, "I should like to s·,
	35–18	*if one is obliged to s·*
	35–22	and then s· it at college
	38–25	*Is it necessary to s· your Science*
	54–17	*Must I s· your Science in order to*
	87–24	s· thoroughly the Scriptures
	91–31	to require their pupils to s· the
	92– 7	needs continually to s· this textbook.
	92–20	to s· it before the recitations ;
	315–29	to s· His revealed Word,
	375–20	* s· each illustration thoroughly,
Man.	83–21	to s· the Scriptures and S. AND H.
Ret.	83–26	s· each lesson before the recitation.
	84– 4	should continue to s· this textbook,
	84–12	continue to s· and assimilate this
No.	28–19	S· C. S. and practise it,
'01.	34–23	s· the Bible and the textbook

studying
Mis.	5– 9	by s· this scientific method
	48–23	*made insane by s· metaphysics?*
	310– 1	s· Truth through the senses,
Hea.	12–14	When s· the . . . remedies of the Jahr,
My.	323–30	* s· in the second class with you

stuff
Mis.	227–11	to get their weighty s· into the
	354– 7	to overbalance this foul s·.
My.	313–11	Nor do I remember any such s·

stuffed
My.	99–20	* s· and jammed with money.

stultifies
Mis.	288–32	s· and causes him to degenerate
Un.	36–24	This error s· the logic of
No.	3–19	Dishonesty necessarily s· the

stultify
Mis.	221–15	will s· the power to heal mentally.
Un.	25– 3	s· my intellect, insult my

stultifying
Mis.	265– 9	Diverse opinions in Science are s·.

stumble
Mis.	10–12	stronger than before the s·.
	264– 6	others s· over misdeeds,
	328–24	causing to s·, fall, or faint,
Pul.	7–21	s· onward to their doom ;
My.	11– 3	* although we may falter or s·
	152–19	s· into doubt and darkness,

stumbled
Mis.	328–17	hast thou turned back, s·,

stumbling
Mis.	327–29	s· and grumbling, and fighting

stung
Pul.	13–24	dragon is at last s· to death
'01.	31– 1	world-worshipper are always s· by

stunning
My.	71–10	* a s· piece of architecture

stupefied
Mis.	328–19	pleased and s·, until wakened

stupendous
Mis.	99– 7	The risk is s·.
	213–10	No risk is so s· as
	380–11	impelled me to begin this s· work
My.	14– 8	s·, Godlike agency of man.
	97–16	* s·, inexplicable faith
	97–29	* produced by that s· gathering.
	165–17	portion of one s· whole,
	269–12	* parts of one s· whole,

stupid
Mis.	343–22	O s· gardener !
	398– 8	Break earth's s· rest.
Ret.	46–14	Break earth's s· rest.
Pul.	17–13	Break earth's s· rest.
Po.	14–12	Break earth's s· rest.

sturdy
Mis.	240–17	while the s· oak, with form
Ret.	2– 2	s· Calvinistic devotion to
	17–19	s· horse-chestnut for centuries
Po.	63– 5	s· horse-chestnut for centuries

Stygian
No.	22–14	as S· night to the kindling dawn.
My.	350–21	S· shadow of a world of glee) ;

style
Mis.	294–27	terse, graphic, and poetic s·
	366–17	new s· of imposition in the field
Pul.	59–20	* in a clear emphatic s·.
No.	10– 8	The former is the highest s· of man ;
My.	68– 1	* Italian Renaissance s·,
	309–24	prevailing s· of architecture
	318– 2	constituted a new s· of language.

styled
'01.	24– 6	s· the laws of nature.

subdivide
Ret.	56–23	does not s· Mind, or good,
Un.	44–16	would multiply and s· personality

subdivided
No.	26– 4	s· into spirits, or souls,

subdivides
Ret.	28–19	which divides, s·, increases,

subdivision
Ret.	56–20	by the reflection, not the s·,

subdue
Un.	42–17	ability to s· material conditions.
Pul.	84– 2	* shall s· the whole earth with the
No.	11–26	Revelation must s· the sophistry of

subdued
Mis.	2–12	s· and recompensed by justice,
	200–30	s· it with this understanding.
	354–17	a character s·, a life consecrated,
Ret.	58– 8	sense of power that s· matter
My.	290–26	him who suffered and s· sorrow.

subdues
Mis.	74– 3	new-born sense s· not only the
My.	131– 2	removes fear, s· sin, and

subduing
'02.	10–13	subjugating the body, s· matter,
Po.	68–11	Enchant deep the senses, — s·,

subject (noun)
abstract
Mis.	38–15	*such a dry and abstract s·?*

considering a
Mis.	271–15	considering a s· that is unworthy

following
Mis.	349–22	a question on the following s·,

for lessons
Man.	62–24	S· for Lessons.
My.	231–29	By-law, "S· for Lessons"

general
My.	107– 6	general s· under discussion,

given out
Mis.	350– 8	s· given out for consideration
	350–15	s· given out at that meeting was,

gives the
My.	234–20	gives the s· quite another aspect.

great
Mis.	7–32	enlightened on this great s·.
Hea.	1–12	great s· of Christian healing ;
My.	339– 8	great s· of C. S.

greater
Mis.	65– 9	greater s· of human weal and woe

her
My.	346– 3	* as one who has lived with her s·

important
Un.	1– 8	reason together on this important s·,

inexhaustible
Ret.	84–13	assimilate this inexhaustible s·

interest in the
My.	322–28	* Seeing my great interest in the s·,

leaves the
Mis.	188–19	and right there he leaves the s·.

leave the
Ret.	63–25	and leave the s· there.
Un.	1–16	better leave the s· untouched,

my
Pan.	13–27	only traversed my s· that you may
'02.	4–13	My s· to-day embraces the

new
Un.	7– 2	apprehension of this new s·,

of Christian Science
Mis.	382– 3	No works on the s· of C. S.
My.	125–24	looking into the s· of C. S.,
	339– 8	the great s· of C. S.

of mental practice
Man.	90–20	s· of mental practice and *malpractice.*

of sin
Mis.	115– 4	s· of sin and mental malpractice,

of the Trinity
My.	338– 7	* upon the s· of the Trinity,

our
Mis.	188–16	On our s·, St. Paul first reasons

said
Man.	67–16	conferred with her on said s·.
	70– 6	first consulting her on said s·
	90–22	shall prepare a paper on said s·

same
My.	322–13	* letter to you on the same s·;

scarcely awakes
Mis.	222–18	the s· scarcely awakes in time,

settle the
Pul.	9–15	and helped settle the s·.

silence on the
My.	104–21	reason for his silence on the s·,

takes up the
My.	217–29	Jesus . . . first takes up the s·.

that
Mis.	306– 6	* any ideas on that s·
Man.	94–13	depart in quiet *thought* on that s·.

this
Mis.	32–14	will find my views on this s·;
	44– 4	are ready to investigate this s·,
	76–18	his authority on this s·
	115–11	ignorance of the community on this s·
	130– 9	What do we find . . . on this s·?
	130–15	Note the Scripture on this s· :
	156–17	read "Retrospection" on this s·.
	185–29	When reasoning on this s· of man
	192–25	Mark is emphatic on this s·;
	193–18	modification of silence on this s·,
	269– 6	Hear the Master on this s· :
	310–24	action of the church on this s·.
	348–32	consulted me on this s·,
	382–16	the first books on this s·;
Man.	59– 4	at random on this s·,
	87– 7	not to be consulted on this s·.
Ret.	35– 9	before a work on this s· could
Un.	5–16	force conclusions on this s·
	7–17	views here promulgated on this s·
	31–21	This s· can be enlarged.
Pul.	80–16	* On this s· we have no opinion
Rud.	15–20	grapple with this s·,
No.	32–11	Frequently when I touch this s·
'01.	14–11	Our only departure . . . on this s· is,
	21–25	knows more than any man on this s·,

subject (noun)
this
'01. 26–25 this s· of the old metaphysicians,
      27–11 correct on this s·
'02.   5–30 silences all questions on this s·,
My. 250–24 favored moment to act on this s·.
    256–13 close the door of mind on this s·,
    303– 6 Scriptures relative to this s·.
this very
Mis. 32–12 and in my books, on this very s·.
whole
Un. 36–10 This whole s· is met
My. 363–23 gist of the whole s· was not to
works on the
Mis. 382– 3 No works on the s· of C. S.
———
Mis. 4–20 on the s· of metaphysical healing,
    116–10 S·: Obedience.
    132– 2 on a s· the substance whereof you
    146–11 regarding both sides of the s·,
    161– 4 S·: The Corporeal and Incorporeal
    299–26 this question on the s·,
Man. 58–11 The s· of the Lesson-Sermon
Ret. 35– 7 so unfamiliar with the s·
Pul. 72– 7 * conversations upon the s·.
Rud. 11–26 the s· of human anatomy ;
      15–25 a s· laid bare for anatomical
No.   13–23 on the s· of mediumship,
Pan.   1– 4 S·: Not Pantheism, but C. S.
'01. 26–29 on the s· of metaphysical healing
My.   33– 8 * s· of the special Lesson-Sermon
      53–31 * address them on the s·.
      60– 4 * to instruct them on the s·
      97–10 * kept no books on the s·,
    151–22 S·: "Not Matter, but Spirit"
    281–22 * on some phase of the s·,
    294– 2 on the s· of divine metaphysics ;
    305– 8 the s· of "vulgar metaphysics,"
    338–12 s· "The Unknown God Made Known,"
subject (adj. and verb)
Mis. 36–25 not s· to the law of God, — Rom. 8 : 7.
      39– 4 To avoid being s· to disease,
      54–22 But not to be s· again to
      82–31 not s· to growth, change, or
    104– 4 not s· to the temptations of
    264–22 Such students are more or less s· to
    284– 5 C. S., . . . is s· to abuses.
    338–15 will s·,one to deception ;
    341–25 is s· to terrible torture if the
Man. 25– 9 s· to the approval of
      28– 1 s· to the approval of
      46–17 failure to do this shall s· the
      63–22 s· to the approval of
      65–23 shall be s· to the approval of
      78–14 and be s· to the approval of
      80– 7 hold this money s· to the order of
      80–21 s· to her approval.
      88–14 shall be s· to the approval of
      93– 7 s· to the approval of
Ret. 48– 8 s· to the one builder and maker,
No.   41–15 to s· them to severe scrutiny.
'01. 19–24 to s· mankind unwarned and
'02. 11– 5 s· to sin, disease, and death.
Peo. 11–11 is made s· to his Maker.
subjected
Ret. 71–15 Who is willing to be s· to such
subjection
Mis. 67–28 without his s· to death,
    201– 6 into s· to Spirit.
subjective
Mis. 24–18 s· state which it names matter,
      73–20 s· states of false sensation
      86–26 s· state of high thoughts.
    102–26 s· state of mortal . . . thought.
    105–25 their own s· state of thought.
    260–16 sickness, and death are its s· states ;
    266– 8 s· state of his own mind
    286–22 s· states of the human . . . mind ;
    367– 5 Matter and evil are s· states of
Rud. 10–10 from the s· states of thought,
No.   14– 7 s· states of mortal mind.
      16–11 The s· states of evil,
My. 109– 1 s· state of mortal mind.
    265–26 reflect this purified s· state
subject-matter
Ret. 82–29 makes the s· clearer than any
subjects
Mis. 146–13 declined to be consulted on these s·,
    317–21 s· of such earnest import.
    339– 2 confine their talk to s· that are
    350–20 misconception of those s·
Man. 53–13 trouble her on s· unnecessarily
      88–20 s· essential to their progress.
Rud.   2– 6 s·, or agents, constituting the

subjects
Hea.   9–12 s· they would gladly discontinue to
      16–17 leave our abstract s· for this time.
      16–26 that we look into these s·,
Peo.   7–25 appeal to mind to improve its s·
My. 242–22 not to make inquiries on these s·,
    338–16 their s· or the handling thereof,
    345–31 * We talked on many s·,
subjugate
Un.   50– 9 s· it as Jesus did,
subjugated
Mis. 118– 1 Human will must be s·.
subjugates
Mis. 260–17 s· and destroys any suppositional
'02. 10– 1 Whatever . . . s· matter, has a fight
subjugating
'02. 10–13 it is s· the body,
subjugation
Mis. 361– 1 rather was it their s·,
sublime
Mis. 131–10 substance of our s· faith,
    137–22 the s· ends of human life.
    163– 7 a s· and everlasting victory !
    227–25 s· summary of an honest life
    369– 8 to stand erect on s· heights,
    393– 5 Soul, s· 'mid human débris,
Ret. 92– 2 not too simple to be s·,
Un.   58–14 Master's s· triumph over all
Pul.   2–25 would overthrow this s· fortress,
'02. 16–21 The meek might, s· patience,
Po.   39– 4 Temperance and truth in song s·
      51–10 Soul, s· 'mid human débris,
      68–11 rock and the sea . . . subduing, s· ;
My. 121– 8 strength of peace . . . is s·,
    189– 3 started in this s· ascent,
    277–12 answer to the s· question
sublimity
Mis. 88–24 * those who do not enter into its s·
My.   25–25 s· of this superb superstructure,
sublunary
Pul.   2–11 Turning the attention from s·
Hea. 11– 2 survey the cost of s· joy,
submarine
'02. 11–13 a steam engine, a s· cable,
submerge
My. 259–28 too much to s· itself
submerged
Mis. 184–32 s· in the humane and divine,
'01.   9– 8 s· them in a sense so pure
My. 179– 8 power and . . . are s· in matter.
submit
Mis. 65– 8 s· to the affirmations of Science
    208–11 Mortals have only to s· to the
Man. 77– 6 Treasurer of this Church shall s· them
My.   26–19 enclosed notice I s· to you,
    219–30 that an individual s· to this process,
    220– 3 s· to the providence of God,
    299–10 I s· that C. S. has been widely
submitted
Mis. 271–29 * statistics are officially s· :
My. 195–10 so have s· to necessity,
    213–29 three quotations . . . are s·
    314–19 After the evidence had been s·
subordinate
Mis. 29–30 matter is proven powerless and s· to
Un.   46–11 would s· the fleshly perceptions
Rud. 16– 6 s· to thorough class instruction
My. 265– 6 less s· to material sight
subordinated
'02.   5–12 s· to this commandment,
My. 303–21 His life-work s· the material
subordinates
Mis. 23– 8 s· so-called material laws ;
    189–24 spiritual power that s· matter
Un.   40– 9 s· the belief in death,
No.   24–13 evil s· good in personality.
subordination
Ret. 50–20 s· of the human to the divine,
Rud. 12–25 from any sense of s· to their
My.   48–23 * the s· of merely material
    194–12 in a complete s· of self.
subscribe
Man. 44–18 to s· for the periodicals
My. 299–20 firmly s· to this statement ;
    353– 1 s· for and read our daily newspaper.
    360–15 cheerfully s· these words of love :

subscribed
Pul. 52– 3 * no sums except those already s·
My. 10–14 * donation to be specifically s·
     57–30 * no sums except those already s·
     72–25 * two million dollars has been s·

subscribing
Mis. 281–27 responsibility you assume when s· to

subscription
Mis. 144– 9 s· list on which appear your
My. 77–30 * secured by voluntary s·.

subscriptions
Pul. 50–15 * no . . . sums outside of the s·
My. 14–16 * further payments or s· were not
     89–16 * s· are not solicited.

subsequent
Mis. xi– 4 the initial "G" on my s· books.
Man. 104–16 s· editions of the Church Manual ;
Pul. 31–10 * s· development of some degree of
My. 86–12 * s· ceremonies and exercises.
     303–28 her duplicate, antecedent, or s·.
     304–20 for ten s· years he
     320–22 * several times s· thereto,

subsequently
Mis. 35– 4 and s· her recovery,
     191– 5 S·, the ancients changed the meaning
Po. v–21 * which was s· mailed to them.

subserve
Mis. 246– 8 to s· the interests of wealth,
My. 147–14 May this little sanctum . . . s· it.
     339– 1 s· the interest of mankind,

subserved
My. 278– 3 s· by the battle's plan

subserves
My. 4–17 such an individual s· the

subsidence
My. 40– 8 * imply the s· of criticism

subsides
Pul. 50–25 * after a little skirmishing, finally s·.
Rud. 15–11 until this impulse s·.

subsist
My. 216– 8 s· on demand and supply,

substance
actual
  Hea. 16– 7 which to you hath the most actual s·,
all
  Mis. 199–26 all s·, Life, and intelligence
and immortality
  Un. 60–23 s·, and immortality be lost.
and intelligence
  Mis. 309–12 spiritual s· and intelligence.
  Hea. 16– 5 Life, s·, and intelligence
and life
  Mis. 187–21 s·, and life of man are one,
and mind
  Ret. 21–21 false sense of life, s·, and mind
and penmanship
  My. 137– 9 * in both s· and penmanship :
and practicality
  Mis. 193– 8 s· and practicality of all
and reality
  My. 109– 2 no more s· and reality in our
becomes the
  Mis. 391–13 And Love becomes the s·,
  Po. 38–12 Love becomes the s·,
called matter
  Un. 33– 5 existence of a s· called matter.
constant
  Ret. 32–17 * Whose most constant s· seems
divine
  Mis. 68– 1 fact of divine s·, intelligence,
falls short of
  My. 260–15 sense that falls short of s·,
her
  My. 19–21 her s·, the immortal fruition of
his
  Mis. 167–11 His s· outweighs the material
intelligence, nor
  Mis. 21–17 intelligence, nor s· in matter.
its
  Ret. 23–22 its s·, cause, and currents
  My. 295– 5 holds its s· safe in the
Life, and
  Mis. 55–25 the only Mind, Life, and s·.
life, . . . and intelligence
  Mis. 175– 6 sense of life, s·, and intelligence,
     218– 9 of life, s·, and intelligence,
  Ret. 67– 7 that life, s·, and intelligence are
Life's
  My. 290–20 passed earth's shadow into Life's s·.
make room for
  My. 260– 7 to make room for s·,

substance
material
  Un. 24–16 There is no material s·,
means more
  Mis. 47– 6 s· means more than matter :
mortal sense of
  Mis. 28– 1 Take away the mortal sense of s·,
nor intelligence
  Ret. 93–20 s·, nor intelligence in matter."
of Christian Science
  Mis. 357–31 Divine Love is the s· of C. S.,
  My. 37–22 * the s· of C. S.,
of form
  Mis. 87– 9 spiritual reality and s· of form,
of God
  Mis. 104– 7 yea, the s· of God,
     187–24 Did the s· of God, Spirit,
of good
  Mis. 103–12 who knoweth the s· of good?"
  Ret. 57–16 is . . . the s· of good.
  Un. 61–18 is . . . not the s· of good.
of life
  Mis. 103–11 say . . . "The s· of life is sorrow
of my Address
  Mis. 98– 7 S· of my Address at the National
of my reply
  Mis. 287–23 the s· of my reply is :
of Soul
  Mis. 104– 6 safe in the s· of Soul,
of Spirit
  Mis. 56– 8 s· of Spirit is divine Mind.
     104– 7 the s· of Spirit, . . .of God,
  Un. 45–25 It lacks the s· of Spirit,
of the truth
  My. 130–30 s· of the truth that is taught ;
of things
  Mis. 27–30 s· of things hoped for." — Heb. 11 : 1.
     103– 9 s· of things not hoped for.
     175–11 s· of things hoped for." — Heb. 11 : 1.
  Pan. 15– 8 "s· of things hoped for" — Heb. 11 : 1.
  My. 226–18 "s· of things hoped for ;" — Heb. 11 : 1.
of this textbook
  Ret. 75–24 the s· of this textbook
of Truth
  '01. 18–14 s· of Truth transcends the
or intelligence
  My. 235–19 Matter as s· or intelligence never was
or law
  '02. 6– 3 knowledge of life, s·, or law,
or Life
  Mis. 367– 8 error is not Mind, s·, or Life.
or mind
  Mis. 198–10 claim to . . . s·, or mind in matter,
  My. 296–16 dream of life, s·, or mind in matter,
people of
  My. 80– 3 * people of s· and of standing,
physical
  '01. 23–27 declared physical s· to be "only
real
  Un. 34–26 Immortal Mind is the real s·,
reality and
  Un. 49–10 reality and s· of being are good,
reflection is
  Ret. 57–16 and this reflection is s·,
sense of
  Mis. 86–20 gain the glorified sense of s·
  Un. 60–27 This false sense of s· must yield to
sign and
  My. 354–18 Sweet sign and s·
so-called
  Un. 34–22 its own so-called s·,
solid
  Mis. 5–30 can seem solid s· to this thought.
Soul and
  Mis. 145– 7 to express Soul and s·.
Soul, is
  Mis. 103– 4 Spirit, Soul, is s·,
Spirit is
  Ret. 57–17 Spirit is s· in Truth.
spiritual
  Mis. 27–30 a type of spiritual s·,
     309–12 spiritual s· and intelligence.
  Rud. 5–12 who has ever seen spiritual s·
  My. 226–18 spiritual "s· of things — Heb. 11 : 1.
the only
  Mis. 47–21 Spirit, is the only s· ;
     200– 9 while God was the only s·,
     361–26 the only s· and divine Principle
  Un. 24–17 and hence is the only s·.
     25– 6 Spirit is the only s·.
     25– 5 good is the only s·,
to translate
  Mis. 74–16 mission was to translate s·
true
  Mis. 103–15 dwell . . . as tangible, true s·,

substance

visionary

Un. 45–24 the visionary *s·* of matter.

Mis. 18–14 in every God-quality, even in *s·* ;
27–31 know a stone as *s·*, only by
47– 5 adipose belief of yourself as *s·* ;
56– 7 If Mind is not *s·*, form, and
74–23 theory that matter is *s·* ;
74–31 matter is neither *s·*, intelligence,
103– 3 which say that . . . *s·* is perishable.
103– 8 as . . . mortals virtually name *s·* ;
103–10 lack of knowing what *s·* is,
131–10 *s·* of our sublime faith,
132– 2 subject the *s·* whereof you had
239– 8 *s·* is taking larger proportions.
272–11 * "The *s·* of this Act is at present
301– 8 periodicals whose *s·* is made up of
349–20 My counsel to all of them was in *s·*
350–15 The subject . . . was, in *s·*,
378–17 He answered . . . in *s·*,
381–14 and he replied, in *s·*,
Ret. 25–14 Soul I denominated *s·*,
57–17 Matter is *s·* in error,
93–18 This statement is in *s·* identical
Un. 24–23 *Evil.* . . . I am *s·*.
31–13 claim . . . that matter is *s·* ;
32–13 destroys all sense of matter as *s·*,
34–20 could not feel what it calls *s·*.
34–25 What is *s·* ?
Pul. 20–16 whose *s·* is the divine Spirit,
Rud. 1– 8 It is *s·*, Spirit, Life, Truth,
No. 20–10 This Principle is Mind, *s·*, Life,
35–18 Life, *s·*, Soul, and intelligence
35–21 God is the only Mind, Life, *s·*,
Pan. 12–24 Life, Truth, Love, *s·*, Spirit,
My. 81–32 * people of standing and of *s·*,
146– 9 The statement in my letter . . . in *s·*
339–20 he answered them in *s·* :

substanceless

Mis. 56– 8 If . . . God is *s·* ;
361– 5 its substances are found *s·*,

substances

Mis. 361– 5 its *s·* are found substanceless,

substantial

Mis. 27–32 first admitting that it is *s·*.
247–24 seems, . . . solid and *s·*.
Ret. 25–15 Soul alone is truly *s·*.
Un. 34–19 What evidence . . . that matter is *s·*,
Pul. 45– 2 * and some *s·* sums.
49–22 * there to build a *s·* home
My. 24–23 * *s·* and enduring character of its

substantially

Ret. 89– 5 preaching and teaching were *s·*

substantiated

Ret. 35–20 and its claim is *s·*,

substantiates

Mis. 47–23 *s·* man's identity,
No. 38– 5 God *s·* their evidence
44– 1 *s·* his ignorance of its Principle

substitute

Mis. 278–25 *s·* my own for their growth,
Man. 65– 1 and to *s·* Leader,
92– 6 nothing can *s·* this demonstration.
Ret. 58– 6 false, and finite *s·*.
No. 8– 5 whenever it can *s·* censure.
21–13 and *s·* matter and evil
'01. 2–10 to *s·* good words for good deeds,
My. 226– 2 use it only where you can *s·*

substituted

Mis. 92–25 cannot be *s·* for God's revelation.
Ret. 84–14 cannot be *s·* for God's revelation.

substitutes

Mis. 122–22 nor *s·* the suffering of the
No. 5–12 *s·* for Truth an unreal belief,
My. 197–16 those whose words are but the *s·*

substituting

Mis. 233–18 *S·* good words for a good life,
310– 4 misused by *s·* personality

substitution

Mis. 75–19 a *s·* of *sense* for *soul*
121–32 *s·* of a good man to suffer
334–26 *s·* of Truth demonstrated,
Pul. 62– 5 * They are a *s·* of tubes

substratum

No. 16–26 matter is the *s·* of evil,

subterfuge

Ret. 78–17 a resort to *s·* in the statement

subtle

Mis. 24–30 put down all *s·* falsities
26– 7 in the most *s·* ether,
108–19 evil and its *s·* workings
191– 5 "more *s·* than— *Gen.* 3 : 1.
335–12 for opposing the *s·* lie,
363–27 exposes the *s·* sophist.
Ret. 63–20 more *s·*, more difficult to heal.
My. 14–22 * *s·* lie with which to ensnare
128–25 as does a *s·* conspirator ;
150–31 to call this "a *s·* fraud,"

subtler

Mis. 115–23 against the *s·* forms of evil,
Rud. 7– 5 *s·* conceptions and consistencies
No. 31– 6 appear to-day in *s·* forms

subtlest

No. 41–16 *s·* forms of sin are trying

subtleties

Mis. 112– 2 with the *s·* of sin !
196– 6 in all manner of *s·*

subtlety

Mis. 36–13 passions, anger, revenge, *s·*,
361–22 *s·* of speculative wisdom
Ret. 64–27 forms, methods, and *s·* of error,
Rud. 6–15 * this is not "any metaphysical *s·*,"
No. 35–10 also the drear *s·* of death.

subtly

Ret. 85–13 the *s·* hidden suggestion
My. 213–16 working so *s·* that we mistake

subtracted

'00. 10–19 not added but *s·* from

subtraction

Mis. 60–16 to say that addition is not *s·*
Ret. 59– 9 saying that addition means *s·*
Un. 53–18 assertion that . . . is the rule of *s·*,

suburbs

Ret. 17– 2 in the beautiful *s·* of Boston.
Po. vii– 2 * *in the beautiful s· of Boston*);
My. 56–10 * churches in such *s·* of Boston
56–23 * established in other *s·*,

subversion

Mis. 31–10 *s·* of right is not scientific.

subvert

Mis. 302–30 to *s·* or to liquidate.

subverts

Mis. 31– 7 *s·* the scientific laws

succeed

Mis. 6–16 Truth must ultimately *s·*
31–22 *s·* with his wrong argument,
216–28 * the attempt . . . may *s·*,
Pul. 83–19 * She must and will *s·*,
My. 166– 4 fail to *s·* and fall to the earth.

succeeded

Mis. 110–27 defense of Truth, and have *s·*.
Ret. 6–23 In 1837 he *s·* to the law-office
Pul. 45–25 * *s·* by the grandest of ministers
My. 31– 1 * *s·* by the following hymns
340–29 *s·* by our time of abundance,

succeeding

Pul. 38– 6 * During these *s·* twenty years
My. 177–18 *s·* years show in livid lines that

succeeds

My. 108– 2 *s·* as well . . . without drugs
193–23 * if it *s·*, it is a right thing."

success

achieving
Mis. 266–23 toiling and achieving *s·*
Christian
Mis. 120–14 Christian *s·* is under arms,
conspicuous
My. 272–26 * leads with such conspicuous *s·*
desires
Mis. 32– 1 if indeed he desires *s·* in this
doctor's
Mis. 229–11 doctor's *s·*, and the clergyman's
each
'02. 13– 3 each *s·* incurred a sharper fire from
element of
Pul. 53–20 * essential element of *s·* in
essential to
Pul. 54–21 * conditions . . . that are essential to *s·*.
fail of
Mis. 147–30 rather fail of *s·* than attain it by
genuine
'02. 14–11 The only genuine *s·* possible
good
My. 246– 9 practised C. S. . . . with good *s·*.
her
My. 64–18 * her *s·* in so doing is what

success
his
My. 165– 1 promote and pervade all his s·
honor and
'01. 29–22 All honor and s· to those who
in healing
No. 2–22 and some marked s· in healing
in life
Mis. 230– 2 S· in life depends upon
in sin
Mis. 354– 4 sanguine of s· in sin,
'00. 10– 1 S· in sin is downright defeat.
insures
My. 287–23 systematizes action, and insures s· ;
is dangerous
My. 283–29 Lured by fame, . . . s· is dangerous,
its
Mis. 365–14 secret of its s· lies in supplying
labor and
My. 197–11 labor and s· in completing
motive and
My. 236–19 a far-reaching motive and s·,
never-ending
My. 357–20 to their never-ending s·,
no
Ret. 79–17 cometh no s· in Truth.
of a student
Mis. v– 6 CONSTITUTE THE S· OF A STUDENT
of Christian Science
My. 234–16 s· of C. S. in benighted
of honesty
Mis. 252–29 secures the s· of honesty.
of others
My. 212–28 hindering . . . the s· of others.
of this church
My. 195–24 praiseworthy s· of this church,
secures
Mis. 135–11 conquers all . . . and secures s·.
social
My. 184–23 rural chapel is a social s·
sure of
My. 203–19 sincerity is sure of s·,
temporary
Mis. 43–26 occasional temporary s· of such
tend to
My. 274–12 tend to s·, intellectuality,
their
My. 219– 6 honor of their s· in teaching
357–17 estimate their s· and glory
the only
'02. 14–12 the only s· I have ever achieved
thy
Mis. 340–23 however slow, thy s· is sure :
without
Ret. 21– 6 employed . . . but without s·.
your own
Ret. 78–24 against your own s·
zenith of
My. 225– 4 rising to the zenith of s·,

Mis. 59–23 s· that one individual has with
204–27 gives . . . s· to endeavor.
228–14 momentary s· of all villainies,
267–29 crowns them with s· ;
My. 244–31 s· of this Christian system of
282–22 interest you manifest in the s· of

successful
Mis. 5–20 metaphysics comes in, . . . and is s·.
43–12 make safe and s· practitioners.
171– 4 first effort . . . was not wholly s· ;
230– 6 If one would be s· in the future,
230–14 s· individuals have become such
305–13 * in making the undertaking s·.
340–20 The conscientious are s·.
Ret. 7–16 * s· practice of a very large
42–12 remarkably s· in Mind-healing,
53– 3 had been made s· and prosperous
Un. 17– 1 one chance of s· deception,
No. 6–15 mistaken healer is not s·,
'00. 2–29 he answers : "I am not so s·
9–18 Sincerity is more s· than
'01. 28–29 After a hard and s· career
'02. 14–15 s· end could never have been
My. 28–28 * It speaks for the s· labors
42–28 * and how s· she is in the
51–32 * s· instructions to heal the sick,
111–19 become s· healers and models of
213–13 they will be proportionately s·
227–20 whether s· or not,
352–28 thanks for your s· plans

successfully
Mis. 243– 7 students treat sprains, . . . s·.
Man. 89–21 practised C. S. healing s·
'00. 8–22 before we can s· war with

succession
My. 360–23 for forty years in s·.
successive
Mis. 26– 4 Each s· period of progress
56–27 and have had s· stages of
80–25 doctors, who, in s· generations
Ret. 40– 1 four s· years I healed,
52– 1 For many s· years I have
'01. 30– 6 s· utterances of reformers
successor
My. 343– 7 ask, perhaps, whether my s·
343–12 * that Mrs. Eddy's immediate s· would,
346–18 * chapter sub-title
346–22 * stated that her s· would be a
346–27 a man would be my future s·.
347– 3 and reveal my s·,
successors
Pan. 12–10 closing century, and its s·,
My. 172–22 * myself and my s· in office."
succor
Pan. 14–22 May the divine Love s· and
succored
Peo. 10– 8 s· a fugitive slave in 1853,
such
Mis. 6–24 uselessness of s· material methods,
11–26 to s· as hate me,
31–10 s· a subversion of right is
31–12 S· false faith finds no place in,
32– 8 s· as have strayed from the
38–15 s· a dry and abstract subject ?
39– 9 of s· beware.
40– 2 demands s· cooperation ;
43–21 s· sinister rivalry does a vast
43–26 success of s· an one is
43–28 to recognize, as s·, the . . . errors
46–12 There are no s· indications
46–13 s· a misconception of Truth
47– 1 there is no s· thing as matter,
48– 8 If s· be its power, I am opposed
48–25 S· an occurrence would
49–31 never created error, or s· a
52– 1 to s· as seek the material
63–15 to save s· as believe in the
76– 9 s· as the mortal belief that
80– 3 By rendering error s· a service,
82– 9 S· Christians as John
95–22 to s· as are "waiting — Rom. 8 : 23.
97–11 S· suppositional healing
97–28 s· must be the personality of
103– 7 destructive forces, s· as sin,
122– 9 s· a monstrous work?
122–16 S· an inference were impious.
123–32 sensation s· as attends eating
124–15 comforting s· as mourn,
130–20 s· Herculean tasks as they
134– 5 reiterate s· words of apology
134–13 blessing s· as you never before
136– 3 routine of s· material modes
137–12 s· opportunity might have been
139– 5 blessing s· as you even yet
140– 1 s· as error could not control.
142–17 s· varying types of true affection,
145–22 s· as Isaiah prophesied :
148–11 nor dictatorial demands, s· as
155–20 write s· excellent letters to her
162– 4 of s· wonderful spiritual import
168–12 only s· as are pure in spirit,
187–32 s· as crucified our Master,
192–13 S· are the words of him who
195–15 authority for s· a conclusion,
197–15 s· an action of mind would
221–21 S· denial dethrones demonstration,
221–23 S· denial also contradicts the
226–25 s· as manages to evade the law,
230–14 have become s· by hard work ;
231–28 s· tones of heartfelt joy
233– 6 are s· in name only,
234–18 on s· unfamiliar ground,
234–21 against s· odds,
237–11 gives them s· a cup of gall
242–25 I cured precisely s· a case
262–21 opening the prison doors to s·
264–22 S· students are more or less
270– 4 of s· as barter integrity
272–21 * s· as any stock company may
272–24 * institutions, under s· charters,
276–28 S· an error and loss will
292–10 s· as eternity is ever sounding.
294–19 Love s· specimens of mortality
294–23 to help even s· as these.
295–25 s· an organization as the
295–29 with s· dignity, clemency, and
296–23 Why fall into s· patronage,
297–22 unless s· claims are relinquished

such

Mis.	306–19	* having been made s· by the
	314–31	this Lesson shall be s·
	315–14	s· as have promising proclivities
	317–21	subjects of s· earnest import.
	317–27	S· students should not pay the
	335–24	S· people say,
	337–24	s· as lived according to
	344–13	s· a material science
	344–19	S· philosophy can never
	344–22	S· philosophy is far from the
	349– 7	S· a course with s· a teacher
	350–29	teach the use of s· arguments
	351–18	nor benefit mankind by s· endeavors.
	370– 4	s· deeds of mercy,
	370–26	sophistry that s· is the true fold
	372–15	s· replies as the following :
	375–27	* gave me s· a thrill of joy
	376– 1	* attention to s· matters,
	377– 1	fashions forever s· forms,
	378–22	removed from s· thoughts
	380– 2	outward sign of s· a practice :
	385–17	diviner sense, that spurns s· toys,
	393–12	Crowns life's Cliff for s· as we.
	394–18	* S· old-time harmonies *retune*,
Man.	3– 8	dictatorial demands, s· as
	32–15	S· announcement shall be made
	37–11	notice of s· rejection ;
	46–15	also s· information as may
	48– 2	who do believe in s· doctrines,
	48–15	for s· a purpose.
	49–14	The cards of s· persons
	51– 4	to accept s· admonition.
	57– 2	transaction of s· other business
	63– 5	s· questions and answers
	64–21	s· as sister or brother.
	69– 9	s· student shall pay to Mrs. Eddy
	69–12	during the time of s· service.
	71– 8	in naming s· churches.
	71–14	to assume s· position would
	72–15	services of s· a church
	73–11	at s· university or college,
	74–18	required to acknowledge as s·
	78– 8	except s· debts as are specified
	78–23	for the payment of s· bills.
	78–23	S· payments shall be reported,
	79– 6	shall transact . . . s· business
	80–15	for s· reasons as to the Board may
	83–10	shall carefully select for pupils s·
	85–18	S· members who have not been
	89–15	s· credentials as are required
	95– 7	at s· places and at s· times
	98–12	read the *last proof sheet* of s·
	98–15	papers containing s· an article,
	102–18	incorporated in all s· deeds
Chr.	55–18	s· as I have give I thee :— *Acts* 3 : 6.
Ret.	21–27	s· narrations may be admissible
	22–10	endured s· contradiction— *Heb.* 12 : 3.
	38–13	not thought of s· a result,
	44– 4	first s· church ever organized.
	50–29	s· obstacles as were encountered
	57–27	s· opposite effects as good and evil,
	57–29	s· methods can never reach the
	59– 7	S· an inference is unscientific.
	64– 4	s· is the unity of evil ;
	65–17	constituted of s· elements as
	70–13	the recurrence of s· events.
	70–29	S· a post of duty, . . . exalts
	71–15	subjected to s· an influence?
	73–23	S· errancy betrays a
	78–13	s· works and words becloud the
	81–28	s· as first led me to the feet of
	87–26	Truth beams with s· efficacy
	88–11	It implies s· an elevation
	88–26	in s· a spiritual attitude
	90–28	to find, in s· a student,
	91–17	with s· fidelity, we see Jesus
Un.	1– 3	knows no s· thing as sin.
	1– 4	s· as the apostle Peter
	4–25	Surely from s· an understanding
	4–26	Surely from . . . s· knowing,
	6–17	far from ready to assimilate s·
	7–20	here is one s· conviction :
	13–21	S· a view would bring us upon
	14– 1	which contains s· planks as
	15–21	S· vagaries are to be found
	16– 2	s· terms as *divine sin*
	18–27	If s· knowledge of evil were
	23– 8	and Truth knows only s·.
	26–11	which leads to s· teaching
	38–12	s· misbelief must enthrone
	41–27	s· a theory implies
	50–13	really there is no s· thing as
	53–16	not built on s· false foundations,
	56–26	S· mental conditions as
	60– 1	s· thoughts — mortal inventions,

such

Un.	64–10	nearer we approximate to s· a Mind,
Pul.	3– 1	S· being its nature, how can
	3–13	S· . . . assurance ends all warfare,
	3–30	unfitness for s· a spiritual animus
	5–11	S· was the founder of the
	9– 6	the full chords of s· a rest.
	32– 9	* Of course s· a personality,
	36–10	* and s· earnestness of attention
	41–28	* others s· — were chimed until
	46– 7	* no s· inference is to be drawn
	57–15	* organization of s· a church,
	57–20	* S· is the excellent name given to
	64– 6	* s· was not the experience of
	66–21	* S· a rapid departure from
	75– 8	S· a statement would not only be
Rud.	5– 1	spiritual senses afford no s·
	5–15	If there is any s· thing as matter,
	8–26	If by s· lower means the health
	15–26	lectures cannot be s· lessons
	16– 5	to fit students for practice by s· means,
No.	2–14	through s· an admission,
	2–20	Institutes furnished with s· teachers
	3–26	s· compilations, instead of
	22– 1	S· philosophy has certainly not
	22–10	S· miscalled metaphysical systems
	23–22	can have no s· warfare
	26– 9	s· material and mortal views
	27–25	In presence of s· thoughts
	29–16	impute s· doctrines to mortal opinion
	29–18	s· a statement is a shocking
	29–22	S· sermons, though clad in soft
	32– 1	misinterpretation of s· passages
	32–10	chapter sub-title
	35– 4	demonstrate the Principle of s· Life ;
	39–14	S· prayer humiliates, purifies,
	41–18	will never admit s· as come to steal
	42– 2	* s· manifestations of God's power
	42– 3	S· sentiments are wholesome
	43–22	S· students come to my College
	45– 9	S· an attempt indicates weakness,
	45–10	s· efforts arise from a
Pan.	9–19	kiss the feet of s· a messenger,
	9–20	to help s· a one is to help
'00.	1–19	cities, s· as Boston, New York,
	2–23	doom of S· workers will come,
	10– 8	S· conflict never ends till
	13–16	A glad promise to s· as wait
'01.	12– 1	to s· a one our mode of worship
	12– 9	would be seen in s· company."
	13–11	with s· a sense of its nullity
	15–18	to waken s· a one from his deluded
	19–23	s· as mesmerism, hypnotism,
	19–26	flow through no s· channels.
	21–16	s· foreseeing is not foreknowing,
	22– 8	I do not believe in s· a compound.
	25–14	or required in s· metaphysics,
	25–18	all s· gilded sepulchres.
	25–28	Jesus likened s· self-contradictions to
	26–18	Let it be left to s· as see God
	27–14	healed hopeless cases, s· as
	32–21	S· churchmen and the Bible,
	33–10	* influence in s· things ;
'02.	10–18	If s· is man's ultimate,
Hea.	3– 1	S· Christianity requires neither
	4–23	s· self-evident contradictions
	5–18	S· hypotheses ignore Biblical
Peo.	2–19	S· a theory has overturned empires
	3–25	s· as dependence on personal
	4–26	grown out of s· false ideals
Po.	vi–16	*assailed . . . Garrison with s· fury*
	32–15	S· physical laws to obey,
	48–11	diviner sense, that spurns s· toys,
	51–17	Crowns life's Cliff for s· as we.
	57– 4	* S· old-time harmonies *retune*,
My.	4–17	* s· an individual subserves the
	14–25	* but it is in s· a healthy state
	21– 2	* expended in s· an event.
	22– 8	* to erect s· a building
	29– 6	* S· was the closing incident of
	29–10	* s· was the scene repeated six times
	41–31	* supports s· selfless devotion
	45–21	* results of s· following have been
	48–21	* build s· truth as they do gain
	51–12	* s· an interest manifested
	56–10	* in s· suburbs of Boston as would
	59–30	* has accomplished s· a work
	61–30	* in s· an immense undertaking,
	62–10	* thank God . . . for s· an one.
	66–30	* never before has s· a grand church
	69– 6	* s· meetings presenting an oval
	71–30	* with s· . . . acoustic properties
	74–25	a belief in s· emancipation.
	74–26	* as s· they are welcome.
	82–27	* came to Boston in s· numbers
	82–28	* with s· remarkable expedition,

such

My.	86–24	* most notable of *s·* occasions.
	87–23	* *s·* serene, beautiful expressions,
	89– 9	* an open space about it, *s·* as
	89–11	* A sect that leaves *s·* a monument
	92–29	* some *s·* comfort as it promises.
	95–29	* *s·* a wonderful demonstration
	96–21	* money was sent in *s·* quantities
	98– 9	* *s·* as religious annals hardly parallel
	99–24	* hundreds of *s·* churches.
	113– 5	Can *s·* a book be ambiguous,
	118–14	*s·* circumstances embarrass the
	119– 3	on *s·* a basis to demonstrate the
	119–12	C. S. destroys *s·* tendency.
	122–13	was *s·* as to command respect
	126– 6	*s·* as drink of the living water.
	132–31	comforts *s·* as mourn,
	150– 9	joy and crown of *s·* a pilgrimage
	150–10	the service of *s·* a mission.
	154–30	*S·* communing uplifts man's being;
	162–10	the bond of blessedness *s·* as
	164– 1	knowing that *s·* an effort
	175–16	if, indeed, *s·* must remain
	176– 8	grant that *s·* great goodness,
	179–30	They afford *s·* expositions of
	185– 2	To *s·* as have waited patiently
	196–20	endured *s·* contradiction — *Heb.* 12 : 3.
	197–15	Comparing *s·* students with
	197–21	of *s·* is the kingdom — *Matt.* 19 : 14.
	201–11	*S·* elements of friendship, faith,
	204– 8	that mutual friendships *s·* as ours
	208–15	expectation of just *s·* blessedness,
	218–26	*S·* labor is impartial,
	219– 3	*S·* practice would be erroneous,
	219– 4	*s·* an anticipation on the part of
	223–17	All *s·* questions are superinduced
	228–31	*s·* a one was never called to
	229– 4	I have no use for *s·*,
	230–13	to comfort *s·* as mourn,
	230–21	fitness and fidelity *s·* as thine
	230–23	*s·* as the Christian education of
	231– 2	*s·* purposes only as God indicates.
	231–10	*s·* uncertain, unfortunate investments.
	233–23	watch against *s·* a result?
	249–17	should countenance *s·* evil tendencies.
	260– 6	would flee before *s·* reality,
	272–26	* leads with *s·* conspicuous success
	276–19	* in *s·* matters no one should
	278–20	civilization destroys *s·* illusions
	284–16	* that *s·* an event has occurred."
	295– 2	our dear God comforts *s·*
	297– 3	shrink from *s·* salient praise.
	306– 7	*s·* was Ralph Waldo Emerson ;
	311– 7	tenderness and sympathy were *s·* that
	312–23	would need on *s·* an excursion.
	313–11	Nor do I remember any *s·* stuff
	316–16	*S·* a dignified, eloquent appeal
	316–23	*s·* sound appreciation of the rights
	317–11	It was for no *s·* purpose.
	318–25	* that there ever was *s·* a man
	319– 1	*s·* a person as the Galilean
	322–24	* to banter me on *s·* enthusiasm,
	323–21	* giving this age *s·* a Leader
	331– 4	* *S·* watchful solicitude
	331–14	* extend *s·* unrestrained hospitality
	340–17	immediately annulling *s·* bills
	343–15	I have sought no *s·* distinction.
	345– 1	see that your mind is in *s·* a state
	348–14	writer's departure from *s·* a religion
	362–22	* our intention to take *s·* action

(see also **cases**)

suckling

My.	113–19	a *s·* in the arms of divine Love,

sucklings

Pul.	8–22	mouths of babes and *s·* — *Matt.* 21 : 16.

sudden

Mis.	48–21	tragic events and *s·* deaths
Man.	49–23	*S·* Decease.
Pan.	3–10	silent as the storm's *s·* hush ;
’00.	2–23	more *s·*, severe, and lasting
My.	201–17	that its *s·* sallies may help us,
	289–14	world's loss, in the *s·* departure of
	290– 3	*s·* international bereavement,
	294–23	sad, *s·* announcement of the decease of
	336–17	* seizure of disease was so *s·*

suddenly

Mis.	162– 7	stepped *s·* before the people
	328– 1	but *s·* the Stranger shouts,
Man.	49–24	If a member . . . shall decease *s·*,
Ret.	19– 9	*s·* attacked by this insidious
Pul.	33–19	* *s·* appeared at his side,
	34–11	* she *s·* became aware of a divine
	35– 1	*s·* I apprehended the spiritual
	53–11	* Can drugs *s·* cure leprosy?

suddenly

Rud.	15– 6	glad surprise of *s·* regained health
My.	291–25	she is *s·* stricken,
	312–20	*s·* seized with yellow fever

sue

Man.	46–20	shall not, . . . *s·* his patient

suffer

Mis.	8–20	however much we *s·* in the process.
	11– 1	to *s·* for his evil intent ;
	66– 3	innocent to *s·* for the guilty.
	73– 2	material body is said to *s·*,
	91–10	"*S·* it to be so now." — *Matt.* 3 : 15.
	93–31	even if you *s·* for it
	99–16	ready to *s·* for a righteous cause,
	118–18	willing to *s·* patiently for error
	121–15	innocent shall *s·* for the guilty,
	122– 1	good man to *s·* for evil-doers
	123–24	sinners *s·* for their own sins,
	141– 7	no one can *s·* from it,
	157– 3	worthy to *s·* for Christ, Truth.
	157– 4	"If we *s·*, we shall also — *II Tim.* 2 : 12.
	184–21	must *s·* for this error until he
	198–32	therefore he must *s·* for it.
	209–21	*s·* for having "other gods — *Exod.* 20 : 3.
	210–27	it may *s·* long, but has neither
	210–31	lest it should *s·* from an encounter.
	211–16	break his peace and cause him to *s·*
	211–19	are you afraid to do this lest he *s·*,
	222–18	*s·* its full penalty after death.
	237–13	impossible . . . to sin and not *s·*.
	261– 9	mortals *s·* from the wrong they
	278–27	learn by the things they *s·*,
	291–25	worthy to *s·* for righteousness,
	328– 3	learn from the things they *s·*.
	380–22	"*S·* it to be so now," — *Matt.* 3 : 15.
Ret.	48–27	"*S·* it to be so now," — *Matt.* 3 : 15.
	61–23	has no sensation and cannot *s·*.
Un.	57–23	was found worthy to *s·* for Christ ;
	57–24	to *s·* with him is to reign
	59–14	to *s·* before Pilate and on Calvary,
Pul.	3–11	what can cause you to sin or *s·* ?
	5–10	bravest to endure, firmest to *s·*,
No.	30– 6	to *s·*, or to be punished.
	32– 8	must *s·*, until it is self-destroyed.
Po.	41–16	And this life but one given to *s·*
My.	41–15	* hatred he may practise and *s·* from.
	140–21	"*S·* it to be so now," — *Matt.* 3 : 15.
	162– 3	"*S·* it to be so now — *Matt.* 3 : 15.
	165– 8	righteous *s·* for the unrighteous ;
	218– 3	"*S·* it to be so now : — *Matt.* 3 : 15.
	220–29	That the innocent should *s·* for
	222– 6	how long shall I *s·* you? — *Matt.* 17 : 17.
	357– 2	"*S·* it to be so now" — *Matt.* 3 : 15.

suffered

Mis.	71– 3	John B. Gough is said to have *s·* from
	84–16	mind, not the immortal Mind, *s·*.
	162–20	*s·* in the flesh,
	198–30	*s·* from inclement weather,
	212– 9	had *s·*, and seen their error.
	235–29	Who . . . has not *s·* from the
	267–17	*s·* temporary shame and loss
Ret.	40–19	"I never before *s·* so little
Un.	56– 3	If Jesus *s·*, as the Scriptures
	56–18	Prophets and apostles *s·*
No.	33–24	Jesus *s·* for all mortals
	35–13	to show the allness of Love . . . Jesus *s·*.
	35–14	He *s·*, to show mortals the
	35–17	*s·* because of the shocking
’00.	7–14	my great reward for having *s·*,
’01.	11– 2	never *s·* and never died.
Hea.	11–14	he who has *s·* from intolerance
My.	43– 9	in the wilderness they *s·* defeats
	166–16	Had I never *s·* for The Mother Church,
	196–16	"Christ also *s·* for us, — *I Pet.* 2 : 21.
	196–18	when he *s·*, — *I Pet.* 2 : 23.
	231– 6	she has *s·* most from
	232–16	not have *s·* his house — *Luke* 12 : 39.
	290–26	the words of him who *s·*

sufferer

Mis.	72– 3	to be born a lifelong *s·*
	241–18	to the bedridden *s·*
	332–25	supposer, false believer, *s·*
’01.	17– 2	to awaken the *s·* from the

sufferers

Mis.	326– 6	and *s·* shriek for help :

suffereth

Mis.	338–12	charity that *s·* long and is kind,
Ret.	79–26	kingdom . . . *s·* violence, — *Matt.* 11 : 12.
Un.	56–14	He also *s·* in the flesh,
No.	45– 5	"Charity *s·* long, — *I Cor.* 13 : 4.
My.	231–17	"Charity *s·* long — *I Cor.* 13 : 4.
	260–23	love that "*s·* long, — *I Cor.* 13 : 4.

suffering (noun)
abating
  Mis. 8– 2 If we can aid in abating s·
above the
  My. 99– 4 * above the s· of petty ills ;
all
  Mis. 185–13 destroying all s·,
  198–21 All s· is the fruit of
  200–23 pain, and all s· of the flesh,
  Ret. 69–21 prolific source of all s·
  Un. 56– 4 all s· comes from mind,
  My. 288–22 all s· is commensurate with sin ;
and death
  Un. 41– 6 unreal sense of s· and death.
  My. 161–32 their ultimatum, sin, s·, and death.
and sacrifice
  Mis. 350–31 through nameless s· and sacrifice,
baptism of
  No. 34– 2 through the baptism of s·,
brings
  Mis. 12– 4 brings s· upon suffering to its
casts out the
  Mis. 73– 4 when Mind casts out the s·.
disease and
  Ret. 61–24 every sense of disease and s·
dis-ease and
  Mis. 219–18 consciousness of dis-ease and s·
dream of
  Mis. 70–14 startle him from the dream of s·.
driven by
  Mis. 328–15 Hast thou been driven by s·
fear or
  Ret. 61–11 you cannot awake in fear or s·
  My. 267–22 relief from fear or s·,
fervent heat of
  No. 28– 5 melt in the fervent heat of s·,
fires of
  Mis. 125– 2 the fires of s· ;
for others
  No. 34–13 unseen glory of s· for others.
for sin
  Mis. 15–27 By s· for sin, . . . thought is
from sin
  Mis. 14–32 not sheltered from s· from sin :
gospel of
  Ret. 30–20 through the gospel of s·,
  Un. 57–17 gospel of s· brought life and bliss.
his
  My. 161– 6 were it not that his s· reforms
human
  Mis. 179– 3 rolled away by human s·.
  Ret. 62– 2 and human s· will increase.
identical with
  Mis. 66–15 sin is identical with s·,
its
  '01. 16– 5 sense of sin and its s·,
loss of
  Mis. 219–19 ease and loss of s· ;
no
  Mis. 125– 6 to know . . . that there is no s· ;
  Po. 31–19 which deems no s· vain
physical
  Mis. 222– 7 causes the victim great physical s· ;
  No. 33–23 physical s· and human woe.
real
  Mis. 288–24 and real s· would stop the farce.
sacrifice and
  Mis. 257–15 repays . . . with sacrifice and s·.
Science or
  Mis. 362–27 won through Science or s· :
self-extinguished by
  Mis. 362–21 until self-extinguished by s· !
self-imposed
  Mis. 361– 4 dissolves through self-imposed s·,
sick and
  My. 153– 4 send these . . . to the sick and s·.
sickness and
  Rud. 10–17 which causes sickness and s·.
sin and
  Mis. 261– 4 and the sin and s· it occasions
  261– 6 sin and s· are not cancelled by
  My. 248–24 of exterminating sin and s·
sin or
  Un. 56– 6 no sin or s· in the Mind which
summary of
  My. 203–15 the summary of s· here
through
  Mis. 356– 8 that they be destroyed through s· ;
  Ret. 94–10 his purification through s·,
  Pul. 13–20 expiate their sin through s·.
  Peo. 9–16 destroyed only through s·.
vicarious
  Mis. 123–22 not through vicarious s·,
which leads
  Un. 55–12 s· which leads out of the flesh.

  Mis. 12– 4 **brings suffering upon s· to its**

suffering (noun)
  Mis. 66–16 s· is the lighter affliction.
  102–23 Science supports harmony, denies s·,
  122–23 the s· of the Godlike
  122–23 the s· due to sin.
  124–28 it gives to s·, inspiration ;
  165–28 example, and s· of our Master.
  198–27 S· is the supposition of another
  209–27 s· is self-inflicted,
  211–15 is unconscious of s·.
  213– 5 S· or Science, or both,
  237– 3 s· is a thing of mortal mind
  261– 2 s· is commensurate with evil,
  262–16 giving joy to the s· and hope to
  265–32 until s· compels the downfall of
  299– 1 s· and mistakes recur until one is
  307– 9 to s· of every sort.
  323–11 privation, temptation, toil, s·.
  332–23 second, a false belief ; third, s· ;
  350–27 which consign people to s·.
  362–28 And s· has no reward, except
  Man. 47–19 description of symptoms or of s·,
  Ret. 61–21 the fact that, if s· exists,
  Un. 57–20 S· was the confirmation of Paul's
  Po. 47–12 Will the hereafter from s· free
  My. 121– 8 strength of peace and of s· is
suffering (adj.)
  Mis. 156– 1 in behalf of a s· race,
  Ret. 92– 3 for the needs of s· mortals,
  My. 132–27 dreaming of s· matter ;
  190– 4 larger sympathy for s· humanity
suffering (verb)
  Mis. 332–27 Supposing, false believing, s· are
  Un. 56–10 s· from mentality in opposition to
  No. 42–26 * "I am s· from nervous prostration,
  Pan. 8–27 s· because of it,
  My. 29–30 * without s· the inconveniences of
sufferings
  Mis. 83– 7 *cause of his own s·."*
  89–12 or alleviate his s·,
  105– 8 His physical s·, which
  122–29 his s·, self-imposed ;
  221– 7 Error produces physical s·,
  221– 7 these s· show the fundamental
  Ret. 30– 8 relieve the s· of humanity
  60–21 when will my s· cease?
  Un. 3–11 through the s· of the flesh
  55–18 s· of the flesh are unreal.
  '01. 11–10 sins and s· of the flesh,
  17– 1 self-inflicted s· of mortals
suffers
  Mis. 66– 9 for the offender alone s·,
  268–16 hence he s· no shipwreck
  276–21 When a false sense s·,
  312– 7 alone, ... s· all inflictions,
  Ret. 25–12 That which sins, s·, and dies,
  Un. 30– 9 this lower sense sins and s·,
  56–21 he s· least from sin who
  No. 43–26 Science often s· blame through
  '01. 14–10 something that enjoys, s·,
  20–22 till he s· up to its extinction
suffice
  '01. 17– 2 s· so to awaken the sufferer
  My. 20–16 let this s· for her rich portion
  28–12 * S· it to say, however,
suffices
  My. 303– 5 It s· me to learn the Science of
  340–27 s· for the Christian era.
sufficiency
  My. 156– 8 all s· in all things, — *II Cor.* 9 : 8.
sufficient
  Mis. 5–11 have not s· faith
  41–28 is s· for all emergencies.
  100–28 Who is s· for these things?
  111– 2 is scarcely s· to demonstrate
  341–11 Seeking is not s· whereby to
  349–25 When the church had s· members
  352–21 not s· spiritual power in the human
  Man. 15– 4 our s· guide to eternal Life.
  39–19 when s· time has elapsed
  45– 2 dutiful and s· occupation for all
  52–15 deemed s· . . . for forgiveness
  53–22 shall be considered a s· evidence
  55–10 For s· reasons it may be decided
  60– 7 One meeting on Sunday . . . is s·.
  65–18 s· cause for the removal of
  111–19 refuse, without s· cause, to sign
  Ret. 15–18 not s· to seat the audience
  40–17 s· to add her babe was safely born,
  55– 4 gain s· knowledge of error to
  57–19 infinite Mind is s· to supply all
  Un. 43–13 "s· for these things." — *II Cor.* 2 : 16.
  57–22 learned that spiritual grace was s·
  Pul. 64– 5 * in securing s· funds

sufficient

No.	23–23	not *s·* to inform us as to the
My.	12– 8	* accumulation of a sum *s·* to
	27–14	* *s·* funds have been received
	27–23	* *s·* funds have been received
	58– 8	* *s·* refutation of the statements
	104–21	a *s·* reason for his silence
	123–22	My little hall, . . . is less *s·* to
	130–23	Quotation-marks are not *s·*.
	161–22	*s·* unto each day is the duty
	161–26	do not afford a *s·* defence against
	179–20	*s·* to authenticate Christ's
	223–14	First, because I have not *s·* time
	231–21	more . . . than one woman is *s·* to
	263– 5	A word to the wise is *s·*.
	279–13	is *s·* to still all strife.
	297–27	not had *s·* interest in the matter
	339–26	not *s·* to meet his demand.

sufficiently

Mis.	7–31	is not *s·* enlightened
	11– 4	I used to think it *s·* just
	40–20	possess *s·* the Christ-spirit
	43– 8	C. S. is not *s·* understood
	44–11	one who understands this Science *s·*
	91–30	*s·* to do this, and also to
	92– 5	become *s·* understood to
	194–32	*s·* to exclude all faith in
	223–12	*s·* strong to discern
	302–11	*s·* to discriminate between
	334–31	*s·* to understand this Golden Rule
	340–31	not *s·* enlightened mankind.
Ret.	28– 6	*s·* to demonstrate, even in part,
	84– 2	*s·* understood to be fully
Pul.	22–13	*s·* to heal the sick in his name.
Rud.	15– 4	understanding *s·* the Science
'02.	7–10	*s·* to fulfil the First Commandment.
My.	161–17	drink *s·* of the cup of
	310– 2	education, *s·* advanced
	348– 9	solved *s·* to give a reason for

suffocate

Hea.	8–18	*s·* reason by materialism.

suffocated

Mis.	274–27	the *vox populi* is *s·*,

suffrage

Mis.	295– 7	* from female *s·*, past a
	296–27	a wish to promote female *s·*?

suffused

Mis.	239–18	red nose, *s·* eyes, cough,

sugar

Hea.	12–27	giving the unmedicated *s·*
	13–16	using only the *s·* of milk ;

sugar-tongs

Mis.	250–15	to be taken down . . . with *s·*

suggest

Mis.	54–27	*does it not s· the possibility*
	240–26	*s·* to them that the habit
	263– 5	*s·* the sweetest similes
Pul.	76–17	* *s·* the tribute of loving friends.
'02.	14– 6	I *s·* as a motto for
	15–21	to *s·* a name for the book
My.	236–14	for the one which I *s·*,
	347–14	*s·* that nature had reproduced

suggested

Mis.	22–28	falling apple *s·* to Newton
Ret.	52–11	I *s·* to my students,
My.	21– 7	* course *s·* will not only hasten
	25– 1	* and it is *s·* to our readers
	57– 7	* she *s·* the need of a larger
	121– 2	I have *s·* a change
	145– 8	*s·* the details outside and
	236– 5	Because I *s·* the name for
	319–23	* you *s·* that I call on the
	340–22	has *s·* to his constituents

suggestion

Man.	42– 6	against aggressive mental *s·*,
Ret.	85–13	the subtly hidden *s·*
'01.	20–13	*s·* of the inaudible falsehood,
'02.	15–25	recorded the hallowed *s·*.
My.	243– 5	This is a *s·* of error,
	324– 4	* and he scorned the *s·*

suggestions

Mis.	113–16	and rises superior to *s·*
	114–24	Scientists will silence evil *s·*,
	118– 3	false *s·*, self-will,
	119– 1	If malicious *s·* whisper
	306– 7	* welcome *s·* of events
Pul.	61–15	* Beautiful *s·* greet you in
My.	128–31	evil *s·*, in whatever guise,
	130– 3	guard . . . against evil *s·*
	213–16	we mistake its *s·* for the
	223–18	wrong motives or by "evil *s·*,"

suggestive

Pul.	29–24	* helpful in its *s·* interpretation.
Pan.	2–13	Webster's *derivation* . . . is most *s·*.
My.	50–22	* simple but *s·* words,
	131–21	There is something *s·* to me

suggests

Mis.	28–21	First Commandment, . . . *s·* the inquiry,
	85–23	*s·* pleasure and pain in matter ;
Pul.	65–17	* *s·* to recollection the story of
'01.	5–13	This *s·* another query :

suicidal

Mis.	129– 9	To avenge . . . wrong, is *s·*.

suicide

Mis.	52–20	*why not commit s·?*
	53– 4	Committing *s·* to dodge the
	53– 7	Not through sin or *s·*,
	122–31	and he ends — with *s·*.
	212– 3	betrays you, and commits *s·*.
'01.	16–11	outdoes itself and commits *s·*.
My.	128–17	Men cannot punish a man for *s·* ;

suing

My.	204–25	the *s·* for payment, hypnotism,

suit

Mis.	xi–18	to *s·* and savor all literature.
	283– 7	*s·* one's self in the arrangement
	381–19	her cost of *s·*, taxed at
Ret.	39– 3	I entered a *s·* at law,
'01.	2–11	may *s·* the weak or the worldly
My.	136–15	Henry M. Baker, who won a *s·*
	138– 6	This *s·* was brought without my
	250–18	branch churches to follow *s·* ;
	309–10	and my father won the *s·*.

suitable

Mis.	228–17	as the only *s·* fabric
	258–28	only *s·* or true idea of Him ;
	302–23	so elect and give *s·* notice,
Man.	27–13	to provide a *s·* building
	27–20	to provide *s·* rooms,
	29–14	five *s·* members of this Church
	31– 6	*s·* portion of their time
	31–19	*S·* Selections.
	61–22	in a dignified and *s·* manner.
	81– 5	*S·* Employees.
	81– 8	is not accepted . . . as *s·*,
	100–25	If a *s·* man is not obtainable
	100–27	a *s·* woman shall be elected.
Rud.	14– 5	*s·* price for their services,
	15–17	*s·* and thorough guardianship
My.	54–18	* no place *s·* could be found
	55– 5	* church, in a *s·* location.
	57–11	* building a *s·* edifice.

suitably

Man.	30–19	*s·* furnish the house,
Pul.	77– 5	* *s·* engraved, and encased

suited

Ret.	11– 1	Poetry *s·* my emotions
Pul.	66–17	* well *s·* to satisfy a taste

suits

Mis.	ix– 2	*s·* my sense of doing good.
	340–15	instead of delving into *s·*,
Pan.	3– 2	while pantheism *s·* not at all

sulphate

My.	108– 1	carbonate and *s·* of lime ;

sum

Mis.	30– 8	*s·* total of transcendentalism.
	52–29	Mortals have the *s·* of being
	105–32	God is the *s·* total of the
	143–23	*s·* of forty-two thousand dollars
	242– 6	*s·* of one thousand dollars
	293–21	*s·* total of Love reflected
	378–18	the *s·* of what he taught her
	386–30	to reap, . . . Of bliss the *s·*.
Man.	78–21	deposit the *s·* of $500
Ret.	50– 6	a startling *s·* for tuition
'02.	13–18	paying for it the *s·* of $4,963.50
Po.	50–17	to reap, . . . Of bliss the *s·*.
My.	12– 8	* accumulation of a *s·* sufficient
	13–29	pledged this munificent *s·*
	16– 7	* the *s·* of $199,607.93,
	22– 8	* *s·* of money adequate to erect
	23–14	* the *s·* of $2,000,000
	26–12	gift is the largest *s·* of money
	30–24	* Scientists gave a *s·* surpassing
	146–10	lengthens my *s·* of years
	157–23	conveyed to them the *s·* of
	164–25	*s·* of all reality and good.
	165–13	*s·* of ten thousand dollars
	177–10	lengthens my *s·* of years
	212–13	complete the *s·* total of sin.
	217– 7	*s·* of four thousand dollars
	217–10	This *s·* is to remain on interest

summarily
　Mis. 12–23　s· dealt with by divine justice.
　　211– 9　dealt with s· by the good judgment of
　Pan. 5–27　Jesus treated the lie s·.

summarized
　Ret. 22– 8　St. Paul s· the character of Jesus

summary
　Mis. 35–11　complete, s· of the matter :
　　227–25　sublime s· of an honest life
　Un. 34–10　s· of the whole matter,
　My. 203–14　s· of suffering here and of heaven

summed
　No. 214–13　s· up its demonstration in

summer
　Mis. 136–23　close your meetings for the s· ;
　　144–24　fresh as a s· morn,
　　329–28　back to their s· homes.
　　394– 8　our tears, as the soft s· rain,
　Man. 48–14　or make a s· resort near
　Pul. 48– 8　* lights and shades of spring and s·
　'02. 18–19　like the s· brook, soon gets dry.
　Po. 24– 2　Breathe through the s· air
　　45–11　our tears, as the soft s· rain,
　　46– 3　Within life's s· bowers !
　　53–18　To empty s· bowers,
　My. 54–17　* During the s· vacation,
　　61– 8　* before the end of s·,
　　133–11　Message from me this s·,
　　134–18　tears like a soft s· shower,
　　158– 8　upon the glories of s· ;
　　196–29　Over the glaciers . . . the s· glows.
　　314–11　fancied, for a s· home.

summer-house
　Pul. 48– 4　* with . . . a fountain or s·.

summing
　Mis. 62–10　s· up positive and negative

summit
　Mis. 41–16　gains the s· in Science
　　66–16　To reach the s· of Science,
　　162– 6　dazzling, God-crowned s·,
　　215–19　walks on the s· of the roof
　　266– 2　s· of unselfish and pure aims
　　323– 7　Then from this sacred s·
　　327–19　Despairing of gaining the s·,
　　328– 9　from the s· of bliss surveys
　　347–23　the s· can be gained.
　　358–18　reach the heaven-crowned s·
　　392– 1　poem
　　392– 8　And from thy lofty s·,
　Ret. 4–10　situated on the s· of a hill,
　　76–23　gains the God-crowned s·
　Un. 64–16　on the s· of Mont Blanc ;
　Po. page 20　poem
　　20–11　And from thy lofty s·,
　My. 133– 6　God-crowned s· of divine Science ;
　　300–18　striving to reach the s·

summits
　Mis. 303– 2　shine from their home s·

summoned
　Ret. 8–22　asked her if she had s· me?
　　13–11　family doctor was s·,

summons
　Chr. 53–54　away from sin Christ s· thee!
　My. 103– 3　s· the severest conflicts
　　148–29　Christianity is the s· of divine Love

sumptuous
　'00. 15– 3　you have come to a s· feast,

sums
　Un. 53–19　s· done under both rules
　Pul. 45– 2　* some giving . . . substantial s·.
　　50–14　* no additional s· outside of the
　　52– 2　* no s· except those already subscribed
　　64–10　* others donating large s·.
　My. 57–30　* no s· except those already subscribed
　　67–23　* vaster s· of money were spent
　　231– 8　to whom she has given large s·

Sun
　Pul. 88–23　* S·, Attleboro, Mass.
　　89–12　* S·, New York City.

sun (*see also* **sun's**)
　before the
　　Mis. 251–30　mountain mists before the s·.
　bright as the
　　Pul. 83–13　* as bright as the s·, — *see Song* 6 : 10.
　clothed with the
　　Pul. 83–28　* clothed with the s·, — *Rev.* 12 : 1.
　detains the
　　Pul. 87–24　church's tall tower detains the s·,
　full-orbed
　　'01. 8–10　but it is not the full-orbed s·.

sun
　great
　　Pul. 81–18　* soars and sings to the great s·.
　his eye on the
　　Mis. 354–26　his eye on the s·,
　in the centre
　　My. 13–10　* like a s· in the centre of its system,
　like the
　　'02. 17–29　like the s· beneath the horizon,
　midnight
　　Mis. 88–17　glows . . . like a midnight s·.
　　Un. 58–20　midnight s· shines over the
　moonbeams to the
　　No. 22–13　they are as moonbeams to the s·,
　no need of the
　　No. 27–10　There will be no need of the s·,
　　My. 206–20　city had no need of the s·, — *Rev.* 21 : 23.
　nor need of the
　　Mis. 323– 5　nor need of the s·,
　one with the
　　'02. 12–18　a ray of light one with the s·,
　outlives the
　　'02. 17–20　Then thy gain outlives the s·,
　reflects the
　　Pul. 4–14　A dewdrop reflects the s·.
　rising of the
　　My. 114–20　until the rising of the s·.
　sends forth
　　Ret. 56–22　The s· sends forth light,
　shines
　　'02. 17–20　the s· shines but to show man
　smiled
　　My. 29–25　* the s· smiled kindly upon the
　standing in the
　　'02. 16–18　the angel, standing in the s·,
　under the
　　Mis. 267–27　cause of all . . . under the s·,
　　Pul. 53– 6　* no new thing under the s·." — *Eccl.* 1 : 9.
　　Pan. 9– 8　a religion under the s· that hath
　　Hea. 6– 5　something new under the s·
　　My. 324–28　* one woman under the s· who could
　worshipped the
　　Mis. 333–24　worshippers of Baal worshipped the s·.

　　Mis. 54– 4　Has the s· forgotten to shine,
　　　192–16　as long as the s·." — *Psal.* 72 : 17.
　　　330–29　unveils its regal splendor to the s· ;
　　Un. 14– 7　plants, the s·, the moon, and
　　　64– 4　than the s· can coexist with
　　No. 6–17　evidence that . . . the s· revolves
　　　6–21　error of the revolution of the s·
　　Pan. 8– 4　find expression in s· worship,
　　My. 344– 3　If we say that the s· stands for

sunbeams
　Hea. 11– 1　fountains play in borrowed s·,
　Po. 32– 8　s· enkindling the sky

sunburst
　Pul. 25–17　* In the ceiling is a s·
　　25–29　* s· in the centre of the ceiling
　　58–22　* In the ceiling is a beautiful s·

Sunday
　service
　　(*see* **service**)
　services
　　(*see* **services**)

　　Mis. 120–23　love to be with you on S·,
　　　161– 3　S· BEFORE CHRISTMAS, 1888.
　　　314– 5　formed for S· worship,
　　　314–31　On the first S· of each month,
　　　314–32　except Communion S·,
　　　315– 5　S· following Communion Day.
　　　349–28　each S· when I preached.
　　Man. 31– 7　reading of the S· lesson,
　　　40–19　the first S· of each month.
　　　56–12　Monday following the first S·
　　　57– 4　preceding the first S· in June,
　　　58–15　repeated at the other services on S·.
　　　59–18　listen to the S· sermon
　　　60– 6　One meeting on S· during
　　　61–13　on the second S· in January
　　Ret. 10– 7　I had to repeat every S·.
　　　16– 1　One memorable S· afternoon,
　　　44–10　in the pulpit every S·,
　　Pul. 29– 8　* Last S· I gave myself the
　　　34– 8　* a S· morning when her pastor
　　　56–26　* dedicated in Boston on S·,
　　　59– 3　* dedicated on New Year's S·
　　　60– 3　* next S· the new order of service
　　　68–19　* The dedication in Boston last S·
　　　74– 7　* meets every S· in Hodgson Hall,
　　　75–19　* ceremonies at Boston last S·
　　　87–18　* I already speak to you each S·
　　'01. 11–17　Sermon on the Mount, read each S·
　　'02. 12–28　their presence on Communion S·.

Sunday
Po.	11– 5	*Boston Herald, S·,* May 15, 1898.
My.	7–11	their presence on Communion S·.
	26– 6	* communion, S·, June 10, 1906.
	50–20	* Communion S·, however,
	50–22	* "S·, January 4, 1880.
	53–17	* preach . . . for ten dollars a S·,
	54–25	* Hawthorne Rooms, S· after S·."
	56–29	* services were held each S·,
	58–30	* services at the C. S. church last S·
	66–22	* elaborate observances of S·,
	66–27	* services of S· will mark an epoch
	82–15	* dedicatory services . . . on S·,
	84–28	* to take place on S·,
	85–26	* Last S· it was entirely credible
	88–10	* The dedication, S·, in Boston,
	92–24	* entered its portals S·.
	94– 8	* entered its portals S·,"
	96– 1	* zeal . . . exhibited at Boston, S·,
	100– 7	* On the S· of the dedication,
	141– 7	* services . . . S· [June 14]
	147– 8	my childhood's S· noons.
	170– 8	my annual Message to the church last S·
	289–24	on S· evening, February 3,
	337– 1	[*Boston Herald, S·,* May 15, 1898]

Sunday Lesson
Mis.	106–17	Your S· L·, composed of

Sunday Lessons
Mis.	114– 1	our S· L·, are of inestimable value
	314–19	referred to in the S· L·.

Sundays
My.	51–17	* remain with us for a few S·
	90– 2	* S· or on week-days

Sunday School
Order of Exercises
Man.	127– 1	heading

Mis.	382–29	form of Sunday services, S· S·,
Man.	62– 7	S· S·.
	62– 8	The S· S·.
	62– 9	received in the S· S· classes
	62–13	S· S· of any Church of Christ,
	62–16	attend the S· S· exercises.
Ret.	42– 8	C. S. S· S·, which he superintended.
Pul.	9–20	together with the S· S·
	46–29	* organizer of a C. S. S· S·,
Po.	page 43	poem
My.	25– 8	* S· S· of The Mother Church
	25–11	* report of the secretary of the S· S·
	55– 2	* date . . . the S· S· was formed.
	69–22	* S· S· and the . . . offices,
	155–26	May the dear S· S· children
	162–11	dear S· S· children,
	230–15	chapter sub-title
	230–17	Teachers of The Mother Church S· S·
	231–25	chapter sub-title
	231–26	S· S· of Second Church . . . New York

Sunday School Lesson
Mis.	314–12	S· S· L· of the *C. S. Quarterly,*

Sunday School Lessons
Mis.	114– 3	Committee on S· S· L·

Sunday Schools
Pul.	5–29	sermons, S· S·, and literature of

Sunday Services
Man.	120– 4	heading

sunder
My.	185–16	the trinity no man can s·.
	268–10	God hath joined . . . man cannot s·.

sunders
Ret.	31– 1	s· the dominant ties of earth

sundries
My.	133–12	in s· already given out.

sung
Ret.	16– 7	she has not s· before since she
Un.	26–12	hymn-verse so often s· in church :
Pul.	16– 1	and S· on This Occasion
	43–16	* s· by the congregation.
Hea.	20– 1	The following hymn was s·
Po.	vi– 7	* was s· by the audience

sun god
Pan.	8– 3	s· g·, moon god, and sin god

sunk
Peo.	5–28	* s· to the bottom of the sea,
My.	53– 3	* were s· into the bottomless sea of
	350–23	S· from beneath man,

sunken
Mis.	234–26	an age so s· in sin and sensuality,

sunlight
Mis.	202– 4	into the s· of Soul.
	331– 9	s· of prayer and praise

sunlight
Mis.	376–23	deeply dazzling s·, softened,
Ret.	4–14	waving gracefully in the s·,
Pul.	82– 5	* and her smiles are the s·
	83– 7	* and the s· cannot long be delayed.
Hea.	19–26	in the s· of our deeds ;
My.	19–19	our shadows follow us in the s·
	114–22	as gloriously as the s·
	202–22	The taper unseen in s·
	282–25	the s· of the law and gospel.

sunlit
Po.	77–19	Bears hence its s· glow

sunny
Mis.	329–29	fair earth and s· skies.
	395–26	Of s· days and cloudless skies,
Pul.	49– 1	* This big, s· room
Po.	41–13	From the green s· slopes
	58–11	Of s· days and cloudless skies,
My.	189–25	erected in the s· South
	194–30	* Ne'er in a s· hour fall off."

sunrise
Mis.	304–23	* It shall ring at s· and sunset ;
	376–16	chapter sub-title
Ret.	23–12	could not prophesy s· or starlight.

sun's
Po.	2–17	the s· more genial, mighty ray ;

suns
Ret.	56–22	sun sends forth light, but not s· ;

sunset (*see also* sunset's)
Mis.	304–23	* It shall ring at sunrise and s· ;
	356– 1	radiant s·, beautiful as blessings
Pul.	39–15	* The s·, burning low,
My.	114–19	I could not write these notes after s·.

sunset's
Po.	70– 4	At s· radiant hour,

sunshine (*see also* sunshine's)
Mis.	51–27	* s· of the world's new spring,
	231– 5	had seen s· and shadow fall
	231–27	brought s· to every heart.
	279– 8	s· and joy unspeakable.
	343–10	Warmed by the s· of Truth,
	343–19	freshness and s· of enlightened faith
	390–18	When s· beautifies the shower,
Ret.	20–17	as s· o'er the sea,
	87–26	s· of Truth beams with such efficacy
Pul.	9–12	as s· from the clouds ;
'00.	9–15	his lightning, thunder, and s·
Po.	15–16	Here smileth the blossom and s·
	42– 1	never a shadow where s· is not,
	42– 3	never the s· without a dark spot ;
	55–19	When s· beautifies the shower,
My.	87–22	* make s· on the grayest day.
	91–13	* cheerful and shed s· about them
	252–13	not work in the s· and run away in
	252–21	rays from the eternal s· of Love,

sunshine's
Po.	53– 7	With s· lovely ray

sun-worshippers
My.	151–24	Baalites or s· failed to

sup
Chr.	55–27	will s· with him, — *Rev.* 3 : 20.

superb
Mis.	276– 1	The floral offerings . . . were s·,
Pul.	42–13	* a s· apartment intended for
	62–15	* quality of tone is something s·,
	76– 4	* s· archway of Italian marble
	76–13	* s· mantel of Mexican onyx
My.	25–25	sublimity of this s· superstructure,

superbly
Pul.	39–10	poem that I consider s· sweet

supercilious
'00.	15–12	s· consciousness that saith

superficial
No.	46– 5	material medicine and s· religion

superfine
Mis.	285–28	in the *rôle* of a s· conjugality ;

superfluous
Mis.	107– 5	Christianity is not s·.
My.	276– 6	to be criticized . . . is s·.

superinduced
Mis.	66–23	Disease that is s· by sin
	117– 6	act s· by the wrong motive
My.	223–17	All such questions are s· by

superintended
Ret.	42– 8	C. S. Sunday School, which he s·.

superintendent
Pul.	46–30	* of which he was the s·,
My.	230–16	To the S· and Teachers

superintends
Pul. 37–10 * *s·* the church in Boston,

superior
Mis. 104– 3 His unseen individuality, so *s·* to
113–16 rises *s·* to suggestions
Pan. 11–14 will demonstrate man to be *s·*
'01. 25–24 good and evil, and the latter *s·*,
Hea. 15–21 as if drugs were *s·* to Deity.

Superior Court
My. 137– 3 * Robert N. Chamberlin of the *S· C·*,

superiority
Mis. 28–30 *s·* of the higher law ;
30–18 proved the *s·* of Mind
109–32 your *s·* to a delusion is won.
140– 9 *s·* of the claims of Spirit
286–12 the *s·* of spiritual power
379–29 Mind and its *s·* over matter,
Ret. 26–10 *s·* of Spirit over matter.
34–16 *s·* of metaphysics over physics.

superlative
Mis. 223–29 To punish ourselves . . . is *s·* folly.

super-modest
My. 115– 8 I cannot be *s·* in

supernal
Mis. 160– 9 meet and mingle in bliss *s·*.
387–23 Whence joys *s·* flow,
Ret. 85–15 the order prescribed by *s·* grace.
Un. 5–27 left to the *s·* guidance.
Po. 6–18 Whence joys *s·* flow,

supernatural
Mis. 3– 4 we shall claim . . . no *s·* power.
88–22 * that Christian healing is *s·*, or
104–11 sin is miraculous and *s·* ;
199–28 neither *s·* or preternatural.
Ret. 26–13 had before seemed to me *s·*,
Pul. 72– 1 * as though inspired . . . by *s·* power.
My. 95–24 * can banish faith in the *s·*,

supernaturally
Pan. 3–20 who reveals Himself *s·* to

superscription
My. 170–17 it has His image and *s·*.

supersede
My. v–10 * threatens to *s·* persecution,

supersedes
Un. 40– 8 As Truth *s·* error,

supersensible
Mis. 86–31 to reach the glory of *s·* Life ;
Ret. 73–17 evil is lost in *s·* good.
Un. 10–11 God, or Spirit, the *s·* eternal.

supersensual
Mis. 77–19 *s·*, impartial, and unquenchable Love.

superstition
Mis. 30–24 wisdomless wit, weakness, and *s·*,
123– 7 *s·*, lust, hypocrisy, *witchcraft.*
199–18 denied and defied their *s·*.
'02. 9–30 counteracts ignorance and *s·*?
My. 245–13 devouring beasts, *s·* and jealousy.

superstitions
Mis. 235–24 Christianity unbiased by the *s·* of

superstitious
My. 313–23 * nor did "the *s·* country folk

superstructure
Mis. 140– 2 God's gift, foundation and *s·*,
140–29 though the material *s·* should crumble
341– 5 *s·* that is real, right, and eternal
357–32 yea, its foundation and *s·*.
Pul. 2–29 *s·* of Truth, reared on the
'01. 25– 4 *s·* eternal in the heavens,
Hea. 11– 9 immortal *s·* is built on Truth ;
My. 6–23 a *s·* high above the work of
25–25 sublimity of this superb *s·*,
94–27 a *s·* high above the work of

supervision
Man. 74– 4 neither shall he exercise *s·* or

supine
Mis. 312–23 reason too *s·* or misemployed

supper
Mis. 90–26 the Passover, or last *s·*,
170– 8 drinking of wine at the Lord's *s·*,

supplant
Pul. 66–26 * are eventually to *s·* those

supplemented
Pul. 60–10 * Each paragraph he *s·* first with

supplied
Mis. 148–16 must be *s·* to maintain the dignity
Man. 3–13 must be *s·* to maintain the dignity
30–10 and the vacancy *s·*.

supplied
Man. 65–21 vacancy shall be *s·* by a
78– 4 vacancy *s·* by the Board.
Un. 51–11 *s·* by the pretentious usurpation,
My. 23– 5 * *s·* the means to consummate the
53–20 * The pulpit was *s·* by Mrs. Eddy,
309–30 * *s·* the only social diversions,

supplies
Mis. 211– 8 *s·* criminals with bouquets
307– 2 they give you daily *s·*.
313–22 garner the *s·* for a world.
Man. 45– 1 *s·* within the wide channels of
No. 42– 8 divine Spirit *s·* all human needs.
My. 12–26 Love *s·* the ever-present help
91– 2 * proof positive that it *s·* these
260–26 *s·* every need of man.

supply
Mis. 45–16 *s·* invariably meets demand,
365–19 what immortal Mind alone can *s·*.
Man. 96–12 he is at liberty to *s·* that need
102– 8 elect, dismiss, or *s·* a vacancy
Ret. 57–20 infinite Mind is sufficient to *s·* all
82–17 ample to *s·* many practitioners,
Pul. 10– 5 power and purpose to *s·* them.
15–17 God will *s·* the wisdom
No. 18–25 for what Mind alone can *s·*.
'01. 7–16 and *s·* the differing needs of
16– 9 *s·* sacrilegious gossip with the
My. 118–21 to *s·* the blessings of the infinite,
186–14 will *s·* all your needs
216– 8 subsist on demand and *s·*,
231–21 more . . . than . . . is sufficient to *s·*.
261– 7 the full *s·* of juvenile joy.
312– 2 to *s·* the place of his leading

supplying
Mis. 193–19 *s·* the word Science to Christianity,
263–20 responsible for *s·* this want,
365–14 *s·* the universal need of
Ret. 56–20 *s·* all Mind by the reflection,
Un. 29–12 *s·* all that is absolutely immutable
My. 349–30 *s·* all the needs of man.

support
Mis. 38– 6 to *s·* one's self and a Cause
39–22 Scientist . . . needs *s·* at times ;
52– 2 *s·* God's power to heal
66–32 to *s·* the liberated thought
77–14 to *s·* their ideal man.
80– 7 in *s·* and defense of
193–11 *s·* unequivocally the proof
381–11 evidence to *s·* his claim
383– 5 approval and *s·* of . . . Scientists.
Ret. 19–15 sympathy helped to *s·* me
26– 3 *s·* the divine power which heals.
Un. 43–15 words of the Master in *s·* of
Rud. 14– 8 The author never sought charitable *s·*,
No. 15–11 *s·* the Christianity that heals
38–15 basis and *s·* of creation,
42–17 * drink strong coffee to *s·* me
My. 8– 3 * In *s·* of the motion,
51– 9 * has not met with the *s·* that she
76–16 * in the *s·* of their church work,
153–23 seeks personality for *s·*,
227–13 turn to divine justice for *s·*
276–24 to help *s·* a righteous government ;
290–13 your *s·*, consolation, and victory.
292–10 O may His love shield, *s·*, and
312–16 * entirely without means of *s·*.
312–29 writing gave me ample *s·*.
330–27 sympathy helped to *s·* me
360–18 *s·* the Directors of The

supported
Mis. xii– 5 *S·*, cheered, I take my pen
66–12 is *s·* in the Scripture by
93–17 *s·* by the unerring Principle
93–20 nor *s·* by facts,
96–30 is not *s·* by the evidence
Ret. 64–14 this view is *s·* by the Scripture,
'00. 13– 8 were part of a system *s·* by
'01. 26– 5 *s·* it by his words and deeds.
My. 68– 4 * ceiling, *s·* on four arches

supporting
Un. 57–18 *s·* the ladder which reaches
Peo. 2–13 by revelation *s·* reason.
My. 355–11 a strong *s·* arm to religion
360–19 *s·* The Mother Church Directors.

supports
Mis. 71–14 never averts law, but *s·* it.
102–23 Science *s·* harmony,
200–32 *s·* the entire wisdom of the
220– 7 he *s·* this silent mental force
My. 41–31 * *s·* such selfless devotion,

Supreme Being

'01.   3–12 * S· B·, self-existent and eternal."
Hea. 15– 4 the omnipotence of the S· B·
Peo.   2– 5 improved views of the S· B·.
       4–27 false ideals of the S· B·
    (see also **Being**)

Supreme God

My. 36–30 * our S· G·, through His power

supremely

Mis. 50–30 one God and loving Him s·,
    206–27 if you love good s·,
    328–30 loving God s· and thy neighbor
    360– 9 s· natural transforming power
    367– 4 and to love God s·.
My.   6– 4 Do we love God s·?
    276–25 love God s·, and my neighbor
    286– 7 love God s·, and love their neighbor

surcease

My. 230–22 give my solitude sweet s·.

sure

Mis. 11–12 the s· way of salvation,
    81– 1 broad and s· foundation of Science ;
    82–10 reach the s· foundations of time,
    90–18 be s· that your means for doing good
   109– 6 a s· pretext of moral defilement.
   117–31 Be s· that God directs your way ;
   143– 2 broad basis and s· foundation
   146–23 I feel s· that as Christian Scientists
   152– 7 Of this we may be s· :
   152–23 against this s· foundation,
   229–28 is a s· defense.
   237–25 but it is s· to follow.
   252–27 with safe and s· medicine ;
   288– 5 s· of being a fit counsellor.
   337–20 Where these exist, C. S. has no s·
   340–23 however slow, thy success is s· :
Man. 28–15 Directors to watch and make s·
Ret. 60–24 the only s· basis of harmony.
   73–21 s· victim of his own corporeality.
   83–14 is s· to be corrected.
   91– 1 God is their s· defense
Pul. 65– 7 * small and new, to be s·,
No. 28– 3 but this is s·, that the mists
   31–12 the s· destruction of sin ;
Pan. 10– 7 we are s· the honest verdict
'01.   2–26 fearless wing and a s· reward.
   33–11 * the s· precursor that they
'02. 15–28 feeling s· that God had led
Hea. 14–10 be s· he is a learned man
My.   8–13 * "Now I am s· that I have
   16–26 a s· foundation : — Isa. 28 : 16.
   21–10 * We therefore feel s· that all
   40– 5 * we are s· that now
   44– 8 * our progress . . . will be s·,
  143– 3 s· that they are blessed in
  146–20 s· that what I wrote is true,
  175–27 I am s· that the . . . letters
  203– 2 s· precursor that its possessor is
  203–19 sincerity is s· of success,
  203–20 I am s· that He will
  224–14 Also be s· that you are not
  230–11 Of this I am s·,
  247–26 be s· that after many . . . days
  254–11 s· reward of right thinking
  256– 4 not specially musical to be s·,
  275–16 Life — is s· and steadfast.
  324–15 * s· that neither Mr. Wiggin nor
  325– 7 * s· Back Bay property would never
  363–25 to be s· that one is not

surely

Mis.   6–13 it s· does, to many thinkers,
   29–24 S· the people of the Occident
   37–23 yields to Science as directly and s·
   57–17 thou shalt s· die." — Gen. 2 : 17.
   81– 8 wait on God to decide, as s· He will,
  173–27 S· not from God,
  208– 2 "Thou shalt s· die." — Gen. 2 : 17.
  229– 7 quite as s· and with better effect
  261–14 S· "the way of — Prov. 13 : 15.
  367–17 thou shalt s· die." — Gen. 2 : 17.
Ret. 81– 7 our friendship will s· continue.
Un.   4–25 S· from such an understanding
  15–28 S· this is no Christian worship !
  17–23 declares . . . they must s· die.
  31– 5 s· there can be no matter ;
Pul. 44– 9 * S· it marks an era in the
  80– 1 * as s· as of a ship
  80– 3 * will s· find the other.
  85–14 * s· she, as the one chosen of God
No. 27–26 S· the probation of mortals
'00. 10–18 S· the wisdom of our forefathers
  10–28 S· it is enough for a soldier
My. 111– 2 S· "the wrath of man — Psal. 76 : 10.

surely

My. 184–28 S·, the Word that is God must
  187– 1 S·, your fidelity, faith, and
  188–19 He s· will not shut me out
  233– 9 I s· should.
  300–30 as s· it is not,
  343–14 s· I have sought no such

surety

Pul. 3–11 Our s· is in our confidence

surf

'02. 19–19 heaving s· of life's troubled sea

surface

Mis. 65– 5 that the earth's s· is flat,
My. 69– 8 * gently curved and panelled s·,
  225– 2 come to the s· to pass off,

surge (see also surge's)

Mis. 339–27 s· dolefully at the door of

surged

My. 11– 6 * storms that have s· against her

surgeon (see also surgeon's)

Mis. 311–25 as a s· who wounds to heal.
Peo.   6– 8 * not a single physician, s·,
My. 106–14 impossible for the s· or
  294–16 If the skilful s· or the
  345–21 "The work done by the s·

Surgeon Extraordinary to the King

Peo.   6– 5 Dr. James Johnson, S· E· to the K·,

surgeon's

My. 105–12 s· instruments were lying on

surgery

Mis. 243– 5 not yet made s· one of the
Ret. 24–14 neither medicine nor s· could
My. 345–20 * "But s·?"
  348– 2 s·, hygiene, electricity,

surge's

Ret. 20–18 new beauty in the s· roll !

surges

Po. 73–11 Laving with s· thy silv'ry beach !

surgical

Mis. 244– 4 even a "s· operation"
  244– 6 before s· instruments were
  349– 5 the s· part of midwifery.
Ret. 40–15 received from a s· operation
My. 345–24 about advice on s· cases."

surging

Pul. 13–17 in the s· sea of error,
My. 189–27 song and the dirge, s· my being,

surly

Mis. 297–12 a s· censor ventilating his

surmounting

My. 68– 7 * dome s· the building

surmounts

Mis. 135–11 s· all obstacles,

surpass

Mis. xi–17 found to s· imagination,
My. 67–26 * s· any church edifice

surpassing

My. 30–24 * Scientists gave a sum s·

surplus

Man. 91–15 S· Funds.
  91–15 Any s· funds left

surprise

Mis. 387– 5 waiting, in what glad s·,
Rud. 15– 6 glad s· of suddenly regained health
'00.   4–14 ought not this to be an agreeable s·,
Po. 50–23 waiting, in what glad s·,
My. 31–15 * expressions of s· and of admiration
  122–14 created s· in our good city
  310–31 * It does not s· me,

surprised

Ret.   8–17 Greatly s·, my cousin turned to
  38–18 We met . . . and were both s·,
Pul. 71–11 * SCIENTISTS OF SYRACUSE S·
'00.   4–11 s· at the new . . . steps in religion,
Hea. 13–19 you cannot be s· that we
My. 322–26 * so clearly stated that I was s·
  330– 3 * I presume we should not be s·

surprises

'00.   3–21 To-day it s· us that
My. 248– 3 its grandeur almost s· me.

surprising

Mis. 66– 5 s· wisdom of these words
  224– 9 * s·, but I don't feel hurt
My. 276–12 recommends this s· privilege
  346– 2 * her views, . . . were continually s·.

surrender
Mis. 15–14 moments of *s·* to God,
231–15 caused unconditional *s·*.
Ret. 29– 1 cause a *s·* of this effort.
My. 127–24 forts of C. S. . . . can never *s·*.

surrendered
My. 127–28 not . . . *s·* in conquest,

surrenders
Mis. 257–30 where the good man *s·* to death
289–13 *s·* independent action
Po. 22–19 dark domain of pain and sin *S·*

surrounded
My. 312–23 I was *s·* by friends,

surrounding
Mis. 30–27 any seeming mysticism *s·* realism
Pul. vii–17 *s·* the cradle of this grand verity
47–27 * Concord and its *s·* villages.
My. 173–27 green *s·* the high school ;
174– 1 beautiful lawn *s·* their church

survey
Mis. xi–26 *s·* the fields of the slain
Hea. 11– 2 *s·* the cost of sublunary joy,
My. 316–14 *S·* of the C. S. Movement,"

surveying
Mis. 324–11 *s·* him who waiteth at the door.
369– 8 *s·* the immeasurable universe

surveys
Mis. 328– 9 *s·* the vale of the flesh,

survival
No. 25–13 * "the *s·* of the fittest."

survive
Mis. 26– 1 can *s·* the wreck of time ;
140–30 the fittest would *s·*,

survived
My. 191– 1 if there *s·* more of the wisdom

survives
My. 166– 6 but the fittest *s·* ;

surviving
'01. 16–12 *s·* defamers share our pity.

susceptibility
'01. 4–10 *s·* of scientific proof.

susceptible
Mis. 27–26 and is *s·* of proof.
52–13 Marriage is *s·* of many definitions.
200–12 rule that is *s·* of proof,
No. 13–17 Science is not *s·*
'01. 19–23 *s·* misuse of the human mind,
'02. 17–30 cheer the heart *s·* of light
My. 349– 8 *s·* of both ease and dis-ease,

suspect
Mis. 328– 6 Dear reader, dost thou *s·*

suspects
Hea. 1–16 * man *s·* himself a fool ;

suspend
My. 104–18 that men *s·* judgment

suspended
Man. 54– 3 the offender shall be *s·*

suspending
My. 69– 3 * *s·* seventy-two lamps,

suspicion
Mis. 257–17 *s·* where confidence is due,

suspicious
My. 211–21 fosters *s·* distrust where

sustain
Mis. 138– 1 students will *s·* themselves
Ret. 48– 3 Who else could *s·* this institute,
Rud. 17–13 miraculous vision to *s·* her,
No. 43– 7 Truth to stimulate and *s·*
My. 52–10 * to *s·* her in her work.
216–11 without a cent to *s·* it?
359– 1 maintain them and *s·* them.

sustained
Mis. 175– 7 says, I am *s·* by bread,
'02. 1–20 should be welcomed and *s·*.
Peo. 10–11 followed her example and *s·*
My. 226–20 the cosmos is *s·* by the
330–19 * *s·* by Masonic records

sustaining
Ret. 33– 2 *s·* my final conclusion

sustains
Mis. 50–23 belief that . . . *s·* life,
126–12 dignity of Soul which *s·* us,
Ret. 28–20 *s·*, according to the law of God.
Un. 48– 7 He *s·* my individuality.
52– 5 reveals and *s·* the unbroken
No. 3–13 *s·* the genuine practice,
33–19 *s·* man's at-one-ment with God ;
Po. 1– 6 What power *s·* thee in thy

swaddling-clothes
No. 45–25 clamor to leave cradle and *s·*.
My. 257– 8 his *s·* (material environments)

swallow
Mis. 257–24 Floods *s·* up homes and households ;
297–11 the public cannot *s·* reports of
My. 235– 5 Straining at gnats, one may *s·* camels.
276– 9 strain at gnats or *s·* camels

swallowed
Mis. 61– 8 *s·* up by the reality and
361– 6 death itself is *s·* up in Life,
Pul. 14–12 *s·* up the flood — *Rev.* 12 : 16.
No. 13– 7 death must be *s·* up in Life,
'01. 15–24 * *s·* up in everlasting destruction.
My. 107–13 pellets can be *s·* without harm
127–15 Aaron's rod *s·* up the rods of
133–11 Message is *s·* up in sundries

swallowing
My. 211– 3 straining at gnats and *s·* camels.
218–20 straining at gnats and *s·* camels.

swallows
Po. 53–13 Bid faithful *s·* come

Swampscott, Mass.
Po. 28–18 *S·*, *M·*, *January* 1, 1868.

sway
Mis. 204–21 holding *s·* over human consciousness.
240–23 slight *s·* over the fresh, unbiased
Ret. 91–20 *s·* of his own perfect understanding.
Hea. 18–23 will cease to assert their Cæsar *s·*
Po. 70–23 Give God's idea *s·*,
My. 89–31 * movement of international *s·* ;

swayed
Mis. 294– 2 *s·* by the maëlstrom of human

sways
Mis. 368– 8 * Yet that scaffold *s·* the future,
'00. 10–19 whatever *s·* the sceptre of self

swearer
My. 106–25 tobacco user, a profane *s·*,

sweareth
My. 33–23 *s·* to his own hurt, — *Psal.* 15 : 4.

sweep
Mis. 99–23 winds of time *s·* clean the centuries,
329–23 *s·* in soft strains her Orphean lyre.
387– 1 the heart-strings gently *s·*,
Pul. 26– 9 * following the *s·* of its curve,
Po. 50–19 the heartstrings gently *s·*
68–15 To *s·* o'er the heartstrings
My. 16–29 hail shall *s·* away — *Isa.* 28 : 17.
78–13 * semi-circular *s·* of mahogany pews
149–10 tides of truth that *s·* the

sweeping
My. 49– 7 * stands a great chance of *s·* the

sweeps
Mis. 396–19 There *s·* a strain,
Pul. 18– 3 There *s·* a strain,
Po. 12– 2 There *s·* a strain,
66–11 No melody *s·* o'er its strings !

sweet
Mis. 8–21 * "*S·* are the uses of adversity."
9– 4 *S·*, indeed, are these uses of
15–30 it drinks in the *s·* revealings
27–18 *s·* water and bitter?" — *Jas.* 3 : 11.
106–26 *s·* sigh of angels answering,
116–18 gain of its *s·* concord,
130–12 "rolling sin as a *s·* morsel
135– 9 *s·* sense of journeying on
144–23 *s·* as the rest that remaineth
145–21 *s·* memorial such as Isaiah
146– 1 'T is *s·* to remember thee,
148–28 invitation to this *s·* converse
160– 8 flow on in the same *s·* rhythm
196–17 *s·*, sacred sense and permanence
200–21 *s·* sincerity of the apostle,
202– 2 the *s·* harmonies of C. S.
224–25 *s·* enough to neutralize
227–25 isles of *s·* refreshment.
239–17 a tiny, *s·* face appeared
239–26 What if that *s·* child,
240– 6 must not take the *s·* freshness
240–30 a *s·* something which belongs
307– 8 This *s·* assurance is the
316–19 accumulative, *s·* demands
320–15 *s·* immunity these bring
329–11 restoring in memory the *s·* rhythm
333–20 the *s·* harmonies of Spirit
385–13 gales celestial, in *s·* music
388–11 life most *s·*, as heart to heart
388–24 To nurse the Bethlehem babe so *s·*,
389–19 *s·* secret of the narrow way,
392–21 To my sense a *s·* refrain ;
394–20 * So full of *s·* enchantment

sweet

Mis.	395– 9	When *s· rondeau* Doth play a part,
	396–12	Are poured in strains so *s·*,
	396–20	sweeps a strain, Low, sad, and *s·*,
	397– 1	His unveiled, *s·* mercies show
Man.	40– 9	reflects the *s·* amenities of Love,
Ret.	27–21	As *s·* music ripples in one's
Un.	35– 1	this is *s·*, this is sour."
	35– 3	and say that sour is *s·*,
	35– 4	believed *s·* to be sour,
	41–15	*s·* and sacred sense of the
Pul.	8–24	S· society, precious children,
	11– 2	*s·* song of silver-throated singers,
	13–13	*s·* and certain sense that God is
	18– 4	sweeps a strain, Low, sad, and *s·*,
	18–10	His unveiled, *s·* mercies show
	39–10	that I consider superbly *s·*
	61–25	* *s·*, musical tones attracted
Rud.	4–12	"bind the *s·* influences — *Job* 38 : 31.
	6– 3	*s· sounds and glories of earth*
No.	14–13	the *s·* breath of springtide,
	45–20	with all its *s·* amenities
Pan.	3– 8	to whisper, "Solitude is *s·*."
'01,	34–18	*s·* charity which seeketh not
Po.	4–18	*s·* secret of the narrow way,
	7–11	life most *s·*, as heart to heart
	12– 3	sweeps a strain, Low, sad, and *s·*,
	12–10	His unveiled, *s·* mercies show
	21–13	To nurse the Bethlehem babe so *s·*,
	31– 7	peace of Soul's *s·* solitude !
	33–17	*s·* when I ponder the days
page 34		poem
	34– 1	O for thy wings, *s·* bird !
	46–14	S· as the poetry of heaven,
	48– 6	gales celestial in *s·* music
	51– 3	To my sense a *s·* refrain ;
	53– 1	Come to thy bowers, *s·* spring,
	57– 6	* So full of *s·* enchantment
	57–16	When *s· rondeau* Doth play a part,
	59– 4	poured in strains so *s·*,
	65–10	O sing me "S· hour of prayer" !
	65–16	moments most *s·* are fleetest alway,
	66– 6	S· spirit of love, at soft eventide
	68– 5	*s·* pledge to my lone heart
My.	37–28	* deeply touched by its *s·* entreaty,
	152–31	I have the *s·* satisfaction of
	153–30	*s·* flowers should be to us His
	155–28	*s·* scents and beautiful blossoms
	159– 3	Never more *s·* than to-day,
	163– 2	*s·* sense of angelic song
	173–21	*s·* to observe with what unanimity
	216–16	your *s·* industry and love
	230– 6	as both *s·* and bitter,
	230– 6	*s·* in expectancy and bitter in
	230–22	give my solitude *s·* surcease.
	236–15	*s·* alacrity and uniformity
	247–17	Then I fed these *s·* little
	252– 5	bee, always distributing *s·* things
	271–15	* with *s·* smile and snowy hair
	284– 4	'tis *s·* to be remembered.
	347–20	with all its *s·* associations.
	354–18	S· sign and substance

sweeten

Mis.	9–16	seem to *s·* life's cup

sweeter

Mis.	227–20	the *s·* the odor they send forth
	356–14	*s·* than the sound of vintage bells.
Pul.	12–18	A louder song, *s·* than has
My.	175–22	S· than the balm of Gilead,
	201– 6	*s·* than a sceptre,

sweetest

Mis.	263– 5	suggest the *s·* similes
	343–27	Among the manifold . . . this is the *s·* :
My.	259– 2	will see the *s·* sculptured face

sweetheart

Mis.	329–10	Spring is my *s·*,

sweetly

Mis.	120–18	come more *s·* to our ear
Pul.	61–20	* chapter sub-title
Po.	25–11	S· to shed Fragrance fresh
	47– 2	As *s·* they came of yore,

sweetness

Mis.	107– 1	but even the *s·* and beauty
Pul.	62–14	* purity and *s·* of their tones.
	81–14	* beauty, *s·*, and nobility

sweet-smelling

Ret.	65– 9	not the *s·* savor of Truth

swell

Mis.	107–13	should *s·* the lyre of human love.
Po.	16–21	hear the glad voices that *s·*,
My.	19–27	*s·* the hearts of the members

swell-box

(*see* **organ**)

swelled

Mis.	388– 2	Which *s·* creation's lay :
'02.	20–11	Which *s·* creation's lay,
Po.	7– 2	Which *s·* creation's lay :

swelling

Mis.	116–14	*s·* the harmony of being
My.	81–23	* rose . . . *s·* as one voice.
	186–12	*s·* the loud anthem
	332– 4	* feelings of a *s·* bosom.

swell organ

(*see* **organ**)

swells

Chr.	53–59	*s·* Christ's music-tone,

(*see also* **organ**)

swept

Mis.	79– 4	*s·* clean by the winds
Pul.	23–11	* that has *s·* over the country,
	52–21	* bigotry that *s·* over the world
'02.	20–13	That *s·* the clouds away ;
Peo.	8–21	*s·* by the divine *Talitha cumi*,
My.	111–10	he *s·* away their illogical

swerved

Pul.	6–30	whose mind never *s·* from

swerves

No.	44– 8	*s·* not from the highest ethics

swift

Mis.	156– 2	pages of this *s·* vehicle
My.	92–13	* *s·* growth of the new faith
	115– 1	on the *s·* and mighty chariot
	124–14	waiting only your *s·* hands,
	196– 9	be *s·* to hear, — *Jas.* 1 : 19.
	229–23	thanks for their *s·* messages
	238–16	*s·* pinions of spiritual thought

swimmer

My.	126– 5	*s·* struggling for the shore,

swimming

'02.	10–30	*s·* the ocean with a letter

swindler

Mis.	226–30	*s·*, who sells himself in a

swine

Mis.	7–14	Cast not your pearls before *s·* ;
	89–17	"pearls before *s·*" — *Matt.* 7 : 6.
	369–23	which he shared with the *s·*,
My.	227–24	pearls before *s·*, — *Matt.* 7 : 6.

swing

My.	149–27	Clouds . . . that *s·* in the sky

swinging

Pul.	48– 7	* she can sit in her *s·* chair,

Switzerland

My.	30–16	* from Germany, from *S·*,

sword

Mis.	214– 1	chapter sub-title — *John* 18 : 11.
	214– 6	not . . . but a *s·*. — *Matt.* 10 : 34.
	214–14	"Put up thy *s·*." — *John* 18 : 11.
	214–16	"Put up thy *s·* ;" — *John* 18 : 11.
	214–16	*s·* must have been drawn
	215–26	use the *s·* of Spirit.
Ret.	2–11	a heavy *s·*, encased in
	11– 9	The *s·* is sheathed,
Pul.	46–19	* a heavy *s·*, encased in
	46–20	* the *s·* had been bestowed
	65–23	* parted his mantle with his *s·*
	83–15	* the ruthless *s·* of injustice.
'01.	31–10	not . . . but a *s·*." — *Matt.* 10 : 34.
Po.	26– 8	While Justice grasped the *s·*
	60– 6	The *s·* is sheathed,
My.	185– 8	*s·* of the Spirit is drawn ;
	189– 2	grasping the *s·* of Spirit,
	278–28	pierced by its own *s·*.

swords

Mis.	10–18	crossing *s·* with temptation,
	285–15	crossed *s·* with free-love,

swordsmen

Mis.	195–22	stroke of unskilled *s·*.

sworn

Mis.	177–11	*s·* enmity against the lives of
My.	34– 4	nor *s·* deceitfully. — *Psal.* 24 : 4.

swung

Pul.	80– 3	* pendulum that has *s·* to one extreme

Sydney

My.	208– 2	chapter sub-title

syllogism

Mis.	195–20	That perfect *s·* of Jesus
Un.	34– 6	What then is the line of the *s·*

syllogisms

My.	111–11	swept away their illogical *s·*

sylvan
Ret. 17– 5 I worship in deep s· spot,
Pan. 3– 3 preside over s· solitude,
Po. 62– 5 I worship in deep s· spot,

symbol
Mis. 170–11 This is the reality behind the s·.
191– 7 serpent became a s· of wisdom.
Un. 61–18 sign and s·, not the substance
My. 8–11 * let us have the best material s·
28–22 * s· of a religion which heals
86– 5 * find pleasure in this new s·,
131–12 given to me in a little s·,
131–14 above the s· seize the spirit,
151–27 to look no higher than the s·.
172–13 material s· of my spiritual call
248–19 No fetishism with a s·
355– 3 * a s· of the glad New Year

symbolic
Mis. 61– 5 material s· counterfeit sciences.
Ret. 42– 6 s· words on his office sign.
Pul. 58–21 * pictures s· of the tenets of
'00. 11–28 His s· ethics bravely rebuke
12–27 s·, rather than personal

symbolisms
My. 88–13 * architectural s· of aspiration

symbolize
Mis. 170– 8 s· the spiritual refreshment
My. 24– 7 * to s· your unmeasured love for
63–24 * s· this revelation,
89– 3 * may be held to s· that faith

symbolized
Mis. 82– 5 brings the peace s· by a dove ;

symbols
Mis. 82–10 cognize the s· of God,
142–10 a number of masonic s·.
142–26 s· of freemasonry depicted on
Pul. 30–13 * outward s· of bread and wine,
My. 185–30 are rich in signs and s·,

symmetrical
Mis. 167– 6 He is wholly s· ;
My. 45–32 * In solid foundation, in s· arches,
85–28 * its s· and appropriate design.

sympathetic
Mis. 312– 5 Love is consistent, uniform, s·,
Ret. 16– 2 clear, strong, s·,
My. 291–17 uniform, consistent, s·,

sympathies
Mis. 32–15 My s· extend to the
317–24 My s· are deeply enlisted for

sympathize
Mis. 371–21 To s· in any degree with error,
My. 151– 4 I s· with their ignorance
295– 1 I s· with those who mourn,

sympathizing
Ret. 5–23 * a s· heart, and a placid spirit.

sympathy
Mis. 102–19 s· of His eternal Mind,
118–14 one's s· can neither atone for error,
208–12 come into s· with it,
253–23 should it not appeal to human s·
379–18 his rare humanity and s·
Ret. 19–15 s· helped to support me
95– 8 * set apart Unto a life of s·.
Un. 18–18 My s· with and My knowledge of
Pul. 35–29 s· with her own views,
No. 30–17 His s· is divine, not human.
30–24 S· with sin, sorrow, and
30–25 Truth has no s· for error.
Hea. 14–27 in s· with all that is right
Po. 74– 6 when parting thy s· glowed !
My. 30– 9 * from curiosity, and from s·, too.
190– 4 s· for suffering humanity
287– 5 enlists my hearty s·.
289–13 s· with the bereaved nation,
311– 6 my tenderness and s· were such
320–17 * in s· with the movement,
330–27 whose kindness and s· helped to
331–24 * extended their care and s·
331–30 * s· extended to her after his

symphonies
My. 155–24 heaven's s· that come to earth.

Symphony Hall
My. 57– 3 * in S· H·, and in the Mechanics Building,

symposium
My. 347–22 contribution to "Bohemia." A s·

symptom
My. 116–19 not a s· of this contagious malady,

symptoms
Mis. 100–30 s· by which our Father indicates
Man. 47–19 description of s· or of suffering,
Ret. 26– 1 as to their disease or its s·.
Hea. 12–16 the general and moral s·
My. 116–17 Its s· are based upon personal

synagogue
Mis. 326–13 crept unseen into the s·,
Ret. 89–17 once again entered the s·
'00. 12–25 he labored in the s·,
14– 3 s· of Satan — Rev. 3 : 9.

synagogues
Mis. 133–12 love to pray standing in the s·
159– 1 He spake in their s·,
373–22 Christianity entered into s·,
Ret. 65–17 ruled Christ out of the s·,
89– 9 s·, scattered about in cities
'01. 28–17 have been scourged in the s·
Hea. 2– 4 s· as of old closed upon it,
My. 285–23 neither in the s·, — Acts 24 : 12.

Syndicates
Man. 27–25 Trusteeships and S·.
27–26 Boards of Trustees and S·

synonym
Mis. 75–11 Soul is a s· of Spirit,
Ret. 57–10 Soul is the s· of Spirit,

synonymous
Mis. 23–22 terms s· for the one God,
27– 4 terms God and good, . . . are s·.
248–10 made the word s· with devil.
'00. 5–10 Father and Mother are s· terms ;
My. 5– 4 marriage s· with legalized

synonyms
Un. 27– 4 used as if they were s·,
My. 225–28 His s· are Love, Truth, Life,

synopsis
Mis. 95–12 insufficient for even a s· of C. S.,

synoptic
My. 179– 2 s· Scriptures, as set forth in the

syntax
Ret. 10–16 S· was spiritual order and unity.

Syracuse
New York
Pul. 71– 9 * The Post, S·, New York,
N. Y.
Pul. 69– 3 * Miss Cross came from S·, N. Y.,

Pul. 71–11 * Christian Scientists of S·

system
barmaid
Mis. 295– 5 * "cursed barmaid S·"
best
Mis. 233– 4 a malpractice of the best s·
complete
My. 113–10 truth of the complete s· of C. S.
educational
Mis. 263–23 educational s· of C. S.
My. 245– 6 This Christian educational s·
312–31 educational s· in New Hampshire.
entire
Mis. 382–30 entire s· of teaching and
gospel-opposing
Mis. 301–11 gospel-opposing s· of authorship,
homœopathic
My. 107– 8 namely, the homœopathic s·,
107–19 efficiency of the homœopathic s·.
human
Mis. 48–16 effect of alcohol, . . . on the human s·,
244– 6 Mind alone constructing the human s·,
hygienic
No. 10–14 My hygienic s· rests on Mind,
its
My. 13–10 * like a sun in the centre of its s·,
learn a
No. 43–22 come to my College to learn a s·
medical
Mis. 80–31 to understand the medical s· of
mental
Mis. 35– 9 this mental s· of treating disease.
Hea. 13–25 this mental s· of healing
metaphysical
Ret. 43– 1 the first purely metaphysical s·
Un. 9–28 difference in my metaphysical s·
mighty
Mis. 234–20 mighty s· of metaphysical healing,
my
Mis. 243–19 since my s· of medicine is not
Un. 10– 2 separates my s· from all others.
No. 4–17 and the efficacy of my s·,
11– 8 my s· of Christian metaphysics
24– 8 at variance with my s· of metaphysics,

system

my
No. 44– 7 My *s·* of Mind-healing
My. 105–26 a work describing my *s·* of healing.
nebulous
Mis. 378–22 than the nebulous *s·* is from the earth.
of Christianity
'01. 34–13 new *s·* of Christianity,
of faith
My. 59– 8 * a new *s·* of faith and worship,
of healing
Mis. 33–21 *advantages of your s· of healing,*
255–19 advantages of your *s·* of healing?
Ret. 43– 1 purely metaphysical *s·* of healing
Pul. 85–13 * the *s·* of healing of Jesus
Hea. 13–25 this mental *s·* of healing
My. 105–26 describing my *s·* of healing.
244–31 Christian *s·* of healing all manner of
of medicine
Mis. 81– 9 which is the true *s·* of medicine.
243–13 every *s·* of medicine claims more than
243–19 since my *s·* of medicine is not
My. 105–31 misrepresenting a *s·* of medicine
of metaphysics
No. 24– 8 at variance with my *s·* of metaphysics,
'01. 26– 4 founded his *s·* of metaphysics
My. 105–28 curative *s·* of metaphysics.
of ministry
Pul. 20–11 *s·* of ministry and church
of religion
Mis. 284– 4 any other *s·* of religion,
296– 1 *s·* of religion, — widely known ;
My. 129– 4 and a lax *s·* of religion.
258– 3 that lifts a *s·* of religion to
of truth
Pul. 51– 1 * not strike all as a *s·* of truth.
part of a
'00. 13– 8 part of a *s·* supported by
proper
Man. 28– 7 Without a proper *s·* of government
public school
'02. 3–16 improved her public school *s·*
sanitary
Ret. 30– 9 a sanitary *s·* that should include
scientific
My. 127–12 Comparing our scientific *s·* of
solar
Mis. 174–13 broader than the solar *s·*
speak of the
Pul. 80–19 * speak of the *s·* it sets forth,
stellar
Mis. 65– 6 man's *ipse dixit* as to the stellar *s·*
this
Mis. 235– 1 By this *s·*, too, man has
296– 1 Founder of this *s·* of religion,
369–11 "method" in the "madness" of this *s·*,
Un. 10– 4 this *s·* is built on Him
No. 11–11 As a Science, this *s·* is held back by
My. 107–20 identifies this *s·* with mind,
type, and
'00. 11–28 human action, type, and *s·*.
whole
Mis. 38– 7 our whole *s·* of education,

system

your
Mis. 33–21 *advantages of your s· of healing,*
255–19 advantages of your *s·* of healing

Mis. 34– 2 "after effects" of these in the *s·* ;
243–14 If the *s·* is Science, it includes
'02. 1–19 a *s·* that honors God
Hea. 19– 4 proved that every organ of the *s·*,

systematic
Ret. 87– 9 settled and *s·* workers,
87–11 *s·* and law-abiding people on earth,
Rud. 15–10 deep *s·* thinking is

systematically
My. 245– 5 cautiously, *s·*, scientifically.

systematized
Mis. 113–28 *s·* centres of C. S.

systematizes
Mis. 235–15 *s·* action, gives a keener sense of
My. 287–23 *s·* action, and insures success ;

systems

and practices
My. 221– 6 *s·* and practices of their times.
and spheres
My. 13–26 all cycles of *s·* and spheres.
erudite
Ret. 31–28 Erudite *s·* of philosophy
four
Pul. 25– 5 * four *s·* with motor electric power.
human
Mis. 74–10 all human *s·* of etiology
Ret. 57–24 Human *s·* of philosophy
material
Mis. 232–14 part with material *s·* and theories,
Peo. 8–25 fossils of material *s·*,
materialistic
Ret. 78–13 which advocate materialistic *s·* ;
medical
Mis. 252– 3 medical *s·* of allopathy
metaphysical
No. 22–11 Such miscalled metaphysical *s·*
modern
My. 103–22 nothing in ancient or in modern *s·*
of crime
Mis. 246– 3 all unmitigated *s·* of crime ;
of *materia medica*
Peo. 4– 2 to all *s·* of *materia medica*
of religion
Mis. 27– 8 and other *s·* of religion
'00. 5–25 foundation of all *s·* of religion.
Peo. 4–25 *S·* of religion and of medicine
My. 216– 4 All *s·* of religion stand on this basis.
ordinary
'02. 1–16 ordinary *s·* of religious beliefs
other
Mis. 27– 8 other *s·* of religion abandon
No. 4–17 beyond other *s·* of medicine,
Hea. 11–28 excellence above other *s·*.
pathological
Mis. 297– 4 pathological *s·* for physical and
sects and
'01. 2–17 feverish pride of sects and *s·*

Pan. 11– 8 *s·*, doctrines, and dogmas of men

T

T——, Professor
Mis. 242– 2 The article of Professor *T·*,

tabernacle
Mis. 152–17 those who worship in this *t·* :
362–26 in the *t·* of Spirit.
My. 33–15 abide in thy *t·* ? — *Psal.* 15 : 1.
36–28 * and set up this *t·*,
188–12 your *t·* of the congregation

tabernacles
Mis. 227–22 abide in *t·* of their own,
Pul. 7–21 their *t·* crumble with dry rot.

table
Mis. 106–20 crumbs fallen from this *t·* of Truth,
231– 9 would I have had the *t·* give a
311– 7 ready for the *t·* of our Lord :
369–20 crumb that falleth from his *t·*.
Pul. 62–23 * might be placed on a small centre *t·*.
No. 9–20 a *t·* in the wilderness" — *Psal.* 78 : 19.
Pan. 14– 5 commune at the *t·* of our Lord
15– 6 spread for us a *t·* in the wilderness
'00. 15– 5 To sit at this *t·* of their Lord
'01. 22–16 with the numeration *t·* of C. S.
22–21 numeration *t·* of C. S.,

table
'01. 22–25 they have learned its numeration *t·*,
22–28 Even the numeration *t·* of C. S.
23– 2 losing the numeration *t·*
My. 105–13 instruments were lying on the *t·*
178–22 on a *t·* in a burning building.
178–24 *t·* sank a charred mass.

tables
Mis. 270– 2 "overthrew the *t·* of — *Matt.* 21 : 12.

tablet
Pul. 24–12 * On the front is a marble *t·*,
26–22 * golden letters on a marble *t·*,
63–25 * a *t·* imbedded in its wall
'02. 2– 6 *t·* of one's own heart,

tablets
Mis. 121– 3 are engraved upon eternity's *t·*.
295–25 ideas are inscribed on *t·* of
No. 1–17 read more clearly the *t·* of Truth.

tabret
Chr. 55–12 The *t·*, and pipe, and wine, — *Isa.* 5 : 12.

tacit
Mis. 291–10 *t·* acquiescence with others' views

tacitly

Mis. 109– 3   *t·* assent where they should dissent ;

tail

Mis. 216–21   * beginning with the end of the *t·*,

taint

Mis. 223–23   or *t·* their examples.
Un.   4– 2   without a single *t·* of our mortal,
Po.   29–19   cruel creed, or earth-born *t·* :

tainted

'00.   3–30   has it not *t·* the religious sects

taints

My. 228–20   washing it clean from the *t·* of

take

Mis. vii– 1   * *t·* care, that tak'st my book in hand,
  xii– 5   I *t·* my pen and pruning-hook,
  6–29   *T·* a large family of children
  14– 4   *t·* in only the immortal facts
  17– 8   you *t·* off your shoes
  27–32   *T·* away the mortal sense
  30–26   *T·* courage, dear reader,
  37–25   *Does Mrs. Eddy t· patients ?*
  39– 2   to *t·* a course of instruction
  39–13   *Can you t· care of yourself ?*
  39–17   not afraid to *t·* their own medicine,
  47– 9   material senses cannot *t·* in.
  52– 2   may refer to such as . . . *t·* drugs
  58–25   *T·* away the theology of
  58–26   and you *t·* away its science,
  64– 9   *t·* for preliminary studies ?
  79–26   *What course should . . . Scientists t·*
  87– 3   To *t·* all earth's beauty into one
  90– 3   *T·* away this pleasure,
  91–25   did not *t·* his textbook with him
  92–12   He will *t·* the textbook of C. S.
  97– 3   *t·* hold of the eternal energies
  99–15   *t·* not back the words of Truth.
  99–17   *t·* the front rank, face the foe,
  109– 4   *t·* me as authority for what I
  115–13   to *t·* up the cross as I have done,
  120– 2   *t·* off their shoes at our altars ;
  129–11   *t·* the next Scriptural step :
  132– 3   *t·* this as a favorable omen,
  135–15   *t·* this cross, and the crown
  137–17   dear ones, if you *t·* my advice
  138–28   all shall *t·* step and march on
  180– 2   to *t·* the side of Spirit,
  191– 4   senses are supposed to *t·* in,
  193–22   next step for ecclesiasticism to *t·*,
  199–11   *t· pleasure in infirmities,— II Cor.* 12 : 10.
  200–21   *t· pleasure in infirmities,"— II Cor.* 12 : 10.
  205–11   "shall *t·* of mine — *John* 16 : 15.
  205–32   *t·* rapid transit to heaven,
  210–10   shall *t·* up serpents ;"— *Mark* 16 : 18.
  214–26   cannot . . . *t·* error along with Truth,
  215–11   if we *t·* the end for the beginning
  215–27   cannot . . . *t·* the attitude, nor
  218–13   can *t·* no cognizance of Spirit
  227–32   *t·* this to be a safer guide
  228– 5   is to *t·* a new standpoint
  231– 8   I *t·* no stock in spirit-rappings
  236–20   "*T·* no counsel of a mortal,
  239–13   alight, and *t·* from his carriage the
  239–15   "somebody has to *t·* it ;
  240– 6   doctors must not *t·* the sweet
  240–14   nature would *t·* it out as gently,
  243–24   "*T·* a little wine for— *see I Tim.* 5 : 23.
  245– 3   "*T·* no thought,— *Matt.* 6 : 31.
  248–16   That I *t·* opium ; . . . is not more true
  254–19   *t·* away a third part of the stars
  262–29   because I *t·* so much pleasure
  264–29   *t·* its hue from the divine Mind.
  270– 1   let us *t·* the side of him who
  271–10   should *t·* our magazine,
  271–16   *t·* in this axiomatic truism :
  275– 3   would you *t·* away even
  294–22   thank God and *t·* courage,
  298– 3   St. Paul's words *t·* in the
  299–18   *t·* from it his garments
  308–10   *t·* their proper place in history,
  309–28   *t·* things too intensely.
  311–11   to *t·* this advanced step
  311–28   *t·* the cup, drink all of it,
  316– 6   When will you *t·* a class
  319–22   *T·* thither thy saintly offerings,
  326–24   *t·* them up the mountain.
  327– 2   to *t·* something out of it,
  327– 6   *t·* nothing of thine own
  327–21   only to *t·* them up again,
  336–28   only to *t·* away its frailty.
  347–16   *T·* the opposite direction !
  347–18   *t·* a few steps, then halt.
  347–26   Those who . . . *t·* His hand,
  349– 2   to *t·* lessons outside of my College,
  356– 1   when they *t·* their flight,

take

Mis. 368–11   chapter sub-title
  398–16   *T·* them in Thine arms ;
Man. 15– 3   we *t·* the inspired Word
  49–13   *t·* proper care of the sick.
  62– 3   required to *t·* the collection.
  63–20   *t·* charge of the Reading Rooms
  67–12   nor *t·* legal action on a case
  69–23   not *t·* care of their churches or
  71– 2   *t·* the title of First Church
Chr. 53–55   Just *T·* Me in !
Ret. 14–15   to trust God, and *t·* my chance
  24–24   should *t·* the things of God
  40– 2   refusing to *t·* any pay for my
  46–22   *T·* them in Thine arms ;
  60–26   *t·* no cognizance of the
  65–12   Mortals must *t·* up the cross
  70–14   No person can *t·* the . . . place of
  70–16   No person can *t·* the place of
  79–27   violent *t·* it by force !"— *Matt.* 11 : 12.
  83–21   Scientists should *t·* their textbook
  84–27   teacher should *t·* charge only of
  89–23   to *t·* charge of their students,
Un. 15–18   *t·* precedence as the infinite sinner,
  25–25   evil can never *t·* away.
  28–18   five senses *t·* no cognizance of Soul,
  28–19   they *t·* no cognizance of God.
  34–14   *T·* another train of reasoning.
  34–19   *T·* away mortal mind,
  34–21   *T·* away matter,
  38– 1   *t·* no cognizance of spiritual
Pul. 13–25   how many periods of torture it may *t·*
  17–21   *T·* them in Thine arms ;
  31– 8   * and *t·*, as the point of departure,
  51–28   * can only aspire to *t·* its place
  69–16   * It would *t·* a small book
  72–26   * we *t·* Christ as an example.
  79–12   * one cannot *t·* up a daily paper
  81–19   * they want no time to *t·*,
  87– 1   * and *t·* charge of any services
Rud. 12–23   "*T·* no thought — *Matt.* 6 : 25.
  14–14   to *t·* the full price of tuition
  16– 2   then public lectures can *t·* the place of
No. v–11   *t·* the unadulterated milk of
  2–11   and *t·* up the cross.
  6– 8   *t·* cognizance of their own phenomena,
  16–21   can *t·* in no more than all.
  19–22   sinner can *t·* no cognizance of
  27–25   *t·* off thy shoes and tread lightly,
  38–18   they *t·* hold of harmony,
  40–17   never to *t·* away the rights,
  43–18   who *t·* it up from mercenary motives,
'00. 2–26   to *t·* some time for myself ;
  9–26   to have some one *t·* my place
  14– 5   that no man *t·* thy crown."— *Rev.* 3 : 11.
'01. 13–10   *t·* possession of us and
  13–11   *t·* possession of sin with such a
  16– 4   *t·* in a poignant present sense of
  32–28   *t·* in the spirit and understanding
'02. 13–25   nor to *t·* the property off my hands,
  17–26   *t·* its answer as to thy aims,
Hea. 1– 3   shall *t·* up serpents ;— *Mark* 16 : 18.
  1–14   "Then there were no cross to *t·* up,
  6–10   they *t·* pleasure in calling me a medium.
  7–25   shall *t·* up serpents ;— *Mark* 16 : 18.
  10–21   *t·* the side you wish to carry,
  15–10   shall "*t·* up serpents" — *Mark* 16 : 18.
Peo. 12–18   we shall *t·* in the remaining
Po. v–15   * *began to t· form in her thought,*
  14–20   *T·* them in Thine arms ;
  27–21   and may *t·* thy rest,
  35– 1   O *t·* me to thy bower !
My. 31–19   * can *t·* a place in the front rank
  47–31   * shall *t·* up serpents ;— *Mark* 16 : 18.
  51– 2   * no one . . . who could *t·* her place
  62– 8   * *t·* this precious truth and give
  75–17   * *t·* it all very good-naturedly.
  84–28   * to *t·* place on Sunday.
  86–12   * to *t·* part in the . . . ceremonies
  96–12   * *t·* joy in attesting their faith
  128–31   that evil suggestions, . . . *t·* no root
  135–14   *t·* the charge of my property ;
  137–21   to *t·* charge of my property ;
  138– 2   gave them my property to *t·* care of
  138– 4   to *t·* care of my property
  140–18   *T·* courage. God is leading you
  146– 4   shall *t·* up serpents ;— *Mark* 16 : 18.
  146–27   Others who *t·* the side of error
  154–30   *t·* it in whatever sense you may.
  155–10   *t·* step with the twentieth century,
  160–27   This may *t·* millions of cycles,
  173–17   to *t·* a peep at this church edifice
  177– 9   I am quite able to *t·* the trip
  180–27   *T·* it up,— it wins the crown ;
  193–16   Love gives nothing to *t·* away.
  215–24   bade them *t·* no scrip

take

My.	215–26	Next, . . . he bade them *t*· scrip.
	217–12	disbursal will *t*· place when the
	236–23	chapter sub-title
	237– 4	chapter sub-title
	237–12	chapter sub-title
	237–20	chapter sub-title
	242–15	chapter sub-title
	243–14	who are adequate to *t*· charge
	251– 8	* to *t*· both Primary and Normal
	258–32	*t*· a peep into my studio ;
	335–22	* to *t*· the remains to Charleston.
	336– 5	* to *t*· her back to the North.
	351–22	chapter sub-title
	358–29	chapter sub-title
	362–22	* to *t*· such action as will unite the

taken

Mis.	67–31	footsteps requisite have been *t*·
	95– 7	* which reply was *t*· in full
	117–21	then watch that each step be *t*·,
	124–20	C. S. has *t*· expressive silence
	144– 1	granite for this church was *t*· from
	172–18	evidences whereof are *t*· in by the
	225–14	clergyman's son was *t*· . . . ill.
	231–21	grandpa was *t*· napping.
	242–23	having *t*· it twenty years ;
	248–28	I have not *t*· drugs,
	250–14	*t*· down . . . with sugar-tongs
	285–16	We have *t*· the precaution to
	311–13	and if it be not *t*· thus,
	314–29	shall be *t*· from the *Quarterly*,
	315– 1	selections *t*· from the Scriptures
	349–11	*t*· the above-named course
	376– 8	* having been *t*· by Fra Angelico
	381– 5	Testimony was *t*· on the part of
Man.	27– 6	no special action to be *t*·
	36– 6	loyal students who have *t*·
	66–10	before action is *t*· it shall be
	85–15	or has *t*· a Normal Course
Ret.	13– 5	Before this step was *t*·,
	20–12	night before my child was *t*·
	20–15	are *t*· from my poem,
Un.	14–23	model would be *t*· away.
	28–20	Whatever cannot be *t*· in by
Pul.	29–22	* lesson was to be *t*· spiritually
	72–17	* "I have not *t*· any medicine
	79– 6	* no debt had to be *t*· care of
	79–19	* had *t*· possession of men's minds,
Rud.	14–10	The only pay *t*· for her labors
	15–13	Few were *t*· besides invalids
'00.	13–13	it was *t*· and sacked.
'01.	7–19	have not *t*· away their Lord,
	24–10	* having *t*· this medicine
	27–23	*t*· out of its metaphysics all matter
'02.	19–21	its treasures, *t*· away from you?
Hea.	5– 8	if a man has *t*· cold by
	13– 9	they have *t*· no medicine,
Peo.	5– 5	have not *t*· away our Lord,
My.	10–12	* *t*· steps in this direction,
	22–25	* position *t*· by our Pastor Emeritus
	25–10	* figures are *t*· from the report
	31–27	* congregation had *t*· their seats,
	43–16	* stones *t*· from the midst of the
	65–22	* deed being *t*· by Ira O. Knapp
	78–14	* offertory *t*· at the beginning
	137–19	affairs carefully *t*· care of
	141–16	* *t*· steps to abolish its
	172– 2	* *t*· from the old Yale College
	217–30	last step to be *t*· first.
	311–22	*t*· in connection with her own
	312–13	* *t*· to her father's home
	317–23	The liberty that I have *t*·
	329– 2	* was accordingly *t*· out.
	329–15	* *t*· from the . . . *Chronicle*

takes

Mis.	5–19	*t*· up the case hopefully
	28– 8	Matter *t*· no cognizance of matter.
	42– 1	*After the change called death t*· *place*,
	72–21	*imply that Spirit t*· *note of*
	84–27	*t*· them away, and teaches Life's
	138– 3	time it *t*· yearly to prepare for
	175– 3	*t*· of the things of God
	175– 3	one belief *t*· the place of another.
	189–17	quickening spirit *t*· it away :
	210–14	handles it, and *t*· away its sting.
	218– 1	spiritual sense *t*· in new views,
	222– 1	It *t*· away a man's proper sense of
	228–21	or in any way *t*· cognizance of,
	240–15	*t*· the frost out of the ground
	240–29	"Battle-Axe Plug" *t*· off men's heads ;
	240–30	*t*· from their bodies a sweet something
	304–15	* *t*· place at Paris, France.
	341–24	*t*· the most solemn vow of celibacy
Man.	68–21	This By-Law *t*· effect on Dec. 15, 1908.
Un.	2– 9	*t*· away man's fondness for sin

takes

Un.	30–10	understanding *t*· away this belief
	53– 1	lie *t*· its pattern from Truth,
	61– 2	*t*· hold of eternal Truth.
Pul.	25–29	* *t*· the place of chandeliers.
	37– 9	* she *t*· a daily walk
	46–12	* Mrs. Eddy *t*· delight in going back to
	50– 2	* in whom she *t*· a vital interest.
Rud.	2–20	*t*· away the trammels assigned to
	6–10	to the material senses, evil *t*· the
	11–21	*t*· away every human belief,
No.	13–18	It *t*· hold of eternity,
Pan.	10– 1	it *t*· away man's personality
'00.	2–13	He *t*· no time for amusement,
	6–14	he *t*· in its spiritual sense
	8–13	till God's discipline *t*· it off
'01.	9–22	Holy Spirit *t*· of the things of God
	14–11	our faith *t*· hold of the fact
My.	26– 3	* Board of Directors *t*· pleasure in
	83–22	* *t*· on a tone of deserved satisfaction,
	120–11	*t*· away all sin, disease, and death,
	129–24	good man's heart *t*· hold on heaven,
	146–26	*t*· the side of sin, disease, or
	166– 8	God *t*· care of our life.
	203–19	for God *t*· care of it.
	217–29	Jesus of Nazareth, first *t*· up the
	229–31	it *t*· life profoundly ;
	247–22	*persuasion that t*· *away their fear,*

taketh

'01.	9–17	*t*· away the sin of — *John* 1 : 29.
My.	4– 8	*t*· not his cross, — *Matt.* 10 : 38.
	33–20	nor *t*· up a reproach — *Psal.* 15 : 3.
	33–26	nor *t*· reward against — *Psal.* 15 : 5.
	196–11	he that *t*· a city." — *Prov.* 16 : 32.
	233–24	*t*· not his cross, — *Matt.* 10 : 38.

taking

Mis.	11–16	save it only . . . by *t*· another's,
	11–31	*t*· by the hand all who love me not,
	13– 4	*t*· special care to mind my
	19–18	*t*· the livery of heaven wherewith to
	78–20	*t*· its money in exchange for this
	136– 5	*t*· forward marches,
	169–28	* *T*· several Bible passages,
	223–24	chapter sub-title
	239– 8	substance is *t*· larger proportions.
	241–13	*t*· a dose of error big enough
	242–21	*t*· morphine . . . at the rate of
	249– 2	experimented by *t*· some large doses
	292–21	enjoins *t*· them by the hand
	297– 1	*T*· into account the short time
	300– 4	*t*· this copy into the pulpit,
	327–13	insisted upon *t*· all of it with them,
	329– 7	*t*· up the white carpets
	371– 5	*t*· them out of the care of
	381– 7	The time for *t*· testimony
Ret.	19– 3	*t*· place under the paternal roof
	36– 5	after *t*· out my first copyright,
	58– 2	*t*· the rule of finite matter,
	86–18	*t*· up his cross and following Truth.
Un.	11–18	*t*· away the material evidence.
Pul.	56–12	* *t*· place on the 6th of January,
	70–19	* *T*· her text from the Bible,
	72–30	* ever hear of Jesus' *t*· medicine
Rud.	17–13	*t*· the first footsteps in this
No.	2–25	*T*· advantage of the present ignorance
'02.	10–14	*t*· steps outward and upwards.
Hea.	13– 2	*t*· hold of both horns of the
My.	13– 2	*t*· no thought for the morrow,
	129– 7	*t*· strong hold of the public thought
	193–24	*t*· the first by the forelock
	212– 6	*t*· the place of older . . . sins,
	214–17	*t*· pay for their labors,
	214–20	*t*· no remuneration for my labors,
	217–25	aids in *t*· the next step
	224–22	not be as *t*· to those ignorant of
	227–15	*t*· a case of malignant disease.
	229–20	*t*· in the Ten Commandments
	233–19	*t*· the name of God in vain.

tak'st

Mis.	vii– 1	* that *t*· my book in hand,

tale

Ret.	21–16	"as a *t*· that is told," — *Psal.* 90 : 9.
Un.	23– 9	How well the Shakespearean *t*· agrees
	48– 2	to repeat my twice-told *t*·,
	48– 3	*t*· already told a hundred times,
My.	186– 8	tells the *t*· of your little church,

talent

Un.	9–12	*t*· and genius of the centuries
'00.	9–19	more successful than genius or *t*·.
My.	195–17	the one *t*· that we all have,
	195–18	only means of adding to that *t*·

talented
Ret. 6–16 reputed one of the most *t*·,
Pul. 39–11 Miss Whiting, the *t*· author
My. 338–18 The *t*· author of this lecture

talents
Mis. 317–26 having already seen . . . their *t*·,
Ret. 7–21 * from his *t*· and acquirements.
11–17 laud the land whose *t*·
Po. 60–14 laud the land whose *t*·
My. 104–26 of the highest *t*·, scholarship,
117–26 their *t*· and loving hearts

tales
Pul. 8– 3 Like the winds telling *t*·
My. 81–31 * *t*· of people of standing

talisman
Po. 68–17 Of the past 'tis the *t*·,

Talitha cumi·
Peo. 8–21 swept by the divine *T*· *c*·,

talk
Mis. 23–17 Matter cannot even *t*· ;
32–17 If I had the time to *t*· with
127–27 Wise sayings and garrulous *t*·
159–22 Here I *t*· once a year,
174– 3 it is a lie, claiming to *t*·
239– 3 I can *t*· — and laugh too !
330–19 *t*· with our past hours,
339– 2 confine their *t*· to subjects that
397– 8 and tenderly, Divinely *t*·.
Un. 6–21 will *t*· to her babe about the
21– 7 good and evil *t*· to one another ;
25–10 Matter cannot *t*· ;
33–11 it cannot *t*· or testify ;
60– 7 *t*· of sin and sinners as real.
Pul. 18–17 and tenderly, Divinely *t*·.
74–22 as I have heard her *t*·.
No. 26– 5 infantile *t*· about Mind-healing
Hea. 9–11 moral advisers *t*· for them
10–22 careful not to *t*· on both sides,
Po. 12–17 and tenderly, Divinely *t*·.
My. 59–27 * I heard her *t*· it before
158–22 Most men and women *t*· well,
189– 8 nor *t*· of unknown love.
321–12 * with whom he had occasion to *t*·,

talked
Mis. 293–27 Truth *t*· and not lived,
312– 2 may the love that is *t*·,
345–27 *t*· of the crucified Saviour ;
Pul. 49–18 * Mrs. Eddy *t*· earnestly
My. 65–12 * It was not even *t*· over,
287–11 Love *t*· and not lived
291–15 not *t*· but felt and lived.
321–15 * differing from what he *t*·
345–31 * We *t*· on many subjects,

talker
Mis. 23–17 Satan, the first *t*· in its behalf,
191–24 original devil was a great *t*·,
295– 9 anonymous *t*· further declares,
My. 210–14 evil thinker is the proud *t*·

talking
Mis. 24–28 not to believe the *t*· serpent,
88–18 task of *t*· to deaf ears
130–10 *t*· about it, thinking it over,
230– 4 time is consumed in *t*· nothing,
230–30 *t*· when they have nothing to say,
Ret. 73–23 is like the sick *t*· sickness.
Un. 44–11 a false, personality, — a *t*· snake,
Pan. 6–12 in the form of a *t*· serpent,
Hea. 9– 5 *t*· on the wrong side
My. 343– 2 * She has a rapt way of *t*·,

talks
Un. 27– 6 one who *t*· much of himself.
Pul. 36–11 * was given to her morning *t*·
Rud. 11–28 He never *t*· about the structure of
My. 341–19 * chapter sub-title
346– 2 * She *t*· as one who has lived with

tall
Pul. 31–28 * Her figure was *t*·, slender,
87–24 church's *t*· tower detains the sun,
Po. 67–11 winds bow the *t*· willow's head !
68– 9 the sea and the *t*· waving pine
My. 308–15 * my father's "*t*·, gaunt frame"

Talmage, Rev. Dr.
Mis. 117–11 I agree with Rev. Dr. *T*·,

Talmudical
Mis. ix– 1 apothegm of a *T*· philosopher

taming
Mis. 323–20 *t*· the beasts of prey,

tampered
Mis. 282–13 would we have our minds *t*· with.
Ret. 83– 9 ought not to be *t*· with.

tampering
No. 5–24 *t*· with the realities of God

tan-bark
My. 313–10 his house with *t*· and straw,

tangibility
Mis. 56– 7 substance, form, and *t*·,

tangible
Mis. 103–15 as *t*·, true substance,
Un. 54– 7 as *t*· as any reality.
Pul. 63–20 * *t*· and material manner
Rud. 6– 4 *are they not* *t*· *and material ?*
'01. 7–21 there must be something *t*·
Hea. 6–16 were evolved and made *t*· ;
My. 98–10 * church, . . . is a *t*· reality,

tape
Un. 11–23 neither red *t*· nor indignity hindered

taper
My. 202–22 The *t*· unseen in sunlight

tapestried
Mis. 324– 7 the gorgeously *t*· parlors,

tapestry
Pul. 76–13 * upholstery is in white and gold *t*·.

tap-rooms
Mis. 296–19 Do manly Britons patronize *t*·

tardy
Mis. 275– 2 Oh, *t*· human justice !
358– 9 naught but *t*· justice,

tares
Mis. 111–16 the *t*· cannot hinder it.
117– 5 separate the *t*· from the wheat ;
172– 4 separating the *t*· from the wheat,
214–29 possibility of destroying the *t*· :
Ret. 71–23 *t*· growing side by side with the wheat,
'02. 18–12 nor spared . . . the consuming *t*·.
My. 124–30 separate the *t*· from the wheat,
249–12 burns the wheat, spares the *t*·,
269–18 separating the *t*· from the wheat.
316– 2 separated the *t*· from the wheat,

targets
Mis. 347–31 Loyal Scientists are *t*· for envy,

tariff
My. 216– 7 manufacture, agriculture, *t*·,

tarried
Mis. 328–18 *t*· in the habitation of the senses,
329–25 snow-bird that *t*· through the storm,

tarry
Pul. 4– 6 I'll *t*· in the sky.' ''
My. 38–14 * visitors showed a tendency to *t*·

tarrying
Mis. 340– 2 faithless *t*·, has torn the laurel from

tar-water
No. 22– 7 on the healing properties of *t*·,
'01. 24– 9 descanting on the virtues of *t*·,
24–16 from divine metaphysics to *t*· !

task
Mis. 19– 8 The *t*· of healing the sick
88–18 closes the *t*· of talking to
114– 4 time and attention to their *t*·,
256–11 severe of remaining at present
302–12 thus sparing their teacher a *t*·
Ret. 38–11 to fulfil this painful *t*·,
Pul. 72– 1 * inspired in her great *t*· by
Rud. 2–27 this *t*·, sometimes, may be harder
No. 4– 2 the *t*· of learning thoroughly
Hea. 14–18 most arduous *t*· I ever performed.
My. 39–19 * my modest *t*· will be ended.
64–24 * holy *t*· of overcoming
234–10 and not *t*· themselves with
258–12 resurrection and *t*· of glory,

tasks
Mis. 130–20 such Herculean *t*· as they have
242–14 I performed more difficult *t*·
273–10 so capable of relieving my *t*·
Ret. 90–24 those first sacred *t*·,
Pul. 9– 5 when your tireless *t*· are done
No. 7–18 God has appointed . . . high *t*·,
My. 42–29 * performance of her daily *t*·.
231–22 for her to undertake new *t*·,

taste
Mis. 28– 3 neither see, hear, feel, *t*·,
86–28 hear, see, feel, *t*·, smell.
Un. 22– 8 would *t*· and know error
24–25 to see, *t*·, hear, feel, smell.
35– 1 *T*·. Mortal mind says, "I *t*· ;
Pul. 36–24 * one of the utmost *t*· and luxury,
66–18 * satisfy a *t*· for the mystical
Rud. 5–20 does not see, hear, smell, or *t*·.
'01. 26–27 a native or an acquired *t*· for
Hea. 16–21 feel, *t*·, nor smell God ;

tasted

Mis.	9–19	having *t·* its tempting wine,
My.	17– 8	"If so be ye have *t·* — I Pet. 2 : 3.

tasteless

Mis.	9–23	set it aside as *t·*

tastes

Mis.	119–13	its habits, *t·*, and indulgences.
	224–13	ambitions, *t·*, and loves ;
Un.	25– 9	feels, *t·*, smells as Mind,

tasting

Ret.	30–24	without *t·* this cup.

tatters

Po.	79–12	fears are foes — truth *t·* those,

taught

Mis.	3–11	his demonstration hath *t·* us
	11– 8	if I *t·* indigent students
	29–15	In 1867, I *t·* the first student in
	35–25	*t·* its Science by the author of
	38–16	Metaphysics, as *t·* by me at the
	43–29	the barefaced errors that are *t·*
	48– 4	should neither be *t·* nor practised,
	65–23	and I have *t·* them both
	78– 7	*t·* to those who are absent ?
	78– 9	can no more be *t·* thus, than
	87–22	*t·* the divine Principle and rules
	87–28	the truth they have been *t·*.
	91–28	as authority for what he *t·*.
	111– 3	to demonstrate what you have . . . *t·* ;
	150–20	as *t·* by our great Master.
	163–10	He healed and *t·* by the wayside,
	166– 6	Truth he has *t·* and spoken lives,
	174–25	and *t·* us to pray,
	189–27	*t·* them as one having — *Matt. 7 : 29.*
	213– 3	All that I have written, *t·*, or
	229–16	would teach man as David *t·* :
	239–28	had been *t·* the value of
	243– 6	mental branches *t·* in my college ;
	247–15	are unwilling to be *t·* it,
	264–15	*t·* their first lessons by my
	273–27	When these were *t·*,
	291–25	*t·* the truth which is energizing,
	308–22	*t·* me more than it has others),
	308–28	C. S. is *t·* through its divine
	317–13	to be *t·* in a class,
	331–16	*t·* them the Lord's Prayer
	337–26	him who *t·* — by the wayside,
	340–19	by practising what he was *t·*.
	349–10	obstetrics *t·* in my College.
	357–25	no matter who has *t·* them.
	357–25	If they have been *t·* wrongly,
	371– 1	*t·* by our great Master.
	378–18	sum of what he *t·* her
	380–24	*t·* me the impossibility of
	382–14	I *t·* the first student in C. S.
Man.	17–17	*t·* and demonstrated by our Master,
	62–19	children shall be *t·* the Scriptures,
	62–23	divine Principle that they are *t·*.
	69–11	charge for what she has *t·* him
	85–14	that he has been *t·* by Mrs. Eddy
	88– 9	Obstetrics will not be *t·*.
	89–12	*t·* in a Primary class by Mrs. Eddy
	90–15	no . . . *t·* under the auspices of
Chr.	53–13	What the Beloved knew and *t·*,
Ret.	10– 1	*t·* to believe that my brain was
	15–10	*t·* me from my youth :— *Psal. 71 : 17.*
	36– 5	I *t·* the Science of Mind-healing,
	40– 2	and *t·* in a general way,
	42– 9	He also *t·* a special Bible-class ;
	43– 9	Asa G. Eddy, *t·* two terms in my
	43–16	*t·* the Primary, Normal,
	43–18	*t·* one Primary class, in 1889,
	58–10	*t·* them as one having — *Matt. 7 : 29.*
	61–28	however little be *t·* or learned,
	65–22	as *t·* in the four Gospels.
	75–12	understood or *t·* by those who
	83– 7	Students whom I have *t·*
	87– 7	Experience has *t·* me that the
	90– 8	*t·* a few hungry ones,
Un.	1– 5	*t·* by his fellow-apostle Paul,
	10– 7	apostles, who have thus *t·*.
	17–13	Jesus distinctly *t·* the arrogant
	42–19	*t·* them as one having — *Matt. 7 : 29.*
	44–12	pretender *t·* the opposite of Truth.
	46–13	He *t·* no selfhood as existent in
	58–10	after the manner that he had *t·*,
Pul.	36– 2	* College in Boston, in which he *t·*.
	46– 4	* in search of the truth as *t·*
	52–19	* *t·* and practised by Jesus
	52–25	* revived belief in what he *t·*
	68– 5	* and here she *t·* the principles
	74–22	it is not what I have *t·* her,
Rud.	14–13	She has never *t·* . . . without
	15–21	assimilate what has been *t·*
No.	2–10	*t·* his students to deny self,

taught

No.	2–19	what he has been *t·*.
Pan.	8–14	Christianity, as *t·* and demonstrated
	8–21	as he *t·* and demonstrated it,
	10–17	utility of what they had been *t·*.
'00.	4–17	as *t·* by our great Master ;
'01.	2– 2	Christ Jesus *t·* and demonstrated
	9–15	*t·* his followers to do likewise.
	18–12	*t·* his disciples none other.
	21–10	* which are now *t·* in C. S."
	22–29	C. S. is not *t·* correctly by those who
	23–19	*t·* his disciples and followers
	25–21	He demonstrated what he *t·*.
	25–22	he *t·* the power of Spirit,
	31–27	*t·* by some grand old divines,
	33–22	after the manner *t·* by Jesus,
'02.	2–30	*t·* the student to overcome evil
	15– 8	indigent students that I *t·*
Peo.	7–28	*t·* me that the health and character
My.	52–13	* *t·* and expressed by our pastor,
	54– 5	* the eternal truth she *t·* them."
	61–24	* *t·* me that I should be willing to
	109–10	Christ *t·* his followers to heal
	112– 9	doctrines *t·* by divine Science
	130–30	substance of the truth that is *t·*;
	163– 4	won the way and *t·* mankind
	180– 7	*t·* his disciples the healing
	182–11	I *t·* a class in C. S.
	215– 7	*t·* students for a tuition of
	215– 9	I seldom *t·* without having
	219–21	what Christ Jesus *t·* and did;
	230–27	all *t·* of God." — *John 6 : 45.*
	239–14	*and all are t· of God*
	251– 7	* students, whom I have *t·*,
	251–14	is *t·* in the Board of Education
	261– 8	children should not be *t·* to
	292– 4	All good that ever was written, *t·*,
	310– 3	they all *t·* school acceptably
	312–17	* For a brief season she *t·* school."
	327–30	* *t·* and practised in C. S.,
	343–15	I have simply *t·* as I learned
		(see also **Jesus**)

taunt

Un.	11–16	He heeded not the *t·*,

tax

Ret.	71– 2	with the *t·* it raises on calamity
My.	80– 8	* *t·* upon frail human credulity,
	309–20	paid the largest *t·* in the colony.

taxed

Mis.	381–19	her cost of suit, *t·* at ($113.09)
My.	82–24	* were *t·* to the utmost

taxes

Man.	30–17	*t·* and rent on this property ;
My.	327–21	* act in the Legislature regulating *t·*,

taxing

Mis.	140– 8	to the end of *t·* their faith

tea

Mis.	348–19	not even coffea (coffee), thea (*t·*),

teach

Mis.	35–16	*t· its readers to heal the sick,*
	43– 7	*Do all . . . t· it correctly ?*
	43–25	to practise or *t·* C. S.
	44– 4	*t·* people, who are ready
	46–10	*Do you t· that you are equal with God ?*
	51–13	*t· him life in matter ?*
	66–14	Truth and Love *t·*, through divine
	78–11	to *t·* either Euclid or the
	87–19	to *t·* students of mine.
	91–23	*in his schoolroom and t· from it ?*
	93– 3	Beloved students, so *t·* that
	98–27	* if thou the truth would'st *t·* ;
	100–18	and *t·* the eternal.
	114–14	and *t·* others to practise,
	115–15	to practise, *t·*, and live C. S. !
	128– 4	too vast . . . to *t·* briefly ;
	132–23	as to what I believe and *t·*,
	137–28	*t·* with increased confidence.
	151–27	heal, and *t·*, and preach,
	161–21	that none should *t·* or preach
	163– 4	preparing to heal and *t·*
	169–15	truths they *t·* must be spiritually
	174–26	did not *t·* us to pray for death
	209– 4	wouldst *t·* God not to punish sin ?
	229–15	would *t·* man as David taught :
	240–24	*T·* the children early
	240–24	*t·* them nothing that is wrong.
	244–23	not to *t·* himself, but others,
	247– 8	I found health in just what I *t·*.
	273–29	if I should *t·* that Primary class,
	293– 1	safe not to *t·* prematurely the
	315–11	*t·* annually three classes
	315–11	*t·* from the C. S. textbook.

teach

Mis.	315–32	*t·* their students how to defend
	330–24	*t·* man to be kind,
	338–21	* If thou the truth wouldst *t·* ;
	350–29	*t·* the use of such arguments
	366– 5	demonstrate what they *t·*
	380–12	and *t·* the first student in C. S.
Man.	55–22	or to *t·* C. S. contrary to the
	84– 8	shall *t·* but one class yearly,
	84–24	not *t·* another loyal teacher's pupil,
	85– 6	*t·* and receive into his association
	85–12	not *t·* pupils C. S. unless he
	85–20	not *t·* C. S. without the approval of
	86– 3	Authorized to *T·*.
	86–17	shall *t·* from the chapter "Recapitulation"
	86–22	*t·* nothing contrary thereto.
	87– 3	Neither . . . shall *t·* Roman Catholics
	87–10	authorized by its By-Laws to *t·*
	92–13	duly qualified to *t·* C. S.,
	92–14	should *t·* yearly one class.
Ret.	83–25	to corroborate what they *t·*.
Un.	9–25	healing, as I *t·* it, has not been
	59–16	*t·* mankind only through this
Pul.	39– 5	* *t·* that one great truth,
Rud.	12–26	*t·* them that the divine Mind,
	15–22	to *t·* thorough C. S.
No.	7–23	speak, *t·*, and write the truth of
	10–11	postulate of all that I *t·*,
	11–20	demonstrate what these works *t·*,
	11–21	because they *t·* divine Science,
	33– 9	demonstrate what these volumes *t·*,
	36– 2	He did not *t·* that there are two
	37–21	Scriptures *t·* an infinite God,
'01.	33–23	enjoined his students to *t·* and
Hea.	5–27	*t·* him that "whatsoever a man — *Gal.* 6 : 7.
	14–21	you must *t·* them how to learn,
	14–24	to reach the ability to *t·* ;
My.	51–24	* to go into new fields to *t·*
	218–23	can either *t·* or heal by
	220–13	I practise and *t·* this obedience,
	234–27	to *t·* and to demonstrate C. S.
	235– 2	To *t·* the truth of life
	235– 8	Can I *t·* my child the correct
	235–12	and *t·* truth scientifically.
	245–24	all who claim to *t·* C. S.
	251–18	can *t·* pupils the practice of C. S.,
	300–23	*t·* the Christianity which heals,
	301–10	*t·* us the life of Love.
	303– 2	I believe in one Christ, *t·* one Christ,
	364–13	And he should *t·* his students to

Teacher

Mis.	121–32	*T·* of both law and gospel
'02.	18–23	prophecy of the great *T·* is fulfilled
My.	190–15	asked their great *T·*,
	267–28	Our great *T·* hath said :
	338–26	great *T·* of Christianity,
		(*see also* **Eddy**)

teacher (*see also* teacher's)

and guide
Pul.	30–19	* *t·* and guide to salvation ;

and members
Man.	90–13	None but the *t·* and members

and preacher
Mis.	252–26	inspires the *t·* and preacher ;

and student
Man.	87–21	for both *t·* and student."
Ret.	84–26	for both *t·* and student.

authorized
Man.	111–11	with an authorized *t·* ;

error in the
Mis.	265– 7	error in the *t·* also predisposes

every
No.	3–16	Every *t·* must pore over it

faithful
My.	254–14	the faithful *t·* of this class

former
Mis.	264–23	influence of their former *t·*.
Man.	86– 8	jurisdiction of his former *t·*.

given to the
Man.	91– 1	this paper shall be given to the *t·*,

great
'01.	26– 3	The great *t·*, preacher, and

healer and
Ret.	47–17	is a better healer and *t·*

his
Mis.	283–31	seldom calls on his *t·* or
	340–18	Is a musician made by his *t·*?
Ret.	75–22	a textbook written by his *t·*,

in Christian Science
Mis.	114–30	*t·* in C. S. who does not

leading
My.	312– 2	supply the place of his leading *t·*

new
Mis.	171–17	works by which the new *t·* would

teacher

of Christian Science
Mis.	91–21	*Should not the t· of C. S.*
	92– 6	*t·* of C. S. needs continually
	264–32	If a *t·* of C. S. unwittingly
Man.	55–13	or a *t·* of C. S.
	84–24	loyal *t·* of C. S. shall not
	85– 5	loyal *t·* of C. S. may
	86– 5	authorized to be a *t·* of C. S.,
	88– 8	vice-president, and *t·* of C. S.
Ret.	30–22	Discoverer and *t·* of C. S. ;
	70–26	right *t·* of C. S.

of divine metaphysics
Mis.	293– 8	*t·* of divine metaphysics should

of Mind-healing
Rud.	9– 3	*t·* of Mind-healing who is not a

one
Man.	73–25	the pupils of one *t·*.

or healer
Rud.	11–25	lecturer, *t·*, or healer who is

replied
Mis.	344– 4	"Very well," the *t·* replied ;

seaside
Ret.	91–28	this hillside priest, this seaside *t·*,

shall be elected
Man.	88–13	*t·* shall be elected every third year

should require
Mis.	92–22	*t·* should require each member to

signature of the
Man.	91– 5	signature of the *t·* and of the

such a
Mis.	349– 7	Such a course with such a *t·*

that
Mis.	92–31	That *t·* does most for his students
Ret.	84–19	That *t·* does most for his students

well qualified
Man.	90–18	lessons by a well qualified *t·*

your
Mis.	136–20	your *t·* and guide.
My.	360–30	God is above your *t·*,

Mis.	32–20	seekers after Truth whose *t·* is
	92–15	*t·* should strictly adhere to the
	115– 8	this state of mind in the *t·*
	315–15	*t·* shall hold himself . . . obligated to
Man.	55–11	it may be decided that a *t·* has
	83–12	*t·* shall not assume personal control
	86–10	whose *t·* have left them,
	87–18	"The less the *t·* personally controls
	91–13	presentation of the card to the *t·*.
	111–13	have not studied C. S. with a *t·*.
Ret.	84– 4	The *t·* himself should continue to
	84–24	The less the *t·* personally controls
	84–27	A *t·* should take charge only of
No.	18–20	but the *t·* is morally responsible.
My.	130–29	your public ministrations, as *t·*
		(*see also* **Eddy**)

teacher's

Mis.	115– 6	even the *t·* own deficiency
	263–16	The need of their *t·* counsel,
	264–26	The tone of the *t·* mind
Man.	84–25	not teach another loyal *t·* pupil,

teachers (*see also* teachers')

and healers
My.	218–25	My published works are *t·* and healers.

and practitioners
Man.	74–11	*T·* and practitioners of C. S.
Ret.	82– 7	even if they are *t·* and practitioners

and preachers
Ret.	82–17	practitioners, *t·*, and preachers

and pupils
Man.	62–16	except the officers, *t·*, and pupils

are deceased
Man.	36–15	Scientists whose *t·* are deceased,
	111–17	Those whose *t·* are deceased,

assistant
Ret.	43–20	assistant *t·* in the College.

association of
My.	251–23	chapter sub-title
	253–10	chapter sub-title

become
Mis.	318–24	all those who become *t·*.
My.	251– 9	* in order to become *t·* of

Canadian
My.	253–14	chapter sub-title

children's
Man.	63– 9	children's *t·* must not deviate from

faithful
My.	244–23	your wise, faithful *t·*

false
Mis.	32– 8	the students of false *t·*,
	39– 9	false *t·* of what they term C. S. ;
	271–27	* false *t·* of mental healing,

fitted for
Mis.	315–10	spiritually fitted for *t·*,

teachers

her
Pul. 82–11   * far better than her *t*·.
loyal
Man. 84–17   the pupils of loyal *t*·
     92–25   loyal *t*· of C. S.
must conform
Mis. 114–10   *T*· must conform strictly to
Normal
Man. 89–11   Normal *T*·.
of Christian Science
Mis. 114– 7   *t*· of C. S. need to watch
Man. 84– 7   *t*· of C. S. shall teach
     87–14   *T*· of C. S. must have the
     92–25   loyal *t*· of C. S.
Ret. 85– 3   *T*· of C. S. will find
My. 251– 4   chapter sub-title
other
Mis. 91–29   my example, and that of other *t*·,
Ret. 83–22   the same as other *t*· ;
     85– 1   other *t*· who should be specially
our
'02. 2–11   making the children our *t*·.
previous
Un. 10– 6   to name any previous *t*·,
refuse
Man. 111–18   *t*· refuse, without sufficient cause,
religious
Pul. 43–28   * which religious *t*· so often receive.
Pan. 10–22   other religious *t*· are unable to
shall instruct
Man. 84– 2   *T*· shall instruct their pupils
such
No. 2–20   Institutes furnished with such *t*·
superintendent and
My. 230–16   To the Superintendent and *T*·
their
Man. 36–12   signature of their *t*·,
     88–20   can confer with their *t*·
without
Man. 86– 9   Without *T*·.

———

Mis. 143–20   physicians, *t*·, editors, and
     315–21   *T*· shall form associations
     315–24   *T*· shall not silently mentally
Man. 36–16   whose *t*·, for insufficient cause,
     55– 9   *T*·.
     83– 3   *T*·.
     83– 9   Christian Scientists who are *t*·
     84–20   *T*· shall not call their pupils
     85–11   *T*· must have Certificates.
     86–16   *t*· of the Normal class shall
     86–22   *t*· of the Primary class
No. 2–21   and many who are not *t*· have

teachers'

Man. 74–10   *T*· and Practitioners' Offices.
     84–19   not by their *t*· personal views.
My. 252–18   chapter sub-title

teaches

Mis. 19– 6   carrying out what He *t*·
     40–22   *t*· her students that they
     54– 6   demonstrated, and *t*· C. S.
     84–27   *t*· Life's lessons aright.
     211– 4   *t*· mortals to handle serpents
     219– 4   nor *t*· that nature and her laws
     358– 4   student who . . . *t*· by healing,
Man. 68–13   members whom she *t*· the course
Ret. 64–10   which *t*· that good is equally
     70–27   lives the truth he *t*·.
'01. 18–20   *t*· that a human hypothesis
Hea. 16– 4   *t*· us there is no other Life,
My. 41–19   * It *t*· us to rise from
     90–15   * *t*· that hate is atheism,
     114– 3   C. S. *t*· : Owe no man ;
     167– 7   Spirit *t*· us to resign what
     188–26   C. S. *t*· the majesty of man.
     212–30   saying . . . that Mrs. Eddy *t*·

teacheth

Mis. 392–12   A lesson grave, of life, that *t*· me
Po. 20–16   A lesson grave, of life, that *t*· me

teaching (noun)

and demonstrating
Ret. 79–20   requisite for *t*· and demonstrating
and demonstration
Ret. 25– 7   Jesus' *t*· and demonstration
and healing
Mis. 162–13   good will, love, *t*·, and healing.
Rud. 15–16   *T*· and healing should have
and life
Un. 9–17   simple *t*· and life of Jesus
and practice
Ret. 65– 4   the *t*· and practice of Jesus,
My. 190–27   declared that his *t*· and practice

teaching (noun)

and preaching
Mis. 359– 4   Christly method of *t*· and preaching
and proof
'01. 23–16   the Master's *t*· and proof.
basis for
Man. 86–16   Basis for *T*·.
better than
Man. 92– 3   Healing Better than *T*·.
books and
Ret. 85– 9   books and *t*· are but a ladder
Christ's
Ret. 65–21   Christ's *t*· and example,
'01. 28–16   followed exclusively Christ's *t*·,
class
Mis. 87–20   After class *t*·, he does best
Man. 87– 8   Class *T*·.
My. 240–22   * chapter sub-title
     240–25   * Does Mrs. Eddy approve of class *t*· :
     241– 2   * Class *t*· will not be abolished until
correct
My. 241–15   * absolute and correct *t*·.
     297–19   clear, correct *t*· of C. S.
exclusive
Mis. 273–32   call is for my exclusive *t*·.
false
Mis. 368–17   false *t*· and false practice
gave up
Ret. 43–10   After I gave up *t*·,
healing and
Ret. 78– 4   In healing and *t*· the student has
     83– 1   scientific healing and *t*·.
immortal
Ret. 91–22   his immortal *t*· was the bread of
incorrect
Mis. 263–26   hampered by incorrect *t*· ;
its
'01. 21–13   in its *t*· and authorship
less
Mis. 355– 6   Less *t*· and good healing
motive in
Man. 83– 4   Motive in *T*·.
motives for
Rud. 16– 2   If . . . are the motives for *t*·,
Mrs. Eddy's
My. 334–15   * Mrs. Eddy's *t*· on the unreality of
my
Mis. 274– 9   my *t*· would advance it :
     317–10   door to my *t*· was shut
Un. 10– 8   If there be any *monopoly* in my *t*·,
of Christian Science
Mis. 302–10   to know the *t*· of C. S.
My. 4– 6   practice or efficient *t*· of C. S.,
     212–17   the *t*· of C. S. Mind-healing.
     297–19   correct *t*· of C. S.
of Jesus
Pul. 35– 2   spiritual meaning of the *t*· of Jesus
or lecturing
Mis. 266–24   in *t*· or lecturing on C. S.,
platform and
Man. 34– 9   according to the platform and *t*·
scientific
Ret. 94–17   scientific *t*·, preaching, and
spurious
Mis. 43–16   spurious *t*· of those who are
stop
Mis. 274– 6   I must stop *t*· at present.
     358–21   not require . . . Scientists to stop *t*·,
St. Paul's
Ret. 93–23   If C. S. reiterates St. Paul's *t*·,
success in
My. 219– 7   their success in *t*· or in healing.
such
Un. 26–11   leads to such *t*· as we find in
that matter
Un. 45–13   falsity is the *t*· that matter can
this
Mis. 38– 5   as this *t*· certainly does,
     292– 4   he chronicles this *t*·,

———

Mis. 38– 3   When *t*· imparts the ability to
     165–27   *t*·, example, and suffering of our
     179–13   In the new religion the *t*· is,
Ret. 48–27   the *t*· was a purely spiritual and
     89– 5   In those days preaching and *t*· were
'00. 4– 7   *t*· of the righteous Galilean,
My. 230–15   chapter sub-title
     240–26   * when the *t*· is done by those who
     246–15   *t*· and letter of Christianity

teaching (verb)

Mis. 11– 9   did not cease *t*· the wayward ones
     19– 9   *t*· the divine Principle and rules
     38– 1   *Why do you charge for* *t*· *C. S.,*
     38–21   *T*· metaphysics at other colleges
     43– 6   *Do all who . . . claim to be* *t*· *C. S.,*

teaching (verb)

Mis.	64– 5	relinquished his earth-task of *t* and
	132–20	editing a magazine, *t* C. S.,
	232–29	*t* and practising in the *name* of
	239– 7	Lecturing, writing, preaching, *t*,
	302– 7	*t* the name without the Spirit,
	303– 8	in *t* and guiding their students.
	315–20	*T* C. S. shall be no question of
	318–18	the gospel work of *t* C. S.,
	358– 4	The student who heals by *t*
	358–24	College for *t* C. S. Mind-healing,
	380–16	I . . . commenced *t*.
	382–30	system of *t* and practising C. S.
	393–21	Isle of beauty, thou art *t*
Man.	34–15	for *t* . . . metaphysical healing.
	43– 7	as auxiliaries to *t* C. S.
	62–18	*T* the Children.
	83– 1	heading
	83– 4	*T* C. S. shall not be a question of
	84–14	A student's price for *t* C. S.
Ret.	43– 3	I began by *t* one student C. S.
	43– 7	*t* the pathology of spiritual power,
	47–22	the gospel work of *t* C. S.,
	49–20	*t* the Science of Mind-healing ;
Pul.	58– 4	* about 1880, she began *t*,
'01.	15– 9	through Christ, Truth, *t* him
Po.	52– 5	Isle of beauty, thou art *t*
	77–13	*T* us thus of Thee,
My.	51– 3	* in *t* us the Science of Life."
	64–16	* she has been *t* her followers
	109–11	*t* them the same heavenly
	147–15	C. S. kindergarten for *t* the
	234–23	*t* C. S. in her country.
	343–19	*t* and organizing,

Teaching Christian Science

Man.	83– 1	heading
Pul.	38–14	"C. S. Practice," "*T C S*,"

teachings

accepted

Mis.	81–10	*in the commonly accepted t*

and demonstration

Mis.	244–26	*t* and demonstration of Jesus

and demonstrations

Mis.	187–18	later *t* and demonstrations of
My.	103–23	except the *t* and demonstrations of

and example

Pul.	75– 5	my writings, *t*, and example
My.	127–10	more of Christ's *t* and example
	129–31	*t* and example of Christ Jesus.

and life

Mis.	25–15	*t* and life of our Lord.

books and

Pul.	74–23	"My books and *t* maintain but

Christ's

Mis.	141–25	ambassador of Christ's *t*,
	193– 8	practicality of all Christ's *t*
	311– 8	so, should we follow Christ's *t* ;
Pul.	9–30	enlightened faith is Christ's *t*
'01.	25– 3	on the rock of Christ's *t*,
My.	127–10	possesses more of Christ's *t*
	228–10	and yet depart from Christ's *t*.
	232–18	Are Christ's *t* the true authority

counsel and

My.	129–29	Accept my counsel and *t* only as

divine

Mis.	302–29	divine *t* contained in "S. and H.

exalted

Ret.	91– 6	No purer and more exalted *t*

false

Peo.	11–14	are clasped by the false *t*,

her

My.	40–32	* as well as by her *t*,
	273– 4	* the value of her *t*.

His

Pul.	72–23	* faith in Him and His *t*.

his

Un.	11– 4	His *t* beard the lions
	43–21	with the power of his *t*,
Pul.	52–24	* all vital belief in his *t*.
My.	111– 8	They disputed his *t*

its

Mis.	50–14	no . . . secret outside of its *t*,
My.	50–27	* and few knew of its *t*,
	112– 7	those who abide in its *t*
	114–30	You can trace its *t* in

Jesus'

Ret.	94–29	Jesus' *t* bore much fruit,
'01.	24–25	necessary to follow Jesus' *t*,

life and

Mis.	244–18	life and *t* of Jesus?
No.	21– 1	contrary to the life and *t* of

literal

Pul.	66–14	* the literal *t* of the Bible

metaphysical

Pul.	6–27	* in Mrs. Eddy's metaphysical *t*

teachings

Mrs. Eddy's

Mis.	48–29	* by Mrs. Eddy's *t*,"
	49– 9	"Mrs. Eddy's *t* had not produced
Man.	42–15	in accord with all of Mrs. Eddy's *t*,

my

Mis.	249–11	and especially through my *t*,
	265–23	My *t* are uniform.
No.	15– 6	comprehension of my *t* would
My.	237–10	accept only my *t* that

obedience to the

My.	43–25	* Obedience to the *t* of this book

of Christ

Pul.	38–25	* the literal *t* of Christ.

of Christian Science

Man.	49– 4	understand the *t* of C. S.
Ret.	43–15	embraced the *t* of C. S.,
My.	130– 4	disloyal to the *t* of C. S.
	272–32	* indorsement to the *t* of C. S.,
	352–13	* so reflect . . . the *t* of C. S.

of Jesus

Mis.	53–23	The *t* of Jesus were simple ;
	195–26	the practice and *t* of Jesus
	244–18	from the life and *t* of Jesus?
	310– 4	Even the *t* of Jesus would
No.	21–21	reproduces the *t* of Jesus,

of John

Mis.	81–11	*mingled with the t of John*

of the Bible

'01.	8–22	if we follow the *t* of the Bible.
My.	251–29	Adhere to the *t* of the Bible,

of the textbook

Man.	35–21	loyal to the *t* of the textbook,

of this book

Ret.	83– 5	to the *t* of this book,
My.	113– 4	practises the *t* of this book

pastor's

My.	52–18	* our pastor's *t*, namely,

practical

Mis.	v– 4	DEDICATE THESE PRACTICAL *t*

practice and

Mis.	195–26	practice and *t* of Jesus relative to

prayer and

Pul.	85–18	* prayer and *t* of Jesus Christ.

sacred

My.	46–25	* obedience to the sacred *t*

these

My.	114– 8	the maximum of these *t* ?

your

My.	44–29	* continued loyalty to your *t*,
	215–14	* "Your *t* are worth much

Mis.	188– 1	whose *t* opposed the doctrines of
Ret.	83– 8	benefited by the *t* of other students,
	84–10	*t* in the chapter on Recapitulation.

tear

Mis.	110– 3	had not the value of a single *t*.
	119–28	should *t* up your landmarks,
	339–28	pour forth the unavailing *t*.
	343–23	*t* them away from their native soil,
	354–30	No *t* dims his eye,
	389–14	glad for every scalding *t*,
	398–14	*T* or triumph harms,
Ret.	18–12	earth yields you her *t*,
	46–20	*T* or triumph harms,
	81– 2	The unavailing *t* is shed
Pul.	17–19	*T* or triumph harms,
'00.	11– 1	cost me a *t* !
'02.	19–15	repentance seen in a *t*
Po.	4–13	glad for every scalding *t*,
	14–18	*T* or triumph harms,
	18– 7	Would a *t* dim his eye,
	27–15	Though thou must leave the *t*,
	29– 9	No natal hour and mother's *t*,
	64– 2	earth yields you her *t*,
	65–23	*man is the cause of its t*.
My.	132–32	the unavailing, tired *t*,
	294–31	shed "the unavailing *t*."
	350–14	heed'st Thou not the scalding *t*

tear-dews

Po.	8– 4	Where *t* of night seek the

teardrops

Mis.	390–19	As smiles through *t* seen,
Po.	55–20	As smiles through *t* seen,

tear-drops

Mis.	389–24	aftersmile earth's *t* gain,
Po.	5– 4	aftersmile earth's *t* gain,

tear-filled

Mis.	231–30	*t* eyes looking longingly
'00.	15– 9	*t* sea of repentance
Po.	31– 8	*t* tones of distant joy,

tearful
Mis.	249– 4	I say with *t·* thanks,
	329–13	touching tenderly its *t·* tones.
Ret.	31–27	the *t·* lips of a babe.

tearfully
Ret.	14–20	but *t·* I had to respond

tearless
My.	124–12	bloodless sieges and *t·* triumphs,

tears
Mis.	11–28	though with *t·* have I striven
	116–23	struggles, *t·*, and triumph.
	120– 6	or repeat their work in *t·*.
	203–22	*T·* flood the eyes,
	210–24	*t·* the black mask from the
	385– 1	* "Faith, hope, and *t·*, triune,
	394– 8	It comes through our *t·*,
	399– 2	Love wipes your *t·* all away,
Ret.	16– 5	*t·* of joy flooding her eyes
	20–17	Thy smile through *t·*,
	86–13	wipe . . . the *t·* from his eyes,
Un.	18–12	wipe the *t·* from the eyes of
	57–27	divine Science wipes away all *t·*.
Pul.	7–12	O ye *t·*! Not in vain did ye flow.
	33–10	* This caused her *t·* of remorse
Peo.	9– 4	but *t·* of repentance,
Po.	16– 1	gentle cypress, in evergreen *t·*,
	22– 9	bliss that wipes the *t·* of time
	37– 1	* "Faith, hope, and *t·*, triune,
	45–10	It comes through our *t·*,
	47– 6	Ever to gladness and never to *t·*,
	47–15	Over the *t·* it has shed;
	54– 3	O come to clouds and *t·*
	67– 7	*t·* be bedewing these fresh-smiling
	67–18	mourn with her evergreen *t·*,
	75– 9	Love wipes your *t·* all away,
	77–12	joy and *t·*, conflict and rest,
	78–10	*T·* of the bleeding slave
My.	36–16	* exchanged the *t·* of sorrow
	44– 4	* *t·* are being wiped away,
	134–18	Love comes to our *t·*
	161– 4	washing the . . . feet with *t·* of joy.
	191–17	Love, which wipes away all *t·*.
	228–20	with *t·* of repentance
	291–27	*T·* blend with her triumphs.
	314–27	told me that with *t·* of gratitude
	332– 4	* silent gush of grateful *t·*

teaspoonful
Ret.	33–16	one *t·* of the water mixed with
Hea.	13–13	administering one *t·* of this water

technical
My.	149–23	Losing the comprehensive in the *t·*,

Te Deum
My.	275–28	unite in one *T· D·* of praise.

tedious
My.	122–10	Now I am done with . . . *t·* prosaics.

teeth
Mis.	72–15	*t·* are set on edge — *Ezek.* 18 : 2.
Pul.	80–14	* fairly broken our mental *t·*
My.	161–11	weeping and gnashing of *t·*, — *Luke* 13 : 28.

Telegram
Pul.	89–13	* *T·*, Philadelphia, Pa.
	89–14	* *T·*, Troy, N. Y.
	89–20	* *T·*, New Orleans, La.
	90– 8	* *T·*, Portland, Ore.

telegram
My.	36– 3	* The *t·* from the church
	44–14	* heading
	194–19	Your *t·*, in which you present
	207– 6	* chapter sub-title
	253–22	thanks for your letter and *t·*.
	281–17	* [*T·*]
	361–15	chapter sub-title
	361–16	[*T·*]

telegrams
My.	234– 1	fifty *t·* per holiday
	234– 4	cannot . . . while reading *t·*;
	259–13	*t·* to me are refreshing

telegraph
Pul.	74– 3	* [By *T·* to the *Herald*]
'02.	11–14	a submarine cable, a wireless *t·*,
My.	73–24	* *t·* and telephone service.

telegraphs
Un.	45–19	it *t·* and telephones

telegraphy
'02.	9–26	Morse's discovery of *t·*?
My.	110–14	*t·*, navigation of the air;

teleology
Mis.	74–10	systems of etiology and *t·*.
	218–30	* "The recognition of *t·*
	219– 1	*t·* is the science of the final cause

telephone
My.	73–24	* telegraph and *t·* service.
	345–10	* the *t·*, the steam engine

telephones
Un.	45–19	it telegraphs and *t·*

telescope
Ret.	65–27	to determine, without a *t·*,
Pul.	vii–11	to turn backward the *t·*

tell
Mis.	121–26	"If I *t·* you, ye will— *Luke* 22 : **67.**
	125–28	to *t·* the towers thereof
	129–10	to *t·* thy brother his fault
	168– 3	*t·* what things ye shall see
	181–14	who can *t·* what is the form
	221–30	Who would *t·* another of a crime
	226–20	* when he shall *t·* the truth."
	242–28	*t·* you that he was my student
	243–27	the medical faculty will *t·* you
	253–23	Can a mother *t·* her child
	311–24	and my necessity was to *t·* it;
	316–17	My juniors can *t·* others
Ret.	8– 7	to *t·* me what she wanted.
	14–19	minister then wished me to *t·* him
	38–19	come to *t·* me he wanted more,
Pul.	15– 7	when you *t·* them their virtues
	15– 8	when you *t·* them their vices.
	15– 9	to *t·* a man his faults,
	34–22	"How, I could not *t·*,
	84–21	* the future will *t·* the story
Rud.	17–10	could *t·* you of timidity,
'00.	7–11	will *t·* you they never loved the Bible
	9–25	My loyal students will *t·* you
'01.	12– 4	If St. John should *t·* that man
Hea.	3–26	We cannot *t·* what is the person of
Po.	1– 5	Beyond the ken of mortal e'er to *t·*
	17– 2	O *t·* of their radiant home
	66–10	And *t·* how that heart is silent
	71–16	can *t·* The holy meaning
My.	15–18	* I love to *t·* the story,
	15–22	* I love to *t·* the story,
	15–26	* I love to *t·* the story;
	60–27	* to *t·* you of the interesting
	63–29	* to *t·* by their presence that
	111–12	will *t·* you that he has found the
	112–16	its readers . . . will *t·* you this.
	112–25	student of this book will *t·* you
	123–12	"*T·* it not in Gath"!— *II Sam.* 1 : 20.
	124–17	What more . . . pen may not *t·*.
	133–22	I have a secret to *t·* you
	134– 2	*t·* my long-kept secret
	313– 5	* *T·* her I love her;
	317–16	he will *t·* you that Mr. Wiggin
	323–17	* My heart has been too full to *t·* you
	332– 5	* grateful tears alone can *t·* the

telling
Pul.	8– 3	Like the winds *t·* tales
	15–11	Who is *t·* mankind of the foe
My.	95–20	* *t·* of miracles performed
	324–12	* I remember *t·* you of this,

tells
Mis.	62–26	especially when she *t·* them that
Un.	14–17	but the New Testament *t·* us of
Pul.	27–20	* window *t·* its pictorial story
My.	81–30	* *t·* his or her experience.
	84–20	* story which the gathering here *t·*.
	107–16	he *t·* you, and you believe him,
	186– 8	neither dome nor turret *t·* the tale
	345– 5	But every thought *t·*,

temerity
Pul.	3–29	to reach out for . . . savors of *t·*.

temper
Mis.	126–10	when struggling . . . his *t·*,
	224–20	with a *t·* so genial
Po.	43–18	*T·* every trembling footfall,
My.	29–27	* cooling breeze to *t·* the heat,
	75–21	* not the slightest evidence of *t·*,
	215–32	should *t·* human affairs,
	310–26	* "hysteria mingled with bad *t·*."

temperament
Pul.	32– 7	* the *t·* to dominate, to lead,

temperance
Mis.	201–27	*t·*, virtue, and truth,
	288–26	cause of *t·* receives a strong impulse
	288–27	*t·* and truth are allies,
	288–31	to promote the ends of *t·*;
	289– 4	only *t·* is total abstinence.
	297– 5	In the direction of *t·*
Ret.	45–22	long-suffering and *t·*,
	79–23	Meekness and *t·* are the jewels
Po.	vi– 5	* poem
	page 39	poem
	39– 3	*T·* and truth in song sublime

temperance
Po. 39–17 Since *t·* makes your laws.
   39–20 blazoned, brilliant *t·* hall
   40– 3 We dedicate this *t·* hall

temperate
Ret. 79–22 Be *t·* in thought, word, and deed.
My. 114– 3 Owe no man ; be *t·* ;

temperately
Mis. 289– 3 evil cannot be used *t·* :

temperature
Hea. 5– 5 by changes of *t·*,

tempered
Pul. 82– 6 *steel *t·* with holy resolve,

tempers
Mis. 275–14 * "*t·* the wind to the shorn lamb,"

tempest (*see also* tempest's)
Mis. ix–17 darkness of storm and cloud and *t·*,
   144–17 a covert from the *t·* ; — *Isa.* 32 : 2.
   152–23 when storm and *t·* beat against
   362–26 shelter from the storm and *t·*
Un. 46–25 earthquake, thunderbolt, and *t·*.
'02. 20– 3 voice of him who stilled the *t·*
Hea. 2– 6 stills the *t·* of error ;
My. 106–20 expressed . . . in *t·* and in flood,
   182–29 a covert from the *t·*.

tempest's
Po. 28–11 Above the *t·* glee ;

tempests
Un. 52–20 its unkind forces, its *t·*,

temple
ample
My. 13–19 an ample *t·* dedicate to God,
beautiful
Pul. 23– 5 * Beautiful *T·* and Its Furnishings
My. 88–19 * this beautiful *t·*, striking as
   187–23 to consecrate your beautiful *t·*
   202–14 builders of this beautiful *t·*,
build a
My. 13–24 to build a *t·* the spiritual spire
cathedral or
My. 71–14 * this new cathedral or *t·*
Christian Science
Pul. 79– 4 * a C. S. *t·* costing over
   81– 1 * The chimes on the C. S. *t·*
My. 70–11 * The chimes for the new C. S. *t·*
   72–19 * fund of the new C. S. *t·*,
   91–16 * The dedication of a C. S. *t·*
   100– 1 * dedication of a C. S. *t·*
church
Mis. 141– 8 and against this church *t·*
earlier
'00. 12–15 The earlier *t·* was burned
erection of the
Pul. 56–11 * erection of the *t·*, in Boston,
giant
My. 76–24 * chapter sub-title
God is
Mis. 323– 5 for God is the *t·* thereof ;
godly
Pul. 3– 1 how can our godly *t·* possibly be
God's
Mis. 140–17 to know who owned God's *t·*,
goodly
My. 162–31 towering top of its goodly *t·*
great
My. 45–13 * The great *t·* is finished !
   45–28 * The great *t·* is finished !
   86–15 * building fund of the great *t·*
her
Pul. 59– 2 * has not yet visited her *t·*,
holy
My. 24–14 * unto an holy *t·* — *Eph.* 2 : 21.
idol's
My. 192– 1 Ye sit not in the idol's *t·*.
its
My. 88–21 * finds its *t·* in the heart of
lofty
My. 193–25 lofty *t·*, dedicated to God
magnificent
Pul. 25–17 * entrance to this magnificent *t·*.
My. 6–14 magnificent *t·* wherein to enter
   43–31 * dedication of our magnificent *t·*,
   59–13 * gallery of that magnificent *t·*,
   77–20 * magnificent *t·* of the C. S. church,
massive
Pul. 52–11 * erection of a massive *t·* in Boston
'neath the
My. 151–19 * 'neath the *t·* of uplifted sky
new
My. 67–25 * new *t·*, begun nearly two years ago,
   73–17 * dedication of the new *t·*.
   83–25 * construction of the new *t·*

temple
new
My. 84–13 * new *t·* is something to be proud of.
   88– 5 * opening of their great new *t·*.
   92–11 * a new *t·* to Isis and Osiris
   94–18 * magnificent new *t·* of the cult.
   97–27 * to dedicate the new *t·*, just built
new-built
Pul. 41–11 * to view the new-built *t·*
no
Mis. 323– 4 having no *t·* therein,
of Diana
'00. 12–14 *t·* of Diana, the tutelary divinity
of Spirit
My. 64–26 * in the universal *t·* of Spirit,
of thought
Mis. 369–13 at the portals of the *t·* of thought,
one
Ret. 89– 7 Men assembled in the one *t·*
our
Mis. 145–11 in this corner-stone of our *t·* :
Pul. 84–24 * our *t·* is completed as God intended
My. 13–32 a foundation for our *t·*,
   63–24 * Grandly does our *t·* symbolize this
sacred
Pul. 11– 4 Word spoken in this sacred *t·*
this
Mis. 107– 2 beauty in and of this *t·*
   144–23 His people in this *t·*,
   144–32 the spire of this *t·*.
Pul. 3– 4 Referring to this *t·*,
   3– 5 "Destroy this *t·*, — *John* 2 : 19.
   27– 8 * remarkable feature of this *t·*.
   51–23 * erection of this *t·* will doubtless
   85– 2 * to lay the foundation of this *t·*,
My. 23–24 * that this *t·*, . . . is being built
   71–20 * have been set aside in this *t·*,
   77– 3 * This *t·* is one of the largest
true
Pul. 2–29 true *t·* is no human fabrication,
vast
My. 79– 9 * dedication of the vast *t·*
   92–21 * dedication of this vast *t·*.
veil of the
Mis. 364–31 C. S. rends this veil of the *t·*
white
My. 202– 2 white wings overshadow this white *t·*
wonderful
My. 60–13 * corner-stone of this wonderful *t·*
your
My. 158–27 may your *t·* and all who worship
   193– 1 dedicate your *t·* in faith unfeigned,

Mis. 149–29 first *t·* for C. S. worship
   166–19 to go to the *t·* and be purified,
Ret. 51– 6 *t·* for C. S. worship.
Pul. 40– 9 * chapter sub-title
   75–25 * The *t·* is believed to be the most
'02. 18– 1 Be faithful at the *t·* gate of
Po. 39– 6 A *t·*, whose high dome
My. 77–27 * *t·* . . . absolutely free of debt,
   78– 1 * seating capacity of the *t·* is
   78–23 * acoustic properties of the *t·*,
   79–13 * to gain admission to the *t·*
   91–26 * *t·* which has just been dedicated
   100– 4 * *t·* recently dedicated at Boston
   158–25 chief corner-stone of the *t·*
   194– 6 a *t·* but foreshadows the idea of
   285–21 neither found me in the *t·* — *Acts* 24 : 12.

temples
Ret. 13–18 she bathed my burning *t·*,
My. 195–26 *t·* erected first in the hearts of
   195–30 fill these spiritual *t·* with grace,

Temples of Honor
Po. 39–18 " *T·* of *H·*," all,

temporal
Mis. 21–20 matter is the unreal and *t·*.
   87– 1 clear ether of the blue *t·* sky.
   93–13 Evil is *t·* : it is the illusion of
   103– 5 one is *t·*, while the other is
   103–18 and knows not the *t·*.
   103–19 Neither does the *t·* know the eternal.
Ret. 25–17 its antipodes, or the *t·*,
   59– 5 Life is not *t·*, but eternal,
   68–12 One is *t·*, but the other is eternal.
   73– 3 material, corporeal, and *t·*.
Un. 40–27 regard all things as *t·*.
   62– 7 which are seen are *t·* ; — *II Cor.* 4 : 18.
Pul. 2–10 Material light and shade are *t·*,
   13–23 Scriptures declare that evil is *t·*,
Rud. 9–12 false and *t·* sense of Truth,
No. 37– 8 evil is *t·* and God is eternal,
'01. 9– 3 referring to . . . his *t·* manhood.
   24–11 *greatest of all *t·* blessings,

temporal
Peo. 4– 8 belief that . . . the eternal entered the *t.*
My. 134– 1 spiritual bespeaks our *t.* history.
143–18 cannot be a *t.* fraud.
193–15 The spiritual dominates the *t.*

temporarily
Mis. 85–10 though his power is *t.* limited.
350– 3 I *t.* organized a secret society
No. 1–12 turn *t.* from the tumult,

temporary
Mis. 43–25 *t.* success of such an one
84– 9 the world's *t.* esteem ;
99– 8 *t.* loss of his self-respect.
247–23 That which is *t.* seems,
267–17 *t.* shame and loss
356– 7 need no *t.* indulgence
Ret. 89–29 is human, fallible, and *t.* ;
Un. 4– 7 To gain a *t.* consciousness of
41– 9 involves a *t.* loss of God,
Hea. 4–18 after a *t.* lapse,
My. 87– 5 * *t.* increase of the population
159–20 towards the *t.* and finite.
188–13 will not be *t.*,
259–29 merely *t.* means and ends.
312– 2 during her *t.* absence.

temptation
Mis. 10–18 crossing swords with *t.*,
12–20 danger of yielding to *t.*
53– 7 *overcoming t.* and sin,
85–21 *T.*, . . . suggests pleasure
85–24 so long as this *t.* lasts,
114–28 He will deliver us from *t.*
115–17 that you enter not into *t.*
198–17 the *t.* will disappear.
278–20 seem stronger to resist *t.*
301–16 to be long led into *t.* ;
302–13 the *t.* to be misled.
312– 2 to guard against that *t.*
321–21 treading each *t.* down,
323–11 beset with peril, privation, *t.*,
343– 2 that we enter not into the *t.*
344–15 sinner struggling with *t.*,
Ret. 45–24 the *t.* of popularity
Un. 50– 7 that we enter not into the *t.*
57–10 Without it there is neither *t.* nor
'01. 14–22 that he enter not into *t.*
My. 6– 9 the tempter and *t.*,
358– 6 enter not into *t.*." — *Matt.* 26 : 41.
359–27 arise from this *t.*

temptations
Mis. 12–16 *t.* to sin are increased
104– 4 was not subject to the *t.* of
Ret. 71– 7 Great *t.* beset an ignorant

tempted
Mis. 198–13 When *t.* to sin, we should
Un. 58–16 "in all points *t.* — *Heb.* 4 : 15.
Pul. 31– 7 * *t.* to "begin at the beginning"
50–18 * *t.* to examine its principles,
My. 122–11 my church *t.* me tenderly

tempter
Ret. 85–22 The *t.* is vigilant,
My. 6– 8 *t.* and temptation, the smile and

tempting
Mis. 9–20 having tested its *t.* wine,
No. 3–28 are *t.* and misleading.

tempts
My. 211–16 *t.* into the committal of acts

ten
Mis. 95– 6 * allowed *t.* minutes in which to reply
221–26 five times *t.* are fifty
221–26 while *t.* times five are not
341–21 *t.* virgins" — *Matt.* 25 : 1.
353–16 bucket of water every *t.* minutes
Man. 52– 8 within *t.* days thereafter,
68– 3 to go in *t.* days to her,
Ret. 10– 4 At *t.* years of age I was as
Pul. 53–11 * When the *t.* lepers were cleansed
'00. 10–27 *t.* five-dollar gold pieces
My. 10– 6 * externalized itself, *t.* years ago,
30–30 * admission at the *t.* o'clock service,
38–30 * Tuesday, June 12, at *t.* o'clock
66– 7 * *t.* estates having been conveyed
76– 3 * Up to within *t.* days
80–24 * it took *t.* meetings to accommodate
82–18 * in something like *t.* minutes.
127–18 the *t.* of *materia medica.*
304–19 and for *t.* subsequent years
310–23 * Mary, a child *t.* years old,
(*see also* **numbers, values**)

tenants
My. 231–24 to receive more *t.*

Ten Commandments
Mis. 303–18 help them to obey the *T. C.*
Man. 62–25 should be the *T. C.*
Rud. 12– 3 keeps unbroken the *T. C.*,
My. 129–30 the letter of the *T. C.*,
229–21 taking in the *T. C.*

tend
Mis. 47–13 *t.* to elucidate your day-dream,
124– 2 *t.* to disturb the divine order,
181– 9 *t.* to obscure the order of Science,
209–19 *t.* to rebuke appetite
353–18 Some people try to *t.* folks,
Ret. 21–23 lessons of Love which *t.* to this
My. 159–18 Material theories *t.* to check spiritual
256–22 whence they came and whither they *t.*
259–24 *t.* to give the activity of man
263– 1 *t.* to obliterate the spiritual idea
274–11 in youth *t.* to success,
340–24 should *t.* to enhance their confidence
345–26 They all *t.* to newer, finer,

tended
Mis. 341–32 must be *t.* to keep aglow the flame
'02. 9–22 not whence it came nor whither it *t.*,

tendencies
Mis. 10–25 material *t.* of human affections
245–19 in all the good *t.*, charities,
My. 151–30 discerned its idolatrous *t.*,
249–18 should countenance such evil *t.*

tendency
Mis. 3–29 *t.* of mental healing is to uplift
4– 4 marked *t.* of mortal mind
49– 2 had a *t.* to monomania,
214–23 their motives, aims, and *t.*
215– 2 The *t.* of mortal mind is to
Un. 31– 7 *t.* of Christianity is to spiritualize
Pul. 14– 4 present apathy as to the *t.* of
No. 46–21 unfolding of this upward *t.*
'02. 10–14 This upward *t.* of humanity will finally
Hea. 1–21 more spiritual basis and *t.*
My. 38–14 * visitors showed a *t.* to tarry
119–12 C. S. destroys such *t.*
159–19 the *t.* towards God,
320–19 * but his *t.* was friendly.

tender
Mis. xi–24 With *t.* tread, thought sometimes
127–28 *t.* sentiment felt, or a kind word
142–27 touched *t.* fibres of thought,
230–28 to render it pathetic, *t.*, gorgeous.
250–23 *t.*, unselfish deed done in secret ;
254– 5 brooded tireless over their *t.* years
311– 6 I would extend a *t.* invitation to
319–18 Scientists accept my *t.* greetings
391–17 Share God's most *t.* mercies,
Man. 64–21 *t.* term such as sister or brother.
Chr. 53– 5 In *t.* mercy, Spirit sped
Ret. 5– 8 object of their *t.* solicitude.
19–19 *t.* devotion to his young bride
Pul. 82– 6 * Her hand is *t.*
'00. 7–26 *t.*, loving Christ is found near,
'01. 29– 7 *t.* care of those who want to help
Po. 38–16 Share God's most *t.* mercies,
44– 1 Then, O *t.* Love and wisdom,
My. 13–22 lovingkindness and *t.* — *Psal.* 103 : 4.
36–27 * in *t.* affection for the cause of
51– 7 * her duty to *t.* her resignation,
51–28 * *t.* . . . the heartfelt thanks
64– 7 * were thrilled with *t.* gratitude
150– 1 where its *t.* lesson is not awaiting
158–21 makes the heart *t.*, faithful, true.
186– 5 like *t.* nestlings in the crannies
194–13 *t.* memorial engraven on your grand
196– 7 accept my *t.* counsel in these words
206– 5 *t.* grace of spiritual understanding,
235– 6 *t.* mother, guided by love,
247–21 *t. persuasion* that takes away their
289–26 may be read on that *t.* occasion.
290–19 Thy *t.* husband, our nation's chief
292–19 in which one earnest, *t.* desire
312–25 provisions in my behalf were most *t.*
326–18 in long procession with *t.* dirge
330–30 *t.* devotion to his young bride
351–14 It was truly Masonic, *t.*, grand
352– 9 * with its years of *t.* ministry,
352–20 I thank you . . . for your *t.* letter

tendered
My. 173–25 thanks are due and are hereby *t.*

tenderest
My. 37– 8 * from the depths of *t.* gratitude,
258– 8 the *t.* tendril of the heart

tenderly
Mis. 249–25 more *t.* to save and bless.
329–12 touching *t.* its tearful tones.
354–16 a few truths *t.* told,

tenderly
Mis.	397– 7	and *t·*, Divinely talk.
Pul.	v– 7	BOOK IS *t·* DEDICATED
	18–16	and *t·*, Divinely talk.
Rud.	v– 3	*t·* AND RESPECTFULLY DEDICATED
No.	v–10	saith *t·*,"Come and drink ;"
Po.	12–16	and *t·*, Divinely talk.
	27–12	heal her wounds too *t·*
My.	122–11	tempted me *t·* to be proud !
	204–17	I congratulate you *t·* on the
	216–15	*T·* thanking you for your

tenderness
Mis.	251– 7	my heart will with *t·*
	331–14	in tones tremulous with *t·*,
'02.	8–15	inspired with *t·*, Truth, and Love.
Po.	35– 7	Or pining *t·*
My.	215–11	Afterwards, with touching *t·*,
	247–30	patient, unfaltering *t·*.
	257–11	with ineffable *t·*.
	291–15	*t·* not talked but felt
	311– 6	my *t·* and sympathy were
	343–28	I wrote to each church in *t·*,

tendeth
Mis.	254– 8	mother-bird *t·* her young

tending
Mis.	353–20	*t·* the action that He adjusts.
	353–23	folly of *t·* it is no mere jest.
	354–12	the children are *t·* the regulator ;
	393–19	As the rock, whose upward *t·*
Ret.	90– 5	salary for *t·* the home flock
'02.	10–18	his predicate *t·* thereto is correct,
Po.	52– 3	As the rock, whose upward *t·*
My.	129– 9	*t·* to counteract the trend of

tendril
My.	258– 8	tenderest *t·* of the heart

tendrils
My.	125– 7	to bend upward the *t·*

tends
Mis.	52–16	*t·* to lift mortals higher.
	85–29	*t·* to destroy error :
	88– 1	*t·* to blight the fruits of my
	115–27	whatever *t·* to impede progress.
	301–28	error *t·* to harden the heart,
	303– 5	*t·* his own flock.
	319–12	*t·* to make sin less or more
	337–32	*t·* to hide from an individual
	341–26	if the lamp she *t·* is not replenished
	369–27	vine which our Father *t·*.
Man.	43–19	*t·* to prevent C. S. from
Ret.	81– 9	*t·* to demoralize mortals,
My.	119–10	Think not that C. S. *t·* towards
	218–18	*t·* to confuse the mind of the reader,
	266–16	*t·* in one ultimate
	267–24	Material thought *t·* to obscure
	316–19	*t·* to turn back the foaming torrents

Tenet
Man.	105– 2	No new *T·* or By-Law shall be
	105– 3	*T·* or By-Law amended or annulled,

tenet
Ret.	14– 2	as John Calvin . . . called his own *t·*

Tenets
Man.	page 15 heading	
	17–15	to draft the *T·* of The Mother Church
	28– 6	ultimate in annulling its *T·*
	33– 7	shall maintain the *T·*, Rules, and
	50–13	Departure from *T·*.
	50–15	If a member . . . depart from the *T·*
	54– 8	The Mother Church of Christ, . . . *T·*.
	54–11	*T·* as to unjust and unmerciful
	61–14	*T·* of The Mother Church are to be
	71–20	*T·* Copyrighted.
	71–21	not write the *T·* of The Mother Church
	71–24	as *T·* of The Mother Church,
My.	vi–14	* wrote its Church Manual and *T·*,
	32–22	* Reading of *T·* of The Mother Church.

tenets
Mis.	285–12	impersonal in its tenor and *t·*.
Pul.	38–23	* which are the *t·* of theosophy.
	57–13	* *t·* of the Christian Scientists,
	58–21	* pictures symbolic of the *t·* of
My.	49–14	* also the *t·* and church covenant.
	59–10	* *t·* be accepted wholly or in part
	84–23	* methods and *t·* of the sect.
	94–13	* in the interpretation of its *t·*,
	95– 4	* *t·* first presented by Mrs. Eddy
	178– 2	Your . . . pastor and ethical *t·*,
	182–30	beloved church adhere to its *t·*,

tenfold
Mis.	11– 2	its punishment is *t·*.

Tennessee and Tenn.
Pul.	25–25	* base and cap are of pink *T·* marble.

(see also Chattanooga)

Tennyson's
Mis.	106– 5	poor parody on *T·* grand verse,

tenor
Mis.	285–12	impersonal in its *t·* and tenets.
Ret.	65–21	*t·* of Christ's teaching and example,

tension
Mis.	339–14	moral *t·* is tested,

tenth
My.	319–20	* On the *t·* day of January, 1887,

tents
Pul.	84– 6	* shall dwell in the *t·* of hate ;

tenure
'02.	17–24	what we give . . . through His *t·*,
My.	201–18	to a *t·* of unprecarious joy.

term (noun)
class
Mis.	11–10	at close of the class *t·*,
	315–17	not only through class *t·*,
Man.	83–16	not only during the class *t·*

"devil"
Mis.	190–13	meaning of the *t·* "devil" — *Luke* 11 : 14.
	191– 2	Hebrew embodies the *t·* "devil"—*Luke* 11 : 14.
No.	22–18	the *t·* devil is generic,

divine Principle
No.	20– 8	When the *t·* divine Principle is used

employed
Ret.	37– 3	*t·* employed by me to express

for Deity
Mis.	75–15	Because Soul is a *t·* for Deity,
	192– 2	Hebrew *t·* for Deity was "good,"

for God
Mis.	13–28	Anglo-Saxon *t·* for God,
	26–29	Saxon *t·* for God is also good.
Pul.	6– 7	Good, the Anglo-Saxon *t·* for God,
My.	185–14	Love is the generic *t·* for God.

generic
Un.	51–14	generic *t·* for all humanity.
	51–16	generic *t·* for all women ;
'01.	10–11	generic *t·* for both male and female.
My.	185–14	Love is the generic *t·* for God.
	239–19	generic *t·* for men and women.
	347– 5	man the generic *t·* for mankind."

God
Hea.	3–14	*t·* God was derived from the

Hebrew
Mis.	192– 2	Hebrew *t·* for Deity was "good,"
Peo.	2– 8	Hebrew *t·* that gives another letter

implies
Pan.	12–25	includes all that the *t·* implies,

Life is a
Ret.	59–12	*Life* is a *t·* used to indicate Deity ;

meaning of the
Mis.	53–19	meaning of the *t·* and of C. S.
	190–13	meaning of the *t·* "devil" — *Luke* 11 : 14.
	191– 6	changed the meaning of the *t·*,

of Mother
Man.	64–17	endearing *t·* of Mother.

of office
Man.	25–15	*t·* of office for the Clerk
	80–22	*t·* of office for the editors
	94–16	His *t·* of office, if approved,

of Readership
Man.	30–14	during his *t·* of Readership,
	95–21	during his *t·* of Readership.

of service
Man.	69– 5	Incomplete *T·* of Service.

one
Ret.	43–17	taught the Primary, . . . class one *t·*.

opening
Mis.	256–19	previous to the opening *t·*.

pantheism
Pan.	2–23	stand, in the *t·* pantheism, for the

pope
My.	343–21	*t·* pope is used figuratively.

serpent
Mis.	191– 3	in another *t·*, serpent,

soul
Mis.	76–20	exchange the *t· soul* for *sense*

"spirits"
Pan.	9– 4	*t·* "spirits" means more than

tender
Man.	64–21	tender *t·* such as sister or

that
Rud.	4–14	if by that *t·* you mean material

the only
No.	20–11	found to be the only *t·* that fully

this
Mis.	75–16	this *t·* should seldom be employed
	75–19	if this *t·* is warped to signify
	180–28	This *t·*, as applied to man,
Man.	65– 7	when this *t·* is used in connection
Rud.	2–19	This *t·* enlarges our sense of Deity,

term (noun)
  three years'
    My. 250– 3   three years' *t·* for church Readers,
  winter's
    My. 327–14   * winter's *t·* of our Legislature,

    Mis. 191–20   *t·*, being here employed in its
    Man. 90– 8   *t·* of the . . . Metaphysical College
    Ret. 89– 7   in the modern sense of the *t·*.
    My. 250–17   as the *t·* for its Readers,
term (verb)
    Mis. 39– 9   false teachers of what they *t·* C. S. ;
    Pul. 31– 4   * C. S., as they *t·* her work
    66– 1   * they *t·* the divine art of healing,
termed
    Mis. 36– 1   *t·* material or mortal man,
    45–26   intelligence or mind *t·* evil.
    172–17   That which is *t·* "natural science,"
    205–20   *t·* in Christian metaphysics the
    233–15   force of mortal mind, *t·* hypnotism,
    Ret. 32–10   *t·* mortal and material existence
    64–20   in belief an illusion *t·* sin,
    Pul. 24– 7   * is *t·* by its Founder,
    70–25   * Mind-healing, which she *t·* C. S.
    No. 10–15   What is *t·* matter,
    Hea. 18–26   what is *t·* death has been produced
    My. 41–23   * hourly application what Paul *t·*
    226– 6   What are *t·* in common speech
terming
    Mis. 233–17   *t·* it metaphysics !
terms
  and nature
    Mis. 192– 9   *t·* and nature of Deity and devil
  belief and understanding
    Pul. 47–18   * upon the *t·* belief and understanding,
  better
    My. 334–16   * in no better *t·* than to quote
  class
    Mis. 256–17   intervals between my class *t·*,
  finite
    Ret. 59–11   even as mortals apply finite *t·*
  its
    Mis. 190–16   spiritual signification of its *t·*
  loving
    My. 224–27   speak in loving *t·* of their efforts,
  lowest
    No. 32–26   reduce this evil to its lowest *t·*,
  material
    No. 11– 9   is hampered by material *t·*,
  obsolete
    Mis. 318– 2   Mine and thine are obsolete *t·*
  opprobrious
    My. 104–10   vented their . . . in opprobrious *t·*.
  other
    My. 307–11   that word, as well as other *t·*
  physical
    Mis. 50–13   the metaphysical in physical *t·*.
    171–12   expressed in literal or physical *t·*,
  proper
    Mis. 365–27   hampered by lack of proper *t·*
  scientific
    Ret. 59– 4   Scientific *t·* have no contradictory
  such
    Un. 16– 2   such *t·* as *divine sin* and
  synonymous
    Mis. 23–22   Spirit, Mind, are *t·* synonymous
    '00. 5–11   Father and Mother are synonymous *t·* ;
  these
    Mis. 190–18   these *t·* will be found to include
  those very
    My. 324–13   * those very *t·* revealed to you.
  three
    Peo. 4–19   three *t·* for one divine Principle
  two
    Ret. 43– 9   taught two *t·* in my College.

    Mis. 27– 3   the *t·* God and good, as Spirit, are
    No. 27–21   what St. Paul *t·* "the old man — *Col.* 3 : 9.
terrace
    Pul. 48– 1   * well placed upon a *t·*
    49– 9   * tree-tops on the lower *t·*,
terra cotta
    Pul. 25–12   * roof is of *t· c·* tiles,
Terre Haute* (Ind.) *Star
    My. 90–21   * [*T· H· (I·.) S·*]
terrestrial
    Mis. 100–24   They unite *t·* and celestial joys,
    376–19   According to *t·* calculations,
terrible
    Mis. 69–17   barely alive, and in *t·* agony.
    246–20   conflict more *t·* than the battle of
    341–25   subject to *t·* torture if the lamp

terrible
    Mis. 350– 4   * not "*t·* and too shocking to relate."
    356– 5   need no *t·* detonation to free them.
    Ret. 19–16   in this *t·* bereavement.
    Pul. 83–13   * *t·* as an army with banners" — *Song* 6 : 10.
    No. 28– 7   purifying processes and *t·* revolutions
    35–15   He atoned for the *t·* unreality of
    My. 330–28   in this *t·* bereavement.
    335–25   * attended cases of this *t·* disease
terrifies
    Ret. 73–20   wrongs it, or *t·* people over it,
Territory
    Mis. 305– 1   * representing each State and *T·*,
territory
    Pul. 41–10   * *t·* that lies between,
Territory of Dakota
    Ret. 21–12   Marshal of the *T· of D·*.
terrors
    Ret. 72–10   consumed with *t·*." — *Psal.* 73 : 19.
terse
    Mis. 294–27   *t·*, graphic, and poetic style
tersely
    Mis. 212– 7   he *t·* reminded his students
test
    Mis. 93–25   does not *t·* sin and the fact of
    114–27   will *t·* all mankind on all questions ;
    158–17   to *t·* your humility and obedience in
    241– 7   *T·*, if you will, metaphysical healing
    249– 1   to *t·* that malpractice
    351– 1   called on students to *t·* their ability
    Man. 39–11   thoroughly to *t·* his sincerity,
    Ret. 62– 3   *T·* C. S. by its effect
    Un. 58–15   to *t·* the full compass of human woe,
    No. 2–13   to *t·* the feasibility of
    '02. 17– 4   obedience is the *t·* of love ;
    Hea. 19– 1   to *t·* the power of mind over body ;
    19– 2   and they did *t·* it,
    My. vii–10   * Deeds, . . . are the sound *t·* of love ;
    92– 3   * until it has stood the *t·* of time.
    138–10   present proceedings *t·* my trust
    215–29   Doubtless to *t·* the effect of both
Testament
  (*see* **Greek, Old,** *and* **New Testament**)
Testaments
  Old and New
    Pan. 7–18   study of the Old and New *T·*
  Old and the New
    My. 179–13   The Old and the New *T·* contain
tested
    Mis. 22–26   He who has not *t·* it,
    46– 6   needs only to be *t·* scientifically
    76– 8   can never be *t·* or proven true upon
    201–23   *t·* and developed latent power.
    339–14   moral tension is *t·*,
    My. 70–15   * were being *t·* the other day.
testified
    Ret. 15–22   persons who feelingly *t·*
    My. vii– 8   * *t·* to by Jesus and the prophets.
testifies
    Un. 33–10   matter *t·* of itself,
    My. 331–11   * *t·* to the love and respect
testify
    Ret. 15–30   were too timid to *t·* in public.
    25–24   material senses *t·* falsely,
    Un. 1–17   able to *t·*, by their lives,
    2–14   is ready to *t·* of God
    23–16   when they *t·* concerning Spirit,
    33– 6   *t·* from their own evidence,
    33–11   it cannot talk or *t·* ;
    33–14   Brain, thus assuming to *t·*,
    37–16   Evil and disease do not *t·* of Life
    39–22   senses, which *t·* that man dies.
    39–24   The material senses *t·* falsely.
    Rud. 4–26   senses *t·* to the existence of matter.
    No. 9– 1   as my Christian students can *t·* ;
    My. 81– 7   * bursting with a desire to *t·*
    84– 5   * Many a clergyman can *t·* from
testifying
    Mis. 54–16   the sick, unasked, are *t·* thereto.
    361–11   spiritual concepts *t·* to one creator,
    No. 17–14   witness, *t·* of Himself.
testimonial
    Man. 75– 3   Church Edifice a *T·*.
    75– 8   church edifice as a *T·*
    Pul. 24–15   * A *t·* to our beloved teacher,
    27–10   * the entire church is a *t·*,
    40–21   * *t·* to the Discoverer
    56–27   * intended to be a *t·*
    63–26   * *t·* to our beloved teacher,
    70–14   * as a *t·* to her labors,

testimonial
Pul. 75–23 * a t· to the Discoverer
77–13 * built as a t· to Truth,
77–16 * formally accept this t·
77–24 * chapter sub-title
78– 1 * a t· which is probably
78–11 * built as a t· to Truth,
78–14 * formally accept this t·
78–23 * t· is encased in a white
85–21 * chapter sub-title
85–26 * a beautiful and unique t·
86–13 * Accompanying the stone t·
86–22 * t· of love and gratitude
My. 58–15 * fitting t· in stone,

testimonials
Mis. 54– 9 lives are worthy t·,
Man. 47–11 T·.
47–21 This By-Law applies to t·

testimony
against sensualism
Mis. 325–27 a t· against sensualism
bear
Man. 48– 3 to bear t· to Truth
93–13 to bear t· to the facts
'02. 3– 2 bear t· to this fact.
beareth
Man. 42–18 the Scripture beareth t·.
bears
Mis. 21– 8 C. S. now bears t·.
bore
Mis. 225–11 bore t· to the power of Christ,
brief
Ret. 22– 3 Gospel narratives bear brief t·
death-bed
Mis. 24– 6 I give it to you as death-bed t·
deny the
Rud. 5– 2 deny the t· of the material
entire
My. 301–19 entire t· of the material
false
Mis. 66– 2 false t· or mistaken evidence
Ret. 30–12 false t· of the physical senses.
Un. 36– 8 reverses false t· and gains a
fitting
My. 352–14 * daily living may be a fitting t·
give
My. 80–26 * throngs who wanted to give t·
His
Rud. 17–16 are the paths of His t·
his
Hea. 2–15 Christian hero, . . . added his t· :
loving
'01. 31–18 church would bear loving t·.
mingle the
Mis. 73– 7 mingle the t· of immortal Science
my
My. 59–29 * Now my t· is not needed.
of material sense
Mis. 218– 6 The t· of material sense
of spiritual sense
Mis. 188–18 the t· of spiritual sense ;
of the five senses
Un. 25– 5 the t· of the five senses.
of the physical senses
No. 6–26 the t· of the physical senses.
of the senses
Mis. 103– 1 annuls the t· of the senses,
105– 9 from the t· of the senses,
164–30 from the t· of the senses,
No. 6– 7 refutes . . . the t· of the senses,
overturns the
Mis. 13–22 overturns the t· of the five erring
pretended
Un. 33– 4 give the only pretended t·
put in
Mis. 381– 9 he should not put in t·.
receive
My. 81–12 * were ready to receive t·,
reverses the
Un. 30– 6 Science reverses the t·
taking
Mis. 381– 7 taking t· on the part of the
their
Un. 33–22 the foundations of their t·,
Pul. 12–10 by the word of their t· ; — Rev. 12 : 11.
Hea. 16–19 how can we rely on their t·
this
Man. 47–18 This t·, however, shall not
was taken
Mis. 381– 5 T· was taken on the part of
which
Rud. 5– 3 Which t· is correct?

Mis. 73–30 t· of the so-called material senses.
Man. 47–13 T· in regard to the healing

testimony
Ret. 67–15 t· of material personal sense
My. 79–29 * at the t· meetings that marked
315–26 t· they have thereby given
tests
Mis. 119–23 t· and discriminates between
156–27 the aids and t· of growth
My. 90– 8 * and is given very real t·.
251–25 armors, and t· in His service,
Tex. (State)
(see **Dallas**)
text
Hebrew
Mis. 180–26 In the Hebrew t·, the word "son"
her
Pul. 70–19 * Taking her t· from the Bible,
My. 324–29 * who could keep to her t·.
meaning of the
Mis. 197–12 comprehend the meaning of the t·,
misinterprets the
Ret. 83–15 misinterprets the t· to his pupils,
my
'01. 22–19 my t·, that one and one are two
original
Mis. 192– 5 the original t· defines devil as a
Pan. 7–19 the original t· indicates,
'01. 16–16 original t· defines devil
Hea. 3–14 In the original t· the term God
our
Mis. 161–15 we have chosen for our t·,
164–17 In our t· Isaiah foretold,
191–23 our t· refers to the devil as
195–17 divine logic, as seen in our t·,
Scriptural
Mis. 194–19 the foregoing Scriptural t·
St. Paul's
Ret. 94– 6 contradicts . . . St. Paul's t·,
their
My. 225–24 expected to stick to their t·,
this
Mis. 52– 1 This t· may refer to such as
197– 7 the full import of this t· is not
wisdom of the
Mis. 201– 1 the entire wisdom of the t· ;
written
Man. 43–12 strengthen the faith by a written t·

Mis. 21–23 has been conformed to the t· of
27– 8 C. S. sticks to its t·,
84–19 the t·, "For to me to live — Phil. 1 : 21.
161– 5 T· : For unto us a child is — Isa. 9 : 6.
168–22 T· : Ye do err, — Matt. 22 : 29.
171–23 T· : The kingdom of heaven — Matt. 13 : 33.
178–11 * t·, "If ye then be risen — Col. 3 : 1.
181–21 His sonship, referred to in the t·,
182–26 The t· is a metaphysical statement
194–31 first condition set forth in the t·,
197– 4 t· is one more frequently used
200–12 that we have chosen for a t· ;
Pul. 1– 1 T· : They shall be — Psal. 36 : 8.
Hea. 1– 1 T· : And these signs shall — Mark 16 : 17.
Peo. 1– 1 T· : One Lord, one faith, — Eph. 4 : 5.

textbook
author of its
Pul. 64– 2 * author of its t·, 'S. and H.
70– 7 * author of its t·, "S. and H.
86–24 * author of its t·, "S. and H.
My. 23–22 * Founder of . . . and author of its t·.
author of the
Pul. 52–14 * Mary Baker Eddy, . . . author of the t·
Christian Science
Mis. 92–29 C. S. t· is the Key.
130– 8 and in the C. S. t·,
314–26 and add to this . . . "the C. S. t·."
314–29 Bible and the C. S. t·
315–12 teach from the C. S. t·.
317–16 the Scriptures and the C. S. t·,
383– 2 Bible, and . . . the C. S. t·,
Man. 34–10 contained in the C. S. t·,
37–20 loyal . . . to the C. S. t·,
60– 9 Scriptures or the C. S. t·.
69–14 author of the C. S. t·
72–10 Scriptures and the C. S. t·.
81–22 where the C. S. t· is published
Pul. 7–25 Bible and the C. S. t·,
43–21 * given in the C. S. t·.
'00. 6–30 In that year the C. S. t·,
'01. 24–23 S. and H., the C. S. t·.
My. v–21 * C. S. t·, "S. and H.
17–27 * given in the C. S. t·,
32–19 * given in the C. S. t·.
115– 9 my estimate of the C. S. t·,
147–15 Bible and the C. S. t·

textbook
Christian Science
My. 178–21 C. S. *t·* lay on a table
305–15 author of the C. S. *t·*,
her
My. 48– 9 * With the reading of her *t·*,
his
Mis. 91–25 did not take his *t·* with him
My. 111–14 he has found . . . through his *t·*.
my
Ret. 25– 3 The Bible was my *t·*.
my only
Pul. 34–27 "the Bible was my only *t·*.
of Christian Science
Mis. 50–10 complete *t·* of C. S. ;
92–12 take the *t·* of C. S.
364– 1 consonance with the *t·* of C. S.
372– 5 *t·* of C. S. is transforming
Ret. 38–27 S. and H. is the *t·* of C. S.
68–16 S. and H., the *t·* of C. S.,
My. 111–15 The *t·* of C. S. maintains
232–19 *t·* of C. S., "S. and H."
our
Mis. 91–22 *Should not the teacher . . . have our t·*,
356–27 must be had to understand our *t·* ;
Man. 53– 9 the author of our *t·*
105– 5 author of our *t·*, S. AND H.
My. 43–23 * later she gave us our *t·*,
46–25 * the Bible and our *t·*,
163–21 to revise our *t·*, "S. and H."
Science and Health
Mis. 91–22 *t·*, "S. and H. with Key to the
114–12 Bible and their *t·*, "S. and H."
144–10 your *t·*, "S. and H. with Key to the
Man. 34–10 *t·*, S. AND H. WITH KEY TO THE
35–21 teachings of the *t·*, S. AND H.
38– 3 students of the *t·*, S. AND H.
55–24 in its *t·*, S. AND H.
105– 5 author of our *t·*, S. AND H.
Pul. 7–25 C. S. *t·*, "S. and H."
64– 2 * author of its *t·*, "S. and H."
70– 7 * author of its *t·*, "S. and H."
86–24 * author of its *t·*, "S. and H."
'00. 6–30 C. S. *t·*, "S. and H."
My. v–21 * C. S. *t·*, "S. and H."
43–23 * gave us our *t·*, "S. and H."
48– 9 * reading of her *t·*, "S. and H."
163–21 to revise our *t·*, "S. and H."
305–15 author of the C. S. *t·*, " S. and H."
their
Mis. 114–12 Bible and their *t·*, "S. and H."
115– 3 With S. and H. for their *t·*,
Man. 63–11 C. S. contained in their *t·*.
64–16 given to the author of their *t·*,
Ret. 83–21 should take their *t·* into the
Pul. 60– 5 * no explanation of . . . their *t·*.
My. 225–27 In their *t·* it is clearly stated
this
Mis. 92– 7 continually to study this *t·*.
92–24 continue the study of this *t·*.
Ret. 75–24 the substance of this *t·* ?
84– 4 should continue to study this *t·*,
My. 114–11 the treasures of this *t·* are
your
Mis. 144–10 your *t·*, "S. and H. with Key
Pul. 87–17 Through my book, your *t·*,
My. 178– 1 Your Bible and your *t·*,
214– 3 would write your *t·* on the walls
320–18 * the statements in your *t·* ;

Mis. 309–27 My Christmas poem . . . not a *t·*.
Ret. 75–22 a *t·* written by his teacher,
'01. 34–24 study the Bible and the *t·*
My. 112–23 better . . . than the *t·* itself, is not

textbooks
Man. 34–14 his only *t·* for self-instruction
42–12 the C. S. *t·*,
Pul. 45–21 * declarations of our *t·*,
My. 103– 5 demanded of man in our *t·*,
203– 4 all is in your *t·*.

texts
Mis. 191–26 the original *t·* define him as
300–27 spiritual meaning of BIBLE *t·* ;
Man. 32– 3 correlative *t·* in S. AND H.
32– 5 Second Readers shall read the BIBLE *t·*.
58–16 correlative Biblical *t·* in the
Chr. 55– 1 These Scriptural *t·* are the basis
Pul. 25–27 * illuminated *t·* from the Bible
My. 317–20 quoting corroborative *t·* of Scripture.

textual
Ret. 78– 5 *t·* explanation of this practice

thank
Mis. 13–11 what *t·* have ye? — *Luke* 6 : 32.
167–23 "I *t·* Thee, O Father, — *Luke* 10 : 21.
218–29 "Pretty well, I *t·* you !"

thank
Mis. 262–13 I just want to say, I *t·* you,
275–17 we *t·* Thee that Thy light
308–18 I *t·* you, each and all,
313–12 I *t·* the contributors to *The*
Ret. 49–19 *Resolved*, That we *t·* the State
49–21 that we *t·* the public for its
No. 44–28 "I *t·* Thee, O Father, — *Luke* 10 : 21.
Peo. 8–24 We *t·* our Father that to-day
My. 6–16 deeply do I *t·* you for this proof
38– 4 * we *t·* you and renew the story of
62–10 * ever *t·* you enough
118– 9 I beg to *t·* you for your
127– 6 We *t·* the Giver of all good
142–26 I *t·* you for your kind
157–12 * We *t·* you for this renewed
163–27 and *t·* their ancestors for helping
165–12 I beg to *t·* the dear brethren
173– 6 *t·* the citizens of Concord
174–10 I *t·* the distinguished editors
194–23 profoundly *t·* you for it,
197–20 I *t·* divine Love for the hope
201–12 I *t·* you out of a full heart.
202–21 I *t·* you for the words of cheer
253–11 *Beloved Brethren:* — I *t·* you.
254–14 I *t·* the faithful teacher
265–31 we *t·* our Father-Mother God.
282–21 Deeply do I *t·* you for the
295–16 I *t·* you for it.
298– 8 I *t·* Miss Wilbur and the Concord
315–25 allow me to *t·* the enterprising
327–27 * We *t·* our heavenly Father
352–20 I *t·* you not only for
357–29 I *t·* you for acknowledging
358–18 I *t·* you for the money
(*see also* **God**)

thanked
Mis. 112–21 The jailer *t·* me, and said,
Un. 11–22 he never *t·* Jesus for restoring
My. 308–23 My father *t·* the Governor,

thankful
Mis. 193–17 I am *t·* even for his allusion to
245–27 it is a thing to be *t·* for
273– 2 I am *t·* that the neophyte
My. 62–23 * *t·* appreciation of your wise
332– 5 * emotions of the *t·* heart,

thankfulness
My. 9– 8 * to turn in loving *t·* to

thanking
Mis. 203– 1 In *t·* you for your gift
My. 5–25 lovingly *t·* your generosity
15–15 *t·* you for your gracious reception
174–17 I have the pleasure of *t·* you
216–15 Tenderly *t·* you for your

thanks (noun)
bankrupt in
My. 9–20 I am bankrupt in *t·* to you,
breath of
My. 256–10 heartfelt breath of *t·* for
card of
My. 173– 1 chapter sub-title
Christian Science
My. 264– 8 * chapter sub-title
cordial
My. 184–14 and to return my cordial *t·*
deep
My. 167– 1 Accept my deep *t·* therefor,
208– 3 Accept my deep *t·* for your
give
Mis. 311–29 drink all of it, and give *t·* ?
Pul. 12–16 we give *t·* and magnify the Lord
14–23 Those ready for . . . will give *t·*.
53–12 * one returned to give *t·*
My. 131–11 for the cup . . . we give *t·*.
giving
Mis. 211–28 He drank this cup giving *t·*,
'02. 11–19 which he drank, giving *t·*,
My. 131– 7 we unite in giving *t·*.
206–26 "Giving *t·* unto the Father, — *Col.* 1 : 12.
heartfelt
My. 51–29 * the heartfelt *t·* and gratitude
knelt in
My. 302–29 knelt in *t·* upon the steps
Leader's
My. 9–18 chapter sub-title
letter of
My. 295– 9 LETTER OF *T·* FOR THE GIFT OF A
331–10 * The following letter of *t·*,
love and
My. 257–27 two words enwrapped, — *love* and *t·*.
many
My. 62–26 * We acknowledge with many *t·*
198– 6 received with many *t·* to you
332– 9 * Many *t·* are due Mr. Cooke,

thanks (noun)

merited the
My. 49–27 * merited the *t·* of the society
Mrs. Eddy's
My. 352–26 chapter sub-title
my
Mis. 137– 2 Accept my *t·* for your card
142–11 my *t·* for the beautiful boat
242–10 Will the gentleman accept my *t·*
Pul. 8– 5 repeat my *t·* to the press.
My. 42–15 * opportunity to express my *t·*
142–10 Accept my *t·* for your approval
164– 9 yearned to express my *t·*
172–18 You will please accept my *t·*
186–25 Accept my *t·* for your cordial
191–30 Accept my *t·*.
231–28 You will accept my *t·* for your
274–20 my *t·* for their magnificent gifts,
285– 2 my *t·* for your kind invitation,
352–27 my *t·* for your successful plans
our
My. 331–21 * to return our *t·* and express
poor in
My. 9–25 never before felt poor in *t·*,
profound
Pul. 87–14 accept my profound *t·*.
My. 229–22 accept profound *t·* for their
253–22 accept my profound *t·*
sends
My. 274–17 * chapter sub-title
special
My. 173–25 Special *t·* are due
speechless
Mis. 275–25 moved me to speechless *t·*.
tearful
Mis. 249– 4 I say with tearful *t·*,
the word
Mis. 160– 4 uttering the word *t·*,
to God
'00. 2– 4 and, *t·* to God,
your
My. 252–26 It expressed your *t·*,

———

Mis. 280–25 fellow-students' *t·* to their teacher.
My. 183–24 *T·* for invitation to your

thanks (verb)
My. 118– 1 My soul *t·* the loyal,

Thanksgiving
Mis. 230–26 chapter sub-title
Man. 67–21 letters to the Pastor Emeritus on *T·*,
Po. page 77 poem
My. 25– 1 * the present *T·* season ;

thanksgiving
Mis. 110–21 We may well unite in *t·*
369– 3 look up with shouts and *t·*,
My. 27–22 * will read with much joy and *t·*
77–21 * a first hymn of *t·*

Thanksgiving Day
Mis. 231–26 his first sitting-at-table on *T· D·*
231–29 heartfelt joy on *T· D·*
Man. 123– 1 heading
My. 167–14 chapter sub-title
167–15 first *T· D·*, . . . in our new church
252–24 "*T· D·*," instituted in England on
264–11 * the birthplace of *T· D·*,
264–12 * last *T· D·* of the nineteenth
264–15 last *T· D·* of this century
322–14 * *T· D·* twenty years ago,

The
Man. 71– 6 "*T·*" must not be used before
112– 5 capitalized (*T·*), or small (the),

the
Man. 112– 4 The article "*t·*" . . . must not be used
112– 5 capitalized (The), or small (*t·*),

thea
Mis. 348–19 not even coffea (coffee), *t·* (tea),

The Arena
My. 316–11 January number of *T· A·*

theatres
Pul. 62–21 * *t·*, concert halls, and

The Board of Education
(*see* **Board of Education**)

The Christian Science Board of Directors
(*see* **Board of Directors**)

The Christian Science Board of Lectureship
(*see* **Board of Lectureship**)

The Christian Science Publishing Society
(*see* **Publishing Society**)

The Church of Christ, Scientist
Mis. 139–21 to be called *T· C· of C·, S·*.
145–31 *T· C· of C·, S·*, in Boston,
154– 3 branches of *T· C· of C·, S·*,
193–14 Referring to *T· C· of C·, S·*,
300–23 *T· C· of C·, S·*, in Boston,
314– 1 pastor of *T· C· of C·, S·*,
My. vii– 3 * *T. C· of C·, S·*, can never
48– 7 * of *T· C· of C·, S·*.
51–28 * members of *T· C· of C·, S·*,
54– 6 * "*T· C· of C·, S·*, had their
243–10 Readers of *T· C· of C·, S·*,
249–23 First Reader in *T· C· of C·, S·*,
342–19 continuity of *T· C· of C·, S·*,"
(*see also* **Church of Christ, Scientist**)

Thee and **thee**
Mis. 83–25 Son also may glorify *T·*."— *John* 17 : 1.
151–16 in heaven but *t·* ?— *Psal.* 73 : 25.
151–17 desire beside *t·*."— *Psal.* 73 : 25.
159–25 grown to behold *T·* !
167–23 "I thank *T·*, O Father,— *Luke* 10 : 21.
275–17 we thank *T·* that Thy light
397–14 From . . . grief afar, And nearer *T·*,
397–18 To Thine, for *T·* ;
400–18 Guide my little feet Up to *T·*.
400–21 lovingly *T·* I seek,
400–25 Be it slow or fast, Up to *T·*.
Pul. 18–23 From . . . grief afar, And nearer *T·*,
19– 2 To Thine, for *T·* ;
No. 44–28 "I thank *T·*, O Father,— *Luke* 10 : 21.
'02. 1–13 shall praise *T·* :— *Psal.* 76 : 10.
Po. 13– 2 From . . . grief afar, And nearer *T·*,
13– 6 To Thine, for *T·* ;
24–11 The Life that lives in *T·* !
28–13 The dove's to soar to *T·* !
39– 5 An offering bring to *T·* !
39–21 temperance hall To *T·* we dedicate.
69– 6 Guide my little feet Up to *T·*.
69– 9 lovingly *T·* I seek,
69–13 Be it slow or fast, Up to *T·*.
77– 1 to *T·* we raise A nation's holiest
77–13 of *T·*, who knowest best !
77–14 to *T·* we'll meekly bow,
My. 4–30 Glory be to *T·*, Thou God
31– 5 * "I need *T·* every hour ;"
31– 7 * "Still, still with *T·*,"
109–18 [spiritual sense] seeth *T·*."— *Job* 42 : 5.
111– 3 shall praise *T·*."— *Psal.* 76 : 10.
151–11 shall praise *T·* :— *Psal.* 76 : 10.
185–27 * we bless *T·*, Our God,
253–12 world hath not known *T·* :— *John* 17 : 25.
253–12 but I have known *T·*,— *John* 17 : 25.
290–15 whose mind is stayed on *T·* :— *Isa.* 26 : 3.
290–16 because he trusteth in *T·*."— *Isa.* 26 : 3.
290–16 I cried unto *T·*."— *Psal.* 130 : 1.

The Evening Press
My. 271–11 * *T· E· P·*, Grand Rapids, Mich.,
271–20 * editor of *T· E· P·*
271–28 *Editor of T· E· P·* :

The First Church of Christ, Scientist
Mis. 131–15 of the edifice of *T· F· C· of C·, S·*,
139– 8 chapter sub-title
141– 1 *T· F· C· of C·, S·*, our prayer
143–16 "*T· F· C· of C·, S·*," in Boston.
146– 4 chapter sub-title
147– 1 chapter sub-title
148– 8 Manual of *T· F· C· of C·, S·*,
310–12 gone out of *T· F· C· of C·, S·*,
Man. 3– 4 Manual of *T· F· C· of C·, S·*,
15– 1 *uniting with T· F· C· of C·, S·*,
18–16 named it, *T· F· C· of C·, S·*.
19– 1 *T· F· C· of C·, S·*, IN BOSTON,
34– 6 *T· F· C· of C·, S·*, in Boston,
37– 8 membership with *T· F· C· of C·, S·*,
45–15 member of *T· F· C· of C·, S·*,
58– 7 *T· F· C· of C·, S·*, in Boston,
65– 4 member of *T· F· C· of C·, S·*,
70–21 "*T· F· C· of C·, S·*," is the legal
72–26 branch church of *T· F· C· of C·, S·*,
75– 5 in behalf of *T· F· C· of C·, S·*,
77–21 Mother Church, *T· F· C· of C·, S·*,
92–19 not a member of *T· F· C· of C·, S·*,
102–11 land for *T· F· C· of C·, S·*,
103– 1 *T· F· C· of C·, S·*, in Boston,
103– 4 *T· F· C· of C·, S·*, in Boston,
104– 4 Manual of *T· F· C· of C·, S·*,
Pul. v– 5 ROOM IN *T· F· C· of C·, S·*,
1— chapter heading
7–26 pastor of *T· F· C· of C·, S·*,
8–27 Room in *T· F· C· of C·, S·*,
20– 1 whereon stands *T· F· C· of C·, S·*,
23– 3 * COMPLETION OF *T· F· C· of C·, S·*.
24– 6 * *T· F· C· of C·, S·*.
24–14 * "*T· F· C· of C·, S·*, erected
40–20 * home for *T· F· C· of C·, S·*,

The First Church of Christ, Scientist
Pul. 61–23 * tower of *T· F· C· of C·, S·,*
63–21 * "*T· F· C· of C·, S·,*" erected
65–15 * of "*T· F· C· of C·, S·.*"
76–26 * members of *T· F· C· of C·, S·,*
77–18 * "*T· F· C· of C·, S·,* at Boston,
77–25 * Members of *T· F· C· of C·, S·,*
78–16 * *T· F· C· of C·, S·,* at Boston,
84–12 * *T· F· C· of C·, S·,* in Boston,
85–22 * *T· F· C· of C·, S·,* in Boston
86–18 * completion of *T· F· C· of C·, S·,*
87–12 pastorate of "*T· F· C· of C·, S·,*"
'02. 13–13 to build *T· F· C· of C·, S·,*
My. vi–11 * organized *T· F· C· of C·, S·,*
15–6 *T· F· C· of C·, S·,* in Boston,
22–30 * edifice of *T· F· C· of C·, S·,*
23–18 * *T· F· C· of C·, S·,* in Boston,
27–3 *T· F· C· of C·, S·. in Boston:*
27–12 * *T· F· C· of C·, S·,* in Boston,
29–8 * *T· F· C· of C·, S·,* at the corner
38–28 *' meeting of *T· F· C· of C·, S·,*
44–24 * *T· F· C· of C·, S·,* in Boston,
47–2 * Brethren of *T· F· C· of C·, S·,*
55–15 * named it *T· F· C· of C·, S·.*
65–5 * members of *T· F· C· of C·, S·,*
67–19 * addition to *T· F· C· of C·, S·,*
134–22 * *T· F· C· of C·, S·,* in Boston,
135–25 * *T· F· C· of C·, S·,* in Boston,
140–11 * service of *T· F· C· of C·, S·,*
141–4 * annually in *T· F· C· of C·, S·,*
141–15 * *T· F· C· of C·, S·,* in Boston,
172–9 * her church, *T· F· C· of C·, S·,*
216–17 *T· F· C· of C·, S·,* Boston,
(*see also* First Church of Christ, Scientist)

theft
Mis. 61–14 * *What commits t·?*
300–11 law defines and punishes as *t·.*
300–21 increasing the record of *t·*

thefts
'01. 20–27 will handle its *t·,* adulteries, and

The Galaxy
Mis. 376–10 * from a description, in *T· G·,*

The Independent
My. 269–15 [*T· I·,* November, 1906]

The Interpretation of Life
My. 351–23 book title

Theism
Mis. 13–13 chapter sub-title
216–7 chapter sub-title

theism
Mis. 76–11 not *t·,* but pantheism.
217–25 This is neither Science nor *t·.*
Pan. 2–25 and *t·* for a belief concerning Deity
3–18 *T·* is the belief in the personality
6–11 Mosaic *t·* introduces evil,
6–15 criticism is not satisfied with this *t·,*
6–21 what becomes of *t·* in Christianity?
7–8 *t·* . . . that after God, Spirit, had
7–21 *t·* seems meaningless,

theist
Mis. 22–1 I am strictly a *t·*

theistic
Pan. 4–7 A *t·* theological belief
7–13 chapter sub-title
7–14 know of but three *t·* religions,

theists
'01. 4–21 Scientists are *t·* and monotheists.

The Ladies' Home Journal
My. 261–21 [*T· L· H· J·*]

"The Lamp"
Mis. 313–16 "*T· L·,*" by Walter Church,

The Life of Mary Baker Eddy
My. 298–1 book title

The Master
Pul. 54–1 * a poem entitled "*T· M·,*"

theme
Mis. 176–6 great *t·* so deeply and solemnly
Ret. 10–18 no earthly or inglorious *t·.*
Un. 5–1 *t·* involving the All of infinity.
'00. 2–5 old-new *t·* of redeeming Love
'02. 5–19 the *t·* for time and for eternity ;
My. 319–23 * about the preparation of a *t·*
320–4 * presented my matter for a *t·*

themes
Ret. 5–27 * *t·* at once pleasing and profitable.
Po. 22–8 New *t·* seraphic, Life divine,

thence
Mis. 64–3 *t·,* the way he made for
123–25 *t·* to receive the reward of
188–18 *t·,* up to the unseen,

thence
Mis. 195–2 *T·* will follow the absorption of
199–5 *t·* comes man's ability to annul
288–14 and *t·* achieves the absolute.
326–9 *t·* they spread to the house of
345–28 *t·* arose the rumor that it
379–22 *t·* to a mental standpoint
'00. 15–14 *t·* to see that sin has no claim,
'01. 23–7 *t·* it would follow that
My. 333–12 * *t·* to the Episcopal burying-ground,

thenceforth
Mis. vii–13 *T·* to evolution's Geology,
My. 182–6 *t·* to exemplify my early love

The New Century
Pul. 81–8 *[*T· N· C·,* Boston, February, 1895]

"The New Pastor"
Mis. 313–15 articles entitled "*T· N· P·,*"

theocracy
Mis. 121–13 Stalled *t·* would make this

theologian
Un. 11–19 If his patient was a *t·*

theologians
Mis. 102–4 lexicographers and scholastic *t·,*
362–10 *T·* make the mortal mistake
No. 46–11 *T·* descant pleasantly

theological
Un. 13–21 an outworn *t·* platform,
Pul. 51–18 * implements of *t·* warfare,
Pan. 4–7 A theistic *t·* belief may agree
'01. 5–28 *t·* God as a Person necessitates
6–25 departure from *t·* personality
My. 307–16 my *t·* belief was offended

theology (*see also* theology's)
and *materia medica*
'01. 30–17 critics in *t·* and *materia medica,*
My. 266–25 points in *t·* and *materia medica,*
and medicine
No. 1–18 *t·* and medicine of Jesus were one,
and philosophy
Un. 45–16 certain forms of *t·* and philosophy,
divine
My. 180–30 divine *t·* and C. S.
doctrine of
Mis. 366–6 to learn the doctrine of *t·,*
God of
'01. 6–3 Who says the God of *t·* is a Person,
6–10 Is the God of *t·* a finite
healing
Mis. 59–2 of the healing *t·* of Mind,
material
'01. 26–2 false philosophy and material *t·*
materia medica **and**
Peo. 5–9 *materia medica* and *t·* were one.
medicine and
My. 28–32 * whole aspect of medicine and *t·.*
metaphysical
Mis. 68–20 meaning of . . . metaphysical *t·?*
needs Truth
No. 43–6 *t·* needs Truth to stimulate
of Christian Science
Mis. 58–19 *Does the t· of C. S. aid its*
62–17 The *t·* of C. S. is Truth ;
62–28 The *t·* of C. S. is based on
of mental healing
Mis. 58–26 Take away the *t·* of mental healing
pantheism in
Pan. 2–26 preferable to pantheism in *t·.*
popular
Un. 13–3 Popular *t·* makes God tributary
pure
Mis. 63–8 triune Principle of all pure *t· ;*
relentless
Ret. 13–13 My father's relentless *t·*
scholastic
Mis. 13–14 Scholastic *t·* elaborates the
173–9 pagan philosophy, or scholastic *t·,*
194–15 which scholastic *t·* has hidden.
340–30 human ethics, scholastic *t·,*
No. 24–11 false philosophy and scholastic *t·,*
Pan. 5–2 pantheism is found in scholastic *t·.*
'01. 7–3 Scholastic *t·* makes God manlike ;
12–20 which scholastic *t·* has obscured,
24–28 *materia medica,* and scholastic *t·*
My. 149–21 deeply read in scholastic *t·*
205–22 Scholastic *t·* at its best touches but the
307–31 want of divinity in scholastic *t·,*
sound
No. 29–13 Is this . . . statement sound *t·,*
speculative
Peo. 3–3 crudest ideals of speculative *t·*
to learn
No. 11–20 to learn *t·,* physiology, or physics ;

theology

would teach
Mis. 229–15   *t·* would teach man as David taught :

Mis. 58–21   Without its *t·* there is no
    62–14   *that their t· is essential to heal*
  203–13   *T·* religiously bathes in water,
Un. 13– 1   evidence of the senses in *t·*,
Pul. 55–21   * *t·* . . . of C. S. is contained in
Pan. 2–25   belief concerning Deity in *t·*.
'01. 6– 6   Person is defined differently by *t·*,

theology's
'01. 6– 2   *t·* three divine persons,

theorems
Mis. 173– 2   man's *t·*, misstate mental Science
  312–22   human *t·* or hypotheses,
My. 248–16   rising above *t·* into the

theoretic
Mis. 369–22   we are tired of *t·* husks,

theoretically
Mis. 48– 1   no . . . mesmerism, practically or *t·*,
  264–24   Their knowledge . . . may be right *t·*,
'01. 10–19   *T·* and practically man's salvation
My. 136– 4   cannot be fully understood, *t·* ;

theories

and practice
No. 2–28   with conflicting *t·* and practice.
crude
My. 111– 5   crude *t·* or modes of metaphysics.
difference in the
Pul. 47–17   * difference in the *t·* between
false
Mis. 366–31   false *t·* whose names are legion,
Peo. 11–15   false *t·*, false fears,
finite
Ret. 56– 2   antagonized by finite *t·*,
human
Mis. 365– 5   Human *t·* weighed in the
Un. 44–15   Human *t·* call, or miscall,
No. 18–13   Human *t·*, when weighed in the
man-made
Mis. 64–15   Man-made *t·* are narrow,
material
Un. 28–15   material *t·* are built on the
My. 159–18   Material *t·* tend to check
of agnosticism
Mis. 55–31   *t·* of agnosticism and pantheism,
other
Mis. 25–13   rejects all other *t·* of causation,
No. 32–15   but other *t·* make sin true.
speculative
Ret. 70–12   speculative *t·* as to the recurrence
systems and
Mis. 232–15   part with material systems and *t·*,

theorist
Mis. 265–15   egotistical *t·* or shallow moralist

theorizing
'02. 18–24   effective healers and less *t·* ;

theory

abjure a
Mis. 197–29   Let man abjure a *t·* that is in
and practice
Ret. 79– 2   *honest* metaphysical *t·* and practice.
No. 5–27   in both *t·* and practice,
'01. 26– 1   consistency of Jesus' *t·* and practice
Peo. 2– 3   *t·* and practice of religion
  5– 1   *t·* and practice of medicine
bacteria
My. 344–16   * reject utterly the bacteria *t·*
embraced in the
Un. 6–19   is embraced in the *t·* of God's
fallacy of the
Mis. 74–22   he proved the fallacy of the *t·*
its
'01. 6–21   its *t·* even seldom named.
man-made
Mis. 38–22   elaborating a man-made *t·*,
may be sound
No. 13–25   A *t·* may be sound in spots,
mere
No. 13–17   being held as a mere *t·*.
metaphysical
Ret. 79– 2   as against *honest* metaphysical *t·*
No. 22– 6   Berkeley ended his metaphysical *t·*
opposite
Ret. 64– 9   any opposite *t·* is heterodox
practice more than
Mis. 195–29   practice more than *t·*,
  281–32   need, . . . *practice* more than *t·*.
same
Pul. 73–19   * same *t·* as Mrs. Copeland.
speculative
Mis. 29–14   between it and any speculative *t·*.

theory

such a
Un. 41–28   such a *t·* implies perpetual
Peo. 2–19   Such a *t·* has overturned
their
Ret. 54–21   far in advance of their *t·*.

Mis. 76–14   The *t·* that death must occur,
  102– 5   a *t·* to me inconceivable.
  198–24   belief, fear, *t·*, or bad deed,
No. 6– 5   *t·* that God's formations are
Peo. 2–16   that make a Christian only in *t·*,

theosophy
Mis. 296–15   with *t·* and spiritualism ;
Man. 41– 7   gulf between C. S. and *t·*,
  47–26   *t·*, hypnotism, or spiritualism,
Ret. 23–21   pantheism, and *t·* were void.
Pul. 38–24   * which are the tenets of *t·*.
Rud. 13– 3   pantheism and *t·* are not Science.
No. 13–16   chapter sub-title
  13–21   C. S., spiritualism, and *t·*.
  14– 8   *T·* is a corruption of Judaism.
  14–11   *T·* is no more allied to C. S. than

therapeutics
Mis. 5–22   *t·* can seem a miracle
  80–27   pathology, hygiene, and *t·*,
  268–23   His *t·* are antidotes for
  378–21   *t·*, as in C. S.,
Pul. 54–20   * in his practice of mental *t·*,
Pan. 4–27   hygiene, and medical *t·*,
'01. 30–16   Even religion and *t·* need
My. 127–12   system of metaphysical *t·*
  179–31   They afford such expositions of the *t·*,
  204–29   *t·*, based as aforetime on
  265–16   religion and scientific *t·*
  267– 1   the only religion and *t·*
  306–31   on my views of mental *t·*.
  349–11   divine metaphysics or its *t·*.

thereabout
My. 100–11   * twenty-five years, or *t·*,

thereabouts
Mis. 381–28   thirty-eight hundred or *t·*,

thereafter
Mis. x–26   *t·* adopted that form of
  24–10   On the third day *t·*,
  87–24   What they need *t·* is to
  129–13   *t·* "let the dead — *Matt. 8 : 22.*
Man. 52– 8   within ten days *t·*, the Clerk
Ret. 83–16   *t·* he will find it more difficult
'02. 16– 1   Six months *t·* Miss Dorcas Rawson
My. 158–26   *t·* dedicate to Truth and Love.
  296–29   *t·* gave her discovery to

thereby
Mis. 9– 7   *t·* numbering them, and giving them
  10–19   they *t·* have tried their strength
  14–30   and *t·* destroys all error,
  24–19   *t·* shutting out the true sense
  33– 4   *t·* they lost, and he won, heaven.
  45– 8   *t·* avoiding the fatal results
  50–25   live *t·*, and have being.
  84– 5   and *t·* hasten or permit it.
  85–30   sick often are *t·* led to Christ,
  109–29   lest *t·* it master you ;
  121–20   *t·* giving the signet of God
  129–10   tell thy brother his fault and *t·* help
  130– 1   hope remained of *t·* benefiting
  155–23   *t·* give to us all the pleasure
  169– 5   insight had been darkened *t·*,
  221– 6   *t·* learns more of its divine
  287–10   on a false basis and *t·* lose it.
  382–10   sinner and the sick are helped *t·*,
Ret. 33–19   matter is *t·* rarefied to
  51– 5   the premises *t·* conveyed,
Pul. vii–16   impetus *t·* given to Christianity ;
  81–17   * the moth to be destroyed *t·*,
Pan. 6–12   and *t·* obtaining social prestige,
'00. 3–10   he is not *t·* worshipped
'01. 7–27   nor can they gain any . . . *t·*.
'02. 6–12   *t·* showing that God made
My. 6–16   impressed and encouraged *t·*,
  17– 7   that ye may grow *t·* : — *I Pet. 2 : 2.*
  21–12   * *t·* aid the progress of our Cause
  52– 5   * *t·* giving in her Christian example,
  113– 5   and *t·* is healed of disease.
  164– 4   I consented, hoping *t·* to
  210–11   but all . . . are *t·* benefited.
  229–15   *t·* help themselves and
  315–26   testimony they have *t·* given

The Recent Reckless and Irresponsible Attacks on Christian Science etc.
My. 316–12   *T· R· R· and I· A· on C· S·*

therefor

Mis.	107–26	and of *repentance t·*,
	119–31	and escape the penalty *t·*?
	301– 3	and receive pay *t·*,
Man.	67–23	and are amenable *t·*.
	69–17	appoint a proper member . . . *t·*,
	89–23	evidence of their eligibility *t·*,
Un.	64– 2	If . . . God is responsible *t·*;
My.	167– 1	Accept my deep thanks *t·*,

therefore

Mis.	2–23	*t·* evil must be mortal
	14–17	*t·* to him evil is as real and
	14–28	*t·*, wholly problematical.
	16–18	*t·*, we must entertain a higher sense
	18– 5	*t·* rejoice in tribulation,
	21–21	*T·* man is not material ;
	22–18	*t·* these are null and void.
	24–22	*t·* it cannot be true.
	27– 2	*T·* the Science of good calls evil *nothing.*
	31– 8	*t·*, is not the use but the abuse of
	45–15	*t·*, under the deific law that
	50– 2	*t·* your answer is, that error is
	50–21	"Be ye *t·* perfect ;"— *Matt.* 5 : 48.
	72–29	*t·* it cannot cognize aught material,
	73–14	Human wisdom *t·* can get no
	85–14	"Be ye *t·* perfect,— *Matt.* 5 : 48.
	96–10	*t·*, I worship that of which I can
	103–31	*t·* is forever with the Father.
	119–31	"*T·* all things whatsoever— *Matt.* 7 : 12.
	128– 5	*T·* I close here,
	155– 1	*t·*, . . . there is but one cause and
	182– 8	*t·*, . . . they lose their false sense
	184–19	If he says, "I am of God, *t·* good,"
	186–15	*t·* divine Love is the
	188–13	*t·* now no condemnation— *Rom.* 8 : 1.
	190–21	*t·* the devil herein referred to
	196–12	*t·* that saying came not from Mind,
	197–26	*t·* cannot stand.
	198–31	*t·* he must suffer for it.
	199–11	*T· I take pleasure in*— *II Cor.* 12 : 10.
	210–10	"Be ye *t·* wise— *Matt.* 10 : 16.
	254–25	"What shall, *t·*, the Lord— *Mark* 12 : 9.
	273–19	*t·* they should continue,
	274–10	*t·* I leave all for Christ.
	292–20	who know not . . . and *t·* curse him ;
	293– 3	*t·* it is best to leave the
	303–11	*t·* no queries should arise as to
	311–25	*t·* I did this even as a surgeon
	313–21	pray ye *t·* the God of harvest
	322–18	*T·*, beloved, my often-coming is
	328–26	*T·*, give up thy earth-weights ;
	350–28	*t·* I teach the use of
	384–17	You *t·* cannot part.
Man.	59– 6	*T·* it is the duty of every member
	71–15	*T·*, no Church of Christ, Scientist,
Ret.	25–25	is *t·* inadequate to form any
	45–15	*T·*, in accord with my special request,
	49–18	*t· Resolved,* That we thank the State
	60–13	*t·* evil is unreal
	67–21	*T·* the lie was, and *is*, collective
	72– 4	*t·* it deteriorates one's ability
	75–18	and is *t· honest.*
	76–10	*T·* the mind to which this
	78–16	*T·* the adoption of a worldly policy
	79–27	*T·* are its spiritual gates
	81– 5	*T·* we should guard thought
	82–23	*t·* their examples either excel or
	82–30	it is *t·* better adapted to
	87–24	can *t·* bear the weight of
	94–11	*T·* this purgation of
Un.	8–10	not absolute, and *t·* not real,
	15–24	whom *t·* they wish to bribe
	18– 3	*t·* I know not evil.
	19–14	"If *t·* the light— *Matt.* 6 : 23.
	20–14	We *t·* need not fear it.
	25–23	*t·* has no groundwork in Life,
	27–10	An *egoist*, *t·*, is one
	29– 7	*T·* there is, . . . no spiritual death.
	34– 8	*t·* that the whole function
	34–11	*t·* there is nothing but Spirit ;
	38– 4	*t·* it is not in accordance with
	40–13	*t·* mortals can no more receive
	41–23	Life, *t·*, is deathless, because
	60–11	its opposite, and *t·* unreal ;
Pul.	4– 8	and *t·* whole number,
	4–15	*t·* is the seer's declaration true,
	12–11	*T·* rejoice, ye heavens, — *Rev.* 12 : 12.
	20– 4	*t·* I paid it,
	25– 7	* *t·* as literally fire-proof as
	55–12	* We do not, *t·*, regard it as a
	80–19	* We do not, *t·*, speak of
	86–26	* We *t·* respectfully extend
Rud.	2–14	*t·* I prefer to retain the
	5– 6	*T·* in divine Science there is
	11– 8	*t·* good is one and All.
No.	5–10	*T·* this material sense,

therefore

No.	5–22	*t·* the mind that attacks a
	23– 9	and *t·* was not a *devil*,
	24– 4	He is in all things, and *t·*
	36– 4	and *t·* as the All-in-all ;
Pan.	2– 5	*t·* is neither hypothetical nor
	5–19	*T·* we should neither believe
	9–11	"Be ye *t·* perfect,— *Matt.* 5 : 48.
	10–25	*t·* no pleasure in loathsome
	10–30	*T·* it required the divinity of
	11–30	"Be ye *t·* perfect,"— *Matt.* 5 : 48.
'00.	9– 6	*t·*, not ready— to obey.
'01.	3–26	*t·* it is illogical
	5–11	*t·* divine metaphysics
	5–21	*t·* man reflects Spirit,
	8–10	*T·* we have the authority of
	8–15	"Be ye *t·* perfect,— *Matt.* 5 : 48.
	8–24	*t·* Christ existed prior to Jesus,
	10– 6	Fear them not *t·* :— *Matt.* 10 : 26.
	10–10	*t·* the son of man only in
	12–23	*t·* the nothingness of matter.
	13–14	*t·* is nothing and the father of
	14–15	*t·* as unreal as a mirage
	14–27	*t·* man is its master.
	15– 6	to prove it false, *t·* unreal.
	16–17	*t·*, according to Holy Writ
	22– 6	*T·* I do not try to mix
	22–13	*t·* matter cannot be a reality.
	23–20	*t·* he demonstrated his power
	26– 8	the metaphysician . . . that combines
'02.	11–20	*T·* it is thine, advancing Christian,
	14–24	*T·*, I ask : What has shielded
Hea.	3–18	*T·* Christ Jesus was an honorary title ;
	10– 9	*t·* evil is impotent.
	17– 9	*t·* the so-called material man
	17–21	and *t·* are not TRUE.
Peo.	5–24	*t·* a Truth-filled mind makes a
Po.	vii–10	* *With grateful acknowledgment, t·*,
	36–16	You *t·* cannot part.
My.	11–25	* The location is, *t·*, determined.
	16–24	"*T·* thus saith the— *Isa.* 28 : 16.
	21–10	* We *t·* feel sure that all
	22–26	* Is it not *t·* the duty of all
	24–30	* It *t·* occurs to us that
	56–11	* *t·* three branch churches
	56–28	* *T·*, beginning October 1, 1905,
	83–13	* *T·*, with the exception of
	100– 8	* is *t·* the property of
	109–19	*T·* there can be but one God,
	113–11	"There is *t·* now no— *Rom.* 8 : 1.
	126–20	*T·* shall her plagues — *Rev.* 18 : 8.
	128– 3	"*T·* . . . let us go on — *Heb.* 6 : 1.
	128–22	*T·* be wise and harmless,
	130–15	*T·* I ask the help of others
	136– 4	*t·* it is best explained by
	146–25	*T·* a Christian Scientist never
	150– 2	*T·* despair not nor murmur,
	150–28	"Be ye *t·* wise— *Matt.* 10 : 16.
	153–21	"whom *t·* ye ignorantly — *Acts* 17 : 23.
	161–19	*T·*, said Jesus, " Ye shall drink — *Matt.* 20 : 23.
	171–11	*T·* I hereby invite all my
	178–16	*t·* if evil exists, it exists without
	202– 8	"Render *t·* to all — *Rom.* 13 : 7.
	205– 1	"There is *t·* now no— *Rom.* 8 : 1.
	205– 4	"Stand fast *t·* — *Gal.* 5 : 1.
	205– 5	"Be ye *t·* wise as— *Matt.* 10 : 16.
	214–25	I *t·* halted from necessity.
	218–28	*T·* an individual should not
	224–23	less correct and *t·* less profound.
	231– 9	She has, *t·*, finally resolved
	231–21	It would *t·* be as unwise
	269–11	This, *t·*, is Christ's plan
	273–23	ever-present good, and *t·*
	276– 5	*t·* to be criticized or judged
	288–22	*t·*, he cast out devils
	299–17	*T·* I query :
	351–24	*t·* I have not endorsed it,
	357–22	*t· Spirit is all.*
	358– 2	*t·*, if you are sincere

therefrom

Mis.	vii–15	Nothing have we gained *t·*,
	33–20	recognize the help they derive *t·*.
	115– 1	to protect themselves *t·*,
	162–17	*t·* rise to his nativity in Spirit.
	288–12	any conclusion drawn *t·*
Man.	110– 4	confusion that might result *t·*.
Ret.	50–28	the blessings which arose *t·*.
Pul.	46– 7	* no such inference is to be drawn *t·*
'02.	13–11	I receive no personal benefit *t·*
My.	133–14	fragments gathered *t·* should
	242– 7	and must be practised *t·*.

therein

Mis.	28–26	find neither pleasure nor pain *t·*.
	146–17	be governed *t·* by the spirit
	158–27	order *t·* given corresponds to

therein

Mis.	169– 3	way of her researches *t·*,
	189– 5	interpretation *t·* will be found to be the
	323– 4	having no temple *t·*,
	323–18	saith unto the patient toilers *t·* :
	325– 2	saith unto the dwellers *t·*,
	344–26	shall in no wise enter *t·*.'' — *Luke* 18 : 17.
Man.	68–19	or allows to visit or to locate *t·*
	69– 9	expiration of the time *t·* mentioned
	79–23	manage the property *t·* conveyed,
	91–20	Students of C. S., duly instructed *t·*
Ret.	26–16	seeing *t·* the operation of the divine
	37–15	Science of Mind-healing as *t·* stated.
	82–16	in large cities, . . . and *t·* abide.
	94–30	the Father was glorified *t·*.
Un.	14–22	if . . . all cannot be good *t·*.
	28–11	never a light . . . was discerned *t·*,
	33–17	and you find no mind *t·*.
	36–19	(instead of acquiescence *t·*)
Pul.	58–29	* *T·* is a portrait of her
	87– 2	* any services that may be held *t·*.
No.	17–17	*t·* is no inverted image of God,
My.	33–29	they that dwell *t·*. — *Psal.* 24 : 1.
	150–16	See *t·* the mirrored sky
	158–28	your temple and all who worship *t·*
	199–14	joint resolutions contained *t·*
	298– 6	the good acomplished *t·*,

thereof

Mis.	28– 2	reappear in the spiritual sense *t·*.
	30– 3	some feeble demonstration *t·*,
	30–12	The gates *t·* he declared were
	55– 4	understanding and demonstration *t·*
	57–16	day that thou eatest *t·* — *Gen.* 2 : 17.
	67–21	you shall, . . . inform them *t·*.
	84–29	a new and higher sense *t·*,
	91–24	I never dreamed, until informed *t·*,
	93– 1	and by reason *t·* is able to
	100–13	may lose sight *t·* ;
	121–31	from the divine Principle *t·*,
	125–28	to tell the towers *t·*
	131–27	let her state the value *t·*,
	144– 5	and the name *t·*,
	156–10	daily Christian demonstration *t·*.
	158–10	comes the interpretation *t·*.
	189–18	revealing, in place *t·*, the power
	244– 1	closed up the wound *t·*, — *see Gen.* 2 : 21.
	291–16	If any are not partakers *t·*,
	291–19	if the spirit *t·* be lacking.
	302–27	received from his reading *t·* ;
	306–21	* was at that time the President *t·*.
	323– 5	for God is the temple *t·* ;
	330–13	consciousness *t·* is here and now
	358–32	leaving the material forms *t·*
	365– 9	gets things wrong, and is ignorant *t·*.
	367–17	day that thou eatest *t·*, — *Gen.* 2 : 17.
Man.	29–10	shall complain *t·* to the Clerk
	36–21	signed by three members *t·*
	50– 1	and the cause *t·* be unknown,
	53–22	considered a sufficient evidence *t·*.
	55–24	contrary to the statement *t·*
	66–13	to await her explanation *t·*.
	68– 8	upon Mrs. Eddy's complaint *t·*
	75–10	with grateful acknowledgments *t·*,
	78– 1	demand that each member *t·*
	110– 9	and become a part *t·*.
Ret.	35–12	spiritual interpretations *t·*.
	83– 5	and the healing efficacy *t·*,
	84–20	and by reason *t·* is able to
	87–14	in the orderly demonstration *t·*.
Un.	19– 8	must have had foreknowledge *t·* ;
	44–20	''In the day ye eat *t·* — *Gen.* 3 : 5.
Pul.	1–13	great is the value *t·*.
	5– 7	we kindle in place *t·*
No.	7–26	discriminations and guidance *t·*.
	8–14	the remainder *t·* He will restrain.
Pan.	1–17	waiteth patiently the appearing *t·*.
	14–21	and their faithful service *t·*,
'00.	6–10	dawns the spiritual meaning *t·* ;
'01.	27–16	rejoice in being informed *t·*.
'02.	5–28	Love and the manifestation *t·*
	8–21	Love is the Principle *t·*.
	9–21	heard the life-giving sound *t·*,
Hea.	3– 5	more than a profession *t·* ;
Peo.	5–21	the demonstration *t·* in healing
My.	8– 5	* outgrowing the institutional end *t·*.
	33–28	and the fulness *t·* ;— *Psal.* 24 : 1.
	161–23	unto each day is the duty *t·*.
	184–13	to wire an acknowledgment *t·*
	186–20	eat the fruit *t·*.
	197–21	in the Word and in the doers *t·*,
	206–22	Lamb is the light *t·*.'' — *Rev.* 21 : 23.
	207– 5	remainder *t·* He will restrain.
	225– 1	the present persecution *t·*.
	230– 8	senses' assimilation *t·*.
	237– 9	understanding of the principle *t·*,
	275–14	(and I trust the desire *t·*)

thereof

My.	338–17	subjects or the handling *t·*,
	348–20	demonstration *t·* was made,

thereon

Mis.	124–19	As we think *t·*, man's true sense
	139–21	erected *t·* a church edifice
Man.	70– 6	adhering strictly to her advice *t·*.
My.	217–14	with interest *t·* up to date,

thereto

Mis.	54–16	the sick, unasked, are testifying *t·*.
	66– 1	obedience *t·* may be found faulty,
	85–12	regeneration leading *t·* is gradual,
	119–23	or strict obedience *t·*,
	124– 9	will not be reconciled *t·*.
	296–27	or are they incited *t·* by their
Man.	83–23	habitually to study . . . as a help *t·*.
	86–22	shall teach nothing contrary *t·*.
Ret.	14–13	if assent . . . was essential *t·*.
	53– 3	and the funds belonging *t·*.
Un.	38– 5	but antagonistic *t·*.
Pul.	84–19	* All who are awake *t·*
Pan.	9– 9	four first rules pertaining *t·*,
'01.	35–18	walk in Patient faith the way *t·*
'02.	10–19	his predicate tending *t·* is correct,
My.	233–15	can you . . . by indifference *t·*?
	237–14	and give daily attention *t·*.
	241–13	* and Mrs. Eddy's reply *t·*.
	284–22	I consented *t·* only as other
	320–22	* several times subsequent *t·*,

thereunto

Mis.	272– 3	* privileges pertaining *t·*

thereupon

Man.	77– 8	decide *t·* by a unanimous vote,
Un.	44– 6	like the structure raised *t·*,
Pul.	58– 2	* and *t·* devoted herself to

therewith

Mis.	296–19	is by no means associated *t·*.
	309–20	whatever is connected *t·*,
Man.	27–24	other literature connected *t·*.
	37– 3	application for membership *t·*
	66– 5	then act in accordance *t·*.
	74–14	nor in rooms connected *t·*.
Ret.	24– 3	would associate *t·*,
Un.	60–14	and *t·* curse we men, — *Jas.* 3 : 9.
'02.	13–20	the note *t·* became due,
My.	175– 4	organizations connected *t·*,
	210– 8	clad *t·* you are completely shielded
	253–25	and my joy *t·*.

The Science of Man

Ret.	35– 2	entitled ''*T· S· of M·*.''

"The Temptation"

Mis.	313–17	''*T· T·*,'' a poem by J. J. Rome,

The Unknown God Made Known

My.	338–12	subject ''*T· U· G· M· K·*,''

The World Beautiful

Pul.	39–11	* author of ''*T· W· B·*.''

thick

Pul.	78– 5	* an eighth of an inch *t·*.
My.	191–22	Mortality's *t·* gloom is pierced.

thicken

Mis.	243–28	cause the coats of the stomach to *t·*

thief (see also thief's)

Mis.	70–10	*when he said to the dying t·*,
	70–17	*t·* was not equal to the demands
	70–25	*t·* would be with Jesus only in a
'02.	18– 2	wilt know when the *t·* cometh.
My.	232–15	hour the *t·* would come, — *Luke* 12 : 39.

thief's

Mis.	70–20	the poor *t·* prayer for help
	70–22	The *t·* body, as matter,

thieves

'01.	14–23	against the approach of *t·*.

thin

Mis.	291–23	will at length dissolve into *t·* air.

Thine

Mis.	212–21	''Not my will, but *T·*, — *Luke* 22 : 42.
	348– 7	It is not *mine* but *T·* they seek.
	397–15	where *T·* own children are,
	397–18	To *T·*, for Thee ;
	398–12	And Thou know'st *T·* own ;
	398–16	Take them in *T·* arms ;
Ret.	15– 9	even of *T·* only. — *Psal.* 71 : 16.
	46–18	And Thou know'st *T·* own.
	46–22	Take them in *T·* arms ;
Pul.	17–17	And Thou know'st *T·* own.
	17–21	Take them in *T·* arms ;
	18–24	where *T·* own children are,
	19– 2	To *T·*, for Thee ;
Po.	13– 3	where *T·* own children are,
	13– 6	To *T·*, for Thee ;
	14–16	And Thou know'st *T·* own ;

Thine

Po.	14–20	Take them in *T·* arms ;
	24–13	This heart of *T·*
	43–11	Ever thus as *T·* !
My.	253–16	through *T·* own name— *John* 17 : 11.

thing

any
Mis.	259– 2	was not any *t·* made.''— *John* 1 : 3.
My.	202–10	Owe no man any *t·*,— *Rom.* 13 : 8.
	267– 8	was not any *t·* made— *John* 1 : 3.

any other
Un.	48– 7	no faith in any other *t·* or being.

any such
Rud.	5–15	If there is any such *t·* as matter,

bad
My.	87–24	* it would not be a bad *t·* if

best
'*00.*	9– 5	not because it is the best *t·* to do,

deadly
Mis.	28–32	drink any deadly *t·*,— *Mark* 16 : 18.
	249– 6	drink any deadly *t·*,— *Mark* 16 : 18.
Hea.	1– 3	*drink any deadly t·,— Mark* 16 : 18.
	7–26	drink any deadly *t·*,— *Mark* 16 : 18.
	15–11	drink any deadly *t·*,— *Mark* 16 : 18.
Peo.	12– 4	drink any deadly *t·*,— *Mark* 16 : 18.
My.	48– 1	* drink any deadly *t·*,— *Mark* 16 : 18.
	146– 5	drink any deadly *t·*,— *Mark* 16 : 18.

every high
Mis.	139–12	*every high t· that exalteth*— *II Cor.* 10 : 5.

first
Mis.	375–17	* ''The first *t·* that impressed me

great
Mis.	38–11	is it a great *t·* if we— *I Cor.* 9 : 11.
	157– 2	great *t·* to be found worthy

holy
Mis.	51–28	* walk transparent like some holy *t·*.''

instead of a
Mis.	271– 4	a thought, instead of a *t·*.

made
My.	205–18	* as the *t·* made is good or bad,

most important
My.	289– 1	The *t·* most important is

no new
Pul.	53– 6	* no new *t·* under the sun.''— *Eccl.* 1 : 9.

no such
Mis.	47– 1	*there is no such t· as matter*
Un.	1– 3	God knows no such *t·* as sin.
	50–13	there is no such *t·* as *mortal mind,*

of mortal mind
Mis.	237– 4	suffering is a *t·* of mortal mind

of the past
Mis.	375–30	* a *t·* of the past,

of thought
Rud.	10–15	Disease is a *t·* of thought

one
Mis.	48– 5	One *t·* is quite apparent ;
	99–19	In no other one *t·* seemed Jesus
	127– 7	One *t·* I have greatly desired,
	163–16	In no one *t·* seemed he less human
	230– 4	more than upon any other one *t·*.
No.	9– 8	but this one *t·* can be done,
'*00.*	6– 5	this one *t·* I do,—*Phil.* 3 : 13.
Hea.	4–25	model is one *t·* at one time,
My.	18– 4	''One *t·* I have greatly desired,
	44– 8	* one *t·* is certain, it will be sure,
	70– 3	* One *t·* is certain:
	87–26	* There is one *t·* about it:
	126–28	One *t·* is eternally here;
	126–32	This is that needful one *t·*
	236–11	Too much of one *t·* spoils the
	271–10	the one *t·* needful and the sole proof
	325– 4	* One *t·* more, that I think will

person and
Un.	45– 6	mind and matter, person and *t·*?''

place or a
'*01.*	13– 1	a man or a woman, a place or a *t·*,

proper
Ret.	90–27	* ''I believe the proper *t·* for us to do

remarkable
My.	89–13	* remarkable *t·* in this building

right
Mis.	71–10	is a very right *t·* to do.
My.	193–23	* if it succeeds, it is a right *t·*.''

same
Mis.	381–32	* discoverer of the same *t·*.''

such
No.	32–10	chapter sub-title

that
Ret.	94–18	that *t·* which he alloweth. — *Rom.* 14 : 22.

the very
Un.	58– 8	This was the very *t·* he *was* doing,

vain
My.	103–17	imagine a vain *t·*?''— *Psal.* 2 : 1.
	200– 5	imagine a vain *t·* ;''— *Psal.* 2 : 1.
	270–14	Let error rage and imagine a vain *t·*.

thing

worse
My.	288–26	lest a worse *t·* come— *John* 5 : 14.

Mis.	8–10	*t·* outside thine own creation?
	245–27	it is a *t·* to be thankful for
Pul.	53– 4	* ''The *t·* that hath been,— *Eccl.* 1 : 9.
No.	3–22	How good and pleasant a *t·* it is
My.	14– 1	in the *t·* whereto— *Isa.* 55 : 11.
	164–11	a *t·* focusing light where love,
	193–22	* Carlyle writes, ''Give a *t·* time ;

things

above
Mis.	391– 4	For *t·* above the floor,
Pan.	14– 4	Set your affections on *t·* above ;
Po.	38– 3	For *t·* above the floor,
My.	15–19	* tell the story, Of unseen *t·* above,

all
Mis.	10–24	and all *t·* become new.
	45–28	''All *t·* were made— *John* 1 : 3.
	59–13	God *has* given all *t·* to those who
	68–27	* causes of all *t·* existing,''
	71–25	to Him, are all *t·*,''— *Rom.* 11 : 36.
	119–31	all *t·* whatsoever— *Matt.* 7 : 12.
	159–13	where all *t·* are pure
	217–14	specific nature of all *t·* is unchanged,
	222– 4	It reverses C. S. in all *t·*.
	232–17	maximum of perfection in all *t·*.
	235–28	''All *t·* whatsoever— *Matt.* 7 : 12.
	258–17	infinite Mind governs all *t·*.
	259– 1	''all *t·* were made— *John* 1 : 3.
	310–16	''Let all *t·* be done— *I Cor.* 14 : 40.
	367–13	Error says that knowing all *t·*
	373–25	gave man dominion over all *t·* ;
Man.	42–22	''All *t·* whatsoever— *Matt.* 7 : 12.
Ret.	23– 3	All *t·* earthly must ultimately
	26–25	Principle of all *t·* pure ;
	28–18	reduce all *t·* real to their own
Un.	10–10	the one God, to whom belong all *t·*.
	15– 8	God created all *t·*,
	17–21	because He knows all *t·* ;
	40–26	and regard all *t·* as temporal.
	56–26	and endureth all *t·*.
Pul.	85–12	* divine Principle of all *t·*
No.	24– 4	He is in all *t·*,
	42– 2	* to believe all *t·* written in the
	43– 8	* ''Only He who knows all *t·*
Pan.	5– 4	''all *t·* were made— *John* 1 : 3.
	7– 9	had created all *t·* spiritually,
	5– 3	nature, and government of all *t·*
'*00.*	11–10	''all *t·* work together— *Rom.* 8 : 28.
'*01.*	21–26	for did He not know all *t·*
Peo.	1– 9	reality and Soul of all *t·*,
My.	52–15	* bring out the perfection of all *t·*,
	123–28	ministry of righteousness in all *t·*,
	143–25	all *t·* work together— *Rom.* 8 : 28.
	152–23	an ever-present help in all *t·*,
	154– 9	Send flowers in all *t·* fair
	156– 8	sufficiency in all *t·*,— *II Cor.* 9 : 8.
	158–12	it endureth all *t·* ;
	180–15	to whom all *t·* are possible ;
	181–19	and thus exemplify in all *t·*
	194– 5	dies, as do all *t·* material,
	266–17	final spiritualization of all *t·*,
	267– 7	''All *t·* were made— *John* 1 : 3.
	285–27	believing all *t·*— *Acts* 24 : 14.
	293– 1	knowledge that all *t·* are possible
	349– 3	to whom all *t·* are possible.

all the
My.	280– 8	* all the *t·* which make for

better
No.	34–18	blood of Christ speaketh better *t·*

carnal
Mis.	38–12	reap your carnal *t·*?''— *I Cor.* 9 : 11.

cause of
Mis.	219– 2	the final cause of *t·* ;

certain
'*00.*	8–30	advise students not to do certain *t·*

childish
Mis.	359–10	I put away childish *t·*.— *I Cor.* 13 : 11.
My.	135– 5	I put away childish *t·*.''— *I Cor.* 13 : 11.
	261–18	I put away childish *t·*.''— *I Cor.* 13 : 11.

crooked
My.	140– 5	crooked *t·* straight.— *Isa.* 42 : 16.

divine
Ret.	31–10	and thirst after divine *t·*,

few
Mis.	116–29	''faithful over a few *t·*.''— *Matt.* 25 : 23.
	339–18	faithful over a few *t·*.''— *Matt.* 25 : 23.
	340–17	not been faithful over a few *t·*.
	340–25	been faithful over a few *t·*.
	342–32	faithful over the few *t·* of Spirit,
Pul.	13– 7	faithful over a few *t·*,— *Matt.* 25 : 23.

fitness of
Mis.	316–11	depend on the fitness of *t·*,

things

glorious
Mis. 151–22 Glorious *t·* are spoken of you
good
Un. 15– 9 Was evil among these good *t·*?
My. 13–23 thy mouth with good *t·* ; — *Psal.* 103 : 5.
99– 2 * good *t·* that this sect is doing.
197– 1 Enjoying good *t·* is not evil,
hard
Mis. 266–18 assertion that I have said hard *t·*
Un. 1– 4 "*t·* hard to be understood," — *II Pet.* 3 : 16.
hidden
My. 124– 1 hidden *t·* of dishonesty, — *II Cor.* 4 : 2.
holy
Mis. 280– 7 not the holy *t·* of Truth.
hoped for
My. 260–16 *t·* hoped for and the evidence
many
Mis. 117– 1 over many *t·*." — *Matt.* 25 : 23.
341– 9 made ruler over many *t·*.
375–22 * resemblance in many *t·*,
Pul. 82–11 * many *t·* dear to the soul
material
(*see* **material**)
material basis of
Mis. 341– 4 unreal material basis of *t·*,
material sense of
Mis. 120– 3 unclasp the material sense of *t·*
mortal
Hea. 19–12 the origin of all mortal *t·*.
mortal sense of
Mis. 188–26 unreal or mortal sense of *t·* ;
Un. 30–23 change in the mortal sense of *t·*,
most essential
Mis. 232–11 in *t·* most essential,
234–12 *t·* most essential and divine.
new
'00. 8–14 *t·* new and old." — *Matt.* 13 : 52.
of earth
Mis. 390–24 like *t·* of earth,
Po. 56– 3 like *t·* of earth,
of God
Mis. 175– 3 takes of the *t·* of God
Ret. 24–24 should take the *t·* of God
'01. 9–23 takes of the *t·* of God
of man
Mis. 332–17 pondered the *t·* of man and God.
of Spirit
Mis. 342–32 faithful over the few *t·* of Spirit,
'01. 9–28 liveth most the *t·* of Spirit,
My. 260–10 *t·* of Spirit, not of matter.
old
Mis. 10–24 wherein old *t·* pass away
personal sense of
Mis. 290–22 from a personal sense of *t·*.
Principle of
Mis. 232– 7 the perfect Principle of *t·* ;
prove the
My. 285–24 prove the *t·* whereof they — *Acts* 24 : 13.
reality of
'01. 1–19 portion of the primal reality of *t·*.
20– 9 alone . . . with the reality of *t·*.
small
My. 123–28 not overlook small *t·* in goodness
spiritual
(*see* **spiritual**)
stubborn
My. 99–27 * Facts and figures are stubborn *t·*,
substance of
(*see* **substance**)
such
'01. 33–10 * originating influence in such *t·* ;
sweet
My. 252– 5 always distributing sweet *t·*
that are Caesar's
Mis. 374–25 "the *t·* that are Cæsar's ;" — *Mark* 12 : 17.
Ret. 71– 5 the *t·* that are Cæsar's, — *Mark* 12 : 17.
My. 220–10 the *t·* that are Cæsar's,' — *Mark* 12 : 17.
344–25 the *t·* that are Cæsar's.' — *Mark* 12 : 17.
that are God's
Ret. 71– 6 the *t·* that are God's." — *Mark* 12 : 17.
My. 220–11 the *t·* that are God's.' " — *Mark* 12 : 17.
these
Mis. 72–21 *need of all these t·*," — *Matt.* 6 : 32.
73–18 We have need of *these t·* ;
100–28 Who is sufficient for these *t·*?
128–11 think on these *t·*. — *Phil.* 4 : 8.
167–24 hid these *t·* from the wise — *Luke* 10 : 21.
270–15 these *t·* shall be added — *Matt.* 6 : 33.
Chr. 55–10 these *t·* shall be added — *Matt.* 6 : 33.
Ret. 13–16 of these *t·* he now spoke,
Un. 43–13 "sufficient for these *t·*." — *II Cor.* 2 : 16.
60–17 these *t·* ought not so to be." — *Jas.* 3 : 10.
No. 45– 1 hid these *t·* from the wise — *Luke* 10 : 21.
'01. 9–24 and these *t·* being spiritual,
10– 3 "For all these *t·* — *see Matt.* 10 : 17.

things

these
'02. 19–23 need of all these *t·*." — *Matt.* 6 : 32.
My. 33–27 He that doeth these *t·* — *Psal.* 15 : 5.
90– 5 * all these *t·* are new,
140– 6 These *t·* will I do — *Isa.* 42 : 16.
143–23 when these *t·* cease to bless
143–28 say to these *t·*? — *Rom.* 8 : 31.
153– 9 "these *t·* saith He — *Rev.* 3 : 7.
229– 5 "For all that do these *t·* — *Deut.* 18 : 12.
300–20 these *t·*, inseparable from C. S.,
they suffer
Mis. 278–27 must learn by the *t·* they suffer,
328– 2 learn from the *t·* they suffer.
those
Mis. 128–11 Those *t·*, which — *Phil.* 4 : 9.
178–12 those *t·* which are above, — *Col.* 3 : 1.
328–28 "Forgetting those *t·* — *Phil.* 3 : 13.
'00. 6– 6 forgetting those *t·* — *Phil.* 3 : 13.
6– 7 those *t·* which are before, — *Phil.* 3 : 13.
My. 155–11 those *t·* that are behind,
256–10 thanks for those *t·* of beauty
thought as
Mis. 331–26 nature as thought, and thought as *t·*.
thoughts are
Pul. 80–26 * belief that "thoughts are *t·*,"
two
My. 92–26 * two *t·* to be said in favor of
165– 2 Of two *t·* fate cannot rob us ;
unseen
My. 15–19 Of unseen *t·* above,
95–25 * without faith in the *t·* unseen.
what
Mis. 168– 3 tell what *t·* ye shall see
My. 293–30 "What *t·* soever ye desire, — *Mark* 11 : 24.
whatsoever
Mis. 128– 7 whatsoever *t·* are true, — *Phil.* 4 : 8.
128– 7 whatsoever *t·* are honest, — *Phil.* 4 : 8.
128– 8 whatsoever *t·* are just, — *Phil.* 4 : 8.
128– 8 whatsoever *t·* are pure, — *Phil.* 4 : 8.
128– 9 whatsoever *t·* are lovely, — *Phil.* 4 : 8.
128– 9 whatsoever *t·* are of — *Phil.* 4 : 8.
which are not seen
Mis. 66–21 *t·* which are not seen." — *II Cor.* 4 : 18.
Un. 62– 7 *t·* which are not seen are — *II Cor.* 4 : 18.
which are seen
Mis. 66–20 at the *t·* which are seen, — *II Cor.* 4 : 18.
Un. 62– 6 *t·* which are seen are — *II Cor.* 4 : 18.
wrong
Mis. 365– 8 gets *t·* wrong, and is ignorant
No. 18–20 gets *t·* wrong, and knows it not ;

———

Mis. 28– 8 In dreams, *t·* are only what
263–15 chapter sub-title
309–28 sometimes take *t·* too intensely.

think

Mis. 7–28 they *t·* that health and strength
11– 4 I used to *t·* it sufficiently just
52–11 *What do you t· of marriage?*
124–18 As we *t·* thereon, man's true sense
128–11 *t·* on these things. — *Phil.* 4 : 8.
158–25 forthcoming completion (as I now *t·*)
171– 7 is as absurd as to *t·*, . . . that
178–15 * "I *t·* it was about a year ago
214– 4 "*T·* not that I am come to — *Matt.* 10 : 34
219–12 admitted that mortals *t·* wickedly
219–14 mortals *t·* also after a sickly
233–21 weak and worldly who *t·* the
233–23 What *t·* you of a scientist
251–20 *T·* of this inheritance !
256–22 accustomed to *t·* and to speak
263– 9 blessed it is to *t·* of you as
280–13 As we commonly *t·*, we imagine
281–20 *t·* instead, of our poverty
338–26 * "*T·* truly, and thy thoughts
344– 6 do you *t·* it possible for you
353–28 *t·* of helping others, go their way.
Man. 59– 4 *t·* at random on this subject,
Ret. 50– 2 I could *t·* of no financial equivalent
74– 9 I desire never to *t·* of it,
74– 9 it cannot *t·* of me.
Un. 18– 2 let us *t·* of God as saying,
46– 2 which neither *t·* nor speak.
Pul. 2–12 *t·* for a moment with me
3– 8 power to *t·* and act rightly,
74–20 "I *t·* Mrs. Lathrop was not understood.
75– 7 But to *t·* or speak of me in
Rud. 2–12 if we *t·* of Him as less
No. 7–22 *t·*, speak, teach, and write
39– 1 that we can *t·* more lucidly
43–19 *t·* to build a baseless fabric
Pan. 10– 3 "If a man *t·* himself — *Gal.* 6 : 3.
'02. 5–23 "*T·* not that I am — *Matt.* 5 : 17.
Hea. 5–14 Does any one *t·* the departed
9– 9 *t·* most of sickness and of sin ;

think

Peo.	12– 1	should *t·* for one moment
Po.	3– 6	I *t·* of thee, I *t·* of thee !
	17– 3	Then I'll *t·* of its glory,
	74– 2	*T·* kindly of me,
My.	3–21	compels him to *t·* genuine,
	41– 2	* so that they *t·* rightly
	87– 7	* And so, we *t·*, must be
	87–20	* I do not *t·* I have ever seen
	95–23	* may *t·* they can banish
	100–16	* who *t·* for themselves.
	119–10	*T·* not that C. S. tends
	133– 3	Ofttimes I *t·* of this in the
	156– 6	that we ask or *t·*,"— *Eph.* 3 : 20.
	163–15	which I *t·* do them more good.
	171–10	I *t·* you would enjoy seeing it.
	187– 5	to *t·* of doing so at present.
	212– 2	*t·* or do voluntarily.
	219–14	"*T·* not that I am— *Matt.* 5 : 17.
	259–16	to *t·* and work for others.
	291–28	She stops to *t·*, to mourn,
	302–17	I still must *t·* the name
	307–23	still *t·* that it was profane.
	313–14	everything they could *t·* of
	321– 2	* He seemed very proud to *t·*
	325– 5	* I *t·* will amuse you :
	335–26	* (Dr. McRee we *t·* it was),
	344–19	I should *t·* myself in danger of
	360–14	as many students *t·* I can,

thinker

Mis.	374–29	between the *t·* and his thought
Un.	14– 5	Can it be seriously held, by any *t·*,
'00.	2– 9	the right *t·* and worker,
	2–11	The right *t·* works ;
	3– 4	The right *t·* and worker
	3– 9	If the right *t·* and worker's
	3–14	what the best *t·* and worker has
	3–18	Only the good man loves the right *t·*
My.	210–12	self-seeking pride of the evil *t·*
	210–14	The evil *t·* is the proud talker
	210–15	right *t·* abides under the shadow of

thinkers

Mis.	6–13	it surely does, to many *t·*,
	112– 3	Even honest *t·*, not knowing
	219–13	beginning to be seen by *t·*,
	234–23	grave wonderment to profound *t·*.
	383–15	rise higher in the estimation of *t·*
Un.	6–14	even the *t·* are not prepared to
	8– 2	much trouble to many earnest *t·*
	9–22	spiritual *t·* in all ages.
No.	9– 5	errors of one class of *t·*
	13–23	revolution in the minds of *t·*
'00.	9–21	will challenge the *t·*,
'01.	17–15	the respect of our best *t·*.
'02.	9–25	Did the age's *t·* laugh long
My.	113–31	the deep *t·*, the truly great
	162– 7	A small group of wise *t·*
	347–24	Most *t·* concede that Science

thinketh

Mis.	70– 7	"*t·* in his heart,— *Prov.* 23 : 7.
	311–13	charity which *t·* no evil ;
No.	45– 6	*t·* no evil,— *I Cor.* 13 : 5.
Peo.	3– 2	"*t·* in his heart,— *Prov.* 23 : 7.

thinking

Mis.	x–22	*t·* that otherwise the name
	19– 1	Envy, evil *t·*, evil speaking,
	117–14	basis of all right *t·* and acting ;
	130–11	*t·* it over, and how to meet it,
	204–32	evil *t·*, evil speaking and acting ;
	230–10	*t·* of nothing or planning for some
	233–13	*t·* to put into the old garment of
	245–23	*t·* that it was following Christ ;
	365–12	Its genius is right *t·*
Man.	59– 5	weight in the scale of right *t·*.
Ret.	81–11	false *t·*, feeling, and acting ;
Pul.	6–12	mistake of *t·* she caught her notions
Rud.	15–10	systematic *t·* is impracticable until
No.	12– 4	essence of this Science is right *t·*
	15–23	*T·* otherwise is what estranges
	18– 9	Right *t·* and right acting,
'00.	3– 5	does the *t·* for the ages.
	9– 8	secret of C. S. in right *t·*
'01.	30– 4	in *t·* the object of vital Christianity
Hea.	3– 7	foundation of right *t·*
	9– 5	*t·* and talking on the wrong side
Po.	8–20	I'm *t·* alone of a fair young bride,
My.	vii–11	* consistent and constant right *t·*
	vii–12	* intelligent *t·* untainted by the
	41– 5	* the law of right *t·*,
	209– 5	right *t·* and right acting,
	233–31	*T·* of person implies that
	234– 1	is not *t·* of Principle,
	234– 2	signalize the *t·* of person.
	254–11	of right *t·* and acting,

thinking

My.	273–14	spiritual sense of *t·*, feeling,
	274–10	right *t·*, right feeling,
	346–14	* looking forward, *t·*, *t·*,

thinks

Mis.	71– 6	one writer *t·* that he was
	88– 8	* "*What Quibus T·.*"
	107–32	Mankind *t·* either too much or
	108– 1	saint *t·* too much of it :
	108– 2	sinner, . . . *t·* too little of sin.
	145–11	And if he *t·* that he is,
	215–20	*t·* he is where he is not,
	298–29	one *t·* he is not mistaken,
Ret.	76–25	He *t·* of every one in his real
Pul.	81–12	* she *t·* so much of herself
Hea.	6–18	*t·* he is a medium of disease ;
My.	271– 9	what a man *t·* or believes

third

Mis.	24–10	On the *t·* day thereafter,
	34– 4	*T·* : One who has been healed
	76– 4	*T·* : Jesus said,
	101–12	Now cometh a *t·* struggle ;
	109–23	through the second to the *t·* stage,
	142–16	my second, a psalm ; my *t·*, a letter.
	162– 3	*t·* event of this eventful period,
	205–13	*T·* : The baptism of Spirit,
	210– 6	the remaining *t·* kills itself.
	217–21	a *t·* quality unlike God.
	219–16	A *t·* person knows that if
	242– 3	in *Zion's Herald,* December *t·*,
	254–19	take away a *t·* part of the
	256– 1	*T·* : Persons who have been healed
	276–12	*t·* convention of our National
	280– 3	The *t·* picture-lesson is from
	290– 1	A *t·* person is not a party to
	301–28	*T·* : All error tends to harden
	309–25	*t·* and fourth paragraphs,
	318–10	must go on *ad libitum* unto the *t·*
	332–13	*t·* chapter and ninth verse,
	332–23	*t·*, suffering ; fourth, death.
	355–14	the last *t·* pierces itself,
	357–19	*t·* stage of mental growth
Man.	26–12	Every *t·* year Readers shall be
	88–13	shall be elected every *t·* year
Ret.	34–17	*T·* : A person healed by C. S.
	88–17	*T·* : This leads inevitably to
Un.	20– 9	*T·* : I am afraid of it.
	20–14	*T·* : We therefore need not fear it.
	31–13	*t·*, that matter has intelligence ;
	43–24	*t·* chapter of Philippians,
Pan.	7–19	in the *t·* chapter of Genesis,
'01.	8– 6	*t·* person in the Godhead?
Peo.	4–14	would form a *t·* person,
My.	56–30	* second and *t·* being repetitions
	146– 7	since the *t·* century.
	305– 7	S. and H., page 68, *t·* paragraph,
	335–23	* the *t·* day of her husband's illness,
	353–13	*t·*, *Der Herold der C. S.*,

Third Church of Christ, Scientist
London, England

My.	205–13	chapter sub-title

      ―――

My.	363– 1	* signature

thirst

Mis.	369–26	*t·* for inspiring wine from
Ret.	31–10	and *t·* after divine things,
My.	40– 4	* to those who hunger and *t·*

thirsteth

Mis.	148–29	"Ho, every one that *t·*,— *Isa.* 55 : 1.

thirsting

Mis.	235–18	*t·* after a better life,
My.	15–28	* Seem hungering and *t·*

thirteen

Ret.	4– 1	grandmother had *t·* children,
		(*see also* **values**)

thirtieth

Ret.	33–14	One drop of the *t·* attenuation

thirty

Mis.	161–19	when he was *t·* years of age ;
	163– 4	He had for *t·* years been preparing
	341–24	vow of celibacy for *t·* years,
	382– 7	has cost more than *t·* years of
Man.	84– 9	consist of not more than *t·* pupils.
	84–12	Normal class not exceeding *t·* pupils.
Pul.	vii– 4	during the ensuing *t·* years.
	32–21	* elastic bearing of a woman of *t·*,
	75–19	* to the number of *t·*,
	85– 1	* nearly *t·* years ago began to
'01.	27–16	could start *t·* years ago
Hea.	1–16	* "At *t·*, man suspects himself a **fool** ;
	13– 6	shaking the preparation *t·* times
My.	70– 4	* organized only *t·* years,
	85– 4	* *T·* years ago it was comparatively

thirty
My.	104–28	learn of her who, *t·* years ago,
	181–21	*T·* years ago (1866) C. S.
	181–25	*t·* years ago the death-rate was
	182– 1	*T·* years ago Chicago had
	182– 3	*T·* years ago at my request
	182– 7	and a membership of *t·* years
		(*see also* **numbers**)

thirty-eight
(*see* **numbers**)

thirty-eighth
Mis.	191–12	ninth chapter and *t·* verse,

thirty-five
Pul.	43– 3	* numbering *t·* singers in all

thirty-four
Ret.	21– 7	had· reached the age of *t·*,

thirty-one
Ret.	7– 3	passed away at the age of *t·*,
		(*see also* **numbers**)

thirty-six
(*see* **numbers**)

thirty-third
Mis.	32–13	commencing at the *t·* verse,

thirty-three
Mis.	315–13	shall consist of not over *t·*

thirty-two
My.	69– 3	* lamp of *t·* candle-power.
	70–30	* which is *t·* feet long.

thistle-down
Mis.	231–21	baby has tumbled, soft as *t·*

thistles
Mis.	27–17	or figs of *t·*?" — *Matt.* 7 : 16.
	336–18	grapes of thorns, nor figs of *t·*.

thither
Mis.	319–22	Take *t·* thy saintly offerings,
My.	124–23	pointing upward, — *T·*!
	229–13	incentive for going *t·*.

thitherward
My.	124–25	facts relating to the *t·*,

Thomas
Mis.	28–15	his doubting disciple, *T·*.
'01.	7–27	"*T·*, because thou hast — *John* 20 : 29.

thorn
Mis.	71– 6	Paul had a *t·* in the flesh :
Un.	57–21	"a *t·* in the flesh" — *II Cor.* 12 : 7.

Thorne, John C.
My.	174–15	Edward A. Moulton, John C. *T·*,

thorns
Mis.	27–17	gather grapes of *t·*, — *Matt.* 7 : 16.
	336–18	we gather not grapes of *t·*,
'02.	18– 9	helped crown with *t·* the life of
My.	201–13	Even the crown of *t·*, which

thorny
Un.	58– 5	walked with bleeding feet the *t·*

thorough
Man.	90– 2	must be *t·* English scholars.
	90–18	Not less than two *t·* lessons
Ret.	6–17	one of the most . . . *t·* scholars
	48–19	*t·* understanding of metaphysics,
Rud.	15–18	*t·* guardianship and grace.
	15–22	impossible to teach *t·* C. S. to
	16– 3	a *t·* knowledge of C. S.,
	16– 7	subordinate to *t·* class instruction
My.	245– 8	*t·* preparation of the student

thoroughly
Mis.	43–19	time is required *t·* to qualify
	87–24	to study *t·* the Scriptures
	92–19	require the students *t·* to study it
	114–18	They cannot arm too *t·*
	242–29	*t·* addicted to the use of opium
	265–21	After *t·* explaining spiritual Truth
	318–16	afterwards studied *t·* "S. and H.
	375–13	* studied the old masters . . . *t·*,
	375–20	* study each illustration *t·*,
Man.	39–10	*t·* to test his sincerity,
	49–11	*t·* understands the practical wisdom
	76–22	and keep themselves *t·* informed
	90–23	*t·* discussed, and understood ;
Ret.	47–20	afterwards studied *t·* S. and H.,
	83–28	necessity of *t·* understanding
	87– 8	more *t·* and readily acquired
Un.	6–26	are not yet *t·* drilled in
Pul.	50–21	* *t·* carried away with the
No.	4– 2	task of learning *t·* the Science
'02.	5–12	For man to be *t·* subordinated
My.	59–31	* so *t·* endorsed or so completely
	96–11	* Scientists are *t·* in earnest
	204–19	*t·* recommend it

Thou
Mis.	63–23	hast *T·* forsaken me ?" — *Mark* 15 : 34.
	167–24	*T·* hast hid these things — *Luke* 10 : 21.
	331–20	*T·* Love that guards the nestling's
	331–21	Keep *T·* my child on upward wing
	334– 4	What doest *T·*?" — *Dan.* 4 : 35.
	347–28	None can say . . . What doest *T·*?
	384– 1	poem
	384– 6	Come *T·*! and now, anew,
	385– 5	*T·* hast heard my prayer ;
	385– 8	*T·*, here and *everywhere*.
	388– 7	*T·* to whose power our hope we **give**,
	389– 8	*T·* Love that guards the nestling's
	389– 9	Keep *T·* my child on upward wing
	398– 5	*T·* wilt bind the stubborn will,
	398–12	And *T·* know'st Thine own ;
	399–13	*T·* the Christ, and not the creed ;
	399–14	*T·* the Truth in thought and deed ;
	399–15	*T·* the water, the bread, and the
	400–23	In the way *T·* hast,
Ret.	15–10	*T·* hast taught me — *Psal.* 71 : 17.
	46–11	*T·* wilt bind the stubborn will,
	46–18	And *T·* know'st Thine own.
Pul.	1– 2	*T· shalt make them drink* — *Psal.* 36 : 8.
	3–17	*T·* shalt make them drink — *Psal.* 36 : 8.
	7–30	*T·* shalt make them drink — *Psal.* 36 : 8.
	8–22	*T·* hast perfected — *Matt.* 21 : 16.
	10–27	breathe *T·* Thy blessing
	17–10	*T·* wilt bind the stubborn will,
	17–17	*T·* know'st Thine own.
No.	45– 1	*T·* hast hid these things — *Luke* 10 : 21.
'02.	1–13	wrath shalt *T·* restrain." — *Psal.* 76 : 10.
Po.	4– 5	*T·* Love that guards the nestling's
	4– 7	Keep *T·* my child on upward wing
	7– 7	*T·* to whose power our hope we give,
	14– 9	*T·* wilt bind the stubborn will,
	14–16	And *T·* know'st Thine own ;
	22–14	how great, how good *T·* art
	28– 9	Knowing *T·* knowest best.
	28–17	In knowing what *T·* art !
	30–10	*T·* gildest gladdened joy,
	30–12	fan *T·* the flame
	30–17	Lift *T·* a patient love above
	33– 3	Increase *T·* my faith
	page 36	poem
	36– 5	Come *T·*! and now, anew,
	37– 5	*T·* hast heard my prayer ;
	37– 8	*T·*, here and *everywhere*.
	43–21	Just the way *T·* hast :
	69–11	In the way *T·* hast,
	75–20	*T·* the Christ, and not the creed ;
	75–21	*T·* the Truth in thought and deed ;
	75–22	*T·* the water, the bread, and
	77– 8	*T·* who, impartial, blessings
	77–10	*T·* wisdom, Love, and Truth,
	77–15	learned of Truth what *T·* doest
	77–19	*T·* knowest best !
	78– 6	*T·* knowest best !
	78–12	*T·* knowest best !
My.	4–30	*T·* God most high and nigh.
	151–11	wrath shalt *T·* restrain." — *Psal.* 76 : 10.
	229–27	*T·* knowest best what we need
	253–13	*T·* hast sent me." — *John* 17 : 25.
	253–17	*T·* hast given me, — *John* 17 : 11.
	280–21	nor say unto Him, What doest *T·*?
	290–14	"*T·* wilt keep him — *Isa.* 26 : 3.
	290–25	*T·* hearest me always," — *John* 11 : 42.
	350–12	*T·* the dark wave treading
	350–14	heed'st *T·* not the scalding tear
	350–15	know'st *T·* not the pathway
	350–19	*T·* all, *T·* infinite — dost doom above.

thought (noun)
accompanies
Mis.	47–16	sense of the body accompanies *t·*

according to
Mis.	247–28	reflects . . . according to *t·*.

Adam's
Ret.	67–23	in no way contingent on Adam's *t·*,

address the
Mis.	315–24	not silently mentally address the *t·*,

advancing
Mis.	2– 1	evolutions of advancing *t·*,

and action
Mis.	255– 8	*t·* and action on the side of right,
	264–12	demands oneness of *t·* and action.
Ret.	28– 5	guiding our every *t·* and action ;
Un.	31– 7	to spiritualize *t·* and action.
Rud.	2–24	bugle-call to *t·* and action,
	8–16	higher condition of *t·* and action,
Peo.	3–23	limits human *t·* and action
My.	153–29	to all human *t·* and action,

and conduct
My.	161–25	because one's *t·* and conduct

thought (noun)

and deed
　Mis. 384– 7　To *t·* and deed Give sober speed,
　　　399–14　Thou the Truth in *t·* and deed ;
　Po. 36– 6　To *t·* and deed Give sober speed,
　　　75–21　Thou the Truth in *t·* and deed ;
　　　79– 8　raise up seed — in *t·* and deed
and desire
　Mis. 15–10　Christianization — of *t·* and desire,
and knowledge
　Mis. 68–23　* necessary to *t·* and knowledge ;
and method
　No. 12–21　spiritualization of *t·* and method,
another's
　Mis. 97– 6　transmitted to another's *t·* from the
any other
　My. 324–16　* any other *t·* but that you were
ascends
　Mis. 96–12　as *t·* ascends the scale of being
atmosphere of
　Mis. 12–32　radius of our atmosphere of *t·*.
awakened
　Mis. 123–20　there has risen to the awakened *t·*
begins
　Peo. 3–20　*t·* begins wrongly to apprehend the
budding
　Mis. 330–18　arranging . . . each budding *t·*.
　Man. 104– 8　adapted to form the budding *t·*
causes
　Mis. 138– 4　if it causes *t·* to wander
chambers of
　My. 156–19　upper chambers of *t·* prepared for
child's
　Mis. 51–17　make clear to the child's *t·*
classifies
　Mis. 252– 8　C. S. classifies *t·* thus :
collisions of
　Un. 6–12　forcible collisions of *t·*
continue in
　Mis. 42– 2　*or does life continue in t· only*
continuity of
　My. 53–30　* even though the continuity of *t·*
deed and
　My. 9–10　* glory in every good deed and *t·*
desire and
　Pul. 55–20　* has its origin in desire and *t·*.
destroy the
　Mis. 37–20　can and does destroy the *t·* that
　　　105–28　Destroy the *t·* of sin, sickness, death,
divine
　Un. 5– 5　toward the perfect *t·* divine.
dominant
　Ret. 20–24　My dominant *t·* in marrying again
dwell in
　Mis. 309– 1　and not to dwell in *t·* upon their
dwells in God
　Mis. 290–23　When *t·* dwells in God,
early
　Mis. 240–19　easier to incline the early *t·*
encompass
　Ret. 68–21　Darkness and doubt encompass *t·*,
enlightened
　My. 187– 7　lighteth every enlightened *t·*
error in
　Hea. 7– 3　and, correcting error in *t·*,
error of
　No. 4–13　error of *t·* becomes fable
　My. 211–16　impels . . . into error of *t·*,
errors of
　Rud. 10–13　ills are but errors of *t·*,
every
　Mis. 85– 9　every *t·* and act leading to good.
　　　139–13　*into captivity every t· — II Cor.* 10: 5.
　Ret. 28– 5　guiding our every *t·*
　My. 345– 5　But every *t·* tells,
evil
　Pul. 29–23　* cast out the demons of evil *t·*.
exist in
　'01. 14– 9　evil, . . . does exist in *t·* ;
expressed the
　My. 60–10　* He only expressed the *t·* of
faith-lighted
　Mis. 15–22　What a faith-lighted *t·* is this !
fibres of
　Mis. 142–27　touched tender fibres of *t·*,
finite
　Rud. 2–21　assigned to God by finite *t·*,
flow of
　'00. 9–20　in the ebb and flow of *t·*
footsteps of
　Peo. 1– 8　footsteps of *t·*, as they pass
forbids the
　'02. 6– 1　forbids the *t·* of any other
forms of
　Mis. 91–19　forms of *t·* and worship

thought (noun)

freer breath to
　Hea. 4– 4　give freer breath to *t·*
gardens of
　Mis. 343–13　clearing the gardens of *t·*
general
　Mis. 8– 4　bring to the general *t·*
　My. 159–28　general *t·* chiefly regards
great
　No. 25– 1　Simply uttering this great *t·*
guide
　Mis. 64–17　ethics which guide *t·* spiritually
harmonious
　Mis. 220–13　the harmonious *t·* has the full
has shrunk
　Mis. 236– 6　until *t·* has shrunk from
heavens of
　Mis. 355–31　will span thy heavens of *t·*.
helm of
　Mis. 113–26　when Love is at the helm of *t·*,
her
　Po. v–15　* *began to take form in her t·*,
higher
　Pul. 2– 9　there is a *t·* higher and deeper
his
　Mis. 374–29　between the thinker and his *t·*
his own
　Mis. 93– 1　spiritualizes his own *t·*,
　　　265– 1　intentionally offers his own *t·*,
holding in
　Mis. 62– 5　holding in *t·* the form of a
human
　　　(*see* **human**)
imagery of
　Mis. 142–20　imagery of *t·* gave place to
images of
　Mis. 96–29　transference of human images of *t·*
improve the
　My. 10– 3　* C. S. should improve the *t·*,
inclining
　My. 261–12　and inclining *t·* of childhood.
individual
　Un. 5–18　or enlighten the individual *t·*.
　No. 1–21　correcting the individual *t·*,
infant
　Mis. 293– 2　the infant *t·* in C. S.
infantile
　Mis. 167– 2　the infantile *t·* of God's man,
involuntary
　Hea. 12–22　without the involuntary *t·*,
is developed
　Mis. 15–28　By suffering . . . *t·* is developed
is spiritualized
　My. 126–32　whereby *t·* is *spiritualized*,
is the essence
　Peo. 10– 1　*T·* is the essence of an act,
jewels of
　Mis. 313–13　jewels of *t·*, so adapted to
labors, and
　My. 137–18　my time, labors, and *t·*,
let loose
　My. 110–17　luxury of *t·* let loose,
liberated
　Mis. 41– 3　power of liberated *t·* to do good,
　　　67– 1　to support the liberated *t·*
line of
　Mis. 3–16　this line of *t·* or action.
　　　186–28　proceeds in this line of *t·*,
　　　188–20　in the intermediate line of *t·*,
lines of
　Mis. 291–29　sentinels along the lines of *t·*,
　My. 124–20　between these lines of *t·* is written
little
　My. 288– 4　gives little *t·* to self-defence ;
lofty trend of
　Po. vii– 3　* *by the same lofty trend of t·*
loving
　Mis. xii– 4　interluding with loving *t·*
made manifest
　Mis. 34– 8　physique is simply *t·* made manifest.
master's
　Mis. 373–19　This master's *t·* presents a sketch
material
　Mis. 102–26　state of mortal and material *t·*.
　Peo. 3–17　Truth meets the old material *t·*
　My. 267–24　Material *t·* tends to obscure
moment's
　My. 144– 5　spare not a moment's *t·* to
more
　Mis. 7–32　More *t·* is given to material
mortal
　　　(*see* **mortal**)
mounted
　My. 115– 1　mounted *t·* on the swift and
movement of
　Mis. 235–21　This movement of *t·* must push on

thought (noun)

must be spiritualized
Ret. 28– 9   *t·* must be spiritualized,
Pul. 35–13   *t·* must be spiritualized

my
Mis. vii– 4   * my *t·* looks Upon thy
279–14   present themselves to my *t·* ;
357–22   clear to my *t·* that those students
'00. 11–21   Adelaide A. Proctor breathes my *t·* :
'01. 32–24   educated my *t·* many years,
My. 268–20   flutters in my *t·* as an unreal shadow,

nature as
Mis. 331–25   Science evolved nature as *t·*,

night
My. 110–20   night *t·*, methinks, should unfold
110–23   night *t·* should show us

no
Mis. 391–12   It stirs no *t·* of strife ;
Po. 38–11   It stirs no *t·* of strife ;
My. 13– 2   taking no *t·* for the morrow,

objects of
Peo. 7–26   its subjects and objects of *t·*,

ocean of
No. 29–23   driftwood on the ocean of *t·* ;

of contempt
My. 324– 3   * a *t·* of contempt for the unlearned,

of fleshly sacrifice
Mis. 345–31   away from the *t·* of fleshly sacrifice,

of sin
Mis. 105–28   Destroy the *t·* of sin,
Un. 15–17   if the *t·* of sin could be possible

or action
Mis. 3–16   this line of *t·* or action.
260– 7   the line of Jesus' *t·* or action.
My. 278–30   brings into human *t·* or action
308– 7   aroused to *t·* or action

or word
Mis. 387–15   By *t·* or word unkind,
Po. 6–10   By *t·* or word unkind,

our
Un. 49–21   masquerades as the real, in our *t·*.

our own
Mis. 224– 1   unless our own *t·* barbs it.
My. 213–17   impulses of our own *t·*,

pearls of
Mis. 211–20   trample on your pearls of *t·*,

phases of
Mis. 60–18   in different phases of *t·*,

pleasant
No. 39–27   to portray the face of pleasant *t·*.

power of
Hea. 12–18   power of *t·* brought to bear on the

power was the
Hea. 12– 24   prove that the power was the *t·*,

preoccupied in
Mis. 47–10   preoccupied in *t·* when moving your

present to the
Un. 54– 6   If the claim be present to the *t·*,

procurator of the
Rud. 10–16   fear is the procurator of the *t·*

public
Mis. 78–23   public *t·* concerning it.
Peo. 11–23   leaders of public *t·* who are mistaken
My. 129– 7   taking strong hold of the public *t·*
224– 9   Hurried conclusions as to the public *t·*
226–28   until the public *t·* becomes

purest
Po. vii–12   * these gems of purest *t·*

purify
Mis. 341– 6   purify *t·*, then put thought into

purifying
Mis. 7–24   with healing, purifying *t·*.

quality of
My. 249–29   devout, unselfed quality of *t·*

quiet
Man. 94–12   in quiet *t·* on that subject.

random
Mis. 264– 2   every random *t·* in line with mine.

reaches the
Hea. 8–13   reaches the *t·* that has produced this,

reach, in
Un. 49–12   I reach, in *t·*, a glorified

realms of
Ret. 73–11   and purer realms of *t·*.

reciprocal
Mis. 265–19   whole line of reciprocal *t·*.

reflects
Peo. 10–22   the images that *t·* reflects

replenish
Mis. 92– 8   His work is to replenish *t·*,

ridding the
Ret. 79–11   ridding the *t·* of effete doctrines,

right
Rud. 9–21   power of a scientific, right *t·*,

satisfies the
Rud. 15– 7   this holds and satisfies the *t·*

thought (noun)

scale of
My. 152– 7   far lower in the scale of *t·*,

scientific
Mis. 156– 2   swift vehicle of scientific *t·* ;
Un. 5–25   shadowed forth in scientific *t·*.

second
No. 19– 8   sober second *t·* of advancing

seed of
Mis. 83– 9   *springing from a seed of t·*,

sensuous
No. 26–10   Theirs is the sensuous *t·*,

serious
Pul. 33–20   * high counsel and serious *t·*.

shadows of
Mis. 352–12   human shadows of *t·* lengthen

silent
Ret. 61– 6   unconsciously in the silent *t·*,

spiritual
My. 136–28   peace, and time for spiritual *t·*
238–16   swift pinions of spiritual *t·*

spiritualization of
Mis. 42–11   spiritualization of *t·* is not attained by
Un. 32–12   spiritualization of *t·* destroys
No. 12–21   impels a spiritualization of *t·*

spiritualize
Ret. 82–30   better adapted to spiritualize *t·*
Un. 31– 7   to spiritualize *t·* and action.
Hea. 19–17   We need it . . . to spiritualize *t·*,

spiritualized
My. 355– 3   * to see in her spiritualized *t·*

standpoint of
Mis. 185–31   spake from their standpoint of *t·* ;

state of
Mis. 105–25   their own subjective state of *t·*.
My. 221–26   correct or incorrect state of *t·*,

states of
Rud. 10–10   the subjective states of *t·*,

status of
Mis. 264–25   moral and spiritual status of *t·*

struggling
No. 40–22   the *t·* struggling for freedom.

student's
Mis. 349– 9   materialization of a student's *t·*,

take no
Mis. 245– 3   "Take no *t·*, — Matt. 6 : 31.
Rud. 12–23   "Take no *t·* — Matt. 6 : 25.

temperate in
Ret. 79–22   Be temperate in *t·*, word, and

temple of
Mis. 369–13   portals of the temple of *t·*,

thing of
Rud. 10–15   Disease is a thing of *t·*

this
Mis. 5–30   seem solid substance to this *t·*.
346– 2   carries this *t·* even higher,

throes of
Peo. 1–15   throes of *t·* are unheard,

thy
Pul. 55– 4   * Nature's marvel in thy *t·*."

time and
Mis. 112– 7   occupy time and *t·* ;
Hea. 12–20   To prepare . . . requires time and *t·* ;

time nor
Un. 11–24   neither cycles of time nor *t·*

to lift
Ret. 73–14   I endeavored to lift *t·* above

touches
My. 287–22   touches *t·* to spiritual issues,

transference of
Ret. 68–18   and the transference of *t·*,

transfigures
No. 26–12   idea which transfigures *t·*.

treasures of
'01. 1–13   to add to your treasures of *t·*

trend of
My. 305–31   was not the trend of *t·*,

true
Mis. 156–23   the basis of all true *t·*
My. 159–15   true *t·* escapes from the inward

unanimity of
My. 29–18   * unanimity of *t·* and of purpose.

unbiased
Mis. 240–23   over the fresh, unbiased *t·*.

unconscious
Hea. 6–24   back in the unconscious *t·*,

underlying
Un. 50–15   express the underlying *t·*.

unfolds the
My. 164–24   unity, which unfolds the *t·*

unity of
My. 24–12   * unity of *t·* and purpose

unprepared
Mis. 307–22   before the unprepared *t·*.

unspoken
Mis. 55–11   power of the unspoken *t·*,

thought (noun)

unworthy of
Mis. 271–16   subject that is unworthy of *t*,

vein of
Mis. 379–11   usually ran in the vein of *t*

vocabulary of
No. 10– 6   words in the vocabulary of *t*

waiting
Un. 7–19   pour into my waiting *t*

weight of
My. 146–30   lays his whole weight of *t*,

white-robed
Peo. 5–18   white-robed *t* points away from

will enable
Ret. 88–12   as will enable *t* to apprehend

woman's
Un. 57–12   influence of the woman's *t* ;

world's
Pul. 51–27   * cannot absorb the world's *t*.

your
Mis. 14– 2   Divest your *t*, then, of
     290–16   * I felt the influence of your *t*
     322–16   your *t* must not be diverted
My. 8– 7   * beyond resistance in your *t*."
     128–32   take no root in your *t*
     216–20   which I present to your *t*.

your own
Mis. 83– 9   *your own t* or another's."
     83–14   at the door of your own *t*

Mis. xi–24   *t* sometimes walks in memory,
     4– 1   *T* imbued with purity, Truth, and
     46–27   *t* has not yet wholly attained unto
     53–27   *t* educated away from it
     88–11   whose *t* is appreciated by many
     117– 5   discern between the *t*, motive, and
     271– 4   a *t*, instead of a thing.
     331–26   evolved . . . *t* as things.
     341– 6   then put *t* into words,
     343– 7   *T* must be made better,
     364–15   *t*, extension, cause, and effect ;
Pul. 79–26   * the *t* of the world's scientific
No. 21– 9   all time, space, immortality, *t*,
'01. 28–30   Has the *t* come to . . . Scientists,
'02. 19–18   The *t* of it stills complaint ;
Po. 23– 4   a *t* of vanished hours
     67– 5   And *t* be at work with
My. 55– 7   * the *t* of obtaining a church
     131–15   may *t* soar and Soul be.
     154– 9   to infringe . . . even in *t*.
     205–17   * "As the *t* is, so is the deed ;
     271–18   * followers of the *t* that has
     272–30   * in this presentation of the *t* of
     324–18   * too honorable to allow the *t*

thought (verb)

Mis. 11– 7   I *t*, also, that if I
     44–17   What you *t* was pain in the bone
     58– 6   proves to him who *t* he died
     67–15   nor cause it to be *t*.
     108–29   What would be *t* of a
     108–32   What should be *t* of an individual
     109– 5   or mayhap never have *t* of,
     138–17   I once *t* that in unity
     158– 6   I little *t* of the changes
     239–15   *t* I, "somebody has to take it ;
     239–28   and which mamma *t* must be
     263–15   chapter sub-title
     265– 4   in order to be *t* original,
     290–18   I had not *t* of the writer
     307–14   *t* best to stop its publication.
     359– 9   I *t* as a child :— *I Cor.* 13 : 11.
     376–30   Then *t* I, What are we,
Ret. 8– 5   I *t* this was my mother's voice,
     38–13   I had not *t* of such a result,
Pul. 34–15   "and they *t* I had died,
     44– 7   * I *t* you would willingly pause
     57–13   * Whatever may be *t* of the peculiar
'01. 14–24   Wrong is *t* before it is acted ;
Hea. 9– 6   The less said or *t* of sin,
My. 26–16   I *t* it better to be brief
     56– 1   * it was *t* the seating capacity
     59– 6   * we *t* this might be true
     59–21   * I *t* of the little melodeon
     60– 4   * if Mrs. Eddy *t* it wise to
     61– 6   * At first I *t* that, since
     61–27   * I have often stood . . . and *t*,
     64– 1   * As one *t* upon the significance
     104– 3   *t* that the learned St. Paul,
     104–11   what would be *t* to-day of
     104–12   what will be *t* to-morrow of
     135– 4   I *t* as a child :— *I Cor.* 13 : 11.
     185–11   wherever *t*, felt, spoken,
     306–11   than to be *t* great.
     319–15   * what he himself *t*
     324–10   * he often hinted that he *t*

thought (verb)

My. 324–20   * the impression that he *t*
     324–21   * always *t* that Mr. Wiggin
     345– 4   not . . . *t* to matter much.

thoughtful

Pul. 80–24   * more *t* and devout ;

thought-leaflet

Mis. 360–19   shall lift every *t* Spiritward ;

thoughts

adverse
My. 41– 9   * *t* adverse to the law of love.

all
Mis. 37– 5   all *t* and desires that draw
My. 114–19   All *t* in the line of Scriptural

and actions
Mis. 280– 5   to weigh the *t* and actions
     291–10   other people's *t* and actions.

and acts
Mis. 46–18   weight of his *t* and acts
     119– 3   responsible for our *t* and acts ;
Hea. 5–22   of our own *t* and acts ;
My. 352–13   * so reflect in our *t* and acts

and being
Mis. 42– 9   with *t*, and being, as material as

angelic
Ret. 85–11   angelic *t* ascend and descend,

are outlined
Mis. 103–13   *t* are outlined, individualized

are things
Pul. 80–26   * belief that "*t* are things,"

aroused
Ret. 13–10   perturbed was I by the *t* aroused

borrows the
My. 224–17   when he borrows the *t*,

crowding
My. 323–20   * crowding *t* of gratitude

evil
Mis. 18–26   into a state of evil *t*,
     252–11   evil *t* are impotent,

first
Ret. 27–21   ripples in one's first *t*

good
Mis. 252–10   Good *t* are potent ;
Pul. 69–12   * so fill the mind with good *t*
'00. 8–11   he may steal other people's good *t*,
My. 210– 7   Good *t* are an impervious armor ;

healthy
Mis. 252–14   healthy *t* are reality and

her
Mis. 169– 3   whenever her *t* had wandered

high
Mis. 86–26   subjective state of high *t*.

his
Mis. 46–18   to throw the weight of his *t*
     59–24   leading his *t* away from the
     283– 5   upset, and adjust his *t*
'00. 3– 2   his *t* are right, active, and
My. 210–16   His *t* can only reflect peace,
     324– 1   * He often spoke his *t* freely

his own
Mis. 126– 9   has his own *t* to guard,
Ret. 84– 5   to spiritualize his own *t*

holy
Mis. 280– 7   messengers of pure and holy *t*
     387–18   holy *t* and heavenly strain,
Po. 6–13   holy *t* and heavenly strain,

human
Mis. 393–10   the misty Mine of human *t*,
Un. 21– 2   wherein human *t* are
Po. 51–15   the misty Mine of human *t*,

illumed
Mis. 396–23   throng Of *t*, illumed By faith,
Pul. 18– 7   throng Of *t*, illumed By faith,
Po. 12– 7   throng Of *t*, illumed By faith,

imperative
Mis. 288– 6   Positive and imperative *t*

indicate
No. 11–10   which must be used to indicate *t*

kind
My. 236– 3   love for them and their kind *t*.

little
My. 247–17   Then I fed these sweet little *t*

my
Mis. 291–15   to be benefited by my *t*
Ret. 14–26   and know my *t* :— *Psal.* 139 : 23.
     48– 7   recent experience . . . fresh in my *t*,
Po. 65–12   My *t* 'neath thy drap'ry
My. 33–11   and know my *t* :— *Psal.* 139 : 23.
     39–21   * My *t* revert to a former

no sinful
Mis. 198– 2   When . . . man has no sinful *t*

of men
Peo. 3–18   while it inscribes on the *t* of men

thoughts

of others
Un. 56–18 suffered from the *t·* of others.
'01. 20– 3 influencing the *t·* of others,
of the practitioner
Rud. 9–24 *t·* of the practitioner should be
of you
Pul. 40– 2 * *t·* of you forever cling to me :
our
Mis. 119– 3 responsible for our *t·* and acts ;
136–17 All our *t·* should be given to
'02. 4–28 Our *t·* of the Bible utter our lives.
Hea. 9– 4 employed our *t·* more in
Peo. 7–30 our *t·* must spiritualize
7–32 to accord with our *t·*.
14– 3 clothe our *t·* of death with
My. 203–15 Our *t·* beget our actions ;
352–13 * so reflect in our *t·* and acts
overflowing
Mis. 310–25 chapter sub-title
people's
Ret. 89–27 upon other people's *t·*,
right
Mis. 252– 8 Right *t·* are reality and power ;
My. 283–14 Right *t·* and deeds are the
scientific
Ret. 68–26 scientific *t·* are true thoughts,
self-respected
Mis. 227–21 wherein calm, self-respected *t·* abide
sick
Mis. 252–13 learn that sick *t·* are unreality
sick man's
Mis. 220–10 to refute the sick man's *t·*,
sick-producing
Pul. 69–11 * from evil and sick-producing *t·*,
spiritual
My. 261–28 Virgin Mary's spiritual *t·* of Life
such
Mis. 378–22 are farther removed from such *t·*
Un. 60– 1 From such *t·* — mortal inventions,
No. 27–25 In presence of such *t·*
that express
'01. 7–13 the *t·* that express the different
their
Mis. 92–21 for this spiritualizes their *t·*.
My. 186– 6 preen their *t·* for upward flight.
355–24 their *t·* are upward ;
their own
Mis. 114– 8 the trend of their own *t·* ;
Un. 43–21 unite the influence of their own *t·*
Pul. vii– 8 inclination given their own *t·*
My. vii– 6 * can so protect their own *t·*
thy
Mis. 338–26 * "Think truly, and thy *t·*
transcribing
Mis. 187–15 their transcribing *t·* were not
true
Mis. 22–16 true *t·* revolve in God's orbits :
Ret. 68–26 scientific thoughts are true *t·*,
woman's
'02. 3–24 woman's *t·* . . . hallow the
works and
Ret. 64–18 God's ways and works and *t·*
wrong
Mis. 252– 9 wrong *t·* are unreality and powerless,
Rud. 12– 6 Wrong *t·* and methods
your
My. 210–10 all whom your *t·* rest upon
213–20 Watch your *t·*, and see whether
256–11 forming themselves in your *t·*
your own
My. 130– 2 guard your own *t·*

Mis. 152– 7 *t·* winged with peace and love
169–29 * *t·* when rightly understood.
Ret. 76– 9 *T·* touched with the Spirit
No. 40–11 *t·* are our honest conviction.

Thoughts on the Apocalypse
My. 13– 4 * book title

thought-tired
Mis. 125–27 *t·*, turns to-day to you ;

thousand
My. 91–21 * The few *t·* persons who followed
332– 2 * more than a *t·* miles,
(see also **numbers, values**)

thousandfold
My. 164–23 *t·* expansion that will engirdle the

thousands
Mis. ix– 7 among my *t·* of students
54– 8 *T·* in the field of metaphysical
Pul. 58– 5 * *t·* of believers throughout this
60–14 * among the *t·* of adherents
71–21 * *t·* throughout the United States
No. 32–25 Cause which is healing its *t·*

thousands
My. 24–10 * prayers and offerings of the *t·*
28–15 * influence upon the lives of *t·*
29–19 * emanating from the *t·* who
29–27 * *t·* who began to congregate
31–15 * *t·* had been seated,
47– 4 * *t·* of Christian Scientists
58–28 * Of the many *t·* who attended
59–10 * by the hundreds of *t·*
63–27 * the *t·* who had come,
76–11 * by the *t·* of church members
80– 4 * assure *t·* of auditors
85–23 * its *t·* of worshippers,
86– 9 * *T·* of Christian Scientists
90– 1 * should number many *t·*
90–8, 9 * *T·* upon *t·* believe that it
92–17 * from . . . to hundreds of *t·*,
93–31 * number hundreds of *t·*,
100–14 * members are numbered by *t·*
111–30, 31 *t·* upon *t·* attest with their
113– 1 and in *t·* of homes,
173–13 *t·* here yesterday ;
228– 3 *t·* are healed by learning that
271–17 * beloved of *t·* of believers
293– 9 *t·* of others believed the same,
293–10 Hundreds of *t·* who prayed for him

thousandth
(see **numbers**)

thraldom
Mis. 86–30 even this pleasing *t·*,
101– 4 departing from the *t·* of the senses

thraldoms
Pul. 55–11 * *t·*, prejudices, and oppressions

thrall
No. 11–26 rescue reason from the *t·* of error.
'00. 6–22 lifts him from the stubborn *t·* of sin
Po. 79–15 lifteth me, Ayont hate's *t·* :

thread
Mis. 99– 5 To weave one *t·* of Science

threaten
Ret. 81– 2 *t·* to paralyze its beneficence.

threatened
Peo. 13–18 *t·* to let loose the wild beasts
My. 196–18 he *t·* not ; — I Pet. 2 : 23.

threatening
My. 129– 3 danger *t·* our nation,

threatens
My. v–10 * popularity *t·* to supersede

threats
'02. 15– 2 contained *t·* to blow up the hall

three
Mis. 51– 7 All mesmerism is of one of *t·* kinds;
69–15 *t·* doses of Croton oil,
107–14 *T·* cardinal points must be gained
107–19 false senses pass through *t·* states
133–22 *T·* times a day, I retire to
136–24 hold *t·* sessions annually,
143–22 within about *t·* months,
166–22 hid in *t·* measures of meal,
171–24 *in t· measures of meal,* — Matt. 13 : 33.
172–13 until the *t·* measures be
174–30 hid in *t·* measures of meal,
175– 5 The *t·* measures of meal may well be
177–23 * *t·* o'clock, the hour for the
230– 8 *T·* ways of wasting time,
231–19 walking ! one, two, *t·* steps,
242–24 to cure that habit in *t·* days,
273–29 *t·* classes . . . would be delayed.
279–13 *t·* picture-stories from the Bible
279–14 *t·* of those pictures from which we
315–11 teach annually *t·* classes only.
315–23 as often as once in *t·* months.
349– 5 twelve lessons, *t·* weeks' time,
355–11 through *t·* stages of growth.
Man. 36–20 recommendation signed by *t·* members
68–14 remain with her *t·* consecutive years,
76–17 shall consist of *t·* members
79– 4 not less than *t·* loyal members
88– 7 consisting of *t·* members,
91–24 once in *t·* years
91–25 for *t· consecutive* years under
98–25 the *t·* largest branch churches
99– 8 its *t·* largest branch churches,
102– 5 consisting of not less than *t·* members,
Ret. 4–12 undulating lands of *t·* townships.
8– 5 *t·* times, in an ascending scale.
8–10 call *Mary, t·* times !''
50– 7 tuition lasting barely *t·* weeks.
Un. 20– 5 Through these *t·* statements,
33–24 two or *t·* witnesses — Matt. 18 : 16.
Pul. vii– 4 *T·* quarters of a century hence,
3– 5 and in *t·* days — John 2 : 19.
6–14 * I had not read *t·* pages before I

three

Pul.	27– 7	* *t·* large class-rooms and the pastor's
	27–30	* composed of *t·* separate panels,
	61–11	* *t·* affecting great and pedal
	61–11	* *t·* affecting swell and pedal
Rud.	2– 6	one of the *t·* subjects,
	8– 1	the *t·* great kingdoms.
No.	30–11	God's law is in *t·* words,
Pan.	7–14	We know of but *t·* theistic religions,
'00.	2– 9	*t·* types of human nature
'01.	4– 5	four times *t·* is twelve,
	4– 5	*t·* times four is twelve.
	4–23	One instead of *t·*,
	4–26	these *t·* are one in essence
	6– 2	theology's *t·* divine persons
	6– 6	which reckons *t·* as one
	6–12	Who can conceive . . . of *t·* infinites?
	6–15	must be One although He is *t·*.
	17–17	in from one to *t·* interviews,
	22–17	do not say that one added to one is *t·*,
	23– 1	neither more nor less than *t·* ;
	27–14	in one to *t·* interviews
	27–28	* truth goes through *t·* stages.
'02.	2–16	hid in *t·* measures of meal,
Hea.	3–26	*t·* statements of one Principle.
Peo.	4–19	*t·* terms for one divine Principle
	4–19	are the *t·* in one
Po.	68–17	when *we t· met,*
My.	56–12	* *t·* branch churches were organized,
	56–19	* *t·* foregoing named churches
	56–29	* *t·* services were held each Sunday,
	69–17	* and *t·* at the back,
	70–27	* *t·* balanced swells,
	74– 4	* within two or *t·* days' ride,
	80–29	* *t·* o'clock in the afternoon
	157–22	deed of trust to *t·* individuals
	213–28	*t·* quotations from "S. and H.
	214–11	Jesus' *t·* days' work in the sepulchre
	227–11	one out of *t·* of their patients,
	243–15	to take charge of *t·* or more churches.
	244–26	not exceed *t·* in number.
	250– 3	*t·* years' term for church Readers,
	253–23	a store of wisdom in *t·* words :
	304–25	* truth goes through *t·* stages.
		(*see also* **dates, numbers, persons, values, years**)

threefold

Un.	55–15	This *t·* Messiah reveals the

three-in-one

Mis.	163– 1	sought to conquer the *t·* of error :

three-manual

Pul.	60–22	* It is of *t·* compass,

three-years

Mis.	163– 5	his *t·* mission was a marvel of

threshold

Mis.	120– 3	at the very *t·* of C. S. :
	324– 4	Pausing at the *t·* of a palatial
My.	264– 9	* *t·* of the twentieth century,

thrice

Ret.	8–19	same call was *t·* repeated.

thrifty

Mis.	329– 6	nature like a *t·* housewife

thrill

Mis.	106–29	strains that *t·* the chords of feeling
	132–26	with a *t·* of pleasure that I read
	375–27	* "It gave me such a *t·* of joy
Ret.	12– 5	echoes still my day-dreams *t·*,
Po.	16–17	send a *t·* To the heart of the leaves
	61– 3	echoes still my day-dreams *t·*,
	66– 4	like the *t·* of that mountain rill,

thrilled

Pul.	31–17	* largely *t·* and pervaded by a
No.	1–10	So men, when *t·* by a new idea,
My.	39–25	* hearts were *t·* by her compassion,
	64– 6	* *t·* with tender gratitude

thrills

My.	125–18	which always *t·* the soul.

thrive

Mis.	80–21	Tyranny can *t·* but feebly under our
My.	4–19	they *t·* together,

thrives

My.	139–10	Scientist *t·* in adversity ;
	165– 9	by this spirit man lives and *t·*,

throb

Mis.	152–13	pulsates with every *t·* of theirs

throbbing

My.	159– 8	the *t·* of every pulse

throbbings

Peo.	1–15	ceaseless *t·* and throes of thought

throe

Mis.	285–22	some extra *t·* of error

throes

Un.	57–25	Mortal *t·* of anguish
Peo.	1–15	throbbings and *t·* of thought

throne

Mis.	67–31	taken up to the very *t·*,
	73–24	*t·* of his glory,— *Matt.* 19 : 28.
	328–31	up to the *t·* of everlasting glory.
	368– 7	* Wrong forever on the *t·*.
	388–16	Her dazzling crown, her sceptred *t·*,
Ret.	22–13	the *t·* of God." — *Heb.* 12 : 2.
Pul.	82– 2	* brain for its great white *t·*.
Rud.	10– 1	unjust usurper of the *t·*
No.	34–24	mounting to the *t·* of glory
'00.	10–22	habitation of His *t·* forever.
Po.	21– 5	Her dazzling crown, her sceptered *t·*,
	26– 9	grasped the sword to hold her *t·*,
	31– 4	seed dropped from Love's *t·*.
	39– 8	from its altar to Thy *t·*
My.	258–16	the *t·* of God." — *Heb.* 12 : 2.

thrones

Mis.	73–25	*shall sit upon twelve t·,— Matt.* 19 : 28.
Po.	79– 6	of these stones, or tyrants' *t·*,
My.	200–22	on crumbling *t·* of justice

throng

Mis.	396–22	wake a white-winged angel *t·*
Ret.	8– 2	*t·* the chambers of memory.
Pul.	18– 6	wake a white-winged angel *t·*
	29–14	* for the overflowing *t·*.
	39–24	* I see the hurrying *t·*
	41–18	* incapable of receiving this vast *t·*,
	54– 4	* We touch him in life's *t·*
	61–25	* attracted quite a *t·* of people,
Po.	12– 6	wake a white-winged angel *t·*
	25– 6	What a shadowy *t·*
My.	79–18	* not a gathering of "the vulgar *t·* ;"
	86–29	* could accommodate the *t·*
	189–28	why *t·* in pity round me?

thronged

Pul.	29–10	* was *t·* with a congregation
	57– 7	* was *t·* at the four services

throngs

My.	80–25	* to accommodate the great *t·*

throttle

My.	26–21	Now is the time to *t· the lie*

throttled

Mis.	286– 5	can neither be obscured nor *t·*.

throughout

Mis.	12– 4	*t·* time and beyond the grave.
	92–15	*T·* his entire explanations,
	113–32	spiritual animus is felt *t·* the land.
	127– 3	*T·* my entire connection with The
	192–27	extends . . . *t·* all Christendom.
	204– 7	attended *t·* with doubt, hope,
	217–13	Nature declares, *t·* the mineral,
	236– 3	*T·* our experience since
	278– 8	*t·* my labors, and in my history
	312–26	emphasis *t·* the entire centuries,
	314– 1	*t·* our land and in other lands.
	364–24	*t·* time and eternity.
Man.	60– 3	Continued *T·* the Year.
	97– 8	*t·* the United States, Canada,
Ret.	7–10	* incessant study *t·* his short life.
	20–13	I knelt by his side *t·* the dark
	21–10	*t·* the war for the Union,
	84– 9	*T·* his entire explanations
Un.	46–22	extend *t·* the universe,
	51–21	eternally radiating *t·* all space
Pul.	8– 2	*t·* our land the press has spoken
	24–25	* The architecture is Romanesque *t·*.
	58– 8	* believers *t·* this country
	60–21	* pneumatic wind-chests *t·*,
	63– 5	* AN IMMENSE FOLLOWING *T·* THE
	71–21	* thousands *t·* the United States
'01.	11–18	and obeyed *t·* the week,
My.	17–31	*T·* my entire connection with The
	20– 1	*t·* the whole world, — *Mark* 14 : 9.
	31– 2	* following hymns *t·* the day :
	111–16	*t·* is logical in premise and in
	129– 7	*t·* our beloved country
	174– 9	courtesy . . . extended to me *t·*.
	175–21	to macadamize North State Street *t·*
	185– 1	acceptance *t·* the earth,
	240– 3	acknowledged *t·* the earth.
	301–19	*t·* the entire testimony of the
		(*see also* **world**)

throw

Mis.	46–17	*t·* the weight of his thoughts
	255– 7	to *t·* the weight of thought
	275–19	*t·* wide the gates of heaven.
	313– 9	*t·* the light of penetration on
	325–11	*t·* them away, and afterwards try to
Un.	15– 5	which God never can *t·* off?
'02.	16–16	and they *t·* a light upon the

throwing

My.	174– 2	*t·* open their doors for the
	221–28	thus *t·* the door wide open

thrown

Mis.	23–28	likeness *t·* upon the mirror
	264– 8	*t·* upon the mists of time,
My.	31–10	* doors of the church were *t·* open
	73–18	* headquarters was *t·* open

throws

Pul.	39–16	* *T·* o'er the Charles its flood of

thrust

Mis.	84– 7	prophets *t·* disputed points
Ret.	90– 1	not to *t·* aside Science,
'02.	18– 4	spectacle of sin *t·* upon the
My.	161–13	yourselves *t·* out." — *Luke* 13 : 28.
	269–17	God hath *t·* in the sickle,

Thummim

Mis.	194– 7	*T·* of priestly office,
Ret.	35–23	*T·* of priestly office,
'01.	12–13	*T·* of priestly office,

thunder

Mis.	277–29	I *t·* His law to the sinner,
	374–13	hatred — earth's harmless *t·*
'00.	9–15	his lightning, *t·*, and sunshine
'02.	5–21	voiced in the *t·* of Sinai,

thunderbolt

Un.	46–24	earthquake, *t·*, and tempest.
'01.	15–21	*t·* of Jonathan Edwards :
Hea.	2– 6	hurls the *t·* of truth,

thunderbolts

My.	149–28	in the sky with dumb *t·*,
	265–27	clearer skies, less *t·*, tornadoes,

thundered

Mis.	106–10	Volleyed and *t·* !

thunderings

Mis.	17– 2	You hear and record the *t·* of

thunders

Ret.	9–21	* where dying *t·* roll

Thursday

My.	333–21	* died on *T·* night,

thwarted

Mis.	11– 2	*t·*, its punishment is tenfold.

Thy and thy

Mis.	83–25	glorify *T·* Son, — *John* 17 : 1.
	83–25	*T·* Son also may glorify — *John* 17 : 1.
	159–25	*T·* children grown to behold *Thee!*
	174–25	" *T·* kingdom come ;" — *Matt.* 6 : 10.
	208– 1	chapter sub-title — *Matt.* 6 : 10.
	208–23	kept *T·* word." — *Psal.* 119 : 67.
	211–30	"*T·* kingdom come." — *Matt.* 6 : 10.
	248– 7	works of *T·* hands." — *Psal.* 92 : 4.
	275–27	*T·* light and *T·* love reach earth,
	384– 9	*T·* will to know, and do.
	385– 7	This is *T·* high behest :
	387– 8	Brood o'er us with *T·* shelt'ring
	388– 9	Fed by *T·* love divine we live,
	397–25	How to feed *T·* sheep ;
	398– 1	I will listen for *T·* voice,
	398–15	Lead *T·* lambkins to the fold,
Man.	41–21	"*T·* kingdom come ;" — *Matt.* 6 : 10.
	41–23	may *T·* Word enrich the affections
Ret.	9–11	*T·* servant heareth." — *I Sam.* 3 : 9.
	15– 9	mention of *T·* righteousness, — *Psal.* 71 : 16.
	15–11	*T·* wondrous works." — *Psal.* 71 : 17.
	46– 6	How to feed *T·* sheep ;
	46– 7	I will listen for *T·* voice,
	46–21	Lead *T·* lambkins to the fold,
Un.	5–28	parts of *T·* ways," — see *Job* 26 : 14.
Pul.	1– 1	*fatness of T· house;* — *Psal.* 36 : 8.
	1– 2	*river of T· pleasures.* — *Psal.* 36 : 8.
	3–16	fatness of *T·* house ; — *Psal.* 36 : 8.
	3–17	river of *T·* pleasures." — *Psal.* 36 : 8.
	4–26	fatness of *T·* house." — *Psal.* 36 : 8.
	7–29	fatness of *T·* house ; — *Psal.* 36 : 8.
	7–30	river of *T·* pleasures." — *Psal.* 36 : 8.
	10–27	breathe Thou *T·* blessing
	17– 5	How to feed *T·* sheep ;
	17– 6	I will listen for *T·* voice,
	17–20	Lead *T·* lambkins to the fold,
	22– 7	"*T·* kingdom come. — *Matt.* 6 : 10.
	22– 7	*T·* will be done — *Matt.* 6 : 10.
	33– 8	* *T·* servant heareth." — *I Sam.* 3 : 9.
Po.	6– 1	Brood o'er us with *T·* shelt'ring
	7– 9	Fed by *T·* love divine we live,
	14– 4	How to feed *T·* sheep ;
	14– 5	I will listen for *T·* voice,
	14–19	Lead *T·* lambkins to the fold,
	24–21	Send us *t·* white-winged dove.
	28– 7	To *T·* all-wise behest
	30–15	cast on *T·* blest name,
	36– 8	*T·* will to know, and do.

Thy and thy

Po.	37– 7	This is *T·* high behest :
	39– 8	And from its altar to *T·* throne
	43–10	in *T·* great heart hold them
	44– 3	With the guerdon of *T·* bosom,
	77– 5	peace abound at *T·* behest,
	77– 6	wherefore this *T·* love?
My.	33–15	abide in *t·* tabernacle? — *Psal.* 15 : 1.
	33–16	dwell in *t·* holy hill? — *Psal.* 15 : 1.
	201–21	I will listen for *T·* voice,
	220–22	make them *T·* friends ;
	225–26	"Hallowed be *T·* name." — *Matt.* 6 : 9.
	228–23	dwell in *T·* holy hill? — *Psal.* 15 : 1.
	229–27	*T·* ways are not as ours.
	281– 4	"*T·* kingdom come. — *Matt.* 6 : 10.
	281– 4	*T·* will be done — *Matt.* 6 : 10.

Thyatira

'00.	13–24	deity in the city of *T·*

tide

Mis.	162–14	to stem the *t·* of Judaism,
	316–11	*t·* which flows heavenward,
Pul.	41– 3	* *t·* of contributions which
Po.	16–10	and roll on with its *t·*,
My.	54–10	* the *t·* of men and women

tides

Mis.	292– 3	overwhelming *t·* of revelation,
	360–23	*t·* of spiritual sensation
My.	149–10	the ever-flowing *t·* of truth

tidings

Mis.	369– 4	the gospel of glad *t·*
	386– 7	"Bearest thou no *t·* from our
Ret.	45– 3	"bringeth good *t·*, — *Isa.* 52 : 7.
Po.	49–11	"Bearest thou no *t·* from our
My.	184–27	bringeth good *t·*, — *Isa.* 52 : 7.

ties

Ret.	31– 2	sunders the dominant *t·* of earth
Un.	17– 9	evil *t·* its wagon-load of offal to
'02.	19–21	Are earth's pleasures, its *t·* and

tiles

Pul.	25–12	* the roof is of terra cotta *t·*,

till

Mis.	vii–11	*T·* time shall end more timely,
	115–18	*t·* you intelligently know and
	140–17	*t·* mortal man sought to know
	145– 5	*T·* then, this form of godliness
	152–26	*t·* the storm has passed.
	160– 9	*t·* they meet and mingle in bliss
	169– 5	*t·* she was God-driven back
	171–24	*t· the whole is leavened.* — *Matt.* 13 : 33.
	227–27	*t·* it grows into the full stature
	264– 7	*t·*, like camera shadows
	272– 9	* *t·* the repealing of said Act
	302–18	*t·* this permission was *withdrawn,*
	384–10	Stay ! *t·* the storms are o'er
	398–18	*T·* the morning's beam ;
Man.	55–16	shall not be counted loyal *t·*
Ret.	8–19	but I answered not, *t·*
	15– 4	*t·* I founded a church
	15–27	*t·* the persons who divulged their
	22–15	*t·* its involved errors are vanquished
	33– 6	*t·* I was weary of "scientific guessing,"
	46–24	*t·* the morning's beam ;
	90–24	*t·* her children can walk steadfastly
	94–16	not *t·* then, will immortal Truth
Un.	30– 9	*t·* divine understanding takes
	43–16	*t·* all be fulfilled." — *Matt.* 5 : 18.
Pul.	6– 3	And it will continue *t·* the
	17–23	*T·* the morning's beam ;
	21–11	struggle *t·* it be accomplished?
No.	1– 8	*t·* they rise in floods
Pan.	13–16	*t·* God's will be witnessed
'00.	7–29	*t·* the long night is past
	8– 3	*t·* we awake in His likeness.
	8–12	*t·* God's discipline takes it off
	9–15	*t·* the mental atmosphere is clear.
	10– 9	Such conflict never ends *t·*
	15–27	Watch ! *t·* the storms are o'er
'01.	16– 6	*t·* the sin is destroyed.
	20–22	*t·* he suffers up to its extinction
	29–20	no excuse for waiting *t·* the wind
Po.	3– 9	*T·* sleep sets drooping fancy free
	3–13	*T·* bursting bonds our spirits part
	8– 9	*T·* vestal pearls that on leaflets
	14–22	*T·* the morning's beam ;
	17– 3	rest *t·* I see My loved ones
	36– 9	Stay ! *t·* the storms are o'er
	43–19	*T·* they gain at last
	53–11	*T·* heard at silvery eve
	65–18	*T·* darkness and death like mist
	72– 3	*T·* God is God no longer
	78– 6	*T·* molds the hero form
My.	9–26	*t·* I am satisfied with what my
	18–24	*t·* God's will be witnessed

till

My.	104–19	*t·* they know of what and of whom
	148–13	unthought of *t·* the day had passed !
	149–13	*t·* you make their treasures yours.
	155–14	*t·*, home at last, it finds the
	183– 7	* "When Christ reigns, and not *t·* then,
	185– 9	*t·* Truth shall reign triumphant
	189–12	*t·* truth and love, commingling in
	216– 1	*T·* Christian Scientists give all
	217–10	*t·* it is disbursed in equal shares
	240– 1	*t·* all men shall know Him
	307– 5	*t·* one day I declared to him
	335– 7	* membership in both *t·* his decease.
	338–13	unknown to me *t·* after the lecture

Tilton
N. H.

My.	174–24	Congregational Church in *T·*, N. H.
	310–12	establishment in *T·*, N. H.
	312–28	to my father's home in *T·*, N. H.
Ret.	5– 9	my parents removed to *T·*,
	5–19	for many years had resided in *T·*
	19– 4	under the paternal roof in *T·*.
My.	310–10	* workman in a *T·* woolen mill."
	314– 3	* "lived for a short time at *T·*,
	314– 6	* from *T·* to North Groton

Tilton, Alexander

My.	310–11	joint partner with Alexander *T·*,
	310–30	Dr. Ladd said to Alexander *T·* :

Tilton Congregational Church

My.	311–13	I joined the *T· C· C·*

Time

Mis.	390– 5	Old *T·* gives thee her palm.
Po.	55– 6	Old *T·* gives thee her palm.

time *(see also* time's*)*

six o'clock

My.	77–22	* at *s· o·* this morning.

7 : 30 a. m.

Pul.	41–23	* At *7 : 30 a. m.* the chimes in the

eight o'clock

My.	16–13	* at *e· o·* in the forenoon.

9. a. m.

Pul.	41–30	* At *9 a. m.* the first congregation gathered.

nine o'clock

Mis.	304–23	* *n· o·* in the morning
	304–28	* It will always ring at *n· o·*

nine to four o'clock

Pul.	59– 6	* were held from *n· to f· o·*,

ten o'clock

My.	30–30	* admission at the *t· o·* service,
	38–30	* Tuesday, June 12, at *t· o·*

10 : 30 a. m.

Pul.	42– 8	* at *10 : 30 a. m.*, however,

10 : 30 o'clock

Pul.	42– 3	* At *10 : 30 o·* another service began,

twelve o'clock

Mis.	304–26	* at *t· o·* on the birthdays of

12 . 30 P. M.

My.	169– 4	on July 5, at *12 . 30 P. M.*,

two o'clock

My.	39–3	* at *t· o·* in the afternoon.
	171–13	at *t· o·* in the afternoon,

3 p. m.

Pul.	42– 5	* at *3 p. m.* the service was repeated

three o'clock

Mis.	177–23	* said that at *t· o·*,
My.	80–29	* *t· o·* in the afternoon

four o'clock

Mis.	304–27	* at *f· o·* it will toll

about the

My.	27– 5	about the *t·* of our annual meeting

acceptable

No.	28–11	now is the most acceptable *t·*

accepted

My.	12–18	now is the accepted *t·*." — *II Cor.* 6: 2.

advance of the

'02.	10– 8	or in advance of the *t·*,

all

Mis.	189–30	it extends to all *t·*,
	244–27	for all peoples and for all *t·* ;
	364–14	all *t·*, space, immortality,
Ret.	26– 9	demonstrated for all *t·* and peoples
	36– 1	or its application in all *t·*
No.	21– 9	all *t·*, space, immortality,
Pan.	5–11	the proper answer for all *t·*
'01.	25–18	of his time and of all *t·*.
Po.	30– 8	To glorify all *t·* — eternity
My.	28–24	* Jesus' gospel was for all *t·*
	158–28	stand through all *t·* for God and

all the

Mis.	32–23	all the *t·* and attention that they
	223– 3	I was saying all the time,

almost perfect

My.	38–21	* in almost perfect *t·*.

time

ample

Man.	82–20	devote ample *t·* for faithful practice.

and attention

Mis.	32–23	all the *t·* and attention that they
	112–11	demands our *t·* and attention.
	114– 4	cannot give too much *t·* and attention
	138– 7	to give *t·* and attention to hygiene
Ret.	44–20	*t·* and attention must be given to
My.	163–14	demands on my *t·* and attention
	192–25	demands upon my *t·* and attention
	231–20	demands on her *t·* and attention
	243–17	give all possible *t·* and attention

and circumstance

Mis.	160– 6	through *t·* and circumstance,

and eternity

Mis.	68– 3	it requires both *t·* and eternity.
	147– 6	victory won for *t·* and eternity?
	264– 5	They build for *t·* and eternity.
	364–24	or quarrel throughout *t·* and eternity,
	382–10	*t·* and eternity bear witness to
Ret.	70–19	fill his own niche in *t·* and eternity.
'01.	25– 5	encompassing *t·* and eternity.
My.	19–26	vibrant through *t·* and eternity

and for eternity

'02.	5–19	the theme for *t·* and for eternity ;

and goodness

My.	306–12	*T·* and goodness determine greatness.

and immortality

'00.	1– 6	all space, *t·*, and immortality

and joy

My.	166–23	let our measure of *t·* and joy

and labor

My.	193–24	you have grasped *t·* and labor,

and place

My.	169–20	beauty of *t·* and place

and retirement

My.	117– 8	*t·* and retirement to pursue the

and space

Mis.	110–17	*t·* and space, when encompassed by
No.	16–13	destitute of *t·* and space ;
My.	110–13	forces annihilating *t·* and space,

and thought

Mis.	112– 7	occupy *t·* and thought ;
Hea.	12–20	requires *t·* and thought ;

another

Mis.	29– 7	At another *t·* he prayed,

any

Mis.	321–25	at any *t·* during the great wonder
Man.	30– 6	be found at any *t·* inadequate
	32–21	no remarks . . . at any *t·*,
	57– 6	meetings may be held at any *t·*
	81–15	shall at any *t·* be published
	101– 1	any *t·* the C. S. Board of Directors
My.	325–14	* Command me at any *t·*,

approaches

Mis.	2–17	*t·* approaches when divine Life,

appropriate

My.	24–31	* no more appropriate *t·* for

at one

Ret.	3– 2	at one *t·* held the position of
	40– 4	At one *t·* I was called to speak

attention and

My.	175– 5	my constant attention and *t·*,

awakes in

Mis.	222–18	subject scarcely awakes in *t·*,

babe of

Pul.	1– 4	a nursling, a babe of *t·*,

before the

'00.	9–12	before the *t·* ?" — *Matt.* 8 : 29.
'02.	10– 6	before the *t·* ?" — *Matt.* 8 : 29.

began

My.	116–22	growth spiritual, since *t·* began,

bells of

My.	31– 7	* clanging bells of *t·* ;"

best

Mis.	80–20	at the best *t·*, will redress

boundary of

Un.	37–11	no boundary of *t·* can separate

cannot quench

Po.	15–22	*t·* cannot quench in oblivion's wave.

cannot spare

Mis.	155–24	cannot spare *t·* to write to God,

change in the

My.	121– 3	change in the *t·* for holding

cometh

Mis.	145– 3	But the *t·* cometh when the
	286–19	The *t.* cometh, and now is,

complete

'00.	14– 8	signifies a complete *t·* or number

consumed

My.	25–17	Owing to the *t·* consumed

consumes

Mis.	117–21	To point out . . . consumes *t·*,

time

corridors of
'02.   4–16   adown the corridors of *t*,
My. 189–10   through the dim corridors of *t*,

cycles of
Un.   11–24   required neither cycles of *t* nor

dated
Mis. 163– 8   He who dated *t*, the Christian era,
My. 180– 8   by him who . . . dated *t*.

dial of
Mis. 71–29   flitting across the dial of *t*.

due
Mis. 373–21   in due *t* Christianity entered into
Ret.   1–17   in due *t* was married

during the
My. 323–30   * during the *t* of our studying

easel of
Mis. ix–10   easel of *t* presents pictures

expiration of the
Man. 69– 9   before the expiration of the *t*

first
Mis. 16–31   behold for the first *t* the
    17–16   behold for the first *t* the divine
   344–30   Christianity for the first *t*
   352– 6   able for the first *t* to discern the
Ret. 25– 6   I apprehended for the first *t*,
My. 166–27   I am for the first *t* informed of
   284–15   * first *t* in the history of
   362–14   * first *t* gathered in one place

flourishes for a
My. 112– 4   false philosophy flourishes for a *t*

flourish for a
My. 95– 2   * cults which flourish for a *t*

footsteps of
Po. 15– 4   moans from the footsteps of *t* !

foundations of
Mis. 82–10   reach the sure foundations of *t*,

fulness of
Pul. 85– 7   * will, in the fulness of *t*, see

future
Mis.   7–20   to be depicted in some future *t*

give a thing
My. 193–22   * Carlyle writes, "Give a thing *t* ;

God's
Mis. 117–23   God's *t* and mortals' differ.
My.   13– 3   act in God's *t*.

God's own
My. 306–19   and that in God's own *t*.

have kept
Mis. 110–18   Our hearts have kept *t* together,

have not had
My. 195– 9   privileges I have not had *t* to

her
Mis. 37–26   Her *t* is wholly devoted to
Rud. 14– 9   gave fully seven-eights of her *t*
My. 231–20   demands on her *t* and attention

his
Mis. 214– 4   mortal thought, of his *t*.
Pul. 13–22   devil knoweth his *t* is short.
'01.   25–18   of his *t* and of all time.

hoary with
No. 13–18   It is hoary with *t*.

illusion of
Mis. 93–13   it is the illusion of *t* and mortality.

improved
Pul.   1–10   *t* improved is eloquent

indefinite
Pul. 58–24   * but for an indefinite *t*

is at hand
My.   10–13   * but the *t* is at hand, now,

is consumed
Mis. 230– 4   great amount of *t* is consumed

is money
'00.   3– 7   to him *t* is money,

is required
Mis. 43–18   *t* is required thoroughly to

Jesus'
My. 211–10   even as in Jesus' *t*

lack of
Mis. 256–16   the old impediment, lack of *t*,

last
Pul. 42– 6   * service was repeated for the last *t*.

less
Man. 68– 6   member who leaves her in less *t*

little
Mis.   4–15   but little *t* has been devoted to
   6– 3   but little *t* free from complaints
'00.   2–11   he gives little *t* to society

looms of
Mis. 99– 6   through the looms of *t*,

many a
Pul. 80–12   * has many a *t* been sent us

matures
Mis. 286– 6   Until *t* matures human growth,

time

may commence
Mis. 15–18   *T* may commence, but it

mean
My. 55– 8   * In the mean *t*, not only was the
   55–19   * In the mean *t* Sunday services

mists of
Mis. 264– 8   shadows thrown upon the mists of *t*,

more
My. 259–16   and give me more *t* to think

most
Mis. 267– 7   I have sacrificed the most *t*,

moth of
My. 230– 1   the sacrilegious moth of *t*,

much
Mis. 137–23   give much *t* to self-examination
Ret. 44–20   much *t* and attention must be given

my
Mis.   x–10   manifold demands on my *t*
   132–16   great demand upon my *t*,
My. 135–11   increasing demands upon my *t*
   137–17   increasing demands upon my *t*,
   163–14   demands on my *t* and attention
   192–25   demands upon my *t* and attention
   275–19   demands upon my *t* at home,

next
Ret.   9–14   resolving to do, next *t*, as my mother

no
Mis. 230–17   spend no *t* in sheer idleness,
   238– 7   reformer has no *t* to give in
   282–27   when there is no *t* for ceremony
   299– 8   no *t* for detailed report
   357– 1   no *t* for idle words,
Pul. 81–19   * they want no *t* to take,
'00.   2–13   He takes no *t* for amusement,
'01.   32–10   no *t* or desire to defame

no better
My. 329–21   * At no better *t* than now,

of contagious disease
My. 116– 2   At a *t* of contagious disease,

of election
Man. 26– 5   from the *t* of election to office.
   80–25   dating from the *t* of election

of such service
Man. 69–12   during the *t* of such service.

of the dedication
My. 76–14   * at the *t* of the dedication
   320–30   * at the *t* of the dedication

of the divorce
My. 314–30   up to the *t* of the divorce.

of the occurrence
Mis. 290–15   naming the *t* of the occurrence,

of times
Pul. 84– 1   * "The *t* of times" is near

olden
My. 147–20   to-day, as in olden *t*,
   162–19   which spake thus in olden *t*

one
Hea.   4–25   is one thing at one *t*,
My. 308–20   One *t* when my father was visiting
   309–14   justice of the peace at one *t*.
   343–26   I found at one *t* that they had

one's
My. 234– 3   absorbing one's *t* writing or

one week's
Mis. 135–14   give one week's *t* and expense

or attention
Mis. 366– 2   the *t* or attention that

or money
My. 231–10   spend no more *t* or money in

our
Mis. 112–11   demands our *t* and attention.
   123– 1   same spirit that in our *t* massacres
Ret. 70–10   in our *t* no Christian Scientist
My. 111– 8   same class of . . . as we have in our *t*.
   340–29   succeeded by our *t* of abundance,

outweighs
'02.   17–15   that which outweighs *t* ;

past
Pul.   1– 9   *T* past and time present,

posterns of
Mis. 383–13   go down the dim posterns of *t*

precise
Ret. 14–21   could not designate any precise *t*.

present
Mis. 56–28   *stages of existence to the present t* ?
Pul.   1– 9   Time past and *t* present,
My. 24–21   * and at the present *t* there are
   110– 5   At the present *t* this Bethlehem star

Queen Elizabeth's
No. 44–13   In Queen Elizabeth's *t* Protestantism

question of
Mis. 348–12   It is only a question of *t*

required
Man. 62– 2   *t* required to take the collection.

time

requires
Mis.	6–22	it requires *t·* to overcome
Un.	43–10	requires *t·* and immense . . . growth.
Hea.	12–20	To prepare the medicine requires *t·*

requisite
My.	285– 6	I cannot spare the *t·* requisite

right
Mis.	359–23	and is available at the right *t·*.

ripeness of
Mis.	164– 6	appeared in the ripeness of *t·*,

sacred
My.	36– 9	* have assembled at this sacred *t·*

same
Mis.	109– 1	at the same *t·* declaring the unity
	256– 3	at the same *t·* improved morally.
Ret.	38–14	at the same *t·*, finished printing
	52– 7	At the same *t·* I have worked to
Pul.	37–14	* At the same *t·* it is her most earnest aim
•*Hea.*	15–16	when at the same *t·* he calls God
My.	vi–23	* at the same *t·* she presented to
	70– 6	* edifices to its credit in the same *t·*
	82– 9	* to get away at the same *t·*.
	131– 4	refines character at the same *t·*
	224–19	at the same *t·* giving full credit

shores of
Mis.	205–31	Mortals who on the shores of *t·*
'02.	11– 3	to wander on the shores of *t·*

short
Mis.	297– 1	Taking into account the short *t·*
Pul.	12–15	he hath but a short *t·*.— *Rev.* 12 : 12.
My.	47–25	* the years . . . seem but a short *t·*.
	314– 3	* "lived for a short *t·* at Tilton,

some
Mis.	78–22	will some *t·* appear all the clearer
	87– 9	shall know, some *t·*, the spiritual
	136–13	as they must some *t·*,
	147–17	by affections which may some *t·*
	216–22	* some *t·* after the rest of it had
	273– 1	some *t·*, as . . . Scientists,
	278–24	I have felt for some *t·* that
	339–27	will some *t·* flood thy memory,
	357–21	For some *t·* it has been clear
	368–28	this earth shall some *t·* rejoice
Ret.	89–16	when he had been some *t·* absent
Un.	9– 6	some *t·* and in some way,
Pul.	62– 2	* for some *t·* well . . . known in
No.	28–10	must be learned some *t·*,
'00.	2–26	to take some *t·* for myself ;
My.	142–18	some *t·* learn this and rejoice with me,
	184–29	must at some *t·* find utterance

space of
Mis.	147– 5	another space of *t·* has been given

specified
Man.	69– 3	*t·* specified in the Church Manual.

storms of
Mis.	392–15	to wrestle with the storms of *t·* ;
Po.	20–19	to wrestle with the storms of *t·* ;

strain of
Mis.	365– 1	will bear the strain of *t·*
No.	21–22	bears the strain of *t·*,

sufficient
Man.	39–10	when sufficient *t·* has elapsed
My.	223–14	because I have not sufficient *t·*

tears of
Po.	22– 9	bliss that wipes the tears of *t·*

test of
My.	92– 4	* until it has stood the test of *t·*.

that
Mis.	137–13	but that *t·* has passed.
	193– 5	deemed it safe to say at that *t·*.
	290–19	not thought of the writer at that *t·*.
	306–20	* was at that *t·* the President
Ret.	27–13	Up to that *t·* I had not fully
	44–14	no student, at that *t·*, was found able
Un.	9– 7	That *t·* has partially come,
Pul.	34– 4	* and from that *t·* until 1866
My.	29–31	* From that *t·*, until the close of
	56– 1	* at that *t·* it was thought
	60–11	* Christian (?) people at that *t·*.
	61– 3	* every night since that *t·*.
	61– 9	* postponed until that *t·*.
	73– 5	* in other countries since that *t·*,
	145– 7	From that *t·*, October 29, 1897,
	181–26	Since that *t·* it has steadily decreased.
	314–11	At that *t·*, he owned a house in
	315–11	* At that *t·* I had no knowledge of
	321–22	* During that *t·*, from my
	323–32	* were at that *t·* some eight days in
	331– 9	* in your city at that *t·*.
	334– 4	* disease was raging at that *t·*.

their
Mis.	xi– 6	in advance of their *t·* ;
	296–12	give their *t·* and strength
Man.	31– 7	suitable portion of their *t·*
Rud.	13–26	give all their *t·* to C. S. work,

time

their
Rud.	14– 2	giving only a portion of their *t·*
My.	62–30	* gave freely of their *t·* and efforts
	216– 2	all their *t·* to spiritual things,

this
Mis.	324–28	this *t·* he struggles on,
	327–23	All this *t·* the Stranger is
Ret.	47– 6	At this *t·* there were over three
Pul.	34–11	* During this *t·* she suddenly
	34–26	"During this *t·*," she said,
'00.	15–17	all this *t·* divine Love
Hea.	16–17	will leave our . . . for this *t·*.
My.	11–11	* in all this *t·* she has never
	21–11	* a visit to Boston at this *t·*,
	47– 3	* It seems meet at this *t·*,
	54–15	* At this *t·* the Hawthorne Rooms,
	55–24	* At this *t·* the church removed
	89–25	* not to this *t·* alone,
	132–12	in all this *t·* and in every heart
	145– 2	by this *t·* acquainted with
	244– 5	gladly give it at this *t·*

this very
Mis.	54–15	curing hundreds at this very *t·* ;

three weeks'
Mis.	349– 5	twelve lessons, three weeks' *t*,

throughout
Mis.	12– 5	throughout *t·* and beyond the grave.

to follow
Mis.	359– 1	*t·* to follow the example of the

to preach
My.	53–21	* when she could give the *t·* to preach,

to receive
My.	163– 9	Not having the *t·* to receive all

to rest
My.	83–16	* will have *t·* to rest and sleep,

to talk
Mis.	32–17	If I had the *t·* to talk with all

to throttle
My.	26–20	Now is the *t·* to *throttle the lie*

touches
Mis.	336–28	touches *t·* only to take away its

to work
Mis.	340– 5	the *t·* to work, is *now*.

treasure of
Mis.	394–10	the treasure of *t·* ;
Po.	45–13	the treasure of *t·* ;

veil of
My.	256–20	veil of *t·* springs aside

want of
Mis.	351– 4	for want of *t·*, . . . I neglect myself.

wasting
Mis.	230– 8	Three ways of wasting *t·*,

whole
Pul.	81–13	* spends her whole *t·* helping others.

will remove
My.	223–28	burdens that *t·* will remove.

will show
My.	52–22	* "Whatever is . . . *t·* will show.

winds of
Mis.	99–23	winds of *t·* sweep clean the

wreck of
Mis.	26– 1	can survive the wreck of *t·* ;

your
Mis.	230– 1	chapter sub-title
My.	60–27	* I ask a little of your *t·* to tell you

Mis.	vii–11	Till *t·* shall end more timely,
	95–11	*t·* so kindly allotted me is
	107–18	it never started with *t·*,
	111–26	in *t·*, that church will love C. S.
	138– 3	The *t·* it takes yearly to
	155–16	Because Mother has not the *t·*
	182– 9	in *t·* they lose their false sense
	248–27	since which *t·* I have not
	267–10	there never was a *t·* when I
	281–12	in the *t·* of the French Huguenots,
	349–27	I accepted, for a *t·*, fifteen dollars
	380– 5	governs the universe, *t·*, space,
	381– 7	The *t·* for taking testimony
Man.	44– 7	possible loss, for a *t·*, of C. S.
Pul.	23– 9	* of the *t·* of Jonathan Edwards
	32–19	* At the *t·* I met her
	45– 7	* get their buildings finished on *t·*,
	51–21	* but as *t·* has gone on,
Pan.	13– 1	every hour in *t·* and in eternity
'00.	12–10	in the *t·* of . . . Emperor Augustus.
'02.	10– 5	molecule, space, *t·*, mortality ;
Po.	31– 2	not of *t·*, nor yet by nature sown,
My.	22–17	* *t·* has put its seal of affirmation
	51–12	* at a *t·* when there is such an
	55– 8	* although given up for a *t·*,
	56–19	* From the *t·* that the three foregoing
	61–13	* I fought hard . . . for a *t·* ;
	74– 8	* in *t·* for the first Sunday service.
	116– 6	In *t·* of religious . . . prosperity,

time
My.	130–14	I have neither the *t·* nor the
	136–27	and *t·* for spiritual thought
	142–16	might in *t·* lose its sacredness
	160–28	but of the *t·* no man knoweth.
	214–12	set the seal of eternity on *t·*.
	235–28	Had I known . . . in *t·* to have
	239–29	going on since ever *t·* was.
	250–22	But if now is not the *t·*,
	319–27	* considered the *t·* an important one
	320–21	* at the *t·* above referred to
	342–31	"In *t·* its present rules
	355– 1	* were with her at the *t·*,
	358–14	I have not the *t·* to do so.

time-honored
My.	174–19	our *t·* First Congregational Church

timely
Mis.	vii–11	Till time shall end more *t·*,
	4–11	chapter sub-title
	17–24	according to the *t·* or untimely
Ret.	80–17	he will not scorn the *t·* reproof,
Pul.	10–24	the *t·* shelter of this house,
My.	62–23	* wise counsel, *t·* instruction, and

time's
Mis.	xi–16	and thus may *t·* pastimes become
Pul.	1– 8	An old year is *t·* adult,
Po.	27–23	Pillow thy head on *t·* untired

Times
Pul.	89–15	* *T·*, Trenton, N. J.
	89–21	* *T·*, New Orleans, La.
	90– 9	* *T·*, Chicago, Ill.
	90–10	* *T·*, Minneapolis, Minn.

times
abreast of the
Man.	44–22	and kept abreast of the *t·*.

all
Mis.	96– 4	help in all *t·* of trouble,
My.	127–32	all *t·*, climes, and races.

apostolic
Pul.	54–11	* as were necessary in apostolic *t·*.

at all
Mis.	44–23	is but a dream at all *t·*.
	91–13	It is imperative, at all *t·*
	147–22	at all *t·* the trusty friend,
Pul.	15–16	At all *t·* and under all circumstances,
'00.	14–24	At all *t·* respect the character and

behind the
Mis.	232–11	will never do to be behind the *t·*

demand of the
Mis.	232–22	C. S., is a demand of the *t·*.

different
My.	315– 5	* at different *t·*, I had conversation

five
Mis.	221–26	five *t·* ten are fifty

four
Pul.	40–13	* Service Repeated Four *T·*
	40–16	* simple ceremonies, four *t·* repeated,
	59– 8	* these exercises four *t·* repeated.
'01.	4– 5	four *t·* three is twelve,

hundred
Un.	48– 3	tale already told a hundred *t·*,

like these
Mis.	275– 7	In *t·* like these it were well to lift the

many
Mis.	375–24	* how many *t·* have I seen these hands
Pul.	36–18	* met Mrs. Eddy many *t·* since then,
	55–15	* she has revised it many *t·*,
My.	130–11	has been made too many *t·*

million
No.	33–15	million *t·* greater than the brief agony
Peo.	8–28	proved a million *t·* unskilful.

modern
My.	98–10	* annals hardly parallel in modern *t·*,

ninety-nine
Mis.	118– 9	ninety-nine *t·* in one hundred

of hate
Mis.	277–27	especially near in *t·* of hate,

of need
'01.	26–13	for help in *t·* of need.

of persecution
'02.	1– 2	His people in *t·* of persecution

of trouble
Mis.	10–13	God, their help in *t·* of trouble.
	96– 4	help in all *t·* of trouble,
'01.	19– 3	is given to them in *t·* of trouble,

olden
Pul.	82–12	* In olden *t·* the Jews claimed to be
	83–16	* In olden *t·* it was the Amazons

our
Mis.	176–25	what of ourselves, and our *t·*

pagan
Pul.	65–22	* the spot where, in pagan *t·*,

times
past
Mis.	92–26	not be forgotten that in *t·* past,
Ret.	84–15	In *t·* past, arrogant pride,
No.	9– 2	if it had been heeded in *t·* past
Pan.	15– 5	God, who in *t·* past hath
My.	323–27	* not . . . able to appreciate in *t·* past.

Phariseeism of the
Mis.	234–13	the Phariseeism of the *t·*,

seven
Mis.	279–17	seven *t·* around these walls,
	279–17	seven *t·* corresponding to the

several
My.	320–20	* I called on Mr. Wiggin several *t·*
	320–22	* and several *t·* subsequent thereto,
	320–28	* I saw Mr. Wiggin several *t·*

signs of the
(see **signs***)*

signs of these
Mis.	2– 6	signs of these *t·* portend a
	278– 3	and are the signs of these *t·* ;
	347–10	discern the mental signs of these *t·*,
My.	270– 5	repeat the signs of these *t·*.

six
My.	29–11	* repeated six *t·* during the day.

stirring
My.	v– 4	* stirring *t·* of church building,

such
Man.	95– 7	such *t·* as the cause of C. S. demands.

support at
Mis.	39–23	needs support at *t·* ;

ten
Mis.	221–26	ten *t·* five are not

their
My.	221– 7	systems and practices of their *t·*.

thirty
Hea.	13– 6	shaking the preparation thirty *t·*

three
Mis.	133–22	Three *t·* a day, I retire to
Ret.	8– 5	three *t·*, in an ascending scale.
	8–10	heard somebody call . . . three *t·* !"
'01.	4– 6	three *t·* four is twelve.

time of
Pul.	84– 1	* "The time of *t·*" is near

two thousand
Hea.	13– 5	reducing . . . two thousand *t·*,

various
My.	310– 3	at various *t·* and places.

Mis.	111– 5	At *t·*, your net has been so full
	162– 1	at *t·* of special enlightenment,
'00.	2–25	intermediate worker works at *t·*.
My.	266–11	chapter sub-title
	320–25	* Our conversations were at *t·*

Times-Herald
Pul.	89–22	* *T·*, Dallas, Tex.

time-table
My.	124–24	produce thy records, *t·*, log,

time-tables
My.	167–16	Thanksgiving Day, according to *t·*,

time-world
My.	268–20	This *t·* flutters in my thought

time-worn
My.	295–12	your *t·* Bible in German.

timid
Mis.	329–15	nursing the *t·* spray,
	390–17	The *t·*, trembling leaves.
Ret.	15–30	were too *t·* to testify in public.
Po.	53–10	The patient, *t·* grass,
	55–18	The *t·*, trembling leaves.
My.	340–19	paltering, *t·*, or dastardly policy,

timidity
Mis.	x–18	*T·* in early years
Rud.	17–11	could tell you of *t·*,

Timothy
Mis.	243–23	alludes to Paul's advice to *T·*.

tincture
Mis.	369–16	higher than a rhubarb *t·*
Pul.	48–24	* a *t·* of blue and brave blood,
'01.	18– 1	"mother *t·*" of one grain

tinged
Ret.	32– 8	hope, if *t·* with earthliness,

tingling
My.	81–23	* rose *t·* to the great dome,

tinkling
No.	45– 4	or a *t·* cymbal ;" — *I Cor.* 13 : 1.
'01.	26–23	or a *t·* cymbal." — *I Cor.* 13 : 1.

tinsel
Po.	27– 2	pomp and *t·* of unrighteous

tint
Mis. 264–28   *t·* of the instructor's mind
Ret. 31–24   and a *t·* of humility,
Pul. 32– 3   * transparency and rose-flush of *t·*
My. 85–30   * noble dome of pure gray *t·*,

tints
Pul. 25–24   * wainscoting repeats the same *t·*.
26– 5   * prisms which reflect the rainbow *t·*.
Po. 25– 3   Soft *t·* of the rainbow and skies

tiny
Mis. 239–17   Just then a *t·*, sweet face appeared
My. 83– 6   * wore *t·* white, unmarked buttons,

tip
Mis. 119–14   material nature strives to *t·* the beam
My. 146–24   beliefs of mortals *t·* the scale

tipping
'02. 20– 5   hues of heaven, *t·* the dawn

tips
My. 277–19   mercy *t·* the beam on the right side,

tire
My. 165–25   Goodness and benevolence never *t·*.

tired
Mis. 52–19   *if one gets t· of it, why not*
52–23   if, when *t·* of mathematics
239–18   suffused eyes, cough, and *t·* look,
316–20   *t·* aphorisms and disappointed ethics ;
324–18   his own heart *t·* of sin,
368–29   *t·* watchmen on the walls of Zion,
369–22   we are *t·* of theoretic husks,
369–22   as *t·* as was the prodigal son of the
397–13   From *t·* joy and grief afar,
Ret. 84–23   *t·* tongue of history be enriched.
Pul. 18–22   From *t·* joy and grief afar,
'01. 26– 2   my *t·* sense of false philosophy
Peo. 8– 7   for the sins of a few *t·* years
Po. 13– 1   From *t·* joy and grief afar,
16–12   *t·* wings flitting through
47–14   sobbing, like some *t·* child
My. 132–32   wipes away the unavailing, *t·* tear,
165–23   Human reason becomes *t·*

tireless
Mis. 254– 5   love which brooded *t·* over their
386– 8   The toiler *t·* for Truth's new birth
Pul. 9– 5   when your *t·* tasks are done
Hea. 19–18   *T·* Being, patient of man's
Po. 49–13   toiler *t·* for Truth's new birth
My. 51–26   * of Mrs. Eddy's *t·* labors,

tithe
Mis. 253–24   one *t·* of the agonies that
'01. 29–26   under a *t·* of my own difficulties,
My. 191– 5   Injustice has not a *t·* of the power

tithes
Mis. 139– 4   bring your *t·* into the storehouse,
My. 14– 2   brought their *t·* into His storehouse.
20–13   all your *t·* into His storehouse,
131–24   "Bring ye all the *t·* — *Mal.* 3 : 10.

title
Mis. 140– 3   hold a wholly material *t·*.
140–26   Our *t·* to God's acres will be
140–27   * when we can "read our *t·* clear"
314–24   announcing the full *t·* of this book,
314–27   unnecessary to repeat the *t·*
Man. 18–25   changed the *t·* of "First Members"
32–14   announce the full *t·* of the book
64–13   The *T·* of Mother Changed.
70–22   legal *t·* of The Mother Church.
71– 2   *t·* of First Church of Christ,
Ret. 91–10   this *t·* really indicates more the
Pul. 46– 9   * under the *t·* of "Retrospection and
53–24   * earned the *t·* of Saviour of
'00. 15– 4   are distinguished above human *t·*
'02. 15–22   Its *t·*, S. and H., came to me
15–27   to drop both the book and the *t·*.
Hea. 3–19   Christ Jesus was an honorary *t·* ;
My. 87–11   * visitors of *t·* and distinction,
310–13   His military *t·* of Colonel
351–10   the *t·* of your gem quoted,

titled
My. 72– 8   * members of the *t·* aristocracy
113–31   among the scholarly and *t·*,

titles
Mis. 140–10   or merely legal *t·*.
Man. 45–23   Legal *T·*.
45–24   must drop the *t·* of Reverend
45–26   *t·* under the *laws* of the *State*.
70–21   *T·*.
71– 6   must not be used before *t·*
112– 6   before *t·* of branch churches.
Pul. 38– 9   * whose *t·* are as follows :

to and fro
Mis. 266–29   running *t· and f·* in the earth,
277– 5   walking *t· and f·* in the earth,
'02. 11– 4   tossed *t· and f·* by adverse

tobacco
Mis. 240–28   nothing but a . . . worm *naturally* chews *t·*.
Ret. 65– 9   persecution, *t·*, and alcohol
Pan. 10–21   cases of intemperance, *t·* using,
'00. 6–19   to a man who uses *t·*,
My. 106–25   an alcohol drinker, a *t·* user,
114– 4   abstain from alcohol and *t·* ;

tocsin
My. 199–19   sounded the *t·* of a higher hope,

to-day (noun)
Mis. 175–24   But this ism of *t·* has
245–20   charities, and reforms of *t·*.
310– 9   is the lesson of *t·*.
339– 8   to-morrow starts from *t·*
Ret. 65–16   If the religion of *t·* is
85–27   will crown the effort of *t·*
Pul. vii– 5   when the children of *t·* are the
Rud. 8– 4   the lion of *t·* is the lion of
No. 28–13   *t·* is none too soon for entering
'01. 2–22   his followers of *t·* will prove,
'02. 4–21   yesterday, and *t·*, and forever.
5– 2   as the dulness of *t·* prophesies
Hea. 1– 6   to-morrow grows out of *t·*.
11–13   burn upon the altars of *t·* ;
Po. 27–13   let *t·* grow difficult and vast
My. 119–15   The Mary of *t·* looks up
158–11   for all mankind *t·* hath its
158–14   *t·* lends a new-born beauty

to-day (adv.)
Mis. 2–14   *T·* we behold but the first
12–12   should be *t·* a law to himself, herself,
30–23   is *t·* the fossil of wisdomless wit,
70–11   "*T· shalt* thou be with me — *Luke* 23 : 43.
99–25   speak louder than *t·*.
99–25   They are *t·* as the voice of one
111–24   no greater difference . . . than *t·* exists
116–12   This question, . . . is *t·* uppermost :
120–28   whose character we *t·* commemorate,
125–27   thought-tired, turns *t·* to you ;
144–21   *T·*, be this hope in each of
144–29   *T·* I pray that divine Love,
150–12   *t·* are repeating their joy
178–18   * had said to me that *t·*
178–28   to be excused from speaking *t·*,
178–32   has been given to the world *t·*.
179–10   He is saying to us *t·*,
179–16   Can we say this *t·* ?
194– 1   How many *t·* believe that the
200–20   Christians *t·* should be able to say,
251– 7   my hand may not touch yours *t·*,
251–12   *T·* we commemorate not only our
258–32   nature and man are as harmonious *t·*
279–27   We, *t·*, in this class-room,
286–18   although it is *t·* problematic.
316–27   *t·* there would be on earth
320–28   *t·* christening religion undefiled,
336– 9   His highest idea as seen *t·*
355– 6   good healing is *t·* the acme of
375–28   * to see produced *t·* that art
Chr. 53–53   *T·*, as oft, away from sin
Ret. 94–23   *t·*, and forever." — *Heb.* 13 : 8.
Un. 61– 4   *t·*, and forever." — *Heb.* 13 : 8.
Pul. 1–18   *T·*, being with you in spirit,
7– 5   *T·*, as of yore, her laws
10–21   If you are less appreciated *t·*
34–19   * it is as true *t·* as it was
35– 8   * as operative in the world *t·*
44–23   * church which will be dedicated *t·*
49–27   * a strikingly well-kept estate
54–11   * conditions . . . *t·* are the same
66– 2   * exists as much *t·* as it did
67–10   * which are to be found there *t·*
67–16   * but *t·* it numbers over a
74– 9   * shown to Mrs. Mary Baker Eddy, . . . *t·*.
82–10   * and *t·* she knows many things
82–22   * *T·* there are ten thousand Esthers,
No. 31– 6   appear *t·* in subtler forms
38– 2   what C. S. is *t·* proving
41–26   * and it is doing it *t·* ;
44–25   * "Heretics of . . . are martyrs *t·*."
Pan. 9–14   What mortal *t·* is wise enough
'00. 3–21   *T·* it surprises us that during the
4–11   *T·* people are surprised at
15– 2   *T·* you have come to a
15–18   *T·* you have come to Love's feast,
'01. 1– 1   brethren, *t·* I extend my
1–10   *T·* you meet to commemorate
9–13   Truth that is persecuted *t·*,
17–14   that *t·* commands the respect
18– 8   more honored and respected *t·*

to-day (adv.)

'01.	32–27	if those . . . Christians were here t·,
	33– 2	holiness that t· seems to be
'02.	4–13	My subject t· embraces the
	11–29	while t· Jew and Christian can
	16– 7	T· I am the happy possessor
Hea.	7–21	would not have done t·,
Peo.	8–24	We thank our Father that t·
	14– 2	T· we clothe our thoughts
Po.	vi–18	T·, by order of Governor Andrew,
	29–20	Fill us t· With all thou art
My.	vi– 6	* That no one on earth t·,
	24– 3	* truth . . . is t· being proven
	28–25	* as effective t· as it was
	39–27	* realize her presence with us t·.
	43–26	* t· we rejoice that we have
	47–16	* T· we look back over the
	57–17	* membership of this church t·
	64– 8	* If t· we feel a pardonable pride
	73–14	* flocking . . . to Boston t·,
	82–21	* at noon t· [June 14]
	85– 7	* T· its adherents number
	93–30	* T· its adherents number
	98– 4	* C. S. army in this country t·,
	99–23	* T· there are hundreds of such
	100–14	* numbered by thousands t·,
	104– 5	t· all sorts of institutions
	104–11	what would be thought t·
	109–11	he is t· teaching them the
	109–13	t·, and forever.'' — Heb. 13 : 8.
	112– 6	C. S. makes practical t·
	115– 2	t· is circling the whole world.
	122–23	Can we say with the angels t· :
	123–10	T· in Concord, N. H., we have
	124– 9	who would say t·,
	126–28	it reigns supreme t·,
	146–18	as true t· as they will be
	147–20	speak the truth that t·,
	148–17	T·, with the large membership
	152–20	T·, if ye would hear His voice,
	153–11	T· our great Master would say
	155–23	May those who discourse music t·,
	155–28	T· may they find some sweet
	158–26	temple which t· you commemorate,
	159– 3	Never more sweet than t·,
	170–15	present a gift to you t·,
	171– 3	T· is fulfilled the prophecy of Isaiah :
	174–25	T· my soul can only sing and soar.
	177–20	T· the glory of His presence
	182– 2	T· it is said to have a majority
	183–11	T· a nation is born.
	184– 8	T· I am privileged to congratulate
	190–30	wherefore vilify His prophets t·
	199– 6	reward . . . is given thee t·.
	220–31	seems more divine t· than
	246–28	the same t· as yesterday
	257– 4	T· the watchful shepherd shouts his
	257–13	T· the Christ is, more than
	257–28	T· Christian Scientists have their
	271–22	* dearest to your heart t· ?''
	292–28	same yesterday, t·, and forever ;
	294–11	if he were personally with us t·,
	296–15	He is wiser t·, healthier and
	314–16	Individuals are here t· who were
	324–17	* were he here t· he would
	346–28	did not mean any man t· on earth.

together

Mis.	xi–22	grant us peace, t· with pardon
	10– 6	''work t· for good — Rom. 8 : 28.
	22–24	t· with the sick, the lame,
	28–27	t· with his divine Love,
	47–23	t· with his immortality and
	59–20	let us reason t·.'' — Isa. 1 : 18.
	94– 8	which God hath not joined t·.
	98–10	brought us t· to minister and to be
	110–18	Our hearts have kept time t·,
	134–10	Meet t· and meet en masse,
	135– 9	sweet sense of journeying on t·,
	138– 9	For students to work t·
	145–25	lion and the fatling t· ; — Isa. 11 : 6.
	145–26	hearts of . . . Scientists are woven t·
	156–24	Assembling themselves t·,
	177– 6	leagued t· in secret conspiracy
	188– 4	when the stars first sang t·,
	231–24	little palms patting t·,
	259–24	morning stars sang t·, — Job 38 : 7.
	275–12	little ones, wondering, huddle t·,
	279–22	met t· in an upper chamber ;
	279–25	they had all to shout t·
	296– 7	t· with unfamiliarity with the
	310–28	t· with those who never have
Man.	34–12	The Bible, t· with S. and H.
	84–21	shall not call their pupils t·,
Ret.	64– 4	and t· both sinner and sin
	82–25	found dwelling t· in harmony,
	85– 4	advisable to band t· their students

together

Un.	1– 8	Let us then reason t·
	42–14	morning stars sang t·, — Job 38 : 7.
Pul.	9–19	t· with the Sunday School
	21–27	spirit of Christ calling us t·.
	64–26	* drawing t· six thousand people
'00.	11–10	work t· for good — Rom. 8 : 28.
Hea.	14–22	t· with what they learn.
	18–10	good and evil never dwelt t·.
Po.	vi– 2	* t· with ''The Valley Cemetery,''
My.	vii– 1	* t· with The C. S. Journal,
	4–19	and they thrive t·,
	21–20	* and shaken t·, — Luke 6 : 38.
	24–14	* ''fitly framed t· — Eph. 2 : 21.
	32– 5	* began all t·, and their voices
	48–24	* t· with the discouragement of
	69– 5	* roof and side walls come t·
	81–28	* two or more of them are met t·,
	104–27	that brought t· this class
	143–25	work t· for good — Rom. 8 : 28.
	163–23	t· with the retirement
	166–22	let us t· sing the old-new song
	174–30	may we not t· rejoice in the
	175– 3	t· with the organizations connected
	243– 4	come t· and form one church.
	268–10	What God hath joined t·,
	310–11	t· they owned a large manufacturing

toil

Mis.	212–17	darkness, and unrequited t·.
	323–11	peril, privation, temptation, t·,
	340– 7	unremitting, straightforward t· ;
	340–24	t· is triumph ;
	382– 8	years of unremitting t·
Ret.	30– 5	Ceaseless t·, self-renunciation, and
	86– 3	to crown patient t·, and
Rud.	17–11	of friendlessness, t·, agonies,
'01.	2–24	doubt, and unrequited t·
Po.	16–11	And bustle and t· for its pomp
My.	64– 6	* and her years of t·,
	136–25	the fruits of honest t·,
	154–20	*''If the poor . . . t· that we have food,
	154–21	* t· for him in return,
	196–27	The poor t· for our bread,
	217– 5	reward your hitherto unselfish t·,

toiled

Mis.	111– 4	you have t· all night ;
Pul.	44– 4	* worked, t·, prayed for.
'00.	14–23	in other words, he that t· for
'01.	29–14	nurtured them, t· for them,

toiler

(see **Eddy**)

toilers

Mis.	323–17	He saith unto the patient t·
Pul.	50– 7	* do something for the t·,
My.	252– 4	you will be t· like the bee,

toilet

Pul.	27– 1	* are t· apartments, with

toiling

Mis.	266–22	who are t· and achieving
Po.	47– 8	Never to t· and never to fears,

token

Mis.	132– 4	t· that heavy lids are opening,
	160– 6	may give no material t·,
	320–30	white stone in t· of purity
No.	24–12	By the same t·, evil is not
'00.	10–23	I received a touching t·
My.	107– 1	as a t· of their Christianity.
	172–28	as a simple t· of love.''
	194–21	t· of your gratitude and love.

told

Mis.	28–11	so-called life is a dream soon t·.
	57–21	t· in the name of Truth,
	170–30	he had just t· them.
	224– 7	A courtier t· Constantine
	239–18	tired look, t· the story ;
	284–17	t· him his fault,
	354–16	a few truths tenderly t·,
	391–20	Some good ne'er t· before,
Ret.	9– 4	Mother t· Mehitable all about
	21–16	It is ''as a tale that is t·,'' — Psal. 90 : 9.
	40– 6	t· me that her next-door neighbor
	40–13	t· me that her physicians had
Un.	17–21	t· our first parents that
	48– 3	already t· a hundred times,
Pul.	2– 4	the half was not t· me : — I Kings 10 : 7.
	8–11	t· their privileged joy
	29–27	* Later I was t· that almost the entire
	30– 2	* I was further t· that once
	30– 6	* I was t· he replied that the C. S.
	32–14	* She t· me the story of her life,
	32–22	* this, she t· me, was due to the
	33–24	* so a friend has t· me,
	46–10	* much is t· of herself in detail

told

Pul. 49–19   * She *t·* something of her domestic
    72–28   * Christ has *t·* us to do his work,
'00. 14–29   being *t·* they are distinguished
'01. 16–27   commence with one truth *t·*
    16–28   one hundred falsehoods *t·* about it
Hea. 6– 3   When I was *t·* the other day,
Po. 38–19   Some good ne'er *t·* before,
My. 43–19   * it was *t·* them :
    59– 4   * When you *t·* us that the truth
    60– 8   * when *t·* that I had studied with you.
    79–28   * *t·* of cures from diseases,
    81–13   * They had been *t·* to name,
  226–26   *t·* by the alert editor-in-chief
  313– 3   so I have been *t·* :
  313– 8   *t·* by *McClure's Magazine*
  314–26   A Christian Scientist has *t·* me
  319–30   * You *t·* me that he had done
  320– 8   * agreed with what you had *t·* me
  321–11   * *t·* the same story to every one
  321–32   * *t·* me of their knowledge of your
  322– 2   * she *t·* me she knew you
  322–16   * I was surprised when he *t·* me
  322–28   * *t·* me of his acquaintance with you
  324–26   * *t·* us laughingly why he accepted
  328–16   * is *t·* in the *Kinston Free Press*
  335–26   * was *t·* by him that he could not
  335–31   * was *t·* by the expert physician

Toledo

Pul. 56– 3   * Detroit, *T·*, Milwaukee, Madison,

tolerant

Mis. 247– 6   familiar with my history are more *t·* ;

toll

Mis. 304–27   * it will *t·* on the anniversaries of
My. 189–30   Wherefore, pray, the bell did *t·*?

tolling

'02. 17– 2   knells *t·* the burial of Christ.

tomb

Mis. 70–28   even in the silent *t·*,
   74–20   the door of his own *t·*.
  388–21   First at the *t·* to hear his word :
  395–25   A requiem o'er the *t·*
Ret. 88– 7   called the physical man from the *t·*
Pul. 10– 8   silent Aventine is glory's *t·* ;
'02. 19– 3   burst the bonds of the *t·*
Po. 21–10   at the *t·* to hear his word :
  39–11   First at the *t·*,
  58–10   A requiem o'er the *t·*
  78– 4   will spread over their *t·* ;
My. 191–18   from the *t·* of the past,
  290– 6   lose their lustre in the *t·*,

to-morrow

Mis. 99–25   *t·* speak louder than to-day.
  307– 2   Never ask for *t·* :
  339– 7   *t·* starts from to-day
Pul. 50–13   * will be dedicated *t·*.
'02. 5– 2   renewed energy for *t·*,
Hea. 1– 6   *t·* grows out of to-day.
My. 75–27   * dedicated *t·* free from debt.
  76–25   * dedicated in Boston *t·*
  104–12   what will be thought *t·*
  126–29   it reigns supreme to-day, *t·*,
  146–18   true to-day as they will be *t·*.
  158–26   *t·* complete, and thereafter dedicate
  161–22   cannot boast ourselves of *t·* ;

tone

Mis. 264–26   The *t·* of the teacher's mind
  282–15   metaphysical *t·* of his command,
  292–10   new *t·* on the scale ascending,
  312–25   he touched a *t·* of Truth
  366–11   this is the prolonged *t·* :
Ret. 5–25   * the *t·* of conversation in the
Pul. 26–18   * fine range and perfect *t·*.
  62–14   * quality of *t·* is something superb,
'00. 1– 2   *t·* of your happy hearts,
  11–18   quantity, and variation in *t·*,
  11–19   if the divine *t·* be lacking,
  11–20   human *t·* has no melody for me.
My. 32–10   * above the usual platform *t·*.
  50–13   * *t·* of this meeting for deliberation
  83–22   * naturally takes on a *t·* of
  202–25   From the dear *t·* of your letter,
  291–19   May his history waken a *t·*

toned

Pul. 26–25   * room is *t·* in pale green

tones

Mis. 46–27   idea of sound, in *t·*, represents
  106–31   organ, in imitative *t·*
  116–14   with *t·* whence come glad echoes
  126– 6   in *t·* that leap for joy,
  151–10   to the unfruitful in *t·* of Sinai :
  213–21   These are its inspiring *t·*

tones

Mis. 231–28   How many homes echo such *t·*
  295–24   high and pure ethical *t·*
  329–13   touching tenderly its tearful *t·*.
  331–13   in *t·* tremulous with tenderness,
Ret. 9– 6   name pronounced in audible *t·*.
Pul. 60– 8   * clear, manly, and intelligent *t·*,
  61–25   * The sweet, musical *t·*
  62–14   * purity and sweetness of their *t·*.
'00. 11–14   besieges you with *t·* intricate,
'02. 9–16   consciousness that leaves the minor *t·*
Po. 31– 8   tear-filled *t·* of distant joy,
  65–22   life hath its music in low minor *t·*,
My. 39–25   * harmonious *t·* of her gentle voice.
  59–20   * sonorous *t·* of the powerful organ

tongue
and pen
My. 146–31   weight of thought, *t·*, and pen
Anglo-Saxon
Mis. 216–13   given to the Anglo-Saxon *t·*,
Christian
'01. 28–12   into almost every Christian *t·*,
examines the
Hea. 12– 5   feels the pulse, examines the *t·*,
her
My. 42– 3   * in her *t·* is the law of — *Prov.* 31 : 26.
his
Mis. 126–10   guard, . . . in society his *t·* ?
new
Mis. 18–12   translated into the new *t·*,
  25–16   religion's "new *t·*," — see *Mark* 16 : 17.
  248– 1   This is the "new *t·*," — see *Mark* 16 : 17.
  248– 6   found in the "new *t·*," — see *Mark* 16 : 17.
  364– 3   in the "new *t·*," — see *Mark* 16 : 17.
Ret. 25– 5   a new meaning, a new *t·*.
Rud. 16–11   into the "new *t·* ;" — see *Mark* 16 : 17.
No. 44– 6   It is the "new *t·*" — see *Mark* 16 : 17.
Hea. 7– 7   "The new *t·*" is the — see *Mark* 16 : 17.
My. 131–15   speak the "new *t·*" — see *Mark* 16 : 17.
  147–11   teaching the "new *t·*" — see *Mark* 16 : 17.
  225– 8   the old "new *t·*," — see *Mark* 16 : 17.
  238–14   C. S. . . . or "new *t·*" — see *Mark* 16 : 17.
  306–15   in the "new *t·*," — see *Mark* 16 : 17.
  318– 1   express the "new *t·*," — see *Mark* 16 : 17.
of angels
My. 354–23   The *t·* of angels
original
My. 180–10   restores their original *t·*
their
Mis. 368–22   under their *t·*." — see *Rom.* 3 : 13.
tired
Ret. 84–23   tired *t·* of history be enriched.
your
Mis. 130–12   sweet morsel under your *t·*,"

Un. 60–13   With the *t·* "bless we God, — *Jas.* 3 : 9.
My. 33–19   backbiteth not with his *t·*, — *Psal.* 15 : 3.
  93–20   * with the *t·* of facetiousness.

tongues

Ret. 10– 9   lessons in the ancient *t·*,
Pan. 13–22   all nations, peoples, and *t·*,
'01. 26–22   speak with the *t·* of men — *I Cor.* 13 : 1.
Hea. 1– 2   *speak with new t· ; — Mark* 16 : 17.
My. 47–22   * many of different races and *t·*
  47–31   * speak with new *t·* ; — *Mark* 16 : 17.

tonic

Mis. 252– 1   Truth is the *t·* for the sick,
My. 152– 8   said, "My material *t·* has

to-night

Mis. 331–21   on upward wing *t·*.
  389– 9   on upward wing *t·*.
  393–22   Lessons long and grand, *t·*,
Chr. 53–55   Truth pleads *t·* : Just take Me in !
Po. 4– 8   on upward wing *t·*
  52– 6   Lessons long and grand, *t·*,
My. 73–28   * due to arrive in Boston *t·*,
  82–23   * more visitors by midnight *t·*.

took

Mis. 77– 5   *believe t·* its original meaning,
  139–30   I *t·* care that the provisions for
  171–24   *leaven, which a woman t·*, — *Matt.* **13 : 33.**
  174–30   leaven which a woman *t·* and hid
  201–16   Paul *t·* pleasure in infirmities,
  201–19   he *t·* pleasure in
  201–23   he *t·* pleasure in
  212–30   *t·* down from the cross
  223– 4   *t·* up the research
  242–29   he *t·* a patient
  243–32   "He *t·* a bone — see *Gen.* 2 : 21.
  248–25   prescribed morphine, which I *t·*,
  339– 3   *t·* place once in heaven,
  345–23   *t·* their infants to a place of
  370– 5   they went away and *t·* counsel
  383– 4   *t·* effect the same year,

took

Ret.	37– 6	critics *t·* pleasure in saying,
Pul.	38– 4	* ceremony *t·* place in 1881.
	48– 5	* *t·* the writer straight to her beloved
	75–19	* *t·* part in the ceremonies
Pan.	7– 9	that . . . material creation *t·* place,
'01.	31–27	what He *t·* away.
My.	45–24	* "He *t·* not away the— *Exod.* 13 : 22.
	64– 3	* *t·* on a larger and truer meaning.
	80–24	* it *t·* ten meetings
	117–14	a stranger, and *t·* thee in?— *Matt.* 25 : 38.
	151–30	it *t·* a step higher ;
	312– 6	* *t·* his bride to Wilmington,
	312–22	He *t·* with him the usual amount
	312–28	*t·* me to my father's home
	313–19	when I *t·* an evening walk,
	313–19	but I seldom *t·* one.
	342– 5	* *t·* a seat on a sofa.

tools

My.	211–18	lend themselves as willing *t·*

tooth

Mis.	44–14	*until I have the t· extracted,*
	44–24	if the *t·* were extracted,

toothache

Mis.	44–13	*If I have the t·,*
	45– 6	more than to heal a *t·* ;

top

Mis.	165–12	rends . . . from *t·* to bottom.
Pul.	9–14	to the *t·* of the tower,
My.	68–10	* The *t·* of the dome is
	69–29	* view is on *t·* of the tower
	122– 7	To cut off the *t·* of a plant
	162–31	towering *t·* of its goodly temple

topaz

Mis.	376–27	*t·*, opal, garnet, turquoise,

Topeka (Kan.) *Daily Capital*

My.	93–16	*[T· (K·) D· C·]*

Topeka, Kans.

Pul.	89–34	*Journal, T·, K·.*

topic

Mis.	280–28	allude briefly to a *t·*
	309–26	elucidates this *t·*.

topically

Mis.	203–16	metaphysics appropriates it *t·*

topics

Mis.	76–18	other *t·* less important.
	92– 5	inexhaustible *t·* of that book
	236– 9	giving advice on personal *t·*.
	350–19	consideration of these two *t·*.
Man.	93–12	*t·* condemning C. S.,
Ret.	42–10	lectured so ably on Scriptural *t·*
	84– 2	inexhaustible *t·* of S. and H.
Pul.	47– 2	* lectures upon Scriptural *t·*.
My.	319–25	* analyzing and arranging the *t·*,

topmost

Mis.	376–22	*t·* pall, drooping over a deeply

tops

My.	68– 5	* *t·* of great stone piers,

torches

Ret.	23–17	the midnight *t·* of Spirit.

torment

Mis.	293–18	brings greater *t·* than ignorance.
'00.	9–12	come hither to *t·* me— *see Matt.* 8 : 29.
'02.	10– 6	come hither to *t·* us— *Matt.* 8 : 29.

tormentor

Mis.	278– 6	the presence of its *t·*.
'00.	3–18	to shun him as their *t·*.

torments

Mis.	210–25	belief in . . . *t·* its victim,

torn

Mis.	186–21	idea cannot be *t·* apart from
	340– 2	has *t·* the laurel from many a brow
My.	110–31	*t·* from their necessary contexts,

tornado

Mis.	240–18	the sturdy oak, . . . breasts the *t·*

tornadoes

My.	265–27	less thunderbolts, *t·*, and

Toronto

Canada

Mis.	142– 6	chapter sub-title
	157– 8	Mrs. Stewart, of *T·*, Canada
Pul.	75–13	* *The Globe, T·*, Canada,
My.	184– 2	chapter sub-title

Mis.	142– 8	presented by Christian Scientists in *T·*,
Pul.	56– 4	* Scranton, Peoria, Atlanta, *T·*,
	67–20	* *T·* and Montreal have strong churches,
	75–17	* MANY *T·* SCIENTISTS PRESENT
	75–18	* Christian Scientists of *T·*,

torpid

Mis.	206– 4	from foul to pure, from *t·* to serene,

torrents

My.	316–20	foaming *t·* of ignorance, envy,

torrid

'00.	10–29	serving his country in that *t·* zone

torture

Mis.	244–13	are they bodily penance and *t·*,
	341–25	and is subject to terrible *t·*
Pul.	13–25	how many periods of *t·* it may take
No.	34–14	Physical *t·* affords but a slight
Peo.	3– 9	sacrifice and *t·* of His favorite Son,
My.	160–26	burning in *t·* until the sinner

tortured

Mis.	123–12	or *t·* to appease the anger of

tortures

Ret.	26– 7	to allay the *t·* of crucifixion.

tossed

'02.	11– 4	*t·* to and fro by adverse

tosses

Mis.	331– 3	*t·* earth's mass of wonders into

total

Mis.	2–10	admit the *t·* depravity of mortals,
	30– 9	sum *t·* of transcendentalism.
	105–32	God is the sum *t·* of the universe.
	112–29	ends in a *t·* loss of moral,
	112–32	exemplification of *t·* depravity,
	289– 4	temperance is *t·* abstinence.
	293–21	sum *t·* of Love reflected
'02.	1– 8	members have been added . . . making *t·*
My.	16– 4	* *t·* of $425,893.66 had been received
	23– 3	* *t·* membership of The Mother Church
	23–12	* *t·* receipts . . . $891,460.49.
	25–14	* *t·*, $2,579.19.
	57–21	* *t·* number admitted during the
	57–22	* *t·* number of branch churches
	212–13	to complete the sum *t·* of sin.
	256– 8	*t·* exemption from Christmas gifts.

totally

No.	30–16	could not destroy our woes *t·* if
My.	311– 4	a girl, *t·* blind, knocked

touch

Mis.	ix–11	the *t·* of God's right hand.
	97–17	*t·* the hem of His garment ;
	143– 1	*t·* of heart to heart
	175–13	increase by every spiritual *t·*,
	180–12	"*T·* me not."— *John* 20 : 17.
	200–22	the *t·* of weakness, pain,
	230–28	canvas and the *t·* of an artist
	251– 6	my hand may not *t·* yours
	294–14	with sting ready for each kind *t·*,
	306–24	*t·* of the breast of a dove ;
	306–26	Oh, may you feel *this t·*,
	372–24	to reproduce, with reverent *t·*,
Ret.	27–19	* *T·* God's right hand
	95–12	* Of Christlike *t·*.
Un.	22– 7	ye shall not *t·* it, lest ye die.
	34–14	*T·*. Take another train of
Pul.	54– 4	* We *t·* him in life's throng
No.	32–11	when I *t·* this subject
	40–15	never to *t·* the human thought save to
'00.	11–25	* With a *t·* of infinite calm.
	15–20	*t·* of the hem of this garment
'01.	9–19	foams at the *t·* of good ;
	21–27	felt the incipient *t·* of divine Love
Hea.	16–14	*t·* but the hem of Truth's garment.
	20– 5	* We'd soar and *t·* the heavenly
Peo.	11–26	that they themselves will not *t·*
My.	26–11	emotion at the *t·* of memory.
	93–19	* too often disposed to *t·* upon it
	108–20	slang, and malice *t·* not the hem
	108–21	for if they did once *t·* it,
	121–11	yielding to the *t·* of a finger.
	125–16	I have felt the *t·* of the spirit
	147– 3	moments when at the *t·* of memory
	152– 4	the *t·* of Jesus' robe
	186– 9	song and sermon will *t·* the heart,
	256–21	springs aside at the *t·* of Love.

touched

Mis.	75– 1	you will have *t·* the hem of
	112–19	My few words *t·* him ;
	142–27	*t·* tender fibres of thought,
	312–24	he *t·* a tone of Truth
	395–20	*T·* by the finger of decay
Ret.	23–17	I had *t·* the hem of C. S.
	76– 9	Thoughts *t·* with the Spirit and
Un.	28– 5	was never *t·* by the scalpel
	29–21	weighed or *t·* by physicality.
	57–11	"Who hath *t·* me ?"— *see Mark* 5 : 31.
Pul.	46–10	* detail that can only be *t·* upon
No.	22– 2	certainly not *t·* the hem of the
'00.	1– 1	methinks even I am *t·* with

touched
Po.	58– 5	T· by the finger of decay
My.	22–27	* t· the healing hem of C. S.,
	37–28	* deeply t· by its sweet entreaty,
	47–11	* t· by its influence for good,
	47–18	* t· by each landmark of progress
	150–11	A heart t· and hallowed by
	192– 7	Thou hast t· its hem,
	319– 5	My saying t· him,
	345–32	* which are here t· upon,

touches
Mis.	29– 6	t· universal humanity.
	174– 9	t· the religious sentiment
	235–15	t· mind to more spiritual issues,
	253–22	mother's love t· the heart of God,
	289–26	Science t· the conjugal question
	336–28	t· time only to take away its
Pul.	13–11	t· the hem of Christ's robe
My.	66–18	* chapter sub-title
	205–22	t· but the hem of C. S.,
	287–22	it t· thought to spiritual issues,
	294–24	t· the heart and will move the pen
	351–12	t· the hem of his garment

touching
Mis.	60–18	even if t· each other corporeally ;
	143–29	t· letter breathing the donor's
	275–24	love and loyalty were very t·.
	329–12	t· tenderly its tearful tones.
Pul.	49–14	* t· my sleeve and pointing,
'00.	10–23	t· token of unselfed manhood
My.	215–10	Afterwards, with t· tenderness,
	347–11	illustrated by Keats' t· couplet,

touchingly
Pul.	8–11	t· told their privileged joy

tourists
Po.	v–17	* Some t· who were passing,

toward
Mis.	13– 2	mercy and charity t· every one,
	13– 3	exercise these sentiments t· them,
	37– 6	desires that draw mankind t· purity,
	63–24	reaching t· a higher goal,
	74– 5	enmity of mortal man t· God.
	133–23	with my face t· the Jerusalem of
	143–24	t· building The Mother Church.
	169–26	carnal mind, which is enmity t· God,
	250–27	door that turns t· want and woe,
	265–28	disaffections t· C. S. growing out of
	272–29	I have endeavored to act t· all
	304–25	* the world's progress t· liberty ;
	315–14	promising proclivities t· C. S.
	316–18	turn them slowly t· the haven.
	338– 4	to be able to lift others t·
Man.	48– 1	cherish no enmity t· those who
	74–20	maintain t· them an attitude of
	83–11	promising proclivities t· C. S.
Ret.	76–10	gravitate naturally t· Truth.
Un.	2–24	their lives have grown so far t· the
	5– 5	t· the perfect thought divine.
	10–13	Spiritual phenomena never converge t·
	61–12	Human perception, advancing t·
Pul.	8–19	earn a few pence t· this
	37– 3	* attitude t· all questions.''
	50– 7	* t· the advancement of
	65– 9	* attitude Rome may assume t· it.
	72– 4	* t· the reported deification of
'00.	6– 7	press t· the mark — Phil. 3 : 14.
My.	156– 7	grace abound t· you ; — II Cor. 9 : 8.
		(see also men)

towards
Mis.	32– 3	How shall we demean ourselves t·
	32– 7	in what manner they should act t·
	32–15	admissible t· friend and foe.
	32–19	do my best t· helping
	232– 6	reaching out t· the perfect
	232– 7	pushing t· perfection in art,
	290–20	involuntarily flow out t· all.
	336–11	right obligations t· him.
	348– 2	press forward t· the mark
Man.	48– 9	impertinent t· religion,
Chr.	53–35	grace t· you and me,
Ret.	3–12	t· the close of the War
	13–15	merciless t· unbelievers ;
No.	9–15	t· some of my students
'02.	10–12	advancing above itself t· the
	18–26	ignoble conduct of his disciples t·
My.	9–22	t· the purchase of more land
	10–11	* paid in t· the fund,
	19–29	t· its church building fund.
	46– 4	* beckoning us on t· a
	50–16	* looked t· the spiritual,
	86–20	* maintain t· their church.
	96–17	* generosity of its adherents t·
	97– 4	* t· making the patient well.
	119–11	Think not that C. S. tends t·

towards
My.	125– 7	incline the vine t· the
	159–19	the tendency t· God,
	159–20	t· the temporary and finite.
	176– 3	FIFTY DOLLARS IN GOLD t·
	189–23	we are drawn t· God.
	191– 4	Be patient t· persecution.
	199–15	t· me and t· the Cause
	201– 2	Press on t· the high calling
	242– 6	nor advancing t· it ;
	244–14	contribute my part t· this result.
	245–13	T· the animal elements
	261–11	t· guarding and guiding
	262–28	letting good will t· man.
	282–11	helped onward t· justice,
	322–11	* work for and attitude t·
	331–22	* gratitude we owe and cherish t·
	338–19	love t· God and man.
	338–29	instructed to be, charitable t·
		(see also men)

tower
Mis.	144– 4	in the second story of the t·
	152–24	safely sheltered in the strong t·
	203– 6	From my t· window,
	252–30	dear children's toy and strong t· ;
Pul.	9–14	climbed . . . to the top of the t·,
	24–10	* Romanesque t· with a circular front
	24–25	* t· is one hundred and twenty feet
	39–21	* angels, on the gray church t·,
	41–23	* chimes in the great stone t·,
	58–27	* In the t· is a room devoted to
	61–22	* first peal of the chimes in the t·
	87–24	church's tall t· detains the sun,
Hea.	11–10	her modest t· rises slowly,
My.	69–29	* t· in Mt. Auburn cemetery
	145–10	from the foundations to the t·,

towering
My.	46– 3	* in t·, overshadowing dome,
	162–31	t· top of its goodly temple

towers
Mis.	125–28	to tell the t· thereof the
My.	71– 1	* stationed in one of the t·,

town
Ret.	5– 1	small t· situated near Concord,
Pul.	79–13	* daily paper in t· or village
My.	72–10	* streaming into t· lords and
	87– 3	* transportation facilities of the t·
	87–10	* multitude that has invaded the t·.
	92– 1	* every important t· and city
	134–16	happifies life in the hamlet or t· ;
	309– 4	to do much business for his t·,
	346–11	* Mrs. Eddy's carriage drove into t·

towns
Mis.	81–18	cities and t· of Judea,
Ret.	4– 5	adjoining t· of Concord and Bow,
	90– 7	t· whither he sent his disciples ;
Pul.	67–21	* in many t· and villages
My.	309– 6	between the t· of Loudon and Bow,
	314– 6	* doctor practised in several t·,

townships
Ret.	4–12	undulating lands of three t·.

toy
Mis.	231–23	a look of cheer and a t· from mamma
	252–29	children's t· and strong tower ;

toys
Mis.	385–17	diviner sense, that spurns such t·,
Po.	48–11	diviner sense, that spurns such t·,

trace
Ret.	24– 8	trying to t· all physical effects to
My.	79–25	* without a t· of fanaticism,
	96– 7	* none . . . with the slightest t· of
	114–29	You can t· its teachings

traceable
My.	349–25	lawless and t· to mortal mind

traced
Mis.	388– 5	Love whose finger t· aloud
'01.	21– 9	* may be t· many of the ideas
	27–11	the basis whereof cannot be t· to
'02.	20–14	Love whose finger t· aloud
Po.	7– 5	Love whose finger t· aloud
My.	296–26	t· its emotions, motives, and object.

tracing
Pul.	46–13	* t· those branches which are

track
Po.	26– 2	t· behind thee is with glory crowned ;

tractable
Rud.	15– 9	inquisitive, plastic, and t· ;

trade
'00.	2–20	his stock in t·, the wages of sin ;

trades
  My. 24–22 * fifteen different *t·* represented.
tradition
  Mis. 370– 8 risen from the grave-clothes of *t·*
  My. 260–19 not because of *t·*, usage, or
       340–19 Not the *t·* of the elders,
traditional
  Ret. 22– 7 legendary and *t·* history
traditions
  No. 8–20 enmity over doctrines and *t·*,
  My. 71–19 * nearly all the *t·* of church
       72– 3 * *t·* of interior church architecture.
       340– 7 *t·*, old-wives' fables, and
traduced
  Mis. 233–12 metaphysical healing is *t·* by
  '01. 2– 7 standard of C. S. was and is *t·* by
traffic
  Mis. 227– 1 *t·* by which he can gain nothing.
trafficking
  Mis. 356–32 it has no moments for *t·*
tragedy
  Mis. 124–24 last act of the *t·* on Calvary
  Un. 22–23 In Shakespeare's *t·* of King Lear,
tragic
  Mis. 48–21 hidden nature of some *t·* events
  My. 312– 4 the *t·* death of my husband,
train
  Un. 34–14 Take another *t·* of reasoning.
  Pan. 14– 3 righteousness with its triumphant *t·*.
  My. 233–21 dishonesty, sin, follow in its *t·*.
       331– 8 * accompanied her to the *t·*
trained
  Mis. 9–28 *t·* in treacherous peace
  Ret. 7– 8 * he *t·* and schooled them
  Pul. 80–27 * *t·* into harmony with the laws of God,
  Po. 2– 8 *t·* falcon in the Gallic van,
  My. 31–30 * As though *t·* carefully under
       38– 8 * carefully *t·* corps of ushers,
training
  Mis. 169– 7 Early *t·*, . . . had been the underlying
  Ret. 20–11 had no *t·* for self-support
  My. 310– 5 In addition to my academic *t·*,
trainloads
  My. 77–13 * daily *t·* of pilgrims
trains
  My. 73–26 * chapter sub-title
       73–27 * Special *t·* and extra sections of *t·*
       74– 5 * night *t·* of Saturday will bring
       82–25 * *t·* pulled out of the city
traitorous
  Un. 23– 1 *t·* and cruel treatment
traitors
  Mis. 106– 7 *T·* to right of them,
  Po. 27–14 With *t·* unvoiced yet?
traits
  Mis. 72– 8 bad *t·* of the parents
       191–17 evils, apparent wrong *t·*,
trammels
  Rud. 2–20 takes away the *t·*
tramping
  My. 308–16 * old man *t·* doggedly along
trample
  Mis. 211–19 *t·* on your pearls
  My. 227–24 lest they *t·* them under — *Matt.* 7 : 6.
trampled
  Mis. 227–19 the more *t·* upon,
       247– 5 treated not as pearls *t·* upon.
  No. 40–10 lest your pearls be *t·* upon.
  Peo. 12–10 *t·* under the feet of Truth.
  My. 139–10 flourish when *t·* upon,
tramples
  Ret. 75– 4 *t·* upon Jesus' Sermon on the
trampling
  Po. 72– 2 *t·* right in dust !
trance
  My. 313–25 I never went into a *t·*
tranquillity
  My. 280– 7 * peaceful *t·* of the race.
transact
  Man. 79– 5 shall *t·* . . . such business as
transacted
  Man. 27– 2 The business . . . shall be *t·* by
  My. 358–22 through whom all my business is *t·*.
transaction
  Mis. 139–26 this *t·* will in future be
       141–23 divine will . . . rule this business *t·*,
  Man. 57– 1 *t·* of such other business

transaction
  Man. 70– 3 nor enter into a business *t·* with
       78–20 not exceeding $200 for any one *t·*,
       79–10 *t·* of the business assigned to them
  Pul. 54–14 * *t·* was in perfect obedience to
  My. 135–19 of this, the aforesaid *t·*.
transactions
  Mis. 350–11 no *t·* at those meetings which I
  '02. 12–23 financial *t·* of this church,
  My. 7– 7 financial *t·* of this church,
transcended
  Pul. 45–13 * *t·* human possibility.
       54–13 * no law of nature violated or *t·*
transcendent
  Mis. 199–20 his *t·* goodness is manifest
transcendental
  '01. 6– 1 more *t·* than theology's three divine
        8– 5 scientific statement more *t·* than
        8–14 more *t·* than God made him?
        8–22 makes man none too *t·*,
       11–21 nor too *t·* to be heard
       12– 7 reply, "That is too *t·* for me
       18–13 C. S. seems *t·* because the
  My. 248–16 above theorems into the *t·*,
transcendentalism
  Mis. 30– 9 revealed the sum total of *t·*.
  '01. 18– 9 who laugh at or pray against *t·*
  My. 3–14 nor a *t·* that heals only the sick.
transcendentalists
  '01. 5–23 We are not *t·* to the extent of
transcending
  Un. 29– 9 *T·* the evidence of the material
  My. 154– 5 *t·* the law of death.
transcends
  '01. 18–14 Truth *t·* the evidence of the
  My. 262–22 a gift which so *t·* mortal, . . . **giving**
transcribed
  Mis. 95– 8 * and is *t·* below.
       187–31 *t·* by pagan religionists,
  '00. 3–23 afterwards *t·* Jehovah ;
transcribes
  Mis. 294– 8 *t·* on the page of reality
transcribing
  Mis. 187–15 because their *t·* thoughts were
       311–27 who can refrain from *t·*
transept
  My. 71–21 * neither nave, aisles, nor *t·*
transfer
  Man. 62–11 by *t·* from another Church
       94–20 nor *t·* this sacred office.
  '02. 13– 9 (which was a part of this *t·*)
transference
  Mis. 96–29 it is not the *t·* of
  Ret. 68–17 the *t·* of thought,
       68–24 no *t·* of mortal thought
transferred
  Mis. 139–23 this desirable site *t·*
  Ret. 28–13 *t·* to a perception of
  Pul. 35–17 *t·* to a perception of
  '02. 13– 5 *t·* to The Mother Church,
  My. 332–27 * Masonic records were *t·* **to**
transferring
  My. 21– 4 * *t·* to this fund the money
transfiguration
  Mis. 360– 5 hammering, chiselling, and *t·*
  Un. 2–26 ready for a spiritual *t·*,
transfigures
  No. 26–12 spiritual idea which *t·* thought.
  My. 183–12 unfolds, *t·*, heals.
transform
  Mis. 220–19 practitioner undertook to *t·* it,
       294–20 to reform and *t·* them,
  Un. 17–17 *t·* the universe into a home
  My. 15–13 *t·* you into His own image
transformation
  My. 61– 3 * To watch the *t·* has been
transformed
  My. 37–19 * the philosophy of the ages *t·*.
transforming
  Mis. 360–10 *t·* power of Truth ;
       372– 5 textbook . . . is *t·* the universe.
  Rud. 7–26 *t·* minerals into vegetables
  My. 10– 2 * *t·* influence of C. S.
transfused
  My. 306–14 wait to be *t·* into the practical
transgress
  My. 160– 3 which it were impious to *t·*,

transgressing
Ret. 71–17 knowingly t· Christ's command.

transgression
Mis. 293–18 wilful t· brings greater torment

transgressor
Mis. 261–15 way of the t·— see Prov. 13 : 15.

transient
Mis. 291– 1 t· views are human :
Ret. 69–14 t·, false sense of an existence

transit
Mis. 125–30 rapid t· from halls to churches,
205–32 take rapid t· to heaven,
'02. 10–22 t· from matter to Spirit

transition
Mis. 84–28 t· from our lower sense of
Un. 2–28 reach this t·, called *death*,
38–11 t· called *material death*,
No. 14– 5 have not passed the t· called death,
28– 2 after the t· called death.

transitory
Un. 36–14 matter is erroneous, t·,

translate
Mis. 74–16 t· substance into its original
Pul. 32–15 * may t· those inner experiences
My. 306–13 almost unutterable truths to t·,

translated
Mis. 18–11 t· into the new tongue,
Un. 31– 1 or, more accurately t·,
'01. 28–11 t· into almost every
My. 206–29 hath t· us into the— Col. 1 : 13.

translates
Mis. 22–10 C. S. t· Mind, God,
25–12 t· matter into Mind,
124–28 it t· love ;
Hea. 7– 8 t· matter into its original language,

translation
Mis. 67–24 *Do you believe in t·?*
68– 2 This t· is not the work of
97–23 I commend the Icelandic t· :
373– 8 t· of the New Testament,
Rud. 16–10 in their t· of the Scriptures
'02. 16– 3 Wyclif's t· of the New Testament,
Peo. 1– 6 t· of law back to its original
My. 295–10 MARTIN LUTHER'S T· INTO GERMAN

translations
Mis. 171–11 spiritual t· of God's messages,
No. 15– 8 Bible t· and voluminous commentaries
My. 178–31 reported as his sayings are t·.
179–14 being t·, the Scriptures are
179–24 renderings or t· of Scripture
238–11 Uninspired knowledge of the t· of
299–15 undiscovered in the t· of the Bible

translator
Mis. 188– 5 It is the t·, not the original Word,

translators
Mis. 187–13 t· of the older Scriptures
187–17 both writers and t· in that age
Ret. 91– 9 compilers and t· of the Bible,

translucent
My. 197–17 t· atmosphere of the former

transmigration
Mis. 22–13 refutes the amalgamation, t·,

transmission
Mis. 71–11 *law of t·, prenatal desires,* and

transmit
Mis. 72– 1 can t· to man . . . nothing evil,
Ret. 68–19 can matter originate or t· mind?

transmitted
Mis. 72– 8 t· to their helpless offspring,
97– 6 not one mortal thought t· to
My. 258–26 A t· charm rests on them.

transmitting
Mis. 22–15 impossibility of t· human ills,

transparency
Mis. 59–27 becomes a t· for the divine Mind,
183–34 Through the t· of Science we learn
330–16 looking through Love's t·,
Pul. 32– 2 * had the t· and rose-flush

transparent
Mis. 51–28 * walk t· like some holy thing.''
No. v– 7 t· to the hearts of all

transpired
My. 321–28 * t· during the past twenty years.

transportation
My. 82–24 * T· facilities at the two stations
87– 2 * t· facilities of the town

transported
'02. 4–25 Alternately t· and alarmed by

transverse
Mis. 348–14 Hence, Solomon's t· command :

trash
Mis. 67– 9 money, which is but t·,

travail
Mis. 15–20 sore t· of mortal mind
17–29 through the t· of mortal mind,
253–16 of the woman in t·,
253–28 spiritual Mother's sore t·,

travel
Mis. 88–13 reading, writing, extensive t·,
230–11 t· of limb more than mind.
My. 25–18 time consumed in t·,
124–26 rate of speed, the means of t·,

traveling
Man. 96– 6 The lecturer's t· expenses

travelled and **traveled**
Mis. 385–16 ''You've t· long, and far
'00. 12–12 elders t· to meet St. Paul,
Po. 48– 9 ''You've t· long, and far
My. 75–21 * no matter how far they had t·

Traveller
Pul. 39–14 * [Written for the T·]

traveller (see also **traveller's**)
Mis. 84–24 turn one, like a weary t·,
177–28 t· in foreign lands
'01. 14–15 misleads the t· on his way home.
Peo. 1–10 a long night to the t· ;

traveller's
My. 124–24 time-table, log, t· companion,
257–29 the Christian t· resting-place.

travellers
Mis. 327–15 The encumbered t· halt
'02. 11– 4 t·, tossed to and fro

travels
My. 75–22 * might have endured in their t·.

traversed
Mis. 320–19 it hath t· night,
Pan. 13–26 I have only t· my subject
My. 257– 5 This truth has t· night,

travesties
Mis. 260– 9 the t· of mortal mind.
My. 288–13 partook not of the t· of

treacherous
Mis. 9–28 trained in t· peace?
82–27 t· glare of its own flame
Un. 64–16 scale the t· ice, and stand on
Po. 43–17 Rough or t· way.

treachery
'02. 19– 1 injustice, ingratitude, t·,

tread
Mis. xi–24 With tender t·, thought sometimes
324– 7 gayly t· the gorgeously tapestried
395–17 The turf, whereon I t·,
Pul. 56–21 * We t· upon life's broken laws,
No. 27–26 take off thy shoes and t· lightly,
Peo. 13–12 iron t· of merciless invaders,
Po. 58– 2 The turf, whereon I t·,
My. 306– 4 to t· on the ashes of the dead
308–11 t· not ruthlessly on their ashes.

treading
Mis. 321–21 Still t· each temptation down,
Un. 58– 6 t· ''the winepress— Isa. 63 : 3.
'00. 10– 2 that is t· on its head
My. 350–12 did'st not Thou the dark wave t·

treason
Mis. 341–20 implicit t· to divine decree.
Peo. 6–23 no longer be deemed t· to understand

treasure
Mis. 394–10 harp of the minstrel, the t· of time ;
Po. 45–13 harp of the minstrel, the t· of time ;
My. 184–17 I t· it next to your compliments.
347–20 I shall t· my loving-cup

treasured
Ret. 6– 9 Among the t· reminiscences of

Treasurer and **treasurer** (see also **Church Treasurer, Treasurer's** and **treasurer's**)
Man. 25– 6 a President, a Clerk, a T·,
25–15 Clerk and T·,
25–16 Clerk and the T· of this Church
56–15 reports of T·, Clerk, and
76–24 T· of The Mother Church,
77– 6 T· of this Church shall
77–13 Board of Directors and the T·
78–16 The T·, personally, or
80– 6 T· of The Mother Church.
91–17 paid over annually to the T·
Pul. 52– 2 * Here is a church whose t· has
My. 16– 2 * t· of the building fund

Treasurer and treasurer
My. 23– 4   * amount each shall send the *T·.*
    27–18   * *T· of the Building Fund.*
    27–24   * *t·* of the building fund,
    39–15   * *T·*, Stephen A. Chase, C.S.D. ;
    57–29   * Here is a church whose *T·* has
    72–18   * *t·* of the building fund
    86–15   * *t·* of the building fund

Treasurer's and treasurer's
My. 16– 1   * chapter sub-title
    23– 9   * *Extract from the T· Report*
    28– 8   * *t·* books will show the

treasures
Mis. 165–20   nor appropriate his *t·*
    165–30   their *t·* reproduced
Ret. 2–21   Among grandmother's *t·*
Pul. 9–25   purity, and love are *t·* untold
'01. 1–13   to add to your *t·* of thought
'02. 19–21   its *t·*, taken away from you?
My. 114–11   the *t·* of this textbook are
    149–13   till you make their *t·* yours.
    149–31   with the *t·* of rain,

treasure-troves
Mis. 22–32   concealed in the *t·* of Science.

treasury
Mis. 140–16   generously poured into the *t·.*
Hea. 7–18   dropped her mite into the *t·*,
My. 214–27   cast my all into the *t·* of Truth,
    291–25   sheaves garnered, her *t·* filled,

treat
Mis. 71– 1   *Is it right for me to t· others,*
    88–27   *a Scientist to t· with a doctor ?*
    89– 6   *would it be right to t· this*
    89–10   that Scientists do not *t·* them,
    243– 6   although students *t·* sprains,
    282–21   to *t·* him without his knowing it,
    283–15   For a student of mine to *t·*
    284–13   How shall I *t·* malicious
    334–13   Why do . . . *t·* disease *as* disease,
    334–22   How shall we *t·* a negation,
Man. 53– 8   to *t·* the author of our textbook
Rud. 13–18   not Science to *t·* every organ
My. 359–29   *T·* yourself for it and get your
    364– 5   *t·* this mind to be Christly.

treated
Mis. 42–29   *Can I be t· without being present*
    90– 8   *to have a husband t· for sin,*
    198–18   disease also is *t·* and healed.
    247– 4   *t·* not as pearls trampled upon.
    282– 7   *t·* . . . without their knowledge
    284–15   for this evil to be *t·* personally,
Ret. 15–25   *t·* and given over by physicians
    71–11   knowledge of the individual *t·*,
Pul. 82–13   * they *t·* woman as a chattel,
Rud. 7– 4   the most difficult case so *t·.*
No. 31–19   but he *t·* them both,
Pan. 5–26   Jesus *t·* the lie summarily.
Hea. 14– 4   until disease is *t·* mentally
My. 97– 9   * those who were medically *t·*,
    330– 6   * his followers would be so *t·.*

treaties
My. 277– 9   and sound, well-kept *t·.*

treating
Mis. 35– 9   mental system of *t·* disease.
    45–17   effectual in *t·* moral ailments.
    65–18   *right way of t· disease*
    97–14   other methods of *t·* disease.
    368–18   Science of *t·* disease through Mind.
    379– 1   After *t·* his patients, Mr. Quimby
Rud. 13–18   When *t·* a patient, it is not
Hea. 14– 4   the science of *t·* disease
My. 363–27   patient whom he is *t·*,

treatise
No. 22– 6   *t·* on the healing properties of

Treatise Concerning the Principle of Human Knowledge
'01. 23–24   book title

treatment
Mis. 31– 8   the abuse of mental *t·*,
    33–16   when they began *t·*, had no faith
    42–29   *without being present during t·?*
    49– 7   restored by C. S. *t·.*
    54–19   *after one month's t· by one of your*
    66–23   as to the scientific *t·* of the sick.
    89– 9   under material medical *t·*,
    315–26   needing it asks for mental *t·.*
    378–12   His *t·* seemed at first to relieve her,
Ret. 71– 9   mental *t·*, without the consent or
    71–12   indications of mental *t·*,
Un. 23– 1   cruel *t·* received by old Gloster
Pul. 30– 2   * healed by C. S. *t·* ;

treatment
Pan. 5–28   His *t·* of evil and disease,
Hea. 14–21   metaphysical *t·* of disease ;
My. 103–19   application to the *t·* of disease
    204–23   The too long *t·* of a disease,
    204–24   a full fee for *t·*,
    237–17   charges for *t·* equal to those of
    307– 6   his magnetic *t·* and manipulation of
    307–26   improved . . . under his *t·*,
    363–26   avoid naming, in his mental *t·*,

treats
Mis. 69– 1   *t·* of the existence of God,
Man. 42–26   malpractises upon or *t·* our Leader
Ret. 68–17   *t·* of the human concept,

treaty
My. 281–23   * parties to the *t·* of Portsmouth,
    281–29   *t·* of Portsmouth is not an executive

trebles
My. 38–20   * their shrill *t·* rising with the

tree (see also tree's)
Mis. 37–17   axe at the root of the *t·.*
    198–22   the fruit of the *t·* of
    223– 9   *t·* is known by its fruit ;
    235–12   axe at the root of the *t·*
    356–20   carry the fruit of this *t·* into
    367–16   this fruit of the *t·* of
    392–13   the Hebrew figure of a *t·.*
Ret. 95– 1   this "*t·* of life"— *Rev.* 22 : 2.
Un. 3–16   the "*t·* of life."— *Gen.* 2 : 9.
    21–10   every *t·* of the garden."— *Gen.* 3 : 1.
    55– 7   own body on the *t·*."— *I Pet.* 2 : 24.
Pul. 4–19   or crown the *t·* with blossoms.
    46–13   * going back to the ancestral *t·*
'00. 8– 8   characteristics of *t·* and flower,
Po. 20–17   the Hebrew figure of a *t·.*
My. 3– 9   have right to the *t·* of life, — *Rev.* 22 : 14.
    111–21   Is not the *t·* known by its fruit?
    112–24   The *t·* is known by its fruit.
    287–21   axe at the root of the *t·*
    300–28   The *t·* is known by its fruit.

tree's
Mis. 264–18   * twig is bent, the *t·* inclined."

trees
Pul. 63– 8   the strength to nourish *t·*
Po. 16–14   Which steepeth the *t·* when the
    53– 2   paint the gray, stark *t·*,
My. 296– 4   the root of the *t·*," — *Matt.* 3 : 10.

tree-tops
Pul. 49– 8   * *t·* on the lower terrace,

tremble
Ret. 17– 8   *t·* with accents of bliss.
Po. 62– 8   *t·* with accents of bliss.
My. 344–27   I should *t·* for mankind ;

trembled
My. 62– 6   * that *t·* in one human heart

trembler
Mis. 341–14   is joy a *t·*?

trembling
Mis. 275– 3   woman's *t·*, clinging faith
    390–17   The timid, *t·* leaves.
Peo. 8–20   *t·* chords of human hope
Po. 43–18   Temper every *t·* footfall,
    55–18   The timid, *t·* leaves.
My. 153–22   This *t·* and blind faith,
    293–13   of *t·* faith, hope, and of fear,
    300– 5   with fear and *t·.*— *Phil.* 2 : 12.

tremendous
My. 90–24   * its *t·* outpouring of eager
    93–24   * missed entirely its *t·* growth

Tremont Street
My. 54–28   * Chickering Hall on *T· S·.*

Tremont Temple
Mis. 95– 1   chapter sub-title
    95– 3   * Monday lectureship in *T· T·*,
My. 57– 2   * were overcrowded in *T· T·*,

tremor
Ret. 14–12   which I answered without a *t·*,

tremulous
Mis. 331–13   tones *t·* with tenderness,
Po. 27– 6   *t·* with shadowy night !
My. 121– 9   neither *t·* nor relapsing.

trenchant
My. 160–14   *t·* truth that cuts its way

trend
Mis. 21–13   to depart from the *t·* of other
    114– 8   the *t·* of their own thoughts ;
Ret. 23– 1   *t·* of human life was too eventful
    65–20   *t·* and tenor of Christ's teaching
Po. vii– 3   * *same lofty t· of thought*

trend
 My. 100— 4 * unmistakable in their *t·*.
   129— 9 counteract the *t·* of mad ambition.
   305—30 was not the *t·* of thought,

Trenton, N. J.
 Pul. 89—15 * *Times, T·, N. J.*

trespass
 Mis. 184—15 would *t·* upon divine Science,
   283—18 conscious *t·* on the rights of
 Ret. 87—18 to *t·* upon the rights of
   89—26 *t·* not intentionally upon
 Pul. ?— 9 nothing can . . . *t·* on Love.
 No. 40—16 never to *t·* mentally on

trespassers
 Mis. 119—26 *t·* upon the sparse individual rights

trespasses
 My. 133—14 "dead in *t·* and sins,"— *Eph.* 2: 1.
   150—22 spiritually dead in *t·* and sins

trespassing
 Ret. 76— 5 student can write . . . without *t·*, if
 No. 3— 4 *t·* error murders either friend or

tresses
 Mis. 330—15 to shake out their *t·*

triad
 Mis. 63— 9 infinite remedy for the opposite *t·*,
 '01. 18—28 popular *t·* — sin, sickness, and death

trial
 Mis. x— 3 sincere in *t·* or in triumph.
   121—21 arrest, *t·*, and crucifixion of
   160—14 every *t·* of our faith in God
   335—24 when the hour of *t·* comes
 Man. 67— 4 cases of those on *t·*
 Ret. 20—14 vision of relief from this *t·*.
 My. 21—16 * every seeming *t·* and deprivation
   143—23 I do not regard this . . . as a *t·*,
   270—17 proven under *t·*, and evidences

trials
 Mis. 107— 5 redemptive power is seen in sore *t·*,
   126—11 have learned that *t·* lift us
   298—18 *T·* purify mortals
 No. 36—16 could find rest from unreal *t·*
 My. 47—15 * memories of *t·*, progress, and
   50— 9 * knew not the *t·* before them,

triangle
 My. 65—20 * in the shape of a *t·*,
   66— 3 * also in the shape of a *t·*,

triangular
 Pul. 24— 9 * on a *t·* plot of ground,
 My. 67— 7 * Shape, *t·* . . . 220x220x236 ft.

tribal
 Mis. 123—16 Jehovah, was the Jewish *t·* deity.
 '02. 5— 3 pagan philosophies and *t·* religions
 My. 288—14 pagan mysticisms, *t·* religion,

tribe
 Mis. 329—27 calling the feathered *t·* back to

tribes
 Mis. 73—26 *twelve t· of Israel.*"— *Matt.* 19: 28.

tribulation
 Mis. 18— 5 therefore rejoice in *t·*,
 No. 25— 3 Having won through great *t·*
 Peo. 14—14 be patient in *t·*,
 My. 132— 6 ye shall have *t·* ;— *John* 16: 33.

tribunals
 Mis. 121—29 Human *t·*, if just,
 My. 277— 8 by means of their wholesome *t·*,

Tribune
 Pul. 90—11 * *T·*, Minneapolis, Minn.
   90—12 * *T·*, Salt Lake City, Utah.

tributary
 Mis. 127—17 the *t·* of divine Love,
 Un. 13— 3 makes God *t·* to man,
 Pul. 3—21 a *t·* of divine Love,
 My. 18—14 the *t·* of divine Love,

tribute
 Pul. 76—17 * the *t·* of loving friends.
 My. 202— 8, 9 *t·* to whom *t·* is due ;— *Rom.* 13: 7.
   291— 1 chapter sub-title
   295— 8 chapter sub-title
   332— 6 * meagre *t·* for so noble an effort
   332— 8 * as a *t·* of grateful hearts?
   333— 8 * the last *t·* of respect
   351— 5 * beautiful *t·* to Free Masonry.

tributes
 My. 289— 6 chapter sub-title

tried
 Mis. xi—27 I have *t·* to remove the
   10—19 *t·* their strength and proven it ;
   24—16 *t·* to make plain to others,
   235—27 *t·* to follow the divine precept,

tried
 Mis. 278—17 who are *t·* in the furnace
   348—26 I *t·* several doses of medicine,
 Man. 50—20 offender's case shall be *t·*
 My. 11— 9 * not *t·* to guide us by means of
   16—25 a stone, a *t·* stone, — *Isa.* 28: 16.
   121— 8 a true, *t·* mental conviction
   290— 4 the *t·* and true seem few.
   306—26 *t·* to get them published

triennial
 My. 141—10 * except on the *t·* gatherings,

triennially
 Mis. 120—20 Association hereafter meet *t·* :
 Man. 84—11 shall have one class *t·*,

tries
 Mis. 43—21 If one student *t·* to undermine
   212—28 *t·* to show his errors to him
 My. 212—26 He *t·* to compensate himself for

trifle
 Mis. 257—16 code whose modes *t·* with joy,
 My. 123—21 a *t·* over two hundred people,

trifles
 My. 75—18 * do not get excited over *t·*.
   123—29 * "*t·* make perfection,"

trifling
 Mis. 43—11 a *t·* sense of it as being

trimmed
 Mis. 92—11 keeps his own lamp *t·*
   276—25 shall have their lamps *t·*
 Ret. 84— 8 his own lamp *t·* and burning.
 My. 125—27 Are our lamps *t·* and burning?

trimmings
 Pul. 24—23 * with *t·* of the pink granite

Trinitarian
 Ret. 13— 2 Congregational (*T·*) Church,
 Rud. 2— 5 He adds, that among *T·* Christians

Trinity
 My. 338— 7 * upon the subject of the *T·*,

trinity
 Mis. 63— 9 divine *t·* is one infinite remedy
 Un. 62—17 Destroy this *t·* of error,
   63— 4 *t·* of Love lives and reigns
 Rud. 3— 8 Life, Truth, and Love— this *t·* of good
   4— 2 Life, Truth, and Love are this *t·*
 No. 1—19 divine oneness of the *t·*,
   1—20 *t·* in unity, correcting the
 '01. 7— 4 *t·* of the Godhead in C. S.
 Hea. 3—25 "God is . . . a *t·* in unity ;
 My. 185—15 Love formed this *t·*,
   185—15 the *t·* no man can sunder.

trip
 Mis. 329—18 her little feet *t·* lightly on,
 My. 169— 4 so long a *t·* for so small a
   177—10 I am quite able to take the *t·*
   312—19 While on a business *t·*
   312—21 I was with him on this *t·*.

triple
 My. 78—13 * and in *t·* galleries.

tripping
 Mis. 250—26 little feet *t·* along the sidewalk ;

triturations
 My. 107—11 same *t·* of medicine have not

triumph
 and rest
  Po. 78— 5 their reward, *t·* and rest,
 crowning
  My. 323—22 * Your crowning *t·* over error
 defeat, and
  Mis. 204— 8 sorrow, joy, defeat, and *t·*.
 of art
  '00. 11—16 his composition is the *t·* of art,
 of good
  Mis. 201—31 *t·* of good that has pleasure in
 of mind
  Peo. 13—17 *t·* of mind over the body,
  My. 74—13 * *t·* of mind over matter.
 of Soul
  Hea. 10—19 *t·* of Soul over sense.
 of Spirit
  Ret. 56—14 *t·* of Spirit in immutable harmony.
 over death
  Un. 43—10 complete *t·* over death,
 over sin
  No. 36—20 *t·* over sin, sickness, and death.
 over the grave
  Mis. 74—25 His *t·* over the grave
 sublime
  Un. 58—14 The Master's sublime *t·*

triumph

tear or
Mis. 398–14 Tear or *t·* harms,
Ret. 46–20 Tear or *t·* harms,
Pul. 17–19 Tear or *t·* harms,
Po. 14–18 Tear or *t·* harms,

tears and
Mis. 116–24 prayer, struggles, tears, and *t·*.

this
Ret. 22–16 but this *t·* will come !

toil is
Mis. 340–24 Be active, . . . toil is *t·* ;

to the truth
Po. 23–21 Give peaceful *t·* to the truth,

Mis. x– 3 sincere in trial or in *t·*.
200–26 *t·* of a reasonable faith
201–17 enabled him to *t·* over them,
248– 7 "I will *t·* in the works of — *Psal.* 92 : 4.
'02. 3–23 *t·* canker not his coronation,
My. 134– 8 To *t·* in truth, to keep the faith
161–31 can *t·* over their ultimatum,
227–28 I abide by this rule and *t·* by it.

triumphal
Mis. 130–30 *t·* march out of the wilderness,
Po. 30–18 Piercing the clouds with its *t·*

triumphant
Man. 19– 6 Church Universal and *T·*
Mis. 100–20 the evermore of Truth is *t·*.
124–30 to understanding, Love *t·* !
138–25 equal to the march *t·*,
153– 5 Truth is restful, and Love is *t·*.
374–12 and its art will rise *t·* ;
385–25 faith *t·* round thy death-couch
Pul. 3–19 of the church *t·* ;
Pan. 14– 2 righteousness with its *t·* train.
Po. 48–21 faith *t·* round thy death-couch
My. 133– 8 rise to the church *t·*,
154–27 foreshadowing of the church *t·*.
174–30 rejoice in the church *t·*
185–10 till Truth shall reign *t·*
259–18 a lowly, *t·* trust,

triumphantly
No. 29–14 walks *t·* over the waves of sin,
My. 273– 7 * emerging *t·* from all attacks

triumphed
'02. 19–26 great Master *t·* in furnace fires.

triumphs
Mis. 260– 3 By conflicts, defeats, and *t·*,
281– 2 chant hymns of victory for *t·*.
298–23 faith vested in righteousness *t·* !
321–11 *t·* of Truth over error,
356–23 This virtue *t·* over the flesh ;
Un. 3–12 and the *t·* of Spirit.
Po. 25–19 Wreaths for the *t·* o'er ill !
My. 124–13 bloodless sieges and tearless *t·*,
291–27 Tears blend with her *t·*.

triune
Mis. 63– 8 *t·* Principle of all pure theology ;
385– 1 * "Faith, hope, and tears, *t·*,
'01. 4–25 *t·*, because He is Life, Truth, Love,
5– 7 one divine infinite *t·* Principle,
Po. 37– 1 * "Faith, hope, and tears, *t·*,

trod
Po. 26– 4 The turf where thou hast *t·*
My. 151–18 * aisles by flaunting folly *t·*,

trodden
Mis. 274–28 individual rights are *t·* under
301–31 *t·* the winepress alone ; — *Isa.* 63 : 3.
My. 139–13 belied, and *t·* upon.

troddest
Pul. 1–16 This spot whereon thou *t·*

tropic
Mis. 394– 4 An infinite essence from *t·* to pole,
Po. 45– 5 An infinite essence from *t·* to pole,

troth
Mis. 298–12 my best friend break *t·* with me?

trouble
Mis. 10–13 their help in times of *t·*.
54–18 *I was healed of a chronic t·*
80–18 and full of *t·*." — *Job.* 14 : 1.
96– 4 help in all times of *t·*,
Man. 53–12 If a member, . . . shall *t·* her
Chr. 55–14 and full of *t·*. — *Job.* 14 : 1.
Un. 2– 5 present help in *t·*." — *Psal.* 46 : 1.
8– 2 much *t·* to many earnest thinkers
'01. 19– 4 given to them in times of *t·*,
My. 162– 3 present help in *t·*'' — *Psal.* 46 : 1.
167– 9 ever-present help in *t·*,
359– 3 neither do they *t·* me with their

troubled
Mis. 71– 7 thinks that he was *t·* with
277– 2 their hearts are not *t·*.
324–20 growing more and more *t·*,
389–23 drops down upon the *t·* breast,
397– 5 o'er earth's *t·*, angry sea
Ret. 13– 6 predestination, greatly *t·* me ;
50– 7 This amount greatly *t·* me.
Un. 50–22 awake from the *t·* dream,
Pul. 18–14 o'er earth's *t·*, angry sea
'00. 7–22 walking the wave of earth's *t·* sea,
'02. 19–19 heaving surf of life's *t·* sea
Po. 5– 2 drops down upon the *t·* breast,
12–14 o'er earth's *t·*, angry sea
My. 152– 3 anchored its faith in *t·* waters.
325– 6 * Mr. Wiggin was very much *t·*

troubles
Mis. 236– 5 little else than the *t·*,
Ret. 3– 6 Indian *t·* of 1722–1725,
Un. 18–15 console others in *t·* that you
My. 212–29 animal magnetism never *t·* him,
311– 9 * she *t·* me so much."

troublesome
Mis. 370–22 braying donkey . . . is less *t·*.
'01. 31– 9 truths . . . that now seem *t·*.

trow
Mis. 395– 8 And yet I *t·*,
Po. 57–15 And yet I *t·*,
My. 20– 9 I *t·* you are awaiting

trowel
Man. 61– 1 No special *t·* should be used.

Troy, N. Y.
Pul. 89–14 * *Telegram, T·, N. Y.*

truant
Pul. 48–13 * little *t·* river, as it wanders

true
Mis. 15–10 can give the *t·* perception of God
18–15, 16 the *t·* man and *t·* woman,
22–16 all *t·* thoughts revolve in
22–32 *T·*, Newton named it gravitation,
23– 4 Is pantheism *t·* ?
24–23 therefore it cannot be *t·*.
40–14 All *t·* healing is governed by,
41–31 Principle that he knows to be *t·*.
46– 7 tested scientifically to be found *t·*,
47–30 accepts as either useful or *t·*.
57– 3 If the first record is *t·*,
57– 8 the *t·* creation was finished,
57–17 opposite error said, "I am *t·*,"
62–12 aggregate positive, or *t·* quantity,
65– 7 this is because Science is *t·*,
65–15 to gain the *t·* solution of Life
69– 5 the unfolding of *t·* metaphysics ;
70– 2 That the Bible is *t·*
72– 6 the only living and *t·* origin, God.
73–10 separates the false sense from the *t·*,
74– 6 the *t·* basis of being,
76– 6 statement of our Master is *t·*,
76– 8 never be tested or proven *t·* upon a
79–21 *t·* ideal of immortal man's divine
80–19 promotes and impels all *t·* reform ;
81– 9 which is the *t·* system of medicine.
91– 2 as a type of the *t·* worship,
93–15 This being *t·*, sin has no power ;
98–27 * "Thou must be *t·* thyself,
103–15 as tangible, *t·* substance,
104–24 How shall we reach our *t·* selves?
104–28 would not gain the *t·* ideal
104–31 on the side of good, my *t·* being.
108–15 This *t·* conception would remove
113– 4 If, as is indisputably *t·*,
113–23 resisted by *t·* Christianity.
117– 7 the wrong motive or the *t·*
128– 7 whatsoever things are *t·*, — *Phil.* 4 : 8.
135– 1 Christians, and all *t·* Scientists,
139–26 like all *t·* wisdom,
140– 5 the *t·* nature of the gift ;
142–18 varying types of *t·* affection,
143– 2 *t·* friendship's "level"
156–23 the basis of all *t·* thought
157–12 Every *t·* Christian Scientist
171– 2 never be wrested from its *t·* meaning
171–18 By these signs are the *t·* disciples
176–23 establish a nation in *t·* freedom,
179–15 more *t·*, more spiritual."
181–15 understand man's *t·* birthright,
183–30 will arrive at the *t·* status
185–14 the *t·* image and likeness.
187– 2 must be accepted as *t·*
189–12 brings to light the *t·* reflection :
193– 2 Are they *t·* ?
193– 4 that the Scripture is *t·* ;
206–16 of what constitutes *t·* manhood.

true

Mis.	216– 3	There *remaineth*, it is *t*,
	217– 1	*T*· idealism is a divine Science,
	222–15	because the false seems *t*·.
	226–15	* To thine own self be *t*·,
	228–16	a kind, *t*·, and just person,
	233–20	the practice of *t*· medicine,
	233–27	having a *t*· standard,
	238– 5	for all who dare to be *t*·,
	248–19	is not more *t*· than
	250–20	having no ring of the *t*· metal.
	264–27	must be pure, grand, *t*·,
	266– 9	The *t*· leader of a *t*· cause
	271–27	* between *t*· and false teachers
	278–31	on the part of *t*· followers,
	291–22	the *t*· and unswerving course
	294–28	the *t*· ideas of humanity
	298–25	*t*· consciousness is the *t*· health.
	299–27	*T*·, it saves your purchasing these
	309–10	*t*· contemplation of his character.
	309–13	Experience proves this *t*·.
	311– 3	*t*· . . . Scientists will be welcomed,
	321–13	*t*· worshippers shall — *see John* 4 : 23.
	336– 4	a lie is never *t*·
	336–22	cognomen of all *t*· religion,
	338–20	* "Thou must be *t*· thyself,
	344– 1	chapter sub-title
	346–14	is not more *t*· or real than
	352–10	*t*· consciousness of God,
	357– 6	having strayed from the *t*· fold,
	357–28	lambs that have sought the *t*· fold
	363– 3	divine Mind and *t*· happiness.
	366– 4	*T*·, it requires more study to
	369– 1	*t*· . . . Scientist at the foot of
	370–26	*t*· fold for Christian healers,
	372–28	*t*· hue and character of the
	375–14	* idea of what constitutes *t*· art.
	375–19	* is the foundation of *t*· art.
	375–28	* the only *t*· art
	376– 2	* *t*· art of the oldest, most revered,
	384– 4	And *t*· hearts greet,
Man.	40–10	in *t*· brotherliness, charitableness,
	93–12	a *t*· and just reply to public
Ret.	21–20	*t*· estimate of being.
	25–28	witness is not *t*·." — *John* 5 : 31.
	35–16	speaking of his *t*· followers
	44–29	that hour holds this *t*· record.
	52– 8	a home for every *t*· seeker
	68–11	while the other is *t*·.
	68–26	scientific thoughts are *t*·
	73–16	in the *t*· Mind,
	81–24	* To thine own self be *t*· ;
	86– 4	we must ourselves be *t*·.
	87– 4	so eternally *t*·, so axiomatic,
	90–16	The *t*· mother never willingly neglects
	93–22	but it is nevertheless *t*·.
	94– 5	seems *t*·, and yet contradicts
	94– 8	acknowledging the *t*· way,
	94–16	immortal Truth be found *t*·,
Un.	1–18	closer to the *t*· understanding of God
	2–14	The *t*· man, really *saved*,
	4–13	God is all *t*· consciousness ;
	9–18	*t*· solution of the perplexing problem
	13– 4	the reverse is *t*· in Science.
	13–12	*t*· understanding of Deity.
	17– 2	to be accounted *t*·.
	21–20	belonging to *t*· individuality,
	23– 2	which makes *t*· the lines :
	26–17	Now if it be *t*· that God's power
	26–18	can it be also *t*· that *chance*
	32–16	*T*· Mind is immortal.
	33– 9	witness is not *t*·." — *John* 5 : 31.
	42–28	*t*· manhood and womanhood go forth
	49– 8	The more I understand *t*· humanhood,
	53–22	he has lost his *t*· individuality
	61– 1	the *t*· evidence of Life,
	62–12	the *t*· ideal of omnipotent and
Pul.	2–28	*t*· temple is no human fabrication,
	4–16	seer's declaration *t*·,
	9–11	Woman, *t*· to her instinct,
	10–17	Christ, the *t*·, the spiritual idea,
	33–25	* It is certainly *t*· that many
	34–19	* and that it is as *t*· to-day
	80–20	* but this much is *t*· :
	81–24	* She is the apostle of the *t*·,
	82–19	* *T*·, there were Miriam and Esther,
Rud.	3–19	Mind, which gives all *t*· volition,
	5– 4	"Let God be *t*·, — *Rom.* 3 : 4.
	6–19	*t*· evidence of spiritual sense
	7–15	*t*· evidence of the being of God
	8–11	be *t*· to thyself, and *t*· to others ;
	11–20	based on a *t*· understanding of God
	17– 5	*t*· character of C. S.,
	17– 8	*t*· understanding of C. S.
No.	v– 9	life-giving waters of a *t*· divinity,
	4–22	*t*· constituency of being.

true

No.	5– 1	All *t*· Christian Scientists are
	7– 2	to be wise and *t*· rejoices every
	9– 4	It is *t*· that the mistakes,
	10– 3	C. S. is demonstrably as *t*·,
	11–18	It is *t*· that it requires more study
	12–14	*t*· Christianity in all ages,
	12–18	Living a *t*· life, casting out evil,
	13– 7	If this be *t*·, then death must be
	13–13	declaration is nevertheless *t*·,
	17– 8	it is impossible for the *t*· man
	28–21	demonstrably *t*· cannot be gainsaid ;
	32–15	other theories make sin *t*·.
	34–10	the *t*· worshippers shall — *John* 4 : 23.
	34–13	who discern his *t*· merit,
	36– 6	Jesus' *t*· and conscious being
	38– 6	established the only *t*· idealism
	38– 9	*t*· philosophy and realism.
	39–17	*T*· prayer is not asking God for love ;
	42–20	declaring itself both *t*· and good.
Pan.	9–26	chapter sub-title
	11–28	man is the *t*· image of God,
	12–28	It is divinely *t*·,
'00.	15– 7	start forward with *t*· ambition.
'01.	1–18	All that is *t*· is a sort of necessity,
	5–24	anything that is real, good, or *t*· ;
	11–13	*T*·, I have made . . . the pastor
	22– 1	That God is good, that Truth is *t*·,
	22–11	so if one is *t*·, the other is false.
	22–12	If Truth is *t*·, its opposite,
	22–13	if Spirit is *t*· and infinite,
'02.	3–28	the only *t*· ambition is to
	7– 1	the *t*· nature of Love intact
	8– 9	shows what *t*· spirituality is,
	12– 5	Messiah, the *t*· spiritual idea,
	17–17	Who . . . ever found her *t*· ?
	18–13	Jesus was compassionate, *t*·,
	19– 4	*T*· to his divine nature,
Hea.	10–27	*t*· fount and Soul's baptism.
	17–21	and therefore are not *T*·
Peo.	2– 2	*t*· glory of immortality.
	6–18	spiritual and *t*· ideal of Deity
Po.	36– 3	And *t*· hearts greet,
My.	4–20	Thus unfolding the *t*· metal
	4–32	natural and demonstrably *t*·,
	6– 4	Are we *t*· to ourselves?
	15–23	* Because I know 'tis *t*· ;
	26–24	the *t*· animus of our church
	28– 6	* this has been proved *t*·
	42– 2	* We have found it *t*· that
	46–14	* work of *t*· Christian Scientists.
	59– 6	* we thought this might be *t*·
	91–13	* element in *t*· Christianity.
	118– 3	go on promoting the *t*· Principle
	119–31	*t*· image and likeness of God.
	121– 8	a *t*·, tried mental conviction
	121–18	found in a *t*· character,
	123–24	the *t*· Christian Scientist is not
	130– 1	correct the false with the *t*·
	138–29	that the statements . . . are *t*·.
	146–17	if they are *t*· at all,
	146–18	as *t*· to-day as they will be
	146–21	what I wrote is *t*·,
	150– 6	the character of *t*· greatness :
	158–21	the heart tender, faithful, *t*·.
	159–15	the *t*· thought escapes from the
	179–23	a *t*· divinity and humanity.
	181–13	the motive of *t*· religion,
	204– 9	C. S. unites its *t*· followers
	213–21	harmony with His *t*· followers.
	229– 9	*t*· that loyal Christian Scientists,
	232–18	the *t*· authority for C. S.?
	233– 1	the spirit of *t*· watching,
	235–30	commemorated . . . what is not *t*·,
	252–11	purpose of *t*· education
	259–19	a *t*· heart, and a helping hand
	260–24	The *t*· spirit of Christmas
	266–29	undoubtedly *t*· that C. S.
	267–25	to darken the *t*· conception
	290– 4	the tried and *t*· seem few.
	306–10	making the *t*· apparent.
	315–18	* statement by him signed is *t*·.
	334– 2	* that the rumor is not *t*·.
	357–23	the axiom of *t*· C. S.
	357–30	I know that every *t*· follower
	358– 2	the *t*· following of their Leader ;
		(*see also* **Christian, God, idea, knowledge, likeness, Science, sense**)

true-hearted

Mis.	301–19	question of my *t*· students,

truer

Mis.	17–31	gains a *t*· sense of Spirit
	47–17	which is the *t*· sense of being.
No.	34– 5	when we gain the *t*· sense of
'01.	9– 7	*t*· sense of Christ baptized them

truer
  Peo. 12–17 advance to *t·* conceptions,
  My. 64– 3 * a larger and *t·* meaning.

truest
  Mis. 375– 5 *t·* art of C.· S. is to be a
  '00. 10– 6 the *t·* signs that can be given
  My. 213–10 the *t·* friends of mankind,

truism
  Mis. 46– 6 *t·* needs only to be tested
      259–24 *t·* that Truth demonstrates good,
      271–16 take in this axiomatic *t·* :
      382– 1 either a *t·* or a rule,
  Ret. 87– 4 that it has become a *t·* ;
  No. 39– 1 It is a *t·* that we can think

truisms
  My. 160–11 willingly accept dead *t·*

truly
  Mis. ix–18 *T·* may it be said :
      98–25 *T·* is it written :
     108–21 that which is *t·* conceived of,
     126– 4 *T·*, I half wish for society again ;
     134– 7 Very *t·*,
     170– 2 for by following Christ *t·*,
     338–26 * "Think *t·*, and thy thoughts
     338–28 * Speak *t·*, and each word of thine
     338–30 * Live *t·*, and thy life shall be
     372–17 * are *t·* a work of art,
  Ret. 14–22 that I *had* been *t·* regenerated,
     25–15 Soul alone is *t·* substantial.
  Un. 3– 6 before it can be *t·* said of them :
     45–28 Matter is not *t·* conscious ;
  No. 3– 6 *T·* it is better to fall into the hands
     16– 2 must *t·* and eternally exist.
  Pan. 13–26 *T·* there is no rest in them,
  '02. 10–24 Rev. Hugh Black writes *t·* :
  My. 4–10 follow *t·*, meekly, patiently,
     42– 1 * to be *t·* grateful to her who
     98– 2 * *t·* make up a mighty host,
    113–32 the *t·* great men and women
    142–21 Most *t·* yours,
    158– 4 Very *t·*,
    282–27 Most *t·* yours,
    351–14 *t·* Masonic, tender, grand in you
    361–21 * *t·* democratic and liberal

trumpet-call
  My. 155–10 May it catch the early *t·*,

trunk
  My. 125– 8 incline . . . towards the parent *t·*.

trunks
  Mis. 274–25 headless *t·*, and quivering hearts
  My. 82–10 * *t·* and smaller articles of baggage

Trust
  Deed of
    (see **Deed of Trust***)*

trust
  childlike
    Mis. 15–15 childlike *t·* and joyful adoption of
  deed of
    My. 157–18 * in her original deed of *t·*,
      157–22 a deed of *t·* to three individuals
  executive
    Pan. 14–16 associated with his executive *t·*,
  feeling of
    My. 50–17 * a feeling of *t·* in the
  fond
    My. 158– 9 in attune with faith's fond *t·*.
  his
    Mis. 197–31 placing his *t·* in this grand Truth,
  my
    My. 138–10 test my *t·* in divine Love.
  no
    Peo. 8–27 trusting where there is no *t·*,
  our
    My. 200– 6 our *t·* is in the Almighty God,
  proclaims the
    My. 58–13 * proclaims the *t·*, the willingness of
  that
    Mis. 284–31 to fulfil that *t·*
  this
    Ret. 31–17 for this *t·* is the unseen sin,
  triumphant
    My. 259–19 a lowly, triumphant *t·*, a true heart,

  Mis. vii–12 There's nothing here to *t·*.
     25–26 if the sick cannot *t·* God for help
     48–19 has, we *t·*, been made in season to
    157–22 *t·* also in Him ; — *Psal.* 37: 5.
    269– 1 *t·* also in Him ; — *Psal.* 37: 5.
    269–27 Error is vending itself on *t·*,
    271–16 * "*T·* her not, she's fooling thee ;"
    297–28 *T·* Truth, not error ;
    298– 1 "*T·* in the Lord with — *Prov.* 3: 5.
    320– 1 *t·* the divine Providence,

trust
  Mis. 369–17 *t·* Christ more than it does drugs.
  Man. 96–13 *t·* to contributions for his fee.
  Ret. 14–15 I was willing to *t·* God,
  No. v– 7 import of this edition is, we *t·*,
     3–24 *t·* Love's recompense of love.
  '01. 34–29 "*T·* in the Lord — *Prov.* 3: 5.
  '02. 19–27 Then, Christian Scientists, *t·*,
  Hea. 14–11 never *t·* yourself in the hands of
  My. 26–19 *t·* that you will see, as I foresee,
    120– 4 *t·* that you and I may meet in truth
    129–28 *T·* God to direct your steps.
    161–26 *T·* in God, and "He shall — *Prov.* 3: 6.
    167–27 will, I *t·*, never be marred by
    170–20 "*T·* in the Lord, — *Psal.* 37: 3.
    170–23 *t·* also in Him ; — *Psal.* 37: 5.
    171– 1 *T·* in Truth, and have no other
    217– 6 deeded in *t·* to The Mother Church
    275–14 (and I *t·* the desire thereof)
    290–13 *T·* in Him whose love enfolds thee.
    343–20 and *t·* in me grew.

trusted
  My. 138–12 students and *t·* personal friends

trustee-deed
  Mis. 140–13 and I supposed the *t·* was legal ;

Trustees and **trustees** *(see also* **Board of Trustees***)*
  Man. 27–26 Boards of *T·* and Syndicates
    65–13 *T·* of The C. S. Publishing Society,
    80–20 remaining *t·* shall fill the vacancy,
  Pul. 20– 4 and through *t·* gave back the land
    20– 6 to recover the land from the *t·*,
  '02. 13–29 gave to my church through *t·*,
  My. vi–22 * she made over to *t·* under agreement
    66– 1 * taken by Ira O. Knapp *et al.*, *t·*.
    136–24 To my aforesaid *T·* I have
    137–27 I selected said *T·* because I had
    137–30 able to select the *T·* I need
    199–11 Directors and *T·* of this church
    362–12 * The *T·* and Readers of all the

Trusteeship and **trusteeship**
  Man. 80–12 Vacancies in *T·*.
    80–14 to declare vacancies in said *t·*,

Trusteeships
  Man. 27–25 *T·* and Syndicates.

trusteth
  My. 290–15 because he *t·* in Thee." — *Isa.* 26: 3.

trustful
  Mis. 127–14 If this heart, humble and *t·*,
  Pul. 45–17 * heaped upon the hopeful, *t·* ones,
  My. 18–10 If this heart, humble and *t·*,

trusting
  '02. 19–27 and *t·*, you will find divine Science
  Peo. 8–27 *t·* where there is no trust,
  My. 138–19 *T·* that I have not exceeded the

trustingly
  My. 182–19 gratefully, *t·*, I dedicate

trusts
  Man. 87–19 *t·* them to the divine Truth
    102–13 shall have named in them all the *t·*
  Ret. 84–25 *t·* them to the divine Truth
  '02. 4– 2 dishonesty in *t·*, begin with
  My. 171– 2 *and have no other t·*.
    230–23 faithful over foundational *t·*,
    265– 8 invests less in *t·*, loses capital,
    266– 8 ritual, creed, and *t·* in place of

trustworthiness
  Mis. 118–17 meritorious faith or *t·*
    153–20 positive proof of *t·*.
  Hea. 5–13 * *t·* of the communications,

trustworthy
  Rud. 13–23 *methods of t· Christian Scientists*

trusty
  Mis. 147–22 at all times the *t·* friend,

Truth *(see also* **Truth's***)*
  abiding in
    Mis. 331– 8 abiding in *T·*, the warmth and
  above
    Mis. 277– 6 trying to be heard above *T·*,
    My. 249– 5 error strives to be heard above *T·*,
  absolute
    Mis. 311–24 The works . . . contain absolute *T·*,
    My. 293–16 prevented the power of absolute *T·*
  according as
    Mis. 147–15 according as *T·* and the voice of
  adherents of
    Mis. 213–19 the faithful adherents of *T·*
    Man. 15– 3 As adherents of *T·*, we take
  admits
    Ret. 54–14 admits *T·* without understanding it.
  advent of
    Ret. 81–15 After the supreme advent of *T·*

Truth

against
Mis. 328–14   and closed it against T·,
aiming for
My. 126– 6   human mind . . . aiming for T·,
all
Mis. 163–27   which leadeth into all T·
     174–32   that leadeth into all T· ;
Un.   46– 3   All T· is from inspiration
No.   9–24   it . . . includes all T·.
alone
No.   5– 7   As T· alone is real,
alterative
Mis. 241–10   the great alterative, T· :
     241–19   administer this alterative T· :
and error
Mis. 65–10   question between T· and error,
     188–12   contest between T· and error ;
'01. 22–10   T· and error, Spirit and matter,
and Life
Mis. 320–22   words of T· and Life.
Chr. 53–10   God anoints Of T· and Life ;
Un.   32– 2   false to T· and Life.
No.   16–10   negations of Spirit, T·, and Life,
Hea.   3–24   "God is Love, T·, and Life,"
My. 221–30   divine Mind, T· and Life,
     257–21   and the reign of T· and Life
     261–26   T· and Life born of God
and Love
Mis.   2– 2   T· and Love to heal the sick.
       3– 8   the power of T· and Love.
       4– 1   imbued with purity, T·, and Love,
       5–13   healing power is T· and Love,
      19–13   divine claims of T· and Love
      36–29   that intelligence, T·, and Love,
      40–23   possess the spirit of T· and Love,
      66–14   law and gospel of T· and Love
      92– 9   open fount of T· and Love.
     100– 1   spake of T· and Love
     103–30   Life, infinite T· and Love.
     135– 5   watchwords are T· and Love ;
     157–13   as free in T· and Love,
     164–16   manifestation of T· and Love.
     165–21   his treasures of T· and Love.
     166– 8   T· and Love — is still with us.
     166–15   understanding of T· and Love.
     189–11   Spiritual insight of T· and Love
     205– 4   T· and Love, shining through the
     205–10   of the spirit of T· and Love
     241–28   divine T· and Love heal,
     260–28   vital functions of T· and Love.
     284–18   vindicated divine T· and Love
     285–11   hold high the banner of T· and Love,
     317– 3   When born of T· and Love,
     320–14   beckons him on to T· and Love
     333–29   exemplify the power of T· and Love.
     336–24   Part and parcel of T· and Love,
     354–25   by wisdom, T·, and Love.
     356–31   the way of T· and Love.
     371–15   more and more of T· and Love ;
     373–32   demonstration of T· and Love.
Man. 60–10   T· and Love rest the weary
      87–20   to the divine T· and Love,
Ret. 30–14   infinite energies of T· and Love,
      31–14   spontaneous motion of T· and Love,
      49– 2   advancement . . . in T· and Love ;
      50–21   adherence to divine T· and Love.
      64–25   deathless T· and Love.
      65– 2   their opinions of T· and Love
      65–10   savor of T· and Love.
      66– 1   ever-present T· and Love,
      84– 6   open fount of T· and Love.
      84–25   to the divine T· and Love,
      85–10   from the heaven of T· and Love,
      92·– 4   he healed by T· and Love.
Un.   2–23   a knowledge of T· and Love
      48–20   able to demonstrate T· and Love.
Pul.   3–12   dwellers in T· and Love,
      75– 2   spirit of T· and Love,
Rud.   3– 5   spiritual T· and Love,
       8–13   Heal through T· and Love ;
No.   7–15   rescue and refuge in T· and Love.
       8–18   commandments of Christ, — T· and Love.
      11–28   demonstration of T· and Love.
      34– 7   efficacy of T· and Love,
      40–23   It is T· and Love that cast out fear
      44–19   healing balm of T· and Love.
'02.   8–16   with tenderness, T·, and Love.
Hea. 16– 7   wealth and fame, or T· and Love?
Po.   31–15   T· and Love attest The solemn
My.   60–14   * temple of "wisdom, T·, and Love."
     114–24   divine power of T· and Love,
     129– 1   a deterrent of T· and Love,
     153– 5   power of T· and Love will fulfil
     158–27   thereafter dedicate to T· and Love.
     210– 3   minds so filled with T· and Love,

Truth

and Love
My. 232– 7   even the way of T· and Love
     245–17   voice of T· and Love be heard
     264–17   T· and Love made more practical ;
     323–12   * living witness to T· and Love,
and the Life
Ret. 36– 2   Christ as the T· and the Life,
Un.   63– 3   The Way, the T·, and the Life
'00.   7–16   Christ, the Way, the T·, and the Life.
My. 139–12   nearing the Way, the T·, and the Life,
     260–29   the Way, the T·, and the Life.
and Truth
'01. 22– 9   T· and Truth is not a compound ;
and wisdom
Mis. 391– 9   And learn that T· and wisdom
Po.   38– 8   And learn that T· and wisdom
animus of
Mis. 38–18   Science that has the animus of T·.
announcing
No.   35–24   Jesus came announcing T·,
anoints with
My. 270–27   C. S., which anoints with T·,
appearing of
My. 185– 3   for the appearing of T·,
ark of
Mis. 92–28   attempting to steady the ark of T·,
Ret. 84–16   attempting to steady the ark of T·,
armor of
Peo. 14–14   put on the whole armor of T· ;
as attested
My. 194–16   T· as attested by the Founder of
as demonstrated
No.   28–18   T·, as demonstrated by Jesus,
attribute of
Mis.   2–13   justice, the eternal attribute of T·,
auxiliaries of
Mis. 260–26   not always the auxiliaries of T·.
availability of
My. 353–15   activity and availability of T· ;
being the cure
Mis. 221–18   If error . . . T· being the cure,
believe in
My. 193–18   unite with all who believe in T·.
bestows
Rud. 10– 3   the power that T· bestows,
betrays
My. 128–24   A lack of wisdom betrays T·
birth of
My. 262–15   the birth of T·, the dawn of
bright gold of
Un.   54– 1   bright gold of T· is dimmed by
built on
Hea.   2–26   his name who built, on T·,
      11–10   superstructure is built on T· ;
can know
Un.   19–17   actuality which T· can know.
canonized
My. 268–24   T·, canonized by life and love,
casting out evils
Ret. 65–23   T·, casting out evils and healing
casts out
Mis. 68–17   error which T· casts out.
     191–17   that Christ, T·, casts out.
Cause of
Un.   5–17   promote the Cause of T·
No.   9– 4   hindrance of the Cause of T·.
cause of
My.   49–28   * labors in the cause of T·,"
challenged by
My. 233– 7   when challenged by T·,
channels of
Mis. 220–11   turn them into channels of T·.
chariot-wheels of
My. 127– 7   speed of the chariot-wheels of T·
Christ is
Mis. 180– 9   I replied ; "Christ is T·,
comes
Mis. 215– 3   T· comes into the intermediate space,
     218–16   T· comes to the rescue
'01.   1–19   T· comes from a deep sincerity
coming anew of
My. 307–19   referred to the coming anew of T·,
conception of
Ret. 83–13   mistake in his conception of T·,
confirms
Un.   36– 7   it unwittingly confirms T·,
conflict against
My. 358– 9   conflict against T· is engendered
consciousness of
My.   63–14   * expanding consciousness of T·,
controvert
Mis. 109– 6   invert, or controvert, T· ;
crucible of
Mis. 79– 3   dissolved in the crucible of T·,

Truth

crushed to earth
My. 128– 9   *T·* crushed to earth springs
currents of
Mis. 135–16   Sending forth currents of *T·*,
    157–28   the eternal currents of *T·*.
dawned
Mis. 24–12   *T·* dawned upon my sense ;
    169– 9   before *T·* dawned upon her
defeat in
My. 278–26   Victory in error is defeat in *T·*.
defense of
Mis. 110–27   dared the perilous defense of *T·*,
delightful
My. 350–26   *T·* delightful, crowned with endless
delivers
Mis. 298–21   then *T·* delivers you from
demands
Chr. 53–19   To celebrate As *T·* demands,
demands of
Mis. 201– 3   immortal demands of *T·*.
demonstrated
Mis. 251–27   will fall before *T·* demonstrated,
    334–26   substitution of *T·* demonstrated,
'02. 6– 9   Christ, *T·*, demonstrated
demonstrates
Mis. 116–26   Obeying . . . demonstrates *T·*.
    259–24   truism that *T·* demonstrates good,
Man. 92– 4   *T·* demonstrates what we affirm
My. 288– 9   it demonstrates *T·* and reflects
demonstrating
Mis. 116–22   the Word — demonstrating *T·*
demonstration of
Mis. 192– 7   to his demonstration of *T·*
    373–32   demonstration of *T·* and Love.
Ret. 75–11   and demonstration of *T·*,
No. 11–28   demonstration of *T·* and Love.
denial by
Mis. 247–32   met, . . . with a denial by *T·*.
denial of
Mis. 31– 2   malpractice is a bland denial of *T·*,
denying
Un. 25–12   denying *T·* and its demonstration
destroyed by
Mis. 37–22   sin . . . is destroyed by *T·*.
destroy it with
Ret. 55– 5   to destroy it with *T·*.
destroys
Mis. 56–21   an error . . . that *T·* destroys.
    62–19   error . . . that *T·* destroys.
    65–13   which the positive *T·* destroys ;
    105–24   *T·* destroys error.
    241–20   *T·* destroys the error that insists
My. 349– 6   state or error that *T·* destroys.
disclaim against
Mis. 174– 4   to talk and disclaim against *T·* ;
discoveries of
No. 41–23   by new discoveries of *T·*
dispensation of
My. 221– 7   the new dispensation of *T·*
divides
My. 316– 3   *T·* divides between sect and Science
divine
    (*see* **divine**)
divinity of
Mis. 102–24   destroys it with the divinity of *T·*.
effects of
Mis. 188–17   effects of *T·* on the material senses ;
My. 103–21   effects of *T·* on the health,
efficacy of
Mis. 89–30   avail himself of the efficacy of *T·*,
No. 34– 7   meaning and efficacy of *T·*
embodiment of
'00. 7–25   far from the embodiment of *T·*
energies of
Mis. 97– 4   eternal energies of *T·*,
Ret. 30–14   infinite energies of *T·* and Love,
engrounds me
Mis. 397– 9   *T·* engrounds me on the rock,
Pul. 18–18   *T·* engrounds me on the rock,
Po. 12–18   *T·* engrounds me on the rock,
epoch of
Mis. 363–31   every advancing epoch of *T·*
equipped with
Hea. 14–13   In proportion as . . . equipped with *T·*,
error and
Mis. 302–11   to discriminate between error and *T·*,
error is not
'01. 14–17   self-evident that error is not *T·* ;
error versus
Mis. 332–22   Error versus *T·* : first, a supposition ;
eternal
Mis. 182–30   eternal *T·* will be understood ;
Un. 17– 3   make the lie seem part of eternal *T·*.
    61– 2   takes hold of eternal *T·*.
No. 10–14   rests on Mind, the eternal *T·*.

Truth

eternal as
Mis. 163–23   are as eternal as *T·*,
Ret. 69–11   as real and eternal as *T·*.
ethics of
Ret. 21–27   they illustrate the ethics of *T·*.
evangel of
Mis. 251–30   flee before the evangel of *T·*
evermore of
Mis. 100–20   evermore of *T·* is triumphant.
expression of
My. 248–30   nearest the scientific expression of *T·*.
eyes of
Mis. 233–17   is still worse in the eyes of *T·*
facts of
Mis. 352– 8   able to behold the facts of *T·*
faith in
Mis. 111–18   Jesus' faith in *T·* must not exceed
falchion of
Ret. 30– 3   smite error with the falchion of *T·*.
fall short of
'01. 2–16   if some fall short of *T·*,
false to
Un. 32– 2   false to *T·* and Life.
feast of
Mis. 233– 8   the death's-head at the feast of *T·* ;
fed them with
Mis. 254– 6   love that hath fed them with *T·*,
feet of
Peo. 12–10   trampled under the feet of *T·*.
My. 228–19   The meek, who sit at the feet of *T·*,
fidelity to
Pul. 22–10   attest their fidelity to *T·*,
filled with
Mis. 93– 2   that they may be filled with *T·*.
Ret. 84–22   that they may be filled with *T·*.
My. 210– 3   keep your minds so filled with *T·*
follow
My. 4–10   We follow *T·* only as we follow truly,
following
Ret. 86–19   taking up his cross and following *T·*.
follows
My. 160– 3   and follows *T·* fearlessly.
footsteps of
Mis. 81–13   *footsteps of T· being baptized of*
Hea. 17– 1   through the footsteps of *T·*.
forces of
Un. 35–17   forces of *T·* are moral and spiritual,
foretelling
Mis. 82– 7   He who knew the foretelling *T·*,
form of
Mis. 310– 6   impersonal form of *T·*,
forthcoming
Mis. 82– 7   beheld the forthcoming *T·*,
foundation in
'01. 2–25   Only a firm foundation in *T·* can
friends to
Mis. 319–29   faith and resolve are friends to *T·* ;
full
Un. 51–23   full *T·* is found only in divine
fusion of
No. 5–26   Any contradictory fusion of *T·* with
genuine as
Un. 22–15   *Evil.* . . . A lie is as genuine as *T·*,
give utterance to
Mis. 183–19   to give utterance to *T·*.
glorious
Mis. 159–24   "O glorious *T·* ! O Mother Love !
God as
No. 30–25   would dethrone God as *T·*,
God is
Mis. 25– 9   God is *T·*, and All-in-all.
    49–30   God is *T·*, the Scriptures aver ;
Un. 35–16   But God is *T·*,
good and
Mis. 36– 4   in contradistinction to good and *T·*,
Peo. 3–16   spiritual idea of good and *T·*
good, or
Mis. 196–13   came not from Mind, good, or *T·*.
gospel of
Mis. 66–14   law and gospel of *T·* and Love
No. 12–19   preaching the gospel of *T·*,
grace and
Mis. 164–26   full of grace and *T·*,
grand
Mis. 197–31   placing his trust in this grand *T·*,
great
Mis. 47–22   This great *T·* does not destroy but
guest-chamber of
Mis. 342– 9   entering the guest-chamber of *T·*,
happifies life
My. 134–16   *T·* happifies life in the hamlet or
has become
Mis. 179–14   *T·* has become more to us,
has reappeared
No. 28–20   will know that *T·* has reappeared.

Truth

has spoken
Mis. 266– 28   Because *T·* has spoken aloud,
healing
Mis.   24–12   healing *T·* dawned upon my sense ;
heals
Mis. 241–16   *T·* heals him of the moral malady.
Hea. 18–21   Christ, *T·* heals the sick.
heart of
Ret. 75–21   strikes at the heart of *T·*.
higher sense of
Mis. 113–12   gaining a higher sense of *T·*
his
Mis. 214–14   The very conflict his *T·* brought,
horizon of
Pan.   1–18   not distant in the horizon of *T·*
idea of
    (see **idea**)
identical with
Un. 33–13   Mind that is identical with *T·*.
imbued with
Hea. 11–26   requires mind imbued with *T·*
immortal
Mis. 21–19   Spirit is immortal *T·* ;
Ret. 94–16   then, will immortal *T·* be found true,
No. 40– 7   spiritual and immortal *T·*.
Po. 70–17   Immortal *T·*,— since heaven rang,
immortality of
Mis. 163–17   faith in the immortality of *T·*.
impartation of
Ret. 48–28   scientific impartation of *T·*,
in divine Science
Un. 61–25   *T·*, in divine Science, is the
infinite
Mis.   1–12   welling up from infinite *T·*
     103–30   eternal Life, infinite *T·* and Love.
     245–27   seeking to stereotype infinite *T·*,
Hea.   4– 7   the power of infinite *T·*.
     4–14   expect infinite *T·* to mix with
Po. 29–17   *T·* infinite,— so far above
inspiration of
Peo.   7–28   discovery and the inspiration of *T·*
in thought
Mis. 399–14   Thou the *T·* in thought and deed ;
Po. 75–21   Thou the *T·* in thought and deed ;
is admitted
Ret. 54–17   if *T·* is admitted, but not understood,
is All
Un.   4– 6   This law declares that *T·* is All,
is always here
Mis. 180–10   and *T·* is always here,
is God
Un.   4– 5   *T·* is God, and in God's law.
is immortal
My. 269–30   *T·* is immortal.
is moulding
No. 20– 6   *T·* is moulding a Godlike man.
is neutralizing
Pul.   6– 1   when *T·* is neutralizing error
is not in matter
Mis. 179–14   *T·* is not in matter ;
is not lost
Peo.   5–11   *T·* is not lost in the mists of
is restful
Mis. 153– 4   *T·* is restful, and Love is triumphant.
is speaking
Mis. 277– 4   *T·* is speaking louder, clearer,
is strong
My. 229–30   *T·* is strong with destiny ;
issues of
No. 40–16   never . . . save to issues of *T·* ;
is supreme
Mis. 260–19   *T·* is supreme and omnipotent.
is the power
Mis. 259–27   *T·* is the power of God
is the real
Hea. 10–14   *T·* is the real ; error is the unreal.
     18–11   *T·* is the real ; error, the unreal.
is the tonic
Mis. 251–30   *T·* is the tonic for the sick,
is the way
'02. 10–24   Christ, *T·*, is the way.
is true
'01. 22– 1   *T·* is true, and Science is
     22–12   If *T·* is true, its opposite,
is won
Mis. 362–27   *T·* is won through Science or
knowledge of
Mis. 160–11   knowledge of *T·* and divine Love.
Ret. 86–17   growth in the knowledge of *T·*,
Un.   2–23   knowledge of *T·* and Love
knows
Un. 23– 7   and *T·* knows only such.
last appearing of
Mis. 165– 7   The last appearing of *T·* will be

Truth

law of
Mis. 208– 2   This is the law of *T·* to error,
Un.   4– 6   This law of *T·* destroys every
Rud. 10–22   His law of *T·*, when obeyed,
learned of
Po. 77–15   When we have learned of *T·*
leaven of
Mis. 39–20   with enough of the leaven of *T·* to
Life and
    (see **Life**)
Life, and Love
Mis.   5–27   perfect in God, in *T·*, Life, and Love,
     12–31   imparting, . . . *T·*, Life, and Love
Man. 16– 2   through *T·*, Life, and Love,
     19– 4   divine *T·*, Life, and Love,
     41–22   reign of divine *T·*, Life, and Love
Rud.   9–12   sense of *T·*, Life, and Love.
Hea. 15– 5   *T·*, Life, and Love, understood,
     16–23   understanding of *T·*, Life, and Love
     17–19   never . . . from *T·*, Life, and Love.
My. 134–14   *T·*, Life, and Love will never lose
     185–10   *T·*, Life, and Love are formidable,
     195–31   with grace, *T·*, Life, and Love.
     353–13   to hold guard over *T·*, Life, and Love ;
Life, . . . and Love
    (see **Life**)
life of
Peo.   9–11   bathes us in the life of *T·*
Life, . . . or Love
Mis. 67– 6   not adulterate Life, *T·*, or Love,
Life that is
My. 214– 9   demonstrating the Life that is *T·*,
light of
Mis. 320–11   light of *T·*, to cheer, guide, and
My. 241–26   * after coming to the light of *T·*,
line of
Mis. 268–16   lie in the line of *T·* ;
lips of
Mis. 51–22   * "When from the lips of *T·*
living
Mis. 115– 1   through Christ, the living *T·*,
logic of
'01.   5–25   or the logic of *T·*,
lost sight of
Mis. 179– 5   believing we have lost sight of *T·*,
love
My. 316– 3   uniting . . . those who love *T·* ;
Love and
    (see **Love**)
love of
Mis. 235–11   the light and love of *T·*.
loyalty to
My. 21–16   * deprivation in our loyalty to *T·*,
makes haste
'02.   2– 9   *T·* makes haste to meet and to
mandate of
Mis. 283–29   Science is the mandate of *T·*
manifest as
Mis. 185– 5   is made manifest as *T·*,
manifestation of
Mis. 164–16   manifestation of *T·* and Love.
Rud.   3–22   manifestation of *T·* upon the body
march of
My. 155–13   in the onward march of *T·*,
meekness and
My. 247–11   meekness and *T·* enthroned.
meets error with
My. 180–17   C. S. meets error with *T·*,
methods of
Mis. 141–12   the bonds and methods of *T·*,
might of
Mis. 52– 8   even the might of *T·*,
     100– 9   the word and might of *T·*
My.   3– 5   The divine might of *T·*
mighty
Mis. 43–27   unacquainted with the mighty *T·*
Mind is
Mis. 332– 3   this Mind is *T·*,
misconception of
Mis. 46–14   a misconception of *T·* is not
Ret. 83–16   his misconception of *T·*,
must be
No. 16– 6   made manifest, and must be *T·*.
name of
Mis. 57–21   must be told in the name of *T·*,
     59– 4   will practise . . . in the name of *T·*.
naturalness of
Mis. 200– 1   naturalness of *T·* in the mind of
nature of
'01. 31– 6   from the very nature of *T·*,
needs
No. 43– 7   theology needs *T·* to stimulate
never created error
Mis. 49–30   that *T·* never created error,

Truth

never dies
  Un. 45–22 But *T·* never dies,
never engraft
  No. 43–21 can never engraft *T·* into error.
never falters
  My. 130–19 *T·* never falters nor fails ;
"new tongue" of
  No. 44– 6 "new tongue" of *T·*,— see Mark 16 : 17.
no
  Mis. 285–29 having no *T·*, it will have no past,
no basic
  Un. 49–19 Standing in no basic *T·*,
not error
  Mis. 71–16 Law brings out *T·*, not error ;
    297–28 Trust *T·*, not error ;
  My. 239– 1 *T·*, not error ; Love, not hate.
of divine Science
  Un. 10–18 in the *T·* of divine Science,
of existence
  Mis. 182– 7 receive the *T·* of existence ;
of healing
  Rud. 9–17 Science . . . is the *T·* of healing.
of Life
  Un. 39– 2 *T·* of Life is rendered practical
omnipotence of
  Mis. 61– 9 omnipotence of *T·* over error,
    192–14 well knowing the omnipotence of *T·*.
omnipresent
  Mis. 105–18 unknown to the omnipresent *T·*.
one
  Ret. 60–28 one *T·*, Life, Love,
opposed to
  Un. 22– 6 ungodliness, which is opposed to *T·*,
    38– 6 Death, then, is error, opposed to *T·*,
opposite of
  Mis. 24–22 error, the opposite of *T·* ;
  Ret. 69– 9 the opposite of *T·*, saying,
  Un. 44–12 pretender taught the opposite of *T·*.
opposition to
  Un. 56–10 mentality in opposition to *T·*,
or Christ
  Pul. 12–23 we lay down all for *T·*, or Christ,
  My. 118–27 in which *T·*, or Christ, finds its
or Life
  Un. 62–20 *T·* or Life in divine Science
outcomes of
  Mis. 267–17 the vital outcomes of *T·*
outtalk
  '01. 16–21 was supposed to outtalk *T·*
outtalked even
  Mis. 191–25 supposed to have outtalked even *T·*,
over error
  Mis. 61– 9 omnipotence of *T·* over error,
    97– 1 it is *T·* over error ;
    321–11 triumphs of *T·* over error,
  Pul. 30–21 * power of *T·* over error,
  My. 154– 3 power of *T·* over error.
    362– 5 right over wrong, of *T·* over error.
part of
  Un. 5–26 of this wonderful part of *T·*
  No. 21– 4 one-hundredth part of *T·*,
pattern from
  Un. 53– 2 a lie takes its pattern from *T·*,
penetration of
  Un. 2–15 in the infinite penetration of *T·*,
perceive
  Mis. 179–29 perceive *T·*, and say with Mary,
person of
  Hea. 3–27 person of *T·*, the body of the
perverted
  Mis. 293–22 *T·* perverted, in belief, becomes the
pleads
  Chr. 53–55 *T·* pleads to-night :
postulate of
  '01. 21–21 predicate nor postulate of *T·*,
potency of
  Mis. 222–31 ways, means, and potency of *T·*
power and
  Mis. 334– 8 Whatever simulates power and *T·*
power of
    (*see* **power**)
practical
  Mis. 90– 6 practical *T·* saves from sin,
premises of
  Mis. 93– 9 to be the premises of *T·*,
prerogative of
  My. 218– 9 power and prerogative of *T·*
price of
  Mis. 342–27 if you pay the price of *T·*,
prism of
  Ret. 35–13 Science is the prism of *T·*,
proclaim
  My. 248–11 to proclaim *T·* so winningly

Truth

proclaims
  Mis. 277– 8 Whosoever proclaims *T·* loudest,
propositions of
  Ret. 31– 6 self-evident propositions of *T·*
question of
  Un. 5–11 to seek . . . this question of *T·*
ray of
  Mis. 333– 4 every ray of *T·*, of infinity,
rays of
  Mis. 194–14 to divide the rays of *T·*,
  '01. 12–21 to divide the rays of *T·*,
real fruits of
  Mis. 265–20 bring forth the real fruits of *T·*.
reality of
  No. 4–14 demonstrates the reality of *T·*
    5– 4 In . . . thought the reality of *T·* has
realize
  Mis. 171– 3 Jesus' first effort to realize *T·*
reappearing of
  No. 13–11 before this reappearing of *T·*,
rebukes error
  No. 43– 5 *T·* rebukes error ;
receive
  Mis. 168–14 only such . . . receive *T·*.
reception of
  My. 156–20 prepared for the reception of *T·*
reflecting
  Mis. 77–27 that man, . . . reflecting *T·*,
remedy of
  Mis. 45–15 demands the remedy of *T·*
replies
  Mis. 367–29 *T·* replies that God is too pure to
resist
  Ret. 80–14 to stir the human heart to resist *T·*,
restores
  No. 10–17 *T·* restores that lost sense,
revealed
  Mis. 302–16 in interpreting revealed *T·*,
reversing
  Un. 53– 2 lie takes its . . . by reversing *T·*.
rock of
  No. 38–10 godliness was the rock of *T·*,
said
  Mis. 363–13 *T·* said, and said from the beginning,
saith
  Mis. 109–28 Christ, *T·*, saith unto you,
sanctuary of
  Mis. 77–23 the spiritual sanctuary of *T·*,
Saviour, which is
  Mis. 164– 9 Saviour, which is *T·*, be comprehended.
Science of
  Mis. 14–29 Science of *T·* annihilates error,
  My. 353–12 the divine Science of *T·* ;
seed of
  Mis. 111–15 Leaving the seed of *T·* to its own
  My. 182–13 small sowing of the seed of *T·*,
seeds of
  Mis. 357–13 seeds of *T·* fall by the wayside,
seek
  Mis. 342–24 Seek *T·*, and pursue it.
seeker after
  Mis 89–22 for I am a seeker after *T·*.
  My. 178– 2 not mislead the seeker after *T·*.
seekers after
  Mis. 32–20 seekers after *T·* whose teacher is
    114– 2 value to all seekers after *T·*.
    156– 4 readers, and seekers after *T·*.
  Man. 17– 2 band of earnest seekers after *T·*
seekers for
  Pul. 14–15 simple seekers for *T·*,
seeking
  My. vi– 3 * who are earnestly seeking *T·* ;
seeks
  Un. 45–23 not the goal which *T·* seeks.
sense of
    (*see* **sense**)
servant of
  Pul. 6–24 seeker, and servant of *T·*,
shall reign
  My. 185– 9 till *T·* shall reign triumphant
side of
  Mis. 46–18 and acts on the side of *T·*,
  '02. 6–25 victory on the side of *T·*.
signs of
  Mis. 156–10 you will see clearly the signs of *T·*
silence
  Mis. 277–17 can the present mode . . . silence *T·*?
Spirit, and
  Mis. 363–25 Word that *is* God, Spirit, and *T·*.
Spirit is
  Un. 36–12 Thus we see that Spirit is *T·*
spirit of
    (*see* **spirit**)

Truth

Spirit, or
No. 5–15   avers that Spirit, or *T·*, cannot
spiritual
Mis. 265–21   thoroughly explaining spiritual *T·*
Ret. 54– 5   than to understand spiritual *T·*.
Rud. 3– 5   through Christ, spiritual *T·*
spirituality of
No. v–13   the pure spirituality of *T·*.
springtide of
No. 27– 7   the springtide of *T·* in C. S.
standard of
My. 180–11   that primordial standard of *T·*.
steadfast in
Mis. 172– 2   lives steadfast in *T·*.
studying
Mis. 310– 1   of studying *T·* through the senses,
substance in
Ret. 57–18   Spirit is substance in *T·*.
substance of
'01. 18–14   substance of *T·* transcends the
substitutes for
No. 5–12   substitutes for *T·* an unreal belief,
success in
Ret. 79–17   cometh no success in *T·*.
sunshine of
Mis. 343–10   Warmed by the sunshine of *T·*,
Ret. 87–26   the sunshine of *T·* beams with
supersedes error
Un. 40– 8   As *T·* supersedes error,
superstructure of
Pul. 2–30   superstructure of *T·*, reared on
supremacy of
Pul. 13– 8   conscious of the supremacy of *T·*,
table of
Mis. 106–21   fallen from this table of *T·*,
tablets of
No. 1–17   read more clearly the tablets of *T·*.
talked
Mis. 293–27   *T·* talked and not lived,
testimonial to
Pul. 77–13   * built as a testimonial to *T·*,
     78–12   * built as a testimonial to *T·*,
testimony to
Man. 48– 4   to bear testimony to *T·*
that destroys
Mis. 194–26   *T·* that destroys all error,
Ret. 61–19   *T·* that destroys error
that is Life
My. 214– 9   and the *T·* that is Life.
the rock
Pan. 15– 8   on *T·*, the rock of Christ,
the victor
Mis. 336– 1   *T·*, the victor over a lie.
things of
Mis. 280– 8   hurt not the holy things of *T·*.
this
No. 38–13   This *T·* is the rock which
through
Mis. 364– 8   to have healed, through *T·*, the sick
Man. 16– 2   through Christ, through *T·*,
Un. 41–21   not through error, but through *T·*.
to bring out
Mis. 346–25   requisite to bring out *T·*.
to error
Mis. 208– 2   This is the law of *T·* to error,
     268–11   from *T·* to error, in pursuit of
tone of
Mis. 312–25   he touched a tone of *T·*
toward
Ret. 76–10   gravitate naturally toward *T·*.
treasury of
My. 214–27   into the treasury of *T·*,
trust in
My. 171– 2   *Trust in T·, and have no*
understanding of
Mis. 166–15   the scientific understanding of *T·*
Un. 40– 9   understanding of *T·* subordinates
Hea. 16–23   can gain no understanding of *T·*,
My. 232–23   understanding of *T·* which destroys
unfit for
Mis. 268–10   He is unfit for *T·*,
unfolding of
Ret. 50–25   furtherance and unfolding of *T·*,
unity of
Mis. 109– 2   declaring the unity of *T·*,
unknown to
No. 31– 9   are unreal, *unknown* to *T·*,
utilize
Ret. 26–28   utilize *T·*, and absolutely reduce
versus error
Mis. 346–22   chapter sub-title
views of
Mis. 234– 5   speculative views of *T·*.
No. 21– 6   Jesus . . . whose views of *T·*

Truth

vineyard of
Ret. 52– 9   worker in this vineyard of *T·*.
vision of
No. 27–12   vision of *T·* is fully interpreted
voice of
     (see voice)
walks triumphantly
No. 29–24   *T·* walks triumphantly over the
way of
Mis. 356–31   or you will miss the way of *T·*
Un. 55–16   and the life-giving way of *T·*.
My. 104– 2   the strait and narrow way of *T·*.
     232– 7   even the way of *T·* and Love
will arise
'02. 9– 9   *T·* will arise in human thought
will destroy
Rud. 10–25   is an error which *T·* will destroy.
will give
Mis. 297–28   *T·* will give you all that belongs to
will soar
Mis. 277– 3   but *T·* will soar above it.
with us
My. 109–24   it is *T·* with us,
Word of
No. 22–13   meaning of the Word of *T·*,
word of
Mis. 100–17   to grasp the word of *T·*,
     334–16   without one word of *T·* in it.
words of
Mis. 99–15   take not back the words of *T·*.
     320–22   words of *T·* and Life.
you find
Un. 62–17   Destroy . . . and you find *T·*.
your
Mis. 241–14   apparently to neutralize your *T·*,

Mis. 6–16   *T·* must ultimately succeed
     7–13   for if serving Christ, *T·*,
     18– 7   law and gospel of Christ, *T·*.
     23–26   reflects good, Life, *T·*, Love
     33– 6   ministries of Christ, *T·*.
     40– 6   *T·* is as effectual in
     41–11   is purged through Christ, *T·*,
     53– 6   only as we master error with *T·*.
     57–14   *T·*, God, denounced it,
     59–26   guiding them with *T·*.
     61–27   of error, not of *T·* ;
     62–17   The theology of C. S. is *T·* ;
     63– 7   Life, *T·*, Love are the triune
     66–19   and *T·* be enthroned,
     77–18   *T·* that knows no error,
     81–21   *has not T· yet reached the shore?*
     84–25   is to live in Christ, *T·*,
     85–30   are thereby led to Christ, *T·*,
     100–10   for *T·* to deny or to destroy.
     124–14   ever-living Life, *T·*, Love :
     150–11   I am with all who are with *T·*,
     157– 3   worthy to suffer for Christ, *T·*.
     166– 5   The *T·* he has taught and spoken
     187– 2   one is God, — Life, *T·*, Love.
     188– 2   demonstrated the opposite, *T·*.
     190– 3   infinite Spirit, *T·*, Life,
     193–24   of our Lord and His Christ, *T·* ;
     195– 1   *T·* that antidotes all error.
     204– 4   *T·*, searching the heart,
     214–27   cannot . . . take error along with *T·*,
     218– 6   by reversion, as error declares *T·*.
     221– 9   and *T·* is their remedy.
     222–25   Error is more abstract than *T·*.
     225–11   power of Christ, *T·*, to heal
     264– 3   who are loyal to Christ, *T·*,
     268–32   and *T·* is used to waiting.
     274–16   *T· is fallen in the street,* — *Isa.* 59 : 14.
     281–22   always as debtors to Christ, *T·*.
     322–13   the *T·* they illustrate,
     334–23   Is matter *T·*? No !
     351–20   it says, "I am *T·*,"
     352– 4   error of regarding Life, *T·*, Love as
     354–11   error to *T·*, and evil to good,
     365– 4   which is Christ, *T·*.
     366–28   is the office of Christ, *T·*,
     368– 7   * "*T·* forever on the scaffold,
     371–23   with *T·*, to give it buoyancy.
     398–24   'T was the *T·* that made us free,
Chr. 53–41   The Way, the *T·*, the Life
Ret. 88– 6   In him, *T·* called the physical man
     93–11   *T·* is not fragmentary,
Un. 16– 2   In *T·*, such terms . . . are unheard-of
     17–15   the would-be murderer of *T·*.
     18–14   *T·*, God, says you oftenest console
     25–25   the eternal All, — Life, *T·*, Love,
     29–13   eternal, — *T·*, Life, Love.
     42–24   *T·*, defiant of error or matter,
     45– 3   as *T·* and "the woman" — *Gen.* 3 : 15.
Pul. 3– 3   Can *T·* be uncertain?

Truth

Pul.	13– 2	*T·*, represented by the Son ;
	55–28	* *T·* is the sole recognized authority.
Rud.	2–19	supreme good, Life, *T·*, Love.
	8–16	In . . . *T·* is in the minority
	8–21	This falsity shuts against him the *T·*
No.	1– 4	must be done gradually, for *T·* is as
	5– 7	To *T·* there is no error.
	5– 9	would be to make it *T·*.
	20–10	Mind, substance, Life, *T·*,
	28–16	*T·* is never understood too soon.
	30–25	*T·* has no sympathy for error.
	42–24	would make a lie the author of *T·*,
	42–24	and so make *T·* itself a
	44– 9	by some other way than *T·*
	45–27	*T·* cannot be stereotyped ;
Pan.	7– 5	demonstration that . . . *T·*, gave
	11–10	his stature in Christ, *T·*,
	12–24	Life, *T·*, Love, substance, Spirit,
	14– 7	living the divine Life, *T·*, Love,
'01.	4–26	because He is Life, *T·*, Love,
	5– 8	named in the Bible Life, *T·*, Love
	7– 5	in C. S. being Life, *T·*, Love,
	11– 8	Through this redemptive Christ, *T·*,
	15– 9	overcomes them through Christ, *T·*,
	18–26	The divine Life, *T·*, Love
	20– 6	guided by no other mind than *T·*,
	22– 5	Is *T·* material? No !
	26– 5	founded his system . . . on Christ, *T·*,
	28–22	beyond a doubt that Christ, *T·*,
	31– 4	*T·* opposed to all error,
'02.	6–23	Through Christ, *T·*,
Hea.	16–20	senses afford no evidence of *T·*
	17–20	not *T·*, and therefore are not TRUE.
Peo.	2–11	divine Principle, — Life, *T·*, Love ;
	2–24	*T·* without a lapse or error, and
Po.	40– 4	To God, to *T·*, and you !
	47– 9	Ever to *T·* and to Love
	page 70	poem
	70–10	*T·* is eternal light,
	70–13	In *T·*, the Life, the Principle of
	75– 4	'Twas the *T·* that made us free,
My.	52–13	* Mind, *T·*, Life, and Love,
	52–23	* if only . . . *T·* may be glorified.
	63–30	* had been healed by Christ, *T·*,
	104–15	healer of men, the Christ, the *T·*,
	105– 1	the words of Christ, *T·*,
	119–17	to the ascended Christ, to the *T·*
	119–23	*T·*, which destroys the false sense
	119–32	St. John found Christ, *T·* in the
	122–26	but is *T·*, even as Jesus declared ;
	122–28	Christ, *T·*, again healing the sick
	126– 1	the body of Christ, *T·* ;
	129–19	plant thy steps in Christ, *T·*,
	161–16	is saved through Christ, *T·*.
	165– 7	for the cause of Christ, *T·*,
	182– 9	Christ, *T·*, as the chief corner-stone.
	185–15	this trinity, *T·*, Life, Love,
	190–25	become students of the Christ, *T·*,
	191–17	Christ, *T·*, has come forth from
	206–17	fact that portrays Life, *T·*, Love.
	219–15	Christ, *T·*, the ever-present spiritual
	225–28	Love, *T·*, Life, Spirit, Mind,
	262–11	Christ, *T·*, never born and never
	339–22	have not the Christ, *T·*, within
	348–29	Divine Life, *T·*, Love is the
	349– 5	gained through Christ, *T·* ;

truth

abode not

Un.	32–22	The *t·* abode not in you.
Rud.	7–17	"the *t·* abode not — see *John* 8 : 44.
No.	24–23	the *t·* abode not — see *John* 8 : 44.

abode not in the

Pan.	5–14	abode not in the *t·* — *John* 8 : 44.

absolute

My.	146–19	absolute *t·* of his sayings

adopt as

My.	235–25	adopt as *t·* the above statements?

advancing

Mis.	247– 3	*proofs* of advancing *t·*

all

Mis.	49–19	spirit of Truth leads into all *t·*,
	189– 7	that leadeth into all *t·*.

allusion to

Mis.	193–17	even for his allusion to *t·* ;

and error

Un.	60– 5	he articulates *t·* and error.
Pan.	8–25	matter and Spirit, *t·* and error,

and love

My.	148– 7	God of all grace, *t·*, and love
	189–13	*t·* and love, commingling
	272– 3	justice, mercy, *t·*, and love.
	280–22	with His own *t·* and love.
	289– 3	through grace, *t·*, and love.

truth

and the life

Mis.	74–12	the *t·*, and the life," — *John* 14 : 6.
No.	12–17	the *t·*, and the life." — *John* 14 : 6.
Hea.	16–28	the *t·*, and the life. — *John* 14 : 6.
My.	257–14	the *t·*, and the life," — *John* 14 : 6.
	349–19	the *t·*, and the life." — *John* 14 : 6.

any

My.	299– 6	* have any *t·* to reveal

basic

Mis.	6–20	with that basic *t·* we conquer

beginnings of

My.	303– 1	beginnings of *t·* fell mysteriously

brightness of

Pul.	81–17	* those who seek the brightness of *t·*

clothed in

My.	349–14	at the feet of Jesus clothed in *t·*,

contemplating

Man.	94–11	should go away contemplating *t·* ;

declares the

My.	113– 9	Paul declares the *t·* of the complete

declaring the

My.	116–18	Declaring the *t·* regarding an

define

My.	235– 4	impossible as to define *t·* and not

demonstrable

Mis.	193– 7	self-evident demonstrable *t·*.
My.	260–21	fundamental and demonstrable *t·*,

demonstrate

My.	3– 6	in order to demonstrate *t·*,

demonstrated its

Mis.	70– 3	*demonstrated* its *t·* when I

demonstrates the

'01.	22– 3	whosoever demonstrates the *t·*

demonstration of the

Mis.	87–27	demonstration of the *t·*

deride

Man.	94–10	goes to hear and deride *t·*,

discovers the

Mis.	352–10	when it discovers the *t·*,

dogma and

Pul.	56–17	* dogma and *t·* could not unite,

elucidation of

'01.	31– 1	stung by a clear elucidation of *t·*,

establishing the

Mis.	177–17	great work of establishing the *t·*,

eternal

My.	54– 4	* for the sake of the eternal *t·*
	143–18	the discoverer of an eternal *t·*

evangelic

Ret.	65–20	C. S. is the pure evangelic *t·*.

every

Pul.	51–11	* Every *t·* is more or less in a state of

exclusive

No.	4–25	rests on the exclusive *t·* that

faith in

My.	292–30	faith in *t·* and faith in error.

find the

Mis.	176– 1	find the *t·* that breaks the dream of

found it

Mis.	178–23	* if I had not found it *t·*,

fountains of

Mis.	113–29	are life-giving fountains of *t·*.

full of

Mis.	147–27	full of *t·*, candor, and humanity.

give the

My.	241–29	* give the *t·* in the *Sentinel*,

glorious

No.	24–27	another and more glorious *t·*,
	35–20	The glorious *t·* of being

grace and

Mis.	292–25	C. S., full of grace and *t·*,

grand

Hea.	5–19	obscure the one grand *t·*
	9–28	shall learn this grand *t·* of being.
My.	37–20	* grand *t·* that God is the supreme

great

Mis.	28–17	and this great *t·* was shown by
	83–26	the avowal of this great *t·*,
	258– 9	the great *t·* that God is All
	321– 3	over the cradle of a great *t·*,
Pul.	39– 5	* all teach that one great *t·*,
Pan.	13–19	great *t·* that Spirit is infinite,
Peo.	12–21	Master demonstrated this great *t·*
My.	52–13	* spreading world wide of this great *t·*,
	117–20	great *t·* of God's impersonality
	279–16	this great *t·*, when understood

he speaks

Rud.	9– 5	Even the *t·* he speaks

his

My.	216–12	or his *t·* not worth a cent.

impart

My.	165–20	able to impart *t·*, health, and

in Christian Science

Mis.	195–23	to try the edge of *t·* in C. S.,
Rud.	6–12	*t·* in C. S. met a response

truth

in the Scriptures
  My. 179–20   the *t·* in the Scriptures,
is leading
  Pul. 6–21   * I feel the *t·* is leading us
it represents
  My. 24– 6   * vastness of the *t·* it represents,
justice and
  Peo. 10–14   Justice and *t·* make man free,
  My. 316–17   in behalf of common justice and *t·*
know the
  Mis. 241–22   'Ye shall know the *t·*, — *John* 8: 32.
     316– 3   to know the *t·* that makes free,
  Man. 84– 5   to know the *t·* that makes free,
  '01. 10– 1   "Ye shall know the *t·*, — *John* 8: 32.
  My. 252–11   to make one not only know the *t·*
learned the
  My. 271– 7   learned the *t·* of what I had written.
legacy of
  My. 303–22   he left his legacy of *t·*
life in
  My. 273–21   life in *t·*, is a scientific knowledge
light and
  My. 154–24   light and *t·*, emanating from the
live
  My. 160–12   a live *t·*, . . . frightens people.
lives the
  Ret. 70–26   lives the *t·* he teaches.
manifestation of the
  My. 124– 3   but by manifestation of the *t·*
     207–12   * perfect manifestation of the *t·*
meet in
  My. 120– 5   trust that you and I may meet in *t·*
mercy and
  Mis. 151–24   May mercy and *t·* go before you:
metaphysical
  My. 52– 1   * by metaphysical *t·* or C. S.,
mirrored in
  Po. 23– 9   Mirrored in *t·*, in light and joy,
new-old
  '02. 9–29   new-old *t·* that counteracts ignorance
no
  Mis. 371–20   has no *t·* to defend.
  Pan. 5–15   no *t·* [reality] in him — *John* 8: 44.
of being
  Mis. 3–23   as seen in the *t·* of being,
     182–18   beholding the *t·* of being ;
     185–17   accept the *t·* of being,
     190–24   cast out by the spiritual *t·* of being ;
     260–17   pure Mind is the *t·* of being
  Un. 55–20   and behold the *t·* of being,
  Rud. 13–11   it is not the *t·* of being,
  No. 4–11   harmony is the *t·* of being,
     35–20   The glorious *t·* of being
  Hea. 9–28   learn this grand *t·* of being.
     13–23   *t·* of being that casts out error
  My. 275–16   keenly alive to the *t·* of being
of Christian Science
  Ret. 61– 9   conscious of the *t·* of C. S.,
  No. 7–23   write the *t·* of C. S.
  My. 111– 4   nature and *t·* of C. S.
     297–23   fundamental *t·* of C. S.
of God
  No. 8– 6   utter the *t·* of God
  '00. 4–19   *t·* of God, and of man and the
of its statements
  My. 112–17   the *t·* of its statements,
of Jesus' words
  Mis. 133–29   attest to the *t·* of Jesus' words.
of Life
  Peo. 9–11   life of Truth and the *t·* of Life.
of life
  My. 235– 2   To teach the *t·* of life
     273–20   The *t·* of life, or life in truth,
of Love
  Mis. 287–11   corrects . . . with the *t·* of Love,
     337– 2   reveals the *t·* of Love,
of man
  Mis. 57–12   *t·* of man had been demonstrated,
of man's being
  My. 4– 7   the *t·* of man's being.
of Mind-healing
  Mis. 260–22   *t·* of Mind-healing uplifts
of prophecy
  Mis. 192–21   to prove the *t·* of prophecy.
of Science
  Rud. 16–12   novices, in the *t·* of Science,
of the axiom
  My. 58– 6   * proves the *t·* of the axiom,
of the Scripture
  No. 17–20   and the *t·* of the Scripture,
of the Scriptures
  My. 299–12   entire *t·* of the Scriptures,
of the soul
  Po. 73–20   the bright *t·* of the soul.

truth

of this statement
  My. 270–23   to the *t·* of this statement.
old
  My. 257– 5   new cradle of an old *t·*.
one
  '01. 16–27   commence with one *t·* told
order and
  Mis. 215–13   C. S. demands order and *t·*.
or science
  My. 107–25   classification as *t·* or science
page of
  Po. 28– 5   to write a deathless page Of *t·*,
portions of
  My. 299–12   whatever portions of *t·* may be found
practical
  Mis. 246–32   earnest seeking after practical *t·*
  Pan. 13– 2   steadfastly to its practical *t·*.
precious
  My. 62– 8   * may I not take this precious *t·*
realizes the
  Rud. 13–22   if the *healer realizes* the *t·*,
rejoiceth in the
  No. 45– 7   rejoiceth in the *t·*." — *I Cor.* 13: 6.
religious
  Pul. 51–10   * searching after religious *t·*.
saw the
  Pul. 53–26   * Whittier, . . . saw the *t·* :
scientific
  Mis. 113–19   escape . . . through scientific *t·* ;
  No. 10–13   for all scientific *t·*.
  '01. 27–27   * "Every great scientific *t·*
  My. 304–25   * "Every great scientific *t·*
search of
  Pul. 51–25   * will go there in search of *t·*,
search of the
  Pul. 46– 4   * in search of the *t·* as taught.
self-evident
  Mis. 26– 3   will be known as self-evident *t·*,
shall seem
  Un. 45– 2   this lie shall seem *t·*
sincerity and
  Mis. 175–17   bread of sincerity and *t·*." — *I Cor.* 5: 8.
speaketh the
  My. 33–18   speaketh the *t·* in his heart. — *Psal.* 15: 2.
     228–25   speaketh the *t·* in his heart." — *Psal.* 15: 2.
speaking the
  Mis. 227–23   speaking the *t·* in the heart ;
speak the
  Mis. 44– 1   Honest students speak the *t·*
     283– 3   can to advantage speak the *t·*
  My. 147–19   speak the *t·* that . . . is found able
spirit and in
  (*see* **spirit**)
spiritual
  Mis. 101– 5   and accepting spiritual *t·*,
     190–24   by the spiritual *t·* of being ;
  Ret. 79– 3   spiritual *t·* learned and loved ;
  Peo. 12–15   when imbued with the spiritual *t·*
spoke the
  My. 146– 3   that Jesus spoke the *t·*.
standard of
  My. 41–18   * maintains the perfect standard of *t·*
state
  My. vi– 4   * to state *t·* absolutely in a
substance of the
  My. 130–30   substance of the *t·* that is taught ;
such
  My. 48–21   * such *t·* as they do gain
system of
  Pul. 51– 1   * does not strike all as a system of *t·*.
tatters
  Po. 79–12   fears are foes — *t·* tatters those,
taught the
  Mis. 291–26   taught the *t·* which is energizing,
teach
  My. 235–12   and teach *t·* scientifically.
tell the
  Mis. 226–20   * when he shall tell the *t·*."
temperance and
  Mis. 288–28   temperance and *t·* are allies,
  Po. 39– 3   Temperance and *t·* in song sublime
that is Life
  My. 260– 2   in the *t·* that is Life,
this
  Un. 61–27   contrite heart soonest discerns this *t·*,
  No. 36– 5   shall know this *t·* when we awake
  Hea. 5–20   This *t·* is, that we are to work out
  Peo. 9–27   This *t·* of Deity, understood,
  My. 257– 5   This *t·* has traversed night,
thunderbolt of
  Hea. 2– 6   hurls the thunderbolt of *t·*,
tides of
  My. 149–10   the ever-flowing tides of *t·*
tone of
  My. 291–20   waken a tone of *t·* that shall

truth

to seek
Man. 94–11 he who goes to seek *t·* should
trenchant
My. 160–14 trenchant *t·* that cuts its way
triumph in
My. 134– 8 triumph in *t·*, to keep the faith
triumph to the
Po. 23–21 Give peaceful triumph to the *t·*,
understanding the
Hea. 8– 5 Understanding the *t·* regarding mind
unfolding
No. 45– 8 To hinder the unfolding *t·*,
untrammelled
'02. 2–18 with the glory of untrammelled *t·*.
uttered
Mis. 165–17 *t·* uttered and lived by Jesus,
veils the
Mis. 62– 9 Believing a lie veils the *t·*
violation of
Mis. 226–23 that from the violation of *t·*
virtue, and
Mis. 201–27 temperance, virtue, and *t·*,
waves of
Po. 8–15 Its starry hopes and its waves of *t·*.
whole
Mis. 84– 2 by speaking, the whole *t·*.
whole of
Pul. 50–26 * No . . . holds the whole of *t·*,
word of
My. 132–16 with the word of *t·*." — *Jas.* 1 : 18.
worshipper in
Mis. 152–20 meek in spirit, the worshipper in *t·*,
write
'02. 2– 5 to write *t·* first on the tablet of
you expounded
My. 59– 4 * the *t·* you expounded

Mis. 21–16 no life, *t·*, intelligence, nor
  98–27 * the *t·* would'st teach ;
  177–14 equally in earnest for the *t·*?
  241–23 *t·* shall make you free.'" — *John* 8 : 32.
  277–18 open the eyes to the *t·* of
  338–21 * If thou the *t·* wouldst teach ;
  379–17 commingled error with *t·*,
Ret. 93–19 no life, *t·*, substance, nor
Un. 22–12 to admit the *t·* of a lie.
  37– 2 "the way" and "the *t·*," — *John* 14 : 6.
'01. 10– 1 *t·* shall make you free." — *John* 8 : 32.
My. 24– 2 * *t·* which Christ Jesus revealed
  24– 2 * the *t·* which makes free
  159–21 *T·*, life, and love are the only
  177–23 direct their work in *t·*, — *Isa.* 61 : 8.
  216–10 What, then, can a man do with *t·*
  316– 1 the *t·* I have promulgated has
  323– 9 * identified yourself with the *t·*

Truth-bearers
Ret. 91– 1 and He anoints His *T·*,

Truth-filled
Peo. 5–24 therefore a *T·* mind makes

truthful
Mis. 87–26 honest, earnest, loving, and *t·*,
Un. 53– 5 be *t·* to call itself a lie ;

truthfully
Mis. 165–31 *t·* conclude that he has

truthfulness
Un. 25– 2 then I deny your *t·*.

Truth-healing
Mis. 259–22 chapter sub-title

Truth-healing's
Mis. 262– 7 clad in *T·* . . . spring dress.

Truth's
Mis. 33– 9 shadow of *T·* appearing
  208–18 divine *T·* negativing error
  261–21 by *T·* destroying error.
  267– 1 heard above *T·* voice.
  277– 9 archers aim at *T·* mouthpiece ;
  320– 5 the history of *T·* idea,
  320–24 the zenith of *T·* domain,
  321– 8 gain of *T·* idea, in C. S. ;
  386– 8 toiler tireless for *T·* new birth
Chr. 53–58 no moan, *T·* fane can dim ;
Ret. 27–15 express in feeble diction *T·* ultimate.
Un. 45–17 error's affirmative to *T·* negative.
  52–13 presents *T·* spiritual idea,
No. 30–18 *T·* knowledge of its own infinitude
Hea. 16–15 touch but the hem of *T·* garment.
Po. 49–13 toiler tireless for *T·* new birth
My. 45–32 * material type of *T·* permanence.
  118–18 of *T·* presence and power.

Truth's
My. 188–15 *T·* evangel, enunciating,
  206–10 they divide *T·* garment
  262–30 my conception of *T·* appearing.

truths
Mis. 77– 6 great *t·* asserted of the Messiah :
  169–15 *t·* they teach must be spiritually
  196–31 acceptance of the *t·* they present ;
  197– 2 these *t·* become the motive-power of
  354–16 a few *t·* tenderly told,
Ret. 27– 8 Mind-healing, like all great *t·*,
  35–11 *t·* of C. S. are not interpolations
Pul. 57–10 * the *t·* which will find emphasis
No. 9–28 * referred to general *t·* and principles
'01. 31– 8 learn and love the *t·* of C. S.
'02. 11–28 for the *t·* he said and did :
  14–16 *t·* so counter to the common convictions
My. vii– 8 * immortal *t·* testified to by Jesus
  88–23 * have found the *t·* of C. S.
  111– 1 and thus reveal *t·* which otherwise
  179–14 self-evident *t·* that cannot be lost,
  180– 4 its life-giving *t·* were preached
  181– 6 at long intervals with elementary *t·*,
  203–26 immortal *t·* in the bosom of earth
  306–13 unutterable *t·* to translate,

truth-telling
My. 130–19 with the help of *t·*.

Truth-traducers
Mis. 63– 3 It was said of old by *T·*,

try
Mis. 10– 6 whatever these *t·* to do,
  11–19 even *t·* not to expose their faults,
  32–29 slander, hate, or *t·* to injure,
  32–29 but always should *t·* to bless
  109– 5 and *t·* to reverse, invert, or controvert,
  129–19 and *t·* to push him aside ;
  171–13 "*t·* the spirits" — *I John* 4 : 1.
  195–23 *t·* the edge of truth in C. S.,
  215–30 you must not *t·* to gather the
  237– 8 serve God (or *t·* to) from fear ;
  241–12 and *t·* to make others do likewise,
  284– 2 and never *t·* to hinder others from
  325–11 and afterwards *t·* to kill him.
  353–18 Some people *t·* to tend folks,
Ret. 14–26 *t·* me, and know my — *Psal.* 139 : 23.
  83– 6 rather than *t·* to centre their
Un. 20–15 *T·* this process, dear inquirer,
  45–15 I *t·* to show its all-pervading
Pul. 83–21 * When we *t·* to praise her later works
No. 38–26 if the lips *t·* to express it.
'01. 22– 6 I do not *t·* to mix matter and Spirit,
My. 33–10 *t·* me, and know my — *Psal.* 139 : 23.
  98– 6 * its foes *t·* to prove it to be,
  163–12 I always *t·* to be just,
  276–10 *t·* to be composed and resigned

trying
Mis. 48–31 *t·* to make capital out of the
  233–14 *t·* to twist the fatal . . . force of
  277– 6 *t·* to be heard above Truth,
Man. 55–22 *t·* to practise or to teach C. S.
Ret. 24– 8 *t·* to trace all physical effects to
  58– 4 this is like *t·* to compensate for
No. 6–15 *t·* to heal on a material basis.
  41–16 *t·* to force the doors of Science
'01. 2– 7 *t·* to put into the *old* garment the
  28–19 my only apology for *t·* to follow it
Hea. 15–19 *t·* everything else besides God,
My. 82– 8 * *t·* to get away at the same

tubes
Pul. 62– 5 * substitution of *t·* of drawn brass
  62–15 * The *t·* are carefully tuned,

tubular
Pul. 58–13 * In the belfry is a set of *t·* chimes.

Tuesday
My. 38–30 * *T·*, June 12, at ten o'clock
  82–16 * sessions of the annual meeting, *T·*,
  346–17 * Concord, N. H., *T·*, April 30, 1901.

tuition
Man. 84–13 Pupil's *T·*.
  91– 8 *T·* of class instruction in the
Ret. 50– 6 for *t·* lasting barely three weeks.
  80–21 scholarship of experimental *t·*.
Rud. 14–15 *t·* only from those who were able to
  14–18 No discount on *t·* was made
  14–20 paying for their *t·* in the higher
'01. 29–30 * our *t·* for the college course."
My. 215– 8 *t·* of three hundred dollars each,
  215–12 sent me the full *t·* money.

tulip
Ret. 17–18 *t·*, magnolia, and fragrant
Po. 63– 3 *t·*, magnolia, and fragrant

tumble
Mis. 134–28 blind to its own fate, it will *t·* into
My. 200–23 will *t·* from this scheme into

tumbled
Mis. 231–21 baby has *t·*, soft as thistle-down,

tumbler-full and tumblerful
Ret. 33–15 in a *t·* of water,
Hea. 13–12 dropped into a *t·* of water a single

tumor
Mis. 313–14 without ill-humor or hyperbolic *t·*.

tumult
Pul. 3–13 ends all warfare, and bids *t·* cease,
       32–10 * wonderful *t·* in the air
No. 1–13 turn temporarily from the *t·*,
Hea. 2–3 a *t·* on earth,

tune
Mis. 395–3 out of *t·* With love and God ;
Po. 57–10 out of *t·* With love and God ;

tuned
Pul. 62–16 * The tubes are carefully *t·*,

turf
Mis. 395–17 The *t·*, whereon I tread,
Po. 26–4 The *t·* where thou hast trod
       58–2 The *t·*, whereon I tread,

turkey
Mis. 231–12 mammoth *t·* grew beautifully less.

turmoil
Po. 73–17 afar from life's *t·* its goal.

turn
Mis. 28–11 In proportion as mortals *t·* from
       52–27 to *t·* back and work out the previous
       80–22 "*t·* and overturn" — see Ezek. 21 : 27.
       84–24 *t·* one, like a weary traveller,
       98–4 should *t·* away from inharmony,
       119–10 Evil is impotent to *t·* the righteous
       124–10 We *t·*, with sickened sense, from
       133–27 I *t·* constantly to divine Love for
       138–1 until, in *t·*, their students will
       156–22 preys, and in *t·* becomes a prey.
       181–6 Principle, which in *t·* is requisite
       194–21 *t·* from matter to Spirit for healing ;
       197–5 to exhort people to *t·* from sin
       211–20 *t·* on you and rend you?
       220–11 *t·* them into channels of Truth.
       244–20 *t·* the water into wine,
       246–18 to invite its prey, then *t·* and
       292–14 causes mortals to *t·* away from
       307–2 in *t·*, they give you daily supplies.
       307–30 human thought must *t·*
       316–17 *t·* them slowly toward the haven.
       335–1 shall you *t·* away from this
       343–5 Too soon we cannot *t·* from disease
       345–21 To *t·* the popular indignation
       353–25 *t·* from the metaphor of the mill
Man. 48–20 *t·* away from personality
       67–18 *t·* their attention from the divine
Ret. 21–19 *t·* it gladly from a material,
       45–21 *t·* to him the other — Matt. 5 : 39.
Un. 23–6 God has no bastards to *t·* again
       64–17 can never *t·* back what Deity knoweth,
Pul. vii–11 *t·* backward the telescope of
       82–8 * but you could no more *t·* her
       85–5 * *t·* their hearts in gratitude to her
No. 1–12 They should then *t·* temporarily
       8–24 lest it *t·* and rend you ;
Pan. 11–12 to *t·* from clay to Soul
'02. 4–26 we are liable to *t·* from them
       11–14 each in *t·* has helped mankind,
Peo. 7–6 *t·* often from marble to model,
My. 9–8 * to *t·* in loving thankfulness
       63–17 * as friend met friend at every *t·*
       88–25 * *t·* with respect and affection.
       139–19 It was to *t·* your sense of worship
       182–26 *t·* hither with satisfied hope.
       227–13 we naturally *t·* to divine justice
       227–25 *t·* again and rend you." — Matt. 7 : 6.
       227–27 *t·* to him the other — Matt. 5 : 39.
       311–10 to *t·* the blind girl out,
       316–19 tends to *t·* back the foaming

turned
Mis. 11–29 I have *t·* the other :
       74–17 he *t·* the water into wine ;
       206–1 on which have *t·* all revolutions,
       309–10 it has *t·* many from the true
       327–1 *t·* my misnamed joys to sorrow.
       328–17 hast thou *t·* back, stumbled,
       345–31 Christianity *t·* men away from the
       380–15 in faith, *t·* to divine help,
Ret. 8–17 my cousin *t·* to me
Un. 11–5 He *t·* the water into wine,
       57–11 When Jesus *t·* and said,
Pul. 6–18 * *t·* to the 'great Physician.'

turned
Po. 9–2 *T·* to his star of idolatry.
My. 6–2 knows will be *t·* against himself.
       30–28 * hundreds had to be *t·* away,
       50–15 * *t·* steadfastly from the mortal
       54–11 * was *t·* from the door with the
       79–4 * solemn little faces *t·* upward.
       87–25 * if all the world *t·* to the new
       119–20 He *t·* to the person,
       152–1 *t·* to another form of idolatry,

turnest
Mis. 333–17 *t·* away from the divine source of

turneth
Man. 41–9 *t·* away wrath." — Prov. 15 : 1.

turning
Mis. 136–10 in *t·* aside for one hour
       198–5 *t·* away from material gods ;
       232–2 *t·* from it, in a bumper of
       329–19 *t·* up the daisies,
       333–14 are *t·* away from the
       340–7 *t·* neither to the right nor
Un. 14–18 neither shadow of *t·*." — Jas. 1 : 17.
       20–3 then *t·* it or *t·* from it.
       63–9 variableness or shadow of *t·*,
Pul. 2–11 *T·* the attention from sublunary
My. 326–20 in *t·* the hearts of the noble

turns
Mis. 101–19 *t·* to the body for evidence,
       115–23 *t·* us more unreservedly to Him
       125–27 Mother, . . . *t·* to-day to you ;
       125–27 *t·* to her dear church,
       128–1 and given a variety of *t·*,
       129–21 lens that he never *t·* on himself.
       250–27 *t·* toward want and woe,
       324–23 he departs ; then *t·* back,
       325–26 the Stranger *t·* quickly,
       351–29 *t·* it into the opposite channels.
       386–16 waking with a love that steady *t·*
Ret. 80–24 sees the door and *t·* away
No. 10–24 *t·* like the needle to the pole
'00. 11–9 *t·* mortals away from earth
'01. 26–11 *t·* away from Christ's
Po. 1–16 the bitter draft which *t·*
       49–24 waking with a love that steady *t·*
My. 346–12 * and made several *t·* about the

turquoise
Mis. 376–28 garnet, *t·*, and sapphire

turret
My. 186–8 neither dome nor *t·* tells

turreted
Pul. 24–11 * porticos and *t·* corners.

turtle
Mis. 329–24 "The voice of the *t·* — Song 2 : 12.

tutelary
'00. 12–14 *t·* divinity of Ephesus.

tutored
My. 310–6 I was privately *t·* by him.

Twain, Mark
My. 302–13 chapter sub-title

twain
Mis. 94–7 the *t·* that are one flesh,
       289–17 *t·* shall be one flesh." — Matt. 19 : 5.

Twain's, Mark
My. 303–13 Mark *T·* wit was not wasted

twelve
Mis. 29–7 prayed, not for the *t·* only,
       73–25 upon *t·* thrones, — Matt. 19 : 28.
       73–26 *t·* tribes of Israel." — Matt. 19 : 28.
       191–10 chosen you *t·*, — John 6 : 70.
       304–26 * *t·* o'clock on the birthdays of
       349–4 included about *t·* lessons,
Man. 18–13 *t·* of her students and
       35–1 Children when *T·* Years Old.
       35–2 arrived at the age of *t·* years,
       54–18 branch church for *t·* years.
       60–5 continued *t·* months each year.
Ret. 8–3 For some *t·* months,
       13–1 At the age of *t·* I was
       40–18 and weighed *t·* pounds.
       50–14 my instruction during *t·* half-days,
       90–14 one of the *t·* whom he kept near
Pul. 69–8 * cured . . . some *t·* years ago,
       81–25 * all that the *t·* have left undone.
       83–29 * crown of *t·* stars." — Rev. 12 : 1.
No. 22–25 chosen you *t·*, — John 6 : 70.
Pan. 10–15 With *t·* lessons or less,
'01. 4–5 four times three is *t·*,
       4–6 three times four is *t·*.
My. 38–13 * and was emptied in *t·*,
       38–17 * the service at half past *t·*

twelve
   My. 43–16 * *t·* stones taken from the midst of
         55–13 * *t·* of the members of the church
         55–31 * *T·* years ago . . . the corner-stone
         68–15 * built *t·* years ago,
         68–28 * There are *t·* exits and
         70– 5 * its first church only *t·* years ago,
         72–29 * first church in Boston *t·* years ago
         78– 9 * passed through the *t·* entrances
         78–28 * the half past *t·* service ;
        169– 6 Busy Bees, under *t·* years of age,
      311–15 seemed to culminate at *t·* years
      347–16 *t·* beautiful pearls that crown this
             (*see also* **numbers**)

twentieth
   Pul. vii– 6 the elders of the *t·* century,
          8–30 They belong to the *t·* century.
       22–10 I predict that in the *t·* century
       77–16 * on the *t·* day of February,
   '00.   9–20 *t·* century in the ebb and flow
   '02.   5– 4 spiritual dawn of the *t·* century
   My. 95–20 * performed in this *t·* century
        98– 3 * a *t·* of the C. S. army
      155–10 take step with the *t·* century,
      199–18 on the verge of the *t·* century,
      229–23 the *t·* century Church Manual
      248–15 sponsors for the *t·* century,
      264– 9 * the threshold of the *t·* century,
      319–25 * the *t·* of the above-named month.

twentieth-century
   My. 316–21 * "*t·* review of opinion"

twenty
   Mis. 88–13 *t·* years in the pulpit,
      242–23 having taken it *t·* years ;
   Man. 18–18 *t·* others of Mrs. Eddy's students
       62–11 up to the age of *t·* years,
       62–15 after reaching the age of *t·*.
   Ret. 24– 7 During *t·* years prior to my
   Pul. 38– 7 * these succeeding *t·* years
   My. 38–12 * in about *t·* minutes,
      321–21 * It will soon be *t·* years
      321–29 * during the past *t·* years.
      322–14 * Thanksgiving Day *t·* years ago,
      342–16 * portraits of *t·* years ago,
             (*see also* **numbers, values**)

twenty-eighth
   My. 333– 6 * *t·* day of June, 1844,

twenty-fifth
   Man. 79–21 on January *t·*, 1898,
   My. 60–29 * On the *t·* of last March

twenty-first
   My. 55–31 * the *t·* of last month,

twenty-five
   Pul. 67–15 * Founded *t·* years ago,
   My. 100–11 * It is only *t·* years,
      237– 5 What I wrote . . . *t·* years ago
             (*see also* **numbers, values**)

twenty-four
   Mis. 243– 1 if she went without it *t·* hours
   My. 359–20 * by *t·* of her students
             (*see also* **numbers**)

twenty-fourth
   Pul. 87– 3 * on the *t·* day of March,

twenty-nine
   My. 68–11 * altitude *t·* feet higher

twenty-one
   Pul. 26– 2 * *t·* inches from point to point,
             (*see also* **numbers, values**)

twenty-seven
   My. 76–28 * *t·* years ago was founded

twenty-seventh
   My. 333– 9 * died on the night of the *t·*.
      333–21 * Thursday night, the *t·* of June.

twenty-six
   Man. 18– 4 members, *t·* in number,
   Ret. 16–18 members, *t·* in number,
       44– 6 members, *t·* in number,
   Pul. 30–27 * It opened with *t·* members,
       37–28 * was founded with *t·* members,
       66– 5 * with a membership of only *t·*,
       67–27 * founded . . . with *t·* members,
       78– 4 * gold scroll, *t·* inches long,
   My. 48–14 * and *t·* years later the
       50–29 * more than *t·* years ago,
       76–30 * membership of *t·* persons.
             (*see also* **numbers**)

twenty-third
   Man. 18–12 On the *t·* day of September, 1892,
   My. 55–13 * *t·* day of September, 1892,

twenty-two
   My. 305–19 * eighth in a list of *t·*

twice
   Mis. 350– 8 The P. M. . . . Society met only *t·*.
   Man. 39–17 *t·* notified of his excommunication,
   My. 68– 7 * more than *t·* the size of the
      275–18 *t·* since I came to Massachusetts.

twice-told
   Un. 48– 2 to repeat my *t·* tale,

twig
   Mis. 264–18 * "As the *t·* is bent, the **tree's**

twilight
   Un. 61–10 *t·* and dawn of earthly vision,
   '00. 11–22 * It flooded the crimson *t·*
   My. 155–22 a dawn that knows no *t·*
      189–21 *t·* of the world's pageantry,

twin
   Po. 65–11 *t·* sister of death and of night !

twined
   Ret. 11–19 wreaths are *t·* round Plymouth Rock,
   Po. 60–16 wreaths are *t·* round Plymouth Rock,

twines
   Mis. 370–16 babe that *t·* its loving arms

twist
   Mis. 233–14 or by trying to *t·* the
   '01.   2– 8 to *t·* the fatal magnetic element of

two
   Mis. 6–32 families of one or *t·* children,
       11–30 I have but *t·* to present.
       60–17 of *t·* individual sleepers,
       89– 2 serve *t·* masters ;" — *Matt.* **6 : 24.**
      101– 9 We already have had *t·*
      168– 5 halting between *t·* opinions
      191–28 These *t·* opposite characters
      221–27 multiplication of the same *t·*
      231–16 *t·* incisors, in a big pippin,
      231–19 one, *t·*, three steps,
      241– 7 metaphysical healing on *t·* patients :
      242–23 one ounce in *t·* weeks,
      256–19 notice from one to *t·* weeks
      263– 5 These *t·* words in Scripture
      268– 3 *T·* personal queries give point
      269– 6 serve *t·* masters : — *Matt.* **6 : 24.**
      273–30 one Primary and *t·* Normal
      278–29 For *t·* years I have been gradually
      280–12 There are not *t·*,
      289– 9 of *t·* evils choose the less ;
      289–16 by the marriage contract *t·* are made **one,**
      289–20 has *divorced t·* minds in one.
      290– 1 the compact of *t·* hearts.
      290– 2 *t·* persons only, should be
      302–16 of *t·* evils the less would be
      305–18 * They are to be of *t·* kinds :
      307–12 rapid sale already of *t·* editions
      314– 6 shall elect *t·* Readers :
      318–26 *T·* points of danger beset mankind ;
      332–14 *t·* mortals, walking in the cool of the
      347–14 *T·* individuals, with all the
      347–16 Between the *t·* I stand still ;
      350–19 consideration of these *t·* topics,
      350–28 I cannot serve *t·* masters ;
      355– 3 presents *t·* opposite aspects,
      372– 8 In *t·* weeks from the date
      375–14 * I spent *t·* years in Paris,
      384– 3 When *t·* hearts meet.
   Man. 25– 6 a Treasurer, and *t·* Readers.
       61– 4 *t·* or more Sunday services
       63–16 *t·* or more churches may unite
       72–17 not more than *t·* small churches
       90–18 Not less than *t·* thorough lessons
       99– 4 as though it were *t·* States,
     111– 9 There are *t·* regular forms
   Ret. 6–18 *t·* or three years he read law
       6–22 admitted to the bar in *t·* States,
       6–26 for *t·* consecutive years.
      16– 3 *t·* ladies pushing their way
      21– 7 had a wife and *t·* children,
      43– 9 taught *t·* terms in my College.
   Un. 21– 6 mortal is not *t·* personalities,
      21– 8 yet they are not *t·* but one,
      27– 3 There are *t·* English words,
      33–24 "In the mouth of *t·* or three — *Matt.* **18 : 16.**
      49–17 There are not *t·* realities of being,
      49–17 *t·* opposite states of existence.
   Pul. 25– 3 * generated by *t·* large boilers
      27–12 * In the auditorium are *t·* rose windows
      27–17 * Beneath are *t·* small windows
      28–20 * reading is from the *t·* alternately ;
      28–26 * For the past year or *t·*
      37–19 * and one or *t·* other friends
      43– 1 *T·* combined choirs — that of First
      45–29 * read from the *t·* books by Readers.

two

Pul.	47–20	* definitions of these *t·* healing arts.
	49–13, 14	"*t·* and a half, only *t·* and a half
	67–28	* charter was obtained *t·* months later.
	75–20	* and for the day or *t·* following,
	76– 8	* *t·* alcoves are separated
	76–18	* One of the *t·* alcoves is a
	79–16	* We believe there are *t·* reasons
Rud.	14– 1	Neither can they serve *t·* masters.
No.	10– 6	*t·* largest words in the vocabulary
	17–21	If mortals could grasp these *t·* words
	23–16	Which of the *t·* is the more important
	27–18	the *t·* should not be confounded.
	36– 1	infinite as one, and not as *t·*.
	36– 2	not teach that there are *t·* deities,
Pan.	2–11	is derived from *t·* Greek words
	4–17	making *t·* creators ;
	6–19	Did one Mind, or *t·* minds,
	6–21	if *t·* minds, what becomes of
	6–23	Christian religion has at least *t·* Gods.
	8– 7	Does not the belief . . . imply *t·* Gods,
'00.	5–13	essence and source of the *t·* latter,
	12–24	St. Paul's stay in that city — over *t·* years
'01.	22–19	my text, that one and one are *t·*
	23– 1	one and *t·* are neither more nor less
	28– 1	passed through the first *t·* stages,
'02.	4–22	consider these *t·* commandments
	16– 8	gift of *t·* Christian Scientists,
Hea.	7–24	his understanding of these *t·* facts,
Peo.	9–21	serve *t·* masters." — *Matt.* 6 : 24.
Po.	36– 2	When *t·* hearts meet,
My.	6– 3	We cannot serve *t·* masters.
	32– 2	* *t·* of the most striking features
	39– 3	* at *t·* o'clock in the afternoon.
	50–24	* *t·* new members were added
	56– 4	* *t·* services were held,
	56– 7	* *t·* Sunday services
	65–12	* beyond *t·* brief explanations
	66– 5	* During the past *t·* weeks
	67–25	* begun nearly *t·* years ago,
	69–10	* *T·* large marble plates
	69–11	* on the *t·* sides of the organ.
	69–16	* *t·* on either side
	71–26	* *t·* Readers who conduct the services
	74– 4	* within *t·* or three days' ride,
	74–28	* Within *t·* weeks we have had here
	74–29	* the *t·* poles of healing,
	81–23	* wherever *t·* or more of them are met
	82–24	* facilities at the *t·* stations
	92–26	* *t·* things to be said in favor of
	123–23	"five loaves and *t·* fishes" — *Matt.* 14 : 17.
	137–15	except in one or *t·* instances,
	138–16	"serve *t·* masters." — *Matt.* 6 : 24.
	145–17	past year and *t·* months,
	165– 2	Of *t·* things fate cannot rob us ;
	171–13	at *t·* o'clock in the afternoon,
	179– 3	in *t·* distinct manuscripts.
	181–31	first *t·* years of my discovery of
	243–11	and *t·* individuals would
	243–14	*t·* students who are adequate to
	257–26	*t·* words enwrapped,
	268–14	*T·* commandments of the
	281–23	* *t·* parties to the treaty of
	318– 6	and for only *t·* of my books.
	328–18	* *t·* C. S. healers in this city.
	347– 2	His *t·* witnesses.
	356–22	serve *t·* masters : — *Matt.* 6 : 24.
		(*see also* **numbers, values**)

two-sided

Mis.	266– 4	To be *t·*, when these sides are
My.	210–20	notion that . . . should be *t·*,

two-thirds and **two thirds**

Mis.	210– 6	found out, is *t·* destroyed,
	355–14	found out is *t·* destroyed,
Peo.	12–18	we shall take in the remaining **t· t·**

tympanum

Mis.	119– 2	through the mind's *t·*,
	168– 8	"*t·* on the brain"

Tyndall

Mis.	361–15	Locke, Berkeley, *T·*, Darwin,
My.	349–10	Berkeley, *T·*, and Spencer

type

Mis.	27–29	a *t·* of spiritual substance,
	33– 9	present the *t·* and shadow of
	61– 2	*t·* and representative of verities
	88–21	* Jesus was the highest *t·* of
	91– 2	as a *t·* of the true worship,
	140– 4	must be conveyed through a *t·*
	140– 5	*t·* morally and spiritually
	140–31	*t·* of the divine Principle it reflects.
	141–11	proposed *t·* of universal Love ;
	184–29	a *t·* of physical cleanliness
	203–16	topically as *t·* and shadow,
	253–20	*t·* and shadow of this hour.
	261–21	No greater *t·* of divine Love
Ret.	2–18	printed in olden *t·* and replete with
	93–13	best spiritual *t·* of Christly method
Pul.	20–14	*t·* and shadow of the warfare between
'00.	11–28	human action, *t·*, and system.
My.	45–31	* *t·* of Truth's permanence.
	52– 7	* highest *t·* of womanhood,
	335–17	* yellow fever of the worst *t·*.

types

Mis.	91–15	*t·* of these mental conditions,
	91–17	all *t·* employed in the service of
	142–18	varying *t·* of true affection,
'00.	2– 9	three *t·* of human nature
	11–29	His *t·* of purity pierce corruption
'01.	16– 7	St. John's *t·* of sin scarcely equal

typical

Pul.	27–18	* lamps, *t·* of S. and H.
	28– 1	* *t·* of the work of Mrs. Eddy.

typified

Mis.	261–19	*t·* in the law of Moses,

typifies

Mis.	86–15	that beauty *t·* holiness,

typify

Mis.	144–15	there to *t·* the prophecy

tyrannical

Pul.	6– 4	a national or *t·* religion,
Peo.	10– 9	a *t·* prohibitory law
My.	265–20	no longer *t·* and proscriptive ;

Tyrannus

'00.	12–25	in the school of *T·*,

tyranny

Mis.	80–21	*T·* can thrive but feebly under our
	297–27	unmercifulness, *t·*, or lust.
No.	44–16	Ecclesiastical *t·* muzzled the

tyrant (*see also* **tyrant's**)

Peo.	2–22	no longer a personal *t·*

tyrant's

Po.	71–11	Feared for an hour the *t·* heel !

tyrants (*see also* **tyrants'**)

Mis.	99–11	weapon in the hands of *t·*.
My.	191– 7	Persecution is the weakness of *t·*

tyrants'

Po.	79– 6	these stones, or *t·* thrones,

U

ulceration

Mis.	243–29	*u·*, bleeding, vomiting,

ultimate

Mis.	14– 7	the origin or *u·* of good?
	68–28	* the *u·* grounds of being,
	103– 5	*u·* and predicate of being.
	116–20	*u·* of scientific research
	190– 8	nor does the material *u·* in
	257–16	immediate or *u·* death.
	286–32	at the spiritual *u·* :
	364–28	This error, carried to its *u·*,
Man.	28– 5	*u·* in annulling its Tenets
Ret.	27–15	express in feeble diction Truth's *u·*.
	69– 3	*u·* source of being ;
	70–23	scientific *u·* of this God-idea
'02.	10–18	If such is man's *u·*,
My.	6–22	Its crowning *u·* rises to
	45– 4	* in the *u·* regeneration of its

ultimate

My.	94–26	"crowning *u·*" of the church
	123– 9	as the *u·* of C. S.
	181– 6	*u·* in unsolved problems
	239–12	the *u·* of the millennium
	266–16	flux and flow . . . tends in one *u·*
	272– 8	This predicate and *u·* of
	273–13	his *u·* or spiritual sense

ultimately

Mis.	6–16	Truth must *u·* succeed
	9–13	Primarily and *u·*, they are
	26– 2	*u·* will be known as
	30– 6	despair of *u·* reaching them,
	290– 6	must *u·* break all bonds
Ret.	23– 4	must *u·* yield to the
Peo.	3– 1	lift man *u·* to the understanding
My.	270–30	will *u·* be seen to control

ultimates
  Mis. 123– 9   *u·* in a religion of pagan priests
       186–10   and *u·* in the opposite of
  Ret. 64– 1   Sin *u·* in sinner,
  My. 218–19   *u·* in what Jesus denounced,
ultimating
  Mis. 122–16   nor good *u·* in evil.
ultimatum
  Mis. 76– 7   the *u·* of C. S. ;
       79–10   man is the *u·* of perfection,
       113–18   the latter-day *u·* of evil,
       212–13   *u·* of their human sense
  Un. 43– 9   achievement of this *u·* of Science,
  My. 161–31   can triumph over their *u·*,
       273–18   *u·* of life here and hereafter
ultra
  '01. 23–16   He was *u·* ; he was a reformer ;
umpire
  Mis. 14–18   evil's *u·* and empire,
       348– 1   is well paid by the *u·*.
unable
  Mis. 168–29   * had to go away *u·* to obtain seats.
       195– 6   is *u·* to demonstrate this Science ;
       238–25   * *u·* to speak a loud word,''
  Man. 96–11   *u·* to meet the expense,
  Pul. 20– 3   they were *u·* to pay the mortgage ;
  No. 42– 5   God is not *u·* or unwilling to heal,
  Pan. 10–22   religious teachers are *u·* to effect.
  My. 41–21   * *u·* to cherish any enmity.
       74–13   * are *u·* to accompany them
       74–22   * if those outside are *u·* to believe
       336–17   * he was *u·* to make a will.
unaccountable
  My. 90– 7   * *U·*? Hardly so.
unaccustomed
  My. 86– 2   * *u·* to fine architectural effects,
unacknowledged
  Mis. 266– 9   is the *u·* servant of mankind.
  No. 45–11   spiritual lack, felt, though *u·*.
unacquainted
  Mis. 43–27   *u·* with the mighty Truth
  Ret. 86– 7   Art thou still *u·* with thyself?
unadored
  Mis. 106–24   most adorable, but most *u·*,
unadorned
  My. 83–12   * and the men go entirely *u·*.
unadulterated
  No. v–12   *u·* milk of the Word,
unambitious
  Pul. 21– 4   *u·*, impartial, universal,
unanimity
  My. 29–18   * *u·* of thought and of purpose.
       32– 1   * *u·* and repetition in unison
       65–11   * passed with both *u·* and assurance.
       173–22   with what *u·* my fellow-citizens
unanimous
  Man. 26– 8   *u·* vote of the C. S. Board
       36–22   *u·* vote of the Board of Directors
       39–14   *u·* vote of the C. S. Board
       73–16   *u·* vote of, the active members
       77– 8   decide thereupon by a *u·* vote,
       81– 2   *u·* vote of the C. S. Board
       97–10   *u·* vote of the C. S. Board
  My. 49–11   * *u·* invitation to Mrs. Eddy
unanimously
  Ret. 47–14   *u·* voted that the school be
       48–15   presented and passed *u·* :
       49–27   it was *u·* voted :
  My. 8–22   * motion was carried *u·*.
       44–18   * The motion was carried *u·*
       49–26   * it was *u·* voted that
unannounced
  Mis. 283– 1   *u·* mental practice where
unapproachable
  Mis. 377– 4   so *u·*, and yet so near
unasked
  Mis. 54–15   the sick, *u·*, are testifying thereto.
  Ret. 88–23   to enter *u·* another's pulpit,
unattractive
  Mis. 369–24   wholesome but *u·* food.
unauthorized
  Man. 50– 7   No *U·* Debating.
       66–23   *U·* Reports.
       67–10   *U·* Legal Action.
unavailable
  Ret. 92– 3   nor was his power . . . *u·*

unavailing
  Mis. 59–17   that is *u·* in divine Science.
       339–28   pour forth the *u·* tear.
  Ret. 81– 2   The *u·* tear is shed
  My. 132–32   wipes away the *u·*, tired **tear,**
       294–31   relatives shed ''the *u·* tear.''
unaware
  Ret. 71–11   People *u·* of the indications
       71–28   one who is *u·* of this attempt,
unawares
  Peo. 5–22   not entertain the angel *u·*.
unbar
  Mis. 394–16   * The gates of memory *u·* :
  Po. 57– 2   * The gates of memory *u·* :
unbarred
  Mis. 325–30   without watchers and the doors *u·* !
unbecoming
  Mis. 243–17   Boasting is *u·* a mortal's
unbelief
  Mis. 169–23   often is the foundation of *u·*
  My. 222– 9   ''Because of your *u·*'' — *Matt.* 17 : 20.
       294– 8   because of their *u·*,'' — *Matt.* 13 : 58.
unbelievers
  Ret. 13–15   a Jehovah merciless towards *u·* ;
       14– 7   to have *u·* in these dogmas
  Pul. 54–23   * He kept the *u·* away,
unbelieving
  Pul. 65–25   * whose *u·* exemplar afterward .
unbiased
  Mis. 43–13   *u·*, contemplative reading of
       226– 4   *u·* youth and the aged Christian
       235–24   *u·* by the superstitions of a
       240–23   over the fresh, *u·* thought.
  My. 96–14   * intelligent and *u·* study
       316–23   manifesting its *u·* judgment **by**
unbidden
  Mis. 396–13   My heart *u·* joins rehearse ;
  Po. 59– 5   My heart *u·* joins rehearse,
unborn
  Mis. 71–12   *influences on the u· child*
unbridled
  Ret. 71–15   Ask the *u·* mind-manipulator if **he**
  '01. 19–25   *u·* individual human will.
unbroken
  Mis. 208–13   *u·* motion of the law of divine
  Ret. 80–27   and an *u·* friendship.
  Un. 52– 5   the *u·* and eternal harmony
  Rud. 12– 3   keeps *u·* the Ten Commandments,
  Po. 2–19   thy deep silence is *u·* still.
  My. 37–24   * *u·* activity of your labors,
       200–12   chain of Christian unity, *u·*,
unburdened
  My. 192– 4   unto the possession of *u·* bliss.
uncalled
  Mis. 87–28   obsequious helpers, who, *u·* for,
uncapitalized
  Pan. 2–13   His *u·* word ''god''
uncarved
  Mis. 360– 2   Human lives are yet *u·*,
  Peo. 7–17   * With our lives *u·* before us,
unceasing
  Ret. 80–19   welling up into *u·* spiritual rise
unceasingly
  My. 47–13   * labored *u·* for the work
uncertain
  Mis. 372–21   gives no *u·* declaration
  Un. 27–10   An *egoist*, therefore, is one *u·* of
  Pul. 3– 3   Can Truth be *u·*?
  My. 231–10   in such *u·*, unfortunate investments.
       282– 9   is no *u·* ray of dawn.
unchained
  My. 201– 5   Satan is *u·* only for a season,
unchangeable
  Mis. 124–13   *u·*, all-wise, all-just,
  Un. 43– 2   perfections, unchanged and *u·*.
       61–15   Spirit and spiritual man are *u·*,
unchangeableness
  Un. 13– 9   His universal laws, His *u·*,
unchanged
  Mis. 217–15   nature of all things is *u·*,
  Ret. 82– 3   law of the chord remains *u·*,
  Un. 43– 1   perfections, *u·* and unchangeable.
unchanging
  Mis. 328–12   *u·*, unquenchable Love
  Ret. 94–24   Science is eternally one, and *u·*,

uncharitable
Mis. 129– 3 is inclined to be *u*,
211– 4 His mode is not cowardly, *u*,
227–12 Some *u* one may give it a
Man. 48– 6 *U* Publications.
48– 8 article that is *u* or impertinent

unchristian
Mis. 68–12 It is *u* to believe that pain
81– 4 all unpleasant and *u* action
89–14 it is humane, and not *u*,
266–17 chapter sub-title
372– 2 contradictory, unscientific, *u* ;
Man. 53– 7 No *U* Conduct.
Un. 37–14 Is it *u* to believe there is no
38–11 It is *u* to believe in the
Rud. 8–22 may say the *u* practitioner
12–15 because the relief is *u*
16–25 springing up among *u* students,

unchristly
Pul. 21–23 Go not into the way of the *u*,

uncivil
Mis. 295–21 as both untrue and *u*.
My. 278–25 burlesque of *u* economics.

unclasp
Mis. 120– 2 *u* the material sense of things

uncle
My. 60– 6 * remember the words of my *u*,

unclean
My. 126–27 cage of every *u* — *Rev.* 18 : 2.
211–10 the *u* spirits cried out,

uncleanness
Mis. 185–13 cleansing mortals of all *u*,

uncomfortable
Mis. 128– 2 *u* whereon to repose.

uncomforted
My. 41– 8 * proud are lonely and *u*,

uncommon
Mis. 95–18 phenomena of an *u* order,
Ret. 7– 7 * young man of *u* promise.
16–11 not an *u* occurrence
Pul. 66–19 * shown an *u* development

uncomplaining
'02. 16–16 *u* agony in the life of

uncomprehended
No. 16–15 *u*, yet forever giving forth

unconceived
'02. 5– 9 this almost *u* light

uncondemned
'01. 15– 4 Error *u* is not nullified.

unconditional
Mis. 231–14 caused *u* surrender.
Ret. 13– 5 doctrine of *u* election,

unconfined
Mis. 30–16 illustrated Life *u*,

unconquerable
'00. 10– 9 till *u* right is begun anew,

unconquered
'01. 13–20 man's fear, *u*, conquers him,

unconscious
Mis. 209–32 Love, as *u* as incapable of
211–15 is *u* of suffering.
298–26 relief from pain in *u* sleep.''
298–29 When *u* of a mistake,
Un. 25– 2 If you say that matter is *u*,
No. 36–12 Christ was *u* of matter,
Hea. 6–24 back in the *u* thought,

unconsciously
Mis. 78–18 that some people employ the . . . *u*,
152– 9 brood *u* o'er the work of
208– 9 enters *u* the human heart
212–24 If, consciously or *u*, one is
Ret. 61– 5 This fear is formed *u*
'00. 8– 6 exhales consciously and *u*
My. 22–10 * let us not be *u* blind
292–17 desire works *u* against the

unconsciousness
Mis. 298–27 through *u* one no more gains

unconstitutional
Mis. 80–16 *U* and unjust coercive

uncontaminated
Mis. 30–16 *u*, untrammelled, by matter.
110– 6 faithful affection, *u* lives.
Man. 31–11 unspotted . . . *u* with evil,

uncover
Mis. 3–32 to meet sin, and *u* it ;
114–24 *u* their methods, and stop their
210–21 to *u* and kill this lurking serpent,

uncover
Mis. 348– 8 When God bids one *u* iniquity,
My. 211– 5 too ignorant, or too wicked to *u*,
235–12 name the error, *u* it,

uncovered
Mis. 12–23 *u* and summarily dealt with
210– 2 evil, *u*, is self-destroyed.
334–28 Because I have *u* evil,
352–29 *u* before it can be destroyed,
No. 24–18 evil . . . is *u* by Science ;
24–19 evil, being thus *u*, is found out,
My. 114–11 treasures of . . . are not yet *u*

uncovering
Mis. 293– 6 This *u* and punishing of sin
343–16 *u* the secrets of sin
Ret. 30–11 as one intelligence, analyzing, *u*,

uncovers
Mis. 67–19 Justice *u* sin of every sort ;
352–10 this *u* the error and quickens the
Un. 32–27 a claim which C. S. *u*,
'02. 10– 3 *u* new ideas, unfolds spiritual
My. 126– 9 *u* and kills this mystery of iniquity
133–28 *u* my life, even as your heart has
288– 3 Love . . . *u* hidden evil.

uncremated
Peo. 8–24 *u* fossils of material systems,

unction
'00. 11–18 but the *u* of Love.

unctuous
Pan. 1–11 In *u* unison with nature,

uncultivated
My. 168– 1 *u* understanding has passed.

undefended
'01. 19–25 to subject mankind unwarned and *u*

undefiled
Mis. 98–20 that pure and *u* religion
320–28 to-day christening religion *u*,
Ret. 71–20 according to pure and *u* religion.
No. 46–16 Puritan standard of *u* religion.
My. 41–26 * "incorruptible and *u*" — *I Pet.* 1 : 4.

undemonstrable
Un. 49–23 it is *u*, without proof.

undeniable
No. 33– 3 The sacrifice . . . is *u*,
'00. 4–21 being demonstrable, they are *u* ;

under
Mis. 9– 6 passes all His flock *u*
17–16 redeems man from *u* the curse
18– 6 *u* the law and gospel of Christ,
33–17 place themselves *u* my care,
35–17 *u* your personal instruction?
35–18 if one is obliged to study *u* you,
37–11 *u* the control of God,
45–15 therefore, *u* the deific law
50–12 *u* the necessity to express
53–16 *u* difficulties the former is not
59–16 to admit that it has been lost *u*
79–31 they chance to be *u* arrest
80–21 thrive but feebly *u* our Government.
89– 9 *u* material medical treatment,
90–11 *u* circumstances exceptional,
91–13 *u* every circumstance,
117–32 follow *u* every circumstance.
118– 7 Honesty . . . *u* every circumstance,
120–15 Christian success is *u* arms,
127–22 know yourself, *u* God's direction,
129–20 to magnify *u* the lens
130–12 sweet morsel *u* your tongue,''
131–18 did not act at that By-law ;
132–13 March 18, *u* the heading,
135– 1 marching *u* whatsoever ensign,
138–27 *u* the banner of His love,
140–20 I redeemed from *u* mortgage.
157–14 *u* the shadow of His wing.
160– 2 *u* the *régime* of C. S. !
161–21 preach in public *u* that age.
185–15 no other way *u* heaven
210–22 hides itself *u* the false pretense
212–16 *u* the reign of difficulties,
222–22 *u* this new *régime* of mind-power,
229– 1 *u* certain predisposing or
231–11 *U* the skilful carving of the
272– 4 * *u* Act of 1874,
272–24 * *u* such charters, *colleges*,
274–28 rights are trodden *u* foot,
288–14 nearest right *u* the circumstances,
298– 9 *U* the same circumstances,
304–10 * *u* the care of our society.
304–18 * *u* the care of the Daughters of
311–26 I was a scribe *u* orders ;
326–16 *u* every hue of circumstances,
331–13 nestles them *u* her wings.

under

Mis.	348–23	*u·* this new *régime* of medicine,
	358– 5	will graduate *u·* divine honors,
	368–21	poison of asps is *u·* their — *Rom.* 3 : 13.
	371–24	What is *u·* the mask,
	381–21	*u·* the seal of the said Court,
	381–28	*u·* the edge of the knife,
Man.	18–15	reorganized, *u·* her jurisdiction,
	25–17	See *u·* "Deed of Trust"
	45–26	*u·* the *laws* of the *State.*
	46–20	shall not, *u·* pardonable circumstances,
	49–15	*u·* rules established by the
	69– 1	shall come *u·* a signed agreement
	72–18	*u·* one church government
	85– 8	*u·* the provisions of Article XII,
	86– 5	*u·* the personal instruction of
	86– 7	no longer *u·* the jurisdiction of
	88– 5	*u·* the auspices of Mary Baker Eddy,
	90–15	*u·* the auspices of this Board.
	91–26	*u·* Mrs. Eddy's daily conversation
	98–22	*u·* the direction of this Committee
Ret.	15–29	had been healed *u·* my preaching,
	19– 3	*u·* the paternal roof in Tilton.
	20– 9	*u·* the care of our family nurse,
	27–28	*u·* the guidance of the great Master.
	48– 3	*u·* all that was aimed at its
	53– 4	prosperous *u·* difficult circumstances,
	80–24	*u·* his compelling rod.
	84–29	place themselves *u·* his direction ;
	87–29	*u·* the care of a regular physician,
	91–19	placed themselves *u·* his care,
	91–20	*u·* the sway of his own perfect
Un.	10–28	hide from His presence *u·* their
	30– 4	This it does *u·* the delusion that
	53–19	sums done *u·* both rules
	57– 7	"*u·* the shadow of the — *Psal.* 91 : 1.
Pul.	6–20	* He went out *u·* the auspices of
	15–16	At all times and *u·* all circumstances,
	23–12	* *u·* several different aspects
	23–12	* and *u·* various names,
	23–14	* *u·* the guise of C. S.,
	26– 4	* each ray *u·* prisms which reflect
	29–20	* could, *u·* certain conditions,
	39–26	* *U·* the meadow grass.
	43– 4	* led the singing, *u·* the direction,
	46– 9	* published *u·* the title of
	66–11	* *u·* the injunction to
	69– 4	* were *u·* the instruction of
	80– 2	* ship when *u·* stress of storm
	83–14	* *u·* the black flag of oppression
	83–28	* the moon *u·* her feet, — *Rev.* 12 : 1.
	86– 8	* On the *u·* side of the cover
Rud.	17–12	agonies, and victories, *u·* which she
Pan.	14–12	for her victory *u·* arms ;
'00.	5–15	I see no other way *u·* heaven
	12–21	*U·* the influence of St. Paul's
'01.	2–23	costs a return *u·* difficulties ;
	16–23	*u·* sanction of the gown,
	20–23	The crimes committed *u·* this
	24–12	* *u·* Providence I owe my life to it."
	29–26	*u·* a tithe of my own difficulties,
	30–27	*u·* all circumstances to obey the
'02.	3–13	self-government *u·* improved laws.
Peo.	10– 6	*u·* the microscope of Mind.
	12–10	trampled *u·* the feet of Truth.
Po.	vi– 9	* *u· the date of February* 3, 1865.
	10–20	Is marching *u·* orders ;
My.	vi–22	* made over to trustees *u·* agreement
	28–18	* *u·* the consecrated leadership of
	29–20	* *u·* the dome of the great edifice
	31–31	* trained carefully *u·* one leader,
	61–26	* stood *u·* the great dome,
	104– 5	*u·* the name of this
	107– 6	general subject *u·* discussion,
	107–23	*u·* the shadow of the — *Psal.* 91 : 1.
	125–19	*u·* the auspices of the
	169– 6	*u·* twelve years of age,
	188–14	*u·*the wings of the cherubim,
	195–11	hidden *u·* an appearance of
	200– 1	*u·* the Constitution of our nation
	204–20	recommend it *u·* the circumstances.
	210–15	*u·* the shadow of the Almighty.
	212–20	impossible *u·* other conditions,
	224–32	*u·* the present persecution
	227– 9	*u·* the protection of State
	227–24	*u·* their feet, — *Matt.* 7 : 6.
	246– 6	examined *u·* its auspices
	266– 5	*u·* the warrant of the Scriptures ;
	270–16	Her life is proven *u·* trial,
	282–24	*u·* the sunlight of the law
	304– 5	*u·* Professor Dyer H. Sanborn,
	307–25	*u·* his treatment.
	316–22	*u·* Mr. Flower's able guardianship
	319–17	* have not come *u·* the observation of
	337–21	Is marching *u·* orders ;
	343–26	five churches *u·* discipline.

under

My.	354– 7	Scientists are *u·* no obligation to
	359–17	* *u·* the heading "None good but
		(*see also* **sun**)

underived

Mis.	46–16	no power *u·* from its creator.
	249–29	the *u·*, the incomparable,
	255– 6	and has no *u·* power.
Un.	39–14	Man has no *u·* power.
Hea.	9–19	not a faculty or power *u·* from
My.	202–24	*u·* glory, the divine *Esse.*

underlie

My.	93–22	* *u·* many of the practices

underlying

Mis.	169– 8	had been the *u·* cause of
Un.	50–14	to express the *u·* thought.
My.	71– 8	* *u·* spirit that built the

undermine

Mis.	43–21	If one student tries to *u·*
'00.	10–11	would *u·* the civic, social, and

undermines

Mis.	101–16	It *u·* the foundations

undermining

My.	211–26	*u·* his health, and sealing his

underneath

'02.	19–20	*u·* is a deep-settled calm.

understand

Mis.	vii– 2	* To read it well ; that is, to *u·*.
	5–23	to those only who do not *u·*
	7–27	because people do not *u·*
	30– 1	Do we really *u·* the
	33– 7	may not *u·* the illustrations
	34–14	so far as I *u·* it,
	50–19	We do believe, and *u·*
	53–22	*so that all can readily u· it?*
	53–24	difficult to make the rulers *u·*,
	54– 7	does *u·* something of what
	58–17	I must spiritually *u·* them
	59– 3	can neither *u·* nor demonstrate
	63–18	*u·* the final fact, — that God is
	65–20	those who *u·* my instructions
	75–21	assists one to *u·* C. S.
	77– 6	to *u·* those great truths
	80–30	not until it shall come to *u·*
	88–24	* who do not . . . *u·* its modes
	90– 7	will save all who *u·* it.
	94– 4	to *u·* me, or himself.
	95–15	I *u·* the impossibility of
	95–19	I clearly *u·* that no human
	96– 3	I *u·* that God is an ever-present
	99– 5	neither can you *u·*." — *see Mark* 8 : 17.
	109–26	To *u·* good, one must discern
	116–25	you profess to *u·* and love,
	130– 6	Do we yet *u·* how much better
	136–13	*u·* the necessity for my seclusion,
	141–16	I believe, — yea, I *u·*,
	159– 6	and he will *u·*
	181– 7	in order to *u·* his sonship,
	181–15	*u·* man's true birthright,
	181–17	*u·* that man is the offspring of
	197–17	to *u·* the beauty of holiness,
	197–23	does not *u·* life in, Christ.
	206–27	*u·* and obey the Way-shower,
	214–20	to *u·* the personal Jesus' labor
	214–22	need to do this even to *u·* my works,
	215–13	first *u·* the Principle
	217– 5	*u·* that Spirit cannot become less
	220–23	should *u·* with equal clearness,
	247–13	do not *u·* my statement of the
	247–15	If they did *u·* it, they could
	247–19	*u·* that Spirit controls body.
	271– 6	*u·* enough of this to keep out of
	293–15	not *u·* all your instructions ;
	311–19	As I now *u·* C. S.
	325– 4	But they *u·* not his saying.
	334–31	to *u·* this Golden Rule
	344– 6	to *u·* aught of that which leads to
	355–13	*u·* the mental state of his patient.
	356–27	to *u·* our textbook ;
	366– 4	to *u·* and demonstrate what they
Man.	16– 6	uplift faith to *u·* eternal Life,
	49– 4	all who *u·* the teachings of C. S.
	66– 2	which he does not fully *u·*,
Ret.	28– 5	*u·* the omnipresence of good
	29– 1	As I *u·* it, spiritualism is the
	36– 2	*u·* Christ as the Truth
	54– 4	to *u·* spiritual Truth.
Un.	3– 3	not ready to *u·* immortality.
	4– 1	To *u·* Him, . . . is to approach Him
	9–20	by those who fail to *u·* me,
	49– 2	I *u·* that man is as
	49– 8	The more I *u·* true humanhood,
	59–10	*u·* Christ to be the divine idea

understand

Un.	62–10	Mortals can *u·* this only as they
Pul.	30– 9	* this estimate, as I *u·*,
	69–23	* must *u·* these laws aright.
	80–15	* That we could not *u·* it might be
	85– 5	* who now, in part, *u·* her mission,
	85– 7	* those who do not *u·* it
Rud.	6–21	so far as you perceive and *u·* this
	6–26	question of how much you *u·* of
No.	6–11	as all *u·* who practise the
	11–19	more study to *u·* and demonstrate
	12– 5	to *u·* and to demonstrate God.
	16–17	Mortals do not *u·* the All ;
	19–20	A sinful sense is incompetent to *u·*
	33– 9	to *u·* and demonstrate what
'00.	6–13	can measurably *u·* C. S.,
	6–26	accept it, *u·* and practise it,
'01.	4–17	*u·* that God is personal in a
	4–18	We *u·* that God is not finite ;
	4–22	misjudge us because we *u·*
	15– 3	in order to *u·* and demonstrate
Hea.	3–22	we must *u·* in part this
	7– 5	signifies those who *u·*
	8–19	When we *u·* that God is
	16– 3	having ears, hear and *u·*.
Peo.	6–25	we should *u·* something of that
My.	13–16	I *u·* that the members of
	41–30	* *u·* how illimitable is the Love
	111–28	professionals who fail to *u·*
	135–27	you *u·* the Scripture,
	135–29	scientifically *u·* that God is
	146– 6	believe this saying because I *u·*
	151– 7	can or does *u·* this Science
	167– 8	and to *u·* what we are
	195–15	nor *u·* what is not ripening in us.
	224– 1	*u·* the importance of that demand
	242– 4	*u·* that you are so.
	253–26	We *u·* best that which begins in
	299–21	*u·* it and the law governing it,
	300–14	*u·* or aver that there is no death,
	303–19	it is essential to *u·* the
	313– 1	but is, I *u·*, a paraphrase
		(*see also* **God**)

understandable

My.	238–21	God is *u·*, knowable,

understandeth

Ret.	64–16	Man that . . . *u·* not, — *Psal.* 49 : 20.

understanding (noun)

absolute
My.	293–15	absolute *u·* of God's omnipotence,

affections and
Un.	2–26	their affections and *u·*.

all
Mis.	125–14	that passeth all *u·* ;
No.	8– 8	passeth all *u·*," — *Phil.* 4 : 7.

all-important
Peo.	13– 8	This all-important *u·*

and demonstration
Mis.	55– 4	*u·* and demonstration thereof
Man.	19– 3	*u·* and demonstration of divine Truth,

and obedience
Mis.	160–15	firmer in *u·* and obedience.

and works
'01.	21– 2	Science, *u·*, and works

belief and
Pul.	47–19	* the terms belief and *u·*,

better
Pul.	69–24	* patient may gain a better *u·*

brought to the
Mis.	3–13	divine Science, brought to the *u·*

clear
Man.	66– 4	obtain a clear *u·* of the matter,

clearer
My.	207–11	* clearer *u·* and more perfect

darkens the
Mis.	291– 6	and darkens the *u·*

divine
Mis.	40–30	requires more divine *u·* to conquer
Un.	30–10	divine *u·* takes away this belief

ears of
Mis.	301–29	stop the ears of *u·*,

elevation of the
Ret.	88–12	implies such an elevation of the *u·*

enlightened
No.	45–17	highest measure of enlightened *u·*
My.	128–17	conscience and enlightened *u·*.

enraptured
Mis.	17–18	opens to the enraptured *u·*

faith and
	(*see* **faith**)

faith with
Mis.	97–16	combines faith with *u·*,

feeble
Un.	61–19	faith and a feeble *u·* make

understanding (noun)

full
Mis.	45– 3	full *u·* that God is Mind,
My.	237– 8	has not attained the full *u·*

get
My.	60–19	* get *u·*." — *Prov.* 4 : 7.

glow and
Mis.	356– 4	with spiritual glow and *u·*.

growth and
Mis.	156–28	tests of growth and *u·*

guides the
Mis.	81–30	It . . . guides the *u·*,

her
Mis.	169–10	Truth dawned upon her *u·*,

higher
Mis.	342–11	wedded to a higher *u·* of God.
My.	51–14	* to lead us to the higher *u·* of
	246–14	higher *u·* of the absolute

highest
Mis.	146–25	highest *u·* of justice and mercy.
'01.	28–10	life up to his highest *u·*

his
Mis.	31–21	parts with his *u·* of good,
Hea.	7–23	his *u·* of these two facts,

human
	(*see* **human**)

implies
Mis.	193–32	the Hebrew of which implies *u·*.

is required
Mis.	334–25	No : *u·* is required to do this.

lack of
Mis.	195– 8	by reason of the lack of *u·*.
Rud.	10–27	It is only a lack of *u·* of the

life and
Pan.	15– 9	life and *u·* of God,

life-giving
No.	46– 8	life-giving *u·* C. S. imparts,

means, and
Ret.	48–29	to higher ways, means, and *u·*,

measure of
Pul.	84–20	* have some measure of *u·* of

misguides the
My.	153–19	Faith in . . . misguides the *u·*;

my
Mis.	25– 5	to my *u·* it is the heart of
My.	344– 2	to my *u·* of Christ

not
Ret.	54– 3	faith is belief, and not *u·* ;

of Christ
Mis.	164–20	Wisemen grew in the *u·* of Christ,
My.	344– 2	to my *u·* of Christ

of Christian Science
Un.	56–11	actual *u·* of C. S.
Pul.	22–12	approximate the *u·* of C. S.
Rud.	17– 8	true *u·* of C. S. Mind-healing
No.	38–17	approximate the *u·* of C. S.,
'01.	32–28	spirit and *u·* of C. S.

of divine Love
Mis.	125–13	rest, in the *u·* of divine Love
My.	162–28	their *u·* of divine Love.

of divine Principle
Man.	83–15	in the *u·* of divine Principle,

of God
	(*see* **God**)

of good
Mis.	31–21	parts with his *u·* of good,
	107–17	(3) the *u·* of good.

of His presence
Un.	4–10	the *u·* of His presence,

of Life
My.	273–22	spiritual *u·* of Life

of Love
My.	278–11	faith armed with the *u·* of Love,

of Mind-healing
Mis.	356–26	to the *u·* of Mind-healing ;

of mortals
Mis.	260– 4	reduced to the *u·* of mortals,

of omnipotence
My.	294–18	his conscious *u·* of omnipotence,

of Science
Un.	4–25	such an *u·* of Science,

of Spirit
Un.	50– 9	by a dominant *u·* of Spirit.

of the Science
Mis.	54–23	require an *u·* of the Science
	96–22	this *u·* of the Science of God,
	221–20	saps one's *u·* of the Science

of Truth
Mis.	166–14	*u·* of Truth and Love.
Un.	40– 9	*u·* of Truth subordinates
Hea.	16–22	gain no *u·* of Truth, Life,
My.	232–22	precede that *u·* of Truth

passeth
Mis.	133–30	peace that passeth *u·*,

patience, and
No.	8–27	power, patience, and *u·*

understanding (noun)

peace, and
  Mis. 290–18 * illumination, peace, and *u·* ; "
perfect
  Ret. 91–20 his own perfect *u·*.
praise and
  Mis. 331– 9 prayer and praise and *u·*
present
  Un. 6– 1 Our present *u·* is but
presents to the
  Pul. 6– 8 presents to the *u·*, not matter,
priceless
  Mis. 30–13 priceless *u·* of man's real
proper
  Un. 8–14 proper *u·* of the unreality of
reach the
  No. 35– 6 to reach the *u·* of this
resurrect the
  Mis. 154–16 Love to resurrect the *u·*,
scientific
  Mis. 118– 5 scientific *u·* guides man.
      166–14 scientific *u·* of Truth and Love.
small
  Un. 5– 3 rejoice in the small *u·* they have
spiritual
  (*see* **spiritual**)
that matter
  Mis. 198– 8 *u·* that matter has no sense ;
their
  Mis. 170–10 whose entrance into their *u·*
  Man. 62–21 according to their *u·*
  My. 162–28 their *u·* of divine Love.
thine own
  Mis. 298– 2 unto thine own *u·*." — *Prov.* 3 : 5.
  '01. 34–30 unto thine own *u·*. — *Prov.* 3 : 5.
this
  Mis. 96–22 this *u·* of the Science of God,
      200–31 subdued it with this *u·*.
      281–21 helplessness without this *u·*,
  Un. 40– 9 this *u·* of Truth subordinates
thorough
  Ret. 48–19 to impart a thorough *u·*
true
  Un. 1–18 closer to the true *u·* of God
     13–12 the true *u·* of Deity.
  Rud. 11–20 based on a true *u·* of God
     17– 8 The true *u·* of C. S.
uncultivated
  My. 168– 1 or of an uncultivated *u·*
upright
  Mis. 265– 6 cannot regain, . . . upright *u·*.
your
  My. 36–30 * a sign of your *u·*

  Mis. 39– 5 the *u·* of how you are healed.
     50–24 the *u·* that God is our Life,
     59–12 pray . . . with the *u·* that God *has*
    114–15 the *u·* . . . according to Christ.
    124–30 to hope, faith ; to faith, *u·* ;
    124–30 to *u·*, Love triumphant !
    169–11 With the *u·* of Scripture-meanings,
    182–19 the *u·* that man was never lost
    193–30 the *u·* of man's capabilities
    307– 6 through the *u·* of omnipresent Love !
    360–22 the divine energies, *u·*, and
  Chr. 53–15 Through *u·*, dearly sought,
  Un. 48–20 I believe . . . through the *u·*,
  '01. 34–23 abound in faith, *u·*, and good works ;
  Peo. 1–17 the *u·* that we are spiritual beings
     3– 1 the *u·* that our ideals form our
  My. 3–18 highway of hope, faith, *u·*.
    170–29 faith, *u·*, prayer, and praise
    240–14 highway of hope, faith, *u·*."

understanding (ppr.)

  Mis. 82– 4 *U·* this fact in C. S.,
     92– 2 necessity for *u·* Science,
    201–16 *U·* this, Paul took pleasure in
    333–19 to aid in *u·* and securing
  Man. 65–25 *U·* Communications.
  Ret. 54–15 admits Truth without *u·* it.
    83–28 the necessity of thoroughly *u·*
  Pul. 69–27 * *u·* and demonstrating the
  Rud. 15– 4 *u·* sufficiently the Science of
  Hea. 8– 5 *U·* the truth regarding mind and
    15– 8 By rightly *u·* the power
  My. 5–21 Him whom, *u·* even in part,
    78–31 * apparently *u·* all they heard,
    112–16 student of this book, *u·* it,
    217–26 *u·* the situation in C. S."
    248–23 The Christ mode of *u·* Life
    349–10 afford little aid in *u·*

understandingly

  Mis. 352–17 act more *u·* in destroying this
  Man. 32–19 They shall read *u·*
  No. 4– 3 and demonstrating it *u·*

understands

  Mis. 19–22 as high a basis as he *u·*,
    43– 9 student of this Science who *u·* it
    44–10 conducted by one who *u·* this Science
    52– 7 Whosoever *u·* the power of Spirit,
    85– 7 demonstrates what he *u·*.
    100–27 He *u·* this Principle, — Love.
    183–20 Who *u·* these sayings?
    243–16 in proportion as he *u·* it.
    265–12 *u·* a single rule in Science,
    269–14 Who is it that *u·*, unmistakably,
  Man. 49–11 thoroughly *u·* the practical wisdom
    52–25 what she *u·* is advantageous to this Church
    75–11 she now *u·* the financial situation
  Un. 39– 9 Who *u·* these sayings?
    40–21 to him who fully *u·* Life.
  No. 16–20 He who is All, *u·* all.
  Pan. 11–15 who *u·* not this Science.
  '01. 15–11 in proportion as one *u·* it
  Peo. 13– 5 *u·* that the Divine Being is more than
  My. 180– 3 Whosoever *u·* C. S. knows

understood

  Mis. 1–13 infinite Truth needs to be *u·*.
    4–23 specialty and . . . are not *u·*.
    5– 5 This should be *u·*.
    9– 2 through affliction rightly *u·*,
    12–19 in a manner least *u·* ;
    14–19 that good, God, *u·*, . . . destroys.
    25–12 Science, *u·*, translates matter into
    36– 3 to be *u·*, we shall classify evil
    43– 8 C. S. is not sufficiently *u·*
    53–26 readily *u·* by the children ;
    56–22 Science of Life needs only to be *u·* ;
    59– 7 divine power *u·*, as in C. S. ;
    63– 7 Our Master *u·* that Life, Truth, Love
    74– 2 noumenon and phenomenon *u·*,
    75–10 includes a rule that must be *u·*,
    92– 5 become sufficiently *u·*
    97– 2 Truth . . . that *u·*, gives man ability
    100–21 The spiritual monitor *u·* is
    101– 3 how the divine Mind is *u·*
    154–21 healing Christ . . . *u·* and glorified.
    156–17 best *u·* through the study of my
    164– 8 until it be acknowledged, *u·*,
    164–22 continue, as it shall become *u·*,
    166–18 the idea of man was not *u·*.
    169–30 * thoughts when rightly *u·*.
    172–21 spiritually *u·*, and demonstrated
    172–24 spiritually discerned, *u·*, and
    172–29 rule of Science must be *u·*
    175–19 mental healing must be *u·*.
    182–30 this eternal Truth will be *u·* ;
    190–15 When the Scripture is *u·*,
    190–16 signification of its terms will be *u·*,
    192– 9 nature of Deity and devil be *u·*.
    196–27 not through death, but Life, God *u·*.
    200– 6 *u·* omnipotence to be All-power :
    232–27 *u·* to be of God,
    233–10 if not *u·* and withstood,
    233–30 Matter must be *u·* as a
    243–20 is not generally *u·*.
    250–10 no sentiment less *u·*.
    278–12 when my motives and acts are *u·*
    286–20 recognized and *u·* in Science.
    286–26 It should be *u·* that Spirit,
    286–29 is seen, *u·*, and demonstrated
    287– 1 *u·* as the most exalted
    288–19 before it is *u·* is impossible,
    292–29 *u·* my instructions on this point
    331–31 hieroglyphics of Love, are *u·* ;
    333–32 the prophet better *u·* Him
    337–17 harmony is not *u·* unless
    337–25 *u·* the concrete character
    344–21 the Science which Paul *u·*
    346– 4 God is *u·* and illustrated.
    352–20 must be *u·* in order to
    358–20 Be it *u·* that I do not require
    359– 9 I *u·* as a child, — *I Cor.* 13 : 11.
    360–30 and this idea is *u·*,
    361–13 *u·* in startling contradiction of
    365–31 must be conscientiously *u·*
    367–10 in the proportion that Science is *u·*,
    369– 4 shall be finally *u·* ;
    379–22 a mental standpoint not *u·*,
    399–26 God is Love, and *u·*
  Man. 90–23 thoroughly discussed, and *u·* ;
  Ret. 28–25 but I have since *u·* it.
    33–24 methods of medicine, when *u·*,
    54–18 admitted, but not *u·*,
    69–19 When will it be *u·* that
    75–12 cannot be, *u·* or taught by
    81–14 so apparent as to be well *u·*.
    84– 2 sufficiently *u·* to be fully
    87–28 *u·* that Christian Scientists
  Un. 1– 4 "things hard to be *u·*," — *II Pet.* 3 : 16.

understood

Un.	6– 5	selfhood of God is *u·*,
	30–24	*u·* the meaning of the declaration
	39– 3	Eternal Life is partially *u·* ;
	48–12	best *u·* as Supreme Being,
	51– 5	neither seen, felt, heard, nor *u·*.
Pul.	14–22	the spiritual idea will be *u·*.
	16–11	God is Love, and *u·*
	54–15	* He *u·* the law perfectly,
	54–16	* as no one before him *u·* it ;
	74–20	"I think Mrs. Lathrop was not *u·*.
	74–21	intention to be thus *u·*,
Rud.	6–23	*u·* in practical demonstration.
	13–16	propositions *u·* in their Science,
No.	11–10	are to be *u·* metaphysically.
	11–14	*u·* and conscientiously introduced.
	14– 3	*u·* the Science of Mind-healing,
	20–11	When *u·*, Principle is found to be
	28–17	Truth is never *u·* too soon.
	31– 8	*u·* that disease and sin are unreal,
	34–22	atonement . . . needs to be *u·*.
Pan.	10–24	the effect of God *u·*.
	11–13	Science of being, *u·* and obeyed,
'00.	5–27	spiritual sense of the Scriptures *u·*
'01.	11–21	to be heard and *u·*.
	22–24	as if they *u·* its Principle
'02.	5–14	intelligently considered and *u·*.
	9– 8	significance of this saying is *u·*,
	12–14	This declaration of Christ, *u·*,
Hea.	9– 3	if we *u·* the Principle better
	14–24	included more than they *u·*.
	15– 5	Truth, Life, and Love, *u·*,
	16– 1	Prayer, *u·* in its spiritual sense,
	17–14	allegory of Adam, when spiritually *u·*,
	18–24	when metaphysics is *u·* ;
Peo.	4–20	three in one that can be *u·*,
	6–21	divine Principle, *u·* in part,
	9–27	This truth of Deity, *u·*,
	12– 8	When this great fact is *u·*,
Po.	76–10	God is Love, and *u·*
	79–13	truth tatters those, When *u·*.
My.	52–15	* *u·*, does bring out the perfection
	103–11	Science, until *u·*, has been persecuted
	109– 7	scientific classification is *u·*,
	112–19	is demonstrable when *u·*,
	112–20	is fully *u·* when demonstrated.
	113–26	as this Principle and rule are *u·*,
	124–29	seen of men, and spiritually *u·* ;
	135– 3	I *u·* as a child, — *I Cor.* 13 : 11.
	136– 4	cannot be fully *u·*, theoretically ;
	146– 2	It is *u·* by all Christians
	152–24	and C. S. will be *u·*.
	152–28	God, . . . when *u·* and demonstrated,
	153–24	Love, which can be *u·*,
	154– 5	Life *u·* by the practitioner
	170– 1	desirous that it should be *u·*
	178– 7	Christianity is not generally *u·*,
	225– 9	C. S. is not *u·* by the
	232–25	*u·* and recognized as the true
	238– 9	discerned, *u·*, and demonstrated.
	239– 7	ratio that C. S. is studied and *u·*,
	261–16	I *u·* as a child, — *I Cor.* 13 : 11.
	261–23	secret, *u·* by few — or by none
	264–16	the Bible better *u·*
	265–21	as *u·* in divine Science,
	271– 5	little *u·* all that I indited ;
	275–27	spiritually *u·* and demonstrated,
	279–17	*u·* in its divine metaphysics,
	298– 4	if correctly narrated and *u·*,
	302–14	It is a fact well *u·* that I
	303– 9	*u·* as following the divine Principle
	306–15	*u·* in the "new tongue." — *see Mark* 16 : 17.
	307–21	*u·* what I said better than some
	342–15	* not be *u·* that I mean weak,
	348– 7	*u·* through divine Science.
	349–12	*u·* by and divinely natural to him
	349–17	Thus the great Way-shower, . . . is *u·*,
	357–10	and this must be *u·*.

undertake

Pul.	84–18	* we shall not *u·* to speak
Rud.	8– 7	*How should I u· to demonstrate*
	16– 5	*u·* to fit students for practice
My.	231–22	unwise for her to *u·* new tasks,

undertaken

Mis.	249– 1	first *u·* by a mesmerist,
No.	4– 4	had better be *u·* in health

undertakes

Ret.	86–19	*u·* to carry his burden

undertaking

Mis.	236– 3	since *u·* the labor of
	305–13	* making the *u·* successful.
My.	61–30	* in such an immense *u·*,

undertook

Mis.	220–19	when the mental practitioner *u·* to

undeserving

My.	231– 7	also from the *u·* poor

undeveloped

No.	21–15	philosophy has an *u·* God,

undisciplined

Mis.	320–21	to dull ears and *u·* beliefs

undiscovered

My.	299–15	hitherto *u·* in the translations of

undisturbed

Ret.	23– 2	too eventful to leave me *u·*
Un.	5–12	*u·* by the frightened sense of
	62–20	*u·* by human error,
My.	68–16	* Mrs. Eddy's famous room will be *u·*.
	266–26	at that date *u·*, are now agitated,

undivided

Mis.	341– 3	an *u·* affection that leaves the
My.	353–16	to spread *u·* the Science

undo

Un.	20– 4	*u·* the statements of error by

undone

Mis.	274– 8	left *u·* might hinder the progress
Pul.	81–25	* all that the twelve have left *u·*.
My.	124–14	the *u·* waiting only your

undoubtedly

Mis.	121– 4	*U·* our Master partook of
	186–29	*u·* refers to the last Adam
Pul.	65– 7	* but is *u·* an interesting faith
My.	179– 1	*u·* the beginning of the gospel
	266–29	It is *u·* true that C. S.

undulating

Ret.	4–12	*u·* lands of three townships.

unduly

Ret.	73–23	or accuse people of being *u·* personal,

unearthed

My.	130– 6	will ere long be *u·* and punished

uneducated

My.	305– 1	(an obscure, *u·* man),

unemployed

Pul.	8– 8	*u·* in our money centres,

unenvironed

My.	122–22	spiritual idea *u·* by materiality

unequal

Mis.	195–24	is *u·* to the conflict,
No.	18–14	found *u·* to the demonstration

unequivocally

Mis.	193–11	support *u·* the proof

unerring

Mis.	3–19	God, *u·* and immortal Mind.
	22– 4	the *u·* manifesto of Mind,
	27–28	but to *u·* spiritual sense,
	93–17	supported by the *u·* Principle
	172–12	*u·* Mind measures man,
	232–24	The *u·* and fixed Principle
	293– 6	*u·* modes of divine wisdom.
	315–28	*u·* wisdom and law of God,
Man.	83–20	in conformity with the *u·* laws
Ret.	34– 2	the unmixed, *u·* source,
	56– 8	*u·* divine Principle of Science,
Un.	53–24	the immortal and *u·* Mind, God,
No.	8– 1	the Father, whose wisdom is *u·*
	39–16	in the direction that is *u·*.
My.	vi–16	* wise and *u·* counsellor.
	3–16	a persuasive animus, an *u·* impetus,
	44–29	* *u·* wisdom of your leadership,
	205–28	demonstrated by perfect rules ; it is *u·*.

unexpected

Pul.	79–17	* has shown a vitality so *u·*.
My.	26–14	quite *u·* at this juncture,
	194–21	*u·* token of your gratitude
	228– 6	I am always saying the *u·*

unexpectedly

My.	42–13	* Most *u·* to me came the call
	343– 5	* reaching an answer often *u·*

unexplained

My.	218–18	divine Principle of C. S. *u·*,
	243–21	in Concord at my *u·* call

unexplored

Mis.	xi–13	hitherto *u·* fields of Science.

unfailing

My.	62– 1	* unflinching faith and *u·* fidelity
	348–22	an actual, *u·* causation,

unfair

My.	323– 5	* answer to an *u·* criticism

unfaithful

Pul.	15–13	designate those as *u·* stewards
'02.	19– 3	console his *u·* followers

unfallen
Mis. 79–23   that perfect and *u·* likeness,
Pul. 8– 4   leaves of an ancient oak, *u·*,
Pan. 11–26   man's *u·* spiritual perfectibility.
Po. 1– 1   *u·* still thy crest !

unfaltering
Mis. 163–17   *u·* faith in the immortality of
'02. 20– 8   glorifying thy *u·* faith
My. 155– 6   *u·* faith in the prophecies,
247–29   patient, *u·* tenderness.

unfamiliar
Mis. 234–18   ventured on such *u·* ground,
347–19   A true sense not *u·*
Ret. 35– 6   men were so *u·* with the subject
My. 338–21   *u·* with his broad views

unfamiliarity
Mis. 296– 7   *u·* with the work and career

unfathomable
Mis. 323– 4   in serene azure and *u·* glory :
Ret. 57– 2   the *u·* sea of possibilities.
Un. 28–21   must be the *u·* Mind,

unfeasted
Mis. 231–10   groan for the *u·* ones.

unfeigned
Mis. 136–11   and of the faith *u·*.
My. 187–13   and of faith *u·* ;" — *I Tim.* 1 : 5.
193– 1   dedicate your temple in faith *u·*,

unfettered
Ret. 9–26   * And won, . . . her own *u·* way !

unfinited
Peo. 2–21   has been dematerialized and *u·*

unfit
Mis. 25–29   then they are bad and *u·* for man ;
195–24   and *u·* to judge in the case ;
268–10   He is *u·* for Truth,
Hea. 4–12   to bless what is *u·* to be blessed.

unfitness
Mis. 309– 8   this declares its *u·* for
Pul. 3–30   *u·* for such a spiritual animus
'01. 21–18   a manifest *u·* to criticise it
'02. 18–26   showing their *u·* to follow

unflinching
My. 61–32   * *u·* faith and unfailing fidelity

unfold
Un. 5–16   *u·* in us a higher sense of Deity ;
Pul. 84–21   * *u·* it to the comprehension of
Po. 16– 8   These vaults will *u·*
My. 110–21   *u·* in part the facts of day,

unfolded
Mis. 189– 5   as *u·* in divine Science,
Pul. 85– 9   * *u·* and demonstrated divine Love,
My. 103–13   Infinite perfection is *u·*
207–12   * truth which you have *u·*
348–19   God *u·* the way,

unfoldeth
No. 45–28   Truth . . . *u·* forever.

unfolding
Mis. 69– 5   C. S. is the *u·* of true
82–17   *u·* the endless beatitudes
83– 2   rhythmic round of *u·* bliss,
293– 4   the righteous *u·* of error
Man. 15–15   *u·* man's unity with God
Ret. 50–25   furtherance and *u·* of Truth,
Pul. 4–23   *u·* its eternal Principle.
No. 45– 8   To hinder the *u·* truth,
46–21   *u·* of this upward tendency
Po. 18– 6   *u·* a quenchless desire.
My. 3–18   *u·* the highway of hope,
4–20   Thus *u·* the true metal
216–21   your present *u·* capacity.
240–13   *u·* the highway of hope,
261–14   and in *u·* the immortal model,

unfolds
Mis. 71–16   *u·* divine Principle,
72– 5   *u·* the eternal harmonies
100–14   Science . . . *u·* infinite good,
117– 2   that *u·* its immortal Principle.
183–22   divine Science *u·* omnipotence,
218– 2   Science *u·* the fact that
218–17   *u·* the real nature of God
Chr. 53–51   same hand *u·* His power,
No. 10– 9   aggregates, amplifies, *u·*,
21–15   *u·* Himself through material modes,
37–12   *u·* the full-orbed glory
'02. 10– 3   *u·* spiritual forces,
My. 42–24   * only as infinite good *u·*
164–24   *u·* the thought most within us
183–12   *u·*, transfigures, heals.
288– 3   Love *u·* marvellous good

unforgotten
Mis. 329–12   sweet rhythm of *u·* harmonies,
Po. 34–22   O'er joys departed, *u·* love.

unfortunate
Mis. 9–12   those *u·* individuals are virtually
32–19   *u·* seekers after Truth
Ret. 20–21   My second marriage was very *u·*,
My. 231–10   uncertain, *u·* investments.
301–20   *u·* people who are committed to
332– 7   * an effort in behalf of the *u·*,

unfruitful
Mis. 151–10   He speaketh to the *u·*
311–14   impractical, *u·*, Soul-less.

unfurling
My. 232– 2   *u·* your banner to the breeze

ungodliness
Un. 22– 6   but as to the fruit of *u·*,

ungodly
Mis. 53–30   to the unspiritual, the *u·*, it is dark

ungrammatical
My. 318– 9   as *u·* as it was misleading.

unharmed
Mis. 383–13   down the dim posterns of time *u·*,
Hea. 15–10   "take up serpents" *u·*, — *Mark* 16 : 18.

unhealing
Ret. 65–30   unspiritual and *u·* religion.

unheard
Peo. 1–15   throes of thought are *u·*,

unheard-of
Un. 16– 3   *u·* contradictions, — absurdities ;

unholiness
Un. 11– 1   mountains of *u·* to shield them

uniform
Mis. ix–15   long course of years still and *u·*,
ix–16   amid the *u·* darkness of storm
265–24   My teachings are *u·*.
312– 4   Love is consistent, *u·*,
365–19   If the *u·* moral and spiritual,
Man. 55–19   proved by *u·* maintenance of
No. 19– 1   If the *u·* moral and spiritual,
My. 291–17   His public intent was *u·*,

uniformity
My. 236–15   with the sweet alacrity and *u·*

uniformly
Mis. 309– 9   The face of Jesus has *u·* been
Pul. 88– 5   *u·* kind and interesting articles
My. 112–21   because of their *u·* pure morals
309– 2   was *u·* dignified
338– 8   * *u·* held and expressed by her.

unify
'00. 11– 5   harmonize, *u·*, and unself you.

unimpeachable
My. 103– 2   Because Science is *u·*,

uninspired
Ret. 26–14   though *u·* interpreters ignorantly
My. 238–11   *U·* knowledge of the translations of

unintentionally
Mis. 40–31   *u·* harms himself or another.
Ret. 83–16   and communicates, even *u·*,

uninterrupted
Man. 60– 2   SERVICES *u·*.

uninvited
Ret. 88–21   to signify that we . . . may go, *u·*, to

Union
Ret. 21–11   throughout the war for the *U·*,
Pul. 41– 5   * From every State in the *U·*,
57– 5   * from every State in the *U·*,
Po. 78– 8   the *U·* now is one,
My. 94–22   * from every State in the *U·*
340–13   In many of the States in our *U·*

union
Mis. 42–12   by a conscious *u·* with God.
52–16   a *u·* of the affections
77–13   indissoluble bond of *u·*,
98–18   and to find strength in *u·*,
254–12   strength of *u·* grows weak
Ret. 42– 2   a blessed and spiritual *u·*,
Un. 17– 9   *u·* predestined from all eternity ;
My. 343–30   brought all back to *u·* and love

Union Chapter, Number 3
Ret. 19–12   *U· C·, N·* 3, of Royal Arch masons.
My. 330–24   *U· C·, N·* 3, of Royal Arch Masons.
335– 6   * Royal Arch Mason in "*U· C·, N· 3*,"

Union Signal, The
Pul. 79– 1   *[The U· S·, Chicago]

unique
Man.	71– 9	Mother Church *U·*.
Pul.	v– 6	THIS *u·* BOOK IS TENDERLY DEDICATED
	5– 5	read by . . . in that *u·* assembly.
	23– 5	* MOST *u·* STRUCTURE IN ANY CITY
	24– 5	* most *u·* structure in any city.
	27–29	* windows are of still more *u·* interest.
	40–18	* the *u·* and costly edifice
	61–16	* in every part of this *u·* church,
	85–26	* a beautiful and *u·* testimonial
My.	71–13	* chapter sub-title
	85–28	* absolutely *u·* in its symmetrical
	320–12	* as being a very *u·* book,
	324–25	* as entirely *u·* and original.

uniquely
Man.	104– 8	*u·* adapted to form the budding

unison
Mis.	40– 3	but this *u·* and its power
	266–23	toiling and achieving success in *u·*
Pan.	1–11	In unctuous *u·* with nature,
'00.	11–13	Music is more than sound in *u·*.
My.	29– 5	* rising in *u·* from the vast congregation,
	32– 1	* unanimity and repetition in *u·*
	78–22	* congregation singing in perfect *u·*.

unit
Mis.	65–24	They are a *u·* in restoring the
Pul.	4– 8	mathematically number one, a *u·*,

Unitarian
Pul.	28–25	* hymn-books of the *U·* churches.
My.	171–22	* on the lawn of the *U·* church
	173–29	committee of the *U·* church,

unite
Mis.	100–24	They *u·* terrestrial and celestial joys,
	110–21	We may well *u·* in thanksgiving
	142–29	I may not *u·* with you in freemasonry,
	152– 6	*u·* in the purposes of goodness.
	160– 3	Never did . . . *u·* more honestly
	311–23	to come and *u·* with The Mother Church
	371–23	but error always strives to *u·*,
Man.	35–19	can *u·* with this Church only by
	44–24	shall not *u·* with organizations which
	63–17	may *u·* in having Reading Rooms,
	94– 3	to *u·* in their attendance
	109– 4	approve candidates to *u·* with this Church.
Ret.	14–12	never could I *u·* with the church, if
Un.	43–20	*u·* the influence of their own thoughts
Pul.	15–20	*u·* all interests in the one divinity.
	21–10	Who will *u·* with me in this
	22– 5	rejoicing that we *u·* in love,
	30– 5	* to *u·* with churches already established
	30–12	* and to *u·* in communion
	56–18	* dogma and truth could not *u·*,
No.	44–21	will again *u·* Church and State,
'02.	11–29	Jew and Christian can *u·* in doctrine
Po.	11– 2	*U·* your battle-plan ;
My.	131– 7	we *u·* in giving thanks.
	193–18	*u·* with all who believe in Truth.
	206– 1	would *u·* dead matter with
	207– 9	* *u·* in loving greetings to you,
	275–28	*u·* in one *Te Deum* of praise.
	283–21	*u·* harmoniously on the basis of
	285–14	*u·* with us in the grand object
	301–10	*u·* as brethren in one prayer :
	338– 2	*U·* your battle-plan ;
	360–18	*u·* with those in your church
	362–22	* will *u·* the churches and societies

united
Ret.	19– 1	I was *u·* to my first husband,
	90–13	on their *u·* pilgrimages.
Pul.	21–18	*u·* to only that which
Pan.	13–14	churches are *u·* in purpose,
'02.	12–25	before making another *u·* effort
My.	7– 8	before making another *u·* effort
	18–22	churches are *u·* in purpose,
	50– 6	* *u·* themselves into a little band
	195–25	*u·* efforts to build an edifice
	333–27	* to whom he had been *u·*

unitedly
My.	362–16	* confer harmoniously and *u·*

United States
Mis.	305–31	* the first President of the *U· S·*,
Man.	27– 5	The manager . . . in the *U· S·*
	60–12	In the *U· S·* there shall be
	94–18	shall lecture in the *U· S·*,
	97– 8	*U· S·*, Canada, Great Britain
	98–26	in each State of the *U· S·*
Ret.	6–20	afterwards President of the *U· S·* ;
Pul.	44–25	* from all parts of the *U· S·*
	63– 5	* THROUGHOUT THE *U· S·*.
	64– 8	* from all parts of the *U· S·*.
	67–18	* majority of whom are in the *U· S·*,

United States
Pul.	68–22	* church edifices in the *U· S·*
	71–21	* thousands throughout the *U· S·*
Pan.	14–28	war between *U· S·* and Spain
'00.	7– 2	From that year the *U· S·*
	10–26	first lieutenant of the *U· S·* infantry
'02.	2–12	religion in the *U· S·* has
	3– 7	the President of the *U· S·*
Po.	vi–21	slavery in the *U· S·*."
	page 10	poem
My.	65– 5	* largest ever held in the *U· S·*
	92– 1	* town and city of the *U· S·*
	96–29	* from all parts of the *U· S·*.
	112–30	the President of the *U· S·*,
	128– 7	Constitution of the *U· S·*,
	182– 3	over any other city in the *U· S·*.
	222–22	Constitution of the *U· S·*
	227– 9	protection of State or *U· S·*
	250–19	churches in the *U· S·* and Canada.
	277– 4	between the *U· S·* and Spain
	278– 4	by the intervention of the *U· S·*,
	290– 2	of New England and the *U· S·*.
	292–14	of every sect in the *U· S·*
	309– 8	afterwards President of the *U· S·*,
	337– 2	poem

United States Circuit Court
Mis.	300–22	record of theft in the *U· S· C· C·*.
	380–27	was filed in the *U· S· C· C·*

United States Marshall
Ret.	21–12	was appointed *U· S· M·*

United States Tubular Bell Company
Pul.	61–27	* *U· S· T· B· C·*, of Methuen, Mass.,

unites
Mis.	205–24	*u·* all periods in the divine design.
Pul.	6– 7	*u·* Science to Christianity.
'02.	12– 9	Jew *u·* with the Christian idea
	12–12	*u·* with the Jew's belief in one God,
Peo.	2– 9	*u·* Science and Christianity,
My.	167– 6	and *u·* us to one another.
	204– 9	C. S. *u·* its true followers

uniting
Man.	15– 1	*To be signed by those u· with The*
Ret.	49–25	*u·* them in one common brotherhood.
Pul.	30–11	* ceremonial of *u·* is to sign a
	30–14	* by *u·* in silent prayer.
My.	279–10	*u·* all periods in the design of
	291– 6	a *u·* of breaches soon to widen,
	291–11	*u·* the interests of all people ;
	316– 2	*u·* . . . those who love Truth

unity
among brethren
My.	274–24	*u·* among brethren, and love to God

and consistency
'01.	26– 1	*u·* and consistency of Jesus' theory

and harmony
My.	270–31	religion and art in *u·* and harmony.

and love
My.	6–17	your progress, *u·*, and love.

and power
My.	162– 6	*u·* and power are not in atom

and progress
My.	123– 1	Our *u·* and progress are proverbial,

and the purity
'00.	13– 1	*u·* and the purity of the church.

any
My.	306– 5	any *u·* that may exist between

bond of
Pul.	22– 3	one bond of *u·*, one nucleus

Christian
My.	200–11	The chain of Christian *u·*, unbroken,

commemorate in
'01.	1–10	you meet to commemorate in *u·*

communicants in
'00.	1–13	sixteen thousand communicants in *u·*,

eternal
Mis.	77–11	eternal *u·* of man and God,

final
Peo.	1– 7	final *u·* between man and God.

fourfold
My.	199–20	of fourfold *u·* between the churches of

in Christian Science
My.	251–28	namely, the *u·* in C. S.

individual
Man.	70–19	on individual *u·* and action

inherent
My.	262– 3	inherent *u·* with divine Love,

is divine might
Mis.	138–19	*u·* is divine might,

its
Mis.	307–16	as to Christianity and its *u·*

love and
My.	39–28	* our own growth in love and *u·*
	205–15	Love and *u·* are hieroglyphs

unity

man's
Mis. 196–18 man's *u·* with his Maker,
Man. 15–16 unfolding man's *u·* with God
Un. 41–16 man's *u·* with his Maker
meet in
Mis. 147– 7 Do you meet in *u·*,
mere
Mis. 80– 4 more than can be gained by mere *u·*
moral
Un. 19–14 would be the end of infinite moral *u·*.
of action
My. 212–18 there would be *u·* of action.
of doctrine
Ret. 15–20 if not in full *u·* of doctrine.
of eternal Love
Mis. 286–10 the *u·* of eternal Love.
of faith
My. 170–28 *u·* of faith, understanding,
of God
Mis. 266–16 inseparable from the *u·* of God.
369–10 strong in the *u·* of God and man.
'02. 9–18 *u·* of God and man is not the dream
of good
Mis. 135–19 noble offering to the *u·* of good,
319– 2 true sense of the *u·* of good
366–21 evil insists on the *u·* of good and evil
Ret. 76–19 *u·* of good and bond of perfectness.
No. 38–16 the infinity and *u·* of good.
of man
Un. 5–24 marvellous *u·* of man with God
of Mind
Peo. 13–11 *u·* of Mind and oneness of Principle.
of Spirit
Mis. 198– 4 at this point of *u·* of Spirit,
My. 167– 8 what we are in the *u·* of Spirit
of spirit
Mis. 145–21 visible *u·* of spirit remains,
Pul. 22–18 there will be *u·* of spirit,
of thought
My. 24–12 * rejoice in the *u·* of thought
of Truth
Mis. 109– 1 declaring the *u·* of Truth,
order and
Ret. 10–17 was spiritual order and *u·*.
perfect
Mis. 21– 4 It goes on in perfect *u·*
preserve
Mis. 131–10 Christian Scientists preserve *u·*,
prevailed
Mis. 140–16 *U·* prevailed, till mortal man
Principle of
Mis. 117–14 Love is the Principle of *u·*,
question of
My. 236–17 seals the question of *u·*,
rests on
Ret. 75–19 excludes opposites, and rests on *u·*.
scientific
My. 246–14 absolute scientific *u·* which
sense of
Pul. 4–10 positive sense of *u·* with
spiritual
Mis. 358–32 higher spiritual *u·* is won,
My. 243–22 your spiritual *u·* with
suppositional
Mis. 217–20 suppositional *u·* and personality,
this
My. 164–27 This *u·* is reserved wisdom
195–29 grant that this *u·* remain,
trinity in
Rud. 4– 2 are this trinity in *u·*,
No. 1–21 This trinity in *u·*,
Hea. 3–25 a trinity in *u·*;
with churches
Pul. 21–26 Our *u·* with churches of other
with God
Mis. 181– 7 his sonship, or *u·* with God,
Man. 15–16 unfolding man's *u·* with God
with Rome
Pul. 65– 5 * In inviting . . . to *u·* with Rome,

Mis. 138–17 I once thought that in *u·* was
185– 1 man in *u·* with . . . his Maker.
264–10 *U·* is the essential nature of C. S.
Ret. 64– 4 for such is the *u·* of evil;
Un. 54–15 a *u·* which sin recognizes as
'02. 1– 5 increase in number, *u·*, steadfastness.
My. 162– 9 *U·* is spiritual cooperation.
164–22 *u·*, the bond of perfectness,
164–24 *u·*, which unfolds the thought

universal

Man. 19– 6 Church *U·* and Triumphant
Mis. 29– 6 touches *u·* humanity.
55– 9 *u·* claim of evil that seeks the
99–28 health, holiness, *u·* harmony,
102–12 He is *u·* and primitive.

universal

Mis. 134–19 the reign of *u·* harmony,
141–11 proposed type of *u·* Love;
144–31 *u·* dawn shall break upon
150–25 God is *u·*; confined to no spot,
150–29 Principle, with its *u·* manifestation,
155–30 to contemplate the *u·* charge
186–14 He is the *u·* Father and Mother
208– 8 the *u·* law of God has no
213–28 God's *u·* kingdom will appear,
252–18 C. S. . . . is *u·*.
259–29 the *u·*, intelligent Christ-idea
288–21 To reckon the *u·* cost and gain,
290–28 from individual as from *u·* love:
318– 3 *u·* brotherhood of man
365–14 *u·* need of better health
383– 4 *u·* approval and support of
Un. 6–23 the assertion of *u·* salvation
13– 9 His *u·* laws, His unchangeableness,
26–18 can it be . . . *chance* and *change* are *u·*
Pul. 21– 4 unambitious, impartial, *u·*,
Rud. 1– 4 Principle and rule of *u·* harmony.
No. 8– 2 and whose love is *u·*.
18–11 *u·* need of better health and
Pan. 3–24 * Pan stood for "*u·* nature
12– 5 * Spirit, is ever in *u·* nature."
'01. 13–25 hence the hope of *u·* salvation.
23–30 * by the operations of the *u·* mind,
31– 5 all error, specific or *u·*.
Peo. 2–10 we learn that God, good, is *u·*,
2–25 Love *u·*, infinite, eternal.
Po. 1– 9 far the *u·* fiat ran,
My. 8–13 * expressed the *u·* voice of
37–15 * before the gaze of *u·* humanity.
64–25 * in the *u·* temple of Spirit,
141–29 communion *u·* and divine.
165–18 identifies man with *u·* good.
181–19 the *u·* equity of Christianity.
186– 1 refuge in mountains, and good *u·*.
226– 9 an effect of one *u·* cause,
245– 3 demand for this *u·* benefice
247– 2 inalienable, *u·* rights of men.
248–15 reaching deep down into the *u·*
248–28 to challenge *u·* indifference,
254–23 inalienable, *u·* rights of men.
265–21 divine Love, impartial and *u·*,
275– 2 chapter sub-title
275– 3 and does produce *u·* fellowship.
280– 9 * the establishment of a *u·*, loving
291–12 it ended with a *u·* good
301–18 There is a *u·* insanity which
348– 5 the offspring of a *u·* cause.
353–14 *u·* activity and availability of Truth;

Universalist

Pul. 60–18 * gift of a wealthy *U·* gentleman,

universality

Mis. 102–32 defines *omnipresence* as *u·*,

universally

Man. 31–13 spiritual *animus* so *u·* needed.
Rud. 6–16 * fact "almost *u·* accepted,
My. 225–20 Mankind almost *u·* gives to
236–24 I request the Christian Scientists *u·*

universe

and man
Mis. 65–13 God's *u·* and man are immortal.
Un. 10–12 *u·* and man are the spiritual
beauty of the
Mis. 86–15 My sense of the beauty of the *u·*
coexistent
'02. 7–18 the *u·* coexistent with God.
conceive the
Mis. 216–27 * to conceive the *u·* as a *phenomenon*
created the
Mis. 56–30 first spiritually created the *u·*,
doctrine that the
Pan. 2–15 * doctrine that the *u·*, . . . is God;
4– 2 doctrine that the *u·* owes its origin
evolves the
Mis. 364–21 self-created or evolves the *u·*.
existing
Pan. 2–18 * manifested in the existing *u·*."
facts of the
Ret. 60–27 the spiritual facts of the *u·*,
Father of the
My. 148–15 Father of the *u·* and the father of
fresh
Ret. 27–30 a fresh *u·* — old to God, but
from the
Un. 60–22 from Himself nor from the *u·*.
God, and the
(*see* **God**)
God's
Mis. 65–13 God's *u·* and man are immortal.

universe

governs the
Mis. 41–27 Principle which governs the *u·*,
258–15 He governs the *u·*.
380– 5 as well as governs the *u·*,
No. 13–19 voices the infinite, and governs the *u·*.
Pan. 3–30 by which he governs the *u·* ;
Peo. 8–18 Mind, that governs the *u·*,
My. 182–22 created and governs the *u·*

grasping the
Mis. 364–14 right hand grasping the *u·*,

harmonies of the
Pul. 81–22 * all the harmonies of the *u·*

His
Mis. 186–26 sense of God and His *u·*
'00. 5–24 Science of God and His *u·*,
My. 109–21 individually but specks in His *u·*,

includes
Pan. 12– 7 for the *u·* includes man

including man
Mis. 23–20 The *u·*, including man, is not a
333–21 relate to the *u·*, including man

including the
Un. 32– 6 man, including the *u·*, is His

indestructibility of the
Mis. 206–10 scientific indestructibility of the *u·*

informing the
Mis. 332– 3 Wisely governing, informing the *u·*,

is spiritual
Rud. 4– 2 and their *u·* is spiritual,

laws of the
My. 340–30 beneficence of the laws of the *u·*

logical
Pul. 67– 8 * the hub of the logical *u·*,

made the
Un. 14– 6 long after God made the *u·*,

man and
'01. 5–19 real spiritual man and *u·*.
My. 253– 4 perfect original man and *u·*.

man and the
Mis. 57–24 sense of man and the *u·*
72– 1 can transmit to man and the *u·*
Rud. 1– 7 the Soul of man and the *u·*.
5–25 believe man and the *u·* to be the
'00. 4–19 truth of God, and of man and the *u·*.
4–26 Man and the *u·* coexist with God
'02. 2– 8 Science of man and the *u·*,
7– 4 manifestations of love — man and the *u·*.
7–18 man and the *u·* coexistent with God.
My. 106–15 Without Mind, man and the *u·*
226–15 Withdraw God, . . . from man and the *u·*,
226–16 man and the *u·* would no longer exist.
226–17 man and the *u·* would remain
262–21 His spiritual idea, man and the *u·*,
266–18 spiritualization . . . of man and the *u·*.
267–10 Alpha and Omega of man and the *u·* ;
294–15 conditions of man and the *u·*,
348–23 the laws of man and the *u·*,

man or the
Mis. 37– 3 creating or governing man or the *u·*.
164–12 Principle of man or the *u·*,

material
(*see* **material**)

mingling with the
Mis. 396–15 When mingling with the *u·*,
Po. 59– 7 When mingling with the *u·*,

miracle in the
Mis. 294– 7 miracle in the *u·* of mortal mind.

of God
Mis. 217– 6 the *u·* of God is spiritual,

of Mind
Mis. 369– 8 immeasurable *u·* of Mind,

reduce the
Un. 13–14 would . . . reduce the *u·* to chaos.

rhythm of the
Ret. 61–11 than the rhythm of the *u·*,

rules the
My. 278– 8 Love rules the *u·*,

sensuous
Mis. 87– 8 beauties of the sensuous *u·* :

spiritual
Mis. 21– 8 spiritual *u·*, whereof C. S.
361–25 spiritual *u·*, including man
Un. 14–14 rectify His spiritual *u·* ?
No. 26–24 in the spiritual *u·* he is

stellar
No. 6–23 true Science of the stellar *u·*.

throughout the
Un. 46–22 must extend throughout the *u·*,

transforming the
Mis. 372– 6 C. S. is transforming the *u·*.

transform the
Un. 17–18 transform the *u·* into a home of

visible
Mis. 218– 5 visible *u·* declares the invisible

universe

whole
My. 269– 1 whole *u·* included in one infinite Mind

would disappear
Un. 60–22 Without Him, the *u·* would disappear,

Mis. 4– 8 and of the *u·* as His idea,
57–22 the *u·* with man created spiritually.
64–30 or of a material state and *u·*,
106– 1 God is the sum total of the *u·*.
235– 7 Mind whence sprang the *u·*.
257– 2 excludes God from the *u·*, or
368– 1 a *u·* in His own image and likeness.
Un. 29–11 only Mind and intelligence in the *u·*.
No. 21– 8 it grasped in spiritual law the *u·*,
My. 149–10 tides of truth that sweep the *u·*,
248–18 reality of God, man, nature, the *u·*.
287–18 Mind whence springs the *u·*.

universities
Pul. 5–23 colleges, and *u·* of America ;

University
Ret. 75–23 when he leaves the *U·*,

university
Man. 73–10 students in any *u·* or college,
73–12 at such *u·* or college,
73–14 graduates of said *u·* or college,
73–18 rules of the *u·* or college
73–20 said *u·* or college organization.
Ret. 91–27 nature's haunts were the Messiah's *u·*.

University Avenue
Pul. 72– 8 * Mrs. D. W. Copeland of *U· A·*

University Press
My. 318–11 proofreader for the *U· P·*,

unjust
Mis. 18–31 that aught that God sends is *u·*,
19– 1 bring to . . . that which is *u·*,
80– 4 opposition to *u·* medical laws.
80–16 *u·* coercive legislation and
87– 5 which is *u·* to human sense
123–23 the just obtain a pardon for the *u·*,
290–12 partial, unmerciful, or *u·*,
Man. 53–23 Publications *U·*.
53–25 an article that is false or *u·*,
54–11 as to *u·* and unmerciful conduct
Un. 44– 2 which are as unkind and *u·* as
54–12 any claim whatever, just or *u·*,
Pul. 7–19 *u·*, unmerciful, and oppressive
Rud. 10– 1 an *u·* usurper of the throne
'02. 14–28 all *u·* public aspersions,

unjustly
Man. 51– 8 member who shall *u·* aggrieve
My. 138–13 *u·*, and wrongfully accused.

unkind
Mis. 387–15 By thought or word *u·*,
Un. 44– 2 which are as *u·* and unjust as
52–19 its *u·* forces, its tempests,
Po. 6–10 By thought or word *u·*,
My. 180–26 and calls them *u·*.
231–18 else . . . giving is *u·*.

unknow
Un. 13–20 which He must learn to *u·*,

unknowingly
'00. 8– 4 imparts knowingly and *u·* goodness ;

unknown
Mis. xi–10 not *u·* to nor unrewarded by Him.
105–18 *u·* to the omnipresent Truth.
295–19 statements of the great *u·*
296– 8 *u·* author cited by Mr. Wakeman
296–21 in this *u·* gentleman's language,
296–29 What manner of man *is* this *u·*
368– 8 * and, behind the dim *u·*
385–21 never of the dead : The dark *u·*.
Man. 50– 1 and the cause thereof be *u·*,
Ret. 31–17 the unseen sin, the *u·* foe,
38–25 motives and circumstances *u·* to me.
Un. 5–15 *mystery* involves the *u·*.
50– 6 and is *u·* to the Divine.
Pul. 67–16 * practically *u·* a decade since,
No. 31– 9 unreal, *u·* to Truth,
Hea. 6–23 wholly *u·* to the individual,
Po. 48–15 never of the dead : The dark *u·*.
My. 5–20 to worship, not an *u·* God,
43– 2 * An *u·* wilderness
85– 5 * years ago it was comparatively *u·* ;
153–20 appeals to an *u·* power
167– 3 mysticism of good is *u·* to the
189– 8 nor talk of *u·* love.
192– 2 Ye build not an *u·* God.
193– 2 not to the *u·* God, but unto
251–11 question from *u·* questioners :
338–12 "The *U·* God Made Known,"
338–13 *u·* to me till after the lecture

unlawful
  Mis. 380–29 the *u·* publishing and use of an
        381–29 their *u·* existence destroyed,
unlearned
  Un. 1– 6 *u·* and unstable— *II Pet.* 3 : 16.
  My. 307–22 For one so *u·*, he was a remarkable
       324– 4 * a thought of contempt for the *u·*,
unleavened
  Mis. 175–16 *u·* bread of sincerity— *I Cor.* 5 : 8.
unless
  Mis. 12–15 *u·* one be watchful and steadfast
     112–10 *u·* he knows *how* to be just ;
     112–28 *U·* this mental condition be
     181–10 *u·* that requirement should express
     197– 9 *u·* this be so, no man can be
     221–12 *u·* he believes that sin has
     224– 1 *u·* our own thought barbs it.
     224–27 *u·* the offense be against God.
     249–18 *u·* it was something to remove stains
     250–18 *U·* these appear, I cast aside the
     296–23 *u·* from their affinity for the
     297–21 *u·* such claims are relinquished
     337–17 *u·* it produces a growing affection
     345– 9 * *u·* you yield your religion,"
     346–25 never to repeat error *u·*
  Man. 30–11 *U·* Mrs. Eddy requests otherwise,
      51–17 *u·* a By-Law governing the
      70–16 *u·* it be when our churches,
      85–13 *u·* he has a certificate
  Ret. 21–26 *u·* they illustrate the ethics of
      61–30 *U·* this method be pursued,
  Un. 10–27 *u·*, pursued by their fears,
     23–20 *u·* God has created them?
     33–11 *u·* matter is mind, it cannot
     37–15 Not *u·* it be a sin to believe
  '00. 3– 3 *u·* he loses the chord.
  '02. 8–11 *u·* he is actuated by love
  Hea. 16–11 *u·* you do this you are not
  Peo. 9–26 *u·* omnipotence is the *All*-power.
  Po. 15– 5 Break not on the silence, *u·*
  My. 87–11 * *u·* they are pointed out.
     152–18 *U·* this be so, the blind is
     211–27 *u·* the cause of the mischief is
     213–15 *U·* one's eyes are opened to
     219– 1 *u·* I am personally present.
     229– 2 *u·* I mistake their calling.
     242– 8 *U·* you fully perceive that
     249–11 *U·* withstood, the heat of hate
     347–27 *u·* it be the manifestation of

unlike
  Mis. 39–16 *U·* the M. D.'s, Christian Scientists
     55–23 all that is *u·* Spirit.
     55–30 in something *u·* Him ;
     72– 2 nothing evil, or *u·* Himself.
    103–16 *U·* mortal mind, which must
    217–21 a third quality *u·* God.
    259–12 good as being *u·* itself,
    292–18 *u·* the risen, immortal Love ;
    355–22 what in thine own mentality is *u·*
    366–13 He is in nothing *u·* Himself ;
  Ret. 49–17 conquering all that is *u·*
  Un. 3–25 of anything *u·* Himself ;
     18– 8 everything that is *u·* Myself.
     23–21 anything so wholly *u·* Himself
     35–25 can form nothing *u·* itself,
     38–22 in aught which is *u·* God,
  No. 15–25 in nothing is He *u·* Himself.
     16–19 of something *u·* Him.
     37–16 what is *u·* God demands His
     37–26 null and void whatever is *u·* God ;
  Pan. 14– 1 of whatever is *u·* good,
  '01. 8–20 image of Spirit is not *u·* Spirit.
  '02. 6– 2 to have aught *u·* the infinite.
     6–30 producing nothing *u·* Himself,
  My. 64–24 * overcoming all that is *u·* God,
    127–25 *U·* Russia's armament, ours is
    240–17 all that is *u·* God, good

unlimited
  Mis. 102– 5 infinite finite being, an *u·* man,
    102– 6 the *u·* and immortal Mind
    103–17 the eternal Mind is free, *u·*,
  Pul. 73– 4 * His *u·* and divine power.
  Hea. 4– 1 *u·* Mind cannot start from a
unlock
  Mis. 283– 7 *u·* the desk, displace the furniture,
  Ret. 37–19 to *u·* this "mystery— *I Tim.* 3 : 16.
unlooked-for
  Mis. 380–10 *u·*, imperative call for help
  Pul. 65– 3 * has penetrated . . . to an *u·* extent.
unloose
  Mis. 341–15 *u·* the latchet of thy sandals ;
  Ret. 92– 6 May we *u·* the latchets of

unloose
  My. 222–20 *u·* the sandals of thy Master's feet.
    338–27 whose sandals none may *u·*.
unlovely
  '02. 6–30 Love, including nothing *u·*,
unloving
  '02. 8– 8 mortals hating, or *u·*,
unmanageable
  Mis. 326–11 until they became *u·* ;
unmarked
  My. 83– 7 * wore tiny white, *u·* buttons,
unmarried
  Man. 111– 8 *u·* women must sign "Miss."
unmasked
  Ret. 69–19 "When will the error . . . be *u·*?
unmeasured
  My. 24– 7 * your *u·* love for humanity,
unmedicated
  Hea. 12–27 giving the *u·* sugar
unmentioned
  Mis. 238–12 reformer works on *u·*,
unmerciful
  Mis. 19– 7 never *u·*, never unwise.
    121–29 Love,— that cannot be *u·*.
    290–12 partial, *u·*, or unjust,
  Man. 54–11 unjust and *u·* conduct
  Pul. 7–19 *u·*, and oppressive priesthood
  My. 41–10 * arrogance, and self-will are *u·*,
unmercifulness
  Mis. 297–26 *u·*, tyranny, or lust.
  Peo. 8– 7 *u·*, that for the sins of a few
unmindful
  Mis. 310–15 not *u·* that the Scriptures enjoin,
  My. 153–23 *u·* of the divine law of Love,
unmistakable
  Mis. 193– 6 His words are *u·*, for they
    193–28 *u·* declaration of the right
    297–16 I hereby state, in *u·* language,
    366– 8 given rule, and *u·* proof.
  No. 11–22 given rule, and *u·* proof.
    33–11 given rule, and *u·* proof.
  My. 100– 4 * they are *u·* in their trend.
    342–10 * The likeness . . . was *u·*.
unmistakably
  Mis. 269–14 Who is it that understands, *u·*,
  My. 266–14 points *u·* to the
    305– 8 express myself *u·* on the subject of
    348–21 I had found *u·* an actual,
unmitigated
  Mis. 246– 3 all *u·* systems of crime ;
unmixed
  Ret. 34– 2 more of the *u·*, unerring source,
unmolested
  Mis. 303– 7 *u·*, be governed by divine Love
unnatural
  Mis. 74– 4 *u·* enmity of mortal man toward God.
  My. 288–10 Evil is *u·* ; it has no origin
unnaturally
  Mis. 309– 9 has uniformly been so *u·* delineated
unnecessarily
  Man. 53–13 trouble her on subjects *u·*
unnecessary
  Mis. 314–26 *u·* to repeat the title or page.
    322–18 my often-coming is *u·* ;
  My. 42–11 * further words of mine are *u·*.
unnoticed
  My. 67–28 * its massiveness is *u·*
unnumbered
  Pul. 80–25 * homes of *u·* invalids.
unparalleled
  My. v–23 * an *u·* record for a work of
unpierced
  Ret. 70–29 post of duty, *u·* by vanity,
  Pan. 12–26 *u·* by bold conjecture's sharp
unpleasant
  Mis. 81– 4 *u·* and unchristian action
unplucked
  Po. 46– 9 *U·* by ruthless hands.
unprecarious
  My. 201–19 a tenure of *u·* joy.
unprecedented
  Mis. 110–22 *u·* prosperity of our Cause.
    246–19 in this most *u·* warfare.
  Ret. 45–16 followed that noble, *u·* action
    47– 4 *u·* popularity of my College.

unprecedented
'00.   1–11   crowned with u· prosperity ;
My.   86–27   * u·, as regards numbers.
       134– 5   u· progress of C. S.
       246–12   in the midst of u· prosperity,

unprejudiced
Pul.   14–14   Millions of u· minds

unprepared
Mis.   84– 8   on minds u· for them.
       307–21   pearls before the u· thought.
Rud.   14–23   u· to enter higher classes.

unpretentious
Mis.   360– 7   u· yet colossal characters,
My.   178– 3   These u· preachers cloud not

unprincipled
Mis.   263–26   especially by u· claimants,
       265–29   self-satisfied, u· students.
       274–21   inordinate, u· clans.
Ret.   71– 7   an ignorant or an u· mind-practice

unprofitable
My.   113– 6   self-contradictory, or u· to mankind

unprohibited
Mis.   286– 7   will continue u· in C. S.

unpromising
Pul.   49–11   * barren waste of most u· ground

unprotected
Man.   28– 8   individuals, and religion are u· ;

unprovided
My.   75–29   * with any part of the . . . u· for,

unpublished
Ret.   36– 9   and u· manuscripts extant,

unpunished
Mis.   12–14   sinning unseen and u·
       93–27   because it cannot go u·
       281–30   shall not go u· :— see Prov. 11 : 21.
My.   160–24   u· sin is this internal fire,

unqualified
Mis.   43–16   those who are spiritually u·.
Hea.   7–26   This is an u· statement of
My.   359–25   * with the latter's u· approval.

unquenchable
Mis.   77–19   impartial, and u· Love.
       328–12   unchanging, u· Love

unquestionable
Mis.   249–15   whose morals are not u·.
My.   286–10   u·, however, that at this hour

unquestionably
Mis.   71– 9   u· right to do right ;
       289– 2   Strong drink is u· an evil,
       295–28   u· the best queen on earth ;
Ret.   70–20   second appearing of Jesus is, u·,
Pul.   71–23   * u· looked upon as having
My.   244–15   u· man's spiritual state
       287– 5   They were u· used in a

unready
Mis.   116–28   never u· to work for God,

unreal
absolutely
No.   6–25   appears real, . . . is absolutely u·.
and temporal
Mis.   21–20   matter is the u· and temporal.
and the real
Mis.   86–14   of the u· and the real.
belief
No.   5–13   substitutes . . . an u· belief,
called
My.   334–18   * while being called u·.
cast out the
Pan.   11– 2   cast out the u· or counterfeit.
concept
'01.   24– 2   * an impossible and u· concept."
discord is the
Rud.   13–20   and discord is the u·,
disease
No.   4– 5   chapter sub-title
       13– 3   It makes disease u·,
disease is
Rud.   13– 1   in Science, disease is u· ;
No.   4–16   that disease is u· ;
error is the
Hea.   10–15   error is the u·.
error, the
Hea.   18–11   Truth is the real ; error, the u·.
evil as
Man.   15–12   that casts out evil as u·.
evil is
Ret.   60–14   therefore evil is u·
'01.   15– 1   declaration that evil is u·,
Hea.   9–23   statement that evil is u· ;
My.   178–19   that evil is u· ;

unreal
matter is
My.   217–18   * "If all matter is u·, why do we
mortal as
No.   36–18   holding the mortal as u·,
necessarily
Mis.   346–21   opposite is necessarily u·,
real and the
Mis.   49–20   between the real and the u·.
       119–24   the real and the u· Scientist.
sense
Un.   41– 6   u· sense of suffering and death.
No.   5–12   this u· sense substitutes for Truth
shadow
My.   268–20   in my thought as an u· shadow,
small and
No.   32–19   must be small and u·.
something
No.   17– 2   something u·, material, and mortal.
to Jesus
Mis.   200–29   were alike u· to Jesus ;
trials
No.   36–16   find rest from u· trials

Mis.   27–12   sin, disease, death) are u·.
       42–23   the former is a dream and u·,
       46– 5   evil, good's opposite, is u·.
       63–16   such as believe in the . . . u· ;
       73–21   states of false sensation — are u·.
       89–20   If mortal man is u·, how can he
       122–29   The hater's pleasures are u· ;
       188–25   the u· or mortal sense of things ;
       218–15   they make Deity u· and
       341– 3   u· material basis of things,
Ret.   25–18   the temporal, I described as u·.
       68–10   human material concept is u·,
Un.   9– 6   they must, . . . be reckoned u·.
       36–15   matter is erroneous, transitory, u·.
       49–18   and the other u·,
       49–20   the u· masquerades as the real,
       55–18   sufferings of the flesh are u·.
       60–11   its opposite, and therefore u· ;
Rud.   11–13   These illusions are not real, but u·.
No.   5–12   is of necessity u·.
       6–20   in both cases to be u·.
       31– 9   disease and sin are u·,
       35–28   is nowhere, and must be u·.
'01.   14–15   u· as a mirage that misleads the
       14–18   and if untrue, u· ; and if u·, to
       14–20   from believing in what is u·,
       14–26   it must become u· to us :
       15– 6   prove it false, therefore u·.
Hea.   11– 3   gladly waken to see it was u·.

unrealities
Mis.   60– 7   as the woeful u· of being,

unreality
Mis.   58– 4   one learns its u· ;
       60–10   make the u· of both apparent
       63–14   on the basis of its u·
       73–11   and the u· of materiality.
       187– 9   opposite of man, hence the u· ;
       187–11   and discord the u·.
       252– 9   wrong thoughts are u·
       252–13   sick thoughts are u· and weakness ;
       319– 2   true sense of . . . the u· of evil
       363– 2   more conscious . . . of its own u·,
Ret.   25–19   and matter, the u·.
       62– 7   demonstration of the u· of evil
Un.   8–14   u· of matter and evil
       9–28   by knowing the u· of disease,
       38– 7   even the u· of mortal mind,
       58–18   u· of sin, sickness, and death
Rud.   11–14   consciousness of the u· of pain
No.   4–15   demonstrates . . . the u· of the error.
       4–24   u· of sin, disease, and death,
       17–19   Hence the u· of error,
       35–15   He atoned for the terrible u· of
'01.   13–29   disappears, and its u· is proven.
       15– 2   his belief in this awful u·,
       15– 4   understand and demonstrate its u·.
My.   334–15   * on the u· of evil

unreasonable
Mis.   38– 5   is it u· to expect

unrelenting
Mis.   258– 5   u· false claim of matter

unreliable
Pul.   45–22   * the evidence . . . is u·."

unremitting
Mis.   340– 6   u·, straightforward toil ;
       382– 8   years of u· toil and unrest ;

unrent
'01.   26–15   to preserve Christ's vesture u· ;

unrequited
Mis. 212–16 difficulties, darkness, and *u·* toil.
'01. 2–24 darkness, doubt, and *u·* toil
unreservedly
Mis. 115–24 turns us more *u·* to Him for help,
unrest
Mis. 382– 8 of unremitting toil and *u·* ;
Pul. 23–20 * manifested in *u·* or in
unrestrained
My. 331–14 * to extend such *u·* hospitality
unrewarded
Mis. xi–10 not unknown to nor *u·* by Him.
unrighteous
Po. 27– 2 pomp and tinsel of *u·* power ;
My. 165– 8 righteous suffer for the *u·* ;
294– 9 *u·* contradicting minds of
unrolled
Po. 26–15 dark record of our guilt *u·*,
unsafe
No. 21– 4 *u·* decoction for the race.
unsatisfying
Ret. 57–21 as *u·* as it is unscientific.
unscientific
Mis. 217–10 fallacy of an *u·* statement
372– 2 incorrect, contradictory, *u·*,
Ret. 57–22 as unsatisfying as it is *u·*.
59– 8 Such an inference is *u·*.
Rud. 12–15 the relief is unchristian and *u·*.
My. 111–20 book itself be absurd and *u·* ?
111–23 Were the apostles absurd and *u·*
111–29 absurd, ambiguous, *u·*.
113–23 is that *u·* which all around us is
303–10 *u·* worshippers of a human being.
unscriptural
My. 113–18 Neither is it presumptuous or *u·*
unscrupulous
My. 212–32 in furtherance of *u·* designs.
unsealed
Ret. 31–28 Frozen fountains were *u·*.
Pul. 7–14 God has now *u·* their receptacle
Po. 9– 5 *u·* fountains of grief and joy
unseemly
No. 45– 6 not behave itself *u·*,— *I Cor.* 13 : 5.
My. 308–27 attributes to my father language *u·*,
Unseen
Un. 7–21 perfection of the infinite *U·*
unseen
Mis. xi–12 pointing the path, dating the *u·*,
12–14 The means for sinning *u·*
47– 8 that which is hoped for but *u·*,
104– 3 His *u·* individuality, so superior
188–18 thence, up to the *u·*,
260–30 lawless mind, with *u·* motives,
292–26 great good, both seen and *u·* ;
301–24 an *u·* form of injustice
307–27 should beware of *u·* snares,
318–25 chapter sub-title
326–13 crept *u·* into the synagogue,
Ret. 31–17 for this trust is the *u·* sin,
Un. 37–21 this *u·* individuality is real
Pul. 14– 4 active yet *u·* mental agencies
No. 10– 4 the *u·* verities of being,
34–13 *u·* glory of suffering for others.
'01. 20–19 This *u·* evil is the sin of sins ;
My. 15–19 * Of *u·* things above,
95–26 * without faith in the things *u·*.
164–19 buried in the depths of the *u·*,
202–22 The taper *u·* in sunlight
211– 3 The *u·* wrong to individuals
211–13 by *u·*, silent arguments
260–16 and the evidence *u·*.
unself
'00. 11– 5 harmonize, unify, and *u·* you.
My. 161–18 *u·* mortality and to destroy its
unselfed
Mis. 238– 9 What has not *u·* love achieved
'00. 10–23 touching token of *u·* manhood
'01. 30–26 heart of the *u·* Christian hero.
'02. 16–16 watch fires of *u·* love,
My. 6– 7 To abide in our *u·* better self
19–21 fruition of her *u·* love,
62–10 * for your *u·* love.
165–28 The best man . . . is the most *u·*.
195–27 *u·* love that builds without hands,
200–19 honesty, purity, and *u·* love.
249–29 devout, *u·* quality of thought
265– 3 It signifies that love, *u·*,
291–19 was wise, brave, *u·*.
298– 9 for their *u·* labors in
306–16 patience and *u·* love,

unselfish
Mis. 35–14 * so *u·* an individual.''
100–14 Science voices *u·* love,
232–27 spiritual and *u·* motives.
250–23 *u·* deed done in secret ;
263– 2 I shall have the *u·* joy of
266– 2 *u·* and pure aims
Ret. 28–10 It must become honest, *u·*,
79–10 in *u·* motives and acts,
80– 1 *u·* affection or love,
Pul. 21– 3 a love *u·*, unambitious,
35–14 It must become honest, *u·*,
84–27 * *u·*, and zealous effort
My. 19–12 * chapter sub-title
28–10 * a hint of the *u·* efforts,
52–16 * *u·* labor to establish these
157–13 * evidence of your *u·* love.''
217– 5 your hitherto *u·* toil,
unselfishly
Ret. 49–16 the bliss of loving *u·*,
unselfishness
Mis. 110– 6 innocence, *u·*, faithful affection,
Ret. 87–25 through the lens of their *u·*
My. 87–27 * spirit of *u·* and helpfulness,
274–11 honesty, purity, *u·*
unselfs
Mis. 204–26 it *u·* the mortal purpose,
My. 288– 2 *u·* men and pushes on the ages.
unsettled
Mis. 125–30 from *u·* questions to permanence,
Ret. 87– 9 *u·* and spasmodic efforts.
unshaken
My. 44–29 * their *u·* confidence in the
unsheathed
Mis. 195–22 He who never *u·* his blade
unshod
Mis. 77–29 to enter *u·* the Holy of Holies,
unsipped
Mis. 324– 9 music is dull, the wine is *u·*,
unskilful
Peo. 8–28 skill proved a million times *u·*.
unskilled
Mis. 195–22 beneath the stroke of *u·* swordsmen.
unsolved
Ret. 79–15 inscrutable problem of being *u·*.
My. 181– 6 and ultimate in *u·* problems
unsought
Mis. 282–26 which may call for aid *u·*,
unsoundness
Mis. 49– 5 had manifested some mental *u·*,
unsparingly
Ret. 36– 8 and distributing them *u·*.
unspeakable
Mis. 279– 8 eternal sunshine and joy *u·*.
unspent
My. 353–16 the Science that operates *u·*.
unspiritual
Mis. 53–30 to the *u·*, the ungodly,
124– 1 It is plain that aught *u·*,
Ret. 65–29 *u·* and unhealing religion.
Peo. 3–25 has implanted . . . certain *u·* shifts,
4–15 *u·* and mysterious ideas of God
unspoken
Mis. 55–11 power of the *u·* thought,
302–17 *not* to leave the Word *u·*
No. 2–15 by the spoken than the *u·* word.
unspotted
Man. 31–10 They must keep themselves *u·*
Ret. 65–24 keeping man *u·* from the world,
unstable
Mis. 147–18 a loose and *u·* character.
Un. 1– 6 are unlearned and *u·* — *II Pet.* 3 : 16.
unstained
Mis. 110– 8 preserve these virtues *u·*,
unstimulating
My. 309–29 * lonely and *u·* existence.
310– 1 * ''lonely and *u·* existence.''
unsubstantial
Pan. 13–27 prove for yourselves the *u·* nature of
unsubstantiality
Mis. 264– 7 stumble over . . . their own *u·*,
unsurpassed
Pul. 20–13 prosperity of this church is *u·*.
unswerving
Mis. 291–22 *u·* course of a Christian Scientist,

unswervingly
   My. 45–18   * followed *u·* the guidance
unsystematic
   Ret. 93–11   fragmentary, disconnected, *u·*,
untainted
   My. vii–12   * *u·* by the emotionalism
untalkable
   Mis. 251– 7   my heart will with tenderness *u·*.
untamed
   Ret. 31–18   the heart's *u·* desire
untaught
   Mis. 302–18   *not* to leave the Word . . . *u·*.
untempered
   Ret. 79–24   Restrain *u·* zeal.
   Un. 5–21   Let no enmity, no *u·* controversy,
untested
   Mis. 264–17   abstract Science is somewhat *u·*.
unthought
   My. 148–13   Memorable date, all *u·* of till
until
   Mis. 7– 4   *u·* their bodies become dry,
   15– 3   *u·* he awakes from it.
   15–23   *u·* man is found to be the image
   44–13   *u· I have the tooth extracted,*
   67– 1   *u·* its altitude reaches beyond the
   71– 4   suffered from . . . *u·* his death ;
   79– 6   *u·* it is clear to human comprehension
   80–22   *u·* right is found supreme.
   80–30   *u·* it shall come to understand
   86– 5   *U·* this be attained,
   86–19   *u·* we gain the glorified sense
   91–24   I never dreamed *u·* informed thereof,
   104–20   false selfhood *u·* self-destroyed.
   118–19   *u·* all error is destroyed
   138– 1   *u·*, in turn, their students will sustain
   148–23   *U·* recently, I was not aware
   164– 8   *u·* it be acknowledged, understood,
   164–22   *u·* man be found in the actual
   165–21   *u·* lifted to these by their own
   166–25   *u·* the whole shall be leavened
   172–12   *u·* the three measures be
   175– 4   *u·* the whole sense of being
   184–21   *u·* he learns that all power is good
   220–12   *u·* the patient's mind yields,
   225–30   * "Wait *u·* we get home,
   229–23   *u·* the whole human race would
   231–14   *u·* delicious pie, pudding, and
   236– 6   *u·* thought has shrunk from contact
   237–10   *u·* earth gives them such a cup
   242– 4   came not to my notice *u·* January
   253–25   *u·* she herself is become a mother?
   261–12   *u·* he pays his full debt
   265–32   *u·* suffering compels the downfall
   276–16   *u·* "no night is there." — *see Rev.* 21 : 25.
   286– 4   * "*u·* death do us part ;"
   286– 6   *U·* time matures human growth,
   286–28   *U·* this absolute Science of being
   287–15   *u·* progress lifts mortals to discern
   299– 1   *u·* one is awake to their cause
   299– 5   but never *u·* then.
   304–14   * *u·* 1900, when it will be sent to
   304–16   * *u·* that Exhibition closes.
   308– 1   *U·* this be done, man will never
   316–12   *U·* minds become less worldly-minded,
   326–10   *u·* they became unmanageable ;
   328–19   *u·* wakened through the baptism of fire
   338–13   cancels not sin *u·* it be destroyed,
   342– 7   *u·*, the midnight gloom upon them,
   343–24   *u·* no seedling be left to propagate
   352–12   *u·* they are lost in light
   353–10   gained the right one— and never *u·*
   356–24   *u·* one has gone down
   358–13   and they never should be *u·* then.
   359– 6   *u·* you can cure without it
   359–17   *u·* we can walk on the water.
   362–20   *u·* self-extinguished by suffering !
   364–24   *u·* this impossible partnership
   Man. 34–20   *u·* that membership is dissolved.
   37– 4   *u·* after the blank has been
   51–15   *u·* the requirements according to
   102– 6   shall not be dissolved *u·*
   Ret. 5–11   there the family remained *u·*
   7–12   * *u·* he had explored their
   8–10   *u·* I grew discouraged,
   20– 3   remained with my parents *u·*
   21– 6   We never met again *u·* he
   27– 9   *u·* S. and H. was written.
   35– 8   I did not venture . . . *u·* later,
   37–18   *u·* our heavenly Father saw fit,
   56–14   must go on *u·* peace be declared
   67–16   *u·* the false claim called sin
   87–30   *u·* he has done with the case

until
   Ret. 90–12   *u·* they were able to fulfil
   Un. 1–16   *u·* they draw nearer to the
   6–13   *U·* the heavenly law of health,
   45–21   *u·* it finally dies in order to
   45–26   *u·* it becomes non-existent.
   56–21   *U·* he awakes from his delusion,
   64–12   *u·* the hope of ever eluding
   Pul. 34– 4   * from that time *u·* 1866
   39– 4   * *u·* it finds the peace of the Lord
   41–20   * *u·* all who wished had heard
   41–28   * *u·* the hour for the dedication
   44–27   * kept coming *u·* the custodian
   66– 7   * *u·* now there are societies in
   Rud. 12– 9   *u·* they hold stronger than before
   15–10   *u·* this impulse subsides.
   15–14   *u·* there were enough practitioners
   No. v–12   *u·* you grow to apprehend
   20– 9   *u·* better apprehended.
   25– 2   *u·* God becomes the All
   27–11   *U·* centuries pass,
   30– 5   will not let sin go *u·* it is
   30– 5   *u·* nothing is left to be forgiven,
   31– 8   *u·* it is understood that disease
   31–18   *u·* a perfect consciousness is
   32– 8   suffer, *u·* it is self-destroyed.
   Pan. 6– 7   fight it *u·* it disappears,
   '00. 10–17   *u·* it is exterminated.
   '01. 10–26   *u·* there shall be nothing left
   13– 3   *u·* it annihilates its own
   '02. 15–15   *u·*, declining dictation as to what
   Hea. 1–10   wait *u·* the age advanced
   11–20   "*u·* you arrive at no medicine."
   13– 8   *u·* the fact is found out
   13–11   *u·* it was no longer aconite,
   14– 4   *u·* disease is treated mentally
   18–17   *u·* it became popular.
   Po. v–23   * *u· the poem finally found its*
   My. 14–27   * *u·* the church is finished.
   29–31   * From that time, *u·* the close
   38–11   * no more were admitted *u·*
   48– 4   * Not *u·* nineteen centuries had
   53– 4   * not *u·* the authoress was satisfied
   53–12   * held there *u·* November, 1883,
   55–20   * continued there *u·* March, 1894,
   55–27   * *u·* The Mother Church edifice was ready
   56– 3   * *u·* every seat was filled
   61– 9   * be postponed *u·* that time.
   74– 3   * From now *u·* Saturday night
   84– 8   * *u·* it be wholly free from debt.
   87– 1   * early morning *u·* the evening,
   92– 3   * *u·* it has stood the test of time.
   103–11   Science, *u·* understood, has
   114–20   leave me *u·* the rising of the sun.
   145– 7   *u·* the remodelling of the house
   160–15   *u·* compelled to glance at it.
   160–26   *u·* the sinner is consumed,
   174–22   *u·* I had a church of my own,
   220–20   *u·* He whose right it is shall reign.
   226–28   *u·* the public thought becomes better
   232–23   destroys error, *u·* the entire
   239–13   *u· every man and woman comes into*
   241– 3   * not be abolished *u·* it has
   242– 3   *u·* you declare yourself to be
   264– 5   *u·* mankind learn more of
   273–26   *u·* at length they are consigned to
   275– 6   *u·* they are controlled by divine
   283–17   *u·* his grasp of goodness grows
   318–21   *u·* I began my attack on
   318–23   *u·* he could control himself no longer
   327–18   * stayed on the field *u·* the last.
   332–11   * or remit his kind attention *u·* he
   336–14   *u·* after my mother's decease."
   345–13   *u·* they had no effect on me.
   357– 3   *u·* we arrive at the spiritual

untimely
   Mis. 17–24   timely or *u·* circumstances,
untired
   Po. 27–23   thy head on time's *u·* breast.
untiring
   Mis. 321–20   * *U·* in your holy fight,
   Ret. 5–28   * she was *u·* in her efforts to
   42–12   *u·* in his chosen work.
   Pul. 84–26   * *u·*, unselfish, and zealous effort
   My. 42–27   * how *u·* are her efforts,
   355–13   the *u·* spiritual armament.
unto
   Mis. 20– 4   "Come *u·* me, — *Matt.* 11 : 28.
   38–10   have sown *u·* you — *I Cor.* 9 : 11.
   46–28   attained to the Science of being,
   73–22   *Jesus said u·* them, — *Matt.* 19 : 28.
   73–22   *Verily I say u· you,* — *Matt.* 19 : 28.
   98–11   and to be ministered *u·* ;
   109–28   Christ, Truth, saith *u·* you,

unto

Mis.	120– 9	whether of sin *u·* death, — *Rom.* 6 : 16.
	120– 9	obedience *u·* righteousness — *Rom.* 6 : 16.
	122– 2	"Woe *u·* the world — *Matt.* 18 : 7.
	131–22	May God give *u·* us all that loving
	134– 2	"wise *u·* salvation" — *II Tim.* 3 : 15.
	135– 9	doing *u·* others as ye
	135–10	would they should do *u·* you,
	146–19	should do *u·* you, — *see Matt.* 7 : 12.
	154–19	word that is spoken *u·* you,
	157–22	thy way *u·* the Lord ; — *Psal.* 37 : 5.
	161– 5	*u· us a child is born,* — *Isa.* 9 : 6.
	161– 5	*u· us a son is given* : — *Isa.* 9 : 6.
	166–10	*u·* us a child is born, — *Isa.* 9 : 6.
	166–11	*u·* us a son *is* given : — *Isa.* 9 : 6.
	167–25	revealed them *u·* babes !" — *Luke* 10 : 21.
	168–17	"*U·* us a son is given." — *Isa.* 9 : 6.
	171–23	*is like u· leaven,* — *Matt.* 13 : 33.
	175– 4	showeth them *u·* the creature,
	192–11	*I go u· my Father,* — *John* 14 : 12.
	194–20	I go *u·* my Father." — *John* 14 : 12.
	196–25	does go *u·* the Father,
	205–12	show it *u·* you." — *John* 16 : 15.
	213–23	give *u·* them eternal life ; — *John* 10 : 28.
	215– 6	not as the . . . give I *u·* thee. — *John* 14 : 27.
	223–18	doing *u·* others what we would resist
	223–18	if done *u·* ourselves.
	235–28	should do *u·* you, — *see Matt.* 7 : 12.
	254–27	vineyard *u·* others." — *Mark* 12 : 9.
	260–29	Mind, . . . is a law *u·* itself,
	268–32	thy way *u·* the Lord ; — *Psal.* 37 : 5.
	270–15	be added *u·* you." — *Matt.* 6 : 33.
	278– 4	my peace returns *u·* me.
	279– 1	woe *u·* him, — *Luke* 17 : 1.
	292– 5	I give *u·* you, — *John* 13 : 34.
	298– 2	lean not *u·* thine own — *Prov.* 3 : 5.
	301– 6	would have others do *u·* you
	316– 4	a law not *u·* others, but themselves.
	317–32	by measure *u·* him." — *John* 3 : 34.
	318– 9	*u·* the third and fourth and final
	321– 3	"*U·* us a child is born," — *Isa.* 9 : 6.
	323–17	He saith *u·* the patient toilers
	325– 2	saith *u·* the dwellers therein,
	325–31	saith *u·* them, "Go ye into — *Mark* 16 : 15.
	326–27	which are sent *u·* thee, — *Matt.* 23 : 37.
	326–27	left *u·* you desolate." — *Matt.* 23 : 38.
	326–31	the Stranger saith *u·* him,
	327– 5	the Stranger saith *u·* him,
	328–29	reaching forth *u·* those — *Phil.* 3 : 13.
	331– 3	committing their way *u·* Him
	334– 3	or say *u·* Him, — *Dan.* 4 : 35.
	337–12	little child *u·* him, — *Matt.* 18 : 2.
	343– 1	make us wise *u·* salvation !
	347– 2	be like *u·* him." — *Prov.* 26 : 4.
	347–28	None can say *u·* Him,
	351–25	life that leads *u·* death,
	361–20	looking *u·* Jesus — *Heb.* 12 : 2.
	370–10	"*U·* us a child is born, — *Isa.* 9 : 6.
	370–10	*u·* us a son is given." — *Isa.* 9 : 6.
	373–26	power is given *u·* me — *Matt.* 28 : 18.
	374–24	one renders not *u·* Cæsar
	387– 4	mount upward *u·* purer skies ;
	390–12	*u·* the laughing hours,
Man.	16–11	to do *u·* others as we would
	16–12	would have them do *u·* us ;
	41–12	do good *u·* your enemies
	84– 6	a law, not *u·* others, but to
Chr.	55– 6	verily, I say *u·* you, — *John* 5 : 25.
	55–11	be added *u·* you. — *Matt.* 6 : 33.
	55–21	made like *u·* the — *Heb.* 7 : 3.
	57– 2	keepeth my works *u·* — *Rev.* 2 : 26.
Ret.	25–21	personal being, like *u·* man ;
	87–23	become a law *u·* themselves.
	88–27	as will draw men *u·* us.
	89–20	guarded them *u·* the end,
	92–10	shall be done *u·* you." — *John* 15 : 7.
	93– 9	draw all men *u·* me." — *John* 12 : 32.
	95– 8	* *U·* a life of sympathy.
Un.	1– 7	*u·* their own destruction." — *II Pet.* 3 : 16.
	24– 8	but verily I say *u·* you,
	60–19	and He will be *u·* them All-in-all.
Pul.	12–11	their lives *u·* the death. — *Rev.* 12 : 11.
	12–13	devil is come down *u·* you, — *Rev.* 12 : 12.
	13–28	cast *u·* the earth, — *Rev.* 12 : 13.
No.	7– 8	continue to do so *u·* the end.
	43– 4	"Come *u·* me, — *Matt.* 11 : 28.
	45– 2	revealed them *u·* babes." — *Luke* 10 : 21.
Pan.	14–21	be *u·* them life-preservers !
'00.	11–27	saith *u·* the churches. — *Rev.* 2 : 7.
	13–15	"Be thou faithful *u·* death, — *Rev.* 2 : 10.
	14–10	what the Spirit saith *u·* the churches ;
	14–20	The angel that spake *u·* the churches
'01.	9–23	showeth them *u·* the creature ;
	11–27	thou also be like *u·* him." — *Prov.* 26 : 4.
	19–10	it shall be given *u·* you ;
	34–30	lean not *u·* thine own — *Prov.* 3 : 5.

unto

'02.	7–25	I give *u·* you, — *John* 13 : 34.
	18–14	*u·* one of the least — *Matt.* 25 : 40.
	18–15	have done it *u·* me." — *Matt.* 25 : 40.
	19–16	"Come *u·* me." — *Matt.* 11 : 28.
Hea.	2–17	"Come *u·* me, — *Matt.* 11 : 28.
	16–28	cometh *u·* the Father, — *John* 14 : 6.
Peo.	5–16	angel form, saying *u·* us,
	8–22	I say *u·* thee, arise." — *Mark* 5 : 41.
Po.	v–14	* *through nature, u· nature's God,"*
	34–17	*U·* thy greenwood home
	50–22	mount upward *u·* purer skies ;
	55–13	Looks love *u·* the laughing hours,
My.	13–30	returns it *u·* them
	17– 9	as *u·* a living stone, — *I Pet.* 2 : 4.
	19–31	"Verily I say *u·* you, — *Mark* 14 : 9.
	24–14	* *u·* an holy temple — *Eph.* 2 : 21.
	34– 4	his soul *u·* vanity, — *Psal.* 24 : 4.
	36–12	* that shall be acceptable *u·* God.
	44–12	* even *u·* the — *Matt.* 28 : 20.
	46–28	* "*u·* the city of the — *Heb.* 12 : 22.
	80– 7	* when wasted *u·* death
	114– 5	Do *u·* others as ye would have
	117–16	and came *u·* thee?" — *Matt.* 25 : 39.
	126–16	reached *u·* heaven, — *Rev.* 18 : 5.
	126–17	double *u·* her double — *Rev.* 18 : 6.
	128– 3	go on *u·* perfection — *Heb.* 6 : 1.
	140– 6	will I do *u·* them, — *Isa.* 42 : 16.
	150–25	shall be done *u·* you." — *John* 15 : 7.
	150–26	what our Master said *u·* his disciples,
	150–28	I say *u·* you :
	153– 8	*U·* "the angel of — *Rev.* 3 : 7.
	156–10	have committed *u·* Him — *II Tim.* 1 : 12.
	156–14	Master saith *u·* thee, — *Luke* 22 : 11.
	159– 5	even *u·* the end." — *Matt.* 28 : 20.
	161–22	sufficient *u·* each day is the duty
	170–23	thy way *u·* the Lord ; — *Psal.* 37 : 5.
	184–28	that saith *u·* Zion, — *Isa.* 52 : 7.
	187–26	to build a house *u·* Him
	188– 6	attent *u·* the prayer — *II Chron.* 7 : 15.
	191–19	Spirit is saying *u·* matter :
	192– 4	press on *u·* the possession of
	193– 2	*u·* Him whom to know aright
	206–19	shall be *u·* thee — *Isa.* 60 : 19.
	206–26	"Giving thanks *u·* the — *Col.* 1 : 12.
	222–11	say *u·* this mountain, — *Matt.* 17 : 20.
	225–13	giving *u·* His holy name
	228–29	have committed *u·* him — *II Tim.* 1 : 12.
	229– 6	abomination *u·* the Lord : — *Deut.* 18 : 12.
	232–13, 14	say *u·* you I say *u·* all, — *Mark* 13 : 37.
	247–13	will draw all men *u·* you.
	252– 8	the good you do *u·* others
	258–13	"Looking *u·* Jesus — *Heb.* 12 : 2.
	269– 9	equal *u·* the angels ; — *Luke* 20 : 36.
	275–24	Doing *u·* others as we would
	279– 4	peace I give *u·* you : — *John* 14 : 27.
	279– 5	give I *u·* you." — *John* 14 : 27.
	280–20	nor say *u·* Him, What doest Thou?
	282– 7	"Look *u·* me, — *Isa.* 45 : 22.
	285–18	keepeth my works *u·* — *Rev.* 2 : 26.
	285–25	I confess *u·* thee, — *Acts* 24 : 14.
	288–26	worse thing come *u·* — *John* 5 : 14.
	290–16	I cried *u·* Thee." — *Psal.* 130 : 1.
	296– 3	"*u·* the root of the trees," — *Matt.* 3 : 10.
	349–16	"looking *u·* Jesus — *Heb.* 12 : 2.
	350–20	Oft mortal sense is darkened *u·* death

untold

Pul.	9–25	purity, and love are treasures *u·*
'02.	9– 1	gives man power with *u·* furtherance.

untouched

Mis.	125–25	hitherto *u·* problems of being,
	153– 8	*u·* by the billows.
Un.	1–16	leave the subject *u·*, until they

untrammelled

Mis.	30–17	uncontaminated, *u·*, by matter.
'02.	2–18	with the glory of *u·* truth.

untranslated

My.	179–29	the *u·* revelations of C. S.

untrodden

Mis.	xi–13	enabling him to walk the *u·*

untrue

Mis.	57–14	That this addendum was *u·*, is seen
	108–28	that which we know to be *u·*.
	109– 1	believing in that which is *u·*,
	295–21	as both *u·* and uncivil.
Ret.	56–22	Whatever else claims to be . . . is *u·*.
	81–19	or else that heart is consciously *u·*
Un.	44– 3	as unkind and unjust as they are *u·* :
No.	5–11	this material sense, which is *u·*,
'01.	14–18	then it follows that it is *u·* ;
	14–18	and if *u·*, unreal.
'02.	6–14	false claim, an *u·* consciousness,

untruthful
   Rud. 9–18 If one is *u·*,

untruths
   Mis. 22–18 *u·* belong not to His creation,

unusual
   Pul. 46–24 * though perhaps with an *u·* zest,
   My. 69–20 * Another *u·* feature is the foyer,
      333–31 * reports of *u·* sickness in the
      341–21 * *u·* public interest centres in the

unusually
   My. 69– 1 * church is *u·* well lighted,

unutterable
   Mis. 133–31 As to the peace, it is *u·* ;
   My. 134– 4 and *u·* in love.
      261–24 and *u·* except in C. S.
      306–13 with almost *u·* truths to translate,

unutterably
   Mis. 312– 5 self-sacrificing, *u·* kind ;
   My. 203–14 but he is *u·* valiant,

unveil
   Un. 39–12 *u·* the Messiah, whose name is
      45–15 This pantheism I *u·*.
   No. 10–22 *u·* the true idea,— namely, that

unveiled
   Mis. 124–25 *u·* Love's great legacy
      159–27 *u·* to us, and to the age !"
      326–32 sight of thee *u·* my sins,
      397– 1 His *u·*, sweet mercies show
   Ret. 31–29 Love *u·* the healing promise
   Pul. 18–10 His *u·*, sweet mercies show
   No. 12–24 *u·* spiritual signification of
   Po. 12–10 His *u·*, sweet mercies show
   My. 199–20 of *u·* hearts, of fourfold unity

unveils
   Mis. 330–29 *u·* its regal splendor

unvoiced
   No. 39– 3 intercession and *u·* imploring
   Po. 27–14 With traitors *u·* yet?

unwarned
   '01. 19–25 mankind *u·* and undefended

unwary
   Mis. 119– 6 If a criminal coax the *u·*

unwearied
   My. 184–25 Love, holding *u·* watch

unweary
   Mis. 393– 7 Art and Science, all *u·*,
   Po. 51–12 Art and Science, all *u·*,

unwilling
   Mis. 233–24 *u·* to work hard enough
      247–14 and are *u·* to be taught it,
   Ret. 13– 7 was *u·* to be saved, if
   No. 42– 5 God is not unable or *u·* to heal,

unwinged
   Mis. 124–16 marking the *u·* bird,

unwise
   Mis. 19– 7 are never unmerciful, never *u·*.
      211– 4 not cowardly, uncharitable, nor *u·*,
   Ret. 86–24 To the *u·* helper our Master said,
   No. 8–26 let the *u·* pass by,
   My. 231–22 *u·* for her to undertake new tasks,
      306– 7 I deem it *u·* to enter into a

unwisely
   Mis. 281–10 if one cherishes ambition *u·*,

unwittingly
   Mis. 264–32 If a teacher of C. S. *u·*
   Un. 36– 6 it *u·* confirms Truth,
   '00. 4– 4 *u·* consents to many minds
   Peo. 11–27 conspires *u·* against the liberty
   My. vii– 6 * *u·* made to deprive their Leader
      111–22 and *u·* misguide his followers
      292–21 *u·* neutralizing another,
      363–24 was not to malpractise *u·*.

unworldliness
   Ret. 91–30 His holy humility, *u·*, and
   Pul. 22– 1 fills the sentiment with *u·*,

unworthy
   Mis. 9–24 tasteless and *u·* of human aims.
      147–21 abhor whatever is base or *u·* ;
      271–15 subject that is *u·* of thought,
      291– 7 above personal motives, *u·* aims and
   Man. 30– 7 If . . . at any time inadequate or *u·*,
   My. 331–14 * unrestrained hospitality to an *u·*

unwritten
   Pul. 81–23 * the *u·* anthems of love.

upas-tree
   Mis. 368–16 more deadly than the *u·*
   No. 14–12 than the odor of the *u·* is to the

upborne
   Po. 23–15 Thy soul, *u·* on wisdom's wings,

upbuilding
   Mis. 140–25 means for *u·* the Church of Christ
      169–12 the *u·* of the body.

upheaval
   Pul. 6– 1 *u·* produced when Truth is

upheaves
   Mis. 331–24 having all power, *u·* the earth.

up-hill
   Mis. 347–22 and if it be *u·* all the way,

uphold
   Pan. 14–17 *u·* our nation with the right arm of

upholds
   Mis. 105–15 It *u·* being, and destroys the

upholstered
   Pul. 25–21 * *u·* in old rose plush.

upholstery
   Pul. 76–12 * the *u·* is in white and gold tapestry.

uplift
   Mis. 3–29 mental healing is to *u·* mankind ;
      317–26 singleness of purpose to *u·* the
      328–25 *u·* the fallen and strengthen the
   Man. 16– 6 his resurrection served to *u·* faith
   '00. 9–14 else they *u·* them.
   My. 130–11 and striven to *u·* morally

uplifted
   Mis. 356–18 the *u·* desires of the human heart,
   Un. 29–28 Virgin-mother's sense being *u·* to
   No. 34–25 over the steps of *u·* humanity,
   My. 151–19 * 'neath the temple of *u·* sky
      180–25 mind, not ready to be *u·*, rebels,
      248–20 only as *u·* by God's power,

uplifting
   Mis. 169–12 The *u·* of spirit was the
      236– 4 labor of *u·* the race,
      245–12 *u·* influence upon the health,
      315–21 of morals and of *u·* the race.
   Man. 83– 7 healing and *u·* the race.
   Ret. 93–13 method for *u·* human thought
   No. 37–24 *u·* the human understanding,
      39–14 Truth, *u·* us to Him.
   Pan. 10– 8 will attest its *u·* power,
   My. 113–27 *u·* human consciousness to a
      268–14 *u·* the motives of men.
      350– 7 revelation, *u·* human reason,

uplifts
   Mis. 260–22 truth of Mind-healing *u·* mankind,
   Ret. 76–24 never abuses the . . . but *u·* it.
   No. 45– 9 to ostracize whatever *u·* mankind,
   My. 155– 1 Such communing *u·* man's being ;

upper
   Mis. 159–13 *u·* chamber, where all things are pure
      279–23 met together in an *u·* chamber ;
   My. 156–16 show you a large *u·* room— *Luke* 22 : 12.
      156–19 the *u·* chambers of thought prepared

uppermost
   Mis. 116–12 This question . . . is to-day *u·* :

upreared
   Mis. 141– 2 will be . . . the monument *u·*,

upright
   Mis. 79–15 If God is *u·* and eternal,
      99– 2 it upsets all that is not *u·*.
      147–19 *u·* man is guided by a
      185–21 man infinitely blessed, *u·*, pure,
      258–16 which saveth the *u·* — *Psal.* 7 : 10.
      265– 6 an *u·* understanding.
   Ret. 42–15 and behold the *u·* :— *Psal.* 37 : 37.
   Pan. 11–17 he is not *u·*, and must regain his

uprightly
   My. 33–17 He that walketh *u·*,— *Psal.* 15 : 2.
      228–24 He that walketh *u·*,— *Psal.* 15 : 2.
      342– 4 * walking *u·* and with light step,

uprightness
   Mis. 119–11 impotent to turn . . . man from his *u·*.

uproar
   My. 310–24 * set the house in an *u·*,"

uproot
   Mis. 118–24 they will *u·* all happiness.
   Ret. 79–14 which *u·* the germs of growth

uprooted
   Ret. 71–25 that must be recognized, and *u·*,
   Un. 8–17 All forms of error are *u·*

uprooting
   Mis. 343–13 *u·* the noxious weeds of passion,
      343–21 not always destroyed by the first *u·* ;

upset
   Mis. 283– 5 *u·*, and adjust his thoughts

upsets
   Mis. 99– 2   *u·* all that is not upright.
upspringing
   My. 192–10   Thine is the *u·* hope,
up-to-date
   My. 175–14   *u·* academies, humane institutions,
upturned
   Po. 9– 4   *U·* to his mother's in playful grace ;
upward
   Mis. 9–30   path that winds *u·*.
   159–26   weary wings sprung *u·* !
   166– 3   monument whose finger points *u·*,
   204–14   new affections, all pointing *u·*.
   228– 6   standpoint whence to look *u·* ;
   267–21   plumed for . . . *u·* flight.
   320– 1   push·*u·* our prayer in stone,
   328– 5   the path that goeth *u·*."
   330– 5   looking *u·*, does it patiently pray
   331–21   on *u·* wing to-night.
   343– 9   to move it onward and *u·*.
   343–12   spring *u·*, and away from
   386–17   a hope that ever *u·* yearns,
   387– 4   mount *u·* unto purer skies ;
   389– 9   on *u·* wing to-night.
   393–19   rock, whose *u·* tending
   Un. 5–11   following *u·* individual convictions,
   Pul. 11– 1   bear you outward, *u·*,
   No. 46–21   unfolding of this *u·* tendency
   '02. 10–14   *u·* tendency of humanity
   Peo. 14–10   * white fingers pointing *u·*."
   Po. vi–27   * poem
   4– 7   on *u·* wing tonight.
   page 18   poem
   19– 4   *u·* and heavenward borne.
   50– 1   hope that ever *u·* yearns,
   50–22   mount *u·* unto purer skies ;
   52– 3   rock, whose *u·* tending
   My. 79– 4   * little faces turned *u·*.
   110–12   *u·* in the scale of being.
   124–23   with finger pointing *u·*,
   125– 7   to bend *u·* the tendrils
   127– 1   reaching outward and *u·*
   128–10   springs spontaneously *u·*,
   129–27   where faith mounts *u·*,
   140–19   leading you onward and *u·*.
   186– 7   preen their thoughts for *u·* flight.
   200–12   rises *u·* to the realms of
   202–18   onward and *u·* chain of being.
   215–10   a dozen or *u·* in one class.
   258–29   may you move onward and *u·*,
   339– 3   whose every link leads *u·*
   355–24   their thoughts are *u·* ;
upwards
   '02. 10–14   taking steps outward and *u·*.
   My. 45– 9   * *u·* of thirty thousand
urchin
   Mis. 391–15   *u·*, With bare feet soiled or sore,
   Po. 38–14   *u·*, With bare feet soiled or sore,
urge
   Mis. 13– 9   *u·* upon the solemn consideration of
   75– 8   *First :* I *u·* this fundamental fact
   Un. 43–18   I *u·* Christians to have more faith
   Pul. 82–19   * and no one to *u·* them.
   My. 123– 8   continue to *u·* the perfect model
urged
   Mis. 14– 8   It is *u·* that, . . . man has fallen
   140–18   and *u·* only the material side
   281–15   He replied to his wife, who *u·* him
   Po. vii– 8   * *they u· her to allow a*
   My. 11–12   * she has never *u·* upon us a
   22–12   * nor wait to be *u·* or to be shown
   105–27   he *u·* me immediately to write a
urgent
   My. 62–31   * there was *u·* need of both.
urges
   Mis. 181–23   apostle *u·* upon our acceptance
   My. 277–11   mental animus goes on, and *u·* that
urging
   Pul. 8–13   no *u·*, begging, or borrowing ;
   No. 45–26   *u·* its highest demands on mortals,
   '02. 9–15   *u·* a state of consciousness that
Urim
   Mis. 194– 7   *U·* and Thummim of priestly office,
   Ret. 35–23   *U·* and Thummim of priestly office,
   '01. 12–13   *U·* and Thummim of priestly office,
Us
   Mis. 18–20   divine idea, even the divine " *U·*' "
   57– 5   The creative " *U·*' " made all,
usage
   Mis. 170–32   "Hand," in Bible *u·*, — *Isa.* 59 : 1.
   My. 226– 4   an intelligent *u·* of the word

usage
   My. 260–19   not because of tradition, *u·*, or
   340– 5   *u·* of special days and seasons
usages
   My. 220– 5   and to governmental *u·*.
use (noun)
  beauty and
   My. 256–11   those things of beauty and *u·*
  correct
   My. 225– 7   A correct *u·* of capital letters in
  dexterous
   Mis. 231–13   dexterous *u·* of knife and fork,
  exclusive
   Pul. 25–10   * for the exclusive *u·* of Mrs. Eddy ;
  future
   Pul. 7–13   enshrined for future *u·*,
  human
   '01. 6–21   as impracticable for human *u·*,
  its
   Mis. 304–32   * and the direction of its *u·*,
   Pul. 28–19   * its *u·* of the Bible.
   My. 219– 9   preventing the occasion for its *u·* ;
   219– 9   otherwise its *u·* is abuse.
  lack of
   My. 213–25   will not rust for lack of *u·*
  medical
   '01. 18–17   If God created drugs for medical *u·*,
  no
   My. 229– 4   I have no *u·* for such,
  of drugs
   Mis. 108–30   believed in the *u·* of drugs,
   My. 301–24   supposition that . . . by the *u·* of drugs
  of hands
   Mis. 242– 8   without the *u·* of hands,
  of medicine
   My. 97– 6   * getting well without the *u·* of medicine.
  of notes
   Mis. 158–16   command, to drop the *u·* of notes,
  of opium
   Mis. 242–30   addicted to the *u·* of opium
  of such arguments
   Mis. 350–29   teach the *u·* of such arguments only
  of the knife
   My. 294–17   by a fruitless *u·* of the knife
  of the rod
   Mis. 51–13   *Doesn't the u· of the rod teach him*
   51–14   The *u·* of the rod is virtually a
  of the word
   My. 302–16   the *u·* of the word spread like
  press
   Pul. 31–21   * favor of an interview for press *u·*,
  proposed
   Mis. 304–22   * the proposed *u·* of the bell :
  slightest
   Mis. 289– 3   its slightest *u·* is abuse ;
  sole
   Pul. 42–13   * intended for the sole *u·* of Mrs. Eddy.
  Wyclif's
   '02. 16– 6   Wyclif's *u·* of that combination of words,
  your
   My. 147–23   prepared for your *u·* work-rooms

   Mis. 31– 8   not the *u·* but the abuse of mental
   45– 9   follow the *u·* of that drug
   304–17   * When not in *u·* in other places,
   380–29   unlawful publishing and *u·* of an
   Man. 46– 7   *U·* of Initials "C. S."
   Un. 36– 6   *u·* of a lie is that it unwittingly
   Pul. 28–17   * the *u·* of Mrs. Eddy's book,
   58–15   * by the *u·* of movable partitions.
   Pan. 4–13   will is capable of *u·* and of abuse,
   '01. 19–22   from the *u·* of inanimate drugs to
   My. 66–11   * *u·* the society will make of the
   171–29   * contained a gavel for the *u·* of
   212–11   The alcoholic habit is the *u·* of

use (verb)
   Mis. 11–22   those who . . . despitefully *u·* one,
   53–11   *Do you sometimes . . . u· medicine*
   55–12   *u·* it to harm rather than to heal,
   58–12   *She had to u· her eyes to read.*
   72–13   that ye *u·* this proverb — *Ezek.* 18 : 2.
   72–16   to *u·* this proverb in — *Ezek.* 18 : 3.
   147–13   and despitefully *u·* you
   215–25   *u·* the sword of Spirit.
   241– 9   *U·* as your medicine the . . . Truth :
   245– 2   or recommended others to *u·*,
   348–18   I *u·* no drugs whatever,
   376– 3   * I *u·* the words *most authentic* in
   Man. 43– 6   No member shall *u·* written formulas,
   43– 7   nor permit his . . . pupils to *u·* them,
   Ret. 29– 4   "despitefully *u·* you — *Matt.* 5 : 44.
   Un. 50–14   *u·* the phrase in the endeavor to
   Pul. 5– 3   in the words I *u·*,
   53–28   * Who *u·* it in his name ;

use (verb)

Pul.	55–21	* theology — if we may *u·* the word — of
	69– 9	* He says they *u·* no medicines,
No.	9– 9	*u·* no influence to prevent their
'01.	3–17	we *u·* this phrase for God
	31–14	can *u·* the power that God gives
'02.	7–13	*U·* these words to define God,
My.	6–11	revile us and despitefully *u·* us,
	52– 5	* loving them that despitefully *u·* her,
	52–16	* we must *u·* more energy and
	174– 1	to *u·* the beautiful lawn
	195–16	*u·* in God's service the one talent
	204– 3	to *u·* their hidden virtues,
	226– 2	*u·* it only where you can substitute
	308–24	* saying, "I never *u·* a cane."
	345–29	We *u·* them, we make them our

used

Mis.	11– 4	I *u·* to think it sufficiently just
	40–10	that Jesus and the apostles *u·*,
	69–23	with the means *u·*
	75–17	where the word *God* can be *u·*
	75–18	*Soul* may sometimes be *u·*
	75–24	name of Deity *u·* in that place
	158–30	no record that he *u·* notes
	180–28	term, as applied to man, is *u·*
	197– 4	one more frequently *u·*
	215–28	the words, that Jesus *u·*
	216– 1	*u·* in your application
	245– 1	that our Master ever *u·*,
	268–32	Truth is *u·* to waiting.
	270–12	those the Master *u·*
	277–11	and is *u·* to waiting ;
	289– 3	evil cannot be *u·* temperately :
	350–23	soundness of the argument *u·*.
	350–26	and cause none to be *u·*
Man.	41–10	However despitefully *u·*
	61– 1	No special trowel should be *u·*.
	65– 2	already *u·* in our periodicals.
	65– 7	when this term is *u·*
	71– 6	"The" must not be *u·*
	76– 3	to be hereafter *u·* for
	78–22	*u·* by him for the payment
	112– 6	must not be *u·* before
Ret.	15–18	and benches were *u·*
	51– 6	to be *u·* as a temple
	59–12	term *u·* to indicate Deity ;
Un.	27– 3	two English words, often *u·*
Pul.	4–29	*u·*, in all its public sessions,
	6–18	* false remedy I had vainly *u·*,
	47–20	* *u·* in the definitions of
	76– 1	* material *u·* in its construction
	76– 1	* being that *u·* in the doors
Rud.	2– 8	*u·* by the best authorities,
No.	11–10	which must be *u·*
	20– 8	term divine Principle is *u·*
	22–19	*u·* in the plural number.
'01.	10–15	mysticism that *u·* to enthrall
	18–18	disciples would have *u·* them
	23–18	He *u·* no material medicine,
	25–19	he never *u·* them.
	31–25	*u·* faithfully God's Word,
'02.	2–30	*u·* no other means
	7–11	*u·* as an English prefix
My.	67–20	* *u·* in giving Boston an edifice
	68–31	* *u·* in the lighting fixtures,
	69–13	* white marble was *u·*,
	121–20	may be *u·* to disguise
	130–28	*u·* as a companion to the Bible
	157– 6	to be *u·* at once to build a
	219– 8	*u·* in preventing the occasion
	225–10	capital letters should be *u·*
	225–31	should not be written or *u·*
	287– 5	*u·* in a remarkable degree
	307– 5	the word science was not *u·*
	307–10	I noticed he *u·* that word,
	308–19	He never *u·* a walking-stick.
	317–21	diction, as *u·* in explaining C. S.,
	343–21	the term pope is *u·* figuratively.
	361– 6	to be *u·* as a model.

useful

Mis.	47–30	accepts as either *u·* or true.
	299–29	new patterns which are *u·*
Ret.	85– 7	commend itself as *u·* to the Cause
'01.	25–26	avowed to be as . . . *u·*, as
My.	49–24	* giving some *u·* hints

usefulness

Mis.	284– 9	sphere of his present *u·*.
'00.	2–13	by his example and *u·*.
	8–17	*U·* is doing rightly by yourself and
'01.	1–13	essential to your growth and *u·* ;
My.	250–10	higher *u·* in this vast vineyard

useless

Mis.	17–12	hygiene as worse than *u·*
	234–16	Empirical knowledge is worse than *u·* :

uselessness

Mis.	6–23	*u·* of such material methods,

user

My.	106–25	tobacco *u·*, a profane swearer,

uses

Mis.	8–21	* "Sweet are the *u·* of adversity."
	9– 5	Sweet, . . . are these *u·* of His rod !
	41– 4	*u·* it to accomplish an evil purpose.
	284– 6	Its infinite nature and *u·*
	338–16	the *u·* of good, to abuses from
Ret.	45–15	*u·* and abuses of organization.
Un.	30– 3	Human language constantly *u·* the word
Pul.	62–19	* practically no limit to the *u·*
'00.	2–17	but he *u·* them evilly.
	6–19	to a man who *u·* tobacco,
'01.	20–12	every opportunity . . . and he *u·* it.
My.	183– 1	infinite *u·* of Christ's creed,
	216–29	money for your own *u·*.

usher

Mis.	174–28	Death can never *u·* in the dawn of
	286–13	*u·* in the dawn of God's creation,

ushering

My.	352–21	*u·* into our church the hearers and

ushers

My.	38– 8	* carefully trained corps of *u·*,
	352– 4	* we, the *u·* of your church,

Ushers of The Mother Church

My.	352–16	* signature
	352–19	*Beloved U· of T· M· C·*

using

Mis.	55–12	and who are *u·* that power against
	59– 6	It is *u·* the power of human will,
	115–31	*U·* mental power in the right direction
	269– 3	By *u·* falsehood to regain his
Ret.	34– 1	utility of *u·* a material curative.
Pul.	50– 1	* *u·* her money to promote the
Rud.	2–15	*u·* the phrase *an individual* God,
Pan.	10–21	intemperance, tobacco *u·*, and
Hea.	13–16	*u·* only the sugar of milk ;
My.	226– 1	To avoid *u·* this word incorrectly,
	235– 2	without *u·* the word death,

usual

Mis.	156– 8	send in your contributions as *u·*
	350–13	deliberations were, as *u·*, Christian,
	373– 6	but, as *u·*, he finally yielded.
My.	20–29	omit this year the *u·* large gathering
	32–10	* above the *u·* platform tone.
	88–12	* ceremonial of far more than *u·*
	134–29	* her *u·* mental and physical vigor."
	145–18	I have worked even harder than *u·*,
	148–18	I, as *u·*, at home and alone,
	312–26	took with him the *u·* amount of money
	333–14	* interred with the *u·* ceremonies.
	341–23	* granting of interviews is not *u·*,

usually

Mis.	379–11	his writings *u·* ran in the vein of
Ret.	10– 4	less labor than is *u·* requisite.
Pul.	64– 5	* There is *u·* considerable difficulty
'01.	28–29	reformers *u·* are handsomely provided for.
My.	83–10	* *u·* hidden away in the laces of

usurpation

Un.	51–11	ill supplied by the pretentious *u·*,

usurper

Rud.	10– 1	an unjust *u·* of the throne

usurpest

Mis.	209– 3	*u·* the prerogative of divine wisdom,

usurps

Ret.	70– 6	*u·* the deific prerogatives
Un.	31–17	matter *u·* the authority of God,
	32– 3	matter *u·* the prerogative of God,

usury

My.	33–25	his money to *u·*, — *Psal.* 15 : 5.

Utah

(see **Salt Lake City**)

utility

Mis.	60–27	power, wisdom, and *u·* of good ;
	86–23	beauty, grandeur, and *u·*
	108–12	hence the *u·* of knowing evil aright,
	233–26	is what constitutes its *u·* :
	365–11	proof of its goodness and *u·*,
Ret.	34– 1	*u·* of using a material curative.
Pan.	10–17	thus proving the *u·* of what they
'01.	2–14	Absolute certainty . . . constitutes its *u·*,

utilization

No.	39–19	Prayer is the *u·* of the love

utilize

Mis.	69– 8	man shall *u·* the divine power.
Ret.	26–28	*u·* Truth, and absolutely reduce the
'00.	5–28	*u·* the power of divine Love

utilized
Mis.	84–31	to those who have *u·* the present,
	238–13	*u·* in the interest of somebody.
Ret.	66– 1	to be *u·* in healing the sick,
My.	222–27	the Golden Rule *u·*,
	340–31	which man's diligence has *u·*.

utilizes
Mis.	55– 7	*u·* its power to overcome sin.

utilizing
'02.	10– 2	*U·* the capacities of the human mind

utmost
Mis.	170–26	expressing the *u·* contempt.
Pul.	36–24	* of the *u·* taste and luxury,
	43–13	* *u·* simplicity marked the exercises.
Hea.	16–25	Friends, it is of the *u·* importance
My.	24–21	* pushed with the *u·* energy,
	82–25	* stations were taxed to the *u·*
	87– 3	* have been strained to their *u·*
	104–17	*u·* concern to the world
	147–28	to the *u·* parts of the earth,

utter
Mis.	67–14	not *u·* a lie, either mentally or
	114–29	even its *u·* nothingness.
	375–10	* I did not *u·* all I felt
Un.	10– 9	*u·* reliance upon the one God,
No.	8– 6	*u·* the truth of God
'01.	14– 8	false entity, and *u·* falsity,
'02.	4–28	Our thoughts of the Bible *u·* our
Po.	73–14	Witness my presence and *u·* my
My.	9–11	* move us to *u·* our gratitude

utterance
Mis.	183–19	to give *u·* to Truth.
	312–20	In honest *u·* of veritable history,

utterance
Ret.	91– 4	our Master's greatest *u·*
Po.	23–12	With *u·* deep and strong,
My.	184–29	must at some time find *u·*

utterances
Un.	17–16	wonderful *u·* of him who
Pul.	vii– 2	*u·* which epitomize the story of
'01.	30– 6	successive *u·* of reformers
My.	97–19	* their teacher and her *u·*."

uttered
Mis.	165–17	truth *u·* and lived by Jesus,
	248–11	falsehoods *u·* about me
No.	13–10	after those words were originally *u·*,
My.	170– 7	sentiments *u·* in my annual
	180– 6	*u·* Christ's Sermon on the Mount,

uttering
Mis.	160– 3	in *u·* the word *thanks*,
	226–19	by *u·* a falsehood,
Rud.	8–19	*u·* falsehood about good.
No.	25– 1	*u·* this great thought

utterly
Mis.	266–20	*u·* false and groundless.
Ret.	72–10	They are *u·* consumed — *Psal.* 73 : 19.
No.	13– 3	destroys sin quickly and *u·*.
'01.	17–26	the drug is *u·* expelled,
My.	90– 5	* these things are new, *u·* new,
	144– 7	either . . . is *u·* false.
	273–18	*u·* apart from a material
	344–16	* "Do you reject *u·* the

utters
Mis.	81–27	Truth *u·* the divine verities
	296–29	unknown individual who *u·*

V

vacancies
Man.	80–12	*V·* in Trusteeship.
	80–14	to declare *v·* in said trusteeship,
My.	266–13	consequent *v·* occuring in the

vacancy
Man.	26–21	shall fill a *v·* occurring on that
	29–15	shall appoint . . . to fill the *v·*.
	30–10	and the *v·* supplied.
	65–21	The *v·* shall be supplied by a
	78– 4	the *v·* supplied by the Board.
	80–17	Whenever a *v·* shall occur,
	80–21	trustees shall fill the *v·*,
	89– 8	shall be elected to fill the *v·*.
	100–19	another Committee to fill the *v·* ;
	102– 8	elect, dismiss, or supply a *v·*

vacant
Mis.	231–32	*v·* seat at fireside and board
	275–11	looks in dull despair at the *v·* seat,

vacate
Man.	89– 2	or *v·* her office of President

vacation
Mis.	239– 5	I have had but four days' *v·*
My.	54–17	* During the summer *v·*,

vacations
Ret.	10–11	during his college *v·*.

vaccinated
My.	345– 1	let your children be *v·*,

vaccination
My.	219–29	"Rather than quarrel over *v·*,
	344–29	Were *v·* of any avail,
	344–30	Where *v·* is compulsory,
	345– 2	*v·* will do the children no harm.

vacillating
Mis.	268–29	*v·* good or self–assertive error

vacuity
Mis.	87– 3	into one gulp of *v·*
Ret.	81–16	overwhelming sense of error's *v·*,

vagaries
Mis.	78–30	human *v·*, formulated views
Un.	15–21	Such *v·* are to be found in
No.	24– 8	All these *v·* are at variance with

vagary
Mis.	200–30	as only a *v·* of mortal belief,

vague
Mis	14–11	admit this *v·* proposition,
	86–13	and *v·* human opinions,
Un.	28–14	are even more *v·* than
Pan.	7–21	*v·* apology for contradictions.
'01.	31–14	no *v·*, fruitless, inquiring wonder.
Peo.	10– 6	matter will become *v·*,
My.	262–18	*v·* human philosophy

vaguely
Mis.	103–10	the senses say *v·* :

vain
Mis.	61– 6	knowledge and *v·* strivings
	78–14	* These "ways that are *v·*"
	145–14	forbids man to be *v·* ;
	153–22	cleansed my heart in *v·*." — *Psal.* 73 : 13.
	168–13	vainglory and *v·* knowledge,
	209– 3	Who art thou, *v·* mortal,
	234– 3	We spread our wings in *v·*
	234–13	What hinders . . . is his *v·* conceit,
	268– 5	Earthly glory is *v·* ;
	268– 5	not *v·* enough to attempt
	357– 2	*v·* amusements, and all the
	362–27	O *v·* mortals ! which shall it be?
	383–11	elements of earth beat in *v·*
Ret.	38– 6	All efforts . . . were in *v·*.
Un.	11– 1	call in *v·* for the mountains
	11–17	he cut off this *v·* boasting
	44– 6	are *v·* shadows, repeating
	60–25	your faith is *v·* ; — *I Cor.* 15 : 17.
Pul.	7–12	Not in *v·* did ye flow.
	70–20	* she endeavored in *v·* to find
No.	41–12	*v·* to look for perfection
	42–11	the *v·* power of dogma
Peo.	5– 8	we look in *v·* for their
Po.	15–13	soft as the vision more *v·*
	31–20	which deems no suffering *v·*
	34–21	Nor pinest thou in *v·*
My.	89–12	* has not lived in *v·*.
	103–17	imagine a *v·* thing?" — *Psal.* 2 : 1.
	113–18	Neither is it . . . *v·* for another,
	128– 1	words are not *v·* when the
	162–31	waves and winds beat in *v·*.
	164–29	enmity, or malice beat in *v·*.
	200– 5	imagine a *v·* thing ;" — *Psal.* 2 : 1.
	210–18	chapter sub-title
	233–19	taking the name of God in *v·*.
	270–14	and imagine a *v·* thing.

vainglorious
My.	37– 2	* No *v·* boast, no pride of

vainglory
Mis.	168–13	emptied of *v·* and vain knowledge,
	267–14	chapter sub-title
	268–17	on the shoals of *v·*.
	326–12	fed by the fat of hypocrisy and *v·*,
Ret.	86– 2	to rebuke *v·*, to offset boastful
My.	155–12	lay down the low laurels of *v·*,

vainly
Pul.	6–18	* false remedy I had *v·* used,
My.	80–28	* hundreds waiting in the streets.
	149–14	When a young man *v·* boasted,
	265–12	and justice plead not *v·*

vale
  Mis. 328– 9   surveys the *v·* of the flesh,
   Po. 32– 4   home where I dwell in the *v·*,
    53– 6   On *v·* and woodland deep ;

valiant
  Mis. 155–11   be *v·* in the Christian's warfare,
  My. 203–14   but he is unutterably *v·*,

valiantly
  Mis. 120–12   ye that have wrought *v·*,
   176–12   strive *v·* for the liberty of the

valid
  Mis. 109–10   this claim you admit as *v·*,
   261–30   or else make the claim *v·*.
  Man. 29–11   the complaint be found *v·*,
   54–13   complaint being found *v·*,
  Pan. 12– 1   Christ's dear demand, . . . is *v·*,
  My. 108–27   the words of . . . are *v·*.
   111–30   C. S. is *v·*, simple, real,

validity
  Mis. 194– 8   yet should deny the *v·*
   195–10   the *v·* of those words
  Man. 52–10   as to the *v·* of the charge.
  Ret. 93–24   convincing proof of the *v·*
  No. 4–18   the *v·* of that statement.
   6– 7   refutes the *v·* of the testimony
   6–14   cannot be healed by denying its *v·* ;
  '01. 12–15   the *v·* and permanence of
  My. 239– 9   prove the practicality, *v·*, and

valley
  Mis. 323– 8   a few laborers in a *v·*
   323–16   *v·* at the foot of the mountain.
   323–22   winds and widens in the *v·* ;
   324– 2   watchers and workers in the *v·*
   324–29   pleasant path of the *v·*
   326–19   would be led to the *v·*
   326–23   Stranger returned to the *v·* ;
   327–10   had entered the *v·* to speculate
   328– 6   the *v·* is humility,
  Pul. 48–12   * the woods that skirt the *v·*
  Po. vi– 2   * poem
   page 15   poem
  My. 186–10   point the path above the *v·*,

Valley Cemetery, The
  Po. vi– 2   * poem
   page 15   poem

Valley of Decision
  Mis. 270– 1   We are in the *V· of D·*.

valleys
  Mis. 203–11   waters that run among the *v·*,

valor
  Mis. 287–32   venturing on *v·* without discretion,
  My. 270–10   records . . . attest honesty and *v·*.

valuable
  Mis. 109–24   *v·* sequence of knowledge
   169–23   makes them nothing *v·*,
  Ret. 27–10   These early comments are *v·*
  My. 62–26   * *v·* services rendered to this Board
   63– 5   * and for their *v·* services,

value
  Mis. 39– 1   would be of less practical *v·*.
   110– 2   had not the *v·* of a single *tear*.
   114– 2   of inestimable *v·* to all seekers
   131–27   let her state the *v·* thereof,
   139–20   at $20,000 and rising in *v·*
   232–24   its infinite *v·* and firm basis.
   239–29   taught the *v·* of saying
   253– 5   its *v·*, and the price that he paid
   269–28   to buy error at par *v·*.
   273– 2   know the *v·* of these rebukes.
   365–22   shows the real *v·* of C. S.
  Ret. 45– 6   organization has its *v·* and peril,
   51– 3   and rising in *v·*,
  Pul. 1–13   great is the *v·* thereof.
  No. 19– 5   shows its real *v·* to the race.
  '02. 13– 7   property and funds, to the *v·* of
  My. 28–15   * has been of immense *v·* to them.
   75– 1   * of the *v·* of the latter,
   99–30   * at their face *v·*.
   172–12   gift that has no intrinsic *v·*
   190–18   relative *v·*, skill, and certainty of
   226–22   even as you *v·* His all-power,
   265– 8   and is bought at par *v·* ;
   273– 4   * *v·* of her teachings.
   348–21   *v·* to the race firmly established.

valued
  Mis. 139–20   now *v·* at $20,000 and rising
  Ret. 51– 2   *v·* in 1892 at about
  Pul. 28–12   * *v·* at some forty thousand dollars.
  '00. 3– 9   worker's servitude is duly *v·*,
  '02. 13–27   now *v·* at twenty thousand dollars,
  My. vi–21   * *v·* at forty-five thousand dollars,
   vi–26   * *v·* at twenty-five thousand dollars,

values
  one cent
   Mis. 305–25   * contribute *o· c·* to be fused into
  twenty-five cents
   Mis. 305–25   * *t· c·* to pay for it.
  fifty cents
   '01. 29–27   *f· c·* on every book
  one dollar
   Man. 44–14   tax of not less than *o· d·*,
   '02. 15–11   paid me not *o· d·* of royalty
  two dollars
   Mis. 305–26   * asked to collect *t· d·*
  three dollars
   Mis. 35–16   *you offer for sale at t· d·*,
  five-dollar
   '00. 10–27   ten *f·* gold pieces
  five dollars
   My. 328–14   * license of *f· d·* annually,
   328–30   * a license fee of *f· d·*."
  ten dollars
   My. 53–17   * preach for the society for *t· d·*
  fifteen dollars
   Mis. 349–27   accepted, for a time, *f· d·*
  fifty dollars
   Mis. 280–20   elegant album costing *f· d·*,
   My. 176– 3   A GIFT OF *F· D·* IN GOLD
  $100.00
   Man. 84–15   shall not exceed $100.00 per pupil.
   91– 9   Tuition . . . shall be $100.00.
  one-hundred-dollar bills
   My. 30–23   * contributions were *o· b·*.
  ($113.09)
   Mis. 381–20   cost of suit, taxed at ($113.09)
  one hundred thirteen and 9/100 dollars
   Mis. 381–20   taxed at . . . *o· h· t·* and $\frac{9}{100}$ *d·*.
  one hundred and seventy-five dollars
   My. 166–28   cabinet, costing *o· h· and s· d·*,
  $200
   Man. 78–19   not exceeding $200 for any one
  three hundred dollars
   Ret. 50– 4   I was led to name *t· h· d·*
   50–12   if they consider *t· h· d·*
   My. 215– 8   tuition of *t· h· d·* each,
  $500
   Man. 78–21   keep on deposit the sum of $500
  five hundred dollars
   Mis. 272–17   * fine not less than *f· h· d·*
   My. 175– 6   enclosed check for *f· h· d·*,
   289– 4   enclose a check for *f· h· d·*
  $621.10
   My. 25–12   * contributions . . . $621.10 ;
  seven hundred dollars
   Ret. 38– 4   already paid him *s· h· d·*,
  $845.96
   My. 25–13   * contributions . . . $845.96 ;
  one thousand dollars
   Mis. 143–21   contributions of *o· t· d·* each,
   242– 6   liberal sum of *o· t· d·*
   272–18   not more than *o· t· d·*.
   Man. 68–11   at the rate of *o· t· d·*
  $1,112.13
   My. 25–14   * to February 28, 1906, $1,112.13 ;
  $1,489.50
   Mis. 350– 1   I hold receipts for $1,489.50
  two thousand dollars
   Mis. 242– 8   *t· t· d·* if either
   349–32   church-fund about *t· t· d·*
  two thousand five hundred dollars
   Man. 29–16   at present *t· t· f· h· d·*
  $2,579.19
   My. 25–14   * total $2,579.19.
  three thousand dollars
   Mis. 242–19   I offer him *t· t· d·*
  four thousand dollars
   Man. 97–14   not less than *f· t· d·*.
   My. 217– 7   the sum of *f· t· d·*
  $4,460
   Pul. v– 4   CONTRIBUTIONS OF $4,460 WERE
   9– 1   have come $4,460.
  $4,963.50
   '02. 13–18   paying for it the sum of $4,963.50
  five thousand dollars
   '02. 14– 1   About *f· t· d·* had been paid
   My. 26– 9   check of *f· t· d·*,
  ten thousand dollars
   Mis. 381–25   on penalty of *t· t· d·*.
   My. 73– 3   * to return more than *t· t· d·*
   164–10   munificent gift . . . of *t· t· d·*.
   165–13   for the sum of *t· t· d·*
   166–10   Your munificent gift of *t· t· d·*,
  eleven thousand dollars
   Pul. 26–14   * and cost *e· t· d·*.
   60–17   * at a cost of *e· t· d·*,
  fourteen thousand dollars
   My. 123–16   cost of the estate was *f· t· d·*.

values

$20,000
Mis. 139–20 now valued at $20,000
twenty thousand dollars
Ret. 51– 3 at about *t· t· d·*,
'*02.* 13–28 now valued at *t· t· d·*,
My. 123–18 amount is now about *t· t· d·*.
twenty-five thousand dollars
My. vi–26 * valued at *t· t· d·*,
forty thousand dollars
Pul. 28–13 * valued at some *f· t· d·*.
forty-two thousand dollars
Mis. 143–23 munificent sum of *f· t· d·*
forty-five thousand dollars
My. vi–21 * valued at *f· t· d·*,
eighty thousand dollars
My. 162–13 gifts to me of about *e· t· d·*,
one hundred thousand dollars
My. 157– 5 your generous gift of *o· h· t· d·*
157–23 the sum of *o· h· t· d·*
one hundred and twenty thousand dollars
'*02.* 13– 7 value of about *o· h· and t· t· d·*;
$191,012.
Pul. 8–10 responded . . . with $191,012.
$199,607.93
My. 16– 7 * paying out the sum of $199,607.93,
two hundred thousand dollars
Pul. 30–29 * costing over *t· h· t· d·*,
50–13 * It has cost *t· h· t· d·*,
52–12 * at a cost of over *t· h· t· d·*,
57– 3 * cost over *t· h· t· d·*.
58–10 * at a cost of over *t· h· t· d·*,
68–20 * cost over *t· h· t· d·*,
79– 5 * costing over *t· h· t· d·*,
two hundred and twenty-one thousand dollars
Pul. 28–11 * The cost . . . is *t· h· and t· t· d·*,
$226,285.73
My. 16– 6 * balance of $226,285.73 on hand
$250,000
Pul. 63– 6 * A CHURCH COSTING $250,000
two hundred and fifty thousand dollars
Pul. 63–22 * a cost of *t· h· and f· t· d·*,
70–15 * cost *t· h· and f· t· d·*
quarter of a million dollars
Pul. 44–23 * with a *q· of a m· d·* expended
71– 6 * contribution of a *q· of a m· d·*
$303,189.41
My. 23–11 * Amount on hand . . . $303,189.41;
$388,663.15
My. 23–12 * expenditures . . . $388,663.15;
$425,893.66
My. 16– 4 * $425,893.66 had been received
$891,460.49
My. 23–13 * total receipts . . . $891,460.49.
$1,108,539.51
My. 23–15 * pledged . . . $1,108,539.51.
$2,000,000
My. 23–14 * to complete the sum of $2,000,000
67– 6 * Cost . . . $2,000,000
two-million-dollar
My. 76– 2 * this new *t·* edifice,
76–26 * the new *t·* cathedral,
86–11 * their new *t·* church,
92–22 * the *t·* stone edifice
94– 7 * the *t·* stone edifice
98–28 * erection . . . of the *t·* church
two million dollars
My. 7–13 chapter sub-title
8– 1 * any portion of *t· m· d·*
9– 5 * any portion of *t· m· d·*
11–30 * "any portion of *t· m· d·*
65– 8 * any part of *t· m· d·*
67–18 * *T· m· d·* was set aside for
72–24 * *t· m· d·* has been subscribed
77–28 * *t· m· d·* required to build
83–24 * *t· m· d·* needed for the
89–14 * although it cost *t· m· d·*,
90–23 * its paid-up cost of *t· m· d·*
91–27 * temple . . . cost *t· m· d·*,
95–13 * cost them about *t· m· d·*,
96–19 * approximately *t· m· d·*.
97–27 * at a cost of *t· m· d·*,
98–18 * cost about *t· m· d·*,
99–15 * at a cost of *t· m· d·*,
100– 5 * cost about *t· m· d·*
two millions of dollars
My. 9–22 any part of *t· m· of d·*
31–12 * approximates *t· m· of d·*,
57–10 * any part of *t· m· of d·*
two millions of money
My. 13–18 any part of *t· m· of m·*
millions of dollars
Pul. 8– 7 *m· of d·* unemployed

My. 48–24 * material to spiritual *v·*,

van
Po. 2– 8 trained falcon in the Gallic *v·*,
Vanderbilt Hall
My. 172– 4 * to make room for *V· H·*.
vane
Un. 14–19 not the shifting *v·* on the spire,
vanguard
My. 31–14 * *v·* of the thousands had been seated,
vanish
Mis. 30–29 mist of materialism will *v·*
205–29 mortal molecules, . . . *v·* as a dream;
vanished
Mis. 216–20 * "*v·* quite slowly,
Ret. 10–13 *v·* like a dream.
Po. 23– 4 a thought of *v·* hours
vanisheth
'*00.* 10– 4 *v·* with the new birth of the
vanity
Mis. 145–14 *v·* forbids man to be vain;
173–18 *v·* to pretend that it is man?
265– 3 makes the venture from *v·*,
363– 8 by Him who compensateth *v·*
Ret. 70–29 post of duty, unpierced by *v·*,
Un. 27– 7 *Egotism* implies *v·* and self-conceit.
No. 39– 8 no dishonesty or *v·* influences the
40– 3 Because of *v·* and self-righteousness,
Hea. 11– 2 plucked from the wings of *v·*.
Po. 2–10 all the strength of weakness— *v·*!
33– 8 *v·*, folly, and all that is wrong
My. 25–26 *v·* of victory disappears
34– 4 his soul unto *v·*,—*Psal.* 24: 4.
vanquished
Mis. 74–20 virtually *v·* matter
339– 6 Experience is victor, never the *v·*;
Ret. 22–15 till its involved errors are *v·*
My. 185–14 victors never to be *v·*.
vanquishment
Mis. 105–17 *v·* is unknown to the
vapors
Peo. 3– 6 roasting amidst noxious *v·*;
vapory
Mis. 38–23 too *v·* and hypothetical for
variableness
Un. 14–18 with whom is no *v·*,—*Jas.* 1: 17.
63– 9 no *v·* or shadow of turning,
variance
Mis. 148– 3 one part of his character at *v·*
214– 7 at *v·* against his father,—*Matt.* 10: 35.
324–14 drunkenness, witchcraft, *v·*,
No. 24– 8 All these vagaries are at *v·* with
variation
Pul. 42– 7 * scarcely even a minor *v·*
'*00.* 11–17 quality, quantity, and *v·* in tone,
varied
Mis. 116–16 *v·* strains of human chords
128– 4 are too vast and *v·* to
198– 7 *v·* forms of pleasure and pain.
374– 5 in most of its *v·* manifestations.
varies
No. 31–11 Our phraseology *v·*.
variety
Mis. 128– 1 and given a *v·* of *turns*,
Pul. 52– 4 * faith of the mustard-seed *v·*.
My. 57–32 * faith of the mustard-seed *v·*.
various
Mis. x–19 to assume *v· noms de plume.*
132–24 refer you . . . to my *v·* publications,
149– 8 presenting the *v·* offerings,
329– 8 her *v·* apartments are
Ret. 33– 9 and from *v·* humbugs,
75– 1 *v·* forms of book-borrowing
Un. 27– 1 From *v·* friends comes inquiry
Pul. 23–13 * and under *v·* names,
53– 7 * on *v·* occasions during the
71–17 * *v·* dignitaries of the faith.
Po. vi–25 * *in v· publications of that day.*
My. 310– 3 at *v·* times and places.
313– 8 *v·* stories told by *McClure's Magazine*
346–22 * *V·* conjectures having arisen
variously
Mis. 180–27 the word "son" is defined *v·*;
varying
Mis. 142–18 *v·* types of true affection,
Un. 26– 8 for my *v·* manifestations.
My. 170–14 but not to *v·* views.
vascular
Rud. 11–27 *v·*, or nervous operations of the

vase
   Pul.   42–29   * a *v·* filled with . . . pink roses.

vassal
   Po.   31–14   *v·* of the changeful hour,

vast
   Mis.   43–22   does a *v·* amount of injury
       77–20   *v·* idea of Christ Jesus,
      128– 3   too *v·* . . . to teach briefly ;
      156– 3   reaches a *v·* number of earnest
      312–26   into the *v·* forever.
   Ret.   9–20   * *v·* and dim And whispering woods,
      82– 4   with the *v·* Wagner Trilogy.
   Pul. vii–19   *v·* problem of eternal life,
      26–13   * It is one of *v·* compass,
      37–10   * attends to a *v·* correspondence ;
      41–18   * receiving this *v·* throng,
      41–21   * each of the four *v·* congregations
   Po.   1– 8   when first creation *v·* began,
      27–13   let today grow difficult and *v·*
   My.   29– 6   * from the *v·* congregation,
      50– 8   * *v·* gloom of the mysterious forests,
      69–18   * anywhere in the *v·* space
      71–21   * just one *v·* auditorium
      78–23   * in spite of its *v·* interior,
      79– 9   * dedication of the *v·* temple
      92–20   * dedication of this *v·* temple.
     100– 9   * representing a *v·* number
     141–19   * *v·* multitudes of . . . Scientists
     250–10   this *v·* vineyard of our Lord.
     291–21   bear its banner into the *v·*
     354–22   Science *v·*, to which belongs

vaster
   My.   67–22   * *v·* sums of money were spent

vastly
   Mis.   52– 6   he could do *v·* more.
   Un.   14– 9   could *v·* improve upon
   My. 190–12   *v·* excelling the former.

vastness
   Mis.   4–22   *v·* of its worth
   My.   24– 6   * *v·* of the truth it represents,
      31–13   * first impression was of *v·*,
      63–25   * purity, stateliness, and *v·* ;

Vatican
   Pul.   5–27   and the *V·* at Rome.
   My. 294–30   The court of the *V·* mourns him ;

vault
   Pul.   27– 4   * *v·* for the safe preservation of

vaulted
   My. 151–18   * *v·* aisles by flaunting folly trod,

vaults
   Po.   16– 7   These *v·* will unfold

vegetable
   Mis. 217–13   *v·*, and animal kingdoms,
   Un.   38–24   *v·*, or animal kingdoms.
   No.   24– 6   animal *v·*, developed through the

vegetables
   Rud.   7–26   transforming minerals into *v·*

vehicle
   Mis. 156– 2   swift *v·* of scientific thought ;
   My. 302– 1   *v·* of all modes of healing

veil
   Mis. 124–24   rent the *v·* of matter,
      165–12   rends the *v·* of the flesh
      203–22   *v·* that hides mental deformity.
      275– 7   it were well to lift the *v·*
      352–32   covered with the *v·* of harmony,
      364–31   C. S. rends this *v·*
      374–28   Looking behind the *v·*,
   No.   21–20   rends this *v·* in the pantheon
   My. 256–20   *v·* of time springs aside at the

veiled
   Mis. 250–25   *v·* form stealing on an errand of
      395–15   *V·* is the modest moon
   Po.   57–19   *V·* is the modest moon

veils
   Mis.   62– 9   Believing a lie *v·* the truth
   Po.   31–11   *v·* the leaflet's wondrous

vein
   Mis. 379–11   *v·* of thought presented by these.
   Un.   7–12   eaten its way to the jugular *v·*.
   Hea.   19– 9   a *v·* had not been opened,
   My. 105–15   and exposed the jugular *v·*

veins
   Pul.   7– 2   * "Had I young blood in my *v·*,
   No.   20–25   have run through the *v·* of all

velvet
   Pul.   78–24   * satin-lined box of rich green *v·*.

venal
   Un.   15–26   criminal appeases, . . . the *v·* officer.

vending
   Mis. 269–27   Error is *v·* itself on trust,

vendors
   Mis.   79–31   *v·* of patent pills, mesmerists,

venerable
   Mis. 225–16   he said to this *v·* Christian :
   Ret.   4– 1   This *v·* grandmother had thirteen
   '01.   32–27   I believe, if those *v·* Christians
   My. 290– 8   Few sovereigns have been as *v·*,
      297– 1   if Miss Barton were not a *v·* soldier,

venereal
   Mis. 210–24   belief in *v·* diseases

vengeance
   Mis. 130–15   "*V·* is mine ;— *Rom.* 12 : 19.

venomous
   Mis. 323–11   *V·* serpents hide among the rocks,

vent
   Mis.   41– 2   given *v·* in the diabolical practice of

vented
   My. 104– 9   *v·* their hatred of Jesus

ventilating
   Mis. 297–12   censor *v·* his lofty scorn

ventilation
   Mis.   78–18   witless *v·* of false statements

venture
   Mis. 265– 3   makes the *v·* from vanity,
   Ret.   35– 7   I did not *v·* upon its publication
   Pul.   29– 6   * of whose work I shall *v·* to speak,
   No.   34– 6   we shall no longer *v·* to
   My.   51– 9   * we *v·* to hope she will remain
      154– 7   I shall scarcely *v·* to send

ventured
   Mis. 234–18   That one should have *v·*

venturing
   Mis. 287–32   *v·* on valor without discretion,
      339–21   *v·* its all of happiness

veracity
   My. 311–23   I never doubted the *v·* of

verb
   Mis.   77– 4   Here the *v· believe* took its
   Rud.   1–14   *v· personare* is compounded of

verbally
   Mis. 127– 9   not *v·*, nor on bended knee,
   My.   18– 6   not *v·*, nor on bended knee,

verbatim
   Mis. 300– 3   Copying my published works *v·*,

verbiage
   '01.   16–10   with the *v·* of hades.

verdant
   Mis. 390–15   The *v·* grass it weaves ;
   Po.   16–23   breath from the *v·* springtime,
      55–16   The *v·* grass it weaves ;
   My. 129–11   The oracular skies, the *v·* earth
      252–20   They point to *v·* pastures,

verdict
   Mis.   73–18   Hence the *v·* of experience :
   Un.   57–15   rendered this infallible *v·* ;
   Rud.   5–24   *v·* of these material senses,
   Pan.   10– 7   the honest *v·* of humanity
   My. 105– 9   by *v·* of the stethoscope

verdure
   Po.   16– 4   My heart hath thy *v·*,
      31–11   Love's *v·* veils the leaflet's
   My. 139– 9   Like the *v·* and evergreen

verge
   Mis. 202– 7   * Quite on the *v·* of heaven."
      357–10   quite on the *v·* of heaven.
   My. 199–18   This year, standing on the *v·* of

veriest
   Mis. 172–11   cover with her feathers the *v·* sinner.

verification
   My. 179–16   *v·* of our Master's sayings.

verified
   Mis.   66–11   precept is *v·* in all directions
   Man.   46– 5   *v·* according to the laws of our land.
   My.   95– 3   * predictions have not been *v·*.
      186–21   Here let His promise be *v·* :
      266–20   since this great fact is to be *v·*
      329–17   * photographs are *v·* by the

verifies
   My.   3–22   Christian Scientist *v·* his calling.

verify
   Man.   89–15   are required to *v·* this fact,
   '01.   13–13   and we *v·* Jesus' words,
   My. 183– 5   *v·* what John Robinson wrote

verifying
My. 58–23 * v· Jesus' words,
190–31 v· his last promise,

verily
Mis. 73–22 V· I say unto you,— Matt. 19 : 28.
Chr. 55– 6 V·, v·, I say unto you,— John 5 : 25.
Un. 24– 8 v· I say unto you, God is All-in-all ;
My. 19–30 "V· I say unto you,— Mark 14 : 9.
113–17 Was it profane . . . Nay, v·.
170–21 v· thou shalt be fed.— Psal. 37 : 3.

veritable
Mis. 243–32 of material methods, and as v· :
312–20 honest utterance of v· history,
No. 27–13 but it is just as v· now
My. 119–22 proof of his Saviour, the v· Christ,
315–22 Is it myself, the v· Mrs. Eddy,

veritably
My. 297–20 is here now as v· as when he

Veritas Odium Parit
Mis. 245– 7 chapter sub-title

verities
of being
Mis. 81–27 utters the divine v· of being
97– 5 the grand v· of being.
136–12 When the v· of being seem to
183– 4 the v· of being exist,
No. 10– 4 relative to the unseen v· of being,

————

Mis. 55–21 v· of Spirit assert themselves
61– 2 representative of v· priceless,
79– 5 The grand v· of Science
112– 4 may deem these delusions v·,
192–22 grand v· of Christian healing
312–19 * v· of the sacred Scriptures.''
363–19 in glimpses of the eternal v·.
No. 27–15 eternal v· of God and man

verity
Mis. 28–27 knowledge of this grand v·,
31–15 grand v· of this Science,
75– 8 grand v· of C. S.,
103– 1 This v· annuls the testimony
181– 5 Man's knowledge of this grand v·
252–16 satisfy himself of their v·.
261– 8 demonstrates this v· of being ;
286– 4 this v· in human economy
286–27 recognize this v· of being,
338– 1 this grand v· in Science,
Ret. 59– 1 C. S. reveals the grand v·,
93–21 as yet this grandest v· has not
Un. 6–17 grand and all-absorbing v·
43–16 in support of this v·,
Pul. vii–17 the cradle of this grand v·
3–27 "The evidence of spiritual v·
No. 5– 3 Principle of this grand v·
17–16 divine consciousness and God's v·.
24–20 appears the grand v· of C. S. :
31– 1 this grand v· of C. S.,
'01. 13–12 neither entity, v·, nor power
14–29 apprehension of this grand v·.
31–17 To this v· every member of my
'02. 6–10 demonstrate this grand v·,
Peo. 10–17 It assures us, of a v·,
My. 37–12 * revealed the v· and rule of
46– 8 * it stands in prophetic v·
105– 2 which had of a v· stirred
146– 6 v· has not been acknowledged
180–20 refuses to see this grand v·
232–24 eternal v·, . . . is understood
251–27 convince yourselves of this grand v· :

vermin
Mis. 249–19 to remove stains or v·.

Vermont
(see Londonderry)

vernal
Mis. 343–18 v· freshness and sunshine
Po. 53–20 The v· songs and flowers.

verse
Mis. 32–14 commencing at the thirty-third v·,
106– 5 parody on Tennyson's grand v·,
191– 9 sixth chapter and seventieth v·,
191–13 ninth chapter and thirty-eighth v·,
332–14 third chapter and ninth v·,
400–12 poem
Po. page 69 poem
My. 189–28 from which I copy this v· :

versed
Pul. 73–21 * perfectly v· in all their beliefs

verse-maker
Ret. 11– 1 From childhood I was a v·.

verses
Mis. 314–22 the book, chapter, and v·.
Chr. 55– 1 the sentiments in the v·,
Ret. 1– 9 other v· and enigmas

version
Mis. 26–26 common v· of Hebrews
Hea. 16– 2 given its spiritual v·,
My. 356–28 the only possible correct v·

versus
Mis. 332–22 What was this sense? Error v· Truth :
346–22 chapter sub-title
My. 232– 9 chapter sub-title

vertebræ
Mis. 171–10 to filter from v· to v·.

vertebrata
My. 271– 3 no v·, mollusca, or radiata.

very
Mis. 3–11 taught them for this v· purpose ;
4–24 "You must have a v· strong
7–19 so loaded . . . seems the v· air.
16– 7 so v· much requisite to
26–18 it is the v· opposite of Spirit,
32–12 in my books, on this v· subject.
54–15 curing hundreds at this v· time ;
56– 1 the v· antipodes of C. S.
61–30 Mortals seem v· material ;
67–31 taken up to the v· throne,
68–14 the penalty . . . is the v· pain and
71–10 is a v· right thing to do.
78–16 deceive, if possible, the v· elect.
99– 2 revolutionary in its v· nature ;
120– 3 at the v· threshold of C. S. :
134– 7 V· truly,
175–20 the v· elect,"— Matt. 24 : 24.
184– 1 v· opposite of that Maker.
185–11 opens the v· flood-gates of heaven ;
214–14 The v· conflict his Truth brought,
215– 1 through this v· process,
224– 9 * "It is v· surprising,
237–25 v· streets through which Garrison
242–21 where the patient is v· low
275–24 love and loyalty were v· touching.
306– 9 * V· cordially yours,
316– 8 I shall speak . . . v· seldom.
338–17 But the v· heavens shall laugh
339– 4 would happen v· frequently
344– 4 "V· well," the teacher replied ;
346– 1 v· centre of its faith.
350– 5 with advice of the v· student who
354– 3 Sin in its v· nature is marvellous !
376– 5 * v· closely resemble in detail the
Ret. 2–22 were not v· ancient,
5– 3 was a v· religious man,
6–12 the v· dearest of my kindred.
7–16 practice of a v· large business.
20–12 my home I regarded as v· precious.
20–21 My second marriage was v· unfortunate,
20–28 v· soon removed to . . . the Far West.
31– 9 From my v· childhood I was
50–15 my list of . . . is v· large,
60– 2 v· far from the divine likeness.
82– 8 exception . . . should be v· rare.
Un. 2– 4 "a v· present help— Psal. 46 : 1.
11–16 withered hand looks v· real
11–17 and feels v· real ;"
13–16 in the v· fibre of His being,
15–13 comes through the v· knowledge
29–20 a soul which that v· sense declares
42–11 for the v· opposite of this error
45– 9 v· far from God's likeness."
54–20 God forbade . . . at the v· beginning,
58– 8 This was the v· thing he was doing,
59–19 rescue men from these v· illusions
Pul. 5– 1 and one of the v· clergymen
9–19 with his better half, is a v· whole man
24–28 * windows of stained glass are v· rich
27– 3 * directors' room is v· beautiful
31– 2 * a v· remarkable retrospect.
36– 4 * in the v· zenith of its prosperity
37–16 * Mrs. Eddy feels v· strongly,"
37–21 * "Mother feels v· strongly,"
47–25 * she lives v· much retired,
51–18 * is v· well known.
63–20 * v· tangible and material manner
70–13 * v· recently saw completed in Boston,
72– 6 * number of v· interesting conversations
72– 9 * Mrs. Copeland is a v· pleasant
72–10 * v· much absorbed in the work
73–17 * is also a v· prominent member
Rud. 15–19 Only a v· limited number of students
No. 40–15 to pursue . . . v· sacredly,
'01. 13–16 on the v· basis of nothingness.
31– 6 from the v· nature of Truth,
'02. 11–30 on the v· basis of his words

very
Hea.	9–12	the v· subjects they would gladly
My.	14–18	* Our friend v· promptly and
	21–23	* meeting v· many of them this year,
	29–16	* lay in its v· simplicity ;
	50–24	* it was a v· inspiring season
	51–25	* relative to this v· early work
	53–27	* some v· interesting statements,
	53–30	* must have been v· much broken
	61– 3	* has been v· interesting indeed,
	61– 6	* lessons . . . have been v· precious.
	73– 6	* v· few of them owe a cent.
	74–12	* v· interesting and agreeable visitors,
	75–17	* take it all v· good-naturedly.
	75–18	* v· patient and good-natured.
	81– 6	* at the v· height of fervor,
	84–20	* Its v· magnitude and
	90– 8	* and is given v· real tests.
	91–19	* It has not been v· many years
	100–15	* are v· generally of a class who
	106–27	the v· antipode of all these?
	122–30	the v· hearts that rejected it
	131–20	this meeting is v· joyous to me.
	147–26	with you personally v· seldom.
	158– 4	V· truly,
	162– 3	"v· present help — *Psal.* 46 : 1.
	175–29	the v· opposite of my real sentiments.
	184–24	prosperity of Zion is v· precious
	208–26	reaching the v· acme of C. S.
	215–11	those v· students sent me the
	272–26	* her v· great following.
	272–28	* Mrs. Eddy writes v· rarely for
	273– 8	* a v· great organization
	319–26	* These dates are v· well fixed
	319–28	* I also recall v· plainly the
	320– 5	* He also seemed v· much pleased
	320–12	* as being a v· unique book,
	320–32	* spoke in a v· animated manner
	321– 2	* He seemed v· proud to
	321–26	* v· glad that I was among your
	324– 9	* so original and so v· decided
	324–13	* to have those v· terms revealed
	324–15	* I am v· sure that neither
	325– 6	* Mr. Wiggin was v· much troubled
	325– 7	* v· sure Back Bay property would
	355– 9	men are v· important factors

vesper
Ret.	17–11	And v· reclines
'02.	4–15	ringing like soft v· chimes
Po.	62–13	And v· reclines

vesper-call
Po.	8– 3	In somber groups at the v·,

vespers
Pan.	3–12	the evening's closing v·,
Po.	34– 9	Wouldst chant thy v·

vessel
My.	149–17	A v· full must be emptied

Vesta
Mis.	341–23	the sad history of V·,

vestal
Po.	8– 9	v· pearls that on leaflets lay,

vested
Mis.	258–12	law was v· in the Lawgiver,
	298–22	faith v· in righteousness

vestibule
Mis.	239–17	sweet face appeared in the v·,
Pul.	25–16	* The v· is a fitting entrance
	59–30	* the front v· and street
My.	159–13	stands at the v· of C. S.,
	320–31	* I met him in the v· of the

vestry
Ret.	15–21	Our last v· meeting was
Pul.	25–11	* "directors' room," and the v·.
	27– 6	* The v· seats eight hundred people,
	42– 1	* had closed the large v· room
My.	80–11	* in the extension v·,
	80–12	* in The Mother Church v·,

vesture
Mis.	302– 5	"cast lots for his v·," — *see Psal.* 22 : 18.
'01.	26–15	to preserve Christ's v· unrent ;
My.	154–17	weaving the new-old v·

vestures
Mis.	358–15	Christ's v· are put on

Veterans
My.	284–21	When the V· indicated their desire to

vexed
Man.	66–12	to report to her the v· question

vial
My.	107–13	a v· full of the pellets can be

viands
Mis.	231– 7	rich v· made busy many appetites ;

vibrant
My.	19–25	v· through time and eternity

vibrate
Ret.	17– 8	v· and tremble with accents of
Po.	62– 8	v· and tremble with accents of

vibrating
My.	189–11	v· from one pulpit to another

vibration
My.	226– 7	principle of harmonious v·,

vicarious
Mis.	123–22	not through v· suffering,
No.	37–11	interpretation of the v· atonement

vice
Mis.	81–29	depths of ignorance and v·.
	296–24	affinity for the worst forms of v·
	388–15	won from v·, by virtue's smile,
Un.	52–26	is sometimes the home of v·.
Rud.	11–11	seem to be disease, v·, and
Po.	21– 2	won from v·, by virtue's smile,
	22–20	peace is won, and lost is v· :
My.	36–15	* reclaimed from v· or redeemed from

Vice-President
My.	245–30	conferred by the President or V·

vice-president
Man.	88– 8	a president, v·, and
	88–10	v· shall be elected annually
	89– 6	v· of the Board of Education

vices
Mis.	226–28	more than do most v·.
Un.	23– 3	* and of our pleasant v·
Pul.	15– 8	when you tell them their v·.
Rud.	9–20	lust, and all fleshly v·.
No.	42–22	cleaving to their own v·.

vice versa
Mis.	45–18	not the master . . . but v· v·;
	192– 3	term for Deity was "good," and v· v·;
	218– 4	never produced Mind, and v· v·.
	219–26	manifest on the body, and v· v·;
	294–12	v· v· of this man is sometimes
	340– 4	never the reward of evil, and v· v·.
	352– 9	v· v· . . . this uncovers the error
Ret.	64– 3	sin is the sinner, and v· v·,
	67– 4	does not constitute sin, but v· v·,

vicious
Un.	42– 9	That man must be v·

vicissitudes
Pul.	10–24	chill v· have not withheld the
	58– 1	* after many v·,

victim
Mis.	112–19	regarded . . . himself as the v·.
	115–30	you will fall the v· of
	210–25	torments its v·, and thus
	222– 5	causes the v· to believe that
	222– 7	in many cases causes the v·
	246–18	then turn and refuse the v· a
	250– 7	so-called affection pursuing its v·
	254–13	The v· of mad ambition
	355–20	its v· is responsible for
Ret.	73–21	v· of his own corporeality.
Peo.	6–14	Believing that man is the v·
My.	211–13	entices its v· by unseen,
	211–29	the v· is in a state of
	212– 1	the v· is led to believe
	213–17	the v· will allow himself to
	220–27	and fell a v· to those laws.

victims
Mis.	123–11	demands human v· to be
	254–24	filling with hate its . . . v·,
Ret.	64–29	will become the v· of error.
My.	211–17	The v· lose their individuality,

victor
Mis.	105–17	C. S. is an everlasting v·,
	336– 2	Truth, the v· over a lie.
	339– 6	Experience is v·,
Po.	42– 4	Yet there's one will be v·,

Victoria (see also Queen Victoria)
My.	289–15	the late lamented V·,
	289–29	the late lamented V·,

Victoria Institute
Mis.	295–26	V· I·, or Philosophical Society
	296– 3	life-member of the V· I·,
Pul.	5–26	and the V· I·, England ;

victories
Mis.	131–32	with perils past and v· won.
	268– 7	The imaginary v· of rivalry
Rud.	17–12	toil, agonies, and v·,
No.	34–26	Nameless woe, everlasting v·,
My.	47–15	* trials, progress, and v·
	202–17	endless hopes, and glad v·

victorious

Un.	30–19	made humanity *v·* over death
Po.	11– 3	|*V·*, all who live it,
My.	186–13	God, o'er all *v·* !
	338– 3	*V·*, all who live it,

victoriously

Pan.	14–25	sailed *v·* through the jaws of death

victors

My.	185–13	*v·* never to be vanquished.

victory

another

Mis.	147– 6	another *v·* won for time and

consolation and

My.	290–13	support, consolation, and *v·*.

defeat and

Mis.	267–26	cause of all defeat and *v·*

everlasting

Mis.	74–26	an everlasting *v·* for Life ;
	118–28	crowns . . . with everlasting *v·*.
	163– 7	sublime and everlasting *v·* !
	277–12	right wins the everlasting *v·*.

final

'00.	10–10	fresh energy and final *v·*.

get the

Mis.	241–16	you get the *v·* and Truth heals
'01.	13–29	get the *v·*, sin disappears,

hymns of

Mis.	281– 2	chant hymns of *v·* for triumphs.

in error

My.	278–26	*V·* in error is defeat in Truth.

its

Un.	48–11	robs the grave of its *v·*.
My.	5–18	rob the grave of its *v·*.
	191–23	and the grave its *v·*.

Love's

My.	62–13	* with the joy of Love's *v·*.

mighty

Mis.	120–13	mighty *v·* is yet to be won,

of right

My.	362– 4	*v·* of right over wrong,

over evil

Pul.	15–18	occasion for a *v·* over evil.

over himself

My.	268–23	gives man the *v·* over himself.

over self

Ret.	79–21	demonstrating the *v·* over self
'01.	10–23	*v·* over self, sin, disease,

over sin

My.	156–23	*v·* over sin, disease, and death.

over the flesh

Pul.	3–28	so far from *v·* over the flesh

palms of

Pul.	27–18	* bearing palms of *v·*,
My.	176–10	palms of *v·* and songs of glory.

ready for

Mis.	41–11	ready for *v·* in the ennobling strife.

secret of

Mis.	339– 7	of defeat comes the secret of *v·*.

sense of

Pul.	3–15	Love gives us the true sense of *v·*.

this

Peo.	11– 7	and this *v·* is achieved,

under arms

Pan.	14–11	for her *v·* under arms ;

vanity of

My.	25–26	wherein all vanity of *v·* disappears

Mis.	96– 3	robbed the grave of *v·*
Pul.	12–16	For *v·* over a single sin,
'00.	15–11	after this Passover cometh *v·*,
'02.	6–25	*v·* on the side of Truth.
My.	134–10	Defeat need not follow *v·*.
	204– 6	awaken to vigor and to *v·*.

victory-bringing

Ret.	22–16	vanquished by *v·* Science ;

vie

Mis.	231–13	to *v·* with guests in the dexterous
Hea.	20– 6	* *v·* with Gabriel, while he sings,

vied

Pul.	8–16	children *v·* with their parents
My.	173–22	my fellow-citizens *v·* with each other

view

accepted

Mis.	75–29	accepted *v·* is that *soul* is deathless.

another

My.	346– 5	* another *v·* of her religion.

brings to

Mis.	208–20	His rod brings to *v·* His love,
	292– 2	brings to *v·* overwhelming tides of
Chr.	53–45	For C. S. brings to *v·*

correct

Mis.	81–19	*if all this be a fair or correct v·*

view

drink in the

Po.	32– 2	and drink in the *v·*

end in

My.	68– 2	* with the end in *v·* of impressing

faint

Mis.	2–15	we behold but the first faint *v·*

human

Mis.	282– 3	to human *v·* an enlarged sense of

interrupts the

My.	69–18	* not a single . . . interrupts the *v·*

limited

Mis.	164–30	The limited *v·* of God's ideas

material

Mis.	14– 3	material *v·* which contradicts the

my

Un.	8–22	it proves my *v·* conclusively,

picturesque

Ret.	4–11	picturesque *v·* of the Merrimac

point of

Mis.	241– 1	From a religious point of *v·*,
Pul.	81– 9	* chapter sub-title
My.	69–29	* best point of *v·* is on top of the
	304–22	* From every point of *v·* a woman of

popular

No.	36–10	popular *v·* of Jesus' nature.

speculative

Mis.	38–23	some speculative *v·* too vapory and

such a

Un.	13–21	Such a *v·* would bring us upon an

this

Ret.	64–14	this *v·* is supported by the
Pul.	69–20	* We find in this *v·* of the Bible

Mis.	374– 8	In *v·* of this, Jesus said,
Ret.	47–12	In *v·* of all this, a meeting was
Pul.	41–10	* to *v·* the new-built temple
Po.	v– 5	* *with a v· of making a book,*
My.	20–23	* In *v·* of the fact that a general
	83–22	* in *v·* of the announcement,
	171–13	and *v·* this beautiful structure,
	354– 2	In *v·* of complaints from the field,

views

advanced

Mis.	379–16	had advanced *v·* of his own,

better

Mis.	175– 9	giving better *v·* of Life ;
	218–27	What can illustrate Dr.——'s *v·* better

broad

My.	338–22	* unfamiliar with his broad *v·*

decided

Mis.	2–32	While we entertain decided *v·* as to

dissolving

Mis.	290– 9	ought to be dissolving *v·*,

false

Mis.	291–21	False *v·*, however engendered,

following

My.	338– 6	* The following *v·* of the Rev. . . . Eddy

formulated

Mis.	78–30	human vagaries, formulated *v·*

her

My.	345–32	* her *v·*, strictly and always

her own

Pul.	35–29	* into sympathy with her own *v·*,

higher

Mis.	136– 6	broader and higher *v·*,

his

Ret.	14–10	depended, according to his *v·*, upon
'01.	24–24	In contradistinction to his *v·*

human

My.	221– 5	with certain purely human *v·*.

illiberal

My.	167–30	day of heathenism, illiberal *v·*,

improved

Peo.	2– 4	improved *v·* of the Supreme Being.

mistaken

Mis.	248–13	mistaken *v·* of Mrs. Eddy's book,
	290– 9	Mistaken *v·* ought to
Hea.	8–17	mistaken *v·* entertained of Deity

mortal

No.	26– 9	such material and mortal *v·*

my

Mis.	32–14	find my *v·* on this subject ;
	247–12	charges against my *v·* are false,
Ret.	44–24	No sooner were my *v·* made known,
'01.	16– 4	My *v·* of a future and eternal
My.	306–31	my *v·* of mental therapeutics.

new

Mis.	218– 1	spiritual sense takes in new *v·*,

of Truth

Mis.	234– 4	by speculative *v·* of Truth.
No.	21– 5	whose *v·* of Truth Confucius and

others'

Mis.	291–11	acquiescence with others' *v·*

views

personal
Man. 84–20 not by their teachers' personal *v*.

political
My. 276–22 * an expression of her political *v*,

popular
Un. 38–26 the popular *v* to this effect

realistic
Mis. 217–17 material realistic *v* presuppose that
218–14 False realistic *v* sap the Science

religious
No. 40–25 If a change in the religious *v*

respected
Pul. 66–21 * departure from long respected *v*

severe
Mis. 203–21 gain severe *v* of themselves ;

sublunary
Pul. 2–11 Turning from sublunary *v*,

these
Mis. 3–2 and shall express these *v*

transient
Mis. 291–1 transient *v* are human :

varying
My. 170–14 but not to varying *v*.

Ret. 62–4 find that the *v* here set forth
Un. 7–17 *v* here promulgated on this subject
My. 281–20 * *v* by representative persons.

vigilant
Ret. 85–22 The tempter is *v*,
My. 213–13 more watchful and *v*.

vigor
My. 84–19 * numbers, wealth, *v*,
134–30 * mental and physical *v*."
204–6 awaken to *v* and to victory.
355–3 * mental *v* a symbol of the

vile
My. 33–22 *v* person is contemned ;— Psal. 15 : 4.

vileness
Ret. 86–10 Behold its *v*, and remember
Un. 17–11 *v* may be christened purity,

vilify
Mis. 246–17 stop free speech, slander, *v* ;
Man. 51–9 aggrieve or *v* the Pastor
My. 190–30 wherefore *v* His prophets to-day

village
Ret. 5–13 Park Cemetery of that beautiful *v*.
Pul. 79–13 * a daily paper in town or *v*
My. 262–9 herds of a Jewish *v*.

villagers
Mis. 120–18 to *v* on the Rhine.

villages
Ret. 89–9 scattered about in cities and *v*,
Pul. 47–27 * Concord and its surrounding *v*.
67–21 * while in many towns and *v*

villainy
My. 121–20 internal vulgarity and *v*.

villainies
Mis. 228–14 momentary success of all *v*,

vindicate
Mis. 141–15 I *v* both the law of God and
No. 2–1 only Mind-healing I *v* ;
My. 125–14 divine Principle they so ably *v*,
273–4 * *v* in her own person the value of

vindicated
Mis. 284–18 *v* divine Truth and Love
No. 45–18 *v* by the noblest of both sexes.
Peo. 10–27 *v* but in a single instance
My. 59–31 * or so completely *v*.

vindicates
Ret. 55–7 *v* the divine Principle,
Hea. 15–9 *v* the omnipotence of the Supreme

vindicating
Ret. 31–5 *v* "the ways of God" to man.— Job 40 : 19.
No. 5–1 All true Christian Scientists are *v*,

vindication
Mis. 246–19 *v* in this most unprecedented

Vine
Chr. 53–19 this living *V* Ye demonstrate.

vine
Mis. 154–13 beneath your own *v* and fig-tree
154–14 *v* whereof our Father is husbandman.
369–27 from the *v* which our Father tends.
Po. 15–2 zephyrs through foliage and *v* !
My. 125–7 to incline the *v* towards the
159–9 fruit of this branch of his *v*,
182–28 this *v* of His husbanding,
202–29 God bless this *v* of His planting.
269–20 The *v* is bringing forth its fruit ;

vinegar
Ret. 26–5 "*v* and gall," — see Matt. 27 : 34.

vines
My. 123–30 spoil the *v*." — Song 2 : 15.

vineyard
Mis. 7–16 faithful laborers in His *v*.
120–12 in the *v* of our Lord ;
254–26 Lord of the *v* — Mark 12 : 9.
254–27 *v* unto others." — Mark 12 : 9.
Ret. 52–9 worker in this *v* of Truth.
Un. 12–3 in this *v* of Mind-sowing
'01. 33–5 not be admitted to the *v* of our
Hea. 19–22 work more earnestly in His *v*,
My. 186–20 may those that plant the *v*
250–10 vast *v* of our Lord.

vineyards
Ret. 88–22 to work in other *v* than our own.

vintage
Mis. 120–18 sound of *v* bells to villagers
356–15 sweeter than the sound of *v* bells.

vintage-time
Mis. 311–10 go forth to the full *v*,

violated
Mis. 198–31 or *v* a law of matter
Pul. 54–13 * "There was no law of nature *v*

violates
Man. 37–5 A member who *v* this By-Law
Ret. 75–3 This error *v* the law

violating
Man. 50–23 *v* any of the By-Laws

violation
Mis. 79–27 for *v* of medical statutes
226–23 that from the *v* of truth
Man. 50–22 *V* of By-Laws.
51–7 *V* of Christian Fellowship.
Pul. 54–7 * not in defiance, suppression, or *v*

violations
Mis. 107–23 oft-repeated *v* of divine law,

violence
Mis. 153–16 wherein *v* coverth men
274–20 gives impulse to *v*, envy, and hate,
Ret. 75–5 it does *v* to the ethics of
79–26 heaven suffereth *v*, — Matt. 11 : 12.

violent
Mis. 182–4 *v* means or material methods.
Man. 41–12 in return employ no *v* invective,
Ret. 73–24 a *v* and egotistical personality,
79–27 *v* take it by force !" — Matt. 11 : 12.
'02. 18–28 *v* death of all his disciples
My. 107–30 most *v* stages of organic and
222–3 a *v* case of lunacy.
336–17 * so *v* that he was unable to

violently
Mis. 225–14 was taken *v* ill.

violet
Mis. 330–28 *v* lifts its blue eye to heaven,
376–27 orange, pink, crimson, *v* ;

virgin
Mis. 165–32 mode, and *v* origin of man
'01. 8–27 was born of a *v* mother,

Virgin Mary
Ret. 70–14 individual place of the *V* *M*.

Virgin Mary's
My. 261–28 *V* *M* spiritual thoughts of Life

Virgin-mother (see also Virgin-mother's)
Mis. 166–19 required the *V* to go to the
Ret. 70–9 Scriptural narrative of the *V*
My. 303–27 to be a first or second *V*

Virgin-mother's
Un. 29–28 *V* sense being uplifted to

virgins
Mis. 341–21 "the ten *v*" — see Matt. 25 : 1.
342–3 The foolish *v* had no oil
342–22 wise *v* had no oil to spare,

virtually
Mis. 9–12 are *v* thy best friends.
19–12 *v* accepted the divine claims
51–14 The use of the rod is *v*
53–15 which is *v* acknowledging that
74–20 *v* vanquished matter and its
101–24 *v* destroys matter and evil,
103–8 mortals *v* name *substance*;
269–3 Galileo *v* lost it.
288–1 which is *v* meddlesomeness.
Ret. 54–14 Belief is *v* blindness, when it
70–27 *v* stands at the head
Un. 19–8 must *v* have intended it,
32–18 *v* saying, "I am the opposite of
38–8 is *v* without existence.

virtually

Pan.	8–15	*v·* annulled the so-called laws
'02.	6–21	all devout desire, *v·* petition,
	12–11	*v·* unites with the Jew's belief
My.	5–26	*v·* what the prophet said :
	13–28	Christian Scientists *v·* pledged
	340–24	which *v·* belongs to the past,

virtue (see also virtue's)

activities of
Mis.	362–32	or lessens the activities of *v·*.

and heaven
Mis.	238–15	health, *v·*, and heaven ;

and truth
Mis.	201–27	temperance, *v·*, and truth,

any
Mis.	128–10	if there be any *v·*, — *Phil.* 4 : 8.

clemency, and
Mis.	295–30	dignity, clemency, and *v·*

color of
Mis.	147–18	give the color of *v·* to a

goodness and
No.	13–24	impulse to . . . goodness and *v·*.

had gone out
Un.	57–13	"*v·* had gone out of him." — *Mark* 5 : 30.

increasing
'01.	3– 2	increasing *v·*, fervor, and fidelity.

in the shambles
Mis.	285–24	puts *v·* in the shambles,

of this nature
Mis.	208– 5	by *v·* of this nature and allness

place of a
Mis.	227– 3	may stand in the place of a *v·* ;

this
Mis.	356–23	This *v·* triumphs over the flesh ;

Mis.	329– 5	a weakness, or a — *v·*?
	367–30	by *v·* of His ignorance of
No.	30– 8	by *v·* of the allness of God.

virtue's

Mis.	388–15	won from vice, by *v·* smile,
Po.	21– 2	won from vice, by *v·* smile,
	41– 4	for the lambkin soft *v·* repose,

virtues

Mis.	110– 8	preserve these *v·* unstained,
	271– 1	foremost *v·* of homœopathy
Ret.	33–23	mental *v·* of the material methods
Pul.	15– 7	when you tell them their *v·*
No.	1–14	quiet practice of its *v·*.
	42–21	false claimants, aping its *v·*,
'01.	24– 9	descanting on the *v·* of tar-water,
My.	166–18	*v·* that lie concealed in the
	204– 4	to use their hidden *v·*,
	290– 6	her personal *v·* can never be lost.

virtuous

Un.	42– 9	before he can be *v·*,
My.	93– 2	* happy, gentle, and *v·*.

virus

Mis.	12– 3	spreads its *v·* and kills at last.

visible

Mis.	68– 6	*v·* to those beholding him here.
	90–27	conferred by a *v·* organization
	91–20	worship that can be made *v·*.
	144–25	our *v·* lives are rising to God.
	145–20	*v·* unity of spirit remains,
	205–18	*v·* being is invisible to the physical
	218– 5	*v·* universe declares the invisible
	244–16	* *v·* agencies for specific ends
	363–18	shines through the *v·* world
Pul.	50–12	* erection of a *v·* house of worship
'01.	13– 4	The *v·* sin should be invisible :
My.	28–21	* *v·* symbol of a religion
	69– 6	* no sharp angles are *v·*,
	78– 7	* *v·* from every quarter of the city.
	154–26	embodied in a *v·* communion,
	338–25	the *v·* discoverer, founder,

vision

earthly
Un.	61–11	twilight and dawn of earthly *v·*,

far-seeing
'01.	30–25	far-seeing *v·*, the calm courage,

illusive
Mis.	206–14	no emasculation, no illusive *v·*,

is fled
Po.	9– 8	weeping alone that the *v·* is fled,

Jacob's
'02.	10–16	gain the scope of Jacob's *v·*,

miraculous
Rud.	17–12	she needed miraculous *v·* to

mortal
My.	59– 7	* distant day beyond our mortal *v·*.

must be clear
Mis.	211– 5	Our own *v·* must be clear

vision

my
Mis.	136– 9	so grow upon my *v·*
	347–11	Where my *v·* begins and is clear,
Po.	33– 3	my faith and my *v·* enlarge,

never clears the
Mis.	355–17	To strike out . . . never clears the *v·* ;

no
Mis.	354–33	No *v·* more bright than the

of envy
Hea.	10– 3	the *v·* of envy, sensuality,

of heaven
My.	155–19	a clear *v·* of heaven here,

of life
Hea.	9–28	St. John saw the *v·* of life

of relief
Ret.	20–14	hoping for a *v·* of relief

of sin
Un.	4–26	*v·* of sin is wholly excluded.

of the Apocalypse
No.	21– 2	and the *v·* of the Apocalypse.

of the Revelator
Mis.	277–32	The *v·* of the Revelator

of the Wisemen
Mis.	164–11	To the *v·* of the Wisemen,

of Truth
No.	27–12	this *v·* of Truth is fully interpreted

our
Mis.	62– 9	veils the truth from our *v·* ;

renewed
My.	202–16	burst . . . with renewed *v·*,

Revelator's
Mis.	113– 8	and the Revelator's *v·*,
'00.	14–11	import of the Revelator's *v·*

so bright
Po.	18–11	What *v·* so bright as the dream

soft as the
Po.	15–12	Their wooings are soft as the *v·*

spiritual
Mis.	373–13	spiritual *v·* that should, does, guide
Un.	61– 6	to immortal and spiritual *v·*
My.	126–23	the Revelator saw in spiritual *v·*

voice and
My.	265– 5	spiritual voice and *v·*,

Mis.	149–23	a *v·* of the new church,

visionary

Un.	45–24	*v·* substance of matter.
My.	93– 7	* if their opinions seem *v·*,

visions

Ret.	18–15	real joy and of *v·* divine ;
Pul.	33– 2	* saw *v·* and dreamed dreams.
	33–27	* *v·* in their early youth.
Po.	64– 6	real joy and of *v·* divine ;

visit

Mis.	69–14	called to *v·* a sick man
	306–23	When angels *v·* us, we do not
Man.	68–18	to *v·* or to locate therein
	77–25	shall *v·* the Board of Directors,
	85– 2	may *v·* each other's churches,
Pul.	54–29	healed Mr. Whittier with one *v·*,
	77–15	* to *v·* and formally accept
	78–13	* most lovingly invited to *v·*
My.	21–11	* gladly forego a *v·* to Boston
	21–18	* forego their anticipated *v·*
	80– 1	* close of their *v·* to Boston ;
	105–14	healed at one *v·* a cancer
	169– 7	are requested to *v·* me at a
	169–14	chapter sub-title
	171– 8	chapter sub-title
	173– 3	* *v·* of the Christian Scientists
	187– 4	at some near future *v·* your city,
	192–22	give me pleasure to *v·* you,
	302–25	first *v·* to The Mother Church
	318–16	I invited Mr. Wiggin to *v·*

visitant

Peo.	5–22	then heed this heavenly *v·*,

visited

Mis.	112–15	I *v·* in his cell the assassin
	237–29	and he *v·* my father,
	265–17	*v·* upon himself and his students,
	297–17	that perhaps he has never *v·*.
Pul.	59– 2	* has not yet *v·* her temple,
'01.	29– 2	housed, fed, clothed, or *v·*
My.	153–12	flowers *v·* his bedside :
	185–22	I *v·* these mountains
	297–21	he *v·* me a year ago.
	306–22	when I first *v·* Dr. Quimby

visiting

Ret.	8–14	Mehitable Huntoon, was *v·* us,
	17– 1	while *v·* a family friend
Po.	vii– 1	* *while v· a family friend*
	page 67	poem
My.	308–20	was *v·* Governor Pierce,

visitor

Pul. 33–24 * that his v· was a spiritual form
49–28 * first impression given to the v·

visitors

Mis. 112–22 * "Other v· have brought
Man. 69–27 shall hereafter be closed to v·.
My. 24–25 * v· who have recently inspected the
30–14 * v· from Australia,
31–21 * first sight which the v· caught of
38–14 * v· showed a tendency to tarry
73–18 * was thrown open to v·
73–21 * v· will receive all information
74–10 * chapter sub-title
74–12 * interesting and agreeable v·,
75–14 * a great number of v·
77–15 * twenty-five thousand v·
82–22 * twenty thousand and more v·
83–27 * The thirty thousand v·
87– 7 * characteristics of this crowd of v·.
87–10 * v· of title and distinction,
173–19 The number of v·,
173–27 allowing the v· to assemble
353–23 shall hereafter be closed to v·.

vital

Mis. 132–29 v· spark of Christianity.
260–27 v· functions of Truth and Love.
267–16 the v· outcomes of Truth
Ret. 48– 4 was aimed at its v· purpose,
Pul. 50– 2 * in whom she takes a v· interest.
52–23 * all v· belief in his teachings.
No. 3– 1 in some v· points lack Science.
34–27 v· currents of Christ Jesus' life,
'01. 16–22 to carry a most v· point.
30– 4 We err in thinking the object of v·
32– 6 student of v· Christianity.
My. 128–13 v· heritage of freedom
146–23 Scientists hold as a v· point

vitality

Mis. 111–15 seed of Truth to its own v·,
Ret. 66– 3 C. S. gives v· to religion,
Pul. 79–17 * has shown a v· so unexpected.
My. 95–25 * religion of growth and v·
139–14 their v· involves Life,

vitals

Mis. 131– 4 gnawing at the v· of humanity.

vivacity

Mis. 117–12 * enduring v· among God's people."

vividly

Ret. 72– 7 The Psalmist v· portrays

vivify

My. 125– 6 and to v· the buds,

vocabulary

No. 10– 6 two largest words in the v·

vocal

Mis. 146– 2 May her walls be v· with

vocations

Man. 82–17 or pursue other v·,

vogue

My. 85– 6 * measured its v·.

voice

called
Ret. 9–10 when the v· called again,
came
Ret. 9–11 The v· came ; but I was afraid,
clear
My. 342–20 * she said, in her clear v·,
dissenting
Ret. 44–26 without a dissenting v·.
from heaven
Mis. 168–15 v· from heaven seems to say,
gentle
My. 39–25 * harmonious tones of her gentle v·.
God's
Mis. 134–27 neither silence nor disarm God's v·.
heard a
Ret. 8– 4 I repeatedly heard a v·,
heard the
Ret. 8–24 my cousin had heard the v·,
Pul. 33– 7 * if she heard the v· again
hear the
Chr. 55– 7 dead shall hear the v· — John 5 : 25.
His
Ret. 9–23 * learned at last to know His v·
Un. 2– 4 no place where His v· is not heard ;
My. 152–21 To-day, if ye would hear His v·,
his
Mis. 81–24 his v· be heard divinely
its
Mis. 277– 7 its v· dies out in the distance.
loud
Pul. 12– 5 I heard a loud v· saying — Rev. 12 : 10.

voice

mother's
Ret. 8– 6 I thought this was my mother's v·,
my
Mis. 151– 3 "My sheep hear my v·, — John 10 : 27.
213–22 "My sheep hear my v·, — John 10 : 27.
Chr. 55–26 if any man hear my v·, — Rev. 3 : 20.
Po. 34– 4 Like thee, my v· had stirred
mysterious
Ret. 9– 5 this mysterious v·,
of his conscience
Mis. 147–16 Truth and the v· of his conscience
of their leader
My. 43–11 * obedient to the v· of their leader.
of the night-bird
Po. 16–16 The v· of the night-bird
of the turtle
Mis. 329–24 v· of the turtle — Song 2 : 12.
of Truth
Mis. 81–27 v· of Truth utters the divine
134–26 "still, small v·" of Truth ; — I Kings 19 : 12.
360–26 "still, small v·" of Truth — I Kings 19 : 12.
Ret. 69–26 v· of Truth still calls :
My. 245–17 Let the v· of Truth and Love
one
My. 81–23 * swelling as one v·.
organ's
Pul. 11– 3 organ's v·, as the sound of many waters,
spiritual
My. 265– 5 revelation, spiritual v· and vision,
still, small
Mis. 134–26 "still, small v·" — I Kings 19 : 12.
138–28 "still, small v·" — I Kings 19 : 12.
175– 1 "still, small v·" — I Kings 19 : 12.
360–25 "still, small v·" — I Kings 19 : 12.
No. 1– 4 still, small v·," — I Kings 19 : 12.
'02. 15–30 "still, small v·" — I Kings 19 : 12.
My. 249– 5 "still small v·" — I Kings 19 : 12.
their
Ret. 61–19 where their v· is not — Psal. 19 : 3.
this
Mis. 81–20 why does not John hear this v·,
Ret. 61–19 this v· is Truth that destroys error
Thy
Mis. 398– 1 I will listen for Thy v·,
Ret. 46– 7 I will listen for Thy v·,
Pul. 17– 6 I will listen for Thy v·,
Po. 14– 5 I will listen for Thy v·,
My. 201–21 I will listen for Thy v·,
Truth's
Mis. 267– 1 make itself heard above Truth's v·.
universal
My. 8–14 * universal v· of Christian Scientists,
was heard
Mis. 246–22 v· was heard crying in the wilderness,
My. 126–13 And a v· was heard, saying,
your
Pul. 14–20 He can neither drown your v·

Mis. 99–13 v· a higher order of Science
99–26 v· of one crying in the wilderness,
'02. 20– 2 v· of him who stilled the tempest

voiced

Mis. 64– 2 cry which v· that struggle ;
336– 2 Hath not Science v· this
Ret. 27–13 not fully v· my discovery.
Pan. 3–11 v· with a hum of harmony,
'02. 5–21 v· in the thunder of Sinai,

voiceless

Po. 35–10 An aching, v· void,

voices

Mis. 100–14 Science v· unselfish love,
133– 9 v· my impressions of prayer :
329– 1 chapter sub-title
329–10 whose v· are sad or glad,
333–10 C. S. v· this question :
372– 7 v· C. S. through song and
396– 8 It v· beauty fled.
Pul. 33– 4 * like Jeanne d'Arc, to hear "v·,"
33–27 * experiences of v· or visions
No. 13–18 v· the infinite, and governs
Po. 15–11 whispering v· are calling away
16–20 the glad v· that swell,
58–20 It v· beauty fled.
My. 32– 5 * their v· rose as one
32–10 * did not have to lift their v·
59–21 * chorus of five thousand v·,
79– 1 * joining with their shrill v·
81–20 * occasionally the v· would
146–29 Scientist v· the harmonious

voicing

Mis. 251– 9 v· the friendship of this city
Ret. 10–15 v· the idea of God
No. 8– 6 Avoid v· error ;

void

Mis.	22–19	therefore these are null and *v.*
	76–16	is rendered *v* by Jesus'
Man.	39– 6	their applications shall be *v*.
Ret.	23–21	pantheism, and theosophy were *v*.
No.	37–25	Jesus rendered null and *v* whatever
Po.	35–10	An aching, voiceless *v*,
My.	219–22	annul nor make *v* the laws

Vol. 1

My.	353– 6	*V.* 1, No. 1, of *The C. S. Monitor*,
		(*see also* **Science and Health**)

volcanoes

Mis.	316–24	warming marble and quenching *v*!
My.	291–10	the *v* of partizanship,

volition

Mis.	28– 7	Destroy the belief . . . *v* ceases;
	117– 7	God-given intent and *v*
	156–24	all true thought and *v*.
Rud.	3–20	*v*, impulse, and action;

volleyed

Mis.	106–10	*V*· and thundered!

Voltaire

Peo.	6–11	*V*· says: "The art of medicine

volume

Mis.	xi–11	May this *v* be to the reader
	29–21	perusal of my *v* is healing
	262– 7	now entering upon its fifth *v*,
Ret.	37–	chapter sub-title
	83– 2	proven that this *v* is accomplishing
Pul.	vii– 1	*v* contains scintillations from
	55–22	* is contained in the *v* entitled
	73–26	* large *v* which Mrs. Eddy had herself
Po.	v– 1	* *garnered up in this little v*
	vii–11	* *little v· is presented to the public*,
My.	81–22	* the *v* of holy song rose
	256–13	open the *v* of Life

volumes

No.	33– 9	demonstrate what these *v* teach,
Po.	vii– 6	* *to prepare a few bound v*

voluminous

Ret.	76– 4	student can write *v* works
Pul.	88– 7	too *v* for these pages.
No.	15– 8	translations and *v* commentaries

voluntarily

Mis.	9–23	we *v* set it aside
	289–13	each party *v* surrenders
	297–18	having *v* entered into wedlock,
Man.	38–21	but who have *v* withdrawn,
Ret.	84–28	those who *v* place themselves
My.	30–24	* Without ostentation and quite *v*
	212– 3	never, otherwise, think or do *v*.

voluntary

Man.	62– 1	eight or nine minutes for the *v*
Pul.	43–14	* After an organ *v*,
	44–21	* building a church by *v* contributions,
	63–24	* *v* contributions of Christian Scientists
	71– 5	* not borne out by the *v* contribution
No.	v– 5	involuntary as well as *v* error.
My.	32–11	* Following the organ *v*
	76–22	* all contributions have been *v*.
	77–30	* secured by *v* subscription.
	98–23	* Contributions were entirely *v*.
	118–19	One's *v* withdrawal from society,

Volunteer

Un.	14–10	boatbuilder, remedies in the *V·* the

volunteer

Ret.	21–10	he had served as a *v*

volunteered

My.	331–31	* *v* to restore her to her friends

wading

Mis.	320–19	*w* through darkness and gloom,

waft

Po.	19– 2	breezes that *w* o'er its sky!
	33–19	*w* me away to my God.

waged

Ret.	56–12	War is *w* between the evidences of
Pul.	3–14	good fight we have *w* is over,

wages

Mis.	76–27	*w* of sin is death."— *Rom.* 6: 23.
	104–16	*w* feeble fight with his individuality,
Ret.	22–14	mortal life-battle still *w*,
Rud.	13–27	receiving no *w* in return,
	14– 6	*conscientiously earn their w*,
'00.	2–20	his stock in trade, the *w* of sin;

Wagner Trilogy

Ret.	82– 4	or with the vast *W· T·*.

vomit

Mis.	353–32	"return to their *v*,"— *see Prov.* 26: 11.

vomiting

Mis.	243–30	induce ulceration, bleeding, *v*,

votaries

Mis.	196–15	*v* to "other gods"— *Exod.* 20: 3.
My.	75– 3	* Its *v* are certainly holding the
	93–11	* which it holds out to its *v*;

vote

Mis.	132– 1	motion was made, and a *v* passed,
Man.	26– 9	by a unanimous *v* of the
	26–23	A majority *v* . . . shall dismiss a
	30– 8	majority *v* of the Board of Directors
	36–22	unanimous *v* of the Board
	38–12	elected by majority *v* of the
	39–14	unanimous *v* of the C. S. Board of
	52– 1	*v* on cases involving The
	65–22	supplied by a majority *v*
	73–17	by the unanimous *v* of,
	77– 9	by a unanimous *v*,
	81– 2	officers elected, by a unanimous *v*
	82–12	except by a majority *v*
	97–10	by a unanimous *v* of the
	102– 9	by a majority *v*.
Ret.	7– 1	majority *v* of seven thousand,
	7– 2	the largest *v* of the State;
My.	44–19	* carried unanimously by a rising *v*.
	276–18	* those who are entitled to *v*

voted

Man.	17–10	on motion of Mrs. Eddy, it was *v*,
Ret.	44– 1	it was *v* to organize a church
	47–14	*v* that the school be discontinued.
	49–28	it was unanimously *v*:
My.	49–27	* it was unanimously *v* that
	49–30	* *v* to instruct the Clerk to
	53– 9	* it was *v* that the church
	53–15	* church *v* to wait upon Mrs. Eddy,
	57– 9	* church *v* to raise any part of
	65– 7	* *v* yesterday afternoon to

votes

Ret.	44–26	*v* passing without a dissenting

votive

Pul.	26–15	* a *v* offering of gratitude

vouches

Mis.	295–20	Mr. Wakeman strongly *v*,
No.	4–18	*v* for the validity of that

vouchsafed

My.	345–22	last healing that will be *v*

vow

Mis.	286– 4	solemn *v* of fidelity,
	290– 4	nuptial *v* is never annulled so long as
	341–24	takes the most solemn *v* of celibacy
My.	268– 3	The nuptial *v* should never

vows

Mis.	285–25	notifies the public of broken *v*.

vox populi

Mis.	xi–21	*v· p·* is inclined to grant us peace,
	80–18	*v· p·*, through the providence of God,
	245–11	calling forth the *v· p·*
	274–27	the *v· p·* is suffocated,

vulgar

My.	79–18	* not a gathering of "the *v* throng;"
	104–22	atone for the *v* denunciation
	305– 9	* subject of "*v* metaphysics,"
	305–10	which "*v*" defamers have

vulgarity

My.	121–20	used to disguise internal *v*
	121–21	no *v* in kindness.

W

wagon

Un.	17– 4	* "Hitch your *w* to a star."
My.	313–13	cradle for me in his *w*.

wagon-load

Un.	17– 9	evil ties its *w* of offal to

wagons

My.	82–12	* secured express *w* enough to

waif

Ret.	93–10	no longer impersonated as a *w*

waifs

No.	29–23	spiritless *w*, literary driftwood

wail

Mis.	267– 2	*w* of evil never harms Scientists,
'01.	14– 4	Publican's *w* won his humble desire,
My.	334–22	Publican's *w* won his humble desire,

wainscoting
Pul. 25–23 * w· repeats the same tints.

wait
Mis. 81– 8 patiently w· on God to decide,
225–30 * "W· until we get home,
230–25 * Learn to labor and to w·."
307– 4 if you w·, never doubting,
331– 6 cause them to w· patiently
364– 5 "W· patiently on the— see Isa. 40 : 31.
389–16 W·, and love more for every hate,
Ret. 79–24 * "Learn to labor and to w·."
85–18 w· for God's finger to point
Un. 6–27 "W· patiently on the— see Psal. 37 : 7.
Pul. 4–23 W· patiently on illimitable Love,
10–21 If you are less appreciated . . . w·
No. 46–23 continue to labor and w·.
Pan. 12–18 not w· by the roadside,
'00. 7–28 w· for the full appearing of
9–10 shut their eyes and w· for a
13–16 promise to such as w· and weep.
'01. 34–20 brethren, w· patiently on God ;
'02. 2– 5 to w· on divine Love ;
17–17 to be willing to w· on God,
Hea. 1–10 to w· until the age advanced
5– 9 must w· for the reward
Po. 4–15 W·, and love more for every hate,
My. 22–12 * nor w· to be urged or to be shown
29–29 * were able to w· patiently for the
53–16 * voted to w· upon Mrs. Eddy,
119–29 look and w· and watch and pray
184– 6 for them that w· upon Him
185– 7 * Learn to labor and to w·."
224– 4 w· on the logic of events?
224–31 * who only stand and w·."
227–13 we naturally . . . w· on God.
227–18 lying in w· to catch them
239–12 Must mankind w· for the ultimate
250–23 the branch churches can w· for
252–15 w· on God, the strong deliverer,
305–22 I still w· at the cross to
306–14 must w· to be transfused

waited
Mis. 84– 2 he w· for a preparation of
'02. 15–21 Six weeks I w· on God
Hea. 14–23 w· many years for a student to
Po. 41–23 w· to welcome the murmur
78– 5 Why w· their reward,
My. 11–10 * but has w· for us to grow
185– 2 To such as have w· patiently
324–13 * w· on the Lord to have those

waiteth
Mis. 324–11 him who w· at the door.
Pan. 1–16 w· patiently the appearing

waiting
Mis. 15– 5 "w· for the adoption,— Rom. 8 : 23.
22–25 have proven to a w· world.
95–22 "w· for the adoption,— Rom. 8 : 23.
125–12 not stand w· and weary ;
158–20 w· for the watchword
268–32 Truth is used to w·.
273–28 w· for the same class instruction ;
276–13 assemblage found w· and watching
277–11 Justice waits, and is used to w· ;
331– 2 looking up, w· on God,
331–19 Life divine, that owns each w· hour ;
384–14 Be patient, w· heart :
387– 5 w·, in what glad surprise,
389– 7 Life divine, that owns each w· hour,
396–18 O'er w· harpstrings of the mind
Ret. 23–15 I was w· and watching ;
79–25 were saved by patient w·.
80–10 * with patience He stands w·,
Un. 7–18 pour into my w· thought
12– 4 let them apply to the w· grain
Pul. 14–15 w· and watching for rest
18– 2 O'er w· harpstrings of the mind
42– 3 * filled with a w· multitude.
60– 1 * with others, w· for admission.
Rud. v– 5 LOYAL STUDENTS, WORKING AND w·
No. 2–18 w· and working to mature
Pan. 1–14 and the sackcloth of w·
'01. 29–20 w· till the wind shifts.
'02. 15–29 to my w· hope and prayer.
Peo. 7–18 * W· the hour when at God's command
10–25 "w· for the adoption,— Rom. 8 : 23.
Po. 4– 4 Life divine, that owns each w· hour,
8– 7 I'm w· alone for the bridal hour
12– 1 O'er w· harpstrings of the mind
17– 4 still w· for me.
36–13 Be patient, w· heart :
39–16 And be your w· hearts elate,
50–23 * w·, in what glad surprise,
My. 31– 8 * "O'er w· harpstrings of the mind ;"

waiting
My. 80–28 * w· vainly in the streets.
124–14 w· only your swift hands,
208–14 my w· heart,— w· in due expectation
232– 4 w· waves will weave for you
270–12 I am rewarding your w·,
322–21 * w· months in Boston

waits
Mis. 130–28 w· on God, renews his strength,
154–10 God only w· for man's worthiness
277–10 Justice w·, and is used to waiting ;
324– 5 he knocks and w·.
330–31 patient corn w· on the elements
Ret. 90–21 w· with her hope,
Pul. 83–12 * with the patience of genius she w·.
'00. 15–15 it w· in the desert
'02. 11– 6 Divine Love w· and pleads to save
Po. 39–11 First at the tomb, who w·
My. 103– 4 and w· on God.
306–16 Age, . . . w· on God.

waive
Mis. 131–16 I recommend that you w· the

wake
Mis. 11– 1 will w· from his delusion
23– 6 * dream in the animal, and w· in man"?
144–30 w· the long night of materialism,
390– 6 shrill song doth w· the dawn :
396–22 w· a white-winged angel throng
397– 3 w· to know A world more bright.
Chr. 53– 7 rouse the living, w· the dead,
Ret. 12– 2 W· freedom's welcome,
17– 7 W· chords of my lyre,
Pul. 18– 6 w· a white-winged angel throng
18–12 w· to know A world more bright.
Po. 12– 6 w· a white-winged angel throng
12–12 w· to know A world more bright.
55– 7 shrill song doth w· the dawn :
60–22 W· freedom's welcome,
62– 7 W· chords of my lyre,
66– 7 W· gently the chords of her lyre,
79–18 centuries break, the earth-bound w·,
My. 61–12 * somebody had to w· up.
189–18 human senses w· from their long

wakefully
'02. 18– 2 gate of conscience, w· guard it ;

Wakeman, Mr.
Mis. 295– 3 Mr. W· writes from London,
295–12 Is Mr. W· awake,
295–19 Mr. W· strongly vouches,
296– 9 author cited by Mr. W·

Wakeman's, Edgar L.
Mis. 294–27 become an admirer of Edgar L. W·

waken
'01. 15–18 to w· such a one from his deluded
'02. 17–13 awake and w· the world.
Hea. 9–27 w· from the dream of life in matter,
11– 3 gladly w· to see it was unreal.
Po. 16–25 w· my joy, as in earliest prime.
65–15 We w· to life's dreary sigh.
My. 132–25 w· the dreamer— the sinner,
133–14 should w· the sleeper,
149–29 which w· the stagnant waters
258–19 w· prophecy, gleams of glory,
291–19 w· a tone of truth
356– 4 w· to the privilege of knowing God,

wakened
Mis. 142–27 The symbols . . . w· memory,
328–19 w· through the baptism of fire?

wakening
Po. 30– 5 w· murmurs from the drowsy rills

wakens
My. 287–20 w· lofty desires, new possibilities,

wakes
Mis. 257– 5 and w· in a wicked man.
Pan. 9– 2 * dreams in . . . and w· in man."
Po. 10– 9 That w· thy laureate's lay.
My. 337–10 That w· thy laureate's lay.

waking
Mis. 36–27 as much in our w· moments
47–11 If never in your w· hours,
58– 4 W· from a dream, one learns
58– 5 W· from the dream of death,
329–14 Spring . . . w· up the world ;
386–16 w· with a love that steady turns
Hea. 10–19 and your w· the reality,
Po. 49–24 w· with a love that steady turns
My. 110–19 if w· to bodily sensation
160–25 w· to a true sense of itself,
296–18 w· out of his Adam-dream of evil

Waldron, Mr. George D.
  My. 173–28 Mr. George D. *W·*, chairman of

walk
Mis.	xi–13	enabling him to *w·* the untrodden
	28– 6	Destroy the belief that you can *w·*,
	51–28	* *w·* transparent like some holy
	146–22	counsel and help him to *w·*
	162– 9	*w·* serenely over their fretted,
	168– 6	how the lame, . . . *w·* ;
	188–14	*w·* not after the flesh,— *Rom.* 8 : 1.
	231–20	papa knew that he could *w·*,
	244–19	causing him to *w·* the wave,
	244–21	deaf to hear, the lame to *w·*,
	245–27	that one can *w·* alone
	311– 4	to *w·* with us hand in hand,
	358–17	we must *w·* in the way which
	359–15	For Jesus to *w·* the water
	359–18	until we can *w·* on the water.
	359–24	*way* is absolute . . . *w·* ye in it ;
	370– 1	"Rise and *w·*." — *see John* 5 : 8.
	396– 2	To scare my woodland *w·*,
	397– 6	I see Christ *w·*,
Chr.	55–19	rise up and *w·*. — *Acts* 3 : 6.
Ret.	90–24	till her children can *w·* steadfastly
Un.	9– 9	all are without excuse who *w·* not
	11– 3	Jesus taught us to *w·* over, not *into*
Pul.	18–15	I see Christ *w·*,
	37– 9	* she takes a daily *w·*
No.	8–26	while you *w·* on in equanimity,
	42– 9	rise up and *w·* !"— *see Luke* 5 : 23.
Pan.	12–18	and *w·*, not wait by the roadside,
'00.	7–23	*w·* more closely with Christ ;
	7–28	Thus it is we *w·* here below,
'01.	29–25	will *w·* in his footsteps.
	35–17	*w·* in patient faith the way thereto
Po.	12–15	I see Christ *w·*, And come to me,
	58–14	To scare my woodland *w·*,
	66– 3	we *w·* by that murmuring stream ;
	67–13	Beside thee they *w·* while you weep,
My.	105–18	have made the lame *w·*.
	113–12	*w·* not after the flesh,— *Rom.* 8 : 1.
	187– 9	perfect path wherein to *w·*,
	202–28	expands as we *w·* in it.
	205– 2	*w·* not after the flesh,— *Rom.* 8 : 1.
	206–31	*w·* as children of light."— *Eph.* 5 : 8.
	254– 8	not be, weary, *w·* and not faint.
	283–24	to *w·* humbly"— *Mic.* 6 : 8.
	313–19	when I took an evening *w·*,

walked
Mis.	74–17	He *w·* upon the waves ;
Chr.	55– 8	people that *w·* in darkness — *Isa.* 9 : 2.
Un.	58– 5	Jesus *w·* with bleeding feet
Pul.	33–19	* *w·* with him as he worked,
	34–14	* she *w·* into the adjoining room,
	34–20	* Jesus of Nazareth *w·* the earth.
	36–17	* *w·* any conceivable distance.

walketh
'00.	12– 4	*w·* in the midst of the— *Rev.* 2 : 1.
'02.	20– 1	Christ *w·* over the wave ;
My.	33–17	He that *w·* uprightly,— *Psal.* 15 : 2.
	228–23	He that *w·* uprightly,— *Psal.* 15 : 2.

walking
Mis.	74–21	*W·* the wave, he proved the
	231–19	Then he was caught *w·* !
	277– 5	Error is *w·* to and fro in the earth,
	332–14	*w·* in the cool of the day
Man.	18– 7	Although *w·* through deep waters,
'00.	7–22	*w·* the wave of earth's troubled sea,
'02.	10–30	*w·* every step over the land route,
My.	124– 1	not *w·* in craftiness,
	342– 4	* *w·* uprightly and with light step,

walking-stick
My.	308–18	* with a huge *w·*."
	308–19	He never used a *w·*.
	308–22	handed him a gold-headed *w·*

walks
Mis.	xi–24	thought sometimes *w·* in memory,
	125–24	common *w·* of mankind,
	202– 6	* beyond the *w·* of common life,
	215–18	as when a child in sleep *w·*
	357–10	beyond the *w·* of common life,
Ret.	5–20	in all the *w·* of life.
No.	29–24	Truth *w·* triumphantly over the
'00.	7–11	in all the *w·* of life,
My.	189– 6	in the common *w·* of life,

wall
Mis.	178–29	*w·* between the old and the new ;
Pul.	42–19	* On the *w·* of the choir gallery
	63–26	* tablet imbedded in its *w·*
	76– 5	* Italian marble set in the *w·*.
	76–14	* superb mantel . . . adorns the south *w·*,

Wallace
Sir William
Ret.	2–14	bestowed by Sir William *W·*,
Pul.	46–21	* bestowed by Sir William *W·*

Ret.	2–16	"Scots wha hae wi' *W·* bled."

wallow
'00.	8–25	not Science for the wicked to *w·*

walls
Mis.	146– 2	May her *w·* be vocal
	279–16	before the *w·* of Jericho.
	279–17	seven times around these *w·*,
	279–25	in order that the *w·* might fall ;
	324–21	the odious company and the cruel *w·*,
	369– 1	watchmen on the *w·* of Zion,
Pul.	2–21	and remain within the *w·*
	25–25	* On the *w·* are bracketed oxidized
	49– 5	* Mrs. Eddy has hung its *w·* with
	58–19	* steps marble, and the *w·* stone.
	76– 8	* green and gold decoration of the *w·*.
'00.	1– 4	storied *w·* of The Mother Church.
Po.	vi–18	*nowhere but in the w· of a jail.*
My.	23–23	*w·* of our new edifice are rising,
	24– 9	* As the *w·* are builded by the
	36–25	* By these stately *w·* ;
	58–14	* the erection of these mighty *w·*.
	69– 5	* roof and side *w·* come together
	188–20	*w·* of your grand cathedral
	193–28	Within its sacred *w·*
	214– 1	to place on the *w·* of their church.
	214– 3	textbook on the *w·* of your churches.

wander
Mis.	138– 5	if it causes thought to *w·*
'02.	11– 3	to *w·* on the shores of time

wandered
Mis.	169– 3	whenever her thoughts had *w·*
	328–18	stumbled, and *w·* away?
Ret.	33– 5	I *w·* through the dim mazes
	93– 2	evangelists of those days *w·* about.

wanderer (see also wanderer's)
Mis.	155– 8	woo the weary *w·* to your door,
Ret.	93–11	impersonated as a waif or *w·* ;
My.	132–32	brings back the *w·* to the Father's
	182–25	May the *w·* in the wilderness

wanderer's
Ret.	86–12	this *w·* soiled garments,

wanderers
Mis.	298– 7	we also are *w·*.
	326–17	*w·* in a beleaguered city,
Pul.	14–15	weary *w·*, athirst in the desert

wandering
Mis.	371– 4	*w·* about without a leader,
Ret.	4–17	*w·* winds sigh low

Wanderings
Mis.	294–28	poetic style in his "*W·*,"

wanderings
My.	313–16	* long and lonely *w·*,

wanders
Pul.	48–13	* truant river, as it *w·* eastward.

waneth
Un.	26–15	* But His mercy *w·* never,
	26–17	God's power *never w·*,

waning
Mis.	312–18	* to restore the *w·* faith of many

want
Mis.	69–32	His *w·* of control over
	250–27	door that turns toward *w·* and woe,
	262–13	I just *w·* to say, I thank you,
	263–20	responsible for supplying this *w·*,
	307– 7	more we do not *w·* :
	351– 4	The fact is, that for *w·* of time,
	355– 4	a full-orbed promise, and a gaunt *w·*.
	365–17	form the common *w·*,
	365–17	this *w·* has worked out a moral
Pul.	8– 7	Notwithstanding . . . the *w·* and woe
	81–19	* have so much to give they *w·* no
No.	42– 7	to meet a mental *w·*.
'00.	11–17	I *w·* not only quality, quantity, and
'01.	29– 7	those who *w·* to help them.
My.	145–11	* said to me : "I *w·* to be let off
	162– 2	question our *w·* of more faith
	216–29	*w·* money for your own uses.
	217– 1	You will *w·* it for academics,
	281– 2	and awakened a wiser *w·*,
	307–30	*w·* of divinity in scholastic

wanted
Mis.	178– 6	*w·* to become a God-like man.
	348–24	I *w·* to satisfy my curiosity
Ret.	8– 7	to tell me what she *w·*.
	9– 1	said that mother *w·* me.
	38–20	to tell me he *w·* more,

wanted
Pul. 33– 6 * questioning if she were *w*.
My. 80–25 * *w*· to give testimony
80–26 * *w*· to hear it.
138– 2 because I *w*· it protected
215– 1 but nobody then *w*· C. S.,
302–27 *w*· to greet me with escort
324–27 * He said he *w*· to see if there was

wanting
Mis. 288– 8 and not be found *w*·,
312– 4 we be not found *w*·.
365– 6 Human theories . . . are found *w*· ;
My. 291–16 was not found *w*·.

wantonly
'01. 34–15 *w*· bereft of the Word of God.

wants
Mis. 67– 2 Above physical *w*·, lie the higher
104–28 Who *w*· to be mortal, or
365–25 met the growing *w*· of humanity.
Ret. 52–10 the broader *w*· of humanity,
No. 18–23 Good health and . . . are the common *w*· ;
18–23 and these *w*· have wrought this
19– 7 have never met the growing *w*· of
Peo. 12–23 application of its Principle to human *w*·.
My. 216–30 Contemplating these important *w*·,

War
Lovewell's
Ret. 3– 8 known historically as Lovewell's *W*·.
of 1812
Ret. 3–12 towards the close of the *W*· of 1812.

war
and oppression
My. 285–10 Bloodshed, *w*·, and oppression
beginning of
'02. 3–21 than the beginning of *w*·.
close the
Pan. 13–15 to close the *w*· between flesh and Spirit,
My. 18–23 to close the *w*· between flesh and Spirit,
divorce and
My. 268–11 Divorce and *w*· should be exterminated
268–17 will eliminate divorce and *w*·.
ending of the
My. 281–22 * on the ending of the *w*·,
formidable in
Pan. 15– 3 will be as formidable in *w*· as
for the Union
Ret. 21–11 throughout the *w*· for the Union,
is waged
Ret. 56–12 *W*· is waged between the evidences of
learn
Mis. xii– 6 "learn *w*· no more,"— *see Isa. 2 : 4.*
make
My. 278– 5 may learn to make *w*· no more,
no more
My. 286– 4 that there be no more *w*·,
on religion
My. 234–24 a *w*· on religion in China
opposed to
My. 284–24 and religiously opposed to *w*·,
preventing
My. 286–12 for the purpose of preventing *w*·
refers to the
Pan. 14–28 refers to the *w*· between United States and
will end
My. 281–28 *W*· will end when nations are ripe for
with Spirit
Un. 36–14 as the flesh at *w*· with Spirit ;

Mis. xii– 1 pioneer signs and ensigns of *w*·,
2–29 beliefs that *w*· against Spirit,
101– 8 C. S. and the senses are at *w*·.
134–22 at *w*· with the omnipotent !
172–26 Science, and the . . . senses, are at *w*· ;
188–11 *w*· between the flesh and Spirit,
217–23 that death is at *w*· with Life,
Pul. 2–16 *w*· between China and Japan ;
No. 6–26 at *w*· with the testimony of the
'00. 8–22 before we can successfully *w*· with
Hea. 15–15 at *w*· with this Mind,
Po. 27– 1 "Convulsion, carnage, *w*· ;
My. 93– 3 * in no wise at *w*· with society ;
277– 2 chapter sub-title
278–25 *W*· is in itself an evil,
278–27 *W*· is not in the domain of good ;
278–27 *w*· weakens power and must finally
279–24 *w*· between Russia and Japan ;
286– 2 chapter sub-title

wardrobe
Mis. 159–16 In this chamber is memory's *w*·,

wares
My. 151– 1 I am patient with the newspaper *w*·

warfare
all
Pul. 3–13 heavenly assurance ends all *w*·,
Christian
Mis. 40–26 In this Christian *w*· the student
281–19 whatever . . . in the Christian *w*·
Ret. 44–23 which must always lie in Christian *w*·.
Christian's
Mis. 155–11 be valiant in the Christian's *w*·,
ends the
Mis. 102–30 outmasters it, and ends the *w*·.
inhuman
Peo. 11– 8 not by inhuman *w*·, but in
is not ended
Mis. 85–24 so long as . . . the *w*· is not ended
long
Mis. 215–24 they have a long *w*· with error
my
Mis. 180– 3 and strive to cease my *w*·.
no such
No. 23–22 no such *w* against Himself.
our
Mis. 139–10 *weapons of our w*·— II Cor. 10 : 4.
Pul. 12–23 in our *w*· against error,
perpetual
Mis. 56–17 mingling in perpetual *w*·
shadow of the
Pul. 20–15 type and shadow of the *w*· between
spiritual
Ret. 86– 1 energize wholesome spiritual *w*·,
theological
Pul. 51–18 * implements of theological *w*·,
this
'00. 10– 7 provided this *w*· is honest
unprecedented
Mis. 246–19 in this most unprecedented *w*·.
whole
Mis. 285–16 the whole *w*· of sensuality

Mis. 118–25 the *w*· with one's self is grand ;
My. 180–30 No *w*· exists between divine

warm
Pul. 9– 9 appliances *w*· this house,
49–16 brought here in *w*· weather,
63–13 brought here in *w*· weather,
Po. 10– 3 We proffer thee *w*· welcome
46– 2 thy rosebud heart rests *w*·
53– 9 More softly *w*· and weave
My. 68–18 * auditorium is of a *w*· gray,
75–20 * and *w*· as the day was,
124– 9 willing hands, and *w*· hearts,
337– 5 We proffer thee *w*· welcome

warmed
Mis. 343–10 *W*· by the sunshine of Truth,
Pul. 9–10 *w*· also our perishless hope,

warmest
My. 189– 1 *w*· wish of men and angels.

warming
Mis. 316–23 *w*· marble and quenching volcanoes !
My. 268–28 heart of humanity *w*· and winning.
291– 9 *w*· the marble of politics

warmth
Mis. 331– 8 *w*· and sunlight of prayer
342– 5 their fading *w*· of action ;
My. 342– 1 * to the pleasant *w*· within

warn
Mis. 309–18 *w*· students against falling into the
Un. 57– 4 *w*· mortals of the approach of danger
My. 64–20 * Fearlessly does she *w*· all her

warned
Mis. 24–27 God *w*· man not to believe
No. 41– 3 *w*· the people to beware of

warning
Mis. 210– 8 placards *w*· people not to
212–10 remember the reiterated *w*·
254– 3 Should not the loving *w*·,
301–17 without this word of *w*·
Man. 28–10 and the *w*· of Holy Writ :
Ret. 80–18 this *w*· will be within him
Pul. 15–15 and yet have given no *w*·.

warnings
'01. 18– 4 woeful *w*· concerning C. S.

warns
Ret. 73–19 *w*· you of "personality,"

warped
Mis. 75–19 if this term is *w*· to signify
Ret. 88–20 should not be so *w*· as to
No. 14– 1 neither *w*· nor misconceived,

warrant

Ret.	65–11	have no *w·* in the gospel
	75–24	There is no *w·* in common law
'02.	11– 7	awaits with *w·* and welcome,
My.	266– 5	under the *w·* of the Scriptures ;

Warren Street

My.	175–20	macadamize a portion of *W· S·*

war-rent

Po.	71–20	O *w·* flag ! O soldier-shroud !

warreth

Mis.	124– 8	which *w·* against Spirit,

warring

Pul.	83–29	* to *w·* men the Prince of Peace,
My.	40–15	* became divided into *w·* sects ;

warriors

Mis.	177–15	real and consecrated *w·*?

wars

Mis.	102–28	Mortal thought *w·* with this
Ret.	47– 2	*w·* with Love's spiritual compact,
'00.	13–13	after a series of *w·* it was taken
My.	279–18	will . . . end *w·*, and demonstrate
	339–28	all that *w·* against Spirit

Wash. (State)

(see **Seattle**)

wash

Mis.	326–23	to *w·* their feet,
	398–20	Shepherd, *w·* them clean.
Ret.	46–26	Shepherd, *w·* them clean.
Pul.	7–16	and with power to *w·* away,
	17–25	Shepherd, *w·* them clean.
Po.	14–24	Shepherd, *w·* them clean.

washed

Mis.	153–13	*w·* in the waters of Meribah,
	246–11	would have *w·* it divinely away
	358–16	"*w·* in the blood of— see *Rev.* 7 : 14.
Un.	3–11	and have *w·* their robes white

washes

Peo.	9– 9	baptism of Spirit that *w·* our robes

washing

Pul.	27–22	* Mary *w·* the feet of Jesus,
Peo.	9– 4	*w·* away the motives for sin ;
My.	161– 3	*w·* the Way-shower's feet
	228–20	*w·* it clean from the taints of

Washington

D. C.

Mis.	304– 2	* 1505 Penna. Ave., *W·*, D. C.
	306–15	* 1505 Penna. Ave., *W·*, D. C.,
Ret.	4– 9	Henry Moore Baker of *W·*, D. C.
Pul.	63– 1	* *The Republic, W·*, D. C.,
	89–19	* *Post, W·*, D. C.
My.	136–16	suit at law in *W·*, D. C.,
	199– 9	chapter sub-title
	203– 2	chapter sub-title
	311–25	When I was last in *W·*, D. C.,

Mis.	304–17	* it will return to *W·*
	304–19	* *W·* will be its home,
'00.	1–20	Philadelphia, *W·*, Baltimore,
My.	157–15	* National Library Building in *W·*

Washington (see also **Washington's**)

George

Mis.	305–30	* the inauguration of George *W·*
Ret.	2–25	death and burial of George *W·*.

Washington's

My.	148–12	February 22 — *W·* birthday.

waste

Mis.	127– 6	watering her *w·* places,
	230–21	and worse than *w·* its years.
Pul.	22–20	her *w·* places budded
	49–10	* and yet from a barren *w·*
My.	3–11	abroad in Zion's *w·* places,
	18– 3	watering her *w·* places,
	166– 6	Religions may *w·* away,
	223–15	not sufficient time to *w·* on them ;

waste-basket

My.	231–16	committed to the *w·* by

wasted

Mis.	127–30	kind word . . . is never *w·*.
	138– 4	The time . . . is worse than *w·*,
	324–25	only to find the lights all *w·*
My.	80– 7	* when *w·* unto death
	231– 9	sums of money, worse than *w·*.
	303–13	not *w·* in certain directions.

wasting

Mis.	230– 8	Three ways of *w·* time,

watch

Mis.	87–26	To *w·* and pray,
	98–14	to *w·* with eager joy the
	109–30	*W·* and pray for self-knowledge ;

watch

Mis.	110– 7	You need also to *w·*, and pray
	114– 7	teachers of C. S. need to *w·*
	114– 8	*w·* that these be not
	114–21	Scientists cannot *w·* too sedulously,
	117–21	*w·* that each step be taken,
	154–26	*W·* diligently ; never desert the post
	291–31	keeps not *w·* over his emotions
	315–17	*w·* well that they prove sound in
	335–23	when the Watcher bids them *w·*,
	342–29	they *w·* the market,
	343– 1	Let us *w·* and pray
	343–23	*w·* their reappearing,
	356–30	Cherish humility, "*w·*," — *Matt.* 26 : 41.
	368– 9	* keeping *w·* above His own."
	387–13	not from those who *w·* and love.
	389–21	*w·* and pray.
Man.	16– 9	we solemnly promise to *w·*, and pray
	28–15	to *w·* and make sure that the
	40–12	should daily *w·* and pray
	83–17	*w·* well that they prove sound in
Un.	50– 6	We should *w·* and pray
Pul.	39–17	* I *w·* the flow Of waves of light.
No.	8–21	*w·*, and pray for the amelioration of
'00.	2– 8	"Work — work — work — *w·* and pray."
	15–27	*W·* ! till the storms are o'er
'01.	14–21	one must *w·* and pray
Po.	3– 8	*w·* thy chair, and wish thee here ;
	4–20	*w·* and pray.
	6– 8	not from those who *w·* and love.
	39–12	will *w·* to cleanse from dross
My.	61– 3	* To *w·* the transformation
	119–29	*w·* and pray for the spirit of Truth
	128–30	*W·*, and pray daily that
	130– 2	*W·* and guard your own thoughts
	143– 1	*W·* and pray that God directs your
	184–25	Love, holding unwearied *w·* over a
	193– 5	privilege remains mine to *w·*
	195– 8	to work more, to *w·* and pray ;
	213–20	*W·* your thoughts, and see whether
	232–14	I say unto all, *W·*" — *Mark* 13 : 37.
	232–28	does that *w·* accord with
	232–31	watching against a negative *w·*,
	233– 1	*alias*, no *w·*,
	233– 3	something to *w·* in yourself,
	233– 5	prevents an effective *w·*?
	233– 9	instead of *putting out your w·*?
	233–21	*w·* to know what his errors are ;
	233–23	*w·* against such a result?
	234– 4	I cannot *w·* and pray while
	254– 6	*W·*, pray, demonstrate.
	358– 5	"*W·* and pray, — *Matt.* 26 : 41.
	358–10	you need to *w·* and pray

watch-care

Ret.	6– 3	* especially entrusted to her *w·*,

watched

Mis.	1– 3	*w·* the appearing of a star ;
Ret.	89–20	he *w·* and guarded them
'02.	15–23	when the steadfast stars *w·*
Po.	18– 1	*w·* in the azure the eagle's
My.	232–16	he would have *w·*, — *Luke* 12 : 39.
	276– 3	Since Mrs. Eddy is *w·*,

Watcher

Mis.	335–23	when the *W·* bids them watch,

watcher

Mis.	117–27	of the more provident *w·*.

watchers

Mis.	324– 1	His converse with the *w·*
	325–30	without *w·* and the doors unbarred !

watches

My.	276– 3	as one *w·* a criminal

watch-fires

'02.	16–15	Kindle the *w·* of unselfed love,

watchful

Mis.	12–15	unless one be *w·* and steadfast
	319–11	Scientists must be most *w·*.
	321– 1	*w·* shepherd chants his welcome
'01.	29– 6	*w·* and tender care
Po.	9– 1	glance of her husband's *w·* eye
My.	213–12	more *w·* and vigilant.
	257– 4	To-day the *w·* shepherd shouts
	280– 5	* your *w·* care and guidance
	331– 4	* Such *w·* solicitude as Mrs. Eddy

watchfulness

Mis.	115–16	constant *w·* and prayer
	116–23	*w·*, prayer, struggles, tears,
No.	33– 8	struggle, prayer, and *w·*.

watching

Mis.	12–19	hence the need of *w·*,
	150– 3	Shepherd of Israel *w·* over you.
	276–13	assemblage found waiting and *w·*
	323– 9	working and *w·* for his coming.

watching

Ret.	23–15	I was waiting and w· ;
Pul.	14–16	and w· for rest and drink.
'00.	9– 2	but, w· them, I discern
'01.	28– 4	praying, w·, and working
Po.	8–11	w· alone o'er the starlit glow,
	47–17	W· the husbandman fled;
My.	60–30	* if I would care to do a little w·
	232– 9	chapter sub-title
	232–27	If so-called w· produces fear
	232–29	Can w· as Christ demands
	232–30	should not "w· out" mean,
	232–31	w· against a negative watch,
	233– 1	gaining the spirit of true w·,
	233–10	are you not made better by w·?
	233–22	if this w· destroys his peace
	254–12	reward . . . of w· and praying,

watchman

My.	221–27	like a w· forsaking his post,

watchmen

Mis.	368–29	tired w· on the walls of Zion,

watch-towers

Mis.	370– 9	sentinels of Zion's w·

watchword

Mis.	158–21	waiting for the w·
No.	44–27	must be the w· of Christianity.
My.	248– 3	Let your w· always be:

watchwords

Mis.	135– 5	Our w· are Truth and Love;

water

as a flood
Pul.	14– 9	w· as a flood, — Rev. 12 : 15.

as a river
Mis.	373–10	w· as a river, that he might cause

baptizing with
Mis.	184–29	John came baptizing with w·.

bathes in
Mis.	203–14	Theology religiously bathes in w·,

bucket of
Mis.	353–16	to pour a bucket of w·

cold
Pul.	14–17	Give them a cup of cold w·

drop of
Pul.	4–18	A single drop of w· may help to
'02.	12–17	drop of w· is one with the ocean,

drunk on
Mis.	48–14	made a man drunk on w·,

first
My.	121–19	a diamond of the first w· ;

into wine
Mis.	74–17	he turned the w· into wine ;
Un.	11– 5	He turned the w· into wine,

living
My.	126– 7	such as drink of the living w·.

sweet
Mis.	27–18	sweet w· and bitter?" — Jas. 3 : 11.

this
Hea.	13–13	one teaspoonful of this w·

tumbler-full of
Ret.	33–16	in a tumbler-full of w·,

tumblerful of
Hea.	13–12	into a tumblerful of w·

walk on the
Mis.	359–18	until we can walk on the w·.

walk the
Mis.	359–15	to walk the w· was scientific,

Mis.	88–26	* had never seen w· freeze."
	152– 3	in w· face answereth to — Prov. 27 : 19.
	154– 8	w· it with the dews of heaven,
	203– 9	in w· face answereth to — Prov. 27 : 19.
	244–20	turn the w· into wine,
	298–16	material rite of w· baptism,
	345–25	baptism not of w· but of blood,
	399–15	w·, the bread, and the wine.
Ret.	33–16	one teaspoonful of the w·
Hea.	10–26	hart panteth for the w· brooks,
Peo.	10– 3	steam is more powerful than w·,
Po.	75–22	w·, the bread, and the wine.

watercresses

Mis.	329–19	paddling the w·,

water-cup

Po.	39– 7	Rose from a w· ;

water-cure

Mis.	378–10	left the w·, en route for

watered

Mis.	343–10	w· by the heavenly dews of Love,
Ret.	95– 1	w· by dews of divine Science,

Waterhouse, Dr. Benjamin

Peo.	6– 2	Dr. Benjamin W· writes :

watering

Mis.	127– 5	w· her waste places,
My.	18– 2	w· her waste places,

water-mirrors

Mis.	330–15	shake out their tresses in the w· ;

water-pots

Pul.	27–15	* emblematic of the six w·

waters

bitter
My.	132–10	waters of Meribah here — bitter w· ;

come ye to the
Mis.	149– 1	come ye to the w·, — Isa. 55 : 1.

cool
Mis.	227–27	bathes it in the cool w·
Ret.	18– 3	Cool w· at play with the
Po.	63–10	Cool w· at play with the

deep
Mis.	393–14	Those who fish in w· deep,
Man.	18– 8	Although walking through deep w·,
Pul.	14–21	deep w· of chaos and old night.
'01.	26–14	I have passed through deep w·
Po.	51–19	Those who fish in w· deep,

life-giving
No.	v– 9	are athirst for the life-giving w·

living
Mis.	207– 3	drink with me the living w·
Pul.	3–22	living w· have their source in God,

many
Pul.	11– 4	as the sound of many w·,

music of
Po.	41–15	music of w· had fled to the sea,

of Meribah
Mis.	153–13	washed in the w· of Meribah,
My.	132– 9	pass through the w· of Meribah

ritualistic
Mis.	81–15	the ceremonial (or ritualistic) w·

shall overflow
My.	17– 1	w· shall overflow the — Isa. 28 : 17.

shout
Po.	73– 6	When w· shout,

stagnant
My.	149–30	which waken the stagnant w·

still
Mis.	207– 1	"beside the still w·," — Psal. 23 : 2.
	227–24	green pastures, beside the still w·,
	322–15	"beside the still w·." — Psal. 23 : 2.
	357– 8	rest beside still w·.
My.	129–26	green pastures beside still w·,
	162–26	beside the still w·." — Psal. 23 : 2.

troubled
My.	152– 3	anchored its faith in troubled w·.

upon the
My.	247–25	cast your bread upon the w·

will be pacified
Pul.	14–24	The w· will be pacified,

Mis.	203–11	w· that run among the valleys,
Po.	70– 7	Making its w· wine,
My.	126– 4	pour wormwood into the w·

Waterville College

My.	304–14	Boston, Portland, and at W· C·,

Watt's "On the Mind and Moral Science."

My.	304– 8	W· "O· the M· and M· S·."

wave

Mis.	74–22	Walking the w·, he proved
	211–14	rescued from the merciless w·
	244–20	causing him to walk the w·,
	257–25	in the death-dealing w·.
	339–26	a w· that will some time flood
Ret.	60–15	C. S. saith to the w·
Pul.	13–18	above the drowning w·.
	14–25	Christ will command the w·.
	23–11	* w· of idealism that has swept
	52–21	* w· of materialism and bigotry
'00.	7–22	the w· of earth's troubled sea,
'02.	20– 1	Christ walketh over the w· ;
Po.	15–22	cannot quench in oblivion's w·.
	24–10	A w· of welcome birth,
	41–22	that flowed as the w·,
	73– 4	hoarse w· revisits thy shore !
	73–16	By the "Rock" or w·,
My.	350–12	Thou the dark w· treading

waver

No.	7– 3	evil influences w· the scales

wavering

Mis.	263–21	poise the w· balance

waves

Mis.	23– 9	winds, and w·, obey this
	74–17	He walked upon the w· ;
	206– 5	Above the w· of Jordan,
	313–19	field w· its white ensign,
	397–11	'Gainst which the winds and w·
Pul.	18–20	'Gainst which the winds and w·

waves

Pul.	39–18	* I watch the flow Of *w·* of light.
No.	29–24	*w·* of sin, sickness, and death.
'01.	19–18	even the winds and *w·*,
Po.	2–18	*w·* kiss the murmuring rill
	8–15	starry hopes and its *w·* of truth.
	12–20	'Gainst which the winds and *w·*
My.	162–30	*w·* and winds beat in vain.
	189–10	go forth in *w·* of sound,
	226–12	commands the *w·* and the winds,
	232– 4	the waiting *w·* will weave
	291–24	*w·* over land and sea,

waving

Ret.	4–14	bending grain *w·* gracefully
Po.	68– 9	the sea and the tall *w·* pine

wavy

Mis.	329–15	weaving the *w·* grass,
Po.	67–16	shade o'er the dark *w·* grass.

Way

Mis.	355– 1	chapter sub-title
Chr.	53– 8	And point the *W·*
	53–11	The *W·* in Science He appoints,
	53–41	The *W·*, the Truth, the Life
Un.	63– 3	The *W·*, the Truth, and the Life
'00.	7–16	Christ, the *W·*, the Truth, and the
My.	139–12	nearing the *W·*, the Truth, and the Life,
	260–28	the *W·*, in word and in deed,
	260–29	the *W·*, the Truth, and the Life.

way

after the

My.	285–25	after the *w·* which they — *Acts* 24 : 14.

all the

Mis.	39–16	alway'' — *all the w·*. — *Matt.* 28 : 20.
	214–16	meant, all the *w·* through,
	251– 4	all the *w·* from the Pacific
	347–23	if it be uphill all the *w·*,
'01.	22–19	that one and one are two all the *w·*
	32–25	all the *w·* up to its preparation for
My.	109– 3	All the *w·* mortals are experiencing

along the

Mis.	169– 2	all along the *w·* of her researches

another's

Mis.	213–16	chastened and illumined another's *w·*

any

Mis.	79–30	which in any *w·* obligates you to
	115–29	if you in any *w·* indulge in sin ;
	132–27	* "If we have in any *w·* misrepresented
	138– 6	conforming to society, in any *w·*,
	228–21	or in any *w·* takes cognizance of,
	381–24	or in any *w·* or manner disposing of,
Ret.	87–18	never, in any *w·*, to trespass upon
My.	138– 8	not for my benefit in any *w·*,
	325–14	* Command me at any time, in any *w·*,

best

Mis.	236–17	best *w·* to overcome them,
My.	195–18	best *w·* to silence a deep discontent

better

'01.	21–23	Does this critic know of a better *w·*

demonstrate "the

Un.	55–10	demonstrate "the *w·*" — *John* 14 : 6.

divine

Ret.	54– 9	and learn the divine *w·*,
No.	12–20	This divine *w·* impels a

effectual

Mis.	263–19	met in the most effectual *w·*.

everlasting

My.	33–12	in the *w·* everlasting.'' — *Psal.* 139 : 24.

every

Pul.	80–10	* socially, indeed every *w·*.
My.	62–28	* to assist us in every *w·* possible ;
	212–27	by hindering in every *w·*

every step of the

My.	234–12	and guide them every step of the *w·*

general

Ret.	40– 2	and taught in a general *w·*,
My.	92–14	* has in a general *w·* been familiar ;

God's

My.	293– 8	believed that . . . was God's *w·*.

her own

My.	343– 4	* works around a question in her own *w·*,

His

My.	323–22	* to reveal to us His *w·*.

his

Mis.	113–16	commits his *w·* to God,
	129–19	will always find somebody in his *w·*,
	323– 7	Stranger wending his *w·* downward,
	324– 2	and he makes his *w·* into the streets
	326–30	groped his *w·* from the dwelling of
'01.	14–16	misleads the traveller on his *w·*
	17– 8	to meet the sad sinner on his *w·*

honorable

My.	277– 5	in a *w·* honorable and satisfactory

in Christian Science

My.	200–20	for you know the *w·* in C. S.

way

in divine Science

Mis.	358– 2	to mark the *w·* in divine Science.

in no

Mis.	97–12	It is in no *w·* allied to divine power.
Ret.	67–22	It was in no *w·* contingent on

in Spirit

Un.	55–13	"The *w·*," in Spirit, is — *John* 14 : 6.

interesting

My.	332–21	* in a most interesting *w·*.

in the

Mis.	197–10	in the *w·* which Jesus marked out
	208–18	in the *w·* of God's appointing.
	215–16	in the *w·* of His appointment,
	358–17	in the *w·* which Jesus marked out,
	400–23	In the *w·* Thou hast,
Ret.	14–28	in the *w·* everlasting.'' — *Psal.* 139 : 24.
Pul.	59–12	* in the *w·* peculiar to
Peo.	3–28	in the *w·* that our Lord has appointed ;
Po.	69–11	In the *w·* Thou hast,
My.	45–20	* to lead you in the *w·*,
	91–24	* despite the obstacles put in the *w·*
	93–12	* in the *w·* of gratifying the passions

in the flesh

Un.	55–11	"The *w·*," in the flesh, is — *John* 14 : 6.

I see the

Mis.	347–19	I see the *w·* now.

is narrow

My.	202–27	The *w·* is narrow at first,

its

Mis.	267–20	while the left beats its *w·* downward,
Un.	7–12	which had eaten its *w·* to the
No.	3– 6	foe who stands in its *w·*.
Po.	vi– 1	* *found its w· into print*,
My.	112–29	has won its *w·* into the
	160–15	cuts its *w·* through iron

lead the

Mis.	389– 4	* point to heaven and lead the *w·*.''
Po.	21–18	* point to heaven and lead the *w·*.''

light the

My.	345–28	light the *w·* to the Church of Christ.

literal

Mis.	169–15	interpreted in a literal *w·*.

living

My.	191–25	lights the living *w·* of Life.
	192–12	lights the living *w·* to Life,

loiter by the

My.	11– 4	* stumble or loiter by the *w·*,

Love is the

'01.	35–10	Love is the *w·* alway.

make

Mis.	99–27	make *w·* for health, holiness,

mistaken

My.	211– 6	This mistaken *w·*, of hiding sin

mysterious

My.	205– 9	* "God moves in a mysterious *w·*

narrow

Mis.	245–28	the straight and narrow *w·* ;
	389–19	sweet secret of the narrow *w·*,
'01.	28– 6	enter the strait and narrow *w·*,
Po.	4–18	sweet secret of the narrow *w·*,
My.	104– 2	strait and narrow *w·* of Truth.

no

Ret.	82–18	This fact interferes in no *w·*
'01.	31–15	in no *w·* except in the interest of
My.	280–28	In no *w·* nor manner did I request

no other

Mis.	11–28	since they permit me no other *w·*,
	185–15	no other *w·* under heaven
	234–10	in no other *w·* can we reach
Ret.	86–21	this manner and in no other *w·*
'00.	5–15	I see no other *w·*
My.	277– 7	no other *w·* of settling difficulties

novel

Mis.	139–24	in a circuitous, novel *w·*,
Pul.	59– 4	* in a somewhat novel *w·*.

obstructs the

Mis.	39–27	*what most obstructs the w·?*
	328–23	Whatever obstructs the *w·*,

of escape

Mis.	113–18	there is a *w·* of escape from
Pan.	12–14	the *w·* of escape from sin,

of healing

Mis.	244–23	*w·* of healing and salvation.

of Life

Un.	55–13	"the *w·*" of Life, Truth, — *John* 14 : 6.
No.	35–10	He who pointed the *w·* of Life
My.	191–25	lights the living *w·* of Life.

of salvation

Mis.	11–12	the sure *w·* of salvation.
	211– 3	Christ points the *w·* of salvation.
Pul.	70–22	* *w·* of salvation demonstrated by Jesus
No.	28–14	C. S. is the *w·* of salvation
'01.	28–22	is indeed the *w·* of salvation from all
My.	9–16	* *w·* of salvation through Christ.''

way

of salvation
My. 37– 1   * *w·* of salvation of all men
     58–20   * demonstrable *w·* of salvation.
of talking
My. 343– 2   * She has a rapt *w·* of talking,
of the Lord
Mis. 246–24   the *w·* of the Lord, — *Matt.* 3 : 3.
of the transgressor
Mis. 261–14   *w·* of the transgressor — *see Prov.* 13 : 15.
of the unchristly
Pul. 21–23   Go not into the *w·* of the unchristly,
of Truth
Mis. 356–31   miss the *w·* of Truth and Love.
Un. 55–16   the life-giving *w·* of Truth.
My. 104– 2   strait and narrow *w·* of Truth.
     232– 6   even the *w·* of Truth and Love
of wisdom
My. 356–21   chapter sub-title
one
Mis. 220– 3   a good rule works one *w·*,
Ret. 86– 4   but one *w·* of *doing* good,
     86– 5   but one *w·* of *being* good,
Hea. 5–19   in one *w·* or another,
one's
Mis. 117–28   He illumines one's *w·*
opens a
Rud. 8–21   but opens a *w·* whereby,
open the
Mis. 317–29   divine Love will open the *w·*
My. 357–19   open the *w·*, widely and impartially,
opposite
Mis. 220– 3   a false rule the opposite *w·*.
other
Mis. 215–10   not seek to climb up some other *w·*,
No. 44– 9   To climb up by some other *w·*
Pan. 6– 4   never disappear in any other *w·*.
My. 152–15   or do I climb up some other *w·* ?
     359–10   any other *w·* than through my
our
Mis. 215–18   infantile conception of our *w·* ;
out of the flesh
No. 33–26   show them that the *w·* out of the flesh,
paved the
My. 176– 6   the dear South paved the *w·*
perfect
'00. 14–16   perfect *w·*, or Golden Rule :
plain
Un. 9– 8   Jesus has made the *w·* plain,
pointing the
Mis. 327–23   the Stranger is pointing the *w·*,
No. 28–12   If Science is pointing the *w·*,
points the
'02. 6–24   metaphysics points the *w·*,
point the
Mis. 213– 7   point the *w·*, shorten the process,
     357–30   to help them and point the *w·*.
Ret. 85–19   God's finger to point the *w·*.
prepares the
My. 12–24   * God prepares the *w·* for
preparing the
My. 345–30   They are preparing the *w·* for us."
reveal "the
Mis. 308– 9   reveal "the *w·*," — *John* 14 : 6.
right
Mis. 65–17   the right *w·* of treating disease?
My. 232– 6   The right *w·* wins the right
right of
My. 232– 6   wins the right of *w·*,
rugged
Mis. 398– 4   All the rugged *w·*.
Ret. 46–10   All the rugged *w·*.
Pul. 17– 9   All the rugged *w·*.
Hea. 19–24   along the rugged *w·*,
Po. 14– 8   All the rugged *w·*.
My. 201–24   All the rugged *w·*.
some
Mis. 236–26   in some *w·* or at some step
     300–19   liable, in some *w·*, to be printed
Ret. 1– 5   in some *w·* related to
     94– 4   At some period and in some *w·*
Un. 9– 6   some time and in some *w·*,
spiritual
'02. 10–20   finds the more spiritual *w·*,
that
My. 317–19   * wouldn't express it that *w·*."
their
Mis. 85–31   to learn their *w·* out of both
     265– 8   make mistakes and lose their *w·*.
     284–12   no danger of mistaking their *w·*.
     331– 3   committing their *w·* unto Him
     342– 4   their *w·* was material ;
     353–29   helping others, go their *w·*.
Ret. 16– 4   pushing their *w·* through the crowd
My. 355–24   their *w·* is onward,

way

the only
Mis. 60– 8   the only *w·* to destroy them ;
Ret. 73–17   This is the only *w·* whereby
thereto
'01. 35–18   Patient faith the *w·* thereto?
thine own
Mis. 328– 3   Make thine own *w·* ;
this
Mis. 347–15   One says, Go this *w·* ;
Ret. 24– 7   discovery came to pass in this *w·*.
Un. 9–10   but this *w·* is not the path of
My. 145–22   if in this *w·* I can serve
     360–21   in this *w·* God will bless
Thou hast
Po. 43–21   Just the *w·* Thou hast :
thy
Mis. 157– 6   He . . . will direct thy *w·*.
     157–22   "Commit thy *w·* unto — *Psal.* 37 : 5.
     268–32   "Commit thy *w·* unto — *Psal.* 37 : 5.
Pul. 53–13   * "Arise, go thy *w·* : — *Luke* 17 : 19.
Po. 29– 3   Pursue thy *w·*,
My. 170–23   Commit thy *w·* unto — *Psal.* 37 : 5.
     274–27   thy *w·* may be known — *Psal.* 67 : 2.
to escape
Mis. 105–11   showing us the *w·* to escape
to heaven
Mis. 268– 6   pointing the *w·* to heaven,
     344–27   point out the *w·* to heaven
to holiness
'01. 14–14   so hinder our *w·* to holiness.
treacherous
Po. 43–17   Rough or treacherous *w·*.
true
Ret. 94– 8   acknowledging the true *w·*,
Truth, is the
'02. 10–24   Truth, is the *w·*.
unfettered
Ret. 9–26   * her own unfettered *w·* !
unfolded the
My. 348–19   God unfolded the *w·*,
weary
Mis. 395–22   to shun my weary *w·*,
Po. 58– 7   to shun my weary *w·*,
wicked
Ret. 14–27   any wicked *w·* in me, — *Psal.* 139 : 24.
My. 33–11   any wicked *w·* in me, — *Psal.* 139 : 24.
'wildered
Po. 70–22   Shine on our 'wildered *w·*,
wisdom's
Po. 23–20   Guide him in wisdom's *w·* !
wise
Mis. 90–18   Break the yoke . . . in every wise *w·*.
My. 248–11   put an end to falsities in a wise *w·*
won the
My. 163– 4   won the *w·* and taught mankind
your
Mis. 117–31   Be sure that God *directs* your *w·* ;
My. 164–22   guiding, and guarding your *w·*

Mis. 39–25   *In what w· is a Christian Scientist an*
     64– 3   *w·* he made for mortals' escape.
     74–12   "the *w·*, the truth, — *John* 14 : 6.
     75– 2   Christ was "the *w·*;" — *John* 14 : 6.
     75– 3   Life and Truth were the *w·*
     96– 1   the *w·* of man's salvation
     132–15   * by the *w·*, from Mrs. Eddy, also."
     155–26   by *w·* of *The C· S· Journal;*
     323–22   The *w·* winds and widens
     359–23   The *w·* is absolute divine Science :
Un. 37– 1   declared himself "the *w·*" — *John* 14 : 6.
     58–13   Christ as "the *w·*;" — *John* 14 : 6.
No. 7–11   and the *w·* out of it ;
No. 12–17   "the *w·*, the truth, — *John* 14 : 6.
'02. 2– 9   The Science . . . is on the *w·*,
     16–15   "I am the *w·*." — *John* 14 : 6.
Hea. 16–27   "I am the *w·*, — *John* 14 : 6.
My. 43–32   * The *w·* out of the wilderness
     72–28   * *w·* the Christian Scientists began
     81–20   * in a *w·* there was no mistaking.
     140– 3   a *w·* that they knew not ; — *Isa.* 42 : 16.
     257–14   "the *w·*, the truth, — *John* 14 : 6.
     292– 6   the *w·* pointed out,
     321– 3   * in a *w·* connected with your work,
     349–18   "the *w·*, the truth, — *John* 14 : 6.

wayfarer
Ret. 79– 9   signs for the *w·* in divine Science
waymarks
Mis. 213–15   so profit by these *w·*,
Ret. 27–11   valuable to me as *w·* of progress,
ways
and means
Mis. 66–17   God's perfect *w·* and means,
     98–11   in finding *w·* and means for
     153– 1   his material *w·* and means,

ways
and means
Mis.	204–17	human policy, *w*·, and means.
	212–13	human sense of *w*· and means
	215– 8	sense of God's *w*· and means,
	357– 3	*w*· and means of personal sense.
Ret.	52– 2	to find new *w*· and means
'01.	29– 5	providing *w*· and means for others.
My.	208–26	confidence in His *w*· and means
	253– 3	with the *w*· and means of the

God's
Mis.	102–17	God's *w*· are not ours.
	158– 3	God's *w*· are not as our ways ;
	215– 8	material sense of God's *w*·
Ret.	64–17	God's *w*· and works and thoughts
No.	21–18	because by it we lose God's *w*·

higher
Ret.	48–29	has led to higher *w*·, means, and

His
Mis.	361–32	His *w*· are not as our ways.
Rud.	10–26	acknowledge God in all His *w*·.
No.	18– 3	nor acknowledged God in all His *w*·.
My.	208–26	confidence in His *w*· and means

many
My.	84–28	* is notable in many *w*·.

mental
Pul.	15– 4	and expose evil's hidden mental *w*·

mighty
Un.	10–21	calculation of His mighty *w*·,

multitudinous
Ret.	50–10	shown me, in multitudinous *w*·,

of Christianity
Rud.	17–15	*w*· of Christianity have not changed.

of God
Ret.	31– 5	vindicating "the *w*· of God" — *Job* 40 : 19.

of living
My.	345–27	more etherealized *w*· of living.

other
'02.	10–29	in other *w*· than by walking
My.	277– 2	chapter sub-title

our
Mis.	158– 3	God's ways are not as our *w*· ;
	361–32	His ways are not as our *w*·.

self-destroying
Un.	55–16	self-destroying *w*· of error

social
My.	163–13	canno*t* show my love . . . in social *w*·

three
Mis.	230– 8	Three *w*· of wasting time,

Thy
Un.	5–28	parts of Thy *w*·," — *see Job* 26 : 14.
My.	229–27	Thy *w*· are not as ours.

thy
Mis.	175–32	remember God in all thy *w*·,
'01.	35– 1	In all thy *w*· acknowledge Him, — *Prov.* 3 : 6.
Peo.	12–12	acknowledge only God in all thy *w*·,

wisdom's
Ret.	90–25	walk steadfastly in wisdom's *w*·.

your
Mis.	236–14	follow God in all your *w*·."

Mis.	78–14	* "*w*· that are vain"
	138– 5	wilderness or *w*· of the world.
	222–30	*w*·, means, and potency of Truth
My.	210–18	chapter sub-title

way-seeker
Pan.	12–19	*w*· gains and points the path.

Way-shower (*see also* Way-shower's)
Mis.	30–16	*W*· illustrated Life unconfined,
	162–19	He was the *W*·,
	206–28	understand and obey the *W*·,
	328–22	He . . . who follows the *W*·,
Man.	15–16	through Christ Jesus the *W*·
Ret.	26– 8	Our great *W*·, steadfast to the end
Un.	55– 9	He was the *W*·;
My.	4–10	how many are following the *W*·?
	19–25	Those words of our holy *W*·,
	140–22	God's *W*·, Christ,
	349–17	great *W*·, invested with glory,

Way-shower's
My.	161– 3	washing the *W*· feet

wayside
Mis.	99–32	Jesus taught by the *w*·,
	150–22	the *w*· is a sanctuary,
	163–10	and taught by the *w*·,
	337–26	by the *w*·, in humble homes,
	357–13	seeds of Truth fall by the *w*·,
No.	3–23	to sow by the *w*· for the way-weary,
Po.	47–16	Weary of sowing the *w*·
My.	185–12	by the *w*·, or in our homes.

wayward
Mis.	11–10	did not cease teaching the *w*· ones

way-weary
No.	3–23	to sow by the wayside for the *w*·,

weak
Mis.	227–15	*w*·, pitifully poor objects
	233–21	is a poor shift for the *w*· and worldly
	254–12	grows *w*· with wickedness
	262–18	strengthening the *w*·,
	288–10	A rash conclusion . . . is *w*· and wicked ;
	328–26	and strengthen the *w*·.
	345–15	* fit only for women and *w*· men ;"
	385–23	the flesh was *w*·, and doomed
Man.	55–15	this *w*· member shall not be
Pul.	4– 1	* "*w*· and infirm of purpose."
No.	44–17	*w*· hand outstretched to God.
'00.	10–20	individuals, *w*· provinces, or peoples.
'01.	2–11	may suit the *w*· or the worldly
	18– 4	*w*· criticisms and woeful warnings
Po.	48–18	the flesh was *w*·, and doomed
My.	287–12	poor shift for the *w*· and worldly.
	342–15	* not be understood that I mean *w*·,
	342–15	* for *w*· she was not.

weaken
Mis.	53–14	You only *w*· your power to heal
Hea.	13– 1	so *w*· both points of action ;

weakened
My.	227– 4	as one who never *w*· in his

weakens
'01.	15–10	The resistance to C. S. *w*·
My.	278–27	war *w*· power and must finally fall,

weakly
Po.	43–16	Beacon beams — athwart the *w*·,

weak-minded
Peo.	13–24	* fit only for women and *w*· men."

weakness
Mis.	10–21	their strength made perfect in *w*·,
	30–24	fossil of . . . *w*·, and superstition.
	64– 1	Jesus assumed . . . the *w*· of flesh,
	138–18	to know that human strength is *w*·,
	200–22	the touch of *w*·, pain, and
	206–13	scientific growth manifests no *w*·,
	245–15	Their movements indicate fear and *w*·,
	252–13	sick thoughts are unreality and *w*· ;
	292–13	that brings to human *w*· might
	329– 4	a *w*·, or a — virtue?
	358–14	Human pride is human *w*·.
Un.	39–12	removes human *w*· by divine strength,
Rud.	9– 8	will lead to *w*· in practice,
No.	45–10	indicates *w*·, fear, or malice ;
Po.	2–10	With all the strength of *w*·
My.	191– 7	Persecution is the *w*· of tyrants
	287– 8	giving to human *w*· strength,

weal
Mis.	65– 9	greater subject of human *w*·
Po.	3–11	Since first we met, in *w*· or woe
My.	36–28	* for the cause of human *w*·,
	213– 9	lurking foe to human *w*·,

wealth
Mis.	246– 8	to subserve the interests of *w*·,
	327–12	search for *w*· and fame.
Pul.	44–18	* chapter sub-title
No.	43–18	from mercenary motives, for *w*· and
'02.	17–21	to show man . . . the *w*· of love.
Hea.	16– 7	*w*· and fame, or Truth and Love?
My.	84–18	* in numbers, *w*·, vigor,
	91–26	* even stranger is its increase in *w*·.
	252–28	allurements of *w*·, pride, or power ;
	265–29	*w*· should be governed by honesty,
	291–14	enfolded a *w*· of affection,

wealthy
Mis.	ix– 7	among my . . . students few were *w*·.
Pul.	60–18	* gift of a *w*· Universalist
'02.	15–17	My husband, . . . was considered *w*·,
My.	97–18	* evidently *w*· congregation

weaned
'00.	11– 7	*w*· me from this love

weapon
Mis.	99–10	Fear is the *w*· in the hands of
Ret.	2–13	*w*· had been bestowed by

weapons
Mis.	139–10	*w*· of our warfare — *II Cor.* 10 : 4.
	204– 9	error yields up its *w*·
	351– 7	*w*· of the silent mental malpractice.
Pul.	84– 3	* with the *w*· of peace.

wear
Mis.	224–21	shall not *w*· upon our sensibilities ;
	303–16	If ever I *w*· out from serving
	340– 9	win and *w*· the crown of the faithful.
'00.	8–12	*w*· the purloined garment as his own,
My.	83–10	* Scientists frequently *w*· a small pin,
	339–23	only those . . . should *w*· sackcloth.

wearied
Pan. 13–25 Have I w· you with the mysticism
My. 196–21 lest ye be w· — *Heb.* 12 : 3.

weariness
Mis. 53– 8 w· and wickedness of mortal existence,
Man. 60–10 Amusement or idleness is w·.
Po. 35– 2 Beguile the lagging hours of w·

wearing
Po. 34–19 W· no earthly chain,

wearisome
Po. 32–20 comfort my soul all the w· day,
My. 189–19 fables flee and faith grows w·,

weary
Mis. 84–24 turn one, like a w· traveller, to
85– 2 To the battle-worn and w·
125–12 not stand waiting and w· ;
144–18 great rock in a w· land :"— *Isa.* 32 : 2.
153– 4 not w· in well doing."— *see Gal.* 6 : 9.
155– 8 woo the w· wanderer to your door,
159–26 w· wings sprung upward !
208–14 to the w· and heavy-laden, rest.
236– 7 w· with study to counsel wisely
263–10 great rock in a w· land,"— *Isa.* 32 : 2.
341–15 w· pilgrim, unloose the latchet of
395–22 For joy, to shun my w· way,
Man. 60–11 rest the w· and heavy laden.
Ret. 33– 6 till I was w· of "scientific guessing,"
Pul. 14–15 w· wanderers, athirst in the desert
20–19 great rock in a w· land."— *Isa.* 32 : 2.
56–15 * hope and comfort to many w· souls.
Pan. 12–17 may run and not w·,
'02. 19–16 To the burdened and w·,
Hea. 2–10 * "I am w· of the world,
2–11 * and the world is w· of me ;
11– 8 w· of matter, it would catch the
Po. vii–14 * a balm to the w· heart.
34– 5 dear remembrance in a w· breast.
41– 5 Where the w· and earth-stricken
47–13 The w· of body and brain?
47–14 W· of sobbing, like some tired
47–16 W· of sowing the wayside
58– 7 to shun my w· way,
My. 93–14 * rare lures for w· hearts,
106–16 the winds would w·,
150–13 never w· of struggling to
182–27 rest their w· wings amid the
254– 8 shall run and not be w·,
355–24 their footsteps are not w· ;

weather
Mis. 198–31 suffered from inclement w·,
Pul. 49–16 brought here in warm w·,
63–13 brought here in warm w·,
My. 275–20 Either my work, . . . or the w·,

weave
Mis. 99– 5 To w· one thread of Science
228–18 to w· an existence fit for
377– 2 to w· a web of words
Po. 53– 9 More softly warm and w·
My. 232– 4 waiting waves will w· for you

weaves
Mis. 390–15 The verdant grass it w· ;
Po. 55–16 The verdant grass it w· ;
My. 252– 6 w· webs that ensnare.

weaving
Mis. 329–15 w· the wavy grass,
My. 154–17 w· the new-old vesture

web
Mis. 145–27 woven . . . in the w· of history,
377– 2 to weave a w· of words

webs
My. 232– 5 their winning w· of life
252– 7 which weaves w· that ensnare.

Webster (*see also* **Webster's**)
Daniel
Mis. 345–18 Daniel W· said, "My heart has
Peo. 13–27 Daniel W· said : "My heart has

Mis. 68–21 According to W·, metaphysics is
Rud. 2– 1 definitions . . . as given by W·,
No. 9–27 according to W·, it is
Pan. 2–10 According to W· the word "pantheism"

Webster's
Pan. 2–12 W· derivation of the English word
'01. 3–10 W· definition of God,

wedded
Mis. 151–25 w· to the spiritual idea,
276–22 w· to a purer, higher affection
277– 1 is w· to their love,
342–10 w· to a higher understanding
'00. 11– 7 w· me to spiritual music,
My. 269– 4 man w· to the Lamb,

wedding
'00. 15–19 a w· garment new and old,
My. 153–28 the w· of this Word to all

wedlock
Mis. 285–13 chapter sub-title
297–19 voluntarily entered into w·,
My. 268–26 the Science of w·,

Wednesday
Man. 31–18 W· evening meetings.
31–20 part of the W· evening services,
47–23 at the W· evening meeting.
90–11 on the first W· of December.
96– 1 No W· Evening Lectures.
96– 3 shall not appoint a lecture for W·
My. 79–24 * chapter sub-title
134–21 * At the W· evening meeting

Wednesday Meetings
Man. 122– 1 heading

weds
Un. 17– 8 man thus w· himself with God,

weeds
Mis. 343–14 noxious w· of passion, malice, envy,
343–20 w· of mortal mind are not always

week (*see also* **week's**)
Mis. 243–11 in less than one w·.
350–14 convened in about one w·
Man. 90–12 will continue not over one w·.
Pul. 45–23 * A w· ago Judge Hanna withdrew
60–13 * having remained over a w·
'00. 10–23 Only last w· I received a
'01. 11–18 and obeyed throughout the w·,
My. 25– 3 * special effort during the coming w·
75– 4 * centre of the stage this w·.
81–25 * fitting close to a memorable w·.
82– 8 * crowding Boston the last w·
97–26 * descended upon Boston . . . last w·
97–30 * incidents witnessed during the w·

week-days
My. 90– 3 * Sundays or on w·

weekly
My. 152–31 sending to you w· flowers
334– 9 * w· issue of the *C· S· Sentinel,*

week's
Mis. 135–14 Is it a cross to give one w· time

weeks (*see also* **weeks'**)
Mis. 110–15 W· have passed into months,
242–23 one ounce in two w·,
243– 9 bandages to remain six w·,
256–19 from one to two w· previous
372– 8 In two w· from the date
378– 4 in a few w· returned
Ret. 50– 7 lasting barely three w·.
'02. 15–21 Six w· I waited on God
My. 52–32 * w· lengthened into months ;
66– 5 * During the past two w·
74–28 * Within two w· we have had
237– 3 in the *Sentinel* a few w· ago,

weeks'
Mis. 349– 5 included about . . . three w· time,

ween
Mis. 393– 6 Paints the limner's work, I w·,
Po. 51–11 Paints the limner's work, I w·,

weep
Mis. 170– 5 w· over the graves of their
279– 6 and am too apt to w·
279– 7 with those who w·,
Pul. 7–11 he would not w· over it,
'00. 8– 25 not Science for . . . the good to w·.
13–16 promise to such as wait and w·.
Po. 67–13 Beside you they walk while you w·,

weepeth
Mis. 275– 8 where w· the faithful, stricken

weeping
Po. 9– 8 w· alone that the vision is fled,
My. 161–10 There shall be w· — *Luke* 13 : 28.

weigh
Mis. 47– 2 w· over two hundred pounds
167–10 How much does he w·?
280– 5 w· the thoughts and actions
280–10 I would not w· you,
Ret. 71– 1 monuments which w· dust,
Pan. 14– 1 w· a sigh, and rise into

weighed
Mis. 5–28 w· down as is mortal thought
280– 9 You have come to be w· ;
280–10 nor have you w·.
288– 7 and w· by spiritual Love,
312– 3 w· in the scale of God
365– 5 w· in the balances of God
Ret. 40–18 and w· twelve pounds.

weighed

Un.	29–21	*w·* or touched by physicality.
No.	18–13	when *w·* in the balance,
My.	291–16	*w·* in the scales of divinity,

weighing

Mis.	46–19	not *w·* equally with Him,

weighs

Mis.	119–16	*w·* mightily in the scale
	293–12	*w·* in the scales of God
Rud.	9–18	*w·* against his healing power;
My.	277–18	Whatever *w·* in the eternal scale

weight

Mis.	46–17	to throw the *w·* of his thoughts
	47– 3	*and carry about this w· daily?*
	47–11	without consciousness of its *w·*?
	255– 7	to throw the *w·* of thought and action
	281–25	I felt the *w·* of this yesterday,
	361–18	lay aside every *w·*,— *Heb.* 12 : 1.
	372– 4	had not one feather's *w·*
Man.	59– 5	lose some *w·* in the scale of
Ret.	87–24	bear the *w·* of others' burdens,
	95– 9	* For heavy is the *w·* of ill
No.	34–16	falls with its leaden *w·*
My.	146–30	He lays his whole *w·* of thought,
	350–16	*w·* of anguish which they blindly

weights

Mis.	327–20	lay down a few of the heavy *w·*,

weighty

Mis.	227–11	to get their *w·* stuff into the

welcome

Mis.	18– 5	and *w·* these spiritual signs
	206– 6	the Father and Mother's *w·*,
	306– 7	* *w·* suggestions of events
	321– 2	chants his *w·* over the cradle
Man.	59–15	The Leader's *W·*.
	59–20	The Local Members' *W·*.
Ret.	6– 7	The needy were ever *w·*,
	12– 2	Wake freedom's *w·*.
	41– 2	contrasted with its present *w·*
Pul.	51–13	* *w·* others who have different
'01.	17– 9	and to *w·* him home.
'02.	2– 9	haste to meet and to *w·* it.
	11– 7	awaits with warrant and *w·*,
	20–25	good people *w·* Christian Scientists.
Po.	10– 3	We proffer thee warm *w·*
	24–10	A wave of *w·* birth,
	41–23	to *w·* the murmur it gave?
	60–22	Wake freedom's *w·*,
My.	24– 8	* inspires you to *w·* all mankind
	42–20	* affords me great pleasure to *w·*
	52–12	* *w·* the fact of the spreading
	72– 6	* open wide in *w·* to nobility.
	74–27	* and as such they are *w·*.
	154–23	I *w·* the means and methods,
	170–12	*Beloved Brethren :— W· home !*
	170–13	*W·* to Pleasant View,
	257– 4	watchful shepherd shouts his *w·*
	290–22	*w·* you where no arrow wounds
	313–31	not *w·* in my father's house.
	337– 5	We proffer thee warm *w·*

welcomed

Mis.	251– 8	has *w·* you to Concord
	311– 3	Christian Scientists will be *w·*,
Pul.	51–22	* compromises have been *w·*.
'02.	1–20	be *w·* and sustained.
My.	86– 1	* is doubly *w·*.
	99– 8	* is *w·* within our midst
	173–20	my heart *w·* each and all.
	188–22	heart of a Southron has *w·* me.

welcomes

Man.	59–16	*w·* to her seats in the church,
My.	133– 2	*w·*, many pardons for the penitent.
	346– 4	* *w·* it as another opportunity for

welcoming

Man.	59–14	*w·* STRANGERS.
My.	21–21	* *w·* their brethren from far and near,
	66–25	* *w·* her children and giving

welding

Pul.	56–16	* *W·* Christianity and Science,

welfare

Mis.	152–14	for the *w·* of her children,
	228– 4	whose *w·* thou hast promoted,
	315–16	to look after the *w·* of his students,
Man.	45–11	strive to promote the *w·* of all
Ret.	72– 4	To disregard the *w·* of others
	82–21	ease and *w·* of the workers.
	90–22	*w·* and happiness of her children
Pul.	21–19	not indifferent to the *w·* of any one.
	50– 1	* to promote the *w·* of
	82–26	* upon which depends the *w·* of
My.	10–30	* their own individual *w·* is closely
	10–31	* general *w·* of the Cause.

welfare

My.	11–13	* result in our *w·*.
	280– 6	* solicitude for the *w·* of the nations
	325– 3	* called to inquire of his *w·*

well

Mis.	vii– 2	* To read it *w·* ;
	vii– 5	* thy *w·* made choice of friends
	5– 1	This work *w·* done will elevate
	9– 5	*W·* is it that the Shepherd of Israel
	25–25	omniscience means as *w·*, all-science.
	33–10	as *w·* as in the manhood of God,
	33–28	for sickness, as *w·* as for sin,
	36– 7	Beasts, as *w·* as men,
	38–26	*to be healed by it and keep w·*
	42–18	proves to have been *w·* done,
	51– 2	physically as *w·* as spiritually,
	54–17	*Must I study . . . in order to keep w·*
	69–18	In one hour he was *w·*,
	70– 9	belief, was removed, the man was *w·*.
	71– 2	*when I am not entirely w· myself?*
	72–23	as *w·* as the material universe,
	84– 2	as *w·* as by speaking, the whole truth.
	96–19	from sickness as *w·* as from sin.
	110–21	We may *w·* unite in thanksgiving
	111– 3	work, *w·* done, would dignify angels.
	115–31	of your own as *w·* as of others' sins.
	122–25	"*W·* done, good and— *Matt.* 25 : 23.
	124–20	It is *w·* that C. S. has taken
	130–21	should know *w·* whereof he speaks.
	136–18	You can *w·* afford to give me up,
	143–19	*w·* known physicians, teachers,
	153– 4	not weary in *w·* doing." — see *Gal.* 6 : 9.
	156– 8	All is *w·* at headquarters,
	175– 6	may *w·* be likened to the
	184– 7	in body as *w·* as in mind.
	192–13	*w·* knowing the omnipotence of
	216–14	"laying on of hands," as *w·*. — *Heb.* 6 : 2.
	218–29	"Pretty *w·*, I thank you !"
	219–23	and immortal Mind makes *w·* ;
	220– 6	"You are *w·*, and you know it ;"
	220–15	"I am *w·*, and I know it."
	224– 4	*W·* may we feel wounded by our
	226– 7	clergyman's son returned home— *w·*.
	238–20	Let one's life answer *w·* these
	241– 6	as *w·* as sin of every sort.
	242–24	leaving the patient *w·*.
	248–27	C. S. . . . made me *w·*,
	249–11	*w·* known that I am not a spiritualist,
	249–13	as *w·* as my intimate acquaintances.
	252–20	physically, as *w·* as spiritually,
	253–12	* chapter sub-title
	255–23	for sickness, as *w·* as for sin,
	265–24	Those who abide by them do *w·*.
	269–27	*w·* knowing the willingness of
	273–12	as *w·* as the better part of
	273–31	more than one person can *w·* accomplish.
	275– 7	it were *w·* to lift the veil
	280–14	we imagine all is *w·* if we
	283–19	as *w·* as its morals and Christianity.
	284– 2	each one to do his own work *w·*,
	288–21	as *w·* as thine own,
	290–19	knew that this person was doing *w·*,
	315–18	watch *w·* that they prove sound
	326–24	*W·* might this heavenly messenger
	333–12	in matter as *w·* as Spirit?
	334– 5	Astrology is *w·* in its place,
	344– 4	"Very *w·*," the teacher replied ;
	347–32	is *w·* paid by the umpire.
	354–27	strength for a flight *w·* begun,
	355– 7	the acme of "*w·* done ;"— *Matt.* 25 : 21.
	365–20	spiritual, as *w·* as physical, effects
	378– 5	returned apparently *w·*,
	380– 5	as *w·* as governs the universe,
Man.	28–17	perform the functions . . . *w·*.
	32–20	They shall . . . be *w·* educated.
	63–18	provided these rooms are *w·* located.
	64– 1	shall be *w·* educated,
	83–17	watch *w·* that they prove sound
	90–18	lessons by a *w·* qualified teacher
Ret.	21–13	It is *w·* to know, dear reader,
	24–15	discovery how to be *w·* myself,
	33– 6	as it has been *w·* called.
	34–12	all sickness, as *w·* as sin,
	40–11	dressed herself, and was *w·*.
	65–27	As *w·* expect to determine,
	67–21	collective as *w·* as individual.
	79– 1	against . . . the human race as *w·* as
	81–14	so apparent as to be *w·* understood.
	85– 2	doing their own work *w·*.
	86– 9	Note *w·* the falsity of this
	91– 5	utterance may *w·* be called
Un.	23– 9	How *w·* the Shakespearean tale
	28– 9	As *w·* might you declare
Pul.	9– 5	tasks are done— *w·* done
	9– 9	It was *w·* that the brother

well

Pul.	13–15	serpent of sin as *w* as of sickness !
	25– 2	* cooling . . . as *w* as heating
	36– 8	* Europe as *w* as this country.
	46–25	* as *w* as looking into the
	48– 1	* *w* placed upon a terrace
	48–29	* as *w* as the hero who killed the
	51–19	* is very *w* known.
	59–17	* *w* adapted for its purpose,
	61–16	* practical as *w* as poetic,
	62– 2	* *w* and favorably known
	62– 7	* economy of space, as *w* as
	63– 8	nourish trees as *w* as souls,''
	66–17	* *w* suited 'o satisfy a taste
	71–19	* It is *w* known that Mrs. Eddy
	72–18	* yet have been perfectly *w*.''
Rud.	1–12	misapprehension, as *w* as definition.
	15–20	*w* assimilate what has been taught
No.	v– 5	as *w* as voluntary error.
	3–17	to keep himself *w* informed.
	9–11	God will *w* regenerate
	19– 2	spiritual, as *w* as physical,
	28–15	I consider *w* established.
	28–16	present, as *w* as the future,
	42–28	Here a skeptic might *w* ask
'00.	2–27	*W*, all that is good.
	12–23	It were *w* if we had a St. Paul
'01.	7–19	as *w* as infinite Person,
	9–30	worketh *w* and healeth quickly,
	13– 9	not *w* to maintain the position
	13–10	*w* that we take possession of
	21– 2	understanding, and works as *w*.
	28–24	*w* to know that even Christ
'02.	3–14	It is *w* that our government,
Hea.	8– 7	sickness as *w* as sin,
Peo.	2–28	nations as *w* as individuals,
	7– 3	on the body as *w* as on history
	10–10	It were *w* if the sister States
	10–16	divine as *w* as human.
	11– 6	disease as *w* as sin ;
Po.	vi–23	* as *w* as many poems
	27–20	Thy work is done, and *w* :
My.	v–10	* *w* for earnest . . . Scientists to
	24–28	* as *w* as this can be done
	30– 5	* *w* over thirty thousand people
	40–32	* as *w* as by her teachings,
	41–29	* for our sakes as *w* as for her own ;
	45– 3	* as *w* as in the ultimate
	46–25	* Bible and our textbook, as *w* as
	52– 6	* as *w* as her instructions,
	59– 9	* as *w* as of healing,
	62– 2	* ''*W* done, good and — *Matt.* 25 : 23.
	66–15	* so *w* situated for church purposes
	69– 1	* church is unusually *w* lighted,
	75– 1	* we cannot *w* withhold our
	90–17	* readily grasped by sick or *w*.
	97– 5	* making the patient *w*.
	97– 6	* *w* without the use of medicine.
	98–26	* might *w* be proud.
	108– 2	succeeds as *w* in healing his cases
	124–13	''*w* done'' — *Matt.* 25 : 23.
	134–11	work *w* done should not be eclipsed
	145–16	* ''I am as *w* as I ever was.''
	158–22	Most men and women talk *w*,
	162–21	''*W* done, good and — *Matt.* 25 : 23.
	180–21	in justice, as *w* as in mercy,
	187– 2	spiritually as *w* as literally,
	190–32	It were *w* for the world if
	202–13	''*W* done, good and — *Matt.* 25 : 23.
	207–21	''*W* done, thou good and — *Matt.* 25 : 21.
	215– 3	knew *w* the priceless worth of
	222–20	It is *w* that thou canst unloose
	225– 4	''*W* done, good and — *Matt.* 25 : 23.
	227–16	consider *w* their ability to cope with
	246– 7	must be *w* educated
	252– 9	you do to yourselves as *w*,
	256– 6	strict observance or note *w*.
	261–11	guarding and guiding *w* the
	264– 4	kind enough to speak *w* of me
	268–31	*man* meaning woman as *w*,
	275–15	Whereas the fact that I am *w*
	302–14	It is a fact *w* understood
	307–10	that word, as *w* as other terms
	318–20	He held himself *w* in check
	319–26	* These dates are very *w* fixed
	323– 1	* what Mr. Bates has so *w* written
	330–19	* as *w* as by Wilmington newspapers
	345–10	* ''*W*, electricity, engineering,
	355–12	to religion as *w* as to politics,

well-behaved

My.	93– 9	* the intelligent, and the *w*.

well-being

Mis.	170–20	no more important to our *w*
Rud.	12–20	requisite for the *w* of man.
My.	81– 2	* air of *w* and of prosperity

well-born

Pul.	48–26	* many another *w* woman's.

well-bred

'01.	30–29	* honest, sensible, and *w* man

well-conducted

My.	175–15	*w* jail and state prison,

well-defined

My.	301–21	*w* instances of the baneful

well-doing

My.	3– 5	demands *w* in order to

well-dressed

My.	95–17	* *w* body of people.
	97–17	* *w*, good-looking, eminently

well-earned

My.	47–20	* *w* joy that is with us now.

well-equipped

My.	319– 9	and *w* scholarship.

Wellesley College

Un.	6–20	though a graduate of *W C*,

well-established

Pul.	51–16	* will affect the *w* methods.

well-informed

My.	309– 2	a *w*, intellectual man,

welling

Mis.	1–12	*w* up from infinite Truth
Ret.	80–19	*w* up into unceasing spiritual
My.	186–11	*w* up from the infinite

well-kept

Pul.	49–27	* to-day a strikingly *w* estate
My.	277– 9	and sound, *w* treaties.

well-known

Pul.	72–14	* a number of *w* physicians.
My.	145–20	*w* fact makes me the servant of

well-mannered

Mis.	275–28	The servants are *w*,

well-meaning

Pul.	80–21	* caused an army of *w* people
'01.	29–12	because *w* people sometimes

well-nigh

My.	v–25	* revealed God to *w* countless
	318– 2	*w* constituted a new style of

well-to-do

My.	87– 8	* congenial, quietly happy, *w*,
	93– 8	* save the moderately *w*,

well-tried

Mis.	200–25	calm of Paul's *w* hope

wending

Mis.	323– 7	*w* his way downward,

went

Mis.	30–28	''There *w* up a mist — *Gen.* 2 : 6.
	61–15	* I *w* once to a place where
	153– 6	*w* forth before His people,
	162–30	like him he *w* forth, simple as
	163– 3	he *w* about doing good.
	180–11	my heart *w* out to God,
	208–22	I *w* astray :— *Psal.* 119 : 67.
	242–30	if she *w* without it twenty-four hours
	279–17	They *w* seven times around
	327– 1	When I *w* back into the house
	370– 5	they *w* away and took counsel
	375–19	* I *w* on to study each
Man.	17– 2	*w* into deliberations over forming a
	18– 8	little Church *w* steadily on,
Ret.	8– 6	*w* to her, beseeching her
	8–21	*w* to my mother, and once more
	13–20	if I *w* to Him in prayer,
	16–13	Many pale cripples *w* into
	16–13	who *w* out carrying them
	19– 5	I *w* with him to the South ;
	38–23	while this *w* on.
	40– 8	I *w* to the invalid's house.
	89–10	they *w* for liturgical worship,
	93– 1	Jesus *w* about doing good.
Pul.	6–19	* I *w* with my husband,
	6–20	* He *w* out under the auspices
	33–22	* or whither he *w*
	36–15	* *w* to her peculiarly fatigued.
	60– 3	* new order . . . *w* into operation.
Hea.	11–22	as matter *w* out and Mind came in
Peo.	13–21	his pure faith *w* up through
My.	45–19	* Him who *w* before you
	76– 1	* it *w* without saying that the
	117– 3	''What *w* ye out for — *Matt.* 11 : 8.
	302–28	*w* alone in my carriage
	313–24	I never *w* into a trance
	320–25	* *w* into matters of detail
	343–22	* she *w* on,

wept
Mis.	386–22	She that has w· o'er thee,
Ret.	9–12	Afterward I w·, and prayed
	14–30	the oldest church-members w·.
Pul.	7–11	as he w· over Jerusalem !
Po.	50– 7	She that has w· o'er thee,
	71–16	Ye who have w· fourscore
My.	119–13	Mary of old w· because

Wesley
Pul.	28–23	* Robertson, W·, Bowring,

West
My.	74– 2	* from abroad and from the far W·
	193– 6	work for all, from East to W·,
	241–13	* from a Christian Scientist in the W·,
	323– 7	* by some minister in the far W·.

west
My.	63–28	* "from the w·, — Psal. 107 : 3.

Westerly, Rhode Island
Ret.	40– 5	Lyceum Club, at W·, R· I·.

Western and western
Mis.	275–26	wonder of the w· hemisphere.
	276– 4	like all else, was purely W·
My.	74– 1	* w· sections of this country.
	197–13	ready hands of our far W· students,

Western States
Pul.	89–23	* heading

Westminster Catechism
Ret.	10– 6	as with the W· C· ;

wet
Po.	27–18	with bright eye w·,
My.	326–16	where with w· eyes the Free Masons

whate'er
Mis.	392–10	W· thy mission, mountain
Po.	20–14	W· thy mission, mountain
	28– 8	W· the gift of joy or woe,
	79– 5	peace is thine, W· betide.

Whateley's Logic
My.	304– 8	book title

whatever (see also whate'er)
Mis.	8–19	W· purifies, sanctifies, and
	10– 4	W· envy, hatred, revenge
	10– 6	w· these try to do,
	12–26	W· manifests aught else in its
	26– 2	w· is of God, hath life
	33– 2	W· is wrong will receive its
	33–16	had no faith w· in the Science,
	40–18	discord of w· sort.
	71–21	W· is humanly conceived
	71–30	W· is real is right and eternal ;
	89–26	from itself, from w· is false.
	102–24	W· seems material,
	115–27	w· tends to impede progress.
	119–16	w· or whoever opposes evil,
	121–17	w· belittles, befogs, or belies
	147–21	abhor w· is base or unworthy ;
	183–13	w· is possible to God, is possible to
	190–22	impersonal evil, or w· worketh ill.
	198–29	w· seems to punish man for
	199–17	w· denied and defied their
	216–14	W· his nom de plume means,
	228–21	W· man sees, feels, or
	236–28	w· else may appear,
	236–29	and at w· cost.
	249– 5	drug had no effect upon me w·."
	259– 3	W· appears to be law,
	260–19	w· else seemeth to be intelligence
	281–18	So, w· we meet that is hard
	281–28	w· may come to you, remember the
	288–32	W· intoxicates a man,
	289– 5	in w· form it is made manifest.
	290–10	since w· is false should disappear.
	292–17	w· is unlike the risen, immortal Love ;
	300–30	pays w· he is able to pay
	309–19	w· is connected therewith,
	328–23	W· obstructs the way,
	329– 3	a satisfaction with w· is hers.
	329–18	W· else droops, spring is gay :
	334– 8	W· simulates power and Truth
	348–19	I use no drugs w·,
	367– 9	w· is wrongfully-minded will
	367–28	would say that w· saves from sin,
	374– 7	w· rebuked hypocrisy
Man.	43– 9	W· is requisite for either
Ret.	32– 5	learned that w· is loved materially,
	47–10	C. S. shuns w· involves material
	56– 5	W· diverges from the one divine Mind,
	56–21	W· else claims to be mind,
	59–15	W· errs is mortal,
	65–18	to avoid w· follows the example of
Un.	22–16	W· exists must come from God,
	22–19	W· cometh not from . . . Spirit,

whatever
Un.	24–25	W· matter thus affirms is
	25–10	w· it appears to say of itself is
	28–19	W· cannot be taken in by mortal mind
	54–12	To admit that sin has any claim w·,
Pul.	21–16	shun w· would isolate us from
	50–26	* and w· is likely to
	57–13	* W· may be thought of the peculiar
	57–14	* w· difference of opinion
	65– 9	* w· attitude Rome may assume
	73–23	* She placed no credit w· in the
Rud.	9–28	w· militates against health,
	13– 4	W· saps, with human belief,
	16–17	W· is said and written correctly
	16–26	snatch at w· is progressive,
No.	7–22	draw no lines w· between
	16– 5	w· He knows is made manifest,
	24– 5	He is extension, of w· character.
	27– 4	is in reality no claim w·.
	37–25	w· is unlike God ;
	45– 8	to ostracize w· uplifts mankind,
Pan.	10–27	W· promotes statuesque being,
	11–22	w· strips off evil's disguise
	14– 1	nature of w· is unlike good,
'00.	4–24	w· is real must proceed from
	10–19	w· sways the sceptre of self
	11– 9	w· turns mortals away from
	14– 8	w· is spoken of in the Scriptures.
	15– 1	you purchase, at w· price, a
'01.	13–21	conquers him, in w· direction.
	22–27	receive no sense w· of it.
	31–25	held fast to w· is good,
'02.	1–15	W· seems calculated to displace
	9–30	W· enlarges man's facilities
Hea.	6–20	w· manifestation we see.
My.	4–31	W· is not divinely natural
	12–22	W· needs to be done
	52–21	* "W· is to be Mrs. Eddy's future
	74–31	* W· opinions we may entertain
	87–27	* w· one's special creed may be,
	90– 7	* W· else it is, this faith is real
	107–25	w· is entitled to a classification
	128–27	w· the shaft aimed at you
	128–31	evil suggestions, in w· guise,
	154–30	take it in w· sense you may.
	158–17	w· manifests love for God
	180–12	no element w· of hypnotism
	220– 1	W· changes come to this century
	250–27	w· is done in this direction
	271–24	* w· their religious beliefs,
	277–18	W· weighs in the eternal scale
	278–30	W· brings into human thought
	285– 8	W· adorns Christianity
	294–11	would rebuke w· accords not with
	296– 4	w· hinders the Science of being.
	299–12	w· portions of truth may be found
	301–26	or affect . . . in any manner w·.
	321–14	* that he has ever said anything w·

whatsoever
Mis.	54–23	not . . . to any disease w·,
	66– 6	"W· a man soweth, — Gal. 6 : 7.
	105–29	"W· a man soweth, — Gal. 6 : 7.
	119–31	w· ye would that men — Matt. 7 : 12.
	128– 6	w· things are true, — Phil. 4 : 8.
	128– 7	w· things are honest, — Phil. 4 : 8.
	128– 8	w· things are just, — Phil. 4 : 8.
	128– 8	w· things are pure, — Phil. 4 : 8.
	128– 9	w· things are lovely, — Phil. 4 : 8.
	128– 9	w· things are of good report ; — Phil. 4 : 8.
	135– 1	marching under w· ensign,
	146–18	"W· ye would that men — Matt. 7 : 12.
	235–28	w· ye would that men — Matt. 7 : 12.
	348– 4	w· a man soweth, that shall he
Man.	42–23	w· ye would that men — Matt. 7 : 12.
	69–10	w· she may charge
Ret.	87–20	"W· ye would that men — Matt. 7 : 12.
	94– 5	that w· seems true,
	94– 7	w· seems to be good,
	94–10	consumes w· is of sin.
	94–19	w· is not of faith — Rom. 14 : 23.
No.	31–28	"W· thou shalt bind — Matt. 16 : 19.
	32– 9	"W· a man soweth, — Gal. 6 : 7.
Hea.	5–27	"w· a man soweth, — Gal. 6 : 7.
My.	6– 5	w· a man soweth, — Gal. 6 : 7.
	41–14	* w· lawlessness of hatred he may
	266– 8	"W· ye would that men — Matt. 7 : 12.

wheat
Mis.	79– 6	sift the chaff from the w·,
	117– 5	separate the tares from the w· ;
	172– 4	separating the tares from the w·,
	214–29	must be separated from the w·
Ret.	71–24	growing side by side with the w·,
	71–25	before the w· can be garnered
My.	111–11	chaff is separated from the w·.
	124–30	to separate the tares from the w·,

wheat
My. 249–12 heat of hate burns the w`,
269–18 separating the tares from the w`.
316– 2 separated the tares from the w`,

wheels
Mis. 234– 3 clog the w` of progress.
235–22 start the w` of reason aright,
Rud. 17– 4 clogging the w` of progress
My. 145–20 keeps the w` revolving.
215–22 from clogging the w` of C. S.
288– 1 it starts the w` of right reason,

whence
Mis. 22– 6 W`, then, is it, if not from
23– 3 W` or what is the power back of
26–13 W` came the first seed,
26–14 W` came the infinitesimals,
37–19 mortal thought, w` cometh all evil.
66–17 w` to discern God's perfect ways
112– 3 not knowing w` they come,
116–14 tones w` come glad echoes
173–25 w`, then, is something besides Him
173–28 W`, then, is the atom or molecule
185–11 w` good flows into every avenue
218–12 w` to reason out God,
228– 6 standpoint w` to look upward ;
233–31 w` we learn that sensation is not
235– 7 Mind w` sprang the universe.
289–31 w` they can choose only good.
316–26 w` they could have derived
324–30 w` he may hopefully look for
346–10 w` comes the evil?
387–23 W` joys supernal flow,
390– 2 W` are thy wooings, gentle June?
Un. 45–18 w` it telegraphs and telephones
Pul. 33–21 as to w` the stranger came
Rud. 11–23 w` emanate health, harmony
'00. 12–12 w` the Ephesian elders travelled
'02. 9–22 and knew not w` it came
Po. 6–18 W` joys supernal flow,
25– 2 W` the dewdrop is born,
55– 1 W` are thy wooings, gentle June?
My. 5–10 W`, then, came the creation of
62– 5 * W` did it come?
124–21 W` and whither?
180–31 the w` and why of the cosmos
256–22 and see w` they came
287–18 Mind w` springs the universe.
302– 7 corpse, w` mind has departed.

whenever
Mis. 11–20 w` opportunity occurs.
76–20 w` this word means the
138–24 but w` they are equal to the
169– 3 w` her thoughts had wandered
229– 3 w` there appear the circumstances
236– 8 counsel wisely w` giving advice
354–32 W` he soareth to fashion his nest,
383– 5 W` and wherever a church of C. S.
Man. 48– 3 But w` God calls a
80–17 W` a vacancy shall occur,
No. 8– 5 w` it can substitute censure.
'01. 29–17 w` they return to the old home
My. 99–13 * w` their form of religion

Where Art Thou?
Mis. 332–12 chapter sub-title— Gen. 3 : 9.

whereas
Mis. 6–31 w`, in small families of one or two
34–13 w` spiritualism, so far as I
39–11 w` the Founder of genuine C. S.
47– 6 w`, substance means more than
62– 3 w`, the opposite image of man,
62–30 w`, "mind-cure" rests on the notion
70–23 w` the body of the holy Spirit
186–26 w`, the spiritual sense of God
240– 9 w` forecasting liberty and joy
296–16 w`, they are by no means identical
Man. 75– 4 W`, on March 20, 1895,
Ret. 48–16 W`, The Massachusetts Metaphysical
48–25 W`, The material organization
49– 4 W`, Other institutions for
49–11 W`, The fundamental principle for
49–14 W`, Mortals must learn to
60–13 w`, good is God ever-present,
Un. 13– 4 w` the reverse is true in Science.
30– 5 w` Science reverses the testimony of
31–23 w`, evil does, according to belief,
51– 8 w` the demonstration of God,
No. 9–12 w` you may err in effort,
11– 1 w` matter and human will,
'01. 5–29 w` God explains Himself in C. S.
Peo. 6–15 w` "perfect Love— I John 4 : 18.
My. 117– 7 w` helping a leader
119–21 w` the discharged evidence of
181– 3 w` philosophy and so-called
212–12 w` animal magnetism is the

whereas
My. 275–15 W` the fact that I am well
284–24 w` I do believe implicitly in
292–28 w` the human mind is a

whereby
Mis. 2– 1 w` we discern the power of
11–18 w` we love our friends ;
17–20 w` man reflects the divine power
18–18 w` Father, Mother, and child are
28–18 w` he arose above the illusion of
29–29 w` matter is proven powerless
42–17 w` we meet the dear departed,
67–25 w` one expresses the sense of
79– 8 reflects all w` we can know God.
98– 2 w` to improve his present condition ;
123–22 w` the just obtain a pardon for
127–21 condition w` to become blessed,
174–26 w` to gain heaven.
185–15 w` we can be saved,
194– 3 w` sin, sickness, . . . are destroyed ;
202– 2 w` the sweet harmonies of C. S. are
252–15 w` any man can satisfy himself of
260–31 w` it may injure the race,
318– 3 wherein and w` the universal brotherhood
341–11 w` to arrive at the results of
342– 1 w` to enter into the joy of divine
364– 3 w` the sick are healed,
Man. 60–20 w` to exemplify our risen Lord.
Ret. 73–18 w` the false personality is laid off.
Un. 3–17 w` man is found in the image
8–18 same basis w` sickness is healed,
23–25 no sense w` to cognize evil.
55– 1 Jesus accepted the one fact w`
Rud. 8–22 w`, through will-power, sense may
11– 6 w` you learn that God is good,
No. 37–19 w` the work of Jesus would
Pan. 12–19 alterative agonies w` the way-seeker
'00. 5–15 w` to have one God,
'01. 7–14 w` we may consistently say,
10–22 w` good destroys evil,
16– 8 w` the demon of this world,
21–23 w` to benefit the race
25– 7 and w` is won the crown
34– 2 w` Christendom saves sinners,
'02. 6–16 w` the mortal concept and
8–24 w` man is Godlike.
Peo. 2–10 w` we learn that God, good,
3–27 w` we grow out of sin
9–25 w` we learn the great fact
My. 43– 6 * w` to order aright the affairs of
51–15 * w` to heal the sick
117–29 w` and wherein to show others
126–32 w` thought is spiritualized,
154–28 w` we are looking heavenward,
159–17 w` we reach our higher nature.
178– 5 w` the sick are healed
180– 1 w` man can prove God's love,
187– 9 w` to demonstrate the perfect man
232– 7 w` all our debts are paid,
238–18 w` the Science is reached
247– 4 w` man governed by his creator
254–26 w` man governed by his creator
267–27 w` soul is emancipate
277–16 w` wrong and injustice are righted
358– 8 w` the conflict against Truth

wherefor
Mis. vii–20 W`, have much to pay.
Un. 62–13 wherein and w` there is no evil.

wherefore
Mis. 9–25 w` our failure longer to relish
64–27 quite as possible to know w`
136–15 "W` come out from— II Cor. 6: 17.
138–23 it is not so adapted . . . And w`?
326–31 "W` comest thou hither?"
351–22 w` it is hate instead of Love ;
Chr. 53–25 Yet w` signalize the birth
'02. 7–28 called his disciples' . . . And w`?
10–19 W`, then, smite the reformer
Po. 34–15 Yet w` ask thy doom?
67– 9 w` the memory of dear ones
77– 6 Yet w` this Thy love?
My. 17– 4 "W` laying aside all— I Pet. 2: 1.
17–14 "W` also it is contained— I Pet. 2: 6.
189–30 W`, pray, the bell did toll?
190–30 w` vilify His prophets to-day
226–24 chapter sub-title
233– 5 Otherwise, w` the Lord's Prayer,
302–22 than others before me— and w`?

wherein
Mis. x– 2 life w` dwelleth peace,
9–10 W` is this conclusion relative to
10–23 w` old things pass away
11–18 w` and whereby we love our friends ;
18–18 w` and whereby Father, Mother, and

wherein

Mis.	27–13	natural science, w· no species ever
	46–29	w· man is perfect even as the Father,
	57–31	Mind that is God, w· man is
	108–19	w· evil seems as real as good,
	113– 2	w· is no darkness.
	121– 7	w· Spirit and matter, good and evil,
	123–24	w· sinners suffer for their own sins,
	124–21	w· to muse His praise,
	150–18	w·, . . . Scientists may worship
	153–16	w· violence covereth men as a
	155–18	and less w· to answer it
	182–27	w· man and his Maker are inseparable
	190– 6	w· the mortal evolves not the
	190– 8	w· man is coexistent with Mind,
	203–20	w· mortals gain severe views of
	227–21	w· calm, self-respected thoughts
	227–23	a life w· the mind can rest
	262– 2	w· it is permitted to enter,
	286–14	w· they neither marry nor are
	318– 3	w· and whereby the universal
	319– 1	w· the true sense of the unity of
	330– 6	w· no arrow wounds the dove
	354–24	w· all is controlled, not by man
	361–29	w· Principle and idea, God and man,
	362– 4	w· God and man, are perfect,
Ret.	49– 8	hour has come w· the great need
Un.	21– 2	mental processes w· human thoughts
	42–26	w· the mortal does not develop the
	42–27	w· true manhood and womanhood
	51– 1	w· man is the reflection of
	62–13	an ideal w· . . . there is no evil.
No.	21–16	w· the human and divine mingle
	21–26	w· Principle heals and saves.
	25– 5	w· we were held ;— *Rom. 7 : 6.*
	30–20	light w· there is no darkness.
	36–22	w· there is no consciousness of
Pan.	7–20	w· theism seems meaningless,
'02.	2–21	w· Christ is Alpha and Omega.
	6–29	w· God is infinite Love,
	15–12	w· the connection between justice and
	17–16	w· joy is real and fadeless.
Peo.	11–11	w· man cooperates with . . . his Maker.
My.	6–15	temple w· to enter and pray.
	25–25	w· all vanity of victory disappears
	117–30	w· to show others the footsteps
	118– 6	w· the remedy is worse than the
	129–24	harmony w· the good man's heart
	154–28	w· . . . we are looking heavenward,
	187– 9	perfect path w· to walk,
	208–19	w· to gather in praise and prayer
	234– 8	every hour w· to express this love
	239– 4	primitive proof, w· reason,
	247– 4	w· and whereby man
	254–25	w· and whereby man governed by
	267–26	w· and whereby soul is emancipate
	357– 5	w· matter has neither part nor portion,

whereof

Mis.	vii–19	W·, I've more to glory,
	21– 1	w· C. S. now bears testimony.
	66– 5	the genius w· is displayed in
	88–14	critic who knows w· he speaks.
	130–22	know well w· he speaks.
	132– 2	on a subject the substance w·
	139–24	wisdom w· a few persons
	154–14	even that vine w· our Father
	172–18	the evidences w· are taken
	195–16	premises w· are not to be found in
	251–15	w· our Master said :
	252–31	w· our Master said,
	296–31	but knew w· he speaks,
	350– 4	the workings w· were not
Man.	17–16	chief corner stone w· is,
	42–17	Christ w· the Scripture
	52–12	that w· he is accused
Un.	10–19	w· God is the Alpha and Omega,
	23–13	w· all are partakers,—*Heb. 12 : 8.*
	23–17	w· they are confessedly
Pul.	7– 4	w· this city is the capital.
Pan.	2– 4	who know w· they speak
'00.	12– 3	the spiritual import w·
	14–13	the name w· signifies
'01.	27–11	the basis w· cannot be traced to
	28– 6	w· our Master said,
My.	131– 9	the bread of heaven w·
	188–11	w· the Psalmist sang,
	244–15	w· David sang,
	285–24	w· they now accuse me.—*Acts 24 : 13.*

whereon

Mis.	128– 2	uncomfortable w· to repose.
	225–21	sofa w· lay the lad
	341–16	place w· thou standest
	395–17	The turf, w· I tread,
Man.	75–17	the land w· they stand,
Pul.	1–16	This spot w· thou troddest

whereon

Pul.	20– 1	land w· stands The First Church
'02.	14– 5	the land w· it stands.
Po.	44– 4	W· they may rest !
	58– 2	The turf, w· I tread,
My.	69– 8	* w· are placed inscriptions

whereout

Mis.	150–19	halls . . . wherein, as w·,

wheresoever

Pul.	21–24	but w· you recognize a
My.	19–31	W· this gospel shall be— *Mark 14 : 9.*

whereto

Mis.	397–19	w· God leadeth me.
Chr.	55– 2	w· their number corresponds.
Ret.	85–16	no position w· you do not
Pul.	19– 3	w· God leadeth me.
Po.	13– 7	w· God leadeth me.
My.	14– 1	"prosper in the thing w·— *Isa. 55 : 11.*

whereunto

Po.	35–11	Hushed in the heart w· none reply,
My.	201– 2	w· divine Love has called us

whereupon

Mis.	225– 9	w· the mother, . . . bore testimony to
My.	328–24	* w· application for license was

wherever

Mis.	256–26	W· law is, Mind is ;
	277–32	I rebuke it w· I see it.
	306– 3	* accompany the bell w· it goes.
	336–24	w· one ray of its effulgence
	383– 6	w· a church of C. S. is established,
Pul.	86–21	* contributors w· they may be,
Pan.	13–12	condemnation of all error, w· found.
My.	18–20	condemnation of all error, w· found.
	19–19	follow us in the sunlight w· we go ;
	81–28	* w· two or more of them are met
	185–11	w· thought, felt, spoken, or
	257–30	W· the child looks up in prayer,

wherewith

Mis.	9–27	w· mortals become educated to
	10– 2	w· to obstruct life's joys
	19–18	w· to cover iniquity,
	104–32	w· to overcome all error.
	155–30	w· divine Love has entrusted us,
	176–28	divine energy w· we are armored
	380–21	evidence w· to satisfy the sick
Un.	34–10	summary of the whole matter, w· we
Pul.	2–13	of the house w·
	21– 3	love w· Christ loveth us ;
No.	39–19	love w· He loves us.
Hea.	3– 2	w· to heal both mind and body ;
	9–19	w· to make himself wicked.
My.	205– 4	liberty w· Christ hath— *Gal. 5 : 1.*
	212–11	w· to do evil ;
	212–13	w· to complete the sum total of sin.
	214–22	no monetary means left w· to

whether

Mis.	25–32	w· in philosphy, medicine, or
	48– 9	w· of ignorance of fanaticism,
	120– 9	w· of sin unto death, — *Rom. 6 : 16.*
	224–31	w· there is enough of a flatterer,
	239– 3	judge for yourself w· I can talk
	261–10	w· intentionally or ignorantly ;
	264–21	w· those be correct or incorrect.
	290–25	w· it be friend or foe,
Man.	110–10	w· of applicants, approvers, or
Ret.	82– 3	chord remains unchanged, w· we
Un.	44–17	W· expressive or not expressive
Pul.	7– 9	I wonder w·, were our dear Master
	66–25	* w· some of the pre-Christian ideas
No.	43– 6	w· stall-fed or famishing,
Pan.	14–20	w· in camp or in battle.
Hea.	6–17	w· that ideal is a flower or
Po.	68–22	w· near or afar.
My.	213–20	w· they lead you to God
	227–19	w· successful or not,
	342–13	* w· blue-gray or grayish brown,
	343– 7	w· my successor will be
	346–23	* as to w· she had in mind
	358–15	w· or not they shall publish

whichever

Mis.	221–28	w· might serve as the
My.	117– 4	W· it be, determines the

while

Mis.	xi– 8	W· no offering can liquidate
	2–32	W· we entertain decided views
	3–22	w· the supreme and perfect Mind,
	21– 6	w· on earth and in the flesh,
	26–11	even w· the Scripture declares
	42–23	w· the latter is real and
	49–12	w· acknowledged and notable
	66–20	and Truth be enthroned, w·
	70–26	w· our Lord would soon be rising
	103– 5	w· the other is eternal.

while

Mis.	103–32	*w·* his personality was on earth
	108–30	*w·* declaring that they have no
	110–20	*w·* leagues have lain between us.
	117–19	*w·* participating in the movements,
	126–13	ordeal refines *w·* it chastens.
	148– 1	*w·* he meditates evil against us
	155–10	*W·* pressing meekly on,
	162–12	*w·* the central point of his
	183–23	*w·* it shames human pride.
	184– 2	claiming that God is Spirit, *w·* man
	187– 8	*w·* discord, as seen in disease
	200– 9	*w·* God was the only substance,
	204–10	*w·* white-winged peace sings
	214– 2	*W·* Jesus' life was full of Love,
	215–31	*w·* the corn is in the blade,
	219–19	*w·* in the other he must change
	219–24	*w·* immortal Mind makes saints ;
	219–26	*w·* one person feels wickedly
	221–26	*w·* ten times five are not
	222– 5	*w·* injuring himself and others.
	222–30	*W·* the ways, means, and potency of
	223– 7	*w·* impure streams flow from
	223–17	*w·* doing unto others what
	224–30	*w·* it is a question in my mind,
	228–11	*w·* seeking to raise those barren
	238–29	*W·* I accord these evil-mongers
	240–17	*w·* the sturdy oak, with form
	252–13	*w·* healthy thoughts are reality
	256– 7	*W·* gratefully acknowledging the
	256–23	*w·* every quality of matter
	259–11	*w·* iniquity, too evil to
	259–25	*w·* error, or evil, is really
	263–29	*w·* they quote from other authors
	267–19	*w·* the left beats its way downward,
	267–29	*w·* disobedience to this divine Principle
	288–17	*w·* Science indicates that it *is not.*
	295–12	*W·* praising the Scotchman's
	302– 6	*w·* the perverter preserves in his own
	310–13	*W·* my affections plead for all
	324– 8	a little *w·*, and the music is dull,
	352–31	*w·* sickness must be covered with the
	363–11	*w·* the immortal modes of Mind
	368–26	But *w·* the best, perverted,
	369–10	*w·* we are strong in the unity of
	369–13	*w·* the leaders of materialistic
	375–12	* Years ago, *w·* in Italy,
	376–26	*w·* the lower lines of light kindled
	378– 1	*w·* the author of this work
Man.	47–24	*W·* members of this Church
	79– 8	*W·* the members of this Committee
Ret.	17– 1	*w·* visiting a family friend
	17– 5	*w·* I worship in deep sylvan spot,
	17–17	*W·* palm, bay, and laurel,
	18– 4	*W·* cactus a mellower glory receives
	38–23	*w·* this went on.
	49–12	*w·* in human growth
	65–21	*w·* it demonstrates the power of Christ
	68–11	One is false, *w·* the other is true.
	75– 7	*w·* appropriating my language and ideas,
	80–25	*w·* innocence strayeth yearningly.
	90– 5	*w·* he is serving another fold
Un.	6–25	*w·* the platoons of C. S. are
	11–27	*w·* ye say, There are yet four months,
	21– 3	mean *w·* accusing— *Rom.* 2 : 15.
	27–14	*w·* God is *egoistic,*
	46– 6	*w·* ours is man's man.
Pul.	7–21	*w·* their tabernacles crumble
	21–14	*W·* we entertain due respect
	28– 4	* *w·* the star of Bethlehem shines down
	29–20	* *w·* all these injunctions
	34– 5	* In 1866, *w·* living in Lynn, Mass.,
	44–11	* *W·* we all rejoice,
	48– 2	* *w·* they themselves are in
	50–24	* opposition . . . keeps up a *w·*,
	51–19	* *W·* it has done this, it may,
	67–21	* *w·* in many towns and villages
	79– 7	* *W·* we are not, . . . devotees of
	81–22	* *w·* her own soul plays upon
	82–16	* *w·* the Jews themselves have
	83– 2	* *w·* we recklessly promise as lover
	84– 6	* *w·* side by side, equal partners in
	87–15	*w·* I fully appreciate your
Rud.	3– 1	*w·* mortals love to sin,
No.	3– 4	*w·* the trespassing error
	8–26	*w·* you walk on in equanimity,
	13–26	*w·* other parts of it have no
	19–16	*W·* material man and the
	20– 6	*w·* Truth is moulding a
	29–24	*w·* Truth walks triumphantly
	36– 7	even *w·* mortals believed it
	36–28	*w·* the divine and ideal Christ
	42–15	*W·* Science is engulfing error
	43–27	*w·* envy and hatred bark
Pan.	3– 1	*w·* pantheism suits not at all
	4–14	*w·* God is incapable of evil ;

while

'01.	14– 4	*w·* the Pharisee's self-righteousness
	24– 9	*w·* descanting on the virtues of
	29– 4	*w·* he was providing ways and means
'02.	1– 9	*w·* our branch churches are
	1–20	*W·* C. S., engaging the
	11–29	*w·* to-day Jew and Christian can
	15– 9	*w·* dependent on the income from
	20–23	*w·* gratefully appreciating the
Hea.	2– 5	*w·* it reasons with the storm,
	5– 2	*W·* admitting that God is omnipotent,
	12– 4	*W·* the matter-physician feels the
	13–26	*w·* it is supposed to cure
	20– 6	* vie with Gabriel, *w·* he sings,
Peo.	3–17	*w·* it inscribes on the thoughts
	6–12	* *w·* nature cures the disease.''
	11–19	*w·* the body, obedient to
Po.	v–10	* *was written w· the author*
	vii– 1	* *w· visiting a family friend*
	26– 8	*W·* Justice grasped the sword
	30–19	*W·* sacred song and loudest breath
	46–17	*W·* beauty fills each bar.
	62– 5	*w·* I worship in deep sylvan spot,
	63– 1	*W·* palm, bay, and laurel,
	63–12	*W·* cactus a mellower glory
	67–13	Beside you they walk *w·* you weep,
	70–18	The *w·* the glad stars sang
	78–14	O meekest of mourners, *w·* yet
My.	12–24	*w·* that which can be done
	38– 4	* *w·* we thank you and renew the
	51– 8	* *w·* we feel that she has not
	52– 2	* *w·* she had many obstacles
	52– 8	* *w·* we sincerely acknowledge
	52–11	* *w·* we realize the rapid growth,
	56–15	* For a *w·* it seemed that there
	61–13	* but after a *w·*, in the night,
	67–22	* *w·* vaster sums of money
	69–22	* *w·* in the basement is a
	70–14	* *w·* the chimes were being tested
	82– 6	* For a *w·* this morning it looked
	90–13	* *w·* health-seeking is the door
	94–20	* *W·* the dedicatory services
	149–29	*w·* those with a mighty rush,
	152–27	*w·* God, the divine Principle
	171–20	* *W·* on her regular afternoon drive
	186–22	*w·* they are yet speaking,— *Isa.* 65 : 24.
	194– 8	*w·* a silent, grand man or woman,
	204–27	*w·* returning good for evil,
	214–19	*w·* taking no remuneration for my
	220–10	even *w·* you render
	225– 2	*w·* the loyal at heart
	227–12	dies *w·* the others recover,
	234– 4	I cannot watch and pray *w·*
	246–19	*W·* revising "S. and H.
	282– 4	*W·* I admire the faith and friendship
	291–23	*W·* our nation's ensign of peace
	291–24	*w·* her reapers are strong,
	291–29	*w·* they work for their own country,
	306–29	*w·* I was his patient in Portland
	311– 3	*W·* I was living with Dr. Patterson
	312–19	*W·* on a business trip to Wilmington,
	320–20	* *w·* I was in your Primary class
	330–17	* *w·* on business in 1844,
	334–18	* *w·* being called unreal.
	334–22	* *w·* the Pharisee's self-righteousness
	335–15	* *W·* at Wilmington, N. C.,
	341–10	*w·* The bird of hope is singing
	343–16	*w·* healing the sick.
	349– 5	*w·* disease is a mental state or error

whilst

My.	331–29	* *w·* recounting the kind attention

whine

Mis.	210– 7	Do men *w·* over a nest of serpents,

whining

Mis.	119– 5	and then *w·* over misfortune,

whirlwind

Mis.	51–23	* Shall, like a *w·*, scatter
Un.	10–25	God was not in the *w·*.
Po.	18–19	He rides on the *w·*

whisper

Mis.	119– 1	If malicious suggestions *w·* evil
	144–18	to *w·* our Master's promise,
Pan.	3– 8	*w·*, "Solitude is sweet."
'02.	20– 6	*w·*, "No drunkards within,
Po.	10–14	List, brother ! angels *w·*
	66– 8	*w·* of one who sat by her side
My.	192–27	*w·* to you of the divine
	337–15	List, brother ! angels *w·*

whispered

Mis.	99–30	it is *w·*, "This is Science."
'02.	15–29	*w·* that name to my waiting hope
My.	62– 7	* *w·* : "Dear God, may I not

whisperers
Mis. 368–21   these words . . . "*w*," and — *Rom.* 1 : 29.

whispering
Mis. 269–30   heard the great Red Dragon *w*·
Ret. 9–21   * *w*· woods, where dying thunders
    18– 6   nestling alder is *w*· low,
Po. 15–11   *w*· voices are calling away
    63–15   nestling alder is *w*· low,

whispers
My. 128–10   and *w*· to the breeze

whit
My. 38–19   * not a *w*· behind their elders,

Whitcomb
E. Noyes
Man. 102–15   Albert Metcalf and E. Noyes *W*·
Mr.
My. 63– 2   * services of Mr. *W*· as builder
Mr. E. Noyes
My. 16–19   * and Mr. E. Noyes *W*·,

White, James T.
Mis. 394–22   * signature
    395– 1   poem
Po. 57– 8   * signature

white
Mis. 124–22   adore the *w*· Christ,
    212–22   and Love, the *w*· Christ, is the
    238– 1   * helped 'niggers' kill the *w*· folks !"
    313–19   field waves its *w*· ensign,
    320–29   *w*· stone in token of purity
    329– 7   taking up the *w*· carpets
    398–19   *W*· as wool, ere they depart,
Chr. 53–38   now blends In seven-hued *w*· !
Ret. 32– 2   bearing on its *w*· wings,
    46–25   *W*· as wool, ere they depart,
Un. 3–11   washed their robes *w*·
    12– 1   fields are already *w*· for the harvest ;
    51– 7   never make one hair *w*· or black,
Pul. 1– 5   promise clad in *w*· raiment,
    17–24   *W*· as wool, ere they depart
    25–22   * The floor is in *w*· Italian mosaic,
    26– 3   * centre being of pure *w*· light,
    26–23   * mosaic marble floor of *w*·
    37– 8   * although her hair is *w*·,
    42–15   * each of them wore a *w*· satin badge
    42–22   * with a centre of *w*· immortelles,
    42–27   * with ferns and pure *w*· roses
    42–28   * large basket of *w*· carnations
    76–11   * furniture frames are of *w*· mahogany
    76–13   * upholstery is in *w*· and gold
    77– 6   * plush casket with *w*· silk linings.
    78–21   * Attached by a *w*· ribbon to the
    78–23   * encased in a *w*· satin-lined box
    82– 2   * brain for its great *w*· throne.
No. 41–17   *w*· sanctuary will never admit such
Peo. 9–10   *w*· in the blood of the Lamb ;
    14– 6   smiling fountains, and *w*· monuments.
    14– 9   * *w*· fingers pointing upward."
Po. 2–18   *w*· waves kiss the murmuring rill
    14–23   *W*· as wool, ere they depart,
    78– 3   Peace her *w*· wings will spread
My. 69–13   * pure *w*· marble was used,
    83– 7   * tiny *w*·, unmarked buttons,
    202– 1   May its *w*· wings overshadow
    202– 2   overshadow this *w*· temple
    259– 4   I have named it my *w*· *student.*

white-haired
My. 342– 3   * became aware of a *w*· lady
    342– 7   * Older in years, *w*· and frailer,

White Mountain Church
My. 184– 7   chapter sub-title

White Mountain House
My. 314–32   proprietor of the *W*· *M*· *H*·,

White Mountains
My. 184–11   built First Church . . . at the *W*· *M*·.

whiteness
Mis. 393–24   To thy *w*·, Cliff of Wight.
Po. 52– 8   To thy *w*·, Cliff of Wight.

white-robed
Peo. 5–18   *w*· thought points away from

Whiteside, Florence
My. 323–14   * signature

white-winged
Mis. 172– 9   *w*· charity, brooding over all,
    204–10   *w*· peace sings to the heart
    262–23   through this *w*· messenger,
    331–12   *w*· dove feeds her callow brood,
    369–21   *w*· charity that heals
    396–22   wake a *w*· angel throng
Pul. 18– 6   wake a *w*· angel throng

white-winged
Po. 12– 6   wake a *w*· angel throng
    24–21   Send us thy *w*· dove.
My. 275–26   *w*· charity brooding over all,

whither
Mis. 158–22   revelation of what, how, *w*·.
Man. 94– 2   the city *w*· he is called
Ret. 90– 7   towns *w*· he sent his disciples ;
Pul. 33–22   * or *w*· he went
'02. 2– 2   this daystar, and *w*· it guides.
    9–22   whence it came nor *w*· it tended,
Po. 34– 6   But *w*· wouldst thou rove,
My. 124–21   Where art thou? Whence and *w*·?
    256–22   whence they came and *w*· they tend.
    307–28   drifting *w*· I knew not.
    350–11   poem
    350–23   *w*· shall he flee?

whithersoever
Mis. 327– 4   follow thee *w*· thou goest."

Whiting
Lilian
Pul. 40– 5   * signature
Miss
Pul. 39–10   from my friend, Miss *W*·,

Whittier
Mr.
Pul. 54–29   healed Mr. *W*· with one visit,

Pul. 28–24   * selections from *W*· and Lowell,
    53–25   * *W*·, grandest of mystic poets,
My. 12–19   *W*· mourned it as what

whoever
Mis. 54– 7   That one, *w*· it be,
    113–11   *W*· is mentally manipulating
    119–16   whatever or *w*· opposes evil,
    131– 1   *W*· challenges the errors
    266– 6   *W*· does this may represent
    283–30   *W*· is honestly laboring to
    347–32   *w*· hits this mark is well paid
    371–19   *W*· desires to say,
Pul. 75– 1   *W*· in any age expresses
Pan. 9–16   *W*· demonstrates the highest
My. 3–22   genuine, *w*· did it.

Whole
Mis. 16–21   God is a divine *W*·, and *All*,

whole (noun)
Mis. 102–14   God is not part, but the *w*·.
    166–25   until the *w*· shall be leavened
    171–24   *till the w· was leavened.* — *Matt.* 13 : 33.
    252–19   to the *w*· and not to a portion ;
    289–14   act as a *w*· and per agreement.
    317–15   the *w*· of the Scriptures
Ret. 67– 3   not the *w*· of error.
Un. 6– 1   *w*· is greater than its parts.
Pul. 50–26   * No . . . holds the *w*· of truth,
Rud. 2–22   *Is healing the sick the w· of Science?*
No. 4– 7   the *w*· of mortal existence,
Pan. 2–16   * conceived of as a *w*·,
Hea. 19– 3   not in part, but as a *w*· ;
My. 165–17   portion of one stupendous *w*·,
    236–11   Too much . . . spoils the *w*·.
    269–12   * parts of one stupendous *w*·,

whole (adj.)
Mis. 11–13   my *w*· duty to students.
    18–27   those of the *w*· human family,
    38– 7   our *w*· system of education,
    39–20   Truth to leaven the *w*· lump.
    51–24   * *w*· dark pile of human mockeries ;
    84– 2   by speaking, the *w*· truth.
    96–22   It brings . . . a *w*· salvation.
    98–12   helping the *w*· human family ;
    167–22   dominion over the *w*· earth ;
    175– 4   until the *w*· sense of being
    194–13   for the *w*· human race.
    224–24   to cover the *w*· world's evil,
    229–23   until the *w*· human race
    265–19   the *w*· line of reciprocal thought.
    268–15   His *w*· inquiry and demonstration
    285–16   the *w*· warfare of sensuality
    293–22   includes the *w*· duty of man :
    330–30   grass, inhabiting the *w*· earth,
    334–10   *w*· fabrication is found to be a lie,
    341– 2   When will the *w*· human race have
    370– 3   and be *w*· !" — *see Matt.* 12 : 13.
Man. 44–26   God requires our *w*· heart,
Ret. 31–20   keep the *w*· law, — *Jas.* 2 : 10.
Un. 6– 4   the *w*· human race will learn
    34– 8   *w*· function of material sight
    34–10   summary of the *w*· matter.
    36–10   This *w*· subject is met and
    54– 9   In order to be *w*·,
Pul. 4– 8   and therefore *w*· number,
    9–19   who, . . . is a very *w*· man

whole (adj.)
Pul.	48–10	* coloring of the w· landscape
	53–14	* faith hath made thee w·."— Luke 17 : 19.
	53–16	* the w· law of human felicity
	54– 5	* And we are w· again.
	54–14	* w· transaction was in perfect obedience
	81–13	* spends her w· time helping others.
	84– 2	* shall subdue the w· earth
No.	15– 7	blessings for the w· human family.
	29–20	he is made w·.
'01.	1– 9	nearer the w· world's acceptance.
	32–21	is the w· duty of man.
'02.	12– 4	settles the w· question
Hea.	8–14	then it is willing to be made w·,
Peo.	5–27	* if the w· materia medica
	10–16	battles for man's w· rights,
	12–22	demonstrated . . . God's w· plan,
	14–13	put on the w· armor of Truth ;
My.	28–31	* changed the w· aspect of medicine
	59– 5	* should leaven the w· lump,
	80– 8	* they had been made w·,
	114–29	the w· lump of human thought
	132–30	whose w· head is sick
	132–31	and whose w· heart is faint ;
	146–30	his w· weight of thought,
	152– 6	faith hath made thee w·."— Matt. 9 : 22.
	153– 7	have come to fulfil the w· law.
	196–13	to bridle the w· body."— Jas. 3 : 2.
	208– 4	seem as if the w· import of C. S.
	208–20	prayer for the w· human family.
	269– 1	w· universe included in one infinite
	297–20	an inspiration to the w· field,
	329–22	* when the w· country is recognizing
	363–23	gist of the w· subject
		(see also **world**)

wholeness
Un.	5– 4	understanding . . . the w· of Deity,

wholesome
Mis.	283–13	Any exception to the old w· rule,
	369–24	that w· but unattractive food.
Ret.	86– 1	energize w· spiritual warfare,
No.	42– 4	w· avowals of C. S.
My.	277– 8	by means of their w· tribunals,
	282–10	w· chastisements of Love,

whole-souled
Mis.	224–32	to offend a w· woman.

wholly
Mis.	14–28	therefore, w· problematical.
	16– 8	requisite to become w· Christlike,
	16–24	awakened consciousness is w· spiritual ;
	34–12	They are w· apart from it.
	37–26	Her time is w· devoted to
	46–28	thought has not yet w· attained unto
	53– 3	false claim can be w· dispelled.
	91–11	bond is w· spiritual and inviolate.
	140– 3	hold a w· material title.
	165– 1	a w· spiritual idea of God
	167– 6	He is w· symmetrical ;
	171– 3	first effort . . . was not w· successful ;
	177–16	give yourselves w· and irrevocably
	197– 9	unless this be so, no man can be w·
	198– 1	w· governed by the one perfect Mind,
	295–22	not w· represented by one man.
	344–17	would place Soul w· inside of body,
Man.	92–10	C. S. heals the sick quickly and w·,
Ret.	37– 7	book is indeed w· original,
	78–15	w· Christlike and spiritual.
Un.	4–27	the vision of sin is w· excluded.
	5–23	w· or partially differ from them as to
	10– 2	w· separates my system from all others.
	23–21	anything so w· unlike Himself
	49–14	So long as . . . I cannot be w· good.
Pul.	28– 1	* designed to be w· typical of the
	69–18	* w· from the spiritual . . . standpoint.
Rud.	7–16	material evidence being w· false.
No.	23– 9	could not have been w· evil,
	36–10	w· opposed to the popular view
'00.	13–26	* seems not to have been w·
'01.	8–20	is he not w· spiritual ?
Hea.	6–23	may be w· unknown to the
	11– 5	w· apart from the dream.
My.	5– 7	W· apart from this mortal dream,
	49– 4	* w· drawn over, as by
	53– 5	* that her duty was w· done,
	59–11	* accepted w· or in part
	84– 9	* until it be w· free from debt.
	130– 4	w· disloyal to the teachings
	134– 3	a heart w· in protest
	205–23	w· apart from human hypotheses,
	224–28	any literature as w· C. S.
	238–10	His language and meaning are w·
	293–23	regarded as w· contingent on
	315– 8	* being w· on his part ;

wholly
My.	349–31	W· hypothetical, inductive
	357– 1	w· apart from C. S.,
	357–16	on a w· spiritual foundation,

whoso
Mis.	65–30	"w· sheddeth man's— Gen. 9 : 6.
	335–30	w· departeth from divine Science,
Hea.	1– 8	w· builds on less than

whosoever
Mis.	52– 7	W· understands the power of
	195– 5	W· learns the letter of C. S.
	195– 7	w· hath the spirit without the
	211–22	"W· will save his life— Matt. 16 : 25.
	235–14	w· shall not be offended— Matt. 11 : 6.
	265–12	W· understands a single rule
	277– 7	W· proclaims Truth loudest,
	308– 4	W· looks to me personally
	337–13	W· . . . shall humble himself— Matt. 18 : 4.
	344–25	"W· shall not receive— Luke 18 : 17.
Chr.	55–23	w· shall do the will— Matt. 12 : 50.
	55–28	w· liveth and believeth— John 11 : 26.
Ret.	31–19	"W· shall keep the— Jas. 2 : 10.
	32– 7	w· will save his life— Matt. 16 : 25.
	38–28	W· learns the letter of this book,
	45–20	"W· shall smite thee— Matt. 5 : 39.
	63–18	W· covers iniquity
No.	13– 8	"W· liveth and believeth— John 11 : 26.
Pan.	9–12	"W· liveth and believeth— John 11 : 26.
'00.	9–22	W· attempts to ostracize C. S.
'01.	11–22	W· saith there is no sermon
	22– 2	w· demonstrates the truth of these
My.	180– 3	W· understands C. S.
	227–27	"W· shall smite thee— Matt. 5 : 39.
	229–17	w· doth not bear his cross, — Luke 14 : 27.

wicked
Mis.	19–14	and all the w· endeavors of
	187–32	by pagan religionists, by w· mortals
	191– 9	refers to a w· man as the devil :
	219–15	another feels w·.
	257– 5	wakes in a w· man.
	281–30	the w· shall not— Prov. 11 : 21.
	288–10	rash conclusion . . . is weak and w· ;
Ret.	14–27	if there be any w· way— Psal. 139 : 24.
Pul.	79–20	* a w· but witty writer
'00.	2–16	The w· idler earns little
	8–10	w· man has little real intelligence ;
	8–25	not Science for the w· to wallow
'01.	15–28	* your sinful, w· manner
Hea.	9–18	God never made a w· man ;
	9–20	wherewith to make himself w·.
My.	33–11	if there be any w· way— Psal. 139 : 24.
	128–26	the motive is not as w·,
	161– 1	hung around the necks of the w·.
	211– 5	they are . . . too ignorant, or too w·

wickedly
Mis.	219–12	mortals think w·
	219–13	and act w· :
	219–27	feels w· and acts w·,

wickedness
Mis.	53– 8	weariness and w· of mortal existence,
	116– 4	w· in high places."— Eph. 6 : 12.
	134–27	Spiritual w· is standing in high
	175–16	"the leaven of malice and w· ;— I Cor. 5 : 8.
	254–12	grows weak with w·
Pul.	13–10	is in proportion to its w·.
'01.	15–17	filling up the measure of w·
'02.	11–18	The world's w· gave our
My.	227– 5	because of another's w·

wide
Mis.	196–20	It opens w· the portals of salvation
	224–11	remember that the world is w· ;
	275–19	throw w· the gates of heaven.
	280–31	doors of animal magnetism open w·
Man.	45– 1	supplies within the w· channels of
Un.	7– 2	glorified in the w· extension of belief
	41–17	opening w· the portal from death into
Pul.	58–16	* main auditorium has w· galleries,
	78– 5	* nine inches w·,
My.	52–12	* spreading world w· of this great truth,
	72– 6	* gates of Boston are open w·
	88–15	* its accommodations are so w·,
	200–25	W· yawns the gap between this
	221–28	throwing the door w· open
	236–18	opens w· on the amplitude of liberty
	245– 3	w· demand for this universal

widely
Mis.	296– 1	this system of religion, — w· known ;
Pul.	28–16	* does not differ w· from that of any
My.	40–17	* more w· reassert its pristine
	85– 2	* in its w· international range,
	299–10	C. S. has been w· made known
	322–10	* correcting mistakes w· published
	357–20	open the way, w· and impartially,

widen
Ret.	11–14	That *w·* in their course.
Po.	60–11	That *w·* in their course.
My.	291– 6	a uniting of breaches soon to *w·*,

widened
Mis.	316–22	patching breaches *w·* the next hour ;

widening
Mis.	322–27	laboring in its *w·* grooves

widens
Mis.	265– 5	this divergence *w·*.
	323–22	way winds and *w·* in the valley ;

wider
Mis.	132– 5	opening, even *w·* than before,
	227–17	*w·* aims of a life made honest :

wide-spreading
My.	174– 4	*w·* elms and soft greensward

widest
Ret.	82– 9	*w·* power and strongest growth
Pul.	80–11	* the *w·* outlook.

widow
My.	126–20	I . . . am no *w·*, — *Rev.* 18 : 7.

(*see also* **Eddy**)

widowhood
My.	126–25	mourn over the *w·* of lust,

wield
Pul.	83–15	* *w·* the ruthless sword of injustice.

wielded
Ret.	54–23	salutary power which can be *w·*.

wielding
Mis.	127–26	cannot avoid *w·* it if we reflect Him.

wife
Mis.	90– 8	*Is it wrong for a w· to*
	143–22	husband and *w·* reckoned as one,
	225– 7	clergyman, his *w·* and child.
	236–16	solicitations of husband or *w·*
	275–10	bereft *w·* or husband,
	281–15	He replied to his *w·*,
	287–22	When asked by a *w·* or a husband
	289–23	nature has bestowed on a *w·*
	289–24	if the *w·* esteems not this
	306–20	* Mrs. Harrison, *w·* of the ex-President,
	339–22	Art thou a *w·*, and hast
Man.	46– 4	spiritually adopted husband or *w·*.
	92–12	If both husband and *w·* are
Ret.	1– 4	His *w·*, my great-grandmother,
	2– 7	Joseph Baker and his *w·*,
	4–23	The *w·* of Mark Baker was
	21– 7	had a *w·* and two children,
Pul.	26–16	* healing of the *w·* of the donor.
My.	59–22	* melodeon on which my *w·* played.
	314–20	for eloping with his *w·*,
	314–24	When this husband recovered his *w·*,
	314–27	the *w·* of this husband
	324–16	* Mr. Wiggin nor his estimable *w·*

(*see also* **Eddy**)

Wiggin (*see also* **Wiggin's**)
J. Henry
My.	319–24	* call on the late J. Henry *W·* to

Mr.
My.	317– 5	* to the effect that Mr. *W·*
	317–11	I engaged Mr. *W·* so as to
	317–17	Mr. *W·* left my diction quite out of
	318– 3	every case where Mr. *W·* added words,
	318– 5	Mr. *W·* was not my proofreader
	318–16	I invited Mr. *W·* to visit one of my
	318–22	Mr. *W·* manifested more . . . agitation,
	318–30	"Now, Mr. *W·*," I said,
	319– 8	hold the late Mr. *W·* in loving,
	319–30	* as regards Mr. *W·*.
	320– 3	* Upon calling on Mr. *W·*,
	320–10	* Mr. *W·* spoke of "S. and H."
	320–15	* Mr. *W·* did not claim to be a
	320–20	* called on Mr. *W·* several times
	320–28	* I saw Mr. *W·* several times
	321– 6	* My recollections of Mr. *W·*
	321–11	* Mr. *W·* was an honest man
	322–14	* conversation I had with Mr. *W·*
	322–24	* Mr. *W·* kindly helped me
	323– 3	* Mr. *W·* gave me a pamphlet
	324– 3	* Mr. *W·* had somewhat of a thought of
	324–15	* sure that neither Mr. *W·* nor
	324–21	* Mr. *W·* regarded you as
	325– 5	Mr. *W·* was very much troubled

Mr. and Mrs.
My.	324–32	* Mr. and Mrs. *W·* frequently mentioned

Mrs.
My.	322–23	* Mrs. *W·* seemed inclined to banter me

Rev. James Henry
My.	52–20	* years ago, the Rev. James Henry *W·*,
	52–30	* of the Rev. James Henry *W·*
	317– 3	* Rev. James *W·* of Boston,
	317–10	employed the Rev. James Henry *W·* to

Wiggin
Rev. J. Henry
My.	323–30	* home of the late Rev. J. Henry *W·*

Rev. Mr.
My.	319–14	* work . . . Rev. Mr. *W·* did for her,
My.	322–16	* to dine with the *W·* family.

Wiggin's
Mr. and Mrs.
My.	324– 1	* in Mr. and Mrs. *W·* home.

Rev. James H.
My.	322–11	* the Rev. James H. *W·* work

Wight
Mis.	392–18	poem
	393–24	To thy whiteness, Cliff of *W·*.
Po.	page 51	poem
	52– 8	To thy whiteness, Cliff of *W·*.

Wilbur, Miss
My.	298– 8	I thank Miss *W·* and the

Wilbur's, Sibyl
My.	297–30	have read Sibyl *W·* book,

wild
Mis.	396– 1	The *w·* winds mutter, howl,
Ret.	4–20	brooklets, beautiful *w·* flowers,
	17– 3	*W·* spirit of song,
Peo.	13–18	to let loose the *w·* beasts
Po.	1– 3	where the *w·* winds rest,
	47–16	sowing the wayside and *w·*,
	58–13	The *w·* winds mutter, howl,
	62– 1	*W·* spirit of song,

'wildered
Po.	70–22	Shine on our *'w·* way,

wilderness
Mis.	81–16	*to go up into the w·*,
	99–26	one crying in the *w·*,
	130–31	march out of the *w·*,
	138– 5	to wander in the *w·*
	153– 7	they marched through the *w·* :
	246–23	heard crying in the *w·*,
	325–24	"provoke Him in the *w·*, — *Psal.* 78 : 40.
	373–21	homelessness in a *w·*.
No.	9–21	a table in the *w·*" — *Psal.* 78 : 19.
Pan.	15– 6	spread for us a table in the *w·*
'00.	15–16	and fasts in the *w·*.
Hea.	19–24	bearing . . . into the *w·*,
My.	22–15	* forty years in the *w·*,
	43– 2	* unknown *w·* was before them,
	43– 3	* that *w·* must be conquered.
	43– 9	* During their sojourn in the *w·*
	43–32	* The way out of the *w·*
	47–25	* the *w·* of dogma and creed,
	50–26	* the little church in the *w·*,
	162– 8	better than a *w·* of dullards
	182–25	May the wanderer in the *w·*
	252–20	an oasis in my *w·*.

wildernesses
Mis.	142– 2	her *w·* to bud and blossom

wildfire
My.	302–17	the word spread like *w·*.

wilful
Mis.	293–18	inasmuch as *w·* transgression

wilfully
Mis.	224–29	He who can *w·* attempt to injure

will
caprice of
Pul.	55– 1	* "Not in blind caprice of *w·*,

creative
Un.	19– 5	contrary to His creative *w·*,

divine
Mis.	141–22	the divine *w·* and the nobility of

God's
Pan.	13–16	till God's *w·* be witnessed
My.	18–24	till God's *w·* be witnessed
	258–12	to know and to do God's *w·*,

good
Mis.	145–30	good *w·* toward men." — *Luke* 2 : 14.
	162–13	good *w·*, love, teaching, and
	215–15	peace, and good *w·* toward men.
	369– 5	good *w·* toward men." — *Luke* 2 : 14.
Man.	45– 7	and good *w·* toward men ;
Pul.	22– 1	peace and good *w·* towards men.
	41–25	* good *w·* toward men." — *Luke* 2 : 14.
No.	44–26	good *w·* toward men." — *Luke* 2 : 14.
Pan.	15–10	and good *w·* towards men.
'02.	8–12	by love and good *w·* towards men.
My.	4–20	Mind-power is good *w·* towards men.
	90–19	* good *w·* toward men." — *Luke* 2 : 14.
	127–30	good *w·* toward men," — *Luke* 2 : 14.
	167–12	good *w·* toward men," — *Luke* 2 : 14.
	167–18	peace, and good *w·* for yourselves,
	201– 6	love and good *w·* to man,
	210–16	peace, good *w·* towards men,

will

good
My.	262–28	letting good *w·* towards man,
	279–19	good *w·* toward men.'' — *Luke* 2 : 14.
	281– 9	good *w·* toward men.'' — *Luke* 2 : 14.
	282– 1	its purpose is good *w·* towards men.
	283–11	good *w·* toward men.'' — *Luke* 2 : 14.

His
Mis.	127–23	will do His *w·* even though
	208–12	to let His *w·* be done.
	208–15	do His *w·* or to let it be done
	213–29	*His w·* be done on earth
	334– 1	according to His *w·* — *Dan.* 4 : 35.
	386–18	Bowed to His *w·*.
Po.	50– 2	Bowed to His *w·*.
	79–20	doth His *w·* — His likeness still

his
Man.	28–12	according to his *w·*, — *Luke* 12 : 47.

his own
My.	132–15	''Of His own *w·* — *Jas.* 1 : 18.

human
(*see* **human**)

intellect, and
Pan.	4– 3	to the reason, intellect, and *w·* of

iron
Ret.	5–14	strong intellect and an iron *w·*.

is capable
Pan.	4–13	*w·* is capable of use and of abuse,

last
My.	137–20	I have designated by my last *w·*,

lord's
Man.	28–11	knew his lord's *w·*, — *Luke* 12 : 47.

my
Mis.	212–20	''Not my *w·*, but Thine, — *Luke* 22 : 42.

no
Mis.	347–26	Those who know no *w·* but His
My.	336–15	* Mr. Glover had made no *w·*

of God
Mis.	185– 4	*w·* of God, or power of Spirit,

of his Father
Mis.	167–18	they who do the *w·* of his Father
No.	41– 8	to do the *w·* of his Father

of man
Mis.	180–23	*nor of the w· of man,* — *John* 1 : 13.
	181–17	nor of the *w·* of man, — *John* 1 : 13.
	182–17	''Nor of the *w·* of man.'' — *John* 1 : 13.

of my Father
Chr.	55–23	do the *w·* of my Father — *Matt.* 12 : 50.

of the Father
'01.	18–19	''the *w·* of the Father.'' — see *John* 5 : 30.

of the flesh
Mis.	180–23	*nor of the w· of the flesh,* — *John* 1 : 13.
	181–16	the *w·* of the flesh, — *John* 1 : 13.
	182–14	nor of the *w·* of the flesh.'' — *John* 1 : 13.

of the woman
Pul.	49–26	* the *w·* of the woman set at work,

reason and
Pan.	4– 8	reason and *w·* are properly classified
	4–11	reason and *w·* are human ;

stubborn
Mis.	398– 5	Thou wilt bind the stubborn *w·*,
Ret.	46–11	Thou wilt bind the stubborn *w·*,
Pul.	17–10	Thou wilt bind the stubborn *w·*,
No.	7–13	sinning sense, stubborn *w·*,
Po.	14– 9	Thou wilt bind the stubborn *w·*,

this
Rud.	9–11	this *w·* is an outcome of

Thy
Mis.	208– 1	chapter sub-title — *Matt.* 6 : 10.
	384– 9	Thy *w·* to know, and do.
Pul.	22– 7	Thy *w·* be done — *Matt.* 6 : 10.
Po.	36– 8	Thy *w·* to know, and do.
My.	281– 4	Thy *w·* be done — *Matt.* 6 : 10.

Mis.	265– 6	cannot regain, at *w·*, an upright
My.	10–21	* to contribute money against their *w·*
	160–12	truisms which can be buried at *w·* ;
	300– 6	both to *w·* and to do — *Phil.* 2 : 13.
	336–18	* he was unable to make a *w·*.

Williams, Mrs. Ella E.
My.	16–18	* Mrs. Ella E. *W·*, Second Reader ;

willing
Mis.	xi– 9	the fervent heart and *w·* hand
	5– 6	*w·* to consecrate themselves
	22–27	he who is a *w·* sinner,
	118–17	*w·* to work alone with God
	118–18	*w·* to suffer patiently for
	189– 4	become *w·* to accept the
	208–14	*w·* to do His will
	269–26	are not *w·* to pay the price.
	335–19	*w·* participants in wrong,
	342–25	are *w·* to pay for error
	349–15	I was *w·*, and said so,
Man.	38–23	provided they are *w·*

willing
Ret.	14–15	I was *w·* to trust God,
	20–26	his stepfather was not *w·*
	49– 1	is *w·* to sacrifice all
	71–15	*w·* to be subjected to such
Un.	58–15	*w·* to test the full compass
Pul.	14–29	Many are *w·* to open the eyes of
	15– 2	not so *w·* to point out the
'00.	9– 6	the student is not *w·*
'01.	11–24	*w·* to hear a sermon from
	32–12	*w·* to renounce all for Him.
	35– 4	Are we *w·* to sacrifice self
	35– 5	*w·* to bare our bosom to the
'02.	17–17	It is wise to be *w·* to wait
Hea.	8–14	it is *w·* to be made whole,
	18– 6	*w·* to put new wine into
Po.	26–11	Lincoln's own Great *w·* heart
My.	21–17	* those who are *w·* to forego
	50–28	* were *w·* to labor for the Cause.
	61–25	* should be *w·* to let God work.
	124– 9	*w·* hands, and warm hearts,
	166–19	When we are *w·* to help
	209– 3	this *w·* and obedient church
	211–18	lend themselves as *w·* tools

willingly
Mis.	73– 6	doth not afflict *w·*.'' — *Lam.* 3 : 33.
	231– 8	*W·* — though I take no stock in
Ret.	90–16	mother never *w·* neglects
Pul.	44– 7	* I thought you would *w·* pause
Rud.	10–20	He afflicteth not *w·* the children
Hea.	18–13	it would *w·* adopt the new idea,
Peo.	12–27	not more *w·* than health ;
My.	40–10	* *w·* enter into the blessedness of
	43–11	* *w·* obedient to the voice of
	160–11	Most of us *w·* accept
	323–10	* nor *w·* leave any false impression.

willingness
Mis.	269–27	knowing the *w·* of mortals
	344–21	*w·* ''to be absent — *II Cor.* 5 : 8.
My.	58–13	* *w·* of those who have contributed
	333–24	* assurance of his *w·* to die,

willow's
Po.	67–11	winds bow the tall *w·* head !

willowy
My.	150–15	sleeping amid *w·* banks

will-power
Mis.	4–24	very strong *w·* to heal,''
	4–27	there is no *w·* required,
	45– 2	This is not done by *w·*,
	281– 5	self-asserting mortal *w·*
Ret.	68–24	mortal thought and *w·*.
Un.	22–21	*human intellect* and *w·*,
Rud.	8–22	opens a way whereby, through *w·*,
My.	348– 3	electricity, magnetism, or *w·*,

wills
Mis.	208–16	Mortals obey their own *w·*,
	224–12	million different human *w·*,

Wilmington (*see also* **Wilmington's**)
N. C.
My.	176– 2	chapter sub-title
	197–24	chapter sub-title
	312–19	business trip to *W·*, N. C.,
	335– 1	* Died at *W·*, N. C.,
	335–15	* While at *W·*, N. C., in June, 1844,

North Carolina
Ret.	19– 7	He was in *W·*, North Carolina,

My.	312– 6	* took his bride to *W·*,
	330– 7	* locates Mrs. Eddy in *W·* in 1843,
	330– 9	* was not then a resident of *W·*.
	330–17	* was of Charleston, S. C., not of *W·*,
	330–20	* by *W·* newspapers of that year.
	331–20	* Major George W. Glover of *W·*
	332– 8	* friends at *W·* accept it as a tribute of
	332–18	* Christian Association at *W·*.
	333– 4	* records of St. John's Lodge, *W·*,
	333–32	* reports of unusual sickness in *W·*
	334–11	* her husband's demise at *W·*.

Wilmington Chronicle
My.	331–10	* *W· C·* of August 21, 1844,
	333–19	* The *W· C·* of July 3, 1844,

Wilmington (N. C.) *Chronicle*
My.	329–15	* taken from the *W·* (*N. C.*) *C·*

Wilmington (N. C.) *Despatch*
My.	329–12	* *W·* (*N. C.*) *D·*, October 24, 1903.

Wilmington's
My.	331– 5	* at the hands of *W·* best citizens,
	331–12	* by *W·* best men,

Wilson's, John
Ret.	2– 6	and in John *W·* sketches.

win

Mis.	122–25	neither . . . can w· high heaven,
	155– 8	w· the pilgrim and stranger
	289–26	she may w· a higher.
	340– 9	can you w· and wear the crown
	341–18	to w· the spiritual sense of good.
Ret.	13–16	to w· me from dreaded heresy.
	80–20	w· the golden scholarship of
Un.	55–11	that they may w· the prize.
'00.	9–24	no one can fight against God, and w·.
Hea.	10–24	w· or lose according to your plea.
My.	126–30	for with it w· we the race
	163– 4	to w· through meekness to might,
	188–25	As you work, the ages w· ;

wind

Mis.	144–16	hiding place from the w·, — *Isa.* 32 : 2.
	275–14	* "tempers the w· to the shorn lamb,"
Pul.	82– 3	* she comes like the south w·
No.	22– 1	every w· of doctrine." — *Eph.* 4 : 14.
	22–11	are reeds shaken by the w·.
'01.	29–20	waiting till the w· shifts.
Po.	25–18	w· Wreaths for the triumphs
	53–15	Where w· nor storm can numb
My.	117– 6	reed shaken with the w·," — *Matt.* 11 : 7.

wind-chests

Pul.	60–20	* containing pneumatic w·

winding-sheet

Peo.	5–15	wrapped in a pure w·,

window

Mis.	203– 6	From my tower w·, as I look
	324–10	from the w· of this dwelling
	355–30	rainbow seen from my w·
Ret.	90– 2	God's w· which lets in light,
Pul.	25–13	* the w· frames are of iron,
	26–26	* Before the great bay w·
	27–16	* The other rose w· represents the
	27–20	* great w· tells its pictorial story
	27–25	* w· in the auditorium represents
	27–30	* bay w·, composed of three separate
	39–13	* poem
	58–22	* a beautiful sunburst w·.
	78–25	* w· of J. C. Derby's jewelry store.
My.	178–23	entered the house through a w·

windows

Mis.	283–12	and break through w·
Pul.	24–28	* The w· of stained glass
	27– 8	* The w· are a remarkable feature
	27– 9	* There are no "memorial" w· ;
	27–12	* In the auditorium are two rose w·
	27–14	* with six small w· beneath,
	27–17	* Beneath are two small w·
	27–27	* In the gallery are w· representing
	27–29	* the w· are of still more unique
	49– 8	* Looking down from the w·
	58–20	* all the w· are of colored glass,
My.	131–27	the w· of heaven, — *Mal.* 3 : 10.
	132– 4	the w· of heaven, — *Mal.* 3 : 10.
	259– 3	pedestal between my bow w·,
	269–21	w· of heaven are sending forth
	269–27	the w· of heaven, — *Mal.* 3 : 10.

winds

Mis.	9–30	the path that w· upward.
	23– 9	disease, death, w·, and waves,
	79– 5	swept clean by the w· of history.
	99–23	w· of time sweep clean the centuries,
	237–18	murmuring w· of their forest home.
	277– 3	Falsehood is on the wings of the w·,
	323–22	The way w· and widens
	330– 1	the w· make melody
	396– 1	wild w· mutter, howl, and moan,
	397–11	'Gainst which the w· and waves
Ret.	4–17	and wandering w· sigh low
Un.	11– 6	he commanded the w·,
Pul.	8– 3	Like the w· telling tales
	18–20	'Gainst which the w· and waves
Pan.	1– 6	the winter w· have come and gone ;
	1– 7	rushing w· of March have shrieked
'01.	19–18	w· and waves, which obeyed him
	29–19	and adverse w· are blowing,
	29–22	won for them by facing the w·.
Po.	1– 4	dweller where the wild w· rest,
	12–20	'Gainst which the w· and waves
	16–18	when the w· are all still.
	58–13	wild w· mutter, howl, and moan,
	67–11	w· bow the tall willow's head !
My.	106–16	the w· would weary,
	162–30	waves and w· beat in vain.
	226–12	commands the waves and the w·,

wine

and milk

Mis.	149– 2	buy w· and milk — *Isa.* 55 : 1.

bread and

Pul.	30–14	* symbols of bread and w·,

wine

drinking of

Mis.	170– 7	eating of bread and drinking of w·

inspiring

Mis.	369–27	We thirst for inspiring w·

is unsipped

Mis.	324– 9	music is dull, the w· is unsipped,

little

Mis.	243–25	"Take a little w· — see *I Tim.* 5 : 23.

new

Mis.	178– 7	He found that the new w·
No.	43–20	"new w· into old — *Matt.* 9 : 17.
Hea.	18– 6	put new w· into old bottles.
	18–12	new w· into old bottles.
	18–15	put the new w· into the

tempting

Mis.	9–20	tasted its tempting w·,

water into

Mis.	74–18	he turned the water into w· ;
	244–20	turn the water into w·,
Un.	11– 5	turned the water into w·,

without

Mis.	325– 7	"drunken without w·." — see *Isa* 29 : 9.

Mis.	144–27	w· poured into the cup of Christ.
	399–15	water, the bread, and the w·.
Chr.	55–12	pipe, and w·. — *Isa.* 5 : 12.
Hea.	18– 7	and the w· be spilled.
Po.	70– 7	Making its waters w·,
	75–22	water, the bread, and the w·.
My.	125–32	"drunk with the w· of — *Rev.* 17 : 2.

wine-cup

Mis.	121– 5	drank from their festal w·.

winepress

Mis.	301–31	trodden the w· alone ; — *Isa.* 63 : 3.
Un.	58– 6	"the w· alone." — *Isa.* 63 : 3.

wines

Mis.	278– 1	The w· of fornication, envy,

wing

Mis.	xii– 7	with strong w· to lift
	157–14	under the shadow of His w·.
	213–20	C. S. gives a fearless w·
	267–19	The bird whose right w·
	331–21	on upward w· to-night.
	387– 8	with Thy shelt'ring w·,
	389– 9	on upward w· to-night.
	389–18	shadow of His mighty w· ;
Chr.	53–57	no broken w·, no moan,
'01.	2–26	fearless w· and a sure reward.
Po.	4– 7	on upward w· tonight.
	4–17	shadow of His mighty w· ;
	6– 2	with Thy shelt'ring w·,
	18– 2	the eagle's proud w·,
	28–12	Give us the eagle's fearless w·,
	34– 7	Bird of the airy w·,
	53– 3	The bud, the leaf and w·

winged

Mis.	152– 7	thoughts w· with peace

wings

angel's

Mis.	388–22	To fold an angel's w· below ;
Po.	21–11	To fold an angel's w· below ;

both

Mis.	267–20	Both w· must be plumed for

chimerical

Ret.	70–11	chimerical w· to his imagination,

find

Mis.	86–30	find w· to reach the glory of

healing in its

'02.	9–10	with healing in its w·,

heaven-born

Mis.	374–14	pluck not their heaven-born w·.

her

Mis.	146– 2	with healing on her w·.
	331–13	nestles them under her w·,
	374–32	without *feathers* on her w·,

of divine Science

Ret.	88–28	to clip the w· of divine Science.

of joy

My.	192–26	My love can fly on w· of joy

of morning

Po.	2–16	On w· of morning gladly flit away,

of sense

Mis.	230–19	floating off on the w· of sense :

of the cherubim

My.	188–14	under the w· of the cherubim,

of the winds

Mis.	277– 3	Falsehood is on the w· of the winds,

of vanity

Hea.	11– 2	plucked from the w· of vanity.

our

Mis.	234– 3	We spread our w· in vain

protecting

Mis.	137–16	protecting w· of the mother-bird,

wings

rustle of
Mis. 306–23   we do not hear the rustle of *w*,
thy
Po. page 34   poem
        34– 1   *O for thy w*, sweet bird!
tired
Po. 16–12   The tired *w* flitting through
weary
Mis. 159–26   many weary *w* sprung upward!
My. 182–27   rest their weary *w* amid the
white
Ret. 32– 2   bearing on its white *w*,
Po. 78– 3   Peace her white *w* will spread
My. 202– 1   May its white *w* overshadow this
wisdom's
Po. 23–15   soul, upborne on wisdom's *w*,
your
My. 248–19   fold or falter your *w*.

Mis. 280– 6   not angels with *w*, but messengers
        393– 4   Gives the artist's fancy *w*.
Po. 51– 9   Gives the artist's fancy *w*.

winning
Pul. 31–26   * *w* in bearing and manner,
My. 232– 4   weave for you their *w* webs of life
        257–11   *w* the heart of humanity with
        268–29   heart of humanity warming and *w*.

winningly
My. 248–11   to proclaim Truth so *w*

wins
Mis. 277–11   right *w* the everlasting victory.
My. 180–27   Take it up,— it *w* the crown;
        232– 6   right way *w* the right of way,

winter (*see also* winter's)
Mis. 239–11   upon the sidewalk one *w* morning,
        332– 7   * long *w* of our discontent,"
Pul. 65–22   * one bitter *w* day, a Roman soldier
        82– 9   * than *w* could stop the coming of
Pan. 1– 6   *w* winds have come and gone;
Po. 16– 2   hopeful though *w* appears.
My. 153– 1   despite our *w* snows.
        196–29   Over the glaciers of *w*

winter's
Mis. 329–29   stricken to the heart with *w* snow,
Po. 46– 4   Nor blasts of *w* angry storm,
My. 327–14   * last *w* term of our Legislature,

wipe
Ret. 86–12   *w* the dust from his feet
Un. 18–12   *w* the tears from the eyes of My

wiped
Po. 78–12   When to be *w* away, Thou knowest
My. 44– 4   * tears are being *w* away,

wipes
Mis. 325–26   *w* off the dust from his feet
        327–32   *w* away the blood stains,
        399– 2   Love *w* your tears all away,
Un. 57–27   divine Science *w* away all tears.
Po. 22– 9   bliss that *w* the tears of time
        31–21   *w* away the sting of death
        75– 9   Love *w* your tears all away,
My. 132–31   *w* away the unavailing, tired tear,
        191–16   which *w* away all tears.

wire
My. 184–13   to *w* an acknowledgment thereof
        281–21   * Will you do us the kindness to *w*

wired
My. 105–19   I was *w* to attend the patient of

wireless
'02. 11–13   a submarine cable, a *w* telegraph,
My. 110–14   *w* telegraphy, navigation of the air;
        259–12   I return my heart's *w* love.

Wis. (State)
        (*see* **Milwaukee**)

wisdom (*see also* wisdom's)

according to
My. 291–10   zeal according to *w*,
all
Pan. 4– 4   possesses all *w*, goodness, and
almighty
Mis. 227–32   command of almighty *w*;
and guidance
My. 338–18   higher source for *w* and guidance.
and Love
Mis. 321–29   a world of *w* and Love
and love
Mis. 316–22   *w* and love into sounding brass;
My. 303–29   need much humility, *w*, and love
and might
Mis. 316–28   patterns of humility, *w*, and might

wisdom

and power
Mis. 204–25   wonderful foresight, *w*, and power;
Un. 14– 8   He should so gain *w* and power
and prosperity
Pul. 2– 4   thy *w* and prosperity— *I Kings* 10:7.
and strength
My. 164–27   unity is reserved *w* and strength.
and utility
Mis. 60–26   power, *w*, and utility of good;
aping the
Mis. 61– 7   aping the *w* and magnitude of
beginning of
Mis. 359–30   is the beginning of *w*.
divine
Mis. 209– 4   the prerogative of divine *w*,
        293– 6   unerring modes of divine *w*.
My. 5–32   Human will may . . . divine *w*, **never.**
        215–32   his divine *w* should temper human
experience and
My. 273–16   acquired by experience and *w*,
fair
Pan. 3–17   * We court fair *w*,
far-seeing
Mis. 254– 3   loving warning, the far-seeing *w*,
God is
Un. 26–16   * God is *w*, God is love.
God's
Mis. 362– 5   reason is at rest in God's *w*,
Un. 51–18   in the economy of God's *w*
has shown
My. 22–20   * she has shown *w*, faith, and
His
Mis. 114–26   His *w* will test all mankind
        158– 4   His *w* above ours.
human
        (*see* **human**)
immense
Mis. 223–25   immense *w* in the old proverb,
infinite
Mis. 18–11   These commands of infinite *w*,
Hea. 4–10   We ask infinite *w* to possess our
in human action
Mis. 288–13   *W* in human action begins with
inspired
No. 22–12   Compared with the inspired *w*
inspires
Mis. 360– 1   Meekness, . . . inspires *w*
intelligence and
My. 79–19   * intelligence and *w* of the country
is justified
Mis. 374– 9   "*W* is justified of— *Luke* 7:35.
My. 228–22   "*w* is justified of— *Matt.* 11:19.
is unerring
No. 8– 1   Father, whose *w* is unerring
is wedded
Mis. 276–32   *W* is wedded to their love,
is won
My. 205– 7   *W* is won through faith,
its
Ret. 87– 5   its *w* is as obvious in religion
My. 84–10   * experience . . . has affirmed its *w*.
Jesus'
Mis. 84– 1   Jesus' *w* ofttimes was shown
lack of
My. 128–24   A lack of *w* betrays Truth
least
Mis. 2– 4   who have the least *w* or
lengthens
My. 146–10   "If *w* lengthens my sum of years
        177–10   if *w* lengthens my sum of years
Love and
Po. 44– 1   Then, O tender Love and *w*,
My. 223–28   divine Love and *w* saith,
manifold
Mis. 363–18   His manifold *w* shines through the
my
Mis. 335–18   Those who deny my *w* or
nor Science
Mis. 359–16   but it is neither *w* nor Science
not infallible in
Mis. 66– 1   is not infallible in *w*;
of a serpent
Mis. 210–11   *w* of a serpent is to hide
of God
Mis. 210–12   *w* of God, as revealed in C. S.,
        359–29   To ask *w* of God, is the beginning
My. 261– 5   elders, who seek *w* of God,
of his words
My. 246–27   the *w* of his words,
of Mind-practice
Ret. 78– 4   entire *w* of Mind-practice.
of Nicodemus
My. 191– 1   *w* of Nicodemus of old,
of our forefathers
'00. 10–18   *w* of our forefathers is not

wisdom

of their elder
My. 261– 4 w· of their elders, who seek
of the practitioner
Man. 87– 6 left to the w· of the practitioner,
of the text
Mis. 201– 1 entire w· of the text ;
of this decision
Ret. 50–11 the w· of this decision ;
of withdrawing
Mis. 326–21 Seeing the w· of withdrawing
order of
Mis. 287–18 In the order of w·,
others'
Ret. 71– 3 not the forager on others' w·
practical
Man. 49–12 practical w· necessary in a sick room,
promotes
My. 250– 5 promotes w·, quiets mad ambition,
requires
Man. 77–19 God requires w·, economy,
requisite
Ret. 79–20 w· requisite for teaching
same
My. 162–19 same w· which spake thus
search after
Mis. 364–13 It is not a search after w·,
No. 21– 7 It was not a search after w· ;
set in
Ret. 79–23 jewels of Love, set in w·.
speculative
Mis. 361–22 subtlety of speculative w·
stature of
Mis. 227–28 into the full stature of w·,
store of
My. 253–23 I send with this a store of w·
stores of
Mis. 165–29 secret stores of w· must be
supply the
Pul. 15–17 and God will supply the w·
surprising
Mis. 66– 5 surprising w· of these words
symbol of
Mis. 191– 7 serpent became a symbol of w·.
temple of
My. 60–14 * temple of "w·, Truth, and Love."
this
Mis. 84– 4 This w·, which characterized his
to profit
Mis. 359–28 give not the w· to profit by it.
true
Mis. 139–26 like all true w·,
Truth and
Mis. 391– 9 And learn that Truth and w·
Po. 38– 8 And learn that Truth and w·
unerring
Mis. 315–28 unerring w· and law of God,
My. 44–29 * unerring w· of your leadership,
way of
My. 356–21 chapter sub-title

Mis. 139–24 at the w· whereof a few persons have
303– 9 w· garrisons these strongholds of
339–29 w· that might have blessed the past
354– 9 w· is not "justified of — *Matt.* 11 : 19.
354–25 by w·, Truth, and Love.
364–13 not a search after wisdom, it *is w·* :
369–15 Metaphysical healing seeks a w· that
No. 21– 8 not a search after wisdom ; it was w·,
Pan. 14–17 give to our congress w·,
Po. 77–10 Thou w·, Love, and Truth,
79–16 Life is light, and w· might,
My. 40–19 * w· that is from above — *Jas.* 3 : 17.
42– 3 * her mouth with w· ;— *Prov.* 31 : 26.
150–29 Then, if the w· you manifest
227– 7 Charity is quite as rare as w·,
228– 8 w· to "overcome evil with — *Rom.* 12 : 21.
231–17 w· must govern charity,

wisdomless

Mis. 30–23 the fossil of w· wit,

wisdom's

Mis. 387–20 w· rod is given For faith to kiss,
Ret. 11– 7 On learning's lore and w· might,
90–24 walk steadfastly in w· ways.
Po. 6–15 w· rod is given For faith to kiss,
23–15 soul, upborne on w· wings,
23–20 Guide him in w· way !
27– 8 young year dawn with w· light
43–15 Light with w· ray
60– 3 On learning's lore and w· might,

wise

Mis. 21–14 in no w· except by increase of
73–13 a commandment to the w·.

wise

Mis. 90–16 w· as serpents." — *Matt.* 10 : 16.
90–17 Break the yoke . . . in every w· way.
127–27 W· sayings and garrulous talk
134– 2 "w· unto salvation" !— *II Tim.* 3 : 15.
139–27 be regarded as greatly w·,
167–25 w· and prudent, — *Luke* 10 : 21.
170–14 right and w·, or wrong and foolish,
209–22 To suffer for . . . is divinely w·.
209–30 say . . . it is w· to cover iniquity
210–11 w· as serpents — *Matt.* 10 : 16.
215–32 a w· spiritual discernment
252–30 w· man's spiritual dictionary ;
276–16 The w· will have their lamps aglow,
276–31 w· Christian Scientists stand
281–16 * "It is w· to count the cost
282–23 it is sometimes w· to do so,
301–14 require only a word to be w· ;
312– 1 w· enough to guard against
319–17 chapter sub-title
321– 1 w· men follow this guiding star ;
332– 4 Infinitely just, merciful, and w·,
342–22 w· virgins had no oil to spare,
343– 1 make us w· unto salvation !
344–26 shall in no w· enter — *Luke* 18 : 17.
348–15 w· in his own conceit." — *Prov.* 26 : 5.
363–29 the w· man's directory.
371–20 It is a w· saying that
393–13 Students w·, he maketh now
Man. 41– 8 The w· man saith,
Ret. 22– 5 Writers less w· than the apostles
24– 4 was in no w· connected with
83– 3 The w· Christian Scientist will
Un. 4–28 no w· men or women will
6–20 No w· mother, though a graduate
58–15 He was too w· not to be willing
Pul. 15–13 If so, listen and be w·.
No. 7– 2 to be w· and true rejoices every
40– 8 sometimes w· to hide from
45– 1 w· and prudent, — *Luke* 10 : 21.
Pan. 9–14 What mortal to-day is w· enough
'01. 19–13 notion that . . . is w· or efficient,
'02. 2–14 w· builders will build on the
17–17 w· to be willing to wait on God,
Po. 51–18 Students w·, he maketh now
My. vi–15 * w· and unerring counsellor.
37–29 * its w· counsel and admonition.
41– 5 * nor in any w· alter its effects.
60– 4 * if Mrs. Eddy thought it w· to
62–23 * appreciation of your w· counsel,
93– 3 * they are in no w· at war with
128–22 Therefore be w· and harmless,
135– 2 The w· man has said,
139–16 chapter sub-title
149–14 * "I am w·, for I have conversed
149–15 * conversed with many w· men,"
150–28 w· as serpents, — *Matt.* 10 : 16.
162– 7 A small group of w· thinkers
179–25 in no w· affect C. S.
205– 5 w· as serpents, — *Matt.* 10 : 16.
223–26 chapter sub-title
237–10 Hence, it were w· to accept only
243–16 w· to remain in their own fields
244–23 and your w·, faithful teachers
248–10 to put an end to falsities in a w· way
250– 1 chapter sub-title
253–22 If wishing is w·, I send with this
259–18 w· zeal, a lowly, triumphant trust,
261–10 deceit or falsehood is never w·.
263– 5 word to the w· is sufficient.
273–13 I for one accept his w· deduction,
285– 7 in all your w· endeavors
291–19 was w·, brave, unselfed.
292– 8 sanctify our nation's sorrow in this w·,
339– 8 is specially requested to be w·
362–20 * we rejoice . . . in your w·

wisely

Mis. 117–16 work w·, in proportion as we love.
236– 8 to counsel w· whenever
247– 1 w· demand for man his
332– 2 W· governing, informing the universe,
No. 9–12 and separate w· and finally ;
'00. 2–14 and gives it w· to the world.
'01. 9–28 he speaketh w·,
My. 3–17 for it acts and acts w·,
6–13 dexterously and w· provided for
148– 3 called to do your part w·
201–16 mercifully forgive, w· ponder,
240–13 for it acts and acts w·,
286– 9 and should be, arbitrated w·, fairly ;
304–24 naturalist and author, w· said :

Wisemen

Mis. 164–11 To the vision of the W·,
164–20 As the W· grew in the

wiser

Mis.	265– 4	or *w·* than somebody else,
	281–17	* "It is *w·* to count the cost of
	342–29	*w·* than the children of — *Luke* 16 : 8.
Pul.	1–12	*w·* by reason of its large lessons,
'02.	3–20	*w·* at the close than the beginning
	17–18	and to be *w·* than serpents ;
My.	213–23	you will grow *w·* and better
	281– 2	and awakened a *w·* want,
	296–15	He is *w·* to-day, healthier and

wish

Mis.	69–28	*w·* to apply to him for information
	126– 4	Truly, I half *w·* for society again ;
	132–30	with the hope that you *w·* to be just.
	211–17	you *w·* to save him from death.
	262– 4	If you *w·* to brighten so pure a purpose,
	296–26	a *w·* to promote female suffrage
	344– 3	expressed the *w·* to become one of
	391– 1	poem
Un.	15–25	they *w·* to bribe with prayers
Pul.	10–14	the *w·* to reign in hope's reality
	58–29	* should she *w·* to make it a home
	87–23	This *w·* stops not with my pen
'00.	2–29	not so successful as I could *w·*,
Hea.	7–23	I *w·* the age was up to his understanding
	10–20	If you *w·* to be happy,
	10–21	take the side you *w·* to carry,
Po.	3– 8	watch thy chair, and *w·* thee here ;
	page 38	poem
My.	131–19	I *w·* to say briefly that
	157–17	* expressed *w·* of Mrs. Eddy,
	189– 1	warmest *w·* of men and angels.
	244– 3	*w·* to share this opportunity
	270–16	the father of their *w·*.
	315–10	* happy home as one could *w·* for.
	327–22	* did not *w·* to be "discourteous

wished

Mis.	98–23	* "consummation devoutly to be *w·*."
	178–27	I *w·* to be excused from
	223–27	* "If I *w·* to punish my enemy,
	299–32	*w·* to handle them, does it justify
	312– 1	*w·* I were wise enough to
Ret.	14–19	The minister then *w·* me to tell him
Un.	17–19	* consummation devoutly to be *w·*."
Pul.	41–20	* until all who *w·* had heard and seen ;
	49–20	* she had long *w·* to get away
My.	181–16	* "a consummation devoutly to be *w·*"

wishes

Pul.	47–24	* when she *w·* to catch a glimpse of
My.	138– 7	carried on contrary to my *w·*.
	263– 6	*w·* you all a *happy Christmas*,
	358–23	Give my best *w·* and love to your

wishing

Po.	9–10	*w·* this earth more gifts from above,
My.	253–22	If *w·* is wise, I send with this a

wit

Mis.	15– 6	to *w·*, the redemption of — *Rom.* 8 : 23.
	30–24	fossil of wisdomless *w·*,
	95–22	to *w·*, the redemption of — *Rom.* 8 : 23.
	117–11	* "there are *w·*, humor, and
	182–10	to *w·*, the redemption of the body.
Peo.	10–26	to *w·*, the redemption of — *Rom.* 8 : 23.
My.	303–13	Mark Twain's *w·* was not wasted

witchcraft

Mis.	123– 7	superstition, lust, hypocrisy, *w·*,
	211–11	class legislation, and Salem *w·*,
	324–14	*w·*, variance, envy,

witch-grass

Mis.	343–22	reappear, like devastating *w·*,

withal

My.	261– 4	and profit them *w·*?

withdraw

Mis.	49– 3	to *w·* before its close.
	273– 7	I *w·* from an overwhelming prosperity.
Man.	51–12	shall either *w·* from the Church
Pul.	34–13	* requested those with her to *w·*,
'00.	9– 3	I sometimes *w·* that advice
My.	226–10	*W·* God, divine Principle, from
	260– 5	matter would reverentially *w·*

withdrawal

My.	118–20	voluntary *w·* from society,

withdrawing

Mis.	278–29	I have been gradually *w·* from
	326–21	Seeing the wisdom of *w·* from
'02.	3–12	our military forces *w·*,

withdrawn

Mis.	302–18	till this permission was *w·*,
Man.	38–21	but who have voluntarily *w·*,
My.	344–11	and then *w·* from it,

withdraws

Mis.	324–20	this mortal inmate *w·* ;

withdrew

Man.	38–17	Members who once *W·*.
Ret.	24–22	I then *w·* from society
Pul.	34–24	* Mrs. Eddy *w·* from the world
	45–23	* Judge Hanna *w·* from the pastorate

withered

Mis.	357–16	Much . . . has *w·* away,
Un.	11–16	*w·* hand looks very real

withheld

Pul.	10–24	have not *w·* the timely shelter
My.	36–14	* or *w·* from open graves

withhold

Ret.	75– 7	Why *w·* my name,
My.	75– 1	* we cannot well *w·* our

withholds

Mis.	300–31	he who *w·* a slight equivalent

within

Mis.	12–32	to all *w·* the radius of our
	21–10	kingdom of God is *w·* — *Luke* 17 : 21.
	34–24	*w·* the realm of mortal thought
	75–12	the infinite is not *w·* the finite ;
	97– 7	that holds *w·* itself all evil.
	114–18	resist the foe *w·* and without.
	125–11	the reign of righteousness — *w·* him ;
	125–29	*w·* the past few years :
	128– 5	*w·* the limits of a letter.
	137–14	*w·* the last few years.
	143–22	*w·* about three months,
	145–32	that my heart folds *w·* it,
	154–18	reign of harmony already *w·* us.
	156–10	heaven of Love *w·* your hearts.
	169– 1	*W·* Bible pages she had found
	173–16	Can the infinite be *w·* the finite?
	174– 9	religious sentiment *w·* man.
	174–24	Jesus said it is *w·* you,
	227– 8	crime comes *w·* its jurisdiction.
	251–18	kingdom of God is *w·* — *Luke* 17 : 21.
	251–19	*w·* the present possibilities of
	290– 3	found *w·* their precincts.
	302–32	stay *w·* their own fields
	324–13	*W·* this mortal mansion are
	324–26	Finding no happiness *w·*,
	368– 9	* Standeth God *w·* the shadow,
	391– 5	Will find *w·* its portals
	393– 9	*w·* the misty Mine of human thoughts,
	399– 7	Cleanse the foul senses *w·* ;
Man.	45– 1	*w·* the wide channels of The
	52– 8	*w·* ten days thereafter,
	94– 2	can invite churches *w·* the city
Ret.	14–24	when the new light dawned *w·* me.
	21– 5	Every means *w·* my power
	80– 1	reign of harmony *w·* us,
	80–18	warning will be *w·* him a spring,
	86–11	"stranger that is *w·* thy — *Deut.* 5 : 14.
Un.	3–23	*W·* Himself is every embodiment of
	6– 2	"the seed *w·* itself," — *see Gen.* 1 : 11.
	28– 3	a reality *w·* the mortal body?
	28– 8	dares define Soul as something *w·* man?
	33–14	only matter *w·* the skull,
	48– 1	a reason for the faith *w·*.
Pul.	2– 6	*w·*, the spirit of beauty dominates
	2–21	and remain *w·* the walls
	3– 7	kingdom of God is *w·* — *Luke* 17 : 21.
	8– 9	Scientists, *w·* fourteen months,
	10–30	May the kingdom of God *w·* you,
	11– 8	find *w·* it home, and *heaven*.
	30–27	* *w·* fifteen years it has grown to
	45–13	* completion *w·* the year 1894
	49–25	* *w·* one mile of the "Eton of
	70–11	* *w·* a few years founded a sect
Rud.	6–16	* *w·* the *last few years*,
No.	30–21	not light holding darkness *w·* itself.
	35–26	kingdom of God is *w·* — *Luke* 17 : 21.
Pan.	4–22	disquieted *w·* me? — *Psal.* 42 : 11.
	13– 8	kingdom of God is *w·* — *Luke* 17 : 21.
'00.	1– 3	chinked *w·* the storied walls of
'01.	7–12	include *w·* this Mind the thoughts
	24– 4	not *without* the mind, but *w·* it,
	28– 5	the kingdom of heaven *w·* us
	35– 9	the kingdom of heaven *w·* us
'02.	2–12	*W·* the last decade
	8–27	the kingdom of heaven *w·* him.
	20– 6	"No drunkards *w·*, no sorrow,
Hea.	4– 3	nor remain for a moment *w·* limits.
Po.	38– 4	Will find *w·* its portals
	46– 3	*W·* life's summer bowers !
	51–14	Work ill-done *w·* the misty
	75–14	Cleanse the foul senses *w·* ;
My.	37– 3	* *w·* the sacred confines of this
	49– 8	* sweeping the world *w·* a generation."
	52–27	* *W·* a few months she has made
	63–20	* But *w·* our sacred edifice
	69–12	* Everywhere *w·* the building

within

My.
70–12	* The effect on all *w·* earshot
74– 4	* *w·* two or three days' ride,
74–28	* *W·* two weeks we have had here
76– 3	* Up to *w·* ten days
99– 9	* is welcomed *w·* our midst
118–28	consciousness of heaven *w·* us
145–17	*W·* the past year and two months,
155–19	heaven here, — heaven *w·* us,
160–13	a sapling *w·* rich soil
161–15	*w·* himself, *w·* his own consciousness,
164–12	and all *w·* the human heart
164–25	unfolds the thought most *w·* us
167– 5	suppositional world *w·* us
176– 9	pointing the path to heaven *w·* you,
181–22	*W·* those years it is estimated
191–20	I am not there, am not *w·*
193–28	*W·* its sacred walls may song
260–21	because of the heaven *w·* us.
265–24	kingdom of God is *w·* — *Luke* 17 : 21.
267–29	kingdom of God is *w·* — *Luke* 17 : 21.
267–29	*w·* man's spiritual understanding
276– 8	preference to remain *w·* doors
303–31	foretasting heaven *w·* us.
315–17	* made oath that the *w·* statement
339–23	have not the Christ, Truth, *w·* them
342– 1	*w·* the ample, richly furnished
348– 6	I sought this cause, not *w·*
348–10	the hope that was *w·* me.
356–14	*w·* the last five years

without

Mis.
x–11	*w·* due preparation.
7–30	*w·* any assistance.
9–11	hated thee *w·* a cause
14–23	proven . . . to be *w·* necessity.
28– 7	muscles cannot move *w·* mind.
30–11	*w·* pain, sin, or death.
42–29	*Can I be treated w· being present*
43– 3	*w·* even having seen the individual,
45–29	*w·* Him was not anything — *John* 1 : 3.
47–10	*w·* consciousness of its weight
51–20	*w·* your having to resort to
58–21	*W·* its theology there is no
59– 8	*w·* this Science there had better
62–16	*mind-cure claims to heal w· it?*
67–28	*w·* his subjection to death,
90–26	*w·* this prerogative being conferred by
93–18	fear, . . . is *w·* divine authority.
93–26	*w·* repentance and reformation.
107–22	*W·* a sense of one's oft-repeated
107–29	*W·* a knowledge of his sins,
108– 8	a lie, being *w·* foundation
109–24	*w·* this the valuable sequence of
113–19	so that all are *w·* excuse
114–18	resist the foe within and *w·*.
129– 4	to condemn his brother *w·* cause,
130–19	*w·* one single mistake,
144–13	*w·* pomp or pride,
149– 2	*w·* money — *Isa.* 55 : 1.
149– 3	and *w·* price." — *Isa.* 55 : 1.
154– 6	Your faith has not been *w·* works,
154–25	Pray *w·* ceasing.
158– 7	your speaking *w·* notes,
162–24	*w·* corporeality or finite mind.
165– 8	man, *w·* the fetters of the flesh,
173–17	Does an evil mind exist *w·* space
178– 8	not . . . *w·* bursting them,
193–25	*w·* this enlarged sense of the
195– 7	hath the spirit *w·* the letter,
210– 4	never healed a patient *w·* proving
216–28	* *phenomenon w· a noumenon*
216–29	* a grin *w·* a cat."
217– 3	effect *w·* a cause is inconceivable ;
218–23	the "grin *w·* a cat ;"
227– 4	given up . . . *w·* friend
227– 5	given up . . . *w·* apologist.
228–25	*w·* questioning the reliability of
233– 1	*w·* knowing its fundamental Principle.
240–13	*w·* the assent of mind,
242– 8	reset certain dislocations *w·* the
242–30	if she went *w·* it twenty-four hours
244– 8	*w·* compliance to ordained conditions.
244–22	raised *w·* matter-agencies.
250–21	goodness *w·* activity and power.
259– 1	*w·* Him was not any thing — *John* 1 : 3.
261–27	*w·* apprehending the moral law
263–22	*w·* a full knowledge of the
263–28	*w·* credit, appreciation, or a
264– 7	*w·* the groundwork of right,
269–21	the body is *w·* action ;
279–15	from which we learn *w·* study.
280– 1	when the earth was *w·* form,
281–21	helplessness *w·* this understanding,
282– 8	*w·* their knowledge or consent?
282–21	to treat him *w·* his knowing it,
283– 6	*w·* his knowledge or consent,

without

Mis.
283–15	to treat another student *w·* his
283–22	*w·* incriminating the person
284– 8	may possess a zeal *w·* knowledge,
286– 3	marriage is not *w·* the law,
287–32	venturing on valor *w·* discretion,
295– 4	whom he quotes *w·* naming,
301– 2	*w·* the author's consent,
301–17	*w·* this word of warning
301–22	and read it publicly *w· my consent.*
302– 7	teaching the name *w·* the Spirit,
302– 8	the skeleton *w·* the heart,
302– 8	the form *w·* the comeliness,
302– 9	the sense *w·* the Science,
313–14	*w·* ill-humor or hyperbolic
319–20	*w·* one gift to me.
325– 7	"drunken *w·* wine." — *see Isa.* 29 : 9.
325–30	*w·* watchers and the doors unbarred !
334–16	*w·* one word of Truth in it.
340– 5	There is no excellence *w·* labor ;
344– 7	*w·* having mastered the sciences
356–30	"pray *w·* ceasing," — *I Thess.* 5 : 17.
357–11	*W·* the cross and healing,
359– 6	until you can cure *w·* it
367– 1	letter *w·* law, gospel, or
371– 4	wandering about *w·* a leader,
374–31	an angel is a woman *w· feathers*
380–18	could heal mentally, *w·* a sign
383– 8	In 1896 it goes *w·* saying,

Man.
17– 3	forming a church *w·* creeds,
27– 8	*w·* consulting with the full Board
28– 6	*W·* a proper system of
41– 8	but *w·* hard words.
43– 1	*w·* her or their consent
43–16	copyrighted works *w·* her permission,
48– 5	do it with love and *w·* fear.
49–24	*w·* previous injury or illness,
50– 9	*w·* the consent of the Board of Directors.
50–15	having the name *w·* the life of
53–11	*w·* her having requested the
53–13	unnecessarily and *w·* her consent,
59– 2	*w·* characterizing their origin
67– 9	*w·* her written consent.
67–15	*w·* having personally conferred
68– 6	*w·* the Directors' consent
70– 5	*w·* first consulting her on said
78–10	*w·* the written consent of the Pastor
82– 8	*w·* her knowledge or
82–11	*w·* the request of the advertiser,
85–21	shall not teach C. S. *w·*
86– 9	*W·* Teachers.
103– 7	*w·* the written consent of
104–10	*w·* the written consent of
105– 3	*w·* the written consent of
111–18	*w·* sufficient cause,

Chr.
53–39	*w·* birth and *w·* end,
55–20	*W·* father, *w·* mother, *w·* descent, — *Heb.* 7 : 3.

Ret.
14–11	I answered *w·* a tremor,
21– 3	*W·* my knowledge a guardian was
21– 5	employed . . . but *w·* success.
30–24	gained *w·* tasting this cup.
33– 9	*w·* receiving satisfaction.
41– 5	"*w·* money and *w·* price," — *Isa.* 55 : 1.
41– 6	*w·* even an acknowledgment
44– 2	church, *w·* a creed,
44–26	*w·* a dissenting voice.
52–11	sheep that were *w·* shepherds,
54–12	*w·* bearing the fruits
54–14	admits Truth *w·* understanding it.
61–15	*w·* 'hope, and *w·* God — *Eph.* 2 : 12.
65–27	determine, *w·* a telescope,
71–10	*w·* the consent or knowledge
71–18	*w·* the permission of man
73– 4	*w·* materiality, *w·* finiteness
75– 1	book-borrowing *w·* credit
76– 5	Science *w·* trespassing,
85–17	Never forsake your post *w·*
86–21	No one can save himself *w·*
88–23	preach *w·* the consent of

Un.
2–28	*w·* having rightly improved
4– 2	*w·* a single taint of our
9– 9	all are *w·* excuse who
19–16	*w·* any actuality which
23–12	if ye be *w·* chastisement, — *Heb.* 12 : 8.
34– 8	cannot see *w·* matter ;
38– 8	is virtually *w·* existence.
40–23	which is . . . *w·* end,
49–22	Evil is *w·* Principle.
49–23	undemonstrable, *w·* proof.
56–26	Love which is *w·* dissimulation
57–10	*W·* it there is neither
58–17	yet *w·* sin." — *Heb.* 4 : 15.
60–22	*W·* Him, the universe would

Pul.
2– 6	Both *w·* and within,
9–29	"Faith *w·* works — *Jas.* 2 : 26.
44–26	* *w·* any special appeal,

without

Pul.	47–12	* w· receiving any real satisfaction.
	64–17	* w· finding a clew ;
	70–10	* w· doubt one of the most
	79–14	* w· seeing notices of
Rud.	9–21	w· a direct effort,
	14– 9	w· remuneration, except the
	14–13	She has never taught . . . w· several,
No.	7–24	w· reference to right or wrong
	8–12	w· fear or doubt, knowing that God
	15– 4	Reading my books, w· prejudice,
	17–14	not w· an ever-present witness,
	21–28	like a cloud w· rain,
	35– 2	W· it, how poor the precedents of
	35– 4	were C. S. w· the power to
	40– 1	"Pray w· ceasing"— I Thess. 5 : 17.
	41–16	W· question, the subtlest forms of
	45– 3	St. Paul said that w· charity
Pan.	12–19	w· the alterative agonies
'01.	11–18	read each Sunday w· comment
	11–22	saith there is no sermon w·
	24– 3	argues that matter is not w· the
	27–17	w· a Christian Scientist on earth,
	34–27	man cannot live w· it ;
	34–28	nor happiness w· godliness.
'02.	2– 4	w· clamor for distinction
	7–14	without beginning and w· end,
	15– 6	Healing . . . diseases w· charge,
	15– 8	"w· money and w· price,"— Isa. 55 : 1.
	16–13	w· which no man shall— Heb. 12 : 14.
	18–24	faith w· proof loses its life,
Hea.	4–20	without beginning and w· end.
	12–21	cannot shake the poor drug w· the
Peo.	2–24	Truth w· a lapse or error,
	12–28	w· health there could be no heaven.
Po.	42– 3	never the sunshine w· a dark spot ;
	42– 6	W· heart to define them,
My.	v–17, 18	* "w· money and w· price."— Isa. 55 : 1.
	3–10	sear leaves of faith w· works,
	14–26	* carried on w· interruption
	15– 8	w· the written consent of the
	29–30	* w· suffering the inconveniences of
	30–23	* W· ostentation and quite voluntarily
	31– 4	* "Just as I am, w· one plea ;"
	40–28	* w· regrets and w· resistance,
	41–11	* so receive judgment w· mercy ;
	46– 6	* w· this spiritual significance
	76– 1	* it went w· saying that the
	76–18	* free of debt w· exception.
	79–25	* w· a trace of fanaticism,
	93– 2	* w· efforts at proselytizing ;
	95–25	* w· faith in the things unseen.
	97– 6	* w· the use of medicine.
	105–24	restored by me w· material aid,
	106– 4	and w· this proof of love
	106–29	heals the sick w· drugs
	107–13	can be swallowed w· harm
	107–14	and w· appreciable effect.
	108– 3	healing his cases w· drugs
	128–23	w· the former the latter were
	130–24	Borrowing from . . . w· credit,
	138– 1	w· the help of others.
	138– 6	suit was brought w· my knowledge
	157– 9	* w· regard to class or creed,
	158–19	letter w· the spirit is dead :
	163–13	w· neglecting the sacred demands
	178–16	if evil exists, it exists w· God.
	195–28	unselfed love that builds w· hands,
	197– 4	Attempt nothing w· God's help.
	197– 6	glorious, w· spot or blemish.
	203– 8	laws which are obeyed w· mutiny
	204–15	SCIENTISTS TO PRACTICE w· FEES
	213–18	wrong direction w· knowing it.
	215– 4	bestowed w· money or price.
	215– 9	w· having charity scholars,
	215–28	first w·, and then with, provision
	216– 2	live w· eating,
	216–11	w· a cent to sustain it?
	218–16	abstractions . . . w· their correlatives,
	223– 3	w· previous appointment by letter.
	224–18	one author w· quotation-marks,
	228–30	It goes w· saying that
	235– 2	w· using the word death,
	244–16	do not enter w· a struggle
	249– 1	w· harming any one
	249–27	then w· reference to sex
	263– 2	alone and w· His glory.
	267– 7	w· Him was not any thing— John 1 : 3.
	268–18	w· a living Divina.
	301–28	w· the aid of mind.
	302–16	But w· my consent, the use of
	312– 9	* entirely w· money or friends.
	312–15	* entirely w· means of support.
	320–23	* w· any hesitation or restriction.
	321–10	* w· any restriction.
	334– 8	* The allegation . . . is w· foundation.

without

My.	339–30	w· the observance of a
	340– 4	"Pray w· ceasing."— I Thess. 5 : 17.
	341–26	* raining all day and was damp w·,
	345–17	pellets w· any medication
		(see also **beginning, Mind**)

withstood

Mis.	233–10	if not understood and w·,
Ret.	45–24	w· less the temptation of popularity
My.	249–11	Unless w·, the heat of hate burns

witless

Mis.	78–18	w· ventilation of false statements

witness

Mis.	46–22	beareth w· with our— Rom. 8 : 16.
	54–10	they bear w· to this fact.
	67–13	not bear false w· ;"— Exod. 20 : 16.
	83– 3	w· to and perpetual idea of
	218–19	beareth w· of things spiritual,
	241–11	and w· the effects.
	255–14	beareth w· with our— Rom. 8 : 16.
	382–10	time and eternity bear w·
Man.	53–21	bear w· to the offense
Ret.	25–27	"If I bear w· of— John 5 : 31.
	25–27	my w· is not true."— John 5 : 31.
	67–17	lost for lack of w·.
Un.	7–15	can bear w· to these cures.
	33– 8	"If I bear w· of— John 5 : 31.
	33– 8	my w· is not true."— John 5 : 31.
	36– 4	this lie was the false w·
Pul.	8–28	The children are destined to w·
No.	17–14	not without an ever-present w·,
Pan.	13– 1	w· more steadfastly to its
Po.	73–14	W· my presence and utter
My.	36–19	* bear w· to the abundance
	192–23	to w· your prosperity,
	270–23	I can appeal to Him as my w·
	323–12	* living w· to Truth
	340–11	as w· her schools,

witnessed

Pul.	84–14	* w· the completion of
Pan.	13–17	till God's will be w·
My.	18–25	till God's will be w·
	30– 5	* who w· the opening.
	42– 7	* "w· a good confession"— I Tim. 6 : 13.
	79–14	* seldom w· anywhere
	97–30	* incidents w· during the week
	323–23	* we have so recently w·,

witnesses

Mis.	150–23	peopled with living w·
	250–17	active w· to prove it,
	321– 9	each recurring year w·
	360–17	cloud of false w· ;
Ret.	25–22	senses are so many w· to
Un.	33–21	these w· for error,
	33–24	two or three w·— Matt. 18 : 16.
'02.	10–25	martyrdom of God's best w·
	16–22	self-defense against false w·,
My.	243–21	w· your fidelity
	248–25	to you, my faithful w·.
	347– 2	His two w·.

witnesseth

My.	191–15	w· a risen Saviour,

witnessing

My.	45– 6	* We are w· with joy

wittingly

Ret.	74– 8	afflicteth me not w· :

witty

Mis.	216–22	a w· or a happy hit at idealism,
Pul.	79–20	* a wicked but w· writer has said,

woe

Mis.	65–10	subject of human weal and w·
	122– 2	"W· unto the world— Matt. 18 : 7.
	122– 4	w· to that man by whom— Matt. 18 : 7.
	250–28	want and w·, sickness and sorrow
	279– 1	w· unto him, — Luke 17 : 1.
	361–23	speculative wisdom and human w·.
	388–23	And hover o'er the couch of w· ;
Ret.	31–13	ever-present relief from human w·.
Un.	15– 2	* "death into the world, and all our w·."
	58–16	full compass of human w·,
Pul.	8– 7	Notwithstanding . . . the want and w·
	12–12	W· to the inhabiters— Rev. 12 : 12.
No.	33–23	physical suffering and human w·.
	34–26	Nameless w·, everlasting victories,
'02.	6–13	Here all human w· is seen to
Hea.	18–19	or claimed to reach that w· ;
Po.	3–11	Since first we met, in weal or w·
	21–12	And hover o'er the couch of w· ;
	28– 8	Whate'er the gift of joy or w·,
	35– 6	binds to earth— infirmity of w· !
	47–19	Evermore gathering in w·
My.	190– 2	bring the recompense of human w·,
	283–15	sovereign remedies for all earth's w·.

woeful
Mis. 60– 7 *w·* unrealities of being,
'01. 18– 4 weak criticisms and *w·* warnings

woes
No. 30–13 God pities our *w·*
    30–16 could not destroy our *w·* . . . if He
'02. 20– 7 glory of earth's *w·* is risen upon you,
Peo. 11–23 responsible for all the *w·* of
Po. 8– 6 Her bosom to fill with mortal *w·*.
    41– 6 earth-stricken lay down their *w·*,

woke
Mis. 386–13 I *w·* to Life,
Ret. 12– 6 *W·* by her fancied feet.
Po. 49–19 I *w·* to Life,
    61– 4 *W·* by her fancied feet.

wolf
Mis. 145–22 "The *w·* also shall— *Isa.* 11: 6.
    213–26 fleeth when he seeth the *w·* coming.
    370–20 a *w·* in sheep's clothing

wolves
Mis. 294–18 *w·* in sheep's clothing
    323–12 *w·* in sheep's clothing
My. 215–21 *w·* in sheep's clothing," — see *Matt.* 7: 15.

woman (see also woman's)
acknowledged
Pul. 82–17 * have long acknowledged *w·* as
after
Pul. 14– 9 flood, after the *w·*,— *Rev.* 12: 15.
as a chattel
Pul. 82–13 * they treated *w·* as a chattel,
at the sepulchre
My. 258– 9 To the *w·* at the sepulchre,
Babylonish
My. 125–29 The doom of the Babylonish *w·*,
    126–24 The Babylonish *w·* is fallen,
behind the
Mis. 373– 3 placing the serpent behind the *w·*
    373–10 out of his mouth, *behind* the *w·*,
born of a
Mis. 184– 8 The child born of a *w·*
Chr. 55–14 Man that is born of a *w·* — *Job.* 14: 1.
certain
Mis. 166–22 leaven that a certain *w·* hid
climbed
Pul. 9–13 a *w·* climbed with feet and hands
drunken
My. 125–30 This *w·*, "drunken with — *Rev.* 17: 6.
every
Mis. 232–22 Every man and every *w·*
good
My. 331–16 * the assailant of a good *w·* :
helped the
Pul. 14–11 earth helped the *w·*,— *Rev.* 12: 16.
in travail
Mis. 253–16 metaphors,— of the *w·* in travail,
man and
    (see **man**)
man meaning
My. 268–31 *man* meaning *w·* as well,
man or
    (see **man**)
man or a
'01. 13– 1 a man or a *w·*, a place or a thing,
married
Man. 111– 5 If the applicant is a married *w·*
new
Mis. 253– 6 I am not enough the new *w·*
Pul. 79– 3 * chapter sub-title
    81– 9 * chapter sub-title
    84– 2 * "the new *w·*" shall subdue the
    84– 8 * the new man with the new *w·*.
noble
My. 290– 9 beloved as this noble *w·*,
of the past
Pul. 81–10 * she is simply the *w·* of the past
of thirty
Pul. 32–21 * elastic bearing of a *w·* of thirty,
one
My. 239–15 as one man and one *w·*
    324–28 * one *w·* under the sun who could
or a man
My. 343– 8 will be a *w·* or a man.
or child
Mis. 336–26 a better man, *w·*, or child.
Rud. 2– 3 * corporeal man, *w·*, or child ;
persecuted the
Pul. 13–28 he persecuted the *w·* — *Rev.* 12: 13.
poor
Hea. 7–18 poor *w·* who dropped her mite
remarkable
Pul. 63–15 * made by a remarkable *w·*,
rich
Pul. 50– 1 * rich *w·* is using her money

woman
right of
No. 45–16 right of *w·* to fill the highest
sick
Ret. 40–11 sick *w·* rose from her bed,
suitable
Man. 100–27 a suitable *w·* shall be elected.
took
Mis. 171–23 *which a w· took,* — *Matt.* 13: 33.
    174–30 leaven which a *w·* took
true
Mis. 18–16 true man and true *w·*,
unworthy
My. 331–15 * hospitality to an unworthy *w·*
whole-souled
Mis. 224–32 *to* offend a whole-souled *w·*.
will help the
Pul. 14–22 the earth will help the *w·* ;
work of a
Pul. 55– 9 * should be the work of a *w·*
wroth with the
Hea. 10– 2 was wroth with the *w·*,

          ————

Mis. 100– 5 *w·*, "last at the cross,"
    142–28 If as a *w·* I may not
    175– 2 And *w·*, the spiritual idea,
    244– 2 builded up the *w·*." — *Gen.* 2: 21.
    374–31 an angel is a *w·* without
Man. 29–21 shall be a man and a *w·*,
Ret. 26–23 *W·* must give it birth.
Un. 45– 4 as Truth and "the *w·*" — *Gen.* 3: 15.
    51–13 *What say you of w·?*
    51–14 *W·* is the highest species of man,
Pul. 9–11 *W·*, true to her instinct,
    27–23 * *w·* spoken of in the Apocalypse,
    83– 8 * *W·* must not and will not
    83–27 * *w·* clothed with the sun, — *Rev.* 12: 1.
No. 45–13 *w·*, "last at the cross
    46–10 *W·* should not be ordered to the rear,
Po. 39–12 *W·* — will watch to cleanse from dross
My. 5– 3 supposed . . . *w·* to be the outcome of
    249–23 a man, rather than a *w·*,
    262–15 of God and not of a *w·*
    277–23 *w·* would be armed with power
    334–14 * *w·* whom he had in mind
    (see also **Eddy**)

womanhood
Mis. 16– 6 grows into the manhood or *w·*
    33–10 in the *w·* as well as in the manhood
    166– 8 infancy, manhood, and *w·*
Un. 42–28 manhood and *w·* go forth
Hea. 10– 7 fell before the *w·* of God,
My. 12–30 in the settings of manhood and *w·*.
    52– 7 * highest type of *w·*,
    330–10 * whose *w·* and Christianity are
    346–30 manhood and *w·* of God

woman's
Mis. 210–15 has faith in *w·* special adaptability
    220–30 would be according to the *w·* belief ;
    245–19 This is *w·* hour,
    275– 3 even *w·* trembling, clinging faith
    287–28 home, — which is *w·* world.
    388–13 poem
Un. 57–12 felt the influence of the *w·* thought ;
Pul. 48–26 * as is many another well-born *w·*.
    83– 1 * *w·* love and *w·* help
No. 45–19 This is *w.* hour,
'02. 3–23 *w·* thoughts . . . hallow the ring of state.
Po. page 21 poem
My. 258– 7 seems illuminated for *w·* hope

women (see also women's)
all
Un. 51–16 the generic term for all *w·* ;
American
Mis. 295– 1 certain references to American *w·*
    296– 8 work and career of American *w·*,
and children
Pul. 45– 1 * *w·*, and children lent a helping hand,
    64– 9 * Men, *w·*, and children contributed,
born of
My. 228–13 none greater had been born of *w·*,
committee of
Mis. 305– 1 * committee of *w·* representing each
devoted
My. 30–14 * devoted *w·* members,
leads
Mis. 295– 6 leads *w·* "along a gamut of isms
men and
    (see **men**)
men or
Un. 5– 1 no wise men or *w·* will rudely
myriad of
Pul. 80–24 * myriad of *w·* more thoughtful

women

noble
Mis. 296–11 same category with noble *w*·
remarkable
Pul. 70–11 * most remarkable *w*· in America.
unmarried
Man. 111– 8 unmarried *w*· must sign "Miss."

Mis. 245–18 conclusion . . . that *w*· have no rights
345–15 * fit only for *w*· and weak men ;"
Man. 110–14 *W*· must sign "Miss" or "Mrs."
Pul. 80– 4 * religious sentiment in *w*·
82–18 * *w*· had few lawful claims
Peo. 13–23 * "Christianity is fit only for *w*· and

women's

Pul. 80– 9 * emphatically the *w*· paradise,
'00. 3–24 *w*· names contained this divine
My. 83–11 * laces of the *w*· frocks,

won

Mis. 33– 5 they lost, and he *w*·, heaven.
85–11 is not *w*· in a moment ;
109–32 your superiority to a delusion is *w*·.
120–13 mighty victory is yet to be *w*·,
131–32 perils past and victories *w*·.
147– 6 victory *w*· for time and eternity
319–24 object to be *w*· affords ample
358–32 a higher spiritual unity is *w*·,
362–27 Truth is *w*· through Science or
388–15 *w*· from vice, by virtue's smile,
Ret. 3–11 *w*· distinction in 1814
9–26 * And *w*·, through clouds, to Him,
30– 4 they have *w*· fields of battle
No. 25– 3 Having *w*· through great tribulation
'01. 10–24 victory over self, . . . is *w*·
14– 4 Publican's wail *w*· his humble desire,
25– 7 whereby is *w*· the crown
29–21 mother worked and *w*· for them
35–13 O the Master's glory *w*· thus,
Po. 21– 2 *w*· from vice, by virtue's smile,
22–20 peace is *w*·, and lost is vice :
26–12 Thy purpose hath been *w*· !
My. 62– 2 * and *w*· the reward,
112–28 *w*· its way into the palaces of
114–13 holiness is not yet *w*·.
136–15 *w*· a suit at law
163– 4 *w*· the way and taught mankind
205– 7 Wisdom is *w*· through faith,
273–22 is *w*· only by the spiritual
309–10 my father *w*· the suit.
334–22 wail *w*· his humble desire,
343–19 it *w*· converts from the first.

wonder

Mis. 69–22 though the *w*· was,
225– 9 the seventh modern *w*·,
275–26 Chicago is the *w*· of the
321–26 the great *w*· of the world,
337– 8 *W*· in heaven and on earth,
Un. 37–10 reveal this *w*· of being.
42–18 No *w*· "people were — *Matt.* 7 : 28.
Pul. 7– 9 I *w*· whether, were our
40– 3 * I *w*· how the seasons come
66–23 * may reasonably excite *w*·
83–27 * a great *w*· in heaven, — *Rev.* 12 : 1.
No. 37–10 to regard this *w*· of glory,
'01. 31–14 no vague, fruitless, inquiring *w*·.
'02. 5–15 human question and *w*·.
18– 8 only to mock, *w*·, and perish.
My. 31–20 * no *w*· that the first sight
43–29 * The world looks with *w*·
49– 2 * What *w*· that when these
82–11 * it was a matter of *w*·
92–12 * hardly more than a day's *w*·.
123– 3 they have become a *w*· !
323–28 * I *w*· if you will remember

wondered

Mis. 178–16 * *w*· what sort of people
278–13 *w*· at the Scriptural declaration

Wonderful

Mis. 161– 7 called *W*·, *Counsellor*, — *Isa.* 9 : 6.
164–18 called *W*·, *Counsellor*, — *Isa.* 9 : 6.
321– 5 called *W*·, *Counsellor*, — *Isa.* 9 : 6.
Un. 39–13 Messiah, whose name is *W*·.

wonderful

Mis. 70–28 those *w*· demonstrations of
162– 4 such *w*· spiritual import
164–15 a *w*· manifestation of Truth
167–27 Is he *w*· ?
175–31 done many *w*· works?
204–25 brings with it *w*· foresight,
290–17 * produced a *w*· illumination,
372–11 * pictures in your *w*· book
375–11 * *w*· new book you have given
Un. 1–10 characterized as *w*·.
5–26 this *w*· part of Truth

wonderful

Un. 17–15 *w*· utterances of him who
Pul. 32–10 * *w*· tumult in the air
'00. 15– 8 *w*· passage over a tear-filled sea of
'02. 16–21 sublime patience, *w*· works,
Hea. 3–20 *w*· works of our Master
My. 60–13 * corner-stone of this *w*· temple
60–28 * in this *w*· consummation.
70–22 * nothing more *w*· than the
85–12 * *w*· woman is a world power.
95–29 * such a *w*· demonstration of
98– 4 * *w*· growth of less than a score of
98–30 * has been a *w*· achievement,
193– 9 for His *w*· works— *Psal.* 107 : 8.
323–18 * your *w*· life and sacrifice

wonderfully

Pan. 10–16 *w*· broadened and brightened
My. 92–27 * Its growth has been *w*· rapid,
307–25 At first my case improved *w*·
342–21 It is growing *w*·.

wondering

Mis. 275–12 little ones, *w*·, huddle together,

wonderment

Mis. 234–22 grave *w*· to profound thinkers.
My. v– 7 * general *w*· and frequent comment,

wonders

Mis. 101– 4 He alone knows these *w*· who is
331– 4 tosses earth's mass of *w*· into
Pul. 52– 1 * *W*· will never cease.
My. 57–28 * "*W*· will never cease.
205–10 * His *w*· to perform ;

wonder-worker

Ret. 76–20 constitute the Mind-healer a *w*·,

wondrous

Mis. 214–12 closed — to the senses — that *w*· life,
Ret. 15–11 I declared Thy *w*· works." — *Psal.* 71 : 17.
Po. 31–11 veils the leaflet's *w*· birth

Wonolancet Club

My. 174– 6 courtesy extended . . . by the *W*· *C*·

wont

Ret. 13–20 as I was *w*· to do,

woo

Mis. 155– 8 *w*· the weary wanderer to your door,
Ret. 17– 5 And *w*·, while I worship
Po. 62– 5 And *w*·, while I worship

wood

Mis. 346–15 an image graven on *w*· or stone
Peo. 2–18 form its Deity out of . . . *w*· or stone.
13– 1 worshippers of *w*· and stone
My. 172– 1 * The *w*· of the head of the gavel
172– 5 * The *w*· in the handle was grown

woodland

Mis. 390–13 Through *w*·, grove, and dell ;
396– 2 To scare my *w*· walk,
Po. 8– 8 nymph and naiad from *w*· bower;
41–13 green sunny slopes of the *w*·
53– 6 On vale and *w*· deep ;
55–14 Through *w*·, grove, and dell ;
58–14 To scare my *w*· walk,

Woodlawn Ave., 5020

Mis. 157–20 Chicago, — 5020 *W*· *A*·,

woods

Ret. 9–21 * whispering *w*·, where dying thunders
Pul. 48–12 * *w*· that skirt the valley

woodwork

Pul. 58–17 * Scarcely any *w*· is to be found.
My. 68–32 * pews and principal *w*· are of

Woodworth, Mayor

Mis. 251– 8 Mayor *W*·, has welcomed you

wooed

Po. 34–13 Has *w*· some mystic spot,
My. 90– 3 * *w*· by no eloquence of orator or

wooings

Mis. 390– 2 Whence are thy *w*·, gentle June?
Po. 15–12 Their *w*· are soft as the vision
55– 1 Whence are thy *w*·, gentle June?

wool

Mis. 398–19 White as *w*·, ere they depart,
Ret. 46–25 White as *w*·, ere they depart,
Pul. 17–24 White as *w*·, ere they depart
Po. 14–23 White as *w*·, ere they depart,

woolen

My. 310–10 * workman in a Tilton *w*· mill."

Woolson

(see **Howe and Woolson Halls**)

Woolson Hall

My. 80–24 * *W*· *H*·, and Chickering Hall,

Wooten, Sheriff
My. 328–18 * Sheriff *W·* issued licenses

Worcester
Mis. 68–24 *W·* defines it as "the philosophy of

Word

dispensing the
Mis. 172– 3 Dispensing the *W·* charitably,
divine
Mis. 192–19 practicability of the divine *W·*,
Pul. 73– 9 * meditated over His divine *W·*.
No. 29–17 than to the divine *W·*.
echoing the
My. 186–11 echoing the *W·* welling up
God's
'01. 31–26 used faithfully God's *W·*,
My. 352–22 hearers and the doers of God's *W·*.
His
Mis. 151–22 spoken of you in His *W·*.
159– 4 to elucidate His *W·*.
170– 9 having rightly read His *W·*,
My. 152–21 listen to His *W·* and serve no
immutable
Mis. 72–11 The immutable *W·* saith,
inspired
Man. 15– 4 the inspired *W·* of the Bible
My. 238–17 *morale* of the inspired *W·*
interpreting the
Mis. 364– 3 Interpreting the *W·* in the
is made flesh
Mis. 182–29 When the *W·* is made flesh,
Un. 39– 1 *W·*" is "made flesh"— *John 1 : 14.*
milk of the
Mis. 15–30 on the milk of the *W·*,
No. v–12 unadulterated milk of the *W·*,
must abide
Mis. 270–19 the *W·* must abide in us,
of God
Mis. 111–22 but the *W·* of God abideth.
163–11 explained the *W·* of God,
'01. 11–19 *W·* of God is a powerful preacher,
34–15 bereft of the *W·* of God.
My. 28–26 * when he preached the *W·* of God
of Truth
No. 22–13 meaning of the *W·* of Truth,
original
Mis. 188– 6 not the original *W·*,
power of the
Mis. 398–23 Felt ye the power of the *W·*?
Po. 75– 3 Felt ye the power of the *W·*?
practise the
My. 238–12 little power to practise the *W·*.
revealed
Mis. 315–30 to study His revealed *W·*,
signification of the
No. 12–24 spiritual signification of the *W·*
Spirit and
Ret. 76– 9 touched with the Spirit and *W·*
spirit and the
My. 246–21 concurrence of the spirit and the *W·*
spoken
Pul. 11– 4 *W·* spoken in this sacred temple
that is God
Mis. 363–25 *W·* that *is* God, Spirit, and Truth.
My. 184–28 Surely, the *W·* that is God must
this
Mis. 363–25 This *W·* corrects the philosopher,
My. 153–28 wedding of this *W·* to all human thought
Thy
Man. 41–24 may Thy *W·* enrich the affections of
unspoken
Mis. 302–17 *not* to leave the *W·* unspoken
was God
Mis. 29–11 the *W·* was God."— *John 1 : 1.*
Pan. 5– 4 "The *W·* was God ;"— *John 1 : 1.*
My. 117–19 the *W·* was God"— *John 1 : 1.*
was with God
Mis. 29–11 "the *W·* was with God,— *John 1 : 1.*
My. 117–18 the *W·* was with God,— *John 1 : 1.*

Mis. 61–21 According to the *W·*, man is the
116–22 doing, the *W·*— demonstrating Truth
169– 7 misinterpretation of the *W·*,
184– 6 The *W·* will be made flesh
No. 45–24 Let the *W·* have free course
Pan. 5– 5 made by Him,"— the *W·*.— *John 1 : 3.*
My. 117–18 "In the beginning was the *W·*,— *John 1 : 1.*
119–32 Christ, Truth, in the *W·*
125–26 the bride (*W·*) is adorned,
153–28 the *W·* and the wedding of this
197–21 hope set before us in the *W·*

word

and deed
Mis. 206–20 harmony in *w·* and deed,
Ret. 79–22 temperate in thought, *w·*, and deed.
My. 338–25 stands alone in *w·* and deed,

word

and deeds
My. 350–27 ripe in prayer, in *w·*, and deeds.
and in deed
My. 260–28 the Way, in *w·* and in deed,
and might
Mis. 100– 8 *w·* and might of Truth
and works
Man. 17–11 *w·* and works of our Master,
My. 46–12 *w·* and works of our Master,
awe-filled
No. 10– 2 I employ this awe-filled *w·*
Christian
'01. 12–10 *w·* Christian was anciently an
death
My. 235– 2 without using the *w·* death,
devil
No. 23–17 moral sense of the *w·* devil,
Hea. 6–27 *w· devil* comes from the Greek
each
Mis. 338–28 * Speak truly, and each *w·* of thine
equivalent
Rud. 1–13 In French the equivalent *w·* is
every
Un. 33–25 every *w·* may be— *Matt. 18 : 16.*
My. 78–30 * every *w·* of the exercises
fitly spoken
Mis. 346–23 "A *w·* fitly spoken is like— *Prov. 25 : 11.*
from the Directors
My. 20–22 * chapter sub-title
gave the
Mis. 153–11 "the Lord gave the *w·* :— *Psal. 68 : 11.*
God
Mis. 75–16 except where the *w· God* can be used
Peo. 2– 8 gives another letter to the *w· God*
My. 226– 3 substitute the *w·* God
"god"
Pan. 2–13 His uncapitalized *w·* "god"
God's
My. 47–25 * God's *w·* in the wilderness of
good
Hea. 3–15 derived from the *w· good.*
grandeur of the
Mis. 99–29 grandeur of the *w·*, the power of
her
My. 52–26 * interest of the world to hear her *w·*
His
Mis. 154–19 Abide in His *w·*, and it shall
Chr. 53–41 The Way, the Truth, the Life— His *w·*
My. 159–10 sent forth His *w·* to heal
his
Mis. 262–26 Having his *w·*, you have little need of
388–21 First at the tomb to hear his *w·* :
Po. 21–10 First at the tomb to hear his *w·* :
in defence
My. 264– 2 chapter sub-title
kind
Mis. 127–29 kind *w·* spoken, at the right moment,
Latin
Mis. 25–23 from the Latin *w·* meaning *all,*
Life
Ret. 59– 6 *w· Life* never means that which is
limits with a
My. 106–21 Mind calms and limits with a *w·*.
loud
Mis. 238–26 * unable to speak a loud *w·*,"
Ret. 16– 9 could not speak a loud *w·*,
Love
Pul. 26–22 * on a . . . is the *w·* "Love."
meaning of a
Un. 27– 2 meaning of a *w·* employed
milk of the
My. 17– 6 sincere milk of the *w·*,— *I Pet. 2 : 2.*
mother
Man. 65– 1 to drop the *w· mother*
my
'00. 14– 2 and has kept my *w·*,— *Rev. 3 : 8.*
no
Mis. 250– 9 No *w·* is more misconstrued ;
no idle
Pul. 67– 7 * This is no idle *w·*,
offend not in
My. 196–12 offend not in *w·*,— *Jas. 3 : 2.*
of God
Mis. 191– 1 handling the *w·* of God— *II Cor. 4 : 2.*
Pan. 6–12 contradicting the *w·* of God
'01. 16–15 handling the *w·* of God deceitfully.
My. 124– 2 handling the *w·* of God— *II Cor. 4 : 2.*
240–19 according to the *w·* of God.
of might
Mis. 388– 1 who gave that *w·* of might
'02. 20–10 who gave that *w·* of might
Po. 7– 1 who gave that *w·* of might
of mine
Mis. 322–16 presence, or *w·* of mine,

word

of Scripture
Un. 23– 9 agrees with the w· of Scripture,
of their testimony
Pul. 12–10 w· of their testimony ;— *Rev.* 12 : 11.
of the Lord
Pul. 7–23 w· of the Lord endureth— *I Pet.* 1 : 25.
of Truth
Mis. 100–17 to grasp the w· of Truth,
334–16 without one w· of Truth
of truth
My. 132–16 with the w· of truth." — *Jas.* 1 : 18.
one
Pul. 53–10 * contained in the one w· — *faith.*
Po. 27– 5 One w·, receding year,
My. 178–26 not one w· in the book was
258–10 one w·, "Mary," — *John* 20 : 16.
or work
Man. 54–20 either by w· or work,
"pantheism"
Pan. 2–10 w· "pantheism" is derived from
2–12 English w· "pantheism"
Person
'01. 5– 2 defined strictly by the w· Person,
person
Rud. 1–11 The w· *person* affords a large
personal
Rud. 1–16 Blackstone applies the w· *personal*
personality
Ret. 74– 3 meaning of the w· *personality,*
philosophical
Un. 27– 8 philosphical w·, signifying
popularity
'01. 26–16 shall the w· popularity be
Principle
My. 225–30 The w· Principle, when referring
reflection
Mis. 23–25 means by the w· *reflection.*
reiterates the
Mis. 25–20 as it reiterates the w·,
Science
Mis. 193–20 supplying the w· Science to
science
My. 307– 4 w· science was not used at all,
send out
Pul. 52– 2 * treasurer has to send out w·
sense of the
Un. 8–11 in our sense of the w·.
No. 32– 6 popular sense of the w·,
"son"
Mis. 180–26 the w· "son" is defined
Soul
Mis. 75–17 The w· *Soul* may sometimes
soul
Un. 30– 3 uses the w· *soul* for *sense.*
spoken
Mis. 316–16 w· spoken at this date.
thanks
Mis. 160– 3 in uttering the w· *thanks,*
that
Mis. 303–11 the fullest sense of that w· ;
388– 1 who gave that w· of might
Pul. 53–15 * "That w·, more than any other,
Rud. 2– 8 not a *person,* as that w· is used
'02. 20–10 who gave that w· of might
Po. 7– 1 who gave that w· of might
My. 307–10 After this I noticed he used that w·
this
Mis. 76–21 whenever this w· means the so-called
301–17 without this w· of warning in public,
Un. 51–15 this w· is the generic term for all
My. 226– 2 using this w· incorrectly,
thought or
Mis. 387–15 By thought or w· unkind,
Po. 6–10 By thought or w· unkind,
through the
Mis. 154–18 Through the w· that is spoken
through their
Mis. 29– 9 through their w·." — *John* 17 : 20.
My. 190–29 through their w·." — *John* 17 : 20.
Thy
Mis. 208–23 now have I kept Thy w·." — *Psal.* 119 : 67.
to the wise
Mis. 319–17 chapter sub-title
My. 139–16 chapter sub-title
223–26 chapter sub-title
263– 5 A w· to the wise is sufficient.
unspoken
No. 2–16 than the unspoken w·.
usage of the
My. 226– 4 an intelligent usage of the w·
use of the
My. 302–17 use of the w· spread like wildfire.
use the
Pul. 55–21 * if we may use the w·

word

was conveyed
My. 77–26 * W· was conveyed to them that
written
Mis. 316–15 have profited . . . from the written w·,

———

Mis. 193–20 a w· which the people are now
248–10 w· synonymous with devil.
249–28 What a w· ! I am in awe before it.
250–19 cast aside the w· as a sham
301–14 require only a w· to be wise ;
Ret. 25– 9 in a w·, C. S.
38–22 Not a w· had passed between us,
Pul. 35– 4 in a *w·* — C. S."
Rud. 2– 5 the w· stands for one of the three
Hea. 16–16 A w· about the five personal senses,
My. 6–21 w· which proceedeth out of the
57–30 * Treasurer has sent out w· that
235–30 commemorated in deed or in w·

words

added
My. 318– 3 where Mr. Wiggin added w·,
adopt the
Mis. 215–28 nor adopt the w·, that Jesus used
and actions
Mis. 220–10 sick man's thoughts, w·, and actions,
and classification
My. 224–18 thoughts, w·, and classification of
and the works
My. 148–30 w· and the works of our great Master.
and works
Mis. 21–11 all his w· and works.
120–30 immortality of his w· and works.
Ret. 44– 1 commemorate the w· and works
'02. 11–30 very basis of his w· and works.
My. 349–18 his w· and works illustrate
applicable
My. 19–30 These are applicable w· :
are inadequate
My. 197–10 W· are inadequate to express
are not vain
My. 128– 1 w· are not vain when the
behind
Mis. 160– 5 a mother's love behind w·
beyond
My. 63–22 * of awe and of reverence beyond w·,
combination of
'02. 16– 7 use of that combination of w·,
David's
Ret. 15– 7 I could say in David's w·,
English
Un. 27– 3 two English w·, often used as if
equivalent
Mis. 67–27 by equivalent w· in another,
exact
My. 322–30 * The exact w· I do not recall,
few
Mis. 77– 8 in those few w· of the apostle.
112–19 My few w· touched him ;
133– 4 to build a sentence of so few w·
137– 8 a few w· aside to your teacher.
'01. 32–19 explain in a few w· a good man.
My. 39–20 * a few w· of reminder and prophecy.
289–25 send a few w· of condolence,
360–13 settle this . . . amicably by a few w·,
following
Mis. 35–10 following w· of her husband,
My. 219–28 in the following w· :
for the wise
My. 250– 1 chapter sub-title
further
My. 42–11 * further w· of mine are unnecessary.
good
Mis. 233–18 Substituting good w· for a good life,
'01. 2–10 or to substitute good w· for
Greek
Pan. 2–11 two Greek w· meaning "all" and "god."
hard
Man. 41– 8 but without hard w·.
her
Pul. 82– 4 * her w· are smiles
her own
My. 334–16 * to quote her own w·.
his
Mis. 21–11 makes practical all his w·
29– 3 Do you believe his w· ?
99–20 the immortality of his w·.
99–24 never bear into oblivion his w·.
120–30 the immortality of his w·
121– 1 his w· can never pass away :
163–14 His w· were articulated in
192–17 his w· reveal the great Principle
193– 6 His w· are unmistakable,
195–18 these are his w· :
216– 1 in your application of his w·

words

his
Mis. 245– 3   but we have his *w*·,
344–24   His *w*·, living in our hearts,
'01. 26– 6   supported it by his *w*·
'02. 8–16   his *w*· and his deeds,
11–30   basis of his *w*· and works.
My. 246–27   the wisdom of his *w*·,
349–18   his *w*· and works illustrate

his own
My. 108–29   will close with his own *w*· :

idle
Mis. 357– 2   no time for idle *w*·,

immortal
Mis. 100– 2   His immortal *w*· were articulated
My. 146–17   Yet his immortal *w*·
277–20   the immortal *w*· and deeds

in other
Mis. 14–27   in other *w*·, a lie
36–16   in other *w*·, the nature and
36–24   [in other *w*·, mortal mind]
67– 5   in other *w*·, thou shalt not
112– 1   in other *w*·, the one evil
118– 2   in other *w*·, the material senses,
186–17   in other *w*·, the spiritual Principle
194–31   in other *w*·, understand God
197–20   in other *w*·, to
222–10   in other *w*·, a moral idiot.
375–22   * In other *w*·, the art is perfect.
Un. 33–10   In other *w*· : matter testifies of
Pan. 5–21   in other *w*·, we should not
'00. 14–23   in other *w*·, he that toiled
'02. 9– 6   in other *w*·, Let the world,
My. 179– 9   In other *w*·, soul enters
239–24   in other *w*·, a kind of man

Jesus'
Mis. 133–29   to the truth of Jesus' *w*·.
149–30   in the faith of Jesus' *w*· :
194–20   text explains Jesus' *w*·,
'01. 13–13   and we verify Jesus' *w*·,
My. 58–24   * verifying Jesus' *w*·,
300–18   the summit of Jesus' *w*·,

Jesus' own
Mis. 20– 3   aroma of Jesus' own *w*·,

key
Pul. 47–19   * which are the key *w*·

largest
No. 10– 6   largest *w*· in the vocabulary

little need of
Mis. 262–27   little need of *w*· of approval

loving
Mis. 292–22   by loving *w*· and deeds.

Master's
Un. 44– 4   only repeat the Master's *w*· :

may belie desire
No. 40–10   *W*· may belie desire,

mere
My. 78–27   * No mere *w*· can convey the

more than
Mis. 110–11   your example, more than *w*·,
126–21   Works, more than *w*·, should
250–22   affection is more than *w*· :
Hea. 2– 2   works more than *w*· ;
15–28   and works more than *w*·,
My. 58–16   * speaks more than *w*· can

Mother's Room
Pul. 42–17   * the *w*·, "Mother's Room,"

my
Mis. 99–22   my *w*· shall not — *Matt.* 24 : 35.
111–17   my *w*· shall not — *Matt.* 24 : 35.
163–19   my *w*· shall not — *Matt.* 24 : 35.
Ret. 92– 9   my *w*· abide in you, — *John* 15 : 7.
Un. 9– 7   my *w*· would not have been spoken.
My. 150–23   my *w*· abide in you, — *John* 15 : 7.

no
Mis. 375–27   * no *w*· can express,
Po. 8–18   love, that no *w*· could speak

of cheer
My. 202–21   thank you for the *w*· of cheer

of Christ
My. 105– 1   more than the *w*· of Christ,

of commendation
Mis. 313– 1   chapter sub-title

of David
Mis. 196–23   and, in the *w*· of David,

of encouragement
My. 62–24   * and *w*· of encouragement

of God
Mis. 317–31   speaketh the *w*· of God : — *John* 3 : 34.

of Jesus
Mis. 37–14   meaning of those *w*· of Jesus,
198–10   with the *w*· of Jesus ;
My. 253–15   and these *w*· of Jesus :

of Life
Mis. 337–27   taught . . . the *w*· of Life.

words

of Mary Baker Eddy
My. 66–23   * *w*· of Mary Baker Eddy will

of Mrs. Hemans
My. 185–26   with the *w*· of Mrs. Hemans :

of my Master
Mis. 180–12   in the *w*· of my Master,

of my uncle
My. 60– 6   * remember the *w*· of my uncle,

of our Master
Mis. 83–17   In the *w*· of our Master,
196–14   hence the *w*· of our Master :
317–22   These *w*· of our Master explain
Ret. 67–23   In the *w*· of our Master,
No. 14–18   Hear the *w*· of our Master :
'00. 5– 6   Here note the *w*· of our Master
My. 147–27   in the *w*· of our Master

of Paul
Hea. 18– 3   In the *w*· of Paul,

of rejoicing
My. 63–17   * with *w*· of rejoicing ;

of Samuel
Ret. 9–15   in the *w*· of Samuel,

of Solomon
Mis. 281–29   remember the *w*· of Solomon.

of St. John
Mis. 205–11   in the *w*· of St. John,
'00. 15–22   In the *w*· of St. John,

of St. Paul
Mis. 120– 6   In the *w*· of St. Paul,
Pan. 13–22   in the *w*· of St. Paul,
'00. 6– 4   In the *w*· of St. Paul :
My. 151–15   And in the *w*· of St. Paul,
153–20   in the *w*· of St. Paul,
187–11   In the *w*· of St. Paul :
202– 7   In the *w*· of St. Paul :
258–13   in the *w*· of St. Paul :
285–19   In the *w*· of St. Paul,

of strange import
Mis. 275–13   *w*· of strange import.

of the Book
My. 183–20   deaf hear the *w*· of the Book,

of the judge
Pul. 46– 6   * *w*· of the judge speak to the point,

of the Master
Un. 43–15   *w*· of the Master in support of this
My. 114– 1   In the *w*· of the Master,

of the prophet
Mis. 148–28   in the *w*· of the prophet Isaiah :
308–15   In the *w*· of the prophet,
Pul. 20–18   In the *w*· of the prophet :

of the Psalmist
Mis. 153–11   In the *w*· of the Psalmist,
Ret. 14–25   in the *w*· of the Psalmist :
Pul. 10– 5   in the *w*· of the Psalmist,

of the Scripture
My. 156– 3   to reply in *w*· of the Scripture :
196– 7   in these *w*· of the Scripture,

of Truth
Mis. 99–15   take not back the *w*· of Truth.
320–22   *w*· of Truth and Life.

of Wendell Phillips
Mis. 245–28   in the *w*· of Wendell Phillips,

our
'02. 4–12   that our works be as worthy as our *w*·.
Hea. 19–25   making our *w*· golden rays

plain
Ret. 90–12   and gave in plain *w*·,

power of
Pul. 26– 7   * beyond the power of *w*· to depict.

redemptive
Mis. 331–16   redemptive *w*· from a mother's lips

remarkable
No. 36–10   remarkable *w*·, as wholly opposed to

sacred
Man. 60–17   sacred *w*· of our beloved Master,

sense of
Mis. 67–26   expresses the sense of *w*·

some
My. 306–31   Some *w*· in these quotations

Soul-full
My. 201–10   Your Soul-full *w*· and song

St. Paul's
Mis. 298– 3   St. Paul's *w*· take in the situation :

such
Mis. 134– 5   To reiterate such *w*· of apology as

suggestive
My. 50–22   * these simple but suggestive *w*·,

symbolic
Ret. 42– 6   symbolic *w*· on his office sign.

their
Ret. 76– 1   an author's ideas and their *w*·.
'00. 13– 6   their *w*· were brave and their
My. 125–15   History will record their *w*·,

words

these
Mis. 66– 6	these *w·* of the New Testament :
83–23	"These *w·* spake Jesus, — *John* 17 : 1.
132–27	I read in your article these *w·* :
298–12	These *w·* of St. Matthew
317–22	These *w·* of our Master explain
368–20	portrayed in these *w·* of the apostle,
Ret. 22– 9	summarized . . . in these *w·* :
72– 8	portrays the result . . . in these *w·* :
Pan. 13– 6	according to Christ, in these *w·* :
'02. 5–18	in these *w·* : "God is Love." — *I John* 4 : 8.
7–13	Use these *w·* to define God,
My. 161– 9	Hence these *w·* of Christ Jesus :
196– 7	in these *w·* of the Scripture,
206–18	May these *w·* of the Scriptures comfort
253–15	and these *w·* of Jesus :
360–15	subscribe these *w·* of love :

those
Mis. 100– 7	infinite meaning of those *w·*.
132–30	those *w·* inspire me with
169–32	those *w·* are salvation
188–32	beheld the meaning of those *w·*
195–11	the validity of those *w·*
No. 13–10	those *w·* were originally uttered,
My. 19–25	Those *w·* of our holy Way-shower,
159– 4	those *w·* of our loved Lord,
270–18	Those *w·* of our dear,

three
No. 30–11	God's law is in three *w·*,
My. 253–23	wisdom in three *w·* :

thy
My. 196–14	"By thy *w·* thou shalt — *Matt.* 12 : 37.

too deep for
Mis. 142–21	chords of feeling too deep for *w·*.

two
Mis. 263– 5	These two *w·* in Scripture
No. 17–21	could grasp these two *w·*
My. 257–26	Christmas gift, two *w·* enwrapped,

use the
Mis. 376– 3	* I use the *w·* most authentic

web of
Mis. 377– 3	to weave a web of *w·*

works and
Ret. 78–13	such works and *w·* becloud

your
My. 59–15	* your *w·* explaining the Scriptures,

Mis. 86–11	*Nothing* and *something* are *w·* which
151– 2	In the *w·* of the loving disciple,
161–14	prophet whose *w·* we have chosen
192–13	*w·* of him who spake divinely,
260–26	*W·* are not always the auxiliaries of
262–10	however simple the *w·*,
262–22	more grateful than *w·* can express,
338– 5	proved to myself, not by "*w·*,"
341– 6	then put thought into *w·*,
341– 7	and *w·* into deeds ;
373–31	presents not *w·* alone, but works,
Un. 43–16	*w·* which can never "pass — *Matt.* 5 : 18.
Pul. 5– 3	in the *w·* I use,
42–23	* in letters of red were the *w·*
Pan. 4–21	in the *w·* of the Hebrew singer,
'01. 34–28	In the *w·* of the Hebrew writers :
'02. 7–12	prefix to the *w·* potence, presence,
My. vii–10	* Deeds, not *w·*, are the sound test
29– 6	* *w·* of the Lord's Prayer !
32–13	* *W·* by the Rev. Mary Baker Eddy.
32–24	* *w·* by the Rev. Mary Baker Eddy,
108–26	*w·* of the New York press
172–15	In the *w·* of our great Master,
197–15	*w·* are but the substitutes for
270–15	*w·* of those who say that she
290–25	*w·* of him who suffered and
306–29	purporting to be Dr. Quimby's own *w·*,
307– 1	read like *w·* that I said to him,
323–18	* to tell you in *w·* all that your
332– 5	* *w·* are indeed but a meagre tribute

wore
Pul. 42–15	* *w·* a white satin badge
My. 83– 6	* *w·* tiny white, unmarked buttons,

work (noun)

absorbed in the
Pul. 72–11	* much absorbed in the *w·*

accumulating
Ret. 44–13	because of accumulating *w·*
My. 276– 7	accumulating *w·* requires it,

actual
My. 86–14	* the actual *w·* was completed,

and career
Mis. 296– 7	unfamiliarity with the *w·* and career

applied for
Mis. 353–15	man who applied for *w·*,

work (noun)

at
Mis. 212–24	at *w·* in a wrong direction,
230–10	and mere motion when at *w·*,
257–12	so-called force, or law, at *w·*
262–14	students, who are at *w·*
276–27	or at *w·* erroneously,
284– 7	the humanitarian at *w·*
285–18	is still at *w·*, deep down in
334–19	evil at *w·* in the name of good,
Pul. 33–17	* at *w·* in a field one day
'01. 20–17	individual knew what was at *w·*
Po. 67– 5	And thought be at *w·* with
My. 145–14	He remained at *w·*,
200–21	Pale, sinful sense, at *w·*

begin with
My. 203– 9	begin wth *w·* and never stop

best
Mis. 273–26	I cannot do my best *w·* for
My. 108–23	designated as his best *w·*,
108–25	best *w·* of a Christian Scientist.

bless the
My. 197–28	God will bless the *w·* of your

charity
Rud. 14–21	doing charity *w·* besides.

chosen
Ret. 42–13	untiring in his chosen *w·*.

Christian
Mis. 5– 7	to this Christian *w·*.
242–16	department of Christian *w·*,

Christian Science
Ret. 88–18	another part of C. S. *w·*,
Rud. 13–26	to give all their time to C. S. *w·*,

church
Pul. 44–19	* chapter sub-title
My. 76–17	* in the support of their church *w·*,
84– 1	* necessary expense of church *w·*,
352– 7	* privileges . . . in this church *w·*.

College
Mis. 274– 8	outside of College *w·*,

commenced
Ret. 15–16	I accepted . . . and commenced *w·*.

commencing
My. 12–12	* and the date of commencing *w·*,

doing the
Mis. 266–11	doing the *w·* that nobody else can
'00. 8–19	when doing the *w·* that belongs to

done
My. 345–21	"The *w·* done by the surgeon is

earnest
My. 61–32	* earnest *w·* of our noble Board

editorial
Pul. 31–16	* resulting from editorial *w·*

extraordinary
My. vi–10	* full credit for this extraordinary *w·*.

field of
My. 216–19	indicates another field of *w·*

God's
Mis. 317– 3	if you are doing God's *w·*.
My. 231–13	in order to help God's *w·*

good
'00. 3–12	love a good *w·* or good workers
My. 156– 9	to every good *w·*," — *II Cor.* 9 : 8.

gospel
Mis. 318–15	gospel *w·* of teaching C. S.,
Ret. 47–21	gospel *w·* of teaching C. S.,

gratuitous
Rud. 14–12	in order to do gratuitous *w·*.

great
Mis. 7–25	great *w·* already has been done,
177–17	great *w·* of establishing the truth,
Ret. 55– 1	true sense of the great *w·*
Pul. 85– 6	* gratitude to her for her great *w·*,
'01. 11– 3	because of Jesus' great *w·* on earth,
My. 22–12	* to complete this great *w·*,
321– 5	* accomplished this great *w·*.

greater
Mis. 7–25	greater *w·* yet remains to be done.

greatest
Mis. 358–25	greatest *w·* of the ages,

growth of the
Mis. 6–14	rapid growth of the *w·* shows.

hard
Mis. 230–15	have become such by hard *w·* ;
234–14	to steal from others and avoid hard *w·* ;
237–27	hero who did the hard *w·*,

healing
Man. 49– 2	endeavor to monopolize the healing *w·*

her
Mis. 62–21	her *w·* entitled "Mind-cure on a
Pul. 31– 5	* C. S., as they term her *w·*
59–16	* were read from . . . her *w·*
My. 52–10	* to sustain her in her *w·*.
52–23	* if only through her *w·*

His
Un. 14– 3	do His *w·* over again,

work (noun)

his
Mis.	92– 8	His w· is to replenish thought,
	212– 6	Jesus did his w·, and
	221–23	divorces his w· from Science.
	238–13	or his w· is utilized
Ret.	38–13	resumed his w· at the same time,
	86–20	carry his burden and do his w·,
Pul.	72–28	* Christ has told us to do his w·,
No.	41– 9	repeat his w· to the best advantage
'00.	3–28	improved on his w· of creation,
My.	291– 7	His w· began with heavy strokes,

his own
Mis.	284– 1	for each one to do his own w·

holds back
My.	84– 6	* holds back w· that would otherwise

holy
Man.	49– 5	privileged to enter into this holy w·,

ill-done
Mis.	393– 9	W· ill-done within the misty
Po.	51–14	W· ill-done within the misty

immortal
Mis.	237–27	immortal w·, of loosing the fetters

important
My.	241– 2	* to perform this important w·.

inspected the
My.	24–25	* have recently inspected the w·,
	145– 8	I inspected the w· every day,

is done
Ret.	33–13	the better the w· is done ;
Po.	27–20	Thy w· is done, and well :

its
Mis.	297– 7	bases its w· on ethical conditions
	308–21	little messenger has done its w·,
	359– 3	when it has done its w·,
My.	50–27	* few saw the grandeur of its w·
	245– 7	Law and order characterize its w·

James H. Wiggin's
My.	322–11	* Rev. James H. Wiggin's w·

limner's
Mis.	393– 6	Paints the limner's w·, I ween,
Po.	51–11	Paints the limner's w·, I ween,

literary
My.	320– 1	had done some literary w· for you

little
No.	9–18	first edition of this little w·

mental
Mis.	350–10	no advice given, no mental w·,

monstrous
Mis.	122– 9	such a monstrous w·?

mosaic
Pul.	25– 6	* marble in mosaic w·,
	26– 9	* mosaic w·, with richly carved

most derided
No.	41– 7	Is it the w· most derided

most important
Ret.	37– 1	most important w·, S. and H.,

Mrs. Eddy's
Pul.	23– 6	* MRS. EDDY'S W· AND HER INFLUENCE

my
Mis.	29–19	first publication of my w·,
	300–26	from my w· S. and H.,
Ret.	27– 3	so laid the foundation of my w·
	38– 3	could not go on with my w·.
	38– 4	and yet he stopped my w·.
Pul.	7– 1	speaking of my w·, said :
Rud.	7– 6	set forth in my w· S. and H.
No.	33– 5	If the Bible and my w· S. and H.
'01.	24–22	published my w· S. and H.,
My.	202–23	My w· is reflected light,
	275–19	Either my w·, the demands upon

needful
No.	1– 3	is a most needful w· ;

noble
Ret.	49–23	for her great and noble w·,

noblest
Mis.	294– 1	The noblest w· of God is man
Ret.	77– 3	* honest man's the noblest w· of God ;"
	77– 5	* honest God's the noblest w· of man."

of a Reader
Man.	55–12	not to be fit for the w· of a Reader

of art
Mis.	372–17	* are truly a w· of art,

of a woman
Pul.	55– 9	* That it should be the w· of a woman

of Christianity
My.	30–25	* for the w· of Christianity.

of Christian Science
Man.	82–19	engaged in the w· of C. S.,
Pul.	44– 9	* blessed onward w· of C. S.

of creation
'00.	3–28	improved on his w· of creation,

of healing
Mis.	7– 7	is necessary in this w· of healing.
	37–27	leaving to . . . the w· of healing ;
Ret.	54–22	w· of healing, in the Science of Mind,

work (noun)

of her life
Pul.	31–11	* familiarity with the w· of her life

of His hand
Mis.	152–10	o'er the w· of His hand.

of its erection
My.	23–28	* in the w· of its erection.

of Jesus
No.	37–19	whereby the w· of Jesus would

of moments
Mis.	68– 2	is not the w· of moments ;

of Mrs. Eddy
Pul.	28– 1	* typical of the w· of Mrs. Eddy.

of the church
My.	51–25	* very early w· of the church,

of the devil
My.	60– 9	* it is the w· of the devil."

of the Lord
Chr.	55–12	w· of the Lord, — *Isa.* 5 : 12.

on this doctrine
Mis.	382– 5	my first w· on this doctrine,

on this subject
Ret.	35– 9	before a w· on this subject could be

our
Mis.	180–18	Let us do our w· ;
	215–14	Principle and object of our w·,
	216– 5	we must first have done our w·,
Hea.	5–23	to do our w· for us,

pioneer
Ret.	50–30	in the beginning of pioneer w·.
My.	148– 1	to do your pioneer w· in this city.

plaster
My.	68–26	* plaster w· for the great arches

present
Mis.	358–28	do their present w·, awaiting,

previous
Un.	14– 9	improve upon His own previous w·,

progress of the
My.	24–18	* progress of the w· on the extension

regarding the
My.	319–13	* her statement regarding the w·

relief
Pul.	26– 5	* richly panelled in relief w·.

religious
Pul.	36– 6	* foundation of her religious w·
	68– 9	* for the interests of her religious w·

result of the
My.	327–14	* This is the result of the w· done

scientific
Pul.	2–27	do this Christianly scientific w·

stupendous
Mis.	380–12	to begin this stupendous w· at once,

such a
My.	59–30	* has accomplished such a w· or

that
Mis.	35–26	the author of that w·,
	62–23	In that w· the author grapples with
My.	319–15	* what he himself thought of that w·

their
Mis.	120– 6	or repeat their w· in tears.
My.	66–20	* hurrying on with their w·
	177–23	direct their w· in truth, — *Isa.* 61 : 8.

their own
Mis.	317– 6	Scientists to do their own w· ;
Ret.	85– 2	doing their own w· well.
Un.	13– 5	doing their own w· in obedience to

this
Mis.	xi–27	In compiling this w·, I have
	4–18	periodical devoted to this w·
	5– 1	This w· well done will elevate
	7– 7	in this w· of healing.
	57– 8	This w· had been done ;
	378– 1	while the author of this w· was
Pul.	60– 7	* before coming into this w·,
My.	v–17	* this w· "without money — *Isa.* 55 : 1.
	234–10	give me the holidays for this w·
	298–11	to publish and circulate this w·.

three days'
My.	214–11	three days' w· in the sepulchre

well done
My.	134–11	good achievements and w· well done

word or
Man.	54–20	either by word or w·,

would be accomplished
My.	61–15	* that the w· would be accomplished

years of
My.	22–20	* In these years of w· she has

your
Mis.	111– 3	your w·, well done, would dignify
My.	59– 1	* grandeur and magnitude of your w·
	194– 5	The letter of your w· dies,
	248– 3	satisfied with your w· :
	320– 6	* converse about you and your w·,
	320–26	* detail regarding your w·,
	321– 3	* connected with your w·,
	321–32	* their knowledge of your w·.

work (noun)
your
My.	322–30	* of you and your *w·*.
	324– 2	* about you and your *w·*,

Mis.	5– 3	devote our best energies to the *w·*.
	15–13	is not the *w·* of a moment.
	224–15	that human life is the *w·*, the play,
	273– 7	where none other can do the *w·*.
	273–31	The *w·* is more than one person can
	274– 6	*w·* that needs to be done,
Ret.	82–18	ample to supply many . . . with *w·*.
Pul.	29– 6	* of whose *w·* I shall venture to
	36– 3	* The *w·* in the Metaphysical College
	49–26	* the will of the woman set at *w·*,
Rud.	16–19	a *w·* which I published in 1875
'01.	17–20	a difficult stage of the *w·*,
My.	v–24	* an unparalleled record for a *w·* of
	6–24	above the *w·* of men's hands,
	12– 2	* *w·* should be commenced as soon as
	12– 6	* those having the *w·* in charge
	14–28	* rapidity with which the *w·*
	16–15	* have the *w·* directly in charge,
	42–26	* *w·* that has been inaugurated by
	46–14	* *w·* of true Christian Scientists.
	47–10	* After a *w·* has been established,
	47–13	* labored unceasingly for the *w·*
	61–21	* One feature about the *w·*
	61–22	* admit that the *w·* could be done,
	72–26	* paid in before the *w·* was
	94–28	above the *w·* of men's hands,
	105–25	*w·* describing my system of healing.
	147–26	I have a *w·* to do
	166–21	would be more irksome than *w·*.
	216–20	*w·* by which you can do much good
	242–18, 19	publication committee *w·*, reading-room *w·*,
	289– 1	All education is *w·*.

work (verb)
Mis.	10– 6	"*w·* together for good — *Rom.* 8 : 28.
	22– 9	must *w·* for the discovery of
	39–29	when claiming to *w·* with God
	52–24	should attempt to *w·* out a rule
	52–27	*w·* out the previous example,
	52–29	have the sum of being to *w·* out,
	52–30	They must *w·* out of this dream
	85–20	and *w·* out his own salvation.
	116–28	never unready to *w·* for God,
	117–16	reciprocate kindness and *w·* wisely,
	118–17	being willing to *w·* alone with God
	137–21	to *w·* out individually and alone,
	138– 2	sustain themselves and *w·* for others.
	138– 9	For students to *w·* together
	175–28	to *w·* by means of both animal
	233–25	unwilling to *w·* hard enough
	237–21	can only *w·* out its own destruction ;
	271–10	take our magazine, *w·* for it,
	273– 5	to *w·* in other directions,
	283–24	*w·* out his own problem
	288– 4	*w·* out the greatest good to the
	303– 1	to *w·* for the race ;
	333–18	to *w·* out the problem of Mind,
	340– 6	the time to *w·*, is *now.*
	340–21	they *w·* on to the achievement of
	353–22	makes the machinery *w·* rightly ;
	389– 3	the right to *w·* and pray,
Ret.	38–10	Accordingly, I set to *w·*,
	49–10	adapted to *w·* this result ;
	55– 2	and *w·* conscientiously.
	58– 3	with which to *w·* out the problem
	88–21	to *w·* in other vineyards
Un.	5– 5	*w·* gradually and gently up
Pul.	69–13	* they can *w·* a cure.
	69–22	* to *w·* a cure the practitioner must
No.	2– 7	leaves you to *w·* against that
	8–12	*w·* out his own salvation,
	8–21	*w·*, watch, and pray for
'00.	2–7, 8	"*W·* — *w·* — *w·* — watch and pray."
	2–22	leave . . . to *w·* for me."
	2–30	I *w·* hard enough to be so."
	11–10	*w·* together for good — *Rom.* 8 : 28.
Hea.	5–21	*w·* out our own salvation,
	8–25	*w·* to become Christians
	13– 2	taking . . . we should *w·* at opposites
	19–22	But let us *w·* more earnestly
Peo.	9–13	*w·* out our own salvation,
Po.	21–17	the right to *w·* and pray,
	39–15	*W·* for our glorious cause !
My.	61–25	* be willing to let God *w·*.
	63–15	* to *w·* out the purposes of
	143–25	*w·* together for good — *Rom.* 8 : 28.
	184– 6	wait upon Him and work righteousness.
	188–25	As you *w·*, the ages win ;
	193– 5	to watch and *w·* for all,
	195– 8	to love more, to *w·* more,
	196–26	*W·* and pray for it.
	196–28	*w·* for their health and holiness.

work (verb)
My.	216–23	*w·* in your own several localties,
	252–13	not *w·* in the sunshine and run away
	252–14	*w·* midst clouds of wrong,
	259–16	to think and *w·* for others.
	291–29	*w·* for their own country,
	300– 4	"*W·* out your own salvation — *Phil.* 2 : 12.

worked
Mis.	365–17	*w·* out a moral result ;
Ret.	52– 8	I have *w·* to provide a
Pul.	33–20	* walked with him as he *w·*,
	44– 3	* you have *w·*, toiled, prayed
	51–12	* *w·* in the mine of knowledge
'01.	29–21	*w·* and won for them
My.	145–17	I have *w·* even harder
	195– 6	new problems to be *w·* out

worker (*see also* **worker's**)
Mis.	147–24	the pious *w·*, the public-spirited
Ret.	52– 9	*w·* in this vineyard of Truth.
	82–19	the prosperity of each *w·* ;
'00.	2–10	the right thinker and *w·*,
	2–25	intermediate *w·* works at times.
	3– 4	The right thinker and *w·*
	3–14	the best thinker and *w·*
	3–19	the right thinker and *w·*,
My.	225– 3	*w·* in the spirit of Truth

worker's
'00.	3– 9	If the right thinker and *w·* servitude

workers
Mis.	324– 1	converse with the watchers and *w·*
Ret.	82–21	ease and welfare of each *w·*
	87– 9	settled and systematic *w·*,
Pul.	8–23	youthful *w·* were called "Busy Bees."
'00.	2–21	are my busiest *w·* ;
	2–23	doom of such *w·* will come,
	3–12	love a good work or good *w·*
	3–12	are themselves *w·* who appreciate a
	9–21	challenge the thinkers, . . . and *w·*
My.	40– 9	* subsidence of criticism among *w·*.
	50– 7	* little band of prayerful *w·*.
	161–10	all ye *w·* of iniquity. — *Luke* 13 : 27.

worketh
Mis.	118–26	divine Principle *w·* with you,
	137–26	that *w·* or maketh a lie.
	174–18	nothing that maketh or *w·* a lie.
	190–22	impersonal evil, or whatever *w·* ill.
	283–25	God *w·* with him,
	366–14	nothing that *w·* or maketh a lie
No.	15–26	"*w·* or maketh a lie" — *see Rev.* 21 : 27.
'00.	10– 2	All that *w·* good is
'01.	9–30	*w·* well and healeth quickly,
	10–25	for God *w·* with us,
	19– 4	He *w·* with them to save sinners.
	28–22	all that *w·* or maketh a lie.
My.	33–17	and *w·* righteousness, — *Psal.* 15 : 2.
	228–24	and *w·* righteousness, — *Psal.* 15 : 2.
	300– 6	God which *w·* in you — *Phil.* 2 : 13.
	348–31	nothing that *w·* ill can enter

working
Mis.	29–31	*w·* up to those higher rules of Life
	44– 3	not *w·* for emoluments,
	53– 4	suicide . . . is not *w·* it out.
	70–27	*w·* out, . . . wonderful demonstrations
	87–17	*that no one there was* w· *in Science,*
	197–31	*w·* from no other Principle,
	263–17	*w·* assiduously for our common Cause,
	280–16	*w·* on one side and in Science.
	302–19	*w·* faithfully for Christ's cause
	323– 9	*w·* and watching for his coming.
	325–22	and seen *w·* for it !
	343– 7	its cure, in *w·* for God.
	368–25	*w·* out the destinies of the
Man.	52–20	*W·* Against the Cause.
	52–22	in *w·* against the interests of
	72– 6	Christian Scientist *w·* in the Field,
Ret.	49– 5	*w·* out their periods of organization,
	49–16	loving unselfishly, *w·* patiently
Pul.	5–29	palpably *w·* in the sermons,
Rud.	v– 5	LOYAL STUDENTS, *w·* AND WAITING
No.	2–18	*w·* to mature what he has been taught.
	12– 2	*w·* from a . . . Christian standpoint.
Pan.	1–12	mortals are hoping and *w·*,
'00.	2–27	*w·* when it is convenient."
'01.	10–25	*w·* out our own salvation,
	28– 4	by praying, watching, and *w·*
	30–24	*w·* alone with God,
	35–16	And the *w·* hitherto
Peo.	4– 1	*w·* out our own salvation.
	7– 2	*w·* out our own ideals,
My.	66–19	* Artisans and artists are *w·*
	203– 9	begin with work and never stop *w·*.
	213–16	*w·* so subtly that we mistake its
	231– 5	liability of *w·* in wrong directions.

working
My. 275–21   W· and praying for my dear friends'
   298– 7   distinguished all my w· years.

workingmen
My. 70–13   * w· stopped in the street

workings
Mis. 51– 8   the malicious w· of error
  108–19   evil and its subtle w·
  115– 5   culpable ignorance of the w· of
  290–13   its w· in the human heart.
  350– 4   w· whereof were not "terrible
My. 236–28   the w· of animal magnetism,

workman
Mis. 353–13   one day a w· in his mills,
Pul. 45–14   * predictions of w· and onlooker
My. 310– 9   * "a w· in a Tilton woolen mill."

workmen
Ret. 35–22   beneath the stroke of artless w·.
Pul. 50– 2   * the welfare of industrious w·,
My. 61–22   * as soon as the w· began to admit

work-rooms
My. 147–23   w· and a little hall,

works (noun)
accomplished the
Mis. 171–17   upon which are accomplished the w·
according to
'01. 10–29   faith according to w·.
and words
Ret. 78–13   such w· and words becloud the
beneficial
My. 99– 8   * good and beneficial w·,
copyrighted
Mis. 381– 1   copyrighted w· of Mrs. Eddy
Man. 43–16   Mary Baker Eddy's copyrighted w·
My. 130–23   Borrowing from my copyrighted w·,
dead
My. 128– 4   repentance from dead w·." — Heb. 6 : 1.
doing the
My. 28–20   * doing the w· which Jesus said
  245–20   doing the w· of primitive Christianity,
faith and
My. 103– 5   faith and w· demanded of man
faith by
Mis. 138–13   should he prove his faith by w·,
God's
My. 294–21   is shown him by God's w·
good
Mis. 203– 9   love, loyalty, and good w·.
  358– 1   Love impels good w·.
'00. 15–11   victory, faith, and good w·.
'01. 32– 9   Full of charity and good w·,
  34–23   understanding, and good w· ;
'02. 20– 9   thy unfaltering faith and good w·
My. 155– 6   abounding in love and good w·,
  191– 9   steadfast in love and good w·.
greater
Mis. 192–11   greater w· than these— John 14 : 12.
her
Mis. 35– 1   healing embodied in her w·.
My. vi–28   * for the publishing of her w· ;
  126–18   according to her w· : — Rev. 18 : 6.
his
Mis. 167–28   His w· thus prove him.
Man. 42– 9   By his w· he shall be judged,
My. 105– 6   prove one's faith by his w·.
  246–28   his w· are the same to-day as
  296–13   and his w· do follow him.
  305–25   simply how to do his w·.
illumined by
Mis. 338– 9   Faith illumined by w· ;
later
Pul. 83–21   * When we try to praise her later w·
marvellous
Mis. 199–23   Principle of these marvellous w·
mighty
My. 294– 8   not many mighty w· — Matt. 13 : 58.
Mrs. Eddy's
Mis. 35–13   * "Mrs. Eddy's w· are the outgrowths
my
Mis. 156–18   through the study of my w·
  214–22   even to understand my w·,
  247–11   departure in one of my w·
  249– 9   false report that . . . in my w·,
  300– 9   publish your copy of my w·,
  300–15   You literally publish my w·
  301–14   have read copies of my w·
  302–20   copying and reading my w·
  310– 2   is neither the intent of my w· nor
  318–21   the latest editions of my w·,
Chr. 57– 2   and keepeth my w· — Rev. 2 : 26.
Ret. 47–24   the latest editions of my w·,
'01. 27– 9   My w· are the first ever
Hea. 5–25   my faith by my w·." — Jas. 2 : 18.

works (noun)
my
My. 130– 8   to keep my w· from public recognition
  130–21   quotations from my w· must have
  285–18   and keepeth my w· — Rev. 2 : 26.
my published
Mis. x–27   in connection with my published w·.
  89–24   will find . . . in my published w·.
of art
Mis. 375–13   * and their great w· of art
of Christ
Mis. 196 –22   we shall do the w· of Christ,
of darkness
Rud. 4–24   extinguishes . . . the w· of darkness
of masters
Mis. 372–13   w· of masters in France
of other authors
Ret. 75– 8   the w· of other authors?
of Satan
Mis. 68–16   to know that the w· of Satan
of the devil
No. 31–15   the w· of the devil" — I John 3 : 8.
of the Spirit
Ret. 65– 4   the w· of the Spirit.
of Thy hands
Mis. 248– 7   the w· of Thy hands." — Psal. 92 : 4.
on science
Mis. 64–21   W· on science are profitable ;
on the subject
Mis. 382– 3   No w· on the subject of C. S.
other
Mis. 144–12   other w· written by the same author,
Man. 34–13   and other w· by Mrs. Eddy,
our
'02. 4–11   that our w· be as worthy
public
Mis. 335–16   In my public w·
published
Mis. 300– 3   Copying my published w·
My. 218–24   My published w· are teachers
  321– 9   * as regards your published w· ;
  321–15   * relations to your published w·
repeats the
Mis. 25–20   repeats the w·, and manifests
scientific
Ret. 78–12   so-called scientific w·,
spurious
Mis. 80– 2   spurious w· on mental healing.
substitutes for
My. 197–16   are but the substitutes for w·,
that I do
Mis. 21– 9   "The w· that I do — John 14 : 12.
  192–10   the w· that I do — John 14 : 12.
  193–27   the w· that I do — John 14 : 12.
  195–19   the w· that I do — John 14 : 12.
  251–15   "The w· that I do — John 14 : 12.
'02. 18–21   "The w· that I do — John 14 : 12.
My. 221–22   the w· that I do — John 14 : 12.
their
Mis. 243–19   their w· alone should declare them,
Pul. 57–17   * proved their faith by their w·.
'01. 33–17   they ask to be known by their w·,
  33–18   to be judged (if at all) by their w·.
My. 125–15   their w· will follow them.
  127– 5   judged according to their w·,
  128–30   according to their w·.
these
No. 11–20   demonstrate what these w· teach,
  41– 6   "For which of these w· — see John 10 : 32.
My. 103– 8   of this faith and these w·,
  149– 1   To attain to these w·, men must
those
'01. 27–12   be traced to some of those w·.
My. 108–24   "For which of those w· — John 10 : 32.
  227– 1   "For which of those w· — John 10 : 32.
thy
'00. 15–24   I know thy w·, — Rev. 2 : 19.
  15–25   thy patience, and thy w· ; — Rev. 2 : 19.
My. 3–12   by thy w·." — see Jas. 2 : 18.
understanding, and
'01. 21– 2   Science, understanding, and w·
voluminous
Ret. 76– 5   write voluminous w· on Science
ways and
Ret. 64–18   God's ways and w· and thoughts
without
Mis. 154– 6   Your faith has not been without w·,
Pul. 9–29   "Faith without w· — Jas. 2 : 26.
My. 3–10   sear leaves of faith without w·,
wonderful
Mis. 175–31   done many wonderful w·
'02. 16–21   sublime patience, wonderful w·,
Hea. 3–20   wonderful w· of our Master
My. 193– 9   for His wonderful w· — Psal. 107 : 8.
wondrous
Ret. 15–11   Thy wondrous w·." — Psal. 71 : 17.

works (noun)
  word and
    Man. 17–11 word and *w·* of our Master,
    My. 46–11 word and *w·* of our Master,
  words and
    (*see* **words**)
  words and the
    My. 148–30 words and the *w·* of our great Master.
  your
    Mis. 299–13 * "Is it right to copy your *w·*
        301–20 "Is it right to copy your *w·*
    My. 148– 4 your faith be known by your *w·*.
       194–27 reward you according to your *w·*,
       320–15 * and the author of all your *w·*.
       320–23 * as the author of your *w·*
       321–25 * of the authorship of your *w·*

    Mis. 126–21 *W·*, more than words,
       311–23 *w·* I have written on C. S.
       373–31 presents not words alone, but *w·*,
    Hea. 2– 2 *w·* more than words ;
       15–27 and *w·* more than words,
    My. 70–21 * *w·* of both ancient and modern
       104–32 *w·* even more that the words of

works (verb)
  Mis. 12–17 *w·* in the interest of both
    19–21 *w·* upon as high a basis
    48– 2 and avoid all that *w·* ill.
    117–24 *w·* somewhat in the dark ;
    220– 3 a good rule *w·* one way,
    238–12 reformer *w·* on unmentioned,
    288–10 this error *w·* out the results
    292–24 *w·* out the purposes of Love.
  Pul. 83–11 * with the certainty of . . . she *w·*,
  '00. 2–11 The right thinker *w·* ;
    2–25 intermediate worker *w·* at times.
  '02. 8–21 *w·* out the rule of
  My. 153–25 Principle of which *w·* intelligently
    292–17 *w·* unconsciously against the
    343– 3 * *w·* around a question

world (*see also* **world's**)
  advancement of the
    Ret. 49– 2 advancement of the *w·* in Truth
  advance the
    Mis. 366– 4 they would advance the *w·*.
  against the
    My. 134–2 constant battle against the *w·*,
  all over the
    Mis. 315– 9 Scientists, all over the *w·*,
    My. 30– 7 * Scientists from all over the *w·*,
    72–23 * members . . . all over the *w·*.
    73–14 * from all over the *w·*
    77– 9 * From all over the *w·*
    84–13 * Scientists all over the *w·*.
  all parts of the
    Pul. 68– 7 * from all parts of the *w·*,
    My. 47– 5 * from all parts of the *w·*,
    141–20 * from all parts of the *w·*.
  all the
    Mis. 37–14 "Go ye into all the *w·* — *Mark* 16 : 15.
    325–32 "Go ye into all the *w·* ; — *Mark* 16 : 15.
    No. 14–19 "Go ye into all the *w·*" ! — *Mark* 16 : 15.
    41–20 "Go ye into all the *w·*, — *Mark* 16 : 15.
    '01. 28–20 more than all the *w·*,
    My. 11– 7 * the one of all the *w·* who has
    47–28 * "Go ye into all the *w·*, — *Mark* 16 : 15.
    63–19 * all the *w·* was in some degree
    87–25 * if all the *w·* turned to the
    128–21 go into all the *w·*, preaching
    172–16 'Go ye into all the *w·*,' — *Mark* 16 : 15.
    271–15 * most discussed woman in all the *w·*.
    300–25 "Go ye into all the *w·*, — *Mark* 16 : 15.
  another
    Pul. 33–25 * spiritual form from another *w·*.
  applause of the
    Mis. 325– 9 with the applause of the *w·* :
  arguing with the
    Hea. 1–12 before arguing with the *w·*
  aroused
    '01. 26–15 land is reached and the *w·* aroused,
  at large
    My. 169–16 and of the *w·* at large,
  back to the
    Hea. 6– 3 and so come back to the *w·*
  before the
    My. 29–24 * different status before the *w·* !
    64–10 * name an honored one before the *w·*.
    64–19 * standing of C. S. before the *w·*.
  below
    Pul. 39–22 * Gaze on the *w·* below.
  brighter
    Ret. 6– 4 * to follow her to the brighter *w·*.
  brought to the
    My. 28–29 * brought to the *w·* the spiritual

world
  business
    My. 96– 6 * the social and business *w·*,
  came to the
    My. 217–30 He came to the *w·* not to destroy
  celestial
    Pan. 3–32 his man-face, the celestial *w·*.
  challenge the
    Mis. 247– 9 I calmly challenge the *w·*
  Christian
    My. 60–12 * What a change in the Christian *w·* !
    103 chapter sub-title
  civilized
    Pul. 79–12 * every part of the civilized *w·*,
    My. 59–12 * accepted . . . in the civilized *w·*.
    90–25 * from all over the civilized *w·*,
    273– 9 * covers practically the civilized *w·*.
  cleave to the
    Mis. 2– 7 to cleave to the *w·*, the flesh, and
  come to the
    Un. 59– 2 why did the Messiah come to the *w·*,
  conqueror of a
    '02. 19–15 happier than the conqueror of a *w·*.
  contact with the
    Mis. 110– 9 not through contact with the *w·*.
    Pul. 36– 7 * to retire from . . . the *w·*.
    68–10 * to retire from . . . the *w·*.
  convert the
    Mis. 279–28 are enough to convert the *w·*
  doctrines of the
    My. 92– 3 * position in the doctrines of the *w·*
  drops the
    Mis. 1–18 gathers fresh . . . and drops the *w·*.
  end of the
    My. 44–13 * unto the end of the *w·*." — *Matt.* 28 : 20.
  engirdle the
    My. 164–24 expansion that will engirdle the *w·*,
  enlightening the
    '02. 2– 18 enlightening the *w·* with the glory of
    My. 245–21 and enlightening the *w·*.
  entire
    Mis. 154– 5 shelter to the entire *w·*.
    My. 31–13 * contributed from over the entire *w·*.
  era of the
    My. 154–23 in our era of the *w·* I welcome
  evil
    My. 297–12 gust of evil in this evil *w·*
  explain to the
    My. 105–28 book which should explain to the *w·*
  fills the
    Mis. 228–10 fills the *w·* with its fragrance,
  floods the
    '02. 5– 8 floods the *w·* with the baptism of
  forefront of the
    '02. 14–21 blazoned on the forefront of the *w·*
  foundation of the
    My. 185–18 foundation of the *w·*," — *Rev.* 13 : 8.
  friction of the
    Mis. 224–21 so genial that the friction of the *w·*
  from the
    Hea. 6– 1 the more are we separated from the *w·* ;
  given to the
    Mis. 165–30 reproduced and given to the *w·*,
    178–32 has been given to the *w·* to-day.
    '01. 26–29 What I have given to the *w·*
  giveth
    Mis. 215– 6 not as the *w·* giveth, — *John* 14 : 27.
    My. 279– 4 not as the *w·* giveth, — *John* 14 : 27.
  give to the
    Mis. 137–27 Then you can give to the *w·* the benefit
    Ret. 93–24 should give to the *w·* convincing proof of
  glimpse of the
    Pul. 47–24 * wishes to catch a glimpse of the *w·*.
  gross
    Po. 47– 7 Ever the gross *w·* above ;
  has need
    Mis. 110– 4 the *w·* has need of you,
  hidden from the
    Pul. 9–24 bounty hidden from the *w·*.
  ideal
    Mis. 74–15 immortal sense of the ideal *w·*.
    217– 7 even the ideal *w·* whose cause is the
  in general
    Mis. 291–14 and the *w·* in general ;
  interest of the
    My. 52–26 * interest of the *w·* to hear her word
  into the
    Un. 15– 2 * came "death into the *w·*,
    19–10 how could it have come into the *w·*?
    Pan. 5–26 sickness, and death into the *w·*,
    '01. 21–22 not to bring death but life into the *w·*.
    '02. 6– 8 into the *w·* on the basis of a lie,
    My. 257–16 that cometh into the *w·*," — *John* 1 : 9.
  is bereft
    Un. 51–10 In pantheism the *w·* is bereft of
  is better
    My. 355–25 *w·* is better for this happy group

world

is far from ready
Un. 6–16 *w·* is far from ready to
is slow
Hea. 8–12 The *w·* is slow to perceive
is weary
Hea. 2–10 * and the *w·* is weary of me;
is wide
Mis. 224–11 remember that the *w·* is wide;
known to the
My. 299– 8 * let them make it known to the *w·*,
299–11 widely made known to the *w·*,
looks
My. 43–29 * *w·* looks with wonder upon this
loved the
Mis. 292– 6 Jesus, who so loved the *w·* that he
malice of the
Hea. 2–20 beneath the malice of the *w·*.
material
(see **material)**
more bright
Mis. 397– 4 A *w·* more bright.
Pul. 18–13 A *w·* more bright.
Po. 12–13 A *w·* more bright.
my
Mis. vii–17 My *w·* has sprung from Spirit,
new
Ret. 27–29 led me into a new *w·* of light
nowhere in the
My. 70–23 * Nowhere in the *w·* is there a
of flowers
Mis. 390–10 The fairy-peopled *w·* of flowers,
Po. 55–11 The fairy-peopled *w·* of flowers,
of glee
My. 350–21 (The Stygian shadow of a *w·* of glee);
of letters
Mis. 364– 5 paraphrase from the *w·* of letters.
of sense
No. 34–15 upon whom the *w·* of sense falls
of wisdom
Mis. 321–29 I have a *w·* of wisdom and Love to
old
My. 72– 9 * titled aristocracy of the old *w·*
operative in the
Pul. 35– 8 * a law as operative in the *w·* to-day
over
My. 47–11 * people the *w·* over have been
overcome the
Mis. 125– 7 enables him to overcome the *w·*,
My. 132– 7 I have overcome the *w·*." — *John* 16 : 33.
overcometh the
Mis. 168– 2 and overcometh the *w·* !
parts of the
My. 95– 7 * in different parts of the *w·*.
96– 2 * Scientists from all parts of the *w*
99–18 * coming from all parts of the *w·*,
physical
Pul. 53–20 * dominion over the physical *w·*.
presented to the
My. 40–24 * Mrs. Eddy, has presented to the *w·*
present to the
'02. 14–17 with truths . . . to present to the *w·*.
proclaims to the
My. 28–24 * proclaims to the *w·* that Jesus' gospel
real
Pul. 80–27 * the invisible is the only real *w·*,
reform the
No. 11–17 revolutionize and reform the *w·*,
rejoices
'02. 3–18 *w·* rejoices with our sister nation
resistance of the
Mis. 74–29 conquered the resistance of the *w·*.
retreat from the
My. 117–29 I left . . . to *retreat* from the *w·*,
revolutionize the
No. 33– 7 they would revolutionize the *w·*
rolling of a
Mis. 174–12 to the rolling of a *w·*.
salvation of a
Mis. 122– 7 salvation of a *w·* of sinners,
salvation of the
Mis. 177–18 necessary to the salvation of the *w·*
saving the
Man. 19– 5 saving the *w·* from sin and death;
sink the
Pul. 14–20 nor again sink the *w·* into the
sin of the
'01. 9–18 the sin of the *w·* ;" — *John* 1 : 29.
sins of the
Mis. 246– 3 covers the sins of the *w·*,
Un. 56– 7 but the sins of the *w·*,
spiritual
'01. 21–10 * many of the ideas about the spiritual *w·*
My. 167– 5 separates us from the spiritual *w·*,
stand still
My. 106–16 and the *w·* stand still.

world

suppositional
My. 167– 5 suppositional *w·* within us
swept over the
Pul. 52–22 * that swept over the *w·*
that
My. 269– 7 to obtain that *w·*, — *Luke* 20 : 35.
this
Mis. 155– 4 this *w·* that has nothing in Christ.
190–29 serpent, liar, the god of this *w·*,
190–31 god of this *w·* ;" — *II Cor.* 4 : 4.
341–30 neither the cares of this *w·*
342–28 children of this *w·* — *Luke* 16 : 8.
Un. 52–19 self-destroying elements of this *w·*,
Pul. 45– 4 * never be known in this *w·*.
53–17 * felicity and power in this *w·*,
'01. 16– 8 whereby the demon of this *w·*,
16–14 *the god of this w·*;
My. 4–24 the prince of this *w·* that hath
throughout the
Mis. 304– 8 * will pass . . . throughout the *w·*
304–21 * its mission throughout the *w·*.
Pul. 30–24 * Scientists throughout the *w·*
My. 8–25 * Scientists from throughout the *w·*,
21–13 * our Cause throughout the *w·*,
143–21 prospering throughout the *w·*
191– 7 steadily throughout the *w·*.
to come
Pul. 53–17 * salvation in the *w·* to come.
unfolded to the
My. 207–13 * which you have unfolded to the *w·*,
unspotted from the
Man. 31–10 themselves unspotted from the *w·*,
Ret. 65–24 keeping man unspotted from the *w·*,
visible
Mis. 363–19 shines through the visible *w·*
waiting
Mis. 22–25 have proven to a waiting *w·*.
waken
My. 356– 4 When will the *w·* waken to the
waken the
'02. 17–13 should . . . awake and waken the *w·*.
waking up the
Mis. 329–15 Spring passes . . . waking up the *w·*;
was dark
Ret. 23–10 The *w·* was dark.
was not worthy
'01. 30– 3 *w·* was not worthy." — *Heb.* 11 : 38.
watched over the
'02. 15–24 stars watched over the *w·*,
watch over a
My. 184–26 holding unwearied watch over a *w·*.
ways of the
Mis. 138– 5 in the wilderness or ways of the *w·*.
weary of the
Hea. 2–10 * "I am weary of the *w·*,
well for the
My. 191– 1 It were well for the *w·* if
whole
Mis. 279–29 whole *w·* will feel the influence of
'01. 19–28 The whole *w·* needs to know
32–11 shield the whole *w·* in their hearts,
My. v– 5 * attention of the whole *w·* is fixed on
20– 1 throughout the whole *w·*, — *Mark* 14 : 9.
115– 3 is circling the whole *w·*.
229–16 help themselves and the whole *w·*,
withdrew from the
Pul. 34–25 * withdrew from the *w·* to meditate,
woe unto the
Mis. 122– 3 "Woe unto the *w·* — *Matt.* 18 : 7.
woman's
Mis. 287–29 home, — which is woman's *w·*.
wonder of the
Mis. 321–26 during the great wonder of the *w·*,
would accept
Hea. 18–13 the *w·* would accept our sentiments;

Mis. 98–25 and call the *w·* to acknowledge its
163– 2 the *w·*, the flesh, and the devil.
169–19 most eminent divines of the *w·* have
281– 7 I learned long ago that the *w·*
290–21 When will the *w·* cease to judge of
295–23 Nor is the *w·* ignorant of
305– 3 * from each Republic in the *w·*,
313–23 garner the supplies for a *w·*.
316–29 patterns of humility, . . . for the *w·*.
353–32 *w·* worship, pleasure seeking, and
Man. 58–10 preach for this Church and the *w·*.
Ret. 26–19 gave the *w·* a new date
61–16 without God in the *w·*.' — *Eph.* 2 : 12.
94– 3 we owe to ourselves and to the *w·*
Pul. 39–11 * author of "The *W·* Beautiful."
53–25 * Saviour of the *W·*."
73– 8 * secluded herself from the *w·*
73–15 * His promises to her and to the *w·*.
80– 7 * freest country in the *w·*

world

'00.	2–15	gives it wisely to the w·
'02.	9– 6	Let the w·, popularity, pride, and
Hea.	2–20	why should the w· hate Jesus,
My.	7–19	* Christian Scientists of the w·,
	8– 9	* the best church in the w·,
	8–12	* in the best city in the w·
	33–29	w·, and they that dwell — Psal. 24 : 1.
	36–27	* Christian Scientists of the w·,
	49– 8	* chance of sweeping the w·
	51– 2	* no one in the w· who could
	52–12	* spreading w· wide of this great
	53– 6	* send forth her book to the w·."
	70– 7	* any other denomination in the w·,
	71–17	* in the country — yes, in the w·.
	71–19	* from any other church in the w·.
	77– 4	* one of the largest in the w·.
	79–14	* seldom witnessed anywhere in the w·
	79–17	* leading newspapers of the w·.
	85–13	* this wonderful woman is a w· power.
	89– 7	* one of the largest organs in the w·.
	89–25	* not to . . . but to the w· ;
	90–18	* w· is enormously richer for this
	91–28	* one of the finest . . . in the w·,
	104–17	of the utmost concern to the w·
	117– 1	the w· would not have lost
	122– 2	for one's self and for the w·
	132– 6	"In the w· ye shall have — John 16 : 33.
	150– 7	rendering the w· happier and
	178–26	If the w· were in ashes,
	183– 7	* will the w· have rest."
	184– 4	Since the w· was, men have
	253–12	w· hath not known Thee :— John 17 : 25.
	268–22	"the w·, the flesh and the devil,"
	272–26	* plays so great a part in the w·
	300–22	make known his doctrine to the w·,
	344–26	cannot force perfection on the w·.

world-great
My.	269–20	world-wide, world-known, w·.

world-imposed
'00.	10– 8	honest and a w· struggle.

world-known
My.	269–19	world-wide, w·, world-great.

worldliness
Mis.	162–25	w·, human pride, or self-will,
'02.	17– 1	selfishness, w·, hatred, and

worldlings
'01.	28–26	not popular among the w·

worldly
Mis.	10–25	w· or material tendencies of
	212– 8	reminded . . . of their w· policy.
	233–21	poor shift for the weak and w·
	312–22	must have risen above w· schemes,
	327–11	to speculate in w· policy,
	354–29	genius inflated with w· desire.
Ret.	78–16	the adoption of a w· policy
	79–16	w· policy, pomp, and pride,
	79–19	quicksands of w· commotion,
'01.	2–12	may suit the weak or the w·
My.	203– 7	not clamorous for w· distinction.
	287–12	poor shift for the weak and w·.

worldly-minded
Mis.	316–13	Until minds become less w·,

worldly-wise
Un.	46–19	as is still claimed by the w·.

world's
Mis.	51–27	* sunshine of the w· new spring,
	84– 9	cost them . . . the w· temporary esteem;
	110–23	obvious that the w· acceptance
	224–24	to cover the whole w· evil,
	304–25	* w· progress toward liberty ;
	338–27	* Shall the w· famine feed ;
Pul.	vii–10	in the glass of the w· opinion.
	51–26	* cannot absorb the w· thought.
	79–27	* thought of the w· scientific leaders
	82–13	* conservators of the w· morals
'01.	1– 9	nearer the whole w· acceptance.
	16–14	St. Paul defines this w· god
'02.	11–18	The w· wickedness
	17–16	Who of the w· lovers ever found
	17–28	w· soft flattery or its frown.
Po.	23–10	Above the w· control?
My.	4– 4	w· nolens volens cannot enthrall
	31–19	* front rank of the w· houses
	124–11	w· arms outstretched to us,
	189–21	twilight of the w· pageantry,
	289–14	its loss and the w· loss,

worlds
Mis.	vii– 9	If w· were formed by matter,
	26– 7	from the rolling of w·,
	184– 4	from the revolving of w· to the

worlds
Mis.	249–29	Over what w· on w· it hath range
	332– 1	kindling the stars, rolling the w·,

World's Congress Auxiliary
Mis.	312–11	President of the W· C· A·,

World's Exhibition
Mis.	304–14	* sent to the next W· E·,

World's Exposition
Mis.	304– 6	* coming W· E· at Chicago.

World's Fair
Mis.	321–26	wonder of the world, the W· F·,

World's Parliament of Religions
Pul.	4 –28	W· P· of R·, held in Chicago,

world-wide
My.	269–19	Its harvest song is w·,
	271–19	* woman of w· renown

world-wish
Ret.	18– 1	Here the poet's w·,
Po.	63– 9	Here the poet's w·,

world-worshipper
'01.	30–30	The sensualist and w·

worm
Mis.	240–28	nothing but a loathsome w·

wormwood
My.	126– 3	would pour w· into the waters

worn
Mis.	295–30	w· the English crown
Pul.	50–21	* many who have w· off the novelty

wornout
Pan.	1–12	outgrown, w·, or soiled garments

worry
Pul.	73– 2	* "Then why should we w· ourselves
My.	48–25	* discouragement of care and w·,

worse
Mis.	17–12	hygiene as w· than useless
	59– 9	in which the last state . . . is w· than
	138– 4	convention is w· than wasted, if
	230–20	and w· than waste its years.
	233–17	still w· in the eyes of Truth
	234–16	Empirical knowledge is w· than
	293–17	last error will be w· than the first
Ret.	63–23	Sin is w· than sickness ;
Un.	49–20	* we make "the w· appear the better
Rud.	8–24	he makes morally w· the invalid
	9– 2	w· than the first." — Matt. 12 : 45.
No.	6– 1	makes the last . . . w· than the first.
	11–13	(w· still) by those who come falsely
	31– 8	and will multiply into w· forms,
Hea.	13–27	and that one is w· than the first ;
Peo.	6– 1	* all the w· for the fishes."
My.	118– 6	remedy is w· than the disease.
	231– 8	money, w· than wasted.
	245–15	Babel of confusion w· confounded,
	288–26	lest a w· thing come — John 5 : 14.

worship (noun)
Christian
Mis.	345–29	that it was a part of Christian w·
Un.	15–28	Surely this is no Christian w· !
My.	47–27	* opened an era of Christian w·

Christian Science
Mis.	149–29	first temple for C. S. w·
Ret.	51– 6	as a temple for C. S. w·.

edifice of
Pul.	77– 1	* magnificent new edifice of w·

faith and
My.	59– 9	* a new system of faith and w·,

home for
My.	31–17	* The new home for w·

house of
Pul.	50–12	* erection of a visible house of w·
My.	182–20	dedicate this beautiful house of w·

houses of
My.	31–20	* the world's houses of w·,
	66–29	* many beautiful houses of w·

liturgical
Ret.	89–10	they went for liturgical w·,

meetings of
My.	53–10	* hold its meetings of w· in the

mode of
'01.	12– 1	mode of w· may be intangible,

my
'01.	12– 8	for me to believe, or for my w·.

of God
Pul.	40–23	* dedicated to the w· of God.

of Spirit
My.	23–25	* which represents the w· of Spirit,

perfect
'00.	4–10	the perfect w· of one God.

worship (noun)

personal
Ret. 76–16 so far from being personal w·,
Pul. 43–28 * that sort of personal w·
My. 116–13 and there is no personal w·,
234– 6 personal w· which C. S. annuls.
place of
Mis. 325–31 Next he enters a place of w·,
345–23 took their infants to a place of w·
places of
My. 91–28 * one of the finest places of w·
public
My. vi–13 * originated its form of public w·,
real
My. 262–25 in mimicry of the real w·
reverence of
My. 98– 9 * enthusiasm and reverence of w·
sense of
My. 139–19 It was to turn your sense of w·
sensual
'00. 13–17 was devoted to a sensual w·.
solemn
'01. 15–29 * attending His solemn w·.
spiritual
My. 152–13 spiritual w·, spiritual power.
sun
Pan. 8– 4 find expression in sun w·,
Sunday
Mis. 314– 5 society formed for Sunday w·,
thought and
Mis. 91–19 spiritual forms of thought and w·
true
Mis. 91– 2 as a type of the true w·,
world
Mis. 353–32 world w·, pleasure seeking, and

My. 187–23 w· of the only true God.

worship (verb)

Mis. 96–10 I w· that of which I can conceive,
96–15 divine Principle, — which I w·;
96–15 so w· I God." — see Acts 24 : 14.
106–23 How shall mankind w· the
123–30 who w· Him must w· Him spiritually,
124– 4 must w· Him in spirit.
152–17 those who w· in this tabernacle :
219– 9 they that w· Him — John 4 : 24.
219– 9 w· Him in spirit — John 4 : 24.
388–18 The right to w· deep and pure,
Ret. 2– 8 seeking "freedom to w· God ;"
9–18 * Is it not much that I may w· Him,
17– 5 I w· in deep sylvan spot,
Un. 15–22 devotees who w· not the good Deity,
31– 3 they that w· Him — John 4 : 24.
31– 3 w· Him in spirit — John 4 : 24.
Pan. 14– 6 w· in spirit and in truth ;
'00. 3–16 not apt to w· the pioneer
3–19 cannot w· him, for that would
'01. 7–24 The God whom all Christians . . . w·
Po. 21– 7 The right to w· deep and pure,
62– 5 I w· in deep sylvan spot,
My. 5–20 to w·, not an unknown God,
26–21 throttle the lie that students w· me
151–20 * Go forth, and w· God."
152–14 w· only Spirit and spiritually,
153–21 ye ignorantly w·." — Acts 17 : 23.
158–28 temple and all who w· therein
162–23 that in them Christians may w· God,
162–23 not that Christians may w· church
168– 2 Freedom to w· God according to
189– 8 You w· no distant deity,
192– 2 Ye w· Him whom ye serve.
192–14 the infinite Person whom we w·,
195–25 an edifice in which to w·
270–32 "they that w· Him — John 4 : 24.
270–32 w· Him in spirit — John 4 : 24.
285–26 so w· I the God — Acts 24 : 14.
341– 7 * "Freedom to w· God."
(see also **Father**)

worshiping (see also worshipping)

Po. 71– 5 Knelt w· at mammon's shrine.

worshipped

Mis. 333–24 worshippers of Baal w· the sun.
'00. 3–10 he is not thereby w·.
My. 29–19 * thousands who w·
55–29 * congregation w· in Copley Hall

worshipper

Mis. 152–20 meek in spirit the w· in truth,
Ret. 89–11 If one w· preached to
My. 163– 1 call the w· to seek the haven

worshippers

Mis. 178–17 * of what you were w·.
321–13 when the true w· — see John 4 : 23.
333–24 w· of Baal worshipped the sun.
No. 34–10 true w· shall worship — John 4 : 23.

worshippers

Peo. 13– 1 w· of wood and stone have a
13– 3 But the w· of a person have
My. 78– 5 * w· saw an imposing structure
85–23 * not merely for its thousands of w·,
90– 3 * w·, wooed by no eloquence
92–23 * or the thirty thousand w·
94– 8 * or the thirty thousand w·
100– 7 * thirty thousand w· were present
303–10 unscientific w· of a human being.

worshipping (see also worshiping)

My. 151–28 w· of matter in the name of
152– 2 w· person instead of

worst

Mis. 233– 4 the w· form of medicine.
237– 9 the w· of human passions
267– 5 w· enemies are the best friends
296–24 affinity for the w· forms of vice?
319–16 sinners of the w· sort.
368–27 perverted, . . . may become the w·,
Peo. 2–17 the w· human qualities,
My. 165– 8 The best help the w· ;
190– 8 in healing the w· forms of
211–19 designs of their w· enemies,
335–17 * yellow fever of the w· type,
335–28 * yellow fever in its w· form,

worth

Mis. 4–22 the vastness of its w·
226–30 assassin of radical w· ;
273– 4 in proportion to its w·.
Chr. 53–27 rehearse the glorious w·
Pul. 84– 7 * all that is w· living for,
'00. 7–12 appreciated its w· as they did
'02. 17–24 conscious w· satisfies the
Hea. 20– 2 * speak the matchless w·,
My. 166– 7 life is w· living and God takes care
203–10 All that is w· reckoning
215– 3 knew well the priceless w·
215–14 * teachings are w· much more
216–13 his truth not w· a cent.
258– 9 to all of holiest w·.
325– 8 * would never be w· what you

worthies

Mis. 246– 4 enlightenment of these w·,
'01. 9– 6 The ancient w· caught glorious

worthily

My. 9–16 * desire that we may w· follow
202–14 rest w· on the builders of

worthiness

Mis. 154–10 God only waits for man's w·
My. 64–25 * and thus prove our w·

worthless

No. 27– 3 and the claim, being w·,

worthy

Mis. 54– 9 whose lives are w· testimonials,
147–10 records w· to be borne heavenward?
157– 3 w· to suffer for Christ, Truth.
291–25 w· to suffer for righteousness,
Man. 39– 4 If, . . . they are found w·,
39– 6 but if not found w·
69–19 is not w· of me." — Matt. 10 : 37.
89– 7 the vice-president . . . being found w·
Ret. 49– 7 accomplished the w· purpose
Un. 57–23 rejoiced that he was found w·
Pul. 48–27 * long list of w· ancestors
50– 3 * w· of his hire," — Luke 10 : 7.
'01. 30– 3 the world was not w·." — Heb. 11 : 38.
'02. 4–11 our works be as w· as our words.
My. 4– 8 is not w· of me." — Matt. 10 : 38.
24–27 * the structure is w· of our Cause
64–26 * w· members of The Mother Church
70–12 * The chimes . . . are w· of the dome.
92–10 * a portent w· of perhaps even
215–17 home for the poor w· student,
215–25 w· of his hire." — Luke 10 : 7.
233–25 is not w· of me — Matt. 10 : 38.
258– 4 Nothing is w· the name of
269– 6 shall be accounted w· — Luke 20 : 35.
358–19 a w· and charitable purpose.

would-be

Un. 17–14 the w· murderer of Truth.

wound

Mis. 215– 4 saying, "I w· to heal ;
244– 1 closed up the w· thereof, — see Gen. 2 : 21.
387–12 arrow that doth w· the dove
398– 6 W· the callous breast,
Ret. 46–12 W· the callous breast,
Pul. 17–11 W· the callous breast,
No. 44–20 healing balm . . . into every w·.
Po. 6– 7 arrow that doth w· the dove
14–10 W· the callous breast,
22–16 probe the w·, then pour the balm
33–10 To kindly pass over a w·,

wounded

Mis. 145–16	a *w·* sense of its own error,
224– 5	Well may we feel *w·* by
258– 8	anointing the *w·* spirit with the
My. 257– 3	love that heals the *w·* heart.
313–27	but I *w·* her pride

wounds

Mis. 209– 7	healest the *w·* of my people slightly
275–15	binds up the *w·* of bleeding hearts,
296–15	the *w·* of the broken-hearted,
311–25	even as a surgeon who *w·* to heal.
327–32	and kindly binds up their *w·*,
330– 6	wherein no arrow *w·* the dove
Ret. 92– 4	*w·* he healed by Truth and Love.
Un. 55–15	false sense of . . . the *w·* it bears.
Po. 27–12	heal her *w·* too tenderly
My. 290–22	where no arrow *w·* the eagle

woven

Mis. 145–26	When the *hearts* . . . are *w·* together

wrapped

Peo. 5–14	*w·* in a pure winding-sheet,

wrapping

Mis. 326–14	*w·* their altars in ruins.

wraps

My. 69–24	* capacity of three thousand *w·*.

wrath

Mis. 41– 6	*w·* of man"— *Psal.* 76 : 10.
324–15	emulation, hatred, *w·*, murder.
Man. 41– 9	turneth away *w·*."— *Prov.* 15 : 1.
Pul. 12–14	having great *w·*,— *Rev.* 12 : 12.
No. 7–17	*w·* of man cannot hide it from Him.
8–13	make the *w·* of man to praise Him,
33– 1	*w·* of man shall praise Him.
35–11	not to appease the *w·* of God,
'02. 1–12	*w·* of man— *Psal.* 76 : 10.
1–13	*w·* shalt Thou restrain."— *Psal.* 76 : 10.
Peo. 3– 8	*w·* of God, . . . false beliefs
My. 111– 2	*w·* of man— *Psal.* 76 : 10.
151–10	*w·* of man— *Psal.* 76 : 10.
151–11	*w·* shalt Thou restrain."— *Psal.* 76 : 10.
196–10	slow to *w·*."— *Jas.* 1 : 19.
207– 4	*w·* of men shall praise God,

wreath

Mis. 388–17	Affection's *w·*, a happy home ;
Po. 21– 6	Affection's *w·*, a happy home ;
65–21	gathers a *w·* for his bier ;
My. 190– 2	falling upon the bridal *w·*

wreathed

Pul. 42–26	* The desk was *w·* with ferns

wreaths

Ret. 11–19	*w·* are twined round Plymouth Rock,
Peo. 14– 9	* are *w·* of immortelles,
Po. 25–19	*W·* for the triumphs o'er ill !
60–16	*w·* are twined round Plymouth Rock,

wreck

Mis. 26– 1	survive the *w·* of time ;

wrecks

Mis. 280–30	by which so many *w·* are made.
No. 43–25	or reconstruct the *w·* of "*isms*"

wrench

Mis. 246– 7	to *w·* from man both human and

wrest

Un. 1– 7	*w·* . . . unto their own— *II Pet.* 3 : 16.

wrested

Mis. 171– 2	can never be *w·* from its

wrestle

Mis. 336– 4	your province to *w·* with error,
392–15	to *w·* with the storms of time ;
Po. 20–19	to *w·* with the storms of time ;

wrestler

Mis. 385–18	Brave *w·*, lone.
Po. 48–12	Brave *w·*, lone.

wrestling

'02. 1–16	*w·* only with material observation,
Peo. 1–12	intellectual *w·* and collisions

wrestlings

Mis. 339–14	the strain of intellectual *w·*,
Ret. 57– 1	mighty *w·* with mortal beliefs,
No. 45–21	Drifting into intellectual *w·*,

wretched

Mis. 52–15	*w·* condition of human existence.

wriggles

Mis. 296–22	* *w·*" itself into publicity

wrist-joint

Mis. 243– 8	In the case of sprain of the *w·*,

writ

Mis. 381–21	A *w·* of injunction was issued
Po. 22–12	'Tis *w·* on earth, on leaf and flower :

write

Mis. 106– 4	and if I could *w·* the history
141–32	O recording angel ! *w·* :
142–13	Let me *w·* to the donors,
155–20	students, who *w·* such excellent letters
155–24	cannot spare time to *w·* to God,
157– 7	or caused my secretary to *w·*,
157–26	*W·* me when you need me.
271–10	*w·* for it, and read it.
285–20	to *w·* briefly on marriage,
379– 2	and *w·* at his desk.
379–18	one could *w·* a sonnet.
Man. 71–21	shall not *w·* the Tenets of
Ret. 75–23	to *w·* out as his own the
76– 4	student can *w·* voluminous works
No. 7–23	and *w·* the truth of C. S.
39– 2	than we can *w·* or speak.
Pan. 11– 3	It caused St. Paul to *w·*,
14– 4	Once more I *w·*,
'00. 13–30	bidden to *w·* the approval of
15–23	may the angel . . . *w·* of this church :
'02. 2– 5	to *w·* truth first on the tablet
3–17	learning to read and *w·*.
15–15	dictation as to what I should *w·*,
15–28	had led me to *w·* that book,
Po. v–17	* seated herself . . . and began to *w·*.
28– 3	to *w·* a deathless page
32–12	inspires my pen as I *w·* ;
My. 59–25	* "Did Mrs. Eddy really *w·* S. and H.?
105–27	urged me immediately to *w·*
114–18	I could not *w·* these notes
115– 4	I should blush to *w·* of "S. and H.
214– 3	would *w·* your textbook on the
258–32	To the children . . . I *w·* :
324–19	* that he had helped you *w·* it.

writer

Mis. 71– 6	one *w·* thinks that he was
290–18	I had not thought of the *w·*
296–15	This *w·* classes C. S. with
Man. 43–26	the spirit in which the *w·*
Pul. 48– 5	* Mrs. Eddy took the *w·*
67– 6	* by a great American *w·*.
79–20	* wicked but witty *w·* has said,
My. 59– 2	* the *w·*, whom you will recall
93– 1	* so far as the *w·* knows them,
225– 9	the *w·* or the reader who does not
(*see also* **Eddy**)	

writer's

(*see* **Eddy**)

writers

Mis. 29–22	*w·* of chronic and acute diseases
169–21	what the inspired *w·* left
187–17	both *w·* and translators
Ret. 22–5	*W·* less wise than the apostles
'01. 28– 8	Of the ancient *w·* since
34–29	words of the Hebrew *w·* :

writes

Mis. 8–21	Shakespeare *w·* : "Sweet are the
24– 3	St. Paul *w·* : " For to be— *Rom.* 8 : 6.
153–25	Sir Edwin Arnold, . . . *w·* :
226–14	Shakespeare, . . . *w·* : — To thine own
295– 3	Mr. Wakeman *w·* from London,
317–30	St. John *w·* : — *John* 3 : 34.
373–23	and, as St. Mark *w·*,
Chr. 53–52	And *w·* the page.
Ret. 76– 5	if he *w·* honestly,
Un. 30–13	In his first epistle . . . Paul *w·* :
Pan. 12– 5	Lyman Abbott, D.D., *w·*,
'00. 13–14	*w·* of this church of Smyrna :
13–25	Smith *w·* : "In this city the
'01. 21– 8	Rev. —— *w·* : "To the famous
24–10	he *w·* : "I esteem my
27– 3	My critic also *w·* :
33– 6	Carlyle *w·* : "Quackery and dupery do
'02. 6–27	St. Paul *w·* : "For to be— *Rom.* 8 : 6.
10–10	Rev. Hugh Black *w·* truly :
16–12	St. Paul *w·* : "Follow peace— *Heb.* 12 : 14.
Hea. 1–15	A classic *w·*, — " At thirty, man
Peo. 6– 2	Dr. Benjamin Waterhouse *w·* :
6– 4	Dr. Abercrombie, . . . *w·* :
My. 3– 7	St. John *w·* : "Blessed are they — *Rev.* 22 : 14.
159–27	*w·*, "What is the essence of God?
186– 3	that *w·* in living characters
193–22	Carlyle *w·*, "Give a thing time ;
194– 2	which Christianity *w·* in broad facts
240– 6	An earnest student *w·* to me :
272–28	* Mrs. Eddy *w·* very rarely for
293–28	St. Paul *w·* : "For the law of — *Rom.* 8 : 2.
299– 5	*w·* : "If they . . . have any truth

writing

Mis.	43–17	sad fact at this early w· is,
	88–12	reading, w·, extensive travel,
	239– 7	Lecturing, w·, preaching, teaching,
Ret.	36– 7	w· out my manuscripts for students
Pul.	35–12	* In w· of this experience,
'02.	15–22	name for the book I had been w·.
Po.	v–19	* asked her what she was w·,
My.	114–27	have been learning . . . since w· it.
	150– 7	* w· what deserves to be read ;
	225–10	used in w· about C. S.
	225–25	either in speaking or in w·,
	234– 3	w· or reading congratulations
	304–10	w· for the leading newspapers,
	312–29	My salary for w·
	322– 2	* when you were w· S. and H.,

writings

Mis.	x– 6	to collect my miscellaneous w·
	46–11	A reader of my w· would not
	291–16	by my thoughts and w·.
	300–20	printed as your original w·,
	301–12	w· cf a few professed . . . Scientists.
	302–24	desist from further copying of my w·
	379–11	I inferred that his w· usually
	381–12	the author of her w· !
Man.	43–17	shall not plagiarize her w·.
	44– 2	His w· must show strict adherence to
	59– 3	w· of authors who think at random
	64– 7	other w· by this author ;
Ret.	75–10	and one's w· on ethics,
Pul.	37–12	* further w· on C. S.
	75– 5	my w·, teachings, and example
No.	3–25	Plagiarism from my w·
'01.	24–21	not read one line of Berkeley's w·
	25– 1	mysticism, so called, of my w·
	26–26	I have read little of their w·.
	28–11	Some of his w· have been
	34–11	and the canonical w· of the Fathers,
My.	vi– 8	* learned it from her and from her w· ;
	17–28	* extracts from Mrs. Eddy's w·
	18–31	* w· of the Rev. Mary Baker Eddy,
	48–19	* the Bible and her own w·,
	64–15	* In all her w·, through all the
	114–14	My first w· on C. S.
	120– 1	the sainted Revelator in his w·,
	120– 3	or elsewhere than in my w·,
	179– 2	the beginning of the gospel w·.
	270–20	My w· heal the sick,
	317–16	Calvin A. Frye copied my w·,
	338– 9	* her w· will fully corroborate

written

Mis.	x–11	were originally w· in haste,
	xi– 6	reproduction of what has been w·,
	98–26	Truly is it w· :
	121– 1	w· in a decaying language,
	142– 7	W· on receipt of a beautiful
	144–12	w· by the same author,
	148–13	were w· at different dates,
	157– 7	I have w·, or caused my
	172–20	which law is w· on the heart,
	185–27	And so it is w·,— I Cor. 15 : 45.
	213– 3	All that I have w·, taught, or lived,
	286– 1	above prophecy, w· years ago,
	306–14	* a duplicate letter w·,
	311–23	works I have w· on C. S.
	315– 6	No copies . . . are allowed to be w·,
	316–15	have profited . . . from the w· word,
	317–14	by the study of what is w·.
	381–31	has been w· that "nobody can
	391– 2	W· to the Editor of the Item,
	392–19	W· on receiving a painting of
	395–15	W· in childhood, in a maple grove
	399–17	W· on laying the corner-stone of
Man.	3–10	were w· at different dates,
	27–10	the w· consent of said Board.
	28–24	shall be w· on the Church records.
	43– 6	No member shall use w· formulas,
	43–12	strengthen the faith by a w· text
	44– 1	spirit in which the writer has w·
	65–16	comply with any w· order,
	67– 9	without her w· consent.
	67–25	w· request of the Pastor
	71– 7	nor w· on applications
	78–10	without the w· consent
	79–14	for her w· approval.
	82– 9	knowledge or w· consent.
	87– 4	w· consent of the authority
	94–14	w· request of Mrs. Eddy,
	103– 7	without the w· consent
	104– 5	w· by Mary Baker Eddy
	104–10	without the w· consent
	105– 4	without the w· consent
	109–16	that names are legibly w·,
	110–12	must be plainly w·,
	110–13	names of each, w· in full.

written

Man.	110–16	All names must be w·
	111– 3	names must be w· in full.
Ret.	1–10	my grandmother said were w·
	17– 1	W· in youth, while visiting
	20–16	w· after this separation :
	27–10	until S. and H. was w·.
	27–27	its w· expression increases
	75–22	textbook w· by his teacher,
Un.	57–13	it is w· that he felt that
Pul.	30–12	* "confession of faith," w· by
	39–14	* [W· for the Traveller]
	43–15	* w· by Mrs. Eddy for the
	73–27	* which Mrs. Eddy had herself w·,
	74–10	* w· answer to the interrogatory,
Rud.	16–18	Whatever is said and w·
No.	42– 2	* things w· in the Scriptures,
'00.	13– 6	It is w· of this church
Peo.	13–25	* history of Christianity was w·,
Po.	v– 2	* w· at different periods
	v– 4	* They were not w· with a
	v–10	* w· while the author was
	vi– 6	* was w· for that occasion,
	vi–24	* poems w· in girlhood
	vi–28	* (w· in a maple grove),
	vi–29	* (w· while visiting a . . . friend
	3–15	W· many years ago.
	19– 6	W· in early years.
	33–20	W· in girlhood.
	35–15	W· more than sixty years ago
	59– 9	W· in girlhood,
My.	15– 9	without the w· consent
	31–29	* Hymn 161, w· by Mrs. Eddy,
	59–28	* before it was ever w·.
	114–32	either w· or indicated in
	124–20	w· in luminous letters,
	150– 6	* "Doing what deserves to be w·,
	151–10	Because it is w· :
	178–30	w· in A.D. 145,
	179–18	narratives had never been w·,
	179–26	contingent on nothing w·
	184–15	birch bark on which it was w·
	185–12	wherever thought, . . . or w·,
	189–28	gave expression to a poem w· in 1844,
	190–23	Bible was w· in order that
	217–23	w· in "S. and H. with Key to the
	225–31	should not be w· or used as a
	271– 8	learned the truth of what I had w·.
	285–27	which are w· in the law — Acts 24 : 14.
	292– 3	All good that ever was w·,
	306–29	w· while I was his patient
	317–19	dissented from what I had w·,
	323– 2	* with what Mr. Bates has so well w·
	323– 5	* he said he had w· in answer to
	354–26	* w· extemporaneously by Mrs. Eddy
	359–10	through my w· and published rules,
	359–20	* had been w· to Mrs. Augusta E. Stetson
	361–10	not w· to her since August 30, 1909.

wrong (noun)

actual
Mis.	129– 9	an imaginary or an actual w·,

all
'01.	14–26	To overcome all w·, it must

all that is
Po.	33– 8	vanity, folly, and all that is w·

amplification of
Mis.	261–11	every effect and amplification of w·
My.	288–24	every effect or amplification of w·.

and injustice
My.	277–16	whereby w· and injustice are righted

be robbed
Pul.	84– 3	* Then shall w· be robbed of her

childhood's
Mis.	238– 4	to contrast with that childhood's w·

clouds of
My.	252–14	midst clouds of w·, injustice, envy,

commit
Mis.	130– 7	how much better . . . than to commit w·?

crouching
Mis.	246–21	crouching w· that refused to

human
Mis.	340–32	Human w·, sickness, sin, and

ignorant
Mis.	300– 8	it is an ignorant w·.

iron heel of
Pul.	82–30	* ceased to kiss the iron heel of w·.

is done
Mis.	391–11	That when a w· is done us,
Po.	38–10	That when a w· is done us,

is thought
'01.	14–23	W· is thought before it is acted ;

jubilant
Po.	27–17	W· jubilant and right with

no
Mis.	224–26	when no w· is meant,

wrong (noun)

nothingness of
Mis. 267– 4 nothingness of *w·* and the supremacy of

or imperfection
My. 41–17 * with sin, *w·*, or imperfection,

participants in
Mis. 335–20 either willing participants in *w·*,

rebuke to
Po. 23–14 A stern rebuke to *w·* !

recompense this
Mis. 12– 7 God will recompense this *w·*,

right over
My. 362– 5 in the victory of right over *w·*,

suffer from the
Mis. 261– 9 suffer from the *w·* they commit,

unseen
My. 211– 3 The unseen *w·* to individuals

Mis. 13– 6 real wrongs (if *w·* can be real)
　　 33– 2 *w·* will receive its own reward.
　287–27 pleasanter to do right than *w·*
　368– 7 * *W·* forever on the throne.
　371–19 * "good right, and good *w·*,"
'01. 14–27 *w·* has no divine authority;
　 31– 2 of truth, of right, and of *w·*.
My. 117– 5 determines the right or the *w·* of
　252– 9 the *w·* you may commit must,
　283–16 *W·* may be a man's highest idea of
　306– 1 to lift the curtain on *w·*,

wrong (adj.)

Mis. 19– 1 is unjust, — is *w·* and cruel.
　 19– 3 hatred, malice, are always *w·*,
　 32– 1 so succeed with his *w·* argument,
　 49–17 *can it be w·, sinful, or an error?*
　 59–11 *Is it w· to pray for . . . the sick?*
　 67–22 *w·* practice discerned, disarmed, and
　 80– 9 individual rights in a *w·* direction
　 80–14 with a *w·* class of people.
　 90– 8 *Is it w· for a wife to*
　117– 6 superinduced by the *w·* motive
　133–18 I hope I am not *w·* in
　170–14 *w·* and foolish, conceptions of God
　179–11 We are *w·* if our consciousness is
　190–26 *w·* power, or the lost sense,
　191–17 evils, apparent *w·* traits,
　212–25 If, . . . one is at work in a *w·*
　215–12 or start from *w·* motives.
　222– 8 conviction of his *w·* state of feeling
　240–25 teach them nothing that is *w·*.
　252– 9 *w·* thoughts are unreality
　263– 3 knowing that the *w·* motives are not
　279– 4 prevent the *w·* action?
　283–11 *w·* to burst open doors
　288–11 If the premise . . . is *w·*,
　351–17 never can place it in the *w·* hands
　365– 8 gets things *w·*, and is
Ret. 57– 9 it is practice that is *w·*.
　 81–17 arise from *w·* apprehension.
Rud. 12– 6 *W·* thoughts and methods
No. 7–24 right or *w·* personality
　 18–20 If . . . the school gets things *w·*,
Pan. 4–13 of right and *w·* action,
Hea. 9– 6 on the *w·* side of the question.
　 14–28 opposed to all that is *w·*,
My. 146–25 in the right or in the *w·* direction.
　213–18 to drift in the *w·* direction
　223–18 superinduced by *w·* motives
　224–11 its right or its *w·* concept,
　231– 5 working in *w·* directions.
　241–22 * said that my statement was *w·*,

wrong (verb)

Mis. 130–25 is to *w·* one of God's

wrong-doer

Mis. 261–11 wrong will revert to the *w·*,
My. 288–24 wrong will revert to the *w·*;

wrong-doing

Mis. 298– 3 Nothing is gained by *w·*.

wronged

Mis. 12– 6 If you have been badly *w·*,
　 12– 9 not fancy that you have been *w·*
　130– 7 how much better it is to be *w·*,

wrongfully

Rud. 10– 9 beliefs, which govern mortals *w·*.
My. 138–13 cruelly, unjustly, and *w·* accused.

wrongfully-minded

Mis. 367– 9 whatever is *w·* will disappear

X-rays

Mis. 112– 6 Hypnotism, microbes, *X·*.

wrongly

Mis. 357–26 If they have been taught *w·*,
Un. 9–12 the centuries have *w·* reckoned.
　 49– 7 sinner, *w·* named *man*.
Peo. 3–21 begins *w·* to apprehend the infinite,

wrongs

done
My. 160–32 *w·* done to others, are mill-stones

existing
No. 9–18 existing *w·* of the nature referred to.

forgiving
Mis. 107–12 forgetting self, forgiving *w·* and

of human life
My. 6– 8 the *w·* of human life,

of mankind
No. 40–18 but only the *w·* of mankind.

real
Mis. 13– 6 real *w·* (if wrong can be real)

will redress
Mis. 80–20 will redress *w·* and rectify injustice.

Ret. 73–20 *w·* it, or terrifies people over it,

wrote

Mis. 189–26 insomuch that St. Matthew *w·*,
　290–15 *w·* to me, naming the time of
　298– 1 The Hebrew bard *w·*,
　330–10 St. Paul *w·*, "Rejoice— *Phil. 4: 4.*
　372–11 A mother *w·*, "Looking at the
　382–25 * its constitution and bylaws,
Ret. 1–12 *w·* a stray sonnet and an
　 7– 5 *w·* of my brother as follows :
　 27– 1 I *w·* also, at this period, comments
　 32–12 the famous Spanish poet who *w·*,
　 40–19 The mother afterwards *w·* to me,
　 90–26 One of my students *w·* to me :
Pul. 6–13 *w·* to me in 1894,
　 31–20 * To a note which I *w·* her,
　 54– 1 * Again, in a poem . . . he *w·* :
'01. 29–29 students *w·* me, "quite quickly we
My. v–20 * *w·* and published the C. S. textbook,
　 vi–13 * *w·* its Church Manual and Tenets,
　 19–15 * Mrs. Eddy *w·* as follows :
　 52–21 * *w·* as follows : "Whatever is to be
　114–17 What I *w·* had a strange coincidence
　146–21 sure that what I *w·* is true,
　154–18 Carlyle *w·* : "Wouldst thou
　183– 6 what John Robinson *w·* in 1620
　215– 6 I *w·* "S. and H· with Key to the
　237– 5 What I *w·* on C. S.
　261–15 St. Paul *w·*, "When I— *I Cor.* 13 : 11.
　271– 4 When I *w·* "S. and H.
　304–11 I *w·* for the best magazines
　319– 6 he *w·* a kind little pamphlet,
　343–17 In 1875 I *w·* my book.
　343–28 I *w·* to each church in tenderness,
　359–26 * Mrs. Eddy *w·* to Mrs. Stetson

wroth

Hea. 10– 2 dragon that was *w·* with the woman,

wrought

Mis. 13– 8 *w·* out for me the law of
　 24– 8 it *w·* my immediate recovery
　 52–21 problem to be *w·* in divine Science,
　 96– 2 salvation . . . as *w·* out by Jesus,
　110–19 our hands have *w·* steadfastly
　120–11 ye that have *w·* valiantly,
　187– 4 The great Metaphysician *w·*,
　201–21 so many proofs that he had *w·*
　237– 7 *w·* a change in the actions of men.
　333–26 believed . . . God *w·* through matter
Ret. 24–20 divine Spirit had *w·* the miracle
　 54– 2 some of the cures *w·* through
　 92– 1 *w·* infinite results.
Pul. 14–27 great benefit which Mind has *w·*.
　 26–11 * richly *w·* oxidized silver lamps,
　 34–21 divine Spirit had *w·* a miracle,"
　 55– 3 * Not for show of power, was *w·*
　 78– 3 * ever *w·* in this country.
Rud. 3–18 He *w·* the cure of disease
No. 18–23 have *w·* this moral result,
　 33–17 and the good it *w·*.
My. 164–19 has *w·* a resurrection among you,
　292– 4 that ever was written, taught, or *w·*

Wyclif

'02. 16– 8 happy possessor of a copy of *W·*,

Wyclif's

'02. 16– 2 brought to me *W·* translation of
　 16– 6 *W·* use of that combination of

X, Y

Yahwah (see also Yawa)

'00. 3–23 the divine name *Y·*,
　 3–26 *Y·*, misnamed Jehovah,

Yale College Athenæum

My. 172– 2   * taken from the old *Y· C· A·,*

Yawa (*see also* Yahwah)

Mis. 123–15   Babylonian *Y·,* or Jehovah,

yawns

My. 200–25   Wide *y·* the gap between

yea

Mis. 13– 6   *y·,* the real wrongs
     15– 9   *y·,* the highest Christianization
     23–27   *y·,* which manifests all His
     63–19   *y·,* "that the Lord He is — *Deut. 4 : 35.*
     66–28   *y·,* it is "the blind — *Matt. 15 : 14.*
     73–20   *y·,* that all subjective states of
     77– 5   *y·,* to *understand* those
    104– 7   *y·,* the substance of God,
    108– 7   *y·,* nothingness — of evil :
    126– 2   *y·,* from darkness to daylight,
    141–16   I believe, — *y·,* I understand,
    149– 2   *y·,* come, buy wine — *Isa. 55 : 1.*
    197–26   *y·,* that is divided against itself,
    209– 6   *y·,* that healest the wounds
    252–31   *y·,* it is the pearl priceless
    333– 1   that sin — *y·,* selfhood
    333– 7   falsity, *y·,* nothingness ;
    336– 6   resort to stones and clubs, — *y·,*
    357–32   *y·,* its foundation and superstructure.
Ret. 88–15   *y·,* its power to demonstrate
Pan. 12–18   *y·,* pass gently on without the
'01.   9–12   *Y·,* it is the healing power
    15–29   * *Y·,* there is nothing else
    17– 5   *y·,* quickly to return to divine Love,
    18–21   *y·,* above the grandeur of
    30–24   working alone with God, *y·,*
    32–25   *y·,* all the way up to its
    34–19   *y·,* which *knoweth no evil.*
'02.   6–15   *y·,* something that is not of God.
    10–23   *y·,* from sin to holiness?
Peo.   3–12   *y·,* that make a mysterious God
    5–20   *y·,* to the Principle that is God,
    9– 5   *y·,* it is love leaving self
Po. 67–21   *Y·,* flowers of feeling may blossom
My. 139–21   *y·,* from the human to the divine.
    248–17   *y·,* to the reality of God,
    291–28   to think, to mourn, *y·,* to pray,
    293–19   *y·,* the spirit and the flesh
    299–20   *y·,* they understand it

year (*see also* year's)

about the
Mis. 285–14   It was about the *y·* 1875
    378– 1   About the *y·* 1862,
'02. 18–28   downfall of . . . about the *y·* 325,
My. 105–19   About the *y·* 1869, I was wired to
    315– 3   * About the *y·* 1874, Dr. Patterson,
ago
Mis. 178–15   * it was about a *y·* ago
Pul. 68–16   * in this city about a *y·* ago.
My. 11–14   * A *y·* ago she quietly alluded to
    297–21   when he visited me a *y·* ago.
all of the
Mis. 131–19   was not in existence all of the *y·.*
another
Mis. 147– 3   Another *y·* has rolled on,
    395–18   Ere autumn blanch another *y·,*
'02.   1– 1   another *y·* of God's loving providence
Po. 58– 3   Ere autumn blanch another *y·,*
brief
Ret. 19– 7   spared to me for only one brief *y·.*
by year
My. 266–23   have increased *y·* by year.
close of the
Pul. 45–12   * one month before the close of the *y·*
    84–14   * close of the *y·,* Anno Domini 1894,
coming
My. 42– 6   * the President for the coming *y·,*
dawning
Po. 28– 5   Of truth, this dawning *y·* !
during the
Pul. 77– 9   * During the *y·* eighteen hundred and
    78– 8   * During the *y·* 1894 a church
'02.   1– 7   during the *y·* ending June, 1902,
each
Mis. 159–17   grand collections once in each *y·.*
Man. 44–15   forwarded each *y·* to the Church
    57– 5   first Friday in November of each *y·.*
    60– 5   continued twelve months each *y·.*
    61–14   in January and July of each *y·,*
    93– 9   shall begin July 1 of each *y·.*
    98–18   published each *y·* in a leading
Pul. 45–30   * elected each *y·* by the congregation.
ensuing
My. 39–13   list of officers for the ensuing *y·*
    51–21   * pastorate for the ensuing *y·* ;

year

expiring
Po. 27–19   Thou fast expiring *y·,*
financial
Mis. 131–14   report of the first financial *y·*
    131–28   After this financial *y·,* when you **call**
fixed the
My. 181–28   fixed the *y·* 1866 or 1867
illustrious
Po. 27–24   Illustrious *y·,* farewell !
last
Man. 76–14   expenditures for the last *y·.*
'00.   1– 9   last *y·* of the nineteenth century
My. 55–21   * during the last *y·* the hall was
    57–22   * admitted during the last *y·*
lecture
Man. 93– 8   The lecture *y·* shall begin July 1
new
Pul.   1– 4   A new *y·* is a nursling,
next
My. 141–11   * would have been held next *y·.*
old
Pul.   1– 8   An old *y·* is time's adult,
Po. page 26   poem
once a
Mis. 159–23   Here I talk once a *y·,*
one
Man. 25–13   shall hold office for one *y·,*
    26– 4   term of office . . . is one *y·* each,
    26– 6   have served one *y·* or more,
    39– 4   at the expiration of said one *y·,*
    80–24   term of office . . . is one *y·* each,
    80–26   Incumbents who have served one *y·*
My. 229–11   can acquire in one *y·* the
only a
Pul. 34– 2   * who lived only a *y·.*
over a
My. 361– 9   not seen Mrs. Stetson for over a *y·,*
past
Mis. 160–12   progress, the past *y·,* has been
    239– 5   four day's vacation for the past *y·,*
Pul. 28–26   * For the past *y·* or two Judge Hanna,
My. 52– 2   * during the past *y·.*
    145–17   Within the past *y·* and two months,
receding
Mis. 310–26   receding *y·* of religious jubilee,
    321– 7   each receding *y·* sees the steady gain
Po. 27– 5   One word, receding *y·,*
recurring
Mis. 321– 9   each recurring *y·* witnesses the
returning
Mis. 330–21   With each returning *y·,* higher joys,
returnless
Pul.   1–14   Pass on, returnless *y·* !
Po. 26– 1   Pass on, returnless *y·* !
rolling
Po. 77– 1   God of the rolling *y·* !
same
Mis. 383– 4   took effect the same *y·,*
My. 49–29   * December 1 of the same *y·,*
    51– 4   * May 26 of the same *y·*
    57– 9   * annual meeting of the same *y·*
    327– 5   they have the same *y·,*
some
Pul. 31–14   * It was during some *y·* in the
son of a
Mis. 180–28   month is called the son of a *y·.*
spent a
Ret.   6–20   later Albert spent a *y·* in
that
'00.   6–30   In that *y·* the C. S. textbook,
    7– 2   From that *y·* the United States
My. 330–20   * newspapers of that *y·.*
third
Man. 26–12   Every third *y·* Readers shall
    88–13   elected every third *y·*
this
Mis. 131–17   this *y·* of your firstfruits.
My. 20–29   * omit this *y·* the usual
    21–18   * this *y·* will receive a greater
    21–23   * very many of them this *y·,*
    57–18   * admitted June 5 of this *y·*
    199–18   This *y·,* standing on the verge
    256– 7   This *y·,* my beloved Christian
throughout the
Man. 60– 3   Continued Throughout the *Y·.*
within the
Pul. 45–13   * completion within the *y·*
young
Po. 27– 8   will the young *y·* dawn with

Man. 64–14   In the *y·* eighteen hundred and
    64–22   *y·* nineteen hundred and three

year

Ret.	15–13	In the y· 1878 I was called to
	42– 4	at Lynn, . . . in the y· 1877.
Pul.	33– 4	* for a y· she heard her name
	36– 1	* a y· after her founding of the
'00.	6–29	cites 1875 as the y· of the second
My.	22– 3	* In the y· 1902 our Leader
	53–26	* y· ending December 7, 1885,
	246–11	In the y· 1889, to gain a higher

yearly

Mis.	138– 3	time it takes y· to prepare for
Man.	68–12	rate of one thousand dollars y·
	84– 8	shall teach but one class y·,
	92–14	should teach y· one class.

yearn

Mis.	118–12	y· to forgive a mistake,
	357– 7	y· to find living pastures

yearned

My.	164– 8	I have y· to express my thanks
	214–24	which I y· to do,

yearning

Mis.	178– 5	a y· of the heart ;
Ret.	48– 2	but I was y· for retirement.
My.	135–12	my y· for more peace
	137–18	and y· for more peace

yearningly

Ret.	80–25	while innocence strayeth y·.

yearnings

Mis.	386– 4	Where mortal y· come not,
Po.	49– 6	Where mortal y· come not,

yearns

Mis.	386–17	a hope that ever upward y·,
Ret.	90–20	What other heart y· with
Po.	50– 1	a hope that ever upward y·,

year's

Mis.	131–31	last y· records immortalized,
Man.	38–23	on one y· probation,

years (see also years')

advancing

My.	135–13	for more peace in my advancing y·,
	135–27	cheer my advancing y·.

afterward

Po.	v–23	* Similar requests . . . y· afterward,

ago

Mis.	242–14	more difficult tasks fifteen y· ago.
	248–23	Many y· ago my regular physician
	286– 1	above prophecy, written y· ago,
	375–11	* Y· ago, while in Italy,
Pul.	35– 9	* nineteen hundred y· ago.
	36–20	* y· ago Mrs. Eddy removed from
	53– 3	* nineteen hundred y· ago,
	66– 5	* founded fifteen y· ago
	67–15	* Founded twenty-five y· ago,
	69– 2	* about three y· ago
	69– 8	* some twelve y· ago,
	72–13	* a number of y· ago
	79–10	* starting fifteen y· ago,
	85– 1	* nearly thirty y· ago
Rud.	8– 5	lion of six thousand y· ago ;
'01.	18– 6	the sneers forty y· ago
	27–16	start thirty y· ago
Po.	3–15	Written many y· ago.
	35–15	more than sixty y· ago
My.	10– 6	* externalized itself, ten y· ago,
	22–14	* almost forty y· ago,
	43–21	* Forty y· ago the Science of
	50–29	* more than twenty-six y· ago,
	52–20	* Eighteen y· ago, the Rev. . . . Wiggin,
	55–31	* Twelve y· ago the twenty-first
	59– 3	* nearly forty y· ago.
	67–25	* begun nearly two years ago,
	68–15	* built twelve y· ago,
	70– 5	* only twelve y· ago,
	72–29	* in Boston twelve y· ago
	76–28	* twenty-seven y· ago was founded
	85– 5	* Thirty y· ago it was comparatively
	92–14	* it is but a few y· ago that
	94–31	* But a few y· ago, men there were
	104–28	learn of her who, thirty y· ago,
	109–10	If nineteen hundred y· ago
	181–21	Thirty y· ago (1866)
	181–25	show that thirty y· ago
	182– 1	Thirty y· ago Chicago
	182– 4	Thirty y· ago at my request
	237– 6	some twenty-five y· ago
	313– 2	a silly song of y· ago.
	322–15	* Thanksgiving Day twenty y· ago,
	325–12	* Y· ago I offered my services
	342– 9	* portraits of twenty y· ago,

allotted

My.	273– 7	* beyond the allotted y· of man,

years

all the

Man.	60–17	each day of all the y·.
My.	64–15	* all the y· of her leadership,

awaited the

My.	318–13	confidently awaited the y· to

beginning of

Un.	13–17	"without beginning of y· — see Heb. 7 : 3.

closing

Pul.	23–19	* closing y· of every century are

desired for

My.	40– 3	* She has desired for y· to

during the

Po.	vi–24	* during the y· she resided in Lynn,

early

Mis.	x–19	Timidity in early y· caused me,
Pul.	68– 2	* the church during its early y·,
Po.	19– 6	Written in early y·.

earthly

'01.	29–10	all the best of his earthly y·.

eight

Mis.	341–24	a little girl of eight y·,
Ret.	8– 3	when I was about eight y· old,
Pul.	33– 3	* When eight y· of age

eighteen

My.	52–20	* Eighteen y· ago, the Rev. . . . Wiggin,

1893

'00.	7– 8	in all the other 1893 y·.

eighty-seven

My.	272–25	* nearly eighty-seven y· of age,

eighty-six

My.	271–14	* lives at eighty-six y· of age

eleven

Pul.	72–16	* "And for the past eleven y·,"

few

Mis.	125–30	within the past few y· :
	137–15	within the last few y·.
	315–23	and for the first few y·,
Pul.	70–12	* She has within a few y·
Rud.	6–17	* within the last few y·,
My.	43–23	* A few y· later she
	91–31	* After but a few y·,
	92–14	* it is but a few y· ago that
	94–31	* a few y· ago, men there were who

fifteen

Mis.	242–14	more difficult tasks fifteen y· ago.
Pul.	30–27	* within fifteen y· it has grown
	66– 5	* was founded fifteen y· ago
	79–10	* starting fifteen y· ago,
My.	309–28	* passed her first fifteen y· at

fifty

Un.	7– 1	in less than another fifty y·

first

My.	91–22	* during the first y· of

five

Ret.	36– 5	Five y· after . . . my first copyright,
	44– 9	I had preached five y· before
Pul.	38– 2	* preached in other parishes for five y·
My.	356–15	within the last five y·

former

My.	141–17	* In former y·, the annual communion

forty

'01.	18– 6	the sneers forty y· ago
My.	22–14	* Since 1866, almost forty y· ago,
	22–15	* almost forty y· in the wilderness,
	37–14	* your obedience during forty y·
	43–15	* forty y· before.
	43–21	* Forty y· ago the Science of
	59– 3	* nearly forty y· ago.
	59– 8	* in less than forty y·
	137–11	It is over forty y· that I have
	174–22	For nearly forty y·
	270–21	for the past forty y·
	360–23	for forty y· in succession.

four

Mis.	349–23	preached four y·, . . . before I
Ret.	20– 8	about four y· of age,
Pul.	49–10	* "You have lived here only four y·,
	49–13	"Four y· !" she ejaculated ;
My.	214–19	Four y· after my discovery of C. S.,

four hundred

Mis.	345– 3	four hundred y· before,

glide on

Mis.	110–25	increase rapidly as y· glide on.

goes on with

Mis.	15–14	and goes on with y· ;

gone by

My.	59–24	* In y· gone by I have been asked,

had passed

Mis.	386–19	" Y· had passed o'er thy broken
Po.	50– 3	" Y· had passed o'er thy broken

her

Mis.	39–12	all her y· in giving it birth.

impart

Po.	23– 3	A look that y· impart?

years

increasing
'01. 29–16 parents' increasing y· and needs
intervening
Pul. 85– 3 * during the intervening y·
its
Mis. 230–21 and worse than waste its y·.
My. 352– 9 * with its y· of tender ministry,
late
My. 141– 8 * Of late y· members of the church
long
Mis. 169– 8 the long y· of invalidism
Pul. 84–26 * the result of long y· of untiring,
My. 41–28 * through long y· of consecration
many
Mis. 178– 2 my own sojourning for many y·,
248–23 Many y· ago my regular physician
300–24 I had for many y· been pastor,
Ret. 5–18 who for many y· had resided in
'00. 9–25 for many y· I have desired
15– 3 for many y· has been awaiting you.
'01. 32–25 educated my thought many y·,
'02. 15– 9 struggled on through many y· ;
Hea. 14–23 waited many y· for a student to reach
Po. 3–15 Written many y· ago.
My. 42– 7 * one who has for many y·
91–19 * It has not been very many y· since
163–19 many y· of incessant labor
250–29 filled this sacred office many y·,
283–10 Many y· have I prayed and labored
286– 3 For many y· I have prayed
304–11 for many y· I .wrote for the best
335–15 * for many y· after his death.
months or
Po. 54– 1 It may be months or y·
nine
Pul. 36– 3 * The work in . . . lasted nine y·,
68– 6 * taught the principles . . . for nine y·.
My. v–19 * in 1875, after nine y· of arduous
314– 5 * During the following nine y·
nineteen hundred
Pul. 35– 9 * nineteen hundred y· ago.
53– 3 * nineteen hundred y· ago,
My. 109–10 If nineteen hundred y· ago
ninety-six
Mis. 231– 6 had seen . . . ninety-six y·.
number of
Pul. 72–13 * healed a number of y· ago
My. 335–12 * a number of y· a resident
of toil
My. 64– 6 * attainments and her y· of toil,
older in
My. 342– 7 * Older in y·, white-haired and
one hundred
Pul. 67–23 * exactly one hundred y·
Po. 22– 5 One hundred y·, aflame with
oracle of
'02. 17–27 this oracle of y· will put to flight
our
My. 166–20 If all our y· were holidays,
recent
Mis. 312–15 * has come in recent y·,
Po. v– 4 * up to recent y·.
My. 83–29 * steady gains in recent y·.
riper
Mis. 238– 5 the reverence of my riper y·
score of
Ret. 2–10 more than a score of y·
My. 98– 5 * less than a score of y·.
seven
Mis. 348–18 once in about seven y·
'02. 13– 5 During the last seven y·
several
Pul. 36–20 * Several y· ago Mrs. Eddy
58– 6 * For several y· past
'01. 29–27 I allowed them for several y·
My. 134–29 * been familiar for several y· ,
304–17 for several y· was the proprietor
309–12 For several y· father was
shadows of
My. 184–19 which stays the shadows of y·.
sixteen
My. 304– 9 At sixteen y· of age,
six thousand
Rud. 8– 5 lion of six thousand y· ago ;
sixty
Pul. 32–20 * some sixty y· of age,
Po. 35–15 Written more than sixty y· ago
subsequent
My. 304–20 and for ten subsequent y·
succeeding
My. 177–18 but succeeding y· show
successive
Ret. 40– 1 Through four successive y·
52– 1 many successive y· I have

years

sum of
My. 146–10 "If wisdom lengthens my sum of y·
177–11 if wisdom lengthens my sum of y·
ten
Ret. 10– 4 At ten y· of age I was
My. 10– 6 * externalized itself, ten y· ago,
310–23 * Mary, a child ten y· old,
tender
Mis. 254– 6 brooded . . . over their tender y·
that have passed
My. 47–17 * over the y· that have passed
47–23 * y· that have passed since Mrs. Eddy
these
My. 11– 9 * during these y· she has
22–20 * In these y· of work she has
thirty
Mis. 161–19 when he was thirty y· of age ;
163– 4 had for thirty y· been preparing
341–15 vow of celibacy for thirty y·,
382– 8 has cost more than thirty y·.
Pul. vii– 4 during the ensuing thirty y·.
85– 1 * nearly thirty y· ago began to lay the
'01. 27–16 could start thirty y· ago
My. 70– 4 * organized only thirty y·,
85– 5 * Thirty y· ago it was comparatively
104–28 thirty y· ago, was met with the
181–21 Thirty y· ago (1866) C. S. was discovered
181–25 thirty y· ago the death-rate was
182– 1 Thirty y· ago Chicago had few
182– 4 Thirty y· ago at my request
182– 7 a membership of thirty y·
three
Mis. 120–24 once in three y· is perhaps as often
139– 2 three y· from this date ;
139– 3 to meet again in three y·.
163– 3 Three y· he went about doing good.
163–22 Only three y· a personal Saviour !
349–31 accepted no . . . for about three y·,
353–27 at about three y· of scientific age,
Man. 25–14 but once in three y·.
54– 4 suspended for not less than three y·
55–16 three y· of exemplary character.
68– 2 member of this Church at least three y·
68– 5 to remain with Mrs. Eddy three y·
89–14 healing acceptably three y·,
89–22 healing successfully three y·
91–24 three y· beginning A.D. 1907 ;
94–17 shall not be less than three y·.
Ret. 6–18 two or three y· he read law
24–22 withdrew from society about three y·,
Pul. 53– 8 * three y· of his ministry on earth,
69– 2 * came to Baltimore about three y· ago
73– 8 * from the world for three y·
'00. 7– 7 during the past three y·
My. 98–20 * in a little less than three y·.
114–16 consulted no other . . . for about three y·.
246– 2 for three y· as practitioners
246– 8 practised C. S. three y·
250– 9 three y· of acceptable service
250–16 stipulating three y· as the term for
251–19 after three y· of good practice,
255– 9 removed every three y·,
three consecutive
Man. 68–15 remain with her three consecutive y·,
91–25 are for three consecutive y·
tired
Peo. 8– 8 for the sins of a few tired y·
to come
My. 22–23 * In y· to come the moral and
56– 2 * adequate for y· to come.
twelve
Man. 35– 1 Children when Twelve Y· Old.
35– 3 at the age of twelve y·,
54–18 not be received . . . for twelve y·.
Pul. 69– 8 * some twelve y· ago,
My. 55–31 * Twelve y· ago the twenty-first of
68–15 * built twelve y· ago,
70– 5 * its first church only twelve y· ago,
72–29 * in Boston twelve y· ago
169– 6 under twelve y· of age,
311–15 at twelve y· of age.
twenty
Mis. 88–13 twenty y· in the pulpit,
242–23 having taken it twenty y· ;
Man. 62–11 up to the age of twenty y·,
Ret. 24– 7 During twenty y· prior to
Pul. 38– 7 * During these succeeding twenty y·
My. 321–11 * twenty y· since I first saw you
321–29 * during the past twenty y·
322–15 * Thanksgiving Day twenty y· ago,
342– 9 * portraits of twenty y· ago,
twenty-five
Pul. 67–15 * Founded twenty-five y· ago,
My. 100–11 * It is only twenty-five y·,
237– 6 some twenty-five y· ago

years

twenty-seven
My. 76–28 * which twenty-seven *y·* ago

twenty-six
My. 48–14 * and twenty-six *y·* later
       50–29 * more than twenty-six *y·* ago,

two
Mis. 278–29 For two *y·* I have been gradually
       375–14 * I spent two *y·* in Paris,
'00. 12–24 over two *y·* — he labored in the
My. 67–25 * begun nearly two *y·* ago,
       181–31 first two *y·* of my discovery of

two and a half
Pul. 49–14 * only two and a half *y·*.''

two consecutive
Ret. 6–27 for two consecutive *y·*.

two hundred
Pul. 26–27 * over two hundred *y·* old,
'01. 24–17 more than two hundred *y·* old.

working
My. 298– 7 distinguished all my working *y·*.

Mis. ix–15 To preserve a long course of *y·*
       xi–25 through the dim corridors of *y·*,
       35– 1 *Y·* of practical proof,
       110–16 and months into *y·*,
Pul. 23–20 * *y·* of more intense life,
Po. 67–20 change not with *y·* ;
My. vi–18 * for *y·* the principal contributor to
       181–22 Within those *y·* it is estimated
       321–31 * who knew you *y·* before I did,

years'
Pul. 6–17 * ailment of seven *y·* standing.
My. 250– 3 relative to a three *y·* term

yellow
Ret. 2–22 newspapers, *y·* with age.

yellow-fever and yellow fever
Ret. 19– 8 *y·* raged in that city,
My. 312– 8 * he died of *y· f·*.
       312–20 suddenly seized with *y· f·*
       335–17 * *y· f·* of the worst type,
       335–27 * case was one of *y· f·*

yesterday
Mis. 281–25 I felt the weight of this *y·*,
Ret. 94–22 ''the same *y·*, — *Heb.* 13 : 8.
Un. 61– 4 ''the same *y·*, — *Heb.* 13 : 8.
Pul. 40–22 * was *y·* dedicated to the
       61–24 * Church . . . dedicated *y·*.
       72– 6 * called upon a few . . . *y·*
       73–18 * When seen *y·* she emphasized
No. 31– 7 than they did *y·*.
       44–25 * ''Heretics of *y·* are martyrs
'02. 4–21 statute for *y·*, and to-day,
       5– 3 tribal religions of *y·*
My. 29–10 * closing incident . . . *y·*
       31–18 * opened . . . in Boston *y·*
       65– 7 * voted *y·* afternoon to raise
       75– 7 * *Y·* was a busy day
       75–19 * Crowded as the hall was *y·*,
       86–11 * present at the dedication *y·*
       86–26 * attendance at the ceremonies *y·*
       109–12 ''the same *y·*, — *Heb.* 13 : 8.
       173– 7 hospitality extended *y·*
       173–13 would bring thousands here *y·* ;
       220–32 to-day than it did *y·*.
       246–28 are the same to-day as *y·*
       292–28 same *y·*, to-day, and forever ;
       296–16 healthier and happier, than *y·*.
       328–18 * issued licenses *y·*

yet
Mis. 4–15 *y·* but little time has been
       7–26 greater work *y·* remains to be done.
       12–23 are *y·* to be uncovered
       35–15 most concise, *y·* complete,
       46–28 has not *y·* wholly attained unto
       53–23 *y·* he found it difficult to
       69–27 The man is living *y·* ;
       71– 4 *y·* he saved many a drunkard
       81–21 *or has not Truth y· reached the*
       86– 4 but it doth not *y·* appear.
       105– 7 *y·* this demonstration is the
       120–13 mighty victory is *y·* to be won,
       126–15 church is not *y·* quite sensible of
       126–23 *y·* nothing circulates so rapidly :
       130– 6 Do we *y·* understand
       139– 5 such as you even *y·* have not
       142–30 *y·* as friends we can
       163–22 *y·* the foundations he laid
       179–26 *y·* we look into matter and the earth
       184–19 *y·* persists in evil,
       190–13 needs *y·* to be learned.
       194– 8 *y·* should deny the validity
       197– 7 is not *y·* recognized.
       212–32 had not *y·* drunk of his cup,

yet
Mis. 215–32 nor *y·* when it is in the ear ;
       222–24 for it is not *y·* known.
       227– 9 with malice aforethought
       228– 4 and *y·* not to avenge thyself,
       236–25 *Y·*, notwithstanding one's
       238–11 more than history has *y·* recorded.
       238–17 *Y·* the good done, and the love that
       243– 5 not *y·* made surgery one of the
       262–24 *y·* were our burdens heavy but for
       270–22 *y·* follow him in healing.
       273–18 not *y·* accomplished all the
       280– 9 *y·*, I would not weigh you,
       286–17 *y·* this is possible in *Science*,
       306– 5 * motto has not *y·* been decided upon,
       309–31 more than they have *y·* learned.
       317–16 is *y·* assimilated spiritually
       317–17 *y·* this assimilation is indispensable
       360– 2 Human lives are *y·* uncarved,
       360– 7 unpretentious *y·* colossal characters,
       368– 8 * *Y·* that scaffold sways the future,
       377– 4 *y·* so near and full of radiant relief
       379–30 *Y·*, there remained the difficulty of
       395– 8 *y·* I trow, When sweet *rondeau*
       396– 9 *Y·* here, upon this faded sod,
Chr. 53–25 *Y·* wherefore signalize the birth
Ret. 18–12 *Y·*, dwellers in Eden,
       21–22 awakening . . . is as *y·* imperfect ;
       26–27 know *y·* more of the nothingness of
       31–20 *y·* offend in one point, — *Jas.* 2 : 10.
       38– 4 *y·* he stopped my work.
       67– 8 and *y·* are separate from God.
       78– 4 student has not *y·* achieved the
       80– 4 *y·* it may seem severe.
       80– 9 * *Y·* they grind exceeding small ;
       82– 1 *y·* their core is constantly
       93–21 as *y·* this grandest verity has not
       94– 5 and *y·* contradicts divine Science
       94– 7 seems to be good, and *y·* errs,
Un. 6–26 are not *y·* thoroughly drilled
       9–24 *y·* healing, as I teach it,
       11–27 There are *y·* four months,
       19– 6 *y·* which He cannot avert.
       21– 5 *y·* each mortal is not two
       21– 7 *y·* they are not two but one,
       29–25 I shall *y·* praise Him, — *Psal.* 42 : 11.
       33– 7 *y·* we have it on divine authority :
       34–15 *y·* put your finger on a burning
       35–10 *y·*, strictly speaking, there is no
       36–21 *y·* admit the reality of moral evil,
       36–23 *y·* is not conscious of matter,
       48– 3 *y·* ask, and I will answer.
       55–21 ''*Y·* in my flesh — *Job.* 19 : 26.
       58–17 *y·* without sin.'' — *Heb.* 4 : 15.
       59– 9 *y·* as ''the Son of man — *John* 3 : 13.
       60–11 *y·* we descant upon sickness,
       60–25 are *y·* in your sins.'' — *I Cor.* 15 : 17.
       62– 4 *y·* God dies not,
Pul. 3–20 ''*Y·* in my flesh — *Job* 19 : 26.
       7– 7 *Y·* when I recall the past,
       14– 4 active *y·* unseen mental agencies
       15–14 *y·* have given no warning.
       32–20 * *y·* she had the coloring and the
       38–26 * *Y·* each and all these movements,
       44–11 * *y·* the mother in Israel, alone
       49–10 * and *y·* from a barren waste
       51– 8 * *y·* they are to be numbered
       59– 2 * she has not *y·* visited her temple,
       72–18 * *y·* have been perfectly well.''
       73–27 * no more complete and *y·* concise
       83– 6 * has not *y·* the moral strength
Rud. 8–19 *y·* is false to God and man,
       14–17 *y·* will expect and require others to
No. 5–19 and *y·* is arrayed against being,
       16–16 *y·* forever giving forth more light,
       27–19 * ''No man living hath *y·* seen man.''
       31– 5 they are *y·* sick and sinful.
       34–22 Life of Spirit is not *y·* discerned.
       34–23 *y·* mounting to the throne of glory
       35–19 and *y·* governs mankind.
Pan. 4–23 I shall *y·* praise Him, — *Psal.* 42 : 11.
'01. 6–14 *y·* God must be One
       7–29 and *y·* have believed.'' — *John* 20 : 29.
       9–18 *y·* Christ is rejected of men !
       12–14 *y·* should not have charity,
       14– 2 and *y·* commit sin,
       23– 5 *y·* that God has an opposite
       23– 7 *y·* that evil exists and is real,
       27–13 If any one as *y·* has healed
'02. 12– 1 has not *y·* come ;
       15– 2 *y·* I never lost my faith
       18–21 *Y·* he said, ''The works — *John* 14 : 12.
       19– 2 *Y·* behold his love !
Peo. 8–16 *y·* we make more of matter,
       10–28 *y·* that hour was a prophecy of
Po. vii– 2 * *y·*, *even these are characterized*

yet

Po.	23– 7	give those earnest eyes y· back
	27–14	With traitors unvoiced y·?
	27–16	ere they break in silence y·,
	31– 2	nor y· by nature sown,
	34–15	Y· wherefore ask thy doom?
	42– 4	Y· there's one will be victor,
	57–15	And y· I trow,
	59– 1	Y· here, upon this faded sod,
	64– 1	Y·, dwellers in Eden,
	68–13	Y· stronger than these is the spell
	74– 4	Smile on me y·,
	77– 6	Y· wherefore this Thy love?
	78–14	O meekest of mourners, while y·
My.	v– 1	* God of Hosts, be with us y·;
	11– 2	* we are as y· but imperfect
	45– 9	* Y· the upwards of thirty thousand
	50–17	* "y· there was a feeling of trust
	53– 4	* y· not until the authoress
	55– 6	* y· the thought of obtaining
	60–15	* I have y· the little Bible
	69–17	* y· not a single pillar or post
	75–27	* No church has ever y· been
	80– 9	* y· they were believed.
	82– 1	* Y· they all have the same
	93–13	* y· it has rare lures for
	97– 7	* It has y· to be shown that
	97–28	* Boston has not y· recovered
	99–25	* and the end is not y·.
	107–14	Y· the homœopathist administers
	109–16	y· we may sometimes say
	111–20	and y· the book itself be
	114– 7	y· reached the maximum
	114–11	not y· uncovered to the gaze
	114–13	is not y· won.
	118–17	y· have believed." — John 20 : 29.
	121–10	y· yielding to the touch of
	121–15	Y· peace is desirable,
	134–13	imperative demand not y· met.
	146–15	has not y· been reached.
	146–16	Y· his immortal words
	152–10	human race has not y· reached
	186–22	while they are y· speaking, — Isa. 65 : 24.
	228– 9	y· depart from Christ's teachings.
	243–13	not y· had the privilege of
	251– 2	I cannot y· say.
	273–11	y· have I not seen — Psal 37 : 25.
	292– 3	more than history has y· recorded.
	294– 2	are y· in a large minority
	302–23	Because C. S. is not y· popular,
	323– 7	* I have his little book y·.
	331–28	* y· when we listen to Mrs. Glover
	332– 7	* y· it is all we can award :
	334–20	and y· commit sin,
	352– 9	* y· we know that the real gratitude

yield

Mis.	46– 3	"To whom ye y· — Rom. 6 : 16.
	120– 7	to whom ye y· — Rom. 6 : 16.
	178–28	but will y· to circumstances.
	182–31	sin, and death will y· to it,
	184–16	y· to material sense, and lose his
	190–26	must y· to the right sense,
	221–28	y· the same product
	236–11	and y· obedience to them
	246–21	wrong that refused to y· its prey
	345– 9	* unless you y· your religion,"
	346–18	"to whom ye y· — Rom. 6 : 16.
	395–24	The languid brooklets y· their sighs,
Ret.	23– 4	y· to the irony of fate,
Un.	39– 4	y· to holiness, health, and Life,
	60–28	y· to His eternal presence,
	64–13	must y· to despair,
No.	35– 8	y· lovingly to the purpose of divine
'02.	13–10	y· this church a liberal income.
Hea.	18– 2	y· to the government of God,
Po.	2–17	Y· to the sun's more genial,
	46–12	And y· its beauty and perfume
	58– 9	languid brooklets y· their sighs,
	67–22	y· earth the fragrance of goodness

yielded

Mis.	237– 3	y· somewhat to the metaphysical
	373– 7	but, as usual, he finally y·.
Ret.	38– 7	I y· to a constant conviction
	57–14	would have y· to Science
'01.	31–26	and y· up graciously

yielding

Mis.	12–20	danger of y· to temptation
	107–20	three states . . . before y· error.
	236–15	y· to constant solicitations of
'01.	20– 1	y· to its aggressive features.
Hea.	11– 6	physics are y· slowly to metaphysics ;
Peo.	7–20	* If we carve it then on the y· stone
Po.	23–13	Y· a holy strength to right,
My.	121–11	y· to the touch of a finger.

yields

Mis.	37–23	appetite for alcohol y· to Science
	84–30	y· a clearer and nearer sense of Life
	204– 9	error y· up its weapons
	220–12	until the patient's mind y·,
	339–15	if it y· not, grows stronger.
Ret.	18–12	earth y· you her tear,
	49– 1	which y· a large income,
Pul.	6– 4	y· to the church established by
'00.	15–15	y· to sharp conviction
Peo.	2– 6	y· its grosser elements,
Po.	64– 1	earth y· you her tear,

yoke

Mis.	90–17	Break the y· of bondage in every
	262–26	and renders the y· easy.

yon

Mis.	392– 6	majestic oak, from y· high place
Po.	1–13	Proud from y· cloud-crowned
	20– 8	majestic oak, from y· high place

yonder

My.	222–12	hence to y· place ; — Matt. 17 : 20.

yore

Mis.	360–27	is heard as of y· saying
Pul.	7– 5	To-day, as of y·, her laws
Po.	47– 2	As sweetly they came of y·,
My.	110– 8	and it shines as of y·,

York, Pa.

Pul.	88–27	* Daily, Y·, P·.

young

Mis.	49– 1	A y· lady entered the College class
	49– 5	this y· lady had manifested
	145–24	y· lion and the fatling — Isa. 11 : 6.
	201–28	y· man is awakened to bar his door
	254– 8	mother-bird tendeth her y·
	390–24	Ne'er perish y·, like things of earth,
Ret.	7– 7	* Albert Baker was a y· man
	19–19	tender devotion to his y· bride
Un.	61– 8	neither y· nor old,
Pul.	7– 2	* "Had I y· blood in my veins,
Rud.	6–13	Langley, the y· American astronomer
Hea.	2–12	* too strong for y· Melanchthon."
Po.	8–20	thinking alone of a fair y· bride,
	9– 3	picturing alone a glad y· face,
	27– 8	will the y· year dawn with wisdom's
	56– 3	Ne'er perish y·, like things of earth,
	66–12	but a y· heart and glad
My.	122–19	where the y· child lies,
	149–14	When a y· man vainly boasted,
	272–19	* chapter sub-title
	273–11	"I have been y·, — Psal. 37 : 25.
	312– 8	* He left his y· wife in a
	330–31	tender devotion to his y· bride
	335–30	* y· wife prayed incessantly

younger

My.	146–11	may then be even y· than now."
	177–12	I shall then be even y·

youngest

Ret.	4– 2	y· of whom was my father,
	5– 6	y· of my parents' six children
My.	309–17	Mark Baker was the y· of
	310– 9	my y· brother, George Sullivan Baker,

Young Men's Christian Association

My.	332–17	* Y· M· C· A· at Wilmington.

youth

Mis.	ix–19	a y· that never grows old ;
	ix–21	fleeting freshness of y·,
	226– 4	unbiased y· and the aged
	241– 1	faith of both y· and adult
	324– 6	y·, manhood, and age gayly tread
Ret.	15–10	taught me from my y·: — Psal. 71 : 17.
	17– 1	Written in y·, while visiting
	18– 1	Here is y·!
Pul.	33–28	* visions in their early y·.
Po.	8–14	the heaven of my y·
	63– 8	Here is y·!
My.	13–23	thy y· is renewed — Psal. 103 : 5.
	261– 2	parents and guardians of y·
	272–19	* chapter sub-title
	273–16	be early presented to y·
	274–11	in y· tend to success,

youthful

Pul.	8–23	The resident y· workers

youward

My.	216–18	The purpose of God to y·

Yule-fires

My.	256–23	the Y· burn,

Z

zeal

Mis.	177–15	doff your lavender-kid *z·*,
	284– 8	a *z·* without knowledge,
Ret.	79–24	Restrain untempered *z·*.
My.	85–14	* the *z·* and enthusiasm of
	95–30	* religious faith and enlightened *z·*
	97–22	* *z·* of its membership.
	187– 1	faith, and Christian *z·*
	259–18	an honest, wise *z·*,
	291–10	*z·* according to wisdom,

zealots

Mis.	335–22	is a fault of *z·*,

zealous

Mis.	322–26	compensate your *z·* affection
Pul.	84–27	* *z·* effort on the part of
My.	213–12	more *z·* to do good,

zenith

Mis.	320–24	the *z·* of Truth's domain,
Pul.	36– 4	* very *z·* of its prosperity,
My.	225– 4	rising to the *z·* of success,

zephyr

Mis.	394– 2	'T is borne on the *z·*
Po.	45– 1	'Tis borne on the *z·*

zephyrs

Ret.	17– 3	midst the *z·* at play
Po.	15– 1	soft sighing *z·*
	62– 2	midst the *z·* at play

zest

Pul.	46–24	* perhaps with an unusual *z·*,

Zeus

My.	159–26	*Z·*, the master of the **gods,**

Zion (*see also* **Zion's**)

Mis.	126–28	this daughter of *Z·* :
	146– 1	remember thee, and God's *Z·*,
	150–14	loveth the gates of *Z·*.
	154–12	the prosperity of His *Z·*.
	369– 1	watchmen on the walls of *Z·*,
Pul.	22–19	Then shall *Z·* have put on her
'01.	35– 8	upon the hill-tops of *Z·*.
My.	16–25	Behold, I lay in *Z·* — *Isa.* 28 : 16.
	125–24	*Z·* must put on her beautiful
	133– 8	church triumphant, and *Z·* be glorified.
	171– 4	come to *Z·* with songs — *Isa.* 35 : 10.
	184–24	prosperity of *Z·* is very precious
	184–28	that saith unto *Z·*, — *Isa.* 52 : 7.
	270–25	I love the prosperity of *Z·*,

Zion's

Mis.	370– 9	sentinels of *Z·* watch-towers
My.	3–11	in *Z·* waste places,

Zion's Herald

Mis.	132–12	your communication to *Z· H·*,
	242– 3	published in *Z· H·*,
My.	97–15	* *Z· H·*, a rather bitter critic

zone

Chr.	53– 1	circling on, from *z·* to *z·*,
'00.	10–29	serving his country in that torrid *z·*

Appendix A
Index to the Chapter Sub-titles and Headings of the Writings of Mary Baker Eddy
other than Science and Health
and to the Titles of the Poems

Index to the Chapter Sub-titles and Headings of the Writings of Mary Baker Eddy

other than Science and Health

and to the Titles of the Poems

Appendix B
Index to the Scriptural Quotations
in the Writings of Mary Baker Eddy
other than Science and Health

Index to the Scriptural Quotations

OLD TESTAMENT

NEW TESTAMENT

Matthew

10 : 39
My. 233–25
10 : 42
Ret. 27–30
11 : 3
No. 46–9
11 : 6
Mis. 235–14
11 : 7
My. 117–6
11 : 8
My. 117–3
11 : 11
My. 228–14
11 : 12
Ret. 79–26
11 : 19
Mis. 354–9
My. 228–22
11 : 28
Mis. 20–4
No. 43–4
'02. 19–16
Hea. 2–17
11 : 30
My. 161–29
12 : 13
Mis. 370–2
12 : 25
Mis. 89–2
12 : 37
My. 196–14
12 : 39
Mis. 242–16
12 : 45
Rud. 9–1
12 : 50
Chr. 55–23
'01. 18–19
13 : 32
Mis. 356–17
13 : 33
Mis. 171–23
13 : 52
'00. 8–14
13 : 58
My. 294–7
14 : 17
My. 123–23
14 : 27
Mis. 109–28
Pul. 4–2
'02. 20–3
15 : 11
Mis. 118–31
15 : 14
Mis. 66–28
16 : 3
Mis. 1–7
My. 114–1
266–14
266–22
16 : 6
Mis. 366–18
16 : 13
Mis. 83–20
16 : 18
Mis. 141–8
144–19
263–7
16 : 19
No. 31–28
16 : 23
No. 23–7
16 : 25
Mis. 211–22
Ret. 32–6
17 : 17
My. 222–5
17 : 19
My. 190–15
17 : 20
My. 222–9
222–10
17 : 21
Mis. 156–20
My. 190–16
222–13
339–24
18 : 2
Mis. 337–12
18 : 3
My. 4–26
18 : 4
Mis. 337–13

Matthew

18 : 6
Mis. 122–11
127–2
130–25
My. 17–30
18 : 7
Mis. 122–2
18 : 11
Mis. 195–11
18 : 16
Un. 33–24
19 : 5
Mis. 289–17
19 : 10
Mis. 298–14
19 : 14
My. 197–21
19 : 19
Mis. 7–9
18–10
311–21
Pan. 9–10
'00. 5–21
My. 109–9
196–14
265–1
278–9
281–11
19 : 28
Mis. 73–22
19 : 30
Un. 30–25
20 : 12
'00. 9–29
20 : 16
Mis. 189–1
20 : 23
Mis. 211–26
My. 161–19
21 : 12
Mis. 270–2
21 : 16
Pul. 8–21
21 : 42
Man. 18–1
Pul. 10–19
No. 38–14
My. 48–7
60–12
129–20
22 : 14
My. 244–20
22 : 29
Mis. 168–22
219–6
No. 37–4
23 : 4
Peo. 11–25
11–26
23 : 9
Mis. 181–1
287–6
Ret. 68–13
Un. 53–26
Pan. 8–18
23 : 17
Mis. 275–2
23 : 37
Mis. 326–25
23 : 38
Mis. 326–27
24 : 24
Mis. 175–20
24 : 35
Mis. 99–21
111–17
163–18
24 : 48
Mis. 335–3
24 : 49
Mis. 328–14
335–5
24 : 50
Mis. 335–7
24 : 51
Mis. 335–10
25 : 1
Mis. 341–21
25 : 6
Mis. 342–17
25 : 8
Mis. 342–19
25 : 9
Mis. 342–23

Matthew

25 : 21
Mis. 116–28
355–7
My. 124–13
207–21
25 : 23
Mis. 116–28
117–1
122–25
339–17
343–27
Pul. 13–6
My. 62–2
124–13
162–21
202–13
225–4
25 : 38
My. 117–13
25 : 39
My. 117–15
25 : 40
'02. 18–14
26 : 27
Mis. 211–29
26 : 41
Mis. 356–30
My. 358–5
27 : 34
Ret. 26–5
27 : 35
Mis. 302–5
27 : 63
'01. 9–12
28 : 6
Mis. 179–14
28 : 18
Mis. 373–26
28 : 20
Mis. 39–15
389–21
Ret. 89–21
No. 46–1
Po. 4–20
My. 44–12
58–24
159–5
190–32

Mark

1 : 15
No. 35–24
1 : 17
Mis. 111–10
1 : 24
'01. 9–20
My. 211–10
4 : 22
Mis. 348–11
4 : 28
Ret. 92–5
4 : 39
Mis. 307–9
Ret. 60–15
5 : 30
Un. 57–13
5 : 31
Un. 57–11
5 : 41
Peo. 8–22
6 : 50
Mis. 109–28
Pul. 4–2
'02. 20–3
8 : 17
Mis. 99–5
8 : 18
Mis. 58–13
99–4
8 : 33
No. 23–7
8 : 35
Mis. 211–22
Ret. 32–6
9 : 25
No. 31–25
9 : 34
Mis. 303–12
'02. 4–2
My. 305–28
9 : 38
Mis. 191–13
9 : 39
Ret. 75–13
9 : 40
My. 224–26

Mark

11 : 24
My. 293–30
12 : 9
Mis. 254–25
12 : 17
Mis. 374–25
Ret. 71–5
My. 220–9
220–11
344–25
12 : 32
Mis. 22–20
12 : 43
Hea. 7–19
13 : 9
'01. 10–3
13 : 31
Mis. 99–21
111–17
13 : 37
My. 232–13
14 : 9
My. 19–30
15 : 30
Un. 58–7
15 : 34
Mis. 63–22
16 : 3
Mis. 179–2
16 : 6
My. 122–23
16 : 15
Mis. 37–14
325–32
No. 14–18
41–20
My. 47–27
172–16
300–24
16 : 17
Mis. 25–16
28–31
192–28
248–1
248–6
364–3
Ret. 16–14
Rud. 16–11
No. 44–5
Hea. 1–1
6–26
7–4
7–6
19–26
My. 47–29
131–15
147–11
225–8
238–14
306–15
318–1
16 : 18
Mis. 28–32
192–29
210–10
248–2
249–6
Ret. 35–17
Hea. 1–2
7–25
8–10
15–10
15–11
19–27
Peo. 12–3
My. 47–31
146–3
16 : 20
Mis. 25–16
133–31
133–32
154–24
No. 37–20
My. 147–11
190–27
258–2

Luke

1 : 46
Mis. 75–22
Un. 30–1
1 : 77
'02. 16–5
2 : 14
Mis. 145–29
369–5

Luke

2 : 14
Pul. 41–25
No. 44–26
My. 90–19
127–30
167–11
279–18
281–9
283–11
4 : 23
Mis. 355–26
5 : 23
No. 42–8
6 : 27
Mis. 9–9
6 : 31
Mis. 90–13
146–18
282–10
'00. 14–16
6 : 32
Mis. 13–11
6 : 38
My. 21–19
7 : 35
Mis. 374–9
8 : 54
Pul. 54–23
9 : 24
Mis. 211–22
Ret. 32–6
9 : 46
Mis. 303–12
9 : 60
My. 353–25
10 : 7
Pul. 50–3
My. 215–24
10 : 21
Mis. 167–23
No. 44–28
10 : 27
My. 183–1
10 : 37
My. 149–3
11 : 14
Mis. 190–11
190–13
190–28
191–2
11 : 17
No. 5–21
12 : 2
Mis. 348–11
12 : 32
Mis. 149–30
321–16
Pul. 9–22
12 : 39
My. 232–14
12 : 47
Man. 28–10
13 : 7
Mis. 151–11
13 : 27
My. 161–9
13 : 28
My. 161–10
14 : 27
My. 229–17
14 : 30
My. 162–16
15 : 32
My. 185–18
16 : 8
Mis. 342–28
17 : 1
Mis. 279–1
17 : 19
Pul. 53–13
17 : 20
Mis. 251–16
17 : 21
Mis. 21–10
251–18
Ret. 94–21
Pul. 3–6
No. 35–25
Pan. 13–6
My. 265–23
267–28
18 : 8
Mis. 83–20